STANLEY GIBBONS
British Commonwealth Stamp Catalogue
1978

Eightieth edition

Including post-independence issues of Ireland, Pakistan, Rhodesia and South Africa

STANLEY GIBBONS PUBLICATIONS LTD
391 Strand London WC2R 0LX

Retail Price in UK £6·95

By appointment to H.M. the Queen, Stanley Gibbons Ltd., Philatelists

ISSN: 0068–1903 ISBN: 0 85259 935 8

Made and Printed in Great Britain by William Clowes & Sons Limited London, Beccles & Colchester.

PREFACE TO THE

1978 Edition

The Silver Jubilee

The Silver Jubilee of Her Majesty's accession to the throne is being celebrated as this edition goes to press. As with earlier Royal events there is a great deal to interest the philatelist and the Jubilee has been marked by the appearance of a particularly well designed omnibus issue for Crown Agents' territories. These stamps are proving deservedly popular with collectors and there is little doubt that the Silver Jubilee will give a great fillip to the hobby. Many newcomers will be attracted to stamp collecting, developing into more advanced philatelists in course of time and ensuring its continued healthy state.

Price Changes

The market in fine stamps flourishes as never before and collector demand seems stronger than ever. Repricing of the present volume has been undertaken with the usual thoroughness but particular note should be taken of the very substantial rises for classic material. Such is today's market in stamps of the early period that prices here can truly be described as an accurate reflection of the real worth of these issues.

Improvements in the Listings and Acknowledgments

The following are the more important changes in this edition:

" SPECIMEN " STAMPS. A thorough check of our listing was made in consultation with Mr. Marcus Samuel, F.R.P.S.,L., and his recently published book *Specimen Stamps of the Crown Colonies, 1857–1948*. Our listing is limited to those stamps which were sent to the U.P.U. for distribution and the review occasioned some additions and deletions.

KING GEORGE VI DEFINITIVES. Continuing our examination of printings and shades following the publications of the King George VI Collectors Society, which are based on Crown Agents records, attention has been paid to *Bechuanaland, Hong Kong* and *Seychelles*.

GREAT BRITAIN. The Postal Fiscal stamps have been rewritten in normal style, replacing the previous condensed tabulated list. We felt that the growing interest in these stamps warranted a fuller treatment. In the Used Abroad section there have been some changes, notably the extended listing and transfer of the obscure wavy lines cancellation from the Crimea to Malta.

BRITISH SOLOMON ISLANDS. This now appears under Solomon Islands, its title since 1975.

BURMA (Japanese Occupation). Some interesting political notes contributed by the late B. St. G. Drennan, F.R.P.S.,L., have been incorporated.

INDIAN FEUDATORY STATES. The listing of *Jasdan* has been extended, again at the suggestion of Basil Drennan and based on the published findings of Mr. R. F. Stoney. The 1893 issue of *Nawanagar* has been simplified.

Travancore. This was completely rewritten only last year but we were not satisfied with it. In that list we showed the three types of the Conch Shell watermark of which only one is distinctively different, so we did not attempt to distinguish between the other two as we felt it would be difficult to identify single stamps. Mr. Philip Kinns demonstrated that this was not so if one took other factors into consideration. The complete country has therefore been again rewritten with fuller information to enable the three types of watermark to be positively identified. Consequential changes have also been made in *Travancore-Cochin*. This has been a considerable undertaking and we are greatly indebted to both Mr. Philip Kinns for the subdivision of the watermarks and help with the Official stamps and to Mr. C. T. Sturton once again for identifying the errors and varieties according to watermark.

LABUAN. Some additional perforation varieties have been introduced in the Crown type on the recommendation of Mr. J. A. Naylor.

NEW ZEALAND. It was decided to give catalogue recognition to the three types of single " N Z and Star " watermark, which are now widely collected. This entailed a complete revision of the 1882–97 " POSTAGE & REVENUE " issue, together with consequential changes in the Postage Dues, Officals, Life Insurance and Postal Fiscal stamps. In the 1882–97 issue we now illustrate and list the dies of the 1d., 2d. and 6d. and have added the rare mixed perforation varieties.

We have inserted clearer notes concerning the different papers of the twenties produced by De La Rue, Jones, Cowan and Wiggins, Teape and now give catalogue recognition to the latter for the first time. This also affected the subsidiary groups.

The Postal Fiscal section has been completely revised. The long-standing controversy over the status of some of these issues has been resolved so far as this Catalogue is concerned. The 1867 issue has been omitted on the grounds that postally used copies were philatelically inspired. In the 1882 period some stamps of under 2s. face value have been admitted as there is evidence that they were needed for postal purposes because of temporary shortages of the corresponding postage stamps. On the other hand certain high values have been dropped because evidence of postal use is lacking. Naturally this list has been greatly expanded by the inclusion of the types of watermark. As the later arms types have the same status as the earlier issues they have been transferred to the Postal Fiscal section and fully listed according to papers.

In all this we have had the fullest collaboration with Dr. K. J. McNaught, F.R.P.S.,L., who is Editor of the forthcoming Vol. VI of *The Postage Stamps of New Zealand* and we acknowledge with thanks the permission of the Royal Philatelic Society of New Zealand to use material included there for the first time.

COOK ISLANDS, NIUE and SAMOA. On the advice of Dr. McNaught a few additions have been made in the 1893–1900 issue of *Cook Islands*. The changes in the Postal Fiscal stamps of New Zealand, particularly the inclusion of the Wiggins, Teape paper, affected all three island groups, but for the sake of convenience we left them in with the postage stamps.

The subdivision of the watermark types entailed a completely revised list of the issues from 1886 to 1900 of *Samoa* and here we must acknowledge the enormous amount of help given by Mr. A. R. Burge, F.R.P.S.,N.Z., who is co-editor of the New Zealand handbook mentioned above and responsible for the island issues.

NOVA SCOTIA. On the suggestion of Mr. Max Guggenheim, R.D.P., F.R.P.S.,L., we list the 1s. deep purple of the 1851 printing, which is sometimes taken for the 1s. purple of 1856.

RHODESIA. Some additional shades have been introduced and others renamed in the period of 1898 to 1908, based on recently revealed official records of printings. The listing is derived from an article by Mr. Robson Lowe in the December 1975 issue of *The Philatelist*.

SOUTH AUSTRALIA. Some clarification of the listing of the value types of the 2s. 6d. and 5s. denominations of 1904 to 1912 was effected on the advice of Mr. J. R. W. Purves, F.R.P.S.,L.

R.G.P.

Personal Note

Since 1966 successive editions of this catalogue have been edited by Rex Phillips and this is his last following his retirement. All collectors owe him a great debt of gratitude for the substantial improvements and revisions he has introduced over the twelve years of his editorship. His term of office involved pleasant collaboration with the many eminent specialists whose names are recorded in successive prefaces and correspondence with innumerable collectors making helpful contributions to the lists. He has provided very secure foundations on which the future success of the catalogue can be built.

James Negus

List of catalogue numbers of stamps

Added to this edition but not listed in Gibbons *Stamp Monthly* Supplements

Great Britain. 26a, 843b/c, 857a, 860b, 864a, 896b, 931b, 948h, 997a, 1009a, 1018a, 1020a, 1022a, W13a
G.B. Used Abroad. ZM1/2a, ZM4, Z9a, Z51*b*, Z1337*b*
Aden. 44a
Aden (Kathiri State of Seiyun). 65a
Antigua. 70a
Australia. 495a, 550a, 552b, 554a, 556a, 557a, 563a, 614b
Bechuanaland. 118*b*, 127*a*, F3a
Belize. 437a
Bermuda. 116d, 164c, 237a
Canada. 199a, 241a, 345a
Cook Islands. 10*a*/*b*, 13a, 122/3*a*, **MS**535a
Falkland Is. (S. Georgia). 19b
Fiji. 26aa, **MS**525a
Gibraltar. 49a, 59a, 69a, 79a, 79ba, 94a
Gilbert Is. 6, 8/10a, 22a
Grenada. 335a
Grenadines of Grenada. 2a
Guyana. 431b, 435a, F4a
Hong Kong. 145*b*, 148*a*, 156*a*, D1a/5a
India. 688a, 722a, 749a, O198
Indian Convention States. Jind. 15a
Indian Feudatory States.
Bhopal. 348e
Jasdan. 1
Nawanagar. 11b
Travancore. *Relisted*
Ireland. 299*a*, 391a, 394a, **MS**395a, D15a
Jamaica. 59b
Labuan 105a, 116d, 117a, 119a, 120b, 121a, 124a, 125a
Malaya.
Kelantan. 103a
Perak. 15ab, 82b, 164b
Straits Settlements. 142a, 144b/ba, 149a, 151a
Japanese Occupation. J205c
Thai Occupation. TK2a, TK3a, TK4a
Malta. 71aa, 477c
Montserrat. **MS**367a
Morocco Agencies 146a
Newfoundland. D3b
New Republic. 35a
New Zealand. 127, 187/245 *rewritten*, 449aa, 1017a, 1083a, E4, D37/40, O82, O85, L2a, L3a, L9*a*/*b*, L13a, L14a, L15b, Postal Fiscals *rewritten*
Aitutaki. 37*a*/*c*
Nigeria (Biafra). 13a, 14a, 16d, 32a, 36a
North Borneo. 6a, 117d, 235a, F3a (old F3a deleted), D1a
Nova Scotia. 7*c*, 8a
Pakistan. 178a, 206a
Queensland. 283*a*
Rhodesia. 75*a*, 80b, 84c/d, 86a, 90a, 100*b*
St. Christopher. 22ab
St. Lucia. 229a
St. Vincent. 441a
Samoa. 194*a*/*d*
Seychelles. 139*d*, 143*a*
South Africa. 350ab, 399a, 409a
South West Africa. 245a
Sri Lanka. 605a/b, 611a
Tanzania. O28a, O29a, O33a, O34a, O36b, O47a
Transvaal (Pietersburg). 19e, 19l, 21c
Trinidad & Tobago. 341b/ba, 354a
Turks & Caicos Is. 104e/f
Western Australia. 139c, 140a, 145b, 151b, 170a, 172a, 173a

Catalogue numbers altered in this edition

Old	New
Great Britain	
830a	*deleted*
831aa	*deleted*
831b	*deleted*
F1/56	*rewritten*
Isle of Man	
74/7	75/8
G.B. Used Abroad	
Z1584*b*	ZM3
Z1584*c*	ZM5
Z1526/31	*deleted*
Z1540	*deleted*
Anguilla	
225/9	226/30
230/**MS**245	232/**MS**247
Bahamas	
448/9	449/50
Bangladesh	
53/62	51/60
67/8	65/6
73	71
Bechuanaland	
54b	54d
54c	54b
54d	54c
118*b*	118*c*
British Honduras	
D5/6	D4/5
Canada	
598a, c	*deleted*
598b, d	598a, b
604a, c	*deleted*
604b, d, e	604a, b, c
604f, h	*deleted*
604g, i	604d, e
605a	*deleted*
608a	*deleted*
693a, b	*deleted*
693c, d	693a, b
701/10	702/11
725/36	727/38
Cayman Islands	
352	351
351	369
353/**MS**364	352/**MS**363
365/6	364/5
Cook Islands	
22b	*deleted*
122/3	98*a*/*b*
131/9	137/45
140/5	131/6
Falkland Islands	
270a/b	264a/b
Gibraltar	
79*a*	79*b*
346/7	344/5
376/90	346/60
Gilbert & Ellice Is.	
204/12	203/7
218/69	208/59
Grenada	
445/**MS**451	455/**MS**461
452/**MS**461	445/**MS**454
Grenadines of Grenada	
MS100/**MS**160	**MS**102/**MS**162
Guyana	
620/52	630/53
Hong Kong	
145b	145c
334/8	335/9
341	342
343	344
349/50	350/1
D1a	D1b
India	
O198/9	O199/200
Indian Feudatory States	
Jasdan	
1	5
1*a*/b	2/3
Nawanagar	
8B	8a
11B	11b
12B	12b
13bB	13ba
Travancore and Travancore-Cochin	
Relisted entirely	
Ireland	
299*a*	299*b*
343/51	342/9
352	351
354/7	356/9
Kenya, Uganda and Tanganyika	
131*ae*/af	*deleted*
131*ag*	131*ae*
Labuan	
105a	105b
117*a*	117*b*
D9*b*	D9a/*ab*
D9a	D9c
Malawi	
514/**MS**518	515/**MS**519
Mauritius	
R2*a*/3	R3/4
Montserrat	
301/3	300/2
308/66	303/61
New Zealand	
115b	129
126a	129a
126b	130c
127/a	128/a
128/b	130/b
129/32a	131/32b
187/245	*rewritten*
544*a*	545
544b/z	*rewritten as* F145/85
545/*c*	F187/90
545*d*	F186
603*a*/5*b*	604/9
606/33	610/37
634/60	F191/218
863/6	F219/22
1018/19	1019/20
1095/9	1110/1114
E3/4	E2/3
D37/44	D41/7
O78/81	O76/9
O82/3	O80/1
O84/5	O83/4
O122/40*b*	O118/40
F1/101	*deleted*
F102/43 and F149/77	F5/144
F144/5	F1/2
F146/7	F3/4
F148	*deleted*
Aitutaki	
83a	87
84a	88
87/99	89/101
Nigeria (Biafra)	
14*a*	14*b*
North Borneo	
253dd	253dd/de
253de	253df
253k	253k/l
Nova Scotia	
5b	*deleted*
8a	7d
Rhodesia	
75a	75aa
75b	75ab
397a/c	*deleted*
400a	*deleted*
399a	*deleted*
401a	*deleted*
403a/b	*deleted*
441a	*deleted*
441*b*	441*c*
496	497
497	499
498	500
499	503
500/518	505/23
St. Helena	
312	309
323/6	310/13
St. Lucia	
368/9	367/8
381/406	369/94
409/13	395/8
422/**MS**437	399**MS**414
St. Vincent	
432/78	433/84
Samoa	
21/73	*rewritten*
133	*deleted*
Sierra Leone	
124b	*deleted*
South Australia	
261	*deleted*
Swaziland	
230/3	232/5
234/5	230/1
Transvaal (Pietersburg)	
19e/j	19f/k
21c	21d
Trinidad & Tobago	
433/5	432/4
448/**MS**480	435/**MS**467

Stanley Gibbons International

Stanley Gibbons Ltd

391 Strand, London WC2R 0LX. Sales and buying departments for popular stamps, albums, catalogues and accessories ; new issues and approvals.

RETAIL SHOP : 391 Strand, London WC2R 0LX.

SPECIALIST AND RARE STAMP DEPARTMENTS : Romano House, 399 Strand, London WC2R 0LX. Classic and rare material, Specialist Register, investment advice, the Gibbons Gallery of changing exhibitions.

Stanley Gibbons Publications Ltd

EDITORIAL OFFICES : Drury House, Russell Street, Drury Lane, London WC2B 5HD. The S.G. catalogues, books and albums. Mail order service (hotline 01–836 0974).

WHOLESALE AND TRADE : Stangib House, Sarehole Road, Hall Green, Birmingham B28 8EE.

Stanley Gibbons Auctions Ltd

Drury House, Russell Street, Drury Lane, London WC2B 5HD. Valuations and sales by auction and private treaty.

Stanley Gibbons Magazines Ltd

Drury House, Russell Street, Drury Lane, London WC2B 5HD. Editorial offices for *Stamp Monthly* and *Flora*.

Stanley Gibbons Currency Ltd

395 Strand, London WC2R 0LX. Fine banknotes and coins of the world, publications and accessories.

Stanley Gibbons Products Ltd
Birmingham Envelope Co Ltd

Stangib House, Sarehole Road, Hall Green, Birmingham B28 8EE. Manilla and plastic folders, specialised envelopes, box and other files, binders, filing trays, cabinets and office equipment.

Stanley Gibbons Advertising Services Ltd

Drury House, Russell Street, Drury Lane, London WC2B 5HD. Advertising for the S.G. Group and the Crown Agents.

Mapsellers Ltd

37 Southampton Street, London WC2E 7HE. Antiquarian map specialists.

StanGib Ltd

601 Franklin Avenue, Garden City, New York, NY, 11530, U.S.A. Stamp sales for the British Post Office and the Crown Agents, retail and wholesale publications.

Stanley Gibbons Merkur GmbH

D–6000 Frankfurt am Main, Zeil 83, West Germany. Rare stamps, covers, postal history material, expertising and auctions.

	Telephone numbers	*Telex numbers*
All London addresses	01–836 8444	28883
Birmingham offices	021–777 7255	—
New York office	(516) 746—4666 and 4667	96–7733
Frankfurt office	0611–287477 and 287454	4189148

Index

Colonial Types

Types of the General Plates used by Messrs. De La Rue & Co. for printing British Colonial Stamps

I. Victorian Key Type

Die I

Die II

Die I

1. The ball of decoration on the second point of the Crown appears as a dark mass of lines.
2. Dark vertical shading separates the front hair from the bun.
3. The vertical line of colour outlining the front of the throat stops at the sixth line of shading on the neck.
4. The white space in the coil of the hair above the curl is roughly the shape of a pin's head.

Die II

1. There are very few lines of colour in the ball and it appears almost white.
2. A white vertical strand of hair appears in place of the dark shading.
3. The line stops at the eighth line of shading.
4. The white space is oblong, with a line of colour partially dividing it at the left end.

Plates numbered 1 and 2 are both Die I. Plates 3 and 4 are Die II.

II. Georgian Key Type

Die I

Die II

Die I

A. The second (thick) line below the name of the country is cut slanting, conforming roughly to the shape of the Crown on each side.

B. The labels of solid colour bearing the words " POSTAGE " and " & REVENUE " are square at the inner top corners.

C. There is a projecting " bud " on the outer spiral of the ornament in each of the lower corners.

Die II

A. The second line is cut vertically on each side of the Crown.

B. The labels curve inwards at the top.

C. There is no " bud " in this position.

Unless otherwise stated in the lists, all stamps with wmk. Multiple Crown CA are Die I while those with wmk. Multiple Script CA are Die II.

Crown Agents 'Chalky', Coloured and Glazed Papers

' Ordinary ' and ' Chalk-surfaced ' Papers

In Great Britain and its Colonies the availability of many postage stamps for revenue purposes made it necessary to provide some safeguard against the illegitimate re-use of stamps with removable cancellations. This was at first secured by the use, where necessary, of fugitive inks and later by the introduction of chalk-surfaced paper, both of which made it difficult to remove any form of obliteration without also damaging the stamp design.

With some exceptions we *do not list* the varieties on chalk-surfaced paper separately, but we have indicated the existence of the papers by the letters " O " (ordinary) and " C " (*chalky*) after the description of all stamps where the chalky paper may be found. The two letters together, signify that the stamp exists on both papers; if a date is given it is that of the first-mentioned paper and the price quoted is that of the cheaper variety. Where no indication is given, the paper is " ordinary ".

Our definition of chalk-surfaced paper applies to a coated paper which shows a black line when touched with silver. The paper used during the Second World War for high values, as in Bermuda, the Leeward Is., etc., was thinly coated with some kind of surfacing which does not react to silver and is therefore regarded (and listed) as " ordinary ". Stamps on chalk-surfaced paper can easily lose this coating through immersion in water.

Another paper introduced during the war as a substitute for " chalky " is rather thick, very white, and glossy, and shows little or no watermark, nor does it show a black line when touched with silver. In the Bahamas high values this paper might be mistaken for the " chalky " (which is thinner and poorer-looking) but for the silver test.

Green and Yellow Papers

These belong to the First World War and immediate post-war period. The issue of stamps printed on paper with coloured surface and white back (commonly called " white-backs ") necessitated a special method of indicating their existence in the Catalogue lists. Owing to further variations in the green and yellow papers the lists were extended, as many of these stamps show one colour on the surface of the paper and another at the back. While there are many variations which will not fall within any hard-and-fast classification, we have adopted the following grouping as being the least likely to cause confusion.

Yellow Paper

(*a*) The original *yellow* paper, usually bright in colour.

(*b*) The " *white backs* ".

(*c*) A bright *lemon* paper. Only stamps with the greenish tinge of true lemons have been put in this group, otherwise they belong to Group (*a*). Stamps of Group (*a*) printed in green sometimes make the paper appear *lemon*, and allowance must be made for this.

(*d*) An *orange-buff* paper, with a distinct brownish (coffee) tinge, not to be confused with a muddy yellow belonging to Group (*a*).

(*e*) The *pale yellow* paper, which has a creamy tone.

Green Paper

(*m*) The original *green* paper, varying considerably through shades of bluish and yellowish green.

(*n*) The " *white backs* ".

(*p*) A paper bluish green on the surface, with " *pale* " or " *olive* " *back*.

(*q*) Paper with a bright green surface, commonly called " *emerald-surfaced* ", with the olive back of Group (*p*).

(*r*) The paper with " *emerald back* ". As (*q*), but with the bright colour at back and front.

Glazed Paper

In 1969 the Crown Agents introduced a new general purpose paper intended for use in conjunction with all current printing processes. It generally has a marked glossy surface but the degree varies according to the process used, being more marked in recess-printed stamps. As it does not respond to the chalky test this presents a further test where previous printings were on chalk-surfaced paper.

Watermarks

Perkins, Bacon

w. 1

w. 2

w. 3

The watermarks in the stamps printed by Messrs. Perkins, Bacon and Co. for various British possessions were (w. 1) *Large Star,* measuring from 15 to 16 mm. across the star from point to point, and about 27 mm. from centre to centre vertically; (w. 2) *Small Star* of similar design, but measuring from 12 to 13½ mm. from point to point, and 24 mm. from centre to centre vertically; and (w. 3) Broad Star, in which the points are broader. The Large Star paper was made for long stamps like Ceylon and St. Helena, the Small Star paper for ordinary size stamps, as Grenada, Barbados, etc.; consequently, when the former was used for the smaller stamps, the watermark only occasionally comes in the centre of the paper, and frequently is so misplaced as to show portions of two stars above and below (this eccentricity will very often determine the watermark when it would be difficult otherwise to test it).

De La Rue and other printers

w. 4

w. 5

w. 6

The watermarks in the stamps printed by Messrs. De La Rue and Co. for various British possessions—not exclusively used for one colony—are (w. 4) a Crown over " CC " (Crown Colonies) for the stamps of ordinary size, (w. 5) for the stamps of larger size and (w. 6) a Crown over " CA " (Crown Agents).

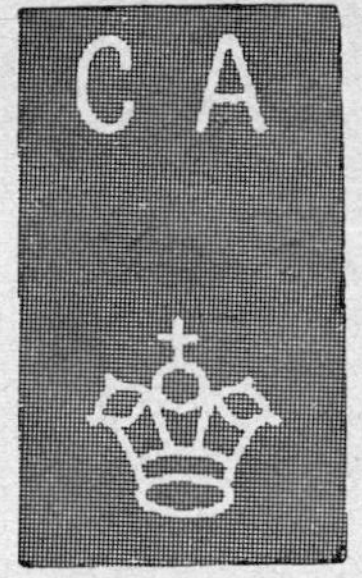

w. 7

w. 8

w. 9

There is another (w. **7**) properly described as " CA over Crown". This watermark was specially made for paper on which it was intended to print long fiscal stamps of the size and shape of those (which have been used postally) in Sierra Leone, Western Australia, etc. It occupies twice the space of the ordinary Crown CA watermark. When stamps of normal size are printed on paper with this watermark, the watermark is *sideways*, and it takes a horizontal pair of postage stamps to show the entire watermark.

In 1904 the watermark described as " Multiple Crown CA " (w. **8**), was introduced. On stamps of the ordinary size portions of two or three watermarks appear, and on the large-sized stamps a greater number can be observed.

In **1921** yet another change was made, resulting in what is known as the " Multiple Script CA " watermark, in which the letters are in Script character, while the Crown is of distinctly different shape (Type w. **9**).

w. **9***a*

w. **9***b*

w. **9** *Watermark Errors*
As a result of a crown falling away from two of the dandy rolls (the rolls which impress the watermark in the paper pulp) and their subsequent replacement by crowns of a different type known as St. Edward's crown, four varieties of the Script CA watermark recur among the 1950–52 printings of several colonies. On one dandy roll the mishap occurred in a " Crown " row as shown in Types w. **9***a* and w. **9***b* and the resulting faulty paper was used for Seychelles, Johore and the postage due stamps of nine colonies. On the other dandy roll the error was in a " Crown CA " row and produced varieties in Bahamas, St. Kitts-Nevis and Singapore.

w. **12**

w. **13**

The " Multiple St. Edward's Crown CA " watermark (Type w. **12**) was introduced for Colonial issues in 1957. Besides the change in the Crown the " CA " reverted to the block capitals. In 1966 the block watermark began to appear sideways and these are generally listed as separate sets.
Type w. **13**, " Multiple PTM ", was introduced for new Malayan issues in November, 1961.

w. **14**

The " Multiple Crown CA Diagonal " watermark was introduced in 1974, being used first for some of the Churchill Centenary stamps.

Australian States

w. **10**

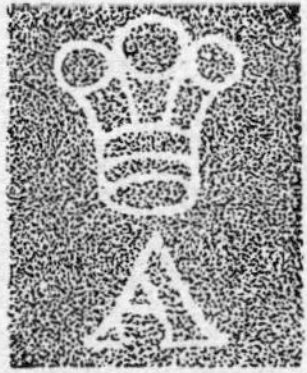

w. **11**

We illustrate here two watermarks which are found in the stamps of the Australian states, to avoid frequent repetition of them in the text.

KINDLY NOTE
Watermarks are normally shown as seen from the FRONT of the stamp. Where no watermark is noted, the stamps are without distinctive watermark.
We do not normally list inverted or reversed watermarks as separate varieties in this Catalogue but such varieties in the Commonwealth stamps of the present reign are listed in the more specialised *Elizabethan Catalogue* and, of course, in the *Great Britain Specialised Catalogue*.

Information for the collector

The anatomy of a postage stamp is made up of the following parts: paper, watermark, printing process, separation and gum which are briefly dealt with in the following notes.

Paper

Many of the early issues were printed on hand-made paper, which was produced sheet by sheet, but most stamps are printed on machine-made paper which is turned out in continuous rolls. The greatest variation in paper is, therefore, to be found on the early issues. The following is a description of the main types of paper used in stamp production:—

Wove paper, on which the great majority of stamps are printed, has a plain, even texture which is created when the wet pulp is brought into contact with finely-netted wire gauze mesh (i.e., the " dandy roll ") of the paper-making machine. Unless otherwise stated in the catalogue, it can be assumed that all stamps are on wove paper.

Laid paper is similarly impressed in the wet state, but with closely-set parallel lines, either vertically or horizontally laid.

Quadrillé (or squared) paper is a form of laid paper where crossed lines produce squares or rectangles.

Bâtonné paper is a thin, " bank " letter paper water-marked with well-spaced parallel lines (intended as a guide to neat writing). This can be either wove or laid and in the latter case the laid lines come between the " batons " (French for a staff).

Granite paper, used for many of the stamps of Switzerland, can be easily distinguished by the coloured lines in its texture.

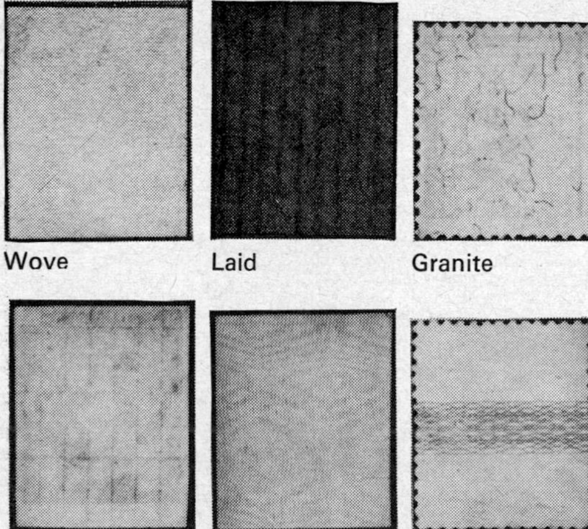

Wove Laid Granite

Quadrillé Moiré Burelé band

Kinds of Paper

Paper is sometimes coated or *chalk-surfaced* and this was often used to make it difficult to clean off post-marks and use the stamps again. In the Catalogue all stamps are deemed to be on " ordinary paper " unless described as " chalky " or " chalk-surfaced ". There are degrees of coating and our definition of chalk-surfaced paper applies to paper which shows a black line when touched with silver. For further notes about Crown Agents " chalky" , coloured and glazed papers see pages xi and xii. *Enamel* and *glazed* papers are other forms of coating often found in the stamps of Portugal and Colonies.

Coloured paper. Unless otherwise stated, stamps are printed on white paper, but where a coloured paper is used (and by this we mean coloured right through), the colour of the paper is given in italics, thus:—

Black/*yellow* (= black on yellow).

Toned paper can be expressed as paper which is off-white but which could not be described as being of any definite colour. There is a tendency nowadays, to introduce specially white paper (either ordinary or chalky), as in Great Britain, Australia, New Zealand, etc.

Native papers, made from rice or silk fibre, are very distinctive and are found in early issues of China, Japan and Indian Native States.

Manilla paper, made from manilla hemp or wood fibre, is normally used for cheap envelopes and news-paper wrappers. It is coarse, usually brown in colour, and may be wove or laid.

Moiré consists of a very fine pattern and examples of this are found on the backs of early Mexican stamps.

Burelage is a fine pattern or network *printed* on the face of the stamp beneath the design or on the back, another device to discourage forgery or tampering with the postmark. There are examples in the early issues of Denmark, in Queensland and the 1932 issue of Venezuela.

Ribbed paper is distinguished by very fine parallel lines on the front and back, and there are examples of this on the first issue of Austria, and in many stamps of Switzerland.

Silk threads. Coloured silk threads embodied in the paper. This was used as an experiment by John Dickinson but the best known examples are in the early issues of Switzerland.

Papers come in a wide range of thicknesses from *pelure*, a very thin, hard, tough paper which is trans-lucent, to thick " *carton* " paper.

The recognition of paper assumes importance when classifying stamps which were successively printed on different kinds of paper.

Watermarks

A watermark is a device or pattern produced by pressure on the wet paper pulp during manufacture thereby thinning the paper. It can usually be seen when a stamp is held up to the light or laid face down on a black watermark detector or tray. If still obscure, a few drops of benzine (petroleum ether 40/60) on the stamp should reveal the watermark, but note that this can affect the colours of a photogravure stamp. Remember also that benzine is highly inflammable.

A device which occurs once on every stamp is called a *single* watermark; a *multiple* watermark is a device repeated closely throughout the sheet so that each stamp shows parts of several devices. A *sheet* watermark is a pattern extending over a part of a sheet, sometimes repeated several times in the sheet. In sheet watermarks there are usually a number of stamps in the sheet without watermark. A *papermakers'* watermark usually consists of a name or a device without postal significance (in contradistinction to a sheet watermark supplied to the order of the postal authority) and only occupies a very small part of the sheet. These are normally ignored as most of the stamps would be without watermark, although copies bearing a portion of the watermark may be worth a premium. Some British Colonial issues have watermarks in the sheet margins in addition to those on the stamps, such as the words " CROWN AGENTS " or the name of the Colony. These are ignored in the Catalogue as they do not normally affect the stamps unless the watermark is misplaced and individual letters happen to fall on the row of stamps adjoining the margin.

Normal

Inverted

Reversed

Reversed and inverted

Sideways

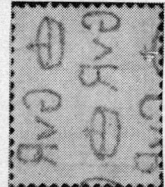

Sideways inverted

The above illustrations showing positions of watermarks are as seen when looking at the backs of the stamps.

Watermarks normally read correctly through the front of the stamp, showing in reverse on the back. Hence in the Catalogue they are always described as seen from the *front* of the stamp. Sometimes watermarks occur sideways, inverted or reversed, etc. We normally list sideways watermarks, but *inverted and reversed watermarks are outside the scope of this catalogue*. They are, however, included in the *Elizabethan Catalogue* as this is more detailed and they are, of course, listed in our *Great Britain Specialised Catalogue*. They are caused through feeding the paper incorrectly and in the older issues sheets were often fed quite indiscriminately so that inverted and reversed watermarks in these issues are often relatively common. In the manufacture of Great Britain booklets from specially prepared sheets about half the stamps have the watermark inverted.

Printing Processes

There are four main processes used for printing postage stamps: Recess-printing, Photogravure, Typography and Lithography.

Recess-printing. In this process, also known as Line-engraving, Intaglio, or *Taille douce*, the design is cut into the plate which is then inked and wiped so that the ink remains only in the recesses. The paper is then placed against the plate under great pressure, whereby the ink is picked up from the grooves and, in the form of the stamp design, stands out in relief on the paper. The raised image can usually be felt with the finger.

The *Die* is the engraved original from which printing plates (or cylinders) are produced in recess-printing, photogravure or typography. New plates made from the original die sometimes show slight differences from the original plates and dies are sometimes re-engraved, often producing marked differences.

Photogravure, also called Rotogravure, Heliogravure, etc., is basically another form of recess-printing. The photograph design is chemically treated and transferred to a copper plate and etched. The surface of the plate holds the ink in a number of tiny cells (or dots) caused by the superimposition of a fine grid or screen; the intensity of colour varies according to the depth of the cells. In modern photogravure the " plate " is usually a cylinder in high-speed, multicolour rotary presses. Some of these print individually cut sheets but in really fast printing the paper is fed " in the web " from large rolls and is cut into sheets afterwards.

Typography, also called Surface-printing or Letterpress-printing, is the opposite to recess-printing in that the image is in "relief" on the plate. When the ink is applied by a roller only the raised portions, i.e. the design, receive the ink. The effect of pressure in printing usually causes the design to stand out in relief on the back of the stamp.

Lithography. Here the design is transferred to the plate or "stone" in a special greasy ink. The flat surface is then moistened so that when the printing ink is applied it adheres only to the greased portion which may then be impressed on the paper. In *offset-lithography,* the image is taken up by a rubber "blanket" which "offsets" it onto the paper, while in modern *photo-lithography* the stamp design is photographically processed onto an etched zinc plate which is attached to the cylinder of a rotary press. *Delacryl* is an advanced and refined form of lithography using improved screens which was developed by De La Rue and Co. in 1966.

Embossing was used in some early issues, notably in the 1847–54 issue of Great Britain, Gambia, Heligoland, Sardinia, etc. The relief effect is achieved by the use of two dies, one engraved in relief and the other in recess, between which the paper is pressed. This can be done with or without colour.

This is the process often used for printing postal stationery. Embossed stamps cut from envelopes etc. should not be confused with embossed postage stamps, which must be adhesive to qualify for listing in the Catalogue.

Gold Blocking and Embossing. Gold blocking is the transfer and adhesion of foil to paper under heat and pressure. Embossing on stamps raises the design above the surrounding areas of paper. This may be achieved either on foil blocking and embossing machines or by printing and embossing on the photogravure machine. Examples are found in modern commemorative issues of Great Britain.

Type-set is the term given to stamps printed from movable type so that each stamp in the sheet is set up separately, generally producing a number of varieties. This process is sometimes resorted to when the ordinary facilities for stamp production are lacking and examples are found in the Postmasters' stamps of United States and Confederate States. A few stamps have been produced on *typewriters,* notably Long Island and Uganda.

In recent times it is not unusual to find stamps produced by a combination of two or more processes.

Recess-printing	Typography	Lithography

Appearance of the Printing Unit:

Design is recessed	Design is raised	Design is level

Sectional View through Middle showing Shape of Printing Surface:

Sectional View of stamp showing effect of Pressure on the Paper:

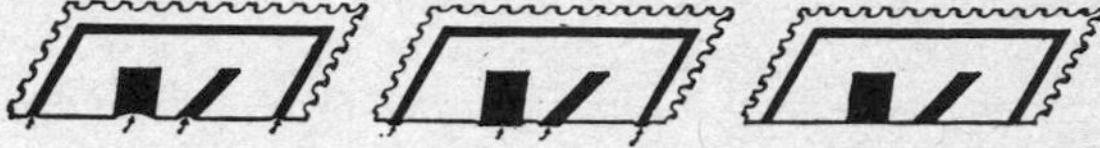

Design indented on Back	Design embossed on Back	Whole Stamp quite flat

Separation

The very first postage stamps were *imperforate* as there were no means available for perforating stamps. They had to be separated by scissors, hence the importance of wide margins when collecting imperf. stamps, particularly where the stamps later appeared with perforations which could be trimmed off so as to create imperf. stamps. Imperf. errors of stamps which normally exist only perforated are usually listed in pairs where pairs are known to exist.

Rouletting was the next form of separation to be introduced. It is a form of perforation in which the paper is partly cut through but no paper is removed. This may be done with a wheel or a series of wheels with small points on their circumference. The various types of roulette are usually expressed in French terms descriptive of the type of cut or the appearance of the edges of the stamps when separated. Thus *Percé* ("pierced") *en arc* is a roulette in which the cuts are curved; *Percé en lignes* implied straight cut; *Percé en croix* means cuts in the shape of little crosses, forming lozenges with the outer corners open; and *Percé en scie* is applied to the distinctive saw-toothed roulette, where the edges of the stamps are like the edge of a saw. *Percé en points* means pin roulette, often called pin perforation in error. In addition there are oblique roulette, serpentine roulette and zig-zag roulette. Roulettes are sometimes indicated by the measurements of a perforation gauge.

Perforation was invented by Henry Archer and first used in Great Britain stamps in 1850. It differs from rouletting in that a part of the paper is punched out by a series of holes between the stamps.

Forms of Separation

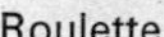

Roulette

Imperforate

Percé en arc

Serpentine roulette

Zig-zag roulette

Perforation

A *line perforation* is produced by a machine with one line of pins which punches a single row of holes at a time. A *comb perforation* is the result of a machine punching three sides of each stamp in a row at the same time. When a whole sheet of stamps is perforated in one operation by punches arranged in transverse rows, the result is called a *harrow* perforation.

As a general rule a line perforation produces irregular corners on a stamp and a comb perforation regular ones, but sometimes a line-perforated stamp has perfect corners, because of a chance matching intersection of the rows of holes. Also, a comb-perforated stamp may have irregular corners due to an imperfection in the comb. Difficulties in distinguishing line or comb perforated stamps can usually be resolved by the study of a corner marginal block of four.

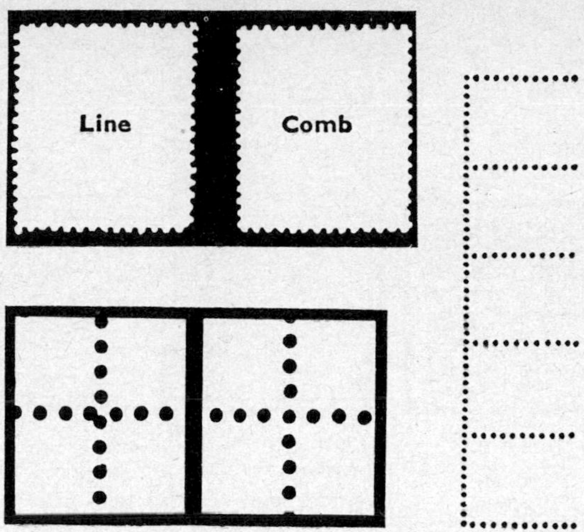

Examples of Line and Comb Perforation

Comb Perforation

The " gauge " of a perforation is measured by the number of holes in a space of two centimetres, indicated by a perforation gauge. In the Catalogue they are normally given to the nearest half and the *Instanta Gauge* is our standard. Where perforations are exactly on the Quarter or Three-quarter measurement, the Catalogue quotes the higher figures, i.e. $11\frac{3}{4} \times 12\frac{1}{4} = 12 \times 12\frac{1}{2}$.

The various perforations are expressed as follows:—

Perf. 14: Perforated alike on all sides.

Perf. 14×15: Compound perforation. The first figure refers to top and bottom, the second to left and right sides.

Perf. 14, $14\frac{1}{2}$: Perforated approximately $14\frac{1}{4}$.

Perf. 14–15: Perforations are irregular in the sheet, and stamps may measure anything between 14 and 15.

Perf. compound of 14 *and* 15: This is a general description indicating that two gauges of perforation have been used, but not *necessarily* on opposite sides of the stamp. It could be one side in one gauge and three in the other; or two adjacent sides with the same gauge.

Perf. 11 *and* 14 *mixed*: This indicates stamps that were perforated in one gauge, and re-perforated in another.

Imperf. × *perf.* 14 means imperf. at top and bottom and perf. 14 at sides, whilst *Perf.* 14 × *imperf.* means the reverse.

Perf. × imperf.

Imperf. between (vertical pair)

Imperf. horizontally (vertical pair)

Imperf. between is a common type of variety in which one row of perforations has been missed. Thus *Imperf. between* (*vert. pair*) means a vertical pair which is imperf. horizontally between the stamps. *Imperf. horiz.* (*vert. pair*) means a vertical pair which is imperf. horizontally not only between the two stamps but also on the top and bottom, showing that it comes from a sheet on which several of the rows were not perforated horizontally. Naturally the missing perforations can just as easily occur in the vertical rows and these are collected in horizontal pairs.

In this Catalogue we do not list stamps which are merely imperf. between stamp and margin.

Gum

The gum normally used on stamps has been Gum Arabic until the late sixties when synthetic adhesives were introduced. Harrison and Sons Ltd. for instance use *Polyvinyl Alcohol,* known as PVA. This is almost invisible except for a slight yellowish tinge which was incorporated to make it possible to see that the stamps have been gummed. Because of its advantages in hot countries, as stamps do not curl and sheets are less likely to stick together, it is probable that it will be used by other printers. Gum arabic and PVA are not distinguished in the lists except that where a stamp exists with both forms this is indicated in footnotes. The *Elizabethan Catalogue* does provide separate listing of PVA gum for Great Britain. Stamps described as being *Self-adhesive* are issued on backing paper from which they are peeled off and reaffixed to mail. There are examples of this in Sierra Leone.

As most stamps are issued with gum we only mention the exceptions in our lists and gum is only described where this helps to identify different printings. One or two countries still issue stamps without gum and these are covered by catalogue notes.

'Specimen' stamps

Originally stamps overprinted "SPECIMEN" were for distribution to post offices or for official records but after the Universal Postal Union was established, supplies were sent to the U.P.U. for distribution to member countries.

British Commonwealth stamps were overprinted "SPECIMEN" in various types and sizes, generally by machine but handstamps are also known. They are normally applied horizontally but some read vertically. From the late 1920's the stamps were mostly perforated with the word, usually horse-shoe shaped, but they are also known in a straight line, normally applied diagonally. The distribution of Specimen stamps by British Commonwealth countries ceased in 1948. Examples of some of the more usual types of overprints and perforations are shown here.

Types of Specimen Overprints

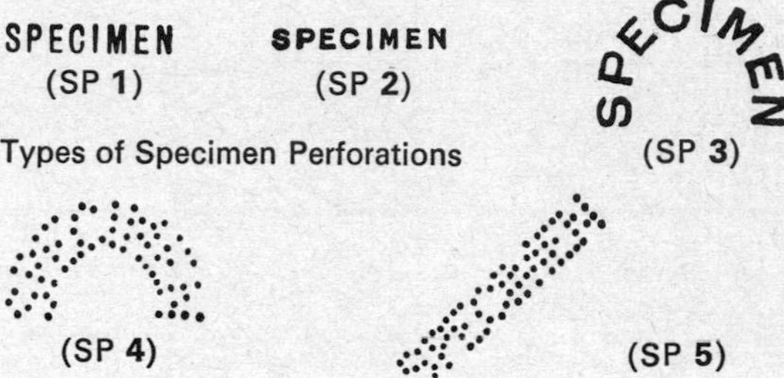

Prices for stamps up to £1 are quoted in sets; higher values are priced singly after the colours, thus "(S. £20)".

We have indicated whether individual high value stamps are overprinted, handstamped or perforated but where we have not done so for lack of space this can be inferred from the date or it can be assumed to be the same as for the lower values quoted as a set. Where more than one type exists our price is for the cheapest. Some sets are mixed, overprinted and perforated, and are indicated as "Optd./Perf.". "H/S" denotes handstamped.

Specimens are not quoted in Great Britain as these are fully listed according to their types in the *Great Britain Specialised Catalogue*.

We only record specimen stamps distributed through the U.P.U., and not printers' samples nor special or irregular Specimen issues. Specimen stamps may be found in pairs or strips of three, four or five but their survival in multiples (even pairs) is most unusual and these command substantial premiums.

Used Stamps

Our used prices are normally for stamps postally used but may be for stamps "cancelled-to-order" where this practice exists.

Pen-cancellation usually denotes fiscal use and such stamps are outside the scope of this catalogue but occasionally postally used copies were pen-cancelled, as in the first issue of Finland.

Luminescence

This term refers to stamps issued overprinted with *fluorescent* or *phosphorescent* bands or printed on paper or with ink containing fluorescence or phosphorescence. These stamps are for use in connection with electronic mail-sorting machines and are now issued by a number of countries which have a very heavy flow of mail. Where this is applied in the form of bands, as in Great Britain, Canada and Japan, they are visible to the naked eye and so are listed. The general practice is now to treat the whole stamp and these can be distinguished by the use of ultra-violet lamps of the correct range. Such stamps are listed only when there are also some other means of distinguishing them. Where this is not so, they are recorded in footnotes or headings.

Colours

Where two or more colours are used, the central portion of the stamp is in the first colour given and other colours are in the order of appearance moving from the centre of the stamp unless otherwise stated. Where four or more colours are used the term multi-coloured is usually employed. Where more than one colour is used the stamps are usually printed in more than one operation. This frequently produces some variation in registration resulting sometimes in unusual varieties, but these are outside the scope of this catalogue. However, major errors such as inverted centres are listed. Aniline colours are derived from coal-tar and have a particular brilliance which generally shows through the back of the stamp.

The following and similar abbreviations are in general use throughout the catalogue to avoid unnecessary overrunning of lines:—Bl. (blue); blk. (black); bwn., brn. (brown); car., carm. (carmine); choc.(chocolate); clar. (claret); emer. (emerald); grn. (green); ind. (indigo); mag. (magenta); mar. (maroon); mve. (mauve); ol. (olive); orge. (orange); pk. (pink); pur. (purple); scar. (scarlet); sep. (sepia); turq. (turquoise); ultram. (ultramarine); verm. (vermilion); vio. (violet); yell. (yellow).

Colours of overprints and surcharges are in black unless otherwise stated. Other colours are given either in the heading or by the following abbreviations in brackets after the description of the stamp, thus (B.)=blue, (Br.)=brown, (C.)=carmine, (G.)=green, (Mag.)=magenta, (Mve.)=mauve, (Ol.)=olive, (O.)=orange, (P.)=purple, (Pk.)=pink, (R.)=red, (Sil.)=silver, (V.)=violet, (Vm.) or (Verm.)=vermilion, (W.)=white, (Y.)=yellow.

Booklets

Booklet stamps are only listed where they can be distinguished by their perforations. In the Br. Commonwealth Catalogue booklet panes are listed where they contain different stamps *se-tenant* or where they contain an attached label.

Coils

Coil stamps are issued in rolls for use in automatic vending machines. They are only listed where there are perforation differences to distinguish them or where the watermark appears sideways, as in Great Britain.

Fiscals

This catalogue is restricted to stamps which are valid for postal use. Many stamps have validity for both postal and fiscal use, i.e. on documents, as revenue or receipt stamps, etc. Others are issued for fiscal use only and these are only listed where they have been expressly authorised for use as postage stamps, usually owing to a temporary shortage. Where fiscal stamps are overprinted for postal use they are included in the ordinary listing but where this is not the case they are known as *Postal Fiscal* stamps and listed under this heading.

Double Prints

This results from a sheet of stamps going through the press twice and such authenticated errors are listed. However, a similar effect can be obtained in offset-litho where the second impression is obtained by contact with the " blanket " and the impression is usually fainter. " Blanket " offsets are outside the scope of this Catalogue.

Bisects

Occasionally during a temporary shortage of stamps of a particular value stamps of a higher denomination are bisected (or trisected etc.) and used on the mail. These are only listed where the practice has been expressly authorised and the prices quoted are for stamps used on large piece or cover and dated during the period of authorisation.

Re-entry

A kind of variety found on recess-printed stamps in which the whole or part of the design is duplicated or deepened. If the roller-die is incorrectly rocked on the plate the impression can be scraped off and the roller-die is " re-entered " in the correct position and may thus produce a double impression of part of the design.

Tête-bêche

Stamps or overprints printed upside down in relation to one another. These are sometimes errors in the positioning of clichés within the plate, or come about through special arrangements of sheets used for making up into booklets.

Se-tenant

(=joined together) Stamps of different denominations joined together or a variety in pair with normal, etc.

Prices

The prices in the left-hand column are for unused stamps and those in the right-hand column for used. Prices are given in pence and pounds: 100 pence (p) = 1 pound (£1). For further notes about prices, see page xxi.

Set prices are generally for one of each value in the set excluding shades, dies, etc., but including major colour changes. Where there are alternative shades, etc., generally the cheapest is included and the number of stamps in the set is always stated.

Value Added Tax

Stanley Gibbons Ltd announce that stamp pricing in this and all other current S.G. catalogues is on a tax inclusive basis as at the date of going to press. They are able to absorb V.A.T. due to their vast exports and the fact that much of their business is in stamps over 100 years old. However, as in the past, price changes will reflect the international market and in addition, if there is any change in the rate of V.A.T. this may be reflected in an increase or decrease in the quoted prices.

Printers

The names of the following printers are often given in abbreviated form:—

A.B.N. Co.	American Bank Note Co., New York.
A. & M.	Alden & Mowbray Ltd., Oxford.
Aspioti-Elka (Aspiotis)	Aspioti-Elka, Corfu, Greece.
B.A.B.N.	British American Bank Note Co., Ottawa.
B.W.	Bradbury Wilkinson & Co., Ltd.
C.B.N.	Canadian Bank Note Co., Ottawa.
Continental B.N. Co.	Continental Bank Note Co.
Courvoisier	Imprimerie Courvoisier S.A., Le-Chaux-de-Fonds, Switzerland.
D.L.R.	De La Rue & Co., Ltd., London.
Edila	Editions de l'Aubetin, S.A.
Enschedé	Joh. Enschedé en Zonen, Haarlem, Netherlands.
Format	Format International Security Printers, Ltd., London.
Harrison	Harrison & Sons, Ltd., London.
Heraclio Fournier	Heraclio Fournier S.A., Vitoria, Spain.
J.W.	John Waddington of Kirkstall, Ltd.
P.B.	Perkins Bacon Ltd., London.
Questa	Questa Colour Security Printers, Ltd.
Walsall	Walsall Security Printers, Ltd.
Waterlow	Waterlow & Sons, Ltd., London.

Illustrations

Illustrations of stamps, overprints, surcharges and watermarks are actual size. In the case of stamps that are too large to fit the catalogue column the illustrations are reduced and the actual measurements of the design are given.

Stamps in sets that are not illustrated are the same size and format as the value shown unless otherwise indicated.

Abbreviations Used

Anniv.	Anniversary.
B.A.	Buenos Aires.
C, c	Chalky paper.
Des.	Designer; designed.
Diag.	Diagonal; diagonally.
Eng.	Engraver; engraved.
F.C.	Fiscal Cancellation.
H/S	Handstamped.
Horiz.	Horizontal; horizontally.
Imp., Imperf.	Imperforate (not Perforated).
Inscr.	Inscribed.
L.	Left.
Litho.	Lithographed.
mm.	Millimetres.
MS	Miniature sheet.
N.Y.	New York.
O, o	Ordinary paper.
Opt(d).	Overprint(ed).
P or P-c.	Pen-cancelled.
P., Pf. or Perf.	Perforated.
Pr.	Pair.
Percé en arc.	Perforated in curves.
Percé en scie.	Perforated with a saw-edge.
Photo.	Photogravure.
Pin Perf.	Perforated without removing any paper.
Ptd.	Printed.
R.	Right.
Recess	Recess-printed.
Roto.	Rotogravure.
Roul.	Rouletted—a broken line of cuts.
S.	SPECIMEN (overprint).
Surch.	Surcharge(d).
T.C.	Telegraph Cancellation.
T.	Type.
Typo.	Typographed.
Un.	Unused.
Us.	Used.
Vert.	Vertical; Vertically.
W. or wmk.	Watermark.
Wmk. s.	Watermark sideways.

(†)=Does not exist.

(—) (or a blank price column)=Exists, or may exist, but price cannot be quoted.

/ between colours means "on" and the colour following is that of the paper on which the stamp is printed.

Building Your Collection

We would like to help you build your collection and Stanley Gibbons offers an unrivalled range of services which make this possible.
To see our world-famous stock we hope you can arrange a visit to our 391 Strand shop or our Specialist and Rare Stamp showrooms at Romano House, 399 Strand. The Specialist Register is available to record your special requirements if we cannot offer immediately.

If you would prefer to examine stamps in your own home the Approval Service can send you attractive selections of fine stamps in various price ranges, no matter where you live.
Our auctions frequently include material of interest and *Stamp Monthly* carries hundreds of offers every month. Brochures with full details of all these services are available on request.

Prices quoted in this catalogue are our selling prices at the time the book went to press. They are for stamps in fine average condition; in issues where condition varies we may ask more for the superb and less for the sub-standard. In the case of unused stamps, our prices are for stamps lightly hinged. Prices for used stamps refer to postally used copies (or cancelled-to-order in some modern issues). All prices are subject to change without prior notice and we give no guarantee to supply all stamps priced, since it is not possible to keep every catalogued item perpetually in stock. We will be pleased, however, to forward lists of current offers on request.

We are proud that we are helping many thousands of people throughout the world build their collections and enjoy a lifetime's hobby. We would welcome hearing from you so that we may be of service.

Stanley Gibbons Ltd.

For your Information . . .

Minimum Price

The minimum price quoted is 5p. This represents a handling charge rather than a basis for valuing common stamps. Where the actual value of a stamp is less than 5p this may be apparent when set prices are shown, particularly for sets including a number of 5p stamps. It therefore follows that in valuing common stamps the 5p catalogue price should not be reckoned automatically since it covers a variation in real scarcity.
For further notes about prices, see page xx.

Guarantee

All stamps are guaranteed genuine originals in the following terms:—
If not as described, and returned by the purchaser within six years, we undertake to refund the price paid to us and our liability will thereby be discharged. If any stamp is certified as genuine by the Expert Committee of the Royal Philatelic Society, London, or of the British Philatelic Federation Ltd. the purchaser shall not be entitled to make any claim against us for any error, omission or mistake in such certificate.

Finally please note . . .

Stanley Gibbons catalogue numbers are recognised universally and any individual stamp can be identified by quoting the catalogue number (the one at the left of the column) prefixed by the country name and the letters "S.G." Do not confuse the catalogue number with the bold face Type numbers which refer to illustrations.

Whilst we welcome information and suggestions we must ask correspondents to include the cost of postage for the return of any stamps submitted plus registration where appropriate.
Where information is solicited purely for the benefit of the enquirer we regret we cannot undertake to reply unless stamps or reply coupons are sent to cover the postage.

Stamps not listed in this catalogue (unless they are new issues) are almost certainly not adhesive postage stamps but Revenue, Local or other issues outside its scope.

The recognised Expert Committees in this country are those of the Royal Philatelic Society, 41 Devonshire Place, London, W1N 1PE, and of the British Philatelic Federation Ltd., 1 Whitehall Place, London SW1A 2HE. These Expert Committees do not undertake valuations under any circumstances and fees are payable for their services.

We regret we do not give opinions as to the genuineness of stamps, nor do we identify stamps or number them by our Catalogue.

INTERNATIONAL PHILATELIC GLOSSARY

English	*French*	*German*	*Spanish*	*Italian*
Agate	Agate	Achat	Agata	Agata
Air stamp	Timbre de la poste aérienne	Flugpostmarke	Sello de correo aéreo	Francobollo per posta aereo
Apple-green	Vert-pomme	Apfelgrün	Verde manzana	Verde mela
Barred	Annulé par barres	Balkenentwertung	Anulado con barras	Sbarrato
Bisected	Timbre coupé	Halbiert	Partido en dos	Frazionato
Bistre	Bistre	Bister	Bistre	Bistro
Bistre-brown	Brun-bistre	Bisterbraun	Castaño bistre	Bruno-bistro
Black	Noir	Schwarz	Negro	Nero
Blackish Brown	Brun-noir	Schwärzlichbraun	Castaño negruzco	Bruno nerastro
Blackish Green	Vert foncé	Schwärzlichgrün	Verde negruzco	Verde nerastro
Blackish Olive	Olive foncé	Schwärzlicholiv	Oliva negruzco	Oliva nerastro
Block of four	Bloc de quatre	Viererblock	Bloque de cuatro	Bloco di quattro
Blue	Bleu	Blau	Azul	Azzurro
Blue-green	Vert-bleu	Blaugrün	Verde azul	Verde azzurro
Bluish Violet	Violet bleuâtre	Bläulichviolett	Violeta azulado	Violetto azzurrastro
Booklet	Carnet	Heft	Cuadernillo	Libretto
Bright Blue	Bleu vif	Lebhaftblau	Azul vivo	Azzurro vivo
Bright Green	Vert vif	Lebhaftgrün	Verde vivo	Verde vivo
Bright Purple	Mauve vif	Lebhaftpurpur	Púrpura vivo	Porpora vivo
Bronze-green	Vert-bronze	Bronzegrün	Verde bronce	Verde bronzo
Brown	Brun	Braun	Castaño	Bruno
Brown-lake	Carmin-brun	Braunlack	Laca castaño	Lacca bruno
Brown-purple	Pourpre-brun	Braunpurpur	Púrpura castaño	Porpora bruno
Brown-red	Rouge-brun	Braunrot	Rojo castaño	Rosso bruno
Buff	Chamois	Sämisch	Anteado	Camoscio
Cancellation	Oblitération	Entwertung	Cancelación	Annullamento
Cancelled	Annulé	Gestempelt	Cancelado	Annullato
Carmine	Carmin	Karmin	Carmín	Carminio
Carmine-red	Rouge-carmin	Karminrot	Rojo carmín	Rosso carminio
Centred	Centré	Zentriert	Centrado	Centrato
Cerise	Rouge-cerise	Kirschrot	Color de ceresa	Color Ciliegia
Chalk-surfaced paper	Papier couché	Kreidepapier	Papel estucado	Carta gessata
Chalky Blue	Bleu terne	Kreideblau	Azul turbio	Azzurro smorto
Charity stamp	Timbre de bienfaisance	Wohltätigkeits-marke	Sello de beneficenza	Francobollo di beneficenza
Chestnut	Marron	Kastanienbraun	Castaño rojo	Marrone
Chocolate	Chocolat	Schokolade	Chocolate	Cioccolato
Cinnamon	Cannelle	Zimtbraun	Canela	Cannella
Claret	Grenat	Weinrot	Rojo vinoso	Vinaccia
Cobalt	Cobalt	Kobalt	Cobalto	Cobalto
Colour	Couleur	Farbe	Color	Colore
Comb-perforation	Dentelure en peigne	Kammzähnung, Reihenzähnung	Dentado de peine	Dentellatura e pettine
Commemorative stamp	Timbre commémoratif	Gedenkmarke	Sello conmemorativo	Francobollo commemorativo
Crimson	Cramoisi	Karmesin	Carmesí	Cremisi
Deep Blue	Bleu foncé	Dunkelblau	Azul oscuro	Azzurro scuro
Deep Bluish Green	Vert-bleu foncé	Dunkelbläulichgrün	Verde azulado oscuro	Verde azzurro scuro
Design	Dessin	Markenbild	Diseño	Disegno
Die	Matrice	Urstempel, Type, Platte	Cuño	Conio, Matrice
Double	Double	Doppelt	Doble	Doppio

English	French	German	Spanish	Italian
Drab	Olive terne	Trüboliv	Oliva turbio	Oliva smorto
Dull Green	Vert terne	Trübgrün	Verde turbio	Verde smorto
Dull Purple	Mauve terne	Trübpurpur	Púrpura turbio	Porpora smorto
Embossing	Impression en relief	Prägedruck	Impresión en relieve	Impressione a relievo
Emerald	Vert-eméraude	Smaragdgrün	Esmeralda	Smeraldo
Engraved	Gravé	Graviert	Grabado	Inciso
Error	Erreur	Fehler, Fehldruck	Error	Errore
Essay	Essai	Probedruck	Ensayo	Saggio
Express letter stamp	Timbre pour lettres par exprès	Eilmarke	Sello de urgencia	Francobollo per espresso
Fiscal stamp	Timbre fiscal	Stempelmarke	Sello fiscal	Francobollo fiscale
Flesh	Chair	Fleischfarben	Carne	Carnicino
Forgery	Faux, Falsification	Fälschung	Falsificación	Falso, Falsificazione
Frame	Cadre	Rahmen	Marco	Cornice
Granite paper	Papier avec fragments de fils de soie	Faserpapier	Papel con filamentos	Carta con fili di seta
Green	Vert	Grün	Verde	Verde
Greenish Blue	Bleu verdâtre	Grünlichblau	Azul verdoso	Azzurro verdastro
Greenish Yellow	Jaune-vert	Grünlichgelb	Amarillo verdoso	Giallo verdastro
Grey	Gris	Grau	Gris	Grigio
Grey-blue	Bleu-gris	Graublau	Azul gris	Azzurro grigio
Grey-green	Vert gris	Graugrün	Verde gris	Verde grigio
Gum	Gomme	Gummi	Goma	Gomma
Gutter	Interpanneau	Zwischensteg	Espacio blanco entre dos grupos	Ponte
Imperforate	Non-dentelé	Geschnitten	Sin dentar	Non dentellato
Indigo	Indigo	Indigo	Azul indigo	Indaco
Inscription	Inscription	Inschrift	Inscripción	Dicitura
Inverted	Renversé	Kopfstehend	Invertido	Capovolto
Issue	Emission	Ausgabe	Emisión	Emissione
Laid	Vergé	Gestreift	Listado	Vergato
Lake	Lie de vin	Lackfarbe	Laca	Lacca
Lake-brown	Brun-carmin	Lackbraun	Castaño laca	Bruno lacca
Lavender	Bleu-lavande	Lavendel	Color de alhucema	Lavanda
Lemon	Jaune-citron	Zitrongelb	Limón	Limone
Light Blue	Bleu clair	Hellblau	Azul claro	Azzurro chlaro
Lilac	Lilas	Lila	Lila	Lilla
Line perforation	Dentelure en lignes	Linienzähnung	Dentado en linea	Dentellatura lineare
Lithography	Lithographie	Steindruck	Litografía	Litografia
Local	Timbre de poste locale	Lokalpostmarke	Emisión local	Emissione locale
Lozenge roulette	Percé en losanges	Rautenförmiger Durchstich	Picadura en rombos	Perforazione a losanghe
Magenta	Magenta	Magentarot	Magenta	Magenta
Margin	Marge	Rand	Borde	Margine
Maroon	Marron pourpré	Dunkelrotpurpur	Púrpura rojo oscuro	Marrone rossastro
Mauve	Mauve	Malvenfarbe	Malva	Malva
Multicoloured	Polychrome	Mehrfarbig	Multicolores	Policromo
Myrtle-green	Vert myrte	Myrtengrün	Verde mirto	Verde mirto
New Blue	Bleu ciel vif	Neublau	Azul nuevo	Azzurro nuovo
Newspaper stamp	Timbre pour journaux	Zeitungsmarke	Sello para periódicos	Francobollo per giornali
Obliteration	Oblitération	Abstempelung	Matasello	Annullamento
Obsolete	Hors (de) cours	Ausser Kurs	Fuera de curso	Fuori corso

English	*French*	*German*	*Spanish*	*Italian*
Ochre	Ocre	Ocker	Ocre	Ocra
Official stamp	Timbre de service	Dienstmarke	Sello de servicio	Francobollo di servizio
Olive-brown	Brun-olive	Olivbraun	Castaño oliva	Bruno oliva
Olive-green	Vert-olive	Olivgrün	Verde oliva	Verde oliva
Olive-grey	Gris-olive	Olivgrau	Gris oliva	Grigio oliva
Olive-yellow	Jaune-olive	Olivgelb	Amarillo oliva	Giallo oliva
Orange	Orange	Orange	Naranja	Arancio
Orange-brown	Brun-orange	Orangebraun	Castaño naranja	Bruno arancio
Orange-red	Rouge-orange	Orangerot	Rojo naranja	Rosso arancio
Orange-yellow	Jaune-orange	Orangegelb	Amarillo naranja	Giallo arancio
Overprint	Surcharge	Aufdruck	Sobrecarga	Soprastampa
Pair	Paire	Paar	Pareja	Coppia
Pale	Pâle	Blass	Pálido	Pallido
Pane	Panneau	Gruppe	Grupo	Gruppo
Paper	Papier	Papier	Papel	Carta
Parcel post stamp	Timbre pour colis postaux	Paketmarke	Sello para paquete postal	Francobollo per pacchi postali
Pen-cancelled	Oblitéré à plume	Federzugentwertung	Cancelado a pluma	Annullato a penna
Percé en arc	Percé en arc	Bogenförmiger Durchstich	Picadura en forma de arco	Perforazione ad arco
Percé en scie	Percé en scie	Bogenförmiger Durchstich	Picado en sierra	Foratura a sega
Perforated	Dentelé	Gezähnt	Dentado	Dentellato
Perforation	Dentelure	Zähnung	Dentar	Dentellatura
Photogravure	Photogravure, Heliogravure	Rastertiefdruck	Fotograbado	Rotocalco
Pin perforation	Percé en points	In Punkten durchstochen	Horadado con alfileres	Perforato a punti
Plate	Planche	Platte	Plancha	Lastra, Tavola
Plum	Prune	Pflaumenfarbe	Color de ciruela	Prugna
Postage Due stamp	Timbre-taxe	Portomarke	Sello de tasa	Segnatasse
Postage stamp	Timbre-poste	Briefmarke, Freimarke, Postmarke	Sello de correos	Francobollo postale
Postal fiscal stamp	Timbre fiscal-postal	Stempelmarke als Postmarke verwendet	Sello fiscal-postal	Fiscale postale
Postmark	Oblitération postale	Poststempel	Matasello	Bollo
Printing	Impression, Tirage	Druck	Impresión	Stampa, Tiratura
Proof	Epreuve	Druckprobe	Prueba de impresión	Prova
Provisionals	Timbres provisoires	Provisorische Marken, Provisorien	Provisionales	Provvisori
Prussian Blue	Bleu de Prusse	Preussischblau	Azul de Prusia	Azzurro di Prussia
Purple	Pourpre	Purpur	Púrpura	Porpora
Purple-brown	Brun-pourpre	Purpurbraun	Castaño púrpura	Bruno porpora
Recess-printing	Impression en taille douce	Tiefdruck	Grabado	Incisione
Red	Rouge	Rot	Rojo	Rosso
Red-brown	Brun-rouge	Rotbraun	Castaño rojizo	Bruno rosso
Reddish Lilac	Lilas rougeâtre	Rötlichlila	Lila rojizo	Lilla rossastro
Reddish Purple	Pourpre-rouge	Rötlichpurpur	Púrpura rojizo	Porpora rossastro
Reddish Violet	Violet rougeâtre	Rötlichviolett	Violeta rojizo	Violetto rossastro
Red-orange	Orange rougeâtre	Rotorange	Naranja rojizo	Arancio rosso
Registration stamp	Timbre pour lettre chargée (recommandée)	Einschreibmarke	Sello de certificado	Francobollo per lettere raccomandate

English	*French*	*German*	*Spanish*	*Italian*
Reprint	Réimpression	Neudruck	Reimpresión	Ristampa
Reversed	Retourné	Umgekehrt	Invertido	Rovesciato
Rose	Rose	Rosa	Rosa	Rosa
Rose-red	Rouge rosé	Rosarot	Rojo rosado	Rosso rosa
Rosine	Rose vif	Lebhaftrosa	Rosa vivo	Rosa vivo
Roulette	Perçage	Durchstich	Picadura	Foratura
Rouletted	Percé	Durchstochen	Picado	Forato
Royal Blue	Bleu-roi	Königblau	Azul real	Azzurro reale
Sage-green	Vert-sauge	Salbeigrün	Verde salvia	Verde salvia
Salmon	Saumon	Lachs	Salmón	Salmone
Scarlet	Ecarlate	Scharlach	Escarlata	Scarlatto
Sepia	Sépia	Sepia	Sepia	Seppia
Serpentine roulette	Percé en serpentin	Schlangenliniger Durchstich	Picado a serpentina	Perforazione a serpentina
Shade	Nuance	Tönung	Tono	Gradazione de colore
Sheet	Feuille	Bogen	Hoja	Foglio
Slate	Ardoise	Schiefer	Pizarra	Ardesia
Slate-blue	Bleu-ardoise	Schieferblau	Azul pizarra	Azzurro ardesia
Slate-green	Vert-ardoise	Schiefergrün	Verde pizarra	Verde ardesia
Slate-lilac	Lilas-gris	Schieferlila	Lila pizarra	Lilla ardesia
Slate-purple	Mauve-gris	Schieferpurpur	Púrpura pizarra	Porpora ardesia
Slate-violet	Violet-gris	Schieferviolett	Violeta pizarra	Violetto ardesia
Special delivery stamp	Timbre pour exprès	Eilmarke	Sello de urgencia	Francobollo per espressi
Specimen	Spécimen	Muster	Muestra	Saggio
Steel Blue	Bleu acier	Stahlblau	Azul acero	Azzurro acciaio
Strip	Bande	Streifen	Tira	Striscia
Surcharge	Surcharge	Aufdruck	Sobrecarga	Soprastampa
Tête-bêche	Tête-bêche	Kehrdruck	Tête-bêche	Tête-bêche
Tinted paper	Papier teinté	Getöntes Papier	Papel Coloreado	Carta tinta
Too-late stamp	Timbre pour lettres en retard	Verspätungsmarke	Sello para cartas retardadas	Francobollo per le lettere in ritardo
Turquoise-blue	Bleu-turquoise	Türkisblau	Azul turquesa	Azzurro turchese
Turquoise-green	Vert-turquoise	Türkisgrün	Verde turquesa	Verde turchese
Typography	Typographie	Buchdruck	Tipografia	Tipografia
Ultramarine	Outremer	Ultramarin	Ultramar	Oltremare
Unused	Neuf	Ungebraucht	Nuevo	Nuovo
Used	Oblitéré, Usé	Gebraucht	Usado	Usato
Venetian Red	Rouge-brun terne	Venezianischrot	Rojo veneciano	Rosso veneziano
Vermilion	Vermillon	Zinnober	Cinabrio	Vermiglione
Violet	Violet	Violett	Violeta	Violetto
Violet-blue	Bleu-violet	Violettblau	Azul violeta	Azzurro violetto
Watermark	Filigrane	Wasserzeichen	Filigrana	Filigrana
Watermark sideways	Filigrane couché	Wasserzeichen liegend	Filigrana acostado	Filigrana coricata
Wove paper	Papier ordinaire, Papier uni	Einfaches Papier	Papel avitelado	Carta unita
Yellow	Jaune	Gelb	Amarillo	Giallo
Yellow-brown	Brun-jaune	Gelbbraun	Castaño amarillo	Bruno giallo
Yellow-green	Vert-jaune	Gelbgrün	Verde amarillo	Verde giallo
Yellow-olive	Olive jaunâtre	Gelboliv	Oliva amarillo	Oliva giallastro
Yellow-orange	Orange jaunâtre	Gelborange	Naranja amarillo	Arancio giallastro
Zig-zag roulette	Percé en zigzag	Sägezahnartiger Durchstich	Picado en zigzig	Perforazione a zigzag

Gibbons Catalogues for *every* Collector

The Stanley Gibbons Great Britain Specialised Catalogue

Comprises four heavily illustrated volumes, uniform in style and format.

Queen Victoria — Volume 1

A detailed and authoritative listing and pricing of the postage stamps of Queen Victoria.

New 5th Edition to be published during 1977.

The Four Kings — Volume 2

Incorporates a detailed listing and pricing of the adhesive postage stamps of King Edward VII, King George V, King Edward VIII and King George VI.

New 4th Edition in preparation.

Queen Elizabeth II Pre-decimal Issues — Volume 3

All Queen Elizabeth stamps denominated in £. s. d., with every significant variety and type of issue.

3rd Edition. £5.00.

Queen Elizabeth II Decimal Issues — Volume 4

Highly detailed coverage of decimal stamp issues to mid-1976, incorporating much absorbing detail.

1st Edition. £5.00.

Elizabethan Catalogue

Provides illustrated specialised listings of all Commonwealth issues of the reign of Queen Elizabeth II. In large size format it lists over 20,400 stamps, over 5,100 varieties, and has over 8,000 illustrations.

1978 Edition due for publication in October 1977.

Stamps of the World

Stanley Gibbons *Stamps of the World* is widely accepted as the standard work of reference; it is a unique, one-volume straightforward priced listing of the postage stamps of the whole world.

1978 Edition due for publication in September 1977.

Collect British Stamps

The concise priced check list of all Great Britain stamps since 1840, illustrated in colour. Over 1,500,000 copies sold to date. 20th Edition. **90p.**

Collect Channel Islands Stamps

Independent issues, Regionals and Occupation stamps, and a good guide to postal history markings. Up-to-date prices and colour check list throughout. 6th Edition. **85p.**

Collect Isle of Man Stamps

Detailed all-colour check list for stamps and postal history, priced in line with today's market. 2nd Edition. **85p.**

Gibbons Foreign Stamp Catalogue

There are three volumes of **Europe** and the four **Overseas** volumes cover the countries of the rest of the world.

Europe 1 (Countries A—F), *3rd Edn.* **£6.00**
Europe 2 (Countries G—P), *3rd Edn.* **£6.50**
Europe 3 (Countries Q—Z), *2nd Edn.* **£3.50**
Overseas 1 (Countries A—C), *2nd Edn.* **£6.25**
Overseas 2 (Countries D—J), *2nd Edn.* **£6.50**
Overseas 3 (Countries K—O), *2nd Edn.* **£6.50**
Overseas 4 (Countries P—Z), **£6.00**

Obtainable from your usual Stanley Gibbons stockist or in case of difficulty direct from:

Stanley Gibbons Publications Ltd., 391 Strand, London, WC2R 0LX

Postage and packing extra: 15p for each check list, 50p for each catalogue.

STANLEY GIBBONS PRICED CATALOGUE

UNUSED AND USED POSTAGE STAMPS OF

BRITISH COMMONWEALTH

IRELAND, PAKISTAN, RHODESIA AND SOUTH AFRICA

80th Edition

GREAT BRITAIN.

GENERAL NOTES.—LINE-ENGRAVED ISSUES.

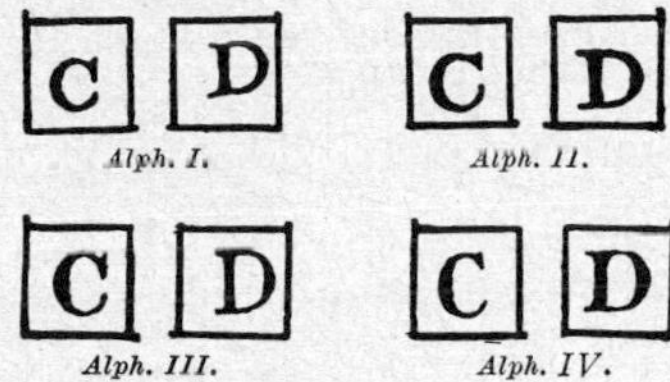

Typical Corner Letters of the four Alphabets.

Alphabets. Four different letterings were used for the corner letters on stamps prior to the issue with letters in all four corners, these being known to collectors as:—

Alphabet I. Used for all plates made from 1840 to the end of 1851. Letters small.

Alphabet II. Plates from 1852 to mid-1855. Letters larger, heavier and broader.

Alphabet III. Plates from mid-1855 to end of period. Letters tall and more slender.

Alphabet IV. 1861. 1d. Die II, Plates 50 and 51 only. Letters were hand-engraved instead of being punched on the plate. They are therefore inconsistent in shape and size but generally larger and outstanding.

While the general descriptions and the illustrations of typical letters given above may be of some assistance, only long experience can enable every stamp to be allocated to its particular Alphabet without hesitation, as certain letters in each are similar to those in one of the others.

Blued Paper. The blueing of the paper of the earlier issues is believed to be due to the presence of prussiate of potash in the printing ink, or in the paper, which, under certain conditions, tended to colour the paper when the sheets were damped for printing.

Corner Letters. The corner letters on the early British stamps were intended as a safeguard against forgery, each stamp in the sheet having a different combination of letters. Taking the first 1d. stamp, printed in 20 horizontal rows of 12, as an example, we have lettering as follows—

Row 1. A A, A B, A C, etc. to A L.
Row 2. B A, B B, B C, etc. to B L.
and so on to
Row 20. T A, T B, T C, etc. to T L.

On the stamps with four corner letters, those in the upper corners are in the reverse positions to those in the lower corners. Thus in a sheet of 240 (12 × 20) we have:—

Row 1. A A B A C A / A A A B A C etc. to L A / A L
Row 2. A B B B C B / B A B B B C etc. to L B / B L
and so on to
Row 20. A T B T C T / T A T B T C etc. to L T / T L

Dies. (*See illustrations on page 4.*) The first Die of the 1d. was used for making the original Die of the 2d. which was used for both the No Lines and White Lines issues. In 1855 the 1d. Die I was amended by retouching the head and deepening the lines on a transferred impression of the original. This later version, known to collectors as Die II, was used for making the dies for the 1d. and 2d. with letters in all four corners and also for the $1\frac{1}{2}$d.

Double letter.

Guide line in corner.

Guide line through value.

NOTE.—*The above illustrations and that illustrating a re-entry below, show marked examples of the varieties described, but there are numerous stamps showing double letters, guide lines or re-entries of differing importance, intensity and value.*

Double Corner Letters. These are due to the workman placing his letter-punch in the wrong position at the first attempt, when lettering the plate, and then correcting the mistake, or to a slight shifting of the punch when struck. If a wrong letter was struck in the first instance, traces of a wrong letter may appear in a corner in addition to the correct one.

Guide Lines and Dots. When laying down the impressions of the design on the early plates, fine vertical and horizontal guide lines were marked on the plates to assist the operative. These were usually removed from the gutter margins, but could not be removed from the stamp impressions without damage to the plate, so that in such cases they appear on the printed stamps, sometimes in the corners, sometimes through "POSTAGE" or the value. (*See illustrations.*)

Guide dots or cuts were similarly made to indicate the spacing of the guide lines. These too sometimes appear on the stamps.

Inverted "S". The corner letter "S" is inverted on the 1d. red-brown (and shades) as follows:—

DIE I (Imperf.)	DIE II (Perf. 16 and 14, Small and Large Crown, Blue paper)
Plates 78, 105, 107: S A to S L	Plate 5: S D to S L
Plate 140: S A and S B	
Plate 142: S B	
Plate 143: S A	

Ivory Head.

"Ivory Head." The so-called "ivory head" variety (*see illustration*) in which the Queen's Head shows white on the back of the stamp is due to the comparative absence of ink in the head portion of the design, with consequent absence of blueing. (*See* "Blued Paper" note on previous page.)

Plates. Until the introduction of the stamps with letters in all four corners, the number of the plate was not indicated in the design of the stamp, but was printed on the sheet margin. By long study of identifiable blocks and the minor variations in the design, coupled with the position of the corner letters, philatelists are now able to allot many of these stamps to their respective plates.

Maltese Cross. Type of Town postmark. Type of 1844 postmark.

Postmarks. The so-called "Maltese Cross" design was the first employed for obliterating British postage stamps and was in use from 1840 to 1844. Being hand-cut, the obliterating stamps varied greatly in detail and some distinctive types can be allotted to particular towns or offices. Local types, such as those used at Manchester, Norwich, Leeds, etc., are keenly sought for. A red ink was first employed, but was superseded by black, after some earlier experiments, in February, 1841. Maltese Cross obliterations in other colours are rare.

Obliterations of this type, numbered 1 to 12 in the centre, were used at the London Chief Office in 1843 and 1844.

In 1844 the Maltese Cross design was superseded by numbered obliterators of various types, one of which is illustrated above. This is naturally comparatively scarce on the first 1d. and 2d. stamps. Like the Maltese Cross it is found in various colours, some of which are rare.

Re-cut "R". On several plates the letter "R" is formed from the letter "P", the tail having been hand cut. It occurs on the Penny Plate 10 in black and in red and also on Plates 30, 31, 32, 33, 58, 83, 86 and 87.

Re-entry.

"Union Jack" re-entry.

Re-entries. Re-entries on the plate show as a doubling of part of the design of the stamp generally at top or bottom. Many re-entries are very slight while others are most marked. (*See illustration.*)

The "*Union Jack*" *re-entry*, so called owing to the effect of the re-entry on the appearance of the corner stars (*see illustration*) occurs on stamp L K of Plate 75 of the 1d. red, Die I.

T A (T L) M A (M L)
Varieties of the Large Crown Watermark.

I

II

Two states of the Large Crown Watermark.

Watermarks. Two watermark varieties, consisting of crowns of entirely different shape, are found in sheets of the Large Crown paper and fall on stamps lettered M A and T A (or M L and T L when the paper is printed on the wrong side). Both varieties are found on the 1d. rose-red of 1857, while the M A (M L) variety comes also on some plates of the 1d. of 1864 (Nos. 43, 44) up to about Plate 96. On the 2d. the T A (T L) variety is known on plates 8 and 9, and the M A (M L) on later prints of plate 9. These varieties may exist inverted, or inverted reversed on stamps lettered A A and A L and H A and H L, and some are known. (*See illustrations.*)

In 1861 a minor alteration was made in the Large Crown watermark by the removal of the two vertical strokes, representing *fleurs-de-lis*, which projected upwards from the uppermost of the three horizontal curves at the base of the Crown. (*See illustration.*)

QUEEN VICTORIA, 1837-1901.

MULREADY ENVELOPES AND COVERS, which were issued concurrently with the first British adhesive stamps, can be supplied as follows:

1d. black.

Envelopes: £40 *unused;* £40 *used.*
Covers: £35 *unused;* £35 *used.*

2d. blue.

Envelopes: £80 *unused;* £225 *used.*
Covers: £70 *unused;* £200 *used.*

I.—LINE-ENGRAVED STAMPS

1

2. Small Crown.

(Eng. Frederick Heath. Printed by Perkins, Bacon & Co.)

1840 (6–8 MAY). *Letters in lower corners. Wmk. Small Crown, T* **2**. *Imperf.*

No.	*Type.*		*Un.*	*Used.*
1	**1**	1d. intense black	£850	55·00
2	,,	1d. black	£550	35·00
3	,,	1d. grey-black (worn plate)	£600	45·00
4	,,	2d. deep full blue (8 May)	£2750	£120
5	,,	2d. blue	£2000	£100
6	,,	2d. pale blue	£3000	£125

The 1d. stamp in black was printed from Plates 1 to 11. Plate 1 was printed from in two states (known to collectors as 1*a* and 1*b*), the latter being the result of extensive repairs.

Repairs were also made to plates 2, 5, 6, 8, 9, 10 and 11, and certain impressions exist in two or more states. See *Stanley Gibbons Specialised Cat., Vol. I.*

Plates. 1d. black.

Plate	Un.	Used.	Plate	Un.	Used.	Plate	Un.	Used.
1*a*.	£1000	45·00	4.	£600	35·00	8.	£750	45·00
1*b*.	£550	35·00	5.	£550	40·00	9.	£900	55·00
2.	£550	35·00	6.	£550	35·00	10.	£1000	60·00
3.	£750	45·00	7.	£650	40·00	11.	£1100	£375

Varieties. 1d. black.

			Un.	Used.
a.	*On bleuté paper (Plates 1 to 8)*	*from*	—	45·00
b.	*Double letter in corner*	*from*	£700	50·00
bb.	*Re-entry*	*from*	£700	55·00
bc.	*"PB" re-entry (Plate 5, 3rd state)*		—	£1750
cc.	*Large letters in each corner* (E J, I L, J C *and* P A) *(Plate 1b)*	*from*	—	75·00
c.	*Guide line in corner*		£600	40·00
d.	*,, ,, through value*		£600	40·00
e.	*Watermark inverted*		£900	£150
f.	*Reconstructed plate of 240 stamps*	*from*	—	£4500
g.	*Obliterated red Maltese Cross*			35·00
h.	*,, black ,,*			35·00
i.	*,, blue ,,*			£350
k.	*,, magenta ,,*			£225
m.	*,, yellow ,,*			£1500
n.	*Number (1 to 12) in Maltese Cross*	*from*		£450
o.	*Town obliteration without Maltese Cross in black on stamp*	*from*		£450
p.	*Town obliteration without Maltese Cross in yellow ,,*	*from*		£2250
q.	*Town obliteration without Maltese Cross in red ,,*	*from*		£450
r.	*"Penny Post" obliteration in black on stamp*	*from*		£450
s.	*Obliteration of 1844 in black ,,*	*from*		90·00

The so-called "Royal reprint" of the 1d. black was made in 1864, from Plate 66, Die II, on paper with Large Crown watermark, inverted. A printing was also made in carmine, on paper with the same watermark, normal.

For 1d. black with "VR" in upper corners see No. V1 under Official Stamps.

The 2d. stamps were printed from Plates 1 and 2.

Plates.	2d. blue.	Un.	Used.
Plate 1	*Shades from*	£2000	£100
Plate 2	*Shades from*	£2500	£125

Varieties. 2d. blue.

			Un.	Used.
a.	*Double letter in corner*		—	£125
aa.	*Re-entry*		—	£140
b.	*Guide line in corner*		—	£110
c.	*,, ,, through value*		—	£110
d.	*Watermark inverted*		£2750	£250
e.	*Obliterated red Maltese Cross (Plate 1)*			£100
f.	*,, black ,,*			£100
g.	*,, blue ,,*			£700
h.	*,, magenta ,,*			£500
i.	*,, number (1 to 12) in Maltese Cross*	*from*		£750
k.	*Town obliteration without Maltese Cross in black on stamp*			£500
l.	*Obliteration of 1844 in black on stamp*			£150
m.	*,, ,, ,, blue ,,*			£450
n.	*"Penny Post" obliteration in black on stamp*			£500

1841 (10 Feb.). *Printed from "black" plates. Wmk. T* **2.** *Paper more or less blued. Imperf.*

			Un.	Used.
7 **1**	1d. red-brown (*shades*)		£125	9·00
	a. *"PB" re-entry (Plate 5, 3rd state)*		—	£400

The first printings of the 1d. in red were made from Plates 1b, 2, 5 and 8 to 11 used for the 1d. black.

Plates. 1d. red-brown.

Plate	Un.	Used.	Plate	Un.	Used.	Plate	Un.	Used.
1*b*.	£1000	55·00	8.	£175	14·00	10.	£150	15·00
2.	£600	30·00	9.	£150	10·00	11.	£125	9·00
5.	£200	15·00						

1841 (Late Feb.). *Plates 12 onwards. Wmk. T* **2.** *Paper more or less blued. Imperf.*

			Un.	Used.
8	**1**	1d. red-brown	45·00	80
8*a*	,,	1d. red-brown on very blue paper	50·00	1·00
9	,,	1d. pale red-brown (worn plates)	60·00	3·00
10	,,	1d. deep red-brown	45·00	2·00
11	,,	1d. lake-red	£175	40·00
12	,,	1d. orange-brown	£100	16·00

Error. No letter "A" *in right lower corner,* (*Stamp* B (A), *Plate 77*).

			Un.	Used.
12*a*	**1**	1d. red-brown	—	£2750

Varieties. 1d. red-brown, etc.

			Un.	Used.
a.	*Re-entry*	*from*	—	8·00
b.	*Double letter in corner*	*from*	—	6·00
ba.	*Double Star (Plate 75) "Union Jack" re-entry (see page 2)*		—	£160
c.	*Guide line in corner*		—	1·25
d.	*,, ,, through value*		—	6·00
e.	*Thick outer frame to stamp*		—	4·00
f.	*Ivory head*		65·00	2·00
g.	*Watermark inverted*		£175	15·00
ga.	*Left corner letter "S" inverted (Plates 78, 105, 107)*	*from*	—	25·00
gb.	*P converted to R (Plates 30, 33, 83, 86)*	*from*	—	15·00
h.	*Obliterated red Maltese Cross*			£300
i.	*,, black ,,*			2·50
k.	*,, blue ,,*			28·00
m.	*Obliteration No. 1 in Maltese Cross*			10·00
	,, ,, 2 ,, ,,			10·00
	,, ,, 3 ,, ,,			18·00
	,, ,, 4 ,, ,,			35·00
	,, ,, 5 ,, ,,			10·00
	,, ,, 6 ,, ,,			9·00
	,, ,, 7 ,, ,,			8·00
	,, ,, 8 ,, ,,			8·00
	,, ,, 9 ,, ,,			11·00
	,, ,, 10 ,, ,,			14·00
	,, ,, 11 ,, ,,			18·00
	,, ,, 12 ,, ,,			25·00
n.	*Obliteration "Penny Post" in black on stamp*			65·00
o.	*Town obliteration without Maltese Cross in black on stamp*	*from*		22·00
p.	*,, ,, ,, ,, blue ,,*	*from*		60·00
q.	*,, ,, ,, ,, green ,,*	*from*		£125
r.	*,, ,, ,, ,, yellow ,,*	*from*		£2000
ra.	*,, ,, ,, ,, red ,,*	*from*		£750
s.	*Obliteration of 1844 in blue on stamp*	*from*		12·00
t.	*,, ,, ,, red ,,*	*from*		£350
u.	*,, ,, ,, green ,,*	*from*		16·00
v.	*,, ,, ,, violet ,,*	*from*		£160
w.	*,, ,, ,, black ,,*	*from*		80

NOTES. The error "No letter A in right corner" was due to the omission to insert this letter on stamp B A of Plate 77. The error was discovered some months after the plate was registered and was then corrected.

Stamps with thick outer frame to the design are from plates on which the frame-lines have been strengthened or recut, particularly Plates 76 and 90.

There are innumerable variations in the colour and shade of the 1d. "red" and those given in the above list represent colour groups each covering a wide range.

For "Union Jack" re-entry, "Inverted S", etc., see General Note on page 2.

3. White lines added.

1841 (13 March). *White lines added. Wmk. T* **2.** *Paper more or less blued. Imperf.*

			Un.	Used.
13	**3**	2d. pale blue	£500	22·00
14	,,	2d. blue	£350	13·00
15	,,	2d. deep full blue	£500	18·00
15*aa*	,,	2d. violet-blue	£2750	£150

The 2d. stamp with white lines was printed from Plates 3 and 4.

Plates.	2d. blue.	Un.	Used.
Plate 3.	*Shades from*	£350	16·00
,, 4.	*Shades from*	£400	13·00

Varieties. 2d. blue.

			Un.	Used.
a.	*Guide line in corner*		—	16·00
b.	*,, ,, through value*		£400	16·00
bb.	*Double letter in corner*		—	20·00
be.	*Re-entry*		—	30·00
c.	*Ivory head*		£450	16·00
d.	*Watermark inverted*		£700	90·00
e.	*Obliterated red Maltese Cross*			£1500
f.	*,, black ,,*			25·00
g.	*,, blue ,,*			£250
i.	*Obliteration No. 1 in Maltese Cross*			65·00
	,, ,, 2 ,, ,,			65·00
	,, ,, 3 ,, ,,			65·00
	,, ,, 4 ,, ,,			60·00
	,, ,, 5 ,, ,,			90·00
	,, ,, 6 ,, ,,			60·00
	,, ,, 7 ,, ,,			£120
	,, ,, 8 ,, ,,			90·00
	,, ,, 9 ,, ,,			£120
	,, ,, 10 ,, ,,			£160
	,, ,, 11 ,, ,,			90·00
	,, ,, 12 ,, ,,			40·00
k.	*Obliteration of 1844 in black on stamp*			13·00
l.	*,, ,, ,, blue ,,*			£125
m.	*,, ,, ,, red ,,*			£1500
n.	*,, ,, ,, green ,*			90·00
p.	*Town obliteration in black ,,*			£125
q.	*,, ,, blue ,,*			£200

1841 (April). *Trial printing (unissued) on Dickinson silk-thread paper. Imperf.*

			Un.	Used.
16	**1**	1d. red-brown (Plate 11)	£600	

Eight sheets were printed on this paper, six being gummed, two ungummed.

1848. *Rouletted 12 by Henry Archer.*

			Un.	Used.
16*a*	**1**	1d. red-brown (Plates 70, 71)	£1250	

1850. *P 16, by Henry Archer.*

			Un.	Used.
16*b*	**1**	1d. red-brown (Alph. I) (from Plates 71, 79, 90–101 and 105. Also Pl. 8, unused only)	£225	55·00

Stamp on cover, dated prior to Feb. 1854 (*price* £125); dated Feb. and after 1854 (*price* £85).

1853. *Government Trial Perforations.*

			Un.	Used.
16*c*	**1**	1d. red-brown (*perf.* 16) (Alph. II) (*on cover*)	†	£2000
16*d*	,,	1d. ,, (*perf.* 14) (Alph. I)	£1500	

NOTES. Although the various trials of machines for rouletting and perforating were unofficial, Archer had the consent of the authorities in making his experiments, and sheets so experimented upon were afterwards put in use by the Post Office.

As Archer ended his experiments in 1850 and plates with corner letters Alphabet II did not come into issue until 1852, perforated stamps with corner letters of Alphabet I may safely be assumed to be Archer productions, if genuine.

The Government trial perforations were done on Napier machines in 1853. As Alphabet II was by that time in use, the trials can only be distinguished from the perforated stamps listed below by being dated prior to January 28th, 1854, the date when the perforated stamps were officially issued.

Die I.

Die II.

Die I is the original die, used from 1840 to 1855. The features of the portrait are lightly shaded and consequently lack emphasis.

Die II is Die I retouched by Mr. William Humphrys in which the lines of the features have been deepened and appear stronger.

The eye is deeply shaded and made more lifelike. The nostril and lips are more clearly defined, the latter appearing much thicker. A strong downward stroke of colour marks the corner of the mouth. There is a deep indentation of colour between lower lip and chin. The band running from the back of the ear to the chignon has a bolder horizontal line below it than in Die I.

1854–57. *Paper more or less blued.* (i) *Wmk. Small Crown, T* **2**. *P* 16.

No.	Type	Description	Un.	Used
17	**1**	1d. red-brown (Die I) (February, 1854)	45·00	1·00
18	,,	1d. yellow-brown (Die I)	50·00	2·00
19	**3**	2d. deep blue (Plate 4) (1 March, 1854)	£400	10·00
20	,,	2d. pale blue (Plate 4)	£450	18·00
20*a*	,,	2d. blue (Plate 5) (28 August, 1855)	£600	45·00
21	**1**	1d. red-brown (Die II) (1 March, 1855)	50·00	3·50
		a. Imperf.		

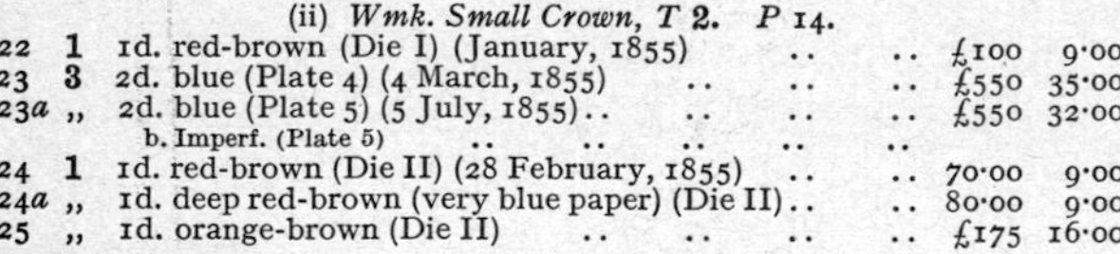

(ii) *Wmk. Small Crown, T* **2**. *P* 14.

No.	Type	Description	Un.	Used
22	**1**	1d. red-brown (Die I) (January, 1855)	£100	9·00
23	**3**	2d. blue (Plate 4) (4 March, 1855)	£550	35·00
23*a*	,,	2d. blue (Plate 5) (5 July, 1855)	£550	32·00
		b. Imperf. (Plate 5)		
24	**1**	1d. red-brown (Die II) (28 February, 1855)	70·00	9·00
24*a*	,,	1d. deep red-brown (very blue paper) (Die II)	80·00	9·00
25	,,	1d. orange-brown (Die II)	£175	16·00

4. Large Crown.

FOR WELL CENTRED LIGHTLY USED COPIES ADD 100%
(Nos. 17/53)

(iii) *Wmk. Large Crown, T* **4**. *P* 16.

No.	Type	Description	Un.	Used
26	**1**	1d. red-brown (Die II) (15 May, 1855)	£150	14·00
		a. Imperf. (Plate 7)		
27	**3**	2d. blue (Plate 5) (20 July, 1855)	£750	50·00
		a. Imperf.	—	£1000

(iv) *Wmk. Large Crown, T* **4**. *P* 14.

No.	Type	Description	Un.	Used
29	**1**	1d. red-brown (Die II) (18 August, 1855)	40·00	45
		a. Imperf. (*shades*) (Plates 22, 25, 43)	£300	£250
30	,,	1d. brick-red (Die II)	50·00	4·50
31	,,	1d. plum (Die II) (February, 1856)	£250	40·00
32	,,	1d. brown-rose (Die II)	50·00	4·00
33	,,	1d. orange-brown (Die II) (March, 1857)	75·00	6·00
34	**3**	2d. blue (Plate 5) (20 July, 1855)	£275	9·00
35	,,	2d. blue (Plate 6) (2 July, 1857)	£275	10·00
		a. Imperf.	—	£1000

1856–62. *Paper no longer blued.* (i) *Wmk. Large Crown, T* **4**. *P* 16.

No.	Type	Description	Un.	Used
36	**1**	1d. rose-red (Die II) (26 December, 1857)	£225	12·00
36*a*	,,	2d. blue (Plate 6) (1 February 1858)	£800	45·00

(ii) (Die II) *Wmk. Large Crown, T* **4**. *P* 14.

No.	Type	Description	Un.	Used
37	**1**	1d. red-brown (November, 1856)	60·00	7·50
38	,,	1d. pale red (9 April, 1857)	28·00	1·75
		a. Imperf.	£250	£200
39	,,	1d. pale rose (March, 1857)	25·00	90
40	,,	1d. rose-red (September, 1857)	14·00	30
		a. Imperf.	£250	£200
		b. Reserve plates 15 or 16 (Alphabet II) (1862) .. *from*	40·00	2·25
41	,,	1d. deep rose-red (July, 1857)	25·00	30

1861. *Letters engraved on plate instead of punched* (Alphabet IV).

No.	Type	Description	Un.	Used
42	**1**	1d. rose-red (Die II) (Plates 50 and 51)	50·00	3·00
		a. Imperf.	—	£1000

NOTES. 1d. The numbering of the 1d. plates recommenced at 1 on the introduction of Die II. Plates 1 to 21 were Alphabet II from which a scarce plum shade exists. Corner letters of Alphabet III appear on Plate 22 and onwards.

As an experiment, the corner letters were engraved by hand on Plates 50 and 51 in 1856, instead of being punched (Alphabet IV), but punching was again resorted to on Plate 52 and onwards. Plates 50 and 51 were not put into use until 1861.

2d. Plates 3 and 4 of the 2d. had corner letters of Alphabet I, Plate 5 Alphabet II and Plate 6 Alphabet III. In Plate 6 the white lines are thinner than before.

In both values varieties may be found as described in the preceding issues—ivory heads, inverted watermarks, re-entries, and double letters in corners.

The change of perforation from 16 to 14 was decided upon late in 1854 owing to the fact that the closer holes of the former gauge tended to cause the sheets of stamps to break up when handled, but for a time both gauges were in concurrent use. Owing to faulty alignment of the impressions on the plates and to shrinkage of the paper when damped, badly perforated stamps are plentiful in the line-engraved issues.

5

6

Plate 191.

Showing position of the plate number on the 1d. *and* 2d. *values.*

1858–79. *Letters in all four corners. Wmk. Large Crown, T* **4**. *Die* II (1*d. and* 2*d.*). *P* 14.

No.	Type	Description	Un.	Used
43	**5**	1d. rose-red (1 April, 1864)	4·50	35
44	,,	1d. lake-red	4·50	35
		a. Imperf. .. *from*	£300	£250

Plate No.	*Un.*	*Used*	*Plate No.*	*Un.*	*Used*	*Plate No.*	*Un.*	*Used*
71.	10·00	35	123.	4·50	55	176.	8·00	85
72.	8·00	35	124.	4·50	35	177.	4·50	35
73.	9·00	35	125.	7·00	35	178.	8·00	85
74.	9·00	40	127.	7·00	35	179.	8·00	85
76.	10·00	35	129.	6·00	35	180.	9·00	85
77.	£14000	£9000	130.	6·00	35	181.	8·00	35
78.	6·00	35	131.	8·00	35	182.	8·00	1·50
79.	6·00	35	132.	60·00	5·50	183.	6·00	35
80.	9·00	35	133.	55·00	5·00	184.	4·50	35
81.	15·00	35	134.	4·50	40	185.	8·00	70
82.	55·00	1·40	135.	5·50	35	186.	8·00	70
83.	90·00	3·00	136.	6·00	35	187.	7·00	35
84.	6·00	35	137.	8·00	35	188.	8·00	35
85.	8·00	35	138.	5·50	35	189.	9·00	70
86.	15·00	35	139.	5·50	35	190.	4·50	35
87.	5·50	35	140.	4·50	35	191.	4·50	35
88.	70·00	4·50	141.	18·00	1·00	192.	4·50	35
89.	7·00	35	142.	8·00	35	193.	4·50	35
90.	13·00	35	143.	10·00	35	194.	8·00	35
91.	5·50	35	144.	15·00	35	195.	8·00	35
92.	8·00	35	145.	4·50	35	196.	5·50	35
93.	8·00	55	146.	6·00	35	197.	8·00	35
94.	9·00	35	147.	6·00	35	198.	5·50	35
95.	8·00	35	148.	4·50	35	199.	4·50	35
96.	13·00	40	149.	8·00	35	200.	6·00	35
97.	8·00	35	150.	5·50	35	201.	4·50	35
98.	8·00	35	151.	9·00	40	202.	5·50	40
99.	9·00	35	152.	7·00	35	203.	5·50	35
100.	8·00	35	153.	28·00	3·00	204.	7·00	35
101.	13·00	35	154.	8·00	35	205.	7·00	35
102.	8·00	35	155.	8·00	70	206.	7·00	35
103.	9·00	35	156.	8·00	35	207.	5·50	35
104.	13·00	1·40	157.	8·00	35	208.	7·00	35
105.	28·00	3·00	158.	5·50	35	209.	8·00	35
106.	8·00	40	159.	6·00	35	210.	9·00	35
107.	13·00	35	160.	5·50	35	211.	20·00	2·00
108.	15·00	70	161.	15·00	1·40	212.	7·00	40
109.	45·00	60	162.	8·00	35	213.	6·00	40
110.	9·00	35	163.	8·00	35	214.	8·00	40
111.	8·00	35	164.	7·00	35	215.	8·00	40
112.	15·00	70	165.	6·00	35	216.	6·00	40
113.	8·00	35	166.	8·00	35	217.	8·00	2·25
114.	45·00	40	167.	5·50	35	218.	7·00	1·75
115.	45·00	70	168.	6·00	35	219.	15·00	12·00
116.	16·00	40	169.	8·00	1·25	220.	5·50	1·75
117.	8·00	35	170.	7·00	35	221.	15·00	3·50
118.	4·50	35	171.	4·50	35	222.	13·00	3·50
119.	5·50	35	172.	6·00	35	223.	20·00	8·00
120.	4·50	35	173.	4·50	35	224.	28·00	15·00
121.	4·50	35	174.	4·50	35	225.	£600	£130
122.	4·50	35	175.	4·50	35			

Error. Imperf. Issued at Cardiff (Plate 116).

44*b* **5** 1d. rose-red (18.1.70) £450 £300

The following plate numbers are also known imperf. and used (No. 44a): 72, 79, 80, 81, 82, 83, 86, 87, 88, 90, 91, 92, 93, 96, 97, 100, 102, 103, 104, 105, 107, 108, 109, 112, 114, 117, 120, 121, 122, 136, 137, 142, 146, 148, 158, 162, 164, 166, 171, 174 and 191.

45 **6** 2d. blue (thick lines) (July, 1858) .. .. .. 45·00 1·25
a. Imperf. (Plate 9) .. .. — £1600

Plate No.	*Un.*	*Used.*	*Plate No.*	*Un.*	*Used.*
7.	£150	8·00	9.	45·00	1·25
8.	£150	7·00	12.	£200	10·00

46 **6** 2d. blue (thin lines) (1 July, 1869) .. .. .. 45·00 1·50
47 ,, 2d. deep blue (thin lines) .. .. 45·00 1·50
a. Imperf. (Plate 13) £600

Plate No.	*Un.*	*Used.*
13.	45·00	1·50
14.	65·00	3·00
15.	65·00	3·00

NOTES ON 1d. The numbering of this series of plates follows after that of the previous 1d. stamp, last printed from Plate 68.

Plates 69, 70, 75, 126 and 128 were prepared for this issue but rejected owing to defects, and stamps from these plates do not exist, so that specimens which appear to be from these plates (like many of those which optimistic collectors believe to be from Plate 77) bear other plate numbers. Owing to faulty engraving or printing it is not always easy to identify the plate number. Plate 77 was also rejected but some stamps printed from it were used. One specimen is in the Tapling Collection and six or seven others are known. Plates 226 to 228 were made but not used.

Specimens from most of the plates are known with inverted watermark. The variety of watermark described in the General Notes occurs on stamp M A (or M L) on plates up to about 96. (*Prices from £60 used.*)

Re-entries in this issue are few, the best being on stamps M K and T K of Plate 71 and on S L and T L, Plate 83.

NOTES ON 2d. Plates 10 and 11 were prepared but rejected. Plates 13 to 15 were laid down from a new roller impression on which the white lines were thinner.

There are some marked re-entries and repairs, particularly on Plates 7, 8, 9 and 12.

Stamps with inverted watermark may be found and also the T A (T L) and M A (M L) watermark varieties (see General Notes).

Though the paper is normally white, some printings showed blueing and stamps showing the " ivory head " may therefore be found.

7

Showing the plate number (20).

9

1870 (1 Oct.). *Wmk. T* **9**, *extending over three stamps. P* 14.

48 **7** ½d. rose-red .. .. 15·00 1·40
49 ,, ½d. rose .. .. 15·00 1·40
a. Imperf. (Plates 1, 4, 5, 6, 8, 14) .. from £500 £300

Plate No.	*Un.*	*Used.*	*Plate No.*	*Un.*	*Used.*	*Plate No.*	*Un.*	*Used.*
1.	35·00	8·00	8.	32·00	11·00	13.	15·00	1·40
3.	18·00	2·00	9.	£400	60·00	14.	15·00	1·40
4.	15·00	1·40	10.	15·00	1·50	15.	15·00	2·00
5.	15·00	1·40	11.	15·00	1·50	19.	25·00	2·25
6.	15·00	1·40	12.	15·00	1·50	20.	20·00	3·00

NOTES. The ½d. was printed in sheets of 480 (24 × 20) so that the check letters run from A A / A A to X T / T X.

Plates 2, 7, 16, 17 and 18 were not completed while Plates 21 and 22, though made, were not used.

Owing to the method of perforating, the outer side of stamps in either the A or X row (i.e. the left or right side of the sheet) is imperf.

Stamps may be found with watermark inverted or reversed, or without watermark, the latter due to misplacement of the paper when printing.

8

1870 (1 Oct.). *Wmk. T* **4**. *P* 14.

51 **8** 1½d. rose-red .. .. .. 55·00 5·00
52 ,, 1½d. lake-red .. .. .. 55·00 5·00
a. Imperf. (Plates 1 and 3) *from* £600 †

Error of lettering. **OP-PC** *for* **CP-PC** (*Plate* 1).

53 **8** 1½d. rose-red £1500 £200

Plate No.	*Un.*	*Used.*
(1)	£110	8·00
3	55·00	5·00

NOTES. Owing to a proposed change in the postal rates, 1½d. stamps were first printed in 1860, in rosy mauve, No. 53*a*, but the change was not approved and the greater part of the stock was destroyed.

In 1870 a 1½d. stamp was required and was issued in rose-red.

Plate 1 did not have the plate number in the design of the stamps, but on stamps from Plate 3 the number will be found in the curved pattern a little above the lower corner letter at each side.

Plate 2 was defective and was not used.

The error of lettering O P-P C on Plate 1 was apparently not noticed by the printers, and therefore not corrected. It was not noticed by collectors until 1894.

1860. *Prepared for use but not issued; blued paper. Wmk. T.* **4**. *P* 14.

53*a* **8** 1½d. rosy mauve (Plate 1) £700
b. Error of lettering, OP-PC for CP-PC .. .. ..

II.—EMBOSSED STAMPS.

PRICES. The prices quoted are for stamps with average to fine embossing. Stamps with exceptionally clear embossing are worth more.

10 11 12

V R

13

Showing position of die number.

(Primary die engraved at the Royal Mint by Mr. William Wyon. Stamps printed at Somerset House.)

1847–54. *Imperf.* (For paper and wmk. see footnote.) *Cut square*

54	**10**	1s. pale green (11 September, 1847)	£1000	65·00
55	,,	1s. green	£1000	75·00
56	,,	1s. deep green	£1200	£110
		Die 1. **1847**	£1000	65·00
		Die 2. **1854**	£1100	65·00
57	**11**	10d. brown (6 November, 1848)	£700	£110
		Die 1. **1848**	£900	£130
		Die 2. **1850**	£700	£110
		Die 3. **1853**	£700	£110
		Die 4. **1854**	£800	£130
		Die 5.	£10000	
58	**12**	6d. mauve (1 March, 1854)	£900	75·00
59	,,	6d. dull lilac	£900	65·00
60	,,	6d. purple	£900	65·00
61	,,	6d. violet	£1200	£130

NOTES. The 1s. and 10d. are on " Dickinson " paper with silk threads. The 6d. is on paper watermarked V R in single-lined letters, Type **13**, which may be found in four ways—upright, inverted, upright reversed, and inverted reversed; none is scarce.

The die numbers are indicated on the base of the bust. Only Die 1 (1 WW) of the 6d. was used for the adhesive stamps. The 10d. is from Die 1 (W.W.1 on stamps), and Dies 2 to 4 (2 W.W., 3 W.W., 4 W.W.) but the number and letters on stamps from Die 1 are seldom clear and many specimens are known without any trace of them. Because of this the stamp we previously listed as "No die number" has been deleted. That they are from Die 1 is proved by the existence of blocks showing stamps with and without the die number. The 1s. is from Dies 1 and 2 (W.W.1, W.W.2).

The normal arrangement of the silk threads in the paper was in pairs running down each vertical row of the sheet, the space between the threads of each pair being approximately 5 mm. and between pairs of threads 20 mm. Varieties due to misplacement of the paper in printing show a single thread on the first stamp from the sheet margin and two threads 20 mm. apart on the other stamps of the row. Faulty manufacture is the cause of stamps with a single thread in the middle.

Through bad spacing of the impressions, which were handstruck, all values may be found with two impressions more or less overlapping. Owing to the small margin allowed for variation of spacing, specimens with good margins on all sides are not common.

Double impressions are known of all values.

Later printings of the 6d. had the gum tinted green to enable the printer to distinguish the gummed side of the paper.

GENERAL NOTES.—SURFACE-PRINTED ISSUES.

" Abnormals ". The majority of the great rarities in the surface-printed group of issues are the so-called " abnormals ", whose existence is due to the practice of printing six sheets from every plate as soon as made, one of which was kept for record purposes at Somerset House, while the others were perforated and usually issued. If such plates were not used for general production or if, before they came into full use, a change of watermark or colour took place, the six sheets originally printed would differ from the main issue in plate, colour or watermark and, if issued, would be extremely rare.

The abnormal stamps of this class listed in this Catalogue and distinguished, where not priced, by a star (*) are:—

3d. Plate 3 (with white dots). 4d. vermilion, Plate 16. 4d. sage-green, Plate 17. 6d. mauve, Plate 10. 6d. pale chestnut, Plate 12. 6d. pale buff, Plate 13. 9d., Plate 3 (hair lines). 9d., Plate 5 (*see* footnote to No. 98). 10d., Plate 2. 1s., Plate 3 (Plate No. 2). 1s. green, Plate 14. 2s. blue, Plate 3.

Those which may have been issued, but of which no specimens are known, are 2½d. wmk. Anchor, Plates 4 and 5; 3d. wmk. Emblems, Plate 5; 3d. wmk. Spray, Plate 21; 6d. grey, wmk; Spray, Plate 18; 8d. orange, Plate 2; 1s. wmk. Emblems, Plate 5. 5s. wmk. Maltese Cross, Plate 4.

The 10d. Plate 1, wmk. Emblems, is sometimes reckoned among the abnormals, but was probably an error, due to the use of the wrong paper.

Imprimaturs and Imperforate Stamps. The post office retained in their records (now in the Postal Museum) one imperforate sheet from each plate, known as the Imprimatur (or officially approved) sheet. Some stamps were removed from time to time for presentation purposes and have come on to the market, but these imperfs. are not listed as they were not issued.

However, other imperforate stamps are known to have been issued and these are listed where it has been possible to prove that they do not come from the Imprimatur sheets. It is therefore advisable to purchase these only when accompanied by an Expert Committee certificate of genuineness.

Corner Letters. With the exception of the 4d., 6d. and 1s. of 1855-57, the ½d., 1½d., 2d. and 5d. of 1880, the 1d. lilac of 1881 and the £5 (which had letters in lower corners only, and in the reverse order to the normal), all the surface-printed stamps issued prior to 1887 had letters in all four corners, as in the later line-engraved stamps. The arrangement is the same, the letters running in sequence right across and down the sheets, whether these were divided into panes or not. The corner letters existing naturally depend on the number of stamps in the sheet and their arrangement.

Plate Numbers. All stamps from No. 75 to No. 163 bear in their designs either the plate number or, in one or two earlier instances, some other indication by which one plate can be distinguished from another. With the aid of these and of the corner letters it is thus possible to " reconstruct " a sheet of stamps from any plate of any issue or denomination—a task undertaken by many collectors.

Wing Margins. As the vertical gutters (spaces) between the panes, into which sheets of stamps of most values were divided until the introduction of the Imperial Crown watermark, were perforated through the centre with a single row of holes, instead of each vertical row of stamps on the inner side of the panes having its own line of perforation as is now usual, a proportion of the stamps in each sheet have what is called a " wing margin " about 5 mm. wide on one or other side.

The stamps with " wing margins " are the watermark Emblems and Spray of Rose series (3d. 6d. 9d. 10d. 1s. and 2s.) with letters D, E, H or I in S.E. corner, and the watermark Garter series (4d. and 8d.) with letters F or G in S.E. corner. Knowledge of this lettering will enable collectors to guard against stamps with wing margin cut down and re-perforated, but note that wing margin stamps of Nos. 62 to 73 are also to be found re-perforated.

Perforations. All the surface-printed issues of Queen Victoria are Perf. 14, with the exception of Nos. 126 to 129.

III.—SURFACE-PRINTED STAMPS.

(Printed by Messrs. De La Rue & Co., until 1911.)

14

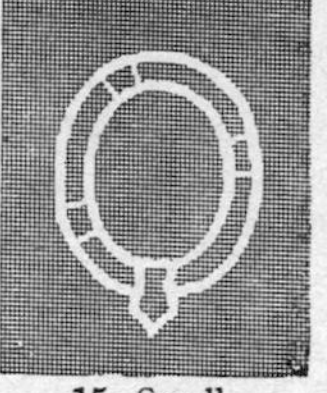
15. Small.

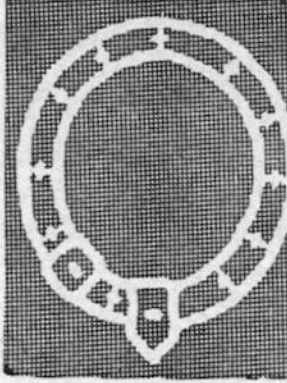
16. Medium.

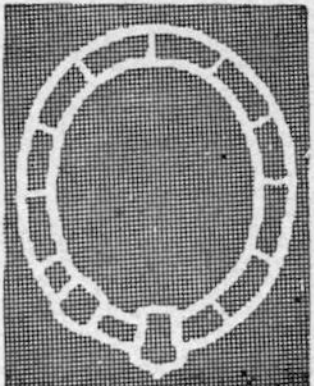
17. Large.

FOR WELL CENTRED LIGHTLY USED COPIES ADD 100% (Nos. 62/73)

1855–57

I. *Wmk. SMALL Garter, T* **15.** *Highly glazed, deeply blued paper* (31 July 1855).

62	**14**	4d. carmine (*shades*)	£1100	55·00
		a. Paper slightly blued	£1100	55·00
		b. White paper	£1500	£150

II. *Wmk. MEDIUM Garter, T* **16.**

(*a*) *Thick, blued highly glazed paper* (25 Feb. 1856).

63	**14**	4d. carmine (*shades*)	£1400	60·00
		a. White paper	£1100	

(*b*) *Ordinary thin white paper* (Sept. 1856).

64	**14**	4d. pale carmine	£600	45·00

(*c*) *Ordinary white paper, specially prepared ink* (1 Nov. 1856).

65	**14**	4d. rose *or* deep rose	£700	50·00

II. *Wmk. LARGE Garter, T* **17.** *Ordinary white paper* (Jan. 1857).

66	**14**	4d. rose-carmine	£200	10·00
		a. Rose	£170	10·00
		b. Thick glazed paper	£500	25·00

18

19

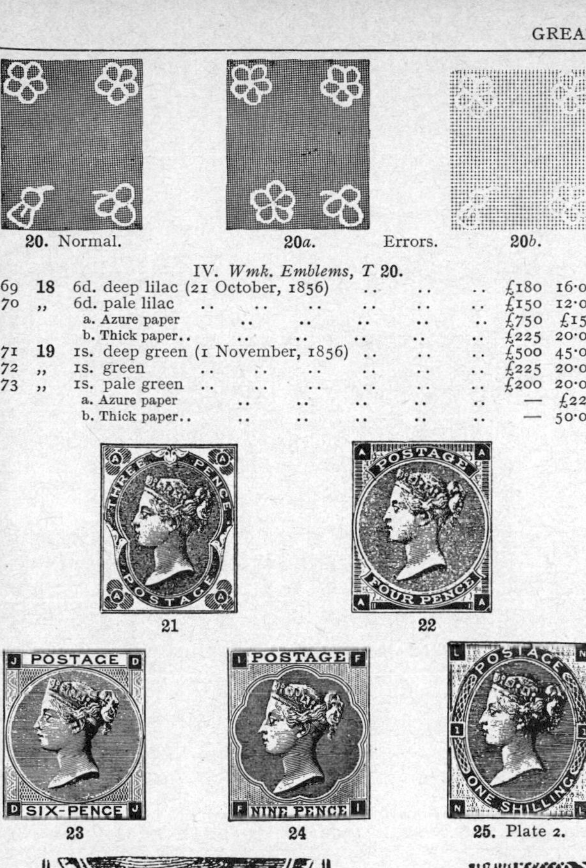

20. Normal. 20*a*. Errors. 20*b*.

IV. *Wmk. Emblems, T* **20**.

69	**18**	6d. deep lilac (21 October, 1856)	£180	16·00
70	,,	6d. pale lilac	£150	12·00
		a. Azure paper	£750	£150
		b. Thick paper..	£225	20·00
71	**19**	1s. deep green (1 November, 1856)	£500	45·00
72	,,	1s. green	£225	20·00
73	,,	1s. pale green	£200	20·00
		a. Azure paper	—	£225
		b. Thick paper..	—	50·00

21 22

23 24 **25.** Plate 2.

A. White dots added.

B. Hair lines.

FOR WELL CENTRED LIGHTLY USED COPIES ADD 75%

1862–64. *A small uncoloured letter in each corner, the 4d. wmk. Large Garter,* T **17**, *the others Emblems, T* **20**.

75	**21**	3d. deep carmine-rose (Plate 2) (1 May, 1862) ..	£400	55·00
76	,,	3d. bright carmine-rose	£190	30·00
77	,,	3d. pale carmine-rose	£190	30·00
		b. Thick paper	—	40·00
78	,,	3d. rose (with white dots, Type A, Plate 3) (Aug. '62)	*	£1100
		a. Imperf. (Plate 3)	£700	
79	**22**	4d. bright red (Plate 3) (15 January, 1862) ..	£225	17·00
80	,,	4d. pale red	£130	11·00
81	,,	4d. bright red (Hair lines, Type B, Plate 4) (16 October, 1863)	£160	12·00
82	,,	4d. pale red (Hair Lines, Type B, Plate 4) ..	£140	10·00
		a. Imperf. (Plate 4)	£300	
83	**23**	6d. deep lilac (Plate 3) (1 December, 1862) ..	£200	22·00
84	,,	6d. lilac	£160	11·00
		a. Azure paper..	—	£125
		b. Thick paper..	—	15·00
		c. Error. Wmk. three roses and thistle (Type 20b) (Stamp TF) ..		
85	,,	6d. lilac (Hair lines, Plate 4) (20 April, 1864) ..	£250	25·00
		a. Imperf.	£350	
		c. Thick paper..	£375	30·00
86	**24**	9d. bistre (Plate 2) (15 January, 1862) ..	£300	35·00
87	,,	9d. straw	£300	35·00
		a. On azure paper		
		b. Thick paper..	£950	50·00
88	,,	9d. bistre (Hair lines, Plate 3) (May, 1862) ..	£3250	£700
89	**25**	1s. deep green (Plate No. 1 = Plate 2) (1 Dec. 1862)..	£225	28·00
90	,,	1s. green (Plate No. 1 = Plate 2)	£200	16·00
		a. " K " in lower left corner in white circle (stamp KD) ..	£1500	£175
		aa. " K " normal (stamp KD)	—	£200
		b. On azure paper		
		c. Thick paper	—	40·00
		ca. Thick paper, " K " in circle as No. 90a	—	£275
91	,,	1s. deep green (Plate No. 2 = Plate 3)	£6500	
		a. Imperf.	£500	*

NOTES. The 3d. as **T21**, but with network background in the spandrels, which is found overprinted " SPECIMEN ", was never issued.

The plates of this issue may be distinguished as follows:—

3d. Plate 2. No white dots. Plate 3. White dots as Illustration A.
4d. Plate 3. No hair lines. Roman I next to lower corner letters. Plate 4. Hair lines in corners. (Illustration B.) Roman II.
6d. Plate 3. No hair lines. Plate 4. Hair lines in corners.
9d. Plate 2. No hair lines. Plate 3. Hair lines in corners. Beware of faked lines.
1s. Plate 2. Numbered 1 on stamps. Plate 3. Numbered 2 on stamps and with hair lines.

The variety " K " in circle, found on stamps lettered K D, is due to the K plug not being driven home when the plate was being lettered, so that there was a slight circular indentation which appeared as an uncoloured line on the stamps. Unused, only two copies are known.

The 9d. on azure paper (No. 87*a*) is very rare, only one specimen being known.

The watermark variety " three roses and a shamrock " illustrated in Type **20***a* was evidently due to the substitution of an extra rose for the thistle in a faulty watermark bit. It is found on stamp T A of Plates 2 and 4 of the 3d., Plates 5 and 6 of the 6d., Plate 4 of the 9d. and Plate 4 of the 1s.

26

27

28
(Without hyphen between "SIX PENCE".)

29

30

31

FOR WELL CENTRED LIGHTLY USED COPIES ADD 75%

1865–67. *Large uncoloured corner letters. Wmk. Large Garter, (4d.); others Emblems.*

92	**26**	3d. rose (Plate No. 4) (1 March, 1865)	£160	12·00
		a. Error. Wmk. three roses and shamrock (Type 20a) ..	£350	£110
		b. Thick paper	£180	14·00
93	**27**	4d. dull vermilion (4 July, 1865)	90·00	8·00
94	,,	4d. vermilion	80·00	8·00
		a. Imperf. (Plates 11, 12)	£100	
95	,,	4d. deep vermilion	80·00	11·00

Plate No.				Plate No.			
7 ..	**1865** ..	£120	10·00	11 ..	**1869** ..	90·00	8·00
8 ..	**1866** ..	90·00	10·00	12 ..	**1870** ..	80·00	8·00
9 ..	**1867** ..	90·00	8·00	13 ..	**1872** ..	90·00	10·00
10 ..	**1868** ..	£140	11·00	14 ..	**1873** ..	£125	11·00

96	**28**	6d. deep lilac (with hyphen) (1 April, 1865)	£165	13·00
97	,,	6d. lilac (with hyphen)	£130	10·00
		a. Thick paper	£140	14·00
		b. Stamp doubly printed (Plate 6)	—	£1500
		c. Error. Wmk. three roses and shamrock (Type 20*a*, Pl. 5, 6) *from*	—	£140
		Pl. 5 .. **1865** .. £130 10·00 | Pl. 6 .. **1867** ..	£450	25·00
98	**29**	9d. straw (Plate No. 4) (1 December, 1865) ..	£300	75·00
		a. Thick paper	£400	£130
		b. Error. Wmk. three roses and shamrock (Type 20*a*) ..	—	£190
99	**30**	10d. red-brown (Plate No. 1) (11.11.67)	*	£5500
101	**31**	1s. green (Plate No. 4) (1 February, 1865).. ..	£140	9·00
		a. Error. Wmk. three roses and shamrock (Type 20*a*) ..	—	£140
		b. Thick paper	£160	30·00
		c. Imperf. between (vert. pr.)	—	£1400

NOTES ON 1865–67 ISSUE. From mid-1866 to about the end of 1871 4d. stamps of this issue appeared generally with watermark inverted.

Unused copies of No. 98 from Plate No. 5 exist, but this was never put to press and all evidence points to the existing copies being from a portion of the Imprimatur sheet which was perforated by De La Rue in 1887 for insertion in albums to be presented to members of the Stamp Committee (*Price £6500 un.*).

The 10d. stamps, No. 99, were printed in *error* on paper wmkd. " Emblems " instead of on paper wmkd. " Spray ".

32

33

34

FOR WELL CENTRED LIGHTLY USED COPIES ADD 75% (Nos. 102/121)

1867–80. *Wmk. Spray of Rose, T* **33.**

102 **26** 3d. deep rose (12 July, 1867) .. .. .. 90·00 10·00
103 ,, 3d. rose .. .. 80·00 5·00
a. Imperf. (Plates 6, 8) .. .. *from* £250

Plate No.				Plate No.			
4	**1867**	£140	19·00	8	**1872**	£100	7·00
5	**1868**	80·00	5·00	9	,,	£100	8·00
6	**1870**	85·00	5·00	10	**1873**	£120	11·00
7	**1871**	£100	7·00				

104 **28** 6d. lilac (with hyphen) (Pl. 6) (21 June, 1867) .. £190 11·00
105 ,, 6d. deep lilac (with hyphen) (Pl. 6) .. .. £190 11·00
106 ,, 6d. purple (with hyphen) (Pl. 6) .. .. .. £190 14·00
107 ,, 6d. bright violet (with hyphen) (Pl. 6) (22 July, '68) £190 11·00
108 ,, 6d. dull violet (without hyphen) (Pl. 8) (13 Mar., '69) £110 10·00
109 ,, 6d. mauve (without hyphen) .. .. £110 9·00
a. Imperf. (Plate Nos. 8 and 9) £250 £200

Plate No.				
8	**1869**	mauve	£110	10·00
,, 9	**1870**	mauve	£110	9·00
,, 10	**1869**	mauve	*	£5500

110 **29** 9d. straw (Plate No. 4) (3 October, 1867) .. £200 28·00
111 ,, 9d. pale straw (Plate No. 4) .. .. .. £200 28·00
a. Imperf. (Plate 4) £600
112 **30** 10d. red-brown (1 July, 1867) .. .. .. £350 32·00
113 ,, 10d. pale red-brown .. .. £350 32·00
114 ,, 10d. deep red-brown .. .. £450 55·00
a. Imperf. (Plate 1) £500

Pl. 1 .. **1867** .. £350 32·00 | Pl. 2 .. **1867** .. £7000 £1400

115 **31** 1s. deep green (13 July, 1867) .. .. .. £120 3·50
117 ,, 1s. pale green .. .. £110 2·50
a. Imperf. between (pair) (Plate 7) .. .. ..
b. Imperf. (Plate 4) £300 £200

Plate No.				Plate No.			
4	**1867**	£110	2·50	6	**1872**	£150	3·50
5	**1871**	£130	3·00	7	**1873**	£150	10·00

118 **32** 2s. dull blue (1 July, 1867) .. .. .. £400 22·00
119 ,, 2s. deep blue .. .. £400 22·00
a. Imperf. (Plate 1) £500
120 ,, 2s. pale blue .. .. £550 28·00
aa. Imperf. (Plate 1) £600
120*a* ,, 2s. cobalt £2000 £250
120*b* ,, 2s. milky blue.. .. .. £1000 85·00

Pl. 1 .. **1867** .. £400 22·00 | Pl. 3 **1868** .. * £1600

121 **32** 2s. brown (Plate No. 1) (27 February, 1880) .. £1800 £300
a. Imperf. £1600

FOR WELL CENTRED LIGHTLY USED COPIES ADD 50%

1872–73. *Uncoloured letters in corners. Wmk. Spray, T* **33.**

122 **34** 6d. deep chestnut (12 April, 1872) .. .. .. £140 7·00
123 ,, 6d. chestnut (23 May, 1872) .. .. .. £100 7·00
124 ,, 6d. pale buff (26 October, 1872) .. .. .. £120 13·00

Plate No.				
11	**1872**	deep chestnut	£140	7·00
,, 11	,,	chestnut	£100	7·00
,, 11	,,	pale buff	£120	13·00
,, 12	,,	pale chestnut†	*	£550
,, 12	,,	chestnut†	*	£550
,, 12	,,	pale buff	£250	25·00

(†) The prices quoted are for the true pale chestnut and chestnut shades which are very rare (in this plate).

125 **34** 6d. grey (Plate No. 12) (24 April, 1873) .. .. £150 14·00
a. Imperf. £400

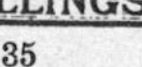
35

36

37

38

39

40

FOR WELL CENTRED LIGHTLY USED COPIES ADD 50%

1867–83. *Uncoloured letters in corners.*

(i.) *Wmk. Maltese Cross, T* **39.** *P* 15½ × 15.

126 **35** 5s. rose (1 July, 1867) .. .. £550 45·00
127 ,, 5s. pale rose .. .. £650 45·00
a. Imperf. (Plate 1) £900

Pl. 1 .. **1867** .. £550 45·00 | Pl. 2 .. **1874** .. £800 60·00

128 **36** 10s. greenish grey (Pl. 1) (26 Sept., '78) £5000 £250
129 **37** £1 brown-lilac (Pl. 1) (26 Sept., '78) £6000 £450

(ii.) *Wmk. Anchor. T* **40.** *P* 14. (*a*) *Blued paper.*

130 **35** 5s. rose (Plate No. 4) (25 November, 1882) .. £2000 £200
131 **36** 10s. grey-green (Plate No. 1) (February, 1883) .. £6000 £350
132 **37** £1 brown-lilac (Plate No. 1) (December, 1882) .. £8000 £900
133 **38** £5 orange (Plate No. 1) (21 March, 1882) £5500 £750

(*b*) *White paper.*

134 **35** 5s. rose (Plate No. 4) £1800 £175
135 **36** 10s. greenish grey (Plate No. 1) £6000 £375
136 **37** £1 brown-lilac (Plate No. 1) £7000 £800
137 **38** £5 orange (Plate No. 1) £2000 £500

41

42

43

44

45

46

47

48

FOR WELL CENTRED LIGHTLY USED COPIES ADD 50%
(Nos. 138/163)

1873–80. *Large coloured letters in the corners.*

(i.) *Wmk. Anchor, T* **47**.

138 **41** 2½d. rosy mauve (*blued paper*) (1 July, 1875) .. £120 16·00
a. Imperf. .. ..
139 ,, 2½d. rosy mauve (*white paper*) .. .. .. 90·00 7·00

Plate No.				
1 (*blued paper*)	**1875**	..	£120	16·00
,, 1 (*white paper*)	,,	..	90·00	7·00
,, 2 (*blued paper*)	,,	..	£1200	£175
,, 2 (*white paper*)	,,	..	90·00	7·00
,, 3 (*white paper*)	,,	..	£120	12·00
,, 3 (*blued paper*)	,,	..	—	£500

Error of Lettering L H—F L *for* L H—H L (*Plate No.* 2).

140 **41** 2½d. rosy mauve £4000 £200

(ii.) *Wmk. Orb, T* **48**.

141 **41** 2½d. rosy mauve (16 May, 1876) .. .. .. 70·00 5·00

Plate No.				Plate No.			
3	**1876**	£120	12·00	11	**1878**	70·00	5·00
4	,,	70·00	5·00	12	,,	70·00	7·00
5	,,	70·00	7·00	13	,,	70·00	7·00
6	,,	70·00	5·00	14	**1879**	70·00	5·00
7	**1877**	70·00	5·00	15	,,	70·00	5·00
8	,,	70·00	7·00	16	,,	70·00	5·00
9	,,	70·00	5·00	17	**1880**	£140	25·00
10	**1878**	85·00	7·00				

142 **41** 2½d. blue (5 February, 1880) .. .. .. 60·00 2·75

Plate No.				Plate No.			
17	**1880**	60·00	5·00	19	**1880**	60·00	2·75
18	,,	75·00	4·00	20	,,	60·00	2·75

(iii.) *Wmk. Spray, T* **33**.

143 **42** 3d. rose (5 July, 1873) .. .. .. 80·00 5·00
144 ,, 3d. pale rose .. .. 80·00 5·00

Plate No.				Plate No.			
11	**1873**	80·00	5·00	17	**1875**	90·00	6·00
12	,,	90·00	6·00	18	,,	90·00	6·00
14	**1874**	£100	7·00	19	**1876**	80·00	6·00
15	,,	80·00	6·00	20	**1879**	90·00	10·00
16	**1875**	80·00	6·00				

145 **43** 6d. pale buff (Plate No. 13) (15 March, 1873) .. * £1200
146 ,, 6d. deep grey (31 March, 1874) .. .. .. 70·00 6·00
147 ,, 6d. grey .. .. 70·00 6·00

Plate No.				Plate No.			
13	**1874**	70·00	7·00	16	**1878**	70·00	6·00
14	**1875**	70·00	7·00	17	**1880**	£100	10·00
15	**1876**	70·00	6·00				

148 **44** 1s. deep green (1 September, 1873) .. .. £110 9·00
150 ,, 1s. pale green .. .. 75·00 7·50

Plate No.				Plate No.			
8	**1873**	£110	9·00	12	**1875**	75·00	7·50
9	**1874**	£110	9·00	13	**1876**	75·00	7·50
10	,,	£100	9·00	14	—		* £5500
11	**1875**	£100	9·00				

151 **44** 1s. orange-brown (Plate No. 13) (14 Oct., '80) .. £350 40·00

(iv.) *Wmk. Large Garter, T* **17**.

152 **45** 4d. vermilion (1 March, 1876) .. .. .. £185 35·00

Pl. 15	**1876**	£185	35·00	Pl. 16	**1874**		* £5500

153 **45** 4d. sage-green (12 March, 1877) .. .. .. £100 20·00

Plate No.				Plate No.			
15	**1877**	£125	22·00	17	**1877**		* £3000
16	,,	£100	20·00				

154 **45** 4d. grey-brown (Plate No. 17) (15 Aug., '80) .. £175 25·00
a. Imperf. .. ..
156 **46** 8d. orange (Plate No. 1) (11 Sept., '76) .. .. £175 22·00

1876 (July). *Prepared for use but not issued.*

156*a* **46** 8d. purple-brown (Plate No. 1) £1000

49

3d
(50)

1880–83. *Wmk. Imperial Crown, T* **49**.

157 **41** 2½d. blue (23 March, 1881) .. .. 55·00 1·75

Plate No.				Plate No.			
21	**1881**	75·00	2·00	23	**1881**	55·00	1·75
22	,,	55·00	1·75				

158 **42** 3d. rose (February, 1881) .. .. 65·00 4·00

Pl. 20	**1881**	85·00	10·00	Pl. 21	**1881**	65·00	4·00

159 **42** 3d. on 3d. lilac (T **50**) (C.) (Pl. 21) (1 Jan., '83) .. 60·00 18·00
160 **45** 4d. grey-brown (9 December, 1880) .. .. .. 55·00 4·00

Pl. 17	**1880**	55·00	4·00	Pl. 18	**1882**	55·00	4·00

161 **43** 6d. grey (1 January, 1881) .. .. 55·00 4·50

Pl. 17	**1881**	65·00	4·50	Pl. 18	**1882**	55·00	4·50

162 **43** 6d. on 6d. lilac (as T **50**) (C.) (Pl. 18) (1 Jan., '83) .. 60·00 18·00
a. Slanting dots (various) .. .. .. *from* 70·00 20·00
b. Opt. double .. .. — £1800
163 **44** 1s. orange-brown (29 May, 1881) .. .. .. 70·00 9·00

Pl. 13	**1881**	80·00	11·00	Pl. 14	**1881**	70·00	9·00

The 1s. Plates 13 and 14 are known in purple, but were not issued thus. They come from the Souvenir Album prepared for members of the "Stamp Committee of 1884".

52

53

54

55

56

FOR WELL CENTRED LIGHTLY USED COPIES ADD 50%
(Nos. 164/74)

1880–81. *Wmk. Imperial Crown, T* **49**.

164 **52** ½d. deep green (14 October, 1880) .. .. .. 5·00 90
a. Imperf. .. .. 90·00
165 ,, ½d. pale green .. .. 6·00 1·00
166 **53** 1d. Venetian red (1 January, 1880) .. .. 2·00 25
a. Imperf. .. .. 90·00
167 **54** 1½d. Venetian red (14 October, 1880) .. .. 22·00 6·00
168 **55** 2d. pale rose (8 December, 1880) .. .. 32·00 7·50
168*a* ,, 2d. deep rose .. .. 32·00 7·50
169 **56** 5d. indigo (15 March, 1881) .. .. .. £140 14·00
a. Imperf. £200

Die I.

57

Die II.

1881. *Wmk. Imperial Crown, T* **49**. (*a*) 14 *dots in each corner, Die* I (12 July).

170 **57** 1d. lilac .. .. 32·00 3·50
171 ,, 1d. pale lilac .. .. 32·00 3·50

(*b*) 16 *dots in each corner, Die* II (12 December).

172 **57** 1d. lilac 40 15
172*a* ,, 1d. bluish lilac .. .. 65·00 15·00
b. Blued paper £500
173 ,, 1d. deep purple 40 15
a. Printed both sides .. .. .. £175 †
b. Frame broken at bottom .. .. .. £175 65·00
c. Printed on gummed side .. .. .. £140 †
d. Imperf. three sides (pair) .. .. .. £700 †
e. Printed both sides but impression on back inverted .. £175 †
f. No watermark .. .. 80·00 †
174 ,, 1d. mauve 40 15
a. Imperf. (pair) £250

1d. stamps with the words "PEAR'S SOAP" printed on back in *orange*, *blue* or *mauve* price *from* £110, *unused.*

The variety "frame broken at bottom" shows a white space just inside the bottom frame-line from between the "N" and "E" of "ONE" to below the first "N" of "PENNY", breaking the pearls and cutting into the lower part of the oval below "PEN".

58

59

60

FOR WELL CENTRED LIGHTLY USED COPIES ADD 50% (Nos. 175/86).

1883–84. *Coloured letters in the corners. Wmk. Anchor, T* **40.**

(i) *Blued paper.*

175	**58**	2s. 6d. lilac (2 July, 1883)	£250	65·00
176	**59**	5s. rose (1 April, 1884)	£900	£180
177	**60**	10s. ultramarine (1 April, 1884)	£3250	£450
177*a*	,,	10s. cobalt (May, 1884)	£4500	£1100

(ii) *White paper.*

178	**58**	2s. 6d. lilac	£140	18·00
179	,,	2s. 6d. deep lilac	£140	18·00
		a. Deep lilac, blued paper (issued during "white paper" period)	£400	90·00
180	**59**	5s. rose	£175	25·00
181	,,	5s. crimson	£175	25·00
182	**60**	10s. cobalt	£4000	£800
183	,,	10s. ultramarine	£300	60·00
183*a*	,,	10s. pale ultramarine	£300	60·00

61

A.
B.

1884 (1 APRIL). *Wmk.* 3 *Imperial Crowns, T* **49.**

185	**61**	£1 brown-lilac	£2750	£250
		a. Frame broken. Plate 2, letters JC (ill. A) or TA (ill. B)	£3500	£400

1888 (1 FEB.). *Wmk.* 3 *Orbs, T* **48.**

186	**61**	£1 brown-lilac	£6000	£450
		a. Frame broken. Plate 2, letters JC (ill. A) or TA (ill. B)	—	£600

62

63

64

65

66

FOR WELL CENTRED LIGHTLY USED COPIES ADD 100%

1883 (1 AUG.) (9*d.*) *or* **1884** (1 APRIL) (*others*). *Wmk. Imperial Crown, T* **49** (*sideways on horiz. designs*).

187	**52**	½d. slate-blue	2·50	40
		a. Imperf.	£100	
188	**62**	1½d. lilac	18·00	4·00
		a. Imperf.	£140	
189	**63**	2d. lilac	20·00	5·50
		a. Imperf.	£140	
190	**64**	2½d. lilac	15·00	1·50
		a. Imperf.	£175	
191	**65**	3d. lilac	35·00	9·00
		a. Imperf.	£175	
192	**66**	4d. dull green	45·00	18·00
		a. Imperf.	£175	
193	**62**	5d. dull green	40·00	18·00
		a. Imperf.	£175	
194	**63**	6d. dull green	45·00	20·00
		a. Imperf.	£175	
195	**64**	9d. dull green (1 August, 1883)	£175	65·00
196	**65**	1s. dull green	£125	40·00
		a. Imperf.	£175	

The above prices are for stamps in the true dull green colour. Stamps which have been soaked, causing the colour to run, are virtually worthless.

Stamps of the above set and No. 180 are also found perf. 12; these are official perforations, but were never issued. A second variety of the 5d. is known with a line instead of a stop under the "d" in the value; this was never issued and is therefore only known *unused.* (*Price* £1500.)

71

72

73

74

75

76

77

78

79

80

81

82

Plate I

Plate II

Plate I: Square dots to right of " d ".
Plate II: Thin vertical lines to right of " d ".

FOR WELL CENTRED LIGHTLY USED COPIES ADD 50% (Nos. 197/214)

1887 (1 Jan.)–**1892.** " *Jubilee* " *issue. New types. The bicoloured stamps have the value tablets, or the frames including the value tablets, in the second colour. Wmk. Imperial Crown, T* **49** (*Three Crowns on £1*).

No.	Type	Description	Unused	Used
197	**71**	½d. vermilion	30	15
		a. Printed on gummed side	£225	†
		b. Printed both sides		
		c. Doubly printed	£650	
		d. Imperf.	£100	
197*e*	,,	½d. orange-vermilion	30	15
198	**72**	1½d. dull purple and green	5·00	40
		a. Purple part of design double		
199	**73**	2d. green and vermilion	£140	35·00
200	,,	2d. green and carmine	6·00	1·25
201	**74**	2½d. purple/*blue*	2·00	15
		a. Printed on gummed side	—	†
		b. Imperf. three sides	£250	
202	**75**	3d. purple/*yellow*	6·00	50
		a. Imperf.		
203	,,	3d. deep purple/*yellow*	6·00	50
204	,,	3d. purple/*orange* (1891)	£190	30·00
205	**76**	4d. green and purple-brown	10·00	2·00
		aa. Imperf.		
205*a*	,,	4d. green and deep brown	10·00	2·00
206	**77**	4½d. green and carmine (15 September, 1892)	1·50	5·00
206*a*	,,	4½d. green and deep bright carmine	90·00	25·00
207	**78**	5d. dull purple and blue (Duty-plate I)	£150	10·00
207*a*	,,	5d. dull purple and blue (Duty-plate II)	12·00	1·50
208	**79**	6d. purple/*rose-red*	5·50	1·50
208*a*	,,	6d. deep purple/*rose-red*	5·00	1·50
209	**80**	9d. dull purple and blue	15·00	6·00
210	**81**	10d. dull purple and carmine (24 February, 1890)	13·00	6·00
		aa. Imperf.	£300	
210*a*	,,	10d. dull purple and deep bright carmine	£160	18·00
211	**82**	1s. green	70·00	10·00
212	**61**	£1 green (27 January, 1891)	£650	£110
		a. Frame broken. Plate 2, letters JC (ill. A) or TA (ill. B)	£850	£200

½d. stamps with " PEARS SOAP " printed on back in *orange, blue,* or *mauve*, price *from* £110 each.

1900. *Wmk. Imperial Crown, T* **49.** *Colours changed.*

No.	Type	Description	Unused	Used
213	**71**	½d. blue-green* (17 April)	45	20
		a. Printed on the gummed side		
		b. Imperf.	£300	
214	**82**	1s. green and carmine (11 July)	18·00	15·00

* The ½d. No. 213, in bright blue, is a colour changeling.

KING EDWARD VII, 1901 (22 Jan.)–1910 (6 May).

83

84

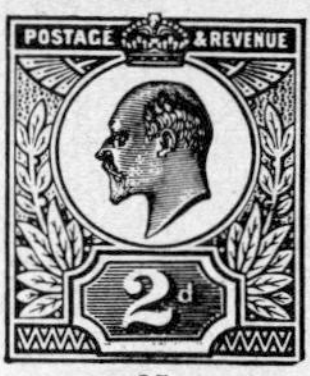

85

86

87

88

89

90

91

92

93

97*a*

94

95

96

97

1902 (1 Jan.)–**10.** *Printed by De La Rue & Co. Wmks. Imperial Crown (½d. to 1s.); Anchor (2s. 6d. to 10s.); Three Crowns (£1). P 14.*

O = "Ordinary" paper. C = Chalk-surfaced paper.

No.	Type	Description	Unused	Used
215	**83**	½d. dull blue-green, O (1 January, 1902)	40	25
216	,,	½d. blue-green, O	40	25
217	,,	½d. pale yellowish green, O (26 November, 1904)	30	15
218	,,	½d. yellowish green, O	30	15
		a. Stamp from booklet with cross attached (pair)	65·00	40·00
		b. Doubly printed (bottom row on one pane) (Control H9)	£1000	
219	**83**	1d. scarlet, O (1 January, 1902)	20	10
220	,,	1d. bright scarlet, O	20	10
		a. Imperf. (pair)	£1000	
221	**84**	1½d. dull purple and green, O (21 March, 1902)	9·00	90
222	,,	1½d. slate-purple and green, O	8·00	80
223	,,	1½d. pale dull purple & green C (6 September, 1905)	11·00	1·25
224	,,	1½d. slate-purple and bluish green, C	10·00	1·10
225	**85**	2d. yellowish green & carmine, O (25 March, 1902)	12·00	1·10
226	,,	2d. grey-green and carmine, O (March, 1903)	13·00	1·10
227	,,	2d. grey-green and carmine, C (6 September, 1905)	13·00	1·40
228	,,	2d. deep grey-green & scarlet, C (July, 1910)	14·00	2·00
229	,,	2d. pale blue-green and carmine, C	30·00	10·00
230	**86**	2½d. ultramarine, O (1 January, 1902)	1·50	50
231	,,	2½d. pale ultramarine, O	3·00	75
232	**87**	3d. dull purple/*orange-yellow*, O (20 March, 1902)	9·00	75
232*a*	,,	3d. deep purple/*orange-yellow*, O	10·00	75
232*b*	,,	3d. pale reddish pur./*orange-yell.*, C (31 March '06)	40·00	4·00
233	,,	3d. dull purple/*orange-yellow*, C	60·00	6·00
233*a*	,,	3d. dull reddish purple/*yellow* (*lemon* back), C	40·00	5·00
233*b*	,,	3d. pale purple/*lemon*, C	8·00	1·00
234	,,	3d. purple/*lemon*, C	8·00	1·10
235	**88**	4d. green and grey-brown, O (27 March, 1902)	22·00	3·00
236	,,	4d. green and chocolate-brown, O	25·00	3·00
237	,,	4d. green and chocolate-brown, C (19 Jan., 1906)	22·00	3·00
238	,,	4d. deep green and chocolate-brown, C	25·00	4·00
239	,,	4d. brown-orange, O (1 November, 1909)	70·00	18·00
240	,,	4d. pale orange, O (December, 1909)	5·00	2·00
241	,,	4d. orange-red, O (December, 1909)	5·00	2·00
242	**89**	5d. dull purple & ultramarine, O (14 May, 1902)	16·00	2·00
243	,,	5d. dull purple and ultramarine, C	20·00	2·50
244	,,	5d. slate-purple & ultramarine, C (19 May, 1906)	16·00	2·50
245	**83**	6d. pale dull purple, O (1 January, 1902)	8·00	1·00
246	,,	6d. slate-purple, O	8·00	1·00
247	,,	6d. pale dull purple, C (1 October, 1905)	14·00	90
248	,,	6d. dull purple, C	10·00	90
249	**90**	7d. grey-black, O (4 May, 1910)	1·00	2·00
249*a*	,,	7d. deep grey-black, O	55·00	18·00
250	**91**	9d. dull purple and ultramarine, O (7 April, 1902)	22·00	7·00
251	,,	9d. slate-purple and ultramarine, O	22·00	7·00
252	,,	9d. dull purple and ultramarine, C (29 June, 1905)	25·00	8·00
253	,,	9d. slate-purple and ultramarine, C	25·00	8·00
254	**92**	10d. dull purple and carmine, O (3 July, 1902)	24·00	4·00
		a. No cross on crown	60·00	25·00
255	,,	10d. slate-purple and carmine, C (6 September, 1905)	24·00	6·00
		a. No cross on crown	50·00	20·00
256	,,	10d. dull purple and scarlet, C (September, 1910)	25·00	7·50
		a. No cross on crown	50·00	22·00
257	**93**	1s. dull green and carmine, O (24 March, 1902)	20·00	2·00
258	,,	1s. dull green and carmine, C (6 September, 1905)	24·00	2·50
259	,,	1s. dull green and scarlet, C (September, 1910)	24·00	2·50
260	**94**	2s. 6d. lilac, O (5 April, 1902)	£100	18·00
261	,,	2s. 6d. pale dull purple, C (7 October, 1905)	£100	18·00
262	,,	2s. 6d. dull purple, C	£100	18·00
263	**95**	5s. bright carmine, O (5 April, 1902)	£150	22·00
264	,,	5s. deep bright carmine, O	£150	22·00
265	**96**	10s. ultramarine, O (5 April, 1902)	£300	65·00
266	**97**	£1 dull blue-green, O (16 June, 1902)	£650	£110

1910 (May). *Prepared for use, but not issued.*

No.	Type	Description	Unused	Used
266*a*	**97*a***	2d. Tyrian plum	£6000	

One copy of this stamp is known used, but it was never issued to the public.

To distinguish De La Rue printings from the provisional printings of the same values made either by Messrs. Harrison & Sons or at Somerset House, the following hints may be helpful. The 6*d.* is the only value on *chalk-surfaced paper*, printed by De La Rue and also at Somerset House. The latter printing can be distinguished by the shade and impression.

Of the stamps *on ordinary paper*, the De La Rue impressions are usually clearer and of a higher finish than those of the other printers. The shades are markedly different except in some printings of the 4*d.*, 6*d.*, and 7*d.* and in the 5*s.*, 10*s.*, and £1. With a little experience the collector should have no difficulty in allotting unused specimens of any value to their respective printings.

1911. *Printed by Harrison & Sons. "Ordinary" paper. Wmk. Imperial Crown.* (*a*) *P 14.*

No.	Type	Description	Unused	Used
267	**88**	½d. dull yellow-green (3 May, 1911)	85	20
268	,,	½d. dull green	1·50	20
269	,,	½d. deep dull green	6·00	1·50
270	,,	½d. pale bluish green	12·00	5·00
		a. From booklet, with cross attached (pair)	65·00	40·00
		b. Wmk. sideways		
		c. Imperf. (pair)		
271	,,	½d. bright green (fine impression) (June, 1911)	£125	35·00
272	,,	1d. rose-red (3 May, 1911)	75	20
		a. No wmk.	50·00	40·00
273	,,	1d. deep rose-red	1·50	30
274	,,	1d. rose-carmine	18·00	3·50
275	,,	1d. aniline pink (May, 1911)	£140	35·00
275*a*	,,	1d. aniline rose	60·00	20·00
276	**86**	2½d. bright blue (10 July, 1911)	10·00	4·50
277	**87**	3d. purple/*lemon* (12 September, 1911	18·00	18·00
277*a*	,,	3d. grey/*lemon*	£1750	
278	**88**	4d. bright orange (13 July, 1911)	22·00	16·00

(*b*) *P* 15 × 14.

No.	Type	Description	Unused	Used
279	**83**	½d. dull green (30 October, 1911)	6·00	5·00
279*a*	,,	½d. deep dull green	7·50	6·00
280	,,	1d. rose-red (5 October, 1911)	10·00	4·00
281	,,	1d. rose-carmine	2·00	90
282	,,	1d. pale rose-carmine	2·00	1·50
283	**86**	2½d. bright blue (14 October, 1911)	7·50	1·25
284	,,	2½d. dull blue	6·00	1·25
285	**87**	3d. purple/*lemon* (22 September, 1911)	5·00	50
285*a*	,,	3d. grey/*lemon*	£1750	
286	**88**	4d. bright orange (22 November, 1911)	6·00	1·25

1911–13. *Printed at Somerset House. Ordinary paper, unless marked* C (*=chalk-surfaced paper*). *Wmks. as 1902–10. P 14.*

No.	Type	Description	Unused	Used
287	**84**	1½d. reddish purple and bright green (13 July, 1911)	14·00	4·00
288	,,	1½d. dull purple and green	5·00	1·00
289	,,	1½d. slate-purple and green (September, 1912)	6·00	1·50
290	**85**	2d. deep dull green and red (8 August, 1911)	5·00	1·00
291	,,	2d. deep dull green and carmine	5·00	1·00
292	,,	2d. grey-green and bright carmine (11 March, 1912) (carmine shows clearly on back)	5·00	2·25
293	**89**	5d. dull reddish purple & bright blue (7 Aug., 1911)	7·00	2·00
294	,,	5d. deep dull reddish purple and bright blue	7·00	2·00
295	**83**	6d. Royal purple, O (31 October, 1911)	16·00	16·00
296	,,	6d. bright magenta, C (31 October, 1911)	£900	
297	,,	6d. dull purple, O	5·00	1·75
298	,,	6d. reddish purple, O (November, 1911)	5·50	1·75
		a. No cross on crown (*various shades*)	50·00	
299	,,	6d. very deep reddish purple, O (November, '11)	16·00	2·25
300	,,	6d. dark purple, O (March, 1912)	9·00	2·50
301	,,	6d. dull purple "Dickinson" coated paper* (March, 1913)	75·00	20·00
303	,,	6d. deep plum, C (July, 1913)	9·00	9·00
		a. No cross on crown	75·00	
305	**90**	7d. slate-grey (1 August, 1912)	3·00	3·00
306	**91**	9d. reddish purple and light blue (24 July 1911)	22·00	9·00
306*a*	,,	9d. deep dull reddish purple and deep bright blue (September, 1911)	18·00	7·00
307	,,	9d. dull reddish purple and blue (Oct., 1911)	14·00	7·00
307*a*	,,	9d. deep dull reddish purple and blue (July, 1913)	14·00	7·00
308	,,	9d. slate-purple and cobalt-blue (March, 1912)	22·00	9·00
309	**92**	10d. dull purple and scarlet (9 October, 1911)	16·00	6·00
310	,,	10d. dull reddish purple and aniline pink	£125	35·00
311	,,	10d. dull reddish purple and carmine (May, 1912)	14·00	6·00
		a. No cross on crown	70·00	
312	**93**	1s. dark green and scarlet (17 July, 1911)	20·00	7·50
313	,,	1s. deep green and scarlet (9 October, 1911)	20·00	3·00
314	,,	1s. green and carmine (15 April, 1912)	7·00	2·00
315	**94**	2s. 6d. dull greyish purple (27 September, 1911)	£130	28·00
316	,,	2s. 6d. dull reddish purple (October, 1911)	£100	16·00
317	,,	2s. 6d. dark purple	£100	16·00
318	**95**	5s. carmine (29 February, 1912)	£150	22·00
319	**96**	10s. blue (14 January, 1912)	£300	65·00
320	**97**	£1 deep green (3 September, 1911)	£600	£100

* No. 301 was on an experimental coated paper which does not respond to the silver test.

KING GEORGE V,

1910 (6 May)–**1936** (20 Jan.).

PRINTERS. T **98** to **102** were typographed by Harrison & Sons, with the exception of certain preliminary printings, referred to in the footnote below No. 343.

> ☞ WATERMARK VARIETIES.
> For note *re* watermark varieties see after No. 429.

98

99

For type differences see notes below T **101/2**.

Die A

Die B

½d.

Die A. The three upper scales on the body of the right hand dolphin form a triangle; the centre jewel of the cross inside the crown is suggested by a comma.
Die B. The three upper scales are incomplete; the centre jewel is suggested by a crescent.

Die A

Die B

1d.

Die A. The second line of shading on the ribbon to the right of the crown extends right across the wreath; the line nearest to the crown on the right hand ribbon shows as a short line at the bottom of the ribbon.
Die B. The second line of shading is broken in the middle; the first line is little more than a dot.

(Des. Bertram Mackennal and G. W. Eve. Head from photograph by W. & D. Downey. Die eng. J. A. C. Harrison.)

1911–12. *Wmk. Imperial Crown*, *T* **49.** *P* 15×14.

321 **98** ½d. pale green (Die A) (22.6.11) .. .. 1·75 40
322 ,, ½d. grn. (Die A) (22.6.11) 1·00 40
323 ,, ½d. bluish green (Die A) .. £150 15·00
a. Error. Perf. 14 .. .. £1500 £100
324 ,, ½d. yellow-green (Die B) .. 1·25 35
325 ,, ½d. bright green (Die B) .. 1·25 30
a. Wmk. sideways .. .. — £600
326 ,, ½d. bluish green (Die B) .. £100 20·00
327 **99** 1d. carmine-red (Die A) (22.6.11) .. .. 1·60 35
a. Error. Perf. 14 .. .. £2200
b. Experimental ptg. chalk-surfaced paper (Control A.11) £160
c. Wmk. sideways .. .. † —
328 ,, 1d. pale carmine (Die A) (22.6.11) .. .. 2·50 35
a. No Cross on Crown .. £125 30·00
329 ,, 1d. carmine (Die B) .. 80 25
330 ,, 1d. pale carmine (Die B) .. 85 25
a. No Cross on Crown .. £125 25·00
331 ,, 1d. rose-pink (Die B) .. 16·00 2·50
332 ,, 1d. scarlet (Die B) (6.12) .. 9·00 2·50
333 ,, 1d. aniline scarlet (Die B)* 60·00 18·00

* For note *re* anilines see below No. 343.

100

1912 (Aug.). *Wmk. Royal Cypher* ("*Simple*"), *T* **100.** *Booklet stamps. P* 15×14.

334 **98** ½d. pale green (Die B) .. 6·00 3·50
335 ,, ½d. green (Die B) .. .. 6·00 3·50
336 **99** 1d. scarlet (Die B) .. 5·00 3·50
337 ,, 1d. bright scarlet (Die B) 5·00 3·50

101

102

Type differences.

½d. In T **98** the ornament above "P" of "HALFPENNY" has two thin lines of colour; beard is undefined. In T **101** the ornament has one thick line and the beard is well defined.
1d. In T **99** the body of the lion is unshaded and in T **102** it is shaded.

1912 (1 Jan.). *Wmk. Imperial Crown*, *T* **49.** *P* 15×14.

338 **101** ½d. deep green .. .. 2·75 1·00
339 ,, ½d. green 75 15
340 ,, ½d. yellow-green .. .. 1·00 20
a. No Cross on Crown 30·00 5·00
341 **102** 1d. bright scarlet .. 35 15
a. No Cross on Crown .. 22·00 4·00
b. Ptd. double, one albino .. 70·00
342 ,, 1d. scarlet 35 15
343 ,, 1d. aniline scarlet* .. 85·00 20·00
a. No Cross on Crown .. £300

A preliminary printing, from the plates of the 1d. (both types), was made at Somerset House before the plates were handed over to Messrs. Harrison & Sons, but these can only be distinguished with certainty when the control is attached, this being lettered "A. 11," "B. 11," or "B. 12," whereas the Harrison control lacks the period after the letter. The ½d. and 1d. wmk., T **103**, with period after the letter, were also printed at Somerset House.

* Our prices for the aniline scarlet 1d. stamps, Nos. 333 and 343, are for specimens in which the colour is suffused on the surface of the stamp and shows through clearly on the back. Specimens without these characteristics, but which show "aniline" reactions under the quartz lamp are relatively common.

1912 (Aug.). *Wmk. Royal Cypher* ("*Simple*"), *T* **100.** *P* 15×14.

344 **101** ½d. green 50 20
a. No Cross on Crown .. 40·00 9·00
345 **102** 1d. scarlet 40 15
a. No Cross on Crown .. 30·00 6·00

103

1912 (Oct.). *Wmk. Royal Cypher* ("*Multiple*"), *T* **103.** *P* 15×14.

346 **101** ½d. green 60 50
a. No Cross on Crown .. 40·00 12·00
b. Imperf. .. .. 40·00
c. Wmk. sideways .. .. † £300
347 **101** ½d. yellow-green .. .. 2·50 2·00
348 ,, ½d. pale green .. .. 1·25 1·75
349 **102** 1d. bright scarlet .. 2·00 1·25
350 ,, 1d. scarlet .. .. 2·00 1·25
a. No Cross on Crown .. 40·00 7·00
b. Imperf. .. .. 30·00
c. Wmk. sideways .. 55·00 30·00
d. Wmk. sideways. No Cross on Crown £200

No. 357a.

104

No. 357ab.

No. 357ac.

105

106

107

108

Die I.

Die II.

2d. Die I.—Inner frame-line at top and sides close to solid of background. *Four* complete lines of shading between top of head and oval frame-line. White line round "TWOPENCE" thin.
Die II.—Inner frame-line farther from solid of background. *Three* lines between top of head and oval. White line round "TWOPENCE" thicker.

(Des. Bertram Mackennal and G. W. Eve. Head from Coinage Head by Mackennal. Dies eng. J. A. C. Harrison.)

(Typo. by Harrison & Sons, except the 6d. printed by the Stamping Department of the Board of Inland Revenue, Somerset House. The latter also made printings of the following which can only be distinguished by the controls: ½d. B.13; 1½d. A.12; 2d. C.13; 2½d. A.12; 3d. A.12, B.13, C.13; 4d. B.13; 5d. B.13; 7d. C.13; 8d. C.13; 9d. agate B.13; 10d. C.13; 1s. C.13.)

1912–22. *Wmk. Royal Cypher, T* **100.** *P* 15×14.

351 **105** ½d. green (Jan. 1913) 10 10
a. Doubly printed .. £900
352 „ ½d. bright green .. 10 10
353 „ ½d. deep green .. 1·40 30
354 „ ½d. yellow-green .. 4·00 50
355 „ ½d. very yellow (Cyprus) green ('14) .. £1000
356 „ ½d. blue-green .. 20·00 7·00
357 **104** 1d. brt. scar. (10.12) .. 10 10
a. "Q" for "O" (R.1/4) (Control E14) .. 75·00 30·00
ab. "Q" for "O" (R. 4/11) (Control T22) .. £175 40·00
ac. Reversed "Q" for "O" (R. 15/9) (Control T22) £175 40·00
ad. Inverted "Q" for "O" (R. 20/3) .. £200
b. Tête-bêche (pair) .. £4000
358 „ 1d. vermilion .. .. 1·00 25
359 „ 1d. pale rose-red .. 1·50 12
360 „ 1d. carmine-red .. 5·00 1·25
361 „ 1d. scarlet-vermilion 30·00 10·00
a. Printed on back† .. 90·00 †
362 **105** 1½d. red-brn. (Oct., '12) 10 10
a. Error "PENCF" .. 80·00 25·00
b. Booklet pane. Four stamps plus two printed labels .. .. 40·00
363 „ 1½d. chocolate-brown .. 20 15
a. Without wmk. .. 70·00
364 „ 1½d. chestnut 75 12
a. Error. "PENCF" .. 45·00 20·00
365 „ 1½d. yellow-brown .. 10·00 4·00
366 **106** 2d. orange-yellow (Die I.) (Aug., 1912) .. 4·00 80
367 „ 2d. reddish orange (Die I.) (Nov., 1913) 60 12
368 „ 2d. orange (Die I.) .. 35 12
369 „ 2d. bright oran. (Die I.) 70 15
370 „ 2d. orange (Die II.) (Sept., 1921) .. 1·25 40
371 **104** 2½d. cobalt-blue (10.12) 2·50 40
371*a* „ 2½d. bright blue (1914) 2·00 40
372 „ 2½d. blue .. .. 2·50 40
373 „ 2½d. indigo-blue* (toned paper) ('20) £500
373*a* „ 2½d. dull Prussian blue* ('21) £300
374 **106** 3d. dull reddish violet (Oct., 1912) .. 5·00 60
375 „ 3d. violet .. .. 1·50 30
376 „ 3d. bluish violet (11.13) 2·00 30
377 „ 3d. pale violet .. 3·00 30
378 „ 4d. dp. grey-grn. (1.13) 8·00 2·00
379 „ 4d. grey-green .. 1·50 35
380 „ 4d. pale grey-green .. 2·50 1·00
381 **107** 5d. brown (June, 1913) 3·00 1·75
382 „ 5d. yellow-brown .. 2·75 1·75
a. Without wmk. £200
383 „ 5d. bistre-brown .. 22·00 3·00
384 „ 6d. dull pur., **C** (Aug., 1913) .. .. 7·50 2·50
385 „ 6d. reddish purple, **C** 2·00 40
a. Perf. 14 (1921) .. 30·00 18·00
386 „ 6d. deep reddish pur., **C** 3·00 75
387 „ 7d. olive (Aug., '13) .. 7·00 2·25
388 „ 7d. bronze-green (1915 18·00 5·00
389 „ 7d. sage-green (1917)) 12·00 2·75
390 „ 8d. black/*yellow* (Aug., 1913) .. .. 16·00 4·50
391 „ 8d. black/*yellow-buff* (*granite*) (May, '17) 20·00 5·00
392 **108** 9d. agate (June, 1913) 4·00 1·50
393 „ 9d. deep agate .. 6·00 1·75
393*a* „ 9d. olive-green (Sept., 1922) .. .. 45·00 10·00
393*b* „ 9d. pale olive-green 55·00 10·00
394 „ 10d. turq.-bl. (Aug. '13) 7·00 6·00
394*a* „ 10d. deep turq.-blue .. 11·00 7·50
395 „ 1s. bistre-brown (Aug., 1913) .. .. 5·00 50
396 „ 1s. olive-bistre .. 20·00 1·00

Imperf. stamps of this issue exist but may be war-time colour trials.

† The impression of No. 361a is set sideways and is very pale.

* No. 373 comes from Control O 20 and also exists on white paper.

No. 373*a* comes from Control R 21 and also exists on toned paper, but both are unlike the rare Prussian blue shade of the 2½d. Jubilee issue.

See also Nos. 418/29.

For the 2d., T **106** bisected, see "Channel Islands".

1913 (Aug.). *Wmk. Royal Cypher ("Multiple"), T* **103.** *P* 15×14.

397 **105** ½d. bright green .. .. 45·00 25·00
398 **104** 1d. dull scarlet .. .. 85·00 50·00

Both these stamps were originally issued in rolls only. Subsequently sheets were found, so that horizontal pairs and blocks are known but are of considerable rarity.

109

A

110

Nos. 400a and 408a.

No. 415b.

Major Re-entries on 2s. 6d.

(Des. Bertram Mackennal. Dies eng. J. A. C. Harrison. Recess.)

T **109.** *Background around portrait consists of horizontal lines. Wmk. Single Cypher, T* **110.** *P* 11×12.

1913 (July). *Printed by Waterlow Bros. & Layton.*

399 2s. 6d. deep sepia-brown .. 75·00 20·00
400 2s. 6d. sepia-brown .. 70·00 18·00
a. Re-entry (R.2/1) £350 £100
401 5s. rose-carmine .. .. £150 35·00
402 10s. indigo-blue .. .. £300 75·00
403 £1 green £800 £250
404 £1 dull blue-green £700 £250

1915 (Dec.)–**1918.** *Printed by De La Rue & Co.*

405 2s. 6d. deep yellow-brown .. 70·00 18·00
406 2s. 6d. yellow-brown .. 70·00 17·00
407 2s. 6d. pale brown (worn pl.) 70·00 17·00
408 2s. 6d. seal-brown .. .. 70·00 22·00
a. Re-entry (R.2/1) £350 £100
409 5s. bright carmine .. .. £160 35·00
410 5s. pale carmine (worn pl.) £160 35·00
411 10s. deep blue .. .. £750 80·00
412 10s. blue .. .. .. £650 65·00
413 10s. pale blue .. .. £650 65·00

1918 (Dec.). *Printed by Bradbury, Wilkinson & Co., Ltd.*

413*a* 2s. 6d. olive-brown .. .. 40·00 10·00
414 2s. 6d. chocolate-brown .. 45·00 10·00
415 2s. 6d. reddish brown .. 50·00 12·00
415*a* 2s. 6d. pale brown .. .. 40·00 10·00
b. Major re-entry (R.1/2) .. £350 £100
416 5s. rose-red .. .. .. 45·00 12·00
417 10s. dull grey-blue .. .. £100 28·00

For (1934) re-engraved Waterlow printings, see Nos. 450/2.

In the De La Rue printings the gum is usually patchy and yellowish, and the colour of the stamp, particularly in the 5s., tends to show through the back.

The distinguishing characteristics of the Bradbury printings are as follows:—The paper appears whiter owing to use generally of a pure white gum. The holes of the perforation are larger.

In the majority of copies of the Bradbury printings a minute coloured dot appears in the margin just above the middle of the upper frame-line.

A further test for the Bradbury printings is the size; the stamps printed by Waterlow and De La Rue being almost invariably 22 mm. high, while those printed by Bradbury, Wilkinson measure between 22¾ and 23 mm.

111

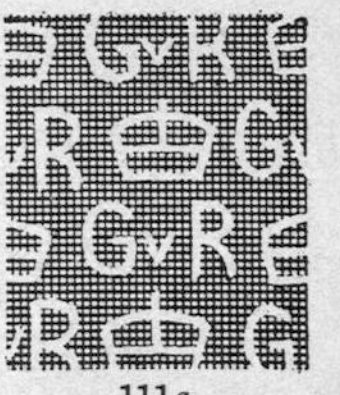

111*a*

TYPE 111*a*, as compared with Type **111**, differs as follows: Closer spacing of horizontal rows to 12½ mm. instead of 14½ mm. Letters shorter and rounder. Wmk. thicker.

(Typo. by Waterlow & Sons, Ltd. (all values except 6d.) and later, 1934–5, by Harrison & Sons, Ltd. (all values). Until 1934 the 6d. was printed at Somerset House where a printing of the 1½d. was also made in 1926 (identifiable only by control E.26). Printings by Harrison & Sons, Ltd., in 1934–35 can be identified, when in mint condition, by the fact that the gum shows a streaky appearance vertically, the Waterlow gum being uniformly applied, but Harrison also used up the balance of the Waterlow "smooth gum" paper.)

1924 (April)–**26.** *W* **111.** *P* 15×14.

418 **105** ½d. green 10 10
a. Wmk. sideways .. 4·00 2·50
b. Doubly printed .. £600
419 **104** 1d. scarlet 40 12
a. Wmk. sideways .. 12·00 5·00
b. Experimental paper, W 111a .. .. 25·00
c. Inverted "Q" for "O" (R 20/3) £225
420 **105** 1½d. red-brown 20 10
a. Tête-bêche (pair) .. £175 £140
b. Wmk. sideways .. 3·00 1·50
c. Printed on the gummed side .. .. £175 †
d. Booklet pane. Four stamps plus two printed labels .. .. 16·00
e. Ditto. Wmk. sideways £300
f. Experimental paper, W 111a .. .. 25·00
g. Double impression ..
421 **106** 2d. orange (Die II) .. 80 25
a. No wmk. £175
b. Wmk. sideways .. 50·00 30·00
422 **104** 2½d. blue .. .. .. 3·00 50
a. No wmk. £175
423 **106** 3d. violet .. .. 3·00 35
424 „ 4d. grey-green .. 6·00 30
a. Printed on the gummed side .. .. £500 †
425 **107** 5d. brown .. .. 9·00 50
426 „ 6d. reddish purple, **C** .. 5·00 75
426*a* „ 6d. purple, **O** (1926) .. 2·00 15
427 **108** 9d. olive-green .. .. 8·00 75
428 „ 10d. turquoise-blue .. 15·00 6·00
429 „ 1s. bistre-brown .. 18·00 50

There are numerous shades in this issue.

The 6d. on both chalky and ordinary papers was printed by both Somerset House and Harrison. The Harrison printings have streaky gum, differ slightly in shade, and that on chalky paper is printed in a highly fugitive ink. The prices quoted are for the commonest (Harrison) printing in each case.

WATERMARK VARIETIES.

☞ Many *modern* British stamps exist without watermark owing to misplacement of the paper, and with either inverted, reversed, or inverted and reversed watermarks. A proportion of the low value stamps issued in booklets have the wmk. inverted in the normal course of printing. We do not list such wmk. varieties here, but they are listed in the *Great Britain Specialised Catalogue*. The 1½d. and 5d. 1912–22, and 2d. and 2½d., 1924–26, listed here, are from *whole* sheets without wmk.

Low values with *watermark sideways* are normally from stamp rolls used in machines with sideways delivery or, from June 1940, certain booklets.

112

(Des. H. Nelson. Eng. J. A. C. Harrison. Recess. Waterlow.)

1924–25. *British Empire Exhibition.* W **111.** *P* 14. (*a*) *Dated* " 1924 " (23.4.24).

430	**112**	1d. scarlet	6·00	6·00
431	,,	1½d. brown	10·00	10·00
		(*b*) *Dated* " 1925 " (9.5.25).		
432	**112**	1d. scarlet	10·00	10·00
433	,,	1½d. brown	35·00	30·00

113

114

115

116. St. George and the Dragon.

117

(Des. J. Farleigh (T **113** and **115**), E. Linzell (T **114**) and H. Nelson (T **116**). Eng. J. A. C. Harrison (1d., 1½d., £1). Typo. by Waterlow from plates made at the Royal Mint, except T **116**, recess by Bradbury, Wilkinson from die and plate of their own manufacture.)

1929 (10 May). *Ninth U.P.U. Congress, London.* *W* **111.** *P* 15 × 14.

434	**113**	½d. green	1·75	10
		a. Wmk. sideways ..	30·00	15·00
435	**114**	1d. scarlet	1·25	50
		a. Wmk. sideways ..	30·00	20·00
436	,,	1½d. purple-brown ..	75	10
		a. Wmk. sideways ..	25·00	10·00
		b. Booklet pane. Four stamps plus two printed labels ..	22·00	
437	**115**	2½d. blue	10·00	3·50
		W **117.** *P* 12.		
438	**116**	£1 black	£425	£275

PRINTERS. All subsequent issues are printed in photogravure by Harrison and Sons, Ltd., *except where otherwise stated.*

118

119

120

121

122

B

1934–36. *W* **111.** *P* 15 × 14.

439	**118**	½d. green (19.11.34) ..	8	8
		a. Wmk. sideways ..	2·00	75
		b. Imperf. three sides* ..	£275	
440	**119**	1d. scarlet (24.9.34) ..	20	10
		a. Imperf. (pair)	£400	
		b. Ptd. on the gummed side	£200	
		c. Wmk. sideways.. ..	4·00	2·25
		d. Double impression ..	£500	
441	**118**	1½d. red-brown (20.8.34)	8	8
		a. Imperf. (pair)	£125	
		b. Imp. (three sides) (pair) ..	£160	
		c. Wmk. sideways ..	3·00	1·50
		d. Booklet pane. Four stamps plus two printed labels ..	9·00	
442	**120**	2d. orange (21.1.35) ..	20	15
		a. Imperf. (pair)	£500	
		b. Wmk. sideways ..	55·00	25·00
443	**119**	2½d. ultramarine (18.3.35)	2·00	35
444	**120**	3d. violet (18.3.35) ..	1·50	30
445	,,	4d. deep grey-grn. (2.12.35)	1·50	30
446	**121**	5d. yellow-brn. (17.2.36)	3·50	40
447	**122**	9d. dp. olive-grn. (2.12.35)	10·00	40
448	,,	10d. turq.-blue (24.2.36)	10·00	3·00
449	,,	1s. bistre-brn. (24.2.36)	18·00	40

*** This is known in a block of four in which the bottom pair is imperf. at top and sides. It is believed that these come from a sheet, not a booklet.**

Owing to the need for wider space for the perforations the size of the designs of the ½d. and 2d. were once, and the 1d. and 1½d. twice reduced from that of the first printings.

There are also numerous minor variations, due to the photographic element in the process.

For No. 442 bisected, see " Channel Islands ".

(Eng. J. A. C. Harrison. Recess. Waterlow.)

1934 (Oct.). *T* **109** (*re-engraved*). *Background around portrait consists of horizontal and diagonal lines, Type* B. *W* **110.** *P* 11 × 12.

450	**109**	2s. 6d. chocolate-brown	60·00	2·00
451	,,	5s. bright rose-red ..	90·00	5·00
452	,,	10s. indigo	£150	12·00

There are numerous other minor differences in the design of this issue.

123

(Des. B. Freedman.)

1935 (7 May). *Silver Jubilee.* *W* **111.** *P* 15 × 14.

453	**123**	½d. green	5	5
454	,,	1d. scarlet	75	50
455	,,	1½d. red-brown	50	5
456	,,	2½d. blue	4·75	4·00
456*a*	,,	2½d. Prussian blue ..	£1600	£1200

The 1d., 1½d. and 2½d. values differ from *T* **123** in the emblem in the panel at right.

KING EDWARD VIII,

1936 (20 Jan.–10 Dec.).

124

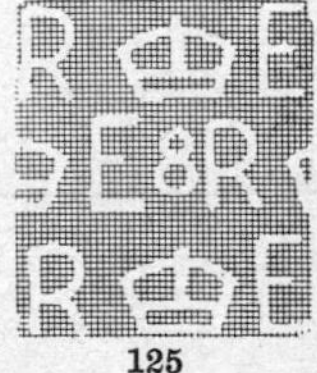
125

1936. *W* **125.** *P* 15 × 14.

457	**124**	½d. green (1.9.36) ..	8	5
		a. Double impression ..	—	85·00
458	,,	1d. scarlet (14.9.36) ..	12	5
459	,,	1½d. red-brown (1.9.36) ..	15	5
		a. Booklet pane. Four stamps plus two printed labels ..	3·00	
460	,,	2½d. bright blue (1.9.36) ..	30	30

KING GEORGE VI,

1936 (11 Dec.)–**1952** (6 Feb.).

126. King George VI and Queen Elizabeth.

(Des. E. Dulac.)

1937 (13 May). *Coronation.* *W* **127.** *P* 15×14.

No.	Type	Description		Unused	Used
461	**126**	1½d. maroon	.. ..	8	5

127

128

129

130

King George VI and National Emblems.

(Des. T **128/9**, E. Dulac (head) and E. Gill (frames). T **130**, E. Dulac (whole stamp).)

1937–47. *W* **127.** *P* 15×14.

No.	Type	Description	Unused	Used
462	**128**	½d. green (10.5.37) ..	10	8
		a. Wmk. sideways (1.38) ..	35	50
		b. Wmk. sideways. Block of 4 (booklet pane)	6·00	
463	,,	1d. scarlet (10.5.37) ..	10	8
		a. Wmk. sideways (2.38) ..	5·00	3·00
		b. Wmk. sideways. Block of 4 (booklet pane)	25·00	
464	,,	1½d. red-brown (30.7.37) ..	10	8
		a. Wmk. sideways (2.38) ..	70	50
		b. Booklet pane. Four stamps plus two printed labels ..	12·00	
		c. Imperf. three sides (pair) ..		
465	,,	2d. orange (31.1.38) ..	60	8
		a. Wmk. sideways (2.38) ..	25·00	15·00
		b. Bisected (on cover)	†	8·00
466	,,	2½d. ultramarine (10.5.37)	20	10
		a. Wmk. sideways (6.40) ..	20·00	12·00
		b. Tête-bêche (horiz. pr.) ..		
467	,,	3d. violet (31.1.38)	1·50	20
468	**129**	4d. grey-green (21.11.38)	45	15
		a. Imperf. (pair)	£275	
		b. Imperf. three sides (pair) ..		
469	,,	5d. brown (21.11.38) ..	1·25	20
		a. Imperf. (pair)	£300	
		b. Imperf. three sides (pair) ..	£240	
470	,,	6d. purple (30.1.39) ..	1·50	15
471	**130**	7d. emerald-grn. (27.2.39)	2·75	20
		a. Imperf. three sides (pair) ..	£240	
472	,,	8d. bright carm. (27.2.39)	5·00	20
473	,,	9d. deep ol.-grn. (1.5.39)	3·50	20
474	,,	10d. turquoise-blue (1.5.39)	3·00	30
		aa. Imperf. (pair)		
474*a*	,,	11d. plum (29.12.47) ..	2·50	50
475	,,	1s. bistre-brown (1.5.39)	4·00	10

For later printings of the lower values in apparently lighter shades and different colours, see Nos. 485/90 and 503/8.

No. 465b was authorised for use in Guernsey. See notes at beginning of Channel Islands.

131. King George VI.

132. King George VI.

133

(Des. E. Dulac (T **131**) and Hon. George R. Bellew, M.V.O. (T **132**). Eng. J. A. C. Harrison. Recess. Waterlow.)

1939–48. *W* **133.** *P* 14.

No.	Type	Description	Unused	Used
476	**131**	2s. 6d. brown (4.9.39) ..	22·00	4·00
476*a*	,,	2s. 6d. yell.-grn. (9.3.42)	6·00	30
477	,,	5s. red (21.8.39)	15·00	70
478	**132**	10s. dark blue (3.10.39)	£100	8·00
478*a*	,,	10s. ultram. (30.11.42) ..	12·00	1·00
478*b*	,,	£1 brown (1.10.48) ..	12·00	10·00

134. Queen Victoria and King George VI.

(Des. H. L. Palmer.)

1940 (6 May). *Centenary of First Adhesive Postage Stamps.* *W* **127.** *P* 14½×14.

No.	Type	Description	Unused	Used
479	**134**	½d. green	12	10
480	,,	1d. scarlet	20	10
481	,,	1½d. red-brown	40	40
482	,,	2d. orange	20	20
		a. Bisected (on cover) ..	†	6·00
483	,,	2½d. ultramarine	50	10
484	,,	3d. violet	4·00	3·50

No. 482a was authorised for use in Guernsey. See notes at beginning of Channel Islands.

1941–42. *Head as Nos. 462/7, but lighter background.* *W* **127.** *P* 15×14.

No.	Type	Description	Unused	Used
485	**128**	½d. pale green (1.9.41) ..	12	8
		a. Tête-bêche (horiz. pr.) ..	£200	
		b. Imperf. (pair)	£225	
486	,,	1d. pale scarlet (11.8.41)	15	8
		a. Wmk. sideways (10.42) ..	3·00	2·00
		b. Imperf. (pair)	£250	
		c. Imperf. three sides (pair) ..	£150	
		d. Imp. between (vert. pr.) ..		
487	,,	1½d. pale red-brn. (28.9.42)	40	20
488	,,	2d. pale orange (6.10.41)	30	8
		a. Wmk. sideways (6.42) ..	5·00	4·00
		b. Tête-bêche (horiz. pr.) ..	£400	
		c. Imperf. (pair) ..	£600	
489	,,	2½d. light ultram. (21.7.41)	20	8
		a. Wmk. sideways (8.42) ..	4·00	2·50
		b. Tête-bêche (horiz. pr.) ..	£400	
		c. Imperf. (pair)	£225	
490	,,	3d. pale violet (3.11.41) ..	75	15
		a. Top margin imperf. ..		

The *tête-bêche* varieties are from defectively made-up stamp booklets.

WATERMARK VARIETIES.

Please note that *inverted watermarks* are outside the scope of this Catalogue but are fully listed in the *Great Britain Specialised Catalogue*. See also the notes about watermarks on page 15.

135

136. Symbols of Peace and Reconstruction.

(Des. H. L. Palmer (T **135**) and Reynolds Stone (T **136**).)

1946 (11 June). *Victory.* *W* **127.** *P* 15×14.

No.	Type	Description	Unused	Used
491	**135**	2½d. ultramarine ..	10	10
492	**136**	3d. violet	10	10

137

138. King George VI and Queen Elizabeth.

(Des. G. T. Knipe and Joan Hassall from photographs by Dorothy Wilding.)

1948 (26 Apr.). *Royal Silver Wedding. W* **127.** *P* 15×14 (2½d.) *or* 14×15 (£1).

493	**137**	2½d. ultramarine	10	10
494	**138**	£1 blue	20·00	20·00

1948 (10 May). Stamps of 1d. and 2½d. showing seaweed-gathering were on sale at eight Head Post Offices elsewhere in Great Britain, but were primarily for use in the Channel Islands and are listed there (see after Great Britain Postal Fiscals).

139. Globe and Laurel Wreath.

140. " Speed ".

141. Olympic Symbol.

142. Winged Victory.

Des. Percy Metcalfe, C.V.O., Abram Games, Stanley D. Scott and Edmund Dulac.)

1948 (29 July). *Olympic Games. W* **127.** *P* 15×14.

495	**139**	2½d. ultramarine	5	5
496	**140**	3d. violet	20	20
497	**141**	6d. bright purple ..	30	35
498	**142**	1s. brown	45	50

143. Two Hemispheres.

144. U.P.U. Monument, Berne.

145. Goddess Concordia, Globe and Points of Compass.

146. Posthorn and Globe.

(Des. Mary Adshead (T **143**), Percy Metcalfe, C.V.O. (T **144**), H. Fleury (T **145**) and the Hon. George R. Bellew, M.V.O. (T **146**).)

1949 (10 Oct.). *75th Anniv. of Universal Postal Union. W* **127.** *P* 15×14.

499	**143**	2½d. ultramarine ..	5	5
500	**144**	3d. violet	15	30
501	**145**	6d. bright purple ..	45	50
502	**146**	1s. brown	80	1·00

1950–51. *4d. as No. 468 and others as Nos. 485/9, but colours changed.*

503	**128**	½d. pale orange (3.5.51)	10	5
		a. Imperf. (pair)		
		b. Tête-bêche (horiz. pr.) ..	£1000	
504	,,	1d. light ultram. (3.5.51)	10	5
		a. Wmk. sideways (-.5.51)	15	20
		b. Imperf. (pair) ..	£275	
		c. Imperf. three sides (pr.)	90·00	
		d. Booklet pane. Three stamps plus three printed labels	4·00	
		e. Do. Partial tête-bêche pane	£1000	
505	,,	1½d. pale green (3.5.51) ..	40	15
		a. Wmk. sideways (-.9.51)	30	30
506	,,	2d. pale red-brn. (3.5.51)	60	15
		a. Wmk. sideways (-.5.51)	50	50
		b. Tête-bêche (horiz. pr.) ..	£850	
		c. Imperf. three sides (pr.)	£125	
507	,,	2½d. pale scarlet (3.5.51)	25	5
		a. Wmk. sideways (-.5.51)	70	60
		b. Tête-bêche (horiz. pr.)		
508	**129**	4d. lt. ultram. (2.10.50)	1·00	20

147. H.M.S. *Victory*.

148. White Cliffs of Dover.

149. St. George and the Dragon.

150. Royal Coat-of-Arms.

(Des. Mary Adshead (T **147/8**), Percy Metcalfe, C.V.O. (T **149/50**). Recess. Waterlow & Sons.)

1951 (3 May). *W* **133.** *P* 11×12.

509	**147**	2s. 6d. yellow-green ..	6·50	30
510	**148**	5s. red	15·00	70
511	**149**	10s. ultramarine	8·00	4·00
512	**150**	£1 brown	25·00	6·00

151. " Commerce and Prosperity ".

152. Festival Symbol.

(Des. E. Dulac (T **151**), A. Games (T **152**).)

1951 (3 May). *Festival of Britain. W* **127.** *P* 15×14.

513	**151**	2½d. scarlet	10	10
514	**152**	4d. ultramarine	25	25

QUEEN ELIZABETH II, 6 February, 1952.

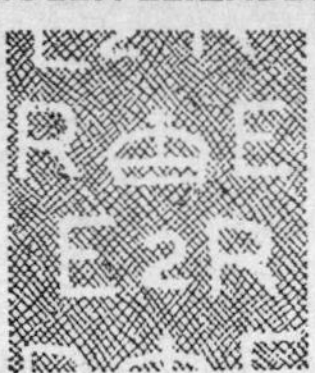

153. Tudor Crown.

154

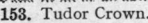

155

156

157

158

159

160

Queen Elizabeth II and National Emblems.

I. II.

Types of 2½d. Type I:—In the frontal cross of the diadem, the top line is only half the width of the cross. Type II:—The top line extends to the full width of the cross and there are signs of strengthening in other parts of the diadem.

(Des. Miss E. Marx, R.D.I. (T **154**), M. C. Farrar-Bell (T **155/6**), G. Knipe (T **157**), Miss M. Adshead (T **158**), E. Dulac (T **159/60**). Portrait by Dorothy Wilding.)

1952–54. *W* **153.** *P* 15 × 14.

No.	Type	Description	Unused	Used
515	**154**	½d. orange-red (31.8.53)	8	8
516	,,	1d. ultramarine (31.8.53)	20	8
		a. Booklet pane. Three stamps plus three printed labels	4·50	
517	,,	1½d. green (5.12.52) ..	5	8
		a. Wmk. sideways (15.10.54)	35	45
		b. Imperf. pane*	£200	
518	,,	2d. red-brown (31.8.53)	50	8
		a. Wmk. sideways (8.10.54)	70	70
519	**155**	2½d. carmine-red, Type I (5.12.52)	10	8
		a. Wmk. sideways (15.11.54)	2·00	1·50
		b. Type II (Booklets) ..	50	40
520	,,	3d. deep lilac (18.1.54) ..	60	8
521	**156**	4d. ultramarine (2.11.53)	80	30
522	**157**	5d. brown (6.7.53) ..	90	80
523	,,	6d. reddish pur. (18.1.54)	1·75	15
		a. Imperf. three sides (pr.)		
524	,,	7d. bright green (18.1.54)	3·00	75
525	**158**	8d. magenta (6.7.53) ..	1·00	40
526	,,	9d. bronze-green (8.2.54)	12·00	50
527	,,	10d. Prussian bl. (8.2.54)	11·00	1·25
528	,,	11d. brn.-purple (8.2.54)	20·00	4·50
529	**159**	1s. bistre-brown (6.7.53)	75	12
530	**160**	1s. 3d. green (2.11.53) ..	2·50	35
531	**159**	1s. 6d. grey-bl. (2.11.53)	18·00	40

See also Nos. 540/56, 561/6, 570/94 and 599/618*a*.

In the above issue Type II is only found in booklets.

* Booklet Errors.—This pane of 6 stamps is *completely* imperf. (cf. No. 540*a*, etc.).

161

162

163

164

(Des. E. G. Fuller (2½d.), M. Goaman (4d.), E. Dulac (1s. 3d.), M. C. Farrar-Bell (1s. 6d.), Portrait (except 1s. 3d.) by Dorothy Wilding.)

1953 (3 June). *Coronation.* *W* **153.** *P* 15 × 14.

No.	Type	Description	Unused	Used
532	**161**	2½d. carmine-red	15	5
533	**162**	4d. ultramarine ..	75	75
534	**163**	1s. 3d. deep yellow-grn.	2·50	3·50
535	**164**	1s. 6d. deep grey-blue ..	3·50	3·50

165. St. Edward's Crown.

166. Carrickfergus Castle.

167. Caernarvon Castle.

168. Edinburgh Castle.

169. Windsor Castle.

(Des. L. Lamb. Portrait by Dorothy Wilding Ltd. Recess. Waterlow (until 31.12.57) and De La Rue (subsequently).)

1955–58. *W* **165.** *P* 11 × 12.

No.	Type	Description	Unused	Used
536	**166**	2s. 6d. blk.-brn. (23.9.55)	6·00	50
		a. De La Rue ptg. (17.7.58)	20·00	60
537	**167**	5s. rose-carmine (23.9.55)	12·00	1·50
		a. De La Rue ptg. (30.4.58)	35·00	3·50
538	**168**	10s. ultramarine (1.9.55)	35·00	5·00
		a. De La Rue ptg. *Dull ultramarine* (25.4.58) ..	80·00	7·00
539	**169**	£1 black (1.9.55) ..	85·00	5·00
		a. De La Rue ptg. (28.4.58)	£240	10·00

See also Nos. 595/8a and 759/62.

On January 1st, 1958, the contract for printing the high values, T **166** to **169** was transferred to De La Rue & Co., Ltd.

The work of the two printers is very similar, but the following notes will be helpful to those attempting to identify Waterlow and De La Rue stamps of the W **165** issue.

The De La Rue sheets are printed in pairs and have a ⊣ or ⊢ shaped guide-mark at the centre of one side-margin opposite the middle row of perforations, indicating left- and right-hand sheets respectively.

The Waterlow sheets have a small circle (sometimes crossed) instead of a "⊢" and this is present in both side-margins opposite the 6th row of stamps, though one is sometimes trimmed off. Short dashes are also present in the perforation gutter between the marginal stamps marking the middle of the four sides and a cross is at the centre of the sheet. The four corners of the sheet have two lines forming a right-angle as trimming marks, but some are usually trimmed off. All these gutter marks and sheet-trimming marks are absent in the De La Rue printings.

De La Rue used the Waterlow die and no alterations were made to it, so that no difference exists in the design or its size, but the making of new plates at first resulted in slight but measurable variations in the width of the gutters between stamps, particularly the horizontal, as follows:

	W.	D.L.R.
Horiz. gutters, mm. ..	3.8 to 4.0	3.4 to 3.8

Later D.L.R. plates were however less distinguishable in this respect.

For a short time in 1959 the D.L.R. 2s. 6d. appeared with one dot in the bottom margin below the first stamp.

It is possible to sort singles with reasonable certainty by general characteristics. The individual lines of the D.L.R. impression are cleaner and devoid of the whiskers of colour of Waterlow's, and the whole impression lighter and softer.

Owing to the closer setting of the horizontal rows the strokes of the perforating comb are closer; this results in the topmost tooth on each side of De La Rue stamps being narrower than the corresponding teeth in Waterlow's which were more than normally broad.

Shades also help. The 2s. 6d. D.L.R. is a warmer, more chocolate shade than the blackish brown of W.; the 5s. a lighter red with less carmine than W's; the 10s. more blue and less ultramarine; the £1 less intense black.

The paper of D.L.R. printings is uniformly white, identical with that of W. printings from February 1957 onwards, but earlier W. printings are on paper which is creamy by comparison.

In this and later issues of T **166/9** the dates of issue given for changes of watermark or paper are those on which supplies were first sent by the Supplies Department to Postmasters.

1955–58. *W* **165.** *P* 15×14.

No.	Type	Description	Unused	Used
540	**154**	½d. orange-red (booklets 8.55, sheets 12.12.55)	10	5
		a. Part perf. pane* ..	70·00	
541	,,	1d. ultramarine (19.9.55)	10	5
		a. Booklet pane, 3 stamps plus 3 printed labels ..	4·50	
		b. Tête-bêche (horiz. pr.) ..	75·00	
542	,,	1½d. green (booklets 8.55, sheets 11.10.55) ..	10	5
		a. Wmk. sideways (7.3.56)	15	25
		b. Tête-bêche (horiz. pr.) ..	£300	
543	,,	2d. red-brown (6.9.55) ..	35	5
		aa. Imperf. between (vert. pr.)	£300	
		a. Wmk. sideways ('56) ..	50	35
		ab. Imperf. between, Wmk. sideways (horiz. pr.) ..	£250	
543*b*	,,	2d. light red-brown (17.10.56)	20	5
		ba. Tête-bêche (horiz. pr.) ..	£100	
		bb. Imperf. pane*.. ..	£130	
		bc. Part perf. pane* ..		
		d. Wmk. sideways (5.3.57)	60	60
544	**155**	2½d. carmine-red (Type I) (28.9.55)	15	5
		a. Wmk. sideways (Type I) (23.3.56)	1·25	75
		b. Type II (booklets 9.55, sheets '57)	25	20
		ba. Tête-bêche (horiz. pr.) ..	40·00	
		bb. Imperf. pane*.. ..	£130	
		bc. Part perf. pane* ..	£175	
545		3d. deep lilac (17.7.56)..	15	5
		aa. Tête-bêche (horiz. pr.) ..	60·00	
		a. Imp. three sides (pair) ..	45·00	
		b. Wmk. sideways (22.11.57)	6·00	5·00
546	**156**	4d. ultram. (14.11.55) ..	1·50	15
547	**157**	5d. brown (21.9.55) ..	2·00	75
548	,,	6d. reddish purple (20.12.55)	4·50	50
		aa. Imperf. three sides (pr.)		
		a. *Deep claret* (8.5.58) ..	2·25	50
		ab. Imperf. three sides (pr.)	85·00	
549	,,	7d. bright green (23.4.56)	30·00	1·00
550	**158**	8d. magenta (21.12.55)..	8·00	40
551	,,	9d. bronze-grn. (15.12.55)	15·00	40
552	,,	10d. Prussian bl. (22.9.55)	15·00	40
553	,,	11d. brn.-purple (28.10.55)	1·00	1·50
554	**159**	1s. bistre-brn. (3.11.55)	12·00	12
555	**160**	1s. 3d. green (27.3.56) ..	18·00	35
556	**159**	1s. 6d. grey-bl. (27.3.56)	22·00	40

The dates given for Nos. 540/556 are those on which they were first issued by the Supplies Dept. to postmasters.

In December 1956 a completely imperforate sheet of No. 543*b* was noticed by clerks in a Kent post office, one of whom purchased it against P.O. regulations. In view of this irregularity we do not consider it properly issued.

Types of 2½d. In this issue, in 1957, Type II formerly only found in stamps from booklets, began to replace Type I on sheet stamps.

*BOOKLET ERRORS. Those listed as "imperf. panes" show one row of perforations either at top or bottom of the booklet pane; those as "part perf. panes" have one row of 3 stamps imperf. on three sides.

170. Scout Badge and "Rolling Hitch".

171. "Scouts coming to Britain".

172. Globe within a Compass.

(Des. Mary Adshead (2½d.), Pat Keely (4d.), W. H. Brown (1s. 3d.).)

1957 (1 AUG.). *World Scout Jubilee Jamboree. W* **165.** *P* 15×14.

No.	Type	Description	Unused	Used
557	**170**	2½d. carmine-red.. ..	15	8
558	**171**	4d. ultramarine	1·50	75
559	**172**	1s. 3d. green	5·50	7·50

173

1957 (12 SEPT.). *46th Inter-Parliamentary Union Conference. W* **165.** *P* 15×14.

No.	Type	Description	Unused	Used
560	**173**	4d. ultramarine	2·00	3·00

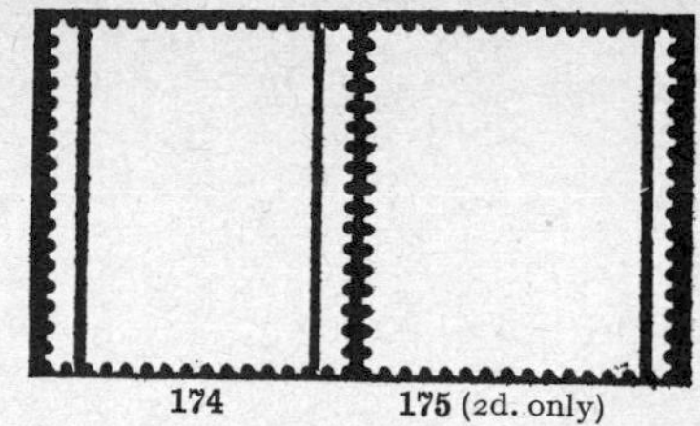

174 **175** (2d. only)

(Stamps viewed from back)

GRAPHITE-LINED ISSUES. These were used in connection with automatic sorting machinery, first introduced experimentally at Southampton.

The graphite lines were printed in black on the back, beneath the gum; two lines per stamp, except for the 2d. (*see* T **174/5**).

In November 1959 phosphor bands were introduced (*see* notes after No. 598).

1957 (19 NOV.). *Graphite-lined issue. Two graphite lines on the back, except* 2d. *value, which has one line. W* **165.** *P* 15×14.

No.	Type	Description	Unused	Used
561	**154**	½d. orange-red	15	15
562	,,	1d. ultramarine ..	25	20
563	,,	1½d. green	35	40
		a. Both lines at left ..	85·00	60·00
564	,,	2d. light red-brown ..	2·50	1·00
		a. Line at left ..	75·00	75·00
565	**155**	2½d. carmine-red (Type II)	6·00	4·00
566	,,	3d. deep lilac	1·50	20

No. 564*a* results from a misplacement of the line and horizontal pairs exist showing one stamp without line. No. 563*a* results from a similar misplacement.

See also Nos. 587/94.

176. Welsh Dragon.

177. Flag and Games Emblem.

178. Welsh Dragon.

(Des. Reynolds Stone (3d.), W. H. Brown (6d.), Pat Keely (1s. 3d.).)

1958 (18 JULY). *Sixth British Empire and Commonwealth Games, Cardiff. W* **165.** *P* 15×14.

No.	Type	Description	Unused	Used
567	**176**	3d. deep lilac	15	8
568	**177**	6d. reddish purple ..	75	45
569	**178**	1s. 3d. green	2·50	2·00

179. Multiple Crowns.

1958–65. *W* **179.** *P* 15 × 14.

570	**154**	½d. orange-red (25.11.58)	5	5
		a. Wmk. sideways (26.5.61)	20	20
		c. Part perf. pane* ..	70·00	
		k. Chalky paper (15.7.63) ..	1·25	1·25
		l. Booklet pane (570k × 3 *se-tenant* with 574k) ..	4·00	
		m. Booklet pane (570a × 2 *se-tenant* with 574l × 2) ..	1·00	
571	,,	1d. ultram. (booklets 11.58, sheets 24.3.59)	5	5
		aa. Imperf. (vert. pair from coil)	£150	
		a. Wmk. sideways (26.5.61)	45	30
		b. Part perf. pane* ..	50·00	
		c. Imperf. pane	£400	
		l. Booklet pane (571a × 2 *se-tenant* with 575a × 2)†	1·25	
572	,,	1½d. green (booklets 12.58, sheets 30.8.60) ..	5	5
		a. Imperf. three sides (horiz. strip of 3)		
		b. Wmk. sideways (26.5.61)	6·00	4·00
573	,,	2d. lt. red-brn. (4.12.58)	5	5
		a. Wmk. sideways (3.4.59)	50	20
574	**155**	2½d. carm.-red (Type II) (booklets 11.58, sheets 15.9.59)	5	5
		aa. Imperf. strip of 3 ..	50·00	
		ab. Tête-bêche (horiz. pr.) ..	£175	
		a. Wmk. sideways (Type I) (10.11.60)	15	15
		b. Type I (wmk. upright).. (4.10.61)	30	15
		ba. Imperf. strip of 6 ..		
		k. Type II. Chalky paper (15.7.63)	15	20
		l. Wmk. sideways (Type II) Ord. paper (1.7.64) ..	75	75
575	,,	3d. deep lilac (booklets 11.58, sheets 8.12.58)	8	5
		a. Wmk. sideways (24.10.58)	20	15
		b. Imperf. pane* ..	£110	
		c. Part perf. pane* ..	75·00	
		d. Phantom "R" (Cyl. 41 no dot)	£130	
		e. Phantom "R" (Cyl. 37 no dot)	25·00	
576	**156**	4d. ultram. (29.10.58)	60	25
		a. *Dp. ultram.*†† (28.4.65)	25	15
		ab. Wmk. sideways (30.4.65)	25	20
		ac. Imperf. pane*		
		ad. Part perf. pane* ..		
577	,,	4½d. chestnut (9.2.59) ..	10	8
578	**157**	5d. brown (10.11.58) ..	45	8
579	,,	6d. dp. claret (23.12.58)	45	8
		a. Imperf. three sides (pr.)		
580	,,	7d. brt. green (26.11.58)	40	10
581	**158**	8d. magenta (24.2.60)	40	10
582	,,	9d. bronze-grn. (24.3.59)	45	8
583	,,	10d. Prussian bl. (18.11.58)	40	12
584	**159**	1s. bistre-brn. (30.10.58)	30	8
585	**160**	1s. 3d. green (17.6.59) ..	75	8
586	**159**	1s. 6d. grey-bl. (16.12.58)	2·50	8

* Booklet Errors. See note after No. 556.

† Booklet pane No. 571l comes in two forms, with the 1d. stamps on the left or on the right.

†† This "shade" has been brought about by making more deeply etched cylinders, resulting in apparent depth of colour in parts of the design. There is no difference in the colour of the ink.

Sideways watermark. The 2d., 2½d., 3d. and 4d. come from coils and the ½d., 1d., 1½d., 2½d., 3d. and 4d. come from booklets. In *coil* stamps the sideways watermark shows the top of the watermark to the left. In the *booklet* stamps it comes equally to the left or right.

Nos. 570k and 574k come only from 2s. "Holiday Resort" Experimental undated booklets issued in 1963, in which one page contained 1 × 2½d. *se-tenant* with 3 × ½d. (*See* No. 570l.)

No. 574l comes from coils, and the "Holiday Resort" Experimental booklets dated "1964" comprising four panes each containing two of these 2½d. stamps *se-tenant* vertically with two ½d. No. 570a. (*See* No. 570m.)

2½d. *imperf.* No. 574aa comes from a booklet with watermark upright. No. 574ba is from a coil with sideways watermark.

No. 574b comes from *sheets* bearing cylinder number 42 and is also known on vertical delivery coils.

Nos. 575d and 615a occurred below the last stamp of the sheet from Cyl. 41 (no dot), where an incomplete marginal rule revealed an "R". The cylinder was later twice retouched. The stamps listed show the original, unretouched "R". The rare variety, No. 575d, is best collected in a block of 4 or 6 with full margins in order to be sure that it is not No. 615a with phosphor lines removed.

No. 575e is a similar variety but from Cyl. 37 (no dot). The marginal rule is much narrower and only a very small part of the "R" is revealed. The cylinder was later once retouched. The listed variety is for the original, unretouched state.

In *Coil* stamps (2d., 2½d., 3d.) the sideways watermark shows the top of the watermark to the left. In the Booklet stamps (½d., 1d., 1½d., 3d.) it comes equally to left or right.

Whiter paper. On 18th May 1962 the Post Office announced that a whiter paper was being used for the current issue (including Nos. 595/8). This is beyond the scope of this catalogue, but the whiter papers are listed in Vol. 3 of the *Stanley Gibbons Specialised Catalogue of Great Britain.*

1958 (24 Nov.)–**61.** *Graphite-lined issue. Two graphite lines on the back, except 2d. value, which has one line.* *W* **179.** *P* 15 × 14.

587	**154**	½d. orange-red (15.6.59)	2·00	2·50
588	,,	1d. ultramarine (18.12.58)	1·00	30
		a. Misplaced Graphite lines (7.61)*	75	75
589	,,	1½d. green (4.8.59)† ..	25·00	15·00
590	,,	2d. lt. red-brn. (24.11.58)	4·00	3·00
591	**155**	2½d. carm.-red (Type II) (9.6.59)	10·00	8·00
592	,,	3d. deep lilac (24.11.58)	60	75
		a. Misplaced Graphite lines (5.61)*	60·00	35·00
593	**156**	4d. ultramarine (29.4.59)	3·50	3·00
		a. Misplaced Graphite lines ('61)*	£100	
594	,,	4½d. chestnut (3.6.59) ..	3·50	4·50

Nos. 587/9 were only issued in booklets or coils (587/8).

* No. 588*a* (in coils), and Nos. 592a and 593a (both in sheets) result from the use of a residual stock of graphite-lined paper. As the use of graphite lines had ceased, the register of the lines in relation to the stamps was of no importance and numerous misplacements occurred—two lines close together, one line only, etc. No. 588a refers to two lines at left or at right; No. 592a refers to stamps with two lines only at left and both clear of the perforations and No. 593a to stamps with two lines at left (with left line down perforations) and traces of a third line down the opposite perforations.

† The prices quoted are for stamps with the watermark inverted. (*Prices for upright watermark £45 un., £30 us.*)

(Recess. D.L.R. (until 31.12.62), then B.W.)

1959–68. *W* **179.** *P* 11 × 12.

595	**166**	2s. 6d. blk.-brn. (22.7.59)	6·00	30
		a. B.W. ptg. (1.7.63) ..	60	10
		k. Chalky paper (30.5.68) ..	60	75
596	**167**	5s. scarlet-verm. (15.6.59)	12·00	60
		a. B.W. ptg. *Red (shades)* (3.9.63)	1·75	30
		ab. Printed on the gummed side	90·00	
597	**168**	10s. blue (21.7.59) ..	26·00	1·50
		a. B.W. ptg. *Bright ultramarine* (16.10.63) ..	5·00	60
598	**169**	£1 black (23.6.59) ..	55·00	5·00
		a. B.W. ptg. (14.11.63) ..	5·00	2·50

The B.W. printings have a marginal Plate Number. They are generally more deeply engraved than the D.L.R., showing more of the Diadem detail and heavier lines on Her Majesty's face. The vertical perf. is 11.9 to 12 as against D.L.R. 11.8.

See also Nos. 759/62.

PHOSPHOR BAND ISSUES. These are printed on the front and are wider than graphite lines. They are not easy to see but show as broad vertical bands at certain angles to the light.

Values representing the rate for printed papers (and when this was abolished in 1968 for second class mail) have one band and others two, three or four bands as stated, according to the size and format.

In the small size stamps the bands are on each side with the single band at left (*except where otherwise stated*). In the large-size commemorative stamps the single band may be at left, centre or right, varying in different designs. The bands are vertical on both horizontal and vertical designs *except where otherwise stated.*

The phosphor was originally applied typographically but later usually by photogravure and sometimes using flexography, a typographical process using rubber cylinders.

Three different types of phosphor have been used, distinguishable by the colour emitted under an ultra-violet lamp, the first being green, then blue and now violet. Different sized bands are also known. All these are fully listed in Vol. 3 of the *Stanley Gibbons Specialised Catalogue of Great Britain.*

Varieties. Misplaced and missing phosphor bands are known but such varieties are beyond the scope of this Catalogue.

1959 (18 Nov.). *Phosphor-Graphite issue. Two Phosphor bands on front and two graphite lines on back, except 2d. value, which has one band on front and one line on back.* *P* 15 × 14.

(*a*) *W* **165.**

599	**154**	½d. orange-red	1·75	2·50
600	,,	1d. ultramarine ..	1·75	2·50
601	,,	1½d. green	1·50	2·50

(*b*) *W* **179.**

605	**154**	2d. lt. red-brn. (1 band)	3·00	3·50
		a. Error. W 165 ..	£150	£100
606	**155**	2½d. carmine-red (Type II)	9·00	7·50
607	,,	3d. deep lilac	12·00	6·00
608	**156**	4d. ultramarine ..	5·50	5·00
609	,,	4½d. chestnut	40·00	25·00

1960 (22 June)–**68.** *Phosphor issue. Two phosphor bands on front, except where otherwise stated.* *W* **179.** *P* 15 × 14.

610	**154**	½d. orange-red ..	12	12
		a. Wmk. sideways (26.5.61)	2·00	2·00
611	,,	1d. ultramarine ..	5	5
		a. Wmk. sideways (14.7.61)	15	15
		l. Booklet pane (611a × 2 *se-tenant* with 615d × 2)†	3·00	
		m. Booklet pane (611a × 2 *se-tenant* with 615b × 2)†† (10.67)	1·25	
612	,,	1½d. green	8	8
		a. Wmk. sideways (14.7.61)	6·00	4·00
613	,,	2d. lt. red-brn. (1 band)	16·00	6·00
613*a*	,,	2d. iight red brown (two bands) (4.10.61)	5	5
		aa. Imperf. three sides***		
		ab. Wmk. sideways (6.4.67)	20	15
614	**155**	2½d. carmine-red (Type II) (2 bands)* ..	10	12
614*a*	,,	2½d. carmine-red (Type II) (1 band) (4.10.61)	60	25
614*b*	,,	2½d. carmine-red (Type I) (1 band) (7.11.61) ..	20·00	18·00
615	,,	3d. deep lilac (2 bands)	60	10
		a. Phantom "R" (Cyl. 41 no dot)	15·00	
		b. Wmk. sideways (14.7.61)	75	60
615*c*	,,	3d. dp. lilac (1 side band) (29.4.65)	35	15
		d. Wmk. sideways (16.8.65)	1·50	1·25
		e. One centre band (8.12.66)	20	12
		ea. Wmk. sideways (19.6.67)	25	35
616	**156**	4d. ultramarine ..	4·00	3·00
		a. *Dp. ultramarine* (28.4.65)	15	5
		aa. Part perf. pane** ..		
		ab. Wmk. sideways (16.8.65)	15	20
616*b*	,,	4½d. chestnut (13.9.61)	15	12

616c	157	5d. brown (9.6.67) ..	15	10
617	"	6d. deep claret (27.6.60)	15	8
617a	"	7d. bright grn. (15.2.67)	25	10
617b	158	8d. magenta (28.6.67) ..	25	10
617c	"	9d. bronze-grn. (29.12.66)	25	10
617d	"	10d. Prussian bl. (30.12.66)	25	10
617e	159	1s. bistre-brn. (28.6.67)	50	8
618	160	1s. 3d. green	70	30
618a	159	1s. 6d. grey-bl. (12.12.66)	90	40

The automatic facing equipment was brought into use on 6th July 1960 but the phosphor stamps may have been released a few days earlier.

The stamps with watermark sideways are from booklets except Nos. 613ab and 615ea which are from coils. No. 616ab comes from booklets and coils.

No. 615a. See footnote after No. 586.

***No. 614 with two bands on the creamy paper was originally from cylinder 50 dot and no dot. When the change in postal rates took place in 1965 it was reissued from cylinder 57 dot and no dot on the whiter paper. Some of these latter were also released in error in districts of S.E. London in September 1964. The shade of the reissue is slightly more carmine.**

**Booklet error. Two stamps at bottom left imperf. on three sides and the third imperf. on two sides.

***This comes from the bottom row of a sheet which is imperf. at bottom and both sides.

†Booklet pane No. 611l comes in two forms, with the 1d. stamps on the left or on the right. This was printed in this manner to provide for 3d. stamps with only one band.

††Booklet pane No. 611m comes from 2s. booklets of October 1967 (part supply only) and January and March 1968. The two bands on the 3d. stamp thus created are intentional because of the technical difficulty of producing a single band on one stamp *se-tenant* with a two-banded stamp, as this requires perfect registration of the bands. It was felt that this predominantly 3d. booklet was mainly sold at holiday resorts for use on postcards which were entitled to first-class service.

Unlike previous one-banded phosphor stamps, No. 615c has a broad band extending over two stamps so that alternate stamps have the band at left or right (same prices either way).

180. Postboy of 1660.

181. Posthorn of 1660.

(Des. Reynolds Stone (3d.), Faith Jacques (1s. 3d.).)

1960 (7 July). *Tercentenary of Establishment of "General Letter Office". W* **179** *(sideways on 1s. 3d.). P* 15×14 *(3d.) or* 14×15 *(1s. 3d.).*

619	180	3d. deep lilac	25	5
620	181	1s. 3d. green	6·50	6·00

182. Conference Emblem.

(Des. Reynolds Stone (emblem, P. Rahikainen).)

1960 (19 Sept.). *First Anniv. of European Postal and Telecommunications Conference. Chalky paper. W* **179**. *P* 15×14.

621	182	6d. bronze-grn. & purple	1·00	1·00
622	,,	1s. 6d. brown and blue ..	6·00	6·00

183. Thrift Plant.

184. " Growth of Savings ".

185. Thrift Plant.

(Des. P. Gauld (2½d.), M. Goaman (others).)

1961 (28 Aug.). *Centenary of Post Office Savings Bank. Chalky paper. W* **179** *(sideways on 2½d.). P* 14×15 *(2½d.) or* 15×14 *(others).*

I. " TIMSON " Machine.

II. " THRISSELL " Machine.

			I.		II.	
623	183	2½d. blk. & red	20	15	2·00	1·50
624	184	3d. orge.-brn. & violet	30	10	60	10
		a. Oran.-brn. omitted	45·00	—	75·00	—
		x. Perf. through side sheet margin ..	25·00	—	†	
		xa. Oran.-brn. omitted	—	—	†	
625	185	1s. 6d. red & blue ..	2·50	2·50	†	

2½d. TIMSON. Cyls. 1E–1F. Deeply **shaded** portrait (brownish black).

2½d. THRISSELL. Cyls. 1D–1B or 1D (**stop**)–1B. Lighter portrait (grey-black).

3d. TIMSON. Cyls. 3D–3E. Clear, well-defined portrait with deep shadows and bright high-lights.

3d. THRISSELL. Cyls. 3C–3B or 3C (**stop**)–3B (**stop**). Dull portrait, lacking in contrast.

NOTE. Sheet marginal copies *without* single extension perf. hole on the short side of the stamp are always " Timson ", as are those with large punch-hole *not* coincident with printed three-sided box guide mark.

The 3d. "Timson" perforated completely through the right-hand side margin comes from a relatively small part of the printing perforated on a sheet-fed machine.

Normally the " Timsons " were perforated in the reel, with three large punch-holes in both long margins and the perforations completely through both short margins. Only one punch-hole coincides with the guide-mark.

The " Thrissells " have one large punch-hole in one long margin, coinciding with guide-mark and one short margin imperf. (except sometimes or encroachments).

186. C.E.P.T. Emblem.

187. Doves and Emblem.

188. Doves and Emblem.

(Des. M. Goaman (doves, T. Kurpershoek).)

1961 (18 Sept.). *European Postal and Telecommunications (C.E.P.T.) Conference, Torquay. Chalky paper. W* **179**. *P* 15×14.

626	186	2d. orge., pink & brown	8	8
627	187	4d. buff, mve. & ultram.	15	20
628	188	10d. turquoise, pale green and Prussian blue ..	60	60
		a. Green omitted	£400	
		b. Turquoise omitted ..	£400	

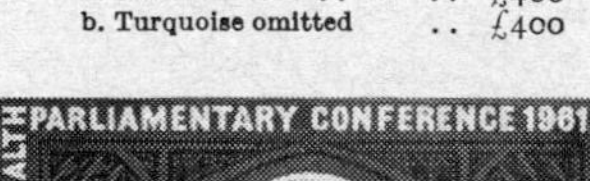

189. Hammer Beam Roof, Westminster Hall.

MINIMUM PRICE

The minimum price quoted is 5p which represents a handling charge rather than a basis for valuing common stamps. For further notes about prices see introductory pages.

190. Palace of Westminster.

(Des. Miss F. Jacques.)

1961 (25 Sept.). *Seventh Commonwealth Parliamentary Conference. Chalky paper. W* **179** *(sideways on 1s. 3d.). P 15 × 14 (6d.) or 14 × 15 (1s. 3d.).*

629 **189** 6d. purple and gold .. 50 50
a. Gold omitted £175
630 **190** 1s. 3d. green and blue .. 3·00 3·00
a. Blue (Queen's head) omitted £350

191. " Units of Productivity ".

192. " National Productivity ".

193. " Unified Productivity ".

(Des. D. Gentleman.)

1962 (14 Nov.). *National Productivity Year. Chalky paper. W* **179** *(inverted on 2½d. and 3d.).) P 15 × 14.*

631 **191** 2½d. myrtle-green and carmine-red (*shades*) .. 10 5
p. One phosphor band .. 50 1·00
632 **192** 3d. light blue and violet (*shades*) 25 10
a. Light blue (Queen's head) omitted.. .. .. £350
p. Three phosphor bands .. 1·50 2·00
633 **193** 1s. 3d. carmine, lt. blue and deep green .. 2·25 2·25
a. Light blue (Queen's head) omitted £500
p. Three phosphor bands.. 22·00 20·00

194. Campaign Emblem and Family.

195. Children of Three Races.

(Des. M. Goaman.)

1963 (21 Mar.). *Freedom from Hunger. Chalky paper. W* **179** *(inverted). P 15 × 14.*

634 **194** 2½d. crimson and pink .. 25 10
p. One phosphor band .. 2·00 2·00
635 **195** 1s. 3d. bis-brn. & yell. 2·25 1·75
p. Three phosphor bands .. 18·00 18·00

196. " Paris Conference ".

(Des. Reynolds Stone.)

1963 (7 May). *Paris Postal Conference Centenary. Chalky paper. W* **179** *(inverted). P 15 × 14.*

636 **196** 6d. green and mauve .. 1·25 75
a. Green omitted .. £375
p. Three phosphor bands 3·75 3·25

197. Posy of Flowers.

198. Woodland Life.

(Des. S. Scott (3d.), M. Goaman (4½d.).)

1963 (16 May). *National Nature Week. Chalky paper. W* **179**. *P 15 × 14.*

637 **197** 3d. yell., grn., brn. & blk. 8 5
p. Three phosphor bands .. 60 60
638 **198** 4½d. black, blue, yellow, magenta & brown-red 85 40
p. Three phosphor bands .. 3·00 2·50

199. Rescue at Sea.

200. 19th-century Lifeboat.

201. Lifeboatmen.

(Des. D. Gentleman.)

1963 (31 May). *Ninth International Lifeboat Conference, Edinburgh. Chalky paper. W* **179**. *P 15 × 14.*

639 **199** 2½d. blue, black and red .. 15 5
p. One phosphor band .. 50 50
640 **200** 4d. red, yellow, brown, black and blue .. 75 1·00
p. Three phosphor bands .. 1·50 2·00
641 **201** 1s. 6d. sepia, yellow and grey-blue .. 3·00 2·25
p. Three phosphor bands .. 25·00 22·00

202. Red Cross.

203

204

(Des. H. Bartram.)

1963 (15 Aug.). *Red Cross Centenary Congress. Chalky paper.* W **179**. *P* 15 × 14.

642 **202** 3d. red and deep lilac .. 8 5
 a. Red omitted £475
 p. Three phosphor bands .. 1·00 1·50
 pa. Red omitted £550
643 **203** 1s. 3d. red, blue and grey 3·00 4·00
 p. Three phosphor bands .. 20·00 18·00
644 **204** 1s. 6d. red, blue & bistre 4·00 3·00
 p. Three phosphor bands .. 20·00 18·00

205. "Commonwealth Cable".

(Des. P. Gauld.)

1963 (3 Dec.). *Opening of COMPAC (Trans-Pacific Telephone Cable). Chalky paper.* W **179**. *P* 15 × 14.

645 **205** 1s. 6d. blue and black .. 2·25 1·75
 a. Black omitted £300
 p. Three phosphor bands .. 18·00 18·00

206. Puck and Bottom. (*A Midsummer Night's Dream*).

207. Feste (*Twelfth Night*).

208. Balcony Scene (*Romeo and Juliet*).

209. "Eve of Agincourt" (*Henry V*).

210. Hamlet contemplating Yorick's Skull (*Hamlet*) and Queen Elizabeth II.

(Des. D. Gentleman. Photo. Harrison & Sons (3d., 6d., 1s. 3d., 1s. 6d.). Des C. and R. Ironside. Recess. B.W. (2s. 6d.).)

1964 (23 April). *Shakespeare Festival. Chalky paper.* W **179**. *P* 11 × 12 (2s. 6d.) *or* 15 × 14 (*others*).

646 **206** 3d. yellow-bistre, black & dp. violet-blue (*shades*) 8 5
 p. Three phosphor bands .. 30 30
647 **207** 6d. yellow, orange, black & yell.-olive (*shades*) 35 30
 p. Three phosphor bands .. 90 80
648 **208** 1s. 3d. cerise, blue-green, black & sepia (*shades*) 2·00 1·75
 p. Three phosphor bands .. 5·00 4·00
649 **209** 1s. 6d. violet, turquoise, black & blue (*shades*) 2·00 2·00
 p. Three phosphor bands .. 15·00 10·00
650 **210** 2s. 6d. deep slate-purple (*shades*) .. .. 3·00 2·50

211. Flats near Richmond Park ("Urban Development").

212. Shipbuilding Yards, Belfast ("Industrial Activity").

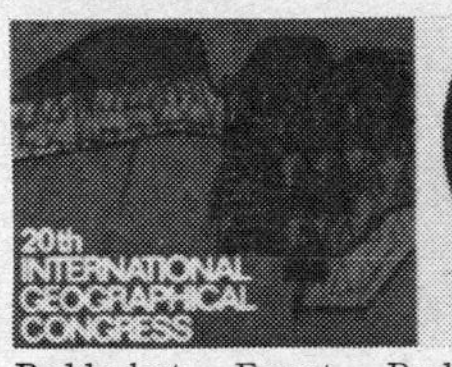

213. Beddgelert Forest Park, Snowdonia ("Forestry").

214. Nuclear Reactor, Dounreay ("Technological Development").

(Des. D. Bailey.)

1964 (1 July). *20th International Geographical Congress, London. Chalky paper.* W **179**. *P* 15 × 14.

651 **211** 2½d. black, olive-yellow, olive-grey & turq.-bl. 8 5
 p. One phosphor band .. 45 45
652 **212** 4d. orge.-brn, red-brown, rose, black and violet 35 75
 a. Violet omitted .. £130
 b. Red-brown omitted .. £200
 c. Violet and red-brown omitted .. .. 60·00
 p. Three phosphor bands .. 1·50 1·50
653 **213** 8d. yellow-brn., emerald, green and black .. 1·75 1·75
 a. Green (lawn) omitted .. £150
 p. Three phosphor bands .. 6·00 6·00
654 **214** 1s. 6d. yellow-brn., pale pink, black & brown 2·50 2·25
 p. Three phosphor bands .. 16·00 14·00

215. Spring Gentian.

216. Dog Rose.

217. Honeysuckle.

218. Fringed Water Lily.

(Des. M. and Sylvia Goaman.)

1964 (5 Aug.). *Tenth International Botanical Congress. Edinburgh. Chalky paper.* W **179**. *P* 15 × 14.

655 **215** 3d. violet, blue & sage-grn. 8 5
 a. Blue omitted £250
 p. Three phosphor bands .. 45 45
656 **216** 6d. apple-green, rose, scarlet and green .. 35 50
 p. Three phosphor bands .. 1·50 1·50
657 **217** 9d. lemon, green, lake and rose-red .. .. 2·00 1·75
 a. Green (leaves) omitted .. £225
 p. Three phosphor bands .. 6·00 6·00
658 **218** 1s. 3d. yell., emerald, reddish violet & grey-grn. 2·00 1·75
 p. Three phosphor bands .. 16·00 14·00

219. Forth Road Bridge.

220. Forth Road and Railway Bridges.

(Des. A. Restall.)

1964 (4 Sept.). *Opening of Forth Road Bridge. Chalky paper. W* **179.** *P* 15 × 14.

659 **219** 3d. blk., bl. & reddish vio. .. 10 5
p. Three phosphor bands .. 75 75
660 **220** 6d. black, light blue and carmine-red 80 60
a. Light blue omitted .. £500 £500
p. Three phosphor bands .. 3·75 3·25

221. Sir Winston Churchill.

(Des. D. Gentleman and Rosalind Dease, from photograph by Karsh.)

1965 (8 July). *Churchill Commemoration. Chalky paper. W* **179.** *P* 15 × 14.

I. "REMBRANDT" Machine.

661 **221** 4d. black & olive-brown 10 10
p. Three phosphor bands .. 50 50

II. "TIMSON" Machine.

661a **221** 4d. black & olive-brown 10 10

III. "L. & M. 4" Machine.

662 – 1s. 3d. black and grey .. 80 80
p. Three phosphor bands .. 4·50 4·00

The 1s. 3d. shows a closer view of Churchill's head.

4d. REMBRANDT. Cyls. 1A–1B dot and no dot. Lack of shading detail on Churchill's portrait. Queen's portrait appears dull and coarse. This is a new rotary machine which is sheet-fed.

4d. TIMSON. Cyls. 5A–6B no dot. More detail on Churchill's portrait—furrow on forehead, his left eyebrow fully drawn and more shading on cheek. Queen's portrait lighter and sharper. This is a reel-fed, two-colour 12-in. wide rotary machine and the differences in impression are due to the greater pressure applied by this machine.

1s. 3d. Plate Nos. 1A–1B no dot. The "Linotype and Machinery No. 4" machine is an ordinary sheet-fed rotary press machine. Besides being used for printing the 1s. 3d. stamps it was also employed for overprinting the phosphor bands on both values.

Two copies of the 4d. value exist with the Queen's head omitted, one due to something adhering to the cylinder and the other due to a paper fold. The stamp also exists with Churchill's head omitted, also due to a paper fold.

222. Simon de Montfort's Seal.

223. Parliament Buildings (after engraving by Hollar, 1647).

(Des. S. R. Black (6d.), Prof. R. Guyatt (2s. 6d.).)

1965 (19 July). *700th Anniv. of Simon de Montfort's Parliament. Chalky paper. W* **179.** *P* 15 × 14.

663 **222** 6d. olive-green 25 25
p. Three phosphor bands .. 1·00 1·00
664 **223** 2s. 6d. black, grey and pale drab .. .. 1·50 1·75

224. Bandsmen and Banner.

225. Three Salvationists.

(Des. M. C. Farrar Bell (3d.), G. Trenaman (1s. 6d.).)

1965 (9 Aug.). *Salvation Army Centenary. Chalky paper. W* **179.** *P* 15 × 14.

665 **224** 3d. indigo, grey-blue, cerise, yellow & brown 15 10
p. One phosphor band .. 50 50
666 **225** 1s. 6d. red, blue, yellow and brown .. .. 1·50 1·25
p. Three phosphor bands .. 4·00 4·00

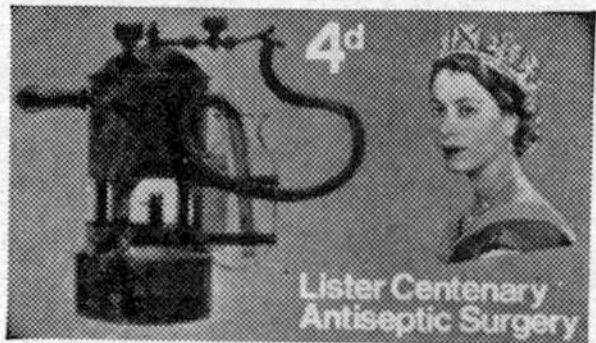

226. Lister's Carbolic Spray.

227. Lister and Chemical Symbols.

(Des. P. Gauld (4d.), F. Ariss (1s.).)

1965 (1 Sept.). *Centenary of Joseph Lister's Discovery of Antiseptic Surgery. Chalky paper. W* **179.** *P* 15 × 14.

667 **226** 4d. indigo, brown-red and grey-black 8 5
a. Brown-red (tube) omitted 60·00
b. Indigo omitted .. .. 80·00
p. Three phosphor bands .. 25 25
pa. Brown-red (tube) omitted 75·00
668 **227** 1s. black, pur. & new blue 1·00 85
p. Three phosphor bands .. 1·50 1·50

228. Trinidad Carnival Dancers.

229. Canadian Folk-dancers.

(Des. D. Gentleman and Rosalind Dease.)

1965 (1 Sept.). *Commonwealth Arts Festival Chalky paper. W* **179.** *P* 15 × 14.

669 **228** 6d. black and orange .. 50 35
p. Three phosphor bands .. 1·25 1·00
670 **229** 1s. 6d. black and light reddish violet .. 1·75 1·50
p. Three phosphor bands .. 4·00 3·50

230. Flight of Spitfires.

231. Pilot in Hurricane.

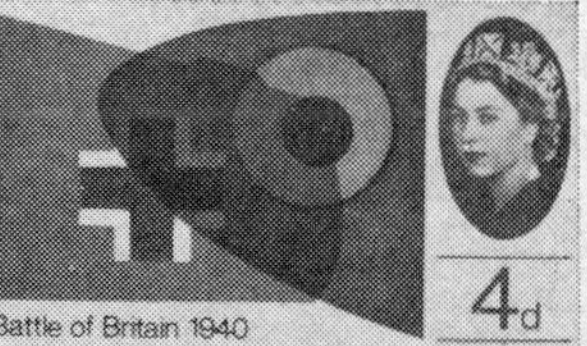

232. Wing-tips of Spitfire and Messerschmitt "ME-109".

233. Spitfires attacking Heinkel "HE-111" Bomber.

234. Spitfire attacking Stuka Dive-bomber.

235. Hurricanes over Wreck of Dornier "DO-17z2" Bomber.

236. Anti-aircraft Artillery in Action.

237. Air-battle over St. Paul's Cathedral.

(Des. D. Gentleman and Rosalind Dease (4d. × 6 and 1s. 3d.), A. Restall (9d.).)

1965 (13 Sept.). *25th Anniv. of Battle of Britain. Chalky paper. W* **179.** *P* 15 × 14.

671	**230**	4d. yellow-olive & black	25	20
		p. Three phosphor bands ..	35	30
672	**231**	4d. yellow-olive, olive-grey and black ..	25	20
		p. Three phosphor bands ..	35	30
673	**232**	4d. red, new blue, yellow-olive, olive-grey & blk.	25	20
		p. Three phosphor bands ..	35	30
674	**233**	4d. olive-grey, yellow-olive and black	25	20
		p. Three phosphor bands ..	35	30
675	**234**	4d. olive-grey, yellow-olive and black	25	20
		p. Three phosphor bands ..	35	30
676	**235**	4d. olive-grey, yellow-olive, new blue and black ..	25	20
		a. New blue omitted ..	—	£125
		p. Three phosphor bands ..	35	30
677	**236**	9d. bluish violet, orange and slate-purple ..	3·00	3·00
		p. Three phosphor bands ..	5·00	5·00
678	**237**	1s. 3d. light & deep grey, black and light and bright blue	3·00	3·00
		p. Three phosphor bands ..	3·00	3·00

Nos. 671/6 were issued together *se-tenant* in blocks of 6 (3 × 2) within the sheet.

238. Tower and Georgian Buildings.

239. Tower and "Nash" Terrace, Regent's Park.

(Des. C. Abbott.)

1965 (8 Oct.). *Opening of Post Office Tower. Chalky paper. W* **179** *(sideways on* 3*d.). P* 14 × 15 (3*d.*) *or* 15 × 14 (1*s.* 3*d.*).

679	**238**	3d. olive-yellow, new blue and bronze-green ..	8	5
		a. Olive-yellow (Tower) omitted	£175	
		p. One phosphor band ..	8	8
680	**239**	1s. 3d. bronze-green, yellow-green and blue	80	80
		p. Three phosphor bands ..	45	40

240. U.N. Emblem.

241. I.C.Y. Emblem.

(Des. J. Matthews.)

1965 (25 Oct.). *20th Anniv. of U.N.O. and International Co-operation Year. Chalky paper. W* **179.** *P* 15 × 14.

681	**240**	3d. black, yellow-orange and light blue ..	12	8
		p. One phosphor band	15	15
682	**241**	1s. 6d. black, brt. purple and light blue ..	1·50	1·25
		p. Three phosphor bands ..	1·50	1·50

242. Telecommunications Network.

243. Radio Waves and Switchboard.

(Des. A. Restall.)

1965 (15 Nov.). *I.T.U. Centenary. Chalky paper. W* **179.** *P* 15 × 14.

683	**242**	9d. red, ultram., dp. slate, violet, black and pink	65	50
		p. Three phosphor bands ..	2·00	2·00
684	**243**	1s. 6d. red, greenish blue, indigo, blk. & lt. pink	85	85
		a. Pink omitted	£130	
		p. Three phosphor bands ..	7·00	6·00

Originally scheduled for issue on May 17th, 1965, supplies from the Philatelic Bureau were sent in error to reach a dealer on that date and another dealer received his supply on May 27th.

244. Robert Burns (after Skirving chalk drawing).

245. Robert Burns (after Nasmyth portrait).

(Des. G. F. Huntly.)

1966 (25 Jan.). *Burns Commemoration. Chalky paper. W* **179.** *P* 15 × 14.

685	**244**	4d. black, deep violet-blue and new blue ..	10	5
		p. Three phosphor bands ..	25	15
686	**245**	1s. 3d. black, slate-blue and yellow-orange ..	80	70
		p. Three phosphor bands ..	1·75	1·50

246. Westminster Abbey.

247. Fan Vaulting, Henry VII Chapel.

(Des. Sheila Robinson. Photo. Harrison (3d.). Des. and eng. Bradbury, Wilkinson. Recess. (2s. 6d.).)

1966 (28 Feb.). *900th Anniv. of Westminster Abbey. Chalky paper* (3d.). *W* **179**. *P* 15×14 (3d.). *or* 11×12 (2s. 6d.).

687 **246** 3d. black, red-brown and new blue 8 5
p. One phosphor band .. 35 20
688 **247** 2s. 6d. black .. .. 1·25 1·00

248. View near Hassocks, Sussex.

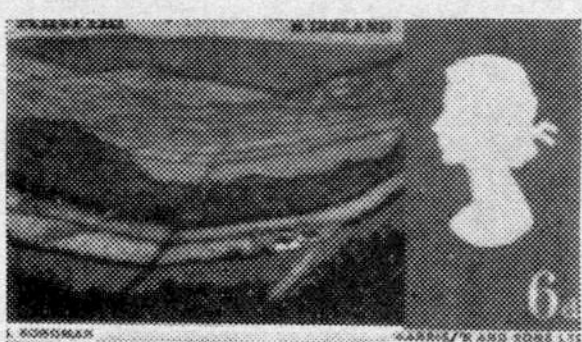

249. Antrim, Northern Ireland.

250. Harlech Castle, Wales.

251. Cairngorm Mountains, Scotland.

(Des. L. Rosoman. Queen's portrait, adapted by D. Gentleman from coinage.)

1966 (2 May). *Landscapes. Chalky paper. W* **179**. *P* 15×14.

689 **248** 4d. black, yellow-green and new blue .. 8 5
p. Three phosphor bands .. 10 10
690 **249** 6d. blk., emer. & new blue 15 10
p. Three phosphor bands .. 25 25
691 **250** 1s. 3d. black, greenish yellow & greenish blue 50 50
p. Three phosphor bands .. 60 60
692 **251** 1s. 6d. black, orange and Prussian blue .. 50 50
a. Three phosphor bands .. 60 60

252. Players with Ball.

253. Goalmouth Mêlée.

254. Goalkeeper saving Goal.

(Des. D. Gentleman (4d.), W. Kempster (6d.). D. Caplan (1s. 3d.). Queen's portrait adapted by D. Gentleman from coinage.)

1966 (1 June). *World Cup Football Competition. Chalky paper. W* **179** (*sideways on* 4*d*.). *P* 14×15 (4*d*.) *or* 15×14 (*others*).

693 **252** 4d. red, reddish purple, brt. blue, flesh & blk. 8 5
p. Two phosphor bands .. 10 8
694 **253** 6d. black, sepia, red, apple-green and blue 20 15
a. Black omitted .. .. 45·00
b. Apple-green omitted .. £125
c. Red omitted £125
p. Three phosphor bands .. 25 25
pa. Black omitted .. .. 75·00
695 **254** 1s. 3d. black, blue, yell., red & lt. yell.-olive 50 40
a. Blue omitted £180
p. Three phosphor bands .. 50 50

255. Black-headed Gull.

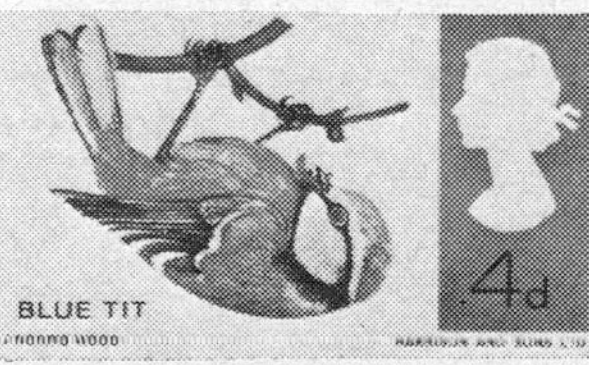

256. Blue Tit.

257. Robin.

258. Blackbird.

(Des. J. Norris Wood.)

1966 (8 Aug.). *British Birds. Chalky paper. W* **179**. *P* 15×14.

696 **255** 4d. grey, black, red, emerald-green, bright blue, greenish yellow and bistre 15 12
a. Black (value), etc. omitted* (*block of four*) .. £425
b. Black only omitted* ..
p. Three phosphor bands .. 15 15
697 **256** 4d. black, greenish yellow, grey, emerald-green, bright blue and bistre 15 12
p. Three phosphor bands .. 15 15
698 **257** 4d. red, greenish yellow, black, grey, bistre, reddish brown and emerald-green .. 15 12
p. Three phosphor bands .. 15 15
699 **258** 4d. black, reddish brown, greenish yell. & grey 15 12
p. Three phosphor bands .. 15 15

Nos. 696/9 were issued together ***se-tenant*** in blocks of four within the sheet.

* In No. 696a the blue, bistre and reddish brown are also omitted but in No. 696b only the black is omitted.

Other missing colours known are greenish yellow, red, emerald-green, bright blue, bistre and reddish brown on ordinary paper and emerald-green, bright blue, bistre and reddish brown on phosphor.

MISSING COLOURS IN MULTI-COLOURED ISSUES. We only actually list the most outstanding errors, but make footnote mention of others known to us which have full listing in the *Elizabethan Catalogue*.

259. Cup Winners.

1966 (18 Aug.). *England's World Cup Football Victory. Chalky paper. W* **179**, *sideways. P* 14×15.

700 **259** 4d. red, reddish purple, brt. blue, flesh & black 12 25

The above was only put on sale at post offices in England, the Channel Islands and the Isle of Man, and at the Philatelic Bureau in London and also, on August 22nd, in Edinburgh on the occasion of the opening of the Edinburgh Festival as well as at Army post offices at home and abroad.

260. Jodrell Bank Radio Telescope.

261. British Motor-cars.

262. SRN 6 Hovercraft.

263. Windscale Reactor.

(Des. D. and A. Gillespie (4d., 6d.), J. A. Restall (others).)

1966 (19 Sept.). *British Technology. Chalky paper. W* **179.** *P* 15 × 14.

701	**260**	4d. black and lemon ..	8	5
		p. Three phosphor bands ..	8	5
702	**261**	6d. red, dp. blue & orange	15	15
		a. Red (Mini-cars) omitted ..	£200	
		b. Blue (Jaguar and inscr.) omitted	£275	
		p. Three phosphor bands ..	20	20
703	**262**	1s. 3d. black, orge.-red, slate, & lt. grn'sh blue	40	40
		p. Three phosphor bands ..	40	40
704	**263**	1s. 6d. black, yell.-green, bronze-green, lilac and deep blue	40	40
		p. Three phosphor bands ..	50	50

264

265

266

267

268

269

(All the above show battle scenes and they were issued together *se-tenant* in horizontal strips of six within the sheet).

270. Norman Ship.

271. Norman Horsemen attacking Harold's Troops.

(All the above are scenes from the Bayeux Tapestry.)

(Des. D. Gentleman. Photo., Queen's head die-stamped.)

1966 (14 Oct.). *900th Anniv. of Battle of Hastings. Chalky paper. W* **179** *(sideways on* 1s. 3*d.). P* 15 × 14.

705	**264**	4d. multicoloured ..	10	8
		p. Three phosphor bands ..	25	25
706	**265**	4d. multicoloured ..	10	8
		p. Three phosphor bands ..	25	25
707	**266**	4d. multicoloured ..	10	8
		p. Three phosphor bands ..	25	25
708	**267**	4d. multicoloured ..	10	8
		p. Three phosphor bands ..	25	25
709	**268**	4d. multicoloured ..	10	8
		p. Three phosphor bands ..	25	25
710	**269**	4d. multicoloured ..	10	8
		p. Three phosphor bands ..	25	25
711	**270**	6d. multicoloured ..	30	20
		p. Three phosphor bands ..	30	25
712	**271**	1s. 3d. multicoloured ..	60	50
		p. Four phosphor bands ..	50	50

Missing colours known on the 4d. are olive-green, bistre, deep blue, orange, magenta, green, blue and grey on ordinary paper and olive-green, bistre, deep blue, orange, magenta, green and grey on phosphor. In addition the magenta and green are known both omitted on phosphor. On the 1s. 3d. the lilac is known omitted on ordinary and phosphor.

Nos. 705 and 709, with grey and blue omitted, have been seen commercially used, posted from Middleton-in-Teesdale.

MISSING GOLD HEADS. The 6d. and 1s. 3d. were also issued with the die-stamped gold head omitted but as these can also be removed by chemical means we are not prepared to list them unless a way is found of distinguishing the genuine stamps from the fakes which will satisfy the Expert Committees.

The same remarks apply to Nos. 713/4.

272. King of the Orient.

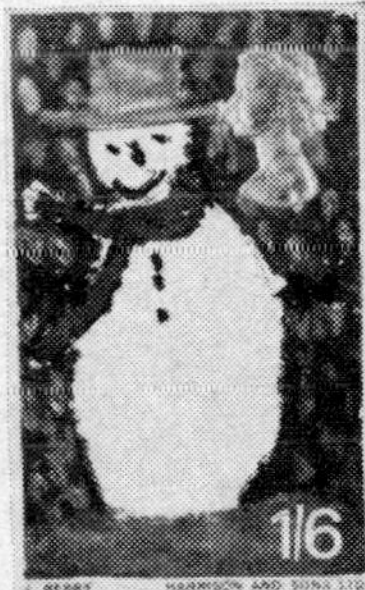

273. Snowman.

(Des. T. Shemza (3d.), J. Berry (1s. 6d.) (winners of children's design competition). Photo., Queen's head die-stamped.)

1966 (1 Dec.). *Christmas. Chalky paper. W* **179** *(sideways on 3d.). P* 14 × 15.

713	**272**	3d. multicoloured ..	8	5
		a. Queen's head double ..		
		p. One phosphor band	10	10
714	**273**	1s. 6d. multicoloured ..	25	30
		p. Two phosphor bands ..	50	50

Missing colours known are the green on the 3d. and the pink (snowman's hat) on the 1s. 6d., both on ordinary paper.

274. Sea Freight.

275. Air Freight.

(Des. C. Abbott.)

1967 (20 Feb.). *European Free Trade Association (EFTA). Chalky paper.* W **179.** *P* 15×14.

715 **274** 9d. multicoloured .. 20 20
  a. Black (Queen's head, etc.), brown, new blue and yellow omitted.. .. £250
  p. Three phosphor bands .. 15 15
716 **275** 1s. 6d. multicoloured .. 25 25
  p. Three phosphor bands .. 20 20

The following missing colours are known:—9d. Lilac, green, brown, new blue and yellow on ordinary paper and lilac, green, brown, new blue and yellow on phosphor, 1s. 6d. Red, deep blue, brown, new blue, yellow and blue-grey on ordinary paper and red, deep blue, brown, new blue and blue-grey on phosphor.

276. Hawthorn and Bramble.

277. Larger Bindweed and Viper's Bugloss.

278. Ox-eye Daisy, Coltsfoot and Buttercup.

279. Bluebell, Red Campion and Wood Anemone.

(The above were issued together *se-tenant* in blocks of four within the sheet.)

280. Dog Violet.

281. Primroses.

(Des. Rev. W. Keble Martin (T **276/9**), Mary Grierson (others).)

1967 (24 Apr.). *British Wild Flowers. Chalky paper.* W **179.** *P* 15×14.

717 **276** 4d. multicoloured .. 20 10
  a. Grey double* .. ..
  p. Three phosphor bands .. 10 10
718 **277** 4d. multicoloured .. 20 10
  a. Grey double* .. ..
  p. Three phosphor bands .. 10 10
719 **278** 4d. multicoloured .. 20 10
  a. Grey double* .. ..
  p. Three phosphor bands .. 10 10
720 **279** 4d. multicoloured .. 20 10
  a. Grey double* .. ..
  p. Three phosphor bands .. 10 10
721 **280** 9d. multicoloured .. 40 45
  p. Three phosphor bands .. 40 35
722 **281** 1s. 9d. multicoloured .. 40 40
  p. Three phosphor bands .. 40 40

The following missing colours are known:—4d. red and reddish purple on ordinary paper and agate, violet and slate-purple on phosphor.

*The double impression of the grey printing affects the Queen's head, value and inscription.

PHOSPHOR BANDS. All issues from No. 723 are normally with phosphor bands only, except for the high values. However, most stamps have appeared with the phosphor bands omitted in error and are relatively common in this state, but they are outside the scope of this catalogue. They are listed in Volumes 3 and 4 of the *Stanley Gibbons Specialised Catalogue of Great Britain.*

"ALL-OVER" PHOSPHOR. Stamps with phosphor applied over the whole area react under an ultra violet lamp. No. 743b was the first experimental use of this and it came into general use for commemorative stamps with the Royal Wedding issue of 1972. They should not be confused with stamps printed on paper with phosphor coating (see note after No. 874).

PVA GUM. Polyvinyl alcohol was introduced by Harrisons in place of gum Arabic in 1968. It is almost invisible except that a small amount of pale yellowish colouring matter was introduced to make it possible to see that the stamps have been gummed. Although this can be distinguished from gum arabic in unused stamps there is, of course, no means of detecting it in used copies and so it is outside the scope of this catalogue, but they are listed in the *Elizabethan Specialised Catalogue.* See further notes *re* gum after Nos. 744 and 762.

282

282a

I. II.

Two types of the 2d.

I. Value spaced away from left side of stamp (cylinders 1 no dot and dot).

II. Value close to left side from new multi-positive used for cylinders 5 no dot and dot onwards. The portrait appears in the centre, thus conforming to the other values.

(Des. after plaster cast by **Arnold Machin.**)

1967–70. *Chalky paper. Two phosphor bands except where otherwise stated. No wmk. Perf.* 15×14.

723 **282** ½d. orange-brown .. 5 10
724 ,, 1d. light olive (*shades*) (2 bands) 8 5
  a. Imperf. (coil strip)† .. £200
  b. Uncoated paper ('70)** 35·00
  l. Booklet pane (724×2 *se-tenant* with 730×2) (6.4.68) 90
  m. Booklet pane (724×4 *se-tenant* with 734×2) (6.1.69) .. .. 1·75
  n. Booklet pane (724×6, 734×6 and 735×3 *se-tenant*) (1.12.69) .. 8·50
  na. Uncoated paper ('70)**
725 1d. yellowish olive (1 centre band) .. 30 30
  l. Booklet pane (725×4 *se-tenant* with 732×2).. 1·50
  m. Coil strip (728×2 *se-tenant* with 729, 725 and 733) (27.8.69) .. .. 2·00
726 ,, 2d. lake-brown (Type I) (2 bands) 15 15
727 ,, 2d. lake-brown (Type II) (2 bands) 12 10
728 ,, 2d. lake-brown (Type II) (1 centre band) .. 40 40
729 ,, 3d. violet (*shades*) (1 centre band) .. 10 5
  a. Imperf. (pair).. .. £325
730 ,, 3d. violet (2 bands) .. 35 5
  a. Uncoated paper** ..
731 ,, 4d. deep sepia (*shades*) (2 bands) 12 5
  a. Part perf. pane* ..
732 ,, 4d. dp. ol.-brn. (*shades*) (1 centre band) .. 12 5
  a. Part perf. pane* ..
  l. Booklet pane. Two stamps plus two printed labels 60
733 ,, 4d. bright vermilion (1 centre band) .. 12 5
  a. Tête-bêche (horiz. pr.)..
  b. Uncoated paper ('70)** 10·00
  l. Booklet pane. Two stamps plus two printed labels (3.3.69) 50
734 ,, 4d. bright vermilion (1 side band) .. .. 75 1·00
  a. Uncoated paper ('70)** 35·00
735 ,, 5d. Royal blue (*shades*) 12 5
  a. Imperf. pane* .. £150
  b. Part perf. pane* .. 70·00
  c. Imperf. (pair)†† .. 30·00
  d. Uncoated paper ('70)** 10·00
736 ,, 6d. bright reddish purple (*shades*) 20 5
737 **282a** 7d. bright emerald .. 35 12
738 ,, 8d. bright vermilion .. 20 30
739 ,, 8d. light turquoise-blue 75 20
740 ,, 9d. myrtle-green .. 40 15
741 **282** 10d. drab.. .. .. 50 20
  a. Uncoated paper ('69)** 20·00
742 ,, 1s. lt. bluish vio. (*shades*) 40 8
743 ,, 1s. 6d. greenish blue and deep blue (*shades*) .. 50 5
  a. Greenish blue omitted.. 25·00
  b. "All-over" phosphor (10.12.69) .. .. 2·00 1·50
  ba. Greenish blue omitted.. 50·00
744 ,, 1s. 9d. dull orange and black (*shades*) .. 75 25

* Booklet errors. See note after 556.

**Uncoated paper. This does not respond to the chalky test, and may be further distinguished from the normal chalk-surfaced paper by the fibres which clearly show on the surface, resulting in the printing impression being rougher, and by the screening dots which are not so evident. The 1d., 4d. and 5d. come from the £1 "Stamps for Cooks" Booklet; the 3d. and 10d. from sheets.

†No. 724a occurs in a vertical strip of four, top stamp perforated on three sides, bottom stamp imperf. three sides and the two middle stamps completely imperf.

††No. 735c comes from the original state of cyl. 15 which is identifiable by the screening dots which extend through the gutters of the stamps and into the margins of the sheet. This must not be confused with imperforate stamps from cyl. 10, a large quantity of which was stolen from the printers early in 1970.

Dates of issue:
5.6.67 4d. (731), 1s., 1s. 9d.
8.8.67 3d. (729), 9d., 1s. 6d.
5.2.68 ½d., 1d. (724), 2d. (726), 6d.
6.4.68 3d. (730) Booklets
1.7.68 5d., 7d., 8d. (738), 10d.
16.9.68 1d. (725), 4d. (732)
12.68 3d. (730) Coils.
6.1.69 4d. (733/4), 8d. (739)
1969 2d. (727)
1.69 3d. (730) Sheets
27.8.69 2d. (728)

The 1d. with centre band (725) only came in the Sept. 1968 booklets (PVA gum) and the coil strip (725m) (gum arabic); the 2d. with centre band (728) was only issued in the coil strip (725m); and the 4d. with one side band (734) only in 10s. and £1 booklets.

Gum. The 1d. (725), 3d. (729), 4d. (731 and 733), 9d., 1s., 1s. 6d. and 1s. 9d. exist with gum arabic as well as the PVA gum; the 2d. (728) and coil strip (725m) exist only with gum arabic; and the remainder exist with PVA gum only.

The 4d. (731) in shades of washed out grey are colour changelings which we understand are caused by the concentrated solvents used in modern dry cleaning methods.

For decimal issue, see Nos. 841/73.

283. "Master Lambton" (after Sir Thomas Lawrence).

284. "Mares and Foals in a Landscape" (after George Stubbs).

285. "Children Coming Out of School" (after L. S. Lowry).

1967 (10 July). *British Paintings. Chalky paper. Two phosphor bands. No wmk. P 14×15 (4d.) or 15×14 (others).*

748 **283** 4d. multicoloured .. 8 5
a. Gold omitted (value and Queen's head) £100
749 **284** 9d. multicoloured .. 20 20
a. Black (Queen's head and value) omitted £150
750 **285** 1s. 6d. multicoloured .. 30 30
a. Gold (Queen's head) omitted £100

The 4d. is known with the blue omitted, the 9d. with the greenish yellow omitted and the 1s. 6d. with the blue, and pale grey omitted.

286. *Gipsy Moth IV.*

(Des. M. and S. Goaman.)

1967 (24 July). *Sir Francis Chichester's World Voyage. Chalky paper. Three phosphor bands. No wmk. P 15×14.*

751 **286** 1s. 9d. black, brown-red, light emerald & blue 30 30

287. Radar Screen.

288. Penicillin Mould.

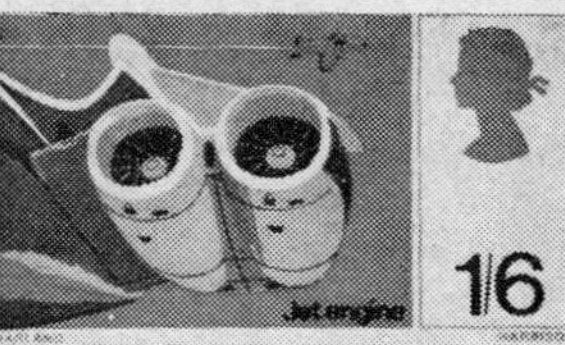

289. "VC-10" Jet Engines.

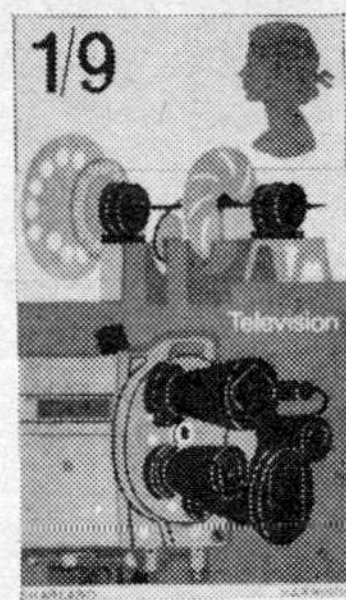

290. Television Equipment.

(Des. C. Abbott (4d., 1s.), Negus-Sharland team (others).)

1967 (19 Sept.). *British Discovery and Invention. Chalky paper. Three phosphor bands (4d.) or two phosphor bands (others). W* **179** *(sideways on 1s. 9d.). P 14×15 (1s. 9d.) or 15×14 (others).*

752 **287** 4d. greenish yellow, black and vermilion .. 8 5
753 **288** 1s. blue-green, light greenish blue, slate-purple and bluish violet .. 20 20
754 **289** 1s. 6d. black, grey, Royal blue, ochre and turquoise-blue 25 25
755 **290** 1s. 9d. black, grey-blue, pale olive-grey, violet and orange 25 25

The 1s. 9d. exists with the grey-blue omitted.

WATERMARK. All issues from this date are on unwatermarked paper.

291. "The Adoration of the Shepherds" (School of Seville).

292. "Madonna and Child" (Murillo).

293. " The Adoration of the Shepherds " (Louis Le Nain).

1967. *Christmas. Chalky paper. One phosphor band (3d.) or two phosphor bands (others). P 15 × 14 (1s. 6d.) or 14 × 15 (others).*

756	**291**	3d. multicoloured (27.11)	8	5
		a. Gold omitted (value and Queen's head)	40·00	
		b. Printed on the gummed side	20·00	
757	**292**	4d. multicoloured (18.10)	8	5
		a. Gold omitted (value and Queen's head)	45·00	
		b. Yellow (Child, robe and Madonna's face) omitted ..		
758	**293**	1s. 6d. mult. (27.11) ..	25	25
		a. Gold omitted (value and Queen's head)		

Distinct shades exist of the 4d. value but are not listable as there are intermediate shades. Stamps emanating from one machine show a darker background and give the appearance of the yellow colour being omitted but this is not so and these should not be confused with No. 757b.

The 3d. is known with the rose colour omitted and the 1s. 6d. is known with the ultramarine colour omitted.

(Recess. Bradbury, Wilkinson.)

1967–68. *No wmk. White paper. P 11 × 12.*

759	**166**	2s. 6d. blk.-brn. (1.7.68)	60	20
760	**167**	5s. red (10.4.68)	1·40	40
761	**168**	10s. brt. ultram. (10.4.68)	5·00	1·25
762	**169**	£1 black (4.12.67) ..	6·00	2·50

PVA GUM. All the following issues from this date have PVA gum *except where footnotes state otherwise.*

294. Tarr Steps, Exmoor.

295. Aberfeldy Bridge.

296. Menai Bridge.

297. M4 Viaduct.

(Des. A. Restall (9d.), L. Rosoman (1s. 6d.), J. Matthews (others).)

1968 (29 Apr.). *British Bridges. Chalky paper. Two phosphor bands. P 15 × 14.*

763	**294**	4d. multicoloured ..	8	5
		a. Printed on the gummed side	10·00	
764	**295**	9d. multicoloured ..	25	25
		a. Gold (Queen's head) omitted	75·00	
765	**296**	1s. 6d. multicoloured ..	25	25
		a. Gold (Queen's head) omitted	90·00	
766	**297**	1s. 9d. multicoloured ..	40	50
		a. Gold (Queen's head) omitted	£100	

The 9d. is known with ultramarine omitted and the 1s. 6d. with red-orange omitted.

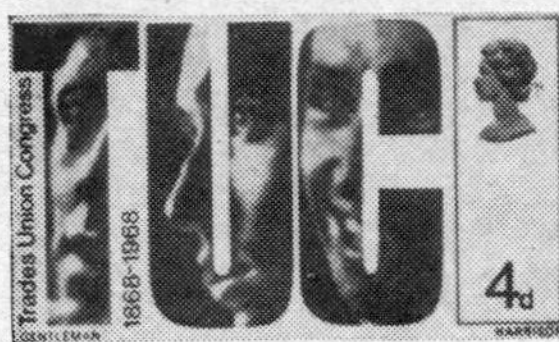

298. " T U C " and Trades Unionists.

299. Mrs. Emmeline Pankhurst (statue).

300. Sopwith " Camel " and " Lightning " Fighters.

301. Captain Cook's *Endeavour* and Signatur

(Des. D. Gentleman (4d.), C. Abbott (others)

1968 (29 May). *British Anniversaries. Event described on stamps. Chalky paper. Tw phosphor bands. P 15 × 14.*

767	**298**	4d. emerald, olive, blue and black	8	
768	**299**	9d. reddish violet, bluish grey and black ..	25	2
769	**300**	1s. olive-brown, blue, red, slate-blue and black ..	25	2
770	**301**	1s. 9d. yellow-ochre and blackish brown ..	40	3

302. " Queen Elizabeth I " (Unknown Artist).

303. " Pinkie " (Lawrence).

304. "Ruins of St. Mary Le Port " (Piper).

305. "The Hay Wain" (Constable).

1968 (12 Aug.). *British Paintings. Queen's head embossed. Chalky paper. Two phosphor bands. P* 15×14 (1s. 9d.) *or* 14×15 (*others*).

771 **302** 4d. multicoloured .. 8 5
  a. Gold omitted (value and Queen's head) .. .. 75·00
772 **303** 1s. multicoloured .. 15 15
  a. Gold omitted (value and Queen's head) £100
  b. Gold (value and Queen's head) and embossing omitted £100
773 **304** 1s. 6d. multicoloured .. 30 30
  a. Gold omitted (value and Queen's head) £100
774 **305** 1s. 9d. multicoloured .. 45 45
  a. Gold (value and Queen's head) and embossing omitted .. .. 80·00

The 4d. is known with the vermilion omitted. Nos. 772b and 774a are only known with the phosphor also omitted.

307. Girl with Doll's House.

308. Boy with Train Set.

(Des. Rosalind Dease. Head printed in gold and then embossed.)

1968 (25 Nov.). *Christmas. Chalky paper. One centre phosphor band* (4*d.*) *or two phosphor bands* (*others*). *P* 15×14 (4*d.*) *or* 14×15 (*others*).

775 **306** 4d. multicoloured .. 5 5
  a. Gold omitted .. ..
  b. Vermilion omitted* .. 60·00
776 **307** 9d. multicoloured .. 15 15
777 **308** 1s. 6d. multicoloured .. 25 25

* The effect of the missing vermilion is shown on the rocking horse, saddle and faces which appear orange instead of red.

The 4d. is known with the ultramarine and phosphor omitted, the 9d. with the yellow omitted and all values with the embossing of Queen's head omitted.

306. Boy and Girl with Rocking Horse.

(Des. D. Gentleman.)

1969 (15 Jan.). *British Ships. Chalky paper. Two vertical phosphor bands at right* (1*s.*), *one horizontal phosphor band* (5*d.*), *or two phosphor bands* (9*d.*). *P* 15×14.

778 **309** 5d. blk., grey, red & turq. 10 5
  a. Black (Queen's head, value, hull and inscr.) omitted £140
  b. Grey (decks, etc.) omitted 50·00
779 **310** 9d. red, blue, ochre, brown, black and grey 25 35
  a. Red and blue omitted .. £170
  b. Blue omitted £145
780 **311** 9d. ochre, brown, black and grey 25 35
781 **312** 9d. ochre, brown, black and grey 25 35
782 **313** 1s. brn., blk., grey, green and greenish yellow 30 40
783 **314** 1s. red, black, brown, carmine and grey .. 30 40

The 9d. and 1s. values were arranged in horizontal strips of three and pairs respectively throughout the sheet.

The 5d. is known with the red omitted and the 1s. (No. 782) with the greenish yellow omitted.

No. 779a is known only with the phosphor also omitted.

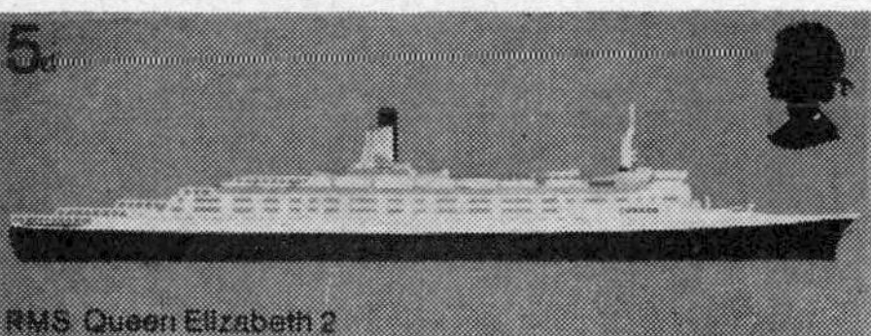

309. R.M.S. *Queen Elizabeth 2.*

310. Elizabethan Galleon.

311. East Indiaman.

313. S.S. *Great Britain.*

312. *Cutty Sark.*

314. R.M.S. *Mauretania.*

315. "Concorde" in Flight.

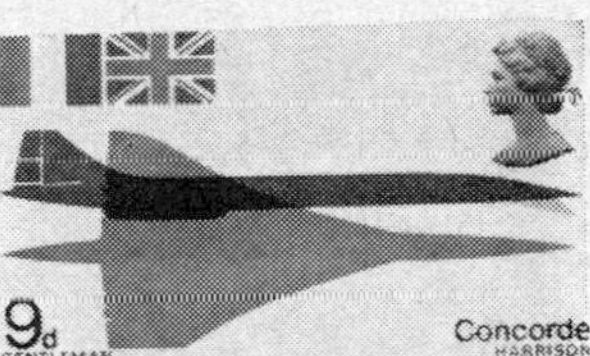

316. Plan and Elevation Views.

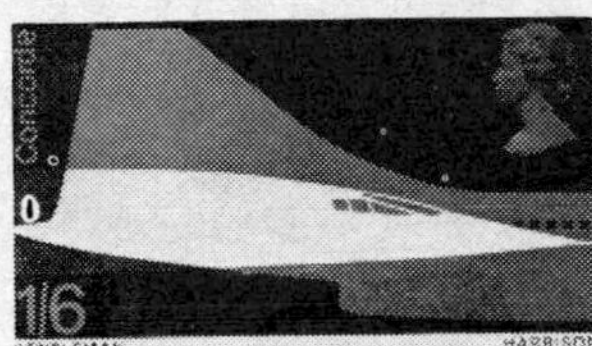

317. "Concorde's" Nose and Tail.

(Des. M. and Sylvia Goaman (4d.), D. Gentleman (9d., 1s. 6d.).)

1969 (3 Mar.). *First Flight of "Concorde". Chalky paper. Two phosphor bands. P* 15×14.

784 **315** 4d. yellow-orange, violet, greenish blue, blue-green and pale green 8 5
  a. Violet (value, etc.) omitted 75·00
785 **316** 9d. ultramarine, emerald, red and grey-blue .. 20 20
786 **317** 1s. 6d. deep blue, silver-grey and light blue 25 30
  a. Silver-grey omitted .. £150

No. 786a affects the Queen's head which appears in the light blue colour.

The 4d. is known with the yellow-orange omitted.

318. Queen Elizabeth II. (See also Type **357.**)

(Des. after plaster cast by Arnold **Machin.** Recess. Bradbury, Wilkinson.)

1969 (5 Mar.). *P* 12.

787	**318**	2s. 6d. brown	1·00	15
788	,,	5s. crimson-lake ..	2·50	30
789	,,	10s. deep ultramarine ..	11·00	10·00
790	,,	£1 bluish black	2·00	1·50

For decimal issue, see Nos. 829/31*a* and notes after No. 831*a*.

319. Page from *Daily Mail*, and Vickers " Vimy " Aircraft.

320. Europa and CEPT Emblems.

321. ILO Emblem.

322. Flags of NATO Countries.

323. Vickers " Vimy " Aircraft and Globe showing Flight.

(Des. P. Sharland (5d., 1s., 1s. 6d.) and M. and Sylvia Goaman (9d., 1s. 9d.)

1969 (2 Apr.). *Anniversaries. Events described on stamps. Chalky paper. Two phosphor bands. P* 15 × 14.

791	**319**	5d. black, pale sage-green, chestnut and new blue	8	5
792	**320**	9d. pale turq., deep blue, light emer.-grn. & blk.	20	20
793	**321**	1s. bright purple, deep blue and lilac ..	25	25
794	**322**	1s. 6d. red, Royal blue, yellow-green, black, lemon and new blue	30	30
795	**323**	1s. 9d. yell.-ol., greenish yell. & pale turq.-grn.	30	30
		a. Uncoated paper* ..	75·00	

* Uncoated paper. The second note after No. 744 also applies here.

The 1s. 6d. is known with black and also with yellow-green omitted.

324. Durham Cathedral.

325. York Minster.

326. St. Giles' Cathedral, Edinburgh.

327. Canterbury Cathedral.

MINIMUM PRICE

The minimum price quoted is 5p which represents a handling charge rather than a basis for valuing common stamps. For further notes about prices see introductory pages.

328. St. Paul's Cathedral.

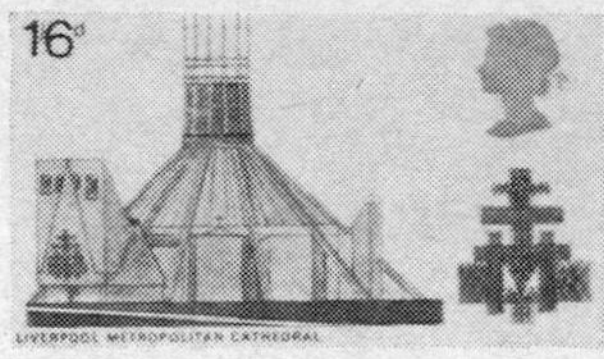

329. Liverpool Metropolitan Cathedral.

(Des. P. Gauld.)

1969 (28 May). *British Architecture* (*Cathedrals*). *Chalky paper. Two phosphor bands. P* 15 × 14.

796	**324**	5d. grey-blk., orge., pale bluish violet & black	8	8
		a. Pale bluish violet omitted	75·00	
797	**325**	5d. grey-blk., pale-bluish violet, new blue & blk.	8	8
		a. Pale bluish violet omitted	75·00	
798	**326**	5d. grey-black, purple, green and black ..	8	8
799	**327**	5d. grey-black, green, new blue and black ..	8	8
800	**328**	9d. grey-black, ochre, pale drab, violet and black	25	25
		a. Black (value) omitted ..	30·00	
801	**329**	1s. 6d. grey-black, pale turq., pale reddish vio. pale yell.-olive & blk.	35	35
		a. Black (value) omitted ..	90·00	
		b. Black (value) double ..		

The 5d. values were issued together *se-tenant* in blocks of four throughout the sheet.

The 5d. (No. 798) is known with green omitted.

330. The King's Gate, Caernarvon Castle.

331. The Eagle Tower, Caernarvon Castle.

332. Queen Eleanor's Gate, Caernarvon Castle.

333. Celtic Cross, Margam Abbey.

334. H.R.H. The Prince of Wales (after photo by G. Argent).

(Des. D. Gentleman.)

1969 (1 July). *Investiture of H.R.H. The Prince of Wales. Chalky paper. Two phosphor bands. P* 14 × 15.

802 **330** 5d. multicoloured .. 8 8
a. Black (value and inscr.) omitted .. .. 80·00
803 **331** 5d. multicoloured .. 8 8
a. Black (value and inscr.) omitted .. .. 80·00
804 **332** 5d. multicoloured .. 8 8
a. Black (value and inscr.) omitted .. .. 80·00
805 **333** 9d. deep grey, light grey, black and gold .. 30 30
806 **334** 1s. blackish yellow-olive and gold 30 30

The 5d. values were issued together *se-tenant* in strips of three throughout the sheet.

The 5d. values are known with red, green and also deep grey omitted.

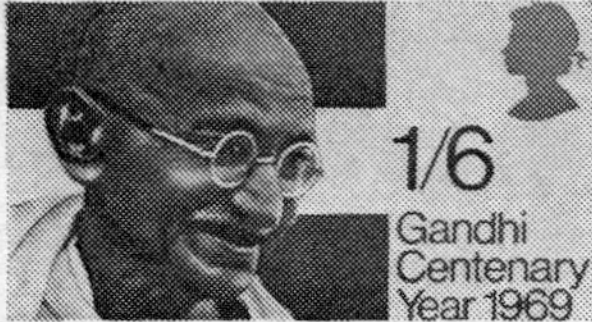

335. Mahatma Gandhi.

(Des. Biman Mullick.)

1969 (13 Aug.). *Gandhi Centenary Year. Chalky paper. Two phosphor bands. P* 15 × 14.

807 **335** 1s. 6d. black, green, red-orange and grey .. 25 25
a. Printed on the gummed side .. .. .. 50·00

336. National Giro "G" Symbol.

337. Telecommunications—International Subscriber Dialling.

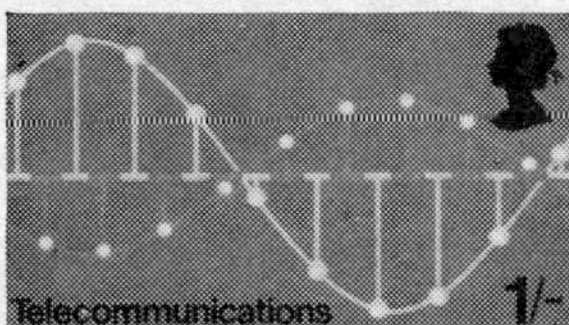

338. Telecommunications—Pulse Code Modulation.

339. Postal Mechanisation—Automatic Sorting.

(Des. D. Gentleman. Litho. De La Rue.)

1969 (1 Oct.). *Post Office Technology Commemoration. Chalky paper. Two phosphor bands. P* 13½ × 14.

808 **336** 5d. new blue, greenish blue, lavender & black 8 5
809 **337** 9d. emerald, violet-blue and black .. 20 20
810 **338** 1s. emerald, lavender and black 20 20
811 **339** 1s. 6d. bright purple, light blue, grey-blue & blk. 25 25

340. Herald Angel.

341. The Three Shepherds.

342. The Three Kings.

(Des. F. Wegner. Queen's head (and stars 4d., 5d. and scroll-work 1s. 6d.) printed in gold and then embossed.)

1969 (26 Nov.). *Christmas. Chalky paper. Two phosphor bands* (5*d.,* 1*s.* 6*d.*) *or one centre band* (4*d.*). *P* 15 × 14.

812 **340** 4d. multicoloured .. 8 5
a. Gold (Queen's head etc.) omitted £100
813 **341** 5d. multicoloured .. 10 8
a. Light blue (sheep, etc.) omitted .. .. 30·00
b. Red omitted* .. .. 50·00
814 **342** 1s. 6d. multicoloured .. 35 35
a. Gold (Queen's head etc.) omitted .. .. 60·00
b. Deep slate (value) omitted 60·00

*The effect of the missing red is shown on the hat, leggings and purse which appear as dull orange.

The 5d. is known with the green omitted and the 1s. 6d. exists with either the greenish yellow or the bluish violet missing. Both values are known with the embossing omitted.

Used copies of the 5d. have been seen with the olive-brown or yellow omitted.

343. Fife Harling.

344. Cotswold Limestone.

345. Welsh Stucco.

346. Ulster Thatch.

(Des. D. Gentleman (5d., 9d.), Sheila Robinson (1s., 1s. 6d.).)

1970 (11 Feb.). *British Rural Architecture. Chalky paper. Two phosphor bands. P* 15 × 14.

815 **343** 5d. multicoloured .. 8 5
a. Yellow omitted .. 10·00
816 **344** 9d. multicoloured .. 25 25
817 **345** 1s. deep blue, reddish lilac, drab and new blue .. 30 30
818 **346** 1s. 6d. greenish yellow, black, turquoise-blue and lilac 45 35

The 1s. is known with the new blue omitted.

Used copies of the 5d. have been seen with the grey-black or greenish blue colours omitted.

347. Signing the Declaration of Arbroath.

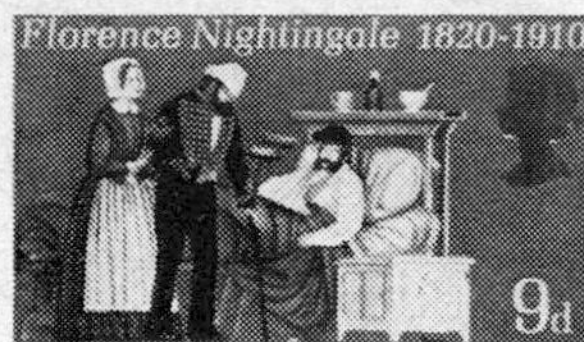

348. Florence Nightingale attending Patients.

349. Signing of International Co-operative Alliance.

350. Pilgrims and *Mayflower*.

351. Sir William Herschel, Francis Baily Sir John Herschel and Telescope.

(Des. F. Wegner (5d., 9d., and 1s. 6d.) and Marjorie Saynor (1s., 1s. 9d.). Queen's head printed in gold and then embossed.)

1970 (1 Apr.). *Anniversaries. Events described on stamps. Chalky paper. Two phosphor bands. P* 15 × 14.

819 **347** 5d. multicoloured .. 8 5
a. Gold (Queen's head) omitted .. .. 70·00
820 **348** 9d. multicoloured .. 25 25
821 **349** 1s. multicoloured .. 25 25
a. Gold (Queen's head) omitted .. .. 20·00
822 **350** 1s. 6d. multicoloured .. 30 30
a. Gold (Queen's head) omitted 35·00
823 **351** 1s. 9d. multicoloured .. 35 35

The following missing colours are known: 5d. emerald, 9d. ochre, 1s. green, brown, 1s. 6d. emerald. The 9d., 1s. and 1s. 6d. are also known with the embossing omitted.

The 1s. 9d. with the lemon colour omitted has been seen used on a First Day Cover.

352. " Mr. Pickwick and Sam " (*Pickwick Papers*).

353. " Mr. and Mrs. Micawber " (*David Copperfield*).

354. " David Copperfield and Betsy Trotwood " (*David Copperfield*).

355. " Oliver asking for more " (*Oliver Twist*).

(The above were issued together *se-tenant* in blocks of four throughout the sheet.)

356. " Grasmere" (from engraving by J. Farrington, R.A.).

357. (Value redrawn).

(Des. Rosalind Dease. Queen's head printed in gold and then embossed.)

1970 (3 June). *Literary Anniversaries. Death Centenary of Charles Dickens (novelist)* (5*d.* × 4) *and Birth Bicentenary of William Wordsworth (poet)* (1s. 6*d*.). *Chalky paper. Two phosphor bands. P* 14 × 15.

824 **352** 5d. black, orange, silver, gold and magenta .. 12 10
a. Imperf. (*block of four*) .. £300
825 **353** 5d. black, magenta, silver, gold and orange .. 12 10
826 **354** 5d. black, light greenish blue, silver, gold and yellow-bistre .. 12 10
a. Yellow-bistre (value) omitted .. ..
827 **355** 5d. black, yellow-bistre, silver, gold and light greenish blue .. 12 10
a. Yellow-bistre (background) omitted ..
b. Light greenish blue (value) omitted* .. 30·00
828 **356** 1s. 6d. light yellow-olive, black, silver, gold and bright blue 60 70
a. Gold (Queen's head) omitted .. .. 50·00
b. Silver (" Grasmere ") omitted .. .. 25·00

*No. 827b (unlike No. 826a) results from a partial missing colour. Although it is completely missing on No. 827, it is only partially omitted on No. 826.

The 1s. 6d. is known with embossing omitted.

(Des. after plaster cast by Arnold Machin. Recess. B.W.)

1970 (17 June)–**72**. *Decimal Currency. Chalky paper or phosphorised paper* (10*p*). *P* 12.

829 **357** 10p. cerise .. .. 1·75 20
830 ,, 20p. olive-green 30 15
831 ,, 50p. deep ultramarine .. 75 35
831*a* ,, £1 bluish black (6.12.72) 1·50 75

The 20p and 50p exist on thinner, uncoated paper and are listed in the *Elizabethan Specialised Catalogue*.

A whiter paper was introduced in 1973. The £1 appeared on 27 Sept. 1973, the 20p. on 30 Nov. 1973 and the 50p. on 20 Feb. 1974.

The 50p. was issued on 1 Feb. 1973 on phosphorised paper. This cannot be distinguished from No. 831 with the naked eye.

The £1, T **318**, was also issued, on 17 June 1970, in sheets of 100 (10 × 10) instead of panes of 40 (8 × 5) but it is not easy to distinguish from No. 790 in singles. It can be readily differentiated when in large strips or marginal pieces showing sheet markings or plate numbers.

358. Runners.

359. Swimmers.

360. Cyclists.

(Des. A. Restall. Litho. D.L.R.)

970 (15 JULY). *Ninth British Commonwealth Games. Chalky paper. Two phosphor bands. P* 13½ × 14.

32 **358** 5d. pink, emerald, greenish yell. & dp. yell.-green — 10 — 5
33 **359** 1s. 6d. light greenish blue, lilac, bistre-brown and Prussian blue .. — 40 — 40
34 **360** 1s. 9d. yell.-orange, lilac, salmon & dp. red-brn. — 40 — 40

361. 1d. Black (1840). **362.** 1s. Green (1847).

363. 4d. Carmine (1855).

(Des. D. Gentleman.)

970 (18 SEPT.). *"Philympia 70" Stamp Exhibition. Chalky paper. Two phosphor bands. P* 14 × 14½.

35 **361** 5d. grey-black, brownish bistre, blk. & dull pur. — 8 — 8
36 **362** 9d. light drab, bluish grn., stone, blk. & dull pur. — 20 — 20
37 **363** 1s. 6d. carm., light drab, black and dull purple — 30 — 35

364. Shepherds and Apparition of the Angel.

365. Mary, Joseph, and Christ in the Manger.

366. The wise men bearing gifts.

(Des. Sally Stiff after De Lisle Psalter. Queen's head printed in gold and then embossed.)

1970 (25 Nov.). *Christmas. Chalky paper. One centre phosphor band (4d.) or two phosphor bands (others). P* 14 × 15.

838 **364** 4d. brn.-red, turq.-green, pale chestnut, brown, gry-blk., gold & verm. — 8 — 5
839 **365** 5d. emerald, gold, blue, brown-red, ochre, grey-black and violet — 8 — 5
a. Emerald omitted .. — 35·00
b. Imperf. (pair) .. .. — £150
840 **366** 1s. 6d. gold, grey-black, pale turq.-grn., salmon, ultram., ochre and yellow-green .. — 45 — 50
a. Salmon omitted .. — 50·00

The 1s. 6d. exists with the ochre colour omitted. The 4d. and 5d. are known with embossing omitted, and the 1s. 6d. is known with embossing and phosphor omitted.

INVALIDATION. All stamps with value expressed in £sd from 1911 (the beginning of the reign of King George V) except No. 790 were invalidated as from 1st March 1972. This includes Regional and Postage Due stamps.

(New Currency. 100 new pence = £1.)

367

(Des. after plaster cast by Arnold Machin.)

1971 (15 FEB.)–77. *Decimal Currency. Chalky paper. Two phosphor bands, except where otherwise stated. P* 15 × 14.

841 **367** ½p. turquoise-blue .. — 5 — 5
a. Imperf. (pair)† .. .. — £100
l. Booklet pane (841 × 2 *se-tenant* vert. with 845 × 2) — 90
la. Do. *se-tenant* horiz. (14.7.71) .. .. — 30
m. Booklet pane (841 × 5 plus *se-tenant* label) .. — 35
n. Coil strip (845 *se-tenant* with 841 × 2 and 843 × 2) — 50
o. Booklet pane (841 × 3, 846 × 3, 847 × 6 *se-tenant*) (24.5.72) .. .. — 4·00
p. Booklet pane (841 × 3, 842, and 847 × 2 *se-tenant*) (24.5.72) .. .. — 13·00
q. Coil strip (858 *se-tenant* with 845, 843 and 841 × 2) (3.12.75) — 20
r. Booklet pane (841 × 2 *se-tenant* with 843 × 3 and 858) (10.3.76) .. — 15
s. Booklet pane (841 × 2, 843 × 2, 860*c* × 2 and 864 × 4 *se-tenant*) (8½p. values at right) (26.1.77) .. — 75
sa. Do. 8½p. values at left — 75
842 „ ½p. turq.-blue (1 band at left) (24.5.72) .. — 12·00 — 12·00
843 „ 1p. crimson .. .. — 5 — 5
a. Imperf. (vert. coil) ..
b. Pair, one imperf. 3 sides (vert. coil) .. ..
c. Imperf. (pair) .. ..
l. Booklet pane (843 × 2 *se-tenant* vert. with 844 × 2) — 90
m. Do. *se-tenant* horiz. (14.7.71) .. .. — 30
844 „ 1½p. black .. .. — 5 — 5
a. Uncoated paper ('72)* — 25·00
845 „ 2p. myrtle-green .. — 5 — 5
846 „ 2½p. magenta (1 centre band) .. .. — 5 — 5
a. Imperf. (pair)† .. — 75·00
l. Booklet pane (846 × 5 plus *se-tenant* label) .. — 40
m. Booklet pane (846 × 4 plus two *se-tenant* labels) — 40
n. Booklet pane (846 × 3, 847 × 3 and 849 × 6 *se-tenant*) (24.5.72) .. .. — 4·00
847 „ 2½p. magenta (1 band at side) .. .. .. — 35 — 35
l. Booklet pane (847 × 2 *se-tenant* with 849 × 4).. — 1·50
848 „ 2½p. magenta (2 bands) (21.5.75) .. .. — 5 — 8
849 „ 3p. ultramarine (2 bands) — 5 — 5
a. Imperf. coil strip of 5 ..
b. Imperf. (pair)† .. .. — £200
c. Uncoated paper ('72)* .. — 8·00
l. Booklet pane (849 × 5 plus *se-tenant* label) .. — 30
850 „ 3p. ultram. (1 centre band) (10.9.73) .. — 8 — 8
a. Imperf. (pair)† .. — 80·00
b. Imp. between (vert. pr.)† .. — 60·00
c. Imperf. horiz. (vert. pr.)† .. — 75·00
851 „ 3½p. pale olive-grey (*shades*) (2 bands) .. .. — 25 — 15
852 „ 3½p. bronze-grn. (1 centre band) (24.6.74) .. — 35 — 15
853 „ 4p. ochre-brown .. — 8 — 8
a. Imperf. (pair)† .. — £250
854 „ 4½p. grey-blue (24.10.73) — 35 — 15
a. Imperf. (pair) .. .. — 70·00
855 „ 5p. pale violet .. .. — 8 — 5
856 „ 5½p. violet (2 bands)(24.10.73) — 8 — 5

857	**367**	5½p. violet (1 centre band) (17.3.75) .. .	8	5
		a. Uncoated paper* ..	45·00	
858	„	6p. light emerald ..	10	5
		a. Uncoated paper* ..	3·00	
859	„	6½p. greenish blue (2 bands) (4.9.74)	10	5
860	„	6½p. greenish bl. (1 centre band) (24.9.75) ..	10	5
		a. Imperf. (vert. pair) ..	£150	
		b. Uncoated paper* ..		
860*c*	„	6½p. greenish blue (1 side band) (26.1.77) ..	10	10
861	„	7p. purple-brn. (15.1.75)	12	8
862	„	7½p. pale chestnut ..	12	8
863	„	8p. rosine (24.10.73) ..	12	8
		a. Uncoated paper* ..	9·00	
864	„	8½p. light yellowish green (*shades*) (24.9.75) ..	12	5
		a. Imperf. (pair) ..		
865	„	8½p. yellowish green (*phosphor paper*) (24.3.76)	12	8
866	„	9p. yell.-orange & black	20	8
867	„	9p. deep violet (25.2.76)	15	8
868	„	9½p. purple (25.2.76) ..	15	10
869	„	10p. orange-brown & deep orange-brn. (11.8.71)	20	10
		a. Orange-brown omitted	22·00	
		b. Imperf. (horiz. pair) ..		
870	„	10p. orange-brown (25.2.76)	15	10
871	„	10½p. yellow (25.2.76) ..	15	12
872	„	11p. brown-red (25.2.76)	15	10
873	„	20p. dull purple (25.2.76)	30	12
874	„	50p. ochre-brown (2.2.77)	75	35

*See footnote after No. 744.

†These come from sheets with gum arabic.

No. 842 comes from £1 booklets, No. 847 from 50p. or £1 booklets and No. 860*c* from 50p. booklets.

Nos. 843a/b come from a strip of eight of the vertical coil. It comprises two normals, one imperforate at sides and bottom, one completely imperforate, one imperforate at top, left and bottom and partly perforated at right due to the bottom three stamps being perforated twice. No. 843b is also known from another strip having one stamp imperforate at sides and bottom.

No. 843c comes from the upper part of an imperf. sheet of which only about the top quarter was completely free of perforation indentations and some of the lower rows contained occasional perforation holes.

WHITE PAPER. From 1972 printings appeared on fluorescent white paper giving a stronger chalk reaction than the original ordinary cream paper.

GUM ARABIC. The following exist with gum arabic as well as PVA gum (with or without added dextrin): Nos. 841, 841n, 846, 849, 850, 853 and 858. See notes after No. 722.

DEXTRIN GUM. From 1973 printings appeared with PVA gum to which dextrin, a bluish green substance, had been added, giving a very mottled appearance.

PHOSPHOR-COATED PAPER. On 13 Nov. 1974 the 4½p. with phosphor bands was printed on paper with phosphor coating as an experiment. This cannot be distinguished from No. 854 with the naked eye. No. 876 exists with two phosphor bands and printed on phosphorised paper in error.

No. 865 was an experimental issue to test the efficacy of stamps containing a phosphor coating in the paper without the normally overprinted phosphor bands.

VARNISH COATING. No. 867 exists with and without a varnish coating. This cannot easily be detected without the use of an ultra-violet lamp as it merely reduces the fluorescent paper reaction.

368. " A Mountain Road " (T. P. Flanagan).

369. " Deer's Meadow " (Tom Carr).

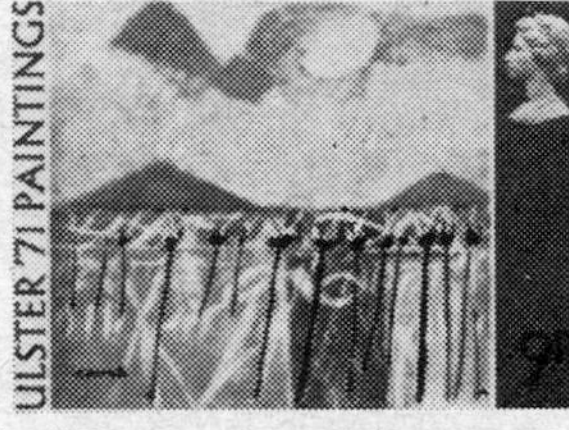

370. " Slieve na brock " (Colin Middleton).

(Layout des. Stuart Rose.)

1971 (16 June). *" Ulster '71 " Paintings. Chalky paper. Two phosphor bands. P* 15×14.

881	**368**	3p. yellow-buff, pale yellow, Venetian red, black, blue and drab	10	5
882	**369**	7½p. olive-brn., brownish grey, pale ol.-grey, deep blue, cobalt and grey-blue ..	1·00	1·00
883	**370**	9p. greenish yell., orange, grey, lav.-grey, bis., black, pale ochre-brn., and ochre-brn.	75	75

A used example of the 3p. has been seen with the Venetian red omitted.

The 7½p. is known with the pale olive-grey omitted (boulder in foreground), and the 9p. is known with orange omitted.

371. John Keats (150th Death Anniv.).

372. Thomas Gray (Death Bicentenary).

373. Sir Walter Scott (Birth Bicentenary).

(Des. Rosalind Dease. Queen's head printed in gold and then embossed.)

1971 (28 July). *Literary Anniversaries. Chalky paper. Two phosphor bands. P* 15×14.

884	**371**	3p. black, gold and greyish blue	15	
		a. Gold (Queen's head) omitted	30·00	
885	**372**	5p. blk., gold & yell.-ol.	40	40
		a. Gold (Queen's head) omitted	50·00	
886	**373**	7½p. blk., gold & yell.-brn.	1·00	1·00

The 7½p. exists with embossing omitted.

374. Servicemen and Nurse of 1921.

375. Roman Centurion.

376. Rugby Football, 1871.

(Des. F. Wegner.)

1971 (25 Aug.). *British Anniversaries. Events described on stamps. Chalky paper. Two phosphor bands. P* 15×14.

887	**374**	3p. red-orge., grey, deep blue, ol.-grn., ol.-brn., blk., rosine & vio.-bl.	10	5
		a. Deep blue omitted* ..	90·00	
		b. Red-orange (nurse's cloak) omitted ..	50·00	
		c. Olive-brown (faces, etc.) omitted	20·00	
		d. Black omitted		
888	**375**	7½p. grey, yellow-brown, verm., mauve, grey-blk., blk., silver, pale ochre and ochre ..	85	85
889	**376**	9p. new bl., myrtle-grn., grey-blk., lemon, ol.-brn., mag. & yell.-ol.	1·25	1·25
		a. Olive-brown omitted ..	30·00	
		b. New blue omitted ..		

*The effect of the missing deep blue is shown on the sailor's uniform, which appears as grey.

The 7½p. exists with grey omitted.

Used copies have been seen of the 3p. with grey omitted and the 9p. with myrtle-green omitted.

377. Physical Sciences Building, University College of Wales, Aberystwyth.

378. Faraday Building, Southampton University.

379. Engineering Department, Leicester University.

380. Hexagon Restaurant, Essex University.

(Des. N. Jenkins.)

1971 (22 Sept.). *British Architecture (Modern University Buildings). Chalky paper. Two phosphor bands. P* 15 × 14.

890 **377**	3p.	ol.-brn., ochre, lemon, black and yell.-olive	15	8
891 **378**	5p.	rose, black, chestnut and lilac	20	20
892 **379**	7½p.	ochre, black and purple-brown ..	85	85
893 **380**	9p.	pale lilac, blk., sepia-brown and deep blue	1·25	1·25

The 3p. exists with lemon omitted.

381. " Dream of the Wise Men ".

382. " Adoration of the Magi ".

383. " Ride of the Magi ".

(Des. Clarke-Clements-Hughes design team, from stained-glass windows, Canterbury Cathedral. Queen's head printed in gold and then embossed.)

1971 (13 Oct.). *Christmas. Ordinary paper. One centre phosphor band* (2½p.) *or two phosphor bands (others). P* 15 × 14.

894 **381**	2½p.	new bl., blk., lemon, emer., reddish violet, carmine-red, carmine-rose and gold	10	5
		a. Imperf. (pair)	£175	
895 **382**	3p.	black, reddish violet, lemon, new blue, carm.-rose, emerald, ultram. and gold ..	12	5
		a. Gold (Queen's head) omitted	70·00	
		b. Carmine-rose omitted ..	70·00	
896 **383**	7½p.	black, lilac, lemon, emerald, new blue, rose, green and gold	85	85
		a. Gold (Queen's head) omitted	30·00	

The 3p. exists with lemon omitted and with embossing omitted; used copies have been seen with reddish violet and embossing omitted, with lemon and carmine-rose omitted, and with new blue omitted. The 7½p. is known with embossing omitted, embossing double, lilac omitted and emerald omitted.

WHITE CHALKY PAPER. From No. 897 all issues, with the exception of Nos. 904/8, were printed on fluorescent white paper giving a stronger chalk reaction than the original cream paper.

384. Sir James Clark Ross.

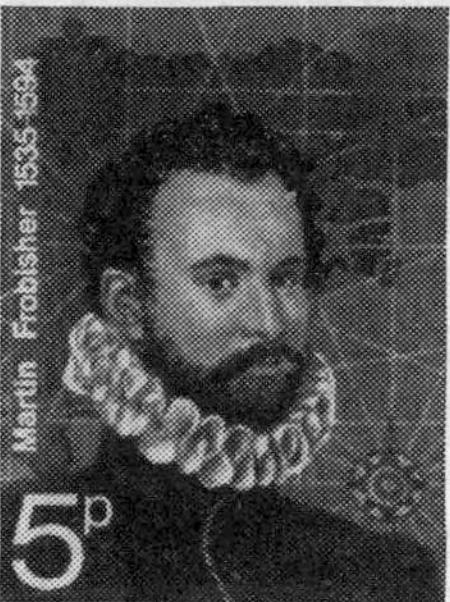

385. Sir Martin Frobisher.

386. Henry Hudson.

387. Capt. Scott.

(Des. Miss M. Saynor. Queen's head printed in gold and then embossed.)

1972 (16 Feb.). *British Polar Explorers. Two phosphor bands. P* 14 × 15.

897 **384**	3p.	yellow-brn., indigo, slate-black, flesh, lemon, rose, bright blue and gold ..	10	8
		a. Gold (Queen's head) omitted	20·00	
		b. Slate-black (hair etc.) omitted	£100	
898 **385**	5p.	salmon, flesh, pur.-brn., ochre, black & gold	25	25
		a. Gold (Queen's head) omitted	28·00	
899 **386**	7½p.	reddish vio., blue, dp. slate, yell.-brn., buff, black and gold	85	85
		a. Gold (Queen's head) omitted	18·00	
900 **387**	9p.	dull blue, ultram., black, greenish yell., pale pink, rose-red and gold	1·25	1·25

The 3p. and 5p. are known with embossing omitted. The 3p. exists with lemon omitted and with gold and embossing omitted. A copy of the 3p. is known used on piece with the flesh colour omitted.

388. Statuette of Tutankhamun.

389. 19th-Century Coastguard.

390. Ralph Vaughan Williams and Score.

(Des. Rosalind Dease (3p.), F. Wegner ($7\frac{1}{2}$p.), C. Abbott (9p.). Queen's head printed in gold and then embossed ($7\frac{1}{2}$p., 9p.).)

1972 (26 APR.). *General Anniversaries. Events described on stamps. Two phosphor bands. P* 15 × 14.

901 **388** 3p. black, grey, gold, dull bistre-brown, blackish brown, pale stone and light brown .. 10 5

902 **389** $7\frac{1}{2}$p. pale yellow, new blue, slate-blue, violet-blue, slate and gold 60 60

903 **390** 9p. bistre-brown, black, sage-green, deep slate, yellow-ochre, brown and gold .. 85 85
- a. Gold (Queen's head) omitted .. .. 70·00
- b. Brown (facial features) omitted

The $7\frac{1}{2}$p. exists with embossing omitted.

391. St. Andrew's, Greensted-juxta-Ongar, Essex.

392. All Saints, Earls Barton, Northants.

393. St. Andrew's, Letheringsett, Norfolk.

394. St. Andrew's, Helpringham, Lincs.

395. St. Mary the Virgin, Huish Episcopi, Somerset.

(Des. R. Maddox. Queen's head printed in gold and then embossed.)

1972 (21 JUNE). *British Architecture (Village Churches). Ordinary paper. Two phosphor bands. P* 14 × 15.

904 **391** 3p. vio.-blue, black, light yell.-olive, emerald-green, orange-verm. and gold 10 8
- a. Gold (Queen's head) omitted .. .. 38·00

905 **392** 4p. dp. yell.-olive, blk., emerald, vio.-blue, orge.-verm. and gold 25 25

906 **393** 5p. deep emerald, black, royal blue, lt. yell.-olive, orange-verm. and gold 50 30
- a. Gold (Queen's head) omitted .. .. 50·00

907 **394** $7\frac{1}{2}$p. orge.-red, blk., dp. yell.-olive, royal blue, lt. emerald and gold 1·00 1·00

908 **395** 9p. new blue, black, emer.-green, deep yellow-olive, orange-vermilion and gold .. 1·00 1·00

The 4p. exists with violet-blue omitted. The 3p., 4p., 5p. and 9p. exist with embossing omitted.

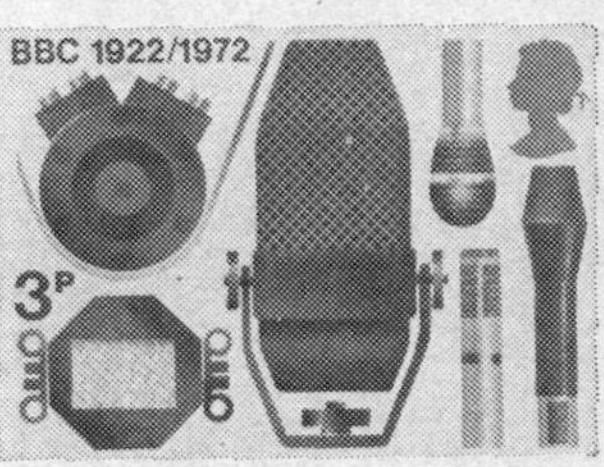

396. Microphones, 1924–69.

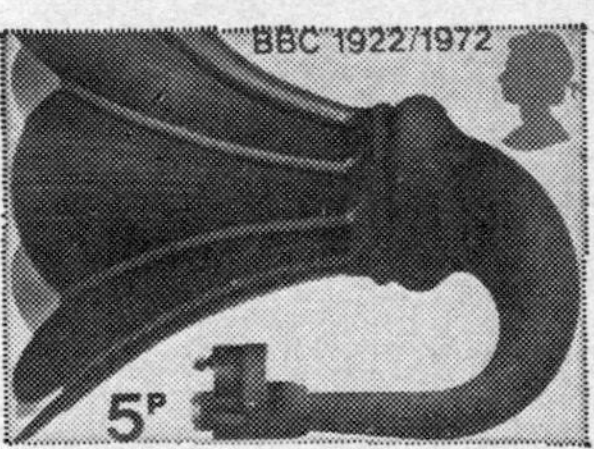

397. Horn Loudspeaker.

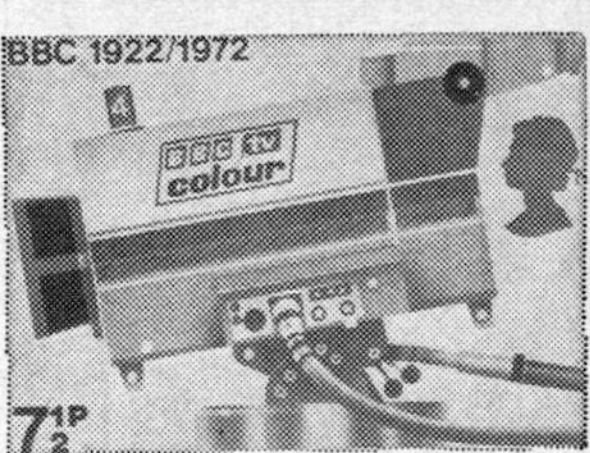

398. T.V. Camera, 1972.

399. Oscillator and Spark Transmitter, 1897.

(Des. D. Gentleman.)

1972 (13 Sept.). *Broadcasting Anniversaries. 75th Anniv. of Marconi and Kemp's Radio Experiments* (9p.), *and 50th Anniv. of Daily Broadcasting by the B.B.C.* (others). *Two phosphor bands. P* 15×14.

909 **396** 3p. pale brown, black, grey, greenish yellow and brownish slate 10 8
910 **397** 5p. brownish slate, lake-brown, salmon, light brown, black and red-brown 30 30
911 **398** 7½p. light grey, slate, brownish slate, mag. and black 60 60
912 **399** 9p. lemon, brown, brownish slate, deep brownish slate, bluish slate and black .. 85 85
a. Brownish slate (Queen's head) omitted £100

The 3p. exists with yellow omitted.

400. Angel holding Trumpet.

401. Angel playing Lute.

402. Angel playing Harp.

(Des. Sally Stiff. Photo. and embossed.)

1972 (18 Oct.). *Christmas. One centre phosphor band* (2½p.) *or two phosphor bands* (others). *P* 14×15.

913 **400** 2½p. cerise, pale reddish brown, yellow-orge., orge.-vermilion, lilac, gold, red-brown and deep grey 8 5
a. Gold omitted £125
914 **401** 3p. ultram., lavender, lt. turquoise-bl., bright green, gold, red-brown and bluish violet 15 5
a. Red-brown omitted .. £100
915 **402** 7½p. deep brown, pale lilac, light cinnamon, ochre, gold, red-brown and blackish violet 60 60

The 2½p. exists with deep grey omitted; the 3p. exists with bright green missing and bluish violet missing; the 7½p. exists with ochre omitted; the 2½p., 3p. and 7½p. exist with embossing omitted.

403. Queen Elizabeth and Duke of Edinburgh.

(Des. J. Matthews from photo by N. Parkinson.)

1972 (20 Nov.). *Royal Silver Wedding. "All-over" phosphor* (3p.) *or no phosphor* (20p.). *P* 14×15.

I. "Rembrandt" Machine.

916 **403** 3p. brownish black, deep blue and silver .. 15 12
a. Silver omitted .. £125
917 ,, 20p. brownish black, reddish purple and silver .. .. 1·00 1·00

II. "Jumelle" Machine.

918 **403** 3p. brownish black, deep blue and silver .. 15 12

The 3p. "Jumelle" has a lighter shade of the brownish black than the 3p. "Rembrandt". It also has the brown cylinders less deeply etched, which can be distinguished in the Duke's face which is slightly lighter, and in the Queen's hair where the highlights are sharper.

3p. "Rembrandt". Cyls. 3A–1B–11C no dot. Sheets of 100 (10×10).

3p. "Jumelle". Cyls. 1A–1B–3C dot and no dot. Sheets of 100 (two panes 5×10, separated by gutter margin.

404. "Europe".

(Des. P. Murdoch.)

1973 (3 Jan.). *Britain's Entry into European Communities. Two phosphor bands. P* 14×15.

919 **404** 3p. dull orge., brt. rose-red, ultram., lt. lilac and black 15 5
920 ,, 5p. new blue, brt. rose-red, ultram., cobalt-blue and black .. 45 45
921 ,, 5p. lt. emer.-grn., brt. rose-red, ultram., cobalt-blue and black 45 45

Nos. 920/1 were printed horizontally *se-tenant* throughout the sheet.

405. Oak Tree.

(Des. D. Gentleman.)

1973 (28 Feb.). *Tree Planting Year. British Trees* (1st issue). *Two phosphor bands. P* 15×14.

922 **405** 9p. brownish blk., apple-green, deep olive, sepia, blackish grn. and brownish grey .. 50 50
a. Brownish black (value and inscr.) omitted .. 75·00
b. Grey (Queen's head) omitted .. .. 70·00

See also No. 949.

CHALKY PAPER. The following issues are printed on chalky paper but where "all-over" phosphor has been applied there is no chalk reaction except in the sheet margins outside the phosphor area.

406. David Livingstone.

407. H. M. Stanley.

(T **406/7** were printed together, horizontally *se-tenant* within the sheet).

408. Sir Francis Drake.

409. Walter Raleigh.

410. Charles Sturt.

(Des. Marjorie Saynor. Queen's head printed in gold and then embossed.)

1973 (18 Apr.). *British Explorers. "All-over" phosphor. P* 14×15.

923 **406** 3p. orge.-yell., lt. orge.-brn., grey-blk., lt. turq.-bl., turq.-bl. & gold 15 12
 a. Gold (Queen's head) omitted .. .. 15·00
 b. Turq.-blue (background and inscr.) omitted .. £100

924 **407** 3p. orge.-yell., lt. orge.-brn., grey-blk., lt. turq.-bl., turq.-bl. & gold 15 12
 a. Gold (Queen's head) omitted .. .. 15·00
 b. Turq.-blue (background and inscr.) omitted .. £100

925 **408** 5p. lt. flesh, chrome-yell., orge.-yell., sepia, brownish grey, grey-blk., vio.-blue & gold 25 25
 a. Gold (Queen's head) omitted .. .. 40·00
 b. Grey-black omitted .. £125

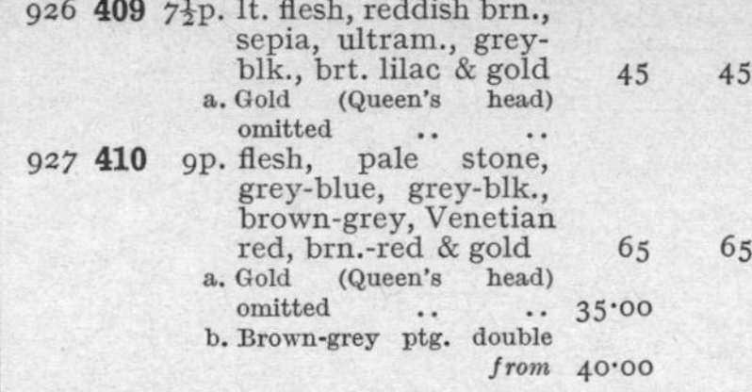

926 **409** 7½p. lt. flesh, reddish brn., sepia, ultram., grey-blk., brt. lilac & gold 45 45
 a. Gold (Queen's head) omitted .. ..

927 **410** 9p. flesh, pale stone, grey-blue, grey-blk., brown-grey, Venetian red, brn.-red & gold 65 65
 a. Gold (Queen's head) omitted .. .. 35·00
 b. Brown-grey ptg. double *from* 40·00

Caution is needed when buying missing gold heads in this issue as they can be removed by using a hard eraser, etc., but this invariably affects the "all-over" phosphor. Genuine copies have the phosphor intact. Used copies off cover cannot be distinguished as much of the phosphor is lost in the course of floating.

In the 5p. value the missing grey-black affects the doublet, which appears as brownish grey, and the lace ruff, which is entirely missing. The missing sepia affects only Drake's hair, which appears much lighter.

The double printing of the brown-grey (cylinder 1F) on the 9p. is a most unusual type of error to occur in a multicoloured photogravure issue. Two sheets are known and it is believed that they stuck to the cylinder and went through a second time. This would result in the following two sheets missing the colour but at the time of going to press this error has not been reported. The second print is slightly askew and more prominent in the top half of the sheets. Examples from the upper part of the sheet showing a clear double impression of the facial features are worth a substantial premium over the price quoted.

The 3p. values exist with the light orange-brown missing, the 5p. exists with the sepia omitted, the 7½p. with the ultramarine omitted and the 9p. with grey-black omitted; the 3p. values, the 5p. and the 9p. exist with embossing omitted.

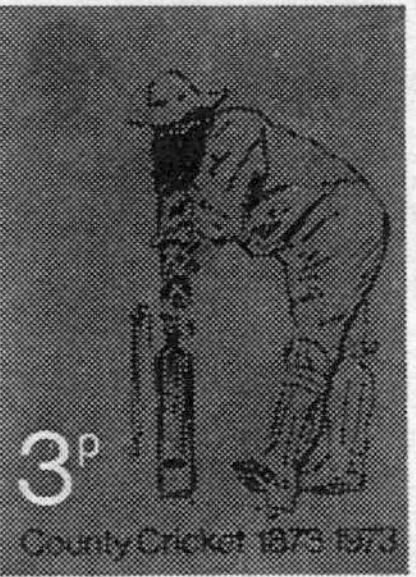

411

412

413

(T **411/413** show sketches of W. G. Grace by Harry Furniss.)

(Des. E. M. Ripley. Queen's head printed in gold and then embossed.)

1973 (16 May). *County Cricket* 1873–1973. *"All-over" phosphor. P* 14×15.

928 **411** 3p. black, ochre and gold 10 10
 a. Gold (Queen's head) omitted .. .. 40·00

929 **412** 7½p. black, lt. sage-green and gold 40 35

930 **413** 9p. black, cobalt and gold 50 45

The 3½p. and 7½p. exist with embossing omitted.

414. "Self-portrait" (Reynolds).

415. "Self-portrait" (Raeburn).

416. "Nelly O'Brien" (Reynolds).

417. " Rev. R. Walker (The Skater) " (Raeburn).

(Des. S. Rose.)

1973 (4 July). *British Paintings. 250th Birth Anniv. of Sir Joshua Reynolds and 150th Death Anniv. of Sir Henry Raeburn.* " *All-over* " *phosphor.* *P* 14 × 15.

931	**414**	3p. rose, new blue, jet-blk., mag., grnsh. yell., blk., ochre & gold	8	5
		a. Gold (Queen's head) omitted	40·00	
		b. Greenish yellow omitted	75·00	
932	**415**	5p. cinnamon, greenish yell., new blue, lt. mag., blk., yell.-ol. & gold	20	20
		a. Gold (Queen's head) omitted	35·00	
933	**416**	7½p. grnsh. yell., new blue, lt. mag., blk., cinnamon & gold	40	40
		a. Gold (Queen's head) omitted	30·00	
		b. Cinnamon omitted	£100	
934	**417**	9p. brownsh rose, blk., dull rose, pale yell., brnsh. grey, pale blue & gold	45	45

No. 931a is also known with the embossing also omitted or misplaced.

The 7½p. is known with the embossing omitted.

The 9p. is known with the brownish rose omitted. It is also known with the embossing and phosphor both omitted.

418. Court Masque Costumes.

419. St. Paul's Church, Covent Garden.

420. Prince's Lodging, Newmarket.

421. Court Masque Stage Scene.

(T **418/19** and T **420/1** were printed horizontally *se-tenant* within the sheet.)

(Des. Rosalind Dease. Litho. and typo. B.W.)

1973 (15 Aug.). *400th Birth Anniv. of Inigo Jones (architect and designer).* " *All-over* " *phosphor.* *P* 15 × 14.

935	**418**	3p. dp. mve., blk. & gold	10	10
936	**419**	3p. dp. brn., blk. & gold	10	10
937	**420**	5p. blue, black and gold	35	35
938	**421**	5p. grey-ol., blk. & gold	35	35

422. Palace of Westminster seen from Whitehall.

423. Palace of Westminster seen from Millbank.

(Des. R. Downer. Recess and typo. B.W.)

1973 (12 Sept.). *19th Commonwealth Parliamentary Conference.* " *All-over* " *phosphor.* *P* 15 × 14.

939	**422**	8p. black, brownish grey and stone	40	40
940	**423**	10p. gold and black	45	45

424. Princess Anne and Capt. Mark Phillips.

(Des. Collis Clements and Ted Hughes.)

1973 (14 Nov.). *Royal Wedding.* " *All-over* " *phosphor.* *P* 15 × 14.

941	**424**	3½p. dull violet & silver	10	5
		a. Imperf. (pair)	£200	
942	„	20p. deep brown & silver	1·00	1·00

425

426

427

428

429

(T **425/9** depict the carol " Good King Wenceslas " and were printed horizontally *se-tenant* within the sheet.)

430. " Good King Wenceslas, the Page and Peasant ".

(Des. D. Gentleman.)

1973 (28 Nov.). *Christmas. One centre phosphor band* (*3p.*) *or " all-over " phosphor* (*3½p.*). *P* 15 × 14.

943 **425** 3p. grey-black, blue, brownish grey, lt. brn., brt. rose-red, turq.-grn., salmon-pink and gold .. 20 12

944 **426** 3p. grey-blk., violet-bl., slate, brn., rose-red, rosy mve., turq.-grn., salmon-pink & gold 20 12
a. Rosy mauve omitted ..

945 **427** 3p. grey-black, vio-bl., slate, brn., rose-red, rosy mve., turq.-grn., salmon-pink & gold 20 12
a. Rosy mauve omitted ..

946 **428** 3p. grey-blk., violet-bl., slate, brn., rose-red, rosy mve., turq.-grn., salmon-pink & gold 20 12
a. Rosy mauve omitted ..

947 **429** 3p. grey-blk., vio.-blue, slate, brn., rose-red, rosy mve., turq.-grn., salmon-pink & gold 20 12
a. Rosy mauve omitted ..

948 **430** 3½p. salmon-pink, grey-blk., red-brn., blue, turq.-grn., brt. rose-red, rosy mauve, lav.-grey & gold 20 12
a. Imperf. (pair) £150
b. Grey-black (value and inscr. etc.) omitted .. 25·00
d. Blue (leg, robes) omitted .. 30·00
e. Rosy mauve (robe at right) omitted .. .. 35·00
f. Blue and rosy mauve omitted .. .. 60·00
g. Bright rose-red (King's robe) omitted .. 35·00
h. Red-brown (logs, basket etc.) omitted .. ..

The 3½p. also exists with salmon-pink omitted affecting the faces, hands and knees.

A copy of the 3½p. with the gold background colour omitted has been seen used on cover.

The 3p. and 3½p. are normally with PVA gum with added dextrin but the 3½p. also exists with normal PVA gum and the 3p. with gum arabic.

431. Horse Chestnut.

(Des. D. Gentleman.)

1974 (27 Feb.). *British Trees* (*2nd issue*). *" All-over " phosphor. P* 15 × 14.

949 **431** 10p. lt. emer., brt. grn., grnsh. yell., brn.-ol., blk. & brownish grey 45 45

432. First Motor Fire-engine, 1904.

433. Prize-winning Fire-engine, 1863.

434. First Steam Fire-engine, 1830.

435. Fire-engine, 1766.

(Des. D. Gentleman.)

1974 (24 Apr.). *Bicentenary of the Fire Prevention* (*Metopolis*) *Act. " All-over " phosphor. P* 15 × 14.

950 **432** 3½p. grey-blk., orge.-yell., grnsh. yell., dull rose, ochre & grey .. 10 8
a. Imperf. (pair) .. ..

951 **433** 5½p. grnsh. yell., dp. rosy mag., orge.-yell., lt. emer., grey-blk. & grey 15 12

952 **434** 8p. grnsh. yell., lt. bl.-grn., lt. grnsh. bl., lt. chest., grey-blk. & grey 50 50

953 **435** 10p. grey-blk., pale reddish brn., lt. brn., orange-yellow & grey 50 50

The 3½p. exists with ordinary PVA gum.

436. P & O Packet, *Peninsular*, 1888.

437. Farman Biplane, 1911.

438. Airmail-blue Van and Postbox, 1930.

439. Imperial Airways "C" Class Flying-boat, 1937.

(Des. Rosalind Dease.)

1974 (12 June). *Centenary of Universal Posta Union. " All-over " phosphor. P* 15 × 14.

954 **436** 3½p. dp. brnsh. grey, brt. mauve, grey-blk. & gold 10

955 **437** 5½p. pale orge., lt. emer., grey-black & gold 15 1

956 **438** 8p. cobalt, brown, grey-black & gold .. 50 5

957 **439** 10p. dp. brownish grey, orange, grey-black and gold 50 5

440. Robert the Bruce.

441. Owain Glyndŵr.

442. Henry the Fifth.

443. The Black Prince.

(Des. F. Wegner.)

974 (10 July). *Medieval Warriors.* "*All-over*" *phosphor.* *P* 15 × 14.

58	**440**	4½p. grnsh. yell., verm., sl.-bl., red-brn., reddish brn., lilac-grey & gold	10	10
59	**441**	5½p. lemon, verm., sl.-bl., red-brn., reddish brn., ol.-drab & gold	12	12
60	**442**	8p. dp. grey, verm., grnsh. yell., new blue, red-brn., dp. cinnamon & gold	45	45
61	**443**	10p. verm., grnsh. yell., new blue, red-brn., reddish brn., lt. blue & gold	45	45

444. Lord Warden of the Cinque Ports, 1942.

445. Prime Minister, 1940.

446. Secretary for War and Air, 1919.

447. War Correspondent, South Africa, 1899.

(Des. C. Clements and E. Hughes.)

1974 (9 Oct.). *Birth Centenary of Sir Winston Churchill.* "*All-over*" *phosphor.* *P* 14 × 15.

962	**444**	4½p. Prussian blue, pale turq.-green & silver	10	10
963	**445**	5½p. sepia, brnsh grey & silver	60	60
964	**446**	8p. crimson, lt. clar. & silver	45	45
965	**447**	10p. lt. brn., stone & sil.	45	45

448. "Adoration of the Magi" (York Minster, *c.* 1355)

449. "The Nativity" (St. Helen's Church, Norwich, *c.* 1480).

450. "Virgin and Child" (Ottery St. Mary Church, *c.* 1350).

451. "Virgin and Child" (Worcester Cathedral, *c.* 1224).

(Des. Peter Hatch Partnership.)

1974 (27 Nov.). *Christmas. Church Roof* Bosses. *One phosphor band* (3½*p.*) *or* "*all-over*" *phosphor* (*others*). *P* 15 × 14.

966	**448**	3½p. gold, lt. new blue, lt. brn., grey-blk. & lt. stone	8	8
967	**449**	4½p. gold, yell.-orge., rose-red, lt. brn., grey-blk. & light new blue ..	10	10
968	**450**	8p. blue, gold, lt. brn., rose-red, dull grn. & grey-black	30	30
969	**451**	10p. gold, dull rose, grey-blk., lt. new blue, pale cinnamon & lt. brn.	30	30

The phosphor band on the 3½p. was first applied down the centre of the stamp but during the printing this was deliberately placed to the right between the roof boss and the value; however, intermediate positions, due to shifts, are known.

452. Invalid in Wheelchair.

(Des. P. Sharland.)

1975 (22 Jan.). *Health and Handicap Funds.* "*All-over*" *phosphor.* *P* 15 × 14.

970	**452**	4½p. + 1½p. azure and grey-blue	20	20

453. "Peace—Burial at Sea".

454. "Snowstorm—Steamer off a Harbour's Mouth".

455. "The Arsenal, Venice".

456. "St. Laurent".

(Des. Stuart Rose.)

1975 (19 Feb.). *Birth Bicentenary of J. M. W. Turner (painter). "All-over" phosphor. P* 15×14.

971	**453**	4½p.	grey-blk., salmon, stone, blue and grey	12	12
972	**454**	5½p.	cobalt, grnsh. yell., lt. yell-brn., grey-black and rose ..	15	15
973	**455**	8p.	pale yell-orge., grnsh. yell., rose, cobalt & grey-black	25	25
974	**456**	10p.	dp. blue, lt. yell.-ochre, lt. brn., dp. cobalt & grey-black	40	40

457. Charlotte Square, Edinburgh.

458. The Rows, Chester.

T **457/8** were printed horizontally *se-tenant* within the sheet.

459. Royal Observatory, Greenwich.

460. St. George's Chapel, Windsor.

461. National Theatre, London.

(Des. P. Gauld.)

1975 (23 Apr.). *European Architectural Heritage Year. "All-over" phosphor. P* 15×14.

975	**457**	7p.	greenish yellow, bright orange, grey-black, red-brown, new blue, lavender and gold	20	20
976	**458**	7p.	grey-black, greenish yellow, new blue, bright orange, red-brown and gold ..	20	20
977	**459**	8p.	magenta, deep slate, pale magenta, light yellow-olive, grey-black and gold ..	20	20
978	**460**	10p.	bistre-brown, grnsh. yellow, deep slate, emerald-green, grey-black and gold ..	30	30
979	**461**	12p.	grey-black, new blue, pale magenta & gold	35	35

462. Sailing Dinghies.

463. Racing Keel Yachts.

464. Cruising Yachts.

465. Multihulls.

(Des. A. Restall. Recess and photo.)

1975 (11 June). *Sailing. "All-over" phosphor P* 15×14.

980	**462**	7p.	black, bluish violet, scarlet, orange-vermilion, orange and gold	15	15
981	**463**	8p.	black, orange-verm. orge., lavender, brt. mauve, bright blue, deep ultram. & gold	15	15
			a. Black omitted	30·00	
982	**464**	10p.	black, orange, bluish emerald, light olive-drab, choc. & gold	30	25
983	**465**	12p.	black, ultramarine, turquoise-blue, rose, grey, steel-bl. & gold	1·00	1·25

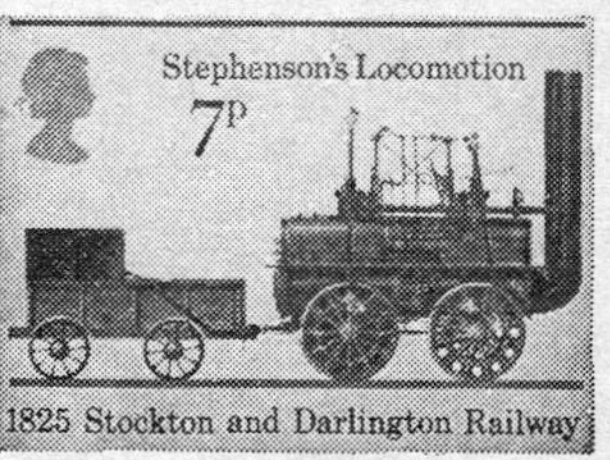

466. Stephenson's "Locomotion", 1825.

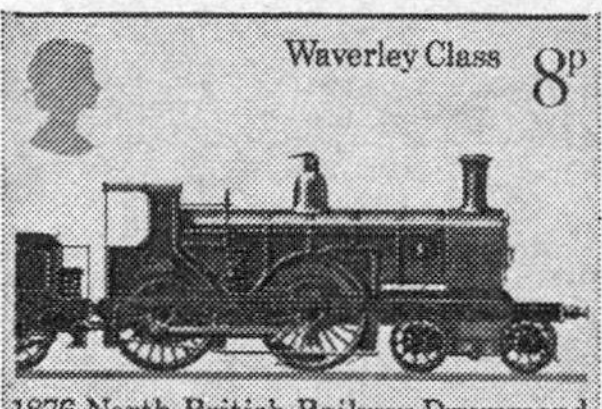

467. "Abbotsford", 1876.

468. "Caerphilly Castle", 1923.

469. High Speed Train, 1975.

(Des. B. Craker.)

1975 (13 Aug.). *150th Anniv. of Public Railways. "All-over" phosphor. P* 15×14.

984	**466**	7p. red-brown, grey-black, greenish yellow, grey and silver	15	15
985	**467**	8p. brown, orange-yellow, vermilion, grey-black, grey & silver	20	20
986	**468**	10p. emerald-green, grey-black, yellow-orange, verm. grey & silver	25	25
987	**469**	12p. grey-black, pale lemon, vermilion, blue, grey and silver	30	30

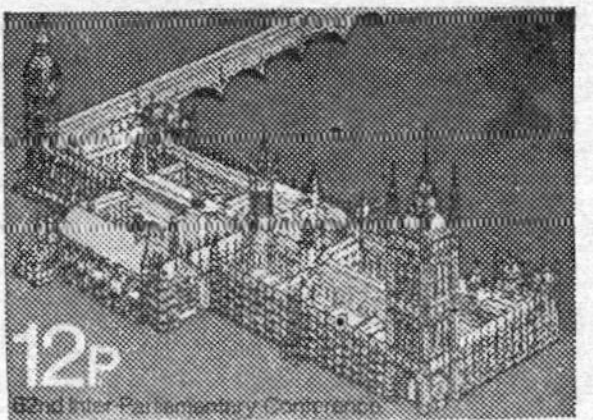

470. Palace of Westminster.

(Des. R. Downer.)

1975 (3 Sept.). *62nd Inter-Parliamentary Union Conference. "All-over" phosphor. P* 15×14.

988	**470**	12p. lt. new blue, black, brownish grey & gold	25	30

471. " Emma and Mr. Woodhouse " (*Emma*).

472. " Catherine Morland " (*Northanger Abbey*).

473. " Mr. Darcy " (*Pride and Prejudice*).

474. " Mary and Henry Crawford " (*Mansfield Park*).

(Des. Barbara Brown.)

1975 (22 Oct.). *Birth Bicentenary of Jane Austen (novelist). "All-over" phosphor. P* 14×15.

989	**471**	8½p. blue, slate, rose-red, light yellow, dull grn, grey-blk. & gold	15	15
990	**472**	10p. slate, bright magenta, grey, light yellow, grey-black & gold ..	25	25
991	**473**	11p. dull blue, pink, olive-sepia, slate, pale greenish yellow, grey-black and gold ..	30	30
992	**474**	13p. bright magenta, light new blue, slate, buff, dull blue-green, grey-black and gold ..	35	35

475. Angels with Harp and Lute.

476. Angel with Mandolin.

477. Angel with Horn.

478. Angel with Trumpet.

(Des. R. Downer.)

1975 (26 Nov.). *Christmas. One phosphor band* (6½*p.*), *phosphor-inked* (8½*p.*) *(background), "all-over" phosphor (others). P* 15×14.

993	**475**	6½p. bluish violet, bright reddish violet, light lavender and gold ..	15	15
994	**476**	8½p. turq.-green, bright emer.-grn., slate, lt. turq.-green & gold	20	20
995	**477**	11p. vermilion, cerise, pink and gold ..	25	25
996	**478**	13p. drab, brown, bright orange, buff & gold	30	30

479. Housewife.

480. Policeman.

481. District Nurse.

482. Industrialist.

(Des. P. Sharland.)

1976 (10 Mar.). *Telephone Centenary.* "*All-over*" *phosphor.* *P* 15 × 14.

997 **479**	8½p. greenish blue, deep rose, blk. and blue	15	20
	a. Deep rose omitted ..		
998 **480**	10p. greenish blue, black and yellow-olive ..	20	20
999 **481**	11p. greenish blue, deep rose, blk. and bright mauve	20	25
1000 **482**	13p. olive-brown, deep rose, black and orange-red ..	25	30

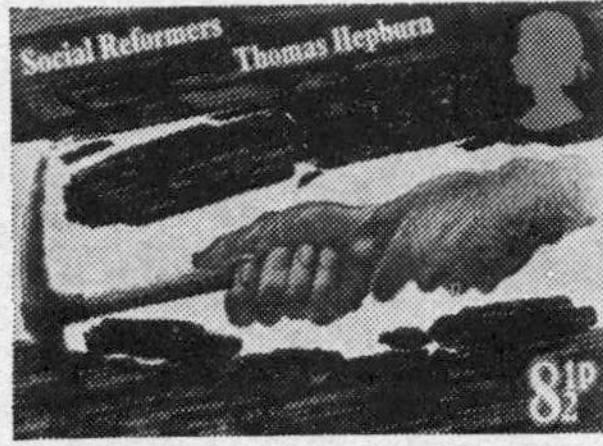

483. Hewing Coal (Thomas Hepburn).

484. Machinery (Robert Owen).

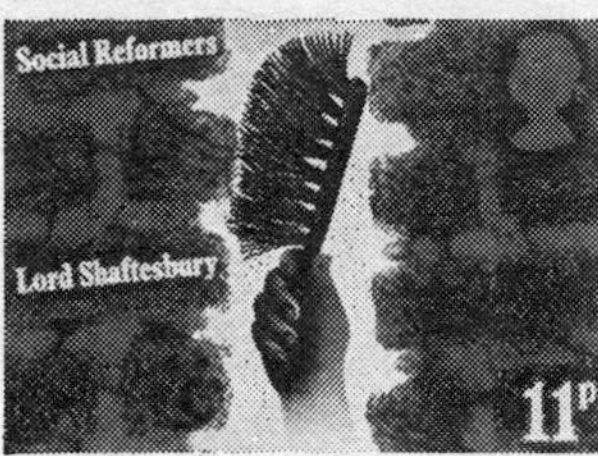

485. Chimney Cleaning (Lord Shaftesbury).

486. Hands clutching Prison Bars (Elizabeth Fry).

(Des. D. Gentleman.)

1976 (28 Apr.). *Social Reformers.* "*All-over*" *phosphor.* *P* 15 × 14.

1001 **483**	8½p. lavender-grey, grey-blk., blk. & sl.-grey	15	20
1002 **484**	10p. lavender-grey, grey-blk., grey & slate-violet	20	20
1003 **485**	11p. black, slate-grey and drab	20	25
1004 **486**	13p. slate-grey, black and deep dull green	25	30

487. Benjamin Franklin (bust by Jean-Jacques Caffieri).

(Des. P. Sharland.)

1976 (2 June). *Bicentenary of American Revolution.* "*All-over*" *phosphor.* *P* 14 × 15.

1005 **487**	11p. pale bistre, slate-vio., pale bl.-grn., black and gold ..	20	25

488. "Elizabeth of Glamis".

489. "Grandpa Dickson".

490. "*Rosa Mundi*".

491. "Sweet Briar".

(Des. Kristin Rosenberg.)

1976 (30 June). *Centenary of Royal National Rose Society.* "*All-over*" *phosphor.* *P* 14 × 15.

1006 **488**	8½p. brt. rose-red, greenish yell., emer., grey-black and gold ..	15	20
1007 **489**	10p. greenish yell., brt. grn., reddish brn., grey-black and gold	20	20
1008 **490**	11p. brt. mag., greenish yell., emer., grey-bl., grey-blk. & gold	20	25
1009 **491**	13p. rose-pink, lake-brn., yell.-grn., pale greenish yell., grey-blk. and gold	25	30
	a. Value omitted* ..	†	—

*The value was not engraved in one position of the cylinder but the error was discovered before issue and the stamps were removed from the sheets. However one copy of the error is known in used condition.

492. Archdruid.

493. Morris Dancing.

494. Scots Piper.

495. Welsh Harpist.

(Des. Marjorie Saynor.)

1976 (4 Aug.). *British Cultural Traditions. "All-over" phosphor. P* 14×15.

1010	**492**	8½p.	yell., sepia, brt. rose, dull ultram., black and gold ..	15	20
1011	**493**	10p.	dull ultram., brt. rose-red, sepia, greenish yell., blk. and gold	20	20
1012	**494**	11p.	bluish green, yell.-brown, yell.-orge., blk., brt. rose-red and gold	20	25
1013	**495**	13p.	dull vio.-bl., yell.-orge., yellow-brn., black, bluish green and gold	25	30

The 8½p. and 13p. commemorate the 800th Anniv. of the Royal National Eisteddfod.

496. Woodcut from *The Canterbury Tales.*

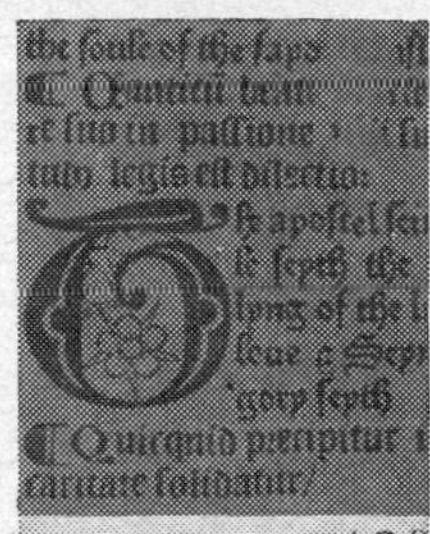

497. Extract from *The Tretyse of Love.*

498. Woodcut from *The Game and Playe of Chesse.*

499. Early Printing Press.

(Des. R. Gay.)

1976 (29 Sept.). *500th Anniv. of British Printing. "All-over" phosphor. P* 14×15.

1014	**496**	8½p.	black, light new blue and gold ..	12	15
1015	**497**	10p.	blk., ol.-grn. & gold	15	20
1016	**498**	11p.	black, brownish grey and gold ..	15	20
1017	**499**	13p.	chocolate, pale ochre and gold	20	25

500. Virgin and Child.

501. Angel with Crown.

502. Angel appearing to Shepherds.

503. The Three Kings.

(Des. Enid Marx.)

1976 (24 Nov.). *Christmas. English Medieval Embroidery. One phosphor band* (6½*p.*), *"all-over" phosphor* (*others*). *P* 15×14.

1018	**500**	6½p.	bl., bistre-yell., brn. and bright orange ..	10	12
			a. Imperf. (pair) ..		
1019	**501**	8½p.	sage-grn., yell., brn.-ochre, chest. and olive-black ..	12	15
1020	**502**	11p.	dp. mag., brn.-orge., new blue, black & cinnamon	15	20
			a. Uncoated paper* ..	35·00	
1021	**503**	13p.	brt. pur., new bl., cinnamon, bronze-green & olive-grey	20	25

*See footnote after No. 744.

504. Lawn Tennis.

505. Table Tennis.

506. Squash.

507. Badminton.

(Des. A. Restall.)

1977 (12 Jan.). *Racket Sports. Phosphorised paper.* P 15×14.

1022	**504**	8½p. emer.-grn., black, grey & bluish green	12	15
		a. Imperf. (horiz. pair) ..		
1023	**505**	10p. myrtle-grn., black, grey-black & deep blue-green	15	20
1024	**506**	11p. orge., pale yell., blk., slate-black and grey	15	20
1025	**507**	13p. brn., grey-blk., grey & brt. reddish vio.	20	25

508

(Des. after plaster cast by Arnold Machin.)

1977 (2 Feb.). P 14×15.

1026	**508**	£1 blackish olive and bright yellow-green ..	1·50	85
1027	,,	£2 purple-brn. & lt. emer.	3·00	1·50
1028	,,	£5 chalky blue & salmon	7·50	4·00

509. Steroids – Conformational Analysis.

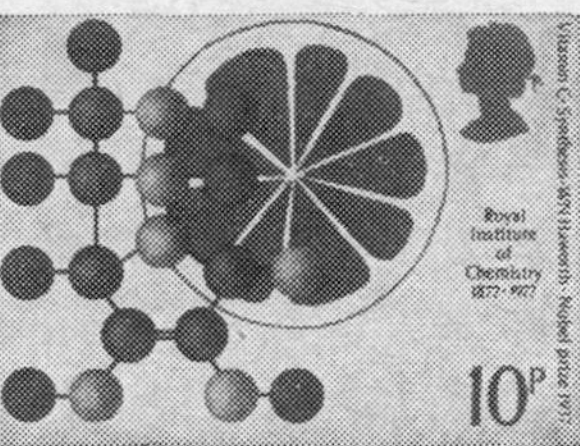

510. Vitamin C – Synthesis.

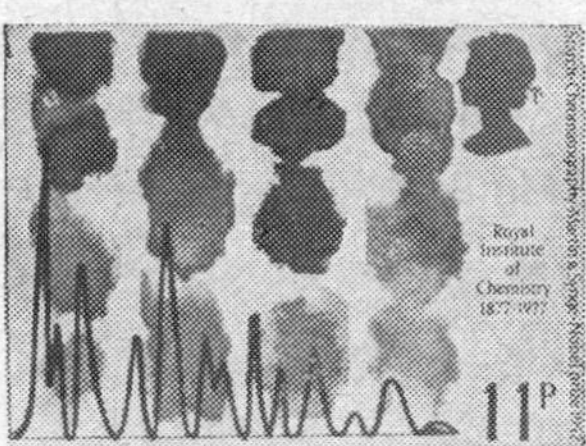

511. Starch – Chromatography.

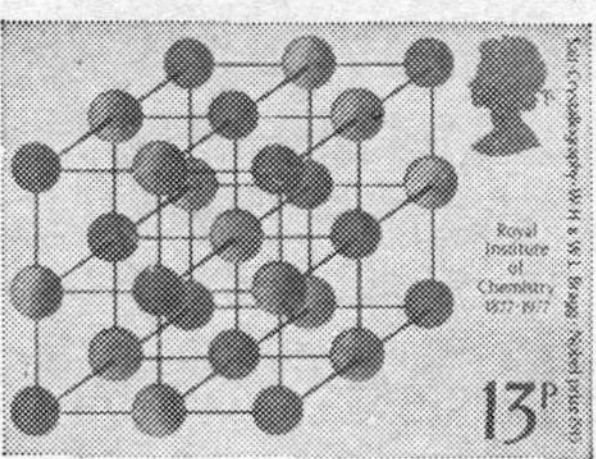

512. Salt – Crystallography.

(Des. Jerzy Karo.)

1977 (2 Mar.). *Royal Institute of Chemistry Centenary. "All-over" phosphor.* P 15×14.

1029	**509**	8½p. rosine, new bl., ol.-yellow, brt. mve., yellow-brn., blk. & gold	12	15
1030	**510**	10p. brt. orange, rosine, new bl., brt. bl., blk. and gold	15	20
1031	**511**	11p. rosine, grnish-yell., new blue, dp. violet, black and gold ..	15	20
1032	**512**	13p. new blue, brt. grn., black and gold ..	20	25

The British Post Office have announced the following further issues for 1977:

11 May	Silver Jubilee
8 June	Commonwealth Heads of Government Meeting
5 October	British Wildlife
23 November	Christmas

Collectors are advised to check dates of issue and other details with their nearest Head Post Office.

ISLAND ISSUES.

Many islands off the coast of Great Britain have issued local carriage labels to cover the cost of ferrying mail to the nearest mainland post office. As they are not recognised as valid for national or international mail they are not listed here. They are classed as British Private Local Issues and the following places are known to have issued them: Alderney, Brecquou, Calf of Man, Davaar, Drake's Is., Gugh Is., Herm, Jethou, Lihou, Lundy, Pabay, Sanda, Sark-Alderney-Guernsey (The Commodore Shipping Co.), Shuna, Stroma and the Summer Isles.

Issues inscribed Carn Iar, Eynhallow, Heston, Hilbre, St. Kilda and Staffa are Tourist Souvenir Labels.

Labels inscribed Soay are bogus and those incribed Canna are charity labels.

REGIONAL ISSUES.

For Regional Issues of Guernsey, Jersey and the Isle of Man, see after Great Britain Postal Fiscals.

Printers (stamps of all regions) :—Photo. Harrison & Sons. Portrait by Dorothy Wilding Ltd. or after plaster cast by Arnold Machin (decimal issues).

DATES OF ISSUE. Conflicting dates of issue have been announced for some of the regional issues, partly explained by the stamps being released on different dates by the Philatelic Bureau in Edinburgh or the Philatelic Counter in London and in the regions. We have adopted the practice of giving the earliest known dates, since once released the stamps could have been used anywhere in the U.K.

I. NORTHERN IRELAND.

N 1

N 2

N 3

(Des. W. Hollywood (3rd., 4d., 5d.), L. Pilton (6d., 9d.), T. Collins (1s. 3d., 1s. 6d.).)

1958–67. *W* **179.** P 15×14.

NI1	**N 1**	3d. dp. lilac (18.8.58) ..	15	8
		p. One centre phosphor band (9.6.67)	10	8
NI2	,,	4d. ultramarine (7.2.66)	15	10
		p. Two phosphor bands (10.67)	12	10
NI3	**N 2**	6d. deep claret (29.9.58)	15	10
NI4	,,	9d. bronze-green (2 phosphor bands) (1.3.67)	20	15
NI5	**N 3**	1s. 3d. green (29.9.58) ..	30	30
NI6	,,	1s. 6d. grey-blue (2 phosphor bands) (1.3.67)	35	35

1968–69. *No wmk. Chalky paper. One centre-phosphor band* (Nos. NI8/9) *or two phosphor bands* (*others*). P 15×14.

NI 7	**N 1**	4d. deep bright blue (27.6.68)	10	12
NI 8	,,	4d. olive-sepia (4.9.68) ..	10	20
NI 9	,,	4d. brt. verm. (26.2.69)	25	10
NI10	,,	5d. Royal blue (4.9.68)	20	8
NI11	**N 3**	1s. 6d. grey-bl. (20.5.69)	4·00	3·00

No. NI7 was only issued in Northern Ireland with gum arabic. After it had been withdrawn from Northern Ireland but whilst still on sale at the philatelic counters elsewhere, about fifty sheets with PVA gum were sold over the London Philatelic counter on 23 October 1968, and some were also on sale at the British Philatelic Exhibition Post Office in October, without any prior announcement. The other values exist with PVA gum only.

N 4

(Des. J. Matthews.)

1971 (7 July)–**76.** *Decimal Currency. Chalky paper. Two phosphor bands, except where otherwise stated. P 15 × 14.*

NI12	**N 4**	2½p. bright magenta (1 centre band) ..	20	15
NI13	,,	3p. ultram. (2 bands) ..	25	15
NI14	,,	3p. ultram. (1 centre band) (23.1.74) ..	8	8
NI15	,,	3½p. olive-grey (2 bands) (23.1.74)	15	12
NI16	,,	3½p. olive-grey (1 centre band) (6.11.74) ..	15	12
NI17	,,	4½p. grey-blue (6.11.74)	15	12
NI18	,,	5p. reddish violet ..	40	30
NI19	,,	5½p. violet (2 bands) (23.1.74) ..	10	10
NI20	,,	5½p. violet (1 centre band) (21.5.75) ..	10	10
NI21	,,	6½p. greenish blue (1 centre band) (14.1.76)	10	10
NI22	,,	7½p. chestnut	60	60
NI23	,,	8p. rosine (23.1.74)	12	12
NI24	,,	8½p. yellow-green (14.1.76) ..	12	12
NI25	,,	10p. orge.-brn. (20.10.76)	15	20
NI26	,,	11p. scarlet (20.10.76) ..	15	20

From 1972 printings were made on the fluorescent white paper and from 1973 printings had dextrin added to the PVA gum (see notes after No. 874 of Great Britain).

II. SCOTLAND.

S 1

S 2

S 3

(Des. G. F. Huntly (3d., 4d., 5d.), J. B. Fleming (6d., 9d.), A. B. Imrie (1s. 3d., 1s. 6d.).)

1958–67. *W* **179.** *P* 15 × 14.

S1	**S 1**	3d. deep lilac (18.8.58) ..	15	5
		p. Two phosphor bands (29.1.63)	4·00	2·50
		pa. One side phosphor band (30.4.65)	15	30
		pb. One centre phosphor band (9.11.67)	12	20
S2	**S 1**	4d. ultramarine (7.2.66) ..	12	15
		p. Two phosphor bands ..	12	8
S3	**S 2**	6d. deep claret (29.9.58) ..	12	5
		p. Two phosphor bands (29.1.63)	25	35
S4	,,	9d bronze-green (2 phosphor bands) (1.3.67) ..	15	30
S5	**S 3**	1s. 3d. green (29.9.58) ..	30	20
		p. Two phosphor bands (29.1.63)	30	65
S6	,,	1s. 6d. grey-blue (2 phosphor bands) (1.3.67) ..	30	45

1967–70. *No wmk. Chalky paper. One centre phosphor band* (S7, S9/10) *or two phosphor bands* (*others*). *P* 15 × 14

S 7	**S 1**	3d. deep lilac (16.5.68) ..	12	20
S 8	,,	4d. dp. brt. blue (28 11.67)	12	8
S 9	,,	4d. olive-sepia (4.9.68) ..	12	8
S10	,,	4d. bright verm. (26.2.69)	20	8
S11	,,	5d. Royal blue (4.9.68) ..	25	12
S12	**S 2**	9d. bronze-green (28.9.70	10·00	7·50
S13	**S 3**	1s. 6d. grey-bl. (12.12.68)	3·50	2·00

Nos. S7/8 exist with both gum arabic and PVA gum; others with PVA gum only.

S 4

(Des. J. Matthews.)

1971 (7 July)–**76.** *Decimal Currency. Chalky paper. Two phosphor bands except where otherwise stated. P 15 × 14.*

S14	**S 4**	2½p. bright magenta (1 centre band) ..	20	15
S15	,,	3p. ultram. (2 bands) ..	25	15
		a. Imperf. (pair)†		
S16	,,	3p. ultramarine (1 centre band) (23.1.74) ..	8	8
S17	,,	3½p. olive-grey (2 bands) (23.1.74)	15	12
S18	,,	3½p. olive-grey (1 centre band) (6.11.74) ..	15	12
S19	,,	4½p. grey-blue (6.11.74)	15	12
S20	,,	5p. reddish violet ..	40	30
S21	,,	5½p. violet (2 bands) (23.1.74)	10	10
S22	,,	5½p. violet (1 centre band) (21.5.75) ..	10	10
		a. Imperf. (pair)		
S23	,,	6½p. greenish blue (1 centre band (14.1.76)	10	10
S24	,,	7½p. chestnut	60	60
S25	,,	8p. rosine (23.1.74) ..	12	12
S26	,,	8½p. yellow-green (14.1.76)	12	12
S27	,,	10p. orge.-brn. (20.10.76)	15	20
S28	,,	11p. scarlet (20.10.76) ..	15	20

†Exists only with gum arabic.

From 1972 printings were on fluorescent white paper. Nos. S14/15 exist with PVA and gum arabic and the remainder with PVA only; from 1973 printings had dextrin added (see notes after No. 874 of Great Britain).

III. WALES

From the inception of the Regional stamps, the Welsh versions were tendered to members of the public at all Post Offices within the former County of Monmouthshire but the English alternatives were available on request. Offices with a Monmouthshire postal address but situated outside the County, namely Beachley, Brockweir, Redbrook, Sedbury, Tutshill, Welsh Newton and Woodcroft, were not supplied with the Welsh Regional stamps.

With the re-formation of Counties, Monmouthshire became known as Gwent and was also declared to be part of Wales. From 1st July 1974, therefore, except for the offices mentioned above, only Welsh Regional stamps were available at the offices under the jurisdiction of Newport, Gwent.

W 1

W 2

W 3

(Des. Reynolds Stone.)

1958–67. *W* **179.** *P* 15 × 14.

W1	**W 1**	3d. deep lilac (18.8.58) ..	15	5
		p. One centre phosphor band (16.5.67)	10	25
W2	,,	4d. ultramarine (7.2.66)	15	5
		p. Two phosphor bands (10.67)	10	8
W3	**W 2**	6d. deep claret (29.9.58)	30	15
W4	,,	9d. bronze-green (2 phosphor bands) (1.3.67)	15	30
W5	**W 3**	1s. 3d. green (29.9.58) ..	30	20
W6	,,	1s. 6d. grey-blue (2 phosphor bands) (1.3.67)	30	20

1967–69. *No wmk. Chalky paper. One centre phosphor band* (W7, W9/10) *or two phosphor bands* (*others*). *P* 15 × 14.

W 7	**W 1**	3d. deep lilac (6.12.67)	8	12
W 8	,,	4d. dp. bright bl. (21.6.68)	12	10
W 9	,,	4d. olive-sepia (4.9.68)	12	5
W10	,,	4d. bright verm. (26.2.69)	20	8
W11	,,	5d. Royal blue (4.9.68)	25	12
W12	**W 3**	1s. 6d. grey-bl. (1.8.69)	4·50	1·50

The 3d. exists with gum arabic only; the remainder with PVA gum only.

W 4

(Des. J. Matthews.)

1971 (7 July)–**76.** *Decimal Currency. Chalky paper. Two phosphor bands, except where otherwise stated. P 15 × 14.*

W13	**W 4**	2½p. bright magenta (1 centre band) ..	20	15
		a. Imperf. (pair)† ..		
W14	,,	3p. ultramarine (2 bands)	25	15
W15	,,	3p. ultram. (1 centre band) (23.1.74) ..	8	8
W16	,,	3½p. olive-grey (2 bands) (23.1.74)	15	12
W17	,,	3½p. olive-grey (1 centre band) (6.11.74) ..	15	12
W18	,,	4½p. grey-blue (6.11.74)	15	12
W19	,,	5p. reddish violet ..	40	30
W20	,,	5½p. violet (2 bands) (23.1.74) ..	10	10
W21	,,	5½p. violet (1 centre band) (21.5.75) ..	10	10
W22	,,	6½p. greenish blue (1 centre band) (14.1.76)	10	10
W23	,,	7½p. chestnut ..	60	60
W24	,,	8p. rosine (23.1.74)	12	12
W25	,,	8½p. yellow-green (14.1.76)	12	12
W26	,,	10p. orge.-brn. (20.10.76)	15	20
W27	,,	11p. scarlet (20.10.76) ..	15	20

†Exists only with gum arabic.

From 1972 printings were on fluorescent white paper. Nos. W13/14 exist with PVA and gum arabic and the remainder with PVA only; from 1973 printings had dextrin added (see notes after No. 874 of Great Britain).

POSTAGE DUE STAMPS.

D 1

D 2

Typo. by Somerset House (early trial printings of ½d., 1d., 2d. and 5d.; all ptgs. of 1s.) and by Harrison (later ptgs. of all values except 1s.). Not easily distinguishable except by the control.)

1914–23. *Wmk. Royal Cypher, sideways* (*"Simple"*), *T* **100**. *P* 14×15.

D1	D 1	½d. emerald	40	20
D2	,,	1d. carmine	40	8
		a. Pale carmine ..	40	8
D3	,,	1½d. chestnut (1923) ..	15·00	6·00
D4	,,	2d. agate	60	15
D5	,,	3d. violet (1918) ..	2·00	50
		a. Bluish violet ..	1·75	50
D6	,,	4d. dull grey-green (1921)	3·50	70
D7	,,	5d. brownish cinnamon	4·00	90
D8	,,	1s. bright blue (1915) ..	12·00	1·25
		a. Deep bright blue ..	14·00	1·25

The 1d. is known bisected and used to make up 1½d. rate on understamped letters from Ceylon (1921).

1924. *As* 1914–23, *but on thick chalk-surfaced paper.*

D9	D 1	1d. carmine	3·00	1·50

(Typo. Waterlow and (from 1934) Harrison.)

1924–31. *W* **111**, *sideways. P* 14×15.

D10	D 1	½d. emerald	40	15
D11	,,	1d. carmine	50	10
D12	,,	1½d. chestnut	15·00	6·00
D13	,,	2d. agate	1·00	15
D14	,,	3d. dull violet	1·75	20
		a. Printed on gummed side	35·00	†
		b. Experimental paper W 111a	17·00	12·00
D15	,,	4d. dull grey-green	3·50	50
D16	,,	5d. brownish cinna. ('31)	12·00	5·00
D17	,,	1s. deep blue ..	4·50	45
D18	D 2	2s. 6d. purple/*yellow* ..	14·00	75

1936–37. *W* **125** (E 8 R) *sideways. P* 14×15.

D19	D 1	½d. emerald (June, '37) ..	90	60
D20	,,	1d. carmine (May, '37) ..	90	50
D21	,,	2d. agate (May, '37) ..	2·00	90
D22	,,	3d. dull violet (Mar., '37)	90	50
D23	,,	4d. dull grey-green (Dec., '36) ..	2·75	2·50
D24	,,	5d. brnsh. cinna. (11.36)	8·00	5·00
		a. Yellow-brown ('37) ..	8·00	5·00
D25	,,	1s. deep blue (Dec., '36)	3·50	3·00
D26	D 2	2s. 6d. pur./*yell.* (5.37) ..	30·00	9·00

The 1d. is known bisected (Solihull, 3 July, 1937).

1937–38. *W* **127** (G VI R) *sideways. P* 14×15.

D27	D 1	½d. emerald ('38) ..	50	25
D28	,,	1d. carmine ('38) ..	75	25
D29	,,	2d. agate ('38)	90	20
D30	,,	3d. violet ('38)	90	20
D31	,,	4d. dull grey-green ('37)	4·00	1·50
D32	,,	5d. yellow-brown ('38) ..	1·25	30
D33	,,	1s. deep blue ('37) ..	6·00	50
D34	D 2	2s. 6d. pur./*yellow* ('38) ..	12·00	1·40

The 2d. is known bisected in June 1951 (Harpenden and St. Albans) and on 30 October 1954 (Harpenden).

DATES OF ISSUE.—The following dates are those on which stamps were first issued by the Supplies Dept. to postmasters.

1951–52. *Colours changed and new value* (1½*d.*). *W* **127** (G VI R) *sideways. P* 14×15.

D35	D 1	½d. orange (18.9.51) ..	75	75
D36	,,	1d. violet-blue (6.6.51)	75	40
D37	,,	1½d. green (11.2.52) ..	1·25	75
D38	,,	4d. blue (14.8.51) ..	2·75	1·60
D39	,,	1s. ochre (6.12.51) ..	8·00	1·00

The 1d. is known bisected (Camberley, 6 April, 1954).

1954–55. *W* **153** (*Mult. Tudor Crown and* E 2 R) *sideways. P* 14×15.

D40	D 1	½d. orange (8.6.55) ..	1·50	50
D41	,,	2d. agate (28.7.55) ..	2·50	60
D42	,,	3d. violet (4.5.55) ..	12·00	3·50
D43	,,	4d. blue (14.7.55) ..	4·00	2·00
		a. Imperf. (pair) ..	70·00	
D44	,,	5d. yellow-brn. (19.5.55)	10·00	2·75
D45	D 2	2s. 6d. purple/*yell.* (11.54)	30·00	4·00

1955–57. *W* **165** (*Mult. St. Edward's Crown and* E 2 R) *sideways. P* 14×15.

D46	D 1	½d. orange (16.7.56) ..	2·50	50
D47	,,	1d. violet-blue (7.6.56)	2·00	30
D48	,,	1½d. green (13.2.56) ..	3·50	1·00
D49	,,	2d. agate (22.5.56) ..	5·00	1·00
D50	,,	3d. violet (5.3.56) ..	4·00	1·00
D51	,,	4d. blue (24.4.56) ..	6·00	1·00
D52	,,	5d. brn.-ochre (23.3.56)	6·00	1·00
D53	,,	1s. ochre (22.11.55) ..	10·00	1·50
D54	D 2	2s. 6d. pur./*yell.* (28.6.57)	50·00	3·75
D55	,,	5s. scar./*yellow* (25.11.55)	35·00	5·00

The 2d. is known bisected (June 1956), and also the 4d. (Poplar, London, April 1959).

1959–63. *W* **179** (*Mult. St. Edward's Crown*) *sideways. P* 14×15.

D56	D 1	½d. orange (18.10.61)	15	10
D57	,,	1d. violet-blue (9.5.60)	15	8
D58	,,	1½d. green (5.10.60) ..	90	75
D59	,,	2d. agate (14.9.59) ..	1·10	15
D60	,,	3d. violet (24.3.59) ..	40	10
D61	,,	4d. blue (17.12.59) ..	40	10
D62	,,	5d. yell.-brown (6.11.61)	40	15
D63	,,	6d. purple (29.3.62) ..	40	12
D64	,,	1s. ochre (11.4.60) ..	60	15
D65	D 2	2s. 6d. pur./*yell.* (11.5.61)	1·25	25
D66	,,	5s. scarlet/*yell.* (8.5.61)	1·50	45
D67	,,	10s. blue/*yellow* (2.9.63)	4·00	2·00
D68	,,	£1 black/*yellow* (2.9.63)	25·00	2·50

Whiter paper. The note after No. 586 also applies to Postage Due stamps.

The 1d. is known bisected (Newbury, Dec. 1962).

1968–69. *Typo. No wmk. Chalky paper. P* 14×15.

D69	D 1	2d. agate (11.4.68) ..	30	25
D70	,,	3d. violet (9.9.68) ..	30	25
D71	,,	4d. blue (6.5.68) ..	60	25
D72	,,	5d. orange-brown (3.1.69)	1·50	40
D73	,,	6d. purple (9.9.68) ..	80	35
D74	,,	1s. ochre (19.11.68) ..	90	25

The 2d. exists with gum arabic and PVA gum, the 4d. with gum arabic only and the remainder with PVA gum only.

1968–69. *Photo. No wmk. Chalky paper. PVA gum. P* 14×15.

D75	D 1	4d. blue (12.6.69) ..	2·50	90
D76	,,	8d. red (3.10.68) ..	75	40

Nos. D75/6 are smaller, 21½×17½ mm.

D 3

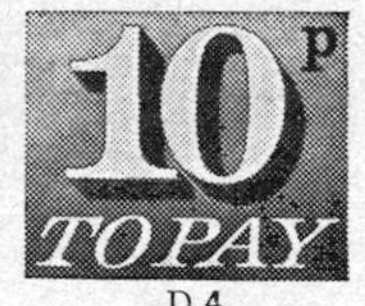

D 4

(Des. J. Matthews. Photo. Harrison.)

1970–75. *Decimal Currency. Chalky paper. P* 14×15.

D77	D 3	½p. turquoise-blue ..	5	10
D78	,,	1p. deep reddish purple	5	5
D79	,,	2p. myrtle-green ..	5	5
D80	,,	3p. ultramarine ..	5	8
D81	,,	4p. yellow-brown ..	8	10
D82	,,	5p. violet ..	8	10
D83	,,	7p. red-brown ..	12	15
D84	D 4	10p. carmine ..	15	15
D85	,,	11p. slate-green ..	15	20
D86	,,	20p. olive-brown ..	30	20
D87	,,	50p. ultramarine ..	75	30
D88	,,	£1 black	1·50	50
D89	,,	£5 orange-yell. & black	7·50	3·50

Dates of issue:—10p. and 20p. to £1, 17.6.70; ½p. to 5p., 15.2.71; £5, 2.4.73; 7p., 21.8.74; 11p., 18.6.75.

Later printings were on fluorescent white paper, some with dextrin added to the PVA gum (see notes after No. 874 of Great Britain).

OFFICIAL STAMPS.

In 1840 the 1d. black (Type **1**), with "V R" in the upper corners, was prepared for official use, but never issued for postal purposes. Obliterated specimens are those which were used for experimental trials of obliterating inks, or those that passed the post by oversight.

V 1

Prepared for use but not issued.

"V" "R" in upper corners. Imperf.

V1	V 1	1d. black	£2000	£1800

All the following were overprinted by De La Rue.

1. INLAND REVENUE.

I.R. I. R.

OFFICIAL OFFICIAL

(O 1) (O 2)

FOR WELL CENTRED LIGHTLY USED COPIES ADD 25% (Nos. O1/19)

Optd. with Types O **1** *or* O **2** (5*s.*, 10*s.*, £1).

1882–1901. *Stamps of Queen Victoria.*

Issues of **1880–81.**

O 1	½d. green (28.10.82) ..	3·50	1·00
O 3	1d. lilac (Die II) (27.9.82) ..	60	45
	a. Optd. in blue-black	35·00	10·00
	b. "OFFICIAL" omitted ..	£300	
	c. Lines of opts. transposed ..		
O 4	6d. grey (30.10.82)	28·00	9·00

Issues of **1884–88.**

O 5	½d. slate-blue (8.5.85) ..	5·50	1·00
O 6	2½d. lilac (12.3.85)	18·00	9·00
O 7	1s. green (12.3.85)	£900	£200
O 8	5s. rose (12.3.85)	£500	£120
	a. Raised stop after "R" ..	£600	£150
	b. Optd. in blue-black	£750	£200
O 9	5s. rose (*blued* paper) (12.3.85)	£900	£200
O 9*a*	10s. cobalt (12.3.85) ..	£1600	£275
O 10	10s. ultramarine (12.3.85) ..	£600	£140
	a. Raised stop after "R" ..	£750	£175
	b. Optd. in blue-black	£1000	£300
O 10*c*	10s. ultramarine (*blued* paper)	£1800	£600
O 11	£1 brn.-lilac (wmk. Crowns) (12.3.85)	£3500	£1500
	a. Frame broken	£4000	£1800
O 12	£1 brn.-lil. (wmk. Orbs) ('90)	£3000	£1400
	a. Frame broken	£3500	£1600

Issues of **1887–92.**

O 13	½d. vermilion (21.1.88) ..	75	20
	a. Without "I.R."		
	b. Imperf.	£200	
	c. Opt. double (imperf.) ..	£275	
O 14	2½d. purple/*blue* (20.10.91) ..	18·00	1·25
O 15	1s. green (15.3.89)	50·00	9·00
O 16	£1 green (13.4.92)	£800	£160
	a. No stop after "R"	—	£400
	b. Frame broken	£1000	£500

Nos. O 3, O 13, O 15 and O 16 may be found with two varieties of overprint, viz. 1887 printings, *thin* letters, and 1894 printings, *thicker* letters.

Issues of **1887** *and* **1900.**

O 17	½d. blue-green (4.01) ..	1·75	50
O 18	6d. purple/*rose-red* (14.6.01)	40·00	7·00
O 19	1s. green & carmine (12.01)	£160	35·00

1902–4. *Stamps of King Edward VII.*

O 20 ½d. blue-green, O (4.2.02) .. 2·00 50
O 21 1d. scarlet, O (4.2.02) .. 1·00 25
O 22 2½d. ultramarine, O (19.2.02) £150 25·00
O 23 6d. dull purple, O (14.3.04) £22000 £12000
O 24 1s. green & car., O (29.4.02) £125 25·00
O 25 5s. carmine, O (29.4.02) .. £1500 £550
a. Raised stop after "R" £1750 £650
O 26 10s. ultram., O (29.4.02) .. £7000 £4500
a. Raised stop after "R" .. £7500 £5000
O 27 £1 dull blue-green, O (20.4.02) £4000 £1200

2. OFFICE OF WORKS.

O. W.

OFFICIAL
(O 3)

Optd. with Type O 3.
Stamps of Queen Victoria.

1896.
O 31 ½d. vermilion (24.3.96) .. 14·00 5·00
O 32 1d. lilac (Die II) (24.3.96) .. 11·00 4·00

1901.
O 33 ½d. blue-green (5.11.01) .. 16·00 10·00

1902.
O 34 5d. pur. & blue (II) (29.4.02) £150 55·00
O 35 10d. purple & carm. (28.5.02) £350 £110

1902–03. *Stamps of King Edward VII.*
O 36 ½d. blue-green, O (11.2.02) 20·00 3·00
O 37 1d. scarlet, O (11.2.02) .. 20·00 2·50
O 38 2d. green & car., O (29.3.02) 80·00 15·00
O 39 2½d. ultramarine, O (20.3.02) £180 18·00
O 40 10d. pur. & carm., O (18.5.03) £800 £275

3. ARMY.

ARMY OFFICIAL (O 4) ARMY OFFICIAL (O 5) ARMY OFFICIAL (O 6)

Optd. with Type O **4** (*½d., 1d.*) *or* O **5** (*2½d., 6d.*).
Stamps of Queen Victoria.

1896 (1 Sept.).
O 41 ½d. vermilion 50 25
a. "OFFICIAI" .. .. 12·00 7·00
b. Lines of opt. transposed ..
O 42 1d. lilac (Die II) 50 25
a. "OFFICIAI" .. .. 12·00 7·00
O 43 2½d. purple/*blue* .. .. 1·50 65

1900–1.
O 46 ½d. blue-green (4.00) .. 75 25
O 47 6d. pur./*rose-red* (7.11.01) .. 6·00 4·00

1902. *Stamps of King Edward VII optd. with Type* O **4.**
O 48 ½d. blue-green, O (11.2.02) 75 30
O 49 1d. scarlet, O (11.2.02) .. 50 25
a. "ARMY" omitted ..
b. "OFFICIAI" .. ..
O 50 6d. dull purple, O (23.8.02) 20·00 12·00

1903 (Sept.). *Optd. with Type* O **6.**
O 52 6d. dull purple, O £300 £100

4. GOVERNMENT PARCELS.

GOVT PARCELS
(O 7)

FOR WELL CENTRED LIGHTLY USED COPIES ADD 100% (Nos. O61/72)

Optd. as Type O **7.**
Stamps of Queen Victoria.

1883 (1 July)–**86.**
O 61 1½d. lilac (30.4.86) .. .. 28·00 7·00
a. No dot under "T" .. — 13·00
b. Dot to left of "T" .. 35·00 10·00
O 62 6d. dull green (30.4.86) .. £110 30·00
O 63 9d. dull green (1.8.83) .. £180 75·00
O 64 1s. brown (w. Crown, Pl. 13) £125 30·00
a. No dot under "T".. .. £140 35·00
b. Dot to left of "T".. .. £140 35·00
O 64c 1s. brown (Pl. 14) .. .. £180 35·00
d. No dot under "T".. .. £210 40·00

1887–90.
O 65 1½d. purple & grn. (29.10.87) 5·00 90
a. No dot under "T" .. 9·00 1·75
b. Dot to right of "T" .. 6·00 1·00
c. Dot to left of "T" .. 6·00 1·00
O 66 6d. pur./*rose-red* (19.12.87) 10·00 4·00
a. No dot under "T" .. 14·00 6·00
b. Dot to right of "T" .. 14·00 6·00
c. Dot to left of "T" .. 14·00 5·00
O 67 9d. purple and blue (21.8.88) 22·00 7·00
O 68 1s. dull green (25.3.90) .. 38·00 30·00
a. No dot under "T" .. 45·00 35·00
b. Dot to right of "T" .. 45·00 35·00
c. Dot to left of "T" .. 45·00 35·00
d. Optd. in blue-black ..

1891–1900.
O 69 1d. lilac (Die II) (6.97) .. 2·00 30
a. No dot under "T" .. 7·00 2·50
b. Dot to left of "T" .. 7·00 2·50
c. Opt. inverted .. £275 £150
d. Ditto. Dot to left of "T" .. £300 £175
O 70 2d. green & carm. (24.10.91) 15·00 2·00
a. No dot under "T" .. 18·00 2·25
b. Dot to left of "T" .. 18·00 3·00
O 71 4½d. green & carmine (9.92) 18·00 25·00
O 72 1s. green & carmine (11.00) 55·00 20·00
a. Opt. inverted .. .. — £1800

1902. *Stamps of King Edward VII.*
O 74 1d. scarlet, O (30.10.02) .. 4·00 3·00
O 75 2d. green & car., O (29.4.02) 25·00 6·50
O 76 6d. dull purple, O (19.2.02) 40·00 6·50
O 77 9d. pur. & ult., O (28.8.02) 90·00 18·00
O 78 1s. grn. & car., O (17.12.02) £160 35·00

5. BOARD OF EDUCATION.

BOARD OF EDUCATION
(O 8)

Overprinted with Type O **8,** *in black.*

1902 (19 Feb.). *Stamps of Queen Victoria.*
O 81 5d. purple and blue (II) .. £120 30·00
O 82 1s. green and carmine .. £275 £160

1902–4. *Stamps of King Edward VII.*
O 83 ½d. blue-green, O (19.2.02) 7·00 1·75
O 84 1d. scarlet, O (19.2.02) .. 7·00 1·50
O 85 2½d. ultramarine, O (19.2.02) £110 22·00
O 86 5d. pur. and blue, O (6.2.04) £350 £140
O 87 1s. grn. & car., O (23.12.02) £8000 £4250

6. ROYAL HOUSEHOLD.

R.H. OFFICIAL
(O 9)

1902. *King Edward VII stamps optd. with Type* O **9.**
O 91 ½d. blue-green, O (29.4.02) 40·00 30·00
O 92 1d. scarlet, O (19.2.02) .. 35·00 25·00

7. ADMIRALTY.

ADMIRALTY OFFICIAL (O 10) ADMIRALTY OFFICIAL (O 11)

1903 (3 Mar.). *Stamps of King Edward VII optd. with Type* O **10.**
O 101 ½d. blue-green, O .. 3·00 1·25
O 102 1d. scarlet, O .. .. 2·00 1·00
O 103 1½d. purple and green, O 22·00 12·00
O 104 2d. green and carmine, O 28·00 15·00
O 105 2½d. ultramarine, O .. 20·00 12·00
O 106 3d. purple/*yellow*, O .. 32·00 12·00

1903–4. *Stamps of King Edward VII optd. with Type* O **11.**
O 107 ½d. blue-green, O, (9.03) 3·50 1·50
O 108 1d. scarlet, O (11.03) .. 2·25 1·00
O 109 1½d. purple & grn. O (2.04) 50·00 20·00
O 110 2d. green & carm. O (3.04) £110 45·00
O 111 2½d. ultramarine, O (3.04) £200 90·00
O 112 3d. purple/*yellow*, O (2.04) £110 12·00

Stamps of various issues perforated with a Crown and initials ("H.M.O.W.", "O.W.", "B.T." or "S.O.") or with initials only ("H.M.S.O." or "D.S.I.R.") have been used for official purposes, but we do not catalogue or deal in this class of stamp.

CONTROL LETTERS.

Stamps with Control Letters formerly listed here will now be found listed in greater detail in the first two volumes of our *Great Britain Specialised Catalogue.*

POSTAL FISCAL STAMPS.

PRICES. Prices in the used column are for stamps with genuine postal cancellations dated from the time when they were authorised for use as postage stamps. Beware of stamps with fiscal cancellations removed and fraudulent postmarks applied.

VALIDITY. The 1d. Surface-printed stamps were authorised for postal use from 1st June 1881 and the 3d. and 6d. values, together with the Embossed issues, from 1st January 1883.

A. Surface-Printed Issues.

(Printed by De La Rue and Co.)

F 1
Rectangular Buckle.

F 2

F 3
Octagonal Buckle

F 4

F 5
Double-lined Anchor

F 6
Single-lined Anchor

1853–57. *P* $15\frac{1}{2} \times 15$.

(*a*) *Wmk. Type* F **5** (*inverted*) (1853–55).

No.	Type	Description	Unused	Used
F1	F **1**	1d. light blue (10.10.53)	5·00	7·00
F2	F **2**	1d. ochre (10.53)	25·00	15·00
		a. Tête-bêche (in block of four)	£6000	
F3	F **3**	1d. pale turquoise-blue (1854)	6·00	6·50
F4	,,	1d. light blue/*blue* (1854)	18·00	14·00
F5	F **4**	1d. reddish lilac/*blue glazed paper* (25.3.55)	28·00	7·00

Only one example is known of No. F2a outside the National Postal Museum and the Royal Collection.

(*b*) *Wmk. Type* F **6** (1856–57).

No.	Type	Description	Unused	Used
F6	F **4**	1d. reddish lilac (*shades*)	4·00	3·00
F7	,,	1d. reddish lilac/*bluish* (*shades*) (1857)	4·00	3·00

INLAND REVENUE

(F **7**)

1860 (3 Apr.). *No.* F7 *optd. with Type* F **7**, *in red.*

No.	Type	Description	Unused	Used
F8	F **4**	1d. dull reddish lilac/*blue*	£100	£100

BLUE PAPER. In the following issues we no longer distinguish between bluish and white paper. There is a range of papers from white or greyish to bluish.

F 8

F 9

F 10

1860–67. *Bluish to white paper.* *P* $15\frac{1}{2} \times 15$.

(*a*) *Wmk. Type* F **6** (1860).

No.	Type	Description	Unused	Used
F 9	F **8**	1d. reddish lilac (May)	3·50	3·50
F10	F **9**	3d. reddish lilac (June)	£120	40·00
F11	F **10**	6d. reddish lilac (Oct.)	45·00	28·00

(*b*) *W* **40** (*Anchor* 16 *mm. high*) (1864).

No.	Type	Description	Unused	Used
F12	F **8**	1d. pale reddish lilac (Nov.)	3·50	3·50
F13	F **9**	3d. pale reddish lilac	40·00	30·00
F14	F **10**	6d. pale reddish lilac	45·00	28·00

(*c*) *W* **40** (*Anchor* 18 *mm. high*) (1867).

No.	Type	Description	Unused	Used
F15	F **8**	1d. reddish lilac	9·00	4·50
F16	F **9**	3d. reddish lilac	28·00	28·00
F17	F **10**	6d. reddish lilac	45·00	25·00

For stamps perf. 14, see Nos. F24/7.

F 11

F 12

Four Dies of Type F **12**.

Die 1. Corner ornaments small and either joined or broken; heavy shading under chin.

Die 2. Ornaments small and always broken; clear line of shading under chin.

Die 3. Ornaments larger and joined; line of shading under chin extended half way down neck.

Die 4. Ornaments much larger; straight line of shading continued to bottom of neck.

1867–81. *White to bluish paper. P* 14.

(*a*) *W* **47** (*Small Anchor*).

No.	Type	Description	Unused	Used
F18	F **11**	1d. purple (1.9.67)	4·00	3·00
F19	F **12**	1d. purple (Die 1) (6.68)	1·25	1·10
F20	,,	1d. purple (Die 2) (6.76)	1·75	2·00
F21	,,	1d. purple (Die 3) (3.77)	1·60	1·75
F22	,,	1d. purple (Die 4) (7.78)	1·40	1·25

(*b*) *W* **48** (*Orb.*)

No.	Type	Description	Unused	Used
F23	F **12**	1d. purple (Die 4) (1.81)	1·40	1·10

1881. *White to bluish paper. P* 14.

(*a*) *W* **40** (*Anchor* 18 *mm. high*) (Jan.).

No.	Type	Description	Unused	Used
F24	F **9**	3d. reddish lilac	£175	£125
F25	F **10**	6d. reddish lilac	90·00	30·00

(*b*) *W* **40** (*Anchor* 20 *mm. high*) (May).

No.	Type	Description	Unused	Used
F26	F **9**	3d. reddish lilac	£110	28·00
F27	F **10**	6d. reddish lilac	60·00	40·00

B. Issues Embossed in Colour.

(Made at Somerset House.)

The embossed stamps were struck from dies not appropriated to any special purpose on paper which the words "INLAND REVENUE" had previously been printed, and thus became available for payment of any duties for which no special stamps had been provided.

The die letters are included in the embossed designs and holes were drilled for the insertion of plugs showing figures indicating dates of striking.

F 13

F 14

INLAND
REVENUE
(F **15**)

INLAND
REVENUE
(F **16**)

1860 (3 Apr.)–**71.** *Types* F **13/14** *and similar types embossed on bluish paper. Underprint Type* F **15.** *No wmk. Imperf.*

No.	Description	Unused	Used
F28	2d. pink (Die A) (1.1.71)	60·00	60·00
F29	3d. pink (Die C)	45·00	40·00
	a. Tête-bêche (vert. pair)	£550	
F30	3d. pink (Die D)	£150	
F31	6d. pink (Die T)	£400	
F32	6d. pink (Die U)	50·00	40·00
	a. Tête-bêche (vert. pair)	£600	
F33	9d. pink (Die C) (1.1.71)	£140	
F34	1s. pink (Die E) (28.6.61)	£200	85·00
F35	1s. pink (Die F) (28.6.61)	60·00	15·00
	a. Tête-bêche (vert. pair)	£250	
F36	2s. pink (Die K) (6.8.61)	£160	£100
F37	2s. 6d. pink (Die N) (28.6.61)	£300	
F38	2s. 6d. pink (Die O) (28.6.61)	40·00	35·00

1861–71. *As last but perf.* 12½.

No.	Description	Unused	Used
F39	2d. pink (Die A) (8.71)	£130	75·00
F40	3d. pink (Die C)		
F41	3d. pink (Die D)		
F42	9d. pink (Die C) (8.71)	£150	85·00
F43	1s. pink (Die E) (8.71)	£110	75·00
F44	1s. pink (Die F) (8.71)	£100	60·00
F45	2s. 6d. pink (Die O) (8.71)	60·00	35·00

1874 (Nov.). *Types as before embossed on white paper. Underprint Type* F **16,** *in green. W* **47** (*Small Anchor*). *P* 12½.

No.	Description	Unused	Used
F46	2d. pink (Die A)	—	£110
F47	9d. pink (Die C)		
F48	1s. pink (Die F)	£100	65·00
F49	2s. 6d. pink (Die O)	—	90·00

1875 (Nov.)–**80.** *As last but colour changed and on white or bluish paper.*

No.	Description	Unused	Used
F50	2d. vermilion (Die A) (1880)	£150	60·00
F51	9d. vermilion (Die C) (1876)	£150	85·00
F52	1s. vermilion (Die E)	90·00	40·00
F53	1s. vermilion (Die F)	90·00	40·00
F54	2s. 6d. vermilion (Die O) (1878)	£110	60·00

1882 (Oct.). *As last but W* **48** (*Orbs*).

No.	Description	Unused	Used
F55	2d. vermilion (Die A)		
F56	9d. vermilion (Die C)		
F57	1s. vermilion (Die E)		
F58	2s. 6d. vermilion (Die O)	£250	£120

The sale of Inland Revenue stamps up to the 2s. value ceased from 30th December 1882 and stocks were called in and destroyed. The 2s. 6d. value remained on sale until 2nd July 1883 when it was replaced by the 2s. 6d. "Postage & Revenue" stamp. Inland Revenue stamps still in the hands of the public continued to be accepted for revenue and postal purposes.

CHANNEL ISLANDS.

A. GENERAL ISSUE.

C **1.** Gathering Vraic.

C **2.** Islanders gathering Vraic.

(Des. 1d. J. R. R. Stobie. 2½d. from drawing by E. Blampied. Photo. Harrison.)

1948 (10 May). *Third Anniv. of Liberation. W* **127** *of Great Britain. P* 15 × 14.

C1 C **1** 1d. scarlet 10 10
C2 C **2** 2½d. ultramarine 15 15

B. GUERNSEY.

(a) War Occupation Issues.

Stamps issued under British authority during the German Occupation.

BISECTS. On December 24th, 1940 authority was given, by Post Office notice, that prepayment of penny postage could be effected by using half a British 2d. stamp, diagonally bisected. Such stamps were first used on December 27th, 1940.

The 2d. stamps generally available were those of the Postal Centenary issue, 1940 (S.G. 482) and the first colour of the King George VI issue (S.G. 465). These are listed under Nos. 482a and 465b. A number of the 2d. King George V, 1912–22, and of the King George V photogravure stamp (S.G. 442) which were in the hands of philatelists, were also bisected and used.

1

(Des. E. W. Vaudin. Typo. Guernsey Press Co. Ltd.)

1941–44. *Rouletted.* (*a*) *White paper. No wmk.*

1 **1** ½d. light green (7.4.41) .. 2·50 1·00
a. Emerald-green (6.41) .. 2·00 2·00
b. Bluish green (11.41) .. .. 17·00 10·00
c. Bright green (2.42) .. .. 6·00 1·50
d. Dull green (9.42) .. .. 2·50 1·50
e. Olive-green (2.43) .. .. 17·00 9·00
f. Pale yellowish green (7.43 and later) (*shades*) .. .. 1·75 1·50
g. Imperf. between (horiz. pair) £250
h. Imperf. between (vert. pair).. £300
2 ,, 1d. scarlet (18.2.41).. .. 1·50 30
a. Pale vermilion (7.43) (etc.) .. 3·00 1·25
b. Carmine ('43) .. .. 6·00 2·00
c. Imperf. (pair) .. .. 55·00 40·00
d. Imperf. between (horiz. pair) £250
e. Imperf. between (vert. pair).. £300
3 ,, 2½d. ultramarine (12.4.44) .. 3·00 2·75

(*b*) *Bluish French bank-note paper. Wmk. loops*

4 **1** ½d. bright green (11.3.42) .. 7·00 8·50
5 ,, 1d. scarlet (9.4.42) .. .. 5·00 8·50

The dates given for the shades of Nos. 1 and 2 are the months in which they were printed as indicated on the printers' imprints. Others are issue dates.

(b) Regional Issues.

DATES OF ISSUE. Conflicting dates of issue have been announced for some of the regional issues, partly explained by the stamps being released on different dates by the Philatelic Bureau in Edinburgh or the Philatelic Counter in London and in the regions. We have adopted the practice of giving the earliest known dates, since once released the stamps could have been used anywhere in the U.K.

2

3

(Des. E. A. Piprell. Portrait by Dorothy Wilding Ltd. Photo. Harrison & Sons.)

1958 (18 Aug.)–**67.** *W* **179** *of Great Britain. P* 15 × 14.

6 **2** 2½d. rose-red (8.6.64) 65 85
7 **3** 3d. deep lilac.. .. .. 60 8
p. One centre phosphor band (24.5.67) 12 30
8 ,, 4d. ultramarine (7.2.66) .. 20 15
p. Two phosphor bands (24.10.67) 12 15

1968–69. *No wmk. Chalky paper. PVA gum*. One centre phosphor band* (*Nos.* 10/11) *or two phosphor bands* (*others*). *P* 15 × 14.

9 **3** 4d. pale ultram. (16.4.68) .. 12 40
10 ,, 4d. olive-sepia (4.9.68) .. 15 15
11 ,, 4d. bright vermilion (26.2.69) 40 35
12 ,, 5d. Royal blue (4.9.68) .. 35 12

No. 9 was not issued in Guernsey until 22nd April.

* *PVA Gum.* See note after No. 722 of Great Britain.

(c) Independent Postal Administration.

4. Castle Cornet and Edward the Confessor.

5. Map and William I.
6. Martello Tower and Henry II.
7. Arms of Sark and King John.
8. Arms of Alderney and Edward III.
9. Guernsey Lily and Henry V.
10. Arms of Guernsey and Elizabeth I.
11. Arms of Alderney and Charles II.
12. Arms of Sark and George III.
13. Arms of Guernsey and Queen Victoria.
14. Guernsey Lily and Elizabeth I.
15. Martello Tower and King John.

16. View of Sark.

17. View of Alderney.
18. View of Guernsey.

T **5/15** are as T **4** and T **17/18** are as T **16.**

Two Types of 1d. and 1s. 6d.
I. Latitude inscr. " 40° 30′ N ".
II. Corrected to " 49° 30′ N ".

(Des. R. Granger Barrett. Photo. Harrison (½d. to 2s. 6d.); Delrieu (others).)

1969 (1 Oct.).–**70.** *P* 14 (*½d. to 2s. 6d.*) *or* 12½ (*others*).

13 **4** ½d. deep magenta & black 8 8
14 **5** 1d. bright blue & black (I) 10 15
14*b* ,, 1d. bright blue and black (II) (12.12.69) 25 25
c. Booklet stamp with blank margins 35 35
15 **6** 1½d. yellow-brown and black 10 10
16 **7** 2d. gold, bright red, deep blue and black .. 10 10
17 **8** 3d. gold, pale greenish yellow, orange-red & black 10 10
a. Error Wmk. w.12 ..
18 **9** 4d. multicoloured .. 10 15
a. Booklet stamp with blank margins 35 35
ab. Yellow omitted .. .. 90·00
19 **10** 5d. gold, bright vermilion, bluish violet and black 25 25
a. Booklet stamp with blank margins 50 50
b. Gold inscr. etc. omitted (booklets) £175
20 **11** 6d. gold, pale greenish yell., lt. bronze-grn. & black 40 40
21 **12** 9d. gold, bright red, crimson and black.. .. 85 85
22 **13** 1s. gold, bright vermilion, bistre and black .. 85 85
23 **5** 1s. 6d. turq.-grn. & blk. (I) 90 90
23*b* ,, 1s. 6d. turquoise-green and black (II) (4.2.70) .. 4·00 2·00
24 **14** 1s. 9d. multicoloured .. 4·00 3·00
25 **15** 2s. 6d. bright reddish violet and black .. .. 8·00 6·00
26 **16** 5s. multicoloured .. 8·00 9·00
27 **17** 10s. multicoloured .. 40·00 30·00
a. Perf. 13 (17.3.70) .. 85·00 60·00
28 **18** £1 multicoloured .. 14·00 15·00
a. Perf. 13 (17.3.70) .. 2·00 3·00

The booklet panes consist of single perforated stamps with wide margins all round intended to fit automatic machines designed for the Great Britain 2s. booklets. They are therefore found with three margins when detached from booklets of four margins when complete.

There was no postal need for the ½d. and 1½d. values as the ½d. coin had been withdrawn prior to their issue in anticipation of decimalisation. These values were only on sale at the Philatelic Bureau and the Crown Agents as well as in the U.S.A.

Nos. 18a and 24 are known with blue-green omitted.

Nos. 14*b* and 23*b* are known only on thin paper and Nos. 13, 14, 16, 17, 20, 21, 22, 23, 24 and 25 also exist on thin paper.

19. Isaac Brock as Colonel.

20. Sir Isaac Brock as Major-General. (*Vert.*)
21. Isaac Brock as Ensign. (*Vert.*)
22. Arms and Flags. (*Horiz.*)

(Litho. Format International.)

1969 (1 Dec.). *Birth Bicentenary of Sir Isaac Brock. P 13½×14 (2s. 6d.) or 14×13½ (others).*

29	**19**	4d. multicoloured	20	20
30	**20**	5d. multicoloured	20	20
31	**21**	1s. 9d. multicoloured ..	2·75	3·00
32	**22**	2s. 6d. multicoloured ..	2·75	3·50

23. Landing Craft entering St. Peter's Harbour.

24. British Ships entering St. Peter's Port. (*Horiz.*)

25. Brigadier Snow reading Proclamation. (*Vert.*)

(Des. and photo. Courvoisier.)

1970 (9 May). *25th Anniv. of Liberation. P 11½.*

33	**23**	4d. blue and pale blue ..	30	30
34	**24**	5d. brown-lake & pale grey	30	30
35	**25**	1s. 6d bistre-brown and buff	6·00	6·00

26. Guernsey " Toms ".

27. Guernsey Cow.

28. Guernsey Bull.

29. Freesias.

(Des. and photo. Courvoisier.)

1970 (12 Aug.). *Agriculture and Horticulture. P 11½.*

36	**26**	4d. multicoloured	25	25
37	**27**	5d. multicoloured	25	25
38	**28**	9d. multicoloured	6·00	4·00
39	**29**	1s. 6d. multicoloured ..	7·50	6·00

30. St. Anne's Church, Alderney. (*Horiz.*)

31. St. Peter's Church. (*Horiz.*)

32. St. Peter Church, Sark.

33. St. Tugual Chapel, Herm. (*Vert.*)

(Des. and photo. Courvoisier.)

1970 (11 Nov.). *Christmas. P 11½.*

40	**30**	4d. multicoloured	25	20
41	**31**	5d. multicoloured	25	25
42	**32**	9d. multicoloured	2·50	2·00
43	**33**	1s. 6d. multicoloured ..	4·00	4·00

INVALIDATION. The regional issues for Guernsey were invalidated for use in Guernsey and Jersey on 1st October 1969 but remained valid for use in the rest of the United Kingdom. Nos. 13/43 (except Nos. 28/a) and Nos. D1/7 were invalidated on 14th February 1972.

34. Martello Tower and King John.

(Photo. Harrison (½p. to 10p.), Delrieu (others).)

1971–73. *Decimal Currency. Designs as T* **4** *etc., but values inscr. in decimal currency as in T* **34.** *Chalk-surfaced paper. P 14 (½p. to 10p.) or 13 (20p., 50p.).*

44	**4**	½p. deep magenta & black	15	15
		a. Booklet stamp with margins. *Glazed, ordinary paper* ..	8	15
		ab. Ditto. *Chalk-surfaced paper* (2.4.73)	8	15
45	**5**	1p. bright blue & blk. (II)	10	8
46	**6**	1½p. yellow-brown & black	12	12
47	**9**	2p. multicoloured ..	12	12
		a. Booklet stamp with margins *Glazed, ordinary paper* ..	15	15
		ab. Ditto. *Chalk-surfaced paper* (2.4.73)	12	15
		b. Glazed, ordinary paper (15.2.71)	20	20
48	**10**	2½p. gold, bright vermilion, bluish violet and black	15	5
		a. Bright vermilion omitted ..	£175	
		b. Booklet stamp with margins *Glazed, ordinary paper* ..	20	20
		ba. Ditto. *Chalk-surfaced paper* (2.4.73)	15	15
49	**8**	3p. gold, pale greenish yellow, orange-red & black	20	20
50	**14**	3½p. mult. (*glazed, ord. paper*)	20	20
51	**7**	4p. multicoloured ..	30	25
52	**5**	5p. turq.-green & blk. (II)	25	25
53	**11**	6p. gold, pale greenish yell., lt. bronze-grn. & black	35	35
54	**13**	7½p. gold, bright vermilion, bistre and black	45	45
55	**12**	9p. gold, bright red, crimson and black	2·50	2·50
56	**34**	10p. bright reddish violet and black ..	2·50	2·50
		a. Ordinary paper. *Brt. reddish violet & dp. black* (1.9.72)	2·00	1·50
57	**16**	20p. mult. (*glazed, ord. paper*)	2·00	2·00
		*a. Shade** (25.1.73)	75	75
58	**17**	50p. mult. (*glazed, ord. paper*)	2·50	2·00

*No. 57 has the sky in a pale turquoise-blue; on No. 57*a* it is pale turquoise-green.

Dates of issue:—10p. to 50p., 6.1.71; ½p. to 9p., 15.2.71.

35. Hong Kong 2 c. of 1862.

(Des. and recess. D.L.R.)

1971 (2 June). *Thomas De La Rue Commemoration. T* **35** *and similar horiz. designs. P 14×13½.*

59	2p. dull pur. to brown-pur.*	20	20
60	2½p. carmine-red	20	20
61	4p. deep bluish green ..	3·50	3·00
62	7½p. deep blue	3·50	3·00

Designs: (Each incorporating portraits of Queen Elizabeth II and Thomas De La Rue as in T **35**)—2½p. Great Britain 4d. of 1855–7; 4p. Italian 5 c. of 1862; 7½p. Confederate States 5 c. of 1862.

*These colours represent the extreme range of shades of this value. The majority of the printing, however, is in an intermediate shade.

36. Ebenezer Church, St. Peter Port.

(Des. and photo. Courvoisier.)

1971 (27 Oct.). *Christmas. T* **36** *and similar multicoloured designs. P 11½.*

63	2p. Type **36**	20	20
64	2½p. Church of St. Pierre du Bois	20	20
65	5p. St. Joseph's Church, St. Peter Port (*vert.*) ..	3·00	2·50
66	7½p. Church of St. Philippe de Torteval (*vert.*)	3·00	3·50

37. *Earl of Chesterfield* (1794).

(Des. and photo. Courvoisier.)

1972 (10 Feb.). *Mail Packet Boats (1st series). T* **37** *and similar horiz. designs. Multicoloured. P 11½.*

67	2p. Type **37**	20	20
68	2½p. *Dasher* (1827)	20	20
69	7½p. *Ibex* (1891)	2·75	3·00
70	9p. *Alberta* (1900)	2·75	3·00

See also Nos. 80/3.

38. Guernsey Bull.

(Photo. Courvoisier.)

1972 (22 May). *World Conference of Guernsey Breeders, Guernsey. P 11½.*

71	**38**	5p. multicoloured ..	2·00	1·75

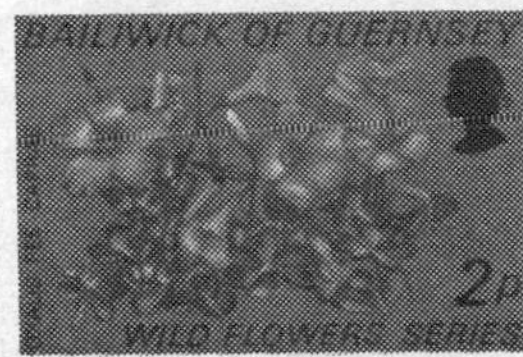

39. Bermuda Buttercup.

(Des. and photo. Courvoisier.)

1972 (24 May). *Wild Flowers. T* **39** *and similar multicoloured designs. P 11½.*

72	2p. Type **39**	15	15
73	2½p. Heath Spotted Orchid (*vert.*)	15	15
74	7½p. Kaffir Fig (*horiz.*) ..	1·25	1·25
75	9p. Scarlet Pimpernel (*vert.*)	2·00	1·50

40. Angels adoring Christ.

(Des. and photo. Courvoisier.)

1972 (20 Nov.). *Royal Silver Wedding and Christmas. T* **40** *and similar vert. designs showing stained-glass windows from Guernsey Churches. Multicoloured. P* 11½.

76	2p. Type **40**	8	8
77	2½p. The Epiphany	10	10
78	7½p. The Virgin Mary ..	75	75
79	9p. Christ	1·00	1·00

See also Nos. 89/92.

(Des. and photo. Courvoisier.)

1973 (9 Mar.). *Mail Packet Boats (2nd series). Multicoloured designs as T* **37**. *P* 11½.

80	2½p. *St. Julien* (1925) ..	12	12
81	3p. *Isle of Guernsey* (1930) ..	30	30
82	7½p. *St. Patrick* (1947) ..	2·00	2·00
83	9p. *Sarnia* (1961)	2·00	2·00

41. Supermarine " Sea Eagle ".

(Des. and photo. Courvoisier.)

1973 (4 July). *50th Anniv. of Air Service. T* **41** *and similar horiz. designs. Multicoloured. P* 11½.

84	2½p. Type **41**	12	12
85	3p. Westland " Wessex " ..	15	15
86	5p. De Havilland " Rapide "	25	25
87	7½p. Douglas " Dakota " ..	85	85
88	9p. Vickers " Viscount " ..	85	85

42. " The Good Shepherd ".

(Des. and photo. Courvoisier.)

1973 (24 Oct.). *Christmas. T* **42** *and similar vert. designs showing stained-glass windows from Guernsey Churches. Multicoloured. P* 11½.

89	2½p. Type **42**	10	10
90	3p. Christ at the well of Samaria	15	15
91	7½p. St. Dominic	25	25
92	20p. Mary and the Child Jesus	50	50

43. Princess Anne and Capt. Mark Phillips.

(Des. G. Anderson. Photo. Courvoisier.)

1973 (14 Nov.). *Royal Wedding. P* 11½.

93	**43** 25p. multicoloured ..	1·00	1·10

44. *John Lockett*, 1875.

(Des. and photo. Courvoisier.)

1974 (15 Jan.). *150th Anniv. of Royal National Life-boat Institution. T* **44** *and similar horiz. designs. Multicoloured. P* 11½.

94	2½p. Type **44**	10	10
95	3p. *Arthur Lionel*, 1912 ..	15	15
96	8p. *Euphrosyne Kendal*, 1954	50	50
97	10p. *Arun*, 1972	50	50

45. Private, East Regt., 1815.

46. Driver, Field Battery, Royal Guernsey Artillery, 1848.

(Photo. Courvoisier (½ to 10p.) or Delrieu (others).)

1974 (2 Apr.)–**77**. *Designs as T* **45/6**. *Multicoloured.*

(*a*) *Vert. designs as T* **45**. *P* 11½.

98	½p. Type **45**	5	5
	a. Booklet strip of 8 (98×5 and 102×3)†	30	
	b. Booklet pane of 16 (98×4, 102×6 and 103×6)† ..	1·00	
	c. Red omitted*		
99	1p. Officer, 2nd North Regt., 1825	5	5
	a. Booklet strip of 8 (99×4, 103, 105×2 and 105*a*) (8.2.77)†	35	
100	1½p. Gunner, Guernsey Artillery, 1787	5	5
101	2p. Gunner, Guernsey Artillery, 1815	5	5
102	2½p. Corporal, Royal Guernsey Artillery, 1868	5	5
	a. Red omitted*		
103	3p. Field Officer, Royal Guernsey Artillery, 1895	5	5
104	3½p. Sergeant, 3rd Regt., 1867	5	8
105	4p. Officer, East Regt., 1822	8	8
105*a*	5p. Field Officer, Royal Guernsey Artillery, 1895 (29.5.76)	8	10
106	5½p. Colour-Sergeant of Grenadiers, East Regt., 1833 ..	10	10
107	6p. Officer, North Regt., 1832	10	10
107*a*	7p. Officer, East Regt., 1822 (29.5.76)	12	15
108	8p. Field Officer, Rifle Company, 1868	15	15
109	9p. Private, 4th West Regt., 1785	15	15
110	10p. Field Officer, 4th West Regt., 1824	20	20

(*b*) *Size as T* **46**. *P* 13×13½ (20, 50*p*.) *or* 13½×13 (£1).

111	20p. Type **46** (1.4.75)	35	35
112	50p. Officer, Field Battery, Royal Guernsey Artillery, 1868 (1.4.75)	85	85
113	£1 Cavalry Trooper, Light Dragoons, 1814 (*horiz.*) (1.4.75)	1·75	1·75

†Nos. 98a/b and 99a come from special booklet sheets of 80 (two panes 8×5). These sheets were put on sale in addition to the normal sheets. The strips and panes have the left-hand selvedge stuck into booklet covers and then folded and supplied in plastic wallets.

* These come from the 10p. booklet.

47. Badge of Guernsey and U.P.U. Emblem.

(Photo. Courvoisier.)

1974 (7 June). *U.P.U. Centenary. T* **47** *and similar horiz. designs. Multicoloured. P* 11½.

114	2½p. Type **47**	5	5
115	3p. Map of Guernsey ..	8	8
116	8p. U.P.U. Building, Berne, and Guernsey flag ..	35	40
117	10p. "Salle des Etats" ..	45	50

48. "Cradle Rock".

(Des. and photo. Delrieu.)

1974 (21 Sept.). *Renoir Paintings. T* **48** *and similar multicoloured designs. P* 13.

118	3p. Type **48**	15	8
119	5½p. "Moulin Huet Bay" ..	25	12
120	8p. "Au Bord de la Mer" (*vert.*)	50	50
121	10p. Self-portrait (*vert.*) ..	75	60

49. Guernsey Spleenwort.

(Des. and photo. Courvoisier.)

1975 (7 Jan.). *Guernsey Ferns. T* **49** *and similar vert. designs. Multicoloured. P* 11½.

122	3½p. Type **49**	8	8
123	4p. Sand Quillwort .. .	10	10
124	8p. Guernsey Quillwort ..	20	20
125	10p. Least Adder's Tongue ..	50	50

50. Victor Hugo House.

(Des. and photo. Courvoisier.)

1975 (6 June). *Victor Hugo's Exile in Guernsey. T* **50** *and similar multicoloured designs. P* 11½.

126	3½p. Type **50**	8	8
127	4p. Candie Gardens (*vert.*) ..	8	8
128	8p. United Europe Oak, Hauteville (*vert.*)	20	20
129	10p. Tapestry Room, Hauteville	30	50
MS130	114 × 143 mm. Nos. 126/9	60	

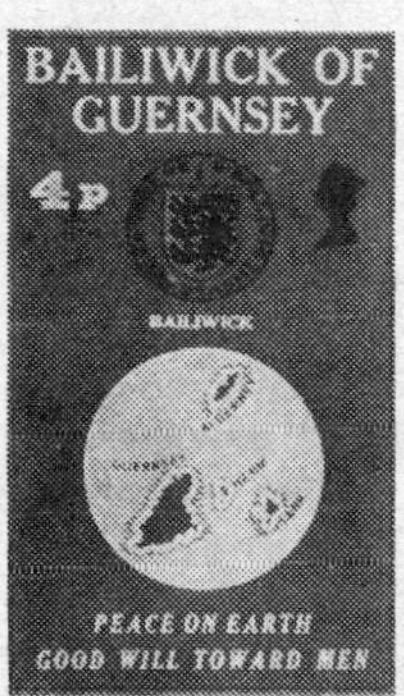

51. Globe and Seal of Bailiwick.

(Des. and photo. Delrieu.)

1975 (7 Oct.). *Christmas. Multicoloured designs each showing Globe as T* **51**. *P* 13.

131	4p. Type **51**	8	10
132	6p. Guernsey flag	12	15
133	10p. Guernsey flag and Alderney shield (*horiz.*) ..	20	20
134	12p. Guernsey flag and Sark shield (*horiz.*)	25	30

52. Les Hanois.

(Des. and photo. Courvoisier.)

1976 (10 Feb.). *Lighthouses. T* **52** *and similar horiz. designs. Multicoloured. P* 11½.

135	4p. Type **52**	8	10
136	6p. Les Casquets	12	15
137	11p. Quesnard	20	25
138	13p. Point Robert	25	30

53. Milk Can.

(Des. and photo. Courvoisier.)

1976 (29 May). *Europa. T* **53** *and similar horiz. design. P* 11½.

139	10p. chestnut & greenish black	55	55
140	25p. slate and deep dull blue ..	1·25	1·25

Design:—25p. Christening Cup.

54. Pine Forest, Guernsey.

(Des. and photo. Courvoisier.)

1976 (3 Aug.). *Views. T* **54** *and similar multicoloured designs. P* 11½.

141	5p. Type **54**	10	12
142	7p. Herm and Jethou ..	15	15
143	11p. Grand Greve Bay, Sark (*vert.*)	20	25
144	13p. Trois Vaux Bay, Alderney (*vert.*)	25	30

55. Royal Court House, Guernsey.

(Des. and photo. Courvoisier.)

1976 (14 Oct.). *Buildings. T* **55** *and similar horiz. designs. Multicoloured. P* 11½.

145	5p. Type **55**	10	12
146	7p. Elizabeth College, Guernsey	15	15
147	11p. La Seigneurie, Sark ..	20	25
148	13p. Island Hall, Alderney ..	25	30

56. Queen Elizabeth II.

(Des. R. Granger-Barrett. Photo. Courvoisier.)

1977 (8 Feb.). *Silver Jubilee. T* **56** *and similar vert. design. Multicoloured. P* 11½.

149	7p. Type **56**	15	15
150	35p. Queen Elizabeth (half-length portrait)	70	80

The States of Guernsey Post Office Board have announced the following further issues for 1977:

17 May	Europa
2 August	Dolmens and Menhirs
2 August	Postage Due Stamps
25 October	Centenary of St. John's Ambulance

For full information on all future Guernsey issues, collectors should write to the States Philatelic Bureau, Head Post Office, Guernsey.

POSTAGE DUE STAMPS.

D 1. Castle Cornet.

(Des. R. Granger Barrett. Photo. Delrieu.)

1969 (1 Oct.). *Value in black; background colour given. No wmk. P* 12½ × 12.

D1	**D 1**	1d. plum	1·00	1·00
D2	,,	2d. bright green	1·50	1·00
D3	,,	3d. vermilion	3·00	2·00
D4	,,	4d. ultramarine	4·00	3·50
D5	,,	5d. yellow-ochre	5·00	4·00
D6	,,	6d. turquoise-blue ..	7·00	6·50
D7	,,	1s. lake-brown	17·00	16·00

1971 (15 Feb.)–**76**. *As Type* D **1** *but values in decimal currency.*

D 8	**D 1**	½p. plum	5	5
D 9	,,	1p. bright green ..	5	5
D10	,,	2p. vermilion	5	5
D11	,,	3p. ultramarine ..	5	8
D12	,,	4p. yellow-ochre ..	8	10
D13	,,	5p. turquoise-blue ..	8	10
D14	,,	6p. violet (10.2.76) ..	10	12
D15	,,	8p. light yellow-orange (7.10.75)	15	15
D16	,,	10p. lake-brown ..	20	20
D17	,,	15p. grey (10.2.76) ..	25	30

C. JERSEY.

(a) War Occupation Issues.

Stamps issued under British authority during the German Occupation.

1

(Des. Major N. V. L. Rybot. Typo. *Evening Post*, Jersey.)

1941–42. *White paper. No wmk. P* 11.

1	1	½d. bright green (29.1.42) ..	1·60	60
		a. Imperf. between (vert. pair) ..	£275	
		b. Imperf. between (horiz. pair) ..	£225	
		c. Imperf. (pair)	40·00	
		d. On greyish paper	2·00	1·75
2	,,	1d. scarlet (1.4.41)	1·50	1·00
		a. Imperf. between (vert. pair) ..	£275	
		b. Imperf. between (horiz. pair) ..	£225	
		c. On chalk-surfaced paper ..	25·00	15·00
		d. On greyish paper	1·75	1·50

2. Old Jersey Farm.

3. Portelet Bay.

4. Corbière Lighthouse.

5. Elizabeth Castle.

6. Mont Orgueil Castle.

7. Gathering Vraic (seaweed).

(Des. E. Blampied. Eng. H. Cortot. Typo. French Govt. Works, Paris.)

1943. *No wmk. P* 13½.

3	2	½d. green (1 June)	4·00	1·25
4	3	1d. scarlet (1 June)	40	15
		a. On newsprint	1·00	1·00
5	4	1½d. brown (8 June)	1·00	1·50
6	5	2d. orange-yellow (8 June) ..	1·00	1·50
7	6	2½d. blue (29 June)	2·50	1·00
		a. On newsprint	1·25	1·00
8	7	3d. violet (29 June)	1·50	2·00

(b) Regional Issues.

DATES OF ISSUE. The note at the beginning of the Guernsey Regional Issues also applies here.

8

9

(Des E. Blampied (T **8**), W. M. Gardner (T **9**). Portrait by Dorothy Wilding Ltd. Photo. Harrison & Sons.)

1958 (18 Aug.)–**67.** *W* **179** *of Great Britain. P* 15 × 14

9	8	2½d. carmine-red (8.6.64) ..	70	85
		a. Imperf. three sides (pair) ..	£250	
10	9	3d. deep lilac	75	5
		p. One centre phosphor band (9.6.67)	12	15
11	,,	4d. ultramarine (7.2.66) ..	25	15
		p. Two phosphor bands (5.9.67)	15	20

1968–69. *No wmk. Chalky paper. PVA gum*. One centre phosphor band (4d. values) or two phosphor bands (5d.). P* 15 × 14.

12	9	4d. olive-sepia (4.9.68) ..	20	20
13	,,	4d. brt. vermilion (26.2.69)	35	30
14	,,	5d. Royal blue (4.9.68) ..	35	15

* *PVA Gum.* See note after No. 722 of Great Britain.

MINIMUM PRICE

The minimum price quoted is 5p which represents a handling charge rather than a basis for valuing common stamps. For further notes about prices see introductory pages.

(c) Independent Postal Administration.

10. Elizabeth Castle.

11. La Hougue Bie (Prehistoric Tomb). (*Horiz.*)
12. Portelet Bay. (*Horiz.*)

13. La Corbière Lighthouse. (*Horiz.*)
14. Mont Orgueil Castle by Night. (*Horiz.*)
15. Arms and Royal Mace. (*Horiz.*)
16. Jersey Cow. (*Horiz.*)
17. Chart of English Channel. (*Horiz.*)
18. Mont Orgueil Castle by Day. (*Horiz.*)

19. Queen Elizabeth II (after Cecil Beaton).

20. Jersey Airport.

21. Legislative Chamber. (*Horiz.*)
22. The Royal Court. (*Horiz.*)

23. Queen Elizabeth II (after Cecil Beaton).

T **11/18** are as T **10** and T **21/22** are as T **20**.

(Des. V. Whiteley. Photo. Harrison (½d. to 1s. 9d.); Courvoisier (others).)

1969 (1 Oct.). *P* 14 (*½d. to 1s. 9d.*) *or* 12 (*others*).

15 **10** ½d. multicoloured .. 30 35
16 **11** 1d. multicoloured (*shades*) 25 20
a. Booklet stamp with blank margins 50 60
17 **12** 2d. multicoloured .. 10 12
18 **13** 3d. multicoloured .. 10 12
19 **14** 4d. multicoloured .. 10 10
a. Booklet stamp with blank margins 30 30
20 **15** 5d. multicoloured .. 20 12
21 **16** 6d. multicoloured .. 50 50
22 **17** 9d. multicoloured .. 1·00 1·00
23 **18** 1s. multicoloured .. 1·00 1·00
24 **17** 1s. 6d. multicoloured .. 1·50 1·50
25 **19** 1s. 9d. multicoloured .. 1·75 1·75
26 **20** 2s. 6d. multicoloured .. 2·50 3·00
27 **21** 5s. multicoloured .. 15·00 14·00
28 **22** 10s. multicoloured .. 30·00 25·00
a. Error. Green border* .. £1750
29 **23** £1 multicoloured (*shades*) 2·00 2·50

*During the final printing of the 10s. a sheet was printed in the colours of the 50p., No. 56, i.e. green border instead of slate.

The 3d. is known with the orange omitted.

There was no postal need for the ½d. value as the ½d. coin had been withdrawn prior to its issue in anticipation of decimalisation.

Nos. 16a and 19a come from 2s. booklets for the automatic machines formerly used for the Great Britain 2s. booklets (see also note after Guernsey No. 28).

Various papers have been used by Harrisons. The ½d. and 1d. exist on much thicker paper from 2s. booklets and the 2d. to 1s. 9d. exist on thinner paper having white instead of creamy gum.

24. First Day Cover.

(Des. R. G. Sellar. Photo. Harrison.)

1969 (1 Oct.). *Inauguration of Post Office.* *P* 14.

30 **24** 4d. multicoloured 25 20
31 ,, 5d. multicoloured 50 30
32 ,, 1s. 6d. multicoloured .. 3·25 3·00
33 ,, 1s. 9d. multicoloured .. 3·25 3·00

25. Lord Coutanche, former Bailiff of Jersey.

26. Sir Winston Churchill. (*Vert.*)

27. " Liberation " (Edmund Blampied) (*Horiz.*)

28. S.S. *Vega.* (*Horiz.*)

(Des. Rosalind Dease. Photo. Courvoisier.)

1970 (9 May). *25th Anniv. of Liberation.* *P* 11½.

34 **25** 4d. multicoloured 20 20
35 **26** 5d. multicoloured 25 25
36 **27** 1s. 6d. multicoloured .. 3·00 3·00
37 **28** 1s. 9d. multicoloured .. 3·00 3·00

29. " A Tribute to Enid Blyton ".

30. " Rags to Riches " (Cinderella and pumpkin).

31. " Gourmet's Delight " (lobster and cornucopia).

32. " We're the Greatest " (ostriches).

(Des. Jennifer Toombs. Photo. Courvoisier.)

1970 (28 July). *" Battle of Flowers " Parade.* *P* 11½.

38 **29** 4d. multicoloured 20 20
39 **30** 5d. multicoloured 30 20
40 **31** 1s. 6d. multicoloured .. 9·00 5·00
41 **32** 1s. 9d. multicoloured .. 9·00 5·00

INVALIDATION. The regional issues for Jersey were invalidated for use in Jersey and Guernsey on 1st October 1969 but remained valid for use in the rest of the United Kingdom. Nos. 15/41 (except No. 29) and Nos. D1/6 were invalidated on 14th February 1972.

33. Jersey Airport.

(Des. V. Whiteley. Photo. Harrison (½ to 9p.); Courvoisier (others).)

1970–74. *Decimal Currency. Designs as T* **10** *etc., but with values inscr. in decimal currency as in T* **33**, *and new design* (*6p.*).

42 **10** ½p. multicoloured .. 5 5
a. Booklet stamp with blank margins 60 60
43 **13** 1p. multicoloured (*shades*) 5 5
44 **16** 1½p. multicoloured .. 5 5
45 **14** 2p. multicoloured .. 5 5
a. Booklet stamp with blank margins 50 50
46 **15** 2½p. multicoloured .. 8 8
a. Booklet stamp with blank margins 60 60
ab. Gold (Mace) omitted .. £150
47 **11** 3p. multicoloured .. 8 8
a. Booklet stamp with blank margins (1.12.72) .. 20 20
48 **12** 3½p. multicoloured .. 10 10
a. Booklet stamp with blank margins (1.7.74) 20 20
49 **17** 4p. multicoloured 10 10
49*a* **15** 4½p. multicoloured 10 10
50 **18** 5p. multicoloured 15 12
50*a* **16** 5½p. multicoloured 12 12
51 – 6p. multicoloured 15 15
52 **17** 7½p. multicoloured 20 20
52*a* **14** 8p. multicoloured 20 20
53 **19** 9p. multicoloured 25 25
54 **33** 10p. multicoloured 30 30
55 **21** 20p. multicoloured 50 50
56 **22** 50p. multicoloured .. .. 1·50 1·50

Design: *As T* **10**—6p. Martello Tower, Archirondel.

Dates of issue:—10p. to 50p., 1.10.70; 4½p., 5½p., 8p., 1.11.74; others, 15.2.71.

Original printings of the ½p. to 4p., 5p. and 6p. to 9p. were with PVA gum; printings from 1974 (including original printings of the 4½p. and 5½p.) have dextrin added (see notes after No. 873 of Great Britain). The 10p. to 50p. have gum arabic.

The border of No. 56 has been changed from turquoise-blue to dull green.

34. White-eared Pheasant.

(Des. Jennifer Toombs. Photo. Courvoisier.)

1971 (12 Mar.). *Wildlife Preservation Trust* (*1st series*). *T* **34** *and similar multicoloured designs.* *P* 11½.

57 2p. Type **34** 20 20
58 2½p. Thick-billed Parrot .. 25 25
59 7½p. Ursine Colobus Monkey 8·00 5·00
60 9p. Ring-tailed Lemur .. 8·00 5·00

The 2½p and 7½p are vertical designs.

See also Nos. 73/6.

35. Poppy Emblem and Field.

(Des. G. Drummond. Litho. Questa.)

1971 (15 June). *50th Anniv. of Royal British Legion.* *T* **35** *and similar horiz. designs. Multicoloured.* *P* 14.

61 2p. Royal British Legion Badge 15 15
62 2½p. Type **35** 20 20
63 7½p. Jack Counter, V.C., and Victoria Cross .. .. 3·50 3·00
64 9p. Crossed Tricolour and Union Jack .. .. 3·50 3·00

36. " Tante Elizabeth " (E. Blampied).

(Des. and photo. Courvoisier.)

1971 (5 Oct.). *Paintings* (*1st series*). *T* **36** *and similar multicoloured designs.* *P* 11½.

65 2p. Type **36** 15 15
66 2½p. " English Fleet in the Channel " (P. Monamy) 20 20
67 7½p. " The Boyhood of Raleigh " (Millais) .. .. .. 5·00 4·00
68 9p. " The Blind Beggar " (W. W. Ouless) .. .. 5·00 4·00

The 2½p. and 7½p. are horizontal designs.

See also Nos. 115/118.

37. Jersey Fern.

38. Artillery Shako.

(Des. G. Drummond. Photo. Courvoisier.)

1972 (18 Jan.). *Wild Flowers of Jersey. T* **37** *and similar vert. designs. Multicoloured. P* 11½.

69 3p. Type **37** 15 15
70 5p. Jersey Thrift 50 50
71 7½p. Jersey Orchid .. .. 3·00 2·50
72 9p. Jersey Viper's Bugloss .. 3·00 2·50

(Des. Jennifer Toombs. Photo. Courvoisier.)

1972 (17 Mar.). *Wildlife Preservation Trust (2nd series). Multicoloured designs similar to T* **34**. *P* 11½.

73 2½p. Cheetah (*horiz.*) 15 15
74 3p. Rothschild's Mynah (*vert.*) 20 20
75 7½p. Spectacled Bear (*horiz.*) .. 2·50 2·00
76 9p. Tuatara (*horiz.*) .. .. 2·50 2·00

(Des. and photo. Courvoisier.)

1972 (27 June). *Royal Jersey Militia. T* **38** *and similar vert. designs. Multicoloured. P* 11½.

77 2½p. Type **38** 15 15
78 3p. Shako (2nd North Regt.) 20 20
79 7½p. Shako (5th South-West Regt.) .. .. .. 2·00 1·50
80 9p. Helmet (3rd Jersey Light Infantry) .. .. 2·00 1·50

39. Princess Anne.

(Des. G. Drummond from photographs by D. Groves. Photo. Courvoisier.)

1972 (1 Nov.). *Royal Silver Wedding. T* **39** *and similar multicoloured designs. P* 11½.

81 2½p. Type **39** 5 5
82 3p. Queen Elizabeth and Prince Philip (*horiz.*) .. 8 8
83 7½p. Prince Charles (*vert.*) .. 60 65
84 20p. The Royal Family (*horiz.*) 60 75

40. Armorican Bronze Coins.

(Des. G. Drummond. Photo. Courvoisier.)

1973 (23 Jan.). *Centenary of La Société Jersiaise. T* **40** *and similar multicoloured designs. P* 11½.

85 2½p. Silver cups 15 15
86 3p. Gold torque (*vert.*) 20 20
87 7½p. Royal Seal of Charles II (*vert.*) .. .. .. 1·00 1·00
88 9p. Type **40** .. .. .. 1·00 1·00

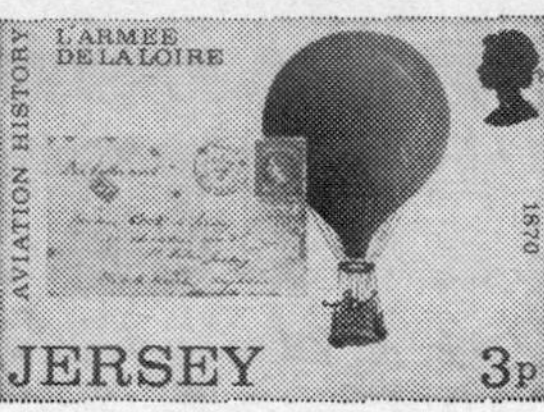

41. Balloon and Letter.

(Des. and photo. Courvoisier.)

1973 (16 May). *Jersey Aviation History. T* **41** *and similar horiz. designs. Multicoloured. P* 11½.

89 3p. Type **41** 15 15
90 5p. Seaplane "Astra" .. 20 20
91 7½p. Supermarine "Sea Eagle" 1·00 1·00
92 9p. De Havilland "Express" 1·00 1·00

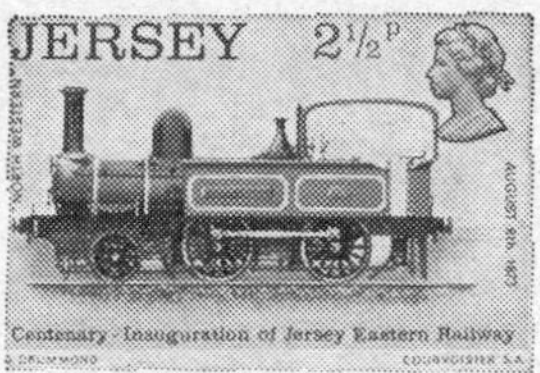

42. " North Western ".

(Des. G. Drummond. Photo. Courvoisier.)

1973 (6 Aug.). *Centenary of Jersey Eastern Railway. T* **42** *and similar designs showing early locomotives. Multicoloured. P* 11½.

93 2½p. Type **42** 15 15
94 3p. " Calvados " 20 20
95 7½p. " Carteret " 85 85
96 9p. " Caesarea " 85 85

43. Princess Anne and Capt. Mark Phillips.

(Des. and photo. Courvoisier.)

1973 (14 Nov.). *Royal Wedding. P* 11½.

97 **43** 3p. multicoloured .. 8 8
98 „ 20p. multicoloured .. 85 85

44. Spider Crab.

(Des. Jennifer Toombs. Photo. Courvoisier.)

1973 (15 Nov.). *Marine Life. T* **44** *and similar horiz. designs. Multicoloured. P* 11½.

99 2½p. Type **44** 8 8
100 3p. Conger eel 8 8
101 7½p. Lobster 35 45
102 20p. Ormer 35 45

45. Freesias.

(Des. G. Drummond. Photo. Courvoisier.)

1974 (13 Feb.). *Spring Flowers. T* **45** *and similar vert. designs. Multicoloured. P* 11½.

103 3p. Type **45** 8 8
104 5½p. Anemones 12 12
105 8p. Carnations and Gladioli 25 45
106 10p. Daffodils and Iris .. 25 45

46. First Letter Box and Contemporary Cover.

(Des. G. Drummond. Photo. Courvoisier.)

1974 (7 June). *U.P.U. Centenary. T* **46** *and similar horiz. designs. Multicoloured. P* 11½.

107 2½p. Type **46** 5 5
108 3p. Postmen, 1862 and 1969 8 8
109 5½p. Letter-box and letter, 1974 .. .. .. 20 20
110 20p. R.M.S. *Aquila* (1874) and aeroplane (1974) 80 80

47. John Wesley.

(Des., recess and litho. D.L.R.)

1974 (31 July). *Anniversaries. T* **47** *and similar vert. designs. P* 13×14.

111 3p. light cinnamon and black 5 8
112 3½p. light azure and black .. 8 8
113 8p. lt. mauve & deep ultram. 20 20
114 20p. pinkish stone and black .. 80 80

Portraits and Events:—3p. Type **47** (Bicentenary of Methodism in Jersey); 3½p. Sir William Hillary, founder (150th Anniv. of R.N.L.I.); 8p. Canon Wace, poet and historian (800th Death Anniv.); 20p. Sir Winston Churchill (Birth Centenary).

48. Royal Yacht.

(Des. and photo. Courvoisier.)

1974 (22 Nov.). *Paintings (2nd series).* *T* **48** *and similar multicoloured designs showing works by Peter Monamy.* *P* 11½.

115	3½p. Type **48**	8	8
116	5½p. French two-decker ..	12	12
117	8p. Dutch vessel (*horiz.*) ..	40	40
118	25p. The Battle of Cap La Hague (*55 × 27 mm.*) ..	80	80

49. Potato Digger.

(Des. G. Drummond. Photo. Courvoisier.)

1975 (25 Feb.). *19th-Century Farming.* *T* **49** *and similar horiz. designs. Multicoloured.* *P* 11½.

119	3p. Type **49**	5	5
120	3½p. Cider Crusher	8	8
121	8p. Six-horse plough	20	20
122	10p. Hay cart	30	30

50. H.M. Queen Elizabeth, the Queen Mother (photograph by Cecil Beaton).

(Des. and photo. Courvoisier.)

1975 (30 May). *Royal Visit.* *P* 11½.

123	**50**	20p. multicoloured ..	45	45

51. Shell.

(Des. A. Games. Photo. Courvoisier.)

1975 (6 June). *Jersey Tourism.* *T* **51** *and similar vert. designs based on holiday posters. Multicoloured.* *P* 11½.

124	5p. Type **51**	10	12
125	8p. Parasol	15	20
126	10p. Deckchair	20	20
127	12p. Sandcastle with flags of Jersey and the U.K. ..	30	30
MS128	146 × 68 mm. Nos. 124/7	70	70

52. Common Tern.

(Des. Jennifer Toombs. Photo. Courvoisier.)

1975 (28 July). *Sea Birds.* *T* **52** *and similar vert. designs. Multicoloured.* *P* 11½.

129	4p. Type **52**	8	10
130	5p. Storm Petrel	10	10
131	8p. Brent Geese	15	20
132	25p. Shag	50	50

53. Siskin "3-A".

(Des. A. Theobald. Photo. Courvoisier.)

1975 (30 Oct.). *50th Anniv. of Royal Air Forces Association, Jersey Branch.* *T* **53** *and similar horiz. designs. Multicoloured.* *P* 11½.

133	4p. Type **53**	8	10
134	5p. "Southampton" flying-boat	10	12
135	10p. Mk. I "Spitfire" ..	20	20
136	25p. Folland "Gnat" ..	50	60

54. Map of Jersey Parishes.

55. Parish Arms and Island Scene.

(Des. G. Drummond. Litho. Questa (½ to 15p.). Photo. Courvoisier (others).

1976. *Various multicoloured designs as T* **54/5.**

(*a*) *Paris Arms and Views as T* **54.** *P* 14½. (29 Jan.).

137	½p. Type **54**	5	5
138	1p. Zoological Park	5	5
	a. Booklet pane of 4 (No. 138) plus 2 *se-tenant* labels ..	10	
	b. Booklet pane. No. 138 × 4 ..	20	
139	5p. St. Mary's Church ..	8	10
	a. Booklet pane of 4	50	
140	6p. Seymour Tower	10	12
141	7p. La Corbière Lighthouse	12	15
	a. Booklet pane of 4	50	
142	8p. St. Saviour's Church ..	15	15
143	9p. Elizabeth Castle	15	20
144	10p. Gorey Harbour	20	20
145	11p. Jersey Airport	20	25
146	12p. Grosnez Castle	20	25
147	13p. Bonne Nuit Harbour ..	25	25
148	14p. Le Hocq Tower	25	25
149	15p. Morel Farm	25	30

(*b*) *Emblems as T* **55.** *P* 12. (20 Aug.).

150	20p. Type **55**	35	40
151	30p. Flag and map	55	65
152	40p. Postal H.Q. and badge ..	70	80
153	50p. Parliament, Royal Court and arms	85	95
154	£1 Lieutenant-Governor's flag and Government House ..	1·75	2·00

Nos. 155/9 have been reserved for further additions to this issue.

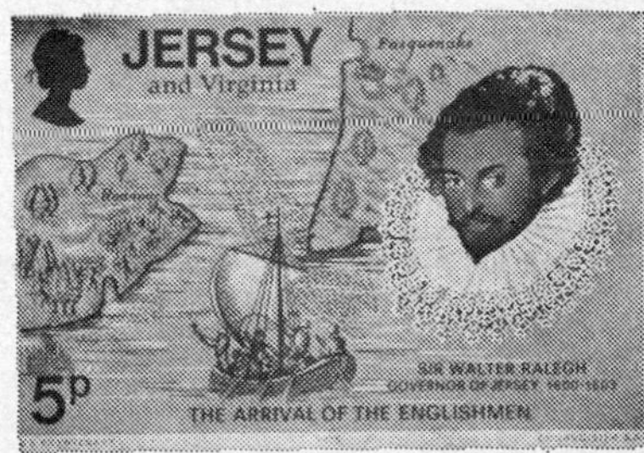

56. Sir Walter Ralegh and Map of Virginia.

(Des. M. D. Orbell. Photo. Courvoisier.)

1976 (29 May). *"Links with America".* *T* **56** *and similar horiz. designs. Multicoloured.* *P* 11½.

160	5p. Type **56**	10	12
161	7p. Sir George Carteret and map of New Jersey ..	15	15
162	11p. Philippe Dauvergne and Long Island Landing ..	25	25
163	13p. John Copley and sketch ..	25	30

57. Dr. Grandin and Map of China.

(Des. Jennifer Toombs. Photo. Courvoisier.)

1976 (25 Nov.). *Birth Centenary of Dr. Lilian Grandin (medical missionary). T* **57** *and similar horiz. designs. P* $11\frac{1}{2}$.

164	5p. multicoloured	10	10
165	7p. light yellow, yellow-brown and black..	15	15
166	11p. multicoloured	20	25
167	13p. multicoloured	25	30

Designs:—7p. Sampan on the Yangtze; 11p. Overland trek; 13p. Dr. Grandin at work.

58. Coronation, 1953 (photographed by Cecil Beaton).

(Des. G. Drummond. Photo. Courvoisier.)

1977 (7 Feb.). *Silver Jubilee. T* **58** *and similar vert. designs. Multicoloured. P* $11\frac{1}{2}$.

168	5p. Type **58**	10	12
169	7p. Visit to Jersey, 1957	15	15
170	25p. Queen Elizabeth II (photo by Peter Grugeon) ..	50	60

59. Coins of 1871 and 1877 (38 × 24 *mm.*).

(Des. D. Henley. Litho. Questa.)

1977 (25 Mar.). *Centenary of Currency Reform. T* **59** *and similar horiz. designs. Multicoloured. P* 14.

171	5p. Type **59**	10	12
172	7p. One-twelfth shilling, 1949	15	15
173	11p. Silver Crown, 1966 ..	25	25
174	13p. £2 piece, 1972	25	30

The Jersey Post Office have announced the following further issues for 1977:

24 June	Centenary of St. John's Ambulance
29 September	125th Anniv. of Victoria College

For full information on all future Jersey issues, collectors should write to the Jersey Philatelic Bureau, P.O. Box 304, St. Helier, Jersey.

POSTAGE DUE STAMPS.

D 1

D 2. Map.

(Des. F. W. Guenier. Litho. Bradbury, Wilkinson.)

1969 (1 Oct.). *P* $14 \times 13\frac{1}{2}$.

D1	D 1	1d. bluish violet	1·00	1·00
D2	,,	2d. sepia	1·00	1·00
D3	,,	3d. magenta	2·00	1·50
D4	D 2	1s. bright emerald ..	7·50	5·00
D5	,,	2s. 6d. olive-grey ..	20·00	12·00
D6	,,	5s. vermilion	35·00	28·00

1971 (15 Feb.)–**75.** *As Type* D **2** *but values in decimal currency.*

D 7	$\frac{1}{2}$p. black	5	5
D 8	1p. violet-blue	5	5
D 9	2p. olive-grey	5	5
D10	3p. reddish purple	5	8
D11	4p. pale red	8	10
D12	5p. bright emerald ..	8	10
D13	6p. yellow-orange (12.8.74)	10	12
D14	7p. bistre-yellow (12.8.74) ..	10	12
D15	8p. lt. greenish blue (1.5.75)	15	20
D16	10p. pale olive-grey	20	25
D17	11p. ochre (1.5.75)	20	25
D18	14p. violet	25	30
D19	25p. myrtle-green (12.8.74) ..	45	50
D20	50p. dull purple (1.5.75) ..	85	95

ISLE OF MAN.

(a) Regional Issues.

Although specifically issued for use in the Isle of Man, these issues were also valid for use throughout Great Britain.

DATES OF ISSUE: The note at the beginning of Guernsey also applies here.

Nos. 8/11 and current stamps of Great Britain were withdrawn from sale on the island from 5th July 1973 when their independent postal administration was established but remained valid for use there for a time. They also remained on sale at the Philatelic Sales counters in the United Kingdom until 4th July 1974.

1

2

(Des. J. H. Nicholson. Portrait by Dorothy Wilding Ltd. Photo. Harrison.)

1958 (18 Aug.)–**68.** *W* **179.** *P* 15×14.

1	**1**	$2\frac{1}{2}$d. carmine-red (8.6.64) ..	90	90
2	**2**	3d. deep lilac	20	8
		a. Chalky paper (17.5.63) ..	20·00	10·00
		p. One centre phosphor band (27.6.68)	15	30
3	,,	4d. ultramarine (7.2.66) ..	1·50	40
		p. Two phosphor bands (5.7.67)	15	12

No. 2a was released in London sometime after 17th May 1963, this being the date of issue in Douglas.

1968–69. *No wmk. Chalky paper. PVA gum. One centre phosphor band (Nos. 5/6) or two phosphor bands (others). P* 15×14.

4	**2**	4d. blue (24.6.68)	15	25
5	,,	4d. olive-sepia (4.9.68) ..	40	30
6	,,	4d. brt. vermilion (26.2.69) ..	90	50
7	,,	5d. Royal blue (4.9.68) ..	1·50	20

3

(Des. J. Matthews. Portrait after plaster cast by Arnold Machin. Photo. Harrison.)

1971 (7 July). *Decimal Currency. Chalky paper. One centre phosphor band* ($2\frac{1}{2}$*p.*) *or two phosphor bands (others). P* 15×14.

8	**3**	$2\frac{1}{2}$p. bright magenta ..	15	15
9	,,	3p. ultramarine	25	25
10	,,	5p. reddish violet	30	30
11	,,	$7\frac{1}{2}$p. chestnut..	40	40

All values exist with PVA gum on ordinary cream paper and the $2\frac{1}{2}$p. and 3p. also on fluorescent white paper.

(b) Independent Postal Administration.

4. Castletown.

5. Manx Cat.

(Des. J. H. Nicholson. Photo. Courvoisier.)

1973 (5 July)–**75**. *Horiz. designs as T* **4** (*½p. to 9p.*) *or vert. designs as T* **5** (*others*). *Multicoloured. P* 11½.

12	½p. Type **4**	5	5
13	1p. Port Erin	5	5
14	1½p. Snaefell	5	5
15	2p. Laxey	5	5
16	2½p. Tynwald Hill	5	5
17	3p. Douglas Promenade	5	5
18	3½p. Port St. Mary	5	5
19	4p. Fairy Bridge	8	8
20	4½p. As 2½p. (8.1.75)	8	8
21	5p. Peel	8	8
22	5½p. As 3p. (28.5.75)	10	10
23	6p. Cregneish	10	10
24	7p. As 2p. (28.5.75)	12	12
25	7½p. Ramsey Bay	12	12
26	8p. As 7½p. (8.1.75)	15	15
27	9p. Douglas Bay	15	15
28	10p. Type **5**	20	20
29	11p. Monk's Bridge, Ballasalla (29.10.75)	20	20
30	13p. Derbyhaven (29.10.75)	25	25
31	20p. Manx Loaghtyn Ram	35	35
32	50p. Manx Shearwater	85	85
33	£1 Viking Longship	1·75	1·75

Printings from late 1973 have invisible gum.

6. Viking landing on Man, A.D. 938.

(Des. J. H. Nicholson. Photo. Harrison.)

1973 (5 July). *Inauguration of Postal Independence. P* 14.

34 **6** 15p. multicoloured .. .. 1·75 1·75

7. " Sutherland ".

(Des. J. H. Nicholson. Photo. Harrison.)

1973 (4 Aug.). *Steam Railway Centenary. T* **7** *and similar horiz. designs. Multicoloured. P* 15 × 14.

35	2½p. Type **7**	10	10
36	3p. " Caledonia "	10	10
37	7½p. " Kissack "	1·75	1·75
38	9p. " Pender "	1·75	1·75

8. Leslie Randles, First Winner, 1923.

(Des. J. H. Nicholson. Litho. J.W.)

1973 (4 Sept.). *Golden Jubilee of the Manx Grand Prix. T* **8** *and similar horiz. design. Multicoloured. P* 14.

39	3p. Type **8**	30	30
40	3½p. Alan Holmes, Double Winner, 1957	30	30

9. Princess Anne and Capt. Mark Phillips.

(Des. A. S. Larkins. Litho. and recess. D.L.R.)

1973 (14 Nov.). *Royal Wedding. P* 13½.

41 **9** 25p. multicoloured .. .. 2·00 1·75

10. Badge, Citation and Sir William Hillary (Founder).

(Des. J. H. Nicholson. Photo. Courvoisier.)

1974 (4 Mar.). *150th Anniv. of Royal National Lifeboat Institution. T* **10** *and similar horiz. designs. Multicoloured. P* 11½.

42	3p. Type **10**	10	10
43	3½p. Wreck of *St. George*, 1830	12	12
44	8p. R.N.L.B. *Manchester & Salford*, 1868–87	70	70
45	10p. R.N.L.B. *Osman Gabriel*	70	70

11. Stanley Woods, 1935.

(Des. J. H. Nicholson. Litho. D.L.R.)

1974 (29 May). *Tourist Trophy Motor-cycle Races* (1*st issue*). *T* **11** *and similar horiz. designs. Multicoloured. P* 13 × 13½.

46	3p. Type **11**	8	8
47	3½p. Freddy Frith, 1937	8	8
48	8p. Max Deubel and Emil Horner, 1961	45	45
49	10p. Mike Hailwood, 1961	45	45

See also Nos. 63/6.

12. Rushen Abbey and Arms.

(Des. J. H. Nicholson from ideas by G. V. H. Kneale. Litho. Questa (3½p., 10p.) or J.W. (others).)

1974 (18 Sept.). *Historical Anniversaries. T* **12** *and similar horiz. designs. Multicoloured. P* 14.

50	3½p. Type **12**	8	8
51	4½p. Magnus Haraldson rows King Edgar on the Dee	12	12
52	8p. King Magnus and Norse fleet	35	35
53	10p. Bridge at Avignon and bishop's mitre	35	35

Nos. 50 and 53 mark the 600th Death Anniv. of William Russell, Bishop of Sodor and Man, and Nos. 51/2 the 1000th Anniv. of the rule of King Magnus Haraldson.

13. Churchill and Bugler Dunne at Colenso, 1899.

(Des. G. V. H. Kneale. Photo. Courvoisier.)

1974 (22 Nov.). *Birth Centenary of Sir Winston Churchill. T* **13** *and similar horiz. designs. Multicoloured. P* 11½.

54	3½p. Type **13**	8	8
55	4½p. Churchill and Government Buildings, Douglas	10	10
56	8p. Churchill and Manx ack-ack crew	50	50
57	20p. Churchill as Freeman of Douglas	50	50
MS58	121 × 91 mm. Nos. 54/7	1·00	1·00

MS58 is inscribed " 30th Nov. 1974 ".

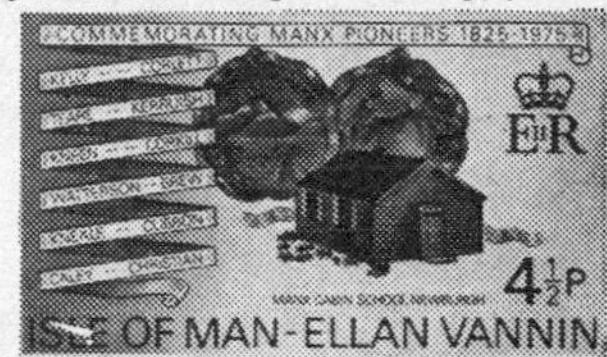

14. Cabin School and Names of Pioneers.

(Des. J. H. Nicholson. Photo. Courvoisier.)

1975 (14 Mar.). *Manx Pioneers in Cleveland, Ohio. T* **14** *and similar horiz. designs. Multicoloured. P* 11½.

59	4½p. Type **14**	10	10
60	5½p. Terminal Tower Building, J. Gill and R. Carran	12	12
61	8p. Clague House Museum, and Robert and Margaret Clague	20	20
62	10p. S.S. *William T. Graves* and Thomas Quayle	30	30

ISLE OF MAN 5½p

15. Tom Sheard, 1923.

(Des. J. H. Nicholson. Litho. J.W.)

1975 (28 May). *Tourist Trophy Motor-cycle Races (2nd issue). T* **15** *and similar horiz. designs. Multicoloured. P* 13½.
63 5½p. Type **15** 10 12
64 7p. Walter Handley, 1925 .. 15 15
65 10p. Geoff Duke, 1955 .. .. 20 25
66 12p. Peter Williams, 1973 .. 25 30

16. Sir George Goldie and Birthplace.

(Des. G. V. H. Kneale. Photo. Courvoisier).

1975 (9 Sept.). *50th Death Anniv. of Sir George Goldie. T* **16** *and similar multicoloured designs. P* 11½.
67 5½p. Type **16** 10 12
68 7p. Goldie and map of Africa (*vert.*) 15 15
69 10p. Goldie as President of Geographical Society (*vert.*) .. 20 25
70 12p. River scene on the Niger .. 25 30

17. Title Page of Manx Bible.

(Des. J. H. Nicholson. Litho. Questa.)

1975 (29 Oct.). *Christmas and Bicentenary of Manx Bible. T* **17** *and similar horiz. designs. Multicoloured. P* 14.
71 5½p. Type **17** 10 12
72 7p. Rev. Philip Moore and Ballaugh Old Church .. 15 15
73 11p. Bishop Hildesley and Bishops Court 20 25
74 13p. John Kelly saving Bible manuscript 25 30

18. William Christian listening to Patrick Henry.

(Des. and Litho. J.W.)

1976 (12 Mar.). *Bicentenary of American Revolution. T* **18** *and similar vert. designs. Multicoloured. P* 13½.
75 5½p. Type **18** 10 12
76 7p. Conveying the Fincastle Resolutions 15 15
77 13p. Patrick Henry and William Christian 25 30
78 20p. Christian as an Indian fighter 40 45
MS79 153×89 mm. Nos. 75/8. P 14 .. .. 1·00

19. First Horse Tram, 1876.

(Des. J. H. Nicholson. Photo. Courvoisier.)

1976 (26 May). *Douglas Horse Trams Centenary. T* **19** *and similar horiz. designs. Multicoloured. P* 11½.
80 5½p. Type **19** 10 12
81 7p. "Toast-rack" tram, 1890 15 15
82 11p. Horse-bus, 1895 .. .. 20 25
83 13p. Royal tram, 1972 .. .. 25 30

20. Barrose Beaker.

21. Diocesan Banner.

(Des. J. H. Nicholson. Photo. Courvoisier.)

1976 (28 July). *Europa. Ceramic Art. T* **20** *and similar multicoloured designs. P* 11½.
84 5p. Type **20** 50 50
85 5p. Souvenir teapot 50 50
86 5p. Laxey jug 50 50
87 10p. Cronk Aust food vessel (*horiz.*) 80 80
88 10p. Sansbury bowl (*horiz.*) .. 80 80
89 10p. Knox urn (*horiz.*) 80 80

Nos. 84/6 and 87/9 were each printed in sheets of 9 (3×3) the three designs being horizontally and vertically *se-tenant*.

(Des. G. V. H. Kneale. Litho. Questa.)

1976 (14 Oct.). *Christmas and Centenary of Mothers' Union. T* **21** *and similar vert. designs. Multicoloured. P* 14½.
90 6p. Type **21** 12 15
91 7p. Onchan banner 15 15
92 11p. Castletown banner .. 25 25
93 13p. Ramsey banner 25 30

22. Queen Elizabeth II. (41×25 *mm.*).

(Des. A. Larkins. Litho. and recess. D.L.R.)

1977 (1 Mar.). *Silver Jubilee. T* **22** *and similar multicoloured designs. P* 14×13 (*7p.*) *or* 13×14 (*others*).
94 6p. Type **22** 12 15
95 7p. Queen Elizabeth and Prince Philip (*vert.*) 15 15
96 25p. Queen Elizabeth 50 55

The 25p. is similar to T **22** but has the portrait on the right.

The Isle of Man Post Office have announced the following further issues for 1977:

25 May — Europa (landscapes)
25 May — Anniversaries
Sept./Oct. — 200th Anniv. of John Wesley's Visit

For full information on all future issues, collectors should write to the Isle of Man Philatelic Bureau, P.O. Box IOM, Douglas.

POSTAGE DUE STAMPS

D 1

D 2

(Litho. Questa.)

1973 (5 July). *P* 13½×14.
D1 D **1** ½p. red, black and bistre-yellow 15 20
D2 „ 1p. red, blk. & cinnamon 20 20
D3 „ 2p. red, black and light apple-green 40 30
D4 „ 3p. red, black and grey . 60 45
D5 „ 4p. red, blk. & carm.-rose 80 60
D6 „ 5p. red, black & cobalt 1·00 75
D7 „ 10p. red. black & lt. lav. 2·00 1·50
D8 „ 20p. red, black & pale turquoise-green .. 4·00 3·00

A second printing of all values was released on 1 September 1973. These can be distinguished by the addition of a small "A" after the date "1973" in the bottom left margin of the stamps. Spurious examples of the second printing exist with the "A" removed.

Prices quoted above are for the second printing. Prices for set of 8 original printing £22 un., £18 us.

(Des. and litho. Questa.)

1975 (8 Jan.). *Arms and inscriptions in black and red; background colour given. P* 14×13½.
D 9 D **2** ½p. greenish yellow .. 5 5
D10 „ 1p. flesh 5 5
D11 „ 4p. rose-lilac 8 8
D12 „ 7p. light greenish blue .. 12 12
D13 „ 9p. brownish grey .. 15 15
D14 „ 10p. bright mauve .. 20 20
D15 „ 50p. orange-yellow .. 85 85
D16 „ £1 turquoise-green .. 1·75 1·75

GREAT BRITAIN STAMPS USED ABROAD.

INDEX

STAMPS OF GREAT BRITAIN OBLITERATED WITH ONE OF THE FOLLOWING TYPES:—

I. Horizontal oval.

(1) (2) (3) (4)

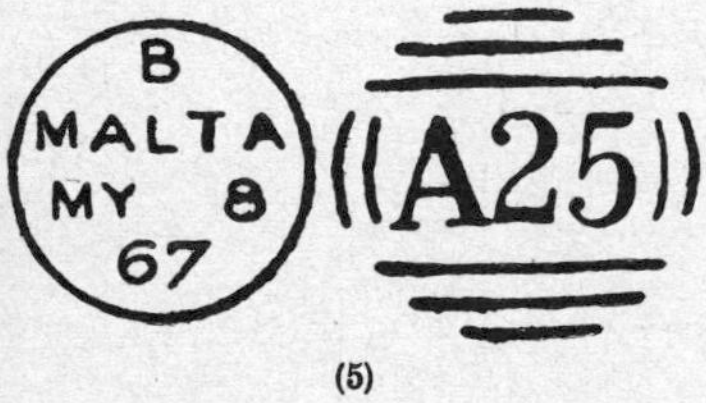

(5) (6) (7)

II. Vertical oval.

(8)

(9)

(or with stop after " S ")
(10)

(11)

(12)

(13)

(14)

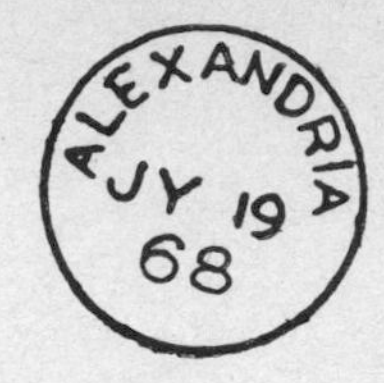

(15)

III. Circular date stamps.

(16)

(17)

(18)

(19)

(20)

NOTE.—Prices quoted for British stamps used abroad are for single stamps not on envelopes unless otherwise stated. Stamps on envelopes are worth considerably more in most instances.

In many instances obliterators allotted to post offices abroad were, at a later date, re-allotted to post offices at home. Later issues than those included in our lists can therefore safely be regarded as *not* " used abroad ".

I.

Used in British Possessions in Europe.

MALTA.

Wavy Lines.

1855–58. *Wavy lines obliteration.*

ZM 1 1d. red-brown (1854), Die I, *wmk.* Small Crown, *perf.* 16 .. ..
ZM 2 1d. red-brown (1855), Die II, *wmk.* Small Crown, *Perf.* 14 ..
a. Very blued paper .. .. ..
ZM 3 1d. red-brown (1855), Die II, *wmk.* Large Crown, *perf.* 16 ..
ZM 4 2d. blue (1855), *wmk.* Large Crown, *perf.* 14 (Plate 5) ..
ZM 5 1s. (1847) embossed .. .. ..

It is now established that this obliterator was sent to Malta in February 1855 but it was mainly used on mail in transit emanating from the Crimea.

1857–85.

" M " *Obliteration, T* 1.

Z 1 1d. red-brown (1841) £200
Z 1*a* 1d. red-brown, Die I, *wmk.* Small Crown, *perf.* 16 .. .. 22·00
Z 1*b* 1d. red-brown, Die II, *wmk.* Small Crown, *perf.* 16 .. .. £225
Z 1*c* 1d. red-brown, Die II (1855), *wmk.* Small Crown, *perf.* 14 .. 40·00
Z 2 1d. red-brown, Die II (1855), *wmk.* Large Crown, *perf.* 14 .. 18·00
Z 3 1d. rose-red (1857), *wmk.* Large Crown, *perf.* 14 .. .. 7·00
Z 3*a* 2d. blue (1841), *imperf.* £550
Z 3*b* 2d. blue (1854), *wmk.* Small Crown, *perf.* 16 (Plate 4) £200
Z 4 2d. blue (1855), *wmk.* Large Crown, *perf.* 14 (Plates, 5, 6) .. .. 22·00
Z 5 2d. blue (1858), *wmk.* Large Crown, *perf.* 16 (Plate 6) .. .. 65·00
Z 6 2d. bl. (1858) (Pl. Nos. 7, 8, 9) *From* 9·00
Z 7 4d. rose (1857) .. .. .. 14·00
a. Thick glazed paper .. .. 50·00
Z 8 6d. violet (1854), embossed .. £500
Z 9 6d. lilac (1856) .. .. .. 15·00
a. Thick paper .. .. 55·00
Z 10 6d. lilac (1856) (blued *paper*) .. £275
Z 11 1s. green (1856) .. .. .. 45·00

" A 25 " *Obliteration as T* 1, 2, 5, 6, 8 *or* 11.

Z 12 ½d. rose-red (1870–79) .. *From* 6·50
Plate Nos. 4, 5, 6, 8, 9, 10, 11, 12, 13, 14, 15, 19, 20.
Z 13 1d. red-brown (1841), *imperf.* .. £275
Z 13*a* 1d. red-brown (1854), *wmk.* Small Crown, *perf.* 16 .. .. 65·00
Z 14 1d. red-brown (1855), *wmk.* Large Crown, *perf.* 14 .. .. 20·00
Z 15 1d. rose-red (1857), *wmk.* Large Crown, *perf.* 14 .. .. 3·50
Z 15*a* 1d. rose-red (1861), Alphabet IV ..
Z 15*b* 1d. rose-red (1862), Alphabet II (Res. Pl. 16) .. .. 24·00
Z 16 1d. rose-red (1864–79) .. *From* 5·50
Plate Nos. 71, 72, 73, 74, 76, 78, 79, 80, 81, 82, 83, 84, 85, 86, 87, 88, 89, 90, 91, 92, 93, 94, 95, 96, 97, 98, 99, 100, 101, 102, 103, 104, 105, 106, 107, 108, 109, 110, 111, 112, 113, 114, 115, 116, 117, 118, 119, 120, 121, 122, 123, 124, 125, 127, 129, 130, 131, 132, 133, 134, 135, 136, 137, 138, 139, 140, 141, 142, 143, 144, 145, 146, 147, 148, 149, 150, 151, 152, 153, 154, 155, 156, 157, 158, 159, 160, 161, 162, 163, 164, 165, 166, 167, 168, 169, 170, 171, 172, 173, 174, 175, 176, 177, 178, 179, 180, 181, 182, 183, 184, 185, 186, 187, 188, 189, 190, 191, 192, 193, 194, 195, 196, 197, 198, 199, 200, 201, 202, 203, 204, 205, 206, 207, 208, 209, 210, 212, 213, 214, 215, 216, 217, 218, 219, 220, 221, 222, 223, 224.
Z 17 1½d. lake-red (1870–79) (Plates, 1, 3) 65·00
Z 17*a* 2d. blue (1841), *imperf.* £500
Z 17*b* 2d. blue (1855), *wmk.* Large Crown, *perf.* 14 .. .. .. 13·00
Z 18 2d. blue (1858–69) .. *From* 7·00
Plate Nos. 7, 8, 9, 12, 13, 14, 15.
Z 19 2½d. rosy mauve (1875) (blued *paper*) Plate Nos. 1, 2 .. *From* 20·00
Z 20 2½d. rosy mauve (1875–76) *From* 8·50
Plate Nos. 1, 2, 3 .. ..
Z 21 2½d. rosy mauve (*Error of Lettering*) £700
Z 22 2½d. rosy mauve (1876–79) *From* 6·00
Plate Nos. 3, 4, 5, 6, 7, 8, 9, 10, 11, 12, 13, 14, 15, 16, 17.
Z 23 2½d. blue (1880–81) .. *From* 3·50
Plate Nos. 17, 18, 19, 20.
Z 24 2½d. blue (1881) .. .. *From* 2·75
Plate Nos. 21, 22, 23.
Z 25 3d. carmine-rose (1862) .. .. 38·00
Z 26 3d. rose (1865) (Plate No. 4) .. 14·00
Z 27 3d. rose (1867–73) .. *From* 6·00
Plate Nos. 4, 5, 6, 7, 8, 9, 10.
Z 28 3d rose (1873–76) .. *From* 6·00
Plate Nos. 11, 12, 14, 15, 16, 17, 18, 19, 20.
Z 29 3d. rose (1881) (Plate Nos. 20, 21) 7·00
Z 30 3d. lilac (1883) (3d. *on* 3d.) ..
Z 31 4d. rose (or rose-carmine) (1857) 11·00
a. Thick glazed paper .. .. 35·00
Z 32 4d. red (1862) (Plates 3, 4) *From* 12·00
Z 33 4d. vermilion (1865–73) .. „ 9·00
Plate Nos. 7, 8, 9, 10, 11, 12, 13, 14.
Z 34 4d. vermilion (1876) (Plate No. 15) 65·00
Z 35 4d. sage-grn. (1877) (Pl. 15, 16) .. 22·00
Z 36 4d. grey-brown (1880) *wmk.* Large Garter. (Plate No. 17) .. 27·00
Z 37 4d. grey-brown (1880) *wmk.* Crown 6·50
Plate Nos. 17, 18.
Z 37*a* 6d. violet (1854), embossed ..
Z 38 6d. lilac (1856) .. .. .. 14·00
Z 39 6d. lilac (1862) (Plates 3, 4) *From* 13·00
Z 40 6d. lilac (1865–67) (Pl. 5, 6) „ 12·00
Z 40*a* 6d. lilac (1865–67) (*Wmk. error*) ..
Z 41 6d. lilac (1867) (Plate No. 6) .. 13·00
Z 42 6d. violet (1867–70) .. *From* 11·00
Plate Nos. 6, 8, 9.
Z 43 6d. buff (1872–73) (Pl. 11, 12) „ 50·00
Z 44 6d. chestnut (1872) (Plate No. 11) 8·00
Z 45 6d. grey (1873) (Plate No. 12) .. 16·00
Z 46 6d. grey (1873–80) .. .. *From* 7·00
Plate Nos. 13, 14, 15, 16, 17.
Z 47 6d. grey (1881–82) (Pl. 17, 18) *From* 5·50
Z 48 6d. lilac (1883) (6d. *on* 6d.) .. 35·00
Z 49 8d. orange (1876) £100
Z 50 9d. straw (1862) £140
Z 51 9d. bistre (1862) £150
Z 51*a* 9d. straw (1865) £150
Z 51*b* 9d. straw (1867) £200
Z 52 10d. red-brown (1867) .. .. 85·00
Z 52*a* 1s. (1847), embossed £350
Z 53 1s. green (1856) .. .. .. 22·00
Z 53*a* 1s. green (1856) (thick *paper*) .. 80·00
Z 54 1s. green (1862) .. .. .. 18·00
Z 55 1s. green (" K " *variety*) £700
Z 56 1s. green (1865) (Plate No. 4) .. 11·00
Z 57 1s. green (1867–73) .. *From* 3·50
Plate Nos. 4, 5, 6, 7.
Z 58 1s. green (1873–77) .. *From* 11·00
Plate Nos. 8, 9, 10, 11, 12, 13.

z 59 1s. orange-brown (1880) (Pl. 13) .. 75·00

z 60 1s. orange-brown (1881) .. *From* 10·00
Plate Nos. 13, 14.

z 61 2s. blue (*shades*) (1867) .. *From* 24·00

z 62 2s. brown (1880) £550

z 63 5s. rose (1867–74) (Pl. 1, 2) *From* 55·00

z 64 5s. rose (1882) (Plate No. 4), blue *paper* £300

z 65 5s. rose (1882) (Plate No. 4), white *paper* £300

z 66 10s. grey-green (1878) £500

1880

z 67 ½d. deep green .. .. .. 3·00

z 68 ½d. pale green .. .. .. 3·00

z 69 1d. Venetian red .. .. .. 2·25

z 69a 1½d. Venetian red .. .. .. 9·00

z 70 2d. pale rose .. .. .. 10·00

z 71 2d. deep rose .. .. .. 10·00

z 72 5d. indigo .. .. .. 16·00

1881

z 73 1d. lilac (14 *dots*) .. .. .. 5·00

z 74 1d. lilac (16 ,,) .. .. .. 2·00

1883–4

z 75–z 79 ½d. slate-blue; 1½d., 2d., 2½d., 3d. .. .. .. *From* 3·50

z 80–z 83a 4d., 5d., 6d., 9d., 1s. ,, 20·00

z 84 5s. rose (blued *paper*) £375

z 85 5s. rose (white ,,) £250

POSTAL FISCALS.

z 86 1d. purple (1871), *wmk.* Anchor .. £200

z 86a 1d. purple (1881) ,, Orb .. £160

GIBRALTAR.

1857

"G" *Obliteration as T* **1a.**

z 87 1d. red-brown (1854) Die I .. 80·00

z 87a 1d. red-brown (1855), Die II, *wmk.* Small Crown, *perf.* 16. £140

z 88 1d. red-brown (1855), Die II, *wmk.* Small Crown, *perf.* 14.. 65·00

z 89 1d. red-brown (1855), Die II, *wmk.* Large Crown, *perf.* 14 20·00

z 90 1d. rose-red (1857), Die II, *wmk.* Large Crown, *perf.* 14 .. 7·00

z 91 2d. blue (1855), *wmk.* Small Crown, *perf.* 14 .. .. 80·00

z 92 2d. blue (1855–58), *wmk.* Large Crown, *perf.* 16 .. .. 80·00

z 93 2d. blue (1855), *wmk.* Large Crown, *perf.* 14 (Plate Nos. 5, 6) .. .. .. *From* 17·00

z 94 2d. blue (1858) (Plate No. 7) .. 50·00

z 95 4d. rose (1857) .. .. .. 14·00

z 96 6d. lilac (1856) .. .. .. 14·00

z 96a 6d. lilac (1856) (blued *paper*) .. £200

z 97 1s. green (1856) .. .. .. 24·00

z 97a 1s. green (1856) (blued *paper*) .. £400

"A 26" *Obliteration as T* **2, 5, 11** *or* **14.**

z 98 ½d. rose-red (1870–79) .. *From* 4·50
Plate Nos. 4, 5, 6, 8, 10, 11, 12, 13, 14, 15, 19, 20.

z 98a 1d. red-brown (1841), *imperf.*

z 99 1d. red-brown (1855), *wmk.* Large Crown, *perf.* 14 .. .. 40·00

z 100 1d. rose-red (1857), *wmk.* Large Crown, *perf.* 14 .. .. 4·00

z 101 1d. rose-red (1864–79) .. *From* 6·00
Plate Nos. 71, 72, 73, 74, 76, 78, 79, 80, 81, 82, 83, 84, 85, 86, 87, 88, 89, 90, 91, 92, 93, 94, 95, 96, 97, 98, 99, 100, 101, 102, 103, 104, 105, 106, 107, 108, 109, 110, 111, 112, 113, 114, 115, 116, 117, 118, 119, 120, 121, 122, 123, 124, 125, 127, 129, 130, 131, 132, 133, 134, 135, 136, 137, 138, 139, 140, 142, 143, 144, 145, 146, 147, 148, 149, 150, 151, 152, 153, 154, 155, 156, 157, 158, 159, 160, 161, 162, 163, 164, 165, 166, 167, 168, 169, 170, 171, 172, 173, 174, 175, 176, 177, 178, 179, 180, 181, 182, 183, 184, 185, 186, 187, 188, 189, 190, 191, 192, 193, 194, 195, 196, 197, 198, 199, 200, 201, 202, 203, 204, 205, 206, 207, 208, 209, 210, 211, 212, 213, 214, 215, 216, 217, 218, 219, 220, 221, 222, 223, 224, 225.

z 102 1½d. lake-red (1870) (Pl. 3) ..

z 103 2d. blue (1855), *wmk.* Large Crown, *perf.* 14 (Plate No. 6) 30·00

z 104 2d. blue (1858–69) .. *From* 6·00
Plate Nos. 7, 8, 9, 12, 13, 14, 15.

z 105 2½d. rosy mauve (1875) (blued *paper*) (Plate Nos. 1, 2) *From* 30·00

z 106 2½d. rosy mauve (1875–76) ,, 8·50
Plate Nos. 1, 2, 3.

z 107 2½d. rosy mauve (*Error of Lettering*)

z 108 2½d. rosy mauve (1876–79) *From* 7·00
Plate Nos. 3, 4, 5, 6, 7, 8, 9, 10, 11, 12, 13, 14, 15, 16, 17.

z 109 2½d. blue (1880–81) .. *From* 4·50
Plate Nos. 17, 18, 19, 20.

z 110 2½d. blue (1881) .. *From* 3·50
Plate Nos. 21, 22, 23.

z 111 3d. carmine-rose (1862) .. .. 40·00

z 112 3d. rose (1865) (Plate No. 4) .. 14·00

z 113 3d. rose (1867–73) .. *From* 6·00
Plate Nos. 4, 5, 6, 7, 8, 9, 10.

z 114 3d. rose (1873–76) .. .. *From* 7·00
Plate Nos. 11, 12, 14, 15, 16, 17, 18, 19, 20.

z 115 3d. rose (1881) (Plate Nos. 20, 21)

z 116 3d. lilac (1883) (3d. *on* 3d.) .. 20·00

z 117 4d. rose (1857) .. .. .. 14·00

z 118 4d. red (1862) (Plates 3, 4) *From* 15·00

z 119 4d. vermilion (1865–73) .. ,, 11·00
Plate Nos. 7, 8, 9, 10, 11, 12, 13, 14.

z 120 4d. vermilion (1876) (Plate No. 15) 60·00

z 121 4d. sage-green (1877) .. .. 25·00
Plate Nos. 15, 16.

z 122 4d. grey-brown (1880) *wmk.* Large Garter (Plate No. 17) .. 30·00

z 123 4d. grey-brown (1880) *wmk.* Crown (Plate Nos. 17, 18) .. *From* 6·00

z 124 6d. lilac (1856) .. .. .. 13·00

z 125 6d. lilac (1862) (Plates 3, 4) *From* 13·00

z 126 6d. lilac (1865–67) .. *From* 11·00
Plate Nos. 5, 6.

z 127 6d. lilac (1867) (Plate No. 6) .. 14·00

z 128 6d. violet (1867–70) .. *From* 11·00
Plate Nos. 6, 8, 9.

z 129 6d. buff (1872–73) .. *From* 50·00
Plate Nos. 11, 12.

z 130 6d. chestnut (1872) (Plate No. 11) 8·00

z 131 6d. grey (1873) (Plate No. 12) .. 18·00

z 132 6d. grey (1874–80) .. *From* 6·00
Plate Nos. 13, 14, 15, 16, 17.

z 133 6d. grey (1881) (Plates 17, 18) ..

z 134 6d. lilac (1883) (6d. on 6d.) .. 25·00

z 135 8d. orange (1876) .. .. .. 40·00

z 136 9d. bistre (1862) .. .. .. 45·00

z 137 9d. straw (1862) £150

z 138 9d. straw (1865) £120

z 139 9d. straw (1867) .. .. .. 32·00

z 140 10d. red-brown (1867) .. .. 35·00

z 141 1s. green (1856) .. .. .. 22·00

z 142 1s. green (1862) .. .. .. 18·00

z 143 1s. green (1862) ("K" *variety*) .. £500

z 144 1s. green (1865) (Plate No. 4) .. 11·00

z 145 1s. green (1867–73) .. *From* 4·50
Plate Nos. 4, 5, 6, 7.

z 146 1s. green (1873–77) .. *From* 11·00
Plate Nos. 8, 9, 10, 11, 12, 13.

z 146a 1s. orange-brown (1880) (Pl. 13) 50·00

z 147 1s. orange-brown (1881) .. *From* 11·00
Plate Nos. 13 and 14.

z 148 2s. blue (1867) .. .. .. 30·00

z 149 5s. rose (1867) (Plate No. 1) .. £120

1880.

z 150 ½d. deep green .. .. .. 4·50

z 151 ½d. pale green .. .. .. 4·50

z 152 1d. Venetian red .. .. .. 4·50

z 153 1½d. Venetian red .. .. ..

z 154 2d. pale rose .. .. .. 18·00

z 155 2d. deep rose .. .. ..

z 156 5d. indigo .. .. ..

1881.

z 157 1d. lilac (14 *dots*) .. .. .. 5·00

z 158 1d. lilac (16 *dots*) .. .. .. 2·00

1884.

z 159–62 ½d. slate-blue; 2d., 2½d., 3d. *From* 4·50

z 163–64 4d., 6d. .. .. .. ,, 24·00

POSTAL FISCAL.

z 173 1d. purple (1881), *wmk.* Orb .. £250

IONIAN ISLANDS.

"PAID AT CORFU"

z 174 1d. red-brown (1855) Die II, *wmk.* Large Crown, *perf.* 14 .. £200

VARIOUS TOWNS IN CYPRUS.

LARNACA.

"**942**" *Obliteration as T* **9.**

1878 *to* 1881.

z 176 ½d. rose-red (1870–79) .. *From* 75·00
Plate Nos. 11, 12, 13, 14, 15, 19, 20.

z 177 1d. rose-red (1864–79) .. *From* 35·00
Plate Nos. 129, 131, 146, 154, 170, 171, 174, 175, 176, 177, 178, 179, 181, 182, 183, 184, 187, 188, 190, 191, 192, 193, 194, 195, 196, 197, 198, 199, 200, 201, 202, 203, 204, 205, 206, 207, 208, 209, 210, 212, 213, 214, 215, 216, 217, 218, 220, 221, 222, 225.

z 177a 1½d. lake-red (1870) (Pl. 3) .. £225

z 178 2d. blue (1858–69) .. .. 20·00
Plate Nos. 9, 13, 14, 15.

z 179 2½d. rosy mauve (1876–79) *From* 10·00
Plate Nos. 4, 5, 6, 8, 10, 11, 12, 13, 14, 15, 16, 17.

z 180 2½d. blue (1880–81) £120
Plate Nos. 17, 18, 19, 20.

z 181 2½d. blue (1881) (Plate No. 21) .. £100

z 182 4d. sage-green (1877) £150
Plate Nos. 15, 16.

z 183 6d. grey (1874–76) .. .. 65·00
Plate Nos. 15, 16, 17.

z 183a 8d. orange (1876) £800

z 184 1s. green (1873–77) .. .. 90·00
Plate Nos. 12, 13.

z 184a 1s. orange-brown (1881) (Pl. 14) £350

z 184b 5s. rose (1874) (Pl. 2) £700

NICOSIA.

"**969.**" *Obliteration as T* **9.**

1878 *to* 1881.

z 185 ½d. rose-red (1870–79) .. .. 65·00
Plate Nos. 12, 13, 14, 15, 20.

z 186 1d. rose-red (1864–79) .. *From* 22·00
Plate Nos. 170, 171, 174, 189, 190, 192, 193, 195, 196, 198, 200, 202, 203, 205, 206, 207, 210, 212, 214, 215, 218, 221, 222, 225.

z 187 2d. blue (1858–69) .. ..
Plate Nos. 14 and 15.

z 188 2½d. rosy mauve (1876–79) *From* 25·00
Plate Nos. 10, 11, 12, 13, 14, 15, 16.

z 188a 2½d. blue (1880) (Plate No. 20) ..

z 188b 2½d. blue (1881) (Plate No. 21) ..

z 188c 4d. vermilion (1876) (Pl. No. 15) ..

z 189 4d. sage-green (1877) (Plate No. 16) £150

z 190 6d. grey (1873) (Plate No. 16) .. £125

KYRENIA.

"**974.**" *Obliteration as T* **9.**

1878 *to* 1880.

z 190a ½d. rose-red (1870–79) (Plate No. 1)

z 191 1d. rose-red (1864–79) .. *From* 55·00
Plate Nos. 168, 171, 193, 196, 206, 207, 209, 220.

z 192 2d. blue (1858–69) .. *From* £150
Plate Nos. 13, 15.

z 193 2½d. rosy mauve (1876–79) *From* 40·00
Plate Nos. 12, 13, 14, 15.

z 193a 4d. sage-grn. (1877) (Pl. No. 16) ..

z 193b 6d. grey (1874–80) (Pl. No. 16) ..

LIMASSOL.

"**975.**" *Obliteration as T* **9.**

1878 *to* 1880.

z 194 ½d. rose-red (1870–79) .. .. 60·00
Plate Nos. 11, 13, 15, 19.

z 195 1d. rose-red (1864–79) .. *From* 25·00
Plate Nos. 160, 171, 173, 174, 177, 179, 184, 187, 190, 193, 195, 196, 197, 198, 200, 202, 206, 207, 208, 209, 210, 213, 215, 216, 218, 220, 221, 222, 225.

z 196 1½d. lake-red (1870–74) (Plate 3) .. £450

z 197 2d. blue (1858–69) .. .. *From* 35·00
Plate Nos. 14, 15.
z 198 2½d. rosy-mauve (1876–80) *From* 24·00
Plate Nos. 11, 12, 13, 14, 15, 16.
z 198*a* 2½d. blue (1880) .. .. *From* £350
Plate Nos. 17, 19, 20.
z 198*b* 4d. sage-green (Plate No. 16) .. 70·00

PAPHO (PAPHOS).

"**981.**" *Obliteration as T* **9.**

1878 *to* **1881.**
z 198*c* ½d. rose-red (1870–79) .. ..
Plate Nos. 13, 15.
z 199 1d. rose-red (1864–79) .. *From* 60·00
Plate Nos. 196, 201, 202, 204, 206, 213, 217.
z 200 2d. blue (1858–69) (Plate No. 15) £140
z 201 2½d. rosy mauve (1876–79) .. *From* 75·00
Plate Nos. 13, 14, 15.

FAMAGUSTA.

"**982.**" *Obliteration* as *T* **9.**

1878 *to* **1881.**
z 202 ½d. rose-red (1870–79) £100
Plate Nos. 11, 13.
z 203 1d. rose-red (1864–70) .. ..
Plate Nos. 145, 174, 181, 193, 202, 206, 215.
z 204 2d. blue (1858–69) £225
Plate Nos. 13, 14, 15.
z 204*a* 2½d. rosy mauve (1876) £200
Plate Nos. 13, 16.
z 204*b* 6d. grey (1874–80) (Pl. 15)
z 204*c* 1s. green (1873–77) (Pl. 12) .. £425
z 205 1s. orange-brown (1881) £475
Plate No. 14.

POLYMEDIA (POLEMIDHIA).

(Nr. Limasol.)

"**D 47.**" *Obliteration T* **8.**

1881–?
z 205*a* ½d. rose-red (1870–79) (Pl. 11) .. £450
z 206 1d. rose-red (1864–79) *From* £150
Plate Nos. 78, 99, 110, 132, 175, 192, 197, 205, 206, 207, 208, 209.
z 207 2d. blue (1858–69) (Plate No. 15) £250

HEAD-QUARTER CAMP.

(Near Nicosia.)

"**D 48.**" *Obliteration as T* **8.**

1881–?
z 207*a* ½d. rose-red (1870–79) (Pl. 13, 20) £275
z 208 1d. rose-red (1864–79) .. *From* £140
Plate Nos. 171, 174, 177, 201, 204, 205, 214, 218.
z 209 2d. blue (1858–69) (Plate No. 15) £325

"**D 48**" differs from Type **8** in that the "D" is taller and narrower and the "**4**" has pronounced serifs. Stamps with "**D47**" and "**D 48**" having four bars instead of three were used in Great Britain before the altered cancellers were sent to Cyprus in 1881. These camps were administrative centres where Great Britain stamps continued to be used after overprinted stamps had been issued.

II.

British Offices in Turkish Empire.

CONSTANTINOPLE.

"C" *Obliteration on circular postmarks as T* **1, 10,** *or* **19.**

1857.
z 210 ½d. rose-red (1870–79) .. *From* 3·00
Plate Nos. 5, 6, 10, 11, 12, 14, 15, 20
z 211 1d. red-brown (1854), Die I, *wmk.* Small Crown, *perf.* 16 ..
z 211*a* 1d. red-brown (1855), Die II, *wmk.* Small Crown, *perf.* 14 ..
z 211*b* 1d. red-brown, (1855), Die II, *wmk.* Large Crown, *perf.* 14 3·75
z 212 1d. rose-red (1857) .. .. 1·50
z 212*a* 1d. rose-red (1861) Alphabet IV
z 213 1d. rose-red (1864–79) .. *From* 1·50
Plate Nos. 71, 72, 73, 74, 76, 78, 79, 80, 81, 83, 85, 87, 89, 90, 92, 93, 94, 95, 96, 97, 99, 101, 102, 105, 106, 108, 109, 110, 113, 116, 118, 119, 120, 121, 122, 123, 124, 125, 127, 129, 130, 131, 134, 135, 136, 137, 138, 140, 141, 143, 144, 145, 146, 147, 148, 149, 150, 151, 152, 155, 156, 157, 158, 159, 160, 161, 162, 163, 164, 166, 167, 170, 171, 172, 173, 174, 175, 176, 177, 178, 179, 180, 181, 183, 184, 186, 187, 188, 189, 190, 191, 192, 193, 194, 195, 196, 198, 200, 201, 208, 204, 205, 206, 207, 208, 210, 212, 214, 215, 216, 220, 222, 224.
z 214 1½d. rose-red (1870) (Plate 1) .. 70·00
z 214*a* 2d. blue (1855), *wmk.* Large Crown, *perf.* 14. (Pl. Nos. 5, 6) ..
z 215 2d. blue (1858–69) .. *From* 2·00
Plate Nos. 8, 9, 12, 13, 14, 15.
z 216 2½d. rosy mauve (1875–76) (*blued paper*) (Pl. Nos. 1, 2) *From* 18·00
z 217 2½d. rosy mauve (1875–76) *From* 8·00
Plate Nos. 1, 2, 3.
z 218 2½d. rosy mauve (*Error of Lettering*)
z 219 2½d. rosy mauve (1876–79) *From* 6·00
Plate Nos. 3 to 17. ..
z 220 2½d. blue (1880–81) .. *From* 3·50
Plate Nos. 17, 18, 19, 20.
z 221 2½d. blue (1881) (Pl. 21, 22, 23) .. 2·50
z 221*a* 3d. carmine-rose (1862) (Plate 2) 32·00
z 221*b* 3d. rose (1865) (Plate 4) .. 22·00
z 222 3d. rose (1867–73) (Pl. 4 to 10) .. 6·00
z 223 3d. rose (1873–76) .. 6·00
Plates, 12, 15, 16, 17, 18, 19.
z 224 3d. rose (1881) (Plate No. 21) ..
z 224*a* 3d. on 3d. lilac (1883) (Pl. No. 21)
z 225 4d. rose (1857) .. .. .. 13·00
z 226 4d. red (1862) (Plates 3, 4) *From* 11·00
z 227 4d. vermilion (1865–73) .. *From* 9·00
Plate Nos. 7 to 14.
z 228 4d. vermilion (1876) (Plate No. 15) 40·00
z 229 4d. sage green (1877) .. .. 20·00
Plate Nos. 15, 16.
z 230 4d. grey-brown (1880) *wmk.* Large Garter (Plate No. 17) ..
z 231 4d. grey-brown (1880) *wmk.* Crown (Plate Nos. 17, 18) *From* 5·00
z 232 6d. lilac (1856) .. .. .. 14·00
z 233 6d. lilac (1862) (Plates 3, 4) *From* 12·00
z 234 6d. lilac (1865–67) .. " 11·00
Plate Nos. 5, 6.
z 235 6d. lilac (1867) (Plate No. 6) .. 12·00
z 236 6d. violet (1867–70) .. *From* 10·00
Plate Nos. 6, 8, 9.
z 237 6d. buff (1872–73) .. .. 18·00
Plate Nos. 11, 12.
z 238 6d. chestnut (1872) (Plate No. 11) 8·00
z 239 6d. grey (1873) (Plate No. 12) .. 16·00
z 240 6d. grey (1874–76) .. *From* 7·00
Plate Nos. 13, 14, 15, 16.
z 241 6d. grey (1881–82) (Pls. 17, 18) .. 5·50
z 242 6d. lilac (1883) 6d. on 6d. .. 20·00
a. Dots slanting (Letters MI or SJ) 38·00
z 243 8d. orange (1876) £100
z 244 10d. red-brn. (1867), *wmk.* Embs. £5500
z 244*a* 10d. red-brown (1867) .. .. 35·00
z 245 1s. green (1856) .. .. .. 22·00
z 246 1s. green (1862) .. .. .. 18·00
z 247 1s. green (1862) ("K" *variety*) ..
z 247*a* 1s. green (1862) (thick *paper*) ..
z 248 1s. green (1865) (Plate No. 4) .. 10·00
z 249 1s. green (1867–73) .. *From* 3·00
Plate Nos. 4, 5, 6, 7.
z 250 1s. green (1873–77) .. *From* 8·50
Plate Nos. 8, 9, 10, 11, 12, 13.
z 251 1s. orange-brown (1880) (Pl. 13) 42·00
z 252 1s. orange-brown (1881) *From* 10·00
Plate Nos. 13, 14.
z 253 2s. blue (1867) .. .. .. 24·00
z 254 5s. rose (1867–74) .. *From* 50·00
Plate Nos. 1, 2.
z 255 5s. rose (1882) (white *paper*) .. £200
z 256 5s. rose (1882) (blued *paper*) .. £225

1880.
z 257 ½d. deep green .. .. .. 1·25
z 258 ½d. pale green .. .. .. 1·40
z 259 1d. Venetian red 85
z 260 2d. pale rose .. .. .. 8·50
z 261 2d. deep rose .. .. .. 9·00
z 261*a* 5d. indigo .. ..

1881.
z 262 1d. lilac (14 *dots*) .. ..
z 263 1d. lilac (16 *dots*) 85

1883 *to* **1884.**
z 264 ½d. slate .. .. .. 1·50
z 265–68 1½d., 2d., 2½d., 3d. .. *From* 2·50
z 269–72*a* 4d., 5d., 6d., 9d., 1s. .. *From* 20·00
z 273 2s. 6d. lilac (blued *paper*) ..
z 274 2s. 6d. lilac (white *paper*) .. 20·00
z 275 5s. rose (blued *paper*) ..
z 276 5s. rose (white *paper*) ..

1887.
z 276*a*–*l* ½d., 1½d., 2d., 2½d., 3d., 4d., 4½d., 5d., 6d., 9d., 10d., 1s. .. .. .. *From* 90

1900.
z 277–77*a* ½d., 1s. .. .. .. *From* 90

1902.
z 278–90*c* ½d., 1d., 1½d., 2d., 2½d., 3d., 4d., 4d. orange, 5d., 6d., 7d., 9d., 10d., 1s., 2s. 6d., 5s. *From* 75

1911–18.
z 290*d*–*u* ½d. (No. 339), ½d. (No. 351), 1d. (No. 330), 1d. (No. 343), 1d. (No. 357), 1½d., 2d., 2½d., 3d., 4d., 5d., 6d., 9d. (No. 392), 9d. (No. 393*a*), 1s., 2s. 6d. (No. 413*a*), 5s. (No. 416), 10s. (No. 417) *From* 90

SALONICA.

Office opened in 1900. *Date-stamp with double circle. Issues of* 1887–1900.
z 290*v* ½d. vermilion .. .. .. 2·25
z 291 ½d. green .. .. 2·75
z 292 1d. lilac .. .. 3·00
z 293 6d. purple/*red* .. .. .. 4·50
z 293*a* 1s. green and carmine .. .. 15·00
z 293*b* 5s. rose (white *paper*) (1883) .. 35·00

1902.
z 293*c* ½d. blue-green .. .. .. 3·50
z 293*d* ½d. yellow-green .. .. .. 2·25
z 293*e* 1d. scarlet .. .. 2·50
z 293*f* 2½d. blue .. .. 3·25
z 293*g* 1s. green and carmine .. .. 6·00

1911–12.
z 293*h* ½d. (*T* **98**) .. .. 2·25
z 293*i* 1d. (*T* **99**) .. .. 2·75
z 293*j* 1d. (*T* **102**) .. .. .. 3·50

1912–13.
z 293*k* ½d. (*T* **105**) .. .. .. 2·25
z 293*l* 1d. (*T* **104**) .. .. .. 2·75

STAMBOUL (CONSTANTINOPLE).

"S" *Obliteration as T* **10.**

1884.
z 294 ½d. slate .. .. 4·50
z 294*a* 1d. lilac .. .. 3·00
z 294*b* 2d. lilac .. ..
z 295 2½d. lilac .. .. 3·50
z 296 5d. green .. .. 20·00

1887.
z 296*a* ½d. vermilion .. .. .. 3·50

1911.
z 296*b* ½d. (*T* **98**) etc., and other values of K.G.V. to 1s. .. ..

Circular postmark as T **18.**
z 298 1d. lilac (1881) .. .. .. 2·25
z 299 2½d. lilac (1884) .. .. .. 2·50
z 300 5d. green (1884) .. .. .. 20·00

1887.
z 301–301*k* ½d., 1½d., 2d., 2½d., 3d., 4d., 4½d., 5d., 6d., 9d., 10d., 1s. *From* 1·40

1900.
z 302 ½d. .. .. 1·75
z 303 1s. .. ..

1902–10.
z 304–15*d* ½d., 1d., 1½d., 2d., 2½d., 3d., 4d., 4d. orange, 5d., 6d., 7d., 9d., 10d., 1s., 2s. 6d., 5s. .. .. .. *From* 1·00

1911–13.
z 316–29*d* ½d. (*T* **98**), ½d. (*T* **101**), 1d. (*T* **99**), ½d. (*T* **105**), 1d. (*T* **104**), 1½d., 2d., 2½d., 3d., 4d., 5d., 6d., 7d., 8d., 9d., 10d., 1s., 2s. 6d., 5s. *From* 1·75

ALEXANDRIA (EGYPT).

"B 01." *Obliteration as T* **2, 8, 12** *or* **15.**

1860 *to* **1879.**

z 330 ½d. rose-red (1870–79) .. *From* 3·00
Plate Nos. 5, 6, 8, 10, 13, 15, 20.

z 331 1d. rose-red (1857) .. .. 2·00

z 331*a* 1d. rose-red (1861) (Alph. IV) ..

z 332 1d. rose-red (1864–79) .. *From* 2·00
Plate Nos. 71, 72, 73, 74, 76, 78, 79, 80, 81, 82, 83, 84, 85, 86, 87, 88, 89, 90, 91, 92, 93, 94, 95, 96, 97, 98, 99, 101, 102, 103, 104, 106, 107, 108, 109, 110, 111, 112, 113, 114, 115, 117, 118, 119, 120, 121, 122, 123, 125, 127, 129, 130, 131, 133, 134, 136, 137, 138, 139, 140, 142, 143, 144, 145, 146, 147, 148, 149, 152, 154, 156, 157, 158, 159, 160, 162, 163, 165, 168, 169, 170, 171, 172, 174, 175, 177, 179, 180, 181, 182, 183, 185, 188, 190, 198, 200, 203, 210, 220.

z 333 2d. blue (1858–69) .. .. *From* 2·25
Plate Nos. 7, 8, 9, 13, 14, 15.

z 334 2½d. rosy mauve (1875) (blued *paper*)
Plate Nos. 1, 2. .. *From* 18·00

z 335 2½d. rosy mauve (1875–6) .. .. 8·00
Plate Nos. 1, 2, 3.

z 336 2½d. rosy mauve (*Error of Lettering*) £400

z 337 2½d. rosy mauve (1876–79) .. *From* 6·00
Plate Nos. 3, 4, 5, 6, 7, 8, 9.

z 338 3d. carmine-rose (1862) .. .. 32·00

z 339 3d. rose (1865) (Plate No. 4) .. 14·00

z 340 3d. rose (1867–73) .. .. *From* 6·00
Plate Nos. 4, 5, 6, 7, 8, 9.

z 341 3d. rose (1873–76) .. *From* 6·00
Plate Nos. 11, 12, 14, 15, 16, 18, 19.

z 341*a* 3d. rose (1881) (Plate No. 20) ..

z 342 4d. rose (1857) .. .. .. 13·00

z 343 4d. red (1862) (Plates 3, 4) *From* 11·00

z 344 4d. vermilion (1865–73) .. .. 9·00
Plate Nos. 7, 8, 9, 10, 11, 12, 13, 14.

z 345 4d. vermilion (1876) (Plate No. 15) 38·00

z 346 4d. sage-green (1877) .. .. 22·00
Plate No. 15.

z 347 6d. lilac (1856) .. .. .. 14·00

z 348 6d. lilac (1862) (Plates 3, 4) *From* 12·00

z 349 6d. lilac (1865–67) .. .. *From* 11·00
Plate Nos. 5, 6.

z 350 6d. lilac (1867) (Plate No. 6) .. 12·00

z 351 6d. violet (1867–70) .. *From* 10·00
Plate Nos. 6, 8, 9.
a. Imperf. (Plate No. 8) £350

z 352 6d. buff (1872–73) .. .. *From* 20·00
Plate Nos. 11, 12.

z 353 6d. chestnut (1872) (Plate No. 11) 8·00

z 354 6d. grey (1873) (Plate No. 12) .. 15·00

z 355 6d. grey (1874–76) .. *From* 7·00
Plate Nos. 13, 14, 15.

z 356 9d. straw (1862) .. .. .. 38·00

z 357 9d. bistre (1862) .. .. ..

z 357*a* 9d. straw (1865) .. .. ..

z 358 9d. straw (1867) .. .. ..

z 359 10d. red-brown (1867) .. .. 35·00

z 360 1s. green (1856) .. .. 22·00

z 361 1s. green (1862) .. .. 18·00

z 361*a* 1s. green (1862) ("K" *variety*) ..

z 362 1s. green (1865) (Plate No. 4) .. 10·00

z 363 1s. green (1867–73) .. *From* 3·00
Plate Nos. 4, 5, 6, 7.

z 364 1s. green (1873–77) .. *From* 8·50
Plate Nos. 8, 9, 10, 11, 12, 13.

z 365 2s. blue (1867) .. .. .. 24·00

z 366 5s. rose (1867–74) .. .. *From* 50·00
Plate Nos. 1, 2.

PORT SAID.

Stamps issued after 1877 can be found with the Egyptian cancellation "Port Said", but these are on letters posted from British ships.

SUEZ (EGYPT).

"B 02." *Obliteration as T* **2, 8** *and circular date stamp as in T* **5.**

1860 *to* **1879.**

z 367 ½d. rose-red (1870–79) .. ..
Plate Nos. 6, 10, 11, 12, 13, 14.

z 368 1d. rose-red (1857) .. .. 3·50

z 369 1d. rose-red (1864–79) .. *From* 3·00
Plate Nos. 73, 74, 79, 80, 81, 83, 84, 86, 87, 90, 91, 93, 94, 96, 97, 100, 101, 106, 107, 108, 110, 113, 119, 120, 121, 122, 123, 124, 125, 129, 131, 134, 137, 138, 140, 143, 144, 145, 147, 148, 149, 150, 151, 153, 154, 156, 158, 159, 161, 162, 163, 164, 165, 166, 167, 168, 170, 174, 176, 177, 178, 179, 180, 181, 182, 184, 185, 186, 187, 189, 190, 205.

z 370 2d. blue (1858–69) .. *From* 5·00
Plate Nos. 8, 9, 13, 14, 15.

z 371 2½d. rosy mauve (1875) (blued *paper*)
Plate Nos. 1, 2 and 3. *From* 18·00

z 372 2½d. rosy mauve (1875–76) *From* 8·00
Plate Nos. 1, 2, 3.

z 373 2½d. rosy mauve (*Error of Lettering*) £450

z 374 2½d. rosy mauve (1876–79) *From* 6·00
Plate Nos. 3, 4, 5, 6, 7, 8, 9.

z 375 3d. carmine-rose (1862) .. .. 32·00

z 376 3d. rose (1865) (Plate No. 4) .. 14·00

z 377 3d. rose (1867–73) .. .. ..
Plate Nos. 5. 6, 7, 8, 10.

z 378 3d. rose (1873–76) .. .. *From* 6·00
Plate Nos. 12, 16.

z 379 4d. rose (1857) .. .. .. 11·00

z 380 4d. red (1862) (Plates 3, 4) *From* 11·00

z 381 4d. vermilion (1865–73) .. *From* 9·00
Plate Nos. 7, 8, 9, 10, 11, 12, 13, 14.

z 382 4d. vermilion (1876) (Plate No. 15)

z 383 4d. sage-green (1877) (Plate No. 15) 22·00

z 384 6d. lilac (1856) .. .. .. 14·00

z 385 6d. lilac (1862) (Plates 3, 4) *From* 12·00

z 386 6d. lilac (1865–67) .. *From* 11·00
Plate Nos. 5, 6.

z 387 6d. lilac (1867) (Plate No. 6) .. 12·00

z 388 6d. violet (1867–70) .. *From* 10·00
Plate Nos. 6, 8, 9.

z 389 6d. buff (1872–73) .. .. *From* 24·00
Plate Nos. 11, 12.

z 389*a* 6d. pale chestnut (Plate No. 12) £700

z 390 6d. chestnut (1872) (Plate No. 11) 8·00

z 391 6d. grey (1873) (Plate No. 12) .. 16·00

z 392 6d. grey (1874–76) .. .. *From* 7·00
Plate Nos. 13, 14, 15, 16.

z 393 8d. orange (1876) .. .. ..

z 394 9d. straw (1862) .. .. .. 40·00

z 395 9d. bistre (1862) .. .. ..

z 396 9d. straw (1867) .. .. ..

z 397 10d. red-brown (1867) .. .. 35·00

z 398 1s. green (1856) .. .. 25·00

z 399 1s. green (1862) .. .. 20·00

z 400 1s. green (1862) ("K" *variety*) ..

z 401 1s. green (1865) (Plate No. 4) .. 10·00

z 402 1s. green (1867–73) .. *From* 3·00
Plate Nos. 4, 5, 6, 7.

z 403 1s. green (1873–77) .. *From* 8·50
Plate Nos. 8, 9, 10, 11, 12.

z 404 2s. blue (1867) .. .. .. 25·00

z 405 5s. rose (1867–74) .. .. *From* 48·00
Plate Nos. 1, 2.

SMYRNA.

"F 87" *Obliteration or circular postmark as T* **8, 16, 18** *or* **19.**

1872.

z 406 ½d. rose-red (1870–79) .. *From* 5·00
Plates 11, 12, 13, 14, 15.

z 407 1d. rose-red (1864–79) .. *From* 2·25
Plate Nos. 120, 124, 134, 137, 138, 139, 140, 142, 143, 145, 146, 148, 149, 150, 151, 152, 153, 155, 156, 157, 158, 159, 160, 161, 162, 163, 164, 166, 167, 168, 169, 170, 171, 172, 173, 174, 175, 176, 177, 178, 183, 184, 185, 186, 187, 188, 191, 193, 195, 196, 198, 200, 201, 204, 210, 215, 217, 218.

z 408 1½d. lake-red (1870–74) (Plates 1, 3) *From* 70·00

z 409 2d. blue (1858) *wmk.* Large Crown, *perf.* 16 .. .. ..

z 410 2d. blue (1858–69) .. *From* 3·50
Plate Nos. 13, 14, 15.

z 411 2½d. rosy mauve (1875) (blued *paper*) 18·00
Plate No. 1.

z 412 2½d. rosy mauve (1875–76) *From* 8·00
Plate Nos. 1, 2, 3.

z 413 2½d. rosy mauve (*Error of lettering*)

z 414 2½d. rosy mauve (1876–79) *From* 6·00
Plate Nos. 3, 4, 5, 6, 7, 8, 9, 10, 11, 12, 13, 14, 15, 16, 17.

z 415 2½d. blue (1880) .. .. *From* 3·50
Plate Nos. 17, 18, 19, 20.

z 416 2½d. blue (1881) .. .. 3·00
Plate Nos. 21, 22, 23.

z 417 3d. rose (1867–73) .. .. .. 6·00
Plate Nos. 5, 7, 9, 10.

z 418 3d. rose (1873–76) (Plate No. 14)

z 419 4d. vermilion (1865–73) .. .. 9·00
Plate Nos. 12, 13, 14.

z 420 4d. vermilion (1876) (Plate No. 15) 38·00

z 421 4d. sage-green (1877) .. .. 22·00
Plate Nos. 15, 16.

z 422 4d. grey-brown (1880) *wmk.* Large Garter (Plate No. 17) .. ..

z 423 4d. grey-brown (1880) *wmk.* Crown (Plate Nos. 17, 18) .. *From* 5·00

z 424 6d. buff (1872–73) .. .. *From* 25·00
Plate Nos. 11, 12.

z 425 6d. chestnut (1872) (Plate No. 11)

z 426 6d. grey (1873) (Plate No. 12) .. 16·00

z 427 6d. grey (1874–80) .. .. *From* 7·00
Plate Nos. 13, 14, 15, 16, 17.

z 428 6d. grey (1881–82) .. .. ..
Plate Nos. 17, 18.

z 429 6d. lilac (1883) (6d. on 6d.) .. 20·00

z 429*a* 8d. orange (1876) .. .. ..

z 430 9d. straw (1867) .. .. 30·00

z 431 10d. red-brown (1867) .. .. 35·00

z 432 1s. green (1867–73) (Pl. Nos. 6, 7)

z 433 1s. green (1873–77) .. *From* 8·50
Plate Nos. 8, 9, 10, 11, 12, 13.

z 434 1s. orange-brown (1880) .. .. 42·00
Plate No. 13.

z 434*a* 1s. orange-brown (1881) (Plate No .13, 14) .. .. 10·00

z 435 5s. rose (1867–74) (Plate No. 2) ..

1880.

z 436 ½d. deep green .. .. .. 1·50

z 437 ½d. pale green .. .. .. 1·50

z 438 1d. Venetian red .. .. .. 2·75

z 439 1½d. Venetian red .. .. .. 20·00

z 440 2d. pale rose .. .. .. 8·50

z 441 2d. deep rose .. .. .. 8·50

z 442 5d. indigo .. .. 15·00

1881.

z 443 1d. lilac (16 *dots*) .. .. .. 1·50

1884.

z 444 ½d. slate-blue .. .. .. 2·50

z 445–6 2d., 2½d. .. .. .. *From* 2·25

z 447–9 4d., 5d., 1s. .. .. *From* 20·00

1887.

z 450–7*a* ½d., 1½d., 2d., 2½d., 3d., 4d., 5d., 6d., 1s. .. .. *From* 1·00

1900.

z 458–9 ½d., 1s. .. .. .. *From* 1·25

1902–10.

z 460–71*b* ½d., 1d., 1½d., 2d., 2½d., 3d., 4d., 5d., 6d., 7d., 9d., 10d., 1s., 2s. 6d. .. *From* 1·25

1911–23.

z 472–86 ½d., 1d., 1½d., 2d., 2½d., 3d., 4d., 5d., 6d., 7d., 8d., 9d., 10d., 1s., 2s. 6d. .. *From* 1·00

BEYROUT (LEVANT).

"G 06." *Obliteration or circular postmark as T* **8, 19,** *or* **20.**

1873.

z 487 ½d. rose-red (1870–79) .. *From* 3·00
Plate Nos. 12, 13, 14, 19, 20.

z 488 1d. rose-red (1864–79) .. *From* 2·50
Plate Nos. 107, 118, 130, 140, 145, 148, 155, 157, 162, 167, 177, 179, 180, 184, 185, 186, 195, 198, 200, 204, 211, 213, 215, 218, 220, 222.

z 489 1½d. lake-red (1870–74) (Plate 3) .. 12·00

z 490 2d. blue (1858–69) .. .. *From* 2·75
Plate Nos. 13, 14, 15.

z 491 2½d. rosy mauve (1875) (blued *paper*) 18·00
Plate No. 1.

z 492 2½d. rosy-mauve (1875–76) *From* 8·00
Plate Nos. 1, 2, 3.

z 493 2½d. rosy mauve (1876–79) *From* 6·00
Plate Nos. 3, 4, 5, 6, 7, 8, 9, 10, 11, 12, 13, 14, 15, 16, 17.

z 494 2½d. blue (1880) .. .. *From* 3·50
Plate Nos. 17, 18, 19, 20.

z 495 2½d. blue (1881) .. .. *From* 2·50
Plate Nos. 21, 22, 23.

z 496 3d. rose (1867–73) (Plate No. 10)

z 497 3d. rose (1873–76)
Plate Nos. 12, 15, 18, 19, 20.
z 498 3d. rose (1881) (Plate Nos. 20, 21)
z 499 4d. vermilion (1865–73) *From* 9·00
Plate Nos. 11, 12, 13, 14.
z 500 4d. vermilion (1876) (Plate No. 15) 38·00
z 501 4d. sage-green (1877)
Plate Nos. 15, 16.
z 502 4d. grey-brown (1880) *wmk.* Large Garter (Plate No. 17)
z 503 4d. grey-brown (1880) *wmk.* Crown
Plate Nos. 17, 18.
z 503*a* 6d. mauve (1870) (Plate Nos. 8, 9)
z 504 6d. buff (1872–73) *From* 25·00
Plate Nos. 11, 12.
z 505 6d. chestnut (1872) (Plate No. 11) 8·00
z 506 6d. grey (1873) (Plate No. 12)
z 507 6d. grey (1874–80) *From* 7·00
Plate Nos. 13, 14, 15, 16, 17.
z 507*a* 8d. orange (1876)
z 508 10d. red-brown (1867) 35·00
z 509 1s. green (1867–73) 4·00
Plate Nos. 6, 7.
z 510 1s. green (1873–77) *From* 8·50
Plate Nos. 8, 9, 10, 12, 13.
z 511 1s. orge.-brn. (1880) (Plate No. 13)
z 512 1s. orange-brown (1881) 10·00
Plate Nos. 13, 14.
z 513 2s. blue (1867) 24·00
z 514 5s. rose (1867) (Pl. 1, 2) *From* £125

1880.
z 515 ½d. deep green 1·50
z 516 ½d. pale green 1·50
z 517 1d. Venetian red 2·25
z 518 1½d. Venetian red 35·00
z 519 2d. pale rose 8·50
z 520 2d. deep rose 8·50
z 521 5d. indigo 16·00

1881.
z 522 1d. lilac (14 *dots*)
z 523 1d. lilac (16 *dots*)

1884.
z 524–529*a* ½d., 1½d., 2d., 2½d., 4d., 5d., 1s. *From* 1·25

1887.
z 530–7*a* ½d., 1½d., 2d., 2½d., 3d., 4½d., 5d., 6d., 1s. *From* 1·00

1900.
z 538–9 ½d., 1s. *From* 1·00

1902–12.
z 540–5 ½d., 1d., 2½d., 5d., 10d., 1s. *From* 70

1912–13.
z 545*a–b* ½d., 1d. (*T* **105, 104**)

POSTAL FISCALS

z 546 1d. purple (*wmk.* Anchor)
z 547 1d. purple (*wmk.* Orb)

III.

British West Indies.

VARIOUS TOWNS IN JAMAICA.

British stamps were issued to several District post offices between 8 May, 1858, and 1 March, 1859 (i.e. before the Obliterators A 27–A 78 were issued). These can only be distinguished (off the cover) when they have the Town's date-stamp on them. They are worth about three times the price of those with an obliteration number.

KINGSTON.

"A **01**." *Obliteration as T* **2**.

1858 (8 May)–**1860** (25 Aug.).
J 1 1d. rose-red (1857), *perf.* 16 70·00
J 2 1d. rose-red (1857), *perf.* 14 9·00
J 4 4d. rose (1857) 14·00
J 5 6d. lilac (1856) 14·00
J 6 1s. green (1856) 27·00

"A **01**." *Obliteration as T* **7** (*Duplex*).

1859 (26 May)–**1860** (24 Aug.).
J 7 1d. rose-red (1857), *perf.* 14 65·00
J 9 4d. rose (1857) 14·00
J 10 6d. lilac (1856) 14·00
J 11 1s. green (1856) 85·00

"A **01**." *Obliteration as T* **3**.

1859 (26 May)–**1860** (24 Aug.).
J 12 1d. rose-red (1857), *perf.* 14 85·00
J 14 4d. rose (1857) 50·00
a. Thick glazed paper £150
J 15 6d. lilac (1856) 50·00
J 16 1s. green (1856) £140

Note:—For A **02**, etc., see after A **78**.

"A **27**" *to* "A **78**". *Obliteration as T* **2**.

1859 (1 Mar.)–**1860** (24 Aug.).

A 27. ALEXANDRIA.
J 17 1d. rose-red (1857), *perf.* 14 £150
J 17*a* 2d. blue (1855) Large Crown, *perf.* 14 (Plate 6) £160
J 18 4d. rose (1857) 65·00
J 19 6d. lilac (1856) £140

A 28. ANNOTTO BAY.
J 20 1d. rose-red (1857), *perf.* 14 £110
J 21 4d. rose (1857) 27·00
J 22 6d. lilac (1856) 60·00

A 29. BATH.
J 23 1d. rose-red (1857), *perf.* 14 50·00
J 24 4d. rose (1857) 32·00
J 25 6d. lilac (1856) £150

A 30. BLACK RIVER.
J 26 1d. rose-red (1857), *perf.* 14 50·00
J 27 4d. rose (1857) 22·00
J 28 6d. lilac (1856) 50·00

A 31. BROWN'S TOWN.
J 29 1d. rose-red (1857), *perf.* 14 65·00
J 30 4d. rose (1857) 65·00
J 31 6d. lilac (1856) 65·00

A 32. BUFF BAY.
J 32 1d. rose-red (1857), *perf.* 14 50·00
J 33 4d. rose (1857) 40·00
J 34 6d. lilac (1856) 50·00

A 33. CHAPLETON.
J 35 1d. rose-red (1857), *perf.* 14 65·00
J 36 4d. rose (1857) 36·00
J 37 6d. lilac (1856) 65·00

A 34. CLAREMONT.
J 38 1d. rose-red (1857), *perf.* 14 £110
J 39 4d. rose (1857) 60·00
J 40 6d. lilac (1856) £120

A 35. CLARENDON.
(Near four paths.)
J 41 1d. rose-red (1857), *perf.* 14 95·00
J 42 4d. rose (1857) 40·00
J 43 6d. lilac (1856) 65·00

A 36. DRY HARBOUR.
J 44 1d. rose-red (1857), *perf.* 14 £140
J 45 4d. rose (1857) £110
J 46 6d. lilac (1856) 90·00

A 37. DUNCANS.
J 47 1d. rose-red (1857), *perf.* 14
J 48 4d. rose (1857) £140
J 49 6d. lilac (1856) 95·00

A 38. EWARTON.
A38 was sent out to Ewarton but it is believed that this office was closed early in 1858 before it arrived as no genuine used specimens have been found on British stamps.

A 39. FALMOUTH.
J 53 1d. rose-red (1857), *perf.* 14 30·00
J 54 4d. rose (1857) 14·00
J 55 6d. lilac (1856) 24·00
J 56 1s. green (1856) £140

A 40. FLINT RIVER.
(Near hopewell.)
J 57 1d. rose-red (1857), *perf.* 14 65·00
J 58 4d. rose (1857) 42·00
J 59 6d. lilac (1856) 65·00
J 60 1s. green (1856) £140

A 41. GAYLE.
J 61 1d. rose-red (1857), *perf.* 14 £150
J 62 4d. rose (1857) 45·00
J 63 6d. lilac (1856) 50·00
J 64 1s. green (1856) 70·00

A 42. GOLDEN SPRING.
(Near stony hill.)
J 65 1d. rose-red (1857), *perf.* 14 65·00
J 66 4d. rose (1857) 60·00
J 67 6d. lilac (1856) £150
J 68 1s. green (1856) £150

A 43. GORDON TOWN.
J 69 1d. rose-red (1857), *perf.* 14
J 70 4d. rose (1857)
J 71 6d. lilac (1856) £160

A 44. GOSHEN.
(Near santa cruz.)
J 72 1d. rose-red (1857), *perf.* 14 45·00
J 73 4d. rose (1857) 40·00
J 74 6d. lilac (1856) 18·00

A 45. GRANGE HILL.
J 75 1d. rose-red (1857), *perf.* 14 65·00
J 76 4d. rose (1857) 14·00
J 77 6d. lilac (1856) 22·00
J 77*a* 1s. green (1856) £140

A 46. GREEN ISLAND.
J 78 1d. rose-red (1857), *perf.* 14 £120
J 79 4d. rose (1857) 60·00
J 80 6d. lilac (1856) 90·00
J 81 1s. green (1856) £150

A 47. HIGHGATE.
J 82 1d. rose-red (1857), *perf.* 14 75·00
J 83 4d. rose (1857) 40·00
J 84 6d. lilac (1856) 75·00

A 48. HOPE BAY.
J 85 1d. rose-red (1857), *perf.* 14 £150
J 86 4d. rose (1857) 60·00
J 87 6d. lilac (1856) £150

A 49. LILLIPUT.
(Near balaclava.)
J 88 1d. rose-red (1857), *perf.* 14 65·00
J 89 4d. rose (1857) 65·00
J 90 6d. lilac (1856) 27·00

A 50. LITTLE RIVER.
A50 was sent out for use at Little River, but no specimen has yet been found used on British stamps.

A 51. LUCEA.
J 91 1d. rose-red (1857), *perf.* 14 90·00
J 92 4d. rose (1857) 20·00
J 93 6d. lilac (1856) 65·00

A 52. MANCHIONEAL.
J 94 1d. rose-red (1857), *perf.* 14 £120
J 95 4d. rose (1857) 70·00
J 96 6d. lilac (1856)

A 53. MANDEVILLE.
J 97 1d. rose-red (1857), *perf.* 14 70·00
J 98 4d. rose (1857) 20·00
J 99 6d. lilac (1856) 55·00

A 54. MAY HILL.
(Near spur tree.)
J 100 1d. rose-red (1857), *perf.* 14 32·00
J 101 4d. rose (1857) 32·00
J 102 6d. lilac (1856) 18·00

A 55. MILE GULLY.
J 103 1d. rose-red (1857), *perf.* 14 £100
J 104 4d. rose (1857) 65·00
J 105 6d. lilac (1856) 65·00

A 56. MONEAGUE.
J 106 1d. rose-red (1857), *perf.* 14 65·00
J 107 4d. rose (1857) 80·00
J 108 6d. lilac (1856) £150

A 57. MONTEGO BAY.
J 109 1d. rose-red (1857), *perf.* 14 70·00
J 110 4d. rose (1857) 14·00
J 111 6d. lilac (1856) 18·00
J 112 1s. green (1856) £150

A 58. MONTPELIER.

J 113 1d. rose-red (1857), *perf.* 14 .. ..
J 114 4d. rose (1857) .. ..
J 115 6d. lilac (1856) £240

A 59. MORANT BAY.

J 116 1d. rose red (1857), *perf.* 14 .. £120
J 117 4d. rose (1857) .. .. .. 20·00
J 118 6d. lilac (1856) .. .. .. 20·00

A 60. OCHO RIOS.

J 119 1d. rose-red (1857), *perf.* 14 ..
J 120 4d. rose (1857) .. .. .. 32·00
J 121 6d. lilac (1856) .. .. .. 55·00

A 61. OLD HARBOUR.

J 122 1d. rose-red (1857), *perf.* 14 .. 65·00
J 123 4d. rose (1857) .. .. .. 40·00
J 124 6d. lilac (1856) .. .. .. 45·00

A 62. PLANTAIN GARDEN RIVER.
(Now called GOLDEN GROVE.)

J 125 1d. rose-red (1857), *perf.* 14 .. 45·00
J 126 4d. rose (1857) .. .. .. 32·00
J 127 6d. lilac (1856) .. .. .. 45·00

A 63. PEAR TREE GROVE.

No genuine specimen of A 63 has been found on a British stamp.

A 64. PORT ANTONIO.

J 131 1d. rose-red (1857), *perf.* 14 .. £140
J 132 4d. rose (1857) .. .. .. 90·00
J 133 6d. lilac (1856) .. .. .. 90·00

A 65. PORT MORANT.

J 134 1d. rose-red (1857), *perf.* 14 .. 90·00
J 135 4d. rose (1857) .. .. .. 38·00
J 136 6d. lilac (1856) .. .. .. 90·00

A 66. PORT MARIA.

J 137 1d. rose-red (1857), *perf.* 14 .. 60·00
J 138 4d. rose (1857) .. .. .. 20·00
J 139 6d. lilac (1856) .. .. .. 90·00

A 67. PORT ROYAL.

J 140 1d. rose-red (1857), *perf.* 14 .. £120
J 141 4d. rose (1857) £120
J 142 6d. lilac (1856) £120

A 68. PORUS.

J 143 1d. rose-red (1857), *perf.* 14 .. 65·00
J 144 4d. rose (1857) .. .. .. 25·00
J 145 6d. lilac (1856) £120

A 69. RAMBLE.

J 146 1d. rose-red (1857), *perf.* 14 .. 65·00
J 147 4d. rose (1857) .. .. .. 65·00
a. Thick glazed paper £140
J 149 6d. lilac (1856) .. .. .. 90·00

A 70. RIO BUENO.

J 150 1d. rose-red (1857), *perf.* 14 ..
J 151 4d. rose (1857) .. .. .. 55·00
J 152 6d. lilac (1856) .. .. .. 32·00

A 71. RODNEY HALL.
(Now called LINSTEAD.)

J 153 1d. rose-red (1857), *perf.* 14 .. 45·00
J 154 4d. rose (1857) .. .. .. 27·00
J 155 6d. lilac (1856) .. .. .. 40·00

A 72. SAINT DAVID.
(Now called YALLAHS.)

J 156 1d. rose-red (1857), *perf.* 14 .. 65·00
J 157 4d. rose (1857) £110
J 158 6d. lilac (1856) .. ..

A 73. ST. ANN'S BAY.

J 159 1d. rose-red (1857), *perf.* 14 .. 65·00
J 160 4d. rose (1857) .. .. .. 32·00
J 161 6d. lilac (1856) .. .. .. 65·00

A 74. SALT GUT.
(Near ORACABESSA.)

J 162 1d. rose-red (1857), *perf.* 14 .. 55·00
J 163 4d. rose (1857) .. .. .. 40·00
J 164 6d. lilac (1856) .. .. .. 65·00

A 75. SAVANNA-LA-MAR.

J 165 1d. rose-red (1857), *perf.* 14 .. 20·00
J 166 4d. rose (1857) .. .. .. 14·00
J 167 6d. lilac (1856) .. .. .. 65·00
J 168 1s. green (1856) £140

A 76. SPANISH TOWN.

J 169 1d. rose-red (1857), *perf.* 14 .. 35·00
J 170 4d. rose (1857) .. .. .. 14·00
J 171 6d. lilac (1856) .. .. .. 35·00
J 172 1s. green (1856) .. .. .. 90·00

A 77. STEWART TOWN.

J 173 1d. rose-red (1857), *perf.* 14 .. £150
J 174 4d. rose (1857) .. .. .. 90·00
J 175 6d. lilac (1856) .. .. .. 65·00

A 78. VERE.
(Now called ALLEY.)

J 176 1d. rose-red (1857), *perf.* 14 .. 90·00
J 177 4d. rose (1857) .. .. .. 32·00
J 178 6d. lilac (1856) .. .. .. 20·00
J 179 1s. green (1856) £150

The use of British stamps in JAMAICA after August, 1860, was unauthorised by the P.M.G. of Great Britain.

OTHER TOWNS IN THE WEST INDIES.
"A 02" *to* "A 15" *and* "A 18."
Obliterations as T 2.

A 02. ST. JOHN'S (ANTIGUA).

z 553 1d. rose-red (1857), *perf.* 14 .. £110
z 553*a* 2d. blue (1855) *perf.* 14 (Plate 6).
z 554 2d. blue (1858) (Plate Nos. 7, 8, 9) £140
z 555 4d. rose (1857) .. .. .. 75·00
z 556 6d. lilac (1856) .. .. .. 75·00
z 557 1s. green (1856) £250

A 03. GEORGETOWN *or* DEMERARA (BRITISH GUIANA).

z 558 1d. rose-red (1857), *perf.* 14 .. 48·00
z 559 4d. rose (1857) .. .. .. 45·00
z 560 6d. lilac (1856) .. .. .. 40·00
z 561 1s. green (1856) £225

A 04. NEW AMSTERDAM *or* BERBICE (BRITISH GUIANA).

z 562 1d. rose-red (1857), *perf.* 14 ..
z 563 2d. blue (1858) (Plate Nos. 7, 8).. £110
z 564 4d. rose (1857) .. .. .. 70·00
z 565 6d. lilac (1856) .. .. .. 70·00
z 566 1s. green (1856) £250

A 05. NASSAU (BAHAMAS).

z 567 1d. rose-red (1857), *perf.* 14 .. £180
z 568 2d. blue (1858) (Plate Nos. 7, 8).. £250
z 569 4d. rose (1857) .. .. .. 90·00
z 570 6d. lilac (1856) .. .. .. 90·00
z 571 1s. green (1856) .. .. ..

A 06. BRITISH HONDURAS.

z 572 1d. rose-red (1857), *perf.* 14 .. £225
z 573 4d. rose (1857) .. .. .. 85·00
z 574 6d. lilac (1856) .. .. .. 85·00
z 575 1s. green (1856) £250

A 07. DOMINICA.

z 576 1d. rose-red (1857), *perf.* 14 ..
z 576*a* 2d. blue (1858) (Plate No. 7) .. £125
z 577 4d. rose (1857) .. .. .. 80·00
z 578 6d. lilac (1856) .. .. .. 80·00
z 579 1s. green £300

A 08. MONTSERRAT.

z 580 1d. rose-red (1857), *perf.* 14 .. £275
z 581 4d. rose (1857) .. ..
z 582 6d. lilac (1856) £140
z 583 1s. green (1856) .. ..

A 09. NEVIS.

z 584 1d. rose-red (1857), *perf.* 14 .. £100
z 585 2d. blue (1858) (Plate Nos. 7, 8) ..
z 586 4d. rose (1857) .. .. .. 80·00
z 587 6d. lilac (1856) .. .. .. 70·00
z 588 1s. green (1856) .. ..

A 10. KINGSTOWN (ST. VINCENT).

z 589 1d. rose-red (1857), *perf.* 14 .. £175
z 590 2d. blue (1855) .. ..
z 591 4d. rose (1857) £140
z 592 6d. lilac (1856) .. .. .. 95·00
z 594 1s. green (1856) £325

A 11. CASTRIES (ST. LUCIA).

z 595 1d. rose-red (1857), *perf.* 14 .. £500
z 596 2d. blue (1855) .. ..
z 597 4d. rose (1857) £110
z 598 6d. lilac (1856) .. .. .. 70·00
z 599 1s. green (1856) £275

A 12. BASSE-TERRE (ST. CHRISTOPHER).

z 600 1d. rose-red (1857), *perf.* 14 ..
z 600*a* 2d. blue (1858) (Plate No. 7) .. £300
z 601 4d. rose (1857) £100
z 602 6d. lilac (1856) .. .. .. 70·00
z 603 1s. green (1856) £275

A 13. TORTOLA (VIRGIN IS.)

z 604 1d. rose-red (1857), *perf.* 14 .. £1100
z 604*a* 4d. rose (1857) £1000
z 605 6d. lilac (1856) £400
z 606 1s. green (1856) .. .. ..

A 14. SCARBOROUGH (TOBAGO).

z 607 1d. rose-red (1857), *perf.* 14 .. £250
z 608 4d. rose (1857) .. .. .. 85·00
z 609 6d. lilac (1856) .. .. .. 75·00
z 610 1s. green (1856) £275

A 15. ST. GEORGE (GRENADA).

z 611 1d. rose-red (1857), *perf.* 14 .. £100
z 612 2d. blue (1858) (Plate No. 7) ..
z 613 4d. rose (1857) .. .. .. 90·00
z 614 6d. lilac (1856) .. .. .. 70·00
z 615 1s. green (1856) £275

A 18. ENGLISH HARBOUR (ANTIGUA).

z 616 6d. lilac £400
z 616*a* 1s. green (1856) .. .. ..

IV.

VARIOUS FOREIGN TOWNS IN SOUTH AND CENTRAL AMERICA AND THE WEST INDIES.

BUENOS AIRES (ARGENTINA).
"B 32." *Obliteration as T* 2, 12, *or* 13.

1860 *to* 1873.

z 736 1d. rose-red (1857) .. ..
z 737 1d. rose-red (1864) .. *From* 4·50
Plate Nos. 71, 72, 73, 74, 76, 78, 79, 80, 81, 85, 87, 89, 90, 91, 92, 93, 94, 95, 96, 97, 99, 101, 103, 104, 107, 108, 110, 112, 113, 114, 117, 118, 119, 120, 121, 123, 129, 130, 131, 135, 138, 139, 140, 142, 143, 145, 147, 149, 150, 151, 155, 159, 163, 164, 166, 169, 172.
z 738 2d. blue (1858–69) .. *From* 6·00
Plate Nos. 8, 9, 12, 13, 14.
z 739 3d. carmine-rose (1862) .. 32·00
z 740 3d. rose (1865) (Plate No. 4) .. 15·00
z 741 3d. rose (1867–73) .. *From* 6·00
Plate Nos. 4, 5, 6, 7, 8, 9, 10.
z 742 4d. rose (1857) .. .. 13·00
z 743 4d. red (1862) (Plate Nos. 3, 4) .. 16·00
z 744 4d. vermilion (1865–73) .. *From* 9·00
Plate Nos. 7, 8, 9, 10, 11, 12, 13.
z 745 6d. lilac (1856) .. .. 13·00
z 746 6d. lilac (1862) (Plate Nos. 3, 4) ..
z 747 6d. lilac (1865–67) .. *From* 11·00
Plate Nos. 5, 6.
z 748 6d. lilac (1867) (Plate No. 6) .. 13·00
z 749 6d. violet (1867–70) .. *From* 10·00
Plate Nos. 6, 8, 9.
z 750 6d. buff (1872) (Plate No. 11) .. 32·00
z 751 6d. chestnut (1872) (Plate No. 11) 8·00
z 752 9d. bistre (1862) .. ..
z 753 9d. straw (1862) .. .. 38·00
z 754 9d. straw (1865) £100
z 755 9d. straw (1867) .. .. 30·00
z 756 10d. red-brown (1867) .. 35·00
z 757 1s. green (1856) .. .. 22·00
z 758 1s. green (1862) .. .. 18·00
z 759 1s. green (1865) (Plate No. 4) .. 10·00
z 760 1s. green (1867–73) .. *From* 4·00
Plate Nos. 4, 5, 6, 7.
z 760*a* 1s. grn. (1873–77) (Plate No. 8)
z 761 2s. blue (1867) .. .. 24·00
z 762 5s. rose (1867) (Plate No. 1) .. 48·00

MONTEVIDEO (URUGUAY).

"C 28." *Obliteration as T* **4** *or* **12**.

1862 *to* **1872.**

z 763 1d. rose-red (1864) 16·00
Plate Nos. 73, 93, 94, 119, 148, 171.
z 764 2d. blue (1858–69) (Plate Nos. 9, 13) 16·00
z 764*a* 3d. rose (1865) Plate No. 4)
z 765 3d. rose (1867–71) (Plate Nos. 4, 5, 7) 9·00
z 765*a* 3d. rose (1873–79) (Plate No. 19)
z 766 4d. rose (1857)
z 766*a* 4d. red (1862) (Plate 4)
z 767 4d. vermilion (1865–70) *From* 9·00
Plate Nos. 7, 8, 9, 10, 11, 12.
z 768 6d. lilac (1856)
z 768*a* 6d. lilac (1862) (Pl. 4)
z 769 6d. lilac (1865–67) (Plate Nos. 5, 6) 11·00
z 770 6d. lilac (1867) (Plate No. 6)
z 771 6d. violet (1867–70) *From* 10·00
Plate Nos. 8, 9.
z 772 6d. buff (1872)
z 773 6d. chestnut (1872)
z 774 9d. straw (1862)
z 775 9d. straw (1865)
z 776 9d. straw (1867) 30·00
z 777 10d. red-brown (1867) 35·00
z 778 1s. green (1862) 18·00
z 779 1s. green (1865) (Plate No. 4) 10·00
z 780 1s. green (1867–73) (Plate Nos. 4, 5) 8·00
z 781 2s. blue (1867) 24·00
z 782 5s. rose (1867) (Plate No. 1) 50·00

VALPARAISO (CHILE).

"C 30." *Obliteration as T* **12** *or as T* **14**.

1865 *to* **1881.**

z 783 ½d. rose-red (1870–79) *From* 20·00
Plate Nos. 6, 11, 12, 13.
z 783*a* 1d. rose-red (1864–79) *From* 6·00
Plate Nos. 80, 84, 85, 91, 122, 123, 140, 149, 152, 157, 158, 162, 167, 175, 178, 181, 185, 186, 187, 189, 190, 195, 197, 198, 200, 201, 207, 209, 210, 211, 212, 214, 215, 217.
z 784 1½d. lake-red (1870–74) *From* 20·00
Plate Nos. 1 and 3.
z 785 2d. blue (1858–69) 16·00
Plate Nos. 9, 13, 14, 15.
z 785*a* 2½d. rosy mauve (1875), white paper (Plate No. 2) 26·00
z 785*b* 2½d. rosy mauve (1876) (Pl. No. 4) 20·00
z 785*c* 3d. carmine-rose (1862)
z 785*d* 3d. rose (1865) (Plate No. 4)
z 786 3d. rose (1867–73) *From* 6·50
Plate Nos. 5, 6, 7, 8, 9, 10.
z 787 3d. rose (1873–76) *From* 7·00
Plate Nos. 11, 12, 14, 16, 17, 18, 19.
z 788 4d. vermilion (1865–73) *From* 9·00
Pl. Nos. 9, 10, 11, 12, 13, 14.
z 789 4d. vermilion (1876) (Plate No. 15)
z 790 4d. sage-green (1877) (Pls. 15, 16) 22·00
z 791 4d. grey-brown (1880) *wmk.* Large Garter (Plate No. 17)
z 792 6d. lilac (1862) (Plates 3, 4) *From* 13·00
z 793 6d. lilac (1865) (Plate Nos. 5, 6)
z 794 6d lilac (1867) (Plate No. 6)
z 795 6d. violet (1867–70) *From* 10·00
Plate Nos. 6, 8, 9.
z 796 6d. buff (1872–73) *From* 20·00
Plate Nos. 11, 12.
z 797 6d. chestnut (1872) (Plate No. 11) 8·00
z 798 6d. grey (1873) (Plate No. 12) 16·00
z 799 6d. grey (1874–80) *From* 7·00
Plate Nos. 13, 14, 15, 16, 17.
z 800 6d. grey (1881) (Plate No. 17)
z 801 8d. orange (1876) 40·00
z 802 9d. straw (1862)
z 803 9d. straw (1865)
z 804 9d. straw (1867) 30·00
z 805 10d. red-brown (1867) 35·00
z 805*a* 1s. green (1865) (Plate No. 4)
z 806 1s. green (1867–73) *From* 4·00
Plate Nos. 4, 5, 6, 7.
z 807 1s. green (1873–77) *From* 8·50
Plate Nos. 8, 9, 10, 11, 12, 13.
z 808 1s. orange-brn. (1880) (Pl. No. 13) 50·00
z 809 2s. blue (1867) 25·00
z 810 2s. brown (1880) £375
z 811 5s. rose (1867–74) *From* 50·00
Plate Nos. 1, 2.
z 812 10s. grey-green (1878) (*wmk.* Cross) £300
z 813 £1 brown-lilac (1878) (*wmk.* Cross) £800

1880.

z 814 1d. Venetian red
z 814*a* 1½d. Venetian red

ARICA (*then in* Peru).

"C 36." *Obliteration as T* **4**, **12** *or* **14**.

1865 *to* **1879.**

z 815 ½d. rose-red (1870–79) *From* 10·00
Plate Nos. 5, 6, 10, 11, 13.
z 816 1d. rose-red (1864–79) *From* 6·00
Plate Nos. 102, 139, 163, 167.
z 817 1½d. lake-red (1870–74) (Plate No. 3)
z 817*a* 2d. blue (1858–69) (Plate No. 14) 32·00
z 817*b* 3d. rose (1867–73) (Plate No. 5)
z 818 3d. rose (1873–76) *From* 8·00
Plate Nos. 11, 12, 17, 18, 19.
z 819 4d. vermilion (1865–73) *From* 9·00
Plate Nos. 10, 11, 12, 13, 14.
z 820 4d. vermilion (1876) (Plate No. 15)
z 821 4d. sage-green (1877) 22·00
Plate Nos. 15, 16.
z 822 6d. lilac (1862) (Plates 3, 4)
z 822*a* 6d. lilac (1865–67) (Plate No. 5)
z 823 6d. violet (1867–70) 10·00
Plate Nos. 6, 8, 9.
z 824 6d. buff (1872) (Plate No. 11) 32·00
z 825 6d. chestnut (1872) (Plate No. 11)
z 825*a* 6d. grey (1873) (Plate No. 12) 16·00
z 826 6d. grey (1874–76) *From* 7·50
Plate Nos. 13, 14, 15, 16.
z 827 8d. orange (1876)
z 828 9d. straw (1862)
z 828*a* 9d. straw (1865)
z 828*b* 9d. straw (1867) 30·00
z 829 10d. red-brown (1867)
z 830 1s. green (1862)
z 830*a* 1s. green (1865)
z 831 1s. green (1867–73) *From* 5·50
Plate Nos. 4, 5, 6, 7.
z 832 1s. green (1873–77) *From* 9·00
Plate Nos. 8, 9, 10, 11, 12, 13.
z 833 2s. blue (1867) 65·00
z 834 5s. rose (1867–74) (Plate Nos. 1, 2) 95·00

CALDERA (CHILE).

"C 37." *Obliterated as T* **4**.

1865 *to* **1881.**

z 835 1d. rose-red (1864–79) *From* 6·00
Plate Nos. 71, 72, 88, 90, 95, 195.
z 836 1½d. lake-red(1870–74) (Plate No)
z 837 2d. blue (1858–69) (Plate No. 9) 6·50
z 838 3d. rose (1865) (Plate No. 4) 14·00
z 839 3d. rose (1867–73) (Plate Nos. 5, 7)
z 840 3d. rose (1873–76) *From* 6·50
Plate Nos. 11, 12, 16, 17, 18, 19.
z 841 4d. red (1862) (Plate 4)
z 842 4d. vermilion (1865–73) *From* 9·00
Plate Nos. 8, 12, 13, 14.
z 843 4d. sage-green (1877) (Plate No. 16)
z 843*a* 6d. lilac (1862) (Plate 4) 27·00
z 844 6d. lilac (1865–67) (Plate No. 6)
z 845 6d. violet (1867–70) *From* 10·00
Plate Nos. 6, 8, 9.
z 846 6d. buff (1872) (Plate No. 11)
z 847 6d. chestnut (1872) (Plate No. 11)
z 848 6d. grey (1873) (Plate No. 12)
z 849 6d. grey (1874–80) *From* 7·00
Plate Nos. 13, 14, 15, 16, 17.
z 850 8d. orange (1876) 65·00
z 851 9d. straw (1867) 38·00
z 852 10d. red-brown (1867) 35·00
z 852*a* 1s. green (1865) (Plate No. 4)
z 853 1s. green (1867–73) *From* 7·00
Plate Nos. 4, 5, 6.
z 854 1s. green (1873–77) *From* 8·50
Plate Nos. 8, 10, 11, 12, 13.
z 855 2s. blue (1867) 70·00
z 856 2s. brown (1880) £375
z 857 5s. rose (1867–74) (Plate No. 2) £120

COBIJA (*then in* Bolivia).

"C 39." *Obliteration* as *T* **4**, **8** *or* **12**.

1865 *to* **1878.**

z 857*a* 1d. rose-red (Plate Nos. 93, 95)
z 858 2d. blue (1858–69) (Plate No. 14)
z 859 3d. rose (1867–73) (Plate No. 6)
z 860 3d. rose (1873–76) (Plate No. 16)
z 860*a* 4d. sage-green (1877) (Plate 15)
z 860*b* 6d. violet (1867–79) (Plate No. 9) 80·00
z 861 6d. buff (1872) (Plate No. 11)
z 862 6d. grey (1874–76) 80·00
Plate Nos. 13, 14, 15, 16.
z 863 1s. green (1867–73) (Pl. Nos. 4, 5)
z 864 1s. green (1873–77) £110
Plate Nos. 10, 11, 12, 13.
z 865 2s. blue (1867) £120
z 866 5s. rose (1867–74) (Plate No. 2)

COQUIMBO (CHILE).

"C 40." *Obliteration as T* **4**.

1865 *to* **1881.**

z 866*a* ½d. rose-red (1870–79) (Pl. No. 14)
z 867 1d. rose-red (1857)
z 867*a* 1d. rose-red (1864–79) (Pl. No. 204)
z 868 2d. blue (1858–69) (Plate Nos. 9, 14)
z 869 3d. rose (1865)
z 869*a* 3d. rose (1872) (Plate No. 8)
z 870 3d. rose (1873–76) *From* 7·00
Plate Nos. 18, 19.
z 870*a* 4d. red (1863) (Plate No. 4) 25·00
z 871 4d. verm. (1865–73) (Pl. Nos. 12, 14)
z 872 4d. sage-green (1877)
Plate Nos. 15, 16.
z 873 6d. lilac (1862) (Plate Nos. 3, 4)
z 873*a* 6d. lilac (1865–67) (Plate No. 5)
z 873*b* 6d. lilac (1867) (Plate No. 6) 27·00
z 874 6d. violet (1867–70) *From* 10·00
Plate Nos. 6, 8, 9.
z 875 6d. buff (1872–73) *From* 27·00
Plate Nos. 11, 12.
z 876 6d. chestnut (1872) (Plate No. 11)
z 877 6d. grey (1873) (Plate No. 12) 19·00
z 878 6d. grey (1874–76) *From* 7·00
Plate Nos. 13, 14, 15, 16.
z 878*a* 8d. orange (1876)
z 878*b* 9d. straw (1862)
z 879 9d. straw (1867) 30·00
z 880 10d. red-brown (1867)
z 881 1s. green (1865) (Plate No. 4) 11·00
z 882 1s. grn. (1867–73) Pl. Nos. 4, 5, 6. 8·00
z 883 1s. green (1873–77) *From* 9·00
Plate Nos. 8, 10, 11, 12, 13.
z 884 2s. blue (1867) 70·00
z 885 2s. brown (1880) £375
z 886 5s. rose (1867–74) (Pl. Nos. 1, 2) 95·00

IQUIQUE (*then in* Peru).

"D 87." *Obliteration as T* **12**.

1868 *to* **1878.**

z 886*a* ½d. rose-red (1870–79) (Pl. 5, 6, 14) 16·00
z 886*b* 1d. rose-red (1864–79) (Pl. No. 179) 13·00
z 887 2d. blue (1858–69) (Plate Nos. 9, 13)
z 888 3d. rose (1867–73) *From* 10·00
Plate Nos. 5, 6, 7, 8, 9.
z 889 3d. rose (1873–76) 27·00
Plate Nos. 12, 18, 19.
z 890 4d. vermilion (1865–73)
Plate Nos. 12, 13.
z 890*a* 4d. vermilion (1876) (Plate No. 15) 55·00
z 890*b* 4d. sage-green (1877) *From* 35·00
Plate Nos. 15, 16.
z 890*c* 6d. mauve (1869) (Plate Nos. 8, 9)
z 891 6d. buff (1872–73) *From* 27·00
Plate Nos. 11, 12.
z 891*a* 6d. chestnut (1872) (Plate No. 11)
z 892 6d. grey (1873) (Plate No. 12) 25·00
z 893 6d. grey (1874–76)
Plate Nos. 13, 14, 15, 16.
z 893*a* 8d. orange (1876) 80·00
z 894 9d. straw (1867) 50·00
z 895 10d. red-brown (1867)
z 896 1s. green (1867–73) *From* 8·00
Plate Nos. 4, 6, 7.
z 897 1s. green (1873–77) *From* 13·00
Plate Nos. 8, 9, 10, 11, 12, 13.
z 898 2s. blue (1867)

CALLAO (PERU).

"C 38." *Obliteration as T* **4**, **12** *or circular date stamp as in T* **5**.

1865 *to* **1879.**

z 899 ½d. rose-red (1870–79) *From* 7·00
Plate Nos. 5, 6, 10, 11, 12, 13, 14.
z 900 1d. rose-red (1864–79) *From* 4·25
Plate Nos. 88, 89, 93, 97, 127, 130, 137, 139, 140, 141, 143, 144, 145, 146, 148, 149, 156, 160, 163, 171, 172, 175 180, 181, 182, 185, 190, 193, 195, 198, 200, 201, 206, 209.
z 901 1½d. lake-red (1870–74) (Plate No. 3)
z 902 2d. blue (1858–69) *From* 3·75
Plate Nos. 9, 12, 13, 14, 15.
z 903 3d. carmine-rose (1862)

z 903a 3d. rose (1865) (Plate No. 4) .. 14·00

z 904 3d. rose (1867–73) .. .. *From* 6·00 Plate Nos. 5, 6, 7, 8, 9, 10.

z 905 3d. rose (1873–76) .. .. *From* 6·50 Plate Nos. 11, 12, 14, 15, 16, 17, 18, 19.

z 906 4d. red (1862) (Plate Nos. 3, 4) ..

z 907 4d. vermilion (1865–73) .. *From* 9·00 Plate Nos. 8, 10, 11, 12, 13, 14.

z 908 4d. vermilion (1876) (Plate No. 15) 45·00

z 909 4d. sage-green (1877) .. .. 22·00 Plate Nos. 15, 16.

z 910 6d. lilac (1862) (Plate Nos. 3, 4) ..

z 911 6d. lilac (1867) .. .. ..

z 912 6d. violet (1867–70) .. *From* 10·00 Plate Nos. 6, 8, 9.

z 913 6d. buff (1872–73) .. .. *From* 28·00 Plate Nos. 11, 12.

z 914 6d. chestnut (1872) (Pl. No. 11) .. 8·00

z 915 6d. grey (1873) (Pl. No. 12) .. 16·00

z 916 6d. grey (1874–80) .. .. *From* 7·00 Plate Nos. 13, 14, 15, 16.

z 918 8d. orange (1876) .. .. .. 42·00

z 918a 9d. straw (1862) .. .. ..

z 919 9d. straw (1865) £110

z 920 9d. straw (1867) .. .. .. 30·00

z 921 10d. red-brown (1867) .. .. 35·00

z 922 1s. green (1865) .. .. ..

z 923 1s. green (1867–73) .. *From* 4·00 Plate Nos. 4, 5, 6, 7.

z 924 1s. green (1873–77) .. *From* 8·50 Plate Nos. 8, 9, 10, 11, 12, 13.

z 925 2s. blue (1867) .. .. .. 24·00

z 926 5s. rose (1867–74) .. *From* 50·00 Plate Nos. 1, 2.

ISLAY (PERU).

" C **42**." *Obliteration as T* **4**.

1865 *to* **1879**.

z 927 1d. rose-red (1864–79) .. *From* 6·50 Plate Nos. 78, 84, 87, 88, 96, 103, 134.

z 928 1½d. lake-red (1870–74) (Plate No. 3)

z 929 2d. blue (1858–69) .. .. .. 5·00 Plate Nos. 9, 15.

z 929a 3d. carmine-rose (1862) .. ..

z 930 3d. rose (1865) .. .. ..

z 931 3d. rose (1867–73) .. .. .. 7·00 Plate Nos. 4, 5, 6, 10.

z 932 4d. red (1862) (Plate Nos. 3, 4) ..

z 933 4d. vermilion (1867–73) .. *From* 9·00 Plate Nos. 9, 10, 11, 12, 13.

z 934 4d. vermilion (1876) (Pl. No. 15) ..

z 935 4d. sage-green (1877) .. .. 22·00 Plate Nos. 15, 16.

z 936 6d. lilac (1862) (Plate Nos. 3, 4) .. 27·00

z 937 6d. lilac (1865) (Plate No. 5) .. 12·00

z 938 6d. violet (1867–60) .. *From* 10·00 Plate Nos. 6, 8, 9.

z 938a 6d. buff (1873) (Plate No. 12) ..

z 939 6d. grey (1873) (Plate No. 12) ..

z 940 6d. grey (1874–76) .. .. *From* 7·00 Plate Nos. 13, 14, 15, 16.

z 941 9d. straw (1865) £110

z 941a 9d. straw (1867) .. .. .. 32·00

z 942 10d. red-brown (1867) .. .. 75·00

z 943 1s. green (1865) (Plate No. 4) ..

z 944 1s. green (1867–73) .. *From* 6·00 Plate Nos. 4, 5, 6, 7.

z 945 1s. green (1873–77) .. *From* 8·50 Plate Nos. 10, 12, 13.

z 946 2s. blue (1867) .. .. ..

z 947 5s. rose (1867) (Plate No. 1) ..

PAITA (PERU).

" C **43**." *Obliteration as T* **4**.

1861 *to* **1879**.

z 947a 1d. rose-red (1864–79) (Pl. No. 127)

z 948 2d. blue (1858–69) (Plate Nos. 9, 14)

z 949 3d. rose (1867–73) (Plate Nos. 5, 6) 14·00

z 949a 3d. rose (1876) (Plate Nos. 17, 19) 14·00

z 950 4d. vermilion (1865–73) .. *From* 10·00 Plates Nos. 10, 11, 12, 13, 14.

z 951 4d. sage-green (1877) (Plate No. 15)

z 952 6d. lilac (1862) (Plate No. 3) .. 16·00

z 953 6d. lilac (1865–67) (Plates 5, 6) .. 14·00

z 954 6d. violet (1867—70) .. .. 14·00 Plate Nos. 6, 8, 9.

z 955 6d. buff (1872–73) .. .. *From* 24·00 Plate Nos. 11, 12.

z 955a 6d. chestnut (Plate No. 11) ..

z 956 6d. grey (1873) .. .. ..

z 957 6d. grey (1874–76) .. .. .. Plate Nos. 13, 14, 15.

z 957a 9d. straw (1862) .. .. ..

z 958 10d. red-brown (1867) .. .. 80·00

z 959 1s. green (1865) (Plate No. 4) ..

z 960 1s. green (1867–73) (Plate No. 4) 13·00

z 961 1s. green (1873–77) .. .. 13·00 Plate Nos. 8, 9, 10, 13.

z 962 2s. blue (1867) .. .. .. 75·00

z 963 5s. rose (1867) (Plate No. 1) .. 90·00

PISAGUA? (PERU).

" D **65**." *Obliteration as T* **12**.

z 963a 2s. blue (1867) .. .. ..

PISCO (PERU).

" D **74**." *Obliteration as T* **12**.

1868 *to* **1870**.

z 963b 2d. blue (1858–69) (Plate No. 9) ..

z 964 4d. vermilion (1865–73) .. .. Plate Nos. 10, 12.

z 965 6d. violet (1868) (Plate No. 6) .. £225

z 965a 1s. green (1867) (Plate No. 4) ..

z 966 2s. blue (1867) £100

PANAMA (COLOMBIA).

" C **35**." *Obliterations as T* **4**, **11** *or* **14**.

1865 *to* **1884**.

z 967 ½d. rose-red (1870–79) .. .. Plate Nos. 10, 11 12, 13, 14, 15, 19.

z 968 1d. rose-red (1864–79) .. *From* 3·50 Plate Nos. 72, 76, 81, 85, 87, 88, 93, 95, 101, 104, 114, 124, 130, 138, 139, 142, 159, 168, 171, 172, 174, 177, 179, 180, 184, 185, 189, 191, 192, 193, 196, 200, 203, 204, 205, 207, 208, 209, 210, 211, 213, 214, 215, 218, 224.

z 969 1½d. lake-red (1870–74) (Plate No. 3) 7·00

z 970 2d. blue (1858–69) .. .. *From* 4·00 Plate Nos. 9, 12, 13, 14, 15.

z 971 2½d. rosy mauve (1875) (Plate 1) ..

z 971a 2½d. rosy mauve (1876–80) .. Plate Nos. 4, 12, 16.

z 971b 2½d. blue (1880) (Plate No. 19) ..

z 972 2½d. blue (1881) (Plate Nos. 22, 23)

z 972a 3d. carmine-red (1862) .. ..

z 973 3d. rose (1865) (Plate No. 4) ..

z 974 3d. rose (1867–73) .. .. *From* 6·00 Plate Nos. 4, 5, 6, 7, 8, 9.

z 975 3d. rose (1873–76) .. .. *From* 6·50 Plates 14, 15, 16, 17, 18, 19, 20.

z 976 3d. rose (1881) (Plate Nos. 20, 21)

z 977 4d. red (1863) (Plate No. 4) ..

z 978 4d. vermilion (1865–73) .. *From* 9·00 Pl. Nos. 7, 8, 9, 10, 11, 12, 13, 14.

z 979 4d. vermilion (1876) (Plate No. 15) 42·00

z 980 4d. sage-green (1877) .. .. 22·00 Plate Nos. 15, 16.

z 981 4d. grey-brn. (1880) *wmk.* Crown (Plate Nos. 17, 18) .. *From* 6·00

z 982 6d. lilac (1862) (Plates 3, 4) *From* 13·00

z 983 6d. lilac (1865–67) .. .. *From* 12·00 Plate Nos. 5, 6.

z 984 6d. lilac (1867) (Plate No. 6) ..

z 985 6d. violet (1867–70) .. .. 10·00 Plate Nos. 6, 8, 9.

z 986 6d. buff (1872–73) .. .. *From* 25·00 Plate Nos. 11, 12.

z 987 6d. chestnut (Plate No. 11) .. 8·00

z 988 6d. grey (1873) (Plate No. 12) .. 16·00

z 989 6d. grey (1874–80) .. .. *From* 7·00 Plate Nos. 13, 14, 15, 16, 17.

z 990 6d. grey (1881) (Plate No. 17) .. 20·00

z 991 8d. orange (1876) .. .. .. 42·00

z 992 9d. straw (1862) .. .. .. 40·00

z 992a 9d. straw (1867) .. .. .. 30·00

z 993 10d. red-brown (1867) .. .. 35·00

z 994 1s. green (1865) (Plate No. 4) .. 10·00

z 995 1s. green (1867–73) .. *From* 3·50 Plate Nos. 4, 5, 6, 7.

z 996 1s. green (1873–77) .. *From* 9·00 Plate Nos. 8, 9, 10, 11, 12, 13.

z 997 1s. orange-brown (1880) (Pl. 13) .. 48·00

z 998 1s. orge.-brn. (1881) (Plate No. 13) 10·00

z 999 2s. blue (1867) .. .. .. 25·00

z 1000 2s. brown (1880) £375

z 1001 5s. rose (1867–74) .. .. *From* 50·00 Plate Nos. 1, 2.

1880.

z 1001a 1d. Venetian red .. .. .. 3·50

z 1002 2d. rose .. .. 7·50

z 1003 5d. indigo .. .. 16·00

1881.

z 1004 1d. lilac (14 *dots*) .. .. .. 9·50

z 1005 1d. lilac (16 *dots*) .. .. .. 8·00

1884.

z 1006–z 1010 1½d., 2d., 2½d., 4d., 5d *Fr.* 6·00

1887.

z 1010a 2d. green and carmine .. ..

The Panama Office was closed to the public in 1881, but remained open as a " transit office " until, at least, 1888.

CARTAGENA (COLOMBIA)

" C **56**." *Obliterations as T* **4**.

1865 *to* **1881**.

z 1010b ½d. rose-red (1870–79) (Pl. No. 10)

z 1010c 1d. rose-red (1864–79) .. *From* 9·50 Plate Nos. 87, 100, 111, 113, 117, 119, 125, 189, 217.

z 1011 2d. blue (1858–69) .. *From* 6·00 Plate Nos. 9, 11, 14.

z 1011a 3d. "*Emblems*" (1865) (Plate No. 4)

z 1012 3d. rose (1865–68) .. .. Plate Nos. 4, 5.

z 1012a 3d. rose (1873–79) .. *From* 18·00 Plate Nos. 17, 18.

z 1013 4d. vermilion (1865–73) .. *From* 9·00 Plate Nos. 7, 8, 9, 10, 11, 12, 13, 14.

z 1014 4d. vermilion (1876) (Pl. No. 15) 38·00

z 1014a 4d. sage-green .. .. *From* 22·00 Plate Nos. 15, 16.

z 1015 6d. lilac (1865–67) (Plate Nos. 5, 6)

z 1016 6d. vio. (1867–70) (Pl. 6, 8) *From* 24·00

z 1017 6d. grey (1873) (Plate No. 12) .. 16·00

z 1018 6d. grey (1874–76) .. *From* 7·50 Plate Nos. 13, 14, 15, 16.

z 1019 8d. orange (1876) .. .. .. 48·00

z 1019a 9d. straw (1865) .. .. ..

z 1020 1s. green (1865) .. .. ..

z 1021 1s. green (1867–73) .. .. Plate Nos. 4, 5, 7.

z 1022 1s. green (1873–77) .. .. 9·50 Plate Nos. 8, 9, 10, 11, 12, 13

z 1023 1s. orange-brown (1880) .. ..

z 1023a 2s. blue (1867) .. .. .. 80·00

z 1024 5s. rose (1867) (Plate No. 1) .. £110

" C **65** " *error for* " C **56**."

1866 *to* **1881**.

z 1024a ½d. rose-red (1870–79) (Pl. 10) ..

z 1024b 1d. rose-red (1864–79) .. *From* 25·00 Plate Nos. 100, 111.

z 1025 2d. blue (1858–69) (Plate No. 9) 8·00

z 1025aa 2d. rose (1880) .. .. ..

z 1025a 2½d. blue (1880) (Pl. 19) .. ..

z 1025b 3d. rose (1867–73) (Plate No. 9)

z 1026 3d. rose (1873–79) (Pl. 17, 19, 20)

z 1027 4d. vermilion (1865–73) .. *From* 9·00 Plate Nos. 7, 9, 11, 12, 13, 14.

z 1028 4d. vermilion (1876) (Plate No. 15) 42·00

z 1028a 4d. sage-green (1877) .. *From* 22·00 Plate Nos. 15, 16.

z 1029 6d. violet (1867–70) (Plates 6, 8)

z 1029a 6d. pale buff (1872) (Plate No. 11)

z 1029b 6d. grey (1873) (Plate No. 12) .. 25·00

z 1029c 6d. grey (1874–80) .. .. 25·00 Plate Nos. 13, 15, 16, 17.

z 1030 8d. orange (1876) .. .. ..

z 1031 9d. straw (1865) £120

z 1032 1s. green (1865) (Plate No. 4) ..

z 1032a 1s. green (1867) (Pls. 4, 5, 6, 7) 8·00

z 1032b 1s. green (1873–77) .. *From* 10·00 Plate Nos. 8, 11, 12, 13.

z 1032c 1s. orange-brown (1880) .. ..

z 1032d 2s. blue (1867) .. .. ..

z 1033 2s. brown (1880) £375

z 1034 5s. rose (1867) (Plate No. 1) .. £110

SANTA MARTHA (COLOMBIA).

" C **62**." *Obliteration as T* **4**.

1865 *to* **1881**.

z 1034a ½d. rose-red (1870–79) (Plate 6) 20·00

z 1035 1d. rose-red (1864–79) (Pl. No. 106) 20·00

z 1036 2d. blue (1858–69) (Plate No. 9) 20·00

z 1037 4d. vermilion (1865–73) .. *From* 13·00 Plate Nos. 7, 8, 9, 11, 12, 13, 14.

z 1037a 4d. sage-green (1877) (Plate 15) 22·00

z 1037b 4d. grey-brown (1880) *wmk.* Large Garter (Plate No. 17) .. 27·00

z 1037c 4d. grey-brown (1880) *wmk.* Crown (Plate No. 17) .. .. 20·00

z 1038 6d. lilac (1865–67) (Plate No. 5)

z 1038a 6d. grey (1873) (Plate No. 12) ..

z 1038b 6d. grey (1874–76) (Plate No. 14)

z 1039 8d. orange (1876) .. .. 45·00

z 1040 1s. green (1865) (Plate No. 4) .. 17·00

z 1040a 1s. green (1867–73) (Pl. Nos. 5, 7) 17·00

z 1040b 1s. green (1873–77) (Plate No. 8)
z 1041 2s. blue (1867) .. .. .. 85·00
z 1041a 5s. rose (1867) (Plate No. 2) .. £110

ASPINWALL, COLON (COLOMBIA).

"E 88." *Obliteration as T* 12.

1870 to 1881.

z 1042 1d. rose-red (1864–79) .. *From* 6·50
Plate Nos. 107, 121, 122, 123, 125, 127, 130, 133, 136, 142, 150, 151, 152, 153, 155, 156, 157, 158, 160, 171, 174, 176, 178, 184, 187, 194, 195, 201, 209, 213, 214, 217.
z 1042a 1d. Venetian red (1880) .. ..
z 1043 1½d. lake-red (1870–74) (Pl. No. 3) 35·00
z 1044 2d. blue (1858–69) (Pl.Nos. 14,15) 8·00
z 1044a 2d. pale brown (1880) .. ..
z 1045 3d. rose (1867–73) (Plate No. 9)
z 1046 3d. rose (1873–76) .. .. 12·00
Plate Nos. 12, 16, 18, 19, 20.
z 1047 4d. vermilion (1865–73) .. *From* 9·00
Plate Nos. 10, 11, 12, 13, 14.
z 1048 4d. vermilion (1876) (Plate No. 15)
z 1049 4d. sage-grn. (1877) (Pl. Nos. 15,16) 24·00
z 1050 4d. grey-brown (1880) *wmk.* Large Garter (Plate No. 17) .. 27·00
z 1051 4d. grey-brown (1880) *wmk.* Crown (Plate No. 17)
z 1052 6d. vio. (1867–70) (Plates 6, 8, 9)
z 1052a 6d. buff (1872) (Plate No. 11) ..
z 1053 6d. chestnut (1872) (Plate No. 11) 18·00
z 1054 6d. grey (1873) (Plate No. 12) ..
z 1055 6d. grey (1874–80) .. *From* 7·50
Plate Nos. 13, 14, 15, 16, 17.
z 1055a 8d. orange (1876) .. .. ..
z 1056 9d. straw (1867) .. .. ..
z 1057 1s. green (1867–73) .. .. 6·50
Plate Nos. 4, 5, 6, 7.
z 1058 1s. green (1873–77) .. *From* 9·00
Plate Nos. 8, 9, 10, 11, 12, 13.
z 1059 1s. orange-brown (1880) (Plate 13) 45·00
z 1060 1s. orange-brown (1881) (Plate 13) 13·00
z 1061 2s. blue (1867) .. .. .. 35·00
z 1061a 2s. brown (1880) £400
z 1061b 5s. rose (1867) (Plate Nos. 1, 2) 80·00

SAVANILLA (COLOMBIA).

"F 69." *Obliteration as T* 12.

1872 to 1881.

z 1062 ½d. rose-red (1870–79) (Plate 6) 17·00
z 1063 1d. rose-red (1864–79) .. .. 17·00
Plate Nos. 122, 171.
z 1064 1½d. lake-red (1870–74) (Pl. No. 3) 35·00
z 1065 3d. rose (1867–73) (Plate No. 7) ..
z 1066 3d. rose (1873–76) (Plate No. 20)
z 1066a 3d. rose (1881) (Plate No. 20) ..
z 1067 4d. vermilion (1865–73) .. .. 12·00
Plate Nos. 12, 13, 14.
z 1068 4d. vermilion (1876) (Plate No. 15)
z 1069 4d. sage-green (1877) .. .. 22·00
Plate Nos. 15, 16.
z 1070 4d. grey-brn. (1880) *wmk.* Large Garter (Plate No. 17)
z 1071 4d. grey-brn. (1880) *wmk.* Crown (Plate No. 17) .. ..
z 1072 6d. buff (1872) (Plate No. 11) ..
z 1072a 6d. grey (1878) (Plate No. 16) .. 25·00
z 1072b 8d. orange (1876) .. .. 50·00
z 1073 1s. green (1867–73) (Pl. Nos. 5,7) 8·00
z 1074 1s. green (1873–77) .. ..
Plate Nos. 8, 11, 12 and 13.
z 1075 1s. orange-brown (1880) ..
z 1076 2s. blue (1867) .. .. ..
z 1077 5s. rose (1867–74) (Plate No. 2) .. £110

GUAYAQUIL (ECUADOR).

"C 41." *Obliteration as T* 4.

1865 to 1880.

z 1078 ½d. rose-red (1870–79) .. .. 16·00
Plate Nos. 5, 6.
z 1079 1d. rose-red (1857) .. ..
z 1080 1d. rose-red (1864–79) .. *From* 6·00
Plate Nos. 74, 78, 85, 92, 94, 105, 110, 115, 133, 140, 145, 166, 174, 216.
z 1081 1½d. lake-red (1870–74) .. .. 13·00
Plate No. 3.
z 1082 2d. blue (1858–69) .. *From* 6·00
Plate Nos. 9, 13, 14.
z 1082a 3d. carmine-rose (1862) .. .. 70·00
z 1083 3d. rose (1865) (Plate No. 4) .. 16·00
z 1084 3d. rose (1867–73) .. *From* 6·00
Plate Nos. 6, 7, 9, 10.
z 1085 3d. rose (1873–76) .. *From* 6·50
Plate Nos. 11, 12, 15, 16, 17, 18, 19.
z 1086 4d. red (1862) (Plate Nos. 3, 4) .. 18·00
z 1087 4d. vermilion (1865–73) .. *From* 10·00
Plate Nos. 7, 8, 9, 10, 11, 12, 13, 14.
z 1088 4d. vermilion (1876) (Pl. No. 15) 42·00
z 1089 4d. sage-green (1877) .. .. 24·00
Plate Nos. 15, 16.
z 1090 6d. lilac (1864) (Plate No. 4) .. 27·00
z 1091 6d. lilac (1865–67) (Pl. Nos. 5, 6) 11·00
z 1092 6d. lilac (1867) (Plate No. 6) ..
z 1093 6d. violet (1867–70) .. *From* 10·00
Plate Nos. 6, 8, 9.
z 1094 6d. buff (1872–73) (Pl. Nos. 11, 12)
z 1095 6d. chestnut (1872) .. ..
z 1096 6d. grey (1873) (Plate No. 12) ..
z 1097 6d. grey (1874–76) .. *From* 7·00
Plate Nos. 13, 14, 15, 16.
z 1098 8d. orange (1876) .. .. 50·00
z 1098a 9d. straw (1862) .. .. .. 80·00
z 1098b 9d. straw (1867) .. .. .. 30·00
z 1099 10d. red-brown (1867) .. .. 40·00
z 1100 1s. green (1865) (Plate No. 4) .. 11·00
z 1101 1s. green (1867–73) .. *From* 5·00
Plate Nos. 4, 5, 6, 7.
z 1102 1s. green (1873–77) .. *From* 8·50
Plate Nos. 8, 9, 10, 11, 12, 13.
z 1103 2s. blue (1867) .. .. .. 35·00
z 1104 2s. brown (1880) £400
z 1105 5s. rose (1867–74) .. *From* £100
Plate Nos. 1, 2.

GREYTOWN (NICARAGUA).

"C 57." *Obliteration as T* 4, 12 *or* 14.

1865 to 1882.

z 1106 ½d. rose-red (1870–79) .. .. 16·00
Plate Nos. 5, 11.
z 1106a 1d. rose-red (1864–79) .. ..
Plate Nos. 197, 210.
z 1107 1½d. lake-red (1870) (Plate No. 3) 9·00
z 1108 2d. blue (1858–69) .. ..
Plate Nos. 9, 14, 15.
z 1109 3d. rose (1873–76) .. ..
Plate Nos. 17, 18, 19, 20.
z 1110 3d. rose (1881) (Plate No. 20) ..
z 1111 4d. vermilion (1865–73) .. *From* 10·00
Plate Nos. 8, 10, 11, 12, 13, 14.
z 1112 4d. vermilion (1876) (Plate No. 15)
z 1113 4d. sage-green (1877) .. .. 25·00
Plate Nos. 15, 16.
z 1114 4d. grey-brn. (1880) *wmk.* Large Garter (Plate No. 17) .. 30·00
z 1115 4d. grey-brown (1880) *wmk.* Crown (Plate No. 17) .. 10·00
z 1116 6d. grey (1874–76) .. ..
Plate Nos. 14, 15, 16.
z 1117 8d. orange (1876) .. ..
z 1117a 1s. green (1865) (Plate No. 4) ..
z 1118 1s. green (1867–73) .. ..
Plate Nos. 6, 7.
z 1119 1s. green (1873–77) .. .. 8·50
Plate Nos. 8, 12, 13.
z 1120 1s. orange-brown (1880) .. 45·00
Plate No. 13.
z 1121 1s. orange-brown (1881) .. 20·00
Plate No. 13.
z 1122 2s. blue (1867) .. .. .. 27·00
z 1123 2s. brown (1880) £400
z 1124 5s. rose (1867–74) (Plate Nos. 1, 2) 50·00
z 1124a 5s. rose (1882) (Plate No. 4), blue *paper* £375
z 1124b 10s. greenish grey (1878) £375

1880.

z 1125 1d. Venetian red .. .. ..
z 1126 1½d. Venetian red .. .. .. 25·00

TAMPICO (MEXICO).

"C 63." *Obliteration as T* 4.

1865 to 1876.

z 1127 1d. rose-red (1864–79) .. *From* 35·00
Plate Nos. 81, 89, 103, 117, 139, 147.
z 1128 2d. blue (1858–69) .. .. 35·00
Plate Nos. 9, 14.
z 1129 4d. vermilion (1865–73) .. *From* 25·00
Plate Nos. 7, 8, 10, 11, 12, 13, 14.
z 1130 1s. green (1867–73) .. ..
Plate Nos. 4, 5, 7.
z 1130a 2s. blue (1867) .. .. .. 95·00

LA GUAYRA (VENEZUELA).

"C 60." *Obliteration as T* 4, *circular postmark as T* 16 *or Crowned Circle undated postmark.*

1865 to 1880.

z 1135 ½d. rose-red (1870) (Plate 6) ..
z 1135a 1d. rose-red (1864–79) .. *From* 6·50
Plate Nos. 92, 96, 98, 111, 113, 115, 131, 138, 145, 154, 177, 178, 180, 196.
z 1136 1½d. lake-red (1870–74) (Plate 3)
z 1137 2d. blue (1858–69) (Plate No. 14) 12·00
z 1138 3d. rose (1873–76) .. *From* 18·00
Plate Nos. 14, 15, 17, 18, 19.
z 1139 4d. vermilion (1865–73) .. *From* 10·00
Plate Nos. 9, 11, 12, 13, 14.
z 1140 4d. vermilion (1876) (Plate No. 15) 40·00
z 1141 4d. sage-green (1877) .. .. 24·00
Plate Nos. 15, 16.
z 1142 6d. lilac (1865) (Plate No. 5) ..
z 1143 6d. violet (1867–70) (Pl. Nos. 6, 8)
z 1144 6d. buff (1872–73) .. *From* 35·00
Plate Nos. 11, 12.
z 1145 6d. grey (1873) (Plate No. 12) .. 20·00
z 1146 6d. grey (1874–76) .. .. 20·00
Plate Nos. 13, 15, 16.
z 1146a 8d. orange (1876) .. .. .. 55·00
z 1146b 9d. straw (1862) .. .. ..
z 1146c 9d. straw (1867) .. .. ..
z 1147 10d. red-brown (1867) .. ..
z 1147a 1s. green (1865) (Plate No. 4) .. 32·00
z 1148 1s. green (1867–73) (Pl. Nos. 4, 7)
z 1149 1s. green (1873–77) .. *From* 10·00
Plate Nos. 8, 9, 10, 11, 12, 13.
z 1150 2s. blue (1867) .. .. .. 85·00
z 1151 5s. rose (1867–74) (Pl. 1, 2) *From* £110

CIUDAD BOLIVAR OR ANGOSTURA (VENEZUELA).

"D 22." *Obliteration or circular postmark as T* 12 *or* 17.

1868 to 1880.

z 1152 1d. rose-red (1864–79) (Pl. No. 133) 25·00
z 1152a 2d. blue (1858–69) (Plate No. 13)
z 1153 3d. rose (1867–73) (Plate No. 5)
z 1153a 3d. rose (1873–79) (Plate No. 11) 35·00
z 1154 4d. vermilion (1865–73) .. .. 20·00
Plate Nos. 9, 12, 14.
z 1155 4d. sage-green (1877) .. *From* 45·00
Plate Nos. 15, 16.
z 1155a 4d. grey-brn. (1880) *wmk.* Crown (Plate No. 17) .. ..
z 1155b 9d. straw (1867) .. .. ..
z 1155c 10d. red-brown (1867) .. ..
z 1156 1s. green (1867–73) .. *From* 35·00
Plate Nos. 4, 5, 7.
z 1157 1s. green (1873–77) .. ..
Plate Nos. 10, 12, 13. .. 25·00
z 1158 2s. blue (1867) £120
z 1158a 5s. rose (1867–74) (Pl. Nos. 1, 2) £120

BAHIA (BRAZIL).

"C 81." *Obliteration as T* 12.

1866 to 1874.

z 1159 1d. rose-red (1864–79) .. *From* 7·50
Plate Nos. 90, 108, 113, 117, 135, 140, 147, 155.
z 1160 1½d. lake-red (1870–74) (Pl. No. 3) 20·00
z 1161 2d. blue (1858–69) .. .. 13·00
Plate Nos. 9, 12, 13, 14.
z 1162 3d. rose (1865) (Plate No. 4) ..
z 1163 3d. rose (1867–73) .. .. 12·00
Plate Nos. 4, 6, 8, 9, 10.
z 1163a 3d. rose (1873–79) (Plate No. 11)
z 1164 4d. vermilion (1865–73) .. *From* 10·00
Plate Nos. 8, 9, 11, 12, 13.
z 1164a 6d. lilac (1865–67) (Plate No. 5)
z 1165 6d. lilac (1867) (Plate No. 6) .. 13·00
z 1166 6d. violet (1867–70) .. *From* 10·00
Plate Nos. 6, 8, 9.
z 1166a 6d. buff (1872–73) .. *From* 38·00
Plate Nos. 11, 12.
z 1167 6d. chestnut (1872) (Plate No. 11)
z 1168 6d. grey (1873) (Plate No. 12) ..
z 1169 6d. grey (1874–76) (Plate No. 13)
z 1170 9d. straw (1865) £110
z 1170a 9d. straw (1867) .. .. .. 35·00
z 1171 1s. green (1865) (Plate No. 4) .. 12·00
z 1172 1s. green (1867–73) .. *From* 7·50
Plate Nos. 4, 5, 6, 7.
z 1173 1s. green (1873–77) .. *From* 10·00
Plate Nos. 8, 9.
z 1174 2s. blue (1867) .. .. .. 55·00
z 1175 5s. rose (1867) (Plate No. 1) .. 95·00

PERNAMBUCO (BRAZIL).

"C 82." *Obliteration as T* 12.

1866 *to* **1874.**

z 1176 1d. rose-red (1864–79) .. *From* 15·00
Plate Nos. 85, 108, 111, 130, 132, 149, 159, 160.
z 1177 2d. blue (1858–69) .. *From* 16·00
Plate Nos. 9, 12, 13, 14.
z 1178 3d. rose (1867–73) .. .. 15·00
Plate Nos. 4, 5, 6, 7, 10.
z 1178*a* 3d. rose (1873–77) (Plate No. 11)
z 1179 4d. vermilion (1865–73) .. *From* 10·00
Plate Nos. 9, 10, 11, 12, 13, 14.
z 1180 6d. lilac (1865–67) (Plate Nos. 5, 6)
z 1181 6d. lilac (1867) (Plate No. 6) .. 13·00
z 1182 6d. violet (1867–70) .. *From*
Plate Nos. 8, 9.
z 1183 6d. buff (1872–73) .. ..
Plate Nos. 11, 12.
z 1184 6d. chestnut (1872) (Plate No. 11)
z 1185 6d. grey (1873) (Plate No. 12) ..
z 1186 9d. straw (1865) £110
z 1187 9d. straw (1867) .. .. .. 35·00
z 1188 10d. red-brown (1867) .. ..
z 1189 1s. green (1865) (Plate No. 4) ..
z 1190 1s. green (1867–73) .. .. 32·00
Plate Nos. 4, 5, 6, 7.
z 1191 2s. blue (1867) .. .. .. 36·00
z 1192 5s. rose (1867–74) (Plate Nos. 1, 2) £110

RIO DE JANEIRO (BRAZIL).

"C 83." *Obliteration as T* 12.

1866 *to* **1874.**

z 1193 1d. rose-red (1857) .. .. 13·00
z 1194 1d. rose-red (1864–79) .. *From* 7·00
Plates 71, 76, 113, 117, 123, 132, 134, 135, 159, 161, 166.
z 1195 2d. blue (1858–69) .. *From* 10·00
Plate Nos. 9, 12, 13, 14.
z 1196 3d. rose (1867–73) .. *From* 10·00
Plate Nos. 4, 5, 6, 7, 8.
z 1197 3d. rose (1873–77) (Pl. No. 11) ..
z 1198 4d. vermilion (1865–73) .. *From* 9·00
Pl. Nos. 8, 9, 10, 11, 12, 13, 14.
z 1199*a* 6d. lilac (1865–67) (Plate No. 5)
z 1200 6d. lilac (1867) (Plate No. 6) .. 13·00
z 1201 6d. violet (1867–70) .. *From* 10·00
Plate Nos. 6, 8, 9.
z 1202 6d. buff (1872) (Plate No. 11) ..
z 1203 6d. chestnut (1872) (Plate No. 11)
z 1204 6d. grey (1873) (Plate No. 12) ..
z 1205 9d. straw (1865) £100
z 1206 9d. straw (1867) .. .. .. 40·00
z 1207 10d. red-brown (1867) .. ..
z 1208 1s. green (1865) (Plate No. 4) .. 10·00
z 1209 1s. green (1867–73) .. *From* 5·00
Plate Nos. 4, 5, 6, 7.
z 1210 1s. green (1873–77) (Pl. Nos. 8, 9) 9·00
z 1211 2s. blue (1867) .. .. .. 35·00
z 1212 5s. rose (1867–74) .. *From* 55·00
Plate Nos. 1, 2.

JACMEL (HAITI).

"C 59." *Obliteration as T* 4.

1865 *to* **1881.**

z 1213 ½d. rose-red (1870–79) .. *From* 9·00
Plate Nos. 4, 5, 6, 10, 11, 12, 14, 15.
z 1214 1d. rose-red (1864–79) .. *From* 6·00
Plate Nos. 74, 87, 95, 107, 109, 122, 136, 137, 139, 148, 150, 151, 152, 156, 157, 159, 160, 162, 164, 166, 170, 171, 179, 181, 186, 187, 189, 192, 194, 200, 204, 215, 219.
z 1215 1½d. lake-red (1870–74) (Plate 3) .. 9·00
z 1216 2d. blue (1858–69) .. .. 7·50
Plate Nos. 9, 13, 14, 15.
z 1217 2½d. rosy mauve (1876) (Plate 4)
z 1217*a* 3d. rose (1867–73) .. *From* 7·50
Plate Nos. 5, 6, 8, 9, 10.
z 1218 3d. rose (1873–76) .. .. 7·50
Plate Nos. 11, 12, 14, 16, 17, 18, 19.
z 1218*a* 4d. red (1863) (Pl. No. 4) (*Hair lines*) .. .. 30·00
z 1219 4d. vermilion (1865–73) .. *From* 10·00
Plate Nos. 7, 8, 9, 10, 11, 12, 13, 14.
z 1220 4d. vermilion (1876) (Plate No. 15) 40·00
z 1221 4d. sage-green (1877) .. .. 24·00
Plate Nos. 15, 16.
z 1222 4d. grey-brn. (1880) *wmk.* Large Garter (Plate No. 17) .. 32·00
z 1223 4d. grey-brn. (1880) *wmk.* Crown (Plate No. 17) .. .. 6·50
z 1224 6d. lilac (1867) (Plate No. 6) .. 14·00
z 1225 6d. vio. (1867–70) (Plate Nos. 8, 9) 10·00
z 1226 6d. buff (1872–73) .. *From* 25·00
Plate Nos. 11, 12.
z 1227 6d. chestnut (1872) (Plate No. 11)
z 1228 6d. grey (1873) (Plate No. 12) ..
z 1229 6d. grey (1874–76) .. *From* 7·00
Plate Nos. 13, 14, 15, 16, 17.
z 1230 8d. orange (1876) .. .. 55·00
z 1230*a* 9d. straw (1862) .. .. .. 40·00
z 1231 9d. straw (1867) .. .. .. 32·00
z 1232 10d. red-brown (1867) .. ..
z 1233 1s. green (1865) (Plate No. 4) .. 11·00
z 1234 1s. green (1867–73) .. *From* 5·00
Plate Nos. 4, 5, 6, 7.
z 1235 1s. green (1873–77) .. *From* 9·00
Plate Nos. 8, 9, 10, 11, 12, 13.
z 1236 1s. orange-brown (1880) .. .. 45·00
Plate No. 13.
z 1237 2s. blue (1867) .. .. .. 38·00
z 1238 2s. brown (1880) £350
z 1239 5s. rose (1867–74) .. *From* 50·00
Plate Nos. 1, 2.

1880.

z 1239*a* ½d. green (1880) .. .. .. 7·50
z 1240 1d. Venetian red .. .. .. 6·00
z 1241 1½d. Venetian red .. .. .. 8·00
z 1242 2d. rose .. .. 14·00

PORT-AU-PRINCE (HAITI).

"E 53." *Obliteration as T* 11, 12 *or* 14.

1869 *to* **1881.**

z 1243 ½d. rose-red (1870–79) .. *From* 7·00
Plate Nos. 5, 6, 10, 11, 12, 13.
z 1244 1d. rose-red (1864–79) .. *From* 4·25
Plate Nos. 87, 134, 154, 167, 171, 174, 183, 187, 189, 193, 199, 200, 201, 202, 206, 209, 210, 218.
z 1245 1½d. lake-red (1870–74) (Plate 3) .. 9·00
z 1245*a* 2d. blue (1858–69) (Pl. No. 9) ..
z 1246 2d. blue (1855–69) .. .. 7·50
Plate Nos. 14, 15.
z 1247 2½d. rosy mauve (1876–79) .. 32·00
Plate Nos. 3, 9.
z 1247*a* 3d. rose (1867–73) (Pl. Nos. 6, 7)
z 1248 3d. rose (1873–79) .. .. 7·50
Plate Nos. 17, 18, 20.
z 1249 4d. vermilion (1865–73) .. *From* 10·00
Plate Nos. 11, 12, 13, 14.
z 1250 4d. vermilion (1876) (Plate No. 15) 48·00
z 1251 4d. sage-green (1877) .. *From* 24·00
Plate Nos. 15, 16.
z 1252 4d. grey-brn. (1880) *wmk.* Large Garter (Plate No. 17) .. 30·00
z 1253 4d. grey-brown (1880) *wmk.* Crown (Plate No. 17) .. .. 9·00
z 1254 6d. grey (1874–76) (Pl. 15, 16.)
z 1255 8d. orange (1876) .. .. .. 36·00
z 1256 1s. green (1867–73) .. *From* 5·50
Plate Nos. 4, 5, 6, 7.
z 1257 1s. green (1873–77) .. *From* 10·00
Plate Nos. 9, 10, 11, 12, 13.
z 1258 1s. orge.-brn. (1880) (Plate No. 13) 45·00
z 1259 1s. orge-brn. (1881) (Plate No. 13) 12·00
z 1260 2s. blue (1867) .. .. .. 32·00
z 1261 2s. brown (1880) £400
z 1262 5s. rose (1867–74) £100
Plate Nos. 1, 2.
z 1262*a* 10s. greenish grey (1878) .. £375

1880.

z 1263 ½d. green .. .. 12·00
z 1264 1d. Venetian red .. .. .. 7·50
z 1265 1½d. Venetian red .. .. .. 13·00
z 1265*a* 2d. rose .. ..

PORTO PLATA (DOMINICAN REPUBLIC).

"C 86." *Obliteration or circular postmark as T* 8, 12 *or* 17.

1867 *to* **1869.**

z 1266 ½d. rose-red (1870–79) .. *From* 14·00
Plate Nos. 10, 12, 14.
z 1267 1d. rose-red (1864–79) .. *From* 7·00
Plate Nos. 123, 130, 136, 146, 151, 178, 199, 200, 205, 217.
z 1268 1½d. lake-red (1870–74) (Pl. 3) .. 20·00
z 1269 2d. blue (1858–69) (Plate No. 15) 9·00
z 1270 2½d. rosy mauve (1876–79) *From* 48·00
Plate Nos. 13, 14.
z 1270*a* 3d. rose (1873–76) (Plate No. 18) 25·00
z 1270*b* 4d. vermilion (1873) (Plate No. 14) 25·00
z 1271 4d. vermilion (1876) (Plate No. 15) 38·00
z 1272 4d. sage-green (1877) (Plate 15) .. 25·00
z 1272*a* 6d. violet (1867–70) (Plate No. 8)
z 1273 6d. grey (1874–76) (Plate No. 15) 20·00
z 1273*a* 8d. orange (1876) .. .. .. 50·00
z 1274 1s. green (1867–73) .. *From* 9·00
Plate Nos. 4, 7.
z 1275 1s. green (1873–77) .. *From* 9·00
Plate Nos. 11, 12, 13.
z 1276 2s. blue (1867) .. .. .. 50·00

SAN DOMINGO (DOMINICAN REP.).

"C 87." *Obliteration or circular postmark as T* 12.

1867 *or* **1879.**

z 1277 ½d. rose-red (1870–79) .. *From* 15·00
Plate Nos. 5, 6, 8, 10, 11, 13.
z 1278 1d. rose-red (1864–79) .. *From* 9·00
Plate Nos. 146, 154, 171, 173, 174, 176, 178, 186, 190, 197, 220.
z 1279 1½d. lake-red (1870–74) (Plate 3) 18·00
z 1280 2d. blue (1858–69) (Pl. 13, 14) .. 13·00
z 1280*a* 3d. rose (1873–76) (Plate No. 18)
z 1281 4d. vermilion (1865–73) .. *From* 13·00
Plate Nos. 11, 12, 14.
z 1282 4d. vermilion (1876) (Plate No. 15) 42·00
z 1282*a* 4d. sage-green (1877) (Plate 15) ..
z 1282*b* 6d. grey (1874–76) (Plate No. 15)
z 1283 9d. straw (1867) .. .. ..
z 1284 1s. green (1867) (Plate No. 4) ..
z 1285 1s. green (1873–77) .. *From* 10·00
Plate Nos. 10, 11, 12, 13.
z 1285*a* 2s. blue (1867) .. .. ..

ST. THOMAS (D.W.I.).

"C 51." *Obliteration as T* 4, 12 *or* 14.

1865 *to* **1879.**

z 1286 ½d. rose-red (1870–79) .. .. 14·00
Plate Nos. 5, 6, 8, 10, 11, 12.
z 1286*a* 1d. rose-red (1857) .. ..
z 1287 1d. rose-red (1864–79) .. *From* 5·00
Plate Nos. 71, 72, 79, 81, 84, 85, 86, 87, 88, 89, 90, 93, 94, 95, 96, 97, 98, 99, 100, 101, 102, 105, 106, 107, 110, 112, 113, 114, 116, 117, 118, 119, 120, 121, 122, 123, 124, 125, 127, 129, 130, 131, 133, 134, 136, 137, 138, 139, 140, 141, 142, 144, 145, 146, 147, 148, 149, 150, 151, 152, 154, 155, 156, 157, 158, 159, 160, 161, 162, 163, 164, 165, 166, 167, 169, 170, 171, 172, 173, 174, 175, 176, 177, 178, 179, 180, 181, 182, 184, 185, 186, 187, 189, 190, 197.
z 1288 1½d. lake-red (1870–74) (Pls. 1, 3) 10·00
z 1289 2d. blue (1858–69) .. *From* 4·75
Plate Nos. 9, 12, 13, 14, 15.
z 1290 3d. rose (1865) (Plate No. 4) .. 18·00
z 1291 3d. rose (1867–73) .. *From* 8·00
Plate Nos. 4, 5, 6, 7, 8, 9, 10.
z 1291*a* 3d. rose (1873–76) .. *From* 10·00
Plate Nos. 11, 12, 14, 15, 16, 17, 18, 19.
z 1292 4d. red (1862) (Plate Nos. 3, 4) ..
z 1293 4d. vermilion (1865–73) .. *From* 9·00
Plate Nos. 7, 8, 9, 10, 11, 12, 13, 14.
z 1294 4d. verm. (1876) (Plate No. 15) .. 55·00
z 1295 4d. sage-green (1877) .. *From* 25·00
Plate Nos. 15, 16.
z 1295*a* 4d. grey-brown (1880) *wmk.* Large Garter (Plate No. 17) .. 30·00
z 1296 6d. lilac (1864) (Plate No. 4) .. 30·00
z 1297 6d. lilac (1865–67) .. *From* 12·00
Plate Nos. 5, 6.
z 1298 6d. lilac (1867) (Plate No. 6) .. 12·00
z 1299 6d. violet (1867–70) .. *From* 10·00
Plate Nos. 6, 8, 9.
z 1300 6d. buff (1872–73) .. *From* 30·00
Plate Nos. 11, 12.
z 1301 6d. chestnut (1872) (Plate No. 11) 9·00
z 1302 6d. grey (1873) (Plate No. 12) .. 18·00
z 1303 6d. grey (1874–76) .. .. 7·50
Plate Nos. 13, 14, 15, 16.
z 1304 8d. orange (1876) .. .. .. 30·00
z 1305 9d. straw (1862) .. .. ..
z 1306 9d. bistre (1862) .. .. .. 48·00
z 1307 9d. straw (1865) £120
z 1308 9d. straw (1867) .. .. .. 32·00
z 1309 10d. red-brown (1867) .. .. 35·00
z 1310 1s. green (1865) (Plate No. 4) .. 11·00

No.	Stamp	Price
z 1311	1s. green (1867–73) .. *From* Plate Nos. 4, 5, 6, 7.	4·00
z 1312	1s. green (1873–77) .. *From* Plate Nos. 8, 9, 10, 11, 12, 13.	9·00
z 1313	2s. blue (1867)	32·00
z 1314	5s. rose (1867–74) .. *From* Plate Nos. 1, 2.	55·00

SPANISH MAIL PACKET ST. THOMAS.

"**D 26.**" *Obliteration as T* **12.**

1868 *to* **1879** (?).

No.	Stamp	Price
z 1315	1d. rose-red (1864) (Pls. 98, 125)	
z 1316	4d. vermilion (1865–73) Plate Nos. 9, 10, 11.	£250
z 1317	6d. violet (1867–70) (Plate No. 8)	
z 1317a	1s. green (1867) (Plate No. 4)	

HAVANA (CUBA).

"**C 58.**" *Obliteration as T* **4** *or* **14.**

1867 *to* **1877.**

No.	Stamp	Price
z 1318	½d. rose-red (1870) (Pl. 12)	16·00
z 1319	1d. rose-red (1864–79) Plate Nos. 86, 90, 93, 115, 120, 123, 144, 146, 171, 208.	
z 1320	2d. blue (1858–69) Plate Nos. 9, 14, 15.	
z 1321	3d. rose (1867–73) (Plate No. 4)	
z 1321a	3d. rose (1873–76) (Pls. 18, 19)	
z 1322	4d. vermilion (1865–73) .. *From* Plate Nos. 7, 10, 11, 12, 13, 14.	10·00
z 1323	4d. verm. (1876) (Plate No. 15)	
z 1324	6d. lilac (1865) (with hyphen) Plate No. 5.	
z 1324a	6d. grey (1874–76) (Pl. No. 15)	
z 1325	8d. orange (1876)	
z 1325a	9d. straw (1867)	85·00
z 1326	10d. red-brown (1867)	
z 1327	1s. green (1865) (Plate No. 4)	
z 1328	1s. green (1867–73) .. *From* Plate Nos. 4, 5, 7.	9·00
z 1329	1s. green (1873–77) .. *From* Plate Nos. 10, 12, 13.	10·00
z 1330	2s. blue (1867)	60·00
z 1331	5s. rose (1867–74) (Plate Nos. 1, 2)	90·00

SANTIAGO DE CUBA.

"**C 88.**" *Obliteration as T* **14.**

1866 *to* **1877.**

No.	Stamp	Price
z 1331a	½d. rose-red (1870–79) (Plate Nos. 4, 6, 14)	
z 1332	1d. rose-red (1864–79) .. *From* Plate Nos. 100, 105, 106, 109, 120, 123, 144, 146, 171, 208.	27·00
z 1333	1½d. lake-red (1870–74) (Pl. No. 3)	
z 1334	2d. blue (1858–69) Plate Nos. 9, 12, 13, 14.	
z 1334a	3d. rose (1867) (Plate No. 5)	
z 1335	4d. vermilion (1865–73) .. *From* Plate Nos. 9, 10, 11, 12, 13, 14.	27·00
z 1336	4d. verm. (1876) (Plate No. 15)	50·00
z 1337	6d. violet (1867–70) .. *From* Plate Nos. 6, 8, 9.	40·00
z 1337a	6d. buff (Plate No. 11)	
z 1337b	9d. straw (1865)	
z 1338	10d. red-brown (1867)	75·00
z 1339	1s. green (1867–73) .. *From* Plate Nos. 4, 5, 6.	75·00
z 1340	1s. green (1873—77) Plate Nos. 9, 10, 12, 13.	
z 1341	2s. blue (1867)	
z 1341a	5s. rose (1867) (Plate 1)	

PUERTO RICO.

"**C 61.**" *Obliterations as T* **4, 8** *or* **14.**

1865 *to* **1877.**

No.	Stamp	Price
z 1342	½d. rose-red (1870) .. *From* Plate Nos. 5, 10, 15.	9·00
z 1343	1d. rose-red (1857)	
z 1344	1d. rose-red (1864–79) .. *From* Plate Nos. 73, 81, 84, 90, 100, 102, 107, 122, 124, 125, 127, 130, 137, 138, 139, 140, 145, 146, 149, 153, 156, 159, 160, 162, 163, 169, 171, 172, 173, 175, 179, 180, 182, 186.	3·50
z 1345	1½d. lake-red (1870–74) .. *From* Plate Nos. 1, 3.	32·00
z 1346	2d. blue (1858–69) .. *From* Plate Nos. 9, 13, 14.	5·00
z 1347	3d. rose (1865) (Plate No. 4)	15·00
z 1348	3d. rose (1867–73) .. *From* Plate Nos. 5, 6, 7, 8, 9. 10.	6·50
z 1349	3d. rose (1873–76) .. *From* Plate Nos. 11, 12, 14, 15, 16, 17, 18.	6·50
z 1350	4d. vermilion (1865–73) .. *From* Plate Nos. 7, 8, 9, 10, 11, 12, 13, 14.	9·00
z 1351	4d. verm. (1876) (Plate No. 15)	50·00
z 1352	6d. lilac (1865–67) .. *From* Plate Nos. 5, 6.	12·00
z 1353	6d. lilac (1867) (Plate No. 6)	13·00
z 1354	6d. violet (1867–70) .. *From* Plate Nos. 6, 8, 9.	10·00
z 1355	6d. buff (1872–73) (Pl. Nos. 11, 12)	22·00
z 1356	6d. chestnut (1872) (Plate No. 11)	9·00
z 1357	6d. grey (1873) (Plate No. 12)	
z 1358	6d. grey (1874–76) .. *From* Plate Nos. 13, 14, 15.	7·00
z 1359	9d. straw (1862)	40·00
z 1359a	9d. straw (1865)	£110
z 1360	9d. straw (1867)	32·00
z 1361	10d. red-brown (1867)	35·00
z 1362	1s. green (1865) (Plate No. 4)	11·00
z 1363	1s. green (1867–73) .. *From* Plate Nos. 4, 5, 6, 7.	4·00
z 1364	1s. green (1873–77) .. *From* Plate Nos. 8, 9, 10, 11, 12, 13.	10·00
z 1365	2s. blue (1867)	25·00
z 1366	5s. rose (1867) (Pls. 1, 2) *From*	50·00

ARROYO (PUERTO RICO).

"**F 83.**" *Obliteration or circular postmark as T* **8** *or* **17.**

1872 *to* **1877.**

No.	Stamp	Price
z 1366a	½d. rose-red (Plate No. 5)	20·00
z 1367	1d. rose-red (1864–79) Pl. Nos. 150, 151, 156, 164, 174, 175.	16·00
z 1367a	1½d. lake-red (1870) (Plate No. 1)	
z 1368	2d. blue (1858–69) (Plate No. 14)	
z 1369	3d. rose (1867–73) (Pl. Nos. 7, 10)	13·00
z 1370	3d. rose (1873–76) Plate Nos. 12, 14, 18.	16·00
z 1371	4d. vermilion (1865–73) Plate Nos. 12, 13, 14.	16·00
z 1372	4d. verm. (1876) (Plate No. 15)	50·00
z 1372a	6d. chestnut (1872) (Plate No. 11)	
z 1372b	6d. pale buff (1872) (Plate No. 11)	
z 1373	6d. grey (1874–76) Plate Nos. 13, 14, 15.	16·00
z 1374	9d. straw (1867)	£100
z 1375	10d. red-brown (1867)	35·00
z 1376	1s. green (1865) (Plate No. 4)	
z 1377	1s. green (1867–73) (Pls. 4, 5, 6, 7)	8·00
z 1378	1s. green (1873–77) Plate Nos. 8, 9, 10, 11, 12, 13.	9·00
z 1379	2s. blue (1867)	£100
z 1379a	5s. rose (1867–74) (Plate No. 2)	

AGUADILLA (PUERTO RICO).

"**F 84.**" *Obliteration or circular postmark as T* **8** *or* **17.**

1873 *to* **1877.**

No.	Stamp	Price
z 1380	½d. rose-red (1870) (Plate No. 6)	20·00
z 1380a	1d. rose-red (1864–79) Plate Nos. 119, 122, 139, 156.	16·00
z 1381	2d. blue (1858–69) (Plate No. 14)	
z 1382	3d. rose (1867–73) (Pl. Nos. 7, 8, 9)	
z 1383	3d. rose (1873–76) (Plate No. 12)	
z 1384	4d. vermilion (1865–73) Plate Nos. 12, 13, 14.	13·00
z 1385	4d. verm. (1876) (Plate No. 15)	50·00
z 1386	6d. grey (1874–76) (Pl. Nos. 13, 14)	
z 1387	9d. straw (1867)	£100
z 1388	10d. red-brown (1867)	38·00
z 1389	1s. green (1867–73) .. *From* Plate Nos. 4, 5, 6, 7.	9·00
z 1390	1s. green (1873–77) .. *From* Plate Nos. 8, 9, 10, 11, 12.	10·00
z 1390a	2s. blue (1867)	£100

MAYAGUEZ (PUERTO RICO).

"**F 85.**" *Obliteration or circular postmark as T* **8** *or* **17.**

1873 *to* **1877.**

No.	Stamp	Price
z 1391	½d. rose-red (1870) .. *From* Plate Nos. 4, 5, 6, 8, 10, 11.	16·00
z 1392	1d. rose-red (1864–79) .. *From* Plate Nos. 76, 120, 121, 122, 124, 134, 137, 140, 149, 150, 151, 154, 155, 156 160, 167, 170, 171, 174, 176, 178, 180, 182, 185, 186, 189.	7·00
z 1393	1½d. lake-red (1870–74) Plate Nos. 1, 3.	
z 1394	2d. blue (1858–69) Plate Nos. 13, 14, 15.	9·00
z 1395	3d. rose (1867–73) Plate Nos. 7, 8, 9.	9·00
z 1396	3d. rose (1873–76) Plate Nos. 11, 12, 14, 15, 16, 17, 18, 19.	9·00
z 1397	4d. vermilion (1865–73) Plate Nos. 11, 12, 13, 14.	9·50
z 1398	4d. verm. (1876) (Plate No. 15)	50·00
z 1398a	4d. sage-green (1877) (Pl. No. 15)	
z 1398b	6d. mauve (1870) (Plate No. 9)	
z 1399	6d. buff (1872) (Plate No. 11)	
z 1400	6d. chestnut (1872) (Plate No. 11)	
z 1401	6d. grey (1873) (Plate No. 12)	
z 1402	6d. grey (1874–80) Plate Nos. 13, 14, 15, 16.	
z 1403	8d. orange (1876)	50·00
z 1404	9d. straw (1867)	50·00
z 1405	10d. red-brown (1867)	35·00
z 1406	1s. green (1867–73) Plate Nos 4, 5, 6, 7.	4·50
z 1407	1s. green (1873–77) .. *From* Plate Nos. 8, 9, 10, 11. 12.	9·00
z 1408	2s. blue (1867)	
z 1409	5s. rose (1867–74) (Plate No. 2)	

PONCE (PUERTO RICO).

"**F 88.**" *Obliteration or circular postmark as T* **8** *or* **17.**

1873 *to* **1877.**

No.	Stamp	Price
z 1409a	½d. rose-red (1870) Plate Nos. 5, 10, 12.	18·00
z 1410	1d. rose-red (1864–79) .. *From* Plate Nos. 121, 122, 123, 124, 146, 148, 154, 156, 157, 158, 160, 167, 171, 174, 175, 186, 187.	5·50
z 1411	1½d. lake-red (1870–74) (Pl. 3)	50·00
z 1412	2d. blue (1858–69) (Pl. Nos. 13, 14)	7·50
z 1413	3d. rose (1867–73) (Pl. Nos. 7, 8, 9)	
z 1414	3d. rose (1873–76) Plate Nos. 16, 17, 18, 19.	7·50
z 1415	4d. vermilion (1865–73) .. *From* Plate Nos. 8, 9, 12, 13, 14.	9·00
z 1416	4d. verm. (1876) (Plate No. 15)	45·00
z 1417	4d. sage-green (1877) (Pls. 15, 16)	
z 1418	6d. buff (1872–73) (Pls. 11, 12)	
z 1419	6d. chestnut (1872) (Plate No. 11)	10·00
z 1420	6d. grey (1873) (Plate No. 12)	
z 1421	6d. grey (1874–76) .. *From* Plate Nos. 13, 14, 15.	8·00
z 1421a	9d. straw (1867)	95·00
z 1422	10d. red-brown (1867)	35·00
z 1423	1s. green (1867–73) Plate Nos. 4, 6, 7.	8·00
z 1424	1s. green (1873–77) .. *From* Plate Nos. 8, 9, 10, 11, 12, 13.	10·00
z 1425	2s. blue (1867)	
z 1426	5s. rose (1867–74) .. *From* Plate Nos. 1, 2.	£120

NAGUABO (PUERTO RICO).

"**582.**" *Obliteration as T* **9.**

1875 *to* **1877** (?).

No.	Stamp	Price
z 1428	½d. rose-red (1870–79) Plate Nos. 5, 12, 14.	
z 1429	1d. rose-red (1864–70) Plate Nos. 159, 165.	
z 1430	3d. rose (1873–76) (Plate No. 18)	£100
z 1430a	4d. vermilion (1872–73) .. *From* Plate Nos. 13, 14.	90·00
z 1430b	4d. verm. (1876) (Plate No. 15)	
z 1431	6d. grey (1874–76) (Pls. 14, 15)	
z 1432	9d. straw (1867)	
z 1433	10d. red-brown (1867)	£150
z 1434	1s. green (1873–77) (Pls. 11, 12)	
z 1435	2s. dull blue (1867) (Plate No. 1)	£120

V.

Miscellaneous

FERNANDO POO.

"**247.**" *Obliteration as T* **9.**

1874 *to* **1877.**

No.	Stamp	Price
z 1436	4d. vermilion (1865–72) Plate Nos. 13, 14.	£275
z 1437	4d. vermilion (1876) (Plate No. 15)	
z 1438	6d. grey (1874–76) Plate Nos. 13, 14, 15, 16.	£250

MAURITIUS.

We no longer list the Great Britain stamps with obliteration " B **53** " as Type **4** as there is no evidence that this obliteration was issued to Mauritius and it is now regarded as a mail boat obliteration.

HONG KONG.

We no longer list the Great Britain stamps with obliteration " B **62** " as Type **4**. The Government notification dated 29 November 1862 stated that only the Hong Kong stamps to be issued on 6 December would be available for postage and the stamps formerly listed were all issued in Great Britain later than the date of the notice.

SEYCHELLES.

We no longer list the 6d. lilac (1862) (Plate No. 3) with obliteration " B **64** " as Type **4** as there is no evidence that this obliterator was issued to Seychelles and it is now regarded as a mail boat obliteration.

ASCENSION.

Circular postmarks of various sizes as *T* 16 or oval Registration postmark.

z 1541 1d. red-brown (1855) £250
z 1542 1d. rose-red (1864–79) .. *From* £160
Plate Nos. 74, 78, 83, 85, 96, 100, 102, 103, 104, 122, 134, 138, 154, 155, 157, 160, 168, 178.
z 1543 6d. lilac (1865) (Plate No. 5) .. £300
z 1544 1s. green (1865) (Plate No. 4) ..
z 1545 1s. green (1867) (Plate No. 7) ..
z 1546 6d. grey (1880) (Plate No. 17) .. £250
z 1547 1d. lilac (1881) (16 *dots*) .. 8·00
z 1548 ½d. vermilion (1887–92) .. 8·00
z 1549 1½d. purple and green .. 13·00
z 1550 2d. green and carmine .. 14·00
z 1551 2½d. purple/*blue* .. .. 8·00
z 1552 3d. purple/*yellow* .. .. 20·00
z 1553 4d. green and brown .. 20·00
z 1553*a* 4½d. green and carmine .. 40·00
z 1553*b* 5d. dull purple and blue.. 25·00
z 1554 6d. purple/*rose-red* .. 22·00
z 1555 9d. purple and blue .. 22·00
z 1556 1s. green .. .. .. 24·00
z 1557 ½d. blue-green (1900) .. 6·00
z 1558 1s. green and carmine .. 22·00
z 1559 ½d. green (1902 etc.) .. 6·00
z 1560 1d. red (1902 etc.) .. 6·00
z 1561 1½d. purple and green (1902 etc.).. 11·00
z 1562 2d. green & carmine (1902 etc.).. 11·00
z 1563 2½d. blue (1902 etc.) .. 11·00
z 1564 3d. purple/*yellow* (1902 etc.) .. 13·00
z 1565 4d. green and brown (1902 etc.).. 30·00
z 1566 4d. orange (1902 etc.) .. 25·00
z 1567 5d. purple and blue (1902 etc.) .. 22·00
z 1568 6d. purple (1902 etc.) .. 24·00
z 1568*a* 7d. grey-black (1902 etc.)
z 1569 9d. purple and blue (1902 etc.) .. 25·00
z 1570 1s. green and carmine (1902 etc.) 16·00
z 1571 ½d. yellow-green (1911–12) .. 8·00
z 1572 ½d. green (1911–12) .. 16·00
z 1573 1d. scarlet (1911–12) .. 16·00
z 1574 ½d. green (1912–22) .. 6·00
z 1575 1d. carmine (1912–22) .. 6·00
z 1576 1½d. red-brown (1912–22) .. 6·00
z 1577 2d. orange (1912–22) .. 6·00
z 1578 2½d. blue (1912–22) .. 7·00
z 1579 3d. violet (1912–22) .. 7·00
z 1580 4d. grey-green (1912–22) .. 8·00
z 1580*a* 5d. brown (1912–22) .. 8·00
z 1581 6d. purple (1912–22) .. 8·00
z 1582 9d. agate (1912–22) .. 22·00
z 1583 9d. olive-green (1912–22) .. 27·00
z 1583*a* 10d. turquoise-blue (1912–22) .. 22·00
z 1584 1s. bistre (1912–22) .. 22·00
z 1584*a* 2s. 6d. brown (1918–30).. .. 40·00

MAIL BOAT OBLITERATIONS.

For many years it was supposed that obliterations numbered A **80** to A **99**, B **03**, B **12**, B **53**, B **56**, B **57**, B **64** and C **79** were used on mail boats or at Naval Stations abroad (the whereabouts of which were not known), owing to the fact that they are almost invariably found on sailor's letters.

It is definitely known that these obliterations were allotted to mail boats and they are therefore omitted from this Catalogue.

VI.

ARMY FIELD OFFICES.
CRIMEA.

1854 *to* **1857.**

Crown between Stars.

z 1585 1d. red-brown (1841), *imperf.* .. 95·00
z 1586 1d. red-brown (1854), Die I, *wmk.* Small Crown, *perf.* 16
z 1587 1d. red-brown (1855), Die II, *wmk.* Small Crown, *perf.* 16 .. 50·00
z 1588 1d. red-brown, Die I, *wmk.* Small Crown, *perf.* 14
z 1589 1d. red-brown (1855), Die II, Small Crown, *perf.* 14 ..
z 1590 2d. blue (1841) *imperf.* £250
z 1591 2d. blue, Small Crown (1854), *perf.* 16, Plate No. 4.. ..
z 1592 1s. green (1847), embossed .. £250

Star between Cyphers.

z 1593 1d. red-brown (1841), *imperf.* .. £160
z 1594 1d. red-brown (1854), Die I, *wmk.* Small Crown, *perf.* 16 .. 25·00
z 1595 1d. red-brown (1855), Die II, *wmk.* Small Crown, *perf.* 16 .. 25·00
z 1596 1d. red-brown (1855), Die I, *wmk.* Small Crown, *perf.* 14 .. 25·00
z 1597 1d. red-brown (1855), Die II, *wmk.* Small Crown, *perf.* 14 .. 25·00
z 1597*a* 1d. red-brown (1855), Die II, *wmk.* Large Crown, *perf.* 16 .. 42·00
z 1598 1d. red-brown (1855), Die II, *wmk.* Large Crown, *perf.* 14 .. 14·00
z 1599 2d. blue (1841), *imperf.* .. £200
z 1600 2d. blue (1854) *wmk.* Small Crown *perf.* 16, Plate Nos. 4, 5 *From* 55·00
z 1601 2d. blue (1855) *wmk.* Small Crown *perf.* 14, Plate No. 4.. .. 48·00
z 1602 2d. blue (1855) *wmk.* Large Crown *perf.* 16, Plate No. 5.. .. 80·00
z 1603 2d. blue (1855) *wmk.* Large Crown. *perf.* 14, Plate No. 5.. .. 48·00
z 1604 4d. rose (1857) £200
z 1605 6d. violet (1854), embossed .. £250
z 1606 1s. green (1847), embossed .. £250

EGYPT AND SUDAN.

1882. *Tel-el-Kebir Campaign.*

z 1607 ½d. rose-red (Plate No. 20) ..
z 1608 ½d. green (1880) £110
z 1609 1d. Venetian red (1880) .. ..
z 1610 1d. lilac (1881) .. .. 50·00
z 1611 2½d. blue (1881) (Plate Nos. 21, 22, 23) .. .. 25·00

1885. *Suakim Campaign.*

z 1611*a* 1d. lilac (1881) £110
z 1612 2½d. lilac (1884) .. .. 85·00
z 1613 5d. green (1884) £120

SOUTH AFRICAN WAR.

1899 *to* **1902.**

z 1613*a–n* ½d., 1d., 1½d., 2d., 2½d., 3d., 4d., 4½d., 5d., 6d., 9d., 10d., 1s., 5s. (1881–92) *From* 3·50
z 1614*a–b* ½d., 1s. (1900) .. *From* 7·00
z 1615*a–l* ½d., 1d., 1½d., 2d., 2½d., 3d., 4d., 5d., 6d., 9d., 10d., 1s. (1902) .. *From* 5·00

Many types of **cancellation exist** besides those shown.

ARMY OFFICIAL.

z 1616 ½d. vermilion .. .. .. 40·00
z 1617 ½d. green .. .. .. 40·00
z 1618 1d. lilac .. .. .. 35·00
z 1619 6d. purple/*red* .. .. ..

VII.

VARIOUS TOWNS ON THE NIGER COAST AND RIVER

(Dates given are those of earliest known postmarks. Colour of postmarks in brackets. Where two or more colours are given, price is for cheapest. Illustrations are reduced to two-thirds linear of the actual size.)

AKASSA.

1. 2.

1888 (6 MAY). *As T* **2** *but with Maltese cross each side of* " AKASSA ". *Size* 36 × 22 *mm.*
1 2 6d. deep purple/*red* .. .. .. 85·00

1890 (24 JUNE). *Size* 39 × 24 *mm.*
1*a* **1** 2½d. purple/*blue* (V.) .. .. 18·00
1*b* 3d. purple/*yellow* (V.) .. ..
1*c* 5d. dull purple and blue (V.) ..
2 6d. deep purple/*red* (V.) .. .. 40·00
2*a* 10d. dull purple & carmine (V.) ..
2*b* 2s. 6d. lilac (V.) .. .. ..

1895 (7 MARCH). *Size* 39 × 25 *mm.*
3 **2** 2½d. purple/*blue* (V.) .. .. .. 40·00

3.

1894.
4 **3** 1d. lilac (V.) (July, '94) .. .. 15·00
5 2½d. purple/*blue* (V.) (3.10.94) .. 15·00

THE ROYAL NIGER COMPANY
CHARTERED & LIMITED.
7- AUG. 98
POST OFFICE
AKASSA.

4.

1895 (1 JUNE)–**1899.**
6 **4** ½d. vermilion (V.) .. .. .. 6·00
7 1d. lilac (V.) .. .. 6·00

7a 2d. green and vermilion (V.) .. 48·00
8 2½d. purple/*blue* (V.) .. .. .. 6·00
9 3d. purple/*yellow* (V.) .. .. 32·00
10 5d. dull purple and blue (V.) .. 6·00
11 6d. deep purple/*red* (V.) .. .. 14·00
12 9d. dull purple and blue (V.) .. 28·00
13 10d. dull purple and carmine (V.) .. 14·00
14 2s. 6d. deep lilac (V.) .. .. 25·00

1899 (20 MAY). *As T* **4**, *but* "CUSTOMS DEPT" *in place of* "POST OFFICE".
15 1d. lilac (V.) .. .. 30·00
16 2½d. purple/*blue* (V.) .. .. .. 30·00

THE ROYAL NIGER COMPANY,
CHARTERED & LIMITED.
4 NOV. 1899
POST OFFICE,
AKASSA.

5.

1897 (JAN.)–**1899** (DEC.).
17 **5** ½d. vermilion (V.) .. .. .. 7·00
18 1d. lilac (V.) .. .. .. 6·50
19 2d. green and vermilion (V.) .. 15·00
20 2½d. purple/*blue* (V.) .. .. 9·00
21 3d. purple/*yellow* (V.) .. .. 25·00
22 4d. green and brown (V.) .. .. 15·00
23 4½d. green and carmine (V.) .. 80·00
24 5d. dull purple and blue (V.) .. 11·00
25 6d. deep purple/*red* (V.) .. .. 25·00
26 9d. dull purple and blue (V.) .. 32·00
27 10d. dull purple and carmine (V.) .. 15·00
28 1s. green (V.) .. .. .. 50·00
29 2s. 6d. deep lilac (V.) .. .. 25·00

Error. As T **5**, *but* "RECD" *in place of year.*
30 1d. lilac (V.) .. ..

THE ROYAL NIGER COMPANY
Chartered & Limited.
9 JUL 1898
BURUTU

6.

1899 (9 JAN.). *As T* **6**, *but inscribed* "AKASSA".
31 5d. dull purple and blue (V.) ..

BURUTU.

1898 (9 JULY)–**1899** (FEB.).
31a **6** 1d. lilac (V.) .. .. ..
32 2½d. purple/*blue* (V.) .. .. 42·00

THE ROYAL NIGER COMPANY
CHARTERED & LIMITED.
31 MAR 1898
POST OFFICE.
BURUTU.

7.

1897 (20 JAN.)–**1898** (30 OCT.). *T* **7**, "BURUTU" *in sans-serif caps. Size* 44 × 24 *mm.*
33 **7** ½d. vermilion (V.) .. .. .. 11·00
34 1d. lilac (V.) .. .. .. 10·00
35 1½d. dull purple and green (V.) .. 28·00
36 2d. green and carmine (V.) .. 15·00
37 2½d. purple/*blue* (V.) .. .. 6·00
38 3d. purple/*yellow* (V.) .. .. 22·00
39 4d. green and brown (V.) .. .. 15·00
40 5d. dull purple and blue (V.) .. 11·00
41 6d. deep purple/*red* (V.) .. .. 22·00
42 9d. dull purple and blue (V.) .. 28·00
43 10d. dull purple and carmine (V.) .. 14·00
44 1s. green (V.) .. .. .. 50·00
45 2s. 6d. lilac (V.) .. .. .. 22·00

The 2½d. is also known with this postmark in blue (6.9.97) and violet-black (Apl. 1898) and the ½d., 2½d., 3d., 5d. and 10d. with it in black.

1898–99. *As T* **4**, *but inscribed* "BURUTU" *in seriffed caps. Size* 44 × 27 *mm.*
46 ½d. vermilion (V., Bk.) .. .. 11·00
47 1d. lilac (V., Bk.) .. .. .. 11·00
48 2d. green and vermilion (V.) .. 25·00
49 2½d. purple/*blue* (V., Bk.) .. .. 9·00
50 3d. purple/*yellow* (V.) .. .. 24·00
51 4d. green and brown (V.) .. .. 18·00
52 4½d. green and carmine (V.) .. 90·00
53 5d. dull purple and blue (V.) .. 12·00
54 6d. deep purple/*red* (V.) .. .. 25·00
55 9d. dull purple and blue (V.) .. 30·00
56 10d. dull purple and carmine (V., Bk.) 16·00
57 2s. 6d. lilac (V., Bk.) .. .. 30·00

1899 (20 MAY). *As T* **4**, *but inscribed* "CUSTOM DEPT. BURUTU".
58 1d. lilac (V.) .. .. 55·00

1900 (9 JAN.). *Small circular postmark with* "BURUTU" *at top, date in centre and ornament below.*
59 1d. lilac (Bk.) .. ..

LOKOJA.

8.

1899 (30 JUNE)–**1900.**
60 **8** ½d. vermilion (V.) .. .. .. 14·00
61 1d. lilac (V.) .. .. .. 12·00
62 2½d. purple/*blue* (V.) .. .. 40·00
63 5d. dull purple and blue (V.) .. 40·00
64 10d. dull purple and carmine (V.) 40·00
64a 2s. 6d. deep lilac (V.) .. ..

ABUTSHI.

1899 (4 OCT.). *As T* **8**, *but inscribed* "THE ROYAL NIGER CO. C. & L. ABUTSHI" *with* "CUSTOMS (date) OFFICE" *in central oval.*
65 ½d. vermilion (V.) .. .. .. 50·00
66 1d. lilac (V.) .. .. .. 40·00
67 2½d. purple/*blue* (V.) .. .. 50·00
68 5d. dull purple and blue (V.) .. 60·00
69 10d. dull purple and carmine (V.) .. 85·00
70 2s. 6d. deep lilac (V.) .. .. 80·00

BENIN.

1892. *Oval with double-lined frame inscribed* "OIL RIVERS PROTECTORATE BENIN" *with date in central oval.*
71 2½d. purple/*blue* (V.) £425

BONNY RIVER.

1892. *Name and date in circle.*
72 ½d. vermilion (Bk.) .. .. ..
73 2½d. purple/*blue* (Bk.) .. .. 40·00
74 5d. dull purple and blue (Bk.) ..
75 6d. deep purple/*red* (Bk.) .. ..

BRASS RIVER.

1892. *Name and date in circle.*
76 2½d. purple/*blue* (Bk.) £225
77 6d. purple/*red* (Bk.) .. .. ..

FORCADOS RIVER.

1892. *Name and date in circle.*
78 1d. lilac (Bk.) £125
79 5d. dull purple & blue (Bk.) ..
80 10d. dull purple & carmine (Bk.) ..

OLD CALABAR RIVER.

1891. *Name and date in circle.*
81 ½d. vermilion (Bk.) .. .. ..
82 1d. lilac (Bk.) .. .. ..
82a 1½d. dull purple & green (Bk.) ..
83 2d. green & vermilion (Bk.) ..
84 2½d. purple/*blue* (Bk.) .. ..
85 5d. dull purple & blue (Bk.) ..
85a 6d. purple/*red* (Bk.) .. ..
86 1s. green (Bk.) .. .. ..

BRITISH VICE-CONSULATE, OLD CALABAR.

1891. *Double-lined circle, with Royal Arms in centre, inscribed as above.*
87 2½d. purple/*blue* (V.) .. .. 75·00
88 5d. dull purple & blue (V.) .. ..

VARIOUS OFFICIAL DATE STAMPS.

1894–99. *As T* **8** *but inscribed* "AGENT GENERAL NIGER TERRITORIES".
89 1d. lilac (V.) (1.6.99) .. .. 20·00
90 2½d. purple/*blue* (V.) (3.10.94) .. 20·00

1895. (4 AUG.). *As T* **6** *but inscribed as last.*
91 2½d. purple/*blue* (V.) .. .. .. 20·00

These "AGENT GENERAL" marks were used at Akassa.

ABU DHABI.

An independent Arab Shaikhdom (one of the Trucial States), with a British postal administration until 31st December, 1966. The postal service was introduced on 30th March, 1963 and the stamps of the British Postal Agencies in Eastern Arabia were at first used.

1. Shaikh Shakhbut bin Sultan.

2. Arabian Gazelle.

3. Ruler's Palace.

4. Oil Rig and Camels.

(Des. M. C. Farrar-Bell. Photo. Harrison (T **1/2**). Des. C. T. Kavanagh (T **3**), Miss P. M. Goth (T **4**). Recess. B.W.)

1964 (30 MAR.). *P* 14½ (5 *to* 75 *n.p.*) *or* 13 × 13½ (*others*).

1 **1**	5 n.p. green		15	15
2 ,,	15 n.p. red-brown		15	15
3 ,,	20 n.p. ultramarine		15	15
4 ,,	30 n.p. red-orange		15	25
5 **2**	40 n.p. reddish violet		15	12
6 ,,	50 n.p. bistre		20	25
7 ,,	75 n.p. black		30	30
8 **3**	1 r. emerald		35	35
9 ,,	2 r. black		95	1·10
10 **4**	5 r. carmine-red		2·25	2·75
11 ,,	10 r. deep ultramarine ..		4·50	5·00
1/11	.. ..	*Set of* 11	8·00	9·00

5

6

7.

Falcons on Gloved Hand.

Fils فلس
(8)

(Des. V. Whiteley. Photo. Harrison.)

1965 (30 Mar.). *Falconry. P* 14½.

No.	Type	Description	Unused	Used
12	**5**	20 n.p. lt. brown & grey-blue	20	20
13	**6**	40 n.p. light brown and blue	30	30
14	**7**	2 r. sepia & turquoise-grn.	1·00	1·00

(New currency. 1,000 fils = 1 dinar.)

1966 (1 Oct.). *Nos.* 1/11 *surch. as T* **8** ("fils" *only on T* **2**, *with new value expressed on remainder*), *by Arabian Printing and Publishing House, Bahrain. P* 13×13½ (20 *f.*), *others as before.*

No.	Type	Description	Unused	Used
15	**1**	5 f. on 5 n.p. green ..	8	25
16	,,	15 f. on 15 n.p. red-brown ..	8	35
17	,,	20 f. on 20 n.p. ultram. ..	10	35
		a. Surch. inverted	45·00	75·00
18	,,	30 f. on 30 n.p. red-orange ..	15	45
		a. Arabic "2" for "3" in surch.	£400	
19	**2**	40 f. reddish violet	15	45
20	,,	50 f. bistre	2·00	2·25
21	,,	75 f. black	2·00	2·25
22	**3**	100 f. on 1 r. emerald ..	2·00	2·25
23	,,	200 f. on 2 r. black	3·75	5·00
24	**4**	500 f. on 5 r. carmine-red ..	7·00	9·00
25	,,	1 d. on 10 r. deep ultram. ..	12·00	14·00
15/25		.. .. *Set of* 11	27·00	32·00

The Abu Dhabi Post Department took over the postal services on January 1st, 1967. Later stamp issues will be found in Vol. 1 of the Stanley Gibbons Foreign Overseas Catalogue.

ADEN.

1. Dhow.

(Recess. D.L.R.)

1937 (1 Apr.). *Wmk. Mult. Script CA sideways. P* 13×12.

No.	Type	Description	Unused	Used
1	**1**	½ a. yellow-green	30	30
2	,,	9 p. deep green	40	40
3	,,	1 a. sepia	35	30
4	,,	2 a. scarlet	60	65
5	,,	2½ a. bright blue	80	1·00
6	,,	3 a. carmine	1·00	1·50
7	,,	3½ a. grey-blue	95	1·40
8	,,	8 a. pale purple	1·75	2·75
9	,,	1 r. brown	3·25	3·25
10	,,	2 r. yellow	9·00	9·00
11	,,	5 r. deep purple	30·00	32·00
12	,,	10 r. olive-green	70·00	75·00
1/12		.. .. *Set of* 12	£100	£110
1/12		Perf. "Specimen" *Set of* 12	£100	

2. King George VI and Queen Elizabeth.

(Des. and recess. D.L.R.)

1937 (12 May). *Coronation. Wmk. Mult. Script CA. P* 14.

No.	Type	Description	Unused	Used
13	**2**	1 a. sepia	10	10
14	,,	2½ a. light blue	15	20
15	,,	3½ a. grey-blue	30	30
3/15		Perf. "Specimen" *Set of* 3	10·00	

3. Aidrus Mosque, Crater.

4. Adenese Camel Corps.

5. The Harbour.

6. Adenese Dhow.

7. Capture of Aden, 1839.

8. Mukalla.

(Recess. Waterlow.)

1939 (19 Jan.)–**48.** *Wmk. Mult. Script CA. P* 12½.

No.	Type	Description	Unused	Used
16	**3**	½ a. yellowish green ..	10	12
		a. Bluish green (9.48) ..	35	60
17	**4**	¾ a. red-brown	10	20
18	**5**	1 a. pale blue	15	12
19	**6**	1½ a. scarlet	30	25
20	**3**	2 a. sepia	12	12
21	**8**	2½ a. deep ultramarine ..	20	15
22	**7**	3 a. sepia and carmine ..	35	25
23	**8**	8 a. red-orange	35	15
23*a*	**7**	14 a. sepia and light blue (15.1.45)	85	70
24	**6**	1 r. emerald-green ..	30	55
25	**5**	2 r. deep blue and magenta	1·25	1·10
26	**4**	5 r. red-brown & olive-grn.	3·25	3·25
27	**7**	10 r. sepia and violet ..	4·50	5·00
16/27		.. .. *Set of* 13	10·00	11·00
16/27		Perf. "Specimen" *Set of* 13	30·00	

9. Houses of Parliament, London.

(Des. and recess. D.L.R.)

1946 (15 Oct.). *Victory. Wmk. Mult. Script CA. P* 13½×14.

No.	Type	Description	Unused	Used
28	**9**	1½ a. carmine	12	12
29	,,	2½ a. blue	20	20
28/9		Perf. "Specimen" *Set of* 2	12·00	

10

11

King George VI and Queen Elizabeth.

(Des. and Photo. Waterlow & Sons (T **10**). Design recess; name typo. Bradbury, Wilkinson (T **11**).)

1949 (17 Jan.). *Royal Silver Wedding. Wmk. Mult. Script CA.*

No.	Type	Description	Unused	Used
30	**10**	1½ a. scarlet (*p* 14×15) ..	15	15
31	**11**	10 r. mauve (*p* 11½×11) ..	7·50	8·50

1949 (10 Oct.). *75th Anniv. of Universal Postal Union. As Nos.* 114/7 *of Antigua, surch. with new values by Waterlow.*

No.	Description	Unused	Used
32	2½ a. on 20 c. ultramarine ..	20	30
33	3 a. on 30 c. carmine-red ..	40	40
34	8 a. on 50 c. orange	75	85
35	1 r. on 1s. blue	1·25	1·40

5
CENTS
(12)

13. Queen Elizabeth II.

1951 (1 Oct.). *Currency changed. Surch. with new values, in cents or shillings, as T* **12**, *or in one line between bars* (30 *c.*) *by Waterlow.*

No.	Type	Description	Unused	Used
36	**5**	5 c. on 1 a. pale blue ..	10	15
37	**3**	10 c. on 2 a. sepia	10	15
38	**8**	15 c. on 2½ a. deep ultram.	25	35
		a. Surch. double	£130	
39	**7**	20 c. on 3 a. sepia & carmine	15	20
40	**8**	30 c. on 8 a. red-orange (R.)	30	35
41	,,	50 c. on 8 a. red-orange ..	30	25
42	**7**	70 c. on 14 a. sepia & lt. blue	35	30
43	**6**	1s. on 1 r. emerald-green ..	40	35
44	**5**	2s. on 2 r. dp. blue & mag.	1·25	1·10
		a. Surch. albino		
45	**4**	5s. on 5 r. red-brown and olive-green	2·50	2·25
46	**7**	10s. on 10 r. sepia & violet ..	5·00	5·50
36/46		.. .. *Set of* 11	9·50	10·00

(Des. & eng. B.W. Recess. D.L.R.)

1953 (2 June). *Coronation. Wmk. Mult. Script CA. P* 13½×13.

No.	Type	Description	Unused	Used
47	**13**	15 c. black and green ..	35	35

14. Minaret.

15. Camel Transport.

16. Crater.

18. Dhow.

17. Mosque.

19. Map.

20. Salt Works.

21. Dhow Building.

21a. Colony's Badge.

22. Aden Protectorate Levy.

23. Crater Pass.

24. Tribesman.

25. Aden in 1572.

(Recess. Waterlow, until 1961, then D.L.R.)

1953 (15 June)–**59.** *Wmk. Mult. Script CA. P* 13½ × 13 (20s.), 12 × 13½ (*Nos.* 57, 64, 66, 68) *or* 12 (*others*).

48	**14**	5 c. yellowish green ..	5	5
49	„	5 c. bluish green (1.6.55)	5	8
		a. Perf. 12 × 13½ (12.4.56) ..	5	10
50	**15**	10 c. orange	5	5
51	„	10 c. vermilion (1.2.55) ..	5	10
52	**16**	15 c. blue-green	5	5
53	„	15 c. greenish grey (26.4.59) (*shades*)	15	15
54	**17**	25 c. carmine-red	5	5
55	„	25 c. deep rose-red (15.3.56) (*shades*)	5	8
56	**18**	35 c. deep ultramarine ..	10	12
57	„	35 c. deep blue (15.10.58) (*shades*)	20	20
58	**19**	50 c. dull blue	25	25
59	„	50 c. deep blue (1.7.55) ..	35	35
		a. Perf. 12 × 13½ (12.4.56) ..	20	20
60	**20**	70 c. brown-grey	25	30
61	„	70 c. black (20.9.54) ..	25	40
		a. Perf. 12 × 13½ (12.4.56) ..	15	12
62	**21**	1s. sepia & reddish violet	25	25
63	„	1s. black & violet (1.7.55)	15	20
64	**21a**	1s. 25, blue and black (16.7.56) (*shades*) ..	35	35
65	**22**	2s. sepia and rose-carmine	95	95
66	„	2s. black and carmine-red (1.3.56) (*shades*) ..	40	35
67	**23**	5s. sepia and dull blue ..	3·00	3·00
68	„	5s. black and deep dull blue (11.4.56) (*shades*)	95	95
69	**24**	10s. sepia and olive ..	6·00	8·00
70	„	10s. black & bronze-green (20.9.54)	2·25	1·75
71	**25**	20s. choc. & reddish lilac ..	9·50	9·50
72	„	20s. black and deep lilac (7.1.57) (*shades*) ..	4·50	4·50
48/72		.. .. *Set of* 25	27·00	29·00

On No. 70 the tribesman's skirt is shaded with cross-hatching instead of with mainly diagonal lines as in No. 69.

1954 (27 Apr.). *Royal Visit. As No.* 62 *but inscr.* "ROYAL VISIT 1954" *at top.*

73	**21**	1s. sepia and reddish violet	30	35

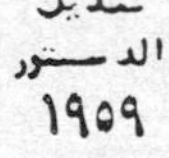

(26)

REVISED
CONSTITUTION
1959

(27)

1959 (26 Jan.). *Revised Constitution. No.* 53 *optd. with T* **26**, *and No.* 64 *optd. with T* **27**, *in red, by Waterlow.*

74	**16**	15 c. slate-green	20	20
75	**21a**	1s. 25 c. blue and black ..	55	55

28. Protein Foods.

(Des. M. Goaman. Photo. Harrison.)

1963 (4 June). *Freedom from Hunger. W* w.12. *P* 14 × 14½.

76	**28**	1s. 25 c. bluish green ..	55	65

For Red Cross issue see under South Arabian Federation.

1964 (5 Feb.)–**65.** *As* 1953–59 *but wmk.* w.12. *P* 12 (10 *c.*, 15 *c.*, 25 *c.*, 1*s.*) *or* 12 × 13½ (*others*).

77	**14**	5 c. green (16.2.65) ..	12	15
78	**15**	10 c. bright orange ..	15	15
79	**16**	15 c. greenish grey ..	15	15
80	**17**	25 c. carmine-red	12	12
81	**18**	35 c. indigo-violet	20	20
82	**19**	50 c. indigo-blue (*shades*)	25	25
83	**20**	70 c. black (*shades*) ..	30	30
84	**21**	1s. black and violet (10.3.64)	35	40
85	**21a**	1s. 25 c. ultramarine and black (10.3.64) ..	45	50
86	**22**	2s. black and carmine-rose (16.2.65) ..	80	95
77/86		.. .. *Set of* 10	2·75	3·00

The stamps of Aden were withdrawn on 31 March 1965 and superseded by the stamps of the South Arabian Federation.

KATHIRI STATE OF SEIYUN.

1. Sultan of Seiyun.

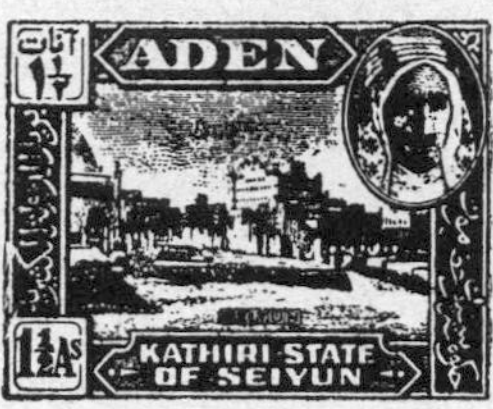

2. Seiyun.

Designs as T **2**:—

3. Tarim. (*Vert.*)
4. Mosque, Seiyun. (*Vert.*)
5. Fortress, Tarim. (*Horiz.*)
6. Mosque, Seiyun. (*Horiz.*)
7. South Gate, Tarim. (*Vert.*)
8. A Kathiri House. (*Horiz.*)
9. Mosque Entrance, Tarim. (*Vert.*)

(Recess. D.L.R.)

1942 (July–Oct.). *Wmk. Mult. Script CA. T* **1**, *perf.* 14; *others, perf.* 12 × 13 (*vert.*) *or* 13 × 12 (*horiz.*).

1	**1**	½ a. blue-green	10	20
2	„	¾ a. brown	10	20
3	„	1 a. blue	10	20
4	**2**	1½ a. carmine	10	25
5	**3**	2 a. sepia	10	30
6	**4**	2½ a. blue	12	35
7	**5**	3 a. sepia and carmine ..	15	30
8	**6**	8 a. red	20	35
9	**7**	1 r. green	30	40
10	**8**	2 r. blue and purple ..	75	1·50
11	**9**	5 r. brown and green ..	1·40	2·50
1/11		.. .. *Set of* 11	3·00	6·00
1/11		Perf. "Specimen" *Set of* 11	19·00	

VICTORY

ISSUE

8TH JUNE 1946

(10)

1946 (15 Oct.). *Victory. No.* 4 *optd. with T* **10**, *and No.* 6 *optd. similarly but in four lines, by De La Rue.*

12	**2**	1½ a. carmine	5	5
13	**4**	2½ a. blue (R.)	8	8
		a. Opt. inverted	£200	
12/13		Perf. "Specimen" *Set of* 2	22·00	

No. 13 is known with surcharge double but the second impression is almost coincident with the first.

1949 (17 Jan.). *Royal Silver Wedding. As Nos.* 30/1 *of Aden.*

14		1½ a. scarlet	8	8
15		5 r. green	2·00	2·50

1949 (10 Oct.). *75th Anniv. of U.P.U. As Nos. 114/17 of Antigua, but inscr.* "ADEN KATHIRI STATE OF SEIYUN" *and surch. with new values, by Waterlow.*

No.	Description		Unused	Used
16	2½ a. on 20 c. ultramarine	..	12	30
17	3 a. on 30 c. carmine-red	..	12	35
18	8 a. on 50 c. orange ..	..	45	1·10
19	1 r. on 1s. blue ..	..	75	1·75

5 CTS
(11)

50 CENTS
(12)

5/-
(13)

1951 (1 Oct.). *Currency changed. Surch. as* **T 11** *(5 c.),* **12** *(20 c. and 50 c.) or* **13** *(1s. to 5s.). 10 c. and 15 c. are as* **T 12**, *but abbrev.* ("CTS"), *by Waterlow.*

No.	Type	Description	Unused	Used
20	**1**	5 c. on 1 a. blue (R.) ..	10	20
21	**3**	10 c. on 2 a. sepia ..	10	20
22	**4**	15 c. on 2½ a. blue ..	10	30
23	**5**	20 c. on 3 a. sepia & carm.	10	30
24	**6**	50 c. on 8 a. red ..	12	35
25	**7**	1s. on 1 r. green ..	30	60
26	**8**	2s. on 2 r. blue & purple	60	1·40
27	**9**	5s. on 5 r. brown & green	1·40	2·25
20/27		.. .. *Set of* 8	2·50	4·75

1953 (2 June). *Coronation. As No. 47 of Aden.*

No.	Description	Unused	Used
28	15 c. black and deep green ..	25	35

14. Sultan Hussein.

15. Tarim.

(Des. Miss Freya Stark and H. Ingram. Recess. D.L.R.)

1954 (15 Jan.). *As* **T 1/9** *(but with portrait of Sultan Hussein as in* **T 14/5**). *Wmk. Mult. Script CA.* **T 14**, *perf.* 12½; *others, perf.* 12 × 13 *(vert.) or* 13 × 12 *(horiz.).*

No.	Type	Description	Unused	Used
29	**14**	5 c. sepia	12	12
30	,,	10 c. deep blue	12	12
31	**2**	15 c. deep bluish green ..	12	15
32	**15**	25 c. carmine-red ..	12	15
33	**4**	35 c. deep blue	12	15
34	**5**	50 c. dp. brown & carm.-red	15	20
35	**6**	1s. brown-orange ..	25	30
36	**7**	2s. deep yellow-green ..	60	70
37	**8**	5s. deep blue and violet	1·10	1·75
38	**9**	10s. yellow-brown & violet	2·25	2·00
29/38		.. .. *Set of* 10	4·50	5·00

16. Qarn Adh Dhabi.

17 Seiyun.

18. Gheil Omer. *(Horiz.)*

(Recess. De La Rue & Co.)

1964 (1 July). *W* **w.12.** *P* 12 × 13 *(70 c.) or* 13 × 12 *(others).*

No.	Type	Description	Unused	Used
39	**16**	70 c. black	12	25
40	**17**	1s. 25 c. blue-green ..	20	35
41	**18**	1s. 50 c. dp. reddish violet	30	45

(New currency. 1000 fils = 1 dinar.)

(19) (20) (21)

1966 (1 Apr.). *New Currency. Nos. 29/41 surch as* **T 19/21.**

No.	Type	Description	Unused	Used
42	**14**	5 f. on 5 c. (19)	5	5
		a. Surch. quadruple, one inverted	40·00	
43	,,	5 f. on 10 c. (19) (R.) ..	5	5
44	**2**	10 f. on 15 c. (21) (R.) ..	5	5
45	**15**	15 f. on 25 c. (20) ..	5	5
46	**4**	20 f. on 35 c. (20) (R.) ..	5	5
47	**5**	25 f. on 50 c. (21) (R.) ..	5	5
48	**16**	35 f. on 70 c. (20) (R.) ..	8	8
49	**6**	50 f. on 1s. (21)	8	10
50	**17**	65 f. on 1s. 25 (21) ..	10	12
51	**18**	75 f. on 1s. 50 (21) ..	15	20
52	**7**	100 f. on 2s. (20) (R.) ..	1·50	2·25
53	**8**	250 f. on 5s. (21) (R.) ..	60	1·00
54	**9**	500 f. on 10s. (20)	1·00	1·50
42/54		.. .. *Set of* 13	3·25	4·50

SOUTH ARABIA

5FILS 50FILS 15 FILS

(22) (23) (24)

1966. *Nos. 29/41 surch. with* **T 22/4.**

No.	Type	Description	Unused	Used
55	**14**	5 f. on 5 c. (22) (B.) ..	5	5
		a. Surch. inverted.. ..		
56	,,	5 f. on 10 c. (22) (R.) ..	5	5
57	**2**	10 f. on 15 c. (23) (Y.) ..	5	5
58	**15**	15 f. on 25 c. (24) (B.) ..	5	5
		a. Surch. inverted ..	40·00	
59	**4**	20 f. on 35 c. (24) (Y.) ..	5	5
60	**5**	25 f. on 50 c. (23) (B.) ..	5	5
61	**16**	35 f. on 70 c. (24) (Br.) ..	8	5
62	**6**	50 f. on 1s. (23) (G.) ..	10	10
		a. Stop after "FILS" ..	7·00	
63	**17**	65 f. on 1s. 25 (23) (Y.) ..	15	20
64	**18**	75 f. on 1s. 50, (23) (G.) ..	20	25
65	**7**	100 f. on 2s. (24) (Y.) ..	25	35
		a. Surch. inverted ..		
66	**8**	250 f. on 5s. (23) (Y.) ..	60	90
67	**9**	500 f. on 10s. (24) (G.) ..	1·25	2·00
55/67		.. .. *Set of* 13	2·25	3·25

HELSINKI 1952
(25)

INTERNATIONAL COOPERATION THROUGH OLYMPICS
(26)

1966. *Nos. 57, 59, 61/7 optd. as* **T 25** *or* **26** *(35 f.), in red.*

No.	Description	Unused	Used
68	10 f. on 15 c. ("LOS ANGELES 1932")	5	5
69	20 f. on 35 c. ("BERLIN 1936")	5	5
70	35 f. on 70 c. (26)	5	5
71	50 f. on 1s. ("LONDON 1948")	10	12
	a. Stop after "FILS" ..	7·00	
72	65 f. on 1s. 25 (25)	12	15
73	75 f. on 1s. 50 ("MELBOURNE 1956")	15	20
74	100 f. on 2s. ("ROME 1960")	25	35
75	250 f. on 5s. ("TOKYO 1964")	50	75
76	500 f. on 10s. ("MEXICO CITY 1968")	1·00	1·75
68/76	.. .. *Set of* 9	1·75	2·50

CHAMPION: ENGLAND
(27)

FOOTBALL 1966
(28)

1966 (19 Sept.). *World Cup Football Championships. Nos. 57, 59, 61/2, 65/7 optd. with* **T 27** *or* **28.**

No.	Description	Unused	Used
77	10 f. on 15 c. (27)	5	5
78	20 f. on 35 c. (28)	5	5
79	35 f. on 70 c. (28)	8	10
80	50 f. on 1s. (27)	10	10
	a. Stop after "FILS" ..	7·00	
81	100 f. on 2s. (28)	25	30
82	250 f. on 5s. (27)	50	60
83	500 f. on 10s. (28)	1·00	1·25
77/83	.. .. *Set of* 7	1·75	2·00

29. "Telstar".
30. "Relay".
31. "Ranger".

(Photo. State Ptg. Wks., Vienna.)

1966 (25 Oct.). *I.T.U. Centenary* (1965). *P* 13½.

No.	Type	Description	Unused	Used
84	**29**	5 f. blackish green, black and reddish violet ..	5	5
85	**30**	10 f. maroon, black and bright green	5	5
86	**31**	15 f. Prussian blue, black and orange	5	5
87	**29**	25 f. blackish green, black and orange-red ..	8	8
88	**30**	35 f. maroon, black and deep olive-yellow	12	12
89	**31**	50 f. Prussian blue, black and orange-brown	20	20
90	**29**	65 f. blackish green, black and orange-yellow ..	25	25
84/90		.. .. *Set of* 7	65	65

32. Churchill at Easel.
33. " Antibes ". (*Horiz.*)
34. " Flowers ". (*Vert.*)
35. " Tapestries ". (*Horiz.*)
36. " Village, Lake Lugano ". (*Horiz.*)
37. " Church, Lake Como ". (*Vert.*)
38. " Flowers at Chartwell ". (*Vert.*)

(Photo. State Ptg. Wks., Vienna.)

1966 (Dec.). *Sir Winston Churchill's Paintings. P* 13½.

91 **32**	5 f. black and gold	..	5	5
92 **33**	10 f. multicoloured	..	5	5
93 **34**	15 f. multicoloured	..	8	8
94 **35**	20 f. multicoloured	..	10	10
95 **36**	25 f. multicoloured	..	12	12
96 **37**	35 f. multicoloured	..	20	20
97 **38**	50 f. multicoloured	..	25	25
98 **32**	65 f. multicoloured	..	30	30
91/8	.. ..	*Set of* 8	75	75

WORLD PEACE
PANDIT NEHRU

(**39**)

1967. " *World Peace* ". *Nos.* 57, 59, 61/7 *optd. as T* **39** *in various sizes of type.*

99	10 f. on 15 c. (Type **39**) (R.)		5	5
100	20 f. on 35 c. (" WINSTON CHURCHILL ") (R.)	..	5	5
101	35 f. on 70 c. (" DAG HAMMARSKJOLD ") (B.)	..	8	5
102	50 f. on 1s. (" JOHN F. KENNEDY ") (R.)	..	12	12
	a. Stop after " FILS "	..	7·00	
103	65 f. on 1s. 25, (" LUDWIG ERHARD ") (Pk.)	..	15	15
104	75 f. on 1s. 50, (" LYNDON JOHNSON ") (B.)	..	20	20
105	100 f. on 2s. (" ELEANOR ROOSEVELT ") (B.)	..	25	25
106	250 f. on 5s. (" WINSTON CHURCHILL ") (R.)	..	60	60
107	500 f. on 10s. (" JOHN F. KENNEDY ") (R.)	..	1·25	1·25
99/107	.. ..	*Set of* 9	2·25	2·25

40. " Master Crewe as Henry VIII " (Sir Joshua Reynolds).

41. " The Dancer " (Degas).
42. " The Fifer " (Manet).
43. " Stag at Sharkey's " (boxing-match, G. Burrows).
44. " Don Manuel Osorio " (Goya).
45. " St. Martin Distributing His Cloak " (A. van Dyck).
46. " The Blue Boy " (Gainsborough).
47. " The White Horse " (Gauguin).
48. " Mona Lisa " (Da Vinci).

All designs vert. as T **40** but T **48** is larger (45 × 61½ *mm.*).

(Photo. State Ptg. Wks., Vienna.)

1967. *Paintings. P* 13½.

108 **40**	5 f. multicoloured	..	5	5
109 **41**	10 f. multicoloured	..	5	5
110 **42**	15 f. multicoloured	..	5	5
111 **43**	20 f. multicoloured	..	8	8
112 **44**	25 f. multicoloured	..	8	8
113 **45**	35 f. multicoloured	..	12	12
114 **46**	50 f. multicoloured	..	15	15
115 **47**	65 f. multicoloured	..	20	20
116 **48**	75 f. multicoloured	..	25	25
108/16	.. ..	*Set of* 9	1·00	1·00

SCOTT CARPENTER

(**49**)

1967. *American Astronauts. Nos.* 57, 59, 61/2 *and* 65/6 *optd. as T* **49** *in various sizes of type, in red.*

117	10 f. on 15 c. (" ALAN SHEPARD, JR.")	..	5	5
118	20 f. on 35 c. (" VIRGIL GRISSOM ")	..	5	5
119	35 f. on 70 c. (" JOHN GLENN, JR.")	..	8	8
120	50 f. on 1s. (Type **49**)	..	15	15
	a. Stop after "FILS"	..	7·00	
121	100 f. on 2s. (" WALTER SCHIRRA, JR.")	..	30	30
122	250 f. on 5s. (" GORDON COOPER, JR.")	..	75	75
117/122	..	*Set of* 6	1·00	1·00

50. Churchill Crown.

1967 (Mar.). *Churchill Commemoration. Photo. P* 13½.

123 **50**	75 f. multicoloured	..	20	20

The National Liberation Front are said to have taken control on 1 October 1967 and full independence was granted by Great Britain on 30 November 1967. Later issues prior to 1st October are recorded in the Appendix to this volume and those issued after independence was granted will be found listed under Yemen (People's Democratic Republic) in Vol. 4 of the Stanley Gibbons Foreign Overseas Catalogue.

QU'AITI STATE IN HADHRAMAUT.

I. Issues inscr. " SHIHR AND MUKALLA ".

1. Sultan of Shihr and Mukalla. **2.** Mukalla Harbour.

Designs as T **2**:—

3. Gateway of Shihr. (*Vert.*)
4. Shibam. (*Horiz.*)
5. Outpost of Mukalla. (*Vert.*)
6. 'Einat. (*Horiz.*)
7. Du'an. (*Vert.*)
8. Mosque in Hureidha. (*Horiz.*)
9. Meshhed. (*Horiz.*)

(Recess. De La Rue & Co.)

1942 (July)–**46.** *Wmk. Mult. Script CA. T* **1**, *perf.* 14; *others, perf.* 12 × 13 (*vert.*) *or* 13 × 12 (*horiz.*).

1 **1**	½ a. blue-green	..	10	15
	a. Olive-green (Dec. '46)	..	2·50	3·50
2 „	¾ a. brown	..	10	15
3 „	1 a. blue	..	10	15
4 **2**	1½ a. carmine	..	10	25
5 **3**	2 a. sepia	..	10	35
6 **4**	2½ a. blue	..	10	30
7 **5**	3 a. sepia and carmine	..	12	30
8 **6**	8 a. red	..	20	50
9 **7**	1 r. green	..	30	55
10 **8**	2 r. blue and purple	..	1·00	1·50
11 **9**	5 r. brown and green	..	1·40	2·50
1/11	.. ..	*Set of* 11	3·25	6·00
1/11	Perf. " Specimen "	*Set of* 11	19·00	

VICTORY
ISSUE
8TH JUNE
1946

(**10**)

1946 (15 Oct.). *Victory. No.* 4 *optd. with T* **10** *and No.* 6 *optd. similarly, but in three lines, by De La Rue.*

12 **2**	1½ a. carmine	..	8	8
13 **4**	2½ a. blue (R.)	..	8	8
12/13	Perf. " Specimen "	*Set of* 2	22·00	

1949 (17 Jan.). *Royal Silver Wedding. As Nos.* 30/1 *of Aden.*

14	1½ a. scarlet	..	10	12
15	5 r. green	..	1·75	2·50

1949 (10 Oct.). *75th Anniv. of Universal Postal Union. As Nos.* 114/7 *of Antigua, but surch. with new values, by Waterlow.*

16	2½ a. on 20 c. ultramarine	..	15	30
17	3 a. on 30 c. carmine-red	..	45	50
18	8 a. on 50 c. orange	..	75	1·00
19	1 r. on 1s. blue	..	1·25	1·60
	a. Surch. omitted	..	£300	

1951 (1 Oct.). *Currency changed. Surch. with new values in cents or shillings as T* **11** *to* **13** *of Seiyun, by Waterlow.*

20 **1**	5 c. on 1 a. blue (R.)	..	10	12
21 **3**	10 c. on 2 a. sepia	..	10	12
22 **4**	15 c. on 2½ a. blue	..	10	12
23 **5**	20 c. on 3 a. sepia & carmine	..	10	15
24 **6**	50 c. on 8 a. red	..	10	20
25 **7**	1s. on 1 r. green	..	20	70
26 **8**	2s. on 2 r. blue and purple	..	60	1·25
27 **9**	5s. on 5 r. brown & green	..	1·25	1·90
20/27	.. ..	*Set of* 8	2·25	4·00

1953 (2 June). *Coronation. As No.* 47 *of Aden.*

28	15 c. black and deep blue	..	20	35

II. Issues inscr. " HADHRAMAUT ".

11. Metal Work.

12. Mat-Making. (*Vert.*)
13. Weaving. (*Vert.*)
14. Pottery. (*Vert.*)
15. Building. (*Vert.*)
16. Date Cultivation. (*Vert.*)
17. Agriculture. (*Vert.*)
18. Fisheries. (*Horiz.*)
19. Lime Burning. (*Horiz.*)
20. Dhow Building. (*Horiz.*)
21. Agriculture. (*Horiz.*)

(Des. Mme. M. de Sturler Raemaekers. Recess. De La Rue & Co.)

1955 (1 SEPT.). *Wmk. Mult. Script CA. P* 11½×13–13½ (*vert.*) *or* 14 (*horiz.*).

29	**11**	5 c. greenish blue	12	12
30	**12**	10 c. grey-black	12	12
31	**13**	15 c. deep green (*shades*) ..	12	12
32	**14**	25 c. carmine-red	12	12
33	**15**	35 c. blue	12	12
34	**16**	50 c. orange-red (*shades*) ..	20	15
35	**17**	90 c. sepia	20	25
36	**18**	1s. black and deep lilac ..	20	25
37	**19**	1s. 25, black & red-orange	30	35
38	**20**	2s. black and indigo ..	55	70
39	**21**	5s. black and bluish green	1·50	1·75
40	**19**	10s. black and lake ..	2·50	3·25
29/40		.. .. *Set of* 12	5·50	6·50

22. Metal Work.

1963 (20 OCT.). *As T* **11/21**, *but with inset portrait of Sultan Awadh bin Saleh el-Qu'aiti as in T* **22** *and wmk.* w.**12**.

41	**22**	5 c. greenish blue ..	5	5
42	**12**	10 c. grey-black	5	5
43	**13**	15 c. bronze-green ..	5	5
44	**14**	25 c. carmine-red	5	5
45	**15**	35 c. blue	5	5
46	**16**	50 c. red-orange	5	8
47	**17**	70 c. deep brown	8	12
48	**18**	1s. black and deep lilac	10	20
49	**19**	1s. 25, black & red-orange	20	30
50	**20**	2s. black and indigo-blue	40	50
51	**21**	5s. black and bluish green	75	1·40
52	**19**	10s. black and lake ..	1·40	2·25
41/52		.. .. *Set of* 12	2·75	4·75

(New currency. 1000 fils=1 dinar.)

1966 (1 APR.). *New currency. Nos.* 41/52 *surch. as T* **20/21** *of Kathiri State of Seiyun.*

53	**22**	5 f. on 5 c. (**20**) (R.) ..	5	5
54	**12**	5 f. on 10 c. (**20**) (R.) ..	5	5
55	**13**	10 f. on 15 c. (**20**) (R.) ..	5	5
56	**14**	15 f. on 25 c. (**20**)	5	5
57	**15**	20 f. on 35 c. (**20**) (R.) ..	5	5
58	**16**	25 f. on 50 c. (**20**)	5	8
59	**17**	35 f. on 70 c. (**20**) (R.) ..	8	10
60	**18**	50 f. on 1s. (**21**) (R.) ..	10	15
61	**19**	65 f. on 1s. 25 (**21**) (R.) ..	20	30
62	**20**	100 f. on 2s. (**21**) (R.) ..	40	60
63	**21**	250 f. on 5s. (**21**) (R.) ..	1·00	1·50
64	**19**	500 f. on 10s. (**21**) (R.) ..	2·00	3·00
53/64		.. .. *Set of* 12	3·00	4·50

1874–1965 WINSTON CHURCHILL (23)

1917–1963 JOHN F. KENNEDY (24)

1966. *Churchill Commemoration. Nos.* 54/6 *optd. with T* **23**.

65	5 f. on 10 c. (R.)	10	15
66	10 f. on 15 c. (R.)	20	30
67	15 f. on 25 c. (B.)	30	45

1966. *President Kennedy Commemoration. Nos.* 57/9 *optd. with T* **24**.

68	20 f. on 35 c. (R.)	40	60
69	25 f. on 50 c. (B.)	55	80
70	35 f. on 70 c. (B.)	70	1·25

25. World Cup Emblem.
(*Illustration reduced. Actual size* 55×55 *mm.*)

26. Wembley Stadium.
27. Footballers.
28. Jules Rimet Cup and Football.

(Photo. State Ptg. Wks., Vienna.)

1966. *World Cup Football Championships. P* 13½.

71	**25**	5 f. maroon & yell.-orange	5	5
72	**26**	10 f. slate-violet & lt. green	5	5
73	**27**	15 f. maroon & yell.-orange	5	5
74	**28**	20 f. slate-violet & lt. green	8	8
75	**25**	25 f. blackish green and orange-red	8	8
76	**26**	35 f. blue and yellow ..	12	12
77	**27**	50 f. blackish green and orange-red	20	20
78	**25**	65 f. blue and yellow ..	25	25
71/78		.. .. *Set of* 8	70	70

29. Mexican Hat and Blanket.
(*Illustration reduced. Actual size* 63×63 *mm.*)

(Photo. State Ptg. Wks., Vienna.)

1966 (25 OCT.). *Pre-Olympic Games, Mexico* (1968). *P* 13½.

79	**29**	75 f. sepia & lt. yell.-green	30	30

30. Telecommunications Satellite.

31. Olympic Runner (inscr. " ROME 1960 ").
32. Fishes.
33. Tobacco Plant.

(Photo. State Ptg. Wks., Vienna.)

1966 (DEC.). *International Co-operation Year* (1965). *P* 13½.

80	**30**	5 f. maroon, bright purple and emerald	5	5
81	**31**	10 f. violet, orange, blue-green and new blue ..	5	5
82	**32**	15 f. maroon, new blue & red	5	5
83	**30**	20 f. Prussian blue, purple and red	8	8
84	**31**	25 f. violet, olive-yellow, red and emerald	8	8
85	**30**	35 f. maroon, rose-red and new blue	12	12
86	**33**	50 f. maroon, green and red	20	20
87	**30**	65 f. chocolate, bluish violet and red ..	25	25
80/87		.. .. *Set of* 8	70	70

No. 84 is inscribed " TOKIO 1964 ".

The National Liberation Front took control on 17 September 1967 and full independence was granted by Great Britain on 30 November 1967. Later issues prior to 17th September are recorded in the Appendix to this volume and those issued after independence was granted will be found listed under YEMEN (PEOPLE'S DEMOCRATIC REPUBLIC) in Vol. 4 of the Stanley Gibbons Foreign Overseas Catalogue.

MAHRA SULTANATE OF QISHN AND SOCOTRA.

(Currency. 1000 fils=1 dinar.)

1. Mahra Flag.

(Des. and litho. Harrison & Sons.)

1967 (12 MAR.). *Flag in green, black and vermilion; inscriptions in black; background colours given. P* 14×14½.

1	**1**	5 f. mauve	5	5
2	,,	10 f. buff	5	5
3	,,	15 f. sage-green	5	5
4	,,	20 f. red-orange	5	5
5	,,	25 f. yellow-brown	5	5
6	,,	35 f. turquoise-green ..	8	5
7	,,	50 f. new blue	8	8
8	,,	65 f. blackish brown ..	10	10
9	,,	100 f. violet	15	15

10 **1** 250 f. rose-red 50 35
11 „ 500 f. grey-green .. .. 1·00 75
1/11 .. .. .. *Set of* 11 2·00 1·60

The National Liberation Front are said to have taken control on 1 October 1967 and full independence was granted by Great Britain on 30 November 1967. Later issues prior to 1st October are recorded in the Appendix to this volume and those issued after independence was granted will be found listed under YEMEN (PEOPLE'S DEMOCRATIC REPUBLIC) in Vol. 4 of the Stanley Gibbons Foreign Overseas Catalogue.

ANGUILLA.

St. Christopher, Nevis and Anguilla were granted Associated Statehood on 27 February 1967 but following a referendum Anguilla declared her independence and the St. Christopher authorities withdrew. The following stamps were issued by the governing Council and have been accepted for international mail. On 7 July 1969 the Anguilla post office was officially recognised by the Government of St. Christopher, Nevis and Anguilla and normal postal communications via St. Christopher were resumed. By the Anguilla Act of 28 July 1971, Anguilla was restored to direct British control.

A degree of internal self-government with an Executive Council was introduced on 10th February 1976.

Independent Anguilla

(1)

1967 (4 SEPT.). *Stamps of St. Kitts-Nevis, Nos. 129/44, optd. as T* **1**, *by Island Press, Inc., St. Thomas, U.S. Virgin Islands.*

1 **32** ½ c. sepia and light blue .. 16·00 18·00
2 **33** 1 c. multicoloured .. .. 13·00 11·00
3 **34** 2 c. multicoloured .. .. 16·00 10·00
4 **35** 3 c. multicoloured .. .. 16·00 11·00
5 **36** 4 c. multicoloured .. .. 16·00 11·00
6 **37** 5 c. multicoloured .. .. 60·00 22·00
7 **38** 6 c. multicoloured .. .. 24·00 13·00
8 **39** 10 c. multicoloured .. .. 16·00 11·00
9 **40** 15 c. multicoloured .. .. 32·00 14·00
10 **41** 20 c. multicoloured .. .. 50·00 17·00
11 **42** 25 c. multicoloured .. .. 42·00 21·00
12 **43** 50 c. multicoloured .. .. — £350
13 **44** 60 c. multicoloured .. .. — £450
14 **45** $1 greenish yellow & blue — £275
15 **46** $2.50 multicoloured .. — £275
16 **47** $5 multicoloured .. .. — £275
1/16 .. .. *Set of* 16 £3000 £1600

Owing to the limited stocks available for overprinting, the sale of the above stamps was personally controlled by the Postmaster and no orders from the trade were accepted.

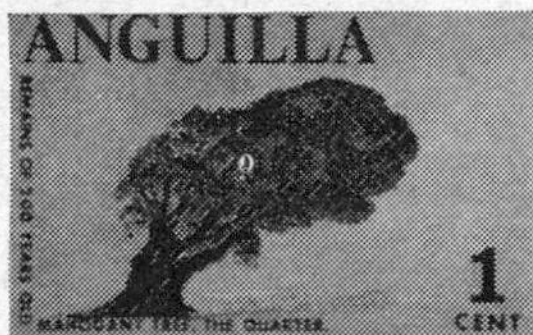

2. Mahogany Tree, The Quarter.

3. Sombrero Lighthouse.
4. St. Mary's Church.
5. Valley Police Station.
6. Old Plantation House, Mt. Fortune.
7. Valley Post Office.
8. Methodist Church, West End.
9. Wall-Blake Airport.
10. Aircraft over Sandy Ground.
11. Island Harbour.
12. Map of Anguilla.
13. Hermit Crab and Starfish.
14. Hibiscus.
15. Local Scene.
16. Spiny Lobster.

(Des. John Lister Ltd. Litho. A. & M.)

1967 (27 Nov.)–**68.** *P* $12\frac{1}{2} \times 13$.

17 **2** 1 c. dull green, bistre-brown and pale orange 12 12
18 **3** 2 c. bluish green and black (21.3.68) 12 12
19 **4** 3 c. black and light emerald (10.2.68) 12 12
20 **5** 4 c. cobalt-blue and black (10.2.68) 12 12
21 **6** 5 c. multicoloured .. 12 12
22 **7** 6 c. light vermilion and black (21.3.68) .. 12 12
23 **8** 10 c. multicoloured .. 15 15
24 **9** 15 c. multicoloured (10.2.68) 20 25
25 **10** 20 c. multicoloured .. 25 30
26 **11** 25 c. multicoloured .. 25 30
27 **12** 40 c. apple grn., lt. greenish blue and black .. 50 50
28 **13** 60 c. multicoloured (10.2.68) 65 75
29 **14** $1 multicoloured (10.2.68) 95 1·25
30 **15** $2.50, mult. (21.3.68) .. 2·00 2·50
31 **16** $5 multicoloured (10.2.68) 3·50 5·00
17/31 .. .. *Set of* 15 8·00 10·00

On 9th January 1969 Anguilla reaffirmed her independence from St. Kitts and issued Nos. 17/31 overprinted in black "INDEPENDENCE JANUARY 1969" in two lines. These are outside the scope of this catalogue.

17. Yachts in Lagoon.

(Des. John Lister Ltd. Litho. A. & M.)

1968 (11 MAY). *Anguillan Ships. T* **17** *and similar horiz. designs. Multicoloured. P* 14.

32 10 c. Type **17** 15 15
33 15 c. Boat on beach 20 25
34 25 c. Schooner *Warspite* .. 35 35
35 40 c. *Atlantic Star* 55 55

18. Purple-throated Carib.

(Des. John Lister Ltd. Litho. A. & M.)

1968 (8 JULY). *Anguillan Birds. T* **18** *and similar multicoloured designs. P* 14.

36 10 c. Type **18** 10 12
37 15 c. Bananaquit 15 20
38 25 c. Black-necked Stilt (*horiz.*) 30 35
39 40 c. Royal Tern (*horiz.*) .. 40 45

19. Guides' Badge and Anniversary Years.

(Des. John Lister Ltd. Litho. A. & M.)

1968 (14 OCT.). *35th Anniv. of Anguillan Girl Guides. T* **19** *and similar multicoloured designs. P* $13 \times 13\frac{1}{2}$ *(horiz.) or* $13\frac{1}{2} \times 13$ *(vert.).*

40 10 c. Type **19** 12 12
41 15 c. Badge and silhouettes of Guides (*vert.*) 15 25
42 25 c. Guides' badge and Headquarters 25 35
43 40 c. Association and Proficiency badges (*vert.*) .. 40 45

20. The Three Kings.

(Des. John Lister Ltd. Litho. A. & M.)

1968 (18 Nov.). *Christmas. T* **20** *and similar designs. P* 13.

44 1 c. black and cerise .. 8 8
45 10 c. black & lt. greenish blue 12 12
46 15 c. black and chestnut .. 25 25
47 40 c. black and blue 40 40
48 50 c. black and dull green .. 60 60
44/8 .. .. .. *Set of* 5 1·25 1·25

Designs: *Vert.*—10 c. The Wise Men; 15 c. Holy Family and manger. *Horiz.*—40 c. The Shepherds; 50 c. Holy Family, and donkey.

21. Bagging Salt.

(Des. J. Lister Ltd. Litho. A. & M.)

1969 (4 JAN.). *Anguillan Salt Industry. T* **21** *and similar horiz. designs. Multicoloured. P* 13.

49 10 c. Type **21** 12 12
50 15 c. Packing salt 25 25
51 40 c. Salt pond 35 35
52 50 c. Loading salt 45 45

22. "The Crucifixion" (Studio of Massys).

(Des. J. Lister Ltd. Litho. Format International.)

1969 (31 MAR.). *Easter Commemoration. T* **22** *and similar vert. design. P* $13\frac{1}{2}$.

53 25 c. multicoloured 30 30
54 40 c. multicoloured 40 40

Design:—40 c. "The Last Supper" (ascribed to Roberti).

23. Amaryllis.

(Des. J. Lister Ltd. Litho. Format International.)

1969 (10 JUNE). *Flowers of the Caribbean. T* **23** *and similar horiz. designs. Multicoloured. P* 14.

55	10 c. Type **23**	12	12
56	15 c. Bougainvillea	20	20
57	40 c. Hibiscus	35	35
58	50 c. *Cattleya* orchid	50	50

24. Turbans and Star Shells.

(Des. J. Lister Ltd. Litho. A. & M.)

1969 (22 SEPT.). *Sea Shells. T* **24** *and similar horiz. designs. Multicoloured. P* 14.

59	10 c. Type **24**	12	12
60	15 c. Spiny oysters	20	20
61	40 c. Scotch, Royal and Smooth Scotch bonnets	45	45
62	50 c. Triton trumpet	60	60

(25)

(26)

(27)

(28)

(29)

1969 (OCT.). *Christmas. Nos.* 17, 25/8 *optd. with T* **25/29.**

63	**2**	1 c. dull green, bistre-brn. and pale orange ..	8	8
64	**10**	20 c. multicoloured ..	35	30
65	**11**	25 c. multicoloured ..	40	35
66	**12**	40 c. apple-grn., lt. greenish blue and black ..	65	55
67	**13**	60 c. multicoloured ..	1·40	95
63/7		.. .. *Set of* 5	2·50	2·00

30. Red Goatfish.

(Des. J. Lister Ltd. Litho. A. & M.)

1969 (1 DEC.). *Fishes. T* **30** *and similar horiz. designs. Multicoloured. P* 14.

68	10 c. Type **30**	12	12
69	15 c. Blue Striped grunts ..	20	20
70	40 c. Mutton grouper	45	45
71	50 c. Banded Butterfly fish ..	50	50

31. " Morning Glory ".

(Des. John Lister Ltd. Litho. A. & M.)

1970 (23 FEB.). *Flowers. T* **31** *and similar vert. designs. Multicoloured. P* 14.

72	10 c. Type **31**	12	12
73	15 c. Blue Petrea	20	20
74	40 c. Hibiscus	35	35
75	50 c. " Flame Tree "	50	50

32. " Deposition " (Rosso Fiorentino).

(Des. J. Lister Ltd. Litho. Format.)

1970 (26 MAR.). *Easter. T* **32** *and similar multicoloured designs. P* 13½.

76	10 c. " The Ascent to Calvary " (Tiepolo) (*horiz.*) ..	12	12
77	20 c. " The Crucifixion " (Masaccio)	25	25
78	40 c. Type **32**	45	45
79	60 c. " The Ascent to Calvary " (Murillo) (*horiz.*) ..	55	55

33. Scout Badge and Map.

(Des. J. Lister Ltd. Litho.)

1970 (10 AUG.). *40th Anniv. of Scouting in Anguilla. T* **33** *and similar horiz. designs. Multicoloured. P* 13.

80	10 c. Type **33**	12	12
81	15 c. Scout camp and cubs practising first-aid ..	20	20
82	40 c. Monkey Bridge ..	35	35
83	50 c. Scout H.Q. Building and Lord Baden-Powell ..	50	50

34. Boatbuilding.

(Des. J. Lister Ltd. Litho. Format.)

1970 (23 NOV.). *Various horiz. designs as T* **34.** *Multicoloured. P* 14.

84	1 c. Type **34**	5	5
85	2 c. Road Construction ..	5	5
86	3 c. Quay, Blowing Point ..	5	5
87	4 c. Broadcaster, Radio Anguilla	8	8
88	5 c. Cottage Hospital Extension	8	8
89	6 c. Valley Secondary School	12	12
90	10 c. Hotel Extension ..	12	15
91	15 c. Sandy Ground	15	20
92	20 c. Supermarket and Cinema	20	25
93	25 c. Bananas and Mangoes ..	25	30
94	40 c. Wall Blake Airport ..	35	40
95	60 c. Sandy Ground Jetty ..	45	50
96	$1 Administration Buildings	80	85
97	$2.50, Livestock	2·00	2·25
98	$5 Sandy Hill Bay	3·50	3·75
84/98	.. .. *Set of* 15	7·00	8·00

35. " The Adoration of the Shepherds " (Reni).

(Des. J. Lister Ltd. Litho. Questa.)

1970 (11 DEC.). *Christmas. T* **35** *and similar vert. designs. Multicoloured. P* 13½.

99	1 c. Type **35**	12	12
100	20 c. " The Virgin and Child " (Gozzoli)	30	30

101 25 c. " Manger Scene " (detail, Botticelli) 30 30
102 40 c. "The Santa Margherita Madonna " (detail, Mazzola) 35 35
103 50 c. " L'Adorazione dei Magi " (detail, Tiepolo) .. 50 50
99/103 .. .. *Set of* 5 1·25 1·25

36. " Ecce Homo " (detail, Correggio).

(Des. J. Lister Ltd. Litho. Format.)

1971 (29 MAR.). *Easter.* *T* **36** *and similar designs.* *P* 13½.
104 10 c. multicoloured 12 12
105 15 c. multicoloured 20 20
106 40 c. multicoloured 40 40
107 50 c. multicoloured 50 50

Designs: *Vert.*—15 c. " Christ appearing to St. Peter " (detail, Carracci). *Horiz.*—40 c. " Angels weeping over the Dead Christ " (detail, Guercino); 50 c. " The Supper at Emmaus " (detail, Caravaggio).

37. *Hypolimnas missipus.*

(Des. J. Lister Ltd. Litho. Questa.)

1971 (21 JUNE). *Butterflies.* *T* **37** *and similar horiz. designs. Multicoloured.* *P* 14 × 14½.
108 10 c. Type **37** 10 10
109 15 c. *Junonia lavinia* .. 15 15
110 40 c. *Agraulis vanillae* .. 30 30
111 50 c. *Danaus plexippus* .. 40 40

38. *Magnanime* and *Amiable* in Battle.

(Des. J. Lister Ltd. Litho. Format.)

1971 (30 AUG.). *Sea-battles of the West Indies.* *T* **38** *and similar vert. designs. Multicoloured.* *P* 14.
112 10 c. Type **38** 10 10
113 15 c. H.M.S. *Duke*, *Glorieux* and H.M.S. *Agamemnon* 15 15
114 25 c. H.M.S. *Formidable* and H.M.S. *Namur* against *Ville de Paris* 25 25
115 40 c. H.M.S. *Canada* .. 40 40
116 50 c. H.M.S. *St. Albans* and wreck of *Hector* .. 50 55
Strip of 5 .. .. 1·40 1·40

Nos. 112/116 were issued in horizontal *se-tenant* strips within the sheet, to form a composite design in the order listed.

ADMINISTRATION BY BRITISH COMMISSION.

39. " The Ansidei Madonna " (detail, Raphael).

(Des. J. Lister Ltd. Litho. Questa.)

1971 (29 NOV.). *Christmas.* *T* **39** *and similar vert. designs.* *P* 13½.
117 20 c. multicoloured 20 20
118 25 c. multicoloured 25 25
119 40 c. multicoloured 35 40
120 50 c. multicoloured 45 45

Designs:—25 c. " Mystic Nativity " (detail, Botticelli); 40 c. " Adoration of the Shepherds " (detail; ascr. to Murillo); 50 c. " The Madonna of the Iris " (detail; ascr. to Dürer).

40. Map of Anguilla and St. Martins by Thomas Jefferys (1775).

(Litho. Format.)

1972 (24 JAN.). *Maps.* *T* **40** *and similar multicoloured designs showing maps by the cartographers given.* *P* 14.
121 10 c. Type **40** 5 5
122 15 c. Samuel Fahlberg (1814) 15 15
123 40 c. Thomas Jefferys (1775) 30 30
124 50 c. Capt. E. Barnett (1847) 35 40

The 40 and 50 c. are horiz. designs.

41. " Jesus Buffeted ".

(Des. J. Lister Ltd. from stained-glass windows at Bray, Berkshire. Litho. Format.)

1972 (14 MAR.). *Easter.* *T* **41** *and similar vert. designs. Multicoloured.* *P* 14 × 13½.
125 10 c. Type **41** 10 10
126 15 c. " The Way of Sorrows " 15 15
127 25 c. " The Crucifixion " .. 25 25
128 40 c. " Descent from the Cross " 35 40
129 50 c. " The Burial " 40 50
125/9 .. .. *Strip of* 5 1·10 1·25

Nos. 125/9 were printed horizontally *se-tenant* within the sheet.

42. Loblolly Tree.

(Litho. Questa ($10), Format (others).)

1972 (30 OCT.)–**75.** *T* **42** *and similar multicoloured designs (horiz., except* 2, 4 *and* 6 *c.).* *P* 13½.
130 1 c. Spear fishing 5 5
131 2 c. Type **42** 5 5
132 3 c. Sandy Ground 5 5
133 4 c. Ferry at Blowing Point 5 5
a. Gold (frame and ornaments) double .. .. ..
134 5 c. Agriculture 5 5
135 6 c. St. Mary's Church .. 8 10
136 10 c. St. Gerard's Church .. 10 10
137 15 c. Cottage Hospital extension 10 10
138 20 c. Public library 12 15
139 25 c. Sunset at Blowing Point 15 20
140 40 c. Boat building 25 30
141 60 c. Hibiscus 30 35
142 $1 Man-o'-War (bird) .. 45 50
143 $2.50, Frangipani .. .. 1·25 1·40
144 $5 Brown Pelican .. .. 2·25 2·50
144*a* $10 Green-back turtle .. (20.5.75) .. .. .. 4·00 4·25
130/44*a* .. .. *Set of* 16 8·50 9·00

43. Schooner and Dolphin.

(Des. (from photograph by D. Groves) and photo. Harrison.)

1972 (20 Nov.). *Royal Silver Wedding. Multi-coloured; background colour given.* W w.**12**. P 14×14½.

145 **43** 25 c. yellow-olive (*shades*) 1·75 2·00
146 ,, 40 c. chocolate .. .. 3·00 3·25

44. Flight into Egypt.

(Des. J. Lister Ltd. Litho. Questa.)

1972 (4 Dec.). *Christmas.* T **44** *and similar vert. designs. Multicoloured.* P 13½.

147 1 c. Type **44** 5 5
148 20 c. Star of Bethlehem .. 15 15
149 25 c. Holy Family 20 20
150 40 c. Arrival of the Magi .. 25 25
151 50 c. Adoration of the Magi.. 35 35
147/51 *Set of* 5 90 90

Nos. 148/51 were printed vertically *se-tenant* within a sheet of 20 stamps.

45. " The Betrayal of Christ ".

(Des. J. Lister Ltd. Litho. Questa.)

1973 (26 Mar.). *Easter.* T **45** *and similar vert. designs. Multicoloured; bottom panel in gold and black.* P 13½.

152 1 c. Type **45** 5 5
153 10 c. " The Man of Sorrows " 5 5
154 20 c. " Christ bearing the Cross " 12 12
155 25 c. " The Crucifixion " .. 15 15
156 40 c. " The Descent from the Cross " 25 25
157 50 c. " The Resurrection " 30 30
152/7 .. .. *Set of* 6 90 90
MS158 140×141 mm. Nos. 152/7
Bottom panel in gold and mauve 1·00 1·00

The 10 to 50 c. were printed within one sheet, vertically *se-tenant*.

46. *Santa Maria.*

(Des. J. Lister Ltd. Litho. Questa.)

1973 (10 Sept.). *Columbus Discovers the West Indies.* T **46** *and similar horiz. designs. Multicoloured.* P 13½.

159 1 c. Type **46** 5 5
160 20 c. Early map 15 15
161 40 c. Map of voyages .. 30 30
162 70 c. Sighting land 45 45
163 $1.20, Landing of Columbus.. 75 75
159/63 .. .. *Set of* 5 1·50 1·50
MS164 193×93 mm. Nos. 159/63 2·00 2·00

Nos. 160/3 were printed horizontally *se-tenant* within the sheet.

47. Princess Anne and Captain Mark Phillips.

(Des. PAD Studio. Litho. Questa.)

1973 (14 Nov.). *Royal Wedding. Centre multi-coloured.* W w.**12** (*sideways*). P 13½.

165 **47** 60 c. turquoise-green .. 40 40
166 ,, $1.20, deep mauve .. 75 75

48. "The Adoration of the Shepherds" (Reni).

(Des. J. Lister Ltd. Litho. Questa.)

1973 (2 Dec.). *Christmas.* T **48** *and similar horiz. designs. Multicoloured.* P 13½.

167 1 c. Type **48** 5 5
168 10 c. "The Virgin and Child" (Filippino Lippi) .. 8 8
169 20 c. "The Nativity" (Meester Van de Brunswijkse Diptiek) 12 12
170 25 c. "Madonna of the Meadow" (Bellini) .. 15 20
171 40 c. "Virgin and Child" (Cima).. .. .. 25 25
172 50 c. "Adoration of the Magi" (Geertgen) .. 30 30
167/72 *Set of* 6 80 90
MS173 148×149 mm. Nos. 167/72 90 95

Nos. 168/72 were printed within the sheet, horizontally *se-tenant*.

49. "The Crucifixion" (Raphael).

(Des. J. Lister Ltd. Litho. Questa.)

1974 (30 Mar.). *Easter.* T **49** *and similar vert. designs showing various details of Raphael's "Crucifixion".* P 13½.

174 **49** 1 c. multicoloured .. 5 5
175 – 15 c. multicoloured .. 10 10
176 – 20 c. multicoloured .. 12 12
177 – 25 c. multicoloured .. 15 15
178 – 40 c. multicoloured .. 20 25
179 – $1 multicoloured .. 45 50
174/9 .. .. *Set of* 6 95 1·00
MS180 123×141 mm. Nos. 174/9 .. 1·10 1·10

Nos. 175/9 were printed vertically *se-tenant* within one sheet.

50. Churchill making "Victory" Sign.

(Des. J. Lister Ltd. Litho. Questa.)

1974 (24 June). *Birth Centenary of Sir Winston Churchill.* T **50** *and similar horiz. designs. Multicoloured.* P 13½.

181 1 c. Type **50** 5 5
182 20 c. Churchill with Roosevelt 12 12
183 25 c. Wartime broadcast 12 15
184 40 c. Birthplace, Blenheim Palace 20 25
185 60 c. Churchill's statue .. 25 30
186 $1.20, Country residence, Chartwell 50 60
181/6 .. .. *Set of* 6 1·10 1·25
MS187 195×96 mm. Nos. 181/6 .. 1·50

Nos. 182/6 were printed horizontally *se-tenant* within the sheet.

51. U.P.U. Emblem.

(Des. John Lister Ltd. Litho. Questa.)

1974 (27 Aug.). *Centenary of Universal Postal Union. P* 13½*

No.	Type	Description	Unused	Used
188	**51**	1 c. black and bright blue	5	5
189	„	20 c. black and pale orange	12	12
190	„	25 c. black and light yellow	12	15
191	„	40 c. black & brt. mauve	20	25
192	„	60 c. black and light emer.	25	30
193	„	$1.20, black & lt. bl.	50	55
188/93		*Set of* 6	1·10	1·25
MS194		195×96 mm. Nos. 188/93	1·25	

Nos. 189/93 were printed horizontally *se-tenant* within the sheet.

*In No. **MS**194 the lower row of three stamps, 40c., 60c. and $1·20 values, are line-perforated 15 at foot, the remaining 3 stamps being comb-perforated 13½.

52. Anguillan pointing to Star.

(Litho. Questa.)

1974 (16 Dec.). *Christmas. T* **52** *and similar horiz. designs. Multicoloured. P* 14.

No.	Description	Unused	Used
195	1 c. Type **52**	5	5
196	20 c. Child in Manger	12	12
197	25 c. King's offering	12	15
198	40 c. Star over Map of Anguilla	20	25
199	60 c. Family looking at star	25	30
200	$1.20, Angels of Peace	50	55
195/200	*Set of* 6	1·10	1·25
MS201	177×85 mm. Nos. 195/200	1·25	

Nos. 195/200 were printed horizontally *se-tenant* within the sheet.

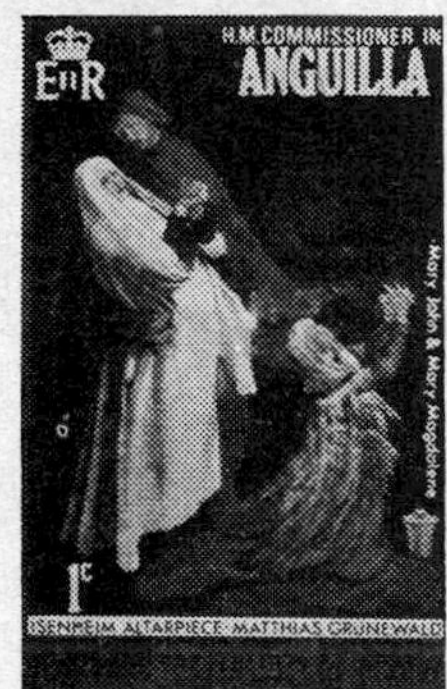

53. "Mary, John and Mary Magdalene" (Matthias Grünewald).

(Litho. Questa.)

1975 (25 Mar.). *Easter. T* **53** *and similar multicoloured designs showing details of the Isenheim altarpiece. P* 14.

No.	Description	Unused	Used
202	1 c. Type **53**	5	5
203	10 c. "The Crucifixion"	5	5
204	15 c. "St. John the Baptist"	8	10
205	20 c. "St. Sebastian and Angels"	10	12
206	$1 "The Entombment"	40	45
207	$1·50, "St. Anthony the Hermit"	60	70
202/7	*Set of* 6	1·10	1·25
MS208	134×127 mm. Nos. 202/7	1·25	

Nos. 203/7 were printed horizontally *se-tenant* within the sheet.

54. Statue of Liberty.

(Des. J. Lister Ltd. Litho. Questa.)

1975 (10 Nov.). *Bicentenary of American Revolution. T* **54** *and similar horiz. designs. Multicoloured. P* 13½.

No.	Description	Unused	Used
209	1 c. Type **54**	5	5
210	10 c. The Capitol	5	8
211	15 c. Congress voting for independence	5	8
212	20 c. Washington and map	8	10
213	$1 Boston Tea Party	40	45
214	$1.50, Bicentenary logo	60	70
209/14	*Set of* 6	1·10	1·25
MS215	198×97 mm. Nos. 209/14	1·25	

Nos. 210/14 are *se-tenant* within one sheet.

55. " Madonna, Child and St. John " (Raphael).

(Des. J. Lister Ltd. Litho. Questa.)

1975 (8 Dec.). *Christmas. T* **55** *and similar vert. designs showing the " Madonna and Child". Multicoloured. P* 13½.

No.	Description	Unused	Used
216	1 c. Type **55**	5	5
217	10 c. Cima	5	8
218	15 c. Dolci	5	8
219	20 c. Dürer	8	10
220	$1 Bellini	40	45
221	$1.50, Botticelli	60	70
216/21	*Set of* 6	1·10	1·25
MS222	130×145 mm. Nos. 216/21	1·25	

Nos. 217/21 are *se-tenant* within one sheet.

EXECUTIVE COUNCIL.

NEW CONSTITUTION 1976

(**56**)

1976 (10 Feb.–1 July). *New Constitution. Nos.* 130, *etc. optd. with T* **56** *or surch. also.*

No.	Description	Unused	Used
223	1 c. Spear fishing	5	5
224	2 c. on 1 c. Spear fishing	5	5
225	2 c. Type **42** (1.7.76)	5	5
226	3 c. on 40 c. Boat building	5	5
	a. Typo. "3 c"*		
227	4 c. Ferry at Blowing Point	5	5
228	5 c. on 40 c. Boat building	5	5
229	6 c. St. Mary's Church	5	5
230	10 c. on 20 c. Public Library	5	5
231	10 c. Gerard's Church (1.7.76)	5	5
232	15 c. Cottage Hospital extension	5	5
233	20 c. Public Library	8	8
234	25 c. Sunset at Blowing Point	10	10
235	40 c. Boat building	15	15
236	60 c. Hibiscus	20	25
237	$1 Man-'O-War (bird)	35	40
238	$2.50, Frangipani	90	1·00
239	$5 Brown Pelican	1·75	2·00
240	$10 Green-back turtle	3·50	4·00
223/40	*Set of* 18	6·50	7·50

*No. 226a occurs on R. 5/2, the " 3c " having been omitted during the normal litho. surcharging.

57. Almond.

(Des. J. Lister Ltd. Litho. Questa.)

1976 (16 Feb.). *Flowering Trees. T* **57** *and similar horiz. designs. Multicoloured. P* 13½.

No.	Description	Unused	Used
241	1 c. Type **57**	5	5
242	10 c. Autograph	5	5
243	15 c. Calabash	5	8
244	20 c. Cordia	8	10
245	$1 Papaya	40	45
246	$1.50, Flamboyant	60	70
241/6	*Set of* 6	1·10	1·25
MS247	194×99 mm. Nos. 241/6	1·25	

Nos. 242/6 are *se-tenant* within one sheet.

58. The Three Marys.

(Litho. Questa.)

1976 (5 Apr.). *Easter. T* **58** *and similar multicoloured designs showing portions of the Altar Frontal Tapestry, Rheinau. P* 13½.

No.	Description	Unused	Used
248	1 c. Type **58**	5	5
249	10 c. The Crucifixion	5	5
250	15 c. Two Soldiers	5	8
251	20 c. The Annunciation	8	10
252	$1 The complete tapestry (*horiz.*)	40	45
253	$1.50, The Risen Christ	60	70
248/53	*Set of* 6	1·10	1·25
MS254	138 × 130 mm. Nos. 248/53. Imperf.	1·25	

Nos. 249/53 are *se-tenant* within one sheet.

ANTIGUA.

For GREAT BRITAIN stamps used in Antigua with "A 02" and "A 18" obliterations, see index to Great Britain Used Abroad list.

I. CROWN COLONY.

1

3 (Die I)

(Des. E. H. Corbould, probably eng. C. H. Jeens. Recess. Perkins, Bacon & Co.)

1862 (Aug.). *No wmk.* (*a*) *Rough perf.* 14 *to* 16.
1 **1** 6d. blue-green £350 £200

(*b*) *P* 11 *to* 12½.
2 **1** 6d. blue-green £1300

(*c*) *P* 14 *to* 16×11 *to* 12½.
3 **1** 6d. blue-green £700

(*d*) *P* 14 *to* 16 *compound with* 11 *to* 12½.
4 **1** 6d. blue-green £1000
(Nos. 2 to 4 have not been found *used.*)

1863 (Jan.)–**1867**. *Wmk. Small Star. T* w.**2**. *Rough perf.* 14 *to* 16.
5 **1** 1d. rosy mauve .. .. 35·00 16·00
6 ,, 1d. dull rose (1864) .. .. 28·00 18·00
a. Imperf. between (vert. pair) £3000
7 ,, 1d. vermilion (1867) .. .. 24·00 14·00
a. Imperf. between (pair) .. £3000
8 ,, 6d. green (*shades*) .. .. 70·00 16·00
9 ,, 6d. dark green .. .. 50·00 15·00
10 ,, 6d. yellow-green .. .. £800 25·00

Caution is needed in buying No. 10 as some of the shades of No. 8 verge on yellow-green.

The 1d. rosy mauve exists perf. compound of 11, 12 and 14 to 16. This is believed to be a trial perforation and it is not known used.

(Recess. De La Rue & Co. from Perkins, Bacon plates.)

1872. *Wmk. Crown CC. P* 12½.
13 **1** 1d. lake .. .. .. 25·00 15·00
14 ,, 1d. scarlet .. .. .. 32·00 15·00
15 ,, 6d. blue-green .. .. .. £150 7·00

1876. *Wmk. Crown CC. P* 14.
16 **1** 1d. lake .. .. .. 20·00 9·00
a. Bisected (½d.) (on cover) .. — £400
17 ,, 1d. lake-rose .. .. .. 20·00 8·50
18 ,, 6d. blue-green .. .. .. 90·00 9·50

(Recess (T **1**); typo. (T **3**) De La Rue & Co.)

1879. *Wmk. Crown CC. P* 14.
19 **3** 2½d. red-brown .. .. £160 48·00
a. Large "2" in "2½" with slanting foot £1500 £600
20 ,, 4d. blue .. .. £100 15·00

1882. *Wmk. Crown CA. P* 14.
21 **3** ½d. dull green .. .. 3·00 7·00
22 ,, 2½d. red-brown .. .. 30·00 18·00
a. Large "2" in "2½" with slanting foot £350 £275
23 ,, 4d. blue .. .. 80·00 17·00

1884. *Wmk. Crown CA. P* 12.
24 **1** 1d. carmine-red .. .. 12·00 10·00

The 1d. scarlet is a colour changeling.

1884–86. *Wmk. Crown CA. P* 14.
25 **1** 1d. carmine-red .. .. 1·25 5·00
26 ,, 1d. rose .. .. .. 13·00 13·00
27 **3** 2½d. ultramarine .. .. 7·00 8·00
a. Large "2" in "2½" with slanting foot .. .. 60·00 £120
28 ,, 4d. chestnut .. .. 3·25 5·00
29 **1** 6d. deep green .. .. 20·00 27·00
30 **3** 1s. mauve .. .. £100 70·00
27/28, 30 Optd. "Specimen" *Set of* 3 40·00

Nos. 25 and 26 postmarked "A 12" in place of "A 02" were used in St. Christopher *q.v.*

2½ 2½ 2½
A B C

The variety "Large '2' in '2½' with slanting foot" occurs on the first stamp of the seventh row in both left (A) and right (B) panes (in which positions the "NN" of "PENNY" have three vertical strokes shortened) and on the first stamp of the third row of the right-hand pane (C). The "2" varies slightly in each position.

From 31 Oct. 1890 until 1903 Leeward Islands general issues were used. Subsequently both general issues and the following separate issues were in concurrent use, until 1 July, 1956, when the general L.I. stamps were withdrawn.

4

5

(Typo. De La Rue & Co.)

1903–9. *T* **4** *and* **5** (5s.). *Wmk. Crown CC. P* 14.
31 ½d. grey-black & grey-grn., O 1·10 2·25
32 1d. grey-black & rose-red, O 2·50 60
a. Blue paper (1903) .. .. 20·00 20·00
33 2d. dull purple & brown, O .. 5·50 8·00
34 2½d. grey black & blue, OC .. 5·00 7·50
35 3d. grey-grn. & orange-brn., O 7·50 9·00
36 6d. purple and black, O .. 14·00 15·00
37 1s. blue and dull purple, OC 14·00 15·00
38 2s. grey-grn. & pale violet, O 21·00 26·00
39 2s. 6d. grey-black & pur., O 17·00 20·00
40 5s. grey-green & violet, OC.. 30·00 35·00
31/40 .. .. *Set of* 10 £110 £120
31/40 Optd. "Specimen" *Set of* 10 55·00

1908–17. *T* **4**. *Wmk. Mult. Crown CA. P* 14.
41 ½d. green, O .. .. .. 65 1·00
42 ½d. blue-green, O (1917) .. 80 1·00
43 1d. red, O .. .. .. 1·60 85
44 1d. scarlet, O (5.8.15) .. 1·25 1·25
45 2d. dull pur. & brn., C (1912) 3·00 3·50
46 2½d. ultramarine, O .. .. 3·00 3·75
a. Blue, O .. .. .. 6·00 7·00
47 3d. grey-green and orange-brown, C (1912) .. 5·00 7·00
48 6d. purple & black, C (1911) 7·50 9·50
49 1s. blue and dull purple, C.. 9·00 11·00
50 2s. grey-grn. & vio., C (1912) 25·00 27·00
41/50 .. .. *Set of* 8 50·00 60·00
41,43,46 Optd. "Specimen" *Set of* 3 18·00

1913. *As T* **5**, *but portrait of King George V. Wmk. Mult. Crown CA. P* 14.
51 5s. grey-green and violet, C (Optd. S. £25) .. .. 25·00 28·00

8

WAR STAMP
(7)

1916 (Sept.)–**17**. *No.* 41 *optd. in London with T* **7**.
52 **4** ½d. deep green (Bk.) .. 25 55
53 ,, ½d. green (R.) (1.10.17) .. 20 55

1918. *Optd. with T* **7**. *Wmk. Mult. Crown CA. P* 14.
54 **4** 1½d. orange 15 35
52/4 Optd. "Specimen" *Set of* 3 22·00

(Typo. De La Rue & Co.).

1921–29. *T* **8**. *P* 14.

(*a*) *Wmk. Mult. Crown CA.*
55 3d. purple/*pale yellow,* C .. 2·00 4·50
56 4d. grey-black and red/*pale yellow,* C (Jan., '22) .. 2·50 4·00
57 1s. black/*emerald,* C .. .. 3·25 5·50
58 2s. purple and blue/*blue,* C .. 5·50 8·50
59 2s. 6d. black and red/*blue,* C.. 6·50 9·00
60 5s. green and red/*pale yellow,* C (Jan., '22) .. .. 11·00 15·00
61 £1 purple & black/*red,* C ('22) 80·00 95·00
55/61 .. .. *Set of* 7 £100 £130
55/61 Optd. "Specimen" *Set of* 7 70·00

(*b*) *Wmk. Mult. Script CA.*
62 ½d. dull green, O 25 35
63 1d. carmine-red, O 50 15
64 1d. bright scarlet, O ('29) .. 35 30
65 1d. bright violet, O .. .. 1·40 1·40
66 1d. mauve, O 80 80
67 1½d. dull orange, O ('22) .. 2·75 4·50
68 1½d. carmine-red, O ('26) .. 50 85
69 1½d. pale red-brown, O ('29) .. 1·00 1·25
70 2d. grey, O .. .. .. 80 1·00
a. Wmk. sideways .. ..
71 2½d. bright blue, O .. .. 3·50 5·00
72 2½d. ultramarine, O ('27) .. 2·75 2·75
73 2½d. orange-yellow, O .. 1·00 3·75
74 3d. purple/*pale yellow,* C ('25) 2·00 3·50
75 6d. dull and bright purple, C 1·40 2·50
76 1s. black/*emerald,* C ('29) 3·50 6·50
77 2s. pur. & blue/*blue,* C ('27).. 7·00 11·00
78 2s. 6d. blk. & red/*blue,* C ('27) 7·00 11·00
79 3s. green and violet, C ('22).. 10·00 13·00
80 4s. grey-black & red, C ('22).. 12·00 15·00
62/80 .. .. *Set of* 16 50·00 75·00
62/80 Optd./Perf. "Specimen" *Set of* 18 65·00

9. Old Dockyard, English Harbour.

12. Sir Thomas Warner's Vessel.

10. Government House, St. John's.

11. Nelson's *Victory.*

(Des. and recess Waterlow & Sons, except 5s. des. by Mrs. J. Goodwin.)

1932 (27 Jan.). *Tercentenary. Wmk. Mult. Script CA. P* 12½.
81 **9** ½d. green 55 70
82 ,, 1d. scarlet 70 85
83 ,, 1½d. brown .. .. .. 1·40 1·50

84	10	2d. grey	3·00	5·00
85	,,	2½d. deep blue	3·25	5·00
86	,,	3d. orange	5·50	8·00
87	11	6d. violet	11·00	12·00
88	,,	1s. olive-green	12·00	14·00
89	,,	2s. 6d. claret	23·00	25·00
90	12	5s. black and chocolate ..	48·00	60·00
81/90		.. .. *Set of* 10	£100	£120
81/90 Perf. " Specimen "		*Set of* 10	90·00	

13. Windsor Castle.

(Des. H. Fleury. Recess. D.L.R.)

1935 (6 May). *Silver Jubilee. Wmk. Mult. Script CA. P* 13½ × 14.

91	13	1d. deep blue and carmine	90	90
92	,,	1½d. ultramarine and grey	1·10	1·10
93	,,	2½d. brown and deep blue ..	2·75	4·00
94	,,	1s. slate and purple ..	7·50	9·00
91/4 Perf. "Specimen"		*Set of* 4	14·00	

1937 (12 May). *Coronation. As Nos.* 13/15 *of Aden, but ptd. by B.W. P* 11 × 11½.

95	1d. carmine	20	20
96	1½d. yellow-brown	25	25
97	2½d. blue	75	75
95/7 Perf. "Specimen"	*Set of* 3	10·00	

14. English Harbour.

15. St. John's Harbour.

16. Nelson's Dockyard.

17. Fort James.

(Recess. Waterlow.)

1938 (15 Nov.)–**51.** *Wmk. Mult. Script CA. P* 12½.

98	14	½d. green	12	12
99	16	1d. scarlet	35	35
		a. Red (8.42 and 11.47) ..	15	15
100	,,	1½d. chocolate-brown ..	50	55
		a. Dull reddish brown (12.43)	35	40
		b. Lake-brown (7.49) ..	5·00	5·50
101	14	2d. grey	12	12
		a. Slate-grey (6.51)	65	65
102	16	2½d. deep ultramarine ..	20	20
103	17	3d. orange	20	20
104	15	6d. violet	30	30
105	,,	1s. black and brown ..	60	50
		a. Black and red-brown (7.49)	5·00	4·50
106	17	2s. 6d. brown-purple ..	1·10	1·25
		a. Maroon (8.42)	90	1·00
107	15	5s. olive-green	2·25	3·25
108	16	10s. magenta (Apr. '48) ..	7·00	8·00
109	17	£1 slate-green (Apr. '48)	12·00	13·00
98/109		.. .. *Set of* 12	21·00	24·00
98/109 Perf. " Specimen "		*Set of* 12	45·00	

1946 (1 Nov.). *Victory. As Nos.* 28/9 *of Aden.*

110	1½d. brown	12	15
111	3d. red-orange	12	15
110/11 Perf. "Specimen"	*Set of* 2	12·00	

1949 (3 Jan.). *Royal Silver Wedding. As Nos.* 30/1 *of Aden.*

112	2½d. ultramarine	10	12
113	5s. grey-olive	3·00	5·00

18. Hermes, Globe and Forms of Transport.

19. Hemispheres, Aeroplane and Steamer.

20. Hermes and Globe.

21. U.P.U. Monument.

(Recess, Waterlow (T **18**, **21**). Design recess, name typo., B.W. (T **19**, **20**).)

1949 (10 Oct.). *75th Anniv. of Universal Postal Union. Wmk. Mult. Script. CA.*

114	18	2½d. ultram. (*p.* 13½–14) ..	20	30
115	19	3d. orange (*p.* 11 × 11½) ..	80	60
116	20	6d. purple (*p.* 11 × 11½) ..	1·40	1·40
117	21	1s. red-brown (*p.* 13½–14)	1·40	1·75

(New Currency. 100 cents = 1 dollar.)

22. Arms of University.

23. Princess Alice.

(Recess. Waterlow.)

1951 (16 Feb.). *Inauguration of B.W.I. University College. Wmk. Mult. Script CA. P* 14 × 14½

118	22	3 c. black and brown ..	15	35
119	23	12 c. black and violet ..	35	45

1953 (2 June). *Coronation. As No.* 47 *of Aden*

120	2 c. black & dp. yellow-green	25	35

24. Martello Tower.

(Recess. Waterlow until 1961, then De La Rue.)

1953 (2 Nov.)–**61.** *As T* **14/17**, *but with portrait of Queen Elizabeth II in place of King George VI, as in T* **24**. *Wmk. Mult. Script CA P* 13 × 13½ (*horiz.*) *or* 13½ × 13 (*vert.*).

120*a*	17	½ c. brown (3.7.56) ..	5	5
121	14	1 c. slate-grey	5	5
		a. Slate (7.11.61) ..	5	5
122	16	2 c. green	5	5
123	,,	3 c. black & orge.-yellow	8	8
		a. Blk. & yell.-orge. (5.12.61)	8	8
124	14	4 c. scarlet (*shades*) ..	10	10
125	16	5 c. black and slate-lilac	12	12
126	17	6 c. yellow-ochre (*shades*)	12	12
127	24	8 c. deep blue	12	15
128	15	12 c. violet	25	15
129	,,	24 c. black and chocolate	30	25
130	24	48 c. purple & deep blue	80	60
131	17	60 c. maroon	1·75	90
132	15	$1.20 olive-green (*shades*)	2·75	3·25
133	16	$2.40 brt. reddish purple	4·50	5·50
134	17	$4.80 slate-blue ..	8·00	9·50
120*a*/134		.. .. *Set of* 15	17·00	18·00

See also Nos. 149/58.

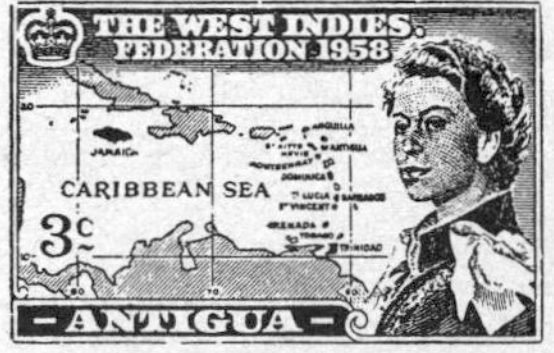

25. Federation Map.

(Recess. B.W.)

1958 (22 Apr.). *Inauguration of British Caribbean Federation. W* w.**12**. *P* 11½ × 11.

135	25	3 c. deep green	10	10
136	,,	6 c. blue	30	30
137	,,	12 c. scarlet	45	45

II. MINISTERIAL GOVERNMENT.

COMMEMORATION
ANTIGUA
CONSTITUTION
1960

(**26**) **27.** Nelson's Dockyard and Admiral Nelson.

1960 (1 Jan.). *New Constitution. Nos.* 123 *and* 128 *optd. with T* **26.**

138	**16**	3 c. black & orge.-yell. (R.)	15	20
139	**15**	12 c. violet	30	25

(Recess. Bradbury, Wilkinson & Co.)

1961 (14 Nov.). *Restoration of Nelson's Dockyard. W* w.**12.** *P* 11½ × 11.

140	**27**	20 c. purple and brown ..	30	35
141	,,	30 c. green and blue ..	45	50

28. Stamp of 1862 and R.M.S.P. *Solent* at English Harbour.

(Des. A. W. Morley. Recess. B.W.)

1962 (1 Aug.). *Stamp Centenary. W* w.**12.** *P* 13½.

142	**28**	3 c. purple and deep green	12	12
143	,,	10 c. blue and deep green ..	20	20
144	,,	12 c. dp. sepia & dp. green	25	25
145	,,	50 c. orge.-brn. & dp. green	65	70

1963 (4 June). *Freedom from Hunger. As No.* 76 *of Aden.*

146	12 c. bluish green	55	55

29. Red Cross Emblem.

(Des. V. Whiteley. Litho. B.W.)

1963 (2 Sept.). *Red Cross Centenary. W* w.**12.** *P* 13½.

147	3 c. red and black	45	45
148	12 c. red and blue	1·75	1·75

(Recess. D.L.R.)

1963 (16 Sept.)–**65.** *As* 1953–61 *but wmk.* w.**12.**

149	**17**	½ c. brown (13.4.65) ..	5	5
150	**14**	1 c. slate (13.4.65) ..	5	5
151	**16**	2 c. green	8	8
152	,,	3 c. black & yell.-orange	10	10
153	**14**	4 c. brown-red	15	15
154	**16**	5 c. black and slate-lilac (*shades*)	15	15
155	**17**	6 c. yellow-ochre	15	15
156	**24**	8 c. deep blue	20	20
157	**15**	12 c. violet	30	30
158	,,	24 c. black and deep chocolate (*shades*)	40	40
149/158		.. .. *Set of* 10	1·40	1·40

30. Shakespeare and Memorial Theatre, Stratford-upon-Avon.

(Des. R. Granger-Barrett. Photo. Harrison.)

1964 (23 April). *400th Anniv. of Birth of William Shakespeare. W* w.**12.** *P* 14×14½.

164	**30**	12 c. orange-brown ..	40	40

(**31**)

1965 (1 April). *No.* 157 *surch. with T* **31.**

165	**15**	15 c. on 12 c. violet ..	30	30

32. I.T.U. Emblem.

(Des. M. Goaman. Litho. Enschedé.)

1965 (17 May). *I.T.U. Centenary. W* w.**12.** *P* 11×11½.

166	**32**	2 c. light blue & light red	12	12
167	,,	50 c. orange-yell. & ultram.	85	90

33. I.C.Y. Emblem.

(Des. V. Whiteley. Litho. Harrison.)

1965 (25 Oct.). *International Co-operation Year. W* w.**12.** *P* 14½.

168	**33**	4 c. reddish purple and turquoise-green ..	12	12
169	,,	15 c. deep bluish green and lavender	40	35

34. Sir Winston Churchill, and St. Paul's Cathedral in Wartime.

(Des. Jennifer Toombs. Photo. Harrison.)

1966 (24 Jan.). *Churchill Commemoration. Printed in black, cerise and gold and with background in colours stated. W* w.**12.** *P* 14.

170	**34**	½ c. new blue	5	5
171	,,	4 c. deep green	20	20
172	,,	25 c. brown	45	50
173	,,	35 c. bluish violet ..	65	70

35. Queen Elizabeth II and Duke of Edinburgh.

(Des. H. Baxter. Litho. Bradbury, Wilkinson).

1966 (4 Feb.). *Royal Visit. W* w.**12.** *P* 11×12.

174	**35**	6 c. black & ultramarine	30	30
175	,,	15 c. black and magenta ..	55	55

36. Footballer's Legs, Ball and Jules Rimet Cup.

(Des. V. Whiteley. Litho. Harrison.)

1966 (1 July). *World Football Cup Championships. W* w.**12** *(sideways). P* 14.

176	**36**	6 c. violet, yellow-green, lake & yellow-brown	15	15
177	,,	35 c. chocolate, blue-green, lake & yellow-brown	50	50

37. W.H.O. Building.

(Des. M. Goaman. Litho. Harrison.)

1966 (20 Sept.). *Inauguration of W.H.O. Headquarters, Geneva. W* w.**12** *(sideways). P* 14.

178	**37**	2 c. black, yellow-green and light blue ..	5	5
179	,,	15 c. black, light purple and yellow-brown ..	35	40

38. Nelson's Dockyard.

39. Old Post Office, St. John's.
40. Health Centre.
41. Teachers' Training College.
42. Martello Tower, Barbuda.
43. Ruins of Officers' Quarters, Shirley Heights.
44. Government House, Barbuda.
45. Princess Margaret School.
46. Air Terminal Building.
47. General Post Office.
48. Clarence House.
49. Government House, St. John's.
50. Administration Building.
51. Courthouse, St. John's.
52. Magistrates' Court.
53. St. John's Cathedral.

(Des. and eng. Bradbury, Wilkinson. Recess.)

1966 (1 Nov.). *W* w.**12**. *P* 11½×11.

180	**38**	½ c. green & turq.-blue	5	5
181	**39**	1 c. purple and cerise ..	5	5
182	**40**	2 c. slate-blue and yellow-orange	5	5
183	**41**	3 c. rose-red and black ..	5	5
184	**42**	4 c. slate-violet & brown	5	5
185	**43**	5 c. ultram. & yellow-olive	8	8
186	**44**	6 c. salmon and purple ..	10	12
187	**45**	10 c. emerald & rose-red ..	12	15
188	**46**	15 c. brown and new blue	15	20
189	**47**	25 c. slate-blue and sepia	30	35
190	**48**	35 c. cerise & blkish. brown	45	50
191	**49**	50 c. dull green and black	70	85
192	**50**	75 c. greenish blue and ultramarine	90	90
193	**51**	$1 cerise and yellow-olive (*shades*) ..	1·40	1·60
194	**52**	$2.50, black and cerise ..	2·50	3·00
195	**53**	$5 olive-green and slate-violet	5·00	5·50
180/195		.. .. *Set of* 16	10·00	12·00

See also Nos. 234/48.

54. " Education ".

55. " Science ".

56. " Culture ".

(Des. Jennifer Toombs. Litho. Harrison.)

1966 (1 Dec.). *20th Anniv. of U.N.E.S.C.O.* *W* w.**12** (*sideways*). *P* 14.

196	**54**	4 c. slate-violet, red, yellow and orange ..	5	5
197	**55**	25 c. orange-yellow, violet and deep olive ..	30	35
198	**56**	$1 black, bright purple and orange	1·10	1·25

III. ASSOCIATED STATEHOOD.

57. State Flag and Maps.

58. State Flag.

59. Premier's Office and State Flag.

(Des. W. D. Cribbs. Photo. Harrison.)

1967 (27 Feb.). *Statehood.* *W* w.**12** (*sideways*). *P* 14.

199	**57**	4 c. multicoloured ..	5	5
200	**58**	15 c. multicoloured ..	20	25
201	**59**	25 c. multicoloured ..	30	35
202	**58**	35 c. multicoloured ..	35	40

60. Gilbert Memorial Church.

61. Nathaniel Gilbert's House.

62. Caribbean and Central American Map.

(Des. G. Drummond (from sketches by W. D. Cribbs). Photo. Harrison.)

1967 (18 May). *Attainment of Autonomy by the Methodist Church.* *W* w.**12**. *P* 14½×13½.

203	**60**	4 c. black and orange-red	5	5
204	**61**	25 c. black & bright green	30	30
205	**62**	35 c. black and bright blue	40	45

63. Coat-of-Arms.

(Des. V. Whiteley (from sketches by W. D. Cribbs). Photo. Harrison.)

1967 (21 July). *300th Anniv. of Treaty of Breda and Grant of New Arms.* *W* w.**12** (*sideways*). *P* 14½×14.

206	**63**	15 c. multicoloured ..	15	15
207	,,	35 c. multicoloured ..	30	35

64. Settlers' Ship.

65. Blaeu's Map of 1665.

(Des. and eng. Bradbury, Wilkinson. Recess.)

1967 (14 Dec.). *300th Anniv. of Barbuda Settlement.* *W* w.**12**. *P* 11½×11.

208	**64**	4 c. deep ultramarine ..	5	5
209	**65**	6 c. purple	12	12
210	**64**	25 c. emerald	30	30
211	**65**	35 c. black	35	40

66. Tracking Station.

67. Antenna and Spacecraft taking off.
68. Spacecraft approaching Moon.
69. Re-entry of Space Capsule.

(Des. G. L. Vasarhelyi. Photo. Harrison.)

1968 (29 Mar.). *N.A.S.A. Apollo Project Inauguration of Dow Hill Tracking Station* *W* w.**12** (*sideways*). *P* 14½×14.

212	**66**	4 c. deep blue, orange-yellow and black ..	5	5
213	**67**	15 c. deep blue, orange-yellow and black ..	20	25
214	**68**	25 c. deep blue, orange-yellow and black ..	30	3[illegible]
215	**69**	50 c. deep blue, orange-yellow and black ..	35	55

70. Limbo-dancing.

71. Water-skiing and Bathers.
72. Yachts and beach.
73. Underwater Swimming.

(Des. and photo. Harrison.)

1968 (1 July). *Tourism.* *W* w.**12**. *P* 14½×14.

216	**70**	½ c. multicoloured ..	5	5
217	**71**	15 c. multicoloured ..	20	20
218	**72**	25 c. multicoloured ..	30	35
219	**73**	35 c. multicoloured ..	35	35
220	**70**	50 c. multicoloured ..	45	45
216/20		.. .. *Set of* 5	1·25	1·25

74. Old Harbour in 1768.

75. Old Harbour in 1829.
76. Freighter and Chart of New Harbour.
77. New Harbour, 1968.

(Des. R. Granger Barrett. Recess. Bradbury, Wilkinson.)

1968 (31 Oct.). *Opening of St. John's Deep Water Harbour. W* **w.12**. *P* 13.

221	**74**	2 c. light blue & carmine	5	5
222	**75**	15 c. lt. yell.-grn. & sepia	20	20
223	**76**	25 c. olive-yellow and blue	25	25
224	**77**	35 c. salmon and emerald	30	35
225	**74**	$1 black	65	70
221/5		.. .. *Set of* 5	1·25	1·40

78. Parliament Buildings.

79. Antigua Mace and Bearer.
80. House of Representatives' Room.
81. Arms and Seal of Antigua.

(Des. R. Granger Barrett. Photo. Harrison.)

1969 (3 Feb.). *Tercentenary of Parliament. W* **w.12** *(sideways). P* 12½.

226	**78**	4 c. multicoloured ..	12	12
227	**79**	15 c. multicoloured ..	20	20
228	**80**	25 c. multicoloured ..	30	30
229	**81**	50 c. multicoloured ..	50	50

82. Freight Transport.

83. Crate of Cargo. (*Vert.*)

(Des. Jennifer Toombs. Litho. De La Rue.)

1969 (14 Apr.). *1st Anniv. of CARIFTA (Caribbean Free Trade Area). W* **w.12** *(sideways on 4 c., 15 c.). P* 13.

230	**82**	4 c. blk. & reddish pur.	5	5
231	,,	15 c. black & turquoise-bl.	20	20
232	**83**	25 c. chocolate, black and yellow-ochre	25	25
233	,,	35 c. chocolate, black and yellow-brown ..	35	35

1969–70. *As Nos.* 180/91 *and* 193/5 *but perf.* 13½.
A. *Ordinary paper* (24.6.69).
B. *Glazed paper* (30.9.69 *or* 6.4.70 (4 c.)).

			A.		B.	
234	**38**	½ c.	5	5	†	
235	**39**	1 c.	5	5	12	12
236	**40**	2 c.	5	5	12	12
237	**41**	3 c.	5	5	†	
238	**42**	4 c.	10	10	70	80
239	**43**	5 c.	12	12	12	15
240	**44**	6 c.	15	15	†	
241	**45**	10 c.	25	25	20	25
242	**46**	15 c.	†		25	30
243	**47**	25 c.	†		30	35
244	**48**	35 c.	†		45	45
245	**49**	50 c.	†		55	60
246	**51**	$1	†		1·75	2·25
247	**52**	$2.50 ..	†		4·00	4·50
248	**53**	$5	†		12·00	14·00
234/41A		.. *Set of* 8	70	70	†	
235/48B		.. *Set of* 12	†		18·00	21·00

84. Island of Redonda (Chart).

85. Redonda from the Sea.

(Des. R. Granger Barrett. Photo. Enschedé).

1969 (1 Aug.). *Centenary of Redonda Phosphate Industry. W* **w.12** *(sideways). P* 13×13½.

249	**84**	15 c. multicoloured ..	25	25
250	**85**	25 c. multicoloured ..	35	40
251	**84**	50 c. multicoloured ..	55	60

86. "The Adoration of the Magi" (Marcillat).

87. "The Nativity" (Unknown German, 15th-cent.).

(Des. adapted by V. Whiteley. Litho. Enschedé.)

1969 (15 Oct.). *Christmas. W* **w.12** *(sideways). P* 13×14.

252	**86**	6 c. multicoloured ..	12	12
253	**87**	10 c. multicoloured ..	20	20
254	**86**	35 c. multicoloured ..	35	35
255	**87**	50 c. multicoloured ..	45	50

20¢

(88)

89. Coat-of-Arms.

1970 (2 Jan.). *No.* 189 *surch. with T* **88**.

256	**47**	20 c. on 25 c. slate-blue and sepia	30	30

(Des. and photo. Harrison.)

1970–73. *Coil Stamps. W* **w.12**. *P* 14½×14.
A. *Chalk-surfaced paper. Wmk. upright* (30.1.70).
B. *Glazed paper. Wmk. sideways* (8.3.73).

			A.		B.	
257	**89**	5 c. blue ..	5	5	5	5
258	,,	10 c. emerald	10	10	5	5
259	,,	25 c. crimson	20	20	10	12

90. Sikorsky "S-38".

(Des. R. Granger Barrett. Litho. J. W.)

1970 (16 Feb.). *40th Anniv. of Antiguan Air Services. T* **90** *and similar horiz. designs. Multicoloured. W* **w.12** *(sideways). P* 14½.

260	5 c. Type **90**	15	15
261	20 c. Dornier "DO-X" ..	35	35
262	35 c. Hawker Siddeley "HS-748"	45	45
263	50 c. Douglas "C-124C" (Globemaster II) ..	55	55
264	75 c. Vickers "VC-10" ..	60	65
260/264	.. .. *Set of* 5	1·90	1·90

91. Dickens and Scene from *Nicholas Nickleby*.

(Des. Jennifer Toombs. Litho. Walsall Security Printers Ltd.)

1970 (19 May). *Death Centenary of Charles Dickens. T* **91** *and similar horiz. designs. W* **w.12** *(sideways). P* 14.

265	5 c. bistre, sepia and black	12	12
266	20 c. light turquoise-blue, sepia and black ..	30	30
267	35 c. violet-blue, sepia & blk.	35	40
268	$1 rosine, sepia and black	75	85

Designs: 20 c. Dickens and Scene from *Pickwick Papers*; 35 c. Dickens and Scene from *Oliver Twist*; $1 Dickens and Scene from *David Copperfield*.

92. Carib Indian and War Canoe.

(Des. J. Waddington Ltd. Litho. Questa.)

1970 (19 Aug.)–**75**. *T* **92** *and similar horiz. designs. Multicoloured. Toned paper. W* **w.12** *(sideways). P* 14.

269	½ c. Type **92**	5	5
270	1 c. Columbus and *Nina* ..	5	5
271	2 c. Sir Thomas Warner's emblem and ship	5	5
	a. Whiter paper (20.10.75) ..	5	5
272	3 c. Viscount Hood and H.M.S. *Barfleur*	5	5
273	4 c. Sir George Rodney and H.M.S. *Formidable* ..	8	8

274 5 c. Nelson and H.M.S. *Boreas* 10 10
275 6 c. William IV and H.M.S. *Pegasus* 10 12
276 10 c. " Blackbeard " and pirate ketch 12 15
277 15 c. Captain Collingwood and H.M.S. *Pelican* .. 15 20
278 20 c. Nelson and H.M.S. *Victory* 20 25
279 25 c. R.M.S.P. *Solent* .. 25 25
280 35 c. George V (when Prince George) and H.M.S *Canada* 35 40
281 50 c. H.M.S. *Renown* .. 40 50
282 75 c. *Federal Maple* 65 75
283 $1 Yacht and Class Emblem 75 90
284 $2.50, H.M.S. *London* .. 2·25 2·50
285 $5 Tug *Pathfinder* .. 4·50 5·00
269/85 .. .. *Set of* 17 9·00 10·00

See also Nos. 323/34 and 426.

93. " The Small Passion " (detail) (Dürer).

(Des. G. Drummond. Recess and litho. D.L.R.)

1970 (28 Oct.). *Christmas. T* **93** *and similar vert. design. W* w.**12**. *P* 13½×14.

286 **93** 3 c. black and turq.-blue 12 12
287 – 10 c. dull purple and pink 15 15
288 **93** 35 c. black and rose-red .. 30 30
289 – 50 c. black and lilac .. 50 55

Design:—10 c., 50 c. " Adoration of the Magi " (detail) (Dürer).

94. 4th King's Own Regt., 1759.

(Des. P. W. Kingsland. Litho. Questa.)

1970 (14 Dec.). *Military Uniforms* (1*st series*). *T* **94** *and similar vert. designs. Multicoloured. W* w.**12**. *P* 14×13½.

290 ½ c. Type **94** 20 20
291 10 c. 4th West India Regt., 1804 .. .. .. 30 30
292 20 c. 60th Regt., The Royal American, 1809 .. 45 45
293 35 c. 93rd Regt., Sutherland Highlanders, 1826–34 .. 75 75
294 75 c. 3rd West India Regt., 1851 .. .. .. 1·40 1·40
MS295 128×146 mm. Nos. 290/4 plus label .. .. 3·00 3·00
290/4 .. .. *Set of* 5 2·75 2·75

See also Nos. 303/8, 313/18, 353/8 and 380/5.

95. Market Woman casting Vote.

(Des. Mrs. S. Goaman. Photo. Harrison.)

1971 (1 Feb.). 20*th Anniv. of Adult Suffrage. T* **95** *and similar vert. designs. W* w.**12** (*sideways*). *P* 14½×14.

296 5 c. brown 5 5
297 20 c. deep olive 20 20
298 35 c. reddish purple .. 25 30
299 50 c. ultramarine 35 40

People voting:—20 c. Executive; 35 c. Housewife; 50 c. Artisan.

96. "The Last Supper".

(Des. Jennifer Toombs from woodcuts by Dürer. Litho. Questa.)

1971 (7 Apr.). *Easter. T* **96** *and similar vert. designs. W* w.**12**. *P* 14×13½.

300 5 c. black, grey and scarlet 10 10
301 35 c. blk., grey & bluish vio. 30 30
302 75 c. black, grey and gold .. 50 50

Designs: 35 c. The Crucifixion; 75 c. The Resurrection.

(Des. J. Waddington Ltd. Litho. Questa.)

1971 (12 July). *Military Uniforms* (2*nd series*). *Multicoloured designs as T* **94**. *W* w.**12**. *P* 13½.

303 ½ c. Private, 12th Regt., The Suffolk (1704) 10 10
304 10 c. Grenadier, 38th Regt., South Staffs (1751) .. 20 20
305 20 c. Light Company, 5th Regt., Royal Northumberland Fusiliers (1778) 35 35
306 35 c. Private, 48th Regt., The Northamptonshire (1793) 65 65
307 75 c. Private, 15th Regt., East Yorks (1805) .. 1·40 1·40
MS308 127×144 mm. Nos. 303/7 plus label .. .. 3·25 3·25
303/7 .. .. *Set of* 5 2·40 2·40

97. " Madonna and Child " (detail, Veronese).

(Des. Jennifer Toombs. Litho. Questa.)

1971 (4 Oct.). *Christmas. T* **97** *and similar vert. design. Multicoloured. W* w.**12**. *P* 13½.

309 3 c. Type **97** 5 5
310 5 c. " Adoration of the Shepherds " (detail, Veronese) 12 12
311 35 c. Type **97** 40 40
312 50 c. As 5 c. 45 45

(Des. J. W. Ltd. Litho. Questa.)

1972 (1 July). *Military Uniforms* (3*rd series*). *Multicoloured designs as T* **94**. *W* w.**12** (*sideways*). *P* 14×13½.

313 ½ c. Battalion Company Officer, 25th Foot, 1815 10 10
314 10 c. Sergeant, 14th Foot, 1837 .. .. .. 15 15
315 20 c. Private, 67th Foot, 1853 .. .. .. 35 35
316 35 c. Officer, Royal Artillery, 1854 .. .. .. 65 65
317 75 c. Private, 29th Foot, 1870 .. .. .. 1·40 1·40
313/17 .. .. *Set of* 5 2·40 2·40
MS318 125×141 mm. Nos. 313/17 plus label .. .. .. 3·25 3·25

98. Cowrie-Helmet.

(Des. J. W. Ltd. Litho. Questa.)

1972 (1 Aug.). *Shells. T* **98** *and similar horiz. designs. Multicoloured. W* w.**12** (*sideways*). *P* 14½.

319 3 c. Type **98** 5 5
320 5 c. Measled Cowrie .. 10 10
321 35 c. West Indian Fighting Conch 30 30
322 50 c. Hawk-wing Conch .. 35 40

1972–74. *As No.* 269 *etc., but W* w.**12** (*upright*) *and whiter paper.*

323 ½ c. Type **92** 5 5
324 1 c. Columbus and *Nina* .. 5 5
325 3 c. Viscount Hood and H.M.S. *Barfleur* 5 5
326 4 c. Sir George Rodney and H.M.S. *Formidable* .. 5 5
327 5 c. Nelson and H.M.S. *Boreas* 5 5
328 6 c. William IV and H.M.S. *Pegasus* 5 5
329 10 c. "Blackbeard" and pirate ketch 8 8
330 15 c. Collingwood and H.M.S. *Pelican* 10 12
331 75 c. *Federal Maple* 40 45
332 $1 Yacht and class emblem 55 60

333 $2.50, H.M.S. *London* .. 1·40 1·75
334 $5 Tug *Pathfinder* .. .. 2·75 3·00
323/34 .. .. *Set of* 12 5·00 5·50

Dates of issue:—2.11.72, ½ c., 15 c., 75 c., $1, $5; 2.1.74, 1 to 10 c.; 25.2.74, $2.50.

See also No. 426.

99. St. John's Cathedral, Side View.

(Des. J.W. Ltd. Litho. Format.)

1972 (6 Nov.). *Christmas and 125th Anniversary of St. John's Cathedral. T* **99** *and similar horiz. designs. Multicoloured. W* w.**12** (*sideways*). *P* 14.

335 35 c. Type **99** 40 40
336 50 c. Cathedral interior .. 55 55
337 75 c. St. John's Cathedral .. 80 80
MS338 165 × 102 mm. Nos. 335/7. *P* 15. .. .. 2·00 2·00

100. Floral Pattern.

(Des. (from photograph by D. Groves) and photo. Harrison.)

1972 (20 Nov.). *Royal Silver Wedding. Multicoloured; background colour given. W* w.**12**. *P* 14 × 14½.

339 **100** 20 c. bright blue .. 20 25
340 ,, 35 c. turquoise-blue .. 30 40

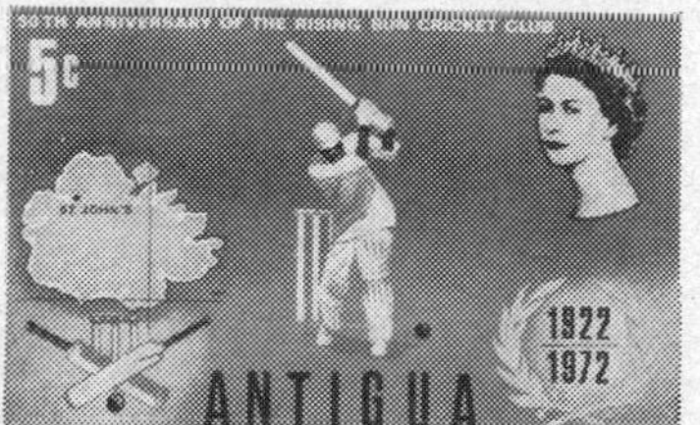

101. Batsman and Map.

(Des. G. L. Vasarhelyi. Litho. Questa.)

1972 (15 Dec.). *50th Anniv. of Rising Sun Cricket Club. T* **101** *and similar horiz. designs. Multicoloured. W* w.**12**. *P* 13½.

341 5 c. Type **101** 5 5
342 35 c. Batsman and wicket-keeper 30 30
343 $1 Club badge 75 75
MS344 88 × 130 mm. Nos. 341/3 .. 1·10 1·10

102. Yacht and Map.

(Des. M. and G. Shamir. Litho. Format.)

1972 (29 Dec.). *Inauguration of Antigua and Barbuda Tourist Office, New York. T.* **102** *and similar square designs. Multicoloured. W* w.**12**. *P* 14½.

345 35 c. Type **102** 35 35
346 50 c. Yachts 40 40
347 75 c. St. John's G.P.O. .. 55 55
348 $1 Statue of Liberty .. 80 80
MS349 100 × 94 mm. Nos. 346, 348 1·40 1·40

103. Stained-glass window.

(Des. PAD Studio. Litho. Format.)

1973 (16 Apr.). *Easter. T* **103** *and similar vert. designs. W* w.**12** (*sideways*). *P* 13½.

350 **103** 5 c. multicoloured .. 5 5
351 – 35 c. multicoloured .. 30 30
352 – 75 c. multicoloured .. 40 45

Nos. 350/2 show different stained-glass windows from St. John's Cathedral.

(Des. J. W. Ltd. Litho. Questa.)

1973 (1 July). *Military Uniforms* (*4th series*). *Multicoloured designs as T* **94.** *W* w.**12** (*sideways*). *P* 13½.

353 ½ c. Private, Zacharia Tiffin's Regt. of Foot, 1701 .. 5 5
354 10 c. Private, 63rd Regt. of Foot, 1759 .. .. 12 12
355 20 c. Light Company Officer, 35th Regt. of Foot, 1828 20 20
356 35 c. Private, 2nd West India Regt., 1853 .. .. 30 30
357 75 c. Sergeant, 49th Regt., 1858 .. .. .. 50 50
353/7 .. .. *Set of* 5 1·00 1·00
MS358 127 × 145 mm. Nos. 353/7 1·40 1·40

104. Butterfly Costumes.

(Des. G. L. Vasarhelyi. Litho. Format.)

1973 (30 July). *Carnival. T* **104** *and similar horiz. designs. Multicoloured. P* 13½.

359 5 c. Type **104** 8 10
360 20 c. Carnival street scene .. 20 20
361 35 c. Carnival troupe .. 30 30
362 75 c. Carnival Queen .. 45 50
MS363 134 × 95 mm. Nos. 359/62 1·00 1·10

105. "Virgin of the Milk Porridge" (Gerard David).

(Des. G. L. Vasarhelyi. Litho. Format.)

1973 (15 Oct.). *Christmas. T* **105** *and similar vert. designs. Multicoloured. P* 14½.

364 3 c. Type **105** 5 5
365 5 c. "Adoration of the Kings" (Stomer) .. 5 5
366 20 c. "The Granduca Madonna" (Raphael) .. 20 20
367 35 c. "Nativity with God the Father and Holy Ghost" (Battista) 30 30
368 $1 "Madonna and Child" (Murillo) 70 70
364/8 .. .. *Set of* 5 1·10 1·10
MS369 130 × 128 mm. Nos. 364/8 1·40 1·40

106. Princess Anne and Captain Mark Phillips.

(Des. G. Drummond. Litho. Format.)

1973 (14 Nov.). *Royal Wedding. T* **106** *and similar horiz. design. P* 13½.

370 **106** 35 c. multicoloured .. 25 25
371 – $2 multicoloured .. 1·10 1·25
MS372 78 × 100 mm. Nos. 370/1 1·40 1·40

The $2 is as T **106** but has a different border.

(107)

1973 (15 Dec.). *Honeymoon Visit of Princess Anne and Captain Phillips. Nos.* 370/**MS**372 *optd. with T* **107** *by lithography.**

373 **106** 35 c. multicoloured .. 25 25
a. Typo opt. 80 80
374 – $2 multicoloured .. 1·10 1·25
a. Typo opt. .. .. 2·50 2·50
MS375 78 × 100 mm. Nos. 373/4 1·60 1·60
a. Typo opt. .. .. 6·50 7·00

*The litho overprints can be distinguished from the typo by the latter being less clear, less intense, and showing through on the reverse.

108. Coats-of-Arms of Antigua and University.

(Des. PAD Studio. Litho. D.L.R.)

1974 (18 Feb.). *25th Anniv. of University of West Indies. T* **108** *and similar horiz. designs. Multicoloured. W* w.**12**. *P* 13.

No.	Value	Description	Unused	Used
376	5 c.	Type **108**	5	5
377	20 c.	Extra-mural art	20	20
378	35 c.	Antigua campus	30	30
379	75 c.	Antigua chancellor	45	50

(Des. J.W. Ltd. Litho. Questa.)

1974 (1 May). *Military Uniforms (5th series). Multicoloured designs as T* **94**. *W* w.**12** *(sideways). P* 13½.

No.	Value	Description	Unused	Used
380	½ c.	Officer, 59th Foot, 1797	5	5
381	10 c.	Gunner, Royal Artillery, 1800	5	5
		a. Error. Wmk. T **55** of Malawi	55·00	
382	20 c.	Private, 1st West India Regt., 1830	20	20
383	35 c.	Officer, 92nd Foot, 1843	30	30
384	75 c.	Private, 23rd Foot, 1846	45	50
380/4		*Set of* 5	80	85
MS385		127×145 mm. Nos. 380/4	1·10	1·25

109. English Postman, Mailcoach and Helicopter.

(Des. G. L. Vasarhelyi. Litho. Format.)

1974 (15 July). *Centenary of Universal Postal Union. T* **109** *and similar horiz. designs. Multicoloured. P* 14½.

No.	Value	Description	Unused	Used
386	½ c.	Type **109**	5	5
387	1 c.	Bellman, mailboat *Orinoco* and satellite	5	5
388	2 c.	Train guard, post-bus and hydrofoil	5	5
389	5 c.	Swiss messenger, Wells Fargo coach and "Concorde"	5	5
390	20 c.	Postillion, Japanese postmen and carrier pigeon	20	20
391	35 c.	Antiguan postman, flying-boat and tracking station	30	30
392	$1	Medieval courier, American express train and Boeing "747"	50	55
386/92		*Set of* 7	1·10	1·10
MS393		141×164 mm. Nos. 386/92 plus label. P 13	1·10	1·10

On the ½ c. "English" is spelt "Enlish", and on the 2 c. "Postal" is spelt "Fostal".

110. Traditional Player.

(Des. C. Abbott. Litho. Questa.)

1974 (1 Aug.). *Antiguan Steel Bands. T* **110** *and similar designs. W* w.**12** *(sideways on 5 c., 75 c. and* **MS**398). *P* 13.

No.	Value	Description	Unused	Used
394	5 c.	rose-red, carm. & blk.	5	5
395	20 c.	brown-ochre, chestnut & black	20	20
396	35 c.	light sage-green, blue-green and black	25	30
397	75 c.	dull blue, dull ultramarine and black	45	45
MS398		115×108 mm. Nos. 394/7	1·00	1·00

Designs: *Horiz.*—20 c. Traditional band; 35 c. Modern band. *Vert.*—75 c. Modern player.

111. Footballers.

(Des. G. L. Vasarhelyi. Litho. Format.)

1974 (23 Sept.). *World Cup Football Championships. T* **111** *and similar vert. designs showing footballers. P* 14½.

No.	Type	Value	Description	Unused	Used
399	**111**	5 c.	multicoloured	5	5
400	–	35 c.	multicoloured	20	25
401	–	75 c.	multicoloured	40	40
402	–	$1	multicoloured	50	50
MS403			135×130 mm. Nos. 399/402 plus two labels. P 13	1·25	1·25

EARTHQUAKE RELIEF

(**112**)

1974 (16 Oct.). *Earthquake Relief Fund. Nos.* 400/2 *and* 397 *optd. with T* **112**, *No.* 397 *surch. also.*

No.	Value	Description	Unused	Used
404	35 c.	multicoloured	25	25
405	75 c.	multicoloured	40	40
406	$1	multicoloured	50	50
407	$5	on 75 c. dull blue, dull ultramarine and black	2·40	2·60

113. Churchill as Schoolboy and School College Building, Harrow.

(Des. V. Whiteley. Litho. Format.)

1974 (20 Oct.). *Birth Centenary of Sir Winston Churchill. T* **113** *and similar horiz. designs. Multicoloured. P* 14½.

No.	Value	Description	Unused	Used
408	5 c.	Type **113**	5	5
409	35 c.	Churchill and St. Paul's Cathedral	25	25
410	75 c.	Coat-of-arms and catafalque	40	40
411	$1	Churchill, "reward" notice and South African escape route	50	50
MS412		107×82 mm. Nos. 408/11. P 13	1·25	1·25

114. "Madonna and Child" (Bellini).

$10

(**115**)

(Des. M. Shamir. Litho. Format.)

1974 (18 Nov.). *Christmas. T* **114** *and similar vert. designs showing "Madonna and Child" by the artists given. Multicoloured. P* 14½.

No.	Value	Description	Unused	Used
413	½ c.	Type **114**	5	5
414	1 c.	Raphael	5	5
415	2 c.	Van der Weyden	5	5
416	3 c.	Giorgione	5	5
417	5 c.	Mantegna	5	5
418	20 c.	Vivarini	15	15
419	35 c.	Montagna	20	20
420	75 c.	Lorenzo Costa	40	40
413/20		*Set of* 8	80	80
MS421		139×126 mm. Nos. 417/20. P 13	80	80

1975 (14 Jan.). *Nos.* 331 *and* 390/2 *surch. as T* **115**.

No.	Value	Description	Unused	Used
422	50 c.	on 20 c. multicoloured	25	30
423	$2.50	on 35 c. multicoloured	1·40	1·60
424	$5	on $1 multicoloured	2·50	2·75
425	$10	on 75 c. multicoloured	4·50	4·75

1975 (21 Jan.). *As No.* 334 *but W* w.**14**.

No.	Value	Description	Unused	Used
426	$5	Tug *Pathfinder*	2·50	2·75

116. Carib War Canoe, English Harbour, 1300.

(Des. G. Drummond. Litho. Format.)

1975 (17 Mar.). *Nelson's Dockyard. T* **116** *and similar horiz. designs. Multicoloured. P* 14½.

No.	Value	Description	Unused	Used
427	5 c.	Type **116**	5	5
428	15 c.	Ship of the line, English Harbour, 1770	8	8
429	35 c.	H.M.S. *Boreas* at anchor, and Lord Nelson, 1787	20	20
430	50 c.	Yachts during "Sailing Week", 1974	25	30
431	$1	Yacht Anchorage, Old Dockyard, 1970	45	50
427/31		*Set of* 5	90	1·00
MS432		130×134 mm. As Nos. 427/31, but in larger format, 43×28 mm., plus *se-tenant* label. P 13½	1·00	

117. Lady of the Valley Church.

(Des. R. Vigus. Litho. Format.)

1975 (19 May). *Antiguan Churches. T* **117** *and similar horiz. designs. Multicoloured. P* 14½.

433	5 c. Type **117**	5	5
434	20 c. Gilbert Memorial	10	10
435	35 c. Grace Hill Moravian	20	20
436	50 c. St. Phillips	25	30
437	$1 Ebenezer Methodist	45	50
433/7	*Set of* 5	90	1·00
MS438	91 × 101 mm. Nos. 435/7. P 13	90	

118. Map of 1721 and Sextant of 1640.

(Des. PAD Studio. Litho. Questa.)

1975 (21 July). *Maps of Antigua. T* **118** *and similar horiz. designs. Multicoloured. W* w. **14** *(sideways). P* 14.

439	5 c. Type **118**	5	5
440	20 c. Map of 1775 and galleon	10	12
441	35 c. Maps of 1775 and 1955	15	15
442	$1 1973 maps of Antigua and English Harbour	45	50
MS443	130 × 89 mm. Nos. 439/42	80	

119. Scout Bugler.

(Des. G. L. Vasarhelyi. Litho. Questa.)

1975 (26 Aug.). *World Scout Jamboree, Norway. T* **119** *and similar horiz. designs. Multicoloured. P* 14.

444	15 c. Type **119**	5	8
445	20 c. Scouts in camp	8	10
446	35 c. Lord Baden-Powell	15	15
447	$2 Scout dancers from Dahomey	85	95
MS448	145 × 107 mm. Nos. 444/7	1·25	

120. *Eurema Elathea.*

(Des. G. L. Vasarhelyi. Litho. Questa.)

1975 (30 Oct.). *Butterflies. T* **120** *and similar horiz. designs. Multicoloured. P* 14.

449	½ c. Type **120**	5	5
450	1 c. *Danaus plexippus*	5	5
451	2 c. *Phoebis philea*	5	5
452	5 c. *Marpesia petreus thetys*	5	5
453	20 c. *Eurema proterpia*	10	12
454	35 c. *Papilio polydamas*	20	20
455	$2 *Vanessa cardui*	90	1·00
449/55	*Set of* 7	1·25	1·25
MS456	147 × 94 mm. Nos. 452/5	1·10	

121. " Virgin and Child " (Correggio).

(Des. G. L. Vasarhelyi. Litho. Questa.)

1975 (17 Nov.). *Christmas. T* **121** *and similar vert. designs showing " Virgin and Child ". Multicoloured. P* 14.

457	½ c. Type **121**	5	5
458	1 c. El Greco	5	5
459	2 c. Dürer	5	5
460	3 c. Antonello	5	5
461	5 c. Bellini	5	5
462	10 c. Dürer	5	5
463	35 c. Bellini	15	15
464	$2 Dürer	90	1·00
457/64	*Set of* 8	1·10	1·25
MS465	138 × 119 mm. Nos. 461/4	1·10	

122. Vivian Richards.

(Des. G. L. Vasarhelyi. Litho. Format.)

1975 (15 Dec.). *World Cup Cricket Winners. T* **122** *and similar multicoloured designs. P* 13½.

466	5 c. Type **122**	5	5
467	35 c. Andy Roberts	15	15
468	$2 West Indies team (*horiz.*)	90	1·00

123. Antillean Crested Hummingbird.

(Des. G. L. Vasarhelyi. Litho. Format.)

1976 (19 Jan.). *Various multicoloured designs as T* **123**.

(*a*) *Size as T* **123**. *P* 14½.

469	½ c. Type **123**	5	5
470	1 c. Imperial Parrot	5	5
471	2 c. Zenaida Dove	5	5
472	3 c. Loggerhead Kingbird	5	5
473	4 c. Red-necked Pigeon	5	5
474	5 c. Rufous-throated Solitaire	5	5
475	6 c. Orchid Tree	5	5
476	10 c. Bougainvillea	5	5
477	15 c. Geiger Tree	5	5
478	20 c. Flamboyant	8	8
479	25 c. Hibiscus	10	10
480	35 c. Flame of the Wood	12	15
481	50 c. Cannon at Fort James	20	20
482	75 c. Premier's Office	25	30
483	$1 Potworks Dam	35	40

(*b*) *Size* 44 × 28 *mm. P* 13½.

484	$2.50, Irrigation Scheme, Diamond Estate	90	1·00
485	$5 Government Estate	1·75	2·00
486	$10 Coolidge Airport	3·50	4·00
469/86	*Set of* 18	6·50	7·50

124. Privates, Clark's Illinois Regt.

(Des. J.W. Ltd. Litho. Format.)

1976 (17 Mar.). *Bicentenary of American Revolution. T* **124** *and similar vert. designs. Multicoloured. P* 14½.

487	½ c. Type **124**	5	5
488	1 c. Riflemen, Pennsylvania Militia	5	5
489	2 c. Powder horn	5	5
490	5 c. Water bottle	5	5
491	35 c. American flags	20	20
492	$1 Privateer *Montgomery*	50	55
493	$5 Sloop *Ranger*	2·50	2·60
487/93	*Set of* 7	3·00	3·25
MS494	71 × 84 mm. $2.50 Congress flag. P 13	1·25	

125. High Jump.

(Des. J.W. Ltd. Litho. Format.)

1976 (17 July). *Olympic Games, Montreal. T* **125** *and similar horiz. designs. P* 14½.

495	½ c. orange-brown, bistre-yellow and black	5	5
496	1 c. lt. reddish vio. & blk.	5	5
497	2 c. light green and black	5	5
498	15 c. bright blue and black	8	10
499	30 c. olive-brown, yellow-ochre and black	15	20
500	$1 red-orange, Venetian red and black	50	55
501	$2 rosine and black	90	1·00
495/501	*Set of* 7	1·60	1·75
MS502	88 × 138 mm. Nos. 498/501. P 13½	1·75	

Designs:—1 c. Boxing; 2 c. Pole vault; 15 c. Swimming; 30 c. Running; $1 Cycling; $2 Shot put.

126. Water Skiing.

(Des. J.W. Ltd. Litho. Questa.)

1976 (26 Aug.). *Water Sports. T* **126** *and similar horiz. designs. Multicoloured. P* 14.

No.	Description	Unused	Used
503	½ c. Type **126** . .	5	5
504	1 c. Sailing . .	5	5
505	2 c. Snorkeling	5	5
506	20 c. Deep sea fishing . .	8	10
507	50 c. Scuba diving	20	25
508	$2 Swimming	80	90
503/8	. . . . *Set of* 6	1·00	1·10
MS509	89 × 114 mm. Nos. 506/8	1·10	

127. French Angelfish.

(Des. G. Drummond. Litho. Questa.)

1976 (4 Oct.). *Fish. T* **127** *and similar horiz. designs. Multicoloured. W* w.**14** *(sideways). P* 13½.

No.	Description	Unused	Used
510	15 c. Type **127** . .	5	8
511	30 c. Yellowfin Grouper	12	15
512	50 c. Yellowtail Snappers	20	25
513	90 c. Shy Hamlet	35	40

128. The Annunciation.

(Des. J.W. Ltd. Litho. Walsall.)

1976 (15 Nov.). *Christmas. T* **128** *and similar vert. designs. Multicoloured. P* 13½.

No.	Description	Unused	Used
514	8 c. Type **128**	5	5
515	10 c. The Holy Family	5	5
516	15 c. The Magi	5	8
517	50 c. The Shepherds	20	25
518	$1 Epiphany scene	40	45
514/18	. . . . *Set of* 5	65	75

BARBUDA.

DEPENDENCY OF ANTIGUA.

BARBUDA

(**1**)

1922 (13 July). *Stamps of Leeward Islands optd. with T* **1**. *All are Die II.*

(a) Wmk. Mult. Script CA.

No.	Type	Description	Unused	Used
1	**11**	½d. deep green, O	90	2·25
2	,,	1d. bright scarlet, O	90	2·25
3	**10**	2d. slate-grey, O	1·10	2·60
4	**11**	2½d. bright blue, O . .	1·10	2·25
5	,,	6d. dull and brt. purple, C	2·50	5·50
6	**10**	2s. purple & blue/*blue*, C	7·50	11·00
7	,,	3s. bright green & violet, C	17·00	20·00
8	,,	4s. black and red, C (R.) . .	20·00	26·00
		(b) Wmk. Mult. Crown CA.		
9	**10**	3d. dull pur./*pale yellow*, C	1·00	2·25
10	**12**	1s. black/*emerald*, C (R.) . .	2·50	4·00
11	,,	5s. grn. & red/*pale yellow*, C	45·00	65·00
1/11		. . . . *Set of* 11	90·00	£130
1/11		Optd. "Specimen" *Set of* 11	£100	

The postage stamps of Antigua were used in Barbuda until 1968.

The following issues of Barbuda were also valid for use in Antigua.

2. Map of Barbuda.

2a. Great Barracuda.
4. French Angelfish.
5. Porkfish.
6. Striped Parrotfish.
7. Longspine Squirrelfish.
8. Catalufa.
9. Blue Chromis.

T **2a** and **4/9** are horiz. designs as T **3**.

3. Great Amberjack.

(Des. R. Granger Barrett. Litho. Format International.)

1968 (19 Nov.)–**70**. *P* 14.

No.	Type	Description	Unused	Used
12	**2**	½ c. brown, black and pink	5	5
13	,,	1 c. orange, black and flesh	5	5
14	,,	2 c. blackish brown, rose-red and rose	5	5
15	,,	3 c. blackish brown, orange-yellow and lemon	5	5
16	,,	4 c. black, bright green and apple-green	5	5
17	,,	5 c. blue-green, black and pale blue-green	5	5
18	,,	6 c. black, bright purple and pale lilac	8	8
19	,,	10 c. blk., ultram. & cobalt	10	12
20	,,	15 c. black, blue-green and turquoise-green	12	15
20*a*	**2a**	20 c. multicoloured (22.7.70)	15	20
21	**3**	25 c. multicoloured (5.2.69) . .	20	25
22	**4**	35 c. multicoloured (5.2.69) . .	25	30
23	**5**	50 c. multicoloured (5.2.69) . .	35	45
24	**6**	75 c. multicoloured (5.2.69) . .	50	60
25	**7**	$1 multicoloured (6.3.69) . .	90	1·40
26	**8**	$2.50 mult. (6.3.69)	2·25	2·50
27	**9**	$5 multicoloured (6.3.69)	4·00	4·50
12/27		. . . . *Set of* 17	8·00	9·50

10. Sprinting and Aztec Sun-stone.
11. High-jumping and Aztec Statue.
12. Yachting and Aztec Lion Mask.
13. Football and Engraved Plate.

(Des. R. Granger Barrett. Litho. Format International.)

1968 (20 Dec.). *Olympic Games, Mexico. P* 14.

No.	Type	Description	Unused	Used
28	**10**	25 c. multicoloured	30	30
29	**11**	35 c. multicoloured	40	40
30	**12**	75 c. multicoloured	65	70
MS31		85 × 76 mm. **13** $1 mult. . .	1·40	1·40

14. "The Ascension" (Orcagna).

(Des. R. Granger Barrett. Litho. Format International.)

1969 (24 Mar.). *Easter Commemoration. P* 14.

No.	Type	Description	Unused	Used
32	**14**	25 c. black and light blue . .	25	25
33	,,	35 c. black & deep carmine	30	35
34	,,	75 c. black and bluish lilac	55	55

15. Scout Enrolment Ceremony.
16. Scouts around Camp Fire.
17. Sea Scouts rowing Boat.

(Des. R. Granger Barrett. Litho. Format International.)

1969 (7 Aug.). *3rd Caribbean Scout Jamboree. P* 14.

No.	Type	Description	Unused	Used
35	**15**	25 c. multicoloured	20	25
36	**16**	35 c. multicoloured	30	35
37	**17**	75 c. multicoloured	50	60

18. " Sistine Madonna " (Raphael).

(Des. R. Granger Barrett. Litho. Format International.)

1969 (20 Oct.). *Christmas. P* 14.

38	**18** ½ c. multicoloured	..	10	10
39	,, 25 c. multicoloured	..	25	30
40	,, 35 c. multicoloured	..	35	35
41	,, 75 c. multicoloured	..	65	80

19. William I (1066–87).

(Des. R. Granger Barrett. Litho. Format (Nos. 42/9) or Questa (others).)

1970–71. *English Monarchs. T* **19** *and similar vert. designs. Multicoloured. P* 14½×14.

42	35 c. Type **19** (16.2.70)	..	35	40
43	35 c. William II (2.3.70)	..	35	40
44	35 c. Henry I (16.3.70)	..	35	40
45	35 c. Stephen (1.4.70)	..	35	40
46	35 c. Henry II (15.4.70)	..	35	40
47	35 c. Richard I (1.5.70)	..	35	40
48	35 c. John (15.5.70)	..	35	40
49	35 c. Henry III (1.6.70)	..	35	40
50	35 c. Edward I (15.6.70)	..	35	40
51	35 c. Edward II (1.7.70)	..	35	40
52	35 c. Edward III (15.7.70)	..	35	40
53	35 c. Richard II (1.8.70)	..	35	40
54	35 c. Henry IV (15.8.70)	..	35	40
55	35 c. Henry V (1.9.70)	..	35	40
56	35 c. Henry VI (15.9.70)	..	35	40
57	35 c. Edward IV (1.10.70)	..	35	40
58	35 c. Edward V (15.10.70)	..	35	40
59	35 c. Richard III (2.11.70)	..	35	40
60	35 c. Henry VII (16.11.70)	..	35	40
61	35 c. Henry VIII (1.12.70)	..	35	40
62	35 c. Edward VI (15.12.70)	..	35	40
63	35 c. Lady Jane Grey (2.1.71)		35	40
64	35 c. Mary I (15.1.71)	..	35	40
65	35 c. Elizabeth I (1.2.71)	..	35	40
66	35 c. James I (15.2.71)	..	35	40
67	35 c. Charles I (1.3.71)	..	35	40
68	35 c. Charles II (15.3.71)	..	35	40
69	35 c. James II (1.4.71)	..	35	40
70	35 c. William III (15.4.71)	..	35	40
71	35 c. Mary II (1.5.71)	..	35	40
72	35 c. Anne (15.5.71)	..	35	40
73	35 c. George I (1.6.71)	..	35	40
74	35 c. George II (15.6.71)	..	35	40
75	35 c. George III (1.7.71)	..	35	40
76	35 c. George IV (15.7.71)	..	35	40
77	35 c. William IV (2.8.71)	..	35	40
78	35 c. Victoria (16.8.71)	..	35	40
42/78	.. .. *Set of* 37		11·00	13·00

20c

(**20**)

21. " The Way to Calvary " (Ugolino).

1970 (26 Feb.). *No.* 12 *surch. with T* **20.**

79	**2** 20 c. on ½ c. brown, black and pink		30	45
	a. Surch. inverted		45·00	

(Des. R. Granger Barrett. Litho. Questa.)

1970 (16 Mar.). *Easter. T* **21** *and similar vert. designs. P* 14.

80	25 c. multicoloured		25	30
81	35 c. multicoloured		30	35
82	75 c. multicoloured		55	65
	Strip of three		1·25	1·40

Paintings: 35 c. " The Deposition from the Cross " (Ugolino); 75 c. Crucifix (The Master of S. Francesco).

The three designs appear *se-tenant*, in horizontal strips throughout the sheet.

22. Oliver is introduced to Fagin (*Oliver Twist*).

(Des. R. Granger Barrett. Litho. Questa.)

1970 (10 July). *Death Centenary of Charles Dickens. T* **22** *and similar horiz. design. Multicoloured. P* 14.

83	20 c. Type **22**		25	30
84	75 c. Dickens and Scene from *The Old Curiosity Shop* ..		55	55

23. " Madonna of the Meadows " (Bellini).

(Des. R. Granger Barrett. Litho. Questa.)

1970 (15 Oct.). *Christmas. T* **23** *and similar horiz. designs. Multicoloured. P* 14.

85	20 c. Type **23**		25	25
86	50 c. " Madonna, Child and Angels " (from Wilton diptych)		35	50
87	75 c. " The Nativity " (della Francesca)		55	70

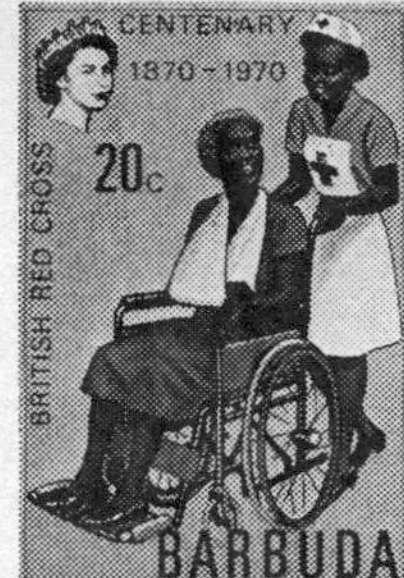

24. Nurse with Patient in Wheelchair.

(Des. R. Granger Barrett. Litho. Questa.)

1970 (21 Dec.). *Centenary of British Red Cross. T* **24** *and similar multicoloured designs. P* 14.

88	20 c. Type **24**		25	25
89	35 c. Nurse giving patient magazines (*horiz.*) ..		35	50
90	75 c. Nurse and Mother weighing baby (*horiz.*)		55	70

25. Angel with Vases.

(Des. R. Granger Barrett from detail of the " Mond " Crucifixion by Raphael. Litho. Questa.)

1971 (7 Apr.). *Easter. T* **25** *and similar vert. designs. Multicoloured. P* 14.

91	35 c. Type **25**		30	30
92	50 c. Christ crucified		40	40
93	75 c. Angel with vase ..		55	55

Nos. 91/3 were issued horizontally *se-tenant* within the sheet.

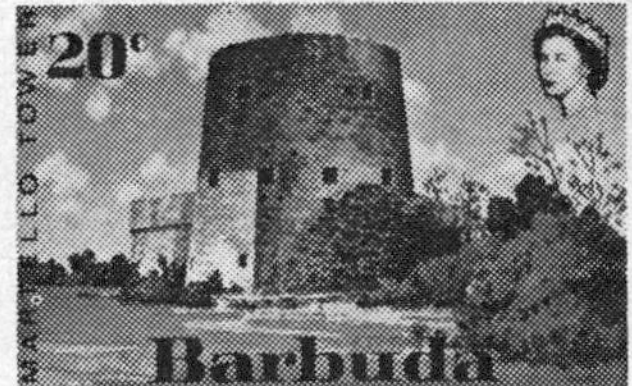

26. Martello Tower.

(Des. R. Granger Barrett. Litho. Questa.)

1971 (10 May). *Tourism. T* **26** *and similar horiz. designs. Multicoloured. P* 14.

94	20 c. Type **26**		25	25
95	25 c. Sailing boats		30	30
96	50 c. Hotel bungalows ..		45	45
97	75 c. Government House and Mystery Stone		65	65

27. " The Granduca Madonna " (Raphael).

(Des. R. Granger Barrett. Litho. Questa.)

1971 (4 Oct.). *Christmas. T* **27** *and similar vert. designs. Multicoloured. P* 14.

98 ½ c. Type **27** 10 10
99 35 c. " The Ansidei Madonna " (Raphael) 30 35
100 50 c. " The Virgin and Child " (Botticelli) 40 45
101 75 c. " The Madonna of the Trees " (Bellini) .. 55 60

The contract with the agency for the distribution of Barbuda stamps was cancelled by the Antiguan Government on 15 August 1971 but the above issue was duly authorised. Four stamps (20, 35, 50 and 70 c.) were prepared to commemorate the 500th anniversary of the birth of Albrecht Dürer but their issue was not authorised.

Barbuda ceased to have separate stamp issues in 1972 but again had stamps of her own on the 14th November 1973 with the following issue.

(28)

1973 (14 Nov.). *Royal Wedding. Nos.* 370/1 *of Antigua optd. with T* **28**.

102 35 c. multicoloured .. .. 5·00 5·50
a. Opt. inverted .. .. 90·00
103 $2 multicoloured .. .. 2·50 3·00
a. Opt. inverted £100

No. **MS**372 of Antigua also exists with this overprint, but was not placed on sale at post offices. Examples of this sheet are known with "Specimen" overprint.

BARBUDA (29) · BARBUDA (30) · BARBUDA (30*a*) · BARBUDA (31)

1973 (26 Nov.)–**74**. *T* **92** *etc. of Antigua optd. with T* **29**.

(*a*) *On Nos.* 270 *etc. W* w.**12** (*sideways*).

104 1 c. Columbus and *Nina* 5 5
105 2 c. Sir Thomas Warner's emblem and ship 5 5
106 4 c. Sir George Rodney and H.M.S. *Formidable* 5 5
107 5 c. Nelson and H.M.S. *Boreas* 5 8
108 6 c. William IV and H.M.S. *Pegasus* 8 10
109 10 c. "Blackbeard" and pirate ketch 10 12
110 20 c. Nelson and H.M.S. *Victory* 12 12
111 25 c. R.M.S.P. *Solent* 20 20
112 35 c. George V (when Prince George) and H.M.S. *Canada* 25 30
113 50 c. H.M.S. *Renown* 30 40
114 75 c. *Federal Maple* .. ..
115 $2.50, H.M.S. *London* .. 40 45
(18.2.74) .. .. .. 1·25 1·60

(*b*) *On Nos.* 323 *etc. W* w.**12** (*upright*). *White paper.*

116 ½ c. Type **92** (11.12.73) .. 8 8
117 3 c. Viscount Hood and H.M.S. *Barfleur* (11.12.73) 8 10
118 15 c. Captain Collingwood and H.M.S. *Pelican* (11.12.73) 15 20
119 $1 Yacht and Class Emblem (11.12.73) 55 60
120 $2.50, H.M.S. *London* (18.2.74) .. .. .. 6·50 6·50
121 $5 Tug *Pathfinder* (26.11.73) 2·50 2·75
104/21 .. .. *Set of* 18 11·00 12·00

1973 (26 Nov.). *Commemorative stamps of Antigua optd.*

(*a*) *Nos.* 353, 355, 357 *and* **MS**358 *optd. with T* **30**.

122 ½ c. Private, Zacharia Tiffin's Regt. of Foot, 1701 .. 8 8
123 20 c. Light Company Officer, 35th Regt. of Foot, 1828 20 20
a. Opt. with T 30*a* 1·50 1·50
124 75 c. Sergeant, 49th Regt., 1858 .. .. .. 45 55
MS125 127 × 145 mm. .. .. 3·00 3·00

(*b*) *Nos.* 360/**MS**363 *optd. with T* **31**, *in red.*

126 20 c. Carnival street scene .. 15 15
127 35 c. Carnival troupe .. 25 25
a. Opt. inverted .. ..
128 75 c. Carnival Queen .. 40 45
MS129 134 × 95 mm. .. .. 2·75 3·00
a. Albino opt. .. ..

Type **30***a* is a typographical overprint, applied locally.

BARBUDA (32) · BARBUDA (33) · BARBUDA (34) · BARBUDA (35)

1973 (11 Dec.). *Christmas. Nos.* 364/**MS**369 *of Antigua optd. with T* **32**.

130 3 c. Type **105** (Sil.) 5 5
a. Opt. inverted .. .. 35·00
b. "BABRDUA" (R.4/2) .. 4·50 4·50
131 5 c. "Adoration of the Kings" (Stomer) (Sil.) 5 5
a. "BABRDUA" (R.4/2) .. 6·50 6·50
132 20 c. "Granduca Madonna" (Raphael) (Sil.) 30 30
a. "BABRDUA" (R.4/2) .. 9·00 9·00
133 35 c. "Nativity with God the Father and Holy Ghost" (Battista) (R.) 40 40
134 $1 "Madonna and Child" (Murillo) (R.) .. .. 1·10 1·25
130/4 .. .. *Set of* 5 1·75 1·75
MS135 130 x 128 mm. Nos. 130/4 (Sil.) .. .. 9·50 9·50

1973 (15 Dec.). *Honeymoon Visit of Princess Anne and Capt. Phillips. Nos.* 373/**MS**375 *of Antigua further optd. with T* **33**.

136 35 c. multicoloured 40 40
137 $2 multicoloured .. .. 1·75 1·75
MS138 78 × 100 mm. Nos. 136/7 5·50 5·50

1974 (18 Feb.). *25th Anniv. of University of West Indies. Nos.* 376/9 *of Antigua optd. with T* **34**.

139 5 c. Coat-of-arms 8 8
140 20 c. Extra-mural art 15 15
141 35 c. Antigua campus 25 25
a. Opt. double .. ..
142 75 c. Antigua Chancellor .. 40 40

1974 (1 May). *Military Uniforms. Nos.* 380/4 *of Antigua optd. with T* **35**.

143 ½ c. Officer, 59th Foot, 1797 8 8
144 10 c. Gunner, Royal Artillery, 1800 .. .. .. 12 12
145 20 c. Private, 1st West India Regt., 1830 .. .. 20 20
146 35 c. Officer, 92nd Foot, 1843 30 30
147 75 c. Private, 23rd Foot, 1846 40 45
143/7 .. .. *Set of* 5 90 95

BARBUDA 13 JULY 1922 (36) · BARBUDA 15 SEPT. 1874 G.P.U. (37. "General Postal Union") · BARBUDA (38)

1974 (15 July). *Centenary of Universal Postal Union (1st issue). Nos.* 386/92 *of Antigua optd. with T* **36** *or* **37**, *in red.*

148 **36** ½ c. multicoloured .. 5 5
149 **37** ½ c. multicoloured .. 5 5
150 **36** 1 c. multicoloured .. 5 5
151 **37** 1 c. multicoloured .. 5 5
152 **36** 2 c. multicoloured .. 5 5
153 **37** 2 c. multicoloured .. 5 5
154 **36** 5 c. multicoloured .. 10 12
155 **37** 5 c. multicoloured .. 10 12
156 **36** 20 c. multicoloured .. 45 50
157 **37** 20 c. multicoloured .. 45 50
158 **36** 35 c. multicoloured .. 90 1·00
159 **37** 35 c. multicoloured .. 90 1·00
160 **36** $1 multicoloured .. 3·00 3·25
161 **37** $1 multicoloured .. 3·00 3·25
148/61 .. .. *Set of* 14 8·00 9·00
MS162 141 × 164 mm. **MS**393 of Antigua optd. "BARBUDA" in red 3·50 3·50
a. Albino opt. .. ..

Types **36** and **37** alternate horizontally throughout the sheet.

1974 (14 Aug.). *Antiguan Steel Bands. Nos.* 394/**MS**398 *of Antigua optd. with T* **38**.

163 5 c. rose-red, carm. & blk. 5 5
164 20 c. brown-ochre, chestnut & black 15 15
165 35 c. light sage-green, blue-green and black 20 25
166 75 c. dull blue, dull ultramarine and black .. 40 40
MS167 115 × 108 mm. Nos. 163/6 1·00 1·00

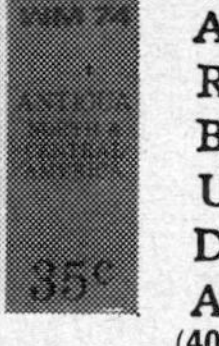

39. Footballers. (40)

(Litho.)

1974 (2 Sept.). *World Cup Football Championships (1st issue). Various horiz. designs as T* **39** *each showing footballers in action. Multicoloured. P* 14.

168 **39** 35 c. multicoloured .. 25 25
169 – $1.20, multicoloured .. 60 70
170 – $2.50, multicoloured .. 1·10 1·25
MS171 70 × 128 mm. Nos. 168/70 2·00

1974 (23 Sept.). *World Cup Football Championships (2nd issue). Nos.* 399/**MS**403 *of Antigua optd. with T* **40**.

172 5 c. multicoloured .. 8 8

173 35 c. multicoloured 20 25
174 75 c. multicoloured 40 40
175 $1 multicoloured 45 50
MS176 135×130 mm. Nos. 172/5 1·25 1·25

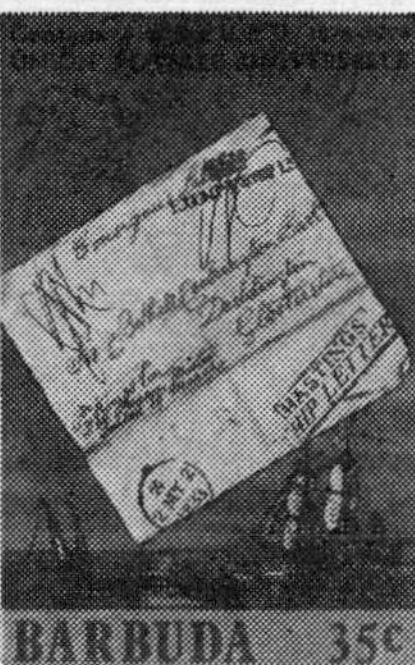

41. Ship Letter of 1833.

(Des. G. Drummond. Litho. Questa.)

1974 (30 Sept.). *Centenary of Universal Postal Union (2nd series).* *T* **41** *and similar vert. designs. Multicoloured. P* 13½.
177 35 c. Type **41** 20 20
178 $1.20, Stamps and postmark of 1922 .. .. 55 60
179 $2.50, Mailplane over map of Barbuda .. .. 1·10 1·40
MS180 128×97 mm. Nos. 177/9 1·90 2·25

42. Greater Amberjack.

(Des. G. Drummond. Litho. Format.)

1974–75. *Various multicoloured designs as T* **42**. *P* 14×14½ (½ *c. to* 3 *c.*, 25 *c.*), 14½×14 (4 *c. to* 20 *c.*, 35 *c.*), 14 (50 *c. to* $1) *or* 13½ (*others*).
181 ½ c. Oleander, Rose Bay (*b*) 5 5
182 1 c. Blue Petrea (*b*) 5 5
183 2 c. Poinsettia (*b*) 5 5
184 3 c. Cassia tree (*b*) 5 5
185 4 c. Type **42** (*a*) 5 5
186 5 c. Holy Trinity School (*a*) 5 5
187 6 c. Snorkeling (*a*) 5 5
188 10 c. Pilgrim Holiness Church (*a*) 5 5
189 15 c. New Cottage Hospital (*a*) 5 5
190 20 c. Post Office and Treasury (*a*) 8 10
191 25 c. Island jetty and boats (*a*) 10 12
192 35 c. Martello Tower (*a*) .. 12 10
193 50 c. Warden's House (*b*) .. 20 25
194 75 c. Inter-island aircraft (*a*) .. 25 30
195 $1 Tortoise (*b*) 35 40
196 $2.50, Spiny lobster (*b*) .. 90 1·00
197 $5 Frigatebird (*b*) .. .. 1·75 2·00
a. Perf. 14×14½ (*c*)* .. .. 10·00
197*b* $10 Hibiscus (*d*) .. .. 3·50 4·00
181/97*b* .. .. *Set of* 18 6·75 7·50

*See footnote below Nos. 227/8.

The 50 c. to $1 are larger, 39×25 mm.; the $2.50 and $5 are 45×29 mm.; the $10 is 34×48 mm. and the ½ c. to 3 c. 25 c. and $10 are vert. designs.

Dates of issue: (*a*) 15.10.74; (*b*) 6.1.75; (*c*) 24.7.75; (*d*) 19.9.75.

1974 (15 Oct.). *Birth Centenary of Sir Winston Churchill (1st issue). Nos.* 408/**MS**412 *of Antigua optd. with T* **38** *in red.*
198 5 c. multicoloured 12 15
199 35 c. multicoloured 40 40
200 75 c. multicoloured 85 90
201 $1 multicoloured .. .. 1·40 1·40
MS202 107×82 mm. Nos. 198/201 7·00 7·00

43. Churchill making Broadcast.

(Litho. Questa.)

1974 (20 Nov.). *Birth Centenary of Sir Winston Churchill (2nd issue). T* **43** *and similar horiz. designs. Multicoloured. P* 13½×14.
203 5 c. Type **43** 5 5
204 35 c. Churchill and Chartwell 20 20
205 75 c. Churchill painting .. 35 40
206 $1 Churchill making "V"-sign 45 50
MS207 146×95 mm. Nos. 203/6 1·10

1974 (25 Nov.). *Christmas. Nos.* 413/**MS**421 *of Antigua optd. with T* **33**.
208 ½ c. multicoloured 5 5
209 1 c. multicoloured 5 5
210 2 c. multicoloured 5 5
211 3 c. multicoloured 5 5
212 5 c. multicoloured 5 5
213 20 c. multicoloured 12 12
214 35 c. multicoloured 15 15
215 75 c. multicoloured 35 35
208/15 *Set of* 8 60 70
MS216 139×126 mm. Nos. 208/15 65 65

BARBUDA
(44)

1975 (17 Mar.). *Nelson's Dockyard. Nos.* 427/**MS**432 *of Antigua optd. with T* **44**.
217 5 c. Type **116** 5 5
218 15 c. Ship of the line, English Harbour, 1770 .. 10 10
219 35 c. H.M.S. *Boreas* at anchor, and Lord Nelson, 1787 .. 20 20
220 50 c. Yachts during "Sailing Week", 1974 .. 25 30
221 $1 Yacht Anchorage, Old Dockyard, 1970 .. 45 50
217/21 .. .. *Set of* 5 90 1·00
MS222 130×134 mm. As Nos. 217/21, but in larger format; 43×28 mm., plus *se-tenant* label .. 1·00 1·10

45. Ships of the Line.

(Des. G. L. Vasarhelyi. Litho. Format.)

1975 (30 May). *Sea Battles. T* **45** *and similar horiz. designs showing scenes from the Battle of the Saints,* 1782. *Multicoloured. P* 13½.
223 35 c. Type **45** 20 20
224 50 c. English three-masters .. 25 30
225 75 c. Ships firing broadsides .. 35 40
226 95 c. Sailors fleeing burning ship 45 50

U.S.A.-U.S.S.R. SPACE COOPERATION 1975

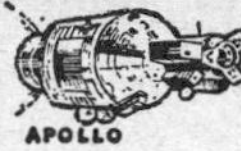

(46)

1975 (24 July). *"Apollo-Soyuz" Space Project. No.* 197a *optd. with T* **46** *and similar ("Soyuz") opt.*
227 $5 mult. ("Apollo") .. .. 2·50 2·75
228 $5 mult. ("Soyuz") .. .. 2·50 2·75
a. *Se-tenant* strip of 3. Nos. 227/8 and 197a .. .. .. 40·00

Nos. 227/8 were issued together *se-tenant* in sheets of 25 (5×5), with the "Apollo" opts. in the first and third vertical rows and the "Soyuz" opts. in the second and fourth vertical rows, the fifth vertical row comprising five unoverprinted stamps, No. 197a.

47. Officer, 65th Foot, 1763.

(Des. G. Drummond. Litho. Questa.)

1975 (17 Sept.). *Military Uniforms. T* **47** *and similar vert. designs. Multicoloured. P* 13½.
229 35 c. Type **47** 20 20
230 50 c. Grenadier, 27th Foot, 1701–10 .. .. .. 25 30
231 75 c. Officer, 21st Foot, 1793–6 35 40
232 95 c. Officer, Royal Regt. of Artillery, 1800 .. .. 40 45

30TH ANNIVERSARY
UNITED NATIONS
1945 — 1975
(48)

1975 (24 Oct.). *30th Anniv. of United Nations. Nos.* 203/206 *optd. with T* **48**.
233 5 c. Churchill making broadcast 5 5
234 35 c. Churchill and Chartwell 20 20
235 75 c. Churchill painting .. 30 35
236 $1 Churchill making "V" sign 45 50

BARBUDA (49)

BARBUDA (50)

1975 (17 Nov.). *Christmas. Nos.* 457/**MS**465 *of Antigua optd. with T* **49**.
237 ½ c. multicoloured 5 5
238 1 c. multicoloured 5 5
239 2 c. multicoloured 5 5
240 3 c. multicoloured 5 5
241 5 c. multicoloured 5 5
242 10 c. multicoloured 8 8
243 35 c. multicoloured 20 20
244 $2 multicoloured 85 95
237/44 .. .. *Set of* 8 1·10 1·25
MS245 138×119 mm. Nos. 241/4 1·25

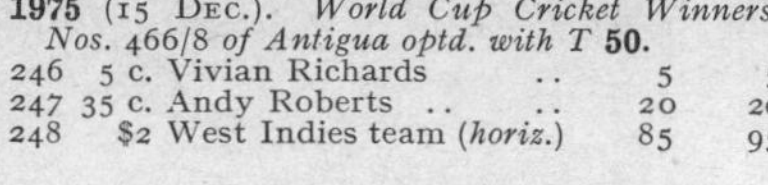

1975 (15 Dec.). *World Cup Cricket Winners. Nos. 466/8 of Antigua optd. with T* **50**.

246 5 c. Vivian Richards .. 5 5
247 35 c. Andy Roberts 20 20
248 $2 West Indies team (*horiz.*) 85 95

51. Surrender of Cornwallis.

(Des. G. L. Vasarhelyi. Litho. Format.)

1976 (8 Mar.). *Bicentenary of American Revolution. T* **51** *and similar horiz. designs. Multicoloured. P* 13½ × 13.

249 15 c. } 5 5
250 15 c. } Type **51** 5 5
251 15 c. } 5 5
252 35 c. } The 12 15
253 35 c. } Battle of 12 15
254 35 c. } Princetown 12 15
255 $1 } Surrender of 35 40
256 $1 } General Burgoyne .. 35 40
257 $1 } at Saratoga 35 40
258 $2 } Jefferson presenting .. 70 80
259 $2 } Declaration of Inde- .. 70 80
260 $2 } pendence 70 80
249/60 .. .. *Set of* 12 3·25 3·75
MS261 140 × 70 mm. Nos. 249/54 and 255/60 (two sheets) .. 3·50

The three designs of each value were printed horizontally *se-tenant* within the sheet to form the composite designs listed. Type **51** shows the left-hand stamp of the 15 c. design.

52. Bananaquits.

(Des. G. L. Vasarhelyi. Litho. Format.)

1976 (30 June). *Birds. T* **52** *and similar horiz. designs. Multicoloured. P* 13½.

262 35 c. Type **52** 15 15
263 50 c. Blue-headed Euphonia .. 20 25
264 75 c. Royal Tern 30 35
265 95 c. Killdeer 35 40
266 $1.25, Glossy Cowbird .. 50 60
267 $2 Purple Gallinule .. 80 90
262/7 .. .. *Set of* 6 2·10 2·40

1976 (12 Aug.). *Royal Visit to the U.S.A. As Nos.* 249/60 *but redrawn and inscr. at top* "H.M. QUEEN ELIZABETH ROYAL VISIT 6TH JULY 1976 H.R.H. DUKE OF EDINBURGH".

268 15 c. } .. 5 8
269 15 c. } As Type **51** 5 8
270 15 c. } .. 5 8
271 35 c. } .. 15 15
272 35 c. } As Nos. 252/4 .. 15 15
273 35 c. } .. 15 15
274 $1 } .. 40 45
275 $1 } As Nos. 255/7 .. 40 45
276 $1 } .. 40 45
277 $2 } .. 80 90
278 $2 } As Nos. 258/60 .. 80 90
279 $2 } .. 80 90
268/79 .. .. *Set of* 12 4·00 4·50
MS280 143 × 81 mm. Nos. 268/73 and 274/9 (two sheets) .. 4·50

The three designs of each value were printed horizontally *se-tenant*, imperf. between.

ASCENSION.

For GREAT BRITAIN stamps used in Ascension, see index to Great Britain Used Abroad list.

DEPENDENCY OF ST. HELENA.

ASCENSION
(1)

2. Badge of St. Helena.

1922 (2 Nov.). *Stamps of St. Helena, optd. with T* **1**.

(*a*) *Wmk. Mult. Script CA.*

1 **14** ½d. black and green .. 60 1·75
2 **15** 1d. green .. .. .. 1·00 1·75
3 ,, 1½d. rose-scarlet .. .. 2·25 6·00
4 **14** 2d. black and grey .. .. 2·25 3·50
5 ,, 3d. bright blue .. .. 2·50 5·50
6 **15** 8d. black and dull purple .. 8·50 8·50
7 ,, 2s. black and blue/*blue* .. 32·00 35·00
8 ,, 3s. black and violet .. 45·00 55·00

(*b*) *Wmk. Mult. Crown CA.*

9 **14** 1s. black/*green* (R.) .. 9·00 11·00
1/9 .. .. .. *Set of* 9 90·00 £110
1/9 Optd. "Specimen" *Set of* 9 £100

(Typo. D.L.R.)

1924–33. *T* **2**. *Wmk. Mult. Script CA. P* 14.

10 ½d. grey-black and black, C .. 45 75
11 1d. grey-blk. & dp. bl.-grn., C 65 90
11*a* 1d. grey-black & bright blue-green, C ('33) .. .. 14·00 17·00
12 1½d. rose-red, C .. .. 1·25 2·25
13 2d. grey-black and grey, C .. 1·25 1·00
14 3d. blue, C .. .. .. 80 1·75
15 4d. grey-blk. & blk./*yellow*, C 9·00 11·00
15*a* 5d. pur. & olive-green, C ('27) 4·50 7·00
16 6d. grey-blk. & bright pur., C 18·00 23·00
17 8d. grey-blk. & bright vio., C 4·00 6·50
18 1s. grey-black and brown, C 7·00 8·50
19 2s. grey-black & blue/*blue*, C 17·00 18·00
20 3s. grey-black & blk./*blue*, C 23·00 25·00
10/20 .. .. *Set of* 12 90·00 £110
10/20 Optd. "Specimen" *Set of* 12 90·00

3. Georgetown.

4. Ascension Island.

5. The Pier.

6. Long Beach.

7. Three Sisters.

8. Sooty Tern and Wideawake Fair.

9. Green Mountain.

(Des. and recess. D.L.R.)

1934 (2 July). *Wmk. Mult. Script CA. P* 14.

21 **3** ½d. black and violet .. 12 25
22 **4** 1d. black and emerald .. 45 45
23 **5** 1½d. black and scarlet .. 45 50
24 **4** 2d. black and orange .. 45 45
25 **6** 3d. black and ultramarine .. 60 85
26 **7** 5d. black and blue .. .. 1·10 1·75
27 **4** 8d. black and sepia .. 2·75 3·25
28 **8** 1s. black and carmine .. 7·00 7·00
29 **4** 2s. 6d. black & bright purple 15·00 16·00
30 **9** 5s. black and brown .. 20·00 23·00
21/30 .. .. *Set of* 10 45·00 48·00
21/30 Perf. "Specimen" *Set of* 10 45·00

1935 (6 May). *Silver Jubilee. As Nos.* 91/4 *of Antigua, but ptd. by Waterlow. P* 11 × 12.

31 1½d. deep blue and scarlet .. 1·75 1·40
32 2d. ultramarine and grey .. 2·00 3·00
33 5d. green and indigo .. .. 6·00 7·00
34 1s. slate and purple .. .. 13·00 17·00
31/4 Perf. "Specimen" *Set of* 4 14·00

1937 (19 May). *Coronation. As Nos.* 13/15 *of Aden. P* 14.

35 1d. green 15 25
36 2d. orange 25 25
37 3d. bright blue 80 80
35/7 Perf. "Specimen" *Set of* 3 10·00

10. The Pier.

(Recess. De La Rue.)

1938 (12 May)–**1953**. *Horiz. designs as T* **3, 6, 7,** *and* **9,** *but modified and with portrait of King George VI as in T* **10.** *Wmk. Mult. Script CA. P* 13½.

No.	Type	Description	Unused	Used
38	**3**	½d. black and violet ..	12	15
		a. Perf. 13. *Black & bluish violet* (1944)	12	15
39	**9**	1d. black and green ..	5·00	2·25
39*a*	,,	1d. black and yellow-orange (8.7.40) ..	1·25	2·75
		b. Perf. 13 (5.42)	12	15
		c. Perf. 14 (17.2.49)	25	40
39*d*	**7**	1d. black and green, *p*. 13 (1.6.49)	12	20
40	**10**	1½d. black & vermilion ..	50	55
		a. Perf. 13 (1944)	25	40
		b. Perf. 14 (2.49)	75	2·25
40*c*	,,	1½d. black and rose-carm. *p*. 14 (1.6.49)	15	25
		ca. Perf. 13 (25.2.53)	35	40
		d. *Black and carmine*, p. 14	85	1·00
41	**9**	2d. black and red-orange	15	25
		a. Perf. 13 (17.5.44)	12	35
		b. Perf. 14 (17.2.49)	2·25	3·25
41*c*	,,	2d. black and scarlet, *p*. 14 (1.6.49)	20	25
42	**6**	3d. black and ultramarine	11·00	6·00
42*a*	,,	3d. black & grey (7.40) ..	40	35
		b. Perf. 13 (17.5.44)	30	15
42*c*	**9**	4d. blk. & ultram. (8.7.40)	25	40
		d. Perf. 13 (17.5.44)	25	40
43	**7**	6d. black and blue ..	40	45
		a. Perf. 13 (17.5.44)	85	60
44	**3**	1s. black and sepia ..	60	90
		a. Perf. 13 (1944)	50	60
45	**10**	2s. 6d. blk. & deep carm.	2·75	2·75
		a. Perf. 13 (1944)	2·75	3·50
46	**6**	5s. blk. & yellow-brown	4·00	2·50
		a. Perf. 13 (17.5.44)	3·50	5·50
47	**7**	10s. black & bright purple	9·00	9·00
		a. Perf. 13 (17.5.44)	5·50	7·00
38/47a		.. .. *Set of* 16	27·00	21·00
38/47		Perf. "Specimen" *Set of* 13	38·00	

1946 (21 Oct.). *Victory. As Nos.* 28/9 *of Aden.*

No.	Description	Unused	Used
48	2d. red-orange	12	20
49	4d. blue	12	20
48/9	Perf. "Specimen" *Set of* 2	10·00	

1948 (20 Oct.). *Royal Silver Wedding. As Nos.* 30/1 *of Aden.*

No.	Description	Unused	Used
50	3d. black	12	20
51	10s. bright purple	6·50	11·00

1949 (10 Oct.). *75th Anniv. of Universal Postal Union. As Nos.* 114/17 *of Antigua.*

No.	Description	Unused	Used
52	3d. carmine	30	30
53	4d. deep blue	60	60
54	6d. olive	1·10	1·10
55	1s. blue-black	1·75	2·00

1953 (2 June). *Coronation. As No.* 47 *of Aden.*

No.	Description	Unused	Used
56	3d. black and grey-black ..	1·10	1·90

15. Water Catchment.

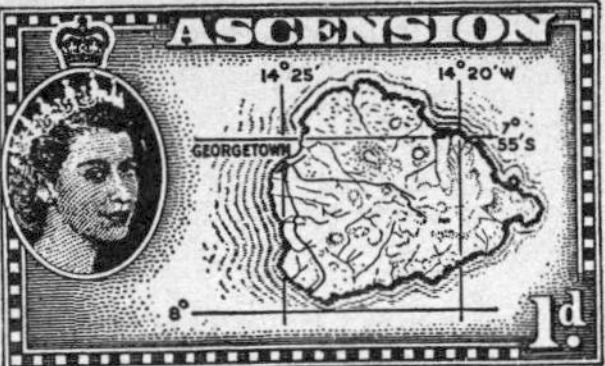

16. Map of Ascension.

17. View of Georgetown.

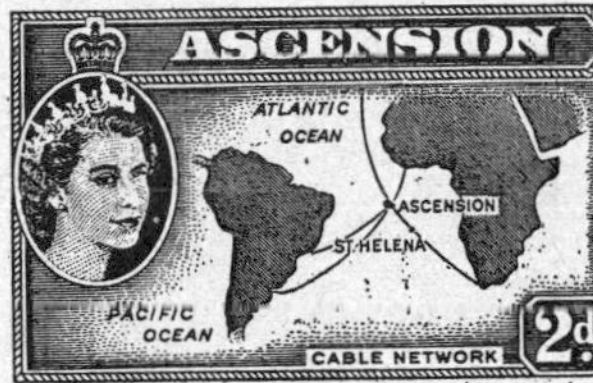

18. Map showing Cable Network.

19. Mountain Road.

20. Boatswain Bird.

21. Long-finned Tunny.

22. Rollers on the Seashore.

23. Young Turtles.

24. Land Crab.

25. Wideawake (Sooty Tern).

26. Perfect Crater.

27. View of Ascension from North-west.

(Recess. Bradbury, Wilkinson & Co.)

1956 (19 Nov.). *Wmk. Mult. Script CA. P* 13.

No.	Type	Description	Unused	Used
57	**15**	½d. black and brown ..	12	12
58	**16**	1d. black and magenta ..	12	12
59	**17**	1½d. black and orange ..	12	12
60	**18**	2d. black and carmine-red	20	20
61	**19**	2½d. black & orange-brown	25	30
62	**20**	3d. black and blue ..	30	30
63	**21**	4d. black & dp. turq.-grn.	35	40
64	**22**	6d. black and indigo ..	45	45
65	**23**	7d. black and deep olive ..	60	65
66	**24**	1s. black and vermilion ..	1·40	1·60
67	**25**	2s. 6d. black & deep dull purple	4·00	4·50
68	**26**	5s. black and blue-green ..	7·00	8·00
69	**27**	10s. black and purple ..	14·00	15·00
57/69		.. .. *Set of* 13	26·00	28·00

28. Brown Booby.

29. Black Noddy.
30. Fairy Tern.
31. Red-billed Tropic Bird.
32. Brown Noddy.
33. Wideawake Tern.
34. Frigate-bird.
35. White Booby.
36. Yellow-billed Tropic Bird.
37. Red-billed Tropic Bird.
38. Madeiran Storm Petrel.
39. Red-footed Booby (brown phase).
40. Frigate-birds.
41. Red-footed Booby (white phase).

(Des. after photos. by N. P. Ashmole. Photo. Harrison.)

1963 (23 May). *W* w.**12**. *P* 14×14½.

70 **28** 1d. blk., lemon & new blue 5 5
71 **29** 1½d. black, cobalt and ochre 5 5
72 **30** 2d. blk., grey & bright blue 8 8
73 **31** 3d. blk., mag. & turq.-blue 10 12
74 **32** 4½d. black, bistre-brown and new blue 12 12
75 **33** 6d. bistre, blk. & yell.-grn. 15 15
76 **34** 7d. blk., brn. & reddish vio. 20 25
77 **35** 10d. black, greenish yellow and blue-green .. 25 25
78 **36** 1s. multicoloured .. 25 35
79 **37** 1s. 6d. multicoloured .. 50 65
80 **38** 2s. 6d. multicoloured .. 90 1·10
81 **39** 5s. multicoloured .. 1·60 1·90
82 **40** 10s. multicoloured .. 2·75 3·25
83 **41** £1 multicoloured .. 5·50 6·50
70/83 .. .. *Set of* 14 11·00 13·00

1963 (4 June). *Freedom from Hunger. As No.* 76 *of Aden.*

84 1s. 6d. carmine .. .. 2·75 2·25

1963 (2 Sept.). *Red Cross Centenary. As Nos.* 147/8 *of Antigua.*

85 3d. red and black 80 80
86 1s. 6d. red and blue .. .. 3·25 3·25

1965 (17 May). *I.T.U. Centenary. As Nos.* 166/7 *of Antigua.*

87 3d. magenta and bluish violet 40 40
88 6d. turq.-blue & light chestnut 75 75

1965 (25 Oct.). *International Co-operation Year. As Nos.* 168/9 *of Antigua.*

89 1d. reddish purple and turquoise-green 15 15
90 6d. dp. bluish green & lavender 55 55

1966 (24 Jan.). *Churchill Commemoration. As Nos.* 170/3 *of Antigua.*

91 1d. new blue 20 20
92 3d. deep green.. .. .. 35 30
93 6d. brown 65 55
94 1s. 6d. bluish violet .. .. 1·90 1·60

1966 (1 July). *World Cup Football Championships. As Nos.* 176/7 *of Antigua.*

95 3d. violet, yellow-green, lake and yellow-brown .. 30 25
96 6d. chocolate, blue-green, lake and yellow-brown .. 50 40

1966 (20 Sept.). *Inauguration of W.H.O. Headquarters, Geneva. As Nos.* 178/9 *of Antigua.*

97 3d. black, yellow-green and light blue 25 20
98 1s. 6d. black, light purple and yellow-brown 85 85

42. Satellite Station.

(Des. V. Whiteley. Photo. Harrison.)

1966 (7 Nov.). *Opening of Apollo Communications Satellite Earth Station. W* w.**12** (*sideways*). *P* 14×14½.

99 **42** 4d. black & reddish violet 20 20
100 „ 8d. black & dp. bluish green 30 30
101 „ 1s. 3d. black & olive-brown 50 50
102 „ 2s. 6d. black & turq.-blue 1·00 1·00

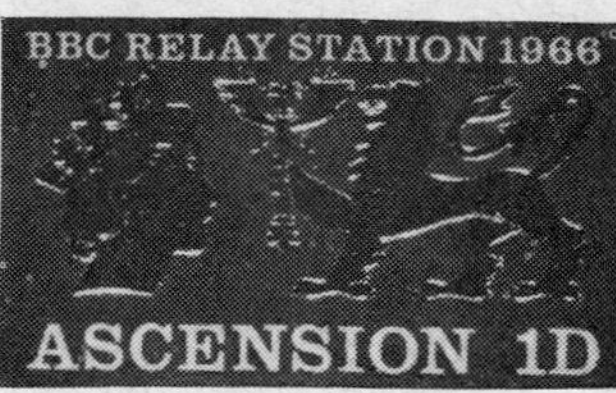

43. B.B.C. Emblem.

(Des. B.B.C. staff. Photo., Queen's head and emblem die-stamped. Harrison.)

1966 (1 Dec.). *Opening of B.B.C. Relay Station. W* w.**12**. *P* 14½.

103 **43** 1d. gold and ultramarine.. 12 12
104 „ 3d. gold and myrtle-green 15 15
105 „ 6d. gold and reddish violet 30 25
106 „ 1s. 6d. gold and red .. 65 65

1967 (1 Jan.). *20th Anniv. of U.N.E.S.C.O. As Nos.* 196/8 *of Antigua.*

107 3d. slate-violet, red, yellow and orange 30 30
108 6d. orange-yellow, violet and deep olive 65 65
109 1s. 6d. black, bright purple and orange .. .. 1·25 1·50

44. Human Rights Emblem and Chain Links.

(Des. and litho. Harrison.)

1968 (8 July). *Human Rights Year. W* w.**12** (*sideways*). *P* 14½×14.

110 **44** 6d. lt. orange, red & black 30 30
111 „ 1s. 6d. light grey-blue, red and black 55 55
112 „ 2s. 6d. lt. grn., red & blk. 85 85

45. Ascension Black-Fish.

(Des. M. C. Farrar Bell. Litho. De La Rue.)

1968 (23 Oct.). *Fishes* (1*st series*). *Multicoloured* (*Nos.* 114/6). *W* w.**12** (*sideways*). *P* 13.

113 **45** 4d. black, slate & turq.-bl. 20 20
114 – 8d. Leather-jacket .. 30 30
115 – 1s. 9d. Tunny .. 70 70
116 – 2s. 3d. Mako Shark .. 80 80

(Des. M. C. Farrar Bell. Litho. D.L.R.)

1969 (3 Mar.). *Fishes* (2*nd series*). *Designs as T* **45**. *Multicoloured. W* w.**12** (*sideways*). *P* 13.

117 4d. Sailfish.. .. .. 12 12
118 6d. Old Wife 20 20
119 1s. 6d. Yellowtail.. .. 50 50
120 2s. 11d. Jack 95 95

See also Nos. 126/9.

46. H.M.S. *Rattlesnake.*

47. H.M.S. *Weston.*
48. H.M.S. *Undaunted.*
49. H.M.S. *Eagle.*

(Des. L. D. Curtis. Photo. Harrison.)

1969 (1 Oct.). *Royal Naval Crests* (1*st series*). *W* w.**12** (*sideways*). *P* 14×14½.

121 **46** 4d. multicoloured 15 15
122 **47** 9d. multicoloured 30 30
123 **48** 1s. 9d. deep blue, pale blue and gold 65 65
124 **49** 2s. 3d. multicoloured .. 80 80
MS125 165×105 mm. Nos. 121/4. P 14½ .. .. 2·00 2·00

See also Nos. 130/4, 149/53, 154/8 and 166/70.

(Des. M. C. Farrar Bell. Litho. De La Rue.)

1970 (6 Apr.). *Fishes* (3*rd series*). *Designs as T* **45.** *Multicoloured. W* w.**12** (*sideways*). *P* 14.

126 4d. Wahoo.. .. .. 10 10
127 9d. Coal-fish 20 25
128 1s. 9d. Dolphin 45 45
129 2s. 3d. Soldier Fish .. 55 55

(Des. L. D. Curtis. Photo. D.L.R.)

1970 (7 Sept.). *Royal Naval Crests* (2*nd series*). *Designs as T* **46.** *Multicoloured. W* w.**12**. *P* 12½.

130 4d. H.M.S. *Penelope* .. 15 15
131 9d. H.M.S. *Carlisle* .. 30 30
132 1s. 6d. H.M.S. *Amphion* .. 55 55
133 2s. 6d. H.M.S. *Magpie* .. 80 80
MS134 153×96 mm. Nos. 130/3 .. 1·90 1·90

50. Early Chinese Rocket.

(Des. V. Whiteley. Litho. Format.)

1971 (15 Feb.). *Decimal Currency. The Evolution of Space Travel. T* **50** *and similar multicoloured designs. W* w.**12** (*sideways on horiz. designs*). *P* 14.

135 ½p. Type **50** 5 5
136 1p. Medieval Arab Astronomers 5 5
137 1½p. Tycho Brahe's Observatory, Quadrant and Supernova 5 5

38 2p. Galileo, Moon and Telescope 5 5
39 2½p. Isaac Newton, Instruments and Apple .. 5 5
40 3½p. Harrison's Chronometer and Ship 10 12
41 4½p. Space Rocket taking-off 12 12
42 5p. World's Largest Telescope, Palomar .. 12 15
43 7½p. World's largest Radio Telescope, Jodrell Bank 20 20
44 10p. Mariner VII and Mars .. 30 30
45 12½p. Sputnik II and Space Dog, Laika 30 35
46 25p. Walking in Space .. 60 70
47 50p. Apollo XI Crew on Moon 1·25 1·40
48 £1 Future Space Research Station .. .. .. 2·50 2·75
35/48 .. .. *Set of* 14 5·00 5·50

The ½p., 1p., 4½p. and 25p. are vertical, and he remainder are horizontal.

(Des. L. D. Curtis. Photo. D.L.R.)

971 (15 Nov.). *Royal Naval Crests* (*3rd series*). *Designs as T* **46.** *Multicoloured. W* w.**12.** *P* 13.
49 2p. H.M.S. *Phoenix* .. 15 15
50 4p. H.M.S. *Milford* .. 30 30
51 9p. H.M.S. *Pelican* .. 55 55
52 15p. H.M.S. *Oberon* 85 85
IS153 151×104 mm. Nos. 149/52 3·00 3·00

(Des. L. D. Curtis. Litho. Questa.)

972 (22 May). *Royal Naval Crests* (*4th series*). *Multicoloured designs as T* **46.** *W* w.**12** (*sideways*). *P* 14.
54 1½p. H.M.S. *Lowestoft* .. 8 8
55 3p. H.M.S. *Auckland* .. 15 20
56 6p. H.M.S. *Nigeria* .. 35 40
57 17½p. H.M.S. *Bermuda* .. 70 75
IS158 157×93 mm. Nos. 154/7 1·40 1·50

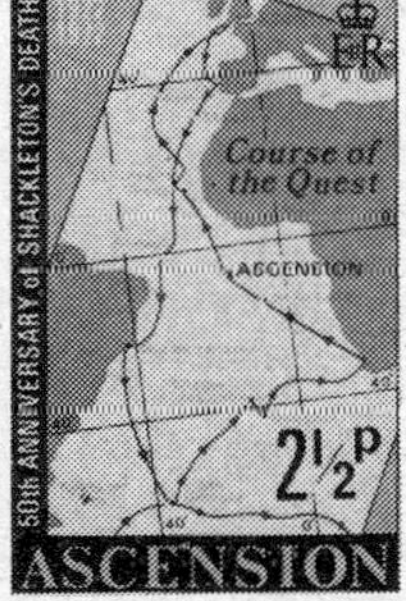

51. Course of the *Quest*.

(Des. J. E. Cooter. Litho. Questa.)

972 (2 Aug.). *50th Anniv. of Shackleton's Death. T* **51** *and similar multicoloured designs. W* w.**12** (*sideways on 4p., 7½p. and* **MS**163). *P* 14.
59 2½p. Type **51** 15 20
60 4p. Shackleton and *Quest* (*horiz.*) 30 35
61 7½p. Shackleton's cabin and *Quest* (*horiz.*) 40 45
62 11p. Shackleton's statue and memorial 60 70
MS163 139×114 mm. Nos. 159/62 1·60 1·75

52. Land Crab and Mako Shark.

(Des. (from photograph by D. Groves) and photo. Harrison.)

1972 (20 Nov.). *Royal Silver Wedding. Multicoloured; background colour given. W* w.**12.** *P* 14×14½.
164 **52** 2p. bright bluish violet .. 10 12
165 ,, 16p. rose-carmine .. 70 80

(Des. L. D. Curtis. Litho. J.W.)

1973 (28 May). *Royal Naval Crests* (*5th series*). *Multicoloured designs as T* **46.** *W* w.**12** (*sideways*). *P* 14.
166 2p. H.M.S. *Birmingham* .. 12 12
167 4p. H.M.S. *Cardiff* 25 25
168 9p. H.M.S. *Penzance* .. 45 50
169 13p. H.M.S. *Rochester* .. 60 65
MS170 109×152 mm. Nos. 166/9 1·40 1·50

53. Green Turtle.

(Des. V. Whiteley Studio. Litho. Enschedé.)

1973 (28 Aug.). *Turtles. T* **53** *and similar triangular designs. Multicoloured. W* w.**12.** *P* 13½.
171 4p. Type **53** 15 15
172 9p. Loggerhead turtle .. 40 40
173 12p. Hawksbill turtle 65 70

54. Sergeant, R.M. Light Infantry, 1900.

(Des. G. Drummond from paintings by C. Stadden. Litho. Walsall Security Printers Ltd.)

1973 (31 Oct.). *50th Anniv. of Departure of Royal Marines from Ascension. T* **54** *and similar vert. designs. Multicoloured. W* w.**12** (*sideways*). *P* 14.
174 2p. Type **54** 8 12
175 6p. R.M. Private, 1816 .. 20 25
176 12p. R.M. Light Infantry Officer, 1880 .. .. 40 45
177 20p. R.M. Artillery Colour Sergeant, 1910 .. .. 65 70

1973 (14 Nov.). *Royal Wedding. As Nos.* 165/6 *of Anguilla. Centre multicoloured. W* w.**12** (*sideways*). *P* 13½.
178 2p. ochre 5 8
179 18p. dull blue-green 55 65

55. Letter and H.Q., Berne.

(Des. PAD Studio. Litho. Questa.)

1974 (27 Mar.). *Centenary of U.P.U. T* **55** *and similar horiz. design. Multicoloured. W* w.**12.** *P* 14½×14.
180 2p. Type **55** 8 8
181 9p. Hermes and U.P.U. monument 35 40

56. Churchill as a Boy, and Birthplace, Blenheim Palace.

(Des. J.W. Ltd. Litho. Questa.)

1974 (30 Nov.). *Birth Centenary of Sir Winston Churchill. T* **56** *and similar horiz. design. Multicoloured. No wmk. P* 14.
182 5p. Type **56** 15 20
183 25p. Churchill as statesman, and U.N. Building .. 55 60
MS184 93×87 mm. Nos. 182/3 .. 75 80

57. "Skylab 3" and Photograph of Ascension.

(Des. PAD Studio. Litho. Questa.)

1975 (20 Mar.). *Space Satellites. T* **57** *and similar horiz. design. Multicoloured. W* w. **12** (*sideways*). *P* 14.
185 2p. Type **57** 5 5
186 18p. "Skylab 4" command module and photograph 45 50

The date "11.1.73" given on the 2p. is incorrect, "Skylab 3" was launched in July 1973 and returned to Earth in September 1973.

58. U.S.A.F. "Starlifter".

(Des. R. Granger Barrett. Litho. Questa.)

1975 (19 June). *Wideawake Airfield. T* **58** *and similar horiz. designs. Multicoloured. W* w. **12** *(sideways) P* 13½.

187 2p. Type **58** 5 5
188 5p. R.A.F. "Hercules" .. 12 15
189 9p. Vickers "VC-10" .. 25 25
190 24p. U.S.A.F. "Galaxy" .. 55 60
MS191 144×99 mm. Nos. 187/90 1·00

APOLLO-SOYUZ
LINK
1975
(59)

1975 (18 Aug.). "*Apollo-Soyuz*" *Space Link. Nos.* 141 *and* 145/6 *optd. with T* **59**.

192 4½p. Space rocket taking-off 25 25
193 12½p. Sputnik II and Space Dog, Laika 55 65
194 25p. Walking in Space .. 1·25 1·40

60. Arrival of Royal Navy, 1815.

(Des. J.W. Ltd. from paintings by Isobel McManus. Litho. Walsall Security Ptrs.)

1975 (22 Oct.). *160th Anniv. of Occupation. T* **60** *and similar horiz. designs. Multicoloured. W* w.**14** *(sideways). P* 14.

195 2p. Type **60** 5 5
196 5p. Water Supply, Dampiers Drip 12 15
197 9p. First landing, 1815 .. 25 25
198 15p. The garden on Green Mountain 35 40

61. Canary.

62. Boatswain Bird Island Sanctuary.

(Des. J.W. Ltd. Litho. Questa.)

1976 (26 Apr.). *Multicoloured designs as T* **61**. *W* w.**14** *(sideways on horiz. designs). P* 13½ *(£2) or* 14 *(others)*.

199 1p. Type **61** 5 5
200 2p. Fairy Tern 5 5
201 3p. Waxbill 5 5
202 4p. Black Noddy 8 8
203 5p. Brown Noddy 8 10
204 6p. Common Mynah 10 12
205 7p. Madeiran Storm Petrel .. 12 15
206 8p. Sooty Tern 15 15
207 9p. White Booby 15 20
208 10p. Red-footed Booby .. 20 20
209 15p. Red-throated Francolin 25 30
210 18p. Brown Booby 30 35
211 25p. Red-billed Bo'sun Bird .. 45 50
212 50p. Yellow-billed Bo'sun Bird 85 95
213 £1 Ascension Frigatebird 1·75 2·00
214 £2 Type **62** .. .. .. 3·50 4·00
199/214 .. .. *Set of* 16 7·50 8·50

The 2, 4, 7, 9, 15, 18p. and £1 are vertical designs.

63. G.B. Penny Red with Ascension Postmark.

(Des. C. Abbott. Litho. J.W.)

1976 (4 May). *Festival of Stamps, London. T* **63** *and similar designs. W* w.**14** *(sideways on 5p., 25p. and* **MS**218). *P* 13 (**MS**218) *or* 13½ *(Nos.* 215/17).

215 5p. rose-red, black and cinnamon 12 15
216 9p. grn., blk. & greenish stone 25 25
217 25p. multicoloured 60 65
MS218 133×121 mm. No. 217 with St. Helena 318 and Tristan da Cunha 206 .. .. .. 2·25

Designs: *Vert.*—9p. ½d. stamp of 1922. *Horiz.*—25p. Cargo vessel *Southampton Castle*.

MS218 is postally valid on each island to the value of 25p.

64. U.S. Base, Ascension.

(Des. V. Whiteley Studio. Litho. J.W.)

1976 (4 July). *Bicentenary of American Revolution. T* **64** *and similar horiz. designs. Multicoloured. W* w.**14** *(sideways). P* 13.

219 8p. Type **64** 20 25
220 9p. NASA Station at Devils Ashpit 25 25
221 25p. *Viking* landing on Mars .. 55 60

MINIMUM PRICE

The minimum price quoted is 5p which represents a handling charge rather than a basis for valuing common stamps. For further notes about prices see introductory pages.

AUSTRALIA.

USTRALIAN STATES. The following States
ombined to form the Commonwealth of Australia
nd their issues are listed in alphabetical order in
is Catalogue:—

NEW SOUTH WALES
QUEENSLAND
SOUTH AUSTRALIA
TASMANIA
VICTORIA
WESTERN AUSTRALIA

RINTERS. Except where otherwise stated, ll Commonwealth stamps have been printed nder Government authority at Melbourne. ntil 1918 there were two establishments (both f the Treasury Dept.)—the Note Printing ranch and the Stamp Printing Branch. The rmer printed T **3** and **4**.

In 1918 the Stamp Printing Branch was closed nd all stamps were printed by the Note Printing ranch. In 1926 control was transferred from e Treasury to the Commonwealth Bank of ustralia, and on 14 Jan. 1960 the branch was ttached to the newly established Reserve Bank f Australia.

Until 1942 stamps bore in the sheet margin e initials or names of successive managers and om 1942 to March 1952 the imprint "Printed y the Authority of the Government of the ommonwealth of Australia". Since November 952 (or Nos. D129/31 for Postage Dues) imprints ave been discontinued.

1

2

Die I.

Die II.

ie I. Break in inner frame line at lower left level with top of words of value.

ie II. Die repaired showing no break.

Die I was only used for the ½d., 1d., 2d. and d. Several plates were produced for each xcept the 3d. When the second plate of the d. was being prepared the damage became ggravated after making 105 out of the 120 units hen the die was returned for repair. This gave se to the *se-tenant* pairs showing the two states the die.

Die II was used until 1945 and deteriorated rogressively with damage to the frame lines nd rounding of the corners. Specialists recog- ise seven states of this die.

(Des. B. Young. Eng. S. Reading. Typo. J. B. Cooke.)

913 (Jan.–Apr.). *W* **2**. *Die II unless otherwise stated. P* 12.

No.	Type	Description	Unused	Used
	1	½d. green (Die I)	3·00	25
	,,	1d. red (Die I)	3·00	20
		a. Wmk. sideways	£200	65·00
		b. Carmine	3·00	20
		c. Die II. *Red*	3·00	20
		ca. Wmk. sideways	£200	65·00
		cb. Carmine	3·00	20
3	**1**	2d. grey (Die I)	7·00	1·00
4	,,	2½d. indigo	11·00	4·50
5	,,	3d. olive (Die I)	12·00	2·50
		a. Imperf. three sides (pair)	£6000	
		b. Yellow-olive	14·00	2·50
		c. *Olive* (Die II)	55·00	25·00
		ca. In pair with Die I	90·00	50·00
		d. *Yellow-olive* (Die II)	55·00	25·00
		da. In pair with Die I	90·00	50·00
6	,,	4d. orange (12 Feb.)	35·00	20·00
		a. Orange-yellow	80·00	40·00
8	,,	5d. chestnut	30·00	20·00
9	,,	6d. ultramarine	15·00	4·00
		a. Retouched "E"	£1000	£350
10	,,	9d. violet	20·00	4·00
11	,,	1s. emerald	20·00	4·25
		a. Blue-green	20·00	3·50
12	,,	2s. brown	80·00	22·00
13	,,	5s. grey & yellow (20 Mar.)	£175	80·00
14	,,	10s. grey and pink (20 Mar.)	£300	£175
15	,,	£1 brown and blue (20 Mar.)	£1000	£750
16	,,	£2 black and rose (8 April)	£2000	£1000
1/16		*Set of* 15	£3500	£2000
14/16		Optd. "Specimen" *Set of* 3	£400	

No. 9*a* shows a badly distorted second "E" in "PENCE", which is unmistakable. It occurs on the last stamp in the sheet.

See also Nos. 20/27 (*W* **5**), 35/45*b* (*W* **6**), 73/5 (*W* **6**, new colours), 107/14 (*W* **7**), 132/8 (*W* **15**), 212 (2s. re-engraved).

INVERTED WATERMARKS are met with in some values in this and subsequent issues.

3

4. Kookaburra.

(Des. R. A. Harrison. Eng. and recess. T. S. Harrison.)

1913 (8 Dec.)–14. *No wmk. P* 11.

No.	Type	Description	Unused	Used
17	**3**	1d. red	3·00	2·50
		a. Pale rose-red	3·00	2·50
		b. Imperf. horiz. (vert. pair)	£600	
19	**4**	6d. claret (26.8.14)	50·00	35·00

All printings from Plate 1 of the 1d. were in the shade of No. 17*a*. This plate shows many retouches.

5

(Typo. J. B. Cooke.)

1915. *W* **5**. *P* 12.

No.	Type	Description	Unused	Used
20	**1**	2d. grey (Die I) (2 Jan.)	18·00	3·00
21	,,	2½d. indigo (July)	22·00	6·00
23	,,	6d. ultramarine (Apr.)	50·00	6·00
		a. Bright blue	£100	30·00
24	,,	9d. violet (9 July)	90·00	8·00
25	,,	1s. blue-green (Aug.)	90·00	7·50
26	,,	2s. brown (Apr.)	£200	40·00
27	,,	5s. grey & yellow (12 Feb.)	£300	£110
		a. Yellow portion doubly printed	£1500	£500
20/27		*Set of* 7	£700	£160

The watermark in this issue is often misplaced as the paper was made for the portrait stamps.

5*a*

Die II.

Die III.

Die II. The flaw distinguishing the so-called Die II is now known to be due to a defective roller-die and occurs in 18 impressions on one of the plates. It appears as a white upward projection to right of the base of figure "**1**" in the shield containing value at left, as shown in the illustration.

Die III. In 1918 a printing (in sheets of 120) was made on paper prepared for printing War Savings Stamps, with wmk. T **5**. A special plate was made for this printing, differing in detail from those previously used. The shading round the head is even; the solid background of the words "ONE PENNY" is bounded at each end by a *white* vertical line; and there is a horizontal white line cutting the vertical shading lines at left on the King's neck. *See* No. 50*c*.

(Dies eng. Perkins Bacon & Co. Typo. J. B. Cooke until 1918, then T. S. Harrison.)

1914–21. *W* **5**. *P* 14.

No.	Type	Description	Unused	Used
29	**5a**	½d. bright green (22.2.15)	1·25	15
		a. Green (13.5.16)	1·25	15
		b. Yellow-green (8.16)	1·75	1·25
		c. Thin "1" in fraction at right	£1000	£550
30	,,	1d. carmine-red (*shades*) (I) (17.7.14)	5·00	20
		a. Rusted cliché (2 vars.)	£1500	£500
		b. Substituted cliché	£400	35·00
		c. Pale carmine (*shades*)	10·00	10
		d. Carmine-pink (1.18)	50·00	3·00
		e. Rose-red (3.18)	7·00	1·75
		f. Carmine (*aniline*) (1921)	8·00	1·75
31	,,	1d. carmine-red (*shades*) (II) (1918)	£150	10·00
		a. Substituted cliché	£600	50·00
		b. Pale red (*shades*)	£125	10·00

32 **5a** 4d. orange (6.1.15) .. .. 15·00 1·50
a. Yellow-orange .. .. 15·00 1·50
b. Pale orange-yellow (10.15) .. 40·00 10·00
c. Lemon-yellow (1916) .. £125 20·00
d. Dull orange .. .. 28·00 1·50
e. Line through "FOUR PENCE" (*all shades*) *From* £250 50·00
34 ,, 5d. brown (22.2.15) .. 12·00 1·75
a. Yellow-brown (1920) .. 12·00 1·75

The variety No. 29*c* was caused by the engraving of a new fraction in a defective electro.

*The two varieties listed under No. 30a were caused by rusting of the steel plate and show as white patches on the design on the back of King's neck and in and beside top of right frame (upper left pane, No. 34); and in left frame, wattles and head and ears of kangaroo (upper left pane, No. 35). These were noticed in late 1916 when the damaged impressions were removed and replaced by a pair of copper electros (Die II for No. 34 and Die I for No. 35), showing rounded corners and some frame damage, the former also showing a white spot under tail of emu. In time the tops of the crown quickly wore away. These substituted clichés (Nos. 30b and 31a) were formerly described as "Top of crown missing".

The 5d. is known printed on the gummed side of the paper.

Two machines were used for the 14 perforation, one an old single line, converted to that gauge, the other a new comb-machine. The former was used mainly for early printings of the 1d. and 5d. and very rarely for later printings of the ½d. and 1d.

See also Nos. 47/50*b* (*W* **5**, rough paper), 51/5*a* (*W* **6***a*), 56/66*b* and 76/84 (*W* **5**, new colours), 85/104 (*W* **7**), 124/31 (*W* **15**).

6

6*a*

Nos. 38ba and 73a (R. 1/6, lower plate).

(Typo. J. B. Cooke (to May 1918), T. S. Harrison (to Feb. 1926), A. J. Mullett (to Jan. 1927) and thereafter J. Ash.)

1915–28. *W* **6** (*narrow Crown*). *P* 12.

35 **1** 2d. grey (Die I) (11.15) .. 6·00 75
a. In pair with Die II ('17)* .. 45·00 15·00
b. Die II (1918) .. .. 11·00 1·25
c. Silver-grey (shiny paper) (Die I) (2.18) .. .. 5·00 1·00
ca. Do. Die II (6.18) .. .. 11·00 1·50
36 ,, 2½d. deep blue .. .. 7·00 1·50
a. Deep indigo (1920) .. 8·00 2·00
ab. "1" of fraction omitted .. £2500 £1100
37 ,, 3d. yellow-olive (I) (12.10.15) 5·00 75
a. Olive-green (1917) .. .. 5·00 75
b. Yellow-olive (Die II) .. 45·00 12·00
ba. In pair with Die I.. .. £120 45·00
c. Olive-green (Die II) .. 45·00 12·00
ca. In pair with Die I .. £120 45·00
d. Light olive (Die II) ('23)† .. 6·00 1·25
38 ,, 6d. ultramarine (15.12.15) .. 12·00 75
a. Dull blue .. .. .. 30·00 2·50
b. Bright ultram. (23.7.21) .. 12·00 75
ba. Leg of kangaroo broken .. £1250 £300

39 **1** 9d. violet (29.7.16) .. .. 10·00 1·00
a. Bright violet .. .. 10·00 1·00
40 ,, 1s. blue-green (6.16) .. 11·00 75
a. Wmk. sideways (1927) .. 35·00 22·00
41 ,, 2s. brown (6.16) .. .. 70·00 12·00
a. Imperf. three sides (pair) .. £5500
b. Red-brown .. .. 70·00 12·00
42 ,, 5s. grey and yellow (4.18) .. £110 30·00
a. Grey and orange (1920) .. £110 30·00
b. Grey and deep yellow .. £110 30·00
ba. Wmk. sideways £700 £700
c. Grey & pale yellow (1928) .. £110 30·00
43 ,, 10s. grey and pink (5.2.17) .. £300 80·00
a. Grey & bright aniline pink £300 80·00
ab. Wmk. sideways £1200 £1000
b. Grey and pale aniline pink (1928) .. .. .. £300 80·00
44 ,, £1 choc. and dull blue (7.16) £700 £300
a. Chestnut & bright blue ('17) £700 £300
b. Bistre-brown and bright blue £700 £300
ba. Wmk. sideways £2000 £1000
45 ,, £2 black and rose (12.19) £1250 £800
a. Grey and crimson (1920) .. £1250 £800
b. Purple-black & pale rose ('24) £1100 £800
35/45*b* .. .. *Set of* 11 £2250 £1200
43/45 Optd. "Specimen" *Set of* 3 £450

*The Die II of No. 35a is a substituted cliché introduced to replace a cracked plate which occurred on No. 55 of the upper left pane (Row 10, No. 1) and this can only be distinguished from the later Die II printings when in pair with Die I.

†No. 37*d* is from new plates entirely from Die II in one of its later stages. It shows a small break in the upper frame over "ST".

All values were printed by both Cooke and Harrison, and the 9d., 1s. and 5s. were also printed by Mullett and Ash.

1916–18. *W* **5.** *Rough paper, locally gummed. P* 14.

47 **5a** 1d. scarlet (I) (14.12.16) .. 9·00 25
48 ,, 1d. deep red (I) (1917) .. 9·00 15
49 ,, 1d. rose-red (I) (1918) .. 18·00 40
a. Substituted cliché .. £300 28·00
49*b* ,, 1d. rosine (I) (1918) .. 30·00 2·50
c. Substituted cliché .. £350 40·00
50 ,, 1d. rose-red (II) (1918) .. £100 10·00
aa. Substituted cliché .. £500 35·00
50*a* ,, 1d. rosine (II) (1918) .. £250 15·00
ab. Substituted cliché .. £700 £100

For explanations of substituted cliché varieties, see 2nd paragraph of note below No. 34*a*.

For illustrations and descriptions of Dies II and III, see after T **5a**.

We no longer list the 5d. bright chestnut perforated "O.S." as we have no evidence of postal use other than on official mail.

1918 (June). *Printed from a new plate* (Die III) *on white unsurfaced paper, locally gummed. W* **5.** *P* 14.

50*c* **5a** 1d. rose-red (III).. . 30·00 10·00
50*d* ,, 1d. rose-carmine (III) . 30·00 10·00

(Typo. J. B. Cooke or T. S. Harrison.)

1918–20. *W* **6a** (*Mult.*). *P* 14.

51 **5a** ½d. green (*shades*) (8.1.18) 60 30
a. "1" in fraction at right thinner.. .. .. 60·00 35·00
52 ,, 1d. carmine-pink (I) (23.1.18) .. .. 75·00 12·00
a. Deep red (I) (1918) .. £280 75·00
53 ,, 1d. carmine (I) (10.12.19) 18·00 1·75
a. Deep red (aniline) (I) (1920) 30·00 10·00
54 ,, 1½d. black-brown (30.1.19) 80 10
a. Very thin paper (3.19) .. 10·00 10·00
55 ,, 1½d. red-brown (4.19) .. 1·75 25
a. Chocolate .. .. 1·75 25

No. 51 was printed by Cooke and Harrison, Nos. 52/*a* by Cooke only and Nos. 53/55*a* by Harrison only. Nos. 52/*a* have rather yellowish gum, that of No. 53 being pure white.

(Typo. T. S. Harrison and also A. J. Mullet for 1s. 4d. from March 1926.)

1918–23. *W* **5.** *P* 14.

56 **5a** ½d. orange (9.11.23) .. 60 1
57 ,, 1d. violet (*shades*) (13.2.22) 1·50 5
a. Imperf. three sides (pair) .. £3500
b. Red-violet .. .. 1·50 5
58 ,, 1½d. black-brown (9.11.18) 1·00 2
59 ,, 1½d. deep red-brown (6.19) 1·75 1
a. Chocolate .. .. 1·75 1
60 ,, 1½d. brt. red-brn. (20.1.22) 3·00 4
61 ,, 1½d. green (7.3.23) .. .. 1·75 1
a. Rough unsurfaced paper .. 50·00 40·0
62 ,, 2d. dull orange (5.10.20) .. 3·00 1
a. Brown-orange .. .. 3·00 1
63 ,, 2d. brt. rose-scar. (17.2.22) 1·75 1
a. Dull rose-scarlet .. .. 1·75 1
64 ,, 4d. violet (21.6.21).. .. 10·00 4·0
a. Line through "FOUR PENCE" £3000 £200
b. "FOUR PENCE" in thinner letters £300 £12
65 ,, 4d. ultramarine (*shades*) (23.3.22) .. .. 25·00 4·0
a. "FOUR PENCE" in thinner letters .. .. £300 85·0
b. Pale milky blue .. .. 28·00 5·0
66 ,, 1s. 4d. pale blue (2.12.20) 55·00 10·0
a. Dull greenish blue ('23) .. 55·00 10·0
b. Deep turquoise .. .. £300 60·0
56/66 .. .. *Set of* 11 80·00 18·0

The 4d. ultramarine was originally printed b Cooke but the plates were worn in mid-1923 an Harrison prepared a new pair of plates. Stam from these plates can only be distinguished b the minor flaws which are peculiar to them.

The variety of Nos. 64 and 65 with "FOU PENCE" thinner, was caused by the correctio of a defective cliché (No. 6, 2nd row, right-han pane), which showed a line running throug these words.

No. 61a was printed on a small residue paper which had been employed for Nos. 47–50

(Typo. T. S. Harrison (to Feb. 1926), A. Mullett (to June 1927), thereafter J. Ash.)

1923–24. *W* **6.** *P* 12.

73 **1** 6d. chestnut (6.12.23) .. 5·00 1·5
a. Leg of kangaroo broken .. 90·00 45·0
74 ,, 2s. maroon (1.5.24) .. .. 16·00 5·0
75 ,, £1 grey (1.5.24) (Optd. S. £60) £275 £1

The 6d. and 2s. were printed by all thr printers, but the £1 only by Harrison.

(Typo. T. S. Harrison (to Feb. 1926), thereaft A. J. Mullett.)

1924. *P* 14.

(*a*) *W* **5** (1 May).

76 **5a** 1d. sage-green 75 1
77 ,, 1½d. scarlet (*shades*).. .. 40 1
a. Very thin paper .. .. 15·00 9·0
b. "HALEPENCE" .. .. 15·00 9·0
c. "RAL" of "AUSTRALIA" thin .. .. .. 15·00 9·0
d. Curved "1" and thin fraction at left .. .. 12·00 9·0
78 ,, 2d. red-brown .. .. 5·00 1·5
a. Bright red-brown .. .. 10·00 1·7
79 ,, 3d. dull ultramarine .. 6·00 4
a. Imperf. three sides (pair) .. £3000
80 ,, 4d. olive-yellow .. .. 6·00 1·0
a. Olive-green .. .. 6·00 1·0
81 ,, 4½d. violet .. .. 6·00 2·0

(*b*) *W* **6a**.

82 **5a** 1d. sage-green (20 May) .. 1·25 7

(*c*) *No wmk.*

83 **5a** 1d. sage-green (18 Aug.) .. 1·85 1·2
84 ,, 1½d. scarlet (14 Aug.) .. 1·75 1·2
76/84 .. .. *Set of* 9 25·00 6·0

Nos. 78/a and 82/4 were printed by Harriso only but the remainder were printed by bot Harrison and Mullett.

In the thin semi-transparent paper of Nos. 54 and 77a the watermark is almost indistinguish able. Nos. 77b, 77c and 77d are typical example of retouching of which there are many others i these issues. In No. 77c the letters "RAL" diff markedly from the normal. There is a whit stroke cutting the oval frame-line above th "L", and the right-hand outer line of the Crow does not cut the white frame-line above th "A". No. 77b is above No. 77c in the shee so that the varieties may be had *se-tenant*.

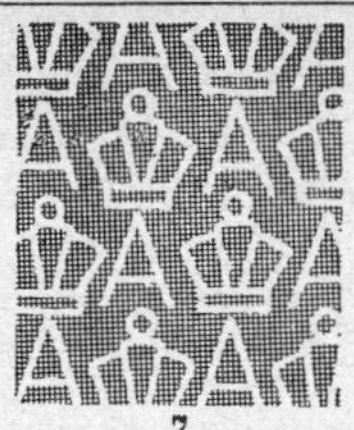

7

I.

II.

New Dies

1d. For differences see note after No. 34*a*.

1½d. From new steel plates made from a new die. Nos. 88 and 98 are the Ash printings, the ink of which is shiny.

2d. Die I. Height of frame 25.6 mm. Die II. Height 25.1 mm.; lettering and figures of value less bold than Die. I.

3d. Die II has bolder letters and figures than Die I, as illustrated above.

5d. Die II has a bolder figure " 5 " with flat top compared with Die I of the earlier issues.

(Typo. by A. J. Mullett or J. Ash.)

1926–30. *W* **7.** (*a*) *P* 14.

85	**5*a***	½d. orange (10.3.27) ..	75	50
86	,,	1d. sage-green (23.10.26)	95	10
87	,,	1½d. scarlet (5.11.26) ..	1·25	10
88	,,	1½d. golden scarlet ('27) ..	2·00	50
89	,,	2d. red-brown (17.8.27) ..	7·00	3·50
90	,,	3d. dull ultram. (12.26) ..	7·00	1·00
91	,,	4d. yellow-olive (17.1.28)	9·00	4·00
92	,,	4½d. violet (26.10.27) ..	5·00	2·00
93	,,	1s. 4d. pale greenish blue (6.9.27)	£125	50·00
85/93		.. .. *Set of* 8	£130	55·00

(*b*) *P* 13½ × 12½.

94	**5*a***	½d. orange (21.11.28) ..	40	20
95	,,	1d. sage-green (Die I) (23.12.26)	40	15
96	,,	1d. sage-green (Die II) ..	30·00	30·00
97	,,	1½d. scarlet (14.1.27) ..	1·00	10
98	,,	1½d. golden scarlet ..	1·00	10
98*a*	,,	1½d. red-brown (16.9.30) ..	1·25	60
99	,,	2d. red-brown (28.4.28) ..	2·25	1·25
99*a*	,,	2d. golden scarlet (Die I) (2.8.30)	1·75	30
99*b*	,,	2d. golden scarlet (Die II) (9.9.30)	1·75	5
		c. No wmk.	£600	£600
		d. Tête-bêche (pair) ..	£10000	
100	,,	3d. dull ultramarine (Die I) (23.2.28)	5·00	75
101	,,	3d. deep ultram. (Die II) (28.9.29)	3·25	30
102	,,	4d. yellow-olive (4.29) ..	5·00	45
103	,,	4½d. violet (Die II) (11.28)	12·00	3·00
103*a*	,,	5d. orange-brown (2.8.30)	6·00	75
104	,,	1s. 4d. turquoise (30.9.28)	40·00	6·00
94/104		.. .. *Set of* 11	60·00	10·00

Owing to defective manufacture, part of a sheet of the 2d. (Die II) escaped unwatermarked; while the watermark in other parts of the same sheet was faint or normal.

Only one example of No. 99d is known.

8. Parliament House, Canberra.

(Des. A. Harrison. R. Die eng. by Waterlow & Sons. Plates and printing by A. J. Mullett.)

1927 (9 May). *Opening of Parliament House, Canberra. No wmk. P* 11.

105	**8**	1½d. brownish lake	30	15
		a. Imp. betwn. (pair) ..	£1200	£750

(Eng. and recess. J. Ash.)

1928 (29 Oct.). *Melbourne Philatelic Exhibition. As T* **4.** *No wmk. P* 11.

106		3d. blue	2·50	1·50
		a. Imperf. (sheet of four) ..	£4500	

Special sheets of 60 stamps divided into 15 blocks of 4 (5 × 3) and separated by wide gutters perforated down the middle, were printed and sold at the Exhibition. Block of 4, *unused*, £75.

(Typo. J. Ash.)

1929–30. *W* **7.** *P* 12.

107	**1**	6d. chestnut	8·00	1·00
108	,,	9d. violet	10·00	1·00
109	,,	1s. blue-green	10·00	1·00
110	,,	2s. maroon	20·00	3·00
111	,,	5s. grey and yellow ..	£150	40·00
112	,,	10s. grey and pink ..	£225	£110
114	,,	£2 black and rose ('30)	£1000	£175
107/114		.. .. *Set of* 7	£1300	£300
112/114		Optd. "Specimen" *Set of* 2	£150	

9. De Havilland Biplane and Pastoral Scene.

(Des. R. A. Harrison and H. Herbert. Eng. A. Taylor. Recess. J. Ash.)

1929 (20 May). *Air. No wmk. P* 11.

115	**9**	3d. green (*shades*)	3·50	3·50

10

(Des. Pitt Morrison. Recess. J. Ash.)

1929 (28 Sept.). *Centenary of Western Australia. No wmk. P* 11.

116	**10**	1½d. dull scarlet	30	20
		a. Re-entry ("T" of "AUSTRALIA" clearly double)	35·00	25·00

11. Capt. Chas. Sturt.

TWO

PENCE

(12)

(Des. R. A. Harrison. Eng. F. D. Manley. Recess. J. Ash.)

1930 (2 June). *Centenary of Exploration of River Murray by Capt. Sturt. No wmk. P* 11.

117	**11**	1½d. scarlet	25	10
118	,,	3d. blue	2·25	2·00

No. 117 with manuscript surcharge " 2d. paid P M L H I " was issued by the Postmaster of Lord Howe Island during a shortage of 2d. stamps. A few copies of the 1½d. value No. 98 were also endorsed. These provisionals are not recognized by the Australian postal authorities. (*Price £175 un. or us., either stamp.*)

1930 (1 Aug.). *T* **5*a*** *surch. as T* **12.** *W* **7.** *P* 13½ × 12½.

119	2d. on 1½d. golden scarlet ..	50	10
120	5d. on 4½d. violet ..	2·50	2·00

No. 120 is from a redrawn die in which the words " FOURPENCE HALFPENNY " are noticeably thicker than in the original die and the figure " 4 " has square instead of tapering serifs.

Stamps from the redrawn die without the surcharge were printed, but not issued thus. A few stamps, *cancelled to order*, were included in sets supplied by the post office. A few mint copies, which escaped the cancellation, were found and some may have been used postally. The stamps cannot, however, be classed as officially issued.

13. The " Southern Cross " above hemispheres.

(Recess-printed by John Ash.)

1931 (19 Mar.). *Kingsford Smith's flights. No wmk. P* 11. (*a*) *Postage.*

121	**13**	2d. rose-red	25	10
122	,,	3d. blue	2·75	2·00

(*b*) *Air. Inscr.* " AIR MAIL SERVICE ".

123	**13**	6d. violet	8·00	5·00
		a. Re-entry ("FO" and "LD" double) ..	35·00	35·00

15

17. Lyre-bird.

(Typo. John Ash.)

1931–36. *W* **15.**

(*a*) *P* 13½ × 12½.

124	**5*a***	½d. orange	1·00	40
125	,,	1d. green (Die I)	30	10
126	,,	1½d. red-brown ('36) ..	3·00	1·50
127	,,	2d. golden scar. (Die II) ..	40	10
128	,,	3d. ultramarine (Die II) ..	4·25	30
129	,,	4d. yellow-olive	7·50	40
130	,,	5d. orange-brown (Die II)	3·00	35
131	,,	1s. 4d. turquoise	35·00	4·50
124/131		.. .. *Set of* 8	45·00	5·50

(*b*) *P* 12.

132	**1**	6d. chestnut	6·00	2·00
133	,,	9d. violet	5·50	60
134	,,	2s. maroon ('35)	3·00	60
135	,,	5s. grey and yellow ..	80·00	18·00
136	,,	10s. grey and pink	£200	50·00
137	,,	£1 grey ('35)	£225	£100
138	,,	£2 black and rose ('34)	£1100	£160
132/138		.. .. *Set of* 7	£1500	£300
136/138		Optd. " Specimen " *Set of* 3	90·00	

Stamps as No. 127, without wmk. and perf. 11 are forgeries made in 1932 to defraud the P.O.

For re-engraved type of No. 134, see No. 212.

(Recess. John Ash.)

1931 (4 Nov.). *Air Stamp. As T* **13** *but inscr.* " AIR MAIL SERVICE " *in bottom tablet. No wmk. P* 11.

139	6d. sepia	11·00	9·00

1931 (17 Nov.). *Air. No.* 139 *optd. with Type* O **1.**

139*a*	6d. sepia	28·00	25·00

This stamp was not restricted to official use but was on general sale to the public.

(Des. F. D. Manley. Recess. John Ash.)

1932 (15 Feb.). *No wmk. P* 11.

140	**17**	1s. green	35·00	1·00
140*a*	,,	1s. yellow-green	45·00	1·00

18. Sydney Harbour Bridge.

(Des. R. A. Harrison. Eng. F. D. Manley. Printed John Ash.)

1932 (14 MAR.). (a) *Recess. No wmk.* P 11.

141 **18** 2d. scarlet 75 40
142 ,, 3d. blue .. .. .. 5·00 3·00
143 ,, 5s. blue-green £400 £225

(b) *Typo.* W **15.** P 10½.

144 **18** 2d. scarlet 75 40

Stamps as No. 144 without wmk., and perf. 11 are forgeries made in 1932 to defraud the P.O.

19. Kookaburra.

(Typo. John Ash.)

1932 (1 JUNE). W **15.** P 13½ × 12½.

146 **19** 6d. red-brown .. .. 10·00 30

20. Melbourne and R. Yarra.

(Recess. John Ash.)

1934 (2 JULY). *Centenary of Victoria.* W **15.**

			I. P 10½.		II. P 11½.	
147	**20**	2d. orge.-verm.	45	25	55	20
148	,,	3d. blue	2·50	2·00	2·50	2·00
149	,,	1s. black	30·00	12·00	30·00	12·00

21. Merino Sheep.

(Recess. John Ash.)

1934 (1 NOV.). *Capt. Macarthur Centenary.* W **15.** P 11½.

150 **21** 2d. carmine-red (A) .. 90 30
150*a* ,, 2d. carmine-red (B) .. 20·00 2·00
151 ,, 3d. blue .. .. .. 6·00 3·00
152 ,, 9d. bright purple .. 28·00 12·00

Type A of the 2d. shows shading on the hill in the background varying from light to dark (as illustrated). Type B has the shading almost uniformly dark.

22. Hermes.

(Recess. John Ash.)

1934–48. (a) *No wmk.* P 11.

153 **22** 1s. 6d. dull pur. (1.12.34) .. 22·00 3·00

(Recess. John Ash or W. C. G. McCracken.)

(b) W **15.** P 13½ × 14.

153*a* **22** 1s. 6d. dull pur. (22.10.37) 3·75 50
b. Thin rough paper ('48) .. 2·50 50

23. Cenotaph, Whitehall.

24. King George V on "Anzac".

(Recess. John Ash.)

1935 (18 MAR.). *20th Anniv. of Gallipoli Landing.* W **15.** P 13½ × 12½ *or* 11 (1s.).

154 **23** 2d. scarlet 20 5
155 ,, 1s. black (*chalk-surfaced*) .. 30·00 20·00

(Recess. John Ash.)

1935 (2 MAY.) *Silver Jubilee. Chalk-surfaced paper.* W **15** *sideways.* P 11½.

156 **24** 2d. scarlet 25 10
157 ,, 3d. blue .. .. .. 2·50 2·00
158 ,, 2s. bright violet .. .. 28·00 18·00

25. Amphitrite and Telephone Cable.

(Recess. John Ash.)

1936 (1 APR.). *Opening of Submarine Telephone to Tasmania.* W **15.** P 11½.

159 **25** 2d. scarlet 20 5
160 ,, 3d. blue .. .. .. 2·50 1·75

26. Site of Adelaide, 1836; Old Gum Tree, Glenelg; King William St., Adelaide.

(Recess. John Ash.)

1936 (3 AUG.). *Centenary of South Australia.* W **15.** P 11½.

161 **26** 2d. carmine 20 5
162 ,, 3d. blue .. .. .. 3·00 2·50
163 ,, 1s. green .. .. .. 15·00 10·00

27. Kangaroo.

28. Queen Elizabeth.

29. King George VI. **30.**

31

32. Koala.

Die I Die Ia Die II

33. Merino Ram. **34.** Kookaburra.

35. Platypus. **36.** Lyre bird.

38. Queen Elizabeth.

39. King George VI.

40. King George VI and Queen Elizabeth.

40*a*. (Background evenly shaded.) **40*b*.**

(Des. R. A. Harrison (T **28/30**), F. D. Manly (T **32**, **34/6**). All recess. With John Ash, W. C. G. McCracken or "By Authority . . ." imprints.)

1937–49. *W* **15** (*sideways on* 5*d.*, 9*d.*, 5*s.* and 10*s.*).

(*a*) *P* 13½ × 14 (*vert. designs*) *or* 14 × 13½ (*horiz.*).

164 **27** ½d. orange (3.10.38) .. 15 5
165 **28** 1d. emerald-grn. (10.5.37) 12 5
166 **29** 1½d. maroon (20.4.38) .. 1·00 20
167 **30** 2d. scarlet (10.5.37) .. 15 5
167*a* **31** 3d. blue (Die I, 1st ptg.) (2.8.37) .. .. 50·00 20·00
168 „ 3d. blue (Die I) (2.8.37).. 10·00 2·00
168*a* „ 3d. blue (Die Ia) (1937).. 18·00 1·75
168*b* „ 3d. blue (Die II) ('38) .. 10·00 75
169 „ 3d. bright blue, *thin paper* (Die II) (21.12.38) .. 10·00 60
170 **32** 4d. green (1.2.38) .. 1·25 5
171 **33** 5d. purple (1.12.38) .. 80 10
172 **34** 6d. purple-brown (2.8.37) 1·50 10
173 **35** 9d. chocolate (1.9.38) .. 1·75 15
174 **36** 1s. grey-green (2.8.37) .. 8·00 25
175 **31** 1s. 4d. deep mag. (3.10.38) 1·25 50
a. Pale magenta .. .. 1·00 40

(*b*) *P* 13½.

176 **38** 5s. claret (1.4.38) .. 8·00 2·00
a. Thin rough paper (4.2.48) 8·00 2·50
177 **39** 10s. dull purple (1.4.38) (Optd. S. £8) .. .. 25·00 12·00
a. Thin rough paper (11.48).. 30·00 25·00
178 **40** £1 blue-slate (1.11.38) (Optd. S. £300) .. .. 75·00 38·00
a. Thin rough paper (4.4.49) £125 75·00
164/178 .. .. *Set of* 14 £125 50·00

(*c*) *P* 15 × 14 (*vert. designs*) *or* 14 × 15 (*horiz.*).

179 **27** ½d. orange (28.1.42) .. 8 5
a. Coil pair .. .. 6·00 6·00
180 **40a** 1d. emerald-green (1.8.38) 12 5
181 „ 1d. maroon (10.12.41) .. 12 5
a. Coil pair .. .. 6·00 6·00
182 **29** 1½d. maroon (21.11.41) .. 1·00 75
183 „ 1½d. emerald-grn. (10.12.41) 15 5
184 **40b** 2d. scarlet (11.7.38) .. 20 5
a. Coil pair.. .. .. £175
185 „ 2d. bright pur. (10.12.41) 12 5
a. Coil pair .. .. 8·00 8·00
186 **31** 3d. bright blue (–.11.40).. 8·00 30
187 „ 3d. pur.-brown (10.1.42) 12 5
188 **32** 4d. green (–.10.42) .. 15 5
188*a* **33** 5d. purple (–.5.46) .. 30 15
189 **34** 6d. red-brown (–.6.42) .. 50 5
a. Purple-brown ('44) .. 30 5
190 **35** 9d. chocolate (1943) .. 25 5
191 **36** 1s. grey-green (–.3.41) .. 35 5
179/191 .. *Set of* 14 7·50 1·50

For unwmkd. issue, see Nos. 228/30*d*.

SPECIAL COIL PERFORATION

This special perforation of large and small holes on the narrow sides of the stamps is intended for stamps issued in coils, to facilitate separation. When they exist we list them as "Coil pairs".

The following with "special coil" perforation were placed on sale in *sheets*: Nos. 222*a* (1952), 228, 230, 237, 262 (1953), 309, 311 and 314. These are listed as "Coil blocks of four".

Dies of the 3d. In Die I the letters "TA" of "POSTAGE" at right are joined by a white flaw; the outline of the chin consists of separate strokes.

Die Ia is similar, but "T" and "A" have been clearly separated by retouches made on the plate.

In Die II "T" and "A" are separate and a continuous line has been added to the chin. The outline of the cheek extends to about 1 mm. above the lobe of the King's right ear.

No. 167*a* is a preliminary printing made with unsuitable ink and may be detected by the absence of finer details; the King's face appears whitish and the wattles are blank. The greater part of this printing was distributed to the Press with advance notices of the issue.

No. 186 is re-engraved and differs from Nos. 167*a* to 169 in the King's left eyebrow which is shaded downwards from left to right instead of from right to left.

Thin paper. Nos. 176a, 177a, 178a. In these varieties the watermark is more clearly visible on the back and the design is much less sharp. Early printings of No. 176a have tinted paper.

41. Governor Phillip at Sydney Cove.

(Recess. J. Ash.)

1937 (1 Oct.). *150th Anniv. of Foundation of New South Wales. W* **15**. *P* 13½ × 14.

193 **41** 2d. scarlet 20 5
194 „ 3d. bright blue .. .. 2·50 2·00
195 „ 9d. purple .. .. .. 12·00 6·00

42. A.I.F. and Nurse.

(**43**)

(**44**)

5½d

(**45**)

(Design from drawing by Virgil Reilly. Recess. W. C. G. McCracken.)

1940 (15 July). *Australian Imperial Forces. W* **15** *sideways. P* 14 × 13½.

196 **42** 1d. green 25 5
197 „ 2d. scarlet 25 5
198 „ 3d. blue .. .. .. 2·50 1·75
199 „ 6d. brown-purple .. .. 12·00 6·00

1941 (10 Dec.). *Nos.* 184, 186 *and* 171 *surch. with T* **43/5**.

200 **40b** 2½d. on 2d. (V.) 15 5
201 **31** 3½d. on 3d. (Y. on Bk.).. 40 25
202 **33** 5½d. on 5d. (V.) .. .. 2·00 1·75

46. Queen Elizabeth. **46a.**

47. King George VI.

48. King George VI.

49. King George VI.

50. Emu.

1942–44. *Recess. W* **15**. *P* 15 × 14.

203 **46** 1d. brn.-purple (1.1.43) 8 5
a. Coil pair .. .. 6·00 6·00
204 **46a** 1½d. green (1.12.42) .. 8 5
204*a* **47** 2d. bright pur. (4.12.44) 8 5
b. Coil pair .. .. 25·00 25·00
205 **48** 2½d. scarlet ('42) .. 8 5
a. Imperf. (pair),* .. £550
206 **49** 3½d. bright blue ('42) .. 10 5
a. Deep blue 35 8
207 **50** 5½d. slate-blue ('42) .. 20 5
203/207 .. .. *Set of* 6 25 10

For stamps as Nos. 204/*a* but without watermark see Nos. 229/30.

*No. 205*a* is in pair with stamp which only has the right-hand side imperf.

52. Duke and Duchess of Gloucester.

1945 (19 Feb.). *Arrival of Duke and Duchess of Gloucester in Australia. Recess. W* **15**. *P* 14½.

209 **52** 2½d. lake 8 5
210 „ 3½d. ultramarine 20 12
211 „ 5½d. indigo.. .. .. 25 12

A.

B.

1946 (3 Jan.). *Kangaroo type, as No.* 134, *but re-engraved as* B. *W* **15**. *P* 12.

212 **1** 2s. maroon.. .. .. 2·75 60

No. 134 has two background lines between the value circle and "TWO SHILLINGS"; No. 212 has only one line in this position. There are also differences in the shape of the letters.

53.

54. Flag and dove. (*Horiz.*)
55. Angel. (*Vert.*)

1946 (18 Feb.). *Victory Commemoration Symbolic designs inscr.* "PEACE 1945". *Recess W* **15** (*sideways on* 5½*d.*). *P* 14½.

213 **53** 2½d. scarlet 8 5
214 **54** 3½d. blue 20 8
215 **55** 5½d. green 25 20

56. Sir Thos. Mitchell and Queensland.

1946 (14 Oct.). *Centenary of Mitchell's Exploration of Central Queensland. Recess. W* **15**. *P* 14½.

216 **56** 2½d. scarlet 8 5
217 „ 3½d. blue 20 10
218 „ 1s. grey-olive 35 20

57. Lt. John Shortland, R.N.

58. Steel Foundry.

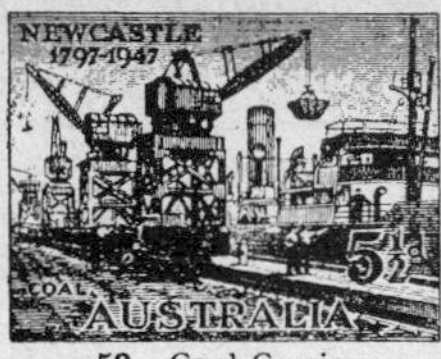

59. Coal Carrier Cranes. **60.** Queen Elizabeth II when Princess.

1947 (8 SEPT.). *Sesquicentenary of City of Newcastle, New South Wales. Recess.* **W 15** *(sideways on 3½d.). P 14½ or 15×14 (2½d.).*

219 **57** 2½d. lake 8 5
a. Imperf. three sides ..
220 **58** 3½d. blue 20 8
221 **59** 5½d. green 25 15

The following items are understood to have been the subject of unauthorised leakages from the Commonwealth Note and Stamp Printing Branch and are therefore not listed by us.

It is certain that none of this material was distributed to post offices for issue to the public.

Imperforate all round. 1d. Princess Elizabeth; 1½d. Queen; 2½d. King; 4d. Koala; 6d. Kookaburra; 9d. Platypus; 1s. Lyre-bird (small); 1s. 6d. Air Mail (Type **22**); 2½d. Newcastle.

Also 2½d. Peace, unwatermarked; 2½d. King, *tête-bêche*; 3½d. Newcastle, in dull ultramarine; 2½d. King on "toned" paper.

(Des. R. A. Harrison. Eng. F. D. Manley. Recess.)

1947 (20 NOV.)–**1948.** *Marriage of Princess Elizabeth. P 14×15.*

(a) **W 15** *sideways.*
222 **60** 1d. purple 5 5
(b) No wmk.
222*a* **60** 1d. purple ('48) 5 5
b. Coil pair .. .. .. 4·00
c. Coil block of four .. 6·00

61. Hereford Bull. **61*a*.** Hermes and Globe.

62. Aboriginal Art. **62*a*.** Commonwealth Coat-of-Arms.

(Des. T **61**/*a*, F. D. Manley; T **62**, G. Sellheim.)

1948 (16 FEB.)–**56.** *Recess.*

(a) **W 15** *sideways. P 14½.*
223 **61** 1s. 3d. brown-purple .. 1·25 35
223*a* **61*a*** 1s. 6d. blackish brown (1.9.49) .. .. 1·00 8
224 **62** 2s. chocolate .. .. 1·00 5
(b) **W 15.** *P14½×13½.*
224*a* **62*a*** 5s. claret (11.4.49) .. 3·00 20
224*b* ,, 10s. purple (3.10.49) .. 12·00 1·25
224*c* ,, £1 blue (28.11.49) .. 30·00 5·00
224*d* ,, £2 green (16.1.50) .. £125 18·00
224*b*/*d* Optd. "Specimen" *Set of* 3 95·00
(c) No wmk. P 14½.
224*e* **61*a*** 1s. 6d. blackish brown (6.12.56) .. .. 6·00 40
224*f* **62** 2s. chocolate (21.7.56) .. 6·00 45
223/224*f* .. *Set of* 9 £175 22·00

63. William J. Farrer. **64.** F. von Mueller.

1948 (12 JULY). *William J. Farrer (wheat research). Recess.* **W 15.** *P 15×14.*
225 **63** 2½d. scarlet 8 5

1948 (13 SEPT.). *Sir Ferdinand von Mueller (botanist). Recess.* **W 15.** *P 15×14.*
226 **64** 2½d. lake 8 5

65. Boy Scout. **66.** Henry Lawson.

Sky retouch (normally unshaded near hill).

1948 (15 NOV.). *Pan-Pacific Scout Jamboree. Recess.* **W 15** *sideways. P 14×15.*
227 **65** 2½d. lake 8 5
See also No. 254.

1948–56. *No wmk. P 15×14 or 14×15 (9d.).*
228 **27** ½d. orange (9.49) .. 5 5
aa. Sky retouch (Rt. pane, R. 6/8) .. .. 4·00
a. Coil pair .. .. 1·25
ab. Sky retouch (in pair)..
b. Coil block of four .. 2·50
229 **46*a*** 1½d. green (29.8.49) .. 12 10
230 **47** 2d. brt. purple (12.48) 12 5
aa. Coil pair .. .. 5·00
ab. Coil block of four ..
230*a* **32** 4d. green (18.8.56) .. 75 8
230*b* **34** 6d. pur.-brn. (18.8.56) 85 8
230*c* **35** 9d. chocolate (13.12.56) 3·00 25
230*d* **36** 1s. grey-grn. (13.12.56) 1·25 5
228/230*d* .. .. *Set of* 7 4·75 60

1949 (17 JUNE). *Anniv. of Birth of Henry Lawson (poet). Recess. P 15×14.*
231 **66** 2½d. maroon 8 5

67. Mounted Postman and Aeroplane.

1949 (10 OCT.). *75th Anniv. of Founding of U.P.U. Recess. P 15×14.*
232 **67** 3½d. ultramarine 25 15

68. Lord Forrest of Bunbury. **69.** King George VI.

1949 (28 NOV.). *Lord Forrest of Bunbury (explorer and politician). Recess.* **W 15** *P 15×14.*
233 **68** 2½d. lake 8 5

1950–51. *Recess. P 15×14. (a)* **W 15.**
234 **69** 2½d. scarlet (12.4.50) .. 8 5
235 ,, 3d. scarlet (28.2.51) .. 10 5
aa. Coil pair .. .. 8·00
(b) No wmk.
235*a* **69** 2½d. pur.-brn. (23.5.51) .. 8 5
235*b* ,, 3d. grey-green (14.11.51) 10 5
c. Coil pair .. .. 18·00

70. Queen Elizabeth. **71.** Aborigine.

1950–51. *Recess. P 15×14.*
236 **70** 1½d. green (19.6.50) .. 8 5
237 ,, 2d. yellow-green (28.3.51) 8 5
a. Coil pair .. .. 3·50
b. Coil block of four .. 6·00

(Des. F. D. Manley.)

1950 (14 AUG.). *Recess.* **W 15.** *P 15×14.*
238 **71** 8½d. brown 25 15

72. Reproductions of First Stamps of New South Wales and Victoria. **73.**

1950 (27 SEPT.). *Centenary of First Adhesive Postage Stamps in Australia. T 72/3 alternately in vertical columns throughout the sheet Recess. P 15×14.*
239 **72** 2½d. maroon 8 5
240 **73** 2½d. maroon 8 5

PRICES for used horizontal pairs of the issues printed alternately in the sheet are four times the price of a single.

74. Sir Edmund Barton. **75.** Sir Henry Parkes

76. Opening First Federal Parliament.

77. Federal Parliament House, Canberra.

1951 (1 May). *Golden Jubilee of Commonwealth of Australia. Recess. P* 15×14.

241	**74**	3d. lake	10	5
242	**75**	3d. lake	10	5
243	**76**	5½d. blue	35	35
244	**77**	1s. 6d. purple-brown	35	35

Nos. 241/2 are printed alternately in vertical columns throughout the sheet.

78. E. H. Hargraves. **79.** C. J. Latrobe.

1951 (2 July). *Centenary of Discovery of Gold in Australia. Recess. P* 15×14.

245	**78**	3d. maroon	8	8

1951 (2 July). *Centenary of Responsible Government in Victoria. Recess. P* 15×14.

246	**79**	3d. maroon	8	8

Nos. 245/6 are printed alternately in vertical columns throughout the sheet.

80. King George VI. **81.**

1951 (31 Oct.). *Recess. W* **15**. *P* 15×14.

247	**80**	7½d. blue	25	15
		a. Imperf. 3 sides (vert. pr.)	£800	

(Des. F. D. Manley. Eng. G. Lissenden.)

1951–52. *Recess. W* **15**. *P* 15×14.

248	**81**	3½d. brown-pur. (28.11.51)	10	8
249	,,	4½d. scarlet (20.2.52)	20	10
250	,,	6½d. brown (20.2.52)	20	15
251	,,	6½d. emerald-green (9.4.52)	20	8

82. King George VI.

(Des. F. D. Manley. Recess.)

1952 (19 Mar.)–**65**. *P* 14½.(*a*) *W* **15** (*sideways*).

252	**82**	1s. 0½d. indigo	45	12
253	–	2s. 6d. deep brown	70	30
		(*b*) *No wmk.*		
253*a*	–	2s. 6d. deep brn. (30.1.57)	7·00	1·00
		b. Sepia (10.65)	12·00	4·00

Design:—2s. 6d. As T **71** but larger (21×25½ *mm.*).

No. 253*b* was an emergency printing and can easily be distinguished from No. 253*a* as it is on white Harrison paper, No. 253*a* being on toned paper.

1952 (19 Nov.). *Pan-Pacific Scout Jamboree, Greystanes. As T* **65**, *but inscr.* "1952–53". *Recess. W* **15** (*sideways*). *P* 14×15.

254		3½d. brown-lake	10	5

83. Butter. **84.** Wheat.

85. Beef. **86.** Queen Elizabeth II.

1953 (11 Feb.). *Food Production. Typo. P* 14½.

255	**83**	3d. emerald	40	15
256	**84**	3d. emerald	40	15
257	**85**	3d. emerald	40	15
		a. Strip of 3. Nos. 255/7	2·50	2·50
258	**83**	3½d. scarlet	40	15
259	**84**	3½d. scarlet	40	15
260	**85**	3½d. scarlet	40	15
		a. Strip of 3. Nos. 258/60	2·50	2·50

The three designs in each denomination appear in rotation, both horizontally and vertically, throughout the sheet.

1953–56. *Recess. P* 15×14. (*a*) *No wmk.*

261	**86**	1d. purple (19.8.53)	5	5
261*a*	,,	2½d. blue (23.6.54)	12	5
262	,,	3d. deep green (17.6.53)	12	5
		aa. Coil pair	4·00	
		ab. Coil block of four	8·00	
262*a*	,,	3½d. brown-red (2.7.56)	10	5
262*b*	,,	6½d. orange (9.56)	40	8
		(*b*) *W* **15**.		
263	**86**	3½d. brown-red (21.4.53)	10	5
263*a*	,,	6½d. orange (23.6.54)	15	8

87. Queen Elizabeth II.

1953 (25 May). *Coronation. Recess. P* 15×14.

264	**87**	3½d. scarlet	8	5
265	,,	7½d. violet	40	40
266	,,	2s. dull bluish green	1·25	1·00

88. Young Farmers and Calf.

1953 (3 Sept.). *25th Anniv. of Australian Young Farmers' Clubs. Recess. P* 14½.

267	**88**	3½d. red-brn. & deep grn.	12	5

89. Lt.-Gov. D. Collins. **90.** Lt.-Gov. W. Paterson.

91. Sullivan Cove, Hobart, 1804.

1953 (23 Sept.). *150th Anniv. of Settlement in Tasmania. Recess. P* 15×14.

268	**89**	3½d. brown-purple	15	10
269	**90**	3½d. brown-purple	15	10
		a. Horiz. pair. Nos. 268/9	40	30
270	**91**	2s. green	3·00	2·25

Nos. 268/9 are printed alternately in vertical columns throughout the sheet.

92. Stamp of 1853.

1953 (11 Nov.). *Tasmanian Postage Stamp Centenary. Recess. P* 14½.

271	**92**	3d. rose-red	12	8

93. Queen Elizabeth II and Duke of Edinburgh.

94. Queen Elizabeth II. Re-entry.

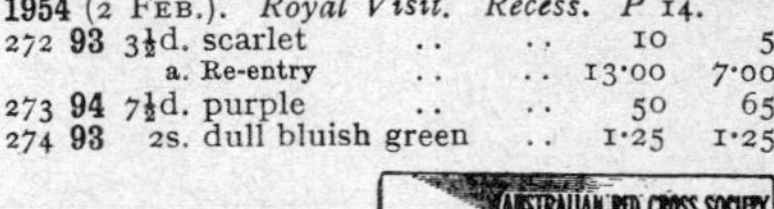

1954 (2 Feb.). *Royal Visit. Recess. P* 14.

272	**93**	3½d. scarlet	10	5
		a. Re-entry	13·00	7·00
273	**94**	7½d. purple	50	65
274	**93**	2s. dull bluish green	1·25	1·25

96. Red Cross and Globe.

95. "Telegraphic Communications".

97. Black Swan.

1954 (7 Apr.). *Australian Telegraph System Centenary. Recess. P* 14.
275 **95** 3½d. brown-red 12 5

1954 (9 June). *40th Anniv. of Australian Red Cross Society. Design recess, cross typo. P* 14½.
276 **96** 3½d. ultramarine & scarlet 12 5

1954 (2 Aug.). *Western Australian Postage Stamp Centenary. Recess. P* 14½.
277 **97** 3½d. black 15 5

98. Locomotives of 1854 and 1954.

1954 (13 Sept.). *Australian Railways Centenary. Recess. P* 14.
278 **98** 3½d. purple-brown .. 12 5

99. Antarctic Map and Indigenous Flora and Fauna.

100. Olympic Games Symbol.

(Des. T. Lawrence. Recess.)

1954 (17 Nov.). *Australian Antarctic Research. P* 14½ × 13½.
279 **99** 3½d. grey-black 20 5

1954–55. *Olympic Games Propaganda. Recess. P* 14.
280 **100** 2s. dp. brt. blue (1.12.54) 90 90
280*a* ,, 2s. dp. bluish grn. (30.11.55) 90 90

101. Rotary Symbol, Globe and Flags.

102. Queen Elizabeth II.

1955 (23 Feb.). *50th Anniv. of Rotary International. Recess. P* 14 × 14½.
281 **101** 3½d. carmine 12 5

(Des. F. D. Manley from bas-relief by W. L. Bowles. Eng. G. Lissenden.)

1955 (9 Mar.)–**57.** *Recess. P* 14½. (*a*) *W* **15** (*sideways*).
282 **102** 1s. 0½d. deep blue .. 70 25
(*b*) *No wmk.*
282*a* **102** 1s. 7d. red-brn. (13.3.57) 1·25 25

103. American Memorial, Canberra.

(Des. R. L. Beck. Recess.)

1955 (4 May). *Australian-American Friendship. P* 14 × 14½.
283 **103** 3½d. violet-blue 12 5

104. Cobb & Co. Coach (from dry-print by Sir Lionel Lindsay).

1955 (6 July). *Mail-coach Pioneers Commemoration. Recess. P* 14½ × 14.
284 **104** 3½d. blackish brown .. 15 5
285 ,, 2s. reddish brown .. 1·25 90

105. Y.M.C.A. Emblem and Map of the World.

(Des. E. Thake. Design recess; emblem typo.)

1955 (10 Aug.). *World Centenary of Y.M.C.A. P* 14½ × 14.
286 **105** 3½d. dp. bluish grn. & red 12 5

106. Florence Nightingale and Young Nurse.

107. Queen Victoria.

1955 (21 Sept.). *Nursing Profession Commemoration. Recess. P* 14 × 14½.
287 **106** 3½d. reddish violet .. 12 5

1955 (17 Oct.). *Centenary of First South Australian Postage Stamps. Recess. P* 14½.
288 **107** 3½d. green 12 5

108. Badges of New South Wales, Victoria and Tasmania.

1956 (26 Sept.). *Centenary of Responsible Government in New South Wales, Victoria and Tasmania. Recess. P* 14½ × 14.
289 **108** 3½d. brown-lake 12 5

109. Arms of Melbourne.

110. Olympic Torch and Symbol.

111. Collins Street, Melbourne.

112. Melbourne across R. Yarra.

(Nos. 290/1. Recess. Govt. Stamp Ptg. Works, Melbourne. No. 292. Des. M. Murphy and L. Coles. Photo. Harrison & Sons, Ltd., London. No. 293. Des. M. Murphy. Photo. Courvoisier, Switzerland.)

1956 (31 Oct.). *Olympic Games, Melbourne. P* 14½ (*4d.*), 14 × 14½ (*7½d.*, 1*s.*) *or* 11½ (2*s.*).
290 **109** 4d. carmine-red.. .. 12 5
291 **110** 7½d. deep bright blue .. 35 35
292 **111** 1s. multicoloured .. 50 30
293 **112** 2s. multicoloured .. 1·10 90

113. Queen Elizabeth II.

114. South Australia Coat-of-Arms.

1957. *Recess. P* 15 × 14.
294 **113** 4d. lake (13 Mar.) .. 15 5
295 ,, 10d. dp. grey-blue (6 Mar.) 25 15

The 4d. exists in booklet panes of six stamps, with imperf. outer edges, producing single stamps with one or two adjacent sides imperf.

1957 (17 Apr.). *Centenary of Responsible Government in South Australia. Recess. P* 14½.
296 **114** 4d. red-brown 12 5

115. Map of Australia and Caduceus.

(Des. J. E. Lyle; adapted B. Stewart. Eng. D. Cameron. Recess.)

1957 (21 Aug.). *Flying Doctor Service. P* 14½ × 14.
297 **115** 7d. ultramarine 30 12

116. "The Spirit of Christmas" (Child, after Sir Joshua Reynolds).

Re-entry (Row 10/1).

1957 (6 Nov.). *Christmas. Recess. P* 14½ × 14.
298 **116** 3½d. scarlet 12 5
a. Re-entry .. .. 4·50 3·50
299 ,, 4d. purple 20 5

117. Queen Elizabeth II.

1957 (13 Nov.). *Recess. P* 15 × 14.
300 **117** 7½d. violet 55 35
a. Double print .. £250

118. Super-Constellation Airliner.

1958 (6 Jan.). *Inauguration of Australian "Round the World" Air Service. Recess. P* 14½ × 14.
301 **118** 2s. deep blue 90 65

119. Hall of Memory, Sailor and Airman.

(Des. and eng. G. Lissenden.)

1958 (10 Feb.). *T* **119** *and similar horiz. design. Recess. P* 14½ × 14.
302 **119** 5½d. brown-red 50 35
303 – 5½d. brown-red 50 35
a. Horiz. pair. Nos. 302/3 2·25 2·25

No. 303 shows a soldier and service-woman respectively in place of the sailor and airman. Nos. 302/3 are printed alternately in vertical columns throughout the sheet.

120. Sir Charles Kingsford Smith and the "Southern Cross".

(Des. J. E. Lyle. Recess.)

1958 (27 Aug.). *30th Anniv. of First Air Crossing of the Tasman Sea. P* 14 × 14½.
304 **120** 8d. deep ultramarine .. 35 35

121. Silver Mine, Broken Hill.

(Des. R. H. Evans. Recess.)

1958 (10 Sept.). *75th Anniv. of Founding of Broken Hill. Recess. P* 14½ × 14.
305 **121** 4d. chocolate 12 5

122. The Nativity.

1958 (5 Nov.). *Christmas. Recess. P* 14½ × 15.
306 **122** 3½d. deep scarlet.. .. 20 5
307 ,, 4d. deep violet 20 5

PHOSPHOR STAMPS ("Helecon").

"Helecon", a chemical substance of the zinc sulphide group, has been incorporated in stamps in two different ways, either in the ink with which the stamps are printed, or included in the surface coating of the stamp paper.

Owing to the difficulty of identification without the use of a U.V. lamp we do not list the helecon stamps separately but when in stock can supply them after testing under the lamp.

The first stamp to be issued was the 11d. Bandicoot from an experimental printing of four millions on helecon paper released to the public in December 1963. The next printing on ordinary paper was released in September 1964. The experimental printing was coarse, showing a lot of white dots and the colour is slate-blue, differing from both the ordinary and the later helecon paper.

The following helecon printings have been reported: 2d. and 3d. (sheets, coils and coil sheets) and 5d. (No. 354) Queen Elizabeth II; 8d. Tiger Cat; 11d. Bandicoot; 1s. Colombo Plan; 1s. 2d. Tasmanian Tiger; 2s. 3d. Wattle (No. 324*a*); and 6d. (No. 363*a*), 9d. and 1s. 6d. Birds (the 2s., 2s. 6d. and 3s. Birds were only issued on helecon paper). The 5d. Queen Elizabeth II in red (No. 354*b*) exists ordinary and with helecon ink. The coil pair was only issued with helecon ink; the booklet is normally with helecon ink but some were printed with ordinary ink by mistake. The Churchill stamp was printed on ordinary and helecon paper. The I.T.U. Centenary, Monash and later commemorative stamps were printed on helecon paper and all issues from No. 382 onwards were on helecon paper or paper coated with Derby Luminescence.

123 124 126 127

128. Queen Elizabeth II. **129.**

Die I. Short break in outer line to bottom right of "4".

Die II. Line unbroken.

Die. A. Four short lines inside "5".

Die B. Five short lines inside "5".

(Des. G. Lissenden from photographs by Baron Studios. Eng. F. D. Manley (2d.). D. Cameron (3d.). P. E. Morriss (others). Recess.)

1959–62. *P* 14 × 15 (*horiz.*), 15 × 14 (*vert.*).
308 **123** 1d. dp. slate-pur. (*shades*) (2.2.59) 5 5
309 **124** 2d. brown (21.3.62) .. 5 5
a. Coil pair (1962) .. 90
b. Coil block of four .. 1·90
311 **126** 3d. blue-green (20.5.59) 5 5
a. Coil pair (8.60) .. 1·25
b. Coil block of four .. 2·50
312 **127** 3½d. deep green (18.3.59) 10 5

313	**128**	4d. carmine-lake (Die I) (*shades*) (2.2.59) ..	25	5
		a. Die II (*shades*)	30	10
314	**129**	5d. deep blue (Die A or B) (1.10.59) ..	15	5
		a. Vert. *se-tenant* pr. (A and B)	40	40
		b. Coil pair (early 1960) ..	2·75	
		c. Coil block of four ..	6·00	

No. 313. Die I occurs in the upper pane and Die II in the lower pane of the sheet.

No. 314. Both dies occur in alternate horizontal rows in the sheet (Die A in Row 1, Die B in Row 2, and so on), and their value is identical.

The Note after No. 295 also applies to Nos. 313/4.

131. Banded Ant-eater.

132. Tiger Cat (Dasyure).

133. Kangaroos.

134. Rabbit Bandicoot.

135. Platypus.

136. Tasmanian Tiger.

137. Christmas Bells.

138. Flannel Flower.

139. Wattle.

140. Banksia.

141. Waratah.

142. Aboriginal Stockman.

(Des. Eileen Mayo (6d., 8d., 9d., 11d., 1s., 1s. 2d.), B. Stewart (5s.), Margaret Stones (others). Recess.)

1959–64. *W* 15 (5s.), *no wmk.* (*others*). *P* 14 × 15 (*T* **136**), 15 × 14 (*T* **131/5**), 14½ × 14 (5s.) *or* 14½ (*others*).

316	**131**	6d. brown (30.9.60) ..	25	5
317	**132**	8d. red-brown (*shades*) (11.5.60)	25	5
318	**133**	9d. deep sepia (21.10.59)	35	12
319	**134**	11d. deep blue (3.5.61) ..	35	15
320	**135**	1s. deep green (9.9.59) ..	90	12
321	**136**	1s. 2d. deep pur. (21.3.62)	45	20
322	**137**	1s. 6d. crim./*yell.* (3.2.60)	55	20
323	**138**	2s. grey-blue (8.4.59) ..	45	8
324	**139**	2s. 3d. grn./*maize* (9.9.59)	65	20
324*a*	,,	2s. 3d. yellow-green (28.10.64)	1·75	80
325	**140**	2s. 5d. brn./*yell.* (16.3.60)	1·25	30
326	**141**	3s. scarlet (15.7.59) ..	90	20
327	**142**	5s. red-brown (26.7.61)	8·00	85
		a. White paper. *Brown-red* (17.6.64)	70·00	6·00
316/327		.. .. *Set of* 13	14·00	3·00

No. 327 is on toned paper. No. 327*a* was a late printing on the white paper referred to in the note below No. 360.

See notes after No. 307 *re* helecon ink.

143. Postmaster Isaac Nichols boarding the brig *Experiment*.

1959 (22 Apr.). *150th Anniv. of the Australian Post Office. Recess. P* 14½ × 14.

331	**143**	4d. slate	12	5

144. Parliament House, Brisbane, and Arms of Queensland.

145. " The Approach of the Magi."

1959 (5 June). *Centenary of Self-Government in Queensland. Recess. P* 14 × 14½.

332	**144**	4d. lilac and green ..	15	5

1959 (4 Nov.). *Christmas. Recess. P* 15 × 14.

333	**145**	5d. deep reddish violet ..	15	5

146. Girl Guide and Lord Baden-Powell.

(Des. and eng. B. Stewart. Recess.)

1960 (18 Aug.). *Golden Jubilee of Girl Guide Movement. P* 14½ × 14.

334	**146**	5d. deep ultramarine ..	15	5

147. "The Overlanders" (after Sir Daryl Lindsay).

(Adapted and eng. P. E. Morriss. Recess.)

1960 (21 Sept.). *Centenary of Northern Territory Exploration. P* 15 × 14½.

335	**147**	5d. magenta	12	5

There are two types in this issue. In Type I the horse's mane is rough and in Type II it is smooth. Type II occurs on 94 stamps in the Printer's sheet of 480.

148. " Archer " and Melbourne Cup.

149. Queen Victoria.

(Des. F. D. Manley. Eng. G. Lissenden. Recess.)

1960 (12 Oct.). *100th Melbourne Cup Race Commemoration. P* 14½.

336	**148**	5d. sepia	12	5

(Des. F. D. Manley. Eng. B. Stewart. Recess.)

1960 (2 Nov.). *Centenary of First Queensland Postage Stamp. P* 14½ × 15.

337	**149**	5d. dp. myrtle-green ..	12	5

150. Open Bible and Candle.

151. Colombo Plan Bureau Emblem.

(Des. K. McKay. Adapted and eng. B. Stewart. Recess.)

1960 (9 Nov.). *Christmas. P* 15 × 14½.

338	**150**	5d. carmine-red	15	5

(Des. and eng. G. Lissenden. Recess.)

1961 (30 June). *Colombo Plan. P* 14 × 14½.

339	**151**	1s. red-brown	35	10

See notes after No. 307 *re* helecon ink.

152. Melba (after bust by Sir Bertram Mackennal).

(Des. and eng. B. Stewart. Recess.)

1961. (20 SEPT.). *Centenary of Birth of Dame Nellie Melba (singer).* P 14½ × 15.

340	**152**	5d. blue	15	8

153. Open Prayer Book and Text.

(Des. G. Lissenden. Eng. P. E. Morriss. Recess.)

1961 (8 Nov.). *Christmas.* P 14½ × 14.

341	**153**	5d. brown	20	5

154. J. M. Stuart. **155.** Flynn's Grave and Nursing Sister.

(Des. Walter Jardine. Eng. P. E. Morriss. Recess.)

1962 (25 JULY). *Centenary of Stuart's Crossing of Australia from South to North.* P 14½ × 15.

342	**154**	5d. brown-red	15	5

(Des. F. D. Manley. Photo.)

1962 (5 SEPT.). *50th Anniv. of Australian Inland Mission.* P 13½.

343	**155**	5d. multicoloured ..	15	5
		a. Red printing omitted ..	—	£120

The note below No. 372b also applies to No. 343a.

156. "Woman". **157.** "Madonna and Child".

(Des. D. Dundas. Eng. G. Lissenden. Recess.)

1962 (26 SEPT.). *"Associated Country Women of the World" Conference, Melbourne.* P 14 × 14½.

344	**156**	5d. deep green	15	5

(Des. and eng. G. Lissenden. Recess.)

1962 (17 OCT.). *Christmas.* P 14½.

345	**157**	5d. violet	20	5

158. Perth and Kangaroo Paw (plant).

159. Arms of Perth and Running Track.

(Des. R. M. Warner (5d.), G. Hamori (2s. 3d.). Photo. Harrison & Sons.)

1962 (1 Nov.). *Seventh British Empire and Commonwealth Games, Perth.* P 14 (5d.) or 14½ × 14 (2s. 3d.).

346	**158**	5d. multicoloured ..	20	10
		a. Red omitted	£200	
347	**159**	2s. 3d. black, red, blue and green	6·00	3·50

160. Queen Elizabeth II. **161.** Queen Elizabeth II and Duke of Edinburgh.

(Des. and eng. after portraits by Anthony Buckley, P. E. Morriss (5d.), B. Stewart (2s. 3d.). Recess.)

1963 (18 FEB.). *Royal Visit.* P 14½.

348	**160**	5d. deep green	15	5
349	**161**	2s. 3d. brown-lake ..	3·50	3·00

162. Arms of Canberra and W. B. Griffin (architect).

(Des. and eng. B. Stewart. Recess.)

1963 (8 MAR.). *50th Anniv. of Canberra.* P 14½ × 14.

350	**162**	5d. deep green	20	12

163. Centenary Emblem.

(Des. G. Hamori. Photo.)

1963 (8 MAY). *Red Cross Centenary.* P 13½ × 13.

351	**163**	5d. red, grey-brn. & blue	15	5

164. Blaxland, Lawson and Wentworth on Mt. York.

(Des. T. Alban. Eng. P. E. Morriss. Recess.)

1963 (28 MAY). *150th Anniv. of First Crossing of Blue Mountains.* P 14½ × 14.

352	**164**	5d. ultramarine	15	5

165. "Export".

(Des. and eng. B. Stewart. Recess.)

1963 (28 AUG.). P 14½ × 14.

353	**165**	5d. red	15	5

No. 354a comes from sheets of uncut booklet panes containing 288 stamps (16 × 18) with wide margins intersecting the sheet horizontally below each third row, alternate rows of stamps imperforate between vertically and the outer left, right and bottom margins imperforate. This means that in each sheet there are 126 pairs of stamps imperf. between vertically, plus a number with wide imperforate margins attached, as shown in the illustration.

166. Queen Elizabeth II.

(Des. and eng. P. E. Morriss from photograph by Anthony Buckley. Recess.)

1963 (9 Oct.)–**65.** *P* 15×14.
354 **166** 5d. deep green 15 5
a. Imperf. between (horiz. pair) (31.7.64) .. .. 1·25 1·25
354*b* „ 5d. red (30.6.65) 35 20
c. Coil pair (30.6.65) .. 6·50
See notes after No. 307 *re* helecon ink.

The above exist in booklet panes of six stamps, with imperf. outer edges, producing single stamps with one or two adjacent sides imperf.

167. Tasman and Ship.

168. Dampier and *Roebuck*.

169. Captain Cook.

170. Flinders and *Investigator*.

171. Bass and whaler.

172. Admiral King and *Mermaid*.

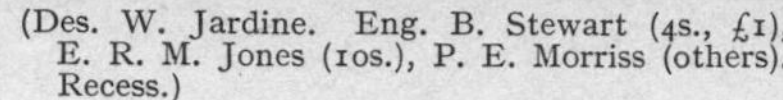
(Des. W. Jardine. Eng. B. Stewart (4s., £1), E. R. M. Jones (10s.), P. E. Morriss (others). Recess.)

1963–65. *No wmk.* (4s.) *or W* **15** (*others*), (*sideways on* 5s., £1). *P* 14½×14 *or* 14½ (5s., £1, £2).
355 **167** 4s. ultramarine (9.10.63) 1·50 90
356 **168** 5s. red-brown (25.11.64) 2·00 90
357 **169** 7s. 6d. olive (26.8.64) .. 7·50 7·50
358 **170** 10s. brown-pur. (26.2.64) 9·00 8·50
a. White paper. *Deep brown-purple* (14.1.65) .. 9·00 4·00
359 **171** £1 deep reddish violet (26.2.64) .. .. 30·00 14·00
a. White paper. *Deep bluish violet* (16.11.64) .. 30·00 14·00
360 **172** £2 sepia (26.8.64) .. 75·00 75·00
355/360 .. .. *Set of* 6 £110 90·00
357/60 Optd. "Specimen" *Set of* 4 £170

Nos. 358 and 359 were printed on a toned paper but all the other values are on white paper, the 4s. being on rather thicker paper.

173. "Peace on Earth. . ."

(Des. R. M. Warner. Eng. B. Stewart. Recess.)

1963 (25 Oct.). *Christmas. P* 14½.
361 **173** 5d. greenish blue .. 25 5

174. "Commonwealth Cable".

(Des. P. E. Morriss. Photo.)

1963 (3 Dec.). *Opening of COMPAC* (*Trans-Pacific Telephone Cable*). *Chalky paper. P* 13½.
362 **174** 2s. 3d. red, blue, black and pale blue .. 3·50 3·00

175. Yellow-tailed Thornbill.

176. Black-backed Magpie.

177. Galah (cockatoo).

178. Golden Whistler (Thickehd).

179. Blue Wren.

180. Scarlet Robin.

181. Straw-necked Ibis.

(Des. Mrs. H. Temple-Watts. Photo.)

1964 (11 Mar.)–**65.** *Chalky paper* (*except No.* 367*a*). *P* 13½.
363 **175** 6d. brown, yellow, black & bluish grn. (19.8.64) 30 15
a. *Brown, yellow, black and emerald-green* (–.12.65) .. 1·40 1·40
364 **176** 9d. black, grey & pale grn. 1·50 1·25
365 **177** 1s. 6d. pink, grey, dull purple and black .. 70 65
366 **178** 2s. yellow, black and pink (21.4.65) .. 80 30
367 **179** 2s. 5d. dp. royal bl., lt. vio.-blue, yell.-orge., grey and black .. 2·50 60
367*a* „ 2s. 5d. dp. blue, lt. blue, orge.-brn., blue-grey and black (8.65) .. 4·50 1·25
368 **180** 2s. 6d. black, red, grey and green (21.4.65) .. 2·50 1·50
a. Red omitted (white breast)
369 **181** 3s. black, red, buff and yellow-green (21.4.65) 1·60 60
363/369 .. .. *Set of* 8 13·00 6·00

No. 367*a* is from a printing on unsurfaced Wiggins Teape paper, the rest of the set being on chalk-surfaced Harrison paper. Apart from the differences in shade, the inscriptions, particularly "BLUE WREN", stand out very much more clearly on No. 367*a*. Although two colours are apparent in both stamps, the grey and black were printed from one plate.

See notes after No. 307 *re* helecon ink.

182. "Bleriot" Aircraft (type flown by M. Guillaux, 1914).

(Des. K. McKay. Adapted and eng. P. E Morriss. Recess.)

1964 1 (July). *50th Anniv. of First Australian Airmail Flight. P* 14½×14.
370 **182** 5d. olive-green 20 5
371 „ 2s. 3d. scarlet .. .. 3·50 2·50

183. Child looking at Nativity Scene.

(Des. P. E. Morriss and J. Mason. Photo.)

1964 (21 Oct.). *Christmas. Chalky paper. P* 13½.
372 **183** 5d. red, blue, buff & blk. 20 5
a. Red omitted £225
b. Black omitted £200

The red ink is soluble and can be removed by bleaching and it is therefore advisable to obtain a certificate from a recognised expert committee before purchasing No. 372a.

184. " Simpson and his Donkey ".

185. " Telecommunications ".

(Des. C. Andrew (after statue, Shrine of Remembrance, Melbourne). Eng. E. R. M. Jones. Recess.)

1965 (14 Apr.). *50th Anniv. of Gallipoli Landing. P* 14×14½.
373 **184** 5d. drab 15 10
374 ,, 8d. blue 70 70
375 ,, 2s. 3d. reddish purple .. 2·50 2·50

(Des. J. McMahon and G. Hamori. Photo.)

1965 (10 May). *I.T.U. Centenary. P* 13½.
376 **185** 5d. black, brown, orange-brown and blue .. 20 5
a. Black (value and pylon) omitted £200

186. Sir Winston Churchill.

187. General Monash.

(Des. P. E. Morriss from photo by Karsh. Photo.)

1965 (24 May). *Churchill Commemoration. Chalky paper. P* 13½.
377 **186** 5d. black, pale grey and light blue 15 15
a. Pale grey ("AUSTRALIA") omitted.. .. £200 £160

About half the printing was on helecon impregnated paper, differing slightly in the shade of the blue.

(Des. O. Foulkes and W. Walters. Photo.)

1965 (23 June). *Birth Centenary of General Sir John Monash (engineer and soldier). Chalky paper. P* 13½.
378 **187** 5d. multicoloured .. 15 5

188. Hargrave and " Seaplane " (1902).

(Des. G. Hamori. Photo.)

1965 (4 Aug.). *50th Death Anniv. of Lawrence Hargrave (aviation pioneer). Chalky paper. P* 13½.
379 **188** 5d. purple-brown, black, yellow-ochre & purple 20 5
a. Purple (value) omitted .. £250

189. I.C.Y. Emblem.

190. " Nativity Scene ".

(Des. H. Fallu from U.N. theme. Photo.)

1965 (1 Sept.). *International Co-operation Year. Chalky paper. P* 13½.
380 **189** 2s. 3d. emer. & lt. blue .. 1·50 1·50

(Des. J. Mason. Photo.)

1965 (20 Oct.). *Christmas. P* 13½.
381 **190** 5d. multicoloured .. 20 5
a. Gold omitted £170
b. Blue omitted .. .. 35·00

No. 381a comes from the bottom row of a sheet in which the gold is completely omitted, the background appearing as black with "CHRISTMAS 1965" and "AUSTRALIA" omitted. The row above had the black missing from the lower two-fifths of the stamp.

(New currency. 100 cents = 1 dollar.)

191. Queen Elizabeth II.

192. Blue-faced Honeyeater.

193. Humbug Fish.

194. Coral Fish.

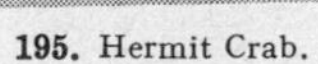

195. Hermit Crab.

196. Anemone Fish.

197. Red-necked Avocet.

198. Azure Kingfisher.

(Des. Mrs. H. Temple-Watts (6 c. T **192**, 13 c., 24 c.), Eileen Mayo (7 c. (No. 388) to 10 c.). Recess. (T **191**, 40 c. to $4). Photo. Chalky paper (others).)

1966 (14 Feb.)–**71**. *Decimal currency. No wmk. P* 15×14 (*T* **191**), 14½×14 (40 c., 75 c., $1), 14½ (50 c., $2, $4) *or* 13½ (*others*).
382 **191** 1 c. deep red-brown .. 5 5
383 ,, 2 c. olive-green 8 5
384 ,, 3 c. slate-green 10 5
385 ,, 4 c. red 5 5
a. Booklet pane. Five stamps plus one printed label .. .. .. 4·00
386 **175** 5 c. brown, yellow, blk., and emerald-green .. 40 10
a. *Brown, yellow, black and blue-green* (Jan '67) .. 20 5
386*b* **101** 5 c. deep blue (29.9.67) 3·25 5
c. Booklet pane. Five stamps plus one printed label .. .. .. 17·00
d. Imperf. in horiz. strip of 3* .. ..
387 **192** 6 c. olive-yellow, black, blue & pale grey .. 70 25
387*a* **191** 6 c. orange (28.9.70) .. 8 5
388 **193** 7 c. black, grey, salmon and brown 30 5
388*a* **191** 7 c. purple (1.10.71) .. 15 5
389 **194** 8 c. red, yell., blue-grn., and blackish green .. 90 15
390 **195** 9 c. brown-red, pur.-brn., black & lt. yell.-olive 90 15
391 **196** 10 c. orge., blackish brn., p. turq.-bl. & ol.-brn. 1·25 12
392 **197** 13 c. red, black, grey and light turquoise-grn. 1·40 35
a. Red omitted .. .. 80·00
393 **177** 15 c. rose carmine, black, grey & lt. bluish grn. 1·40 40
394 **178** 20 c. yellow, black & pink 1·40 25
395 **198** 24 c. ultramarine, yellow, black & light brown 1·75 60
396 **180** 25 c. blk., red, grey & grn. 1·75 30
a. Red omitted £300
397 **181** 30 c. black, red, buff and light yellow-green .. 10·00 30
398 **167** 40 c. ultramarine .. 17·00 60
399 **168** 50 c. red-brown .. .. 17·00 60
400 **169** 75 c. olive .. .. 2·25 1·25
401 **170** $1 brown-pur. (*shades*) 2·50 50
402 **171** $2 deep reddish violet 5·00 2·00
403 **172** $4 sepia .. .. 9·50 5·50
382/403 .. .. *Set of* 25 70·00 12·00
400/3 Optd. "Specimen" *Set of* 4 50·00

*This comprises one stamp imperf. all round, one imperf. on three sides and one normal.

No. 385 is normally printed with helecon ink, the rest being on helecon paper. Early in 1967 experimental printings of No. 385 on different kinds of paper coated with helecon or Derby Luminescents phosphor were put on sale. They cannot be distinguished by the naked eye.

199. Queen Elizabeth II.

1966 (14 Feb.)–**67.** *Coil stamps.* *Photo.* *P* 14½ × *imperf.*

404 **199** 3 c. black, lt. brn. & green 25 20
405 „ 4 c. black, light brown and light vermilion .. 25 20
405*a* „ 5 c. black, light brown and new blue (29.9.67) .. 70 25

200. " Saving Life ".

(Des. L. Mason. Photo.)

1966 (6 July). *75th Anniv. of Royal Life Saving Society.* *P* 13½.

406 **200** 4 c. black, bright blue and blue 20 10

201. " Adoration of the Shepherds ".

(Des. L. Stirling, after medieval engraving. Photo.)

1966 (19 Oct.). *Christmas.* *P* 13½.

407 **201** 4 c. black & yellow-olive 20 10

202. Dutch Ship. **203.** Open Bible.

(Des. F. Eidlitz. Photo.)

1966 (24 Oct.). *350th Anniv. of Dirk Hartog's Landing in Australia.* *P* 13½.

408 **202** 4 c. multicoloured .. 20 10

(Des. L. Stirling. Photo.)

1967 (7 Mar.). *150th Anniv. of British and Foreign Bible Society in Australia.* *P* 13½.

409 **203** 4 c. multicoloured .. 20 10

204. Ancient Keys and Modern Lock.

(Des. G. Andrews. Photo.)

1967 (5 Apr.). *150th Anniv. of Australian Banking.* *P* 13½.

410 **204** 4 c. black, light blue and emerald 20 10

205. Lions Badge and 50 Stars.

(Des. M. Ripper. Photo.)

1967 (7 June). *50th Anniv. of Lions International.* *P* 13½.

411 **205** 4 c. black, gold and blue 25 10

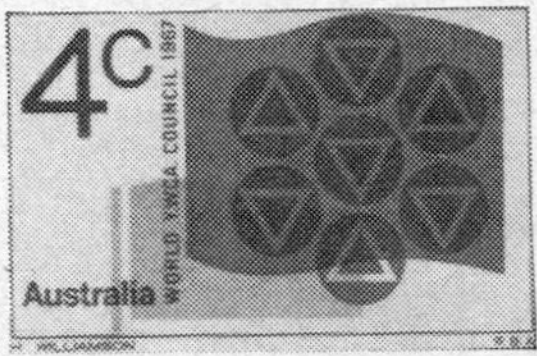

206. Y.W.C.A. Emblem.

(Des. H. Williamson. Photo.)

1967 (21 Aug.). *World Y.W.C.A. Council Meeting, Monash University, Victoria.* *P* 13½.

412 **206** 4 c. dp. blue, ultramarine, light purple & lt. blue 20 10

207. Anatomical Figures.

5c
(208)

(Des. R. Ingpen. Photo.)

1967 (20 Sept.). *Fifth World Gynaecology and Obstetrics Congress, Sydney.* *P* 13½.

413 **207** 4 c. black, blue and light reddish violet .. 20 10

1967 (29 Sept.). *No.* 385 *surch. with T* **208.**

414 **191** 5 c. on 4 c. red 25 5
a. Booklet pane. Five stamps plus one printed label .. 1·75

No. 414 was only issued in booklets and so only occurs with one or two adjacent sides imperforate. It only exists printed with normal ink on helecon paper.

209. Christmas Bells and Gothic Arches.

210. Religious Symbols.

(Des. M. Ripper (5 c.), Erica McGilchrist (25 c.). Photo.)

1967. *Christmas.* *P* 13½.

415 **209** 5 c. mult. (18.10.67) .. 15 5
a. Imperf three sides ..
416 **210** 25 c. mult. (27.11.67) .. 1·25 1·25

211. Satellite in Orbit.

212. World Weather Map. **213.** Radar Antenna.

(Des. J. Mason. Photo.)

1968 (20 Mar.). *World Weather Watch.* *P* 13 × 13½.

417 **211** 5 c. orange-brown, pale blue, blue and ochre 20 10
418 **212** 20 c. orge.-brn., bl. & blk. 2·25 1·25

(Des. R. Ingpen. Photo.)

1968 (20 Mar.). *World Telecommunications Intelsat II.* *P* 13½ × 13.

419 **213** 25 c. greenish blue, black and light blue-green 2·25 1·50

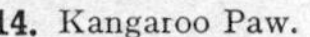

214. Kangaroo Paw. **215.** Pink Heath.

216. Tasmanian Blue Gum. **217.** Sturt's Desert Pea.

218. Cooktown Orchid.

219. Waratah.

(Des. Nell Wilson (6 c., 30 c.); R. and P. Warner (13 c., 25 c.); Dorothy Thornhill (15 c., 20 c.). Photo.)

1968 (10 July). *State Floral Emblems. Multi-coloured. P 13½.*

420	**214**	6 c. Western Australia ..	25	15
421	**215**	13 c. Victoria	35	20
422	**216**	15 c. Tasmania	45	15
423	**217**	20 c. South Australia ..	60	12
424	**218**	25 c. Queensland ..	1·00	25
425	**219**	30 c. New South Wales (*shades*)	1·50	12
		a. Green (leaves) omitted		
420/25		.. .. *Set of* 6	3·50	90

No. 425 was reprinted in 1971, and this resulted in shade variations; particularly in the petals, which showed greater areas of white.

220. Soil Sample Analysis.

221. Rubber-gloved Hands, Syringe and Head of Hippocrates.

(Des. R. Ingpen. Photo.)

1968 (6 Aug.). *International Soil Science Congress and World Medical Association Assembly. P 13 × 13½.*

426	**220**	5 c. orange-brown, stone, greenish blue & black	25	15
427	**221**	5 c. greenish blue, dull ol.-yellow, rose and black	25	15
		a. Nos. 426/7 *se-tenant* with gutter margin between ..	2·50	2·00

The above were printed in sheets of 100 containing a pane of 50 of each design.

The major shades formerly listed have been deleted as there is a range of intermediate shades.

222. Athlete carrying Torch, and Sunstone Symbol.

223. Sunstone Symbol and Mexican Flag.

(Des. H. Williamson. Photo.)

1968 (2 Oct.). *Olympic Games, Mexico City. P 13½ × 13 (5 c.) or 13 × 13½ (25 c.).*

428	**222**	5 c. multicoloured ..	20	10
429	**223**	25 c. multicoloured ..	1·00	1·00

224. Houses and Dollar Signs.

225. Church Window and View of Bethlehem.

(Des. Erica McGilchrist. Photo.)

1968 (16 Oct.). *Building and Savings Societies Congress. P 13½ × 13.*

430	**224**	5 c. multicoloured ..	20	10

(Des. G. Hamori. Photo.)

1968 (23 Oct.). *Christmas. P 13½ × 13.*

431	**225**	5 c. multicoloured ..	25	5
		a. Green window (gold omitted)		

226. Edgeworth David (geologist).

227. A. B. Paterson (poet).

228. Albert Namatjira (artist).

229. Caroline Chisholm (social worker).

(Des. Note Ptg. Branch (Nos. 432, 434), A. Cook (others). Recess, background litho.)

1968 (6 Nov.). *Famous Australians (First Series). P 14½ × 14.*

432	**226**	5 c. myrtle-grn./*pale green*	85	12
		a. Booklet pane. Five stamps plus one printed label	4·50	
433	**227**	5 c. black/*pale blue* ..	85	12
		a. Booklet pane. Five stamps plus one printed label	4·50	
434	**228**	5 c. blackish brn./*pale buff*	85	12
		a. Booklet pane. Five stamps plus one printed label	4·50	
435	**229**	5 c. deep violet/*pale lilac*	85	12
		a. Booklet pane. Five stamps plus one printed label	4·50	

Nos. 432/5 were only issued in booklets and only exist with one or two adjacent sides imperf.

See also Nos. 446/9, 479/82, 505/8, 537/40, 590/5, 602/7 and 637/40.

230. Macquarie Lighthouse.

1968 (27 Nov.). *150th Anniv. of Macquarie Lighthouse. Recess, background litho. P 14½ × 13½.*

436	**230**	5 c. black/*pale yellow* ..	20	12

Used examples are known with the pale yellow background colour omitted.

231. Pioneers and Modern Building, Darwin.

(Des. Mrs. M. Lyon. Photo.)

1969 (5 Feb.). *Centenary of Northern Territory Settlement. P 13½.*

437	**231**	5 c. blackish brown, yellow-olive & yell.-ochre	20	12

232. Melbourne Harbour.

(Des. J. Mason. Photo.)

1969 (26 Feb.) *Sixth Biennial Conference of International Association of Ports and Harbours. P 13½.*

438	**232**	5 c. multicoloured ..	20	12

233. Concentric Circles (symbolising Management, Labour and Government).

(Des. G. Hamori. Photo.)

1969 (4 June). *50th Anniv. of International Labour Organization. P 13½.*

439	**233**	5 c. lt. grn'sh bl., ultram., gold & blackish grey	20	12

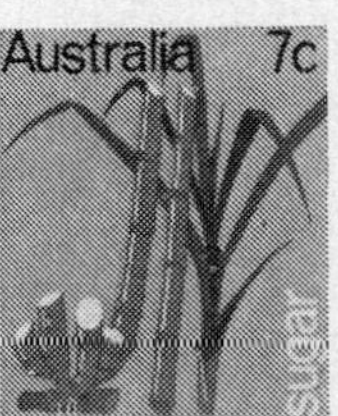

234. Sugar Cane.

235. Timber.

236. Wheat.

237. Wool.

(Des. R. Ingpen. Photo.)

1969 (17 Sept.). *Primary Industries. P* 13½×13.
440 **234** 7 c. multicoloured .. 65 50
441 **235** 15 c. multicoloured .. 1·25 1·00
a. Black ("Australia" and value) omitted ..
442 **236** 20 c. multicoloured .. 85 50
443 **237** 25 c. multicoloured .. 1·25 75

238. " The Nativity" (stained-glass window).

239. " Tree of Life ", Christ in Crib and Christmas Star (abstract).

(Des. G. Hamori (5 c.), J. Coburn (25 c.). Photo.)

1969 (15 Oct.). *Christmas. P* 13½×13 (5 *c.*) *or* 13×13½ (25 *c.*).
444 **238** 5 c. multicoloured .. 20 10
445 **239** 25 c. orange-red, light crimson, black & gold 1·50 1·25

240. Edmund Barton.

241. Alfred Deakin.

242. J. C. Watson.

243. G. H. Reid.

(Des. from drawings by J. Santry. Recess, background litho.)

1969 (22 Oct.). *Famous Australians* (*Second Series*). *Prime Ministers. P* 14½×14.
446 **240** 5 c. black/*pale green* .. 60 10
a. Booklet pane. Five stamps plus one printed label .. 3·50
447 **241** 5 c. black/*pale green* .. 60 10
a. Booklet pane. Five stamps plus one printed label .. 3·50
448 **242** 5 c. black/*pale green* .. 60 10
a. Booklet pane. Five stamps plus one printed label .. 3·50
449 **243** 5 c. black/*pale green* .. 60 10
a. Booklet pane. Five stamps plus one printed label .. 3·50

Nos. 446/9 were only issued in booklets and only exist with one or two adjacent sides imperf.

244. Capt. Ross Smith's Vickers " Vimy ", 1919.

245. Lt. H. Fysh and Lt. P. McGinness 1919 survey with Ford Car.

246. Capt. Wrigley and Sgt. Murphy in " BE 2E " take off to meet the Smiths.

(Des. E. Thake. Photo.)

1969 (12 Nov.). *50th Anniv. of First England–Australia Flight. P* 13½.
450 **244** 5 c. olive-green, pale blue, black and red .. 25 12
451 **245** 5 c. blk., red & olive-grn. 25 12
452 **246** 5 c. olive-green, black, pale blue and red .. 25 12
a. Strip of 3. Nos. 450/2.. 1·25 1·25

The three designs appear *se-tenant*, both horizontally and vertically, throughout the sheet.

247. Symbolic Track and Diesel Locomotive.

(Des. B. Sadgrove. Photo.)

1970 (11 Feb.). *Sydney–Perth Standard Gauge Railway Link. P* 13×13½.
453 **247** 5 c. multicoloured .. 15 10

248. Australian Pavilion, Osaka.

249. " Southern Cross " and " from the Country of the South with warm feelings " (message).

(Des. J. Copeland (5 c.), A. Leydin (20 c.). Photo.)

1970 (16 Mar.). *World Fair, Osaka. P* 13½.
454 **248** 5 c. multicoloured .. 12 12
455 **249** 20 c. orange-red & black 70 60

250. Queen Elizabeth II and Prince Philip.

251. Australian Flag.

(Des. Staff Artists (5 c.), J. Mason (30 c.). Photo.)

1970 (31 Mar.). *Royal Visit. P* 13×13½.
456 **250** 5 c. black & deep ochre 15 12
457 **251** 30 c. multicoloured .. 1·25 1·00

252. Lucerne Plant, Bull and Sun.

(Des. R. Ingpen. Photo.)

1970 (13 Apr.). *Eleventh International Grasslands Congress. P* 13×13½.
458 **252** 5 c. multicoloured .. 15 12

253. " Cook, giant among navigators, enters the Pacific . . ."

254. ". . . and fixes the position of the eastern part of Australia . . ."

255. ". . . where he finds new people and strange animals ".

256. " He and his scientists chart the shores and sketch the flora . . ."

257. ". . . and sovereignty is proclaimed over the land discovered ".

258. Captain Cook, H.M.S. *Endeavour*, Quadrant, Aborigines and Kangaroo. (*Horiz.* 84 × 30 *mm.*)

(Des. R. Ingpen and " Team " (T. Keneally, A. Leydin, J. R. Smith). Photo.)

1970 (20 Apr.). *Bicentenary of Captain Cook's Discovery of Australia's East Coast. P* 13½ × 13.

459 **253** 5 c. multicoloured .. 25 25
460 **254** 5 c. multicoloured .. 25 25
461 **255** 5 c. multicoloured .. 25 25
462 **256** 5 c. multicoloured .. 25 25
463 **257** 5 c. multicoloured .. 25 25
a. Strip of 5. Nos. 459/63 .. 1·50 1·50
464 **258** 30 c. multicoloured .. 1·50 1·50
MS465 157 × 129 mm. Nos. 459/64. Imperf. .. .. 2·50 2·50
459/64 .. .. *Set of* 6 2·50 2·50

The 5 c. stamps were issued horizontally *se-tenant* within the sheet, to form a composite design in the order listed.

50,000 miniature sheets were made available by the Post Office to the organisers of the Australian National Philatelic Exhibition which overprinted them in the white margin at each side of the 30 c. stamp with "Souvenir Sheet AUSTRALIAN NATIONAL PHILATELIC EXHIBITION" at left and "ANPEX 1970 SYDNEY 27 APRIL—1 MAY" at right in light-red-brown and they were also serially numbered. These were put on sale at the exhibition on the basis of one sheet to each visitor paying 30 c. for admission. Although still valid for postage, since the stamps themselves had not been defaced, these sheets were not sold at post offices.

Subsequently further supplies were purchased and similarly overprinted and numbered by a private firm without the authority of the Post Office and ANPEX took successful legal action to stop their further sale to the public. This firm also had the unoverprinted sheets rouletted in colour between the stamps whilst further supplies of the normal sheets were overprinted with reproductions of old coins and others with an inscription commemorating the opening of Melbourne Airport on 1st July 1970, but all these are private productions. Further private productions have been reported.

260. Golden Wattle.

260*a*. Sturt's Desert Pea.

259. Sturt's Desert Rose.

AUSTRALIA AUSTRALIA
I. II.

Two types of 2c.

I. "AUSTRALIA" thin; "2c" thin; flower name lightly printed.

II. Redrawn. "AUSTRALIA" thicker; "2c" much more heavily printed; flower name thicker and bolder.

(Des. Note Ptg. Branch. Photo.)

1970–75. *Coil Stamps. Perf.* 14½ × *imperf.*

465*a* **259** 2 c. mult. (I) (1.10.71) 20 5
ab. Type II (1973) .. 5 5
466 ,, 4 c. mult. (27.4.70) .. 25 10
467 **260** 5 c. mult. (27.4.70) .. 5 5
468 **259** 6 c. mult. (28.9.70) .. 30 5
a. Green (leaves) omitted
468*b* **260*a*** 7 c. mult. (1.10.71) .. 10 5
c. Green (leaves) omitted 80·00
468*d* ,, 10 c. mult. (15.1.75) .. 12 5
465*a*/8*d* .. .. *Set of* 6 70 35

Nos. 465*a*/8*d* have horizontal coil perforations described after No. 191.

The 2 c. (No. 465*a*), 5 c. and 7 c. also exist on fluorescent paper; the 2 c. (No. 465ab) and 10 c. exist only on fluorescent paper (see note after No. 504).

261. Snowy Mountains Scheme.
262. Ord River Scheme.
263. Bauxite to Aluminium.

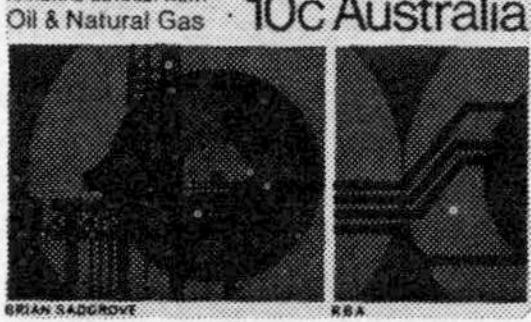

264. Oil and Natural Gas.

(Des. L. Mason (7 c.), R. Ingpen (8 c., 9 c.) B. Sadgrove (10 c.). Photo.)

1970 (31 Aug.). *National Development* (1st *series*). *P* 13 × 13½.

469 **261** 7 c. multicoloured .. 65 30
470 **262** 8 c. multicoloured .. 10 8
471 **263** 9 c. multicoloured .. 10 5
472 **264** 10 c. multicoloured .. 65 12

See also Nos. 541/4.

265. Rising Flames.

(Des. G. Hamori. Photo.)

1970 (2 Oct.). *16th Commonwealth Parliamentary Association Conference, Canberra. P* 13½.

473 **265** 6 c. multicoloured .. 20 5

266. Milk Analysis and Dairy Herd.

(Des. R. Honisett. Photo.)

1970 (7 Oct.). *18th International Dairy Congress, Sydney. P* 13½.

474 **266** 6 c. multicoloured .. 20 5

267. " The Nativity ".

268. U.N. " Plant " and Dove of Peace.

(Des. W. Beasley. Photo.)

1970 (14 Oct.). *Christmas. P* 13½.

475 **267** 6 c. multicoloured .. 20

(Des. Monad Ltd. Photo.)

1970 (19 Oct.). *25th Anniv. of United Nations. P* 13½.

476 **268** 6 c. multicoloured .. 20 5

269. Boeing " 707 " and Avro " 504 ".

(Des. G. Hamori. Photo.)

1970 (2 Nov.). *50th Anniv. of QANTAS Airline. T* **269** *and similar horiz. design. Multicoloured. P* 13½.

477 6 c. Type **269** 20 8
478 30 c. Avro " 504 " and Boeing " 707 " 95 80

270. The Duigan Brothers (Pioneer Aviators).

(Des. A. Cook (No. 480), T. Adams (No. 482), Note Ptg. Branch (others.). Recess (background litho).)

1970 (16 Nov.). *Famous Australians* (*Third Series*). *T* **270** *and similar vert. designs. P* 14½ × 14.

479 6 c. blue 55 8
a. Booklet pane. Five stamps plus one printed label .. 3·25
480 6 c. black/*flesh* 55 8
a. Booklet pane. Five stamps plus one printed label .. 3·25
481 6 c. purple/*pink* 55 8
a. Booklet pane. Five stamps plus one printed label .. 3·25
482 6 c. brown-lake/*pink* .. 55 8
a. Booklet pane. Five stamps plus one printed label .. 3·25

Designs:—No. 479 Type **270**; No. 480 Lachlan Macquarie (Governor of N.S.W.); No. 481 Adam Lindsay Gordon (poet); No. 482 E. J. Eyre (explorer).

Nos. 479/82 were only issued in booklets and only exist with one or two adjacent sides imperf.

271. " Theatre ".

(Des. D. Annand. Photo.)

1971 (6 Jan.). *" Australia-Asia ". T* **271** *and similar horiz. designs. Multicoloured. P* 13½ × 13.

483 7 c. Type **271** 25 12
484 15 c. " Music " 45 40
485 20 c. " Sea Craft " 60 55

272. The Southern Cross.

(Des. R. Beck. Photo.)

1971 (21 Apr.). *Centenary of Australian Natives' Association. P* 13 × 13½.

486 **272** 6 c. blk., verm. & brt. blue 20 5

273. Market " Graph ".

(Des. Monad Ltd. Photo.)

1971 (5 May). *Centenary of Sydney Stock Exchange. P* 13½ × 13.

487 **273** 6 c. multicoloured .. 20 5

274. Rotary Emblem.

(Des. H. Williamson. Photo.)

1971 (17 May). *50th Anniv. of Rotary International in Australia. P* 13 × 13½.

488 **274** 6 c. multicoloured .. 20 5

275. " Mirage " Jet and " D.H.9a " Biplane. **276.** Draught-horse, Cat and Dog.

(Des. R. Honisett. Photo.)

1971 (9 June). *50th Anniv. of R.A.A.F. P* 13½ × 13.

489 **275** 6 c. multicoloured .. 20 5

(Des. R. Ingpen. Photo.)

1971 (5 July). *Animals. T* **276** *and similar vert. designs. Multicoloured. P* 13½ × 13.

490 6 c. Type **276** 20 12
491 12 c. Vet and lamb (" Animal Science ") 35 20
492 18 c. Red Kangaroo (" Fauna Conservation ") .. 45 30
493 24 c. Guide-dog (" Animals Aid to Man ") .. 65 40

The 6 c. commemorates the Centenary of the Australian R.S.P.C.A., and the others are short-time definitives.

277. Bark Painting.

(Des. J. Mason. Photo.)

1971 (29 Sept.). *Aboriginal Art. T* **277** *and similar multicoloured designs. P* 13 × 13½ (20, 25 *c.*) *or* 13½ × 13 (*others*).

494 20 c. Type **277** 45 20
495 25 c. Body decoration .. 55 40
a. Black omitted* .. ..
496 30 c. Cave painting (*vert.*) .. 65 40
497 35 c. Grave posts (*vert.*) .. 45 35

*The omission of the black results in the stamp being without face-value and " AUSTRALIA ".

Nos. 494/7 also exist on fluorescent paper.

278. The Three Kings and the Star.

(Des. J. Lee. Photo.)

1971 (13 Oct.). *Christmas. Colours of star and colour of* " AUSTRALIA " *given. P* 13 × 13½.

498 **278** 7 c. Royal bl., pale mauve and pale lake-brown 1·00 25
499 ,, 7 c. pale lake-brown, pale mauve and white .. 1·00 25
500 ,, 7 c. p. mve., white & blk. 1·00 25
501 ,, 7 c. black, green and black 1·00 25
502 ,, 7 c. lilac, green and lilac 1·00 25
503 ,, 7 c. blk., pale lake-brn. & white .. .. 1·00 25
504 ,, 7 c. Royal blue, pale mauve and green .. 1·00 25
a. Block of 7. Nos. 498/504 10·00 10·00
498/504 .. .. *Set of* 7 6·00 1·50

Nos. 498/504, which also exist on fluorescent paper, were issued in sheets having two panes of 50 stamps. Each half pane had its stamps arranged thus:—

498	499	500	499	498
503	502	501	502	503
504	501	500	501	504
503	502	501	502	503
498	499	500	499	498

FLUORESCENT VERY WHITE CHALKY PAPER. As an experiment 10% of the above issue was printed on very white paper which fluoresces back and front under an ultraviolet lamp; it also has a strong coating of chalk on the surface. Late in 1972 this paper began to be introduced more generally and a number of stamps exist on both types of paper. The normal helecon paper does not fluoresce under the lamp but does react to the chalky test to a lesser degree.

Stamps reprinted on the white fluorescent paper are recorded below in footnotes and are listed in the *Elizabethan Catalogue*.

279. Andrew Fisher. **280.** Cameo Brooch.

(Des. J. Sandry. Recess.)

1972 (8 Mar.). *Famous Australians* (*Fourth Series*). *Prime Ministers. T* **279** *and similar vert. designs. P* 14½ × 14.

505 7 c. ultramarine (Type **279**) 35 5
a. Booklet pane. Five stamps plus one printed label .. 2·00
506 7 c. ultram. (W. M. Hughes) 35 5
a. Booklet pane. Five stamps plus one printed label .. 2·00
507 7 c. red (Joseph Cook) .. 35 5
a. Booklet pane. Five stamps plus one printed label .. 2·00
508 7 c. red (S. M. Bruce) .. 35 5
a. Booklet pane. Five stamps plus one printed label .. 2·00

Nos. 505/8 were issued only in booklets and exist only with one or two adjacent sides imperf.

(Des. Mrs. V. Mason. Photo.)

1972 (18 Apr.). *50th Anniv. of Country Women's Association. P* 13½ × 13.

509 **280** 7 c. multicoloured .. 20 5

281. Fruit.

(Des. D. Annand. Photo.)

1972 (14 June). *Primary Industries. T* **281** *and similar horiz. designs. Multicoloured. P* 13½.

510 20 c. Type **281** .. .. 1·75 1·00
511 25 c. Rice .. .. .. 1·75 1·10
512 30 c. Fish .. .. .. 1·90 1·40
513 35 c. Beef .. .. .. 6·50 4·50

282. Worker in Wheelchair. **284.** Athletics.

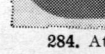

283. Telegraph Line.

(Des. from photographs by Barbara Ardizzone. Photo.)

1972 (2 Aug.). *Rehabilitation of the Disabled. T* **282** *and similar designs. P* $13\frac{1}{2}\times13$ (18 *c.*) *or* $13\times13\frac{1}{2}$ (*others*).

514 12 c. yellow-brown & emer. 15 10
515 18 c. sage-grn. & yell.-orge. 30 20
516 24 c. blue & yellow-brown .. 30 20

Designs: *Horiz.*—18 c. Patient and teacher. *Vert.*—24 c. Boy playing with ball.

The 12 c. and 24 c. also exist on fluorescent paper and these are scarce.

(Des. J. Copeland. Photo.)

1972 (22 Aug.). *Centenary of Overland Telegraph Line. P* $13\times13\frac{1}{2}$.

517 **283** 7 c. multicoloured .. 20 5

1972 (28 Aug.). *Olympic Games, Munich. T* **284** *and similar vert. designs. Multicoloured. P* $13\frac{1}{2}\times13$.

518 7 c. Type **284** 20 12
519 7 c. Rowing 20 12
520 7 c. Swimming 20 12
521 35 c. Equestrian .. .. 2·25 1·75

285. Numerals and Computer Circuit.

(Des. G. Andrews. Photo.)

1972 (16 Oct.). *Tenth International Congress of Accountants, Sydney. P* $13\times13\frac{1}{2}$.

522 **285** 7 c. multicoloured .. 20 5

286. Australian-built Harvester.

(Des. R. Ingpen. Photo.)

1972 (15 Nov.). *Pioneer Life. T* **286** *and similar multicoloured designs. P* $13\frac{1}{2}\times13$ (5, 10 *and* 60 *c.*) *or* $13\times13\frac{1}{2}$ (*others*).

523 5 c. Pioneer family (*vert.*) 5 5
524 10 c. Water-pump (*vert.*) .. 12 8
525 15 c. Type **286** 20 12
526 40 c. House 50 30
527 50 c. Stage-coach 60 40
528 60 c. Morse key (*vert.*) .. 75 50
529 80 c. Paddle-steamer .. 1·00 70
523/9 .. .. *Set of* 7 2·75 1·90

All values also exist on fluorescent paper.

287. Jesus with Children.

(Des. from drawing by Wendy Tamlyn. (7 c.), L. Stirling (35 c.). Photo.)

1972 (29 Nov.). *Christmas. T* **287** *and similar vert. design. Multicoloured. P* $14\frac{1}{2}\times14$ (7 *c.*) *or* $13\frac{1}{2}\times13$ (35 *c.*).

530 7 c. Type **287** 15 5
a. Brown-red ("Australia 7c") omitted .. .. ..
b. Red-brown (inscr.) omitted
531 35 c. Dove and spectrum motif .. .. .. 3·25 85

The 7c. was printed on fluorescent paper only.

288. "Length".

(Des. Weatherhead & Stitt Pty. Ltd. Photo.)

1973 (7 Mar.). *Metric Conversion. T* **288** *and similar multicoloured designs. Fluorescent paper. P* $14\frac{1}{2}\times14$ (No. 535) *or* $14\times14\frac{1}{2}$ (*others*).

532 7 c. Type **288** 45 12
533 7 c. "Volume" 45 12
a. Yellow-olive omitted*
534 7 c. "Mass" 45 12
535 7 c. "Temperature" (*horiz.*) 45 12

*This results in the man's drink and shorts appearing white, and the colour of the stool being the same as the background.

289. Caduceus and Laurel Wreath.

(Des. H. Williamson. Photo.)

1973 (4 Apr.). *25th Anniv. of W.H.O. Fluorescent paper. P* $14\frac{1}{2}\times14$.

536 **289** 7 c. multicoloured .. 15 5

290. William Wentworth (statesman and explorer). **291.** Shipping.

(Des. J. Santry. Recess and litho.)

1973 (16 May). *Famous Australians* (5*th series*). *T* **290** *and similar vert. designs. P* $14\frac{1}{2}\times14$.

537 7 c. yellow-bistre and black 30 5
538 7 c. lilac and black .. 30 5
539 7 c. yellow-bistre and black 30 5
540 7 c. lilac and black 30 5
a. Block of 4. Nos. 537/40 1·75 90

Portraits:—No. 537, Type **290**; No. 538, Isaac Isaacs (first Australian-born Governor-General); No. 539, Mary Gilmore (writer); No. 540, Marcus Clarke (author).

Nos. 537/40 were printed in *se-tenant* blocks of four within the sheet. They also exist on fluorescent paper.

(Des. J. Copeland. Photo.)

1973 (6 June). *National Development* (2*nd series*). *T* **291** *and similar vert. designs. Multicoloured. P* $13\frac{1}{2}\times13$.

541 20 c. Type **291** 65 45
542 25 c. Iron ore and steel .. 85 60
543 30 c. Beef roads 80 60
544 35 c. Mapping .. .. 1·60 1·40

292. Banded Coral Shrimp.

(Des. Printing Bureau artists (1 to 4 c.), J. Mason (others). Photo.)

1973 (11 July)–**74**. *Marine Life and Gemstones. T* **292** *and similar multicoloured designs. Fluorescent paper. Horiz. designs, P* $14\times14\frac{1}{2}$ (1 *to* 4 *c.*), *or vert., P* $14\frac{1}{2}\times14$ (*others*).

545 1 c. Type **292** 5 5
546 2 c. Fiddler crab 5 5
547 3 c. Coral crab 5 5
548 4 c. Mauve stinger 5 5
549 6 c. Chrysoprase 8 5
550 7 c. Agate 10 5
a. Black (value and "agate") omitted .. .. ..
551 8 c. Opal 10 5
552 9 c. Rhodonite 12 8
552*a* 10 c. Star sapphire (16.10.74) 12 8
b. Black (value, inscr., etc.) omitted .. .. ..
545/52*a* .. .. *Set of* 9 55 35

The 3 c. and 7 c. exist with PVA gum as well as gum arabic.

293. Children at Play.

(Des. G. Hamori. Photo.)

1973 (5 Sept.). *50th Anniv. of Legacy* (*Welfare Organisation*). *P* $13\times13\frac{1}{2}$.

553 **293** 7 c. cinnamon, deep claret and emerald .. 15 8

PAPER. From No. 554 onwards all issues are on white fluorescent paper, *unless otherwise stated.*

PERFORATIONS. From No. 554 onwards two different perforating machines were used for some issues, giving gauges of 14 or $14\frac{1}{2}\times14$ (on horizontal stamps), the exact measurement being 14.2×13.8 or 14.6×13.8. Other unrecorded examples may exist.

294. John Baptising Jesus.

(Des. G. Hamori. Photo.)

1973 (3 Oct.). *Christmas. T* **294** *and similar vert. design. Multicoloured. P* 14 (7 *c.*) *or* $13\frac{1}{2}\times13$ (30 *c.*).

554 7 c. Type **294** 20 10
a. Perf. $14\times14\frac{1}{2}$ 25 20
555 30 c. The Good Shepherd .. 1·00 80

295. Sydney Opera House.

(Des. A. Leydin. Photo.)

1973 (17 Oct.). *Architecture. T* **295** *and similar designs. P* 14 (7, 10 *c.*), 13 × 13½ (40 *c.*) *or* 13½ × 13 (50 *c.*).

556	7 c. pale turquoise-blue and new blue	20	12
	a. Perf. 14½ × 14	25	20
557	10 c. light ochre and sepia ..	35	35
	a. Perf. 14½ × 14	40	40
558	40 c. light grey, grey-brown and grey-black ..	85	85
559	50 c. multicoloured	1·10	1·10

Designs: *Horiz.*—10 c. Buchanan's Hotel, Townsville; 40 c. Como House, Melbourne. *Vert.*—50 c. St. James' Church, Sydney.

296. Wireless Receiver and Speaker.

(Des. E. Thake. Photo.)

1973 (21 Nov.). *50th Anniv. of Regular Radio Broadcasting. P* 13 × 13½.

560	**296**	7 c. lt. turq.-blue, brown-red & black	15	12

297. Wombat.

(Des. R. Bates.)

1974 (13 Feb.). *Animals. T* **297** *and similar vert. designs. Multicoloured. P* 14 × 14½ (20, 30 *c.*) *or* 13½ × 13 (*others*).

561	20 c. Type **297**	25	15
562	25 c. Spiny Ant-eater ..	35	15
563	30 c. Brushtail Possum ..	35	20
	a. Carmine-red (face-value, etc.) omitted		
564	75 c. Feather-tailed Glider ..	90	60

298. "Sergeant of Light Horse" (G. Lambert).

(Des. P.O. artists. Photo.)

1974 (24 Apr.). *Australian Paintings. T* **298** *and similar horiz. designs. Multicoloured. P* 13 × 13½ ($1) *or* 13½ × 13 (*others*).

565	$1 Type **298**	1·25	25
566	$2 "Red Gums of the Far North" (H. Heysen) ..	2·40	80
567	$4 "Shearing the Rams" (Tom Roberts)	5·00	2·25

209. Supreme Court Judge.

(Des. T. Thompson. Photo.)

1974 (15 May). *150th Anniv. of Australia's Third Charter of Justice. P* 14 × 14½.

568	**299** 7 c. multicoloured	10	12

300. Rugby Football.

(Des. A. Leydin from drawings by D. O'Brien. Photo.)

1974 (24 July). *Non-Olympic Sports. T* **300** *and similar multicoloured designs. P* 14½ × 14 (*Nos.* 569/70) *or* 14 × 14½ (*others*).

569	7 c. Type **300**	20	12
570	7 c. Bowls (*horiz.*)	20	12
571	7 c. Australian football (*vert.*)	20	12
572	7 c. Cricket (*vert.*)	20	12
573	7 c. Golf (*vert.*)	20	12
574	7 c. Surfing (*vert.*)	20	12
575	7 c. Tennis (*vert.*)	20	12
569/75	.. .. *Set of 7*	1·25	75

301. "Transport of Mails".

(Des. J. Copeland. Photo.)

1974 (9 Oct.). *Centenary of Universal Postal Union. T* **301** *and similar vert. design. Multicoloured. P* 14 (7 *c.*) *or* 13½ × 13 (30 *c.*).

576	7 c. Type **301**	15	12
	a. Perf. 14½ × 14	15	12
577	30 c. Three-part version of Type **301**	65	65

302. Letter "A" and W. C. Wentworth (co-founder).

= 9c (**303**)

(Des. I. Dalton. Typo. and litho.)

1974 (9 Oct.). *150th Anniv. of First Independent Newspaper, "The Australian". P* 14.

578	**302** 7 c. black/*light cinnamon*	8	5

1974 (16 Oct.). *No.* 551 *surch. with T* **303**, *in red.*

579	9 c. on 8 c. Opal	12	12

304. "The Adoration of the Magi".

306. "Road Safety".

305. "Pre-School Education".

(Des. and recess R.B.A.)

1974 (13 Nov.). *Christmas. Woodcuts by Dürer. T* **304** *and similar vert. designs. P* 14 × 14½.

580	10 c. black/*cream*	15	15
581	35 c. black/*cream*	60	60

Design:—35 c. "The Flight into Egypt".

PROCESS. All the following issues were printed in photogravure, *except where otherwise stated.*

(Des. Vivienne Binns (5 c.), Erica McGilchrist (11 c.), E. Tanner (15 c.), J. Meldrum (60 c.).)

1974 (20 Nov.). *Education in Australia. T* **305** *and similar multicoloured designs. P* 13½×13 (60 *c.*) *or* 13×13½ (*others*).
582 5 c. Type **305** 5 5
583 11 c. "Correspondence Schools" 15 12
584 15 c. "Science Education" .. 20 15
585 60 c. "Advanced Education" (*vert.*) 75 60

(Des. G. Andrews.)

1975 (29 Jan.). *Environment Dangers. T* **306** *and similar horiz. designs. Multicoloured. P* 14.
586 10 c. Type **306** 15 15
587 10 c. "Pollution" 15 15
a. Perf. 14½×14 .. .. 15 15
588 10 c. "Bush Fires" 15 15
a. Perf. 14½×14 .. .. 15 15

307. Australian Women's Year Emblem.

308. J. H. Scullin.

(Des. Leonora Howlett.)

1975 (12 Mar.). *International Women's Year. P* 14×14½.
589 **307** 10 c. deep vio.-blue, grn. and bluish violet 15 15

It is understood that this was issued with PVA gum as well as gum arabic.

(Des. B. Dunlop.)

1975 (26 Mar.). *Famous Australians (6th series). Prime Ministers. T* **308** *and similar vert. designs. Multicoloured. P* 14×15.
590 10 c. Type **308** 15 15
591 10 c. J. A. Lyons 15 15
592 10 c. Earle Page 15 15
593 10 c. Arthur Fadden 15 15
594 10 c. John Curtin 15 15
595 10 c. J. B. Chifley 15 15
590/5 .. .. *Set of* 6 80 80

The above issue exists with both PVA gum and gum arabic.

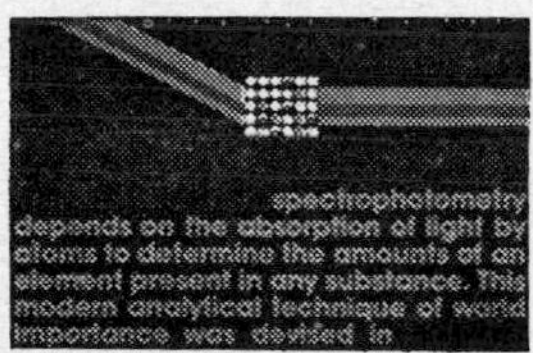

309. Atomic Absorption Spectrophotometry.

(Des. Weatherhead & Stitt.)

1975 (14 May). *Scientific Development. T* **309** *and similar horiz. designs. Multicoloured. P* 13×13½.
596 11 c. Type **309** 12 10
597 24 c. Radio astronomy 30 25
598 33 c. Immunology 40 35
599 48 c. Oceanography 60 50

310. Logo of Australian Postal Commission.

(Des. P. Huveneers.)

1975 (1 July). *Inauguration of Australian Postal and Telecommunications Commissions. T* **310** *and similar horiz. design. P* 14.
600 10 c. blk., rosine & pale grey .. 50 60
a. Perf. 14½×14 .. .. 50 60
601 10 c. black, orange-yellow and pale grey 50 60
a. Perf. 14½×14 .. .. 50 60

Design:—No. 601, Logo of Australian Telecommunications Commission.

Nos. 600/1 were printed together, within the sheet, horizontally and vertically *se-tenant.*

311. Edith Cowan.

312. *Helichrysum thomsonii.*

(Des. D. and J. O'Brien.)

1975 (6 Aug.). *Famous Australians (7th series). Australian Women. T* **311** *and similar vert. designs. Multicoloured.* A. *P* 14. B. *P* 14×14½.

		A.		B.	
602	10 c. Type **311**	12	15	12	15
603	10 c. Louisa Lawson ..	12	15	12	15
604	10 c. Ethel Richardson	12	15	12	15
605	10 c. Catherine Spence	12	15	12	15
606	10 c. Constance Stone	12	15	12	15
607	10 c. Truganini ..	12	15	12	15
602/7	.. .. *Set of* 6	70	80	70	80

No. 602 exists with both PVA gum and gum arabic.

No. 604 is inscr. with the *nom de plume* "Henry Handel Richardson".

(Des. F. Knight.)

1975 (27 Aug.). *Wild Flowers. T* **312** *and similar multicoloured designs. P* 14½×14 (18 *c.*) *or* 14×14½ (45 *c.*).
608 18 c. Type **312** 20 15
609 45 c. *Callistemon teretifolius* (*horiz.*) 55 45

The 18 c. exists with both PVA gum and gum arabic.

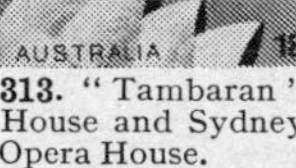

313. "Tambaran" House and Sydney Opera House.

314. Epiphany Scene.

(Des. D. Annand (18 c.) or G. Hamori (25 c.).)

1975 (16 Sept.). *Papua New Guinea Independence. T* **313** *and similar horiz. design. Multicoloured. P* 13½ (18 *c.*) *or* 13×13½ (25 *c.*).
610 18 c. Type **313** 30 25
611 25 c. "Freedom" (bird in flight) 40 40

(Des. D. O'Brien (15 c.) or J. Milne (45 c.).)

1975 (29 Oct.). *Christmas. T* **314** *and similar horiz. design. P* 14×14½ (15 *c.*) *or* 13×13½ (45 *c.*).
612 15 c. multicoloured 20 20
613 45 c. reddish violet, greenish blue and silver .. .. 2·75 2·25

Design:—45 c. "Shining Star".

315. Australian Coat of Arms.

(Des. J. Spatchurst.)

1976 (5 Jan.). *75th Anniv. of Nationhood. P* 15×14.
614 **315** 18 c. multicoloured .. 20 25
b. Buff (supporters) omitted .. ..

316. Telephone-user, *c.* 1878.

(Des. R. Ingpen.)

1976 (10 Mar.). *Telephone Centenary. P* 13×13½.
615 **316** 18 c. multicoloured .. 25 5

317. John Oxley.

(Des. B. Dunlop.)

1976 (9 June). *19th Century Explorers. T* **317** *and similar horiz. designs. Multicoloured. P* 13×13½.
616 18 c. Type **317** 25 25
617 18 c. Hume and Hovell .. 25 25
618 18 c. John Forest 25 25
619 18 c. Ernest Giles 25 25
620 18 c. William Gosse 25 25
621 18 c. Peter Warburton .. 25 25
616/21 .. .. *Set of* 6 1·40 1·40

318. Measuring Stick, Graph and Computer Tape.

(Des. R. Ingpen.)

1976 (15 June). *50th Anniv. of Commonwealth Scientific and Industrial Research Organisation. P* 14½×14.

622 **318** 18 c. multicoloured .. 25 25

319. Football.

(Des. A. Leydin.)

1976 (14 July). *Olympic Games, Montreal. T* **319** *and similar multicoloured designs. P* 13×13½ (*Nos.* 623 *and* 626) *or* 13½×13 (*others*).

623	18 c.	Type **319** ..	25	30
624	18 c.	Gymnastics (*vert.*)	25	30
625	25 c.	Diving (*vert.*)	35	40
626	40 c.	Cycling	55	65

320. Richmond Bridge, Tasmania.

(Des. O. Borchert.)

1976 (23 Aug.). *Australian Scenes. T* **320** *and similar designs. Multicoloured. P* 14×14½ (50 *c.*) *or* 14½×14 (*others*).

627	5 c.	Type **320** ..	5	8
628	25 c.	Broken Bay, N.S.W.	30	35
629	35 c.	Wittenoom Gorge, W.A.	45	50
630	50 c.	Mt. Buffalo, Victoria (*vert.*)	60	70
631	70 c.	Barrier Reef	85	95
632	85 c.	Ayers Rock, N.T.	1·00	1·10
627/32		*Set of* 6	3·00	3·25

321. Blamire Young (designer of first Australian stamp).

(Des. R. Honisett.)

1976 (27 Sept.). *National Stamp Week. P* 13½×13.

633 **321** 18 c. multicoloured .. 25 30

MS634 101×112 mm. No. 633×4 1·00

MS634 contains one stamp coloured as No. 633; the others, showing the different colour separations used in the printing, are each differently coloured.

322. "Virgin and Child" (detail, Simone Cantarini).

(Des. C. Medlycott (15 c.), Wendy Tamlyn (45 c.).)

1976 (1 Nov.). *Christmas. T* **322** *and similar horiz. design. P* 14½×14 (15 *c.*) *or* 13×13½ (45 *c.*).

635	15 c.	brt. magenta & lt. azure	20	25
636	45 c.	multicoloured ..	55	65

Design:—45 c. Toy koala and decorations.

323. John Gould.

(Des. B. Weatherhead.)

1976 (10 Nov.). *Famous Australians (8th series). T* **323** *and similar horiz. designs. Multicoloured. P* 14½×14.

637	18 c.	Type **323**	20	25
638	18 c.	Thomas Laby ..	20	25
639	18 c.	Sir Baldwin Spencer	20	25
640	18 c.	Griffith Taylor ..	20	25

POSTAGE DUE STAMPS.

POSTAGE DUE PRINTERS. Nos. D1/62 were typographed at the New South Wales Government Printing Office, Sydney.

D 1

D 2

Type D **1** adapted from New South Wales Type D **1**. No space at foot.

1902 (From July). *Chalk-surfaced paper. Wmk. Type* D **2**.

(*a*) *P* 11½, 12.

D1	D **1**	½d. emerald-green ..	1·25	1·25
D2	,,	1d. emerald-green ..	2·25	1·00
D3	,,	2d. emerald-green ..	2·25	1·00
D4	,,	3d. emerald-green ..	3·75	1·50
D5	,,	4d. emerald-green ..	3·75	1·50
D6	,,	6d. emerald-green ..	3·75	1·50
D7	,,	8d. emerald-green ..	18·00	12·00
D8	,,	5s. emerald-green ..	42·00	14·00

(*b*) *P* 11½, 12, *compound with* 11.

D 9	D **1**	1d. emerald-green ..	6·00	3·00
D10	,,	2d. emerald-green ..	6·00	3·00

(*c*) *P* 11.

D12	D **1**	1d. emerald-green ..	35·00	10·00

The ½d., 6d. and 8d. exist in dull green.

Stamps may be found showing portions of the letters "N S W" at foot.

D 3

D 4

1902–4. *Type* D **3**, *space at foot filled in. Chalky paper. Wmk.* D **2**. (*a*) *P* 11½, 12.

D13	1d. emerald-green ..	6·00	1·75
D14	2d. emerald-green ..	8·00	4·50
D15	3d. emerald-green ..	12·00	5·00
D17	5d. emerald-green ..	3·00	65
D18	10d. emerald-green ..	4·50	1·00
D19	1s. emerald-green ..	4·50	1·00
D20	2s. emerald-green ..	9·00	1·50
D21	5s. emerald-green ..	65·00	20·00

(*b*) *P* 11½, 12, *compound with* 11.

D22	½d. emerald-green ..	1·10	35
D23	1d. emerald-green ..	60	15
D24	2d. emerald-green ..	1·10	25
D25	3d. emerald-green ..	1·25	30
D26	4d. emerald-green ..	3·50	60
D27	5d. emerald-green ..	4·50	75
D28	6d. emerald-green ..	3·50	80
D29	8d. emerald-green ..	10·00	1·50
D30	10d. emerald-green ..	6·00	1·40
D31	1s. emerald-green ..	7·50	1·40
D32	2s. emerald-green ..	22·00	5·00
D33	5s. emerald-green ..	22·00	2·00

(*c*) *P* 11.

D34	½d. emerald-green ..	7·50	4·50
D35	1d. emerald-green ..	3·00	1·00
D36	2d. emerald-green ..	2·25	75
D37	3d. emerald-green ..	1·00	60
D38	4d. emerald-green ..	4·50	1·25
D39	5d. emerald-green ..	12·00	3·00
D40	6d. emerald-green ..	6·00	1·50
D41	1s. emerald-green ..	15·00	3·25
D42	5s. emerald green ..	50·00	7·00
D43	10s. emerald-green ..	£325	£200
D44	20s. emerald-green ..	£625	£400

Most values exist in dull green.

1906 (From JAN.)–**08.** *Chalky paper. Wmk. Type* D **4**.

(*a*) *P* 11½, 12, *compound with* 11.

D45 D **3** ½d. green (1907)	75	30
D46 „ 1d. green	60	15
D47 „ 2d. green	60	20
D48 „ 3d. green	5·00	3·00
D49 „ 4d. green (1907)	3·00	90
D50 „ 6d. green (1908)	3·25	90

(*b*) *P* 11.

D51 D **3** 1d. dull green	7·50	3·00
D52 „ 4d. dull green	15·00	7·50

Shades exist.

1907 (From JULY). *Chalky paper. Wmk. Type* w.**11** (*see Introduction*). *P* 11½×11.

D53 D **3** ½d. dull green	1·50	1·00
D54 „ 1d. dull green	1·50	1·00
D55 „ 2d. dull green	3·50	2·25
D56 „ 4d. dull green	10·00	4·50
D57 „ 6d. dull green	10·00	4·50

D 6

D 7

1908 (SEPT.)–**09.** *Stroke after figure of value. Chalky paper. Wmk. Type* D **4**.

(*a*) *P* 11½×11.

D58 D **3** 1s. dull green (1909) ..	10·00	3·00
D59 „ 5s. dull green	55·00	12·00

(*b*) *P* 11.

D60 D **6** 2s. dull green	£150	£120
D61 „ 10s. dull green	£350	£225
D62 „ 20s. dull green	£750	£500

Die I. Die II.

1d.

Die I. Die II.

2d.

(Typo. J. B. Cooke, Melbourne.)

1909 (JULY)–**1911.** *Type* D **7**. *Wmk. Crown over A, Type* w.**11**.

(*a*) *P* 12×12½ (*comb.*) *or* 12½ (*line*).

D63 ½d. rosine and yellow-green	30	30
D64 1d. rosine & yellow-grn. (I) ..	75	30
a. Die II (1911)		
D65 2d. rosine & yellow-grn. (I) ..	1·00	60
a. Die II (7.10)		
D66 3d. rosine and yellow-green	1·00	50
D67 4d. rosine and yellow-green	1·00	50
D68 6d. rosine and yellow-green	1·25	50
D69 1s. rosine and yellow-green	2·50	60
D70 2s. rosine and yellow-green	4·00	1·50
D71 5s. rosine and yellow-green	10·00	2·50
D72 10s. rosine and yellow-green	65·00	30·00
D73 £1 rosine and yellow-green	£110	55·00

(*b*) *P* 11.

D74 1d. rose & yellow-grn. (II) (1911)	50·00	50·00
D74*a* 2d. rose & yell.-grn. (II) (7.10)	£1250	
D75 6d. rose and yellow-green ..	£200	£175

The 1d. of this printing is distinguishable from No. D78 by the colours, the green being very yellow and the rose having less of a carmine tone. The paper is thicker and slightly toned, that of No. D78 being pure white; the gum is thick and yellowish, No. D78 having thin white gum.

All later issues of the 1d. and 2d. are Die II.

(Typo J. B. Cooke and T. S. Harrison (from May 1918).)

1912–23. *Type* D **7**. *Thin paper. White gum. W* w.**11**. (*a*) *P* 12½.

D76 ½d. scar. & p. yell.-grn. (12.12)	1·10	45

(*b*) *P* 11.

D77 ½d. rosine and bright apple-green (11.14)	30	30
a. Wmk. sideways	1·50	1·50
D78 1d. rosine and bright apple-green (1913)	30	30
a. Wmk. sideways	40	40

(*c*) *P* 14.

D79 ½d. rosine and bright apple-green (1916)	2·75	1·50
a. Carmine and apple-green (Harrison) (1918)	40	30
D80 1d. rosine and bright apple-green (10.14)	2·25	1·50
a. Scarlet and pale yellow-green (1916)	60	35
b. Carmine and apple-green (Harrison) (1918)	45	45
D81 2d. scarlet and pale yellow-green (1915)	75	50
a. Carmine and apple-green (Harrison) (1918)	1·10	60
D82 3d. rosine & apple-grn. (5.16)	3·00	3·00
a. Wmk. sideways	35·00	35·00
D83 4d. rosine & apple-grn. ('16)	4·50	4·50
a. Wmk. sideways	25·00	25·00
b. Carmine and apple-green (Harrison) (1918)	3·00	3·00
c. Carmine and pale yellow-green (Harrison) (26.4.21) ..	1·25	1·00
D85 1s. scarlet and pale yellow-green (7.23)	1·50	1·50
D86 10s. scarlet and pale yellow-green (5.21)	60·00	45·00
D87 £1 scarlet and pale yellow-green (5.21)	£110	65·00

Although printed by Cooke, the three higher values were not issued until some years later.

(Typo. T. S. Harrison (to Feb. 1926), A. J. Mullett (to June 1927) and J. Ash (later).)

1919–30. *Type* D **7**. *W* **6**. (*a*) *P* 14.

D91 ½d. carm. & yell.-grn. (7.23)	30	30
D92 1d. carm. & yell.-grn. (28.3.22)	30	15
D93 1½d. carm. & yell.-grn. (3.25)	3·00	3·00
D94 2d. carm. & yell.-grn. (20.3.22)	75	50
D95 3d. carm. & yell.-grn. (12.11.19)	1·10	1·00
D96 4d. carm. & yell.-grn. (13.2.22)	3·00	1·10
D97 6d. carm. & yell.-grn. (13.2.22)	3·00	1·50

(*b*) *P* 11.

D98 4d. carm. & yell.-grn. (10.30)	35	35

All values perf. 14 were printed by Harrison and all except the 4d. by Mullett and Ash. There is a wide variation of shades in this issue.

(Typo. J. Ash.)

1931–37. *Type* D **7**. *W* **15**. (*a*) *P* 14.

D100 1d. carm. & yell.-grn. (10.31)	1·50	40
D102 2d. carm. & yell.-grn. (19.10.31)	1·50	40

(*b*) *P* 11.

D105 ½d. carm. & yell.-grn. (4.34)	75	30
D106 1d. carm. & yell.-grn. (1.33)	35	5
D107 2d. carm. & yell.-grn. (29.9.32)	30	10
D108 3d. carm. & yell.-grn. (4.37)	30·00	25·00
D109 4d. carm. & yell.-grn. (26.7.34)	1·25	60
D110 6d. carm. & yell.-grn. (8.36)	£150	45·00
D111 1s. carm. & yell.-grn. (8.34)	6·00	2·50

MINIMUM PRICE

The minimum price quoted is 5p which represents a handling charge rather than a basis for valuing common stamps. For further notes about prices see introductory pages.

D 8

D 9

A. B. C.

The differences are found in the middle of the "D".

D.

E.

Type E. Larger "1" with only three background lines above; hyphen more upright.

(Frame recess. Value typo. J. Ash.)

1938. *W* **15**. *P* 14½×14.

D112 D **8** ½d. carmine & green (A)	25	5
D113 „ 1d. carmine & green (A)	25	8
D114 „ 2d. carmine & green (A)	25	8
D115 „ 3d. carmine & green (B)	80	70
D116 „ 4d. carmine & green (A)	50	25
D117 „ 6d. carmine & green (A)	1·50	1·50
D118 „ 1s. carmine & green (D)	5·00	1·50

Shades exist.

1946–57. *Redrawn as Type* C *and* E (1s.). *W* **15**. *P* 14½×14.

D119 D **9** ½d. carmine and green (9.56)	35	40
D120 „ 1d. carmine and green (11.1.47)	15	5
D121 „ 2d. carm. & grn. (9.46)	60	5
D122 „ 3d. carmine and green (25.9.46)	45	5
D123 „ 4d. carm. & grn. (11.52)	60	5
D124 „ 5d. carm. & grn. (12.48)	75	40
D125 „ 6d. carm. & green (9.47)	75	10
D126 „ 7d. carmine and green (26.8.53)	75	40
D127 „ 8d. carmine and green (24.4.57)	1·40	1·50
D128 „ 1s. carm. & green (9.47)	3·00	50
D119/28 .. .. *Set of* 10	7·50	3·00

There are many shades in this issue.

D 10

1953 (26 AUG.)–**60.** *W* **15**. *P* 14½×14.

D129 D **10** 1s. carmine and yellow-green (17.2.54)	1·00	30
a. Carmine and deep green	1·00	30
D130 „ 2s. carmine and yellow-green	1·75	60
a. Carmine and deep green	1·75	60
D131 „ 5s. carmine and green	6·00	1·25
a. Carmine and deep green ('60)	6·00	1·25

I.

II.

Type I. Numeral, "D" and stop, generally unoutlined.

Type II. Clear white line separates numeral, etc. from background.

1958–60. *No wmk.* *P* 14½×14.

D132	D **9**	½d. carmine and deep green (II) (27.2.58)	25	25
D133	,,	1d. carmine and deep green (I) (25.2.58)	50	35
		a. Type II ('59) ..	5	5
D134	,,	3d. carmine and deep green (II) (25.5.60)	10	10
D135	,,	4d. carmine and deep green (I) (27.2.58)	80	30
		a. Type II ('59) ..	5·00	5·00
D136	,,	5d. carmine and deep green (I) (27.2.58)	1·25	75
		a. Type II (–.10.59) ..	35·00	25·00
D137	,,	6d. carmine and deep green (II) (25.5.60)	30	30
D138	,,	8d. carmine and deep green (II) (25.2.58)	2·25	75
D139	,,	10d. carmine and deep green (II) (9.12.59)	75	25
D140	D **10**	1s. carmine and deep green (8.9.58) ..	75	15
		a. *Deep carmine & deep green* ('60)	75	15
D141	,,	2s. deep carmine and deep green (8.3.60)	1·25	20
D132/41		.. .. *Set of* 10	6·50	1·75

Nos. D140*a* and D141. Value tablets are re-engraved and have thicker and sharper printed lines than before.

The use of Postage Due stamps ceased on 31st January, 1963.

OFFICIAL STAMPS.

Postage stamps perforated "O S" in either large or small letters were used for official purposes. We do not list such varieties separately, but can supply when in stock.

O S

(O 1)

1931 (4 May). *Optd. with Type* O **1**.

O1	**13**	2d. rose-red..	25·00	12·00
O2	,,	3d. blue	90·00	30·00

For No. 139 overprinted with Type O **1**, see No. 139*a*.

1932–33. *Optd. as Type* O **1**.

(*a*) *W* **7**. (i.) *P* 13½×12½.

O4	**5a**	2d. golden-scarlet (No. 99*b*)	1·25	60
O5	,,	4d. yellow-olive (Jan. '32)	6·00	3·50

(ii.) *P* 12.

O6	**1**	6d. chestnut	30·00	25·00

(*b*) *W* **15**. (i.) *P* 13½×12½.

O 7	**5a**	½d. orange..	3·00	75
		a. Overprint inverted ..	£600	£450
O 8	,,	1d. sage-green (Feb. '32)..	1·00	30
O 9	,,	2d. golden-scarlet (10.2.32)	1·10	45
O10	,,	3d. ultramarine (Mar. '33)	6·00	4·50
O11	,,	5d. orange-brown.. ..	22·00	15·00

(ii.) *P* 12.

O13	**1**	6d. chestnut	10·00	10·00

(*c*) *Recess.* *No wmk.* *P* 11.

O16	**18**	2d. scarlet..	3·00	1·50
O17	,,	3d. blue	8·00	8·00
O18	**17**	1s. green	25·00	25·00

Issues of specially overprinted Official stamps became obsolete in 1933 when the various States reverted to the use of stamps with perforated initials.

BRITISH COMMONWEALTH OCCUPATION FORCE (JAPAN).

B.C.O.F. JAPAN 1946
(1)

B.C.O.F JAPAN 1946
(2)

1946 (11 Oct.)–**1947** (8 May). *Stamps of Australia optd. as T* **1** (1*d.*, 3*d.*) *or T* **2** (*others*).

B1	**27**	½d. orange (No. 179) ..	1·00	1·25
B2	**46**	1d. brown-purple (No. 203)	1·00	1·25
		a. Error. Blue overprint ..	40·00	48·00
B3	**31**	3d. purple-brown (No. 187)	1·25	1·50
B4	**34**	6d. purple-brown (No. 189*a*)	4·00	5·00
B5	**36**	1s. grey-green (No. 191) ..	5·00	6·00
B6	**1**	2s. maroon (No. 212) ..	18·00	22·00
B7	**38**	5s. claret (No. 176) ..	75·00	85·00
		a. Thin rough paper (No. 176a)	75·00	85·00
B1/B7		.. .. *Set of* 7	95·00	£110

The ½d., 1d. and 3d. values were first issued on 11th October, 1946, and withdrawn two days later, but were re-issued together with the other values on 8th May, 1947.

The following values with T **2** opt. in the colours given were from proof sheets, which however were used for postage: ½d. (red), 1d. (red or black) and 3d. (gold, red or black). (*Price from £250 un.*)

The use of B.C.O.F. stamps ceased on March 28, 1949.

AUSTRALIAN ANTARCTIC TERRITORY.

VALIDITY. All Antarctic Territory stamps are also valid for use in Australia, where they are put on sale for a limited period when first issued.

DATES OF ISSUE. The dates given refer to release dates in Australia. Local release dates are usually later and where known they are given in footnotes.

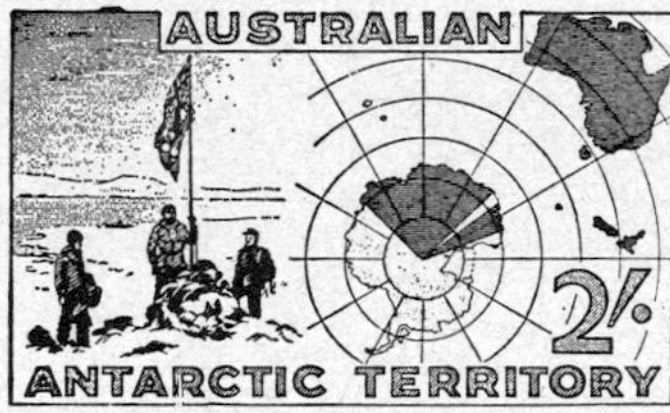

1. 1954 Expedition at Vestfold Hills and Map.

1957 (27 Mar.). *Recess.* *P* 14½.

1	**1**	2s. ultramarine	90	35

The first local use was 11.12.57.

2. Members of Shackleton Expedition at South Magnetic Pole, 1909.

3. Weazel and Team.

4. Dog-team and Iceberg.

5. Map of Antarctica and Emperor Penguins.

1959 (16 Dec.). *Recess; new values surch. typo.* (5*d.*, 8*d.*). *P* 14½ (5*d.*), 14½×14 (8*d.*) *or* 14×14½ (*others*).

2	**2**	5d. sepia and black	25	20
3	**3**	8d. deep blue	40	40
4	**4**	1s. deep green	90	90
5	**5**	2s. 3d. green	1·25	1·10

The first local use was 30.1.60.

6

7. Sir Douglas Mawson (Expedition leader).

1961 (5 July). *Recess.* *P* 14½.

6	**6**	5d. deep blue	35	20

1961 (18 Oct.). 50*th Anniv.* 1911–14 *Australasian Antarctic Expedition.* *Recess.* *P* 14½.

7	**7**	5d. myrtle-green	25	15

(New currency. 100 cents = 1 Australian dollar.)

8. Aurora and Camera Dome.

9. Helicopter.

10. Radio Operator.

(Des. J. Mason. Photo.)

1966 (28 Sept.)–**68.** *T* **8/10** *and similar multi-coloured designs. P* 13½.

8 1 c. Type **8** (*shades*) 5 5
9 2 c. Banding penguins (*shades*) 5 5
10 4 c. Ship and iceberg 8 8
11 5 c. Banding elephant seals (25.9.68) 10 10
12 7 c. Measuring snow strata .. 12 20
13 10 c. Wind gauges 25 25
14 15 c. Weather balloon .. 35 55
15 20 c. Type **9** 60 90
16 25 c. Type **10** .. .. 80 1·25
17 50 c. Ice compression tests .. 1·75 2·00
18 $1 Parahelion ("mock sun") 3·50 4·50
8/18 .. .. *Set of* 11 7·00 8·50

The 1 c. to 15 c. are vert. as Type **8**; the 50 c. and $1 are horiz. as Types **9** and **10** respectively.

The first local use of the 5 c. was 4.12.68, of the others 11.12.67.

11. Sastrugi (Snow Ridges).

(Des. J. Mason. Photo.)

1971 (23 June). *Tenth Anniv. of Antarctic Treaty. T* **11** *and similar horiz. design.*

19 6 c. blue and black 25 25
20 30 c. mult. (Pancake ice) .. 80 80

The first local use was 23.11.71.

12. Capt. Cook, Sextant and Compass.

(Des. J. Mason. Photo.)

1972 (13 Sept.). *Bicentenary of Cook's Circumnavigation of Antarctica. T* **12** *and similar horiz. design. Multicoloured. P* 13½.

21 7 c. Type **12** 20 20
22 35 c. Chart and *Resolution* .. 90 90

The first local use was in December 1972.

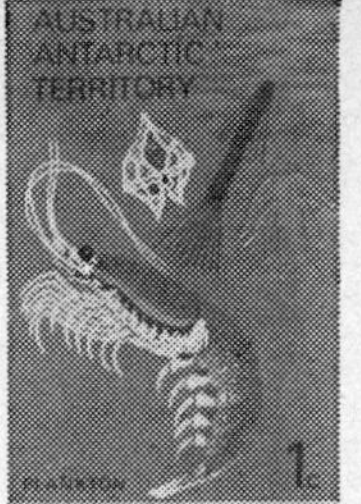

13. Plankton.

(Des. G. Browning (1, 7, 9, 10, 20 c., $1), R. Honisett (others). Photo.)

1973 (15 Aug.). *T* **13** *and similar multicoloured designs. P* 13×13½ (*horiz.*) *or* 13½×13 (*vert.*).

23 1 c. Type **13** 5 5
24 5 c. Mawson's "Gipsy Moth", 1931 .. .. .. 5 8
25 7 c. Adélie penguin .. 8 10
26 8 c. Rymill's "Fox Moth", 1934–7 .. .. .. 10 10
27 9 c. Leopard seal (*horiz.*) .. 10 12
28 10 c. Killer whale (*horiz.*) .. 12 12
29 20 c. Albatross (*horiz.*) .. 25 25
30 25 c. Wilkin's Lockheed "Vega", 1928 (*horiz.*) .. 30 35
31 30 c. Ellsworth's Northrop "Gamma", 1935 .. 35 40
32 35 c. Christensen's Avro "Avian", 1934 (*horiz.*) 40 45
33 50 c. Byrd's "Tri-Motor", 1929 .. .. .. 60 65
34 $1 Sperm whale .. .. 1·25 1·40
23/34 .. .. .. *Set of* 12 3·25 3·50

The first local use was 29.11.73.

BAGHDAD

BRITISH OCCUPATION

IN BRITISH BAGHDAD OCCUPATION
2 Ans
(1)

1917 (Sept.). *Stamps of Turkey, surch. as T* **1.**

(*a*) *Pictorial designs of* 1914. *T* **32**, *etc., and* **31** (*Mosque of Selim*).

1 **32** ½ a. on 2 pa. claret .. 30·00 30·00
a. "IN BRITISH" omitted £1500
2 **34** ½ a. on 5 pa. dull purple .. 25·00 25·00
a. Value omitted £1200
3 **36** ½ a. on 10 pa. green £140 £120
4 **31** ½ a. on 10 pa. green .. £300 £325
5 **37** 1 a. on 20 pa. red £140 £120
a. "BAGHDAD" double .. £500
6 **38** 2 a. on 1 pi. bright blue .. 45·00 45·00

(*b*) *As* (*a*), *but overprinted with small five-pointed Star.*

7 **37** 1 a. on 20 pa. red (B.) .. £110 £110
a. "OCCUPATION" omitted £1000
8 **38** 2 a. on 1 pi. bright blue (R.) £1400 £2400

(*c*) *Postal Jubilee stamps.*

9 **60** ½ a. on 10 pa. carmine .. £110 £110
10 ,, 1 a. on 20 pa. blue .. £250 £250
a. Value omitted £1700
11 ,, 2 a. on 1 pi. blk. & violet .. 25·00 25·00
a. "BAGHDAD" omitted .. £750

(*d*) *T* **30** *with opt. T* **26.**

12 **30** 2 a. on 1 pi. ultramarine .. £100 £100

(*e*) *Stamps optd. with Star and Arabic date* "1331" *within Crescent. T* **53** (*except No.* 16, *T* **57**, *five-pointed Star*).

13 **30** ½ a. on 10 pa. green (R.) .. 25·00 25·00
14 ,, 1 a. on 20 pa. rose .. £110 £110
a. Value omitted £1300 £1500
b. Optd. with T 26 also .. £1500 £1800
c. First "D" of "BAGHDAD" omitted £1100
15 **23** 1 a. on 20 pa. rose (No. 554a) £120 £120
a. Value omitted £1800
16 **21** 1 a. on 20 pa. carmine (No. 732) £1500 £1600
17 **30** 2 a. on 1 pi. ultram. (R.) .. 30·00 30·00
18 **21** 2 a. on 1 pi. dull blue (No. 543) (R.) .. .. 60·00 60·00

(*f*) *Stamps with similar opt., but date between Star and Crescent* (*Nos.* 19 *and* 22, *T* **54**; *others T* **55**, *five-pointed Star*).

19 **23** ½ a. on 10 pa. grey-green (No. 609a) (R.) .. 30·00 30·00
a. "OCCUPATION" omitted £1100
20 **60** ½ a. on 10 pa. carmine (B.) .. 55·00 55·00
21 **30** 1 a. on 20 pa. rose .. 28·00 28·00
22 **28** 1 a. on 20 pa. rose (Pl. II) (No. 617) .. .. 60·00 60·00
23 **15** 1 a. on 10 pa. on 20 pa. claret (No. 630) .. 70·00 70·00
a. "OCCUPATION" omitted £800 £750
24 **30** 2 a. on 1 pi. ultram. (R.) .. 60·00 60·00
a. "OCCUPATION" omitted £1200
b. "BAGHDAD" omitted .. £1200
25 **28** 2 a. on 1 pi. ultramarine (Pl. II) (No. 649) .. £350 £350

The last group (*f*) have the Crescent obliterated in violet-black ink, as this included the inscription, "Tax for the relief of children of martyrs."

BAHAMAS.

For GREAT BRITAIN stamps used in Bahamas with "A 05" obliteration, see index to Great Britain Used Abroad list.

I. CROWN COLONY.

1

2

(Eng. and recess. Perkins, Bacon & Co.)

1859 (10 June). *No wmk. Imperf.*

(*a*) *Thick paper.*

1 **1** 1d. reddish lake £850 £650
a. Brown-lake £550 £550

(*b*) *Thin paper.*

2 **1** 1d. dull lake .. .. .. 18·00 £250

Collectors are warned against false postmarks upon the remainder stamps of 1d., imperf., on thin paper.

1860 (Oct.). *No wmk. Clean-cut perf.* 14 *to* 16.

3 **1** 1d. lake £375 £200

1861 (June–Dec.). *No wmk.*

(*a*) *Rough perf.* 14 *to* 16.

4 **1** 1d. lake £275 £100
5 **2** 4d. dull rose (Dec., 1861) .. £400 £110
a. Imperf. between (pair) .. £2000
6 ,, 6d. grey-lilac (Dec., 1861) .. £475 £120
a. Pale dull lilac £475 £120

(*b*) *P* 11 *to* 12½.

7 **1** 1d. lake £600

No. 7 was not sent out to the Colony. It is also known part perforated.

(Recess. D.L.R.)

1862. *No wmk.** (*a*) *P* 11½, 12.

8 **1** 1d. carmine-lake .. .. £140 35·00
9 ,, 1d. lake .. .. .. £130 42·00
10 **2** 4d. dull rose .. .. £500 70·00
11 ,, 6d. lavender-grey £550 £100

(*b*) *P* 11½, 12, *compound with* 11.

12 **1** 1d. carmine-lake £350 £180
13 ,, 1d. lake £350 £180
14 **2** 4d. dull rose £2000 £500
15 ,, 6d. lavender-grey £2500 £375

(*c*) *P* 13.

16 **1** 1d. lake .. .. .. £150 45·00
17 ,, 1d. brown-lake .. .. £160 42·00
18 **2** 4d. dull rose .. .. £475 95·00
19 ,, 6d. lavender-grey .. .. £475 85·00
a. Lilac £500 £140

*Stamps exist with part of papermarker's sheet wmk. ("T. H. SAUNDERS" and date).

3

(T **3** Typo. D.L.R.)

1863–80. *Wmk. Crown CC.* (*a*) *P* 12½.

20 **1** 1d. brown-lake .. .. 32·00 32·00
21 ,, 1d. carmine-lake .. .. 35·00 38·00
22 ,, 1d. carmine-lake (aniline) 35·00 38·00
23 ,, 1d. rose-red .. .. 20·00 24·00
24 ,, 1d. red .. .. .. 22·00 24·00
25 ,, 1d. vermilion .. .. 22·00 24·00
26 **2** 4d. dull rose .. .. 95·00 32·00
27 ,, 4d. bright rose .. .. 42·00 25·00
28 ,, 4d. brownish rose .. .. 80·00 32·00
28*a* ,, 6d. rose-lilac £1000
29 ,, 6d. lilac (*shades*) .. 70·00 24·00
30 ,, 6d. deep violet (*Pen-c.* £1) 40·00 24·00
31 ,, 6d. violet (aniline) .. 60·00 32·00
32 **3** 1s. green (1865) .. £425 75·00

No. 28*a*, believed to be the shade of the first printing only, is a very rare stamp, not to be confused with No. 29.

(*b*) *P* 14.

33 **1** 1d. scarlet-vermilion .. 16·00 12·00
34 ,, 1d. scarlet (or scarlet-vermilion) (aniline) .. £400 †
35 **2** 4d. bright rose .. .. £200 24·00
36 ,, 4d. dull rose .. .. £425 24·00
37 ,, 4d. rose-lake .. .. £180 25·00
38 **3** 1s. dark green (1863) .. 25·00 14·00
39 ,, 1s. green (thick paper) (1880?) .. .. 3·50 4·00

1882 (March). *Wmk. Crown CA.* (*a*) *P* 12.

40 **1** 1d. scarlet-vermilion .. 16·00 12·00
41 **2** 4d. rose .. .. .. £150 24·00

(*b*) *P* 14.

42 **1** 1d. scarlet-vermilion .. 70·00 22·00
43 **2** 4d. rose .. .. .. £190 24·00
44 **3** 1s. green .. .. .. 14·00 12·00

See also No. 55.

FOURPENCE

(4)

5

1883. *No.* 30 *surch. with T* **4.**

45 **2** 4d. on 6d. deep violet .. £200 90·00
a. Surch. inverted £650 £500

The surcharge is also found placed diagonally and in various other positions.

Caution is needed in buying Nos. 45 and 45a.

(Typo. D.L.R.)

1884–98. *Wmk. Crown CA.* *P* 14.

47 **5** 1d. pale rose .. .. 6·50 4·50
48 ,, 1d. carmine-rose .. .. 3·00 1·60
49 ,, 1d. bright carmine (aniline) 2·50 3·75
50 ,, 2½d. dull blue .. .. 7·50 7·50
51 ,, 2½d. blue .. .. .. 8·00 3·75
52 ,, 2½d. ultramarine .. .. 3·00 2·50
53 ,, 4d. deep yellow .. .. 3·75 2·75
54 ,, 6d. mauve .. .. .. 4·00 4·25
55 **3** 1s. blue-green (1898) .. 15·00 11·00
56 **5** 5s. sage-green .. .. 25·00 25·00
57 ,, £1 Venetian red .. .. £130 85·00
47/57 .. .. *Set of* 7 £170 £120
50 & 54 Optd. "Specimen" *Set of* 2 25·00

6. Queen's Staircase, Nassau. 7

(Recess. De La Rue.)

1901–10. *P* 14

(*a*) *Wmk. Crown CC* (Sept. 1901).

58 **6** 1d. blk. & red (Optd. S. £8) .. 1·90 2·75

(*b*) *Wmk. Mult. Crown CA* (1910).

59 **6** 1d. black and red .. .. 3·25 2·25

For later shades, see Nos. 93/4.

(Typo. De La Rue.)

1902 (Dec.). *Wmk. Crown CA.* *P* 14.

60 **7** 1d. carmine .. .. 1·60 85
61 ,, 2½d. ultramarine .. .. 5·00 3·25
62 ,, 4d. orange .. .. .. 7·50 9·50
63 ,, 4d. deep yellow .. .. 7·50 11·00
64 ,, 6d. brown .. .. .. 7·00 9·00
65 ,, 1s. grey-black & carmine .. 8·00 11·00
66 ,, 1s. brownish grey & carm. 8·00 11·00
67 ,, 5s. dull purple and blue .. 32·00 32·00
68 ,, £1 green and black .. £180 £250
60/68 .. .. *Set of* 7 £225 £300
60/8 Optd. "Specimen" *Set of* 7 80·00

1903. *Wmk. Crown CC.* *P* 14.

69 **6** 5d. black and orange .. 10·00 13·00
70 ,, 2s. black and blue .. .. 10·00 15·00
71 ,, 3s. black and green .. 14·00 17·00
69/71 Optd. "Specimen" *Set of* 3 22·00

1906–11. *Wmk. Mult. Crown CA.* *P* 14.

72 **7** ½d. pale grn. (Optd. S. £15) 2·25 65
73 ,, 1d. carmine-rose .. .. 2·50 50
74 ,, 2½d. ultramarine (1907) .. 8·00 10·00
75 ,, 6d. bistre-brown (1911) .. 13·00 23·00

8

1.1.17.

(9)

(Typo. De La Rue.)

1912–19. *Wmk. Mult. Crown CA.* *P* 14.

76 **8** ½d. green, O 45 50
77 ,, ½d. yellow-green, O .. 75 50
78 ,, 1d. carmine (aniline), O .. 30 35
79 ,, 1d. deep rose, O .. .. 1·25 75
80 ,, 1d. rose, O .. .. .. 2·50 1·25
81 ,, 2d. grey, O (1919) .. 1·25 1·50
82 ,, 2½d. ultramarine, O .. 2·50 3·50
83 ,, 2½d. deep dull blue, O .. 3·75 5·00
84 ,, 4d. orange-yellow, O .. 2·25 4·00
85 **8** 4d. yellow, O .. .. 1·25 3·25
86 ,, 6d. bistre-brown, O .. 1·40 3·25
87 ,, 1s. grey-blk. & carmine, C 1·75 3·25
88 ,, 1s. jet-black & carmine, C 3·75 5·50
89 ,, 5s. dull purple and blue, C 14·00 20·00
90 ,, 5s. p. dull pur. & dp. bl., C 19·00 20·00
91 ,, £1 dull green and black, C 75·00 85·00
92 ,, £1 green and black, C .. 85·00 95·00
76/91 .. .. *Set of* 9 90·00 £110
76/91 Optd. "Specimen" *Set of* 9 80·00

1916–19. *Wmk. Mult. Crown CA.* *P* 14.

93 **6** 1d. grey-black & scarlet ('16) 2·50 3·00
94 ,, 1d. grey-black and deep carmine-red (1919) .. 2·25 3·00
95 ,, 3d. purp./*orange* (*thin*) (1917) 5·00 5·50
96 ,, 3d. reddish purple/*yellow* (*thick*) (1.19) .. 1·50 3·00
97 ,, 5d. black & mauve (18.5.17) 1·50 4·50
98 ,, 2s. black and blue (11.16) .. 10·00 15·00
99 ,, 3s. black and green (8.17) .. 19·00 21·00
93/99 .. .. *Set of* 5 30·00 42·00
95 & 97 Optd. "Specimen" *Set of* 2 17·00

1917 (18 May). *No.* 59 *optd. with T* **9.**

100 **6** 1d. black and red (R.) (Optd. S. £15) 25 60
a. Long stroke to "7" .. 15·00 17·00

The above stamps were to have been on sale on 1st January 1917, but owing to delay in shipment they were not issued till May 1917.

WAR TAX

(10)

1918 (21 Feb.). *Optd. at Nassau with T* **10.**

101 **8** ½d. green .. .. .. 2·00 2·50
a. Opt. double £120 £120
b. Opt. inverted £120
102 ,, 1d. carmine 60 90
a. Opt. double £120 £120
b. Opt. inverted £120
103 **6** 3d. purple/*yellow* .. .. 2·25 2·75
a. Opt. double £120 £120
b. Opt. inverted £120 £120
104 **8** 1s. grey-black and carmine 25·00 32·00
a. Opt. double £350

1918 (10 July). *Wmk. Mult. Crown CA.* *Optd. with T* **10.**

105 **6** 1d. black and red .. .. 1·60 2·50
a. Opt. double, one inverted £150
b. Opt. double £160
c. Opt. inverted £160 £180

No. 105a is from a sheet in which the top row was normal and the other five showed this error. No. 105 was on sale for ten days.

WAR TAX

(11)

WAR CHARITY 3.6.18.

(13)

WAR TAX

(12)

1918 (1 June–20 July). *Optd. in London with T* **11** *or* **12** (3*d.*).

106 **8** ½d. green 20 50
107 ,, 1d. carmine 20 60
a. Wmk. sideways £200
108 **6** 3d. purple/*yellow* (20 July) 45 1·25
109 **8** 1s. grey-black & carm. (R.) 65 1·50
106/9 Optd. "Specimen" *Set of* 4 32·00

1919 (21 Mar.). *Colour changed.* *Wmk. Mult. Crown CA.* *P* 14.

110 **6** 3d. black & brn. (Optd. S. £15) .. .. .. 90 3·00

1919 (21 Mar.). *No.* 110 *optd. with T* **12.**

111 **6** 3d. black & brn. (Optd. S. £15) .. .. .. 50 2·50

1919 (1 Jan.). *No.* 59 *optd. with T* **13.**

112 **6** 1d. black and red (R.) (Optd. S. £15) .. .. .. 30 1·10
a. Opt. double £300

The date is that originally fixed for the issue of the stamp. The year 1918 was also the bicentenary of the appointment of the first Royal governor.

WAR
TAX
(14)

WAR
TAX
(15)

1919 (14 JULY). *Optd. with T* **14.**
113 **8** ½d. green (R.) 20 75
114 ,, 1d. carmine 20 75
115 ,, 1s. grey-blk. & carmine (R.) 2·00 3·75

No. 110 *optd. with T* **15.**
116 **6** 3d. black and brown .. 60 2·25
113/16 Optd. " Specimen " *Set of* 4 32·00

16

(Recess. D.L.R.)

1920 (1 MAR.). *Peace Celebration. Wmk. Mult. Crown CA (sideways). P* 14.
117 **16** ½d. green 25 75
118 ,, 1d. carmine .. .. 1·00 1·10
119 ,, 2d. slate-grey .. .. 2·00 3·00
120 ,, 3d. deep brown .. .. 1·90 4·50
121 ,, 1s. deep myrtle-green .. 11·00 15·00
117/121 .. .. *Set of* 5 14·00 22·00
117/21 Optd. " Specimen " *Set of* 5 42·00

1921–29. *Wmk. Mult. Script CA. P* 14.
(*a*) *Staircase type.*
122 **6** 1d. grey and rose-red (29.3.21) .. .. 1·10 2·00
122*a* ,, 5d. black and purple ('29) 3·00 5·00
123 ,, 2s. black and blue ('22) 10·00 13·00
123*a* ,, 3s. black and green ('24) 17·00 20·00
122/123*a* Optd./Perf. " Specimen " *Set of* 4 35·00

(*b*) *King George V type.*
124 **8** ½d. green, O ('24) .. 12 25
125 ,, 1d. carmine, O (8.9.21) .. 25 25
125*a* ,, 2d. grey, O (1927) .. 45 1·00
126 ,, 2½d. ultramarine, O ('22) .. 50 1·00
127 ,, 4d. orange-yellow, O ('24) 75 2·25
128 ,, 6d. bistre-brown, O ('22) 60 2·25
129 ,, 1s. black & carm., C ('26) 1·75 4·50
130 ,, 5s. dull pur. & bl., C ('24) 15·00 19·00
131 ,, £1 green & black, C ('26) 80·00 £110
124/131 .. .. *Set of* 9 90·00 £120
124/31 Optd. " Specimen " *Set of* 9 75·00

17

(T **17/18** Recess. B.W.)

1930 (2 JAN.). *Tercentenary of Colony. Wmk. Mult. Script CA. P* 12.
132 **17** 1d. black and scarlet .. 1·25 1·90
133 ,, 3d. black and deep brown 2·50 3·50
134 ,, 5d. black and deep purple 5·00 7·00
135 ,, 2s. black and deep blue 13·00 18·00
136 ,, 3s. black and green .. 17·00 23·00
132/136 .. .. *Set of* 5 35·00 48·00
132/6 Perf. " Specimen " *Set of* 5 38·00

18

1931. *Wmk. Mult. Script CA. P* 12.
137 **18** 2s. black & deep blue .. 60 45
a. Slate-purple & deep blue .. 8·50 8·50
138 ,, 3s. black & green .. 70 75
a. Slate-purple & green .. 7·00 7·50
137/8 Perf. " Specimen " *Set of* 2 14·00

1931–7. *Wmk. Mult. Script CA. P* 14.
139 **8** 1½d. red-brown, O ('34) .. 50 60
140 ,, 3d. pur./*pale yellow*, C ('31) 3·00 5·00
a. Purple/orange-yellow, C ('37) 3·00 5·00
139/40 Perf. " Specimen " *Set of* 2 12·00

1935 (6 MAY). *Silver Jubilee. As Nos.* 91/4 *of Antigua. P* 13½×14.
141 1½d. deep blue and carmine 35 35
142 2½d. brown and deep blue .. 1·10 1·10
143 6d. light blue & olive-green 2·50 3·25
144 1s. slate and purple .. 4·00 5·00
141/4 Perf. " Specimen " *Set of* 4 12·00

19. Flamingoes in flight.

(Recess. Waterlow.)

1935 (22 MAY). *Wmk. Mult. Script CA. P* 12½.
145 **19** 8d. ultramarine and scarlet 4·50 3·00
145 Perf. " Specimen " .. .. 12·00

1937 (12 MAY). *Coronation. As Nos.* 13/15 *of Aden. P* 14.
146 ½d. green 15 15
147 1½d. yellow-brown 30 30
148 2½d. bright blue 75 45
146/8 Perf. " Specimen " *Set of* 3 11·00

20. King George VI.

(Typo. De La Rue.)

1938–52. *Wmk. Mult. Script CA. P* 14.
149 **20** ½d. green (11.3.38) .. 12 12
149*a* ,, ½d. brown-pur. (18.2.52) 12 30
c. Error. St. Edward's Crown £200
150 ,, 1d. carmine (11.3.38) .. 1·00 1·10
150*a* ,, 1d. grey (17.9.41) .. 10 10
151 ,, 1½d. red-brown (19.4.38) .. 15 20
a. Pale red-brown (Apr. '48) 30 25
152 ,, 2d. grey (19.4.38) .. 5·50 4·00
152*a* ,, 2d. scarlet (17.9.41) .. 10 20
152*b* ,, 2d. green (1.5.51) .. 30 50
153 ,, 2½d. blue (11.3.38) .. 80 1·00
153*a* ,, 2½d. violet ('43) .. 10 15
154 ,, 3d. violet (19.4.38) .. 70 2·75
154*a* ,, 3d. blue ('43) 10 30
154*b* ,, 3d. scarlet (1.2.52) .. 40 60
154*c* ,, 10d. yell.-orange (18.11.46) 25 25
155 **20** 1s. black and carmine C O (15.9.38) .. 45 45
156 ,, 5s. lilac and blue, C (19.4.38) .. .. 16·00 17·00
a. Purple and blue, O ('42) .. 4·50 4·00
b. Deep purple and bright blue, C ('48) .. .. 6·50 4·00
157 ,, £1 green and black, C O (15.9.38) .. .. 8·00 11·00
149/157 .. .. *Set of* 17 20·00 24·00
149/57 Perf. " Specimen " *Set of* 14 70·00

No. 149*c* occurs on a row in the watermark in which the crowns and letters " C A " alternate.

The ordinary paper of Nos. 155/7 is thick, smooth and opaque, and first appeared in 1942 as a substitute for chalk-surfaced paper.

21. Sea Garden, Nassau.

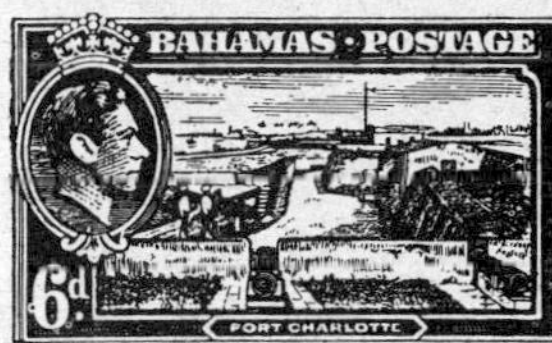

22. Fort Charlotte.

23. Flamingoes in Flight.

(Recess. Waterlow.)

1938 (1 JULY). *Wmk. Mult. Script CA. P* 12½.
158 **21** 4d. light blue & red-orange 25 30
159 **22** 6d. olive-green & light blue 15 20
160 **23** 8d. ultramarine & scarlet 25 45
158/60 Perf. " Specimen " *Set of* 3 14·00

3d.
(24)

1492
LANDFALL
OF
COLUMBUS
1942
(25)

1940 (28 NOV.). *No.* 153 *surcharged with T* **24.**
161 **20** 3d. on 2½d. blue .. 10 40

1942 (12 OCT.). 450*th Anniv. of Landing of Columbus in New World. Optd. locally with T* **25.**
162 **20** ½d. green 10 15
163 ,, 1d. grey 10 15
164 ,, 1½d. red-brown 12 20
165 ,, 2d. scarlet 12 20
166 ,, 2½d. blue 12 20
167 ,, 3d. blue 12 20
168 **21** 4d. light bl. & red-orange 25 35
169 **22** 6d. olive-grn. & light blue 30 40
170 **23** 8d. ultramarine & scarlet 30 35
171 **20** 1s. black & carmine, CO 30 50
172 **18** 2s. black and deep blue .. 2·00 2·50
a. Slate-purple and deep blue 5·00 5·00
173 ,, 3s. black and green .. 7·00 8·00
a. Slate-purple and green 1·50 2·50
174 **20** 5s. purple and blue, CO 1·75 2·50
175 ,, £1 green and black, CO 10·00 11·00
162/175 .. .. *Set of* 14 15·00 19·00
162/75 Perf. " Specimen " *Set of* 14 55·00

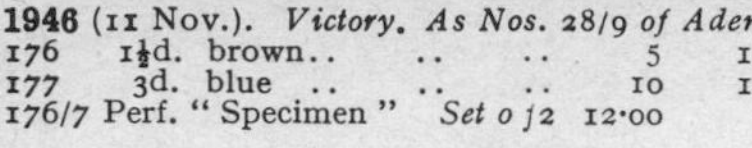

1946 (11 Nov.). *Victory. As Nos. 28/9 of Aden.*
176 1½d. brown 5 10
177 3d. blue 10 12
176/7 Perf. "Specimen" *Set of 2* 12·00

26. Infant Welfare Clinic.

27. Agriculture (Combine Harvester).
28. Sisal.
29. Straw Work.
30. Dairy Farm.
31. Fishing Fleet.
32. Island Settlement.
33. Tuna Fishing.
34. Paradise Beach.
35. Modern Hotels.
36. Yacht Racing.
37. Water Sports—Skiing.
38. Shipbuilding.
39. Transportation.
40. Salt Production.
41. Parliament Buildings.

(Recess. Canadian Bank Note Co.)

1948 (11 Oct.). *Tercentenary of Settlement of Island of Eleuthera.* P 12.
178 **26** ½d. orange 10 20
179 **27** 1d. sage-green 10 20
180 **28** 1½d. yellow 12 25
181 **29** 2d. scarlet 15 25
182 **30** 2½d. brown-lake 15 35
183 **31** 3d. ultramarine 25 35
184 **32** 4d. black 25 50
185 **33** 6d. emerald-green 30 50
186 **34** 8d. violet 30 55
187 **35** 10d. carmine 25 30
188 **36** 1s. sepia 40 50
189 **37** 2s. magenta .. .. .. 4·00 4·50
190 **38** 3s. blue .. .. .. 3·50 4·00
191 **39** 5s. mauve .. .. .. 2·50 3·50
192 **40** 10s. grey .. .. .. 3·00 5·50
193 **41** £1 vermilion .. .. .. 6·00 8·50
178/193 .. .. *Set of* 16 19·00 27·00

1948 (1 Dec.). *Royal Silver Wedding. As Nos.* 30/1 *of Aden.*
194 1½d. red-brown 8 12
195 £1 slate-green .. .. 14·00 17·00

1949 (10 Oct.). *75th Anniv. of Universal Postal Union. As Nos.* 114/7 *of Antigua.*
196 2½d. violet 15 20
197 3d. deep blue 30 30
198 6d. greenish blue 70 70
199 1s. carmine .. .. .. 1·00 1·00

1953 (3 June). *Coronation. As No.* 47 *of Aden.*
200 6d. black and pale blue 40 55

42. Infant Welfare Clinic.

(Recess. B.W.)

1954 (1 Jan.). *As T* **26/41** (*but portrait of Queen Elizabeth II in place of King George VI, as in T* **42**, *and commemorative inscr. omitted*). *Wmk. Mult. Script CA.* P 11×11½.
201 **42** ½d. black and red-orange 10 10
202 **27** 1d. olive-green and brown 10 10
203 **32** 1½d. blue and black 10 10
204 **29** 2d. yellow-brown and myrtle-green (*shades*) 12 12
205 **31** 3d. black and carmine-red 15 15
206 **37** 4d. turquoise-green & dp. reddish purple (*shades*) 15 15
207 **30** 5d. red-brown and deep bright blue 25 25
308 **39** 6d. light blue and black .. 25 20
209 **34** 8d. black & reddish lilac (*shades*) 30 20
210 **35** 10d. blk. & ultram. (*shades*) 30 30
211 **36** 1s. ultramarine and olive-brown (*shades*) .. 40 45
212 **28** 2s. orange-brown & black (*shades*) .. .. 1·10 1·40
213 **38** 2s. 6d. black & deep blue 1·60 1·90
214 **33** 5s. bright emerald and orange (*shades*) .. 2·50 3·00
215 **40** 10s. black and slate-black 5·00 6·00
216 **41** £1 slate-black and violet 9·50 11·00
201/216 .. .. *Set of* 16 20·00 22·00

See also No. 246.

43. Queen Elizabeth II.

(Recess. Waterlow.)

1959 (10 June). *Centenary of First Bahamas Postage Stamp. W* w.**12**. P 13½.
217 **43** 1d. black and scarlet .. 10 12
218 „ 2d. black and blue-green 15 25
219 „ 6d. black and blue .. 30 40
220 „ 10d. black and chocolate .. 50 50

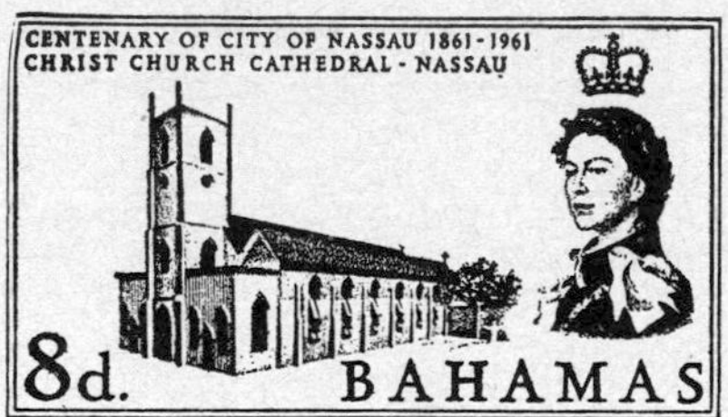

44. Christ Church Cathedral.

45. Nassau Public Library.

(Photo. Enschedé.)

1962 (30 Jan.). *Nassau Centenary.* P 14×13.
221 **44** 8d. green 40 45
222 **45** 10d. bluish violet 40 45

1963 (4 June). *Freedom from Hunger. As No.* 76 *of Aden.*
223 8d. sepia 75 75
a. Name and value omitted .. £400

BAHAMAS TALKS
1962
(**46**)

NEW CONSTITUTION
1964
(**47**)

1963 (15 July). *Bahamas Talks,* 1962. *Nos.* 209/10 *optd. with T* **46**.
224 **34** 8d. black & reddish lilac .. 90 1·00
225 **35** 10d. black & dp. ultram. .. 1·60 1·60

1963 (2 Sept.). *Red Cross Centenary. As Nos.* 147/8 *of Antigua.*
226 1d. red and black 15 20
227 10d. red and blue .. .. 75 1·10

II. SELF-GOVERNMENT

1964 (7 Jan.). *New Constitution. As Nos.* 201/16 *but W* w.**12**, *optd. with T* **47**, *by B.W.*
228 **42** ½d. black and red-orange 8 10
229 **27** 1d. olive-green and brown 8 10
230 **32** 1½d. blue and black .. 10 10
231 **29** 2d. yellow-brown & deep myrtle-green .. 10 10
232 **31** 3d. black and carmine-red 12 12
233 **37** 4d. turquoise-blue & deep reddish purple .. 15 20
234 **30** 5d. red-brn. & dp. brt. bl. 20 25
235 **39** 6d. deep blue and black .. 25 25
236 **34** 8d. black & reddish lilac 30 30
237 **35** 10d. black & deep ultram. 35 35
238 **36** 1s. ultram. & olive-brown 50 55
239 **28** 2s. chestnut and black .. 1·40 1·60
240 **38** 2s. 6d. black & deep blue 1·60 1·90
241 **33** 5s. brt. emerald & orange 2·75 3·00
242 **40** 10s. black and slate-black 4·75 5·50
243 **41** £1 slate-black and violet 9·50 11·00
228/243 .. .. *Set of* 16 20·00 22·00

1964 (23 April). *400th Birth Anniv. of William Shakespeare. As No.* 164 *of Antigua.*
244 6d. turquoise 45 45

(**48**)

1964 (1 Oct.). *Olympic Games, Tokyo. As No.* 211 *but W* w.**12**, *surch. with T* **48**.
245 **36** 8d. on 1s. ultram. & ol.-brn. 40 45

1964 (6 Oct.). *As No.* 204, *but wmk.* w.**12**.
246 **29** 2d. yellow-brown and deep myrtle-green 25 30

49. Colony's Badge.

50. Out Island Regatta.
51. Hospital.
52. High School.
53. Flamingo.
54. R.M.S. *Queen Elizabeth*.
55. "Development".
56. Yachting.
57. Public Square.
58. Sea Garden.
59. Old Cannons at Fort Charlotte.
60. Sikorsky "S–38" seaplane (1929) and Boeing "707" Airliner.
61. Williamson Film Project (1914) and Undersea Post Office (1939).
62. Conch Shell.
63. Columbus's Flagship.

(Queen's portrait by Anthony Buckley. Litho and recess (portrait and "BAHAMAS"), B.W.)

1965 (7 Jan.–14 Sept.). *W* w.**12**. P 13½.
247 **49** ½d. multicoloured .. 5 5
248 **50** 1d. slate, lt. blue & orange 5 5
249 **51** 1½d. rose-red, grn. & brown 5 5
250 **52** 2d. slate, grn. & turq.-bl. 8 8
251 **53** 3d. red, lt. blue & purple 10 8
252 **54** 4d. grn., bl. & org.-brn. 12 20
253 **55** 6d. dull green, light blue and rose 20 15
254 **56** 8d. reddish purple, light blue & bronze-green 30 30
255 **57** 10d. orange-brown, green and violet 25 20
256 **58** 1s. red, yellow, turquoise-blue & deep emerald 40 35
a. *Red, yellow, dull blue and emerald* (14.9.65) .. 35 30
257 **59** 2s. brn., lt. blue & emer. 85 95

258 **60** 2s. 6d. yellow-olive, blue and carmine .. .. 1·00 1·40
259 **61** 5s. orange-brown, ultramarine and green .. 1·90 2·25
260 **62** 10s. rose, blue & chocolate 3·00 3·75
261 **63** £1 chest., bl. & rose-red 5·50 6·00
247/261 .. .. *Set of* 15 12·00 14·00

1965 (17 May). *I.T.U. Centenary. As Nos. 166/7 of Antigua.*
262 1d. light emerald and orange 12 12
263 2s. purple and yellow-olive .. 90 90

9d

(64)

1965 (12 July). *No. 254 surch. with T* **64**.
264 **56** 9d. on 8d. reddish purple, lt. blue & bronze-green 40 40

1965 (25 Oct.). *International Co-operation Year. As Nos. 168/9 of Antigua.*
265 ½d. reddish pur. & turq.-grn. 12 12
266 1s. dp. bluish grn. & lavender 55 55

1966 (24 Jan.). *Churchill Commemoration. As Nos. 170/3 of Antigua.*
267 ½d. new blue 5 5
268 2d. deep green 15 15
269 10d. brown 65 75
270 1s. bluish violet 75 90

1966 (4 Feb.). *Royal Visit. As Nos. 174/5 of Antigua, but* " to the Caribbean " *omitted.*
271 6d. black and ultramarine .. 30 30
272 1s. black and magenta .. 40 40

(New currency. 100 cents=1 dollar.)

(65) **(66)**

1966 (25 May). *Decimal Currency. Nos. 247/6 variously surch. as T* **65/6**, *by Bradbury, Wilkinson & Co.*
273 **49** 1 c. on ½d. multicoloured 5 5
274 **50** 2 c. on 1d. slate, light blue and orange .. 5 5
275 **52** 3 c. on 2d. slate, green and turquoise-blue .. 5 5
276 **53** 4 c. on 3d. red, light blue and purple .. 8 10
277 **54** 5 c. on 4d. green, blue and orange-brown .. 10 12
a. Surch. omitted (vert. strip of 10) £1500
278 **55** 8 c. on 6d. dull green, light blue and rose .. 15 15
279 **56** 10 c. on 8d. reddish purple, lt. blue & bronze-grn. 20 25
280 **51** 11 c. on 1½d. rose-red, green and brown 20 25
281 **57** 12 c. on 10d. orange-brown, green and violet .. 25 25
282 **58** 15 c. on 1s. multicoloured 30 35
283 **59** 22 c. on 2s. brown, light blue and emerald .. 55 65
284 **60** 50 c. on 2s. 6d. yellow-olive, blue and carmine .. 95 1·10
285 **61** $1 on 5s. orange-brown, ultramarine & green 1·90 2·25
286 **62** $2 on 10s. rose, blue and chocolate .. 3·25 3·75
287 **63** $3 on £1 chestnut, blue and rose-red .. .. 6·50 7·50
273/287 .. .. *Set of* 15 13·00 15·00

The above were made on new printings some of which vary slightly in shade and in No. 273 the shield appears as vermilion and green instead of carmine and blue-green due to a different combination of the printing colours.

No. 277a. One sheet exists and the stamp can be distinguished from No. 252 when in a vertical strip of ten as these were printed in sheets of 100 whereas No. 252 was printed in sheets of 60 (six rows of ten across).

1966 (1 July). *World Cup Football Championships. As Nos. 176/7 of Antigua.*
288 8 c. violet, yellow-green, lake and yellow-brown 25 25
289 15 c. chocolate, blue-green, lake and yellow-brown 35 35

1966 (20 Sept.). *Inauguration of W.H.O. Headquarters, Geneva. As Nos. 178/9 of Antigua.*
290 11 c. black, yellow-green and light blue 35 35
291 15 c. black, light purple and yellow-brown 40 45

1966 (1 Dec.). *20th Anniv. of U.N.E.S.C.O. As Nos. 196/8 of Antigua.*
292 3 c. slate-violet, red, yellow and orange 5 5
293 15 c. orange-yellow, violet and deep olive .. 50 60
294 $1 black, bright purple and orange .. .. .. 1·90 1·90

67. *Oceanic.*

68. Conch Shell.

(Portrait by Anthony Buckley. Litho. and recess (portrait, " BAHAMAS " and value), Bradbury, Wilkinson & Co.)

1967 (25 May)–**71**. *Designs as T* **49**, *etc., and T* **67/8**, *but in decimal currency and colours changed. Toned paper. W* **w.12**. *P* 13½.
295 **49** 1 c. multicoloured .. 5 5
a. Whiter paper ('70) 15 15
296 **50** 2 c. slate, light blue and deep emerald .. 8 10
a. Whiter paper ('70) .. 15 15
297 **52** 3 c. slate, green & violet 10 10
a. Whiter paper ('70) .. 7·00 1·50
298 **53** 4 c. red, lt. blue & ultram. 10 12
a. Whiter paper (9.70*) .. 7·00 7·00
299 **67** 5 c. black, greenish blue and purple .. 12 12
a. Whiter paper ('70) 25 25
300 **55** 8 c. dull green, light blue and sepia .. 12 15
a. Whiter paper ('70) .. 30·00 8·00
301 **56** 10 c. reddish purple, greenish blue and carmine 15 12
a. Whiter paper ('70) .. 50 40
302 **51** 11 c. rose-red, green & blue 25 20
a. Whiter paper ('70) .. 60 50
303 **57** 12 c. orge.-brn., grn. & ol. 30 20
a. Whiter paper (4.71) .. 8·00 8·00
304 **58** 15 c. red, yellow, turquoise-blue and carmine .. 40 30
a. Whiter paper ('70) .. 40·00 10·00
305 **59** 22 c. brown, new blue and rose-red 45 45
a. Whiter paper ('70) .. 1·50 1·00
306 **60** 50 c. yellow-olive, new blue and emerald 85 75
a. Whiter paper ('70) .. 2·50 1·50
307 **61** $1 orange-brown, ultramarine & slate-purple 1·75 2·00
a. Whiter paper (4.71) .. 15·00 12·00
308 **68** $2 multicoloured .. 3·25 3·75
a. Whiter paper (4.71) .. 22·00 22·00
309 **63** $3 chestnut, new blue and purple .. 6·00 6·50
a. Whiter paper (4.71) .. 22·00 22·00
295/309 .. .. *Set of* 15 12·00 13·00

*This is the earliest known date recorded in the Bahamas.

The 3 c. has the value at right instead of at left as in T **52**.

The 1970–71 printings on whiter paper were released as needed, the 12 c., $1, $2 and $3 only a week or two before the issue was withdrawn. Due to the marked difference in paper and the use of some new plates there are marked differences in shade in nearly all values.

69. Bahamas Crest.

70. Scout Badge.

(Des. R. Granger Barrett. Photo. J. Enschedé & Sons.)

1967 (1 Sept.). *Diamond Jubilee of World Scouting. W* **w.12** *(sideways). P* 14×13.
310 **69** 3 c. multicoloured .. 5 5
311 **70** 15 c. multicoloured .. 25 25

71. Globe and Emblem.

72. Scales of Justice and Emblem.

73. Bahamas Crest and Emblem.

(Des. R. Granger Barrett. Litho. De La Rue.)

1968 (13 May). *Human Rights Year. W* **w.12**, *sideways (to left on 12 c.). P* 14×13½.
312 **71** 3 c. multicoloured .. 10 10
313 **72** 12 c. multicoloured .. 55 55
314 **73** $1 multicoloured .. 1·40 1·75

74. Golf.

75. Yachting.

76. Horse-racing.

77. Water-skiing.

(Litho. Bradbury, Wilkinson.)

1968 (20 Aug.). *Tourism. P* 13.
315 **74** 5 c. multicoloured .. 10 10

316 **75** 11 c. multicoloured .. 20 30
317 **76** 15 c. multicoloured .. 25 30
318 **77** 50 c. multicoloured .. 60 70

78. Racing Yacht and Olympic Monument.

79. Long-Jumping and Olympic Monument.

80. Running and Olympic Monument.

(Photo. Harrison.)

1968 (29 SEPT.). *Olympic Games, Mexico City. No wmk. P* 14½×13½.
319 **78** 5 c. red-brown, orange-yellow and blue-green 10 10
320 **79** 11 c. multicoloured .. 20 25
321 **80** 50 c. multicoloured .. 90 1·00
322 **78** $1 olive-grey, greenish blue and violet .. 1·75 2·00

It is understood that the above were released by the Philatelic Agency in the U.S.A. on 1st September.

81. Legislative Building.

82. Bahamas Mace and Westminster Clock-Tower. (*Vert.*)

83. Local Straw Market. (*Vert.*)

84. Horse-drawn Surrey. (*Horiz.*)

(Des. J. E. Cooter. Litho. Format International.)

1968 (1 NOV.). *14th Commonwealth Parliamentary Conference. P* 14.
323 **81** 3 c. multicoloured .. 5 5
324 **82** 10 c. multicoloured .. 25 25
325 **83** 12 c. multicoloured .. 25 30
326 **84** 15 c. multicoloured .. 35 35

85. Obverse and reverse of $100 Gold Coin.

86. Obverse and reverse of $50 Gold Coin.

87. Obverse and reverse of $20 Gold Coin.

88. Obverse and reverse of $10 Gold Coin.

(Recess. De La Rue.)

1968 (2 DEC.). *Gold Coins commemorating the first General Election under the New Constitution. P* 13½.
327 **85** 3 c. red/*gold* 10 10
328 **86** 12 c. blue-green/*gold* .. 25 25
329 **87** 15 c. dull purple/*gold* .. 35 35
330 **88** $1 black/*gold* .. .. 1·60 1·60

89. First Flight Postcard of 1919.

90. Sikorsky " S–38 " Seaplane of 1929.

(Des. V. Whiteley. Litho. Format International.)

1969 (30 JAN.). *50th Anniv. of Bahamas Airmail Service. P* 14.
331 **89** 12 c. multicoloured .. 40 50
332 **90** 15 c. multicoloured .. 50 55

91. Game-Fishing Boats.

(Des. J. E. Cooter. Litho. Format.)

1969 (26 AUG.). *Tourism. One Millionth Visitor to Bahamas. T* **91** *and similar horiz. designs. Multicoloured. W* w.**12** (*sideways*). *P* 14½.
333 3 c. Type **91** 5 5
334 11 c. Paradise Beach .. 20 20
335 12 c. Sunfish sailing boats .. 25 25
336 15 c. Rawson Square and Parade 30 30
MS337 130×96 mm. Nos. 333/6 .. 1·50 1·75

92. " The Adoration of the Shepherds " (Louis le Nain).

(Des. G. Drummond. Litho. De La Rue.)

1969 (15 OCT.). *Christmas. T* **92** *and similar vert. designs. W* w.**12**. *P* 12.
338 3 c. multicoloured 8 8
339 11 c. multicoloured 30 30
340 12 c. multicoloured 30 30
341 15 c. multicoloured 40 40

Designs:—11 c. " The Adoration of the Shepherds " (Poussin); 12 c. " The Adoration of the Kings " (Gerard David); 15 c. " The Adoration of the Kings " (Vincenzo Foppa).

93. Badge of Girl Guides.

(Des. Mrs. R. Sands. Litho. Harrison.)

1970 (23 FEB.). *Girl Guides Diamond Jubilee. T* **93** *and similar designs. Multicoloured. W* w.**12**. *P* 14½.
342 3 c. Type **93** 10 10
343 12 c. Badge of Brownies .. 25 25
344 15 c. Badge of Rangers .. 30 30

94. U.P.U. Headquarters and Emblem.

(Des. L. D. Curtis. Litho. J.W.)

1970 (20 MAY). *New U.P.U. Headquarters Building. W* w.**12** (*sideways*). *P* 14
345 **94** 3 c. multicoloured .. 12 12
346 ,, 15 c. multicoloured .. 50 55

95. Coach and Globe.

(Des. G. Drummond. Litho. B.W.)

1970 (14 JULY). " *Goodwill Caravan* ". *T* **95** *and similar horiz. designs. Multicoloured. W* w.**12** (*sideways*). *P* 13½×13.
347 3 c. Type **95** 5 5
348 11 c. Train and globe .. 30 30
349 12 c. Liner, Yacht and globe 35 35
350 15 c. Airliner and globe .. 40 40
MS351 165×125 mm. Nos. 347/50 1·40 1·40

96. Nurse, Patients and Flamingo.

(Photo. Harrison.)

1970 (1 Sept.). *Centenary of British Red Cross. T* **96** *and similar horiz. design. Multicoloured. W* w.**12** *(sideways). P* 14½.

352	3 c. Type **96**	5	5
	a. Gold (" EIIR ", etc.) omitted	90·00	
353	15 c. Hospital and Dolphin ..	35	40

97. "The Nativity" (detail, Pittoni).

(Des. G. Drummond. Litho. D.L.R.)

1970 (3 Nov.). *Christmas. T* **97** *and similar vert. designs. Multicoloured. W* w.**12**. *P* 13.

354	3 c. Type **97**	10	10
355	11 c. " The Holy Family " (detail, Anton Raphael Mengs)	20	20
356	12 c. " Adorazione dei Pastori " (detail, Giorgione) ..	25	30
357	15 c. " The Adoration of the Shepherds " (detail, School of Seville) ..	30	35
MS358	114×140 mm. Nos. 354/7 plus two labels	1·10	1·25

98. " VC–10 " at Airport Terminal.

(Des. Mrs. W. Wasile. Litho. Format.)

1971 (27 Apr.–21 Sept.). *T* **98** *and similar multicoloured designs. W* w.**12** *(sideways on $1, $2 and $3 and upright on others). P* 14½×14 *(½ c. to 50 c.) or* 14×14½ *(others).*

359	1 c. Type **109**	5	5
360	2 c. Breadfruit	8	8
361	3 c. Straw Market	5	5
362	4 c. Hawksbill turtle ..	10	10
363	5 c. Grouper	10	10
364	6 c. As 4 c. (21.9.71) ..	5	5
365	7 c. Hibiscus (21.9.71) ..	8	8
366	8 c. Yellow Elder	12	12
367	10 c. Bahamian sponge boat	12	15
368	11 c. Flamingoes	8	10
369	12 c. As 7 c.	25	20
370	15 c. Bonefish	15	15
371	18 c. Royal Poinciana (21.9.71)	15	20
372	22 c. As 18 c.	30	35
373	50 c. Nassau Post Office ..	60	70
374	$1 Pineapple (*vert.*) ..	1·25	1·40
375	$2 Crawfish (*vert.*) ..	2·50	2·75
376	$3 Junkanoo (*vert.*) ..	3·50	3·75
359/376	.. .. *Set of* 18	8·50	9·00

See also Nos. 398, etc.

99. Snowflake.

(Litho (15 c. additionally die-stamped in gold). Walsall Security Printers Ltd.)

1971 (19 Oct.). *Christmas. T* **99** *and similar horiz. designs. W* w.**12**. *P* 14×14½.

377	3 c. deep reddish purple, orange and gold ..	8	8
378	11 c. light ultram. and gold	25	25
379	15 c. multicoloured	30	30
380	18 c. bluish green, Royal blue and gold	40	40
MS381	126×95 mm. Nos. 377/80 P 15	1·40	1·40

Designs:—11 c. " Peace on Earth " (doves); 15 c. Arms of Bahamas and holly; 18 c. Starlit lagoon.

100. High jumping.

(Des. J. W. Ltd. Litho. B.W.)

1972 (11 July). *Olympic Games, Munich. T* **100** *and similar horiz. designs. Multicoloured. W* w.**12** *P* 13½.

382	10 c. Type **100**	20	20
383	11 c. Cycling	20	20
384	15 c. Running	25	25
385	18 c. Sailing	40	40
MS386	127×95 mm. Nos. 382/5	1·50	1·50

101. Shepherd.

(Des. Jennifer Toombs. Litho. (15 c. additionally embossed). J.W.)

1972 (3 Oct.). *Christmas. T* **101** *and similar vert. designs. Multicoloured. W* w. **12** *(sideways on 6 c., 20 c. and* **MS**391*). P* 14.

387	3 c. Type **101**	8	8
388	6 c. Bells	12	12
389	15 c. Holly and Cross ..	30	35
390	20 c. Poinsettia	40	45
MS391	108×140 mm. Nos. 389/92	1·25	1·25

102. Northerly Bahama Islands.

(Des. M. Shamir. Litho. Format.)

1972 (1 Nov.). *Tourism Year of the Americas. Sheet* 133×105 mm., *containing T* **102** *and similar vert. designs. P* 15.

MS392	11, 15, 18 and 50 c. mult.	1·50	1·50

The four designs are printed horizontally *se-tenant* in **MS**392, forming a composite map design of the Bahamas.

103. Mace and Galleon.

(Des. (from photograph by D. Groves) and photo. Harrison.)

1972 (13 Nov.). *Royal Silver Wedding. Multi-coloured, background colour given. W* w.**12**. *P* 14×14½.

393 **103**	11 c. rose	20	25
394 ,,	18 c. bluish violet ..	30	35

1972–73. *As Nos.* 359 *etc., but W* w.**12** *upright on* $1, $2 *and* $3, *and sideways on others.*

398	5 c. Grouper	5	8
399	8 c. Yellow Elder	10	12
406	50 c. Nassau Post Office ..	65	75
407	$1 Pineapple	1·25	1·40
408	$2 Crawfish	1·90	2·00
409	$3 Junkanoo	3·00	3·25
398/409	.. .. *Set of* 6	6·50	7·00

Dates of issue:—5 c., 23.11.72; 8 c. to $2, 25.7.73; $3, 1973.

Nos. 395/409 have been allocated to this issue.

104. Weather Satellite.

(Des. C. Abbott. Litho. Questa.)

1973 (3 Apr.). *I.M.O./W.M.O. Centenary. T* **104** *and similar horiz. design. Multicoloured. W* w.**12**. *P* 14.

410	15 c. Type **104**	25	25
411	18 c. Weather radar ..	30	30

III. INDEPENDENT.

105. C. A. Bain (national hero).

(Des. PAD Studio. Litho. Questa.)

1973 (10 July–1 Aug.). *Independence. T* **105** *and similar vert. designs. Multicoloured. W* w.**12** (*sideways*). *P* 14½ × 14.

412 3 c. Type **105** 5 5
413 11 c. Coat-of-arms 15 15
414 15 c. Bahamas flag 25 25
415 $1 Governor-General, M. B. Butler (1 Aug.) .. .. 1·10 1·25
MS416 86 × 121 mm. Nos. 412/15 (1 Aug.) .. .. 1·60 1·75

106. " Madonna in Prayer " (Sassoferrato).

(Des. C. Abbott. Litho. Format.)

1973 (16 Oct.). *Christmas. T* **106** *and similar vert. designs. Multicoloured. W* w.**12** (*sideways*). *P* 14.

417 3 c. Type **106** 5 5
418 11 c. " Virgin and Child with St. John " (Filippino Lippi) 15 15
419 15 c. " A Choir of Angels " (Simon Marmion) .. 25 25
420 18 c. " The Two Trinities " (Murillo) 30 30
MS421 120 × 99 mm. Nos. 417/20 75 75

107. "Agriculture and Sciences".

(Des. C. Abbott. Litho. Questa.)

1974 (5 Feb.). *25th Anniv. of University of West Indies. T* **107** *and similar horiz. design. Multicoloured. W* w.**12**. *P* 13½.

422 15 c. Type **107** 25 25
423 18 c. "Arts, Engineering and General Studies" .. 30 30

108. U.P.U. Monument, Berne.

(Des. P. B. Powell. Litho. Questa.)

1974 (23 Apr.). *Centenary of Universal Postal Union. Designs as T* **108** *showing different arrangements of the U.P.U. Monument. W* w.**12** (*upright on* 3 *c.*, 14 *c. and* **MS**428; *sideways on others*). *P* 14.

424 **108** 3 c. multicoloured .. 5 5
425 – 13 c. mult. (*vert.*) 20 20
426 – 14 c. multicoloured .. 25 25
427 – 18 c. mult. (*vert.*) 30 30
MS428 128 × 95 mm. Nos. 424/7 80 80

109. Roseate Spoonbills.

(Des. G. Drummond. Litho. Questa.)

1974 (10 Sept.). *15th Anniv. of Bahamas National Trust. T* **109** *and similar horiz. designs. Multicoloured. W* w.**12** (*sideways*). *P* 13½.

429 13 c. Type **109** 15 20
430 14 c. White-crowned Pigeon .. 20 20
431 21 c. White-tailed Tropic Birds 25 25
432 36 c. Bahamian Parrot .. 40 40
MS433 123 × 120 mm. Nos. 429/32 1·00 1·00

110. "The Holy Family" (Jacques de Stella).

(Des. J. W. Ltd. Litho. Enschedé.)

1974 (29 Oct.). *Christmas. T* **110** *and similar horiz. designs. Multicoloured. W* w.**12** (*sideways*). *P* 13 × 13½.

434 8 c. Type **110** 10 10
435 10 c. "Madonna and Child" (Romanino) 12 12
436 12 c. "Virgin and Child with St. John the Baptist and St. Catherine" (Previtali) 15 15
437 21 c. "Virgin and Child with Angels" (Previtali) .. 30 30
MS438 126 × 105 mm. Nos. 434/7 70 70

111. *Anteos maerula.*

(Des. PAD Studio. Litho. D.L.R.)

1975 (4 Feb.). *Butterflies. T* **111** *and similar horiz. designs. Multicoloured. W* w.**12**. *P* 14 × 13½.

439 3 c. Type **111** 5 5
440 14 c. *Eurema nicippe* .. 20 20
441 18 c. *Papilio andraemon bonhotei* 25 30
442 21 c. *Euptoieta hegesia* .. 25 25
MS443 119 × 94 mm. Nos. 439/42 75 80

112. Sheep Husbandry.

(Des. Daphne Padden. Litho. Questa.)

1975 (27 May). *Economic Diversification. T* **112** *and similar multicoloured designs. P* 14.

444 3 c. Type **112** 5 5
445 14 c. Electric-reel fishing (*vert.*) 15 20
446 18 c. Farming 20 20
447 21 c. Oil Refinery (*vert.*) .. 20 25
MS448 127 × 94 mm. Nos. 444/7 65

113. Rowena Rand (evangelist).

(Des. Jennifer Toombs. Litho. Questa.)

1975 (22 July). *International Women's Year. T* **113** *and similar vert. design. W* w.**14** (*sideways*). *P* 14.

449 14 c. bistre-brown, lt. turq.-bl. & ultramarine .. 20 20
450 18 c. lemon, bright yell.-grn. and sepia 25 30

Design:—18 c. I.W.Y. symbol and Harvest symbol.

BAHAMAS
Perugino: 'Adoration of the Shepherds' (detail)
CHRISTMAS · 1975
3c
MUSÉE DES BEAUX-ARTS, ROUEN

114. " Adoration of the Shepherds " (Perugino).

(Des. Jennifer Toombs. Litho. J.W.)

1975 (2 Dec.). *Christmas. T* **114** *and similar horiz. design. Multicoloured. W* w.**14** (*sideways*). *P* 13.

451 3 c. Type **114** 5 5
452 8 c. " Adoration of the Magi " (Ghirlandaio) 10 10
453 18 c. As 8 c. 20 20
454 21 c. Type **114** 25 25
MS 455 142 × 107 mm. Nos. 451/4 P 13½ 60 60

115. Telephones, 1876 and 1976.

(Des. G. L. Vasarhelyi. Litho. D.L.R.)

1976 (23 Mar.). *Telephone Centenary. T* **115** *and similar horiz. designs. Multicoloured. W* w.**14** *(sideways). P* 14.

456	3 c. Type **115**	5	5
457	16 c. Radio-telephone link, Deleporte	20	25
458	21 c. Alexander Graham Bell	25	30
459	25 c. Satellite	35	40

1976. *As Nos.* 359 *etc., but W* w.**14** *(sideways on* $1 *to* $3).

460	1 c. Type **109** (7.76?) . .	5	5
461	2 c. Breadfruit (4.76) . .	5	5
462	3 c. Straw market (7.76?) . .	5	5
464	5 c. Grouper (7.76?)	5	5
466	8 c. Yellow Elder (4.76) . .	8	8
467	10 c. Bahamian Sponge Boat (4.76)	10	10
471	50 c. Nassau P.O. (4.76)	45	55
472	$1 Pineapple (4.76)	95	1·10
473	$2 Crawfish (7.76?)	1·90	2·10
474	$3 Junkanoo (7.76?) . .	3·00	3·25
460/74	. . . . *Set of* 10	6·00	6·50

116. Map of North America.

(Des. and litho. Walsall.)

1976 (1 June). *Bicentenary of American Revolution. T* **116** *and similar horiz. design. Multicoloured. W* w.**14** *(sideways). P* 14 (C).

475	16 c. Type **116**	15	20
476	$1 John Murray, Earl of Dunmore	1·10	1·25
MS477	127×100 mm. No. 476×4	4·50	

117. Cycling.

(Des. J.W. Ltd. Litho. Questa.)

1976 (13 July). *Olympic Games, Montreal. T* **117** *and similar vert. designs. W* w.**14**. *P* 14.

478	8 c. mag., blue & pale cobalt . .	8	10
479	16 c. orge., brn. & pale cobalt	15	20
480	25 c. blue, deep magenta and pale cobalt	30	35
481	40 c. brn., orge. & pale cobalt	45	50

Designs:—16 c. Jumping; 25 c. Sailing; 40 c. Boxing.

118. " Virgin and Child " (detail, Lippi).

(Des. G. Drummond. Litho. Questa.)

1976 (5 Oct.). *Christmas. T* **118** *and similar vert. designs. Multicoloured. W* w.**14**. *P* 14.

482	3 c. Type **118**	5	5
483	21 c. " Adoration of the Shepherds " (School of Seville)	20	25
484	25 c. " Adoration of the Kings " (detail, Foppa) . .	30	35
485	40 c. " Virgin and Child " (detail, Vivarini)	45	50
MS486	107×127 mm. Nos. 482/5	1·00	

SPECIAL DELIVERY STAMPS.

SPECIAL DELIVERY
(S 1)

1916 (1 May). *Wmk. Crown CC. Optd. locally with Type* S1.

S1 **6**	5d. black and orange	5·00	5·50
	a. Opt. double	£250	£300
	b. Opt. double, one inverted . .	£275	£325
	c. Opt. inverted	£250	£300
	d. Pair, one without opt. . .	£1200	£1500

There were three printings from similar settings of 30, and each sheet had to pass through the press twice. The first printing of 600 was on sale from 1 May, 1916 in Canada at Ottawa, Toronto, Westmount (Montreal) and Winnipeg; and under an agreement with the Canadian P.O. were used in combination with Canadian stamps and were cancelled in Canada. The second printing (number unknown) was made about the beginning of December 1916, and the third of 6000, issued probably on 1 March 1917, were on sale only in the Bahamas. These printings caused the revocation, in mid-December 1916, of the agreement by Canada, which no longer accepted the stamps as payment of the special delivery fee and left them to be cancelled in the Bahamas.

It is not possible to identify the printings of the normal stamps without plating both the basic stamp and the overprint, though, in general, the word " special " is further to the right in relation to " delivery " in the third printing than in the first or second. Our prices for No. S1 are for the third printing and any stamps which can be positively identified as being from the first or second printings would be worth about eight times as much unused, and any on cover are very rare. All the errors appear to be from the third printing.

SPECIAL DELIVERY (S 2) SPECIAL DELIVERY (S 3)

1917 (2 July). *Wmk. Mult. Crown CA. Optd. in London with Type* S **2**.

S2 **6**	5d. blk. & orange (Optd. S. £20)	75	1·50

1918. *Optd. with Type* S **3**.

S3 **6**	5d. black and mauve (R.) (Optd. S. £20)	40	1·00

BAHRAIN.

An independent shaikhdom, with an Indian postal administration from 1884, at first using unoverprinted Indian stamps. A British postal administration operated from 1st April 1948 to 31st December 1965.

BAHRAIN (1) BAHRAIN (2)

Stamps of India overprinted with T **1** *or T* **2** *(rupee values).*

1933 (10 Aug–Dec). *King George V. Wmk. Mult. Star, T* **69**.

1	**55**	3 p. slate (12.33)	30	30
2	**56**	½ a. green	75	60
3	**80**	9 p. deep green . .	65	40
4	**57**	1 a. chocolate	40	40
5	**82**	1 a. 3 p. mauve . .	50	30
6	**70**	2 a. vermilion	80	70
7	**62**	3 a. blue	3·50	3·00
8	**83**	3 a. 6 p. ultramarine . .	45	35
9	**71**	4 a. sage-green . .	3·50	2·00
10	**65**	8 a. reddish purple	50	30
11	**66**	12 a. claret	75	40

12	**67**	1 r. chocolate and green	3·50	1·00
13	,,	2 r. carmine and orange..	7·50	3·50
14	,,	5 r. ultramarine & purple	18·00	14·00
1/14		.. .. *Set of* 14	35·00	24·00

The 9 p. exists both offset-litho and typo.

1934–37. *King George V. Wmk. Mult. Star, T* **69**.

15	**79**	½ a. green (1935).. ..	30	8
16	**81**	1 a. chocolate (1935) ..	75	12
17	**59**	2 a. vermilion (1935) ..	3·00	90
17*a*	,,	2 a. verm. (*small die*) ('37)	4·00	40
18	**62**	3 a. carmine	1·50	15
19	**63**	4 a. sage-green (1935) ..	1·00	20
15/19		.. .. *Set of* 5	6·00	80

1938–41. *King George VI.*

20	**91**	3 p. slate (5.38)	40	30
21	,,	½ a. red-brown (5.38) ..	5	5
22	,,	9 p. green (5.38)	15	12
23	,,	1 a. carmine (5.38) ..	8	5
24	**92**	2 a. vermilion (1939) ..	40	15
26	**94**	3 a. yellow-green (1941)	1·50	50
27	**95**	3½ a. bright blue (7.38) ..	50	75
28	**96**	4 a. brown (1941) ..	7·50	8·50
30	**98**	8 a. slate-violet (1940) ..	14·00	12·00
31	**99**	12 a. lake (1940)	13·00	13·00
32	**100**	1 r. grey & red-brn. ('40)	50	40
33	,,	2 r. purple & brown ('40)	3·25	90
34	,,	5 r. green and blue ('40)	6·00	4·00
35	,,	10 r. purple & claret ('41)	10·00	6·00
36	,,	15 r. brown & green ('41)	8·00	9·00
37	,,	25 r. slate-vio. & pur. ('41)	18·00	14·00
20/37		.. .. *Set of* 16	70·00	60·00

1942–45. *King George VI on white background.*

38	**100*a***	3 p. slate	5	8
39	,,	½ a. purple	5	8
40	,,	9 p. green	5	20
41	,,	1 a. carmine	5	5
42	**101**	1 a. 3 p. bistre	15	45
43	,,	1½ a. dull violet	20	8
44	,,	2 a. vermillion	20	8
45	,,	3 a. bright violet ..	30	40
46	,,	3½ a. bright blue	75	60
47	**102**	4 a. brown	40	15
48	,,	6 a. turquoise-green ..	1·50	90
49	,,	8 a. slate-violet	20	30
50	,,	12 a. lake	50	40
38/50		.. .. *Set of* 13	4·00	3·50

BAHRAIN
1
ANNA
(3)

BAHRAIN
5 RUPEES
(4)

NOTE. All the following issues until 1960 are surcharged on stamps of GREAT BRITAIN.

For similar surcharges without the name of the country, see BRITISH POSTAL AGENCIES IN EASTERN ARABIA.

1948 (1 APR.)–**1949**. *Surch. as T* **3**, **4** (2 *r. and* 5 *r.*) *or similar surch. with bars at foot* (10 *r.*).

51	**128**	½ a. on ½d. pale green ..	5	8
52	,,	1 a. on 1d. pale scarlet ..	5	8
53	,,	1½ a. on 1½d. pale red-brn.	5	15
54	,,	2 a. on 2d. pale orange ..	5	5
55	,,	2½ a. on 2½d. light ultram.	15	20
56	,,	3 a. on 3d. pale violet ..	5	5
57	**129**	6 a. on 6d. purple ..	5	8
58	**130**	1 r. on 1s. bistre-brown	25	25
59	**131**	2 r. on 2s. 6d. yell.-green	65	1·10
60	,,	5 r. on 5s. red	2·00	3·00
60*a*	**132**	10 r. on 10s. ultram. (4.7.49)	11·00	9·00
51/60*a*		.. .. *Set of* 11	13·00	12·00

BAHRAIN
2½
ANNAS
(5)

BAHRAIN
15
RUPEES
(6)

1948 (26 APR.). *Silver Wedding, surch. as T* **5** *or* **6**.

61	**137**	2½ a. on 2½d. ultramarine	5	5
62	**138**	15 r. on £1 blue	6·00	7·00

1948 (29 JULY). *Olympic Games, surch. as T* **5**, *but in one line* (6 *a.*) *or two lines* (*others*).

63	**139**	2½ a. on 2½d. ultramarine..	5	8
		a. Surch. double ..	65·00	£130
64	**140**	3 a. on 3d. violet ..	12	15
65	**141**	6 a. on 6d. bright purple	15	20
66	**142**	1 r. on 1s. brown ..	35	45

The only used copies seen of No. 63a are cancelled with an experimental killer, used out of date.

BAHRAIN
3 ANNAS
(7)

1949 (10 OCT.). *75th Anniv. of U.P.U., surch. as T* **7**, *in one line* (2½ *a.*) *or in two lines* (*others*).

67	**143**	2½ a. on 2½d. ultramarine	10	12
68	**144**	3 a. on 3d. violet ..	12	20
69	**145**	6 a. on 6d. bright purple	25	35
70	**146**	1 r. on 1s. brown ..	40	45

BAHRAIN
2 RUPEES
(7*a*)

BAHRAIN
2 RUPEES
(7*b*)

"2" level with "RUPEES". "BAHRAIN" sharp.

"2" raised. "BAHRAIN" worn.

The third type (No. 77b) is as Type II but the vertical distance between "BAHRAIN" and "2 RUPEES" is 16 mm. instead of 15 mm. and the value is set more to the left of "BAHRAIN".

1950–55. *Surch. as T* **3** *or* **7*a*** (*rupee values*).

71	**128**	½ a. on ½d. pale orange ..	5	10
72	,,	1 a. on 1d. light ultram...	5	10
73	,,	1½ a. on 1½d. pale green ..	5	20
74	,,	2 a. on 2d. pale red-brown	5	5
75	,,	2½ a. on 2½d. pale scarlet ..	5	30
76	**129**	4 a. on 4d. light ultram. ..	12	20
77	**147**	2 r. on 2s. 6d. yell.-grn. ..	1·25	75
		a. Surch. with Type 7*b* (1955)	10·00	7·00
		b. Third type (1955) ..	60·00	12·00
		ba. "1" inverted and raised		
78	**148**	5 r. on 5s. red	1·50	1·75
79	**149**	10 r. on 10s. ultramarine ..	3·00	2·50
71/79		.. .. *Set of* 9	5·00	5·00

Dates of issue:—2.10.50, 4 a.; 3.5.51, others.

1952–54. *Q.E. II* (*W* **153**). *surch. as T* **3**.

80	**154**	½ a. on ½d. orange-red ..	5	5
		a. Fraction "½" omitted ..	20·00	25·00
81	,,	1 a. on 1d. ultramarine ..	5	5
82	,,	1½ a. on 1½d. green ..	5	5
83	,,	2 a. on 2d. red-brown ..	5	5
84	**155**	2½ a. on 2½d. carmine-red..	5	8
85	,,	3 a. on 3d. deep lilac (B.)	8	10
86	**156**	4 a. on 4d. ultramarine ..	12	12
87	**157**	6 a. on 6d. reddish purple	12	15
88	**160**	12 a. on 1s. 3d. green ..	20	20
89	**159**	1 r. on 1s. 6d. grey-blue ..	25	20
80/89		.. .. *Set of* 10	85	80

The word BAHRAIN is in taller letters on the 1½ a., 2½ a., 3 a. and 6 a.

Dates of issue:—5.12.52, 1½ a., 2½ a.; 31.8.53, ½ a., 1 a., 2 a.; 2.11.53, 4 a., 12 a., 1 r.; 18.1.54, 3 a., 6 a.

2½ BAHRAIN
ANNAS
(8)

1963 (3 JUNE). *Coronation. Surch. as T* **8**, *or similarly.*

90	**161**	2½ a. on 2½d. carmine-red..	15	25
91	**162**	4 a. on 4d. ultramarine ..	25	35
92	**163**	12 a. on 1s. 3d. dp. yell.-grn.	70	70
93	**164**	1 r. on 1s. 6d. dp. grey-bl.	75	80

BAHRAIN 2 RUPEES I

BAHRAIN 2 RUPEES II

BAHRAIN 2 RUPEES III

(9)

BAHRAIN 5 RUPEES I

BAHRAIN 5 RUPEES II

(10)

BAHRAIN 10 RUPEES I

BAHRAIN 10 RUPEES II

(11)

TYPE I (T **9/11**). Type-set opt. Bold, thick letters with sharp corners and straight edges.

TYPE II (T **9/11**). Plate-printed opt. Thinner letters, rounded corners and rough edges. Bars wider apart.

Type III (T **9**). Plate-printed opt. Similar to Type II as regards the position of the bars on all 40 stamps of the sheet, but the letters are thinner and with more rounded corners than in II, while the ink of the surcharge is less black.

The general characteristics of Type II of the 2 r. are less pronounced than in the other values, but a distinguishing test is in the relative position of the bars and the "U" of "RUPEES". In Type II (except for the 1st stamp, 5th row) the bars start immediately beneath the left-hand edge of the "U". In Type I they start more to the right.

In the 10 r. the "1" and the "O" are spaced 0.9 mm. in Type I and only 0.6 mm. in Type II.

1955 (23 SEPT.)–**60**. *T* **166/8** (*Waterlow ptgs.*) *surch. as T* **9/11**.

94I	**166**	2 r. on 2s. 6d. black-brn.	50	65
		II. Type II (13.5.58) ..	1·25	1·50
		III. Type III (No. 536*a*, D.L.R.) (29.1.60) ..	5·00	6·00
95I	**167**	5 r. on 5s. rose-red ..	2·00	2·00
		II. Type II (19.8.57) ..	2·75	2·50
96I	**168**	10 r. on 10s. ultramarine	2·50	2·25
		II. Type II (13.5.58) ..	14·00	15·00

1956–7. *Q.E. II* (*W* **165**). *surch. as T* **3**.

97	**154**	½ a. on ½d. orge.-red (1.57)	10	20
98	**156**	4 a. on 4d. ultram. (8.6.56)	45	75
99	**157**	6 a. on 6d. red.-purple (5.12.56)	15	25
100	**160**	12 a. on 1s. 3d. grn. (2.8.56)	90	1·50
101	**159**	1 r. on 1s. 6d grey-bl. (4.3.57)	25	20
		a. Surch. double ..	—	£200
97/101		.. .. *Set of* 5	1·60	2·75

(New currency. 100 naye paise = 1 rupee).

BAHRAIN **BAHRAIN** **BAHRAIN**

NP 1 NP (12) **3 NP** (13) **75 NP** (14)

1957 (1 Apr.)–59. *Q.E. II* (*W* **165**), *surch. as T* **12** (1 *n.p.*, 15 *n.p.*, 25 *n.p.*, 40 *n.p.*, *and* 50 *n.p.*), *T* **14** (75 *n.p.*) *or T* **13** (*others*).

102 **157** 1 n.p. on 5d. brown .. 5 5
103 **154** 3 n.p. on ½d. orange-red 5 8
104 ,, 6 n.p. on 1d. ultramarine 8 8
105 ,, 9 n.p. on 1½d. green 8 8
106 ,, 12 n.p. on 2d. lt. red-brn. 8 8
107 **155** 15 n.p. on 2½d. carmine-red (Type I) .. 10 10
a. Type II ('59) .. 12 15
108 ,, 20 n.p. on 3d. dp. lilac (B.) 8 8
109 **156** 25 n.p. on 4d. ultramarine 12 15
110 **157** 40 n.p. on 6d. reddish pur. 12 15
a. Deep claret ('59) .. 20 25
111 **158** 50 n.p. on 9d. bronze-grn. 25 35
112 **160** 75 n.p. on 1s. 3d. green .. 25 30
102/112 .. .. *Set of* 11 1·00 1·25

BAHRAIN
15 NP

(15)

1957 (1 Aug.). *World Scout Jubilee Jamboree, surch. in two lines as T* **15** (15 *n.p.*), *or in three lines* (*others*).

113 **170** 15 n.p. on 2½d. carm.-red 12 15
114 **171** 25 n.p. on 4d. ultram. 15 20
115 **172** 75 n.p. on 1s. 3d. green .. 30 35

1960. *Q.E. II* (*W* **179**), *surch. as T* **12.**

116 **155** 15 n.p. on 2½d. carmine-red (Type II) .. 25 75

16. Shaikh Sulman bin Hamed al-Khalifa. **17.**

(Des. M. C. Farrar-Bell. Photo. Harrison (T **16**). Des. O. C. Meronti. Recess. D.L.R. (T **17**).)

1960 (1 July). *P* 15 × 14 (*T* **16**) *or* 13½ × 13 (*T* **17**)

117 **16** 5 n.p. bright blue .. 5 5
118 ,, 15 n.p. red-orange .. 5 5
119 ,, 20 n.p. reddish violet .. 5 5
120 ,, 30 n.p. bistre-brown .. 5 8
121 ,, 40 n.p. grey 8 10
122 ,, 50 n.p. emerald-green .. 10 12
123 ,, 75 n.p. chocolate .. 12 15
124 **17** 1 r. black 15 20
125 ,, 2 r. rose-red 30 40
126 ,, 5 r. deep blue .. .. 85 1·10
127 ,, 10 r. bronze-green .. 1·50 1·50
117/127 .. .. *Set of* 11 3·00 3·25

18. Shaikh Isa bin Sulman al-Khalifa.

19. Air Terminal, Muharraq.

20. Deep Water Harbour.

(Des. M. C. Farrar-Bell. Photo. Harrison (5 to 75 n.p.). Des. D. C. Rivett. Recess. B.W. (others).)

1964 (22 Feb.). *P* 15 × 14 *T* **18** *or* 13½ × 13 *T* **19/20.**

128 **18** 5 n.p. bright blue .. 5 5
129 ,, 15 n.p. orange-red .. 5 5
130 ,, 20 n.p. reddish violet .. 5 5
131 ,, 30 n.p. olive-brown .. 5 8
132 ,, 40 n.p. slate 8 8
133 ,, 50 n.p. emerald-green .. 8 8
134 ,, 75 n.p. brown .. 12 10
135 **19** 1 r. black 15 10
136 ,, 2 r. carmine-red .. 30 20
137 **20** 5 r. ultramarine .. 75 65
138 ,, 10 r. myrtle-green .. 1·50 1·10
128/138 .. .. *Set of* 11 3·00 2·25

LOCAL STAMPS.

The following stamps were issued primarily for postage within Bahrain, but apparently also had franking value when used on external mail.

L **1.** Shaikh Sulman bin Hamed al-Khalifa. L **2.**

(Types L **1/2.** Recess. D.L.R.)

1953–56. *P* 12 × 12½.

L1 L **1** ½ a. deep green (1.10.56) 25 25
L2 ,, 1 a. deep blue (1.10.56) .. 25 25
L3 ,, 1½ a. carmine (15.2.53) .. 20 20

1957 (16 Oct.). *As Nos.* L1/3 *but values in new currency.*

L4 L **1** 3 p. deep green 50 50
L5 ,, 6 p. carmine 50 50
L6 ,, 9 p. deep blue 50 50

1961 (20 Mar.). *P* 12 × 12½.

L 7 L **2** 5 p. green 30 35
L 8 ,, 10 p. carmine-red 30 35
L 9 ,, 15 p. grey 15 20
L10 ,, 20 p. blue 20 25
L11 ,, 30 p. sepia 20 25
L12 ,, 40 p. ultramarine .. 20 25
L7/12 .. .. .. *Set of* 6 1·25 1·50

The Bahrain Post Department took over the postal services on 1st January, 1966. Later stamp issues will be found in Vol. 1 of the Stanley Gibbons Foreign Overseas Catalogue.

BANGKOK.

British Post Offices in Siam.

B

(1)

1882–85. *Stamps of Straits Settlements optd. with T* **1.**

On issue of 1867.

1 – 32 c. on 2 a. yellow (No. 9) £1300 £1500

On issues of 1867–82. *Wmk. Crown CC.*

2 **5** 2 c. brown .. .. .. 80·00 £140
3 ,, 4 c. rose .. .. .. 75·00 85·00
a. Opt. double .. .. — £450
4 **18** 5 c. purple-brown .. .. 12·00 12·00
5 **5** 6 c. lilac .. .. .. 11·00 11·00
6 **6** 8 c. orange .. .. .. £140 12·00
7 **19** 10 c. slate .. .. .. 16·[illegible] 11·00
8 **6** 12 c. blue .. .. .. 45·[illegible] 28·00
9 **7** 24 c. green .. .. .. 28·00 11·00
10 **27** 30 c. claret £750 £500
11 **9** 96 c. grey £150 £160

On issue of April, 1883.

12 **9** 2 c. on 32 c. pale red (*Wide* "E" (No. 59)) .. 90·00 £120
13 ,, 2 c. on 32 c. pale red (*Wide* "S" (No. 60)) .. £120 £140

On issues of 1882–84. *Wmk. Crown CA.*

14 **5** 2 c. brown .. .. .. 12·00 12·00
15 ,, 2 c. rose .. .. .. 4·00 3·75
a. Opt. inverted .. .. — £160
b. Opt. double £140
16 ,, 4 c. rose .. .. .. 20·00 16·00
17 ,, 4 c. brown .. .. 7·00 7·00
18 **18** 5 c. blue .. .. .. 18·00 12·00
19 **5** 6 c. lilac .. .. .. 11·00 10·00
20 **6** 8 c. orange .. .. .. 7·00 6·00
a. Opt. inverted .. .. — £250
21 **19** 10 c. slate .. .. .. 11·00 9·00
22 **6** 12 c. dull purple .. .. 16·00 12·00
23 **7** 24 c. green .. .. .. £120 85·00

The use of these stamps ceased on 1 July, 1885.

BANGLADESH.

Prior to the issue of these stamps, various Pakistan issues were overprinted by local postmasters, mainly using handstamps. These are of philatelic interest, but outside the scope of the catalogue.

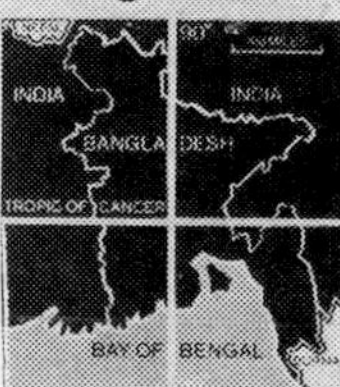

1. Map of Bangladesh.

(Des. Biman Mullick. Litho. Format.)

1971 (29 July). *T* **1** *and similar vert. designs. P* 14 × 14½.

1 10 p. indigo-blue, red-orange and pale blue 5 5
2 20 p. multicoloured 5 5
3 50 p. multicoloured 8 8
4 1 r. multicoloured 12 15
5 2 r. deep greenish blue, light new blue & rose-magenta 25 30
6 3 r. apple-green, dull yellowish green and greenish blue .. 35 40
7 5 r. multicoloured 60 65
8 10 r. gold, rose-magenta and deep greenish blue .. 1·25 1·40
1/8 .. .. .. *Set of* 8 2·40 2·60

Designs: 20 p. "Dacca University Massacre"; 50 p. "75 Million People"; 1 r. Flag of Independence; 2 r. Ballot box; 3 r. Broken chain; 5 r. Shaikh Mujibur Rahman; 10 r. "Support Bangla Desh" and map.

BANGLADESH
LIBERATED
বাংলাদেশের মুক্তি

(2)

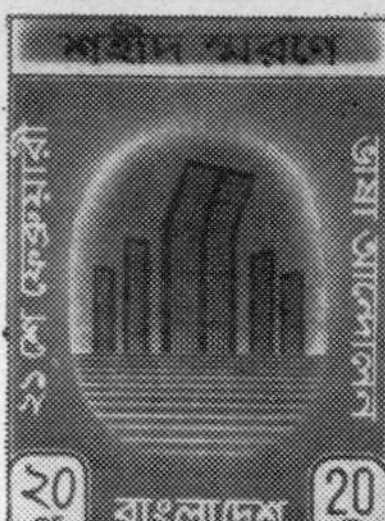

3. " Martyrdom ".

1971 (20 Dec.). *Liberation. Nos.* 1 *and* 7/8 *optd. with T* **2**.

9		10 p. indigo-blue, red-orange and pale blue	10	10
10		5 r. multicoloured (O.) ..	75	75
11		10 r. gold, rose-magenta and deep greenish blue ..	1·40	1·40

The remaining values of the original issue were also overprinted and placed on sale in Great Britain but were not issued in Bangladesh. (*Price for the complete set £2 un.*)

On 1st February 1972 the Agency placed on sale a further issue in the flag, map and Sheikh Mujib designs in new colours and new currency (100 paisas = 1 taka). This issue proved to be unacceptable to the Bangladesh authorities and was not put on sale there and so has no postal validity. The values comprise 1, 2, 3, 5, 7, 10, 15, 20, 25, 40, 50, 75 p. and 1, 2 and 5 t. (*Price for set of* 15 *un.*, £1.)

(Des. and photo. Indian Security Printing Press, Nasik.)

1972 (21 Feb.). *In Memory of the Martyrs. P* 13.

12	**3**	20 p. dull green and rose-red	5	5

4. Flames of Independence.

(Photo. Indian Security Printing Press, Nasik.)

1972 (26 Mar.). *First Anniv. of Independence. P* 13.

13	**4**	20 p. brn.-lake & red ..	5	5
14	,,	60 p. dull ultram. & red ..	8	10
15	,,	75 p. reddish vio. & red ..	10	10

5. Doves of Peace.

(Litho. B.W.)

1972 (6 Dec.). *Victory Day. P* 13.

16	**5**	20 p. multicoloured	5	5
17	,,	60 p. multicoloured	8	10
18	,,	75 p. multicoloured	10	10

(New Currency. 100 paisa = 1 taka.)

6. " Homage to Martyrs ".

(Des. K. G. Mustafa. Litho. B.W.)

1973 (25 Mar.). *In Memory of the Martyrs. P* 13.

19	**6**	20 p. multicoloured	5	5
20	,,	60 p. multicoloured	8	10
21	,,	1 t. 35, multicoloured ..	20	20

7. Embroidered Quilt.

8. Court of Justice.

(Litho. B.W.)

1973 (30 Apr.). *T* **7/8** *and similar designs. P* 14½ × 14 (50 *p.*, 1 *t.*, 5 *t.*, 10 *t.*) *or* 14 × 14½ (*others*).

22		2 p. black	5	5
23		3 p. blue-green	5	5
24		5 p. light brown	5	5
25		10 p. slate-black	5	5
26		20 p. yellow-green	5	5
27		25 p. bright reddish mauve	5	5
28		50 p. bright purple	5	5
29		60 p. greenish slate	5	5
30		75 p. yellow-orange	8	10
31		90 p. orange-brown	8	10
32		1 t. light violet	10	12
33		2 t. olive-green	20	25
34		5 t. grey-blue	50	55
35		10 t. rose	1·00	1·10
22/35		.. .. *Set of* 14	2·00	2·25

Designs:—*As T* **7**—3 p. Jute field; 5 p. Jack fruit; 10 p. Bullocks ploughing; 20 p. Rakta jaba (flower); 25 p. Bengal tiger; 60 p. Bamboo grove; 75 p. Plucking tea; 90 p. Handicrafts. *Horiz.* (28 × 22 *mm.*)—50 p. Hilsa (fish). *Horiz. as T* **8**—5 t. fishing boat; 10 t. Sixty-dome mosque, Bagerhat. *Vert. as T* **8**—2 t. Date tree.

See also Nos. 49/50 and 63 etc.

9. Flame Emblem.

(Des. and litho. Govt. Printer, Dacca.)

1973 (10 Dec.). *25th Anniv. of Declaration of Human Rights. P* 13½.

36	**9**	10 p. multicoloured ..	5	5
37	,,	1 t. 25, multicoloured ..	12	15

10. Family, Map and Graph.

(Des. K. G. Mustafa. Litho. B.W.)

1974 (10 Feb.). *First Population Census. P* 13½.

38	**10**	20 p. multicoloured ..	5	5
39	,,	25 p. multicoloured ..	5	5
40	,,	75 p. multicoloured ..	10	12

11. Copernicus and Heliocentric System.

(Litho. B.W.)

1974 (22 July). *500th Birth Anniv. of Copernicus. P* 13 × 13½.

41	**11**	25 p. yellow-orange, bluish violet and black ..	5	5
42	,,	75 p. orge., yell.-grn. & blk.	8	8

12. U.N. H.Q. and Bangladesh Flag.

(Litho. B.W.)

1974 (25 SEPT.). *Bangladesh's Admission to the U.N. P* 13.

43	**12**	25 p. multicoloured ..	5	5
44	,,	1 t. multicoloured ..	10	10

13. U.P.U. Emblem.

(Des. and litho. B.W.)

1974 (9 OCT.). *Centenary of Universal Postal Union. T* **13** *and similar vert. design. Multicoloured. P* 13×13½.

45	25 p. Type **13**	5	5
46	1 t. 25, Mail runner	12	15
47	1 t. 75, Type **13**	15	20
48	5 t. As 1 t. 25	50	55

The above exist imperforate in a miniature sheet from a restricted printing.

14. Courts of Justice.

1974. *Nos.* 32/3 *redrawn with revised value inscriptions as T* **14**.

49	1 t. light violet	10	12
50	2 t. olive	20	25

15. Royal Bengal Tiger. **16.** Symbolic Family.

(Des. and litho. B.W.)

1974 (4 NOV.). *Wildlife Preservation. T* **15** *and similar vert. designs. Multicoloured. P* 13×13½.

51	25 p. Type **15**	5	5
52	50 p. Tiger whelp	5	8
53	2 t. Tiger in stream	20	25

(Litho. B.W.)

1974 (30 DEC.). *World Population Year. "Family Planning for All". T* **16** *and similar multicoloured designs. P* 14.

54	25 p. Type **16**	5	5
55	70 p. Village family	8	8
56	1 t. 25, Heads of family (*horiz.*)	10	12

17. Radar Antenna.

(Des. and litho. B.W.)

1975 (14 JUNE). *Inauguration of Betbunia Satellite Earth Station. P* 13½.

57	**17**	25 p. blk., silver & dull red..	5	5
58	,,	1 t. blk., silver & ultram...	10	12

18. Woman's Head.

(Des. A. F. Karim. Litho. Asher & Co., Melbourne.)

1975 (31 DEC.). *International Women's Year. P* 15.

59	**18**	50 p. multicoloured ..	5	8
60	,,	2 t. multicoloured ..	20	25

(Litho. Asher & Co., Melbourne.)

1976. *As Nos.* 22 *etc., but redrawn in a smaller size. P* 14½×15 (50*p.*), 14½ (1 *t.*, 2 *t.*) *or* 15×14½ (*others*).

(*a*) 18×23 *mm.*

63	5 p. dp. yell.-grn. (11.2.76) ..	5	5
64	10 p. slate-black (28.4.76) ..	5	5
65	20 p. yellow-green (1.76) ..	5	5
66	25 p. brt. reddish mauve (1·76)	5	5

(*b*) 23×18 *mm.*

67	50 p. light purple (8.6.76) ..	5	5

(*c*) 31 × 20 *mm.*

71	1 t. ultramarine (1.76) ..	10	12
72	2 t. olive-green (8.6.76) ..	20	25
63/72	*Set of* 7	35	40

Nos. 61/74 have been provisionally allocated to this set.

19. Telephones, 1876 and 1976.

(Des. A. F. Karim. Litho. Asher & Co., Melbourne.)

1976 (10 MAR.). *Telephone Centenary. T* **19** *and similar vert. design. P* 15.

75	2 t. 25, multicoloured ..	25	30
76	5 t. dull vermilion, apple-green and black	55	65

Design:—5 t. Alexander Graham Bell.

20. Eye and Nutriments.

(Des. A. F. Karim. Litho. Asher & Co., Melbourne.)

1976 (7 APR.). *Prevention of Blindness. P* 15.

77	**20**	30 p. multicoloured ..	5	5
78	,,	2 t. 25, multicoloured ..	25	30

21. Liberty Bell.

(Des. E. W. Roberts. Photo. Heraclio Fournier.)

1976 (29 MAY). *Bicentenary of American Revolution. T* **21** *and similar horiz. designs. Multicoloured. P* 14.

79	30 p. Type **21**	5	5
80	2 t. 25, Statue of Liberty ..	25	30
81	5 t. *Mayflower*	55	65
82	10 t. Mount Rushmore ..	1·10	1·25
MS83	167×95 mm. Nos. 79/82	2·10	

No. **MS**83 also exists imperforate from a restricted printing.

22. Industry, Science, Agriculture and Education.

(Des. K. G. Mustafa. Litho. Asher & Co., Melbourne.)

1976 (29 JULY). *25th Anniv. of the Colombo Plan. P* 15.

84	**22**	30 p. multicoloured ..	5	5
85	,,	2 t. 25, multicoloured ..	25	30

BARBADOS.

I. CROWN COLONY.

1 Britannia. 2

(Recess. Perkins, Bacon & Co.)

1852 (15 April)–**1855.** *Paper blued. No wmk. Imperf.*

1 **1** (½d.) yellow-green .. .. — £250
2 ,, (½d.) deep green .. .. 42·00 £130
3 ,, (1d.) blue .. .. 9·00 65·00
4 ,, (1d.) deep blue .. .. 5·00 28·00
4*a* ,, (2d.) greyish slate £120
b. Bisected (1d.) (on cover) .. — £1400
5 ,, (4d.) brownish red (1855) .. 13·00 £160

It has now been proved that the stamp in greyish slate was intended for issue as a 2d. stamp. As its use for this rate was extremely limited it was officially bisected and used for the penny rate in August and September, 1854.

Apart from the shade, which is distinctly paler, No. 4*a* can be distinguished from No. 5*b* by the smooth even gum, the gum of No. 5*b* being yellow and patchy, giving a mottled appearance to the back of the stamp. No. 5*a* also has the latter gum.

Prepared for use but not issued.

5*a* **1** (No value), slate-blue (*shades*) 6·00
5*b* ,, (No value), deep slate .. £150

1855–57. *White paper. No wmk. Imperf.*

7 **1** (½d.) yellow-green .. .. £170 50·00
8 ,, (½d.) green .. .. 42·00 80·00
9 ,, (1d.) pale blue .. .. 22·00 22·00
10 ,, (1d.) deep blue .. .. 8·00 24·00

1858. *No wmk. Imperf.*

11 **2** 6d. pale rose-red .. .. £225 50·00
11*a* ,, 6d. deep rose-red .. .. £275 80·00
12 ,, 1s. brown-black .. .. 65·00 42·00
12*a* ,, 1s. black .. .. 45·00 25·00

1860. *No wmk. (a) Pin-perf.* 14.

13 **1** (½d.) yellow-green .. £450 £100
14 ,, (1d.) pale blue .. .. £450 55·00
15 ,, (1d.) deep blue .. .. £450 55·00

(*b*) *Pin-perf.* 12½.

16 **1** (½d.) yellow-green £1100 £180
16*a* ,, (1d.) blue .. .. — £350

(*c*) *Pin-perf.* 14 × 12½.

16*b* **1** (½d.) yellow-green .. .. — £750

1861. *No wmk. Clean-cut perf.* 14 *to* 16.

17 **1** (½d.) deep green .. .. 20·00 6·00
18 ,, (1d.) pale blue .. .. £200 10·00
19 ,, (1d.) blue .. .. .. £250 10·00
a. Bisected (½d.) (on cover) — £550

1861–70. *No wmk. Rough perf.* 14 *to* 16.

20 **1** (½d.) deep green .. .. 5·00 4·25
21 ,, (½d.) green .. .. 3·00 3·00
21*a* ,, (½d.) blue-green .. .. 20·00 28·00
b. Imperf. (pair) £125
22 ,, (½d.) grass-green .. .. 8·00 4·00
a. Imperf. (pair) £125
23 ,, (1d.) blue (1861) .. .. 12·00 3·00
a. Imperf. (pair) £140
24 ,, (1d.) deep blue .. .. 7·00 2·25
a. Bisect. diag. (½d.) (on cover) — £275
25 ,, (4d.) dull rose-red (1861) .. 18·00 9·00
a. Imperf. (pair) £180
26 ,, (4d.) dull brown-red (1865) 30·00 11·00
a. Imperf. (pair) £250
27 ,, (4d.) lake-rose (1868) .. 18·00 14·00
a. Imperf. (pair) £250
28 ,, (4d.) dull vermilion (1869) 50·00 22·00
a. Imperf. (pair) £250
29 **2** 6d. rose-red (1861) .. 55·00 6·00
30 ,, 6d. orange-red (1864) .. 22·00 6·00
31 ,, 6d. brt. orge.-verm. (1868) 14·00 6·00
32 ,, 6d. dull orge.-verm. (1870) 14·00 5·00
a. Imperf. (pair) £100
33 ,, 6d. orange (1870) .. 25·00 8·00
34 ,, 1s. brown-black (1863) .. 12·00 5·00
35 ,, 1s. black (1866) .. .. 7·50 6·00
a. Imperf. between (horiz. pr.) £1300

Variety. P 11 *to* 12.

36 **1** (½d.) green £1700
37 ,, (1d.) blue £750

Nos. 36 and 37 are only known unused.

Error of colour.

38 **2** 1s. blue £6000

No. 38 only exists with manuscript corner to corner cross cleaned off.

1870. *Wmk. Large Star, Type* w. **1**. *Rough perf.* 14 *to* 16.

43 **1** (½d.) green .. .. .. 18·00 5·00
a. Imperf. (pair) £120
43*b* ,, (½d.) yellow-green .. 35·00 20·00
44 ,, (1d.) blue .. .. .. £250 12·00
a. Blue paper .. .. — 18·00
45 ,, (4d.) dull vermilion .. £160 14·00
46 **2** 6d. orange-vermilion .. £140 15·00
47 ,, 1s. black .. .. 60·00 10·00

1871. *Wmk. Small Star, Type* w. **2**. *Rough perf.* 14 *to* 16.

48 **1** (1d.) blue .. .. .. 20·00 2·50
49 ,, (4d.) dull rose-red .. £200 12·00
50 **2** 6d. orange-vermilion .. 85·00 9·00
51 ,, 1s. black .. .. 35·00 9·00

1872. *Wmk. Small Star. Type* w. **2**.

(*a*) *Clean-cut perf.* 14½ *to* 15½.

52 **1** (1d.) blue .. .. .. 55·00 2·00
a. Bisect. diag. (½d.) (on cover) — £250
53 **2** 6d. orange-vermilion .. £120 9·00
54 ,, 1s. black .. .. 32·00 4·00

(*b*) *P* 11 *to* 13 × 14½ *to* 15½.

56 **1** (½d.) green .. .. 50·00 4·00
57 ,, (4d.) dull vermilion .. 70·00 13·00

1873. *Wmk. Large Star, Type* w.**1**. *Clean-cut perf.* 14½ *to* 15½.

58 **1** (½d.) green .. .. 45·00 5·50
59 ,, (4d.) dull rose-red .. £140 35·00
60 **2** 6d. orange-vermilion .. £140 20·00
a. Imperf. between (horiz. pair) £600
b. Imperf. (pair) .. .. 50·00
61 ,, 1s. black .. .. 25·00 4·00
a. Imperf. between (horiz. pair)

Two used singles of No. 60*b* have been seen.

1873 (June). *Wmk. Small Star, Type* w. **2** (*two points upwards*). *P* 14.

63 **2** 3d. brown-purple .. .. £150 40·00

3

1873. *Wmk. Small Star, Type* w. **2**. *P* 15½ × 15.

64 **3** 5s. dull rose (Optd. S. £200) .. £300 £180

1874 (May). *Wmk. Large Star, Type* w. **1**.

(*a*) *Perf.* 14.

65 **2** ½d. deep green .. .. 5·00 3·25
66 ,, 1d. deep blue .. .. 18·00 1·75

(*b*) *Clean-cut perf.* 14½ *to* 15½.

66*a* **2** 1d. deep blue .. .. — £750

(*c*) *Imperf.* (*pair*).

66*b* ,, 1d. deep blue

(Recess. De La Rue.)

1875–78. *Wmk. Crown CC (sideways on 6d. and* 1s.). (*a*) *P* 12½.

67 **2** ½d. bright green .. .. 3·50 2·00
68 ,, 4d. deep red .. .. 55·00 5·50
69 ,, 6d. bright yellow (aniline) .. £300 35·00
70 ,, 6d. chrome-yellow .. £225 32·00
71 ,, 1s. violet (aniline) .. £180 14·00

(*b*) *P* 14.

72 **2** ½d. bright green (1876) .. 2·50 1·40
73 ,, 1d. dull blue .. .. 6·00 60
a. Bisected (½d.) (on cover) .. — £225
74 ,, 1d. grey-blue .. .. 7·00 70
a. Wmk. sideways .. .. — £500
75 ,, 3d. mauve-lilac (1878) .. 28·00 5·50
76 ,, 4d. red (1878) .. .. 32·00 7·50
77 **2** 4d. carmine .. .. 50·00 2·75
78 ,, 4d. crimson-lake .. £120 3·25
79 ,, 6d. chrome-yellow (1876) .. 42·00 2·75
80 ,, 6d. yellow .. .. 55·00 6·50
81 ,, 1s. purple (1876) .. 42·00 2·75
82 ,, 1s. violet (aniline) .. £475 16·00
83 ,, 1s. dull mauve .. 80·00 2·00
a. Bisected (6d.) (on cover) .. — £1000

Variety. Perf. 14 × 12½.

84 **2** 4d. red £3750

Very few specimens of No. 84 have been found unused. One used specimen is known.

1D. (A) 1D. (B) 1D. (C)

1878 (March). *No. 64, with lower label removed, divided vertically by perforation, and each half surch. sideways in black.*

(A) *Large numeral "1", 7 mm. high with curved serif, and large letter "D", 2¾ mm. high.*

(86 **3** 1d. on half 5s. dull rose .. £800 £200
a. Unsevered pair (both No. 86) £3000 £650
b. Ditto, Nos. 86 and 87 .. — £1200
c. Ditto, Nos. 86 and 88 ..
d. As 86b without dividing perf. — £4000

(B) *As last, but numeral with straight serif.*

87 **3** 1d. on half 5s. dull rose .. £1000 £275
a. Unsevered pair .. .. — £875

(C) *Smaller numeral "1", 6 mm. high and smaller "D", 2½ mm. high.*

88 **3** 1d. on half 5s. dull rose .. £1200 £275
a. Unsevered pair £3500 £900

All types of the surcharge are found reading upwards as well as downwards, and there are minor varieties of the type.

4

HALF-PENNY (5)

(Typo. De La Rue.)

1882–86. *Wmk. Crown CA. P* 14.

89 **4** ½d. dull green (1882) .. 2·00 70
90 ,, ½d. green .. .. 1·75 70
91 ,, 1d. rose (1882) .. 5·00 70
a. Bisected (½d.) (on cover) .. — £140
92 ,, 1d. carmine .. .. 1·75 45
93 ,, 2½d. ultramarine (1882) .. 10·00 1·00
94 ,, 2½d. deep blue .. .. 12·00 90
95 ,, 3d. deep purple (1885) .. 25·00 14·00
96 ,, 3d. reddish purple .. 2·75 3·25
97 ,, 4d. grey (1882) .. 55·00 2·25
98 ,, 4d. pale brown (1885) .. 2·00 1·25
99 ,, 4d. deep brown .. 2·00 70
100 ,, 6d. olive-black (1886) .. 14·00 7·00
102 ,, 1s. chestnut (1886) .. 9·00 9·00
103 ,, 5s. bistre (1886) .. 95·00 £100
89/103 .. .. *Set of* 8 £125 £110
95/103, except 97, Optd. "Specimen" *Set of* 5 55·00

1892. *No.* 99 *surch. with T* **5**.

104 **4** ½d. on 4d. deep brown .. 20 55
a. No hyphen .. .. 1·50 2·00
b. Surch. double (R.+Bk.) .. £200 £225
ba. Do. No hyphen £450 £450

6. Seal of Colony.

7

(Typo. D.L.R.)

1892–1903. *Wmk. Crown CA. P* 14.

105 **6** ½d. slate-grey & carm. ('96) 20 30
106 „ ½d. dull green 10 30
107 „ 1d. carmine 20 20
108 „ 2d. slate-black & orange (1899) .. .. .. 2·50 1·50
109 „ 2½d. ultramarine .. .. 2·25 60
110 „ 5d. grey-olive .. .. 3·50 2·50
111 „ 6d. mauve and carmine .. 3·50 2·75
112 „ 8d. orange & ultramarine 1·75 4·00
113 „ 10d. dull blue-grn. & carm. 5·00 6·00
114 „ 2s. 6d. blue-blk. & orange 14·00 15·00
115 „ 2s. 6d. vio. & grn. (1903) 24·00 25·00
105/15 .. .. *Set of* 11 50·00 50·00
105/115 Optd. "Specimen" *Set of* 11 40·00

See also Nos. 135/44 and 163/9.

(Typo. D.L.R.)

1897–98. *Diamond Jubilee. T* **7**. *Wmk. Crown CC. P* 14.

(*a*) *White paper* (1897).

116 ¼d. grey and carmine .. 30 35
117 ½d. dull green 70 35
118 1d. rose .. .. .. 1·25 50
119 2½d. ultramarine .. .. 3·50 75
120 5d. olive-brown .. .. 6·50 7·50
121 6d. mauve and carmine .. 8·00 7·00
122 8d. orange and ultramarine 7·00 6·50
123 10d. blue-green and carmine 12·00 13·00
124 2s. 6d. blue-black & orange 12·00 13·00
116/124 .. .. *Set of* 9 45·00 42·00
116/124 Optd. "Specimen" *Set of* 9 60·00

(*b*) *Paper blued* (1898).

125 ¼d. grey and carmine .. 7·00 8·00
126 ½d. dull green .. .. 7·50 7·50
127 1d. carmine .. .. 8·00 9·00
128 2½d. ultramarine .. .. 9·00 9·00
129 5d. olive-brown .. .. 50·00 50·00
130 6d. mauve and carmine .. 22·00 22·00
131 8d. orange and ultramarine 20·00 22·00
132 10d. dull green and carmine 28·00 32·00
133 2s. 6d. blue-black & orange 20·00 21·00

1904–5. *Wmk. Mult. Crown CA. P* 14.

135 **6** ¼d. slate-grey and carmine 30 30
136 „ ½d. dull green 75 15
137 „ 1d. carmine 55 15
139 „ 2½d. blue .. .. 2·50 45
141 „ 6d. mauve and carmine .. 8·00 7·50
142 „ 8d. orange & ultramarine 13·00 16·00
144 „ 2s. 6d. violet and green .. 21·00 23·00
135/144 .. .. *Set of* 7 40·00 42·00

See also Nos. 163/9.

8. Nelson Monument.

(Des. G. Goodman. Recess. D.L.R.)

1906. *Nelson Centenary. Wmk. Crown CC. P* 14.

145 **8** ¼d. black and grey .. 45 50
146 „ ½d. black and pale green .. 1·60 55
147 „ 1d. black and red .. 1·60 35
148 „ 2d. black and yellow .. 3·50 5·00
149 „ 2½d. black and bright blue 4·00 4·50
150 „ 6d. black and mauve .. 11·00 12·00
151 „ 1s. black and rose .. 12·00 12·00
145/151 .. .. *Set of* 7 30·00 32·00
145/51 Optd. "Specimen" *Set of* 7 55·00

Two sets may be made of the above: one on thick, opaque, creamy white paper; the other on thin, rather transparent, bluish white paper.

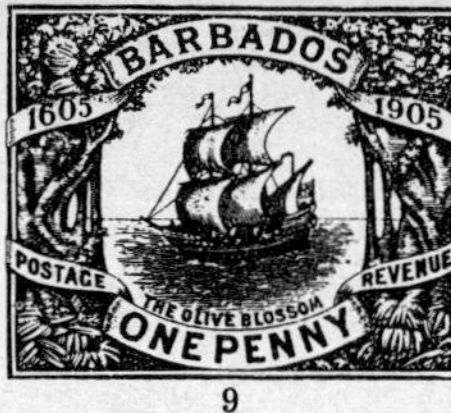

9

Kingston Relief Fund. 1d.

(10)

(Des. Lady Carter. Recess. D.L.R.)

1906 (15 Aug.). *Tercentenary of Annexation. Wmk. Multiple Crown CA (sideways). P* 14.

152 **9** 1d. black, blue and green .. 6·00 1·75
152 Optd. "Specimen" .. .. 30·00

1907 (25 Jan.). *Kingston Relief Fund. No.* 108 *surch. with T* **10**.

153 **6** 1d. on 2d. slate-black and orange (R.) .. .. 1·40 1·75
a. Surch. inverted (25.2.07) .. 1·40 1·75
b. Surch. double £300
c. Surch. double, both inverted .. £300
d. Surch. tête-bêche (pair) .. £350
e. No stop after "1d." .. 5·50 6·00
ea. Do., surch. inverted (25.2.07) 5·00 5·00

The above stamp was sold for 2d., of which 1d. was retained for postal revenue, and the other 1d. given to a fund for the relief of the sufferers by the earthquake in Jamaica.

1907 (6 July). *Nelson Centenary. Wmk. Mult. Crown CA. P* 14.

158 **8** ¼d. black and grey .. 75 75
161 „ 2d. black and yellow .. 6·00 7·50
162 „ 2½d. black & bright blue .. 10·00 11·00
a. Black and indigo £400 £450

1909–10. *Wmk. Mult. Crown CA. P* 14.

163 **6** ¼d. brown 20 25
164 „ ½d. blue-green 70 55
165 „ 1d. red 50 20
166 „ 2d. greyish slate ('10) .. 4·00 5·00
167 „ 2½d. bright blue ('10) .. 6·00 2·25
168 „ 6d. dull & brt. purple ('10) 7·00 7·00
169 „ 1s. black/*green* ('10) .. 12·00 13·00
163/169 .. .. *Set of* 7 27·00 25·00
163, 165/6, 168/9 Optd. "Specimen" *Set of* 5 26·00

11

13

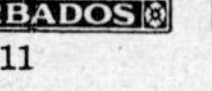

12

14

(Typo. De La Rue.)

1912 (23 July–13 Aug.). *Wmk. Mult. Crown CA. P* 14.

170 **11** ¼d. brown (23 July) .. 8 12
a. Pale brown 30 25
171 „ ½d. green (23 July) .. 8 8
172 „ 1d. red 55 25
a. Scarlet .. .. 2·25 50
173 **11** 2d. greyish slate .. .. 1·25 3·50
174 „ 2½d. bright blue 90 70
175 **12** 3d. purple/*yellow* .. 1·00 2·25
176 „ 4d. red and black/*yellow* 1·00 3·25
177 „ 6d. purple and dull purple 2·25 3·00
178 **13** 1s. black/*green* .. 3·50 5·00
179 „ 2s. blue and purple/*blue* .. 22·00 20·00
180 „ 3s. violet and green .. 22·00 22·00
170/180 .. .. *Set of* 11 50·00 55·00
170/80 Optd. "Specimen" *Set of* 11 45·00

(Recess. De La Rue.)

1916 (16 June)–**20.** *Wmk. Mult. Crown CA. P* 14.

181 **14** ¼d. deep brown 15 20
182 „ ¼d. chestnut-brown (4.18) 25 25
183 „ ¼d. sepia-brown (11.18) .. 45 55
184 „ ½d. green 35 30
185 „ ½d. deep green (4.18) .. 30 30
186 „ ½d. pale green (10.18) .. 30 30
187 „ 1d. deep red .. .. 3·50 2·25
187*a* „ 1d. bright carmine-red .. 1·10 35
188 „ 1d. pale carmine-red (7.17) 1·25 50
189 „ 2d. grey .. .. .. 2·00 3·00
190 „ 2½d. ultramarine 50 75
191 „ 3d. pur./*yellow* (*thin paper*) 1·00 1·10
191*a* „ 3d. deep purple/*yellow* (*thick paper*) ('20) .. 7·00 7·50
192 „ 4d. red/*yellow* (*thin paper*) (23.6.16) .. .. 85 3·25
193 „ 6d. purple .. .. 1·00 1·50
194 „ 1s. black/*green* .. .. 2·50 2·25
195 „ 2s. purple/*blue* .. .. 11·00 11·00
196 „ 3s. deep violet (23.6.16) .. 21·00 23·00
181/196 .. .. *Set of* 11 35·00 42·00
181/96 Optd. "Specimen" *Set of* 11 45·00

WAR TAX

(15)

1917 (10 Oct.)–**18.** *War Tax. Optd. in London with T* **15**.

197 **11** 1d. brt. red (Optd. S. £14) 15 20
a. Imperf. (pair) £500

Thicker bluish paper.

198 **11** 1d. pale red (4.18) .. 35 35

1918 (18 Feb.). *Colours changed. Wmk. Mult. Crown CA. P* 14.

199 **14** 4d. black and red .. 45 1·90
200 „ 3s. green & deep violet .. 10·00 11·00
200*a* „ 3s. green & bright violet 65·00 75·00
199/200 Optd. "Specimen" *Set of* 2 35·00

The centres of these are from a new die having no circular border line.

16

17

(Recess. D.L.R.)

1920 (9 Sept.)–**21.** *Victory.* P 14. (*a*) *Wmk. Mult. Crown CA* (*sideways on T* **17**).

201 **16** ½d. black & bistre-brown 15 35
202 „ ½d. black & brt. yell.-grn. 15 35
203 „ 1d. black and vermilion 20 30
204 „ 2d. black and grey .. 80 2·50
205 „ 2½d. indigo & ultramarine 1·50 2·50
206 „ 3d. black and purple .. 85 1·50
207 „ 4d. black and blue-green 85 2·25
208 „ 6d. black & brown-orange 1·00 2·25
209 **17** 1s. black and bright green 3·25 5·50
210 „ 2s. black and brown .. 6·50 9·50
211 „ 3s. black and dull orange 14·00 17·00

(*b*) *Wmk. Mult. Script CA.*

212 **16** 1d. black & verm. (22.8.21) 2·75 30
201/212 .. .. *Set of* 12 29·00 40·00
201/12 Optd. "Specimen" *Set of* 12 60·00

18

19

(Recess. D.L.R.)

1921 (14 Nov.)–**24.** P 14.

(*a*) *Wmk. Mult. Crown CA.*

213 **18** 3d. purple/*pale yellow* .. 40 1·25
214 „ 4d. red/*pale yellow* .. 70 1·25
215 „ 1s. black/*emerald* .. 3·00 5·50

(*b*) *Wmk. Mult. Script CA.*

217 **18** ¼d. brown 15 5
219 „ ½d. green 15 25
220 „ 1d. red 25 25
a. Bright rose-carmine .. 1·25 35
221 „ 2d. grey 90 25
222 „ 2½d. ultramarine .. 55 1·10
225 „ 6d. reddish purple .. 95 2·25
226 „ 1s. black/*emer.* (18.9.24) 12·00 13·00
227 „ 2s. purple/*blue* .. 12·00 14·00
228 „ 3s. deep violet .. 15·00 18·00
213/228 .. .. *Set of* 12 40·00 50·00
213/28 Optd. "Specimen" *Set of* 12 38·00

1925–35. *T* **19.** *Wmk. Mult. Script CA.* I. *P* 14. II. *P* 13½×12½ ('32).

		I.		II.	
229	¼d. brown ..	5	5	†	
230	½d. green ..	5	5	20	5
231	1d. scarlet ..	5	5	30	5
231*a*	1½d. orange	1·25	35	35	15
232	2d. grey ..	20	65	†	
233	2½d. blue ..	50	25	†	
233*a*	2½d. bt. ultram.	1·50	8	2·00	30
234	3d. pur./*p. yellow*	25	20	†	
234*a*	3d. reddish pur./*yellow* ('35)	1·25	1·25	†	
235	4d. red/*p. yellow*	50	50	†	
236	6d. purple ..	75	75	†	
237	1s. blk./*emerald*	1·50	2·50	4·00	5·00
237*a*	1s. brownish blk./*brt. yell-grn.*	2·00	4·00	†	
238	2s. purple/*blue*	3·00	4·50	†	
238*a*	2s. 6d. car./*blue*	12·00	16·00	†	
239	3s. deep violet	7·00	9·00	†	
229/239	*Set of* 13	24·00	32·00		
229/39	Optd./Perf. "Specimen" *Set of* 13	48·00			

20. King Charles I and King George V.

(Recess. B.W.)

1927 (17 Feb.). *Tercentenary of Settlement of Barbados. Wmk. Mult. Script CA.* P 12½.

240 **20** 1d. carmine (Optd. S. £14) 45 45

1935 (6 May). *Silver Jubilee. As Nos.* 91/4 *of Antigua, but ptd. by Waterlow.* P 11×12.

241 1d. deep blue and scarlet .. 8 12
242 1½d. ultramarine and grey .. 20 30
243 2½d. brown and deep blue .. 85 85
244 1s. slate and purple .. 3·50 4·00
241/4 Perf. "Specimen" *Set of* 4 13·00

1937 (14 May). *Coronation. As Nos.* 13/15 *of Aden.* P 14.

245 1d. scarlet 20 20
246 1½d. yellow-brown 25 20
247 2½d. bright blue 70 70
245/7 Perf. "Specimen" *Set of* 3 10·00

21. Badge of the Colony.

(Recess. De La Rue.)

1938 (3 Jan.)–**1947.** *Wmk. Mult. Script CA.* P 13½×13.

248 **21** ½d. green 15 12
a. Perf. 14 ('42) .. .. 14·00 85
248*b* „ ½d. yellow-bistre ('42) .. 10 15
249 „ 1d. scarlet .. .. 25·00 70
a. Perf. 14 ('38) 85 12
249*b* „ 1d. blue-green (42) .. 20 8
c. Perf. 14 ('42) 8 8
250 „ 1½d. orange 15 8
a. Perf. 14 ('42) 30 8
250*b* „ 2d. claret (June, '41) .. 35 35
250*c* „ 2d. carmine ('43) .. 10 8
d. Perf. 14 ('44) 8 20
251 „ 2½d. ultramarine 20 25
a. Blue ('44) 35 90
252 „ 3d. brown 20 25
a. Perf. 14 ('41) 20 20
252*b* „ 3d. blue (1.4.47) .. 12 12
253 „ 4d. black 20 8
a. Perf. 14 ('44) 20 30
254 „ 6d. violet 12 8
254*a* „ 8d. magenta (9.12.46) .. 45 40
255 „ 1s. olive-green .. .. 2·75 90
a. Brown-olive 60 35
256 „ 2s. 6d. purple .. .. 1·75 75
256*a* „ 5s. indigo (June, '41) .. 2·00 1·25
248/256*a* .. .. *Set of* 16 6·50 4·00
248/56*a* Perf. "Specimen" *Set of* 16 50·00

No. 249*a* was perforated by two machines, one gauging 14.1, the other 13.8×14.1.

22. Kings Charles I, George VI, Assembly Chamber and Mace.

(Recess. De La Rue.)

1939 (27 June). *Tercentenary of General Assembly. Wmk. Mult. Script CA.* P 13½×14.

257 **22** ½d. green 25 15
258 „ 1d. scarlet 25 15
259 „ 1½d. orange 85 55
260 „ 2½d. bright ultramarine .. 1·10 1·25
261 „ 3d. brown .. .. 1·10 2·00
257/261 .. .. *Set of* 5 3·00 3·50
257/61 Perf. "Specimen" *Set of* 5 45·00

1946 (18 Sept.). *Victory. As Nos.* 28/9 *of Aden.*

262 1½d. red-orange 5 5
263 3d. brown 5 5
262/3 Perf. "Specimen" *Set of* 2 12·00

ONE PENNY

(**23**)

(Surch. by Barbados Advocate Co.)

1947 (21 Apr.). *Surch. with T* **23**.

(*a*) *Perf.* 14.

264 **21** 1d. on 2d. carmine .. 30 60

(*b*) *P* 13½×13.

264*a* **21** 1d. on 2d. carmine .. 40 60

1948 (24 Nov.). *Royal Silver Wedding. As Nos.* 30/1 *of Aden.*

265 1½d. orange 8 5
266 5s. indigo .. .. .. 2·50 5·00

1949 (10 Oct.). *75th Anniv. of Universal Postal Union. As Nos.* 114/7 *of Antigua.*

267 1½d. red-orange 10 12
268 3d. deep blue 25 20
269 4d. grey 45 45
270 1s. olive 55 55

24. Dover Fort.

25. Sugar Cane Breeding.

26. Public Buildings.

27. Statue of Nelson.

28. Casting Net.

29. Inter-Colonial Schooner.

30. Flying Fish.

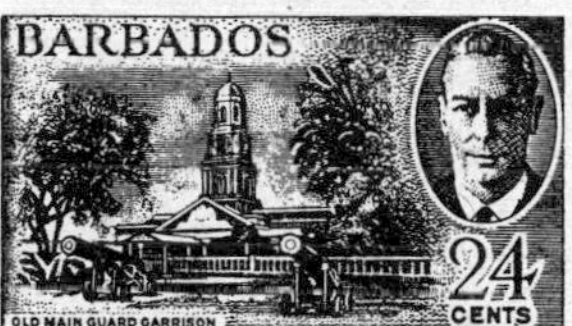

31. Old Main Guard Garrison.

32. The Cathedral.

34. Map of Barbados and Wireless Mast.

33. Careenage.

35. Arms of Barbados.

(Recess. B.W.)

1950 (1 May). *Wmk. Mult. Script CA. P* 11 × 11½ (*horiz.*), 13½ (*vert.*).

No.	Type	Description	Unused	Used
271	**24**	1 c. indigo	12	20
272	**25**	2 c. emerald-green ..	10	12
273	**26**	3 c. reddish brn. & bl.-grn.	12	20
274	**27**	4 c. carmine	12	15
275	**28**	6 c. light blue	10	15
276	**29**	8 c. bright bl. & pur.-brn.	20	20
277	**30**	12 c. greenish blue and brown-olive	50	35
278	**31**	24 c. scarlet and black ..	40	40
279	**32**	48 c. violet	1·25	1·25
280	**33**	60 c. green and claret ..	1·25	1·10
281	**34**	$1.20, carmine & olive-grn.	2·00	1·25
282	**35**	$2.40, black	4·00	5·00
271/282		.. .. *Set of* 12	9·00	9·00

1951 (16 Feb.). *Inauguration of B.W.I. University College. As Nos.* 118/9 *of Antigua.*

No.	Description	Unused	Used
283	3 c. brown and blue-green	5	10
284	12 c. blue-green & brn.-olive	35	40

36. King George VI and Stamp of 1852.

(Recess. Waterlow.)

1952 (15 Apr.). *Barbados Stamp Centenary. Wmk. Mult. Script CA. P* 13½.

No.	Type	Description	Unused	Used
285	**36**	3 c. green and slate-green	12	15
286	„	4 c. blue and carmine ..	12	20
287	„	12 c. slate-grn. & brt. grn.	20	20
288	„	24 c. red-brown & brownish black	35	45

1953 (4 June). *Coronation. As No.* 47 *of Aden*

No.	Description	Unused	Used
289	4 c. black and red-orange	12	12

37. Harbour Police.

(Recess. Bradbury, Wilkinson & Co.)

1953 (13 Apr.)–**57**. *As T* **24/34** (*but with portrait or cypher* ($2.40) *of Queen Elizabeth II in place of that of King George VI, as in T* **37**). *Wmk. Mult. Script CA. P* 11 × 11½ (*horiz.*) *or* 13½ (*vert.*).

No.	Type	Description	Unused	Used
290	**24**	1 c. indigo	12	15
291	**25**	2 c. orange and deep turquoise (15.4.54) ..	12	12
292	**26**	3 c. blk. & emer. (15.4.54)	12	12
293	**27**	4 c. black and orange (*shades*) (15.4.54) ..	12	15
294	**37**	5 c. blue & deep carmine-red (4.1.54)	12	12
295	**28**	6 c. red-brown (15.4.54)	12	12
296	**29**	8 c. blk. & blue (15.4.54)	15	15
297	**30**	12 c. turq.-blue & brn.-olive (*shades*) (15.4.54)	25	25
298	**31**	24 c. rose-red and black (2.3.56)	25	35
299	**32**	48 c. deep violet (2.3.56) ..	80	65
300	**33**	60 c. blue-grn. & brn.-pur. (*shades*) (3.4.56) ..	1·25	1·25
301	**34**	$1.20, carmine & bronze-green (3.4.56) ..	2·75	2·00
302	**35**	$2.40, black (1.2.57) ..	3·75	2·75
290/302		.. .. *Set of* 13	9·00	7·00

See also Nos. 312/19.

1958 (23 Apr.). *Inauguration of British Caribbean Federation. As Nos.* 135/7 *of Antigua.*

No.	Description	Unused	Used
303	3 c. deep green	12	12
304	6 c. blue	25	30
305	12 c. scarlet	30	30

38. Deep Water Harbour, Bridgetown.

(Recess. B.W.)

1961 (6 May). *Opening of Deep Water Harbour, Bridgetown. W* w.**12**. *P* 11 × 12.

No.	Type	Description	Unused	Used
306	**38**	4 c. black and red-orange	12	12
307	„	8 c. black and blue ..	20	20
308	„	24 c. carm.-red and black	40	40

II. SELF-GOVERNMENT.

39. Scout Badge and Map of Barbados.

(Recess. B.W.)

1962 (9 Mar.). *Golden Jubilee of Barbados Boy Scout Association. W* w.**12**. *P* 11½ × 11.

No.	Type	Description	Unused	Used
309	**39**	4 c. black and orange ..	12	12
310	„	12 c. blue & olive-brown ..	30	30
311	„	$1.20, carmine & olive-grn.	1·10	1·40

1964 (14 Jan.)–**65**. *As Nos.* 290, *etc., but wmk.* w.**12**.

No.	Type	Description	Unused	Used
312	**24**	1 c. indigo (6.10.64) ..	20	20
313	**27**	4 c. black and orange ..	15	15
314	**29**	8 c. blk. & blue (29.6.65)	20	20
315	**30**	12 c. turquoise-blue and brown-olive (29.6.65)	20	25
316	**31**	24 c. rose-red and black (6.10.64)	20	20
317	**32**	48 c. deep violet	1·10	1·25
318	**33**	60 c. blue-green & brown-purple (6.10.64) ..	1·10	1·40
319	**35**	$2.40, black (29.6.65) ..	3·75	4·00
312/319		.. .. *Set of* 8	6·50	7·00

The above dates are for Crown Agents releases. The 14.1.64 printings were not released in Barbados until April 1964, the 6.10.64 printings until December 1964 and of the 29.6.65 printings the 8 c. and $2.40 were released from about 15th June 1965 but the 12 c. value was never put on sale in Barbados.

1965 (17 May). *I.T.U. Centenary. As Nos.* 166/7 *of Antigua.*

No.	Description	Unused	Used
320	2 c. lilac and red	8	10
321	48 c. yellow and grey-brown	65	65

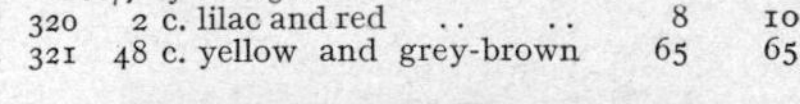

40. Deep Sea Coral.

41. Lobster.

42. Sea Horse (*wrongly inscr.* " Hippocanpus ")

43. Sea Urchin.

44. Staghorn Coral.

45. Butterfly Fish.

46. File Shell.

47. Balloon Fish.

48. Angel Fish.

49. Brain Coral.

50. Brittle Star.

51. Flying Fish.

52. Queen Conch Shell.

53. Fiddler Crab.

(Des. V. Whiteley, from drawings by Mrs. J. Walker. Photo. Harrison.)

1965 (15 July). *W* w.**12** (*upright*). *P* 14×13½.

322	**40**	1 c. black, pink and blue	5	5
323	**41**	2 c. olive-brown, yellow and magenta ..	5	8
324	**42**	3 c. olive-brn. & orange	8	8
325	**43**	4 c. dp. blue & olive-green	8	8
		a. Imperf. (pair)	£125	
326	**44**	5 c. sepia, rose and lilac ..	8	8
327	**45**	6 c. multicoloured ..	8	10
328	**46**	8 c. multicoloured ..	12	15
329	**47**	12 c. multicoloured ..	15	20
		a. Grey printing double ..	35·00	
330	**48**	15 c. black, greenish yellow and red	30	35
331	**49**	25 c. ultramarine and yellow-ochre	45	50
332	**50**	35 c. brown-red & dp. grn.	65	65
333	**51**	50 c. brt. bl. & apple-grn.	90	90
334	**52**	$1 multicoloured ..	1·75	1·75
335	**53**	$2.50, multicoloured ..	3·25	3·25
322/335		.. .. *Set of* 14	7·00	7·00

See also Nos. 342, etc.

1966 (24 Jan.). *Churchill Commemoration. As Nos.* 170/3 *of Antigua.*

336	1 c. new blue	5	5
337	4 c. deep green	8	5
338	25 c. brown	35	45
339	35 c. bluish violet	55	65

1966 (4 Feb.). *Royal Visit. As Nos.* 174/5 *of Antigua.*

340	3 c. black and ultramarine	12	12
341	35 c. black and magenta ..	50	50

53a. Dolphin.

1966 (15 Mar.)–**69.** *As Nos.* 322, *etc., but wmk.* w.**12** *sideways and new value.*

342	**40**	1 c. black, pink and blue	5	5
343	**41**	2 c. olive-brown, yellow and magenta (16.5.67)	5	5
344	**42**	3 c. olive-brown and orange (4.12.67) ..	5	5
345	**43**	4 c. dp. blue & olive-green	5	5
346	**44**	5 c. sepia, rose and lilac (23.8.66)	5	5
347	**45**	6 c. mult. (31.1.67) ..	5	8
348	**46**	8 c. mult. (19.9.67) ..	8	8
349	**47**	12 c. mult. (31.1.67) ..	10	10
350	**48**	15 c. black, greenish yellow and red	10	12
351	**49**	25 c. ultramarine and yellow-ochre (*shades*) ..	15	15
352	**50**	35 c. brown-red and deep grn. (*shades*) (23.8.66)	30	30
353	**51**	50 c. brt. blue & apple-grn.	40	40
354	**52**	$1 mult. (23.8.66) ..	1·00	1·00
355	**53**	$2.50, mult. (23.8.66) ..	1·75	1·75
355a	**53a**	$5 mult. (9.1.69) ..	4·00	4·00
342/55a		.. .. *Set of* 15	7·00	7·00

No. 344 is correctly inscribed "Hippocampus".

All values except the 50 c. exist with PVA gum as well as gum arabic but the $5 exists with PVA gum only.

The $5 was released by the Crown Agents on 6th January but was not put on sale locally until 9th January.

III. INDEPENDENT.

54. Arms of Barbados.

55. Hilton Hotel. (*Horiz.*)

56. G. Sobers (Test cricketer). (*Vert.*)

57. Pine Hill Dairy. (*Horiz.*)

(Des. V. Whiteley. Photo. Harrison.)

1966 (2 Dec.). *Independence. P* 14.

356	**54**	4 c. multicoloured ..	12	12
357	**55**	25 c. multicoloured ..	30	30
358	**56**	35 c. multicoloured ..	40	40
359	**57**	50 c. multicoloured ..	50	55

1967 (6 Jan.). *20th Anniv. of U.N.E.S.C.O. As Nos.* 196/8 *of Antigua.*

360	4 c. slate-violet, red, yellow and orange	12	12
361	12 c. orange-yellow, violet & deep olive	35	35
362	25 c. black, bright purple and orange	55	55

58. Policeman and Anchor.

59. Policeman with Telescope. (*Vert.*)

60. Police Launch. (*Horiz.*)

61. Policemen outside H.Q. (*Vert.*)

(Des. V. Whiteley. Litho. De La Rue.)

1967 (16 Oct.). *Centenary of Harbour Police. P* 14.

363	**58**	4 c. multicoloured ..	10	10
364	**59**	25 c. multicoloured ..	25	25
365	**60**	35 c. multicoloured ..	35	35
366	**61**	50 c. multicoloured ..	55	55

62. Governor-General Sir Winston Scott, G.C.M.

63. Independence Arch. (*Horiz.*)

64. Treasury Building. (*Horiz.*)

65. Parliament Building. (*Horiz.*)

(Des. V. Whiteley. Photo. Harrison.)

1967 (4 Dec.). *First Anniv. of Independence. P* 14½×14 (4 *c.*) *or* 14×14½ (*others*).

367	**62**	4 c. multicoloured ..	8	8
368	**63**	25 c. multicoloured ..	25	25
369	**64**	35 c. multicoloured ..	35	35
370	**65**	50 c. multicoloured ..	55	55

66. U.N. Building, Santiago, Chile.

(Des. G. L. Vasarhelyi. Photo. Harrison.)

1968 (27 Feb.). *20th Anniv. of the Economic Commission for Latin America. P* 14½.

371	**66**	15 c. multicoloured ..	20	20

67. Radar Antenna.

68. Meteorological Institute. (*Horiz.*)

69. Harp Gun and Coat-of-Arms. (*Vert.*)

(Des. G. L. Vasarhelyi. Photo. Harrison.)

1968 (4 June). *World Meteorological Day. P* 14×14½ (25 *c.*) *or* 14×14½ (*others*).

372	**67**	3 c. multicoloured ..	10	20
373	**68**	25 c. multicoloured ..	25	25
374	**69**	50 c. multicoloured ..	40	40

70. Lady Baden-Powell, and Guide at Camp Fire.

71. Lady Baden-Powell and Pax Hill.

72. Lady Baden-Powell and Guides' Badge.

(Des. V. Whiteley (from local designs). Photo. Harrison.)

1968 (29 Aug.). *Golden Jubilee of Girl Guiding in Barbados. P* 14.

375	**70**	3 c. ultram., black & gold	10	10
376	**71**	25 c. turquoise-blue, black and gold	30	30
377	**72**	35 c. orge.-yell., blk. & gold	45	45

73. Hands breaking Chain, and Human Rights Emblem.

74. Human Rights Emblem, and Family enchained.

75. Shadows of Refugees beyond opening Fence.

(Des. V. Whiteley. Litho. Bradbury, Wilkinson.)

1968 (10 Dec.).* *Human Rights Year. P* 11 × 12.

378	**73**	4 c. violet, brn. & lt. grn.	10	10
379	**74**	25 c. blk., blue & orge.-yell.	25	25
380	**75**	35 c. multicoloured ..	40	40

* This was the local release date but the Crown Agents issued the stamps on 29th October.

76. Racehorses in the Paddock.

77. Starting-Gate.

78. On the Flat.

79. The Winning-Post.

(Des. J. E. Cooter. Litho. Format International.)

1969 (20 Mar.).* *Horse-Racing. P* 14.

381	**76**	4 c. multicoloured ..	10	10
382	**77**	25 c. multicoloured ..	25	25
383	**78**	35 c. multicoloured ..	35	35
384	**79**	50 c. multicoloured ..	40	40
MS385		117 × 85 mm. Nos. 381/4 ..	1·10	1·10

* This was the local release date but the Crown Agents issued the stamps on 15th March.

80. Map showing "CARIFTA" Countries.

81. "Strength in Unity".

(Des. J. E. Cooter. Photo. Harrison).

1969 (6 May). *First Anniv. of CARIFTA (Caribbean Free Trade Area). W* w.**12** *(sideways on T* **80**). *P* 14.

386	**80**	5 c. multicoloured ..	10	10
387	**81**	12 c. multicoloured ..	15	20
388	**80**	25 c. multicoloured ..	25	30
389	**81**	50 c. multicoloured ..	40	40

ONE CENT

82. ILO Emblem and "1919–1969". (**83**)

(Des. Sylvia Goaman. Litho. Enschedé.)

1969 (12 Aug.). *50th Anniv. of International Labour Organisation. P* 14 × 13.

390	**82**	4 c. black, emerald and turquoise-blue ..	10	10
391	,,	25 c. black, cerise and brown-red	35	35

Although released by the Crown Agents on 5th August, the above were not put on sale in Barbados until 12th August.

1969 (30 Aug.). *No* 363 *surch. with T* **83**.

392	**58**	1 c. on 4 c. multicoloured ..	15	15
		a. Surch. double	50·00	

84. National Scout Badge.

85. Sea Scouts rowing.

86. Scouts around Camp Fire.

87. Scouts and National Scout Headquarters.

(Des. J. E. Cooter. Litho. Enschedé.)

1969 (16 Dec.). *Independence of Barbados Boy Scouts Association and 50th Anniv. of Barbados Sea Scouts. P* 13 × 13½.

393	**84**	5 c. multicoloured ..	8	8
394	**85**	25 c. multicoloured ..	30	30
395	**86**	35 c. multicoloured ..	35	35
396	**87**	50 c. multicoloured ..	40	45
MS397		155 × 115 mm. Nos. 393/6	1·75	1·75

4 X
(**88**)

1970 (11 Mar.). *No.* 346 *surch. locally with T* **88.**

398	**44**	4 c. on 5 c. sepia, rose and lilac	8	8
		a. Vert. pair, one without surch.	50·00	
		b. Surch. double	35·00	
		c. Vert. pair, one normal, one surch. double		
		d. Surch. triple		
		e. Surch. normal on front, inverted on back ..	10·00	
		f. Surch. omitted on front, inverted on back ..	20·00	

89. Lion at Gun Hill.

90. Trafalgar Fountain.

91. Montefiore Drinking Fountain.

92. St. James' Monument.

93. St. Anne's Fort.

94. Old Sugar Mill, Morgan Lewis.

95. Cenotaph.

96. South Point Lighthouse.

97. Barbados Museum.

98. Sharon Moravian Church.

99. George Washington House.

100. Nicholas Abbey.

101. Bowmanston Pumping Station.

102. Queen Elizabeth Hospital.

103. Modern Sugar Factory.

104. Seawell International Airport.

(*T* **89/96** *are all vert. T* **97/104** *are horiz.*)

(Des. J. Waddington Ltd. Photo. D.L.R.)

1970–71. *W* w.**12** *(sideways on horiz. designs and upright on vert. designs). P* 12½.

A. *Chalk-surfaced paper* (4.5.70)
B. *Glazed, ordinary paper* (13.12.71, 12 *c.*, 15 *c.* *and* $2.50; 15.3.71, *others*).

			A.		B.	
399	**89**	1 c. mult. ..	5	5	5	5
400	**90**	2 c. mult. ..	5	5	5	5
401	**91**	3 c. mult. ..	5	5	5	5
402	**92**	4 c. mult. ..	5	5	5	5
403	**93**	5 c. mult. ..	5	5	5	5
404	**94**	6 c. mult. ..	8	8	†	
405	**95**	8 c. mult. ..	10	10	5	8
406	**96**	10 c. mult. ..	10	10	8	8
407	**97**	12 c. mult. ..	12	12	8	10
408	**98**	15 c. mult. ..	12	12	10	12
409	**99**	25 c. mult. ..	25	25	20	20
410	**100**	35 c. mult. ..	45	45	30	25
411	**101**	50 c. mult. ..	60	60	35	35
412	**102**	$1 mult. ..	1·00	1·00	65	65
413	**103**	$2.50, mult.	2·00	2·25	1·50	1·60
414	**104**	$5 mult. ..	4·50	5·00	2·75	3·00
399/414A		*Set of* 16	8·50	9·50		
399B/414B		*Set of* 15			5·50	6·00

See also Nos. 455 etc.

105. Primary Schoolgirl.

(Des. V. Whiteley. Litho. J.W.)

1970 (26 June). *25th Anniv. of United Nations. T* **105** *and similar horiz. designs. Multicoloured. W* w.**12**. *P* 14.

415	4 c. Type **105**	5	5
416	5 c. Secondary Schoolboy ..	5	5
417	25 c. Technical Student ..	20	20
418	50 c. University Building ..	40	40

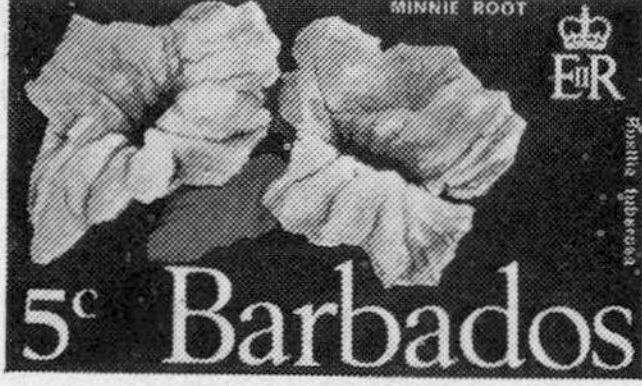

106. Minnie Root.

(Des. and litho. J. Waddington.)

1970 (24 Aug.). *Flowers of Barbados. T* **106** *and similar designs. Multicoloured. W* w.**12** *(sideways on horiz. designs). P* 14½.

419	1 c. Barbados Easter Lily (*vert.*)	5	5
420	5 c. Type **106**	5	5
421	10 c. Eyelash Orchid ..	5	5
422	25 c. Pride of Barbados (*vert.*)	20	20
423	35 c. Christmas Hope ..	30	35
MS424	162×101 mm. Nos. 419/23 Imperf.	60	60
419/23	.. .. *Set of* 5	60	60

107. Window, St. Margaret's Church, St. John.

(Des. Jennifer Toombs. Litho. J.W.)

1971 (7 Apr.). *Easter. T* **114** *and similar vert. design. Multicoloured. W* w.**12**. *P* 14.

425	4 c. Type **107**	8	8
426	10 c. "The Resurrection" (Benjamin West) ..	12	12
427	35 c. Type **107**	35	35
428	50 c. As 10 c.	45	45

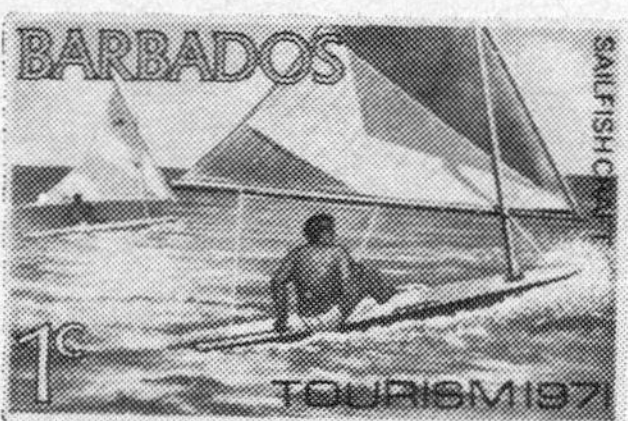

108. Sail-fish Craft.

(Des. and litho. Harrison.)

1971 (17 Aug.). *Tourism. T* **108** *and similar horiz. designs. Multicoloured. W* w.**12** *(sideways on 5 c. and 25 c.). P* 14.

429	1 c. Type **108**	8	8
430	5 c. Tennis	10	10
431	12 c. Horse-riding	15	15
432	25 c. Water-skiing	25	25
433	50 c. Scuba-diving	45	45
429/33	.. .. *Set of* 5	85	85

109. S. J. Prescod (politician).

(Des. J. Waddington Ltd. Litho. Questa.)

1971 (28 Sept.*). *Death Centenary of Samuel Jackman Prescod. W* w.**12**. *P* 14.

434	**109**	3 c. multicoloured ..	8	8
435	,,	35 c. multicoloured ..	30	30

*This is the local date but the Crown Agents released the stamps two days earlier.

110. Arms of Barbados.

(Des. G. Drummond. Litho. Questa.)

1971 (23 Nov.). *Fifth Anniv. of Independence. T* **110** *and similar horiz. design. Multicoloured. W* w.**12** *(sideways). P* 14.

436	4 c. Type **110**	8	8
437	15 c. National flag and map	15	15
438	25 c. Type **110**	30	35
439	50 c. As 15 c.	50	55

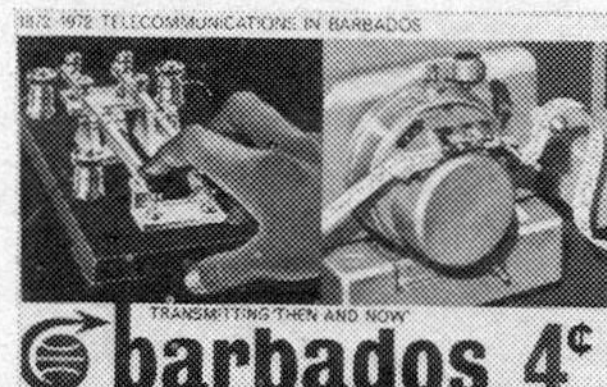

111. Transmitting "Then and Now".

(Des. Cable & Wireless Ltd. Litho. J.W.)

1972 (28 Mar.). *Cable Link Centenary. T* **111** *and similar horiz. designs. Multicoloured. W* w.**12** *(sideways). P* 14.

440	4 c. Type **111**	8	8
441	10 c. Cable Ship *Stanley Angwin*	12	12
442	35 c. Barbados Earth Station and "Intelsat 4" ..	35	35
443	50 c. Mt. Misery and Tropospheric Scatter Station	50	50

HAVE YOU READ THE NOTES AT THE BEGINNING OF THIS CATALOGUE?

These often provide answers to the enquiries we receive

112. Map and Badge.

(Des. Mrs. C. Barrow (50 c.), Major L. Quintyne (others) and adapted by G. Drummond. Litho. Questa.)

1972 (1 Aug.). *Diamond Jubilee of Scouts. T* **112** *and similar horiz. designs. Multicoloured. W* w.**12** *(sideways on* 5 c.*). P* 14.

444	5 c. Type **112**	8	8
445	15 c. Pioneers of scouting ..	15	15
446	25 c. Scouts	30	35
447	50 c. Flags	45	50

113. Mobile Library.

(Des. PAD Studio. Litho. Harrison.)

1972 (31 Oct.). *International Book Year. T* **113** *and similar horiz. designs. Multicoloured. W* w. **12**. *P* 14.

448	4 c. Type **113**	8	8
449	15 c. Visual-aids van ..	12	12
450	25 c. Public library ..	30	30
451	$1 Codrington College ..	1·00	1·25

1972 (17 Nov.)–**74**. *As No.* 399 *etc., but W.* w.**12** *(sideways on vert. designs and upright on horiz. designs). Glazed, ordinary paper.*

455	**92**	4 c. multicoloured ..	5	5
456	**93**	5 c. multicoloured ..	5	5
457	**94**	6 c. multicoloured ..	5	5
458	**95**	8 c. multicoloured ..	5	8
459	**96**	10 c. mult. (21.1.74) ..	8	8
460	**97**	12 c. multicoloured ..	8	10
461	**98**	15 c. multicoloured ..	10	12
462	**99**	25 c. multicoloured ..	15	20
463	**100**	35 c. multicoloured ..	20	25
464	**101**	50 c. multicoloured ..	30	35
465	**102**	$1 multicoloured ..	55	60
466	**103**	$2.50, mult. (2.10.73) ..	1·40	1·60
467	**104**	$5 mult. (2.10.73) ..	2·75	3·00
455/67		.. .. *Set of* 13	5·00	6·00

114. Potter's Wheel.

(Des. PAD Studio. Litho. Questa.)

1973 (1 Mar.). *Pottery in Barbados.* *T* **114** *and similar horiz. designs. Multicoloured.* *W* w.**12**. *P* 14.

468 5 c. Type **114** 8 8
469 15 c. Kilns 12 12
470 25 c. Finished products .. 20 25
471 $1 Market scene 50 60

115. First Flight, 1911.

(Des. C. Abbott. Litho. Enschedé.)

1973 (25 July). *Aviation.* *T* **115** *and similar horiz. designs.* *W* w.**12** (*sideways*). *P* $12\frac{1}{2} \times 12$.

472 5 c. multicoloured 5 5
473 15 c. multicoloured 12 12
474 25 c. grey-blue, black and cobalt 20 20
475 50 c. multicoloured 35 35

Designs:—15 c. First flight to Barbados, 1928; 25 c. Passenger aircraft, 1939; 50 c. Jet airliner, 1973.

116. University Chancellor.

(Des. J.W. Ltd. Litho. Enschedé.)

1973 (11 Dec.). *25th Anniv. of University of West Indies.* *T* **116** *and similar horiz. designs. Multicoloured.* *W* w.**12**. *P* 13×14.

476 5 c. Type **116** 5 5
477 25 c. Sherlock Hall 15 15
478 35 c. Cave Hill Campus .. 25 25

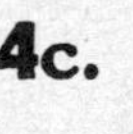

(117)

1974 (30 Apr.). *No.* 462 *surch. with* *T* **117**.

479 4 c. on 25 c. multicoloured .. 8 8
a. "4c." omitted .. .. 7·00

No. 479a occurs on R. 10/1, the overprint being applied to sheets consisting of two horizontal panes, 5×5. The variety occurs on plate 1A, and shows a clear albino impression of the "4c." on the reverse.

118. Old Sail Boat.

(Des. J. E. Cooter. Litho. Questa.)

1974 (11 June). *Fishing Boats of Barbados.* *T* **118** *and similar diamond-shaped designs. Multicoloured.* *W* w.**12**. *P* 14.

480 15 c. Type **118** 12 12
481 35 c. Rowing-boat 25 25
482 50 c. Motor fishing-boat .. 30 30
483 $1 U.N.D.P. vessel, *Calamar* 50 60
MS484 140×140 mm. Nos. 480/3 1·25 1·40

119. *Cattleya Gaskelliana Alba.*

(Des. PAD Studio. Photo. Harrison.)

1974 (16 Sept.). *Orchids.* *T* **119** *and similar multicoloured designs.* *W* w.**12** (*upright on* 1 *c.,* 25 *c.,* $1 *and* $10; *sideways on others*). *P* $14\frac{1}{2} \times 14$ ($1, $10) $14 \times 14\frac{1}{2}$ ($2.50, $5) *or* 14 (*others*).

485 1 c. Type **119**.. .. .. 5 5
486 2 c. *Renanthera storiei* .. 5 5
487 3 c. *Dendrobium* "Rose Marie" 5 8
488 4 c. *Epidendrum ibaguense* .. 75 70
489 5 c. *Schomburgkia humboldtii* 5 5
490 8 c. *Oncidium ampliatum* .. 5 5
491 10 c. *Arachnis maggie oei* 8 8
492 12 c. *Dendrobium aggregatum* 5 5
493 15 c. *Paphiopedilum puddle* .. 12 12
494 25 c. *Epidendrum ciliare* (Eyelash) 12 15
495 35 c. *Bletia patula* 20 25
496 50 c. *Phalaenopsis schilleriana* "Sunset Glow" .. 25 30
497 $1 *Ascocenda* "Red Gem".. 55 60
498 $2.50, *Brassolaeliocattleya* "Nugget" .. .. 1·40 1·50
499 $5 *Caularthron bicornutum*.. 2·75 3·00
500 $10 *Vanda* "Josephine Black" 5·50 6·00
485/500 .. .. *Set of* 16 11·00 12·00

The 1 c., 25 c., $2.50 and $5 are horiz. designs, and the remainder are vert.

See also Nos. 510 etc. and 543 etc.

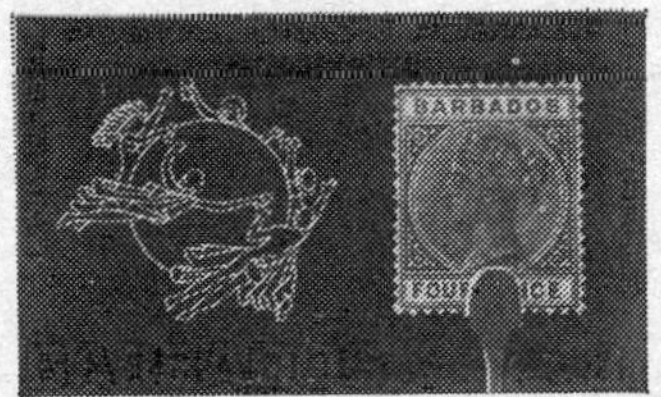

120. 4d. Stamp of 1882, and U.P.U. Emblem.

(Des. Harrison. Litho. Questa.)

1974 (9 Oct.). *Centenary of Universal Postal Union.* *T* **120** *and similar horiz. designs.* *W* w.**12** (*sideways*). *P* 14.

501 8 c. magenta, light orange and light grey-green 8 8
502 35 c. deep rose-red, dull orange and bistre-brown .. 25 25
503 50 c. ultram., cobalt & silver 30 30
504 $1 bright blue, dull brown and grey-black 50 50
MS505 126×101 mm. Nos. 501/4 1·00 1·10

Designs:—35 c. Letters encircling the globe; 50 c. U.P.U. emblem and arms of Barbados; $1 Map of Barbados, sailing-ship and aeroplane.

121. Royal Yacht *Britannia.*

(Des. Jennifer Toombs. Litho. Harrison.)

1975 (18 Feb.). *Royal Visit.* *T* **121** *and similar horiz. design. Multicoloured.* *W* w. **12** (*sideways on* 8 *and* 25 *c.*). *P* 14.

506 8 c. Type **121** 5 5
507 25 c. Type **121** 15 20
508 35 c. Sunset and palms .. 25 25
509 $1 As 35 c. 50 60

1975 (30 Apr.). *As Nos.* 485 *etc., but* *W* w.**14** (*sideways on* 1 *c.,* $1 *and* $10).

510 1 c. Type **119**.. .. .. 5 5
511 2 c. *Renanthera storiei* .. 5 5
512 3 c. *Dendrobium* "Rose Marie" 5 5
513 4 c. *Epidendrum ibaguense* .. 5 5
518 15 c. *Paphiopedilum puddle* .. 8 12
522 $1 *Ascocenda* "Red Gem" 55 60
523 $2.50, *Brassolaeliocattleya* "Nugget" .. .. 1·25 1·40
524 $5 *Caularthron bicornutum* 2·50 2·75
525 $10 *Vanda* "Josephine Black" 5·00 5·50
510/25 .. .. *Set of* 9 8·50 9·50

122. St. Michael's Cathedral.

(Des. R. Granger Barrett. Litho. Questa.)

1975 (29 July). *150th Anniv. of Anglican Diocese.* *T* **122** *and similar square designs. Multicoloured.* *W* w.**12** (*sideways*). *P* $13\frac{1}{2}$.

526 5 c. Type **122**.. .. .. 5 5
527 15 c. Bishop Coleridge .. 8 8
528 50 c. All Saints' Church .. 20 25
529 $1 Stained-glass window, St. Michael's Cathedral .. 45 50
MS530 95×96 mm. Nos. 526/9. Wmk. upright. 85

123. Pony Float.

(Des. R. Granger Barrett. Litho. Questa.)

1975 (18 Nov.). *Crop-over Festival.* *T* **123** *and similar horiz. designs. Multicoloured.* *W* w.**14** (*sideways*). *P* 14.

531 8 c. Type **123** 5 5
532 25 c. Man on stilts .. 12 15
533 35 c. Maypole dancing .. 20 20
534 50 c. Cuban dancers .. 20 25
MS535 127×85 mm. Nos. 531/34 60

124. Barbados Coat of Arms. **125.** 17th-Century Sailing Ship.

(Des. and litho. Harrison.)

1975 (15 Dec.). *Coil Definitives* W w.**14** (*sideways*). *P.* 14½ × 14.
536 **124** 5 c. greenish blue .. 5 5
537 „ 25 c. bluish violet .. 12 15

(Des. PAD Studio. Litho. J.W.)

1975 (17 Dec.). *350th Anniv. of First Settlement. T* **125** *and similar vert. designs. Multicoloured. W* w.**14.** *P* 13½.
538 4 c. Type **125** 5 5
539 10 c. Bearded fig tree and fruit 5 5
540 25 c. Ogilvy's 17th-century map 12 15
541 $1 Captain John Powell .. 45 50
MS542 105 × 115 mm. Nos. 538/41. P 14 × 14½ 70

1976 (20 Feb.). *As Nos.* 485 *etc., but W* w.**12** (*sideways on* 1 *c.,* 25 *c.,* $1) *or upright* (*others*).
543 1 c. Type **119** 5 5
544 2 c. *Rananthera storiei* .. 5 5
545 3 c. *Dendrobium* " Rose Marie " 5 5
546 4 c. *Epidendrum ibaguense* .. 5 5
549 10 c. *Arachnis maggie ori* .. 5 5
551 15 c. *Paphiopedilum puddle* .. 8 8
552 25 c. *Epidendrum ciliare* " Eyelash " 12 15
553 35 c. *Bletia patula* 15 20
555 $1 *Ascocenda* " Red Gem " 50 55
543/55 .. .. *Set of* 9 95 1·10
Nos. 547/8, 550 and 554 have been reserved for further additions to this issue.

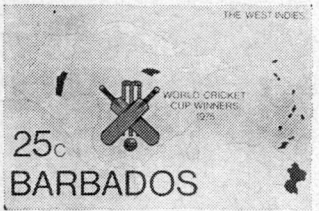

126. Map of the Caribbean.

(Des. PAD Studio. Litho. Questa.)

1976 (7 July). *West Indian Victory in World Cricket Cup. T* **126** *and similar vert. design. No wmk. P* 14.
559 25 c. multicoloured 15 15
560 45 c. black and magenta .. 25 30
Design:—45 c. The Prudential Cup.

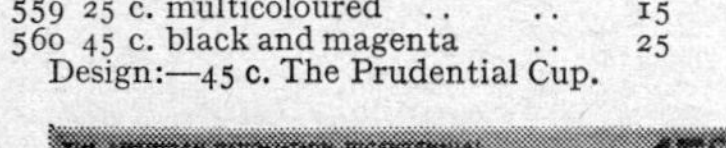

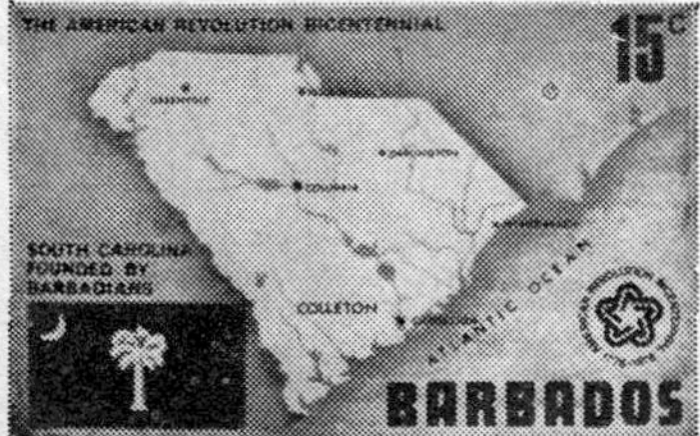

127. Flag and Map of S. Carolina.

(Des. G. L. Vasarhelyi. Litho. Walsall.)

1976 (17 Aug.). *Bicentenary of American Revolution. T* **127** *and similar horiz. designs. Multicoloured. W* w.**14** (*sideways*). *P* 13½.
561 15 c. Type **127** 8 10
562 25 c. George Washington and map of Bridgetown .. 15 15
563 50 c. Independence Declaration 30 35
564 $1 Prince Hall 55 65

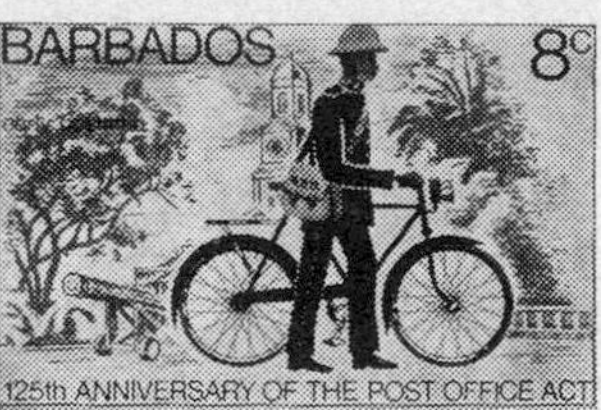

128. Early Postman.

(Des. Jennifer Toombs. Litho. Questa.)

1976 (19 Oct.). *125th Anniv. of Post Office Act. T* **128** *and similar horiz. designs. Multicoloured. W* w.**14** (*sideways*). *P* 14.
565 8 c. Type **128** 5 5
566 35 c. Modern postman .. 20 20
567 50 c. Early letter 30 35
568 $1 Delivery van 55 65

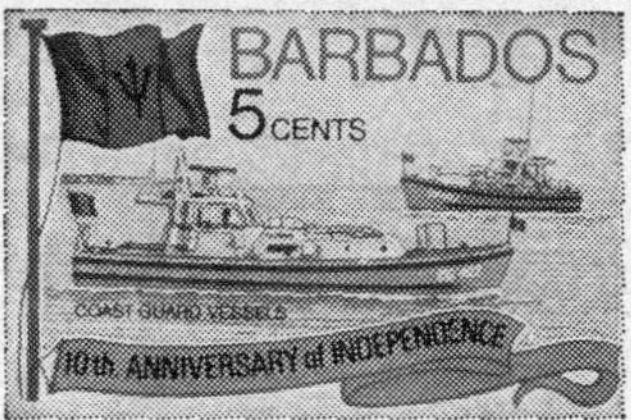

129. Coast Guard Vessels.

(Des. PAD Studio. Litho. J.W.)

1976 (30 Nov.). *Tenth Anniv. of Independence. T* **129** *and similar horiz. designs. Multicoloured. W* w.**14** (*sideways*). *P* 13 × 13½.
569 5 c. Type **129** 5 5
570 15 c. Reverse of currency note 8 10
571 25 c. National anthem .. 15 20
572 $1 Independence Day parade 60 70
MS573 90 × 125 mm. Nos. 569/72. P 14 90

130. Arrival of Coronation Coach at Westminster Abbey.

(Des. C. Abbott. Litho. Walsall.)

1977 (7 Feb.). *Silver Jubilee. T* **130** *and similar vert. designs. Multicoloured. W* w.**14.** *P* 13½.
574 15 c. Garfield Sobers being knighted, 1975 .. .. 8 10
575 50 c. Type **130** 30 35
576 $1 Queen entering abbey .. 60 70

POSTAGE DUE STAMPS.

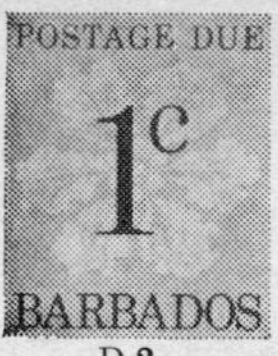

D 1 D 2

(Typo. D.L.R.)

1934–47. *Wmk. Mult. Script CA. P* 14.
D1 D **1** ½d. green (10.2.35) .. 12 10
D2 „ 1d. black (2.1.34) .. 40 25
a. Bisected (½d.) (on cover) — £100
D3 „ 3d. carmine (13.3.47) .. 3·50 90
D1/3 Perf. " Specimen " *Set of* 3 £15

The use of the bisected 1d. stamp was officially authorised March 1934 pending the arrival of supplies of the ½d. received 1935. Some specimens had the value " ½d." written across the half stamp in red or black ink. (*Price on cover* £85.)

1950 (8 Dec.)–**53.** *Values in cents. Wmk. Mult. Script CA. P* 14.
D4 D **1** 1 c. green, O 25 25
a. Deep green, C (29.11.51) .. 8 8
b. Error. Crown missing, W9a, C .. .. — 12·00
c. Error. St. Edward's Crown, W9b, C .. .. 10·00
D5 „ 2 c. black, O 25 35
a. Chalky paper (20.1.53) .. 8 8
c. Error. St. Edward's Crown, W9b, C .. .. 10·00
D6 „ 6 c. carmine, O 60 75
a. Chalky paper (20.1.53) .. 8 8
b. Error. Crown missing, W9a, C .. .. 18·00
c. Error. St. Edward's Crown, W9b, C .. .. 16·00
The 1 c. stamps have no dot below "c".

1965 (3 Aug.). *As Nos.* D4/6 *but wmk.* w.**12** (*upright*). *Chalky paper.*
D7 D **1** 1 c. deep green (*shades*) .. 8 8
D8 „ 2 c. black 8 8
D9 „ 6 c. carmine 8 8
The 1 c. has no dot below "c".

1974 (4 Feb.). *As No.* D9 *but W* w.**12** (*sideways*). *Glazed, ordinary paper. P* 14.
D10 D **1** 6 c. carmine 10 10
1974 (4 Dec.). *W* w.**12** (*sideways*). *P* 13.
D12 D **1** 2 c. black 8 8
D13 „ 6 c. carmine 10 10

(Des. Jennifer Toombs. Litho. Questa.)

1976 (12 May). *Different floral backgrounds. W* w.**14.** *P* 14.
D14 D **2** 1 c. dp. mve. & lt. pink 5 5
D15 – 2 c. ultram. & lt. cobalt 5 5
D16 – 5 c. reddish brn. & yell. 5 5
D17 – 10 c. royal bl. & lt. lilac 5 5
D18 – 25 c. deep green and bright yellow-green 12 15
D19 – $1 rose-carmine & rose 50 60
D14/19 .. .. *Set of* 6 70 80

BARBUDA.

(*See* after ANTIGUA.)

BASUTOLAND.

I. PROTECTORATE.

1. King George V, Crocodile and Mountains.

2. King George VI, Crocodile and Mountains.

(Recess. Waterlow.)

1933 (1 Dec.). *Wmk. Mult. Script CA. P* 12½.

No.	Type	Description	Un.	Used
1	1	½d. emerald	25	30
2	,,	1d. scarlet	15	30
3	,,	2d. bright purple	30	40
4	,,	3d. bright blue	40	1·10
5	,,	4d. grey	90	1·75
6	,,	6d. orange-yellow	1·10	2·25
7	,,	1s. red-orange	2·50	4·00
8	,,	2s. 6d. sepia	6·00	10·00
9	,,	5s. violet	16·00	18·00
10	,,	10s. olive-green	35·00	40·00
1/10		*Set of* 10	55·00	70·00
1/10 Perf. "Specimen"		*Set of* 10	50·00	

1935 (4 May). *Silver Jubilee. As Nos.* 91/4 *of Antigua. P* 13½ × 14.

No.	Description	Un.	Used
11	1d. deep blue and carmine	15	20
12	2d. ultramarine and grey	30	65
13	3d. brown and deep blue	1·10	1·40
14	6d. slate and purple	1·75	2·25
11/14 Perf. "Specimen"	*Set of* 4	14·00	

1937 (12 May). *Coronation. As Nos.* 13/15 *of Aden. P* 14.

No.	Description	Un.	Used
15	1d. scarlet	10	12
16	2d. bright purple	12	20
17	3d. bright blue	20	30
15/17 Perf. "Specimen"	*Set of* 3	11·00	

(Recess. Waterlow.)

1938 (1 Apr.). *Wmk. Mult. Script CA. P* 12½.

No.	Type	Description	Un.	Used
18	2	½d. green	10	12
19	,,	1d. scarlet	12	12
20	,,	1½d. light blue	10	10
21	,,	2d. bright purple	10	10
22	,,	3d. bright blue	10	20
23	,,	4d. grey	40	40
24	,,	6d. orange-yellow	30	35
25	,,	1s. red-orange	40	50
26	,,	2s. 6d. sepia	1·10	1·25
27	,,	5s. violet	2·25	2·75
28	,,	10s. olive-green	4·50	5·00
18/28		*Set of* 11	8·50	10·00
18/28 Perf. "Specimen"		*Set of* 11	30·00	

Basutoland

(3)

1945 (3 Dec.). *Victory. Stamps of South Africa, optd. with T* **3**, *inscr. alternately in English and Afrikaans.*

No.	Type	Description	*Un. pair*	*Used pair*
29	55	1d. brown and carmine	10	10
30	56	2d. slate-blue and violet	10	15
31	57	3d. deep blue and blue	12	30

4. King George VI.

5. King George VI and Queen Elizabeth.

6. Queen Elizabeth II as Princess, and Princess Margaret.

7. The Royal Family.

(Recess. Waterlow.)

1947 (17 Feb.). *Royal Visit. Wmk. Mult. Script CA. P* 12½.

No.	Type	Description	Un.	Used
32	4	1d. scarlet	5	8
33	5	2d. green	5	8
34	6	3d. ultramarine	12	12
35	7	1s. mauve	20	20
32/5 Perf. "Specimen"		*Set of* 4	28·00	

1948 (1 Dec.). *Royal Silver Wedding. As Nos.* 30/1 *of Aden.*

No.	Description	Un.	Used
36	1½d. ultramarine	5	5
37	10s. grey-olive	2·50	3·50

1949 (10 Oct.). *75th Anniv. of Universal Postal Union. As Nos.* 114/7 *of Antigua.*

No.	Description	Un.	Used
38	1½d. blue	12	15
39	3d. deep blue	25	30
40	6d. orange	30	35
41	1s. red-brown	40	45

1953 (3 June). *Coronation. As No.* 47 *of Aden.*

No.	Description	Un.	Used
42	2d. black and reddish purple	15	20

8. Qiloane.

18. Mohair (Shearing Goats).

9. Orange River.
10. Mosuto Horseman.
11. Basuto Household.
12. Maletsunyane Falls.
13. Herd-boy with Lesiba.
14. Pastoral Scene.
15. Aeroplane over Lancers' Gap.
16. Old Fort Leribe.
17. Mission Cave House.

T **9/17** are horiz. designs as T **8**.

(Recess. D.L.R.)

1954 (18 Oct.). *Wmk. Mult. Script CA. P* 13½ *or* 11½ (10s.).

No.	Type	Description	Un.	Used
43	8	½d. grey-black and sepia	8	10
44	9	1d. grey-blk. & bluish grn.	8	10
45	10	2d. dp. brt. blue & orange	10	12
46	11	3d. yellow-green and deep rose-red (*shades*)	15	15
47	12	4½d. indigo & deep ultram.	25	35
48	13	6d. chestnut & dp. grey-grn.	30	25
49	14	1s. bronze-green & purple	35	35
50	15	1s. 3d. brn. & turq.-green	60	70
51	16	2s. 6d. deep ultramarine and crimson (*shades*)	1·40	1·60
52	17	5s. black and carmine-red	1·60	1·90
53	18	10s. black and maroon	3·25	3·50
43/53		*Set of* 11	7·00	8·00

½d.

(19)

1959 (1 Aug.). *No.* 45 *surch. with T* **19**, *by South African Govt. Ptr., Pretoria.*

No.	Type	Description	Un.	Used
54	19	½d. on 2d. deep bright blue and orange	10	12

20. Paramount Chief Moshesh.

21. Council House.

22. Mosuto Horseman.

(Des. from drawings by James Walton. Recess. Waterlow.)

1959 (15 Dec.). *Inauguration of National Council. W* w.**12**. *P* 13 × 13½.

No.	Type	Description	Un.	Used
55	20	3d. black and yellow-olive	12	15
56	21	1s. carm. and yellow-green	30	30
57	22	1s. 3d. ultram. & red-orge.	40	45

(Currency changed. 100 cents = 1 rand.)

½c. (23) 1c. (24) 2c (25)

2½c (I) 2½c (II) 3½c (I) 3½c (II)

5c (I) 5c (II) 10c (I) 10c (II)

12½c (I) 12½c (II) 50c (I) 50c (II)

25c (I) 25c (II) 25c (III)

R1 (I) R1 (II) R1 (III)

(Surch. by South African Govt. Printer, Pretoria.)

1961 (14 Feb.). *T* **8/18** *surch. as T* **23/25.**
58 **23** ½ c. on ½d. 5 5
a. Surch. double £140
59 **24** 1 c. on 1d. 5 5
60 **25** 2 c. on 2d. 8 8
a. Surch. inverted .. .. 55·00
61 ,, 2½ c. on 3d. (Type I) .. 15 20
a. Type II 12 15
b. Type II inverted .. .. — £300
62 ,, 3½ c. on 4½d. (Type I) .. 20 25
a. Type II .. .. .. 3·50 4·00
63 ,, 5 c. on 6d. (Type I) .. 12 20
a. Type II 12 20
64 ,, 10 c. on 1s. (Type I) .. 30 30
a. Type II .. .. .. 20·00 22·00
65 ,, 12½ c. on 1s. 3d. (Type I) .. 55 60
a. Type II 40 55
66 ,, 25 c. 2s. 6d. (Type I) .. 75 1·00
a. Type II .. .. .. 12·00 12·00
b. Type III 75 95
67 ,, 50 c. on 5s. (Type I) .. 2·25 3·00
a. Type II .. .. .. 1·75 2·00
68 ,, 1 r. on 10s. (Type I) .. 9·00 12·00
a. Type II .. .. .. 12·00 17·00
b. Type III .. .. .. 3·00 4·00
58/68b .. .. *Set of* 11 6·50 7·50

There were two printings of the 2½ c. Type II, differing in the position of the surcharge on the stamps.

26. Basuto Household.

(Recess. De La Rue.)

1961–63. *Value in cents. Wmk. Mult. Script CA. P* 13½ *or* 11½ (1 *r.*).
69 **8** ½ c. grey-black and sepia (25.9.62) 5 5
a. Imperf. (pair) £100
70 **9** 1 c. grey-black and bluish green (25.9.62) .. 5 5
71 **10** 2 c. deep bright blue and orange (17.12.62) .. 5 8
72 **26** 2½ c. yellow-grn. & dp. rose-red (*shades*) (14.2.61) .. 5 5
73 **12** 3½ c. indigo and deep ultramarine (25.9.62) .. 8 10
74 **13** 5 c. chestnut & deep grey-green (10.8.62) .. 12 12
75 **14** 10 c. bronze-green & purple (22.10.62) 25 25
76 **15** 12½ c. brown and turquoise-green (17.12.62) .. 35 40
77 **16** 25 c. deep ultramarine and crimson (25.9.62) .. 1·10 1·25
78 **17** 50 c. black and carmine-red (22.10.62) .. 2·50 2·75
79 **18** 1 r. black and maroon (*shades*) (4.2.63) .. 3·75 4·25
69/79 .. .. *Set of* 11 7·50 8·00

1963 (4 June). *Freedom from Hunger. As No.* 76 *of Aden.*
80 12½ c. reddish violet 35 35

1963 (2 Sept.). *Red Cross Centenary. As Nos.* 147/8 *of Antigua.*
81 2½ c. red and black 12 12
82 12½ c. red and blue 40 45

1964. *As Nos.* 70 *etc., but wmk.* w.**12.**
84 **9** 1 c. grey-black and bluish green (11.8.64) .. 5 5
86 **26** 2½ c. pale yellow-green and rose-red (10.3.64) .. 5 5
88 **13** 5 c. chestnut and deep grey-green (10.11.64) 15 20
90 **15** 12½ c. brown and turquoise-green (10.11.64) .. 45 50
92 **17** 50 c. black and carmine-red (29.9.64) .. 1·25 1·60
84/92 .. .. *Set of* 5 1·75 2·25

II. SELF-GOVERNMENT.

27. Mosotho Woman and Child.

28. Maseru Border Post.

29. Mountain Scene.
30. Legislative Buildings.

(Des. V. Whiteley. Photo. Harrison.)

1965 (10 May). *New Constitution. T* **27/28** *and horiz. designs similar to T* **28.** *W* w.**12.** *P* 14×13½.
94 **27** 2½ c. multicoloured .. 5 5
95 **28** 3½ c. multicoloured .. 12 15
96 **29** 5 c. multicoloured .. 15 15
97 **30** 12½ c. multicoloured .. 30 35

1965 (17 May). *I.T.U. Centenary. As Nos.* 166/7 *of Antigua.*
98 1 c. orange-red & brt. purple 5 5
99 20 c. lt. blue & orange-brown 45 55

1965 (25 Oct.). *International Co-operation Year. As Nos.* 168/9 *of Antigua.*
100 ½ c. reddish purple and turquoise-green 8 8
101 12½ c. deep bluish green and lavender 35 45

1966 (24 Jan.). *Churchill Commemoration. As Nos.* 170/3 *of Antigua.*
102 1 c. new blue 5 5
103 2½ c. deep green 8 5
104 10 c. brown 30 35
105 22½ c. bluish violet 55 60

OFFICIAL STAMPS.

1934 (4 May). *Optd.* " official ".
O1 **1** ½d. emerald £400 £450
O2 ,, 1d. scarlet £225 £250
O3 ,, 2d. bright purple £170 £150
O4 ,, 6d. orange-yellow £2600 £900
O1/4 .. .. *Set of* 4 £3000 £1600

Collectors are advised to buy these stamps only from reliable sources. They were not sold to the public.

POSTAGE DUE STAMPS.

D 1

D 2

(Typo. D.L.R.)

1933 (1 Dec.)–**1952.** *Wmk. Mult. Script CA. P* 14.
D1 **D 1** 1d. carmine, O 40 45
a. Scarlet, O ('38) .. .. 2·00 2·50
b. Deep carmine, C (24.10.51) 15 25
c. Error. Crown missing, C .. 15·00
d. Error. St. Edward's Crn., C 15·00
D2 **D 1** 2d. violet, O 70 85
a. Chalky paper (6.11.52) .. 12 25
b. Error. Crown missing, C .. 17·00
c. Error. St. Edward's Crn., C 11·00
D1/2 Perf. " Specimen " *Set of* 2 14·00

(Typo. D.L.R.)

1956 (1 Dec.). *Wmk. Mult. Script CA. P* 14.
D3 **D 2** 1d. carmine 15 25
D4 ,, 2d. deep reddish violet 20 30

5c 5c
(I) (II)

1961 (14 Feb.). *Surch. as T* **24,** *but without stop.*
D5 **D 2** 1 c. on 1d. carmine .. 5 8
D6 ,, 1 c. on 2d. dp. reddish vio. 5 8
D7 ,, 5 c. on 2d. dp. reddish vio. (Type I) 12 12
a. Type II .. .. 10·00

1961 (June). *No.* D2a *surch. as T* **24** (*without stop*).
D8 **D 1** 5 c. on 2d. violet .. 2·00 2·50
a. Error. Missing Crown, W9a £300
b. Error. St. Ed. Crown, W9b £120

1964. *As No.* D3/4 *but values in cents. Chalky paper. W* w.**12** (*sideways on* 1 *c.*). *P* 14.
D 9 **D 2** 1 c. carmine 5 5
D10 ,, 5 c. deep reddish violet 10 15

POSTAL FISCAL

In July 1961 the 10s. stamp, T **18**, surcharged " R1 Revenue ", was used for postage at at least one post office, but such usage was officially unauthorized.

Basutoland attained independence on 4th October 1966, and her stamps were withdrawn on 31st October 1966. For later issues see Lesotho.

BATUM.

(BRITISH OCCUPATION.)

1

БАТУМ. ОБ.
Руб 10 Руб
(2)

1919. *Litho. Imperf.*
1 **1** 5 k. green 12 20
2 ,, 10 k. ultramarine 12 20
3 ,, 50 k. yellow 15 25
4 ,, 1 r. chocolate 15 25
5 ,, 3 r. violet 45 55
6 ,, 5 r. brown 60 70
Russian stamps. Arms types, surch. with T **2.**
7 10 r. on 1 k. orange (*imperf.*) 4·00 4·00
8 10 r. on 3 k. carm.-red (*imp.*) 2·00 2·25
9 10 r. on 5 k. brn.-lilac (*perf.*) 20·00 20·00
10 10 r. on 10 on 7 k. d. bl. (*perf.*) 17·00 17·00

БАТУМ ОБЛАС.
P 10 P.
BRITISH
OCCUPATION
(3)

БАТУМЪ
BRITISH
P. 15 P.
OCCUPATION
О Б Л.
(4)

1919. *Russian stamps, Arms types, surch. with T* **3** *or* **4.** *Imperf.*
11 10 r. on 3 k. carmine-red .. 2·00 2·25
12 15 r. on 1 k. orange .. .. 4·00 4·00
a. Surch. in red .. .. 4·00 4·00
b. Surch. in violet .. .. 4·00 4·00

БАТУМ.ОБЛ.
Р.50Р.

BRITISH OCCUPATION (5)

BRITISH OCCUPATION (6)

919. *T* **1**, *new colours etc., optd. with T* **5**.

3 5 k. yellow-green 35 35
4 10 k. bright blue 35 35
5 25 k. orange-yellow 35 35
6 1 r. pale blue 15 25
7 2 r. pink 15 20
8 3 r. bright violet 15 25
9 5 r. brown 25 40
a. Error. "COCUPATION" .. 12·00 13·00
o 7 r. brownish red 40 50

920. *Russian Arms stamps, surch. as T* **6**.

(*a*) *Perf.*

1 25 r. on 5 k. brown-lilac .. 2·50 2·75
2 25 r. on 5 k. brown-lilac (B.).. 2·25 2·50
3 25 r. on 10 on 7 k. deep blue 3·00 3·00
4 25 r. on 10 on 7 k. dp. bl. (B.) 3·00 3·00
5 25 r. on 20 on 14 k. dp. carmine and blue .. .. 4·00 4·00
6 25 r. on 20 on 14 k. deep carmine and blue (B.) .. 4·00 4·00
7 25 r. on 25 k. deep violet and light green (B.) .. .. 4·00 4·00
8 25 r. on 25 k. dp. vio. & lt. grn. 4·00 4·00
9 25 r. on 50 k. grn. & copper-red 2·00 2·00
o 25 r. on 50 k. green & copper-red (B.) .. .. .. 3·00 3·00
1 50 r. on 2 k. yellow-green 4·50 4·50
2 50 r. on 3 k. carmine-red 4·50 4·50
3 50 r. on 4 k. red .. .. 4·50 4·50
4 50 r. on 5 k. brown-lilac .. 4·00 4·00

(*b*) *Imperf.*

5 50 r. on 2 k. yellow-green .. 15·00 15·00
6 50 r. on 3 k. carmine-red .. 17·00 17·00
7 50 r. on 5 k. brown-lilac .. 25·00 25·00

:omanov issue, as T **25** *of Russia, surch. with T* **6**.

8 50 r. on 4 k. rose-carmine (B.) 5·00 5·00

ussian Arms stamps surch. as T **3**. (*a*) *Imperf.*

9 50 r. on 1 k. orange .. .. 22·00 22·00
o 50 r. on 2 k. yellow-green .. 28·00 28·00

(*b*) *Perf.*

1 50 r. on 2 k. yellow-green .. 32·00 32·00
2 50 r. on 3 k. carmine-red .. 35·00 35·00
3 50 r. on 4 k. red .. .. 30·00 30·00
4 50 r. on 5 k. brown-lilac .. 20·00 20·00
4*a* 50 r. on 10 k. deep blue (C.).. 42·00 42·00
5 50 r. on 15 k. blue & red-brn. 23·00 23·00

РУБ 25 ЛЕЙ

25 РУБ. 25 (7)

R.50R. BRITISH OCCUPATION РУБ. (8)

1920. *Nos.* 13 *and* 15 *surch. with T* **7**.

6 25 r. on 5 k. yellow-green .. 2·50 2·50
7 25 r. on 5 k. yellow-green (B.) 2·75 2·75
8 25 r. on 25 k. orange-yellow .. 2·00 2·25
9 25 r. on 25 k. orange-yell. (B.) 4·50 5·50

1920. *No.* 3 *surch. with T* **8**.

o 50 r. on 50 k. yellow .. .. 2·00 2·00
1 50 r. on 50 k. yellow (B.) .. 4·00 4·00

1920 (JUNE). *T* **1** (*new colours etc.*) *optd. with T* **5**. *Imperf.*

A. *Normal.* B. *Error* "BPITISH."

		A.		B.	
52	1 r. chestnut ..	5	5	1·25	1·75
53	2 r. pale blue ..	5	5	1·25	1·75
54	3 r. pink	5	5	1·25	1·75
55	5 r. black-brown	5	5	1·25	1·75
56	7 r. yellow.. ..	5	5	1·25	1·75
57	10 r. myrtle-green	8	10	2·00	2·50
58	15 r. violet	15	20	2·00	2·50
59	25 r. scarlet ..	25	30	3·00	3·50
60	50 r. deep blue ..	30	40	3·50	4·00

BECHUANALAND.

A. BRITISH BECHUANALAND.

CROWN COLONY.

British Bechuanaland was proclaimed a Crown Colony on 30th September 1885.

British Bechuanaland (1)

BRITISH BECHUANALAND (2)

1885 (DEC.)–**87**. *Stamps of Cape of Good Hope ("Hope" seated) optd. with T* **1**, *by W. A. Richards & Sons, Cape Town.*

1 **6** ½d. slate (R.) (wmk. CA) .. 4·00 4·50
a. Opt. in lake .. .. ..
b. Opt. double (Lake + Bk.) .. £160
2 „ 3d. claret (wmk. CA) .. 7·00 9·00
3 „ 4d. blue (wmk. CC) (12.86?) 15·00 18·00

Wmk. Anchor (*Cape, T* **13**).

4 **6** ½d. grey-black (3·87?) .. 2·50 2·50
a. Error "ritish" .. ..
b. Opt. double £150 £150
5 „ 1d. pale rose-red .. .. 2·50 2·50
a. Error "ritish" £375 £400
b. Opt. double .. .. — £450
6 „ 2d. bistre .. .. .. 8·00 6·50
a. Error "ritish" £1000 £900
b. Opt. double .. .. ..
7 **4** 6d. purple .. .. .. 10·00 12·00
8 „ 1s. green (11.86?) .. 75·00 50·00
a. Error "ritish" £2500 £1700

Overprints with stop after "Bechuanaland" are forged.

1887 (1 Nov.). *Stamp of Gt. Britain optd. with T* **2**, *by D.L.R.*

9 **71** ½d. vermilion (H/S S. £35) .. 45 35
a. Opt. double £500

3

4

5

(Typo. De La Rue.)

1887 (1 Nov.). *P* 13½, 14.

(*a*) *Wmk. Orb.* (G.B. *T* **48**).

10 **3** 1d. lilac and black .. .. 6·00 1·60
11 „ 2d. lilac and black .. .. 6·50 1·60
a. Pale dull lilac and black .. 8·50 6·50
12 „ 3d. lilac and black .. .. 1·60 1·60
a. Pale reddish lilac and black .. 8·50 3·25
13 „ 4d. lilac and black .. .. 12·00 3·25
14 „ 6d. lilac and black .. .. 11·00 8·50

(*b*) *Wmk. Script "V R" sideways, reading up.*

15 **4** 1s. green and black.. .. 11·00 4·00
16 „ 2s. green and black.. .. 13·00 6·50
17 „ 2s. 6d. green and black .. 14·00 10·00
18 **4** 5s. green and black.. .. 32·00 26·00
19 „ 10s. green and black.. .. 55·00 55·00

(*c*) *Wmk. two orbs, sideways.*

20 **5** £1 lilac and black £275 £300
21 „ £5 lilac and black £700 £300
10/21 H/S "Specimen" *set of* 12 £350

Several values of the above series are known on blued paper. No. 11*a* is the first printing of the 2d. (on safety paper?) and has a faded appearance.

When purchasing Nos. 20/21 in used condition beware of copies with fiscal cancellations cleaned off and bearing forged postmarks.

For No. 15 surcharged "£5" see No. F2.

1d. (6)

1s. (7)

1888 (7 AUG.). *Surch. as T* **6** *or* **7**, *by P. Townshend & Co., Vryburg.*

22 **3** 1d. on 1d. lilac and black .. 2·75 1·60
23 „ 2d. on 2d. lilac and blk. (R.) 3·25 2·10
a. Pale dull lilac and black .. 13·00 10·00
b. Curved foot to "2" .. 65·00 65·00
24 „ 2d. on 2d. lilac and blk. (G.) — £250
25 „ 4d. on 4d. lilac and blk. (R.) 26·00 22·00
26 „ 6d. on 6d. lilac and black .. 20·00 10·00
27 „ 6d. on 6d. lilac and blk. (B.) — £300
28 **4** 1s. on 1s. green and black 26·00 18·00

One Half-Penny (8)

British Bechuanaland. (9)

British Bechuanaland. (10)

1888 (DEC.). *No.* 12*a surch. with T* **8**, *by P. Townshend & Co., Vryburg.*

29 **3** ½d. on 3d. pale reddish lilac and black .. .. 22·00 22·00

1889 (JAN.). *T* **6** *of Cape of Good Hope (wmk. Anchor) optd. with T* **9**, *by P. Townshend & Co., Vryburg.*

30 ½d. slate (G.) .. .. .. 2·75 4·00
b. Opt. double, one inverted .. £130
c. Opt. double, one vertical .. £130
d. As Var. c, se-tenant with stamp without opt. £250
e. "British" omitted £325

1891 (Nov.). *T* **6** *of Cape of Good Hope (wmk. Anchor), optd. with T* **10**, *reading upwards.*

31 1d. rose-red .. .. .. 4·00 4·50
a. Pair, one without opt. ..
b. "British" omitted .. .. — 65·00
c. "Bechuanaland." omitted ..
32 2d. bistre .. .. .. 1·40 1·60
a. No stop after "Bechuanaland" 55·00
31/32 H/S "Specimen" *Set of* 2 £120

See also Nos. 38 and 39.

BRITISH BECHUANALAND (11)

1891 (DEC.)–**1894**. *Stamps of Great Britain optd. with T* **11**, *by D.L.R.*

33 **57** 1d. lilac 65 35
34 **73** 2d. green and carmine .. 40 75
35 **76** 4d. green and purple-brown 1·40 80
a. Bisected (2d.) (on cover) .. † £325
36 **79** 6d. purple/*rose-red* .. .. 1·60 1·10
37 **82** 1s. green (July, 1894) .. 3·50 5·50
a. Bisected (6d.) (on cover) .. † —
33/36 H/S "Specimen" *Set of* 4 50·00

1893–95. *As Nos.* 31 *and* 32, *but T* **10** *reads downwards.*

38 1d. rose-red (12.93) 60 60
a. Pair, one without opt. ..
b. "British" omitted .. .. 65·00
c. Optd. "Bechuanaland. British" ..
d. No dots to "i" of "British" .. 13·00 13·00
e. Opt. reading up, no dots to "i" of "British" .. .. ..

39 2d. bistre (15.3.95 .. .. 1·10 60
a. Opt. double £225 £200
b. "British" omitted .. .. 85·00 85·00
c. Optd. "Bechuanaland. British"
d. No dots to "i" of "British" 26·00 29·00

No. 38e was formerly listed as No. 31a but it does not occur on that setting and only exists from sheets fed the wrong way in the 1893 issue.

On 16th November 1895 British Bechuanaland was annexed to the Cape of Good Hope and ceased to have its own stamps, but they remained in use in the Protectorate until superseded in 1897.

B. BECHUANALAND PROTECTORATE.

This large area north of the Molopo River was proclaimed a British Protectorate on 30th September 1885 at the request of the native chiefs.

A postal service using runners was inaugurated in August 1888 and Nos. 40 to 55 were issued as a temporary measure with the object of assessing the cost of this service.

Protectorate (12) 16 mm.

Protectorate 1d (13)

Types 12/17 were applied by P. Townshend & Co., Vryburg.)

1888 (7 Aug.). *No. 9 optd. with T* **12** *and Nos. 10/19 surch. or optd. only as T* **13**.
40 **71** ½d. verm. (H/S S. £30) .. 1·25 2·25
a. "Protectorate" double .. 55·00
41 **3** 1d. on 1d. lilac and black .. 1·40 2·25
a. Small figure "1" .. .. 75·00 75·00
42 ,, 2d. on 2d. lilac and black .. 4·50 4·50
b. Curved foot to "2" .. 65·00 65·00
43 ,, 3d. on 3d. pale reddish lilac and black .. 20·00 21·00
44 ,, 4d. on 4d. lilac and black .. 26·00 26·00
a. Small figure "4" .. ..
45 ,, 6d. on 6d. lilac and black .. 12·00 11·00
46 **4** 1s. grn. & blk. (H/S S. £25) 18·00 12·00
a. First "o" omitted £250 £250
47 ,, 2s. green and black .. 65·00 65·00
a. First "o" omitted £650
48 ,, 2s. 6d. green and black £120 £110
a. First "o" omitted £800
49 ,, 5s. green and black .. £250 £270
a. First "o" omitted £1100
50 ,, 10s. green and black .. £650 £650
a. First "o" omitted £2250

See also Nos. 54/5.

1888 (Dec.). *No. 25 optd. with T* **12**.
51 **3** 4d. on 4d. lilac and black .. 16·00 11·00

Bechuanaland

Protectorate

Protectorate. (14)

Fourpence (15)

1889 (Jan.). *T* **6** *of Cape of Good Hope (wmk. Anchor), optd. with T* **14**.
52 ½d. slate (G.) .. .. .. 1·25 2·10
a. Opt. double .. .. .. 80·00 85·00
b. "Bechuanaland" omitted .. £130
c. Optd. "Protectorate. Bechuanaland" .. ..

1889 (Aug.). *No. 9 surch. with T* **15**.
53 **71** 4d. on ½d. verm. (H/S S. £50) .. .. .. 2·25 2·25
a. Surch. (T 18) inverted .. — £700

Protectorate (16) 15½ mm.

Protectorate (17)

1890. *No. 9 surch.*
54 **16** ½d. vermilion .. .. 12·00 12·00
a. Type 16 inverted .. .. 15·00 15·00
b. Type 16 double .. .. 15·00 15·00
c. Type 16 double and inverted £120 £100
d. Error. "Portectorate" and opt. inverted .. ..
55 **17** ½d. vermilion .. .. 13·00 15·00
a. Type 17 double .. .. 75·00
b. Error. "Protectorrte" ..

These were trial printings made in 1888 which were subsequently issued.

In June 1890 the Bechuanaland Protectorate and the Colony of British Bechuanaland came under one postal administration and the stamps of British Bechuanaland were used in the Protectorate until 1897.

BRITISH

BECHUANALAND

(18)

1897. *T* **6** *of Cape of Good Hope (wmk. Anchor), optd. as T* **18**.

(*a*) *Lines 13 mm. apart, bottom line 16 mm. long, by Taylor & Marshall, Cape Town.*
56 ½d. yellow-green (July?) .. 70 1·25

(*b*) *Lines 13½ mm. apart, bottom line 15 mm. long, by P. Townshend & Co., Vryburg.*
57 ½d. yellow-green (April) .. 5·00 6·00

(*c*) *Lines 10½ mm. apart, bottom line 15 mm. long, by W. A. Richards & Sons, Cape Govt. Printers.*
58 ½d. yellow-green (July?) .. 2·50 3·00

Although issued only in the Protectorate, the above were presumably overprinted "BRITISH BECHUANALAND" because stamps bearing this inscription were in use there at the time.

BECHUANALAND PROTECTORATE (19)

BECHUANALAND PROTECTORATE (20)

1897 (Oct.)–**1902.** *Stamps of Great Britain (Queen Victoria) optd. with T* **19**, *by D.L.R.*
59 **71** ½d. vermilion 30 60
60 ,, ½d. blue-green (25.2.02) .. 30 60
61 **57** 1d. lilac 30 40
62 **73** 2d. green and carmine .. 1·50 1·75
63 **75** 3d. purple/*yellow* (12.97) .. 2·50 2·50
64 **76** 4d. green and purple-brown 3·25 3·50
65 **79** 6d. purple/*rose-red* .. 8·00 8·50
59/65 .. .. *Set of* 7 14·00 16·00
59, 61/5 Optd. "Specimen" *Set of* 660 00

1904–13. *Stamps of Great Britain (King Edward VII) optd. with T* **20**, *by D.L.R.*
66 **83** ½d. blue-green (3.06) .. 1·40 1·25
67 ,, ½d. yellow-green (11.08) .. 1·60 1·60
68 ,, 1d. scarlet (4.05) .. .. 1·60 90
69 **86** 2½d. ultramarine (29.11.04) 3·25 3·25
a. Stop after "P" in "PROTECTORATE" £250
70 **93** 1s. grn. & scarlet (10.12) (H/S S. £10) .. 6·50 9·00
71 ,, 1s. grn. & carmine (1913) 8·50 11·00
66/71 .. .. *Set of* 5 19·00 23·00

Nos. 70 and 71 are the Somerset House printings.

1912 (Sept.). *T* **102** *of Great Britain (King George V, wmk. Crown) optd. with T* **20**.
72 **102** 1d. scarlet .. .. .. 1·10 1·00
a. No cross on crown .. — 24·00
b. Aniline scarlet .. ..

BECHUANALAND PROTECTORATE (21)

1913 (July)–**24.** *Stamps of Great Britain (Kin George V) optd.*

(*a*) *With T* **20** *(wmk. Script Cypher, T* **100**).
73 **105** ½d. green 45 4
74 **104** 1d. scarlet (shades) (4.15) 50 4
75 **105** 1½d. red-brown (12.20) .. 60 8
76 **106** 2d. reddish orange (Die I) 80 1·0
a. Orange (Die I) .. ..
77 ,, 2d. orange (Die II) (1924) 5·00 3·2
78 **104** 2½d. ultramarine .. .. 1·00 1·1
a. Blue (1915) .. ..
79 **106** 3d. blue-violet .. .. 2·50 3·2
80 ,, 4d. slate-green .. .. 1·75 3·0
81 **107** 6d. reddish pur. (*shades*), C 2·00 2·5
a. Purple, C .. ..
82 **108** 1s. bistre-brn. (Optd. S. £15) 3·25 3·5
a. Olive-bistre .. ..
73/82 .. .. *Set of* 9 12·00 15·0

(*b*) *With T* **21.** (*Wmk. T* **110.**)

(i) *Waterlow printings.* (1914-15.)
83 **109** 2s. 6d. deep sepia-brown (1.15) .. .. .. 25·00 32·0
a. Re-entry £200 £25
b. Opt. double, one albino .. £125
84 ,, 5s. rose-carmine (1914) .. 28·00 32·0
a. Opt. double, one albino .. £190
83/84 Optd. "Specimen" *Set of* 2 45·00

(ii) *De La Rue printings.* (1916–20.)
85 **109** 2s. 6d. grey-brown (7.16) 23·00 30·0
a. Re-entry £275
86 ,, 2s. 6d. deep brown (1920) 27·00 32·0
a. Opt. treble, two albino ..
87 ,, 5s. bright carmine (8.19) 45·00 65·0
a. Opt. double, one albino .. £130

(iii) *Bradbury, Wilkinson printings.* (1920–23.
88 **109** 2s. 6d. chocolate-brown .. (7.23) .. .. .. 23·00 29·0
a. Major Re-entry £600
b. Opt. double, one albino. .
89 ,, 5s. rose-red (7.20) .. 25·00 32·0
90 ,, 5s. deep carmine .. 25·00 32·0
a. Opt. treble, two albino .. £170

1925–27. *As* 1913–24, *but W* **111** *(block letters)*
91 **105** ½d. green (1927) 60 7
92 **104** 1d. scarlet (8.25) 60 9
93 **106** 2d. orange (Die II) (7.25) 95 1·1
94 ,, 3d. violet (10.26) .. .. 1·60 2·0
a. Opt. double, one albino ..
95 ,, 4d. grey-green (10.26) .. 1·60 2·4
96 **107** 6d. purple, C (12.25) .. 3·50 4·2
97 ,, 6d. purple, O (1926) .. 4·50 5·0
98 **108** 1s. bistre-brown (10.26) .. 7·00 7·5
91/98 .. .. *Set of* 8 18·00 21·0

22. King George V, Baobab Tree and Cattle drinking.

23. King George VI Baobab Tree and Cattle drinking.

(Des. from photo by Resident Commissioner Ngamiland. Recess. Waterlow.)

1932 (12 Dec.). *Wmk. Mult. Script CA. P* 12½
99 **22** ½d. green 15 3
100 ,, 1d. scarlet 25 4
101 ,, 2d. brown 70 6
102 ,, 3d. ultramarine 80 8
103 ,, 4d. orange 65 8
104 ,, 6d. purple .. .. 80 1·0
105 ,, 1s. black and olive-green 2·00 2·5
106 ,, 2s. black and orange .. 7·00 8·0
107 ,, 2s. 6d. black and scarlet 9·00 11·0
108 ,, 3s. black and purple .. 12·00 14·0
109 ,, 5s. black and ultramarine 15·00 18·0
110 ,, 10s. black and brown .. 27·00 30·0
99/110 .. .. *Set of* 12 70·00 80·0
99/110 Perf. "Specimen" *Set of* 12 50·00

Extra flagstaff variety.

1935 (4 May). *Silver Jubilee. As Nos.* 91/4 *of Antigua but ptd. by B. W. P* 11 × 12.
111 1d. deep blue and scarlet .. 10 20
a. Extra flagstaff .. .. 14·00
112 2d. ultramarine & grey-black 25 40
a. Extra flagstaff .. .. 11·00
113 3d. brown and deep blue .. 30 60
a. Extra flagstaff .. .. 14·00
114 6d. slate and purple .. 60 85
a. Extra flagstaff .. .. 14·00
111/14 Perf. "Specimen" *Set of* 4 15·00

1937 (12 May). *Coronation. As Nos.* 13/15 *of Aden. P* 14.
115 1d. scarlet 12 12
116 2d. yellow-brown 12 15
117 3d. bright blue 15 25
115/7 Perf. "Specimen" *Set of* 3 11·00

(Recess. Waterlow.)

1938 (1 Apr.)–**52**. *Wmk. Mult. Script CA. P* 12½.
118 **23** ½d. green 50 50
a. Light yellowish green (1941) 90 90
b. Yellowish green (4.43) .. 30 30
c. Deep green (4.49) .. 30 30
119 ,, 1d. scarlet 10 12
120 ,, 1½d. dull blue 40 40
a. Light blue (4.43) 15 12
121 ,, 2d. chocolate-brown .. 10 15
122 ,, 3d. deep ultramarine .. 10 15
123 ,, 4d. orange 15 25
124 ,, 6d. reddish purple .. 1·00 90
a. Purple (1944) 90 80
125 ,, 1s. black and brown-olive 30 50
a. Grey-black and olive-green (21.5.52) .. .. 1·50 1·75
126 ,, 2s. 6d. black and scarlet 1·25 1·50
127 ,, 5s. black & dp. ultram. 2·00 2·25
a. Grey-black and deep ultramarine (10.46) .. 7·00 8·00
128 ,, 10s. black and red-brown 6·50 7·00
118/128 .. .. *Set of* 11 11·00 12·00
118/28 Perf. "Specimen" *Set of* 11 32·00

Bechuanaland
(24)

1945 (3 Dec.). *Victory. Stamps of South Africa optd. with T* **24**. *Inscr. alternately in English and Afrikaans.*

Un. pair *Used pair*
129 **55** 1d. brown and carmine .. 10 12
130 **56** 2d. slate-blue and violet .. 12 20
131 **57** 3d. deep blue and blue .. 20 25
a. Opt. omitted (in vert. pr. with normal) .. .. £1000 †

1947 (17 Feb.). *Royal Visit. As Nos.* 32/5 *of Basutoland.*

Un. *Us.*
132 1d. scarlet 5 5
133 2d. green 5 5
134 3d. ultramarine 5 5
135 1s. mauve 25 25
132/5 Perf. "Specimen" *Set of* 4 28·00

1948 (1 Dec.). *Royal Silver Wedding. As Nos.* 30/1 *of Aden.*
136 1½d. ultramarine 10 10
137 10s. black .. .. .. 2·75 4·00

1949 (10 Oct.). *75th Anniv. of Universal Postal Union. As Nos.* 114/17 *of Antigua.*
138 1½d. blue 12 12
139 3d. deep blue.. .. .. 12 15
140 6d. magenta 30 30
141 1s. olive 55 55

1953 (3 June). *Coronation. As No.* 47 *of Aden.*
142 2d. black and brown .. 15 20

25. Queen Elizabeth II, Baobab Tree and Cattle drinking.

(Des. from photo by Resident Commissioner, Ngamiland. Recess. Waterlow.)

1955 (3 Jan.)–**58**. *Wmk. Mult. Script CA. P* 13½ × 14.
143 **25** ½d. green 5 5
144 ,, 1d. rose-red 5 5
145 ,, 2d. red-brown 8 8
146 ,, 3d. ultramarine (*shades*) 10 10
146*a* ,, 4d. red-orange (1.12.58) .. 20 25
147 ,, 4½d. blackish blue .. 25 25
148 ,, 6d. purple 20 20
149 ,, 1s. black & brown-olive 30 30
150 ,, 1s. 3d. black and lilac .. 50 65
151 ,, 2s. 6d. black and rose-red 1·10 1·40
152 ,, 5s. black and violet-blue 1·90 2·25
153 ,, 10s. black and red-brown 3·75 4·25
143/153 .. .. *Set of* 12 7·50 9·00

26. Queen Victoria, Queen Elizabeth II and Landscape.

(Photo. Harrison.)

1960 (21 Jan.). *75th Anniv. of Bechuanaland Protectorate. W* w.**12**. *P* 14½ × 14.
154 **26** 1d. sepia and black .. 5 5
155 ,, 3d. magenta and black .. 12 12
156 ,, 6d. bright blue and black 25 25

Currency changed. 100 cents = 1 rand.

1c **(27)** **1c** (I) **1c** (II) **5c** (I) **5c** (II)

3 (I) **3** (II) **3** (III) (3½ c. on 4d.) **R1** (I) **R1** (II)

(Surch. by South African Govt. Printer, Pretoria.)

1961 (14 Feb.–June). *Surch. as T* **27**.
157 **25** 1 c. on 1d. (Type I) .. 10 10
a. Type II (6.6) 12 15
158 ,, 2 c. on 2d. 10 10
159 ,, 2½ c. on 2d. (*two types*) .. 12 15
b. Pair, one without surch. £200
160 ,, 2½ c. on 3d. 70 70
161 ,, 3½ c. on 4d. (Type I) .. 35 40
a. Type II .. .. 1·10 1·40
b. Wide surch. (I) .. 8·50 8·50
c. Wide surch. (II) .. 22·00
d. Type III (6.6) 12 15
162 ,, 5 c. on 6d. (Type I) .. 40 40
a. Type II (12.5) 25 25
163 ,, 10 c. on 1s. 30 35
a. Pair, one without surch. £200
164 ,, 12½ c. on 1s. 3d. 40 50
165 ,, 25 c. on 2s. 6d. .. .. 85 1·10
166 ,, 50 c. on 5s. .. .. 1·75 2·00
167 ,, 1 r. on 10s. (Type I) .. £100 60·00
a. Type II (1st Ptg.) (17.3).. 5·50 6·50
b. Type II (2nd Ptg.) .. 3·50 4·00
157/167b .. .. *Set of* 11 7·50 8·00

No. 161—3½ c. on 4d. Types I and II of "3" were mixed in the sheet of 60 stamps—38 of Type I, 22 of Type II. The "wide surcharge" measures 9½ mm. overall (with "C" spaced 1½ mm. from "½") and comes on 8 of the 10 stamps in the last vertical row (5 × Type I, 3 × Type II). The surcharge on the remainder of the sheet varies between 8½ and 9¼ mm.

Type III was a later printing.

Nos. 167a/b—1 rand (Type II). The First Printing (No. 167a) had the surcharge at bottom left; in the Second Printing (No. 167b) it was placed towards the bottom of the stamp, either centrally or towards the right.

Later printings of the 2½ c. on 2d. and 12½ c. on 1s. 3d. were from fresh settings of type, but insufficiently different for separate listing here. Later printings of the 10 c. and 25 c. were identical with the originals.

28. Golden Oriole.

29. African Hoopoe.

30. Scarlet-chested Sunbird.

31. Cape Widow-bird.

32. Swallow-tailed Bee-eater.

33. Grey Hornbill.

34. Red-headed Weaver.

35. Brown-hooded Kingfisher.

36. Woman Musician.

38. Woman Grinding Maize.

37. Baobab Tree.

39. Bechuana Ox.

40. Lion.

41. Police Camel Patrol.

(Des. P. Jones. Photo. Harrison & Sons.)

1961 (2 Oct.). *W* w.**12**. *P* 14 × 14½ (*vert.*) *or* 14½ × 14 (*horiz.*).

168 **28** 1 c. yell., red, blk. & lilac 5 5
169 **29** 2 c. orge., blk. & yell.-ol. 5 5
170 **30** 2½ c. carmine, green, black and bistre 5 8
171 **31** 3½ c. yell., blk., sep. & pk. 8 10
172 **32** 5 c. yell., bl., blk. & buff 10 12
173 **33** 7½ c. brown, red, black and apple-green .. 15 20
174 **34** 10 c. red, yellow, sepia and turquoise-green .. 25 25
175 **35** 12½ c. buff, blue, red and grey-black 30 30
176 **36** 20 c. yellow-brown & drab 35 40
177 **37** 25 c. dp. brown and lemon 45 55
178 **38** 35 c. deep blue & orange 65 80
179 **39** 50 c. sepia and olive .. 95 1·40
180 **40** 1 r. black and cinnamon 1·90 2·25
181 **41** 2 r. brown & turq.-blue 3·75 4·25
168/181 .. .. *Set of* 14 8·00 9·50

1963 (4 June). *Freedom from Hunger. As No.* 76 *of Aden.*

182 12½ c. bluish green 35 40

1963 (2 Sept.). *Red Cross Centenary. As Nos.* 147/8 *of Antigua.*

183 2½ c. red and black .. 12 20
184 12½ c. red and blue 35 45

1964 (23 April). *400th Anniv. of Birth of William Shakespeare. As No.* 164 *of Antigua.*

185 12½ c. light brown 25 30

(C) BECHUANALAND.

INTERNAL SELF GOVERNMENT.

42. Map and Gaberones Dam.

(Des. V. Whiteley. Photo. Harrison & Sons.)

1965 (1 Mar.). *New Constitution. W* w.**12**. *P* 14½ × 14.

186 **42** 2½ c. red and gold .. 5 5
187 ,, 5 c. ultramarine & gold 8 8
188 ,, 12½ c. brown and gold .. 25 30
189 ,, 25 c. green and gold .. 35 40

1965 (17 May). *I.T.U. Centenary. As Nos.* 166/7 *of Antigua.*

190 2½ c. red and bistre-yellow .. 8 10
191 12½ c. mauve and brown .. 35 35

1965 (25 Oct.). *International Co-operation Year. As Nos.* 168/9 *of Antigua.*

192 1 c. reddish purple and turquoise-green 5 5
193 12½ c. dp. bluish green & lav. 35 35

1966 (24 Jan.). *Churchill Commemoration. As Nos.* 170/3 *of Antigua.*

194 1 c. new blue 5 5
195 2½ c. deep green 8 8
196 12½ c. brown 30 30
197 20 c. bluish violet 55 60

43. Haslar Smoke Generator.

44. Bugler.
45. Gun-site.
46. Regimental Cap Badge.

(Des. V. Whiteley. Photo. Harrison.)

1966 (1 June). *Bechuanaland Royal Pioneer Corps. W* w.**12**. *P* 14½.

198 **43** 2½ c. Prussian blue, red and light emerald .. 5 5
199 **44** 5 c. brown and light blue 10 12
200 **45** 15 c. Prussian blue, rosine and emerald 30 30
201 **46** 35 c. buff, blackish brown, red and green .. 60 65

POSTAGE DUE STAMPS.

BECHUANALAND (D 1)

PROTECTORATE

BECHUANALAND PROTECTORATE (D 2)

1926 (Jan.). *Type* D **1** *of Great Britain, optd. with Types* D **1** *or* D **2** (*2d.*).

D1 ½d. emerald (No. D10) .. 20 25
D2 1d. carmine (No. D9) .. 25 30
D3 2d. agate (No. D13) .. 40 50

D **3**

1c 1c

I. (Small.) II. (Large.)

(Typo. De La Rue.)

1932 (12 Dec.)–**58**. *Wmk. Mult. Script. CA. P* 14.

D4 D **3** ½d. sage-green 70 80
D5 ,, 1d. carmine, O 35 45
a. Chalky paper (27.11.58) .. 12 15
D6 ,, 2d. violet, O .. .. 90 1·00
a. Chalky paper (27.11.58) .. 15 30
D4/6 Perf. "Specimen" *Set of* 3 16·00

1961 (14 Feb.). *Surch. as T* **27**.

D7 D **3** 1 c. on 1d., C (Type I) .. 15 25
a. Type II (chalky paper) .. 8 10
aa. Double surch. (Type II) .. 45·00
b. Type II (ordinary paper) .. 8·00
D8 ,, 2 c. on 2d., C (Type I) .. 12 20
a. Type II (chalky paper) .. 10 12
b. Type II (ordinary paper) .. 10·00
D9 ,, 5 c. on ½d. 20 30

1961 (15 Nov.). *As Type* D **3** *but values in cents. Chalky paper. Wmk. Mult. Script CA. P* 14.

D10 1 c. carmine 8 10
D11 2 c. violet 8 10
D12 5 c. green 12 25

POSTAL FISCAL STAMPS.

The following stamps issued for fiscal purposes were each allowed to be used for postal purposes for a short time. No. F2 was used by the public because the word "POSTAGE" had not been obliterated and No. F3 because the overprint did not include the words "Revenue only" as did the contemporary fiscal overprints for Basutoland and Swaziland.

Bechuanaland

Protectorate

(F **1**)

£5

(F **2**)

1910 (July). *No.* 266 *of Transvaal, optd. with Type* F **1**.

F1 6d. black and orange, C (B.) .. 25·00 27·00

1918. *No.* 15 *surch. with Type* F **2** *at top.*

F2 **4** £5 on 1s. green and black ..

Bechuanaland

Protectorate.

(F **3**)

1922. *No.* 4*b of South Africa optd. with Type* F **3**, *in varying positions.*

F3 1d. scarlet .. .. .. 13·00 13·00
a. Opt. double, one albino

The stamps of Bechuanaland were withdrawn on 29th September, 1966, when she attained independence. For later issues see Botswana.

BELIZE.

(FORMERLY BRITISH HONDURAS.)

✲BELIZE✲

(81)

1973 (11* JUNE). *Designs as T* **63** *of Br. Honduras optd. with T* **81** *in silver and black by D.L.R. W* w.**12** (*upright*). *P* 13 × 12½.

No.	Description		Unused	Used
347	½ c. Crana Fish (As No. 277)		5	5
348	1 c. Jew Fish ..	.. ..	5	5
349	2 c. Warree ..	.. ..	5	5
350	3 c. Grouper	.. ..	5	8
351	4 c. Ant Bear	.. ..	8	8
352	5 c. Bone Fish	.. ..	8	10
353	10 c. Gibnut ..	.. ..	10	12
	a. Black (value etc.) omitted ..			
354	15 c. Dolphin	.. ..	20	20
355	25 c. Night Walker ..	..	25	30
356	50 c. Mutton Snapper	..	40	50
357	$1 Bush Dog	.. ..	95	1·10
358	$2 Great Barracuda	..	1·90	2·25
359	$5 Mountain Lion	..	3·75	4·25
347/59	.. ..	*Set of* 13	7·00	8·00

* This is the local date of issue: the Crown Agents released the stamps on 1 June.

1973 (14 NOV.). *Royal Wedding. As Nos.* 165/6 *of Anguilla. Centre multicoloured. W* w.**12** (*sideways*). *P* 13½.

No.	Description		Unused	Used
360	26 c. light turquoise-blue	..	20	25
361	50 c. ochre ..	.. ..	35	40

82. Crana.

(Des. and litho. J. W.)

1974 (1 JAN.). *Designs as T* **63** *of Br. Honduras but incr.* "BELIZE" *as T* **82**. *Multicoloured. W* w.**12**. *P* 13½.

No.	Description		Unused	Used
362	½ c. Type **82**	.. ..	5	5
363	1 c. Jew Fish ..	.. ..	5	5
364	2 c. Warree ..	.. ..	5	5
365	3 c. Grouper	.. ..	5	5
366	4 c. Ant Bear	.. ..	5	5
367	5 c. Bone Fish	.. ..	5	5
368	10 c. Gibnut ..	.. ..	8	8
369	15 c. Dolphin	.. ..	10	10
370	25 c. Night Walker ..	..	15	20
371	50 c. Mutton Snapper	..	30	35
372	$1 Bush Dog	.. ..	55	60
373	$2 Great Barracuda	..	1·10	1·25
374	$5 Mountain Lion	..	2·75	3·00
362/74	.. ..	*Set of* 13	4·75	5·25

83. Deer.

(Des. Mrs. Hosek; adapted PAD Studio. Litho. Questa.)

1974 (1 MAY). *Mayan Artefacts. T* **83** *and similar horiz. designs showing pottery motifs. Multicoloured. W* w.**12**. *P* 14½.

No.	Description		Unused	Used
375	3 c. Type **83** ..	.. ..	5	8
376	6 c. Jaguar deity	.. ..	8	10
377	16 c. Sea monster	.. ..	12	15
378	26 c. Cormorant	.. ..	20	20
379	50 c. Scarlet macaw ..	..	40	45
375/9	.. ..	*Set of* 5	75	85

84. *Parides arcas.*

(Des. J. E. Cooter from the collection of P. T. Hill. Litho. Harrison.)

1974 (2 SEPT.)–**75.** *Butterflies of Belize. T* **84** *and similar horiz. designs. Multicoloured. W* w.**12** (*sideways*). *P* 14 (½ *to* 10 *c. and* 26 *c.*) *or* 14 × 14½ (*others*).

No.	Description		Unused	Used
380	½ c. Type **84** ..	.. ..	8	5
381	1 c. *Thecla regalis*	.. ..	5	5
382	2 c. *Colobura dirce*	.. ..	5	5
383	3 c. *Catonephele numilia*	..	5	5
384	4 c. *Battus belus*	.. ..	5	5
385	5 c. *Callicore patelina*	..	5	5
386	10 c. *Callicore astala*	.. ..	5	5
387	15 c. *Nessaea aglaura* ..	..	10	12
388	16 c. *Prepona pseudojoiceyi*	..	8	8
389	25 c. *Papilio thoas*	.. ..	12	15
390	26 c. *Hamadryas arethusa*	..	20	25
391	50 c. *Thecla bathildis*	.. ..	25	30
392	$1 *Caligo uranus*	.. ..	50	55
393	$2 *Heliconius sapho*	..	1·00	1·10
394	$5 *Eurytides philolaus*	..	2·50	2·75
395	$10 *Philaethria dido* (2.1.75)		5·00	5·25
380/95	.. ..	*Set of* 16	9·00	9·50

See also Nos. 403, 426 and 433.

85. Churchill when Prime Minister, and Coronation Scene.

(Des. J.W. Ltd. Litho. Questa.)

1974 (30 NOV.). *Birth Centenary of Sir Winston Churchill. T* **85** *and similar horiz. design. Multicoloured. W* w.**14** (*sideways*). *P* 14.

No.	Description		Unused	Used
396	50 c. Type **85** ..	.. ..	25	30
397	$1 Churchill in stetson, and Williamsburg Liberty Bell		50	55

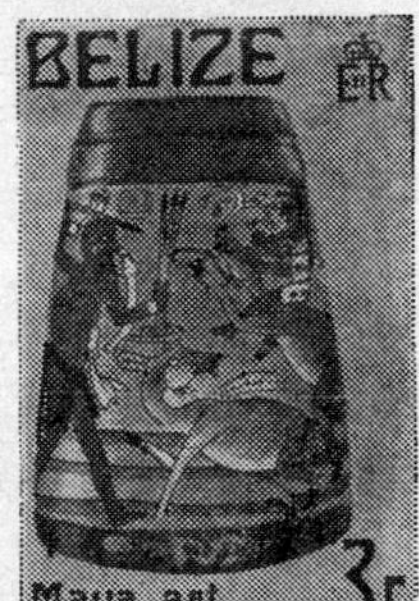

86. The Actun Balam Vase.

(Des. Mrs. Hosek; adapted P. B. Powell. Litho. Questa.)

1975 (2 JUNE). *Mayan Artefacts. T* **86** *and similar vert. designs showing decorated vessels. Multicoloured. W* w.**14**. *P* 14.

No.	Description		Unused	Used
398	3 c. Type **86**	.. ..	5	5
399	6 c. Seated figure ..	.. ..	5	5
400	16 c. Costumed priest	..	10	10
401	26 c. Head with headdress ..		12	15
402	50 c. Layman and priest	..	25	30
398/402		*Set of* 5	50	60

1975 (11 JUNE). *As No.* 380 *but W* w.**14** (*sideways*).

No.	Description		Unused	Used
403	½ c. Type **84**	.. ..	5	5

Nos. 404/18 have been reserved for any further additions to this issue.

1975 (20 OCT.). *As Nos.* 387 *and* 394 *but W* w.**12** *upright.*

No.	Description		Unused	Used
426	15 c. *Nessaea aglaura* ..	..	8	8
433	$5 *Eurytides philolaus*	..	2·75	3·00

Nos. 419/34 have been reserved for any further additions to this issue.

87. Musicians.

(Des. PAD Studio. Litho. Harrison.)

1975 (17 NOV.). *Christmas. T* **87** *and similar multicoloured designs. W* w.**12** (*upright on* 6 *c.,* 26 *c.*) *or sideways* (*others*). *P* 14 × 14½ (*horiz.*) *or* 14½ × 14 (*vert.*).

No.	Description		Unused	Used
435	6 c. Type **87**	.. ..	5	5
436	26 c. Children and "crib"	..	12	15
437	50 c. Dancer and drummers (*vert.*)	.. ..	25	30
	a. Imperf. (pair)	.. ..		
438	$1 Family and map (*vert.*)		50	55

88. William Wrigley Jr. and Chicle Tapping.

(Des. PAD Studio. Litho. Questa.)

1976 (29 MAR.). *Bicentenary of American Revolution. T* **88** *and similar horiz. designs. Multicoloured. W* w.**14** (*sideways*). *P* 14.

No.	Description		Unused	Used
439	10 c. Type **88** ..	.. ..	5	8
440	35 c. Charles Lindbergh	..	20	25
441	$1 J. L. Stephens (archaeologist) ..	.. ..	50	55

89. Cycling.

(Des. J.W. Ltd. Litho. Walsall.)

1976 (17 JULY). *Olympic Games, Montreal. T* **89** *and similar horiz. designs. Multicoloured. W* w.**14** (*sideways*). *P* 14.

No.	Description		Unused	Used
442	35 c. Type **89** ..	.. ..	20	25
443	45 c. Running ..	.. ..	30	35
444	$1 Shooting ..	.. ..	55	65

20c

(90)

1976 (30 Aug.). *No.* 390 *surch. with T* **90.** *W* w.**14** (*sideways*).

445	20 c. on 26 c. *Hamadryas arethusa*	10	12

1976 (18 Oct.). *West Indian Victory in World Cricket Cup. As Nos.* 559/60 *of Barbados.*

446	35 c. Map of the Caribbean ..	20	20
447	$1 The Prudential Cup ..	55	65

POSTAGE DUE STAMPS.

D 2

(Des. P. B. Powell. Litho. Questa.)

1976 (1 July). *Type* D **2** *and similar vert. designs, but with different frames. W* w.**14** (*sideways*). *P* $13\frac{1}{2} \times 14$.

D 6	D **2**	1 c. red and dull green	5	5
D 7	–	2 c. lt. mag. & bluish vio.	5	5
D 8	–	5 c. dull green and orange-brown ..	5	5
D 9	–	15 c. apple-green and dull vermilion ..	8	8
D10	–	25 c. orge. and olive-grn.	12	15
D6/10		.. .. *Set of* 5	20	25

MINIMUM PRICE

The minimum price quoted is 5p which represents a handling charge rather than a basis for valuing common stamps. For further notes about prices see introductory pages.

BERMUDA.

I. COLONY.

O 1

O 2

1848–61. *Postmasters' Stamps. Adhesives prepared and issued by the postmasters at Hamilton and St. Georges. Dated as given in brackets.*

(*a*) *By W. B. Perot at Hamilton.*

O1	O **1**	1d. black/*bluish grey* (1848)	—	£50000
O2	,,	1d. black/*bluish grey* (1849)	—	£50000
O3	,,	1d. red/*thick white* (1853) ..	—	£30000
O4	,,	1d. red/*bluish laid* (1854)	—	£90000
O5	,,	1d. red/*bluish wove* (1856)		
O6	O **2**	(1d.) carmine-red/*bluish laid* (1861)	—	£55000

(*b*) *By J. H. Thies at St. Georges.*
As Type O **2** *but inscr.* " ST. GEORGES ".

O7	–	(1d.) carmine-red/*buff* (1860)	—	£40000

Stamps of Type O **1** bear manuscript value and signature, and the dates given are those inscribed on the known copies existing. Although the franking value is believed to have been 1d., it was not given on Nos. O6/7.

Prices shown reflect our estimation of value based on known copies. For instance of the two copies known of No. O4, one is in the Royal collection and the other is on entire. (There is one recorded copy of No. O5 in existence.)

1

2

3

4

5

(Typo. De La Rue.)

1865-1903. *Wmk. Crown CC.*

(*a*) *P* 14.

1	**1**	1d. rose-red (25.9.65) ..	5·50	1·90
2	,,	1d. pale rose ..	6·50	2·40
3	**2**	2d. dull blue (14.3.66) ..	16·00	4·75
4	,,	2d. bright blue ..	19·00	4·75
5	**3**	3d. yellow-buff (10.3.73) ..	£120	24·00
5*a*	,,	3d. orange ..	£120	24·00
6	**4**	6d. dull purple (25.9.65) ..	£250	24·00
7	,,	6d. dull mauve ..	5·50	6·00
8	**5**	1s. green (25.9.65)	16·00	10·00

(*b*) *Imperf.*

9	**1**	1d. rose-red	£3500	

(*c*) *P* $14 \times 12\frac{1}{2}$.

10	**3**	3d. yellow-buff (1882) ..	45·00	14·00
10*a*	**4**	6d. bright mauve (1903) ..	5·50	6·00
11	**5**	1s. green (1894)	6·50	9·50
		a. Vert. strip of 3, two stamps imperf. horiz.	£2500	

Though manufactured early in 1880, stamps p. $14 \times 12\frac{1}{2}$ were not issued until the dates given above.

THREE PENCE (6) THREE PENCE (6*a*)

THREE PENCE (7) One Penny. (8)

1874 (12 Mar.–19 May). *Nos.* 1 *and* 8 *surch. diagonally.* (*a*) *With T* **6.** (" P " *and* " R " *different type.*)

12	**1**	3d. on 1d. rose-red	£1600	
13	**5**	3d. on 1s. green	£325	£250

(*b*) *With T* **6***a*. (" P " *same type as* " R ".)

13*b*	**5**	3d. on 1s. green	£400	£350

(*c*) *With T* **7** (19 May).

14	**5**	3d. on 1s. green	£325	£275

The 3d. on 1d. was not regularly issued, though a few specimens were used later. Nos. 13, 13*b* and 14, being handstamped, are found with double or partial double surcharges.

(Surch. by Queen's Printer, Donald McPhee Lee.)

1875 (March–May). *Surch. with T* **8.**

15	**2**	1d. on 2d. (No. 4) (23 Apr.) ..	£190	95·00
		a. No stop after " Penny " ..		
16	**3**	1d. on 3d. (No. 5) (8 May) ..	£135	£135
17	**5**	1d. on 1s. (No. 8) (11 Mar.) ..	75·00	75·00
		a. Surch. inverted	—	£1600
		b. No stop after " Penny " ..		

Our prices for Nos. 12/17 are for stamps in average condition; fine examples, which are seldom available, are worth a substantial premium.

9

10

(Typo. D.L.R.)

1880 (23 Mar.). *Wmk. Crown CC. P* 14.

19	**9**	½d. stone	90	1·10
20	**10**	4d. orange-red	2·25	1·40

11

ONE FARTHING

(12)

(Typo. De La Rue.)

1883–98. *Wmk. Crown CA. P 14.*

21	9	½d. dull grn. (Oct., '92)..	80	80
21a	"	½d. dp. grey-green (1893)	80	60
22	1	1d. dull rose (Dec., '83)..	15·00	2·00
23	"	1d. rose-red	12·00	90
24	"	1d. carmine-rose (1886)..	6·50	70
24a	"	1d. aniline carmine (1889)	70	20
25	2	2d. blue (Dec., '86)	6·00	1·25
26	,,	2d. aniline pur. (July, '93)	3·25	1·40
26a	"	2d. brown-purple (1898)	1·25	1·25
27	11	2½d. dp. ultram. (10.11.84)	2·75	30
27a	"	2½d. pale ultramarine ..	2·50	45
28	3	3d. grey (Jan., '86) ..	4·00	1·25
29	5	1s. yellow-brown (1893)	7·00	6·00
29a	"	1s. olive-brown	7·00	6·00
21/29a		*Set of* 7	20·00	10·00
21, 26 & 29 Optd. "Specimen"		*Set of* 3	40·00	

1901. *As Nos. 29/a but colour changed, surch. with T* **12.**

30	5	¼d. on 1s. dull grey (Optd. S. £16)	15	25
30a	,,	¼d. on 1s. bluish grey ..	20	25

13. Dry Dock.

(Typo. D.L.R.)

1902 (Nov.)–**04.** *Wmk. Crown CA. P 14.*

31	13	½d. black & green (12.03)	3·25	1·60
32	,,	1d. brown and carmine ..	3·00	15
33	,,	3d. mag. & sage-grn. (9.03)	1·25	1·75
34	10	4d. orange-brn. (18.1.04)	7·00	9·50
31/33 Optd. "Specimen"		*Set of* 3	27·00	

1906–9. *Wmk. Mult. Crown CA. P 14.*

34a	13	¼d. brown & violet (9.08)	75	1·10
35	,,	½d. black & green (12.06)	2·75	1·60
36	,,	1d. brown & carm. (4.06)	2·25	30
37	,,	2d. grey & orange (10.07)	2·50	3·50
38	,,	2½d. brn. & ultram. (12.06)	4·00	7·00
39	,,	4d. blue & choc. (11.09)	2·25	3·50
34a/39		*Set of* 6	13·00	15·00
34a, 37/39 Optd. "Specimen"		*Set of* 4	32·00	

1908–10. *Wmk. Mult. Crown CA. P 14.*

41	13	½d. green (3.09)	1·75	1·25
42	,,	1d. red (5.08)	1·75	30
43	,,	2½d. blue (14.2.10)	7·50	6·00
41/43 Optd. "Specimen"		*Set of* 3	30·00	

14

15

(Recess. (**14**). Typo. (**15**). De La Rue.)

1910–25. *Wmk. Mult. Crown CA. P 14.*

44	14	¼d. brown (26.3.12) ..	85	75
		a. Pale brown	40	75
45	,,	½d. green (4.6.10)	60	30
		a. Deep green	1·75	85
46	,,	1d. red (I) (15.10.10) ..	70	25
		a. Rose-red	2·25	25
		b. Carmine (12.19)	4·25	1·75
47	,,	2d. grey (1.13)	1·25	2·00
48	,,	2½d. blue (27.3.12)	1·10	1·10
49	,,	3d. purple/*yellow* (1.13) ..	1·60	2·00
49a	,,	4d. red/*yellow* (1.9.19) ..	1·60	2·25
50	,,	6d. purple (26.3.12) ..	5·00	6·50
		a. Pale claret (2.6.24) ..	4·00	4·50
51	,,	1s. black/*green* (26.3.12) ..	4·50	4·50
		a. Jet-black/olive (1925) ..	4·00	5·00
51b	15	2s. purple & blue/*blue*, C (19.6.20)	4·00	8·50
52	,,	2s. 6d. black & red/*blue*, C (1.4.18)	8·50	12·00
52a	,,	4s. black and carmine, C (19.6.20)	16·00	18·00
53	,,	5s. green and red/*yellow*, C (1.4.18)	16·00	18·00
54	,,	10s. green and red/*green*, C (1.4.18)	32·00	38·00
55	,,	£1 purple and black/*red*, C (1.4.18)	80·00	£120
44/55		*Set of* 15	£150	£200
44/55 Optd. "Specimen"		*Set of* 15	£160	

Nos. 44 to 51a are comb-perf. 13.8×14. No. 45 exists also line-perf. 13.75.

Beware of cleaned copies of the 10s. with faked postmarks.

WAR TAX (16) WAR TAX (17)

1918 (4 May). *Nos. 46 and 46a optd. locally with T* **16.**

56	14	1d. red	20	25
		a. Rose-red	12	20

1920 (5 Feb.). *No. 46b optd. with T* **17.**

58	14	1d. carmine	30	40

The War Tax stamps represented a compulsory levy in addition to normal postal fees until 31 Dec. 1920. Subsequently they were valid for ordinary postage.

18

(Des. by the Governor (Gen. Sir James Willcocks.) Typo. De La Rue.)

1920–21. *Tercentenary of Representative Institutions.*

A. 1st Issue. *P 14.*

(a) Wmk. Mult. Crown CA (sideways) (19.1.21).

59	18	¼d. brown, O	35	60
60	,,	½d. green, O	60	1·60
61	,,	2d. grey, O	3·25	4·50
62	,,	3d. dull and deep purple/*pale yellow*, C	4·00	7·00
63	,,	4d. black and red/*pale yellow*, C	7·00	8·50
64	,,	1s. black/*blue-green*, C ..	10·00	11·00
		(b) Wmk. Mult. Script CA (sideways).		
65	18	1d. carmine, O (11.11.20)	55	65
66	,,	2½d. brt. blue, O (11.11.20)	2·75	4·00
67	,,	6d. dull and bright purple, C (19.1.21) ..	9·50	10·00
59/67		*Set of* 9	35·00	45·00
59/67 Optd. "Specimen"		*Set of* 9	70·00	

19

(Des. H. J. Dale. Recess. De La Rue.)

B. *2nd Issue. P 14* (12.5.21).

(a) Wmk. Mult. Crown CA (sideways).

68	19	2d. slate-grey	4·00	5·00
69	,,	2½d. bright ultramarine ..	3·50	2·50
70	,,	3d. purple/*pale yellow* ..	3·50	3·25
71	,,	4d. red/*pale yellow* ..	5·00	4·50
72	,,	6d. purple	5·00	7·00
73	,,	1s. black/*green*	10·00	11·00
		(b) Wmk. Mult. Script CA (sideways).		
74	19	¼d. brown	40	65
75	,,	½d. green	1·25	1·40
76	,,	1d. deep carmine	75	50
68/76		*Set of* 9	30·00	32·00
68/76 Optd. "Specimen"		*Set of* 9	70·00	

I. II. III.

Three Types of the 1d.

I. Scroll at top left very weak and figure "1" has pointed serifs.

II. Scroll weak, "1" has square serifs and "1d" is heavy.

III. Redrawn. Scroll is completed by a strong line and "1" is thinner with long square serifs.

I. II.

Two Types of the 2½d.

I. Short, thick figures, especially of the "1"; small "d".

II. Figures taller and thinner; "d" larger.

1922–34. *Wmk. Mult. Script CA. P 14.*

76a	14	¼d. brown (7.28)	30	40
77	,,	½d. green (11.22)	15	10
78	,,	1d. scarlet (I) (11.12) ..	85	30
		a. Carmine (6.24)	2·50	30
78b	,,	1d. carmine (II) (12.25) ..	2·75	50
		c. Scarlet (8.27)	2·50	30
79	,,	1d. scarlet (III) (10.28) ..	25	20
		a. Carmine-lake (1934) ..	85	30
79b	,,	1½d. red-brown (27.3.34) ..	1·75	55
80	,,	2d. grey (12.23)	55	75
81	,,	2½d. pale sage-grn. (12.22)	4·00	4·50
		a. Deep sage-green ('24) ..	1·40	1·60
82	,,	2½d. ultram. (I) (1.12.26) ..	1·10	40
82a	,,	2½d. ultram. (II) (3.32) ..	1·10	40
83	,,	3d. ultramarine (12.24) ..	7·00	9·50
84	,,	3d. purple/*yellow* (10.26)	60	65
85	,,	4d. red/*yellow* (8.24) ..	65	1·00
86	,,	6d. purple (8.24)	1·10	1·25
87	,,	1s. black/*emerald* (10.27)	5·00	5·00
		a. Brownish black/yellow-green (1934)	11·00	13·00
88	15	2s. purple & bright blue/*pale blue*, C (1.9.27) ..	11·00	12·00
		a. Purple & blue/grey-blue, C (1931)	11·00	13·00

89 **15** 2s. 6d. black & carmine/*pale blue*, C (4.27) .. 14·00 16·00
a. Black and red/blue to deep blue, C (1929) .. .. 14·00 16·00
b. Black and pale orange-verm./grey-blue, C (8.30) .. £200 £225
c. Black and vermilion/deep blue, C (1931) .. .. 14·00 16·00
92 „ 10s. green and red/*pale emerald*, C (12.24) .. 38·00 55·00
a. Green and red/deep emer., C (1931) .. .. 38·00 55·00
93 „ 12s. 6d. grey and orange, CO (8.32) .. .. 70·00 80·00
76*a*/93 .. .. *Set of* 16 £140 £170
76*a*/93 Optd./Perf. " Specimen " *Set of* 16 £130

Nos. 76*a* to 87 exist both line-perf. 13.75 and comb-perf. 13.8 × 14 except Nos. 79*b*, 82*a* and 87*a* which are line-perf. only.

The true No. 89*b* is the only stamp on grey-blue paper; other deeper orange-vermilion shades exist on different papers.

No. 93 on ordinary paper would seem to be an error. Our prices are for the chalky paper.

Beware of fiscally used 2s. 6d., 10s. and 12s. 6d. stamps cleaned and bearing faked postmarks. Large quantities were used for a " head tax " levied on travellers leaving the country.

In 1936 a 12s. 6d. revenue stamp was issued in the same colours (inscribed " REVENUE " at each side) and during a temporary shortage of the 12s. 6d. postage stamp between 1 Feb. and April 1937 it was validated for postal use and postally used copies are known. Postmarks with later dates were obtained by favour.

1935 (6 MAY). *Silver Jubilee. As T* **13** *of Antigua. Recess. W'low. & Sons. Wmk. Mult. Script CA. P* 11 × 12.

94 1d. deep blue and scarlet .. 15 20
95 1½d. ultramarine and grey .. 30 35
96 2½d. brown and deep blue .. 75 1·40
97 1s. slate and purple .. .. 4·00 5·00
94/7 Perf. " Specimen " *Set of* 4 15·00

20. Hamilton Harbour.

22. The *Lucie*.

21. South shore near Spanish Rock.

23. Grape Bay, Paget Parish.

25. House at Par-la-Ville, Hamilton.

24. Point House, Warwick Parish.

(Recess. Bradbury, Wilkinson.)

1936 (14 APR.)–**47**. *Wmk. Mult. Script CA (sideways on horiz. designs). P* 12.

98 **20** ½d. bright green 10 12
99 **21** 1d. black and scarlet .. 15 12
100 „ 1½d. black and chocolate .. 30 25
101 **22** 2d. black and pale blue .. 2·25 2·75
102 **23** 2½d. light and deep blue .. 50 60
103 **24** 3d. black and scarlet .. 1·40 1·60
104 **25** 6d. carmine-lake & violet 30 20
a. Claret & dull violet (6.47) 20 10
105 **23** 1s. green .. .. .. 4·00 4·50
106 **20** 1s. 6d. brown 25 30
98/106 .. .. *Set of* 9 8·00 9·00
98/106 Perf. " Specimen " *Set of* 9 28·00

All are line-perf. 11.9, except printings of the 6d., from July 1951 onwards, which are comb. perf. 11.9 × 11.75.

1937 (14 MAY). *Coronation Issue. As T* **2** *of Aden. Recess. D.L.R. Wmk. Mult. Script CA. P* 14.

107 1d. scarlet 12 15
108 1½d. yellow-brown 20 10
109 2½d. bright blue 50 50
107/9 Perf. " Specimen " *Set of* 3 11·00

26. Ships in Hamilton Harbour.

27. St. David's Lighthouse.

28. Longtail, Arms of Bermuda and Native Flower.

(Des. Miss Higginbotham (T **28**). Recess. B.W.)

1938 (20 JAN.)–**1952**. *T* **22**, *T* **23** *(but with portrait of King George VI) and T* **26** *to* **28**. *Wmk. Mult. Script CA. P* 12.

110 **26** 1d. black and rose-red 7·00 1·10
a. Black and dull red (5.44) 15 15
111 „ 1½d. dp. blue & pur-brn. 30 30
a. Blue and brown (3.43) .. 50 50
b. Lt. blue & pur.-brn. (9.45) 12 12
112 **22** 2d. light blue and sepia 7·00 4·00
112*a* „ 2d. ultram. and scar. (12.11.40) .. .. 90 1·00
113 **23** 2½d. light and deep blue 1·40 55
113*a* „ 2½d. light blue and sepia-black (18.12.41) .. 35 30
b. Pale blue & sepia-black (3.43) 60 50
c. Brt. blue and deep sepia-black (23.9.52) 20 30
114 **27** 3d. black and rose-red 1·40 90
114*a* **27** 3d. black and deep blue (16.7.41) .. 20 15
114*b* **28** 7½d. blk., blue & bright green (18.12.41) .. 40 50
c. Black, blue and yellow-green (3.43) 60 70
115 **23** 1s. green 40 40
a. Bluish green (20.6.52) .. 1·10 1·10

The 1d. (110), 2d. (112), 2½d. (113/3*a*), 3d. (114) and 7½d. (114*b*) are line-perf. 11.9. The others exist line-perf. 11.9 (early printings) and comb-perf. 11.9 × 11.75 (printings from July 1950).

29. King George VI.

HALF
PENNY

X X

(**30**)

(Typo. De La Rue.)

1938 (20 JAN.)–**1953**. *T* **29**. *P* 14.

(*a*) *Wmk. Mult. Script CA.*

116 2s. deep purple & ultramarine/*grey-blue*, C .. .. 9·00 8·00
a. Purple & blue/deep bl., O ('42) 2·00 1·60
b. Purple & deep blue/pale blue, O (5.3.43) .. .. 1·10 1·00
c. Perf. 13. *Dull purple & blue/pale blue*, O (15.2.50) .. 5·00 5·00
d. Perf. 13. *Purple and deep blue/pale blue*, O (10.50) .. 1·50 1·50
117 2s. 6d. blk. & red/*grey-blue*, C 6·00 3·00
a. Black & red/pale blue, O ('42) .. 1·25 2·00
b. Perf. 13. *Black and orange-red/pale blue*, O (10.10.50) .. 1·25 2·50
c. Perf. 13. *Black & red/pale blue*, O (18.6.52) .. .. 2·00 4·00
118 5s. green and red/*yellow*, C .. 10·00 4·50
a. Pale green & red/pale yellow, O (3.43) .. .. 3·00 3·00
b. Perf. 13. *Pale green & red/pale yellow*, OC (15.2.50) .. 2·50 3·25
119 10s. green & dp. lake/*grn.*, C 30·00 28·00
a. Green and red/green, O ('39) .. 6·50 7·00
b. Perf. 13. *Green and vermilion/green*, O (21.9.51) .. 5·50 8·50
ba. Perf. 13. *Green and dull red/green*, O (16.4.53) .. 3·25 5·00
120 12s. 6d. grey and brownish orange, C .. .. 19·00 19·00
a. Grey and pale orange, OC ('43) 7·50 8·50
*b. Grey and yellow**, (O (?'47) .. £120 £130
c. Perf. 13. *Grey and pale orange*, C (10.10.50) .. 7·00 7·50

(*b*) *Wmk. Mult. Crown CA.*

121 £1 purple and black/*red*, C 35·00 32·00
a. Brown-purple and black/salmon, C ('42) .. .. 9·00 9·50
b. Perf. 13. *Violet and black/scarlet*, C (7.12.51) .. .. 7·00 7·50
110*a*/121b .. .. *Set of* 16 30·00 30·00
110/121 Perf. " Specimen " *Set of* 16 £100

In No. 116*a* the coloured surfacing of the paper is mottled with white specks sometimes accompanied by very close horizontal lines.

In Nos. 116*b*, 117*a* and 118*a* the surfacing is the same colour as the back, sometimes applied in widely spaced horizontal lines giving the appearance of laid paper.

In No. 119 the surfacing is bright yellowish green and in No. 119*a* bluish green.

Early printings of the 2s., 2s. 6d., 5s. and 10s. exist perf. 14.2 line in addition to the normal perforation which is 13.9 × 13.8 comb. These are comparatively rare.

*No. 120*b* is the so-called " lemon " shade.

1940 (20 DEC.). *No.* 110 *surch. with T* **30**.

122 **26** ½d. on 1d. black and red (*shades*) 25 35

The spacing between " PENNY " and " X " varies from 12½ mm. to 14 mm.

1946 (6 NOV.). *Victory. As Nos.* 28/9 *of Aden.*

123 1½d. brown 12 12

124 3d. blue 20 15
123/4 Perf. "Specimen" *Set of* 2 12·00

1948 (1 Dec.). *Royal Silver Wedding. As Nos.* 30/1 *of Aden.*
125 1½d. red-brown 15 15
126 £1 carmine .. .. 14·00 15·00

31. Postmaster Perot's Stamp.

(Recess. B.W.)

1949 (11 Apr.). *100th Anniv. of Postmaster Perot's Stamp. Wmk. Mult. Script CA. P* 13½.
127 **31** 2½d. blue and brown .. 25 20
128 ,, 3d. black and blue .. 25 30
129 ,, 6d. violet and green .. 30 40

1949 (10 Oct.). *75th Anniv. of Universal Postal Union. As Nos.* 114/7 *of Antigua.*
130 2½d. blue-black 12 15
131 3d. deep blue.. .. .. 20 30
132 6d. purple 25 35
133 1s. blue-green 45 45

1953 (4 June). *Coronation. As No.* 47 *of Aden, but ptd. by B. W. & Co.*
134 1½d. black and blue 30 30

32. Easter Lilies.

33. Postmaster Perot's Stamp.

34. Easter Lily.

42. Warwick Fort.

35. Bermuda Racing Dinghy.

36. Sir George Somers and *Sea Venture.*

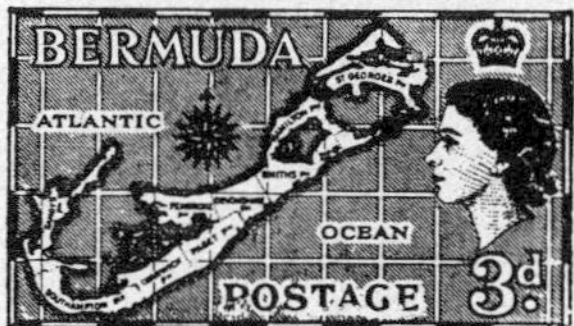

37. Map of Bermuda.

Die I. "Sandy's". Die II. "Sandys".

38. *Sea Venture,* Inter-island Boat, Coin and Perot Stamp.

39. Longtail, or Boatswain Bird.

40. Early Bermudan Coinage.

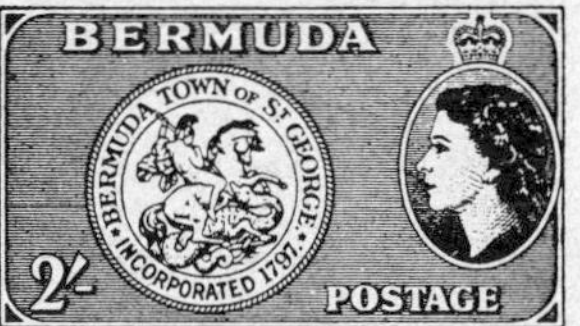

41. Arms of St. George's.

43. Hog Coin.

44. Obverse and Reverse of Hog Coin.

45. Arms of Bermuda.

(Des. C. Deakins (T **32, 37, 43**), J. Berry (T **33, 34, 36, 40**), B. Brown (T **35, 39**), D. Haig (T **38**), Pamela Braley-Smith (T **42**) and E. C. Leslie (T **44**). Recess (except £1, centre typo.), B.W.)

1953 (9 Nov.)–**62.** *Wmk. Mult. Script CA. P* 13½.
135 **32** ½d. olive-green (*shades*) 5 5
136 **33** 1d. black & red (*shades*) 5 5
137 **34** 1½d. green 8 8
138 **35** 2d. ultram. & brown-red 10 10
139 **36** 2½d. rose-red 12 12
140 **37** 3d. deep purple (I) .. 20 20
140*a* ,, 3d. dp. pur. (II) (2.1.57) 10 10
141 **33** 4d. black & bright blue 12 15
142 **38** 4½d. emerald 35 35
143 **39** 6d. black & deep turq. 25 25
143*a* ,, 8d. black & red (16.5.55) 25 30
143*b* **38** 9d. violet (6.1.58) .. 35 35
144 **40** 1s. orange 30 25
145 **37** 1s. 3d. blue (I) (*shades*) 40 35
145*b* ,, 1s. 3d. blue (II) (2.1.57) 45 45
c. Bright blue (II) (14.8.62) 55 40
146 **41** 2s. brown 70 60
147 **42** 2s. 6d. scarlet 80 75
148 **43** 5s. carmine .. .. 2·25 2·00
149 **44** 10s. dp. ultram. (*shades*) 3·75 4·25
150 **45** £1 brown, blue, red, green & bronze-green 8·00 9·50
135/150 .. .. *Set of* 18 17·00 18·00

1953 (26 Nov.). *Royal Visit. As No.* 143 *but inscr.* "ROYAL VISIT 1953" *in top left corner.*
151 **39** 6d. blk. & deep turquoise 25 25

Three Power Talks
December, 1953.
(46)

50th ANNIVERSARY
U S – BERMUDA
OCEAN RACE 1956
(47)

1953 (8 Dec.). *Three Power Talks. Nos.* 140 *and* 145 *optd. with T* **46.**
152 **37** 3d. deep purple (B.) .. 20 20
153 ,, 1s. 3d. blue (R.) 40 45
There are two settings of T **46.**

1956 (22 June). *50th Anniv. United States-Bermuda Yacht Race. Nos.* 143*a and* 145 *optd. with T* **47** *by The Bermuda Press.*
154 **39** 8d. black and red (Bk.) .. 30 30
155 **37** 1s. 3d. greenish blue (R.) 40 40

48. Perot's Post Office.

(Des. W. H. Harrington. Recess. B.W.)

1959 (1 Jan.). *Wmk. Mult. Script CA.* *P* 13½.

156	**48**	6d. black & deep mauve ..	20	25

49. Arms of King James I and Queen Elizabeth II.

(Des. W. H. Harrington. Recess; arms litho. D.L.R.)

1959 (29 July). *350th Anniv. of Settlement. Arms, red, yellow and blue; frame colours below.* *W* w.**12**, *P* 13.

157	**49**	1½d. grey-blue	12	15
158	,,	3d. drab-grey	20	20
159	,,	4d. reddish purple ..	30	30
160	,,	8d. slate-violet	70	85
161	,,	9d. olive-green	70	85
162	,,	1s. 3d. brown	1·25	1·50
157/162		.. .. *Set of* 6	3·00	3·50

50. The Old Rectory, St. George's, *c.* 1730.
51. Church of St. Peter, St. George's.
52. Government House, 1892.
53. The Cathedral, Hamilton, 1894.
54. H.M. Dockyard, 1811.
55. Perot's Post Office, 1848.
56. G.P.O., Hamilton, 1869.
57. Library, Par-la-Ville.
58. Christ Church, Warwick, 1719.
59. City Hall, Hamilton, 1960.
60. Bermuda Cottage, *c.* 1705.
61. Town of St. George.
62. Bermuda House, *c.* 1710.
63. Bermuda House, early 18th century.
64. Colonial Secretariat, 1833.
65. Old Post Office, Somerset, 1890.
66. The House of Assembly, 1815.

(Des. W. H. Harrington. Photo. Harrison.)

1962 (26 Oct.)–**65**. *W* w.**12** (*upright*). *P* 12½.

163	**50**	1d. reddish purple, black and orange	5	8
164	**51**	2d. lilac, indigo, yellow and green (*shades*) ..	8	8
		a. Lilac omitted	£100	70·00
		b. Green omitted		
		c. Imperf. (pair)		
165	**52**	3d. yell.-brown & lt. blue	8	10
		a. Yellow-brown omitted ..		
166	**53**	4d. red-brn. & magenta	10	10
167	**54**	5d. grey-blue and rose ..	20	20
168	**55**	6d. grey-bl., emer. & lt. bl.	12	10
169	**56**	8d. bright blue, bright green and orange ..	20	20
170	**57**	9d. light blue and brown	20	15
170*a*	**60**	10d. violet & ochre (8.2.65)	25	25
171	**58**	1s. black, emerald, bright blue and orange ..	20	20
172	**59**	1s. 3d. lake, grey & bistre	30	25
173	**60**	1s. 6d. violet and ochre..	1·25	1·50
174	**61**	2s. red-brown and orange	80	60
175	**62**	2s. 3d. bistre-brown and yellow-green	1·25	1·40
176	**63**	2s. 6d. bistre-brown, bl'sh green & olive-yellow	65	50
177	**64**	5s. brn.-pur. & bl.-green	1·25	1·40
178	**65**	10s. magenta, deep bluish green and buff	2·25	2·50
179	**66**	£1 black, yellow-olive and yellow-orange ..	5·00	5·50
163/79		.. .. *Set of* 18	12·00	13·00

A single copy of No. 164b is known, used on piece.

See also Nos. 195/200 and 246a.

1963 (4 June). *Freedom from Hunger. As No. 76 of Aden.*

180		1s. 3d. sepia	1·75	1·50

1963 (2 Sept.). *Red Cross Centenary. As Nos. 147/8 of Antigua.*

181		3d. red and black	30	30
182		1s. 3d. red and blue	1·75	1·75

67. Finn Boat.

(Des. V. Whiteley. Photo. D.L.R.)

1964 (28 Sept.). *Olympic Games, Tokyo.* *W* w.**12**. *P* 14×13½.

183	**67**	3d. red, violet and blue ..	20	25

1965 (17 May). *I.T.U. Centenary. As Nos. 166/7 of Antigua.*

184		3d. light blue and emerald ..	25	25
185		2s. yellow and ultramarine ..	1·50	1·50

68. Scout Badge and St. Edward's Crown.

(Des. W. H. Harrington. Photo. Harrison.)

1965 (24 July). *50th Anniv. of Bermuda Boy Scouts Association.* *W* w.**12**. *P* 12½.

186	**68**	2s. multicoloured	60	70

1965 (25 Oct.). *International Co-operation Year. As Nos. 168/9 of Antigua.*

187		4d. reddish purple and turquoise-green	20	15
188		2s. 6d. deep bluish green and lavender	1·00	1·00

1966 (24 Jan.). *Churchill Commemoration. As Nos. 170/3 of Antigua.*

189		3d. new blue	15	15
190		6d. deep green	30	35
191		10d. brown	50	55
192		1s. 3d. bluish violet ..	80	85

1966 (1 July). *World Cup Football Championships. As Nos. 176/7 of Antigua.*

193		10d. violet, yellow-green, lake and yellow-brown ..	30	30
194		2s. 6d. chocolate, blue-green, lake and yellow-brown	70	75

1966 (25 Oct.)–**69**. *As Nos. 164, etc. but wmk.* w.**12** *sideways. 1s. 6d. value also in new colour and changed design.*

195	**51**	2d. lilac, indigo, yellow and green (20.5.69) ..	8	8
196	**56**	8d. bright blue, bright green & orge. (14.2.67)	30	25
197	**60**	10d. violet & ochre (1.11.66)	30	35
198	**58**	1s. black, emerald, bright blue & orange (14.2.67)	30	30
199	**54**	1s. 6d. grey-blue & rose (1.11.66)	35	40
200	**61**	2s. red-brn. & brt. orge.	50	55
195/200		.. .. *Set of* 6	1·60	1·75

The 2d. value exists with PVA gum only, and the 8d. exists with PVA gum as well as gum arabic.

1966 (1 Dec.). *20th Anniv. of U.N.E.S.C.O. As Nos. 196/8 of Antigua.*

201		4d. slate-violet, red, yellow and orange	12	12
202		1s. 3d. orange-yellow, violet and deep olive	50	55
203		2s. black, bright purple and orange	1·00	1·00

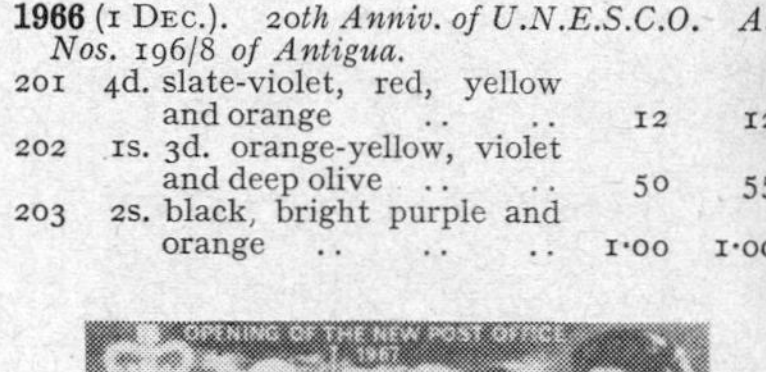

69. G.P.O. Building.

(Des. G. L. Vasarhelyi. Photo. Harrison.)

1967 (23 June). *Opening of New General Post Office, Hamilton.* *W* w.**12**. *P* 14½.

204	**69**	3d. multicoloured ..	10	10
205	,,	1s. multicoloured ..	25	25
206	,,	1s. 6d. multicoloured ..	35	35
207	,,	2s. 6d. multicoloured ..	50	50

70. Cable Ship and Chain Links.

71. Map, Telephone and Microphone.
72. Telecommunications Media.
73. Cable Ship and Marine Fauna.

(Des. V. Whiteley. Photo. Harrison.)

1967 (14 Sept.). *Inauguration of Bermuda-Tortola Telephone Service.* *W* w.**12**. *P* 14½×14.

208	**70**	3d. multicoloured	8	8
209	**71**	1s. multicoloured	30	30
210	**72**	1s. 6d. multicoloured ..	35	40
211	**73**	2s. 6d. multicoloured ..	60	65

74. Human Rights Emblem and Doves.

(Des. R. Farrar Bell. Litho. Harrison.)

1968 (1 FEB.). *Human Rights Year.* W **w.12.** P 14×14½.

212	**74**	3d. indigo, blue & dull grn.	8	8
213	,,	1s. yellow-brown, blue and light blue	30	30
214	,,	1s. 6d. black, blue & rose	40	40
215	,,	2s. 6d. grey-green, blue and yellow	55	55

II. REPRESENTATIVE GOVERNMENT.

75. Mace and Queen's Profile.

76. Houses of Parliament, and House of Assembly, Bermuda.

(Des. R. Granger Barrett. Photo. Harrison.)

1968 (1 JULY). *New Constitution.* W **w.12.** P 14.

216	**75**	3d. multicoloured ..	8	8
217	,,	1s. multicoloured ..	30	30
218	**76**	1s. 6d. greenish yellow, blk. and turquoise-blue ..	40	40
219	,,	2s. 6d. lilac, black and orange-yellow	55	55

77. Football, Athletics and Yachting.

(Des. V. Whiteley. Photo. Harrison.)

1968 (24 SEPT.). *Olympic Games, Mexico.* W **w.12.** P 12½.

220	**77**	3d. multicoloured ..	10	10
		a. Red-brown ("BERMUDA" and value) omitted ..	£350	
221	,,	1s. multicoloured ..	30	30
222	,,	1s. 6d. multicoloured ..	40	40
223	,,	2s. 6d. multicoloured ..	70	70

78. Brownie and Guide.

79. Guides and Badge.

(Des. Harrison & Sons. Litho. Format International.)

1969 (17 FEB.). *50th Anniv. of Bermuda Girl Guides.* P 14.

224	**78**	3d. multicoloured	8	8
225	,,	1s. multicoloured	30	30
226	**79**	1s. 6d. multicoloured ..	45	45
227	,,	2s. 6d. multicoloured ..	70	70

80. Emerald-studded Gold Cross and Sea weed.

81. Emerald-studded Gold Cross and Sea-bed.

(Des. K. Giles adapted by V. Whiteley. Photo. Harrison.)

1969 (29 SEPT.). *Underwater Treasure.* W **w.12** *(sideways).* P 14½×14.

228	**80**	4d. multicoloured	10	10
229	**81**	1s. 3d. multicoloured ..	30	30
230	**80**	2s. multicoloured	40	40
231	**81**	2s. 6d. multicoloured ..	60	60

(New currency. 100 cents=1 dollar.)

1c

(82)

1970 (6 FEB.). *Decimal Currency. T* **50/66** *surch. as T* **82.** *Wmk. upright* (1 *c.*, 3 *c.*, 4 *c.*, 6 *c.*, 9 *c.*, 36 *c.*) *or sideways (others).* P 12½.

232	**50**	1 c. on 1d.	5	5
233	**51**	2 c. on 2d.	5	5
		a. Lilac omitted	95·00	
		b. Pair, one without surch.		
		c. Wmk. upright	55	60
234	**52**	3 c. on 3d.	5	5
235	**53**	4 c. on 4d. (Br.)	5	5
236	**56**	5 c. on 8d.	8	8
237	**55**	6 c. on 6d.	8	10
		a. Horiz. pair, one with albino surch., the other with albino bar		
238	**57**	9 c. on 9d. (Br.)	12	12
239	**60**	10 c. on 10d.	15	15
240	**58**	12 c. on 1s.	20	20
241	**59**	15 c. on 1s. 3d.	40	55
242	**54**	18 c. on 1s. 6d.	25	25
243	**61**	24 c. on 2s.	35	45
244	**63**	30 c. on 2s. 6d.	40	50
245	**62**	36 c. on 2s. 3d.	50	55
246	**64**	60 c. on 5s.	1·10	1·50
		a. Surch. omitted* ..	75·00	
247	**65**	$1.20, on 10s.	2·50	3·00
248	**66**	$2.40, on £1	4·50	5·50
232/48		.. .. *Set of* 17	10·00	12·00

* No. 246a differs from No. 177 in that the watermark is sideways instead of upright and the gum is PVA.

83. Spathiphyllum.

(Des. W. Harrington. Photo. D.L.R.)

1970 (6 JULY)–75. *Flowers. T* **83** *and similar designs. Multicoloured.* W **w.12** *(sideways on horiz. designs).* P 14.

249		1 c. Type **83**	5	5
250		2 c. Bottlebrush	5	5
251		3 c. Oleander (*vert.*) ..	5	5
252		4 c. Bermudiana	5	5
253		5 c. Poinsettia	5	8
254		6 c. Hibiscus	8	8
255		9 c. Cereus	10	8
256		10 c. Bougainvillea (*vert.*) ..	10	8
257		12 c. Jacaranda	25	25
258		15 c. Passion-Flower ..	15	20
258*a*		17 c. As 15 c. (2.6.75) ..	15	20
259		18 c. Coralita	20	20
259*a*		20 c. As 18 c. (2.6.75) ..	20	20
260		24 c. Morning Glory	30	35
260*a*		25 c. As 24 c. (2.6.75) ..	25	30
261		30 c. Tecoma	35	40
262		36 c. Angel's Trumpet ..	35	40
262*a*		40 c. As 36 c. (2.6.75) ..	40	45
263		60 c. Plumbago	75	85
263*a*		$1 As 60 c. (2.6.75) ..	95	1·10
264		$1.20, Bird of Paradise flower	1·50	1·75
264*a*		$2 As $1.20 (2.6.75) ..	1·90	2·10
265		$2.40, Chalice Cup	2·75	3·00
265*a*		$3 As $2.40 (2.6.75) ..	3·00	3·25
249/65*a*		.. .. *Set of* 24	11·00	12·00

See also Nos. 307 etc. and 341 etc.

84. The State House, St. George's.

(Des. G. Drummond. Litho. Questa.)

1970 (12 Oct.). *350th Anniv. of Bermuda Parliament. T* **84** *and similar horiz. designs. Multicoloured.* W **w.12** *(sideways).* P 14.

266		4 c. Type **84**	8	8
267		15 c. The Sessions House, Hamilton	25	25
268		18 c. St. Peter's Church, St. George's	30	30
269		24 c. Town Hall, Hamilton ..	40	40
MS270		131×95 mm. Nos. 266/9 ..	1·10	1·10

85. Street Scene, St. George's.

(Des. G. Drummond. Litho. Questa.)

1971 (8 Feb.). *"Keep Bermuda Beautiful". T* **85** *and similar horiz. designs. Multicoloured. W* w.**12** *(sideways). P* 14.

271	4 c. Type **85**	8	8
272	15 c. Horshoe Bay	30	30
273	18 c. Gibb's Hill Lighthouse	35	35
274	24 c. Hamilton Harbour ..	45	45

86. Building of the *Deliverance.*

(Des. E. Amos. Adapted C. Abbott. Litho. Questa.)

1971 (10 May). *Voyage of the "Deliverance". T* **86** *and similar multicoloured designs. W* w.**12** *(sideways on 4 c. and 24 c.). P* 14.

275	4 c. Type **86**	12	12
276	15 c. *Deliverance* and *Patience* at Jamestown	35	35
277	18 c. Wreck of the *Sea Venture*	35	35
278	24 c. *Deliverance* and *Patience* on the high seas ..	45	45

The 15 c. and 18 c. are vert. designs.

87. Green overlooking Ocean View.

(Des. G. Drummond. Litho. D.L.R.)

1971 (1 Nov.). *Golfing in Bermuda. T* **87** *and similar horiz. designs. Multicoloured. W* w.**12** *(sideways). P* 13.

279	4 c. Type **87**	10	10
280	15 c. Golfers at Port Royal ..	30	30
281	18 c. Castle Harbour ..	35	35
282	24 c. Belmont	50	50

HEATH-NIXON DECEMBER 1971

(88)

1971 (20 Dec.). *Anglo-American Talks. Nos.* 252 *and* 258/60 *optd. with T* **88** *by Format.*

283	4 c. Bermudiana	10	10
284	15 c. Passion Flower ..	25	30
285	18 c. Coralita	35	35
286	24 c. Morning Glory	45	45

89. Bonefish.

(Des. Maynard Reece. Litho. B.W.)

1972 (21 Aug.). *World Fishing Records. T* **89** *and similar horiz. designs. Multicoloured. W* w.**12**. *P* $13\frac{1}{2}\times14$.

287	4 c. Type **89**	8	8
288	15 c. Wahoo	25	25
289	18 c. Yellowfin Tuna ..	30	30
290	24 c. Greater Amberjack ..	45	45

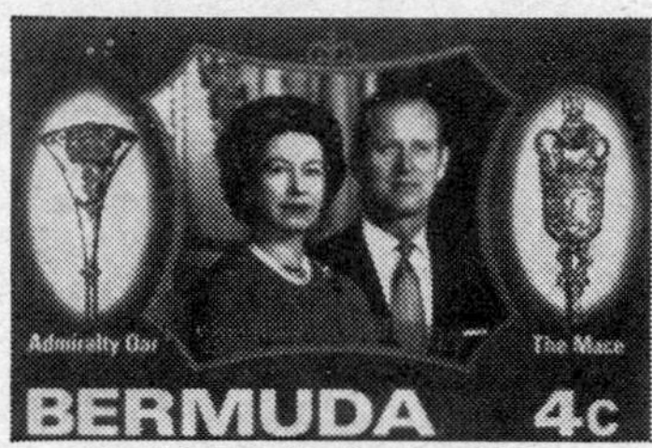

90. "Admiralty Oar" and Mace.

(Des. (from photograph by D. Groves) and photo. Harrison.)

1972 (20 Nov.). *Royal Silver Wedding. Multicoloured; background colour given. W* w.**12**. *P* $14\times14\frac{1}{2}$.

291	**90**	4 c. bright bluish violet	8	10
292	,,	15 c. rose-carmine ..	35	40

91. Palmetto.

(Des. Jennifer Toombs. Litho. J.W.)

1973 (3 Sept.). *Tree Planting Year. T* **91** *and similar vert. designs. Multicoloured. W* w.**12** *(sideways). P* 14.

293	4 c. Type **91**	5	5
294	15 c. Olivewood Bark ..	30	30
	a. Brown (Queen's head and value) omitted		
295	18 c. Bermuda Cedar ..	35	35
296	24 c. Mahogany	40	40

1973 (21 Nov.*). *Royal Wedding. As Nos.* 165/6 *of Anguilla. Centre multicoloured. W* w.**12** *(sideways). P* $13\frac{1}{2}$.

297	15 c. bright mauve	25	25
298	18 c. steel blue	30	35

*This is the local date of issue. The Crown Agents released these stamps on the 14th of November.

92. Bernard Park, Pembroke, 1973.

(Des. J.W. Ltd. Litho. Questa.)

1973 (17 Dec.). *Lawn Tennis Centenary. T* **9** *and similar horiz. designs. Multicoloure W* w.**12**. *P* 14.

299	4 c. Type **92**	8	
300	15 c. Clermont Court, 1873	25	2
301	18 c. Leamington Spa Court, 1872	35	3
302	24 c. Staten Island Courts, 1874	40	3

1974 (13 June)–**76**. *As No.* 249 *etc., but W* w.**12** *upright.*

307	5 c. Poinsettia	5	
308	6 c. Hibiscus	10	1
311	12 c. Jacaranda	12	1
315	30 c. Tecoma (11.6.76) ..	30	3

Nos. 303/319 have been allocated to this issu

93. Weather Vane, City Hall.

(Des. G. Drummond. Litho. Questa.)

1974 (24 June). *50th Anniv. of Rotary in Bermu da. T* **93** *and similar horiz. designs. Mult coloured. W* w.**12** *(sideways). P* 14.

320	5 c. Type **93**	10	1
321	17 c. St. Peter's Church, St. George's	25	2
322	20 c. Somerset Bridge	30	3
323	25 c. Map of Bermuda, 1626 ..	30	3

94. Jack of Clubs and "good bridge hand".

(Des. J.W. Ltd. Litho. Format.)

1975 (27 Jan.). *World Bridge Championship Bermuda. T* **94** *and similar vert. design Multicoloured. W* w. **12**. *P* 14.

324	5 c. Type **94**	10	1
325	17 c. Queen of Diamonds and Bermuda Bowl	25	2
326	20 c. King of Hearts and Bermuda Bowl	30	3
327	25 c. Ace of Spades and Bermuda Bowl	30	3

95. Queen Elizabeth II and the Duke of Edinburgh.

(Des. and photo. Harrison.)

1975 (17 Feb.). *Royal Visit.* W **w.14**. P 14×14½.

328	**95**	17 c. multicoloured ..	25	25
329	,,	20 c. multicoloured ..	30	30

96. " Cavalier " Flying-boat, 1937.

(Des. R. Granger Barrett. Litho. Questa.)

1975 (28 Apr.). *50th Anniv. of Air-mail Service to Bermuda.* T **96** *and similar horiz. designs. Multicoloured.* W **w.14** (*sideways*). P 14.

330	5 c. Type **96** ..	5	5
331	17 c. Airship " Los Angeles ", 1925 ..	25	25
332	20 c. Lockheed " Constellation ", 1946 ..	25	30
333	25 c. Boeing " 747 ", 1970 ..	30	35
MS334	128×85 mm. Nos. 330/3	80	90

97. Supporters of American Army raiding Royal Magazine.

(Des. J. E. Cooter. Litho. J.W.)

1975 (27 Oct.). *Bicentenary of Gunpowder Plot, St. George's.* T **97** *and similar horiz. designs. Multicoloured.* W **w.14** (*sideways*). P 13×13½.

335	5 c. Type **97** ..	8	8
336	17 c. Setting off for raid ..	20	20
337	20 c. Loading gunpowder aboard American ship ..	20	25
338	25 c. Gunpowder on beach	25	30
MS339	165 × 138 mm. Nos. 335/8. P 14 (*sold for* 75 c.) ..	85	

1975 (8 Dec.)–**76.** *As Nos.* 250 *and* 254 *but* W **w.14** (*sideways*).

341	2 c. Bottlebrush ..	5	5
345	6 c. Hibiscus (11.6.76) ..	5	5

Nos. 340/56 have been reserved for any further additions to this issue.

98. Launching Bathysphere.

(Des. G. Drummond. Litho. Questa.)

1976 (29 Mar.). *50th Anniv. of Bermuda Biological Station.* T **98** *and similar multicoloured designs.* W **w.14** (*sideways on* 17 *and* 20 c.). P 14.

357	5 c. Type **98** ..	5	8
358	17 c. View from the sea (*horiz.*)	20	20
359	20 c. H.M.S. *Challenger*, 1873 (*horiz.*) ..	20	25
360	25 c. Beebe's bathysphere descent, 1934 ..	25	30

99. *Christian Radich.*

(Des. R. Granger Barrett. Litho. J.W.)

1976 (15 June). *Tall Ships Race,* 1976. T **99** *and similar horiz. designs. Multicoloured.* W **w.12** (*sideways*). P 13.

361	5 c. Type **99** ..	5	8
362	12 c. *Juan Sebastian de Elcano*	12	15
363	17 c. U.S.C.G. *Eagle* ..	20	20
364	20 c. *Winston S. Churchill* ..	20	25
365	40 c. *Kruzenshtern* ..	45	50
366	$1 *Cutty Sark* trophy ..	1·10	1·25
361/6	.. *Set of* 6	1·90	2·20

100. Silver Trophy and Club Flags.

(Des. C. Abbott. Litho. Questa.)

1976 (16 Aug.). *75th Anniv. of the St. George's v. Somerset Cricket Cup Match.* T **100** *and similar horiz. designs. Multicoloured.* W **w.14** (*sideways*). P 14½ × 14.

367	5 c. Type **100** ..	5	5
368	17 c. Badge and Pavilion, St. George's Club ..	20	20
369	20 c. Badge and Pavilion, Somerset Club ..	20	25
370	25 c. Somerset playing field ..	30	35

BOTSWANA.

(Formerly Bechuanaland.)

INDEPENDENCE.

47. National Assembly Building.

48. Abattoir, Lobatsi. (*As T* **47.**)

49. National Airways " Dakota ".

50. State House, Gaberones. (*As T* **49.**)

(Des. R. Granger Barrett. Photo. Harrison.)

1966 (30 Sept.). *Independence.* P 14½.

202	**47**	2½ c. multicoloured ..	5	5
		a. Imperf. (pair) ..	£100	
203	**48**	5 c. multicoloured ..	12	12
204	**49**	15 c. multicoloured ..	35	35
205	**50**	35 c. multicoloured ..	55	55

REPUBLIC OF BOTSWANA

(51)

1966 (30 Sept.). *Nos.* 168/81 *of Bechuanaland optd. as T* **51.**

206	**28**	1 c. yellow, red, black and lilac ..	5	5
207	**29**	2 c. orange, black and yellow-olive ..	8	8
208	**30**	2½ c. carmine, green, black and bistre ..	10	10
209	**31**	3½ c. yellow, black, sepia and pink ..	12	12
210	**32**	5 c. yellow, blue, black and buff ..	15	15
211	**33**	7½ c. brown, red, black and apple-green ..	20	25
212	**34**	10 c. red, yellow, sepia and turquoise-green	25	25
213	**35**	12½ c. buff, blue, red and grey-black ..	30	30
214	**36**	20 c. yellow-brown & drab	40	40
215	**37**	25 c. dp. brown & lemon	45	50
216	**38**	35 c. deep blue & orange	65	75
217	**39**	50 c. sepia and olive ..	1·25	1·60
218	**40**	1 r. black and cinnamon	2·25	2·75
219	**41**	2 r. brown & turq.-blue	4·00	5·50
206/219		.. *Set of* 14	9·50	11·00

52. Golden Oriole.

53. African Hoopoe.
54. Ground-scraper Thrush. **55.** Blue Waxbill.
56. Secretary Bird. **57.** Yellow-billed Hornbill.
58. Crimson-breasted Shrike. **59.** Malachite Kingfisher.
60. Fish Eagle. **61.** Grey Lory.
62. Scimitar-bill. **63.** Knob-billed Duck.
64. Crested Barbet. **65.** Diederick Cuckoo.

(Des. D. M. Reid-Henry. Photo. Harrison.)

1967 (3 Jan.). P 14×14½.

No.	Type	Description	Unused	Used
220	**52**	1 c. multicoloured ..	5	5
		a. Error. Wmk. **105** of Malta	†	—
221	**53**	2 c. multicoloured ..	5	5
222	**54**	3 c. multicoloured ..	5	8
223	**55**	4 c. multicoloured ..	8	10
224	**56**	5 c. multicoloured ..	10	12
225	**57**	7 c. multicoloured ..	12	15
226	**58**	10 c. multicoloured ..	15	20
227	**59**	15 c. multicoloured ..	30	55
228	**60**	20 c. multicoloured ..	35	45
229	**61**	25 c. multicoloured ..	45	55
230	**62**	35 c. multicoloured ..	55	65
231	**63**	50 c. multicoloured ..	1·40	1·60
232	**64**	1 r. multicoloured ..	2·00	2·50
233	**65**	2 r. multicoloured ..	3·75	4·75
220/33		.. .. *Set of* 14	8·50	11·00

A used copy of the 20 c. has been seen with the pale brown colour missing, resulting in the value (normally shown in white) being omitted.

The 1, 2, 4, 7 and 10 c. values exist with PVA gum as well as gum arabic.

66. Students and University.

(Des. V. Whiteley. Photo. Harrison.)

1967 (7 Apr.). *First Conferment of University Degrees.* P 14×14½.

No.	Type	Description	Unused	Used
234	**66**	3 c. sepia, ultramarine and light orange-yellow ..	5	5
235	,,	7 c. sepia, ultramarine and light greenish blue ..	15	15
236	,,	15 c. sepia, ultram. and rose	30	30
237	,,	35 c. sepia, ultramarine and light violet	50	50

67. Chobe Bush-buck.

68. Sable Antelope.
69. Fishing on the Chobe River.

(Des. G. L. Vasarhelyi. Photo. Harrison.)

1967 (2 Oct.). *Chobe Game Reserve.* P 14.

No.	Type	Description	Unused	Used
238	**67**	3 c. multicoloured ..	5	5
239	**68**	7 c. multicoloured ..	12	15
240	**69**	35 c. multicoloured ..	55	60

70. Arms of Botswana and Human Rights Emblem.

71 and **72.** Arms of Botswana and Human Rights Emblem (*arranged differently*).

(Litho. De La Rue.)

1968 (8 Apr.). *Human Rights Year.* P 13½×13.

No.	Type	Description	Unused	Used
241	**70**	3 c. multicoloured ..	8	8
242	**71**	15 c. multicoloured ..	30	35
243	**72**	25 c. multicoloured ..	45	45

73. Rock Paintings, Tsodilo Hills.

74. Girl wearing Ceremonial Beads. (*Vert.*, 30×48 *mm.*)

75. "Baobab Trees" (Thomas Baines).

76. National Museum and Art Gallery. (*Reduced. Actual size* 72×19 *mm.*)

(Litho. De La Rue.)

1968 (30 Sept.). *Opening of National Museum and Art Gallery.* P 12½ (7 *c.*), 12½×13½ (15 *c.*), *or* 13×13½ (*others*).

No.	Type	Description	Unused	Used
244	**73**	3 c. multicoloured ..	5	5
245	**74**	7 c. multicoloured ..	12	15
246	**75**	10 c. multicoloured ..	20	25
247	**76**	15 c. multicoloured ..	30	35
MS248		132×82 mm. Nos. 244/7. P 13	85	85

77. African Family, and Star over Village.

(Des. Mrs. M. E. Townsend and J. E. Cooter. Litho. Enschedé.)

1968 (11 Nov.). *Christmas.* P 13×14.

No.	Type	Description	Unused	Used
249	**77**	1 c. multicoloured ..	5	5
250	,,	2 c. multicoloured ..	8	8
251	,,	5 c. multicoloured ..	12	15
252	,,	25 c. multicoloured ..	55	60

78. Scout, Lion and Badge in Frame.

79. Scouts cooking over Open Fire. (*Vert.*)
80. Scouts around Camp Fire. (*Horiz.*)

(Des. De La Rue. Litho. Format International.)

1969 (21 Aug.). *22nd World Scout Conference, Helsinki.* P 13½×14.

No.	Type	Description	Unused	Used
253	**78**	3 c. multicoloured ..	8	10
254	**79**	15 c. multicoloured ..	35	45
255	**80**	25 c. multicoloured ..	45	55

81. Woman, Child and Christmas Star.

(Des. V. Whiteley. Litho. Harrison.)

1969 (6 Nov.). *Christmas.* P 14½×14.

No.	Type	Description	Unused	Used
256	**81**	1 c. pale blue & chocolate	5	5
257	,,	2 c. pale yellow-olive and chocolate	8	8
258	,,	4 c. yellow and chocolate	10	12
259	,,	35 c. chocolate & bluish vio.	50	55
MS260		86×128 mm. Nos. 256/9. P 14½ (*shades*)	1·00	1·00

82. Diamond Treatment Plant, Orapa.

Des. J. Waddington Ltd. Litho. Harrison.)

970 (23 MAR.). *Developing Botswana.* T **82** *and similar designs. Multicoloured.* P $14\frac{1}{2}\times14$ (3 *c.*, 7 *c.*) *or* $14\times14\frac{1}{2}$ (*others*).

61	3 c. Type **82**	5	5
62	7 c. Copper-nickel mining ..	15	15
63	10 c. Copper-nickel mine, Selebi-Pikwe (*horiz.*) ..	20	20
64	35 c. Orapa diamond mine, and diamonds (*horiz.*) ..	55	65

83. Mr. Micawber (*David Copperfield*).

Des. V. Whiteley. Litho. Walsall Security Printers Ltd.)

970 (6 JULY). *Death Centenary of Charles Dickens.* T **83** *and similar horiz. designs. Multicoloured.* P 11.

65	3 c. Type **83**	12	12
66	7 c. Scrooge (*A Christmas Carol*)	15	15
67	15 c. Fagin (*Oliver Twist*) ..	30	30
68	25 c. Bill Sykes (*Oliver Twist*)	45	50
IS269	114 × 81 mm. Nos. 265/8	1·10	1·40

84. U.N. Building and Emblem.
Illustration reduced. Actual size 59 × 21 *mm.*)

Des. J. E. Cooter. Litho. Walsall Security Printers Ltd.)

970 (24 OCT.). *25th Anniv. of United Nations.* P 11.

70 **84**	15 c. bright blue, chestnut and silver	35	35

85. Crocodile.

(Des. A. A. Vale. Litho. Questa.)

970 (3 NOV.). *Christmas.* T **85** *and similar horiz. designs. Multicoloured.* P 14.

71	1 c. Type **85**	5	5
72	2 c. Giraffe	8	8
73	7 c. Elephant	15	15
74	25 c. Rhinoceros	55	60
IS275	128 × 90 mm. Nos. 271/4	85	90

86. Sorghum.

(Des. J. Waddington Ltd. Litho. Questa.)

1971 (6 APRIL). *Important Crops.* T **86** *and similar horiz. designs. Multicoloured.* P 14.

276	3 c. Type **86**	5	5
277	7 c. Millet	15	15
278	10 c. Maize	25	25
279	35 c. Groundnuts	55	60

87. Map and Head of Cow.

(Des. L. D. Curtis. Litho. Harrison.)

1971 (30 SEPT.). *Fifth Anniv. of Independence.* T **87** *and similar vert. designs inscr.* "PULA" (*local greeting*). P $14\frac{1}{2}\times14$.

280	3 c. blk., brn. & apple-green	8	8
281	4 c. blk., new blue & pale bl.	10	10
282	7 c. black and red-orange ..	20	20
283	10 c. multicoloured	25	25
284	20 c. multicoloured	35	40
280/4	.. .. *Set of* 5	80	85

Designs:—4 c. Map and cogs; 7 c. Map and zebra; 10 c. Map and sorghum stalk crossed by tusk; 20 c. Arms and map of Botswana.

88. King bringing gift of gold.

(Des. A. A. Vale. Litho. Questa.)

1971 (11 NOV.). *Christmas.* T **88** *and similar vert. designs. Multicoloured.* P 14.

285	2 c. Type **88**	8	8
286	3 c. King bearing frankincense	10	10
287	7 c. King bearing myrrh ..	20	25
288	20 c. Three Kings behold the star	40	45
MS289	85 × 128 mm. Nos. 285/8	90	90

89. Orion.

(Des. R. Granger Barrett. Litho. Questa.)

1972 (24 APR.). *"Night Sky".* T **89** *and similar vert. designs.* P 14.

290	3 c. turquoise-blue, black and red	5	5
291	7 c. dull blue, black and yellow	15	15
292	10 c. dull green, black and orange	20	25
293	20 c. deep violet-blue, black and blue-green	35	45

Constellations:—7 c. The Scorpion; 10 c. The Centaur; 20 c. The Cross.

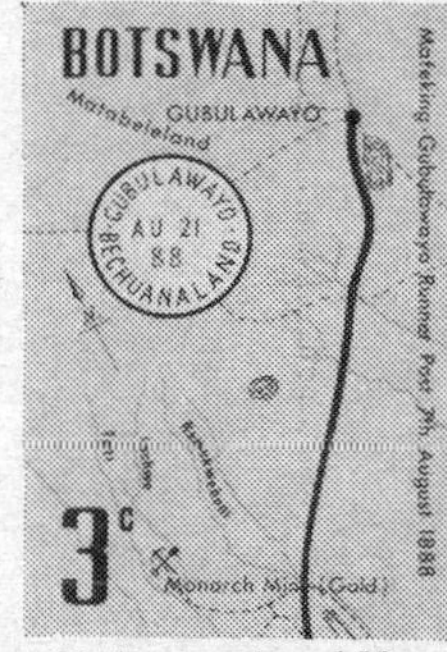

90. Postmark and Map.

(Des. M. F. Bryan; adapted G. Drummond. Litho. A. & M.)

1972 (21 AUG.). *Mafeking-Gubulawayo Runner Post.* T **90** *and similar vert. designs. Multicoloured.* P $13\frac{1}{2}\times13$.

294	3 c. Type **90**	8	8
295	4 c. Bechuanaland stamp and map	10	10
296	7 c. Runners and map ..	20	25
297	20 c. Mafeking postmark and map	55	60
MS298	84 × 216 mm. Nos. 294/7 vertically *se-tenant*, forming a composite map design	1·10	1·10

91. Cross, Map and Bells.

(Des. locally; adapted J. E. Cooter. Litho. Questa.)

1972 (6 NOV.). *Christmas. Vert. designs each with Cross and Map as* T **91.** *Multicoloured.* P 14.

299	2 c. Type **91**	5	5
300	3 c. Candle	8	8
301	7 c. Christmas tree ..	15	20
302	20 c. Star and holly ..	50	55
MS303	96 × 119 mm. Nos. 299/302	70	70

92. Thor.

(Des. Mrs. E. Elphick; adapted Jennifer Toombs. Litho. Questa.)

1973 (23 Mar.). *I.M.O./W.M.O. Centenary. T* **92** *and similar designs showing Norse myths. Multicoloured. P* 14.

304	3 c. Type **92**	5	5
305	4 c. Sun God's chariot (*horiz.*)	8	8
306	7 c. Ymir, the frost giant..	15	15
307	20 c. Odin and Sleipnir (*horiz.*)	35	40

93. Livingstone and River Scene.

(Des. G. L. Vasarhelyi. Litho. Walsall Security Printers, Ltd.)

1973 (10 Sept.). *Death Centenary of Dr. Livingstone. T* **93** *and similar horiz. design. Multicoloured. P* 13½.

308	3 c. Type **93**	8	8
309	20 c. Livingstone meeting Stanley	50	55

94. Donkey and Foal at Village Trough.

(Des. locally; adapted G. L. Vasarhelyi. Litho. Questa.)

1973 (3 Dec.). *Christmas. T* **94** *and similar multicoloured designs. P* 14.

310	3 c. Type **94**	5	5
311	4 c. Shepherd and flock (*horiz.*)	8	8
312	7 c. Mother and child ..	15	15
313	20 c. Kgotla meeting (*horiz.*)	35	40

95. Gaberone Campus.

(Des. locally; adapted P. B. Powell. Litho. Questa.)

1974 (8 May). *Tenth Anniv. of University of Botswana, Lesotho and Swaziland. T* **95** *and similar horiz. designs. Multicoloured. P* 14.

314	3 c. Type **95**	5	5
315	7 c. Kwaluseni Campus ..	10	12
316	20 c. Roma Campus	35	35
317	35 c. Map and flags of the three countries..	55	60

96. Methods of Mail Transport.
(*Illustration reduced. Actual size* 58 × 21 *mm.*)

(Des. locally; adapted G. L. Vasarhelyi. Litho. J.W.)

1974 (29 May). *Centenary of Universal Postal Union. T* **96** *and similar horiz. designs. Multicoloured. P* 14.

318	2 c. Type **96**	5	5
319	3 c. Post Office, Palapye, *circa* 1889	8	8
320	7 c. Bechuanaland Police Camel Post, *circa* 1900 ..	12	15
321	20 c. Mail-planes of 1920 and 1974	40	45

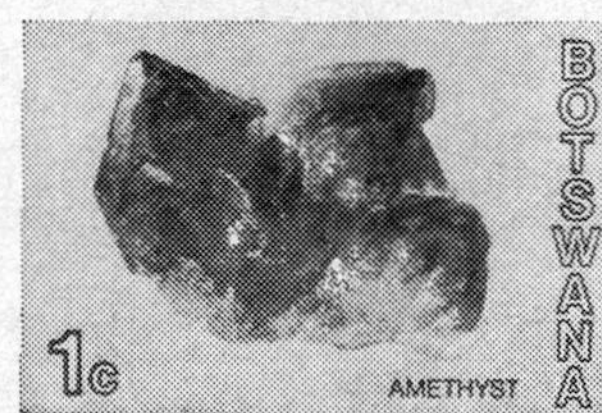

97. Amethyst.

(Des. locally; adapted PAD Studio. Photo. Enschedé.)

1974 (1 July). *Botswana Minerals. T* **97** *and similar horiz. designs. Multicoloured. P* 14 × 13.

322	1 c. Type **97**	5	5
323	2 c. Agate—"Botswana Pink"	5	5
324	3 c. Quartz	5	5
325	4 c. Copper nickel	8	8
326	5 c. Moss agate	8	8
327	7 c. Agate	10	12
328	10 c. Stilbite	12	15
329	15 c. Moshaneng Banded Marble	20	20
330	20 c. Gem diamonds	25	30
331	25 c. Chrysotile	30	35
332	35 c. Jasper	45	50
333	50 c. Moss quartz	60	70
334	1 r. Citrine	1·25	1·40
335	2 r. Chalcopyrite	2·50	2·75
322/35	.. .. *Set of* 14	5·50	6·00

98. *Stapelia variegata.*

(Des. M. F. Bryan. Litho. Questa.)

1974 (4 Nov.). *Christmas. T* **98** *and similar vert. designs showing flowers. Multicoloured. P* 14.

336	2 c. Type **98**	5	5
337	7 c. *Hibiscus lunarifolius* ..	10	12
338	15 c. *Ceratotheca triloba* ..	25	25
339	20 c. *Nerine laticoma*	30	35
MS340	85 × 130 mm. Nos. 336/9	70	80

99. President Sir Seretse Khama.

(Des. M. F. Bryan; adapted G. L. Vasarhelyi. Photo. Enschedé.)

1975 (24 Mar.). *Tenth Anniv. of Self-Government. P* 13½ × 13.

341	**99** 4 c. multicoloured ..	8	8
342	,, 10 c. multicoloured ..	15	20
343	,, 20 c. multicoloured ..	25	30
344	,, 35 c. multicoloured ..	45	50
MS345	93 × 130 mm. Nos. 341/4	95	1·10

100. Ostrich.

(Des. M. F. Bryan. Litho. Questa.)

1975 (23 June). *Rock Paintings, Tsodilo Hills. T* **100** *and similar horiz. designs. Multicoloured. P* 14.

346	4 c. Type **100**	8	8
347	10 c. Rhinocerus	15	20
348	25 c. Hyena	35	40
349	35 c. Scorpion	45	55
MS350	150 × 150 mm. Nos. 346/9	1·10	1·25

101. Map of British Bechuanaland, 1885.

(Des. M. F. Bryan and G. L. Vasarhelyi. Litho. Harrison.)

1975 (13 Oct.). *Anniversaries. T* **101** *and similar multicoloured designs. P* 14×14½ (25 *c.*) *or* 14½×14 (*others*).

51	6 c. Type **101**	8	10
52	10 c. Chief Khama, 1875 ..	15	20
53	25 c. Chiefs Sebele, Bathoen and Khama, 1895 (*horiz.*)	35	35

Events:—6 c. 90th Anniv. of Protectorate; 0 c. Centenary of Khama's Accession; 25 c. oth Anniv. of Chiefs' visit to London.

102. *Aloe marlothii.*

(Des. M. F. Bryan. Litho. Questa.)

975 (3 Nov.). *Christmas. T* **102** *and similar vert. designs showing aloes. Multicoloured. P* 14½.

54	3 c. Type **102**	5	5
55	10 c. *Aloe lutescens*	10	12
56	15 c. *Aloe zebrina*	15	15
57	25 c. *Aloe littoralis*	25	30

103. Drum.

(Des. M. F. Bryan. Litho. Questa.)

976 (1 Mar.). *Traditional Musical Instruments. T* **103** *and similar horiz. designs. Multicoloured. P* 14.

58	4 c. Type **103**	5	5
59	10 c. Hand Piano	10	12
60	15 c. Segankuru (violin) ..	15	15
61	25 c. Kudu Signal Horn ..	25	30

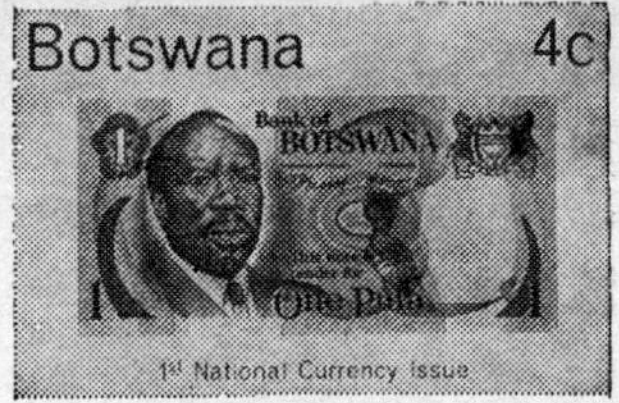

104. One Pula Note.

(Des. M. F. Bryan from banknotes by D.L.R. Litho. Questa.)

1976 (28 June). *First National Currency. T* **104** *and similar horiz. designs. Multicoloured. P* 14.

362	4 c. Type **104**	5	5
363	10 c. Two pula note	12	15
364	15 c. Five pula note	20	20
365	25 c. Ten pula note	30	35
MS366	163 × 107 mm. Nos. 362/5	70	

(New Currency. 100 thebe = 1 pula.)

1t

(**105**)

1976 (23 Aug.). *Nos.* 322/35 *surch. as T* **105** (*Nos.* 369, 374 *and* 380 *in gold*).

367	1 t. on 1 c. Type **97**	5	5
368	2 t. on 2 c. Agate—" Botswana Pink "	5	5
369	3 t. on 3 c. Quartz ..	5	5
370	4 t. on 4 c. Copper nickel ..	5	5
371	5 t. on 5 c. Moss agate ..	5	5
372	7 t. on 7 c. Agate	8	8
373	10 t. on 10 c. Stilbite	12	12
374	15 t. on 15 c. Moshaneng Banded Marble	15	20
375	20 t. on 20 c. Gem diamonds ..	20	25
376	25 t. on 25 c. Chrysotile ..	30	30
377	35 t. on 35 c. Jasper	40	45
378	50 t. on 50 c. Moss quartz ..	55	60
379	1 p. on 1 r. Citrine	1·10	1·25
380	2 p. on 2 r. Chalcopyrite ..	2·25	2·50
367/80	.. .. *Set of* 14	4·75	5·25

106. Botswanan Cattle.

(Des. M. F. Bryan. Litho. Questa.)

1976 (30 Sept.). *Tenth Anniv. of Independence. T* **106** *and similar multicoloured designs. P* 14.

381	4 t. Type **106**	5	5
382	10 t. Deer, Okavango Delta (*vert.*)	12	15
383	15 t. School and pupils ..	20	20
384	25 t. Rural weaving (*vert.*) ..	30	35
385	35 t. Miner (*vert.*)	45	50
381/5	.. .. *Set of* 5	1·00	1·10

Nos. 381/5 were printed on sand-grained paper which has an uneven surface.

107. *Colophospermum mopane.*

(Des. M. F. Bryan. Litho. J.W.)

1976 (1 Nov.). *Christmas. T* **107** *and similar horiz. designs showing trees. Multicoloured. P* 13.

386	3 t. Type **107**	5	5
387	4 t. *Baikiaea plurijuga* ..	5	5
388	10 t. *Sterculia rogersii*	12	15
389	25 t. *Acacia nilotica*	30	35
390	40 t. *Kigelia africana*	50	55
386/90	.. .. *Set of* 5	90	1·00

POSTAGE DUE STAMPS.

REPUBLIC OF

BOTSWANA

(D 4)

BOTSWANA 1c POSTAGE DUE

D **5.** Elephant.

1967 (1 Mar.). *Nos.* D10/12 *of Bechuanaland optd. with Type* D **4**.

D13	1 c. carmine	5	8
D14	2 c. violet	8	10
D15	5 c. green	10	12

(Des. and litho. B.W.)

1971 (9 June). *P* 13½.

D16	D **5**	1 c. carmine	5	5
D17	,,	2 c. bluish violet ..	5	5
D18	,,	6 c. sepia	5	8
D19	,,	14 c. blue-green	15	20

BRITISH ANTARCTIC TERRITORY.

1. M.V. *Kista Dan.*

2. Manhauling
3. Muskeg (tractor).
4. Skiing.
5. Beaver (aircraft).
6. R.R.S. *John Biscoe.*
7. Camp Scene.
8. H.M.S. *Protector.*
9. Sledging.
10. Otter (aircraft).
11. Huskies.
12. Helicopter.
13. Snocat (tractor).
14. R.R.S. *Shackleton.*
15. Antarctic Map.
16. H.M.S. *Endurance.*

(Des. Bradbury, Wilkinson (No. 15*a*), M. Goaman (others). Recess. Bradbury, Wilkinson.)

1963 (1 Feb.)–**69.** *W* w.**12.** *P* 11 × 11½.

1	**1**	½d. deep blue	5	5
2	**2**	1d. brown	5	5
3	**3**	1½d. orge.-red & brn.-pur.	8	8
4	**4**	2d. purple	10	12
5	**5**	2½d. myrtle-green	12	12
6	**6**	3d. deep blue	15	15
7	**7**	4d. sepia	20	20
8	**8**	6d. olive & deep ultram.	20	20
9	**9**	9d. olive-green	30	35
10	**10**	1s. deep turquoise-blue..	40	45
11	**11**	2s. deep vio. & orge.-sepia	1·25	1·75
12	**12**	2s. 6d. blue	1·40	1·90
13	**13**	5s. red-orange & rose-red	2·50	3·00
14	**14**	10s. deep ultram. & emer.	5·50	7·00
15	**15**	£1 black and light blue	11·00	14·00
15*a*	**16**	£1 red and brownish black (1.12.69)	15·00	17·00
1/15*a*		.. .. *Set of* 16	35·00	40·00

1966 (24 Jan.). *Churchill Commemoration. As Nos.* 170/3 *of Antigua.*

16	½d. new blue	12	12
17	1d. deep green..	30	30
18	1s. brown	3·50	4·50
19	2s. bluish violet	4·50	5·50

17. Lemaire Channel and Icebergs.

(Des. R. Granger Barrett. Litho. Format International.)

1969 (6 Feb.). *25th Anniv. of Continuous Scientific Work.* *T* **17** *and similar horiz. designs.* *W* w.12 (*sideways*). *P* 14.

20	3½d. black, pale blue & ultram.	20	25
21	6d. multicoloured	35	45
22	1s. blk., pale blue and verm.	55	65
23	2s. blk., orange & turq.-blue	1·10	1·40

Designs:—6d. Radio Sonde balloon; 1s. Muskeg pulling tent equipment; 2s. Surveyors with theodolite.

≡ ½p

(18)

1971 (15 Feb.). *Decimal Currency. As Nos.* 1/14, *but glazed paper, colours changed and surch. as T* **18.**

24	**1**	½p. on ½d. blue	5	5
25	**2**	1p. on 1d. pale brown ..	5	8
26	**3**	1½p. on 1½d. red and pale brown-purple	8	8
27	**4**	2p. on 2d. bright purple ..	8	10
28	**5**	2½p. on 2½d. green	10	12
29	**6**	3p. on 3d. blue	15	20
30	**7**	4p. on 4d. bistre-brown ..	20	25
31	**8**	5p. on 6d. olive & ultram.	25	30
32	**9**	6p. on 9d. dull green ..	30	30
33	**10**	7½p. on 1s. turquoise-blue ..	30	45
34	**11**	10p. on 2s. violet and orange-sepia	45	65
35	**12**	15p. on 2s. 6d. pale blue ..	90	1·10
36	**13**	25p. on 5s. orange and pale rose-red	1·60	1·90
37	**14**	50p. on 10s. ultram. & emer.	3·25	3·75
24/37		.. .. *Set of* 14	7·00	8·50

19. Setting up Camp.

(Des. M. Goaman. Recess and litho. Enschedé.)

1971 (23 June). *10th Anniv. of Antarctic Treaty. Vert. designs each including Antarctic Map and Queen Elizabeth, as T* **19.** *Multicoloured.* *W* w.12 (*sideways*). *P* 14 × 13.

38	1½p. Type **19**	12	12
39	4p. Snow petrels	45	50
40	5p. Weddell seals	45	50
41	10p. Adelie penguins	90	1·00

20. Seals and Emperor Penguins.

(Des. (from photograph by D. Groves) and photo. Harrison.)

1972 (13 Dec.*). *Royal Silver Wedding. Multicoloured; background colour given.* *W* w.**12.** *P* 14 × 14½.

42	**20**	5p. red-brown	55	1·10
43	,,	10p. brown-olive	1·10	2·50

*This is the local release date; they were issued by the Crown Agents on 20 November.

GIBBONS BUY STAMPS

21. James Cook and *Resolution.*

(Des. J. W. Ltd. Litho. Questa.)

1973 (14 Feb.). *T* **21** *and similar vert. design Multicoloured.* *W* w.**12** (*sideways*). *P* 14 × 14½

44	½p. Type **21** (*shades*)	8	
45	1p. Thaddeus Von Bellingshausen and *Vostok* ..	5	
46	1½p. James Weddell and *Jane*	5	
47	2p. John Biscoe and *Tula* ..	5	
48	2½p. J. S. C. Dumont d'Urville and *Astrolabe*	8	
49	3p. James Clark Ross and *Erebus*	5	
50	4p. C. A. Larsen and *Jason*	8	
51	5p. Adrien de Gerlache and *Belgica*	8	
52	6p. Otto Nordenskjöld and *Antarctic*	10	
53	7½p. W. S. Bruce and *Scotia*	12	
54	10p. Jean-Baptiste Charcot and *Pourquoi Pas?* ..	20	
55	15p. Ernest Shackleton and *Endurance*	25	
56	25p. Hubert Wilkins and "San Francisco" ..	45	
57	50p. Lincoln Ellsworth and "Polar Star"	85	
58	£1 John Rymill and *Penola*	1·75	2·
44/58	.. .. *Set of* 15	4·00	4·

The 25 and 50p. show aircraft; the rest sho ships.

See also No. 64.

1973 (23 Dec.*). *Royal Wedding. As Nos.* 165 *of Anguilla. Centre multicoloured.* *W* w. (*sideways*). *P* 13½.

59	5p. ochre	25	
60	15p. light turquoise-blue ..	45	

*This is the local date of issue: the Crow Agents released the stamps on 14th Novembe

22. Churchill and Churchill Peninsula, B.A.T.

(Des. G. L. Vasarhelyi. Litho. Format.)

1974 (10 Dec.*). *Birth Centenary of Sir Winst Churchill.* *T* **22** *and similar horiz. desig Multicoloured.* *W* w.**12** (*sideways on 5p.* *P* 14.

61	5p. Type **22**	25	
62	15p. Churchill and *Trespassey* ("Operation Tabarin", 1943)	50	
MS63	114 × 88 mm. Nos. 61/2 ..	75	

*This is the local date of issue: the Crow Agents released the stamps on 30th November.

1975 (11 June). *As No.* 44 *but W* w.**14** *uprig*

64	½p. Type **21**	5	

Nos. 65/78 have been reserved for any furth additions to this issue.

BRITISH CENTRAL AFRICA.

See **NYASALAND PROTECTORATE.**

BRITISH COLUMBIA & VANCOUVER ISLAND.

1

(Typo. De La Rue & Co.)

1860. *No wmk. Imperf.*
1 **1** 2½d. pale dull red £1000

1860. *No wmk. P* 14.
2 **1** 2½d. deep reddish rose .. £120 90·00
3 " 2½d. pale reddish rose .. £120 90·00

From June 20, 1864, to Nov. 1, 1865, the 2½d. was sold for 3d., and did duty as a 3d. provisional No. 1 was never actually issued.

VANCOUVER ISLAND.

2 3

(Typo. De La Rue.)

1865 (19 Sept.). *Wmk. Crown CC.* (*a*) *Imperf.*
11 **2** 5 c. rose £11000 £5000
12 **3** 10 c. blue £700 £550

Medium or poor copies of Nos. 11 and 12 can be supplied at much lower prices, when in stock.

(*b*) *P* 14.
13 **2** 5 c. rose .. .. .. 75·00 65·00
14 **3** 10 c. blue .. .. .. 75·00 65·00

BRITISH COLUMBIA.

4

(Typo. De La Rue.)

1865 (1 Nov.)–**67.** *Wmk. Crown CC. P* 14.
21 **4** 3d. deep blue .. .. 24·00 20·00
22 „ 3d. pale blue (1867) .. .. 24·00 20·00

On 19 Nov., 1866, British Columbia and Vancouver Island were consolidated as one territory called British Columbia, after which date the current stamps of each colony were distributed and used throughout the combined territory.

Though bearing the names of both colonies the 2½d. of 1860 was mainly used for inland postage in British Columbia.

TWO CENTS (5) **5.CENTS.5** (6)

1868–71. T **4** *in various colours. Wmk. Crown CC. Surch. as T* **5** *or* **6**.

(*a*) *P* 12½ (March, 1869).
23 5 c. red (Bk.) £200 £200
24 10 c. lake (B.) £180 £150
25 25 c. yellow (V.) £160 £150
26 50 c. mauve (R.) £160 £150
27 1 dol. green (G.) £375 £300

(*b*) *P* 14.
28 2 c. brown (Bk.) (Jan., '68) .. 25·00 22·00
29 5 c. pale red (Bk.) (May, '69) 32·00 30·00
30 10 c. lake (B.) £350
31 25 c. yellow (V.) (July, '69) .. 42·00 38·00
32 50 c. mauve (R.) (Feb., '71) .. £180
33 1 dol. green (G.) £400

Nos. 30 and 33 were not issued.

The stamps of British Columbia were withdrawn from use on July 20, 1871, when the Colony joined the Dominion of Canada.

BRITISH EAST AFRICA.

I. BRITISH EAST AFRICA COMPANY ADMINISTRATION.

BRITISH EAST AFRICA COMPANY HALF ANNA (1)

BRITISH EAST AFRICA COMPANY 1 ANNA (2)

(Surch. De La Rue.)

1890 (May). *Stamps of Great Britain* (*Queen Victoria*). *Surch. as T* **1** *or* **2** (1 *a. and* 4 *a.*).
1 **57** ½ a. on 1d. deep purple .. £150 85·00
2 **73** 1 a. on 2d. green and carm. .. £150 85·00
3 **78** 4 a. on 5d. dull pur. & blue .. £140 70·00

A copy of the ½ a. with the short crossbar of "F" in "HALF" omitted exists in the Royal Collection but is the only known example.

3

4

(Litho. Bradbury, Wilkinson & Co.)

1890 (Oct.)–**1894.** *P* 14.
4 **3** ½ a. dull brown 65 65
a. Imperf. (pair) .. .. 90·00 85·00
b. Deep brown ('93) 60 60
ba. Imperf. (pair) .. .. 85·00 70·00
bb. Imperf. between (horiz. pr.) £350 £190
bc. Imperf. between (vert. pr.) £140 £140
c. Pale brown ('94) 30 30
5 „ 1 a. blue-green .. .. 1·10 1·10
aa. "ANL" (broken "D") .. 17·00 21·00
a. Imperf. (pair) .. .. £110 90·00
ab. "ANL" (broken "D") ..
b. Deep blue-green ('94) .. 30 1·10
ba. Imperf. (pair) .. .. £120 85·00
6 „ 2 a. vermilion .. .. 1·10 1·25
a. Imperf. (pair) £180 £120
7 „ 2½ a. black/*yellow-buff* ('91) .. 8·50 3·00
a. Black/pale buff ('92) .. 5·50 1·10
b. Black/bright yellow ('93) .. 1·75 1·00
bb. Imperf. (pair) £140 £110
bc. Imperf. between (horiz. pr.) £120 £110
bd. Imperf. between (vert. pr.) £180 £120
8 „ 3 a. black/*dull red* ('91) .. 2·00 2·25
a. Black/bright red ('93) .. 60 70
ab. Imperf. (pair) £120 £110
ac. Imperf. between (horiz. pr.) £120 £110
ad. Imperf. between (vert. pr.) £110 £100
9 „ 4 a. yellow-brown .. .. 1·10 1·75
a. Imperf. (pair) £240 £120
10 „ 4 a. grey (*imperf.*) £300 £330
11 „ 4½ a. dull violet ('91) .. .. 6·50 5·00
a. Brown-purple ('93) .. .. 1·10 3·75
ab. Imperf. (pair) £170 £110
ac. Imperf. between (horiz. pr.) £300 £300
ad. Imperf. between (vert. pr.) £130 £120
12 **3** 8 a. blue .. .. .. 1·75 2·25
a. Imperf. (pair) £240 £120
13 „ 8 a. grey .. .. .. 65·00 70·00
14 „ 1 r. carmine .. .. .. 2·10 3·00
a. Imperf. (pair) £375 £120
15 „ 1 r. grey .. .. .. 50·00 60·00
16 **4** 2 r. brick-red .. .. 4·25 4·75
17 „ 3 r. slate-purple .. .. 3·00 4·75
18 „ 4 r. ultramarine .. .. 4·50 5·50
19 „ 5 r. grey-green .. .. 12·00 9·50
4/19 .. .. *Set of* 15 (*perf.*) £140 £145

For the 5 a. and 7½ a. see Nos. 29/30.

The paper of Nos. 7, 7*a*, 7*b*, 8 and 8*a* is coloured on the surface only.

Printings of 1890/92 are on thin paper having the outer margins of the sheets imperf. and bearing sheet watermark "PURE LINEN WOVE BANK" and "W. C. S. & Co." in a monogram, the trademark of the makers, Messrs. William Collins, Sons & Co.

1893/94 printings are on thicker coarser paper with outer margins perforated through the selvedge and without watermark. Single specimens cannot always be distinguished by lack of watermark alone.

Nos. 7 (coloured through) and 16/19 on thick unwatermarked paper are from a special printing made for presentation purposes.

Forgeries of the 4 a., 8 a., 1 r. grey and 2 to 5 r. exist. The latter are common and can be distinguished by the scroll above "LIGHT" where there are five vertical lines of shading in the forgeries and seven in the genuine stamps. Forged cancellations exist on the commoner stamps. Beware of "imperf." stamps made by trimming margins of stamps from marginal rows.

1891. *Provisionals.* (*a*) *New value handstamped in dull violet, and manuscript initials in black.*
20 **3** "½ Anna" on 2 a. vermilion ("A.D.") (Jan.) £280 £130
a. "½ Anna" double .. — £225
21 „ "1 Anna" on 4 a. brown ("A.B.") (Feb.) £550 £225

(*b*) *Manuscript value and initials in black.*
22 **3** "½ Anna" on 2 a. vermilion ("A.B.") (Jan.) £425 £120
a. Error. "½ Annas" ("A.B.") — £225
23 „ "½ Anna" on 2 a. vermilion ("A.D.") .. .. .. — £120
a. Error. "½ Annas" .. — £225
24 „ "½ Anna" on 3 a. black/*dull red* ("A.B.") (May) £350 £170
25 „ "1 Anna" on 3 a. black/*dull red* ("V.H.M.") (June) .. £350 £170
26 „ "1 Anna" on 4 a. brown ("A.B.") (March) .. £325 £160

A.D. = Andrew Dick, representative of the Company in Mombasa.

A.B. = Archibald Brown, cashier of the Company.

V.H.M. = Victor H. Mackenzie, bank manager in Mombasa.

5 ANNAS. (5)

(Surch. Bradbury, Wilkinson.)

1894 (1 Nov.). *Surch. as T* **5**.
27 **3** 5 a. on 8 a. blue .. .. 13·00 28·00
28 „ 7½ a. on 1 r. carmine .. 14·00 28·00
27/28 Handstamped "Specimen" *Set of* 2 30·00

Forgeries exist.

1894 (Dec.). *No wmk. P* 14.
29 **3** 5 a. black/*grey-blue* .. .. 70 3·50
30 „ 7½ a. black .. .. 70 3·50
29/30 Handstamped "Specimen" *Set of* 2 25·00

These two stamps have "LD" after "COMPANY" in the inscription.

The paper of No. 29 is coloured on the surface only.

1895 (19 Feb.). *Surch. with manuscript value and initials* ("T.E.C.R.").
31 **3** "½ anna" on 3 a. black/*dull red* .. .. 42·00 17·00
32 „ "1 anna" on 3 a. black/*dull red* £450 £325

T.E.C.R. = T. E. C. Remington, postmaster.

II. IMPERIAL ADMINISTRATION.

British
East
Africa
(6)

(Handstamped at Mombasa.)

1895 (1 July). *Handstamped with T* **6**.
33 **3** ½ a. brown .. .. .. 10·00 6·50
a. Double .. .. .. 28·00 28·00
34 „ 1 a. green .. .. .. 14·00 15·00
a. Double .. .. .. 30·00 30·00
35 „ 2 a. vermilion .. .. 26·00 26·00
a. Double .. .. .. 40·00 40·00
36 „ 2½ a. black/*yellow* .. .. 23·00 15·00
a. Double .. .. .. 40·00 40·00
37 „ 3 a. black/*dull red* .. .. 12·00 12·00
38 „ 4 a. yellow-brown .. .. 12·00 12·00
a. Double .. .. .. 40·00 40·00
39 „ 4½ a. dull violet .. .. 28·00 26·00
a. Double .. .. .. 50·00 50·00
b. Brown-purple .. .. 80·00 65·00
ba. Double .. .. ..
40 „ 5 a. black/*grey-blue* .. .. 40·00 30·00
a. Double £130 £130
41 „ 7½ a. black .. .. .. 20·00 20·00
a. Double .. .. .. 50·00 50·00
42 „ 8 a. blue .. .. .. 23·00 23·00
a. Double .. .. .. 65·00 65·00
b. Inverted £275
43 „ 1 r. carmine .. .. .. 13·00 14·00
a. Double .. .. .. 50·00 65·00
44 **4** 2 r. brick-red .. .. 30·00 35·00
45 „ 3 r. deep purple .. .. 26·00 30·00
a. Double .. .. .. 90·00 90·00
b. Inverted .. .. ..
46 „ 4 r. ultramarine .. .. 35·00 30·00
a. Double .. .. .. 90·00 90·00
47 „ 5 r. grey-green .. .. 65·00 80·00
a. Double £130 £130
33/47 .. .. *Set of* 15 £350 £350
Forgeries exist.

2½ (7) British East Africa (8) British East Africa (9)

1895 (Oct.). *No.* 39 *surch. locally with T* **7**.
48 **3** 2½ on 4½ a. dull violet (R.) .. 20·00 17·00
a. Opt. (T 6) double .. .. 90·00 80·00

(Overprinted at the offices of *The Gazette for Zanzibar.*)

1895 (Nov.). *Stamps of India* (*Queen Victoria*) *optd. with T* **8** *or* **9** (2 *r.* to 5 *r.*).
49 **23** ½ a. deep green 80 80
a. "Br1tish" for "British" .. £225 £250
b. "Br1tish" for "British" .. 30·00
c. "Afr1ca" for "Africa" .. 30·00
50 **25** 1 a. plum .. .. .. 1·10 1·40
a. "Br1tish" for "British" .. £225
b. "Br1tish" for "British" .. 30·00
c. "Afr1ca" for "Africa" .. 40·00
51 **26** 1½ a. sepia .. .. .. 1·75 1·75
a. "Br1tish" for "British" .. 32·00
b. "Afr1ca" for "Africa" .. 40·00
52 **27** 2 a. ultramarine .. .. 80 1·10
a. "Br1tish" for "British" .. £210
b. "Br1tish" for "British" .. 32·00
c. "Afr1ca" for "Africa" .. 32·00 32·00
53 **36** 2½ a. green .. .. .. 3·00 1·75
a. "B1itish" for "British" .. £275
b. "Bpitish" for "British" .. £360
c. "Br1tish" for "British" .. — £225
d. "Eas" for "East" .. £120 £130
e. "Br1tish" for "British" .. 35·00 35·00
f. "Afr1ca" for "Africa" .. 32·00
54 **28** 3 a. brown-orange .. .. 3·00 3·00
a. "Br1tish" for "British" .. 32·00 32·00
b. "Afr1ca" for "Africa" .. 42·00
55 **29** 4 a. olive-green .. .. 4·50 4·50
a. Slate-green .. .. 4·50 4·50
b. "Br1tish" for "British" .. 32·00 32·00
c. "Afr1ca" for "Africa" .. 42·00
56 **21** 6 a. pale brown .. .. 6·00 7·00
a. "Br1tish" for "British" .. 60·00
b. "Afr1ca" for "Africa" .. 42·00
57 **31** 8 a. dull mauve .. .. 13·00 14·00
a. "Br1tish" for "British" .. 42·00
b. "Afr1ca" for "Africa" .. 50·00
c. Magenta .. .. 9·00 10·00
ca. "Easr" for "East" .. — £250
58 **32** 12 a. purple/*red* .. .. 6·50 8·00
a. "Br1tish" for "British" .. 40·00 38·00
b. "Afr1ca" for "Africa" .. 55·00
59 **33** 1 r. slate .. .. .. 13·00 16·00
60 **37** 1 r. green and carmine .. 7·00 9·00
a. "Easr" for "East" .. £250
b. "Br1tish" for "British" .. 45·00
c. "Afr1ca" for "Africa" .. 50·00
d. Opt. double, one sideways 45·00 50·00
61 **38** 2 r. carmine and yell.-brn. 15·00 20·00
62 „ 3 r. brown and green .. 20·00 22·00
63 „ 5 r. ultramarine & violet .. 22·00 23·00
a. Opt. double £300
49/63 .. .. *Set of* 15 £110 £120

Dates of issue: 11 Nov., ½, 1, 2 and 2½ a.; 25 Nov., remainder.

The 2½ a. is known on cover used on 31 Oct. but as Zanzibar did not take control of the posts until 10 November it was probably released in error.

The relative horizontal positions of the three lines of the overprint vary considerably but the distance vertically between the lines of the overprint is constant.

There are other varieties, such as inverted "s" in "British", wide and narrow "B", and inverted "V" for "A" in "Africa".

The 2, 3, and 5 r., normally overprinted in larger type than the lower values, are also known with a smaller overprint, but were not issued thus for postal purposes (*price £60 un. per set*).

Forgeries exist.

2½ (10)

11

1895 (Dec.). *No.* 51 *surch. locally with T* **10**, *in bright red.*
64 **26** 2½ on 1½ a. sepia .. .. 12·00 12·00
a. Inverted "1" in fraction .. 75·00

No. 51 also exists surcharged with *T* **12**, **13** and **14** in *brown-red*. These stamps were sent to the Postal Union authorities at Berne, but were never issued to the public. (*Price £18 each un.*)

(Recess. D.L.R.)

1896 (19 May)–**1901**. *Wmk. Crown CA. P* 14.
65 **11** ½ a. yellow-green 15 15
66 „ 1 a. carmine-red 35 12
a. Bright rose-red 65 12
b. Rosine (1901) .. .. 4·00 1·00
67 „ 2 a. chocolate 85 65
68 „ 2½ a. deep blue .. .. 1·25 70
a. Violet-blue .. .. 1·25 45
69 „ 3 a. grey .. .. .. 90 1·40
70 „ 4 a. deep green .. .. 1·75 70
71 „ 4½ a. orange-yellow .. .. 1·25 2·00
72 „ 5 a. yellow-bistre .. .. 3·00 2·00
73 „ 7½ a. mauve .. .. .. 3·00 3·50
74 „ 8 a. grey-olive .. .. 1·25 2·10
75 „ 1 r. pale dull blue .. .. 7·00 6·00
a. Ultramarine .. .. 6·50 5·50
76 „ 2 r. orange .. .. 11·00 7·00
77 „ 3 r. deep violet .. .. 11·00 7·00
78 „ 4 r. carmine-lake .. .. 11·00 9·00
79 „ 5 r. sepia .. .. .. 11·00 9·00
a. Thin "U" in "RUPEES" £275
65/79 .. .. *Set of* 15 60·00 45·00
65/79 Optd. "Specimen" *Set of* 15 90·00

1897 (Jan.). *Stamps of Zanzibar* (1896 *issue*) *optd. with T* **8**. *Wmk. Single Rosette.*
80 **13** ½ a. green and red .. 14·00 10·00
81 „ 1 a. indigo and red .. 26·00 26·00
82 „ 2 a. red-brown and red .. 14·00 10·00
83 „ 4½ a. orange and red .. 15·00 10·00
84 „ 5 a. bistre and red .. 15·00 11·00
85 „ 7½ a. mauve and red .. 22·00 17·00
80/85 .. .. *Set of* 6 95·00 75·00

The above six stamps exist with an overprint similar to T **8** but normally showing a stop after "Africa.". These overprints (in red on the 1 a.) were made officially to supply the U.P.U. However, the stop does not always show. Pieces are known showing overprints with and without stop *se-tenant* (including the red overprint on the 1 a.).

Stamps of Zanzibar, wmk. "Multiple Rosettes" and overprinted with T **8** *are forgeries.*

2½ (12) 2½ (13) 2½ (14)

(Surcharged locally.)

1897 (Jan.). *Nos.* 157 *and* 162 *of Zanzibar optd. with T* **8** *and further surch. locally, in red.*
86 **12** 2½ on 1 a. indigo and red .. 20·00 16·00
a. "2" over "1" for "½" £225
b. Opt. Type 8 double .. £1100
87 **13** 2½ on 1 a. indigo and red .. 21·00 17·00
88 **14** 2½ on 1 a. indigo and red .. 21·00 17·00
a. Opt. Type 8 double .. £1400
89 **12** 2½ on 3 a. grey and red .. 17·00 16·00
a. "2" over "1" for "½" £275
90 **13** 2½ on 3 a. grey and red .. 20·00 16·00
91 **14** 2½ on 3 a. grey and red .. 21·00 16·00
86/91 .. .. *Set of* 6 £110 90·00

The setting of the 2½ surcharge on the 1 a. and 3 a. stamps overprinted as T **8** but *with stop* after "Africa." differs from that on Nos. 86/91 and includes a "2" over "1" in T **14**.

Both the notes after No. 85 also apply here.

15

(Recess. De La Rue.)

1897 (Nov.)–**1903**. *Wmk. Crown CC. P* 14.
92 **15** 1 r. grey-blue .. .. 8·50 8·00
a. Dull blue (1901) .. .. 5·50 4·25
b. Bright ultramarine (1903) 20·00 25·00
93 „ 2 r. orange .. .. 20·00 20·00
94 „ 3 r. deep violet .. .. 22·00 25·00
95 „ 4 r. carmine .. .. 35·00 42·00
96 „ 5 r. deep sepia .. .. 42·00 60·00
97 „ 10 r. yellow-bistre (S. £30) .. 80·00 85·00
98 „ 20 r. pale green (S. £45) .. £225 £225
99 „ 50 r. mauve (S. £100) .. £550 £600
92/96 Optd. "Specimen" *Set of* 5 60·00

In 1903 stamps of British E. Africa were superseded by those of East Africa and Uganda Protectorate. (*See* Kenya, Uganda and Tanganyika.)

BRITISH FORCES IN EGYPT.

All issues of Egypt will be found listed in Vol. 2 of the Foreign Overseas Catalogue.

For GREAT BRITAIN stamps used in Army Field Offices in Egypt see Great Britain Index to Stamps Used Abroad list.

From 1st November, 1932, to 29th February, 1936, members of the British Forces in Egypt and their families were allowed to send letters to the British Isles at reduced rates. Special seals which were on sale in booklets at N.A.A.F.I. Institutes and Canteens were used instead of Egyptian stamps, and were stuck on the back of the envelopes, letters bearing the seals being franked on the front with a hand-stamp inscribed "EGYPT POSTAGE PREPAID" in a double circle surmounted by a crown.

A 1

(Des. Lt.-Col. C. Fraser. Typo. Hanbury, Tomsett & Co., London.)

1932 (1 Nov.)–**33.** *P* 11.

(*a*) *Inscr.* " POSTAL SEAL ".

A1 **A 1** 1 p. deep blue and red .. 4·00 2·50

(*b*) *Inscr.* " LETTER SEAL ".

A2 **A 1** 1 p. dp. blue & red (8.33) 4·00 1·60

A 2

(Des. Sgt. W. F. Lait. Litho. Walker & Co., Amalgamated Press, Cairo.)

1932 (26 Nov.)–**35.** *Christmas Seals. P* 11½.

A3 **A 2** 3 m. black/*azure* .. .. 6·00 6·00
A4 „ 3 m. brown-lake (13.11.33) 2·50 2·25
A5 „ 3 m. deep blue (17.11.34) 1·60 1·60
A6 „ 3 m. vermilion (23.11.35) 85 85
a. Pale vermilion (19.12.35) 2·25 2·25

A 3

(Des. Miss Waugh. Photo. Harrison.)

1934 (1 June)–**35.** (*a*) *P* 14½ × 14.

A7 **A 3** 1 p. carmine .. .. 6·00 1·60
A8 „ 1 p. green (5.12.34) .. 1·25 80

(*b*) *P* 13½ × 14.

A9 **A 3** 1 p. carmine (24.4.35) .. 55 30

JUBILEE
COMMEMORATION
1935

(A 4)

1935 (6 May). *Silver Jubilee. As No.* A9, *but colour changed and optd. with Type* A **4**, *in red.*

A10 **A 3** 1 p. ultramarine .. .. 20·00 20·00

Xmas 1935
3 Milliemes

(A 5)

1935 (16 Dec.). *Provisional Christmas Seal. No.* A9 *surch. with Type* A **5**.

A11 **A 3** 3 m. on 1 p. carmine .. 6·50 4·00

The seals and letter stamps were replaced by the following Army Post stamps issued by the Egyptian Postal Administration.

A **6.** King Fuad I.

A **7.** King Farouk.

(Types A **6**/A **7.** Photo. Survey Dept., Cairo.)

1936. *W* **48** *of Egypt* (*Mult. Crown and Arabic* " F "). *P* 13½ × 14.

A12 **A 6** 3 m. green (9.11.36) .. 20 20
A13 „ 10 m. carmine (1.3.36) .. 40 20

1939 (12 Dec.). *W* **48** *of Egypt* (*Mult. Crown and Arabic* " F "). *P* 13 × 13½.

A14 **A 7** 3 m. green 12 12
A15 „ 10 m. carmine 12 12

These stamps were withdrawn in April 1941 but the concession, without the use of special stamps, continued until October 1951 when the postal agreement was abrogated.

BRITISH GUIANA.

For GREAT BRITAIN stamps used in British Guiana with " A 03 " or " A 04 " obliterations, see index to Great Britain Stamps Used Abroad list.

I. CROWN COLONY.

1

(Set up and printed at the office of the *Royal Gazette*, Georgetown, British Guiana.)

1850 (1 July)–**51.** *Type-set. Black impression. Medium wove paper.*

Prices are for—I. Cut square. II. Cut round.

			I *Used.*	II *Used.*
1	**1**	2 c. *rose* (1.3.51)	—	£35000
2	„	4 c. *orange*	£7500	£1500
3	„	4 c. *lemon-yellow* ..	£12000	£2000
4	„	8 c. *green*	£5000	£1200
5	„	12 c. *blue*	£2500	£1100
6	„	12 c. *indigo*	£4500	£1100
7	„	12 c. *pale blue*	£4250	£1400
		a. " 2 " of " 12 " with straight foot		
		b. " 1 " of " 12 " omitted ..	†	£14000

Pelure paper.

8 **1** 4 c. *pale yellow* .. £11000 £1800

These stamps were initialled by the postmaster, or the Post Office clerks, before they were issued. The initials are—E. T. E. D(alton), E. D. W(ight), J. B. S(mith), H. A. K(illikelley), and W. H. L(ortimer). There are several types of each value.

2

3

(Litho. Waterlow & Sons.)

1852 (1 Jan.). *Surface-coloured paper. Imperf.*

			Un.	*Used*
9	**2**	1 c. black/*magenta*	£4000	£2500
10	„	4 c. black/*deep blue* ..	£5000	£2500

There are two types of each value.

Reprints, on thicker paper and perf. 12½, were made in 1865. (*Price* £5 *either value.*)

Reprints with the perforations removed are sometimes offered as genuine originals.

CONDITION.—*Prices for Nos.* 9 *to* 21 *are for fine copies. Poor to medium specimens can be supplied when in stock at much lower rates.*

(Dies eng. and stamps litho. Waterlow & Sons.)

1853–59. *Imperf.*

11 **3** 1 c. vermilion £1200 £300

This 1 c. in *reddish brown* is probably a proof.

ONE CENT
A

ONE CENT
B

ONE CENT
C

ONE CENT
D

A. " O " large and 1 mm. from left corner.
B. " O " small and ¾ mm. from left corner.
C. " O " small and ¾ mm. from left corner. " NT " widely spaced.
D. " ONE " close together, " O " 1¼ mm. from left corner.

Fresh lithographic transfers with varying labels of value. White line above value (1858–59).

12	**3**	1 c. dull red (A)	£800	£350
13	„	1 c. brownish red (A) ..	£1900	£350
14	„	1 c. dull red (B)	£1100	£350
15	„	1 c. brownish red (B) ..	£1900	£350
16	„	1 c. dull red (C)	£1100	£350
17	„	1 c. dull red (D)	£1100	£700

4

5

1853–59. *Imperf.*

18	**4**	4 c. deep blue	£425	£200
		a. Retouched	£550	£240
19	„	4 c. blue (1855)	£350	£200
20	„	4 c. pale blue (1859) ..	£300	£150
		a. Retouched	£450	£200

These stamps are generally found with a white line or traces of it above the label of value and lower corner figures. In some stamps on the sheet this line is missing, owing to having been retouched, and in these cases a line of colour usually appears in its place.

The 1 c. and 4 c. stamps were reprinted in 1865 from fresh transfers of five varieties. These are on *thin* paper and perf. 12½.

1860 (May). *Figures in corners framed. Imperf.*

21 **5** 4 c. blue £850 £225

6

(Type-set and printed at the *Official Gazette* by Baum and Dallas, Georgetown.)

1856. (a) *Surface-coloured paper.*

23	**6**	1 c. black/*magenta*	—	£225000
24	,,	4 c. black/*magenta* (Feb.)	—	£2700
25	,,	4 c. black/*rose-carmine* (Sept.)	—	£3500
26	,,	4 c. black/*blue* (Oct.)	—	£13000

(b) *Paper coloured through.*

27	**6**	4 c. black/*deep blue* (Aug.)	—	£18000

These stamps, like those of the first issue, were initialled before being issued; the initials are—E.T.E.D., E.D.W., C.A. W(atson), and W.H.L.

The 4 c. is known in eight types differing in the position of the inscriptions.

PAPERMAKERS' WATERMARKS. Seven different papermakers' watermarks were used in the period 1860 to 1875 and stamps bearing portions of these are worth a premium.

7

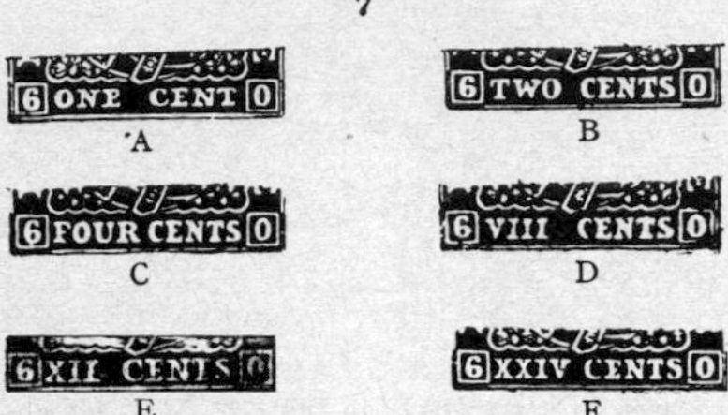

A B C D E F

(Dies eng. and litho. Waterlow.)

1860 (From JUNE). *Tablets of value as illustrated. Thick paper.* P 12.

29	**7**	1 c. pale rose	£225	55·00
30	,,	2 c. deep orange	27·00	12·00
31	,,	2 c. pale orange	27·00	12·00
32	,,	4 c. deep blue	60·00	14·00
33	,,	4 c. blue	55·00	12·00
34	,,	8 c. brownish rose	65·00	15·00
35	,,	8 c. pink	60·00	14·00
36	,,	12 c. lilac	90·00	12·00
37	,,	12 c. grey-lilac	65·00	12·00
38	,,	24 c. deep green	£225	21·00
39	,,	24 c. green	£225	21·00

The 1 c. was reprinted in 1865 on *thin* paper, P 12½—13, and in a different shade. *Price* £2.

The 12 c. in both shades is frequently found surcharged with a large "5d." in *red*; this is to denote the proportion of postage repayable by the colony to Great Britain for oversea letters.

1861 (1 Nov.). *Colour changed. Thick paper.* P 12.

40	**7**	1 c. reddish brown	60·00	23·00

1862–66. (a) *Thin paper.* P 12 (1862).

41	**7**	1 c. brown	75·00	45·00
42	,,	1 c. black	15·00	7·50
43	,,	2 c. orange	15·00	6·00
44	,,	4 c. blue	18·00	7·50
45	,,	4 c. pale blue	15·00	6·00
46	,,	8 c. pink	18·00	11·00
47	,,	12 c. dull purple	18·00	6·00
48	,,	12 c. purple	18·00	6·00
49	,,	12 c. lilac	23·00	9·00
50	,,	24 c. green	£110	18·00

(b) *Thin paper.* P 12½ × 13 (1863).

51	**7**	1 c. black	7·50	3·75
52	,,	2 c. orange	15·00	5·50
53	,,	4 c. blue	15·00	5·50
54	,,	8 c. pink	35·00	15·00
55	,,	12 c. brownish lilac	£100	17·00
56	,,	24 c. green	£110	17·00

Copies are found on *pelure* paper.

(c) *Medium paper.* P 12½–13 (1863).

57	**7**	1 c. black	7·50	5·50
58	,,	2 c. deep orange	7·00	5·50
59	,,	2 c. orange	7·50	4·50
60	,,	4 c. greyish blue	12·00	3·75
61	,,	4 c. blue	14·00	7·50
62	,,	8 c. pink	30·00	9·00
63	,,	12 c. brownish lilac	55·00	15·00
64	,,	24 c. green	30·00	14·00
65	,,	24 c. deep green	55·00	14·00

(d) *Medium paper.* P 10 (March 1866).

65*a*	**7**	12 c. grey-lilac	55·00	15·00

8 9

G H

I K

New transfers for the 1 c., 2 c., 8 c., and 12 c. with the spaces between values and the word "CENTS" about 1 mm.

1863–75. *Medium paper.*

(a) P 12½–13 (1863–64).

66	**8**	1 c. black	6·00	5·00
67	,,	2 c. orange-red	7·50	1·50
68	,,	2 c. orange	6·00	1·50
69	**9**	6 c. blue	18·00	9·00
70	,,	6 c. greenish blue	18·00	11·00
71	,,	6 c. deep blue	18·00	9·00
72	,,	6 c. milky blue	21·00	9·00
73	**8**	8 c. pink	21·00	4·50
74	,,	8 c. carmine	21·00	4·50
75	,,	12 c. grey-lilac	60·00	4·50
76	,,	12 c. brownish purple	75·00	6·00
77	**9**	24 c. green (*perf.* 12)	45·00	6·00
78	,,	24 c. yellow-green (*perf.* 12)	21·00	3·75
79	,,	24 c. yellow-grn. (*p.* 12½–13)	22·00	3·50
80	,,	24 c. green (*perf.* 12½–13)	22·00	4·50
81	,,	24 c. blue-green (*p.* 12½–13)	33·00	7·50
82	,,	48 c. pale red	24·00	11·00
83	,,	48 c. deep red	24·00	11·00
84	,,	48 c. carmine-rose	42·00	11·00

The 4 c. corresponding to this issue can only be distinguished from that of the previous issue by minor plating flaws.

There is a variety of the 6 c. with stop before "VICISSIM".

Varieties of most of the values of issues of 1863–64 and 1866 are to be found on both very thin and thick papers.

(b) P 10 (1866).

85	**8**	1 c. black	3·00	1·50
86	,,	1 c. grey-black	3·75	2·00
87	,,	2 c. orange	2·00	1·50
88	,,	2 c. reddish orange	5·50	1·50
89	,,	4 c. slate-blue	11·00	3·75
90	,,	4 c. blue	12·00	2·75
		a. Bisected (on cover)	†	£500
		b. Do. Imperf. (on cover)	†	—
91	,,	4 c. pale blue	15·00	3·75
92	**9**	6 c. milky blue	23·00	6·00
93	,,	6 c. ultramarine	23·00	9·00
94	,,	6 c. dull blue	23·00	8·50
95	**8**	8 c. pink	23·00	5·50
96	,,	8 c. brownish pink	23·00	5·50
96*a*	,,	8 c. carmine	23·00	6·00
97	,,	12 c. pale lilac	42·00	5·50
98	,,	12 c. grey-lilac	23·00	4·50
99	,,	12 c. brownish grey	23·00	5·50
100	,,	12 c. lilac	23·00	5·50
101	**9**	24 c. dark green	42·00	4·50
102	,,	24 c. bluish green	—	4·25
103	,,	24 c. yellow-green	30·00	3·75
104	,,	48 c. crimson	60·00	11·00
105	,,	48 c. red	55·00	11·00
104		Handstamped "Specimen"	25·00	
104		Perf. "Specimen"	25·00	

(c) P 15 (1875).

106	**8**	1 c. black	5·50	2·25
107	,,	2 c. orange-red	26·00	3·75
108	,,	2 c. orange	26·00	3·75
109	,,	4 c. bright blue	55·00	22·00
111	**9**	6 c. ultramarine	55·00	15·00
112	**8**	8 c. deep rose	33·00	15·00
113	,,	12 c. lilac	85·00	15·00
114	**9**	24 c. yellow-green	£110	15·00
115	,,	24 c. deep green	£110	15·00

There is a variety of the 48 c. *with* stop after "P" in "PETIMUSQUE".

Imperforate stamps of this and of the previous issue are considered to be proofs.

(Type-set and printed by George Melville at the Office of the *Royal Gazette*, Georgetown.)

Printed in sheets of 24, comprising 24 varieties of type. Stamps were initialled in the centre before use by the Acting Receiver-General of the colony, Robert Mather.

1862 (SEPT.). *Black on coloured paper. Roul.* 6.

10

Prices for stamps of this 1862 issue are for good average copies. Copies with roulettes on all sides very seldom occur and do not exist in marginal positions.

116	**10**	1 c. *rose* (12 *in sheet*)	£375	75·00
		a. Unsigned	38·00	
		b. "1" for "I" in "BRITISH"	—	90·00
		c. Wrong ornament on left	—	90·00
117	,,	2 c. *yellow* (12 *in sheet*)	£375	60·00
		a. Unsigned	38·00	
		b. "1" for "I" in "BRITISH"	—	85·00
		c. Wrong ornament on left	—	60·00

11 12

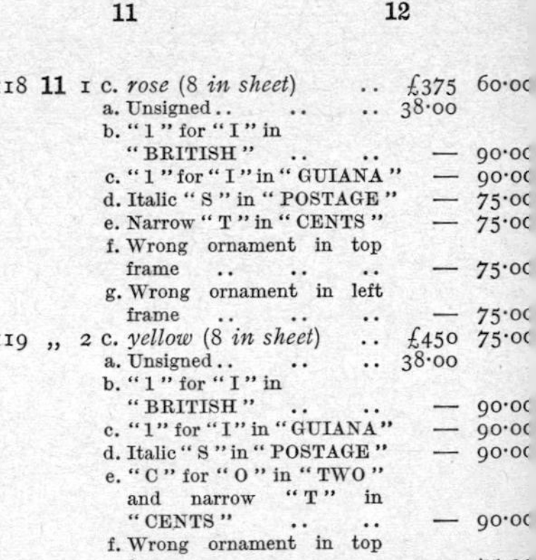

118	**11**	1 c. *rose* (8 *in sheet*)	£375	60·00
		a. Unsigned	38·00	
		b. "1" for "I" in "BRITISH"	—	90·00
		c. "1" for "I" in "GUIANA"	—	90·00
		d. Italic "S" in "POSTAGE"	—	75·00
		e. Narrow "T" in "CENTS"	—	75·00
		f. Wrong ornament in top frame	—	75·00
		g. Wrong ornament in left frame	—	75·00
119	,,	2 c. *yellow* (8 *in sheet*)	£450	75·00
		a. Unsigned	38·00	
		b. "1" for "I" in "BRITISH"	—	90·00
		c. "1" for "I" in "GUIANA"	—	90·00
		d. Italic "S" in "POSTAGE"	—	90·00
		e. "C" for "O" in "TWO" and narrow "T" in "CENTS"	—	90·00
		f. Wrong ornament in top frame	—	75·00
		g. Italic "T" in "TWO"	—	75·00
120	**12**	1 c. *rose* (4 *in sheet*)	£600	£110
		a. Unsigned	90·00	
		b. "1" for "I" in "GUIANA"	—	£110
		c. "C" for "O" in "POSTAGE"	—	£110
121	,,	2 c. *yellow* (4 *in sheet*)	£750	£100
		a. Unsigned		
		b. "1" for "I" in "GUIANA"	—	£110
		c. "C" for "O" in "POSTAGE"	—	£110

13

14

122 **13** 4 c. *blue* (10 *in sheet*) .. £375 60·00
a. Unsigned .. ..
b. Ornament omitted on right — 90·00
123 **14** 4 c. *blue* (6 *in sheet*) .. £450 75·00
a. Unsigned .. .. 85·00

15

124 **15** 4 c. *blue* (6 *in sheet*) .. £450 £110
a. Unsigned .. .. 85·00
b. "1" for "I" in "BRITISH" — £110

As T **15**, *but with four thin inner lines.*

125 – 4 c. *blue* (2 *in sheet*) .. £900 £300
a. Unsigned .. ..

16

(17)

(Typo. D.L.R.)

1876 (1 JULY). *Wmk. Crown CC.* (*a*) *P* 14.
126 **16** 1 c. slate .. .. .. 1·50 35
127 ,, 2 c. orange .. .. .. 6·00 70
128 ,, 4 c. blue .. .. .. 14·00 4·50
129 ,, 6 c. brown .. .. .. 12·00 4·50
130 ,, 8 c. rose .. .. .. 12·00 2·10
131 ,, 12 c. pale violet .. .. 14·00 2·75
132 ,, 24 c. emerald-green .. .. 14·00 4·50
133 ,, 48 c. red-brown .. .. 17·00 6·00
134 ,, 96 c. olive-bistre .. .. 90·00 75·00
126/134 .. .. *Set of* 9 £170 90·00
126/132, 134 Handstamped/Perf. "Specimen" *Set of* 8 .. 80·00
(*b*) *P* 12½.
135 **16** 4 c. blue .. .. .. £275 75·00
(*c*) *Perf. compound of* 14 × 12½.
136 **16** 1 c. slate .. .. .. — 75·00

1878. *Provisionals. Various stamps with old values ruled through with thick bars, in black ink, the bars varying in depth of colour.*

(*a*) *With two horiz. bars* (17 Apr.).
137 **16** (1 c.) on 6 c. brown .. 11·00 12·00
(*b*) *Official stamps with horiz. bars across* "OFFICIAL" (End Aug.).
138 **8** 1 c. black .. .. .. 20·00 11·00
139 **16** 1 c. slate .. .. .. 20·00 7·50
140 ,, 2 c. orange.. .. .. 21·00 11·00
(*c*) *With horiz. and vert. bars as T* **17** (6 Nov.).
141 **9** (1 c.) on 6 c. ultram. (93) 24·00 9·00
142 **16** (1 c.) on 6 c. brown .. 26·00 11·00
(*d*) *Official stamps with bars across* "OFFICIAL" (23 Nov.).
(i) *With two horiz. bars and one vert.*
144 **16** (1 c.) on 4 c. blue.. .. 20·00 11·00
145 ,, (1 c.) on 6 c. brown .. 23·00 11·00
146 **8** (2 c.) on 8 c. rose .. .. 23·00 12·00
(ii) *With one horiz. bar and one vert.*
148 **16** (2 c.) on 8 c. rose .. .. 24·00 14·00

1 (18) 2 (19) 2 (20)

1881 (21 DEC.). *No.* 134 *with old value ruled through with bar in black ink and surch.*
149 **18** 1 on 96 c. olive-bistre .. 1·90 1·90
a. Bar in red.. .. ..
b. Bar omitted .. ..
150 **19** 2 on 96 c. olive-bistre .. 1·90 3·50
a. Bar in red .. .. ..
b. Bar omitted .. ..
151 **20** 2 on 96 c. olive-bistre .. 6·00 6·00

1 (21) 1 OFFICIAL (22) 2 (23) 2 (24)

1881 (28 DEC.). *Various stamps with old value ruled through with bar and surch.*
(*a*) *On No.* 105.
152 **21** 1 on 48 c. red .. .. 5·00 2·10
a. Bar omitted .. ..
(*b*) *On No.* 133.
153 **22** 1 on 48 c. red-brown .. 20·00 14·00
(*c*) *On Official stamps.*
154 **21** 1 on 12 c. brnsh. pur. (O4) 12·00 9·00
155 **23** 2 on 12 c. pale violet (O11) 9·00 6·50
a. Surch. double £140 £120
b. Do. T 23 and 24 .. ..
c. Extra bar through "OFFICIAL" .. ..
156 **24** 2 on 12 c. pale violet (O11) 24·00 21·00
157 **23** 2 on 24 c. emer.-grn. (O12) 12·00 6·50
a. Surch. double £180
158 **24** 2 on 24 c. emer.-grn. (O12) £180 £140
159 **19** 2 on 24 c. green (O5) .. 24·00 21·00

On Nos. 149/59 the bar is found in various thicknesses ranging from 1 to 4 mm.

26 27

(Type-set. Baldwin & Co., Georgetown.)

1882. *Black impression. P* 12. *Perforated with the word* "SPECIMEN" *diagonally.*
162 **26** 1 c. *magenta* .. .. 9·00 7·00
a. Imperf. between (pair) ..
b. Without "SPECIMEN" .. 17·00 17·00
c. "1" with foot .. .. 17·00 17·00
163 ,, 2 c. *yellow* .. .. 11·00 7·00
a. Without "SPECIMEN" .. 17·00 17·00
b. Small "2" .. .. 11·00 11·00
164 **27** 1 c. *magenta* .. .. 7·50 7·50
a. Without "SPECIMEN" .. 18·00 17·00
b. "1" with foot .. .. 12·00 12·00
165 ,, 2 c. *yellow* .. .. 12·00 9·00
a. Bisected diagonally (1 c.) ..
b. Without "SPECIMEN" .. 18·00 18·00
c. Small "2" .. .. 17·00 17·00

These stamps were perforated "SPECIMEN" as a precaution against fraud. Stamps are known with "SPECIMEN" double.

These were printed in sheets of twelve in two settings using the same clichés:—

1st setting. Four rows of three, T **26** being Nos. 5, 6, 7, 8, 11 and 12, and T **27** the remainder.

2nd setting. Six rows of two, T **26** being Nos. 3, 7, 8, 9, 11 and 12, and T **27** the remainder.

Se-tenant pairs are worth about 20% more.

The "1" with foot occurs on T **27** on No. 9 in the first setting and on T **26** on No. 7 in the first printing only of the second setting.

The small "2" appears on T **26** in the first setting on Nos. 6, 7, 8 and 12 in the first printing and on Nos. 7, 8 and 12 only in the second printing; in the second setting it comes on Nos. 3, 9, and 12 in the first printing and on Nos. 9, 11 and 12 in the second printing. On T **27** the variety occurs in the first setting on No. 9 of the second printing only and in the second setting on No. 10 in both printings.

(Typo. D.L.R.)

1882. *Wmk. Crown CA. P* 14.
170 **16** 1 c. slate (27 Jan.) .. 1·40 30
171 ,, 2 c. orange (27 Jan.) .. 3·75 55
a. Value doubly printed ..
172 ,, 4 c. blue .. .. .. 12·00 5·50
173 ,, 6 c. brown .. .. .. 3·00 3·00
174 ,, 8 c. rose .. .. .. 17·00 90

INLAND 4 CENTS (*a*) 4 CENTS (*b*)

Two types of "4"

2 CENTS REVENUE (28) 6 (*c*) 6 (*d*) 2 (29)

Two types of "6"

1888–89. *T* **16** (*without value in lower label*) *optd.* "INLAND REVENUE", *and surch. with value as T* **28**, *by D.L.R. Wmk. Crown CA. P* 14.
175 1 c. dull purple (8.89) .. 40 40
176 2 c. dull purple (25.5.89) .. 40 40
177 3 c. dull purple 40 40
178 4 c. dull purple (*a*) .. 70 55
a. Larger fig. "4" (*b*) .. 7·50 5·50
179 6 c. dull purple (*c*) .. .. 1·40 70
a. Fig. 6 with straight top (*d*) 3·00 1·75
180 8 c. dull purple (8.89) .. 55 55
181 10 c. dull purple .. .. 1·75 1·50
182 20 c. dull purple .. .. 3·50 3·00
183 40 c. dull purple .. .. 5·50 4·25
184 72 c. dull purple (1.10.88) .. 5·50 5·00
185 1 dol. green (1.10.88) .. 85·00 60·00
186 2 dol. green (1.10.88) .. 45·00 38·00
187 3 dol. green (1.10.88) .. 27·00 23·00
188 4 dol. green (*a*) (1.10.88) .. 75·00 60·00
a. Larger fig. "4" (*b*) .. £190 £190
189 5 dol. green (1.10.88) .. 42·00 38·00
175/189 .. .. *Set of* 15 £270 £220

1889 (6 JUNE). *No.* 176 *surch. locally as T* **29**.
192 "2" on 2 c. dull purple (R.) 40 40

The varieties with figure "2" *inverted* or *double* were made privately by a postal employee in Demerara.

30

INLAND One Cent ~~1 DOLLAR~~ REVENUE (31)

(Typo. D.L.R.)

1889 (SEPT.). *Wmk. Crown CA. P* 14.
193 **30** 1 c. dull pur. & slate-grey 55 45
194 ,, 2 c. dull pur. and orange 45 25
195 ,, 4 c. dull pur. and ultram. 1·40 1·40
196 ,, 4 c. dull pur. and cobalt 4·50 1·10
197 ,, 6 c. dull pur. and brown 7·00 3·25
198 ,, 6 c. dull pur. and maroon 3·50 1·90
199 ,, 8 c. dull purple and rose 2·25 90
200 ,, 12 c. dull pur. & brt. pur. 3·50 75
200*a*,, 12 c. dull pur. and mauve 2·75 90
201 ,, 24 c. dull purple and green 3·50 1·25
202 ,, 48 c. dull pur. & orge.-red 7·00 3·00
203 ,, 72 c. dull purple & red-brn. 7·50 4·50
204 ,, 72 c. dull purple & yell.-brn. 12·00 11·00
205 ,, 96 c. dull purple & carmine 20·00 18·00
206 ,, 96 c. dull purple & rosine.. 27·00 21·00
193/205 .. .. *Set of* 10 50·00 30·00
193/206 Optd. "Specimen" *Set of* 10 75·00

1890 (15 JULY). *Stamps of* 1888–89 *surch. locally* " One Cent ", *in red, as in T* **31**.

207 1 c. on 1 dol. (No. 185) .. 75 55
a. Surch. double .. .. — 20·00
208 1 c. on 2 dol. (No. 186) .. 40 75
a. Surch. double .. .. 38·00
209 1 c. on 3 dol. (No. 187) .. 70 60
a. Surch. double .. .. 26·00
210 1 c. on 4 dol. (No. 188) .. 1·50 2·25
a. Surch. double .. .. 30·00
b. Larger fig. " 4 " (*b*) .. 7·50 6·00

1890–91. *Colours changed. Wmk. Crown CA. P* 14.

213 **30** 1 c. sea-green (12.90) .. 15 15
214 ,, 5 c. ultramarine (1.91) .. 1·25 40
215 ,, 8 c. dull purple & greenish black (10.90) .. .. 1·75 2·25
213/215 Optd. " Specimen " *Set of* 3 23·00

32. Mount Roraima.

33. Kaieteur Falls.

TWO CENTS.
(34)

(Recess. De La Rue.)

1898 (18 JULY). *Queen Victoria's Jubilee. Wmk. Crown CC. P* 14.

216 **32** 1 c. blue-black & carmine 1·60 45
217 **33** 2 c. brown and indigo .. 1·75 55
a. Imperf. between (pair) .. £1000
218 ,, 2 c. brown and blue .. 4·00 50
219 **32** 5 c. green and sepia .. 6·00 2·75
a. Imperf. between (pair) ..
220 **33** 10 c. blue-black & orge. red 8·00 5·00
221 **32** 15 c. red-brown and blue .. 8·00 5·50
216/221 .. .. *Set of* 5 23·00 13·00
216/221 Optd. " Specimen " *Set of* 5 40·00

The 1 c. was later retouched, the lines of shading on the mountains in the background being strengthened, and along the ridge distinct from each other, whereas, in the original, they are more or less blurred. In the retouched die the shading of the sky is less pronounced.

(Surch. at Printing Office of the *Daily Chronicle*, Georgetown.)

1899 (22 FEB.). *Surch. with T* **34**.

222 **32** 2 c.on 5 c. (No. 219) .. 70 80
a. No stop after " CENTS " .. 7·50 7·50
223 **33** 2 c. on 10 c. (No. 220) .. 45 60
a. No stop after " CENTS " .. 6·50 6·50
b. " GENTS " for " CENTS " .. 13·00 13·00
c. Surch. inverted .. .. 70·00 80·00
224 **32** 2 c. on 15 c (No. 221) .. 1·00 1·00
a. No stop after " CENTS " .. 11·00 11·00
b. Surch. double .. £130
c. Surch. double one without stop .. .. ..
d. Surch. inverted .. .. 85·00 90·00

The " no stop " variety occurs on the 53rd stamp in sheets of No. 222a and of the first setting of No. 223a and on the 21st stamp in the second setting of No. 223a.

The " GENTS " error is on the 55th stamp in the sheet.

Of 224c only one specimen exists.

1900–7. T **30**. *Wmk. Crown CA. P* 14.

233 1 c. grey-green ('07) 70 20
234 2 c. dull purple and carmine 1·40 25
235 2 c. dull purple & black/*red* 45 12
236 6 c. grey-blk. & ultram. ('02) 3·50 4·00
237 48 c. grey & purple-brn. ('01) 14·00 13·00
a. Brownish grey and brown ('07) 11·00 11·00
238 60 c. green and rosine ('03) .. 25·00 25·00
233/238 .. .. *Set of* 6 38·00 38·00
233/238 Optd. " Specimen " *Set of* 6 38·00

No. 233 is a reissue of No. 213 in non-fugitive ink.

1905–7. T **30**. *Wmk. Multiple Crown CA. P* 14.

240 1 c. grey-green 15 15
241 2 c. purple & black/*red*, O C 30 20
242 4 c. dull pur. & ultram., O C 6·00 5·50
243 5 c. dull pur. & blue/*blue*, O C 2·25 1·60
244 6 c. grey-blk. & ultram., O C 7·00 7·50
245 12 c. dull & bright pur., O C 10·00 9·50
246 24 c. dull pur. & grn., O C ('06) 3·00 3·00
247 48 c. grey & pur.-brown, O C 8·00 8·50
248 60 c. green and rosine, O C .. 8·00 9·00
249 72 c. pur. & orge.-brn., C ('07) 16·00 16·00
250 96 c. blk. & verm./*yell.*, C ('06) (Optd. S. £8) .. .. 17·00 17·00
240/250 .. .. *Set of* 11 70·00 70·00

35

37

War
Tax
(38)

1905. *Optd.* " POSTAGE AND REVENUE ". *Wmk. Multiple Crown CA. P* 14.

251 **35** $2.40, grn. & vio., C (S.£40) 90·00 £100

1907–10. *Colours changed. Wmk. Mult. Crown CA. P* 14.

252 **30** 1 c. blue-green, O ('10) .. 55 25
253 ,, 2 c. rose-red, O .. .. 1·60 25
a. Redrawn ('10) 85 25
254 ,, 4 c. brown and purple, O 1·60 90
255 ,, 5 c. ultramarine, O .. 85 35
256 ,, 6 c. grey and black, O .. 5·00 2·50
257 ,, 12 c. orange and mauve, O 2·50 1·60
252/257 .. .. *Set of* 6 11·00 5·00
253/257 Optd. " Specimen " *Set of* 5 38·00

In No. 253a the flag at the main truck is close to the mast, whereas in the original type it appears to be flying loose from halyards. There are two background lines above the value " 2 CENTS " instead of three and the " S " is farther away from the end of the tablet.

(Typo. D.L.R.)

1913–21. *Wmk. Mult. Crown CA. P* 14.

259 **37** 1 c. yellow-green, O .. 50 30
a. Blue-green, O (1917) .. 35 15
260 ,, 2 c. carmine, O 30 12
a. Scarlet, O (1916) .. 30 12
b. Wmk. sideways ..
261 ,, 4 c. brown and bright purple, C (1914) .. 1·00 55
a. Deep brown & purple, C 1·10 35
262 ,, 5 c. bright blue, O .. 50 50
263 ,, 6 c. grey and black, O .. 55 55
264 ,, 12 c. orange & violet, C .. 85 60
265 ,, 24 c. dull purple & green, O (1915) .. .. 1·60 1·60
266 ,, 48 c. grey & purple-brown, C (1914) .. .. 3·00 3·75
267 ,, 60 c. grn. & rosine, C ('15) 8·50 8·50
268 ,, 72 c. purple & orange-brown, C (1915) .. 10·00 10·00
269 ,, 96 c. black and vermilion/*yellow*, C (1915) .. 12·00 12·00
a. White back (1913) (Optd. S. £6) .. .. 9·50 9·50
b. On lemon (1916) .. 9·50 10·00
c. On pale yellow (1921) (Optd. S. £6) .. .. 11·00 12·00
259/269*c* .. .. *Set of* 11 32·00 32·00
259/69 Optd. " Specimen " *Set of* 11 60·00

1918 (4 JAN.). *No.* 260*a optd. with T* **38**, *by D.L.R.*

271 **37** 2 c. scarlet 15 15

The relative positions of the words " WAR " and " TAX " vary considerably in the sheet.

1921–27. *Wmk. Mult. Script CA. P* 14.

272 **37** 1 c. green, O (1922) .. 15 12
273 ,, 2 c. rose-carmine, O .. 30 15
274 ,, 2 c. bright violet, O ('23) 15 10
275 ,, 4 c. brown and bright purple, O (1922) .. 60 20
276 ,, 6 c. bright blue, O ('22) 60 35
277 ,, 12 c. orange & vio., O ('22) 85 75
278 ,, 24 c. dull pur. & green, C 1·40 1·40
279 ,, 48 c. black & pur., C ('26) 3·25 3·50
280 ,, 60 c. grn. & rosine, C ('26) 6·50 6·50
281 ,, 72 c. dull purple & orange brown, C (1923) .. 7·00 7·00
282 ,, 96 c. blk. & red/*yell.*, C ('27) 8·50 10·00
272/282 .. .. *Set of* 11 26·00 27·00
272/82 Optd. " Specimen " *Set of* 11 60·00

39. Ploughing a Rice Field.

40. Indian shooting Fish.

41. Kaieteur Falls.

42. Public Buildings, Georgetown.

(Recess. Waterlow.)

1931 (21 JULY). *Centenary of County Union. Wmk. Mult. Script CA. P* 12½.

283 **39** 1 c. emerald-green .. 35 35
284 **40** 2 c. brown 55 35
285 **41** 4 c. carmine .. .. 1·50 1·00
286 **42** 6 c. blue .. .. .. 3·00 3·25
287 **41** $1 violet .. .. .. 15·00 17·00
283/287 .. .. *Set of* 5 19·00 20·00
283/7 Perf. "Specimen" *Set of* 5 25·00

43. Ploughing a Rice Field.

44. Gold Mining.

45. Shooting Logs over Falls.

46. Stabroek Market.

47. Sugar Canes in Punts.

48. Forest Road.

49. Victoria Regia Lilies.

50. Mount Roraima.

51. Sir Walter Raleigh and his son.

52. Botanical Gardens.

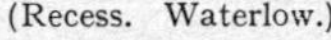
(Recess. Waterlow.)

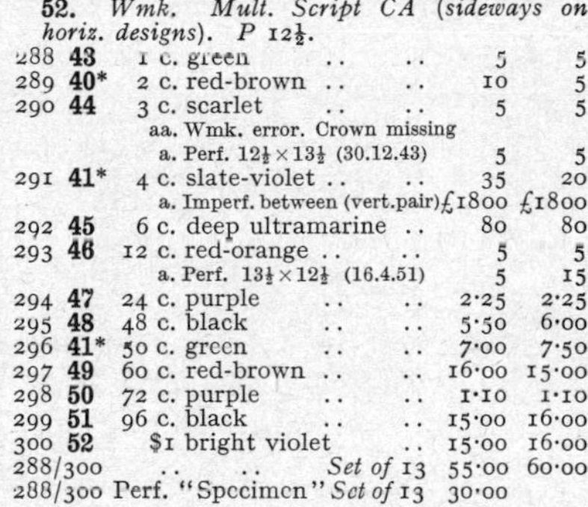
1934–51. *Types as* **40** (2 *c.*) *and* **41** (4 *c. and* 50 *c.*) *but without dates at top of frame* and T* **43** *to* **52.** *Wmk. Mult. Script CA (sideways on horiz. designs). P* 12½.

288 **43** 1 c. green 5 5
289 **40*** 2 c. red-brown 10 5
290 **44** 3 c. scarlet 5 5
aa. Wmk. error. Crown missing
a. Perf. 12½×13½ (30.12.43) 5 5
291 **41*** 4 c. slate-violet 35 20
a. Imperf. between (vert.pair) £1800 £1800
292 **45** 6 c. deep ultramarine .. 80 80
293 **46** 12 c. red-orange 5 5
a. Perf. 13½×12½ (16.4.51) 5 15
294 **47** 24 c. purple .. .. 2·25 2·25
295 **48** 48 c. black .. .. 5·50 6·00
296 **41*** 50 c. green .. .. 7·00 7·50
297 **49** 60 c. red-brown .. .. 16·00 15·00
298 **50** 72 c. purple .. .. 1·10 1·10
299 **51** 96 c. black .. .. 15·00 16·00
300 **52** $1 bright violet .. 15·00 16·00
288/300 .. .. *Set of* 13 55·00 60·00
288/300 Perf. "Specimen" *Set of* 13 30·00

No. 290a was first line-perforated, but from 28.4.49 printings appeared comb-perforated.

1935 (6 May). *Silver Jubilee. As T* **13** *of Antigua. Recess. D.L.R. Wmk. Mult. Script CA. P* 13½×14.

301 2 c. ultramarine and grey .. 5 5
302 6 c. brown and deep blue .. 60 50
303 12 c. green and indigo .. 80 90
304 24 c. slate and purple .. 1·75 1·75
301/4 Perf. "Specimen" *Set of* 4 12·00

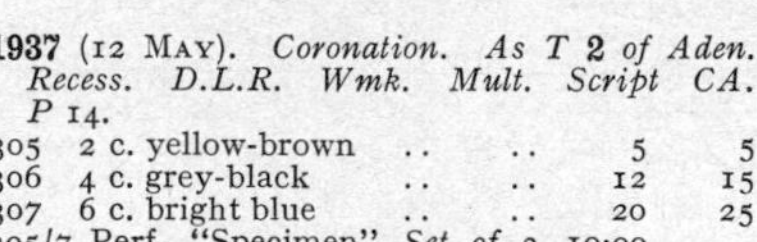
1937 (12 May). *Coronation. As T* **2** *of Aden. Recess. D.L.R. Wmk. Mult. Script CA. P* 14.

305 2 c. yellow-brown 5 5
306 4 c. grey-black 12 15
307 6 c. bright blue 20 25
305/7 Perf. "Specimen" *Set of* 3 10·00

53. South America.

54. Victoria Regia Lilies.

(Recess. Waterlow.)

1938 (1 Feb.)–**1952.** *As earlier types but portrait of King George VI in place of King George V. Wmk. Mult. Script CA. P* 12½.

308 **43** 1 c. yellow-green.. .. 80 15
aa. Green ('44) 5 5
a. Perf. 13½×12½ ('49) .. 5 5
309 **41** 2 c. slate-violet 5 5
a. Perf. 12½×13½ (28.4.49) 5 5
310 **53** 4 c. scarlet and black .. 5 5
a. Imperf. between (vert. pair) £800 £400
b. Perf. 12½×13½ ('52) .. 10 8
311 **40** 6 c. deep ultramarine .. 5 5
a. Perf. 12½×13½ (24.10.49) 8 8
312 **47** 24 c. blue-green .. .. 5·50 3·00
a. Wmk. sideways .. 1·25 20
313 **41** 36 c. bright violet (7.3.38) 25 25
a. Perf. 12½×13½ (13.12.51) 50 35
314 **48** 48 c. orange 35 20
a. Perf. 13½×12½ (14.6.51).. 50 75
315 **45** 60 c. red-brown 40 40
316 **51** 96 c. purple .. .. 1·50 85
a. Perf. 12½×13½ ('44) .. 1·10 1·10
317 **52** $1 bright violet.. .. 1·10 90
a. Perf. 13½×12½ ('51) .. 80·00 75·00
318 **50** $2 purple (11.6.45) .. 2·00 3·00
a. Perf. 13½×12½ (9.8.50) .. 1·75 3·00
319 **54** $3 red-brown (2.7.45) .. 3·00 4·00
a. Bright red-brn. (Dec. '46) 6·00 6·00
b. Perf. 13½×12½. *Red-brown* (29.10.52) .. .. 4·00 4·00
308/319*b* .. .. *Set of* 12 9·00 9·00
308/19 Perf. "Specimen" *Set of* 12 32·00

No. 316a was first line-perforated, but from 8.2.51 printings appeared comb-perforated.

1946 (21 Oct.). *Victory. As Nos.* 28/9 *of Aden.*

320 3 c. carmine 8 5
321 6 c. blue 8 5
320/1 Perf. "Specimen" *Set of* 2 11·00

1948 (20 Dec.). *Royal Silver Wedding. As Nos.* 30/1 *of Aden;* (*recess* $3).

322 3 c. scarlet 8 8
323 $3 red-brown .. .. 4·00 5·00

1949 (10 Oct.). *75th Anniv. of Universal Postal Union. As Nos.* 114/7 *of Antigua.*

324 4 c. carmine 20 15
325 6 c. deep blue 35 30
326 12 c. orange 45 40
327 24 c. blue-green 65 65

1951 (16 Feb.). *University Coll. of B.W.I. As Nos.* 118/9 *of Antigua.*

328 3 c. black and carmine .. 15 12
329 6 c. black and blue 25 20

1953 (2 June). *Coronation. As No.* 47 *of Aden.*

330 4 c. black and scarlet .. 12 8

MINIMUM PRICE

The minimum price quoted is 5p which represents a handling charge rather than a basis for valuing common stamps. For further notes about prices see introductory pages.

55. G.P.O. Georgetown.

56. Botanical Gardens.

57. Victoria Regia Lilies.

59. Map of Caribbean.

58. Amerindian shooting Fish.

60. Rice Combine-harvester.

61. Sugar Cane entering Factory.

62. Felling Greenheart.

63. Mining for Bauxite.

65. Kaieteur Falls.

64. Mount Roraima.

66. Arapaima.

67. Toucan.

69. Arms of British Guiana.

68. Dredging Gold.

(Centre litho., frame recess ($1); recess (others). Waterlow (until 1961), then D.L.R.)

1954 (1 Dec.)–**62.** *Wmk. Mult. Script CA. P* 12½×13* (*horiz.*) *or* 13 (*vert.*).

331	**55**	1 c. black	5	5
332	**56**	2 c. myrtle-green ..	5	5
333	**57**	3 c. brn.-olive & red-brn.	5	5
334	**58**	4 c. violet	5	5
		a. D.L.R. ptg. (*shades*) (5.12.61)	20	20
335	**59**	5 c. scarlet and black ..	5	8
336	**60**	6 c. yellow-green (*shades*)	8	8
337	**61**	8 c. ultramarine (*shades*)	8	10
338	**62**	12 c. black and reddish brown (*shades*) ..	35	30
339	**63**	24 c. black and brownish orange (*shades*) ..	35	30
340	**64**	36 c. rose-carmine & black	30	25
341	**65**	48 c. ultramarine & brown-lake (*shades*)	45	40
		ab. D.L.R. ptg. *Brt. ultram. & pale brown-lake* (19.9.61)	1·25	1·50
342	**66**	72 c. carmine & emerald ..	70	75
		a. D.L.R. ptg. (17.7.62) ..	1·60	1·75
343	**67**	$1 pink, yell., grn. & blk.	75	50
344	**68**	$2 deep mauve (*shades*)	1·50	90
345	**69**	$5 ultramarine & black	3·75	4·00
		a. D.L.R. ptg. (19.9.61) ..	6·00	7·00
331/345*a*		.. .. *Set of* 15	7·00	6·50

The separately listed De La Rue printings are identifiable as singles by the single wide-tooth perfs. at each side at the *bottom* of the stamps. In the Waterlow these wide teeth are at the *top*.

*All the Waterlow printings and early De La Rue printings of the horizontal designs measure 12.3×12.8, but De La Rue printings of 22nd May, 1962 and all later printings (including those on the Block CA watermark), measure 12.3×12.6.

II. SELF-GOVERNMENT.

70

(Photo. Harrison.)

1961 (23 Oct.). *History and Culture Week. W* w.**12.** *P* 14½×14.

346	**70**	5 c. sepia and orange-red	10	12
347	,,	6 c. sepia and blue-green	12	12
348	,,	30 c. sepia & yellow-orange	30	40

1963 (14 July). *Freedom from Hunger. As No. 76 of Aden.*

349	20 c. reddish violet	30	30

1963 (2 Sept.). *Red Cross Centenary. As Nos. 147/8 of Antigua.*

350	5 c. red and black	12	12
351	20 c. red and blue	45	50

1963–65. *As Nos.* 333/44, *but wmk.* w.**12.**

354	**57**	3 c. brown-olive and red-brown (12.65) ..	25	30
356	**59**	5 c. scarlet & blk. (28.5.64)	5	5
359	**62**	12 c. black and yellowish brown (6.10.64) ..	12	5
360	**63**	24 c. black and bright orange (10.12.63) ..	25	5
361	**64**	36 c. rose-carmine & black (10.12.63)	30	5
362	**65**	48 c. brt. ultram. & Venetian red (25.11.63) ..	35	35
363	**66**	72 c. carmine and emerald (25.11.63)	60	1·00
364	**67**	$1 pink, yellow, green and black (10.12.63)	85	1·25
365	**68**	$2 reddish mauve (10.12.63)	1·50	2·50
354/365		.. .. *Set of* 9	3·00	4·50

There was no London release of No. 354.

For 1 c. value, see No. 393aA of Guyana.

71. Weightlifting.

(Photo. D.L.R.)

1964 (1 Oct.). *Olympic Games, Tokyo. W* **w.12.** *P* 13×13½.

No.	Type	Description	Unused	Used
367	**71**	5 c. orange	10	10
368	,,	8 c. blue	12	12
369	,,	25 c. magenta	30	30

1965 (17 May). *I.T.U. Centenary. As Nos.* 166/7 *of Antigua.*

No.	Description	Unused	Used
370	5 c. emerald and yellow-olive	8	8
371	25 c. light blue and magenta	25	25

1965 (25 Oct.). *International Co-operation Year. As Nos.* 168/9 *of Antigua.*

No.	Description	Unused	Used
372	5 c. reddish pur. & turq.-grn.	8	8
373	25 c. deep bluish green & lav.	25	25

72. St. George's Cathedral, Georgetown.

(Des. Jennifer Toombs. Photo. Harrison.)

1966 (24 Jan.). *Churchill Commemoration. W* **w.12.** *P* 14×14½.

No.	Type	Description	Unused	Used
374	**72**	5 c. black, crimson & gold	10	10
375	,,	25 c. black, blue and gold	30	30

1966 (3 Feb.). *Royal Visit. As Nos.* 174/5 *of Antigua.*

No.	Description	Unused	Used
376	3 c. black and ultramarine	8	8
377	25 c. black and magenta	25	25

POSTAGE DUE STAMPS.

D 1

(Typo. De La Rue.)

1940 (Mar.)–**55.** *Wmk. Mult. Script CA. P* 14.

No.	Type	Description	Unused	Used
D1	**D 1**	1 c. green, O	40	45
		a. Deep green, C (30.4.52)	10	10
		b. W9a (Crown missing), C	15·00	
		b. W9b (St. Ed. Crown), C	11·00	
D2	,,	2 c. black, C	45	25
		aa. Chalky paper (30.4.52)	10	10
		a. W9a (Crown missing), C	13·00	
		b. W9b (St. Ed. Crown), C	9·00	
D3	,,	4 c. brt. blue, C (1.5.52)	10	10
		a. W9a (Crown missing), C	10·00	
		b. W9b (St. Ed. Crown), C	9·00	
D4	,,	12 c. scarlet, O	70	85
		a. Chalky paper (19.7.55)	10	10
D1, D2 & D4 Perf. "Specimen"		*Set of* 3	12·00	

OFFICIAL STAMPS.

OFFICIAL (O 1) OFFICIAL (O 2)

1875. *Optd. with Type* O **1** (1 *c.*) *or* O **2** (*others*). *P* 10.

No.	Type	Description	Unused	Used
O1	**8**	1 c. black (R.)	4·25	4·25
		a. Imperf. between (pair)	—	£350
O2	,,	2 c. orange	21·00	4·25
O3	,,	8 c. rose	50·00	22·00
O4	**7**	12 c. brownish purple	£130	70·00
O5	**9**	24 c. green	85·00	35·00

Two types of the word "OFFICIAL" are found on each value. On the 1 c. the word is either 16 or 17 mm. long. On the other values the chief difference is in the shape and position of the letter "o" in "OFFICIAL". In one case the "o" is upright, in the other it slants to the left.

1877. *Optd. with Type* O **2.** *Wmk. Crown CC. P* 14.

No.	Type	Description	Unused	Used
O 6	**16**	1 c. slate	38·00	18·00
		a. Imperf. betwn. (vert. pr.)	—	£1100
O 7	,,	2 c. orange	11·00	4·25
O 8	,,	4 c. blue	17·00	8·50
O 9	,,	6 c. brown	£325	£100
O10	,,	8 c. rose	£300	85·00
		Prepared for use, but not issued.		
O11	**16**	12 c. pale violet	£170	
O12	,,	24 c. green	£225	

The "OFFICIAL" overprints have been extensively forged.

The use of Official stamps was discontinued in 1878.

British Guiana attained independence on 25th May, 1966, her stamps being withdrawn on that date. For later issues see Guyana.

BRITISH HONDURAS.

For GREAT BRITAIN stamps used in British Honduras with "**A 06**" obliteration, see index to Great Britain Stamps Used Abroad list.

CROWN COLONY.

1

(Typo. De La Rue.)

1866 (Jan.). *No wmk. P* 14.

No.	Type	Description	Unused	Used
1	**1**	1d. pale blue	18·00	17·00
		a. Imperf. between (pair)		
2	,,	1d. blue	18·00	17·00
3	,,	6d. rose	55·00	35·00
4	,,	1s. green	60·00	35·00
		a. In horiz. pair with 6d.	£6500	
		b. In vert. pair with 1d.	£10000	

In the first printing all three values were printed in the same sheet separated by horizontal and vertical gutter margins. The sheet comprised two panes of 60 of the 1d. at the top with a pane of 60 of the 1s. at bottom left and another of 6d. at bottom right. Copies of 1d. *se-tenant* with the 6d. are not known. There were two later printings of the 1d. but they were in sheets without the 6d. and 1s.

1872–79. *Wmk. Crown CC.* (*a*) *P* 12½.

No.	Type	Description	Unused	Used
5	**1**	1d. pale blue	20·00	6·50
6	,,	1d. deep blue (1874)	20·00	6·50
7	,,	3d. red-brown	40·00	26·00
8	,,	3d. chocolate (1874)	45·00	32·00
9	,,	6d. rose	55·00	9·50
9*a*	,,	6d. brt. rose-carmine (1874)	90·00	13·00
10	,,	1s. green	90·00	11·00
10*a*	,,	1s. deep green (1874)	65·00	8·00
		b. Imperf. between (pair)	—	£6000

(*b*) *P* 14 (1877–79).

No.	Type	Description	Unused	Used
11	**1**	1d. pale blue (1878)	13·00	6·00
12	,,	1d. blue	12·00	4·50
		a. Imperf. between (pair)	£550	
13	,,	3d. chestnut	32·00	6·50
14	,,	4d. mauve (1879)	45·00	4·50
15	,,	6d. rose (1878)	80·00	65·00
16	,,	1s. green	60·00	6·50
		a. Imperf. between (pair)		

1882–87. *Wmk. Crown CA. P* 14.

No.	Type	Description	Unused	Used
17	**1**	1d. blue (4.84)	8·00	6·50
18	,,	1d. rose (1884)	6·50	5·50
		a. Bisected (½d.) (on cover)		
19	,,	1d. carmine (1887)	12·00	6·50
20	,,	4d. mauve (7.82)	26·00	2·75
21	,,	6d. yellow (1885)	90·00	60·00
22	,,	1s. grey (1.87)	90·00	55·00
18, 22 Optd. "Specimen"		*Set of* 2	45·00	

2 CENTS (2) TWO (3) 2 CENTS (4)

1888 (1 Jan.). *Stamps of* 1872–79 (*wmk. Crown CC*), *surch. locally as T* **2.** (*a*) *P* 12½.

No.	Type	Description	Unused	Used
23	**1**	2 c. on 6d. rose	45·00	45·00
24	,,	3 c. on 3d. chocolate	£2250	£1200

(*b*) *P* 14.

No.	Type	Description	Unused	Used
25	**1**	2 c. on 6d. rose	29·00	29·00
		a. Surch. double	£350	
		b. Bisected (1 c.) (on cover)		45·00
		c. Slanting "2" with curved foot	£200	
26	,,	3 c. on 3d. chestnut	24·00	24·00

There are very dangerous forgeries of these surcharges.

1888. *Stamps of* 1882–87 (*wmk. Crown CA*), *surch. locally as T* **2.** *P* 14.

No.	Type	Description	Unused	Used
27	**1**	2 c. on 1d. rose	3·25	6·00
		a. Surch. inverted	£350	£350
		b. Surch. double	£350	£350
		c. Bisected (1 c.) (on cover)	—	35·00
28	,,	10 c. on 4d. mauve	12·00	5·50
29	,,	20 c. on 6d. yellow	12·00	8·00
30	,,	50 c. on 1s. grey	£110	£130
		a. Error. "5" for "50"	£2000	

1888 (July). *No.* 30 *further surch. locally with T* **3.**

No.	Type	Description	Unused	Used
35	**1**	"TWO" on 50 c. on 1s. grey (R.)	16·00	20·00
		a. Bisected (1 c.) (on cover)	—	40·00
		b. Surch. in black	£3250	£3000
		c. Surch. double (R. + Bk.)	£3000	£2750

1888 (July)–**91.** *Surch. in London as T* **4.** *Wmk Crown CA. P* 14

No.	Type	Description	Unused	Used
36	**1**	1 c. on 1d. dull green (?12.91)	25	25
37	,,	2 c. on 1d. carmine	25	55
		a. Bisected (1 c.) (on cover)	—	26·00
38	,,	3 c. on 3d. red-brown	35	70
39	,,	6 c. on 3d. ultram. (?4.91)	80	2·00
40	,,	10 c. on 4d. mauve	80	80
		a. Surch. double	£325	
41	,,	20 c. on 6d. yellow (2.89)	2·75	5·50
42	,,	50 c. on 1s. grey (11.88)	6·50	12·00
36/42 Optd. "Specimen"		*Set of* 7	£120	

6 ~~10~~ CENTS (5)

FIVE (6) 15 (7)

1891. *Stamps of* 1888–91 *surch. locally.*

(*a*) *With T* **5** (May).

43 **1** 6 c. on 10 c. on 4d. mauve (R.) .. .. .. 45 1·60
a. "6" and bar inverted .. £120 11·00
b. "6" only inverted.. .. — £800
44 „ 6 c. on 10 c. on 4d. mauve (Bk.) .. .. .. 45 1·60
a. "6" and bar inverted .. £800 £250
b. "6" only inverted.. .. — £800

Of variety (b) only six copies of each can exist, as one of each of these errors came in the first six sheets, and the mistake was then corrected. Of variety (a) more copies exist.

Essays are known with "SIX" in place of "6", both with and without bars (*price* £25 *and* £160 *respectively*). Although not issued, we mention them, as two contemporary covers franked with them are known.

(*b*) *With T* **6/7** (23 Oct).

49 **1** 5 c. on 3 c. on 3d. red-brown 75 1·60
a. Wide space between "I" and "V" .. .. .. 10·00 12·00
b. "FIVE" and bar double .. 50·00
50 „ 15 c. on 6 c. on 3d. ultram. 3·75 5·00
a. Surch. double .. ..

8

9

10

11

(Typo. D.L.R.)

1891 (JULY)–**1901**. *Wmk. Crown CA. P* 14.

51 **8** 1 c. dull green (4.95) .. 25 35
52 „ 2 c. carmine-rose 25 30
53 „ 3 c. brown .. .. .. 40 1·10
54 „ 5 c. ultramarine (4.95) .. 5·00 55
55 **11** 5 c. grey-black and ultramarine/*blue* (10.00) .. 85 65
56 **8** 6 c. ultramarine 90 45
57 **9** 10 c. mauve and green (4.95) 3·25 3·00
58 **10** 10 c. dull pur. & grn. (1901) 1·60 3·00
59 **9** 12 c. pale mauve and green 12·00 2·25
a. Violet and green .. .. 3·25 3·00
60 „ 24 c. yellow and blue .. 1·60 3·25
a. Orange and blue .. .. 5·50 7·50
61 „ 25 c. red-brown & grn. (4.95) 8·00 10·00
62 **10** 50 c. green and carmine (3.98) 6·50 8·50
63 **11** $1 grn. & carmine (12.99) 11·00 12·00
64 „ $2 green & ultram. (12.99) 26·00 30·00
65 „ $5 green and black (12.99) £130 £160
51/65 .. .. *Set of* 15 £180 £225
51/65 Optd. "Specimen" *Set of* 15 £100

1899 (1 JULY). *Optd.* "REVENUE". A. *Opt.* 12 *mm. long.* B. *Opt.* 11 *mm. long.*

		A.		B.	
66	5 c. (No. 54) ..	1·25	1·25	1·25	1·40
	a. "BEVENUE"	12·00	13·00		
67	10 c. (No. 57) ..	2·00	2·25	4·00	4·50
	a. "BEVENUE"	45·00	—		†
	b. "REVENU"		†	£100	50·00
68	25 c. (No. 61) ..	1·60	2·25	2·00	2·25
	a. "BEVENUE"	23·00	24·00		†
69	50 c. (No. 41) ..	38·00	38·00	32·00	32·00
	a. "BEVENUE"	£850	—		†

Two minor varieties, a small "U" and a tall, narrow "U" are found in the word "REVENUE".

14

15

(Typo. D.L.R.)

1902 (10 OCT.)–**4**. *Wmk. Crown CA. P* 14.

80 **14** 1 c. grey-green and green (28.4.04) .. .. 1·90 3·25
81 „ 2 c. purple and black/*red* (18.3.03) 35 35
82 „ 5 c. grey-black & blue/*blue* 1·25 1·00
83 **15** 20 c. dull & bright purple (28.4.04) .. .. 4·50 6·00
80/3 Optd. "Specimen" *Set of* 4 27·00

1904–07. *Wmk. Mult. Crown CA. P* 14.

84 **14** 1 c. grey-green & grn., OC 30 40
85 „ 2 c. purple & black/*red*, OC 30 15
86 „ 5 c. grey-blk. & blue/*blue*, C 75 50
87 **15** 10 c. dull pur. & emer.-grn.,C 2·25 3·00
89 „ 25 c. dull pur. & orge., C .. 5·00 5·00
90 „ 50 c. grey-green & carm., C 8·50 9·50
91 **14** $1 grey-green & carm., C 13·00 14·00
92 „ $2 grey-green & blue, C .. 38·00 42·00
93 „ $5 grey-green & black, C £120 £130
84/93 .. .. *Set of* 9 £170 £180
87/93 Optd. "Specimen" *Set of* 6 50·00

Dates of issue:—1 c. 8.05; 2 c. 12.04; 5 c. 5.2.06; others 20.9.07.

1908 (7 DEC.)–**11**. *Colours changed. Wmk. Mult. Crown CA. P* 14.

95 **14** 1 c. blue-green, O (1.7.10) 50 40
96 „ 2 c. carmine, O 30 25
97 „ 5 c. ultram. O (1.6.09) .. 1·10 55
100 **15** 25 c. black/*grn.* C (14.10.11) 4·00 6·50
96/100 Optd. "Specimen" *Set of* 3 23·00

16

17

(Typo. D.L.R.)

1913–21. *Wmk. Mult. Crown CA. P* 14.

101 **16** 1 c. blue-green, O .. 12 12
a. Yellow-green (13.3.17) .. 25 30
102 „ 2 c. red, O 25 30
a. Bright scarlet (1915) .. 25 40
b. Dull scarlet (8.17) .. 60 60
c. Red/bluish .. .. 1·90 1·90
103 „ 3 c. orange, O (16.4.17).. 15 20
104 „ 5 c. bright blue, O .. 70 75
105 **17** 10 c. dull purple and yellow-green, C .. 1·60 1·75
a. Dull purple and bright green (1917) .. .. 1·90 1·90
106 „ 25 c. black/*green*, C .. 1·60 1·90
a. On blue-green, olive back (8.17) .. .. .. 1·60 3·50
b. On emerald back (1921) .. 1·60 3·50
107 „ 50 c. pur. & blue/*blue*, C.. 3·25 3·50
108 **16** $1 black and carm., C 6·00 6.50
109 „ $2 purple and green, C 26·00 28·00
110 „ $5 purple & black/*red*, C £110 £120
101/110 .. .. *Set of* 10 £140 £150
101/10 Optd. "Specimen" *Set of* 10 60·00

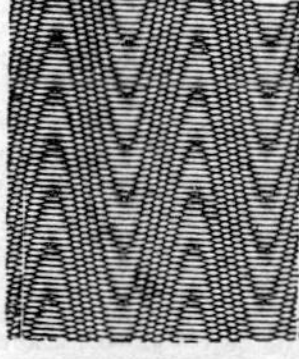
(**18**)

1915–16. *Optd. with T* **18**, *in violet.*

111 **16** 1 c. green (30.12.15) .. 50 1·60
a. Yellow-green (6.6.16) .. 25 90
112 „ 2 c. scarlet (3.11.15) .. 30 40
113 „ 5 c. bright blue (29.7.15).. 35 1·60
111/13 Optd. "Specimen" *Set of* 3 35·00

These stamps were shipped early in the 1914–18 war, and were thus overprinted, so that if seized by the enemy, they could be distinguished and rendered invalid.

WAR
(**19**)

WAR
(**20**)

1916 (23 AUG.). *No.* 111. *Optd. locally with T* **19.**

114 **16** 1 c. green 12 12
a. Opt. inverted .. .. 38·00 40·00

1917. *Nos.* 101 *and* 103. *Optd. with T* **19.**

116 **16** 1 c. blue-green 15 35
a. Yellow-green 15 30
118 „ 3 c. orange.. .. .. 30 40
a. Overprint double .. 75·00

1918. *Nos.* 101 *and* 103. *Optd. with T* **20.**

119 **18** 1 c. blue-green 20 35
a. Yellow-green 50 60
120 „ 3 c. orange.. .. .. 20 50
119/20 Optd. "Specimen" *Set of* 2 32·00

21

(Recess. D.L.R.)

1921 (28 APR.). *Peace Commemoration. Wmk. Mult. Crown CA* (*sideways*). *P* 14.

121 **21** 2 c. rose-red .. .. 1·25 1·00

1922 (4 JAN.). *As T* **21** *but with words* "PEACE" *omitted. Wmk. Mult. Script CA* (*sideways*). *P* 14.

122 4 c. slate .. .. .. 2·50 90
121/2 Optd. "Specimen" *Set of* 2 32·00

1921 (26 NOV.). *Wmk. Mult. Script CA. P* 14.

123 **16** 1 c. green, O (Optd. S. £13) 90 50

22

BELIZE
RELIEF FUND
PLUS
3 CENTS
(**23**)

(Typo. D.L.R.)

1922 (1 AUG.)–**33.** *Ordinary paper* (1 c. *to* 5 c.) *or chalk-surfaced paper* (*others*). *P* 14.

(*a*) *Wmk. Mult. Crown CA.*

124 **22** 25 c. black/*emerald* .. 3·25 5·50
125 „ $5 purple and black/*red* (1.10.24) £110 £130

(*b*) *Wmk. Mult. Script CA.*

126 **22** 1 c. green (2.1.29) .. 15 30
127 „ 2 c. brown (1.3.23) .. 12 12
128 „ 2 c. rose-carmine (10.12.26) 12 12
129 „ 3 c. orange (1933) .. 75 60
130 „ 4 c. grey (1.10.29) .. 65 35
131 „ 5 c. ultramarine 60 35
a. Milky blue (1923) .. 60 1·10
132 „ 10 c. dull purple and sage-green (1.12.22) .. 50 40
133 „ 25 c. black/*emerald* (1.10.24) 90 1·00
134 „ 50 c. purple and blue/*blue* (1.11.23) .. .. 2·75 4·00
136 „ $1 black & scarlet (2.1.25) 7·00 9·00
137 „ $2 yell.-grn. & brt. pur. 15·00 18·00
124/137 .. .. *Set of* 13 £130 £150
124/137 Optd./Perf. "Specimen" *Set of* 13 60·00

1932 (2 May). *Belize Relief Fund. Surch. as T* **23**. *Wmk. Mult. Script CA. P* 14.

138	**22**	1 c.+1 c. green ..	45	1·60
139	,,	2 c.+2 c. rose-carmine ..	65	1·60
140	,,	3 c.+3 c. orange ..	85	2·25
141	,,	4 c.+4 c. grey (R.) ..	1·25	2·75
142	,,	5 c.+5 c. ultramarine ..	2·75	5·50
138/142		.. .. *Set of* 5	5·00	12·00
138/42		Perf. "Specimen" *Set of* 5	42·00	

1935 (6 May). *Silver Jubilee. As Nos.* 91/4 *of Antigua, but ptd. by B.W. & Co. P* 11×12.

143	3 c. ultramarine & grey-black	20	25
	a. Extra flagstaff	12·00	
144	4 c. green and indigo	30	35
	a. Extra flagstaff	45·00	
145	5 c. brown and deep blue ..	85	95
146	25 c. slate and purple ..	1·60	1·90
	a. Extra flagstaff	60·00	
143/6	Perf. "Specimen" *Set of* 4	14·00	

For illustration of "extra flagstaff" variety, see Bechuanaland.

1937 (12 May). *Coronation. As Nos.* 13/15 *of Aden. P* 14.

147	3 c. orange	8	10
148	4 c. grey-black	10	12
149	5 c. bright blue	10	15
147/9	Perf. "Specimen" *Set of* 3	11·00	

24. Maya figures.

25. Chicle tapping.

26. Cohune palm.

27. Local Products.

28. Grapefruit.

29. Mahogany logs in river.

30. Sergeant's Cay.

31. Dorey.

32. Chicle industry.

33. Court House, Belize.

34. Mahogany felling.

35. Arms of Colony.

(Recess. Bradbury, Wilkinson.)

1938–47?. *Wmk. Mult. Script CA* (**sideways on** *horizontal stamps*). *P* $11\frac{1}{2}\times11$ (**horiz. designs**) *or* $11\times11\frac{1}{2}$ (*vert. designs*).

150	**24**	1 c. bright magenta & grn.	10	12
151	**25**	2 c. black and scarlet ..	10	12
		a. Perf. 12	85	70
152	**26**	3 c. purple and brown ..	12	15
153	**27**	4 c. black and green ..	12	15
154	**28**	5 c. mauve and dull blue	12	15
155	**29**	10 c. green & reddish brown	20	15
156	**30**	15 c. brown and light blue	30	25
157	**31**	25 c. blue and green	50	35
158	**32**	50 c. black and purple ..	80	80
159	**33**	$1 scarlet and olive ..	1·40	1·40
160	**34**	$2 deep blue and maroon	3·25	2·50
161	**35**	$5 scarlet and brown ..	9·00	6·50
150/161		.. .. *Set of* 12	15·00	12·00
150/61		Perf. "Specimen" *Set of* 12	26·00	

Dates of issue. 10.1.38, 3 c., 4 c. and 5 c. 14.2.38, 1 c., 2 c. (p. $11\times11\frac{1}{2}$), 10 c., 15 c., 25 c. and 50 c.; 28.2.38, $1, $2, and $5; 1947? 2 c. p. 12).

1946 (9 Sept.). *Victory. As Nos.* 28/9 *of Aden.*

162	3 c. brown	8	5
163	5 c. blue	8	5
162/3	Perf. "Specimen" *Set of* 2	11·00	

1948 (1 Oct.). *Royal Silver Wedding. As Nos.* 30/1 *of Aden.*

164	4 c. green	8	5
165	$5 brown	8·00	10·00

36. Island of St. George's Cay.

37. H.M. Sloop, ***Merlin***.

(Recess. Waterlow.)

1949 (10 Jan.). *150th Anniv. of Battle of St. George's Cay. Wmk. Mult. Script CA. P* $12\frac{1}{2}$.

166	**36**	1 c. ultramarine & green	12	12
167	,,	3 c. blue & yellow-brown	12	15
168	,,	4 c. olive and violet	15	20
169	**37**	5 c. brown and deep blue	25	25
170	,,	10 c. green and red-brown	35	35
171	,,	15 c. emerald and ultram.	45	50
166/171		.. .. *Set of* 6	1·25	1·40

1949 (10 Oct.). *75th Anniv. of U.P.U. As Nos.* 114/17 *of Antigua.*

172	4 c. blue-green	20	20
173	5 c. deep blue	30	40
174	10 c. red-brown	55	60
175	25 c. blue	1·00	1·25

1951 (16 Feb.). *Inauguration of B.W.I. University College. As Nos.* 118/19 *of Antigua.*

176	3 c. reddish violet & brown	15	15
177	10 c. green and brown ..	30	30

1953 (2 June). *Coronation. As No.* 47 *of Aden.*

178	4 c. black and green.. ..	30	35

38. Arms of British Honduras.

39. Mountain Cow.

40. Mace and Legislative Council Chamber.

41. Pine Industry.

42. Spiny Lobster.

43. Stanley Field Airport.

44. Maya Frieze.

45. Blue Butterfly.

46. Maya Indian.

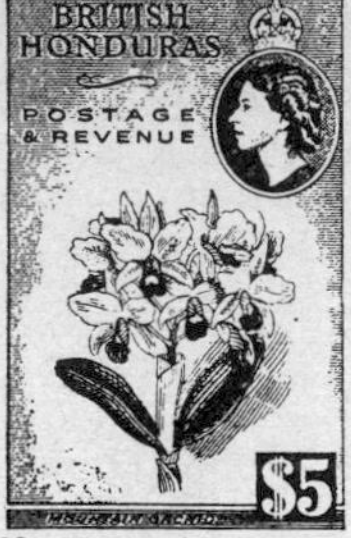

49. Mountain Orchid.

47. Armadillo.

48. Hawkesworth Bridge.

(Recess. Waterlow (until 1961), then De La Rue.)

1953 (2 Sept.)–**57.** *Wmk. Mult. Script CA. P* 13½.

179	**38**	1 c. green and black ..	5	5
180	**39**	2 c. yellow-brn. & black	8	10
		a. Perf. 14 (18.9.57) ..	10	12
181	**40**	3 c. reddish violet and bright purple (*shades*)	5	5
		a. Perf. 14 (18.9.57) ..	5	5
182	**41**	4 c. brown and green ..	5	10
183	**42**	5 c. deep olive-green and scarlet	15	15
		a. Perf. 14 (15.5.57) ..	8	12
184	**43**	10 c. slate & bright blue ..	10	12
185	**44**	15 c. green and violet ..	30	30
186	**45**	25 c. brt. blue & yell.-brn.	35	30
187	**46**	50 c. yellow-brown and reddish purple (*shades*)	90	1·10
188	**47**	$1 slate-blue & red-brn.	1·90	2·75
189	**48**	$2 scarlet and grey ..	3·75	4·75
190	**49**	$5 purple and slate ..	8·50	9·50
179/190		.. .. *Set of* 12	14·00	17·00

Nos. 179/90 were released a day earlier by the Crown Agents in London.

50. Belize from Fort George, 1842.

51. Public Seals, 1860 and 1960.

52. Tamarind Tree, Newtown Barracks.

(Recess. Bradbury, Wilkinson.)

1960 (1 July). *Post Office Centenary. W* w.**12.** *P* 11½×11.

191	**50**	2 c. green	10	10
192	**51**	10 c. deep carmine ..	20	20
193	**52**	15 c. blue	35	35

NEW CONSTITUTION
1960
(**53**)

HURRICANE
HATTIE
(**54**)

1961 (1 Mar.). *New Constitution. Nos.* 180*a*, 181*a and* 184/5 *optd. with T* **53** *by Waterlow.*

194	**39**	2 c. yellow-brown & black	5	8
195	**40**	3 c. red'sh vio. & brt. pur.	12	15
196	**43**	10 c. slate and brt. blue ..	35	35
197	**44**	15 c. green and violet ..	45	50

1962 (15 Jan.). *Hurricane Hattie Relief Fund. Optd. with T* **54** *by De La Rue.*

198	**38**	1 c. green and black ..	5	8
199	**43**	10 c. slate and bright blue	12	20
200	**45**	25 c. brt. blue & yell.-brown	25	30
201	**46**	50 c. yellow-brown & reddish purple	50	55

55. Great Curassow.

(Des. D. R. Eckelberry. Photo. Harrison.)

1962 (2 Apr.). *T* **55** *and similar horiz. designs. Multicoloured. W* w.**12** (*upright*). *P* 14×14½.

202	1 c. Type **55**	5	5
203	2 c. Red-legged Honey-creeper	5	5
204	3 c. American Jacana ..	5	5
	a. Blue-green (legs) omitted ..	70·00	
205	4 c. Great Kiskadee ..	5	8
206	5 c. Scarlet-rumped Tanager	8	10
207	10 c. Scarlet Macaw	10	12
	a. Blue omitted	50·00	
208	15 c. Massena Trogon ..	12	15
209	25 c. Red-footed Booby ..	20	25
210	50 c. Keel-billed Toucan ..	65	80
211	$1 Magnificent Frigate Bird	1·75	2·00
212	$2 Rufous-tailed Jacamar (*shades*)	3·00	3·75
213	$5 Montezuma Oropendola	5·50	6·50
202/213	.. .. *Set of* 12	10·00	12·00

See also Nos. 239/45.

1963 (4 June). *Freedom from Hunger. As No. 76 of Aden.*

214	22 c. bluish green	50	55

1963 (2 Sept.). *Red Cross Centenary. As Nos. 147/8 of Antigua.*

215	4 c. red and black	8	10
216	22 c. red and blue	55	55

II. SELF-GOVERNMENT.

SELF GOVERNMENT
1964
(**56**)

DEDICATION OF SITE
NEW CAPITAL
9th OCTOBER 1965
(**57**)

1964. *New Constitution. Nos.* 202, 204/5, 207 *and* 209 *optd. with T* **56.**

217 1 c. Type **55** (20.4) 5 5
 a. Opt. inverted .. .. 75·00
218 3 c. American Jacana (20.4) 8 8
219 4 c. Great Kiskadee (3.2) .. 10 10
220 10 c. Scarlet Macaw (20.4) .. 25 25
221 25 c. Red-footed Booby (3.2) 40 45
217/21 .. .. *Set of* 5 80 85

1965 (17 MAY). *I.T.U. Centenary. As Nos.* 166/7 *of Antigua.*

222 2 c. orange-red & lt. green .. 5 5
223 50 c. yellow & light purple 45 50

1965 (25 OCT.). *International Co-operation Year. As Nos.* 168/9 *of Antigua.*

224 1 c. reddish pur. & turq.-grn. 8 8
225 22 c. dp. bluish grn. & lavender 35 40

1966 (24 JAN.). *Churchill Commemoration. As Nos.* 170/3 *of Antigua.*

226 1 c. new blue 12 12
227 4 c. deep green 20 20
228 22 c. brown 35 35
229 25 c. bluish violet 45 55

1966 (1 JULY). *Dedication of new Capital Site. Stamps of* 1962 *but with W* w.**12** *sideways, optd. with T* **57** *by Harrison.*

230 1 c. Type **55** 5 5
231 3 c. American Jacana .. 5 5
232 4 c. Great Kiskadee .. 8 8
233 10 c. Scarlet Macaw .. 20 20
234 25 c. Red-footed Booby .. 35 35
230/34 .. .. *Set of* 5 60 60

58. Citrus Grove.

(Des. V. Whiteley. Photo. Harrison.)

1966 (1 OCT.). *Stamp Centenary. T* **58** *and similar horiz. designs. Multicoloured. W* w.**12.** *P* 14 × 14½.

235 5 c. Type **58** 5 5
236 10 c. Half Moon Cay .. 20 20
237 22 c. Hidden Valley Falls .. 35 35
238 25 c. Maya Ruins, Xunantunich 50 50

1967. *As Nos.* 202, *etc., but wmk.* w.**12** *sideways.*

239 1 c. Type **55** (16.2) 5 5
240 2 c. Red-legged Honeycreeper (28.12) .. 5 8
241 4 c. Great Kiskadee (16.2) .. 8 10
242 5 c. Scarlet-rumped Tanager (16.2) 12 15
243 10 c. Scarlet Macaw (28.11) .. 20 25
244 15 c. Massena Trogon (28.11) 30 35
245 50 c. Keel-billed Toucan (16.2) 80 90
239/245 .. .. *Set of* 7 1·40 1·60

The 15 c. value exists with PVA gum as well as gum arabic.

59. Sailfish.

(Des. R. Granger Barrett. Photo. Harrison.)

1967 (1* DEC.). *International Tourist Year. T* **59** *and similar horiz. designs. W* w.**12.** *P* 12½.

246 5 c. deep violet-blue, black and light yellow .. 5 5
247 10 c. brown, black and orange-red 5 8
248 22 c. yellow-orange, black and bright green .. 25 25
249 25 c. light greenish blue, black and greenish yellow .. 30 35

Designs:—10 c. Deer; 22 c. Jaguar; 25 c. Tarpon.

*The stamps were not released by the Crown Agents until 4 December.

60. *Schomburgkia libiscinus.*

(Des. Mrs. S. Goaman. Photo. Harrison.)

1968 (16 APR.). *20th Anniv. of Economic Commission for Latin America. T* **60** *and similar vert. designs. Multicoloured. W* w.**12** *(sideways). P* 14½ × 14.

250 5 c. Type **60** 5 5
251 10 c. *Maxillaria tenuifolia* .. 5 8
252 22 c. *Bletia purpurea* .. 20 25
253 25 c. *Sobralia macrantha* .. 25 30

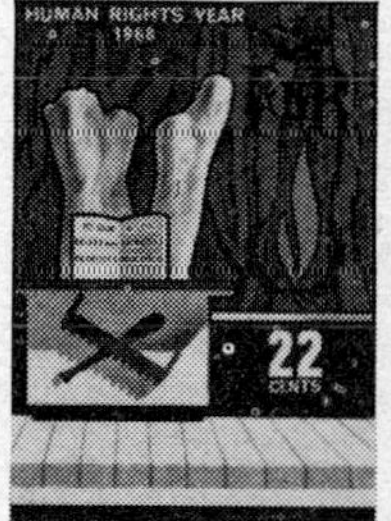

61. Monument to Belizean Patriots.

62. Monument at Site of New Capital.

(Des. G. L. Vasarhelyi. Litho. B.W.)

1968 (15 JULY). *Human Rights Year. W* w.**12.** *P* 13½.

254 **61** 22 c. multicoloured .. 20 20
255 **62** 50 c. multicoloured .. 30 35

63. Jew Fish.

(Des. J. Waddington Ltd. Litho. De La Rue.)

1968 (15 OCT.). *Fishes and Animals. T* **63** *and similar horiz. designs. Multicoloured. No wmk. P* 13 × 12½.

256 1 c. Type **63** 5 5
257 2 c. Warree 5 5
258 3 c. Grouper 5 5
259 4 c. Ant Bear 5 5
260 5 c. Bonefish 8 8
261 10 c. Gibnut 10 12
262 15 c. Dolphin 15 15
263 25 c. Night Walker 25 25
264 50 c. Mutton Snapper .. 45 55
265 $1 Bush Dog .. .. 90 1·10
266 $2 Great Barracuda .. 1·75 2·00
267 $5 Mountain Lion .. 3·25 3·75
256/67 .. .. *Set of* 12 6·50 7·50

See also Nos. 276/8 and 338/40.

64. *Rhyncholaelia digbyana.*

(Des. Mrs. Sylvia Goaman. Photo. Harrison.)

1969 (9 APR.). *Orchids of Belize (First Series). T* **64** *and similar vert. designs. Multicoloured. W* w.**12** *(sideways). P* 14½ × 14.

268 5 c. Type **64** 8 8
269 10 c. *Cattleya bowringiana* .. 15 15
270 22 c. *Lycaste cochteatum* .. 30 35
271 25 c. *Coryanthes speciosum* .. 35 40

See also Nos. 287/90.

65. Ziricote Tree.

(Des. V. Whiteley. Litho. De La Rue.)

1969 (1 SEPT.). *Indigenous Hardwoods (First Series). T* **65** *and similar vert. designs. Multicoloured. W* w.**12.** *P* 14.

272 5 c. Type **65** 8 8
273 10 c. Rosewood 12 12
274 22 c. Mayflower 25 25
275 25 c. Mahogany 30 30

See also Nos 291/4 and 315/8.

1969–72. *As T* **63.** *New value and design* (½ c.). *Others as Nos.* 257/8, 261, 267 *but W* w.**12** *(sideways).*

276 ½ c. Crana Fish (ultramarine background) (1.9.69) .. 10 10
277 ½ c. Crana Fish (yellow-olive background) (1.2.71) .. 5 5
 a. Black (All inscr. and value) omitted ..
277*b* 2 c. Waree (5.5.72) 5 5
277*c* 3 c. Grouper (5.5.72) .. 5 5
277*d* 10 c. Gibnut (5.5.72) .. 10 12
278 $5 Mountain Lion (12.5.70) 3·75 4·25
276/78 .. .. *Set of* 6 3·75 4·25

See also Nos. 338/40.

66. " The Virgin and Child " (Bellini).

POPULATION
CENSUS 1970
(68)

67. " The Adoration of the Magi " (Veronese).

(Des. adapted by G. Drummond. Litho. Format.)

1969 (1 Nov.). *Christmas.* *W* w.**12**. *P* 14 × 14½.

279	**66**	5 c. multicoloured ..	5	5
280	,,	15 c. multicoloured ..	15	15
281	**67**	22 c. multicoloured ..	25	25
282	,,	25 c. multicoloured ..	30	30

Although released by the Crown Agents on 1 October this issue was not put on sale locally until 1 November.

1970 (2 Feb.). *Population Census.* *As Nos.* 260/3, *but W* w.**12** (*sideways*), *optd. with T* **68**.

283	5 c. Bonefish	5	5
284	10 c. Gibnut	12	12
285	15 c. Dolphin	20	20
286	25 c. Night Walker	25	30

(Des. G. Drummond. Litho. Format.)

1970 (2 Apr.). *Orchids of Belize* (*Second Series*). *As T* **64**. *Multicoloured.* *W* w.**12**. *P* 14.

287	5 c. Black Orchid	8	8
288	15 c. White Butterfly Orchid	15	15
289	22 c. Swan Orchid	20	20
290	25 c. Butterfly Orchid ..	25	25

69. Santa Maria.

(Des. Jennifer Toombs. Litho. Questa.)

1970 (7 Sept.). *Indigenous Hardwoods* (*Second Series*). *T* **69** *and similar vert. designs. Multicoloured.* *W* w.**12** (*sideways*). *P* 14 × 14½.

291	5 c. Type **69**	15	12
292	15 c. Nargusta	20	15
293	22 c. Cedar	25	20
294	25 c. Sapodilla	30	25

70. " The Nativity " (A. Hughes).

(Des. J. E. Cooter. Litho. J.W.)

1970 (7 Nov.*). *Christmas.* *T* **70** *and similar vert. design. Multicoloured.* *W* w.**12**. *P* 14.

295	½ c. Type **70**	5	5
296	5 c. " The Mystic Nativity " (Botticelli)	10	10
297	10 c. Type **70**	12	12
298	15 c. As 5 c.	15	15
299	22 c. Type **70**	30	30
300	50 c. As 5 c.	45	45
295/300	.. .. *Set of* 6	1·00	1·00

*These stamps were released by the Crown Agents in London on 2 November.

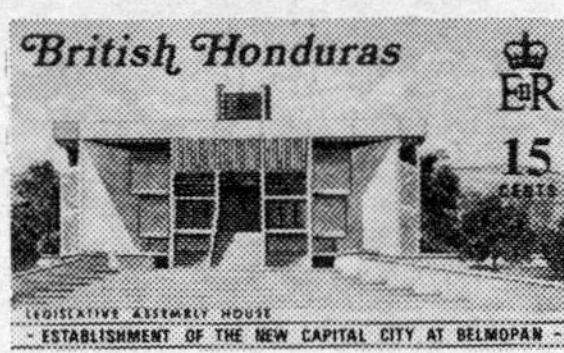

71. Legislative Assembly House.

(Des. G. Drummond. Litho. Enschedé.)

1971 (30 Jan.). *Establishment of New Capital, Belmopan.* *T* **71** *and similar horiz. designs. Multicoloured.* *W* w.**12** *upright* (5 c., 10 c.) *or sideways* (*others*). *P* 13 × 13½.

301	5 c. Old Capital, Belize ..	5	5
302	10 c. Government Plaza ..	10	10
303	15 c. Type **71**	12	12
304	22 c. Magistrates' Court ..	25	25
305	25 c. Police H.Q.	25	25
306	50 c. New G.P.O.	40	40
301/306	.. .. *Set of* 6	1·00	1·00

The 5 c. and 10 c. are larger, 60 × 22 mm.

72. *Tabebuia chrysantha.*

(Des. Sylvia Goaman. Litho. Questa.)

1971 (27 Mar.). *Easter.* *T* **72** *and similar horiz. designs showing flowers. Multicoloured.* *W* w.**12** (*sideways*). *P* 14.

307	½ c. Type **72**	5	5
308	5 c. *Hymenocallis littorallis*	8	8
309	10 c. *Hippeastrum equestre* ..	10	10
310	15 c. Type **72**	12	12
311	22 c. As 5 c.	20	20
312	25 c. As 10 c.	25	25
307/12	.. .. *Set of* 6	70	70

RACIAL EQUALITY
YEAR-1971
(73)

1971 (14 June). *Racial Equality Year.* *As Nos.* 261 *and* 264, *but W* w.**12** (*sideways*) *and optd. with T* **73**.

313	10 c. Gibnut	10	10
314	50 c. Mutton Snapper ..	35	40

74. Tubroos.

(Des. Jennifer Toombs. Litho. Questa.)

1971 (16 Aug.). *Indigenous Hardwoods* (*Third Series*). *T* **74** *and similar vert. designs. Multicoloured.* *W* w. **12**. *P* 13½.

315	5 c. Type **74**	12	12
316	15 c. Yemeri	25	25
317	26 c. Billywebb	30	30
318	50 c. Logwood	45	50
MS319	96 × 171 mm. Nos. 315/8 ..	1·40	1·40

One example of the miniature sheet with the silver (Queen's head) omitted, has been reported.

75. Hawksworth and Belcan Bridges.

(Des. and litho. J.W.)

1971 (23 Sept.). *Bridges of the World.* *T* **75** *and similar horiz. designs. Multicoloured.* *W* w.**12** (*sideways*). *P* 13½.

320	½ c. Type **75**	5	5
321	5 c. Narrows Bridge, N.Y. and Quebec Bridge ..	8	8
322	26 c. London Bridge (1871) and reconstructed, Arizona (1971)	25	25
323	50 c. Belize Mexican Bridge and Swing Bridge ..	50	50

76. *Petrae volubis.* **77.** Seated Figure.

(Des. G. Drummond. Litho. Format.)

1972 (28 FEB.). *Easter. T* **76** *and similar vert. designs showing wild flowers. Multicoloured. W* w.**12**. *P* 14½.

324	6 c. Type **76**	12	12
325	15 c. Yemeri	25	25
326	26 c. Mayflower	30	30
327	50 c. Tiger's Claw	50	50

(Des. Jennifer Toombs. Litho. Questa.)

1972 (22 MAY). *Mayan Artefacts. T* **77** *and similar multicoloured designs. W* w.**12** *(sideways, except* 16 *c.). P* 13½×13 *(*16 *c.) or* 13×13½ *(others).*

328	3 c. Type **77**	10	10
	a. Royal Cypher double	—	75·00
329	6 c. Priest in "dancing" pose	10	10
330	16 c. Sun God's head (*horiz.*) ..	25	25
331	26 c. Priest and Sun God ..	30	30
332	50 c. Full-front figure ..	45	50
328/32	.. .. *Set of* 5	1·10	1·10

Nos. 328/32 are inscribed on the reverse with information about the artefacts depicted.

As well as the 3 c., the 26 c. comes with Royal Cypher double; but this is due to a blanket offset.

78. Banak.

(Des. Jennifer Toombs. Litho. Questa.)

1972 (21 AUG.). *Indigenous Hardwoods (Fourth Series). T* **78** *and similar vert. designs. Multicoloured. W* w.**12** *(sideways). P* 14½.

333	3 c. Type **78**	8	8
334	5 c. Quamwood	10	10
335	16 c. Waika Chewstick ..	15	15
336	26 c. Mamee-Apple	30	30
337	50 c. My Lady	40	45
333/7	.. .. *Set of* 5	90	1·00

1972 (17 NOV.). *As Nos.* 258 *and* 260/1 *but W* w.**12** *(upright).*

338	3 c. Grouper	5	5
339	5 c. Bonefish	8	8
340	10 c. Gibnut	10	10

79. Orchids of Belize.

(Des. (from photograph by D. Groves) and photo. Harrison.)

1972 (20 NOV.). *Royal Silver Wedding. Multicoloured; background colour given. W* w.**12**. *P* 14×14½.

341	**79** 26 c. deep ultramarine ..	25	25
342	,, 50 c. bright bluish violet	40	40

80. Baron Bliss Day.

(Des. J.W. Ltd. Litho. Questa.)

1973 (9 MAR.). *Festivals of Belize. T* **80** *and similar horiz. designs. Multicoloured. W* w.**12**. *P* 14½×14.

343	3 c. Type **80**	5	5
344	10 c. Labour Day	10	10
345	26 c. Carib Settlement Day	15	15
346	50 c. Pan American Day ..	35	35

POSTAGE DUE STAMPS.

D 1

(Typo. D.L.R.)

1923–64. *Wmk. Mult. Script CA. P* 14.

D1	D **1** 1 c. black, O	30	45
	a. Chalky paper (25.9.56) ..	5	8
	b. White uncoated paper (9.4.64)	8	8
D2	,, 2 c. black, O	30	45
	a. Chalky paper (25.9.56) ..	5	8
D3	,, 4 c. black, O	65	75
	a. Chalky paper (25.9.56) ..	5	8
D1/3	Optd. "Specimen" *Set of* 3	15·00	

The early ordinary paper printings were yellowish and quite distinct from No. D1b.

1965 (3 AUG.)–**72.** *As Nos.* D2a *and* D3a, *but Wmk.* w.**12** *(sideways on* 2 *c.). P* 13½×13 *(*2 *c.) or* 13½×14 *(*4 *c.).*

D4	D **1** 2 c. black (10.1.72) ..	8	8
D5	,, 4 c. black	8	8

On 1st June 1973, British Honduras was renamed BELIZE (*q.v.*).

BRITISH INDIAN OCEAN TERRITORY.

This Crown Colony was created on 8th November 1965 and comprises the Chagos Archipelago, previously administered by Mauritius, together with the islands of Aldabra (Diego Garcia), Farquhar and Desroches, previously administered by Seychelles.

(100 cents = 1 rupee.)

B.I.O.T.

(1)

1968 (17 JAN.). *Stamps of Seychelles (Nos.* 196/200, 202/4 *and* 206/12, *but sideways wmk. on all vert. designs) optd. with T* **1**.

1	**24** 5 c. multicoloured	8	8
2	**25** 10 c. multicoloured	8	10
3	**26** 15 c. multicoloured	10	10
4	**27** 20 c. multicoloured	12	12
5	**28** 25 c. multicoloured	12	15
6	**30** 40 c. multicoloured	20	25
7	**31** 45 c. multicoloured	25	25
8	**32** 50 c. multicoloured	25	35
9	**34** 75 c. multicoloured	40	60
10	**35** 1 r. multicoloured	90	1·10
11	**36** 1 r. 50, multicoloured	1·40	1·75
12	**37** 2 r. 25, multicoloured ..	2·25	3·00
13	**38** 3 r. 50, multicoloured ..	3·50	4·50
14	**39** 5 r. multicoloured	4·00	5·00
15	**40** 10 r. multicoloured	9·00	11·00
1/15	.. .. *Set of* 15	20·00	25·00

These were issued by the Crown Agents on 15th January but owing to shipping delays they were not put on sale locally until 17th January.

"Missing stop" varieties occur as follows: after "O" twice in each sheet on the 5, 10, 15, 20, 25, 40 and 50 c. and 1, 1.50, 2.25, 3.50 and 5 r.; after "I" once in the sheet on the same values plus the 45 c.; after "B" once in the sheet on the 10 r. only. Prices for pairs with and without stop after "O" are from three times the normal price for a single and for the other varieties, from four times normal.

We have seen a sheet of the 5 c. and 10 c. with all stops in place so that either the no stop varieties developed during printing or they were discovered and inserted during the printing.

2. Lascar.

(Des. G. Drummond, based on drawings by Mrs. W. Veevers-Carter. Litho. De La Rue.)

1968 (23 OCT.)–**70.** *Sea Creatures. T* **2** *and similar designs. Multicoloured. White paper (Nos.* 20a, 23a, 24a) *or Cream paper (others). W* w.**12** *(sideways on horiz., inverted on vert. designs). P* 14.

16	5 c. Type **2**	15	15
17	10 c. Hammerhead Shark (*vert.*)	12	10
18	15 c. Tiger Shark	12	10
19	20 c. Bat Ray	12	10
20	25 c. Butterfly Fish (*vert.*) ..	12	10
20a	30 c. Robber Crab (7.12.70) ..	12	10
21	40 c. Caranx	12	10
22	45 c. Garfish (*vert.*) ..	30	35
23	50 c. Barracuda	20	15
23a	60 c. Spotted Pebble Crab (7.12.70)	25	20
24	75 c. Parrot Fish	60	60
24a	85 c. Dorade (*Elegatis bipinnulatus*) (7.12.70) ..	30	30
25	1 r. Giant Hermit Crab ..	50	60
26	1 r. 50, Humphead	1·00	1·25
27	2 r. 25, Rock Cod	2·75	3·50
28	3 r. 50, Black Marlin ..	2·25	2·75
29	5 r. blk., blue-grn. & greenish blue (Whale Shark) (*vert.*)	2·25	2·75
30	10 r. Lion Fish	4·50	6·00
	a. Imperf. (pair) ..		
16/30	.. .. *Set of* 18	14·00	17·00

See also No. 52.

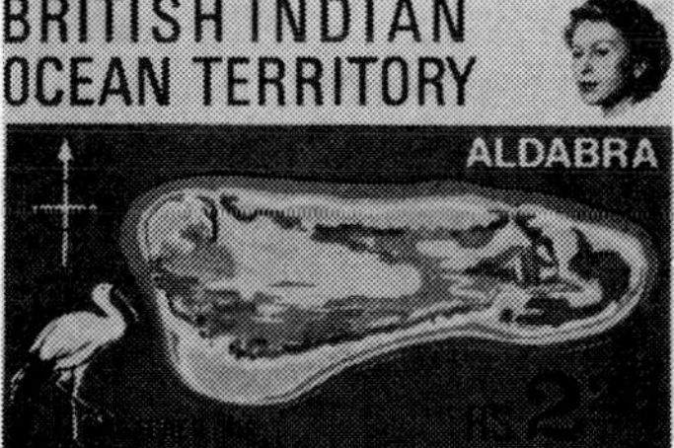

3. Sacred Ibis and Aldabra Coral Atoll.

(Des. and litho. De La Rue.)

1969 (10 JULY). *Coral Atolls. W* w.**12** *(sideways). P* 13½×13.

31	**3** 2 r. 25, multicoloured ..	1·00	1·25

4. Out-rigger.

(Des. Mrs. M. Hayward adapted by V. Whiteley. Litho. De La Rue.)

1969 (15 Dec.). *Ships of the Islands. T* **4** *and similar horiz. designs. Multicoloured. W* w.**12** *(sideways). P* 13½ × 14.

32	45 c. Type **4**	30	30
33	75 c. Pirogue	45	45
34	1 r. M.V. *Nordvaer*	55	55
35	1 r. 50, *Isle of Farquhar* ..	75	80

5. Giant Land Tortoise.

(Des. G. Drummond. Litho. Format.)

1971 (1 Feb.). *Aldabra Nature Reserve. T* **4** *and similar horiz. designs. Multicoloured. W* w.**12** *(sideways). P* 13½.

36	45 c. Type **5**	25	25
37	75 c. Aldabra Lily	40	40
38	1 r. Aldabra Snail	50	50
39	1 r. 50, Dimorphic Egrets ..	75	75

6. Arms of Royal Society and Flightless Rail.

(Des. V. Whiteley. Litho. J.W.)

1971 (30 June). *Opening of Royal Society Research Station on Aldabra. W* w.**12** *(sideways). P* 13½.

40	**6** 3 r. 50, multicoloured ..	2·00	2·00

7. Staghorn Coral.

(Des. V. Whiteley. Litho. A. & M.)

1972 (1 Mar.). *Coral. T* **7** *and similar horiz. designs. Multicoloured. W* w.**12** *(sideways). P* 13½.

41	40 c. Type **7**	20	20
42	60 c. Brain coral	30	30
43	1 r. Mushroom coral ..	50	50
44	1 r. 75, Organ Pipe coral ..	75	80

On some sheets of No. 43 the inks have been applied in a different order, resulting in an almost total absence of blue.

8. Flightless Rail and Sacred Ibis.

(Des. (from photograph by D. Groves) and photo. Harrison.)

1972 (20 Nov.). *Royal Silver Wedding. Multicoloured; background colour given. W* w.**12**. *P* 14 × 14½.

45	**8** 95 c. deep dull green (*shades*)	80	1·25
46	„ 1 r. 50, bright bluish violet	1·25	1·90

9. Christ on the Cross.

(Des. Jennifer Toombs. Litho. Questa.)

1973 (9 Apr.). *Easter. T* **9** *and similar vert. design. Multicoloured. W* w.**12**. *P* 14.

47	45 c. Type **9**	15	15
48	75 c. Joseph and Nicodemus burying Jesus	25	25
49	1 r. Type **9**	40	40
50	1 r. 50, As 75 c.	50	55
MS51	126 × 110 mm. Nos. 47/50 ..	3·00	3·00

1973 (2 Oct.). *As No.* 16 *but white paper and W* w.**12** *upright*.

52	5 c. Type **2**	15	15

No. 52 differs in shade from No. 16 because of the change of paper.

10. Upsidedown Jellyfish.

(Des. G. Drummond. Litho. Walsall Security Printers Ltd.)

1973 (12 Nov.). *Wildlife (1st series). T* **10** *and similar vert. designs. Multicoloured. W* w.**12** *(sideways) P* 14.

53	50 c. Type **10**	20	25
54	1 r. Butterflies	40	45
55	1 r. 50, Spider	50	50

See also Nos. 58/61, 77/80 and 86/9.

11. M.V. *Nordvaer*.

(Des. C. Abbott. Litho. Walsall.)

1974 (14 July). *Fifth Anniv. of "Nordvaer" Travelling Post Office. T* **11** *and similar vert. design. Multicoloured. W* w.**12** *(sideways). P* 14.

56	85 c. Type **11**	30	30
57	2 r. 50, *Nordvaer* off shore ..	65	75

12. Auger Shells.

(Des. PAD Studio. Litho. J.W.)

1974 (12 Nov.). *Wildlife (2nd series). T* **12** *and similar horiz. designs showing shells. Multicoloured. W* w.**12**. *P* 13½ × 14.

58	45 c. Type **12**	12	12
59	75 c. Green Turban	20	20
60	1 r. Drupe Snail	25	25
61	1 r. 50, Helmet Shell	40	40

13. Aldabra Drongo.

(Des. R. Granger Barrett. Litho. Questa.)

1975 (28 Feb.). *Birds. T* **13** *and similar multicoloured designs. W* w. **12** *(sideways on horiz. designs). P* 14.

62	5 c. Type **13**	5	5
63	10 c. Malagasy Coucal	5	5
64	20 c. Red-headed Forest Fody	5	5
65	25 c. Fairy Tern	5	5
66	30 c. Crested Tern	5	5
67	40 c. Brown Booby	5	5
68	50 c. Noddy Tern	8	8
69	60 c. Grey Heron	8	10
70	65 c. Blue-faced Booby ..	8	10
71	95 c. Malagasy White-eye ..	12	12
72	1 r. Green-backed Heron ..	12	15
73	1 r. 75, Lesser Frigate Bird	25	30
74	3 r. 50, White-tailed Tropic Bird	45	50
75	5 r. Souimanga Sunbird ..	65	75
76	10 r. Malagasy Turtle-dove ..	1·25	1·50
62/76	*Set of* 15	2·75	3·00

The 50 c. and 65 c. to 10 r. are horiz. designs, and the remainder are vert.

14. *Grewia salicifolia.*

(Des. Sylvia Goaman. Litho. Questa.)

1975 (10 July). *Wildlife* (*3rd series*). *T* **14** *and similar vert. designs showing seashore plants. Multicoloured. W* w.**12** (*sideways*). *P* 14.

77 50 c. Type **14** 10 12
78 65 c. *Cassia aldabrensis* .. 15 20
79 1 r. *Hypoestes aldabrensis* .. 20 25
80 1 r. 60, *Euphorbia pyrifolia* .. 30 35

15. Map of Aldabra.

(Des. L. D. Curtis. Litho. Questa.)

1975 (8 Nov.). *Maps T* 15 *and similar horiz. designs. Multicoloured. W* w.**12**. *P* 13½.

81 50 c. Type **15** 10 12
82 1 r. Desroches 20 25
83 1 r. 50, Farquhar 30 35
84 2 r. Diego Garcia 35 40
MS85 147×147 mm. Nos. 81/4. W w.**12** (sideways) .. .. 1·00

16. Crimson Speckled Moth.

(Des. PAD Studio. Litho. Questa.)

1976 (22 Mar.). *Wildlife* (*4th series*). *T* **16** *and similar horiz. designs. Multicoloured. W* w.**12** (*sideways*). *P* 13½.

86 65 c. Type **16** 10 12
87 1 r. 20, *Dysdercus fasciatus* (weevil) 20 25
88 1 r. 50, *Sphex torridus* (wasp) 25 30
89 2 r. *Oryctes rhinocerus* (beetle) 30 35

Aldabra (Diego Garcia) is now the only remaining island of this group, the others having been transferred to the Seychelles group when they achieved independence on 29 June 1976. Aldabra is entirely occupied by British and American Servicemen who have no need of a civilian postal service. At the time of going to press the 1975 definitive issue had not been withdrawn.

BRITISH LEVANT.

For GREAT BRITAIN stamps used in the Turkish Empire with "B **01**, B **02**, C, F **87**, G **06**" or "S obliterations," see index to Great Britain Stamps Used Abroad list.

I. British Post Offices in Turkish Empire.

80 PARAS (1) **4 PIASTRES** (2)

12 PIASTRES (3)

Stamps of Great Britain (*Queen Victoria*) *surch. as T* **1** *to* **3**.

1885 (1 April).
1 **64** 40 pa. on 2½d. lilac .. .. 5·50 1·40
2 **62** 80 pa. on 5d. green .. .. 48·00 3·00
3 **58** 12 pi. on 2s. 6d. lilac/*bluish* 60·00 28·00
a. On white paper.. .. 11·00 5·00
1/3 *Optd.* "Specimen" *Set of* 3 45·00

1887 (June)–**96.**
4 **74** 40 pa. on 2½d. purple/*blue* .. 55 20
a. Surch. double .. £500 £700
5 **78** 80 pa. on 5d. purple & blue 1·40 35
a. Small "0" in "80" .. 18·00 12·00
6 **81** 4 pi. on 10d. purple and carmine (10.10.96) .. 4·50 3·00
a. Large, wide "4" .. 8·00 8·00
4/6 Optd. "Specimen" *Set of* 3 30·00

1893 (25 Feb.). *Roughly handstamped at Constantinople, as T* **1**.
7 **71** 40 pa. on ½d. vermilion .. 80·00 42·00

This provisional was in use five days only. As fraudulent copies were made with the original handstamp, this stamp should only be purchased from undoubted sources. It is also known with genuine handstamp inverted.

1902–5. *Stamps of King Edward VII surch. as T* **1** *to* **3**.
8 **86** 40 pa. on 2½d. ultramarine, O (6.2.02) 60 20
9 **89** 80 pa. on 5d. purple and ultram., O (5.6.02) 90 80
a. Small "0" in "80" .. 22·00 11·00
10 **92** 4 pi. on 10d. dull purple & carmine, O (6.9.02) 2·75 1·10
a. No cross on crown .. 30·00
b. Chalky paper .. .. 3·00 2·25
ba. Chalky. No cross on crown.. .. .. 30·00
11 **94** 12 pi. on 2s. 6d. lilac, O (29.8.03) .. .. 11·00 12·00
a. Dull purple, C.. .. 11·00 12·00
12 **95** 24 pi. on 5s. carmine, O (15.8.05) .. .. 19·00 21·00
8/12 .. .. *Set of* 5 30·00 32·00
9/11 H/S "Specimen" *Set of* 3 30·00

LEVANT (4) **1 PIASTRE** (5)

1905 (15 Aug.). *Stamps of King Edward VII optd. with T* **4**.
13 **83** ½d. pale yellowish green, O 35 20
14 ,, 1d. scarlet, O 35 20
15 **84** 1½d. dull purple & green, O 1·90 1·40
a. Chalky paper .. .. 2·75 1·90
16 **85** 2d. grey-green & carm., O 1·90 1·90
a. Chalky paper .. .. 1·40 1·60
17 **86** 2½d. ultramarine, O .. 3·50 3·50
18 **87** 3d. purple/*orge.-yellow*, O 2·50 2·75
19 **88** 4d. green & choc.-brn., O 2·40 2·75
20 **89** 5d. dull pur. & ultram., O 5·50 6·00
21 **83** 6d. pale dull purple, O .. 4·50 5·50
22 **93** 1s. dull green & carm., O 7·50 7·50
a. Chalky paper .. .. 7·50 7·50
13/22 .. .. *Set of* 10 27·00 28·00

1905–08. *Surch. in* "piastres" *instead of* "paras" *as T* **5** *and* **2**.
23 **86** 1 pi. on 2½d. ultramarine, O (19.4.06) 90 15
24 **89** 2 pi. on 5d. dull purple and ultram., O (28.10.05) 2·25 90
a. Chalky paper (1.08) .. 2·25 90

1 Piastre (6) **1 PIASTRE 10 PARAS** (7)

1906 (2 July). *Issued at Beirut. No.* 16 *surch. with T* **6**.
25 **85** 1 pi. on 2d. grey-green and carmine, O .. £500 £200

1909 (16 Nov.–Dec.). *Stamps of King Edward VII surch. as T* **1** (*30 par.*), **7**, *and* **2** (*5 pi.*).
26 **84** 30 pa. on 1½d. dull purple and green, C .. 40 50
a. Surch. double, one albino
27 **87** 1 pi. 10 par. on 3d. purple/*orange-yellow*, C .. 2·75 3·50
28 **88** 1 pi. 30 par. on 4d. green & chocolate-brown, C 2·75 3·25
29 ,, 1 pi. 30 par. on 4d. pale orange, O (16.12.09) 3·00 3·25
30 **83** 2 pi. 20 par. on 6d. dull purple, C .. .. 5·50 6·00
31 **93** 5 pi. on 1s. dull green and carm., C (Optd. S. £18) 2·75 3·00
26/31 .. .. *Set of* 6 15·00 18·00

1¾ PIASTRE (8) **4** Normal "4". **4** Pointed "4".

1910 (24 Jan.). *Stamps of King Edward VII surch. as T* **8**.
32 **87** 1¾ pi. on 3d. purple/*orange-yellow*, C 35 75
33 **88** 1¾ pi. on 4d. orange, O .. 40 60
a. Thin, pointed "4" in fraction .. .. 11·00 12·00
34 **83** 2½ pi. on 6d. dull purple, C 90 90

1 PIASTRE (9) **1 PIASTRE** (10)

Type differences. In T **5** the letters are tall and narrow and the space enclosed by the upper part of the "A" is small.

In T **9** the opening of the "A" is similar, but the letters are shorter and broader, the "P" and the "E" being particularly noticeable.

In T **10** the letters are short and broad, but the "A" is thin and open.

1911–13. *Stamps of King Edward VII, Harrison or Somerset House ptgs., surch. or optd.*

(*a*) *Surch. with T* **5** (20 *July*).
35 **86** 1 pi. on 2½d. brt. blue (*p.* 14) 1·00 55
36 ,, 1 pi. on 2½d. bright blue (*perf.* 15×14) .. 2·00 80

(*b*) *Surch. with T* **9** (1911).
37 **86** 1 pi. on 2½d. bright blue (*perf.* 15×14) .. 3·50 1·40

(*c*) *Surch. with T* **10** (1911).
38 **86** 1 pi. on 2½d. bright blue (*perf.* 15×14) .. 6·00 1·10

(*d*) *Surch. as T* **1** *to* **3** (1911–13).

39 **84** 30 par. on 1½d. reddish purple and bright green (22.8.11) .. 1·10 45
 a. Slate-purple and green .. 90 90
40 **89** 2 pi. on 5d. deep dull reddish purple & bright blue (13.5.12) .. 90 85
41 **92** 4 pi. on 10d. dull purple & scarlet (26.6.12) .. 3·50 4·00
 a. Dull reddish purple and aniline pink .. ..
 b. Dull reddish pur. & carm. 3·75 4·50
 c. No cross on crown ..
42 **93** 5 pi. on 1s. grn. & carmine ('13) .. .. .. 3·00 3·25
43 **94** 12 pi. on 2s. 6d. dull reddish purple (3.2.12) 25·00 23·00
 a. Dull greyish purple .. 11·00 12·00
 b. Pale dull reddish purple .. 11·00 12·00
44 **95** 24 pi. on 5s. carmine ('13) 19·00 21·00
39/44 .. .. *Set of* 6 35·00 38·00

(*e*) *Optd. with T* **4** (14.2.12).

45 **83** ½d. dull yellow-green (*perf.* 14) .. .. 1·40 2·75

1911–13. *Stamps of King George V optd. with T* **4**.

(*a*) *Dies A. Wmk. Crown* (12.9.11).

46 **98** ½d. yellow-green (No. 322) 65 80
47 **99** 1d. deep rose-red (No. 327) 65 80
 a. No cross on crown ..
 b. Opt. double, one albino .. 50·00

(*b*) *Redrawn types. Wmk. Crown* (24.2.12).

48 **101** ½d. green (No. 339) .. 20 10
49 **102** 1d. scarlet (No. 342) .. 20 10
 a. Opt. triple, two albino ..

(*c*) *New types. Wmk. Royal Cypher* (7.13).

50 **105** ½d. green (No. 351) .. 15 15
51 **104** 1d. scarlet (No. 358) .. 25 50

These two stamps were reissued in 1919.

For other values of this series with "LEVANT" overprint see Nos. 68 to 74.

1913 (Apr.)–**14.** *Stamps of King George V, wmk. Royal Cypher, surch. as T* **1** (*30 par.*), **10** (*1 pi.*), **8** *or* **2** (*4 and 5 pi.*).

52 **105** 30 par. on 1½d. red-brown (4.13) .. .. 95 1·25
53 **104** 1 pi. on 2½d. bright blue (6.13) 20 12
54 **106** 1¼ pi. on 3d. violet (9.13) .. 55 1·25
55 „ 1¾ pi. on 4d. grey-green (7.13) .. .. 75 1·60
 a. Thin, pointed "4" in fraction .. 19·00 19·00
56 **108** 4 pi. on 10d. turq.-blue (2.14) .. .. 3·50 3·50
57 „ 5 pi. on 1s. bistre-brown (5.14) .. .. 6·00 8·00
52/7 .. .. *Set of* 6 11·00 14·00

The British P.O.'s in the Turkish Empire were closed in 1914.

II. British Occupation of Turkey.

1½ PIASTRES (11) **15 PIASTRES** (12)

1921. *Stamps of King George V, wmk. Royal Cypher, surch. as T* **1** (*30 pa.*), **11** *and* **12** (*15 and 18¾ pi.*).

58 **105** 30 pa. on ½d. green .. 10 35
59 **104** 1½ pi. on 1d. scarlet .. 10 15
60 „ 3¾ pi. on 2½d. blue .. 20 30
61 **106** 4½ pi. on 3d. bluish violet 35 70
62 **107** 7½ pi. on 5d. yellow-brown 15 15
63 **108** 15 pi. on 10d. turq.-blue 30 20
64 „ 18¾ pi. on 1s. bistre-brown 1·60 1·10

45 PIASTRES (13)

1921. *Stamps of King George V* (*Bradbury, Wilkinson printing*) *surch. as T* **13**.

65 **109** 45 pi. on 2s. 6d. chocolate-brown .. .. 7·50 10·00
66 „ 90 pi. on 5s. rose-red .. 16·00 8·50
67 „ 180 pi. on 10s. dull grey-blue .. .. 38·00 20·00
58/67 .. .. *Set of* 10 60·00 38·00
64/7 H/S "Specimen" *Set of* 4 50·00

1921. *Stamps of King George V optd. as T* **4**.

68 **106** 2d. reddish orange (Die I) 60 1·10
69 „ 3d. bluish violet .. .. 1·40 80
70 „ 4d. grey-green .. .. 1·10 1·25
71 **107** 5d. yellow-brown .. .. 2·25 2·50
72 „ 6d. reddish purple, C .. 2·25 2·75
73 **108** 1s. bis.-brn. (H/S S. £30) 1·60 1·40
74 **109** 2s. 6d. chocolate-brown (H/S S. £38) .. .. 15·00 19·00
68/74 .. .. *Set of* 7 22·00 26·00

On No. 74 the letters of the overprint are shorter, being only 3 mm. high.

BRITISH FIELD OFFICE IN SALONICA.

Levant (S 1)

1916 (End Feb.–9 Mar.). *Stamps of Gt. Britain, optd. with Type* S **1**.

S 1 **105** ½d. green .. .. .. 6·00 11·00
 a. Opt. double .. .. 65·00 65·00
 b. Vert. pr. one without opt. 55·00 60·00
S 2 **104** 1d. scarlet .. .. 6·00 11·00
 a. Opt. double .. .. 85·00 85·00
S 3 **106** 2d. reddish orange (Die I) 22·00 35·00
S 4 „ 3d. bluish violet .. .. 17·00 28·00
 a. Opt. double .. ..
S 5 „ 4d. grey-green .. .. 23·00 35·00
S 6 **107** 6d. reddish purple, C .. 17·00 28·00
 a. Vert. pr., one without opt. 75·00 95·00
S 7 **108** 9d. agate .. .. .. 55·00 75·00
 a. Opt. double £400 £400
S 8 „ 1s. bistre-brown .. 55·00 75·00
S 1/8 .. .. *Set of* 8 £180 £275

There are numerous forgeries of this overprint.

BRITISH NEW GUINEA.

See **PAPUA.**

BRITISH OCCUPATION OF FORMER ITALIAN COLONIES.

MIDDLE EAST FORCES.

For use in territory occupied by British Forces in Eritrea (1942), *Italian Somaliland* (1942), *Cyrenaica* (1943), *Tripolitania* (1943), *and some of the Dodecanese Islands* (1945).

PRICES. Our prices for used stamps with "M.E.F." overprints are for specimens with identifiable postmarks of the territories in which they were issued. These stamps were also used in the United Kingdom, with official sanction, from the summer of 1950 onwards, and with U.K. postmarks are worth about 25 per cent less.

M.E.F. (M 1)

1942 (2 Mar.). *Stamps of Great Britain optd. in London and Cairo with Type* M **1**, *in black, W* **127**. *P* 15 × 14.

M1 **128** 1d. scarlet (No. 463) .. 8 25
M2 „ 2d. orange (No. 465) .. 10 25
M3 „ 2½d. ultram. (No. 466) .. 8 20
M4 „ 3d. violet (No. 467) .. 10 15
 a. Opt. double .. ..
M5 **129** 5d. brown 12 25

These are two printings in the above issue:

I. By Harrison & Sons. Ltd., London. Opt. 14 mm. Sharp lettering with upright oblong stops.

II. By Army Printing Services, Cairo. Opt. 13½ mm. The setting comprises three rows with sharp lettering and square stops, and seven rows with thick rough lettering and rounded stops.

Both printings were issued simultaneously.

1943 (1 Jan.)–**1947.** *Stamps of Great Britain optd. in London as Type* M **1**.

(*a*) *In blue-black. W* **127.** *P* 15 × 14.

M 6 **128** 1d. pale scarlet (No. 486) 5 5
M 7 „ 2d. pale orange (No. 488) 5 5
M 8 „ 2½d. lt. ultram. (No. 489) 5 5
M 9 „ 3d. pale violet (No. 490) 5 8
M10 **129** 5d. brown 5 8
M11 „ 6d. purple 5 20
M12 **130** 9d. deep olive-green .. 25 30
M13 „ 1s. bistre-brown .. 20 20

(*b*) *In black. W* **133.** *P* 14.

M14 **131** 2s. 6d. yellow-green .. 60 60
M15 „ 5s. red ('47) .. .. 1·75 3·00
M16 **132** 10s. ultramarine ('47) .. 3·50 3·75
M6/16 .. .. *Set of* 11 6·00 7·50
M13/16 H/S "Specimen" Set of 4 £100

On Nos. M6 to M13 the overprint measures 13½ mm. and the letters are sharp with square stops. The 5d. is best distinguished by the shade of the opt. which is black in the Cairo printing and blue-black in No. M10.

POSTAGE DUE STAMPS.

M.E.F. (MD 1)

1942. *Postage Due Stamps of Great Britain optd. with Type* MD **1**, *in blue. W* **127** (*sideways*). *P* 14 × 15.

MD1 D **1** ½d. emerald 5 35
MD2 „ 1d. carmine 5 35
MD3 „ 2d. agate 30 70
MD4 „ 3d. violet 20 70
MD5 „ 1s. deep blue (H/S S. £15) 85 1·75
MD1/5 .. .. .. *Set of* 5 1·25 3·50

ERITREA.

British Military Administration.

B. M. A. ERITREA 10 CENTS (E 1) **B. M. A. ERITREA 5 SHILLINGS** (E 2)

1948–9. *Stamps of Great Britain surch. as Types* E **1** *or* E **2**.

E 1 **128** 5 c. on ½d. pale green .. 8 12
E 2 „ 10 c. on 1d. pale scarlet .. 12 35
E 3 „ 20 c. on 2d. pale orange .. 20 50
E 4 „ 25 c. on 2½d. lt. ultram. 8 25
E 5 „ 30 c. on 3d. pale violet. 25 35
E 6 **129** 40 c. on 5d. brown .. 10 35
E 7 „ 50 c. on 6d. purple .. 10 30
E 7a **130** 65 c. on 8d. brt. carmine (1.2.49) 25 50
E 8 „ 75 c. on 9d. dp. ol.-grn. 20 35
E 9 „ 1s. on 1s. bistre-brown 20 25
E10 **131** 2s. 50 c. on 2s. 6d. yellow-green .. .. 1·00 2·75
E11 „ 5s. on 5s. red .. .. 2·50 3·75
E12 **132** 10s. on 10s. ultramarine 3·50 5·00
E1/12 .. .. *Set of* 13 7·50 13·00

BRITISH ADMINISTRATION.

1950 (6 FEB.). *As Nos.* E1/12, *but surch.* "B.A. ERITREA" *and new values instead of* "B.M.A." *etc.*

No.	Type	Description	Unused	Used
E13	**128**	5 c. on ½d. pale green ..	5	20
E14	,,	10 c. on 1d. pale scarlet	5	20
E15	,,	20 c. on 2d. pale orange	5	30
E16	,,	25 c. on 2½d. light ultram.	5	25
E17	,,	30 c. on 3d. pale violet ..	5	25
E18	**129**	40 c. on 5d. brown ..	10	25
E19	,,	50 c. on 6d. purple ..	12	25
E20	**130**	65 c. on 8d. brt. carmine	25	45
E21	,,	75 c. on 9d. dp. olive-grn.	12	20
E22	,,	1 s. on 1s. bistre-brown	15	20
E23	**131**	2 s. 50 c. on 2s. 6d. yellow-green	1·00	1·75
E24	,,	5 s. on 5s. red ..	2·25	3·50
E25	**132**	10 s. on. 10s. ultramarine	5·50	6·50
E13/25		.. .. *Set of* 13	8·50	13·00

1951 (3 MAY). *Nos.* 503/4, 506/7 *and* 509/11 *of Great Britain surch.* "B.A. ERITREA" *and new values.*

No.	Type	Description	Unused	Used
E26	**128**	5 c. on ½d. pale orange	8	25
E27	,,	10 c. on 1d. light ultram.	8	20
E28	,,	20 c. on 2d. pale red-brn.	8	25
E29	,,	25 c. on 2½d. pale scarlet	8	20
E30	**147**	2 s. 5 c. on 2s. 6d. yellow-green	1·40	2·50
E31	**148**	5 s. on 5s. red ..	4·00	4·50
E32	,,	10 s. on 10s. ultramarine	5·00	5·50
E26/32		.. .. *Set of* 7	9·50	12·00

POSTAGE DUE STAMPS.

B. M. A.
ERITREA
10 CENTS
(ED 1)

1948. *Postage Due stamps of Great Britain surch. as Type* ED **1**.

No.	Type	Description	Unused	Used
ED1	D **1**	5 c. on ½d. emerald ..	1·40	2·75
ED2	,,	10 c. on 1d. carmine ..	1·40	2·75
ED3	,,	20 c. on 2d. agate ..	1·40	3·25
ED4	,,	30 c. on 3d. violet ..	1·75	3·25
ED5	,,	1 s. on 1s. deep blue ..	4·00	5·50
ED1/5		.. .. *Set of* 5	9·00	16·00

1950 (6 FEB.). *As Nos.* ED1/5, *but surch.* "B.A. ERITREA" *and new values instead of* "B.M.A." *etc.*

No.	Type	Description	Unused	Used
ED6	D **1**	5 c. on ½d. emerald ..	2·25	2·75
ED7	,,	10 c. on 1d. carmine ..	2·25	2·75
		a. "C" of "CENTS" omitted	£250	
ED8	,,	20 c. on 2d. agate ..	2·25	2·25
ED9	,,	30 c. on 3d. violet ..	2·75	2·50
ED10	,,	1 s. on 1s. deep blue ..	4·00	3·50
ED6/10		.. .. *Set of* 5	12·00	12·00

Stamps of Ethiopia were used in Eritrea after Sept. 15, 1952, following federation with Ethiopia.

SOMALIA.

BRITISH OCCUPATION.

E.A.F.

(S **1**. "East Africa Forces").

1943 (15 JAN.)–**46**. *Stamps of Great Britain optd. with Type* S **1**, *in blue.*

No.	Type	Description	Unused	Used
S1	**128**	1d. pale scarlet	5	15
S2	,,	2d. pale orange	5	15
S3	,,	2½d. light ultramarine ..	5	15
S4	,,	3d. pale violet	5	15
S5	**129**	5d. brown	5	15
S6	,,	6d. purple	8	20
S7	**130**	9d. deep olive-green ..	15	60
S8	,,	1s. bistre-brown ..	15	12
S9	**131**	2s. 6d. yellow-green ('46)	90	1·40
S1/9		.. .. *Set of* 9	1·25	2·75
S8/9		H/S "Specimen" *Set of* 2	45·00	

The note *re* used prices above Type M **1** of Middle East Forces also applies to the above issue.

BRITISH MILITARY ADMINISTRATION.

1948 (27 MAY). *Stamps of Great Britain surch.* "B.M.A./SOMALIA" *and new values, as Types* E **1** *and* E **2** *of Eritrea.*

No.	Type	Description	Unused	Used
S10	**128**	5 c. on ½d. pale green ..	5	15
S11	,,	15 c. on 1½d. pale red-brn.	30	75
S12	,,	20 c. on 2d. pale orange ..	5	35
S13	,,	25 c. on 2½d. lt. ultram. ..	5	15
S14	,,	30 c. on 3d. pale violet ..	35	80
S15	**129**	40 c. on 5d. brown ..	8	45
S16	,,	50 c. on 6d. purple ..	12	55
S17	**130**	75 c. on 9d. dp. ol.-green	45	1·25
S18	,,	1 s. on 1s. bistre-brown	25	55
S19	**131**	2 s. 50 c. on 2s. 6d. yellow-green	1·40	3·25
S20	,,	5 s. on 5s. red	2·75	5·00
S10/20		.. .. *Set of* 11	5·00	12·00

BRITISH ADMINISTRATION.

1950 (2 JAN.). *As Nos.* S10/20, *but surch.* "B.A./SOMALIA" *and new values, instead of* "B.M.A." *etc.*

No.	Type	Description	Unused	Used
S21	**128**	5 c. on ½d. pale green ..	5	12
S22	,,	15 c. on 1½d. pale red-brn.	20	60
S23	,,	20 c. on 2d. pale orange ..	20	50
S24	,,	25 c. on 2½d. lt. ultram. ..	8	40
S25	,,	30 c. on 3d. pale violet ..	30	70
S26	**129**	40 c. on 5d. brown ..	20	35
S27	,,	50 c. on 6d. purple ..	15	35
S28	**130**	75 c. on 9d. dp. ol.-green	35	80
S29	,,	1 s. on 1s. bistre-brown	20	55
S30	**131**	2 s. 50 c. on 2s. 6d. yellow-green	1·75	3·75
S31	,,	5 s. on 5s. red	3·00	4·50
S21/31		.. .. *Set of* 11	6·00	11·00

Somalia reverted to Italian Administration on 1 April, 1950, later becoming independent. Later issues will be found listed in Vol. 4 of the Stanley Gibbons Foreign Overseas Catalogue.

TRIPOLITANIA.

BRITISH MILITARY ADMINISTRATION.

1948 (1 JULY). *Stamps of Great Britain surch.* "B.M.A./TRIPOLITANIA" *and new values, as Types* E **1** *and* E **2** *of Eritrea, but expressed in M(ilitary) A(dministration) L(ire).*

No.	Type	Description	Unused	Used
T 1	**128**	1 l. on ½d. pale green ..	8	30
T 2	,,	2 l. on 1d. pale scarlet	5	20
T 3	,,	3 l. on 1½d. pale red-brown	5	35
T 4	,,	4 l. on 2d. pale orange	8	25
T 5	,,	5 l. on 2½d. lt. ultram.	8	30
T 6	,,	6 l. on 3d. pale violet	5	30
T 7	**129**	10 l. on 5d. brown	5	25
T 8	,,	12 l. on 6d. purple	8	20
T 9	**130**	18 l. on 9d. dp. ol.-green	20	60
T10	,,	24 l. on 1s. bistre-brown	30	75
T11	**131**	60 l. on 2s. 6d. yell.-grn.	85	2·00
T12	,,	120 l. on 5s. red ..	1·75	3·50
T13	**132**	240 l. on 10s. ultramarine	3·25	4·75
T1/13		.. .. *Set of* 13	6·00	12·00

BRITISH ADMINISTRATION.

1950 (6 FEB.). *As Nos.* T1/13, *but surch.* "B.A. TRIPOLITANIA" *and new values, instead of* "B.M.A." *etc.*

No.	Type	Description	Unused	Used
T14	**128**	1 l. on ½d. pale green ..	10	30
T15	,,	2 l. on 1d. pale scarlet	8	25
T16	,,	3 l. on 1½d. pale red-brown	12	35
T17	,,	4 l. on 2d. pale orange	5	30
T18	,,	5 l. on 2½d. lt. ultram.	5	30
T19	,,	6 l. on 3d. pale violet ..	5	30
T20	**129**	10 l. on 5d. brown ..	5	25
T21	,,	12 l. on 6d. purple ..	5	25
T22	**130**	18 l. on 9d. dp. ol.-green	12	40
T23	,,	24 l. on 1s. bistre-brown	15	40
T24	**131**	60 l. on 2s. 6d. yell.-grn.	1·25	2·50
T25	,,	120 l. on 5s. red ..	2·25	4·50
T26	**132**	240 l. on 10s. ultramarine	4·00	7·00
T14/26		.. .. *Set of* 13	7·50	15·00

1951 (3 MAY). *Nos.* 503/7 *and* 509/11 *of Great Britain surch.* "B.A. TRIPOLITANIA" *and new values.*

No.	Type	Description	Unused	Used
T27	**128**	1 l. on ½d. pale orange	5	30
T28	,,	2 l. on 1d. light ultram.	5	30
T29	,,	3 l. on 1½d. pale green	15	30
T30	,,	4 l. on 2d. pale red-brn.	10	30
T31	,,	5 l. on 2½d. pale scarlet	8	30
T32	**147**	60 l. on 2s. 6d. yell.-grn.	1·50	3·25
T33	**148**	120 l. on 5s. red	3·50	4·25
T34	**149**	240 l. on 10s. ultramarine	5·00	7·50
T27/34		.. .. *Set of* 8	9·00	15·00

POSTAGE DUE STAMPS.

1948. *Postage Due stamps of Great Britain surch.* "B.M.A./TRIPOLITANIA" *and new values, as Type* ED **1** *of Eritrea, but expressed in M(ilitary) A(dministration) L(ire).*

No.	Type	Description	Unused	Used
TD1	D **1**	1 l. on ½d. emerald ..	25	75
TD2	,,	2 l. on 1d. carmine ..	30	75
TD3	,,	4 l. on 2d. agate ..	75	1·50
TD4	,,	6 l. on 3d. violet ..	1·50	2·00
TD5	,,	24 l. on 1s. deep blue ..	3·25	3·50
TD1/5		.. .. *Set of* 5	5·50	7·50

1950 (6 FEB.). *As Nos.* TD1/5, *but surch.* "B.A. TRIPOLITANIA" *and new values, instead of* "B.M.A." *etc.*

No.	Type	Description	Unused	Used
TD 6	D **1**	1 l. on ½d. emerald ..	55	90
TD 7	,,	2 l. on 1d. carmine ..	35	85
TD 8	,,	4 l. on 2d. agate ..	45	90
TD 9	,,	6 l. on 3d. violet ..	2·00	2·50
TD10	,,	24 l. on 1s. deep blue ..	3·50	4·00
TD6/10		.. .. *Set of* 5	6·00	8·00

Tripolitania is now part of the Independent Republic of Libya.

BRITISH P.O's IN CRETE.

BRITISH ADMINISTRATION.
(CANDIA PROVINCE (now Iraklion).)

During the provisional Joint Administration by France, Great Britain, Italy, and Russia.

1

2

1898 (25 NOV.). *Handstruck locally. Imperf.*

No.	Type	Description	Unused	Used
1	**1**	20 par. bright violet	85·00	80·00

1898 (3 DEC.). *Litho. by M. Grundmann, Athens. P* 11½.

No.	Type	Description	Unused	Used
2	**2**	10 par. blue	2·25	3·50
		a. Imperf. (pair)	50·00	
3	,,	20 par. green	2·25	3·50
		a. Imperf. (pair)	50·00	

1899. *P* 11½.

No.	Type	Description	Unused	Used
4	**2**	10 par. brown	2·50	4·50
		a. Imperf. (pair)	50·00	
5	,,	20 par. rose	4·50	5·00
		a. Imperf. (pair)	50·00	

The British postal service closed at the end of 1899.

BRITISH POSTAL AGENCIES IN EASTERN ARABIA.

Certain Arab States in Eastern Arabia, whilst remaining independent, had British postal administrations.

Bahrain and Kuwait (from 1948) and Qatar (from 1957) used British stamps overprinted and surcharged in local currency. Abu Dhabi (from 1964) and Trucial States (from 1961 and used only in Dubai) had definitive issues made under the auspices of the British Agencies.

In addition, British stamps were surcharged with value only for use in Muscat and certain other states. They were formerly listed under Muscat as they were first put on sale there, but in view of their more extended use, the list has been transferred here, retaining the same numbering.

The stamps were used in Muscat from 1st April 1948 to 29th April 1966; in Dubai from 1st April 1948 to 6th January 1961; in Qatar: Doha from August 1950, Umm Said from February 1956, to 31st March 1957; and in Abu Dhabi from 30th March 1963 (Das Island from December 1960) to 29th March 1964.

Certain of them were placed on sale in Kuwait Post Offices in 1951 and in 1953 due to shortages of stamps with "KUWAIT" overprint; and they can all be found commercially used from that state and from Bahrain.

Stamps of Great Britain surcharged.

1 ANNA (3) — 2 RUPEES (4)

1948 (1 Apr.). *Surch. with T* **3** (*½ a. to 1 r.*) *or* **4** (*2 r.*).

16 **128** ½ a. on ½d. pale green .. 5 5
17 „ 1 a. on 1d. pale scarlet .. 8 8
18 „ 1½ a. on 1½d. pale red-brn. 8 8
19 „ 2 a. on 2d. pale orange .. 10 15
20 „ 2½ a. on 2½d. light ultram. 8 20
21 „ 3 a. on 3d. pale violet .. 8 8
22 **129** 6 a. on 6d. purple .. 10 10
23 **130** 1 r. on 1s. bistre-brown .. 35 40
24 **131** 2 r. on 2s. 6d. yellow-grn. 2·50 3·50
16/24 .. .. *Set of* 9 3·00 4·00

2½ ANNAS (5) — 15 RUPEES (6)

1948 (26 Apr.). *Royal Silver Wedding. Nos.* 493/4 *surch. with T* **5** *or* **6**.

25 **137** 2½ a. on 2½d. ultramarine .. 8 10
26 **138** 15 r. on £1 blue .. .. 4·50 6·50

1948 (29 July). *Olympic Games. Nos.* 495/8 *surch. with new values in* "ANNAS" *or* "1 RUPEE", *as T* **5/6**, *but in one line on* 2½ *a.* (*vert.*) *or* 6 *a. and* 1 *r.* (*horiz.*) *and grills obliterating former values of all except* 2½ *a.*

27 **139** 2½ a. on 2½d. ultramarine 10 15
28 **140** 3 a. on 3d. violet .. 12 25
29 **141** 6 a. on 6d. bright purple 12 30
30 **142** 1 r. on 1s. brown .. 35 50
a. Surch. double .. .. 85·00

1949 (10 Oct.). *75th Anniv. of Universal Postal Union. Nos.* 499/502 *surch. with new values in* "ANNAS" *or* "1 RUPEE" *as T* **3/4**, *but all in one line, with grills obliterating former values.*

31 **143** 2½ a. on 2½d. ultram. .. 15 15
32 **144** 3 a. on 3d. violet .. 20 25
33 **145** 6 a. on 6d. bright purple 25 30
34 **146** 1 r. on 1s. brown .. 45 45

2 RUPEES (6a)

2 RUPEES (6b)

Type **6a**. "2" and "RUPEES" level and in line with lower of the two bars.

Type **6b**. "2" raised in relation to "RUPEES" and whole surcharge below the lower bar.

1950–55. *Nos.* 503/8 *surch. as T* **3** *and No.* 509 *with T* **6a**.

35 **128** ½ a. on ½d. pale orange .. 8 10
36 „ 1 a. on 1d. light ultram. 8 10
37 „ 1½ a. on 1½d. pale green .. 20 25
38 „ 2 a. on 2d. pale red-brown 8 15
39 „ 2½ a. on 2½d. pale scarlet .. 20 25
40 **129** 4 a. on 4d. light ultram. 15 25
41 **147** 2 r. on 2s. 6d. yellow-grn. 1·50 1·75
a. Surch. with Type 6b ('55) 15·00 13·00
35/41 .. .. *Set of* 7 2·00 2·50

Dates of issue:—2.10.50, 4 a.; 3.5.51, others.

1952–54. *Stamps of Queen Elizabeth II wmk. Tudor Crown, surch. as T* **3**.

42 **154** ½ a. on ½d. orange-red .. 5 5
43 „ 1 a. on 1d. ultramarine .. 5 5
44 „ 1½ a. on 1½d. green .. 5 5
45 „ 2 a. on 2d. red-brown .. 5 5
46 **155** 2½ a. on 2½d. carmine-red 12 12
47 „ 3 a. on 3d. deep lilac (B.) 5 8
48 **156** 4 a. on 4d. ultramarine .. 12 12
49 **157** 6 a. on 6d. reddish purple 15 15
50 **160** 12 a. on 1s. 3d. green .. 30 40
51 **159** 1 r. on 1s. 6d. grey-blue .. 35 50
42/51 .. .. *Set of* 10 1·10 1·40

Dates of issue:—5.12.52, 1½ a., 2½ a.; 31.8.53, ½ a., 1 a., 2 a.; 2.11.53, 4 a., 12 a., 1 r.; 18.1.54, 3 a., 6 a.

1953 (10 June). *Coronation. Nos.* 532/5 *surch. with new values.*

52 **161** 2½ a. on 2½d. carmine-red 25 30
53 **162** 4 a. on 4d. ultramarine .. 30 35
54 **163** 12 a. on 1s. 3d. deep yellow-green 80 90
55 **164** 1 r. on 1s. 6d. deep grey-blue .. .. .. 75 1·10

2 RUPEES I

2 RUPEES II

2 RUPEES III

(7)

5 RUPEES I

5 RUPEES II

(8)

Types of surcharges.

2 rupees.

Type I. *On Waterlow ptg.* Top of "R" level with top of "2" and other letters of "RUPEES". Bars 7 mm. long.

Type II. *On Waterlow ptg.* "R" dropped out of alignment with "2" and other letters of "RUPEES". Bars 6½ mm. long.

Type III. *On De La Rue ptg.* Top of "R" below level of top of "2". Bars 7–7¼ mm. long and with left sides aligned with "S".

5 rupees.

Type I. *On Waterlow ptg.* Ends of letters square and sharp. There were two printings made in March and May 1957.

Type II. *On De La Rue ptg.* Type is thicker and ends of letters are relatively rounded.

For differences between Waterlow and De La Rue printings of the basic stamps see notes in Great Britain after No. 539.

1955–60. *T* **166/7** (*Waterlow ptgs.*) (*W* **165**, *St. Edward's Crown*) *surch. with T* **7/8**.

56 **166** 2 r. on 2s. 6d. black-brown (Type 1) (23.9.55) .. 1·00 1·25
II. Type II (2.57) .. 1·00 1·25
III. Type III (No. 536a D.L.R.) (6.60) .. .. .. 5·00 6·00
57 **167** 5 r. on 5s. rose-red (Type 1) (1.3.57) .. 1·50 1·50
a. Wide surcharge .. 75·00 80·00
II. Type II (No. 537a D.L.R.) (27.1.60) .. .. .. 6·00 5·00

No. 57a ("5" and "R" spaced 2¼ mm. instead of 1¼ mm.) occurred on the last stamp of Row 8 of the first "Waterlow" issue.

1956–57. *Stamps of Queen Elizabeth II, W* **165**, *St. Edward's Crown, surch. as T* **3**.

58 **154** 1 a. on 1d. ultram. (4.3.57) 10 10
58*a* „ 1½ a. on 1½d. green (1956) .. — 75·00
59 „ 2 a. on 2d. red-brn. (8.6.56) 15 15
60 **155** 2½ a. on 2½d. carmine-red (8.6.56) 25 25
61 „ 3 a. on 3d. deep lilac (B.) (3.2.57) 35 40
62 **156** 4 a. on 4d. ultramarine (9.12.56) 40 45
63 **157** 6 a. on 6d. red-purple (10.2.57) 25 40
64 **159** 1 r. on 1s. 6d. grey-blue (2.8.56) 30 30
58/64 .. .. *Set of* 7 1·60 1·75

NP 1 NP (9) — 3 NP NP (10) — 75 NP (11)

1957 (1 Apr.)–**59.** *Value in naye paise. Stamps of Queen Elizabeth II, W* **165**, *St. Edward's Crown, surch. as T* **9** (1, 15, 25, 40, 50 *n.p.*), **11** (75 *n.p.*) *or* **10** (*others*).

65 **157** 1 n.p. on 5d. brown .. 5 5
66 **154** 3 n.p. on ½d. orange-red 5 5
67 „ 6 n.p. on 1d. ultramarine 5 5
68 „ 9 n.p. on 1½d. green .. 5 5
69 „ 12 n.p. on 2d. lt. red-brn. 10 20
70 **155** 15 n.p. on 2½d. carmine-red (Type I) .. 20 20
a. Type II (4.59) .. 8 10
71 „ 20 n.p. on 3d. dp. lilac (B.) 5 5
72 **156** 25 n.p. on 4d. ultramarine 10 8
73 **157** 40 n.p. on 6d. reddish pur. 12 10
a. Deep claret (3.59) .. 15 15
74 **158** 50 n.p. on 9d. bronze-grn. 15 15
75 **160** 75 n.p. on 1s. 3d. green .. 25 25
65/75 .. .. *Set of* 11 95 95

15 NP

(12)

1957 (1 Aug.). *World Scout Jubilee Jamboree. Nos.* 557/9 *surch. in one line as T* **12** (15 *n.p.*), *or in two lines* (*others*).

76 15 n.p. on 2½d. carmine-red 20 20
77 25 n.p. on 4d. ultramarine .. 30 30
78 75 n.p. on 1s. 3d. green .. 30 35

1960–61. *Stamps of Queen Elizabeth II, W* **179**, *Mult. Crown, surch. as T* **9** (*1, 15, 30, 40, 50 n.p.*), **11** (*75 n.p.*), **3** (*1 r.*), **7** (*2 r., 5 r.*) *or* **10** (*others*).

79 **157** 1 n.p. on 5d. brown .. 5 5
80 **154** 3 n.p. on ½d. orange-red 25 25
81 ,, 5 n.p. on 1d. ultramarine 20 20
82 ,, 6 n.p. on 1d. ultramarine 40 40
83 ,, 10 n.p. on 1½d. green .. 10 10
84 ,, 12 n.p. on 2d. lt. red-brown 75 75
85 **155** 15 n.p. on 2½d. carmine-red (Type II) 10 10
86 ,, 20 n.p. on 3d. deep lilac (B.) 10 10
87 **156** 30 n.p. on 4½d. chestnut .. 15 15
88 **157** 40 n.p. on 6d. deep claret 15 15
89 **158** 50 n.p. on 9d. bronze-green 20 20
90 **160** 75 n.p. on 1s. 3d. green .. 20 20
91 **159** 1 r. on 1s. 6d. grey-blue 30 35
92 **166** 2 r. on 2s. 6d. black-brown (No. 595) 60 75
93 **167** 5 r. on 5s. rose-red (No. 596) .. .. 1·50 1·75
79/93 .. .. *Set of* 15 4·50 4·50

Dates of issue: 1960—1 n.p., 15 n.p.; June, 3 n.p., 6 n.p., 12 n.p.; Oct., 20 n.p., 40 n.p. 1961—8, April, others.

Later issues for Muscat will be found listed under OMAN in Vol. 3 of the Stanley Gibbons Foreign Overseas Catalogue.

BRITISH SOLOMON ISLANDS.

See SOLOMON ISLANDS.

BRITISH SOMALILAND.

See SOMALILAND PROTECTORATE.

BRITISH SOUTH AFRICA COMPANY.

See RHODESIA.

BRITISH VIRGIN ISLANDS.

See VIRGIN ISLANDS.

BRUNEI.

BRUNEI.
(1)

BRUNEI. TWO CENTS.
(2)

BRUNEI. 25 CENTS.
(3)

1906 (11 OCT.). *Stamps of Labuan, T* **18** (*Nos. 116c, etc.*), *optd. with T* **1**, *or surch. as T* **2** *or* **3** (*25 c.*), *in red. P 13½ or 14* (*1 c.*).

1 1 c. black and purple .. .. 4·50 6·50
a. Error. Opt. in black £350 £400
2 2 c. on 3 c. black and sepia .. 1·25 1·60
a. "BRUNEI" double £750
3 2 c. on 8 c. black & vermilion 6·50 6·50
a. "TWO CENTS" double .. £1200
b. "TWO CENTS" omitted in vert. pair with normal .. £1300
4 3 c. black and sepia .. .. 6·50 6·50
5 4 c. on 12 c. black and yellow 80 1·60
6 5 c. on 16 c. green and brown 6·50 5·00
7 8 c. black and vermilion .. 2·00 2·75
8 10 c. on 16 c. green and brown 1·60 2·25
9 25 c. on 16 c. green and brown 27·00 32·00
10 30 c. on 16 c. green and brown 22·00 28·00
11 50 c. on 16 c. green and brown 22·00 28·00
12 1 dol. on 8 c. black and verm. 22·00 28·00
1/12 .. .. *Set of* 12 £110 £130

PRINTERS. All Brunei stamps from Nos. 14 to 99 were recess-printed by De La Rue.

4. View on Brunei River.

1907 (26 FEB.). *Wmk. Mult. Crown CA. P* 14.

14 **4** 1 c. grey-blk. & pale green 40 65
15 ,, 2 c. grey-black and scarlet 50 1·00
16 ,, 3 c. grey-blk. and chocolate 2·75 2·75
17 ,, 4 c. grey-black and mauve 2·50 2·75
a. Grey-black and reddish purple 9·00 10·00
18 ,, 5 c. grey-black and blue .. 9·00 10·00
19 ,, 8 c. grey-black and orange 2·00 4·50
20 ,, 10 c. grey-blk. and deep grn. 4·50 5·00
21 ,, 25 c. pale blue and ochre-brn. 6·00 7·00
22 ,, 30 c. violet and black .. 6·00 7·00
23 ,, 50 c. green and deep brown 6·00 7·00
24 ,, $1 red and grey .. .. 20·00 27·00
14/24 *Set of* 11 55·00 70·00
14/24 Optd. "Specimen" *Set of* 11 50·00

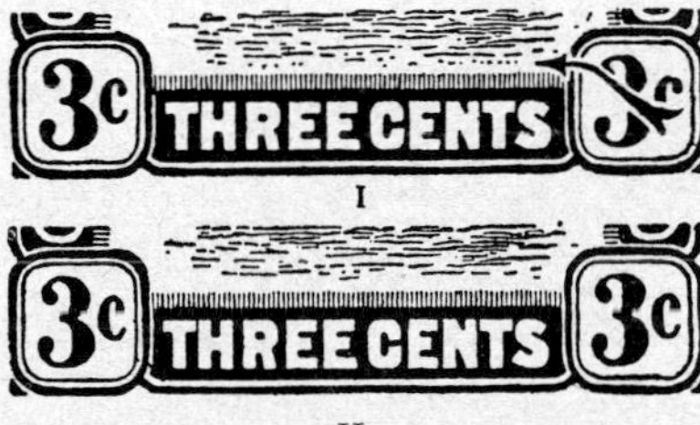

I

II

I. Double plate. Lowest line of shading on water is dotted.

II. Single plate. Dotted line of shading removed.

Stamps printed in two colours are as I.

1908–16. *Colours changed. Double or single plates. Wmk. Mult. Crown CA. P* 14.

25 **4** 1 c. green (I) 30 55
26 ,, 1 c. green (II) (1911) .. 15 20
27 ,, 2 c. black and brown (1911) 35 30
28 ,, 3 c. scarlet (I) 60 60
29 ,, 3 c. scarlet (II) (1916) .. 4·00 4·00
30 ,, 4 c. claret (II) (1912) .. 25 25
31 ,, 5 c. black and orange (1916) 1·60 1·60
32 ,, 8 c. blue & indigo-blue ('16) 1·60 1·60
33 ,, 10 c. purple/*yell.* (II) (1912) 55 55
a. On pale yell. (Optd. S. £4) .. 45 60
34 ,, 25 c. deep lilac (II) (1912) .. 90 90
35 ,, 30 c. pur. & orge.-yell. (1912) 1·75 1·75
36 ,, 50 c. black/*green* (II) (1912) 4·00 6·00
a. On blue-green .. .. 3·00 4·00
37 ,, $1 black & red/*blue* (1912) 6·00 8·00
38 ,, $5 carmine/*green* (I) (1911) 27·00 32·00
39 ,, $25 black/*red* (I) (1911) .. £140 £190
25/38 .. .. *Set of* 12 40·00 45·00
25/39 Optd. "Specimen" *Set of* 13 80·00

Retouch. Normal.

MALAYA-BORNEO EXHIBITION. 1922.
(5)

Retouches. We list the very distinctive 5 c. Retouch (top left value tablet, 1st row, 8th stamp) but there are others of interest, notably in the clouds.

1916. *Colours changed. Single plates. Wmk. Mult. Crown CA. P* 14.

40 **4** 5 c. orange 65 70
a. "5 c." retouch .. .. 32·00 32·00
41 ,, 8 c. ultramarine .. .. 1·10 2·25
40/1 Optd. "Specimen" *Set of* 2 24·00

1922. *Optd. with T* **5**, *in black.*

42 **4** 1 c. green (II) .. .. 90 3·25
43 ,, 2 c. black and brown .. 1·90 3·25
44 ,, 3 c. scarlet (II) .. .. 2·25 6·00
45 ,, 4 c. claret (II) .. .. 2·00 8·50
46 ,, 5 c. orange (II) .. .. 3·00 11·00
a. "5 c." retouch .. .. 60·00 £130
47 ,, 10 c. purple/*yellow* (II) .. 4·00 15·00
48 ,, 25 c. purple (II) .. .. 8·00 20·00
49 ,, 50 c. black/*blue-green* (II) .. 20·00 42·00
50 ,, $1 black and red/*blue* .. 24·00 42·00
42/50 .. .. *Set of* 9 60·00 £130

6. Native houses, Brunei Town.

1924–37. *Printed from single plates as Type* II, *except 30 c. and $1 as Type* I. *Wmk. Mult. Script CA. P* 14.

51 **4** 1 c. black ('26) 12 15
52 ,, 2 c. brown 30 35
52*a* ,, 2 c. green ('33) 15 15
53 ,, 3 c. green .. .. .. 55 1·00
54 ,, 4 c. maroon 85 60
55 ,, 4 c. orange ('29) 55 30
56 ,, 5 c. orange-yellow* 40 40
a. "5 c." retouch .. .. 35·00 35·00
57 ,, 5 c. grey ('31) .. .. 1·75 1·40
a. "5 c." retouch .. .. 70·00 70·00
57*b* ,, 5 c. chocolate ('33) 20 25
a. "5 c." retouch .. .. 20·00 20·00
58 **6** 6 c. intense black** .. 1·25 1·50
59 ,, 6 c. scarlet ('31) .. .. 1·40 2·50
60 **4** 8 c. ultramarine ('27) .. 1·10 1·00
60*a* ,, 8 c. grey-black ('33) .. 90 55
60*b* ,, 10 c. purple/*yellow* ('37) .. 3·00 3·50
61 **6** 12 c. blue .. .. .. 2·00 2·25
a. Pale greenish blue .. .. 25·00 32·00
62 **4** 25 c. slate-purple ('31) .. 1·75 2·00
63 ,, 30 c. pur. & orge.-yell. ('31) 1·60 2·00
64 ,, 50 c. black/*emerald* ('31) .. 2·75 4·00
65 ,, $1 black & red/*blue* ('31) 7·50 9·00
51/65 .. .. *Set of* 19 25·00 30·00
51/65 Optd./Perf. "Specimen" *Set of* 19 80·00

* For 5 c. orange, see No. 69.

** For 6 c. black, see No. 69*d*. Apart from the difference in shade there is a variation in size, No. 58 being 37¾ mm. long and No. 69*d* 39 mm.

The 2 c. orange in Type **4** and the 8 c. red and 15 c. ultramarine in Type **6** were not issued without the Japanese Occupation overprint, although unoverprinted copies may exist.

1947 (2 JAN.)–**51.** *Colours changed and new values. Wmk. Mult. Script CA. P* 14.

66 **4** 1 c. chocolate 12 12
67 ,, 2 c. grey 12 35
a. Perf. 14½×13½ (25.9.50) .. 35 30
ab. Black (27.6.51) 10 25
68 **6** 3 c. green 20 35

No.	Type	Description	Unused	Used
69	4	5 c. orange	25	35
		a. " 5 c." retouch	8·50	8·50
		b. Perf. 14½×13½ (25.9.50)	1·25	1·50
		c. Ditto. " 5 c." retouch	8·50	8·50
69*d*	6	6 c. black*	12	30
70	4	8 c. scarlet	15	12
		a. Perf. 13 (25.1.51)	10	40
71	,,	10 c. violet	5	5
		a. Perf. 14½×13½ (25.9.50)	35	50
72	,,	15 c. ultramarine	20	8
73	,,	25 c. purple	8	15
		a. Perf. 14½×13½ (25.1.51)	15	70
74	,,	30 c. black and orange	15	25
		a. Perf. 14½×13½ (25.1.51)	15	85
75	,,	50 c. black	15	50
		a. Perf. 13 (25.9.50)	50	2·50
76	,,	$1 black and scarlet	45	45
77	,,	$5 grn. & red-orge. (2.2.48)	4·00	5·00
78	,,	$10 black & purple (2.2.48)	8·00	11·00
66/78		*Set of* 14	12·00	18·00
66/78		Perf. " Specimen " *Set of* 14	48·00	

* See also No. 58.

7. Sultan Ahmed Tajudin and Brunei Town.

1949 (22 Sept.). *Sultan's Silver Jubilee. Wmk. Mult.Script CA. P* 13.

No.	Type	Description	Unused	Used
79	7	8 c. black and carmine	35	65
80	,,	25 c. purple and red-orange	35	25
81	,,	50 c. black and blue	50	75

1949 (10 Oct.). *75th Anniv. of Universal Postal Union. As Nos.* 114/7 *of Antigua.*

No.	Description	Unused	Used
82	8 c. carmine	12	25
83	15 c. deep blue	30	30
84	25 c. magenta	35	35
85	50 c. blue-black	50	60

8. Sultan Omar Ali Saifuddin.

9. Native houses, Brunei Town.

1952 (1 Mar.). *Wmk. Mult. Script CA. P* 13.

No.	Type	Description	Unused	Used
86	8	1 c. black	5	10
87	,,	2 c. black and orange	5	12
88	,,	3 c. black and lake-brown	5	10
89	,,	4 c. black and green	5	12
90	,,	6 c. black and grey	8	10
91	,,	8 c. blk. & crim. (*shades*)	8	12
92	,,	10 c. black and sepia	8	8
93	,,	12 c. black and violet	8	12
94	,,	15 c. black and pale blue	10	10
95	,,	25 c. black & pur. (*shades*)	10	10
96	,,	50 c. blk. & ultram. (*shades*)	15	12
97	9	$1 blk. & green (*shades*)	50	55
98	,,	$2 black and scarlet	90	80
99	,,	$5 black & mar. (*shades*)	3·00	3·00
86/99		*Set of* 14	4·25	4·75

See also Nos. 104/117 and 188/95.

10. Brunei Mosque and Sultan Omar.

(Recess. Bradbury, Wilkinson & Co.)

1958 (24 Sept.). *Opening of Brunei Mosque. W* **w.12.** *P* 13½.

No.	Type	Description	Unused	Used
100	10	8 c. black & myrtle-grn.	12	12
101	,,	15 c. black and carmine	15	15
102	,,	35 c. black and deep lilac	30	30

11. " Protein Foods ".

(Des. M. Goaman. Photo. Harrison.)

1963 (4 June). *Freedom from Hunger. W* **w.12.** *P* 14×14½.

No.	Type	Description	Unused	Used
103	11	12 c. sepia	40	50

1964–71. *As Nos.* 86, *etc. but wmk.* **w.12.** *Ordinary paper.*

No.	Type	Description	Unused	Used
104	8	1 c. black (17.3.64)	5	5
		a. Glazed paper. *Grey* (*shades*) (28.11.69)	5	5
105	,,	2 c. black & orge. (17.3.64)	5	5
		a. Glazed paper (27.5.70)	5	5
106	,,	3 c. black and lake-brown (10.11.64)	5	5
		a. Glazed paper (27.5.70)	5	5
107	,,	4 c. black & green (12.5.64)	5	5
		a. Glazed paper (*shades*) (22.4.70)	5	5
108	,,	6 c. black & grey (12.5.64)	5	5
		a. Glazed paper (*shades*) (28.11.69)	5	5
		b. Black (28.11.69)	8	8
109	,,	8 c. black & crimson-lake (12.5.64)	15	15
		a. Glazed paper (*shades*) (27.5.70)	5	5
110	,,	10 c. black & sepia (12.5.64)	8	8
		a. Glazed paper (*shades*) (31.3.70)	8	8
111	,,	12 c. black & violet (12.5.64)	12	10
		a. Glazed paper (5.11.70)	5	5
112	,,	15 c. blk. & p. bl. (12.5.64)	12	12
		a. Glazed paper (28.11.69)	5	5
113	,,	25 c. black & pur. (12.5.64)	15	12
		a. Glazed paper (18.5.70)	10	10
		b. Glazed paper. *Black and reddish violet* (30.4.71)	10	10
114	,,	50 c. black and ultramarine (*shades*) (10.11.64)	25	30
		a. Glazed paper (*shades*) (5.11.70)	25	25
115	9	$1 black and bronze-green (14.5.68)	65	80
		a. Glazed paper (5.11.70)	45	45
116	,,	$2 black and scarlet (*glazed paper*) (5.11.70)	90	80
117	,,	$5 black & maroon (*glazed paper*) (15.11.70)	2·25	2·00
104/115		*Set of* 12	1·60	1·75
104a/115a, 116/7		*Set of* 15	4·00	3·75

Printings of the 6 and 15 c. issued on 28 Nov., 1969 were on both ordinary and glazed paper, the 6 c. on ordinary producing a distinct shade.

See also Nos. 188/95.

12. I.T.U. Emblem.

(Des. M. Goaman. Litho. Enschedé.)

1965 (17 May). *I.T.U. Centenary. W* **w.12.** *P* 11×11½.

No.	Type	Description	Unused	Used
118	4	c. mauve & orange-brown	8	8
119		75 c. orge.-yell. & lt. emerald	40	40

13. I.C.Y. Emblem.

(Des. V. Whiteley. Litho. Harrison.)

1965 (25 Oct.). *International Co-operation Year. W* **w.12.** *P* 14.

No.	Type	Description	Unused	Used
120	13	4 c. reddish purple and turquoise-green	8	8
121	,,	15 c. deep bluish green and lavender	25	25

14. Sir Winston Churchill and St. Paul's Cathedral in Wartime.

(Des. Jennifer Toombs. Photo. Harrison.)

1966 (24 Jan.). *Churchill Commemoration. W* **w.12.** *P* 14.

No.	Type	Description	Unused	Used
122	14	3 c. black, cerise, gold and new blue	5	5
123	,,	10 c. black, cerise, gold and deep green	10	10
124	,,	15 c. black, cerise, gold and brown	12	12
125	,,	75 c. black, cerise, gold and bluish violet	45	45

15. Footballer's Legs, Ball and Jules Rimet Cup.

(Des. V. Whiteley. Litho. Harrison.)

1966 (4 July). *World Football Cup Championships. W* **w.12.** (*sideways*). *P* 14.

No.	Type	Description	Unused	Used
126	15	4 c. violet, yellow-green, lake & yellow-brown	8	8
127	,,	75 c. chocolate, blue-green, lake & yellow-brown	40	40

16. W.H.O. Building.

(Des. M. Goaman. Litho. Harrison.)

1966 (20 Sept.). *Inauguration of W.H.O. Headquarters, Geneva. W* w.**12** *(sideways). P* 14.

128	**16**	12 c. black, yellow-green and light blue ..	8	8
129	,,	25 c. black, light purple and yellow-brown ..	15	15

17. " Education ".

18. " Science ".

19. " Culture ".

(Des. Jennifer Toombs. Litho. Harrison.).

1966 (1 Dec.). *20th Anniv. of U.N.E.S.C.O. W* w.**12** *(sideways). P* 14.

130	**17**	4 c. slate-violet, red, yellow and orange ..	8	8
131	**18**	15 c. orange-yellow, violet and deep olive ..	12	12
132	**19**	75 c. black, bright purple and orange	40	40

20. Bangunan Pejabat Hal Ehwal Ugama (Religious Headquarters building).

(Des. and Photo. Harrison.)

1967 (19 Dec.). *1400th Year of Al-Quran's Descent to Universe. W* w.**12** *(sideways). P* 12½.

133	**20**	4 c. multicoloured ..	5	5
134	,,	10 c. multicoloured ..	8	8
135	–	25 c. multicoloured ..	15	15
136	–	50 c. multicoloured ..	30	30

Nos. 135/6 have sprigs of laurel flanking the main design (which has a smaller circle) in place of flagpoles.

21. Sultan of Brunei, Mosque and Flags.

22. Sultan of Brunei, Mosque and Flags. (*As T* **21** *but horiz.*)

(Des. V. Whiteley. Photo. Enschedé.)

1968 (9 July). *Installation of Y.T.M. Seri Paduka Duli Pengiran Temenggong. P* 14 × 13 (*12 c.*) *or* 13 × 14 (*others*).

137	**21**	4 c. multicoloured ..	5	5
138	**22**	12 c. multicoloured ..	8	8
139	**21**	25 c. multicoloured ..	20	20

23. Sultan of Brunei.

(Des. V. Whiteley. Litho. De La Rue.)

1968 (15 July). *Sultan's Birthday. W* w.**12** *(sideways). P* 12.

140	**23**	4 c. multicoloured ..	5	5
141	,,	12 c. multicoloured ..	8	8
142	,,	25 c. multicoloured ..	20	20

24. Sultan of Brunei.

(Des. V. Whiteley. Photo Harrison.)

1968 (1 Aug.). *Coronation of the Sultan of Brunei. W* w.**12** *(sideways). P* 14½ × 14.

143	**24**	4 c. multicoloured ..	5	5
144	,,	12 c. multicoloured ..	8	8
145	,,	5 c. multicoloured ..	20	20

25. New Building and Sultan's Portrait.

26. New Building and Sultan's Portrait.

(Photo. J. Enschedé.)

1968 (29 Sept.). *Opening of Hall of Language and Culture. W* w.**12** *(sideways). P* 13½ (*10 c.*) *or* 12½ × 13½ (*others*).

146	**25**	10 c. multicoloured ..	5	5
147	**26**	15 c. multicoloured ..	10	10
148	,,	30 c. multicoloured ..	15	15

The above were scheduled for release in 1967, and when finally issued had the year altered by overprinting.

27. Human Rights Emblem and struggling Man.

(Des. V. Whiteley. Litho. Harrison.)

1968 (16 Dec.). *Human Rights Year. W* w.**12**. *P* 14.

149	**27**	12 c. black, yellow & green	5	5
150	,,	25 c. black, yellow and blue	12	12
151	,,	75 c. black, yell. & dull pur.	40	40

28. Sultan of Brunei and W.H.O. Emblem.

(Des. V. Whiteley. Litho. Format International.)

1968 (19 Dec.). *20th Anniv. of World Health Organization. P* 14.

152 **28** 4 c. yellow, black & cobalt .. 5 5
153 ,, 15 c. yellow, black and deep bluish violet .. 10 10
154 ,, 25 c. yellow, black and pale yellow-olive 20 20

29. Deep Sea Oil-Rig, Sultan of Brunei and inset portrait of Di-Gadong Sahibol Mal.

(Des. adapted by V. Whiteley. Photo. Enschedé.)

1969 (10 July). *Installation (9th May, 1968) of Pengiran Shah-bandar as Y.T.M. Seri Paduka Duli Pengiran Di-Gadong Sahibol Mal. W* w.**12**. *P* 14×13.

155 **29** 12 c. multicoloured .. 5 5
156 ,, 40 c. multicoloured .. 20 20
157 ,, 50 c. multicoloured .. 25 25

30. Aerial View of Royal Assembly Hall.

31. Side View of Royal Assembly Hall.

(Des. Harrison & Sons. Litho. De La Rue.)

1969 (23 Sept.). *Opening of Dewan Majlis and Lapau Di-Raja. P* 15.

158 **30** 12 c. multicoloured .. 5 5
159 ,, 25 c. multicoloured .. 12 12
160 **31** 50 c. rose-red and bluish violet 25 25

32. Youth Centre and Sultan's Portrait.

(Des. V. Whiteley. Litho. De La Rue.)

1969 (20 Dec.). *Opening of the New Youth Centre. W* w.**12**. *P* 15×14½.

161 **32** 6 c. flesh, slate-lilac and black 5 5
162 ,, 10 c. olive-yellow, grey-grn. and blackish brown .. 10 10
163 ,, 30 c. yellow-olive, yellow-brown and black .. 30 30

33. Soldier, Sultan and Badge.

(Des. Maj. M. A. Bowman. Adapted V. Whiteley Litho. Questa.)

1971 (31 May). *Tenth Anniv. of Royal Brunei Malay Regiment. Multicoloured designs, each with Badge and Sultan's portrait as T* **33**. *W* w.**12** (*sideways on* 15 *and* 75 *c.*). *P* 14½.

164 10 c. Type **33** 5 5
165 15 c. Helicopter (*horiz.*) .. 8 8
166 75 c. Patrol boat (*horiz.*) .. 35 35

34. Badge, and Officer in Full-dress Uniform.

(Des. T. Swan. Litho. Format.)

1971 (14 Aug.). *50th Anniv. of Royal Brunei Police Force. T* **34** *and similar vert. designs. Multicoloured. W* w.**12**. *P* 14½.

167 10 c. Type **34** 5 5
168 15 c. Badge and Patrol Constable 8 8
169 50 c. Badge and Traffic Constable 25 25

35. Perdana Wazir, Sultan of Brunei and view of Brunei Town.

(Des. and litho. Harrison.)

1971 (27 Aug.). *Installation of the Yang Teramat Mulia as the Perdana Wazir (1970). T* **35** *and similar vert. designs showing different views of Brunei Town. W* w.**12**. *P* 14.

170 **35** 15 c. multicoloured .. 8 8
171 – 25 c. multicoloured .. 15 15
172 – 50 c. multicoloured .. 30 30

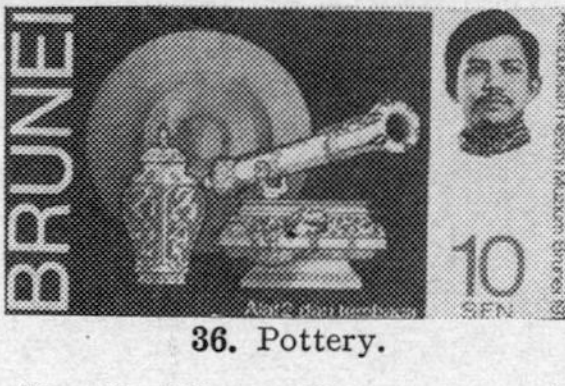

36. Pottery.

(Des. C. Abbott. Litho. Questa.)

1972 (29 Feb.). *Opening of Brunei Museum. T* **36** *and similar horiz. designs. Multicoloured. W* w.**12** (*sideways*). *P* 13½.

173 10 c. Type **36** 5 5
174 12 c. Straw-work 5 5
175 15 c. Leather-work 8 8
176 25 c. Gold-work 12 12
177 50 c. Museum Building (58×21 *mm.*) 30 30
173/7 .. .. *Set of* 5 45 50

37. Modern Building, Queen Elizabeth and Sultan of Brunei.

(Des. locally. Photo. Enschedé.)

1972 (29 Feb.). *Royal Visit. T* **37** *and similar horiz. designs each with portraits of Queen and Sultan. Multicoloured. W* w.**12** (*sideways*). *P* 13×13½.

178 10 c. Type **37** 5 5
179 15 c. Native houses 10 10
180 25 c. Mosque 15 20
181 50 c. Royal Assembly Hall .. 30 25

38. Bangunan Secretariat.

(Des. Harrison. Litho. J.W.)

1972 (4 Oct.). *Renaming of Brunei Town as Bandar Seri Begawan. T* **38** *and similar horiz. designs. W* w.**12** (*sideways*). *P* 13½.

182 10 c. multicoloured .. 5 5
183 15 c. green, light yellow and black 8 8
184 25 c. ultramarine, lemon and black 12 12
185 50 c. rosine, pale turq.-blue and black 25 30

Views:—15 c. Istana Darul Hana; 25 c. Bandar Brunei Lama; 50 c. Bandar Dan Kampong Ayer.

39. Blackburn " Beverley " parachuting Supplies.

(Des. Trident Artists. Litho. Questa.)

1972 (15 Nov.). *Opening of R.A.F. Museum, Hendon. T* **39** *and similar horiz. design. Multicoloured. W* w.**12** (*sideways on* 75 *c.*). *P* $14 \times 13\frac{1}{2}$ (25 *c.*) *or* $13\frac{1}{2} \times 14$ (75 *c.*).

186	25 c. Type **39**	12	12
187	75 c. Blackburn "Beverley" landing	35	35

1972 (17 Nov.)–**73**. *As Nos.* 105 *etc., but W* w.**12** (*sideways*). *Glazed paper.*

188	**8**	2 c. black and orange (9.5.73)	5	5
189	,,	3 c. black and lake-brown	5	5
190	,,	4 c. black and green ..	5	5
191	,,	6 c. black and grey ..	5	5
192	,,	8 c. black and brown-red (9.5.73)	5	5
193	,,	10 c. black and sepia (*shades*)	5	5
194	,,	12 c. black and violet ..	5	5
195	,,	15 c. black and pale blue ..	5	8
188/95		.. .. *Set of* 8	20	20

40. Girl with Traditional Flower-pot, and Boy with Bowl and Pipe.

(Des. (from photograph by D. Groves) and photo. Harrison.)

1972 (20 Nov.). *Royal Silver Wedding. Multicoloured; background colour given. W* w.**12.** *P* $14 \times 14\frac{1}{2}$.

196	**40**	12 c. carmine-red	8	8
197	,,	75 c. deep myrtle-green ..	40	40

41. Interpol H.Q., Paris.

(Des. Shamir Bros. Litho. Harrison.)

1973 (7 Sept.). *50th Anniv. of Interpol. T* **41** *and similar horiz. design. W* w.**12** (*inverted on* 50 *c.*). *P* $14 \times 14\frac{1}{2}$.

198	25 c. bright green, purple and dull blue-black ..	12	12
199	50 c. pale greenish blue, ultramarine and carmine ..	25	25

The 50 c. shows a different view of the H.Q.

42. Sultan, Princess Anne and Capt. Phillips.

(Des. PAD Studio. Litho. Format.)

1973 (14 Nov.). *Royal Wedding. W* w.**12.** *P* 14.

200	**42**	25 c. multicoloured ..	12	12
201	,,	50 c. multicoloured ..	25	25

43. Churchill Painting. **44.** Sultan Sir Muda Hassanal Bolkiah Mu'izzaddin Waddaulah.

(Des. C. Abbott. Litho. Questa.)

1973 (31 Dec.). *Churchill Memorial Exhibition. T* **43** *and similar vert. design. Multicoloured. W* w.**12** (*sideways*). *P* $14 \times 13\frac{1}{2}$.

202	12 c. Type **43**	8	8
203	50 c. Churchill making " V " sign	15	20

(Des. Staff Artists, Dept. of Language and Literature. Photo. Harrison.)

1974–76. *Multicoloured; background colour given.* *P* $13\frac{1}{2} \times 14$.

A. *W* w.**12** *sideways* (15.7.74).
B. *W* w.**12** *upright* (12.4.76).

			A.		B.	
204	**44**	4 c. turq.-green	5	5	†	
205	,,	5 c. pale blue ..	5	5	†	
206	,,	6 c. olive ..	5	5	†	
207	,,	10 c. lavender ..	5	8	5	8
208	,,	15 c. lt. brown ..	8	8	†	
209	,,	20 c. stone ..	8	10	8	10
210	,,	25 c. sage-green ..	12	12	10	12
211	,,	30 c. bright blue	12	15	†	
212	,,	35 c. grey ..	15	20	†	
213	,,	40 c. brt. purple	20	20	†	
214	,,	50 c. cinnamon ..	20	25	†	
215	,,	75 c. lt. yell.-grn.	35	40	†	
216	,,	$1 buff ..	45	50	†	
217	,,	$2 greenish yell.	90	1·00	†	
218	,,	$5 silver ..	2·25	2·50	†	
219	,,	$10 gold ..	4·50	4·75	†	
204/19		.. *Set of* 16	8·50	9 00		

See also Nos. 230/45.

45. Aerial View of Airport.

(Des. Harrison. Litho. B.W.)

1974 (18 July). *Inauguration of Brunei International Airport. T* **45** *and similar horiz. design. Multicoloured. W* w.**12.** *P* $14 \times 14\frac{1}{2}$ (50 *c.*) *or* $12\frac{1}{2} \times 13$ (75 *c.*).

220	50 c. Type **45**	25	25
221	75 c. Sultan in Air Force uniform, and airport (48 × 36 *mm.*)	35	35

46. U.P.U. Emblem and Sultan.

(Des. J.W. Ltd. Litho. Harrison.)

1974 (28 Oct.). *Centenary of Universal Postal Union. W* w.**12** (*sideways*). *P* $14\frac{1}{2}$.

222	**46**	12 c. multicoloured ..	8	8
223	,,	50 c. multicoloured ..	20	20
224	,,	75 c. multicoloured ..	25	30

47. Sir Winston Churchill.

(Des. C. Abbott. Litho. Questa.)

1974 (30 Nov.). *Birth Centenary of Sir Winston Churchill. T* **47** *and similar horiz. design. Multicoloured. W* w.**14** (*sideways*). *P* 14.

225	12 c. Type **47**	8	8
226	75 c. Churchill smoking cigar (profile)	30	30

48. Boeing " 737 " and R.B.A. Crest.

(Des. PAD Studio. Litho. Enschedé.)

1975 (14 May). *Inauguration of Royal Brunei Airlines. T* **48** *and similar horiz. designs. Multicoloured. No wmk. P* $12\frac{1}{2} \times 12$.

227	12 c. Type **48**	5	5
228	35 c. " 737 " over Bandar Seri Begawan Mosque ..	12	12
229	75 c. " 737 " in flight.. ..	25	30

1975 (13 Aug.). *As Nos.* 204/19 *but W* **w.14** (*sideways*). *Background colours given.*

230	**44**	4 c. turquoise-green ..	5	5
231	„	5 c. pale blue	5	5
232	„	6 c. brown	5	5
233	„	10 c. lavender	5	5
234	„	15 c. light brown	5	8
235	„	20 c. stone	8	8
236	„	25 c. sage-green	10	12
237	„	30 c. bright blue	12	12
238	„	35 c. grey	12	15
239	„	40 c. bright purple ..	15	20
240	„	50 c. cinnamon	20	20
241	„	75 c. light yellow-green ..	30	35
242	„	$1 buff	40	45
243	„	$2 greenish yellow ..	75	85
244	„	$5 silver	2·00	2·25
245	„	$10 gold	3·75	4·00
230/45		.. .. *Set of* 16	7·00	7·50

10

sen

(49)

1976 (16 Aug.). *No.* 232 *surch. in silver with T* **49.**

246	10 c. on 6 c. brown	5	5

JAPANESE OCCUPATION OF BRUNEI.

Stamps listed under this heading were valid in Brunei, Labuan, North Borneo and Sarawak.

府政國帝本日大

(" Imperial Japanese Government ")

(1)

1942–45. *Stamps of Brunei handstamped with T* **1** *in violet to blue. Wmk. Mult. Script CA* (*except Nos.* J16/17, *Mult. Crown CA*). *P* 14.

J 1	**4**	1 c. black	2·00	2·50
J 2	„	2 c. green	15·00	20·00
J 3	„	2 c. orange ('45)	1·00	1·25
J 4	„	3 c. green	12·00	14·00
J 5	„	4 c. orange	1·25	2·00
J 6	„	5 c. chocolate	1·25	2·00
		aa. "5 c." retouch	50·00	
J 6*a*	**6**	6 c. greenish grey (*p.* 14×11½)	20·00	22·00
J 6*b*	„	6 c. scarlet	90·00	£110
J 7	**4**	8 c. grey-black	70·00	75·00
J 8	**6**	8 c. red	1·00	1·00
J 9	**4**	10 c. purple/*yellow*	2·00	2·50
J10	**6**	12 c. blue	2·00	2·50
J11	„	15 c. ultramarine ('45) ..	2·00	2·50
J12	**4**	25 c. slate-purple	5·00	6·00
J13	„	30 c. purple & orange-yell.	40·00	50·00
J14	„	50 c. black/*emerald* ..	8·00	8·00
J15	„	$1 black & red/*blue* ..	8·00	8·00
J16	„	$5 carmine/*green* ..	£100	
J17	„	$25 black/*red*	£200	

The overprint varies in shade from violet to blue, and, being handstamped, exists double and treble.

Nos. 3, 8 and 11 were not issued without the overprint.

便郵國帝

(2)

1944. *No.* 51 *of Brunei surch. with T* 2 ("*Imperial Japanese Post* $3"), *in orange-red.*

J18	**4**	$3 on 1 c. black	£300	£250

BURMA.

BRITISH RULE.

From 1 January 1886 Burma was a province of the Indian Empire but was separated from India and came under direct British rule on 1 April 1937.

BURMA (1) **BURMA** (1*a*)

1937 (1 April). *Stamps of India* (*King George V inscr.* "INDIA POSTAGE") *optd. with T* **1** *or* **1a** (*rupee values*). *W* **69.** *P* 14.

1	3 p. slate	12	5
2	½ a. green	12	5
3	9 p. deep green	15	5
4	1 a. chocolate	15	12
5	2 a. vermilion (*small die*) ..	15	12
6	2½ a. orange	25	15
7	3 a. carmine	45	35
8	3½ a. deep blue	45	30
	a. Dull blue	2·00	2·50
9	4 a. sage-green	40	12
10	6 a. bistre	40	25
11	8 a. reddish purple	50	30
12	12 a. claret	65	60
13	1 r. chocolate and green ..	70	30
14	2 r. carmine and orange ..	1·75	55
15	5 r. ultramarine and purple	3·75	3·00
16	10 r. green and scarlet ..	7·50	4·00
17	15 r. blue and olive	30·00	18·00
18	25 r. orange and blue	50·00	35·00
1/18	.. .. *Set of* 19	90·00	60·00

The opt. is at top on all values except the 3 a.

2. King George VI and "Chinthes".

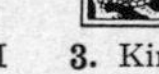

3. King George VI and "Nagas".

4. Royal Barge.

5. Burma Teak.

6. Burma Rice.

7. R. Irrawaddy.

8. King George VI and Peacock.

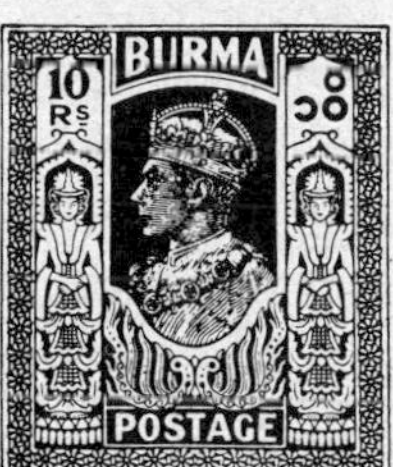

9. King George VI and "Nats".

10. Elephants' Heads.

(Des. Maung Kyi (*T* **4**), Maung Hline (*T* **5**), Maung Ohn Pe (*T* **6**) and N. K. D. Naigamwalla (*T* **7**). Litho. Security Ptg. Press, Nasik.).

1938 (15 Nov.)–**40.** *W* **10.** *P* 14 (*vert.*) or 13½×13 (*horiz.*).

No.	Type	Description	Unused	Used
18*a*	**2**	1 p. red-orange (1.8.40) ..	8	25
19	,,	3 p. bright violet ..	8	12
20	,,	6 p. bright blue	5	5
21	,,	9 p. yellow-green ..	10	20
22	**3**	1 a. purple-brown	5	5
23	,,	1½ a. turquoise-green ..	10	12
24	,,	2 a. carmine	15	12
25	**4**	2 a. 6 p. claret	30	30
26	**5**	3 a. dull violet ..	50	40
27	**6**	3 a. 6 p. light blu[illegible]nd blue	1·00	1·40
28	**3**	4 a. greenish b[illegible] ..	20	20
29	**7**	8 a. myrtle-g[illegible] ..	40	40
30	**8**	1 r. purple an[illegible]e ..	85	45
31	,,	2 r. brown and [illegible]ple ..	2·00	75
32	**9**	5 r. violet and sc[illegible]t ..	6·50	3·50
33	,,	10 r. brown and my[illegible] ..	14·00	13·00
18*a*/33		.. .. *Set* [illegible]6	24·00	19·00

The 1 a. exists lithographed and typographed, the latter having a "Jubilee" line in the sheet margin.

COMMEMORATION
POSTAGE STAMP
6th MAY 1840

(11)

1940 (6 May). *Centenary of First Adhesive Postage Stamps. No.* 25 *surch. with T* **11.**

No.	Type	Description	Unused	Used
34	**4**	1 a. on 2 a. 6 p. claret ..	85	90

For stamps issued in 1942–45 see under Japanese Occupation.

BRITISH MILITARY ADMINISTRATION.

MILY ADMN (12) MILY ADMN (13)

1945 (From 16 June). *Nos.* 18*a to* 33, *optd. with T* **12** (*small stamps*) *or* **13** (*others*).

No.	Type	Description	Unused	Used
35	**2**	1 p. red-orange	5	5
36	,,	3 p. bright violet	5	10
37	,,	6 p. bright blue	5	10
38	,,	9 p. yellow-green	5	10
39	**3**	1 a. purple-brown (16.6) ..	5	10
40	,,	1½ a. turquoise-green (16.6) ..	5	10
41	,,	2 a. carmine	5	10
42	**4**	2 a. 6 p. claret	5	8
43	**5**	3 a. dull violet	5	8
44	**6**	3 a. 6 p. light blue and blue	5	8
45	**3**	4 a. greenish blue	5	10
46	**7**	8 a. myrtle green	5	10
47	**8**	1 r. purple and blue ..	12	20
48	,,	2 r. brown and purple ..	25	30
49	**9**	5 r. violet and scarlet ..	55	65
50	,,	10 r. brown and myrtle ..	1·40	1·40
35/50		.. .. *Set of* 16	2·50	3·00

BRITISH CIVIL ADMINISTRATION.

1946 (1 Jan.). *Colours changed.*

No.	Type	Description	Unused	Used
51	**2**	3 p. brown	5	8
52	,,	6 p. deep violet	5	5
53	,,	9 p. green	8	8
54	**3**	1 a. blue	8	8
55	,,	1½ a. orange	5	5
56	,,	2 a. claret	8	10
57	**4**	2 a. 6 p. greenish blue ..	5	5
57*a*	**5**	3 a. blue-violet	10	8
57*b*	**6**	3 a. 6 p. black and ultram.	5	10
58	**3**	4 a. purple	5	8
59	**7**	8 a. maroon	8	12
60	**8**	1 r. violet and maroon ..	15	12
61	,,	2 r. brown and orange ..	30	30
62	**9**	5 r. green and brown ..	80	80
63	,,	10 r. claret and violet ..	1·75	2·00
51/63		.. .. *Set of* 15	3·25	3·75

14. Burman.

15. Burmese Woman.

16. Chinthe.

17. Elephant.

(Des. A. G. I. McGeogh. Offset-litho, Nasik.)

1946 (2 May). *Victory. P* 13. *W* **10** *sideways.*

No.	Type	Description	Unused	Used
64	**14**	9 p. turquoise-green ..	5	5
65	**15**	1½ a. violet	5	5
66	**16**	2 a. carmine	5	5
67	**17**	3 a. 6 p. ultramarine ..	5	8

INTERIM BURMESE GOVERNMENT.

ကြားဖြတ်
အစိုးရ။

(**18.** *Trans.* "Interim Government.")

1947 (1 Oct.). *Stamps of* 1946 *optd. with T* **18** (*small stamps*) *or larger opt.* (*others*).

No.	Type	Description	Unused	Used
68	**2**	3 p. brown	8	10
69	,,	6 p. deep violet	5	10
70	,,	9 p. green	5	10
		a. Opt. inverted	6·00	6·50
71	**3**	1 a. blue	5	10
72	,,	1½ a. orange	12	10
73	,,	2 a. claret	5	10
74	**4**	2 a. 6 p. greenish blue ..	10	10
75	**5**	3 a. blue-violet	5	10
76	**6**	3 a. 6 p. black and ultram.	5	10
77	**3**	4 a. purple	10	10
78	**7**	8 a. maroon	10	12
79	**8**	1 r. violet and maroon ..	25	20
80	,,	2 r. brown and orange ..	45	35
81	**9**	5 r. green and brown ..	80	85
82	,,	10 r. claret and violet ..	1·40	1·60
68/82		.. .. *Set of* 15	3·25	3·50

The 3 p., 6 p., 2 a., 2 a. 6 p. and 3 a. 6 p. are also known with overprint inverted.

OFFICIAL STAMPS.

BURMA BURMA

SERVICE (O 1) SERVICE (O 1*a*)

1937. (Apr. June). *Stamps of India* (*King George V inscr.* "INDIA POSTAGE") *optd. with Type* O **1** *or* O **1***a* (*rupee values*). *W* **69.** *P* 14.

No.	Description	Unused	Used
O 1	3 p. slate	5	10
O 2	½ a. green	25	12
O 3	9 p. deep green	20	12
O 4	1 a. chocolate	20	12
O 5	2 a. vermilion (*small die*) ..	20	12
O 6	2½ a. orange	25	20
O 7	4 a. sage-green	25	15
O 8	6 a. bistre	60	45
O 9	8 a. reddish purple (1.4.37)	35	25
O10	12 a. claret (1.4.37) ..	55	45
O11	1 r. choc. and green (1.4.37)	60	50
O12	2 r. carmine and orange ..	1·60	1·40
O13	5 r. ultramarine and purple	4·50	4·00
O14	10 r. green and scarlet ..	11·00	8·50
O1/14	.. .. *Set of* 15	18·00	15·00

The bulk of the above issue was overprinted "BURMA" and "SERVICE" by offset-lithography at one operation; but a certain quantity of some values was overprinted at two operations.

SERVICE (O 2) SERVICE (O 3)

1939. *Nos.* 19/24 *and* 28 *optd. with Type* O **2** (*typo.*) *and Nos.* 25 *and* 29/33 *optd. with Type* O **3** (*offset-litho.*).

No.	Type	Description	Unused	Used
O15	**2**	3 p. bright violet	5	10
O16	,,	6 p. bright blue	5	10
O17	,,	9 p. yellow-green	8	10
O18	**3**	1 a. purple-brown ..	8	10
O19	,,	1½ a. turquoise-green ..	30	10
O20	,,	2 a. carmine	12	15
O21	**4**	2 a. 6 p. claret	35	35
O22	**3**	4 a. greenish blue	55	20
O23	**7**	8 a. myrtle-green	60	45
O24	**8**	1 r. purple and blue ..	85	65
O25	,,	2 r. brown and purple ..	1·40	65
O26	**9**	5 r. violet and scarlet ..	4·00	2·25
O27	,,	10 r. brown and myrtle ..	6·00	3·50
O15/27		.. .. *Set of* 13	13·00	8·00

1946. *British Civil Administration. Nos.* 51/6 *and* 58 *optd. with Type* O **2** (*typo*) *and Nos.* 57 *and* 59/63 *optd. with Type* O **3** (*offset-litho.*).

No.	Type	Description	Unused	Used
O28	**2**	3 p. brown	5	10
O29	,,	6 p. deep violet	10	10
O30	,,	9 p. green	5	10

O31	3	1 a. blue	5	10
O32	,,	1½ a. orange	8	10
O33	,,	2 a. claret	5	10
O34	4	2 a. 6 p. greenish blue ..	5	10
O35	3	4 a. purple	5	10
O36	7	8 a. maroon	5	12
O37	8	1 r. violet and maroon ..	10	12
O38	,,	2 r. brown and orange ..	40	45
O39	9	5 r. green and brown ..	80	1·40
O40	9	10 r. claret and violet ..	1·25	2·25
O28/40		.. .. *Set of* 13	2·75	4·50

1947. *Interim Burmese Government. Nos.* O28/40 *optd. with T* **18** *(small stamps) or larger opt. (others).*

O41	2	3 p. brown	5	5
O42	,,	6 p. deep violet	5	5
O43	,,	9 p. green	5	5
O44	3	1 a. blue	12	8
O45	,,	1½ a. orange	15	8
O46	,,	2 a. claret	15	8
O47	4	2 a. 6 p. greenish blue ..	15	10
O48	3	4 a. purple	15	8
O49	7	8 a. maroon	15	10
O50	8	1 r. violet and maroon ..	35	30
O51	,,	2 r. brown and orange ..	60	45
O52	9	5 r. green and brown ..	1·00	1·40
O53	,,	10 r. claret and violet ..	2·00	2·40
O41/53		.. .. *Set of* 13	4·50	4·50

Later stamp issues will be found listed in Vol. 1 of the Stanley Gibbons Foreign Overseas Catalogue.

JAPANESE OCCUPATION OF BURMA.

(March 1942 to March 1945.)

ISSUES OF THE BURMA INDEPENDENCE ARMY.

The Burma Independence Army, formed by Aung San in 1941, took control of the Delta area of the Irrawaddy in May 1942. They re-opened a postal service in the area and were authorised by the Japanese to overprint local stocks of stamps with the Burmese emblem of a peacock.

Postage and Official stamps with the peacock overprints or handstamps were used for ordinary postal purposes with the probable exception of No. J44.

Distinguishing Features. Type **1.** Body and head of Peacock always clearly outlined by broad uncoloured band.

Type **2.** Peacock with slender neck and more delicately detailed tail. Clear spur on leg at right. Heavy fist-shaped blob of ink below and parallel to beak and neck.

Type **4.** No basic curve. Each feather separately outlined. Straight, short legs.

Type **5.** Much fine detail in wings and tail in clearly printed overprints. Thin, long legs ending in claws which, with the basic arc, enclose clear white spaces in well-printed copies. Blob of colour below beak shows shaded detail and never has the heavy fist-like appearance of this portion in Type **2.**

Two sub-types may be distinguished in Type **5**, the basic arc of one having a chord of 14–15 mm. and the other 12½–13 mm.

Type **6.** Similar to Type **5**, but with arc deeply curved and reaching nearly to the top of the wings. Single diagonal line parallel to neck below beak.

Collectors are warned against forgeries of these overprints, often in the wrong colours or on the wrong values.

(1)

(2)

(3)

1942 (May). *Stamps of Burma overprinted with the national device of a Peacock.*

I. *Overprinted at Myaungmya.*

A. *With Type* **1** *in black.*

On Postage Stamps of King George V.

J 1		9 p. deep green (No. 3) ..	9·50	
J 2		3½ a. deep blue (No. 8) ..	4·50	

On Official Stamp of King George V.

J 3		6 a. bistre (No. O8)	9·50	

On Postage Stamps of King George VI.

J 4	2	9 p. yellow-green ..	23·00	
J 5	3	1 a. purple-brown	55·00	
J 6	,,	4 a. greenish blue (opt. black on red) ..	18·00	
		a. Triple opt., black on double red	45·00	

On Official Stamps of King George VI.

J 7	2	3 p. bright violet ..	2·50	4·50
J 8	,,	6 p. bright blue	70	2·00
J 9	3	1 a. purple-brown ..	70	2·00
J 9*a*	,,	1½ a. turquoise-green ..	50·00	
J10	,,	2 a. carmine	2·60	
J11	,,	4 a. greenish blue ..	2·00	2·60

The overprint on No. J6 was apparently first done in red in error, and then corrected in black. Some stamps have the black overprint so accurately superimposed that the red hardly shows. These are rare.

Nos. J5 and J9 exist with the Peacock overprint on both the typographed and the offset printings of the original stamps.

B. *With Types* **2** *or* **3** *(rupee values), in black.*

On Postage Stamps of King George VI.

J12	2	3 p. bright violet	1·60	6·00
J13	,,	6 p. bright blue	3·25	
J14	,,	9 p. yellow-green	1·60	4·50
J15	3	1 a. purple-brown.. ..	80	2·00
J16	,,	2 a. carmine	1·25	2·75
J17	,,	4 a. greenish blue ..	2·00	
		a. Opt. double		
		b. Opt. inverted	40·00	
		c. Opt. double, one inverted..	40·00	
		d. Opt. double, both inverted	40·00	
J18	8	1 r. purple and blue ..	32·00	
J19	,,	2 r. brown and purple ..	21·00	

The Myaungmya overprints (including No. J44) are usually clearly printed.

(4)

II. *Handstamped (at Pyapon?) with T* **4**, *in black (so-called experimental type).*

On Postage Stamps of King George VI.

J19*a*	3	1 a. purple-brown ..	25·00	
J20	,,	2 a. carmine	16·00	
J21	,,	4 a. greenish blue ..	50·00	

Unused specimens of these stamps are usually in poor condition.

Type **5** generally shows the details of the peacock much less clearly and, due to heavy inking, or careless impression, sometimes appears as almost solid colour.

Type **6** was officially applied only to postal stationery. However, the handstamp remained in the possession of a postal official who used it on postage stamps after the war. These stamps are no longer listed.

(5)

(6)

III. *Overprinted at Henzada with T* **5** *in blue, or blue-black.*

On Postage Stamps of King George V.

J22		3 p. slate (No. 1)	35	80
		a. Opt. double..	2·00	3·00
J23		9 p. deep green (No. 3) ..	2·50	4·50
		a. Opt. double..	9·00	
J24		2 a. vermilion (No. 5) ..	15·00	23·00

On Postage Stamps of King George VI.

J25	2	1 p. red-orange	16·00	25·00
J26	,,	3 p. bright violet ..	4·50	9·50
J27	,,	6 p. bright blue	2·50	8·00
		a. Opt. double	13·00	
		b. Clear opt., on back and front	30·00	
J28	,,	9 p. yellow-green ..	45·00	
J29	3	1 a. purple-brown ..	1·40	2·25
		a. Opt. inverted	17·00	
J30	,,	1½ a. turquoise-green ..	2·00	4·50
J31	,,	2 a. carmine	2·00	4·00
J32	,,	4 a. greenish blue ..	6·00	9·50
		a. Opt. double	17·00	
		b. Opt. inverted		

On Official Stamps of King George VI.

J33	2	3 p. bright violet ..	12·00	19·00
J34	,,	6 p. bright blue	8·00	16·00
J35	3	1½ a. turquoise-green ..	15·00	23·00
J35*a*	,,	2 a. carmine	32·00	32·00
J36	,,	4 a. greenish blue ..	50·00	

(6*a*)
("Yon Thon" = "Office use".)

IV. *Official Stamp of King George VI optd. at Myaungmya with Type* **6*a*** *in black.*

J44	7	8 a. myrtle-green	16·00	

No. J44 was probably for official use.

There are two types of T **6*a***, one with base of peacock 8 mm. long and the other with base about 5 mm. long. The neck and other details also vary. The two types are found *se-tenant* in the sheet.

Stocks of the peacock types were withdrawn when the Japanese Directorate-General took control of the postal services in the Delta in August 1942.

ISSUES OF THE JAPANESE ARMY ADMINISTRATION.

7

.942 (1 June). *Impressed by hand.* P 12×11. *No gum.*
J45 7 (no value) red .. .. 9·00 14·00

This device was the personal seal of S. Yano, he Japanese official in charge of the Posts and Telegraphs department of the Japanese Army Administration. Some stamps show part of the papermaker's watermark, either "ABSORBO DUPLICATOR" or "ELEPHANT BRAND", each with an elephant.

8. Farmer.

(Typo. *Rangoon Gazette* Press.)

.942 (15 June). *Value in annas.* P 11×11½. *Laid bâtonné paper. No gum.*
J46 8 1 a. scarlet .. .. .. 5·50 6·00

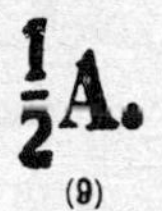

1R.

(9) (10)

.942 (22 Sept.). *Contemporary Japanese stamps (Cat. Nos. in brackets) surch. as T* **9/10.**

J47 **9** ½ a. on 1 s. chestnut (317) 4·50 6·00
 a. Surch. inverted .. .. 20·00 20·00
J48 „ ½ a. on 2 s. scarlet (318) .. 4·50 6·00
 a. Surch. inverted .. .. 13·00
 b. Surch. double, inverted .. 26·00
J49 „ ¾ a. on 3 s. green (319) .. 6·00
 a. Surch. inverted .. .. 20·00 20·00
 b. Surch. double, one inverted — 27·00
J50 „ 1a. on 5 s. claret (396) .. 6·00 8·00
 a. Surch. inverted.. .. 17·00 17·00
 b. Surch. double, one inverted — 22·00
 c. Surch. omitted (in pair with normal) .. .. — 20·00
J51 „ 3 a. on 7 s. green (323) .. 7·50 8·50
 a. Surch. inverted .. .. 17·00
J52 „ 4 a. on 4 s. green (320) .. 7·50 8·50
 a. Surch. inverted .. .. 20·00
J53 „ 8 a. on 8 s. violet (324) .. 25·00 32·00
 a. Surch. inverted .. .. 32·00 38·00
 b. Surch. double, one inverted 65·00
 c. Surch. in red .. .. 40·00 45·00
 d. Red surch. inverted .. 75·00
J54 **10** 1 r. on 10 s. lake (325) .. 4·50 5·50
 a. Surch. inverted .. .. — 17·00
 b. Surch. double .. ..
 c. Surch. double (black and red) 24·00
 d. Surch. omitted (in pair with normal) .. .. — 25·00
J55 „ 2 r. on 20 s. ultram. (328) 9·00 9·00
 a. Surch. inverted .. .. 16·00 20·00
 b. Surch. double, inverted .. 16·00
 c. Surch. omitted (in pair with normal black surch.).. 20·00 20·00
 d. Surch. in red .. .. 9·00 9·00
 e. Red surch. inverted .. 16·00
 f. Red surch. double .. 35·00
 g. Surch. omitted (in pair with normal red surch.) .. — 20·00
J56 **10** 5 r. on 30 s. blue-grn. (330) 3·00 3·50
 a. Surch. inverted .. .. 55·00
 b. Surch. double .. ..
 c. Surch. in red .. .. 6·00 6·50
 d. Red surch. inverted .. 17·00 14·00
 e. J56a and J56c se-tenant .. — 60·00
 f. Surch. omitted (in pair with normal red surch.) .. — 21·00

Japanese stamp commemorating the fall of Singapore similarly surch.

J56g **9** 4 a. on 4+2 s. green and red (386) .. .. 17·00 20·00
 h. Surch. omitted (in pair with normal) £150
 i. Surch. inverted.. .. 32·00

Currency changed. 100 cents=1 rupee.

15 C. 15 C. 15 C.

(11) (12) (13)

1942 (15 Oct.). *Previous issues, with "anna" surcharges obliterated, and handstamped with new value in cents, as T* **11** *and* **12** *(No.* J 57 *handstamped with new value only).*

(a) T **8** *(Farmer).*

J57 5 c. on 1 a. scarlet .. .. 3·50 4·50

(b) Contemporary Japanese issues.

J58 1 c. on ¼ a. on 1 s. (J47) .. 9·00 9·00
 a. "1 c." omitted in pair with normal .. .. ..
J59 2 c. on ½ a. on 2 s. (J48) .. 9·00 9·00
J60 3 c. on ¾ a. on 3 s. (J49) .. 9·00 9·00
 a. Surch. in blue .. ..
J61 5 c. on 1 a. on 5 s. (J50) .. 9·00
J62 10 c. on 3 a. on 7 s. (J51) .. 13·00 13·00
J63 15 c. on 4 a. on 4 s. (J52) .. 4·50 5·00
J64 20 c. on 8 a. on 8 s. (J53) .. 17·00 20·00
 a. 20 c. on 8 a. (R.) on 8 s. (J53a) — 32·00

The "anna" surcharges were obliterated by any means available, in some cases by a bar or bars, and in others by the butt of a pencil dipped in ink. In the case of the fractional surcharges, the letter "A" and one figure of the fraction, were sometimes barred out, leaving the remainder of the fraction to represent the new value, e.g. the "1" of "½" deleted to create the 2 c. surcharge or the "4" of "¾" to create the 3 c. surcharge.

1942. *Contemporary stamps of Japan (Cat. Nos. in brackets) surcharged in cents only, as T* **13.**

J65 1 c. on 1 s. chestnut (317).. 4·00 4·50
 a. Surch. inverted .. .. 9·00 9·00
J66 2 c. on 2 s. scarlet (318) .. 4·50 5·50
J67 3 c. on 3 s. green (319) .. 7·00 8·00
 a. Pair, with and without surch. — 25·00
 b. Surch. inverted .. .. 17·00
 c. Surch. in blue .. .. 25·00 32·00
 d. Surch. in blue (inverted) .. 50·00 60·00
J68 5 c. on 5 s. claret (396) .. 7·50 9·00
 a. Surch. in violet .. .. 35·00
 b. Surch. in violet (inverted).. — 20·00
J69 10 c. on 7 s. green (323) .. 7·00 8·00
J70 15 c. on 4 s. green (320) .. 4·50 6·00
 a. Surch. inverted .. .. 17·00 19·00
 b. Pair, with and without surch. — 20·00
J71 20 c. on 8 s. violet (324) .. 17·00 17·00

Nos. J67*c* and J68*a* were issued for use in the Shan States.

ISSUES OF THE BURMESE GOVERNMENT.

On 1 November 1942 the Japanese Army Administration handed over the control of the postal department to the Burmese Government. On 1 August 1943 Burma was declared by the Japanese to be independent.

14. Burma State Crest.

(Des. U Tun Tin and Maung Tin from drawing by U Ba Than. Typo. Rangoon.)

1943 (15 Feb.). *P* 11. *No gum.*
J72 **14** 5 c. scarlet.. .. .. 4·50 6·00
 a. Imperf.. .. .. 4·50 5·50
 b. Printed on both sides .. 26·00

This stamp was usually sold affixed to envelopes, particularly those with the embossed 1 a. King George VI stamp, which it covered. Unused specimens off cover are rarely met with and blocks are very rare.

15. Farmer.

1943. *P* 11½. *Typo. No gum.*
J73 **15** 1 c. orange (22 Mar.) .. 30 50
 a. Brown-orange 40 70
J74 „ 2 c. yellow-grn. (24 Mar.) 30 60
 a. Blue-green .. .. 1·25
J75 „ 3 c. light blue (25 Mar.) 30
 a. On laid paper .. .. 4·00 5·00
J76 „ 5 c. carmine (small "c") (17 Mar.) .. .. 2·00 2·50
J77 „ 5 c. carmine (large "C") 30 40
 a. Imperf. (pair).. ..
 b. "G" for "C".. ..
J78 „ 10 c. grey-brown (25 Mar.) 50 75
 a. Imperf. (pair) .. .. 15·00
J79 „ 15 c. magenta (26 Mar.) .. 12 45
 a. On laid paper .. .. 3·50 4·50
 b. Reversed "C" in value 25·00 35·00
J80 „ 20 c. grey-lilac (29 Mar.).. 12 45
J81 „ 30 c. dp. blue-grn. (29 Mar.) 12 50

The 1 c., 2 c. and 3 c. have large "C" in value as illustrated. The 10 c. and higher values have small "c". Owing to hurried printing and the method of make-up (the different values being plugged in individually to the same basic plate) numerous varieties may be found in the values, e.g. missing stops and different types of figure or "c".

There are marked varieties of shade in this issue.

Imperf. stamps come from a proof sheet.

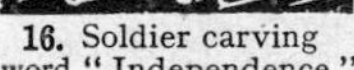

16. Soldier carving word "Independence". **17.** Rejoicing Peasant.

18. Boy with National Flag.

(Des. Maung Ba Thit (**16**), Naung Ohn Maung (**17**), and Maung Soi Yi (**18**). Typo. State Press, Rangoon.)

1943 (1 Aug.). *Independence Day.* (a) *Perf.* 11.
J82 **16** 1 c. orange .. .. 85 1·75
J83 **17** 3 c. light blue .. .. 1·75 2·25
J84 **18** 5 c. carmine .. .. 1·75 2·25

(*b*) *Rouletted.*

No.	Type	Description	Unused	Used
J82*a*	16	1 c. orange	45	70
		b. Perf. × roul.		
		c. Imperf. (pair)	25·00	32·00
J83*a*	17	3 c. light blue	45	70
		b. Perf. × roul.		
		c. Imperf. (pair)	25·00	32·00
J84*a*	18	5 c. carmine	45	70
		aa. Horiz. roulette omitted (vert. pair)		
		b. Perf. × roul.		
		c. Imperf. (pair)	25·00	32·00

The stamps perf. × rouletted may have one, two, or three sides perforated. They are scarce.

The rouletted stamps often appear to be roughly perforated owing to failure to make clean cuts. These apparent perforations are very small and quite unlike the large, clean holes of the stamps perforated 11.

A few imperforate sets, mounted on a special card folder and cancelled with the commemorative postmark were presented to officials. These are rare.

19. Burmese Woman. **20.** Elephant carrying Log.

21. Watch Tower, Mandalay.

(Typo. G. Kolff & Co., Batavia.)

1943 (1 Oct.). *P* 12½.

No.	Type	Description	Unused	Used
J85	19	1 c. red-orange	1·25	1·40
J86	,,	2 c. yellow-green ..	8	30
J87	,,	3 c. deep violet	10	12
		a. Bright violet	15	20
J88	20	5 c. carmine	8	12
J89	,,	10 c. blue	12	12
J90	,,	15 c. red-orange	8	12
J91	,,	20 c. yellow-green ..	8	30
J92	,,	30 c. olive-brown	8	30
J93	21	1 r. red-orange	10	35
J94	,,	2 r. bright violet ..	12	40

22. Bullock Cart. **23.** Shan Woman.

(Typo. G. Kolff & Co., Batavia.)

1943. *Issue for Shan States.* *P* 12½.

No.	Type	Description	Unused
J 95	22	1 c. olive-brown ..	6·00
J 96	,,	2 c. yellow-green ..	6·00
J 97	,,	3 c. bright violet ..	9·00
J 98	,,	5 c. ultramarine ..	80
J 99	23	10 c. blue	6·00
J100	,,	20 c. carmine ..	6·00
J101	,,	30 c. olive-brown ..	6·00

The Shan States were placed under the administration of the Burmese Government on 24 December, 1943, and these stamps were later overprinted as T **24** for use throughout Burma.

ဗမာနိုင်ငံတော်

၂၀ ဆင့်။

(**24.** " Burma State " and value.)

1944 (1 Nov.). *Optd. as T* **24** (*the lower characters differ for each value*).

No.	Type	Description	Unused	Used
J102	22	1 c. olive-brown ..	60	70
J103	,,	2 c. yellow-green ..	8	25
		a. Opt. inverted	60·00	
J104	,,	3 c. bright violet ..	45	65
J105	,,	5 c. ultramarine ..	30	40
J106	23	10 c. blue	45	70
J107	,,	20 c. carmine ..	12	40
J108	,,	30 c. olive-brown ..	12	40

The British 14th Army recaptured Mandalay on 20 March 1945 and Rangoon on 6 May.

BUSHIRE.

(BRITISH OCCUPATION.)

BUSHIRE
Under British
Occupation
(1)

Stamps of Iran (Persia) overprinted with T **1.**

1915 (15 Aug.). *Nos.* 361, *etc.* (*Ahmed Mirza*).

No.	Description	Unused	Used
1	1 ch. orange and green ..	5·00	6·00
	a. No stop	13·00	17·00
2	2 ch. sepia and carmine ..	5·00	6·00
	a. No stop	13·00	17·00
3	3 ch. green and grey	5·00	6·00
	a. No stop	13·00	17·00
4	5 ch. carmine and brown ..	55·00	65·00
5	6 ch. brown-lake and green ..	5·00	6·00
	a. No stop	13·00	17·00
6	9 ch. indigo-lilac and brown	7·00	9·00
	a. No stop	22·00	26·00
	b. Opt. double ..		
7	10 ch. brown and carmine ..	7·00	9·00
	a. No stop	22·00	29·00
8	12 ch. blue and green ..	10·00	12·00
	a. No stop	29·00	32·00
9	24 ch. green and purple ..	9·00	11·00
	a. No stop	29·00	32·00
10	1 kr. carmine and blue ..	9·00	9·00
	a. Double overprint	£1100	
	b. No stop	29·00	29·00
11	2 kr. claret and green ..	22·00	24·00
	a. No stop	55·00	
12	3 kr. black and lilac	55·00	60·00
	a. No stop	£100	
13	5 kr. blue and red	20·00	24·00
	a. No stop	60·00	
14	10 kr. rose and bistre-brown	19·00	20·00
	a. No stop	60·00	

1915 (Sept.). *Nos.* 426, *etc.* (*Coronation of Shah Ahmed*).

No.	Description	Unused
15	1 ch. deep blue and carmine ..	£110
16	2 ch. carmine and deep blue ..	£1100
17	3 ch. deep green	£130
18	5 ch. vermilion	£1000
19	6 ch. carmine and green ..	£950
20	9 ch. deep violet and brown ..	£190
21	10 ch. brown and deep green ..	£325
22	12 ch. ultramarine	£350
23	24 ch. sepia and brown ..	£130
24	1 kr. black, brown and silver	£120
25	2 kr. carmine, slate and silver	£110
26	3 kr. sepia, dull lilac, and silver	£130
27	5 kr. slate, sepia and silver ..	£130
	a. Overprint inverted	
28	1 t. black, violet and gold ..	£120
29	3 t. red, crimson and gold ..	£400

1915. *No.* 414 (" 1 CH 1914 " *provisional*).

No.	Description	Unused
30	1 ch. on 5 ch. carm. & brown	£1000

Bushire, a seaport town of Persia, was occupied by the British on 8th August, 1915. The Persian postal authorities resumed control on 16th October, 1915.

CAMEROONS.

BRITISH OCCUPATION.

(A)

(B)

The above ((A) and (B)) are the types of German Colonial stamps that have been surcharged.

C. E. F. 1d.	C. E. F. 1s.
(1)	(2)

1915. *German Colonial issues of Cameroons, Type* A *surch. as T* **1** *and Type* B *as T* **2**, *in black or blue.*

No.	Type	Description	Unused	Used
1	A	½d. on 3 pf. (No. 7) (B.) ..	1·25	1·25
2	,,	½d. on 5 pf. (No. 21) (B.) ..	50	75
		a. Surch. double	70·00	35·00
		b. Surch. in black	65	80
3	,,	1d. on 10 pf. (No. 22) (B.)	50	65
		a. Thin serif and foot to "1"	5·50	6·50
		b. Surch. double	19·00	
		c. Surch. double with thin serif and foot to "1"		
		d. "1d." double, but "C.E.F." not double	£300	
		e. Surch. in black	2·00	2·75
		f. Surch. in black with thin serif and foot to "1" ..	14·00	
		g. "C.E.F." omitted	£350	
4	,,	2d. on 20 pf. (No. 23) ..	50	85
5	,,	2½d. on 25 pf. (No. 11) ..	90	1·25
		a. Surch. double	£450	
6	"	3d. on 30 pf. (No. 12) ..	90	1·40
7	,,	4d. on 40 pf. (No. 13) ..	90	1·40
		a. Shorter "4"	£110	
8	,,	6d. on 50 pf. (No. 14) ..	90	1·25
9	,,	8d. on 80 pf. (No. 15) ..	90	1·25
10	B	1s. on 1 m. (No. 16) ..	18·00	22·00
		a. "s" inverted	£100	£110
11	,,	2s. on 2 m. (No. 17) ..	18·00	22·00
		a. "s" inverted	£100	£110
12	,,	3s. on 3 m. (No. 18) ..	18·00	22·00
		a. "s" inverted	70·00	80·00
		b. Surch. double	£600	
		c. Surch. double and "s" inverted		
13	,,	5s. on 5 m. (No. 25a) ..	38·00	45·00
		a. "s" inverted	£130	£150
1/13		.. .. *Set of* 13	90·00	£110

The letters "C. E. F." signify "Cameroons Expeditionary Force." British Cameroons was later incorporated in Nigeria and used Nigerian stamps.

For stamps optd. "CAMEROONS U.K.T.T.", see under SOUTHERN CAMEROONS.

CANADA.

CANADIAN PROVINCES. The following Provinces issued their own stamps before joining the Confederation of Canada, whilst the former Dominion of Newfoundland became part of Canada in 1949. Their issues are listed in alphabetical order in this Catalogue:

BRITISH COLUMBIA and VANCOUVER IS.
NEW BRUNSWICK
NEWFOUNDLAND
NOVA SCOTIA
PRINCE EDWARD ISLAND

POSTMASTER'S PROVISIONAL.

NEW CARLISLE, GASPÉ.

ENVELOPE

(1)

1851 (7 April).
1 **1** 3d. black .. .. .. † £16000

Only one example is known, with the impression cancelled by the signature of the postmaster, R. W. Kelly.

COLONY OF CANADA.

1. Beaver.

(Designed by Sir Sandford Fleming.)

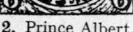

2. Prince Albert.

3

Major re-entry: Line through "EE PEN".

(T **1/6**. Eng. and recess. Rawdon, Wright, Hatch and Edson, New York.)

1851. *Imperf. Laid paper.*
1 **1** 3d. red (23 April) £3750 £225
1*a* 3d. orange-vermilion .. £3750 £225
b. Major re-entry .. .. — £650
2 **2** 6d. slate-violet (15 May) .. £3000 £550
3 ,, 6d. brown-purple £3250 £700
a. Bisected (3d.) on cover .. — £8000
4 **3** 12d. black (14 June) .. £25000 £23000

There are several re-entries on the plate of the 3d. in addition to the major re-entry listed. All re-entries occur in this stamp on all papers.

1852–57. *Imperf.*

A. *Thin wove paper.*
6 **1** 3d. red .. .. .. £675 85·00
7 a. Bisected, on cover .. £12000
,, 3d. deep red .. .. £675 85·00
7*a* ,, 3d. scarlet-vermilion .. £675 85·00
b. Major re-entry .. .. — £375
9*a* **3** 12d. black .. .. .. —£23000

B. *Medium hard wove paper.*
10 **1** 3d. red .. .. .. £350 65·00
11 ,, 3d. deep red .. .. £350 65·00
11*a* ,, 3d. brown-red .. .. £350 65·00
b. Major re-entry .. .. — £225
c. Bisected (1½d.), on cover —
12 **2** 6d. slate-violet £3500 £425
a. Bisected (3d.), on cover .. — £5500
13 ,, 6d. greenish grey £3500 £400
14 ,, 6d. brownish grey .. £3500 £450
14*a* **3** 12d. black .. .. .. —£23000

C. *Thick hard wove paper.*
15 **1** 3d. red £500 £240
a. Bisected, on cover .. — £6500
16 **2** 6d. grey-lilac £5500 £900

D. *Very thick soft wove paper.*
17 **2** 6d. purple (reddish) .. £4000 £1300
a. Bisected (3d.), on cover .. — £8000

We no longer list the 6d. on thin wove paper as there is no record of a printing on this paper. The 12d. exists and comes from a proof sheet. The laid lines on thin paper are often difficult to see, having been pressed out, and these are sometimes mistaken for wove paper.

1857. E. *Thin soft ribbed paper.*
18 **1** 3d. red £1300 £400

F. *Thin brittle wove paper.*
19 **1** 3d. red £1500 £550

4. Jacques Cartier.

1855 (Jan.). *Imperf.*

A. *Thin wove paper.*
20 **4** 10d. bright blue £3500 £475
20*a* ,, 10d. dull blue £3500 £475
aa. Major re-entry* .. .. — £850

B. *Medium wove paper, semi-transparent.*
20*b* **4** 10d. bright blue £4000 £500
20*c* ,, 10d. Prussian blue £4000 £500
d. Major re-entry* .. .. — £850

1857. C. *Stout hard wove paper.*
21 **4** 10d. blue £3500 £650
a. Major re-entry* .. .. — £850

These stamps may be divided into "wide" and "narrow," due to the shrinkage of the paper, which was wetted before printing, and which contracted unevenly when drying. The width varies from 17 mm. to 18 mm., the narrower being the commoner.

* The 10d. Major Re-entry listed shows strong doubling of top frame line and left-hand "8d. stg.", and line through lower parts of "ANAD" and "ENCE". There are other, lesser re-entries.

5

6

1857 (2 June). *Imperf.*
22 **5** 7½d. pale yellow-green .. £3000 £750
22*a* ,, 7½d. deep yellow-green .. £3500 £700

There are several re-entries in these stamps.

The same remarks apply to this stamp as to the 10d. blue. The width varies less, being generally 18 to 8½ mm.

1857 (1 Aug.). *Imperf.*

A. *Stout hard wove paper.*
23 **6** ½d. deep rose £250 £110

B. *Thin soft ribbed paper.*
24 **6** ½d. deep rose (*horiz.*) .. £1400 £650
24*a* ,, ½d. deep rose (*vert.*) .. £1500 £800

1858–59. *P* 11¾. A. *Stout wove paper.*
25 **6** ½d. deep rose (12.58) .. £400 £150
a. *Lilac-rose* £500 £200
26 **1** 3d. red (1.59) £550 £150
27 **2** 6d. brownish grey (1.59) £2000 £850
a. *Slate-violet* £2500 £750

B. *Thin ribbed paper.*
27*b* **6** ½d. deep rose-red .. .. — £900
28 **1** 3d. red .. .. .. — £400

C. *Thick hard paper.*
28*a* **1** 3d. red .. .. .. — £425

The 3d. is known perf. 14, and also *percé en scie* 13, both being unofficial, but used at the period of issue.

7

8. Beaver.

9. Prince Albert.

10

11. Jacques Cartier.

(Recess. American Bank Note Co.)

(On 1st May, 1858, Messrs. Rawdon, Wright Hatch, and Edson altered the name of their firm to "The American Bank Note Co.," and the "imprint" on sheets of the following stamps has the new title of the firm with "New York" added.)

1859 (1 July). *P* 12.
29 **7** 1 c. pale rose (to rose-red) 30·00 6·50
30 ,, 1 c. dp. rose (to carm.-rose) 38·00 8·00
a. Imperf. (pair) £1000
b. Imperf. × perf. .. ..
31 **8** 5 c. pale red .. .. 45·00 6·00
32 ,, 5 c. deep red .. .. 45·00 6·00
a. Re-entry* .. .. — £200
b. Imperf. (pair) £1300
c. Bisected (2½ c.), on cover — £1000
33 **9** 10 c. black-brown £1100 £400
a. Bisected (5 c.), on cover .. — £1700
33*b* ,, 10 c. deep red-purple .. £850 £400
ba. Bisected (5 c.), on cover.. — £1400
34 ,, 10 c. purple (*shades*) .. £140 16·00
a. Bisected (5 c.), on cover .. — £1400
35 ,, 10 c. brownish purple .. £140 16·00
36 ,, 10 c. brown (to pale) .. £140 16·00
a. Bisected (5 c.), on cover — £2000
37 ,, 10 c. dull violet .. .. £110 16·00
38 ,, 10 c. bright red-purple .. £110 16·00
a. Imperf. (pair) £1500

29 **10** 12½ c. deep yellow-green .. 75·00 14·00
30 „ 12½ c. pale yellow-green .. 75·00 14·00
31 „ 12½ c. blue-green .. .. 75·00 14·00
a. Imperf. (pair) £1100
b. Imperf. between (vert. pr.)
32 **11** 17 c. deep blue .. .. £130 20·00
a. Imperf. (pair) £1200
33 „ 17 c. slate-blue .. .. £180 30·00
33*a* „ 17 c. indigo.. .. .. £140 20·00
b. Imperf. (pair) £1200

* The price of No. 32*a* is for the very marked re-entry showing oval frame line doubled above "CANADA". Slighter re-entries are worth from £10 upwards in used condition.

As there were numerous P.O. Dept. orders for the 10 c., 12½ c. and 17 c. and some of these were executed by more than one separate printing, with no special care to ensure uniformity of colour, there is a wide range of shade, especially in the 10 c., and some shades recur at intervals after periods during which other shades predominated. The colour-names given in the above list therefore represent groups only.

It has been proved by leading Canadian specialists that the perforations may be an aid to the approximate dating of a particular stamp, the gauge used measuring 11¾×11¾ from mid-July, 1859, to late 1862, 12×11¾ from early 1863 to mid-1865 and 12×12 from April, 1865 to 1868. Exceptionally in the 5 c. value many sheets were perforated 12×12 between May and October, 1862, whilst the last printings of the 12½ c. and 17 c. perf. 11¾×11¾ were in July 1863, the perf. 12×11¾ starting towards the end of 1863.

12

(Recess. American Bank Note Co.)

1864 (1 Aug.). *P* 12.
44 **12** 2 c. rose-red.. .. .. 95·00 50·00
45 „ 2 c. bright rose .. .. 95·00 50·00
a. Imperf. (pair) £750

DOMINION OF CANADA.

13. *Large types.* 14.

On 1 July, 1867, Canada, Nova Scotia, and New Brunswick were united, the combined territory being termed "The Dominion of Canada". Under the Act of Union provision was made for the admission of Newfoundland, Prince Edward Island, British Columbia, Rupert's Land, and the North-Western Territory.

(Recess. British American Bank Note Co., at Ottawa or Montreal.)

T **13** *and* **14** (*various frames*).

1868 (March). *Ottawa printings. Thin rather transparent crisp paper. P* 12.
46 **13** ½ c. black.. .. .. 45·00 32·00
47 **14** 1 c. red-brown .. .. £140 28·00
48 „ 2 c. grass-green .. .. £180 22·00
49 „ 3 c. red-brown .. .. £240 22·00
50 „ 6 c. blackish brown .. £475 £140
51 „ 12½ c. bright blue £400 £120
52 „ 15 c. deep reddish purple.. £525 £120

In these first printings the impression is generally blurred and the lines of the back-ground are less clearly defined than in later printings.

1868–71. *Ottawa printings. Medium to stout wove paper. P* 12.
53 **13** ½ c. black.. .. .. 14·00 14·00
54 „ ½ c. grey-black .. .. 14·00 14·00
a. Imperf. between (pair) ..
b. Watermarked .. .. — £2000
55 **14** 1 c. red-brown .. .. 85·00 13·00
a. Laid paper £2000 £525
b. Watermarked (1868) .. £750 £130
56 „ 2 c. deep green .. .. £120 9·00
57 „ 2 c. pale emer. grn. (1871) £120 9·00
aa. Bisected (1 c. with 2 c. to make 3 c. rate) (on cover) — £2000
a. Laid paper .. .. — £23000
57*b* „ 2 c. bluish green .. .. 80·00 9·00
c. Watermarked (1868) .. £500 £100
58 „ 3 c. brown-red .. .. £160 5·00
a. Laid paper .. .. £1700 70·00
b. Watermarked (1868) .. £750 80·00
59 „ 6 c. blkish. brn. (to choc.) £150 9·00
a. Watermarked (1868) .. £750 £200
60 „ 6 c. yellow-brown (1870) £150 9·00
a. Bisected (3 c.), on cover.. † £950
61 „ 12½ c. bright blue .. .. 85·00 9·00
a. Imperf. horiz. (vert. pr.) † —
b. Watermarked (1868) .. £1100 £110
62 „ 12½ c. pale dull blue (milky) 80·00 9·00
63 „ 15 c. deep reddish purple.. £160 18·00
63*a* „ 15 c. pale reddish purple .. £140 18·00
b. Watermarked (1868) .. † £700
64 „ 15 c. dull violet-grey .. £100 18·00
a. Watermarked (1868) .. — £400
65 „ 15 c. dull grey-purple .. £110 18·00

For 1 c. orange see Nos. 74/6.

1879–88. *Montreal printings. Medium to stout wove paper. P* 12.
66 **14** 15 c. clear deep violet .. £950 £250
67 „ 15 c. deep slate .. .. 80·00 11·00
68 „ 15 c. slaty blue .. .. 80·00 11·00

The watermark on the stout paper stamps consists of the words "E & G BOTHWELL CLUTHA MILLS," in large double-lined capitals. Portions of one or two letters only may be found on these stamps, which occur in the early printings of 1868.

The papers may, in most cases, be easily divided if the stamps are laid face downwards and carefully compared. The thin hard paper is more or less transparent and shows the design through the stamp; the thicker paper is softer to the feel and more opaque.

The paper of this issue may be still further subdivided in several values into sets on—(a) *Medium to stout wove.* (b) *Thin, soft very white:* and (c) *Thinner and poorer quality, sometimes greyish or yellowish* (*from* 1878 *to end of issue*).

Of the 2 c. laid paper No. 57*a* two examples only are known.

20

1875–78. *Montreal printings. Medium to stout wove paper. P* 11½×12 *or* 11¾×12.
69 **13** ½ c. black .. .. .. 18·00 18·00
70 **20** 5 c. olive-grn. (1 Oct., '75) £350 35·00
a. Perf. 12 .. .. — £2000
71 **14** 15 c. dull grey-purple .. £300 85·00
72 „ 15 c. lilac-grey (Mar., '77).. £375 85·00
a. Script Wmk.* £5000 £600
73 „ 15 c. slate £525 £200

*The watermark on No. 72*a* is part of the words "Alexr. Pirie & Sons" in script lettering, a very small quantity of paper thus watermarked having been used for printing this stamp.

One used copy of the 12½ c. has been reported. See also No. 113/4.

1869. *Ottawa printings. Colour changed. Stout wove paper. P* 12.
74 **14** 1 c. dp. orange (Jan. '69) £200 28·00
75 „ 1 c. orge.-yell. (May (?), '69) £200 22·00
76 „ 1 c. pale orange-yellow .. £200 20·00
a. Imperf. .. .. ..

21 *Small types.* 27

(Nos. 77–114 and 117–120. Recess. British American Bank Note Co., at Montreal or Ottawa.)

1870–88. *T* **21** (*various frames*). *P* 12 (*or slightly under*).

Montreal printings.

Papers. (*a*) 1870–80. *Medium to stout wove.*
(*b*) 1870–72. *Thin, soft, very white.*
(*c*) 1878–97. *Thinner and poorer quality.*

77 **21** 1 c. bright orange (*a, b*) (1870–73) .. .. 50·00 5·00
78 „ 1 c. orange-yellow (*a*) (1876–79) .. .. 12·00 60
79 „ 1 c. pale dull yellow (*a*) (1877–79) .. .. 10·00 20
80 „ 1 c. bright yellow (*a, c*) (1878–97) .. .. 5·50 5
a. Imperf. (pair) (*c*) £130
b. Bisected (½ c.) (on "Railway News") .. .. † £950
c. Printed both sides .. £400
81 „ 2 c. deep green (*a, b*) (1872–73 and 1876–78) .. 24·00 20
82 „ 2 c. grass-grn. (*c*) (1878–88) 9·00 5
a. Imperf. (pair) (1891-93?) .. £130
b. Bisected (1 c.) on cover .. † £425
83 „ 3 c. Indian red (*a*) (1.70) £275 25·00
a. Perf. 12½ .. .. — £425
83*b* „ 3 c. pale rose-red (*a*) (9.70) 80·00 3·75
84 „ 3 c. deep rose-red (*a, b*) (1870–73) .. .. 85·00 4·50
84*a* „ 3 c. deep rose-red (*thick soft paper*) (Jan., '71) .. — 85·00
85 „ 3 c. dull red (*a*) (1876–88) 14·00 35
86 „ 3 c. orange-red (*a, c*) (1876–88) (*shades*) .. 9·00 20
87 „ 5 c. olive-grey (*a, c*) (February, 1876–88) .. 17·00 60
88 „ 6 c. yellowish brown (*a, b, c*) (1872–73 & 1876–90).. 19·00 2·75
a. Bisected (3 c.), on cover .. † £850
89 „ 10 c. pale lilac-magenta (*a*) (1876–?) .. .. 90·00 14·00
90 „ 10 c. deep lilac-magenta (*a, c*) (March 1876–88) .. 85·00 14·00

One used copy of the 10 c. perf. 12½ has been reported.

1873–77. *P* 11½×12. *Medium to stout wove paper.*
90*a* **21** 1 c. bright orange .. 70·00 11·00
91 „ 1 c. orge.-yellow (1873–79) 65·00 6·00
92 „ 1 c. p. dull yell. (1877–79) 55·00 8·00
93 „ 2 c. deep green (1873–78) 60·00 6·00
94 „ 3 c. dull red (1875–79) .. 55·00 5·50
95 „ 3 c. orange-red (1873–79) 55·00 4·25
96 „ 5 c. olive-grey (1876–79) £110 5·50
97 „ 6 c. yellowish brn. (1876–79) .. .. .. £110 5·50
98 „ 10 c. very pale lilac-magenta (1874–79) .. .. £250 70·00
99 „ 10 c. deep lilac-magenta (1876–79) .. .. £140 35·00

1882–97. *P 12. Thinnish paper often toned.*

101 **27** ½ c. black (July, 1882–97) 1·25 1·25
102 „ ½ c. grey-black .. .. 1·25 1·25
a. Imperf. (pair) (1891–93?) £150
b. Imperf. between (pair) .. £250

Ottawa printings.

1888–97. As *T* **14** *and* **21** (various frames). *P* 12.
Thinnish paper of poor quality, often toned grey or yellowish.

103 **21** 2 c. dull sea-green (Jan., 1888) .. .. .. 10·00 12
104 „ 2 c. blue-green (July, 1889–91) .. .. 10·00 15
105 „ 3 c. rose-carmine (Oct., 1888–April, '89) .. 90·00 4·50
106 „ 3 c. bright vermilion (Apr., 1889–97) .. .. 4·00 5
a. Imperf. (pair) (1891–93?) £130
107 „ 5 c. brownish grey (May, '88) .. .. .. 10·00 5
a. Imperf (pair) 1891–93) £130
108 „ 6 c. deep chestnut (Oct., '90) .. .. 10·00 2·50
a. " 5 c." re-entry* ..
109 „ 6 c. pale chestnut .. 10·00 2·25
a. Imperf. (pair) (1891–93?) £200
110 „ 10 c. lilac-pink (Mar., '88) 35·00 8·00
110*a* „ 10 c. salmon-pink .. 80·00 42·00
111 „ 10 c. carmine-pink (1891?) 32·00 4·25
a. Imperf. (pair) (1891–93?) £130
112 „ 10 c. brownish red (1894?) 32·00 3·00
a. Imperf. (pair) £100
113 **14** 15 c. slate-purple (*shades*) (July, '88) .. .. 25·00 9·00
114 „ 15 c. slate-violet (*shades*) (May, '90) .. .. 25·00 9·00
a. Imperf. (brn.-pur.) (pair) £130

* No. 108a shows traces of the 5 c. value 2½ mm. lower than the 6 c. design.

The 1 c. showed no change in the Ottawa printings, so is not included. The 2 c. reverted to its previous grass-green shade in 1891. The 15 c. stamps are generally found with yellowish streaky gum; about 1895 remainders of this value were used concurrently with the 1888 and 1890 shades. They vary from grey and slate to a nearly true blue.

28

29

(Recess. British American Bank Note Co.)

1893 (17 Feb.). *P* 12.

115 **28** 20 c. vermilion .. .. 60·00 15·00
a. Imperf. (pair) £600
116 „ 50 c. blue .. .. .. 80·00 10·00
a. Imperf. (Prussian blue) (pair) £600

1893 (1 Aug.). *P* 12.

117 **29** 8 c. pale bluish grey .. 20·00 1·40
a. Imperf. (pair) £180
118 „ 8 c. bluish slate .. .. 20·00 1·40
119 „ 8 c. slate-purple .. .. 20·00 1·40
120 „ 8 c. blackish purple .. 20·00 1·40

PRINTERS. The following stamps to No. 287 were recess-printed by the American Bank Note Co., Ottawa, which in 1923 became the Canadian Bank Note Co.

30

(Des. L. Pereira and F. Brownell.)

1897 (19 June). *Jubilee issue. P* 12.

121 **30** ½ c. black .. .. .. 30·00 32·00
122 „ 1 c. orange .. .. 2·25 1·50
123 „ 1 c. orange-yellow .. 2·25 1·50
a. Bisected (½ c.) on cover
124 „ 2 c. green .. .. .. 4·00 3·00
125 „ 2 c. deep green .. .. 4·00 3·00
126 „ 3 c. carmine .. .. 2·75 70
127 „ 5 c. slate-blue .. .. 15·00 9·00
128 „ 5 c. deep blue .. .. 15·00 9·00
129 „ 6 c. brown .. .. 60·00 55·00
130 „ 8 c. slate-violet .. .. 12·00 12·00
131 „ 10 c. purple .. .. 20·00 20·00
132 „ 15 c. slate .. .. .. 45·00 45·00
133 „ 20 c. vermilion .. .. 50·00 50·00
134 „ 50 c. pale ultramarine .. 55·00 55·00
135 „ 50 c. bright ultramarine .. 60·00 60·00
136 „ $1 lake £250 £180
137 „ $2 deep violet £425 £200
138 „ $3 bistre £575 £325
139 „ $4 violet £550 £300
140 „ $5 olive-green £550 £300
121/140 .. .. *Set of* 16 £2500 £1400
133/40 Optd. " Specimen " *Set of* 7 £700

No. 123a was used on issues of the *Railway News* of 5, 6 and 8 November 1897 and must be on large part of original newspaper with New Glasgow postmark.

31

32

(From photograph by W. & D. Downey, London.)

1897–98. *P* 12.

141 **31** ½ c. grey-blk. (9 Nov. 1897) 3·00 3·00
142 „ ½ c. black .. .. 3·00 3·00
a. Imperf. (pair) .. £160
143 „ 1 c. blue-grn. (Dec., 1897) 4·00 12
a. Imperf. (pair) £160
144 „ 2 c. violet (Dec., 1897) .. 6·00 12
a. Imperf. (pair) £160
145 „ 3 c. carmine (Jan., 1898) 6·00 10
a. Imperf. (pair) £375
146 „ 5 c. dp. blue/*bluish* (Dec., 1897) .. .. 15·00 2·25
a. Imperf. (pair) £160
147 „ 6 c. brown (Dec., 1897) .. 15·00 11·00
a. Imperf. (pair) £350
148 „ 8 c. orange (Dec., 1897) .. 25·00 5·50
a. Imperf. (pair) £160
149 „ 10 c. brownish purple (Jan., 1898) .. .. 55·00 35·00
a. Imperf. (pair) £175
141/149 .. .. *Set of* 8 £120 50·00

Two types of the 2 c.

Die Ia. Frame consists of four fine lines.
Die Ib. Frame has one thick line between two fine lines.

The die was retouched in 1900 for Plates 11 and 12 producing weak vertical frame lines and then retouched again in 1902 for Plates 15 to 20 resulting in much thicker frame lines. No. 155*b* covers both states of the retouching.

IMPERF. SIDES. Stamps with one side, or two adjacent sides imperf. come from booklet panes.

1898–1902. *P* 12.

150 **32** ½ c. black (Sept., 1898) .. 55 55
a. Imperf. (pair) £140
151 „ 1 c. blue-grn. (June, 1898) 5·00 8
152 „ 1 c. dp. grn./*toned paper* .. 5·00 8
a. Imperf. (pair) £350
153 „ 2 c. purple (Die Ia) (Sept., 1898) .. .. .. 3·75 12
154 „ 2 c. violet (Die Ia) .. 3·75 8
155 „ 2 c. rose-carmine (Die Ia) (20.8.99) .. .. 5·00 8
a. Imperf. (pair) £140
155*b* „ 2 c. rose-carmine (Die Ib) (1900) .. .. 5·00 8
c. Booklet pane of 6 (11.6.00) £400
156 „ 3 c. rose-carm. (June, 1898) .. .. 10·00 8
157 **32** 5 c. slate-blue/*bluish* .. 25·00 1:
a. Imperf. (pair) £350
158 „ 5 c. Prussian blue/*bluish* 25·00 2:
159 „ 6 c. brown (Sept., 1898) .. 30·00 14·0
a. Imperf. (pair) £350
160 „ 7 c. greenish yellow (23.12.02) .. .. 14·00 5·0
161 „ 8 c. orange-yellow (Oct., 1898) (Opt. S. £35) .. 32·00 7·0
162 „ 8 c. brownish orange .. 32·00 7·0
a. Imperf. (pair) £350
163 „ 10 c. pale brownish purple (Nov., 1898) .. 60·00 6·0
164 „ 10 c. deep brownish purple 60·00 6·0
a. Imperf. (pair) £350
165 „ 20 c. olive green (29.12.00) £110 30·0
150/165 .. .. *Set of* 11 £260 50·0

The 7 c. and 20 c. also exist imperf. but unlik the values listed in this condition, they have n gum. (*Price*, 7 c. £100, 20 c. £500 *pair, un.*)

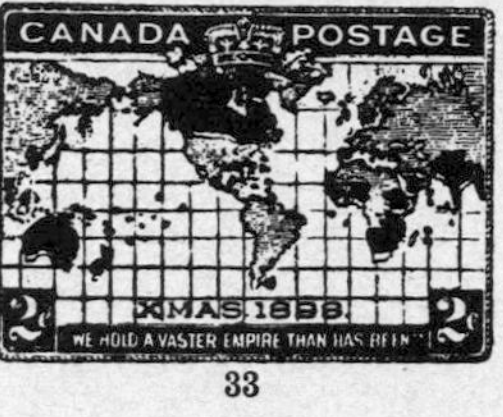

33

(Des. Postmaster-General Mulock; frame, recess colours, typo.)

1898 (7 Dec.). *Imperial Penny Postage. Desig in black. British possessions in red. Oceans i colours given. P* 12.

166 **33** 2 c. lavender .. .. 7·00 2·0
167 „ 2 c. greenish blue .. .. 7·00 2·0
168 „ 2 c. blue .. .. .. 7·00 2·0
a. Imperf. (pair) £250

1899 (5 Jan.). *Provisionals used at Port Hood No.* 156 *divided vertically and handstamped*

169 **32** " 1 " in blue, on ⅓ of 3 c. .. — £160
170 „ " 2 " in violet, on ⅔ of 3 c. — £150

2 CENTS

(**34**)

35. King Edward VII.

1899. *Surch. with T* **34,** *by Public Printing Office.*

171 **31** 2 c. on 3 c. carm. (8 Aug.) 2·25 1·5
a. Surch. inverted £140
172 **32** 2 c. on 3 c. rose-carmine (28 July) .. .. 2·25 1·5
a. Surch. inverted £140

(Des. King George V when Prince of Wales and J. A. Tilleard.)

1903 (1 July)–**12**. *P* 12.

173 **35** 1 c. pale green .. .. 4·00 8
174 „ 1 c. deep green .. .. 4·00 8
175 „ 1 c. green .. .. .. 4·00 8
176 „ 2 c. rose-carmine .. .. 4·50 8
a. Booklet pane of 6 .. £425
177 „ 2 c. pale rose-carmine .. 4·50 8
a. Imperf. (pair) (7.09) .. 8·00 8·00
178 „ 5 c. blue/*bluish* .. .. 20·00 90
179 „ 5 c. indigo/*bluish* .. .. 20·00 90
180 „ 7 c. yellow-olive .. .. 18·00 1·10
181 „ 7 c. greenish bistre (6.12) 25·00 1·10
182 „ 10 c. brown-lilac .. .. 50·00 2·50
183 „ 10 c. pale dull purple .. 50·00 2·50
184 „ 10 c. dull purple .. .. 50·00 2·50
185 „ 20 c. pale ol.-grn. (27.9.04) £110 10·00
186 „ 20 c. deep olive-grn. (S.£40) £110 12·00
187 „ 50 c. deep violet (19.11.08) £180 30·00
173/187 .. .. *Set of* 7 £350 40·00

The 1c., 5 c., 7 c. and 10 c. exist imperforate but are believed to be proofs.

36. King George V and Queen Mary when Prince and Princess of Wales.

37. Jacques Cartier and Samuel Champlain.

38. King Edward VII and Queen Alexandra.

39. Champlain's House in Quebec.

40. Generals Montcalm and Wolfe.

41. Quebec in 1700.

42. Champlain's Departure for the West.

43. Cartier's Arrival before Quebec.

(Des. Machado.)

1908 (16 July). *Quebec Tercentenary. P* 12.

No.	Type	Description	Unused	Used
188	**36**	½ c. sepia	2·25	2·25
		a. Imperf. (pair)	£300	
189	**37**	1 c. blue-green	3·00	2·50
		a. Imperf. (pair)	£300	
190	**38**	2 c. carmine	6·00	55
		a. Imperf. (pair)	£300	
191	**39**	5 c. indigo	18·00	12·00
		a. Imperf. (pair)	£300	
192	**40**	7 c. olive-green	25·00	14·00
		a. Imperf. (pair)	£300	
193	**41**	10 c. violet..	40·00	38·00
		a. Imperf. (pair)	£300	
194	**42**	15 c. brown-orange ..	55·00	50·00
		a. Imperf. (pair)	£300	
195	**43**	20 c. dull brown	70·00	60·00
		a. Imperf. (pair)	£300	
188/195		.. .. *Set of* 8	£200	£150

Some values exist on both *toned* and *white* papers.

44

1912–22. *P* 12.

No.	Type	Description	Unused	Used
196	**44**	1 c. yellow-green	2·00	5
		a. With fine horizontal lines across stamp	13·00	10·00
197	,,	1 c. bluish green ..	2·00	5
		a. Booklet pane of 6 (5.13)	15·00	
198	,,	1 c. deep bluish green ..	2·00	5
199	,,	1 c. deep yellow-green ..	2·00	5
		a. Booklet pane of 6 ..	15·00	
200	,,	2 c. rose-red	2·00	5
201	,,	2 c. deep rose-red ..	2·25	5
		a. Booklet pane of 6 (1.12)	18·00	
202	,,	2 c. pale rose-red ..	2·00	5
		a. With fine horizontal lines across stamp	10·00	4·00
203	,,	2 c. carmine	2·00	5
204	,,	3 c. brown (1918) ..	2·50	8
205	,,	3 c. deep brown ..	2·50	8
		a. Booklet pane of 4+2 labels (12.22) ..	32·00	
205*b*	,,	5 c. deep blue	20·00	12
206	,,	5 c. indigo	24·00	12
206*a*	,,	5 c. grey-blue	20·00	12
206*b*	,,	7 c. straw	38·00	5·00
207	,,	7 c. pale sage-green ('14)	60·00	12·00
208	,,	7 c. olive-yellow (1915)	15·00	45
209	,,	7 c. yellow-ochre (1916)	6·00	45
210	,,	10 c. brownish purple ..	32·00	30
211	,,	10 c. reddish purple ..	40·00	30
212	,,	20 c. olive-green	14·00	25
213	,,	20 c. olive	14·00	20
214	,,	50 c. sepia	14·00	70
215	,,	50 c. grey-black	45·00	2·00
196/215		.. .. *Set of* 8	80·00	1·75

1912 (Nov.)–**1921.** *For use in coil-machines.*

(*a*) *P* 12 × *imperf.*

No.	Type	Description	Unused	Used
216	**44**	1 c. yellow-green ..	2·00	2·00
217	,,	1 c. blue-green ..	9·00	6·00
		a. Two large holes at top and bottom (pair) ..	20·00	20·00
218	,,	2 c. deep rose-red ..	8·00	8·00
218*a*	,,	3 c. brown (1921) ..	3·00	3·00

No. 217a has two large holes about 3½ mm. in diameter in the top and bottom margins. They were for experimental use in a vending machine at Toronto in July 1918 and were only in use for two days.

The 1 c. and 2 c. also exist with two small "V" shaped holes about 9.5 mm. apart at top which are gripper marks due to modifications made in vending machines in 1917.

(*b*) *Imperf.* × *perf.* 8.

No.	Type	Description	Unused	Used
219	**44**	1 c. yellow-green ..	5·00	50
220	,,	1 c. blue-green	5·50	25
		a. With fine horizontal lines across stamp	20·00	
221	,,	2 c. carmine	6·00	15
222	,,	2 c. rose-red	9·00	25
223	,,	2 c. scarlet	10·00	2·50
224	,,	3 c. brown (1918) ..	3·00	15

(*c*) *P* 8 × *imperf.*

No.	Type	Description	Unused	Used
224*a*	**44**	1 c. blue-green ..	32·00	14·00
224*b*	,,	2 c. carmine ..	32·00	14·00

The stamps imperf. × perf. 8 were sold in coils over the counter; those perf. 8 × imperf. were on sale in automatic machines. Varieties showing perf. 12 on 2 or 3 adjacent sides and 1 or 2 sides imperf. are from booklets, or the margins of sheets.

45 **46** **47**

1915 (12 Feb.). *Optd. with T* **45.**

No.	Type	Description	Unused	Used
225	**44**	5 c. blue	90·00	90·00
226	,,	20 c. olive-green ..	20·00	20·00
227	,,	50 c. sepia (R.)	30·00	30·00

These stamps were intended for tax purposes, but owing to ambiguity in an official circular, dated 16 April, 1915, it was for a time believed that their use for postal purposes was authorised.

1915. *P* 12.

No.	Type	Description	Unused	Used
228	**46**	1 c. green	80	8
229	,,	2 c. carmine-red ..	80	12
230	,,	2 c. rose-carmine ..	1·10	1·40

Die I.

Die II.

In Die I there is a long horizontal coloured line under the foot of the "T", and a solid bar of colour runs upwards from the "1" to the "T".

In Die II this solid bar of colour is absent, and there is a short horizontal line under the left side of the "T", with two short vertical dashes and a number of dots under the right-hand side.

1916. (Jan.). *P* 12.

No.	Type	Description	Unused	Used
231	**47**	2 c.+1 c. rose-red (Die I)	3·00	50
232	,,	2 c.+1 c. brt. carm. (Die I)	3·50	50
233	,,	2 c.+1 c. scarlet (Die I) ..	3·50	50

1916 (Sept.). *P* 12.

No.	Type	Description	Unused	Used
234	**47**	2 c.+1 c. carm.-red (Die II)	40·00	1·75

1916. *Imperf.* × *perf.* 8 (*coils*).

No.	Type	Description	Unused	Used
235	**47**	2 c.+1 c. rose-red (Die I)	28·00	2·00

1916. *P* 12 × 8.

No.	Type	Description	Unused	Used
236	**47**	2 c.+1 c. carm.-red (Die I)	7·00	7·00
237	,,	2 c.+1 c. brt. rose-red (Die I)	7·00	7·00

1916 (Sept.). *Colour changed. P* 12.

No.	Type	Description	Unused	Used
238	**47**	2 c.+1 c. brown (Die I) ..	85·00	5·00
239	,,	2 c.+1 c. yell.-brn. (Die II)	1·25	8
240	,,	2 c.+1 c. deep brn. (Die II)	5·00	8

Imperf. × *perf.* 8.

No.	Type	Description	Unused	Used
241	**47**	2 c.+1 c. brown (Die I) ..	40·00	1·50
		a. Pair, 241 and 243 ..		
243	,,	2 c.+1 c. deep brn. (Die II)	6·00	1·50

48. Quebec Conference, 1864, from painting. "The Fathers of Confederation", by Robert Harris.

1917 (15 Sept.). *50th Anniv. of Confederation. P 12.*

244 **48** 3 c. bistre-brown .. .. 7·50 25
  a. Imperf. (pair) (ungummed) £175
245 ,, 3 c. dark brown .. .. 8·00 25

ONE CENT I.

ONE CENT II.

Die I. Space between top of "N" and oval frame line and space between "CENT" and lower frame line.

Die II. "ONE CENT" appears larger so that "N" touches oval and "CENT" almost touches frame line. There are other differences but this is the most obvious one.

Die. I. The lowest of the three horizontal lines of shading below the medals does not touch the three heavy diagonal lines; three complete white spaces over both "E's" of "THREE"; long centre bar to figures "3". Vertical spandrel lines fine.

Die II. The lowest horizontal line of shading touches the first of the three diagonal lines; two and a half spaces over first "E" and spaces over second "E" partly filled by stem of maple leaf; short centre bar to figures "3". Vertical spandrel lines thick. There are numerous other minor differences.

1922–31. *As T* **44**. (*a*) *P* 12.

246 **44** 1 c. chrome-yellow (Die I) (7.6.22) .. 1·75 8
  aa. Booklet pane of 4+2 labels (12.22) .. .. 15·00
  ab. Booklet pane of 6 (12.22) 10·00
  a. Die II (10.24) .. 2·00 15
247 ,, 2 c. dp. yell-grn. (6.6.22) 1·50 5
  aa. Booklet pane of 4+2 labels (12.22) .. 15·00
  ab. Booklet pane of 6 (12.22) £150
  a. *Deep green* .. .. 1·75 5
  b. Thin experimental paper (10.24) .. .. 2·00 1·00
248 ,, 3 c. carm. (Die I) (14.12.23) .. .. 1·25 5
  aa. Booklet pane of 4+2 labels (12.23) .. 10·00
  a. Die II (10.24).. .. 3·50 15
249 ,, 4 c. olive-yellow (3.7.22) 7·00 60
  a. *Yellow-ochre* .. .. 7·00 60
250 ,, 5 c. violet (2.2.22) .. 3·50 25
  a. Thin experimental paper (19.10.24) .. .. 4·00 4·00
  b. *Reddish violet* .. .. 4·00 35
251 ,, 7 c. red-brown (12.12.24) 6·50 2·00
252 ,, 8 c. blue (1.9.25) .. 9·00 2·00
253 ,, 10 c. blue (20.2.22) .. 9·00 25
254 ,, 10 c. bistre-brn. (1.8.25) 9·00 25
  a. *Yellow-brown* .. .. 12·00 35
255 ,, $1 brown-orge. (2.7.23) 35·00 1·50
246/255 .. .. *Set of* 10 70·00 6·00

The $1 differs from T **44** in that the value tablets are oval.

(*b*) *Imperf.* × *perf.* 8 (*horiz. pairs*).

256 **44** 1 c. chrome-yellow (Die I) (1922) .. 5·00 3·00
  a. Thick soft paper (vt.pr.)* £140
  b. Die II (1924) .. 7·00 5·00
  c. Do. Imp. betwn. (vt. pair) 10·00 10·00
257 **44** 2 c. yellow-green (8.22) 5·00 2·00
  a. Thick soft paper (vt.pr.)* £140
  b. Imp. betwn. (vert. pr.) 10·00 10·00
258 ,, 3 c. carm. (Die I) (9.4.24) 12·00 3·00
  a. Thick soft paper (vt.pr.)* £180
  b. Die II (1924) .. 15·00 10·00

Used price of normals are for singles.

*Nos. 256a, 257a and 258a are the first printing in sheets (22 sheets in all), on thick soft paper which can be had in pairs, blocks, etc. Nos. 256c and 257b are a later sheet printing, on the normal paper. The colours differ slightly from those of 256a and 257a and the lettering of the inscription is sharply embossed as seen from the back of the stamps, whereas in the rare printing her e is no embossed effect.

(*c*) *Imperf.*

259 **44** 1 c. chrome-yellow (Die I) (6.10.24) .. .. 18·00 18·00
260 ,, 2 c. deep green (6.10.24) 18·00 18·00
261 ,, 3 c. carmine (Die I) (31.12.23)† .. .. 7·00 7·00

(*d*) *P* 12 × *imperf.*

262 **44** 2 c. deep green (9.24) .. 40·00 40·00

(*e*) *P* 12 × 8.

263 **44** 3 c. carm. (Die II) (24.6.31) 3·00 3·00

Nos. 259 to 261 were on sale only at the Philatelic Branch P.O. Dept., Ottawa.

†Earliest known postmark.

2 CENTS (49)   2 CENTS (50)

1926. *No. 248 surch.*

(*a*) *With T* **49**, *by the Govt. Printing Bureau.*

264 **44** 2 c. on 3 c. carm. (12.10.26) 24·00 24·00
  a. Pair, one without surch. £120
  b. On Die II .. ..

(*b*) *With T* **50**, *by the Canadian Bank Note Co.*

265 **44** 2 c. on 3 c. carm. (26.10.26) 9·00 9·00
  a. Surch. double (partly treble) £100

51. Sir J. A. Macdonald.

54. Sir W. Laurier.

52. "The Fathers of Confederation".

53. Parliament Buildings, Ottawa.

55. Canada, Map 1867–1927.

1927 (29 June). *60th Anniv. of Confederation. P* 12. I. *Commemorative Issue. Inscr.* "1867–1927. CANADA CONFEDERATION".

266 **51** 1 c. orange .. .. 1·00 30
267 **52** 2 c. green 50 8
268 **53** 3 c. carmine .. .. 3·50 2·25
269 **54** 5 c. violet .. .. .. 1·50 1·00
270 **55** 12 c. blue .. .. .. 3·00 1·75
266/270 .. .. *Set of* 5 7·50 4·50

IMPERFORATE STAMPS. With the exception of Nos. 177a and 259/61 it is understood that the imperf. stamps listed up to this point are proofs or imprimaturs which were illicitly removed from the P.O. archives. However, we retain them in our list as they have been on the market a very long time and changed hands in good faith. They remain rare stamps even as proofs. They exist with or without gum but were probably ungummed at the time of their removal.

During the period 1927–46 most contemporary stamps appeared on the market both imperf. and part perf. and generally with original gum. They emanate from six sheets of each which were supplied by the printers for record purposes but which found their way on to the market and we no longer list them. Since 1948 the Post Office has taken effective steps to prevent this practice.

56. Darcy McGee.

57. Sir W. Laurier and Sir J. A. Macdonald.

58. R. Baldwin and L. H. Lafontaine.

II. *Historical Issue.*

271 **56** 5 c. violet .. .. .. 1·50 90
272 **57** 12 c. green .. .. .. 3·00 2·00
273 **58** 20 c. carmine .. .. 5·00 2·00

59

1928 (21 Sept.). *Air. P* 12.

274 **59** 5 c. olive-brown .. .. 2·00 1·00

60. King George V.

61. Mt. Hurd and Indian Totem Poles.

62. Quebec Bridge.

63. Harvesting with Horses.

64. Fishing smack *Bluenose*.

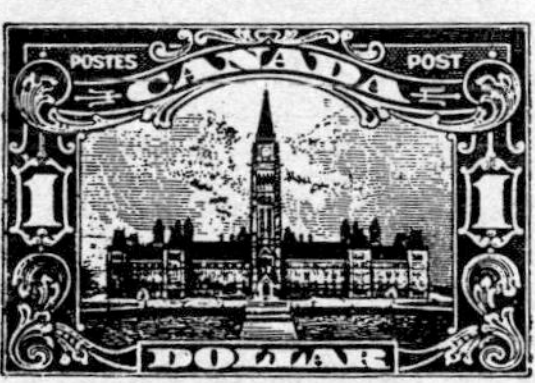

65. Parliament Buildings, Ottawa.

1928–29. (*a*) *P* 12.

275	**60**	1 c. orange (29.10.28) ..	50	12
		a. Booklet pane of 6 (25.10.28)	7·00	
276	,,	2 c. green (16.10.28) ..	20	8
		a. Booklet pane of 6 (16.10.28)	5·50	
277	,,	3 c. lake (12.12.28) ..	5·00	3·00
278	,,	4 c. olive-bistre (16.8.29)	4·00	1·50
279	,,	5 c. violet (12.12.28) ..	2·00	70
		a. Booklet pane of 6 (6.1.29)	32·00	
280	,,	8 c. blue (21.12.28) ..	3·00	1·50
281	**61**	10 c. green (5.11.28) ..	2·25	25
282	**62**	12 c. grey-black (6.1.29) ..	4·00	2·50
283	**63**	20 c. lake (6.1.29)	5·00	3·00
284	**64**	50 c. blue (6.1.29)	£100	20·00
285	**65**	$1 olive-green (6.1.29) ..	£125	30·00
275/285		.. .. *Set of* 11	£225	55·00

(*b*) *Imperf.* × *perf.* 8 (5.11.28).

286	**60**	1 c. orange	6·00	5·00
287	,,	2 c. green	3·00	35

Slight differences in the size of many Canadian stamps, due to paper shrinkage, are to be found.

PRINTERS. The following stamps to No. 334 were recess-printed by the British American Bank Note Co.

66.

67. Parliamentary Library, Ottawa.

68. The Old Citadel, Quebec.

69. Harvesting with Tractor.

70. Acadian Memorial Church and Statue of "Evangeline" Grand Pre, Nova Scotia.

71. Mt. Edith Cavell, Canadian Rockies.

Die I. 1 c. Die II.

Die I. 2 c. Die II.

1 c. Die I. Three thick coloured lines and one thin between "P" and ornament, at right. Curved line in ball-ornament short.

Die II. Four thick lines. Curved line longer.

2 c. Die I. Three thick coloured lines between "P" and ornament, at left. Short line in ball.

Die II. Four thick lines. Curved line longer.

1930–31. (*a*) *P* 11.

288	**66**	1 c. orange (I) (17.7.30) ..	20	10
289	,,	2 c. green (I) (6.7.30) ..	25	8
		a. Booklet pane of 6 (6.7.30)	14·00	
290	**66**	4 c. yell.-bistre (5.11.30) ..	3·00	2·00
291	,,	5 c. violet (18.6.30) ..	90	90
292	,,	8 c. blue (13.8.30) ..	4·50	3·75
293	**67**	10 c. olive-green (15.9.30)	3·00	60
294	**68**	12 c. grey-black (4.12.30) ..	4·00	2·00
295	**69**	20 c. red (4.12.30)	5·00	15
296	**70**	50 c. blue (4.12.30) ..	65·00	5·00
297	**71**	$1 olive-green (4.12.30)	60·00	8·00
288/297		.. .. *Set of* 10	£125	18·00

(*b*) *Imperf.* × *perf.* 8½.

298	**66**	1 c. orange (I)	3·50	3·50
299	,,	2 c. green (I)	1·25	60

Colours changed and new value. (*a*) *P* 11.

300	**66**	1 c. green (I) (6.12.30) ..	30	5
		a. Booklet pane of 6 (5.12.30)	11·00	
		b. Booklet pane of 4+2 labels (13.11.31)	40·00	
		c. Die II	30	5
301	,,	2 c. scarlet (I) (17.11.30) ..	40	5
		a. Booklet pane of 6 (17.11.30)	5·00	
		b. Die II	40	5
302	,,	2 c. dp. brown (I) (4.7.31)	1·00	1·00
		a. Booklet pane of 6 (13.7.31)	9·00	
		b. Die II	25	10
		ba. Booklet pane of 4+2 labels (13.11.31)	50·00	
303	,,	3 c. scarlet (13.7.31) ..	40	5
		a. Booklet pane of 4+2 labels (13.11.31)	15·00	
304	,,	5 c. blue (13.11.30) ..	55	5
305	,,	8 c. red-orange (5.11.30) ..	1·25	1·25
300/305		*Set of* 6	3·00	1·40

(*b*) *Imperf.* × *perf.* 8½.

306	**66**	1 c. green (I)	2·00	2·00
307	,,	2 c. scarlet (I)	2·75	1·25
308	,,	2 c. deep brn. (I) (4.7.31)	3·00	15
309	,,	3 c. scarlet (13.7.31) ..	4·00	12

Some low values in the above and subsequent issues have been printed by both Rotary and "Flat plate" processes. The former can be distinguished by the gum, which has a striped appearance.

For 13 c. bright violet, *T* **68**, see No. 325.

72. Mercury and Western Hemisphere.

1930 (4 Dec.). *Air.* *P* 11.

310	**72**	5 c. deep brown	14·00	9·00

73. Sir Georges Etienne Cartier.

3

(75)

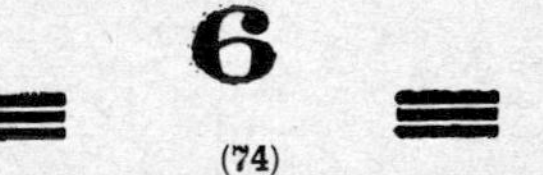

(74)

1931 (30 Sept.). *P* 11.

312	**73**	10 c. olive-green	4·00	8

1932 (22 Feb.). *Air.* *No.* 274 *surch. with T* **74.**

313	**59**	6 c. on 5 c. olive-brown ..	2·25	1·10
		a. Surch. inverted (vert. pair)	70·00	
		b. Triple surcharge ..	70·00	
		c. Double surcharge ..	70·00	

Collectors are warned against forged errors of No. 313, some of which bear unauthorized markings which purport to be the guarantee of Stanley Gibbons Ltd.

1932 (21 June). *Nos.* 301/1*b* *surch. with T* **75.**

314	**66**	3 c. on 2 c. scarlet (I) ..	75	60
314*a*	,,	3 c. on 2 c. scarlet (II) ..	25	5

76. King George V.

77. Duke of Windsor when Prince of Wales.

78. Allegory of British Empire.

6 6

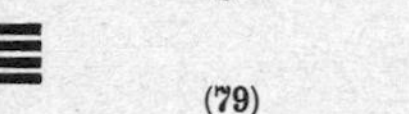

(79)

1932 (12 July). *Ottawa Conference. P* 11.

(*a*) *Postage stamps.*

315	**76**	3 c. scarlet	25	8
316	**77**	5 c. blue	1·75	80
317	**78**	13 c. green	2·25	1·75

(*b*) *Air. No.* 310 *surch. with T* **79.**

318	**72**	6 c. on 5 c. deep brown (B.)	5·50	4·50

80. King George V.

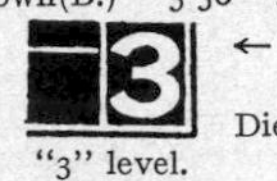

← Die I.

"3" level.

← Die II.

"3" raised.

1932 (1 Dec.)–**33.** (*a*) *P* 11.

319	**80**	1 c. green	25	8
		a. Booklet pane of 6 ..	8·00	8·00
		b. Booklet pane of 4+2 labels (19.9.33)	40·00	40·00
320	,,	2 c. sepia	35	8
		a. Booklet pane of 6 ..	8·00	8·00
		b. Booklet pane of 4+2 labels (19.9.33)	40·00	40·00
321	,,	3 c. scarlet (Die I) ..	40	10
		a. Booklet pane of 4+2 labels	15·00	15·00
		b. Die II (29.11.32) ..	40	8
		ba. Booklet pane of 4+2 labels (19.9.33)	12·00	12·00
322	,,	4 c. yellow-brown ..	10·00	1·50
323	,,	5 c. blue	1·25	8
324	,,	8 c. red-orange	2·00	1·25
325	**68**	13 c. bright violet	6·50	1·00
319/325		.. .. *Set of* 7	18·00	3·50

(*b*) *Imperf.* × *perf.* 8½ ('33).

326	**80**	1 c. green	5·50	90
327	,,	2 c. sepia	5·50	25
328	,,	3 c. scarlet (Die II) ..	2·25	8

81. Parliament Buildings, Ottawa.

1933 (18 May). *U.P.U. Congress Preliminary Meeting. P* 11.

329	**81**	5c. blue	3·25	1·25

WORLD'S
GRAIN EXHIBITION &
CONFERENCE

REGINA 1933

(82)

1933 (24 July). *World's Grain Exhibition and Conference, Regina. Optd. with T* **82.** *P* 11.

330	**69**	20 c. red (B.)	14·00	5·00

83. S.S. *Royal William* (after S. Skillett).

1933 (17 Aug.). *Centenary of First Trans-Atlantic Steamboat Crossing. P* 11.

331	**83**	5 c. blue	3·25	1·25

84. Jacques Cartier approaching Land.

1934 (1 July). *Fourth Centenary of Discovery of Canada.* P 11.

332	**84**	3 c. blue	1·75	65

85. U.E.L. Statue, Hamilton.

1934 (1 July). *150th Anniv. of Arrival of United Empire Loyalists. P* 11.

333	**85**	10 c. olive-green	8·00	3·25

86. Seal of New Brunswick.

1934 (16 Aug.). *150th Anniv. of Province of New Brunswick. P* 11.

334	**86**	2 c. red-brown	80	60

PRINTERS. The following stamps were recess-printed (except where otherwise stated) by the Canadian Bank Note Co., Ottawa, until No. 616.

87. Queen Elizabeth II when Princess.

88. King George VI when Duke of York.

89. King George V and Queen Mary.

90. Duke of Windsor when Prince of Wales.

91. Windsor Castle. (*Size as* 13 *c.*)

92. *Britannia.*

1935 (4 May). *Silver Jubilee. P* 12.

335	**87**	1 c. green	20	8
336	**88**	2 c. brown	35	8
337	**89**	3 c. carmine-red	80	8
338	**90**	5 c. blue	2·25	1·25
339	**91**	10 c. green	2·50	1·25
340	**92**	13 c. blue	3·25	2·50
335/340		.. .. *Set of* 6	8·50	4·75

93. King George V.

94. Royal Canadian Mounted Policeman.

95. Confederation Charlottetown, 1864.

96. Niagara Falls.

97. Parliament Buildings, Victoria, B.C.

98. Champlain Monument, Quebec.

99. Daedalus.

1935 (1 June–5 Nov.). (*a*) *Postage*. (i) *P* 12.

341	**93**	1 c. green	12	8
		a. Booklet pane of 6 ..	8·00	8·00
		b. Booklet pane of 4+2 labels	32·00	32·00
342	,,	2 c. brown	15	8
		a. Booklet pane of 6 ..	8·00	8·00
		b. Booklet pane of 4+2 labels	32·00	32·00
343	,,	3 c. scarlet	30	8
		a. Booklet pane of 4+2 labels	8·00	8·00
344	,,	4 c. yellow	1·25	20
345	,,	5 c. blue	1·25	8
		a. Imp. between (horiz. pr.)	£125	
346	,,	8 c. orange	1·25	40
347	**94**	10 c. carmine	3·25	8
348	**95**	13 c. purple	3·25	20
349	**96**	20 c. olive-green	10·00	25
350	**97**	50 c. deep violet	12·00	2·00
351	**98**	$1 bright blue	30·00	4·00
341/351		.. .. *Set of* 11	55·00	6·50

(ii) *Coil stamps. Imperf.* × *perf.* 8.

352	**93**	1 c. green (5.11.35) ..	5·50	80
353	,,	2 c. brown (14.10.35) ..	5·50	25
354	,,	3 c. scarlet (20.7.35) ..	3·50	12

(*b*) *Air*. *P* 12.

355	**99**	6 c. red-brown	80	60

100. King George VI and Queen Elizabeth.

1937 (10 May). *Coronation*. *P* 12.

356	**100**	3 c. carmine	15	5

101. King George VI.

102. Memorial Chamber Parliament Buildings, Ottawa.

103. Entrance to Halifax Harbour.

104. Fort Garry Gate, Winnipeg.

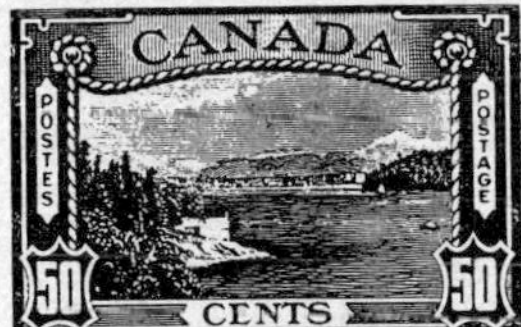

105. Entrance, Vancouver Harbour.

106. Chateau de Ramezay, Montreal.

107. Seaplane over S.S. *Distributor* on R. Mackenzie.

(T **101**. Photograph by Bertram Park.)

1937–38. (*a*) *Postage*. (i) *P* 12.

357	**101**	1 c. green (1.4.37) ..	12	5
		a. Booklet pane of 6 ..	1·00	1·00
		b. Booklet pane of 4+2 labels	4·00	4·00
358	,,	2 c. brown (1.4.37) ..	15	5
		a. Booklet pane of 6 ..	3·25	3·25
		b. Booklet pane of 4+2 labels	4·00	4·00
359	,,	3 c. scarlet (1.4.37) ..	25	5
		a. Booklet pane of 4+2 labels	1·25	1·25
360	,,	4 c. yellow (10.5.37) ..	1·25	15
361	**101**	5 c. blue (10.5.37) ..	70	12
362	,,	8 c. orange (10.5.37) ..	1·25	12
363	**102**	10 c. rose-carm. (15.6.38)	5·00	12
		a. Red	5·00	12
364	**103**	13 c. blue (15.11.38) ..	6·00	20
365	**104**	20 c. red-brown (15.6.38)	12·00	25
366	**105**	50 c. green (15.6.38) ..	17·00	2·50
367	**106**	$1 violet (15.6.38) ..	35·00	3·25
357/367		.. .. *Set of* 11	70·00	6·00

(ii) *Coil stamps. Imperf.* × *perf.* 8.

368	**101**	1 c. green (15.6.37) ..	65	35
369	,,	2 c. brown (18.6.37) ..	85	12
370	,,	3 c. scarlet (15.4.37) ..	1·00	5

(*b*) *Air*. *P* 12.

371	**107**	6 c. blue (15.6.38) ..	80	12

108. Queen Elizabeth II when Princess and Princess Margaret.

109. National War Memorial, Ottawa.

110. King George VI and Queen Elizabeth.

1939 (15 May). *Royal Visit*. *P* 12.

372	**108**	1 c. black and green ..	15	5
373	**109**	2 c. black and brown ..	10	5
374	**110**	3 c. black and carmine ..	10	5

111. King George VI in Naval uniform.

112. King George VI in Military uniform.

113. King George VI in Air Force uniform.

114. Grain Elevator.

115. Farm Scene.

116. Parliament Buildings.

117. Ram Tank.

118. Corvette.

119. Munitions Factory.

120. Destroyer.

121. Air Training Camp.

1942 (1 July)–**1948.** *War Effort.*
(*a*) *Postage.* (i) *P* 12.

375	**111**	1 c. green	12	5
		a. Booklet pane of 6 ..	80	80
		b. Booklet pane of 4+2 labels	3·00	3·00
376	**112**	2 c. brown	20	5
		a. Booklet pane of 6 ..	3·00	3·00
		b. Booklet pane of 4+2 labels	3·00	3·00
377	**113**	3 c. carmine-lake ..	25	5
		a. Booklet pane of 4+2 labels	80	80
378	,,	3 c. purple (30.6.43) ..	25	5
		a. Booklet pane of 6 ..	2·75	2·75
		b. Booklet pane of 4+2 labels	80	80
379	**114**	4 c. slate	80	20
380	**112**	4 c. carmine-lake (9.4.43)	20	5
		a. Booklet pane of 6 ..	1·25	1·25
381	**111**	5 c. blue	50	5
382	**115**	8 c. red-brown	1·00	20
383	**116**	10 c. brown	1·75	5
384	**117**	13 c. dull green	2·50	1·75
385	,,	14 c. dull green (16.4.43)	3·00	20
386	**118**	20 c. chocolate	2·50	10
387	**119**	50 c. violet	11·00	1·00
388	**120**	$1 blue	35·00	3·50
375/388		.. .. *Set of* 14	55·00	6·50

(ii) *Coil stamps.* *Imperf.*×*perf.* 8.

389	**111**	1 c. green (9.2.43) ..	25	15
390	**112**	2 c. brown (24.11.42) ..	35	20
391	**113**	3 c. carmine-lake (23.9.42)	35	20
392	,,	3 c. purple (19.8.43) ..	70	10
393	**112**	4 c. carmine-lake (13.5.43)	85	8

(iii) *Booklet stamps.* *Imperf.*×*perf.* 12.

394	**111**	1 c. green (24.11.42) ..	12	12
395	**113**	3 c. purple (20.8.42) ..	25	25
396	**112**	4 c. carmine-lake (3.5.43)	25	25

Nos. 394/6 are from booklets in which the stamps are in strips of three, imperforate at top and bottom and right-hand end.

(iv) *Coil stamps.* *Imperf.*×*perf.* $9\frac{1}{2}$.

397	**111**	1 c. green (13.7.48) ..	1·10	55
397*a*	**112**	2 c. brown (1.10.48) ..	4·25	2·75
398	**113**	3 c. purple (2.7.48) ..	1·75	70
398*a*	**112**	4 c. carmine-lake (22.7.48)	1·75	70

(*b*) *Air.* *P* 12.

399	**121**	6 c. blue (1.7.42)	1·40	35
400	,,	7 c. blue (16.4.43) ..	35	10

122. Ontario Farm Scene.

123. Great Bear Lake.

124. St. Maurice River Power Station.

125. Combine Harvester.

126. Lumbering in British Columbia.

127. Train Ferry, Prince Edward Is.

128. Canada Geese in flight.

1946 (16 Sept.). *Peace Re-conversion.* *P* 12.
(*a*) *Postage.*

401	**122**	8 c. brown	50	20
402	**123**	10 c. olive-green	85	5
403	**124**	14 c. sepia	1·40	8
404	**125**	20 c. slate	1·75	8
405	**126**	50 c. green	12·00	70
406	**127**	$1 purple	25·00	1·25

(*b*) *Air.*

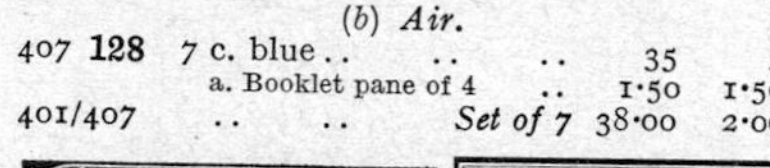

407	**128**	7 c. blue	35	5
		a. Booklet pane of 4 ..	1·50	1·50
401/407		.. .. *Set of* 7	38·00	2·00

129. Alexander Graham Bell and " Fame ".

130. " Canadian Citizenship ".

1947 (3 Mar.). *Birth Centenary of Bell* (*inventor of telephone*). *P* 12.

408	**129**	4 c. blue	10	8

1947 (1 July). *Advent of Canadian Citizenship and Eightieth Anniv. of Confederation.* *P* 12.

409	**130**	4 c. blue	10	8

131. Queen Elizabeth II when Princess.
(From photograph by Dorothy Wilding.)

1948 (16 Feb.). *Princess Elizabeth's Marriage.* *P* 12.

410	**131**	4 c. blue	10	5

132. Queen Victoria, Parliament Building, Ottawa, and King George VI.

1948 (1 Oct.). *One Hundred Years of Responsible Government.* *P* 12.

411	**132**	4 c. grey	10	5

133. Cabot's Ship *Matthew.*

1949 (1 Apr.). *Entry of Newfoundland into Canadian Confederation.* *P* 12.

412	**133**	4 c. green	10	5

134. " Founding of Halifax, 1749 ", after C. W. Jeffries, R.C.A., LL.D.

1949 (21 June). *200th Anniv. of Halifax, Nova Scotia.* *P* 12.

413	**134**	4 c. violet	10	5

135.

136.

137.

138. King George VI. **139.**

(From photographs by Dorothy Wilding.)

1949 (15 Nov.)–**51.** (i) *P* 12.

414	**135**	1 c. green	8	5
415	**136**	2 c. sepia	10	5
415*a*	,,	2 c. olive-green (25.7.51)	10	5
416	**137**	3 c. purple	10	5
		a. Booklet pane of 4+2 labels	70	70
417	**138**	4 c. carmine-lake ..	15	5
		a. Booklet pane of 6 ..	5·00	5·00
417*b*	,,	4 c. vermilion (25.7.51)	15	5
		c. Booklet pane of 6 ..	1·25	1·25
418	**139**	5 c. blue	35	8
		(ii) *Imperf.×perf.* 9½ (*coil stamps*).		
419	**135**	1 c. green (18.5.50) ..	10	8
420	**136**	2 c. sepia (18.5.50) ..	50	35
420*a*	,,	2 c. olive-green (9.10.51)	20	10
421	**137**	3 c. purple (18.5.50) ..	35	8
422	**138**	4 c. carm.-lake (20.4.50)	2·50	20
422*a*	,,	4 c. vermilion (27.11.51)	25	8
		(iii) *Imperf.×perf.* 12 (*booklets*).		
422*b*	**135**	1 c. green (18.5.50) ..	8	8
423	**137**	3 c. purple (12.4.50) ..	10	10
423*a*	**138**	4 c. carmine-lake (5.4.50)	1·25	1·25
423*b*	,,	4 c. vermilion (2.6.51) ..	30	30

These booklet stamps come from strips of three, imperforate at top and bottom and right-hand end.

140. King George VI.

(From photograph by Dorothy Wilding.)

1950 (19 Jan.). *As T* **135/9** *but without* "POSTES POSTAGE", *as T* **140.** (i) *P* 12.

424	1 c. green	8	5
425	2 c. sepia	15	10
426	3 c. purple	12	5
427	4 c. carmine-lake	15	5
428	5 c. blue	40	35
	(ii) *Imperf.×perf.* 9½ (*coil stamps*).		
429	1 c. green	12	12
430	3 c. purple	20	20

141. Oil Wells in Alberta.

1950 (1 Mar.). *P* 12.

431	**141**	50 c. green	5·00	50

142. Drying Furs.

1950 (2 Oct.). *P* 12.

432	**142**	10 c. brown-purple ..	50	5

143. Fisherman.

1951 (1 Feb.). *P* 12.

433	**143**	$1 ultramarine	40·00	4·50

144. Sir R. L. Borden. **145.** W. L. Mackenzie King.

1951 (25 June). *Prime Ministers* (1*st issue*). *P* 12.

434	**144**	3 c. blue-green	12	5
435	**145**	4 c. rose-carmine.. ..	12	5

See also Nos. 444/5, 475/6 and 483/4.

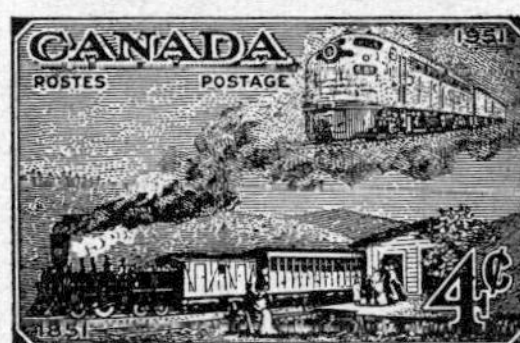

146. Mail Trains, 1851 and 1951.

147. SS. *City of Toronto* and SS. *Prince George.*

148. Mail Coach and Aeroplane.

149. Reproduction of 3d., 1851.

1951 (24 Sept.). *Canadian Stamp Centenary. P* 12.

436	**146**	4 c. black	25	8
437	**147**	5 c. violet	1·00	70
438	**148**	7 c. blue	50	12
439	**149**	15 c. scarlet	50	12

150. Queen Elizabeth II when Princess and Duke of Edinburgh.

1951 (26 Oct.). *Royal Visit. P* 12.

440	**150**	4 c. violet..	12	5

151. Forestry Products.

(Des. A. L. Pollock.)

1952 (1 Apr.). *P* 12.

441	**151**	20 c. grey	70	8

152. Red Cross Emblem.

1952 (26 July). 18*th International Red Cross Conference, Toronto. Design recess; cross litho. P* 12.

442	**152**	4 c. scarlet and blue ..	12	5

153. Canada Goose.

(Des. E. Hahn.)

1952 (3 Nov.). *P* 12.

443	**153**	7 c. blue	20	8

1952 (3 Nov.). *Prime Ministers* (2*nd issue*). *Various portraits as T* **144**. *P* 12.

444	3 c. reddish purple	12	8
445	4 c. orange-red	15	8

Portraits:—3 c. Sir John J. C. Abbott; 4 c. A. Mackenzie.

154. Pacific Coast Indian House and Totem Pole.

(Des. E. Hahn.)

1953 (2 Feb.). *P* 12.

No.	Type	Description	Unused	Used
446	**154**	$1 black	11·00	50

155. Polar Bear.

156. Moose.

157. Bighorn Sheep.

(Des. J. Crosby (2 c.), E. Hahn (others).)

1953 (1 Apr.). *National Wild Life Week.* *P* 12.

No.	Type	Description	Unused	Used
447	**155**	2 c. blue	10	5
448	**156**	3 c. sepia	12	5
449	**157**	4 c. slate	20	5

158. Queen Elizabeth II. **159.**

(From photograph by Karsh, Ottawa.)

1953 (1 May–Sept.). (i) *P* 12.

No.	Type	Description	Unused	Used
450	**158**	1 c. purple-brown ..	5	5
451	,,	2 c. green	8	5
452	,,	3 c. carmine	12	5
		a. Booklet pane. Four stamps and two blank labels (6.7)	85	85
453	,,	4 c. violet..	12	5
		a. Booklet pane of 6 ..	1·10	1·10
454	,,	5 c. ultramarine	15	5
		(ii) *Imperf. × perf.* 9½ (*coil stamps*).		
455	**158**	2 c. green (30.7)	35	25
456	,,	3 c. carmine (27.7) ..	40	30
457	,,	4 c. violet (3.9)	60	40
		(iii) *Imperf. × perf.* 12 (*booklets*).		
458	**158**	1 c. purple-brown (12.8)..	30	30
459	,,	3 c. carmine (17.7) ..	35	35
460	,,	4 c. violet (6.7)	50	50

These booklet stamps come from strips of three, imperforate at top and bottom and right-hand end.

(Des. E. Hahn.)

1953 (1 June). *Coronation.* *P* 12.

No.	Type	Description	Unused	Used
461	**159**	4 c. violet..	12	5

160. Textile Industry.

(Des. A. L. Pollock.)

1953 (2 Nov.). *P* 12.

No.	Type	Description	Unused	Used
462	**160**	50 c. deep bluish green ..	2·50	15

161. Queen Elizabeth II.

162. Walrus.

163. Beaver.

164. Gannet.

(From photograph by Dorothy Wilding.)

1954–62. (i) *P* 12.

No.	Type	Description	Unused	Used
463	**161**	1 c. purple-brn. (10.6.54)	5	5
		a. Booklet pane. Five stamps plus printed label (1.6.56)	35	35
		p. Two phosphor bands (13.1.62)	60	60
464	,,	2 c. green (10.6.54) ..	8	5
		a. Pack. Two blocks of 25	3·50	
		p. Two phosphor bands (13.1.62)	60	60
465	,,	3 c. carmine (10.6.54) ..	10	5
		a. Imperf. vert. (horiz. pr.)	£650	
		p. Two phosphor bands (13.1.62)	55	50
466	,,	4 c. violet (10.6.54) ..	12	5
		a. Booklet pane. Five stamps plus printed label (1.6.56)	1·00	1·00
		b. Booklet pane of 6 ..	2·50	2·50
		p. One phosphor band (13.1.62)	2·25	2·25
467	,,	5 c. bright blue (1.4.54)..	15	5
		a. Booklet pane. Five stamps plus printed label (14.7.54)	1·10	1·10
		b. Pack. One block of 20 ..	3·50	
		p. Two phosphor bands (13.1.62)	2·25	2·25
468	,,	6 c. red-orange (10.6.54)	25	15
463/8		.. .. *Set of* 6	65	35
		(ii) *Imperf. × perf.* 9½ (*coil stamps*).		
469	**161**	2 c. green (9.9.54) ..	12	10
470	,,	4 c. violet (23.8.54) ..	35	15
471	,,	5 c. bright blue (6.7.54)..	50	12

Nos. 464a and 467b are blocks with the outer edges imperf. These come from "One Dollar Plastic Packages" sold at post offices.

WINNIPEG PHOSPHOR BANDS. In 1962 facer-cancelling machines were introduced in Winnipeg which were activated by phosphor bands on the stamps. Under long or short wave ultra-violet light the phosphor glows and there is also a short after-glow when the lamp is turned off. This should not be confused with the fluorescent bands introduced in Ottawa in 1971.

(Des. E. Hahn.)

1954 (1 Apr.). *National Wild Life Week.* *P* 12.

No.	Type	Description	Unused	Used
472	**162**	4 c. slate-black	20	5
473	**163**	5 c. ultramarine	20	5
		a. Booklet pane. Five stamps plus one printed label ..	1·25	1·25

(Des. L. Hyde.)

1954 (1 Apr.). *P* 12.

No.	Type	Description	Unused	Used
474	**164**	15 c. black	50	1

1954 (1 Nov.). *Prime Ministers* (*3rd issue*) *Various portraits as T* **144.** *P* 12.

No.	Description	Unused	Used
475	4 c. violet	20	5
476	5 c. bright blue	20	5

Portraits:—4 c. Sir John Thompson; 5 c Sir Mackenzie Bowell.

165. Eskimo Hunter.

(Des. H. Beament.)

1955 (21 Feb.). *P* 12.

No.	Type	Description	Unused	Used
477	**165**	10 c. purple-brown ..	25	8

166. Musk-ox.

167. Whooping Cranes.

(Des. E. Hahn (4 c.), Dr. W. Rowan (5 c.).)

1955 (4 Apr.). *National Wild Life Week.* *P* 12

No.	Type	Description	Unused	Used
478	**166**	4 c. violet..	20	8
479	**167**	5 c. ultramarine	20	8

168. Dove and Torch.

(Des. W. Lohse.)

1955 (1 June). *Tenth Anniv. of International Civil Aviation Organisation.* *P* 12.

No.	Type	Description	Unused	Used
480	**168**	5 c. ultramarine	25	5

169. Pioneer Settlers.

(Des. L. Hyde.)

955 (30 June). *50th Anniv. of Alberta and Saskatchewan Provinces.* P 12.
81 **169** 5 c. ultramarine 25 5

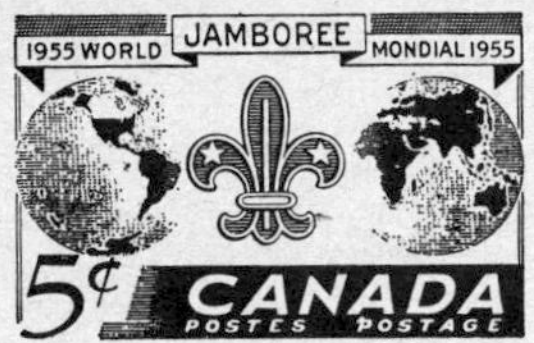

170. Scout Badge and Globe.

(Des. L. Hyde.)

955 (20 Aug.). *Eighth World Scout Jamboree, Niagara-on-the-Lake.* P 12.
82 **170** 5 c. orange-brn. & green 25 8

955 (8 Nov.). *Prime Ministers (4th Issue). Various portraits as T* **144.** P 12.
83 4 c. violet 15 5
84 5 c. bright blue 15 5
Portraits:—4 c. R. B. Bennett; 5 c. Sir harles Tupper.

173. Ice-hockey Players.

(Des. J. Simpkins.)

956 (23 Jan.). *Ice-hockey Commemoration.* P 12.
85 **173** 5 c. ultramarine 20 5

174. Caribou.  **175.** Mountain Goat.

(Des. E. Hahn.)

956 (12 Apr.). *National Wild Life Week.* P 12.
86 **174** 4 c. violet.. .. .. 20 5
87 **175** 5 c. bright blue 20 5

176. Pulp and Paper Industry.

177. Chemical Industry. **178.**

(Des. A. J. Casson (20 c.), A. L. Pollock (25 c.).)

1956 (7 June). P 12.
488 **176** 20 c. green 70 5
489 **177** 25 c. red 90 5

(Des. A. Price.)

1956 (9 Oct.). *Fire Prevention Week.* P 12.
490 **178** 5 c. red and black .. 15 5

179. Fishing.

180. Swimming.

181. Hunting.

182. Skiing.

(Des. L. Hyde.)

1957 (7 Mar.). *Outdoor Recreation.* P 12.
491 **179** 5 c. ultramarine 15 5
492 **180** 5 c. ultramarine 15 5
493 **181** 5 c. ultramarine 15 5
494 **182** 5 c. ultramarine 15 5
Block of 4, *se-tenant* .. .. 1·25 1·25

No. 491/4 are printed together in sheets of 50 (5×10). In the first, second, fourth and fifth vertical rows the four different designs are arranged in *se-tenant* blocks, whilst the central row is made up as follows (reading downwards):—Nos. 491/4, 491/2 (or 493/4), 491/4.

183. Common Loon. **184.** Thompson with Sextant, and North American Map.

(Des. L. Hyde.)

1957 (10 Apr.). *National Wild Life Week.* P 12.
495 **183** 5 c. black 20 5

(Des. G. A. Gundersen.)

1957 (5 June). *Death Centenary of David Thompson (explorer).* P 12.
496 **184** 5 c. ultramarine 20 5

185. Parliament Buildings, Ottawa. **186.** Globe within Posthorn.

(Des. Carl Mangold.)

1957 (14 Aug.). *14th U.P.U. Congress, Ottawa.* P 12.
497 **185** 5 c. grey-blue 20 5
498 **186** 15 c. blackish blue .. 1·10 85

187. Miner.  **188.** Queen Elizabeth II and Duke of Edinburgh.

(Des. A. J. Casson.)

1957 (5 Sept.). *Mining Industry.* P 12.
499 **187** 5 c. black 15 5

(From photographs by Karsh, Ottawa.)

1957 (10 Oct.). *Royal Visit.* P 12.
500 **188** 5 c. black 12 5

189. " A Free Press ".

(Des. A. L. Pollock.)

1958 (22 Jan.). *The Canadian Press.* P 12.
501 **189** 5 c. black 15 5

190. Microscope.

(Des. A. L. Pollock.)

1958 (5 Mar.). *International Geophysical Year.* P 12.
502 **190** 5 c. blue 20 5

191. Miner Panning for Gold.

(Des. J. Harman.)

1958 (8 May.) *Centenary of British Columbia. P 12.*

503 **191** 5 c. deep turquoise-green 15 5

192. La Verendrye (statue).

(Des. G. Trottier.)

1958 (4 June). *La Verendrye (explorer) Commemoration. P 12.*

504 **192** 5 c. ultramarine 15 5

193. Samuel de Champlain and the Heights of Quebec.

(Des. G. Trottier.)

1958 (26 June). *350th Anniv. of Founding of Quebec. P 12.*

505 **193** 5 c. brown-ochre & dp. grn. 15 5

194. Nurse.

(Des. G. Trottier.)

1958 (30 July). *National Health. P 12.*

506 **194** 5 c. reddish purple .. 15 5

195. " Petroleum 1858–1958 ".

(Des. A. L. Pollock.)

1958 (10 Sept.). *Centenary of Canadian Oil Industry. P 12.*

507 **195** 5 c. scarlet and olive .. 15 5

196. Speaker's Chair and Mace.

(Des. G. Trottier and C. Dair.)

1958 (2 Oct.). *Bicentenary of First Elected Assembly. P 12.*

508 **196** 5 c. deep slate 15 5

197. The " Silver Dart ".

1959 (23 Feb.). *50th Anniv. of First Flight of the " Silver Dart " in Canada. P 12.*

509 **197** 5 c. black and ultramarine 15 5

198. Globe showing N.A.T.O. Countries.

(Des. P. Weiss.)

1959 (2 Apr.). *Tenth Anniv. of North Atlantic Treaty Organization. P 12.*

510 **198** 5 c. ultramarine.. .. 15 5

199. **200.** Queen Elizabeth II.

(Des. Helen Fitzgerald.)

1959 (13 May). " *Associated Country Women of the World* " *Commemoration. P 12.*

511 **199** 5 c. black & yellow-olive 15 5

(Des. after painting by Annigoni.)

1959 (18 June). *Royal Visit. P 12.*

512 **200** 5 c. lake-red 15 5

201. Maple Leaf linked with American Eagle.

(Des. A. L. Pollock, G. Trottier (of Canada) W. H. Buckley, A. J. Copeland, E. Metz (of the United States).)

1959 (26 June). *Opening of St. Lawrence Seaway. P 12.*

513 **201** 5 c. ultramarine and red.. 15

a. Centre inverted .. £1700 £130

202. Maple Leaves.

(Des. P. Weiss.)

1959 (10 Sept.). *Bicentenary of Battle of Plains of Abraham (Quebec). P 12.*

514 **202** 5 c. deep green and red.. 15

203. **204.** Dollard des Ormeaux.

(Des. Helen Fitzgerald.)

1960 (20 Apr.). *Golden Jubilee of Canadian Girl Guides Movement. P 12.*

515 **203** 5 c. ultram. & orge.-brn. 15

(Des. P. Weiss.)

1960 (19 May). *Tercentenary of Battle of the Long Sault. P 12.*

516 **204** 5 c. ultram. & lt. brown.. 15

205. Surveyor, Bulldozer and Compass Rose. **206.** E. Pauline Johnson.

(Des. B. J. Reddie.)

1961 (8 Feb.). *Northern Development. P 12.*

517 **205** 5 c. emerald and red .. 15 5

(Des. B. J. Reddie.)

1961 (10 Mar.). *Centenary of Birth of E. Pauline Johnson (Mohawk poetess). P 12.*

518 **206** 5 c. green and red .. 15 5

207. Arthur Meighen (statesman).

61 (19 Apr.). *Arthur Meighen Commemoration.* P 12.
9 **207** 5 c. ultramarine 15 5

208. Engineers and Dam.

(Des. B. J. Reddie.)

61 (28 June). *Tenth Anniv. of Colombo Plan.* P 12.
0 **208** 5 c. blue and brown .. 15 5

09. " Resources for Tomorrow ".

210. " Education ".

(Des. A. L. Pollock.)

61 (12 Oct.). *Natural Resources.* P 12.
21 **209** 5 c. blue-green and brown 15 5

(Des. Helen Fitzgerald.)

962 (28 Feb.). *Education Year.* P 12.
22 **210** 5 c. black and orge.-brown 15 5

211. Lord Selkirk and Farmer.

(Des. Phillips-Gutkin Ltd.)

962 (3 May). *150th Anniv. of Red River Settlement.* P 12.
23 **211** 5 c. chocolate and green .. 15 5

12. Talon bestowing fts on married couple.

213. Br. Columbia & Vancouver Is. 2½d. stamp of 1860, and Parliament Buildings, B.C.

(Des. P. Weiss.)

962 (13 June). *Jean Talon Commemoration.* P 12.
24 **212** 5 c. blue 15 5

(Des. Helen Bacon.)

1962 (22 Aug.). *Centenary of Victoria, B.C.* P 12.
525 **213** 5 c. red and black .. 15 5

214. Highway (map version) and Provincial Arms.

(Des. A. L. Pollock.)

1962 (31 Aug.). *Opening of Trans-Canada Highway.* P 12.
526 **214** 5 c. black & orange-brn. 15 5

215. Queen Elizabeth II.

(From drawing by Ernst Roch.)

1962–64. *T* **215** *and similar horiz. designs with different symbols at top left.* (*i*) P 12.
527 1 c. chocolate (4.2.63) .. 5 5
a. Booklet pane. Five stamps plus one ptd. label (15.5.63) .. 1·25 1·25
p. Two phosphor bands (15.5.63) 12 12
528 2 c. green (2.5.63) 5 5
a. Pack. Two blocks of 25 .. 3·00
p. Two phosphor bands (15.5.63) .. 12 12
529 3 c. reddish violet† (2.5.63) .. 10 5
p. Two phosphor bands (15.5.63) .. 12 12
530 4 c. carmine-red (4.2.63) .. 10 5
a. Booklet pane. Five stamps plus one ptd. label (15.5.63) .. 2·00 2·00
b. Pack. One block of 25 .. 3·00
p. One centre phosphor band (*narrow*)* (2.63) 90 90
pa. One centre phosphor band (*wide*) (8.64) .. .. .. 2·25 2·25
pb. One side phosphor band (12.64) 30 30
531 5 c. ultramarine (3.10.62) .. 15 10
a. Booklet pane. Five stamps plus one ptd. label ('63) .. 2·00 2·00
b. Pack. One block of 20 .. 3·00
c. Imperf. horiz. (vert. pair) ..
p. Two phosphor bands (31.1.63.?) 15 12
pa. Pack. One block of 20 .. 3·50
(*ii*) *P* 9½ × *imperf.* (*coil stamps*).
532 2 c. green ('63) 40 40
532*a* 3 c. reddish violet ('64) .. 20 20
533 4 c. carmine-red (15.5.63) .. 30 20
534 5 c. ultramarine (15.5.63) .. 30 10

Symbols :—1 c. Crystals (Mining); 2 c. Tree (Forestry); 3 c. Fish (Fisheries); 4 c. Electricity pylon (Industrial power); 5 c. Wheat (Agriculture).

Nos. 528a, 530b, 531b and 531pa are blocks with the outer edges imperf. These come from " One Dollar Plastic Packages " sold at post offices.

†This is a fugitive colour which tends to become reddish on drying. In successive printings the violet colour became more and more reddish as the printer tried to match the shade of each previous printing instead of referring back to the original shade. A deep reddish violet is also known from Plate 3. As there is such a range of shades it is not practical to list them.

*On No. 530p the band is 4 mm. wide as against 8 mm. on No. 530pa. No. 530pb exists with the band at either left or right side of the stamp, the bands being applied across alternate vertical perforations.

216. Sir Casimir Gzowski.

(Des. P. Weiss.)

1963 (5 Mar.). *150th Birth Anniv. of Gzowski (engineer).* P 12.
535 **216** 5 c. reddish purple .. 15 5

217. " Export Trade ".

(Des. A. L. Pollock.)

1963 (14 June). P 12.
536 **217** $1 carmine .. .. 18·00 1·50

218. Frobisher and barque *Gabriel.*

(Des. P. Weiss.)

1963 (21 Aug.). *Sir Martin Frobisher Commemoration.* P 12.
537 **218** 5 c. ultramarine 20 5

219. Horseman and Map.

(Des. B. J. Reddie.)

1963 (25 Sept.). *Bicentenary of Quebec-Trois-Rivieres-Montreal Postal Service.* P 12.
538 **219** 5 c. red-brown & dp. grn. 15 5

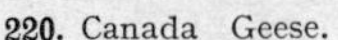

220. Canada Geese.

221. Jet Airliner (composite) and Uplands Airport, Ottawa.

(Des. A. Shortt and P. Arthur.)

1963 (30 Oct.). *P* 12.

539 **220** 15 c. blue .. .. .. 1·40 15

1964. *P* 12.

540 **221** 7 c. blue (11 Mar.) .. 20 20

540*a* „ 8 c. blue (18 Nov.) .. 20 20

222. "Peace on Earth".

1964 (8 Apr.). "*Peace*". *Litho. and recess. P* 12.

541 **222** 5 c. ochre, blue and turquoise-blue 15 5

223. Maple Leaves.

1964 (14 May). "*Canadian Unity*". *P* 12.

542 **223** 5 c. lake-red & light blue 15 8

224. White Trillium and Arms of Ontario.

225. Madonna Lily and Arms of Quebec.

226. Purple Violet and Arms of New Brunswick.

227. Mayflower and Arms of Nova Scotia.

228. Dogwood and Arms of British Columbia.

229. Prairie Crocus and Arms of Manitoba.

230. Lady's Slipper and Arms of Prince Edward Island.

231. Wild Rose and Arms of Alberta.

232. Prairie Lily and Arms of Saskatchewan.

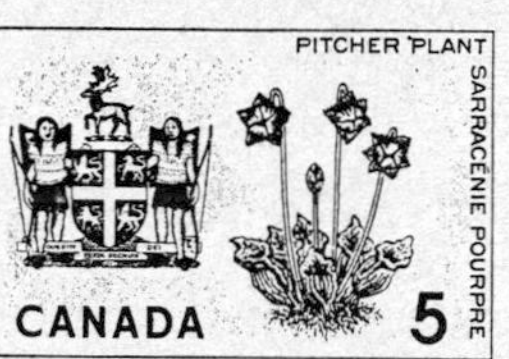

233. Pitcher Plant and Arms of Newfoundland.

234. Mountain Avens and Arms of Northwest Territories.

235. Fireweed and Arms of Yukon Territory

236. Maple Leaf and Arms of Canada.

1964–66. *Provincial Emblems. Recess* (*No.* 555) *or litho. and recess* (*others*). *P* 12.

543 **224** 5 c. green, brown & orange (30.6.64) 20 8

544 **225** 5 c. green, orange-brown and yellow (30.6.64) .. 20 8

545 **226** 5 c. carmine-red, green & bluish violet (3.2.65) 20 8

546 **227** 5 c. bl., red & grn. (3.2.65) 20 8

547 **228** 5 c. purple, green and yellow-brown (28.4.65) 20 8

548 **229** 5 c. red-brown, dp. bluish grn. & mauve (28.4.65) 20 8

549 **230** 5 c. slate-lilac, grn. & lt. reddish pur. (21.7.65) 20 8

550 **231** 5 c. green, yellow and rose-red (19.1.66) .. 20 [illegible]

551 **232** 5 c. sepia, orange and green (19.1.66) .. 20 8

552 **233** 5 c. black, green and red (23.2.66) 20 8

553 **234** 5 c. drab, green and yellow (23.3.66) 20 8

554 **235** 5 c. blue, green and rose-red (23.3.66) 20 8

555 **236** 5 c. red and blue (30.6.66) 20 8

543/55 .. .. *Set of* 13 2·25 90

(**237**)

238. Fathers of the Confederation Memorial, Charlottetown.

1964 (15 July). *No.* 540 *surch. with T* **237.**

556 **221** 8 c. on 7 c. blue 25 20

(Des. P. Weiss.)

1964 (29 July). *Centenary of Charlottetown Conference. P* 12.

557 **238** 5 c. black 15 5

239. Maple Leaf and Hand with Quill Pen.

(Des. P. Weiss.)

1964 (9 Sept.). *Centenary of Quebec Conference. P* 12.

558 **239** 5 c. light red & chocolate 15 5

240. Queen Elizabeth II.

241. " Canadian Family ".

(Portrait by Anthony Buckley.)

1964 (5 Oct.). *Royal Visit.* P 12.
559 240 5 c. reddish purple .. 15 5

1964 (14 Oct.). *Christmas.* P 12.
560 241 3 c. scarlet 12 5
a. Pack. Two blocks of 25 .. 4·00
p. Two phosphor bands .. 40 30
pa. Pack. Two blocks of 25 .. 9·00
561 „ 5 c. ultramarine 15 8
p. Two phosphor bands .. 1·75 1·75

Nos. 560a and 560pa are blocks with the outer edges imperf. These come from " $1.50 Plastic Packages " sold at post offices.

242. " Co-operation ".

1965 (3 Mar.). *International Co-operation Year.* P 12.
562 242 5 c. grey-green 15 8

243. Sir W. Grenfell.

1965 (9 June). *Birth Centenary of Sir Wilfred Grenfell (missionary).* P 12.
563 243 5 c. deep bluish green .. 15 5

244. National Flag.

1965 (30 June). *Inauguration of National Flag.* P 12.
564 244 5 c. red and blue .. 15 5

245. Sir Winston Churchill.

246. Peace Tower, Parliament Buildings, Ottawa.

(Des. P. Weiss from photo by Karsh. Litho.)

1965 (12 Aug.). *Churchill Commemoration.* P 12.
565 245 5 c. purple-brown .. 15 8

(Des. Philips-Gutkin.)

1965 (8 Sept.). *Inter-Parliamentary Union Conference, Ottawa.* P 12.
566 246 5 c. deep green 15 8

247. Parliament Buildings, Ottawa, 1865.

(Des. G. Trottier.)

1965 (8 Sept.). *Centenary of Proclamation of Ottawa as Capital.* P 12.
567 247 5 c. brown 15 5

248. " Gold, Frankincense and Myrrh ".

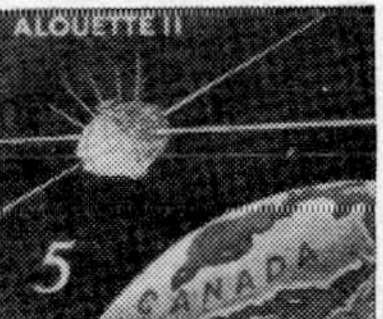

249. " Alouette 2 " over Canada.

(Des. Helen Fitzgerald.)

1965 (13 Oct.). *Christmas.* P 12.
568 248 3 c. olive-green 10 5
a. Pack. Two blocks of 25 3·00
p. Two phosphor bands .. 12 12
pa. Pack. Two blocks of 25 4·00
569 „ 5 c. ultramarine 15 5
p. Two phosphor bands .. 20 15

Nos. 568a and 568pa are blocks with the outer edges imperf. These come from " $1.50 Plastic Packages " sold at post offices.

1966 (5 Jan.). *Launching of Canadian Satellite, " Alouette 2 ".* P 12.
570 249 5 c. ultramarine 15 5

250. La Salle.

251. Road Signs.

(Des. Brigdens Ltd., Toronto.)

1966 (13 Apr.). *300th Anniv. of La Salle's Arrival in Canada.* P 12.
571 250 5 c. deep bluish green .. 15 5

(Des. Helen Fitzgerald.)

1966 (2 May). *Highway Safety. Invisible gum.* P 12.
572 251 5 c. yellow, blue and black 15 5

252. Canadian Delegation and Houses of Parliament.

(Des. P. Pederson (Brigdens Ltd.).)

1966 (26 May). *London Conference Centenary.* P 12.
573 252 5 c. red-brown 15 5

253. Douglas Point Nuclear Power Station.

(Des. A. L. Pollock.)

1966 (27 July). *Peaceful Uses of Atomic Energy.* P 12.
574 253 5 c. ultramarine 15 5

254. Parliamentary Library, Ottawa.

255. " Hands in Prayer", after Dürer.

(Des. Brigdens Ltd.)

1966 (8 Sept.). *Commonwealth Parliamentary Association Conference, Ottawa.* P 12.
575 254 5 c. purple 15 5

(Des. G. Holloway.)

1966 (12 Oct.). *Christmas.* P 12.
576 255 3 c. carmine 8 5
a. Pack. Two blocks of 25 3·00
p. Two phosphor bands .. 10 10
pa. Pack. Two blocks of 25 4·00
577 „ 5 c. orange 15 5
p. Two phosphor bands .. 15 15

Nos. 576a and 576pa are blocks with the outer edges imperf. These come from " $1.50 Plastic Packages " sold at post offices.

256. Flag and Canada on Globe.

(Des. Brigdens Ltd.)

1967 (11 Jan.). *Canadian Centennial. Invisible gum.* P 12.
578 256 5 c. scarlet and blue .. 15 8
p. Two phosphor bands .. 20 20

257. Northern Lights and Dog-team.

258. Totem Pole.

259. Combine-harvester and Oil Derrick.

260. Ship in Lock.

261. Harbour Scene.

261*a*. "Transport".

261*b*. Library of Parliament.

262. "Alaska Highway" (A. Y. Jackson).

263. "The Jack Pine" (T. Thomson).

264. "Bylot Island" (L. Harris).

265. "Quebec Ferry" (J. W. Morrice).

266. "The Solemn Land" (J.E.H. MacDonald).

267. "Summer's Stores" (Grain elevators, J. Ensor).

268. "Oilfield" (near Edmonton, H. G. Glyde).

1967 (8 Feb.)–72.

A. *Recess Canadian Bank Note Co.*

(i) *P* 12.

579 **257** 1 c. brown 5 5
- a. Booklet pane. Five stamps plus one printed label (2.67) 20
- p. Two phosphor bands 20 15
- pa. Centre phosphor band (12.68) 12 10

580 **258** 2 c. green 5 5
- b. Booklet pane. No. 580×4 *se-tenant* with No. 581×4 with gutter margin between (26.10.70) .. .. 1·00
- p. Two phosphor bands 20 12
- pa. Centre phosphor band (12.68) 10 10

581 **259** 3 c. slate-purple .. 8 5
- p. Two phosphor bands 15 15

582 **260** 4 c. red 10 5
- a. Booklet pane. Five stamps plus one printed label (2.67) 70
- b. Pack. One block of 25 (2.67) .. .. 8·00
- p. One side phosphor band 20 12
- pa. Centre phosphor band (3.69) 12 10

583 **261** 5 c. blue 8 5
- a. Booklet pane. Five stamps plus one printed label (3.67) .. .. 2·50
- b. Pack. One block of 20 (2.67) .. .. 13·00
- p. Two phosphor bands 25 15
- pa. Pack. One block of 20 (2.67) .. .. 25·00
- pb. Centre phosphor band (12.68) 15 12

583*c* **261*a*** 6 c. black (2.72) .. 12 5
- cp. Centre phosphor band (2.72) 20 10

584 **262** 8 c. purple-brown .. 15 5

585 **263** 10 c. olive-green .. 15 5
- p. Two phosphor bands (9.12.69) 40 25

586 **264** 15 c. dull purple .. 25 8
- p. Two phosphor bands (9.12.69) 45 35

587 **265** 20 c. deep blue 35 10
- p. Two phosphor bands (9.12.69) 45 35

588 **266** 25 c. myrtle-green .. 50 10
- p. Two phosphor bands (9.12.69) .. .. 1·00 70

589 **267** 50 c. cinnamon .. .. 1·00 20

590 **268** $1 scarlet .. .. 3·50 50

579/90 .. .. *Set of* 13 5·50 2·00

579p/588p .. .. *Set of* 10 3·00 2·00

(ii) *Perf.* 9½ × *imperf.* (*coil stamps*).

591 **259** 3 c. slate-purple (3.67) 20 15

592 **260** 4 c. red (3.67) 35 15

593 **261** 5 c. blue (2.67) .. 35 15

(iii) *Perf.* 10 × *imperf.* (*coil stamps*).

594 **261*a*** 6 c. orange-red (1.69) .. 15 10
- a. Imperf. (vert. pair) .. £150

595 „ 6 c. black (8.70) .. 15 8

596 „ 7 c. green (30.6.71) .. 20 10

597 **261*b*** 8 c. black (30.12.71) .. 15 8

B. *Recess British American Bank Note Co.*

(i) *P* 10 (*sheets* (601/*p*) *or booklets*).

598 **257** 1 c. brown (9.68) .. 12 5
- a. Booklet pane. No. 598 ×5 *se-tenant* with No. 599×5 (9.68) 75
- b. Booklet pane. No. 601 ×4 *se-tenant* with No. 598 plus one printed label (11.68) 90

599 **260** 4 c. red (6.68) 15 10
- a. Booklet pane. 25 stamps plus two printed labels 4·00

600 **261** 5 c. blue (9.68) 10 8

601 **261*a*** 6 c. orange-red (1.11.68) 20 10
- a. Booklet pane. 25 stamps plus two printed labels (1.69) .. .. 7·00
- p. Two phosphor bands (1.11.68) 30 20

602 „ 6 c. black (1.70) .. 40 15
- a. Booklet pane. 25 stamps plus two printed labels 10·00

603 „ 6 c. black (*re-engraved die*) (8.70) 50 30
- a. Booklet pane of 4 .. 2·50

(ii) *P* 12½ × 12 (*sheets* (606/10) *or booklets*).

604 **257** 1 c. brown (30.6.71) .. 8 8
- a. Booklet pane. Nos. 604 ×4, 605×4 and 609 ×12 *se-tenant* .. 3·00
- b. Booklet pane. No. 604 ×3, No. 608 and No. 610×2 *se-tenant* (30.12.71) 70
- c. Booklet pane. No. 604×6, No. 608 and No. 610×11 (*se-tenant*) (30.12.71) .. 2·75
- d. Booklet pane. No. 604, No. 605 and No. 609×3 *se-tenant* plus one printed label 90
- e. Booklet pane. No. 604× 4, No. 608 and No. 610×5 *se-tenant* (8.72) 1·00

605 **259** 3 c. slate-purple (30.6.71) 25 12

606 **261*a*** 6 c. orange-red (3.69) .. 15 5
- p. Two phosphor bands .. 25 20

607 „ 6 c. black (7.1.70) .. 15 5
- a. Booklet pane. 25 stamps plus two printed labels (8.70) .. .. 9·00
- p. Two phosphor bands .. 20 12

608 „ 6 c. black (*re-engraved die*) (9.70) 12 5
- a. Booklet pane of 4 (11.70) 2·00
- p. One centre phosphor band (9.71) 20 12

609 „ 7 c. myrtle-grn. (30.6.71) 12 5
- p. Two phosphor bands 25 15

610 **261*b*** 8 c. slate-black (30.12.71) 12 5
- p. Two phosphor bands .. 20 12

Nos. 582b, 583b and 583pa are blocks with the outer edges imperf. These come from "One Dollar Plastic Packages" sold at post offices.

No. 582p comes with the band to the left or right of the stamp, the phosphor having been applied across alternate vertical perforations.

Normal.

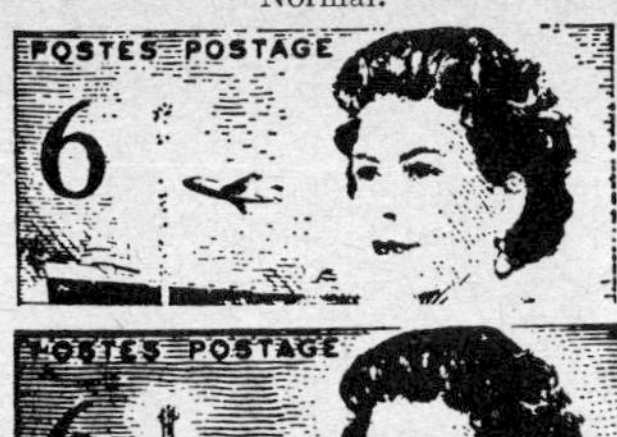

Re-engraved.

When the basic postal rate was changed to 6 c. :he C.B.N. lent their die to B.A.B.N. who made a luplicate die from it by transfer. Parts of this proved to be weak, but it was used for Nos. 601/2 and 606/7. B.A.B.N. later re-engraved their die to make fresh plates which were used for Nos. 603 and 608. No. 608 first appeared on heets from Plate 4.

There are no records of dates of issue of the booklets, packs and coils, but supplies of these were distributed to depots in the months ndicated.

MPERF. BETWEEN PAIRS FROM COIL STAMPS. Nos. 595/6 (and possibly others) are known in blocks or horizontal pairs imperf. between vertically. Coils are supplied to post offices in batches of ten coils held together by roulettes between every fourth stamp so that they can easily be split apart. If two or more unsplit coils are purchased it is possible to obtain blocks or pairs imperf. between vertically.

Vertical coil stamps are also known imperf. between horizontally or with some stamps apparently completely imperf. These can result from blind perforations identifiable by slight indentations.

WHITE FLUORESCENT PAPER. Different papers with varying degrees of whiteness have been used for Canadian stamps, but during 1968–70 a distinctive very white and highly fluorescent paper was used known as "hybrite"; this fluoresces on the back and front. This paper has also been employed for commemorative issues, some of which exist on more than one type of paper. The white fluorescent papers are recorded in the Stanley Gibbons *Elizabethan Catalogue.*

FLUORESCENT BANDS. During the second half of 1971 new sorting machines were installed in the Ottawa area which were activated by stamps bearing fluorescent bands. These differ from the Winnipeg phosphor bands in that there is no after-glow and they are hardly visible to the naked eye and so can only be distinguished by using an ultra-violet lamp. For this reason they are outside the scope of this catalogue but instead are recorded in footnotes. They are, however, fully listed in the Stanley Gibbons *Elizabethan Catalogue.*

In the 1967–72 definitive issue fluorescent bands occur on some printings of Nos. 579, 580, 581, 582, 583*c*, 585, 586, 597, 604, 608 and 610.

The experiments were successful and what was at first called "Ottawa tagging" has since come into more general use and the Winnipeg phosphor was phased out. However, the substance at first used (known as OP–4) was found to migrate to envelopes, documents, album pages, etc. as well as to adjoining stamps. Late in 1972 this fault was cured by using another substance (called OP–2). The migrating bands were used on early printings of Nos. 604, 608 and 610 as well as certain stamps referred to in a footnote after No. 692. It is most advisable to use plastic mounts for housing stamps with migrating bands or else clear acetate should be affixed to the album leaves, such as is used in the Stanley Gibbons Stock Album.

269. Canadian Pavilion.

(Des. Canadian Bank Note Co., Ottawa.)

1967 (28 Apr.). *World Fair, Montreal.* *P* 12.
611 **269** 5 c. blue and red .. 12 5

270. Allegory of "Womanhood" on Ballot-box.

271. Queen Elizabeth II and Centennial Emblem.

(Des. Helen Fitzgerald. Litho.)

1967 (24 May). *50th Anniv. of Women's Franchise.* *P* 12.
612 **270** 5 c. reddish purple & black 12 5

(Portrait from photo by Anthony Buckley.)

1967 (30 June). *Royal Visit.* *P* 12.
613 **271** 5 c. plum & orange-brown 12 5

272. Athlete.

(Des. Brigdens Ltd.)

1967 (19 July). *Fifth Pan-American Games, Winnipeg.* *P* 12.
614 **272** 5 c. rose-red 12 5

273. "World News".

(Des. W. McLauchlan.)

1967 (31 Aug.). *50th Anniv. of the Canadian Press.* *P* 12.
615 **273** 5 c. blue 12 5

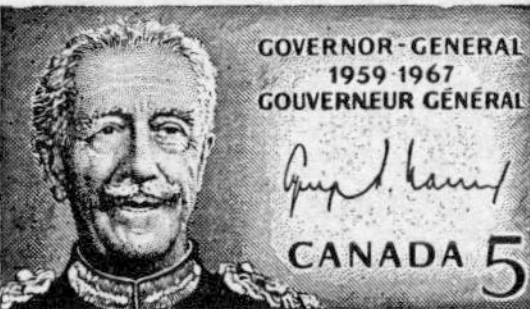

274. Governor-General Vanier.

(Des. from photo by Karsh.)

1967 (15 Sept.). *Vanier Commemoration.* *P* 12.
616 **274** 5 c. black 12 5

PRINTERS. The following were printed either by the Canadian Bank Note Co., Ottawa (C.B.N.) or the British American Bank Note Co., Ottawa (B.A.B.N.), *except where otherwise stated.*

275. People of 1867 and Toronto, 1967.

(Des. and recess C.B.N.)

1967 (28 Sept.). *Centenary of Toronto as Capital City of Ontario.* *P* 12.
617 **275** 5 c. myrtle-grn. & verm. 12 5

276. Carol Singers.

CANADA

5

277. Grey Jays.

(Des. and recess. B.A.B.N.)

1967 (11 Oct.). *Christmas.* *P* 12.
618 **276** 3 c. scarlet 10 5
a. Pack. Two blocks of 25 3·00
p. Two phosphor bands .. 12 8
pa. Pack. Two blocks of 25 3·75
619 ,, 5 c. emerald-green .. 12 5
p. Two phosphor bands .. 15 8

Nos. 618a and 618pa are blocks with the outer edges imperf. These come from "$1.50 Plastic Packs" sold at post offices.

(Des. M. G. Loates. Litho. C.B.N.)

1968 (15 Feb.). *Wild Life.* *P* 12.
620 **277** 5 c. multicoloured .. 20 10

See also Nos. 638/40.

278. Weather Map and Instruments.

(Des. and litho. B.A.B.N.)

1968 (13 Mar.). *200th Anniv. of First Meteorological Readings.* *P* 11.
621 **278** 5 c. multicoloured .. 12 5

279. Narwhal.

(Des. J. A. Crosby. Litho. B.A.B.N.)

1968 (10 Apr.). *Wildlife.* *P* 11.
622 **279** 5 c. multicoloured .. 12 5

No. 622 has a background of yellow-green and pale blue but copies are known with the yellow-green apparently missing. This " yellow-green " is produced by an overlay of yellow on the blue but we have not come across any copies where the yellow is completely missing and the wide range of colour variation is due to technical difficulties in maintaining an exact blend of the two colours.

280. Globe, Maple Leaf and Rain Gauge.

(Des. I. von Mosdossy. Litho. B.A.B.N.)

1968 (8 May). *International Hydrological Decade.* *P* 11.
623 **280** 5 c. multicoloured .. 12 5

IMPERF. EDGES On Nos 624/54, 657 and 659 (stamps printed by the B.A.B.N. Co.) the outer edges of the sheets were guillotined to remove the imprints for P.O. stock so that single stamps may, therefore, be found with either one, or two adjacent sides imperforate.

281. *Nonsuch.*

(Recess and photo. B.A.B.N.)

1968 (5 June). *300th Anniv. of Voyage of the " Nonsuch ".* *P* 10.
624 **281** 5 c. multicoloured .. 12 5

282. Lacrosse Players.

(Des. J. E. Aldridge. Recess and photo. B.A.B.N.)

1968 (3 July). *Lacrosse.* *P* 10.
625 **282** 5 c. blk., red and lemon 12 5

283. Front page of *The Globe,* George Brown and Legislative Building.

(Des. N. Sabolotny. Recess and photo. B.A.B.N.)

1968 (21 Aug.). *150th Birth Anniv. of George Brown (politician and journalist).* *P* 10.
626 **283** 5 c. multicoloured .. 12 5

284. H. Bourassa.

286. Armistice Monument, Vimy.

285. John McCrae, Battlefield and First Lines of " In Flanders Fields ".

(Des. and recess and litho. C.B.N.)

1968 (4 Sept.). *Birth Centenary of Henri Bourassa (journalist and politician).* *P* 12.
627 **284** 5 c. blk., red & pale cream 12 5

(Des. I. von Mosdossy. Litho. C.B.N.)

1968 (15 Oct.). *50th Death Anniv. of John McCrae (soldier and poet).* *P* 12.
628 **285** 5 c. multicoloured .. 12 5

(Des. and recess. C.B.N.)

1968 (15 Oct.). *50th Anniversary of 1918 Armistice.* *P* 12.
629 **286** 15 c. slate-black 40 35

287. Eskimo Family (carving).

288. " Mother and Child " (carving).

(Designs from Eskimo carvings by Munamee (6 c.) and unknown carver (5 c.). Photo. C.B.N.)

1968. *Christmas.* *P* 12.
630 **287** 5 c. black and new blue (1.11.68) 10 5
a. Booklet pane of 10 .. 1·75
p. One centre phosphor band 15 12
pa. Booklet pane of 10 .. 2·00

631 **288** 6 c. black and ochre (15.11.68) 15
p. Two phosphor bands .. 20 1

289. Curling.

(Des. D. Eales. Recess and photo. B.A.B.N.)

1969 (15 Jan.). *Curling.* *P* 10.
632 **289** 6 c. blk., new bl. & scar. 15

290. Vincent Massey.

292. Globe and Tools.

291. " Return from the Harvest Field " (Suzor-Côté).

(Des. I. von Mosdossy. Recess and litho C.B.N.)

1969 (20 Feb.) *Vincent Massey, First Canadian born Governor-General.* *P* 12.
633 **290** 6 c. sepia & yellow-ochre 10

(Photo. C.B.N.)

1969 (14 Mar.). *Birth Centenary of Auréle d Foy Suzor-Côté (painter).* *P* 12.
634 **291** 50 c. multicoloured .. 90 7

(Des. J. Hébert. Recess. B.A.B.N.)

1969 (21 May). *50th Anniv. of Internationa Labour Organization.* *P* 12½×12.
635 **292** 6 c. bronze-green .. 10

293. Vickers " Vimy " Aircraft over Atlantic Ocean.

(Des. R. W. Bradford. Recess and photo B.A.B.N.)

1969 (13 June). *50th Anniv. of First Non-sto Transatlantic Flight.* *P* 12×12½.
636 **293** 15 c. chocolate, bright grn. and pale blue .. 40 3

294. Sir William Osler. **295.** White-throated Sparrows.

296. Ipswich Sparrow. (*Horiz.*)
297. Hermit Thrush. (*Horiz.*)

(Des., recess and photo. B.A.B.N.)

969 (23 JUNE). *50th Death Anniv. of Sir William Osler (physician).* P $12\frac{1}{2}\times 12$.
37 **294** 6 c. deep blue, light blue and chestnut .. 10 5

(Des. M. G. Loates. Litho. C.B.N.)

969 (23 JULY). *Birds.* P 12.
38 **295** 6 c. multicoloured .. 12 8
39 **296** 10 c. multicoloured .. 30 20
40 **297** 25 c. multicoloured .. 55 50

298. Flags of Winter and Summer Games. **300.** Sir Isaac Brock and Memorial Column.

299. Outline of Prince Edward Island showing Charlottetown.

Des. C. McDiarmid. Recess and litho. C.B.N.)

969 (15 AUG.). *Canadian Games.* P 12.
41 **298** 6 c. emer., scarlet & blue 10 5

Des. L. Fitzgerald. Recess and photo. B.A.B.N.)

969 (15 AUG.). *Bicentenary of Charlottetown as Capital of Prince Edward Island.* P $12\times 12\frac{1}{2}$.
42 **299** 6 c. yell.-brn., blk. & blue 10 5

Des. I. von Mosdossy. Recess and litho. C.B.N.)

969 (12 SEPT.). *Birth Bicentenary of Sir Isaac Brock.* P 12.
43 **300** 6 c. orange, bistre and bistre-brown .. 10 5

301. Children of the World in Prayer.

(Des. Rapid Grip and Batten Ltd. Litho. C.B.N.)

1969 (8 OCT.). *Christmas.* P 12.
644 **301** 5 c. multicoloured .. 10 5
a. Booklet pane of 10 .. 1·00
p. One centre phosphor band 15 12
pa. Booklet pane of 10 .. 1·40
645 ,, 6 c. multicoloured .. 10 5
a. Black (inscr. value and frame) omitted .. £1000
p. Two phosphor bands .. 15 12

302. Stephen Butler Leacock, Mask and "Mariposa".

(Des., recess and photo. B.A.B.N.)

1969 (12 NOV.). *Birth Centenary of Stephen Butler Leacock (humorist).* P $12\times 12\frac{1}{2}$.
646 **302** 6 c. multicoloured .. 10 5

303. Symbolic Cross-roads.

(Des. K. C. Lochhead. Litho. C.B.N.)

1970 (27 JAN.). *Centenary of Manitoba.* P 12.
647 **303** 6 c. ultramarine, lemon and vermilion .. 10 8
p. Two phosphor bands .. 20 15

304. "Enchanted Owl" (Kenojuak).

(Des. N. E. Hallendy and Miss S. Van Raalte. Recess. C.B.N.)

1970 (27 JAN.). *Centenary of Northwest Territories.* P 12.
648 **304** 6 c. carmine-red & black 10 5

305. Microscopic View of Inside of Leaf.

(Des. I. Charney. Recess and photo. B.A.B.N.)

1970 (18 FEB.). *International Biological Programme.* P $12\times 12\frac{1}{2}$.
649 **305** 6 c. emerald, orange-yellow and ultramarine 10 5

306. Expo '67 Emblem and Stylized Cherry Blossom.

307. Dogwood.
308. White Trillium.
309. White Garden Lily.

(Des. E. R. C. Bethune. Litho. C.B.N.)

1970 (18 MAR.). *World Fair, Osaka. Stylised Cherry Blossom in colour given in brackets.* P 12.
650 **306** 25 c. multicoloured (*Red*) 85 70
p. Two phosphor bands .. 1·00 85
651 **307** 25 c. mult. (*Violet*) .. 85 70
p. Two phosphor bands .. 1·00 85
652 **308** 25 c. multicoloured (*Green*) 85 70
p. Two phosphor bands .. 1·00 85
653 **309** 25 c. multicoloured (*Blue*) 85 70
p. Two phosphor bands .. 1·00 85

Nos. 650/3 and 650p/3p are printed together in sheets of 50 (5 × 10). In the first, second, fourth and fifth vertical rows the four different designs are arranged in *se-tenant* blocks, whilst the centre row is composed as follows (reading downwards:—650(p)/3(p), 650(p) × 2, 653(p), 652(p), 651(p) and 650(p).

310. Henry Kelsey.

(Des. D. Burton. Recess and photo. B.A.B.N.)

1970 (15 APR.). *300th Birth Anniv. of Henry Kelsey (explorer).* P $12\times 12\frac{1}{2}$.
654 **310** 6 c. multicoloured .. 10 5

311. "Towards Unification".

(Des. B. Fisher. Litho. B.A.B.N.)

1970 (13 MAY). *25th Anniv. of United Nations.* P 11.
655 **311** 10 c. blue 30 25
p. Two phosphor bands .. 40 35
656 ,, 15 c. magenta & bluish lilac 50 40
p. Two phosphor bands .. 65 50

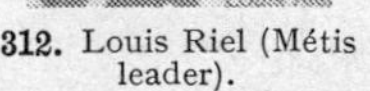

312. Louis Riel (Métis leader). **313.** Mackenzie's Inscription, Dean Channel.

(Des. R. Derreth. Photo. B.A.B.N.)

1970 (19 JUNE). *Louis Riel Commemoration.* P $12\frac{1}{2}\times 12$.
657 **312** 6c. greenish blue and vermilion 10 5

(Design from Government Archives photo. Recess. C.B.N.)

1970 (25 June). *Sir Alexander Mackenzie (explorer). P* 12 × 11½.

658	**313**	6 c. bistre-brown ..	10	5

314. Sir Oliver Mowat (statesman).

(Des. E. Roch. Recess and photo. B.A.B.N.)

1970 (12 Aug.). *Sir Oliver Mowat Commemoration. P* 12.

659	**314**	6 c. vermilion and black	10	5

315. " Isles of Spruce " (A. Lismer).

(Litho. Ashton-Potter, Toronto.)

1970 (18 Sept.). *50th Anniv. of " Group of Seven " (artists). P* 11.

660	**315**	6 c. multicoloured ..	10	5

316. " Horse-drawn Sleigh" (D. Niskala).

317. " Stable and Star of Bethlehem " (L. Wilson).
318. " Snowmen " (M. Lecompte).
319. " Skiing " (D. Durham).
320. " Santa Claus " (A. Martin).
321. " Santa Claus " (E. Bhattacharya).
322. " Christ in Manger " (J. McKinney).
323. " Toy Shop " (N. Whateley).
324. " Christmas Tree " (J. Pomperleau).
325. " Church " (J. McMillan).

326. " Christ in Manger " (C. Fortier).

327. " Trees and Sledge " (J. Dojcak).

(Des. from children's drawings. Litho. C.B.N.)

1970 (7 Oct.). *Christmas. P* 12.

661	**316**	5 c. multicoloured ..	12	5
		p. One centre phosphor band	12	8
662	**317**	5 c. multicoloured ..	12	5
		p. One centre phosphor band	12	8
663	**318**	5 c. multicoloured ..	12	5
		p. One centre phosphor band	12	8
664	**319**	5 c. multicoloured ..	12	5
		p. One centre phosphor band	12	8
665	**320**	5 c. multicoloured ..	12	5
		p. One centre phosphor band	12	8
666	**321**	6 c. multicoloured ..	15	5
		p. Two phosphor bands ..	15	8
667	**322**	6 c. multicoloured ..	15	5
		p. Two phosphor bands ..	15	8
668	**323**	6 c. multicoloured ..	15	5
		p. Two phosphor bands ..	15	8
669	**324**	6 c. multicoloured ..	15	5
		p. Two phosphor bands ..	15	8
670	**325**	6 c. multicoloured ..	15	5
		p. Two phosphor bands ..	15	8
671	**326**	10 c. multicoloured ..	20	20
		p. Two phosphor bands ..	20	20
672	**327**	15 c. multicoloured ..	30	30
		p. Two phosphor bands ..	30	30
661/72		.. .. *Set of* 12	1·50	90
661p/672p		.. .. *Set of* 12	1·50	1·00

The designs of the 5 c. and 6 c. were each issued with the various designs *se-tenant* in a diamond shaped arrangement within the sheet. This generally results in *se-tenant* pairs both vert. and horiz., but due to the sheet arrangement vert. and horiz. pairs of the same design exist from the two centre vert. and horiz. rows.

328. Sir Donald A. Smith.

329. " Big Raven " (E. Carr).

(Des. Dora de Pédery-Hunt. Litho. C.B.N.)

1970 (4 Nov.). *150th Birth Anniv. of Sir Donald Alexander Smith. P* 12.

673	**328**	6 c. yellow, brown and bronze-green ..	10	5

(Litho. C.B.N.)

1971 (12 Feb.). *Birth Centenary of Emily Carr (painter). P* 12.

674	**329**	6 c. multicoloured ..	10	5

330. Laboratory Equipment.

332. Maple " Keys ".

331. " The Atom ".

(Des. R. Webber. Litho. B.A.B.N.)

1971 (3 Mar.). *50th Anniv. of Discovery of Insulin. P* 10½.

675	**330**	6 c. multicoloured ..	10

(Des. R. Webber. Litho. B.A.B.N.)

1971 (24 Mar.). *Birth Centenary of Sir Ernest Rutherford (scientist). P* 11.

676	**331**	6 c. yellow, red and deep chocolate	10

(Des. Alma Duncan. Litho. Ashton-Potter)

1971. *" The Maple Leaf in Four Seasons". T* **332** *and similar vert. designs. Multicoloured. P* 11.

677	6 c. Type **332** (Spring) (14.4)	15
	a. Imperf. (pair)	£500
678	6 c. Green leaves (Summer) (16.6)	15
679	7 c. Autumn leaves (3.9) ..	15
	a. Grey (inscr. and value) omitted	£1500
680	7 c. Withered leaves and snow (Winter) (19.11) ..	15

333. Louis Papineau.

335. " People " and Computer Tapes.

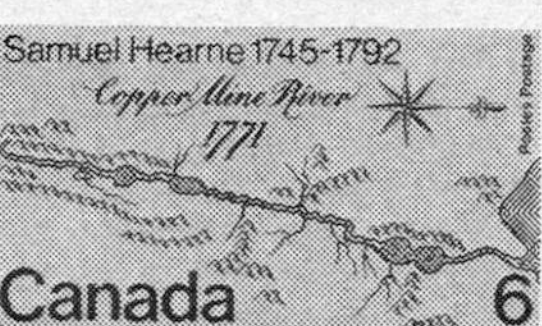

334. Chart of Coppermine River.

(Des. Laurent Marquart. Recess and photo B.A.B.N.)

1971 (7 May). *Death Centenary of Louis-Joseph Papineau (politician). P* 12½ × 12.

681	**333**	6 c. multicoloured ..	10

(Des. Laurent Marquart. Recess and photo B.A.B.N.)

1971 (7 May). *Bicentenary of Samuel Hearne's Expedition to Coppermine. P* 12 × 12½.

682	**334**	6 c. red, sepia & pale buff	10

(Des. H. Kleefeld. Litho. C.B.N.)

1971 (1 June). *Centennial of Census. P* 11½.

683	**335**	6 c. blue, red and black ..	10

336. Maple Leaves.

(Des. B. Kramer. Litho. C.B.N.)

1971 (1 JUNE). *Radio Canada International.* *P* 12.
684 **336** 15 c. red, yellow and black 45 35
p. Two phosphor bands .. 50 40

337. " B C ".

(Des. E. R. C. Bethune. Litho. C.B.N.)

1971 (20 JULY). *Centenary of British Columbia's Entry into the Confederation.* *P* 12.
685 **337** 7 c. multicoloured .. 10 8

338. " Indian Encampment on Lake Huron " (Kane).

(Des. and litho. B.A.B.N.)

1971 (11 AUG.). *Death Centenary of Paul Kane (painter).* *P* 12½.
686 **338** 7 c. multicoloured .. 15 10

339. " Snowflake ". **340.** Pierre Laporte (Quebec Cabinet Minister).

(Des. Lisl Levinsohn. Recess (6 c., 7 c.) or recess and litho (others). C.B.N.)

1971 (6 OCT.). *Christmas.* *T* **379** *and similar design.* *P* 12.
687 **339** 6 c. deep blue .. 10 5
p. One centre phosphor band 12 8
688 „ 7 c. deep emerald .. 10 5
p. Two phosphor bands.. 12 10
689 – 10 c. silver and cerise .. 15 12
p. Two phosphor bands .. 15 12
690 – 15 c. silver, brown-purple and lavender .. 25 20
p. Two phosphor bands .. 30 25

Design:—10 c., 15 c. " Snowflake " design similar to T **339** but square (26×26 mm.).

(Des. G. Gundersen. Recess and litho. B.A.B.N.)

1971 (20 OCT.). *First Anniv. of the Assassination of Pierre Laporte.* *P* 12½×12.
691 **340** 7 c. black/*pale buff* .. 10 8

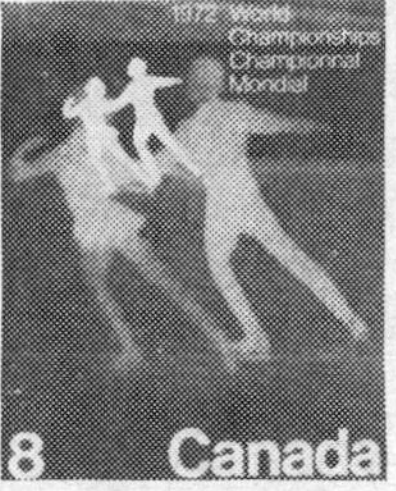

341. Skaters.

(Des. Design Workshop, Toronto. Litho. C.B.N.)

1972 (1 MAR.). *World Figure Skating Championships, Calgary.* *P* 11½×12.
692 **341** 8 c. purple 10 5

MIGRATING FLUORESCENT BANDS. These are referred to in the notes after No. 610. In the following issues they exist on Nos. 719/20 and 723/4 and on early printings only of Nos. 701/5.

342. J. A. MacDonald. **343.** Forest, Central Canada.

344. Vancouver.

(Des. D. Annesley (1 to 8 c.), R. Derreth (others). Recess. C.B.N. (1 to 6 c.). Recess B.A.B.N. (7 c., 8 c.). Recess and photo. B.A.B.N. (10 to 50 c. and No. 706). Recess B.A.B.N. and litho. Ashton-Potter (No. 708 and $2).)

1972–76. *Various designs as T* **342**/**4**.

(*a*) *Vert. as T* **342**. *Two fluorescent bands.* *P* 13 (10 *c.*) *or* 12×12½ (1 *to* 8 *c.*). (1 Oct. 1973).
693 1 c. orange 5 5
a. Booklet pane. No. 693×3, 698 and 700×2 *se-tenant* (10.4.74).. 30
b. Booklet pane. No. 693×6, 698 and 700×11 *se-tenant* (17.1.75) 1·25
c. No. 693×2, 694×4 and 701×4 *se-tenant* (1.9.76.) 50
694 2 c. deep green 5 5
695 3 c. agate 5 5
696 4 c. black 8 5
697 5 c. deep magenta 8 5
698 6 c. Indian red 5 5
699 7 c. reddish brown (8.4.74) .. 5 5
700 8 c dull ultramarine .. 5 8
701 10 c. brown-lake (1.9.76) .. 10 12

(*b*) *Vert. as T* **343** (10 *to* 50 *c.*) *or horiz., T* **344** ($1). *Two fluorescent bands.* *P* 12½×12 (8.9.72).
702 10 c. deep green, blue-green and yellow-orange .. 20 12
b. Perf. 13 (2.76) 10 8
p. Two phosphor bands .. 60 20
703 15 c. dull ultramarine and orange-brown 20 8
a. Perf. 13 (2.76) 15 8
p. Two phosphor bands .. 1·00 35
704 20 c. pale orange, reddish violet and ultramarine.. 30 10
a. Perf. 13 (2.76) 20 8
p. Two phosphor bands .. 1·25 40
705 25 c. deep ultramarine and pale blue.. .. .. 35 10
a. Perf. 13 (2.76) 25 10
p. Two phosphor bands .. 2·00 50
706 50 c. blue-green, Royal blue and buff (*shades*) 80 12
b. Perf. 13 (2.76) 50 50
707 $1 multicoloured (1973) .. 1·10 75

(*c*) *Horiz. as T* **344**. *No fluorescent bands.* *P* 11 (17.3.72).
709 $1 multicoloured .. .. 2·50 1·10
710 $2 multicoloured .. .. 2·10 1·25
693/710 .. .. *Set of* 17 6·50 4·00

(*d*) *As Nos.* 700/1. *Imperf*×*perf.* 10 (*coil stamps*).
711 8 c. dull ultramarine (10.4.74) 5 8
712 10 c. brown-lake (1.9.76) .. 10 12

Designs (1 to 7 c. show Canadian Prime Ministers): 1 c. Type **342**; 2 c. W. Laurier; 3 c. R. Borden; 4 c. W. L. Mackenzie King; 5 c. R. B. Bennett; 6 c. L. B. Pearson; 7 c. Louis St. Laurent; 8 and 10 c. (No. 701), Queen Elizabeth II; 10 c. (No. 702), Type **343**; 15 c. Mountain sheep; 20 c. Prairie landscape from the air; 25 c. Polar Bears; 50 c. Seashore; $1 Type **344**; $2 Quebec.

345. Heart.

1972 (7 APR.). *Heart Disease (World Health Day).* *P* 12×12½.
719 **345** 8 c. carmine 10 5

This stamp exists on two kinds of paper, with or without fluorescent bands.

346. Frontenac and Fort Saint-Louis, Quebec.

(Des. L. Marquart. Recess and photo. B.A.B.N.)

1972 (17 May). *300th Anniv. of Governor Frontenac's Appointment to New France. P 12×12½.*

720 **346** 8 c. brown-red, orange-brown and deep ultramarine .. 10 8

This exists with or without fluorescent bands.

347. Plains Indians' Artefacts.

348. Dancer in Ceremonial Costume.

(Des. G. Beaupré. Sources: photograph by R. Webber (721), print by G. Catlin (722), design by R. Webber (723), print by J. Webber (724), design by R. Webber (725), painting by G. Heriot (726), design by G. Beaupré (727), painting by Gerald Tailfeathers (728), design by G. Beaupré (729), painting by L. Parker (730), painting on a Kwatiutl house-front (731), painting by L. Parker (732), design by R. Webber (733), anonymous painting (734), photograph by R. Webber (735), drawing by A. H. Murray from lithograph by M. & N. Hanhart (736), sketch by L. Parker (737), design by G. Beaupré (738), drawing by L. Parker (739), design by G. Beaupré (740).)

1972–76. *Canadian Indians.*

(*a*) *P 12×12½ (Nos. 721/4) or 13 (Nos. 725/6). Litho. Ashton-Potter. T* **347** *and similar horiz. designs.*

721 8 c. multicoloured (6.7.72) .. 20 8
722 8 c. multicoloured (6.7.72) .. 20 8
723 8 c. multicoloured (16.1.74) 15 8
724 8 c. multicoloured (16.1.74) 15 8
725 10 c. multicoloured (17.9.76) .. 12 15
726 10 c. lt. stone, black and dp. dull green (17.9.76) .. 12 15

(*b*) *P 12½×12. Recess and photo. B.A.B.N. T* **348** *and similar vert. designs.*

727 8 c. light yellow-orange, rose-red and black (4.10.72) .. 20 8
728 8 c. multicoloured (4.10.72) 20 8
729 8 c. light rose-red, violet and black (28.11.73) .. 15 8
730 8 c. multicoloured (28.11.73) 15 8
731 8 c. rose-red and black (22.2.74) 15 8
732 8 c. multicoloured (22.2.74) 15 8

(*c*) *P 12. Litho. B.A.B.N. Horiz. designs similar to T* **347**.

733 8 c. multicoloured (21.2.73) 15 8
734 8 c. multicoloured (21.2.73) 15 8

(*d*) *P 13. Litho. C.B.N. Horiz. designs similar to T* **347**.

735 8 c. multicoloured (4.4.75) .. 12 8
736 8 c. multicoloured (4.4.75) .. 12 8

(*e*) *P 12½. Litho. (Nos. 736 and 740 also embossed). Ashton-Potter. Vert. designs as T* **348**.

737 8 c. multicoloured (4.4.75) .. 10 8
738 8 c. brownish grey and black (4.4.75) 10 8
739 10 c. multicoloured (17.9.76) .. 12 15
740 10 c. olive-bistre, reddish orge. and black (17.9.76) .. 12 15
721/40 .. .. *Set of* 20 2·75 1·25

Designs:—No. 721, Type **347**; No. 722, "Buffalo Chase"; No. 723, Pacific Coast Indians' artefacts; No. 724, "The Inside of a House in Nootka Sound"; No. 725, Iroquoian artefacts; No. 726, Iroquoian encampment; No. 727, Plains Indians' Thunderbird and decorative pattern; No. 728, Type **348**; No. 729, Algonkians' Thunderbird and decorative pattern; No. 730, Algonkian Indians; No. 731, Pacific Coast Indians' Thunderbird and decorative pattern; No. 732, Gitksan Tsimshian chief; No. 733, Algonkian artefacts; No. 734, "Micmac Indians"; No. 735, Sub-arctic Indians' artefacts; No. 736, The Dance of Kutcha-Kutchin; No. 737, Ceremonial costume, Kutchin tribe; No. 738, Ojibwa thunderbird and Naskapi pattern; No. 739, Iroquoian costume; No. 740, Iroquoian thunderbird.

Nos. 721/2 and 727/8 exist with or without fluorescent bands and the remainder only with fluorescent bands.

The pairs of stamps issued on the same date were printed together within the sheet, horizontally and vertically *se-tenant*.

349. Photogrammetric Surveying.

350. Candles.

(Des. Gottschalk & Ash, Ltd. Litho. Ashton-Potter, Toronto.)

1972 (2 Aug.). *Earth Sciences. T* **349** *and similar square designs. P 12.*

741 15 c. multicoloured .. 50 45
742 15 c. pale grey, dull ultram. and black 50 45
743 15 c. multicoloured .. 50 45
744 15 c. light emerald, red-orge. and black 50 45

Designs and Events:—No. 741, Type **349** (12th Congress of International Society of Photogrammetry); No. 742, "Siegfried" lines (6th Conference of International Cartographic Association); No. 743, Earth's crust (24th International Geological Congress); No. 744, Diagram of village at road-intersection (22nd International Geographical Congress).

Nos. 741/4 were issued in sheets of 64, made up of 4 panes of 16, each pane having a marginal commemorative inscription. Within a pane are 4 copies of each design, arranged in *se-tenant* blocks of 4.

This issue exists with or without fluorescent bands.

(Des. R. Webber. Litho. Ashton-Potter, Toronto.)

1972 (1 Nov.). *Christmas. T* **350** *and similar designs. P 12½×12 (6 and 8 c.) or 11×10½ (others).*

745 **350** 6 c. multicoloured .. 10 8
p. One centre phosphor band 12 10
746 ,, 8 c. multicoloured .. 10 8
p. Two phosphor bands .. 10 8
747 – 10 c. multicoloured .. 12 10
p. Two phosphor bands .. 12 12
748 – 15 c. multicoloured .. 20 I
p. Two phosphor bands .. 20 2

Designs: *Horiz.* (36×20 *mm.*)—10 c. Candle with fruits and pine boughs; 15 c. Candles wit prayer-book, caskets and vase.

This issue also exists with fluorescent bands.

351. "The Blacksmith's Shop" (Krieghoff).

(Des. and litho. B.A.B.N. and Saults & Pollar Ltd., Winnipeg.)

1972 (29 Nov.). *Death Centenary of Corneliu Krieghoff (painter). P 12½.*

749 **351** 8 c. multicoloured .. 12

This stamp exists with or without fluorescen bands.

FLUORESCENT BANDS. Stamps from No 750 onwards were issued only with two fluorescent bands, *unless otherwise stated.* Example are known with the bands omitted in error, bu such varieties are outside the scope of th catalogue.

352. François de Montmorency-Laval.

(Des. M. Fog and G. Lorange. Litho. Ashton Potter, Toronto.)

1973 (31 Jan.). *350th Birth Anniv. of Monsigno de Laval (First Bishop of Quebec). P 11*

750 **352** 8 c. ultram., gold & silver 10 8

353. Commissioner French and Route of the March West.

(Des. Dallaire Morin DeVito Inc. Litho. Ashton-Potter, Toronto.)

1973 (9 Mar.). *Centenary of Royal Canadian Mounted Police. T* **353** *and similar horiz. designs. Multicoloured (except 8 c.). P 11.*

751 8 c. Type **353** (dp. reddish brn., dull orge. & orge.-vermilion) 12 8
752 10 c. Spectrograph 15 12
753 15 c. Mounted policeman .. 20 20

354. Jeanne Mance.

(Des. R. Bellemare. Litho. Ashton-Potter.)

973 (18 APR.). *300th Death Anniv. of Jeanne Mance (nurse). P* 11.
54 **354** 8 c. multicoloured .. 10 8

55. Joseph Howe. **356.** " Mist Fantasy " (MacDonald).

(Des. A. Fleming. Litho. Ashton-Potter).

973 (16 MAY). *Death Centenary of Joseph Howe (Nova Scotian politician). P* 11.
55 **355** 8 c. gold and black .. 10 8

(Des. and litho. Ashton-Potter.)

973 (8 JUNE). *Birth Centenary of J. E. H. MacDonald (artist). P* 12½.
56 **356** 15 c. multicoloured .. 20 20

357. Oaks and Harbour.

(Des. A. Mann. Recess and photo. B.A.B.N.)

973 (22 JUNE). *Centenary of Prince Edward Island's Entry into the Confederation. P* 12.
57 **357** 8 c. pale orange and brown-red 10 8

358. Scottish Settlers.

(Des. P. Swan. Litho. Ashton-Potter.)

1973 (20 JULY). *Bicentennial of Arrival of Scottish Settlers at Pictou, Nova Scotia. P* 12×12½.
758 **358** 8 c. multicoloured .. 10 8

359. Queen Elizabeth II.

(Des. A. Fleming from photograph by Anthony Buckley. Eng. G. A. Gundersen. Recess and photo. B.A.B.N.)

1973 (2 AUG.). *Royal Visit and Commonwealth Heads of Government Meeting, Ottawa. P* 12×12½.
759 **359** 8 c. multicoloured .. 10 8
760 „ 15 c. multicoloured (*shades*) 20 15

360. Nellie McClung. **361.** Emblem of 1976 Olympics.

(Des. S. Mennie. Litho. Ashton-Potter.)

1973 (29 AUG.). *Birth Centenary of Nellie McClung (feminist). P* 10½×11.
761 **360** 8 c. multicoloured .. 10 8

(Des. Wallis and Matanovic. Litho. Ashton-Potter.)

1973 (20 SEPT.). *1976 Olympic Games, Montreal (1st issue). P* 12×12½.
762 **361** 8 c. multicoloured .. 12 15
763 „ 15 c. multicoloured .. 20 25
See also Nos. 768/71, 772/4, 786/9, 798/802, 809/11, 814/16, 829/31 and 833/7.

362. Ice-skate. **363.** Diving.

(Des. Arnaud Maggs. Litho. Ashton-Potter.)

1973 (7 NOV.). *Christmas. T* **362** *and similar vert. designs. Multicoloured. P* 12½×12 (6, 8 c.) *or* 11 (*others*).
764 6 c. Type **362** 5 5
765 8 c. Bird decoration .. 10 8
766 10 c. Santa Claus (20×36 *mm.*) 12 10
767 15 c. Shepherd (20×36 *mm.*) 20 15

(Des. Hunter, Straker, Templeton Ltd. Recess. C.B.N.)

1974 (22 MAR.). *1976 Olympics (2nd issue). "Summer Activities". T* **363** *and similar vert. designs. Each deep blue. P* 12.
768 8 c. Type **363** 10 10
769 8 c. " Jogging " 10 10
770 8 c. Cycling 10 10
771 8 c. Hiking 10 10
Nos. 768/71 were printed in *se-tenant* blocks of four throughout the sheet. Each design has a second (latent) image—the Canadian Olympic Games symbol—which appears when the stamp is viewed obliquely to the light.
See also Nos. 786/9.

(Des. Wallis and Mantanovic. Litho. Ashton Potter.)

1974 (17 APR.). *1976 Olympics (3rd issue). As T* **361** *but smaller* (20×36½ *mm.*). *P* 12½.
772 **361** 8 c.+2 c. multicoloured 12 10
773 „ 10 c.+5 c. multicoloured 20 15
774 „ 15 c.+5 c. multicoloured 25 20

364. Winnipeg Signpost, 1872.

(Des. J. R. MacDonald. Litho & embossed. Ashton-Potter.)

1974 (3 MAY). *Winnipeg Centennial. P* 12½×12.
775 **364** 8 c. multicoloured .. 10 8

365. Postmaster and Customer.

(Des. S. Mennie. Litho. Ashton-Potter.)

1974 (11 JUNE). *Centenary of Canadian Letter Carrier Delivery Service. T* **365** *and similar horiz. designs. Multicoloured. P* 13½.
776 8 c. Type **365** 10 8
777 8 c. Postman collecting mail 10 8
778 8 c. Mail handler 10 8
779 8 c. Mail sorters 10 8
780 8 c. Postman making delivery 10 8
781 8 c. Rural delivery by car .. 10 8
776/81 .. .. *Set of* 6 50 40
Nos. 776/81 were printed in *se-tenant* combinations throughout a sheet of 50, giving 6 blocks of 6 and 14 single stamps.

MINIMUM PRICE

The minimum price quoted is 5p which represents a handling charge rather than a basis for valuing common stamps. For further notes about prices see introductory pages.

366. " Canada's Contribution to Agriculture ".

(Des. M. Brett, P. Cowley-Brown, and A. McAllister. Litho. Ashton-Potter.)

1974 (12 July). *" Agricultural Education ". Centenary of Ontario Agricultural College. P* 12½ × 12.
782 **366** 8 c. multicoloured .. 10 8

367. Telephone Development.

(Des. R. Webber. Litho. Ashton-Potter.)

1974 (26 July). *Centenary of Invention of Telephone by Alexander Graham Bell. P* 12½.
783 **367** 8 c. multicoloured .. 10 8

368. Bicycle Wheel.

(Des. Burns and Cooper. Recess and photo. B.A.B.N.)

1974 (7 Aug.). *World Cycling Championships, Montreal. P* 12 × 12½.
784 **368** 8 c. black, rosine and silver 10 8

369. Mennonite Settlers.

(Des. W. Davies. Litho. Ashton-Potter.)

1974 (28 Aug.). *Centenary of Arrival of Mennonites in Manitoba. P* 12½.
785 **369** 8 c. multicoloured .. 10 8

(Des. Hunter, Straker, Templeton Ltd. Recess. C.B.N.)

1974 (23 Sept.). *1976 Olympics (4th issue). " Winter Activities ". Horiz. designs as T* **363**, *each rosine. P* 13½ × 13.
786 8 c. Snow-shoeing 10 8
787 8 c. Skiing 10 8
788 8 c. Skating 10 8
789 8 c. Curling 10 8

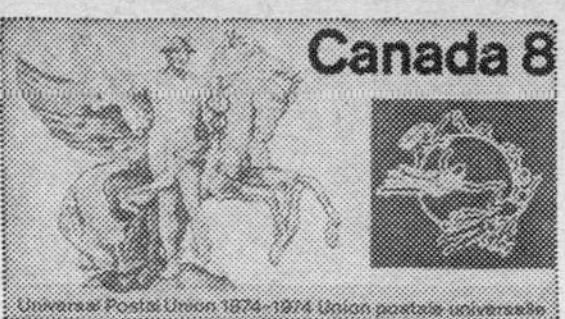

370. Mercury, Winged Horses and U.P.U. Emblem.

(Des. G. Gundersen. Recess and photo. B.A.B.N.)

1974 (9 Oct.). *Centenary of Universal Postal Union. P* 12 × 12½.
790 **370** 8 c. violet, red-orange and cobalt 10 8
791 ,, 15 c. red-orange, violet and cobalt 20 15

371. " The Nativity " (J. P. Lemieux).

(Des. Wallis and Matanovic. Litho. Ashton-Potter.)

1974 (1 Nov.). *Christmas. T* **371** *and similar horiz. designs showing paintings. Multicoloured. P* 13½.
792 6 c. Type **371** 8 5
793 8 c. " Skaters in Hull " (H. Masson) (34 × 31 *mm.*) .. 10 8
794 10 c. " The Ice Cone, Montmorency Falls " (R. C. Todd) 12 10
795 15 c. " Village in the Laurentian Mountains " (C. A. Gagnon) 20 15

372. Marconi and St. John's Harbour, Newfoundland.

(Des. J. Boyle. Litho. Ashton-Potter.)

1974 (15 Nov.). *Birth Centenary of Guglielmo Marconi (radio pioneer). P* 13.
796 **372** 8 c. multicoloured .. 10 8

373. Merritt and Welland Canal.

(Des. W. Rueter. Recess. (B.A.B.N.) and litho (C.B.N.).)

1974 (29 Nov.). *William Merritt Commemoration. P* 13 × 13½.
797 **373** 8 c. multicoloured 10 8

374. Swimming.

(Des. Wallis and Matanovic. Litho. C.B.N.)

1975 (5 Feb.). *1976 Olympics (5th issue) T* **374** *and similar horiz. designs. Multi coloured.*
798 8 c. + 2 c. Type **374** 12 1
799 10 c. + 5 c. Rowing 20 1
800 15 c. + 5 c. Sailing 25 2

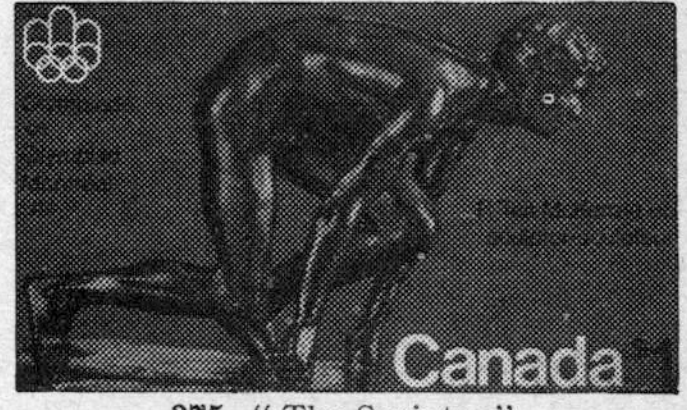

375. " The Sprinter ".

(Des. A. R. Fleming. Litho and embossed Ashton-Potter.)

1975 (14 Mar.). *1976 Olympics (6th issue) T* **375** *and similar multicoloured design showin sculpture by R. T. McKenzie. P* 12½ × 12 ($1 *or* 12 × 12½ ($2).
801 $1 Type **375** .. .. 1·40 1·1
802 $2 " The Diver " (*vert.*) .. 2·75 2·2

376. " Anne of Green Gables " (Lucy Mauc Montgomery).

(Des. P. Swan (No. 803), C. Gagnon (No. 804) Litho. Ashton-Potter.)

1975 (15 May). *Canadian Writers (1st series) T* **376** *and similar vert. design. Multicoloured P* 13½.
803 8 c. Type **376** 10 8
804 8 c. " Maria Chapdelaine " (Louis Hémon) 10 8

Nos. 803/4 were printed horizontally anc vertically *se-tenant* throughout the sheet.

See also Nos. 846/7.

377. Marguerite Bourgeoys (founder of the Ordei of Notre Dame).

78. S. D. Chown (founder of United Church of Canada).

Des. Design & Communication, Montreal. Litho. Ashton-Potter (Nos. 805/6). Des. W. Southern. Eng. G. Gundersen. Recess and photo. B.A.B.N. (Nos. 807/8).)

975 (30 May). *Canadian Celebrities.* T **377/8** *and similar vert. designs.* (*a*) *As* T **377.** *P* 12½×12.

05 8 c. multicoloured 10 8

06 8 c. multicoloured 10 8

(*b*) *As T* **378.** *P* 12×12½.

07 8 c. sepia, flesh & light yellow 10 8

08 8 c. sepia, flesh & light yellow 10 8

Designs:—No. 805, Type **377**; No. 806, lphonse Desjardins (leader of Credit Union novement); No. 807, Type **378**; No. 808, Dr. J. ook (first moderator of Presbyterian Church in anada).

Nos. 807/8 were printed together in the sheet orizontally and vertically *se-tenant.*

379. Pole-vaulting.

(De . P. Swan. Litho. Ashton-Potter.)

975 (11 June). 1976 *Olympics* (7*th issue*). *T* **379** *and similar vert. designs. Multicoloured. P* 12×12½.

09 20 c. Type **379** 25 25

10 25 c. Marathon-running .. 30 30

11 50 c. Hurdling 70 60

380. " Untamed " (photo by Walt Petrigo).

(Des. B. Reilander. Litho. C.B.N.)

975 (3 July). *Centenary of Calgary. P* 12×12½.

12 **380** 8 c. multicoloured .. 10 8

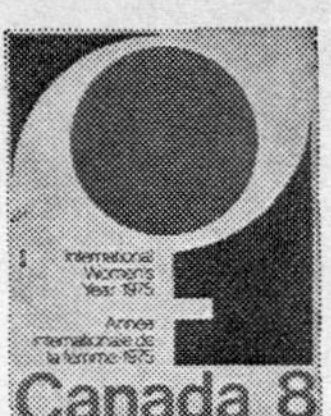

381. I.W.Y. Symbol. **382.** Fencing.

(Des. Susan McPhee. Recess and photo. B.A.B.N.)

1975 (14 July). *International Women's Year. P* 13.

813 **381** 8 c. light grey-brown, bistre-yellow & black 10 8

(Des. J. Hill. Litho. C.B.N.)

1975 (6 Aug.). 1976 *Olympics Funds* (8*th issue*). *T* **382** *and similar vert. designs showing combat sports. Multicoloured. P* 13.

814 8 c.+2 c. Type **382** 12 12

815 10 c.+5 c. Boxing 20 20

816 15 c.+5 c. Judo 25 25

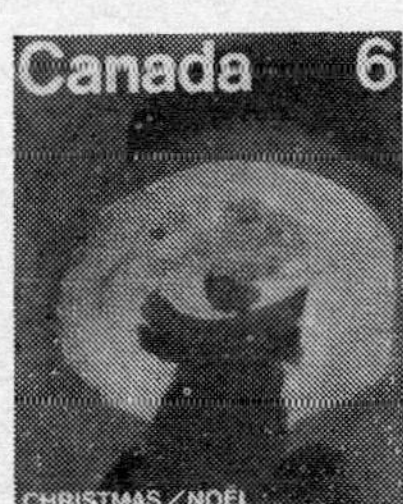

383. " Justice-Justitia" (statue by W. S. Allward). **385.** " Santa Claus " (G. Kelly).

384. The *William D. Lawrence.*

(Des. A. Fleming. Litho. Ashton-Potter.)

1975 (2 Sept.). *Centenary of Canadian Supreme Court. P* 12½.

817 **383** 8 c. multicoloured .. 10 8

(Des. T. Bjarnason. Recess and photo. B.A.B.N.)

1975 (24 Sept.). *Coastal Ships. T* **384** *and similar horiz. designs. P* 13.

818 8 c. yellow-brown and black .. 10 8

819 8 c. yellow-green and black .. 10 8

820 8 c. blue-green and black .. 10 8

821 8 c. yellow-brown and black .. 10 8

Designs:—No. 819, *Beaver*; No. 820, *Neptune*; No. 821, *Quadra.*

Nos. 818/21 were printed in *se-tenant* combinations throughout a sheet of 50, giving 10 blocks of 4 and 10 single stamps.

(Des. B. Reilander from children's paintings. Litho. Ashton-Potter.)

1975 (22 Oct.). *Christmas. T* **385** *and similar multicoloured designs. P* 13.

822 6 c. Type **385** 8 5

823 6 c. " Skater " (Bill Cawsey) 8 5

824 8 c. " Child " (D. Hébert) .. 10 5

825 8 c. " Family " (L. Caldwell) 10 5

826 10 c. " Gift " (D. Lovely) .. 12 10

827 15 c. "Trees " (R. Kowalski) (*horiz.*) 20 15

822/7 .. .. *Set of* 6 60 40

Nos. 822/3 and 824/5 were respectively issued together *se-tenant* in an alternate arrangement within the sheet.

386. Text, Badge and Bugle.

(Des. R. Kavach. Recess and photo. B.A.B.N.)

1975 (10 Nov.). 50*th Anniv. of Royal Canadian Legion. P* 12½×13.

828 **386** 8 c. multicoloured .. 10 5

387. Basketball.

(Des. J. Hill. Litho. Ashton-Potter.)

1976 (7 Jan.). *Olympics* (9*th issue*). *T* **387** *and similar vert. designs. Multicoloured. P* 13.

829 8 c.+2 c. Type **387** .. 12 10

830 10 c.+5 c. Gymnastics .. 20 15

831 20 c.+5 c. Soccer 30 25

388. Games Symbol and Snow Crystal. **389.** " Communications Arts ".

(Des. R. Harder. Litho. Ashton-Potter.)

1976 (6 Feb.). 12*th Winter Olympic Games, Innsbruck. P* 12½.

832 **388** 20 c. multicoloured .. 25 20

(Des. R. Webber. Litho. C.B.N.)

1976 (6 Feb.). *Olympics* (10*th issue*). *T* **389** *and similar vert. designs. Multicoloured. P* 12×12½.

833 20 c. Type **389** 25 20

834 25 c. " Performing Arts " .. 30 25

835 50 c. " Handicrafts " .. 70 55

390. Place Ville Marie and Notre-Dame Church. (*Illustration reduced. Actual size* 57 × 20 *mm.*)

(Des. J. and P. Mercier. Recess and photo. B.A.B.N.).

1976 (12 MAR.). *Olympics* (11*th issue*). *T* **390** *and similar horiz. design. Multicoloured. P* 13.

836 $1 Type **390** .. .. .. 1·25 1·00
837 $2 Olympic Stadium and flags .. .. .. 2·50 2·00

391. Flower and Urban Sprawl.

(Des. I. McLeod. Litho. Ashton-Potter.)

1976 (12 MAY). *U.N. Conference on Human Settlements* (*HABITAT*), *Vancouver. P* 12 × 12½.

838 **391** 20 c. multicoloured .. 25 25

392. Benjamin Franklin and Map.

(Des. B. Reilander. Recess & photo. B.A.B.N.)

1976 (1 JUNE). *Bicentenary of American Revolution. P* 13.

839 **392** 10 c. multicoloured .. 10 12

393. Wing Parade before Mackenzie Building.

(Des. W. Davies. Litho. C.B.N.)

1976 (1 JUNE). *Royal Military College Centenary. T* **393** *and similar vert. design. Multicoloured. P* 12 × 12½.

840 8 c. Type **393** 10 10
841 8 c. Colour party and Memorial Arch 10 10

Nos. 840/1 were printed horizontally and vertically *se-tenant* throughout the sheet.

394. Transfer of Olympic Flame by Satellite.

(Des. P. Swan. Litho. Ashton-Potter.)

1976 (18 JUNE). *Olympics* (12*th issue*). *T* **394** *and similar horiz. designs. Multicoloured. P* 13½.

842 8 c. Type **394** 10 10
843 20 c. Carrying the Olympic flag 25 25
844 25 c. Athletes with medals .. 35 30

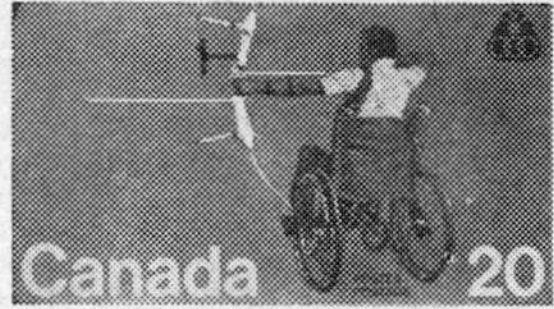

395. Archer.

(Des. T. Bjarnason. Litho. C.B.N.)

1976 (3 AUG.). *Olympiad for the Physically Disabled. P* 12 × 12½ (C).

845 **395** 20 c. multicoloured .. 25 25

396. " Sam McGee " (Robert W. Service).

(Des. D. Bierk (No. 846), A. Dumas (No. 847). Litho. Ashton-Potter.)

1976 (17 AUG.). *Canadian Writers* (2*nd series*). *T* **396** *and similar vert. design. Multicoloured. P* 13.

846 8 c. Type **396** 10 10
847 8 c. " Le Survenant " (Germaine Guèvremont) 10 10

Nos. 846/7 were printed horizontally and vertically *se-tenant* throughout the sheet.

397. " Nativity " (F. Mayer).

(Des. B. Reilander. Litho. Ashton-Potter.)

1976 (3 NOV.). *Christmas. T* **397** *and similar vert. designs showing stained-glass windows. Multicoloured. P* 13½.

848 8 c. Type **397** 10 10
849 10 c. " Nativity " (G. Maile & Son) 12 12
850 20 c. " Nativity " (Yvonne Williams) 25 25

REGISTRATION STAMPS.

R 1

(Eng. & ptd. British-American Bank Note Co Montreal and Ottawa.)

1875 (15 Nov.)–**92.** *White wove paper* (*a*) *P* 1 (*or slightly under*).

R1 R **1** 2 c. orange .. .. 12·00 1·5
R2 ,, 2 c. orange-red (1889) .. 13·00 2·5
R3 ,, 2 c. vermilion .. .. 20·00 2·5
a. Imperf. (pair) ..
R4 ,, 2 c. rose-carmine (1888) 30·00 9·c
R5 ,, 5 c. yellow-green (1878) 17·00 1·c
R6 ,, 5 c. dark green .. .. 15·00 1·c
a. Imperf. (pair) .. £110
R7 ,, 5 c. blue-green (1888) .. 17·00 1·c
R7*a* ,, 5 c. dull sea-green (1892) 20·00 1·7
R8 ,, 8 c. bright blue .. .. 90·00 65·c
R9 ,, 8 c. dull blue .. .. 90·00 65·c

(*b*) *P* 12 × 11½ *or* 12 × 11¾.

R10 R **1** 2 c. orange .. .. — 15·c
R11 ,, 5 c. green (*shades*) .. — 48·c

SPECIAL DELIVERY STAMPS.

PRINTERS. The following Special Deliver and Postage Due stamps were recess-printed b the American Bank Note Co. (to 1928), the Britis American Bank Note Co. (to 1934), and th Canadian Bank Note Co. (1935 onwards).

S 1

1898–1920. *P* 12.

S1 S **1** 10 c. blue-green (28.6.98) .. 12·00 2·5
S2 ,, 10 c. deep green (Dec. '13) 12·00 2·5
S3 ,, 10 c. yellowish green (8.20) 12·00 2·5

The differences between Types I and I (figures " 10 " with and without shading) form erly illustrated were due to wear of the plat There was only one die.

S 2

1922 (21 AUG.). *P* 12.

S4 S **2** 20 c. carmine-red .. .. 14·00 2·5

S **3.** Mail-carrying, 1867 and 1927.

.927 (29 June). *60th Anniversary of Confederation.* *P* 12.

5	S 3	20 c. orange	3·00	3·00

S 4

930 (2 Sept.). *P* 11.

6	S4	20 c. brown-red	14·00	4·50

932 (24 Dec.). *Type as* S 4, *but inscr.* "CENTS" *in place of* "TWENTY CENTS". *P* 11.

7		20 c. brown-red	10·00	5·00

S 5. Allegory of Progress.

935 (1 June). *P* 12.

8	S 5	20 c. scarlet	2·00	1·75

S 6. Canadian Coat of Arms.

.938–39. *P* 12.

9	S 6	10 c. green (1.4.39) ..	2·00	90
10	,,	20 c. scarlet (15.6.38) ..	9·00	6·00

≡10 10≡

(S 7)

.939 (1 Mar.). *Surch. with Type* S 7.

11	S 6	10 on 20 c. scarlet ..	1·50	1·50

S 8. Coat of Arms and Flags.

S 9. Trans-Canada Plane.

1942 (1 July)–**1943**. *War Effort.* *P* 12.

(a) Postage.

S12	S 8	10 c. green	1·00	50

(b) Air.

S13	S 9	16 c. ultramarine ..	90	70
S14	,,	17 c. ultramarine (1.4.43)	1·00	1·00

S 10. Arms of Canada and Peace Symbols.

S 11. Transatlantic plane over Quebec.

1946 (16 Sept.)—**1947**. *P* 12. *(a) Postage.*

S15	S 10	10 c. green	90	40

(b) Air. (i) *Circumflex accent in* "EXPRÊS".

S16	S 11	17 c. ultramarine	1·60	1·40

(ii) *Grave accent in* "EXPRÈS".

S17	S 11	17 c. ultramarine ('47)..	2·00	2·00

POSTAGE DUE STAMPS.

PRINTERS. See note under "Special Delivery Stamps".

D 1

D 2

1906 (1 July)–**28**. *P* 12.

D1	D 1	1 c. dull violet	2·00	1·00
D2	,,	1 c. red-violet	2·00	1·00
		a. Thin paper (10.24) ..	4·00	3·50
D3	,,	2 c. dull violet ..	3·00	35
D4	,,	2 c. red-violet ..	3·00	35
		a. Thin paper (10.24) ..	5·00	3·50
D5	,,	4 c. violet (3.7.28) ..	11·00	6·00
D6	,,	5 c. dull violet ..	3·00	35
D7	,,	5 c. red-violet ..	3·00	35
		a. Thin paper (10.24) ..	5·00	3·50
D8	,,	10 c. violet (3.7.28) ..	9·00	3·00

1930–2. *P* 11.

D 9	D 2	1 c. bright vio. (14.7.30)	2·00	2·00
D10	,,	2 c. bright vio. (21.8.30)	1·00	30
D11	,,	4 c. bright vio. (14.10.30)	2·00	1·50
D12	,,	5 c. bright vio. (12.12.31)	2·00	1·50
D13	,,	10 c. bright vio. (24.8.32)	25·00	3·50

D 3

D 4

1933–4. *P* 11.

D14	D 3	1 c. violet (5.5.34) ..	2·50	2·00
D15	,,	2 c. violet (20.12.33) ..	1·00	40
D16	,,	4 c. violet (12.12.33) ..	2·50	1·75
D17	,,	10 c. violet (20.12.33) ..	3·50	2·00

1935–65. *P* 12.

D18	D 4	1 c. violet (14.10.35) ..	5	5
D19	,,	2 c. violet (9.9.35) ..	5	5
D20	,,	3 c. violet (4.65) ..	70	65
D21	,,	4 c. violet (2.7.35) ..	12	5
D22	,,	5 c. violet (12.48) ..	15	5
D23	,,	6 c. violet ('57) ..	50	45
D24	,,	10 c. violet (16.9.35) ..	15	5
D18/24		.. .. *Set of* 7	1·60	1·25

D 5

1967–74. *Litho. P* 12. *(a) Size* $20\frac{1}{4} \times 17$ *mm.*

D25	D 5	1 c. scarlet (3.67) ..	12	8
D26	,,	2 c. scarlet (3.67) ..	10	8
D27	,,	3 c. scarlet (3.67) ..	10	10
D28	,,	4 c. scarlet (2.67) ..	35	15
D29	,,	5 c. scarlet (3.67) ..	1·25	1·10
D30	,,	6 c. scarlet (2.67) ..	20	15
D31	,,	10 c. scarlet (1.67) ..	30	25
D25/31		.. .. *Set of* 7	2·25	1·75

(b) Size $19\frac{1}{4} \times 15\frac{1}{2}$ *mm.*

D32	D 5	1 c. scarlet (12.70) ..	5	5
D33	,,	2 c. scarlet ('72) ..	5	5
D34	,,	3 c. scarlet (1.74) ..	5	5
D35	,,	4 c. scarlet (4.69) ..	5	5
D36	,,	5 c. scarlet (2.69) ..	10·00	10·00
D37	,,	6 c. scarlet ('72) ..	5	5
D38	,,	8 c. scarlet (1.69) ..	8	5
D39	,,	10 c. scarlet (4.69) ..	10	5
D40	,,	12 c. scarlet (1.69) ..	12	5
D41	,,	16 c. scarlet (1.74) ..	15	5
D32/41		.. .. *Set of* 10	10·00	10·00

There are no records of dates of issue of the above but supplies were distributed to depots in the months indicated.

Both white and ordinary papers have been used for Nos. D32/41. These are listed in Stanley Gibbons *Elizabethan Catalogue.*

OFFICIAL STAMPS.

We do not list stamps perforated "O.H.M.S.".

O.H.M.S.

(O 1)

1949. *Optd. with Type* O 1 *(1 c. to 4 c.) or larger opt., 15 × 2 mm. (others).*

(a) Postage.

O1	111	1 c. green	70	70
O2	112	2 c. brown	5·00	5·00
O3	113	3 c. purple	50	35
O4	112	4 c. carmine-lake ..	70	20
O5	123	10 c. olive-green ..	1·40	20
O6	124	14 c. sepia	1·75	50
O7	125	20 c. slate	4·50	90
O8	126	50 c. green	70·00	65·00
O9	127	$1 purple	20·00	17·00

(b) Air.

O10	128	7 c. blue	2·75	1·75
O1/10		.. .. *Set of* 10	£100	85·00

A variety without stop after "S" is known on Nos. O1/2 and O5/10.

1949–50. *Optd. with Type* O **1** (1 *c. to* 5 *c.*) *or larger.*

O11	**135**	1 c. green	15	10
O12	**136**	2 c. sepia	30	15
O13	**137**	3 c. purple	35	20
O14	**138**	4 c. carmine-lake ..	50	15
O15	**139**	5 c. blue ('49)	70	35
O16	**141**	50 c. green ('50)	12·00	10·00

G (O 2) **G** (O 3) **G** (O 4)

Type O **4** differs from Type O **3** in having a thinner appearance and an upward sloping left serif to the lower arm. It results from a new plate introduced in 1961/62. Variations in thickness are known in Type O **2** but these are due to wear and subsequent cleaning of the plate.

1950 (2 Oct.)–**52.** *Optd. with Type* O **2** (1 *c. to* 5 *c.*) *or* O **3** (*others*).

(*a*) *Postage.*

O17	**135**	1 c. green	5	5
O18	**136**	2 c. sepia	25	15
O19	,,	2 c. olive-green (11.51)	15	5
O20	**137**	3 c. purple	25	12
O21	**138**	4 c. carmine-lake ..	35	5
O22	,,	4 c. vermilion (1.5.52) ..	35	5
O23	**139**	5 c. blue	50	35
O24	**123**	10 c. olive-green	1·00	15
O25	**124**	14 c. sepia	3·50	90
O26	**125**	20 c. slate	5·50	40
O27	**141**	50 c. green	4·50	3·00
O28	**127**	$1 purple	38·00	35·00

(*b*) *Air.*

O29	**128**	7 c. blue	3·00	2·50
O17/29		.. .. *Set of* 13	50·00	38·00

1950–51. *Optd. with Type* O **3.**

O30	**142**	10 c. brown-purple ..	70	10
		a. Opt. omitted in pair with normal	£200	£100
O31	**143**	$1 ultramarine (1.2.51)	38·00	35·00

1952–53. *Optd. with Type* O **3.**

O32	**153**	7 c. blue (3.11.52) ..	1·25	30
O33	**151**	20 c. grey (1.4.52) ..	1·00	15
O34	**154**	$1 black (2.2.53) ..	5·00	3·00

1953 (1 Sept.)–**61.** *Optd. with Type* O **2** (1 *c. to* 5 *c.*) *or* O **3** (50 *c.*).

O35	**158**	1 c. purple-brown ..	10	5
O36	,,	2 c. green	12	5
O37	,,	3 c. carmine	12	5
O38	,,	4 c. violet	20	5
O39	,,	5 c. ultramarine ..	20	8
O40	**160**	50 c. deep bluish green (2.11.53)	2·50	40
		a. Opt. Type O 4 (24.4.61*)	2·50	1·50

* Earliest recorded date.

1955–56. *Optd. with Type* O **2.** *P* 12.

O41	**161**	1 c. pur.-brn. (12.11.56)	10	5
O42	,,	2 c. green (19.1.56) ..	10	5
O43	,,	4 c. violet (23.7.56) ..	30	8
O44	,,	5 c. bright blue (11.1.55)	15	5

1955–62. *Optd. with Type* O **3.**

O45	**165**	10 c. pur.-brn. (21.2.55)	30	5
		a. Opt. Type O 4 (28.3.62*)	50	30
O46	**176**	20 c. green (4.12.56) ..	80	12
		a. Opt. Type O 4 (10.4.62*)	4·50	45

* Earliest recorded date.

1963 (15 May). *Optd. as Type* O **2.** *P* 12.

O47	**215**	1 c. chocolate	40	40
O48	,,	2 c. green	40	40
O49	,,	4 c. carmine-red ..	40	40
O50	,,	5 c. ultramarine ..	25	25

The use of official stamps was discontinued on 31st December, 1963.

OFFICIAL SPECIAL DELIVERY STAMPS.

1950. *Optd. as Type* O **1**, *but larger.*

OS1	S **10**	10 c. green	6·00	6·00

1950 (2 Oct.). *Optd. as Type* O **2**, *but larger.*

OS2	S **10**	10 c. green	10·00	10·00

CAPE OF GOOD HOPE.

PRICES.—*Our prices for early Cape of Good Hope are for stamps in very fine condition. Exceptional copies are worth more, poorer copies considerably less.*

1. Hope.

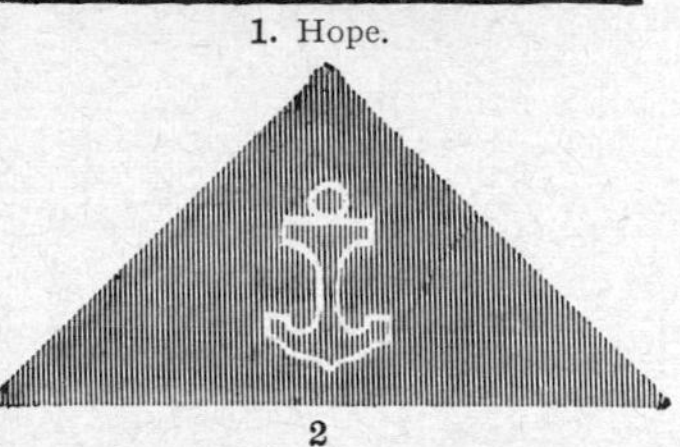

2

(Des. Charles Bell, Surveyor-General; die. eng. W. Humphrys; recess. Perkins, Bacon.)

1853 (1 Sept.). *W* **2.** *Imperf.*

(*a*) *Paper deeply blued.*

1 1d. pale brick-red £1500 £150
a. Deep brick-red £1700 £180
,, 4d. deep blue .. .. .. £900 85·00

Beware of proofs with faked watermarks offered as originals of No. 2

(*b*) *Paper slightly blued* (*blueing not so pronounced at back*).

1 1d. brick-red £1100 £120
a. Brown-red £1200 £130
,, 4d. deep blue .. .. .. £600 65·00
a. Pale blue .. .. .. £650 85·00

Both values are known with wmk. sideways.

1855–8. *White paper.* *W* **2.** *Imperf.*

1 1d. brick-red (1857) £1600 £250
a. Pale rose (1858) £250 £120
b. Deep rose-red £275 £130
,, 4d. deep blue (1855) .. .. £120 30·00
a. Blue .. .. .. £120 30·00
,, 6d. slate-lilac (18.2.58) .. £1800 £225
a. Blued paper £1800 £300
b. Pale rose-lilac £375 £140
c. Deep rose-lilac £800 £180
d. Slate-purple. Blued paper .. £1800 £300
,, 1s. bright yell.-grn. (18.2.58) £750 95·00
a. Deep dark green £140 £300

The method adopted for producing the plate of the 4d., 6d., and 1s. stamps involved the use of two dies, so that there are two types of each of these values, differing slightly in detail, but produced in equal numbers.

All values of this issue are known with watermark sideways. The 6d. is known bisected and used with 1d. for 4d. rate.

The 4d. is known in black, and it was at one time suggested that a small supply of stamps in this colour was issued on the occasion of the death of the Prince Consort, but there is no confirmation of this in the official records. (*Price un.* £5000.)

Varieties. Unofficially rouletted.

1 1d. brick-red .. .. .. — £2000
,, 4d. blue .. .. .. — £1600
,, 6d. rose-lilac .. .. .. — £1200
,, 1s. bright yellow-green .. — £2000
a. Deep dark green .. .. — £2400

These rouletted stamps are best collected on cover.

3. Hope.

(Local provisional (so-called "wood-block") issue. Engraved on steel by C. J. Roberts. Printed from stereotyped plates by Saul Solomon & Co., Cape Town.)

1861 (Feb.–April). *Laid paper.* *Imperf.*

13 **3** 1d. vermilion (27 Feb.) .. £8000 £1200
a. Carmine (7 March) £9000 £1600
b. Brick-red (10 April) .. £10000 £1800
14 ,, 4d. pale milky blue (23 Feb.) £3250 £1100
a. Pale grey-blue (Mar. ?) .. £4000 £1100
b. Pale bright blue (Mar. ?) .. £4000 £1100
c. Deep bright blue (12 April) .. — £2250
d. Blue £5500 £1500

Errors of colour.

15 **3** 1d. pale milky blue .. .. — £14000
a. Pale bright blue .. .. — £14000
16 ,, 4d. vermilion .. .. — £16000
a. Carmine .. .. .. — £18000

Variety. Retouch or repair to right-hand lower corner of stereo.

17 **3** 4d. pale milky blue .. .. — £3000
a. Pale bright blue .. .. — £3000

Both values were officially reprinted in March, 1883, on wove paper. The 1d. is in deep red, and the 4d. in a deeper blue than that of the deepest shade of the issued stamp.

Specimens of the reprints have done postal duty, but their use thus was not intended. There are no reprints of the errors or of the retouched 4d.

Further reprints were made privately but with official permission, in 1940/41, in colours much deeper than those of any of the original printings, and on thick carton paper.

Early in 1863, Perkins Bacon & Co. handed over the four plates used for printing the triangular Cape of Good Hope stamps to De La Rue & Co., who made all the subsequent printings.

(Printed from the Perkins Bacon plates by D.L.R.)

1863–4. *W* **2.** *Imperf.*

18 **1** 1d. deep carmine-red .. 80·00 £120
a. Deep brown-red £160 £150
b. Brownish red £150 £150
19 ,, 4d. dark blue .. .. 60·00 28·00
a. Pale blue .. .. .. 70·00 40·00
b. Slate-blue £750 £225
c. Steel-blue £900 £200
20 ,, 6d. bright mauve £120 £180
21 ,, 1s. bright emerald-green .. £250 £300
a. Pale emerald-green £600

Variety. Wmk. Crown CC (sideways).

22 **1** 1d. deep carmine-red .. £10000

This was a trial printing, and is only known unused.

Our prices for the 4d. pale blue are for stamps which are pale blue by comparison with the other listed shades. An exceptionally pale shade is recognised by specialists and is rare.

All values of this issue are known with watermark lying sideways.

With the exception of the 4d., these stamps may be easily distinguished from those printed by Perkins Bacon & Co. by their colours, which are quite distinct.

The De La Rue stamps of all values are less clearly printed, the figure of Hope and the lettering of the inscriptions standing out less boldly, while the fine lines of the background appear blurred and broken when examined under a glass. The background as a whole often shows irregularity in the apparent depth of colour, due to wear of the plates.

For note regarding the two dies of the 4d., 6d., and 1s. *values, see after* No. 8.

All the triangular stamps were demonetised as from 1st October, 1900.

4. "Hope" seated, with vine and ram. (With outer frame-line.)

Four Pence.

(5)

(Des. Charles Bell; die engraved on steel and stamps typo. by De La Rue.)

1864–77. *With outer frame-line surrounding the design.* *Wmk. Crown CC.* *P* 14.

23 **4** 1d. carmine-red (5.65) .. 12·00 3·25
a. Rose-red .. .. .. 12·00 3·50
24 ,, 4d. pale blue (8.65) .. .. 14·00 80
a. Blue .. .. .. 16·00 80
b. Ultramarine .. .. 48·00 17·00
c. Deep blue (1872) .. .. 20·00 80
25 ,, 6d. pale lilac (before 21.3.64) 16·00 5·50
a. Deep lilac .. .. .. 40·00 3·00
b. Violet (to bright) (1877) .. 16·00 80
26 ,, 1s. deep green (1.64) .. 85·00 4·75
a. Green .. .. .. 12·00 1·25
b. Blue-green .. .. .. 14·00 1·40

The 1d. rose-red, 6d. lilac, and 1s. blue-green are known imperf., probably from proof sheets.

The 1d. and 4d. stamps of this issue may be found with side and/or top outer frame-lines missing, due to wear of the plates.

(Surch. by Saul Solomon & Co., Cape Town.)

1868 (17 Nov.). *No.* 25*a surch. with T* **5.**

27 **4** 4d. on 6d. deep lilac (R.) .. 18·00 4·50
a. "Peuce" for "Pence" .. £350
b. "Fonr" for "Four" .. .. — £150

Specimens may also be found with bars omitted or at the top of the stamp, due to misplacement of the sheet.

The space between the words and bars varies from $12\frac{1}{2}$ to 16 mm., stamps with spacing $15\frac{1}{2}$ and 16 mm. being rare. There were two printings, one of 120,00 in November, 1868, and another of 1,000,000 in December. Stamps showing widest spacings are probably from the earlier printing.

6. (No outer frame-line.)

(Die re-engraved. Typo. D.L.R.)

1871–6. *Outer frame-line removed.* *Wmk. Crown CC.* *P* 14.

28 **6** $\frac{1}{2}$d. pale grey-blk. (12.75) .. 1·25 90
a. Deep grey-black .. .. 1·10 80
29 ,, 1d. pale carmine-red (2.72) .. 2·00 15
a. Deep carmine-red .. .. 2·50 15
30 ,, 4d. dull blue (12.76) .. .. 13·00 25
a. Deep blue .. .. .. 13·00 40
b. Ultramarine .. .. .. 35·00 10·00
31 ,, 5s. yellow-orange (25.8.71) .. 25·00 3·00

The $\frac{1}{2}$d., 1d. and 5s. are known imperf., probably from proof sheets.

For the 3d. of this issue see Nos. 36 and 39.

ONE PENNY (7)

THREE PENCE (8)

(Surch. by Saul Solomon & Co., Cape Town.)

1874–6. *Nos.* 25*a and* 26*a surch. with T* **7.**

32 **4** 1d. on 6d. deep lilac (R.) (1.9.74) .. .. 45·00 7·00
a. "E" of "PENNY" omitted — 90·00
33 ,, 1d. on 1s. green (11.76) .. 5·50 5·50

These provisionals are found with the bar only, either across the centre of the stamp or at top, with value only; or with value and bar close together, either at top or foot. Such varieties are due to misplacement of sheets during surcharging.

1879 (1 Nov.). *No.* 30 *surch. with T* **8.**

34 **6** 3d. on 4d. blue (R.) .. .. 13·00 1·75
a. "PENCB" for "PENCE" .. £325 85·00
b. "THE.EE" for "THREE" .. £350 £100
c. Surch. double .. .. — £350
d. Variety b. double .. ..

The double surcharge must also have existed showing variety a. but only variety b. is known.
There are numerous minor varieties, including letters broken or out of alignment, due to defective printing and use of poor type.
The spacing between the bar and the words varies from 16½ to 18 mm.

THREEPENCE
(9)

(Surch. by D.L.R.)

1880 (Feb.). *Special printing of the 4d. in new colour, surch. with T* **9**. *Wmk. Crown CC.*
35 **6** 3d. on 4d. pale dull rose .. 6·50 85

A minor constant variety exists with foot of "P" in "PENCE" broken off, making the letter appear shorter.

1880 (1 July). *Wmk. Crown CC.* *P* 14.
36 **6** 3d. pale dull rose .. .. 20·00 2·50

3 (10) 3 (11) One Half-penny. (12)

(Surch. by Saul Solomon & Co., Cape Town.)

1880 (Aug.). *No. 36 surch.*
37 **10** "3" on 3d. pale dull rose .. 5·00 50
a. Surch. inverted .. £110 12·00
38 **11** "3" on 3d. pale dull rose .. 15·00 1·50
a. Surch. inverted .. — £275

The "3" (T **10**) is sometimes found broken. Vertical pairs are known showing the two types of surcharge *se-tenant*, and vertical strips of three exist, the top stamp having surcharge T **10**, the middle stamp being without surcharge, and the lower stamp having surcharge T **11** (*price for strip of 3 un. £500*).

1881 (Jan.). *Wmk. Crown CC.* *P* 14.
39 **6** 3d. pale claret .. .. 6·50 75
a. Deep claret .. .. 8·00 65

This was a definite colour change made at the request of the Postmaster-General owing to the similarity between the colours of the 1d. stamp and the 3d. in pale dull rose. Imperf. copies are probably from proof sheets.
Proofs of this value were printed in brown, on unwatermarked wove paper and imperf., but the colour was rejected as unsuitable.

1882 (July). *Wmk. Crown CA.* *P* 14.
40 **6** 3d. pale claret .. .. 1·25 55
a. Deep claret .. .. 1·40 50

(Surch. by Saul Solomon & Co., Cape Town.)

1882 (July). *Nos. 39a and 40a surch. with T* **12**.
41 **6** ½d. on 3d. dp. clar. (Wmk. CC) £400 38·00
a. Hyphen omitted .. .. — £850
42 ,, ½d. on 3d. dp. clar. (Wmk. CA) 1·40 1·10
a. "p" in "penny" omitted .. £475 £225
b. "y" in "penny" omitted .. £200
c. Hyphen omitted .. .. £100 95·00

Varieties also exist with broken and defective letters, and with the obliterating bar omitted or at the top of the stamp.

1882–83. *Wmk. Crown CA.* *P* 14.
43 **6** ½d. black (1.9.82) .. .. 1·75 15
a. Grey-black 85 10
44 ,, 1d. rose-red (7.82) .. .. 4·00 8
a. Deep rose-red .. .. 3·00 8
45 ,, 2d. pale bistre (1.9.82) .. 7·50 10
a. Deep bistre .. .. 10·00 8
46 **4** 6d. mauve (to bright) (8.82) 9·50 50
47 **6** 5s. orange (8.83) .. £250 32·00

Imperf. pairs of the ½d., 1d., and 2d. are known, probably from proof sheets.

For the 3d. stamp with this watermark see No. 40.

13. "Cabled Anchor".

2½d (14)

1884–90. *W* **13**. *P* 14.
48 **6** ½d. black (1.86) 10 8
a. Grey-black 10 8
49 ,, 1d. rose-red (12.85) 15 8
a. Carmine-red 10 8
50 ,, 2d. pale bistre (12.84) .. 65 8
a. Deep bistre 30 8
51 ,, 4d. blue (6.90) 45 10
a. Deep blue 50 10
52 **4** 6d. reddish purple (12.84) .. 5·50 1·00
a. Purple (shades) 80 12
b. Bright mauve .. 4·00 25
53 ,, 1s. yellow-green (12.85) .. 10·00 1·00
a. Blue-green (1889) .. .. 5·50 15
54 **6** 5s. orange (7.87) .. .. 10·00 80
48/54 .. .. *Set of* 7 15·00 1·25

All the above stamps are known in imperf. pairs, probably from proof sheets.

For later shade and colour changes, etc., see Nos. 59, etc.

(Surch. by De La Rue.)

1891 (Mar.). *Special printing of the 3d. in new colour, surch. with T* **14**.
55 **6** 2½d. on 3d. pale magenta .. 1·25 50
a. Deep magenta .. 45 15
b. Fig. "1" with horiz. serif .. 15·00 12·00

Variety b occurs on two stamps (Nos. 8 and 49) of the pane of 60.
Two types of "d" are found in the surcharge, one with square end to serif at top, and the other with pointed serif.

15

ONE PENNY.
(16)

1892 (June). *W* **13**. *P* 14.
56 **15** 2½d. sage-green 55 10
a. Olive-green .. .. 2·00 50

(Surch. by W. A. Richards & Sons, Cape Town.)

1893 (Mar.). *Nos. 50/a surch. with T* **16**.
57 **6** 1d. on 2d. pale bistre .. 70 8
a. Deep bistre 25 8
b. No stop after "PENNY" .. 8·00 6·00
c. Surch. double .. .. — £100

Variety b. occurs on stamp No. 42 of the upper left-hand pane, and on No. 6 of the lower right-hand pane.
Minor varieties exist showing broken letters and letters out of alignment or widely spaced. Also with obliterating bar omitted, due to misplacement of the sheet during surcharging.

17. "Hope" standing. Table Bay in background.

18. Table Mountain and Bay with Arms of the Colony.

(Des. Mr. Mountford. Typo. De La Rue & Co.)

1893 (Oct.). *W* **13**. *P* 14.
58 **17** 1d. rose-red 10 8
a. Carmine 10 8

The above stamp is known in imperf. pairs, probably from proof sheets.

1893–98. *New colours, etc.* *W* **13**. *P* 14.
59 **6** ½d. pale yell.-green (12.96) 10 8
a. Green .. .. 1·10 10
60 ,, 2d. choc.-brown (3.97) .. 20 8
61 **15** 2½d. pale ultram. (3.96) .. 30 10
a. Ultramarine 20 8
62 **6** 3d. bright magenta (9.98) 50 20
63 ,, 4d. sage-green (3.97) .. 70 20
64 ,, 1s. blue-green (12.93) .. 3·50 35
a. Deep blue-green .. 11·00 2·00
65 ,, 1s. yellow-ochre (5.96) .. 1·25 25
66 ,, 5s. brown-orange (6.96) .. 6·00 90
59/66 .. .. *Set of* 8 11·00 1·75

1898–1902. *W* **13**. *P* 14.
67 **17** ½d. green (10.98) 10
68 ,, 3d. magenta (3.02) 85

(Des. E. Sturman. Typo. De La Rue.)

1900 (Jan.). *W* **13**. *P* 14.
69 **18** 1d. carmine 10

19

20

21

22

23

24

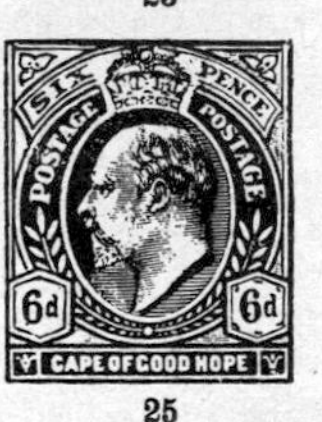

25

26

27

(Typo. De La Rue.)

1902 (Dec.)–**04**. *W* **13**. *P* 14.
70 **19** ½d. green 12
71 **20** 1d. carmine 10
72 **21** 2d. brown (10.04) 45
73 **22** 2½d. ultramarine (3.04) .. 95 1·
74 **23** 3d. magenta (4.03) .. 55
75 **24** 4d. olive-green (2.03) .. 95
76 **25** 6d. bright mauve (3.03) .. 95
77 **26** 1s. yellow-ochre .. 1·50
78 **27** 5s. brown-orange (2.03) .. 7·50 2·
70/78 .. .. *Set of* 9 12·00 4·

All values exist in imperf. pairs, from pro sheets.
When the Union of South Africa came in being in 1910 the stamps of the Cape of Go Hope (except the already demonetised triang lars) became available for postal use througho the Union, until December 31st, 1937, fro which date the stamps of the four provinces the Union were demonetised. For Union issu see under South Africa.

MAFEKING SIEGE STAMPS.

There are numerous forgeries of the Mafeking verprints, many of which were brought home y soldiers returning from the Boer War.

24 MARCH TO 17 MAY, 1900.

MAFEKING,
3d.
BESIEGED.
(1)

MAFEKING
3d.
BESIEGED.
(2)

I. *Surcharged in fancy type as T* **1**.

(A) *On Cape of Good Hope stamps.*

6 1d. on ½d. green .. .. 35·00 14·00
17 1d. on ½d. green .. .. 40·00 15·00
,, 3d. on 1d. carmine .. .. 35·00 14·00
6 6d. on 3d. magenta .. .. £900 90·00
,, 1s. on 4d. sage-green .. £800 90·00

A variety in the setting of each value exists ithout comma after "MAFEKING".

B) *On Bechuanaland Prot. stamps of* 1897–1902.

1d. on ½d. vermilion .. .. 25·00 14·00
a. Surch. inverted .. .. — £1000
b. Vert. pr., surch. tête-bêche .. — £1100
3d. on 1d. lilac .. .. £275 22·00
a. Surch. double .. ..
6d. on 2d. green and carmine £300 22·00
6d. on 3d. purple/*yellow* .. £750 75·00
a. Surch. inverted .. .. — £1100
b. Surch. double .. ..

(C) *On British Bechuanaland stamps.*

6d. on 3d. lilac & blk. (No. 12) £120 20·00
1s. on 4d. green and purple-brown (No. 35) .. .. £400 22·00
a. Surch. double .. .. — £1200
b. Surch. treble .. .. — £1700
c. Surch. double, one inverted .. — £1700

II. *Surcharged in thin block letters as T* **2**.

(A) *On Bechuanaland Protectorate stamps.*

3d. on 1d. lilac (No. 61) .. £250 18·00
a. Surch. double .. .. — £1200
6d. on 2d. grn. & carm. (No. 62) £325 20·00
1s. on 6d. pur./*r.-red* (No. 65) £500 28·00

(B) *On British Bechuanaland stamps.*

1s. on 6d. purple/*r.-red* (No. 36) £1000 £225
2s. on 1s. green (No. 37) .. £900 £100

No. 11a has both surcharges T **1**. Copies exist ith normal surcharge T **1** and the second surarge T **2** but are believed to be trials.

In the stamps overprinted "BECHUANALAND ROTECTORATE" and "BRITISH BECHUANALAND" e local surcharge is so adjusted as not to overlap e original overprint.

3

Cadet Sergt.-major Goodyear.

4

General Baden-Powell.

(Des. Dr. W. A. Hayes.) (Des. Capt. Greener.)

I. *Produce photographically by Mr. D. Taylor. Horiz. laid paper with sheet wmk.* "OCEANA FINE". *P* 12.

(*a*) 18½ *mm. wide.* (*b*) 21 *mm. wide.*

3 1d. pale blue/*blue* £300 £100
,, 1d. deep blue,*blue* £300 £110
a. Imperf. (pair) £2500
4 3d. pale blue/*blue* (*a*) .. £450 £160
,, 3d. deep blue/*blue* (*a*) .. £500 £130
a. Imperf. between (horiz. pair) — £2250
b. Double print .. .. — £2250
,, 3d. pale blue/*blue* (*b*) .. £1500 £350
,, 3d. deep blue/*blue* (*b*) .. £1600 £450

Variety. Reversed design.

4 3d. blue/*blue* (*a*) £4000 £2750

These stamps vary a great deal in colour from ep blue to pale grey.

VRYBURG.

TEMPORARY BOER OCCUPATION.

½ PENCE

Z.A.R.

(1)

1899 (Nov.). *Cape stamps surch. as T* **1**. A. *Surch.* 10 *mm. high.* B. *Surch.* 12 *mm. high.*

			A.		B.	
1	**6**	½ PENCE, green	40·00	25·00	—	90·00
2	**17**	1 PENCE, rose ..	48·00	28·00	—	£110
3	**4**	2 PENCE on 6d. mauve ..	†		£750	£130
4	**15**	2½ pence, blue ..	£500	£100	—	—

Nos. 1A, 2A, 4A, and 3B are known with italic "Z" in the surcharge.

BRITISH REOCCUPATION.

V. R. SPECIAL POST

(2)

1900 (MAY). *Provisionals issued by the Military Authorities. Stamps of Transvaal optd. with T* **2**.

11 **33** ½d. green £225
12 ,, 1d. carmine and green .. £300 £275
13 ,, 2d. deep brown and green
14 ,, 2½d. blue and green ..

CAYMAN ISLANDS.

I. DEPENDENCY OF JAMAICA.

1

(T **1/9** and **12/13** typo. De La Rue & Co.)

1900 (Nov.). *Wmk. Crown CA. P* 14.

1 **1** ½d. deep green.. .. .. 1·50 2·00
a. Pale green .. .. 45 1·00
2 ,, 1d. rose-carmine .. .. 1·75 80
a. Pale carmine .. .. 3·25 3·25
1/2 Optd. "Specimen" *Set of* 2 30·00

2

3

1901 (20 DEC.)–**03**. *Wmk. Crown CA. P* 14.

3 **2** ½d. green (15.9.02) .. .. 1·50 1·50
4 ,, 1d. carmine (6.3.03) .. 3·00 2·75
5 ,, 2½d. bright blue .. .. 4·50 5·50
6 ,, 6d. brown .. .. 12·00 11·00
7 **3** 1s. orange .. .. 25·00 27·00
3/7 .. .. *Set of* 5 42·00 45·00
3/7 Optd. "Specimen" *Set of* 5 65·00

1905 (MAR.–18 OCT.). *Wmk. Mult. Crown CA. P* 14.

8 **2** ½d. green 35 90
9 ,, 1d. carmine (18.10) .. 3·00 4·00
10 ,, 2½d. bright blue .. .. 2·00 3·50
11 ,, 6d. brown .. .. 11·00 13·00
12 **3** 1s. orange .. .. 26·00 30·00
8/12 .. .. *Set of* 5 38·00 45·00

1907 (13 MAR.). *Wmk. Mult. Crown CA. P* 14.

13 **3** 4d. brown and blue .. 15·00 17·00
14 **2** 6d. olive and rose .. .. 15·00 17·00
15 **3** 1s. violet and green .. 28·00 32·00
16 ,, 5s. salmon and green .. £100 £130
13/16 Optd. "Specimen" *Set of* 4 75·00

One
Halfpenny.

(4)

1907 (30 AUG.). *No.* 9 *surch. at Govt. Printing Office, Kingston, with T* **4**.

17 **2** ½d. on 1d. carmine .. .. 25·00 32·00

(5) (6) (7)

1907 (Nov.). *No.* 16 *handstamped at Georgetown P.O. with T* **5** *or* **6**.

18 **3** ½d. on 5s. salmon & grn. (26.11) £100 £130
a. Surch. inverted £3000
b. Surch. double £2000 £2250
c. Surch. double, one inverted ..
d. Surch. omitted (in pair with normal) £4500
19 ,, 1d. on 5s. salmon & grn. (23.11) £100 £130
a. Surch. double £2250

The ½d. on 5s. may be found with the figures "1" or "2" omitted, owing to defective handstamping.

1908 (12 FEB.). *No.* 13 *handstamped locally with T* **7**.

24 2½d. on 4d. brown and blue £900 £1000
a. Surch. double .. .. — £5000

The 1d. on 4d. is a revenue stamp and was never authorised for postal use (*price* £60 *un.*). Exists with surcharge inverted (*price* £400 *un.*).

8

9

1907 (17 DEC.)–**09**. *Ordinary paper* (½*d. to* 2½*d.*) *or chalk-surfaced paper* (*others*). *P* 14.

(*a*) *Wmk. Mult. Crown CA.*

25 **8** ½d. green 60 65
26 ,, 1d. carmine 60 60
27 ,, 2½d. ultramarine (30.3.08) .. 2·50 4·00
28 **9** 3d. purple/*yellow* (30.3.08) 2·50 4·00
29 ,, 4d. black and red/*yellow* (30.3.08) .. .. 30·00 32·00
30 **8** 6d. dull & bright purple (2.10.08) .. .. 3·50 7·50
a. Dull purple and violet-purple 3·50 7·50
31 **9** 1s. blk./*green* (5.4.09) .. 4·00 7·50
32 ,, 5s. grn. & red/*yell.* (30.3.08) 28·00 32·00

(*b*) *Wmk. Crown CA* (30.3.08)

33 **9** 1s. black/*green* .. .. 15·00 20·00
34 **8** 10s. green and red/*green* .. £110 £130
25/34 .. .. *Set of* 10 £180 £225
25/34 Optd. "Specimen" *Set of* 10 £120

11

1908 (30 JUNE)–**09**. *Wmk. Mult. Crown CA. Litho. P* 14.

38 **11** ¼d. brown, O (Optd. S. £18) 12 25
a. Grey-brown (2.09) .. 40 65

12

13

1912 (24 Apr.)–**20.** *Wmk. Mult. Crown CA. Ordinary paper (½d. to 2½d.) or chalk-surfaced paper (others).* P 14.

No.	Type	Description	Unused	Used
40	**13**	½d. brown (10.2.13) ..	15	30
41	**12**	½d. green	30	70
42	,,	1d. red (25.2.13)	60	90
43	**13**	2d. pale grey	60	1·00
44	**12**	2½d. bright blue (26.8.14) ..	2·25	3·50
		a. *Deep bright blue* (9.11.17) ..	2·50	3·50
45	**13**	3d. purple/*yellow* (26.11.14)	3·50	3·75
		a. *White back* (19.11.13) (Optd. S. £12)	1·40	2·00
		b. *On lemon* (12.3.18)	1·40	2·00
		c. *On orange-buff* (1920) ..	1·50	3·50
		d. *On pale yellow* (1920) ..	2·25	3·50
46	,,	4d. blk. & red/*yell.* (25.2.13)	85	1·60
47	**12**	6d. dull & brt. pur. (25.2.13)	1·40	2·50
48	**13**	1s. black/*green* (15.5.16) ..	3·00	3·50
		a. *White back* (19.11.13) (Optd S. £16)	2·75	3·50
49	,,	2s. purple & brt. blue/*blue*	7·50	10·00
50	,,	3s. green and violet ..	10·00	12·00
51	,,	5s. grn. & red/*yell.* (26.8.14)	25·00	35·00
52	**12**	10s. deep green & red/*grn.* (26.11.14)	50·00	65·00
		a. *White back* (19.11.13) (Optd. S. £20)	50·00	65·00
		b. *On blue-green, olive back* (5.10.18)	45·00	65·00
40/52*b*		*Set of* 13	90·00	£120
40/52		Optd. "Specimen" *Set of* 13	£110	

WAR
STAMP.
1½d
(14)

WAR
STAMP.
1½d
(15)

1917 (26 Feb.) *T* **12**, *surch. with T* **14** *or* **15.**

No.	Type	Description	Unused	Used
53	**14**	1½d. on 2½d. deep blue ..	80	1·50
		a. No fraction bar	15·00	18·00
54	**15**	1½d. on 2½d. deep blue ..	45	1·25
		a. No fraction bar	7·50	11·00

In No. 53 the spacing between the word "STAMP" and the top of the figure "1" varies between 1½ mm. and 5 mm.

WAR STAMP 1½d (16)

WAR STAMP 1½d (17)

WAR STAMP 1½d. (18)

1917 (4 Sept.). *T* **12** *surch. with T* **16** *or* **17.**

No.	Type	Description	Unused	Used
55	**16**	1½d. on 2½d. deep blue ..	£225	£300
56	**17**	1½d. on 2½d. deep blue (Optd. S. £20)	12	15

1919–20. *T* **12** *and* **13** *(2½d. special printing), optd. only, or surch. in addition.*

No.	Type	Description	Unused	Used
57	**16**	½d. green (4.2.19)	25	25
58	**18**	1½d. on 2d. grey (10.3.20) ..	60	1·10
59	**17**	1½d. on 2½d. orange (4.2.19)	60	85
57, 59		Optd. "Specimen" *Set of* 2	28·00	

In T **16** the "R" of "WAR" has a curved foot and the other letters vary slightly from T **17**. "1½d." is in thin type. In T **17** the "R" has straight foot, and the "1½d." differs.

The ½d. stamps on *buff* paper, and later consignments of the 2d. T **13** on *pinkish*, derived their colour from the paper in which they were packed for despatch from England.

19

(Recess. D.L.R.)

1921 (4 Apr.)–**26.** P 14.

(*a*) *Wmk. Mult. Crown CA*

No.	Type	Description	Unused	Used
60	**19**	3d. purple/*orange-buff* ..	1·25	2·50
		a. *Purple/pale yellow* ..	15·00	20·00
62	,,	4d. red/*yellow* (1.4.22) ..	75	2·50
63	,,	1s. black/*green*	2·25	4·50
64	,,	5s. yellow-green/*pale yellow*	13·00	22·00
		a. *Blue-green/pale yellow* ..	16·00	32·00
		b. *Deep green/orange-buff* (19.11.21)	22·00	32·00
67	,,	10s. carmine/*green* (19.11.21)	38·00	48·00
60/67		.. .. *Set of* 5	50·00	70·00
60/67		Optd. "Specimen" *Set of* 5	80·00	

(*b*) *Wmk. Mult. Script CA.*

No.	Type	Description	Unused	Used
69	**19**	¼d. yellow-brown (1.4.22)	20	30
70	,,	½d. pale grey-green (1.4.22)	30	40
71	,,	1d. deep carmine-red (1.4.22)	25	50
72	,,	1½d. orange-brown	40	60
73	,,	2d. slate-grey (1.4.22) ..	60	90
74	,,	2½d. bright blue (1.4.22) ..	70	90
75	,,	3d. purple/*yell.* (29.6.23) ..	70	1·00
76	,,	4½d. sage-green (29.6.23) ..	1·10	2·50
77	,,	6d. claret (1.4.22) ..	2·50	4·00
	,,	a. *Deep claret*	6·50	9·00
79	,,	1s. black/*green* (15.5.25) ..	1·75	4·00
80	,,	2s. violet/*blue* (1.4.22) ..	5·50	10·00
81	,,	3s. violet (1.4.22) ..	12·00	16·00
82	,,	5s. green/*yellow* (15.5.25)	16·00	18·00
83	,,	10s. carmine/*green* (5.9.26)	35·00	48·00
69/83		.. .. *Set of* 14	75·00	£100
69/83		Optd. "Specimen" *Set of* 14	£120	

20. King William IV and King George V.

(Recess. Waterlow.)

1932 (5 Dec.). *Centenary of the "Assembly of Justices and Vestry". Wmk. Mult. Script CA.* P 12½.

No.	Type	Description	Unused	Used
84	**20**	¼d. brown	35	55
85	,,	½d. green	50	80
86	,,	1d. scarlet	50	75
87	,,	1½d. red-orange	70	80
88	,,	2d. grey	90	1·10
89	,,	2½d. ultramarine	90	1·10
90	,,	3d. olive-green	1·75	3·50
91	,,	6d. purple	6·00	9·00
92	,,	1s. black and brown ..	11·00	14·00
93	,,	2s. black and ultramarine	22·00	25·00
94	,,	5s. black and green ..	55·00	65·00
95	,,	10s. black and scarlet ..	£140	£180
84/95		.. .. *Set of* 12	£225	£275
84/95		Perf. "Specimen" *Set of* 12	£150	

1935 (6 May). *Silver Jubilee. As Nos.* 91/4 *of Antigua.* P 13½ × 14.

No.	Description	Unused	Used
96	½d. black and green	12	25
97	2½d. brown and deep blue ..	90	1·40
98	6d. light blue and olive-green	1·50	2·25
99	1s. slate and purple	2·25	3·00
96/9	Perf. "Specimen" *Set of* 4	18·00	

21. Cayman Islands.

22. Cat Boat.

23. Booby Birds.

24. Conch Shells and Coconut Palms.

25. Hawksbill Turtles.

(Recess. Waterlow & Sons.)

1935. *Wmk. Mult. Script CA.* P 12½.

No.	Type	Description	Unused	Used
100	**21**	¼d. black and brown ..	8	
101	**22**	½d. ultram. & yell.-green	15	
102	**23**	1d. ultramarine & scarlet	1·50	
103	**24**	1½d. black and orange ..	70	
104	**22**	2d. ultramarine & purple	70	
105	**25**	2½d. blue and black ..	3·00	
106	**21**	3d. black and olive-green	90	
107	**25**	6d. bright purple & black	3·25	3·
108	**22**	1s. ultramarine & orange	3·00	3·
109	**23**	2s. ultramarine & black	18·00	20·
110	**25**	5s. green and black ..	22·00	25·
111	**24**	10s. black and scarlet ..	32·00	38·
100/111		.. .. *Set of* 12	80·00	85·
100/11		Perf. "Specimen" *Set of* 12	65·00	

1937 (13 May). *Coronation Issue. As Nos.* 13/ *of Aden but ptd. by B.W. & Co.* P 11 × 11½.

No.	Description	Unused	Used
112	½d. green	30	
113	1d. carmine	30	
114	2½d. blue	60	
112/14	Perf. "Specimen" *Set of* 3	13·00	

26. Beach View.

27. Dolphin fish (*Coryphaena hippurus*).

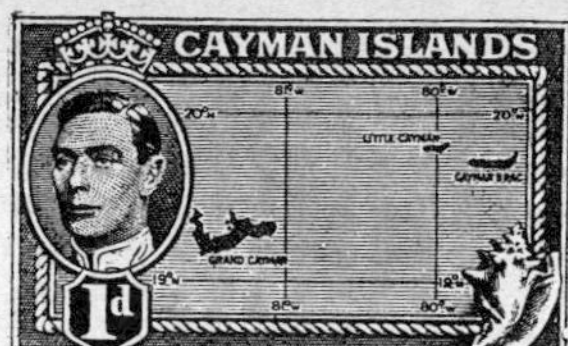

28. Cayman Islands.

29. Cayman Schooner.

30. Hawksbill Turtles.

(Recess. D.L.R. (*T* **27** and **30**), Waterlow (others).)

938 (5 May)–**47**. *Wmk. Mult. Script CA (sideways on T* **26** *and* **28/9**). *Various perfs.*

15	**26**	$\frac{1}{4}$d. red-orange (*p.* 12$\frac{1}{2}$) ..	5	12
		a. Perf. 13$\frac{1}{2}$ × 12$\frac{1}{2}$ (16.7.43)	8	20
16	**27**	$\frac{1}{2}$d. green (*p.* 13 × 11$\frac{1}{2}$) ..	5	12
		a. Perf. 14 (16.7.43) ..	5	15
17	**28**	1d. scarlet (*p.* 12$\frac{1}{2}$) ..	8	15
18	**26**	1$\frac{1}{2}$d. black (*p.* 12$\frac{1}{2}$) ..	10	15
19	**30**	2d. violet (*p.* 11$\frac{1}{2}$ × 13) ..	25	25
		a. Perf. 14 (16.7.43) ..	12	25
20	**29**	2$\frac{1}{2}$d. bright blue (*p.* 12$\frac{1}{2}$) ..	10	25
20*a*	,,	2$\frac{1}{2}$d. orange (*p.* 12$\frac{1}{2}$) (25.8.47)	1·00	35
21	**28**	3d. orange (*p.* 12$\frac{1}{2}$) ..	20	50
21*a*	,,	3d. bright blue (*p.* 12$\frac{1}{2}$) (25.8.47)	45	40
22	**30**	6d. olive-grn. (*p.* 11$\frac{1}{2}$ × 13)	90	1·60
		a. Perf. 14 (16.7.43) ..	45	40
		b. Brownish olive, p. 11$\frac{1}{2}$ × 13 (8.7.47)	75	90
23	**27**	1s. red-brn. (*p.* 13 × 11$\frac{1}{2}$)	1·10	1·50
		a. Perf. 14 (16.7.43) ..	70	85
24	**26**	2s. yellow-green (*shades*) (*p.* 12$\frac{1}{2}$)	4·00	6·00
		a. Deep green (16.7.43) ..	3·50	4·50
25	**29**	5s. crimson (*p.* 12$\frac{1}{2}$) ..	2·50	3·25
26	**30**	10s. chocolate (*p.* 11$\frac{1}{2}$ × 13)	6·00	4·50
		a. Perf. 14 (16.7.43) ..	6·50	4·00
15/126*a*		.. .. *Set of* 14	14·00	14·00
15/26		Perf. "Specimen" *Set of* 14	50·00	

946 (26 Aug.). *Victory. As Nos.* 28/9 *of Aden.*

27	1$\frac{1}{2}$d. black	10	10
28	3d. orange-yellow ..	8	8
27/8	Perf. "Specimen" *Set of* 2	13·00	

948 (29 Nov.). *Royal Silver Wedding. As Nos.* 30/1 *of Aden.*

29	$\frac{1}{2}$d. green	10	10
30	10s. violet-blue	5·50	6·50

949 (10 Oct.). *75th Anniv. of Universal Postal Union. As Nos.* 114/17 *of Antigua.*

31	2$\frac{1}{2}$d. orange	15	25
32	3d. deep blue	25	30
33	6d. olive	30	65
34	1s. red-brown	65	90

31. Cat Boat.

32. Coconut Grove, Cayman Brac.

33. Green Turtle.

34. Thatch Rope Industry.

35. Caymanian Seamen.

36. Cayman Islands (map).

37. Parrot Fish.

38. Bluff, Cayman Brac.

39. Georgetown Harbour.

40. Turtle in "Crawl".

41. Cayman Schooner.

42. Boat-building.

43. Government Offices, Grand Cayman.

(Recess. Bradbury, Wilkinson.)

1950 (2 Oct.). *Wmk. Mult. Script CA. P* 11$\frac{1}{2}$ × 11.

135	**31**	$\frac{1}{4}$d. bt. blue & pale scarlet	15	25
136	**32**	$\frac{1}{2}$d. reddish violet and emerald-green ..	15	25
137	**33**	1d. olive-grn. & deep blue	30	40
138	**34**	1$\frac{1}{2}$d. green and brown ..	20	25
139	**35**	2d. reddish violet and rose-carmine ..	30	40
140	**36**	2$\frac{1}{2}$d. turquoise and black ..	40	20

141	**37**	3d. bt. green & light blue	80	70
142	**38**	6d. red-brown and blue ..	80	80
143	**39**	9d. scarlet and grey-green	1·50	1·40
144	**40**	1s. brown and orange ..	1·40	1·75
145	**41**	2s. violet & reddish purple	2·50	3·25
146	**42**	5s. olive-green and violet	3·50	4·00
147	**43**	10s. black and scarlet ..	5·50	8·00
135/147		.. .. *Set of* 13	16·00	20·00

44. Lighthouse, South Sound, Grand Cayman. **45.** Queen Elizabeth II.

(Recess. B.W.)

1953–59. *As T* **31/43** (*but with portrait of Queen Elizabeth II in place of King George VI*) *and T* **44/5**. *Wmk. Mult. Script CA. P* 11½×11 *or* 11×11½. (*T* **44/5**).

148	**31**	¼d. deep bright blue and rose-red (*shades*) ..	8	10
149	**32**	½d. purple & bluish green	8	10
150	**33**	1d. brown-olive & indigo	8	10
151	**34**	1½d. dp. green & red-brown	8	10
152	**35**	2d. reddish violet & cerise	10	12
153	**36**	2½d. turquoise-blue & black	12	15
154	**37**	3d. bright green and blue	20	25
155	**44**	4d. blk. & dp. blue (*shades*)	30	35
156	**38**	6d. lake-brown & deep blue	25	30
157	**39**	9d. scarlet & bluish green	30	35
158	**40**	1s. brown and red-orange	35	40
159	**41**	2s. slate-vio. & reddish pur.	1·50	1·75
160	**42**	5s. olive-grn. & slate-vio.	3·00	3·75
161	**43**	10s. black and rose-red ..	6·00	7·50
161*a*	**45**	£1 blue	12·00	14·00
148/161*a*		.. .. *Set of* 15	22·00	26·00

Dates of issue:—2.3.53, 4d.; 2.6.54, 2d., 2½d., 9d.; 7.7.54, ½d., 1d., 1½d., 6d.; 6.1.59, £1; 21.2.55, others.

1953 (2 June). *Coronation. As No.* 47 *of Aden but ptd. by B. W.*

162	1d. black and emerald ..	20	30

46. Arms of the Cayman Islands.

(Photo. D.L.R.)

1959 (4 July). *New Constitution. Wmk. Mult. Script CA. P* 12.

163	**46**	2½d. black and light blue ..	35	40
164	,,	1s. black and orange ..	45	45

II. CROWN COLONY.

47. Cayman Parrot.

55. Angler with Kingfish.

48. Cat Boat.

49. *Schomburgkia thomsoniana* (orchid).

50. Cayman Islands (map).

51. Fisherman casting Net.

52. West Bay Beach.

53. Green Turtle.

54. Cayman Schooner.

56. Iguana.

57. Swimming Pool, Cayman Brac.

58. Water Sports.

59. Fort George.

60. Arms.

61. Queen Elizabeth I[illegible]

(Recess. B.W.)

1962 (28 Nov.). *W* w.**12**. *P* 11×11½ (*vert.*) [illegible] 11½×11 (*horiz.*).

165	**47**	¼d. emerald & red (*shades*)	5	
166	**48**	1d. black and yellow-olive	5	
167	**49**	1½d. yellow and purple ..	5	
168	**50**	2d. blue and deep brown	5	
169	**51**	2½d. violet & bluish green	5	
170	**52**	3d. brt. blue and carmine	8	[illegible]
171	**53**	4d. deep green and purple	12	[illegible]
172	**54**	6d. bluish green and sepia	15	[illegible]
173	**55**	9d. ultramarine & purple	20	[illegible]
174	**56**	1s. sepia and rose-red ..	25	[illegible]
175	**57**	1s. 3d. bluish green and orange-brown ..	75	[illegible]
176	**58**	1s. 9d. dp. turq. & violet	85	[illegible]
177	**59**	5s. plum and deep green	1·75	[illegible]
178	**60**	10s. olive and blue ..	2·75	[illegible]
179	**61**	£1 carmine and black ..	5·50	[illegible]
165/79		.. .. *Set of* 15	11·00	[illegible]

1963 (4 June). *Freedom from Hunger. As N*[illegible] *76 of Aden.*

180	1s. 9d. carmine	1·25	[illegible]

1963 (2 Sept.). *Red Cross Centenary. As Nos.* 147/8 *of Antigua.*

181 1d. red and black 5 5
182 1s. 9d. red and blue.. .. 1·50 1·50

1964 (23 April). *400th Anniv. of Birth of William Shakespeare. As No.* 164 *of Antigua.*

183 6d. magenta 15 20

1965 (17 May). *I.T.U. Centenary. As Nos.* 166/7 *of Antigua.*

184 1d. blue and light purple .. 5 5
185 1s. 3d. bright purple & green 45 50

1965 (25 Oct.). *International Co-operation Year. As Nos.* 168/9 *of Antigua.*

186 1d. reddish pur. & turq.-grn. 5 5
187 1s. dp. bluish green & lav. 40 45

1966 (24 Jan.). *Churchill Commemoration. As Nos.* 170/3 *of Antigua.*

188 ½d. new blue 5 5
189 1d. deep green 5 5
190 1s. brown 35 40
191 1s. 9d. bluish violet .. 55 60

1966 (4 Feb.). *Royal Visit. As Nos.* 174/5 *of Antigua.*

192 1d. black and ultramarine .. 5 5
193 1s. 9d. black and magenta .. 40 45

1966 (1 July). *World Cup Football Championships. As Nos.* 176/7 *of Antigua.*

194 1½d. violet, yellow-green, lake and yellow-brown .. 5 5
195 1s. 9d. chocolate, blue-green, lake and yellow-brown .. 35 40

1966 (20 Sept.). *Inauguration of W.H.O. Headquarters, Geneva. As Nos.* 178/9 *of Antigua.*

196 2d. black, yellow-green and light blue 8 8
197 1s. 3d. black, light purple and yellow brown 45 45

62. Telephone and Map.

(Des. V. Whiteley. Litho Harrison.)

1966 (5 Dec.). *International Telephone Links.* W w.**12**. P 14½ × 14.

198 **62** 4d. red, black, greenish blue and olive-green .. 15 15
199 ,, 9d. violet-blue, blk., brown-red and light green .. 30 30

1966 (12 Dec.*). *20th Anniv. of U.N.E.S.C.O. As Nos.* 196/8 *of Antigua.*

200 1d. slate-violet, red, yellow and orange 5 5
201 1s. 9d. orange-yellow, violet and deep olive 40 45
202 5s. black, brt. pur. & orge. .. 1·00 1·10

*This is the local date of issue; the Crown Agents released the stamps on 1st December.

63. BAC 1–11 Airliner over Cayman Schooner.

(Des. V. Whiteley. Photo. Harrison.)

1966 (17 Dec.). *Opening of Cayman Jet Service.* W w.**12**. P 14½.

203 **63** 1s. black, new blue and olive-green 20 25
204 ,, 1s. 9d. deep purple-brown, ultramarine & emerald 30 35

64. Water-skiing.

65. Skin Diving.

66. Sport Fishing.

67. Sailing.

(Des. G. L. Vasarhelyi. Photo. Harrison.)

1967 (1 Dec.). *International Tourist Year.* W w.**12**. P 14½ × 14.

205 **64** 4d. multicoloured .. 5 5
a. Gold omitted .. .. 80·00 55·00
206 **65** 6d. multicoloured .. 10 10
207 **66** 1s. multicoloured .. 20 20
208 **67** 1s. 9d. multicoloured .. 30 30

A used copy of No. 207 is known with yellow omitted.

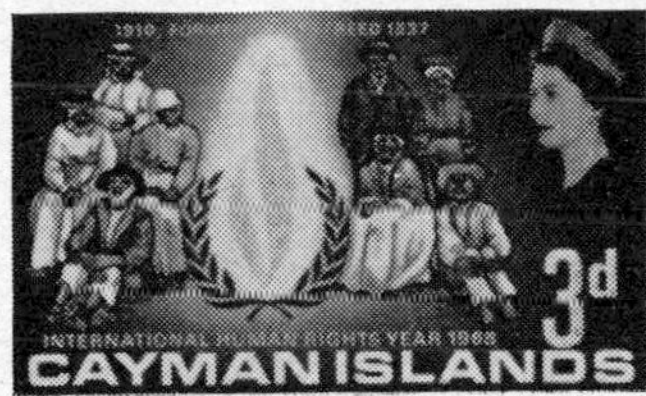

68. Former Slaves and Emblem.

(Des. and photo. Harrison.)

1968 (3 June). *Human Rights Year.* W w.**12**. P 14½ × 14.

209 **68** 3d. deep bluish green, black and gold .. 8 8
210 ,, 9d. brown, gold & myrtle-green 20 20
211 ,, 5s. ultramarine, gold and myrtle-green .. 70 75

69. Long-Jumping.

70. High-Jumping. (*Horiz.*)

71. Pole-Vaulting. (*Vert.*)

(Des. R. Granger Barrett. Litho. Perkins, Bacon Ltd.)

1968 (1 Oct.). *Olympic Games, Mexico.* W w.**12**. P 13½.

212 **69** 1s. multicoloured 25 25
213 **70** 1s. 3d. multicoloured .. 30 30
214 **71** 2s. multicoloured 45 45

72. " The Adoration of the Shepherds " (Fabritius).

73. " The Adoration of the Shepherds " (Rembrandt).

(Des. and photo. Harrison.)

1968–69. *Christmas. Centres multicoloured; country name and frames in gold; value and background in colours given.* P 14 × 14½.

(*a*) W w.**12** (18.11.68).

215 **72** ½d. brown 5 5
a. Gold omitted £125
216 **73** 1d. bluish violet 5 5
217 **72** 6d. bright blue 12 12
218 **73** 8d. cerise 20 20
219 **72** 1s. 3d. bright green .. 25 25
220 **73** 2s. grey 45 45

(*b*) *No wmk.* (8.1.69)

221 **72** ½d. bright purple 5 5
215/21 .. .. *Set of* 7 1·00 1·00

74. Cayman Red-legged Thrush.

75. Brahmin Cattle.

76. Blowholes on the Coast. (*As T* **75**.)

77. Map of Grand Cayman. (*As T* **74**.)

78. Georgetown Scene. (*As T* **74**.)

79. Royal Poinciana. (*As T* **75**.)

80. Cayman Brac and Little Cayman on Chart. (*As T* **74**.)

81. Motor Vessels at Berth. (*As T* **75**.)

82. Basket-Making. (*As T* **75**.)

83. Beach Scene. (*As T* **75**.)

84. Straw-rope Making (*As T* **75**.)

85. Barracuda. (*As T* **74**.)

86. Government House. (*As T* **75**.)

87. Arms of the Cayman Islands.

88. Queen Elizabeth II. (*Vert.*)

(Des. G. L. Vasarhelyi. Litho. Format International.)

1969 (5 June). *No Wmk. P* 14.

222	**74**	½d. multicoloured ..	5	5
223	**75**	1d. multicoloured ..	5	5
224	**76**	2d. multicoloured ..	5	5
225	**77**	2½d. multicoloured ..	8	8
226	**78**	3d. multicoloured ..	10	10
227	**79**	4d. multicoloured ..	12	15
228	**80**	6d. multicoloured ..	15	20
229	**81**	8d. multicoloured ..	20	25
230	**82**	1s. multicoloured ..	25	30
231	**83**	1s. 3d. multicoloured ..	40	50
232	**84**	1s. 6d. multicoloured ..	50	60
233	**85**	2s. multicoloured ..	60	75
234	**86**	4s. multicoloured ..	90	1·10
235	**87**	10s. multicoloured ..	2·25	2·50
236	**88**	£1 black, ochre and red	4·25	4·75
222/36		.. .. *Set of* 15	9·00	10·00

1969 (11 Aug.). *As No.* 222, *but wmk.* w.**12** (*sideways*).

237	**74**	½d. multicoloured	8	15

(New currency. 100 cents=1 dollar.)

C-DAY
8th September 1969
¼c═

(89)

1969 (8 Sept.). *Decimal Currency. No.* 237, *and as Nos.* 223/36, *but wmk.* w.**12** (*sideways on horiz. designs*), *surch as T* **89**.

238	**74**	¼ c. on ½d.	5	5
239	**75**	1 c. on 1d.	5	5
240	**76**	2 c. on 2d.	5	5
241	**79**	3 c. on 4d.	5	5
242	**77**	4 c. on 2½d.	5	8
243	**80**	5 c. on 6d.	8	10
244	**81**	7 c. on 8d.	10	12
245	**78**	8 c. on 3d.	12	15
246	**82**	10 c. on 1s.	15	20
247	**83**	12 c. on 1s. 3d.	30	40
248	**84**	15 c. on 1s. 6d.	40	50
249	**85**	20 c. on 2s.	50	60
250	**86**	40 c. on 4s.	75	85
251	**87**	$1 on 10s.	2·25	2·50
252	**88**	$2 on £1	4·50	5·50
238/52		.. .. *Set of* 15	8·50	10·00

90. " Madonna and Child " (Vivarini).

91. " The Adoration of the Kings " (Gossaert).

(Des. Adapted by G. Drummond. Photo. Harrison.)

1969 (14 Nov.*). *Christmas. Multicoloured; background colours given. W* w.**12** (*sideways on* 1, 7 *and* 20 *c.*). *P* 14½.

253	**90**	¼ c. orange-red	5	5
254	,,	¼ c. magenta	5	5
255	,,	¼ c. emerald	5	5
		a. Gold frame omitted ..	85·00	
256	,,	¼ c. new blue	5	5
257	**91**	1 c. ultramarine	5	5
258	**90**	5 c. orange-red	8	10
259	**91**	7 c. myrtle-green ..	15	20
260	**90**	12 c. emerald	25	30
261	**91**	20 c. brown-purple ..	40	45
253/61		.. .. *Set of* 9	1·00	1·10

*This is the local release date. The Crown Agents released the stamps on 4th November.

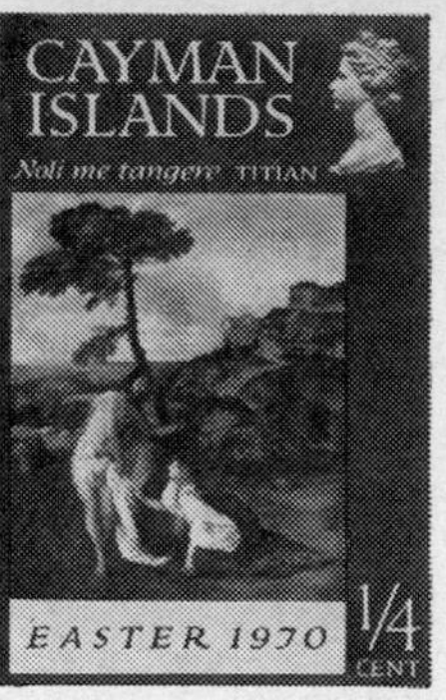

92. " Noli me tangere " (Titian).

(Des. L. D. Curtis. Litho. De La Rue.)

1970 (23 Mar.). *Easter. Paintings multicoloured; frame colours given. P* 14.

262	**92**	¼ c. carmine-red	5	5
263	,,	¼ c. deep green	5	5
264	,,	¼ c. yellow-brown ..	5	5
265	,,	¼ c. pale violet ..	5	5
266	,,	10 c. chalky blue	15	20
267	,,	12 c. chestnut	25	25
268	,,	40 c. plum	55	55
262/68		.. .. *Set of* 7	1·00	1·10

93. Barnaby (*Barnaby Rudge*).

94. Sairey Gamp (*Martin Chuzzlewit*).

95. Mr. Micawber and David (*David Copperfield*).

96. The " Marchioness " (*The Old Curiosity Shop*).

(Des. Jennifer Toombs. Photo. Harrison.)

1970 (17 June). *Death Centenary of Charles Dickens. W* w.**12** (*sideways*). *P* 14½×14.

269	**93**	1 c. black, olive-green and greenish yellow ..	8	8
270	**94**	12 c. black, lake-brown and red	25	25
271	**95**	20 c. black, ochre-brown and gold	35	40
272	**96**	40 c. black, bright ultramarine and new blue	60	65

97. Cayman Red-legged Thrush.

1970 (8 Sept.). *Decimal Currency. Designs as Nos.* 223/37, *but with values inscr. in decimal currency as T* **97**. *W* w.**12** (*sideways on cent values*).

273	**97**	¼ c. multicoloured ..	5	5
274	**75**	1 c. multicoloured ..	5	5
275	**76**	2 c. multicoloured ..	5	5
276	**79**	3 c. multicoloured ..	5	5
277	**77**	4 c. multicoloured ..	5	5
278	**80**	5 c. multicoloured ..	8	8
279	**81**	7 c. multicoloured ..	10	10
280	**78**	8 c. multicoloured ..	10	12
281	**82**	10 c. multicoloured ..	12	15
282	**83**	12 c. multicoloured ..	20	25
283	**84**	15 c. multicoloured ..	30	35
284	**85**	20 c. multicoloured ..	40	40
285	**86**	40 c. multicoloured ..	75	85
286	**87**	$1 multicoloured ..	2·25	2·50
287	**88**	$2 black, ochre and red	4·25	4·75
273/87		.. .. *Set of* 15	8·00	9·00

98. The Three Wise Men.

99. Nativity Scene and Globe.

(Des. G. Drummond. Litho. Format.)

1970 (8 Oct.). *Christmas. W* w.**12** (*sideways*). *P* 14.

288	**98**	¼ c. apple-green, grey and emerald	5	5
289	**99**	1 c. black, lemon and turquoise-green ..	5	5
290	**98**	5 c. grey, red-orange and crimson	10	10
291	**99**	10 c. black, lemon and orange-red	20	20
292	**98**	12 c. grey, pale turquoise and ultramarine ..	25	30
293	**99**	20 c. black, lemon & green	35	40
288/93		.. .. *Set of* 6	85	95

100. Grand Cayman Terrapin.

(Des. V. Whiteley. Photo. Harrison.)

1971 (28 Jan.). *Turtles. T* **100** *and similar diamond-shaped designs. W* w.**12** (*sideways, reading from inscr. to* " islands "). *P* 14½×14.

294	5 c. Type **100**	12	15
295	7 c. Green Turtle ..	20	25
296	12 c. Hawksbill Turtle ..	35	40
297	20 c. Turtle Farm	50	60

101. *Dendrophylax fawcettii.*

(Des. Mrs. S. Goaman. Litho. Questa.)

1971 (7 Apr.). *Orchids.* *T* **101** *and similar vert. designs. Multicoloured.* *W* w.**12**. *P* 14.

298	¼ c. Type **101**	5	5
299	2 c. *Schomburgkia thomsoniana*	8	8
300	10 c. *Vanilla claviculata* ..	25	30
301	40 c. *Oncidium variegatum* ..	65	70

102. "Adoration of the Magi" (Flemish, 15th Cent.).

(Des. Jennifer Toombs. Litho. Questa.)

1971 (15 Oct.*). *Christmas.* *T* **102** *and similar vert. designs. Multicoloured.* *W* w.**12**. *P* 14.

302	¼ c. Type **102**	8	8
303	1 c. "The Nativity" (Parisian, 14th Cent.) ..	8	8
304	5 c. "Adoration of the Magi" (Burgundian, 15th Cent.)	10	10
305	12 c. Type **102**	25	30
306	15 c. As 1 c.	30	35
307	20 c. As 5 c.	40	45
302/7	.. .. *Set of* 6	1·00	1·10
MS308	113 × 115 mm. Nos. 302/7	1·00	1·00

*This is the local date of issue. The Crown Agents released the stamps on 27th September.

103. Turtle and Telephone Cable.

(Des. Anglo Arts Associates. Litho. Walsall Security Printers.)

1972 (10 Jan.). *Co-Axial Telephone Cable.* *W* w.**12** (*sideways*). *P* 14.

309	**103**	2 c. multicoloured ..	8	8
310	,,	10 c. multicoloured ..	25	30
311	,,	40 c. multicoloured ..	90	95

104. Court House Building.

(Des. C. Abbott. Litho. Questa.)

1972 (15 Aug.). *New Government Buildings.* *T* **104** *and similar horiz. designs. Multicoloured.* *W* w.**12**. *P* 13½.

312	5 c. Type **104**	8	8
313	15 c. Legislative Assembly Building	30	30
314	25 c. Type **104**	45	45
315	40 c. As 15 c.	65	65
MS316	121 × 108 mm. Nos. 312/15	2·00	2·00

105. Hawksbill Turtle and Conch Shell.

(Des. (from photograph by D. Groves) and photo. Harrison.)

1972 (20 Nov.). *Royal Silver Wedding. Multicoloured; background colour given.* *W* w.**12**. *P* 14 × 14½.

317	**105**	12 c. deep slate-violet ..	20	20
318	,,	30 c. yellow-olive ..	45	50
		a. Blue omitted* ..	£100	

*The omission of the blue colour results in the Duke's suit appearing sepia instead of deep blue.

106. $1 Coin and Note.

(Des. and photo. D.L.R.)

1973 (15 Jan.). *First Issue of Currency.* *T* **106** *and similar horiz. designs. Multicoloured.* *W* w.**12** (sideways). *P* 13.

319	3 c. Type **106**	5	5
320	6 c. $5 Coin and note ..	12	12
321	15 c. $10 Coin and note ..	25	30
322	25 c. $25 Coin and note ..	35	40
MS323	128 × 107 mm. Nos. 319/22	1·10	1·10

107. "The Way of Sorrow".

(Des. G. Drummond. Litho. Questa.)

1973 (11 Apr.*). *Easter.* *T* **107** *and similar multicoloured designs showing stained-glass windows.* *W* w.**12** (*sideways on* 10 *and* 12 *c*). *P* 14½.

324	10 c. Type **107**	15	15
325	12 c. "Christ Resurrected"	20	20
326	20 c. "The Last Supper" (*horiz.*)	30	30
327	30 c. "Christ on the Cross" (*horiz.*)	40	40
MS328	122 × 105 mm. Nos. 324/7. Imperf.	1·25	1·25

*This is the local date of issue; the Crown Agents released the stamps on 15th March.

108 "The Nativity" (Sforza Book of Hours).

(Des. J. E. Cooter. Litho. Questa.)

1973 (2 Oct.). *Christmas.* *T* **108** *and similar vert. design.* *W* w.**12** (*sideways*). *P* 14.

329	**108**	3 c. multicoloured ..	5	5
330	–	5 c. multicoloured ..	8	8
331	**108**	9 c. multicoloured ..	12	12
332	–	12 c. multicoloured ..	20	20
333	**108**	15 c. multicoloured ..	25	25
334	–	25 c. multicoloured ..	35	35
329/34		.. .. *Set of* 6	90	90

Design:—5, 12, 25 c. "The Adoration of the Magi" (Breviary of Queen Isabella).

1973 (14 Nov.). *Royal Wedding. As Nos.* 165/6 *of Anguilla. Centre multicoloured.* *W* w.**12** (*sideways*). *P* 13½.

335	10 c. sage-green	20	25
336	30 c. bright mauve	45	50

109. White-winged Dove.

(Des. M. Goaman. Litho. Walsall Security Printers, Ltd.)

1974 (2 Jan.). *Birds* (1*st series*). *T* **109** *and similar vert. designs. Multicoloured.* *W* w.**12** (*sideways*). *P* 14.

337	3 c. Type **109**	5	5
338	10 c. Vitelline Warbler ..	12	12
339	12 c. Greater Antillean Grackle	15	15
340	20 c. West Indian Red-bellied Woodpecker ..	25	30
341	30 c. Stripe-headed Tanager	35	40
342	50 c. Yucatan Vireo ..	55	60
337/42	.. .. *Set of* 6	1·25	1·40

See also Nos. 383/8.

110. Old School Building.

(Des. PAD Studio. Litho. Questa.)

1974 (1 MAY). *25th Anniv. of University of West Indies. T* **110** *and similar horiz. designs. Multicoloured. W* w.**12** *(sideways). P* 14.

343	12 c. Type **112**	20	20
344	20 c. New Comprehensive School	25	30
345	30 c. Creative Arts Centre, Mona	35	40

111. Hermit Crab and Staghorn Coral.

(Des. J.W. Ltd. Litho. Kynoch Press.)

1974 (1 AUG.). *T* **111** *and similar multicoloured designs. W* w.**12** *(sideways on* $1 *and* $2). *P* 14.

346	1 c. Type **111**	5	5
347	3 c. Treasure-chest and lion's paw	5	5
348	4 c. Treasure and spotted scorpion-fish	5	5
349	5 c. Flintlock pistol and brain coral	5	8
350	6 c. Blackbeard and green turtle	8	8
351	9 c. Jewelled pomander and pork-fish	10	12
352	10 c. Spiny lobster and treasure	15	20
353	12 c. Jewelled sword and dagger, and sea-fan ..	15	15
354	15 c. Cabrit's Murex and treasure	20	20
355	20 c. Queen Conch and treasure	30	35
356	25 c. Hogfish and treasure ..	30	35
357	40 c. Gold chalice and sea-whip	50	55
358	$1 Coat-of-arms *(vert.)* ..	1·25	1·40
359	$2 Queen Elizabeth II *(vert.)*	2·40	2·60
346/59	.. .. *Set of* 14	5·00	5·50

See also Nos. 364/9 and 413/26.

112. Sea Captain and Ship (Shipbuilding).

(Des. G. L. Vasarhelyi. Litho. D.L.R.)

1974 (7 OCT.). *Local Industries. T* **112** *and similar horiz. designs. Multicoloured. W* w.**12** *(inverted on* 8 *c. and* 12 *c.). P* 14 × 13½.

360	8 c. Type **112**	12	12
361	12 c. Thatcher and cottages	20	20
362	20 c. Farmer and plantation	30	30
MS363	92 × 132 mm. Nos. 360/2	65	65

1974–75. *New value* (8 *c.*); *others as Nos.* 346/7 *but W* w.**12** *sideways.*

364	1 c. Type **111** (29.9.75) ..	5	5
365	3 c. Treasure-chest and lions-paw (12.11.74)	8	5
369	8 c. As No. 351 (16.12.74) ..	12	15

Nos. 366/8 and 370/79 have been reserved for any further additions to this set.

113. Arms of Cinque Ports and Lord Warden's Flag.

(Des. P. B. Powell. Litho. D.L.R.)

1974 (30 NOV.). *Birth Centenary of Sir Winston Churchill. T* **113** *and similar vert. design. Multicoloured. W* w. **12** *(sideways). P* 13½ × 14.

380	12 c. Type **113**	20	20
381	50 c. Churchill's coat-of-arms	60	70
MS382	98 × 86 mm. Nos. 380/1 ..	85	95

(Des. M. Goaman. Litho. Questa.)

1975 (1 JAN.). *Birds (2nd series). Multicoloured designs as T* **109**. *W* w. **12** *(sideways). P* 14.

383	3 c. Yellow-shafted Flicker ..	5	5
384	10 c. West Indian Tree Duck	10	12
385	12 c. Yellow Warbler ..	15	20
386	20 c. White-bellied Dove ..	25	30
387	30 c. Magnificent Frigate Bird	35	40
388	50 c. Cayman Amazon ..	60	70
	a. Error. Wmk. Lesotho T 53 (inverted)	£250	
383/8	*Set of* 6	1·25	1·40

114. " The Crucifixion ".

(Des. PAD Studio. Litho. D.L.R.)

1975 (24 MAR.). *Easter. French Pastoral Staffs. T* **114** *and similar vert. design. Multicoloured. W* w. **12** *(sideways). P* 13½ × 14.

389	**114** 15 c. multicoloured ..	20	25
390	– 35 c. multicoloured ..	35	40
MS391	128 × 98 mm. Nos. 389/90. *W* w. **12** *(upright)*	65	
	a. Error. Imperf. ..		

See also Nos. 396/**MS**398.

115. Israel Hands.

(Des. J.W. Ltd. Litho. Harrison.)

1975 (25 JULY). *Pirates. T* **115** *and similar horiz. designs. Multicoloured. W* w.**12** *(sideways). P* 14.

392	10 c. Type **115**	12	15
393	12 c. John Fenn	20	25
394	20 c. Thomas Anstis	25	30
395	30 c. Edward Low	35	40

(Des. PAD Studio. Litho. Questa.)

1975 (31 OCT.). *Christmas. Vert. designs as T* **114** *but showing " Virgin and Child with Angels " and inscr.* " Christmas 1975 ". *W* w.**14**. *P* 14.

396	12 c. multicoloured	20	25
397	50 c. multicoloured	60	70
MS398	113 × 85 mm. Nos. 396/7	80	

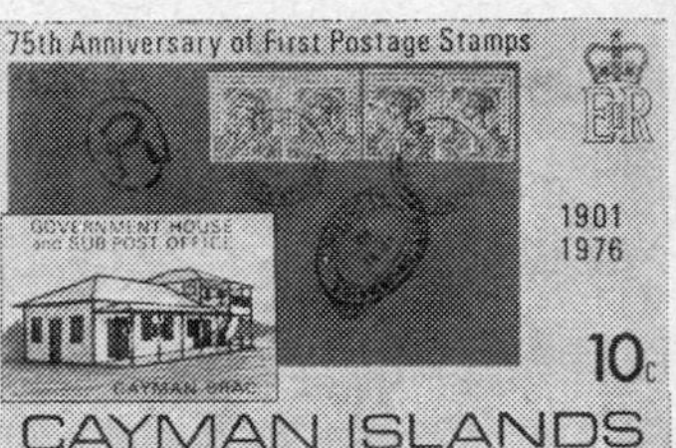

116. Registered Cover, Government House and Sub-Post Office.

(Des. J. Cooter. Litho. Questa.)

1976 (12 MAR.). *75th Anniv. of First Cayman Is. Postage Stamp. T* **116** *and similar horiz. designs. Multicoloured. W* w.**14** *(sideways). P* 13½.

399	10 c. Type **116**	10	12
400	20 c. ½d. stamp and 1890–94 postmark	20	25
401	30 c. 1d. stamp and 1908 surcharge	30	35
402	50 c. ½d. and 1d. stamps ..	50	60
MS403	117 × 147 mm. Nos. 399/402	1·10	

117. Seals of Georgia, Delaware and New Hampshire.

(Illustration reduced. Actual size 58 × 22 *mm.)*

(Des. P. B. Powell. Litho. J.W.)

1976 (29 MAY). *Bicentenary of American Revolution. T* **117** *and similar horiz. designs showing seals of the States given. Multicoloured. W* w.**14** *(sideways). P* 13½ × 14.

404	10 c. Type **117**	12	15
405	15 c. S. Carolina, New Jersey and Maryland	20	25
406	20 c. Virginia, Rhode Is. and Massachusetts ..	25	30
407	25 c. New York, Connecticut and N. Carolina	30	35
408	30 c. Pennsylvania seal, Liberty Bell and U.S. Great Seal	35	40
404/8	.. .. *Set of* 5	1·10	1·25
MS409	166 × 124 mm. Nos. 404/8. P 14	1·25	

118. Racing Dinghies.

(Des. C. Abbott. Litho. D.L.R.)

1976 (16 Aug.). *Olympic Games, Montreal. T* **118** *and similar vert. design. Multicoloured. W* w.**14**. *P* 14.

410	20 c. Type **118**	25	30
411	50 c. Racing dinghy	65	75

1976 (3 Sept.). *As Nos.* 346 *etc., but W* w.**14** (*inverted on* $2, *sideways on others*).

413	3 c. Treasure chest and lion's paw	5	5
417	8 c. Jewelled pomander and porkfish	10	10
419	10 c. Spiny lobster and treasure	12	12
422	20 c. Queen Conch and treasure	25	25
426	$2 Queen Elizabeth II . .	2·40	2·60
413/26	. . . . *Set of* 5	2·50	2·75

Nos. 412/26 have been allocated to this issue.

CEYLON.

I. CROWN COLONY.

PRICES.—*The prices of the imperf. stamps of Ceylon vary greatly according to condition. The following prices are for fine copies with four margins.*

Poor to medium specimens can be supplied at much lower prices.

1

2

(Recess. Perkins Bacon.)

1857 (1 April). *Blued paper. Wmk. Star T* w.**1**. *Imperf.*

1 **1** 6d. purple-brown £3000 £250

Collectors should beware of proofs with faked watermark, often offered as originals.

(Typo. De La Rue.)

1857 (Oct.)–**58.** *No wmk. Imperf.*

(a) Blue glazed paper.

3 **2** ½d. lilac £800 £225

(b) White glazed paper.

4 **2** ½d. lilac (1858) .. .. 50·00 35·00

3

4

(Recess. Perkins Bacon.)

NOTE.—Beware of stamps of Type **3** which are often offered with corners added.

1857–9. *White paper. Wmk. Star, Type* w.**1**. *Imperf.*

5 **1** 1d. blue (24.8.57) .. .. £120 11·00
6 „ 1d. deep blue .. .. £150 11·00
a. Blued paper .. .. — 25·00
7 „ 2d. deep green (24.8.57) .. 60·00 21·00
8 „ 2d. yellow-green .. .. £125 35·00
9 **3** 4d. dull rose (23.4.59) .. £25000 £1900
10 **1** 5d. chestnut (2.7.57) .. £350 50·00
11 „ 6d. purple-brown .. .. £600 90·00
12 „ 6d. brown £1800 £250
12*a* „ 6d. deep brown £2000 £700
13 **3** 8d. brown (23.4.59) .. £3000 £750
14 „ 9d. purple-brn. (23.4.59) .. £5500 £550
15 **4** 10d. orange-verm. (2.7.57) £350 90·00
16 „ 1s. dull violet (2.7.57) .. £2000 £130
17 **3** 1s. 9d. green (23.4.59) .. £250 £200
18 „ 1s. 9d. pale yellow-green £500 £475
19 „ 2s. blue (23.4.59) .. £1750 £550

Varieties. Rouletted.

20 **2** ½d. lilac (*No wmk.*) .. £2000
21 **1** 1d. blue (*Wmk. Star*) .. £2000
22 „ 2d. dp. green (*Wmk. Star*) £750 £425

These rouletted stamps are believed to have been made by some Ceylon firm for their own convenience.

(Recess. Perkins Bacon.)

1861. *Wmk. Star, Type* w. **1**.

(a) Clean-cut perf. 14 *to* 15½.

23 **1** 1d. deep blue .. .. 30·00 7·00
24 „ 1d. pale blue .. .. 50·00 10·00
25 „ 2d. green .. .. 60·00 10·00
27 „ 5d. chestnut .. .. 30·00 7·00
29 **4** 1s. dull violet .. .. 30·00 10·00
30 **3** 2s. deep full blue .. £180 £100

(b) Intermediate perf. 14 *to* 15½.

31 **1** 1d. deep blue .. .. 20·00 7·00
32 „ 1d. blue .. .. 20·00 8·00
33 „ 2d. green .. .. 20·00 17·00
34 **3** 4d. dull rose .. .. £500 75·00
34*a* **1** 5d. chestnut .. .. 85·00 50·00
35 „ 6d. brown .. .. £150 25·00
36 „ 6d. yellowish brown .. — 35·00
36*a* „ 6d. olive-brown .. .. — 25·00
37 **3** 8d. brown .. .. £350 85·00
38 „ 9d. dull purple-brown .. £850 85·00
40 **4** 1s. bright violet .. 25·00 8·00
41 „ 1s. dull violet .. 25·00 7·50

(c) Rough perf. 14 *to* 15½.

42 **1** 1d. blue .. .. 15·00 4·00
43 „ 1d. blue (*bleuté paper*) .. 60·00 8·00
44 **3** 4d. rose-red .. .. 35·00 15·00
45 „ 4d. deep rose-red .. 35·00 15·00
47 **1** 6d. yellowish brown .. £300 38·00
48 „ 6d. blackish brown .. 80·00 21·00
48*a* „ 6d. olive-brown .. .. £100 18·00
49 **3** 8d. brown .. .. £350 70·00
50 „ 8d. yellow-brown .. £300 70·00
51 „ 9d. olive-brown .. .. £100 11·00
52 „ 9d. yellowish brown .. £110 20·00
53 „ 9d. deep brown .. .. 20·00 11·00
53*a* **4** 10d. orange-vermilion .. 50·00 8·00
b. Imperf. between (pair) ..
54 „ 1s. dull violet .. .. 55·00 5·50
55 **3** 2s. blue .. .. £140 28·00
56 „ 2s. deep blue .. .. £140 28·00

Variety. Prepared for use, but not issued.

57 **3** 1s. 9d. green £130

No. 33 is known imperf. between (vert. pair), used.

No. 34 is distinguished from Nos. 44/5 with fraudulently altered perfs. by its colour.

(Recess. or typo. (T **2**). D.L.R.)

1862–64. *No wmk. (a) Smooth paper. P* 13.

58 **1** 1d. blue .. .. .. 20·00 4·25
59 „ 5d. deep red-brown .. £225 50·00
60 „ 6d. reddish brown .. 21·00 10·00
61 „ 6d. deep brown .. .. 28·00 10·00
62 **3** 9d. brown .. .. £110 22·00
63 **4** 1s. cold violet .. .. £225 25·00

(b) Smooth paper. P 11½, 12.

64 **1** 1d. blue .. .. £100 21·00

(c) Glazed paper. P 12½ (1864).

65 **2** ½d. pale lilac .. .. 28·00 21·00

The 1s. is known imperf., but not used. The "no wmk." stamps were printed on paper having the papermaker's name and date, "T H SAUNDERS 1862" across the sheets, and one or more of these letters or figures are often found on the stamps.

(Recess. Perkins, Bacon, perforated by D.L.R.)

1864 (Sept.). *Wmk. Star, Type* w.**1**. *P* 12½.

66 **4** 10d. vermilion .. .. 65·00 10·00
67 „ 10d. orange-red .. .. 65·00 10·00

5

6

T **5**. 23 mm. high. "CC" oval.
T **6**. 21½ mm. high. "CC" round and smaller.

(Recess. or Typo. (T **2**). D.L.R.)

1863–6. *Paper medium thin and slightly soft. W* **5**. *Wmks. arranged in four panes, each of* 60, *with the words* "CROWN COLONIES" *between the panes. Portions of these letters often appear on the stamps.*

(a) P 11½, 12.

68 **1** 1d. blue .. .. .. 55·00 12·00

(b) P 13.

69 **1** 6d. brown .. .. £350 21·00
70 **3** 9d. brown .. .. £550 60·00

(c) P 12½.

71 **2** ½d. mauve .. .. .. 5·50 3·50
72 „ ½d. lilac .. .. .. 7·00 3·50
73 „ ½d. deep lilac .. .. 7·00 4·25
74 **1** 1d. dark blue .. .. 8·50 2·75
75 „ 1d. blue .. .. .. 8·50 2·75
76 „ 2d. yellow-green £1200 £100
77 **1** 2d. deep bottle-green .. — £1300
78 „ 2d. grey-green .. .. 17·00 4·25
79 „ 2d. emerald-green .. 40·00 30·00
80 „ 2d. maize .. .. .. 70·00 15·00
81 **3** 4d. lake-rose .. .. 50·00 10·00
82 „ 4d. rose .. .. .. 30·00 7·00
83 **1** 5d. reddish brown .. 40·00 21·00
84 „ 5d. deep sage-green .. £425 70·00
84*a* „ 5d. olive-green .. .. 25·00 8·00
85 „ 6d. brown .. .. 10·00 5·50
86 „ 6d. reddish brown .. 11·00 5·50
87 „ 6d. deep brown .. .. 8·50 3·50
88 **3** 8d. light carmine-brown .. 10·00 7·00
89 „ 8d. dark carmine-brown .. 10·00 7·00
90 „ 9d. brown .. .. 50·00 10·00
91 **4** 10d. vermilion .. .. £180 8·00
91*a* „ 10d. orange .. .. 50·00 10·00
92 **3** 2s. dark blue .. .. 50·00 7·50

The ½d. lilac; 1d. blue; 2d. grey-green; 2d. maize; and 5d. deep sage-green and olive-green, are known imperf.

1867. *Paper hand-made. Prepared and used only for these Ceylon stamps. W* **6**. *Wmks. arranged in one pane of* 240 *in* 20 *rows of* 12, *with the words* "CROWN COLONIES" *twice in each side margin. P* 12½.

93 **1** 1d. pale blue .. .. 7·50 2·75
94 „ 1d. Prussian blue .. 7·00 3·00
95 „ 2d. maize .. .. 11·00 4·25
96 „ 2d. olive-yellow .. .. 8·00 3·50
97 „ 2d. greenish-yellow .. 50·00 20·00
98 „ 2d. orange-yellow .. 7·50 2·75
99 **3** 4d. pale rose .. .. 11·00 7·00
100 „ 4d. rose .. .. .. 7·00 3·50
101 **1** 5d. pale sage-green .. 8·00 4·50
102 „ 5d. deep olive-green .. 11·00 4·50
103 „ 5d. deep myrtle-green .. 7·50 7·00
104 „ 6d. deep brown .. .. 8·00 3·50
105 „ 6d. blackish brown .. 10·00 3·50
106 „ 6d. red-brown .. .. 8·00 2·75
107 **3** 8d. pale carmine-brown .. 11·00 10·00
108 „ 8d. deep carmine-brown 8·00 5·50
109 „ 9d. bistre-brown .. 50·00 6·00
110 „ 9d. deep brown .. .. 7·00 4·25
111 **4** 10d. vermilion .. .. £170 50·00
111*a* „ 10d. red-orange .. .. 11·00 3·50
112 „ 10d. orange .. .. 11·00 4·00
113 „ 1s. lilac .. .. .. 70·00 7·00
114 „ 1s. violet .. .. 17·00 4·00
115 **3** 2s. pale blue .. .. 24·00 6·50
116 „ 2s. blue .. .. .. 17·00 4·50
117 „ 2s. Prussian blue .. 17·00 4·50

The 1d. pale blue, 6d. deep brown, 9d. deep brown and 10d. orange are known imperf. but only unused.

PRINTERS. All stamps from No. 118 to 367 were typographed by De La Rue & Co.

7

8

1866. *Wmk. Crown CC. P* 12½.

118 **7** 3d. rose .. .. .. 30·00 13·00

1867–8. *Wmk. Crown CC. P* 14.

119 **8** 1d. blue .. .. .. 4·50 2·75
120 **7** 3d. pale rose (1867) .. 13·00 7·00
a. Deep rose. .. 14·00 7·00

9

10

11 12 13 14 15 16 17 18

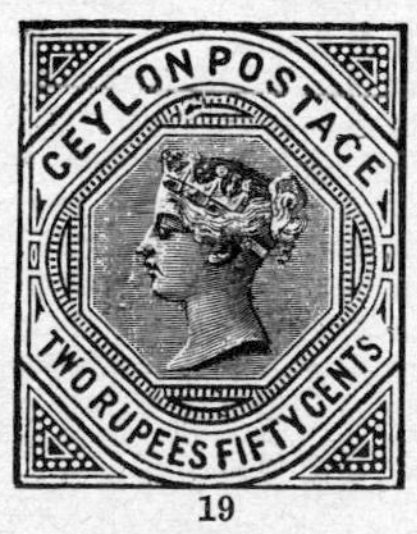

19

1872–80. *Wmk. Crown CC.* (*a*) *P* 14.

No.	Type	Description	Unused	Used
121	**9**	2 c. pale brown (*shades*)	1·10	30
122	**10**	4 c. grey	3·50	30
123	,,	4 c. rosy-mauve (1880)	6·00	70
124	**11**	8 c. orange-yellow ..	6·00	2·00
		a. Yellow	5·50	2·00
126	**12**	16 c. pale violet ..	8·50	1·75
127	**13**	24 c. green	7·00	1·75
128	**14**	32 c. slate (1877) ..	12·00	4·00
129	**15**	36 c. blue	12·00	4·00
130	**16**	48 c. rose	12·00	4·00
131	**17**	64 c. red-brown (1877) ..	24·00	10·00
132	**18**	96 c. drab	18·00	7·00
121/132		.. .. *Set of* 11	£100	32·00
		(*b*) *P* 14×12½.		
133	**9**	2 c. brown	30·00	5·50
134	**10**	4 c. grey	30·00	4·00
135	**11**	8 c. orange-yellow ..	24·00	7·00
		(*c*) *P* 12½.		
136	**9**	2 c. brown	£140	8·00
137	**10**	4 c. grey	90·00	30·00
		(*d*) *P* 12½×14.		
138	**19**	2 r. 50 c. dull-rose ..	75·00	32·00

Prepared for use and sent out to Ceylon, but not issued unsurcharged.

No.	Type	Description	Unused	Used
139	**14**	32 c. slate (*p.* 14×12½) ..	£170	
140	**17**	64 c. red-brn. (*p.* 14×12½)	£275	
141	**19**	2 r. 50, dull rose (*p.* 12½)	£250	

FORGERIES.—Beware of forged overprint and surcharge varieties on Victorian issues.

SIXTEEN

16

CENTS

(20)

1882. *Nos.* 127 *and* 131 *surch. as T* **20.**

No.	Type	Description	Unused	Used
142	**13**	16 c. on 24 c. green ..	7·00	4·00
		a. Surch. inverted ..		
143	**17**	20 c. on 64 c. red-brown ..	4·50	1·75
		a. Surch. double ..	—	£170

1883–98. *Wmk. Crown CA.* *P* 14.

No.	Type	Description	Unused	Used
146	**9**	2 c. pale brown	4·50	45
147	,,	2 c. dull green (1884) (Optd. S. £14) ..	30	10
148	**10**	4 c. rosy mauve ..	35	10
149	,,	4 c. rose (1884) (Optd. S. £20)	1·10	2·40
150	**11**	8 c. orange	1·60	2·40
		a. Yellow (1898)	1·60	2·40
151	**12**	16 c. pale violet	£110	35·00
		Trial perforation. *P* 12.		
151*a*	**9**	2 c. dull green	£225	
151*b*	**10**	4 c. rose	£550	
151*c*	**13**	24 c. brown-purple ..	£350	

Prepared for use and sent out to Ceylon, but not issued unsurcharged. *P* 14.

No.	Type	Description	Unused	Used
152	**13**	24 c. brown-purple (Optd. S. £45)	£160	

Postage &

FIVE
CENTS

Revenue

(21)

TEN
CENTS

(22)

Twenty
Cents

(23)

One Rupee
Twelve
Cents

(24)

1885. *T* **10/19** *surch. locally as T* **21/24.**

I. *Wmk. Crown CC.*

(*a*) *P* 14.

No.	Type	Description	Unused	Used
153	**21**	5 c. on 16 c. pale violet ..	£225	
154	,,	5 c. on 24 c. green ..	£180	14·00
155	,,	5 c. on 32 c. slate ..	7·00	4·00
		a. Surch. inverted ..	—	90·00
		b. Dark grey ..	6·00	4·00
156	,,	5 c. on 36 c. blue ..	8·50	1·75
		a. Surch. inverted ..	—	45·00
157	,,	5 c. on 48 c. rose ..	28·00	6·00
158	,,	5 c. on 64 c. red-brown ..	8·00	1·75
		a. Surch. double ..	—	42·00
159	,,	5 c. on 96 c. drab ..	24·00	8·50
161	**22**	10 c. on 16 c. pale violet ..	£140	£100
162	,,	10 c. on 24 c. green ..	70·00	20·00
163	,,	10 c. on 36 c. blue ..	35·00	25·00
164	,,	10 c. on 64 c. red-brown ..	17·00	10·00
165	,,	20 c. on 24 c. green ..	10·00	5·50
166	**23**	20 c. on 32 c. slate ..	6·00	4·50
		a. Dark grey	6·00	5·50
167	,,	25 c. on 32 c. slate ..	4·00	2·75
		a. Dark grey	4·00	2·10
168	,,	28 c. on 48 c. rose ..	6·00	2·75
		a. Surch. double	—	£100
169	**22**	30 c. on 36 c. blue ..	4·25	4·25
		a. Surch. inverted ..	28·00	17·00
170	,,	56 c. on 96 c. drab ..	6·00	4·50
		(*b*) *P* 14×12½.		
172	**21**	5 c. on 32 c. slate ..	12·00	5·50
173	,,	5 c. on 64 c. red-brown ..	16·00	7·00
174	**22**	10 c. on 64 c. red-brown ..	10·00	10·00
		a. Imperf. betwn. (vert. pr.)	£200	
175	**24**	1 r. 12 c. on 2 r. 50 c., dull rose (*p.* 12½) ..	35·00	10·00
176	,,	1 r. 12 c. on 2 r. 50 c. dull rose (*p.* 12½×14) ..	9·00	8·50
		II. *Wmk. Crown CA.* *P* 14.		
177	**21**	5 c. on 4 c. rosy mauve	50·00	42·00
178	,,	5 c. on 4 c. rose ..	2·10	30
		a. Surch. inverted ..	60·00	45·00
179	,,	5 c. on 8 c. orange-yellow	4·25	1·40
		a. Surch. double	—	30·00
		b. Surch. inverted	—	70·00
180	,,	5 c. on 16 c. pale violet	6·00	3·50
		a. Surch. inverted.. ..	—	21·00
181	,,	5 c. on 24 c. green ..		
182	,,	5 c. on 24 c. brown-purple	50·00	28·00
184	**22**	10 c. on 16 c. pale violet	—	£100
185	,,	10 c. on 24 c. brn.-purple ..	4·00	2·75
186	,,	15 c. on 16 c. pale violet ..	4·00	3·25

REVENUE AND POSTAGE

10 CENTS

(26)

5 CENTS

(25)

1 R. 12 C.

(27)

1885–87. *T* **11/15, 18** *and* **19** *surch. with T* **25/7** *by D.L.R.* *P* 14.

(*a*) *Wmk. Crown CA.*

No.	Type	Description	Unused	Used
187	**25**	5 c. on 8 c. lilac ..	2·00	30
188	**26**	10 c. on 24 c. brown-purple	4·00	2·10
189	,,	15 c. on 16 c. orange-yellow	5·00	2·75
190	,,	28 c. on 32 c. slate ..	4·00	1·25
191	,,	30 c. on 36 c. olive-green	5·50	4·50
192	,,	56 c. on 96 c. drab ..	5·50	4·00
		(*b*) *Wmk. Crown CC* (*sideways*).		
193	**27**	1 r. 12 c. on 2 r. 50, dull rose	10·00	11·00
187/193		Optd. "Specimen" *Set of* 7	35·00	

28

29

5 c. Type (*a*) has thicker lines in the background and masses of solid colour under the chin, in front of the throat, at the back of the neck, and at the base. Type (*b*) has thinner lines in the background, and coil and pendent curl clearer.

1886. *Wmk. Crown CA.* *P* 14.

No.	Type	Description	Unused	Used
194	**28**	5 c. dull purple (*a*) ..	1·00	10
195	,,	5 c. dull purple (*b*) ..	30	8
196	**29**	15 c. sage-green	45	35
197	,,	15 c. olive-green ..	50	20
198	,,	25 c. yellow-brown ..	60	70
		a. Value in yellow ..	17·00	13·00
199	,,	28 c. slate	1·25	65
194, 197/199		Optd. "Specimen" .. .. *Set of* 4	30·00	

30

1887. *Wmk. Crown CC.* *P* 14.

No.	Type	Description	Unused	Used
201	**30**	1 r. 12, dull rose (Optd. S. £20)	4·50	4·50

This stamp comes on both white and bluish paper with wmk. sideways, and, in a different shade, with upright wmk.

TWO CENTS (31) **TWO** (32) **2 Cents** (33)

Two Cents (34) **2 Cents** (35)

1888–90. *Nos.* 148/9 *surch. with T* **31/5.**

202 **31** 2 c. on 4 c. rosy mauve .. 20 15
- a. Surch. inverted .. .. 2·10 1·75
- b. Surch. double, one inverted — 8·00

203 „ 2 c. on 4 c. rose 20 20
- a. Surch. inverted .. .. 2·75 2·10
- b. Surch. double .. .. — 7·00

204 **32** 2 (c.) on 4 c. rosy mauve .. 40 15
- a. Surch. inverted .. .. 5·50 5·00
- b. Surch. double .. .. 7·00 7·00
- c. Surch. double, one inverted 4·25 4·00

205 „ 2 (c.) on 4 c. rose .. 35 15
- a. Surch. inverted .. .. 14·00
- b. Surch. double .. .. 7·00 7·00
- c. Surch. double, one inverted 7·00 7·50

206 **33** 2 c. on 4 c. rosy mauve .. 7·00 6·00
- a. Surch. inverted .. .. — 7·50
- b. Surch. double, one inverted 10·00

207 „ 2 c. on 4 c. rose .. 50 60
- a. Surch. inverted .. .. 4·00 4·25
- b. Surch. double .. ..
- c. Surch. double, one inverted 2·75 2·75

208 **34** 2 c. on 4 c. rosy mauve .. 6·50 8·00
- a. Surch. inverted .. .. 13·00 6·50

209 „ 2 c. on 4 c. rose .. 50 30
- a. Surch. inverted .. .. 2·75 3·00
- b. Surch. double .. .. 6·00 6·50
- c. Surch. double, one inverted 2·75 2·75

210 **35** 2 c. on 4 c. rosy mauve .. 6·00 6·00
- a. Surch. inverted .. .. 11·00 11·00
- b. Surch. double, one inverted 11·00 11·00
- c. Surch. double .. .. — 8·50
- d. "s" of "Cents" inverted
- e. As d. Whole surch. inverted

211 „ 2 c. on 4 c. rose .. 85 35
- a. Surch. inverted .. .. 2·00 2·10
- b. Surch. double .. .. 11·00 11·00
- c. Surch. double, one inverted 4·25 4·25
- d. "s" of "Cents" inverted — 11·00

209, 211 Optd. "Specimen" *Set of* 2 30·00

The 4 c. *rose* and the 4 c. *rosy mauve* are found surcharged "Postal Commission 3 (or 'Three') Cents". They denote the extra commission charged by the Post Office on postal orders which had not been cashed within three months of the date of issue. For a short time the Post Office did not object to the use of these stamps on letters.

POSTAGE

Five Cents

REVENUE

(36)

1890. *No.* 197 *surch. with T* **36.**

233 5 c. on 15 c. olive-green (Optd. S. £6) 35 45
- a. Surch. inverted .. .. 4·00 4·00
- b. Surch. double .. .. 21·00 17·00
- c. "Flve" for "Five" .. 21·00 17·00
- d Variety as c., inverted ..
- e. "REVENUE" omitted .. 20·00 17·00
- f. Inverted "s" in "Cents" .. 4·00 4·25
- g. Variety as f., and whole surch. inverted .. .. .. 90·00
- h. "REVENUE" omitted and inverted "s" in "Cents" .. 42·00
- i. "POSTAGE" spaced between "T" and "A" .. .. 10·00

FIFTEEN CENTS (37) **3 Cents** (38)

1891. *Nos.* 198/9 *surch. with T* **37.**

239 **29** 15 c. on 25 c. yellow-brn. 2·75 2·75
240 „ 15 c. on 28 c. slate .. 2·75 2·75

1892. *Nos.* 148/9 *and* 199 *surch. with T* **38.**

241 **10** 3 c. on 4 c. rosy mauve .. 30 30
242 „ 3 c. on 4 c. rose (Optd. S. £12) 45 85
243 **28** 3 c. on 28 c. slate 30 40
- a. Surch. double .. .. 10·00

39

Six Cents (40)

2 R. 25 C. (41)

1893–99. *Wmk. Crown CA. P* 14.

245 **39** 3 c. terracotta & blue-grn. 40 30
246 **10** 4 c. carmine-rose ('98) .. 1·25 1·60
247 **29** 30 c. brt. mauve & chest. 1·00 70
- *a. Bright violet & chestnut* 70 70

249 **19** 2 r. 50, purple/*red* ('99) .. 8·00 8·50
245, 247/9 Optd. "Specimen" *Set of* 3 20·00

1899. (*a*) *No.* 196 *surch. with T* **40.**

250 **29** 6 c. on 15 c. sage-green .. 25 25

(*b*) *As No.* 138 *but colour changed and perf.* 14, *surch. as T* **41.**

254 **19** 1 r. 50 c. on 2 r. 50, slate.. 7·50 8·50
255 „ 2 r. 25 c. on 2 r. 50, yellow 10·00 11·00
250/255 Optd. "Specimen" *Set of* 3 32·00

43

1899–1900. *Wmk. Crown CA* (1 *r.* 50, 2 *r.* 25 *wmk. Crown CC*). *P* 14.

256 **9** 2 c. pale orange-brown .. 35 15
257 **39** 3 c. deep green 35 15
258 **10** 4 c. yellow 35 45
259 **29** 6 c. rose and black .. 35 15
260 **39** 12 c. sage-green and rose.. 95 1·00
261 **29** 15 c. blue 95 60
262 **39** 75 c. black and red-brown 1·75 1·10
263 **43** 1 r. 50, rose .. .. 8·50 8·50
264 „ 2 r. 25, dull blue.. .. 11·00 11·00
256/264 .. .. *Set of* 9 23·00 21·00
256/264 Optd. "Specimen" *Set of* 9 32·00

44

45

46

47

48

1903–5. *Wmk. Crown CA. P* 14.

265 **44** 2 c. red-brown 35 20
266 **45** 3 c. green 35 20
267 „ 4 c. orange-yellow & blue 40 35
268 **46** 5 c. dull purple .. 40 8
269 **47** 6 c. carmine 45 35
270 **45** 12 c. sage-green & rosine 1·60 1·25
271 **48** 15 c. blue .. .. 1·75 50
272 „ 25 c. bistre .. .. 2·00 1·90
273 „ 30 c. dull violet and green 1·75 1·00
274 **45** 75 c. dull blue & orge. ('05) 1·75 3·50
275 **48** 1 r. 50, greyish slate ('04) 16·00 16·00
276 „ 2 r. 25, brn. & grn. ('04) 19·00 19·00
265/276 .. .. *Set of* 12 42·00 40·00
265/76 Optd. "Specimen" *Set of* 12 50·00

1904–5. *Wmk. Mult. Crown CA. P* 14.

277 **44** 2 c. red-brown, O .. 30 15
278 **45** 3 c. green, O 30 15
279 „ 4 c. orange & ultram., O 20 35
280 **46** 5 c. dull purple, OC .. 70 15
281 **47** 6 c. carmine, O 30 15
282 **45** 12 c. sage-grn. & rosine, O 70 35
283 **48** 15 c. blue, O 35 20
284 „ 25 c. bistre, O ('05) 2·50 1·25
285 „ 30 c. violet & grn. O ('05) 1·10 35
286 **45** 75 c. dull blue and orange, O ('05) .. .. 1·90 2·50
287 **48** 1 r. 50, grey, O ('05) .. 3·25 4·50
288 „ 2 r. 25, brn. & green, O 6·50 5·50
277/288 .. .. *Set of* 12 17·00 14·00

50

51

1908. *Wmk. Mult. Crown CA. P* 14.

289 **50** 5 c. deep purle, O .. 40 12
290 „ 5 c. dull purple, O .. 65 15
291 **51** 6 c. carmine, O .. 40 15
289, 291 Optd. "Specimen" *Set of* 2 14·00

1910–11. *Wmk. Mult. Crown CA. P* 14.

292 **44** 2 c. brn.-orange, O (1911) 25 15
293 **48** 3 c. green, O (1911) .. 40 15
294 „ 10 c. sage-grn. & maroon, O 65 35
295 „ 25 c. grey, O .. .. 1·25 50
296 „ 50 c. chocolate, O .. 2·25 1·75
297 „ 1 r. purple/*yellow*, O .. 3·00 3·00
298 „ 2 r. red/*yellow*, O .. 4·00 4·50
299 „ 5 r. black/*green*, O .. 20·00 20·00
300 „ 10 r. black/*red*, O .. 45·00 42·00
292/300 .. .. *Set of* 9 70·00 65·00
292/300 Optd. "Specimen" *Set of* 9 60·00

52

53

(A)

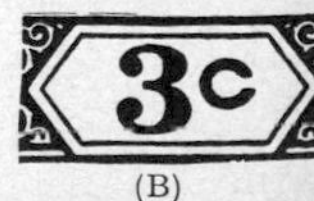

(B)

Stamps of Type **52** were normally printed in two operations, but the 1 c. and 5 c., together with later issues of the 3 c. and 6 c., were printed from special plates at one operation. These plates are distinguished by a large "C" in the value tablet as illustration B. Except for the 5 c. (which is Die I), the frames also differ slightly from Dies I and II described in the Introduction, but the 3 c. is similar to Die I and the 1 c. and 6 c. similar to Die II, except that inner top corners of side panels are square and not curved as in Die II.

All stamps with wmk. Mult. Crown CA are Die I unless otherwise stated.

1912–25. *T* **52** *and* **53** (50 *r. to* 1000 *r.*). *Wmk. Mult. Crown CA. P* 14.

301 1 c. brown, O 8 12
302 2 c. brown-orange, O .. 20 15
303 2 c. dp. orange-brown, O 20 15
304 3 c. yellow-green, O (A) 50 40
305 3 c. deep green, O (A) .. 40 30
306 3 c. blue-green, O (B) .. 20 15
307 5 c. purple, O 30 15
308 5 c. bright magenta, O .. 10 12
a. Wmk. sideways .. 75
309 6 c. scarlet, O (A) .. 75 15
310 6 c. bright scarlet, O (A) 65 15
311 6 c. pale scarlet, O (B) .. 25 15
312 6 c. carmine, O (B) .. 60 20
a. Wmk. sideways .. 75
313 10 c. sage-green, O .. 75 40
314 10 c. deep sage-green, O 85 30
315 15 c. ultramarine, O .. 80 35
316 15 c. deep bright blue, O 85 35
317 25 c. yellow and blue, O .. 80 35
318 25 c. orange and blue, O 85 45
319 30 c. blue-green & violet, C 70 45
320 30 c. yellow-grn. & violet, C 75 85
a. Wmk. sideways .. 55
321 50 c. black and scarlet, C 55 60
322 1 r. purple/*yellow*, C .. 75 1·10
a. White back (1914) (Optd. S. £8) .. .. .. 90 1·25
b. On lemon (1916) (Optd. S. £8) .. .. .. 2·50 2·00
c. On orange-buff .. 4·50 5·00
d. On pale yellow (Optd. S. £8) 3·00 2·50
323 2 r. black & red/*yellow*, C 1·60 2·50
a. White back (Optd. S. £8) .. 1·40 3·25
b. On lemon (Optd. S. £8) .. 5·50 6·00
c. On orange-buff .. .. 7·00 6·50
d. On pale yellow .. .. 6·50 6·50
324 5 r. black/*green*, C 4·00 4·50
a. White back (Optd. S. £9) .. 4·00 4·50
b. On blue-grn., olive back (1921) (Optd. S. £8) .. 5·00 5·50
c. On emerald back (Die II) (Optd. S. £11) .. .. 23·00 26·00
325 10 r. purple & blk./*red*, C 17·00 14·00
a. Die II 18·00
326 20 r. black and red/*blue*, C 32·00 26·00
327 50 r. dull purple, C (S. £45) £200
328 100 r. grey-black, C (S. £160) £850
329 500 r. dull green, C (S. £225) £3000
329*a* 1000 r. purple/*red*, C (1925) (S. £350) £9000
301/325 .. .. *Set of* 14 25·00 24·00
301/26 Optd. "Specimen" *Set of* 15 80·00

WAR STAMP
(54)

WAR STAMP ONE CENT
(55)

1918 (18 Nov.). (*a*) *Optd. with T* **54**.

330 **52** 2 c. brown-orange.. 10 15
a. Opt. inverted .. .. 9·00 9·00
b. Opt. double .. .. 9·00 9·00
c. Opt. omitted in pair with opt. inverted .. ..
331 „ 3 c. green (A) 12 20
a. Opt. double .. .. 16·00 16·00
332 „ 3 c. green (B) 5 12
333 „ 5 c. purple 5 12
a. Opt. double .. .. 9·00 9·00
334 „ 5 c. bright magenta 50 30
a. Opt. inverted .. .. 9·00 9·00
b. Opt. double .. .. 8·50 8·50

(*b*) *Surch. with T* **55**.

335 **52** 1 c. on 5 c. purple .. 8 12
336 „ 1 c. on 5 c. bright magenta 8 12
330/1, 333, 335 Optd. "Specimen" *Set of* 4 20·00

Collectors are warned against forgeries of the errors in the "WAR STAMP" overprints.

1918. *Surch. as T* **55**, *but without* "WAR STAMP".

337 **52** 1 c. on 5 c. purple (Optd. S. £8) 10 15
337*a* „ 1 c. on 5 c. brt. magenta 30 25

1921–34. *Wmk. Mult. Script CA. P* 14.

A. **1921–27.** *The basic issue. Die I for the* 5 *c.,* 10 *c. to* 30 *c. and* 1 *r., Die II remainder in T* **52**.

338 **52** 1 c. brown, O ('27) .. 5 12
339 „ 2 c. brn.-orange, O ('27) 20 20
340 „ 3 c. green, O (B) (5.5.22) 40 20
341 „ 5 c. brt. mag., O ('27).. 5 12
342 „ 6 c. carmine-red, O (B) (3.8.21) 15 15
343 „ 10 c. sage-grn., O (16.9.21) 50 25
344 „ 15 c. ultram., O (30.5.22) 85 1·00
345 „ 20 c. bright blue, O ('22) 1·40 65
346 „ 25 c. yellow and blue, O (17.10.21) .. 50 45
347 „ 30 c. yellow-grn., & violet, C (15.3.22) 90 80
348 „ 50 c. black & scar., C ('22) 1·25 55
349 „ 1 r. pur./*p. yell.*, C ('23) 7·50 4·00
350 „ 2 r. black and red/*pale yellow*, C ('23) .. 2·75 2·25
351 „ 5 r. blk./*emerald*, C ('25) 8·00 6·50
352 „ 20 r. black and red/*blue*, C ('24) .. .. 24·00 28·00
353 **53** 50 r. dull purple, C ('24) (S. £40) £175
354 „ 100 r. grey-black, C ('24) (S. £100) £900
338/351 .. .. *Set of* 14 22·00 16·00
338/52 Optd. "Specimen" *Set of* 15 65·00

B. **1922–27.** *New values and colours changed. Die I for* 3 *c.,* 12 *c. and* 15 *c., Die II remainder in T* **52**.

355 **52** 3 c. slate-grey, O (B) ('23) 5 10
a. Wmk. sideways ..
356 „ 6 c. bright violet, O (B) 8 15
357 „ 9 c. red/*yellow*, O ('26) 15 20
358 „ 12 c. rose-scarlet, O ('24) 1·00 1·25
359 „ 15 c. green/*pale yellow*, O 75 50
360 **53** 100 r. dull purple & blue, C (24.10.27) (S. £160) £750
355/9 Optd. "Specimen" *Set of* 5 30·00

C. **1924–25.** *Change to Die II.*

360*a* **52** 10 c. sage-green, O .. 35 20
360*b* „ 12 c. rose-scarlet, O ('24) 90 1·10
360*c* „ 15 c. green/*pale yellow*, O 60 60
360*d* „ 20 c. bright blue, O .. 30 35
360*e* „ 25 c. yellow and blue, O 70 80
360*f* „ 30 c. yellow-grn. & vio., C 70 75
360*g* „ 1 r. purple/*pale yellow*, C 5·00 3·50

2 Cents.
(56)

(Surch. at Ceylon Govt. Printing Works.)

D. **1926** (27 Nov.). *Surch. as T* **56**.

361 **52** 2 c. on 3 c. slate-grey .. 35 25
a. Surch. double .. .. 15·00
b. Bar omitted .. .. 12·00
362 „ 5 c. on 6 c. bright violet .. 35 30
361/362 Optd. "Specimen" *Set of* 2 16·00

E. **1934.** *Reappearance of Die I (Key Plate* 23).

362*a* **52** 50 c. black and scarlet, C 10·00 7·00

The 30 c. value also reappeared in Die I from Plate 23 but this was identical with No. 347.

57

1927 (27 Nov.)–**29.** *Wmk. Mult. Script CA. P* 14.

363 **57** 1 r. dull and bright purple, C ('28) .. .. 1·60 90
364 „ 2 r. green & carm., C ('29) 3·25 2·00
365 „ 5 r. green & dull purple, C ('28) .. .. 10·00 6·50
366 **57** 10 r. grn. & brn.-orge., C 14·00 13·00
367 „ 20 r. dull purple & blue, C 26·00 21·00
363/367 .. .. *Set of* 5 50·00 40·00
363/7 Optd. "Specimen" *Set of* 5 35·00

No. 364. Collectors are warned against faked 2 r. stamps, showing what purports to be a double centre.

1935 (6 May). *Silver Jubilee. As Nos.* 91/4 *of Antigua. P* 13½ × 14.

368 6 c. ultramarine and grey .. 5 8
369 9 c. green and indigo .. 20 20
370 20 c. brown and deep blue .. 35 35
371 50 c. slate and purple .. 1·10 85
368/71 Perf. "Specimen" *Set of* 4 14·00

58. Tapping Rubber.

59. Colombo Harbour.

60. Adam's Peak.

61. Plucking Tea.

62. Coconut Palms.

63. Hill Paddy (rice).

64. River Scene.

65. Temple of the Tooth, Kandy.

66. Ancient Irrigation Tank.

67. Wild Elephants.

68. Trincomalee.

(Recess. D.L.R. (2, 3, 20, 50 c.), B.W. (others).)

1935 (1 MAY)–**36.** *Wmk. Mult. Script CA (sideways on* 10, 15, 25, 30 *c. and* 1 *r.). Various perfs.*

372 **58** 2 c. black and carmine (*p.* 12×13) 5 8
a. Perf. 14 .. .. 80 30
373 **60** 3 c. black and olive-green (*p.* 13×12) (1.10.35) 12 12
a. Perf. 14 .. .. 80 30
374 **59** 6 c. black and blue (*perf.* 11×11½) (1.1.36) .. 25 15
375 **61** 9 c. green and orange (*p.* 11×11½) (1.1.36) 20 15
376 **63** 10 c. black & purple (*perf.* 11½×11) (1.6.35) .. 20 15
377 **64** 15 c. red-brown and green (*p.* 11½×11) .. 70 35
378 **62** 20 c. black and grey-blue (*p.* 12×13) (1.1.36) .. 50 30
379 **65** 25 c. deep blue & chocolate (*p.* 11½×11) .. 55 30
380 **66** 30 c. carmine and green (*p.* 11½×11) (1.8.35) 55 50
381 **67** 50 c. black & mauve (*p.* 14) (1.1.36) .. 2·25 50
382 **68** 1 r. violet-blue and choc. (*p.* 11½×11) (1.7.35) 2·50 2·25
372/382 *Set of* 11 7·00 4·25
372/382 Perf. "Specimen" *Set of* 11 26·00

1937 (12 MAY). *Coronation. As Nos.* 13/15 *of Aden but ptd. by B.W. & Co.* P 11×11½.

383 6 c. carmine 5 5
384 9 c. green 12 15
385 20 c. blue 25 25
383/5 Perf. "Specimen" *Set of* 3 11·00

69. Tapping Rubber.

71. Ancient Guard-stone, Anuradhapura.

70. Sigiriya (Lion Rock).

72. King George VI.

(Recess. B.W. (stamps perf. 11×11½ or 11½×11), D.L.R. (all others). T **72** typo. D.L.R.)

1938–49. *T* **69**/**72** *and types as* 1935–36, *but with portrait of King George VI instead of King George V and* "POSTAGE & REVENUE" *omitted. Wmk. Mult. Script CA (sideways on* 10, 15, 25, 30 *c. and* 1 *r.). Various perfs.*

386 **69** 2 c. black and carmine (*p.* 11½×13) (25.4.38) 85 12
a. Perf. 13½×13 (1938) .. 2·50 12
b. Perf. 13½ (25.4.38) .. 5 8
c. Perf. 11×11½ (17.2.44) .. 8 10
d. Perf. 12 (22.4.49) 5 10
387 **60** 3 c. black & dp. blue-green (*p.* 13×11½) (21.3.38) 1·40 10
a. Perf. 13×13½ (1938) .. 26·00 35
b. Perf. 13½ (21.3.38) .. 8 8
c. Perf. 14 (7.41) .. .. 5·00 35
d. Perf. 11½×11 (14.5.42) .. 5 8
e. Perf. 12 (14.1.46) 5 8
387*f* **62** 5 c. sage-green and orange (*p.* 13½) (1.1.43) .. 25 8
g. Perf. 12 (1947) 10 10
388 **59** 6 c. black and blue (*p.* 11×11½) (1.1.38) 5 8
389 **70** 10 c. black and light blue (*p.* 11½×11) (1.2.38) 12 10
a. Wmk. upright (1.6.44) .. 8 8
390 **64** 15 c. green and red-brown (*p.* 11½×11) (1.1.38) 5 8
a. Wmk. upright (23.7.45) .. 12 8
391 **61** 20 c. black and grey-blue (*p.* 11½×11) (15.1.38) 10 8
392 **65** 25 c. dp. blue & chocolate (*p.* 11×11½) (1.2.38) 5 8
a. Wmk. upright (1944) .. 10 8
393 **66** 30 c. carmine and green (*p.* 11½×11) (1.2.38) 70 50
a. Wmk. upright (16.4.45) .. 65 20
394 **67** 50 c. black and mauve (*p.* 13×11½) (25.4.38) 14·00 3·25
a. Perf. 13×13½ (1938) .. 15·00 1·25
b. Perf. 13½ (25.4.38) .. 70 25
c. Perf. 14 (4.42) .. .. 3·50 1·50
d. Perf. 11½×11 (14.5.42) .. 25 8
e. Perf. 12 (14.1.46) 40 12
395 **68** 1 r. blue-violet and choc. (*p.* 11½×11) (1.2.38) 1·10 35
a. Wmk. upright (1944) .. 85 35
396 **71** 2 r. black and carmine (*p.* 11×11½) (1.2.38) 80 50
396*a* ,, 2 r. black and violet (*p.* 11×11½) (15.3.47) 70 35
397 **72** 5 r. grn. & pur. (*shades*), C (*p.* 14) (10.10.38) .. 2·50 70
a. Green and pale purple, O (19.2.43) .. .. 2·00 55
386/397*a* (*cheapest*) .. *Set of* 14 5·00 2·50
387/397 Perf. "Specimen" *Set of* 14 35·00

3 CENTS **3 CENTS**
(73) (74)

1940–41. *Nos.* 388 *and* 391 *surch.*

398 **73** 3 c. on 6 c. (10.5.41) .. 12 5
399 **74** 3 c. on 20 c. (5.11.40) .. 12 20

1946 (10 DEC.). *Victory. As Nos.* 28/9 *of Aden.*

400 6 c. blue 5 8
401 15 c. brown 5 10
400/1 Perf. "Specimen" *Set of* 2 12·00

75. Parliament Building.

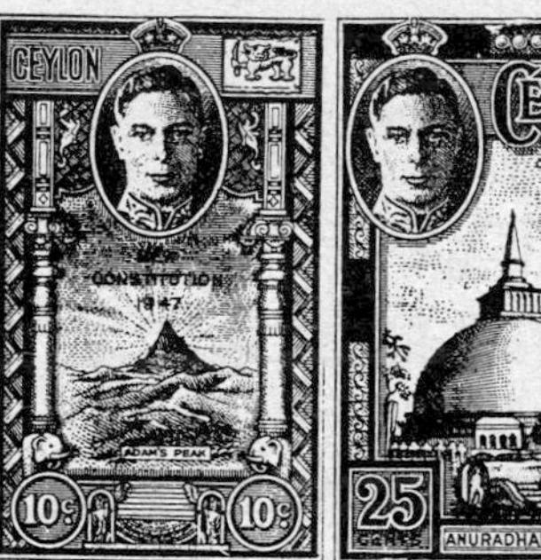

76. Adam's Peak. **77.** Anuradhapura.

78. Temple of the Tooth.

(Des. R. Tenison and M. S. V. Rodrigo. Recess. B.W.)

1947 (25 NOV.). *Inauguration of New Constitution. Wmk. Mult. Script CA.* P 11×12 (*horiz.*) *or* 12×11 (*vert.*).

402 **75** 6 c. black and blue .. 5 10
403 **76** 10 c. blk., orange & carmine 5 12
404 **78** 15 c. green and purple .. 8 12
405 **77** 25 c. ochre & emer.-green 15 15
402/405 Perf. "Specimen" *Set of* 4 32·00

II. DOMINION.

79. Lion Flag of Dominion. **80.** D. S. Senanayake.

81. Lotus Flowers and Sinhalese Letters "Sri".

(Recess. (flag typo.). B.W.)

1949. *First Anniv. of Independence* (*a*) (4 FEB.). *Wmk. Mult. Script CA* (*sideways on* 4 *c.*). *P* 12½×12 (4 *c.*) *or* 12×12½ (5 *c.*).

406	**79**	4 c. yell., carm. & brown	5	10
407	**80**	5 c. brown and green ..	10	12

(*b*) (5 APR.). *W* **81** (*sideways on* 15 *c.*). *P* 13×12½ (15 *c.*) *or* 12×12½ (25 *c.*).

408	**79**	15 c. yell., carm. & verm.	10	12
409	**80**	25 c. brown and blue ..	15	15

The 15 c. is larger, measuring 28×12 mm.

82. Globe and Forms of Transport.

83

84

(Recess. De La Rue & Co.)

1949 (10 OCT.). *75th Anniv. of Universal Postal Union. W* **81.** *P* 13 (25 *c.*) *or* 12 (*others*).

410	**82**	5 c. brown and bluish green	8	8
411	**83**	15 c. black and carmine ..	30	12
412	**84**	25 c. black and ultramarine	35	12

85. Kandyan Dancer. **86.** Kiri Vehera, Polonnaruwa.

87. Vesak Orchid. **88.** Sigiriya (Lion Rock).

89. Octagon Library, Temple of the Tooth.

90. Ruins at Madirigiriya.

(Recess. Bradbury, Wilkinson.)

1950 (4 FEB.). *W* **81.** *P* 11×11½ (75 *c.*), 11½×11 (1 *r.*), 12×12½ (*others*).

413	**85**	4 c. purple and scarlet ..	5	8
414	**86**	5 c. green	8	8
415	**87**	15 c. blue-green and violet	12	8
416	**88**	30 c. carmine and yellow..	12	8
417	**89**	75 c. ultramarine & orange	25	8
418	**90**	1 r. deep blue and brown	30	12
413/418		.. .. *Set of* 6	80	45

91. Ruhuna National Park. **92.** Ancient Guard-stone, Anuradhapura.

93. Harvesting Rice. **94.** Coconut Trees.

95. Sigiriya Fresco. **96.** Star Orchid.

97. Rubber Plantation.

98. Outrigger Canoe. **99.** Tea Plantation.

100. River Gal Dam.

101. Bas-relief, Anuradhapura. **102.** Harvesting Rice.

(Photo. Courvoisier.)

1951–54. *No wmk.* *P* 11½.

419 **91** 2 c. brown and blue-green 5 5
420 **92** 3 c. black and slate-violet 5 5
421 **93** 6 c. brn.-blk. & yell.-grn. 5 5
422 **94** 10 c. green and blue-grey.. 5 5
423 **95** 25 c. orge.-brn. & brt. blue 8 5
424 **96** 35 c. red and deep green (I) 20 5
a. Type II 15 5
425 **97** 40 c. deep brown 12 5
426 **98** 50 c. indigo and slate-grey 12 5
427 **99** 85 c. blk. & dp. blue-green 25 10
428 **100** 2 r. blue and deep brown 50 20
429 **101** 5 r. brown and orange .. 1·25 40
430 **102** 10 r. red-brown and buff .. 4·00 1·25
419/430 .. .. *Set of* 12 6·00 2·00

No. 424a. In Type II of the 35 c. value, a dot has been added above the third Tamil character in the second line of the inscription at the top right corner.

Dates of issue:—1.8.51, 10 c.; 1.2.52, 35 c. (I); '54, 35 c. (II); 15.3.54, 25 c., 50 c., 5 r., 10 r.; 15.5.54, 2 c., 3 c., 6 c., 40 c., 85 c. and 2 r.

103. Ceylon Mace and Symbols of Progress.

(Photo. Harrison.)

1952 (23 Feb.). *Colombo Plan Exhibition. Chalk-surfaced paper.* *W* **81** (*sideways*). *P* 14½ × 14.

431 **103** 5 c. green 8 8
432 ,, 15 c. ultramarine .. 12 15

104. Queen Elizabeth II. **106.** King Coconuts.

105. Ceremonial Procession.

(Recess. Bradbury, Wilkinson.)

1953 (2 June). *Coronation.* *W* **81.** *P* 12 × 13.

433 **104** 5 c. green 8 8

(Recess. De La Rue.)

1954 (10 Apr.). *Royal Visit.* *W* **81** (*sideways*). *P* 13 × 12½.

434 **105** 10 c. deep blue 5 5

(Photo. Courvoisier.)

1954 (1 Dec.). *No wmk.* *P* 11½.

435 **106** 10 c. orange, bistre-brown and buff 5 5

107. Farm Produce.

(Photo. Harrison.)

1955 (10 Dec.). *Royal Agricultural and Food Exhibition.* *W* **81** (*sideways*). *P* 14 × 14½.

436 **107** 10 c. brown and orange.. 5 5

108. Sir John Kotelawala and House of Representatives.

(Photo. Courvoisier.)

1956 (26 Mar.). *Prime Minister's 25 years of Public Service.* *P* 11½.

437 **108** 10 c. deep bluish green .. 5 5

109. Arrival of Vijaya in Ceylon.

110. Lampstand and Dharmachakra. **111.** Hand of Peace and Dharmachakra.

112. Dharmachakra encircling the Globe.

(Photo. Courvoisier.)

1956. *Buddha Jayanti.* *P* 11½.

438 **109** 3 c. blue & brownish grey (23 May) 5 5
439 **110** 4 c.+2 c. greenish yellow & deep blue (10 May) 5 5
440 **111** 10 c.+5 c. carmine, yellow and grey (10 May).. 10 10
441 **112** 15 c. bright blue (23 May) 10 5

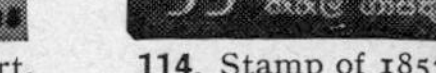

113. Mail Transport. **114.** Stamp of 1857.

(Photo. J. Enschedé & Sons (4 c., 10 c.), Courvoisier (others).)

1957 (1 Apr.). *Centenary of First Ceylon Postag Stamp.* *P* 12½ × 13 (4 *c.*, 10 *c.*) *or* 11½ (*others*

442 **113** 4 c. orange-red and deep bluish-green .. 5
443 ,, 10 c. vermilion and blue 5
444 **114** 35 c. brown, yellow & blue 10
445 ,, 85 c. brn., yell. & grey-grn. 20 1

(**115**) (**116**) **117.** Kandyan Dancer

1958 (15 Jan.). *Nos.* 439/40 *with premiu obliterated as T* **115** (4 *c.*) *or T* **116** (10 *c.*).

446 **110** 4 c. greenish yellow and deep blue .. 5
a. Opt. inverted.. .. 12·00
b. Opt. double .. 15·00
447 **111** 10 c. carmine, yell. & grey 5
a. Opt. inverted.. .. 18·00

The 4 c. exists with opt. misplaced to right s that some stamps show the vertical bar on th left (*Price* £18 *un.*).

(Recess. Bradbury, Wilkinson (4 c., 5 c., 15 c 30 c., 75 c., 1 r.). Photo. Courvoisier (others)

1958 (14 May)–**59.** *As earlier types, but inscri tions redrawn as in T* **117.** *W* **81**; *P* 11 × 1 (75 *c.*), 11½ × 11 (1 *r.*) *or* 12 × 12½ (4 *c.*, 5 *c.*, 15 30 *c.*). *No. wmk.*; *P* 11½ (*others*).

448 **91** 2 c. brown & blue-green 5
449 **92** 3 c. black & slate-violet 5
450 **117** 4 c. purple and scarlet.. 5
451 **86** 5 c. grn. (*shades*) (1.10.58) 5
452 **93** 6 c. brown-black & yellow-green 5
453 **106** 10 c. orange, bistre-brown and buff (1.10.58) .. 5
454 **87** 15 c. blue-green & violet (1.10.58) 5
455 **95** 25 c. orange-brown & brt. blue 5
456 **88** 30 c. carm. & yell. (1.5.59) 5
457 **96** 35 c. red and deep green (II) (15.7.58) .. 5
459 **98** 50 c. indigo and slate-grey (15.7.58) 8
460 **89** 75 c. ultramarine & orange (*shades*) (1.5.59) .. 12
461 **99** 85 c. black & deep blue-green (1.5.59) .. 15
462 **90** 1 r. deep blue & brown (1.10.58) .. 20
463 **100** 2 r. blue and deep brown 35
464 **101** 5 r. brown and orange.. 1·00
465 **102** 10 r. red-brown and buff 2·25 1·
448/65 .. .. *Set of* 17 4·00 2·

118. " Human Rights ".

(Photo. J. Enschedé.)

958 (10 Dec.). *Tenth Anniv. of Declaration of Human Rights. P* 13×12½.
66 **118** 10 c. vermilion & dull pur. 5 5
67 „ 85 c. verm. & dp. blue-grn. 20 20

119. Portraits of Founders and University Buildings.

(Photo. J. Enschedé.)

959 (31 Dec.). *Institution of Pirivena Universities. P* 13×12½.
68 **119** 10 c. red-orge. & ultram. 5 5

120. Uprooted Tree. **121.** S. W. R. D. Bandaranaike.

Des. W. A. Ariyasena. Photo. Courvoisier.)

960 (7 Apr.). *World Refugee Year. P* 11½.
69 **120** 4 c. red-brown and gold 5 5
70 „ 25 c. blackish vio. & gold 5 5

(Photo. Courvoisier.)

961 (8 Jan.). *Prime Minister Bandaranaike Commemoration. P* 11½.
71 **121** 10 c. deep blue & greenish blue 5 5
a. Portrait redrawn ('61) 20 5

No. 471a can be identified by Mr. Bandaranaike's dark hair at temples.

122. Ceylon Scout Badge. **123.** Campaign Emblem.

Des. W. A. Ariyasena. Photo. Courvoisier.) (Photo. Harrison & Sons.)

962 (26 Feb.). *Golden Jubilee of Ceylon Boy Scouts Association. P* 11½.
72 **122** 35 c. buff and blue .. 8 5

1962 (7 Apr.). *Malaria Eradication.* **W 81.** *P* 14½×14.
473 **123** 25 c. red-orange and sepia 5 5

124. Moth and Comet Aircraft.

(Photo. Courvoisier.)

1963 (28 Feb.). *25th Anniv. of Airmail. P* 11½.
474 **124** 50 c. black and light blue 12 12

125. " Produce " and Campaign Emblem.

(Photo. Courvoisier.)

1963 (21 Mar.). *Freedom from Hunger. P* 11½.
475 **125** 5 c. vermilion and blue 5 5
476 „ 25 c. brown & yellow-olive 5 5

ශත
2
சதம்
■ ■

(**126**)

1963 (1 June). *No.* 450 *surch. with T* **126.**
477 **117** 2 c. on 4 c. pur. & scarlet 5 5
a. Surch. inverted .. .. 20·00
b. Surch. double .. .. 18·00

127. " Rural Life ".

(Photo. Harrison & Sons.)

1963 (5 July). *Golden Jubilee of Ceylon Co-operative Movement.* **W 81.** *P* 14×14½.
478 **127** 60 c. rose-red and black 12 12

128. S. W. R. D. Bandaranaike.

(Recess. Courvoisier.)

1963 (26 Sept.). *P* 11½.
479 **128** 10c. light blue 5 5

129. Terrain, Elephant and Tree.

(Photo. Harrison & Sons.)

1963 (2 Dec.). *National Conservation Week.* **W 81** *(sideways). P* 14×14½.
480 **129** 5 c. sepia and blue .. 5 5

130. S. W. R. D. Bandaranaike. **131.** Anagarika Dharmapala (Buddhist missionary).

(T **130**/1. Photo. Courvoisier.)

1964 (1 July). *P* 11½.
481 **130** 10 c. deep violet-blue and greenish grey .. 5 5

1964 (16 Sept.). *Birth Centenary of Anagarika Dharmapala (founder of Maha Bodhi Society). P* 11½.
482 **131** 25 c. sepia & olive-yellow 5 5

134. Grackle.

135. D. S. Senanayake. **136.**

137. Peacock.

138. Ruins at Madirigiriya.

143. Jungle Fowl.

144. Oriole.

146. Tea Plantation.

149. Map of Ceylon.

148. Girls transplanting rice.

(Des. A. Dharmasiri (5 r.); P. A. Miththapala (10 r.). Photo. Courvoisier (10 c. (486), (20 c.), Harrison (10 c. (487), 60 c., 1 r., 5 r., 10 r.), De La Rue (others incl. sheet).)

1964–69. *No wmk.* (*Nos.* 486, 489), *W* **81** (*others; sideways on Nos.* 487, 449, 499) *P* 11½ (*Nos.* 486, 489), 14½ × 14 (*No.* 494) *or* 14 (*others*).

485	**134**	5 c. multicoloured ..	5	5
486	**135**	10 c. myrtle-green ..	5	5
487	**136**	10 c. myrtle-green ..	5	5
		a. Imperf. (pair) ..		
488	**137**	15 c. multicoloured ..	5	5
489	**138**	20 c. brown-purple & buff	5	5
494	**143**	60 c. multicoloured ..	8	5
		a. Red omitted	45·00	
		b. Blue and green omitted* ..	45·00	
495	**144**	75 c. multicoloured ..	8	5
497	**146**	1 r. brown & bluish grn.	12	5
499	**148**	5 r. multicoloured ..	55	25
500	**149**	10 r. multicoloured ..	1·10	50
MS500*a*		148 × 174 mm. 5 c., 15 c., 60 c. & 75 c. Imperf.	50	50
485/500		.. .. *Set of* 10	1·75	90

Dates of issue: 1.10.64, 20 c., 1 r.; 22.3.66, 10 c. (No. 486); 24.9.68 (but released a day earlier by Crown Agents), 10 c. (No. 487); 15.8.69, 5 r., 1.10.69, 10 r.; 5.2.66, others.

The 5 c., 75 c. and 1 r. exist with PVA gum as well as gum arabic.

In the miniature sheet the inscriptions on the 60 c. have been rearranged to conform with the style of the other values.

* Actually only the blue printing is omitted on this sheet, but where this was printed over the yellow to form the leaves it appeared as green.

150. Exhibition Buildings and Cogwheels.

(Photo. State Ptg. Wks., Budapest.)

1964 (1 Dec.). *Industrial Exhibition. T* **150** *and similar horiz. design. No wmk. P* 11.

501	–	5 c. multicoloured ..	5	5
502	**150**	5 c. multicoloured ..	5	5

No. 501 is inscribed "INDUSTRIAL EXHIBITION" in Sinhala and Tamil, No. 502 in Sinhala and English. The stamps were issued together *se-tenant* in alternate vertical rows, producing horizontal pairs.

151. Trains of 1864 and 1964.

(Photo. Harrison & Sons.)

1964 (21 Dec.). *Centenary of Ceylon Railways. T* **151** *and similar horiz. design. W* **81** (*sideways*). *P* 14 × 14½.

503	–	60 c. blue, reddish purple and yellow-green ..	12	15
504	**151**	60 c. blue, reddish purple and yellow-green ..	12	15

No. 503 is inscribed "RAILWAY CENTENARY" in Sinhala and Tamil, No. 504 in Sinhala and English. The stamps were issued together *se-tenant* in alternate horizontal rows, producing vertical pairs.

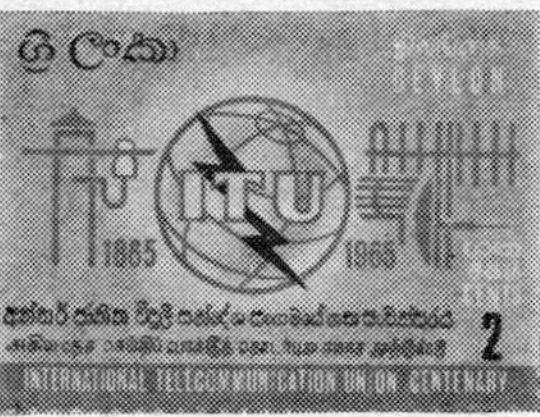

152. I.T.U. Emblem and Symbols.

(Photo. Harrison & Sons.)

1965 (16 May). *I.T.U. Centenary. W* **81** (*sideways*). *P* 14½.

505	**152**	2 c. bright blue and red	5	5
506	,,	30 c. brown and red ..	8	10

153. I.C.Y. Emblem.

(Photo. Courvoisier.)

1965 (26 June). *International Co-operation Year T* **153** *and similar horiz. design. P* 11½

507	3 c. dp. blue & rose-carmine	8	
508	50 c. black, rose-carm. & gold	10	

No. 508 is similar to T **153** but has the multilingual inscription "CEYLON" rearranged.

154. Town Hall, Colombo.

(Photo. Courvoisier.)

1965 (29 Oct.). *Centenary of Colombo Municipal Council. P* 11 × 11½.

509	**154**	25 c. myrtle-green & sepia	8

5 ■

(155)

157. Kandy and Council Crest

1965 (18 Dec.). *No.* 481 *surch. with T* **155.**

510	**130**	5 c. on 10 c. deep violet-blue & greenish grey	8

(Photo. Harrison.)

1966 (15 June). *Kandy Municipal Council Centenary. W* **81.** *P* 14 × 13½.

512	**157**	25 c. multicoloured ..	5	

158. W.H.O. Building.

(Litho. De La Rue.)

1966 (8 Oct.). *Inauguration of W.H.O. Headquarters, Geneva. P* 14.

513	**158**	4 c. multicoloured ..	5	
514	,,	1 r. multicoloured ..	15	

159. Rice Paddy and Map of Ceylon.

160. Rice paddy and Globe.

(Photo. Courvoisier.)

1966 (25 Oct.). *International Rice Year.* P 11½.
515 **159** 6 c. multicoloured .. 5 5
516 **160** 30 c. multicoloured .. 8 8

161. U.N.E.S.C.O. Emblem.

(Litho. State Ptg. Wks., Vienna.)

1966 (3 Nov.). *20th Anniv. of U.N.E.S.C.O.* P 12.
517 **161** 3 c. multicoloured .. 5 5
518 ,, 50 c. multicoloured .. 10 8

162. Water-resources Map.

(Litho. De La Rue.)

1966 (1 Dec.). *International Hydrological Decade.* P 14.
519 **162** 2 c. orange-brown, greenish yellow and blue .. 5 5
520 ,, 2 r. orange-brown, greenish yellow, blue and yellow-green 30 25

163. Devotees at Buddhist Temple.

164. Mihintale.

165. Sacred Bo-tree, Anuradhapura.

166. Adam's Peak.

(Photo. State Ptg. Wks., Vienna.)

1967 (2 Jan.). *Poya Holiday System.* P 12.
521 **163** 5 c. multicoloured .. 5 5
522 **164** 20 c. multicoloured .. 5 5
523 **165** 35 c. multicoloured .. 5 8
524 **166** 60 c. multicoloured .. 12 10

167. Galle Fort and Clock Tower.

(Litho. Rosenbaum Brothers Vienna.)

1967 (5 Jan.). *Centenary of Galle Municipal Council.* P 14.
525 **167** 25 c. multicoloured .. 5 5

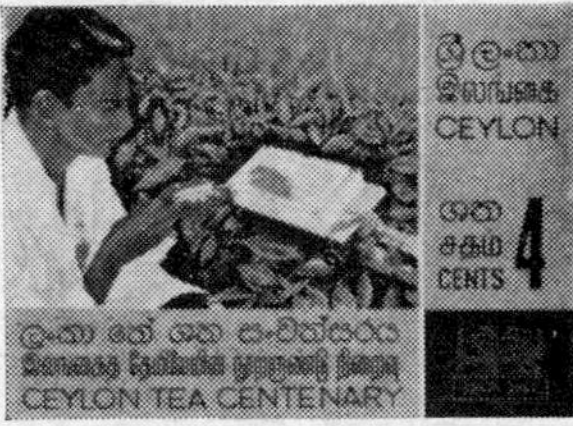

168. Field Research.

169. Tea-tasting Equipment.

170. Leaves and Bud.

171. Shipping Tea.

(Litho. Rosenbaum Bros., Vienna.)

1967 (1 Aug.). *Centenary of Ceylon Tea Industry.* P 14×13½.
526 **168** 4 c. multicoloured .. 5 5
527 **169** 40 c. multicoloured .. 8 8
528 **170** 50 c. multicoloured .. 8 8
529 **171** 1 r. multicoloured .. 15 12

172. Elephant Ride.

(Litho. Rosenbaum Bros., Vienna.)

1967 (15 Aug.). *International Tourist Year.* P 14×13½.
530 **172** 45 c. multicoloured .. 8 8

1967 (15 Sept.). *First National Stamp Exhibition. Sheet No.* **MS**500a *optd.* "FIRST NATIONAL STAMP EXHIBITION 1967".
MS531 148×174 mm. Imperf. .. 30 35

173. Ranger, Jubilee Emblem and Flag.

(Litho. De La Rue.)

1967 (19 Sept.). *Golden Jubilee of Ceylon Girl Guides Association.* P 12½×13.
532 **173** 3 c. multicoloured .. 5 5
533 ,, 25 c. multicoloured .. 8 8

174. Col. Olcott and Buddhist Flag.

(Litho. Rosenbaum Bros., Vienna.)

1967 (8 Dec.). *60th Death Anniv. of Colonel H. S. Olcott (theosophist).* P 14.
534 **174** 15 c. multicoloured .. 5 5

175. Independence Hall.

176. Lion Flag and Sceptre.

(Photo. Harrison.)

1968 (2 Feb.). *20th Anniv. of Independence.* W **81** (*sideways*). P 14.
535 **175** 5 c. multicoloured .. 5 5
536 **176** 1 r. multicoloured .. 15 12

177. Sir D. B. Jayatilleke.

(Litho. De La Rue.)

1968 (14 Feb.). *Birth Centenary of Sir Baron Jayatilleke (scholar and statesman).* P 14.
537 **177** 25 c. yellow-brn. & sepia 5 5

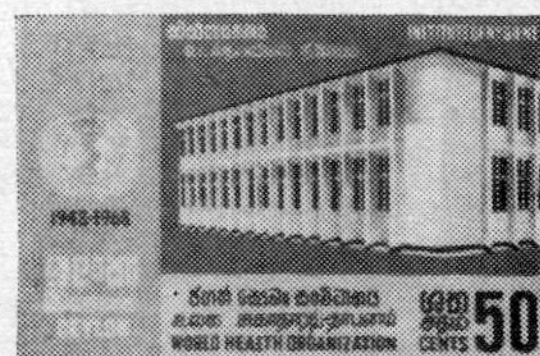

178. Institute of Hygiene.

(Litho. Bradbury, Wilkinson.)

1968 (7 Apr.). *20th Anniv. of World Health Organization.* W **81**. P 12.
538 **178** 50 c. multicoloured .. 8 8

179. Aircraft over Terminal Building.

(Des. and litho. Bradbury, Wilkinson.)

1968 (5 Aug.). *Opening of Colombo Airport. W* **81.** *P* $13\frac{1}{2}$.

539 **179** 60 c. grey-blue, chestnut, red and yellow .. 10 10

181. Open Quran and " 1400 ".

(Des. M. I. M. Mohideen. Photo. Harrison.)

1968 (14 Oct.). *1400th Anniv. of the Holy Quran. W* **81.** *P* 14.

541 **181** 25 c. multicoloured .. 5 5

182. Human Rights Emblem.

(Photo. Pakistan Security Printing Corp.)

1968 (10 Dec.). *Human Rights Year. P* $12\frac{1}{2}\times13\frac{1}{2}$.

542 **182** 2 c. multicoloured .. 5 5
543 „ 20 c. multicoloured .. 5 5
544 „ 40 c. multicoloured .. 8 8
545 „ 2 r. multicoloured .. 25 25

183. All Ceylon Buddhist Congress Headquarters.

(Des. A. Dharmasiri. Litho. Rosenbaum Bros., Vienna.)

1968 (19 Dec.). *Golden Jubilee of All Ceylon Buddhist Congress. P* $14\times13\frac{1}{2}$.

546 **183** 5 c. multicoloured .. 8 5

A 50 c. value showing a footprint was prepared but its release was stopped the day before it was due for issue. However, some are known to have been released in error.

184. E. W. Perera (patriot).

185. Symbols of Strength in Savings.

(Photo. Harrison.)

1969 (17 Feb.). *E. W. Perera Commemoration. W* **81.** *P* $14\times13\frac{1}{2}$.

547 **184** 60 c. brown 12 10

(Des. A. Dharmasiri. Photo. Harrison.)

1969 (20 Mar.). *Silver Jubilee of National Savings Movement. W* **81.** *P* 14.

548 **185** 3 c. multicoloured .. 5 5

186. Seat of Enlightenment under Sacred Bodhi Tree.

187. Buduresmala (Six fold Buddha-Rays).

Des. L. T. P. Manjusree. Litho. De La Rue.)

1969 (10 Apr.). *Vesak Day (inscr. " Wesak "). W* **81** *(sideways). P* 15.

549 **186** 4 c. multicoloured .. 5 5
550 **187** 6 c. multicoloured .. 5 5
551 **186** 35 c. multicoloured .. 5 8

No. 549 exists with the gold apparently omitted. Normally the gold appears (without a separate plate number) over an underlay of olive-green on carmine. In one sheet we have seen, the gold only shows as tiny specks under a strong magnifying glass and as there may be intermediate stages of faint printing we do not list this.

188. A. E. Goonesinghe.

(Des. and photo. Harrison.)

1969 (29 Apr.). *Commemoration of Goonesinghe (founder of Labour Movement in Ceylon). W* **81.** *P* 14.

552 **188** 15 c. multicoloured .. 5 5

189. I.L.O Emblem.

(Photo. Harrison.)

1969 (4 May). *50th Anniv. of International Labour Organization. W* **81** *(sideways). P* 14.

553 **189** 5 c. black & turq.-blue 5 5
554 „ 25 c. black & carmine-red 5 5

190. Convocation Hall, University of Ceylon.

191. Lamp of Learning, Globe and Flags.

192. Uranium Atom.

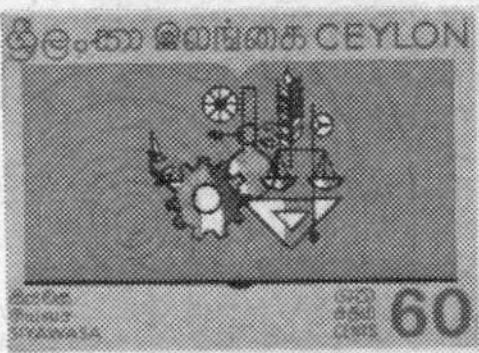

193. Symbols of Scientific Education.

(Des. A. Edward (35 c.); L. D. P. Jayawardena (50 c.); A. Dharmasiri (60 c.); 4 c. from photograph. Litho. Rosenbaum Bros., Vienna.)

1969 (1 Aug.). *Educational Centenary. P* $13\frac{1}{2}$.

555 **190** 4 c. multicoloured .. 5 5
556 **191** 35 c. multicoloured .. 5 5
557 **192** 50 c. multicoloured .. 8 10
558 **193** 60 c. multicoloured .. 10 10

194. Ath Pana (Elephant Lamp).

195. Rock Fortress of Sigiriya.

(Des. from photographs. Litho. Rosenbaum Bros., Vienna.)

1969 (1 Aug.). *Archeological Centenary. P* $13\frac{1}{2}$.

559 **194** 6 c. multicoloured .. 5 5
560 **195** 1 r. multicoloured .. 15 12

196. Leopard.

(Litho. Rosenbaum Bros., Vienna.)

1970 (11 May). *Wildlife Conservation. T* **196** *and similar horiz. designs. Multicoloured. P* 14×13½.

561 5 c. Wild Buffalo 5 5
562 15 c. Slender Loris 5 5
a. Brown-black and orange-brown colours omitted ..
563 50 c. Spotted Deer 8 8
a. Imperf. (in vert. pr. with stamp perf. 3 sides) .. 75·00
564 1 r. Type **196** 15 12

In No. 562a the sky is blue instead of violet and the animal is in green and yellow only.

197. Emblem and Symbols.

(Des. A. Dharmasiri. Litho. Rosenbaum Bros., Vienna.)

1970 (17 June). *Asian Productivity Year. P* 14.

565 **197** 60 c. multicoloured .. 10 10

198. New U.P.U. H.Q. Building.

(Litho. Rosenbaum Bros., Vienna.)

1970 (14 Aug.). *New U.P.U. Headquarters Building. P* 14.

566 **198** 50 c. yellow-orange, black and new blue .. 10 8
a. New blue (Building omitted) .. ..
567 „ 1 r. 10, vermilion, black and new blue .. 20 15

199. Oil Lamp and Caduceus.

(Des. A. Dharmasiri. Litho. Rosenbaum Bros., Vienna.)

1970 (1 Sept.). *Centenary of Colombo Medical School. P* 13½.

568 **199** 5 c. multicoloured .. 5 5
a. Vert. pair, bottom stamp imperf. .. .. 65·00
569 „ 45 c. multicoloured .. 8 8

200. Victory March and S. W. R. D. Bandaranaike.

(Des. A. Dharmasiri. Litho. D.L.R.)

1970 (25 Sept.). *Definitive issue marking establishment of United Front Government. P* 13½.

570 **200** 10 c. multicoloured .. 5 5

201. U.N. Emblem and Dove of Peace.

(Des. A. Dharmasiri. Photo. Pakistan Security Printing Corp.)

1970 (24 Oct.). *25th Anniv. of United Nations. P* 12½×13½.

571 **201** 2 r. multicoloured .. 25 25

202. Keppetipola Dissawa.

(Des. A. Dharmasiri. Litho. Harrison.)

1970 (26 Nov.). *152nd Death Anniv. of Keppetipola Dissawa (Kandyan patriot). P* 14×14½.

572 **202** 25 c. multicoloured .. 5 5

203. Ola Leaf Manuscript.

(Des. A. Dharmasiri. Photo. Pakistan Security Printing Corp.)

1970 (21 Dec.). *International Educational Year. P* 13.

573 **203** 15 c. multicoloured .. 8 5

204. C. H. de Soysa. **205.** D. E. H. Pedris (patriot).

(Des. L. D. P. Jayawardena. Litho. Pakistan Security Printing Corp.)

1971 (3 Mar.). *135th Birth Anniv. of C. H. de Soysa (philanthropist). P* 13½.

574 **204** 20 c. multicoloured .. 8 5

(Des. L. D. P. Jayawardena. Litho. Harrison.)

1971 (8 July). *D. E. H. Pedris Commemoration. P* 14×14½.

575 **205** 25 c. multicoloured .. 5 5

206. Lenin. **207.** Ananda Rajakaruna.

(Des. L. D. P. Jayawardena. Litho. Harrison.)

1971 (31 Aug.). *Lenin Commemoration. P* 14½.

576 **206** 40 c. multicoloured .. 8 8

(Des. A. Dharmasiri (Nos. 577 and 579), P. A. Miththapala (Nos. 578 and 580), L. D. P. Jayawardena (No. 581). Litho. Harrison.)

1971 (29 Oct.). *Poets and Philosophers. T* **207** *and similar vert. designs. P* 14×13½.

577 5 c. Royal blue 5 5
578 5 c. lake-brown 5 5
579 5 c. red-orange 5 5
580 5 c. deep slate-blue 5 5
581 5 c. brown 5 5
577/81 .. .. *Set of* 5 10 10

Portraits: No. 577, Type **207**; No. 578, Arumuga Navalar; No. 579, Rev. S. Mahinda; No. 580, Ananda Coomaraswamy; No. 581; Cumaratunga Munidasa.

15 

(208)

1971. *Various stamps surch. as T* **208** *(obliterating shape differs).*

582 **186** 5 c. on 4 c. mult. .. 8 10
a. Surch. inverted, reading "ς X" .. 20·00
b. Pair, one with "X" omitted .. .. 35·00
c. Surch. double, one inverted
d. Ditto. Pair, one with "X" omitted .. ..
583 **190** 5 c. on 4 c. mult. .. 8 10
a. Surch. inverted .. 15·00
b. Surch. double, one inverted
584 **200** 15 c. on 10 c. mult. .. 5 5
a. Surch. inverted .. 15·00
b. Surch. double .. .. 15·00
585 **187** 25 c. on 6 c. mult. .. 10 12
586 **194** 25 c. on 6 c. mult. .. 10 12
a. Surch. inverted .. 15·00
582/6 .. .. *Set of* 5 35 40

Dates of issue:—No. 584, 2.12.71; others, 26.11.71.

209. Colombo Plan Emblem and Ceylon.

(Des. P. A. Miththapala. Litho. Harrison.)

1971 (28 Dec.). *20th Anniv. of Colombo Plan. P* 14×14½.

587 **209** 20 c. multicoloured .. 8 5

210. Globe and CARE Package.

(Des. A. Dharmasiri. Litho. Harrison.)

1971 (28 Dec.). *20th Anniv. of CARE (Co-operative for American Relief Everywhere). P* 14×13½.

588	**210**	50 c. new blue, lilac & vio.	8	8

211. W.H.O. Emblem and Heart.

(Des. A. Miththapala. Litho. D.L.R.)

1972 (2 May). *World Health Day. P* 13×13½.

589	**211**	25 c. multicoloured ..	8	5

212. Map of Asia and U.N. Emblem.

(Des. L. D. P. Jaywardena. Litho. B.W.)

1972 (2 May). *25th Anniv. of ECAFE (Economic Commission for Asia and the Far East). P* 13.

590	**212**	85 c. multicoloured ..	12	12

OFFICIAL STAMPS.

1869. *Issues of* 1863–68 *overprinted* "SERVICE" *in block letters.*

Although these stamps were prepared for use and sent out to the colony, they were never issued.

Prices:

Narrow "SERVICE"		Wide "SERVICE"	
No. 98. 2d. ..	6·00	No. 119. 1d. ..	5·00
„ 104. 6d. ..	7·00	„ 120. 3d. ..	7·00
„ 108. 8d. ..	8·00		
„ 113. 1s. ..	9·00		
„ 116. 2s. ..	9·00		
„ 116. 2s. *imp.*	30·00		

On

Service

(O 3)

Contemporary issues overprinted with Type O **3.**

1895–96.

O1	**9**	2 c. green	95	12
O2	**39**	3 c. terra cotta & bl.-grn.	85	50
O3	**28**	5 c. dull purple (*b*) ..	35	10
O4	**29**	15 c. sage-green	95	20
O5	„	25 c. yellow-brown ..	75	25
O6	„	30 c. bright mauve & brown	60	15
O7	**30**	1 r. 12, dull rose	4·50	3·50

The varieties of the 1 r. 12 mentioned in note after No. 201 all exist with the "On Service" overprint.

1899–1900.

O 8	**9**	2 c. pale orange-brown ..	30	10
O 9	**39**	3 c. deep green	55	25
O10	**29**	15 c. blue	60	25
O11	**39**	75 c. black and red-brown (R.) ('99)	65	60

1903. *King Edward VII.*

O12	**44**	2 c. orange-brown ..	85	60
O13	**45**	3 c. green	60	60
O14	**46**	5 c. dull purple	80	30
O15	**48**	15 c. blue	1·40	75
O16	„	25 c. bistre	4·00	4·00
O17	„	30 c. dull violet and green	1·60	65

About half a dozen sheets of the 15 c. were overprinted with a space of 3 mm. instead of 4 mm. between the words "On" and "Service".

POSTAL FISCAL.

1952 (1 Dec.). *As T* **72** *but inscr.* "REVENUE" *at sides.*

F1	10 r. dull grn. & yell.-orge., C	5·00	4·50

This revenue stamp was on sale for postal use from December 1st, 1952, until March 14th, 1954.

On May 22nd, 1972, Ceylon became the Republic of Sri Lanka (*q.v.*).

CHANNEL ISLANDS

These issues are now listed under Great Britain after the Postal Fiscal Issues.

CHINA.

BRITISH POST OFFICES.

See after **HONG KONG.**

CHRISTMAS ISLAND.

Formerly a part of the Colony of Singapore: now an Australian territory.

(Malaysian currency.)

1. Queen Elizabeth II.

(Recess; name and value typo. in black. Note Printing Branch, Commonwealth Bank, Melbourne.)

1958 (15 Oct.). *No wmk. P* 14½.

1	**1**	2 c. yellow-orange	8	10
2	„	4 c. brown	10	12
3	„	5 c. deep mauve	12	12
4	„	6 c. grey-blue	15	20
5	„	8 c. black-brown	25	25
6	„	10 c. violet	35	45
7	„	12 c. carmine	60	70
8	„	20 c. blue	1·25	1·50
9	„	50 c. yellow-green	3·25	3·75
10	„	$1 deep bluish green ..	7·50	8·50
1/10		.. .. *Set of* 10	12·00	14·00

PRINTERS. Nos. 11/32 were printed by the Note Printing Branch, Reserve Bank of Australia, Melbourne. From No. 33 onwards all stamps were printed in photogravure by Harrison.

2. Map.

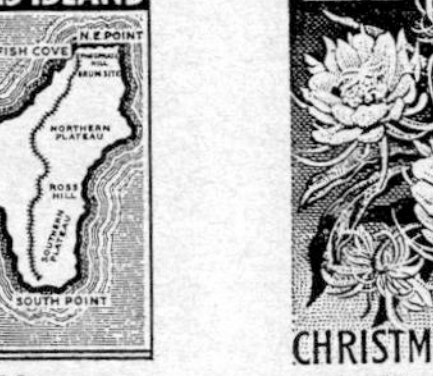

3. Moonflower.

4. Robber Crab.

5. Island Scene.

6. Phosphate Train.

8. Flying Fish Cove.

7. Raising Phosphate.

9. Loading Cantilever.

10. Frigate Bird.

11. Golden Bo'sun Bird.

1963 (28 Aug.). *Recess. P* 14½×14 ($1) *or* 14½ (*others*).

11	**2**	2 c. orange	5	5
12	**3**	4 c. red-brown	5	5
13	**4**	5 c. purple	8	8
14	**5**	6 c. indigo	10	10
15	**6**	8 c. black	12	12
16	**7**	10 c. violet	15	15
17	**8**	12 c. brown-red	25	25
18	**9**	20 c. blue	45	55
19	**10**	50 c. green	90	1·10
20	**11**	$1 yellow	1·75	2·25
11/20		.. .. *Set of* 10	3·50	4·00

I Thick lettering.

II Thinner lettering.

1965. *50th Anniv. of Gallipoli Landing. As T* **181** *of Australia, but slightly larger* (22 × 34½ *mm.*). *Photo.*

21	10 c. sepia, black & emerald (I) (14.4)	30	30
	a. Black-brown, black and light emerald (II) (24.4.)	40	40

(Australian currency.)

12. Golden Striped Grouper.

(Des. G. Hamori. Photo.)

1968 (6 May)–**70.** *Fishes. T* **12** *and similar horiz. designs. Multicoloured. P* 13½.

22	1 c. Type **12**	5	5
23	2 c. Moorish Idol	5	5
24	3 c. Forceps Fish	8	8
25	4 c. Queen Triggerfish ..	10	10
26	5 c. Regal Angelfish	12	12
27	9 c. Surgeon Fish	15	20
28	10 c. Scorpion Fish	20	25
28*a*	15 c. Saddleback Butterfly (fish) (14.12.70) ..	35	40
29	20 c. Clown Butterfly (fish) ..	55	65
29*a*	30 c. Ghost Pipefish (14.12.70)	80	90
30	50 c. Blue Lined Surgeon ..	1·75	2·00
31	$1 Meyers Butterfly (fish) ..	3·25	3·75
22/31	.. .. *Set of* 12	6·50	7·50

13. "Angel" (Mosaic). **14.** "The Ansidei Madonna" (Raphael).

(Des. G. Hamori. Photo.)

1969 (10 Nov.). *Christmas. P* 13½.

32 **13**	5 c. red, deep blue and gold	30	45

(Des. Harrison.)

1970 (26 Oct.). *Christmas. T* **14** *and similar vert. design. P* 14 × 14½.

33 **14**	3 c. multicoloured	12	25
34 –	5 c. multicoloured	20	30

Design:— 5 c. "The Virgin and Child, St. John the Baptist and an Angel" (Morando).

15. "The Adoration of the Shepherds" (ascr. to the School of Seville).

(Des. Harrison.)

1971 (4 Oct.). *Christmas. T* **15** *and similar vert. design. Multicoloured. W* w**12**. *P* 14.

35	6 c. Type **15**	15	15
36	20 c. "The Adoration of the Shepherds" (Reni) ..	40	40

16. H.M.S. *Flying Fish*, 1887.

(Des. V. Whiteley.)

1972–73. *Ships. T* **16** *and similar horiz. designs. Multicoloured. P* 14 × 13½.

37	1 c. *Eagle*, 1714	5	5
38	2 c. H.M.S. *Redpole*, 1890 ..	5	5
39	3 c. M.V. *Hoi Houw*, 1959 ..	5	5
40	4 c. *Pigot*, 1771	5	5
41	5 c. S.S. *Valetta*, 1968 ..	5	8
42	6 c. Type **16**	8	8
43	7 c. *Asia*, 1805	10	10
44	8 c. T.S.S. *Islander*, 1929–60	10	12
45	9 c. H.M.S. *Imperieuse**, 1888	10	12
46	10 c. H.M.S. *Egeria*, 1887 ..	12	15
47	20 c. *Thomas*, 1615	25	30
48	25 c. H.M.S. *Gordon*, 1864 ..	30	35
49	30 c. *Cygnet*, 1688	35	40
50	35 c. S.S. *Triadic*, 1958 ..	45	50
51	50 c. H.M.S. *Amethyst*, 1857	60	70
52	$1 *Royal Mary*, 1643 ..	1·25	1·40
37/52	.. .. *Set of* 16	3·50	4·00

* The design is wrongly inscribed "H.M.S. *Imperious*".

Dates of issue:—7.2.72, Nos. 42/4, 47; 5.6.72, Nos. 37/9, 52; 6.2.73, Nos. 40/1, 45 and 51; 4.6.73, Nos. 46 and 48/50.

17. Angel of Peace.

(Des. Jennifer Toombs.)

1972 (2 Oct.). *Christmas. T* **17** *and similar vert. design. Multicoloured. P* 14.

53	3 c. Type **17**	8	8
54	3 c. Angel of Joy	8	8
55	7 c. Type **17**	15	15
56	7 c. As No. 54	15	15

Nos. 53/4 and 55/6 have the two designs printed horizontally *se-tenant* within sheethet.

18. Virgin and Child, and Map.

(Des. P. L. S. Cheong.)

1973 (2 Oct.). *Christmas. P* 14 × 13.

57 **18**	7 c. multicoloured ..	10	12
58 „	25 c. multicoloured ..	35	40

19. Mary and Holy Child within Christmas Star.

(Des. Harrison.)

1974 (2 Oct.). *Christmas. P* 13 × 14½.

59 **19**	7 c. mauve and grey-black	10	10
60 „	30 c. light orange, bright yellow and grey-black	40	45

20. "The Flight into Egypt".

(Des. Harrison.)

1975 (2 Oct.). *Christmas. P* 14 × 13.

61 **20**	10 c. light greenish yellow, agate and gold.. ..	12	15
62 „	35 c. light rose, deep blue and gold	40	45

21. Dove of Peace and Star of Bethlehem.

(Des. Harrison.)

1976 (2 Oct.). *Christmas. P* 13½.

63 **21**	10 c. cerise, lem. & brt. mve.	15	15
64 –	10 c. cerise, lem. & brt. mve.	15	15
65 **21**	35 c. reddish vio., lt greenish blue & lt. yellow-green	50	55
66 –	35 c. reddish vio., lt. greenish blue & lt. yellow-green	50	55

Nos. 64 and 66 are "mirror-images" of T **21**, the two designs of each value being printed horizontally *se-tenant* throughout the sheet.

COCOS (KEELING) IS.

Formerly incorporated with Singapore: an Australian territory since 1955.

(Australian currency.)

PRINTERS. All the following stamps were printed by the Note Printing Branch, Reserve Bank of Australia, Melbourne, *unless otherwise stated.*

1. Copra Industry.

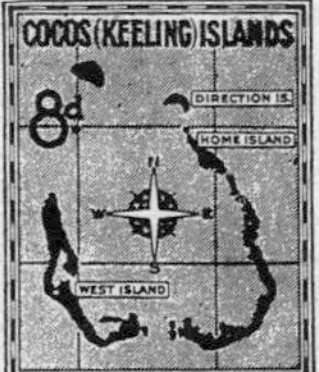

3. Map of Islands.

2. " Super Constellation ".

4. Palms.

5. Dukong (sailboat).

6. White Tern.

1963 (11 June). *Recess. P* $14\frac{1}{2}\times 14$ (*5d., 2s. 3d.*) *or* $14\frac{1}{2}$ (*others*).

1	**1**	3d. chocolate	45	35
2	**2**	5d. ultramarine	45	40
3	**3**	8d. scarlet	75	75
4	**4**	1s. green	2·50	2·50
5	**5**	2s. deep purple	4·00	3·50
6	**6**	2s. 3d. deep green	6·00	5·00
1/6		*Set of* 6	13·00	11·00

I

II

I Thick lettering.

II Thinner lettering.

1965. *50th Anniv. of Gallipoli Landing. As* **T 181** *of Australia, but slightly larger* ($22\times 34\frac{1}{2}$ *mm.*). *Photo.*

7	5d. sepia, black and emerald (I) (14.4)	30	30
	a. Black-brown, black & light emerald (II) (24.4)	40	40

With the introduction of decimal currency on 14th February, 1966, Australian stamps were used in Cocos Islands, until the appearance of the new definitives on 9th July 1969.

(100 cents = $1 Australian.)

7. Reef Clam.

8. Frigate Bird.

(Des. L. Annois (1 c. to 6 c.); P. Jones (10 c. *to* $). Photo.)

1969 (9 July). *Decimal Currency.* **T 7** *and similar designs showing clams, fish or birds and* **T 8.** *Multicoloured. P* $13\frac{1}{2}\times 13$ (*1 c., 2 c., 50 c., $1*) *or* $13\times 13\frac{1}{2}$ (*others*).

8	1 c. Turbo mollusc (*vert.*)	8	8
9	2 c. Burrowing clam (*vert.*)	8	8
10	3 c. Type **7**	8	8
11	4 c. Blenny (fish)	8	10
12	5 c. Coral	10	12
13	6 c. Flying Fish	10	12
14	10 c. Land Rail	20	25
15	15 c. Java Sparrow	25	30
16	20 c. Red-tailed Tropic Bird	35	40
17	30 c. Sooty Tern	55	60
18	50 c. Reef Heron (*vert.*)	90	1·00
19	$1 Type **8**	1·75	2·00
8/19	*Set of* 12	4·00	4·75

9. *Dragon*, 1609.

(Des. R. Honisett. Photo.)

1976 (29 Mar.). **T 9** *and similar multicoloured designs. P* $13\frac{1}{2}\times 13$ (*1, 25, 30, 50 c., $1*) *or* $13\times 13\frac{1}{2}$ (*others*).

20	1 c. Type **9**	5	5
21	2 c. H.M.S. *Juno*, 1857	5	5
22	5 c. H.M.S. *Beagle*, 1836	5	8
23	10 c. H.M.A.S. *Sydney*, 1914	12	12
24	15 c. S.M.S. *Emden*, 1914	20	20
25	20 c. *Ayesha*, 1907	25	25
26	25 c. T.S.S. *Islander*, 1927	30	35
27	30 c. M.V. *Cheshire*, 1951	35	40
28	35 c. Jukung (sailboat)	40	45
29	40 c. C.S. *Scotia*, 1900	45	50
30	50 c. R.M.S. *Orontes*, 1929	60	70
31	$1 Royal Yacht *Gothic*, 1954	1·25	1·40
20/31	*Set of* 12	3·75	4·00

COOK ISLANDS.

(RAROTONGA.)

These are also known as the Hervey Islands. The islands of Manikiki, Rakahanga, and Pukapuka were annexed to the group in October, 1890, and use the same stamps.

I. BRITISH PROTECTORATE.

1

(Des. F. Moss. Typo. Govt. Printing Office Wellington.)

1892 (7 MAY). *No wmk. P* 12½.
A. *Toned paper.* B. *White paper.*

			A.		B.	
1	1	1d. black ..	8·00	10·00	8·00	10·00
		a. Imp. betwn. (vert. pr.) ..	£3000	—		†
2	„	1½d. mauve ..	10·00	12·00	10·00	12·00
		a. Imperf. (pr.)	—	—	£2000	—
3	„	2½d. blue ..	12·00	14·00	12·00	14·00
4	„	10d. carmine	40·00	38·00	40·00	38·00

2. Queen Makea Takau **3.** Torea or Wry-bill.

(Eng. A. E. Cousins. Typo. Govt. Printing Office, Wellington.)

1893–1900. *W* **12b** *of New Zealand* (*N Z and Star wide apart*).
(*a*) *P* 12 × 11½. (7.8.93–'94.)

5 **2** 1d. brown .. .. .. 8·00 10·00
6 „ 1d. blue (2.94) .. .. 3·00 3·00
7 „ 1½d. mauve .. .. .. 3·00 4·00
8 „ 2½d. rose .. .. .. 7·00 10·00
a. Rose-carmine .. .. 20·00 24·00
9 „ 5d. olive-black .. .. 4·00 6·00
10 „ 10d. green .. .. .. 18·00 22·00
5/10 .. .. *Set of* 6 40·00 50·00

(*b*) *Mixed perfs.* 12 × 11½ *and* 12½ (1891–93?).
10*a* **2** 1d. blue .. .. ..
10*b* „ 2½d. rose-carmine .. ..

(*c*) *P* 11. (July, 1896–1900.)
11 **3** ½d. blue (9.99) .. .. 1·50 2·00
12 **2** 1d. blue .. .. .. 1·00 2·00
13 „ 1d. brown/*cream* (4.99) .. 2·00 5·00
a. Wmk. sideways .. ..
14 „ 1½d. deep lilac .. .. 1·50 2·75
a. Deep mauve .. .. 1·40 2·75
15 **3** 2d. brown/*thin toned* (6.98) 1·75 2·75
a. Deep brown (2.1900) .. 1·50 2·75
16 **2** 2½d. pale rose .. .. 8·00 14·00
a. Deep rose .. .. 1·60 3·50
17 „ 5d. olive-black .. .. 6·00 8·00
18 **3** 6d. purple/*thin toned* (6.98) 7·50 8·50
a. Bright purple (2.1900) .. 6·00 7·50
19 **2** 10d. green .. .. .. 6·00 7·00
20 **3** 1s. red/*thin toned* (6.98) 20·00 24·00
a. Deep carmine (2.1900) .. 13·00 15·00
11/20*a* .. .. *Set of* 10 35·00 50·00

ONE
HALF
PENNY
(4)

(5)

1899 (24 APR.). *No.* 12 *surch. with T* **4**.
21 **2** ½d. on 1d. blue .. .. 15·00 18·00
a. Surch. inverted £300 £325
b. Surch. double £300 £275

II. NEW ZEALAND TERRITORY.

1901 (OCT.). *No.* 13 *optd. with T* **5**.
22 **2** 1d. brown .. .. .. 55·00 45·00
a. Crown inverted .. £500 £500
c. Optd. with crown twice .. £500 £500

1902. *No wmk. P* 11.
(*a*) *Medium white Cowan paper.* (Feb.).
23 **3** ½d. blue-green .. .. 2·75 2·50
24 **2** 1d. dull rose .. .. 4·50 4·00
(*b*) *Thick white Pirie paper.* (May).
25 **3** ½d. yellow-green .. .. 1·50 1·75
a. Imperf. betwn. (horiz. pr.) .. £300
26 **2** 1d. rose-red .. .. 3·50 4·50
a. Rose-lake .. .. 2·50 3·00
27 „ 2½d. dull blue .. .. 5·50 7·50

1902 (SEPT.). *W* **41** *of New Zealand* (*single-lined NZ and Star, close together; sideways on T* **2**). *P* 11.
28 **3** ½d. yellow-green .. .. 60 1·25
a. Grey-green .. .. 5·00 6·00
29 **2** 1d. rose-pink .. .. 80 3·00
30 „ 1½d. deep mauve .. .. 1·50 3·00
31 **3** 2d. deep brown .. .. 1·75 3·00
a. No figures of value .. £350 £400
b. Perf. 11 × 14 .. ..
32 **2** 2½d. deep blue .. .. 1·50 2·75
33 „ 5d. olive-black .. .. 7·00 7·50
34 **3** 6d. purple .. .. .. 7·00 7·50
35 **2** 10d. green .. .. .. 20·00 22·00
36 **3** 1s. carmine .. .. 20·00 22·00
a. Perf. 11 × 14 .. .. £110
28/36 .. .. *Set of* 9 55·00 65·00

1909–11. *W* **41** *of New Zealand.*
37 **3** ½d. green (*p.* 14½ × 14) ('11) 2·00 3·00
38 **2** 1d. deep red (*perf.* 14) .. 3·00 4·00

1913–19. *W* **41** *of New Zealand. Chalk-surfaced paper.*
39 **3** ½d. deep green (*p.* 14) ('15) 45 1·00
40 **2** 1d. red (*perf.* 14) (7.13) .. 90 2·00
41 „ 1d. red (*p.* 14 × 14½) ('14) .. 1·50 2·25
42 „ 1½d. dp. mauve (*p.* 14) ('15) 12·00 10·00
43 „ 1½d. dp. mve. (*p.* 14 × 15) ('16) 1·25 1·25
44 **3** 2d. dp. brn. (*p.* 15 × 14) ('19) 5·50 7·50
45 **2** 10d. green (*p.* 14 × 15) ('18) 7·50 9·50
46 **3** 1s. carmine (*p.* 15 × 14) ('19) 7·50 10·00
39/46 .. .. *Set of* 6 20·00 28·00

RAROTONGA

APA PENE
(8)

RAROTONGA
(9)

1919 (APR.–JULY). *Contemporary stamps of New Zealand surch. as T* **8**. (*a*) *Typographed. P* 14 × 15.
50 **60b** ½d. green (R.) (June) .. 8 12
51 **51** 1d. carmine (B.) (June) .. 8 15
52 **60b** 1½d. orange-brn. (R.) (June) 25 55
53 „ 2d. yellow (R.) 35 55
54 „ 3d. chocolate (B.) (July) 45 65

(*b*) *Recess.* (*a*) *P* 14 × 14½. (*b*) *P* 14 × 13½.
55 **60** 2½d. blue (R.) (*a*) (June) .. 60 60
56 „ 2½d. blue (R.) (*b*) .. 65 2·00
a. Vert. pair (55/56) .. 7·00 9·00
57 „ 3d. chocolate (B.) (*a*) .. 45 1·25
58 „ 3d. chocolate (B.) (*b*) .. 65 2·00
a. Vert. pair (57/58) .. 8·00 10·00
59 „ 4d. violet (B.) (*a*) .. 75 1·50
60 „ 4d. violet (B.) (*b*) .. 90 2·50
a. Vert. pair (59/60) .. 5·00 7·50
61 **60** 4½d. deep green (B.) (*a*) .. 75 1·75
62 „ 4½d. deep green (B.) (*b*) .. 75 2·00
a. Vert. pair (61/62) .. 9·00 10·00
63 „ 6d. carmine (B.) (*a*) (June) 90 2·50
64 „ 6d. carmine (B.) (*b*) .. 1·00 2·50
a. Vert. pair (63/64) .. 13·00 15·00
65 „ 7½d. red-brown (B.) (*b*) .. 90 2·50
66 „ 9d. sage-green (R.) (*a*) .. 1·25 2·50
67 „ 9d. sage-green (R.) (*b*) .. 1·40 2·50
a. Vert. pair (66/67) .. 13·00 15·00
68 „ 1s. vermilion (B.) (*a*) (June) 1·40 4·50
69 „ 1s. vermilion (B.) (*b*) .. 2·00 4·50
a. Vert. pair (68/69) .. 16·00 18·00
55(*a*)/68(*a*) .. .. *Set of* 7 5·50 13·00
56(*b*)/69(*b*) .. .. *Set of* 8 7·50 18·00

1921 (OCT.). *Postal Fiscal stamps as Type* F **4** *of New Zealand optd. with T* **9**. *W* **41** (*sideways*). *Chalk-surfaced "De La Rue" paper. P* 14½ × 14.
70 2s. deep blue (R.) .. .. 16·00 20·00
a. Carmine opt. .. .. 40·00 50·00
71 2s. 6d. grey-brown (B.) .. 12·00 15·00
72 5s. yellow-green (R.) .. .. 12·00 15·00
73 10s. maroon (B.) .. .. 24·00 29·00
74 £1 rose-carmine (B.) .. .. 32·00 40·00
70/74 .. .. *Set of* 5 85·00 £100
See also Nos. 85/89.

10. Capt. Cook landing.

11. Wharf at Avarua.

12. Capt. Cook.

13. Palm Tree.

14. Huts at Arorangi.

15. Avarua Harbour.

(Des., eng. and recess. Perkins, Bacon & Co.)

1920 (23 AUG.). *No wmk. P* 14.
75 **10** ½d. black and green .. 90 1·60
76 **11** 1d. black and carmine-red 70 1·40
77 **12** 1½d. black & dull blue .. 1·75 2·50
78 **13** 3d. black and chocolate .. 2·25 3·00
79 **14** 6d. brown & yellow-orange 2·50 3·00
80 **15** 1s. black and violet .. 4·00 6·50
75/80 .. .. *Set of* 6 11·00 16·00

16. Te Po, Rarotongan Chief.

17. Harbour, Rarotonga and Mt. Ikurangi.

(2½d. from a photograph; 4d. des. A. H. Messenger. Plates by Perkins, Bacon. Recess. Govt. Ptg. Office, Wellington.)

1924–27. *W* **41** *of New Zealand. P* 14.
81 **10** ½d. black & green (13.5.26) 85 1·10
82 **11** 1d. black & deep carmine (10.11.24) 85 50
83 **16** 2½d. red-brown & steel-blue (15.10.27) .. .. 1·75 2·50
84 **17** 4d. green & violet (15.10.27) 2·50 3·50

1926 (FEB.–MAY). *As Nos.* 70/4, *but thick, opaque, white chalk-surfaced " Cowan " paper.*
85 2s. blue (C.) .. .. .. 75·00 90·00
86 2s. 6d. deep grey-brown (B.) 32·00 40·00
87 5s. yellow-green (R.) (May) 26·00 32·00
88 10s. brown-red (B.) (May) .. 45·00 60·00
89 £1 rose-pink (B.) (May) .. 60·00 75·00

1926–28. *T* **72** (*"Admiral" Type*) *of New Zealand, overprinted with T* **9**. (*a*) *" Jones " chalk-surfaced paper.*
90 2s. deep blue (R.) (10.26) .. 6·50 12·00
(*b*) *" Cowan " thick chalk-surfaced paper.*
91 2s. light blue (R.) (18.6.27) .. 6·50 11·00
92 3s. bright mauve (R.) (30.1.28) 10·00 11·00

TWO PENCE (18) **COOK ISLANDS.** (19)

1931. *Surch. with T* **18**. *P* 14. (*a*) *No wmk.*
93 **12** 2d. on 1½d. black & blue (R.) 1·25 1·40
(*b*) *W* **41** *of New Zealand.*
94 **12** 2d. on 1½d. blk. & blue (R.) 50 80

1931 (12 NOV.)–**32.** *Postal Fiscal stamps as Type* F **6** *of New Zealand. W* **41**. *Thick, opaque, white chalk-surfaced " Cowan " paper. P* 14.
(*a*) *Optd. with T* **9**.
95 2s. 6d. deep brown (B.) .. 6·00 7·00
96 5s. green (R.) .. .. .. 12·00 14·00
97 10s. carmine-lake (B.) .. .. 22·00 26·00
98 £1 pink (B.) .. .. .. 32·00 35·00
(*b*) *Optd. with T* **19** (3.32).
98*a* £3 green (R.) .. .. .. 50·00 65·00
98*b* £5 blue (R.) £110 £120
The £3 and £5 values were mainly used for fiscal purposes.

20. Capt. Cook landing.

21. Capt. Cook.

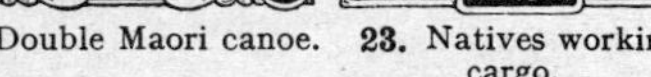
22. Double Maori canoe. **23.** Natives working cargo.

24. Port of Avarua.

25. R.M.S. *Monowai.*

26. King George V.

(Des. L. C. Mitchell. Recess. Perkins, Bacon.)

1932 (16 MAR.). *No wmk. P* 13.
99 **20** ½d. black & deep green .. 40 45
a. Perf. 14 .. .. 10·00 12·00
100 **21** 1d. black and lake .. 65 1·00
a. Centre inverted .. £400 £400
b. Perf. 14 .. .. 5·00 5·50
101 **22** 2d. black and brown .. 1·25 1·25
a. Perf. 14 .. .. 2·50 2·75
102 **23** 2½d. black & deep blue .. 3·50 4·00
a. Perf. 14 .. .. 4·00 4·50
103 **24** 4d. black & bright blue 4·00 4·50
a. Perf. 14 .. .. 3·50 4·50
b. Perf. 14×13 .. .. 18·00 24·00
c. Perf. comp. of 14 and 13
104 **25** 6d. black and orange .. 6·00 8·00
a. Perf. 14 .. .. 1·75 2·75
105 **26** 1s. blk. & violet (*perf.* 14) 4·00 5·00
99/105 .. .. *Set of* 7 14·00 17·00

(Recess from Perkins, Bacon's plates at Govt. Printing Office, Wellington.)

1933–36. *Wmk. T* **41** *of New Zealand (Single N Z and Star). P* 14.
106 **20** ½d. black & deep green .. 15 20
107 **21** 1d. black & scarlet ('35) 15 20
108 **22** 2d. black & brown ('36) 20 15
109 **23** 2½d. black & deep blue .. 25 30
110 **24** 4d. black & bright blue 25 25
111 **25** 6d. blk. & orge.-yell. ('36) 65 65
112 **26** 1s. black & violet ('36) .. 3·75 4·50
106/112 .. .. *Set of* 7 5·00 5·50

SILVER JUBILEE OF KING GEORGE V. 1910-1935. (27)

Normal letters. B K E N
Narrow letters. B K E N

1935 (7 MAY). *Silver Jubilee. Optd. with T* **27** (*wider vertical spacing on 6d.*). *Colours changed. W* **41** *of New Zealand. P* 14.
113 **21** 1d. red-brown and lake .. 12 35
a. Narrow " K " in " KING " 1·25
b. Narrow " B " in " JUBILEE " 1·60
114 **23** 2½d. dull & deep blue (R.) 30 60
a. Narrow first " E " in " GEORGE " .. .. 2·50 2·75
115 **25** 6d. green and orange .. 1·60 2·50
a. Narrow " N " in " KING " 7·50

1936 (15 JULY)–**44.** *Stamps of New Zealand optd. with T* **19**. *W* **41**. *Thick, white, opaque chalk-surfaced " Cowan " paper. P* 14.
(*a*) *As T* **72** (*" Admiral " type*).
116 2s. blue .. .. .. 6·00 8·50
117 3s. mauve .. .. .. 8·00 9·50
(*b*) *As Type* F **6** (*" Arms " type*).
118 2s. 6d. deep brown .. .. 6·50 7·50
119 5s. green (R.) .. .. .. 6·00 8·50
120 10s. carmine-lake .. .. 12·00 16·00
121 £1 pink .. .. .. 20·00 26·00
Thin, hard, chalk-surfaced " Wiggins, Teape " paper.
122 2s. 6d. dull brown (12.40) .. 11·00 13·00
123 5s. green (R.) (10.40) .. 25·00 30·00
123*a* 10s. pale carmine-lake (11.44) 20·00 25·00

COOK IS'DS. (28)

1937 (1 JUNE). *Coronation. Nos.* 599/601 *of New Zealand optd. with T* **28**.
124 **106** 1d. carmine 5 5
125 **106** 2½d. Prussian blue 8 10
126 „ 6d. red-orange 12 20

29. King George VI.

31. Native Canoe.

32. Tropical Landscape.

30. Native Village.

(Des. J. Berry (2s., 3s., and frame of 1s.). Eng. Bradbury, Wilkinson. Recess. Govt. Ptg. Office, Wellington.)

1938 (2 MAY). *W* **41** *of New Zealand. P* 14.
127 **29** 1s. black and violet .. 40 75
128 **30** 2s. black and red-brown .. 1·10 1·60
129 **31** 3s. lt. blue & emerald-grn. 2·25 2·50

(Recess. Bradbury, Wilkinson.)

1940 (2 SEPT.). *Surch. as in T* **32**. *W* **98** *of New Zealand. P* 13½×14.
130 **32** 3d. on 1½d. black & purple 5 8
Type **32** was not issued without surcharge.

1943–50. *Postal Fiscal stamps as Type* F **6** *of New Zealand optd. wih T* **19**. *W* **98**. *" Wiggins, Teape " chalk-surfaced paper. P* 14.
131 2s. 6d. dull brown (3.46) .. 2·25 2·50
132 5s. green (R.) (11.43) .. 1·90 2·50
133 10s. carmine-lake (10.48) .. 6·00 7·50
134 £1 pink (11.47) .. .. 7·00 9·50
135 £3 green (R.) (1946?) .. 22·00 26·00
136 £5 blue (R.) (25.10.50) .. 45·00 50·00
131/136 .. .. *Set of* 6 75·00 90·00
The £3 and £5 were mainly used for fiscal purposes.
All values were later printed with the watermark inverted for technical reasons and the prices quoted are for the cheapest form. They are fully listed in the *Elizabethan Specialised Catalogue.*

(Recess. Govt. Ptg. Office, Wellington.)

1944–46. *W* **98** *of New Zealand (sideways on ½d. 1d., 1s. and 2s.). P* 14.
137 **20** ½d. blk. & dp. grn. (11.44) 20 12
138 **21** 1d. black & scarlet (3.45) 10 10
139 **22** 2d. black & brown (2.46) 30 25
140 **23** 2½d. black & dp. blue (5.45) 25 20
141 **24** 4d. black and blue (4.44) 15 30
142 **25** 6d. black & orange (6.44) 20 20
143 **26** 1s. black & violet (9.44) 30 30
144 **27** 2s. blk. & red-brn. (8.45) 60 70
145 **28** 3s. light blue & emerald-green (6.45) .. .. 1·40 1·75
137/145 .. .. *Set of* 9 3·00 3·50

COOK ISLANDS (33)

1946 (1 JUNE). *Peace. Stamps of New Zealand optd. with T* **33** (*reading up and down at sides on 2d.*).
146 **132** 1d. green 5 5
147 **134** 2d. purple (B.) 5 8
148 **138** 6d. chocolate and verm. 8 10
149 **139** 8d. black & carm. (B.) .. 12 15

34. Ngatangiia Channel, Rarotonga.

35. Capt. Cook and Map of Hervey Islands.

36. Rarotonga and Rev. John Williams.

37. Aitutaki and Palm Trees.

38. Rarotonga Airfield.

39. Penrhyn Village.

40. Native Hut.

41. Map and Statue of Capt. Cook.

42. Native Hut and Palms.

43. M.V. *Matua.*

(Des. J. Berry. Recess. Waterlow.)

1949 (1 Aug.)–**61.** *W* **98** *of New Zealand (sideways on shilling values). P* 13½ × 13 *(horiz.) or* 13 × 13½ *(vert.).*

150 **34** ½d. violet and brown .. 8 15
151 **35** 1d. chestnut and green .. 25 25
152 **36** 2d. reddish brown & scarlet 15 20
153 **37** 3d. green and ultramarine 12 20
a. Wmk. sideways (white opaque paper) (22.5.61) .. 55 80
154 **38** 5d. emerald-green & violet 50 70
155 **39** 6d. black and carmine .. 25 30
156 **40** 8d. olive-green and orange 50 65
157 **41** 1s. light blue and chocolate 85 1·00
158 **42** 2s. yellow-brown & carmine 2·00 2·25
159 **43** 3s. light blue & bluish grn. 2·50 2·75
150/159 .. .. *Set of* 10 6·50 7·50

See note on white opaque paper below No. 736 of New Zealand.

1953 (25 May). *Coronation. As designs of New Zealand, but inscr.* "COOK ISLANDS".

160 **164** 3d. brown 10 12
161 **166** 6d. slate-grey 25 30

1/6

(**44**)

1960 (1 Apr.). *No.* 154 *surch. with T* **44.**

162 **38** 1s. 6d. on 5d. emerald-green and violet 35 45

45. Tiare Maori.

47. Frangipani.

48. Love Tern.

46. Fishing God.

49. Hibiscus.

50. Bonito.

51. Oranges.

52. Queen Elizabeth II.

53. Island Scene.

54. Administration Centre, Mangaia.

55. Rarotonga.

(Des. J. Berry. Recess. (1s. 6d.), litho. (others). B.W.)

1963 (4 June). *Wmk. T* **98** *of New Zealand (sideways). P* 13½×13 (*1d., 2d., 8d.*), 13×13½ (*3d., 5d., 6d., 1s.*) *or* 13½ (*others*).

No.	Type	Description	Unused	Used
163	**45**	1d. emer.-green & yellow ..	5	5
164	**46**	2d. brown-red and yellow	5	5
165	**47**	3d. yellow, yellow-green & reddish violet ..	5	5
166	**48**	5d. blue and black ..	8	10
167	**49**	6d. red, yellow and green ..	10	12
168	**50**	8d. black and blue ..	15	15
169	**51**	1s. orange-yellow and yellow-green	20	20
170	**52**	1s. 6d. bluish violet ..	65	55
171	**53**	2s. bistre-brn. & grey-blue	1·10	80
172	**54**	3s. black and yellow-green	1·40	1·10
173	**55**	5s. bistre-brown and blue	2·40	2·25
163/73		.. .. *Set of* 11	5·50	4·75

56. Eclipse and Palm.

(Des. L. C. Mitchell. Litho. B.W.)

1965 (31 May). *Solar Eclipse Observation, Manuae Island. W* **98** *of New Zealand. P* 13½.

No.	Type	Description	Unused	Used
174	**56**	6d. black, yellow & lt. blue	15	20

III. SELF-GOVERNMENT.

57. N.Z. Ensign and Map.

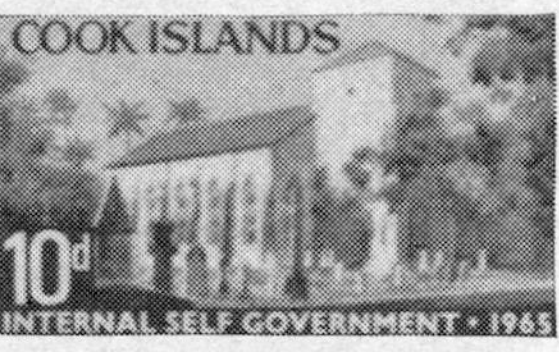

58. London Missionary Society Church.

59. Proclamation of Cession, 1900.

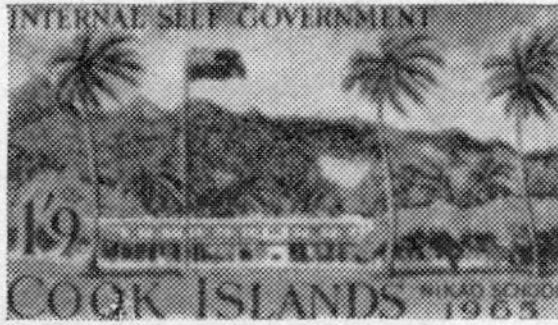

60. Nikao School.

(Des. R. M. Conly (4d.), L. C. Mitchell (10d., 1s.), J. Berry (1s. 9d.). Litho. B.W.)

1965 (16 Sept.). *Internal Self-Government. W* **98** *of New Zealand (sideways). P* 13½.

No.	Type	Description	Unused	Used
175	**57**	4d. red and blue ..	12	12
176	**58**	10d. multicoloured ..	25	25
177	**59**	1s. multicoloured ..	30	30
178	**60**	1s. 9d. multicoloured ..	45	45

In Memoriam
Sir Winston Churchill
1874 - 1965
(61)

Airmail
(62)

1966 (24 Jan.). *Churchill Commemoration. Nos.* 171/3 *and* 175/7 *optd. with T* **61**, *in red.*

No.	Type	Description	Unused	Used
179	**57**	4d. red and blue ..	12	12
180	**58**	10d. multicoloured ..	35	40
		a. Opt. inverted	£200	
181	**59**	1s. multicoloured ..	40	45
182	**53**	2s. bistre-brn. & grey-blue	90	1·10
183	**54**	3s. black & yellow-green	1·40	1·60
184	**55**	5s. bistre-brown and blue	2·25	2·25
179/84		.. .. *Set of* 6	4·50	5·00

1966 (22 Apr.). *Air. Various stamps optd. with T* **62** *or surch. also.*

No.	Type	Description	Unused	Used
185	**49**	6d. red, yellow and green	12	15
186	**50**	7d. on 8d. black and blue	12	15
187	**47**	10d. on 3d. yellow, yellow-green & reddish violet	20	20
188	**51**	1s. org.-yell. & yell.-grn.	25	25
189	**52**	1s. 6d. bluish violet ..	30	30
190	**54**	2s. 3d. on 3s. black and yellow-green ..	45	50
191	**55**	5s. bistre-brown and blue	95	1·10
192	**53**	10s. on 2s. bistre-brown and grey-blue	2·25	3·00
193	–	£1 pink (No. 143) ..	5·00	5·50
		a. Aeroplane omitted ..	16·00	
185/93		.. .. *Set of* 9	8·50	10·00

No. 193a occurred in all stamps of the last vertical row as insufficient aeroplane symbols were available. There are also numerous other varieties on all values, notably aeroplanes of different sizes and broken first "i" with dot missing owing to damaged type.

PRINTERS. The following stamps were printed in photogravure by Heraclio Fournier, Spain *except where otherwise stated.*

63. " Adoration of the Wise Men " (Fra Angelico).

64. " The Nativity " (Memling). (*Vert.*)

65. " Adoration of the Wise Men " (Velazquez). (*Horiz.*)

66. " Adoration of the Wise Men " (H. Bosch). (*Horiz.*)

67. Adoration of the Shepherds " (J. de Ribera).

1966 (28 Nov.). *Christmas.*
A. *P* 13×12 (*horiz.*) *or* 12×13 (*vert.*).
B. *P* 13×14½ (*horiz.*) *or* 14½×13 (*vert.*).

No.	Type	Description	A.		B.	
194	**63**	1d. mult. ..	10	10	5	5
195	**64**	2d. mult. ..	—	—	8	8
196	**65**	4d. mult. ..	30	30	15	15
197	**66**	10d. mult. ..	75	75	35	35
198	**67**	1s. 6d. mult.	1·10	1·10	70	55
194/98B		*Set of* 5			1·10	1·00

68. Tennis, and Queen Elizabeth II.

69. Netball and Games Emblem.

70. Boxing and Cook Islands' Team Badge.

71. Football and Queen Elizabeth II.

72. Running and Games Emblem.

73. Running and Cook Islands' Team Badge.

(Des. V. Whiteley.)

1967 (12 Jan.). *2nd South Pacific Games, Nouméa. P* 13½. (*a*) *Postage.*

No.	Type	Description	Unused	Used
199	**68**	½d. orange-brown, black, dp. brn. & yell.-olive	5	5
200	**69**	1d. orange-brown, black and new blue ..	5	5
201	**70**	4d. orange-brown, black, new bl. & reddish vio.	10	10
202	**71**	7d. orange-brown, black, new blue and brt. red	15	15
		(*b*) *Air.*		
203	**72**	10d. orange-brown, black, new bl. & yell.-orange	20	20
204	**73**	2s. 3d. orge.-brn., black, new blue & yell.-grn.	45	45
199/204		.. .. *Set of* 6	80	80

(New currency. 100 cents = 1 dollar.)

1c (74) **2½c** (I) **2½c** (II)

These occur on alternative vertical rows within the sheet.

1967. *Decimal Currency. Various stamps surch. as T* **74** *by the Government Printer. Sterling values unobliterated except No.* 218.

No.	Type	Description	Unused	Used
205	**45**	1 c. on 1d. (No. 163) ..	20	20
206	**46**	2 c. on 2d. (No. 164) ..	5	5
207	**47**	2½ c. on 3d. (No. 165) (I) ..	5	5
208	,,	2½ c. on 3d. (No. 165) (II)	5	5
209	**57**	3 c. on 4d. (No. 175) ..	5	5
210	**48**	4 c. on 5d. (No. 166) ..	10	10
211	**49**	5 c. on 6d. (No. 167) ..	8	8
212	**56**	5 c. on 6d. (No. 174) ..	40	40

213 **50**	7 c. on 8d. (No. 168) ..		10	10
214 **51**	10 c. on 1s. (No. 169) ..		12	15
215 **52**	15 c. on 1s. 6d. (No. 170) (R.)		65	75
216 **54**	30 c. on 3s. (No. 172) (R.)		3·75	2·75
217 **55**	50 c. on 5s. (No. 173) (R.)		2·75	2·75
218 **58**	$1 and 10s. on 10d. (No. 176) (R.)		6·50	5·50
219 –	$2 on £1 (No. 143) (R.) ..		85·00	85·00
220 –	$6 on £3 (No. 144) (R.) ..		£110	£110
221 –	$10 on £5 (No. 145) (R.) ..		£110	£110
205/18	.. ..	*Set of* 14	13·00	12·00

The surcharge on No. 218 is $1 and its equivalent of 10s. in the old currency. The " 10d. " is obliterated by three bars.

A large number of minor varieties exist in these surcharges, such as wrong fount letter " C " and figures.

Dates of issue:—2 c., 2½ c., 3 c., 5 c., 7 c., 10 c. 3.4.67; $2, $6, $10 6.6.67; others 4.5.67.

75. Village Scene. Cook Islands 1d. Stamp of 1892 and Queen Victoria (from " Penny Black").

76. Post Office, Avarua, Rarotonga and Queen Elizabeth II.

77. Avarua, Rarotonga, and Cook Islands 10d. Stamp of 1892.

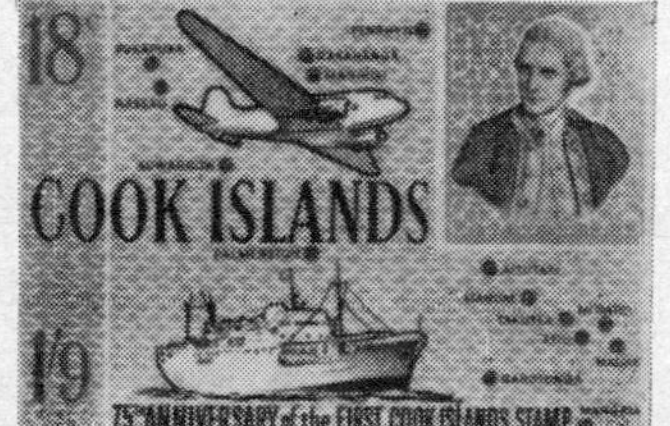

78. S.S. *Moana Roa,* " DC-3 " Aircraft, Map and Captain Cook.

(Des. V. Whiteley.)

1967 (3 JULY). *75th Anniv. of First Cook Islands Stamps.* P 13½.

222 **75**	1 c. (1d.) multicoloured ..	5	5
223 **76**	3 c. (4d.) multicoloured ..	8	8
224 **77**	8 c. (10d.) multicoloured	15	20
225 **78**	18 c. (1s. 9d.) mult.	30	40
MS226	134 × 109 mm. Nos. 222/5	55	55

The stamps are expressed in decimal currency and in the sterling equivalent.

79. Hibiscus.

Designs as T **79**:

80. *Hibiscus syriacus.*
81. Frangipani.
82. *Clitoria ternatea.*
83. " Suva Queen ".
84. Water Lily.
85. *Bauhinia bi-pinnata rosea.*
86. Hibiscus.
87. *Allamanda cathartica.*
88. Stephanotis.
89. *Poinciana regia flamboyant.*
90. Frangipani.
91. Thunbergia.
92. Canna Lily.
93. *Euphorbia pulcherrima poinsettia.*
94. *Gardinia taitensis.*

95. Queen Elizabeth II.

96. Queen Elizabeth and Flowers.
(*Illustration reduced. Actual size* 55 × 34 *mm.*)

Two types of $4.
I. Value 32½ mm. long. Coarse screen.
II. Value 33½ mm. long. Finer screen.

(Floral designs from paintings by Mrs. Kay W. Billings.)

1967–71. P 14 × 13½. A. *Without fluorescent security markings.* B. *With fluorescent security markings.*

		A.		B.	
227 **79**	½ c. mult. ..	8	8	5	5
228 **80**	1 c. mult. ..	8	8	5	5
229 **81**	2 c. mult. ..	8	8	5	5
230 **82**	2½ c. mult. ..	8	8	5	5
231 **83**	3 c. mult. ..	8	8	5	5
232 **84**	4 c. mult. (" WALTER LILY ") ..	30	30	†	
233 ,,	4 c. mult. (" WATER LILY ") ..	8	8	5	5
234 **85**	5 c. mult. ..	8	8	8	8
235 **86**	6 c. mult. ..	10	10	8	8
236 **87**	8 c. mult. ..	10	10	10	10
237 **88**	9 c. mult. ..	12	12	12	12
238 **89**	10 c. mult. ..	15	15	12	12
239 **90**	15 c. mult. ..	20	25	20	20
240 **91**	20 c. mult. ..	25	30	25	25
241 **92**	25 c. mult. ..	30	30	30	30
242 **93**	30 c. mult. ..	35	40	35	40
243 **94**	50 c. mult. ..	65	70	55	60
244 **95**	$1 mult. ..	1·25	1·40	1·25	1·25
245 ,,	$2 mult. ..	2·50	2·75	2·25	2·50
246 **96**	$4 mult (I)	4·75	5·00	25·00	—
246*c* ,,	$4 mult. (II)	†		4·25	4·50
247 ,,	$6 mult. ..	7·50	8·00	6·50	7·00
247*c* ,,	$8 mult. ..	10·00	11·00	8·50	9·00
248 ,,	$10 mult. ..	13·00	14·00	10·00	11·00
227A/243A	*Set of* 17	2·75	3·00		
227B/243B	*Set of* 16			2·10	2·50

Dates of issue:—Nos. 227A/238A, 31.7.67; Nos. 239/243A, 11.8.67; Nos. 244/245A, 31.8.67; Nos. 246/247A, 30.4.68; No. 248A, 12.7.68; No. 247*c*A, 21.4.69; Nos. 227/243B, 9.2.70; Nos. 244/245B, 12.10.70; No. 246*c*B, 14.7.71; No. 246B, 11.11.70; No. 247B, 12.2.71; No. 247*c*B, 3.5.71; No. 248B, 14.6.71.

The " WALTER " spelling error occurred on all stamps in one of the four post office sheets which went to make up the printing sheet and this was corrected in later supplies.

FLUORESCENT PAPER. This is on paper treated with fluorescent security markings, in the form of faint multiple coats of arms. Stamps exist with these markings inverted. In addition an invisible synthetic gum has been used which prevents curling and is suitable for use in the tropics without interleaving the sheets.

Some of the above are known with these markings omitted and can be distinguished when in unused condition from the original printings without markings by their synthetic invisible gum.

97. " Ia Orana Maria ".

1967 (24 OCT.). *Gauguin's Polynesian Paintings.* T **97** *and similar designs. Multicoloured.* P 13.

249	1 c. Type **97**	5	5
250	3 c. " Riders on the Beach "	5	5
251	5 c. " Still Life with Flowers "	8	8
252	8 c. " Whispered Words " ..	12	12
253	15 c. " Maternity "	25	25
254	22 c. " Why are you angry?"	35	40
249/54	.. .. *Set of* 6	85	85
MS255	156 × 131 mm. Nos. 249/54	1·00	1·00

The 5 c. includes an inset portrait of Queen Elizabeth.

98. "The Holy Family" (Rubens).

1967 (4 Dec.). *Christmas. Renaissance Paintings. T* **98** *and similar designs. Multicoloured. P* 12×13.

256	1 c. Type **98**	.. ..	5	5
257	3 c. "The Epiphany" (Dürer)	.. ..	5	5
258	4 c. "The Lucca Madonna" (J. van Eyck)	.. ..	8	8
259	8 c. "The Adoration of the Shepherds" (J. da Bassano)	.. ..	15	15
260	15 c. "The Nativity" (El Greco)	.. ..	30	30
261	25 c. "The Madonna and Child" (Correggio)	..	50	50
256/61	.. ..	*Set of* 6	1·00	1·00

HURRICANE
RELIEF
PLUS 5c

(99)

1968 (12 Feb.). *Hurricane Relief. Nos.* 231A, 233A, 251, 238A, 241A *and* 243/4A *surch., as T* **99** *by Govt. Printer, Rarotonga.*

262 **83**	3 c.+1 c. multicoloured	..	5	5
263 **84**	4 c.+1 c. multicoloured	..	8	8
264 –	5 c.+2 c. mult. (No. 251)		10	10
265 **89**	10 c.+2 c. multicoloured	..	20	20
266 **92**	25 c.+5 c. multicoloured	..	65	65
267 **94**	50 c.+10 c. multicoloured		1·25	1·25
268 **95**	$1+10 c. multicoloured		2·00	2·00
262/8	.. ..	*Set of* 7	4·00	4·00

The surcharge on No. 268 is as T **99**, but with seriffed letters. On No. 264 silver blocking obliterates the design area around the lettering.

100. "Matavai Bay, Tahiti" (S. Parkinson).

101. "*Resolution* and *Discovery*" (J. Webber).

(Des. J. Berry.)

1968 (12 Sept.). *Bicentenary of Captain Cook's First Voyage of Discovery. Multicoloured. Invisible gum. P* 13.

(*a*) *Postage. Vert. designs as T* **100**.

269	½ c. Type **100**	.. ..	5	5
270	1 c. "Island of Huaheine" (John Cleveley)	..	5	5
271	2 c. "Town of St. Peter and St. Paul, Kamchatka" (J. Webber)	.. ..	10	10
272	4 c. "The Ice Islands" (Antarctica: W. Hodges)		15	15

(*b*) *Air. Horiz. designs as T* **101**.

273	6 c. Type **101**	.. ..	15	15
274	10 c. "The Island of Tahiti" (W. Hodges)	.. ..	20	20
275	15 c. "Karakakooa, Hawaii" (J. Webber)	.. ..	30	30
276	25 c. "The Landing at Middleburg" (W. Hodges)	.. ..	55	60
269/76	.. ..	*Set of* 8	1·40	1·40

FLUORESCENT PAPER. From No. 277, *unless otherwise stated*, all issues are printed on paper treated with fluorescent security markings with invisible synthetic gum. These markings may be inverted or omitted in error.

102. Sailing.

1968 (21 Oct.). *Olympic Games, Mexico. T* **102** *and similar horiz. designs. Multicoloured. P* 13.

277	1 c. Type **102**	.. ..	5	5
278	5 c. Gymnastics	.. ..	8	8
279	15 c. High-jumping	.. ..	20	20
280	20 c. High-diving	.. ..	25	25
281	30 c. Cycling	.. ..	40	40
282	50 c. Hurdling	.. ..	65	65
277/82	.. ..	*Set of* 6	1·40	1·40

103. "Virgin and Child" (Titian).

1968 (2 Dec.). *Christmas. Paintings. T* **103** *and similar vert. designs. Multicoloured. P* 13½.

283	1 c. Type **103**	.. ..	5	5
284	4 c. "The Holy Family of the Lamb" (Raphael)		5	5
285	10 c. "The Madonna of the Rosary" (Murillo)	..	15	15
286	20 c. "Adoration of the Magi" (Memling)	..	30	30
287	30 c. "Adoration of the Magi" (Ghirlandaio)	..	45	45
283/7	.. .. ..	*Set of* 5	85	85
MS288	114×177 mm. Nos. 283/7 plus label	.. .. ..	1·25	1·25

104. Camp-fire Cooking.

1969 (6 Feb.). *Diamond Jubilee of New Zealand Scout Movement and Fifth National (New Zealand) Jamboree. T* **104** *and similar designs. Multicoloured. P* 13½.

289	½ c. Type **104**	.. ..	5	5
290	1 c. Descent by rope	..	5	5
291	5 c. Semaphore	.. ..	8	8
292	10 c. Tree-planting	.. ..	15	15
293	20 c. Constructing a shelter	..	30	30
294	30 c. Lord Baden-Powell and island scene	.. ..	50	50
289/94	.. ..	*Set of* 6	1·00	1·00

105. Pole-vaulter.

1969 (7 July). *Third South Pacific Games, Port Moresby. Without fluorescent security markings. T* **105** *and similar designs. Multicoloured. P* 13×13½.

295	½ c. Type **105**	.. ..	5	5
296	½ c. Footballer	.. ..	5	5
297	1 c. Long-jumper	.. ..	5	5
298	1 c. Weightlifter	.. ..	5	5
299	4 c. Tennis-player	.. ..	5	5
300	4 c. Hurdler	.. ..	5	5
301	10 c. Javelin-thrower	..	15	15
302	10 c. Runner	.. ..	15	15
303	15 c. Golfer	.. ..	30	30
304	15 c. Boxer	.. ..	30	30
295/304	.. ..	*Set of* 10	1·00	1·00
MS305	174×129 mm. Nos. 295/304 plus two labels depicting Coat-of-Arms and Games Emblem	.. ..	1·25	1·25

Each value was issued in small sheets of 10 containing two labels and five *se-tenant* pairs of both designs.

106. Flowers, Map and Premier Albert Henry. (*Illustration reduced. Actual size,* 72×26 *mm.*)

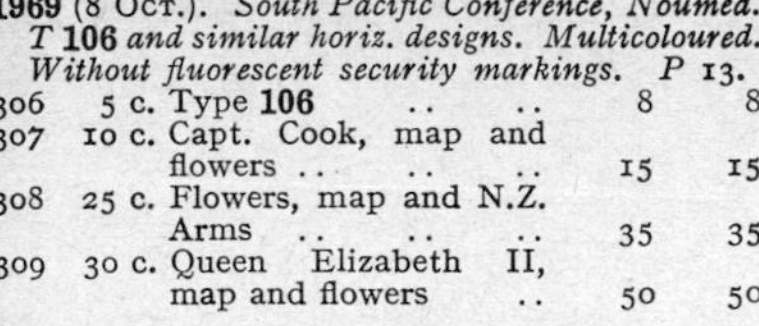

1969 (8 Oct.). *South Pacific Conference, Nouméa. T* **106** *and similar horiz. designs. Multicoloured. Without fluorescent security markings. P* 13.

306	5 c. Type **106**	8	8
307	10 c. Capt. Cook, map and flowers	15	15
308	25 c. Flowers, map and N.Z. Arms	35	35
309	30 c. Queen Elizabeth II, map and flowers ..	50	50

107. " Madonna and Child with Saints " (Lippi).

1969 (21 Nov.). *Christmas. Paintings. T* **107** *and similar designs. Multicoloured. Without fluorescent security markings. P* 13.

310	1 c. Type **107**	5	5
311	4 c. " The Holy Family " (Fra. B. Della Porta) ..	5	5
312	10 c. " Virgin and Child with Saints " (Memling) ..	15	15
313	20 c. " Virgin and Child with Saints " (Robert Campin)	30	30
314	30 c. " Virgin and Child " (Correggio)	55	55
310/14	.. .. *Set of* 5	1·00	1·00
MS315	132 × 97 mm. Nos. 310/14	1·25	1·25

108. Raphael.

1970 (12 Mar.). *Easter. Paintings of " The Resurrection of Christ " as T* **108** *by the artists named. Multicoloured. P* 13.

316	4 c. Type **108**	5	5
317	8 c. Dirk Bouts	10	10
318	20 c. Altdorfer	35	35
319	25 c. Murillo	45	45
MS320	132 × 162 mm. Nos. 316/19 plus two stamp size labels	90	90

KIA ORANA

APOLLO 13

ASTRONAUTS

Te Atua to

Tatou Irinakianga

(109)

1970 (17–30 Apr.). *Apollo 13. 1967–70 Definitives surch. with T* **109** *(4 c. to $2) or with first three lines only in larger type ($4), by Govt. Printer. A. Without fluorescent security markings. B. With fluorescent security markings.*

				A.		B.	
321	**84**	4 c. mult. ..	5	5	†		
322	**87**	8 c. mult. ..	10	10	†		
323	**90**	15 c. mult. ..	20	20	†		
324	**91**	20 c. mult. ..	25	25	†		
325	**93**	30 c. mult. ..	35	35	†		
326	**95**	$2 mult. ..	2·25	2·25	†		
327	**96**	$4 mult. (30.4) ..	50·00	—	6·00	6·00	
321/6A, 327B		*Set of* 7	8·00	8·00			

110. The Royal Family.

111. Captain Cook and H.M.S. *Endeavour*.
112. Royal Visit Commemorative Coin.

(Des. V. Whiteley (5 c.), J. Berry ($1).)

1970 (12 June). *Royal Visit to New Zealand. P* 13.

328	**110**	5 c. multicoloured ..	8	8
329	**111**	30 c. multicoloured ..	50	50
330	**112**	$1 multicoloured ..	1·50	1·50
MS331		145 × 97 mm. Nos. 328/30	2·00	2·00

FIFTH ANNIVERSARY
SELF-GOVERNMENT
AUGUST 1970

(113)

1970 (27 Aug.). *5th Anniv. of Self-Government. Nos. 328/30 optd. with T* **113** *(30 c. and $1), or in single line in silver around frame of stamp (5 c.).*

332	**110**	5 c. multicoloured ..	5	8
333	**111**	30 c. multicoloured ..	75	75
334	**112**	$1 multicoloured ..	2·00	2·00

FOUR

DOLLARS

$4.00

(114)

1970 (11 Nov.). *Nos. 247c and 248 surch. with T* **114** *by Govt. Printer, Rarotonga. A. Without fluorescent security markings. B. With fluorescent security markings.*

			A.		B.	
335	**96**	$4 on $8 mult.	35·00	—	8·00	8·00
336	„	$4 on $10 mult.	35·00	—	8·00	8·00

There are variations in the setting of this surcharge and also in the rule.

HAVE YOU READ THE NOTES AT THE BEGINNING OF THIS CATALOGUE?

These often provide answers to the enquiries we receive.

115. Mary, Joseph and Christ in Manger.

(Des. from De Lisle Psalter. Photo.)

1970 (30 Nov.). *Christmas. T* **115** *and similar square designs. Multicoloured. P* 13.

337	1 c. Type **115**	5	5
338	4 c. Shepherds and Apparition of the Angel ..	5	5
339	10 c. Mary showing Child to Joseph	20	20
340	20 c. The Wise Men bearing Gifts	35	35
341	30 c. Parents wrapping Child in swaddling clothes ..	50	50
337/41	.. .. *Set of* 5	1·00	1·00
MS342	100 × 139 mm. Nos. 337/41 plus label	1·25	1·25

Nos. 337/41 were issued in small sheets of 5 (3 × 2) plus *se-tenant* label in position 1. Stamps from the miniature sheet are smaller, since they do not have the buff parchment border as on the stamps from the sheets.

PLUS 20c

UNITED
KINGDOM

SPECIAL
MAIL SERVICE

(116)

1971. *Nos. 242B and 243B surch. as T* **116.**

343	**93**	30 c. + 20 c. mult. (25.2) ..	2·00	2·50
344	**94**	50 c. + 20 c. mult. (8.3) ..	4·00	5·00

The premium of 20 c. was to prepay a private delivery service fee in Great Britain during the postal strike. The mail was sent by air to a forwarding address in the Netherlands. No. 343 was intended for ordinary airmail ½ oz. letters, and No 344 included registration fee.

The postal strike ended on 8 March and both stamps were withdrawn on 12 March.

117. Wedding of Princess Elizabeth and Prince Philip.

(Des. from photographs. Litho. Format.)

1971 (11 Mar.). *Royal Visit of H.R.H. The Duke of Edinburgh. T* **117** *and similar horiz. designs. Multicoloured. P* 13½.

345	1 c. Type **117**	5	5
346	4 c. Queen Elizabeth, Prince Philip, Princess Anne and Prince Charles at Windsor	5	5

347 10 c. Prince Philip sailing .. 20 20
348 15 c. Prince Philip in polo gear 40 40
349 25 c. Prince Philip in naval uniform, and the royal yacht *Britannia* 60 60
345/9 .. .. *Set of* 5 1·00 1·00
MS350 168 × 122 mm. Nos. 345/9 plus printed labels in positions 1, 3, 4, and 6 .. 1·00 1·00

(118)

(119)

1971 (8 Sept.). *Fourth South Pacific Games, Tahiti. Nos.* 238B, 241B *and* 242B *optd. with T* **118** *in black, or surch. as T* **119** *in blue.*
351 **89** 10 c. multicoloured .. 20 20
352 „ 10 c.+1 c. multicoloured.. 20 20
353 „ 10 c.+3 c. multicoloured.. 20 20
354 **92** 25 c. multicoloured .. 50 60
355 „ 25 c.+1 c. multicoloured.. 50 60
356 „ 25 c.+3 c. multicoloured.. 50 60
357 **93** 30 c. multicoloured .. 75 85
358 „ 30 c.+1 c. multicoloured.. 75 85
359 „ 30 c.+3 c. multicoloured.. 75 85
351/9 .. .. *Set of* 9 3·75 4·00

The stamps additionally surcharged 1 c. or 3 c. helped to finance the Cook Islands' team at the games.

10c ≡

(120)

121. "Virgin and Child" (Bellini).

1971 (20 Oct.). *Nos.* 230B, 233B, 236B/7B *and* 239B *surch. with T* **120.**
360 **82** 10 c. on 2½ c. multicoloured 20 20
361 **84** 10 c. on 4 c. multicoloured 20 20
362 **87** 10 c. on 8 c. multicoloured 20 20
363 **88** 10 c. on 9 c. multicoloured 20 20
364 **90** 10 c. on 15 c. multicoloured 20 20
360/4 .. .. *Set of* 5 85 85

1971 (30 Nov.). *Christmas. T* **121** *and similar vert. designs showing different paintings of the "Virgin and Child", by Bellini. P* 13.
365 **121** 1 c. multicoloured .. 8 8
366 – 4 c. multicoloured .. 8 8
367 – 10 c. multicoloured .. 20 25
368 – 20 c. multicoloured .. 40 45
369 – 30 c. multicoloured .. 60 75
365/9 .. .. *Set of* 5 1·00 1·25
MS370 135 × 147 mm. Nos. 365/9 1·25 1·40
MS371 92 × 98 mm. 50 c.+5 c. "The Holy Family in a Garland of Flowers" (Jan Brueghel and Pieter van Avont) (41 × 41 mm.) .. 1·25 1·25

SOUTH PACIFIC COMMISSION FEB. 1947 - 1972

(122)

1972 (17 Feb.). *25th Anniv. of South Pacific Commission. No.* 244B *optd. with T* **122.**
372 **95** $1 multicoloured .. .. 2·00 2·25

123. Mary Magdalen.

HURRICANE RELIEF PLUS 2c

(124)

Hurricane Relief Plus 5c

(125)

(Des. from De Lisle Psalter. Photo.)

1972 (6 Mar.). *Easter. T* **123** *and similar vert. designs. Multicoloured. P* 13.
373 5 c. Type **123** 10 10
374 10 c. Christ on the Cross .. 20 25
375 30 c. Mary, Mother of Jesus 60 65
MS376 79 × 112 mm. Nos. 373/5 forming triptych of "The Crucifixion" .. .. .. 1·00 1·25

Stamps from the miniature sheet do not have a border around the perforations, and are therefore smaller than stamps from sheets.

1972 (30 Mar.). *Hurricane Relief. Nos.* 373/5 *surch. as T* **124**, *and Nos.* 239B, 241B *and* 243B *surch. as T* **125**, *by Govt. Printer, Rarotonga.*
377 **123** 5 c.+2 c. mult. (R.) .. 10 10
a. Albino surch. .. .. 50·00
378 – 10 c.+2 c. mult. (R.) .. 20 20
379 **90** 15 c.+5 c. mult. .. 30 30
380 **92** 25 c.+5 c. mult. .. 50 50
381 – 30 c.+5 c. mult. (R.) .. 60 60
a. Albino surch. ..
382 **94** 50 c.+10 c. mult. .. 1·00 1·25
377/82 .. .. *Set of* 6 2·50 2·75

126. Rocket heading for Moon. **127.**

(*Illustration reduced. Actual size* 62 × 30 *mm.*)

1972 (17 Apr.). *Apollo Moon Exploration Flights. T* **126/7** *and similar horiz. designs. Multicoloured. P* 13.
383 5 c. Type **126** 8 8
384 5 c. Type **127** 8 8
385 10 c. } Astronauts on Moon .. 15 15
386 10 c. } .. 15 15
387 25 c. } Moon Rover and .. 45 45
388 25 c. } astronauts working .. 45 45
389 30 c. } Splashdown and .. 55 55
390 30 c. } helicopter 55 55
383/90 .. .. *Set of* 8 2·25 2·25
MS391 83 × 205 mm. Nos. 383/90 2·50 2·50

These were issued in horizontal *se-tenant* pairs of each value, forming one composite design.

HURRICANE RELIEF Plus 2c

(128)

129. High-jumping.

1972 (24 May). *Hurricane Relief. Nos.* 383/**MS**391 *surch. as T* **128.**
392 5 c.+2 c. multicoloured .. 8 8
393 5 c.+2 c. multicoloured .. 8 8
394 10 c.+2 c. multicoloured .. 20 20
395 10 c.+2 c. multicoloured .. 20 20
396 25 c.+2 c. multicoloured .. 50 50
397 25 c.+2 c. multicoloured .. 50 50
398 30 c.+2 c. multicoloured .. 60 60
399 30 c.+2 c. multicoloured .. 60 60
392/9 .. .. *Set of* 8 2·50 2·50
MS400 83 × 205 mm. **MS**391 surch. 3 c. on each stamp .. .. 2·75 2·75

1972 (26 June). *Olympic Games, Munich. T* **129** *and similar vert. designs. Multicoloured. P* 13½.
401 10 c. Type **129** 20 20
402 25 c. Running 75 75
403 30 c. Boxing 75 75
MS404 88 × 78 mm. 50 c.+5 c. Pierre de Coubertin .. .. 1·50 1·50
MS405 84 × 133 mm. Nos. 401/3 plus *se-tenant* label .. .. 2·00 2·00

130. "The Rest in Egypt" (Caravaggio).

1972 (11 Oct.). *Christmas T* **130** *and similar vert. designs. Multicoloured. P* 13.
406 1 c. Type **130** 5 5
407 5 c. "Virgin of the Swallow" (Guercino) 10 10
408 10 c. "Virgin with Green Cushion" (Solario) .. 20 20
409 20 c. "Virgin and Child" (di Credi) 40 40
410 30 c. "Virgin and Child" (Bellini) 75 75
406/10 .. .. *Set of* 5 1·25 1·25

MS411	141×152 mm. Nos. 406/10 plus *se-tenant* label in position 1	1·25	1·25
MS412	101×82 mm. 50 c.+5 c. "Christmas" (Bellini) (31×43 mm.)	1·25	1·25

131. Marriage Ceremony.

1972 (20 Nov.). *Royal Silver Wedding. T* **131** *and similar black and silver designs. P* 13.

413	5 c. Type **131**	10	10
414	10 c. Leaving Westminister Abbey	25	25
415	15 c. Bride and Bridegroom (40×41 *mm.*)	35	35
416	30 c. Family Group (67×40 *mm.*)	75	75

132. Taro Leaf.

1973 (15 Mar.). *Silver Wedding Coinage. T* **132** *and similar designs showing coins. P* 13.

417	1 c. blk., rosy carmine & gold	5	5
418	2 c. blk., bright blue & gold	5	5
419	5 c. blk., green and silver ..	5	5
420	10 c. blk., Royal blue & silver	20	20
421	20 c. blk., deep blue-green and silver	45	45
422	50 c. blk., carmine and silver	85	85
423	$1 blk., bright blue and silver	1·75	1·75
417/23	.. .. *Set of* 7	3·25	3·25

Designs: *As T* **132**—2 c. Pineapple; 5 c. Hibiscus. 46×30 *mm.*—10 c. Oranges; 20 c. Fairy Tern; 50 c. Bonito. 32×55 *mm.*—$1 Tangaroa.

133. "Noli me Tangere" (Titian).

1973 (9 Apr.). *Easter. T* **133** *and similar vert. designs. Multicoloured. P* 13.

424	5 c. Type **133**	5	5
425	10 c. "The Descent from the Cross" (Rubens) ..	15	15
426	30 c. "Christ weeping for his People" (Dürer) ..	45	45
MS427	132×67 *mm.* Nos. 424/6 ..	1·00	1·00

1973 (30 Apr.). *Easter. Children's Charity. Designs as Nos.* 424/6 *in separate Miniature Sheets* 67×87 *mm., each with a face value of* 50 *c.*+5 *c. P* 13×14.

MS428 As Nos. 424/6. *Set of* 3 *sheets* 2·40

134. Queen Elizabeth II in Coronation Regalia.

1973 (1 June). *20th Anniv. of Queen Elizabeth's Coronation. P* 14×13½.

429	**134** 10 c. multicoloured ..	1·00	1·00
MS430	64×89 mm. 50 c. as 10 c. *P* 13×14	1·50	1·50

The perforated portion of **MS**430 is similar to No. 429, but has no borders.

TENTH ANNIVERSARY
CESSATION OF
NUCLEAR TESTING
TREATY
(135)

1973 (25 July). *Tenth Anniv. of Treaty Banning Nuclear Testing. Nos.* 234B, 236B, 238B, *and* 240B/242B *optd. with T* **135**.

431	5 c. multicoloured	8	8
432	8 c. multicoloured	12	12
433	10 c. multicoloured	15	15
434	20 c. multicoloured	30	30
435	25 c. multicoloured	40	40
436	30 c. multicoloured	50	55
431/6	.. .. *Set of* 6	1·40	1·40

136. Tipairua.

1973 (17 Sept.). *Maori Exploration of the Pacific. T* **136** *and similar horiz. designs showing sailing craft. Multicoloured. P* 13.

437	½ c. Type **136**	5	5
438	1 c. Wa'a Kaulua	5	5
439	1½ c. Tainui	5	5
440	5 c. War canoe	8	8
441	10 c. Pahi	15	15
442	15 c. Amatasi	20	25
443	25 c. Vaka	35	40
437/443	.. .. *Set of* 7	80	90

137. The Annunciation.

1973 (30 Oct.). *Christmas. T* **137** *and similar vert. designs showing scenes from a* 15*th-cent. prayer-book. Multicoloured. P* 13.

444	1 c. Type **137**	5	5
445	5 c. The Visitation	8	8
446	10 c. Announcement to the Shepherds	15	15
447	20 c. Epiphany	30	30
448	30 c. The Slaughter of the Innocents	45	45
444/8	.. .. *Set of* 5	90	90
MS449	121×128 *mm.* Nos. 444/8 plus *se-tenant* label	1·00	1·00

See also **MS**454.

138. Princess Anne.

1973 (14 Nov.). *Royal Wedding. T* **138** *and similar vert. designs. Multicoloured. P* 14×13½.

450	25 c. Type **138**	35	40
451	30 c. Capt. Mark Phillips ..	50	60
452	50 c. Princess Anne and Capt. Phillips	80	90
MS453	119×100 mm. Nos. 450/2 plus *se-tenant* label. *P* 13 ..	2·00	2·00

1973 (3 Dec.). *Christmas. Children's Charity. Designs as Nos.* 444/8 *in separate Miniature Sheets* 50×70 *mm., each with a face value of* 50 *c.*+5 *c.*

MS454 As Nos. 444/8 *Set of* 5 *sheets* 3·00

139. Running.

1974 (24 Jan.). *British Commonwealth Games, Christchurch. T* **139** *and similar multicoloured designs. P* 14×13½ (1 *and* 3 *c.*) *or* 13½×14 (*others*).

455 1 c. Diving (*vert.*) 5 5
456 3 c. Boxing (*vert.*) 5 5
457 5 c. Type **139** 8 8
458 10 c. Weightlifting 12 15
459 30 c. Cycling 40 50
455/9 .. .. *Set of* 5 60 70
MS460 115×90 mm. 50 c. Discobolus .. .. .. 1·00 1·00

140. " Jesus bearing the Cross " (Raphael).

1974 (25 Mar.). *Easter. T* **140** *and similar vert. designs. Multicoloured. P* 13½.

461 5 c. Type **140** 5 8
462 10 c. " Christ in the Arms of God " (El Greco) .. 12 15
463 30 c. " The Descent from the Cross " (Caravaggio) .. 35 40
MS464 130×70 mm. Nos. 461/3 .. 80 80

1974 (22 Apr.). *Easter. Children's Charity. Designs as Nos.* 461/3 *in separate Miniature Sheets* 59×87 *mm., each with a face value of* 50 *c.*+5 *c.*

MS465 As Nos. 461/3. *Set of* 3 *sheets* 1·75

141. *Phallicium glaucum.*

142. Queen Elizabeth II.

1974 (17 May)–**75.** *T* **141** *and similar horiz. designs showing seashells. Multicoloured. P* 14×13½ ($4 *to* $10) *or* 13½ (*others*).

466 ½ c. Type **141** 5 5
467 1 c. *Vasum turbinellus* 5 5
468 1½ c. *Corculum cardissa* 5 5
469 2 c. *Terebellum terebellum* .. 5 5
470 3 c. *Aulica vespertilio* 5 5
471 4 c. *Strombus gibberulus* .. 5 5
472 5 c. *Cymatium pileare* .. 5 5
473 6 c. *Cypraea caputserpentis* .. 5 5
474 8 c. *Bursa granularis* .. 8 8
475 10 c. *Tenebra muscaria* .. 10 10
476 15 c. *Mitra mitra* 15 15
477 20 c. *Natica alapapillonis* .. 20 20
478 25 c. *Gloripallium pallium* .. 25 25
479 30 c. *Conus miles* 30 35
480 50 c. *Conus textile* (26.8.74) .. 50 55
481 60 c. *Oliva senicea* (26.8.74) .. 60 70
482 $1 Type **142** (26.8.74) .. 95 1·10
483 $2 Type **142** (27.1.75) .. 1·90 2·10
484 $4 Queen Elizabeth II and seashells (17.3.75) .. 3·75 4·00
485 $6 As $4 (29.4.75) .. .. 5·75 6·00
486 $8 As $4 (30.5.75) .. .. 7·50 8·00
487 $10 As $4 (30.6.75) .. .. 9·50 1·000
466/82 .. .. *Set of* 17 2·75 3·25

Nos. 484/7 are horiz., 60 × 39 mm.

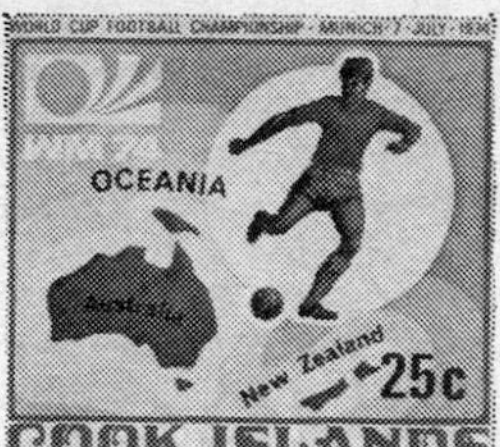

143. Footballer and Australasian Map.

1974 (5 July). *World Cup Football Championships. T* **142** *and similar horiz. designs. Multicoloured. P* 13.

488 25 c. Type **143** 30 35
489 50 c. Map and Munich Stadium 60 65
490 $1 Footballer, stadium and World Cup .. .. 1·25 1·40
MS491 89×100 mm. Nos. 488/90 2·10

144. Obverse and Reverse of Commemorative $2·50 Silver Coin.

1974 (22 July). *Bicentenary of Capt. Cook's Second Voyage of Discovery. T* **144** *and similar vert. design. P* 14.

492 $2.50, silver, black & violet 3·50 3·75
493 $7.50, sil., blk. & dp. turq.-grn. 10·00 11·00
MS494 73×73 mm. Nos. 492/3 .. 15·00

Design:—$7.50, As T **144** but showing $7.50 coin.

145. Early Stamps of Cook Islands.

1974 (16 Sept.). *Centenary of Universal Posta[l] Union. T* **145** *and similar horiz. designs Multicoloured. P* 13½×14.

495 10 c. Type **145** 15 1
496 25 c. Old landing strip, Rarotonga, and stamp of 1898 35 3
497 30 c. Post Office, Rarotonga, and stamp of 1920 .. 40 4
498 50 c. U.P.U. emblem and stamps 65 6
MS499 118×79 mm. Nos. 495/8. P 13 .. .. 1·50

146. " Madonna of the Goldfinch " (Raphael).

1974 (15 Oct.). *Christmas. T* **146** *and simila[r] vert. designs. Multicoloured. P* 13.

500 1 c. Type **146** 5
501 5 c. " The Holy Family " (Andrea del Sarto) .. 5
502 10 c. " Virgin and Child " (Correggio) 10 1
503 20 c. " The Holy Family " (Rembrandt) 20 2
504 30 c. " The Nativity " (Rogier Van Der Weyden) .. 35 4
500/504 .. .. *Set of* 5 70 7
MS505 114×133 mm. Nos. 500/4 plus *se-tenant* label 75

147. Churchill and Blenheim Palace.

1974 (20 Nov.). *Birth Centenary of Sir Winston Churchill. T* **147** *and similar horiz. designs Multicoloured. P* 13½×14.

506 5 c. Type **147** 8
507 10 c. Churchill and Houses of Parliament 20 1
508 25 c. Churchill and Chartwell 35 4
509 30 c. Churchill and Buckingham Palace 45 4
510 50 c. Churchill and St. Paul's Cathedral 90 8
506/10 *Set of* 5 1·75 1·7
MS511 108×114 mm. Nos. 506/10 plus *se-tenant* label .. .. 2·00

1974 (9 Dec.). *Christmas. Children's Charity. Designs as Nos.* 500/504 *in separate miniatur[e] sheets* 53×69 *mm., each with a face-value o[f]* 50 *c.*+5 *c.*

MS512 As Nos. 500/4. *Set of* 5 *sheets* 3·25

148. Vasco Nuñez de Balboa and Discovery of Pacific Ocean (1513).

1975 (3 Feb.). *Pacific Explorers. T* **148** *and similar horiz. designs. Multicoloured. P* 13.

513 1 c. Type **148** 5 5
514 5 c. Fernando de Magellanes and map (1520) .. 8 8
515 10 c. Juan Sebastian de Elcano and *Vitoria* (1520) .. 12 12
516 25 c. Friar de Urdaneta and ship (1564–67) .. 30 35
517 30 c. Miguel Lopez de Legazpi and ship (1564–67) .. 35 40
513/17 .. *Set of* 5 80 90

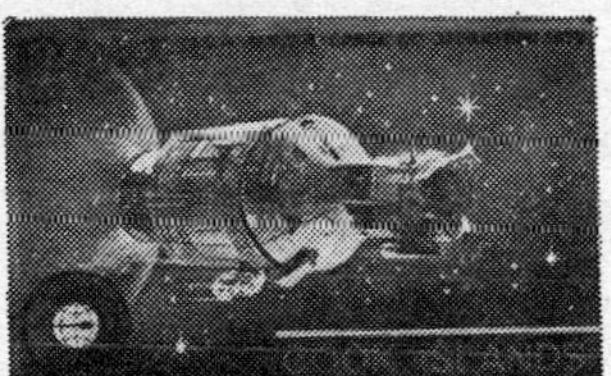

149. " Apollo " Capsule.

1975 (15 July). *" Apollo-Soyuz " Space Project. T* **149** *and similar horiz. designs. Multicoloured. P* $13\frac{1}{2}$.

518 25 c. Type **149** 25 30
519 25 c. " Soyuz " capsule .. 25 30
520 30 c. " Soyuz " crew 30 35
521 30 c. " Apollo " crew 30 35
522 50 c. Cosmonaut within " Soyuz " 50 60
523 50 c. Astronauts within " Apollo " 50 60
518/23 .. *Set of* 6 1·90 2·25
MS524 119×119 mm. Nos. 518/23. P 13×14 .. .. .. 2·10

These were issued in horizontal *se-tenant* pairs of each value, forming one composite design.

150. $100 Commemorative Gold Coin.

1975 (8 Aug.). *Bicentenary of Captain Cook's Second Voyage. P* 13.

525 **150** $2 brn., gold & bluish vio. 2·00 2·25

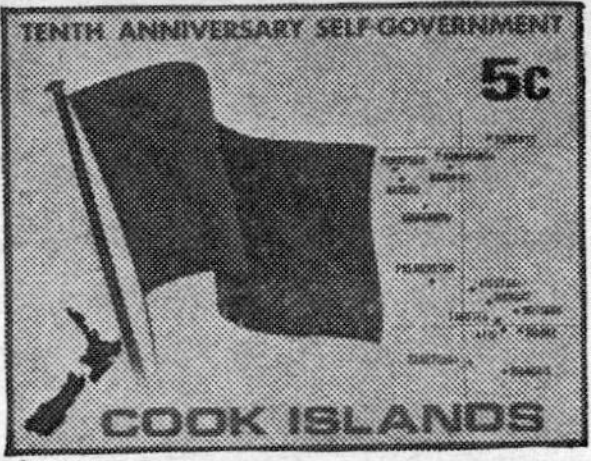

151. Cook Islands' Flag and Map.

1975 (8 Aug.). *Tenth Anniv. of Self-Government. T* **151** *and similar multicoloured designs. P* 13.

526 5 c. Type **151** 5 5
527 10 c. Premier Sir Albert Henry and flag (*vert.*) 10 12
528 25 c. Rarotonga and flag .. 25 30

152. " Virgin and Child " (Flemish Master).

1975 (1 Dec.). *Christmas. T* **152** *and similar vert. designs. Multicoloured. P* $13\frac{1}{2}$.

529 6 c. Type **152** 5 8
530 10 c. " Madonna of the Meadow " (Raphael) 10 12
531 15 c. " Holy Family of Oak " (Raphael) .. 15 20
532 20 c. " Adoration of the Shepherds " (J. B. Mayno) 20 25
533 35 c. " The Annunciation " (Murillo) 30 35
529/33 .. .. *Set of* 5 75 85
MS534 110×124 mm. Nos. 529/33 90

1975 (15 Dec.). *Christmas. Children's Charity. Designs as Nos.* 529/33 *in separate miniature sheets* 53×71 *mm., each with a face value of* 75 *c.*+5 *c.*

MS535 As Nos. 529/33. *Set of 5 sheets* .. .. 4·00
a. Error. Miniature sheet as No. 531 imperf.

153. " The Descent " (Raphael).

1976 (29 Mar.). *Easter. T* **153** *and similar square designs. Multicoloured. P* 13.

536 7 c. Type **153** 8 8
537 15 c. " Pietà " (Veronese) .. 15 20
538 35 c. " Pietà " (El Greco) .. 40 45
MS539 144×57 mm. Nos. 536/8 65

1976 (3 May). *Easter. Children's Charity. Designs as Nos.* 536/8 *in separate miniature sheets* 69×69 *mm., each with a face-value of* 60 *c.* + 5 *c.*

MS540 .. *Set of three sheets* 2·25

154. Benjamin Franklin and *Resolution*.

1976 (29 May). *Bicentenary of American Revolution. T* **154** *and similar horiz. designs. Multicoloured. P* 13.

541 $1 Type **154** .. .. .. 1·10 1·25
542 $2 Capt. Cook and *Resolution* 2·25 2·50
MS543 118×58 mm. $3 Cook, Franklin and *Resolution* (74×31 *mm.*) .. .. 3·25 3·50

1976 (9 July). *Visit of Queen Elizabeth to the U.S.A. Nos.* 541/**MS**543 *optd.* ROYAL VISIT JULY 1976.

544 $1 Type **154** .. 1·10 1·25
545 $2 Capt. Cook and *Resolution* 2·25 2·50
MS546 118×58 mm. $3 Cook, Franklin and *Resolution* (74×31 mm.) .. .. 3·25 3·50

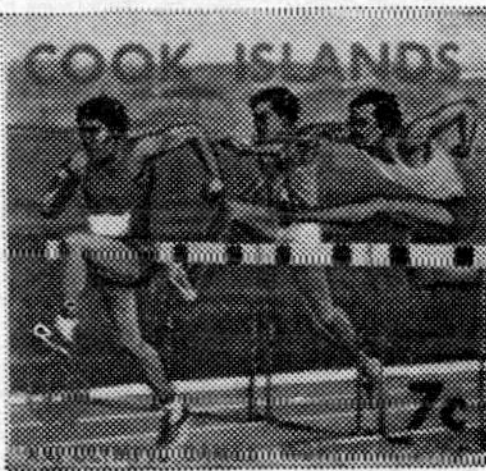

156. Hurdling.

1976 (22 July). *Olympic Games, Montreal. T* **156** *and similar square designs. Multicoloured. P* 13.

547 7 c. Type **156** 8 8
548 7 c. 8 8
549 15 c. Hockey 15 20
550 15 c. 15 20
551 30 c. Fencing 35 40
552 30 c. 35 40
553 35 c. Football 40 45
554 35 c. 40 45
547/54 .. .. *Set of* 8 1·75 2·00
MS555 104×146 mm. Nos. 547/54 2·00

The two designs of each value were printed horizontally *se-tenant* within the sheet to form the design listed. The first stamp has the face-value on the right, the second has it on the left. Illustrated is the left-hand stamp of the 7 c. design.

157. " The Visitation ".

1976 (12 Oct.). *Christmas. T* **157** *and similar vert. designs showing Renaissance sculptures. Multicoloured. P* 14×13½.

556	6 c. Type **157**	5	5
557	10 c. " Adoration of the Shepherds "	10	12
558	15 c. " Adoration of the Shepherds " (*different*) ..	15	20
559	20 c. " The Epiphany " ..	20	20
560	35 c. " The Holy Family " ..	35	40
556/60	.. .. *Set of* 5	80	90
MS561	116×110 mm. Nos. 556/60. P 13	90	

1976 (2 Nov.). *Christmas. Children's Charity. Designs as Nos.* 556/60 *in separate miniature sheets* 66×80 *mm., each with a face-value of* 75 *c.* + 5 *c.*

MS562	As Nos. 556/60. *Set of* 5 *sheets*	4·25	

OFFICIAL STAMPS.

O.H.M.S.

(O 1)

1975 (17 Mar.–19 May). *Nos.* 227B *etc. optd. with Type* O **1** (5, 10, 18, 25 *and* 30 *c. surch. also*), *in black and silver.*

O 1	1 c. multicoloured		
O 2	2 c. multicoloured		
O 3	3 c. multicoloured		
O 4	4 c. mult. (No. 233) ..		
O 5	5 c. on 2½ c. mult.		
O 6	8 c. multicoloured		
O 7	10 c. on 6 c. mult.		
O 8	18 c. on 20 c. mult.		
O 9	25 c. on 9 c. mult.		
O10	30 c. on 15 c. mult.		
O11	50 c. multicoloured		
O12	$1 multicoloured		
O13	$2 multicoloured		
O14	$4 mult. (19.5.75)		
O15	$6 mult. (19.5.75)		
O1/15	.. .. *Set of* 15	†	15·00

These stamps were only sold to the public cancelled to order and not in unused condition.

AITUTAKI

On 9th August 1972, Aitutaki became a Port of Entry into the Cook Islands, and at the close of business on the previous day, Cook Islands stamps were withdrawn from sale there. Whilst remaining part of the Cook Islands, Aitutaki has a separate postal service.

The Aitutaki issues of 1903 to 1927 are listed after New Zealand.

PRINTERS. Stamps of Aitutaki were printed in photogravure by Heraclio Fournier, Spain, *unless otherwise stated.* All issues are on paper treated with fluorescent security markings, and with synthetic gum. The fluorescent markings can be found inverted or omitted.

Aitutaki

(9) (10)

(Optd. by Govt. Printer, Wellington.)

1972 (9 Aug.). *Nos.* 227B *etc. of Cook Is. optd. with T* **9** (*applied horizontally on* $1), *by New Zealand Govt. Printer.*

33	**79**	½ c. multicoloured ..		
34	**80**	1 c. multicoloured ..		
35	**82**	2½ c. multicoloured ..		
36	**84**	4 c. mult. (No. 233B) ..		
37	**85**	5 c. multicoloured ..		
38	**89**	10 c. multicoloured ..		
39	**91**	20 c. multicoloured ..		
40	**92**	25 c. multicoloured ..		
41	**94**	50 c. multicoloured ..		
42	**95**	$1 multicoloured ..		
		*a. Shade**		
33/42		.. .. *Set of* 10	25·00	35·00

*No. 42*a* has the border flowers predominately in a carmine colour instead of scarlet, and may be due to a missing yellow colour.

1972 (27 Oct.). *Christmas. Nos.* 406/8 *of Cook Is. optd. in silver with T* **10.**

43	**130**	1 c. multicoloured ..	5	5
44	–	5 c. multicoloured ..	8	8
45	–	10 c. multicoloured ..	15	20

1972 (20 Nov.). *Royal Silver Wedding. As Nos.* 413 *and* 415 *of Cook Is., but inscr.* " COOK ISLANDS Aitutaki ".

46	**131**	5 c. black and silver ..	3·25	3·00
47	–	15 c. black and silver ..	1·50	1·50

AITUTAKI AITUTAKI

(11) (12)

1972 (24 Nov.). *No.* 245B *of Cook Is. optd. with T* **11** *by Govt. Printer, Rarotonga.*

48	**95**	$2 multicoloured ..	2·50	3·00
		a. Optd. "AJTUTAKI" for "AITUTAKI" (R.2/4) ..	10·00	

1972 (13 Dec.). *Nos.* 227B *etc. of Cook Is. optd. with T* **12**, *by Heraclio Fournier.*

49	**79**	½ c. multicoloured ..	5	5
50	**80**	1 c. multicoloured ..	5	5
51	**82**	2½ c. multicoloured ..	5	5
52	**84**	4 c. mult. (No. 233B) ..	5	8
53	**85**	5 c. multicoloured ..	8	10
54	**89**	10 c. multicoloured ..	15	20
55	**91**	20 c. multicoloured ..	30	40
56	**92**	25 c. multicoloured ..	40	50
57	**94**	50 c. multicoloured ..	75	1·00
58	**95**	$1 multicoloured ..	1·50	2·00
49/58		.. .. *Set of* 10	2·75	3·50

13. " Via Dolorosa " (Grünewald).

1973 (6 Apr.). *Easter. T* **13** *and similar vert. designs. Multicoloured. P* 13.

59	1 c. Type **13**	5	5
60	1 c. " Veronica " (Van der Weyden)	5	5
61	1 c. " Crucifixion " (Raphael)	5	5
62	1 c. " Resurrection " (Piero della Francesca) ..	5	5
63	5 c. " The Last Supper " (Master of Amiens) ..	10	12
64	5 c. " Condemnation " (Holbein)	10	12
65	5 c. " Crucifixion " (Rubens)	10	12
66	5 c. " Resurrection " (El Greco)	10	12
67	10 c. " Via Dolorosa " (El Greco)	20	25
68	10 c. " Veronica " (Coneliz) ..	20	25
69	10 c. " Crucifixion " (Rubens)	20	25
70	10 c. " Resurrection " (Bouts)	20	25
59/70	.. .. *Set of* 12	1·00	1·25

Each value is printed in a separate sheet, throughout which the four designs are printed in *se-tenant* blocks.

AITUTAKI TENTH ANNIVERSARY CESSATION OF NUCLEAR TESTING TREATY

(14) (15)

1973 (14 May). *Silver Wedding Coinage. Nos.* 417/23 *of Cook Is. optd. in silver and black as T* **14.**

71	1 c. blk., rosy carmine & gold	5	5
72	2 c. blk., bright blue and gold	5	5
73	5 c. blk., green and silver ..	10	12
74	10 c. blk., Royal blue and silver	20	25
75	20 c. blk., deep blue-green and silver	35	40
76	50 c. blk., carmine and silver	75	85
77	$1 blk., bright blue & silver	1·75	2·00
71/7	.. .. *Set of* 7	3·00	3·50

1973 (13 Aug.). *Tenth Anniv. of Treaty Banning Nuclear Testing. Nos.* 236B, 238B, 240B, *and* 243B *of Cook Is. optd. with T* **15** *and T* **12** *together.*

78	**87**	8 c. multicoloured ..	12	15
79	**89**	10 c. multicoloured ..	20	25
80	**91**	20 c. multicoloured ..	35	40
81	**94**	50 c. multicoloured ..	75	85

16. Red Hibiscus and Princess Anne.

1973 (14 Nov.). *Royal Wedding. T* **16** *and similar horiz. design. Multicoloured. P* 13½×14.

82	25 c. Type **16**	40	45
83	30 c. Capt. Phillips and Blue Hibiscus	50	60
MS84	114×65 mm. Nos. 82/3. P 13	1·00	1·25

17. "Virgin and Child" (Montagna).

1973 (10 Dec.). *Christmas. T* **17** *and similar vert. designs showing "The Virgin and Child" by the artists listed. Multicoloured. P* 13½.

85	1 c. Type **17**	5	5
86	1 c. Crivelli	5	5
87	1 c. Van Dyck	5	5
88	1 c. Perugino	5	5
89	5 c. Veronese	10	12
90	5 c. Veronese	10	12
91	5 c. Cima	10	12
92	5 c. Memling	10	12
93	10 c. Memling	20	25
94	10 c. Del Colle	20	25
95	10 c. Raphael	20	25
96	10 c. Garofalo	20	25
85/96	.. .. *Set of* 12	1·10	1·25

Each value was printed in separate sheets with the four designs in *se-tenant* blocks throughout.

18. *Murex ramosus.*

1974 (31 Jan.)-**75.** *T* **18** *and similar horiz. designs showing sea-shells. Multicoloured. P* 13.

97	½ c. Type **18**	5	5
98	1 c. *Nautilus macromphallus*	5	5
99	2 c. *Harpa major*	5	5
100	3 c. *Phalium strigatum* ..	5	5
101	4 c. *Cypraea talpa*	5	5
102	5 c. *Mitra stictica* ..	5	5
103	8 c. *Charonia tritonis* ..	8	8
104	10 c. *Murex triremis* ..	10	10
105	20 c. *Oliva sericea*	20	20
106	25 c. *Tritonalia rubeta* ..	25	25
107	60 c. *Strombus latissimus* ..	60	70
108	$1 *Biplex perca*	95	1·10
109	$2 Queen Elizabeth II and *Terebra maculata* (20.1.75)	1·90	2·00
110	$5 Queen Elizabeth II and *Cypraea hesitata* (28.2.75)	4·75	5·00
97/108	.. .. *Set of* 12	2·00	2·25

Nos. 109/110 are larger, 53×25 *mm.*

19. Bligh and *Bounty*.

(Des. G. L. Vasarhelyi.)

1974 (11 Apr.). *William Bligh's Discovery of Aitutaki. T* **19** *and similar horiz. designs. Multicoloured. P* 13½.

114	1 c. Type **19**	5	5
115	1 c. *Bounty*	5	5
116	5 c. Bligh, and *Bounty* at Aitutaki	5	8
117	5 c. Aitutaki chart of 1856 ..	5	8
118	8 c. Capt. Cook and *Resolution*	10	10
119	8 c. Map of Aitutaki and inset location map	10	10
114/119	.. .. *Set of* 6	30	35

Each value is printed in a separate sheet, throughout which the two designs are horizontally and vertically *se-tenant*.

See also Nos. 123/8.

20. Aitutaki Stamps of 1903, and Map.

1974 (15 July). *Centenary of Universal Postal Union. T* **20** *and similar horiz. design. Multicoloured. P* 13½×14.

120	25 c. Type **20**	30	35
121	50 c. Stamps of 1903 and 1920, and map	60	65
MS122	66×75 mm. Nos. 120/1 ..	90	

1974 (9 Sept.). *Air. As Nos.* 114/119 *but larger* (46×26 *mm.*), *denominations changed, and inscr.* "AIR MAIL".

123	10 c. Type **19**	12	15
124	10 c. *Bounty*	12	15
125	25 c. Blight, and *Bounty* at Aitutaki	30	35
126	25 c. Aitutaki chart of 1856 ..	30	35
127	30 c. Capt. Cook and *Resolution*	35	40
128	30 c. Map of Aitutaki and inset location map	35	40
123/8	.. .. *Set of* 6	1·40	1·50

The note beneath No. 119 also applies here.

21. "Virgin and Child" (Hugo van der Goes).

1974 (11 Oct.). *Christmas. T* **21** *and similar vert. designs showing "Virgin and Child" by the artists listed. Multicoloured. P* 13.

129	1 c. Type **21**	5	5
130	5 c. Bellini	5	5
131	8 c. Gerard David	8	10
132	10 c. Antonello de Messina ..	10	12
133	25 c. Joos van Cleve ..	30	35
134	30 c. Maitre Legende St. Catherine	35	40
129/34	.. .. *Set of* 6	80	90
MS135	127×134 mm. Nos. 129/34	90	

22. Churchill as Schoolboy. **(23)**

1974 (29 Nov.). *Birth Centenary of Sir Winston Churchill. T* **22** *and similar vert. designs. Multicoloured. P* 13½.

136	10 c. Type **22**	10	12
137	25 c. Churchill as young man	30	35
138	30 c. Churchill with troops ..	35	40
139	50 c. Churchill painting ..	55	60
140	$1 Giving "V" sign ..	1·10	1·25
136/40	.. .. *Set of* 5	2·10	2·25
MS141	115×108 mm. Nos. 136/40 plus *se-tenant* label. P 13 ..	2·40	

1974 (2 Dec.). *Children's Christmas Fund. Nos.* 129/34 *surch. with T* **23.**

142	1 c.+1 c. multicoloured ..	5	5
143	5 c.+1 c. multicoloured ..	5	8
144	8 c.+1 c. multicoloured ..	10	10
145	10 c.+1 c. multicoloured ..	10	12
146	25 c.+1 c. multicoloured ..	30	35
147	30 c.+1 c. multicoloured ..	35	40
142/7	.. .. *Set of* 6	85	95

24. Soviet and U.S. Flags.

1975 (24 July). *"Apollo-Soyuz" Space Project. T* **24** *and similar horiz. design. Multicoloured. P* 13×14.

148	25 c. Type **24**	25	30
149	50 c. Daedalus and space capsule	50	55
MS150	123×61 mm. Nos. 148/9	80	

25. "Madonna and Child" (Lorenzetti).

26. "The Descent" (detail, Flemish School).

1975 (24 Nov.). *Christmas. T* **25** *and similar vert. designs. Multicoloured. P* 13½.

No.		Design	Unused	Used
151	6 c.		5	8
152	6 c.	Type **25**	5	8
153	6 c.		5	8
154	7 c.	"Adoration of the	8	8
155	7 c.	Magi" (Van der	8	8
156	7 c.	Weyden)	8	8
157	15 c.	"Madonna and Child"	15	20
158	15 c.	(Montagna)	15	20
159	15 c.		15	20
160	20 c.	"Adoration of the	20	25
161	20 c.	Magi" (Reni)	20	25
162	20 c.		20	25
151/62		*Set of* 12	1·25	1·50
MS163		104×201 mm. Nos. 151/62. P 13	1·40	

The three designs of each value were printed horizontally *se-tenant* within the sheet to form the composite designs listed. Type **25** shows the left-hand stamp of the 6 c. design.

1975 (19 Dec.). *Children's Christmas Fund.* Nos. 151/62 *surch. as T* **23**, *in silver.*

No.		Design	Unused	Used
164	6 c.+1 c.		8	8
165	6 c.+1 c.	Type **25**	8	8
166	6 c.+1 c.		8	8
167	7 c.+1 c.	"Adoration of	8	10
168	7 c.+1 c.	the Magi" (Van	8	10
169	7 c.+1 c.	der Weyden)	8	10
170	15 c.+1 c.	"Madonna and	15	20
171	15 c.+1 c.	Child"	15	20
172	15 c.+1 c.	(Montagna)	15	20
173	20 c.+1 c.	"Adoration of	20	25
174	20 c.+1 c.	the Magi"	20	25
175	20 c.+1 c.	(Reni)	20	25
164/75		*Set of* 12	1·40	1·60

1976 (5 Apr.). *Easter. Various vert. designs showing portions of "The Descent" as in T* **26**. *P* 13.

No.			Unused	Used
176	**26**	15 c. multicoloured	15	20
177	–	30 c. multicoloured	35	40
178	–	35 c. multicoloured	40	45
MS179		87×67 mm. Nos. 176/8 forming a complete picture of "The Descent". P 12½×13	95	

Stamps from **MS**179 have no borders and are therefore smaller than stamps from the sheets.

27. "The Declaration of Independence" (detail).

1976 (1 June). *Bicentenary of American Revolution. T* **27** *and similar vert. designs showing paintings by John Trumbull. Multicoloured. P* 13.

No.		Design	Unused	Used
180	30 c.		35	40
181	30 c.	Type **27**	35	40
182	30 c.		35	40
183	35 c.	"The Surrender of	40	45
184	35 c.	Lord Cornwallis	40	45
185	35 c.		40	45
186	50 c.	"The Resignation of	55	60
187	50 c.	General Washington"	55	60
188	50 c.		55	60
180/8		*Set of* 9	3·50	4·00
MS189		132×120 mm. Nos. 180/8. P 13	3·75	

The three designs of each value were printed horizontally *se-tenant* within the sheet to form the composite design listed. Type **27** shows the left-hand stamp of the 30 c. design.

Stamps from **MS**189 have their borders in a different colour and with a different inscription.

28. Cycling.

1976 (15 July). *Olympic Games, Montreal. T* **28** *and similar horiz. designs. Multicoloured. P* 13×14.

No.		Unused	Used
190	15 c. Type **28**	15	20
191	35 c. Sailing	40	45
192	60 c. Hockey	70	80
193	70 c. Sprinting	75	85
MS194	107×97 mm. Nos. 190/3	2·10	

Stamps from **MS**194 have borders of a different colour.

ROYAL VISIT JULY 1976

(29)

1976 (30 July). *Visit of Queen Elizabeth to the U.S.A. Nos.* 190/**MS**194 *optd. with T* **29**.

No.		Unused	Used
195	15 c. Type **28**	15	20
196	35 c. Sailing	40	45
197	60 c. Hockey	70	80
198	70 c. Sprinting	75	85
MS199	107×97 mm. Nos. 195/8	2·10	

30. "The Visitation".

+1c

(31)

1975 (18 Oct.). *Christmas. T* **30** *and similar vert. designs. Figures in gold; background colours given. P* 13.

No.		Colour	Unused	Used
200	6 c.	deep bluish green	5	5
201	6 c.		5	5
202	7 c.	dull brown-purple	8	8
203	7 c.		8	8
204	15 c.	deep blue	15	20
205	15 c.		15	20
206	20 c.	reddish violet	20	25
207	20 c.		20	25
200/207		*Set of* 8	85	95
MS208		128×96 mm. Stamps as Nos. 200/207 but with borders on three sides	95	

Designs:—7 c. "Angel and Shepherds"; 15 c. "The Holy Family"; 20 c. "The Magi".

Each design covers two stamps; Type **30** shows the left-hand stamp of the 6 c. design.

1976 (19 Nov.). *Children's Christmas Fund. Nos.* 200/**MS**208 *surch. in silver as T* **31**.

No.		Design	Unused	Used
209	6 c.+2 c.	"The	8	10
210	6 c.+2 c.	Visitation"	8	10
211	7 c.+2 c.	"Angel and	10	10
212	7 c.+2 c.	Shepherds"	10	10
213	15 c.+2 c.	"The Holy	20	20
214	15 c.+2 c.	Family"	20	20
215	20 c.+2 c.	"The Magi"	20	25
216	20 c.+2 c.		20	25
209/16		*Set of* 8	1·10	1·25
MS217		128×96 mm. Stamps as Nos. 209/16 but with borders on three sides	1·25	

PENRHYN ISLAND

Penrhyn (or Tongareva) belongs to the Northern Group of the Cook Islands. The following issues are for use in all the islands of the group. Earlier issues are listed after New Zealand.

The Penrhyn Island issues of 1902 to 1929 are listed after New Zealand.

PRINTERS.—The note at the beginning of Aitutaki concerning printers, fluorescent security markings and gum also applies here.

PENRHYN

NORTHERN

(8)

PENRHYN NORTHERN

(9)

1973 (24 Oct.–14 Nov.). *Nos.* 228B/45B *of Cook Is. optd. with T* **8** (*without* "NORTHERN" *on* $1, $2).

No.			Unused	Used
41	**80**	1 c. multicoloured	8	10
42	**81**	2 c. multicoloured	10	15
43	**83**	3 c. multicoloured	10	15
44	**84**	4 c. multicoloured (233B)	12	15
45	**85**	5 c. multicoloured	15	20
46	**86**	6 c. multicoloured	50	60
47	**87**	8 c. multicoloured	75	1·00
48	**90**	15 c. multicoloured	1·75	2·00
49	**91**	20 c. multicoloured	3·50	4·00
50	**94**	50 c. multicoloured	7·00	8·00
51	**95**	$1 multicoloured	14·00	16·00
52	,,	$2 multicoloured (14.11)	14·00	16·00
41/52		*Set of* 12	25.00	28·00

1973 (14 Nov.). *Royal Wedding. Nos.* 450/2 *of Cook Is. optd. as T* **9**, *in silver.*

No.			Unused	Used
53	**138**	25 c. multicoloured	1·25	1·40
54	–	30 c. multicoloured	1·50	1·60
55	–	50 c. multicoloured	2·50	2·75

10. *Ostracion sp.*

1974 (15 Aug.)–**75**. *Fishes. T* **10** *and similar horiz. designs. Multicoloured. P* 13½ (½ *c. to* $1) *or* 13×12½ ($2, $5).

No.			Unused	Used
56	½ c.	Type **10**	5	5
57	1 c.	*Monodactylus argenteus*	5	5
58	2 c.	*Pomacanthus imperator*	5	5
59	3 c.	*Chelmon rostratus*	5	5
60	4 c.	*Chaetodon ornatissimus*	5	5
61	5 c.	*Chaetodon melanotus*	5	5
62	8 c.	*Chaetodon raffessi*	8	8
63	10 c.	*Chaetodon ephippium*	10	10
64	20 c.	*Pygoplites diacanthus*	20	20
65	25 c.	*Heniochus acuminatus*	25	25
66	60 c.	*Plectorhynchus chaetodonoides*	60	65
67	$1	*Balistipus undulatus*	95	1·10
68	$2	Birds-eye view of Penrhyn (12.2.75)	1·90	2·10
69	$5	Satellite view of Australasia (12.3.75)	4·75	5·00
56/67		*Set of* 12	2·00	2·25

Nos. 68/9 are larger, 63×25 mm.

11. Penrhyn Stamps of 1902.

1974 (27 Sept.). *Centenary of Universal Postal Union. T* **11** *and similar vert. design. Multicoloured. P* 13.

70 25 c. Type **11** 30 35
71 50 c. Stamps of 1920 .. .. 55 65

12. "Adoration of the Magi" (Memling).

1974 (30 Oct.). *Christmas. T* **12** *and similar horiz. designs. Multicoloured. P* 13.

72 5 c. Type **12** 5 5
73 10 c. "Adoration of the Shepherds" (Hugo van der Goes) 10 12
74 25 c. "Adoration of the Magi" (Rubens) 30 35
75 30 c. "The Holy Family" (Borgianni) 35 45

13. Churchill giving "V" Sign.

KIA ORANA ASTRONAUTS

(14)

1974 (30 Nov.). *Birth Centenary of Sir Winston Churchill. T* **13** *and similar vert. design. P* 13.

76 30 c. agate and gold 35 45
77 50 c. myrtle-green and gold .. 55 65

Design:—50 c. Full-face portrait.

1975 (24 July). *"Apollo-Soyuz" Space Project. No.* 69 *optd. with T* **14.**

78 $5 Satellite view of Australasia .. .. .. 5·00 5·50

15. "Virgin and Child" (Bouts).

1975 (21 Nov.). *Christmas. T* **15** *and similar vert. designs showing the "Virgin and Child". Multicoloured. P* 14 × 13.

79 7 c. Type **15** 8 8
80 15 c. Leonardo da Vinci .. 15 20
81 35 c. Raphael 35 40

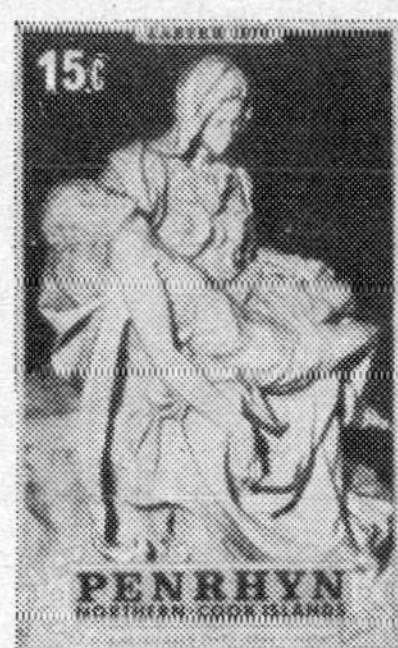

16. "Pietà".

1976 (19 Mar.). *Easter and 500th Birth Anniv. of Michelangelo. T* **16** *and similar vert. designs. P* 14 × 13.

82 15 c. sepia and gold 15 20
83 20 c. blackish purple and gold .. 20 25
84 35 c. myrtle-green and gold .. 40 45
MS85 112 × 72 mm. Nos. 82/4 .. 80

17. "Washington Crossing the Delaware" (E. Leutze).

1976 (20 May). *Bicentenary of American Revolution. T* **17** *and similar vert. designs. Multicoloured. P* 13.

86 30 c. } Type **17** 35 40
87 30 c. } .. 35 40
88 30 c. } .. 35 40
89 50 c. } "The Spirit of '76" (A. M. Willard) 55 65
90 50 c. } .. 55 65
91 50 c. } .. 55 65
86/91 .. .. *Set of* 6 2·40 2·75
MS92 103 × 103 mm. Nos. 86/91. P 13 .. .. 2·75

The three designs of each value were printed horizontally *se-tenant* within the sheet to form the composite design listed. Type **10** shows the left-hand stamp of the 30 c. design.

18. Running.

1976 (9 July). *Olympic Games, Montreal. T* **18** *and similar horiz. designs. Multicoloured. P* 14.

93 25 c. Type **18** 30 35
94 30 c. Long Jump 35 40
95 75 c. Throwing the Javelin .. 80 90
MS96 86 × 128 mm. Nos. 93/5. P 14 × 13 .. .. 1·50

19. "The Flight into Egypt".

1976 (20 Oct.). *Christmas. Dürer Engravings. T* **19** *and similar horiz. designs. P* 13.

97 7 c. black and silver 8 8
98 15 c. steel-blue and silver .. 15 20
99 35 c. violet and silver 35 40

Designs:—15 c. "Adoration of the Shepherds"; 35 c. "The Epiphany".

CYPRUS.

I. BRITISH ADMINISTRATION.

For GREAT BRITAIN stamps used in Cyprus with "**942, 969, 974, 975, 981, 982,** D **47**" or "D **48**" obliterations, see index to Great Britain Stamps Used Abroad list.

PERFORATION. Nos. 1/122 are perf. 14.

Stamps of Great Britain overprinted.

CYPRUS (1) CYPRUS (2)

(Optd. by D.L.R.)

1880 (1 APR.).

1 **1** ½d. rose .. .. .. 28·00 32·00
a. Opt. double (Pl. 15) .. .. — £1000

Plate No.	*Un.*	*Used.*	*Plate No.*	*Un.*	*Used.*
12. ..	35·00	50·00	19. ..	£450	£300
15. ..	28·00	32·00			

2 **2** 1d. red .. .. .. 4·00 7·00
a. Opt. double (Pl. 208) £900
aa. Opt. double (Pl. 218) £700
b. Pair, one without opt. (Pl. 208) £2000

Plate No.	*Un.*	*Used.*	*Plate No.*	*Un.*	*Used.*
174. ..	£300	£250	208. ..	18·00	8·00
181. ..	26·00	28·00	215. ..	4·50	6·50
184. ..	£600	£650	216. ..	4·50	7·00
193. ..	£300	†	217. ..	4·00	7·00
196. ..	£300	†	218. ..	5·50	7·50
201. ..	4·00	7·00	220. ..	£200	60·00
205. ..	6·00	8·00			

3 **2** 2½d. rosy mauve .. .. 90 1·25
a. Large thin "c" (Plate 14) .. 6·50 9·00
b. Large thin "c" (Plate 15) .. 7·00 7·00
14. .. 75 1·00 | 15. .. 1·25 4·50
4 **2** 4d. sage-green (Plate 16) .. 60·00 65·00
5 „ 6d. grey (Pl. 16) £110 £100
6 „ 1s. green (Pl. 13) £300 £150

HALF-PENNY (3) 18 mm. HALF-PENNY (4) 16 or 16½ mm.

HALF-PENNY (5) 13 mm. 30 PARAS (6)

(Optd. by Govt. Ptg. Office, Nicosia.)

1881 (FEB.–JUNE). *No.* 2 *surch.*

7 **3** ½d. on 1d. red (Feb.) .. .. 11·00 13·00
a. "HALFPENN" (*all plates*) *from* £200 £200

Plate No.	*Un.*	*Used.*	*Plate No.*	*Un.*	*Used.*
174. ..	22·00	42·00	215. ..	55·00	£110
181. ..	22·00	27·00	216. ..	11·00	13·00
201. ..	11·00	13·00	217. ..	85·00	90·00
205. ..	13·00	13·00	218. ..	80·00	75·00
208. ..	27·00	30·00	220. ..	35·00	42·00

8 **4** ½d. on 1d. red (Apr.) .. .. 28·00 35·00
a. Surch. double (Pl. 201) .. £500

201. ..	28·00	35·00	218. ..	—	—
216. ..	55·00	85·00			

9 **5** ½d. on 1d. red (June) .. .. 9·00 11·00
a. Surch. double (Pl. 201) ..
aa. Surch. double (Pl. 205) .. £150
ab. Surch. double (Pl. 215) .. £120 £120
b. Surch. treble (Pl. 205) ..
ba. Surch. treble (Pl. 215) .. £160
bb. Surch. treble (Pl. 217) ..
bc. Surch. treble (Pl. 218) ..
c. Surch. quadruple (Pl. 205) .. £450
ca. Surch. quadruple (Pl. 215) .. £400
d. "CYPRUS" double (Pl. 218) .. £750

201. ..	—	—	217. ..	11·00	13·00
205. ..	28·00		218. ..	11·00	13·00
215. ..	9·00	11·00			

10 **6** 30 paras on 1d. red (June) .. 25·00 28·00
a. Surch. double, one invtd. (Pl. 216) £450
aa. Surch. double, one invtd. (Pl. 220) £350 £400

201. ..	28·00	30·00	217. ..	28·00	32·00
216. ..	26·00	30·00	220. ..	35·00	42·00

7

(Typo. De La Rue.)

1881 (1 JULY). *Die I. Wmk. Crown CC.*

11 **7** ½ pi. emerald-green .. .. 60·00 20·00
12 „ 1 pi. rose .. .. .. 65·00 20·00
13 „ 2 pi. blue .. .. .. 65·00 20·00
14 „ 4 pi. pale olive-green .. £200 60·00
15 „ 6 pi. olive-grey .. .. £225 80·00

Stamps of Queen Victoria initialled "J. A. B." or overprinted "POSTAL SURCHARGE" with or without the same initials were employed for accounting purposes between the Chief Post Office and sub-offices. The initials are those of the then Postmaster, Mr. J. A. Bulmer.

1882 (MAY)–**86**. *Die I*. Wmk. Crown CA.*

16 **7** ½ pi. emerald-green (5.82) .. £700 80·00
a. Dull green (4.83) .. 1·60 30
17 „ 30 pa. pale mauve (7.6.82) .. 7·00 5·50
18 „ 1 pi. rose (5.83) .. .. 9·00 1·50
19 „ 2 pi. blue (9.83) .. .. 15·00 1·50
20 „ 4 pi. deep olive-green ('83) 45·00 9·00
a. Pale olive-green .. .. 40·00 9·00
21 „ 6 pi. olive-grey (1.83) .. 12·00 6·00
22 „ 12 pi. orange-brown (1886) (Optd. S. £28) .. 40·00 12·00
16/22 .. .. *Set of* 7 £110 32·00

* For description and illustrations of Dies I and II see Introduction. See Nos. 31/7.

½ (8) ½ 30 PARAS (9)

1882. *Surch. with T* **8/9** *by De La Rue.*

(*a*) *Wmk. Crown CC.*

23 **7** ½ on ½ pi. emer.-grn. (6.82) .. 48·00 14·00
24 30 pa. on 1 pi. rose (22.5.82) £250 70·00

(*b*) *Wmk. Crown CA.*

25 **7** ½ on ½ pi. emer.-grn. (6.82) .. 20·00 5·00
a. Surch. double .. .. — £300

1/2 1/2 (**10**)

(*a*) Fractions approx. 6 mm. apart.
(*b*) Fractions approx. 8 mm. apart.

1886 (APR.). *Surch. locally with T* **10** (*a*).

(*a*) *Wmk. Crown CC.*

26 **7** ½ on ½ pi. emerald-green .. £1100

(*b*) *Wmk. Crown CA.*

27 **7** ½ on ½ pi. emerald-green .. 42·00 20·00

The status of No. 26 remains in doubt as it is not known used.

1886 (MAY). *Surch. locally with T* **10** (*b*).

(*a*) *Wmk. Crown CC.*

28 **7** ½ on ½ pi. emerald-green .. £1100 £150
a. Large "1" at left .. .. — £450
b. Small "1" at right £2000 £650

(*b*) *Wmk. Crown CA.*

29 **7** ½ on ½ pi. emerald-green .. 40·00 5·00
a. Large "1" at left .. .. £300 70·00
b. Small "1" at right .. .. £450 90·00

A third type of this surcharge is known with the fraction spaced approximately 10 mm. apart on CA paper with postmarks from August 1886. This may be due to the shifting of type.

1892–94. *Die II. Wmk. Crown CA.*

31 **7** ½ pi. dull green .. .. 1·10 30
32 „ 30 pa. mauve.. .. .. 1·10 90
33 „ 1 pi. carmine .. .. 3·25 1·10
34 „ 2 pi. ultramarine .. .. 5·00 60
35 „ 4 pi. olive-green .. .. 16·00 3·00
a. Pale olive-green .. .. 8·00 3·00
36 **7** 6 pi. olive-grey (1894) .. 30·00 45·00
37 „ 12 pi. orange-brown .. .. 30·00 30·00
31/37 .. .. *Set of* 7 70·00 75·00

1894 (14 AUG.)–**96**. *Colours changed and new values. Die II. Wmk. Crown CA.*

40 **7** ½ pi. green & carmine ('96) 1·00 20
41 „ 30 pa. brt. mauve & grn. ('96) 1·00 20
42 „ 1 pi. carmine and blue ('96) 1·40 25
43 „ 2 pi. blue and purple ('96) .. 1·40 30
44 „ 4 pi. sage-grn. & pur. ('96) 3·00 1·40
45 „ 6 pi. sepia and green ('96) .. 3·00 2·25
46 „ 9 pi. brown and carmine .. 6·00 3·00
47 „ 12 pi. orge.-brn. & blk. ('96) 5·50 9·00
48 „ 18 pi. greyish slate & brown 14·00 9·00
49 „ 45 pi. grey-purple and blue .. 25·00 25·00
40/49 .. .. *Set of* 10 55·00 45·00
40/49 Optd. "Specimen" *Set of* 10 85·00

11

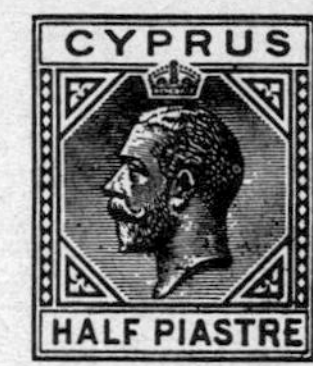

12

(Typo. De La Rue.)

1902–04. *Wmk. Crown CA.*

50 **11** ½ pi. green & carm. (12.02) 1·25 45
51 „ 30 pa. violet & green (2.03) 65 65
a. Mauve and green .. 80 80
52 „ 1 pi. carmine & blue (9.03) 3·50 1·10
53 „ 2 pi. blue and purple (2.03) 8·00 2·50
54 „ 4 pi. olive-grn. & pur. (9.03) 12·00 4·00
55 „ 6 pi. sepia and green (9.03) 22·00 24·00
56 „ 9 pi. brn. & carmine (5.04) 45·00 50·00
57 „ 12 pi. chestnut & blk. (4.03) 6·00 7·50
58 „ 18 pi. black & brown (5.04) 38·00 42·00
59 „ 45 pi. dull purple and ultramarine (10.03) .. £110 £140
50/59 .. .. *Set of* 10 £225 £250
50/59 Optd. "Specimen" *Set of* 10 £110

1904–10. *Wmk. Mult. Crown CA.*

60 **11** 5 pa. bistre & blk. (14.1.08) 20 40
61 „ 10 pa. orange & grn. (12.06) 50 65
a. Yellow and green .. 11·00 5·50
62 „ ½ pi. green & carm. (1.7.04) 40 15
63 „ 30 pa. purple & grn. (1.7.04) 1·90 80
a. Violet and green (1910) .. 2·00 80
64 „ 1 pi. carmine & blue (11.04) 65 30
65 „ 2 pi. blue & purple (11.04) 1·40 30
66 „ 4 pi. ol.-grn. & pur. (2.05) 6·50 2·50
67 „ 6 pi. sepia & grn. (17.7.04) 6·00 3·00
68 „ 9 pi. brn. & carm. (30.5.04) 2·75 3·25
a. Yellow-brown and carmine 2·75 3·25
69 „ 12 pi. chestnut & blk. (4.06) 13·00 8·50
70 „ 18 pi. black & brn. (16.6.04) 16·00 6·00
71 „ 45 pi. dull purple and ultramarine (15.6.04) 26·00 23·00
60/71 .. .. *Set of* 12 70·00 45·00
60/61 Optd. "Specimen" *Set of* 2 35·00

(Typo. De La Rue.)

1912 (JULY)–**15**. *Wmk. Mult. Crown CA.*

74 **12** 10 pa. orange & grn. (11.12) 55 65
a. Wmk. sideways .. ..
b. Orange-yellow and bright green (8.15) 75 65
75 " ½ pi. green and carmine .. 65 55
a. Yellow-green and carmine.. 90 55
76 " 30 pa. violet & green (8.13) 65 50
77 " 1 pi. rose-red & blue (9.12) 90 1·10
a. Carmine and blue (8.15?) 3·50 1·50
78 " 2 pi. blue and purple (7.13) 1·75 75
79 „ 4 pi. olive-green & purple 1·75 80
80 „ 6 pi. sepia and green 1·75 1·10
81 „ 9 pi. brn. & carmine (3.15) 8·00 6·00
a. Yellow-brown and carmine 9·50 7·00
82 „ 12 pi. chestnut & blk. (7.13) 3·25 3·50
83 „ 18 pi. black & brown (3.15) 7·50 7·50
84 „ 45 pi. dull purple and ultramarine (3.15) .. 22·00 22·00
74/84 .. .. *Set of* 11 45·00 40·00
74/84 Optd. "Specimen" *Set of* 11 85·00

1921–23. (*a*) *Wmk. Mult. Script CA.*

85	**12**	10 pa. orange and green ..	40	65
86	,,	10 pa. grey and yellow ('23)	2·00	2·25
87	,,	30 pa. violet and green ..	65	40
88	,,	30 pa. green (1923)	1·00	60
89	,,	1 pi. carmine and blue ..	2·75	4·00
90	,,	1 pi. violet and red ('22) ..	2·00	2·25
91	,,	1½ pi. yellow and black ('22)	1·10	1·75
92	,,	2 pi. blue and purple ..	2·75	2·50
93	,,	2 pi. carmine and blue ('22)	3·25	4·00
94	,,	2¾ pi. blue and purple ('22)	4·00	5·00
95	,,	4 pi. olive-green & purple	2·25	2·75
96	,,	6 pi. sepia and green ('23)	4·50	5·00
97	,,	9 pi. brown & carmine ('22)	7·50	11·00
		a. Yellow-brown and carmine	11·00	14·00
98	,,	18 pi. black & brown ('23)	35·00	40·00
99	,,	45 pi. dull purple and ultramarine (1923) ..	60·00	60·00
85/99		.. .. *Set of* 15	£120	£130
85/99 Optd. "Specimen"		*Set of* 15	£110	

(*b*) *Wmk. Mult. Crown CA* (1923).

100	**12**	10s. green & red/*pale yellow*	£180	£300
101	,,	£1 purple and black/*red*	£500	£600
100/101 Optd. "Specimen		*Set of* 2	£180	

13

1924. *Chalk-surfaced paper.*

(*a*) *Wmk. Mult. Crown CA.*

102	**13**	£1 purple and black/*red*	80·00	90·00

(*b*) *Wmk. Mult. Script CA.*

103	**13**	¼ pi. grey and chestnut ..	20	25
104	,,	½ pi. black	40	65
105	,,	¾ pi. green	40	30
106	,,	1 pi. purple and chestnut	25	25
107	,,	1½ pi. orange and black ..	55	80
108	,,	2 pi. carmine and green..	1·10	1·40
109	,,	2¾ pi. bright blue & purple	55	1·10
110	,,	4 pi. sage-green & purple	1·00	1·40
111	,,	4½ pi. black & orge./*emerald*	1·90	2·50
112	,,	6 pi. olive-brown & green	1·75	2·75
113	,,	9 pi. brown and purple ..	1·75	2·75
114	,,	12 pi. chestnut and black..	2·50	7·00
115	,,	18 pi. black and orange ..	6·00	6·00
116	,,	45 pi. purple and blue ..	10·00	13·00
117	,,	90 pi. green and red/*yellow*	35·00	45·00
117*a*	,,	£5 black/*yellow* ('28) (Optd. S. £400) ..	£1500	£1750

II. CROWN COLONY.

1925–28. *Wmk. Mult. Script CA.*

118	**13**	½ pi. green, C	40	65
119	,,	¾ pi. black, C	40	10
120	,,	1½ pi. scarlet, O	65	45
121	,,	2 pi. yellow and black, C	1·40	1·75
122	,,	2½ pi. bright blue, O ..	1·10	40
102/122		.. ..*Set of* 21 *to* £1	£130	£160
102/22 Optd. "Specimen"		*Set of* 21	£100	

In the above set the fraction bar in the value is horizontal. In Nos. 91, 94, 107 and 109 it is diagonal.

MINIMUM PRICE

The minimum price quoted is 5p which represents a handling charge rather than a basis for valuing common stamps. For further notes about prices see introductory pages.

14. Silver Coin of Amathus.

16. Map of Cyprus.

15. Philosopher Zeno.

17. Discovery of Body of St. Barnabas.

19. Badge of Cyprus.

18. Cloister, Abbey of Bella Paise.

20. Tekke of Umm Haram.

21. Statue of Richard I, London.

22. St. Nicholas, Famagusta.

23. King George V.

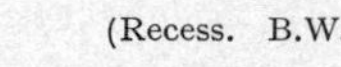
(Recess. B.W.)

1928 (1 Feb.). *50th Anniv. of British Rule. Wmk. Mult. Script CA. P 12.*

123	**14**	¾ pi. deep dull purple ..	45	25
124	**15**	1 pi. black & greenish blue	60	65
125	**16**	1½ pi. scarlet	1·40	1·10
126	**17**	2½ pi. light blue	55	1·00
127	**18**	4 pi. deep brown.. ..	2·50	3·50
128	**19**	6 pi. blue	3·25	4·00
129	**20**	9 pi. maroon	2·75	2·75
130	**21**	18 pi. black and brown ..	5·50	6·50
131	**22**	45 pi. violet and blue ..	12·00	15·00
132	**23**	£1 blue & bistre-brown	55·00	65·00
123/132		.. .. *Set of* 10	75·00	90·00
123/32 Optd. "Specimen"		*Set of* 10	£120	

24. Vouni Palace.

25. Salamis.

26. Peristerona Church.

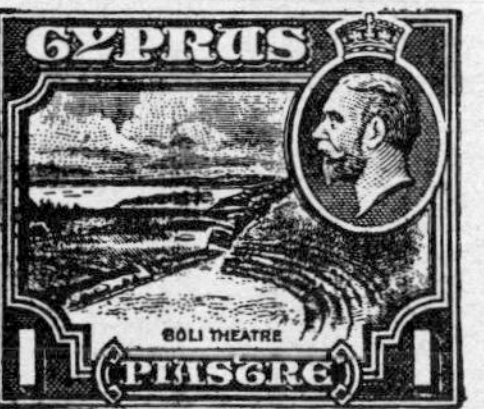

27. Soli Theatre.

28. Kyrenia Harbour.

29. Kolossi Castle.

30. St. Sophia, Nicosia.

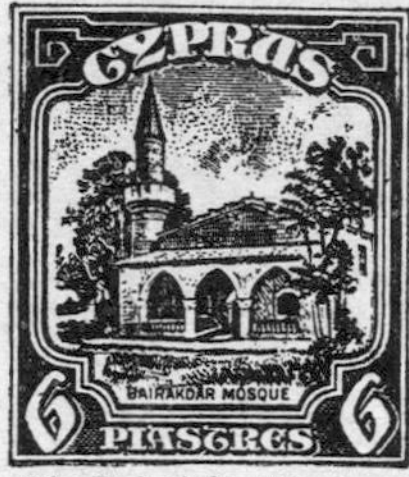

31. Bairakdar Mosque.

32. Queen's Window, St. Hilarion Castle.

33. Buyuk Khan, Nicosia.

34. Forest Scene.

(Recess. Waterlow.)

1934 (1 Dec.). *Wmk. Mult. Script CA (sideways on ½ p., 1½ p., 2½ p., 4½ p., 6 p., 9 p. and 18 p.). P 12½.*

133 **24** ½ p. ultram. & orge.-brn. 12 30
a. Imp. between (vert. pair) £2000
134 **25** ½ p. green 12 30
a. Imp. between (vert. pair) £1800 £1800
135 **26** ¾ p. black and violet .. 15 10
a. Imp. between (pair) .. £2000
136 **27** 1 p. black and red-brown 40 55
a. Imp. between (pair) .. £1800 £1700
137 **28** 1½ p. carmine 35 25
138 **29** 2½ p. ultramarine 40 55
139 **30** 4½ p. black and crimson .. 2·00 85
140 **31** 6 p. black and blue .. 1·75 2·75
141 **32** 9 p. sepia and violet .. 1·50 1·75
142 **33** 18 p. black & olive-green 6·50 4·50
143 **34** 45 p. green and black .. 14·00 13·00
133/143 .. .. *Set of* 11 25·00 22·00
133/43 Perf. "Specimen" *Set of* 11 45·00

1935 (6 May). *Silver Jubilee. As Nos. 91/4 of Antigua, but ptd. by W'low & Sons. P 11 × 12.*

144 ¾ p. ultramarine and grey .. 12 10
145 1½ p. deep blue and scarlet .. 1·00 1·00
146 2½ p. brown and deep blue .. 2·25 2·75
147 9 p. slate and purple .. 4·50 5·50
144/7 Perf. "Specimen" *Set of* 4 16·00

1937 (12 May). *Coronation. As Nos. 13/5 of Aden, but ptd. by B.W. & Co. P 11 × 11½.*

148 ¾ p. grey 20 5
149 1½ p. carmine 40 20
150 2½ p. blue 80 70
148/50 Perf. "Specimen" *Set of* 3 12·00

35. Vouni Palace.

36. Map of Cyprus.

37. "Citadel" (Othello's Tower), Famagusta.

38. King George VI.

(Recess. Waterlow & Sons, Ltd.)

1938 (12 May)–**1951.** *T* **35** *to* **38** *and other designs as 1934, but with portrait of King George VI. Wmk. Mult. Script CA. P 12½.*

151 **35** ¼ p. ultram. & orge.-brn. 10 8
152 **25** ½ p. green 8 5
152*a* ,, ½ p. violet (2.7.51) .. 20 8
153 **26** ¾ p. black and violet .. 60 5
154 **27** 1 p. orange 20 5
a. Perf. 13½ × 12½ ('44) .. 50·00 6·50
155 **28** 1½ p. carmine 35 25
155*a* ,, 1½ p. violet (15.3.43) .. 10 8
155*ab* ,, 1½ p. green (2.7.51) .. 50 12
155*b* **26** 2 p. blk. & car. (30.1.42) 12 5
c. Perf. 12½ × 13½ ('44) .. 20 15
156 **29** 2½ p. ultramarine .. 1·10 1·60
156*a* ,, 3 p. ultram. (30.1.42) .. 15 5
156*b* ,, 4 p. ultram. (2.7.51) .. 60 10
157 **36** 4½ p. grey 12 5
158 **31** 6 p. black and blue .. 40 30
159 **37** 9 p. black and purple .. 25 10
160 **33** 18 p. black & olive-green 50 35
a. *Blk. & sage-green* (19.8.47) 1·75 1·00
161 **34** 45 p. green and black .. 1·25 60
162 **38** 90 p. mauve and black .. 5·00 6·50
163 ,, £1 scarlet and indigo .. 11·00 11·00
151/163 .. .. *Set of* 19 21·00 20·00
151/63 Perf. "Specimen" *Set of* 16 60·00

1946 (21 Oct.). *Victory. As Nos. 28/9 of Aden.*

164 1½ p. deep violet 8 5
165 3 p. blue 8 5
164/5 Perf. "Specimen" *Set of* 2 15·00

1948 (20 Dec.). *Royal Silver Wedding. As Nos. 30/1 of Aden.*

166 1½ p. violet 10 10
167 £1 indigo .. .. .. 17·00 20·00

1949 (10 Oct.). *75th Anniv. of Universal Postal Union. As Nos. 114/7 of Antigua but inscr.* "CYPRUS" *(recess).*

168 1½ p. violet 25 30
169 2 p. carmine-red 40 55
170 3 p. deep blue 75 90
171 9 p. purple .. .. .. 1·50 1·40

1953 (2 June). *Coronation. As No. 47 of Aden, but ptd. by B. W. & Co.*

172 1½ p. black and emerald .. 25 25

(New currency. 1,000 mils. = £1)

39. Carobs.

40. Grapes.

41. Oranges.

42. Copper Pyrites Mine.

43. Troodos Forest.

44. Beach of Aphrodite.

45. Ancient Coin of Paphos.

46. Kyrenia.

47. Harvest in Mesaoria.

48. Famagusta Harbour.

49. St. Hilarion Castle.

50. Hala Sultan Tekke.

51. Kanakaria Church.

52. Coins of Salamis, Paphos, Citium and Idalium.

53. Arms of Byzantium, Lusignan, Ottoman Empire and Venice.

(Recess. B.W.)

1955 (1 Aug.)–**60.** *Wmk. Mult. Script CA. P* 13½ (*Nos.* 183/5) *or* 11½ (*others*).

173 **39** 2 m. blackish brown .. 8 10
174 **40** 3 m. blue-violet .. 8 10
175 **41** 5 m. brn.-orange (*shades*) 8 5
176 **42** 10 m. dp. brn. & dp. grn. 10 5

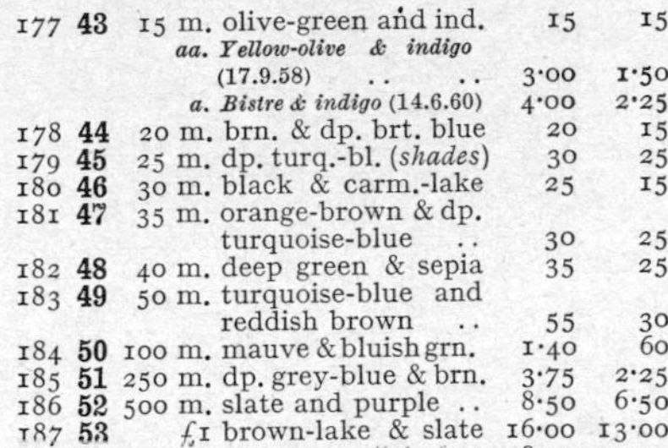
177 **43** 15 m. olive-green and ind. 15 15
aa. Yellow-olive & indigo (17.9.58) .. .. 3·00 1·50
a. Bistre & indigo (14.6.60) 4·00 2·25
178 **44** 20 m. brn. & dp. brt. blue 20 15
179 **45** 25 m. dp. turq.-bl. (*shades*) 30 25
180 **46** 30 m. black & carm.-lake 25 15
181 **47** 35 m. orange-brown & dp. turquoise-blue .. 30 25
182 **48** 40 m. deep green & sepia 35 25
183 **49** 50 m. turquoise-blue and reddish brown .. 55 30
184 **50** 100 m. mauve & bluish grn. 1·40 60
185 **51** 250 m. dp. grey-blue & brn. 3·75 2·25
186 **52** 500 m. slate and purple .. 8·50 6·50
187 **53** £1 brown-lake & slate 16·00 13·00
173/87 .. .. *Set of* 15 28·00 22·00

III. REPUBLIC.

ΚΥΠΡΙΑΚΗ
ΔΗΜΟΚΡΑΤΙΑ
KIBRIS
CUMHURIYETI

(**54.** "Cyprus Republic".)

55. Map of Cyprus.

1960 (16 Aug.). *T* **39**/**53** *optd. as T* **54**, *in blue, by B.W. Opt. larger on Nos.* 191/7 *and in two lines on Nos.* 198/202.

188 **39** 2 m. blackish brown .. 15 25
189 **40** 3 m. blue-violet .. 15 25
190 **41** 5 m. brn.-orange (*shades*) 12 10
191 **42** 10 m. dp. brown & dp. grn. 20 10
192 **43** 15 m. yellow bistre and indigo (*shades*) .. 40 40
a. Olive-green & indigo .. 60·00 50·00
193 **44** 20 m. brn. & dp. brt. blue 40 35
a. Opt. double .. .. † £450
194 **45** 25 m. dp. turquoise-blue (*shades*) 65 45
195 **46** 30 m. blk. & carm.-lake .. 65 30
a. Opt. double .. .. † £450
196 **47** 35 m. orange-brown and dp. turquoise-blue 75 55
197 **48** 40 m. dp. green and sepia 85 65
198 **49** 50 m. turquoise-blue and reddish brown .. 1·00 65
199 **50** 100 m. mauve & bluish grn. 3·50 2·00
200 **51** 250 m. dp. grey-blue & brn. 7·50 6·50
201 **52** 500 m. slate and purple .. 23·00 19·00
202 **53** £1 brown-lake & slate 65·00 65·00
188/202 .. .. *Set of* 15 90·00 85·00

Only one used copy of each of Nos. 193*a* and 195*a* is known.

(Recess. B.W.)

1960 (16 Aug.). *Constitution of Republic. W* w.**12**. *P* 11½.

203 **55** 10 m. sepia & deep green 30 30
204 „ 30 m. ultram. & dp. brn. 80 80
205 „ 100 m. purple & deep slate 2·00 1·75

PRINTERS. All the following were lithographed by Aspioti-Elka, Athens, *unless otherwise stated.*

56. Doves.

(Des. T. Kurpershoek.)

1962 (19 Mar.). *Europa. P* 14×13.

206 **56** 10 m. purple and mauve 8 8
207 „ 40 m. ultram. & cobalt .. 30 30
208 „ 100 m. emerald & pale grn. 60 60

57. Campaign Emblem.

1962 (14 May). *Malaria Eradication. P* 14×13½.

209 **57** 10 m. black & olive-green 15 15
210 „ 30 m. black and brown .. 55 55

WATERMARK VARIETIES. The issues printed by Aspioti-Elka with *W* **58** are known with the vertical stamps having the watermark normal or inverted and the horizontal stamps with the watermark reading upwards or downwards.

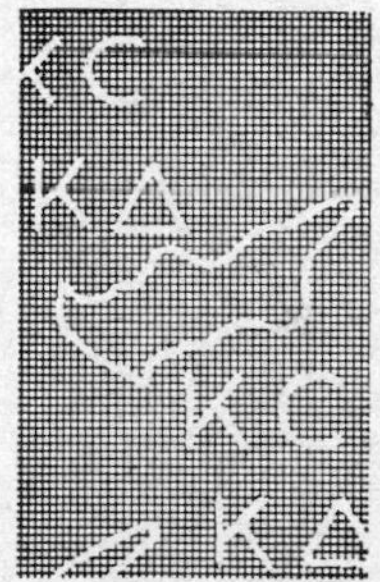

58. Mult. K C K Δ and Map.

59. Iron Age Jug.

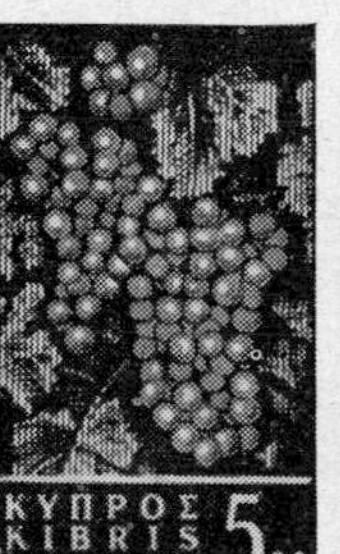

60. Grapes.

61. Bronze Head of Apollo.

62. St. Sophia Church. **65.** Head of Aphrodite.

63. St. Barnabas's Church.

64. Temple of Apollo Hylates.

66. Skiing at Troodos.

67. Salamis Gymnasium.

68. Hala Sultan Tekke. **70.** Cyprus Moufflon.

69. Bellapais Abbey.

71. St. Hilarion Castle.

1962 (17 SEPT.). *W* **58** (*sideways on* 20, 30, 40, 50, 250 *m.*, £1). *P* 13½ × 14 (*vert.*) *or* 14 × 13½ (*horiz.*).

No.	Type	Description	Unused	Used
211	**59**	3 m. dp. brn. & orge.-brn.	10	10
212	**60**	5 m. purple and grey-grn.	10	10
213	**61**	10 m. black & yell.-grn.	10	10
214	**62**	15 m. blk. & reddish pur.	12	10
215	**63**	25 m. dp. brn. & chestnut	25	20
216	**64**	30 m. dp. blue & lt. blue	30	25
217	**65**	35 m. lt. green and blue	35	25
218	**66**	40 m. black & violet-blue	45	35
219	**67**	50 m. bronze-grn. & bistre	60	40
220	**68**	100 m. dp. brn. & yell.-brn.	1·25	50
221	**69**	250 m. black & cinnamon	3·50	1·50
222	**70**	500 m. dp. brn. & lt. grn.	9·00	5·00
223	**71**	£1 bronze-grn. & grey	20·00	15·00
211/23		.. .. *Set of* 13	32·00	21·00

72. Europa "Tree".

(Des. Lex Weyer.)

1963 (28 JAN.). *Europa.* *W* **58** (*sideways*). *P* 14 × 13½.

No.	Type	Description	Unused	Used
224	**72**	10 m. brt. blue and black	10	10
225	„	40 m. carm.-red & black	60	60
226	„	150 m. emerald-grn. & blk.	1·40	1·40

73. Harvester. **75.** Wolf Cub in Camp.

74. Demeter, Goddess of Corn. **76.** Sea Scout. **77.** Scout with Moufflon.

1963 (21 MAR.). *Freedom from Hunger.* *W* **58.** *P* 13½ × 14.

No.	Type	Description	Unused	Used
227	**73**	25 m. ochre, sepia & brt. bl.	30	30
228	**74**	75 m. grey, black and lake	75	80

1963 (21 AUG.). *50th Anniv. of Cyprus Scout Movement and Third Commonwealth Scout Conference, Platres.* *W* **58.** *P* 13½ × 14.

No.	Type	Description	Unused	Used
229	**75**	3 m. brown, black, dull green and turquoise	8	8
230	**76**	20 m. bluish violet, brown, black & light blue ..	30	30
231	**77**	150 m. brn., blk., olive & bl.	1·40	1·50
MS231*a*		110 × 90 mm. Nos. 229/31 (sold at 250 m.). Imperf.	75·00	60·00

78. Nurse tending Child.

79. Children's Home, Kyrenia.

1963 (9 SEPT.). *Centenary of Red Cross.* *W* **58** (*sideways on* 100 *m.*). *P* 13½ × 14 (10 *m.*) *or* 14 × 13½ (100 *m.*).

No.	Type	Description	Unused	Used
232	**78**	10 m. red, blue, grey-blue, chestnut and black	12	12
233	**79**	100 m. red, grn., blk. & bl.	1·40	1·50

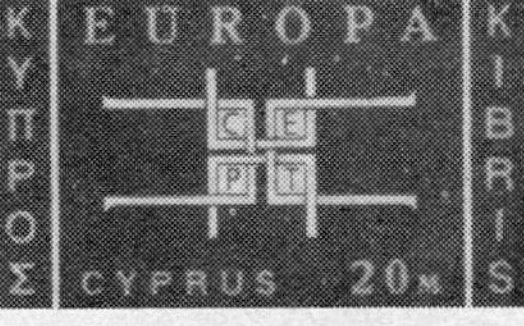

1964

80. "Co-operation" (emblem). **(81)**

(Des. A. Holm.)

1963 (4 NOV.). *Europa.* *W* **58** (*sideways*). *P* 14 × 13½.

No.	Type	Description	Unused	Used
234	**80**	20 m. buff, blue & violet	25	20
235	„	30 m. grey, yellow & blue	40	35
236	„	150 m. buff, blue & orange-brown	1·60	1·60

1964 (5 MAY). *U.N. Security Council's Cyprus Resolutions, March,* 1964. *Nos.* 213, 216, 218/20 *optd. with T* **81** *in blue.*

No.	Type	Description	Unused	Used
237	**61**	10 m. black & yellow-grn.	12	12
238	**64**	30 m. dp. blue & lt. blue	20	25
239	**66**	40 m. black & violet-blue	30	30
240	**67**	50 m. bronze-grn. & bistre	40	40
241	**68**	100 m. dp. brn. & yell.-brn.	70	70
237/41		.. .. *Set of* 5	1·60	1·60

82. Soli Theatre.

964 (15 JUNE). *400th Anniv. of Shakespeare's Birth. T* **82** *and similar horiz. designs. Multicoloured. W* **58**. *P* 13½×13.

42	15 m. Type **82**	10	20
43	35 m. Curium Theatre ..	35	35
44	50 m. Salamis Theatre ..	50	45
45	100 m. Othello Tower and scene from *Othello* ..	85	80

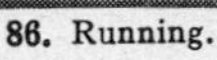

86. Running. **89.** Europa "Flower".

87. Boxing.

88. Charioteers. (*As T* **87**).

964 (6 JULY). *Olympic Games, Tokyo. W* **58** *(sideways, 25 m., 75 m.). P* 13½×14 *(10 m.) or* 14×13½ *(others).*

46 **86**	10 m. brn., blk. & yellow	12	12
47 **87**	25 m. brn., blue & blue-grey	20	20
48 **88**	75 m. brown, black and orange-red ..	50	50
IS248*a*	110×90 mm. Nos. 246/8 (sold at 250 m.). Imperf. ..	2·00	2·25

(Des. G. Bétemps.)

964 (14 SEPT.). *Europa. W* **58**. *P* 13½×14.

49 **89**	20 m. chestnut & lt. ochre	12	12
50 ,,	30 m. ultram. & lt. blue	25	25
51 ,,	150 m. olive and light blue-green	1·50	1·50

90. Dionysus and Acme.

91. Silenus (satyr). **92.** Commandaria Wine.

93. Wine Factory.

1964 (26 OCT.). *Cyprus Wines. W* **58** *(sideways, 10 m., 100 m.). P* 14×13½ *(horiz.) or* 13½×14 *(vert.).*

252 **90**	10 m. multicoloured ..	5	5
253 **91**	40 m. multicoloured ..	35	35
254 **92**	50 m. multicoloured ..	45	45
255 **93**	100 m. multicoloured ..	90	90

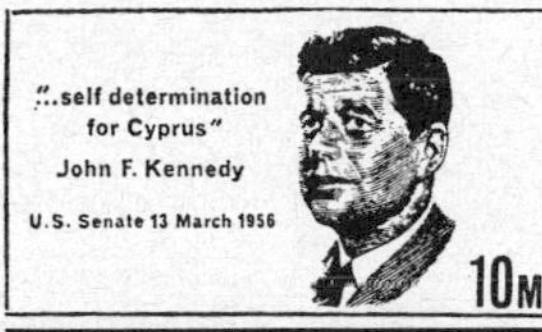

94. President Kennedy.

1965 (15 FEB.). *President Kennedy Commemoration. W* **58** *(sideways). P* 14×13½.

256 **94**	10 m. ultramarine ..	5	5
257 ,,	40 m. green ..	30	30
258 ,,	100 m. carmine-lake ..	85	90
MS258*a*	110×90 mm. Nos. 256/8 (sold at 250 m.) Imperf. ..	1·75	1·75

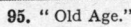

95. "Old Age." **97.** "Maternity".

96. "Accident".

1965 (12 APR.). *Social Insurance Law. W* **58**. *P* 13½×12 *(75 m.) or* 13½×14 *(others).*

259 **95**	30 m. drab and dull green	25	25
260 **96**	45 m. light grey-green, blue and deep ultramarine	40	40
261 **97**	75 m. red-brown and flesh	85	90

98. I.T.U. Emblem and Symbols.

1965 (17 MAY). *I.T.U. Centenary. W* **58** *(sideways). P* 14×13½.

262 **98**	15 m. blk., brn. & yellow	12	12
263 ,,	60 m. blk., grn. & lt. grn.	50	55
264 ,,	75 m. blk., indigo & lt. bl.	70	75

99. I.C.Y. Emblem.

1965 (17 MAY). *International Co-operation Year. W* **58** *(sideways). P* 14×13½.

265 **99**	50 m. brown, deep green and lt. yellow-brn.	45	45
266 ,,	100 m. purple, deep green and light purple ..	80	80

100. Europa "Sprig".

(Des. H. Karlsson.)

1965 (27 SEPT.). *Europe. W* **58** *(sideways). P* 14×13½.

267 **100**	5 m. black, orange-brn. and orange ..	8	8
268 ,,	45 m. black, orange-brn. and lt. emerald ..	40	40
269 ,,	150 m. black, orange-brn. and light grey ..	1·10	1·10

U. N.
Resolution
on Cyprus
18 Dec. 1965
(101)

1966 (31 JAN.). *U.N. General Assembly's Cyprus Resolution, 18 December 1965. Nos.* 211, 213, 216 *and* 221 *optd. with T* **101**, *in blue.*

270 **59**	3 m. dp. brn. & orge.-brn.	5	5
271 **61**	10 m. black & yellow-grn.	8	8
272 **64**	30 m. dp. blue & lt. blue	25	25
273 **69**	250 m. black and cinnamon	1·25	1·25

102. Discovery of St. Barnabas's Body.

103. St. Barnabas's Chapel.

104. St. Barnabas (icon).

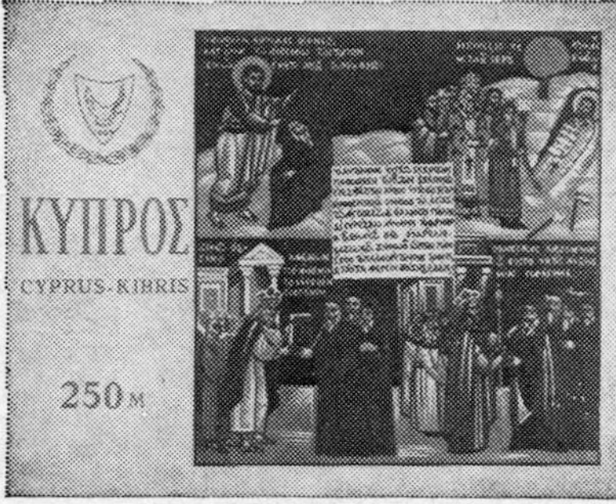

105. "Privileges of Cyprus Church".

(*Illustration ½ size.*)

1966 (25 APR.). *1900th Death Anniv. of St. Barnabas. W* **58** (*sideways on* 15 *m.*, 100 *m.*, 250 *m.*). *P* 14×13 (25 *m.*) *or* 13×14 (*others*).

274	**102**	15 m. multicoloured ..	20	20
275	**103**	25 m. drab, black & blue	30	30
276	**104**	100 m. multicoloured ..	1·25	1·40
MS277	**105**	110×91 mm. 250 m. multicoloured Imperf. ..	3·00	3·00

5 M

Ξ

(106)

107. General K. S. Thimayya and U.N. Emblem.

1966 (30 MAY). *No.* 211 *surch. with T* **106.**

278	**59**	5 m. on 3 m. deep brown and orange-brown ..	10	10

1966 (6 JUNE). *General Thimayya Commemoration. W* **58** (*sideways*). *P* 14×13.

279	**107**	50 m. black & lt. orge.-brn.	25	25

108. Europa "Ship".

(Des. G. and J. Bender.)

1966 (26 SEPT.). *Europa. W* **58.** *P* 13½×14.

280	**108**	20 m. green and blue ..	15	15
281	,,	30 m. brt. purple & blue	25	25
282	,,	150 m. bistre and blue ..	1·10	1·10

109. Stavrovouni Monastery.

110. Church of St. James (Tricomo).

111. Zeno of Citium (marble bust).

113. Silver Coin of Evagoras I.

112. Ancient Ship (painting).

114. Sleeping Eros (marble statue).

115. St. Nicholas' Cathedral, Famagusta.

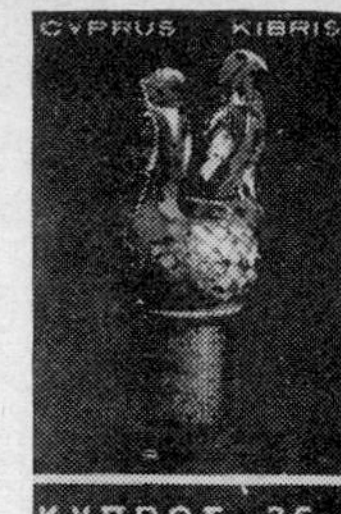

116. Gold Sceptre from Curium.

117. Silver Disc of 7th Century.

119. 7th-Century Jug.

118. Silver Coin of Alexander the Great.

120. Bronze Ingot-stand.

121. "The Rape of Ganymede" (mosaic).

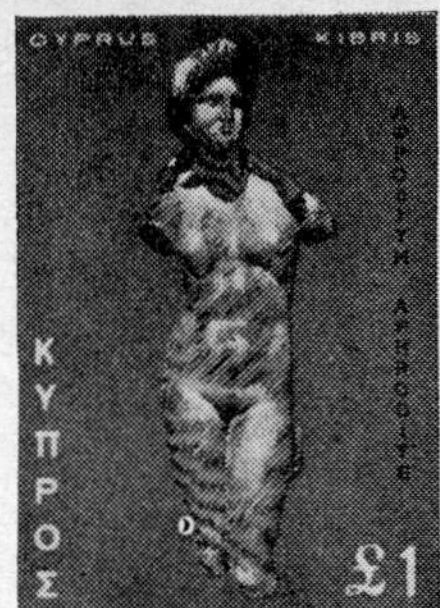

122. Aphrodite (marble statue).

966 (21 Nov.). *W* **58** (*sideways on* 3, 15, 25, 50, 250, 500 *m.*, *£*1). *P* 12×13 (3 *m.*), 13×12 (5, 10 *m.*), 14×13½ (15, 25, 50 *m.*), 13½×14 (20, 30, 35, 40, 100 *m.*) *or* 13×14 (*others*).

83 **109** 3 m. grey-green, buff, black & light blue .. 5 5
84 **110** 5 m. bistre, black and steel-blue (*shades*) 5 5
85 **111** 10 m. black and bistre .. 5 8
86 **112** 15 m. black, chestnut & light orange-brown 8 8
87 **113** 20 m. black, slate & brn. 8 10
88 **114** 25 m. black, drab & lake-brown 12 12
89 **115** 30 m. black, yellow-ochre and turquoise .. 25 12
90 **116** 35 m. yellow, black and carmine-red .. 30 25
91 **117** 40 m. black, grey and new blue .. 30 12
a. Grey background omitted .. ..
92 **118** 50 m. black, slate & brn. 35 20
93 **119** 100 m. black, red, pale buff and grey .. 1·00 40
94 **120** 250 m. olive-green, black and lt. yell.-ochre 1·50 80
95 **121** 500 m. multicoloured 5·00 2·50
96 **122** £1 blk., drab & slate 8·00 8·00
83/96 .. .. *Set of* 14 16·00 11·00

123. Power Station, Limassol.

124. Cogwheels.

967 (10 Apr.). *First Development Programme. T* **123** *and similar designs but horiz. Multi-coloured. W* **58** (*sideways on* 15 *to* 100 *m.*). *P* 13½×14 (10 *m.*) *or* 14×13½ (*others*).

97 10 m. Type **123** 10 10
98 15 m. Arghaka-Maghounda Dam 10 10
99 35 m. Troodos Highway .. 20 20
00 50 m. Hilton Hotel, Nicosia 25 25
01 100 m. Famagusta Harbour .. 45 45
97/301 .. .. *Set of* 5 1·00 1·00

(Des. O. Bonnevalle.)

967 (2 May). *Europa. W* **58**. *P* 13½×14.

02 **124** 20 m. olive-green, green & pale yellow-grn. 12 12
03 „ 30 m. reddish violet, lilac and pale lilac .. 20 20
04 „ 150 m. brn., lt. reddish brn. & p. yell.-brn. 60 60

125. Throwing the Javelin.

126. Running (amphora) and Map of Eastern Mediterranean.

(*Illustration reduced. Actual size* 97×77 *mm.*)

(Des. Aspioti-Elka, Athens.)

1967 (4 Sept.). *Athletic Games, Nicosia. T* **125** *and similar designs and T* **126**. *Multicoloured. W* **58**. *P* 13½×13.

305 15 m. Type **125** 8 8
306 35 m. Running 20 20
307 100 m. High-jumping .. 45 55
MS308 **126** 110×90 mm. 250 m. multicoloured. *W* **58** (sideways). Imperf. .. .. 1·75 1·75

127. Ancient Monuments.

1967 (16 Oct.). *International Tourist Year. T* **127** *and similar horiz. designs. Multicoloured. W* **58**. *P* 13×13½.

309 10 m. Type **127** 8 8
310 40 m. Famagusta Beach .. 20 20
311 50 m. Comet at Nicosia Airport 30 30
312 100 m. Skier and youth hostel 55 55

128. St. Andrew Mosaic.

1967 (8 Nov.). *Centenary of St. Andrew's Monastery. W* **58** (*sideways*). *P* 13×13½.

313 **128** 25 m. multicoloured .. 15 15

129. The Crucifixion.

(Photo. Mint, Paris.)

1967 (8 Nov.). *Cyprus Art Exhibition, Paris. P* 12½×13½.

314 **129** 50 m. multicoloured .. 25 25

130. The Three Magi.

1967 (8 Nov.). *20th Anniv. of U.N.E.S.C.O. W* **58** (*sideways*). *P* 13×13½.

315 **130** 75 m. multicoloured .. 30 35

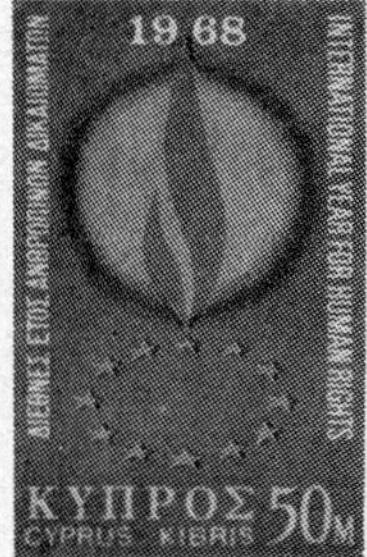

131. Human Rights Emblem over Stars.

132. Human Rights and U.N. Emblems.

HAVE YOU READ THE NOTES AT THE BEGINNING OF THIS CATALOGUE?

These often provide answers to the enquiries we receive

133. Scroll of Declaration.
(*Illustration reduced. Actual size* 95×75½ *mm.*)

1968 (18 Mar.). *Human Rights Year.* *W* **58.** *P* 13×14.
316 **131** 50 m. multicoloured .. 25 25
317 **132** 90 m. multicoloured .. 40 40
MS318 **133** 95×75½ mm. 250 m. mult. *W* **58** (sideways). Imperf. 1·50 1·60

134. Europa " Key ".

(Des. H. Schwarzenbach.)

1968 (29 Apr.). *Europa.* *W* **58** (*sideways*). *P* 14×13.
319 **134** 20 m. multicoloured .. 8 8
320 ,, 30 m. multicoloured .. 20 20
321 ,, 150 m. multicoloured .. 75 75

135. U.N. Children's Fund Symbol and Boy drinking Milk.

(Des. A. Tassos.)

1968 (2 Sept.). *21st Anniv. of U.N.I.C.E.F.* *W* **58** (*sideways*). *P* 14×13.
322 **135** 35 m. yellow-brown, carmine-red and black 20 20

136. Aesculapius. **137.** Throwing the Discus.

(Des. A. Tassos.)

1968 (2 Sept.). *20th Anniv. of W.H.O.* *W* **58.** *P* 13×14.
323 **136** 50 m. blk., grn. & lt. olive 25 25

1968 (24 Oct.). *Olympic Games, Mexico.* *T* **137** *and similar designs. Multicoloured.* *W* **58** (*sideways on* 100 *m.*). *P* 14×13 (100 *m.*) *or* 13×14 (*others*).
324 10 m. Type **137** 12 12
325 25 m. Runners, breasting tape 20 20
326 100 m. Olympic Stadium (*horiz.*) 65 65

138. I.L.O. Emblem.

(Des. Aspioti-Elka.)

1969 (3 Mar.). *50th Anniv. of International Labour Organization.* *W* **58.** *P* 12×13½.
327 **138** 50 m. yellow-brown, blue and light blue .. 20 20
328 ,, 90 m. yellow-brown, black and pale grey .. 45 45

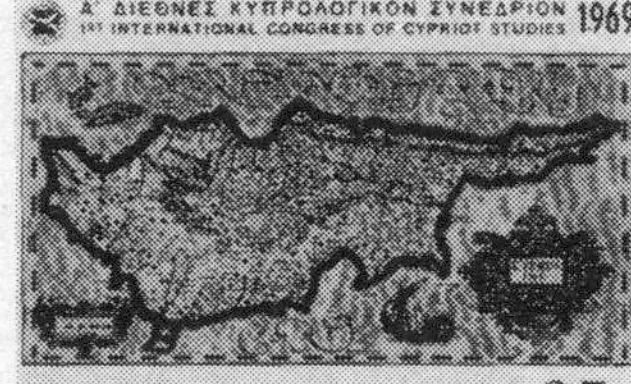

139. Mercator's Map of Cyprus, 1554.

140. Blaeu's Map of Cyprus, 1635.

(Des. Aspioti-Elka.)

1969 (7 Apr.). *First International Congress of Cypriot Studies.* *W* **58** (*sideways*). *P* 14×14½.
329 **139** 35 m. multicoloured .. 25 25
330 **140** 50 m. multicoloured .. 25 25
a. Wmk upright ..

141. Europa Emblem.

(Des. L. Gasbarra and G. Belli.)

1969 (28 Apr.). *Europa.* *W* **58** (*sideways*). *P* 14×13½.
331 **141** 20 m. multicoloured .. 10 10
332 ,, 30 m. multicoloured .. 20 20
333 ,, 150 m. multicoloured .. 65 65

142. Roller.

(Des. Aspioti-Elka.)

1969 (7 July). *Birds of Cyprus.* *T* **142** *a*[cut off] *similar designs. Multicoloured.* *W* **5**[cut off] *P* 13½×12.
334 5 m. Type **142** 8
335 15 m. Audouin's gull .. 10
336 20 m. Cyprus warbler .. 12
337 30 m. Cyprus jay (*vert.*) .. 20
338 40 m. Hoopoe (*vert.*) .. 25
339 90 m. Eleanora's falcon (*vert.*) 80
334/9 .. .. *Set of* 6 1·40 1·
The above were printed on glazed Samu[cut off] Jones paper with very faint watermark.

143. " The Nativity " (12th-century Wall Painting).

144. " The Nativity " (14th-century Wall Painting).

145. " Virgin and Child between Archange[cut off] Michael and Gabriel " (6th–7th-century Mosaic[cut off]
(*Illustration reduced. Actual size* 97×77 *mm.*)

1969 (24 Nov.). *Christmas.* *W* **58.** *P* 13½×1[cut off]
340 **143** 20 m. multicoloured .. 15
341 **144** 45 m. multicoloured .. 40 4
MS342 **145** 110×90 mm. 250 m. multicoloured. Imperf. 2·50 2·5

146. Mahatma Gandhi.

(Des. Aspioti-Elka.)

70 (26 JAN.). *Birth Centenary of Mahatma Gandhi. W* **58** *(sideways). P* 14×13½.

No.	Type	Value	Description	Unused	Used
3	**146**	25 m.	ultramarine, drab and black	12	12
4	„	75 m.	yellow-brown, drab and black	45	45

147. " Flaming Sun ".

(Des. L. le Brocquy.)

70 (4 MAY). *Europa. W* **58** *(sideways). P* 14×13.

No.	Type	Value	Description	Unused	Used
5	**147**	20 m.	brown, greenish yellow and orange	10	10
6	„	30 m.	new blue, greenish yellow and orange	25	25
7	„	150 m.	brt. pur., greenish yellow and orange	65	65

148. Gladioli.

970 (3 AUG.). *European Conservation Year. T* **148** *and similar vert. designs. Multicoloured. W* **58.** *P* 13×13½.

No.	Value	Description	Unused	Used
48	10 m.	Type **148**	5	5
49	50 m.	Poppies	25	25
50	90 m.	Giant fennel	55	55

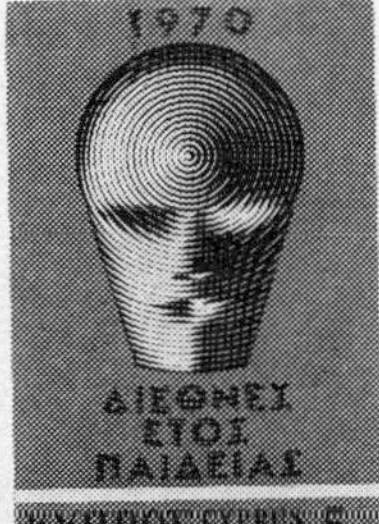

149. I.E.Y. Emblem.

150. Mosaic.

151. Globe, Dove and U.N. Emblem.

1970 (7 SEPT.). *International Events. W* **58.** *P* 13×14 *(5 m.), or* 14×13 *(others).*

No.	Type	Value	Description	Unused	Used
351	**149**	5 m.	black, red-brown & light yellow-brown	5	5
352	**150**	15 m.	multicoloured	8	8
353	**151**	75 m.	multicoloured ..	35	35

Events:—5 m. International Education Year; 15 m. 50th General Assembly of International Vine and Wine Office; 75 m. 25th Anniv. of United Nations.

152. Virgin and Child. **153.** Cotton Napkin.

(Des. from Wall Painting in 16th-cent. Church. Photo. Harrison.)

1970 (23 NOV.). *Christmas. T* **152** *and similar multicoloured designs. P* 14×14½.

No.	Value	Description	Unused	Used
354	25 m.	Archangel (facing right)	12	12
355	25 m.	Type **152**	12	12
356	25 m.	Archangel (facing left)	12	12
357	75 m.	Virgin and Child between Archangels ..	45	45
354/6		.. .. *Strip of* 3	60	60

The 75 m. is horiz., size 42×30 mm., and the 25 m. values are vert., size as T **152.**

Nos. 354/6 were issued in *se-tenant* strips of three, throughout the sheet. The triptych thus formed is depicted in its entirety on the 75 m. value.

1971 (22 FEB.). *T* **153** *and similar multicoloured designs. W* **58** *(sideways on horiz. designs).*

(*a*) *Size* 23×33 *mm. Vert. P* 12×13½.

No.	Value	Description	Unused	Used
358	3 m.	Type **153**	5	5
359	5 m.	St. George and Dragon (19th-cent. bas-relief)	5	5

(*b*) *Size* 24×37 *mm. Horiz., P* 14×13 *(15, 30, 90 m.). Vert., P* 13×14 *(others).*

No.	Value	Description	Unused	Used
360	10 m.	Woman in festival costume	5	5
361	15 m.	Archaic Bychrome Kylix (cup) (*shades*) ..	5	5
362	20 m.	A pair of donors (St. Mamas Church) ..	8	5
363	25 m.	" The Creation " (6th-cent. mosaic)	8	10
364	30 m.	Athena and horse-drawn chariot (5th-cent. B.C. terracotta) ..	8	5
365	40 m.	Shepherd playing pipe (14th-cent. fresco) ..	12	15
366	50 m.	Hellenistic bust (3rd cent. B.C.)	15	20
367	75 m.	Detail of Apse mosaic	25	25
368	90 m.	Mycenaean silver bowl	30	30

(*c*) *Size* 28×41 *mm. Horiz., P* 13½×13 *(250, 500 m.). Vert., P* 13×13½ *(£1).*

No.	Value	Description	Unused	Used
369	250 m.	Moufflon (detail of 3rd-cent. mosaic) (*shades*)	75	80
370	500 m.	Ladies and sacred tree (detail, 6th-cent. amphora)	1·40	1·60
371	£1	Horned god from Enkomi (12th-cent. bronze statue) ..	2·75	3·00
358/71		.. .. *Set of* 14	5·50	6·00

154. Europa Chain.

(Des. H. Haflidason.)

1971 (3 MAY). *Europa. W* **58** *(sideways). P* 14×13.

No.	Type	Value	Description	Unused	Used
372	**154**	20 m.	pale blue, ultram., and black ..	12	12
373	„	30 m.	apple grn., myrtle-green and black ..	20	20
374	„	150 m.	lemon, bright green and black ..	65	65

The above were printed on glazed paper with very faint watermark.

155. Archbishop Kyprianos.

1971 (9 JULY). *150th Anniv. of Greek War of Independence. T* **155** *and similar multi-coloured designs. W* **58** *(sideways on 30 m.). P* 13½×12½ *(30 m.) or* 12½×13½ *(others).*

No.	Value	Description	Unused	Used
375	15 m.	Type **155**	8	8
376	30 m.	" Taking the Oath " ..	20	20
377	100 m.	Bishop Paleon Patron Germanos, flag and freedom-fighters ..	50	50

The 30 m. is a horizontal design.

156. Harbour Castle.

1971 (20 Sept.). *Tourism. T* **156** *and similar multicoloured designs. W* **58** (*sideways on* 15 *and* 100 *m.*). *P* 13½×13 (15 *m.*, 100 *m.*) *or* 13×13½ (*others*).

378 15 m. Type **156** 8 8
379 25 m. Gourd on sunny beach 10 10
380 60 m. Mountain scenery .. 35 35
381 100 m. Church and blue sky .. 50 50

The 25 and 60 m. are vert. designs.

157. Madonna and Child in Stable.

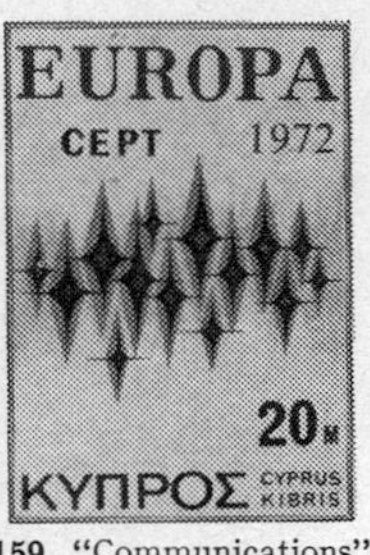

159. "Communications".

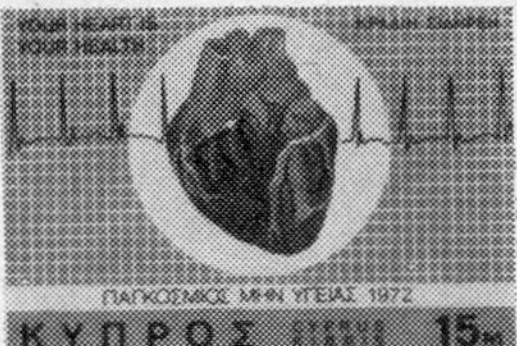

158. Heart.

(Des. A. Tassos.)

1971 (22 Nov.). *Christmas. T* **157** *and similar vert. designs. Multicoloured. W* **58.** *P* 13×14.

382 10 m. Type **157** 8 8
383 50 m. The Three Wise Men .. 25 25
384 100 m. The Shepherds .. 50 50
Strip of three 90 90

The 50, 10 and 100 m. (in that order) were printed horizontally *se-tenant* within each sheet.

1972 (11 Apr.). *World Health Month. W* **58.** *P* 13½×12.

385 **158** 15 m. multicoloured .. 8 8
386 ,, 50 m. multicoloured .. 25 25

(Des. P. Huovinen.)

1972 (22 May). *Europa. W* **58.** *P* 12½×13½.

387 **159** 20 m. yellow-orange, sepia & pale grey-brown 5 5
388 ,, 30 m. yellow-orange, brt. deep ultram. & cobalt 10 10
389 ,, 150 m. yellow-orange, myrtle-grn. & pale turquoise-green .. 55 55

160. Archery.

1972 (24 July). *Olympic Games. T* **160** *and similar horiz. designs. Multicoloured. W* **58** (*sideways*). *P* 14×13.

390 10 m. Type **160** 5 5
391 40 m. Wrestling 15 15
392 100 m. Football 45 45

161. Stater of Marion.

1972 (25 Sept.). *Ancient Coins of Cyprus. T* **161** *and similar horiz. designs. P* 14×13.

393 20 m. pale turquoise-blue, black & silver .. 5 5
394 30 m. pale violet-blue, black & silver 15 15
395 40 m. brownish stone, black & silver 20 20
396 100 m. light salmon-pink, black & silver 60 60

Coins:—30 m. Stater of Paphos; 40 m. Stater of Lapithos; 100 m. Stater of Idalion.

162. Bathing the Child Jesus.

(Des. A. Tassos.)

1972 (20 Nov.). *Christmas. T* **162** *and similar vert. designs showing portions of a mural in the Church of the Holy Cross of Agiasmati. Multicoloured. W* **58** (*sideways on* **MS**400). *P* 13×14.

397 10 m. Type **162** 5 5
398 20 m. The Magi 8 8
399 100 m. The Nativity .. 45 45
MS400 110×90 mm. 250 m. Showing the mural in full. Imperf. .. .. 1·50 1·50

163. Snow-covered Landscape.

1973 (13 Mar.). *29th International Ski Federation Congress. T* **163** *and similar horiz. design. Multicoloured. W* **58** (*sideways*). *P* 14×13.

401 20 m. Type **163** 5 5
402 100 m. Congress emblem .. 45 45

164. Europa "Posthorn".

(Des. L. F. Anisdahl.)

1973 (7 May). *Europa. W* **58** (*sideway*
P 14×13.

403 **164** 20 m. multicoloured .. 5
404 ,, 30 m. multicoloured .. 8
405 ,, 150 m. multicoloured .. 55

165. Archbishopric Palace, Nicosia.

1973 (23 July). *Traditional Architecture. T* 1
and similar multicoloured designs. W **58** (*si*
ways on 20 *and* 100 *m.*). *P* 14×13 (20 *a*
100 *m.*) *or* 14×13 (*others*).

406 20 m. Type **165** 5
407 30 m. Konak of Hajigeorgajis Cornessios, Nicosia (*vert.*) 10
408 50 m. House at Gourri, 1850 (*vert.*) 20
409 100 m. House at Rizokarpaso, 1772 45

20M

(166)

167. Scout Emblem.

1973 (24 Sept.). *No.* 361 *surch. with T* **166.**
410 20 m. on 15 m. mult. (*shades*) 12

1973 (24 Sept.). *Anniversaries. T* **167** *a*
similar designs. W **58** (*sideways on* 25 *a*
35 *m.*). *P* 13×14 (10, 50 *and* 100 *m.*)
14×13 (*others*).

411 10 m. yell.-olive & dp. brn... 8
412 25 m. deep blue, and slate-lilac 10
413 35 m. light brown-olive, stone and sage-green .. 12
414 50 m. dull blue and indigo .. 20
415 100 m. brown and sepia .. 50
411/15 .. .. *Set of* 5 80

Designs and Events: *Vert.*—10 m. Type 1
(60th Anniv. of Cyprus Boy Scouts); 50 m. Airli
emblem (25th Anniv. of Cyprus Airways); 100
Interpol emblem (50th Anniv. of Interpo
Horiz.—25 m. Outline of Cyprus and E.E
nations (Association of Cyprus with the E.E.C
35 m. F.A.O. emblem (Tenth Anniv. of F.A.O.

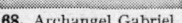

168. Archangel Gabriel.

169. Grapes.

973 (26 Nov.). *Christmas.* *T* **168** *and similar multicoloured designs.* *W* **58** *(sideways on* 100 *m.).* *P* 14 × 13 (100 *m.*) *or* 13 × 14 (*others*).
16 10 m. Type **168** 5 5
17 20 m. Madonna and Child .. 5 5
18 100 m. Arakas Church (*horiz.*) 45 45

974 (18 Mar.). *Products of Cyprus.* *T* **169** *and similar vert. designs. Multicoloured.* *W* **58.** *P* 13 × 14.
19 25 m. Type **169** 8 10
20 50 m. Grapefruit 25 25
21 50 m. Oranges 25 25
22 50 m. Lemons 25 25

Nos. 420/2 were printed together, horizontally *e-tenant* throughout the sheet.

170. " The Rape of Europa " (Silver Stater of Marion).

171. Title Page of A. Kyprianos' " History of Cyprus " (1788).

974 (29 Apr.). *Europa.* *W* **58.** *P* 13½ × 14.
23 **170** 10 m. multicoloured .. 5 5
24 „ 40 m. multicoloured .. 15 15
25 „ 150 m. multicoloured .. 40 45

974 (22 July*). *Second International Congress of Cypriot Studies.* *T* **171** *and similar multicoloured designs.* *W* **58** *(sideways on* 25 *m. and* **MS**429). *P* 14 × 13½ (25 *m.*) *or* 13½ × 14 (*others*).
26 10 m. Type **171** 5 5
27 25 m. Solon (philosopher) in mosaic (*horiz.*) .. 10 10
28 100 m. " St. Neophytos " (wall painting) 35 35
MS429 111 × 90 mm. 250 m. Ortelius' map of Cyprus and Greek Islands, 1584. Imperf... 1·00 1·00

*Although this is the date appearing on first ay covers, it is reported that the stamps were not ut on sale until the 24th.

REFUGEE FUND
ΤΑΜΕΙΟΝ ΠΡΟΣΦΥΓΩΝ
GÖÇMENLER FONU
10M
—
(172)

SECURITY COUNCIL RESOLUTION 353
20 JULY 1974
(173)

974 (1 Oct.). *Obligatory Tax. Refugee Fund. No.* 359 *surch. with* *T* **172.**
30 10 m. on 5 m. St. George and Dragon 8 8

974 (14 Oct.). *U.N. Security Council Resolution* 353. *Nos.* 360, 365, 366 *and* 369 *optd. as* *T* **173.**
31 10 m. Woman in festival costume 5 5
32 40 m. Shepherd playing pipe 12 10
33 50 m. Hellenistic bust .. 12 15
34 250 m. Moufflon (*shades*) .. 70 75

174. " Refugees ".

1974 (2 Dec.). *Obligatory Tax. Refugee Fund.* *W* **58** (*sideways*). *P* 12 × 12½.
435 **174** 10 m. black and light grey 8 8

175. " Virgin and Child between Two Angels ".

1974 (2 Dec.). *Christmas.* *T* **175** *and similar multicoloured designs showing wall-paintings.* *W* **58** (*sideways on* 10 *m. and* 100 *m.*). *P* 13 × 14 (50 *m.*) *or* 14 × 13 (*others*).
436 10 m. Type **175** 5 5
437 50 m. " Adoration of the Magi " (*vert.*) 15 15
438 100 m. " Flight into Egypt " 25 30

176. First Cyprus Mail-coach.

(Des. and photo. Harrison.)

1975 (17 Feb.). *International Events.* *T* **176** *and similar designs. No wmk.* *P* 14.
439 **176** 20 m. multicoloured .. 5 5
440 – 30 m. ultramarine, slate black and dull orge. 8 8
441 **176** 50 m. multicoloured .. 15 15
442 – 100 m. multicoloured .. 30 30

Designs and Events:—20 m., 50 m. Centenary of Universal Postal Union. Vert.—30 m. " Disabled Persons " (Eighth European Meeting of International Society for the Rehabilitation of Disabled Persons); 100 m. Council flag (25th Anniv. of Council of Europe).

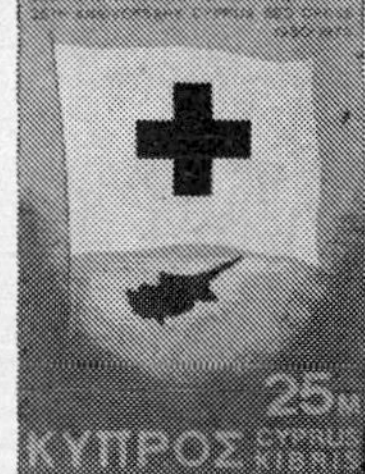

177. " The Distaff " (M. Kashalos).

178. Red Cross Flag over Map.

(Des. and photo. Harrison.)

1975 (28 Apr.). *Europa.* *T* **177** *and similar vert. designs. Multicoloured.* *P* 13½ × 14½.
443 20 m. Type **177** 5 5
444 30 m. " Nature Morte " (C. Savva) 8 8
445 150 m. " Virgin and Child of Liopetri " (G. P. Georghiou) 45 50

Nos. 443/5 were printed horizontally *se-tenant* throughout the sheet.

(Des. and litho. Aspioti-Elka.)

1975 (4 Aug.). *International Events.* *T* **178** *and similar horiz. designs.* *P* 12½ × 13½ (25 *m.*) *or* 13½ × 12½ (*others*).
446 25 m. multicoloured 5 5
447 30 m. turquoise-green and greenish blue 8 8
448 75 m. red-brown, orange-brown and pale blue grey .. 20 25

Designs and events: *Vert.*—25 m. Type **178** (25th Anniversary of Cyprus Red Cross). *Horiz.* 30 m. Nurse and lamp (International Nurses' Day); 75 m. Woman's Steatite Idol (International Women's Year).

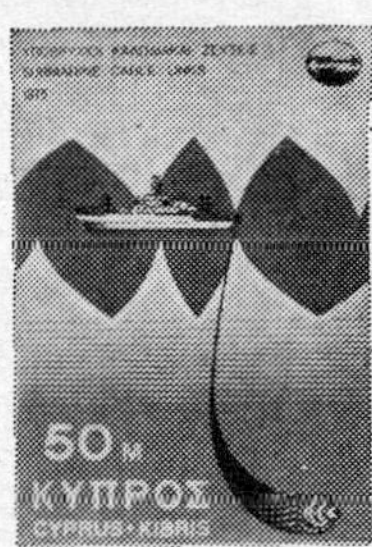

179. Submarine Cable Links.

(180)

1975 (13 Oct.). *Telecommunications Achievements.* *T* **179** *and similar design.* *W* **58** (*sideways on* 100 *m.*). *P* 12 × 13½ (50 *m.*) *or* 13½ × 12 (100 *m.*).
449 50 m. multicoloured.. .. 15 20
450 100 m. orange-yellow, dull violet and lilac .. 30 35

Design: *Horiz.*—100 m. International subscriber dialling.

1976 (5 Jan.). *No.* 358 *surch. with* *T* **180.**
451 10 m. on 3 m. Cotton napkin.. 5 5

181. Human-figured Vessel, 19th-Century.

1976 (3 May). *Europa.* *T* **181** *and similar vert. designs. Multicoloured.* *W* **58.** *P* 13 × 14.
452 20 m. Type **181** 5 5
453 60 m. Composite vessel, 2100–2000 B.C. .. 15 20
454 100 m. Byzantine goblet .. 30 35

182. Self-help Housing.

1976 (3 May). *Economic Reactivication.* *T* **182** *and similar horiz. designs. Multicoloured. W* **58** *(sideways). P* 14 × 13.

455 10 m. Type **182** 5 5
456 25 m. Handicrafts 8 8
457 30 m. Reafforestation .. 8 10
458 60 m. Air Communications .. 15 20

183. Terracotta Statue. **184.** Olympic Symbol.

(Des. A. Tassos.)

1976 (7 June). *Cypriot Treasures. T* **183** *and similar designs. W* **58** *(sideways on horiz. designs, upright on vert. designs). P* 12 × 13½ (5, 10 *m.*), 13 × 14 (20, 25, 30 *m.*), 14 × 13 (40, 50, 60 *m.*), 13½ × 12 (100 *m.*) *or* 13 × 13½ (250 *m. to* £1).

459 5 m. multicoloured 5 5
460 10 m. multicoloured 5 5
461 20 m. red, yellow and black .. 5 5
462 25 m. multicoloured 5 8
463 30 m. multicoloured 8 8
464 40 m. grey-green, light olive-bistre and black 10 10
465 50 m. buff, brown and black 12 12
466 60 m. multicoloured 15 20
467 100 m. multicoloured 25 30
468 250 m. deep dull blue, grey and black 60 65
469 500 m. black, stone and deep blue-green .. .. 1·25 1·40
470 £1 multicoloured .. .. 2·50 2·75
459/70 .. .. *Set of* 12 4·75 5·00

Sizes:—23 × 34 *mm.*, 5 m., 10 m.; 34 × 23 *mm.*, 100 m.; 24 × 37 *mm.*, 20, 25, 30 m.; 37 × 24 *mm.*, 40, 50, 60 m.; 28 × 41 *mm.*, others.

Designs:—10 m. Limestone head; 20 m. Gold necklace; 25 m. Terracotta warrior; 30 m. Statue of a priest; 40 m. Bronze tablet; 50 m. Mycenaean crater; 60 m. Limestone sarcophagus; 100 m. Gold bracelet; 250 m. Silver dish; 500 m. Bronze stand; £1 Statue of Artemis.

(Litho. Harrison.)

1976 (5 July). *Olympic Games, Montreal. T* **184** *and similar designs. P* 14.

471 20 m. carm.-red, blk. & yell. 5 5
472 60 m. multicoloured 15 15
473 100 m. multicoloured 25 30

Designs: *Horiz.*—60, 100 m. Olympic symbols (*different*).

185. George Washington.

1976 (5 July). *Bicentenary of American Revolution. W* **58.** *P* 13 × 13½.

474 **185** 100 m. multicoloured .. 25 30

186. Children in Library.

1976 (27 Sept.). *International Events. T* **186** *and similar vert. designs. W* **58.** *P* 13½ × 12½ (50 *m.*) *or* 13½ (*others*).

475 40 m. multicoloured 12 12
476 50 m. yellow-brown and black 15 20
477 80 m. multicoloured 20 25

Designs and Events:—40 m. Type **186** (Promotion of Children's Books); 50 m. Low-cost housing (HABITAT Conference, Vancouver); 80 m. Eye protected by hands (World Health Day).

187. Archangel Michael.

(Litho. Harrison.)

1976 (15 Nov.). *Christmas. T* **187** *and similar vert. designs, showing icons from Ayios Neophytis Monastery. Multicoloured. P* 12½.

478 10 m. Type **187** 5 5
479 15 m. Archangel Gabriel .. 5 5
480 150 m. The Nativity 45 50

TURKISH CYPRIOT POSTS.

After the inter-communal clashes durin December, 1963, a separate postal service wa established on 6th January 1964 between som of the Turkish Cypriot areas, using handstamp inscribed "KIBRIS TURK POSTALARI". Durin 1964, however, an agreement was reache between representatives of the two communitie for the restoration of postal services. Th agreement, to which the United Nations repre sentatives were a party, was ratified in Novembe 1966 by the Republic's Council of Ministers Under the scheme postal services were provide for the Turkish Cypriot communities in Fama gusta, Limassol, Lefka and Nicosia, staffed b Turkish Cypriot employees of the Cypriot De partment of Posts.

On 8 April 1970 5 m. and 15 m. locally-produce labels, originally designated "Social Ai Stamps", were issued by the Turkish Cyprio community and these can be found on commercia covers. These local stamps are outside the scop of this catalogue.

On 29 October 1973 Nos. 1/7 were placed o sale, but were used only on mail between th Turkish Cypriot areas.

Following the intervention by the Republic o Turkey in July 1974 these stamps replaced issue of the Republic of Cyprus in that part of th island, north and east of the Attila Line, con trolled by the Autonomous Turkish Cypric Administration.

KIBRIS
TÜRK
FEDERE
DEVLETI
13.2.1975

30M

1. 50th Anniversary Emblem. (**2**)

(Des. F. Direkoglu, Miss E. Ata, G. Pir. Litho.

1974 (27 July*). *50th Anniv. of Republic o Turkey. T* **1** *and similar designs. P* 12 × 11 (*vert.*) *or* 11½ × 12 (*horiz.*).

1 3 m. multicoloured .. ..
2 5 m. multicoloured .. ..
3 10 m. multicoloured .. ..
4 15 m. vermilion and black ..
5 20 m. multicoloured .. ..
6 50 m. multicoloured .. ..
7 70 m. multicoloured .. ..
1/7 .. .. *Set of* 7 45·00 45·0

Designs: *Vert.*—3 m. Woman sentry; 10 m. Ma and woman with Turkish flags; 20 m. Atatür statue, Kyrenia Gate, Nicosia; 50 m. "Th Fallen". *Horiz.*—5 m. Military parade, Nico sia; 70 m. Turkish flag and map of Cyprus.

*This is the date on which Nos. 1/7 becam valid for international mail.

On 13 February 1975 a Turkish Cypriot Feder ated State was proclaimed in that part of Cypru under Turkish occupation and later 9,000 Turk ish Cypriots were transferred from the South t the North of the island.

1975 (3 Mar.). *Proclamation of the Turkis Federated State of Cyprus. Nos.* 3 *and* 5 *surch as T* **2.**

8 30 m. on 20 m. multicoloured .. 1·40 1·6
9 100 m. on 10 m. multicoloured .. 5·00 5·5

On No. 9 the surcharge appears at the top c the stamp and the inscription at the bottom.

3. Namik Kemal's Bust, Famagusta.

(Des. Işil Özişik. Litho. Güzel Sanatlar Matbaasi, Ankara.)

1975 (21 Apr.). *T* **3** *and similar multicoloured designs. Imprint at foot with date "1975". P* 13.

10 3 m. Type **3** 5 5
11 10 m. Atatürk Statue, Nicosia 5 5
12 15 m. St. Hilarion Castle .. 5 8
13 20 m. Atatürk Square, Nicosia 10 12
14 25 m. Famagusta Beach .. 10 12
15 30 m. Kyrenia Harbour .. 15 20
16 50 m. Lala Mustafa Pasha Mosque, Famagusta (*vert.*) 20 25
17 100 m. Interior, Kyrenia Castle 35 40
18 250 m. Castle walls, Kyrenia .. 85 95
19 500 m. Othello Tower, Famagusta (*vert.*) .. .. 1·75 2·00
10/19 .. .. *Set of* 10 3·25 3·50

See also Nos. 37 etc.

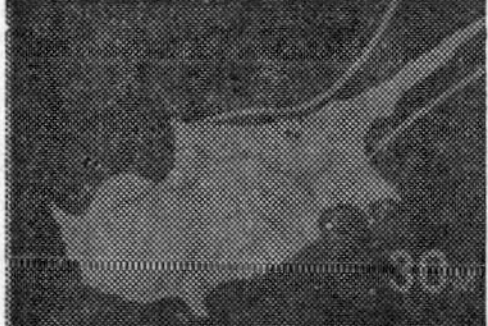

4. Map of Cyprus.

(Des. B. Erkmen (30 m.), S. Tuga (50 m.), N. Güneş (150 m.). Litho. Ajans-Türk Matbaacilik Sanayii, Ankara.)

1975 (20 July). *"Peace in Cyprus". T* **4** *and similar multicoloured designs. P* 13.

20 30 m. Type **4** 8 8
21 50 m. Map, laurel and broken chain 12 15
22 150 m. Map and laurel-sprig on globe (*vert.*) 40 45

5. "Pomegranates" (I. V. Guney).

(Litho. Guzel Sanatlar Matbaasi, Ankara.)

1975 (29 Dec.). *Europa. Paintings. T* **5** *and similar horiz. design. Multicoloured. P* 13.

23 90 m. Type **5** 20 20
24 100 m. "Harvest Time" (F. Direkoglu) 25 25

10 M ——

(**6**)

7. "Expectation".

1976 (28 Apr.). *Nos.* 16/17 *surch. as T* **6** *at Govt. Printing House, Nicosia.*

25 10 m. on 50 m. multicoloured 1·25 1·25
26 30 m. on 100 m. multicoloured 3·75 3·75

(Litho. Ajans-Türk Matbaacilik Sanayii, Ankara.)

1976 (3 May). *Europa. T* **7** *and similar vert. design showing ceramic statuette. Multicoloured. P* 13.

27 60 m. Type **7** 15 20
28 120 m. "Man in Meditation" 35 40

8. Carob.

(Des. Sadettin Atlihan. Litho. Güzel Sanatlar Matbaasi, Ankara.)

1976 (28 June). *Export Products—Fruits. T* **8** *and similar horiz. designs. Multicoloured. P* 13.

29 10 m. Type **8** 8 10
30 25 m. Mandarin 15 20
31 40 m. Strawberry 20 25
32 60 m. Orange 30 35
33 80 m. Lemon 40 45
29/33 .. .. *Set of* 5 1·10 1·25

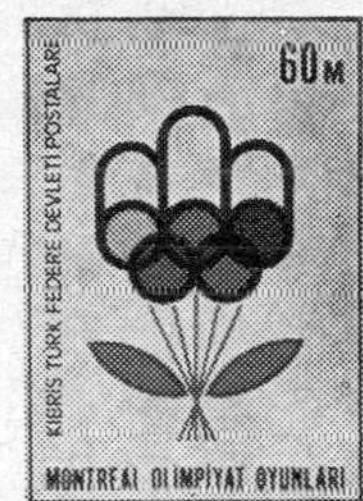

9. Olympic Symbol "Flower".

(Des. C. Mutver (60 m.), A. B. Kocamanoglu (100 m.). Litho. Güzel Sanatlar Matbaasi, Ankara.)

1976 (17 July). *Olympic Games, Montreal. T* **9** *and similar horiz. design. Multicoloured. P* 13.

34 60 m. Type **9** 15 20
35 100 m. Olympic symbol and doves 25 25

10. Kyrenia Harbour.

(Des. Işil Özişik. Litho. Ajans-Türk Matbaacilik Sanayii, Ankara.)

1976 (2 Aug.). *New design* (5 *m.*) *and Nos.* 12/13 *redrawn with lettering altered. New imprint at foot with date "1976".*

37 5 m. Type **10** 5 5
39 15 m. St. Hilarion Castle .. 5 5
40 20 m. Ataturk Square, Nicosia 5 5

Nos. 36/46 have been provisionally reserved for any further additions to this issue.

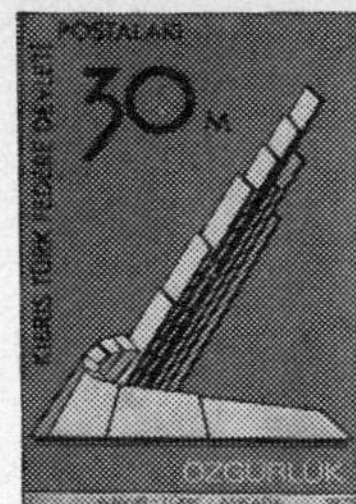

11. Liberation Monument, Nicosia.

(Des. Dincer Erimez and Cahit Gizer. Litho. Ajans-Türk Matbaacilik Sanayii, Ankara.)

1976 (1 Nov.). *Liberation Monument. T* **11** *and similar vert. design. P* 13.

47 **11** 30 m. light turquoise-blue, light flesh and black 8 10
48 – 150 m. light vermilion, lt. flesh and black .. 30 35

No. 48 shows a different view of the Monument.

DOMINICA.

For GREAT BRITAIN stamps used in Dominica with "A 07" obliteration, see Index to Great Britain Stamps Used Abroad list.

CROWN COLONY.

1 (2) (3) (4)

(Typo. D.L.R.)

1874 (4 MAY). *Wmk. Crown CC. P* 12½.
1 **1** 1d. lilac .. .. .. 85·00 18·00
2 ,, 6d. green .. .. .. £120 35·00
3 ,, 1s. dull magenta .. .. £120 28·00

1877–79. *Wmk. Crown CC. P* 14.
4 **1** ½d. olive-yellow (1879) .. .. 5·00 7·50
5 ,, 1d. lilac .. .. .. 2·75 2·00
a. Bisected vert. or diag. (½d.), (on cover or card) .. — £450
6 ,, 2½d. red-brown (1879) .. 48·00 11·00
7 ,, 4d. blue (1879) .. .. 35·00 4·50
a. Malformed "CE" in "PENCE" £900 £110
8 ,, 6d. green .. .. .. 50·00 11·00
9 ,, 1s. magenta .. .. 42·00 19·00

1882 (25 NOV.)–**83.** *No.* 5 *bisected and surch.*
10 **2** ½(d.), in *black*, on half 1d. .. 42·00 17·00
a. Surch. inverted £275 £225
b. Surcharges tête-bêche (pair) £450
11 **3** ½(d.), in *red* on half 1d. .. 13·00 13·00
a. Surch. inverted £250 £120
c. Surch. double £600
14 **4** ½d. in *black*, on half 1d. (3.83) 15·00 17·00
a. Unsevered pair .. .. 45·00 50·00
b. Surch. double £225

Type **4** is found reading up or down.

1883–84. *Wmk. Crown CA. P* 14.
15 **1** ½d. olive-yellow .. .. 2·00 3·75
16 ,, 2½d. red-brown (1884) .. 35·00 6·00

Half Penny (5)   One Penny (6)

1886 (MAR.). *Nos.* 8 *and* 9 *surch.*
17 **5** ½d. on 6d. green .. .. 4·50 6·50
18 **6** 1d. on 6d. green £6000 £5000
a. Thick bar (approx. 1 mm.) .. — £6000
19 ,, 1d. on 1s. magenta .. .. 6·00 7·50
a. Surch. double .. .. — £1100

There are variations in the spacing of the letters of "One Penny" in the surcharge of No. 19.

1886–88. *Wmk. Crown CA. P* 14.
20 **1** ½d. dull green .. .. 60 2·50
21 ,, 1d. lilac .. .. 5·50 6·00
a. Bisected (½d.) (on cover) .. — £500
22 ,, 1d. rose ('87) .. .. 3·00 3·50
a. Deep carmine .. .. 1·00 1·75
b. Bisected (½d.) (on cover) .. — £500
23 ,, 2½d. ultramarine ('88) .. 2·75 2·25
24 ,, 4d. grey .. .. 2·00 2·00
a. Malformed "CE" in "PENCE" .. .. 42·00 55·00
25 ,, 6d. orange ('88) .. .. 7·00 9·50
26 ,, 1s. dull magenta ('88) .. 70·00 80·00
20/26 .. .. *Set of* 7 80·00 95·00
20, 22/25 Optd. "Specimen" *Set of* 5 75·00

The stamps of Dominica were superseded by the general issue for "Leeward Islands" on 31st October, 1890, but the sets following were in concurrent use with the stamps inscribed "LEEWARD ISLANDS" until 31st December, 1939, when the island came under the administration of the Windward Is.

WATERMARKS. Nos. 27/91 all have the watermark *sideways* except Nos. 36, 46, and 54.

9. View of Roseau from the Sea (from photo by Sir Hesketh Bell).

10

(T **9** to **11** typo. D.L.R.)

1903. *T* **9** *and* **10** (5*s*.). *Wmk. Crown CC. P* 14.
27 ½d. green and grey-green, OC 1·40 1·60
28 1d. grey and red, OC .. 1·40 85
29 2d. green and brown, OC .. 6·00 6·00
30 2½d. grey and bright blue, OC 7·00 5·50
31 3d. dull pur. & grey-blk., OC 7·50 7·50
32 6d. grey and chestnut, O .. 9·00 9·00
33 1s. magenta & grey-green, OC 13·00 14·00
34 2s. grey-black and purple, O 14·00 15·00
35 2s. 6d. grey-green & maize, O 15·00 17·00
36 5s. black and brown, O .. 65·00 75·00
27/36 .. .. *Set of* 10 £130 £140
27/36 Optd. "Specimen" *Set of* 10 85·00

1907–8. *T* **9** *and* **10** (5*s*.). *Wmk. Multiple Crown CA. P* 14.
37 ½d. green, OC .. .. 1·00 80
38 1d. grey and red, C 90 45
39 2d. green and brown, C .. 4·00 5·50
40 2½d. grey and bright blue, C .. 7·00 8·00
41 3d. dull pur. & grey-black, C 7·00 8·00
42 6d. black & chestnut, C ('08) 27·00 30·00
43 1s. magenta & grey-green, C 10·00 12·00
44 2s. grey-black & pur., C ('08) 17·00 19·00
45 2s. 6d. grey-green and maize, C ('08) .. .. 19·00 22·00
46 5s. black and brown, C ('08) 32·00 35·00
37/46 .. .. *Set of* 10 £110 £130

11

1908–21. *T* **9** *and* **11** (5*s*.). *Wmk. Mult. Crown CA. P* 14.
47 **9** ½d. blue-green, O .. .. 80 1·10
a. Deep green, O (1918) .. 1·00 1·10
48 ,, 1d. carmine-red, O .. .. 1·00 65
a. Scarlet, O 80 80
49 ,, 2d. grey, O ('09) .. .. 2·75 3·25
a. Slate, O .. .. .. 3·25 4·50
50 **9** 2½d. blue, O .. .. 2·75 4·5
a. Bright blue, O .. .. 2·50 3·7
51 ,, 3d. purple/*yellow*, OC ('09) 2·50 3·7
a. On pale yellow .. .. 4·75 6·0
52 ,, 6d. dull & brt. pur., C ('09) 7·00 8·0
a. Dull purple, O .. .. 3·25 4·7
53 ,, 1s. black/*green*, OC ('10) 4·50 5·0
53*a* ,, 2s. purple and deep blue/*blue*, C (1919) .. 9·50 14·0
53*b* ,, 2s. 6d. blk. & red/*blue*, C ('21) .. .. .. 15·00 18·0
54 **11** 5s. red & green/*yellow*, C ('14) .. .. .. 23·00 27·0
47/54 .. .. *Set of* 10 60·00 75·0
47/54 Optd. "Specimen" *Set of* 10 85·00
53 Optd. "Specimen" in black instead of red .. .. .. 20·00

WAR TAX

ONE HALFPENNY
(12)

1916. *No.* 47 *surch. with T* **12.**
55 **9** ½d. on ½d. blue-green (R.) 15 6
a. Small "O" in "ONE" .. 3·50 5·5

1918 (18 MAR.). *No.* 47 *optd. locally with T* **1**
but with "ONE HALFPENNY" *blanked out.*
56 **9** ½d. blue-green (Bk.) .. 40 1·7

The blanking out of the surcharge was not com pletely successful so that it almost always appear as an albino to a greater or lesser extent.

WAR TAX (14)   WAR TAX ═1½D.═ (15)

1918 (JUNE). *Nos.* 47 *and* 51 *optd. in Londo with T* **14.**
57 **9** ½d. blue-green 8 4
58 ,, 3d. purple/*yellow* (R.) .. 12 1·1

1919. *Special printing of T* **9**, *surch. with T* **15**
59 **9** 1½d. on 2½d. orange (R.) .. 8 8

1920. *As No.* 59, *but without* "WAR TAX".
60 **9** 1½d. on 2½d. orange (Bk.) 90 2·2
55/60 Optd. "Specimen" *Set of* 6 70·00

1921. *Wmk. Mult. Script CA. P* 14.
62 **9** ½d. blue-green .. .. 80 2·2
63 ,, 1d. carmine-red .. .. 80 1·1
64 ,, 1½d. orange .. .. .. 2·00 3·0
65 ,, 2d. grey .. .. .. 4·00 4·0
66 ,, 2½d. bright blue .. .. 1·00 4·0
67 ,, 6d. purple, C .. .. 4·50 6·5
69 ,, 2s. purple and blue/*blue* .. 19·00 22·0
70 ,, 2s. 6d. black and red/*blue* 25·00 27·0
62/70 .. .. *Set of* 8 50·00 65·0
62/70 Optd. "Specimen" *Set of* 8 65·00

The 1½d. has figures of value, in the lowe corners, and no ornamentation below word of value.

16

(Typo. D.L.R.)

1923 (FEB.)–**33.** *Chalk-surfaced paper. P* 14.
(*a*) *Wmk. Mult. Script CA.*
71 **16** ½d. black and green .. 25 35
72 ,, 1d. black and bright violet 50 90
73 ,, 1d. black and scarlet ('33) 1·00 1·10
74 ,, 1½d. black and scarlet .. 65 65
75 ,, 1½d. black & red-brown ('33) 1·60 1·25
76 ,, 2d. black and grey .. 65 90
77 ,, 2½d. black & orange-yellow 1·00 1·75
78 ,, 2½d. black & ultram. ('27) 1·25 1·75
79 ,, 3d. black and ultramarine 1·25 1·75
80 ,, 3d. black & red/*yellow* ('27) 80 1·10
81 ,, 4d. black and brown .. 80 2·00
82 ,, 6d. black & bright magenta 1·50 3·00

No.	Type	Description	Unused	Used
83	**16**	1s. black/*emerald*	1·75	3·00
84	,,	2s. black and blue/*blue*	3·75	6·00
85	,,	2s. 6d. black and red/*blue*	7·00	9·50
86	,,	3s. blk. & pur./*yell.* (1927)	6·00	9·50
87	,,	4s. black and red/*emerald*	7·50	12·00
88	,,	5s. blk. & grn./*yell.* (1927)	12·00	17·00
		(*b*) *Wmk. Mult. Crown CA.*		
89	**16**	3s. black & purple/*yellow*	7·00	14·00
90	,,	5s. black and green/*yellow*	12·00	17·00
91	,,	£1 black and purple/*red*	95·00	£150
71/91		*Set of* 21	£150	£225
71/91		Optd./Perf. "Specimen" *Set of* 21	£150	

1935 (6 May). *Silver Jubilee. As Nos.* 91/4 *of Antigua. P* 13½×14.

No.	Description	Unused	Used
92	1d. deep blue and carmine	25	35
93	1½d. ultramarine and grey	30	45
94	2½d. brown and deep blue	1·50	2·00
95	1s. slate and purple	2·75	3·50
92/5	Perf. "Specimen" *Set of* 4	16·00	

1937 (12 May). *Coronation. As Nos.* 13/15 *of Aden, but printed by B. W. P* 11×11½.

No.	Description	Unused	Used
96	1d. carmine	15	25
97	1½d. yellow-brown	15	15
98	2½d. blue	30	60
96/8	Perf. "Specimen" *Set of* 2	11·00	

17. Fresh Water Lake.

18. Layou River.

19. Picking Limes.

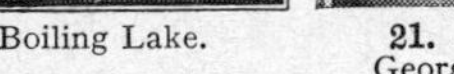

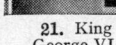

20. Boiling Lake. **21.** King George VI.

(Recess. Waterlow.)

1938 (15 Aug.)–**47**. *Wmk. Mult. Script CA. P* 12½.

No.	Type	Description	Unused	Used
99	**17**	½d. brown and green	8	5
100	**18**	1d. grey and scarlet	10	10
101	**19**	1½d. green and purple	25	12
102	**20**	2d. carmine & grey-black	15	20
103	**19**	2½d. purple & bright blue	2·00	75
		a. Purple & brt. ultram. ('42)	10	12
104	**18**	3d. olive-green & brown	12	20
104*a*	**19**	3½d. ultram. and purple (15.10.47)	35	25
105	**17**	6d. emerald-green & vio.	20	25
105*a*	,,	7d. green & yell.-brown (15.10.47)	30	30
106	**20**	1s. violet & olive-green	55	35
106*a*	**18**	2s. slate and purple (15.10.47)	1·25	1·40
107	**17**	2s. 6d. black & verm.	1·00	1·40
108	**18**	5s. light blue and sepia	2·25	2·50
108*a*	**20**	10s. black and brown-orange (15.10.47)	5·50	7·50
99/108*a*		*Set of* 14	11·00	13·00

(Photo. Harrison.)

1940 (15 Apr.). *Wmk. Mult. Script CA. P* 15×14.

No.	Type	Description	Unused	Used
109	**21**	¼d. chocolate, C O	5	5
99/109		Perf. "Specimen" *Set of* 15	55·00	

1946 (14 Oct.). *Victory. As Nos.* 28/9 *of Aden.*

No.	Description	Unused	Used
110	1d. carmine	8	5
111	3½d. blue	10	8
110/11	Perf. "Specimen" *Set of* 2	14·00	

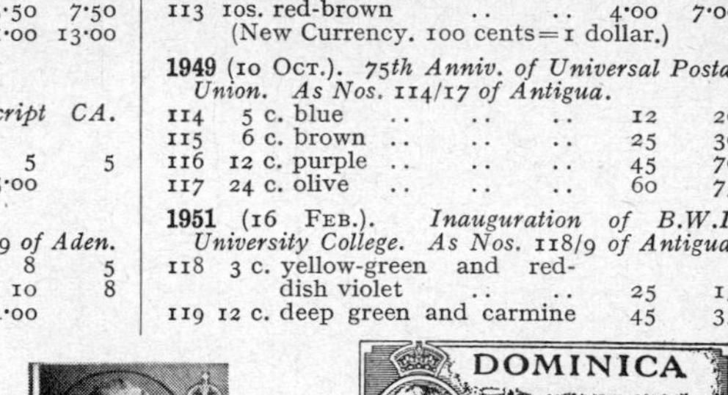

1948 (1 Dec.). *Royal Silver Wedding. As Nos.* 30/1 *of Aden.*

No.	Description	Unused	Used
112	1d. scarlet	8	5
113	10s. red-brown	4·00	7·00

(New Currency. 100 cents=1 dollar.)

1949 (10 Oct.). *75th Anniv. of Universal Postal Union. As Nos.* 114/17 *of Antigua.*

No.	Description	Unused	Used
114	5 c. blue	12	20
115	6 c. brown	25	30
116	12 c. purple	45	70
117	24 c. olive	60	75

1951 (16 Feb.). *Inauguration of B.W.I. University College. As Nos.* 118/9 *of Antigua.*

No.	Description	Unused	Used
118	3 c. yellow-green and reddish violet	25	15
119	12 c. deep green and carmine	45	35

23. Drying Cocoa. **22.** King George VI. **24.** Making Carib Baskets.

25. Lime Plantation.

26. Picking Oranges.

27. Bananas.

28. Botanical Gardens.

29. Drying Vanilla Beans.

30. Fresh Water Lake.

31. Layou River.

33. Picking Oranges.

32. Boiling Lake.

(Photo. Harrison (½ c.). Recess. B.W. (others).)

1951 (1 July). *Wmk. Mult. Script CA. P* 15×14 (½ *c.*), 13½×13 ($2.40), 13×13½ (*others*).

No.	Type	Description	Unused	Used
120	**22**	½ c. chocolate	12	15
121	**23**	1 c. black and vermilion	12	12
122	**24**	2 c. red-brn. & dp. green	10	20
123	**25**	3 c. grn. & reddish violet	12	20
124	**26**	4 c. brown-orange & sepia	15	30
125	**27**	5 c. black and carmine	20	30
126	**28**	6 c. olive and chestnut	15	30
127	**29**	8 c. blue-green and blue	20	40
128	**30**	12 c. black & bright green	20	45
129	**31**	14 c. blue and violet	20	45
130	**32**	24 c. reddish violet and rose-carmine	35	45
131	**25**	48 c. brt. green & red-orge.	70	2·00
132	**24**	60 c. carmine and black	1·10	2·00
133	**30**	$1.20 emerald and black	2·75	4·50
134	**33**	$2.40 orange and black	7·00	7·50
120/134		*Set of* 15	12·00	18·00

(34)

35. Queen Elizabeth II.

1951 (15 Oct.). *New Constitution. Optd. with T* **34** *by B. W.*

No.	Type	Description	Unused	Used
135	**25**	3 c. green & reddish violet	8	15
136	**27**	5 c. black and carmine	10	25
137	**29**	8 c. blue-grn. & blue (R.)	15	20
138	**31**	14 c. blue and violet (R.)	20	25

1953 (2 June). *Coronation. As No.* 47 *of Aden.*

No.	Description	Unused	Used
139	2 c. black and deep green	12	12

36. Mat Making.

37. Picking Oranges.

38. Canoe Making.

39. Bananas. (*As T* **38.**)

(Photo. Harrison (½ c.). Recess. B. W. (others).)

1954 (1 Oct.)–**57.** *As T* **22/23** (*but with portrait of Queen Elizabeth II in place of King George VI, as in T* **35** *and* **37**. *Also new designs, T* **36** *and* **38/9**. *Wmk. Mult. Script CA. P* 15 × 14 (*½ c.*), 13½ × 13 ($2.40), 13 × 13½ (*others*).

140	**35**	½ c. brown	5	8
141	**23**	1 c. black and vermilion	5	5
142	**24**	2 c. chocolate and myrtle-green (*shades*) ..	5	5
143	**25**	3 c. green and purple ..	12	12
144	**36**	3 c. blk. & carm. (15.10.57)	5	5
145	**37**	4 c. brown-orange & sepia	5	5
146	**27**	5 c. black & carmine-red	20	20
147	**38**	5 c. light blue and sepia-brn. (*shades*) (15.10.57)	5	5
148	**28**	6 c. bronze-grn. & red-brn.	8	8
149	**29**	8 c. dp. green & dp. blue	8	8
150	**39**	10 c. green & brown (*shades*) (15.10.57)	25	25
151	**30**	12 c. black and emerald ..	12	12
152	**31**	14 c. blue and purple ..	12	12
153	**32**	24 c. purple and carmine	25	20
154	**25**	48 c. green & red-orange ..	4·50	6·50
155	**36**	48 c. dp. brown and violet (15.10.57)	2·50	3·00
156	**24**	60 c. rose-red and black ..	75	95
157	**30**	$1.20 emerald and black	2·75	3·25
158	**33**	$2.40 yellow-orge. & blk.	4·50	5·00
140/158		.. .. *Set of* 19	15·00	18·00

1958 (22 Apr.). *Inauguration of British Caribbean Federation. As Nos.* 135/7 *of Antigua.*

159	3 c. deep green	8	8
160	6 c. blue	20	20
161	12 c. scarlet	25	25

47. Seashore at Rosalie.

42. Sailing Canoe.

41. Queen Elizabeth II.

43. Sulphur Springs.

44. Road Making.

45. Dug-out Canoe.

46. Crapaud.

47. Scotts Head.

48. Traditional Costume.

49. Bananas.

Two types of 14 c.

I. Eyes of model looking straight ahead.

II. Eyes looking to her right.

51. Goodwill.

50. Sisserou Parrot.

52. Cocoa Tree.

54. Trafalgar Falls.

53. Coat of Arms.

55. Coconut Palm.

(Des. S. Scott. Photo. Harrison.)

1963 (16 May)–**65.** *W* w.**12** (*upright*). *P* $14 \times 14\frac{1}{2}$ (*vert.*), $14\frac{1}{2} \times 14$ (*horiz.*).

No.	Type	Description	Unused	Used
162	**40**	1 c. green, blue and sepia	5	5
163	**41**	2 c. bright blue	5	5
164	**42**	3 c. blackish brown & blue	5	5
165	**43**	4 c. grn., sepia & slate-vio.	5	5
166	**41**	5 c. magenta	5	5
167	**44**	6 c. grn., bistre & violet	8	8
168	**45**	8 c. green, sepia & black	10	10
169	**46**	10 c. sepia and pink	10	12
170	**47**	12 c. green, blue & blackish brown	12	15
171	**48**	14 c. multicoloured (I) ..	25	25
171*a*	,,	14 c. mult. (II) (1.4.65) ..	12	12
172	**49**	15 c. yellow, grn. & brown	15	15
173	**50**	24 c. multicoloured ..	40	40
174	**51**	48 c. green, blue and black	60	65
175	**52**	60 c. orange, green & black	65	80
176	**53**	$1.20, multicoloured ..	2·25	1·60
177	**54**	$2.40, blue, turq. & brn.	2·25	2·75
178	**55**	$4.80, grn., blue & brown	5·50	6·00
162/78		.. .. *Set of* 17	11·00	12·00

See also Nos. 200/4.

1963 (4 June). *Freedom from Hunger. As No. 76 of Aden.*

No.	Description	Unused	Used
179	15 c. reddish violet	35	35

1963 (2 Sept.). *Red Cross Centenary. As Nos. 147/8 of Antigua.*

No.	Description	Unused	Used
180	5 c. red and black	12	12
181	15 c. red and blue	45	45

1964 (23 April). *400th Anniv. of Birth of William Shakespeare. As No. 164 of Antigua.*

No.	Description	Unused	Used
182	15 c. bright purple	35	40

1965 (17 May). *I.T.U. Centenary. As Nos. 166/7 of Antigua.*

No.	Description	Unused	Used
183	2 c. light emerald and blue ..	5	5
184	48 c. turquoise-blue and grey	45	50

1965 (25 Oct.). ***International Co-operation Year. As Nos. 168/9 of Antigua.***

No.	Description	Unused	Used
185	1 c. reddish purple and turquoise-green	5	5
186	15 c. dp. bluish green & lav.	25	25

1966 (24 Jan.). ***Churchill Commemoration. As Nos. 170/3 of Antigua.***

No.	Description	Unused	Used
187	1 c. new blue	5	5
	a. Gold omitted		
188	5 c. deep green	8	8
189	15 c. brown	25	25
190	24 c. bluish violet	40	40

1966 (4 Feb.). ***Royal Visit. As Nos. 174/5 of Antigua.***

No.	Description	Unused	Used
191	5 c. black and ultramarine	10	10
192	15 c. black and magenta ..	25	25

1966 (1 July). ***World Cup Football Championships. As Nos. 176/7 of Antigua.***

No.	Description	Unused	Used
193	5 c. violet, yellow-green, lake and yellow-brown	8	8
194	24 c. chocolate, blue-grn., lake and yellow-brown	25	25

1966 (20 Sept.). ***Inauguration of W.H.O. Headquarters, Geneva. As Nos. 178/9 of Antigua.***

No.	Description	Unused	Used
195	5 c. black, yellow-green and light blue	8	10
196	24 c. black, light purple and yellow-brown	30	30

1966 (1 Dec.). *20th Anniv. of U.N.E.S.C.O. As Nos. 196/8 of Antigua.*

No.	Description	Unused	Used
197	5 c. slate-violet, red, yellow and orange	8	10
198	15 c. orange-yellow, violet and deep olive	20	20
199	24 c. black, bright purple and orange	30	35

1966 (30 Dec.)–**67.** *As Nos. 165, etc. but wmk.* w.**12** *sideways.*

No.	Type	Description	Unused	Used
200	**43**	4 c. green, sepia and slate-violet (16.5.67) ..	5	5
201	**44**	6 c. green, bistre & violet	5	8
202	**45**	8 c. green, sepia & black	10	12
203	**46**	10 c. sepia & pink (16.5.67)	12	15
204	**49**	15 c. yellow, green and brown (16.5.67) ..	25	30
200/4		.. .. *Set of* 5	50	60

56. Children of Three Races.

(Des. and photo. Harrison.)

1967 (2 Nov.). *National Day. T* **56** *and similar horiz. designs. Multicoloured. W* w.**12**. *P* $14\frac{1}{2}$.

No.	Description	Unused	Used
205	5 c. Type **56**	5	5
206	10 c. The *Santa Maria* and motto	5	8
207	15 c. Hands holding motto ribbon	10	10
208	24 c. Belaire dancing ..	20	20

57. John F. Kennedy.

(Des. G. L. Vasarhelyi. Litho. De La Rue.)

1968 (20 Apr.). *Human Rights Year. T* **57** *and similar horiz. designs. Multicoloured. W* w.**12** (*sideways*). *P* $14 \times 13\frac{1}{2}$.

No.	Description	Unused	Used
209	1 c. Type **57**	5	5
210	10 c. Cecil E. A. Rawle ..	5	8
211	12 c. Pope John XXIII ..	8	8
212	48 c. Florence Nightingale ..	30	30
213	60 c. Albert Schweitzer ..	40	45
209/13	.. .. *Set of* 5	70	85

ASSOCIATED STATEHOOD (58)

NATIONAL DAY 3 NOVEMBER 1968 (59)

1968 (8 July). *Associated Statehood. Nos. 163/4, 166, 170, 171a, 173, 175/8, 200/4 and as Nos. 162, 170, 174, but wmk. sideways, optd. with T* **58.**

No.	Type	Description	Unused	Used
214	**40**	1 c. green, bl. & sepia (Sil.)	5	5
215	**41**	2 c. bright blue (Sil.) ..	5	5
216	**42**	3 c. blackish brown and blue (Sil.)	5	5
217	**43**	4 c. green, sepia & slate-violet (Sil.)	5	5
218	**41**	5 c. magenta (Sil.) ..	5	5
219	**44**	6 c. green, bistre & violet	5	5
220	**45**	8 c. green, sepia & black	5	8
221	**46**	10 c. sepia and pink (Sil.)	8	8
222	**47**	12 c. green, blue & blackish brown (Sil.) (wmk. s.)	8	8
		a. Wmk. upright	8	10
224	**48**	14 c. mult. (II) (Sil.) ..	10	10
225	**49**	15 c. yell., grn. & brn. (Sil.)	12	12
226	**50**	24 c. multicoloured (Sil.) ..	20	20
227	**51**	48 c. green, blue and black (Sil.) (wmk. s.)	45	60
		a. Wmk. upright	2·25	2·25
228	**52**	60 c. orange, green & black	50	50
229	**53**	$1.20 multicoloured ..	1·10	85
230	**54**	$2.40 bl., turq. & brn. (Sil.)	1·50	1·60
231	**55**	$4.80 grn., bl. & brn. (Sil.)	2·75	3·00
214/31		.. .. *Set of* 17	6·50	7·00

The 5 c. value exists with PVA gum as well as gum arabic.

1968 (3 Nov.). *National Day. Nos. 162/4, 171 and 176 optd. with T* **59.**

No.	Type	Description	Unused	Used
232	**40**	1 c. green, blue and sepia	5	5
		a. Opt. inverted	50·00	
233	**41**	2 c. bright blue	5	5
		a. Opt. double	40·00	
234	**42**	3 c. blackish brown & blue	10	10
		a. Opt. inverted	40·00	
235	**48**	14 c. multicoloured (I) ..	15	15
236	**53**	$1.20, multicoloured ..	70	70
		a. Opt. double	40·00	
		b. Vert. pair, one opt. omitted, other opt. double	£200	
232/6		.. .. *Set of* 5	95	95

The above set was put on sale by the New York Agency on 1st November but not sold locally until the 3rd November.

60. Forward shooting at Goal.

(Des. M. Shamir (1 c., 60 c.), K. Plowitz (5 c., 48 c.). Litho. Bradbury, Wilkinson.)

1968 (25 Nov.). *Olympic Games, Mexico. T* **60** *and similar horiz. designs. Multicoloured. P* $11\frac{1}{2} \times 11$.

No.	Description	Unused	Used
237	1 c. Type **60**	5	5
238	1 c. Goalkeeper trying to save goal	5	5
239	5 c. Swimmers about to dive	8	8
240	5 c. Swimmers diving ..	8	8
241	48 c. Javelin-throwing ..	30	35
242	48 c. Hurdling	30	35
243	60 c. Basketball	35	40
244	60 c. Basketball players ..	35	40
237/44	.. .. *Set of* 8	1·40	1·60

Nos. 237/44 were issued in sheets of 40 containing two panes of *se-tenant* pairs.

61. " The Small Cowper Madonna " (Raphael).

(Photo. Delrieu, Paris.)

1968 (23 Dec.). *Christmas. P* $12\frac{1}{2} \times 12$.

No.	Type	Description	Unused	Used
245	**61**	5 c. multicoloured ..	5	5

Three other values were issued: **12 c.** " Madonna of the Chair " (Raphael); **24 c.** " Madonna and Child " (Italo-Byzantine, XVI century); $1.20 " Madonna and Child " (Byzantine, XIII century). Size as **T61.**

These only come from miniature sheets, containing two *se-tenant* strips of each value.

62. " Venus and Adonis " (Rubens).

63. " The Death of Socrates " (David).

64. " Christ and the Pilgrims of Emmaus " (Velasquez).

65. " Pilate washing his hands " (Rembrandt).

(Litho. De La Rue.)

1969 (30 Jan.). *20th Anniv. of World Health Organization. W* w.**12**. *P* 15.

246	**62**	5 c. multicoloured ..	5	5
247	**63**	15 c. multicoloured ..	12	12
248	**64**	24 c. multicoloured ..	15	15
249	**65**	50 c. multicoloured ..	25	35

66. Picking Oranges.

(Des. K. Plowitz. Litho. Harrison.)

1969 (10 Mar.). *Tourism. T* **66** *and similar horiz. designs. Multicoloured. W* w.**12**. *P* 14½.

250	10 c. Type **66**	8	8
251	10 c. Woman, child and ocean scene	8	8
252	12 c. Fort Yeoung Hotel ..	10	10
253	12 c. Parrots	10	10
254	24 c. Calypso band	20	25
255	24 c. Women dancing ..	20	25
256	48 c. Underwater life ..	35	40
257	48 c. Skin-diver and turtle ..	35	40
250/7	.. .. *Set of* 8	1·25	1·25

Each denomination was printed *se-tenant* throughout the sheet. The 12 c. stamps are on cream paper.

67. "Strength in Unity" Emblem and Fruit Trees.

68. " HS 748 " Aircraft, Emblem and Island.
69. Chart of Caribbean Sea and Emblem.
70. Steamship unloading, Tug and Emblem.

Litho. Bradbury, Wilkinson.)

1969 (July). *First Anniv. of CARIFTA (Caribbean Free Trade Area). P* 13½ × 13.

258	**67**	5 c. multicoloured ..	5	5
259	**68**	8 c. multicoloured ..	10	10
260	**69**	12 c. multicoloured ..	12	12
261	**70**	24 c. multicoloured ..	25	25

71. " Spinning " (J. Millet).

(Each design is bordered by flags of member-nations of the I.L.O.)

(Litho. Bradbury, Wilkinson.)

1969 (10 July). *50th Anniv. of International Labour Organization. T* **71** *and other vert. paintings by J. Millet. Multicoloured. No wmk. P* 13 × 13½.

262	15 c. Type **71**	10	10
263	30 c. " Threshing "	20	20
264	38 c. " Flax-pulling " ..	25	25

72. Mahatma Gandhi Weaving and Clock Tower, Westminster.

73. Gandhi, Nehru and Mausoleum.
74. Gandhi and Taj Mahal.

(All stamps incorrectly inscribed " Ghandi ".)

(Des. G. L. Vasarhelyi. Litho. Format International.)

1969 (20 Oct.). *Birth Centenary of Mahatma Gandhi. P* 14½.

265	**72**	6 c. multicoloured ..	5	5
266	**73**	38 c. multicoloured ..	25	25
267	**74**	$1.20, multicoloured ..	85	85

75. " Saint Joseph ".

76. " Saint John ".

77. " Saint Peter ".

78. " Saint Paul ".

(Des. G. L. Vasarhelyi (from stained glass windows). Litho. Govt. Printer, Jerusalem.)

1969 (3 Nov.). *National Day. P* 14.

268	**75**	6 c. multicoloured ..	5	5
269	**76**	8 c. multicoloured ..	10	10
270	**77**	12 c. multicoloured ..	15	15
271	**78**	60 c. multicoloured ..	60	60

Nos. 268/71 were printed in sheets of 16 (4 × 4) containing 12 stamps and four printed labels in the top row. The labels each contain two lines of a patriotic poem by W. O. M. Pond, the first letter from each line spelling " DOMINICA ".

79. Queen Elizabeth II.

80. Humming Bird and Flower.

81. Poinsettia.
82. Ramier Pigeon.
83. Sisseron Parrot.
84. Swallowtail Butterfly.
85. Julia Butterfly.
86. Shipping Bananas.
87. Portsmouth Harbour.
88. Copra Processing Plant.
89. Straw Workers.
90. Timber Plant.
91. Pumice Mine.
92. Grammar School and Playing Fields.
93. Roseau Cathedral.

94. Government Headquarters.

95. Melville Hall Airport. (*As T* **96**.)

96. Coat-of-Arms.

(Photo. De La Rue.)

969–72. *Centres multicoloured; colours of* " D " *given.* W **41** *of Singapore* (60 *c. to* $4.80) *or no wmk.* (*others*). P 13½×14 (½ *c.*), 14×13½ (1 *to* 50 *c.*) *or* 14 (*others*).

A. *Chalk-surfaced paper* (26.11.69).

B. *Glazed paper* (1972).

			A.		B.	
72	**79**	½ c. blk. & sil.	5	5	5	5
73	**80**	1 c. blk. and lemon	5	5	5	5
74	**81**	2 c. blk. and lemon	5	5	5	5
75	**82**	3 c. blk. and lemon	5	5	5	5
76	**83**	4 c. blk. and lemon	5	5	5	5
77	**84**	5 c. blk. and lemon	5	5	5	5
78	**85**	6 c. blk. and chest.	8	8	5	8
79	**86**	8 c. blk. and orge.-brn.	10	12	8	8
80	**87**	10 c. blk. and lemon	10	12	8	10
81	**88**	12 c. blk. and ol.-yell.	10	10	10	8
82	**89**	15 c. blk. and blue ..	10	12	8	10
83	**90**	25 c. blk. and rose-red	12	15	10	12
84	**91**	30 c. blk. and yell.-ol.	20	20	12	15
85	**92**	38 c. blk. and deep reddish purple	25	25	12	15
86	**93**	50 c. blk. and chest.	25	30	20	20
87	**94**	60 c. blk. and lemon	30	35	†	
88	**95**	$1.20, blk. and lemon	55	60	†	
89	**96**	$2.40, blk. and gold ..	1·00	1·10	†	
90	**79**	$4.80, blk. and gold ..	2·00	2·25	†	
72A/90A		*Set of* 19	5·00	5·50		
72B/86B		*Set of* 15			1·00	1·10

No. 290 is as T **79** but larger (26×39 mm.).

97. " The Virgin and the Child " (Lippi).
8. " Holy Family with the Lamb " (Raphael).

99. " Virgin and Child " (Perugino).
00. " Madonna of the Rose Hedge " (Botticelli).

Des. G. L. Vasarhelyi. Litho. Bradbury, Wilkinson.)

969 (Dec.). *Christmas. Paintings multi-coloured; frame colours given.* P 14×14½.

91	**97** 6 c. turq.-blue & lt. blue		10	10
92	**98** 10 c. yellow-brown & flesh		12	12
93	**99** 15 c. pale violet & dp. lilac		20	20
94	**100** $1.20, olive-green and pale grey-green		80	1·10
IS295	89×76 mm. Nos. 293/4. Imperf.		1·10	1·25

101. Astronauts First Step onto the Moon.

102. Scientific Experiment on the Moon, and Flag.
103. Astronauts collecting Rocks.
104. Module over the Moon.
105. Moon Plaque.
106. Astronauts.

(Des. G. L. Vasarhelyi. Photo. Banknote Printing Office, Helsinki.)

1970 (6 Feb.).* *Moon Landing. Multicoloured; frame colours given.* P 12½.

296	**101** ½ c. deep lilac	8	8
297	**102** 5 c. pale greenish blue ..	10	10
298	**103** 8 c. pale red	15	15
299	**104** 30 c. new blue	20	20
300	**105** 50 c. reddish brown ..	35	35
301	**106** 60 c. pink..	40	40
MS302	116×112 mm. Nos. 298/301. Imperf.	1·40	1·75
296/301	.. .. *Set of* 6	1·10	1·10

* This is the date of release in Dominica, but the above were released by the Philatelic Agency in the U.S.A. on 2nd February.

107. Giant Green Turtle.

(Des. G. Drummond. Litho. Kyodo Printing Co., Tokyo.)

1970 (7 Sept.). *Flora and Fauna.* T **107** *and similar horiz. designs. Multicoloured.* P 13.

303	6 c. Type **107**	8	8
304	24 c. Flying fish	20	20
305	38 c. Anthurium lily ..	25	25
306	60 c. Imperial and Red-necked parrots.. ..	35	35
MS307	160×111 mm. Nos. 303/6	1·00	1·00

108. 18th-Century National Costume.

(Des. G. Drummond from local designs. Litho. Questa.)

1970 (30 Oct.). *National Day.* T **108** *and similar horiz. designs. Multicoloured.* P 14.

308	5 c. Type **108**.. ..	5	5
309	8 c. Carib Basketry	5	5
310	$1 Flag and Chart of Dominica	55	55
MS311	150×85 mm. Nos. 308/10 plus three labels	60	60

109. Scrooge and Marley's Ghost.

(Des. R. Granger Barrett. Litho. Questa.)

1970 (23 Nov.). *Christmas and Charles Dicken's Death Centenary.* T **109** *and similar vert. designs showing scenes from " A Christmas Carol ". Multicoloured.* P 14×14½.

312	2 c. Type **109**	8	8
313	15 c. Fezziwig's Ball	15	15
314	24 c. Scrooge and his Nephew's Party	25	25
315	$1.20, Scrooge and the Ghost of Christmas Present ..	95	95
MS316	142×87 mm. Nos. 312/5	1·25	1·25

110. " The Doctor " (Sir Luke Fildes).

(Des. G. L. Vasarhelyi. Litho. Questa.)

1970 (28 Dec.). *Centenary of British Red Cross.* T **110** *and similar horiz. designs. Multicoloured.* P 14½×14.

317	8 c. Type **110**	10	10
318	10 c. Hands and Red Cross ..	12	12
319	15 c. Flag of Dominica and Red Cross Emblem ..	15	15
320	50 c. " The Sick Child " (E. Munch)	50	50
MS321	108×76 mm. Nos. 317/20	90	90

111. Marigot School.

(Des. G. L. Vasarhelyi. Litho. Questa.)

1971 (1 Mar.). *International Education Year* (1970). T **111** *and similar horiz. designs. Multicoloured.* P 13½.

322	5 c. Type **111**	5	5
323	8 c. Goodwill Junior High School	8	8
324	14 c. University of West Indies (Jamaica) ..	15	15
325	$1 Trinity College, Cambridge	60	60
MS326	85×85 mm. Nos. 324/5 ..	90	90

112. Waterfall.

(Des. O. Bonnevalle. Litho. Questa.)

1971 (22 Mar.). *Tourism.* *T* **112** *and similar horiz. designs. Multicoloured. P* 13½.

327	5 c. Type **112**	8	8
328	10 c. Boat-building	10	10
329	30 c. Sailing	20	20
330	50 c. Yacht and motor launch	30	35
MS331	130×86 mm. Nos. 327/30	60	60

113. UNICEF Symbol in "D".

(Des. G. Drummond. Litho. Questa.)

1971 (14 June). *25th Anniv. of UNICEF. P* 14.

332 **113**	5 c. bluish violet, black and gold	8	8
333 ,,	10 c. yellow black & gold	10	10
334 ,,	38 c. green, black & gold	20	20
335 ,,	$1.20, orge, blk. & gold	70	70
MS336	84×79 mm. Nos 333 and 335	90	90

114. German Boy Scout.

(Litho. Format.)

1971 (18 Oct). *World Scout Jamboree, Asagiri, Japan. T* **114** *and similar vert. designs showing Boy Scouts from the nations listed. Multi-coloured. W* w.**12**. *P* 11.

337	20 c. Type **114**	12	12
338	24 c. Great Britain	15	15
339	30 c. Japan	20	25
340	$1 Dominica	60	60
MS341	114×102 mm. Nos. 339/40	1·10	1·10

The above were printed on thick paper and the watermark is very faint.

115. Groine at Portsmouth.

(Des. V. Whiteley. Litho. Format.)

1971 (15 Nov.). *National Day. T* **115** *and similar multicoloured designs. P* 13½.

342	8 c. Type **115**	8	8
343	15 c. Carnival scene	8	10
344	20 c. Carifta Queen (*vert.*) ..	15	15
345	50 c. Rock of Atkinson (*vert.*)	30	35
MS346	63×89 mm. $1.20 As 20 c. P 15	1·00	1·00

116. Eight Reals Piece, 1761.

(Des. G. Drummond. Litho. Questa.)

1972 (7 Feb.). *Coins. T* **116** *and similar designs. P* 14.

347	10 c. black, silver and violet	10	10
348	30 c. blk., sil. & yellowish grn.	20	20
349	35 c. blk., sil., & bright blue	25	25
350	50 c. black, silver & vermilion	30	30
MS351	86×90 mm. Nos. 349/50 ..	1·00	1·00

Designs: *Horiz.*—30 c. Eleven and three bitt pieces, 1798. *Vert.*—35 c. Two reals and two bitt pieces, 1770; 50 c. Mocos, Pieces-of-eight and eight reals-eleven bitts piece, 1798.

117. Manicou.

(Des. R. Granger Barrett. Litho. Questa.)

1972 (3 June). *U.N. Conference on the Human Environment, Stockholm. T* **117** *and similar horiz. designs. Multicoloured. W* w.**12** (*sideways*). *P* 14.

352	½ c. Type **117**	5	5
353	35 c. Agouti (rodent) ..	15	15
354	60 c. Orchid	30	35
355	$1.20 Hibiscus	1·00	1·00
MS356	139×94 mm. Nos. 352/5	1·75	1·75

118. Sprinter.

(Des. R. Granger Barrett. Litho. Format.)

1972 (16 Oct.*). *Olympic Games, Munich. T* **11**[8] *and similar multicoloured designs. P* 14.

357	30 c. Type **118**	15	1
358	35 c. Hurdler ..	20	2
359	58 c. Hammer-thrower (*vert.*)	30	3
360	72 c. Long-jumper (*vert.*) ..	50	5
MS361	98×96 mm. Nos. 359/60. P 15	1·50	1·5

*This is the local release date; the America philatelic agency released the stamps on 9th Oc

119. General Post Office.

(Des. G. L. Vasarhelyi. Litho. Format.)

1972 (1 Nov.). *National Day. T* **119** *an similar horiz. designs. Multicoloured. P* 13½

362	10 c. Type **119**	8	
363	20 c. Morne Diablotin ..	12	1
364	30 c. Rodney's Rock ..	20	2
MS365	83×96 mm. Nos. 363/4. P 15	50	5

120. Bananas and Sisserou Parrot.

(Des. (from photograph by D. Groves) and photo Harrison.)

1972 (20 Nov.). *Royal Silver Wedding. Multi-coloured; background colour given. W* w.12 *P* 14×14½.

366 **120**	5 c. yellow-olive (*shades*)	8	1
367 ,,	$1 myrtle-green ..	60	6

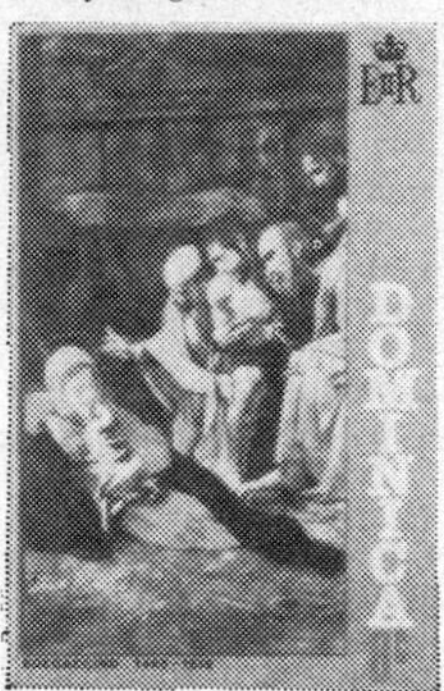

121. "Madonna and Child, and Shepherds (Boccaccino).

(Des. G. L. Vasarhelyi. Litho. Format.)

1972 (4 Dec.*). *Christmas. T* **121** *and simila vert. designs. Multicoloured. P* 13½.

368	8 c. Type **121**	5	
369	14 c. "Madonna and Child" (Rubens)	5	
370	30 c. "Madonna and Child" (Gentileschi)	15	1
371	$1 "Visit of the Magi" (Mostaert)	70	7
MS372	102×79 mm. Nos. 370/1. Imperf.	85	8

*This is the date of release in Dominica; the tamps were put on sale by the Philatelic agency n the U.S.A. on 27th November.

122. Launching of Weather Satellite.

(Des. G. L. Vasarhelyi. Litho. Format.)

1973 (16 July). *I.M.O./W.M.O. Centenary. T* **122** *and similar multicoloured designs. P* 14½.

373	½ c. Type **122**	5	5
374	1 c. Nimbus satellite ..	5	5
375	2 c. Radiosonde balloon ..	5	5
376	30 c. Radarscope (*horiz.*) ..	15	20
377	35 c. Diagram of pressure zones (*horiz.*) ..	20	20
378	50 c. Hurricane shown by satellite (*horiz.*) ..	30	35
379	$1 Computer weather-map (*horiz.*)	55	65
373/9	.. .. *Set of 7*	1·10	1·40
MS380	90×105 mm. Nos. 378/9	1·10	1·25

123. Going to Hospital.

(Des. G. L. Vasarhelyi. Litho. Format.)

1973 (20 Aug.). *25th Anniv. of W.H.O. T* **123** *and similar horiz. designs. Multicoloured. P* 14½.

381	½ c. Type **123**	5	5
382	1 c. Maternity care	5	5
383	2 c. Smallpox inoculation	5	5
384	30 c. Emergency service ..	15	20
385	35 c. Waiting for the doctor	20	20
386	50 c. Medical examination ..	25	30
387	$1 Travelling doctor ..	45	50
381/7	.. .. *Set of 7*	1·00	1·10
MS388	112×110 mm. Nos. 386/7. P 14×14½	1·25	1·40
	a. Perf. 14½		

124. Cyrique Crab.

(Des. G. Drummond. Litho. Format.)

1973 (15 Oct.). *Flora and Fauna. T* **124** *and similar vert. designs. Multicoloured. P* 14½.

389	½ c. Type **124**	5	5
390	22 c. Blue Land-crab ..	10	10
391	25 c. Bread Fruit	15	15
392	$1.20, Sunflower	75	75
MS393	91×127 mm. Nos. 389/92	1·25	1·25

125. Princess Anne and Captain Mark Phillips.

(Des. G. Drummond. Litho. Format.)

1973 (14 Nov.). *Royal Wedding. P* 13½.

394	**125** 25 c. multicoloured ..	12	12
395	– $2 multicoloured ..	1·25	1·25
MS396	79×100 mm. 75 c. as 25 c. and $1.20 as $2	1·25	1·25

No. 395 is as T **125**, but the portrait has a different frame.

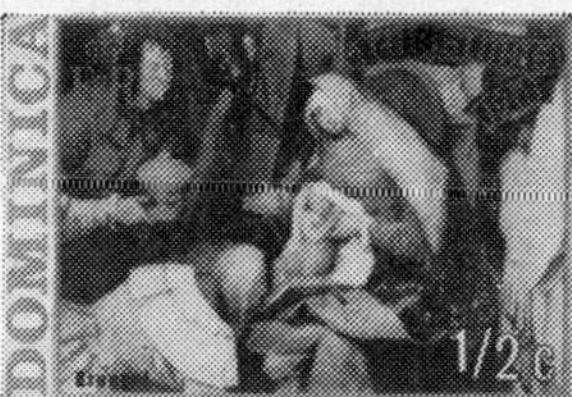

126. Painting by Brueghel.

(Des. M. Shamir. Litho. Format.)

1973 (26 Nov.). *Christmas. T* **126** *and similar horiz. designs showing "The Adoration of the Shepherds" by the artists listed. Multicoloured. P* 14½.

397	½ c. Type **126**	5	5
398	1 c. Botticelli	5	5
399	2 c. Dürer	5	5
400	12 c. Botticelli	5	5
401	22 c. Rubens	10	12
402	35 c. Dürer	20	20
403	$1 Giorgione	45	50
397/403	.. .. *Set of 7*	80	85
MS404	122×98 mm. Nos. 402/3 ..	65	

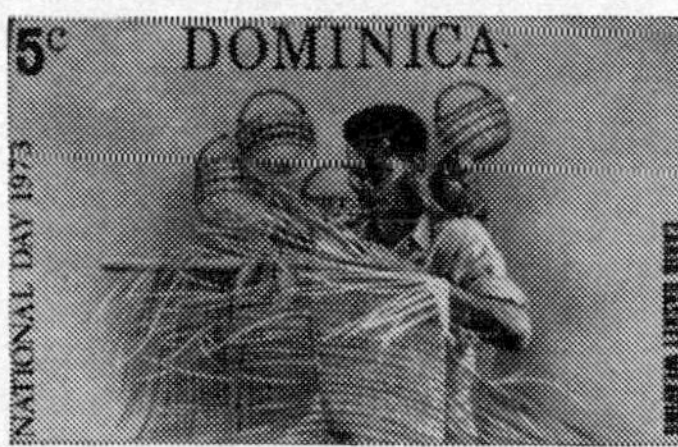

127. Carib Basket-weaving.

(Des. G. Drummond. Litho. Format.)

1973 (17 Dec.). *National Day. T* **127** *and similar multicoloured designs. P* 13½.

405	5 c. Type **127**	5	5
406	10 c. Staircase of the Snake ..	5	5
407	50 c. Miss Caribbean Queen (*vert.*)	25	30
408	60 c. Miss Carifta Queen (vert.)	30	35
409	$1 Dance group	45	50
405/9	.. .. *Set of 5*	95	1·10
MS410	95×127 mm. Nos. 405/6 and 409	40	

128. University of Dominica.

(Des. G. Drummond. Litho. Format.)

1974 (21 Jan.). *25th Anniv. of West Indies University. T* **128** *and similar horiz. designs. Multicoloured. P* 14½.

411	12 c. Type **128**	5	5
412	30 c. Graduation ceremony ..	12	15
413	$1 University coat-of-arms	50	55
MS414	97×131 mm. Nos. 411/13	70	

129. Dominica 1d. Stamp of 1874 and Map.

(Des. G. Drummond. Litho. Format.)

1974 (27 May). *Stamp Centenary. T* **129** *and similar horiz. designs. Multicoloured. P* 14½.

415	½ c. Type **129**	5	5
416	1 c. 6d. stamp of 1874 and posthorn	5	5
417	2 c. 1s. stamp of 1874 and arms	8	8
418	10 c. Type **129**	12	12
419	50 c. As 1 c.	25	30
420	$1.20, As 2 c.	55	60
415/20	.. .. *Set of 6*	1·00	1·10
MS421	105×121 mm. Nos. 418/20	95	

130. Footballer and Flag of Brazil.

(Des. V. Whiteley. Litho. Format.)

1974 (12 Aug.). *World Cup Football Championships. T* **130** *and similar vert. designs showing footballers and flags of the countries given. Multicoloured. P* 14½.

422	½ c. Type **130**	5	5
423	1 c. West Germany	5	5
424	2 c. Italy	5	5
425	30 c. Scotland	15	20
426	40 c. Sweden	20	25
427	50 c. Netherlands	25	30
428	$1 Yugoslavia	45	50
422/8	.. .. *Set of 7*	90	1·00
MS429	89×87 mm. Nos. 427/8 ..	70	

131. Indian Hole.

(Des. G. L. Vasarhelyi. Litho. Format.)

1974 (1 Nov.). *National Day. T* **131** *and similar horiz. designs. Multicoloured. P* $13\frac{1}{2}$.

430 10 c. Type **131** 5 5
431 40 c. Teachers' Training College 20 25
432 $1 Bay Oil distillery plant, Petite Savanne .. 45 50
MS433 96 × 143 mm. Nos. 430/2 70

132. Churchill with "Colonist".

(Des. G. Drummond. Litho. Format.)

1974 (25 Nov.). *Birth Centenary of Sir Winston Churchill. T* **132** *and similar horiz. designs. Multicoloured. P* $14\frac{1}{2}$.

434 $\frac{1}{2}$ c. Type **132** 5 5
435 1 c. Churchill and Eisenhower 5 5
436 2 c. Churchill and Roosevelt 5 5
437 20 c. Churchill and troops on assault-course 10 10
438 45 c. Painting at Marrakesh .. 25 30
439 $2 Giving the "V" sign .. 90 1·00
434/9 .. .. *Set of 6* 1·25 1·40
MS440 126 × 100 mm. Nos. 438/9. P 13 .. .. 1·10

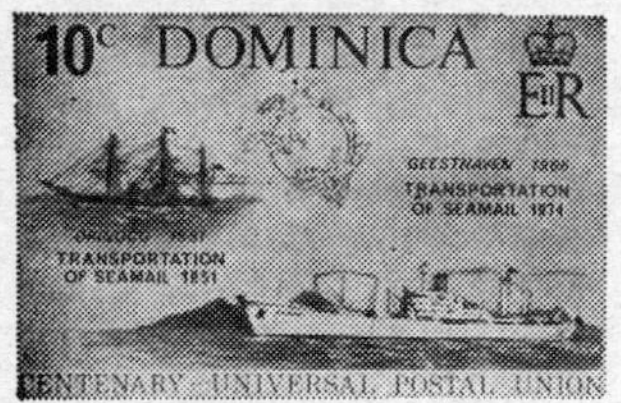

133. Mailboats *Orinoco* (1851) and *Geesthaven* (1974).

(Des. G. Drummond. Litho. Format.)

1974 (4 Dec.). *Centenary of Universal Postal Union. T* **133** *and similar horiz. design. Multicoloured. P* 13.

441 10 c. Type **133** 5 5
442 $2 De Havilland "4" (1918) and Boeing "747" (1974) 90 1·00
MS443 107 × 93 mm. $1.20 as 10 c. and $2.40 as $2 .. .. 1·50

Nos. 442 and **MS**443 are inscr. "De Haviland".

134. "The Holy Family" (Tiso).

(Des. M. Shamir. Litho. Questa.)

1974 (16 Dec.). *Christmas. T* **134** *and similar vert. designs. Multicoloured. P* 14.

444 $\frac{1}{2}$ c. Type **134** 5 5
445 1 c. "Virgin and Child" (Costa) 5 5
446 2 c. "Virgin, Child and Mary Magdalen" (unknown) 5 5
447 10 c. "The Holy Family" (Romanelli) 5 5
448 25 c. "Nativity" (da Sermoneta) 12 15
449 45 c. "The Nativity" (Guido Reni) 25 30
450 $1 "The Adoration of the Kings" (Caselli) .. 45 50
444/50 .. .. *Set of 7* 90 1·00
MS451 114 × 78 mm. Nos. 449/50 70

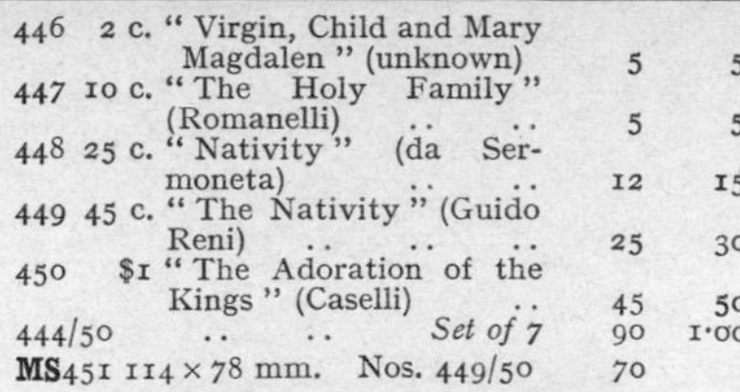

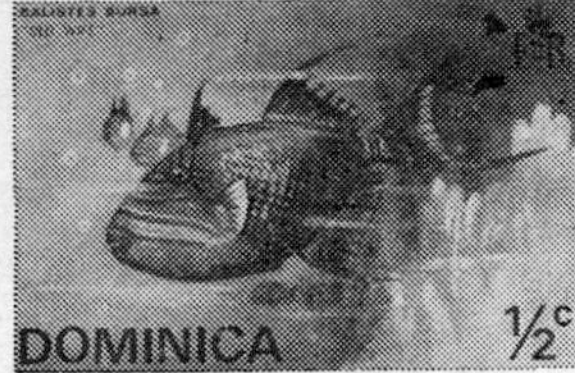

135. Old Wife.

(Des. G. L. Vasarhelyi. Litho. Format.)

1975 (2 June). *Fishes. T* **135** *and similar horiz. designs. Multicoloured. P* 14.

452 $\frac{1}{2}$ c. Type **135** 5 5
453 1 c. Cola 5 5
454 2 c. Billfish 5 5
455 3 c. Vayway 5 5
456 20 c. Bechine 10 12
457 $2 Grouper 85 90
452/7 .. .. *Set of 6* 1·00 1·10
MS458 104 × 80 mm. No. 457. P 13 85

136. *Myscelia antholia.*

(Des. J.W. Ltd. Litho. Format.)

1975 (28 July). *Dominican Butterflies. T* **136** *and similar horiz. designs. Multicoloured. P* $14\frac{1}{2}$.

459 $\frac{1}{2}$ c. Type **136** 5 5
460 1 c. *Lycorea ceres* 5 5
461 2 c. *Siderone nemesis* .. 5 5
462 6 c. *Battus polydamus* .. 5 5
463 30 c. *Anartia lytrea* 15 20
464 40 c. *Morpho peleides* .. 20 25
465 $2 *Dryas julia* 85 90
459/65 .. .. *Set of 7* 1·25 1·40
MS466 108 × 80 mm. No. 465. P 13 85

137. R.M.S. *Yare.*

(Des. J.W. Ltd. Litho. Questa.)

1975 (1 Sept.). *"Ships Tied to Dominica's History". T* **137** *and similar horiz. designs. Multicoloured. P* 14.

467 $\frac{1}{2}$ c. Type **137** 5 5
468 1 c. R.M.S. *Thames* .. 5 5
469 2 c. S.S. *Lady Nelson* .. 5 5
470 20 c. S.S. *Lady Rodney* .. 10 12
471 45 c. M.V. *Statesman* .. 25 30
472 50 c. M.V. *Geestecape* .. 25 30
473 $2 M.V. *Geestestar* .. 85 90
467/73 .. .. *Set of 7* 1·40 1·60
MS474 78 × 103 mm. Nos. 472/3 1·10

138. "Women in Agriculture".

(Litho. Questa.)

1975 (Oct.). *International Women's Year. T* **138** *and similar horiz. designs. Multicoloured. P* 14.

475 10 c. Type **138** 5 5
476 $2 "Women in Industry and Commerce" .. 85 95

139. Miss Caribbean Queen, 1975.

(Litho. Format.)

1975 (6 Nov.). *National Day. T* **139** *and similar multicoloured designs. P* $14 \times 13\frac{1}{2}$ *(vert.) or* $13\frac{1}{2} \times 14$ *(horiz.).*

477 5 c. Type **139** 5 5
478 10 c. Public Library *(horiz.)* 5 5
479 30 c. Citrus Factory *(horiz.)* 12 15
480 $1 National Day Trophy .. 40 45
MS481 130 × 98 mm. Nos. 478/80. Imperf. 60

140. "Virgin and Child" (Montagna).

(Des. M. Shamir. Litho. Questa.)

1975 (24 Nov.). *Christmas. T* **140** *and similar vert. designs showing "Virgin and Child". Multicoloured. P* 14.

482 $\frac{1}{2}$ c. Type **140** 5 5
483 1 c. Fra Filippo Lippi .. 5 5
484 2 c. Bellini 5 5
485 10 c. Botticelli 5 5
486 25 c. Bellini 12 15
487 45 c. Correggio 20 25
488 $1 Dürer 40 45
482/88 .. .. *Set of 7* 80 90
MS489 139 × 85 mm. Nos. 487/88 60

141. Hibiscus.

Des. Waddington Studio. Litho. Format.)

75 (8 Dec.). *T* **141** *and similar multicoloured designs.*

(*a*) *Size as T* **141**. *P* 14½.

o ½ c. Type **141** 5 5
ɪ 1 c. African Tulip 5 5
2 2 c. Castor Oil Tree 5 5
3 3 c. White Cedar Flower .. 5 5
4 4 c. Egg Plant 5 5
5 5 c. Gare 5 5
6 6 c. Ochro 5 5
7 8 c. Mountain Dove .. 5 5
8 10 c. Screw Pine 5 5
9 20 c. Mango Longue 8 0
o 25 c. Crayfish 10 18
ɪ 30 c. Manicou 10 12

(*b*) *Size* 44 × 28 *mm.* *P* 13½.

2 40 c. Bay Leaf Groves .. 12 15
3 50 c. Tomatoes 20 20
4 $1 Lime Factory 35 40
5 $2 Rum Distillery .. 70 80
6 $5 Bay Oil Distillery .. 1·75 2·00
7 $10 Queen Elizabeth II .. 3·50 4·00
o/507 .. .. *Set of* 18 6·50 7·50

142. American Infantry.

(Des. J.W. Ltd. Litho. Format.)

76 (12 Apr.). *Bicentenary of American Revolution. T* **142** *and similar vert. designs. Multicoloured. P* 14½.

8 ½ c. Type **142** 5 5
9 1 c. English three-decker, 1782 .. .. .. 5 5
o 2 c. George Washington .. 5 5
ɪ 45 c. British sailors 20 20
2 75 c. British ensign 30 35
3 $2 Admiral Hood 80 90
8/13 .. .. *Set of* 6 1·25 1·40
5514 105 × 92 mm. Nos. 512/13. P 13 .. .. 1·10

143. Rowing.

(Des. J.W. Ltd. Litho. Format.)

1976 (15 June). *Olympic Games, Montreal. T* **143** *and similar vert. designs. Multicoloured. P* 14½.

515 ½ c. Type **143** 5 5
516 1 c. Shot putting 5 5
517 2 c. Swimming 5 5
518 40 c. Relay 15 20
519 45 c. Gymnastics 20 20
520 60 c. Sailing 25 30
521 $2 Archery 80 90
515/21 .. .. *Set of* 7 1·25 1·50
MS522 90 × 104 mm. Nos. 520/1. P 13 .. .. 1·00

144. Ringed Kingfisher.

(Des. G. Drummond. Litho. Format.)

1976 (28 June). *Wild Birds. T* **144** *and similar multicoloured designs. P* 14½.

523 ½ c. Type **144** 5 5
524 1 c. Mourning Dove 5 5
525 2 c. Green Heron 5 5
526 15 c. Blue-winged Hawk .. 5 8
527 30 c. Blue-headed Humming-bird 12 15
528 45 c. Bananaquit 20 20
529 $2 Imperial Parrot 80 90
523/9 .. .. *Set of* 7 1·00 1·10
MS530 133 × 101 mm. Nos. 527/9. P 13 .. .. 1·10

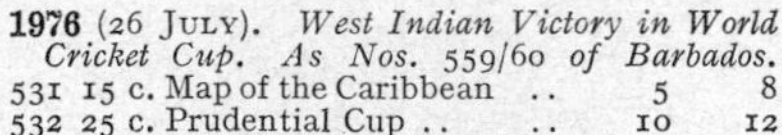

1976 (26 July). *West Indian Victory in World Cricket Cup. As Nos.* 559/60 *of Barbados.*

531 15 c. Map of the Caribbean .. 5 8
532 25 c. Prudential Cup 10 12

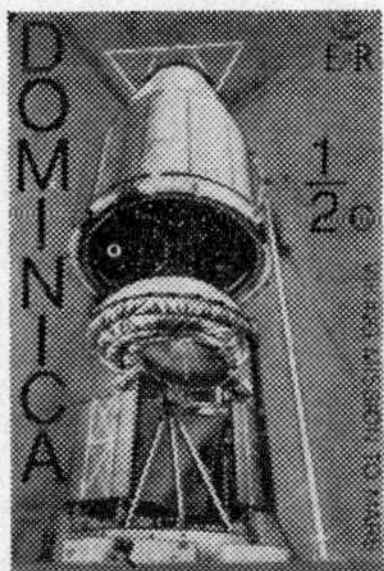

145. Viking Spacecraft System.

(Des. PAD Studio. Litho Format.)

1976 (Sept.). *Viking Space Mission. T* **145** *and similar multicoloured designs. P* 14½.

533 ½ c. Type **145** 5 5
534 1 c. Launching pad 5 5
535 2 c. Titan IIID and Centaur DII 5 5
536 3 c. Orbiter and lander capsule 5 5
537 45 c. Capsule, parachute unopened 20 20
538 75 c. Capsule, parachute opened 30 35
539 $1 Lander descending .. 40 45
540 $2 Space vehicle on Mars .. 80 90
533/40 .. .. *Set of* 8 1·50 1·75
MS541 104 × 78 mm. Nos. 539/40. P 13 .. .. 1·25

The 1 c., $1 and $2 are horizontal designs.

146. "Virgin and Child" (Giorgione).

(Des. M. Shamir. Litho. Questa.)

1976 (10 Oct.). *Christmas. T* **146** *and similar vert. designs showing "Virgin and Child" by the artists named. Multicoloured. P* 14.

542 ½ c. Type **146** 5 5
543 1 c. Bellini 5 5
544 2 c. Mantegna 5 5
545 6 c. Mantegna (*different*) .. 5 5
546 25 c. Memling 10 12
547 45 c. Corregio 20 25
548 $3 Raphael .. .. .. 1·25 1·40
542/8 .. .. *Set of* 7 1·40 1·60
MS549 140 × 85 mm. 50 c. as No. 547 and $1 as No. 548 60

POSTAL FISCALS.

REVENUE	Revenue
(R 1)	(R 2)

1879–86. *Optd. with Type* R **1**.

(*a*) *Wmk. Crown CC.*

R1 **1** 1d. lilac .. .. 12·00 3·00
a. Bisected vert. (½d.) on cover
R2 „ 6d. green .. .. .. 1·60 3·00
R3 „ 1s. magenta .. .. .. 4·50 9·00

(*b*) *Wmk. Crown CA.*

R4 **1** 1d. lilac (1886) 55 65

1888. *Optd. with Type* R **2**. *Wmk. Crown CA.*

R6 **1** 1d. carmine .. .. .. 11·00 9·50

EAST AFRICA.

The following stamps were issued by the East African Postal Administration for use in Uganda, Kenya and Tanganyika (or later, Tanzania, excluding Zanzibar).

PRINTERS. All stamps of East Africa are printed in photogravure by Harrison, *unless otherwise stated.*

1. Chrysanthemum Emblems. **2.**

3. East African " Flags ".

(Des. V. Whiteley.)

1964 (21 Oct.). *Olympic Games, Tokyo.* P 14½.

1	**1**	30 c. yellow and reddish violet	8	8
2	**2**	50 c. dp. reddish violet & yell.	12	12
3	**3**	1s. 30, orange-yellow, deep green and light blue ..	30	30
4	,,	2s. 50, magenta, deep violet-blue and light blue ..	50	50

4. Rally Badge. **5.** Cars *en route.*

1965 (15 Apr.). *13th East African Safari Rally.* P 14.

5	**4**	30 c. black, yellow and turquoise	10	8
6	,,	50 c. black, yellow and brown	12	10
		a. Imperf. (pair)		
7	**5**	1s. 30, dp. bluish green, yellow-ochre and blue	25	25
8	,,	2s. 50, dp. bluish green, brown-red and light blue	50	55

6. I.T.U. Emblem and Symbols.

1965 (17 May). *I.T.U. Centenary.* P 14½.

9	**6**	30 c. gold, choc. & magenta	8	8
10	,,	50 c. gold, chocolate and grey	12	12
11	,,	1s. 30, gold, choc. and blue	15	15
12	,,	2s. 50, gold, chocolate and turquoise-green ..	40	45

7. I.C.Y. Emblem.

1965 (4 Aug.). *International Co-operation Year.* P 14½×14.

13	**7**	30 c. dp. bluish grn. & gold	8	8
14	,,	50 c. black and gold.. ..	12	12
15	,,	1s. 30, ultramarine & gold	15	15
16	,,	2s. 50, carmine-red & gold	40	45

8. Game Park Lodge, Tanzania.

9. Murchison Falls, Uganda.
10. Flamingoes, Lake Nakuru, Kenya.
11. Deep Sea Fishing, Tanzania.

(Des. Mrs. R. M. Fennessy.)

1966 (4 Apr.). *Tourism.* P 14½.

17	**8**	30 c. multicoloured ..	8	8
18	**9**	50 c. multicoloured ..	12	12
		a. Blue omitted		
19	**10**	1s. 30, multicoloured ..	15	15
20	**11**	2s. 50, multicoloured ..	40	45

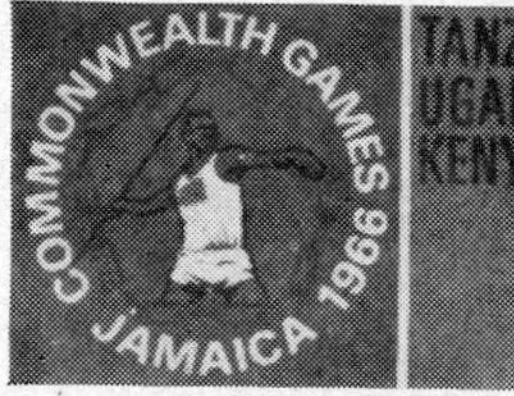

12. Games Emblem.

(Des. Harrison.)

1966 (2 Aug.). *Eighth British Empire and Commonwealth Games, Jamaica.* P 14½.

21	**12**	30 c. black, gold, turquoise-green and grey ..	8	8
22	,,	50 c. black, gold, cobalt and cerise	12	12
23	,,	1s. 30, black, gold, rosine and deep bluish green	15	15
24	,,	2s. 50, black, gold, lake and ultramarine ..	40	45

13. U.N.E.S.C.O. Emblem.

(Des. Harrison.)

1966 (3 Oct.). *20th Anniv. of U.N.E.S.C* P 14½×14.

25	**13**	30 c. black, emerald and red	8
26	,,	50 c. black, emerald & light brown	12
27	,,	1s. 30, black, emerald and grey	15
28	,,	2s. 50, black, emerald and yellow	40

14. D.H. Dragon Rapide.

15. Super VC-10.
16. Comet 4.
17. F-27 Friendship.

(Des. R. Granger Barrett.)

1967 (23 Jan.). *21st Anniv. of East Afri Airways.* P 14½.

29	**14**	30 c. slate-violet, greenish blue and myrtle-green	8
30	**15**	50 c. black, green, yellow, red and new blue ..	12
		a. Red omitted	
31	**16**	1s. 30, black, yellow, red and blue	15
32	**17**	2s. 50, black, red, yellow and new blue	60

18. Pillar Tomb. **19.** Rock painting.

MINIMUM PRICE

The minimum price quoted is 5p whi represents a handling charge rather th a basis for valuing common stamp For further notes about prices s introductory pages.

20. Clay Head. **21.** Proconsul Skull.

(Des. Mrs. R. M. Fennessy.)

67 (2 May). *Archaeological Relics.* P 14½.
18 30 c. ochre, black and deep reddish purple .. 8 8
19 50 c. orange-red, black and greyish brown .. 12 12
20 1s. 30, black, greenish yellow & dp. yellow-green 15 15
21 2s. 50, black, ochre and brown-red 40 45

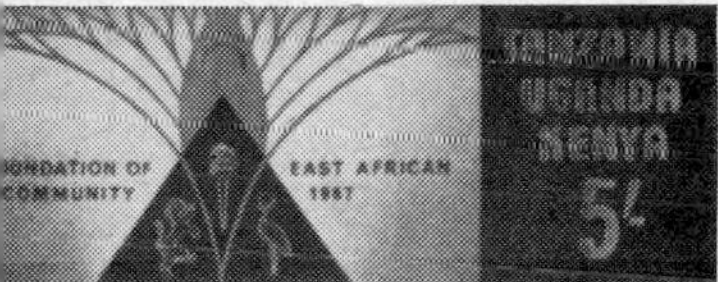

. Unified Symbols of Kenya, Tanzania, and Uganda.

'llustration reduced. Actual size 58 × 21 *mm.*)

(Des. Mrs. R. M. Fennessy.)

37 (1 Dec.). *Foundation of East African Community.* P 14½ × 14.
22 5s. gold, black and grey .. 65 70

23. Mountaineering.

24. Mount Kenya.
25. Mount Kilimanjaro.
26. Ruwenzori Mountains.

(Des. Mrs. R. M. Fennessy.)

38 (4 Mar.). *Mountains of East Africa.* P 14.
23 30 c. multicoloured .. 10 10
24 50 c. multicoloured .. 15 15
25 1 s. 30, multicoloured .. 20 20
26 2 s. 50, multicoloured .. 40 60

27. Family and Rural Hospital.

28. Family and Nurse.
29. Family and Microscope.
30. Family and Hypodermic Syringe.

(Des. Mrs. R. M. Fennessy. Litho. De La Rue.)

1968 (13 May). *20th Anniv. of World Health Organization.* P 13½.
42 **27** 30 c. deep yellow-green, lilac and chocolate .. 5 5
43 **28** 50 c. slate-lilac, lilac & blk. 8 8
44 **29** 1 s. 30, yellow-brown, lilac and chocolate .. 15 15
45 **30** 2 s. 50, grey, black and reddish lilac 40 60

31. Olympic Stadium, Mexico City.

32. High-diving Boards. (*Horiz.*)
33. Running Tracks. (*Horiz.*)
34. Boxing Ring. (*Vert.*)

(Des. V. Whiteley.)

1968 (14 Oct.). *Olympic Games, Mexico.* P 14.
46 **31** 30 c. light green and black 5 5
47 **32** 50 c. black and blue-green 8 8
48 **33** 1 s. 30, carmine-red, black and grey 15 15
49 **34** 2 s. 50, blackish brown and yellow-brown 40 60

35. M.V. *Umoja.*

36. S.S. *Harambee.*
37. M.V. *Victoria.*
38. *St. Michael.*

(Des. Ashley Grosart.)

1969 (20 Jan.). *Water Transport.* P 14.
50 **35** 30 c. deep blue, light blue and slate-grey .. 10 10
51 **36** 50 c. multicoloured .. 15 15
52 **37** 1 s. 30, bronze-grn. greenish blue and blue .. 20 20
53 **38** 2 s. 50, red-orange, deep blue and pale blue .. 50 55

39. I.L.O. Emblem and Agriculture.

40. I.L.O. Emblem and Building-Work.
41. I.L.O. Emblem and Factory-Workers.
42. I.L.O. Emblem and Shipping.

(Des. Mrs. R. M. Fennessy.)

1969 (14 Apr.). *50th Anniv. of International Labour Organization.* P 14.
54 **39** 30 c. black, green and greenish yellow 5 5
55 **40** 50 c. black, plum, cerise and rose 8 8
56 **41** 1 s. 30, black, orange-brown and yellow-orange .. 15 15
57 **42** 2 s. 50, black, ultramarine and turquoise-blue .. 45 45

43. Pope Paul VI and Ruwenzori Mountains.

(Des. Harrison.)

1969 (31 July). *Visit of Pope Paul VI to Uganda.* P 14.
58 **43** 30 c. blk., gold & Royal blue 5 5
59 „ 70 c. black, gold and claret 15 12
60 „ 1 s. 50, blk., gold & dp. bl. 30 30
61 „ 2 s. 50, blk., gold & violet 45 60

44. Euphorbia Tree shaped as Africa and Emblem.

(Des. Mrs. R. M. Fennessy. Litho. Bradbury, Wilkinson.)

1969 (8 Dec.). *Fifth Anniv. of African Development Bank.* P 13½.
62 **44** 30 c. deep bluish green, gold and blue-green .. 5 5
63 „ 70 c. deep bluish green, gold and reddish-purple .. 10 10
64 „ 1 s. 50, deep bluish green, gold & light turq.-blue 20 20
65 „ 2 s. 50, deep bluish green, gold and orange-brown 40 45

45. Marimba.

46. Amadinda.
47. Nzomari.
48. Adeudeu.

(Des. Mrs. R. M. Fennessy. Litho. Bradbury, Wilkinson.)

1970 (16 Feb.). *Musical Instruments.* P 11 × 12.
66 **45** 30 c. buff, yellow-brown and bistre-brown 5 5
67 **46** 70 c. olive-green, yellow-brown and yellow .. 10 10
68 **47** 1 s. 50, chocolate & yellow 20 20
69 **48** 2 s. 50, salmon, yellow and chocolate 40 55

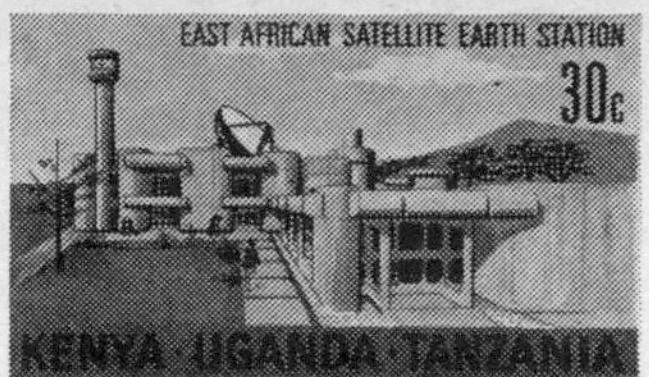

49. Satellite Earth Station.

50. Transmitter—Daytime.
51. Transmitter—Night.
52. Earth and Satellite.

(Des. V. Whiteley. Litho. J.W.)

1970 (18 May). *Inauguration of East African Satellite Earth Station.* P 14½ × 14.

70 **49** 30 c. multicoloured .. 5 5
71 **50** 70 c. multicoloured .. 10 10
72 **51** 1 s. 50, black, slate-violet and pale orange .. 20 20
73 **52** 2 s. 50, multicoloured .. 40 55

53. Athlete.

(Des. Mrs. R. M. Fennessy. Litho. Walsall Security Printers Ltd.)

1970 (13 July). *Ninth Commonwealth Games.* P 14 × 14½.

74 **53** 30 c. orange-brown & black 5 5
75 „ 70 c. olive-green and black 10 10
76 „ 1 s. 50, slate-lilac & black 20 20
77 „ 2 s. 50, turq.-blue & black 55 40

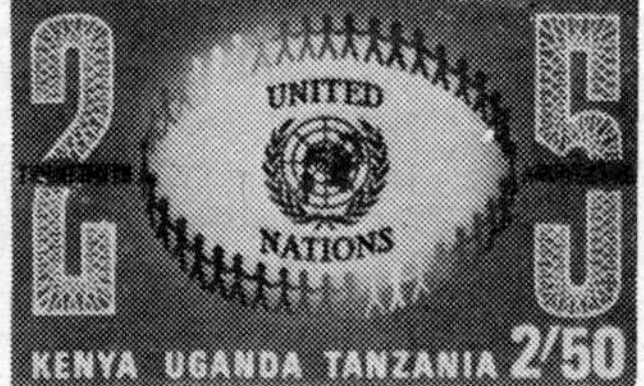

54. " 25 " and U.N. Emblem.

(Des. Mrs. R. M. Fennessy.)

1970 (19 Oct.). *25th Anniv. of United Nations.* P 14½.

78 **54** 30 c. multicoloured .. 5 5
79 „ 70 c. multicoloured .. 10 10
80 „ 1 s. 50, multicoloured .. 20 20
81 „ 2 s. 50, multicoloured .. 55 55

55. Balance and Weight Equivalents.

(Des. and litho. J. Waddington Ltd.)

1971 (4 Jan.). *Conversion to Metric System. T* **55** *and similar horiz. designs. Multicoloured.* P 14½ × 14.

82 30 c. Type **55** 5 5
83 70 c. Fahrenheit and Centigrade Thermometers .. 10 10
84 1 s. 50, Petrol Pump and Liquid Capacities .. 20 20
85 2 s. 50, Surveyors and Land Measures 40 40

56. 11 Class Locomotive.

(Des. Mrs. R. Fennessy.)

1971 (5 Apr.). *Railway Transport. T* **56** *and similar horiz. designs. Multicoloured.* P 14.

86 30 c. Type **56** 10 5
87 70 c. 90 Class Locomotive .. 15 15
88 1 s. 50, 59 Class Locomotive 30 35
89 2 s. 50, 30 Class Locomotive 50 60
MS90 120 × 88 mm. Nos. 86/9 .. 1·25 1·25

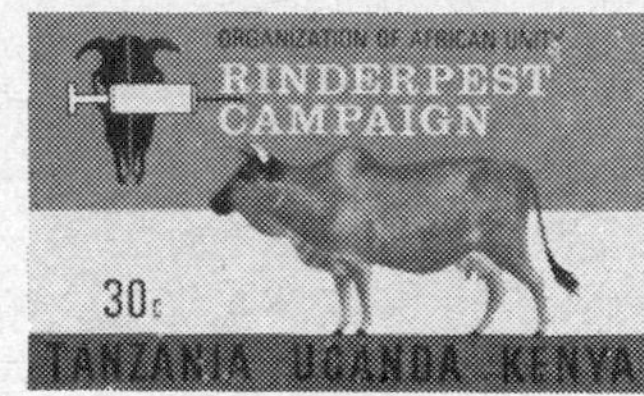

57. Syringe and Cow.

(Des. Mrs. R. Fennessy. Litho.)

1971 (5 July). *O.A.U. Rinderpest Campaign. T* **57** *and similar horiz. design.* P 14.

91 **57** 30 c. black, pale yell.-brown and pale yellow-green 5 5
92 – 70 c. black, pale slate-blue and pale yellow-brown 10 10
93 **57** 1 s. 50, black, plum and pale yellow-brown .. 20 20
94 – 2 s. 50, black, brown-red and pale yellow-brown 45 45

Design:—70 c., 2 s. 50. As T **57**, but with bull facing right.

58. Livingstone meets Stanley.

(*Illustration reduced. Actual size* 58 × 21 *mm.*)

(Des. and litho. J.W.)

1971 (28 Oct.). *Centenary of Livingstone and Stanley meeting at Ujiji.* P 13½ × 14.

95 **58** 5 s. multicoloured .. .. 1·00 1·00

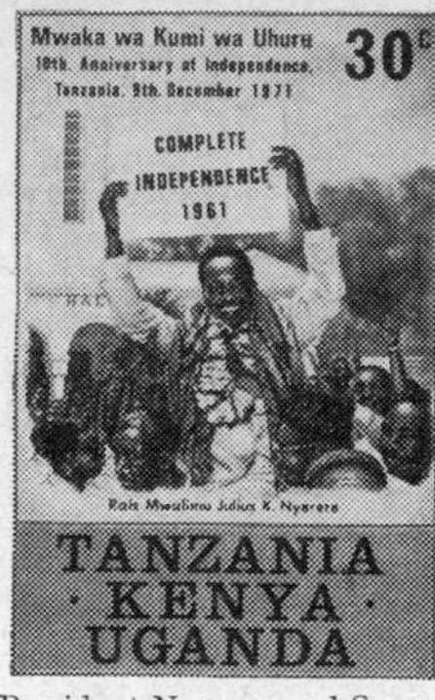

59. President Nyerere and Supporters.

(Des. G. Drummond. Litho. J.W.)

1971 (9 Dec.). *Tenth Anniv. of Tanzani Independence. T* **59** *and similar horiz. desig Multicoloured.* P 13½.

96 30 c. Type **59** 8
97 70 c. Ujamaa village 10
98 1 s. 50, Dar es Salaam University 25
99 2 s. 50, Kilimanjaro airport 45

60. Flags and Trade Fair Emblem.

(Des. Trade Fair Publicity Agents. Lith Questa.)

1972 (23 Feb.). *All-Africa Trade Fa* P 13½ × 14.

100 **60** 30 c. multicoloured .. 8
101 „ 70 c. multicoloured .. 10
102 „ 1 s. 50, multicoloured .. 25
103 „ 2 s. 50, multicoloured .. 45

61. Child with Cup.

(Des. Mrs. R. Fennessy. Litho. Questa.)

1972 (24 Apr.). *25th Anniv. of UNICEF. T and similar horiz. designs. Multicolour* P 14 × 14½.

104 30 c. Type **61** 8
105 70 c. Children with ball .. 10
106 1 s. 50, Child at blackboard 25
107 2 s. 50, Child and tractor .. 45

62. Hurdling.

(Des. G. L. Vasarhelyi. Litho. J.W.)

1972 (28 Aug.). *Olympic Games, Munich. T* **62** *and similar horiz. designs. Multicoloured. P* 14.

108	40 c. Type **62**	10	10
109	70 c. Running	12	12
110	1 s. 50, Boxing	20	20
111	2 s. 50, Hockey	50	50
MS112	131×98 mm. Nos. 108/11	1·25	1·25

63. Ugandan Kobs.

(Des. G. Drummond. Litho. D.L.R.)

1972 (9 Oct.). *Tenth Anniv. of Ugandan Independence. T* **63** *and similar horiz. designs. Multicoloured. P* 14.

113	40 c. Type **63**	5	5
114	70 c. Conference Centre ..	8	8
115	1 s. 50, Makerere University	20	20
116	2 s. 50, Coat-of-Arms ..	45	45
MS117	132×120 mm. Nos. 113/16. P 13×14	1·00	1·00

64. Community Flag.

(*Illustration reduced. Actual size* 58×21½ *mm.*)

(Des. Mrs. R. M. Fennessy. Litho.)

1972 (1 Dec.). *Fifth Anniv. of East African Community. P* 14½×14.

118	**64** 5 s. multicoloured.. ..	70	75

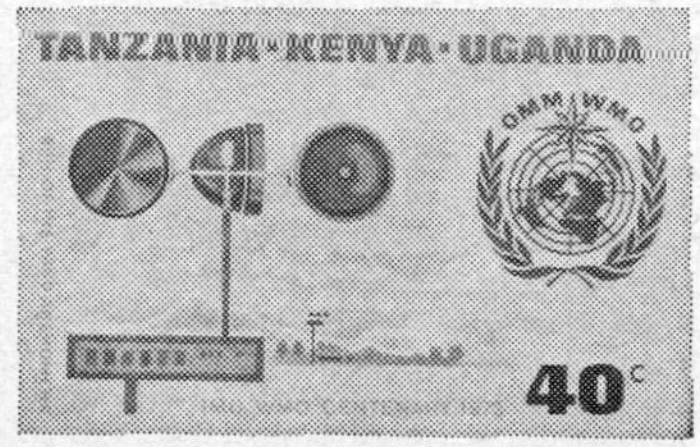

65. Run-of-the-wind Anemometer.

(Des. P. B. Powell. Litho.)

1973 (5 Mar.). *I.M.O./W.M.O. Centenary. T* **65** *and similar multicoloured designs. P* 14½.

119	40 c. Type **65**	10	10
120	70 c. Weather balloon (*vert.*)..	12	12
121	1 s. 50, Meteorological rocket	20	20
122	2 s. 50, Satellite Receiving aerial	45	45

No. 119 exists with country name at foot instead of at top, and also with country name omitted (or with imprint or plate numbers in lieu). These are because of faulty registration of the perforation comb.

66. "Learning by Serving".

(Des. Mrs. R. M. Fennessy. Litho.)

1973 (16 July). *24th World Scout Conference, Nairobi. T* **66** *and similar vert. designs. P* 14.

123	40 c. multicoloured	10	10
124	70 c. Venetian red, reddish violet and black	12	12
125	1 s. 50, cobalt, reddish violet and black	20	25
126	2 s. 50, multicoloured ..	45	45

Designs:—70 c. Baden-Powell's grave, Nyeri; 1 s. 50, World Scout emblem; 2 s. 50, Lord Baden-Powell.

67. Kenyatta Conference Centre.

(Des. Marketing Communications Ltd., Nairobi; adapted J. E. Cooter. Litho. D.L.R.)

1973 (24 Sept.). *I.M.F./World Bank Conference. T* **67** *and similar designs. P* 13½×14 (1 *s.* 50), *or* 14×13½ (*others*).

127	**67** 40 c. sage-green, light greenish grey and black ..	10	10
128	– 70 c. orge.-brn., greenish grey and black ..	12	12
129	– 1 s. 50, multicoloured ..	35	35
130	– 2 s. 50, orange, greenish grey and black ..	30	35
MS131	166×141 mm. Nos. 127/30. Imperf.	75	75

Designs:—Nos. 128/30 show different arrangements of Bank emblems and the Conference Centre, the 1 s. 50 being vertical.

68. Police Dog-handler.

(Des. C. Abbott. Litho. Questa.)

1973 (24 Oct.)–**74.** *50th Anniv. of Interpol. T* **68** *and similar vert. designs. P* 14.

132	40 c. yellow, blue and black..	8	8
133	70 c. turquoise-green, orange-yellow and black ..	10	10
134	1 s. 50, light vio., yell. & blk.	20	25
135	2 s. 50, light yellow-green, red-orange and black (I)	30	35
136	2 s. 50, light yellow-green, red-orge., and black (II) (25.2.74)	30	35

Designs:—70 c. East African Policeman; 1 s. 50, Interpol emblem; 2s. 50, Interpol H.Q.

Nos. 135/6. Type I inscribed "St Clans"; Type II corrected to "St Cloud".

69. Tea Factory.

(Des. G. Drummond. Litho. Enschedé.)

1973 (12 Dec.). *10th Anniv. of Kenya's Independence. T* **69** *and similar horiz. designs. Multicoloured. P* 13×13½.

137	40 c. Type **69**	8	8
138	70 c. Kenyatta Hospital ..	10	10
139	1 s. 50, Nairobi Airport ..	20	25
140	2 s. 50, Kindaruma hydro-electric scheme ..	45	45

70. Party H.Q.

(Des. PAD Studio. Litho. D.L.R.)

1974 (12 Jan.). *Tenth Anniv. of Zanzibar's Revolution. T* **70** *and similar horiz. designs. Multicoloured. P* 13½.

141	40 c. Type **70**	8	8
142	70 c. Housing scheme ..	10	10
143	1 s. 50, Colour T.V.	20	25
144	2 s. 50, Amaan Stadium ..	45	45

71. "Symbol of Union".

(Des. Jennifer Toombs. Litho. Questa.)

1974 (26 Apr.). *Tenth Anniv. of Tanganyika-Zanzibar Union. T* **71** *and similar horiz. designs. Multicoloured. P* 14½.

145	40 c. Type **71**	8	8
146	70 c. Handclasp and map ..	10	10
147	1 s. 50, "Communications"	20	25
148	2 s. 50, Flags of Tanu, Tanzania and Afro-Shirazi Party	30	35

72. East African Family ("Stability of the Home").

(Des. locally; adapted PAD Studio. Litho.)

1974 (15 JULY). *17th Social Welfare Conference, Nairobi. T* **72** *and similar horiz. designs. P* 14½.

149 40 c. greenish yellow, lake-brown and black .. 8 8
150 70 c. multicoloured 10 10
151 1 s. 50, olive-green, yellow-green and black 20 25
152 2 s. 50, light rose, reddish violet and black .. 30 35

Designs:—70 c. Dawn and drummer (U.N. Second Development Plan); 1 s. 50, Agricultural scene (Rural Development Plan); 2 s. 50, Transport and telephone ("Communications").

73. New Postal H.Q., Kampala.

(Des. Mrs. R. Fennessy. Litho.)

1974 (9 OCT.). *Centenary of Universal Postal Union. T* **73** *and similar horiz. designs. Multicoloured. P* 14½.

153 40 c. Type **73** 5 5
154 70 c. Mail-train and post-van 8 10
155 1 s. 50, U.P.U. Building, Berne 20 25
156 2 s. 50, Loading mail into "VC-10" 30 35

74. Family-planning Clinic.

(Des. C. Abbott. Litho. Harrison.)

1974 (16 DEC.). *World Population Year. T* **74** *and similar horiz. designs. P* 14.

157 40 c. multicoloured 8 8
158 70 c. deep reddish violet and scarlet 10 10
159 1 s. 50, multicoloured .. 20 25
160 2 s. 50, apple-green, blue-green and bluish black .. 30 35

Designs:—70 c. "Tug of war"; 1 s. 50, Population "scales"; 2 s. 50, W.P.Y. emblem.

75. Seronera Wild-Life Lodge, Tanzania.

(Des. R. Granger Barrett. Litho. Harrison.)

1975 (24 FEB.). *East Africa Game Lodges. T* **75** *and similar horiz. designs. Multicoloured. P* 14.

161 40 c. Type **75** 8 8
162 70 c. Mweya Safari Lodge, Uganda 10 10
163 1 s. 50, "Ark"–Aberdare Forest Lodge, Kenya .. 20 25
164 2 s. 50, Paraa Safari Lodge, Uganda 30 35

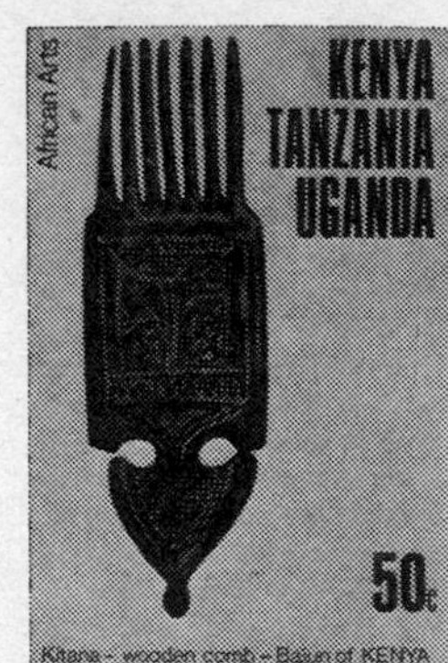

76. Kitana (wooden comb), Bajun of Kenya.

(Des. Mrs. Gombe of the E.A.P.T.; adapted C. Abbott. Litho. Questa.)

1975 (5 MAY). *African Arts. T* **76** *and similar vert. designs. Multicoloured. P* 13½.

165 50 c. Type **76** 5 8
166 1 s. Earring, Chaga of Tanzania 12 15
167 2 s. Okoco (armlet), Acholi of Uganda 25 30
168 3 s. Kitete (Kamba gourd), Kenya 40 45

77. International Airport, Entebbe.

(Des. PAD Studio. Litho. State Ptg. Wks., Warsaw.)

1975 (28 JULY). *O.A.U. Summit Conference, Kampala. T* **77** *and similar multicoloured designs. P* 11.

169 50 c. Type **77** 5 8
170 1 s. Map of Africa and flag (*vert.*) 12 15
171 2 s. Nile Hotel, Kampala .. 25 30
172 3 s. Martyrs' Shrine, Namugongo (*vert.*) 35 40

78. Ahmed ("Presidential" Elephant).

(Des. locally. Litho. State Ptg. Wks., Warsaw.)

1975 (11 SEPT.). *Rare Animals. T* **78** *and similar vert. designs. Multicoloured. P* 11.

173 50 c. Type **78** 5 8
174 1 s. Albino buffalo 12 15
175 2 s. Ahmed in grounds of National Museum .. 25 30
176 3 s. Abbott's Duiker .. 35 40

79. Maasai Manyatta (animal slaughter), Kenya.

(Des. Mrs. R. Fennessy. Litho. Questa.)

1975 (3 NOV.). *Second World Black and African Festival of Arts and Culture. Multicoloured. P* 13½×14.

177 50 c. Type **79** 5 8
178 1 s. "Heartbeat of Africa" (Ugandan dancers) .. 12 15
179 2 s. Makonde sculpture, Tanzania 25 30
180 3 s. "Early Man and Technology" (skinning animal) 35 40

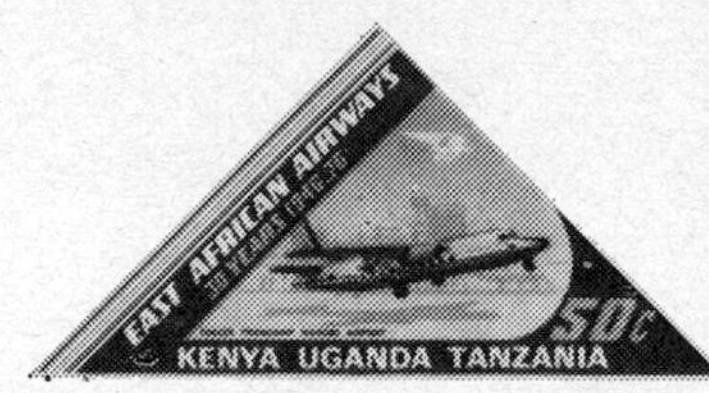

80. Fokker "Friendship" at Nairobi Airport.

(Des. Local Artist. Litho. State Security Ptg. Wks., Warsaw.)

1976 (2 JAN.). *30th Anniv. of East African Airways. T* **80** *and similar triangular designs. Multicoloured. P* 11½.

181 50 c. Type **80** 5 8
182 1 s. "DC 9" at Kilimanjaro Airport 12 15
183 2 s. Super "VC 10" at Entebbe Airport 25 30
184 3 s. East African Airways Crest 35 40

Further commemorative issues were released from 1976 onwards, using common designs, but valid in one republic only. These are listed under Kenya, Tanzania or Uganda.

EAST AFRICA AND UGANDA PROTECTORATES.

See KENYA, UGANDA AND TANGANYIKA.

EAST AFRICA (G.E.A.).

See TANGANYIKA.

EGYPT.

See BRITISH FORCES IN EGYPT.

FALKLAND ISLANDS.

CROWN COLONY.

FALKLAND PAID. ISLANDS

(1)

(2)

861–77. *The Franks.*

'R1	1	In black, *on cover*	£6500
'R2	2	In red, *on cover* (1877)	£8500

On *piece*, FR1 on white or coloured papers £40; 'R2 on white £50. The use of these franks ceased vhen the first stamps were issued.

3

In the ½d., 2d., 2½d. and 9d. the figures of value in the lower corners are replaced by small rosettes and the words of value are in colour.

(Recess. Bradbury, Wilkinson.)

NOTE.—Nos. 1, 2, 3, 4, 10, 26, 35 and 37 exist vith one or two sides imperf. from the margin f the sheets.

878–79. *No wmk.* P 14, 14½.

1	3	1d. claret (19.6.78)	£120	£100
2	,,	4d. grey-black (Sept. 1879)	£250	48·00
		a. On wmkd. paper	£350	£110
3	,,	6d. blue-green (19.6.78)	10·00	13·00
4	,,	1s. bistre-brown (1878)	10·00	13·00

Nos. 2*a* shows portions of the papermaker's vatermark—"R. TURNER, CHAFFORD MILLS"— n double-lined capitals.

883–1902. *Wmk. Crown CA (upright).* P 14, 14½.

5	3	½d. blue-green (10.9.91)	5·00	7·00
6	,,	½d. green (1892)	5·00	5·50
7	,,	½d. deep yellow-green (1894)	5·00	7·00
8	,,	½d. yellow-green (1895)	35	45
9	,,	1d. dull claret (1883)	65·00	28·00
		a. Imperf. between (horiz. pr.)	£9500	
0	,,	1d. red-brown (April 1891)	20·00	20·00
		a. Bisected (on cover) (1891)	†	£1100
1	,,	1d. orange, red-brn. (12.91)	14·00	15·00
2	,,	1d. brown (1892)	13·00	14·00
3	,,	1d. russet brown (1892)	13·00	14·00
4	,,	1d. orange-brown (*Wmk. reversed*) (1894)	8·50	8·50
5	,,	1d. bright claret (1894)	10·00	10·00
16	3	1d. Venetian red (1895)	2·00	2·00
17	,,	1d. pale red (1899)	2·00	2·00
18	,,	1d. orange-red (1902)	2·50	2·50
19	,,	2d. reddish purple (1895)	2·00	5·00
20	,,	2d. pale purple (1898)	2·00	5·00
21	,,	2½d. pale chalky ultramarine (10.9.91)	14·00	8·50
22	,,	2½d. blue (1892)	8·50	9·50
23	,,	2½d. Prussian blue (1894)	60·00	45·00
24	,,	2½d. ultramarine (bright to deep) (1894)	2·75	6·00
25	,,	4d. grey-black (1883)	11·00	13·00
26	,,	4d. olive grey-black (1890)	10·00	11·00
28	,,	4d. olive-black (1895)	5·00	8·50
29	,,	6d. orange-yellow (1892)	5·50	11·00
30	,,	6d. yellow (1896)	5·50	11·00
31	,,	9d. orange-vermilion (1895)	5·00	13·00
32	,,	9d. pale vermilion (1896)	6·50	13·00
33	,,	1s. grey-brown (1895)	5·50	11·00
34	,,	1s. yellow-brown (1896)	5·50	11·00
5/34		*Set of* 8	25·00	50·00
		½d., 2d., 2½d., 6d., 9d. Optd. "Specimen" *Set of* 5	£175	

NOTES.—The plates used for these stamps did not fit the paper, and therefore the wmk. appears in all sorts of positions, a well-centred Crown CA being scarce. Stamps from the edge of the sheet exist without watermark. Also individual letters from "CROWN AGENTS FOR THE COLONIES", which normally appears in the margins, sometimes occur on the stamps.

1d. No. 9 can be distinguished from No. 15 (apart from the shade difference), in that the former has crinkly gum and watermark, normal (or occasionally inverted and reversed), whilst No. 15 has smooth gum, and watermark normally *reversed.*

1885–91. *Wmk. Crown CA sideways (to right or left).* P 14, 14½.

35	3	1d. claret	12·00	11·00
		a. Bisected (on cover) (1891)	†	£1000
36	,,	4d. pale grey-black	48·00	11·00
37	,,	4d. grey-black (1887)	42·00	11·00

In 1891 the postage to the United Kingdom and Colonies was reduced from 4d to 2½d. per ½ oz. As no ½d. or 2½d. stamps were yet available, the 1d. was allowed to be bisected (see Nos. 10*a* and 35*a*) and used for half its value until the following provisionals appeared.

½d.

(4)

1891. *Stamps bisected diagonally and each half surch. diagonally with T* **4**.

38	3	½d. on half of 1d. claret (No. 35)	£110	£100
		a. Unsevered pair	£325	£300
		b. Unsevered pair se-tenant with unsurcharged whole stamp	£2000	
		c. Surch. double	£275	
		d. Surch. inverted	£350	£300
		e. Surch. sideways	£225	£250
39	,,	½d. on half of 1d. red-brown (No. 10)	75·00	42·00
		a. Unsevered pair	—	£150
		b. Surch. double	£275	

Bisected stamps were authorised by decree dated 1 Jan., 1891 and were used until 11 Jan., 1892 when authorisation was withdrawn. Supplies of the ½d. and 2½d. values were available from September 1891 but as it took some time for them to be distributed, unsurcharged bisects were accepted up to 11 July, 1892.

The ½d. on half of 1d. orange-red-brown, previously listed as No. 40 are found only cancelled by favour to bring them within the authorised period.

5

6

(Recess. B.W.)

1898 (JUNE). *Wmk. Crown CC.* P 14, 14½.

41	5	2s. 6d. deep blue	42·00	45·00
42	6	5s. red	35·00	40·00
41/2		Optd. "Specimen" *Set of* 2	85·00	

7

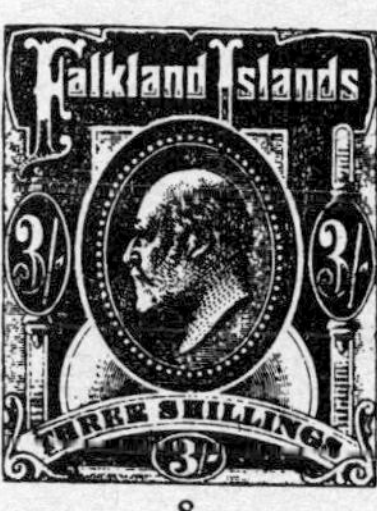

8

(Recess. De La Rue & Co.)

1904–12. *Wmk. Mult. Crown CA.* P 14.

43	7	½d. yellow-green (1904)	65	1·10
44	,,	½d. pale yellow-green on thick paper (1907)	1·75	3·25
45	,,	½d. deep yellow-green (1911)	1·10	1·50
46	,,	1d. vermilion (1904)	1·90	1·10
47	,,	1d. verm., thick paper (1907)	1·50	1·40
48	,,	1d. dull coppery red (1907)	48·00	14·00
49	,,	1d. orange-vermilion (1911)	1·10	55
50	,,	2d. purple (1904)	2·25	10·00
51	,,	2d. reddish purple (1912)	95·00	£120
52	,,	2½d. ultramarine (*shades*)	7·00	7·00
53	,,	2½d. deep blue (1912)	90·00	55·00
54	,,	6d. orange (1904)	9·00	11·00
55	,,	1s. brown (1904)	7·00	10·00
56	8	3s. green (1904)	35·00	32·00
57	,,	3s. deep green (1906)	23·00	28·00
58	,,	5s. red (1904)	45·00	45·00
43/58		*Set of* 8	85·00	£100
43/58		Optd. "Specimen" *Set of* 8	£130	

1906. *Wmk. Mult. Crown CA., sideways.* P 14.

59	7	1d. vermilion	55	1·10

SOUTH GEORGIA "UNDERPRINT". From late 1909 a small handstamp inscribed "South Georgia" was used on mail from that place, the intention being that it should be applied below the stamps, although it sometimes appears across them. It is found in conjunction with all contemporary King Edward VII issues, and some values of the Victorian issue, until its use finally ceased in June, 1912. Examples are scarce, particularly with the Falkland Is. date-stamp.

9

10

(Recess. De La Rue & Co.)

1912–20. *Wmk. Mult. Crown CA. P* 14.

No.	Type	Description	Unused	Used
60	9	½d. yellow-green (1912) ..	65	1·10
61	,,	½d. dp. yellow-green (1914)	8·00	12·00
62	,,	½d. pale green (1918) ..	1·60	3·25
63	,,	½d. green (1919)	1·10	1·60
64	,,	½d. green on thick greyish paper (1920)	1·40	4·00
65	,,	1d. vermilion (1912) ..	1·40	1·60
66	,,	1d. orge.-verm. (1914, 1916)	1·90	1·40
67	,,	1d. scarlet (1919)	1·00	1·25
68	,,	1d. scarlet on thick greyish paper (1920)	2·25	90
69	,,	2d. deep purple (1912) ..	1·40	2·50
69*a*	,,	2d. dp. reddish pur. (1914)	7·00	7·00
69*b*	,,	2d. purple (1918)	8·00	12·00
70	,,	2d. pale purple (1919) ..	1·10	2·25
71	,,	2½d. dark blue (1912) ..	3·00	5·50
72	,,	2½d. bright blue (1914) ..	3·00	4·50
73	,,	2½d. milky blue (1916) ..	80·00	85·00
74	,,	2½d. blue (1919)	1·60	3·25
75	,,	6d. yellow-orange (1912) ..	2·25	5·50
76	,,	6d. brown-orange (1919) ..	2·25	3·50
77	,,	1s. yellow-brown (1912) ..	7·00	9·50
78	,,	1s. pale bistre-brn. (1919)	7·00	11·00
79	,,	1s. brown on thick greyish paper (1920) ..	7·00	14·00
80	,,	1s. deep brown on thick greyish paper (1920) ..	6·00	14·00
81	10	3s. deep green (1912) ..	12·00	14·00
82	,,	5s. red (1912)	22·00	24·00
83	,,	5s. reddish maroon (1914)	24·00	27·00
83*a*	,,	5s. maroon (1916) ..	18·00	20·00
84	,,	10s. red/*green* (1913) ..	60·00	75·00
85	,,	£1 black/*red* (1913) ..	£110	£120
60/85		.. .. *Set of* 11	£200	£250
60/85 (incl. two 5s.) Optd. "Specimen"		.. .. *Set of* 11	£250	

As there was considerable variation in shade in the war-time printings it is useful to know that the 1914, 1916 and 1918 printings of Type **9** were all line perforated instead of comb, i.e. Nos. 61/2, 66, 69*a*/*b*, and 72/3. No. 73 may be distinguished by the very white paper and gum.

The 2½d. No. 74 and 6d. No. 76 were bisected and used as 1d. and 2½d. respectively in S. Georgia in 1923. This procedure was not authorised from Port Stanley. (*Prices on cover:* 2½d. £2000, 6d. £1900.)

The ½d. and 1d. stamps of the above issue, and the 1d. King Edward VII, exist used with a "PORT FOSTER" handstamped overprint, applied at Port Foster, Deception Island, during the 1912–13 whaling season. Unused stamps and higher values bearing the overprint were "made to order". (*Price from £1000 upwards.*)

WAR STAMP
(11)

2½D
(12)

1918–20. *Optd. locally with T* **11**.

No.	Type	Description	Unused	Used
86	9	½d. pale yellow-green (No. 62) (7.10.18)	50	2·25
87	,,	½d. yellow-green (No. 60) (3.19)	3·25	4·00
		a. Albino impression only ..	£350	
88	,,	½d. green (No. 63) (3.19) ..	20	1·10
89	,,	½d. green on thick greyish paper (No. 64) (5.20) ..	3·25	7·50
90	,,	1d. pale scarlet (*) (7.10.18)	1·40	2·50
		a. Opt. double, one albino ..	£110	
91	,,	1d. bright orange-vermilion (No. 66) (3.19) ..	2·25	4·50
92	,,	1d. scarlet (No. 67) (3.19) ..	25	1·00
		a. Opt. double..	£450	
93	,,	1d. scarlet on thick greyish paper (No. 68) (5.20) ..	13·00	24·00
94	,,	1s. yell.-brn. (No. 77) (7.10.18)	12·00	17·00
95	,,	1s. pale bistre-brown (No. 78) (3.19)	2·40	10·00
		a. Opt. double, one albino ..	£350	£150
96	,,	1s. brown on thick greyish paper (No. 79) (5.20) ..	4·50	11·00
		a. Opt. double, one albino ..	£350	£250
97	,,	1s. deep brown on thick greyish paper (No. 80) (5.20)	5·50	13·00

* No. 90 was overprinted on a consignment delivered in 1918 in a distinctive pale scarlet with line perf. and copies without the overprint are not known. Nos. 86 and 91 are also line perf., the rest being comb.

1921–29. *Wmk. Mult. Script CA. P* 14.

No.	Type	Description	Unused	Used
98	9	½d. bright yellow-green ..	65	1·00
99	,,	½d. green (1925)	40	1·00
100	,,	1d. scarlet-verm. (1924) ..	40	65
101	,,	1d. scarlet (1925) ..	1·75	85
102	,,	1d. deep scarlet (1928) ..	1·60	1·00
103	,,	2d. reddish purple (1923)	1·00	1·25
104	,,	2d. purple (1927) ..	80	1·10
105	,,	2½d. indigo	2·25	3·00
106	,,	2½d. dp. pur./*lemon* (1923)	1·10	2·00
107	,,	2½d. pale pur./*yellow* (1925)	1·40	4·00
108	,,	2½d. dark blue (1927) (optd. S. £17)	2·50	4·00
109	,,	2½d. steel-blue (Jan. '28) ..	90	4·00
110	,,	2½d. Prussian blue (1929) ..	80·00	£130
111	,,	6d. orange (*shades*) (1925)	1·25	1·90
113	,,	1s. bistre-brown	5·50	9·00
114	10	3s. green (1923) ..	14·00	17·00
98/114		.. .. *Set of* 9	24·00	35·00
98/114 Optd. "Specimen"		*Set of* 9	£120	

1928. *No.* 104 *surch. with T* **12**.

No.	Type	Description	Unused	Used
115	9	2½d. on 2d. purple	£250	£350
		a. Surch. double	£10000	

13. Whale and Penguins. **14.**

(Recess. Perkins, Bacon & Co.)

1929 (2 SEPT.)**–36.** *P* 14.

(*a*) *Wmk. Mult. Script CA.*

No.	Type	Description	Unused	Used
116	13	½d. green	15	30
117	,,	1d. scarlet	25	25
		a. Deep red (1.35)	2·50	5·00
118	,,	2d. grey	25	50
119	,,	2½d. blue	25	70
120	14	4d. orange ('31) ..	1·10	2·25
		a. Deep orange	5·50	7·00
121	13	6d. purple	1·50	2·25
		a. Reddish purple ('36) ..	4·50	5·50
122	,,	1s. black/*emerald* ..	3·00	4·00
		a. On bright emerald ('36) ..	4·00	4·50
123	,,	2s. 6d. carmine/*blue* ..	9·50	12·00
124	,,	5s. green/*yellow* ..	13·00	18·00
125	,,	10s. carmine/*emerald* ..	27·00	45·00
		(*b*) *Wmk. Mult. Crown CA.*		
126	13	£1 black/*red*	£100	£130
116/126		.. .. *Set of* 11	£140	£200
116/26 Perf. "Specimen"		*Set of* 11	£150	

Two kinds of perforation exist:

A. Comb perf. 13.9:—original values of 1929.

B. Line perf. 13.9, 14.2 or compound:—4d. and 1936 printings of ½d., 1d., 6d. and 1s.

15. Romney Marsh Ram.

16. Iceberg.

17. Whale-catcher *Bransfield*.

18. Port Louis.

19. Map of Falkland Islands.

20. South Georgia.

21. Whale.

22. Govt. House, Stanley.

23. Battle Memorial.

24. King Penguin.

25. Coat of Arms.

26. King George V.

(Des. (except 6d.) by G. Roberts. Eng. and recess. B.W.)

1933 (2 Jan.). *Centenary of British Occupation. Wmk. Mult. Script CA. P* 12.

127	**15**	½d. black and green ..	70	1·00
128	**16**	1d. black and scarlet ..	60	75
129	**17**	1½d. black and blue ..	70	1·60
130	**18**	2d. black and brown ..	1·40	2·25
131	**19**	3d. black and violet ..	1·75	3·00
132	**20**	4d. black and orange ..	3·00	5·00
133	**21**	6d. black and slate ..	11·00	13·00
134	**22**	1s. black and olive-green	14·00	20·00
135	**23**	2s. 6d. black and violet ..	35·00	45·00
136	**24**	5s. black and yellow ..	£130	£150
		a. Black and yellow-orange ..	£300	£325
137	**25**	10s. black and chestnut ..	£170	£200
138	**26**	£1 black and carmine ..	£500	£550
127/138		.. .. *Set of* 12	£800	£900
127/38 Perf. "Specimen"		*Set of* 12	£450	

1935 (7 May). *Silver Jubilee. As Nos.* 91/4 *of Antigua, but printed by B. W. P* 11×12.

139	1d. deep blue and scarlet ..	20	12
140	2½d. brown and deep blue ..	40	65
141	4d. green and indigo ..	50	70
142	1s. slate and purple ..	1·25	2·25
	a. Extra flagstaff ..	£800	£800
139/42 Perf. "Specimen"	*Set of* 4	20·00	

For illustration of "extra flagstaff" variety see Bechuanaland.

1937 (12 May). *Coronation. As Nos.* 13/15 *of Aden, but printed by B. W. & Co. P* 11×11½.

143	½d. green	12	12
144	1d. carmine	15	12
145	2½d. blue	20	30
143/5 Perf. "Specimen"	*Set of* 3	16·00	

27. Whales' Jaw Bones.

28. Black-necked Swan.
29. Battle Memorial.
30. Flock of Sheep.
31. Upland Goose.
32. R.R.S. *Discovery II.*
33. R.R.S. *William Scoresby.*
34. Mount Sugar Top.
34*a*. Turkey Vultures.
35. Gentoo Penguins.
36. Sea Lion.
37. Deception Island.
38. Arms of the Falkland Islands.

(Des. G. Roberts (except 6d. and 9d.). Recess. B.W.)

1938 (3 Jan.)–**50.** *Wmk. Mult. Script CA. P* 12.

146	**27**	½d. black & green (*shades*)	10	10
147	**28**	1d. black and carmine ..	3·50	2·75
		a. Black and scarlet ('40) ..	50	50
148	**29**	1d. black and vio. (14.7.41)	10	12
		a. Black. & purple-vio. (1.43)	15	20
149	,,	2d. black & deep violet ..	55	80
150	**28**	2d. blk. & car.-red (14.7.41)	30	40
		a. Black and red (1.43) ..	10	12
151	**30**	2½d. black and bright blue	35	50
152	**31**	2½d. black & blue (15.6.49)	45	80
153	**30**	3d. black & blue (14.7.41)	25	20
		a. Black & deep blue (1.43)	35	25
154	**31**	4d. black and purple ..	40	40
155	**32**	6d. black and brown ..	1·75	2·25
156	,,	6d. black (15.6.49) ..	80	1·25
157	**33**	9d. black and grey-blue ..	55	55
158	**34**	1s. pale blue	11·00	11·00
		a. Deep blue ('41) ..	1·00	1·00
159	**34*a***	1s. 3d. black & carmine-red (10.12.46) ..	40	55
160	**35**	2s. 6d. slate	8·50	9·00
161	**36**	5s. brt. blue & pale brn.	5·00	5·50
		a. Blue and buff-brown (9.2.50)	5·00	5·50
		b. Indigo & yellow-brn. ('39?)	45·00	30·00
162	**37**	10s. black and orange ..	6·50	7·00
163	**38**	£1 black and violet ..	11·00	12·00
146/163		.. .. *Set of* 18	35·00	38·00
146/63 Perf. "Specimen"		*Set of* 16	80·00	

1946 (7 Oct.). *Victory. As Nos.* 28/9 *of Aden.*

164	1d. dull violet ..	10	12
165	3d. blue	10	15
164/5 Perf. "Specimen"	*Set of* 2 ..	22·00	

1948 (1 Nov.). *Royal Silver Wedding. As Nos.* 30/1 *of Aden.*

166	2½d. ultramarine	10	12
167	£1 mauve	14·00	22·00

1949 (10 Oct.). *75th Anniv. of Universal Postal Union. As Nos.* 114/7 *of Antigua.*

168	1d. violet	15	25
169	3d. deep blue	25	30
170	1s. 3d. deep blue-green ..	65	1·10
171	2s. blue	1·10	2·25

39. Sheep.

40. R.M.S. *Fitzroy.*

41. Upland Goose.

42. Map of Falkland Is.

43. Arms of the Colony.

47. Gentoo Penguins.

44. Auster Aircraft.

45. M.S.S. *John Biscoe.*

46. View of the Two Sisters.

48. Kelp Goose and Gander.

HAVE YOU READ THE NOTES AT THE BEGINNING OF THIS CATALOGUE?

These often provide answers to the enquiries we receive.

49. Sheep Shearing.

50. Battle Memorial.

51. Sea-lion and Female (Clapmatch).

52. Hulk of *Great Britain.*

(Recess. Waterlow.)

1952 (2 Jan.). *Wmk. Mult. Script CA. P* 13×13½ (*vert.*) *or* 13½×13 (*horiz.*).

172	**39**	½d. green	25	25
173	**40**	1d. scarlet	30	25
174	**41**	2d. violet	45	55
175	**42**	2½d. black & light ultram.	20	30
176	**43**	3d. deep ultramarine ..	20	35
177	**44**	4d. reddish purple ..	25	40
178	**45**	6d. bistre-brown	50	55
179	**46**	9d. orange-yellow ..	1·00	1·10
180	**47**	1s. black	1·10	95
181	**48**	1s. 3d. orange ..	55	1·10
182	**49**	2s. 6d. olive-green ..	1·60	2·25
183	**50**	5s. purple	2·25	3·00
184	**51**	10s. grey	4·00	5·50
185	**52**	£1 black	7·00	7·50
172/185		.. .. *Set of* 14	18·00	22·00

1953 (4 June). *Coronation. As No.* 47 *of Aden.*

186	1d. black and scarlet ..	45	50

53. M.S.S. *John Biscoe.*

(Recess. Waterlow & Sons, Ltd.)

1955–57. *As T* **39/47** (*but with portrait of Queen Elizabeth II in place of King George VI as in T* **53**). *Wmk. Mult. Script CA. P* 13×13½ (*vert.*) *or* 13½×13 (*horiz.*).

187	**39**	½d. green (2.9.57)	12	12
188	**40**	1d. scarlet (2.9.57) ..	15	15
189	**41**	2d. violet (3.9.56) ..	30	40
190	**53**	6d. dp. yellow-brn. (1.6.55)	1·40	1·60
191	**46**	9d. orange-yellow (2.9.57)	2·40	3·00
192	**47**	1s. black (15.7.55) ..	2·40	3·00
187/92		.. .. *Set of* 6	6·00	7·00

54. Falkland Islands Thrush.

(Recess. Waterlow (until 1962), then De La Rue.)

1960 (10 Feb.). *Type* **54** *and similar horiz. designs. W* w.**12** (*upright*). *P* 13½.

193	½d. black and myrtle-green (*shades*)	10	12
194	1d. black & scarlet (*shades*) ..	15	15
195	2d. black & blue (*shades*) ..	12	12
196	2½d. black & yellow-brown ..	15	15
197	3d. black and olive	15	20
198	4d. black and carmine ..	15	20
199	5½d. black and violet ..	20	25
200	6d. black and sepia ..	30	25
201	9d. black and orange-red ..	30	30
202	1s. black and maroon ..	20	25
203	1s. 3d. black & ultramarine	60	1·75
204	2s. blk. & brn.-red (*shades*)	70	85
205	5s. black and turquoise ..	2·50	3·00
206	10s. black and purple ..	5·00	6·00
207	£1 black & orange-yellow	10·00	11·00
193/207	.. .. *Set of* 15	18·00	22·00

Designs:—1d. Dominican Gull; 2d. Gentoo Penguins; 2½d. Falkland Islands Marsh Starling; 3d. Upland Geese; 4d. Steamer Ducks; 5½d. Rockhopper Penguin; 6d. Black-browed Albatross; 9d. Silver Grebe; 1s. Pied Oystercatchers; 1s. 3d. Yellow-billed Teal; 2s. Kelp Geese; 5s. King Cormorants; 10s. Carancho; £1 Black-necked Swan.

See also No. 227.

69. Morse Key. **70.** One-valve Receiver.

71. Rotary Spark Transmitter.

(Des. M. Goaman. Photo. Enschedé.)

1962 (5 Oct.). *50th Anniv. of Establishment of Radio Communications. W* w.**12**. *P* 11½×11.

208	**69**	6d. carm.-lake and orange	40	40
209	**70**	1s. deep bluish green and yellow-olive ..	90	90
210	**71**	2s. deep violet & ultram.	1·75	1·75

1963 (4 June). *Freedom from Hunger. As No.* 76 *of Aden.*

211	1s. ultramarine	3·00	3·00

1963 (2 Sept.). *Red Cross Centenary. As Nos.* 147/8 *of Antigua.*

212	1d. red and black	75	75
213	1s. red and blue	3·00	4·50

1964 (23 April). *400th Anniv. of Birth of William Shakespeare. As No.* 164 *of Antigua.*

214	6d. black	50	55

72. H.M.S. *Glasgow.*

73. H.M.S. *Kent.* (*Horiz.*)
74. H.M.S. *Invincible.* (*Horiz.*)
75. Battle Memorial. (*Vert.*)

(Recess. D.L.R.)

1964 (8 Dec.). *50th Anniv. of the Battle of the Falkland Islands. W* w.**12**. *P* 13×14 (2s). *or* 13 (*others*).

215	**72**	2½d. black and red ..	30	30
216	**73**	6d. black and light blue ..	30	30
		a. Centre Type 72 ..	£4500	
217	**74**	1s. black and carmine-red	60	70
218	**75**	2s. black and blue ..	1·25	1·40

It is believed that No. 216a came from a sheet which was first printed with the centre of the 2½d. and then accidentally included among the supply of the 6d. value and thus received the wrong frame. Four copies of the error have been reported.

1965 (26 May). *I.T.U. Centenary. As Nos.* 166/7 *of Antigua.*

219	1d. light blue and deep blue	15	15
220	2s. lilac and bistre-yellow ..	1·75	1·75

1965 (25 Oct.). *International Co-operation Year. As Nos.* 168/9 *of Antigua.*

221	1d. reddish pur. & turq.-grn.	15	15
222	1s. dp. bluish green & lav.	90	1·10

1966 (24 Jan.). *Churchill Commemoration. As Nos.* 170/3 *of Antigua.*

223	½d. new blue	10	10
224	1d. deep green	15	15
225	1s. brown	80	1·10
226	2s. bluish violet	1·60	2·25

1966 (25 Oct.). *As No.* 193 *but wmk.* w.**12** *sideways.*

227	**54**	½d. black & myrtle-green ..	25	25

76. Globe and Human Rights Emblem.

(Des. R. Farrar Bell. Photo. Harrison.)

1968 (4 July). *Human Rights Year. W* w.**12**. *P* 14×14½.

228	**76**	2d. multicoloured ..	10	10
		a. Yellow omitted ("1968" white)	90·00	
229	,,	6d. multicoloured ..	25	25
230	,,	1s. multicoloured ..	40	40
231	,,	2s. multicoloured ..	70	70

77. Dusty Miller.

78. Pig Vine. (*Horiz.*)
79. Pale Maiden. (*Vert.*)
80. Dog Orchid. (*Vert.*)
81. Sea Cabbage. (*Horiz.*)
82. Vanilla Daisy. (*Vert.*)
83. Arrowleaf Marigold. (*Horiz.*)
84. Diddle Dee. (*Horiz.*)
85. Scurvy Grass. (*Horiz.*)
86. Prickly Burr. (*Vert.*)
87. Fachine. (*Vert.*)
88. Lavender. (*Vert.*)
89. Felton's Flower. (*Horiz.*)
90. Yellow Orchid. (*Vert.*)

(Des. Sylvia Goaman. Photo. Harrison.)

1968 (9 Oct.). *Flowers. Chalk-surfaced paper. W* **w.12** *(sideways on vert. designs). P* 14.

No.	Type	Description		
232	**77**	½d. multicoloured ..	5	5
233	**78**	1½d. multicoloured ..	5	5
234	**79**	2d. multicoloured ..	5	5
235	**80**	3d. multicoloured ..	5	8
236	**81**	3½d. multicoloured ..	10	12
237	**82**	4½d. multicoloured ..	12	15
238	**83**	5½d. olive-yellow, brown and yellow-green ..	15	20
239	**84**	6d. carmine, black and yellow-green	15	20
240	**85**	1s. multicoloured ..	25	30
241	**86**	1s. 6d. multicoloured ..	40	1·10
242	**87**	2s. multicoloured ..	70	75
243	**88**	3s. multicoloured ..	90	1·10
244	**89**	5s. multicoloured ..	1·25	1·50
245	**90**	£1 multicoloured ..	1·75	2·00
232/245		.. .. *Set of* 14	5·00	6·50

For stamps inscribed in decimal currency see Nos. 276/88, 293 etc. and 325.

91. DHC–2 Beaver Floatplane.

(Des. V. Whiteley. Litho. Format International.)

1969 (8 Apr.). *21st Anniv. of Government Air Services. T* **91** *and similar horiz. designs. Multicoloured. W.* **w.12** *(sideways). P* 14.

No.	Description		
246	2d. Type **91**	10	10
247	6d. "Norseman"	15	15
248	1s. "Auster"	30	35
249	2s. Falkland Is. Arms ..	60	70

92. Holy Trinity Church, 1869.

93. Christ Church Cathedral, 1969.

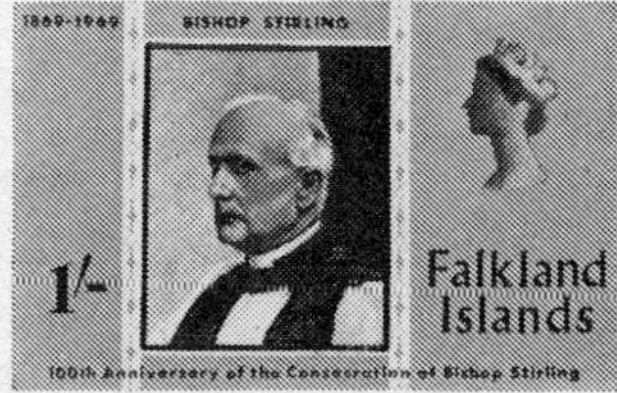

94. Bishop Stirling.

95. Bishop's Mitre.

(Des. G. Drummond. Litho. Format International.)

1969 (30 Oct.). *Centenary of Bishop Stirling's Consecration. W* **w.12** *(sideways). P* 14.

No.	Type	Description		
250	**92**	2d. blk., grey & apple-grn.	8	8
251	**93**	6d. blk., grey & orange-red	12	12
252	**94**	1s. black, grey and lilac ..	20	25
253	**95**	2s. multicoloured ..	40	50

96. Mounted Volunteer.

(Des. R. Granger Barrett. Litho. B.W.)

1970 (30 Apr.). *Golden Jubilee of Defence Force. T* **96** *and similar designs. Multicoloured. W* **w.12** *(sideways on 2d. and 1s.). P* 13.

No.	Description		
254	2d. Type **96**	5	8
255	6d. Defence Post (*horiz.*) ..	12	12
256	1s. Corporal in Number-One Dress Uniform	30	30
257	2s. Defence Force Badge (*horiz.*)	50	55

97. S.S. *Great Britain* (1843).

(Des. V. Whiteley. Litho. J.W.)

1970 (30 Oct.). *Restoration of S.S. "Great Britain". T* **97** *and views of the ship at different dates. Multicoloured. W* **w.12** *(sideways). P* 14½ × 14.

No.	Description		
258	2d. Type **97**	10	10
259	4d. In 1845	20	25
260	9d. In 1876	25	30
261	1s. In 1886	40	50
262	2s. In 1970	80	1·00
258/62	.. .. *Set of* 5	1·50	1·75

½p

(98)

99. Dusty Miller.

1971 (15 Feb.). *Decimal Currency. Nos. 232/44 surch. as T* **98**. *W* **w.12** *(sideways on vert. designs). P* 14.

No.	Type	Description		
263	**77**	½p. on ½d. multicoloured	15	15
264	**78**	1p. on 1½d. multicoloured	5	5
		a. Error. Surch. 5p. ..	75·00	
		b. Do. but surch. at right ..	£150	
265	**79**	1½p. on 2d. multicoloured	5	5
266	**80**	2p. on 3d. multicoloured	8	8
267	**81**	2½p. on 3½d. multicoloured	10	12
268	**82**	3p. on 4½d. multicoloured	12	15
269	**83**	4p. on 5½d. olive-yellow, brown & yellow-green	20	25
270	**84**	5p. on 6d. carmine, black and yellow-green ..	25	30
271	**85**	6p. on 1s. multicoloured ..	25	35
272	**86**	7½p. on 1s. 6d. mult. ..	40	50
273	**87**	10p. on 2s. multicoloured ..	45	55
274	**88**	15p. on 3s. multicoloured ..	65	80
275	**89**	25p. on 5s. multicoloured ..	1·50	1·75
263/75		.. .. *Set of* 13	3·75	4·50

1972 (1 June). *Decimal Currency. As Nos. 232/44 but Glazed, ordinary paper and with values inscr. in decimal currency as T* **99**. *W* **w.12** *sideways on vert. designs* (½, 1½, 2, 3, 7½, 10 *and* 15*p.*) *and upright on horiz. (remainder). P* 14.

No.	Type	Description		
276	**99**	½p. multicoloured ..	8	10
277	**78**	1p. multicoloured ..	5	5
278	**79**	1½p. multicoloured ..	5	5
279	**80**	2p. multicoloured ..	10	10
280	**81**	2½p. multicoloured ..	5	5
281	**82**	3p. multicoloured ..	5	8
282	**83**	4p. olive-yellow, brown & yellow-green ..	10	10
283	**84**	5p. carmine, black and yellow-green ..	12	12
284	**85**	6p. multicoloured ..	20	25
285	**86**	7½p. multicoloured ..	15	20
286	**87**	10p. multicoloured ..	20	25
287	**88**	15p. multicoloured ..	25	30
288	**89**	25p. multicoloured ..	45	50
276/88		.. .. *Set of* 13	1·50	1·60

See also Nos. 293 etc. and 325.

100. Romney Marsh Sheep and Giant Sea Lions.

(Des. (from photograph by D. Groves) and photo. Harrison.)

1972 (20 Nov.). *Royal Silver Wedding. Multicoloured; background colour given. W* **w.12**. *P* 14 × 14½.

No.	Type	Description		
289	**100**	1p. grey-green	12	20
290	,,	10p. bright blue	75	1·10

1973 (14 Nov.). *Royal Wedding. As Nos.* 165/6 *of Anguilla. Centre multicoloured. W* **w.12**. *(sideways). P* 13½.

No.	Description		
291	5p. bright mauve	12	15
292	15p. brown-ochre	45	50

1974 (25 Feb.–18 Oct.). *As Nos. 276 etc., but wmk. upright on ½p. and 2p., and sideways on 6p.* P 14.

293 **99** ½p. multicoloured (18.10.74) .. 5 5
296 **80** 2p. multicoloured 5 5
301 **85** 6p. multicoloured (28.3.74) .. 15 20

Nos. 294/305 have been reserved for further additions to this issue.

101. Fur Seal.

(Des. J. E. Cooter. Litho. Walsall Security Printers Ltd.)

1974 (6 Mar.). *Tourism.* T **101** *and similar horiz. designs. Multicoloured.* W w.**12**. P 14.

306 2p. Type **101** 8 8
307 4p. Trout-fishing 12 12
308 5p. Rockhopper Penguins .. 15 20
309 15p. Military Starling 45 50

102. 19th-Century Mail-coach.

(Des. PAD Studio. Litho. Questa.)

1974 (31 July). *Centenary of Universal Postal Union.* T **102** *and similar vert. designs. Multicoloured.* W w. **12** (*sideways*). P 14.

310 2p. Type **102** 8 8
311 5p. Packet ship, 1841 .. .. 15 15
312 8p. First U.K. aerial post, 1911 .. .. .. 20 25
313 16p. Ship's catapult mail, 1920's 45 45

103. Churchill and Houses of Parliament.

(Des. G. L. Vasarhelyi. Litho. Enschedé.)

1974 (30 Nov.). *Birth Centenary of Sir Winston Churchill.* T **103** *and similar horiz. design. Multicoloured.* W w.**12**. P 13½.

314 16p. Type **103** 40 45
315 20p. Churchill and warships .. 45 50
MS316 108 × 83 mm. Nos. 314/15 90 1·00

104. H.M.S. *Exeter*.

(Des. J.W. Ltd. Litho. Harrison.)

1974 (13 Dec.). *35th Anniv. of the Battle of the River Plate.* T **104** *and similar horiz. designs. Multicoloured.* W w.**12** (*sideways*). P 14.

317 2p. Type **104** 10 10
318 6p. H.M.N.Z. *Achilles* .. 20 25
319 8p. *Admiral Graf Spee* .. 25 30
320 16p. H.M.S. *Ajax* 40 45

105. Seal and Flag Badge.

(Des. PAD Studio, Litho. Walsall Security Ptrs.)

1975 (28 Oct.). *50th Anniv. of Heraldic Arms.* T **105** *and similar vert. designs. Multicoloured.* W w.**14** (*inverted*). P 14.

321 2p. Type **105** 5 5
322 7½p. Coat of arms, 1925 .. 20 20
323 10p. Coat of arms, 1948 .. 25 25
324 16p. Arms of the Dependencies, 1952 .. .. 35 40

1975 (8 Dec.). *As No. 276 but* W w.**14** (*sideways*). P 14.

325 **99** ½p. multicoloured 5 5

Nos. 326/37 have been reserved for future additions to this issue.

106. ½p. Coin and Trout.

(Des. G. Drummond. Litho. Questa.)

1975 (31 Dec.). *New Coinage.* T **106** *and similar horiz. designs each showing coin as* T **106**. *Multicoloured.* W w.**12** (*sideways*). P 14.

338 2p. Type **106** 5 5
339 5½p. Gentoo penguin 12 15
340 8p. Upland goose 20 25
341 10p. Albatross 25 25
342 16p. Sea lion 40 45
338/42 .. .. *Set of* 5 85 95

107. Gathering Sheep.

(Des. PAD Studio. Litho. J.W.)

1976 (28 Apr.). *Sheep Farming Industry.* T **107** *and similar horiz. designs. Multicoloured.* W w.**14** (*sideways*). P 13½.

343 2p. Type **107** 5 5
344 7½p. Shearing 15 15
345 10p. Dipping 20 20
346 20p. Shipping 40 45

108. The Queen awaiting Anointment.

(Des. M. and G. Shamir; adapted J.W. Ltd. Litho. Questa.)

1977 (7 Feb.). *Silver Jubilee.* T **108** *and similar horiz. designs. Multicoloured.* W w.**14** (*sideways*). P 13½.

347 6p. Visit of Prince Philip, 1957 .. .. .. 12 15
348 11p. Queen Elizabeth, ampulla and anointing spoon .. 25 25
349 33p. Type **108** 65 75

FALKLAND ISLANDS DEPENDENCIES.

A. GRAHAM LAND.

GRAHAM LAND

DEPENDENCY OF

(A 1)

1944 (12 FEB.)–**45.** *Stamps of Falkland Is. optd. with Type* A **1**, *in red.*

A 1	**27**	½d. black and green ..	12	15
		a. Blue-black and green ..		
A 2	**29**	1d. black and violet ..	12	20
A 3	**28**	2d. black and carmine-red	12	20
A 4	**30**	3d. black and blue ..	15	25
A 5	**31**	4d. black and purple ..	20	40
A 6	**32**	6d. black and brown ..	65	75
		a. Blue-black and brown ('45) ..	1·75	
A 7	**33**	9d. black and grey-blue	45	60
A 8	**34**	1s. deep blue	50	65
A1/8		Perf. "Specimen" *Set of* 8	40·00	

B. SOUTH GEORGIA.

1944 (3 APR.)–**45.** *Stamps of Falkland Is. optd.* "SOUTH GEORGIA/DEPENDENCY OF", *in red, as Type* A, *of Graham Land.*

B 1	**27**	½d. black and green ..	12	12
B 2	**29**	1d. black and violet ..	12	12
B 3	**28**	2d. black and carmine-red	12	15
B 4	**30**	3d. black and blue ..	15	20
B 5	**31**	4d. black and purple ..	20	25
B 6	**32**	6d. black and brown ..	70	80
		a. Blue-black and brown ('45) ..	2·75	
B 7	**33**	9d. black and grey-blue	45	40
B 8	**34**	1s. deep blue	45	60
B1/8		Perf. "Specimen" *Set of* 8	40·00	

For later issues, see after No. G44.

C. SOUTH ORKNEYS.

1944 (21 FEB.)–**45.** *Stamps of Falkland Is. optd.* "SOUTH ORKNEYS/DEPENDENCY OF", *in red as Type* A **1** *of Graham Land.*

C 1	**27**	½d. black and green ..	12	20
C 2	**29**	1d. black and violet ..	12	20
C 3	**28**	2d. black and carmine-red	12	20
C 4	**30**	3d. black and blue ..	15	25
C 5	**31**	4d. black and purple ..	20	25
C 6	**32**	6d. black and brown ..	70	80
		a. Blue-black and brown ('45)	2·50	
C 7	**33**	9d. black and grey-blue ..	45	70
C 8	**34**	1s. deep blue	45	70
C1/8		Perf. "Specimen" *Set of* 8	40·00	

D. SOUTH SHETLANDS.

1944–45. *Stamps of Falkland Is. optd.* "SOUTH SHETLANDS/DEPENDENCY OF", *in red, as Type* A **1** *of Graham Land.*

D 1	**27**	½d. black and green ..	12	20
D 2	**29**	1d. black and violet ..	12	20
D 3	**28**	2d. black and carmine-red	12	20
D 4	**30**	3d. black and blue ..	15	20
D 5	**31**	4d. black and purple ..	20	40
D 6	**32**	6d. black and brown ..	70	70
		a. Blue-black and brown ('45)	2·50	
D 7	**33**	9d. black and grey-blue ..	45	60
D 8	**34**	1s. deep blue	45	70
D1/8		Perf. "Specimen" *Set of* 8	40·00	
A1/D8		.. .. *Set of* 32	8·50	11·00

E. GENERAL ISSUES.

G 1

(Map litho., frame recess. D.L.R.)

1946 (1 FEB.)–**49.** *Wmk. Mult. Script CA, sideways. P* 12.

(*a*) *Map thick and coarse.*

G 1	G **1**	½d. black and green ..	10	12
G 2	,,	1d. black and violet ..	10	15
G 3	,,	2d. black and carmine ..	10	15
G 4	,,	3d. black and blue ..	12	15
G 5	,,	4d. black and claret ..	15	25
G 6	,,	6d. black and orange ..	20	40
		a. Black and ochre ..	2·50	3·25
G 7	,,	9d. black and brown ..	20	40
G 8	,,	1s. black and purple ..	40	65
G1/8		.. .. *Set of* 8	1·10	2·00
G1/8		Perf "Specimen" *Set of* 8	80·00	

(*b*) *Map thin and clear* (16.2.48).

G 9	G **1**	½d. black and green ..	20	1·00
G10	,,	1d. black and violet ..	20	1·00
G11	,,	2d. black and carmine ..	30	1·25
G11*a*	,,	2½d. black & deep blue (6.3.49)	30	60
G12	,,	3d. black and blue ..	30	1·10
G13	,,	4d. black and claret ..	50	1·75
G14	,,	6d. black and orange ..	65	2·25
G15	,,	9d. black and brown ..	75	2·50
G16	,,	1s. black and purple ..	1·10	5·00
G9/16		.. .. *Set of* 9	4·00	15·00

In Nos. G1/8 a variety with a gap in the 80th parallel occurs six times in each sheet of all values in positions 4, 9, 24, 29, 44, and 49.

In Nos. G9 to G16 the map is redrawn; the "0°" meridian does not touch the "s" of "COATS", the "n" of "Alexander" is not joined to the "L" of "Land" below, and the loops of letters "s" and "t" are generally more open.

1946 (4 OCT.). *Victory. As Nos.* 28/9 *of Aden.*

G17	1d. deep violet	10	10
G18	3d. blue	10	12
G17/18	Perf. "Specimen" *Set of* 2	22·00	

1948 (6 DEC.). *Royal Silver Wedding. As Nos.* 30/1 *of Aden but inscr.* "FALKLAND ISLANDS DEPENDENCIES" (*recess* 1s.).

G19	2½d. ultramarine	10	15
G20	1s. violet-blue	1·10	1·40

1949 (10 OCT.). *75th Anniv. of U.P.U. As Nos.* 114/17 *of Antigua.*

G21	1d. violet	20	30
G22	2d. carmine-red	30	50
G23	3d. deep blue	55	65
G24	6d. red-orange	80	1·10

1953 (4 JUNE). *Coronation. As No.* 47 *of Aden.*

G25	1d. black and violet ..	50	50

G **2.** *John Biscoe*, 1947–52.

G **3.** *Trepassey*, 1945–47.

G **4.** *Wyatt Earp*, 1934–36. (*Horiz.*)
G **5.** *Eagle*, 1944–45. (*Horiz.*)
G **6.** *Penola*, 1934–37. (*Horiz.*)
G **7.** *Discovery II*, 1929–37. (*Horiz.*)
G **8.** *William Scoresby*, 1926–46. (*Horiz.*)
G **9.** *Discovery*, 1925–27. (*Vert.*)
G **10.** *Endurance*, 1914–16. (*Vert.*)
G **11.** *Deutschland*, 1910–12. (*Horiz.*)
G **12.** *Pourquoi-Pas* 1908–10. (*Horiz.*)
G **13.** *Français*, 1903–05. (*Vert.*)
G **14.** *Scotia*, 1902–04. (*Vert.*)
G **15.** *Antarctic*, 1901–03. (*Horiz.*)
G **16.** *Belgica*, 1897–99. (*Vert.*)

(Recess. Waterlow (until 1962), then D.L.R.)

1954 (1 FEB.). *Wmk. Mult. Script CA. P* 12½.

G26	G **2**	½d. black and bluish green (*shades*) ..	12	12
G27	G **3**	1d. black and sepia-brown (*shades*) ..	12	12
G28	G **4**	1½d. blk. & olive (*shades*)	12	15
G29	G **5**	2d. black and rose-red	12	15
G30	G **6**	2½d. blk. & yellow-ochre	12	15
G31	G **7**	3d. blk. & dp. brt. blue	15	20
G32	G **8**	4d. black & bright reddish purple ..	30	35
G33	G **9**	6d. black and deep lilac	40	45
G34	G **10**	9d. black	45	60
G35	G **11**	1s. black and brown ..	70	80
G36	G **12**	2s. black and carmine	1·75	2·00
G37	G **13**	2s. 6d. blk. & pale turq.	2·00	2·25
G38	G **14**	5s. black and violet ..	5·00	6·00
G39	G **15**	10s. black and blue ..	9·00	11·00
G40	G **16**	£1 black	20·00	22·00
G26/40		.. *Set of* 15	35·00	40·00

TRANS-ANTARCTIC EXPEDITION 1955-1958

(G **17**)

1956 (30 JAN.). *Trans-Antarctic Expedition. Nos.* G27, G30/1 *and* G33 *optd. with Type* G **17.**

G41	G **3**	1d. black & sepia-brown	10	10
G42	G **6**	2½d. black & yellow-ochre	15	25
G43	G **7**	3d. black & dp. brt. blue	20	25
G44	G **9**	6d. black and deep lilac	35	45

The stamps of Falkland Islands Dependencies were withdrawn on July 16th, 1963. They were superseded by issues for BRITISH ANTARCTIC TERRITORY and SOUTH GEORGIA.

F. SOUTH GEORGIA.

Issues resumed for the remaining dependencies of South Georgia and South Sandwich Islands.

1. Reindeer.

2. South Sandwich Islands.

3. Sperm Whale. (*Vert.*)
4. Chinstrap and King Penguin. (*Horiz.*)
5. Fur Seal. (*Vert.*)
6. Fin Whale. (*Horiz.*)
7. Elephant Seal. (*Horiz.*)
8. Sooty Albatross. (*Vert.*)
9. Whale-catcher. (*Horiz.*)
10. Leopard Seal. (*Horiz.*)
11. Shackleton's Cross. (*Horiz.*)
12. Wandering Albatross. (*Horiz.*)
13. Elephant and Fur Seal. (*Horiz.*)
14. Plankton and Krill. (*Vert.*)
15. Blue Whale. (*Horiz.*)
16. King Penguins. (*Vert.*)

(Des. De La Rue (No. 16), M. Goaman (others). Recess. De La Rue.)

1963 (17 JULY)–**69.** *Ordinary or glazed paper (No. 16). W* w.**12**. *P* 15.

No.	Type	Description		
1	**1**	½d. brown-red	10	12
		a. P 14 × 15 (13.2.67) ..	12	15
2	**2**	1d. violet-blue	5	5
3	**3**	2d. turquoise-blue ..	5	8
4	**4**	2½d. black	8	10
5	**5**	3d. bistre	10	12
6	**6**	4d. bronze-green	12	15
7	**7**	5½d. deep violet	20	25
8	**8**	6d. orange	20	25
9	**9**	9d. blue	30	35
10	**10**	1s. purple	30	40
11	**11**	2s. yellow-olive & lt. blue	65	80
12	**12**	2s. 6d. blue	1·25	1·50
13	**13**	5s. orange-brown	1·75	2·00
14	**14**	10s. magenta	5·50	7·00
15	**15**	£1 ultramarine	13·00	15·00
16	**16**	£1 grey-black (1.12.69) ..	1·75	2·00
1/16		.. .. *Set of* 16	23·00	25·00

1970 (22 JAN.). *As No.* 1, *but wmk.* w.**12** *sideways and on glazed paper.*

No.	Type	Description		
17	**1**	½d. brown-red	12	15

½p (**17**) ½p (**17*a***) 1½p (**18**) 1½p (**18*a***) 50p (**19**) 50p (**19*a***)

1971 (15 FEB.)–**76.** *Decimal Currency. Nos.* 17 *and* 2/14 *surch. as* T **17/19.** *Nos.* 18/*a wmk. sideways, glazed paper. Others wmk. upright, ordinary paper.*

No.	Type	Description		
18	**1**	½p. on ½d. brown-red (T **17**)	12	15
		a. Surch. with T 17*a* (16.6.72)	12	15
		b. Do. Wmk. upright (24.8.73)	5	5
19	**2**	1p. on 1d. violet-blue ..	10	12
		a. Glazed paper (1.12.72) ..	8	10
		b. Do. but wmk. sideways (9.3.76)	5	5
20	**7**	1½p. on 5½d. dp. vio. (T **18**)	12	15
		a. Surch. with T 18*a*. Glazed paper (24.8.73)	5	5
21	**3**	2p. on 2d. turquoise-blue..	5	5
22	**4**	2½p. on 2½d. black	8	10
23	**5**	3p. on 3d. bistre	8	10
24	**6**	4p. on 4d. bronze-green ..	8	10
25	**8**	5p. on 6d. orange	8	12
26	**9**	6p. on 9d. blue	10	12
27	**10**	7½p. on 1s. purple	12	15
28	**11**	10p. on 2s. yellow-olive and light blue	20	25
29	**12**	15p. on 2s. 6d. blue ..	25	30
30	**13**	25p. on 5s. orange-brown ..	45	50
31	**14**	50p. on 10s. magenta (T **19**)	3·25	3·75
		a. Surch with T 19*a*. Glazed paper (1.12.72)	2·00	2·25
		b. Do. but wmk. sideways. *Deep magenta* (9.3.76) ..	85	95
18b/31b		.. .. *Set of* 14	2·20	2·50

20. *Endurance* beset in Weddell Sea.

(Des. R. Granger Barrett. Litho. A. & M.)

1972 (5 JAN.). *50th Death Anniv. of Sir Ernest Shackleton.* T **20** *and similar horiz. designs. Multicoloured.* W w.**12** (*sideways*). *P* 13½.

No.	Description		
32	1½p. Type **20**	10	15
33	5p. Launching the longboat *James Caird*	30	30
34	10p. Route of the *James Caird*	60	60
35	20p. Sir Ernest Shackleton and the *Quest*	1·25	1·25

21. Elephant Seal and King Penguins.

(Des. (from photograph by D. Groves) and photo. Harrison.)

1972 (20 NOV.). *Royal Silver Wedding. Multicoloured; background colour given.* W w.**12.** *P* 14 × 14½.

No.	Type	Description		
36	**21**	5p. slate-green	55	90
37	,,	10p. bluish violet	1·10	1·75

1973 (1 DEC.*). *Royal Wedding. As Nos.* 165/6 *of Anguilla. Centre multicoloured.* W w.**12** (*sideways*). *P* 13½.

No.	Description		
38	5p. brown-ochre	15	20
39	15p. bright lilac	40	50

* This is the local date of issue: the Crown Agents released the stamps on 14th November.

22. Churchill and Westminster Skyline.

(Des. L. Curtis. Litho. Questa.)

1974 (14 DEC.*). *Birth Centenary of Sir Winston Churchill.* T **22** *and similar horiz. design. Multicoloured.* W w.**12** (*sideways*). *P* 14½.

No.	Description		
40	15p. Type **22**	40	50
41	25p. Churchill and warship ..	60	75
MS42	122 × 98 mm. Nos. 40/1	1·10	1·25

*This is the local date of issue: the Crown Agents released the stamps on 30th November.

23. Captain Cook.

(Des. J. E. Cooter. Litho. Questa.)

1975 (26 APR.). *Bicentenary of Possession by Captain Cook.* T **23** *and similar horiz. designs. Multicoloured.* W w.**12** (*sideways on* 8 *and* 16*p.*). *P* 14.

No.	Description		
43	2p. Type **23**	8	
44	8p. H.M.S. *Resolution* ..	25	2
45	16p. Possession Bay	40	5

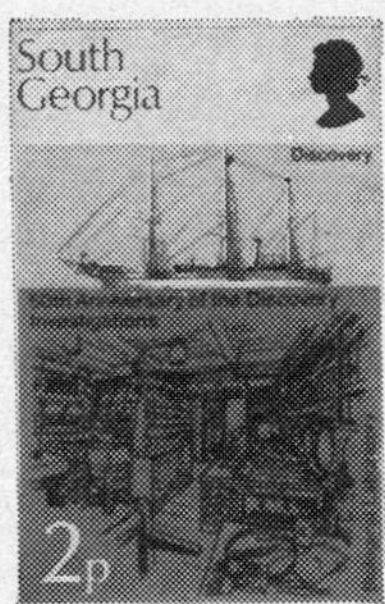

24. *Discovery* and Biological Laboratory.

(Des. J.W. Ltd. Litho. Format.)

1976 (21 DEC.). *75th Anniv. of "Discovery" Investigations.* T **24** *and similar vert. designs. Multicoloured.* W w.**14.** *P* 14.

No.	Description		
46	2p. Type **24**	5	
47	8p. *William Scoresby* and water-sampling bottles ..	15	2
48	11p. *Discovery II* and plankton net	25	2
49	25p. Biological Station and krill	50	5

25. Queen and Retinue after Coronation.

(Des. G. Drummond. Litho. Questa.)

1977 (7 FEB.). *Silver Jubilee.* T **25** *and simila[r] horiz. designs. Multicoloured.* W w.**14** (*side[ways]*). *P* 13½.

No.	Description		
50	6p. Visit by Prince Philip, 1957	12	1
51	11p. Queen Elizabeth and Westminster Abbey	25	2
52	33p. Type **25**	65	7

FIJI.

I. PROTECTORATE.

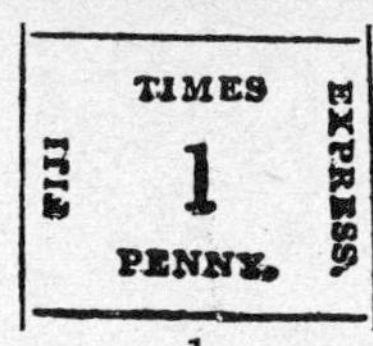

1

(Type-set and printed at the office of *The Fiji Times*, Levuka, Ovalau, Fiji, in sheets of twenty-four stamps arranged in four rows of six stamps of each value in the following order: 6d., 1s., 1d., 3d.)

1870 (1 Nov.)–**71**. *Rouletted in the printing.*

(*a*) *Quadrillé paper.*

1 **1** 1d. black/*rose* £425 £650
2 ,, 3d. black/*rose* £425 £650
3 ,, 6d. black/*rose* £425 £650
4 ,, 1s. black/*rose* £425 £650

(*b*) *Laid bâtonné paper* (1871).

5 **1** 1d. black/*rose* £225 £275
6 ,, 3d. black/*rose* £325 £400
7 ,, 6d. black/*rose* £225 £275
8 ,, 9d. black/*rose* £325 £400
9 ,, 1s. black/*rose* £225 £275

The stamps of the last group were printed from the same plate as the first, but the values of the last three stamps in the bottom row of the sheet were altered to "9d." by inserting figures "9" in place of the figures "3".

There are no reprints of these stamps, but the 1d., 3d., 6d. and 1s. are known in the correct type on *yellow wove* paper and are believed to be proofs.

There are also three different sets of imitations made by the proprietors of *The Fiji Times* to meet the demands of collectors:—

The first was produced in 1876 on *white wove* or *vertically laid* paper, rouletted on dotted lines and arranged in sheets of 40 (5 rows of 8) comprising 1d., 3d., 6d., 9d. and 1s.; the horizontal frame lines are continuous and the vertical ones broken.

The second was produced later on *thick rosy mauve wove* paper, rouletted on dotted lines and arranged in sheets of 30 (5 rows of 6) comprising 1s., 9d., 6d., 3d. and 1d.; the vertical frame lines are continuous and the horizontal ones broken.

The third only came to light in the 1960s and is rare, only one complete sheet being known. The sheet arrangement is the same as Nos. 1/4, which suggests that this was the first imitation to be produced. It is on *off-white wove* paper, rouletted on closely dotted or solid lines, with vertical frame lines continuous and the horizontal ones broken, as in the originals. These differ from the proofs mentioned above in that the lettering is slightly larger and the figures also differ.

King Cakobau, June 1871–Oct. 1874.

2

3

Two Cents (4)

(Eng. and electrotyped by A. L. Jackson. Typo. Govt. Printing Office, Sydney.)

1871 (Nov.). *Wove paper. Wmk.* "FIJI POSTAGE" *in small sans-serif capitals across the middle row of stamps in the sheet.* P $12\frac{1}{2}$.

10 **2** 1d. blue .. .. .. 26·00 35·00
11 ,, 3d. pale yellow-green .. 45·00 70·00
12 **3** 6d. rose .. .. .. 55·00 80·00

The 3d. differs from T **2** in having a white circle containing coloured pearls surrounding the centre.

All three values are known *imperf.*, but were not issued in that condition.

See notes after No. 33b.

1872 (13 Jan.). *Surch. as T* **4**, *at Govt. Ptg. Office, Sydney.*

13 **2** 2 c. on 1d. pale blue .. 8·00 9·00
a. *Deep blue* .. .. 8·00 9·00
14 ,, 6 c. on 3d. yellow-green .. 9·50 12·00
15 **3** 12 c. on 6d. carmine-rose .. 14·00 13·00

II. CROWN COLONY.

Ceded to Great Britain, 10 Oct., 1874.

V.R. (5) V.R. (6) 2d. (7)

Varieties:—

V.R. V.R.

(*Enlarged*).

Cross pattée stop Inverted "A"

Cross pattée stop after "R" (No. 26)
Round raised stop after "V" (No. 28)
Round raised stops after "V" and "R" (No. 29.)
Inverted "A" for "V" (No. 30).
No stop after "R" (No. 13 on T **5**, No. 43 on T**6**).

(Optd. at *Polynesian Gazette* Office, Levuka.)

1874 (10 Oct.). *Nos. 13/15 optd.*

(*a*) *With T* **5**.

16 **2** 2 c. on 1d. blue .. .. 80·00 35·00
a. No stop after "R" .. £275
b. Cross pattée stop after "R" £275
c. Round raised stop after "V" — £275
d. Round raised stops after "V" and "R" £275
e. Inverted "A" for "V" .. — £275
17 ,, 6 c. on 3d. green .. £160 £130
a. No stop after "R" ..
b. Cross pattée stop after "R"
c. Round raised stop after "V"
d. Round raised stops after "V" and "R" ..
e. Inverted "A" for "V" .. £450
18 **3** 12 c. on 6d. rose .. 80·00 35·00
a. No stop after "R" .. £325
b. Cross pattée stop after "R" — £325
c. Round raised stop after "V" £325
d. Round raised stops after "V" and "R" £325
e. Inverted "A" for "V" .. — £325
f. Opt. inverted £650

(*b*) *With T* **6**.

19 **2** 2 c. on 1d. blue .. 85·00 35·00
a. No stop after "R" .. £275 £275
20 ,, 6 c. on 3d. green .. £200 £150
a. No stop after "R" .. £450
21 **3** 12 c. on 6d. rose .. 80·00 45·00
a. No stop after "R" .. — £325
b. Opt. inverted .. £800

1875. *Stamps of 1874 surch. in Levuka with T* **7**.

(*a*) *In red* (May?).

22 **2** 2d. on 6 c. on 3d. green (No. 17) .. .. 45·00 20·00
a. No stop after "R" .. £300 £190
b. Cross pattée stop after "R" £300 £190
c. Round raised stop after "V" £300 £190
d. Round raised stops after "VR" and "R" .. £300 £190
e. Inverted "A" for "V" .. £300 £190
f. No stop after "2d" .. £300 £190
23 ,, 2d. on 6 c. on 3d. green (No. 20) .. .. 70·00 45·00
a. No stop after "R" .. £300 £190
b. Stop between "2" and "d" £300 £190

(*b*) *In black* (30 Sept.).

24 **2** 2d. on 6 c. on 3d. green (No. 17) .. .. £130 65·00
a. No stop after "R" .. £400 £250
b. Cross pattée stop after "R" £400 £250
c. Round raised stop after "V" £400 £250
d. Round raised stops after "V" and "R" .. £400 £250
e. Inverted "A" for "V" .. £400 £250
f. No stop after "2d" .. £400 £250
25 **2** 2d. on 6 c. on 3d. green (No. 20) £250 £110
a. No stop after "R" .. £400 £250
b. Stop between "2" and "d" £400 £500
c. "V.R." double .. .. — £650

1875 (20 Nov.). *No. 15 surch. in Levuka with T 7 and "V.R." at one operation.*

(*a*) "V.R." *T* **5**.

26 **3** 2d. on 12 c. on 6d. rose .. £120 70·00
aa. Round raised stop after "R"
a. Inverted "A" for "V" .. £150 £140
b. Do. and round raised stop after "V" £200 £175
c. As "a" and round raised stops after "R" and "V" £120 90·00
d. Surch. double .. .. — £350

(*b*) "V.R." *T* **6**.

27 **3** 2d. on 12 c. on 6d. rose .. 90·00 70·00
a. Surch. double .. .. — £400

The position of No. 26aa is not known.

(8)

Two Pence (9)

(Typo. Govt. Printing Office, Sydney, from plates of 1871.)

1876–77. *On paper previously lithographed "VR" as T* **8**, *the 3d. surch. with T* **9**. *P* $12\frac{1}{2}$.

(*a*) *Wove paper* (31.1.76).

28 **2** 1d. grey-blue .. .. 6·50 6·50
a. *Dull blue* .. .. 6·50 6·50
b. Doubly printed .. ..
c. Void corner.. .. ..
d. Imperf. between (pair) ..
29 ,, 2d. on 3d. pale green .. 8·00 8·00
a. *Deep green* .. .. 8·00 8·00
30 **3** 6d. pale rose .. .. 12·00 12·00
a. *Dull rose* .. .. 11·00 6·50
b. *Carmine-rose* .. .. 11·00 6·50
c. Doubly printed .. ..

(*b*) *Laid paper* (5.1.77).

31 **2** 1d. blue .. .. .. 3·50 4·00
a. *Deep blue* .. .. 4·00 4·00
b. Void corner .. .. 20·00 13·00
c. Imperf. between (pair) .. £200
32 ,, 2d. on 3d. yellow-green .. 13·00 12·00
a. *Deep yellow-green* .. 13·00 12·00
b. Perf. 10 .. ..
c. Imperf. between (pair) .. £200
d. Perf. 11 .. .. ..
33 **3** 6d. rose .. .. .. 6·50 6·50
a. *Carmine-rose* .. .. 6·50 6·50
b. Imperf. between (pair) .. £200

The 3d. *green* is known without the surcharge T **9** on wove paper and also without the surcharge and the monogram. In this latter condition it can only be distinguished from No. 11 by its colour, which is a fuller, deeper yellow-green.

Stamps on both wove and laid paper *imperf.* are from printer's trial or waste sheets and were not issued.

All values are known on laid paper without the monogram "VR" and the 3d. stamp also without the surcharge but these are also believed to be from printer's trial sheets and were never issued. Being on laid paper they are easily distinguishable from Nos. 10/12.

1877 (12 Oct.). *Optd. with T* **8** *and surch. as T* **9**. *Laid paper. P* $12\frac{1}{2}$.

34 **2** 4d. on 3d. mauve .. .. 9·00 9·00
a. Imperf. between (pair) .. £250

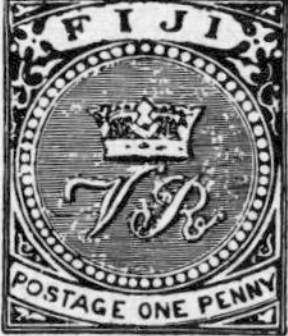

10

11

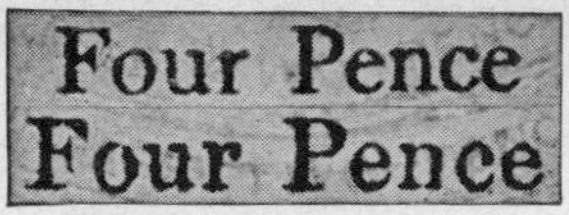

Type A: Length 12½ mm.
Type B: Length 14 mm.
Note also the different shape of the two "e"s.

(Typo. from new plates made from original dies of 1871 with "CR" altered to "VR" at Govt. Printing Office, Sydney. 2d. and 4d. made from old 3d. die.)

1878–1900. *Surcharges as T* **9** *or as Types* A *or* B *for 4d. value. Wove paper with paper-maker's name* "T. H. SAUNDERS" *or* "SANDERSON" *in double-lined capitals extending over seven stamps in each full sheet.*

(*a*) *P* 12½ (1878–80).
35 **10** 1d. pale ultramarine .. 2·00 1·90
a. Ultramarine .. .. 2·75 2·75
36 ,, 2d. on 3d. green .. .. 1·50 1·60
37 ,, 2d. yellow-green .. .. 2·75 2·00
a. Blue-green .. .. 2·75 2·00
b. Error. Ultramarine .. £6500
38 **11** 6d. rose .. .. 13·00 3·50

(*b*) *P* 10 (1881–90).
39 **10** 1d. dull blue .. 5·25 2·00
a. Ultramarine .. .. 2·00 1·25
b. Cambridge blue (12.7.83) .. 3·25 1·25
40 ,, 2d. yellow-green .. .. 1·60 90
a. Blue-green .. .. 1·60 1·25
41 ,, 4d. on 1d. mauve .. .. 2·50 2·00
42 ,, 4d. on 2d. pale mauve (A) 5·25 2·00
a. Dull purple .. .. 5·25 2·00
43 ,, 4d. on 2d. dull purple (B) .. — 32·00
44 ,, 4d. mauve .. .. .. 6·50
a. Deep purple .. .. 6·50 7·00
45 **11** 6d. pale rose .. .. 8·00 2·75
a. Bright rose .. .. 4·00 4·00

(*c*) *P* 10 × 12½ (1882).
46 **10** 1d. ultramarine .. .. 6·50 5·25
47 ,, 2d. green .. .. .. 32·00 6·50
48 **11** 6d. rose .. .. .. 60·00 8·00

(*d*) *P* 12½ × 10 (1890).
49 **10** 1d. ultramarine .. ..

(*e*) *P* 12 × 10 *or* 10 × 12 (1885).
50 **10** 1d. ultramarine .. .. 5·25 2·00
a. Dull blue .. ..
51 ,, 2d. yellow-green .. .. 5·25 2·00
52 **11** 6d. rose .. .. ..

(*f*) *P* 11 × 10 (1893).
53 **10** 1d. ultramarine 65 90
54 ,, 4d. pale mauve .. .. 1·90 1·60
55 **11** 6d. pale rose .. .. 1·90 1·60
a. Rose .. .. .. 2·75 1·60

(*g*) *P* 11 (1897–99).
56 **10** 4d. mauve .. .. .. 2·50 2·50
57 **11** 6d. dull rose .. .. 5·25 5·25
a. Printed both sides (12.99) £130 £110
b. Bright rose .. .. 6·50 4·50

(*h*) *P* 11 × *nearly* 12 (1900).*
58 **10** 4d. deep purple .. .. 4·00
a. Bright purple .. .. 1·60 1·90
59 **11** 6d. rose .. .. .. 8·00
a. Bright rose .. .. 1·90 1·60

(*i*) *Imperf.* (1882–90).
60 **10** 1d. ultramarine .. ..
61 ,, 2d. yellow-green .. ..
62 ,, 4d. on 2d. pale mauve ..
63 **11** 6d. rose .. .. ..

* Under this heading are included all the stamps formerly catalogued as *perfs.* 12 × 11; 11 × 12; 11 × 11½; or 11½ × 11. They are all compounds of *perf.* 11 with that of the machine gauging *nearly* 12, which has sometimes been measured as 11½ and sometimes as 12.

12

13

(Typo. Govt. Printing Office, Sydney.)

1881–99. *Paper-maker's name wmkd. as previous issue.*

(*a*) *P* 10 (19.10.81).
64 **12** 1s. pale brown .. .. 6·50 3·50
a. Deep brown .. .. 6·50 4·00

(*b*) *P* 11 × 10 (1894).
65 **12** 1s. pale brown .. .. 9·00 6·50

(*c*) *P* 11 (1897).
66 **12** 1s. pale brown .. .. 8·00 5·25

(*d*) *P* 11 × *nearly* 12 (5.99).
67 **12** 1s. pale brown .. .. 5·75 4·00
a. Brown .. .. .. 5·75 4·00
b. Deep brown .. .. 8·00 11·00

(*e*) *P nearly* 12 × 11 (3.97).
68 **12** 1s. brown .. .. 9·00 6·50

Dates given are of earliest known use.
Forgeries exist.

(Litho. Govt. Printing Office, Sydney.)

1882 (23 May). *Toned paper wmkd. with paper-maker's name* "Cowan" *in old English outline type once in each sheet. P* 10.
69 **13** 5s. dull red and black .. 23·00 26·00

In July, 1900, an electrotyped plate of a 5s. stamp was made and stamps were printed from it with pale orange-red centre and grey-black frame; these are known *perf.* 10, *perf. nearly* 12, and *imperf.* These stamps were sold as remainders with a special obliteration dated "15 Dec., 00," but were not issued for postal use. The design differs in many particulars from the issued stamp.

2½d. (**14**) **2½d.** (**15**)

T **14.** Fraction bar 1 mm. from "2".
T **15.** Fraction bar 2 mm. from "2".

(Stamps typo. in Sydney and surch. at Govt. Printing Office, Suva.)

1891 (1 Jan.). *T* **10** *surch. P* 10.
70 **14** 2½d. on 2d. green .. 8·00 8·00
71 **15** 2½d. on 2d. green .. 26·00 23·00

½d. (**16**) **5d** (**17**)

FIVE PENCE (**18**) 2 mm. spacing. **FIVE PENCE** (**19**) 3 mm. spacing.

1892. *P* 10. (*a*) *Surch. on T* **10**.
72 **16** ½d. on 1d. dull blue (1.3) .. 11·00 11·00
a. Ultramarine .. .. 6·50 5·25
73 **17** 5d. on 4d. deep purple (25.7) 13·00 13·00
a. Dull purple .. .. 13·00 13·00

(*b*) *Surch. on T* **11**.
74 **18** 5d. on 6d. brownish rose (30.11) .. .. .. 13·00 13·00
a. Bright rose .. .. 11·00 11·00
b. Perf. 10 × 12½ .. ..
75 **19** 5d. on 6d. rose (31.12) .. 18·00
a. Deep rose .. .. 12·00
b. Brownish rose .. .. 11·00

20

21. Native Canoe.

22

(Typo. in Sydney.)

1891–1902. *Wmk. in sheet, either* "SANDERSON" *or* "NEW SOUTH WALES GOVERNMENT" *in outline capitals.*

(*a*) *P* 10 (1891–93).
76 **20** ½d. slate-grey .. .. 1·10 90
77 **21** 1d. black .. .. .. 1·10 90
78 ,, 2d. pale green .. .. 12·00 2·00
79 **22** 2½d. chocolate .. .. 4·50 2·75
80 **21** 5d. ultramarine .. .. 5·25 2·75

(*b*) *P* 11 × 10 (1893–97).
81 **20** ½d. slate-grey .. .. 1·60 2·75
82 **21** 1d. black .. .. .. 1·25 65
83 ,, 2d. green .. .. .. 1·25 65
84 **22** 2½d. chocolate .. .. 4·50 2·75
a. Brown .. .. .. 1·90 1·90
b. Yellowish brown ..
85 **21** 5d. ultramarine .. .. 2·00 2·75

(*c*) *P* 11 (1893–98).
86 **20** ½d. slate-grey .. .. 1·00 1·25
a. Greenish slate .. .. 1·25 1·25
87 **21** 1d. black 65 65
88 ,, 1d. pale mauve 80 55
a. Rosy mauve 80 55
89 ,, 2d. dull green .. .. 1·00 65
a. Emerald-green .. .. 1·00 65
90 **22** 2½d. brown .. .. 1·90 1·90
a. Yellowish brown .. 3·00 3·25
91 **21** 5d. ultramarine .. ..

(*d*) *P* 10 × 12 *or* 12 × 10 (1894–98).
92 **20** ½d. pale grey .. ..
93 **21** 1d. black .. .. .. 1·25 1·25
94 ,, 2d. dull green .. .. — 65·00

(*e*) *Perf. nearly* 12 (1895–97).
95 **20** ½d. greenish slate .. 1·25 1·40
a. Grey .. .. .. 4·00
96 **21** 1d. black .. .. .. 40·00 1·90
97 ,, 1d. rosy mauve 90 90
98 ,, 2d. dull green .. .. 13·00 5·25

(*f*) *P* 11 *and nearly* 12, *compound* (1897–1902).
99 **20** ½d. greenish slate .. 70 80
100 **21** 1d. black .. .. .. 40·00
101 ,, 1d. rosy mauve 80 35
a. Pale rosy mauve 80 80
102 ,, 2d. dull green .. .. 3·25 1·25
103 **22** 2½d. brown .. .. 3·25 3·25
a. Yellow-brown .. .. 2·75 2·75

The 2½d. brown is known *doubly printed*, but only occurs in the remainders and with the special obliteration. It was never issued for postal use.

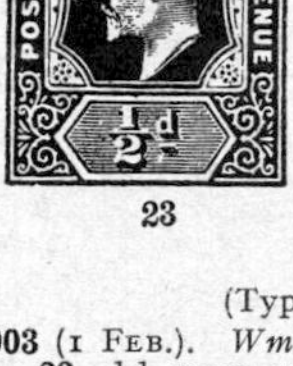

23

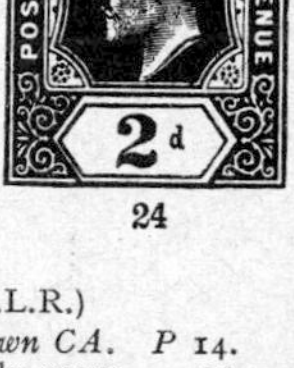

24

(Typo. D.L.R.)

1903 (1 Feb.). *Wmk. Crown CA. P* 14.
104 **23** ½d. green and pale green 25 55
105 ,, 1d. dull pur. & black/*red* 1·25 85
106 **24** 2d. dull purple & orange 60 1·00
107 **23** 2½d. dull pur. & blue/*blue* 4·00 5·50
108 ,, 3d. dull purple and purple 1·40 2·25
109 **24** 4d. dull purple and black 1·60 2·25
110 **23** 5d. dull purple and green 1·60 2·25
111 **24** 6d. dull purple & carmine 2·50 3·50
112 **23** 1s. green and carmine .. 5·50 8·00
113 **24** 5s. green and black .. 24·00 28·00
114 **23** £1 grey-black & ultram. £150 £180
104/14 .. .. *Set of* 11 £180 £225
104/14 Optd. "Specimen" *Set of* 11 £100

904–9. *Wmk. Mult. Crown CA. P* 14.

No.	Type	Description	Unused	Used
5	**23**	½d. green & pale green, O	45	55
6	,,	1d. purple & black/*red*, O	55	25
7	,,	1s. grn. & carm., C (1909)	9·50	11·00

906–12. *Colours changed. Wmk. Mult. Crown CA. P* 14.

No.	Type	Description	Unused	Used
8	**23**	½d. green, O (1908) ..	35	55
9	,,	1d. red, O (1906) ..	35	55
20	,,	2½d. bright blue, O (1910)	1·00	2·75
21	**24**	6d. dull purple, C (1910)	1·60	3·00
22	**23**	1s. black/*green*, C (1911)	3·25	3·50
23	**24**	5s. green and red/*yellow*, C (1911)	23·00	28·00
24	**23**	£1 purple and black/*red*, C (1912)	£110	£140
8/124		.. .. *Set of* 7	£130	£160
8/24 Optd. "Specimen"		*Set of* 7	£120	

25

26

(Typo. D.L.R.)

912 (Oct.)–23. *Ordinary paper (¼d. to 4d.) or chalk-surfaced paper (others). Wmk. Mult. Crown CA. P* 14.

No.	Type	Description	Unused	Used
5	**26**	¼d. brown (1916)	15	40
		a. Deep brown	23	40
6	**25**	½d. green	25	30
		a. Yellow-green (1915) ..	1·40	1·75
		b. Blue-green (1917) ..	60	60
7	,,	1d. carmine	60	15
		a. Bright scarlet (2.16) ..	55	50
		b. Deep rose (1919)	85	20
8	**26**	2d. greyish slate (5.14) ..	55	40
		a. Wmk. sideways		
9	**25**	2½d. bright blue (5.14) ..	1·75	2·50
0	,,	3d. purple/*yellow* (5.14) ..	1·75	2·25
		a. Wmk. sideways	£200	
		b. On lemon (1915)	2·25	2·75
		c. On pale yellow (Die I) ..	1·50	2·25
		d. On pale yellow (Die II) ('23)	2·00	2·25
1	**26**	4d. black and red/*yellow* (5.14)	2·00	3·00
		a. On lemon	2·75	3·50
		b. On orange-buff (1.21) ..	9·50	11·00
		c. On pale yellow (Die I) ('21)	4·00	4·00
		d. On pale yellow (Die II) ('23) (Optd. S. £4)	3·25	5·00
2	**25**	5d. dull purple & ol.-grn. (5.14)	2·50	3·25
3	**26**	6d. dull & bright purple (5.14)	1·60	2·50
4	**25**	1s. black/*green* (10.13) ..	3·25	4·50
		a. White back (4.14) ..	2·25	2·50
		b. On blue-green, olive back (1917)	3·25	4·00
		c. On emerald back (Die I) ('21)	2·25	3·50
		d. On emerald back (Die II) (1923)	2·25	3·00
5	**26**	2s. 6d. black and red/*blue* (29.1.16)	9·00	11·00
6	,,	5s. green and red/*yellow*	19·00	24·00
7	**25**	£1 purple and black/*red* (Die I) (5.14)	£100	£120
		a. Die II	£100	£120
5/37a		.. .. *Set of* 13	£130	£160
5/37 Optd. "Specimen"		*Set of* 13	£130	

WAR STAMP

(27)

915 (Dec.).–19. *Optd. locally with T* **27**.

No.	Type	Description	Unused	Used
8	**25**	½d. blue-green	12	35
		a. Yellow-green	15	45
		b. Opt. inverted	£150	
		c. Opt. double		
9	,,	1d. carmine	6·00	9·50
		a. Bright scarlet	40	1·10
		b. Do. Strip of 12, one without opt.	£2500	
		c. Opt. inverted	£150	
		d. Deep rose (1919)	35	80
8, 139 Optd. "Specimen"		*Set of* 2	22·00	

No. 139b occurred on one pane of 120 only, e overprint being so misplaced that all the amps of the last vertical row escaped it entirely.

Nos. 140/227 no longer used.

1922–27. *Wmk. Mult. Script CA. P* 14.

No.	Type	Description	Unused	Used
228	**26**	¼d. deep brown, O ('23)	70	2·75
229	**25**	½d. green, O ('23) ..	25	45
230	,,	1d. carmine-red, O ..	40	90
231	,,	1d. violet, O ('27) ..	35	12
232	**26**	1½d. scarlet, O ('27) ..	1·00	1·25
233	,,	2d. grey, O	50	12
234	**25**	3d. bright blue, O ('24)	65	1·00
235	**26**	4d. blk. & red/*lemon* O ('24)	1·40	1·90
		a. On orange-buff (1927) ..	1·25	1·75
236	**25**	5d. dull pur. & sage-grn., O	85	1·25
237	**26**	6d. dull & brt. purple, O	70	1·10
238	**25**	1s. black/*emerald*, C ('24)	1·75	2·75
239	**26**	2s. pur. & blue/*blue*, C ('27)	8·00	11·00
240	,,	2s. 6d. blk. & red/*blue*, C ('25)	6·00	10·00
241	,,	5s. grn. & red/*yell.*, C ('26)	15·00	18·00
228/241		.. .. *Set of* 14	35·00	50·00
228/41 Optd. "Specimen"		*Set of* 14	95·00	

The 2d. imperforate with watermark Type **10** of Ireland came from a trial printing and was not issued.

1935 (6 May). *Silver Jubilee. As Nos.* 91/4 *of Antigua. P* 13½ × 14.

No.	Description	Unused	Used
242	1½d. deep blue and carmine ..	20	40
243	2d. ultramarine and grey ..	35	45
244	3d. brown and deep blue ..	95	1·25
245	1s. slate and purple ..	1·75	3·00
242/5	Perf. "Specimen" *Set of* 4	20·00	

1937 (12 May). *Coronation. As Nos.* 13/15 *of Aden, but ptd. by B. W. P* 11 × 11½.

No.	Description	Unused	Used
246	1d. purple	20	20
247	2d. grey-black	25	20
248	3d. Prussian blue	25	20
246/8	Perf. "Specimen" *Set of* 3	14·00	

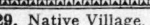

28. Natives Sailing Canoe.

29. Native Village.

30. Native Canoe.

Die I. **30.** Die II.
Empty Canoe. Native in Canoe.

31. Map of Fiji Islands.

Die I. **31.** Die II.
Without "180°" With "180°"

32. Government Offices.

34. Sugar Cane.

33. Canoe and Arms of Fiji.

36. Arms of Fiji.

35. Spearing Fish by Torchlight.

37. Suva Harbour.

38. River Scene.

40. Paw-Paw Tree.

39. Chief's Hut.

41. Police Bugler.

(Des. V. E. Ousey (T **28**, **35** and **38**), C. D. Lovejoy (T **29**, **30** and **34**), I. Stinson (T **33** and **39**) and A. V. Guy (T **31** and **37**). Recess. De La Rue (T **28**, **30**, **31**, **32** and **36**), Waterlow (others).)

1938 (5 Apr.)–**1955.** *Wmk. Mult. Script CA. Various perfs.*

No.	Type	Description	Unused	Used
249	**28**	½d. green (*p* 13½) ..	15	15
		a. Perf. 14	1·10	75
		b. Perf. 12	15	15
250	**29**	1d. brown & blue (*p* 12½)	12	12
251	**30**	1½d. carm. (Die I) (*p* 13½)	2·25	1·10
252	,,	1½d. carm. (Die II) (*p* 13½)	55	55
		a. *Dark carmine*	1·10	1·25
		b. Perf. 14	2·50	3·00
		c. Perf. 12	15	20
253	**31**	2d. brown & green (Die I) (*p* 13½)	2·50	30
254	,,	2d. brown & green (Die II) (*p* 13½)	65	1·40
255	**32**	2d. green & mag. (*p* 13½)	12	15
		a. Perf. 12	15	15
256	**31**	2½d. brown & green (Die II) (*p* 14)	20	20
		a. Perf. 13½	12	12
		b. Perf. 12	12	12
257	**33**	3d. blue (*p* 12½)	15	15
258	**34**	5d. blue & scarlet (*p* 12½)	8·00	6·50
259	,,	5d. yellow-green & scarlet (*p* 12½)	30	35
260	**31**	6d. blk. (Die I) (*p* 13×12)	7·00	6·50
261	,,	6d. blk. (Die II) (*p* 13½)	1·10	30
		a. *Violet-black*	6·50	5·00
		b. Perf. 12. *Black* ..	25	30
261*c*	**36**	8d. carmine (*p* 14) ..	35	45
		d. Perf. 13	30	70
262	**35**	1s. black & yell. (*p* 12½)	40	35
263	**36**	1s. 5d. blk. & carm. (*p* 14)	35	40
263*a*	,,	1s. 6d. ultramarine (*p* 14)	50	70
		b. Perf. 13	65	75
264	**37**	2s. vio. & orge. (*p* 12½)	40	65
265	**38**	2s. 6d. grn. & brn. (*p* 12½)	75	1·10
266	**39**	5s. grn. & pur. (*p* 12½) ..	1·10	1·10
266*a*	**40**	10s. orge. & emer. (*p* 12½)	6·00	7·00
266*b*	**41**	£1 ultram. & car. (*p* 12½)	7·50	8·00
249/266*b*		.. .. *Set of* 22	35·00	32·00
249/66 excl. 261*c* & 263*a* Perf. "Specimen"		.. *Set of* 18	£110	

Dates of issue:—1940, Nos. 252, 254; 1.10.40, Nos. 259, 261; 13.6.40, No. 263; 1941, No. 249*a*; 1942, No. 252*b*; 19.5.42, No. 255; 6.2.42, Nos. 256/*a*; 1.44, No. 261*a*; 1946, No. 255*a*; 1947, No. 261*b*; 1948, Nos. 249*b*, 256*b*; 15.11.48 No. 261*c*; 21.7.49, No. 252*c*; 13.3.50, Nos. 266*a*/*b*; 7.6.50; No. 261*d*, 1.8.50, No. 263*a*; 16.2.55, No. 263*b*; 5.4.38, others.

2½d.

(**42**)

1941 (10 Feb.). *No. 254 surch. with T* **42**.

No.	Type	Description	Unused	Used
267	**31**	2½d. on 2d. brown & green	5	5

1946 (17 Aug.). *Victory. As Nos. 28/9 of Aden.*

No.	Description	Unused	Used
268	2½d. green	8	5
269	3d. blue	15	10
268/9	Perf. "Specimen" *Set of* 2	16·00	

1948 (17 Dec.). *Royal Silver Wedding. As Nos. 30/1 of Aden.*

No.	Description	Unused	Used
270	2½d. green	8	5
271	5s. violet-blue	2·25	4·00

1949 (10 Oct.). *75th Anniv. of U.P.U. As Nos. 114/7 of Antigua.*

No.	Description	Unused	Used
272	2d. bright reddish purple ..	12	15
273	3d. deep blue	20	30
274	8d. carmine-red	35	50
275	1s. 6d. blue	65	60

43. Children Bathing.

44. Rugby Footballer.

(Recess. B.W.)

1951 (17 Sept.). *Health Stamps. Wmk. Mult. Script CA. P* 13½.

No.	Type	Description	Unused	Used
276	**43**	1d.+1d. brown	20	25
277	**44**	2d.+1d. green	25	30

1953 (2 June). *Coronation. As No. 47 of Aden.*

No.	Description	Unused	Used
278	2½d. black and green ..	35	30

45. Arms of Fiji.

(Recess. D.L.R.)

1953 (16 Dec.). *Royal Visit. Wmk. Mu Script CA. P* 13.

No.	Type	Description	Unused	Used
279	**45**	8d. deep carmine-red ..	20	

46. Queen Elizabeth II (after Annigoni).

47. Government Offices.

48. Loading Copra.

49. Sugar Cane Train.

50. Preparing Bananas for Export.

51. Gold Industry.

)es. V. E. Ousey (½d., 1s., 2s. 6d.), A. V. Guy (6d.). Recess. D.L.R. (½d., 2d., 6d., 8d.), Waterlow (1s., 2s. 6d., 10s., £1) and B.W. (others).).

54–56. *T* **46/51** *and designs as T* **28/41** *(but with portrait of Queen Elizabeth II in place of King George VI, as in T* **47**). *Wmk. Mult. Script CA. P* 12 (2*d*.), 13 (8*d*.), 12½ (1*s*., 2*s*. 6*d*., 10*s*., £1), 11½×11 (3*d*., 1*s*. 6*d*., 2*s*., 5*s*.) *or* 11½ (½*d*., *and T* **46**).

0	**28**	½d. myrtle-green	5	5
1	**46**	1d. turquoise-blue ..	5	5
2	,,	1½d. sepia.	8	8
3	**47**	2d. green and magenta ..	10	10
4	**46**	2½d. blue-violet	12	15
5	**48**	3d. brown and reddish violet (*shades*) ..	12	10
7	**31**	6d. black	20	20
8	**36**	8d. dp. carm.-red (*shades*)	25	25
9	**35**	1s. black and yellow ..	30	30
0	**49**	1s. 6d. bl. & myrtle-grn.	90	60
1	**50**	2s. black and carmine ..	70	60
2	**38**	2s. 6d. bluish green and brown (*shades*) ..	70	70
3	**51**	5s. ochre and blue ..	2·00	2·25
4	**40**	10s. orange and emerald	13·00	13·00
5	**41**	£1 ultramarine and carm.	10·00	11·00
0/95		.. .. *Set of* 15	25·00	26·00

Dates of issue: 1954—1 Feb. (2d., 1s., 2s. 6d.). July (½d., 6d., 8d., 10s., £1). 1956–1 June l.), 1 Oct. (others).

52. River Scene.

53. Cross of Lorraine.

(Recess. Bradbury, Wilkinson.)

4 (1 Apr.). *Health Stamps. Wmk. Mult. Script CA. P* 11×11½.

52	1½d.+½d. bistre-brn. & grn.	15	20
53	2½d.+½d. orange and black	20	25

Queen Elizabeth II (after Annigoni).

56. Hibiscus.

55. Fijian beating Lali.

57. Yaqona Ceremony.

58. Location Map.

59. Nadi Airport.

60. Kandavu Parrot.

61. Cutting Sugar-cane.

62. Arms of Fiji.

(Des. M. Goaman: Photo. Harrison (8d., 4s.). Recess. B.W. (others).)

1959–63. *Wmk. Mult. Script CA. P* 11½ (*T* **46** *and* **54**), 11½ × 11 (6*d*., 10*d*., 1*s*., 2*s*. 6*d*., 10*s*., £1), 14½ × 14 (8*d*.) *or* 14 × 14½ (4*s*.).

298	**46**	½d. emer.-green (14.11.61)	5	5
299	**54**	1d. deep ultram. (3.12.62)	5	5
300	,,	1½d. sepia (3.12.62) ..	8	8
301	**46**	2d. rose-red (14.11.61) ..	10	10
302	,,	2½d. orange-brown (3.12.62)	12	12
303	**55**	6d. carm. & blk. (14.11.61)	20	20
304	**56**	8d. scarlet, yellow, green and black (1.8.61) ..	30	35
305	**57**	10d. brown & carm. (1.4.63)	50	60
306	**58**	1s. lt. bl. & bl. (14.11.61)	25	25
307	**59**	2s. 6d. black and purple (14.11.61)	1·50	60
308	**60**	4s. red, green, blue and slate-green (13.7.59) ..	1·60	2·00
309	**61**	10s. emerald and deep sepia (14.11.61) ..	4·00	4·50
310	**62**	£1 blk. & orge. (14.11.61)	8·50	8·50
298/310		.. .. *Set of* 13	15·00	15·00

Nos. 299 and 311 have turtles on either side of "Fiji" instead of shells.

63. Queen Elizabeth II.

65. White Orchid.

64. International Dateline.

66. Orange Dove.

(Des. M. Goaman. Photo. Harrison (3d., 9d. 1s. 6d., 2s., 4s., 5s.). Recess. Bradbury, Wilkinson (others).)

1962 (3 Dec.)–**66.** *W* w.**12** (*upright*). *P* 11½ (1*d*., 2*d*.), 12½ (3*d*.), 11½×11 (6*d*., 10*d*., 2*s*. 6*d*., 10*s*., £1), 14½×14 (9*d*., 2*s*.) *or* 14×14½ (1*s*. 6*d*., 4*s*., 5*s*.).

311	**54**	1d. deep ultram. (14.1.64)	5	5
312	**46**	2d. rose-red (3.8.65) ..	5	5
313	**63**	3d. multicoloured ..	8	8
314	**55**	6d. carm. & blk. (9.6.64)	10	10
315	**56**	9d. scarlet, yellow, green & ultramarine (1.4.63)	15	15
316	**57**	10d. brn. & carm. (14.1.64)	15	15
317	**58**	1s. lt. blue & blue (24.1.66*)	20	15
318	**64**	1s. 6d. red, yellow, gold, black and blue ..	35	35
319	**65**	2s. yellow-green, green and copper (*shades*) ..	60	60
320	**59**	2s. 6d. black and purple (*shades*) (3.8.65) ..	50	50
321	**60**	4s. red, yellow-green, blue and green (1.4.64) ..	1·10	1·10
322	,,	4s. red, green, blue and slate-green (1.3.66) ..	1·00	1·75
323	**66**	5s. red, yellow and grey ..	1·10	1·10
324	**61**	10s. emerald and deep sepia (14.1.64)	2·25	2·25
325	**62**	£1 black & orge. (9.6.64)	4·50	5·00
311/25		.. .. *Set of* 15	10·00	12·00

* This is the earliest known used date in Fiji and it was not released by the Crown Agents until 1 November.

See also No. 359.

ROYAL VISIT

1963

(**67**)

ROYAL VISIT 1963

(**68**)

1963 (1 Feb.). *Royal Visit. Nos.* 313 *and* 306 *optd. with T* **67/8**.

326	**67**	3d. multicoloured ..	15	20
327	**68**	1s. light blue and blue ..	45	50

1963 (4 JUNE). *Freedom from Hunger. As No. 76 of Aden.*
328 2s. ultramarine .. .. 1·50 1·75

69. Running.

70. Throwing the Discus. (*Vert.*)
71. Hockey. (*Vert.*)
72. High-jumping. (*Horiz.*)

(Des. M. Goaman. Photo. Harrison.)

1963 (6 AUG.). *First South Pacific Games, Suva. W* w.**12**. *P* 14½.
329 **69** 3d. red-brn., yell. & black 15 20
330 **70** 9d. red-brn., vio. & black 35 40
331 **71** 1s. red-brn., green & black 35 35
332 **72** 2s. 6d. red-brown, lt. blue and black .. .. 1·10 1·25

1963 (2 SEPT). *Red Cross Centenary. As Nos. 147/8 of Antigua.*
333 2d. red and black 12 12
334 2s. red and blue .. .. 1·40 1·60

COMPAC CABLE
IN SERVICE
DECEMBER 1963

(**73.** Cable-laying ship, *Retriever*.)

1963 (3 DEC.). *Opening of COMPAC (Trans-Pacific Telephone Cable). No. 317 optd. with T* **73** *by Bradbury, Wilkinson.*
335 **58** 1s. light blue and blue .. 60 65

74. Jamborette Emblem.

75. Scouts of Three Races.

(Des. V. Whiteley assisted by Norman L. Joe, Asst. D.C., Fiji Scouts for Jamboree emblem. Photo. Harrison.)

1964 (4 AUG.). *50th Anniv. of Fijian Scout Movement. W* w.**12**. *P* 12½.
336 **74** 3d. red, gold, ultramarine and deep green .. 12 15
337 **75** 1s. violet & yellow-brown 55 60

76. Flying-boat " Aotearoa ".

77. Fiji Airways " Heron ".

78. " Aotearoa " and Map.

(Des. V. Whiteley. Photo. Harrison.)

1964 (24 OCT.). *25th Anniv. of First Fiji-Tonga Airmail Service. W* w.**12**. *P* 14½×14 (1s.) *or* 12½ (*others*).
338 **76** 3d. black and vermilion .. 15 15
339 **77** 6d. vermilion & brt. blue 30 30
340 **78** 1s. black & turquoise-blue 60 65

1965 (17 MAY). *I.T.U. Centenary. As Nos. 166/7 of Antigua.*
341 3d. blue and rose-carmine .. 12 15
342 2s. orange-yellow and bistre 80 85

1965 (25 OCT.). *International Co-operation Year. As Nos. 168/9 of Antigua.*
343 2d. reddish pur. & turq.-grn. 8 10
344 2s. 6d. dp. bluish grn. & lav. 60 70

1966 (24 JAN.). *Churchill Commemoration. As Nos. 170/3 of Antigua.*
345 3d. new blue 8 8
346 9d. deep green 30 35
347 1s. brown 45 50
348 2s. 6d. bluish violet .. .. 1·40 1·60

1966 (1 JULY). *World Cup Football Championships. As Nos. 176/7 of Antigua.*
349 2d. violet, yellow-green, lake and yellow-brown 10 10
350 2s. chocolate, blue-green, lake and yellow-brown .. 50 60

79. H.M.S. *Pandora* approaching Split Island, Rotuma.

80. Rotuma Chiefs.
81. Rotumans welcoming H.M.S. *Pandora*.

(Des. V. Whiteley. Photo. Enschedé.)

1966 (29 AUG.). *175th Anniv. of Discovery of Rotuma. W* w. **12** (*sideways*). *P* 14×13.
351 **79** 3d. multicoloured .. 10 10
352 **80** 10d. multicoloured .. 30 35
353 **81** 1s. 6d. multicoloured .. 60 60

1966 (20 SEPT.). *Inauguration of W.H.O. Headquarters, Geneva. As Nos. 178/9 of Antigua.*
354 6d. black, yellow-green and light blue 15 20
355 2s. 6d. black, light purple and yellow-brown 70 75

III. LEGISLATIVE ASSEMBLY.

82. Running.

83. Putting the Shot. (*Vert.*)
84. Diving. (*Horiz.*)

(Des. V. Whiteley. Photo. Harrison.)

1966 (5 DEC.). *2nd South Pacific Games, Noumé W* w.**12** (*sideways on 9d.*). *P* 14½×14 (*9d.*) 14×14½ (*others*).
356 **82** 3d. black, chestnut and yellow-olive 10
357 **83** 9d. black, chestnut and greenish blue 25
358 **84** 1s. multicoloured .. 30

1967 (16 FEB.). *As No. 321 but wmk.* w. *sideways.*
359 **60** 4s. red, yellow-green, blue and green 80

85. Military Forces Band.

86. Reef Diving.
87. Beqa Fire Walkers.
88. Cruise Liner at Suva.

(Des. G. L. Vasarhelyi. Photo. Enschedé.)

1967 (20 OCT.). *International Tourist Yea W* w.**12** (*sideways*). *P* 14×13.
360 **85** 3d. multicoloured .. 10
361 **86** 9d. multicoloured .. 25
362 **87** 1s. multicoloured .. 30
363 **88** 2s. multicoloured .. 40

89. Bligh (bust), H.M.S. *Providence* and Cha

90. " *Bounty*'s longboat being chased in F waters ".

(*Illustration reduced. Actual size* 54×20 *mm*

91. Bligh's Tomb.

(Des. V. Whiteley. Photo. Harrison.)

1967 (11 DEC.). *150th Death Anniv. of Admi Bligh. W* w.**12** (*sideways on* 1s.). *P* 12½× (1s.) *or* 15×14 (*others*).
364 **89** 4d. multicoloured .. 10
365 **90** 1s. multicoloured .. 25
366 **91** 2s. 6d. multicoloured .. 45

92. Simmonds "Spartan" Seaplane.

93. "HS 748" Aircraft and Airline Insignia.

94. "Southern Cross" and Crew.

95. Lockheed "Altair" Monoplane.

(Des. V. Whiteley. Photo. Harrison.)

.968 (5 June). *40th Anniv. of Kingsford Smith's Pacific Flight via Fiji.* W w.**12**. *P* 14 × 14½.

No.	Type	Description	Unused	Used
67	**92**	2d. black and green ..	8	8
68	**93**	6d. greenish blue, black and lake	15	15
69	**94**	1s. deep violet and turquoise-green	25	25
70	**95**	2s. orange-brown and blue	45	50

96. Bure Huts.

97. Passion Flowers. (*As T* **96.**)

98. Pearly Nautilus. (*As T* **96.**)

99. Reef Heron (after Belcher).

100. Hawk Moth. (*As T* **96.**)

101. Angel Fish. (*As T* **96.**)

102. Bamboo Raft. (*As T* **96.**)

103. Tiger Moth. (*As T* **96.**)

104. Black Marlin. (*As T* **99.**)

105. "Sun Birds" (Orange-breasted Honeyeaters) (after Belcher). (*As T* **99.**)

106. Sea Snake.

107. Outrigger Canoes. (*As T* **106.**)

108. Golden Cowrie Shell. (*As T* **96.**)

109. Mining Industry. (*As T* **99.**)

110. Bamboo Orchids. (*As T* **106.**)

111. Ceremonial Whale's Tooth. (*As T* **99.**)

112. Queen Elizabeth and Arms of Fiji.

(Des. G. Hamori (½d., 1d., 9d.), W. O. Cernohorsky (2d., 4s.), H. S. Robinson (4d., 10d.), D. W. Blair (6d., 5s.), P. D. Clarke (1s.), G. Vasarhelyi (2s. 6d.), W. O. Cernohorsky and E. Jones (3s.), E. Jones and G. Hamori (10s.), E. Jones (£1). Adapted V. Whiteley. Photo. D.L.R.)

1968 (15 July). *W* w.**12** (*sideways on all vert. designs*). *P* 14 × 13½ (2*s*., 2*s*. 6*d*., 5*s*., £1) *or* 13½ × 14 (3*d*., 1*s*., 1*s*. 6*d*., 4*s*., 10*s*.) *or* 13½ × 13 (*others*).

No.	Type	Description	Unused	Used
371	**96**	½d. multicoloured ..	5	5
372	**97**	1d. deep greenish blue, red and yellow ..	5	5
373	**98**	2d. new blue, brown and ochre	5	5
374	**99**	3d. blackish green, blue and ochre	8	8
375	**100**	4d. multicoloured ..	8	8
376	**101**	6d. multicoloured ..	10	10
377	**102**	9d. multicoloured ..	15	20
378	**103**	10d. Royal blue, orange and blackish brown	20	20
379	**104**	1s. Prussian blue and brown-red	25	30
380	**105**	1s. 6d. multicoloured ..	50	60
381	**106**	2s. turquoise, black and rosine	50	65
382	**107**	2s. 6d. multicoloured ..	70	60
383	**108**	3s. multicoloured ..	1·00	1·50
384	**109**	4s. yellow-ochre, black and olive	1·00	1·25
385	**110**	5s. multicoloured ..	1·00	1·25
386	**111**	10s. lake-brown, black and ochre	2·25	2·50
387	**112**	£1 multicoloured ..	5·00	6·00
371/87		.. .. *Set of* 17	11·00	14·00

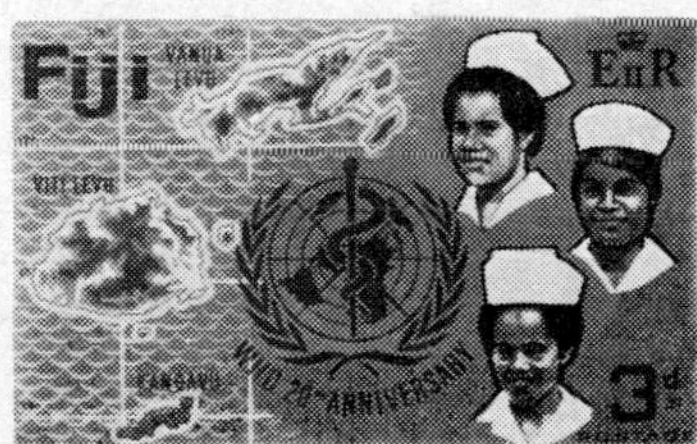

113. Map of Fiji, W.H.O. Emblem and Nurses.

114. Transferring Patient to Medical Ship, *Vuniwai.*

115. Recreation.

(Des. V. Whiteley. Litho. De La Rue.)

1968 (9 Dec.). *20th Anniv. of World Health Organization.* *W* w.**12** (*sideways*). *P* 14.

No.	Type	Description	Unused	Used
388	**113**	3d. multicoloured ..	8	8
389	**114**	9d. multicoloured ..	20	25
390	**115**	3s. multicoloured ..	50	60

(New currency. 100 cents = 1 dollar.)

116. Passion Flowers.

1969 (13 Jan.)–**70.** *Decimal Currency. Designs as T* **96**, *etc., but with values inscr. in decimal currency as in T* **116**. *W* w.**12** (*sideways on all vert. designs*). *Chalk-surfaced paper. P* 14 × 13½ (20 *c*., 25 *c*., 50 *c*., $2), 13½ × 14 (3 *c*., 10 *c*., 15 *c*., 40 *c*., $1) *or* 13½ × 13 (*others*).

No.	Type	Description	Unused	Used
391	**116**	1 c. deep greenish blue, red and yellow ..	5	5
392	**98**	2 c. new bl., brn. & ochre	5	5
393	**99**	3 c. blackish green, blue and ochre	5	5
394	**100**	4 c. multicoloured ..	8	8
395	**101**	5 c. multicoloured ..	10	10
396	**96**	6 c. multicoloured ..	12	12
397	**102**	8 c. multicoloured ..	15	15
398	**103**	9 c. Royal blue, orange and blackish brown	15	15
399	**104**	10 c. Prussian blue and brown-red	20	20
400	**105**	15 c. multicoloured ..	30	40
401	**106**	20 c. turq., blk. & rosine	40	45
402	**107**	25 c. multicoloured ..	45	35
403	**108**	30 c. multicoloured ..	60	80
404	**109**	40 c. yellow-ochre, black and olive	75	80
405	**110**	50 c. multicoloured ..	1·00	75
		a. Glazed, ordinary paper (3.9.70)	1·00	75
406	**111**	$1 lake-brown, black & ochre	2·00	1·75
		a. Glazed, ordinary paper (3.9.70)	2·00	1·75
407	**112**	$2 multicoloured ..	4·50	5·50
391/407		.. .. *Set of* 17	9·50	10·00

117. Fijian Soldiers overlooking the Solomon Islands.

118. Regimental Flags and Soldiers in Full Dress and Battledress.

119. Fijian Soldier and Victoria Cross.

(Des. G. Drummond. Photo. Harrison.)

1969 (23 June). *25th Anniv. of Fijian Military Forces' Solomons Campaign. W* w.**12**. *P* 14.

No.	Type	Description	Unused	Used
408	**117**	3 c. yellow-brown, black and bright emerald	5	5
409	**118**	10 c. multicoloured ..	15	15
410	**119**	25 c. multicoloured ..	40	45

120. Javelin Thrower.

121. Yachting.

122. Games Medal and Winners' Rostrum.

(Des. L. D. Curtis. Photo. Harrison.)

1969 (18 Aug.). *3rd South Pacific Games, Port Moresby. W* w.**12** (*sideways*). *P* 14½ × 14.

No.	Type	Description	Unused	Used
411	**120**	4 c. black, brown and vermilion	5	5
412	**121**	8 c. black, grey and new blue	15	15
413	**122**	20 c. multicoloured ..	30	35

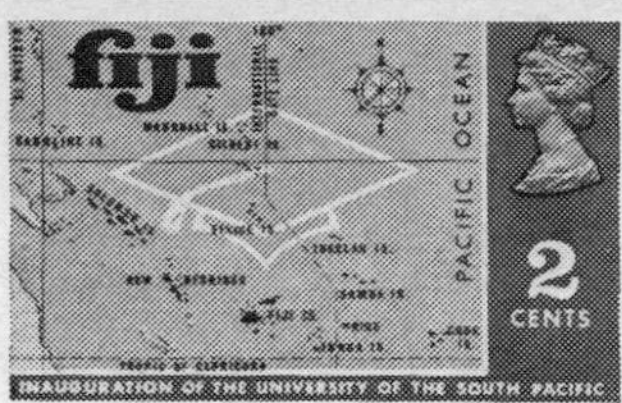

123. Map of South Pacific and "Mortar-board".

124. RNZAF Badge and "Sunderland" Flying-Boat over Laucala Bay (Site of University).

125. Science Students at Work.

(Des. G. Drummond. Photo. Harrison.)

1969 (10 Nov.). *University of the South Pacific Inauguration. W* w.**12**. *P* 14×15.

414	**123**	2 c. multicoloured ..	5	5
415	**124**	8 c. multicoloured ..	15	20
416	**125**	25 c. multicoloured ..	40	45

ROYAL VISIT
1970
(**126**)

1970 (4 Mar.). *Royal Visit. Nos.* 392, 399 *and* 402 *optd. with T* **126**.

417	**98**	2 c. new blue, brown and ochre	5	5
418	**104**	10 c. Prussian blue and brown-red	20	20
419	**107**	25 c. multicoloured ..	45	45

127. Chaulmugra Tree, Makogai.

128. "Cascade" (Semisi Maya). (*Vert.*)

129. "Gasagasau" (Semisi Maya). (*Vert.*)

130. Makogai Hospital. (*Horiz.*)

(Des. G. Drummond. Photo. Harrison.)

1970 (25 May). *Closing of Leprosy Hospital, Makogai. W* w.**12** (*sideways on* 10 *c.*). *P* 14×14½.

420	**127**	2 c. multicoloured ..	5	5
421	**128**	10 c. pale turquoise-green and black ..	20	20
422	**129**	10 c. turquoise-blue, black and magenta ..	20	20
423	**130**	30 c. multicoloured ..	45	45

Nos. 421/2 were printed together *se-tenant* throughout the sheet.

131. Abel Tasman and Log, 1643.

132. Captain Cook and *Endeavour*, 1774.

133. Captain Bligh and Longboat, 1789.

134. Fijian and Ocean-going Canoe.

(Des. V. Whiteley. Litho. D.L.R.)

1970 (18 Aug.). *Explorers and Discoverers. W* w.**12** (*sideways*). *P* 13×12½.

424	**131**	2 c. black, brown & turq.	5	5
425	**132**	3 c. multicoloured ..	8	8
426	**133**	8 c. multicoloured ..	25	25
427	**134**	25 c. multicoloured ..	55	55

IV. INDEPENDENCE.

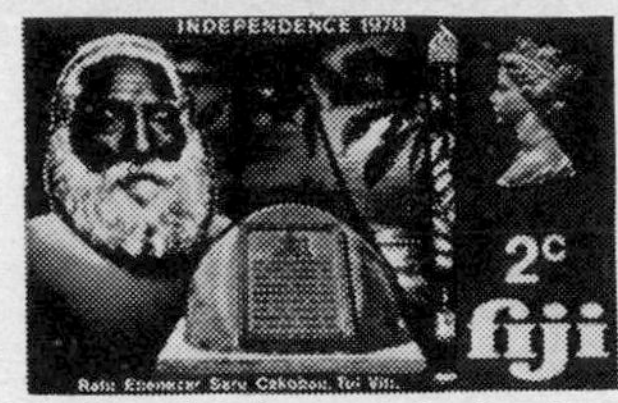

135. King Cakobau and Cession Stone.

136. Children of the World.

137. Prime Minister and Fijian Flag.

138. Dancers in Costume.

(Des. J. Waddington Ltd. Litho. Format.)

1970 (10 Oct.). *Independence. W* w.**12** (*sideways*). *P* 14.

428	**135**	2 c. multicoloured ..	5	5
429	**136**	3 c. multicoloured ..	8	8
430	**137**	10 c. multicoloured ..	20	20
431	**138**	25 c. multicoloured ..	45	45

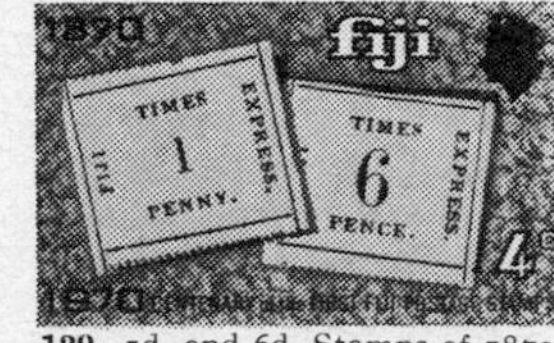

139. 1d. and 6d. Stamps of 1870.

(Des. V. Whiteley. Photo. Harrison.)

1970 (2 Nov.). *Stamp Centenary. T* **139** *and similar horiz. designs. Multicoloured. W* w.**12** (*sideways on* 15 *c.*). *P* 14½×14.

432	4 c. Type **139**	8	8
433	15 c. Fijian Stamps of all Reigns	25	25
434	20 c. *Fiji Times* Office and modern G.P.O.	35	35

The 15 c. is larger, 61×21 mm.

140. Grey-backed White-eye.

141. Yellow-breasted Musk Parrot.

(Des. G. Drummond. Litho. Questa.)

1971–72. *Birds and Flowers. T* **140/1** *and similar vert. designs. Multicoloured. W* w.**12** (*upright*).

(*a*) *Size as T* **140**. *P* 13½×14.

435	1 c. *Cirrhopetalum umbellatum*	5	5
436	2 c. Cardinal Honey-eater ..	5	5
437	3 c. *Calanthe furcata* ..	8	8
438	4 c. *Bulbophyllum sp. nov.* ..	8	8
439	5 c. Type **140** ..	12	12
440	6 c. *Phaius tancarvilliae* ..	12	12
441	8 c. Blue-crested Broadbill	15	15
442	10 c. *Acanthephippium vitiense* ..	15	15
443	15 c. *Dendrobium tokai* ..	25	30
444	20 c. Slaty Flycatcher ..	30	35

(*b*) *Size as T* **141**. *P* 14.

445	25 c. Kandavu Honey-eater	40	40
446	30 c. *Dendrobium gordonii* ..	40	45
447	40 c. Type **141** ..	55	60
448	50 c. White-throated pigeon	85	90
449	$1 Collared Lory	1·75	2·00
450	$2 *Dendrobium platygastrium*	3·50	4·00
435/50	.. .. *Set of* 16	8·00	9·00

Dates of issue:—6.8.71, 5, 20, 40, 50 c.; 22.11.71, 2 c., 8 c., 25 c., $1; 4.1.72, 1 c., 10 c., 30 c., $2; 23.6.72, 3, 4, 6, 15 c.

See also Nos. 459/73 and 505/20.

142. Women's Basketball.

(Des. R. Granger Barrett. Litho. Questa.)

1971 (6 Sept.). *Fourth South Pacific Games, Tahiti. T* **142** *and similar vert. designs. W* w.**12**. *P* 14.

451	8 c. multicoloured ..	12	15
452	10 c. cobalt, black & brown	20	20
453	25 c. pale turquoise-green, black and brown ..	40	45

Designs:—10 c. Running; 25 c. Weightlifting.

143. Community Education.

(Des. V. Whiteley. Litho. Questa.)

1972 (7 Feb.). *25th Anniv. of South Pacific Commission. T* **143** *and similar vert. designs. Multicoloured. W* w.**12**. *P* 14.

454	2 c. Type **143**	8	8
455	4 c. Public Health	10	10
456	50 c. Economic Growth ..	75	85

144. "Native Canoe".

(Des. locally and adapted by A. B. New. Litho Questa.)

1972 (10 Apr.). *South Pacific Festival of Arts, Suva. W* w.**12**. *P* 14.

457	**144**	10 c. blk., orge. & new bl.	15	20

1972–74. *As Nos.* 435 *etc., but W* w.**12** *sideways.*

459	2 c. Cardinal Honey-eater ..	5	5
460	3 c. *Calanthe furcata* ..	8	8
461	4 c. *Bulbophyllum sp. nov.*	8	8
462	5 c. Type **140**	10	10
463	6 c. *Phaius tancarvilliae* ..	8	10
464	8 c. Blue-crested Broadbill	10	12
466	15 c. *Dendrobium tokai* ..	20	25
467	20 c. Slaty Flycatcher ..	25	30
468	25 c. Kandavu Honey-eater	30	35
470	40 c. Type **141**	50	60
471	50 c. White-throated Pigeon..	60	70
472	$1 Collared Lory	1·25	1·40
473	$2 *Dendrobium platygastrium*	2·50	2·75
459/73	.. .. *Set of* 13	5·25	5·75

Dates of issue:—17.11.72, 20 c., $1, $2; 8.3.73, 3 and 5 c.; 11.4.73, 4, 6, 8, 15 and 25 c.; 12.12.73, 2 c.; 15.3.74, 40 and 50 c.

See also Nos. 505/20.

145. Flowers, Conch and Ceremonial Whale's Tooth.

(Des. (from photograph by D. Groves) and photo. Harrison.)

1972 (20 Nov.). *Royal Silver Wedding. Multi coloured; background colour given. W* w.**12.** *P* 14×14½.

474	10 c. slate-green	15	20
475	25 c. bright purple	35	35
	a. Blue printing omitted ..	£100	

*The omission of the blue colour results in the Duke's suit appearing brown instead of deep blue.

HURRICANE RELIEF +10c

(146)

147. Line Out.

1972 (4 Dec.). *Hurricane Relief. Nos.* 400 *and* 403 *surch. as T* **146**, *by the Reserve Bank of Australia.*

476	**105**	15 c.+5 c. multicoloured	35	40
477	**108**	30 c.+10 c. multicoloured	70	80

(Des. J.W. Ltd. Litho. Questa.)

1973 (9 Mar.). *Diamond Jubilee of Fiji Rugby Union. T* **147** *and similar vert. designs. Multicoloured. W* w.**12** *(sideways). P* 14.

478	2 c. Type **147**	8	8
479	8 c. Body tackle	12	15
480	25 c. Conversion	35	40

148. Forestry Development.

(Des. J.W. Ltd. from local ideas. Litho. Questa.)

1973 (23 July). *Development Projects. T* **148** *and similar horiz. designs. Multicoloured. W* w.**12.** *P* 14.

481	5 c. Type **148**	8	8
482	8 c. Rice irrigation scheme ..	12	15
483	10 c. Low income housing ..	15	15
484	25 c. Highway construction ..	35	40

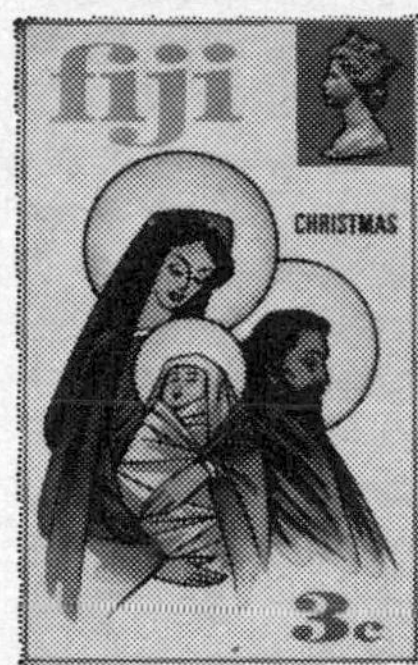

149. Christmas.

(Des. L. D. Curtis. Litho. Questa.)

1973 (26 Oct.). *Festivals of Joy. T* **149** *and similar vert. designs. Multicoloured. W* w.**12.** *(sideways). P* 14.

485	3 c. Type **149**	10	10
486	10 c. Diwali	20	20
487	20 c. Id-ul-Fitar	30	30
488	25 c. Chinese New Year ..	40	40

150. Athletics.

(Des. G. Drummond. Litho. Questa.)

1974 (7 Jan.). *Commonwealth Games, Christchurch. T* **150** *and similar vert. designs. Multicoloured. W* w.**12.** *(sideways). P* 14.

489	3 c. Type **150**	5	5
490	8 c. Boxing	15	20
491	50 c. Bowling	70	80

151. Bowler.

(Des. J.W. Ltd. Litho. Questa.)

1974 (21 Feb.). *Cricket Centenary. T* **151** *and similar multicoloured designs. W* w.**12** *(sideways on* 3 *and* 25 *c.). P* 14.

492	3 c. Type **151**	5	5
493	25 c. Batsman and wicket-keeper	40	40
494	40 c. Fielder (*horiz.*)	60	65

152. Fijian Postman.

(Des. J.W. Ltd. Litho. Questa.)

1974 (22 May). *Centenary of the Universal Postal Union. T* **152** *and similar horiz. designs. Multicoloured. W* w.**12.** *P* 14.

495	5 c. Type **152**	5	8
496	8 c. Loading mail onto ship	12	15
497	30 c. Fijian post office and mail bus	40	45
498	50 c. Modern aircraft	70	80

153. Cubs lighting Fire.

(Des. E. W. Roberts. Litho. Questa.)

1974 (30 Aug.). *First National Scout Jamboree, Lautoka. T* **153** *and similar multicoloured designs. W* w.**12** *(sideways on* 40 *c.). P* 14.

499	3 c. Type **153**	5	5
500	10 c. Scouts reading map ..	15	20
501	40 c. Scouts and Fijian flag (*vert.*)	60	65

154. Cakobau Club and Flag.

(Des. J.W. Ltd. Litho. Enschedé.)

1974 (9 Oct.). *Centenary of Deed of Cession and Fourth Anniv. of Independence. T* **154** *and similar horiz. designs. Multicoloured. W* w.**12** *(sideways on* 8 *and* 50 *c.). P* 13½ × 13 *(*3 *c.) or* 13 × 13½ *(others).*

502	3 c. Type **154**	5	5
503	8 c. King Cakobau and Queen Victoria	12	15
504	50 c. Raising the Royal Standard at Nasova Ovalau ..	65	70

1975–76. *As Nos.* 435 *etc. but W* w.**14** (*sideways on* 1 *and* 10 *c.*).

505	1 c. *Cirrhopetalum umbellatum*	5	5
506	2 c. Cardinal Honey-eater ..	5	5
507	3 c. *Calanthe furcata*	5	5
508	4 c. *Bulbophyllum sp. nov.* ..	5	5
509	5 c. Type **140**	5	5
510	6 c. *Phaius tancarvilliae* ..	5	8
511	8 c. Blue-crested Broadbill ..	8	10
512	10 c. *Acanthephippium vitiense*	10	12
513	15 c. *Dendrobium tokai* ..	15	20
516	30 c. *Dendrobium gordonii* ..	35	40
517	40 c. Type **141**	45	50
518	50 c. White-throated pigeon ..	55	60
519	$1 Collared Lory	1·10	1·25
520	$2 *Dendrobium platygastrium*	2·25	2·50
505/20	.. .. *Set of* 14	4·75	5·25

Dates of issue:—9.4.75, 1, 2, 3, 5, 10 c.; 3.9.76, others.

155. " Diwali" (Hindu Festival).

(Des. Jennifer Toombs. Litho. Walsall.)

1975 (31 Oct.). " *Festivals of Joy* ". *T* **155** *and similar vert. designs. Multicoloured. W* w.**14** (*inverted*). *P* 14.

521	3 c. Type **155**	5	5
522	15 c. " Id-Ul-Fitar " (Muslim Festival)	20	20
523	25 c. Chinese New Year ..	30	35
524	30 c. Christmas	40	45
MS525	121×101 mm. Nos. 521/4. W w.**14** (sideways)	1·00	1·00
	a. Imperf. between (vert.) ..	£250	

156. Steam Loco. No. 21.

(Des. R. Granger Barrett. Litho. Questa.)

1976 (26 Jan.). *Sugar Trains. T* **156** *and similar horiz. designs. Multicoloured. W* w.**14** (*sideways*). *P* 14.

526	4 c. Type **156**	5	5
527	15 c. Diesel Loco. No. 8 ..	20	20
528	20 c. Diesel Loco. No. 1 ..	25	30
529	30 c. Free Passenger Train ..	35	40

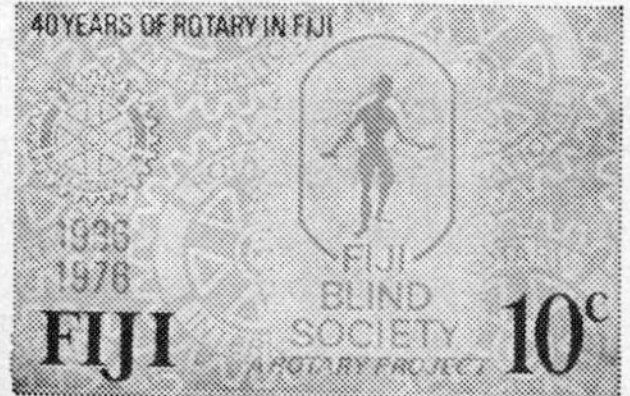

157. Fiji Blind Society and Rotary Symbols.

(Des. V. Whiteley Studio. Litho. J.W.)

1976 (26 Mar.). *40th Anniv. of Rotary in Fiji. T* **157** *and similar horiz. design. W* w.**14** (*sideways*). *P* 13.

530	10 c. ultramarine, pale sage-green and black	12	12
531	25 c. multicoloured	30	35

Design:—25 c. Ambulance and Rotary symbol.

158. D. H. " Drover ".

(*Illustration reduced. Actual size* 57×21 *mm.*)

(Des. P. B. Powell. Litho. Questa.)

1976 (1 Sept.). *25th Anniv. of Air Services. T* **158** *and similar horiz. designs. Multicoloured. W* w.**14.** *P* 13½×14.

532	4 c. Type **158**	5	5
533	15 c. B.A.C. " 1–11 "	20	25
534	25 c. H.S. " 748 "	30	35
535	30 c. Britten-Norman " Trislander "	40	45

159. The Queen's Visit to Fiji, 1970.

(Des. L. D. Curtis. Litho. Questa.)

1977 (7 Feb.). *Silver Jubilee. T* **159** *and similar vert. designs. Multicoloured. W* w.**14.** *P* 13½.

536	10 c. Type **159**	12	15
537	25 c. King Edward's Chair ..	30	35
538	30 c. Queen wearing cloth-of-gold supertunica ..	40	45

MINIMUM PRICE

The minimum price quoted is 5p which represents a handling charge rather than a basis for valuing common stamps. For further notes about prices see introductory pages.

POSTAGE DUE STAMPS.

D 1

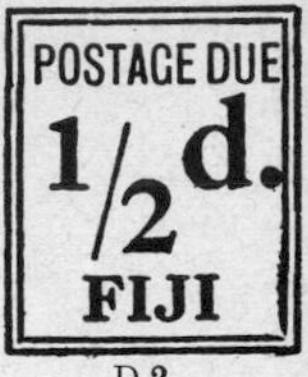

D 2

1917 (1 Jan.). *Typo. locally, on thick yellowish white laid paper. No gum. P* 11.

D1	D **1**	½d. black	£100	90·00
D2	,,	1d. black	32·00	20·00
		a. *Se-tenant* strip of 8: 1d. (×3) + ½d. + 4d. + 3d. (×3) ..	£1100	
D3	,,	2d. black	32·00	17·00
D4	,,	3d. black	42·00	22·00
D5	,,	4d. black	£100	80·00

No. D2a derives from sheets of 96 (8×12) comprising 3×1d., 1×½d., 1×4d., 3×3d. The 2d. was printed separately in sheets of 84 (7×12). On all these sheets marginal copies were imperforate on the outer edge.

1917 (April)–**18.** *Narrower setting, value in* ½*d. as Type* D **2.**

D5*a*	½d. black	£125	50·00
D5*b*	1d. black	40·00	30·00
D5*c*	2d. black (4.18)	£150	£150

1d. and 2d. stamps must have wide margins (3½ to 4 mm.) on the vertical sides to be Nos. D2 or D3. Stamps with narrow margins of approximately the same width on all four sides are Nos. D5*b* or D5*c*.

Nos. D5*a/c* were printed in separate sheets of 84 (7×12). The marginal copies are perforated on all sides.

D 3

D 4

(Typo. D.L.R.)

1917–18. (1 June). *Wmk. Mult. Crown CA. P* 14.

D 6	D **3**	½d. black..	55	55
D 7	,,	1d. black..	55	55
D 8	,,	2d. black..	60	70
D 9	,,	3d. black..	1·10	1·25
D10	,,	4d. black..	1·60	1·75
D6/10		.. .. *Set of* 5	4·00	4·50
D6/10 Optd. " Specimen "		*Set of* 5	40·00	

(Typo. Waterlow.)

1940. *Wmk. Mult. Script CA. P* 12½.

D11	D **4**	1d. emerald-green ..	20	40
D12	,,	2d. emerald-green ..	30	50
D13	,,	3d. emerald-green ..	30	60
D14	,,	4d. emerald-green ..	55	70
D15	,,	5d. emerald-green ..	80	90
D16	,,	6d. emerald-green ..	1·10	1·25
D17	,,	1s. carmine-lake ..	1·60	2·00
D18	,,	1s. 6d. carmine-lake ..	3·00	4·00
D11/18		.. .. *Set of* 8	7·00	9·50
D11/18 Perf. " Specimen "		*Set of* 8	40·00	

GAMBIA.

I. WEST AFRICAN SETTLEMENT.

PRICES.—The prices of Nos. 1 to 8 are for fine copies, with good margins and embossing. Brilliant or poor copies can be supplied at prices consistent with their condition.

DOUBLE EMBOSSING—The majority of the stamps of T 1 with so-called "double embossing" are merely specimens in which the printing and embossing do not register accurately and have no special value. We no longer list "twice embossed" or "twice embossed, once inverted" varieties as they are considered to be outside the scope of this catalogue.

1

(Typo. and embossed by De La Rue & Co.)

1869–72. *No wmk. Imperf.*
1 **1** 4d. brown .. .. .. £225 85·00
2 ,, 4d. pale brown £175 £100
3 ,, 6d. deep blue (19.4.69) .. £175 90·00
3a ,, 6d. blue (30.4.69) .. .. £225 85·00
4 ,, 6d. pale blue (17.2.72) .. £700 £500

Our prices for the 6d., pale blue, No. 4, are for stamps which are pale by comparison with specimens of the "deep blue" and "blue" colour groups listed under Nos. 3 and 3a. An exceptionally pale shade is recognized by specialists and this is rare. The dates given for the 6d. are those of the earliest known postmarks.

1874 (Aug.). *Wmk. Crown CC. Imperf.*
5 **1** 4d. brown .. .. .. £160 90·00
6 ,, 4d. pale brown .. .. .. £160 80·00
7 ,, 6d. deep blue £150 £100
8 ,, 6d. blue .. .. .. £140 90·00

1880 (June). *Wmk. Crown CC. P* 14 (*comb*).
10 **1** ½d. deep orange .. .. 2·00 4·00
11 ,, ½d. dull orange .. .. 2·00 4·00
12 ,, 1d. maroon .. .. .. 3·00 2·50
13 ,, 2d. rose .. .. .. 8·00 5·00
14 ,, 3d. pale dull ultramarine .. 10·00 12·00
14b ,, 3d. bright ultramarine .. 16·00 12·00
15 ,, 4d. brown .. .. .. 75·00 7·00
16 ,, 4d. pale brown .. .. 70·00 8·00
17 ,, 6d. deep blue .. .. 20·00 12·00
18 ,, 6d. blue .. .. .. 20·00 12·00
19 ,, 1s. green .. .. .. 85·00 50·00
20 ,, 1s. deep green .. .. 85·00 50·00
10/20 .. .. *Set of* 7 £180 80·00

The watermark in this issue is found sideways as well as upright. These stamps also exist in line perf. 14, believed to have come from the first delivery to the Colony. Some of them are rare.

1886 (Jan.)–**87.** *Wmk. Crown CA, sideways. P* 14.
21 **1** ½d. myrtle-green (1887) .. 50 60
22 ,, ½d. grey-green (1887) .. 55 75
22b,, 1d. maroon .. .. .. — £5000
23 ,, 1d. crimson (1887) .. .. 1·00 1·25
23a,, 1d. aniline crimson (1887) 5·50 5·00
23b,, 1d. pale carmine (1887) .. 4·00 4·00
24 ,, 2d. orange (1887) .. .. 2·00 2·50
25 ,, 2d. deep orange (1887) .. 1·75 2·00
26 ,, 2½d. ultramarine .. .. 3·00 3·00
27 ,, 2½d. deep bright blue .. 2·50 2·00
28 ,, 3d. slate-grey .. .. 1·75 3·00
29 ,, 3d. grey .. .. .. 1·75 3·50
29a,, 3d. pearl-grey .. .. 2·50 3·00
30 ,, 4d. brown .. .. .. 2·00 2·00
31 ,, 4d. deep brown .. .. 2·00 2·00
32 ,, 6d. yellowish olive-green .. 18·00 12·00
32a,, 6d. olive-green .. .. 22·00 15·00
33 ,, 6d. bronze-green .. .. 7·00 9·00
33a,, 6d. deep bronze-green .. 8·00 10·00
34 ,, 6d. slate-green .. .. 5·50 9·00
35 ,, 1s. violet .. .. .. 4·50 7·00
36 ,, 1s. deep violet .. .. 4·50 8·00
36a,, 1s. aniline violet £300
21/36 .. .. *Set of* 8 18·00 22·00
21/24, 32 Optd. "Specimen" *Set of* 4 30·00

The above were printed in panes of 15 on paper intended for larger panes. Hence the watermark is sometimes misplaced or omitted and letters from "CROWN AGENTS FOR THE COLONIES" from the margin may appear on the stamps.

The ½d., 2d., 3d., 4d., 6d. (No. 32) and 1s. with watermark Crown CA are known imperf. (*price from* £600).

II. CROWN COLONY.

2

(Typo. D.L.R.)

1898 (Jan.)–**1902.** *Wmk. Crown CA. P* 14.
37 **2** ½d. dull green .. .. 90 1·00
38 ,, 1d. carmine .. .. 1·25 90
39 ,, 2d. orange and mauve .. 1·25 2·00
40 ,, 2½d. ultramarine .. .. 1·60 2·40
41 ,, 3d. reddish pur. and blue 3·50 5·00
a. Dp. purple & ultram. ('02) 20·00 25·00
42 ,, 4d. brown and blue .. 3·00 5·50
43 ,, 6d. olive-green and carmine 5·00 8·50
44 ,, 1s. violet and green .. 7·00 11·00
37/44 .. .. *Set of* 8 21·00 32·00
37/44 Optd. "Specimen" *Set of* 8 65·00

3

4

(Typo. D.L.R.)

1902–5. *Wmk. Crown CA. P* 14.
45 **3** ½d. green 40 70
46 ,, 1d. carmine 85 70
47 ,, 2d. orange and mauve .. 1·90 2·50
48 ,, 2½d. ultramarine .. .. 3·75 5·00
49 ,, 3d. purple and ultramarine 3·75 3·75
50 ,, 4d. brown and ultramarine 3·75 5·50
51 ,, 6d. pale sage-grn. & carmine 4·00 6·00
52 ,, 1s. violet and green .. 14·00 17·00
53 **4** 1s. 6d. green and carmine/*yellow* (6.4.05) .. 7·50 11·00
54 ,, 2s. deep slate and orange 10·00 15·00
55 ,, 2s. 6d. purple and brown/*yellow* (6.4.05) .. 11·00 15·00
56 ,, 3s. carmine and green/*yellow* (6.4.05) .. 14·00 17·00
45/56 .. .. *Set of* 12 70·00 90·00
45/56 Optd. "Specimen" *Set of* 12 80·00

1904–6. *Wmk. Mult. Crown CA. P* 14.
57 **3** ½d. green 25 30
58 ,, 1d. carmine 50 30
59 ,, 2d. orange and mauve ('06) 3·50 4·25
60 ,, 2½d. bright blue .. .. 1·60 1·75
a. Bright blue & ultramarine .. 2·75 3·25
61 ,, 3d. purple & ultramarine 3·25 3·75
62 ,, 4d. brown & ultram. ('06) 4·00 5·50
63 **4** 5d. grey and black ('05) .. 3·75 5·00
64 **3** 6d. olive-grn. & carm. ('06) 2·75 4·50
65 **4** 7½d. green & carmine ('05) 3·25 4·50
66 ,, 10d. olive & carmine ('05) 6·00 8·00
67 **3** 1s. violet and green .. 11·00 14·00
68 **4** 2s. deep slate & orange .. 19·00 25·00
57/68 .. .. *Set of* 12 55·00 70·00
63, 65/6 Optd. "Specimen" *Set of* 3 23·00

See also Nos. 72/85.

HALF PENNY
(5)

ONE PENNY
(6)

1906 (April). *Nos.* 55 *and* 56 *surch. with T* **5** *and* **6** *respectively.*
69 ½d. on 2s. 6d. pur. & brn./*yell.* 15·00 17·00
70 1d. on 3s. carm. & green/*yell.* 20·00 21·00
a. Surch. Double. £800

The spacing between the words and bars on No. 69 varies from 4 mm. to 5 mm.

A constant variety with broken "E" is found in the surcharge of No. 69.

1909. *Colours changed. Wmk. Mult. Crown CA. P* 14.
72 **3** ½d. blue-green 25 30
73 ,, 1d. red 25 15
74 ,, 2d. greyish slate .. .. 1·00 90
75 ,, 3d. purple/*yellow* .. .. 1·90 1·60
a. Purple/lemon-yellow .. 3·25 2·75
76 ,, 4d. black and red/*yellow* .. 1·00 1·10
77 **4** 5d. orange and purple .. 1·75 1·60
78 **3** 6d. dull & bright purple .. 1·60 1·90
79 **4** 7½d. brown and blue .. 1·75 1·90
80 ,, 10d. pale sage-green & carm. 1·75 1·90
81 **3** 1s. black/*green* .. .. 1·75 2·50
82 **4** 1s. 6d. violet and green .. 6·50 6·00
83 ,, 2s. purple & brt. blue/*blue* 5·50 6·50
84 ,, 2s. 6d. black and red/*blue* .. 11·00 10·00
85 ,, 3s. yellow and green .. 14·00 14·00
72/85 .. .. *Set of* 14 45·00 45·00
72/85 Optd. "Specimen" *Set of* 14 80·00

7

8

Split "A"

The split "A" variety occurs on No 45 in the left-hand pane in printings to 1918 of all values up to 3s. (*Prices about three times normal.*)

(Typo. De La Rue.)

1912–22. *Wmk. Mult. Crown CA. P* 14.
86 **7** ½d. pale green, O 30 35
a. Green 30 35
b. Deep green 30 30
87 ,, 1d. red, O 30 25
a. Rose-red 30 25
b. Scarlet (1916) 35 25
88 **8** 1½d. olive-grn. & bl.-grn., O 40 65
89 **7** 2d. greyish slate, O .. 35 50
90 ,, 2½d. deep bright blue, O .. 1·25 1·10
a. Bright blue .. .. 1·10 95
91 ,, 3d. purple/*yellow*, O .. 35 45
a. On lemon (1917) .. .. 5·50 7·00
b. On orange-buff (1920) .. 6·00 1·90
c. On pale yellow 40 75
92 ,, 4d. black and red/*yellow*, O 1·60 2·50
a. On lemon .. .. .. 1·00 2·50
b. On orange-buff .. .. 1·90 2·50
c. On pale yellow .. .. 1·60 2·50
93 **8** 5d. orange and purple, O 55 1·00
94 **7** 6d. dull & brt. purple, O 65 90
95 **8** 7½d. brown and blue, O .. 85 1·10
96 ,, 10d. p. sage-grn. & carm., O 2·00 3·25
a. Deep sage-green & carmine 2·00 3·25
97 **7** 1s. black/*green*, O .. .. 75 1·60
a. On emerald back .. .. 1·10 2·75
98 **8** 1s. 6d. violet & green, O 2·75 4·00
99 ,, 2s. purple & blue/*blue*, O 2·75 4·00
100 ,, 2s. 6d. blk. & red/*blue*, O 4·00 5·00
101 ,, 3s. yellow and green, O .. 5·00 6·50
102 ,, 5s. green and red/*pale yellow*, C ('22) .. 12·00 18·00
86/102 .. .. *Set of* 17 32·00 45·00
86/102 Optd. "Specimen" *Set of* 17 £100

1921–22. *Wmk. Mult. Script CA. P* 14.
108 **7** ½d. dull green, O 30 55
109 „ 1d. carmine-red, O .. 30 35
110 **8** 1½d. ol.-grn. & blue-grn., O 1·40 2·25
111 **7** 2d. grey, O .. .. 95 1·60
112 „ 2½d. bright blue, O .. 65 1·60
113 **8** 5d. orange and purple, O 1·40 3·25
114 **7** 6d. dull & brt. purple, O 1·90 3·25
115 **8** 7½d. brown and blue, O .. 1·00 3·25
116 „ 10d. pale sage-grn. & car., O 1·60 3·75
117 „ 4s. black & red, C (1922) 13·00 18·00
108/117 .. .. *Set of* 10 20·00 35·00
108/17 Optd. "Specimen" *Set of* 10 65·00

9

10

(Recess. D.L.R.)

1922–27. *Portrait and shield in black. P* 14.

(*a*) *Wmk. Mult. Crown CA.*
118 **9** 4d. red/*yellow* 45 85
119 „ 7½d. purple/*yellow* .. .. 1·10 2·50
120 **10** 1s. purple/*yellow* .. .. 3·00 5·00
121 „ 5s. green/*yellow* .. .. 18·00 20·00
118/121 Optd./H/S "Specimen" *Set of* 4 40·00

(*b*) *Wmk. Mult. Script CA.*
122 **9** ½d. green 20 15
123 „ ½d. deep green 20 30
124 „ 1d. brown 12 12
125 „ 1½d. bright rose-scarlet .. 25 15
126 „ 2d. grey 35 40
127 „ 2½d. orange-yellow .. 35 1·90
128 „ 3d. bright blue 40 35
129 „ 4d. red/*yellow* (1927) 50 1·60
130 „ 5d. sage-green .. .. 1·10 2·50
131 „ 6d. claret 75 75
132 „ 7½d. purple/*yellow* (1927) .. 1·60 4·25
133 „ 10d. blue .. .. .. 1·90 3·25
134 **10** 1s. purple/*yellow* (1924) .. 1·00 1·25
135 „ 1s. 6d. blue .. .. 2·75 4·25
136 „ 2s. purple/*blue* .. .. 3·75 3·00
137 „ 2s. 6d. deep green .. 3·75 4·25
138 „ 3s. bright aniline violet .. 5·50 7·50
139 „ 3s. slate-purple .. .. 55·00 £120
140 „ 4s. brown .. .. 5·00 7·50
141 „ 5s. green/*yellow* (1926) .. 7·50 11·00
142 „ 10s. sage-green .. .. 25·00 32·00
118/142 .. .. *Set of* 23 75·00 £100
122/40, 142 Optd. "Specimen" *Set of* 19 £175

No. 139 has been faked, but note that this stamp is comb. perf. 13·9 × 13·8 whereas No. 138 is line perf. 14 exactly. There are also shades of the slate-purple.

1935 (6 May). *Silver Jubilee. As T* **13** *of Antigua. Recess. B.W. Wmk. Mult. Script CA. P* 11×12.
143 1½d. deep blue and scarlet .. 25 25
a. Extra flagstaff .. .. 20·00
144 3d. brown and deep blue .. 90 80
a. Extra flagstaff .. .. 35·00
145 6d. light blue & olive-green 1·00 1·10
a. Extra flagstaff .. .. 35·00
146 1s. slate and purple .. 1·10 1·25
a. Extra flagstaff .. .. 55·00
143/6 Perf. "Specimen" *Set of* 4 12·00

For illustration of "extra flagstaff" variety see Bechuanaland.

1937 (12 May). *Coronation. As T* **2** *of Aden. Recess. B.W. Wmk. Mult. Script CA. P* 11×11½.
147 1d. yellow-brown 10 12
148 1½d. carmine 10 12
149 3d. blue 20 30
147/9 Perf. "Specimen" *Set of* 3 11·00

11. Elephant.

(Recess. B.W.)

1938 (1 Apr.)–**46.** *Wmk. Mult. Script CA. P* 12.
150 **11** ½d. black & emer.-green 15 15
151 „ 1d. purple and brown 15 15
152 „ 1½d. lake and carmine .. 6·00 3·50
a. Lake and scarlet ('42) .. 12 15
152*b* „ 1½d. blue & black (2.1.45) 35 40
153 „ 2d. blue and black 20 35
153*a* „ 2d. lake and scarlet ('43) 15 20
154 „ 3d. light blue & grey-blue 12 15
154*a* „ 5d. sage-green & purple-brown (13.3.41) .. 25 40
155 „ 6d. olive-green & claret 35 35
156 „ 1s. slate-blue and violet 70 35
156*a* **11** 1s. 3d. chocolate & light blue (28.11.46) .. 35 50
157 „ 2s. carmine and blue .. 75 1·00
158 „ 2s. 6d. sepia & dull grn. 1·60 1·25
159 „ 4s. vermilion and purple 1·75 1·75
160 „ 5s. blue and vermilion 2·40 2·40
161 „ 10s. orange and black .. 3·50 4·00
150/161 .. .. *Set of* 16 12·00 12·00
150/61 Perf. "Specimen" *Set of* 16 42·00

1946 (6 Aug.). *Victory. As Nos.* 28/9 *of Aden.*
162 1½d. black 25 10
163 3d. blue 25 12
162/3 Perf. "Specimen" *Set of* 2 13·00

1948 (24 Dec.). *Royal Silver Wedding. As Nos.* 30/1 *of Aden.*
164 1½d. black 10 10
165 £1 mauve .. .. .. 5·00 7·50

1949 (10 Oct.). *75th Anniv. of Universal Postal Union. As Nos.* 114/7 *of Antigua.*
166 1½d. blue-black 25 25
167 3d. deep blue 30 30
168 6d. magenta 45 65
169 1s. violet 75 80

1953 (2 June). *Coronation. As No.* 47 *of Aden, but ptd. by B. W.*
170 1½d. black & deep bright blue 10 12

12. Tapping for Palm Wine.

13. Cutter.

14. Wollof Woman.

15. Barra Canoe.

16. S.S. *Lady Wright.*

17. James Island.

18. Woman Hoeing.

19. Elephant and Palm.

(Des. Mrs. O. W. Meronti. Recess. De La Rue.)

1953 (2 Nov.). *Wmk. Mult. Script CA. P* 13½.
171 **12** ½d. carmine-red and bluish green (*shades*) .. 8 8
172 **13** 1d. deep ultramarine and deep brown (*shades*) .. 8 8
173 **14** 1½d. dp. brn. & grey-black 10 10
174 **15** 2½d. black and carmine-red 10 10
175 **16** 3d. deep blue & slate-lilac 12 12
176 **17** 4d. black and deep blue .. 12 15
177 **12** 6d. brn. & reddish purple 15 15
178 **18** 1s. yell.-brn. & yell.-green 20 20
179 **13** 1s. 3d. ultramarine and pale blue (*shades*) .. 30 20
180 **15** 2s. indigo and carmine .. 80 65
181 **18** 2s. 6d. deep bluish green and sepia 80 65
182 **17** 4s. grey-blue & Indian red 1·40 1·40
183 **14** 5s. chocolate & brt. blue 1·50 1·50
184 **16** 10s. dp. bl. & myrtle-green 4·25 3·75
185 **19** £1 green and black .. 7·00 8·00
171/85 .. .. *Set of* 15 15·00 15·00

20. Queen Elizabeth II and Palm.

21. Queen Elizabeth II and West African Map.

(Des. J. R. F. Ithier (T **20**), A. W. Morley (T **21**). Recess. Bradbury, Wilkinson.)

1961 (2 Dec.). *Royal Visit. W* w.**12**. *P* 11½.

186	**20**	2d. green and purple ..	8	8
187	**21**	3d. turq.-blue and sepia ..	12	12
188	,,	6d. blue and cerise ..	15	15
189	**20**	1s. 3d. vio. & myrtle-grn.	30	35

1963 (4 June). *Freedom from Hunger. As No.* 76 *of Aden.*

190	1s. 3d. carmine	50	50

1963 (2 Sept.). *Red Cross Centenary. As Nos.* 147/8 *of Antigua.*

191	2d. red and black	8	10
192	1s. 3d. red and blue	50	50

III. SELF GOVERNMENT.

22. Beautiful Long-tailed Sunbird.

SELF GOVERNMENT
1963
(**35**)

23. Yellow-mantled Whydah.
24. Cattle Egret.
25. Yellow-bellied Parrot.
26. Long-tailed Parakeet.
27. Amethyst Starling.
28. Village Weaver.
29. Rufous-crowned Roller.
30. Red-eyed Turtle Dove.
31. Bush Fowl.
32. Palm-nut Vulture.
33. Orange-cheeked Waxbill.
34. Emerald Cuckoo.

(Des. V. Whiteley. Photo. Harrison.)

1963 (4 Nov.). *W* w.**12**. *P* 12½×13.

193	**22**	½d. multicoloured ..	5	5
194	**23**	1d. multicoloured ..	5	5
195	**24**	1½d. multicoloured ..	5	5
196	**25**	2d. multicoloured ..	8	8
197	**26**	3d. multicoloured ..	10	10
198	**27**	4d. multicoloured ..	10	12
199	**28**	6d. multicoloured ..	12	12
200	**29**	1s. multicoloured ..	25	20
201	**30**	1s. 3d. multicoloured ..	80	90
202	**31**	2s. 6d. multicoloured ..	1·25	1·25
203	**32**	5s. multicoloured ..	2·25	2·25
204	**33**	10s. multicoloured ..	3·50	3·50
205	**34**	£1 multicoloured ..	8·00	9·00
193/205		.. .. *Set of* 13	14·00	16·00

1963 (7 Nov.). *New Constitution. Nos.* 194, 197, 200/1 *optd. with T* **35**.

206	**23**	1d. multicoloured ..	5	5
207	**26**	3d. multicoloured ..	8	8
208	**29**	1s. multicoloured ..	20	25
209	**30**	1s. 3d. multicoloured ..	30	35

1964 (23 April). *400th Anniv. of Birth of William Shakespeare. As No.* 164 *of Antigua.*

210	6d. greenish blue	20	20

IV. INDEPENDENT.

36. Gambia Flag and River. **37.** Arms.

(Des. V. Whiteley. Photo. Harrison.)

1965 (18 Feb.). *Independence. P* 14½.

211	**36**	½d. multicoloured ..	5	5
212	**37**	2d. multicoloured ..	5	5
213	**36**	7½d. multicoloured ..	15	20
214	**37**	1s. 6d. multicoloured ..	25	30

INDEPENDENCE
1965
(**38**)

1965 (18 Feb.). *Nos.* 193/205 *optd. with T* **38** *or with date centred* (1d., 2d., 3d., 4d., 1s., 5s., 10s., £1).

215	**22**	½d. multicoloured ..	5	5
216	**23**	1d. multicoloured ..	5	5
217	**24**	1½d. multicoloured ..	5	5
218	**25**	2d. multicoloured ..	5	8
219	**26**	3d. multicoloured ..	8	8
220	**27**	4d. multicoloured ..	8	10
221	**28**	6d. multicoloured ..	12	15
222	**29**	1s. multicoloured ..	15	25
223	**30**	1s. 3d. multicoloured ..	35	40
224	**31**	2s. 6d. multicoloured ..	50	65
225	**32**	5s. multicoloured ..	1·10	1·10
226	**33**	10s. multicoloured ..	2·25	3·25
227	**34**	£1 multicoloured ..	5·00	7·00
215/27		.. .. *Set of* 13	9·00	12·00

39. I.T.U. Emblem and Symbols.

(Des. V. Whiteley. Photo. Harrison.)

1965 (17 May). *I.T.U. Centenary. P* 14½.

228	**39**	1d. silver and Prussian blue	5	5
229	,,	1s. 6d. gold & bluish violet	25	25

THE GAMBIA. From this point onwards stamps are inscribed " The Gambia ".

40. Sir Winston Churchill and Houses of Parliament.

(Des. Jennifer Toombs. Photo. Harrison.)

1966 (24 Jan.). *Churchill Commemoration. P* 14×14½.

230	**40**	1d. multicoloured ..	5	5
231	,,	6d. multicoloured ..	12	15
232	,,	1s. 6d. multicoloured ..	30	40

41. Cordon Bleu.

42. Whistling Teal.
43. Red-throated Bee-eater.
44. Pied Kingfisher.
45. Napoleon Bishop.
46. River Eagle.
47. Yellow-bellied Fruit Pigeon.
48. Blue-bellied Roller.
49. Pigmy Kingfisher.
50. Spur-winged Goose.
51. Little Woodpecker.
52. Violet Plantain-eater.

53. Pintailed Whydah.

(Des. V. Whiteley. Photo. Harrison.)

1966 (18 Feb.). *P* 14×14½ (£1) *or* 12×13 (*others*).

233	**41**	½d. multicoloured ..	5	5
234	**42**	1d. multicoloured ..	5	5
235	**43**	1½d. multicoloured ..	8	8
236	**44**	2d. multicoloured ..	10	10
237	**45**	3d. multicoloured ..	12	12
238	**46**	4d. multicoloured ..	15	15
239	**47**	6d. multicoloured ..	20	20
240	**48**	1s. multicoloured ..	25	25
241	**49**	1s. 6d. multicoloured ..	30	30
242	**50**	2s. 6d. multicoloured ..	50	50
243	**51**	5s. multicoloured ..	1·00	1·00
244	**52**	10s. multicoloured ..	1·75	1·75
245	**53**	£1 multicoloured ..	3·25	3·50
233/45		.. .. *Set of* 13	7·00	7·00

The ½d., 1d. and 2d. to 1s. values exist with PVA gum as well as gum arabic.

54. Arms, Early Settlement and Modern Buildings.

(*Reduced size illustration. Actual size* 58×21½ *mm.*)

(Photo., arms die-stamped. Harrison.)

1966 (24 June). *150th Anniv. of Bathurst. P* 14½×14.

246	**54**	1d. silver, brn. & yell.-orge.	5	5
247	,,	2d. silver, brown & lt. blue	5	5
248	,,	6d. silver, brn. & lt. emerald	12	12
249	,,	1s. 6d. silver, brown and light magenta	25	25

55. I.T.Y. Emblem and Hotels.

(*Illustration reduced. Actual size* 57×21 *mm.*)

(Des. and photo. (emblem die-stamped). Harrison.)

1967 (20 Dec.). *International Tourist Year.* P 14½×14.
250 **55** 2d. silver, brn. & apple-grn. 5 5
251 ,, 1s. silver, brown & orange 15 15
252 ,, 1s. 6d. silver, brown and magenta 25 25

56. Handcuffs.

57. Fort Bullen.
58. Methodist Church.

(Des. V. Whiteley. Photo. Enschedé.)

1968 (15 July). *Human Rights Year.* P 14×13.
253 **56** 1d. multicoloured 5 5
254 **57** 1s. multicoloured 15 15
255 **58** 5s. multicoloured 70 75

59. Queen Victoria, Queen Elizabeth II and 4d. stamp of 1869.

60. Queen Elizabeth II with 4d. and 6d. stamps of 1869.

(Des. G. Drummond. Photo. and embossing (cameo head). Harrison.)

1969 (20 Jan.). *Gambia Stamp Centenary.* P 14½×13½.
256 **59** 4d. sepia and yellow-ochre 8 8
257 ,, 6d. Prussian blue and deep yellow-green 12 15
258 **60** 2s. 6d. multicoloured .. 50 55

In the 6d. value the stamp illustrated is the 6d. of 1869.

61. Catapult-Ship *Westfalen* launching Dornier "Wal".

62. Dornier "Wal" Flying-Boat.
63. Airship "Graf Zeppelin".

(These designs are all set on a background of the South Atlantic and have the Lufthansa emblem.)

(Des. L. D. Curtis. Litho. Format International.)

1969 (15 Dec.). *35th Anniv. of Pioneer Air Services.* P 13½×14.
259 **61** 2d. black, grey, flesh and brownish red 10 10
260 **62** 1s. black, grey, buff and yellow-ochre 20 25
261 **63** 1s. 6d. cobalt, grey, black and ultramarine .. 35 50

V. REPUBLIC.

64. Athlete and Gambian Flag.

(Des. Jennifer Toombs. Litho. Format.)

1970 (16 July). *Ninth British Commonwealth Games, Edinburgh.* P 14.
262 **64** 1d. multicoloured .. 5 5
263 ,, 1s. multicoloured .. 15 20
264 ,, 5s. multicoloured .. 70 75

65. President and State House.

(Des. G. L. Vasarhelyi. Litho. Questa.)

1970 (2 Nov.). *Republic Day. T* **65** *and similar multicoloured designs.* P 14.
265 2d. Type **65** 5 5
266 1s. President Dauda Jawara 15 15
267 1s. 6d. President and Flag of Gambia 20 25

The 1s. and 1s. 6d. are both vertical designs.

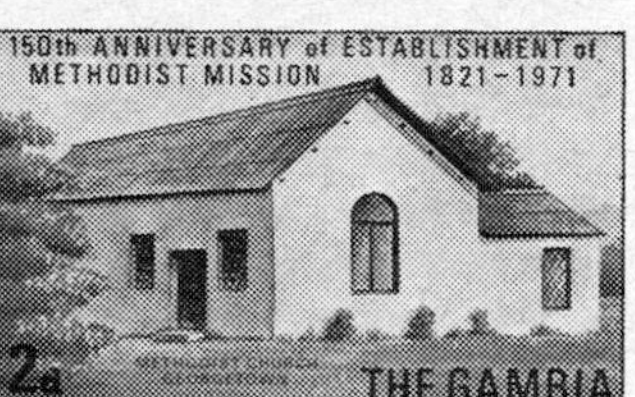

66. Methodist Church, Georgetown.

(Des. J. E. Cooter. Litho. Questa.)

1971 (16 Apr.). *150th Anniv. of Establishment of Methodist Mission. T* **66** *and similar multicoloured designs.* P 14.
268 2d. Type **54** 5 5
269 1s. Map of Africa and Gambian flag (*vert.*) .. 15 15
270 1s. 6d. John Wesley and scroll (*horiz.*) 25 25

(New currency. 100 bututs=1 dalasy.)

67. Yellowfin Tunny.

(Des. J. Waddington Ltd. Litho. Format.)

1971 (1 July). *New Currency. T* **67** *and similar horiz. designs showing fishes. Multicoloured.* P 14.
271 2 b. Type **67** 5 5
272 4 b. Peters' Mormyrid .. 5 5
273 6 b. Tropical Flying Fish .. 5 5
274 8 b. African Sleeper Goby .. 5 5
275 10 b. Yellowtail Snapper .. 5 5
276 13 b. Rock Hind 5 8
277 25 b. Gymnallabes 10 12
278 38 b. Tiger Shark 15 20
279 50 b. Electric Catfish .. 20 25
280 63 b. Black Synbranchus .. 25 30
281 1 d. 25, Smalltooth Sawfish 55 60
282 2 d. 50, Barracuda .. .. 1·10 1·25
283 5 d. Brown Bullhead .. 2·25 2·50
271/83 .. .. *Set of* 13 4·75 5·00

67. Mungo Park in Scotland.

(Des. J. Waddington Ltd. from ideas by P. J. Westwood. Litho. Questa.)

1971 (10 Sept.). *Birth Bicentenary of Mungo Park (explorer). T* **67** *and similar horiz. designs. Multicoloured. W* w.**12** (*sideways*). P 13½×13.
284 4 b. Type **67** 8 8
285 25 b. Dug-out canoe .. 25 25
286 37 b. Death of Mungo Park, Busa Rapids 40 40

68. Radio Gambia.

(Des. G. Drummond. Litho. Questa.)

1972 (1 July). *Tenth Anniv. of Radio Gambia. T* **68** *and similar horiz. design.* P 14.
287 **68** 4 b. orange-ochre and black 8 8
288 – 25 b. light new blue, red-orange and black .. 20 20
289 **68** 37 b. bright green & black 25 25

Design:—25 b. Broadcast-area map.

69. High-jumping.

(Des. and litho. D.L.R.)

1972 (31 Aug.). *Olympic Games, Munich.* P 13.
290 **69** 4 b. multicoloured .. 5 5
291 ,, 25 b. multicoloured .. 20 20
292 ,, 37 b. multicoloured .. 25 25

70. Manding Woman.

(Des. C. Abbott. Litho. Questa.)

1972 (16 Oct.). *International Conference on Manding Studies, London. T* **70** *and similar vert. designs. Multicoloured. P* 14 × 14½.

293 2 b. Type **70** 5 5
294 25 b. Musician playing the Kora 20 20
295 37 b. Map of Mali Empire .. 25 25

71. Children carrying Fanal.

(Des. L. Curtis. Litho. Enschedé.)

1972 (1 Dec.). *Fanals (Model Boats). T* **71** *and similar horiz. design. Multicoloured. P* 13 × 13½.

296 2 b. Type **71** 5 5
297 1 d. 25, Fanal with lanterns 75 85

72. Groundnuts.

(Des. locally; adapted G. Drummond. Litho. Harrison.)

1973 (31 Mar.). *Freedom from Hunger Campaign.*

298 **72** 2 b. multicoloured .. 5 5
299 „ 25 b. multicoloured .. 15 15
300 „ 37 b. multicoloured .. 25 25

73. Planting and Drying Rice.

(Des. PAD Studio. Litho. J.W.)

1973 (30 Apr.). *Agriculture (1st series). T* **73** *and similar vert. designs. Multicoloured. P* 14.

301 2 b. Type **73** 5 5
302 25 b. Guinea Corn 15 15
303 37 b. Rice 25 25

74. Oil Palm.

(Des. PAD Studio. Litho. Format.)

1973 (16 July). *Agriculture (2nd series). T* **74** *and similar vert. designs. Multicoloured. P* 12.

304 2 b. Type **74** 5 5
305 25 b. Limes 15 15
306 37 b. Oil palm (fruits) .. 25 25

75. Cassava.

(Des. PAD Studio. Litho. Questa.)

1973 (15 Oct.). *Agriculture (3rd series). Type* **75** *and similar horiz. design. Multicoloured. P* 14.

307 2 b. Type **75** 5 5
308 50 b. Cotton 30 30

76. O.A.U. Emblem.

(Des. and litho. D.L.R.)

1973 (1 Nov.). *Tenth Anniv. of O.A.U. P* 13½ × 13.

309 **76** 4 b. multicoloured .. 5 5
310 „ 25 b. multicoloured .. 15 15
311 „ 37 b. multicoloured .. 20 25

77. Red Cross.

(Des. J. E. Cooter. Litho. Questa.)

1973 (30 Nov.). *25th Anniv. of Gambian Red Cross. P* 14 × 14½.

312 **77** 4 b. dull orange-red, and black.. .. .. 5 5
313 „ 25 b. dull orange-red, black and new blue .. 15 15
314 „ 37 b. dull orange-red, black & light yellow-green 20 25

78. Arms of Banjul.

(Des. and litho. D.L.R.)

1973 (17 Dec.). *Change of Bathurst's Name to Banjul. P* 13½ × 13.

315 **78** 4 b. multicoloured .. 5 5
316 „ 25 b. multicoloured .. 15 15
317 „ 37 b. multicoloured .. 20 25

79. U.P.U. Emblem.

(Des. and litho. D.L.R.)

1974 (24 Aug.). *Centenary of Universal Postal Union. P* 13½.

318 **79** 4 b. multicoloured .. 5 5
319 „ 37 b. multicoloured .. 25 25

HAVE YOU READ THE NOTES AT THE BEGINNING OF THIS CATALOGUE?

These often provide answers to the enquiries we receive.

80. Churchill as Harrow Schoolboy.

(Des. and litho. J.W.)

1974 (30 Nov.). *Birth Centenary of Sir Winston Churchill. T* **80** *and similar vert. designs. Multicoloured. P* 13½.

320	4 b. Type **80**	5	5
321	37 b. Churchill as 4th Hussars officer	20	25
322	50 b. Churchill as Prime Minister	30	30

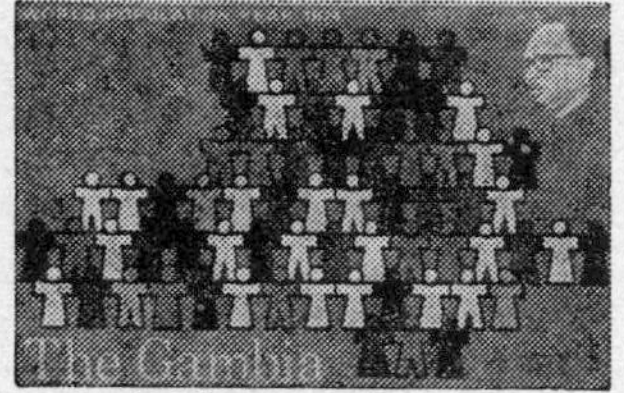

81. " Different Races ".

(Des. G. L. Vasarhelyi. Litho. Questa.)

1974 (16 Dec.). *World Population Year. T* **81** *and similar horiz. designs. Multicoloured. P* 14.

323	4 b. Type **81**	5	5
324	37 b. " Multiplication and Division of Races " ..	20	25
325	50 b. " World Population " ..	25	30

82. Dr. Schweitzer and River Scene.

(Des. G. L. Vasarhelyi. Litho. Walsall Security Printers Ltd.)

1975 (14 Jan.). *Birth Centenary of Dr. Albert Schweitzer. T* **82** *and similar horiz. designs. Multicoloured. P* 14.

326	10 b. Type **82**	5	8
327	50 b. Surgery scene	30	30
328	1 d. 25, River journey ..	65	65

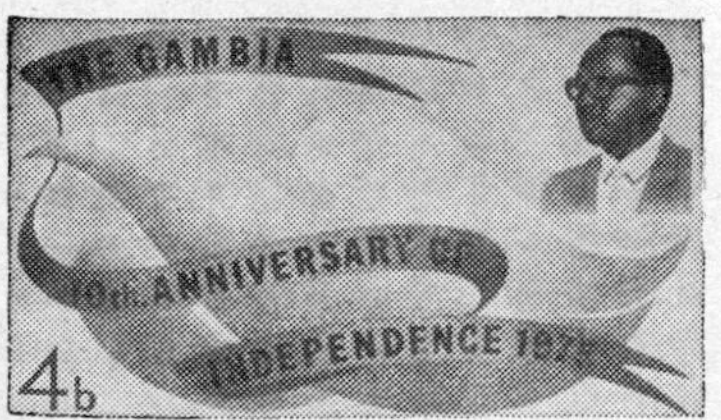

83. Dove of Peace.

(Des. and litho. D.L.R.)

1975 (18 Feb.). *Tenth Anniv. of Independence. T* **83** *and similar horiz. designs. Multicoloured. P* 13.

329	4 b. Type **83**	5	5
330	10 b. Gambian flag	5	8
331	50 b. Gambian arms ..	30	30
332	1 d. 25, Map of The Gambia	65	70

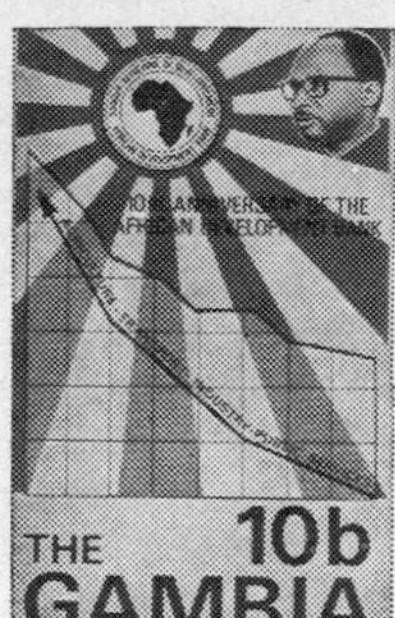

84. Development Graph.

(Des. PAD Studio. Litho. Questa).

1975 (31 Mar.) *Tenth Anniv. of African Development Bank. T* **84** *and similar vert. designs. Multicoloured. P* 14½.

333	10 b. Type **84**	5	8
334	50 b. Symbolic plant	30	30
335	1 d. 25, Bank emblem and symbols	65	70

85. " Statue of David " (Michelangelo).

(Des. C. Abbott. Litho. Walsall.)

1975 (14 Nov.). *500th Birth Anniv. of Michelangelo. T* **85** *and similar multicoloured designs. P* 14½×14 (1 *d.* 25) *or* 14×14½ (*others*).

336	10 b. Type **85**	5	5
337	50 b. " Madonna of the Steps "	30	30
338	1 d. 25, " Battle of the Centaurs " (*horiz.*)	65	70

86. School Building.

(Des. G. L. Vasarhelyi. Litho. Format.)

1975 (17 Nov.). *Centenary of Gambia High School. T* **86** *and similar horiz. designs. Multicoloured. P* 14½.

339	10 b. Type **86**	5	5
340	50 b. Pupil with scientific apparatus	30	30
341	1 d. 50, School crest ..	75	80

87. " Teaching ".

(Des. A. B. Oliver; adapted by Jennifer Toombs. Litho. Questa.)

1975 (15 Dec.). *International Women's Year. T* **87** *and similar horiz. designs. Multicoloured. P* 14½.

342	4 b. Type **87**	5	5
343	10 b. " Planting rice " ..	5	5
344	50 b. " Nursing "	25	30
345	1 d. 50, " Directing traffic "	70	80

88. Woman playing Golf.

(Des. R. Granger Barrett. Litho. J.W.)

1976 (18 Feb.). *11th Anniv. of Independence. T* **88** *and similar horiz. designs. Multicoloured. P* 14½×14.

346	10 b. Type **88**	5	5
347	50 b. Man playing golf ..	25	30
348	1 d. 50, President playing golf	70	80

89. American Militiaman.

(Des. C. Abbott. Litho. Questa.)

1976 (15 May). *Bicentenary of American Revolution. T* **89** *and similar vert. designs. Multicoloured. P* 14×13½.

349	25 b. Type **89**	12	15
350	50 b. Soldier of the Continental Army	25	30
351	1 d. 25, Independence Declaration	60	70
MS352	110×80 mm. Nos. 349/51	1·10	

90. Mother and Child.

(Des. G. L. Vasarhelyi. Litho. Questa.)

1976 (28 Oct.). *Christmas.* *P* 14.

353	**90**	10 b. multicoloured ..	5	8
354	,,	50 b. multicoloured ..	25	30
355	,,	1 d. 25, multicoloured ..	65	75

91. Serval Cat.

(Des. G. Drummond. Litho. Questa.)

1976 (29 Nov.). *Abuko Nature Reserve.* *T* **91** *and similar horiz. designs. Multicoloured.* *P* 13½.

356	10 b. Type **91**	5	5
357	25 b. Harnessed Antelope ..	12	15
358	50 b. Sitatunga (deer) ..	25	30
359	1 d. 25, Leopard	60	70
MS360	137 × 110 mm. Nos. 356/9	1·10	

92. Festival Emblem and Gambian Weaver.

(Des. E. N. Sillah; adapted C. Abbott. Litho. Walsall.)

1977 (12 Jan.). *Second World Black and African Festival of Arts and Culture, Nigeria.* *P* 14.

361	**92**	25 b. multicoloured ..	12	15
362	,,	50 b. multicoloured ..	25	30
363	,,	1 d. 25, multicoloured ..	60	65
MS364		115 × 127 mm. Nos. 361/3	1·00	

MINIMUM PRICE

The minimum price quoted is 5p which represents a handling charge rather than a basis for valuing common stamps. For further notes about prices see introductory pages.

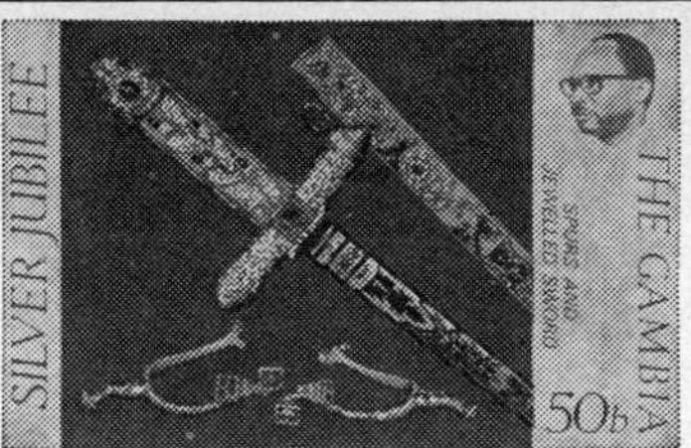

93. The Spurs and Jewelled Sword.

(Des. PAD Studio. Litho. Questa.)

1977 (7 Feb.). *Silver Jubilee.* *T* **93** *and similar horiz. designs. Multicoloured.* *P* 13½.

365	25 b. Queen's visit, 1961 ..	12	15
366	50 b. Type **93**	25	30
367	1 d. 25, Oblation of the sword	60	65

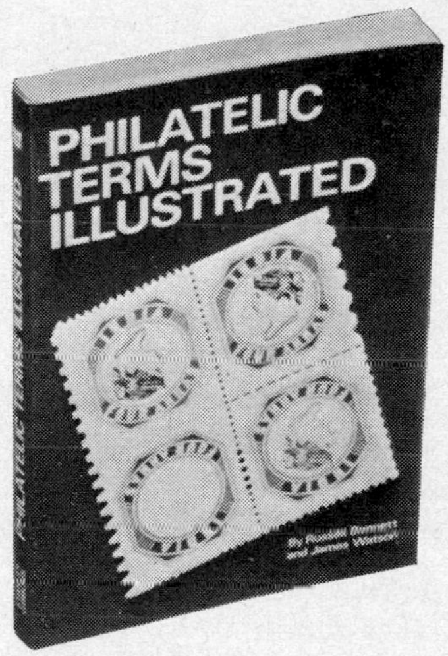

GHANA.

(Formerly Gold Coast.)

I. DOMINION.

✱CANCELLED REMAINDERS. In 1961 remainders of some issues of 1957 to 1960 were put on the market cancelled-to-order in such a way as to be indistinguishable from genuine postally used copies for all practical purposes. Our used quotations which are indicated by an asterisk are the same for cancelled-to-order or postally used copies.

29. Dr. Kwame Nkrumah, Fish Eagle and Map of Africa.

(Photo. Harrison.)

1957 (6 Mar.). *Independence. Wmk. Mult. Script CA. P* 14×14½.

166 **29** 2d. scarlet 5 5*
167 ,, 2½d. green 5 5*
168 ,, 4d. brown 5 5*
169 ,, 1s. 3d. deep blue 15 5*

GHANA
INDEPENDENCE
6TH MARCH,
1957.
(30)

1957 (6 Mar.)–**58.** *Nos.* 153/64 *of Gold Coast optd. as T* **30.**

170 **20** ½d. bis.-brn. & scar. (*shades*) 5 5*
171 **17** 1d. deep blue (R.) .. 5 5*
172 **18** 1½d. emerald-green .. 10 5*
173 **19** 2d. chocolate (26.5.58) .. 12 10
174 **28** 2½d. scarlet (26.5.58) .. 15 15
175 **21** 3d. magenta 5 5*
176 **22** 4d. blue (26.5.58) .. 50 50
177 **23** 6d. black and orange (R.) 8 5*
178 **24** 1s. black and orange-red 12 5*
179 **25** 2s. brn.-olive & carmine 25 10*
180 **26** 5s. purple and black .. 60 25*
181 **27** 10s. black and olive-green 1·25 50*
170/181 .. .. *Set of* 12 3·00 1·25*

The 6d. (No. 177) exists with double overprint.

Nos. 173/4 and 176 were officially issued on May 26th, 1958 although, in error, small quantities were sold at certain post offices when the rest of the set appeared.

31. Viking Ship.

32. Galleon.
33. M.V. *Volta River.*

(Des. W. Wind. Recess. E. A. Wright Bank Note Co., Philadelphia.)

1957 (27 Dec.). *Inauguration of Black Star Shipping Line. No wmk. P* 12.

182 **31** 2½d. emerald-green .. 10 10
a. Imperf. between (vert. pair) £200
b. Imperf. between (horiz. pr.) £200
183 **32** 1s. 3d. deep blue 25 30
a. Imperf. between (vert. pair) £200
184 **33** 5s. bright purple .. 1·10 1·25

PRINTERS. The following stamps were printed in photogravure by Harrison & Sons *except where otherwise stated.*

34. Ambassador Hotel, Accra.

35. State Opening of Parliament. (*Horiz.*)
36. National Monument. (*Horiz.*)

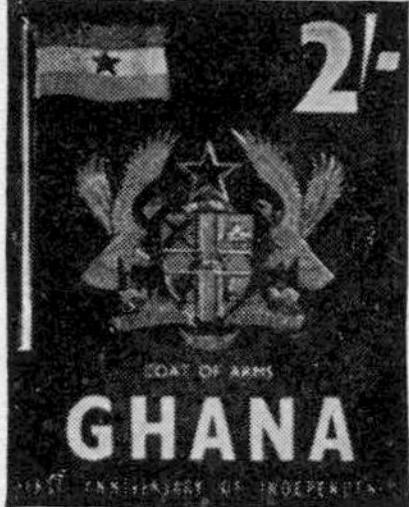

37. Ghana Coat-of-Arms.

1958 (6 Mar.). *First Anniv. of Independence. Wmk. Mult. Script CA. P* 14½×14 (2*s.*) *or* 14×14½ (*others*).

185 **34** ½d. black, red, yellow, green and carmine .. 5 5
186 **35** 2½d. black, red, green and yellow 5 5
187 **36** 1s. 3d. black, red, yellow, green and blue .. 15 15
188 **37** 2s. red, yellow, blue, green, brown & black 25 40

38. Map showing the Independent African States.

39. Map of Africa and Flaming Torch.

(Des. R. Milton.)

1958 (15 Apr.). *First Conference of Independent African States, Accra. Wmk. Mult. Script CA. P* 13½×14½ (2½*d.*, 3*d.*) *or* 14½×13½ (*others*).

189 **38** 2½d. black, bistre & bright carmine-red 5 5
190 ,, 3d. black, bistre, brown and bright green .. 5 5
191 **39** 1s. black, yellow, red and dull blue 12 15
192 ,, 2s. 6d. black, yellow, red and dull violet .. 30 40

40. Eagle over Globe.

41. "Britannia" Airliner.

42. "Stratocruiser" and Albatross.

43. Fish Eagle and Jet Aircraft.

(Des. M. Goaman (2½d., 2s. 6d.), R. Milton (1s. 3d.), W. Wind (2s.).)

1958 (15 July). *Inauguration of Ghana Airways. Wmk. Mult. Script CA. P* 15×14 (2*s.* 6*d.*) *or* 14×15 (*others*).

193 **40** 2½d. black, yellow-bistre and rose-carmine .. 5 5
194 **41** 1s. 3d. multicoloured .. 15 15
195 **42** 2s. multicoloured .. 20 25
196 **43** 2s. 6d. black and bistre .. 25 30

(44)

45

1958 (18 July). *Prime Minister's Visit to the United States and Canada. Nos.* 166/9 *optd. with T* **44.**

197 **29** 2d. scarlet 5 5
198 ,, 2½d. green 5 5
199 ,, 4d. brown 5 8
200 ,, 1s. 3d. deep blue .. 15 15

(Des. W. Wind.)

958 (24 Oct.). *United Nations Day. Wmk. Mult. Script CA. P* 14×14½.

01 **45** 2½d. purple-brown, green and black 5 5
02 ,, 1s. 3d. purple-brown, blue and black 15 15
03 ,, 2s. 6d. purple-brown, violet and black 25 30

46. Dr. Nkrumah and Lincoln Statue, Washington.

47

(Des. M. Goaman.)

959 (12 Feb.). *150th Anniv. of Birth of Abraham Lincoln. W* **47.** *P* 14×14½.

04 **46** 2½d. pink and deep purple 5 5
05 ,, 1s. 3d. light blue and blue 12 12
06 ,, 2s. 6d. orange-yellow and deep olive-green .. 30 30
IS206a 102×77 mm. Nos. 204/6. Imperf. .. .. .. 1·75 1·75

48. Kente Cloth and Traditional Symbols.

9. Talking Drums and Elephant-horn Blower.

50. " Symbol of Greeting ".

51. Map of Africa, Ghana Flag and Palms.

(Des. Mrs. T. Sutherland (½d.), M. Karoly (2½d.), K. Antubam (1s. 3d.), A. M. Medina (2s.).)

1959 (6 Mar.). *Second Anniv. of Independence. W* **47.** *P* 14½×14 (2s.) *or* 14×14½ (*others*).

207 **48** ½d. multicoloured .. 5 5
208 **49** 2½d. multicoloured .. 5 5
209 **50** 1s. 3d. multicoloured .. 12 12
210 **51** 2s. multicoloured .. 25 30

52. Globe and Flags.

(Des. Mrs. H. Potter.)

1959 (15 Apr.). *Africa Freedom Day. W* **47** (*sideways*). *P* 14½×14.

211 **52** 2½d. multicoloured .. 5 5
212 ,, 8½d. multicoloured .. 15 15

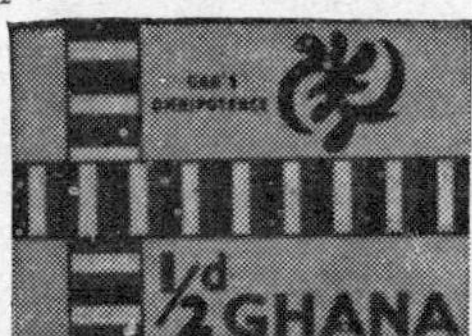

53. " God's Omnipotence ".

54. Nkrumah Statue, Accra.

55. Ghana Timber.

56. Volta River.

57. Cocoa Bean.

58. " God's Omnipotence".

59. Diamond and Mine.

60. Fire-crowned Bishop.

61. Golden Spider Lily.

62. Shell Ginger.

63. Giant Plantain Eater.

64. Tiger Orchid.

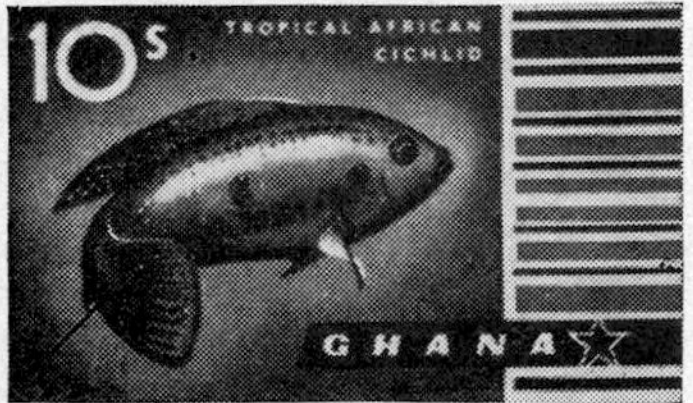

65. Tropical African Cichlid.

65*a*. Leaping Antelope.

66. Pennant-winged Nightjar.

67. Crowned Cranes.

(Des. Mrs. T. Sutherland (½d., 3d.), Ghana Information Bureau (source of 1d. and 2d.), O. Haulkland (1½d.), M. Medina (2½d., 4d.), M. Goaman (6d., 1s. 3d., 2s. 6d.), W. Wind (11d., 1s., 2s., 5s.), W. H. Brown (10s.), M. Shamir (£1).)

1959 (5 Oct.)–**61.** *W* **47** (*sideways on horiz. designs*). *P* 11½ × 12 (½*d.*), 12 × 11½ (1*d.*), 14 × 14½ (1½*d.*, 11*d.*, 1*s.*, 2*s.*, *and* 5*s.*), 14 × 15 (10*s.*) *or* 14½ × 14 (*others*).

		(*a*) *Postage.*		
213	**53**	½d. multicoloured (I) ..	5	5
213*a*	,,	½d. multicoloured (II) (29.4.61)	5	5
214	**54**	1d. multicoloured ..	5	5
215	**55**	1½d. multicoloured ..	5	5
216	**56**	2d. multicoloured ..	5	5
217	**57**	2½d. multicoloured ..	5	5
218	**58**	3d. multicoloured (I) ..	5	5
218*a*	,,	3d. multicoloured (II) (29.4.61)	5	5
219	**59**	4d. multicoloured ..	5	5
220	**60**	6d. multicoloured ..	8	5
221	**61**	11d. multicoloured ..	12	8
222	**62**	1s. multicoloured ..	12	5
223	**63**	2s. 6d. multicoloured ..	30	25
224	**64**	5s. multicoloured ..	60	50
225	**65**	10s. multicoloured ..	1·50	80
225*a*	**65***a*	£1 multicoloured (29.4.61)	3·50	3·25
		(*b*) *Air.*		
226	**66**	1s. 3d. multicoloured ..	15	10
227	**67**	2s. multicoloured ..	25	20
213/27		.. .. *Set of* 16	6·00	5·00

Nos. 213/*a* and 218/*a*. I. inscr. "GOD'S OMNIPOTENCE"; II. inscr. "GYE NYAME".

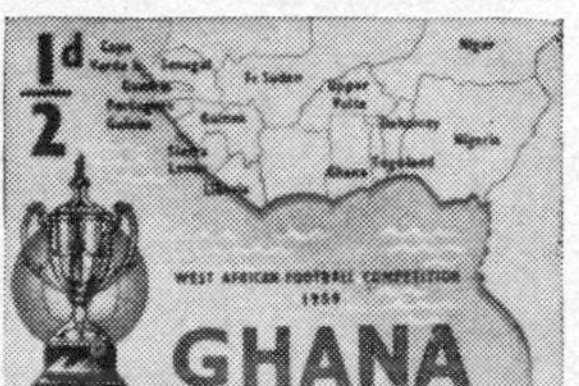

68. Gold Cup and West African Map.

69. Footballers. (*Vert.*)

70. Goalkeeper saving Ball. (*Horiz.*)

71. Forward attacking Goal. (*Horiz.*)

72. "Kwame Nkrumah" Gold Cup. (*Vert.*)

(Des. K. Lehmann (½d., 3d.), M. & G. Shami (1d.), W. Wind (8d.), and R. Antubam 2s. 6d.)

1959 (15 Oct.). *West African Football Competition, 1959.* *W* **47** (*sideways on horiz. designs*). *P* 14 × 14½ (1*d.*, 2*s.* 6*d.*) *or* 14½ × 1 (*others*).

228	**68**	½d. multicoloured ..	5	5
229	**69**	1d. multicoloured ..	5	5
230	**70**	3d. multicoloured ..	5	5
231	**71**	8d. multicoloured ..	15	10
232	**72**	2s. 6d. multicoloured ..	35	30
228/32		.. .. *Set of* 5	55	45

73. The Duke of Edinburgh and Arms of Ghana.

(Des. A. S. B. New.)

1959 (24 Nov.). *Visit of the Duke of Edinburg to Ghana.* *W* **47** (*sideways*). *P* 15 × 14.

233	**73**	3d. black and magenta ..	5	5

74. Ghana Flag and Talking Drums.

75. Ghana Flag and U.N. Emblem.

76. Ghana Flag and U.N. Emblem.

77. " Totem Pole ".

Des. M. Medina (T **74/6**), K. Antubam (T **77**).)

959 (10 Dec.). *United Nations Trusteeship Council. W* **47** *(sideways on 3d.). P* 14½×14 (*3d.*) *or* 14×14½ *(others).*

34 **74** 3d. multicoloured .. 5 5*
35 **75** 6d. multicoloured .. 8 8*
36 **76** 1s. 3d. multicoloured .. 15 12*
37 **77** 2s. 6d. multicoloured .. 30 30*

78. Eagles in Flight.

79. Fireworks.

80. " Third Anniversary ".

81. " Ship of State ".

(Des. M. Medina (½d.), M. Goaman (3d.), W. Wind (1s. 3d., 2s.).)

1960 (6 Mar.). *Third Anniv. of Independence. W* **47.** *P* 14×14½.

238 **78** ½d. multicoloured .. 5 5*
239 **79** 3d. multicoloured .. 5 5*
240 **80** 1s. 3d. multicoloured .. 15 12*
241 **81** 2s. multicoloured .. 25 25*

82

83

84

(Des. W. Wind.)

1960 (15 Apr.). *Africa Freedom Day. W* **47** *(sideways). P* 14½×14.

242 **82** 3d. multicoloured .. 5 5*
243 **83** 6d. multicoloured .. 8 5*
244 **84** 1s. multicoloured .. 12 10*

II. REPUBLIC.

85. President Nkrumah.

86. Ghana Flag. (*Vert.*)
87. Torch of Freedom. (*Vert.*)
88. Arms of Ghana. (*Horiz.*)

(Des. M. Medina (3d., 10s.), W. Wind (1s. 3d., 2s.).)

1960 (1 July). *Republic Day. W* **47.** *P* 14½×14 (*10s.*) *or* 14×14½ *(others).*

245 **85** 3d. multicoloured .. 5 5
246 **86** 1s. 3d. multicoloured .. 12 12
247 **87** 2s. multicoloured .. 25 25
248 **88** 10s. multicoloured .. 1·10 1·25
MS248*a* 102×77 mm. Nos. 245/8. Imperf. .. .. 1·50 1·75

89. Olympic Torch.

90. Athlete.

(Des. A. Medina (T **89**), W. Wind (T **90**).)

1960 (15 Aug.). *Olympic Games. W* **47** *(sideways on T* **90***). P* 14×14½ (*T* **89**) *or* 14½×14 (*T* **90**).

249 **89** 3d. multicoloured .. 5 5
250 ,, 6d. multicoloured .. 5 5
251 **90** 1s. 3d. multicoloured .. 15 20
252 ,, 2s. 6d. multicoloured .. 30 25

91. President Nkrumah.

92. President Nkrumah. (*Vert.*)
93. Flag-draped Column over Map of Africa. (*Vert.*)

(Des. M. Goaman (3d., 6d.), W. Wind (1s. 3d.).)

1960 (21 Sept.). *Founder's Day.* *W* **47** (*sideways on 3d.*). *P* 14½×14 (*3d.*) *or* 14×14½ (*others*).

253	**91**	3d. multicoloured ..	5	5
254	**92**	6d. multicoloured ..	8	5
255	**93**	1s. 3d. multicoloured ..	20	15

94. U.N. Emblem and Ghana Flag.

95. U.N. Emblem and Torch.
96. U.N. Emblem.

(Des. M. Goaman (3d., 1s. 3d.), W. Wind (6d.).)

1960 (10 Dec.). *Human Rights Day.* *W* **47.** *P* 14×14½.

256	**94**	3d. multicoloured ..	5	5
257	**95**	6d. yellow, black and blue	8	5
258	**96**	1s. 3d. multicoloured ..	20	15

97. Talking Drums.

98. Map of Africa. (*Vert.*)
99. Flags and Map. (*Horiz.*)

(Des. M. Goaman (T **97**), A. S. B. New (T **98**), W. Wind (T **99**).)

1961 (15 Apr.). *Africa Freedom Day.* *W* **47** (*sideways on 2s.*). *P* 14½×14 (*2s.*) *or* 14×14½ (*others*).

259	**97**	3d. multicoloured ..	5	5
260	**98**	6d. red, black and green	8	5
261	**99**	2s. multicoloured ..	30	25

100. Eagle on Column.

101. " Flower ".
102. Ghana Flags.

(Des. A. S. B. New (3d.), M. Shamir (1s. 3d.), W. Wind (2s.).).

1961 (1 July). *First Anniv. of Republic.* *W* **47.** *P* 14×14½.

262	**100**	3d. multicoloured ..	5	5
263	**101**	1s. 3d. multicoloured ..	15	12
264	**102**	2s. multicoloured ..	30	35

103. Dove with Olive Branch.

104. World Map, Chain and Olive Branch. (*Horiz.*)
105. Rostrum, Conference Room. (*Horiz.*)

(Des. V. Whiteley.)

1961 (1 Sept.). *Belgrade Conference.* *W* **47.** (*sideways on 1s. 3d., 5s.*) *P* 14×14½ (*3d.*) *or* 14½×14 (*others*).

265	**103**	3d. yellow-green ..	8	8
266	**104**	1s. 3d. deep blue ..	20	20
267	**105**	5s. brt. reddish purple ..	70	85

106. Pres. Nkrumah and Globe.

107. President and Kente Cloth. (*Vert.*)
108. President in National Costume. (*Vert.*)

(Des. M. Medina (3d.), M. Goaman (1s. 3d.), Miriam Karoly (5s.).)

1961 (21 Sept.). *Founder's Day.* *W* **47** (*sideways on 3d.*). *P* 14½×14 (*3d.*) *or* 14×14½ (*others*).

268	**106**	3d. multicoloured ..	5	5
269	**107**	1s. 3d. multicoloured ..	20	20
270	**108**	5s. multicoloured ..	80	85

MS270*a*. Three sheets 106×86 mm. (3d.) or 86×106 mm. (others) each with Nos. 268/70 in block of four. Imperf. Three sheets. 7·00 7·50

The 1s. 3d. Miniature Sheet is known with the brown colour omitted.

109. Queen Elizabeth II and African Map.

1961 (9 Nov.). *Royal Visit.* *W* **47.** *P* 14½×1

271	**109**	3d. multicoloured ..	5	
272	,,	1s. 3d. multicoloured ..	20	
273	,,	5s. multicoloured ..	80	

MS273*a* 106×84 mm. No. 273 in block of four. Imperf. .. 5·50 6·0

110. Ships in Tema Harbour.

111. Aircraft and Ships at Tema.

(Des. C. Bottiau. Litho. Enschedé & Sons.)

1962 (10 Feb.). *Opening of Tema Harbour.* *N wmk.* *P* 14×13. (*a*) *Postage.*

274	**110**	3d. multicoloured ..	5	

(*b*) *Air.*

275	**111**	1s. 3d. multicoloured ..	15	
276	,,	2s. 6d. multicoloured ..	35	

112. Africa and Peace Dove.

(Des. R. Hegeman. Litho. Enschedé.)

1962 (6 Mar.). *First Anniv. of Casablanca Co-ference.* *No wmk.* *P* 13×14. (*a*) *Postage.*

277	**112**	3d. multicoloured ..	5	

(*b*) *Air.*

278	**112**	1s. 3d. multicoloured ..	15	
279	,,	2s. 6d. multicoloured ..	35	

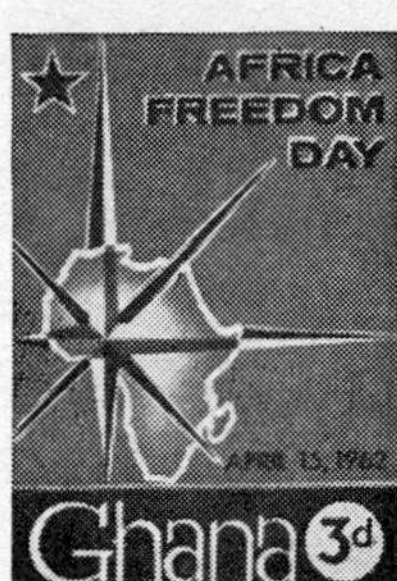

113. Compass over Africa.

(Des. R. Hegeman.)

1962 (24 APR.). *Africa Freedom Day.* *W* **47.** *P* 14×14½.

280	**113**	3d. sepia, blue-green and reddish purple ..	5	5
281	,,	6d. sepia, blue-green and orange-brown ..	8	5
282	,,	1s. 3d. sepia, blue-green and red	20	20

114. Ghana Star and " Five Continents ".

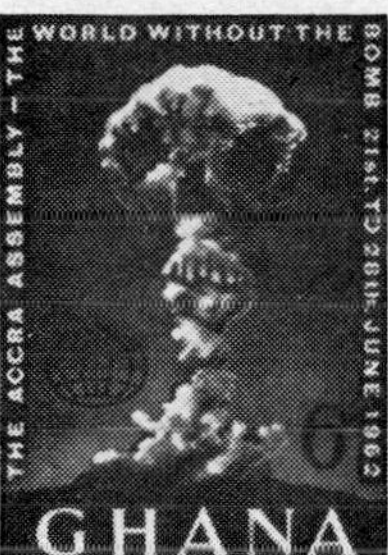

115. Atomic Bomb-burst "Skull".

116. Dove of Peace.

(Des. M. Goaman (3d.), M. Shamir (6d.), W. Wind (1s. 3d.).)

1962 (21 JUNE.) *Accra Assembly.* *W* **47.** *P* 14 × 14½.

283	**114**	3d. black and lake-red ..	5	5
284	**115**	6d. black and scarlet ..	10	10
285	**116**	1s. 3d. turquoise.. ..	25	25

117. Patrice Lumumba.

(Des. A. S. B. New.)

1962 (30 JUNE). *First Death Anniv. of Lumumba.* *W* **47.** *P* 14½×14.

286	**117**	3d. blk. & orange-yellow	5	5
287	,,	6d. black, green and lake	8	8
288	,,	1s. 3d. black, pink and black-green	15	20

118. Star over Two Columns.

119. Flaming Torch. (*Vert.*)

120. Eagle trailing Flag. (*Horiz.*)

(Des. A. S. B. New (3d.), A. Medina (6d.), M. Goaman (1s. 3d.). Litho. Enschedé.)

1962 (1 JULY). *2nd Anniv. of Republic.* *P* 14×13½ (1s. 3d.) *or* 13½×14 (*others*).

289	**118**	3d. violet, black, red, yellow and green ..	5	5
290	**119**	6d. red, yellow, green, black and violet ..	8	8
291	**120**	1s. 3d. red, yellow, green and indigo	25	20

121. President Nkrumah.

122. Nkrumah Medallion.

123. President Nkrumah and Ghana Star.

124. Laying " Ghana " Brick.

(Litho. Enschedé.)

1962 (21 SEPT.). *Founder's Day.* *P* 13 × 14½.

292	**121**	1d. black, red, green and yellow	5	5
293	**122**	3d. orange, black, red, green, yellow & cream	5	5
294	**123**	1s. 3d. black and brt. blue	15	15
295	**124**	2s. black, red, olive-green and yellow	25	25

MINIMUM PRICE

The minimum price quoted is 5p which represents a handling charge rather than a basis for valuing common stamps. For further notes about prices see introductory pages.

125. Campaign Emblem.

1962 (3 DEC.). *Malaria Eradication.* *W* **47.** *P* 14×14½.

296	**125**	1d. cerise	5	5
297	,,	4d. yellow-green	5	5
298	,,	6d. bistre	8	5
299	,,	1s. 3d. bluish violet ..	20	15
MS299*a*		90×115 mm. Nos. 296/9. Imperf.	60	60

126. Campaign Emblem.

127. Emblem in Hands. (*Horiz.*)

128. World Map and Emblem. (*Horiz.*)

1963 (21 MAR.). *Freedom from Hunger.* *W* **47** (*sideways on 4d., 1s. 3d.*). *P* 14×14½ (1d.) *or* 14½×14 (*others*).

300	**126**	1d. yellow, red, green, black and light blue	5	5
301	**127**	4d. sepia, yellow & orange	5	5
302	**128**	1s. 3d. ochre, black & grn.	15	15

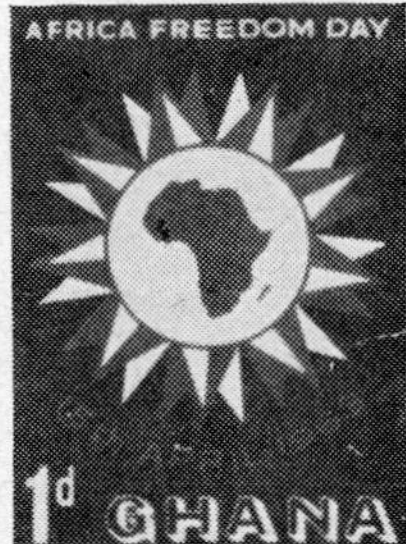

129. Map of Africa.

130. Carved Stool. (*Horiz.*)

131. Map and Bowl of Fire. (*Vert.*)

132. Antelope and Flag. (*Vert.*)

1963 (15 APR.). *Africa Freedom Day.* *W* **47** (*sideways on 4d.*). *P* 14½×14 (4d.) *or* 14×14½ (*others*).

303	**129**	1d. gold and red	5	5
304	**130**	4d. red, black and yellow	5	5
305	**131**	1s. 3d. black, red, yellow and green	15	15
306	**132**	2s. 6d. multicoloured ..	35	35

133. Red Cross.

134. Centenary Emblem. (*Horiz.*)
135. Nurses and Child. (*Horiz.*)
136. Emblem, Globe Laurel. (*Vert.*)

(Des. R. Hegeman (4d.), M. Shamir (others).)

1963 (8 May). *Red Cross Centenary. W* **47** (*sideways on* 1½*d.*, 4*d.*). *P* 14 × 14½ (1*d.*, 1*s.* 3*d.*) *or* 14 × 14½ (*others*).

307	**133**	1d. multicoloured ..	5	5
308	**134**	1½d. multicoloured ..	5	5
309	**135**	4d. multicoloured ..	5	5
310	**136**	1s. 3d. multicoloured ..	15	15
MS310*a*		102 × 127 mm. Nos. 307/10. Imperf.	40	60

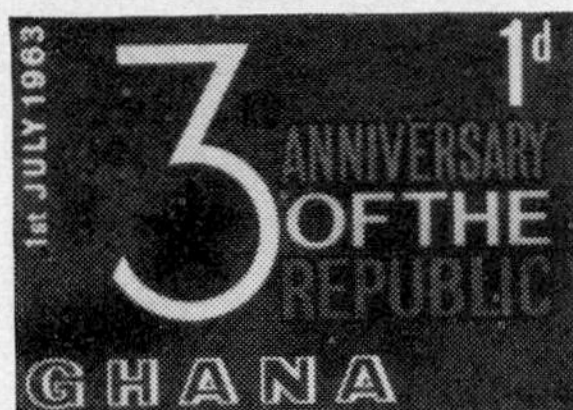

137. "3rd Anniversary".

138. Three Ghanaian Flags. (*Horiz.*)
139. Map, Flag and Star. (*Vert.*)
140. Flag and Torch. (*Vert.*)

(Des. M. Goaman (1d., 4d.), R. Hegeman (others).)

1963 (1 July). *3rd Anniv. of Republic. W* **47** (*sideways on* 1*d.*, 4*d.*). *P* 14½ × 14 (*horiz.*) *or* 14 × 14½ (*vert.*)

311	**137**	1d. red, yellow, green black and sepia ..	5	5
312	**138**	4d. red, yellow, green, black and blue ..	5	5
313	**139**	1s. 3d. green, black, red and yellow	15	15
314	**140**	2s. 6d. red, yellow, green, black & dp. violet-bl.	30	30

141. President Nkrumah and Ghanaian Flag.

142. President Nkrumah and Ghanaian Flag. (*Vert.*) (*different*).
143. Pres. Nkrumah and Fireworks. (*Horiz.*)
144. Native Symbol of Wisdom. (*Horiz.*)

(Des. R. Hegeman (1d., 4d.), M. Shamir (1s. 3d.), G. Rose (5s.).)

1963 (21 Sept.). *Founder's Day. W* **47** (*sideways on* 1*s.* 3*d.*, 5*s.*). *P* 14 × 14½ (*vert.*) *or* 14½ × 14 (*horiz.*).

315	**141**	1d. blk., red, yell. & grn.	5	5
316	**142**	4d. red, yell., grn. & blk.	5	5
317	**143**	1s. 3d. red, yellow, green and brown	15	15
318	**144**	5s yellow & bright reddish purple	65	75

145. Rameses II, Abu Simbel.

146. Rock Paintings. (*Horiz.*)
147. Queen Nefertari. (*Horiz.*)
148. Sphinx, Sebua. (*Vert.*)
149. Rock Temple, Abu Simbel. (*Horiz.*)

(Des. M. C. Farrar-Bell and R. Hegeman. Litho. (1½d., 2d.) or photo. (others). Enschedé.)

1963 (1 Nov.). *Nubian Monument Preservation. No wmk. P* 11½ × 11 (*vert.*) *or* 11 × 11½ (*horiz.*).

319	**145**	1d. multicoloured ..	5	5
320	**146**	1½d. multicoloured ..	5	5
321	**147**	2d. multicoloured ..	5	5
322	**148**	4d. multicoloured ..	5	5
323	**149**	1s. 3d. multicoloured ..	25	25
319/23		.. .. *Set of* 5	40	40

150. Steam and Diesel Locomotives.

(Des. H. L. W. Stevens.)

1963 (1 Dec.). *60th Anniv. of Ghana Railway. W* **47** (*sideways*). *P* 14½ × 14.

324	**150**	1d. multicoloured ..	5	5
325	"	6d. multicoloured ..	8	8
326	"	1s. 3d. multicoloured ..	20	20
327	"	2s. 6d. multicoloured ..	40	40

151. Eleanor Roosevelt and "Flame of Freedom". (*Vert.*)

152. Eleanor Roosevelt. (*Vert.*)
153. Eleanor Roosevelt and Emblems. (*Horiz.*).

(Des. R. Hegeman and F. H. Savage. Photo Enschedé.)

1963 (10 Dec.). *15th Anniv. of Declaration of Human Rights. No wmk. P* 11 × 11½ (1*s.* 3*d.*) *or* 11½ × 11 (*others*).

328	**151**	1d. multicoloured ..	5	5
329	"	4d. multicoloured ..	5	5
330	**152**	6d. multicoloured ..	8	8
331	**153**	1s. 3d. multicoloured ..	20	20

No. 329 differs slightly from No. 328 in the arrangement of the trailing "flame" and of the background within the circular emblem.

154. Sun and Globe Emblem.

1964 (15 June). *International Quiet Sun Years. W* **47** (*sideways*). *Each blue, yellow, red and green; background colours given. P* 14½.

332	**154**	3d. pale brown	5	5
333	"	6d. pale grey	8	8
334	"	1s. 3d. mauve	15	15
MS334*a*		90 × 90 mm. No. 334 in block of four. Imperf. ..	1·00	1·00

Nos. 332/4 each exist in a miniature sheet of 12 in different colours (i.e. 3d. in colours of 6d. 6d. in colours of 1s. 3d.; 1s. 3d. in colours of 3d.) but these were not generally available to the public.

155. Harvesting Corn on State Farm.

156. Oil Refinery, Tema.
157. "Communal Labour".
158. Procession headed by Flag.

(Des. M. Shamir. Photo. Govt. Printer, Israel.)

1964 (1 July). *4th Anniv. of Republic. P* 13 × 14.

335	**155**	3d. olive, brown and yellow-olive	5	5
336	**156**	6d. bluish green, brown and turquoise-green ..	8	8
337	**157**	1s. 3d. brown-red, brown and salmon-red ..	15	15
338	**158**	5s. red, green, brown and light violet-blue ..	70	7[illegible]
MS338*a*		126 × 100 mm. Nos. 335/8. Imperf.	1·00	1·25

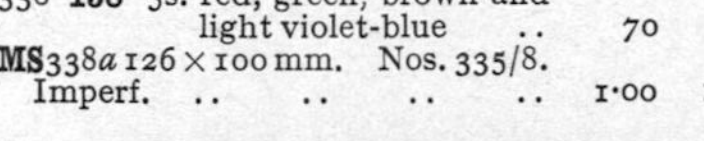

159. Globe and Dove.

160. Map of Africa and Quill Pen. (*Vert.*)
161. Hitched Rope on Map of Africa. (*Horiz.*)
162. Planting Flower. (*Vert.*)

(Des. M. Shamir. Litho. Lewin-Epstein, Ltd., Bat Yam, Israel.)

1964 (15 July). *1st Anniv. of African Unity Charter. P* 14.
339 **159** 3d. multicoloured .. 5 5
340 **160** 6d. dp. bronze-grn. & red 8 5
341 **161** 1s. 3d. multicoloured .. 15 15
342 **162** 5s. multicoloured .. 60 60

163. Pres. Nkrumah and Hibiscus Flowers.

1964 (21 Sept.). *Founder's Day. W* **47** *(sideways). P* 14 × 14½.
343 **163** 3d. sepia, red, deep green and light blue .. 5 5
344 ,, 6d. sepia, red, deep green and yellow 8 8
345 ,, 1s. 3d. sepia, red, deep green and grey .. 15 15
346 ,, 2s. 6d. sepia, red, deep green and lt. emerald 35 35
MS346*a* 90 × 122 mm. No. 346 in block of four. Imperf. .. 1·25 1·50

IMPERF. STAMPS. Many issues, including miniature sheets, from here onwards exist imperf., but these were not sold at post offices.

164. Hurdling.

165. Running. (*Horiz.*)
166. Boxing. (*Vert.*)
167. Long-jumping. (*Vert.*)
168. Football. (*Vert.*)
169. Athlete holding Olympic Torch. (*Vert.*)
170. Olympic " Rings " and Flags. (*Horiz.*)

(No. 352 des. A.S.B. New.)

1964 (25 Oct.). *Olympic Games, Tokyo. W* **47** *(sideways on* 1*d.,* 2½*d.,* 6*d.,* 5*s.). P* 14½ × 14 *(horiz.) or* 14 × 14½ *(vert.).*
347 **164** 1d. multicoloured .. 5 5
348 **165** 2½d. multicoloured .. 5 5
349 **166** 3d. multicoloured .. 5 5
350 **167** 4d. multicoloured .. 5 5
351 **168** 6d. multicoloured .. 8 8
352 **169** 1s. 3d. multicoloured .. 15 15
353 **170** 5s. multicoloured .. 75 75
MS353*a* 128 × 102 mm. Nos. 351/3 Imperf. .. .. 1·50 1·75
347/53 .. *Set of* 7 1·00 1·00

171. G. Washington Carver (botanist) and Plant.

172. Albert Einstein (scientist) and Atomic Symbol.

(Des. M. Shamir.)

1964 (7 Dec.). *UNESCO Week. W* **47**. *P* 14½.
354 **171** 6d. deep blue and green .. 5 5
355 **172** 1s. 3d. reddish purple and greenish blue .. 15 15
356 **171** 5s. sepia and orange-red 70 70
MS356*a* 127 × 77 mm. Nos. 354/6 Imperf. .. .. 1·00 1·25

173. African Elephant.

174. Secretary Bird. (*Horiz.*)
175. Purple Wreath (flower). (*Vert.*)
176. Grey Parrot. (*Vert.*)
177. Mousebird. (*Horiz.*)
178. African Tulip Tree. (*Horiz.*)
179. Amethyst Starling. (*Horiz.*)
180. Hippopotamus. (*Horiz.*)

(No. 360 des. A.S.B. New. Photo. Enschedé.)

1964 (Dec.). *P* 11½ × 11 *(vert.) or* 11 × 11½ *(horiz.).*
357 **173** 1d. multicoloured .. 5 5
358 **174** 1½d. multicoloured .. 8 10
359 **175** 2½d. multicoloured .. 10 12
360 **176** 3d. multicoloured .. 12 15
361 **177** 4d. multicoloured .. 12 15
362 **178** 6d. multicoloured .. 15 12
363 **179** 1s. 3d. multicoloured .. 35 40
364 **180** 2s. 6d. multicoloured .. 70 70
MS364*a* 150 × 86 mm. Nos. 357/9 and 150 × 110 mm. Nos. 360/4. Both Imperf. Two sheets .. .. .. 2·00 2·00
357/64 .. .. *Set of* 8 1·50 1·50

181. I.C.Y. Emblem.

(Litho. Enschedé.)

1965 (22 Feb.). *International Co-operation Year. P* 14 × 12½.
365 **181** 1d. multicoloured .. 5 5
366 ,, 4d. multicoloured .. 5 5
367 ,, 6d. multicoloured .. 10 10
368 ,, 1s. 3d. multicoloured .. 20 20
MS368*a* 100 × 100 mm. No. 368 in block of four. Imperf. .. 75 75

182. I.T.U. Emblem and Symbols.

(Litho. Enschedé.)

1965 (12 Apr.). *I.T.U. Centenary. P* 13½.
369 **182** 1d. multicoloured .. 5 5
370 ,, 6d. multicoloured .. 8 5
371 ,, 1s. 3d. multicoloured .. 15 15
372 ,, 5s. multicoloured .. 65 70
MS372*a* 132 × 115 mm. Nos. 369/72. Imperf. .. .. 1·00 1·10

183. Lincoln's Home.

184. Lincoln's Inaugural Address.
185. Abraham Lincoln.
186. Adaptation of U.S. 90 c. Lincoln Stamp of 1869.

(Des. M. C. Farrar Bell. (6d.), A. S. B. New (1s. 3d., 5s.), R. Hegeman (2s.).)

1965 (17 May). *Death Centenary of Abraham Lincoln. W* **47** *(sideways). P* 12½.
373 **183** 6d. red-brown, greenish yellow, red and green 8 5
374 **184** 1s. 3d. blk., red and blue 15 15
375 **185** 2s. black, orange-brown and greenish yellow .. 30 30
376 **186** 5s. black and red .. 60 60
MS376*a* 115 × 115 mm. Nos. 373/6 Imperf. .. .. .. 1·25 1·75

(New currency. 100 pesewas = 1 cedi.)

187. Obverse (Pres. Nkrumah) and Reverse of 5 p. Coin.

(Photo. Enschedé.)

1965. (19 July). *Introduction of Decimal Currency. T* **187** *and similar horiz. designs. Multicoloured. P* 11 × 13 (5*p.*, 10*p.*), 13 × 12½ (25*p.*) *or* 13½ × 14 (50*p.*)
377 5 p. Type **187** 8 5
378 10 p. As Type **187** 10 10
379 25 p. Size 63 × 39 mm. .. 30 30
380 50 p. Size 71 × 43½ mm. .. 60 65

The coins in Nos. 378/80 are all circular and express the same denominations as on the stamps.

₵2·40
Ghana New Currency
19th July. 1965.

(188)

1965 (19 JULY). *Stamps of* 1959–61 *surch. as T* **188** *diagonally upwards*, (D) *or horizontally*, (H), *by Govt. Printer, Accra. Multicoloured.*

(*a*) *Postage.*

381 **54** 1 p. on 1d. (R.) (D) .. 5 5
a. Surch. inverted .. 30·00
b. Surch. double ..
382 **56** 2 p. on 2d. (Ultram.) (H) 5 5
a. Surch. inverted ..
b. Surch. double .. .. 8·00
c. Surch. on back only ..
d. Surch. on back and face ..
e. Red surch. .. .. 40·00
f. Orange surch. .. .. 40·00
g. Indigo surch. .. ..
383 **58** 3 p. on 3d. (Br.) (H) .. 20 25
a. Surch. inverted .. 30·00
b. Indigo surch. .. ..
384 **59** 4 p. on 4d. (B.) (H) .. 8 5
a. Surch. inverted ..
b. Surch. double ..
c. Red surch. .. ..
385 **60** 6 p. on 6d. (Bk.) (H) .. 8 5
a. Surch. inverted .. 8·00
b. Surch. double .. .. 20·00
386 **61** 11 p. on 11d. (White) (D) .. 12 20
a. Surch. inverted .. 20·00
387 **62** 12 p. on 1s. (B.) (D) .. 12 20
a. Surch. double ..
b. Black surch. ..
ba. Surch. inverted .. 30·00
388 **63** 30 p. on 2s. 6d. (B.) (H) .. 30 40
389 **64** 60 p. on 5s. (B.) (D) .. 60 80
a. Surch. double (G.+B.) .. 25·00
390 **65** ¢1.20 on 10s. (B.) (D) .. 1·25 1·75
a. Surch. double (G.+B.) ..
391 **65*a*** ¢2.40 on £1 (B.) (D) .. 2·50 3·50

(*b*) *Air.*

392 **66** 15 p. on 1s. 3d. (White) (H) 15 20
a. Surch. inverted ..
393 **67** 24 p. on 2s. (G.) (D) .. 35 40
381/93 .. .. *Set of* 13 5·00 7·00

On the diagonal surcharges the values are horizontal.

The 30 p. was not released in Ghana until 30th July and the 3 p. sometime later.

Numerous minor varieties exist.

189. "OAU" and Flag.

190. "OAU", Heads and Flag.

191. "OAU" Emblem and Flag.

(T **189/91.** *Illustrations reduced: actual size* 60×30 *mm.*)

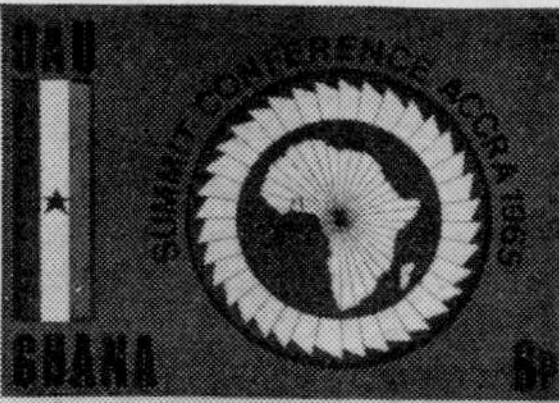

192. African Map and Flag.

193. "Sunburst", Map and Flag.
194. "OAU" on Map, and Flag.

1965 (21 OCT.). *O.A.U. Summit Conference, Accra.* W **47** (*sideways, except on* 6 *p.*). *P* 14 (*T* **189/91**) *or* 14½×14 (*others*).

394 **189** 1 p. multicoloured .. 5 5
395 **190** 2 p. multicoloured .. 5 5
396 **191** 5 p. multicoloured .. 5 5
397 **192** 6 p. multicoloured .. 8 5
398 **193** 15 p. multicoloured .. 15 15
399 **194** 24 p. multicoloured .. 25 30
394/9 .. .. *Set of* 6 50 55

195. Goalkeeper saving Ball.

196. Player with Ball. (*Vert.*)
197. Players, Ball and Soccer Cup. (*Horiz.*)

(Photo. Enschedé.)

1965 (15 NOV.). *African Soccer Cup Competition. P* 13×14 (15 *p.*) *or* 14×13 (*others*).

400 **195** 6 p. multicoloured .. 8 8
401 **196** 15 p. multicoloured .. 20 20
402 **197** 24 p. multicoloured .. 30 30

198. Pres. Kennedy and Grave Memorial.

199. Pres. Kennedy and Eternal Flame.
200. Pres. Kennedy and Memorial Inscription.
201. President Kennedy.

(No. 405 des. A.S.B. New.)

1965 (15 DEC.)–**66.** *2nd Anniv. of President Kennedy's Death.* W **47** (*sideways*). *P* 12½.

403 **198** 6 p. multicoloured .. 8 5
404 **199** 15 p. violet, red & green 20 20
405 **200** 24 p. black & reddish vio. 25 25
406 **201** 30 p. dull purple & black 35 35
MS407 114½×114 mm. Nos. 403/6. Imperf. (21.3.66) .. .. 1·00 1·00

202. Section of Dam and Generators.

203. Dam and Lake Volta.
204. Word "GHANA" as Dam.
205. "Fertility".

(No. 411 des. A.S.B. New. Photo. Enschedé.)

1966 (22 JAN.). *Volta River Project. P* 11×11½.

408 **202** 6 p. multicoloured .. 8 5
409 **203** 15 p. multicoloured .. 20 20
410 **204** 24 p. multicoloured .. 25 25
411 **205** 30 p. black and new blue 35 35

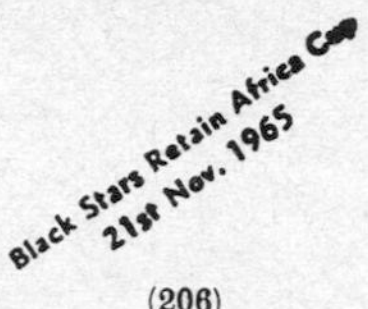

(**206**)

1966 (7 FEB.). *"Black Stars" Victory in African Soccer Cup Competition. Nos.* 400/2 *optd. with T* **206**, *in black.*

412 **195** 6 p. multicoloured .. 8 10
a. Green opt. .. .. 40·00
b. Green opt. double, one inverted .. ..
413 **196** 15 p. multicoloured .. 20 20
414 **197** 24 p. multicoloured .. 30 35
a. Opt. inverted* .. 50·00
b. Error. Opt. for 15 p. on 24 p.* .. ..

*In No. 414a the overprint reads downwards (top right to bottom left), but in No. 414b it reads upwards (bottom right to top left).

DATES OF ISSUE of miniature sheets are approximate as they are generally released some time after the related ordinary stamps, but it is known that the G.P.O. sometimes apply first-day cancellations months after the dates shown on the cancellations.

207. W.H.O. Building and Ghana Flag.

208. W.H.O. Building and Emblem.

1966 (1 JULY). *Inauguration of W.H.O. Headquarters, Geneva. W* **47.** *P* 14½×14.

415	**207**	6 p. multicoloured ..	8	5
416	,,	15 p. multicoloured ..	15	15
417	**208**	24 p. multicoloured ..	25	30
418	,,	30 p. multicoloured ..	30	40
MS419		120×101 mm. Nos. 415/8. Imperf. (11.66)	90	90

209. Herring.

210. Flat Fish.
211. Spade Fish.
212. Red Snapper.
213. Tuna.

(Des. Ole Hamann. Photo. Enschedé.)

1966 (10 AUG.). *Freedom from Hunger. P* 14×13.

420	**209**	6 p. multicoloured ..	8	5
421	**210**	15 p. multicoloured ..	15	12
422	**211**	24 p. multicoloured ..	25	25
423	**212**	30 p. multicoloured ..	35	30
424	**213**	60 p. multicoloured ..	75	75
420/4		.. .. *Set of* 5	1·40	1·25
MS425		126×109 mm. No. 423 in block of four. Imperf. (11.66) ..	1·50	1·50

214. African " Links " and Ghana Flag.

215. Flags as "Quill", and Diamond. (*Horiz.*).
216. Ship's Wheel, Map and Cocoa Bean. (*Horiz.*).

(Photo. Enschedé.)

1966 (11 OCT.). *Third Anniv. of African Charter. P* 13½.

426	**214**	6 p. multicoloured ..	8	5
427	**215**	15 p. multicoloured ..	15	15
428	**216**	24 p. multicoloured ..	25	30

217. Player heading Ball, and Jules Rimet Cup.

218. Goalkeeper clearing Ball.
219. Player and Jules Rimet Cup (replica).
220. Players and Jules Rimet Cup (replica).
221. Players with Ball.

1966 (14 NOV.). *World Cup Football Championships. W* **47.** *P* 14½×14.

429	**217**	5 p. multicoloured ..	8	5
430	**218**	15 p. multicoloured ..	15	15
431	**219**	24 p. multicoloured ..	25	25
432	**220**	30 p. multicoloured ..	35	35
433	**221**	60 p. multicoloured ..	65	65
MS434		120×102 mm. 60 p. (block of four). Imperf.	2·00	2·00
429/33		.. .. *Set of* 5	1·25	1·25

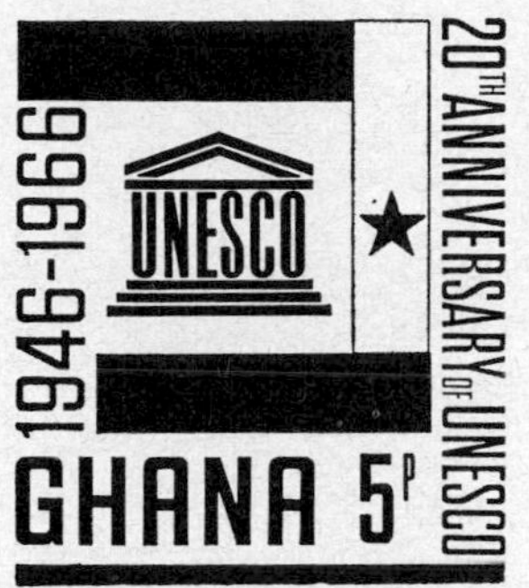

222. U.N.E.S.C.O. Emblem.

1966 (23 DEC.). *20th Anniv. of U.N.E.S.C.O. W* **47** *(sideways). P* 14½.

435	**222**	5 p. multicoloured ..	5	5
436	,,	15 p. multicoloured ..	15	15
437	,,	24 p. multicoloured ..	25	25
438	,,	30 p. multicoloured ..	35	35
439	,,	60 p. multicoloured ..	70	70
MS440		140×115 mm. Nos. 435/9. Imperf.	1·50	1·50
435/9		.. .. *Set of* 5	1·25	1·25

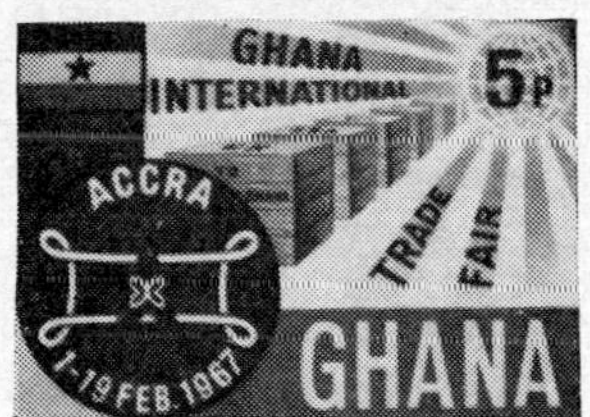

223. Fair Emblem and Crates.

224. Fair Emblem and World Map. (*Horiz.*)
225. Shipping and Flags. (*Vert.*)
226. Fair Emblem and Hand-held Hoist. (*Horiz.*)

1967 (1 FEB.). *Ghana Trade Fair, Accra. W* **47**, *sideways* (24 *p.*) *or upright* (*others*). *P* 14×14½ (24 *p.*) *or* 14½×14 (*others*).

441	**223**	5 p. multicoloured ..	5	5
442	**224**	15 p. multicoloured ..	15	15
443	**225**	24 p. multicoloured ..	25	35
444	**226**	36 p. multicoloured ..	35	45

(New currency. 100 new pesewas = 1 new cedi. = 1·2 (old) cedi.)

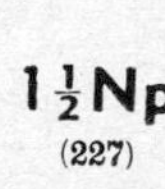

(227)

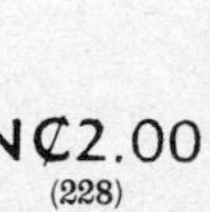

(228)

229. Ghana Eagle and Flag.

1967 (23 FEB.). *Various stamps surch. as T* **227/8.**

(*a*) *Postage.*

445	**56**	1½ n.p. on 2d. (Bk.) (No. 216)	4·00	2·50
446	**59**	3½ n.p. on 4d. (R.) (No. 219)	8	5
447	**60**	5 n.p. on 6d. (R.) (No. 220)	8	5
448	**61**	9 n.p. on 11d. (White) (No. 221)	20	25
449	**62**	10 n.p. on 1s. (White) (No. 222)	20	25
450	**63**	25 n.p. on 2s. 6d. (R.) (No. 223)	1·00	1·25
451	**65**	1 n.c. on 10s. (R.) (No. 225)	3·50	4·00
452	**65*a***	2 n.c. on £1 (R.) (No. 225*a*)	7·00	8·00

(*b*) *Air.*

453	**66**	12½ n.p. on 1s. 3d. (White) (No. 226) ..	50	60
454	**67**	20 n.p. on 24 p. on 2s. (R.) (No. 393) ..	1·00	1·25
445/54		.. .. *Set of* 10	12·00	15·00

Inverted surcharges in a different type face on the 3½, 5 and 25 n.p. are fakes.

(Des. M. Shamir.)

1967 (24 FEB.). *First Anniv. of February 24th Revolution. W* **47** *(sideways). P* 14×14½.

455	**229**	1 n.p. multicoloured ..	5	5
456	,,	4 n.p. multicoloured ..	5	5
457	,,	12½ n.p. multicoloured ..	20	20
458	,,	25 n.p. multicoloured ..	35	40
MS459		89×108 mm. Nos. 455/8 Perf. or imperf.	80	80

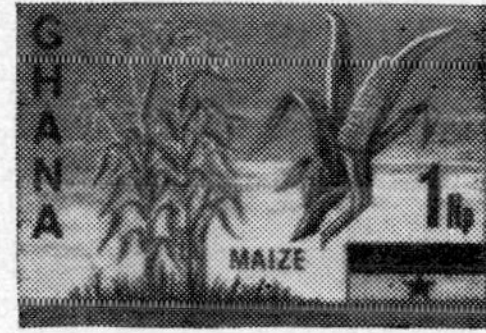

230. Maize.

231. Forest Kingfisher.

232. The Ghana Mace.

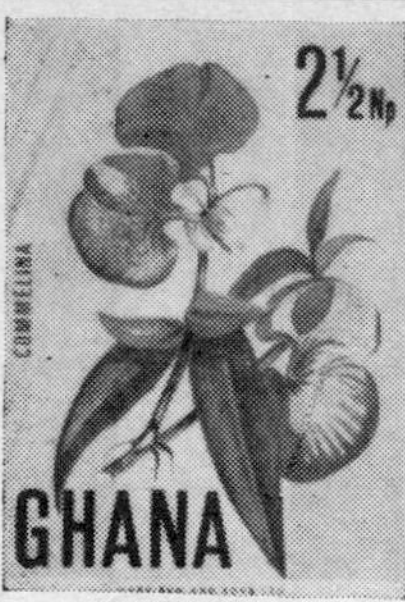

233. Commelina.

235. Rufous-crowned Roller.

234. Mud-fish.

236. Akosombo Dam.

237. Adomi Bridge.

238. Chameleon.

239. Tema Harbour.

240. Hare.

241. Black-winged Stilt.

242. Wooden Stool.

243. Frangipani.

244. Seat of State.

The 2 n.p. and 20 n.p. were officially issued on 4th September but small quantities of both were released in error on 1st June. The 2½ n.p. is also known to have been released in error in June.

1967 (1 June–4 Sept.). *W* **47** (1½, 2, 4, 50 *n.p. and* 1 *n.c.*) *or sideways* (*others*). *P* 11½×12 (1, 8 *n.p.*), 12×11½ (4 *n.p.*), 14×14½ (1½, 2, 2½, 20 *n.p.*, 2 *n.c.*, 2 *n.c.* 50) *or* 14½×14 (*others*).

460	**230**	1 n.p. multicoloured ..	5	5
461	**231**	1½ n.p. multicoloured ..	5	5
		a. Blue omitted* ..		
		b. Green printing double, once inverted† ..		
462	**232**	2 n.p. multicoloured (4.9)	5	5
463	**233**	2½ n.p. multicoloured (4.9)	5	5
		a. Wmk. upright ..		
464	**234**	3 n.p. multicoloured ..	5	5
465	**235**	4 n.p. multicoloured ..	5	5
466	**236**	6 n.p. multicoloured ..	5	5
467	**237**	8 n.p. multicoloured ..	5	8
468	**238**	9 n.p. multicoloured (4.9)	5	8
469	**239**	10 n.p. multicoloured ..	8	8
470	**240**	20 n.p. deep blue and new blue (4.9)	15	15
471	**241**	50 n.p. multicoloured ..	35	40
472	**242**	1 n.c. multicoloured (4.9)	75	85
473	**243**	2 n.c. multicoloured (4.9)	1·50	1·60
474	**244**	2 n.c. 50, multicoloured	1·75	2·00
460/74		.. .. *Set of* 15	5·25	5·50

* In this stamp the blue not only affects the bird but is printed over the yellow background to give the value in green, so that its omission results in the value also being omitted.

† This affects the feather-tips and the flag.

245. Kumasi Fort.

246. Christiansborg Castle and British Galleon.
247. Elimina Castle and Portuguese Galleon.
248. Cape Coast Castle and Spanish Galleon.

(Des. Ole Hamann.)

1967 (1 July). *Castles and Forts. W* **47** (*diagonal*). *P* 14½.

475	**245**	4 n.p. multicoloured ..	5	10
476	**246**	12½ n.p. multicoloured ..	20	30
477	**247**	20 n.p. multicoloured ..	30	50
478	**248**	25 n.p. multicoloured ..	40	70

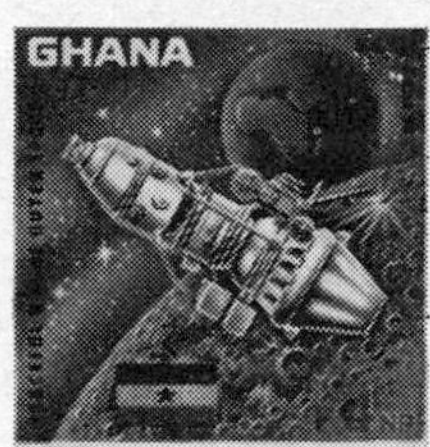

249. "Luna 10".

250. "Orbiter 1".
251. Man in Space.

(Des. M. Shamir. Photo. Enschedé.)

1967 (16 Aug.). *"Peaceful Use of Outer Space". P* 13½×14.

479	**249**	4 n.p. multicoloured ..	5	5
480	**250**	10 n.p. multicoloured ..	12	12
481	**251**	12½ n.p. multicoloured ..	20	20
MS482		140×90 mm. Nos. 479/81. Imperf.	40	40

252. Scouts and Camp-fire.

253. Scout on March.
254. Lord Baden-Powell.

(Photo. Enschedé.)

1967 (18 Sept.). *50th Anniv. of Ghanaian Scout Movement. P* 14½ × 13.

483	**252**	4 n.p. multicoloured ..	5	5
484	**253**	10 n.p. multicoloured ..	12	12
485	**254**	12½ n.p. multicoloured ..	20	20
MS486		167 × 95 mm. Nos. 483/5. Imperf.	40	40

255. U.N. Headquarters Building.

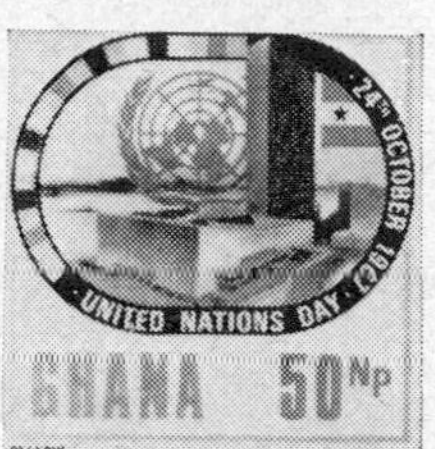

256. General View of U.N. H.Q., Manhattan.

(Litho. De La Rue.)

1967 (20 Nov.). *United Nations Day* (*24th October*). *P* 13½.

487	**255**	4 n.p. multicoloured ..	5	5
488	,,	10 n.p. multicoloured ..	12	10
489	**256**	50 n.p. multicoloured ..	50	50
490	,,	2 n.c. 50, multicoloured	2·50	2·50
MS491		76 × 75 mm. No. 490 Imperf. (4.12.67).	3·75	3·75

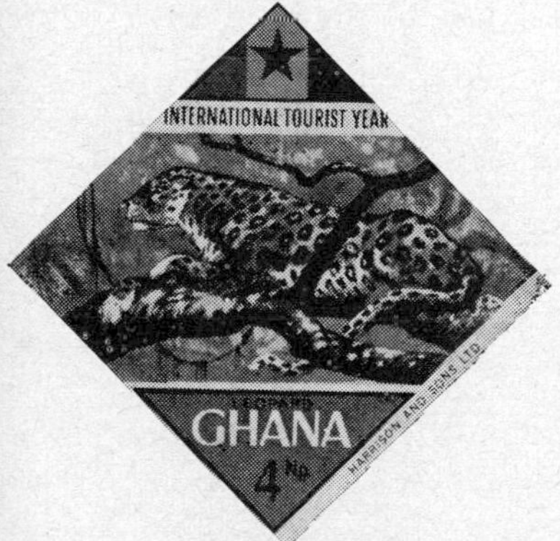

257. Leopard.

258. Christmas Butterfly.
259. Carmine Bee-eater.
260. Water Buck.

1967 (28 Dec.). *International Tourist Year. W* **47** (*diagonal*). *P* 12½.

492	**257**	4 n.p. multicoloured ..	5	5
493	**258**	12½ n.p. multicoloured ..	15	15
494	**259**	20 n.p. multicoloured ..	25	25
495	**260**	50 n.p. multicoloured ..	55	55
MS496		126 × 126 mm. Nos. 493/5. Imperf.	1·00	1·00

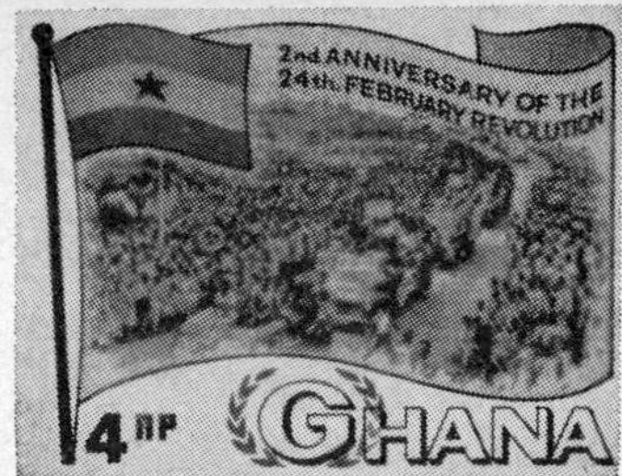

261. Revolutionaries entering Accra.

262. Marching Troops.
263. Cheering People.
264. Victory Celebrations.

(Litho. De La Rue.)

1968 (24 Feb.). *2nd Anniv. of February Revolution. P* 14.

497	**261**	4 n.p. multicoloured ..	5	5
498	**262**	12½ n.p. multicoloured ..	12	15
499	**263**	20 n.p. multicoloured ..	20	25
500	**264**	40 n.p. multicoloured ..	45	50

265. Microscope and Cocoa Beans.

266. Microscope and Cocoa Tree, Beans and Pods.

1968 (18 Mar.). *Cocoa Research. W* **47** (*sideways*). *P* 14½ × 14.

501	**265**	2½ n.p. multicoloured ..	5	5
502	**266**	4 n.p. multicoloured ..	5	5
503	**265**	10 n.p. multicoloured ..	12	12
504	**266**	25 n.p. multicoloured ..	30	40
MS505		102 × 102 mm. Nos. 501/4. Imperf.	50	50

267 Kotoka and Flowers.

268. Kotoka and Wreath. (*Horiz.*)
269. Kotoka in Civilian Clothes. (*Horiz.*)
270. Lt.-Gen. Kotoka. (*Vert.*)

(Des. A. S. B. New (No. 508) and F. Mate (others). Litho. De La Rue.)

1968 (17 Apr.). *1st Death Anniv. of Lt.-Gen. E. K. Kotoka. P* 14.

506	**267**	4 n.p. multicoloured ..	5	5
507	**268**	12½ n.p. multicoloured ..	15	15
508	**269**	20 n.p. multicoloured ..	25	30
509	**270**	40 n.p. multicoloured ..	50	60

271. Tobacco.

272. Porcupine.
273. Rubber.
274. *Cymothoe sangaris* (butterfly).
275. *Charaxes ameliae* (butterfly).

(No. 511 des. A.S.B. New.)

1968 (19 Aug.). *W* **47** (*sideways*). *P* 14 × 14½.

510	**271**	4 n.p. multicoloured ..	5	5
511	**272**	5 n.p. multicoloured ..	5	5
512	**273**	12½ n.p. multicoloured ..	15	15
513	**274**	20 n.p. multicoloured ..	25	25
514	**275**	40 n.p. multicoloured .	45	45
MS515		88 × 114 mm. Nos. 510, 512/4. Imperf. .	95	1·00
510/14		.. .. *Set of* 5	85	85

276. Surgeons, Flag and W.H.O. Emblem.

(Photo. Enschedé.)

1968 (11 Nov.). *20th Anniv. of World Health Organization. P* 14 × 13.

516	**276**	4 n.p. multicoloured ..	5	5
517	,,	12½ n.p. multicoloured ..	15	15
518	,,	20 n.p. multicoloured ..	25	25
519	,,	40 n.p. multicoloured ..	50	50
MS520		132 × 110 mm. Nos. 516/9. Imperf.	90	90

277. Hurdling.

278. Boxing.
279. Torch, Olympic Rings and Flags.
280. Football.

1969 (10 Jan.). *Olympic Games, Mexico* (1968). *W* **47** (*sideways*). *P* 14 × 14½.

521	**277**	4 n.p. multicoloured ..	5	5
522	**278**	12½ n.p. multicoloured ..	15	15
523	**279**	20 n.p. multicoloured ..	25	25
524	**280**	40 n.p. multicoloured ..	50	50
MS525		89 × 114 mm. Nos. 521/4. Imperf. (17.1.69)	90	90

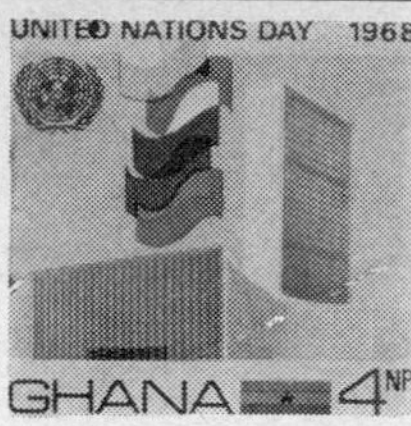

281. U.N. Building.

282. Native Stool, Staff and U.N. Emblem.
283. U.N. Building and Emblem over Ghanaian Flag.
284. U.N. Emblem encircled by Flags.

(Litho. De La Rue.)

1969 (1 Feb.). *United Nations Day* (1968). *P* 13½.

526 **281** 4 n.p. multicoloured .. 5 5
527 **282** 12½ n.p. multicoloured .. 15 15
528 **283** 20 n.p. multicoloured .. 25 25
529 **284** 40 n.p. multicoloured .. 50 50
MS530 127 × 117 mm. Nos. 526/9. Imperf. 95 95

285. Dr. J. B. Danquah.

286. Dr. Martin Luther King.

1969 (7 Mar.). *Human Rights Year.* *W* **47** (*sideways on* **MS**535). *P* 14½ × 14.

531 **285** 4 n.p. multicoloured .. 5 5
532 **286** 12½ n.p. multicoloured .. 15 15
533 „ 20 n.p. multicoloured .. 25 25
534 **285** 40 n.p. multicoloured .. 50 55
MS535 116 × 50 mm. Nos. 531/4. Imperf. (17.4.69) .. .. 1·00 1·00

287. Constituent Assembly Building.

288. Arms of Ghana.

1969 (10 Sept.). *Third Anniv. of the Revolution.* *W* **47** (*sideways on* **MS**540). *P* 14½ × 14.

536 **287** 4 n.p. multicoloured .. 5 5
537 **288** 12½ n.p. multicoloured .. 15 12
538 **287** 20 n.p. multicoloured .. 25 25
539 **288** 40 n.p. multicoloured .. 45 45
MS540 114 × 89 mm. Nos. 536/9. Imperf. .. .. 95 1·00

NEW CONSTITUTION
1969
(289)

1969 (1 Oct.). *New Constitution. Nos.* 460/74 *optd. with T* **289** *by Government Press, Accra.*

541 **230** 1 n.p. mult. (Horiz.) .. 5 5
542 **231** 1½ n.p. mult. (Vt. down) 5 5
 a. Opt. vert. up .. 8·00
543 **232** 2 n.p. mult. (Vt. up) .. 5 5
 a. Opt. vert. down .. 8·00
 b. Opt. double .. 15·00
544 **233** 2½ n.p. mult. (Vt. up) .. 5 5
545 **234** 3 n.p. mult. (Horiz.) .. 5 5
 a. Opt. inverted .. 30·00
546 **235** 4 n.p. mult. (Y.) (Vt. down) 8 5
 a. Black opt. (vert. down) .. .. 7·00 2·00
 b. Black opt. (vert. up) 20·00
 c. Red opt. (vert. down) 40·00
 d. Opt. double (White vert. down + yellow vert. up) .. .. 50·00
547 **236** 6 n.p. mult. (Horiz.) .. 8 5
548 **237** 8 n.p. mult. (Horiz.) .. 10 8
549 **238** 9 n.p. mult. (Horiz.) .. 10 8
550 **239** 10 n.p. mult. (Horiz.) .. 10 8
551 **240** 20 n.p. deep blue and new blue (Vt. up) .. 20 20
 a. Opt. vert. down .. 40·00
552 **241** 50 n.p. mult. (Horiz.) .. 90 90
 a. Opt. double ..
553 **242** 1 n.c. mult. (Horiz.) .. 1·00 95
554 **243** 2 n.c. mult. (R.) (Vt. up) 2·00 1·75
 a. Opt. double (vert. up and down) .. 50·00
555 **244** 2 n.c. 50, multicoloured (Vt. down) .. 2·75 2·50
541/55 .. .. *Set of* 15 6·50 6·00

The 1 n.p. is known with the overprint inverted with "NEW CONSTITUTION" appearing between the stamps across the perforations.

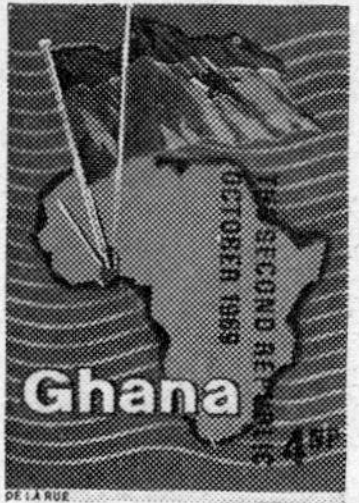

290. Map of Africa and Flags.

291. Figure "2", Branch and Ghanaian Colours.
292. Hands receiving Egg.

(Litho. De La Rue.)

1969 (4 Dec.). *Inauguration of Second Republic.* *P* 14.

556 **290** 4 n.p. multicoloured .. 5 5
557 **291** 12½ n.p. multicoloured .. 15 15
558 **292** 20 n.p. multicoloured .. 25 25
559 **290** 40 n.p. multicoloured .. 45 50

293. I.L.O. Emblem and Cog-wheels.

1970 (5 Jan.). *50th Anniv. of International Labour Organisation.* *W* **47** (*sideways*). *P* 14½ × 14.

560 **293** 4 n.p. multicoloured .. 5 5
561 „ 12½ n.p. multicoloured .. 15 15
562 „ 20 n.p. multicoloured .. 25 25
MS563 117 × 89 mm. Nos. 560/2. Imperf. 55 55

294. Red Cross and Globe.

295. Henri Dunant and Red Cross Emblem. (*Horiz.*)
296. Patient receiving Medicine. (*Horiz.*)
297. Patient having Arm Bandaged. (*Horiz.*)

1970 (2 Feb.). *50th Anniv. of League of Red Cross Societies.* *W* **47** (*sideways on* 4 n.p.). *P* 14 × 14½ (4 n.p.) *or* 14½ × 14 (*others*).

564 **294** 4 n.p. multicoloured .. 5 5
565 **295** 12½ n.p. multicoloured .. 15 12
566 **296** 20 n.p. multicoloured .. 30 30
567 **297** 40 n.p. multicoloured .. 45 45
MS568 114 × 89 mm. Nos. 564/7. Imperf. 85 85

298. General Kotoka, VC-10 and Airport.

299. Control Tower and Tail of VC-10.
300. Aerial View of Airport.
301. Airport and Flags.

(Des. G. Vasarhelyi. Litho. D.L.R.)

1970 (17 Apr.). *Inauguration of Kotoka Airport.* *P* 13 × 13½.

569 **298** 4 n.p. multicoloured .. 5 5
570 **299** 12½ n.p. multicoloured .. 15 15
571 **300** 20 n.p. multicoloured .. 25 25
572 **301** 40 n.p. multicoloured .. 45 45

302. Lunar Module landing on Moon.

303. Astronaut's First Step onto the Moon. (*Vert.*)
304. Astronaut with Equipment on Moon. (*Horiz.*)
305. Astronauts. (*Horiz.*)

(Des. A. Medina (4 n.p., 12½ n.p.,) G. Vasarhelyi (others). Litho. D.L.R.)

1970 (15 June). *Moon Landing. P* 12½.

573	**302**	4 n.p. multicoloured ..	5	5
574	**303**	12½ n.p. multicoloured ..	25	25
575	**304**	20 n.p. multicoloured ..	50	50
576	**305**	40 n.p. multicoloured ..	1·00	1·00
MS577		142×142 mm. Nos. 573/6. Imperf. (with or without simulated perfs.)	2·00	2·00

On 18 September 1970 Nos. 573/6 were issued overprinted "PHILYMPIA LONDON 1970" but it is understood that only 900 sets were made available for sale in Ghana and we do not consider that this is sufficient to constitute normal postal use. The miniature sheet was also overprinted but not issued in Ghana.

306. Adult Education.

307. International Education.
308. "Ntesie" and I.E.Y. Symbols.
309. Nursery Schools.

(Litho. D.L.R.)

1970 (10 Aug.). *International Education Year. P* 13.

578	**306**	4 n.p. multicoloured ..	5	5
579	**307**	12½ n.p. multicoloured ..	15	15
580	**308**	20 n.p. multicoloured ..	25	25
581	**309**	40 n.p. multicoloured ..	45	45

310. Saluting March-Past.

311. Busia Declaration.
312. Doves Symbol.
313. Opening of Parliament.

1970 (1 Oct.). *First Anniv. of the Second Republic. Litho. P* 13×13½.

582	**310**	4 n.p. multicoloured ..	5	5
583	**311**	12½ n.p. multicoloured ..	15	15
584	**312**	20 n.p. multicoloured ..	25	25
585	**313**	40 n.p. multicoloured ..	50	50

314. *Crinum ornatum.*

(Des. G. L. Vasarhelyi).

1970 (2 Nov.). *Flora and Fauna. T* **314** *and similar horiz. designs. Multicoloured. W* **47** *(sideways). P* 14½×14.

586	4 n.p. Type **314**	5	5
587	12½ n.p. Lioness	15	15
588	20 n.p. *Ansellia africana* (flower)	25	25
589	40 n.p. Elephant	50	50

315. Kuduo Brass Casket.

(Des. G. L. Vasarhelyi.)

1970 (7 Dec.). *Monuments and Archaeological Sites in Ghana. T* **315** *and similar horiz. designs. Multicoloured. W* **47** *(sideways on* **MS**594). *P* 14½×14.

590	4 n.p. Type **315**	5	5
591	12½ n.p. Akan Traditional House	15	15
592	20 n.p. Larabanga Mosque ..	25	25
593	40 n.p. Funerary Clay Head	40	50
MS594	89×71 mm. Nos. 590, 592 and 12½ n.p. Basilica of Pompeii; 40 n.p. Pistrinum of Pompeii. Imperf. (2.71)	90	90

316. Trade Fair Building.

(Des. G. Drummond (4 n.p., 50 n.p.), A. S. Larkins (others).)

1971 (5 Feb.). *International Trade Fair, Accra. T* **316** *and similar multicoloured designs. W* **47** *(sideways, except* 50 *n.p.). P* 14×14½ (50 *n.p.) or* 14½×14 *(others).*

595	4 n.p. Type **316**	5	5
596	12½ n.p. Cosmetics and Pharmaceutical Goods ..	15	15
597	20 n.p. Vehicles	25	25
598	40 n.p. Construction Equipment	45	45
599	50 n.p. Transport and Packing Case	60	60
595/9	.. .. *Set of* 5	1·25	1·25

The 50 n.p. is a vertical design.

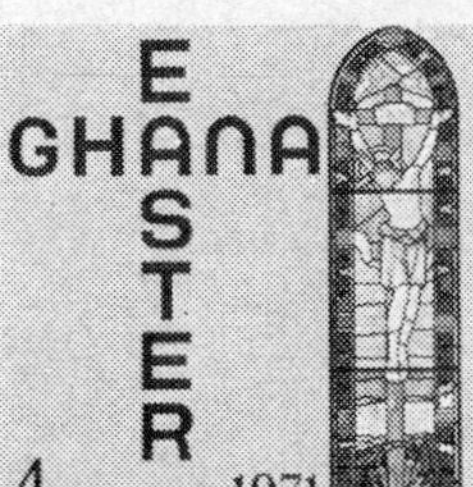

317. Christ on the Cross.

(Des. from stained-glass windows. Litho. D.L.R.)

1971 (19 May). *Easter. T* **317** *and similar square designs. Multicoloured. P* 13.

600	4 n.p. Type **317**	5	5
601	12½ n.p. Christ and Disciples	15	15
602	20 n.p. Christ blessing Disciples	30	30

318. Corn Cob.

1971 (15 June). *Freedom From Hunger Campaign. W* **47**. *P* 14×14½.

603	**318**	4 n.p. multicoloured ..	5	5
604	„	12½ n.p. multicoloured ..	15	15
605	„	20 n.p. multicoloured ..	25	25

Remainder stocks of the above were overprinted on the occasion of the death of Lord Boyd Orr and the 4 n.p. surch. 60 n.p.

It is understood that 8,070 sets from the New York Agency were overprinted locally and returned to the Agency. Limited remainders of these stamps (only 330 of the 60 n.p.) were sold at the G.P.O. We do not list these as they were not freely on sale in Ghana.

319. Guides Emblem and Ghana Flag.

(Des. and litho. Questa.)

1971 (22 July). *Ghana Girl Guides Golden Jubilee. T* **319** *and similar horiz. designs each with Guides Emblem. Multicoloured. P* 14.

606	4 n.p. Type **319**	5	5
607	12½ n.p. Mrs. E. Ofuatey-Kodjoe (founder) and guides with flags ..	15	15
608	20 n.p. Guides laying stones	25	25
609	40 n.p. Camp-fire and tent ..	45	45
610	50 n.p. Signallers	60	60
606/10	.. .. *Set of* 5	1·25	1·25
MS611	133×105 mm. Nos. 606/10 Imperf.	1·40	1·40

320. Child-care Centre.

(Des. and litho. D.L.R.)

1971 (7 Aug.). *Y.W.C.A. World Council Meeting, Accra. T* **320** *and similar horiz. designs. Multicoloured. P* 13×13.

612	4 n.p. Type **320**	5	5
613	12½ n.p. Council meeting ..	15	15
614	20 n.p. School typing-class ..	20	20
615	40 n.p. Building Fund Day ..	40	45
MS616	84×83 mm. Nos. 612/15 Imperf.	1·00	1·00

321. Firework Display. **322.** Weighing Baby.

1971 (22 Nov.). *Christmas. T* **321** *and similar horiz. designs. Multicoloured. W* **47** *(sideways on 3 and 6 n.p.). P* 14 × 14½ (1 *n.p.*) *or* 14½ × 14 *(others).*

617 1 n.p. Type **321** 5 5
618 3 n.p. African Nativity .. 8 8
619 6 n.p. The flight into Egypt 10 10

1971 (20 Dec.). *25th Anniv. of UNICEF. T* **322** *and similar multicoloured designs, each showing the UNICEF symbol. No wmk.* (**MS**624) *or W* **47** *(sideways on 5 and 30 n.p.). P* 13.

620 5 n.p. Type **322** 5 5
621 15 n.p. Mother and child (*horiz.*) 15 15
622 30 n.p. Nurse 30 30
623 50 n.p. Young boy (*horiz.*) .. 50 55
MS624 111 × 120 mm. Nos. 620/3 Imperf. .. .. .. 1·25 1·25

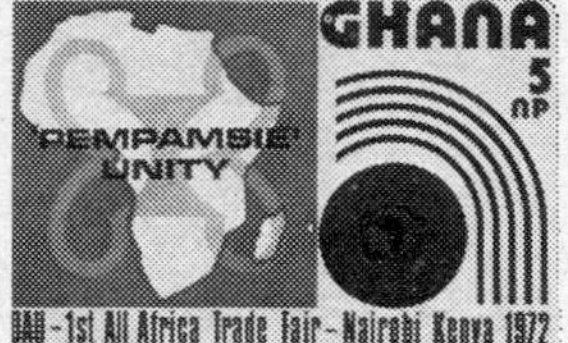

323. Unity Symbol and Trade Fair Emblem.

(Litho. Questa.)

1972 (23 Feb.). *All-Africa Trade Fair. T* **323** *and similar horiz. designs. Multicoloured. W* **47**. *P* 14.

625 5 n.p. Type **323** 5 5
626 15 n.p. Horn of Plenty .. 15 15
627 30 n.p. Fireworks on map of Africa 30 30
628 60 n.p. " Participating Nations " 60 60
629 1 n.c. As No. 628 .. .. 1·00 1·00
625/9 .. .. *Set of* 5 1·90 1·90

All designs include the Trade Fair Emblem as in T **323**.

On 24 June 1972, on the occasion of the Belgian International Philatelic Exhibition, Nos. 625/9 were issued overprinted ' " BELGICA 72 " ' in red. Only very limited supplies were sent to Ghana (we understand not more than 900 sets), and for this reason we do not list them.

(New currency. 100 pesewas = 1 cedi = 0.8 (old) new cedi.)

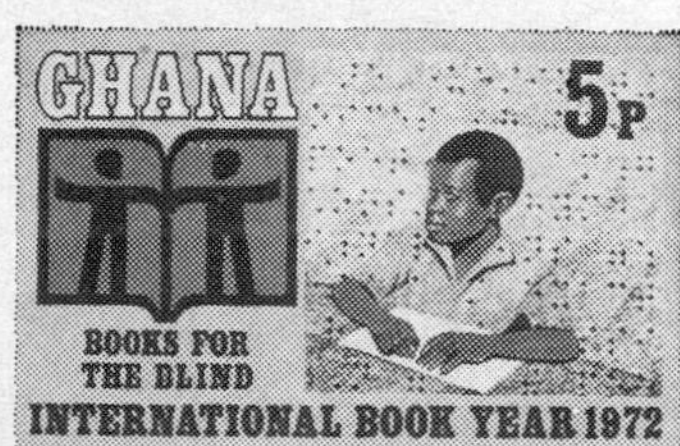

324. Books for the Blind.

(Des. and litho. D.L.R.)

1972 (21 Apr.). *International Book Year. T* **324** *and similar multicoloured designs. P* 13.

630 5 p. Type **324** 5 5
631 15 p. Children's books .. 15 20
632 30 p. Books for recreation .. 30 35
633 50 p. Books for students .. 50 60
634 1 c. Book and flame of knowledge (*vert.*) .. .. 1·00 1·10
630/4 .. .. *Set of* 5 1·75 1·90
MS635 99 × 106 mm. Nos. 630/4. Imperf. .. .. 3·50 3·50

325. *Hypoxis urceolata.*

(Litho. D.L.R.)

1972 (3 July). *Flora and Fauna. T* **325** *and similar horiz. designs. Multicoloured. P* 13½.

636 5 p. Type **325** 5 5
637 15 p. *Cercopithecus mona* (monkey) 15 15
638 30 p. *Crinum ornatum* .. 30 30
639 1 c. *Funisciurus substriatus* (squirrel) .. .. 1·00 1·00

326. Football.

(Litho. D.L.R.)

1972 (5 Sept.). *Olympic Games, Munich. T* **326** *and similar horiz. designs. Multicoloured. P* 13.

640 5 p. Type **326** 5 5
641 15 p. Running 15 15
642 30 p. Boxing 30 30
643 50 p. Long-jumping .. 50 50
644 1 c. High-jumping .. 1·00 1·00
640/4 .. .. *Set of* 5 1·75 1·75
MS645 86 × 43 mm. 40 p. as No. 642 *se-tenant* with 60 p. as No. 640. .. .. 1·75 1·75

327. Senior Scout and Cub.

(Litho. Questa.)

1972 (2 Oct.). *65th Anniv. of Boy Scouts T* **327** *and similar diamond-shaped designs Multicoloured. P* 13½.

646 5 p. Type **327** 5
647 15 p. Scout and tent .. 15 1
648 30 p. Sea scouts 30 3
649 50 p. Leader with cubs .. 50 5
650 1 c. Training school .. 1·00 1·0
646/50 .. .. *Set of* 5 1·75 1·7
MS651 110 × 110 mm. 40 p. as 30 p. and 60 p. as 1 c. .. .. 1·10 1·1

328. "The Holy Night" (Correggio).

(Des. G. L. Vasarhelyi and Lothar Apelt. Litho Questa.)

1972 (1 Dec.). *Christmas. T* **328** *and simila vert. designs. Multicoloured. P* 13½.

652 1 p. Type **328** 5
653 3 p. Epiphany scene (Holbein) 5
654 15 p. Madonna and Child (Andrea Rico) 15 1
655 30 p. King Melchior 30 3
656 60 p. King Gaspar, Mary and Jesus 60 6
657 1 c. King Balthasar .. 1·25 1·2
652/7 .. .. *Set of* 6 2·00 2·0
MS658 139 × 90 mm. Nos. 655/7 Imperf. .. .. 2·50 2·5

Nos. 655/7 are from a 16th-Cent. Normar stained-glass window.

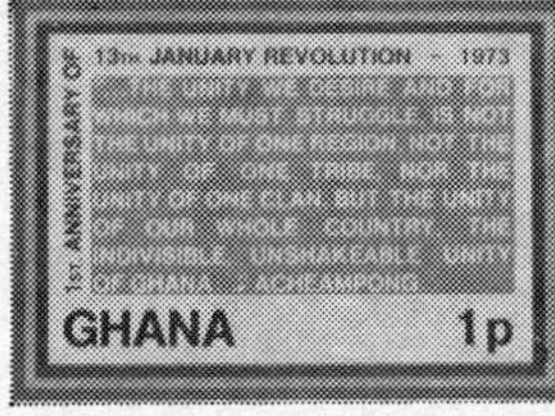

329. Extract from Speech.

(Des. and litho. D.L.R.)

1973 (10 Apr.). *First Anniv. of January 13th Revolution. T* **329** *and similar multicoloured designs. P* 14 × 13 (*horiz. designs*) *or* 13 × 14 (*vert.*).

659 1 p. Type **329** 5 5
660 3 p. Market scene 5 5
661 5 p. Selling bananas (*vert.*) .. 5 5
662 15 p. Farmer with hoe and produce (*vert.*) 15 15
663 30 p. Market traders 30 30
664 1 c. Farmer cutting palm-nuts 90 90
659/64 .. .. *Set of* 6 1·25 1·25
MS665 90 × 55 mm. 40 p. as 1 c. and 60 p. Miners .. .. .. 1·10 1·10

330. Under 5's Clinic.

(Litho. D.L.R.)

1973 (24 July). *25th Anniv. of W.H.O. T* **330** *and similar horiz. designs. Multicoloured. P* 13½.
666 5 p. Type **330** 5 5
667 15 p. Radiography 15 15
668 30 p. Immunisation .. 30 30
669 50 p. Starving child 45 45
670 1 c. W.H.O. H.Q., Geneva .. 90 90
666/70 .. .. *Set of* 5 1·60 1·60

1st WORLD SCOUTING CONFERENCE IN AFRICA
(331)

1973 (14 Aug.). *First World Scouting Conference, Nairobi/Addis Ababa. Nos.* 646/**MS**651 *optd. with T* **331**.
671 5 p. Type **327** 5 5
672 15 p. Scout and tent 15 15
673 30 p. Sea scouts 30 30
674 50 p. Leader with cubs .. 45 45
675 1 c. Training school .. 85 85
671/675 .. .. *Set of* 5 1·60 1·60
MS676 110×110 mm. As **MS**651 .. 1·10 1·10

332. Poultry Farming.

(Litho. Questa.)

1973 (11 Sept.). *Tenth Anniv. of World Food Programme. T* **332** *and similar horiz. designs. Multicoloured. P* 14.
677 5 p. Type **332** 5 5
678 15 p. Mechanisation 15 15
679 50 p. Cocoa harvest .. 45 45
680 1 c. F.A.O. H.Q., Rome .. 90 90
MS681 92×104 mm. 40 p. as 15 p. and 60 p. as 1 c. .. .. 1·00 1·00

333. " Green Alert ".

(Litho. D.L.R.)

1973 (1 Oct.). *50th Anniv. of Interpol. T* **333** *and similar horiz. designs. Multicoloured. P* 13.
682 5 p. Type **333** 5 5
683 30 p. " Red Alert " 30 30
684 50 p. " Blue Alert " 50 50
685 1 c. " Black Alert " .. 90 90

334. Handshake.

1973 (22 Oct.). *Tenth Anniv. of O.A.U. T* **334** *and similar horiz. designs. Multicoloured. P* 14 × 14½.
686 5 p. Type **334** 5 5
687 30 p. Africa Hall, Addis Ababa 30 30
688 50 p. O.A.U. emblem .. 50 50
689 1 c. " X " in colours of Ghana flag 90 90

335. Weather Balloon.

(Des. G. L. Vasarhelyi. Litho. Format.)

1973 (16 Nov.). *I.M.O./W.M.O. Centenary. T* **335** *and similar horiz. designs. Multicoloured. P* 14×14½.
690 5 p. Type **335** 5 5
691 15 p. Satellite "Tiros" .. 15 15
692 30 p. Computer weather map 30 30
693 1 c. Radar 90 90
MS694 120×95 mm. 40 p. as 15 p., and 60 p. as 30 p. .. 1·00 1·00

336. Epiphany Scene.

1973 (10 Dec.). *Christmas. T* **336** *and similar vert. designs. Multicoloured. P* 14.
695 1 p. Type **336** 5 5
696 3 p. Madonna and Child .. 5 5
697 30 p. Madonna and Child (Murillo) 30 30
698 50 p. Epiphany Scene (Tiepolo) 50 50
MS699 77 × 103 mm. Nos. 695/8. Imperf. 90 90

337. "Carrying the Cross" (Thomas de Coloswar).

(Des. M. Shamir and A. S. Larkins. Litho. D.L.R.)

1974 (17 Apr.). *Easter. T* **337** *and similar vert. designs. P* 14.
700 5 p. multicoloured 5 5
701 30 p. brt. bl., sil. & sepia 30 30
702 50 p. light orange-vermilion, silver and sepia 45 45
703 1 c. dull yell.-grn., sil. & sepia 90 90
MS704 111 × 106 mm. 15 p. as No. 700, 20 p. as No. 701, 25 p. as No. 702. Imperf. .. .. 1·00 1·00

Designs (from 15th-century English carved alabaster):—30 p. "The Betrayal"; 50 p. "The Deposition"; 1 c. "The Risen Christ and Mary Magdalene".

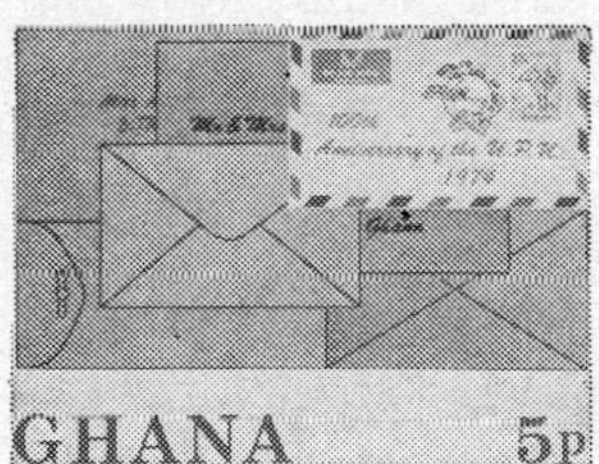

338. Letters.

(Des. A. S. Larkins. Litho. Questa.)

1974 (21 May). *Centenary of Universal Postal Union. T* **338** *and similar horiz. designs. Multicoloured. P* 14½.
705 5 p. Type **338** 5 5
706 9 p. U.P.U. Monument & H.Q. 8 8
707 50 p. Airmail letter 45 45
708 1 c. U.P.U. Monument and Ghana stamp 90 90
MS709 108 × 90 mm. 20 p. as No. 705, 30 p. as No. 706, 40 p. as No. 707, 60 p. as No. 708 .. 1·40 1·40

1974 (7 June). *"Internaba 1974" Stamp Exhibition, Basle. Nos.* 705/**MS**709 *additionally inscribed* "INTERNABA 1974".
710 5 p. Type **338** 5 5
711 9 p. U.P.U. Monument & H.Q. 8 8
712 50 p. Airmail letter 45 45
713 1 c. U.P.U. Monument and Ghana stamp 90 90
MS714 108 × 90 mm. As **MS**709 1·40 1·40

339. Footballers.

(Des. G. L. Vasarhelyi. Litho. Format.)

1974 (17 June). *World Cup Football Championships. Designs as T* **339** *showing footballers in action.*

			A. P 14½.		B. P 13.	
715	**339**	5 p. multicoloured	5	5	5	5
716	–	30 p. multicoloured	30	30	30	30
717	–	50 p. multicoloured	45	45	45	45
718	–	1 c. multicoloured	90	90	90	90
MS719		148 × 94 mm. 25, 40, 55 and 60 p. as Nos. 715/18	1·60	1·60	†	

Nos. 715/8B come from small sheets of 5 stamps plus one *se-tenant* label.

340. Roundabout.

(Des. and litho. B.W.)

1974 (16 July). *Change to Driving on the Right. T* **340** *and similar designs. P* 13½ (5 *and* 15 *p.*) *or* 14½ × 14 (*others*).

720	5 p. bright yellow-green, rose-vermilion and black	8	8
721	15 p. lavender, dull red & blk.	15	15
722	30 p. multicoloured	25	25
723	50 p. multicoloured	40	40
724	1 c. multicoloured	80	80
720/4	.. .. *Set of* 5	1·50	1·50

Designs: *Horiz.*—15 p. Warning triangle sign. *Vert.* (29 × 42 *mm.*)—30 p. Highway arrow and slogan; 50 p. Warning hands; 1 c. Car on symbolic hands.

WEST GERMANY WINNERS

(341)

1974 (30 Aug.). *West Germany's Victory in World Cup. Nos.* 715/**MS**719 *optd. with T* **341.**

			A. P 14½.		B. P 13.	
725	**339**	5 p. mult. ..	5	5	5	5
726	–	30 p. mult. ..	25	30	25	30
727	–	50 p. mult. ..	40	40	40	40
728	–	1 c. mult. ..	80	80	80	80
MS729		148 × 94 mm. As **MS**719	1·50	1·50	†	

342. "Planned Family".

(Des. and litho. D.L.R.)

1974 (12 Sept.). *World Population Year. T* **342** *and similar horiz. designs. Multicoloured. P* 12½.

730	5 p. Type **342**	5	5
731	30 p. Family planning clinic ..	25	25
732	50 p. Immunization	40	40
733	1 c. Population census enumeration	80	80

343. Angel.

APOLLO
SOYUZ
JULY 15, 1975

(344)

(Des. A. Medina (5 and 7 p.), A. Larkins (others). Litho. D.L.R.)

1974 (19 Dec.). *Christmas. T* **343** *and similar multicoloured designs. P* 13½.

734	5 p. Type **343**	5	5
735	7 p. The Magi (*diamond* 47 × 47 *mm.*)	8	8
736	9 p. The Nativity	8	8
737	1 c. The Anunciation ..	85	85
MS738	128 × 128 mm. 15 p. Type **343**; 30 p. as 7 p.; 45 p. as 9 p.; 60 p. as 1 c. Imperf.	1·25	1·25

1975 (15 Aug.). "*Apollo-Soyuz*" *Space Link. Nos.* 715/8 *optd. with T* **344.**

			A. P 14½.		B. P 13.	
739	**339**	5 p. multicoloured	5	5	10	10
740	–	30 p. multicoloured	25	30	50	40
741	–	50 p. multicoloured	40	45	1·00	90
742	–	1 c. multicoloured	85	90	1·50	1·40
MS743		148 × 94 mm. 25, 40, 55 and 60 p. as Nos. 739/42	1·50	1·75	†	

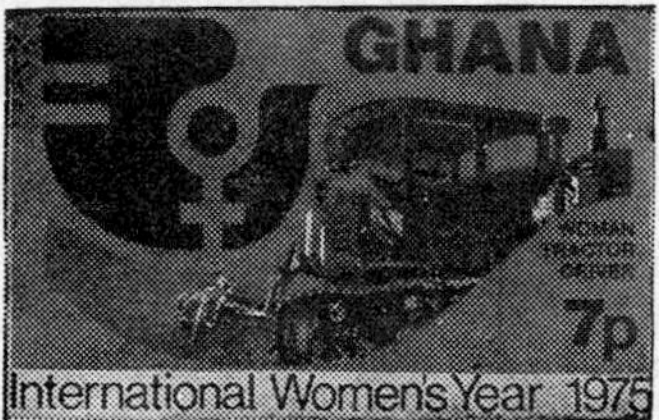

345. Tractor Driver.

(Des. and litho. D.L.R.)

1975 (3 Sept.). *International Women's Year. T* **345** *and similar horiz. designs each showing I.W.Y. emblem. Multicoloured. P* 14 × 13½.

744	7 p. Type **345**	8	8
745	30 p. Motor mechanic ..	25	30
746	60 p. Factory workers ..	50	55
747	1 c. Cocoa research ..	85	90
MS748	136 × 110 mm. 15, 40, 65 and 80 p. as Nos. 744/7. Imperf.	1·75	

346. Angel.

(Litho. D.L.R.)

1975 (31 Dec.). *Christmas. T* **346** *and simila horiz. designs. P* 14 × 13½.

749	**346**	2 p. multicoloured ..	5	
750	–	5 p. greenish yellow and light green	5	
751	–	7 p. greenish yellow and light green	5	
752	–	30 p. greenish yellow and light green	25	3
753	–	1 c. greenish yellow and light green	85	9
749/53		.. .. *Set of* 5	1·10	1·2
MS754		98 × 87 mm. 15, 40, 65 and 80 p. as Nos. 750/3. Imperf. ..	1·75	

Designs:—5 p. Angel with harp; 7 p. Ange with lute; 30p. Angel with viol; 1 c. Angel wit trumpet.

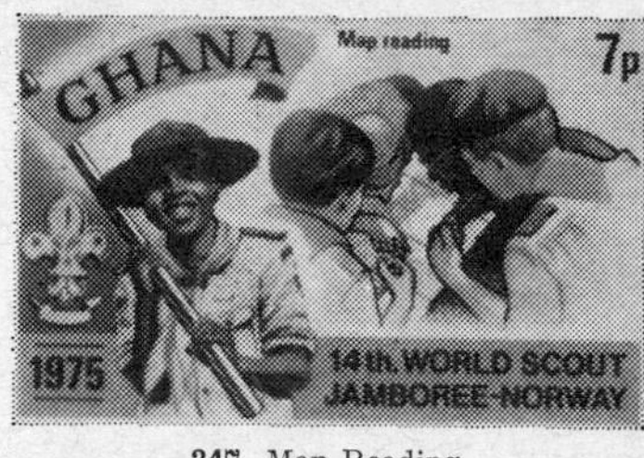

347. Map Reading.

(Litho. Format.)

1976 (5 Jan.). *14th World Scout Jamboree, Nor way. T* **347** *and similar horiz. designs Multicoloured. P* 13½ × 14.

755	7 p. Type **347**	5	
756	30 p. Sailing	25	3
757	60 p. Hiking	50	5
758	1 c. Life-saving	85	9
MS759	133 × 99 mm. 15, 40, 65 and 80 p. as Nos. 755/8	1·75	

348. Bottles (litre).

(Litho. D.L.R.)

1976 (5 Jan.). *Metrication Publicity. T* **34** *and similar horiz. designs. Multicoloured P* 14.

760	7 p. Type **348**	5	
761	30 p. Scales (kilogramme) ..	25	3
762	60 p. Tape measure and bale of cloth (metre)	50	5
763	1 c. Ice, thermometer and kettle (temperature) ..	85	9

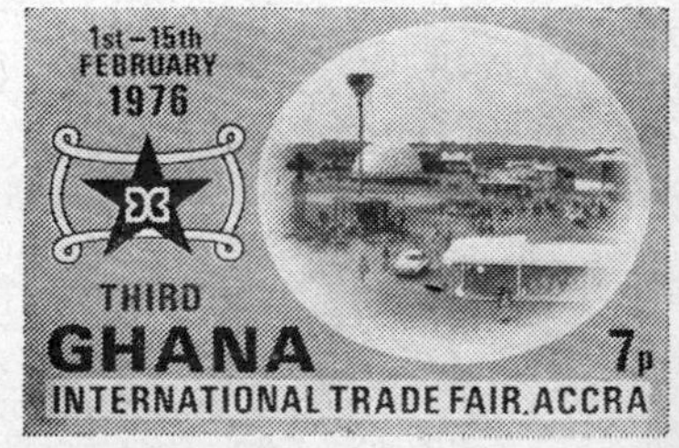

349. Fair Site.

(Litho. Format.)

76 (6 Apr.). *International Trade Fair, Accra. T* **349** *and similar horiz. designs. P* 13½.
4 **349** 7 p. multicoloured .. 5 5
5 – 30 p. multicoloured .. 25 40
6 – 60 p. multicoloured .. 50 55
7 – 1 c. multicoloured .. 85 95
Nos. 765/7 are as T **349** but show different views the Fair.

'INTERPHIL' 76
BICENTENNIAL
EXHIBITION

(**350**)

76 (28 May). *Interphil Stamp Exhibition, Philadelphia. Nos.* 755/9 *optd. with T* **350** *in blue.*
8 7 p. Type **347** 5 5
9 30 p. Sailing 25 30
0 60 p. Hiking 50 55
1 1 c. Life-saving 85 90
S772 133×99 mm. 15, 40, 65 and 80 p. as Nos. 768/71 .. .. 1·75

351. Shot-put.

(Des. PAD Studio. Litho. Format.)

76 (9 Aug.). *Olympic Games, Montreal. T* **351** *and similar vert. designs. Multicoloured.* A. *P* 13½. B. *P* 15.
3 7 p. Type **351** 5 5 5 5
4 30 p. Football 25 30 25 30
5 60 p. Women's 1500 metres 50 55 50 55
6 1 c. Boxing 85 95 85 95
S777 103×135 mm. 15, 40, 65 and 80 p. as Nos. 773/6 1·75 †
Nos. 773/6B come from small sheets of 5 amps plus one *se-tenant* label.

352. Supreme Court.

(Litho. D.L.R.)

76 (7 Sept.). *Centenary of Supreme Court. T* **352** *and similar horiz. designs. P* 14.
8 **352** 8 p. multicoloured .. 5 8
9 – 30 p. multicoloured .. 25 30
0 – 60 p. multicoloured .. 50 55
1 – 1 c. multicoloured .. 85 95
Nos. 779/81 show different views of the Court ilding.

POSTAGE DUE STAMPS.

GHANA
(D 2)

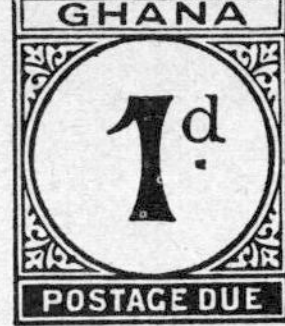

D 3

1958 (25 June). *Postage Due stamps of Gold Coast. Chalk-surfaced paper. Optd. with Type* D **2**, *in red.*
D 9 D **1** 1d. black 5 5
D10 ,, 2d. black 5 5
D11 ,, 3d. black 5 8
D12 ,, 6d. black 12 15
D13 ,, 1s. black 20 25
D9/13 .. .. *Set of* 5 40 50

(Typo. De La Rue.)

1958 (1 Dec.). *Chalk-surfaced paper. Wmk. Mult. Script CA. P* 14.
D14 D **3** 1d. carmine 5 5
D15 ,, 2d. green 5 5
D16 ,, 3d. orange 5 8
D17 ,, 6d. bright ultramarine .. 10 12
D18 ,, 1s. reddish violet .. 15 25
D14/18 .. .. *Set of* 5 30 45

3p.
Ghana New Currency
19th July, 1965.
(D **4**)

1½Np
(D **5**)

1965 (19 July). *Nos.* D14/8 *surch. as Type* D **4** *diagonally upwards* (D) *or horiz.* (H), *by Govt. Printer, Accra.*
D19 D **3** 1 p. on 1d. (D) 5 5
a. Surch. inverted .. 6·00
D20 ,, 2 p. on 2d. (B.) (H) .. 5 5
a. Surch. inverted .. 6·00
D21 ,, 3 p. on 3d. (Indigo) (H) 5 5
a. Surch inverted ..
b. Ultram. surch. ..
ba. Ditto. Surch. inverted 8·00
bb. Ditto. Surch. on back and face .. ..
c. Black surch. .. ..
D22 ,, 6 p. on 6d. (R.) (H) .. 8 8
a. Surch. inverted ..
b. Purple-brn. surch. ..
ba. Ditto. Surch. double .. 40·00
c. Green surch. .. .. 30·00
D23 ,, 12 p. on 1s. (B.) (D) 15 15
D19/23 ,, ... *Set of* 5 30 30
On the diagonal surcharges the figures of value are horizontal.

1968 (Feb.)–**70**. *Nos.* D20/2 *additionally surch. as Type* D **5**, *in red* (1½ *n.p.*, 5 *n.p.*) *or black* 2½ *n.p.*).
D24 D **3** 1½ n.p. on 2 p. on 2d. .. 2·00 1·50
a. Type D 4 double (one albino) ..
D25 ,, 2½ n.p. on 3 p. on 3d. (4.70?) 75
a. Type D 4 double, one albino ..
D26 ,, 5 n.p. on 6 p. on 6d. ('70) 75

The above were three in a series of surcharges, the others being 1 n.p. on 1 p. and 10 n.p. on 12 p., which were prepared, but owing to confusion due to the two surcharges in similar currency it was decided by the authorities not to issue the stamps, however, Nos. D24/6 were issued in error.

(Litho. D.L.R.)

1970. *Inscr. in new currency. P* 14½×14.
D27 D **3** 1 n.p. carmine-red .. 5 5
D28 ,, 1½ n.p. green 5 5
D29 ,, 2½ n.p. yellow-orange .. 5 5
D30 ,, 5 n.p. ultramarine .. 5 5
D31 ,, 10 n.p. reddish violet .. 8 10
D27/31 .. .. *Set of* 5 20 25

GIBRALTAR.

CROWN COLONY.

> For GREAT BRITAIN stamps used in Gibraltar with "G" or "A **26**" obliterations, see index to Great Britain Stamps Used Abroad list.

GIBRALTAR

(**1**)

1886 (1 Jan.). *Contemporary types of Bermuda optd. with T* **1** *by D.L.R. Wmk. Crown CA. P* 14.
1 **9** ½d. dull green .. .. 3·00 3·00
2 **1** 1d. rose-red .. .. 8·00 4·50
3 **2** 2d. purple-brown .. .. 25·00 13·00
4 **11** 2½d. ultramarine .. .. 25·00 3·50
a. Optd. in blue-black .. £120 55·00
5 **10** 4d. orange-red .. .. 32·00 32·00
6 **4** 6d. deep lilac .. .. 70·00 70·00
7 **5** 1s. yellow-brown £130 £140
1/7 .. .. *Set of* 7 £275 £250
1/7 Optd. "Specimen" *Set of* 7 £425

PRINTER. All Gibraltar stamps to No. 109 were typographed by De La Rue & Co., Ltd.

2

3

4

5

1886 (Dec.). *Wmk. Crown CA. P* 14.
8 **2** ½d. dull-green .. .. 1·10 1·10
9 **3** 1d. rose .. .. 4·00 1·00
10 **4** 2d. brown-purple .. .. 11·00 11·00
11 **5** 2½d. blue .. .. 11·00 3·00
12 **4** 4d. orange-brown .. .. 24·00 16·00
13 ,, 6d. lilac .. .. 30·00 27·00
14 ,, 1s. bistre .. .. 70·00 60·00
8/14 .. .. *Set of* 7 £140 £110
8/14 Optd. "Specimen" *Set of* 7 £100
See also Nos. 39 to 45.

5 CENTIMOS

(**6**)

1889 (July). *Surch. as T* **6**.
15 **2** 5 c. on ½d. green .. .. 2·75 2·75
16 **3** 10 c. on 1d. rose .. .. 2·75 2·75
17 **4** 25 c. on 2d. brown-purple .. 2·75 3·00
a. Small "I" .. .. 80·00 80·00
b. Broken "N" £100 £100
18 **5** 25 c. on 2½d. bright blue .. 5·50 2·75
a. Small "I" .. .. 40·00 40·00
b. Broken "N" .. .. 50·00 50·00
19 **4** 40 c. on 4d. orange-brown .. 11·00 12·00
20 ,, 50 c. on 6d. bright lilac .. 12·00 14·00
a. Bisect. diag. (25 c.) (on cover)
21 ,, 75 c. on 1s. bistre .. .. 12·00 15·00
15/21 .. .. *Set of* 7 45·00 48·00
15/21 Optd. "Specimen" *Set of* 7 £110
The small "I" is No. 32 and the broken "N" No. 59 on each pane. Two varieties of the figure "5" of the 5 c., 25 c., 50 c. and 75 c. may also be found.

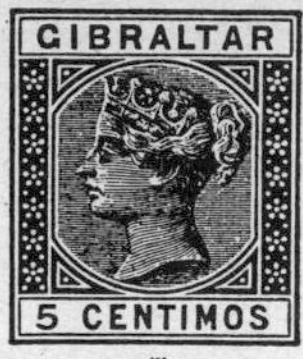

7

1889 (Nov.)–**96.** *Issue in Spanish currency. Wmk. Crown CA. P* 14.

22 **7** 5 c. green 30 35
23 ,, 10 c. carmine 30 35
 a. Bisect. diag. (5 c.) (on cover) † £800
 b. Value omitted £3000
24 ,, 20 c. olive-green (11.95) 1·60 3·00
25 ,, 20 c. olive-grn. & brn. (6.96) 2·75 3·00
26 ,, 25 c. ultramarine .. .. 1·60 55
 a. Deep ultramarine .. .. 3·00 55
27 ,, 40 c. orange-brown .. 1·10 1·60
 a. Bisect. diag. (20 c.) (on cover) † £800
28 ,, 50 c. bright lilac (1890) .. 1·40 2·25
 a. Bisect. diag. (25 c.) (on cover)
29 ,, 75 c. olive-green (1890) .. 11·00 12·00
30 ,, 1 p. bistre (12.89) .. .. 12·00 13·00
31 ,, 1 p. bistre & ultram. (6.95) 2·25 2·75
32 ,, 2 p. black & carmine (11.95) 4·00 4·50
33 ,, 5 p. slate-grey (12.89) .. 17·00 18·00
22/33 *Set of* 11 (excluding No. 25) 48·00 55·00
22/33 Optd. "Specimen" *Set of* 11 £110

The bisects were necessary because of shortages of stamps at different times in various post offices in Morocco.

1898 (1 Oct.). *Reissue in English currency. Wmk. Crown CA. P* 14.

39 **2** ½d. grey-green 25 55
40 **3** 1d. carmine 40 35
41 **4** 2d. brown-purple & ultram. 2·50 2·50
42 **5** 2½d. bright ultramarine .. 2·50 85
43 **4** 4d. orange-brown and green 4·50 4·00
44 ,, 6d. violet and red .. .. 7·00 7·00
45 ,, 1s. bistre and carmine .. 7·00 9·00
39/45 .. .. *Set of* 7 22·00 22·00
39/45 Optd. "Specimen" *Set of* 7 75·00

No. 39 is greyer than No. 8, No. 40 brighter and deeper than No. 9 and No. 42 much brighter than No. 11.

8

9

½ Normal ½ Large "2"

2½d.

This occurs on R. 10/1 in each pane of 60 above Plate No. 1 & 2. The diagonal stroke is longer.

1903 (1 May). *Wmk. Crown CA. P* 14.

46 **8** ½d. grey-green and green .. 90 1·40
47 ,, 1d. dull purple/*red* .. .. 2·25 90
48 ,, 2d. grey-green and carmine 3·25 2·75
49 ,, 2½d. dull purple & black/*blue* 85 1·60
 a. Large "2" in "½" .. 8·00 9·00
50 ,, 6d. dull purple and violet .. 4·00 5·50
51 ,, 1s. black and carmine .. 5·50 7·00
52 **9** 2s. green and blue .. .. 23·00 26·00
53 ,, 4s. dull purple and green .. 23·00 30·00
54 ,, 8s. dull purple & black/*blue* 30·00 35·00
55 ,, £1 dull purple & black/*red* £250 £325
46/55 .. .. *Set of* 10 £325 £400
46/55 Optd. "Specimen" *Set of* 10 £110

1904–7. *Wmk. Mult. Crown CA. P* 14.

56 **8** ½d. dull & bright green, OC 40 40
57 ,, 1d. dull purple/*red*, OC .. 40 40
 a. Bisected (½d.) (on card) .. † £500
58 ,, 2d. grey-grn. & carm., OC 1·60 1·60
59 ,, 2½d. pur. & blk./*blue*, C ('07) 6·00 7·00
 a. Large "2" in "½" .. .. 25·00 30·00
60 ,, 6d. d. pur. & vio., OC ('06) 1·40 2·50
61 ,, 1s. black & carm., OC ('05) 4·00 3·75
62 **9** 2s. green & blue, OC (1905) 19·00 21·00
63 ,, 4s. deep purple & green, C 35·00 38·00
64 ,, £1 dp. pur. & black/*red*, C £275 £350
56/64 .. .. *Set of* 9 £325 £400

1907–11. *Colours changed. Wmk. Mult. Crown CA. P* 14.

66 **8** ½d. blue-green, O 30 30
67 ,, 1d. carmine, O 30 25
 a. Wmk. sideways
68 ,, 2d. greyish slate, O (1910) 1·25 1·90
69 ,, 2½d. ultramarine, O .. 65 1·90
 a. Large "2" in "½" .. 6·00 10·00
70 ,, 6d. dull & bright purple, C 35·00 50·00
71 ,, 1s. black/*green*, C (1910) .. 4·00 6·00
72 **9** 2s. purple & bright blue/*blue*, C (1910) .. .. 19·00 23·00
73 ,, 4s. black & carm., C (1910) 28·00 32·00
74 ,, 8s. purple & grn., C (1911) £110 £120
66/74 .. .. *Set of* 9 £180 £225
66/74 Optd. "Specimen" *Set of* 9 £130

10

11

1912 (17 July)–**24.** *Wmk. Mult. Crown CA. P* 14.

76 **10** ½d. blue-green, O 15 15
 a. Yellow-green (1917) .. 20 15
77 ,, 1d. carmine-red, O 50 25
 a. Scarlet (1916) 85 15
78 ,, 2d. greyish slate, O .. 1·10 55
79 ,, 2½d. deep bright blue, O .. 1·60 50
 a. Large "2" in "½" .. 8·00 5·00
 b. Pale ultramarine .. 2·25 50
 ba. Large "2" in "½" .. 12·00 6·00
80 ,, 6d. dull pur. & mauve, C 2·50 1·60
81 ,, 1s. black/*green*, OC .. 1·60 1·60
 a. On bl.-grn., olive back (1919) 3·25 3·25
 b. On emerald surface (1923) (Optd. S. £10) .. .. 5·50 5·50
 c. On emerald back (1924) C 2·00 5·50
82 **11** 2s. dull pur. & blue/*blue*, C 6·00 4·50
83 ,, 4s. black and carmine, C 12·00 15·00
84 ,, 8s. dull pur. & green, C 23·00 26·00
85 ,, £1 dull pur. & blk./*red*, C 55·00 70·00
76/85 .. .. *Set of* 10 95·00 £110
76/85 Optd. "Specimen" *Set of* 10 £100

WAR TAX

(12)

1918 (15 Apr.). *Optd. locally with T* **12.**

86 **10** ½d. green 25 30

Two printings of this overprint exist, the second being in slightly heavier type on a deeper shade of green.

3 PENCE (I) THREE PENCE (II)

1921–27. *Wmk. Mult. Script CA. P* 14.

89 **10** ½d. green, O (1927) .. 10 15
90 ,, 1d. carmine-red, O ('21) 20 20
91 ,, 1½d. chestnut, O (1922) .. 35 30
 a. Pale chestnut (1924) .. 30 20
93 ,, 2d. grey, O (1921) .. 55 60
94 ,, 2½d. bright blue, O (1921) 2·75 2·50
 a. Large "2" in "½" .. 14·00 14·00

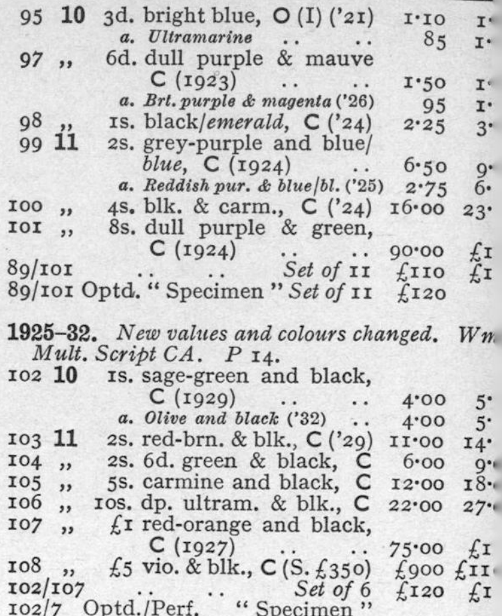

95 **10** 3d. bright blue, O (I) ('21) 1·10 1·
 a. Ultramarine .. .. 85 1·
97 ,, 6d. dull purple & mauve C (1923) .. .. 1·50 1·
 a. Brt. purple & magenta ('26) 95 1·
98 ,, 1s. black/*emerald*, C ('24) 2·25 3·
99 **11** 2s. grey-purple and blue/*blue*, C (1924) .. 6·50 9·
 a. Reddish pur. & blue/bl. ('25) 2·75 6·
100 ,, 4s. blk. & carm., C ('24) 16·00 23·
101 ,, 8s. dull purple & green, C (1924) .. .. 90·00 £1
89/101 .. .. *Set of* 11 £110 £1
89/101 Optd. "Specimen" *Set of* 11 £120

1925–32. *New values and colours changed. Wm Mult. Script CA. P* 14.

102 **10** 1s. sage-green and black, C (1929) .. .. 4·00 5·
 a. Olive and black ('32) .. 4·00 5·
103 **11** 2s. red-brn. & blk., C ('29) 11·00 14·
104 ,, 2s. 6d. green & black, C 6·00 9·
105 ,, 5s. carmine and black, C 12·00 18·
106 ,, 10s. dp. ultram. & blk., C 22·00 27·
107 ,, £1 red-orange and black, C (1927) .. .. 75·00 £1
108 ,, £5 vio. & blk., C (S. £350) £900 £11
102/107 .. .. *Set of* 6 £120 £1
102/7 Optd./Perf. "Specimen" *Set of* 6 £130

1930. *T* **10** *inscribed* "THREE PENCE". *Wm Mult. Script CA. P* 14.

109 3d. ultram. (II) (Perf. S. £17) 4·00 2·

13. The Rock of Gibraltar.

(Des. Capt. H. St. C. Garrod. Recess. D.L.R.

1931–33. *T* **13.** *Wmk. Mult. Script C* A. *P* 14. B. 13½×14.

		A.		B.	
110	1d. scar (1.7.31)	65	65	2·50	
111	1½d. red-brown (1.7.31) ..	95	65	1·25	
112	2d. pale grey (1.11.32) ..	85	65	3·00	
113	3d. blue (1.6.33)	1·40	2·00	4·50	4·

110/13 Perf. "Specimen" *Set of* 4 45·00

Figures of value take the place of both corn ornaments at the base of the 2d. and 3d.

1935 (6 May). *Silver Jubilee. As Nos.* 91/4 *Antigua but ptd. by B. W. & Co. P* 11×1

114 2d. ultramarine & grey-black 95
 a. Extra flagstaff .. .. 18·00
115 3d. brown and deep blue .. 80 1·
 a. Extra flagstaff .. .. 95·00
116 6d. green and indigo .. 2·00 3·
 a. Extra flagstaff .. .. 48·00
117 1s. slate and purple .. .. 5·00 5·
 a. Extra flagstaff .. .. 55·00
114/17 Perf. "Specimen" *Set of* 4 18·00

For illustration of "extra flagstaff" variet see Bechuanaland.

1937 (12 May). *Coronation. As Nos.* 13/5 *Aden, but ptd. by B. W. & Co. P* 11×11½.

118 ½d. green 25
119 2d. grey-black 65
120 3d. blue 85
118/20 Perf. "Specimen" *Set of* 3 14·00

14. King George VI.

15. Rock of Gibraltar.

16. The Rock (North Side).

riz. designs as T **16**:—
. Europa Point. **20.** Eliott Memorial.
Moorish Castle. **21.** Government House.
. Southport Gate. **22.** Catalan Bay.

(Recess. D.L.R.)

38–51. *Wmk. Mult. Script CA.*
1 **14** ½d. deep grn. (*p.* 13½×14) 8 10
2 **15** 1d. yellow-brown (*p.* 14) 80 80
a. Perf. 13½ 70 70
ab. Perf. 13½. Wmk. sideways. 15 55
b. Perf. 13. Wmk. sideways. *Red-brown* ('42) .. 10 35
c. Perf. 13. Wmk. sideways. *Deep brown* ('44) .. 25 90
d. Perf. 13. *Red-brown* ('49) 10 50
3 **15** 1½d. carmine (*p.* 14) .. 1·90 45
a. Perf. 13½. .. .. 24·00 10·00
3*b* ,, 1½d. slate-vio. (*p.* 13) ('43) 12 30
4 **16** 2d. grey (*p.* 14) .. .. 1·25 50
a. Perf. 13½. 12 25
ab. Perf. 13½. Wmk. sideways 60·00 6·50
b. Perf. 13. Wmk. sideways ('42) 30 30
4*c* ,, 2d. carmine (*p.* 13) (*wmk. sideways*) ('44) .. 20 20
5 **17** 3d. light blue (*p.* 13½) .. 70 25
a. Perf. 14 .. .. 8·50 4·00
b. Perf. 13 ('42) 15 20
ba. *Greenish blue* (2.51) .. 65 90
5*c* ,, 5d. red-orge. (*p.* 13) ('47) 45 55
6 **18** 6d. carm. & grey-vio. (*p.* 13½) 1·75 1·10
a. Perf. 14 .. .. 17·00 45
b. Perf. 13 ('42) 25 65
c. Perf. 13. *Scarlet and grey-violet* ('45) .. .. 1·10 1·00
7 **19** 1s. black & green (*p.* 14) 2·75 5·00
a. Perf. 13½ .. .. 7·00 3·25
b. Perf. 13 ('42) 55 55
8 **20** 2s. black & brown (*p.* 14) 10·00 9·50
a. Perf. 13½ .. .. 12·00 8·00
b. Perf. 13 ('42) .. .. 1·10 1·25
9 **21** 5s. black & carm. (*p.* 14) 12·00 13·00
a. Perf. 13½ .. .. 2·75 3·75
b. Perf. 13 ('44) .. .. 2·75 3·75
0 **22** 10s. black and blue (*p.* 14) 8·00 8·50
a. Perf. 13 ('43) .. .. 6·00 7·50
1 **14** £1 orange (*p.* 13½×14) .. 10·00 14·00
1/131 .. .. *Set of* 14 21·00 27·00
1/31 Perf. "Specimen" *Set of* 14 85·00

46 (12 Oct.). *Victory. As Nos.* 28/9 *of Aden.*
2 ½d. green 10 15
3 3d. ultramarine 20 25
2/3 Perf. "Specimen" *Set of* 2 15·00

48 (1 Dec.). *Royal Silver Wedding. As Nos.* 30/1 *of Aden.*
4 ½d. green 10 10
5 £1 brown-orange .. .. 17·00 20·00

49 (10 Oct.). *75th Anniv. of Universal Postal Union. As Nos.* 114/7 *of Antigua.*
6 2d. carmine 65 65
7 3d. deep blue.. .. .. 70 70
8 6d. purple .. .. .. 1·40 1·40
9 1s. blue-green .. .. 2·75 3·25

NEW CONSTITUTION 1950

(**23**)

1950 (1 Aug.). *Inauguration of Legislative Council. Nos.* 124*c*, 125*b*, 126*b* *and* 127*b* *optd. as T* **23**.
140 **16** 2d. carmine 25 35
141 **17** 3d. light blue 30 50
142 **18** 6d. carmine & grey-violet 60 90
a. Opt. double .. .. 80·00
143 **19** 1s. black and green (R.) .. 95 1·75
On stamps from the lower part of the sheet of No. 142a the two impressions are almost coincident.

1953 (2 June). *Coronation. As No.* 47 *of Aden.*
144 ½d. black and bronze-green.. 15 12

24. Cargo and Passenger Wharves.
25. South View from Straits.
26. Tunny Fishing Industry.
27. Southport Gate.
28. Sailing in the Bay.
29. Ocean-going Liner.
30. Coaling Wharf.
31. Airport.
32. Europa Point.
33. Straits from Buena Vista.
34. Rosia Bay and Straits.

35. Main Entrance, Government House.

36. Tower of Homage, Moorish Castle. **37.** Arms of Gibraltar.

(Recess (except £1, centre litho.). De La Rue.)

1953 (19 Oct.). *Wmk. Mult. Script CA. P* 13.
145 **24** ½d. indigo and grey-green 8 8
146 **25** 1d. bluish green (*shades*) 10 8
147 **26** 1½d. black 12 12
148 **27** 2d. dp. olive-brn. (*shades*) 20 15
149 **28** 2½d. carmine (*shades*) .. 35 30
150 **29** 3d. light blue (*shades*) .. 20 10
151 **30** 4d. ultramarine (*shades*).. 30 25
152 **31** 5d. maroon (*shades*) .. 30 25
153 **32** 6d. blk. & p. blue (*shades*) 35 35
154 **33** 1s. pale blue & red-brown (*shades*) .. .. 1·00 85
155 **34** 2s. orange and reddish violet (*shades*) .. 3·50 1·50
156 **35** 5s. deep brown .. .. 6·50 4·50
157 **36** 10s. reddish brn. & ultram. 27·00 20·00
158 **37** £1 scarlet & orge.-yellow 45·00 27·00
145/58 .. .. *Set of* 14 75·00 50·00

1954 (10 May). *Royal Visit. As No.* 150 *but inscr.* "royal visit 1954" *at top.*
159 3d. greenish blue 30 25

38. Gibraltar Candytuft.

39. Moorish Castle.
40. St. George's Hall. (*Horiz.*)
41. The Keys. (*Vert.*)
42. The Rock by Moonlight. (*Horiz.*)
43. Catalan Bay. (*Horiz.*)
44. Map of Gibraltar. (*Vert.*)
45. Air Terminal. (*Vert.*)
46. American War Memorial. (*Vert.*)
47. Rock Ape. (*Horiz.*)
48. Barbary Partridge. (*Horiz.*)
49. Blue Rock Thrush. (*Horiz.*)
50. Rock Lily (*Narcissus niveus*). (*Vert.*)

51. Rock and Badge of Gibraltar Regiment.

(Des. J. Celecia (½d., 2d., 2½d., 2s., 10s.), N. A. Langdon (1d., 3d., 6d., 7d., 9d., 1s.), M. Bonilla (4d.), L. J. Gomez (5s.), Sgt. T. A. Griffiths (£1). Recess (£1) or photo. (others). De La Rue.)

1960 (29 Oct.). *W* w.**12** (*upright*). *P* 14 (£1) *or* 13 (*others*).
160 **38** ½d. brt. pur. & emer.-grn. 5 5
161 **39** 1d. black and yell.-green 5 5
162 **40** 2d. indigo & orange-brn. 8 8
163 **41** 2½d. black and blue (*shades*) 10 10
164 **42** 3d. dp. blue & red-orange 12 20
165 **43** 4d. deep red-brn. & turq. 25 20
166 **44** 6d. sepia and emerald .. 25 10
167 **45** 7d. indigo & carmine-red 35 20
168 **46** 9d. grey-blue & greenish bl. 40 35
169 **47** 1s. sepia and bluish green 35 20
170 **48** 2s. chocolate & ultram. .. 70 70
171 **49** 5s. turq.-blue & olive-brn. 2·25 2·25
172 **50** 10s. yellow and blue .. 5·00 4·50
173 **51** £1 black & brown-orange 10·00 8·00
160/73 .. .. *Set of* 14 18·00 15·00
See also No. 199.

1963 (4 June). *Freedom from Hunger. As No. 76 of Aden.*
174 9d. sepia .. .. .. 6·50 6·00

1963 (2 Sept.). *Red Cross Centenary. As Nos. 147/8 of Antigua.*
175 1d. red and black 20 20
176 9d. red and blue .. .. 6·50 6·00

1964 (23 April). *400th Anniv. of Birth of William Shakespeare. As No. 164 of Antigua.*
177 7d. bistre-brown 30 30

NEW CONSTITUTION 1964.

(52)

1964 (16 Oct.). *New Constitution. Nos. 164 and 166 optd. with T* **52.**
178 **42** 3d. dp. blue and red-orange 15 15
179 **44** 6d. sepia and emerald .. 25 25
a. No stop after "1964" .. 10·00 9·00

1965 (17 May). *I.T.U. Centenary. As Nos. 166/7 of Antigua.*
180 4d. light emerald and yellow 30 25
181 2s. apple-green and deep blue 9·00 7·00

1965 (25 Oct.). *International Co-operation Year. As Nos. 168/9 of Antigua.*
182 ½d. dp. bluish green & lav. 10 10
183 4d. reddish pur. & turq.-grn. 60 60
The value of the ½d. stamp is shown as "1/2".

1966 (24 Jan.). *Churchill Commemoration. As Nos. 170/3 of Antigua.*
184 ½d. new blue 5 5
185 1d. deep green 8 8
186 4d. brown 30 30
187 9d. bluish violet 75 75

1966 (1 July). *World Cup Football Championships. As Nos. 176/7 of Antigua.*
188 2½d. violet, yellow-green, lake and yellow-brown .. 12 12
189 6d. chocolate, blue-grn., lake and yellow-brown .. 40 35

PRINTERS. All stamps from here to No. 239 were printed in photogravure by Harrison.

53. Bream.

54. Scorpion Fish. (*Horiz.*)
55. Stone Bass. (*Vert.*)

(Des. A. G. Ryman.)

1966 (27 Aug.). *European Sea Angling Championships, Gibraltar. W* w.**12.** *P* 13½×14 (1s.) *or* 14×13½ (*others*).
190 **53** 4d. rosine, bright blue and black 5 5
191 **54** 7d. rosine, deep olive-green and black 20 20
a. Black (value and inscr.) omitted £250
192 **55** 1s. lake-brn., emer. & blk. 25 25

1966 (20 Sept.). *Inauguration of W.H.O. Headquarters, Geneva. As Nos. 178/9 of Antigua.*
193 6d. black, yellow-green and light blue 40 40
194 9d. black, light purple and yellow-brown 60 55

56. "Our Lady of Europa".

(Des. A. G. Ryman.)

1966 (15 Nov.). *Centenary of Re-enthronement of "Our Lady of Europa". W* w.**12.** *P* 14×14½.
195 **56** 2s. bright blue and black .. 1·00 95

1966 (1 Dec.). *20th Anniv. of U.N.E.S.C.O. As Nos. 196/8 of Antigua.*
196 2d. slate-violet, red, yellow and orange 5 5
197 7d. orange-yellow, violet and deep olive 15 15
198 5s. black, bright purple and orange 90 90

1966 (23 Dec.). *As No. 165 but wmk.* w.**12** *sideways.*
199 **43** 4d. dp. red-brn. & turquoise 12 12

57. H.M.S. *Victory.*

(Des. A. G. Ryman.)

1967 (3 Apr.)–**69.** *T* **57** *and similar horiz. designs showing ships. Multicoloured. W* w.**12.** *P* 14×14½.
200 ½d. Type **57** 5 5
201 1d. S.S. *Arab* 5 5
202 2d. H.M.S. *Carmania* .. 8 8
203 2½d. M.V. *Mons Calpe* .. 10 12
204 3d. S.S. *Canberra* 10 10
205 4d. H.M.S. *Hood* 10 10
205*a* 5d. Cable Ship *Mirror* (7.7.69) 15 12
206 6d. Xebec (sailing vessel) .. 15 15
207 7d. *Amerigo Vespucci* (training vessel) 15 20
208 9d. T.V. *Raffaello* 25 25
209 1s. H.M.S. *Royal Katherine* 30 30
210 2s. H.M.S. *Ark Royal* .. 50 50
211 5s. H.M.S. *Dreadnought* .. 1·50 1·75
212 10s. S.S. *Neuralia* .. .. 2·75 3·50
213 £1 *Mary Celeste* (sailing vessel) .. .. .. 7·00 7·50
200/13 .. .. *Set of* 15 12·00 13·00

The ½d., 1d., 2d., 3d., 6d., 2s., 5s. and £1 exist with PVA gum as well as gum arabic, but the 5d. exists with PVA gum only.

58. Aerial Ropeway.

(Des. A. G. Ryman.)

1967 (15 June). *International Tourist Yea T* **58** *and similar designs but horiz. Mul coloured. W* w.**12** (*sideways on 7d.*). *P* 14½ 14 (*7d.*) *or* 14×14½ (*others*).
214 7d. Type **58** 12
215 9d. Shark fishing 15
216 1s. Skin-diving 25

59. Mary, Joseph and Child Jesus.

60. Church Window.

1967 (1 Nov.). *Christmas. W* w.**12** (*sidewa on 6d.*). *P* 14.
217 **59** 2d. multicoloured .. 8
218 **60** 6d. multicoloured .. 15

61. Gen. Eliott and Route Map.

62. Heathfield Tower and Monument, Sussex. (*Horiz.*)
63. General Eliott. (*Vert.*)

64. Eliott directing Rescue Operations.

(*Illustration reduced. Actual size* 55×21 *mm*

(Des. A. G. Ryman.)

1967 (11 Dec.). *250th Birth Anniv. of Gener Eliott. W* w.**12** (*sideways on horiz. design P* 14×15 (1s.) *or* 15×14 (*others*).
219 **61** 4d. multicoloured .. 5
220 **62** 9d. multicoloured .. 15
221 **63** 1s. multicoloured .. 20
222 **64** 2s. multicoloured .. 35

65. Lord Baden-Powell.

(Des. A. G. Ryman).

1968 (27 Mar.). *60th Anniv. of Gibraltar Scout Association.* T **65** *and similar horiz. designs.* W **w.12.** *P* 14×14½.

223	4d. buff and bluish violet ..	8	8
224	7d. ochre and blue-green ..	12	12
225	9d. bright blue, yell.-orange and black	15	15
226	1s. greenish yell. & emerald	25	25

Designs:—7d. Scout Flag over the Rock; 9d. Tent, scouts and salute; 1s. Scout badges.

66. Nurse and W.H.O. Emblem.

67. Doctor and W.H.O. Emblem.

(Des. A. G. Ryman.)

1968 (1 July). *20th Anniv. of World Health Organization.* W **w.12.** *P* 14×14½.

227	**66**	2d. ultramarine, black and yellow	10	10
228	**67**	4d. slate, black and pink ..	20	20

68. King John signing Magna Carta.

70. Shepherd, Lamb and Star.

69. "Freedom" and Rock of Gibraltar.

71. Mary holding Holy Child.

(Des. A. G. Ryman.)

1968 (26 Aug.). *Human Rights Year.* W **w.12** (*sideways*). *P* 13½×14.

229	**68**	1s. yellow-orange, brown and gold	20	20
230	**69**	2s. myrtle and gold ..	35	35

(Des. A. G. Ryman.)

1968 (1 Nov.). *Christmas.* W **w.12.** *P* 14½×13½.

231	**70**	4d. multicoloured ..	12	12
232	**71**	9d. multicoloured ..	30	30

72. Parliament Houses.

73. Parliamentary Emblem and Outline of "The Rock". (*Horiz.*)

74. Clock Tower, Westminster (Big Ben) and Arms of Gibraltar. (*Vert.*)

(Des. A. G. Ryman.)

1969 (26 May). *Commonwealth Parliamentary Association Conference.* W **w.12** (*sideways on* 2s.). *P* 14×14½ (2s.) *or* 14½×14 (*others*).

233	**72**	4d. green and gold ..	8	8
234	**73**	9d. bluish violet and gold	15	15
235	**74**	2s. vermilion, gold, blue and pale blue ..	30	30

75. Silhouette of Rock, and Queen Elizabeth.

(Des. A. G. Ryman.)

1969 (30 July). *New Constitution.* W **w.12.** *P* 14×13½ (*in addition, the outline of the Rock is perforated*).

236	**75**	½d. gold and orange ..	5	5
237	,,	5d. silver and bright green	15	15
		a. Portrait and inscr. in gold and silver*		
238	,,	7d. silver and bright purple	20	30
239	,,	5s. gold and ultramarine .. .	90	1·00

*No. 237a was first printed with the head and inscription in gold and then in silver but displaced slightly to lower left.

76. Royal Artillery Officer, 1758 and Modern Cap Badge.

77. Soldier and Cap Badge, Royal Anglian Regiment, 1969.

78. Royal Engineers' Artificer, 1786 and Modern Cap Badge.

79. Private, Fox's Marines, 1704, and Modern Royal Marines' Cap Badge.

(Des. A. G. Ryman. Photo. De La Rue.)

1969 (6 Nov.). *Military Uniforms* (*First Series*). W **w.12.** *P* 14.

240	**76**	1d. multicoloured	5	5
241	**77**	6d. multicoloured	30	30
242	**78**	9d. multicoloured	40	40
243	**79**	2s. multicoloured	1·00	1·00

Nos. 240/3 have a short history of the Regiment printed on the reverse side over the gum, therefore, once the gum is moistened the history becomes removed.

See also Nos. 248/51, 290/3, 300/303, 313/16, 331/4, 340/3 and 363/6.

80. "Madonna della Seggiola" (detail, Raphael).

81. "Virgin and Child" (detail, Morales).

82. "Madonna of the Rocks" (detail, Leonardo da Vinci).

(Des. A. G. Ryman. Photo. Enschedé.)

1969 (1 Dec.). *Christmas.* W **w.12** (*sideways*). *P* 14×*Roulette* 9.

244	**80**	5d. multicoloured	10	10
245	**81**	7d. multicoloured	15	15
246	**82**	1s. multicoloured	30	30
Strip of three		.. .. ..	50	50

Nos. 244/6 were issued together in *se-tenant* strips of three throughout the sheet.

83. Europa Point.

(Des. A. G. Ryman. Photo. Enschedé.)

1970 (8 June). *Europa Point.* W **w.12.** *P* 13½.

247	**83**	2s. multicoloured	30	35

Designs as T **77**:—
84. Royal Scots Officer (1839) and Cap Badge.
85. South Wales Borderers Private (1763) and Cap Badge.
86. Queen's Royal Regiment Private (1742) and Cap Badge.
87. Royal Irish Rangers Piper (1969) and Cap Badge.

(Des. A. G. Ryman. Photo. D.L.R.)

1970 (28 Aug.). *Military Uniforms* (*Second Series*). W **w.12.** *P* 14.

248	**84**	2d. multicoloured	8	8
249	**85**	5d. multicoloured	20	20
250	**86**	7d. multicoloured	30	30
251	**87**	2s. multicoloured	1·00	1·00

Nos. 248/51 have a short history of the Regiment printed on the reverse side under the gum.

88. No. 191a and Rock of Gibraltar.

89. Victorian stamp (No. 23b) and Moorish Castle.

(Des. A. G. Ryman. Litho. D.L.R.)

1970 (18 Sept.). *"Philympia 1970" Stamp Exhibition, London. W* w.**12** *(sideways). P* 13.

252	**88**	1s. verm. & bronze-green	20	20
253	**89**	2s. bright blue & magenta	35	35

The stamps shown in the designs are well-known varieties with values omitted.

90. "The Virgin Mary".

(Des. from stained-glass-window by Gabriel Loire. Photo. Enschedé.)

1970 (1 Dec.). *Christmas. W* w.**12**. *P* 13×14.

254	**90**	2s. multicoloured	50	50

91. Saluting Battery, Rosia.

92. Saluting Battery, Rosia, Modern View.

(Des. A. G. Ryman. Litho. Questa.)

1971 (15 Feb.). *Decimal Currency. T* **91/2** *and similar multicoloured designs. Each value printed se-tenant in two designs showing respectively old and new views of Gibraltar. W* w.**12** *(sideways on horiz. designs). P* 14.

255	½p.	Type **91**	5	5
256	½p.	Type **92**	5	5
257	1p.	Prince George of Cambridge Quarters and	8	5
258	1p.	Trinity Church	8	5
259	1½p.	The Wellington Bust,	5	5
260	1½p.	Alameda Gardens ..	5	5
261	2p.	Gibraltar from the	8	5
262	2p.	North Bastion ..	8	5
263	2½p.	Catalan	5	5
264	2½p.	Bay	5	5
265	3p.	Convent	5	8
266	3p.	Garden	5	8
267	4p.	The Exchange and	15	15
268	4p.	Spanish Chapel ..	15	15
269	5p.	Commercial Square	10	12
270	5p.	and Library ..	10	12
271	7p.	South Barracks and	15	15
272	7p.	Rosia Magazine ..	15	15
273	8p.	Moorish Mosque and	15	20
274	8p.	Castle	15	20
275	9p.	Europa	20	20
276	9p.	Pass Road	20	20
277	10p.	South Barracks from	20	25
278	10p.	Rosia Bay	20	25
279	12½p.	Southport	25	30
280	12½p.	Gates	25	30
281	25p.	The Alameda, Trooping the Guards	50	55
282	25p.	ing the Guards ..	50	55
283	50p.	Europa Pass	95	1·10
284	50p.	Gorge	95	1·10
285	£1	Prince Edward's	2·00	2·10
286	£1	Gate	2·00	2·10
255/86		.. .. *Set of* 32	9·00	10·00

The 50p. and £1 are vertical, and the remainder are horizontal designs.

See also Nos. 317/20 and 344/5.

93

94. Regimental Arms.

(Des. A. G. Ryman. Photo. Harrison.)

1971 (15 Feb.). *Coil Stamps. W* w.**12**. *P* 14½×14.

287	**93**	½p. red-orange	5	5
		a. Coil strip (287×2, 288×2 and 289 *se-tenant*) ..	8	10
288	,,	1p. blue	5	5
289	,,	2p. bright green	5	5

(Des. A. G. Ryman. Litho. Questa.)

1971 (6 Sept.). *Military Uniforms (Third Series). Multicoloured designs as T* **77**, *showing uniform and cap-badge. W* w.**12**. *P* 14.

290	1p.	The Black Watch (1845)	12	12
291	2p.	Royal Regt. of Fusiliers (1971)	20	20
292	4p.	King's Own Royal Border Regt. (1704) ..	40	40
293	10p.	Devonshire and Dorset Regt. (1801)	1·00	1·00

Nos. 290/3 have a short history of the Regiment printed on the reverse side under the gum.

(Des. A. G. Ryman. Litho. Harrison.)

1971 (25 Sept.). *Presentation of Colours to the Gibraltar Regiment. W* w.**12** *(sideways). P* 12½×12.

294	**94**	3p. black, gold and red ..	20	20

95. Nativity Scene.

(Des. A. G. Ryman. Photo. Enschedé.)

1971 (1 Dec.). *Christmas. T* **95** *and similar horiz. design. Multicoloured. W* w.**12**. *P* 13×13½.

295	3p. Type **95**	20	20
296	5p. Mary and Joseph going to Bethlehem	30	30

96. Soldier Artificer, 1773.

(Des. A. G. Ryman. Litho. Questa.)

1972 (6 Mar.). *Bicentenary of Royal Engineer in Gibraltar. T* **96** *and similar multicolourec designs. W* w.**12** *(sideways on* 1 *and* 3 p.). *P* 13½×14 *(5p.) or* 14×13½ *(others).*

297	1p. Type **96**	8	
298	3p. Modern tunneller ..	20	
299	5p. Old and new uniforms and badge *(horiz.)*	30	

(Des. A. G. Ryman. Litho. Questa.)

1972 (19 July). *Military Uniforms (Fourt Series). Multicoloured designs as T* **77** *W* w.**12** *(sideways). P* 14.

300	1p. Duke of Cornwall's Light Infantry, 1704	5	
301	3p. King's Royal Rifle Corps, 1830	20	
302	7p. Officer, 37th North Hampshire, 1825 ..	35	
303	10p. Royal Navy, 1972 ..	60	

Nos. 300/303 have a short history of th Regiment printed on the reverse side under th gum.

97. "Our Lady of Europa".

(Des. A. G. Ryman. Litho. Harrison.)

1972 (4 Oct.). *Christmas. W* w.**12** *(sideways) P* 14½×14.

304	**97**	3p. multicoloured ..	12	
305	,,	5p. multicoloured ..	25	

These stamps have an inscription printed o the reverse side.

98. Keys of Gibraltar and *Narcissus niveus.*

Des. (from photograph by D. Groves) and photo. Harrison.)

972 (20 Nov.). *Royal Silver Wedding. Multicoloured; background colour given.* *W* **w.12.** *P* 14 × 14½.

06 **98** 5p. carmine-red 20 20
07 ,, 7p. deep grey-green .. 25 30

99. Flags of Member Nations and E.E.C. Symbol.

(Des. A. G. Ryman. Litho. Questa.)

973 (22 Feb.). *Britain's Entry into E.E.C.* *W* **w.12** (*sideways*). *P* 14½ × 14.

08 **99** 5p. multicoloured .. 20 20
09 ,, 10p. multicoloured .. 35 40

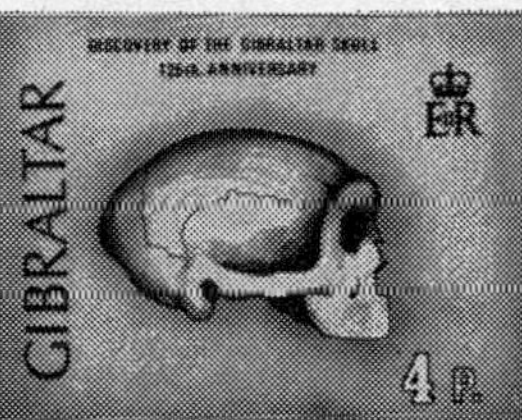

100. Skull.

(Des. A. G. Ryman. Litho. B.W.)

973 (22 May). *125th Anniv. of Gibraltar Skull Discovery.* *T* **100** *and similar horiz. designs. Multicoloured.* *W* **w.12.** *P* 13 (10*p.*) *or* 13½ (*others*).

10 4p. Type **100** 12 12
11 6p. Prehistoric man .. 20 20
12 10p. Prehistoric family (40 × 26 *mm.*) 35 35

(Des. A. G. Ryman. Litho. Questa.)

973 (22 Aug.). *Military Uniforms (5th series). Multicoloured designs as* *T* **77.** *W* **w.12** (*sideways*). *P* 14.

13 1p. King's Own Scottish Borderers, 1770 .. .. 5 5
14 4p. Royal Welch Fusiliers, 1800 .. .. .. 25 25
15 6p. Royal Northumberland Fusiliers, 1736 .. .. 35 35
16 10p. Grenadier Guards, 1898 55 55

Nos. 313/16 have a short history of the Regiment printed on the reverse side under the gum.

973 (12 Sept.). *As Nos.* 261/2 *and* 267/8 *but* *W* **w.12** *upright.*

17 2p. } Gibraltar from .. 5 5
18 2p. } the North Bastion .. 5 5
19 4p. } The Exchange .. 8 10
20 4p. } and Spanish Chapel .. 8 10

See also Nos. 346/7.

101. Nativity Scene (Danckerts).

(Des. and litho. Enschedé.)

1973 (17 Oct.). *Christmas.* *W* **w.12.** *P* 12½ × 12.

321 **101** 4p. violet and Venetian red 15 15
322 ,, 6p. magenta and turq.-blue 25 25

1973 (14 Nov.). *Royal Wedding. As Nos.* 165/6 *of Anguilla. Centre multicoloured.* *W* **w.12** (*sideways*). *P* 13½.

323 6p. turquoise 15 15
324 14p. yellow-green 35 35

102. Victorian Pillar-box.

(Des. A. G. Ryman. Litho. Walsall Security Ptrs. Ltd.)

1974 (2 May). *Centenary of Universal Postal Union.* *T* **102** *and similar vert. designs. Multicoloured.*

(*a*) *W* **w.12** (*sideways*). *P* 14½.

325 2p. Type **102** 10 10
326 6p. Pillar-box of George VI .. 20 20
327 14p. Pillar-box of Elizabeth II 40 40

(*b*) *No wmk. Imperf.* × *roul.* 5. *Self-adhesive.* (*From Booklets.*)

328 2p. Type **102** 40 40
a. Booklet pane. Nos. 328/30 *se-tenant* .. .. .. 4·50
b. Booklet pane. Nos. 328 × 3 and 329 × 3. .. .. 4·00
329 6p. As No. 326 .. .. 1·00 1·00
330 14p. As No. 327 .. .. 3·50 3·50

(Des. A. G. Ryman. Litho. Questa.)

1974 (21 Aug.). *Military Uniforms (6th series). Multicoloured designs as* *T* **77.** *W* **w.12** (*sideways*). *P* 14.

331 4p. East Lancashire Regt., 1742 .. .. .. 15 15
332 6p. Somerset Light Infantry, 1833 .. .. .. 20 25
333 10p. Royal Sussex Regt., 1790 30 30
334 16p. R.A.F. Officer, 1974 .. 45 50

Nos. 331/4 have a short history of the regiment printed on the reverse side under the gum.

103. "Virgin with the Green Cushion" (Solario).

(Des. A. G. Ryman and M. Infante. Litho. Questa.)

1974 (5 Nov.). *Christmas.* *T* **103** *and similar vert. design. Multicoloured.* *W* **w.14.** *P* 14.

335 4p. Type **103** 12 15
336 6p. "Madonna of the Meadow" (Bellini) .. 20 25

104. Churchill and Houses of Parliament.

(Des. L. D. Curtis. Litho. Harrison.)

1974 (30 Nov.). *Birth Centenary of Sir Winston Churchill.* *T* **104** *and similar horiz. design.* *W* **w.12.** *P* 14 × 14½.

337 6p. black, reddish and light lavender 15 15
338 20p. brownish black, lake-brn. and light orange-red .. 45 45
MS339 114 × 93 mm. Nos. 337/8. W **w.12** (sideways). P 14 .. 65 65

Design:—20p. Churchill and battleship.

(Des. A. G. Ryman. Litho. Questa.)

1975 (14 Mar.). *Military Uniforms (7th series). Multicoloured designs as* *T* **77.** *W* **w.12** (*sideways*). *P* 14.

340 4p. East Surrey Regt., 1846 10 10
341 6p. Highland Light Infantry, 1777 .. .. 15 15
342 10p. Coldstream Guards, 1704 25 25
343 20p. Gibraltar Regt., 1974 .. 50 50

Nos. 340/3 have a short history of each regiment printed on the reverse side under the gum.

1975 (9 July). *As Nos.* 257/8 *but* *W* **w.14** (*sideways*).

344 1p. } Prince George of Cambridge Quarters and .. 5 5
345 1p. } Trinity Church .. 5 5

105. Girl Guides' Badge.

(Des. A. G. Ryman. Litho. Harrison.)

1975 (10 Oct.). *50th Anniv. of Gibraltar Girl Guides.* *W* **w. 12.** *P* 13 × 13½.

346 **105** 5p. gold, light blue and dull violet 12 12
347 ,, 7p. gold, sepia and light lake-brown 15 15
348 – 15p. silver, brownish black and yellow-brown .. 35 35

No. 348 is as T **105** but shows a different badge.

106. Child at Prayer.

(Des. A. G. Ryman. Litho. Walsall.)

1975 (26 Nov.). *Christmas.* *T* **106** *and similar vert. designs. Multicoloured.* *W* w.**14** (*sideways*). *P* 14.

349 6p. Type **106** 15 15
350 6p. "Angel" with lute .. 15 15
351 6p. Child singing carols with guitar 15 15
352 6p. Child with toddlers .. 15 15
353 6p. Young girl at prayer with candle 15 15
354 6p. Young boy with lamb .. 15 15
349/54 .. .. *Set of* 6 80 80

Nos. 349/54 were issued together *se-tenant* in small sheets of six (3×2) with the usual plate numbers and marginal inscriptions.

107. Bruges Madonna.

(Des. Jennifer Toombs. Litho. Walsall.)

1975 (17 Dec.). *500th Birth Anniv. of Michelangelo.* *T* **107** *and similar vert. designs. Multicoloured.*

(*a*) *W* w.**14** (*sideways*). *P* 14.

355 6p. Type **107** 15 15
356 9p. Taddei Madonna .. 20 20
357 15p. Pietà 35 35

(*b*) *No wmk. Imperf.* × *roul.* 5. *Self-adhesive.* (*From booklets.*)

358 6p. Type **107** 15 15
a. Booklet pane. Nos. 358/60 *se-tenant* 60
b. Booklet pane. Nos. 358 × 2, 359 × 2 and 360 × 2 1·25
359 9p. As No. 356 .. .. 20 20
360 15p. As No. 357 .. .. 35 35

108. Bicentennial Emblem and Arms of Gibraltar.

(Des. A. G. Ryman. Litho. Walsall.)

1976 (28 May). *Bicentenary of American Revolution.* *W* w.**14** (*inverted*). *P* 14.

361 **108** 25p. multicoloured .. 50 60
MS362 85×133 mm. No. 391×4 2·00

The edges of **MS**362 are rouletted.

(Des. A. G. Ryman. Litho. Walsall.)

1976 (21 July). *Military Uniforms* (*8th series*). *Multicoloured designs as* *T* **77**. *W* w.**14** (*inverted*). *P* 14.

363 1p. Suffolk Regt., 1795 .. 5 5
364 6p. Northamptonshire Regt., 1779 .. .. .. 12 15
365 12p. Lancashire Fusiliers, 1793 25 30
366 25p. Ordnance Corps, 1896 .. 50 50

Nos. 363/6 have a short history of each regiment printed on the reverse side under the gum.

109. The Holy Family.

(Des. A. G. Ryman. Litho. Questa.)

1976 (3 Nov.). *Christmas.* *T* **109** *and similar vert. designs showing stained-glass windows in St. Joseph's Church, Gibraltar. Multicoloured.* *W* w.**14**. *P* 14.

367 6p. Type **109** 12 15
368 9p. The Holy Family (*different*) 20 20
369 12p. Angel with dove 25 30
370 20p. Archangel Michael .. 40 45

110. Queen Elizabeth II, Royal Arms and Gibraltar Arms.

(Des. A. G. Ryman. Litho. J.W.)

1977 (7 Feb.). *Silver Jubilee.* *W* w.1
P 13½.

371 **110** 6p. multicoloured .. 12
372 ,, £1 multicoloured .. 2·00 2·
MS373 124×115 mm. Nos. 371/2 2·10

POSTAGE DUE STAMPS.

D 1

D 2

(Typo. De La Rue.)

1956 (1 Dec.). *Chalky paper. Wmk. Mul*
Script CA. *P* 14.

D1 **D 1** 1d. green 8 1
D2 ,, 2d. sepia 20 2
D3 ,, 4d. blue 50 5

1971 (15 Feb.). *As Nos.* D1/3 *but inscr. i*
decimal currency. *W* w.**12**. *P* 17½×18.

D4 **D 1** ½p. green 5
D5 ,, 1p. sepia 5
D6 ,, 2p. blue 5

(Des. A. G. Ryman. Litho. Questa.)

1976 (13 Oct.). *W* w.**14**. *P* 14×13½.

D 7 **D 2** 1p. light red-orange .. 5
D 8 ,, 3p. bright blue 5
D 9 ,, 5p. orange-vermilion .. 8 1
D10 ,, 7p. reddish violet .. 15 1
D11 ,, 10p. greenish slate .. 20 2
D12 ,, 20p. green 35 4
D7/12 .. .. *Set of* 6 80 9

GILBERT ISLANDS.

On 1st January 1976, the Gilbert Islands and Tuvalu (Ellice) Islands became separate Crown Colonies.

1. Charts of Gilbert Islands and Tuvalu (formerly Ellice) Islands.

(Des. J. E. Cooter. Litho. Questa.)

1976 (2 Jan.). *Separation of the Islands.* *T* **1** *and similar horiz. design. Multicoloured.* *W* w.**14** (*sideways*). *P* 14.

1	4 c. Type **1**	8	8
2	35 c. Maps of Tarawa and Funafuti	50	50

THE GILBERT ISLANDS

(2)

1976 (2 Jan.). *Nos.* 173/86 *of Gilbert & Ellice Is. optd. as T* **2**.

(*a*) *W* w.**12** (*sideways on Nos.* 5/7 *and* 9/10).

3	1 c. Cutting toddy (R.) ..	5	5
4	2 c. Lagoon fishing (R.) ..	12	12
5	2 c. Lagoon fishing (*wmk. sideways*) (R.)	12	12
6	3 c. Cleaning pandanus leaves (R.)	10·00	10·00
7	4 c. Casting nets (R.)	5	8
8	20 c. Beating a pandanus leaf (R.)	†	45·00
9	20 c. Beating a pandanus leaf (*wmk. sideways*) (R.) ..	50	50
10	25 c. Loading copra	20·00	
	a. Opt. double (Blk. + R.) ..	£125	

(*b*) *W* w.**14** (*sideways on* 3, 5, 20, 25 *and* 35 c.; *inverted on others*).

11	1 c. Cutting toddy (R.) ..	5	5
12	3 c. Cleaning pandanus leaves (R.)	5	8
13	5 c. Gilbertese canoe (R.) ..	8	10
14	6 c. De-husking coconuts ..	10	12
15	8 c. Weaving pandanus fronds (R.)	12	15
16	10 c. Weaving a basket ..	15	20
17	15 c. Tiger Shark	20	25
18	20 c. Beating a pandanus leaf (R.)	30	35
19	25 c. Loading copra ..	35	40
20	35 c. Fishing at night (Gold) ..	50	60
21	50 c. Local handicrafts	70	80
22	$1 Weaving coconut screen (R.)	1·40	1·60
	a. Opt. double	50·00	
3, 4, 7 and 12/22	.. *Set of* 14	3·75	4·00

3. M.V. *Teraaka*.

(Des. J. E. Cooter. Litho. Questa.)

1976 (1 July). *T* **3** *and similar horiz. designs. Multicoloured.* *W* w.**14** (*sideways*). *P* 14.

23	1 c. Type **3**	5	5
24	3 c. M.V. *Tautunu*	5	5
25	4 c. Moorish Idol	5	5
26	5 c. Hibiscus	5	8
27	6 c. Reef Egret	8	8
28	7 c. Tarawa Cathedral ..	8	10
29	8 c. Frangipani	10	10
30	10 c. Maneaba building ..	12	12
31	12 c. Betio Harbour	15	15
32	15 c. Evening scene	20	20
33	20 c. Marakei Atoll	25	25
34	35 c. Tanginteba Chapel ..	40	45
35	40 c. Flamboyant tree	45	50
36	50 c. *Hypolimnas bolina elliciana* (butterfly)	60	65
37	$1 Ferry *Tabakea*	1·25	1·40
38	$2 National flag	2·40	2·60
23/38	.. .. *Set of* 16	5·50	6·00

4. Church.

(Des. P. B. Powell. Litho. Questa.)

1976 (15 Sept.). *Christmas.* *T* **4** *and similar multicoloured designs showing children's drawings.* *W* w.**14** (*sideways on* 5 *and* 35 c.). *P* 14.

39	5 c. Type **4**	8	10
40	15 c. Feasting (*vert.*)	20	25
41	20 c. Maneaba (*vert.*)	30	35
42	35 c. Dancing	50	55

5. Porcupine Fish Helmet.

(Des. J. E. Cooter. Litho. J.W.)

1976 (6 Dec.). *Artefacts.* *T* **5** *and similar vert. designs. Multicoloured.* *W* w.**14**. *P* 13.

43	5 c. Type **5**	8	10
44	15 c. Shark's Teeth Dagger ..	20	25
45	20 c. Fighting Gauntlet ..	30	35
46	35 c. Coconut Body Armour ..	50	55
MS47	140×130 mm. Nos. 43/6. P 14.	1·10	

6. Queen in Coronation Robes.

(Des. J. E. Cooter. Litho. Questa.)

1977 (7 Feb.). *Silver Jubilee.* *T* **6** *and similar vert. designs. Multicoloured.* *W* w.**14**. *P* 14.

48	8 c. Prince Charles' visit, 1970	10	12
49	20 c. Prince Philip's visit, 1959	25	30
50	40 c. Type **6**	50	55

GILBERT AND ELLICE ISLANDS.

I. BRITISH PROTECTORATE.

GILBERT&ELLICE

PROTECTORATE

(1)

1911 (1 Jan.). *Stamps of Fiji optd. with* **T 1**. *Wmk. Mult. Crown CA.*

No.	Type	Description	Unused	Used
1	**23**	½d. green, O	3·75	12·00
2	,,	1d. red, O	20·00	22·00
3	**24**	2d. grey, O	5·00	9·00
4	**23**	2½d. ultramarine, O	8·00	11·00
5	,,	5d. pur. and olive-green, C	18·00	17·00
6	**24**	6d. dull & bright purple, C	20·00	18·00
7	**23**	1s. black/*green*, C (R.)	12·00	17·00
1/7		*Set of* 7	75·00	95·00
1/7 Optd. "Specimen"		*Set of* 7	£130	

The 2d. to 6d. are on special printings which were not issued without overprint.

2. Pandanus Pine.

3

(T **2** recess, T **3** typo. D.L.R.)

1911. *Wmk. Mult. Crown CA.* P 14.

No.	Type	Description	Unused	Used
8	**2**	½d. green	80	2·75
9	,,	1d. carmine	95	2·75
10	,,	2d. grey	95	2·75
11	,,	2½d. blue	95	3·25
8/11 Optd. "Specimen"		*Set of* 4	32·00	

1912–24. *Wmk. Mult. Crown CA.* P 14.

No.	Type	Description	Unused	Used
12	**3**	½d. green, O	35	55
		a. *Yellow-green* (1914)	55	80
13	,,	1d. carmine, O	45	80
		a. *Scarlet* (1916)	1·25	1·75
14	,,	2d. greyish slate, O (1916)	3·75	5·00
15	,,	2½d. bright blue, O (1916)	1·40	2·75
16	,,	3d. purple/*yellow*, C (1919)	55	1·60
17	,,	4d. black & red/*yellow*, C	65	1·75
18	,,	5d. dull pur. & sage-grn., C	2·00	5·50
19	,,	6d. dull & bright purple, C	80	4·00
20	,,	1s. black/*green*, C	2·75	5·50
21	,,	2s. purple and blue/*blue*, C	11·00	14·00
22	,,	2s. 6d. black & red/*blue*, C	12·00	15·00
23	,,	5s. green and red/*yellow*, C	15·00	20·00
24	,,	£1 purple and black/*red*, C (Die II) (1924)	£225	£350
12/24		*Set of* 13	£250	£400
12/24 Optd. "Specimen"		*Set of* 13	£150	

II. CROWN COLONY.

WAR TAX

(5)

1918 (June). *Optd. with* **T 5**.

No.	Type	Description	Unused	Used
26	**3**	1d. red (Optd. S. £14)	25	1·00

1922–27. *Wmk. Mult. Script CA.* P 14.

No.	Type	Description	Unused	Used
27	**3**	½d. green, O (1923)	20	55
28	,,	1d. violet, O (1927)	55	80
29	,,	1½d. scarlet, O (1924)	95	1·10
30	,,	2d. slate-grey, O	1·40	2·00
35	,,	10s. grn. & red/*emer.*, C ('24)	60·00	70·00
27/35 Optd. "Specimen"		*Set of* 5	60·00	

1935 (6 May). *Silver Jubilee. As Nos.* 91/4 *of Antigua, but ptd. by B.W.* P 11×12.

No.	Description	Unused	Used
36	1d. ultramarine & grey-black	65	1·75
37	1½d. deep blue and scarlet	65	1·75
38	3d. brown and deep blue	2·50	3·50
39	1s. slate and purple	7·50	9·00
36/9 Perf. "Specimen"	*Set of* 4	18·00	

1937 (12 May). *Coronation. As Nos.* 13/5 *of Aden*

No.	Description	Unused	Used
40	1d. violet	8	12
41	1½d. scarlet	15	25
42	3d. bright blue	25	30
40/2 Perf. "Specimen"	*Set of* 3	12·00	

6. Frigate Bird.

7. Pandanus Pine.

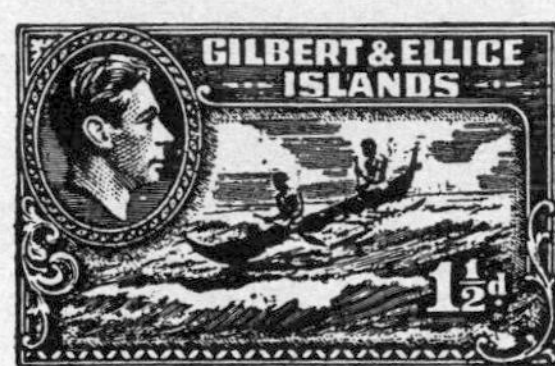

8. Canoe crossing Reef.

9. Canoe and Boat-house.

10. Native House.

11. Seascape.

12. Ellice Is. Canoe.

13. Coconut Palms.

14. Cantilever Jetty, Ocean Is.

15. H.M.C.S. *Nimanoa*.

16. Gilbert Is. Canoe.

17. Coat of Arms.

(Recess. Bradbury, Wilkinson (½d., 2d., 2s. 6d.), Waterlow (1d., 5d., 6d., 2s., 5s.), De La Rue (1½d., 2½d., 3d., 1s.).)

1939 (14 Jan.)–**55.** *Wmk. Mult. Script CA (sideways on ½d., 2d. and 2s. 6d.).*

No.	Type	Description	Unused	Used
43	**6**	½d. slate-blue & blue-green (*p.* 11½×11)	12	25
44	**7**	1d. emerald-green & purple (*p.* 12½)	12	25
45	**8**	1½d. blk. & carm. (*p.* 13½)	25	35
46	**9**	2d. red-brown and black (*p.* 11½×11)	15	40
47	**10**	2½d. blk. & ol.-grn. (*p.* 13½)	15	40
48	**11**	3d. blk. & ultram. (*p.* 13½)	20	30
		a. Perf. 12. *Black and bright blue* (24.8.55)	45	50
49	**12**	5d. brt. bl. & sepia (*p.* 12½)	65	55
50	**13**	6d. ol.-grn. & vio. (*p.* 12½)	45	55

51 **14** 1s. blk. & turq.-bl. (*p.* 13½) 35 55
a. Perf. 12 (8.5.51) .. .. 1·40 1·75
52 **15** 2s. brt. bl. & verm. (*p.* 12½) 2·00 2·35
53 **16** 2s. 6d. blue and emerald-green (*p.* 11½×11) .. 2·50 3·50
54 **17** 5s. scar. & brt. bl. (*p.* 12½) 4·50 5·50
43/54 .. .. *Set of* 12 11·00 14·00
43/54 Perf. "Specimen" *Set of* 12 30·00

1946 (16 Dec.). *Victory. As Nos.* 28/9 *of Aden.*
55 1d. purple 10 12
56 3d. blue 12 12
55/6 Perf. "Specimen" *Set of* 2 10·00

1949 (29 Aug.). *Royal Silver Wedding. As Nos.* 30/1 *of Aden.*
57 1d. violet 10 15
58 £1 scarlet .. .. 9·50 14·00

1949 (10 Oct.). *75th Anniv. of U.P.U. As Nos.* 114/7 *of Antigua.*
59 1d. purple 20 30
60 2d. grey-black 25 40
61 3d. deep blue 40 55
62 1s. blue .. .. 95 1·40

1953 (2 June). *Coronation. As No.* 47 *of Aden.*
63 2d. black and grey-black .. 35 40

18. Frigate Bird.

(Recess. B.W. (½d., 2d., 2s. 6d.), Waterlow (1d., 5d., 6d., 2s., 5s.), D.L.R. (2½d., 3d., 1s., 10s.) and after 1962, 1d., 5d.)

1956 (1 Aug.). *As T* **6/17** (*but Queen's portrait as in T* **18**). *Wmk. Mult. Script CA. P* 11½×11 (*½d., 2d., 2s. 6d.*), 12½ (*1d., 5d., 6d., 2s., 5s.*) *or* 12 (*2½d., 3d., 1s., 10s.*).
64 **18** ½d. black & dp. bright blue 8 8
65 **7** 1d. brn. olive & dp. violet 8 8
66 **9** 2d. bluish green and deep purple (*shades*) .. 10 12
67 **10** 2½d. black & myrtle-green .. 10 12
68 **11** 3d. black and carmine-red 12 15
69 **12** 5d. ultramarine and red-orange (*shades*) .. 20 25
70 **13** 6d. chestnut & black-brown 25 30
71 **14** 1s. black and bronze-green 45 60
72 **15** 2s. dp. bright blue & sepia 1·50 2·00
73 **16** 2s. 6d. scarlet & deep blue 1·50 2·00
74 **17** 5s. grnish. bl. & bluish grn. 4·00 4·50
75 **8** 10s. black and turquoise .. 9·00 10·00
64/75 .. .. *Set of* 12 16·00 18·00
See also Nos. 85/6.

19. Loading Phosphate from Cantilever.

20. Phosphate Rock.

21. Phosphate-mining.

(Des. R. Turrell (2d.), M. Thoma (2½d.), M. A. W. Hook and A. Larkins (1s.). Photo. De La Rue.)

1960 (1 May). *Diamond Jubilee of Phosphate Discovery at Ocean Island. W* w. **12**. *P* 12.
76 **19** 2d. green & carmine-rose 30 30
77 **20** 2½d. black and olive-green .. 35 35
78 **21** 1s. black & dp. turquoise 95 1·10

1963 (1 Aug.). *Freedom from Hunger. As No.* 76 *of Aden.*
79 10d. ultramarine .. .. 2·50 2·50

1963 (5 Oct). *Red Cross Centenary. As Nos.* 147/8 *of Antigua.*
80 2d. red and black 15 20
81 10d. red and blue .. .. 2·00 2·00

22. D.H. "Heron" Aircraft and Route Map.

24. D.H. "Heron" Aircraft over Tarawa Lagoon.

23. Heron in Flight.

(Des. Mrs. Margaret Barwick. Litho. Enschedé.)

1964 (20 July). *First Air Service. W* w.**12** (*sideways, 3d., 3s. 7d.*). *P* 11×11½ (*1s.*) *or* 11½×11 (*others*).
82 **22** 3d. blue, black and lt. blue 15 15
83 **23** 1s. lt. blue, black & dp. blue 30 30
84 **24** 3s. 7d. deep green, black and light emerald .. .. 1·25 1·40

No. 82 exists with watermark showing Crown to right or left of "CA". *Prices same either way.*

(Recess. B.W. (2d.), D.L.R. (6d.).)

1964 (30 Oct.)–**65**. *As Nos.* 66 *and* 70 *but wmk.* w.**12**.
85 **9** 2d. bluish green and purple 15 20
86 **13** 6d. chestnut and black-brown (4.5.65) 30 35

1965 (4 June). *I.T.U. Centenary. As Nos.* 166/7 *of Antigua.*
87 3d. red-orge. & dp. bluish grn. 12 15
88 2s. 6d. turquoise-blue and light purple 85 90

25. Maneaba and Gilbertese Man blowing Bu Shell.

26. Ellice Islanders Reef-fishing by Flare.

27. Gilbertese Girl weaving Head-garland.

28. Gilbertese Woman performing Ruoia.

29. Gilbertese Man performing Kamei.

30. Gilbertese Girl drawing Water.

31. Ellice Islander performing a Fatele.

32. Ellice Youths performing Spear Dance.

33. Gilbertese Girl tending Ikaroa Babai plant.

34. Ellice Islanders dancing a Fatele.

35. Ellice Islanders pounding Pulaka.

(*T* **26/35** *are vert. as T* **25.**)

36. Gilbertese Women's Dance.

37. Gilbertese Boys playing a Stick Game.

38. Ellice Youths beating the Box for the Fatele.

39. Coat-of-Arms.

(*T* **37/9** *are horiz. as T* **36.**)

(Des. V. Whiteley, from drawings by Mrs. D. R. Barwick. Litho. B.W.)

1965 (16 Aug.). *Centres multicoloured. W* w.**12**. *P* 12×11 (*vert.*) *or* 11×12 (*horiz.*).
89 **25** ½d. turquoise-green .. 5 5
90 **26** 1d. deep violet-blue .. 5 5
91 **27** 2d. bistre 5 5
92 **28** 3d. rose-red 8 10
93 **29** 4d. purple 10 12
94 **30** 5d. cerise 12 15
95 **31** 6d. turquoise-blue .. 15 20
96 **32** 7d. bistre-brown 20 25
97 **33** 1s. bluish violet 25 30
98 **34** 1s. 6d. lemon 50 60
99 **35** 2s. yellow-olive 75 90
100 **36** 3s. 7d. new blue .. .. 1·10 1·25
101 **37** 5s. light yellow-olive .. 1·50 1·75
102 **38** 10s. dull green .. .. 3·50 4·00
103 **39** £1 light turquoise-blue .. 7·00 8·00
89/103 .. .. *Set of* 15 14·00 16·00

1965 (25 Oct.). *International Co-operation Year. As Nos.* 168/9 *of Antigua.*
104 ½d. reddish pur. & turq.-grn. 5 5
105 3s. 7d. dp. bluish grn. & lav. 90 95

1966 (24 Jan.). *Churchill Commemoration. As Nos.* 170/3 *of Antigua.*
106 ½d. new blue 5 5
107 3d. deep green 12 12
108 3s. brown 85 90
109 3s. 7d. bluish violet .. .. 95 1·00

(New currency. 100 cents = $1 Australian.)

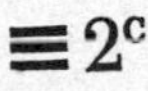

(40)

1966 (14 Feb.). *Decimal currency. Nos.* 89/103 *surch. as T* **40**.
110 **26** 1 c. on 1d. dp. violet-blue 5 5
111 **27** 2 c. on 2d. bistre .. 5 5
112 **28** 3 c. on 3d. rose-red .. 5 5
113 **25** 4 c. on ½d. turquoise-grn. 5 5
114 **31** 5 c. on 6d. turquoise-blue 8 10
115 **29** 6 c. on 4d. purple .. 10 10
116 **30** 8 c. on 5d. cerise .. 12 12
117 **33** 10 c. on 1s. bluish violet .. 15 20
118 **32** 15 c. on 7d. bistre-brown 20 25
119 **34** 20 c. on 1s. 6d. lemon .. 40 50
120 **35** 25 c. on 2s. yellow-olive .. 65 75
121 **36** 35 c. on 3s. 7d. new blue .. 75 90
122 **37** 50 c. on 5s. lt. yellow-olive 1·00 1·10
123 **38** $1 on 10s. dull green .. 2·25 2·50
124 **39** $2 on £1 lt. turq.-blue .. 4·25 4·75
110/124 .. .. *Set of* 15 9·00 10·00

1966 (1 July). *World Cup Football Championships. As Nos.* 176/7 *of Antigua.*
125 3 c. violet, yellow-green, lake and yellow-brown .. 10 10
126 35 c. chocolate, blue-grn., lake and yellow-brown .. 80 85

1966 (20 Sept.). *Inauguration of W.H.O. Headquarters, Geneva. As Nos.* 178/9 *of Antigua.*
127 3 c. black, yellow-green and light blue 10 10
128 12 c. black, light purple and yellow-brown 45 45

1966 (1 Dec.). *20th Anniv. of U.N.E.S.C.O. As Nos.* 196/8 *of Antigua.*
129 5 c. slate-violet, red, yellow and orange 10 12
130 10 c. orange-yellow, violet and deep olive 30 30
131 20 c. black, brt. pur. and orge. 55 55

41. H.M.S. *Royalist.*

42. Trading Post.

43. Island Family.

(Des. V. Whiteley. Photo. Harrison.)

1967 (1 Sept.). *75th Anniv. of the Protectorate. W* **w.12.** *P* 14½.

132	**41**	3 c. red, blue and myrtle-green . .	8	8
133	**42**	10 c. multicoloured . .	25	25
134	**43**	35 c. sepia, orange-yellow and deep bluish green	75	80

44. Gilbertese Women's Dance.

1968 (1 Jan.). *Decimal Currency. Designs as T* **25**, *etc., but with values inscr. in decimal currency as T* **44**. *Centres multicoloured. W* **w.12** *(sideways on horiz. values). P* 12×11 *(vert.) or* 11×12 *(horiz.).*

135	**26**	1 c. deep violet-blue . .	5	5
136	**27**	2 c. bistre	5	5
137	**28**	3 c. rose-red	5	5
138	**25**	4 c. turquoise-green . .	8	8
139	**31**	5 c. turquoise-blue . .	10	10
140	**29**	6 c. purple	12	12
141	**30**	8 c. cerise	15	15
142	**33**	10 c. bluish violet . .	20	25
143	**32**	15 c. bistre-brown . .	25	30
144	**34**	20 c. lemon	35	40
145	**35**	25 c. yellow-olive	50	55
146	**44**	35 c. new blue	70	90
147	**37**	50 c. light yellow-olive . .	1·10	1·25
148	**38**	$1 dull green	2·25	2·50
149	**39**	$2 light turquoise-blue . .	4·25	4·75
135/49		. . . . *Set of* 15	9·00	10·00

45. Map of Tarawa Atoll.

(Des. V. Whiteley. Photo. De La Rue.)

1968 (21 Nov.). *25th Anniv. of the Battle of Tarawa. T* **45** *and similar designs. Multicoloured. W* **w.12** *(sideways). P* 14.

150		3 c. Type **45**	10	10
151		10 c. Marines landing . .	20	20
152		15 c. Beach-head assault . .	30	30
153		35 c. Raising U.S. and British flags	80	80

46. Young Pupil against outline of Abemama Island.

(Des. J. Waddington Ltd. (from original designs by Mrs. V. J. Andersen and Miss A. Loveridge). Litho. De La Rue.)

1969 (2 June). *End of Inaugural Year of South Pacific University. T* **46** *and similar horiz. designs. W* **w.12** *(sideways). P* 12½.

154	3 c. multicoloured	12	12
155	10 c. multicoloured	20	20
156	35 c. blk., brn. & grey-green	75	80

Designs:—10 c. Boy and girl students and Tarawa atoll; 35 c. University graduate and South Pacific islands.

47. "Virgin and Child" in Pacific Setting.

(Des. Jennifer Toombs. Litho. Bradbury, Wilkinson.)

1969 (20 Oct.). *Christmas. W* **w.12** *(sideways). P* 11½.

157	–	2 c. olive-green and multi-coloured *(shades)* . .	30	30
158	**47**	10 c. olive-green and multi-coloured *(shades)* . .	80	80

Design: 2 c. As T **47** but foreground has grass instead of sand.

48. "The Kiss of Life".

(Des. Manate Tenang Manate. Litho. J. Waddington Ltd.)

1970 (9 Mar.*). *Centenary of British Red Cross. W* **w.12** *(sideways). P* 14.

159	**48**	10 c. multicoloured . .	25	25
160	–	15 c. multicoloured . .	35	35
161	–	35 c. multicoloured . .	70	75

Nos. 160/1 are as T **48**, but arranged differently.

*The above were released by the Crown Agents on 2nd March, but not sold locally until the 9th.

49. Foetus and Patients.

50. Nurse and Surgical Instruments.

51. X-ray Plate and Technician.

52. U.N. Emblem and Map.

(Des. Jennifer Toombs. Litho. Enschedé.)

1970 (26 June). *25th Anniv. of United Nations. W* **w.12** *(sideways). P* 12½×13.

162	**49**	5 c. mauve, reddish lilac, black and lilac . .	12	12
163	**50**	10 c. black, grey and red . .	25	25
164	**51**	15 c. blue, green, black and yellow	30	30
165	**52**	35 c. new blue, black and turquoise-green . .	80	85

53. Map of Gilbert Islands.

54. Sailing-Ship *John Williams III.* *(Vert.)*

55. Rev. S. J. Whitmee. *(Vert.)*

56. M.V. *John Williams VII.* *(Horiz.)*

(Des. G. L. Vasarhelyi. Litho. Harrison.)

1970 (1 Sept.). *Centenary of Landing in Gilbert Islands by London Missionary Society. W* **w.12** *(sideways on vert. designs). P* 14½×14 *(2 c., 35 c.) or* 14×14½ *(others.).*

166	**53**	2 c. multicoloured . .	10	10
167	**54**	10 c. black and pale green	25	25
168	**55**	25 c. chestnut and cobalt . .	45	50
169	**56**	35 c. turquoise-blue, black and red	80	85

57. Child with Halo.

58. Sanctuary, Tarawa Cathedral.

59. Three Ships inside Star.

(Des. L. D. Curtis, based on sketches by T. Collis (2 c.), Mrs. A. Burroughs (10 c.), Mrs. C. Barnett (35 c.). Litho. Format.)

1970 (3 Oct.). *Christmas. W* **w.12.** *P* 14½.

170	**57**	2 c. multicoloured . .	5	5
171	**58**	10 c. multicoloured . .	30	30
172	**59**	35 c. multicoloured . .	85	90

60. Casting Nets.

)es. G. Drummond. Litho. Walsall Security Printers.)

71 (31 MAY). *T* **60** *and similar multicoloured designs. W* **w.12** *(sideways on horiz. designs and upright on vert. designs). P* 14.

'3	1 c. Cutting toddy	5	5
'4	2 c. Lagoon fishing	5	5
'5	3 c. Cleaning pandanus leaves	5	5
'6	4 c. Type **60**	5	5
'7	5 c. Gilbertese canoe ..	8	10
'8	6 c. De-husking coconuts ..	10	10
'9	8 c. Weaving pandanus fronds	12	15
o	10 c. Weaving a basket ..	15	20
ı	15 c. Tiger shark and fishermen	30	30
2	20 c. Beating a rolled pandanus leaf	35	40
3	25 c. Loading copra	40	45
4	35 c. Fishing at night ..	55	65
5	50 c. Local Handicrafts ..	85	1·00
6	$1 Weaving coconut screens	1·75	2·00
7	$2 Coat-of-Arms	3·50	3·75
'3/87	.. .. *Set of* 15	7·50	8·50

The 1 c., 6 c. to 15 c., 50 c., $1 and $2 are ertical designs, and the remainder horizontal.

See also No. 203/7.

61. House of Representatives.

(Des. V. Whiteley. Litho. J.W.)

71 (1 AUG.). *New Constitution. T* **61** *and similar horiz. design. Multicoloured. W* **w.12** *(sideways). P* 14.

8	3 c. Type **61**	8	8
9	10 c. Maneaba Betio (Assembly hut) ..	25	30

62. Pacific Nativity Scene.

)es. J. D. Curtis and T. J. Collis. Litho. Questa.)

71 (1 OCT.). *Christmas. T* **62** *and similar vert. designs. W* **w.12.** *P* 14 × 14½.

o	3 c. black, yell. & ultram.	10	10
ı	10 c. black, gold & turq.-blue	30	30
2	35 c. black, gold & magenta	75	80

Designs:—10 c. Star and palm leaves; 35 c. utrigger canoe and star.

63. Emblem and Young Boys.

(Des. G. L. Vasarhelyi. Litho. Questa.)

1971 (11 DEC.). *25th Anniv. of UNICEF. T* **63** *and similar horiz. designs, each showing the UNICEF Emblem. Multicoloured. W* **w.12** *(sideways). P* 14.

193	3 c. Type **63**	8	8
194	10 c. Young boy	30	30
195	35 c. Young boy's face ..	75	80

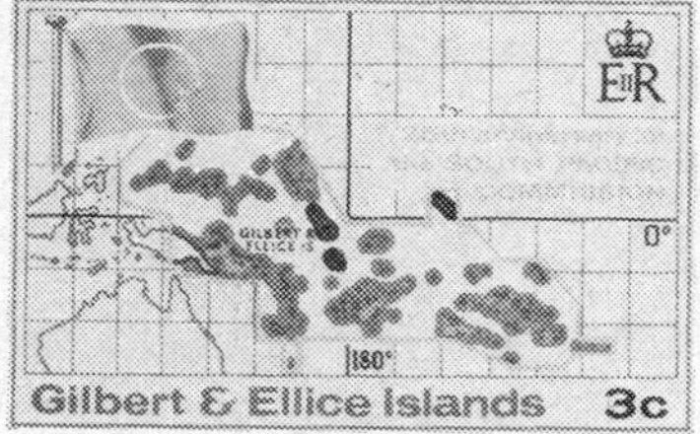

64. Flag and Map of South Pacific.

(Des. A. S. B. New. Litho. Questa.)

1972 (21 FEB.). *25th Anniv. of South Pacific Commission. T* **64** *and similar horiz. designs. Multicoloured. W* **w.12.** *P* 13½.

196	3 c. Type **64**	8	8
197	10 c. Flag and native boats ..	20	20
198	35 c. Flags of member nations	75	75

65. *Alveopora.*

(Des. Sylvia Goaman after original designs by H. Wickison. Litho. Questa.)

1972 (26 MAY). *Coral. T* **65** *and similar horiz. designs. Multicoloured. W* **w.12** *(sideways). P* 14.

199	3 c. Type **65**	5	5
200	10 c. *Euphyllia*	25	25
201	15 c. *Melithea*	30	30
202	35 c. *Spongodes*	75	75

1972 (7 SEPT.)–**73.** *As Nos.* 173 *etc., but W* **w.12** *(sideways on 6, 15 and 20 c. and upright on others).*

203	2 c. Lagoon fishing (13.6.73)	5	5
204	5 c. Gilbertese canoe ..	8	10
205	6 c. De-husking coconuts (13.6.73)	10	10
206	15 c. Tiger shark and fishermen	25	30
207	20 c. Beating a rolled pandanus leaf	40	40
203/7	.. .. *Set of* 5	75	85

66. Star of Peace.

(Des. T. Matarena (35 c.), Father Bermond (others). Adapted by Jennifer Toombs. Litho. Questa.)

1972 (15 SEPT.). *Christmas. T* **66** *and similar multicoloured designs. W* **w.12** *(sideways on 3 and 10 c.). P* 13½.

208	3 c. Type **66**	5	5
209	10 c. The "Nativity" ..	30	30
210	35 c. Baby in "manger" (*horiz.*)	70	75

67. Floral Head-dresses.

(Des. (from photograph by D. Groves) and photo. Harrison.)

1972 (20 NOV.). *Royal Silver Wedding. Multicoloured; background colour given. W* **w.12.** *P* 14 × 14½.

211 **67**	3 c. brown-olive ..	10	10
212 ,,	35 c. lake-brown ..	75	80

68. Funafuti ("The Land of Bananas").

(Des. H. Wickison; adapted J. E. Cooter. Litho. Walsall.)

1973 (5 MAR.). *Legends of Island Names (1st series). T* **68** *and similar horiz. designs. Multicoloured. W* **w.12.** *P* 14½ × 14.

213	3 c. Type **68**	5	5
214	10 c. Butaritari ("The Smell of the Sea")	25	25
215	25 c. Tarawa ("The Centre of the World") ..	45	50
216	35 c. Abemama ("The Land of the Moon") ..	70	75

See also Nos. 252/5.

69. Dancer.

(Des. Sister Juliette (3 c.), R. P. Turner (10 and 35 c.), C. Potts (50 c.); adapted Jennifer Toombs. Litho. Questa.)

1973 (24 SEPT.). *Christmas. T* **69** *and similar vert. designs. Multicoloured. W* **w.12** *(sideways). P* 14.

217	3 c. Type **69**	5	5
218	10 c. Canoe and lagoon ..	25	25
219	35 c. Lagoon at evening ..	60	65
220	50 c. Map of Christmas Island	80	90

1973 (14 Nov.). *Royal Wedding. As Nos.* 165/6 *of Anguilla. Centre multicoloured. W* w.**12** *(sideways). P* 13½.

221	3 c. pale green	5	5
222	35 c. Prussian blue	50	55

70. Meteorological Observation.

(Des. E. S. Cheek; adapted PAD Studio. Litho. Questa.)

1973 (26 Nov.). *I.M.O./W.M.O. Centenary. T* **70** *and similar horiz. designs. Multicoloured. W* w.**12**. *P* 14.

223	3 c. Type **70**	5	5
224	10 c. Island observing-station	20	20
225	35 c. Wind-finding radar ..	55	60
226	50 c. World weather watch stations	90	95

71. Te Mataaua Crest.

(Des. J. E. Cooter. Litho. Questa.)

1974 (4 Mar.). *Canoe Crests. T* **71** *and similar horiz. designs showing sailing craft and the canoe crests given. Multicoloured. W* w.**12**. *P* 13½.

227	3 c. Type **71**	5	5
228	10 c. Te Nimta-wawa.. ..	20	25
229	35 c. Tara-tara-venei-na ..	60	65
230	50 c. Te Bou-uoua	85	90
MS231	154×130 mm. Nos. 227/30	1·75	2·00

72. £1 Stamp of 1924 and Te Koroba (canoe).

(Des. E. S. Cheek; adapted J. E. Cooter. Litho. Questa.)

1974 (10 June). *Centenary of Universal Postal Union. T* **72** *and similar horiz. designs. W* w.**12**. *P* 14.

232	4 c. multicoloured	5	8
233	10 c. multicoloured	20	25
234	25 c. multicoloured	45	50
235	35 c. light vermilion & black	60	65

Designs:—10 c. 5s. stamp of 1939 and sailing vessel *Kiakia*; 25 c. $2 stamp of 1971 and B.A.C. "1–11"; 35 c. U.P.U. emblem.

73. Toy Canoe.

(Des. H. Wickison and G. J. Hayward; adapted J. E. Cooter. Litho. Questa.)

1974 (5 Sept.). *Christmas. T* **73** *and similar horiz. designs. Multicoloured. W* w.**12** *(sideways). P* 14.

236	4 c. Type **73**	5	8
237	10 c. Toy windmill	20	25
238	25 c. Coconut "ball"	45	50
239	35 c. Canoes and constellation Pleiades	55	60

74. North Front Entrance, Blenheim Palace.

(Des. J. E. Cooter. Litho. Questa.)

1974 (30 Nov.). *Birth Centenary of Sir Winston Churchill. T* **74** *and similar vert. designs. Multicoloured. W* w.**14**. *P* 14.

240	4 c. Type **74**	5	5
241	10 c. Churchill painting ..	20	25
242	35 c. Churchill's statue, London	55	60

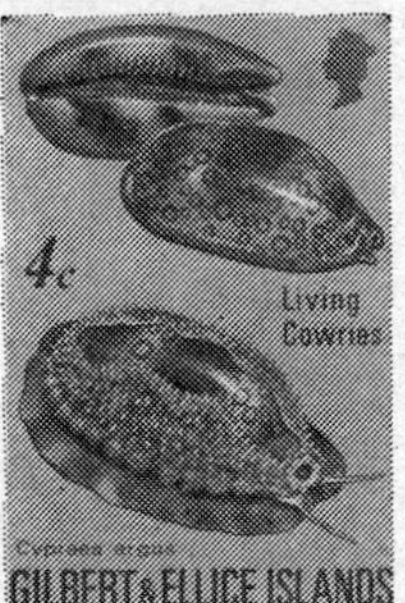

75. *Carpilius maculatus.*

(Des. J. E. Cooter. Litho. Questa.)

1975 (27 Jan.). *Crabs. T* **75** *and similar horiz. designs. Multicoloured. W* w. **12** *(sideways). P* 14.

243	4 c. Type **75**	5	5
244	10 c. *Ranina ranina*	20	25
245	25 c. *Portunus pelagicus* ..	40	45
246	35 c. *Ocypode ceratophthalma*	50	60

76. Eyed Cowrie.

(Des. E. S. Cheek; adapted J. E. Cooter. Litho. Questa.)

1975 (26 May). *Cowrie Shells. T* **76** *and similar vert. designs. Multicoloured. W* w.**14**. *P* 14.

247	4 c. Type **76**	5	5
248	10 c. Sieve Cowrie	15	15
249	25 c. Mole Cowrie	40	40
250	35 c. Map Cowrie	50	55
MS251	146×137 mm. Nos. 247/50	1·10	1·25

(Des. J. E. Cooter. Litho. Questa.)

1975 (1 Aug.). *Legends of Island Names* (2 *series). Horiz. designs as T* **68**. *Mul coloured. W* w.**12** *(sideways). P* 14.

252	4 c. Beru ("The Bud") ..	5	
253	10 c. Onotoa ("Six Giants")	15	
254	25 c. Abaiang ("Land to the North")	40	
255	35 c. Marakei ("Fish-trap floating on eaves") ..	50	

77. "Christ is Born".

(Des. C. J. Barnett (4 and 25 c.), Philatelic A visory Committee (10 c.), P. T. Burangke (35 c. adapted J. E. Cooter. Litho. Questa.)

1975 (22 Sept.). *Christmas. T* **77** *and simil vert. designs. Multicoloured. W* w.**14**. *P* 1

256	4 c. Type **77**	5	
257	10 c. Protestant Chapel, Tarawa	15	
258	25 c. Catholic Church, Ocean Island	40	
259	35 c. Fishermen and star ..	50	

POSTAGE DUE STAMPS.

GILBERT & ELLICE ISLANDS

1d.

POSTAGE DUE

D 1

(Typo. B.W.)

1940. *Wmk. Mult. Script CA. P* 12.

D1	**D 1** 1d. emerald-green ..	15	
D2	„ 2d. scarlet..	20	
D3	„ 3d. brown	25	
D4	„ 4d. blue	30	1·
D5	„ 5d. grey-green	40	1·
D6	„ 6d. purple	50	1·
D7	„ 1s. violet	80	5·
D8	„ 1s. 6d. turquoise-green ..	2·25	10·
D1/8	.. .. *Set of* 8	4·25	19·
D1/8	Perf. "Specimen" *Set of* 8	40·00	

Stamps for the Gilbert and Ellice Islands we withdrawn on 31st December 1975 when t separate colonies of the Gilbert Islands ar Tuvalu were created. For later issues see und these titles.

GOLD COAST.

CROWN COLONY.

1

ONE
PENNY.

(2)

(Typo. De La Rue.)

1875 (JULY). *Wmk. Crown CC. P* 12½.
1 **1** 1d. blue .. .. .. £150 22·00
2 ,, 4d. magenta .. .. .. £180 28·00
3 ,, 6d. orange .. .. .. £225 28·00

1876–79. *Wmk. Crown CC. P* 14.
4 **1** ½d. olive-yellow (1879) .. 11·00 11·00
5 ,, 1d. blue .. .. .. 6·00 3·50
a. Bisected diag. (½d.) (on cover) † £500
6 ,, 2d. green (1879) .. .. 13·00 7·00
a. Bisected diag. (1d.) (on cover) † £550
7 ,, 4d. magenta .. .. .. 70·00 4·50
a. Quartered (1d.) (on cover) .. † £1300
8 ,, 6d. orange .. .. .. 35·00 8·50

1883 (MAY). *No. 7 surch. locally.*
8*a* **1** "1d." on 4d. magenta ..

1883. *Wmk. Crown CA. P* 14.
9 **1** ½d. olive-yellow (Jan.) .. 45·00 13·00
10 ,, 1d. blue (May) .. .. £200 20·00

1884 (AUG.)–**91.** *Wmk. Crown CA. P* 14.
11 **1** ½d. green 25 25
a. Dull green 25 30
12 ,, 1d. rose-carmine 30 30
a. Carmine 30 20
b. Bisected diag. (½d.) on cover † £850
13 ,, 2d. grey .. .. .. 85 1·00
a. Value omitted .. ..
b. Slate 75 65
14 ,, 2½d. ultram. & orge. (13.3.91) 50 50
15 ,, 3d. olive-yellow (9.89) .. 2·00 2·00
a. Olive .. .. .. 1·25 2·00
16 ,, 4d. deep mauve (3.85) .. 85 85
a. Rosy mauve .. .. 1·10 1·00
17 ,, 6d. orange (1.89) .. .. 1·25 1·10
a. Orange-brown .. .. 2·00 1·00
18 ,, 1s. violet (1888) .. .. 6·50 5·50
a. Bright mauve .. .. 2·00 1·10
19 ,, 2s. yellow-brown (1888) .. 25·00 9·50
a. Deep brown .. .. 6·50 5·50
11/19*a* .. .. *Set of* 9 12·00 11·00
14/15, 18/19 Optd. "Specimen" *Set of* 4 38·00

1889 (MAR.). *No.* 17 *surch. with T* **2.**
20 **1** 1d. on 6d. orange .. .. 25·00 13·00

In some sheets examples may be found with the bar and "PENNY" spaced 8 mm., the normal spacing being 7 mm.

3

4

1889 (SEPT.)–**94.** *Wmk. Crown CA. P* 14.
22 **3** 5s. dull mauve and blue .. 12·00 6·50
23 ,, 10s. dull mauve and red .. 25·00 9·00
a. Dull mauve and carmine 45·00 23·00
24 ,, 20s. green and red £1400
25 ,, 20s. dull mauve and black/*red* ('94) 48·00 12·00
22/25 Optd. "Specimen" *Set of* 4 £160

1898–1902. *Wmk. Crown CA. P* 14.
26 **3** ½d. dull mauve and green 15 15
27 ,, 1d. dull mauve and rose .. 20 20
27*a* **4** 2d. dull mauve & orange-red (1902) .. .. 4·50 5·50
28 **3** 2½d. dull mauve & ultram. 1·60 3·00
29 **4** 3d. dull mauve and orange 1·50 1·10
30 ,, 6d. dull mauve and violet 1·10 1·10
31 **3** 1s. green and black .. 2·50 2·75
32 ,, 2s. green and carmine .. 6·50 5·50
33 ,, 5s. green & mauve (1900) 15·00 6·50
34 ,, 10s. green & brown (1900) 30·00 9·50
26/34 .. .. *Set of* 10 55·00 32·00
26/34 Optd. "Specimen" *Set of* 10 65·00

1901 (6 OCT.). *Nos.* 28 *and* 30 *surch. with T* **2.**
35 1d. on 2½d. dull mve. & ultram. 45 1·60
36 1d. on 6d. dull mve. & violet 45 1·60
a. "ONE" omitted £110 £120

6

7

1902. *Wmk. Crown CA. P* 14.
38 **6** ½d. dull purple and green .. 35 40
39 ,, 1d. dull purple and carmine 20 40
40 **7** 2d. dull purple & orge.-red 80 80
41 **6** 2½d. dull purple and ultram. 2·75 2·75
42 **7** 3d. dull purple and orange 1·40 55
43 ,, 6d. dull purple and violet .. 1·50 1·25
44 **6** 1s. green and black .. 1·60 2·00
45 ,, 2s. green and carmine .. 9·00 6·50
46 ,, 5s. green and mauve .. 12·00 9·00
47 ,, 10s. green and brown .. 22·00 18·00
48 ,, 20s. purple and black/*red* .. 55·00 42·00
38/48 .. .. *Set of* 11 95·00 75·00
38/48 Optd. "Specimen" *Set of* 11 65·00

1904–7. *Wmk. Mult. Crown CA. P* 14.
49 **6** ½d. dull pur. & grn., O ('07) 65 30
50 ,, 1d. dull pur. & carm., O C 55 30
51 **7** 2d. dull purple and orange-red, O C .. .. 1·25 65
52 **6** 2½d. dull purple and ultramarine, O (10.06) .. 9·00 6·50
53 **7** 3d. dull purple and orange, O C (10.05) .. .. 3·25 1·00
54 ,, 6d. dull purple and violet, O C (5.07) .. .. 5·00 3·25
57 ,, 2s. 6d. green and yellow, C (3.06) (Optd. S. £22) .. 17·00 20·00
49/57 .. .. *Set of* 7 32·00 29·00

1907–13. *Wmk. Mult. Crown CA. P* 14.
59 **6** ½d. dull green, O 20 30
a. Blue-green 30 30
60 ,, 1d. red, O 40 15
61 **7** 2d. greyish slate, O (1909) 1·00 45
62 **6** 2½d. blue, O.. .. .. 1·10 45
63 **7** 3d. purple/*yellow*, C (1909) 1·50 55
64 ,, 6d. dull & deep pur., C ('08) 3·00 1·25
a. Dull & bright pur., C ('11) 1·10 1·25
65 **6** 1s. black/*green*, C (1909) 4·00 1·00
66 ,, 2s. purple and blue/*blue*, O C ('10) .. .. 9·50 9·50
67 **7** 2s. 6d. bl. & red/*bl.*, C ('11) 14·00 13·00
68 **6** 5s. grn. & red/*yell.*, C ('13) 24·00 26·00
59/68 .. .. *Set of* 10 50·00 48·00
59/68 Optd. "Specimen" *Set of* 10 50·00

A 10s. green and red on green, Type **6**, was prepared for use but not issued. It exists overprinted "Specimen", *price* £140.

8

(Typo. D.L.R.)

1908 (NOV.). *Wmk. Mult. Crown CA. P* 14.
69 **8** 1d. red, O (Optd. S. £14) .. 10 5

9

10

11

WAR TAX

ONE PENNY
(12)

(Typo. D.L.R.)

1913–21. *Ordinary paper* (½*d. to* 2½*d.*) *or chalk-surfaced paper* (*others*). *Wmk. Mult. Crown CA. P* 14.
70 **9** ½d. green 40 20
a. Yellow-green (1916) .. 40 40
72 **10** 1d. red 12 5
a. Scarlet (1919) 25 25
74 **11** 2d. grey .. .. .. 2·25 60
a. Slate-grey .. .. 2·00 60
76 **9** 2½d. bright blue 65 65
77 **11** 3d. purple/*yellow* (8.15) .. 65 25
a. White back (9.13) (Optd. S £12) 35 35
b. On orange-buff (1919) .. 2·25 1·00
c. On pale yellow (Die II) (1919) 2·25 1·60
78 ,, 6d. dull & bright purple .. 1·10 85
79 **9** 1s. black/*green* 70 60
a. On blue green, olive back ('21) 70 90
b. On emerald back (Die I) ('21) 1·60 1·10
c. On emerald back (Die II) ('21) .. .. .. 1·90 70
80 ,, 2s. pur. & blue/*blue* (Die I) 3·25 1·40
a. Die II (1921) .. .. 48·00 27·00
81 **11** 2s. 6d. black and red/*blue* (Die I) .. .. .. 6·00 2·00
a. Die II (1921) .. .. 12·00 12·00
82 **9** 5s. green & red/*yellow* ('16) 6·00 8·50
a. White back (10.13) (Optd. S £14) .. .. .. 4·50 6·50
b. On orange-buff .. .. 8·50 8·00
c. On pale yellow (Die I) ('21) 14·00 15·00
d. Die II (1921) .. .. 8·00 17·00
83 ,, 10s. green and red/*green* .. 12·00 18·00
a. On blue-grn., olive back ('19) 8·00 9·00
b. On emerald back (1921) .. 13·00 17·00
84 ,, 20s. purple & blk./*red* ('16) 45·00 40·00
70/84 .. .. *Set of* 12 65·00 55·00
70/84 Optd. "Specimen" *Set of* 12 75·00
79*a*/*c* Optd. "Specimen" *Set of* 3 18·00

1918 (MAY). *Surch. with T* **12.**
85 **10** 1d. on 1d. red (Optd. S £17) 8 20

1921–24. *Ordinary paper* (½*d. to* 3*d.*) *or chalk-surfaced paper* (*others*). *Wmk. Mult. Script CA. P* 14.
86 **9** ½d. green 8 15
87 **10** 1d. chocolate-brn. (1922) 8 8
88 **11** 1½d. red (1922) 12 10
89 ,, 2d. grey 20 10
90 **9** 2½d. yellow-orange (1922) 20 1·40
91 **11** 3d. bright blue (1922) .. 20 30
94 ,, 6d. dull & bright purple.. 50 95
95 **9** 1s. black/*emerald* (1924) 75 1·25
96 ,, 2s. pur. & blue/*blue* (1923) 2·75 2·75
97 **11** 2s. 6d. black & red/*blue* ('24) .. .. .. 3·00 3·25
98 **9** 5s. green and red/*pale yellow* (1924) .. .. 5·50 5·50
100 **11** 15s. dull pur. & grn. (Die I) 80·00 90·00
a. Die II ('24) (Optd. S £80) 60·00 80·00
102 ,, £2 green & orange (Die I) £150 £200
86/100a .. .. *Set of* 12 65·00 85·00
86/102 Optd. "Specimen" *Set of* 13 £150

In Nos. 88, 100 and 102 the words "GOLD COAST" are in distinctly larger letters.

13. King George V and Christiansborg Castle.

(Photo. Harrison.)

1928 (1 Aug.). *Wmk. Mult. Script CA. P* 13½×15.

No.	Type	Description	Unused	Used
103	**13**	½d. green	8	12
104	,,	1d. red-brown	8	8
105	,,	1½d. scarlet	45	50
106	,,	2d. slate	15	8
107	,,	2½d. orange-yellow ..	65	1·60
108	,,	3d. blue	65	30
109	,,	6d. black and purple ..	70	40
110	,,	1s. black and vermilion ..	1·75	1·25
111	,,	2s. black and violet ..	5·50	3·25
112	,,	5s. carmine & olive-green	14·00	15·00
103/112		.. .. *Set of* 10	22·00	20·00
103/12 Optd. "Specimen"		*Set of* 10	70·00	

1935 (6 May). *Silver Jubilee. As Nos.* 91/4 *of Antigua, but ptd. by B.W. P* 11×12.

No.	Description	Unused	Used
113	1d. ultramarine & grey-black	12	15
	a. Extra flagstaff	27·00	
114	3d. brown and deep blue ..	80	90
	a. Extra flagstaff	20·00	
115	6d. green and indigo	2·00	2·25
	a. Extra flagstaff	20·00	
116	1s. slate and purple	2·25	2·75
	a. Extra flagstaff	20·00	
113/16 Perf. "Specimen"	*Set of* 4	14·00	

For illustration of "extra flagstaff" variety see Bechuanaland.

1937 (12 May). *Coronation. As Nos.* 13/15 *of Aden, but ptd. by B. W. P* 11×11½.

No.	Description	Unused	Used
117	1d. buff	12	12
118	2d. slate	15	15
119	3d. blue	25	25
117/19 Perf. "Specimen"	*Set of* 2	11·00	

14

15. King George VI and Christiansborg Castle, Accra.

(Recess. B.W.)

1938 (1 Apr.)–**41.** *Wmk. Mult. Script CA. P* 11½×12.

No.	Type	Description	Unused	Used
120	**14**	½d. green	5	5
121	,,	1d. red-brown	5	5
122	,,	1½d. scarlet	5	5
123	,,	2d. slate	8	8
124	,,	3d. blue	10	10
125	,,	4d. magenta	10	10
126	,,	6d. purple	10	10
127	,,	9d. orange	25	25
128	**15**	1s. black and olive-green	20	15
129	,,	1s. 3d. brown & turquoise-blue (12.4.41) ..	20	25
130	,,	2s. blue and violet ..	95	85
131	,,	5s. olive-green & carmine	2·00	1·75
132	,,	10s. black & violet (1940)	3·00	3·25
120/132		.. .. *Set of* 13	6·50	6·50
120/32 Perf. "Specimen"		*Set of* 13	42·00	

Nos. 120 to 132, except 1s. 3d. and 10s., exist in two perforations: (*a*) Line-perf. 12, from early printings; (*b*) Comb-perf. 12×11.7 (vertical design) or 11.7×12 (horiz. design), from later printings. The 1s. 3d. and 10s. exist only comb-perf. 11.7×12.

1946 (14 Oct.). *Victory. As Nos.* 28/9 *of Aden. P* 13½×14.

No.	Description	Unused	Used
133	2d. slate-violet	15	15
	a. Perf. 13½	8	8
134	4d. claret	45	30
	a. Perf. 13½	10	12
133/4 Perf. "Specimen"	*Set of* 2	13·00	

16. Northern Territories Mounted Constabulary.

19. Talking Drums.

17. Christiansborg Castle.

18. Emblem of Joint Provincial Council.

20. Map showing position of Gold Coast.

21. Manganese Mine.

22. Lake Bosumtwi.

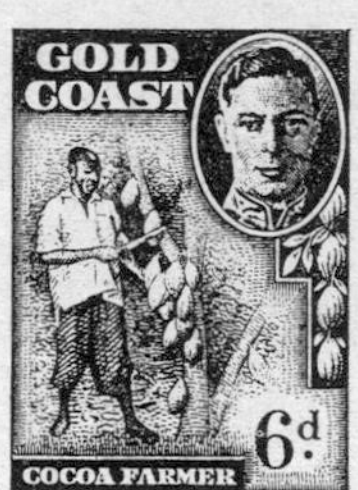

23. Cocoa Farmer. **27.** Forest.

24. Breaking Cocoa Pods.

25. Trooping the Colour.

26. Surfboats.

(Des. B. A. Johnston (1½d.), M. Ziorkley an B. A. Abban (2d.), P.O. draughtsman (2½d.) C. Gomez (1s.), M. Ziorkley (10s.); others fron photographs. Recess. B.W.)

1948 (1 July). *Wmk. Mult. Script CA. P* 12×11 (*vert.*) *or* 11½×12 (*horiz.*).

No.	Type	Description	Unused	Used
135	**16**	½d. emerald-green ..	10	1
136	**17**	1d. blue	8	1
137	**18**	1½d. scarlet	10	1
138	**19**	2d. purple-brown ..	8	
139	**20**	2½d. yellow-brn. & scarlet	15	2
140	**21**	3d. light blue	12	1
141	**22**	4d. magenta	25	2
142	**23**	6d. black and orange ..	25	1
143	**24**	1s. black and vermilion	25	
144	**25**	2s. sage-green & magenta	55	4
145	**26**	5s. purple and black ..	2·00	1·1
146	**27**	10s. black and sage-green	3·00	2·2
135/146		.. .. *Set of* 12	6·50	4·5
135/46 Perf. "Specimen"		*Set of* 12	70·00	

1948 (20 Dec.). *Royal Silver Wedding. As Nos* 30/1 *of Aden.*

No.	Description	Unused	Used
147	1½d. scarlet	8	
148	10s. grey-olive	3·00	4·5

1949 (10 Oct.). *75th Anniv. of U.P.U. As Nos. 114/17 of Antigua.*
149 2d. red-brown 12 25
150 2½d. orange 20 55
151 3d. deep blue.. .. .. 45 95
152 1s. blue-green .. .. 1·00 1·50

28. Northern Territories Mounted Constabulary.

(Recess. B.W.)

1952–54. *As T* **16/27** *(but with portrait of Queen Elizabeth II in place of King George VI, as in T* **28**). *Portrait faces left on ½d., 4d., 6d., 1s., 2s., and 5s. Wmk. Mult. Script CA. P 12×11½ (vert.) or 11½×12 (horiz.).*
153 **20** ½d. yellow-brown & scarlet (*shades*) 5 5
154 **17** 1d. deep blue 5 5
155 **18** 1½d. emerald-green .. 5 8
156 **19** 2d. chocolate 5 8
157 **28** 2½d. scarlet 5 8
158 **21** 3d. magenta 5 5
159 **22** 4d. blue 10 10
160 **23** 6d. black and orange .. 10 8
161 **24** 1s. black and orange-red 20 8
162 **25** 2s. brown-olive and carm. 50 12
163 **26** 5s. purple and black .. 2·00 80
164 **27** 10s. black and olive-green 4·00 1·50
153/64 .. .. *Set of* 12 6·50 2·50

Dates of issue: 19.12.52, 2½d.; 1.4.53, ½d., 1½d., 3d., and 4d.; 1.3.54, other values.

1953 (2 June). *Coronation. As No. 47 of Aden, but ptd. by B. W.*
165 2d. black and sepia 10 5

POSTAGE DUE STAMPS.

D 1

(Typo. D.L.R.)

1923. *Yellowish toned paper. Wmk. Mult. Script CA. P 14.*
D1 D **1** ½d. black .. .. 5·00 4·50
D2 ,, 1d. black 10 20
D3 ,, 2d. black 80 65
D4 ,, 3d. black 80 55
D1/4 Optd. "Specimen" *Set of* 4 22·00

1951–52. *Type* D **1**. *Chalk-surfaced paper. Wmk. Mult. Script CA. P 14.*
D5 2d. black (13.12.51) 5 15
a. Error. Crown missing, W9a .. 20·00
b. Error. St. Edward's Crown, W9b 14·00
D6 3d. black (13.12.51) 10 30
a. Error. Crown missing, W9a .. 20·00
b. Error. St. Edward's Crown, W9b 13·00
D7 6d. black 1.10.52) 20 25
a. Error. Crown missing, W9a .. 17·00
b. Error. St. Edward's Crown, W9b 14·00
D8 1s. black (1.10.52) 40 50
b. Error. St. Edward's Crown, W9b 14·00

On March 6th, 1957 Gold Coast became the Dominion of Ghana (*q.v.*).

GRENADA.

For GREAT BRITAIN stamps used in Grenada with "A 15" obliteration, see index to Great Britain Stamps Used Abroad list.

I. CROWN COLONY.

PRINTERS. Types **1** and **5** recess-printed by Perkins, Bacon and Co.

1

1861–62. *No wmk.* (*a*) *Rough perf.* 14 *to* 16.
1 **1** 1d. bluish green £950 £110
2 ,, 1d. green (May 1862) .. 32·00 32·00
a. Imperf. between (horizontal pair)
3 ,, 6d. rose (*shades*) .. £350 40·00
(*b*) *Wove paper. Perf.* 11 *to* 12½.
3*a* **1** 6d. lake-red £400

No. 3*a* is only known unused, and has also been seen on laid paper. (*Price* £450.)

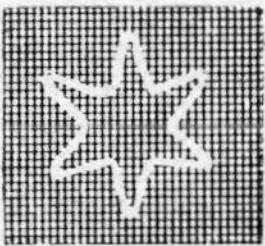

2. Small Star.

Wmk. s = Wmk. sideways (two points of Star downwards).

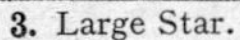

3. Large Star.

4. Broad-pointed Star.

1863–71. *W* **2** (*Small Star*). *Rough perf.* 14 *to* 16.
4 **1** 1d. green (1864) .. .. 25·00 13·00
5 ,, 1d. yellowish green .. 42·00 16·00
6 ,, 6d. rose (*shades*) (2.63) .. £225 16·00
7 ,, 6d. orange-red (*shades*) .. £250 16·00
8 ,, 6d. dull rose-red (wmk. s) .. £1100 85·00
9 ,, 6d. vermilion .. .. £225 16·00
a. Double impression .. .. — £550

The sideways wmk. is an identifying aid to the rare shade, No. 8. Normally in this issue the wmk. is upright, but it also exists sideways.

1873. *W* **2** (*Small Star sideways*). *Clean-cut perf.* 15.
10 **1** 1d. deep green .. .. 30·00 15·00
a. Bisected diag. (on cover) .. † £2000
b. Imperf. between (pair) .. — £1000

1873–74. *W* **3** (*Large Star*). *Intermediate perf.* 15.
11 **1** 1d. blue-grn. (wmk. s) (1874) 28·00 15·00
a. Double impression
12 ,, 6d. orange-vermilion (upright wmk.) .. .. £200 16·00

5 POSTAGE ONE SHILLING (6)

NOTE. The early ½d., 2½d., 4d. and 1s. postage stamps were made by surcharging the undenominated Type **5** design.

The surcharges were from two founts of type—one about 1½ mm. high, the other 2 mm. high—so there are short and tall letters on the same stamp; also the spacing varies considerably, so that the length of the words varies.

1875 (July). *Surch. with T* **6**. *W* **3**. *P* 14.
13 **5** 1s. deep mauve (B.) .. £200 12·00
a. Error. "SHLLIING" .. — £400
b. Error. "NE SHILLING" — £950
c. Error. Inverted "S" in "POSTAGE" £1500 £300
d. Error. "OSTAGE" ..

1875 (Dec.). *W* **3** (*Large Star, upright*).
14 **1** 1d. grn. *to* yell.-grn. (*p.* 14) 15·00 13·00
a. Bisected diag. (on cover) .. † £2000
15 ,, 1d. green (*p.*15) £2750 £750

No. 14 was perforated at Somerset House. 40 sheets of No. 15 were perforated by Perkins, Bacon to replace spoilages and to complete the order.

1878. *W* **2** (*Small Star, sideways*). *Intermediate perf.* 15.
16 **1** 1d. green .. .. .. £100 18·00
17 ,, 6d. deep vermilion .. £300 18·00
a. Double impression .. — £500

1879. *W* **2** (*Small Star, upright*). *Rough perf.* 15.
18 **1** 1d. pale green (*thin paper*) £130 10·00
a. Double impression ..

1881 (April). *W* **2** (*Small Star, sideways*). *Rough perf.* 14½.
19 **1** 1d. green .. .. .. 50·00 10·00
a. Bisected diag. (on cover) .. † £2000

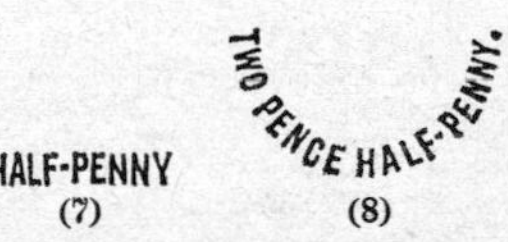

(7) (8) (9)

1881 (April). *Surch. with T* **7/9**. *P* 14½.

(*a*) *Wmk. Large Star, T* **3**.
20 **5** ½d. pale mauve .. .. 14·00 7·00
21 ,, ½d. deep mauve .. .. 6·00 7·00
a. Imperf. (pair) £120
ab. Do. incl. "OSTAGE" .. £1400
b. Surch. double .. 95·00
c. Error. "OSTAGE" .. 60·00 55·00
d. Error. No hyphen .. 55·00 42·00
e. Error. "ALF-PENNY" .. £1000
f. Wmk. upright .. .. — £140
g. Ditto. "OSTAGE" .. £800
22 ,, 2½d. rose-lake .. .. 15·00 8·00
a. Imperf. (pair) £160
b. Imperf. between (horiz. pair) £750
c. Error. No stop .. 65·00 42·00
d. Error. "PENCF" .. 90·00 45·00
23 ,, 4d. blue .. .. .. 40·00 11·00

The watermark is normally *sideways* on the ½d.

(*b*) *Wmk. Broad-pointed Star, T* **4**.
24 **5** 2½d. rose-lake .. .. 55·00 17·00
a. Error. No stop .. £225 85·00
b. Error. "PENCF" .. £275 £110
25 ,, 2½d. claret .. .. £140 50·00
a. Error. No stop .. £350 £180
b. Error. "PENCF" .. £550 £250
25*c* ,, 2½d. deep claret .. £250 90·00
d. Error. No stop .. £1000 £375
e. Error. "PENCF" .. £1300 £500
26 ,, 4d. blue .. .. 80·00 75·00

POSTAGE (12, inverted and diagonal)

ONE PENNY POSTAGE. POSTAGE

(10) (11) (12)

1883 (Jan.). *Revenue stamps* (*T* **5** *with green surcharge as in T* **10**) *optd. for postage. W* **2** (*Small Star*). *P* 14½.

A. *Optd. horizontally with T* **11**.

27 **5** 1d. orange .. .. .. 65·00 18·00
a. "POSTAGE" inverted .. £650 £475
b. "POSTAGE" double £450 £450
c. Invtd. "S" in "POSTAGE" £250 £225
d. Bisected diag. (on cover) .. † £1100

B. *Optd. diagonally with T* **11** *twice on each stamp, the stamp being cut and each half used as ½d.*

28 **5** Half of 1d. orange £225 £100
a. Unsevered pair £1400 £550
b. "POSTAGE." inverted .. — £425

C. *Optd. with T* **12**, *the stamps divided diagonally and each half used as ½d.*

29 **5** Half of 1d. orange .. .. 60·00 45·00
a. Unsevered pair £400 £250

Nos. 27/9 exist with wmk. either upright or sideways.

1d. Revenue stamps are known with "POSTAGE" written by hand, in red or black. These were apparently used, but not officially authorised.

13

d. 1 POSTAGE.

(14)

(Typo. De La Rue.)

1883. *Wmk. Crown CA. P* 14.

30 **13** ½d. dull green (Feb.) .. 1·00 1·00
a. Tête-bêche (pr.) .. .. 2·50 6·00
31 ,, 1d. carmine (Feb.) .. 10·00 3·00
a. Tête-bêche (pr.) .. .. 70·00 80·00
32 ,, 2½d. ultramarine (May) .. 4·00 1·25
a. Tête-bêche (pr.) .. .. 12·00 14·00
33 ,, 4d. greyish slate (May) .. 3·50 4·00
a. Tête-bêche (pr.) .. .. 9·00 10·00
34 ,, 6d. mauve (May) .. 5·00 5·00
a. Tête-bêche (pr.) .. .. 15·00 22·00
35 ,, 8d. grey-brown (Feb.) .. 10·00 10·00
a. Tête-bêche (pr.) .. .. 25·00 35·00
36 ,, 1s. pale violet (April) .. 55·00 40·00
a. Tête-bêche (pr.) £250
30/36 .. .. *Set of* 7 80·00 55·00

Types **13** and **15** were printed in rows tête-bêche in the sheets.

1886. *Revenue stamps* (*T* **5** *with green surch. as T* **10**), *surch. with T* **14**. *P* 14.

A. *Wmk. Large Star, T* **3**.

37 **5** 1d. on 1½d. orange (Oct.) .. 13·00 13·00
a. Type 14 inverted £100 £100
b. Type 14 double £100 £100
c. Error. "THRFE" £100 £100
d. Error. "PFNCE £100 £100
e. Error. "HALH" £100 £100
f. Bisected diag. (on cover) .. † £500
38 ,, 1d. on 1s. orange (Dec.) .. 13·00 13·00
a. Error. "POSTAGE" (no stop)
b. Error. "SHILLNG" .. £160 £180
c. Error. Wide space (3¼ mm.) between "ONE" and "SHILLING" .. £160 £140
d. Bisected diag. (on cover) .. † £500

B. *Wmk. Small Star, T* **2**.

39 ,, 1d. on 4d. orange (Nov.) .. 45·00 32·00

15

1887 (Jan.). *Wmk. Crown CA. P* 14.

40 **15** 1d. carmine (Optd. S. £20) .. 40 40
a. Tête-bêche (pr.) .. .. 1·25 7·00

4d. POSTAGE (16) HALF PENNY POSTAGE (17)

1888–91. *Revenue stamps* (*T* **5** *with green surch. as T* **10**) *surcharged. W* **2**. *P* 14½.

A. **1888** (31 Mar.). *Surch. with T* **16**.

I. *4 mm. between value and* "POSTAGE".

41 **5** 4d. on 2s. orange .. 11·00 11·00
a. Upright "d" £120 £120
b. Wide space (2¼ mm.) between "TWO" & "SHILLINGS" 45·00 45·00
c. First "S" in "SHILLINGS" inverted £120 £120
d. Imp. between (horiz. pr.)

II. *5 mm. between value and* "POSTAGE".

42 **5** 4d. on 2s. orange .. 17·00 18·00
a. Wide spacing (as 41b) .. 75·00 80·00
b. "S" inverted (as 41c) .. £200 £200

B. **1889** (Dec.). *Surch. as T* **17**.

43 **5** ½d. on 2s. orange .. .. 11·00 12·00
a. Type 17 double £110 £120
b. Wide spacing (as 41b) .. 45·00 50·00
c. "S" inverted (as 41c) .. £120 £120

POSTAGE d. AND 1 REVENUE (18) POSTAGE AND REVENUE 1d. (19) 2½d. (20)

C. **1890** (Dec.). *Surch. with T* **18**.

44 **5** 1d. on 2s. orange .. 30·00 30·00
a. Surcharge inverted .. £120
b. Wide spacing (as 41b) .. 85·00 85·00
c. "S" inverted (as 41c) .. £160

D. **1891** (Jan.). *Surch. with T* **19**.

45 **5** 1d. on 2s. orange .. 13·00 13·00
a. No stop after "1d" .. 90·00
b. Wide spacing (as 41b) .. 80·00
c. "S" inverted (as 41c) .. £150

1891 (Jan.). *Surch. with T* **19**.

46 **13** 1d. on 8d. grey-brown .. 11·00 11·00
a. Tête-bêche (pair) .. 30·00
b. Surcharge inverted .. £110 £110
c. No stop after "1d" .. 90·00 85·00

1891 (Dec.). *Surch. with T* **20**.

47 **13** 2½d. on 8d. grey-brown (Optd. S. £40) .. 13·00 11·00
a. Tête-bêche (pair) .. 45·00
b. Inverted surcharge ..
c. Double surcharge .. £200 £300
d. Double surch., one inverted £150 £150
e. Treble surch. .. .. — £300

There are two types of fraction; in one the "1" has horizontal serif and the "2" commences in a ball; in the other the "1" has sloping serif and the "2" is without ball.

Each type occurs 30 times in the pane of 60. See also Nos. D4/7.

21

22

(Typo. D.L.R.)

1895–99. *Wmk. Crown CA. P* 14.

48 **22** ½d. mauve & green (1899) 40 55
49 **21** 1d. mauve & carm. (1896) 65 25
50 ,, 2d. mauve & brown (1899) 9·50 12·00
51 ,, 2½d. mauve & ultramarine 2·75 95
52 **22** 3d. mauve and orange .. 5·00 5·00
53 **21** 6d. mauve and green .. 3·25 4·50
54 **22** 8d. mauve and black .. 8·00 9·50
55 ,, 1s. green and orange .. 9·50 11·00
48/55 .. .. *Set of* 8 35·00 40·00
48/55 Optd. "Specimen" *Set of* 8 55·00

23. Flagship of Columbus.
(Columbus named Grenada "La Concepcion".)

(Recess. D.L.R.)

1898 (15 Aug.). *400th Anniv. of Discovery of Grenada by Columbus. Wmk. Crown CC. P* 14.

56 **23** 2½d. ultram. (Optd. S. £35) 6·00 6·00
a. Bluish paper .. .. 12·00 15·00

24

25

(Typo. D.L.R.)

1902. *Wmk. Crown CA. P* 14.

57 **24** ½d. dull purple and green .. 40 55
58 **25** 1d. dull purple & carmine 45 3[illegible]
59 ,, 2d. dull purple and brown 2·00 2·75
60 ,, 2½d. dull purple and ultram. 2·50 3·25
61 **24** 3d. dull purple and orange 2·00 2·00
62 **25** 6d. dull purple and green .. 3·75 5·00
63 **24** 1s. green and orange .. 6·00 7·50
64 ,, 2s. green and ultramarine 12·00 17·00
65 **25** 5s. green and carmine .. 20·00 25·00
66 **24** 10s. green and purple .. 70·00 85·00
57/66 .. .. *Set of* 10 £110 £130
57/66 Optd. "Specimen" *Set of* 10 90·00

1904–6. *Wmk. Mult. Crown CA. P* 14.

67 **24** ½d. purple & green, O ('05) 4·00 4·5[illegible]
68 **25** 1d. purple & carm., O ('04) 2·50 1·75
69 ,, 2d. pur. & brown, O ('05) 7·50 7·50
70 ,, 2½d. pur. & ultram., O ('05) 7·50 7·50
71 **24** 3d. pur. & orge., OC ('05) 3·00 4·00
72 **25** 6d. purple & grn., OC ('06) 4·00 4·00
73 **24** 1s. green & orge., O ('05) 7·00 7·50
74 ,, 2s. grn. & ultram., OC ('06) 14·00 20·00
75 **25** 5s. green & carm., O ('06) 27·00 32·00
76 **24** 10s. green & pur., O ('06) £100 £120
67/76 .. .. *Set of* 10 £160 £190

26. Badge of the Colony. **27.**

(Recess. D.L.R.)

1906. *Wmk. Mult. Crown CA. P* 14.

77 **26** ½d. green .. .. .. 40 3[illegible]
78 ,, 1d. carmine .. .. .. 25 2[illegible]

9 **26** 2d. orange .. .. .. 1·75 2·25
o ,, 2½d. blue .. .. .. 3·00 2·75
a. Ultramarine .. .. 3·75 3·00

(Typo. De La Rue.)

908. *Wmk. Crown CA. P* 14.
2 **27** 1s. black/*green*, C .. 9·50 12·00
3 ,, 10s. green & red/*green*, C .. 75·00 90·00

908-11. *Wmk. Mult. Crown CA. P* 14.
4 **27** 3d. dull purple/*yellow*, C .. 1·00 2·00
5 ,, 6d. dull purple & purple, C 5·00 6·00
6 ,, 1s. black/*green*, C (1911) .. 2·50 4·00
7 ,, 2s. blue and purple/*blue*, C 8·00 11·00
8 ,, 5s. green and red/*yellow*, C 24·00 30·00
7/88 .. .. *Set of* 11 £110 £140
7/80, 82/88 Optd. "Specimen" *Set of* 11 £100

28

WAR TAX
(29)

WAR TAX
(30)

(Typo. De La Rue & Co.)

913 (Jan.)-**1921.** *Wmk. Mult. Crown CA. P* 14.
89 **28** ½d. yellow-green, O 25 30
90 ,, ½d. green, O 20 30
91 ,, 1d. red, O 25 20
92 ,, 1d. dp. rose-red, O (1916) 40 20
93 ,, 2d. orange, O 40 60
94 ,, 2½d. bright blue, O .. 90 1·10
95 ,, 2½d. dull blue, O .. 1·75 2·25
96 ,, 3d. purple/*yellow*, C .. 45 95
a. White back (Optd. S. £8) 80 2·25
b. On lemon .. .. 1·25 1·75
c. On pale yellow .. 1·75 2·00
97 ,, 6d. dull & bright pur., C 1·10 1·75
98 ,, 1s. black/*green*, C .. 1·75 2·50
a. White back (Optd. S. £8) 1·10 2·50
b. On blue-green, olive back .. 15·00 18·00
c. On emerald surface .. 1·10 2·50
d. On emerald back (Optd. S. £8) .. .. 1·00 2·50
99 ,, 2s. pur. & blue/*blue*, C .. 2·50 3·25
00 ,, 5s. grn. & red/*yell.*, C .. 7·50 11·00
a. On pale yellow (Optd. S. £14) .. .. 12·00 16·00
01 ,, 10s. grn. & red/*green*, C.. 25·00 35·00
a. On emerald back (Optd. S. £17) .. .. 25·00 35·00
9/101*a* .. .. *Set of* 10 35·00 50·00
9/101 Optd. "Specimen" *Set of* 10 70·00

916 (1 June). *Optd. locally with T* **29.**
09 **28** 1d. rose-red (H/S S. £20) 1·60 2·75
a. Opt. inverted .. .. 80·00
10 ,, 1d. red .. .. 6·00 9·00
a. "TΔX" .. .. 15·00 23·00

A small "A" in "WAR", 2 mm. high, is found n Nos. 29, 38 and 48 of the setting of 60 and a ery small "A" in "TAX", 1½ mm. high, on No. 11. Value about twice normal. The noral "A" is 2¼ mm. high.

No. 110*a* is on No. 56 of the setting.

916 (Sept.)-**18.** *Optd. with T* **30** *in London.*
11 **28** 1d. rose-red (Optd. S. £8) 25 30
a. Carmine-red/bluish (5.18) 90 1·10
11 Optd. "Specimen" .. .. 16·00

921-31. *T* **28.** *Wmk. Mult. Script CA. P* 14.
12 ½d. green, O 15 25
13 1d. carmine-red, O 15 25
14 1d. brown, O (1922) 20 20
15 1½d. rose-red, O (1922) 25 30
16 2d. orange, O .. 30 45
17 2d. grey, O (1926) 45 75
18 2½d. bright blue, O .. 45 90
19 2½d. grey, O (1922) .. 50 2·00
20 2½d. chalky blue & blue, O ('26) 7·00 10·00
a. Bright ultramarine (1931) .. 90 1·00
21 3d. bright blue, O .. 1·00 2·00
22 3d. purple/*yellow*, C (1926).. 45 1·10
23 4d. blk. & red/yellow. C ('26) 45 2·25

124 5d. dull purple & sage-green, C (1923) .. .. .. 80 2·50
125 6d. dull and bright purple, C 1·10 2·50
126 6d. black & carmine, C (1926) 1·25 2·25
127 9d. dull pur. & black, C ('23) 1·10 2·50
128 1s. black/*emerald*, C (1923).. 2·25 5·00
129 1s. chestnut, C (1926) .. 5·00 6·50
130 2s. pur. & blue/*blue*, C ('22) 4·50 7·00
131 2s. 6d. black and carmine/*blue*, C (1929) .. .. 7·00 10·00
132 3s. green and violet, C ('23) 7·00 10·00
133 5s. green and red/*pale yellow* C (1923) .. .. .. 12·00 16·00
134 10s. grn. & red/*emerald*, C ('23) 24·00 30·00
112/134 *Set of* 22 (excluding Nos. 120 and 120*a*) .. .. 65·00 95·00
112/34 Optd./Perf. "Specimen" *Set of* 23 £170

31. Grand Anse Beach.

32. Badge of the Colony.

33. Grand Etang.

34. St. George's.

(Recess. Waterlow.)

1934 (23 Oct.)-**36.** *Wmk. Mult. Script CA.* (*sideways on T* **32**). *P* 12½.
135 **31** ½d. green 20 25
a. Perf. 12½×13½ ('36) .. 1·75 4·50
136 **32** 1d. black and sepia 20 20
a. Perf. 13½×12½ ('36) .. 1·10 1·75
137 **33** 1½d. black and scarlet .. 45 45
a. Perf. 12½×13½ ('36) .. 1·75 1·75
138 **32** 2d. black and orange .. 45 55
139 **34** 2½d. blue 25 50
140 **32** 3d. black and olive-green 55 80
141 ,, 6d. black and purple .. 90 1·25
142 ,, 1s. black and brown .. 2·00 2·50
143 ,, 2s. 6d. black & ultram... 7·00 10·00
144 ,, 5s. black and violet .. 11·00 12·00
135/144 .. *Set of* 10 21·00 26·00
135/44 Perf. "Specimen" *Set of* 10 40·00

1935 (6 May). *Silver Jubilee. As T* **13** *of Antigua but ptd. by Waterlow. P* 11×12.
145 ½d. black and green .. 15 15
146 1d. ultramarine and grey .. 20 15
147 1½d. deep blue and scarlet .. 45 45
148 1s. slate and purple .. 3·00 3·25
145/8 Perf. "Specimen" *Set of* 4 16·00

1937 (12 May.). *Coronation. As T* **2** *of Aden but ptd. by B. W. P* 11×11½.
149 1d. violet 10 15
150 1½d. carmine 10 15
151 2½d. blue 12 30
149/51 Perf. "Specimen" *Set of* 3 11·00

35. King George VI.

(Photo. Harrison.)

1937 (12 July). *Wmk. Mult. Script CA. P* 15×14.
152 **35** ¼d. brown, CO 8 8
a. Chocolate, CO 8 8

The ordinary paper is thick, smooth and opaque.

36. Grand Anse Beach.

40. Badge of the Colony.

(Recess. D.L.R. (10s.), Waterlow (others).)

1938 (16 Mar.)-**50.** *As T* **31/4** (*but portrait of King George VI as in T* **36**) *and T* **40.** *Wmk. Mult. Script CA.* (*sideways on T* **32**). *P* 12½ *or* 12×13 (10s.).
153 **36** ½d. yellow-green 45 20
a. Perf. 12½×13½ ('38) .. 55 55
b. Perf. 12½. *Blue-green* ('43) 10 10
ba. Perf. 12½×13½. *Blue-green* 35 1·10
154 **32** 1d. black and sepia .. 5 5
a. Perf. 13½×12½ (1938) .. 5 5
155 **33** 1½d. black and scarlet .. 8 5
a. Perf. 12½×13½ (1938) .. 55 25
156 **32** 2d. black and orange .. 5 5
a. Perf. 13½×12½ (1938) .. 5 5
157 **34** 2½d. bright blue 10 8
a. Perf. 12½×13½ (?Mar. '50) £550 50·00
158 **32** 3d. black and olive-green 90 65
a. Perf. 13½×12½ (16.3.38) .. 1·10 75
ab. Perf. 13½×12½. *Black and brown-olive* ('42).. 35 45
b. Perf. 12½. *Black and brown-olive* (16.8.50) .. 30 30
159 ,, 6d. black and purple .. 15 15
a. Perf. 13½×12½ ('42) .. 25 12
160 ,, 1s. black and brown .. 25 25
a. Perf. 13½×12½ ('41) .. 40 40
161 ,, 2s. black & ultramarine 80 80
a. Perf. 13½×12½ ('41) .. 2·00 75
162 ,, 5s. black and violet .. 1·60 1·40
a. Perf. 13½×12½ ('47) .. 2·00 2·40
163 **40** 10s. slate-blue and carmine (*narrow*) (p. 12×13) 4·50 5·00
a. Perf. 14. *Pale blue and carmine-rose* (*narrow*) .. 20·00 20·00
b. Perf. 14. *Slate-blue and carmine* (*narrow*) ('43) .. 3·00 3·50
c. Perf. 12. *Slate-blue and carmine* (*narrow*) ('43) .. 55·00 55·00
d. Perf. 14. *Slate-blue and claret* (*wide*) ('44) .. 15·00 8·00
e. Perf. 14. *Blue-black and carmine* (*wide*) ('47) .. 7·00 8·00
152/163*b* .. .. *Set of* 12 6·00 6·00
152/63 Perf. "Specimen" *Set of* 12 35·00

In the earlier printings of the 10s. the paper was dampened before printing and the subsequent shrinkage produced narrow frames 23½ to 23¾ mm. wide. Later printings were made on dry paper producing wide frames 24¼ mm. wide.

No. 163*a* is one of the earlier printings line perf. 13.8×14.1

No. 163*b* is line-perf. 14.1.

Nos. 163*a* and 163*b* may be found with gum more or less yellow due to local climatic conditions.

1946 (25 SEPT.). *Victory. As Nos. 28/9 of Aden.*
164 1½d. carmine 8 8
165 3½d. blue 12 10
164/5 Perf. "Specimen" *Set of* 2 14·00

1948 (27 OCT.). *Royal Silver Wedding. As Nos. 30/1 of Aden.*
166 1½d. scarlet 8 8
167 10s. slate-green .. .. 3·50 5·50

(Currency changed. 100 cents=1 West Indian dollar.)

1949 (10 OCT.). *75th Anniv. of Universal Postal Union. As Nos. 114/17 of Antigua.*
168 5 c. ultramarine 12 12
169 6 c. olive 20 20
170 12 c. magenta 40 40
171 24 c. red-brown 65 65

41. King George VI.

42. Badge of the Colony.

43. Badge of the Colony.

(Recess. B.W. (T **41**), D.L.R. (others).)

1951 (8 JAN.). *Wmk. Mult. Script CA. P* 11½ (*T* **41**), 11½×12½ (*T* **42**), *and* 11½×13 (*T* **43**).
172 **41** ½ c. black and red-brown 12 25
173 ,, 1 c. black & emerald-grn. 12 12
174 ,, 2 c. black and brown .. 12 12
175 ,, 3 c. black & rose-carmine 15 12
176 ,, 4 c. black and orange .. 20 35
177 ,, 5 c. black and violet .. 20 20
178 ,, 6 c. black and olive .. 20 12
179 ,, 7 c. black and light blue 20 12
180 ,, 12 c. black and purple .. 80 65
181 **42** 25 c. black and sepia .. 65 65
182 ,, 50 c. black and blue .. 55 55
183 ,, $1.50 black & yell.-orange 6·00 4·00
184 **43** $2.50 slate-blue & carm. 4·00 4·00
172/184 .. .. *Set of* 13 12·00 11·00

1951 (16 FEB.). *Inauguration of B.W.I. University College. As Nos. 118/9 of Antigua.*
185 3 c. black and carmine .. 15 12
186 6 c. black and olive 30 25

NEW CONSTITUTION

1951

(**44**)

1951 (21 SEPT.). *New Constitution. Optd. with T* **44** *by B.W.*
187 **41** 3 c. black & rose-carmine 12 20
188 ,, 4 c. black and orange .. 15 25
189 ,, 5 c. black and violet (R.) 15 25
190 ,, 12 c. black and purple .. 25 40

1953 (3 JUNE). *Coronation. As No. 47 of Aden.*
191 3 c. black and carmine-red .. 12 15

45. Queen Elizabeth II.

46. Badge of the Colony.

47. Badge of the Colony.

(Recess. B.W. (T **45**), D.L.R. (T **46/7**).)

1953–59. *Wmk. Mult. Script CA. P* 11½ (*T* **45**), 11½×12½ (*T* **46**), *or* 11½×13 (*T* **47**).
192 **45** ½ c. black and brown .. 5 5
193 ,, 1 c. black & dp. emerald 5 5
194 ,, 2 c. black and sepia .. 8 8
195 ,, 3 c. black & carmine-red 8 8
196 ,, 4 c. black & brown-orange 8 8
197 ,, 5 c. black and deep violet 8 10
198 ,, 6 c. black and olive-green 10 12
199 ,, 7 c. black and blue .. 12 12
200 ,, 12 c. black & reddish pur. 15 15
201 **46** 25 c. black and sepia .. 25 30
202 ,, 50 c. black and deep blue.. 40 40
203 ,, $1.50, black & brn.-orge. 2·25 2·50
204 **47** $2.50, slate-blue & carm. 5·00 6·00
192/204 .. .. *Set of* 13 8·00 9·00

Dates of issue: 1953—15 June, 1 c., 12 c.; 15 Sept., 2 c.; 28 Dec., ½ c., 6 c. 1954—22 Feb., 3 c., 4 c., 5 c. 1955—10 Jan., 25 c.; 6 June, 7 c.; 2 Dec., 50 c., $1.50. 1959—16 Nov., $2.50.

On 23rd December, 1965 No. 203 was issued surcharged "2" but this was intended for fiscal and revenue purposes and it was not authorised to be used postally, although some are known to have passed through the mail.

1958 (22 APR.). *Inauguration of British Caribbean Federation. As Nos. 135/7 of Antigua.*
205 3 c. deep green 10 10
206 6 c. blue 20 20
207 12 c. scarlet 30 30

48. Queen Victoria, Queen Elizabeth II, Mail Van and Post Office, St. George's.

49. Queen Victoria, Queen Elizabeth II and *La Concepcion.*

50. Queen Victoria, Queen Elizabeth II, R.M.S.P. *Solent* and Dakota aircraft.

(Photo. Harrison.)

1961 (1 JUNE). *Stamp Centenary. W* w.**12.** *P* 14½×14.
208 **48** 3 c. crimson and black .. 15 15
209 **49** 8 c. brt. blue and orange 30 30
210 **50** 25 c. lake and blue .. 50 50

1963 (4 JUNE). *Freedom from Hunger. As No. 76 of Aden.*
211 8 c. bluish green 30 30

1963 (9 JULY)–**64.** *As Nos.* 194/8, 200/1, *but wmk.* w. **12.**
212 **45** 2 c. black and sepia .. 5 5
213 ,, 3 c. black & carmine-red 5 5
214 ,, 4 c. black & brown-orange 5 5
215 ,, 5 c. black and deep violet 8 8
216 ,, 6 c. black and olive-green 45·00 30·00
217 ,, 12 c. black & reddish purple 20 20
218 **46** 25 c. black and sepia .. 35 40

Dates of issue: 1963—9 July, 6 c.; 1964—12 May, remainder.

1963 (2 SEPT.). *Red Cross Centenary. As Nos. 147/8 of Antigua.*
219 3 c. red and black 10 12
220 25 c. red and blue 50 50

1965 (17 MAY). *I.T.U. Centenary. As Nos. 166/7 of Antigua.*
221 2 c. red-orange and yellow-olive 8 8
222 50 c. lemon and light red .. 50 55

1965 (25 OCT.). *International Co-operation Year. As Nos. 168/9 of Antigua.*
223 1 c. reddish pur. & turq.-grn. 8 8
224 25 c. dp. bluish green & lav. 30 35

1966 (24 JAN.). *Churchill Commemoration. As Nos. 170/3 of Antigua.*
225 1 c. new blue 5 5
226 3 c. deep green 8 8
227 25 c. brown 30 30
228 35 c. bluish violet 50 55

1966 (4 FEB.). *Royal Visit. As Nos. 174/5 of Antigua.*
229 3 c. black and ultramarine 10 10
230 35 c. black and magenta .. 40 40

52. Hillsborough, Carriacou.

53. Bougainvillea.
54. Flamboyant Plant.
55. Levera Beach.
56. Careenage, St. George's. (*Inscr.* "CARENAGE".)
57. Annandale Falls.
58. Cocoa Pods.
59. Inner Harbour.
60. Nutmeg.
61. St. George's.
62. Grand Anse Beach.
63. Bananas.

(*T* **53/63** *are horiz. as T* **52.**)

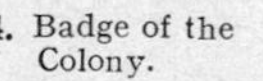

64. Badge of the Colony.

65. Queen Elizabeth II

66. Map of Grenada.

(Des. V. Whiteley. Photo. Harrison.)

1966 (1 Apr.). *W* w.**12**. *P* 14½ ($1, $2, $3) *or* 14½×13½ (*others*).

231	**52**	1 c. multicoloured	5	5
232	**53**	2 c. multicoloured	5	5
233	**54**	3 c. multicoloured	5	5
234	**55**	5 c. multicoloured	5	5
235	**56**	6 c. multicoloured	5	5
236	**57**	8 c. multicoloured	5	8
237	**58**	10 c. multicoloured	8	8
238	**59**	12 c. multicoloured	10	12
239	**60**	15 c. multicoloured	12	15
240	**61**	25 c. multicoloured	15	25
241	**62**	35 c. multicoloured	35	40
242	**63**	50 c. multicoloured	60	70
243	**64**	$1 multicoloured	80	90
244	**65**	$2 multicoloured	2·00	2·25
245	**66**	$3 multicoloured	3·00	3·50
231/45		*Set of* 15	7·00	8·00

1966 (1 July). *World Cup Football Championships. As Nos.* 176/7 *of Antigua.*

246	5 c. violet, yellow-green, lake and yellow-brown	5	10
247	50 c. chocolate, blue-grn., lake and yellow-brown	45	45

1966 (20 Sept.). *Inauguration of W.H.O. Headquarters, Geneva. As Nos.* 178/9 *of Antigua.*

248	8 c. black, yellow-green and light blue	10	10
249	25 c. black, light purple and yellow-brown	30	35

1966 (1 Dec.). *20th Anniv. of U.N.E.S.C.O. As Nos.* 196/8 *of Antigua.*

250	2 c. slate-violet, red, yellow and orange	5	5
251	15 c. orange-yellow, violet and deep olive	20	20
252	50 c. black, bright purple and orange	60	65

II. ASSOCIATED STATEHOOD.

ASSOCIATED STATEHOOD 1967

(67)

1c

(68)

1967 (3 Mar.). *Statehood. Nos.* 232/3, 236 *and* 240 *optd. with T* **67**, *in silver.*

253	**53**	2 c. multicoloured	5	5
254	**54**	3 c. multicoloured	5	5
255	**57**	8 c. multicoloured	10	10
256	**61**	25 c. multicoloured	20	25

1967 (June). *World Fair, Montreal. Nos.* 232, 237, 239 *and* 243/4 *surch. as T* **68** *or optd. with "Expo" emblem only.*

257	**60**	1 c. on 15 c. multicoloured	5	5
		a. Surch. and opt. albino	18·00	
258	**53**	2 c. multicoloured	5	5
259	**58**	3 c. on 10 c. multicoloured	5	5
260	**64**	$1 multicoloured	50	55
261	**65**	$2 multicoloured	95	1·10
257/61		*Set of* 5	1·40	1·60

ASSOCIATED STATEHOOD

(69)

1967 (Oct.). *Statehood. Nos.* 231/45 *optd. with T* **69**.

262	**52**	1 c. multicoloured	5	5
263	**53**	2 c. multicoloured	5	5
264	**54**	3 c. multicoloured	5	5
265	**55**	5 c. multicoloured	5	5
266	**56**	6 c. multicoloured	5	5
267	**57**	8 c. multicoloured	5	5
268	**58**	10 c. multicoloured	8	8
269	**59**	12 c. multicoloured	10	12
270	**60**	15 c. multicoloured	12	12
271	**61**	25 c. multicoloured	20	20
272	**62**	35 c. multicoloured	30	35
273	**63**	50 c. multicoloured	50	60
274	**64**	$1 multicoloured	75	85
275	**65**	$2 multicoloured	1·75	2·00
276	**66**	$3 multicoloured	2·50	3·00
262/76		*Set of* 15	6·00	7·00

See also No. 295.

70. Kennedy and Local Flower.

71. Kennedy and Strelitzia.
72. Kennedy and Roses.

(Des. M. Shamir. Photo. Harrison.)

1968 (13 Jan.). *50th Birth Anniv. of President Kennedy. P* 14½×14.

277	**70**	1 c. multicoloured	5	5
278	,,	15 c. multicoloured	12	12
279	**71**	25 c. multicoloured	20	20
280	**72**	35 c. multicoloured	25	30
281	**71**	50 c. multicoloured	30	35
282	**72**	$1 multicoloured	55	60
277/82		*Set of* 6	1·25	1·40

73. Scout Bugler.

74. Scouts Camping.
75. Lord Baden-Powell.

(Des. K. Plowitz. Photo. Govt. Printer, Israel.)

1968 (17 Feb.). *World Scout Jamboree, Idaho. P* 13×13½.

283	**73**	1 c. multicoloured	5	5
284	**74**	2 c. multicoloured	5	5
285	**75**	3 c. multicoloured	5	5
286	**73**	35 c. multicoloured	25	30
287	**74**	50 c. multicoloured	30	35
288	**75**	$1 multicoloured	55	60
283/8		*Set of* 6	1·10	1·25

76. "Fishing Boat at Moorings".
77. "View overlooking the Sea".
78. "Waterfront Scene".
79. Sir Winston painting.

(Des. G. L. Vasarhelyi. Photo. Harrison.)

1968 (23 Mar.). *Paintings by Sir Winston Churchill. P* 14×14½.

289	**76**	10 c. multicoloured	10	10
290	**77**	12 c. multicoloured	10	10
291	**78**	15 c. multicoloured	12	12
292	**76**	25 c. multicoloured	20	20
293	**78**	35 c. multicoloured	30	30
294	**79**	50 c. multicoloured	35	40
289/94		*Set of* 6	1·00	1·10

$5

(80)

1968 (18 May). *No.* 275 *surch. with T* **80**.

295	**65**	$5 on $2 multicoloured	3·00	3·50

CHILDREN NEED MILK

2cts. + 3cts.

(81)

CHILDREN NEED MILK

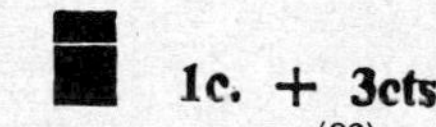

1c. + 3cts.

(82)

1968. "*Children Need Milk*". (*a*) *Nos.* 244/5 *surch. locally as T* **81** (22 *July*).

296	**65**	2 c.+3 c. on $2 mult.	15	20
297	**66**	3 c.+3 c. on $3 mult.	15	25
		a. Surch. inverted	55·00	
		b. Surch. double	35·00	

(*b*) *Nos.* 243/4 *surch. locally as T* **82** (19 *Aug.*).

298	**64**	1 c. +3 c. on $1 mult.	1·40	1·60
		a. Surch. on No. 274	70·00	
		b. Surch. double	65·00	
299	**65**	2 c.+3 c. on $2 mult.	13·00	14·00
		a. Surch. on No. 275	70·00	

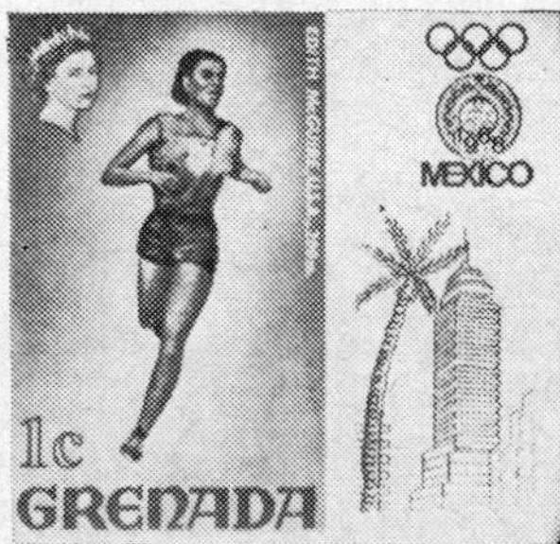

83. Edith McGuire (U.S.A.).

84. Arthur Wint (Jamaica).
85. Ferreira da Silva (Brazil).

(Des. M. Shamir. Photo. Harrison.)

1968 (24 Sept.). *Olympic Games, Mexico. P* 12½.

300	**83**	1 c. brown, black & blue	5	5
301	**84**	2 c. orange, brown, blue and lilac	5	5
302	**85**	3 c. scarlet, brown and dull green	5	5
		a. Scarlet (rings, "MEXICO" etc.) omitted		
303	**83**	10 c. brown, black, blue and vermilion ..	10	10
304	**84**	50 c. orange, brown, blue and turquoise ..	30	35
305	**85**	60 c. scarlet, brown and red-orange	40	50
300/305		.. .. *Set of* 6	85	1·00
2 complete sheets each of 9 stamps			2·75	3·00

Nos. 300/2 were issued in a composite sheet containing three strips of three, each value, adjoining three labels showing an ancient Greek athlete and history of the Olympic Games.

Nos. 303/5 were also issued thus but with labels showing statue of Discobolos.

86. Hibiscus.

(*Nos.* 314*a*, 317*a and the dollar values are larger*—25½ × 48, 29 × 45½ *and* 44 × 28½ *mm. respectively*.)

(Des. G. L. Vasarhelyi (No. 314*a*), V. Whiteley (75 c.), M. Shamir (others). Litho. Format (Nos. 314*a* and 317*a*). Photo. Harrison (others).)

1968 (Oct.)–**71.** *T* **86** *and similar multicoloured designs. P* 13½ (*Nos.* 314*a and* 317*a*), 13½ × 14½ (*vert. except No.* 314*a*) *or* 14½ × 13½ (*horiz. except No.* 317*a*).

306	1 c. Type **86**	5	5
307	2 c. Strelitzia	5	5
308	3 c. Bougainvillea (1.7.69) ..	5	5
309	5 c. Rock Hind (*horiz.*) (4.2.69)	5	5
310	6 c. Sailfish	5	5
311	8 c. Snapper (*horiz.*) (1.7.69)	5	8
312	10 c. Giant Toad (*horiz.*) (4.2.69)	8	10
313	12 c. Turtle	10	12
314	15 c. Tree Boa (*horiz.*) ..	20	20
314*a*	15 c. Thunbergia (1970) ..	20	20
315	25 c. Opossum (4.2.69) ..	25	25
316	35 c. Armadillo (*horiz.*) (1.7.69)	25	25
317	50 c. Mona Monkey	35	35
317*a*	75 c. Yacht in St. George's Harbour (*horiz.*) (9.10.71)	45	50
318	$1 Bananaquit	65	70
319	$2 Pelican (4.2.69) ..	1·25	1·40
320	$3 Frigate Bird	2·00	2·25
321	$5 Bare-eyed Thrush (1.7.69)	3·25	3·50
306/21	.. .. *Set of* 18	8·50	9·50

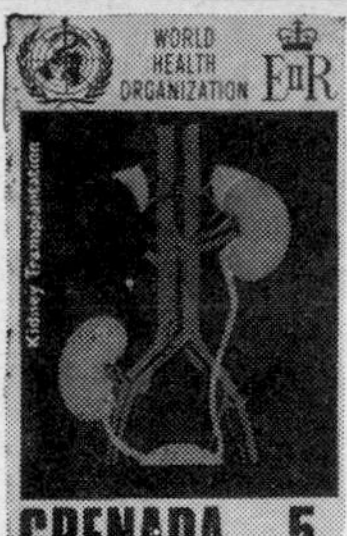

102. Kidney Transplant.

103. Heart Transplant.
104. Lung Transplant.
105. Eye Transplant.

(Des. M. Shamir. Litho. Bradbury, Wilkinson.)

1968 (25 Nov.). *20th Anniv. of World Health Organization. P* 13 × 13½.

322	**102**	5 c. multicoloured ..	5	5
323	**103**	25 c. multicoloured ..	20	25
324	**104**	35 c. multicoloured ..	25	30
325	**105**	50 c. multicoloured ..	35	40

106. " The Adoration of the Magi " (Veronese).

(Photo. Harrison.)

1968 (3 Dec.). *Christmas. T* **106** *and similar square designs. P* 12½.

326	5 c. multicoloured ..	5	5
327	15 c. multicoloured ..	15	15
328	35 c. multicoloured ..	30	30
329	$1 multicoloured ..	65	80

Designs: 15 c. " Madonna and Child with Sts. John and Catherine " (Titian); 35 c. " Adoration of the Magi " (Botticelli); $1 " A Knight adoring " (Catena).

VISIT CARIFTA EXPO '69
April 5-30
5c

(110)

1969 (Feb.). *Caribbean Free Trade Area Exhibition. Nos.* 300/5 *surch. in red as T* **110.**

330	**83**	5 c. on 1 c.	5	5
331	**84**	8 c. on 2 c.	8	8
332	**85**	25 c. on 3 c.	20	20
333	**83**	35 c. on 10 c.	25	25
334	**84**	$1 on 50 c.	60	60
335	**85**	$2 on 60 c.	1·25	1·25
		a. Scarlet (rings, " MEXICO " etc.) omitted	†	—
330/5		.. .. *Set of* 6	2·25	2·25
2 complete sheets each of 9 stamps			8·00	8·00

The centre of the composite sheets is also overprinted with a commemorative inscription publicising CARIFTA EXPO 1969.

111. Dame Hylda Bynoe (Governor) and Island Scene.

112. Premier E. M. Gairy and Island Scene.
113. Emblems of 1958 and 1967 World's Fairs.

(Des. and litho. De La Rue.)

1969 (1 May). *Carifta Expo* '69. *P* 13 × 13½.

336	**111**	5 c. multicoloured ..	5	5
337	**112**	15 c. multicoloured ..	12	15
338	**111**	50 c. multicoloured ..	30	30
339	**113**	60 c. multicoloured ..	35	40

114. Dame Hylda Bynoe.
115. Dr. Martin Luther King. (*Vert.*)

116. " Balshazzar's Feast " (Rembrandt).

(Photo. Enschedé.)

1969 (8 June). *Human Rights Year. P* 12½ × 13 ($1) *or* 13 × 12½ (*others*).

340	**114**	5 c. multicoloured ..	5	5
341	**115**	25 c. multicoloured ..	20	20
342	**114**	35 c. multicoloured ..	25	25
343	**116**	$1 multicoloured ..	60	70

117. Batsman playing Off-drive.

118. Batsman playing defensive Stroke.
119. Batsman sweeping Ball.
120. Batsman playing On-drive.

(Des. M. Shamir and L. W. Denyer. Photo Harrison.)

1969 (1 Aug.). *Cricket. P* 14 × 14½.

344	**117**	3 c. yellow, brown and ultramarine ..	5	5
345	**118**	10 c. multicoloured ..	8	8
346	**119**	25 c. brown, ochre and myrtle-green ..	20	25
347	**120**	35 c. multicoloured ..	25	30

Nos. 344/7 were each issued in small sheets of 9 (3 × 3) with decorative borders.

126. Spacecraft after Lift-Off.

129. Astronaut handling Moon Rock.

121. Astronaut handling Moon Rock.

'his differs from T **129** in the design of the frame and the larger size, 56 × 35½ mm.)

2. Moon Rocket *en route* to the Moon. (*Horiz.*)

3. Space Module landing on Moon. (*Horiz.*)

4. Declaration left on the Moon by Astronauts. (*Horiz.*)

5. Module separating from Space Ship. (*Horiz.*)

127. Spacecraft in Orbit. (*Vert.*)

8. Final descent of Space Module. (*Vert.*)

(Des. G. L. Vasarhelyi. Photo.)

69 (24 Sept.). *First Man on the Moon.* P 13½ (½ c.) *or* 12½ (*others*).

8 **121** ½ c. multicoloured .. 5 5
9 **122** 1 c. multicoloured .. 5 5
0 **123** 2 c. multicoloured .. 5 5
1 **124** 3 c. multicoloured .. 5 5
2 **125** 8 c. multicoloured .. 8 8
3 **126** 25 c. multicoloured .. 15 15
4 **127** 35 c. multicoloured .. 25 25
5 **128** 50 c. multicoloured .. 30 30
6 **129** $1 multicoloured .. 70 70
8/56 .. .. *Set of* 9 1·50 1·50
S357 115 × 90 mm. Nos. 351 and 356. Imperf. 70 80

130. Gandhi.

131. Gandhi (standing). (*Vert.*)

132. Gandhi (walking). (*Vert.*)

133. Head of Gandhi. (*Horiz.*)

)es. A. Robledo. Litho. Bradbury, Wilkinson.)

69 (8 Oct.). *Birth Centenary of Mahatma Gandhi.* P 11½.

8 **130** 6 c. multicoloured .. 5 5
9 **131** 15 c. multicoloured .. 12 12
0 **132** 25 c. multicoloured .. 20 20
1 **133** $1 multicoloured .. 60 65
S362 155 × 122 mm. Nos. 358/61. Imperf. .. .. .. 1·00 1·10

(134) **135.** " Blackbeard " (Edward Teach).

136. Anne Bonney.

137. Jean Lafitte.

138. Mary Read.

1969 (23 Dec.). *Christmas. Nos.* 326/9 *surch. with T* **134** *in black* (2 *c.*) *or optd. with new date only in silver* (*others*).

363 2 c. on 15 c. multicoloured 5 5
364 5 c. multicoloured 5 5
365 35 c. multicoloured 30 35
a. Opt. inverted .. .. 55·00
366 $1 multicoloured 75 80
a. Opt. inverted .. .. 55·00

(Des. K. Plowitz. Recess. Bradbury, Wilkinson.)

1970 (2 Feb.). *Pirates.* P 13½.

367 **135** 15 c. black 12 12
368 **136** 25 c. dull green 20 20
369 **137** 50 c. lilac 40 35
370 **138** $1 carmine 85 75

(139)

(140)

1970 (18 Mar.). *No.* 348 *surch. with T* **139**.

371 **121** 5 c. on ½ c. multicoloured 8 8
a. Surch. double .. 60·00
b. Surch. with T 140 .. 1·25

141. " The Last Supper " (detail, Del Sarto). **142.**

(*Illustration reduced. Actual size* 64 × 45 *mm.*).

143/4. " Christ crowned with Thorns " (detail, Van Dyck).

145/6. " The Passion of Christ " (detail, Memling).

147/8. " Christ in the Tomb " (detail, Rubens).

(Des. and litho. Bradbury Wilkinson Ltd.)

1970 (13 Apr.). *Easter.* P 11½.

372 **141** 5 c. multicoloured .. 5 5
373 **142** 5 c. multicoloured .. 5 5
374 **143** 15 c. multicoloured .. 12 12
375 **144** 15 c. multicoloured .. 12 12
376 **145** 25 c. multicoloured .. 20 20
377 **146** 25 c. multicoloured .. 20 20
378 **147** 60 c. multicoloured .. 40 40
379 **148** 60 c. multicoloured .. 40 40
372/9 .. .. *Set of* 8 1·40 1·40
MS380 120 × 140 mm. Nos. 376/9 1·40 1·40

Nos. 372/9 were issued with each design spread over two *se-tenant* stamps of the same denomination.

149. Girl with Kittens in Pram.

(*Illustration reduced. Actual size* 59 × 34 *mm.*)

150. Girl with Puppy and Kitten.

151. Boy with Fishing-rod and Cat.

152. Boys and Girls with Cats and Dogs.

(Des. A. Robledo. Litho. Questa.)

1970 (27 May). *Birth Bicentenary of William Wordsworth* (*poet*). " *Children and Pets* ". P 11.

381 **149** 5 c. multicoloured .. 5 5
382 **150** 15 c. multicoloured .. 12 12
383 **151** 30 c. multicoloured .. 20 20
384 **152** 60 c. multicoloured .. 35 35
MS385 Two Sheets each 114 × 126 mm. Nos. 381, 383 and Nos. 382, 384. Imperf. .. 90 1·00

153. Parliament of India.

154. Parliament of Great Britain, Westminster.

155. Parliament of Canada.

156. Parliament of Grenada.

(Des. G. L. Vasarhelyi. Litho. Questa.)

1970 (15 June). *Seventh Regional Conference of Commonwealth Parliamentary Association.* P 14.

386 **153** 5 c. multicoloured .. 5 5
387 **154** 25 c. multicoloured .. 20 20
388 **155** 50 c. multicoloured .. 30 35
389 **156** 60 c. multicoloured .. 35 40
MS390 126 × 90 mm. Nos. 386/9 .. 1·00 1·10

157. Tower of the Sun.

158. Livelihood and Industry Pavilion (*Horiz.*)

159. Flower Painting (1634). (*Vert.*)

160. " Adam and Eve " (Titian). (*Horiz.*)

161. Organisation for Economic Co-operation and Development (O.E.C.D.) Pavilion. (*Horiz.*)

162. San Francisco Pavilion. (*Vert.*)

163. Japanese Pavilion. (*Horiz. Size* 56 × 34 *mm.*)

(Litho. Kyodo Printing Co., Tokyo.)

1970 (8 Aug.). *World Fair Osaka. P* 13.

391	**157**	1 c. multicoloured ..	5	5
392	**158**	2 c. multicoloured ..	5	5
393	**159**	3 c. multicoloured ..	5	5
394	**160**	10 c. multicoloured ..	10	10
395	**161**	25 c. multicoloured ..	20	20
396	**162**	50 c. multicoloured ..	35	45
391/6		.. .. *Set of* 6	70	80
MS397	**163**	121 × 91 mm. $1 mult.	65	75

164. Roosevelt and " Raising U.S. Flag on Iwo Jima ".

(*Illustration reduced. Actual size* 60 × 35 *mm.*)

165. Zhukov and " Fall of Berlin ".

166. Churchill and " Evacuation at Dunkirk".

167. De Gaulle and " Liberation of Paris ".

168. Eisenhower and " D–Day Landing ".

169. Montgomery and " Battle of Alamein ".

(Litho. Questa.)

1970 (3 Sept.). *25th Anniv. of Ending of World War II. P* 11.

398	**164**	$\frac{1}{2}$ c. multicoloured ..	5	5
399	**165**	5 c. multicoloured ..	5	5
400	**166**	15 c. multicoloured ..	12	12
401	**167**	25 c. multicoloured ..	20	20
402	**168**	50 c. multicoloured ..	40	40
403	**169**	60 c. multicoloured ..	50	50
398/403		.. .. *Set of* 6	1·10	1·10
MS404		163 × 113 mm. Nos. 398, 400, 402/3	1·50	1·50

PHILYMPIA
LONDON 1970
(**169**)

1970 (18 Sept.). " *Philympia* 1970 " *Stamp Exhibition, London. Nos.* 353/6 *optd., with T* **169**.

405	**126**	25 c. multicoloured ..	15	20
		a. Albino opt.	20·00	
406	**127**	35 c. multicoloured ..	25	25
		a. Opt. inverted	55·00	
407	**128**	50 c. multicoloured ..	35	35
		a. Albino opt.	14·00	
408	**129**	$1 multicoloured (Sil.) (optd. vert. upwards)	55	55
		a. Albino opt.	27·00	

The Miniature sheet was also issued but we understand that only 300 of these were put on sale in Grenada.

170. U.P.U. Emblem, Building and Transport.

(Litho. Questa.)

1970 (17 Oct.). *New U.P.U. Headquarters Building. T* **170** *and similar multicoloured designs. P* 14.

409		15 c. Type **170**	12	12
410		25 c. As Type **170**, but modern transport	20	20
411		50 c. Sir Rowland Hill and U.P.U. Building ..	30	30
412		$1 Abraham Lincoln and U.P.U. Building ..	55	60
MS413		79 × 85 mm. Nos. 411/12	90	1·00

The 50 c. and $1 are both vertical designs.

171. " The Madonna of the Goldfinch " (Tiepolo).

(Des. G. L. Vasarhelyi. Litho. Questa.)

1970 (5 Dec.). *Christmas. T* **171** *and similar vert. designs. Multicoloured. P* $13\frac{1}{2}$.

414	$\frac{1}{2}$ c. Type **171**	5	5
415	$\frac{1}{2}$ c. " The Virgin and Child with St. Peter and St. Paul " (Bouts)	5	5
416	$\frac{1}{2}$ c. " The Virgin and Child " (Bellini)	5	5
417	2 c. " The Madonna of the Basket " (Correggio) ..	5	5
418	3 c. Type **171**	5	5
419	35 c. As No. 415	30	30
420	50 c. As 2 c.	40	40
421	$1 As No. 416	65	65
414/21	.. .. *Set of* 8	1·40	1·40
MS422	102 × 87 mm. Nos. 420/1	1·25	1·25

172. 19th-Century Nursing.

(Des. G. L. Vasarhelyi. Litho. Questa.)

1970 (12 Dec.). *Centenary of British Red Cross. T* **172** *and similar horiz. designs. Multicoloured. P* $14\frac{1}{2} \times 14$.

423	5 c. Type **172**	5	5
424	15 c. Military Ambulance, 1918	12	12
425	25 c. First-Aid Post, 1941 ..	20	20
426	60 c. Red Cross Transport, 1970	40	40
MS427	113 × 82 mm. Nos. 423/6	80	80
	a. Imperf.	11·00	

173. John Dewey and Art Lesson.

(Des. G. L. Vasarhelyi. Litho. Questa.)

1971 (1 May). *International Education Year (1970). T* **173** *and similar horiz. designs. Multicoloured. P* $13\frac{1}{2}$.

427*a*	5 c. Type **173**	5	5
428	10 c. Jean-Jacques Rousseau		
429	and " Alphabetisation "	8	8
430	50 c. Maimonides and laboratory	30	30
431	$1 Bertrand Russell and mathematics class ..	60	65
MS432	90 × 98 mm. Nos. 430/1 ..	95	95

174. Jennifer Hosten and outline of Grenada.

(Adapted by G. Drummond from local design. Litho. Format.)

1971 (1 June). *Winner of " Miss World " Competition* (1970). *P* $13\frac{1}{2}$.

433	**174**	5 c. multicoloured ..	5	5
434	,,	10 c. multicoloured ..	10	8
435	,,	15 c. multicoloured ..	12	10
436	,,	25 c. multicoloured ..	20	15
437	,,	35 c. multicoloured ..	30	25
438	,,	50 c. multicoloured ..	50	45
433/8		.. .. *Set of* 6	1·25	1·40
MS439	**174**	50 c. multicoloured. Printed on silk. Imperf.	45	50

175. French and Canadian Scouts.

(Litho. Format.)

1971 (11 Sept.). *13th World Scout Jamboree, Asagiri, Japan. T* **175** *and similar horiz. designs. Multicoloured. P* 11.

440	5 c. Type **175**	5	5
441	35 c. German and American scouts	20	20
442	50 c. Australian and Japanese scouts	35	35
443	75 c. Grenada and British scouts	45	50
MS444	101 × 114 mm. Nos. 442/3	1·10	1·10

176. " Napoleon reviewing Troops " (Edouard Detaille).

(Des. G. L. Vasarhelyi. Litho. Questa.)

1971 (9 Oct.). *150th Death Anniversary of Napoleon Bonaparte. T* **176** *and similar vert. designs showing paintings. Multicoloured. P* 13½.

445	5 c. Type **176**	5	5
446	15 c. " Napoleon outside Madrid " (Vernet) ..	12	12
447	35 c. " Napoleon crossing Alps " (David) ..	25	25
448	$2 " Napoleon Bonaparte " (David)	1·25	1·40
MS449	101 × 76 mm. No. 447. Imperf.	45	50

177. 1d. Stamp of 1861 and Badge of Grenada.

(*Illustration reduced. Actual size* 59 × 34 *mm.*)

(Des. R. Granger Barrett. Litho. Questa.)

1971 (6 Nov.). *110th Anniv. of the Postal Service. Type* **177** *and similar horiz. designs. Multicoloured. W* w.**12** (*sideways**) *P* 11.

450	5 c. Type **177**	5	5
451	15 c. 6d. stamp of 1861 and Queen Elizabeth II ..	12	12
452	35 c. 1d. and 6d. stamps of 1861 and badge of Grenada	25	25
453	50 c. Scroll and 1d. stamp of 1861	40	40
MS454	96 × 114. Nos. 452/3 ..	70	80

*This issue is printed on thick paper and consequently the watermark is very faint.

178. Apollo Splashdown.

(*Illustration reduced. Actual size* 58 × 35 *mm.*)

(Des. R. Granger Barrett. Litho. Questa.

1971 (13 Nov.). *Apollo Moon Exploration Series. T* **178** *and similar multicoloured designs. P* 11.

455	1 c. Type **178**	5	5
456	2 c. Recovery of Apollo 13	5	5
457	3 c. Separation of Lunar Module from Apollo 14	5	5
458	10 c. Shepard and Mitchell taking samples of moon rock	10	10
459	25 c. Moon Buggy	25	25
460	$1 Apollo 15 blast-off (*vert.*)	85	90
455/60	.. .. *Set of* 6	1·25	1·25
MS461	77 × 108 mm. 50 c. As $1	60	70

179. 67th Regt. of Foot, 1787.

(Des. G. L. Vasarhelyi. Litho. Format.)

1971 (11 Dec.). *Military Uniforms. T* **179** *and similar vert. designs. Multicoloured. P* 13½.

462	½ c. Type **179**	5	5
463	1 c. 45th Regt. of Foot, 1792	5	5
464	2 c. 29th Regt. of Foot, 1794	5	5
465	10 c. 9th Regt. of Foot, 1801	10	10
466	25 c. 2nd Regt. of Foot, 1815	25	25
467	$1 70th Regt. of Foot, 1764	80	90
462/7	.. .. *Set of* 6	1·10	1·25
MS468	108 × 99 mm. Nos. 466/7 P 15	1·75	1·75

180. " The Adoration of the Magi " (Memling).

(Des. G. L. Vasarhelyi. Litho. Questa.)

1972 (15 Jan.). *Christmas* (1971). *T* **180** *and similar vert. designs. Multicoloured. P* 14 × 13½.

469	15 c. Type **180**	12	15
470	25 c. " Madonna and Child " (Michelangelo) ..	20	20
471	35 c. " Madonna and Child " (Murillo)	25	25
472	50 c. " Virgin Mary with the Apple " (Memling) ..	35	40
MS473	105 × 80 mm. $1 " The Adoration of the King " (Mostaert).	75	80

35c 

WINTER OLYMPICS
FEB. 3-13, 1972
SAPPORO, JAPAN

(181)

1972 (3 Feb.). *Winter Olympic Games, Sapporo, Japan. Nos.* 462/4 *and* **MS**468 *surch. or optd. only* (**MS**475).

(*a*) *Postage. As T* **181.**

474	$2 on 2 c. multicoloured ..	1·00	1·25
MS475	108 × 99 mm. Nos. 466/7 (R.)	1·10	1·25

(*b*) *Air. As T* **181**, *but additionally surch.* " AIR MAIL ".

476	35 c. on ½ c. multicoloured	20	20
477	50 c. on 1 c. multicoloured	30	35

VOTE
FEB. 28 1972
(182)

1972 (25 Feb.). *General Election. Nos.* 307/8, 310 *and* 315 *optd. with T* **182.**

478	2 c. multicoloured ..	5	5
479	3 c. multicoloured ..	10	10
480	6 c. multicoloured ..	12	15
481	25 c. multicoloured ..	35	40

183. King Arthur.

(Litho. Questa.)

1972 (4 Mar.). *UNICEF. T* **183** *and similar multicoloured designs. P* 14.

482	½ c. Type **183**	5	5
483	1 c. Robin Hood	5	5
484	2 c. Robinson Crusoe ..	5	5
485	25 c. Type **183**	15	15
486	50 c. As No. 483	30	30
487	75 c. As No. 484	40	40
488	$1 Mary and her little lamb	55	55
482/8	.. .. *Set of* 7	1·40	1·40
MS489	65 × 98 mm. No. 488 ..	60	60

INTERPEX
1972
(184)

(185)

12¢

AIR MAIL
(186)

1972 (17 Mar.). *" Interpex " Stamp Exhibition, New York. Nos.* 433/**MS**439 *optd. with T* **184.**

490	**174** 5 c. multicoloured ..	8	8
491	,, 10 c. multicoloured ..	10	10
492	,, 15 c. multicoloured ..	15	15
493	,, 25 c. multicoloured ..	25	25
494	,, 35 c. multicoloured ..	30	35
495	,, 50 c. multicoloured ..	50	60
490/5	.. .. *Set of* 6	1·25	1·40
MS496	**174** 50 c. multicoloured Printed on silk. Imperf. ..	4·50	5·00

1972 (20 Apr.). *Nos.* 306/8 *surch. with T* **185**, *and No.* 433 *surch. similarly but with obliterating bars under* " 12 ¢ ".

497	12 c. on 1 c. Type **86**	15	15
498	12 c. on 2 c. Strelitzia	15	15
499	12 c. on 3 c. Bougainvillea ..	15	15
500	12 c. on 5 c. Type **174**	15	15

1972. *Air.* (*a*) *Stamps of* 1968 *optd. as T* **186** *or surch. in addition* (2 May).

501	5 c. Rock Hind	5	5
502	8 c. Snapper	5	5
503	10 c. Giant Toad	8	8
	a. Opt. double	45·00	
504	15 c. Thunbergia	10	10
505	25 c. Opossum	20	20
	a. Horiz. pair, one without opt.		
506	30 c. on 1 c. Type **86**	20	20
507	35 c. Armadillo	25	25
508	40 c. on 2 c. Strelitzia	25	25
509	45 c. on 3 c. Bougainvillea ..	30	30
510	50 c. Mona Monkey	30	30
	a. Horiz. pair, one without opt.	60·00	
511	60 c. on 5 c. Rock Hind ..	35	40
512	70 c. on 6 c. Sailfish	40	45
513	$1 Bananaquit	50	60
514	$1·35 on 8 c. Snapper ..	65	75
515	$2 Pelican	1·00	1·25
516	$3 Frigate Bird	1·50	1·75
517	$5 Bare-eyed Thrush ..	2·50	3·00

(*b*) *Nos.* 440/3 *optd. as T* **186** (5 June).

518 **175**	5 c. multicoloured ..	8	8
519 –	35 c. multicoloured ..	20	25
520 –	50 c. multicoloured ..	30	35
521 –	75 c. multicoloured ..	45	50
501/21	.. .. *Set of* 21	9·00	10·00

187. Yachting.

(Litho. Format.)

1972 (8 Sept.). *Olympic Games, Munich. T* **187** *and similar multicoloured designs. P* 14.

(*a*) *Postage.*

522	½ c. Type **187**	5	5
523	1 c. Show-jumping ..	5	5
524	2 c. Running (*vert.*) ..	5	5
525	35 c. As 2 c.	25	25
526	50 c. As 1 c.	35	35

(*b*) *Air.*

527	25 c. Boxing	20	20
528	$1 As 25 c.	75	75
522/8	.. .. *Set of* 7	1·50	1·50
MS529	82 × 85 mm. 60 c. as 25 c. *se-tenant* with 70 c. as 1 c. ..	1·00	1·00

188. Badge of Grenada and Nutmegs.

(Des. (from photograph by D. Groves) and photo. Harrison.)

1972 (20 Nov.). *Royal Silver Wedding. Multi-coloured; background colour given. W* w.**12.** *P* 14 × 14½.

530 **188**	8 c. olive-brown	8	10
531 ,,	$1 ultramarine ..	70	70

189. Boy Scout Saluting.

(Des. R. Granger Barrett. Litho. Questa.)

1972 (2 Dec.). *65th Anniv. of Boy Scouts. T* **189** *and similar horiz. designs. Multicoloured. P* 14.

(*a*) *Postage.*

532	½ c. Type **189**	5	5
533	1 c. Scouts knotting ropes	5	5
534	2 c. Scouts shaking hands	5	5
535	3 c. Lord Baden-Powell ..	5	5
536	75 c. As 2 c.	40	40
537	$1 As 3 c.	55	55

(*b*) *Air.*

538	25 c. Type **189**	20	20
539	35 c. As 1 c.	25	25
532/9	.. .. *Set of* 8	1·40	1·40
MS540	87 × 88 mm. 60 c. as 3 c., and 70 c. as 2 c.	85	85

190. Madonna and Child.

(Des. V. Whiteley. Litho. Format.)

1972 (9 Dec.). *Christmas. T* **190** *and similar vert. designs. Multicoloured. P* 13½.

541	1 c. Type **190**	5	5
542	3 c. The Three Kings ..	5	5
543	5 c. The Nativity ..	5	5
544	25 c. Type **190**	20	20
545	35 c. As 3 c.	25	30
546	$1 As 5 c.	75	85
541/6	.. .. *Set of* 6	1·10	1·25
MS547	102 × 76 mm. 60 c. Type **190**, and 70 c. as 3 c. *P* 15	1·00	1·00

191. Flamingoes.

(Des. Shamir Bros. Litho. Questa.)

1973 (26 Jan.). *National Zoo. T* **191** *and similar horiz. designs. Multicoloured. P* 14½.

548	25 c. Type **191**	15	15
549	35 c. Tapir	25	25
550	60 c. Macaws	30	35
551	70 c. Leopard	35	35

192. Class II Racing Yacht.

(Des. V. Whiteley. Litho. Format.)

1973 (26 Feb.). *Yachting. T* **192** *and simila horizontal designs. Multicoloured. P* 13½.

552	25 c. Type **192**	15	1
553	35 c. Harbour, St. George's	20	2
554	60 c. Yacht *Bloodhound* ..	30	3
555	70 c. St. George's	35	3

193. Helios and Earth Orbiting the Sun.

(Des. G. L. Vasarhelyi. Litho. Format.)

1973 (6 July). *I.M.O./W.M.O. Centenary T* **193** *and similar horiz. designs showing Gree Gods. Multicoloured. P* 13½.

556	½ c. Type **193**	5	
557	1 c. Poseidon and " Normad " storm detector	5	
558	2 c. Zeus and radarscope ..	5	
559	3 c. Iris and weather balloon	5	
560	35 c. Hermes and " ATS-3 " satellite	20	2
561	50 c. Zephyrus and diagram of pressure zones	30	3
562	75 c. Demeter and space photo	45	5
563	$1 Selene and rainfall diagram	50	5
556/63	.. .. *Set of* 8	1·40	1·4
MS564	123 × 92 mm. $2 Computer weather map (42 × 31 mm.). P 13½	1·25	1·2

194. Racing Class Yachts.

(Des. G. Drummond. Litho. Format.)

1973 (3 Aug.). *Carriacou Regatta. T* **194** *an similar horiz. designs. Multicoloured. P* 13½

565	½ c. Type **194**	5	
566	1 c. Cruising Class Yacht ..	5	
567	2 c. Open-decked sloops ..	5	
568	35 c. *The Mermaid* (sloop)	20	2
569	50 c. St. George's Harbour ..	25	3
570	75 c. Map of Carriacou ..	40	4
571	$1 Boat-building	50	5
565/71	.. .. *Set of* 7	1·25	1·4
MS572	109 × 88 mm. $2 End of Race	1·25	1·2

195. Ignatius Semmelweis (Obstetrician).

(Des. G. L. Vasarhelyi. Litho. Format.)

973 (17 Sept.). *25th Anniv. of W.H.O. T* **195** *and similar vert. designs. Multicoloured. P* 14½.

73	½ c. Type **195**	5	5
74	1 c. Louis Pasteur	5	5
75	2 c. Edward Jenner ..	5	5
76	3 c. Sigmund Freud ..	5	5
77	25 c. Emil Von Behring (bacteriologist) ..	15	20
78	35 c. Carl Jung	20	20
79	50 c. Charles Calmette (bacteriologist) ..	30	35
80	$1 William Harvey ..	50	50
73/80	.. .. *Set of* 8	1·25	1·25
IS581	105 × 80 mm. $2 Marie Curie	1·25	1·25

96. Princess Anne and Capt. Mark Phillips.

(Des. G. Drummond. Litho. Format.)

973 (14 Nov.). *Royal Wedding. P* 13½.

82	**196** 25 c. multicoloured ..	15	20
83	„ $2 multicoloured ..	1·25	1·25
IS584	79 × 100 mm. 75 c. and $1 as Nos. 582/3	1·00	1·00

197. " Virgin and Child " (Maratti).

(Litho. Format.)

973 (10 Dec.). *Christmas. T* **197** *and similar vert. designs. Multicoloured. P* 14½.

85	½ c. Type **197**	5	5
86	1 c. " Virgin and Child " (Crivelli)	5	5
87	2 c. " Virgin and Child " (Verrocchio)	5	5
88	3 c. " Adoration of the Shepherds " (Roberti) ..	5	5
589	25 c. " The Holy Family " (Baroccio)	15	15
590	35 c. " The Holy Family " (Bronzino)	20	20
591	75 c. " Mystic Nativity " (Botticelli)	40	40
592	$1 " Adoration of the Magi " (Geertgen)	50	55
585/92	.. .. *Set of* 8	1·25	1·25
MS593	89 × 89 mm. $2 "Adoration of the Magi" (Mostaert) (30 × 45 mm.). *P* 13½..	1·25	1·25

III. INDEPENDENT.

INDEPENDENCE
7TH FEB. 1974

(198)

1974 (7 Feb.). *Independence. Nos.* 306 *etc. optd. as T* **198**.

594	1 c. Hibiscus	5	5
595	2 c. Strelitzia..	5	5
596	3 c. Bougainvillea	5	5
597	5 c. Rock Hind	8	8
598	8 c. Snapper	8	8
599	10 c. Giant Toad	10	10
600	12 c. Turtle	10	10
601	25 c. Opossum..	25	25
602	35 c. Armadillo	30	25
603	75 c. Yacht in St. George's Harbour	70	70
604	$1 Bananaquit	90	80
605	$2 Pelican	1·75	1·50
606	$3 Frigate bird	2·50	2·25
607	$5 Bare-eyed thrush ..	4·00	3·75
594/607	.. .. *Set of* 14	10·00	9·00

199. Creative Arts Theatre, Jamaica Campus.

(Des. G. Drummond. Litho. Format.)

1974 (10 Apr.). *25th Anniv. of University of West Indies. T* **199** *and similar multicoloured designs. P* 13½ × 14.

608	10 c. Type **199**..	10	10
609	25 c. Marryshow House ..	15	20
610	50 c. Chapel, Jamaica Campus (*vert.*)	25	30
611	$1 University arms (*vert.*) ..	55	55
MS612	69 × 86 mm. $2 as No. 611	1·25	1·25

200. Nutmeg Pods and Scarlet Mace.

(Des. G. Drummond. Litho. Format.)

1974 (19 Aug.). *Independence. T* **200** *and similar vert. designs. Multicoloured. P* 13½.

613	3 c. Type **200**..	5	5
614	8 c. Map of Grenada	5	5
615	25 c. Prime Minister Eric Gairy	15	20
616	35 c. Grand Anse Beach and flag	25	25
617	$1 Coat-of-arms	50	60
613/17	.. .. *Set of* 5	90	1·00
MS618	91 × 125 mm. $2 as $1..	1·00	1·25

201. Footballers (West Germany v. Chile).

(Des. G. L. Vasarhelyi. Litho. Format.)

1974 (3 Sept.). *World Cup Football Championships. T* **201** *and similar multicoloured designs showing footballers of the countries given. P* 14½.

619	½ c. Type **201**..	5	5
620	1 c. East Germany v. Australia	5	5
621	2 c. Yugoslavia v. Brazil ..	5	5
622	10 c. Scotland v. Zaire ..	5	5
623	25 c. Netherlands v. Uruguay	15	20
624	50 c. Sweden v. Bulgaria ..	30	35
625	75 c. Italy v. Haiti ..	40	45
626	$1 Poland v. Argentina ..	50	55
619/26	.. .. *Set of* 8	1·40	1·60
MS627	114 × 76 mm. $2 Country flags. P 13	1·00	1·25

202. Early Mail-trains and "Concorde".

(Des. G. L. Vasarhelyi. Litho. Format.)

1974 (8 Oct.). *Centenary of Universal Postal Union. T* **202** *and similar horiz. designs. Multicoloured. P* 14½.

628	½ c. Type **202**..	5	5
629	1 c. Mailboat *Caesar* (1839) and helicopter	5	5
630	2 c. Airmail transport ..	5	5
631	8 c. Pigeon post (1480) and telephone dial	8	8
632	15 c. 18th-century bellman and tracking antenna	12	12
633	25 c. Messenger (1450) and satellite	15	20
634	35 c. French pillar-box (1850) and mail-boat	25	25
635	$1 18th-century German postman and mail-train of the future	50	55
628/35	.. .. *Set of* 8	1·10	1·25
MS636	105 × 66 mm. $2 St. Gotthard mail-coach (1735). P 13	1·10	1·25

203. Sir Winston Churchill.

(Des. G. L. Vasarhelyi. Litho. Format.)

1974 (28 Oct.). *Birth Centenary of Sir Winston Churchill. T* **203** *and similar portrait design. P* 13½.

637	**203**	35 c. multicoloured ..	20	20
638	–	$2 multicoloured ..	90	95
MS639		129×96 mm. 75 c. as 35 c. and $1 as $2	80	85

204. " Madonna and Child " (Botticelli).

(Des. M. Shamir. Litho. Format.)

1974 (18 Nov.). *Christmas. T* **204** *and similar vert. designs showing " The Madonna and Child" by the artists given. Multicoloured. P* 14½.

640	½ c. Type **204**	5	5
641	1 c. Niccolo di Pietro ..	5	5
642	2 c. Van der Weyden ..	5	5
643	3 c. Bastiani	5	5
644	10 c. Giovanni	8	8
645	25 c. Van Der Weyden ..	15	20
646	50 c. Botticelli	30	35
647	$1 Mantegna	50	55
640/7	.. .. *Set of* 8	1·10	1·25
MS648	117×96 mm. $2 as 1 c. P 13	1·10	1·25

205. Yachts, Port Saline.

(Des. G. Drummond. Litho. Format.)

1975 (13 Jan.–Mar.). *T* **205** *and similar horiz. designs. Multicoloured.* (a) *Size as T* **205**. *P* 14½.

649	½ c. Type **205**	5	5
650	1 c. Yacht Club race, St. George's	5	5
651	2 c. Carneenage taxi ..	5	5
652	3 c. Large working boats ..	5	5
653	5 c. Deep-water dock, St. George's	5	5
654	6 c. Cocoa beans in drying trays	5	5
655	8 c. Nutmegs	5	5
656	10 c. Rum distillery, River Antoine Estate *c.* 1785 ..	5	5
657	12 c. Cocoa tree	5	5
658	15 c. Fishermen at Fontenoy ..	5	5
659	20 c. Parliament Building ..	8	10
660	25 c. Fort George cannons ..	10	12
661	35 c. Pearls Airport	12	15
662	50 c. General Post Office ..	20	25

(*b*) *Size* 45×28 *mm. P* 13½.

663	75 c. Caribs Leap, Sauteurs Bay (22.1)	25	30
664	$1 Careenage, St. George's (22.1)	35	40
665	$2 St. George's Harbour by night (22.1)	70	75
666	$3 Grand Anse beach (22.1)	1·10	1·25
667	$5 Canoe Bay and Black Bay (22.1)	1·75	2·00
668	$10 sugar-loaf Island (26.3)	3·50	4·00
649/68	.. .. *Set of* 20	8·00	9·00

206. Sail-fish.

(Des. V. Whiteley. Litho. Format.)

1975 (3 Feb.). *Big Game Fishing. T* **206** *and similar horiz. designs. Multicoloured. P* 14½.

669	½ c. Type **206**	5	5
670	1 c. Blue Marlin	5	5
671	2 c. White Marlin	5	5
672	10 c. Yellowfin Tuna	8	8
673	25 c. Wahoo	15	20
674	50 c. Dolphin	30	35
675	70 c. Grouper	40	45
676	$1 Great Barracuda ..	50	55
669/76	.. .. *Set of* 8	1·40	1·60
MS677	107×80 mm. $2 Blue Pointer or Mako Shark. P 13 ..	1·10	1·25

207. Granadilla Barbadine.

(Des. G.L. Vasarhelyi. Litho. Format.)

1975 (26 Feb.). *Flowers. T* **207** *and similar horiz. designs. Multicoloured. P* 14½.

678	½ c. Type **207**	5	5
679	1 c. Bleeding Heart (Easter Lily)	5	5
680	2 c. Poinsettia	5	5
681	3 c. Cocoa flower	5	5
682	10 c. Gladioli	5	8
683	25 c. Redhead/Yellowhead ..	15	15
684	50 c. Plumbago	25	30
685	$1 Orange flower	45	50
678/85	.. .. *Set of* 8	1·00	1·10
MS686	102×82 mm. $2 Barbados Gooseberry. P 13	95	1·00

MINIMUM PRICE

The minimum price quoted is 5p which represents a handling charge rather than a basis for valuing common stamps. For further notes about prices see introductory pages.

208. Dove, Grenada Flag and U.N. Emblem

(Des. G. Drummond. Litho. Format.)

1975 (19 Mar.). *Grenada's Admission to the U.N.* (1974). *T* **208** *and similar vert. design Multicoloured. P* 14½.

687	½ c. Type **208**	5	
688	1 c. Grenada and U.N. flags	5	
689	2 c. Grenada coat-of-arms ..	5	
690	35 c. U.N. emblem over map of Grenada	20	2
691	50 c. U.N. buildings and flags	25	3
692	$2 U.N. emblem and scroll	90	9
687/92	.. .. *Set of* 6	1·25	1·4
MS693	122×91 mm. 75 c. Type **208** and $1 as 2 c. P 13 ..	75	8

209. Paul Revere's Midnight Ride.

(Des. J. Cornel (½ to 10 c.), PAD Studio (40 c. $1), J.W. Ltd. (**MS**704). Litho. Format.)

1975 (6 May). *Bicentenary of American Revolutic (1st issue). T* **209** *and similar multicolour designs.*

(i) *Postage. Horiz. designs.*

		A.	*P* 14½.	B.	*P* 13.
694	½ c. Type **209**	5	5	5	
695	1 c. Crispus Attucks ..	5	5	5	
696	2 c. Patrick Henry ..	5	5	5	
697	3 c. Franklin visits Washington	5	5	5	
698	5 c. Rebel troops ..	5	5	5	
699	10 c. John Paul Jones ..	5	5	5	

(ii) *Air. Vert. designs.*

700	40 c. John Hancock ..	20	25	20	2
701	50 c. Benjamin Franklin ..	25	30	25	3
702	75 c. John Adams ..	35	40	35	4
703	$1 Lafayette	40	45	40	4
694/703	*Set of* 10	1·25	1·40	1·25	1·4

MS704 Two sheets 131×102 mm.: $2 Grenada arms and U.S. seal; $2 Grenada and U.S. flags. P 13½ .. .. 1·75 2·0

Stamps from **MS**704 are horiz. and large 47½×35 mm.

Nos. 694B/703B come from small sheets 5 stamps plus one *se-tenant* label.

See also Nos. 785/92.

210. "Blood of the Redeemer" (G. Bellini).

(Des. M. Shamir. Litho. Format.)

1975 (21 May). *Easter. T* **210** *and similar vert. designs. Multicoloured. P* 14½.

705 ½ c. Type **210** 5 5
706 1 c. "The Virgin Mary with Christ's Body" (Bellini) 5 5
707 2 c. "The Entombment" (Van der Weyden) .. 5 5
708 3 c. "Christ with the Virgin Mary" (Bellini) .. 5 5
709 35 c. "Christ with the Apostles" (Bellini) .. 15 20
710 75 c. "The Dead Christ" (Bellini) 35 40
711 $1 "The Deposition" (Procaccini) 40 45
705/11 .. .. *Set of* 7 1·00 1·10
MS712 117 × 100 mm. $2 "Pietà" (Botticelli). P 13 .. .. 80 85

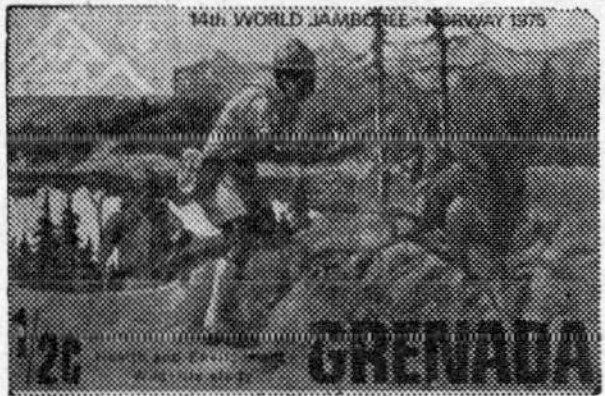

211. Wildlife Study.

(Des. J.W. Ltd. Litho. Questa.)

1975 (2 July). *14th World Scout Jamboree, Norway. T* **211** *and similar horiz. designs. Multicoloured. P* 14.

713 ½ c. Type **211** 5 5
714 1 c. Sailing 5 5
715 2 c. Map-reading 5 5
716 35 c. First-aid 15 15
717 40 c. Physical training .. 20 25
718 75 c. Mountaineering 30 35
719 $2 Sing-song 80 85
713/19 .. .. *Set of* 7 1·40 1·40
MS720 106 × 80 mm. $1 Boat-building 40 45

212. Leafy Jewel Box.

(Des. J.W. Ltd. Litho. Questa.)

1975 (1 Aug.). *Seashells. T* **212** *and similar vert. designs. Multicoloured. P* 14.

721 ½ c. Type **212** 5 5
722 1 c. Emerald Nerite 5 5
723 2 c. Yellow Cockle 5 5
724 25 c. Purple Sea Snail .. 12 12
725 50 c. Turkey Wing 20 25
726 75 c. West Indian Fighting Conch 30 35
727 $1 Noble Wentletrap .. 40 45
721/7 .. .. *Set of* 7 1·00 1·00
MS728 102 × 76 mm. $2 Music Volute 85 90

213. Lady or Large Tiger.

(Des. J.W. Ltd. Litho. Format.)

1975 (22 Sept.). *Butterflies. T* **213** *and similar vert. designs. Multicoloured. P* 14.

729 ½ c. Type **213** 5 5
730 1 c. Five Continent 5 5
731 2 c. Large Striped Blue .. 5 5
732 35 c. Gonatryx 15 15
733 45 c. Spear-winged Cattle-heart 20 20
734 75 c. Rusty Nymula 30 35
735 $2 Blue Night 80 90
729/35 .. .. *Set of* 7 1·40 1·60
MS736 108 × 83 mm. $1 Lycrophon 40 45

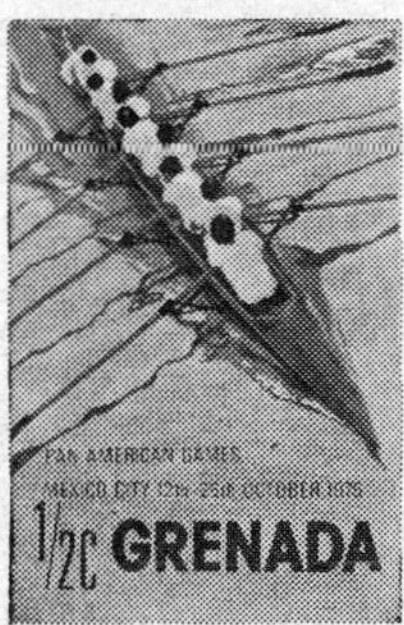

214. Rowing.

(Des. J.W. Ltd. Litho. Questa.)

1975 (13 Oct.). *Pan-American Games, Mexico City. T* **214** *and similar vert. designs. Multicoloured. P* 14.

737 ½ c. Type **214** 5 5
738 1 c. Swimming 5 5
739 2 c. Show-jumping 5 5
740 35 c. Gymnastics 15 15
741 45 c. Football 20 20
742 75 c. Boxing 30 35
743 $2 Cycling 80 90
737/43 .. .. *Set of* 7 1·40 1·60
MS744 106 × 81 mm. $1 Yachting 40 45

215. "The Boy David" (Michelangelo).

(Des. M. and G. Shamir. Litho. J.W.)

1975 (3 Nov.). *500th Birth Anniv. of Michelangelo. T* **215** *and similar vert. designs. Multicoloured. P* 14.

745 ½ c. Type **215** 5 5
746 1 c. "Young Man" (detail) 5 5
747 2 c. "Moses" 5 5
748 40 c. "Zachariah" 20 20
749 50 c. "St. John the Baptist" 20 25
750 75 c. "Judith and Holofernes" 30 35
751 $2 "Doni Madonna" (detail from "Holy Family") 80 85
745/51 .. .. *Set of* 7 1·40 1·60
MS752 104 × 89 mm. $1 "Madonna" (head from Pietà) .. 40 45

The sculpture on No. 749 though ascribed to Michelangelo, shows a work by Francesco Sangallo.

216. "Virgin and Child" (Filippino Lippi).

(Des. M. Shamir. Litho. Questa.)

1975 (8 Dec.). *Christmas. T* **216** *and similar vert. designs showing "Virgin and Child". Multicoloured. P* 14.

753 ½ c. Type **216** 5 5
754 1 c. Mantegna 5 5
755 2 c. Luis de Morales .. 5 5
756 35 c. G. M. Morandi 15 20
757 50 c. Antonello 20 25
758 75 c. Dürer 30 35
759 $1 Velasquez 40 45
753/9 .. .. *Set of* 7 1·00 1·25
MS760 125 × 98 mm. $2 Bellini 75 80

217. Bananaquit.

(Des. G. Drummond. Litho. Questa.)

1976 (20 Jan.). *Flora and Fauna. T* **217** *and similar multicoloured designs. P* 14.

761	½ c. Type **217**	5	5
762	1 c. Orange-rumped Agouti	5	5
763	2 c. Hawksbill Turtle (*horiz.*)	5	5
764	5 c. Dwarf Poinciana	5	5
765	35 c. Albacore (*horiz.*)	15	15
766	40 c. Cardinal's Guard	20	20
767	$2 Antillean Armadillo (*horiz.*)	75	85
761/67	*Set of* 7	1·10	1·25
MS768	82×89 mm. $1 Belted Kingfisher	40	45

218. Carnival Time.

(Des. G. Drummond. Litho. Questa.)

1976 (25 Feb.). *Tourism. T* **218** *and similar horiz. designs. Multicoloured. P* 14.

769	½ c. Type **218**	5	5
770	1 c. Scuba diving	5	5
771	2 c. Cruise Ship *Southward* at St. George's	5	5
772	35 c. Game fishing	15	15
773	50 c. St. George's Golf Course	20	20
774	75 c. Tennis	30	30
775	$1 Ancient rock carvings at Mount Rich	35	40
769/75	*Set of* 7	1·00	1·10
MS776	100×73 mm. $2 Small Boat sailing	70	75

219. " Pietà " (Master of Okolicsno).

(Des. M. & G. Shamir. Litho. Questa.)

1976 (29 Mar.). *Easter. T* **219** *and similar vert. designs by the artists listed. Multicoloured. P* 14.

777	½ c. Type **219**	5	5
778	1 c. Correggio	5	5
779	2 c. Van der Weyden	5	5
780	3 c. Dürer	5	5
781	35 c. Unknown Master	15	15
782	75 c. Raphael	30	35
783	$1 Raphael	40	45
777/83	*Set of* 7	80	90
MS784	108×86 mm. $2 Crespi	80	85

220. Sharpshooters.

(Des. J.W. Ltd. Litho. Questa.)

1976 (15 Apr.). *Bicentenary of American Revolution (2nd issue). T* **220** *and similar vert. designs. Multicoloured. P* 14.

785	½ c. Type **220**	5	5
786	1 c. Defending the Liberty Pole	5	5
787	2 c. Loading muskets	5	5
788	35 c. The fight for Liberty	15	15
789	50 c. Peace Treaty, 1783	20	25
790	$1 Drummers	40	45
791	$3 Gunboat	1·25	1·40
785/91	*Set of* 7	1·75	2·00
MS792	93×79 mm. 75 c. as 35 c. and $2 as 50 c.	1·10	1·25

221. Nature Study.

(Des. G. L. Vasarhelyi. Litho. Questa.)

1976 (1 June). *50th Anniv. of Girl Guides in Grenada. T* **221** *and similar vert. designs. Multicoloured. P* 14.

793	½ c. Type **221**	5	5
794	1 c. Campfire cooking	5	5
795	2 c. First Aid	5	5
796	50 c. Camping	20	25
797	75 c. Home economics	30	35
798	$2 First Aid	80	90
793/8	*Set of* 6	1·25	1·40
MS799	111×85 mm. $1 Painting	40	45

222. Volleyball.

(Des. J.W. Ltd. Litho. Questa.)

1976 (21 June). *Olympic Games, Montreal. T* **222** *and similar vert. designs. Multicoloured. P* 14.

800	½ c. Type **222**	5	5
801	1 c. Cycling	5	5
802	2 c. Rowing	5	5
803	35 c. Judo	15	15
804	45 c. Hockey	20	20
805	75 c. Gymnastics	30	35
806	$1 High jump	40	45
800/6	*Set of* 7	1·00	1·10
MS807	106×81 mm. $3 Equestrian event	1·25	1·40

223. " Cha-U-Kao at the Moulin Rouge ".

(Des. M. Shamir. Litho. Questa.)

1976 (20 July). *75th Death Anniv. of Toulouse Lautrec. T* **223** *and similar vert. designs. Multicoloured. P* 14.

808	½ c. Type **223**	5	5
809	1 c. " Quadrille Beginning "	5	5
810	2 c. " Woman's Bust "	5	5
811	3 c. " Hall at the Moulin Rouge "	5	5
812	40 c. " Launderer Both Albi "	15	20
813	50 c. " Bolero Dancer "	20	25
814	$2 " Signor Boileau at Café "	80	90
808/14	*Set of* 7	1·10	1·25
MS815	152×125 mm. $1 " Lady with Boa "	40	45

1976 (26 July). *West Indian Victory in World Cricket Cup. As Nos.* 559/60 *of Barbados.*

816	35 c. Map of the Caribbean	15	20
817	$1 The Prudential Cup	40	45

224. Piper " Apache ".

(Des. J.W. Ltd. Litho. Questa.)

1976 (18 Aug.). *Aeroplanes. T* **224** *and similar horiz. designs. Multicoloured. P* 14.

818	½ c. Type **224**	5	5
819	1 c. Beech " Twin Bonanza "	5	5
820	2 c. D.H. " Twin Otter "	5	5
821	40 c. Britten Norman " Islander "	15	20
822	50 c. D.H. " Heron "	20	25
823	$2 H.S. " 748 "	80	90
818/23	*Set of* 6	1·10	1·25
MS824	75×83 mm. $3 B.A.C. " 1-11 "	1·25	1·40

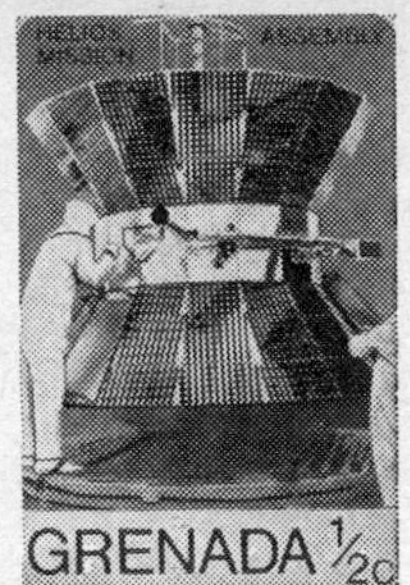

225. Satellite Assembly.

(Des. PAD Studio. Litho. Questa.)

1976 (1 Sept.). *Viking and Helios Space Missions. T* **225** *and similar multicoloured designs. P* 14.

825	½ c. Type **225** . .	5	5
826	1 c. Helios satellite . .	5	5
827	2 c. Helios encapsulation . .	5	5
828	15 c. Systems test . .	5	8
829	45 c. Viking lander (*horiz.*) . .	20	20
830	75 c. Lander on Mars . .	30	35
831	$2 Viking encapsulation . .	80	90
825/31	*Set of* 7	1·25	1·40
MS832	110 × 85 mm. $3 Orbiter and lander . .	1·25	

226. S.S. *Geestland.*

(Des. J.W. Ltd. Litho. Format.)

1976 (3 Nov.). *Ships. T* **226** *and similar horiz. designs. Multicoloured. P* 14½.

833	½ c. Type **226** . .	5	5
834	1 c. M.V. *Federal Palm* . .	5	5
835	2 c. H.M.S. *Blake* . .	5	5
836	25 c. M.V. *Vistafjord* . .	10	12
837	75 c. S.S. *Canberra* . .	30	35
838	$1 S.S. *Regina* . .	40	45
839	$5 S.S. *Arandora Star* . .	2·00	2·25
833/39	*Set of* 7	2·50	2·75
MS840	91 × 78 mm. $2 *Santa Maria* . .	80	

POSTAGE DUE STAMPS.

D 1

1d.

SURCHARGE POSTAGE

(D 2)

(Typo. D.L.R.)

1892. (*a*) *Type* D **1**. *Wmk. Crown CA. P* 14.

D1	D **1** 1d. blue-black . .	3·00	1·60
D2	„ 2d. blue-black . .	4·00	1·60
D3	„ 3d. blue-black . .	5·50	2·00

(*b*) *Nos.* 34 *and* 35 *surch. locally as Type* D **2**.

D4	**13** 1d. on 6d. mauve . .	3·25	1·25
	a. Tête-bêche (pr.) . .	11·00	
	b. Surch. double . .	—	17·00
D5	„ 1d. on 8d. grey-brown . .	24·00	2·75
	a. Tête-bêche (pr.) . .	85·00	
D6	„ 2d. on 6d. mauve . .	6·50	2·00
	a. Tête-bêche (pr.) . .	22·00	
D7	„ 2d. on 8d. grey-brown . .	50·00	6·50
	a. Tête-bêche (pr.) . .	£200	

It seems unlikely that Nos. D4/7 were required or used for postage due purposes as supplies of Nos. D1/3 were received in April or May and the earliest used copy is dated 12 July.

The provisionals were used in the period of August to November but their usage was mainly philatelic. It is known that there was a shortage of 1d. postage stamps from late July to early August, but this was met by the use of Nos. 44/45 which were still available then.

It is therefore believed that the provisionals were intended for use as postage stamps (as indicated by the word "POSTAGE" in the surcharge) but we are left with the fact that their use was purely philatelic.

1906. *Wmk. Mult. Crown CA. P* 14.

D 8	D **1** 1d. blue-black . .	25	35
D 9	„ 2d. blue-black . .	40	40
D10	„ 3d. blue-black . .	65	90

1921–22. *As Type* D **1**, *but inscr.* "POSTAGE DUE". *Wmk. Mult. Script CA. P* 14.

D11	1d. black . .	25	30
D12	1½d. black . .	50	55
D13	2d. black . .	50	55
D14	3d. black . .	60	55
D11/14	Optd. "Specimen" *Set of* 4	28·00	

1952 (1 Mar.). *As Type* D **1**, *but inscr.* "POSTAGE DUE". *Value in cents. Chalk-surfaced paper. Wmk. Mult. Script CA. P* 14.

D15	2 c. black . .	5	5
	a. Error. Crown missing. W9a . .	15·00	
	b. Error. St. Edward Crown, W9b	10·00	
D16	4 c. black . .	8	8
	a. Error. Crown missing. W9a . .	10·00	
	b. Error. St. Edward Crown, W9b	10·00	
D17	6 c. black . .	10	10
	a. Error. Crown missing, W9a . .	15·00	
	b. Error. St. Edward Crown, W9b	18·00	
D18	8 c. black . .	12	12
	a. Error. Crown missing, W9a . .	20·00	
	b. Error. St. Edward Crown, W9b	20·00	

GRENADINES OF GRENADA.

Part of a group of islands north of Grenada, the most important of which is Carriacou. The Grenadine islands further north are administered by St. Vincent, and their stamps are listed after that country.

GRENADINES

(1)

GRENADINES

(2)

1973 (29 Dec.). *Royal Wedding. Nos.* 582/**MS**584 *of Grenada optd. with T* **1**.

1	**196** 25 c. multicoloured . .	20	25
2	„ $2 multicoloured . .	1·25	1·25
	a. Albino opt. . .		
MS3	79 × 100 mm. 75 c. and $1 as Nos. 1/2 . .	1·00	1·00

1974 (29 May). *Nos.* 306 *etc. of Grenada optd. with T* **2**.

4	**86** 1 c. multicoloured . .	5	5
5	**87** 2 c. multicoloured . .	5	5
6	**88** 3 c. multicoloured . .	5	5
7	**89** 5 c. multicoloured . .	5	5
8	**91** 8 c. multicoloured . .	5	5
9	**92** 10 c. multicoloured . .	5	5
10	**93** 12 c. multicoloured . .	8	8
11	**95** 25 c. multicoloured . .	12	15
12	**98** $1 multicoloured . .	40	45
13	**99** $2 multicoloured . .	85	95
14	**100** $3 multicoloured . .	1·25	1·40
15	**101** $5 multicoloured . .	2·10	2·25
4/15	*Set of* 12	4·50	4·75

1974 (17 Sept.). *World Cup Football Championships. As Nos.* 619/**MS**627 *of Grenada but additionally inscr.* "GRENADINES".

16	½ c. Type **201** . .	5	5
17	1 c. East Germany v. Australia . .	5	5
18	2 c. Yugoslavia v. Brazil . .	5	5
19	10 c. Scotland v. Zaire . .	8	8
20	25 c. Netherlands v. Uruguay . .	15	20
21	50 c. Sweden v. Bulgaria . .	30	35
22	75 c. Italy v. Haiti . .	40	45
23	$1 Poland v. Argentina . .	50	55
16/23	*Set of* 8	1·40	1·50
MS24	114 × 76 mm. $2 Country flags . .	1·00	1·10

1974 (8 Oct.). *Centenary of Universal Postal Union. Designs as Nos.* 628 *etc. of Grenada, but additionally inscr.* "GRENADINES".

25	8 c. Mailboat *Caesar* (1839) and helicopter . .	8	8
26	25 c. Messenger (1450) and satellite . .	15	20
27	35 c. Airmail transport . .	20	25
28	$1 Type **202** . .	50	55
MS29	172 × 109 mm. $1 Bellman and antenna & $2 18th-century postman and mail-train of the future . .	1·50	1·60

1974 (11 Nov.). *Birth Centenary of Sir Winston Churchill. As Nos.* 637/**MS**639 *of Grenada but additionally inscr.* "GRENADINES".

30	**203** 35 c. multicoloured . .	15	15
31	– $2 multicoloured . .	85	90
MS32	129 × 96 mm. 75 c. as 35 c. and $1 as $2 . .	75	80

1974 (27 Nov.). *Christmas. As Nos.* 640/**MS**648 *of Grenada but additionally inscr.* "GRENADINES".

33	½ c. Type **204** . .	5	5
34	1 c. Niccolo di Pietro . .	5	5
35	2 c. Van der Weyden . .	5	5
36	3 c. Bastiani . .	5	5
37	10 c. Giovanni . .	8	8
38	25 c. Van der Weyden . .	15	20
39	50 c. Botticelli . .	30	35
40	$1 Mantegna . .	50	55
33/40	*Set of* 8	1·10	1·25
MS41	117 × 96 mm. $2 as 1 c.	1·10	1·25

CANCELLED REMAINDERS*. Some of the following issues have been remaindered, cancelled to order, at a fraction of their face value. For all practical purposes these are indistinguishable from genuine postally used copies. Our used quotations, which are indicated by an asterisk, are the same for cancelled-to-order or postally used copies.

1975 (17 Feb.). *Big Game Fishing. As Nos. 669 etc. of Grenada, but additionally inscr.* "GRENADINES" *and background colours changed.*

42 ½ c. Type **206** 5 5
43 1 c. Blue Marlin 5 5
44 2 c. White Marlin 5 5
45 10 c. Yellow Tuna 8 8
46 25 c. Wahoo 15 20
47 50 c. Dolphin 30 35
48 75 c. Grouper 40 40
49 $1 Great Barracuda 50 55
42/9 .. .. .. *Set of* 8 1·40 1·50
MS50 107×80 mm. $2 Blue Pointer or Mako Shark. P 13 .. 1·10 1·25

1975 (11 Mar.). *Flowers. As Nos.* 678 *etc. of Grenada, but additionally inscr.* "GRENADINES".

51 ½ c. Type **207** 5 5
52 1 c. Bleeding Heart (Easter Lily) 5 5
53 2 c. Poinsettia 5 5
54 3 c. Cocoa flower 5 5
55 10 c. Gladioli 8 8
56 25 c. Redhead/Yellowhead .. 15 20
57 50 c. Plumbago 30 35
58 $1 Orange flower 50 55
51/8 .. .. .. *Set of* 8 1·10 1·25
MS59 102×82 mm. $2 Barbados Gooseberry .. .. .. 1·10 1·25

3. "The Crucifixion" (Titian).

(Des. M. Shamir. Litho. Format.)

1975 (June). *Easter.* T **3** *and similar vert. designs showing Crucifixion and Deposition scenes by the artists listed. Multicoloured.* P 14½.

60 ½ c. Type **3** 5 5*
61 1 c. Giotto 5 5*
62 2 c. Tintoretto 5 5*
63 3 c. Cranach 5 5*
64 35 c. Caravaggio 15 8*
65 75 c. Tiepolo 35 8*
66 $2 Velasquez 80 8*
60/6 .. .. .. *Set of* 7 1·25 40*
MS67 105×90 mm. $1 Titian. P 13 .. .. 40 45

4. "Lorenzo de Medici".

(Des. M. Shamir. Litho. Format.)

1975 (July). *500th Birth Anniv. of Michelangelo.* T **4** *and similar vert. designs. Multicoloured.* P 14½.

68 ½ c. Type **4** 5 5*
69 1 c. "Delphic Sybil" .. 5 5*
70 2 c. "Giuliano de Medici" .. 5 5*
71 40 c. "The Creation" (detail) 15 8*
72 50 c. "Lorenzo de Medici" (*different*) 20 8*
73 75 c. "Artist at work" .. 35 8*
74 $2 "Head of Christ" .. 80 8*
68/74 .. .. .. *Set of* 7 1·40 40*
MS75 118×96 mm. $1 "The Prophet Jeremiah". P 13 .. 40 45

1975 (12 Aug.). *Butterflies. Designs as Nos.* 729 *etc. of Grenada, but additionally inscr.* "GRENADINES". P 14½.

76 ½ c. Emperor 5 5
77 1 c. Queen 5 5
78 2 c. Tiger Pierid 5 5
79 35 c. Cracker 15 15
80 45 c. Scarce Bamboo Page .. 20 20
81 75 c. Apricot 30 35
82 $2 Purple King Shoemaker .. 80 90
76/82 .. .. .. *Set of* 7 1·40 1·60
MS83 104×77 mm. $1 Bamboo Page. P 13 .. .. .. 40 45

5. Progress "Standard" Badge.

(Des. J.W. Ltd. Litho. Format.)

1975 (22 Aug.). *14th World Scout Jamboree, Norway.* T **5** *and similar horiz. designs. Multicoloured.* P 14½.

84 ½ c. Type **5** 5 5
85 1 c. Boatman's badge 5 5
86 2 c. Coxswain's badge 5 5
87 35 c. Interpreter's badge .. 15 15
88 45 c. Ambulance badge .. 20 20
89 75 c. Chief Scout's award .. 30 35
90 $2 Queen's Scout award .. 80 90
84/90 .. .. .. *Set of* 7 1·40 1·60
MS91 106×80 mm. $1 Venture award. P 13 .. .. .. 40 45

6. "The Surrender of Lord Cornwallis".

(Des. J.W. Ltd. Litho. Questa.)

1975 (30 Sept.)–**76**. *Bicentenary of American Revolution* (1*st issue*). T **6** *and similar horiz. designs. Multicoloured.* P 11 (*Nos.* 100/101) *or* 14 (*others*).

92 ½ c. Type **6** 5 5*
93 1 c. Minute-men 5 5*
94 2 c. Paul Revere's ride .. 5 5*
95 3 c. Battle of Bunker Hill .. 5 5*
96 5 c. Fifer and drummers .. 5 5*
97 45 c. Backwoodsman 20 8*
98 75 c. Boston Tea Party .. 30 8*
99 $2 Naval engagement .. 80 8*
100 $2 George Washington (35×60 *mm.*) (16.1.76) .. 80 90
101 $2 White House and flags (35×60 *mm.*) (16.1.76) .. 80 90
92/9 .. .. .. *Set of* 8 1·25 40*
MS102 Two sheets: 113×128 mm., $2 George Washington; 128×113 mm., $2 White House and flags. Imperf. .. .. .. 1·75 2·00

Stamps from **MS**102 are larger, the first being 35×60 mm. and the second 60×34 mm.

See also Nos. 176/**MS**183.

7. Fencing.

(Des. J.W. Ltd. Litho. Format.)

1975 (27 Oct.). *Pan-American Games, Mexico City.* T **7** *and similar horiz. designs. Multicoloured.* P 14½.

103 ½ c. Type **7** 5 5
104 1 c. Hurdling 5 5
105 2 c. Pole-vaulting 5 5
106 35 c. Weightlifting 15 15
107 45 c. Throwing the javelin .. 20 20
108 75 c. Throwing the discus .. 30 35
109 $2 Diving 80 90
103/109 .. .. *Set of* 7 1·40 1·60
MS110 78×104 mm. $1 Sprinter. P 13 .. .. 40 45

1975 (6 Nov.). *Horiz. designs as* T **205** *of Grenada but additionally inscribed* "GRENADINES". *Multicoloured.*

111 ½ c. Yachts, Port Saline .. 5 5
112 1 c. Yacht Club race, St. George's 5 5
113 2 c. Carenage taxi .. 5 5
114 3 c. Large working boats .. 5 5
115 5 c. Deep-water dock, St. George's 5 5
116 6 c. Cocoa beans in drying trays 5 5
117 8 c. Nutmegs 5 5
118 10 c. Rum distillery, River Antoine Estate *c.* 1785 .. 5 5
119 12 c. Cocoa tree 5 5
120 15 c. Fishermen at Fontenoy 5 5
121 20 c. Parliament Building .. 8 8
122 25 c. Fort George cannons .. 10 10
123 35 c. Pearls Airport .. 12 15
124 50 c. General Post Office .. 20 20
125 75 c. Caribs Leap, Sauteurs Bay 20 25
126 $1 Careenage, St. George's 35 40
127 $2 St. George's Harbour by night 70 80
128 $3 Grand Anse beach .. 1·10 1·25
129 $5 Canoe Bay and Black Bay .. .. .. 1·75 2·00
130 $10 Sugar-loaf Island .. 3·50 4·00
111/30 .. .. *Set of* 20 8·00 9·00

8. "Virgin and Child" (Dürer).

(Des. M. Shamir. Litho. Questa.)

1975 (22 Dec.). *Christmas.* T **8** *and similar vert. designs showing* "*Virgin and Child*". *Multicoloured.* P 14.

131 ½ c. Type **8** 5 5
132 1 c. Dürer 5 5
133 2 c. Correggio 5 5
134 40 c. Botticelli 15 15
135 50 c. Niccolla da Cremona .. 20 20
136 75 c. Correggio 25 30
137 $2 Correggio 75 80
131/7 .. .. *Set of* 7 1·25 1·40
MS138 114×102 mm. $1 Bellini 40 45

9. Bleeding Tooth.

(Des. J.W. Ltd. Litho. Questa.)

1976 (13 JAN.). *Shells. T* **9** *and similar horiz. designs. Multicoloured. P* 14.

139 ½ c. Type **9** 5 5
140 1 c. Wedge Clam 5 5
141 2 c. Hawk Wing Conch .. 5 5
142 3 c. *Distorsio clathrata* .. 5 5
143 25 c. Scotch Bonnet 10 10
144 50 c. King Helmet 20 20
145 75 c. Queen Conch 20 25
139/45 .. .. *Set of* 7 65 65
MS146 79 × 105 mm. $2 Atlantic Triton 70 75

10. Cocoa Thrush.

(Des. J.W. Ltd. Litho. Questa.)

1976 (26 JAN.). *Flora and Fauna. T* **10** *and similar horiz. designs. Multicoloured. P* 14.

147 ½ c. *Lignum vitae* .. .. 5 *d*
148 1 c. Type **10** 5 5
149 2 c. Tarantula 5 5
150 35 c. Hooded Tanager .. 15 15
151 50 c. *Nyctaginaceae* 20 20
152 75 c. Grenada Dove 30 30
153 $1 Marine Toad 35 40
147/53 .. .. *Set of* 7 1·00 1·10
MS154 108 × 84 mm. $2 Blue-hooded Euphonia 70 75

11. Hooked Sailfish.

(Des. G. Drummond. Litho. Questa.)

1976 (17 FEB.). *Tourism. T* **11** *and similar horiz. designs. Multicoloured. P* 14.

155 ½ c. Type **11** 5 5
156 1 c. Careened schooner, Carriacou 5 5
157 2 c. Carriacou Annual Regatta 5 5
158 18 c. Boat building on Carriacou 5 8
159 22 c. Workboat race, Carriacou Regatta 10 10
160 75 c. Cruising off Petit Martinique 30 30
161 $1 Water skiing 35 40
155/61 .. .. *Set of* 7 85 90
MS162 $2 Yacht racing at Carriacou 70 75

12. Making a Camp Fire.

(Des. G. L. Vasarhelyi. Litho. Questa.)

1976 (17 MAR.). *50th Anniv. of Girl Guides in Grenada. T* **12** *and similar horiz. designs. Multicoloured. P* 14.

163 ½ c. Type **12** 5 5
164 1 c. First aid 5 5
165 2 c. Nature study 5 5
166 50 c. Cookery 20 25
167 $1 Sketching 40 45
163/7 .. .. *Set of* 5 60 70
MS168 85 × 110 mm. $2 Guide playing guitar 80 80

13. "Christ Mocked" (Bosch.)

(Des. PAD Studio. Litho. Questa.)

1976 (28 APR.). *Easter. T* **13** *and similar vert. designs. Multicoloured. P* 14.

169 ½ c. Type **13** 5 5
170 1 c. "Christ Crucified" (Antonello da Messina) .. 5 5
171 2 c. "Adoration of the Trinity" (Dürer) .. 5 5
172 3 c. "Lamentation of Christ" (Dürer) 5 5
173 35 c. "The Entombment" (Van der Weyden) .. 15 15
174 $3 "The Deposition" (Raphael) .. .. 1·25 1·40
169/74 .. .. *Set of* 6 1·40 1·60
MS175 57 × 72 mm. $2 "Blood of the Redeemer" (G. Bellini) .. 80 80

14. Frigate *South Carolina.*

(Des. J.W. Ltd. Litho. Questa.)

1976 (18 MAY). *Bicentenary of American Revolution (2nd issue). T* **14** *and similar horiz. designs. Multicoloured. P* 14.

176 ½ c. Type **14** 5 5
177 1 c. Schooner *Lee* 5 5
178 2 c. H.M.S. *Roebuck* 5 5
179 35 c. *Andrea Doria* 15 15
180 50 c. Sloop *The Providence* .. 20 25
181 $1 American flagship *Alfred* 40 50
182 $2 Frigate *Confederacy* .. 80 90
176/82 .. .. *Set of* 7 1·50 1·75
MS183 72 × 85 mm. $3 Cutter *Revenge* .. .. 1·25 1·40

15. Piper "Apache".

(Des. J.W. Ltd. Litho. Format.)

1976 (10 JUNE). *Aeroplanes. T* **15** *and similar horiz. designs. Multicoloured. P* 14.

184 ½ c. Type **15** 5 5
185 1 c. Beech "Twin Bonanza" 5 5
186 2 c. D.H. "Twin Otter" .. 5 5
187 40 c. Britten Norman "Islander" 15 20
188 50 c. D.H. "Heron" 20 25
189 $2 H.S. "748" .. .. 90 1·00
184/9 .. .. *Set of* 6 1·25 1·40
MS190 71 × 85 mm. $3 B.A.C. "1-11" .. .. 1·25 1·25

16. Cycling.

(Des. J.W. Ltd. Litho. Format.)

1976 (1 JULY). *Olympic Games, Montreal. T* **16** *and similar horiz. designs. Multicoloured. P* 14.

191 ½ c. Type **16** 5 5
192 1 c. Pommel horse 5 5
193 2 c. Hurdling 5 5
194 35 c. Shot putting 15 20
195 45 c. Diving 20 20
196 75 c. Sprinting 30 35
197 $2 Rowing 80 90
191/7 .. .. *Set of* 7 1·40 1·60
MS198 101 × 76 mm. $3 Sailing 1·25 1·25

17. "Virgin and Child" (Cima).

(Litho. Format.)

1976 (19 OCT.). *Christmas. T* **17** *and similar multicoloured designs. P* 13½.

199 ½ c. Type **17** 5 5
200 1 c. "The Nativity" (Romanino) 5 5
201 2 c. "The Nativity" (Romanino) (*different*) .. 5 5
202 35 c. "Adoration of the Kings" (Bruegel) 15 20
203 50 c. "Madonna and Child" (Girolamo) 20 25
204 75 c. "Adoration of the Magi" (Giorgione) (*horiz.*) .. 30 35
205 $2 "Adoration of the Kings" (Fra Angelico) (*horiz.*) .. 80 90
199/205 .. .. *Set of* 7 1·40 1·60
MS206 120 × 100 mm. $3 "The Holy family" (Garofalo) .. 1·25

GRIQUALAND WEST.

Stamps of the Cape of Good Hope, T **4** *(4d., 6d. and 1s.) and* **6** *(½d., 1d., 4d. and 5s.), wmk. Crown CC, perf. 14, with various overprints.*

1874 (Sept.). *With manuscript surcharge.*

1	1d. in red on 4d. blue (T 4) ..	£200	£275

G. W.

1877 (Mar.). *Optd. "G.W." as above. (a) In black.*

2	1d. carmine-red	£110	25·00
	a. Overprint double	†	£350
	(b) In red.		
3	4d. blue (T 6)	75·00	18·00

G (1) G (2) G (3) G (4) G (5) G (6)

G (7) G (8) G (9) G (10) G (11)

G (12) G (13) G (14)

A. *Overprinted with large capital letter.*

1877 (April). I. *First printing, in black on the 1d. and in red on the other values. SEVEN principal varieties of type (T* **1, 2, 3, 4, 5, 6** *and* **8**).

No.	Type		Unused	Used
4	1	½d. grey-black	3·00	3·00
5	2	½d. grey-black	5·50	6·00
6	3	½d. grey-black	2·00	3·00
7	4	½d. grey-black	5·00	5·00
8	5	½d. grey-black	5·50	5·50
9	6	½d. grey-black	3·00	2·50
10	8	½d. grey black		
11	1	1d. carmine-red	2·00	2·00
12	2	1d. carmine-red	6·00	5·50
13	3	1d. carmine-red	2·75	3·00
14	4	1d. carmine-red	4·50	4·50
15	5	1d. carmine-red	8·00	5·50
16	6	1d. carmine-red	3·00	2·50
17	1	4d. blue (T 4)	20·00	2·75
18	2	4d. blue (T 4)	65·00	16·00
19	3	4d. blue (T 4)	50·00	7·00
20	4	4d. blue (T 4)	55·00	28·00
21	5	4d. blue (T 4)	55·00	35·00
22	6	4d. blue (T 4)	32·00	8·00
23	8	4d. blue (T 4)		
24	1	4d. blue (T 6)	20·00	2·50
25	2	4d. blue (T 6)	—	16·00
26	3	4d. blue (T 6)	25·00	5·00
27	4	4d. blue (T 6)	25·00	5·00
28	5	4d. blue (T 6)	40·00	18·00
29	6	4d. blue (T 6)	18·00	4·50
30	8	4d. blue (T 6)	£250	
31	1	6d. dull violet	11·00	5·00
32	2	6d. dull violet	30·00	10·00
33	3	6d. dull violet	18·00	4·50
34	4	6d. dull violet	35·00	16·00
35	5	6d. dull violet	30·00	16·00
36	6	6d. dull violet	16·00	4·50
37	8	6d. dull violet		
38	1	1s. green	16·00	2·50
		a. Opt. inverted	—	70·00
39	2	1s. green	30·00	9·00
		a. Opt inverted		
40	3	1s. green	9·00	3·00
41	4	1s. green	30·00	4·00
		a. Opt. inverted		
42	5	1s. green	30·00	5·50
43	6	1s. green	16·00	3·75
		a. Opt. inverted		
44	8	1s. green		
45	1	5s. orange	50·00	2·50
46	2	5s. orange	—	7·00
47	3	5s. orange	65·00	2·50
48	4	5s. orange	—	4·00
49	5	5s. orange	£100	5·00
50	6	5s. orange	65·00	2·50
51	8	5s. orange	£350	

The setting of the above was in two panes of 60. Sub-types of Types **1** and **2** are found. The 1d., Type **8**, of this setting can only be distinguished when *se-tenant* with Type **3**.

1878. II. *Second printing, in black for all values. NINE principal varieties of type (T* **6** *to* **14**).

No.	Type		Unused	Used
52	7	1d. carmine-red	2·50	2·50
53	8	1d. carmine-red	3·00	3·00
54	9	1d. carmine-red	5·00	8·00
55	10	1d. carmine-red	20·00	
56	11	1d. carmine-red	5·00	5·00
57	12	1d. carmine-red	20·00	20·00
58	13	1d. carmine-red	18·00	16·00
59	14	1d. carmine-red	85·00	85·00
60	6	4d. blue (T 6)	45·00	15·00
61	7	4d. blue (T 6)	16·00	4·00
62	8	4d. blue (T 6)	45·00	10·00
63	9	4d. blue (T 6)	20·00	5·00
64	10	4d. blue (T 6)	90·00	38·00
65	11	4d. blue (T 6)	45·00	10·00
66	12	4d. blue (T 6)	55·00	18·00
67	13	4d. blue (T 6)	70·00	45·00
68	14	4d. blue (T 6)	—	28·00
69	6	6d. dull violet	70·00	20·00
70	7	6d. dull violet	38·00	16·00
		a. Opt. double		
71	8	6d. dull violet	75·00	18·00
72	9	6d. dull violet	42·00	20·00
		a. Opt. double		
73	10	6d. dull violet	70·00	
74	11	6d. dull violet	£200	70·00
75	12	6d. dull violet	80·00	35·00
76	13	6d. dull violet	90·00	48·00
77	14	6d. dull violet	£200	70·00

The 1d., T **6**, of this printing can only be distinguished from the same variety of the first printing when it is *se-tenant* with another type.

The type without horizontal or vertical serifs, previously illustrated as T **10**, is a broken "G" of the type now shown under that number.

Minor varieties may be found of T **7** and **12**.

Red overprints on the 4d., 1s. and 5s. Type **7** and 1s. and 5s. Type **8** exist but there is no evidence as to their status.

G (15) G (16) G (17)

B. *Overprinted with small capital letters.*

1878 (July). I. *First printing, in red or in black.*

(a) Red overprint.

No.	Type		Unused	Used
78	15	½d. grey-black	1·60	2·00
		a. Opt. inverted	2·00	2·00
		b. Opt. double	11·00	
		c. Opt. double, both inverted ..	18·00	
79	16	½d. grey-black	2·00	2·00
		a. Opt. inverted	2·00	2·50
		b. Opt. double	18·00	18·00
		c. Opt. double, both inverted ..		
80	15	4d. blue (T 6)	55·00	24·00
		a. Opt. inverted	£200	18·00
81	16	4d. blue (T 6)	—	20·00
		a. Opt. inverted	60·00	20·00
		(b) Black overprint.		
82	15	½d. grey-black	45·00	25·00
		a. Opt. inverted	45·00	
		b. Black opt. normal, with additional red opt. T 15 invert.	60·00	
		c. Ditto, but red opt. is T 16 ..	25·00	
83	16	½d. grey-black	9·00	9·00
		a. Optd. inverted	9·00	9·00
		b. Black opt. normal, with additional red opt. T 15 inverted	35·00	
84	15	1d. carmine-red	2·00	1·25
		a. Opt. inverted	2·00	2·00
		b. Ditto, with additional red opt. T 15 inverted	7·00	7·50
		c. Ditto, with additional red opt. T 16 inverted		
		d. Opt. double	40·00	11·00
		e. Opt. double. both inverted ..	40·00	16·00
85	16	1d. carmine-red	2·00	2·00
		a. Opt. inverted	16·00	7·00
		b. Ditto. with additional red opt. T 16 inverted	16·00	16·00
		c. Opt. double	—	22·00
		d. Opt. double, both inverted ..	—	30·00
86	15	4d. blue (T 4)	—	32·00
87	16	4d. blue (T 4)	—	38·00
88	15	4d. blue (T 6)	16·00	5·00
		a. Opt. inverted	45·00	20·00
		b. Opt. double	—	45·00
		c. Opt. double, both inverted ..		
89	16	4d. blue (T 6)	35·00	2·50
		a. Opt. inverted	50·00	7·00
		b. Opt. double	—	48·00
		c. Opt. double, both inverted ..		
90	15	6d. dull violet	18·00	6·00
91	16	6d. dull violet	—	6·00

1879 (?). II. *Second printing, in black only.*

No.	Type		Unused	Used
92	17	½d. grey-black	2·00	1·75
		a. Opt. double	70·00	70·00
93	„	1d. carmine-red	2·00	1·00
		a. Opt. inverted	—	25·00
		b. Opt. double	—	40·00
		c. Opt. treble		
94	„	4d. blue (T 6)	2·00	1·00
		b. Opt. double	—	35·00
95	„	6d. mauve	18·00	2·00
		a. Opt. inverted	—	8·00
		b. Opt. double	90·00	45·00
96	„	1s. green	12·00	1·00
		a. Opt. double	55·00	27·00
97	„	5s. orange	55·00	2·00
		a. Opt. double	70·00	20·00
		b. Opt. treble	—	55·00

Besides the type shown above, which is the normal, there are in this printing three or four minor varieties differing in the shape and size of the body of the letter. In this setting are also found at least two varieties very like the upright "antique" of the first printing in small capitals.

Beware of forged overprints.

The stamps of Griqualand West became obsolete in October, 1880, when the stock on hand of Cape stamps overprinted with small "G" was returned from Kimberley to Cape Town and redistributed among various post offices in Cape Colony, where they were used as ordinary Cape stamps.

GUYANA.

(Formerly British Guiana.)

GUYANA INDEPENDENCE 1966

(73)

1966 (26 May)–**67**. *Various stamps of British Guiana, 1954–65, optd. with T* **73**, *by De La Rue.*

(i) *Wmk. Mult. Script CA.*

No.	Type		Unused	Used
379	56	2 c. myrtle-green ..	5	5
380	57	3 c. brn.-olive & red-brn.	1·00	1·00
381	58	4 c. violet.. ..	8	8
383	60	6 c. yellow-green.. ..	5	5
384	61	8 c. ultramarine	8	8
385	62	12 c. black & reddish-brn.	10	10
392	69	$5 ultramarine & black	15·00	15·00
379/92		.. .. *Set of* 7	16·00	16·00

(ii) *Wmk.* w.**12**. A, *Upright;* B, *Sideways.*

No.	Type		A. Unused	A. Used	B. Unused	B. Used
393	55	1 c.	5	5	5	5
		a. Opt. omitted	—	—	†	
395	57	3 c.	5	5	†	
396	58	4 c.	5	5	5	5
397	59	5 c.	5	5	†	
398	60	6 c.	5	8	†	
399	61	8 c.	8	10	5	8
400	62	12 c.	10	15	15	12
401	63	24 c.	25	25	15	20
402	64	36 c.	30	35	25	30
403	65	48 c.	3·50	3·50	25	25
404	66	72 c.	35	45	35	55
405	67	$1	40	50	45	70
406	68	$2	1·00	1·25	1·10	1·25
407	69	$5	2·25	2·75	2·25	2·75
393A/407A		*Set of* 14	7·50	8·50		
393B/407B		*Set of* 11			4·50	6·00

Dates of issue: Of the above, the 1 c., 4 c., 6 c. (W w.**12** upright) and the 12 c., 36 c., 72 c., $2 and $5 (W w.**12** sideways) were issued on 28.2.67; the 8 c. upright wmk. and the $1 sideways wmk., on 14.3.67; the rest on 26.5.66.

No. 393a is listed here as an error as there is no evidence of the 1 c. having been issued as a printing with Block CA watermark.

See also Nos. 420/40.

74. Flag and Map.

75. Arms of Guyana.

(Des. V. Whiteley. Photo. Harrison.)

966 (26 MAY). *Independence.* P 14½.
o8 **74** 5 c. multicoloured .. 5 5
o9 ,, 15 c. multicoloured .. 10 8
10 **75** 25 c. multicoloured .. 20 20
11 ,, $1 multicoloured .. 60 60

76. Bank Building.

)es. R. Granger Barrett. Photo. Enschedé.)

966 (11 OCT.). *Opening of Bank of Guyana.* P 13½×14.
12 **76** 5 c. multicoloured .. 5 5
13 ,, 25 c. multicoloured .. 15 15

ANCELLED REMAINDERS. *In 1969 emainders of some issues were put on the market ancelled-to-order in such a way as to be inistinguishable from genuine postally used copies r all practical purposes. Our used quotations hich are indicated by an asterisk are the same r cancelled-to-order or postally used copies.

77. British Guiana One Cent Stamp of 1856.

(Des. V. Whiteley. Litho. De La Rue.)

967 (23 FEB.). *World's Rarest Stamp Commemoration.* P 12½.
14 **77** 5 c. black, magenta, silver and light ochre .. 5 5*
15 ,, 25 c. black, magenta, gold and light green .. 15 10*

78. Château Margot.

GUYANA
INDEPENDENCE
1966
(82)

79. Independence Arch. (*Vert.*)
80. Fort Island. (*Horiz.*)
81. National Assembly. (*Horiz.*)

(Des. R. Granger Barrett. Photo. Harrison.)

1967 (26 MAY). *First Anniv. of Independence.* P 14 (6 *c.*) *or* 14×14½ (*others*).
416 **78** 6 c. multicoloured .. 5 5*
417 **79** 15 c. multicoloured .. 10 5*
418 **80** 25 c. multicoloured .. 15 5*
419 **81** $1 multicoloured .. 60 65

1967–68. *Stamps of British Guiana optd. with* T **82** *locally.*

(i) *Wmk. Mult. Script CA.*
420 **55** 1 c. black (3.10.67) .. 5 5
a. Opt. inverted .. .. 30·00
421 **56** 2 c. myrtle-grn. (3.10.67) 5 5
a. "1966" for "GUYANA" 20·00
422 **57** 3 c. brown-olive and red-brown (3.10.67) .. 5 5
a. "1966" for "GUYANA" 15·00
423 **58** 4 c. violet (*shades*) (10.67) 5 5
b. Opt. inverted .. .. 40·00
424 **60** 6 c. yellow-green (11.67) 5 5
a. "1966" for "GUYANA" 20·00
b. Opt. inverted .. .. 35·00
425 **61** 8 c. ultramarine (12.67).. 5 5
426 **62** 12 c. black & brown (12.67) 8 10
426*a* **63** 24 c. black & orange (date?) 30·00 22·00
427 **68** $2 reddish mauve (12.67) 1·40 1·75
428 **69** $5 ultram. & blk. (12.67) 2·00 2·25

(ii) *Wmk.* w.**12** (*upright*).
429 **55** 1 c. black (2.68) 5 5
430 **56** 2 c. myrtle-green (2.68) .. 5 5
431 **57** 3 c. brown-olive and red-brn. (*shades*) (3.10.67) 5 5
a. "1966" for "GUYANA" 60·00
b. Opt. inverted .. ..
432 **58** 4 c. violet (2.68) 5 5
433 **59** 5 c. scarlet & blk. (*shades*) (3.10.67) 10 10
434 **60** 6 c. yellow-green (2.68) .. 10 12
435 **63** 24 c. black & bright orange (11.12.67) 15 15
a. Opt. double, one diagonal (horiz. pair) .. ..
436 **64** 36 c. rose-carmine & black (12.67) 20 25
437 **65** 48 c. bright ultramarine & Venetian red (12.67) 30 40
a. Opt. inverted .. .. 35·00
438 **66** 72 c. carm. & emer. (12.67) 35 40
439 **67** $1 pink, yellow, green and black (12.67) 60 70
440 **68** $2 reddish mauve (12.67) 1·25 1·40
420/40 (*excl.* 426*a*) .. *Set of* 21 6·00 7·00

The "1966" errors occurred on R. 7/10 and were later corrected. Nos. 425/8 and 436/40 were issued in mid-December, but some were cancelled to order with a November date in error.

83. "Millie" (parrot).

84. Wicket-keeping.

85. Batting.
86. Bowling.

(Des. V. Whiteley. Photo. Harrison.)

1967–68. *Christmas.* P 14½×14.

(*a*) *First issue* (6 Nov. '67).
441 **83** 5 c. yellow, new blue, black and bronze-green .. 8 5*
442 ,, 25 c. yellow, new blue, black and violet 20 8*

(*b*) *Second issue. Colours changed* (22 Jan. '68)
443 **83** 5 c. yellow, new blue, black and red 5 5*
444 ,, 25 c. yellow, new blue, black and apple-green .. 20 8*

(Des. V. Whiteley. Photo. Harrison.)

1968 (8 JAN.). *M.C.C.'s West Indies Tour.* P 14.
445 **84** 5 c. multicoloured .. 5 5*
446 **85** 6 c. multicoloured .. 5 5*
447 **86** 25 c. multicoloured .. 15 8*

Nos. 445/7 were issued in small sheets of 9 containing three *se-tenant* strips of each value.
Strips of three values .. 30 15*
Complete sheets of nine stamps .. 1·00 50*

87. Sunfish.

88. Pirai. (*Horiz.*)
89. Lukunani. (*Horiz.*)
90. Hassar. (*Horiz.*)
91. Patua. (*Horiz.*)
92. White-headed Piping Guan. (*Vert.*)
93. Harpy Eagle. (*Vert.*)
94. Hoatzin, or Canje Pheasant. (*Vert.*)
95. Cock of the Rock. (*Vert.*)
96. Great Kiskadee. (*Vert.*)
97. Accouri. (*Horiz.*)
98. Peccary. (*Horiz.*)
99. Labba. (*Horiz.*)
100. Armadillo. (*Horiz.*)
101. Ocelot. (*Horiz.*)

(Des. R. Granger Barrett. Photo. Harrison.)

1968 (4 MAR.). *No wmk.* P 14×14½.
448 **87** 1 c. multicoloured .. 5 5
449 **88** 2 c. multicoloured .. 5 5
450 **89** 3 c. multicoloured .. 5 5
451 **90** 5 c. multicoloured .. 5 5
452 **91** 6 c. multicoloured .. 5 5
453 **92** 10 c. multicoloured .. 8 8
454 **93** 15 c. multicoloured .. 10 10

455	**94**	20 c. multicoloured ..	12	10
456	**95**	25 c. multicoloured ..	15	12
457	**96**	40 c. multicoloured ..	25	20
458	**97**	50 c. multicoloured ..	30	30
459	**98**	60 c. multicoloured ..	30	45
460	**99**	$1 multicoloured ..	60	65
461	**100**	$2 multicoloured ..	1·25	1·50
462	**101**	$5 multicoloured ..	3·00	3·25
448/62		.. .. *Set of* 15	5·50	6·50

For the above issue *W* **106**, see Nos. 485/99.

102. "**Christ of St. John of the Cross**" (**after** Salvador Dali).

(Des. and photo. Harrison.)

1968 (25 Mar.). *Easter Commemoration.* *P* 14.

463	**102**	5 c. multicoloured ..	5	5*
464	,,	25 c. multicoloured ..	20	5*

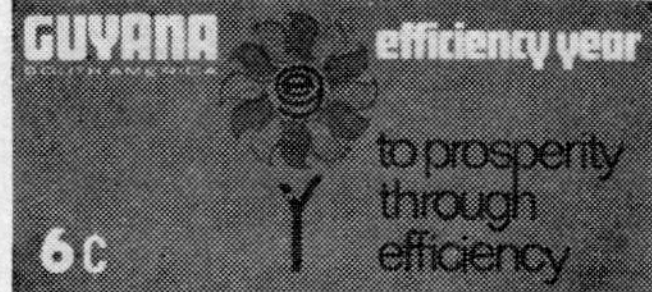

103. "Efficiency Year".

104. "Savings Bonds".

(Des. W. Starzmann. Litho. Bradbury, Wilkinson.)

1968 (22 July). "*Savings Bonds and Efficiency*". *P* 14.

465	**103**	6 c. multicoloured ..	5	5*
466	,,	25 c. multicoloured ..	12	5*
467	**104**	30 c. multicoloured ..	15	5*
468	,,	40 c. multicoloured ..	20	5*

105. Open Book, Star and Crescent.

(Des. R. Gates. Photo. De La Rue.)

1968 (9 Oct.). *1400th Anniv. of the Holy Quran.* *P* 14.

469	**105**	6 c. black, gold and flesh	5	5*
470	,,	25 c. black, gold and lilac	12	5*
471	,,	30 c. black, gold and light apple-green ..	15	5*
472	,,	40 c. black, gold & cobalt	20	5*

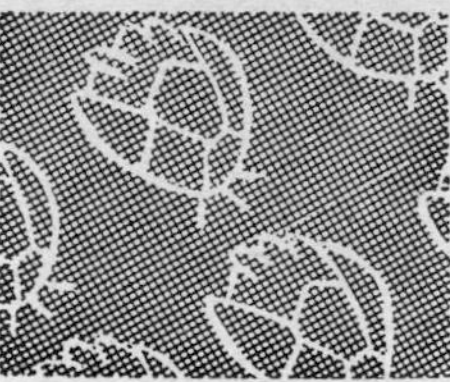

106. Lotus Blossoms.

107. Broadcasting Greetings.

108. Map showing Radio Link, Guyana—Trinidad.

(Des. L. Pritchard; adapted G. L. Vasarhelyi. Litho. De La Rue.)

1968 (11 Nov.). *Christmas.* *W* **106.** *P* 14.

473	**107**	6 c. brown, blue & green	5	5*
474	,,	25 c. brown, reddish violet and green	12	5*
475	**108**	30 c. blue-green and turquoise-green ..	15	5*
476	,,	40 c. red & turquoise-grn.	20	5*

109. Festival Ceremony.

110. Ladies spraying Scent.

(Des. J. E. Cooter. Litho. Perkins Bacon Ltd.)

1969 (26 Feb.). *Hindu Festival of Phagwah.* *W* **106** (*sideways*). *P* 13½.

477	**109**	6 c. multicoloured ..	5	5
478	**110**	25 c. multicoloured ..	12	12
479	**109**	30 c. multicoloured ..	15	15
480	**110**	40 c. multicoloured ..	20	25

111. "Sacrament of the Last Supper" (Dali).

(Photo. De La Rue.)

1969 (10 Mar.). *Easter Commemoration.* *W* **106** (*sideways*). *P* 13½ × 13.

481	**111**	6 c. multicoloured ..	5	5
482	,,	25 c. multicoloured ..	12	12
483	,,	30 c. multicoloured ..	15	15
484	,,	40 c. multicoloured ..	20	25

1969–71. *As Nos. 448/62, but Wmk.* **106** (*sideways on 1 c. to 6 c. and 50 c. to $5*). *Chalk-surfaced paper.*

485	**87**	1 c. multicoloured ..	5	5
486	**88**	2 c. multicoloured ..	5	5
487	**89**	3 c. multicoloured ..	5	5
488	**90**	5 c. multicoloured ..	5	5
489	**91**	6 c. multicoloured ..	5	5
490	**92**	10 c. multicoloured ..	5	5
		a. Glazed paper (21.12.71)	5	8
491	**93**	15 c. multicoloured ..	8	10
		a. Glazed paper (21.12.71)	10	10
492	**94**	20 c. multicoloured ..	10	12
493	**95**	25 c. multicoloured ..	12	12
		a. Glazed paper (21.12.71)	12	15
494	**96**	40 c. multicoloured ..	20	30
495	**97**	50 c. multicoloured ..	25	30
496	**98**	60 c. multicoloured ..	30	30
497	**99**	$1 multicoloured ..	45	50
		a. Glazed paper (21.12.71)	45	50
498	**100**	$2 multicoloured ..	1·25	1·25
499	**101**	$5 multicoloured ..	2·75	2·75
485/99		.. .. *Set of* 15	5·50	6·00

These were put on sale by the Crown Agents on 25 March 1969 but although supplies were sent to Guyana in time they were not released there until needed as ample supplies remained of the stamps without watermark. It is understood that the 3 c. and 5 c. were put on sale in early May 1969 followed by the 25 c. but there are no records of when the remainder were released.

112. Map showing "CARIFTA" Countries.

113. "Strength in Unity". (*Horiz.*)

(Des. J. E. Cooter. Litho. Perkins, Bacon.)

1969 (30 Apr.). *First Anniv. of CARIFTA (Caribbean Free Trade Area).* *W* **106** (*sideways on 25 c.*). *P* 13½.

500	**112**	6 c. rose-red, ultramarine and turquoise-blue	5	5
501	**113**	25 c. lemon, brown and rose-red	15	15

114. First all-Aluminium Ship.

115. Bauxite Processing Plant. (*Horiz.*)

(Des. R. Gates. Litho. Bradbury, Wilkinson.)

1969 (30 APR.). *50th Anniv. of International Labour Organization.* *W* **106** (*sideways on* 40 *c.*). *P* 12×11 (30 *c.*) *or* 11×12 (40 *c.*).

502 **114** 30 c. turquoise-blue, black and silver 15 15
503 **115** 40 c. multicoloured .. 20 20

116. Scouts raising Flag.

117. Camp-fire cooking.

(Des. Jennifer Toombs. Litho. Bradbury, Wilkinson.)

1969 (13 AUG.). *Third Caribbean Scout Jamboree and Diamond Jubilee of Scouting in Guyana.* *W* **106** (*sideways*). *P* 13.

504 **116** 6 c. multicoloured .. 5 5
505 **117** 8 c. multicoloured .. 5 5
506 **116** 25 c. multicoloured .. 12 12
507 **117** 30 c. multicoloured .. 15 15
508 **116** 50 c. multicoloured .. 30 35
504/8 .. .. *Set of* 5 60 65

118. Gandhi and Spinning-wheel.

(Des. G. Drummond. Litho. Format International.)

1969 (1 OCT.). *Birth Centenary of Mahatma Gandhi.* *W* **106** (*sideways*). *P* $14\frac{1}{2}$.

509 **118** 6 c. black, brown and yellowish olive .. 5 5
510 ,, 15 c. black, brown & lilac 12 12

119. " Mother Sally Dance Troupe ".

120. City Hall, Georgetown.

(Des. V. Whiteley (T **119**), J. Waddington Ltd. (T **120**). Litho. Bradbury, Wilkinson (T **119**), De La Rue (T **120**).)

1969 (17 NOV.). *Christmas. Previously unissued stamps optd. as in T* **119** *by Guyana Lithographic Co. Ltd.* *W* **106** (6 *c.*, 60 *c. only*). *P* $13\frac{1}{2}$ (*T* **119**) *or* $13\times13\frac{1}{2}$ (*T* **120**).

511 **119** 5 c. multicoloured .. 5 5
a. Opt. omitted .. .. 35·00
512 **120** 6 c. multicoloured .. 5 5
a. Opt. omitted .. .. 35·00
513 **119** 25 c. multicoloured .. 15 15
a. Opt. omitted .. .. 35·00
514 **120** 60 c. multicoloured .. 45 40

121. Forbes Burnham and Map.

122. " Rural Self-Help ". (*Vert.*)

123. University of Guyana. (*Horiz.*)

124. Guyana House. (*Horiz.*)

(Des. L. D. Curtis. Litho. De La Rue.)

1970 (23 FEB.). *Republic Day.* *W* **106** (*sideways on horiz. designs*). *P* 14.

515 **121** 5 c. sepia, ochre and pale blue .. 5 5
516 **122** 6 c. multicoloured .. 5 5
517 **123** 15 c. multicoloured .. 12 12
518 **124** 25 c. multicoloured .. 12 12

125. " The Descent from the Cross " (Rubens).

126. " Christ on the Cross " (Rubens).

(Des. J. E. Cooter. Litho. Questa.)

1970 (24 MAR.). *Easter.* *W* **106** (*inverted*). *P* $14\times14\frac{1}{2}$.

519 **125** 5 c. multicoloured .. 5 5
520 **126** 6 c. multicoloured .. 5 5
521 **125** 15 c. multicoloured .. 15 15
522 **126** 25 c. multicoloured .. 25 25

127. " Peace " and U.N. Emblem.

(Des. and litho. Harrison.)

1970 (26 OCT.). *25th Anniv. of United Nations. T* **127** *and similar horiz. design. Multicoloured.* *W* **106.** *P* 14.

523 5 c. Type **127** 5 5
524 6 c. U.N. Emblem, Gold-panning and Drilling .. 5 5
525 15 c. Type **127** 12 12
526 25 c. As 6 c. 20 20

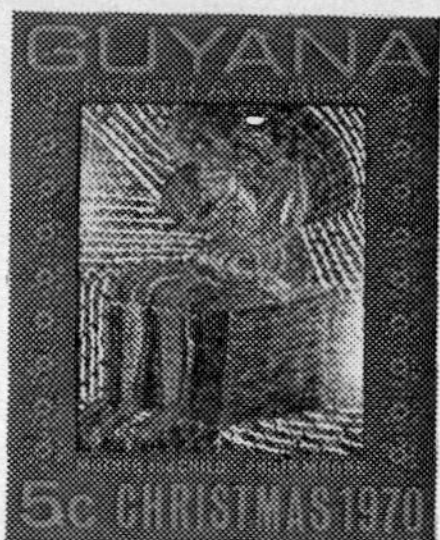

128. " Mother and Child " (Philip Moore).

(Des. Harrison & Sons. Litho. J.W.)

1970 (8 DEC.). *Christmas.* *W* **106.** *P* $13\frac{1}{2}$.

527 **128** 5 c. multicoloured .. 5 5
528 ,, 6 c. multicoloured .. 5 5
529 ,, 15 c. multicoloured .. 12 12
530 ,, 25 c. multicoloured .. 20 20

129. National Co-operative Bank.

(Des. E. Samuels. Litho. J.W.)

1971 (23 FEB.). *Republic Day.* *W* **106** (*sideways*). *P* 14.

531 **129** 6 c. multicoloured .. 5 5
532 ,, 15 c. multicoloured .. 10 12
533 ,, 25 c. multicoloured .. 15 20

130. Racial Equality Symbol.

(Des. E. Samuels. Litho. Harrison.)

1971 (22 MAR.). *Racial Equality Year.* *W* **106.** *P* 14.

534 **130** 5 c. multicoloured .. 5 5
535 ,, 6 c. multicoloured .. 5 5
536 ,, 15 c. multicoloured .. 10 12
537 ,, 25 c. multicoloured .. 15 20

131. Young Volunteer felling Tree.

(Des. from painting by J. Criswick. Litho. Harrison.)

1971 (19 July). *First Anniv. of Self-help Road Project. W* **106.** *P* 14.

No.	Type	Description		Unused	Used
538	**131**	5 c. multicoloured	..	5	5
539	„	20 c. multicoloured	..	12	12
540	„	25 c. multicoloured	..	15	15
541	„	50 c. multicoloured	..	30	30

132. Yellow Allamanda.

Two types of 25 c.:

I. Flowers facing up. Value in centre.

II. Flowers facing down. Value to right. Colours changed.

(Des. V. Whiteley (1 to 40 c.), PAD Studio (others). Litho. D.L.R. (1 to 6 c.), J.W. (10 c. to 40 c.), Format (50 c. to $5).)

1971 (17 Sept.)–**76.** *Flowering Plants. T* **132** *and similar vert. designs. Multicoloured. W* **106.** *P* 13×13½ (*1 to 6 c.*) *or* 13½ (*others*).

No.	Description		Unused	Used
542	1 c. Pitcher Plant of Mt. Roraima (15.1.72)	..	5	5
543	2 c. Type **132** (*shades*)	..	5	5
544	3 c. Hanging Heliconia	..	5	5
545	5 c. Annatto tree ..	..	5	5
546	6 c. Cannon-ball tree	..	5	5
547	10 c. Cattleya (18.9.72)	..	5	8
	a. Perf. 13 (28.1.76) ..	..	5	5
548	15 c. Christmas Orchid (18.9.72)		8	8
	a. Perf. 13 (3.9.76) ..	..	5	8
549	20 c. *Paphinia cristata* (18.9.72)		8	10
	a. Perf. 13 (28.1.76) ..	..	8	10
550	25 c. Marabunta (I) (18.9.72) ..		15	15
550*a*	25 c. Marabunta (II) (20.8.73)		12	12
	ab. Perf. 13 (3.9.76) ..	..	10	12
551	40 c. Tiger Beard (18.9.72)	..	15	20
552	50 c. *Guzmania ligulata* (3.9.73)		20	20
553	60 c. Soldier's Cap (3.9.73)	..	25	25
554	$1 *Chelonanthus uliginoides* (3.9.73)	..	40	45
555	$2 *Norantea guianensis* (3.9.73)	..	75	85
556	$5 *Odontadenia grandiflora* (3.9.73)	..	2·00	2·25
542/56	.. .. *Set of* 16		3·50	3·75

The watermark is often indistinct, particularly on the early printings.

133. Child praying at Bedside.

(Des. V. Bassoo (T **133**), M. Austin (25, 50 c.). Litho. J.W.)

1971 (29 Nov.). *Christmas. T* **133** *and similar vert. design. Multicoloured. W* **106** (*sideways on* 5 *c. and* 20 *c.*). *P* 13½.

No.	Description		Unused	Used
557	5 c. Type **133**	..	5	5
558	20 c. Type **133**	..	15	15
559	25 c. Carnival Masquerader		15	15
560	50 c. As 25 c.	..	30	30

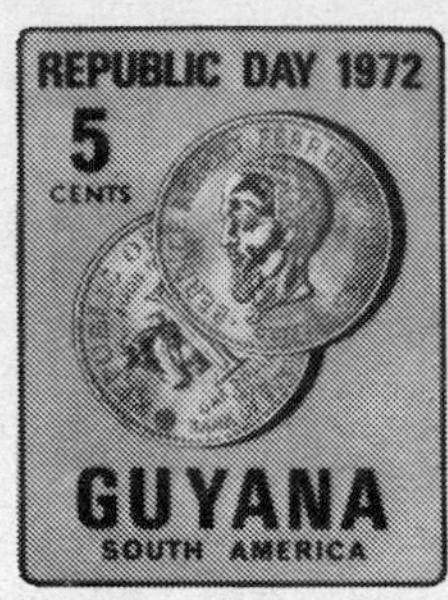

134. Obverse and Reverse of Guyana $1 Coin.

(Des. G. Drummond. Litho. Questa.)

1972 (23 Feb.). *Republic Day. T* **134** *and similar vert. design. W* **106** (*sideways*). *P* 14½×14.

No.	Type	Description	Unused	Used
561	**134**	5 c. sil., blk. & orge.-red	5	5
562	–	20 c. sil., blk. & magenta	10	10
563	**134**	25 c. sil., blk. & ultram.	15	15
564	–	50 c. sil., blk. & yell.-grn.	30	30

Design: 20, 50 c. Reverse and obverse of Guyana $1 coin.

135. Hands and Irrigation Canal.

(Des. J. Criswick. Litho. J.W.)

1972 (3 Apr.). *Youman Nabi* (*Mohammed's Birthday*). *W* **106.** *P* 14.

No.	Type	Description		Unused	Used
565	**135**	5 c. multicoloured	..	5	5
566	„	25 c. multicoloured	..	12	12
567	„	30 c. multicoloured	..	15	15
568	„	60 c. multicoloured	..	35	35

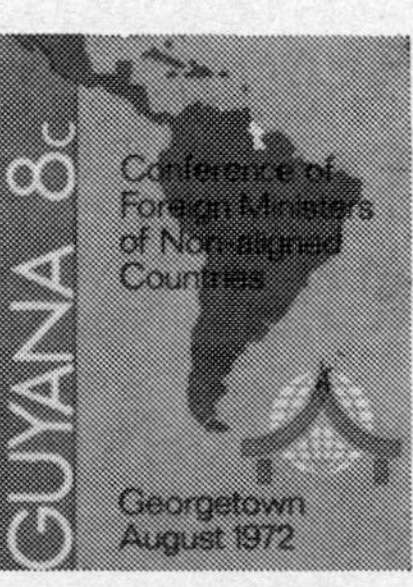

136. Map and Emblem.

(Des. J. Criswick. Litho. J.W.)

1972 (20 July). *Conference of Foreign Ministers of Non-aligned Countries. W* **106.** *P* 13½.

No.	Type	Description		Unused	Used
569	**136**	8 c. multicoloured	..	5	5
570	„	25 c. multicoloured	..	12	12
571	„	40 c. multicoloured	..	20	20
572	„	50 c. multicoloured	..	30	30

137. Hand reaching for Sun.

(Des. G. Bowen. Litho. J.W.)

1972 (25 Aug.). *First Caribbean Festival of Arts. W* **106.** *P* 13½.

No.	Type	Description		Unused	Used
573	**137**	8 c. multicoloured	..	5	5
574	„	25 c. multicoloured	..	12	12
575	„	40 c. multicoloured	..	20	20
576	„	50 c. multicoloured	..	30	30

138. Joseph, Mary, and the Infant Jesus.

(Des. Megan Anderson. Litho. B.W.)

1972 (18 Oct.). *Christmas. W* **106.** *P* 13×13½.

No.	Type	Description		Unused	Used
577	**138**	8 c. multicoloured	..	5	5
578	„	25 c. multicoloured	..	12	12
579	„	40 c. multicoloured	..	20	20
580	„	50 c. multicoloured	..	30	30

139. Umana Yana (Meeting-house).

(Des. J. E. Cooter. Litho. Questa.)

1973 (23 Feb.). *Republic Day. T* **139** *and similar vert. design. Multicoloured. W* **106.** *P* 14.

No.	Description			Unused	Used
581	8 c. Type **139**	..	..	5	5
582	25 c. Bethel Chapel ..	..		12	12
583	40 c. As 25 c.	..	..	20	20
584	50 c. Type **139**	..	..	25	25

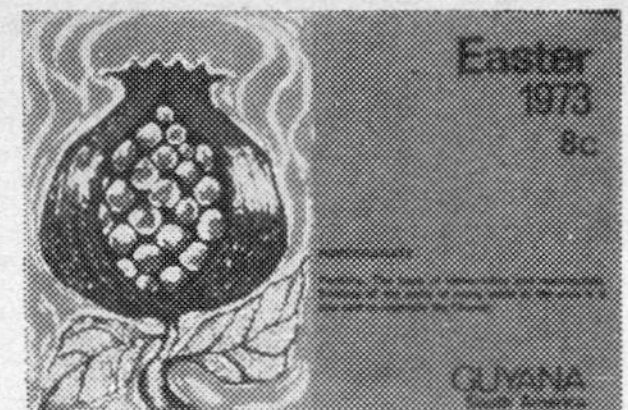

140. Pomegranate.

(Des. E. Samuels. Litho. Format.)

1973 (19 APR.). *Easter.* *T* **140** *and similar multicoloured design.* *W* **106** (*sideways on* 25 *and* 40 *c.*). *P* 14½ (8 *and* 50 *c.*) *or* 13½ (*others*).

585	8 c. Type **140**	5	5
586	25 c. Cross and map (*vert.*, 34 × 47 *mm.*)	12	12
587	40 c. As 25 c.	20	20
588	50 c. Type **140**	25	25

141. Stylized Blood Cell.

(Des. S. Greaves. Litho. Harrison.)

1973 (1 OCT.). *25th Anniv. of Guyana Red Cross.* *W* **106.** *P* 14.

589	**141**	8 c. vermilion and black	5	5
590	,,	25 c. vermilion & bright purple	12	12
591	,,	40 c. vermilion and ultramarine	20	20
592	,,	50 c. vermilion and blackish olive	25	25

142. Steel-Band Players.

(Des. E. Samuels; adapted J. E. Cooter. Litho. Questa).

1973 (20 NOV.). *Christmas.* *T* **142** *and similar vert. design.* *Multicoloured.* *W* **106.** *P* 14 (8, 25 *c.*) *or* 13½ (*others*).

593	8 c. Type **142**	5	5
594	25 c. Type **142**	12	12
595	40 c. Stained-glass window (34 × 47 *mm.*).	20	20
596	50 c. As 40 c.	25	25

143. Symbol of Progress.

(Des. PAD Studio. Litho. Questa.)

1974 (23 FEB.). *Republic Day.* *T* **143** *and similar vert. design.* *Multicoloured.* *W* **106.** *P* 13½.

597	8 c. Type **143**	5	5
598	25 c. Wai-Wai Indian ..	12	12
599	40 c. Type **143**	20	20
600	50 c. As 25 c.	25	25

8c

(**144**)

1974 (18 MAR.). *No.* 546 *surch. with* *T* **144.**

601	8 c. on 6 c. Cannon-ball tree	8	8

See also No. 620.

145. Kite with Crucifixion Motif.

(Des. R. Savory; adapted J. E. Cooter. Litho. Questa.)

1974 (8 APR.). *Easter.* *T* **145** *and similar vert. design.* *W* **106.** *P* 13½.

602	**145**	8 c. multicoloured ..	5	5
603	–	25 c. black and dull green	12	12
604	–	40 c. black and magenta ..	20	20
605	**145**	50 c. multicoloured ..	25	25

Design:—Nos. 603/4, "Crucifixion" in pre-Columbian style.

146. British Guiana 24 c. Stamp of 1874.

(Des. R. Savory. Litho. Harrison.)

1974 (18 JUNE). *Centenary of Universal Postal Union.* *T* **146** *and similar horiz. design.* *W* **106** (*sideways on* 8 *and* 40 *c.*). *P* 13½ × 14 (8, 40 *c.*) *or* 14 (*others*).

606	**146**	8 c. multicoloured ..	5	5
607	–	25 c. bright yellow-green, deep slate-violet and black	12	12
608	**146**	40 c. multicoloured ..	20	20
609	–	50 c. bright yellow-green, reddish chestnut & black	20	25

Design (42 × 25 *mm.*):—25 c., 50 c. U.P.U. emblem and Guyana postman.

147. Guides with Banner.

(Des. M. Broodhagen; adapted J. E. Cooter. Litho. Questa.)

1974 (1 AUG.). *Girl Guides' Golden Jubilee.* *T* **147** *and similar horiz. design.* *Multicoloured.* *W* **106** (*sideways*). *P* 14½.

610	8 c. Type **147**	5	5
611	25 c. Guides in camp	12	12
612	40 c. As 25 c.	20	20
613	50 c. Type **147**	20	25
MS614	170 × 137 mm. Nos. 610/13	55	65

148. Buck Toyeau.

149. Golden Arrow of Courage.

(Des. S. Greaves and R. Granger Barrett. Litho. Enschedé.)

1974 (18 Nov.). *Christmas.* *T* **148** *and similar vert. designs. Multicoloured. W* **106**. *P* 13½ × 13.

615 8 c. Type **148** 5 5
616 35 c. Five-fingers and awaras 15 15
617 50 c. Pawpaw and tangerine .. 20 20
618 $1 Pineapple and sapodilla 40 45
MS619 127 × 94 mm. Nos. 615/618 80 90

1975 (20 Jan.). *No.* 544 *surch. as T* **144**.

620 8 c. on 3 c. Hanging Heliconia 5 5

(Des. L. D. Curtis. Litho. D.L.R.)

1975 (23 Feb.). *Republic Day. Guyana Orders and Decorations. T* **149** *and similar vert. designs. W* **106**. *P* 13½.

621 10 c. Type **149** 5 5
622 35 c. Cacique's Crown of Honour 15 15
623 50 c. Cacique's Crown of Valour 20 25
624 $1 Order of Excellence .. 40 45

150. Old Sluice Gate.

(Des. E. Samuels; adapted PAD Studio. Litho. Questa.)

1975 (2 May). *Silver Jubilee of International Commission on Irrigation and Drainage. T* **150** *and similar horiz. design. Multicoloured. W* **106** *(sideways on* 35 *c. and* $1*). P* 14.

625 10 c. Type **150** 5 5
626 35 c. Modern sluice gate .. 12 15
627 50 c. Type **150** 20 20
628 $1 As 35 c. 40 45
MS629 162 × 121 mm. Nos. 625/8. Wmk. sideways .. 80

151. I.W.Y. Emblem and Rock Drawing.

(Des. C. Henriques; adapted PAD Studio. Litho. Questa.)

1975 (1 July). *International Women's Year. T* **151** *and similar horiz. designs showing different rock drawings. W* **106** *(sideways). P* 14.

630 **151** 10 c. grey-green & yellow 5 5
631 – 35 c. reddish violet and greenish blue .. 12 15
632 – 50 c. royal blue & orange 20 20
633 – $1 brown & bright blue 40 45
MS634 178 × 89 mm. Nos. 630/3 85 90

152. Freedom Monument.

(Des. PAD Studio. Litho. Questa.)

1975 (26 Aug.). *Namibia Day. T* **152** *and similar vert. designs. Multicoloured. W* **106**. *P* 14.

635 10 c. Type **152** 5 5
636 35 c. Unveiling of Monument 12 15
637 50 c. Type **152** 20 20
638 $1 As 35 c. 40 45

153. G.N.S. Emblem.

(Des. C. Henriques; adapted PAD Studio. Litho. Questa.)

1975 (1 Oct.*). *First Anniv. of National Service. W* **106**. *P* 14.

639 **153** 10 c. greenish yell., lt. grn. & lt. reddish violet 5 5
640 – 35 c. orange, light green and reddish violet 12 15
641 – 50 c. lt. vio.-bl., lt. grn. & lt. yellow-brown 20 20
642 – $1 lt. mauve., dull green & lt. emerald 40 45
MS643 196 × 133 mm. Nos. 640/2. W **106** (inverted) 80 90

*This is the local date of issue; the Crown Agents released the stamps a day later.

Nos. 640/2 are as T **153** but have different symbols within the circle.

154. Court Building, 1875 and Forester's Badge.

GIBBONS BUY STAMPS

(Des. R. Savory; adapted PAD Studio. Litho Questa.)

1975 (14 Nov.). *Centenary of Guyanese Ancient Order of Foresters. T* **154** *and similar horiz designs. Multicoloured. W* **106** *(sideways). P* 14.

644 10 c. Type **154** 5 5
645 35 c. Rock drawing of hunter and quarry 12 15
646 50 c. Crossed axes and bugle-horn 20 20
647 $1 Bow and arrow 40 45
MS648 129 × 97 mm. Nos. 644/7 80 90

35c

(155)

1976 (10 Feb.). *No.* 553 *surch. with T* **155**.

649 35 c. on 60 c. Soldier's Cap .. 12 12

156. Shoulder Flash.

(Des. Cletus Henriques; adapted J.W. Ltd. Litho. Questa.)

1976 (29 Mar.). *50th Anniv. of the St. John's Ambulance in Guyana. T* **156** *and similar vert. designs. W* **106**. *P* 14.

650 **156** 8 c. silver, black and magenta 5 5
651 – 15 c. silver, black & orge. 5 5
652 – 35 c. silver, black & grn. 12 12
653 – 40 c. silver, black and new blue .. 15 15

Nos. 651/3 are as T **156** but show different shoulder flashes.

157. Triumphal Arch.

(Des. C. Henriques. Litho. J.W.)

1976 (25 May). *Tenth Anniv. of Independence. T* **157** *and similar vert. designs. Multi-coloured. W* **106**. *P* 13½.

654 8 c. Type **157** 5 5
655 15 c. Stylised Victoria Regia lily 5 8
656 35 c. "Onward to Socialism" 12 15
657 40 c. Worker pointing the way 15 20
MS658 120 × 100 mm. Nos. 654/7. P 14½ 40

1976 (3 Aug.). *West Indian Victory in World Cricket Cup. As Nos.* 559/60 *of Barbados.*

559	15 c. Map of the Caribbean ..	8	8
560	15 c. Prudential Cup	8	8

158. Flame in Archway.

(Des. G. L. Vasarhelyi. Litho. J.W.)

1976 (21 Oct.). *Deepavali Festival. T* **158** *and similar vert. designs. Multicoloured. W* **106**. *P* 14.

661	8 c. Type **158**	5	5
662	15 c. Flame in hand	8	8
663	35 c. Flame in bowl	15	20
664	40 c. Goddess Latchmi ..	20	20
MS665	94×109 mm. Nos. 661/4	50	

POSTAGE DUE STAMPS.

D 2

(Typo. De La Rue.)

1967-68. *Chalky paper. W* w.**12**. *P* 14.

D5 **D 2**	2 c. black (11.12.68) ..	35	35
D6 „	4 c. deep ultramarine ..	10	10
D7 „	12 c. reddish violet ..	10	10

1973 (24 May). *Glazed, ordinary paper. W* **106**. *P* 14.

D 8 **D 2**	1 c. olive	5	5
D 9 „	2 c. black	5	5
D10 „	4 c. dull ultramarine ..	5	5
D11 „	12 c. bright scarlet ..	5	5

POSTAL FISCAL STAMPS.

REVENUE ONLY

*

(F 1)

1975 (1 Nov.). *Nos.* 543/5 *and* 550*a*/56 *optd. with Type* F **1**.

F 1	2 c. Yellow Allamanda ..	5	5
F 2	3 c. Hanging Heliconia ..	5	5
F 3	5 c. Annatto tree	5	5
F 4	25 c. Marabunta (Type II) ..	10	12
	a. Optd. on No. 550 (Type I) ..		
F 5	40 c. Tiger Beard	15	20
F 6	50 c. *Guzmania livgulata* ..	20	25
F 7	60 c. Soldier's Cap	25	25
F 8	$1 *Chelonanthus uliginoides*	40	45
F 9	$2 *Noreantea guianensis* ..	75	85
F10	$5 *Odontadenia grandiflora*	1·90	2·10
F1/F10	.. .. *Set of* 10	3·25	3·75

Although intended for fiscal use Nos. F1/10 were allowed, by the postal authorities, as "an act of grace" to do duty as postage stamps until 30 June, 1976.

HELIGOLAND.

Collectors should be on their guard against reprints of Heligoland stamps, which are very numerous and of little value. Beware also of forgeries.

PRINTERS. All the stamps of Heligoland were typographed at the Imperial Printing Works, Berlin.

1

(Des. Wedding. Die eng. E. Schilling.)

1867. *Head embossed in colourless relief. Roul.*
1 **1** ½ sch. green and rose (Die I) £160 £350
2 „ ½ sch. green and rose (Die II) £400 £650
3 „ 1 sch. rose and blue-green .. 90·00 95·00
4 „ 2 sch. rose and grass-green .. 5·50 35·00
5 „ 6 sch. green and rose .. .. 7·50 £150

In Nos. 1 to 9, the second colour is that of the spandrels in the ½ and 1 sch., and of the central background also in the 2 and 6 sch. In Die I the small curl below the chignon is solid and projects downwards, while in Die II it is in the shape of a hook opening to the left.

1869–72. *P* 13½ × 14½.
6 **1** ½ sch. yellow-green and rose .. 70·00 90·00
7 „ ½ sch. blue-green and rose .. 70·00 90·00
8 „ 1 sch. rose & pale blue-green 65·00 80·00
9 „ 1 sch. rose and yellow-green .. 65·00 80·00

1873. *New values. P* 13½ × 14½.
10 **1** ¼ sch. rose and green .. 14·00 £900
11 „ ¼ sch. deep rose & pale grn. 14·00 £900
12 „ ¾ sch. green and rose .. 14·00 £750
13 „ 1½ sch. green and rose .. 28·00 £150
Error, colours reversed.
14 **1** ¼ sch. green and deep rose .. 40·00 £1300

In Nos. 10, 11, 13, and 14 the second colour is that of the central background.

In No. 12 the second colour is also that of the side labels and side marginal lines.

2

3

(Des. H. Gätke. Die eng. E. Schilling.)

1875. *Head embossed in colourless relief. P* 13½ × 14½.
15 **2** 1 pf. (¼d.) dp. green & rose 5·00 £300
16 „ 2 pf. (½d.) dp. rose & green 5·00 £375
17 „ 5 pf. (¾d.) deep yellow-green and rose .. .. 5·00 10·00
18 „ 5 pf. (¾d.) dp. grn. & rose .. 6·50 25·00
19 „ 10 pf. (1½d.) deep rose and deep green .. .. 5·00 12·00
20 „ 10 pf. (1½d.) scarlet and pale blue-green .. .. 5·00 12·00
21 „ 10 pf. (1½d.) rose aniline and pale yellow-green .. 6·50 14·00
22 „ 25 pf. (3d.) dp. green & rose 6·50 15·00
23 „ 50 pf. (6d.) dp. rose & green 10·00 15·00

The first colour given above is that of the central background, the second that of the frame.

(Des. H. Gätke. Die eng. A. Schiffner.)

1876. *P* 13½ × 14½.
24 **3** 3 pf. (⅜d.) green, red and yellow-orange .. 85·00 £500
24*a* „ 3 pf. (⅜d.) pale green, red and yellow .. .. 85·00 £500
25 „ 20 pf. (2½d.) rose, green and yellow .. .. 8·00 14·00
26 „ 20 pf. (2½d.) rose-carmine, deep green and orange 20·00 20·00
27 „ 20 pf. (2½d.) dull red, pale green and lemon .. 7·00 14·00
28 „ 20 pf. (2½d.) vermilion aniline, brt. grn. & lemon 7·00 14·00

Colours. 3 pf. (1) Frame and top band of shield. (2) Centre band of shield. (3) Border of shield.

20 pf. (1) Frame and centre band. (2) Upper band. (3) Border of Shield.

4

5

(Des. H. Gätke. Die eng. A. Schiffner.)

1879. (*a*) *P* 13½ × 14½.
29 **4** 1 m. (1s.) deep green, scarlet and black .. .. 48·00 £100
30 „ 1 m. (1s.) deep green, rose aniline and black .. 55·00 £100
31 **5** 5 m. (5s.) deep green, rose aniline and black .. 65·00 £550
(*b*) *P* 11½.
32 **4** 1 m. (1s.) deep green, scarlet and black £200
33 **5** 5 m. (5s.) deep green, scarlet and black £200
a. Imperf. between (pair) .. £1200

The stamps perf. 11½ are given above on the ground that specimens exist on the original envelopes and are known to have been genuinely postally used.

Numerous reprints of the ¼ sch. (including the *error*), ½ sch. (Die II), ¾ sch., 1 sch., 1½ sch., 2 sch., 6 sch., 1 pf., 2 pf. and 3 pf. were made between 1875 and 1895. It is impossible to describe them all here. Collectors should exercise caution in purchasing stamps of which reprints exist.

Heligoland was ceded to Germany, 9 Aug., 1890.

HONG KONG.

CROWN COLONY.

PRINTERS. All definitive stamps up to 196 were typographed by De La Rue & Co.

CONDITION. *Mint or fine used specimen of the earlier Hong Kong stamps are rarely me with and are worth considerably more than ou prices which are for stamps in average condition Inferior specimens can be supplied at much lowe prices.*

1

2

HONGKONG
18 CENTS
3

1862 (8 Dec.). *No wmk. P* 14.
1 **1** 2 c. brown .. .. .. 70·00 13·00
a. Deep brown .. .. £120 15·00
2 „ 8 c. yellow-buff .. .. 85·00 15·00
3 „ 12 c. pale greenish blue .. 70·00 13·00
4 **3** 18 c. lilac .. .. .. 75·00 13·00
5 „ 24 c. green .. .. .. 95·00 25·00
6 „ 48 c. rose .. .. .. £225 35·00
7 „ 96 c. brownish grey .. .. £250 35·00

1863–74. *Wmk. Crown CC. P* 14.
8 **1** 2 c. deep brown (1865) .. 17·00 5·00
a. Brown .. .. .. 17·00 1·00
b. Pale yellowish brown .. 20·00 2·75
9 **2** 4 c. grey (1863) .. .. 10·00 2·50
a. Slate .. .. .. 10·00 90
b. Deep slate .. .. 12·00 1·60
c. Greenish grey .. .. 20·00 7·00
d. Bluish slate .. .. 38·00 4·00
e. Variety. Perf. 12½ (1870) .. £600 70·00
10 „ 6 c. lilac (1863) .. .. 40·00 2·25
a. Mauve .. .. .. 40·00 4·00
11 **1** 8 c. pale dull orange (1865) 40·00 2·25
a. Brownish orange .. .. 25·00 3·00
b. Bright orange .. .. 42·00 1·60
12 „ 12 c. pale gr'nish blue ('64?) 60·00 5·50
a. Pale blue .. .. 4·00 2·25
b. Deep blue .. .. 25·00 3·00
13 **3** 18 c. lilac (1866) .. .. £325 80·00
14 „ 24 c. green (1865) .. .. 25·00 3·00
a. Pale green .. .. 45·00 5·50
b. Deep green .. .. 55·00 6·50
15 **2** 30 c. vermilion (1863) .. 60·00 4·50
a. Orange-vermilion .. .. 55·00 4·50
16 „ 30 c. mauve (1871) .. .. 25·00 2·25
17 **3** 48 c. pale rose (1865) .. 40·00 9·00
a. Rose-carmine .. .. 45·00 6·50
b. Bright claret .. .. † —
18 „ 96 c. olive-bistre (1865) .. £1100 £1100
19 „ 96 c. brownish grey (1866) .. 40·00 6·50
a. Brownish black .. .. 65·00 5·50

There is a wide range of shades in this issue, of which we can only indicate the main groups.

No. 12 is the same shade as No. 3 without wmk., the impression having a waxy appearance.

Only one used copy of No. 17*b* is known.

See also Nos. 22 and 28/31.

16 cents.
(4)

28 cents.
(5)

1876–77. *Nos. 13 and 16 surch. with T* **4** *or* **5.**
20 **3** 16 c. on 18 c. lilac (1877) .. £100 20·00
a. Space between "n" and "t" £225
21 **2** 28 c. on 30 c. mauve (11.76) .. 55·00 8·00

1877 (Aug.). *New value. Wmk. Crown CC. P 14.*
22 **3** 16 c. yellow .. .. 70·00 10·00

5 cents. (6)   10 cents. (7)

1880 (Mar.). *Surch. with T* **6** *or* **7.**
23 **1** 5 c. on 8 c. brt. or. (No. 11*b*) 27·00 9·00
a. Surch. inverted .. .. — £2000
b. Surch. double .. ..
24 **3** 5 c. on 18 c. lilac (No. 13) .. 25·00 8·00
25 **1** 10 c. on 12 c. p. bl. (No. 12*a*) 25·00 11·00
a. Blue .. .. 25·00 6·50
26 **3** 10 c. on 16 c. yellow (No. 22) 48·00 22·00
a. Surch. inverted .. .. — £4500
27 ,, 10 c. on 24 c. green (No. 14) .. 30·00 11·00

1880. *Colours changed and new values. Wmk. Crown CC. P 14.*
28 **1** 2 c. dull rose (July) .. .. 5·00 2·25
a. Rose .. .. .. 6·00 2·25
29 **2** 5 c. blue (Nov.) .. .. 9·00 2·75
30 ,, 10 c. mauve (Nov.) .. .. 11·00 2·25
31 **3** 48 c. brown .. .. .. 42·00 18·00

1882–83. *Wmk. Crown CA. P 14.*
32 **1** 2 c. rose-lake .. .. 6·00 3·50
a. Rose-pink .. .. .. 13·00 7·00
b. Variety. Perf. 12 .. .. £2250
33 ,, 2 c. carmine (1883) 65 15
a. Aniline carmine 85 15
34 **2** 5 c. pale blue 85 15
a. Blue 75 12
35 ,, 10 c. dull mauve .. .. 42·00 2·25
36 ,, 10 c. green (1883) .. .. 6·50 45
a. Deep blue-green .. .. £110 3·50

20 CENTS (8)   50 CENTS (9)   1 DOLLAR (10)

1885 (June). *Surch. with T* **8** *to* **10.** *Wmk. Crown CA. P 14.*
37 **2** 20 c. on 30 c. orange-red .. 4·50 1·25
a. Surch. double £475
38 **3** 50 c. on 48 c. yellowish brown 13·00 3·00
39 ,, $1 on 96 c. grey-olive .. 13·00 8·50
37/39 Optd "Specimen" *Set of* 3 70·00

1891–92. *Wmk. Crown CA. P 14.*
(*a*) *Colours changed* (1.1.91).
40 **2** 10 c. purple/*red* 55 12
41 ,, 30 c. yellowish green .. 11·00 7·50
a. Grey-green .. .. 3·25 3·25
40, 41*a* Optd. "Specimen" *Set of* 2 50·00
(*b*) *Colours changed and surch. with T* **8** *to* **10.**
42 **2** 20 c. on 30 c. yellowish green (No. 41) .. .. .. 11·00 9·50
a. Grey-green (No. 41a) .. 5·50 6·00
43 **3** 50 c. on 48 c. dull purple ('92) 12·00 8·00
44 ,, $1 on 96 c. purple/*red* .. 14·00 12·00
42*a*/44 Optd. "Specimen" *Set of* 3 60·00

Nos. 41/2 should not be confused with faded or washed copies of the grey-green, which turns to a very yellow-green shade when dampened.

弍 (11) (20c.)   五十 (12) (50 c.)   五十 (12*a*)   壹員 (13) ($1)

1891. *Surch. with T* **8/10.** *As Nos. 42/4, but handstamped Chinese characters added at top of label at left.* (*T* **11/13.**)
45 **2** 20 c. on 30 c. yellowish green 4·00 1·25
a. Grey-green .. .. 1·40 85
b. "20 CENTS" double ..
46 **3** 50 c. on 48 c. dull purple .. 3·50 1·50
47 ,, $1 on 96 c. purple/*red* .. 11·00 3·00

Type **11** consists of a single character for "2" intended to overstamp the "3" to convert the 30 c. to 20 c. Six different chops were made and three of the 50 c. Type **12.**

The errors of the Chinese surcharges previously listed on the above issue and also on Nos. 52 and 55 are now omitted as being outside the scope of the catalogue. While some without doubt possess philatelic merit, it is impossible to distinguish between the genuine errors and the clandestine copies made to order with the original chops. No. 55c is retained as this represents a distinctly different chop which was used for the last part of the printing.

1841 Hong Kong JUBILEE 1891 (14)   7 cents. (15)   14 cents. (16)

1891 (22 Jan.). *50th Anniv. of Colony. Optd. with T* **14.**
48 **1** 2 c. carmine (No. 33) .. 11·00 11·00
a. Short "J" in "JUBILEE" 35·00 35·00
b. Short "U" in "JUBILEE" 35·00 35·00
c. Broken "1" in "1891" .. 50·00 50·00
d. Tall narrow "K" in "KONG" .. .. 90·00 90·00
e. Opt. double £850 £900
f. Space between "O" and "N" of "HONG" .. .. 70·00 70·00

This overprint was applied in a setting of 12, and other less marked varieties therefore exist.

1891. *Surch. with T* **15** *or* **16.**
49 **2** 7 c. on 10 c. green (No. 36) (Jan.) .. .. .. 7·50 7·00
a. Antique "t" in "cents." .. 55·00 48·00
b. Surch. double £325 £180
50 ,, 14 c. on 30 c. mauve (No. 16) (Apr.) .. .. .. 10·00 11·00
a. Antique "t" in "cents." .. £225 £200

The true antique "t" must not be confused with a small "t" with short foot, which is sometimes mistaken for it. In the antique "t" the cross-bar is accurately bisected by the vertical stroke, the latter being thick at the top. The lower curve bends towards the right and does not turn upwards so far as in the normal.

Dangerous forgeries of these two surcharges exist.

1896. *Wmk. Crown CA. P 14.*
51 **2** 4 c. slate-grey 25 12

1898. *Surch. with T* **10**, *and handstamped Chinese characters as T* **13.** *Wmk. Crown CA. P 14.*
52 **3** $1 on 96 c. black .. .. 6·50 6·00
a. Grey-black .. .. 7·00 6·00
Surch. with T **10** *only.*
53 **3** $1 on 96 c. black (Optd. S. £20) 28·00 30·00
a. Grey-black (Optd. S. £25) .. 30·00

10 CENTS (17)   拾 (18)   拾 (19)

1898 (April). *Surch. with T* **17.**
54 **2** 10 c. on 30 c. grey-green (No. 41*a*) .. .. .. 22·00 70·00
a. Figures "10" widely spaced (1½ mm.) .. ..

As No. 54, but with Chinese character, T **18**, *in addition.*
55 **2** 10 c. on 30 c. grey-green (No. 41*a*) (H/S S. £22) .. 2·75 5·50
a. Yellowish green (Optd. S. £22) 15·00
b. Figures "10" widely spaced (1½ mm.) .. .. 15·00 15·00
c. Chinese character large (Type 19) .. .. 15·00 15·00

1900–02. *Wmk. Crown CA. P 14.*
56 **1** 2 c. dull green 40 15
57 **2** 4 c. carmine 15 15
58 ,, 5 c. yellow 55 60
59 ,, 10 c. ultramarine 65 35
60 **1** 12 c. blue (1902) .. .. 1·10 3·25
61 **2** 30 c. brown (1901) .. .. 1·10 1·75
56/61 .. .. *Set of* 6 3·50 5·50
56/59, 61 Optd. "Specimen" *Set of* 5 35·00

20

21

22

23

1903. *Wmk. Crown CA. P 14.*
62 **20** 1 c. dull purple and brown 12 12
63 ,, 2 c. dull green 30 20
64 **21** 4 c. purple/*red* 12 12
65 ,, 5 c. dull grn. & brn.-orange 40 90
66 ,, 8 c. slate and violet .. 30 25
67 **20** 10 c. purple and blue/*blue* .. 45 20
68 **23** 12 c. green & purple/*yellow* 1·00 40
69 ,, 20 c. slate and chestnut .. 80 65
70 **22** 30 c. dull green and black .. 90 75
71 **23** 50 c. dull green & magenta 2·75 3·25
72 **20** $1 purple and sage-green 6·50 3·50
73 **23** $2 slate and scarlet .. 16·00 18·00
74 **22** $3 slate and dull blue .. 18·00 20·00
75 **23** $5 purple and blue-green 25·00 27·00
76 **22** $10 slate and orange/*blue* .. £120 £140
62/76 .. .. *Set of* 15 £170 £200
62/76 Optd. "Specimen" *Set of* 15 70·00

1904–7. *Wmk. Mult. Crown CA. P 14.*
77 **20** 2 c. dull green, CO .. 8 15
78 **21** 4 c. purple/*red*, CO .. 8 15
79 ,, 5 c. dull green and brown-orange, CO 30 30
80 ,, 8 c. slate & violet, C ('07) 65 30
81 **20** 10 c. purple & blue/*blue*, O 65 25
82 **23** 12 c. grn. & pur./*yell.*, C ('07) 85 85
83 ,, 20 c. slate and chestnut, CO 45 30
84 **22** 30 c. dull grn. & blk., CO 75 75
85 **23** 50 c. grn. & magenta, CO 1·40 1·00
86 **20** $1 pur. & sage-green, CO 4·50 4·00
87 **23** $2 slate and scarlet, CO 14·00 11·00
88 **22** $3 slate and dull blue, C 16·00 17·00
89 **23** $5 purple & blue-green, C 30·00 26·00
90 **22** $10 slate & orge./*blue*, CO £100 £120
77/90 .. .. *Set of* 14 £150 £170

1907–11. *Colours changed and new value. Wmk. Mult. Crown CA. P 14.*

No.	Type	Description		
91	**20**	1 c. brown, O (1910) ..	20	15
92	,,	2 c. deep green, O ..	75	15
		a. Green	55	15
93	**21**	4 c. carmine-red, O ..	40	12
94	**22**	6 c. orge.-verm. & pur., C	85	40
95	**20**	10 c. bright ultramarine, O	35	12
96	**23**	20 c. pur. & sage-grn., C ('11)	3·25	1·60
97	**22**	30 c. pur. & or.-yell., C ('11)	3·25	1·60
98	**23**	50 c. black/*green*, C (1911)	2·00	1·40
99	,,	$2 car.-red & blk., C ('10)	14·00	16·00
91/99		.. .. *Set of* 9	22·00	19·00
91, 93/9		Optd. "Specimen" *Set of* 8	60·00	

24

25

26

27

28

(A)

(B)

In Type A of the 25 c. the upper Chinese character in the left-hand label has a short vertical stroke crossing it at the foot. In Type B this stroke is absent.

1912–21. *Wmk. Mult. Crown CA. P 14.*

No.	Type	Description		
100	**24**	1 c. brown, O	30	12
		a. Black-brown	30	12
		b. Crown broken at right ..	17·00	19·00
101	,,	2 c. deep green, O ..	20	15
		a. Green	40	15
102	**25**	4 c. carmine-red, O ..	25	8
		a. Scarlet	1·10	20
103	**26**	6 c. yellow-orange, O ..	50	55
		a. Brown-orange	90	30
104	**25**	8 c. grey, O	1·60	45
		a. Slate	2·50	30
105	**24**	10 c. ultramarine, O ..	2·00	20
		a. Deep bright ultramarine..	1·00	15
106	**27**	12 c. purple/*yellow*, C ..	65	45
		a. White back (Optd. S. £9)	1·00	65
107	,,	20 c. purple & sage-grn., C	50	25
108	**28**	25 c. purple and magenta, C (Type A) (1914) ..	1·25	1·50
109	,,	25 c. purple and magenta, C (Type B) (1920) ..	4·00	4·50
110	**26**	30 c. pur. & orge.-yell., C	4·00	1·60
		a. Purple and orange.. ..	1·00	40
111	**27**	50 c. black/*blue-green*, C ..	80	40
		a. White back (Optd. S. £9) ..	70	40
		b. On blue-green, olive back..	14·00	1·40
		c. On emerald surface ..	3·25	1·25
		d. On emerald back (Optd. S. £9)	1·10	2·00
112	**24**	$1 purple & blue/*blue*, C	4·00	1·00
113	**27**	$2 car.-red & grey-blk., C	6·00	4·50
114	**26**	$3 green and purple, C	13·00	8·00
115	**27**	$5 green & red/*green*, C	16·00	13·00
		a. White back (Optd. S. £9))	16·00	13·00
		b. On blue-green, olive back (Optd. S. £10)	25·00	12·00
116	**26**	$10 purple & black/*red*, C	30·00	16·00
100/116		.. .. *Set of* 17	70·00	45·00
100/16		Optd. "Specimen" *Set of* 17	£120	

1921–37. *Wmk. Mult. Script CA. P 14.*

No.	Type	Description		
117	**24**	1 c. brown, O ..	8	5
118	,,	2 c. blue-green, O ..	8	10
		a. Yellow-green	35	15
118*b*	,,	2 c. grey, O (4.37) ..	25	30
119	**25**	3 c. grey, O ('31) ..	35	20
120	,,	4 c. carmine-rose, O ..	8	15
		a. Carmine-red	8	15
		b. Top of lower Chinese characters at right broken off	15·00	15·00
121	,,	5 c. violet, O ('31) ..	25	8
122	,,	8 c. grey, O	25	60
123	,,	8 c. orange, O	30	25
124	**24**	10 c. bright ultram., O ..	12	12
124*a*	**27**	12 c. purple/*yellow*, C ('33)	40	35
125	,,	20 c. pur. & sage-grn., C	80	15
126	**28**	25 c. pur. & mag., C (B)	40	30
127	**26**	30 c. pur. & chrome-yell., C	80	25
		a. Purple & orange-yellow	2·25	85
128	**27**	50 c. black/*emerald*, C ('24)	60	25
129	**24**	$1 pur. & blue/*blue*, C	2·00	50
130	**27**	$2 carmine-red & grey-black, C	7·00	3·00
131	**26**	$3 green & dull purple, C ('26)	20·00	5·00
132	**27**	$5 green & red/*emerald*, C ('25)	20·00	6·00
117/132		.. .. *Set of* 18	50·00	16·00
117/32		Optd./Perf. "Specimen" *Set of* 18	£120	

1935 (6 May). *Silver Jubilee. As Nos. 91/4 of Antigua, but ptd. by B.W. P 11 × 12.*

No.	Description		
133	3 c. ultramarine & grey-black	15	20
134	5 c. green and indigo ..	40	25
	a. Extra flagstaff ..	28·00	
135	10 c. brown and deep blue ..	55	40
136	20 c. slate and purple ..	1·25	1·25
133/6	Perf. "Specimen" *Set of* 4	17·00	

For illustration of "extra flagstaff" variety see Bechuanaland.

1937 (12 May). *Coronation. As Nos. 13/5 of Aden, but ptd. by B.W. P 11 × 11½.*

No.	Description		
137	4 c. green	20	20
138	15 c. carmine	20	20
139	25 c. blue	40	40
137/9	Perf. "Specimen" *Set of* 3	12·00	

29. King George VI.

1938–52. *Wmk. Mult. Script CA. P 14.*

No.	Type	Description		
140	**29**	1 c. brown (24.5.38) ..	8	15
		a. Pale brown (27.2.52) ..	8	20
141	,,	2 c. grey (5.4.38) ..	12	12
		a. Perf. 15 × 14 (1942) ..	30	25
142	,,	4 c. orange (5.4.38) ..	12	12
		a. Perf. 15 × 14 (28.9.45) ..	25	15
143	,,	5 c. green (24.5.38) ..	12	12
		a. Perf. 15 × 14 (12.41) ..	8	12
144	,,	8 c. red-brown (1.11.41)	12	20
		a. Error. Imperf. ..		
145	,,	10 c. bright violet (13.4.38)	1·00	50
		a. Dull reddish violet (9.4.46)	15	10
		b. Reddish lilac (9.4.47) ..	30	20
		c. Perf. 15 × 14 *Dull violet* (12.41)	45	20
146	,,	15 c. scarlet (13.4.38) ..	8	8
147	,,	20 c. black (1.2.46) ..	8	10
148	,,	20 c. scar.-verm. (1.4.48)	8	8
		a. Rose-red (25.4.51) ..	25	35
149	,,	25 c. bright blue (5.4.38)	20	15
150	,,	25 c. pale sage-grn. (9.4.46)	30	20
151	,,	30 c. yell.-olive (13.4.38)	6·50	2·50
		a. P 15 × 14. *Sage-green* (12.41)	40	65
152	,,	30 c. blue (9.4.46) ..	8	8
153	,,	50 c. reddish purple, O (13.4.38)	15	15
		a. Bright purple, C (9.4.47) ..	10	8
		b. P 15 × 14. *Deep magenta* (12.41)	15	20
154	,,	80 c. carmine, C (2.2.48)	25	15
155	**29**	$1 dull lilac & blue, C	60	9
		a. Pale reddish lilac and blue, O (11.41) ..	1·25	1·2
156	,,	$1 red-orange & green, OC (9.4.46) ..	25	3
		a. Yellow-orange & green, C (6.11.52)	1·25	1·5
157	,,	$2 red-orange & green, C (25.5.38) ..	8·00	4·c
158	,,	$2 reddish vio. & scar., OC (9.4.46) ..	80	2
159	,,	$5 dull lilac & scar., C (2.6.38)	3·25	2·c
160	,,	$5 green and violet, O (9.4.46)	2·00	1·6
		a. Yellowish grn. & violet, OC (9.4.46)	4·50	9
161	,,	$10 grn. & vio., C (2.6.38)	15·00	5·5
162	,,	$10 brt. lilac & blue, O (9.4.46)	5·50	4·c
		a. Reddish violet & blue, C (9.4.47)	7·00	2·c
140/162		.. .. *Set of* 23	35·00	17·c
140/62		Perf. "Specimen" *Set of* 23	£110	

The varieties perf. 15 × 14 with the exceptio of the 4 c. were printed and perforated b Bradbury, Wilkinson & Co., Ltd. from De L Rue plates and are on rough-surfaced pape The dates quoted for these are London releas dates and it is not known if supplies reache Hong Kong before the Japanese occupation.

The 4 c. is on smoother paper and was printe by Harrison & Sons in 1941 and issued in sheet of 120 (12 × 10) instead of two panes of 60 (6 × 10 it was not released until 1945. It is believed tha Harrison also printed some of the 8 c. on smoot paper at the same time.

Also in 1941 Williams, Lea & Co. printed th 1 c. and $1 to $10 in perf. 14 from De La Ru plates.

Nos. 160/*a* were separate printings release in Hong Kong on the same day.

No. 144a. One imperforate sheet was foun and most of the stamps were sold singly to th public at a branch P.O. and used for postage.

30. Street Scene.

34. The Hong Kong Bank.

31. Liner and Junk.

32. The University.

33. The Harbour.

35. China Clipper and Seaplane.

(Des. W. E. Jones. Recess. B.W.)

1941 (26 FEB.). *Centenary of British Occupation. Wmk. Mult. Script CA (sideways on horiz. designs). P* 13½ × 13 (*2 c. and 25 c.*) *or* 13 × 13½ (*others*).

163 **30** 2 c. orange and chocolate .. 25 30
164 **31** 4 c. brt. purple & carmine 50 90
165 **32** 5 c. black and green .. 12 12
166 **33** 15 c. black and scarlet .. 45 50
167 **34** 25 c. chocolate and blue .. 1·00 1·10
168 **35** $1 blue and orange .. 4·00 2·00
163/168 .. .. *Set of* 6 5·50 4·50
163/8 Perf. "Specimen" *Set of* 6 42·00

36. King George VI and Phoenix.

(Des. W. E. Jones. Recess. D.L.R.)

1946 (29 AUG.). *Victory. Wmk. Mult. Script CA. P* 13.

169 **36** 30 c. blue and red .. 25 25
170 ,, $1 brown and red .. 70 55
169/70 Perf. "Specimen" *Set of* 2 25·00

1948 (22 DEC.). *Royal Silver Wedding. As Nos.* 30/1 *of Aden.*

171 10 c. violet 15 15
172 $10 carmine .. .. 6·00 5·50

1949 (10 OCT.). *75th Anniv. of Universal Postal Union. As Nos.* 114/7 *of Antigua.*

173 10 c. violet 15 15
174 20 c. carmine-red 15 15
175 30 c. deep blue 30 20
176 80 c. bright reddish purple .. 70 70

1953 (2 JUNE). *Coronation. As No.* 47 *of Aden.*

177 10 c. black and slate-lilac .. 8 5

37. Queen Elizabeth II.

38. University Arms.

1954 (5 JAN.)–**60.** *Wmk. Mult. Script CA. P* 14.

178 **37** 5 c. orange 5 5
a. Imperf. (pair) £250
179 ,, 10 c. lilac (*shades*) 5 5
180 ,, 15 c. green (*shades*) .. 5 5
181 ,, 20 c. brown, C 8 12
182 ,, 25 c. scarlet (*shades*), C .. 8 10
183 ,, 30 c. grey (*shades*), C .. 12 8
184 ,, 40 c. bright blue (*shades*), C 15 12
185 ,, 50 c. reddish purple, C .. 25 10
186 ,, 65 c. grey, C (20.6.60) .. 40 45
187 ,, $1 orange and green, C 30 12
188 ,, $1.30, blue & red (*shades*), C (20.6.60) .. 80 30
189 ,, $2 reddish violet and scarlet (*shades*), C .. 1·10 30
190 ,, $5 grn. & pur. (*shades*), C 3·50 60
191 ,, $10 reddish violet and brt. blue (*shades*), C 7·50 2·00
178/191 .. .. *Set of* 14 13·00 4·00

No. 178a. One sheet was found: 90 stamps imperf., 10 perf. three sides only.

(Photo. Harrison.)

1961 (11 SEPT.). *Golden Jubilee of Hong Kong University. W* w.**12**. *P* 11½ × 12.

192 **38** $1 multicoloured .. 1·00 75
a. Gold ptg. omitted .. £300

39. Statue of Queen Victoria.

(Photo. Harrison.)

1962 (4 MAY). *Stamp Centenary. W* w.**12**. *P* 14½.

193 **39** 10 c. black and magenta 10 10
194 ,, 20 c. black and light blue 15 15
195 ,, 50 c. black and bistre .. 35 35

40. Queen Elizabeth II (after Annigoni). **41.**

(Photo. Harrison).

1962 (4 OCT.)–**73.** *W* w.**12** (*upright*). *Chalk-surfaced paper. P* 15 × 14 (*5 c. to $1*) *or* 14 × 14½ (*others*).

196 **40** 5 c. red-orange 5 5
197 ,, 10 c. bright reddish violet (*shades*) 5 5
b. Glazed paper. *Reddish violet* (14.4.72) 5 5
198 ,, 15 c. emerald .. 10 5
199 ,, 20 c. red-brown (*shades*) .. 10 5
b. Glazed paper. *Brown* (27.9.72) 8 5
200 ,, 25 c. cerise 12 12
201 ,, 30 c. dp. grey-blue (*shades*) 12 5
b. Glazed paper. *Chalky blue* (27.9.72) 8 5
202 ,, 40 c. deep bluish green .. 15 10
203 ,, 50 c. scarlet (*shades*) .. 15 5
b. Glazed paper. *Vermilion* (27.9.72) 15 10
204 ,, 65 c. ultramarine 30 25
205 ,, $1 sepia 30 5
206 **41** $1.30, multicoloured .. 60 12
a. Glazed, ordinary paper (3.2.71) 60 15
207 ,, $2 multicoloured .. 80 25
a. Glazed paper (1973)* .. 12·00 1·00
208 ,, $5 multicoloured .. 2·00 40
a. Glazed, ordinary paper (3.2.71) .. .. 2·00 1·25
209 **41** $10 multicoloured .. 3·50 1·25
a. Glazed, ordinary paper (1973)* .. .. 35·00 10·00
210 ,, $20 multicoloured .. 7·50 3·50
196/210 .. .. *Set of* 15 14·00 5·00

*These are from printings which were sent to Hong Kong in March 1973 but not released in London.

The $1.30 to $20 exist with PVA gum as well as gum arabic. The glazed paper printings are with PVA gum only.

See also Nos. 222, etc.

1963 (4 JUNE). *Freedom from Hunger. As No.* 76 *of Aden, but additionally inscr. in Chinese characters.*

211 $1.30 bluish green .. .. 2·25 1·60

1963 (2 SEPT.). *Red Cross Centenary. As Nos.* 147/8 *of Antigua, but additionally inscr. in Chinese characters at right.*

212 10 c. red and black .. 15 15
213 $1.30 red and blue .. 1·50 1·25

1965 (17 MAY) *I.T.U. Centenary. As Nos.* 166/7 *of Antigua.*

214 10 c. light pur. & orge.-yell. 10 10
215 $1·30, olive-yellow and deep bluish green .. 1·25 1·00

1965 (25 OCT.). *International Co-operation Year. As Nos.* 168/9 *of Antigua.*

216 10 c. reddish pur. & turq.-grn. 10 10
217 $1.30, deep bluish green & lavender (*shades*) .. 1·00 1·00

1966 (24 JAN.). *Churchill Commemoration. As Nos.* 170/3 *of Antigua but additionally inscr. in Chinese characters.*

218 10 c. new blue 8 8
219 50 c. deep green 35 35
220 $1.30, brown .. .. 1·50 75
221 $2 bluish violet .. .. 1·75 1·40

1966–72. *As* 1962 *issue but wmk.* w.**12** *sideways. Glazed paper* ($1.30 *to* $20) *or Chalk-surfaced paper* (*others*).

222 40 5 c. red-orange 5 5
223 ,, 10 c. reddish violet .. 5 5
224 ,, 15 c. emerald .. 8 8
225 ,, 20 c. red-brown (6.9.66) .. 10 8
a. Glazed paper (14.4.72) .. 10 8
226 ,, 25 c. cerise .. 12 12
a. Glazed paper (14.4.72) .. 12 12
227 ,, 30 c. dp. grey-blue (31.3.70) 12 8
a. Glazed paper (14.4.72) .. 12 10
228 ,, 40 c. deep bluish green .. 12 10
a. Glazed paper (14.4.72) .. 12 10
229 ,, 50 c. scarlet 15 8
230 ,, 65 c. ultramarine (*shades*) 35 25
231 ,, $1 sepia 35 10
232 **41** $1.30, mult. (14.4.72) .. 45 20
233 ,, $2 mult. (13.12.71) .. 55 30
234 ,, $5 mult. (13.12.71) .. 1·75 90
236 ,, $20 mult. (14.4.72) .. 6·00 4·00
222/36 .. .. *Set of* 14 9·00 5·50

The 5 c. to 25 c., 40 c. and 50 c. exist with PVA gum as well as gum arabic, but the 30 c., and all stamps on glazed paper exist with PVA gum only.

1966 (20 SEPT.). *Inauguration of W.H.O. Headquarters, Geneva. As Nos.* 178/9 *of Antigua, but additionally inscr. in Chinese characters.*

237 10 c. black, yell.-grn. & lt. bl. 5 5
238 50 c. black, lt. pur. & yell.-brn. 35 35

1966 (1 DEC.). *20th Anniv. of U.N.E.S.C.O. As Nos.* 196/8 *of Antigua, but additionally inscr. in Chinese characters.*

239 10 c. slate-vio., red, yell. & orge. 5 5
240 50 c. orange-yell., vio. & dp. ol. 35 35
241 $2 black, lt. purple & orange 1·40 1·25

42. Rams' Heads on Chinese Lanterns.

43. Three Rams (" Year of the Ram ").

(Des. V. Whiteley. Photo. Harrison.)

1967 (17 JAN.). *Chinese New Year* (" *Year of the Ram* "). *W* w.**12** (*sideways*). *P* 14½.

242 **42** 10 c. rosine, olive-green & light yellow-olive .. 8 8
243 **43** $1.30, emerald, rosine & light yellow-olive .. 85 80

44. Cable Route Map.

(Des. V. Whiteley. Photo. Harrison.)

1967 (30 MAR.). *Completion of Malaysia–Hong Kong Link of SEACOM Telephone Cable. W* w.**12.** *P* 12½.

244 **44** $1.30, new blue and red .. 75 75

45. Monkeys in Tree (" Year of the Monkey ").

46. Family of Monkeys.

(Des. R. Granger Barrett. Photo. Harrison.)

1968 (23 JAN.). *Chinese New Year* (" *Year of the Monkey* "). *W* w.**12** (*sideways*). *P* 14.

245 **45** 10 c. gold, black & scarlet 5 5
246 **46** $1.30, gold, blk. & scar. 75 75

47. Liner at Ocean Terminal.

(Des. and litho. De la Rue.)

1968 (24 APR.). *Sea Craft.* *T* **47** *and similar horiz. designs.* *P* 13.

247 10 c. multicoloured 5 5
248 20 c. cobalt-blue, blk. & brn. 10 10
249 40 c. orange, black & mauve 25 25
250 50 c. orange-red, blk. & grn. 30 25
a. Green omitted .. ..
251 $1 greenish yell., blk. & red 1·00 1·00
252 $1.30 Prussian blue, black and pink .. .. 1·50 1·50
247/52 .. .. *Set of* 6 2·00 2·00

Designs:—20 c. Pleasure launch; 40 c. car ferry; 50 c. Passenger ferry; $1, Sampan: $1.30, Junk.

53. *Bauhinia blakeana.* **54.** Arms of Hong Kong.

(Des. V. Whiteley. Photo. Harrison.)

1968 (25 SEPT.)–**72.** *P* 14×14½. *W* w.**12.**

(*a*) *Upright. Chalk-surfaced paper.*

253 **53** 65 c. multicoloured .. 35 35
254 **54** $1 multicoloured .. 50 50

(*b*) *Sideways. Glazed paper.*

254*a* **53** 65 c. mult. (27.9.72) .. 30 25
254*b* **54** $1 mult. (13.12.71) .. 35 30

Nos. 253/4 exist with PVA gum as well as gum arabic; Nos. 254*a*/*b* with PVA gum only.

55. " Aladdin's Lamp " and Human Rights Emblem.

(Des. R. Granger Barrett. Litho. B. W.)

1968 (20 NOV.). *Human Rights Year.* *W* w.**12** (*sideways*). *P* 13½.

255 **55** 10 c. orange, black and myrtle-green .. 5 5
256 ,, 50 c. yellow, black and deep reddish purple 30 30

56. Cockerel.

57. Cockerel. (*Vert.*)

(Des. R. Granger Barrett. Photo. Enschedé.)

1969 (11 FEB.). *Chinese New Year.* (" *Year of the Cock* "). *P* 13×13½ (10 *c.*) *or* 13½×13 ($1.30).

257 **56** 10 c. multicoloured .. 5 5
258 **57** $1.30, multicoloured .. 85 85

58. Arms of Chinese University.

(Des. V. Whiteley. Photo. Govt. Ptg. Bureau, Tokyo.)

1969 (26 AUG.). *Establishment of Chinese University of Hong Kong.* *P* 13½.

259 **58** 40 c. violet, gold and pale turquoise-blue .. 25 25

59. Earth Station and Satellite.

(Des. V. Whiteley. Photo. Harrison.)

1969 (24 SEPT.). *Opening of Communications Satellite Tracking Station.* *W* w.**12.** *P* 14×14½.

260 **59** $1 multicoloured 50 50

60. Chow's Head. **62.** Expo 70 Emblem.

61. Chow standing. (*Horiz.*) **63.** Expo 70 Emblem and Junks. (*Horiz.*)

(Des. R. Granger Barrett. Photo. De La Rue.)

1970 (28 JAN.). *Chinese New Year.* (" *Year of the Dog* "). *W* w.**12** (*sideways on* $1.30). *P* 14.

261 **60** 10 c. lemon-yellow, orange-brown and black .. 10 10
262 **61** $1.30, multicoloured .. 60 60

(Des. and litho. Bradbury, Wilkinson.)

1970 (14 MAR.). *World Fair, Osaka.* *W* w.**12** (*sideways on* 25 *c.*). *P* 13½×13 (15 *c.*) *or* 13×13½ (25 *c.*).

263 **62** 15 c. multicoloured .. 10 10
264 **63** 25 c. multicoloured .. 15 15

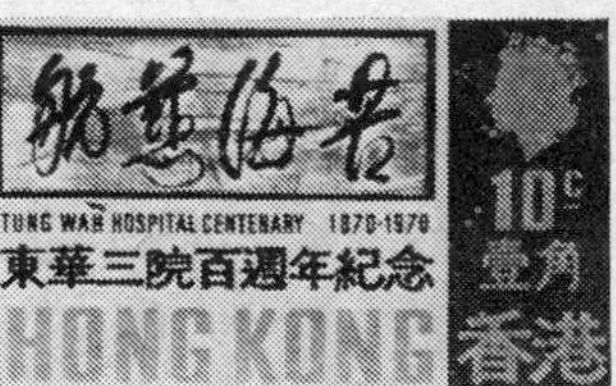

64. Plaque in Tung Wah Hospital.

(Des. M. F. Griffith. Photo. Harrison.)

1970 (9 APR.). *Centenary of Tung Wah Hospital.* *W* w.**12** (*sideways*). *P* 14.

265 **64** 10 c. multicoloured .. 5 5
266 ,, 50 c. multicoloured .. 25 25

65. Symbol.

(Des. J. E. Cooter. Litho. B.W.)

1970 (5 AUG.). *Asian Productivity Year.* *W* w.**12.** *P* 14×13½.

267 **65** 10 c. multicoloured .. 10 10

66. Pig.

(Des. Kan Tai Keung. Photo. Govt. Ptg. Bureau, Tokyo.)

1971 (20 JAN.). *Chinese New Year* (" *Year of the Pig* "). *P* 13½.
268 **66** 10 c. multicoloured .. 8 8
269 ,, $1.30, multicoloured .. 55 55

67. " 60 " and Scout Badge.

(Des. locally. Litho. Harrison.)

1971 (23 JULY). *Diamond Jubilee of Scouting in Hong Kong. W* w.**12** (*sideways*). *P* 14×14½.
270 **67** 10 c. black, scarlet & yell. 8 8
271 ,, 50 c. black, green and blue 20 20
272 ,, $2 black, magenta and bluish violet 70 70

68. Festival Emblem.

(Des. Kan Tai-Keung. Litho. J.W.)

1971 (2 Nov.). *Hong Kong Festival. T* **68** *and similar designs. W* w.**12** (*sideways on* 10 *c. and* 50 *c.*). *P* 13½×14 (10 *c.*) *or* 14 (*others*).
273 **68** 10 c. orange and purple .. 8 8
274 – 50 c. multicoloured .. 15 15
275 – $1 multicoloured .. 35 35

Designs: *Horiz.* (39×23 *mm.*)—50 c. Coloured streamers. *Vert.* (23×39 *mm.*)—$1 " Orchid ".

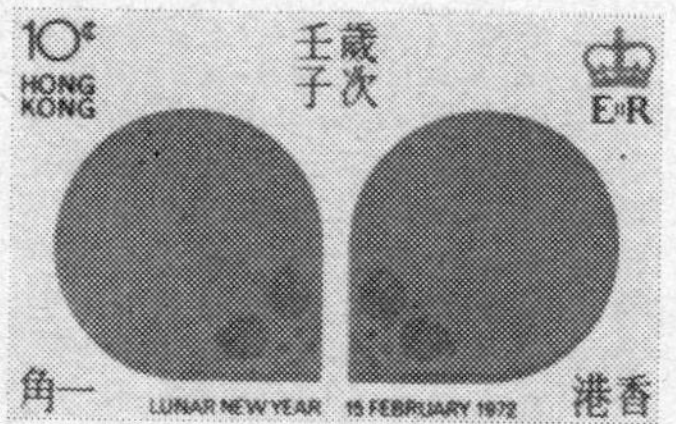

69. Stylised Rats.

(Des. Kan Tai-Keung. Photo. D.L.R.)

1972 (8 FEB.). *Chinese New Year.* (" *Year of the Rat* "). *W* w.**12**. *P* 13½×13.
276 **69** 10 c. red, gold and black .. 8 8
277 ,, $1.30, gold, red & black 45 45

70. Tunnel Entrance.

(Des. G. Drummond from painting by G. Baxter. Litho. Harrison.)

1972 (20 OCT.). *Opening of Cross-Harbour Tunnel. W* w.**12**. *P* 14×14½.
278 **70** $1 multicoloured .. 30 35

71. Phoenix and Dragon.

(Des. (from photograph by D. Groves) and photo. Harrison.)

1972 (20 Nov.). *Royal Silver Wedding. W* w.**12**. *P* 14×14½.
279 **71** 10 c. multicoloured .. 5 5
280 ,, 50 c. multicoloured .. 25 25

72. Ox.

(Des. R. Granger Barrett. Photo. Harrison.)

1973 (25 JAN.). *Chinese New Year* (" *Year of the Ox* "). *W* w.**12** (*sideways on* 10 *c.*). *P* 14.
281 **72** 10 c. reddish orge., brn. & black 5 5
282 – $1.30, lt. yellow, yell.-orge. & black .. 35 30

Design:—$1.30, similar to 10 c., but horiz.

73. Queen Elizabeth II. **74.**

(Des. from coinage. Photo. ($10 and $20 also embossed). Harrison.)

1973 (12 JUNE). *W* w.**12** (*sideways on* 15, 30, 40 *c. and T* **74**). *P* 14½×14 (*T* **73**) or 14×14½ (*T* **74**).
283 **73** 10 c. bright orange .. 5 5
a. Wmk. sideways (from coils) 5 5
284 ,, 15 c. yellow-green 10 10
285 ,, 20 c. reddish violet .. 10 8
286 ,, 25 c. lake-brown 10 10
287 ,, 30 c. ultramarine 10 10
288 ,, 40 c. deep turquoise-blue 12 15
289 ,, 50 c. light orange-vermilion 15 15
290 ,, 65 c. greenish bistre .. 20 20
291 ,, $1 bottle-green .. 30 30
292 **74** $1.30, pale yellow and reddish violet .. 35 35
293 ,, $2 pale green & reddish brown 45 45
294 ,, $5 pink and Royal blue 90 1·00
295 ,, $10 pink & deep blackish olive .. .. 1·90 2·10
296 ,, $20 pink and brownish black .. .. 3·75 4·00
283/96 .. .. *Set of* 14 8·00 8·50

See also Nos. 311/21 and 341 etc.

1973 (14 Nov.). *Royal Wedding. As Nos.* 165/6 *of Anguilla, but additionally inscr. in Chinese characters. Centre multicoloured. W* w.**12** (*sideways*). *P* 13½.
297 50 c. ochre 12 15
298 $2 bright mauve 45 45

75. Festival Symbols forming Chinese Character.

(Des. locally. Litho. B.W.)

1973 (23 Nov.). *Hong Kong Festival. T* **75** *and similar horiz. designs. W* w.**12**. *P* 14.
299 **75** 10 c. brownish red & bright green 5 5
300 – 50 c. deep magenta and reddish orange .. 15 15
301 – $1 bright green and deep mauve 35 35

Each value has the festival symbols arranged to form a Chinese character: " Hong " on the 10 c.; " Kong " on the 50 c.; " Festival " on the $1.

76. Tiger.

(Des. R. Granger Barrett. Litho. Harrison.)

1974 (8 JAN.). *Chinese New Year* (" *Year of the Tiger* "). *W* w.**12** (*sideways on* $1.30). *P* 14.
302 **76** 10 c. multicoloured .. 5 5
303 – $1.30, multicoloured .. 30 30

Design:—$1.30, Similar to *T* **76**, but vert.

77. Chinese Mask.

(Des. R. Hookham. Litho. Enschedé.)

1974 (1 Feb.). *Arts Festival. Vert. designs as T* **77** *showing Chinese opera masks. W* w.**12** *(sideways). P*12 × 12½.

304 **77** 10 c. multicoloured .. 5 5
305 – $1 multicoloured .. 25 25
306 – $2 multicoloured .. 50 50
MS307 159 × 94 mm. Nos. 304/6.
Wmk. upright. P 14 × 13. .. 1·00 1·00

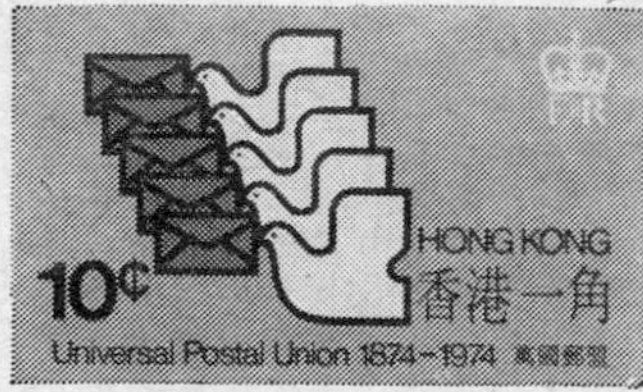

78. Pigeons with Letters.

(Des. Kan Tai-Keung. Litho. Harrison.)

1974 (9 Oct.). *Centenary of Universal Postal Union. T* **78** *and similar horiz. designs. W* w.**12** *(sideways on* 10 *and* 50 *c.). P* 14.

308 10 c. light greenish blue, light yellow-grn. and slate-blk. 5 5
a. No. wmk .. .. .. 20·00
309 50 c. deep mauve, orange and slate-black 12 15
310 $2 multicoloured 45 50

Designs:—50 c. Globe within letter; $2 Hands holding letters.

1975 (21 Jan.–9 Apr.). *As Nos.* 283/93 *but W* w.**14** *(sideways on* 10, 20, 25, 50, 65 *c. and* $1).

311 **73** 10 c. bright orange .. 5 5
312 ,, 15 c. yellow-green 5 5
313 ,, 20 c. reddish violet (19.3) 5 5
314 ,, 25 c. lake-brown (19.3) .. 5 5
315 ,, 30 c. ultramarine (9.4) .. 5 8
316 ,, 40 c. dp. turq.-blue (19.3) 8 10
317 ,, 50 c. lt. orge.-verm. (19.3) 10 12
318 ,, 65 c. greenish bistre (19.3) 12 15
319 ,, $1 bottle-green (19.3) .. 20 25
320 **74** $1.30, pale yellow and reddish violet (19.3) .. 30 30
321 ,, $2 pale green and red-dish brown (19.3) .. 40 45
311/21 .. .. *Set of* 11 1·10 1·25

See also Nos. 431, etc.

79. Stylised Rabbit.

(Des. Kan Tai-Keung. Litho. Harrison.)

1975 (5 Feb.). *Chinese New Year (" Year of the Rabbit "). T* **79** *and similar horiz. design. P* 14. (*a*) *No wmk.*

325 **79** 10 c. silver and light red 5 5
326 – $1.30, gold and lt. green 35 40

(*b*) *W* w.**12**.

327 **79** 10 c. silver and light red 5 5
328 – $1.30, gold and lt. green 35 40

Design:—$1.30, Pair of rabbits.

80. Queen Elizabeth II, the Duke of Edinburgh and Hong Kong Arms.

(Des. PAD Studio. Litho. Questa.)

1975 (30 Apr.). *Royal Visit. W* w.**14** *(sideways). P* 13½.

329 **80** $1.30, multicoloured .. 30 25
330 ,, $2 multicoloured 45 50

81. Mid-Autumn Festival.

(Des. Tao Ho. Litho. De La Rue, Bogotá.)

1975 (31 July). *Chinese Festivals of* 1975. *T* **81** *and similar vert. designs. Multicoloured. No wmk. P* 13½ × 14.

331 50 c. Type **81** 10 12
332 $1 Dragon-boat Festival .. 20 25
333 $2 Tin Hau Festival .. 40 45
MS334 102 × 83 mm. Nos. 331/3 80

82. Hwamei.

(Des. C. Kuan. Litho. Harrison.)

1975 (29 Oct.). *Birds. T* **82** *and similar vert. designs. Multicoloured. W* w.**14**. *P* 14.

335 50 c. Type **82** 10 12
336 $1.30, Chinese Bulbul .. 25 30
337 $2 Black-capped Kingfisher 40 45

83. Dragon.

(Des. local artist. Litho. Questa.)

1976 (21 Jan.). *Chinese New Year (" Year of the Dragon "). T* **83** *and similar horiz. design. W* w.**14** *(sideways). P* 14½.

338 **83** 20 c. mauve, dull lake and gold 5 8
339 – $1.30, light yellow-grn., light red and gold .. 25 30

No. 339 is as T **83** but has the design reversed.

1976 (20 Feb. 1–9 Mar.). *As Nos.* 283 *etc., but no wmk.*

342 **73** 20 c. reddish violet .. 5 5
344 ,, 30 c. ultramarine 5 8
350 **74** $2 pale green & reddish brown 45 50
351 ,, $5 pink and royal blue 1·00 1·10
352 ,, $10 pink and deep blackish olive (19.3.76) .. 2·25 2·50
353 ,, $20 pink and brownish blk. (19.3.76) .. .. 4·50 5·00
342/53 .. .. *Set of* 6 7·50 8·50

84. " 60 " and Girl Guides Badge.

(Des. locally. Photo. Harrison.)

1976 (23 Apr.). *Girl Guides Diamond Jubilee T* **84** *and similar horiz. design. Multicoloured. W* w.**12**. *P* 14.

354 20 c. Type **84** 5 8
355 $1.30, Badge, stylised diamond and " 60 " .. 25 30

85. " Postal Services " in Chinese Characters.

(Des. Tao Ho. Litho. Harrison.)

1976 (11 Aug.). *Opening of new G.P.O. T* **85** *and similar vert. designs. W* w.**14**. *P* 14.

356 20 c. yellow-green, light greenish grey and black .. 5 8
357 $1.30, reddish orange, lt. greenish grey and black .. 25 40
358 $2 yellow, light greenish grey and black .. 40 45

Designs:—$1.30, Old G.P.O.; $2 New G.P.O.

86. Snake on Branch.

(Des. Jennie Wong. Litho. J.W.)

1977 (6 Jan.). *Chinese New Year ("Year of the Snake"). T* **86** *and similar horiz. design. W* w. **14** *(sideways). P* 13½.

359	**86**	20 c. multicoloured	5	8
360	–	$1·30, multicoloured	30	35

The $1·30 shows a snake facing left.

87. Presentation of the Orb.

(Des. Hong Kong Govt. Services Dept.; adapted J.W. Ltd. Litho. Harrison.)

1977 (7 Feb.). *Silver Jubilee. T* **87** *and similar multicoloured designs. W* w.**14** *(sideways on* $1·30 *and* $2). *P* 14½×14 ($2) *or* 14×14½ *(others)*.

361	20 c. Type **78**	5	8
362	$1·30, Queen's visit, 1975 ..	30	35
363	$2 The Orb	50	55

POSTAGE DUE STAMPS.

PRINTERS. Nos. D1/23 were typographed by De La Rue & Co.

D **1.** Post-office Scales.

1923 (Dec.)–**56.** *Wmk. Mult. Script CA. P* 14.

D1 D **1**	1 c. brown, O	15	25
	a. Wmk. sideways (1931) ..	10	15
	b. Chalk-surfaced paper, wmk. sideways (21.3.56)	12	15
D2 ,,	2 c. green	40	50
	a. Wmk. sideways (1928) ..	25	30
D3 ,,	4 c. scarlet	50	70
	a. Wmk. sideways (1928) ..	30	40
D4 ,,	6 c. yellow	1·00	1·75
	a. Wmk. sideways (1931) ..	60	1·00
D5 ,,	10 c. bright ultramarine ..	1·00	1·25
	a. Wmk. sideways (1934) ..	60	70
D1/5	.. .. *Set of* 5	2·75	4·00
D1a/5a	.. .. *Set of* 5	1·60	2·25
D1/5 Optd. "Specimen"	*Set of* 5	38·00	

1938 (Feb.)–**63.** *Wmk. Mult. Script CA (sideways). P* 14.

D 6 D **1**	2 c. grey, O	25	25
	a. Chalky paper (21.3.56)	12	20
D 7 ,,	4 c. orange, O	30	30
	a. Chalky paper. *Orange-yellow* (23.5.61) ..	15	20
D 8 ,,	6 c. scarlet	35	15
D 9 ,,	8 c. chestnut (26.2.46)	35	40
D10 ,,	10 c. violet, O	25	10
	a. Chalky paper (17.9.63)	15	12
D11 ,,	20 c. black (26.2.46) ..	35	50
D12 ,,	50 c. blue (7.47)	50	55
D6a/12	.. .. *Set of* 7	1·75	1·90
D6/12 Perf. "Specimen"	*Set of* 7	42·00	

1965 (15 Apr.)–**72.** *Chalk-surfaced paper. P* 14.

(*a*) *Wmk.* w.**12** *(sideways)*.

D13 D **1**	4 c. yellow-orange ..	5	5
D14 ,,	5 c. red (13.5.69) ..	5	5
	a. Glazed paper (17.11.72)	5	5
D15 ,,	10 c. violet (27.6.67) ..	8	8
D16 ,,	20 c. black ('65) ..	10	10
D17 ,,	50 c. deep blue (*shades*) ('65)	20	25

(*b*) *Wmk.* w.**12** *(upright)*.

D18 D **1**	5 c. red (20.7.67) ..	5	5
D19 ,,	50 c. deep blue (26.8.70)	15	20

The 5 c. is smaller, 21×18 mm.

1972 (17 Nov.)–**74.** *Glazed paper. W* w.**12** *(sideways).* (*a*) *P* 14×14½.

D20 D **1**	10 c. bright reddish violet	5	5
D21 ,,	20 c. grey-black	5	5
D22 ,,	50 c. deep dull blue ..	10	12

(*b*) *P* 13½×14.

D23 D **1**	5 c. brown-red (1.5.74)	5	5

(Typo. Walsall.)

1976 (19 Mar.–1 Apr.). *Smaller design* (21×17 *mm.) with redrawn value-tablet. Glazed paper. W* w.**14.** *P* 14.

D25 D **1**	10 c. bright reddish violet	5	5
D26 ,,	20 c. grey-black	5	5
D27 ,,	50 c. deep dull blue ..	10	12
D28 ,,	$1 yellow (1 Apr.) ..	20	25

FISCALS, ETC., USED FOR POSTAGE.

I. Stamps inscribed "stamp duty."

NOTE—The dated circular "hong kong" cancellation with "paid all" in lower segment normally indicates fiscal, not postal, use, but a few instances are known where it was applied *in red*, for postal purposes.

F 1

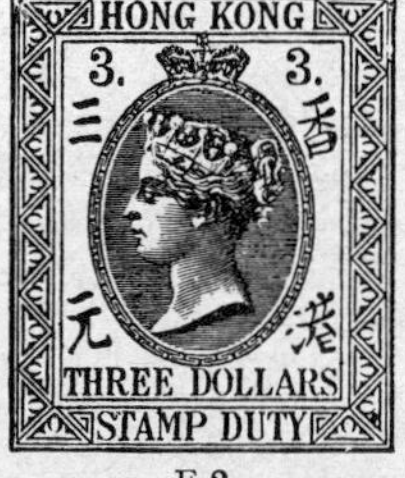

F 2

12
CENTS.
(F 4)

F 3

5
DOLLARS
(F 5)

1874–1902. *Wmk. Crown CC.*

(*a*) *P* 15½×15.

F1 F **1**	$2 olive-green	16·00	1·60
	a. Thin paper	20·00	4·00
F2 F **2**	$3 dull violet	14·00	1·60
	a. Thin paper	16·00	4·00
	b. Bluish paper		
F3 F **3**	$10 rose-carmine	95·00	40·00
F1/3 Optd. "Specimen"	*Set of* 3	55·00	

(*b*) *P* 14.

F4 F **1**	$2 dull bluish grn. (1890)	20·00	5·50
F5 F **2**	$3 dull mauve (1902) ..	20·00	5·50
	a. Bluish paper		
F6 F **3**	$10 grey-green (? 1884) ..	70·00	
F4/5 Optd. "Specimen"	*Set of* 2	35·00	

1882. *No.* F3 *surch. with Type* F **4.**

F7 F **3**	12 c. on $10 rose-carmine	20·00	15·00

1891 (Jan.). *Surch. with Type* F **5.** *Wmk. Crown CA. P* 14.

F8 F **3**	$5 on $10 purple/*red* (Optd. S. £17)	14·00	11·00

F 6

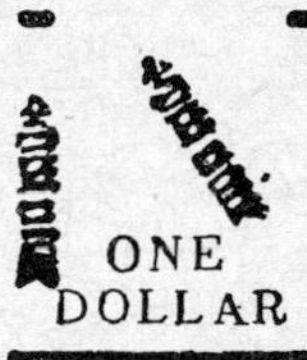

(F 7)

1890. *Wmk. Crown CA. P* 14.

F9 F **6**	2 c. dull purple	1·40	1·10

1897 (Sept.). *Surch. with Type* F **7.**

F10 F **1**	$1 on $2 olive-green (No. F1)	2·25	3·00
	a. Chinese surch. wholly omitted	40·00	35·00
F11 ,,	$1 on $2 dull bluish green (No. F4) (H/S S. £17)	4·00	5·00
	a. Chinese surch. wholly omitted	11·00	8·00
	b. Diag. portion of Chinese surch. omitted		

F 8

1938 (11 Jan.). *Wmk. Mult. Script CA. P* 14.

F12 F **8**	5 c. green	10·00	1·40

Authorised for postal use from Jan. 11th to 20th, 1938 (both dates inclusive).

II. Stamps specially surcharged for use on Postcards.

3
CENTS
(P 1)

THREE
(P 2)

1879. *Nos. 22 and 13 surch. as Type* P **1**.

P1	**3**	3 c. on 16 c. yellow (No. 22)	40·00	80·00
P2	,,	5 c. on 18 c. lilac (No. 13) ..	40·00	80·00

No. P2 *surch. with Type* P **2**.

P3	**3**	3 on 5 c. on 18 c. lilac ..	£150	

III. Stamps overprinted "S.O." (Stamp Office) or "S.D." (Stamp Duty).

S. O. **S. D.**

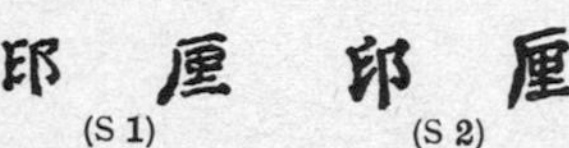

(S 1) (S 2)

1891. *Optd. with Types* S **1** *or* S **2**.

S1	S **1**	2 c. carmine (No. 33) ..	14·00	16·00
S2	S **2**	2 c. carmine (No. 33) ..	5·50	7·00
S3	S **1**	10 c. purple/*red* (No. 40) ..	16·00	20·00

Other fiscal stamps are found apparently postally used, but there is no evidence that this use was authorised.

JAPANESE OCCUPATION OF HONG KONG.

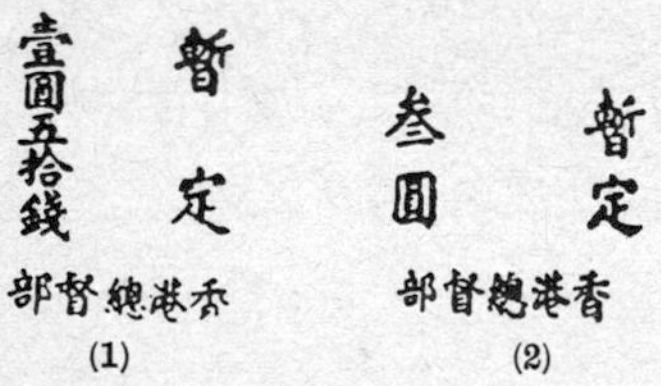

(1) (2)

1945 (Apr.). *Stamps of Japan surch. with T* **1** *(No.* J1*) or as T* **2**.

J1	1.50 yen on 1 s. brown ..	60	1·75
J2	3 yen on 2 s. scarlet	60	1·75
J3	5 yen on 5 s. claret	22·00	6·50

Designs ($18\frac{1}{2} \times 22$ mm.):—1 s. Girl Worker; 2 s. Gen. Nogi; 5 s. Admiral Togo.

No. J3 has four characters of value similarly arranged but differing from T **2**.

CHINA.

BRITISH POST OFFICES.

CHINA

(1)

1917–21. *Stamps of Hong Kong,* 1912–21 *(wmk. Mult. Crown CA), optd. with T* **1**, *at Somerset House.*

1	1 c. brown, O	10	15
	a. Crown broken at side ..	28·00	
	b. Black-brown, O	10	15
2	2 c. green, O	20	20
3	4 c. carmine-red, O	10	10
4	6 c. orange, O	20	15
5	8 c. slate, O	40	20
6	10 c. ultramarine, O	30	10
7	12 c. purple/*yellow*, C	60	45
8	20 c. purple & sage-green, C ..	80	20
9	25 c. purple & magenta, C (A)	1·10	1·40
11	30 c. pur. & orange-yellow, C	1·75	55
12	50 c. blk./*bl.-grn.*, C *(olive back)*	2·25	55
	a. On emerald surface (1917?) ..	1·50	80
	b. On emerald back (1919) ..	1·00	70
	c. On white back (1920) ..	3·25	1·00
13	$1 reddish purple and bright blue/*blue*, C	5·50	80
	a. Grey-pur. & blue/blue, C (1921)	4·50	85
14	$2 car.-red & grey-black, C	12·00	7·00
15	$3 green and purple, C ..	16·00	12·00
16	$5 green and red/*blue-green*, C *(olive back)*	14·00	14·00
17	$10 purple & black/*red.*, C ..	30·00	35·00
1/17	.. .. *Set of* 16	80·00	65·00
12/17	H/S "Specimen" *Set of* 6	£250	

1922–27. *As last, but wmk. Mult. Script CA.*

18	1 c. brown, O	10	20
19	2 c. green, O	20	25
20	4 c. carmine-rose, O	15	15
	a. Lower Chinese character at right broken at top	14·00	12·00
21	6 c. orange-yellow, O ..	25	50
22	8 c. grey, O	25	45
23	10 c. bright ultramarine, O ..	25	35
24	20 c. purple and sage-green, C	35	30
25	25 c. purple & magenta, C (B)	45	1·25
26	50 c. black/*emerald*, C (1927) (H/S S. £30)	1·25	2·25
27	$1 purple & blue/*blue*, C ..	3·00	4·00
28	$2 car.-red & grey-black, C	7·00	9·00
18/28	.. .. *Set of* 11	12·00	18·00

The use of these stamps was discontinued as from 1st Oct., 1930, on the closing of the British P.O's concerned.

INDIA.

1

1852 (1 July). "Scinde Dawk." *Embossed.*

S1 **1** ½ a. white £1200 £400
S2 „ ½ a. blue £3000 £900
S3 „ ½ a. scarlet .. .. .. — £2250

These stamps were issued under the authority of Sir Bartle Frere, Commissioner in Scinde. They were suppressed in October, 1854.

No. S3 is on sealing wax (usually cracked). Perfect copies are very rare.

I. EAST INDIA COMPANY ISSUES.

2 (*Much reduced*).

3

(Actual size of ½ a. and 1 a. stamps.)

The ½ a., 1 a. and 4 a. were lithographed in Calcutta at the office of the Surveyor-General. The die was engraved by Mr. Maniruddin (spelling uncertain). *Ungummed* paper watermarked as T **2** (the "No. 4" paper) with the Arms of the East India Co. in the sheet. The watermark is sideways on the ½ a. and 1 a., and upright on the 4 a. where the paper was trimmed so that only the central portion showing the oval and the arms was used. Imperforate.

1854 (April).

1 **3** ½ a. vermilion £160

This stamp, with 9½ arches in the side border, was prepared for use and a supply was sent to Bombay, but was not officially issued.

4

1854 (1 Oct.). *Die I.*

2 **4** ½ a. blue .. .. .. 9·00 4·50
a. Printed on both sides .. — £750
3 „ ½ a. pale blue .. .. .. 18·00 4·25
4 „ ½ a. deep blue .. .. .. 12·00 5·00
5 „ ½ a. indigo .. .. .. 15·00 6·00

We give the official date of issue, but copies are known which were put on sale as much as a fortnight earlier.

These stamps were printed between 5 May and 29 July, 1854. (Printing 30 millions.)

4*a*.

Die II.

6 **4a** ½ a. blue .. .. .. 14·00 30·00
7 „ ½ a. indigo .. .. .. 14·00 30·00

The bulk were printed between 1 and 12 August, 1854, with some extra sheets on or before 2 Nov. (Printing about 2 millions.)

5

Die III.

8 **5** ½ a. pale blue .. .. £150 13·00
8*a* „ ½ a. blue .. .. £130 12·00
9 „ ½ a. greenish blue .. .. £250 60·00
10 „ ½ a. deep blue .. .. £150 20·00

These stamps were printed between 3 July and 25 August, 1855. (Printing about 4¾ millions.)

The Three Dies of the ½ Anna.

Die I. *Chignon shading* mostly solid blobs of colour. *Corner ornaments*, solid blue stars with long points, always conspicuous. *Band below diadem* always heavily shaded. *Diadem and jewels.* The middle and right-hand jewels usually show a clearly defined cross. *Outer frame lines.* Stamps with white or faintly shaded chignons and weak frame lines are usually Die I (worn state).

Die II. *Chignon* normally shows much less shading. A strong line of colour separates hair and chignon. *Corner ornaments.* The right blue star is characteristic (see illustration) but tends to disappear. It never obliterates the white cross. *Band below diadem.* As Die I but heavier, sometimes solid. *Diadem and jewels.* As Die I but usually fainter. *Outer frame lines.* Always strong and conspicuous.

Die III. *Chignon shading* shows numerous fine lines, often blurred. *Corner ornaments* have a small hollow blue star with short points, which tends to disappear as in Die II. *Band below diadem*, shows light shading or hardly any shading. *Diadem and jewels.* Jewels usually marked with a solid squat star. The ornaments between the stars appear in the shape of a characteristic white "w". *Frame lines* variable.

The above notes give the general characteristics of the three Dies, but there are a few exceptions due to retouching, etc.

6

(*See note below No.* 14.)

Die I.

11 **6** 1 a. deep red .. .. .. 35·00 12·00
12 „ 1 a. red .. .. .. 35·00 11·00

Printing of these stamps commenced on 26 July, 1854, and continued into August. (Printing, see note below No. 14.)

7

Die II. With more lines in the chignon than in Die I, and with white curved line where chignon joins head.*

13 **7** 1 a. deep red .. .. .. 24·00 12·00
14 „ 1 a. dull red .. .. .. 12·00 12·00

* Very worn printings of Die II may be found with chignon nearly as white as in Die I.

In stamps of Die I, however, the small blob of red projecting from the hair into the chignon is always visible.

These stamps were printed in August and September, 1854. (Total printing, Dies I and II together, about 7¾ millions.)

8

Die III. With pointed bust.

15	**8**	1 a. red	£225	50·00
16	,,	1 a. dull red	£225	50·00

These stamps were printed between 7 July and 25 August, 1855. (Printing, about $1\frac{1}{2}$ millions.)

9. (Actual size.)

NOTE. Our catalogue prices for Four Annas stamps are for cut-square specimens, with clear margins and in good condition. Cut-to-shape copies are worth from 3% to 20% of these prices according to condition.

Four Dies of the Head:—

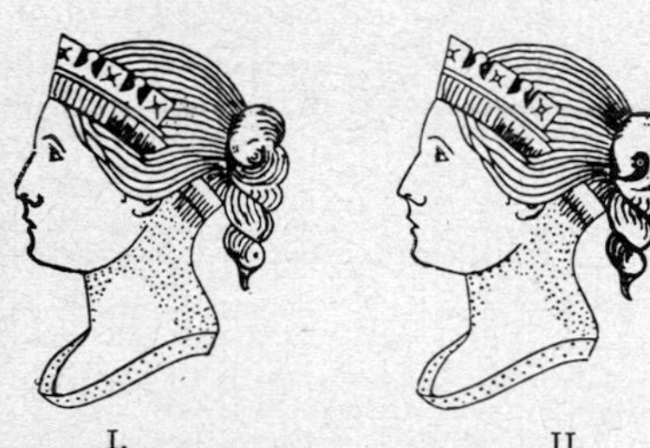

I. II.

DIE I. Band of diadem and chignon strongly shaded.

Die II. Lines in band of diadem worn. Few lines in the upper part of the chignon, which, however, shows a strongly drawn comma-like mark.

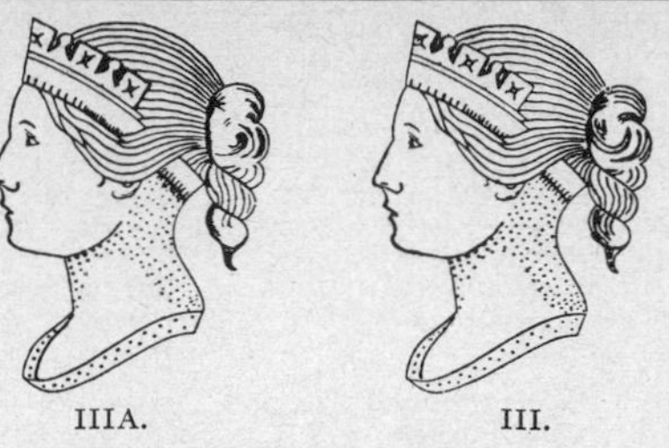

IIIA. III.

Die IIIA. Upper part of chignon partly redrawn, showing two short, curved vertical lines in the NE corner. "Comma" has disappeared.

Die III. Upper part of chignon completely redrawn, but band of diadem shows only a few short lines.

Two Dies of the Frame:—

DIE I. Outer frame lines weak. Very small dots of colour, or none at all, in the "R" and "A's". The white lines to the right of "INDIA" are separated, by a line of colour, from the inner white circle.

DIE II. Outer frame lines strengthened. Dots in the "R" and "A's" strong. White lines to right of "INDIA" break into inner white circle.

1854 (15 OCT.). *W* **2** *upright, central portion only. Imperf.*

1st Printing. Head Die I. Frame Die I. Stamps widely spaced and separated by blue wavy line.

			Un.	*Used*	*Us. pr.*
17	**9**	4 a. indigo & red	£500	£100	£350
18	,,	4 a. blue & pale red ..	£500	£100	£350
		a. Head inverted (*cut to shape*) ..	—	£5000–£15000	—

This printing was made between 13 and 28 Oct., 1854. (Printing, 206,040.)

2nd Printing. Head Die II. Frame Die I. Stamps widely spaced and separated by blue wavy line.

19	**9**	4 a. blue and red..	£400	75·00	£200
20	,,	4 a. indigo & dp. red	£400	75·00	£250

This printing was made between 1 and 13 Dec., 1854. (Printing, 393,960.)

This is known with head double.

3rd Printing. Head, Dies II, IIIA and III. Frame, Dies I and II. Stamps widely spaced and separated by wavy line.

21	**9**	4 a. bt. blue & bt. red (Head III, Frame I) ..	£900	£200	£600
		a. Head II, Frame I	—	£250	—
		b. Head IIIA, Frame I	—	£250	£700
		c. Head III, Frame II			

This printing was made between 10 March and 2 April, 1855. (Printing, 138,960.)

4th Printing. Head Die III. Frame Die II. Stamps closely spaced 2 to $2\frac{1}{2}$ mm. without separating line.

22	**9**	4 a. dp. blue & red	£350	70·00	£200
23	,,	4 a. blue and red ..	£350	65·00	£200
24	,,	4 a. p. blue & p. red	£350	70·00	£200

This printing was made between 3 April and 9 May, 1855. (Printing, 540,960.)

This is known with head double.

5th Printing. Head Die III. Frame Die II. Stamps spaced 4 to 6 mm. without separating line.

25	**9**	4 a. blue & rose-red	£350	80·00	£300
26	,,	4 a. dp. blue & red	£325	75·00	£300

This printing was made between 4 Oct. and 3 Nov., 1855. (Printing, 380,064.)

Serrated perf. about 18, or pin-perf.

27	$\frac{1}{2}$ a. blue (Die I)	
28	1 a. red (Die I)	
29	1 a. red (Die II)	
30	4 a. blue & red (Die II) ..	

This is believed to be an unofficial perforation. Most of the known specimens bear Madras circle postmarks (C122 to C126), but some are known with Bombay postmarks. Beware of fakes.

10

11

(Plate made at Mint, Calcutta. Typo., Stamp Office.)

1854 (6 OCT.). *Sheet wmk. sideways, as W* **2** *but with* " No. 3 " *at top left.* Imperf.*

31	**10**	2 a. green (*shades*)	9·00	3·50
34	,,	2 a. emerald-green	£150	

* The 2 a. was also printed on paper with sheet wmk. incorporating the words " STAMP OFFICE. One Anna ", etc. (Price £10 un. or us.)

Apart from the rare emerald-green shade, there is a range of shades of No. 31 varying from bluish to yellowish green.

Many stamps show traces of lines external to the design shown in our illustration. Stamps with this frame on all four sides are scarce.

Many reprints of the $\frac{1}{2}$, 1, 2, and 4 a. exist.

PRINTERS. All Indian stamps from No. 35 to 200 were typographed by De La Rue & Co.

1855 (OCT.). *Blue glazed paper. No wmk. P* 14.

35	**11**	4 a. black	28·00	3·50
		a. Imperf. (pair) ..	£125	£125
		b. Bisected (on cover) ..	—	£300
36	,,	8 a. carmine (Die I) ..	30·00	5·00
		a. Imperf. (pair) ..	£130	£130
		b. Bisected (on cover) ..	—	£300

The first supply of the 4 a. was on white paper, but it is difficult to distinguish from No. 45.

In the 8 a. the paper varies from deep blue to almost white.

For difference between Die I and Die II in the 8 a., see illustrations above No. 73.

1856–64. *No wmk. Paper yellowish to white. P 14.*

37 **11** ½ a. blue (Die I) .. .. 1·75 12
a. Imperf. (pair) .. .. 50·00 £125
38 „ ½ a. pale blue (Die I) .. 1·50 12
39 „ 1 a. brown .. .. .. 2·75 35
a. Imperf. between (vert. pair)
b. Imperf. (pair) £160
c. Bisected (on cover) .. £500
40 „ 1 a. deep brown .. .. 2·50 40
41 „ 2 a. dull pink .. .. 12·00 3·50
a. Imperf. (pair) £180 £180
42 „ 2 a. yellow-buff .. .. 6·00 2·00
a. Imperf. (pair) £180 £180
43 „ 2 a. yellow .. .. .. 6·00 2·50
44 „ 2 a. orange .. .. .. 9·00 2·50
a. Imperf. (pair) £200 £200
45 „ 4 a. black .. .. .. 6·00 1·50
a Bisected diagonally (2 a.) (on cover) .. .. — £300
b. Imperf. (pair) £250 £250
46 „ 4 a. grey-black .. .. 6·00 1·25
47 „ 4 a. green (1864) .. .. 28·00 6·00
48 „ 8 a. carmine (Die I) .. 6·00 2·50
49 „ 8 a. pale carmine (Die I) .. 6·00 2·50
a. Bisected (4 a.) (on cover) .. — £300

Prepared for use, but not officially issued.

50 **11** 2 a. yellow-green .. .. 30·00 90·00
a. Imperf. (pair) £170

This stamp is known with trial obliterations, and a few are known postally used. It also exists *imperf.*, but is not known used thus.

For difference between Die I and Die II in the ½ a., see illustrations above No. 75.

II. CROWN COLONY.

On the 1 November, 1858, Her Majesty Queen Victoria assumed the government of the territories in India "heretofore administered in trust by the Honourable East India Company".

12

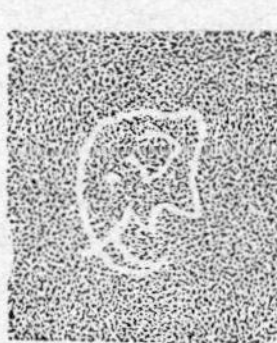
13

1860 (9 May). *No wmk. P 14.*

51 **12** 8 p. purple/*bluish* .. .. 24·00 18·00
52 „ 8 p. purple/*white* .. .. 3·50 1·75
a. Bisected diagonally (4 p.) (on cover) .. .. .. — £400
b. Imperf. (pair) £150 £150
53 „ 8 p. mauve .. .. .. 3·50 2·25

The bisected stamps of the issues of 1855–60 listed above were used exclusively in the Straits Settlements during shortage of stocks of certain values. Prices are for Singapore cancellations on original. Penang marks are considerably rarer.

1865. *Paper yellowish to white. W* **13.** *P 14.*

54 **11** ½ a. blue (Die I) 80 10
a. Imperf. .. .. .. — £150
55 „ ½ a. pale blue (Die I) .. 60 8
56 **12** 8 p. purple .. .. .. 2·75 2·00
57 „ 8 p. mauve .. .. .. 3·00 2·00
58 **11** 1 a. pale brown .. .. 1·10 8
59 „ 1 a. deep brown 65 8
60 „ 1 a. chocolate .. .. 1·25 8
61 „ 2 a. yellow .. .. .. 5·00 1·25
62 „ 2 a. orange .. .. .. 6·00 60
a. Imperf. .. .. .. — £300
63 „ 2 a. brown-orange .. .. 2·75 1·25
64 „ 4 a. green .. .. .. 18·00 7·00
65 „ 8 a. carmine (Die I) .. 50·00 20·00

The 8 p. mauve, No. 57, is found variously surcharged "NINE" or "NINE PIE" by local postmasters, to indicate that it was being sold for 9 pies, as was the case at one period. Such surcharges were made without Government sanction.

The stamps of India, wmk. Elephant's Head surcharged with a crown and value in "cents", were used in the Straits Settlements; *q.v.*

14

POSTAGE
(15)

POSTAGE
(16)

1866 (28 June). *T* **14** *optd. P 14 (at sides only).*

(a) As T **15.**

66 6 a. purple (G.) .. .. 60·00 28·00
a. Overprint inverted .. .. — £1000

There are 20 different types of this overprint.

(b) With T **16.**

68 6 a. purple (G.) .. 90·00 28·00

17

18

Die I

(4 annas.)

Die II

Die I.—Mouth closed, line from corner of mouth downwards only. Pointed chin.

Die II.—Mouth slightly open; lips, chin, and throat defined by line of colour. Rounded chin.

1866 (Sept.)–**1867.** *W* **13.** *P 14.*

69 **17** 4 a. green (Die I) .. .. 4·00 20
70 „ 4 a. deep green (Die I) .. 4·00 20
71 „ 4 a. blue-green (Die II) .. 4·00 15
72 **18** 6 a. 8 p. slate .. .. 8·00 7·00
a. Imperf. (pair) £300

Die I. (8 a.)

Die I. (½ a.)

Die II. (8 a.)

Die II. (½ a.)

1868 (Jan.). *Die II. Profile redrawn and different diadem. W* **13.** *P 14.*

73 **11** 8 a. rose (Die II) .. .. 3·25 2·25
74 „ 8 a. pale rose (Die II) .. 4·00 2·25

1873. *Die II. Features, especially the mouth, more firmly drawn. W* **13.** *P 14.*

75 **11** ½ a. deep blue (Die II) .. 55 8
76 „ ½ a. blue (Die II) 55 8

19

20

1874. *W* **13.** *P 14.*

77 **19** 9 p. bright mauve .. .. 2·50 2·75
78 „ 9 p. pale mauve .. .. 2·50 3·25
79 **20** 1 r. slate .. .. .. 5·00 5·00

21

22

1876 (Oct.). *W* **13.** *P 14.*

80 **21** 6 a. olive-bistre .. .. 1·75 1·00
81 „ 6 a. pale brown .. .. 1·25 95
82 **22** 12 a. Venetian red .. .. 2·00 2·75

III. EMPIRE OF INDIA.

Queen Victoria assumed the title of Empress of India in 1877, and the inscription on the stamps was altered from "EAST INDIA" to "INDIA".

23

24

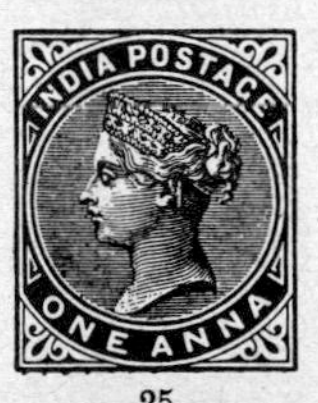

25

26

27

28

29

30

31

32

33

34

1882–88. *W* **34.** *P* 14.

No.	Type	Description	Unused	Used
84	**23**	½ a. deep blue-green ..	8	8
85	,,	½ a. blue-green	8	8
		a. Double impression ..	35·00	
86	**24**	9 p. rose	35	60
87	,,	9 p. aniline carmine ..	35	60
88	**25**	1 a. brown-purple ..	20	8
89	,,	1 a. plum	20	8
90	**26**	1 a. 6 p. sepia	45	25
91	**27**	2 a. pale blue	25	8
92	,,	2 a. blue	45	8
		a. Double impression ..	65·00	65·00
93	**28**	3 a. orange	2·75	1·60
94	,,	3 a. brown-orange ..	90	8
95	**29**	4 a. olive-green	1·50	10
96	,,	4 a. slate-green	1·10	10
97	**30**	4 a. 6 p. yellow-green ..	1·75	1·50
98	**31**	8 a. dull mauve	2·00	90
99	,,	8 a. magenta	2·00	1·00
100	**32**	12 a. purple/*red*	2·00	90
101	**33**	1 r. slate	2·00	1·25

No. 92a is from a sheet of 2 a. stamps with a very marked double impression issued in Karachi in 1896–97. Most of the stamps were used on telegrams.

2½ As.

(35)

1891 (1 Jan.). *No.* 97 *surch. with T* **35.**

No.	Type	Description	Unused	Used
102	**30**	2½ a. on 4½ a. yellow-green	80	1·25

There are several varieties in this surcharge due to variations in the relative positions of the letters and figures.

36

37

1892 (Jan.)–**1897.** *W* **34.** *P* 14.

No.	Type	Description	Unused	Used
103	**36**	2½ a. yellow-green ..	25	25
104	,,	2½ a. pale blue-green (1897)	60	25
105	**37**	1 r. green and rose ..	3·25	2·00
106	,,	1 r. green & aniline carm.	2·00	1·25

38

USED HIGH VALUES. It is necessary to emphasise that used prices quoted for the following and all later high value stamps are for postally used copies.

(Head of Queen from portrait by von Angeli.)

1895. *W* **34.** *P* 14.

No.	Type	Description	Unused	Used
107	**38**	2 r. carmine & yellow-brown	6·00	2·25
107*a*	,,	2 r. carmine and brown ..	6·00	2·25
108	,,	3 r. brown and green ..	7·00	2·75
109	,,	5 r. ultramarine & violet ..	7·00	6·50

(39)

40

1898. *No.* 85 *surch. with T* **39.**

No.	Type	Description	Unused	Used
110	**23**	¼ on ½ a. blue-green ..	8	8
		a. Surch. double	16·00	
		b. Stamp printed double ..	20·00	

1899. *W* **34.** *P* 14.

No.	Type	Description	Unused	Used
111	**40**	3 p. aniline carmine ..	8	8

1900 (1 Oct.)–**02.** *W* **34.** *P* 14.

No.	Type	Description	Unused	Used
112	**40**	3 p. grey	8	8
113	**23**	½ a. pale yellow-green ..	10	8
114	,,	½ a. yellow-green ..	8	8
115	**25**	1 a. carmine	10	8
116	**27**	2 a. pale violet	1·10	30
117	,,	2 a. mauve (1902) ..	1·00	30
118	**36**	2½ a. ultramarine	2·00	2·00

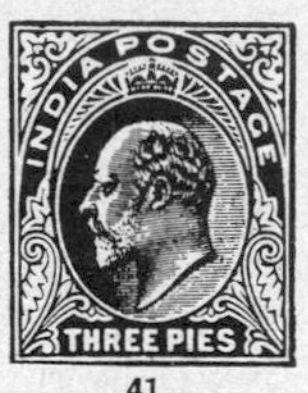

41

42

43

44

45

46

47

48

49

50

51

52

1902–11. *W* **34.** *P* 14.

No.	Type	Description	Unused	Used
119	**41**	3 p. grey	12	12
120	,,	3 p. slate-grey (1904) ..	8	8
121	**42**	½ a. yellow-green	20	12
122	,,	½ a. green	20	12
123	**43**	1 a. carmine	15	8
124	**44**	2 a. violet	95	15
125	,,	2 a. mauve	75	12
126	**45**	2½ a. ultramarine	1·10	12
127	**46**	3 a. orange-brown ..	1·60	15
128	**47**	4 a. olive	1·60	15
129	,,	4 a. pale olive	1·60	15
130	,,	4 a. olive-brown	3·00	1·50
131	**48**	6 a. olive-bistre	3·50	2·00
132	,,	6 a. maize	3·50	2·00
133	**49**	8 a. mauve	2·75	80
134	,,	8 a. magenta (1910) ..	2·75	80
135	**50**	12 a. purple/*red*	3·50	1·75
136	**51**	1 r. green and carmine ..	2·25	50
137	,,	1 r. green & scar. (1911)	5·50	60
138	**52**	2 r. rose-red & yell.-brn.	5·00	2·00
139	,,	2 r. carmine & yell.-brn.	5·00	2·00
140	,,	3 r. brown & grn. (1904)	7·50	6·00
141	,,	3 r. red-brn. & grn. (1911)	7·50	7·00
142	,,	5 r. ultram. & vio. (1904)	18·00	18·00
143	,,	5 r. ultramarine & deep lilac (1911)	18·00	18·00
144	,,	10 r. grn. & carm. (1909) ..	18·00	6·00
146	,,	15 r. blue & ol.-brn. (1909)	50·00	17·00
147	,,	25 r. brownish orge. & blue	£130	£120
119/147		.. .. *Set of* 17	£225	£160

No. 147 is normally telegraphically used; postally used copies are worth much more.

1905. *No.* 122 *surch. with T* **39.**

No.	Type	Description	Unused	Used
148	**42**	¼ on ½ a. green	12	12
		a. Surch. inverted ..	—	£100

It is doubtful if No. 148a exists unused with genuine surcharge.

53

54

1906. *W* **34.** *P* 14.

No.	Type	Description	Unused	Used
149	**53**	½ a. green	10	5
150	**54**	1 a. carmine	10	5

55

56

57 58* 59 60 61 62 63 64 65 66

67

* T 58. Two types of the 1½ a.; (A) As illustrated. (B) Inscribed "1½ As". "ONE AND A HALF ANNAS".

1911 (Dec.)–**1922.** *W* **34.** *P* 14.

151	**55**	3 p. pale grey	10	5
152	,,	3 p. grey	5	5
153	,,	3 p. slate-grey	5	5
154	,,	3 p. blue-slate (1922) ..	12	10
155	**56**	½ a. yellow-green	12	10
		a. Double print	12·00	
156	,,	½ a. pale blue-green ..	12	10
159	**57**	1 a. rose-carmine ..	20	5
160	,,	1 a. carmine	12	5
161	,,	1 a. aniline carmine ..	25	5
162	,,	1 a. pale rose-car., **C** ('18)	40	5
163	**58**	1½ a. choc. (Type A) ('19)	40	5
164	,,	1½ a. grey-brown (Type A)	1·00	40
165	,,	1½ a. choc. (Type B) ('21)	50	40
166	**59**	2 a. dull purple	35	5
167	,,	2 a. mauve	30	10
168	,,	2 a. violet	1·60	10
169	,,	2 a. brt. pur. (Jan. '19)..	1·25	10
170	**60**	2½ a. ultramarine	90	85
171	**61**	2½ a. ultramarine (1913) ..	45	5
172	**62**	3 a. dull orange	75	10
173	,,	3 a. orange-brown ..	65	10
174	**63**	4 a. deep olive	90	10
175	,,	4 a. olive-green	65	5
176	**64**	6 a. bistre	1·25	40
177	,,	6 a. yellow-bistre ..	1·25	40
178	,,	6 a. deep bistre-brown ..	1·75	50
179	**65**	8 a. purple	2·00	25
180	,,	8 a. mauve	4·00	25
181	,,	8 a. deep lilac	3·00	30
182	,,	8 a. brt. aniline mauve..	3·00	30
183	**66**	12 a. dull claret	3·00	50
184	,,	12 a. claret	3·50	50
185	**67**	1 r. brown and green ..	4·00	65
186	,,	1 r. red-brn. & blue-green	3·50	45
187	,,	2 r. carmine & brown ..	4·00	45
188	,,	5 r. ultram. and violet ..	9·50	1·60
189	,,	10 r. green and scarlet ..	15·00	3·50
190	,,	15 r. blue and olive ..	38·00	5·50
191	,,	25 r. orange and blue ..	60·00	10·00
151/191		.. .. *Set of* 17	£130	22·00

A variety of the 3 pies exists with line joining "P" and "S" of value at right, sometimes described as "3 Rs."

NINE

PIES

(68)

NOTE.—*Collectors are warned against forgeries of all the later surcharges of India, and particularly the errors.*

1921. *T* **57** *surch. with T* **68.**

192		9 p. on 1 a. rose-carmine ..	10	5
		a. Error. "NINE—NINE" ..	8·00	
		b. Error. "PIES—PIES" ..	8·00	
		c. Surch. double	15·00	16·00
193		9 p. on 1 a. carmine-pink ..	10	10
194		9 p. on 1 a. aniline carmine..	10	10

1922. *T* **56** *surch. with T* **39.**

195		¼ on ½ a. yellow-green ..	10	10
		a. Surch. inverted	3·00	
		b. Surch. omitted (in pair with normal)	55·00	
196		¼ on ½ a. blue-green ..	10	10

1922–26. *W* **34.** *P* 14.

197	**57**	1 a. chocolate	5	5
198	**58**	1½ a. rose-carm. (Type B)	20	10
199	**61**	2½ a. orange	2·00	1·00
200	**62**	3 a. ultramarine ..	5·00	55

69

70

71

PRINTERS. The following issues of postage and contemporary official stamps were all printed by the Security Printing Press, Nasik, *unless otherwise stated.*

1926–33. *Typo.* *W* **69.** *P* 14.

201	**55**	3 p. slate	5	5
202	**56**	½ a. green	12	5
203	**57**	1 a. chocolate	5	5
		a. Tête-bêche (pair) ..	45	70
204	**58**	1½ a. rose-carm. (Type B)	45	5
205	**59**	2 a. bright purple ..	55	35
206	**70**	2 a. purple	35	10
		a. Tête-bêche (pair) ..	1·90	3·00
207	**61**	2½ a. orange	25	5
208	**62**	3 a. ultramarine ..	1·25	35
209	,,	3 a. blue ('31) ..	1·25	15
210	**63**	4 a. pale sage-green ..	40	5
211	**71**	4 a. sage-green ..	2·00	5
212	**65**	8 a. reddish purple ..	1·25	5
213	**66**	12 a. claret	2·50	10
214	**67**	1 r. chocolate & green ..	1·25	5
215	,,	2 r. carmine & orange ..	2·50	45
216	,,	5 r. ultram. & purple ..	5·00	1·00
217	,,	10 r. green and scarlet ..	15·00	2·00
218	,,	15 r. blue and olive ..	15·00	10·00
219	,,	25 r. orange and blue ..	18·00	12·00
201/219		.. .. *Set of* 16	60·00	24·00

72

(Des. R. Grant. Offset-litho.)

1929 (22 Oct.). *Air.* *W* 69. *P* 14.

220	**72**	2 a. deep blue-green ..	25	25
221	,,	3 a. blue	55	1·00
222	,,	4 a. olive-green	1·50	1·00
223	,,	6 a. bistre	2·00	1·00
224	,,	8 a. purple	2·50	3·50
225	,,	12 a. rose-red	4·50	7·00
220/225		.. .. *Set of* 6	10·00	12·00

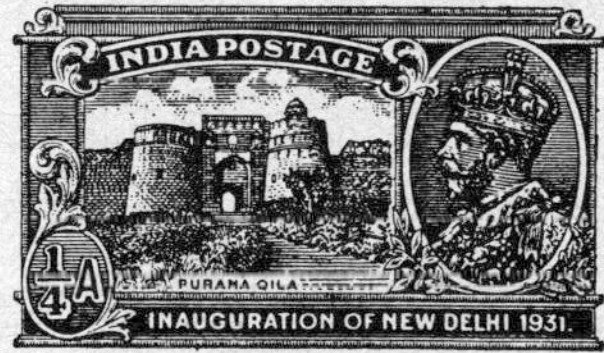

73. Purana Qila.

74. War Memorial Arch.
75. Council House.
76. The Viceroy's House.
77. Government of India Secretariat.
78. Dominion Columns and the Secretariat.

(Des. H. W. Barr. Offset-litho.)

1931 (9 Feb.). *Inauguration of New Delhi.* *W* **69.** *P* 13½×14.

226	**73**	¼ a. olive-grn. & orge.-brn.	10	20
227	**74**	½ a. violet and green ..	10	10
228	**75**	1 a. mauve and chocolate	10	5
229	**76**	2 a. green and blue ..	35	30
230	**77**	3 a. chocolate and carmine	75	90
231	**78**	1 r. violet and green ..	4·50	5·00
226/231		.. .. *Set of* 6	5·00	6·00

79

80

81

82

83

(9 p. litho. and typo.; 1¼ a., 3½ a. litho; others typo.)

1932–36. *W* **69.** *P* 14.

232	**79**	½ a. green ('34)	5	5
233	**80**	9 p. deep grn. (22.4.32)	5	5
234	**81**	1 a. chocolate (1934)	5	5
235	**82**	1¼ a. mauve (22.4.32)	5	5
236	**70**	2 a. vermilion	6·00	3·00
236*a*	**59**	2 a. vermilion (1934)	3·50	50
236*b*	,,	2 a. ver. (*small die*) ('36)	1·25	25
237	**62**	3 a. carmine	40	10
238	**83**	3½ a. ultramarine (22.4.32)	80	15
239	**64**	6 a. bistre (1935)	6·50	2·75
232/239		*Set of* 9	14·00	6·00

No. 236*a* measures 19 × 22.6 mm. and No. 236*b* 18.4 × 21.8 mm.

84. Gateway of India, Bombay.

85. Victoria Memorial, Calcutta.
86. Rameswaram Temple, Madras.
87. Jain Temple, Calcutta.
88. Taj Mahal, Agra.
89. Golden Temple, Amritsar.
90. Pagoda in Mandalay.

1935. *Silver Jubilee. Offset-litho.* *W* **69.** *P* 13½ × 14.

240	**84**	½ a. black & yellow-green	12	5
241	**85**	9 p. black and grey-green	10	5
242	**86**	1 a. black and brown	12	5
243	**87**	1¼ a. black & bright violet	10	10
244	**88**	2½ a. black and orange	25	12
245	**89**	3½ a. black & dull ultram.	40	45
246	**90**	8 a. black and purple	1·25	80
240/246		*Set of* 7	2·00	1·40

91. King George VI.

92. Dak Runner.

93. Dak Bullock Cart.
94. Dak Tonga.
95. Dak Camel.
96. Mail Train.
97. Mail Steamer.
98. Mail lorry.
99. Mail Plane (small head).
(*T* **93/9** *are horiz. as T* **92.**)

100. King George VI.

1937 (23 Aug.–15 Dec.). *Typo.* *W* **69.** *P* 13½ × 14 *or* 14 × 13½ (T **100**).

247	**91**	3 p. slate	10	5
248	,,	½ a. red-brown	10	5
249	,,	9 p. green (23.8.37)	20	12
250	,,	1 a. carmine (23.8.37)	5	5
		a. Tête-bêche (Vert. pair)	20	12
251	**92**	2 a. vermilion	25	5
252	**93**	2½ a. bright violet	20	5
253	**94**	3 a. yellow-green	30	5
254	**95**	3½ a. bright blue	30	25
255	**96**	4 a. brown	35	5
256	**97**	6 a. turquoise-green	35	10
257	**98**	8 a. slate-violet	60	5
258	**99**	12 a. lake	1·60	30
259	**100**	1 r. grey and red-brown	25	5
260	,,	2 r. purple and brown	85	5
261	,,	5 r. green and blue	2·25	10
262	,,	10 r. purple and claret	3·75	35
263	,,	15 r. brown and green	6·50	4·50
264	,,	25 r. slate-vio. & purple	10·00	5·00
247/264		*Set of* 18	25·00	10·00

100*a*. King George VI.

101. King George VI. **102.**

103. Mail Plane (large head).

1940–43. *Typo.* *W* **69.** *P* 13½ × 14.

265	**100*a***	3 p. slate	5	5
266	,,	½ a. purple (1.10.42)	5	5
267	,,	9 p. green	5	5
268	,,	1 a. carmine (1.4.43)	5	5
269	**101**	1 a. 3 p. bistre	30	10
269*a*	,,	1½ a. dull violet (9.42)	12	5
270	,,	2 a. vermilion	5	5
271	,,	3 a. bright violet ('42)	5	5
272	,,	3½ a. bright blue	10	5
273	**102**	4 a. brown	10	5
274	,,	6 a. turquoise-green	12	10
275	,,	8 a. slate-violet	20	5
276	,,	12 a. lake	40	12
277	**103**	14 a. purple (15.10.40)	40	12
265/277		*Set of* 14	1·90	65

The 1½ a. and 3 a. were at first printed by offset-lithography and were of finer execution and without Jubilee lines in the sheet margins.

105. " Victory " and King George VI.

1946 (2 Jan.). *Victory. Offset-litho.* *W* **69** *P* 13.

278	**105**	9 p. yellow-grn. (8.2.46)	10	5
279	,,	1½ a. dull violet	10	5
280	,,	3½ a. bright blue	10	10
281	,,	12 a. claret (8.2.46)	20	20

= =

3 PIES
(**106**)

1946. *Surch. with T* **106.**

282	**101**	3 p. on 1 a. 3 p. bistre	5	5

IV. DOMINION OF INDIA.

301. Asokan Capital.
(Inscr. reads " Long Live India ".)

302. Indian National Flag.

303. Douglas DC4.

947 (21 Nov.–15 Dec.). *Independence. Offset-litho.* *W* **69.** *P* 14 × 13½ (1½ *a.*) *or* 13½ × 14 (*others*).

01	**301**	1½ a. grey-grn. (15 Dec.)	5	5
02	**302**	3½ a. orange-red, blue and green	10	5
03	**303**	12 a. ultram. (15 Dec.) ..	25	5

304. Lockheed Constellation.

948. *Air. Inauguration of India-U.K. Air Service. Offset litho.* *W* **69.** *P* 13½ × 14.

04	**304**	12 a. black & ultramarine	30	25

305. Mahatma Gandhi. **306.**

(Photo. Courvoisier.)

948 (15 Aug.). *First Anniv. Independence.* *P* 11½.

05	**305**	1½ a. brown	12	10
06	,,	3½ a. violet	20	10
07	,,	12 a. grey-green	50	12
08	**306**	10 r. purple-brown & lake	20·00	20·00

307. Ajanta Panel. **308.** Konarak Horse.

309. Trimurti.

310. Bodhisattva.

311. Nataraja.

312. Sanchi Stupa, East Gate.

313. Bodh Gaya Temple.

314. Bhuvanesvara.

315. Gol Gumbad, Bijapur.

316. Kandarya Mahadeva Temple.

317. Golden Temple, Amritsar.

318. Victory Tower, Chittorgarh. **321.** Qutb Minar, Delhi.

319. Red Fort, Delhi.

320. Taj Mahal, Agra.

322. Satrunjaya Temple, Palitana.

(Des. T. I. Archer and I. M. Das. Typo. (low values), offset-litho. (rupee values).)

1949 (15 Aug.). *W* **69** (*sideways on Nos.* 310, 320 *and* 323*a*). *P* 14 (3 *p. to* 2 *a.*), 13½ (3 *a.* to 12 *a.*), 14 × 13½ (1 *r. and* 10 *r.*), 13½ × 14 (2 *r. and* 5 *r.*), 13 (15 *r.*).

309	**307**	3 p. slate-violet ..	5	5
310	**308**	6 p. purple-brown ..	5	5
311	**309**	9 p. yellow-green ..	5	5
312	**310**	1 a. turquoise	5	5
313	**311**	2 a. carmine	5	5
314	**312**	3 a. brown-orange ..	5	5
315	**313**	3½ a. bright blue ..	60	50
316	**314**	4 a. lake	40	5
317	**315**	6 a. violet	40	5
318	**316**	8 a. turquoise-green ..	75	5
319	**317**	12 a. dull blue	45	12
320	**318**	1 r. dull violet & green	1·40	12
321	**319**	2 r. claret and violet ..	1·60	15
322	**320**	5 r. bl.-grn. & red.-brn.	2·50	35
323	**321**	10 r. pur.-brn. & dp. blue	6·00	1·75
		a. Purple-brown and blue ..	7·00	1·40
324	**322**	15 r. brown and claret ..	8·00	2·50
309/324		.. .. *Set of* 16	20·00	5·00

For T **310** with statue reversed, see No. 333.

323. Globe and Asokan Capital.

1949 (Oct.). *75th Anniv. of U.P.U. Offset-litho. W* **69.** *P* 13.

325	**323**	9 p. green ..	15	12
326	,,	2 a. rose	25	25
327	,,	3½ a. bright blue ..	25	30
328	,,	12 a. brown-purple ..	40	45

V. REPUBLIC OF INDIA.

324. Rejoicing Crowds.

325. Quill, Ink-well and Verse. (*Vert.*)
326. Ear of Corn and Plough. (*Horiz.*)
327. Spinning-wheel and Cloth. (*Horiz.*)

(Des. D. J. Keymer & Co. Offset-litho.)

1950 (26 Jan.). *Inauguration of Republic. W* **69** (*sideways on* 3½ *a.*). *P* 13.

329	**324**	2 a. scarlet	15	10
330	**325**	3½ a. ultramarine ..	25	10
331	**326**	4 a. violet	25	15
332	**327**	12 a. maroon	45	30

328. As T **310**, but statue reversed.

1950 (15 July)–**51.** *Typo. W* **69.** *P* 14 (1 *a.*). 13½ (*others*).

333	**328**	1 a. turquoise	8	5
333*a*	**313**	2½ a. lake (30.4.51) ..	10	10
333*b*	**314**	4 a. brt. blue (30.4.51)	15	12

329. *Stegodon Ganesa.*

1951 (13 Jan.). *Centenary of Geological Survey of India. Offset-litho. W* **69.** *P* 13.

334	**329**	2 a. black and claret ..	30	30

330. Torch.

331. Kabir.

1951 (4 Mar.). *First Asian Games, New Delhi. Offset-litho. W* **69** (*sideways*). *P* 14.

335	**330**	2 a. reddish purple and brown-orange ..	15	15
336	,,	12 a. chocolate & lt. blue	35	35

PROCESS. All the following issues were printed in photogravure, *except where otherwise stated.*

1952 (1 Oct.). *Indian Saints and Poets. As T* **331** (*Various portraits; similar frames*). *W* **69.** *P* 14.

337		9 p. bright emerald-green ..	15	10
338		1 a. carmine (Tulsidas) ..	15	10
339		2 a. orange-red (Meera)	20	10
340		4 a. bright blue (Surdas) ..	20	10
341		4½ a. bright mauve (Ghalib)	30	15
342		12 a. brown (Tagore) ..	55	40
337/42		.. .. *Set of* 6	1·40	80

332. Locomotives in 1853 and 1953.

1953 (16 Apr.). *Railway Centenary. W* **69.** *P* 14½×14.

343	**332**	2 a. black	8	8

333. Mount Everest.

1953 (2 Oct.). *Conquest of Mount Everest. W* **69.** *P* 14½×14.

344	**333**	2 a. bright violet ..	10	10
345	,,	14 a. brown	40	30

334. Telegraph Poles of 1851 and 1951.

1953 (1 Nov.). *Centenary of Indian Telegraphs. W* **69.** *P* 14½×14.

346	**334**	2 a. blue-green	10	10
347	,,	12 a. blue..	90	30

335. Postal Transport, 1854.

336. " Airmail ".
337. Postal Transport, 1954.

1954 (1 Oct.). *Stamp Centenary. W* **69** *P* 14½×14.

348	**335**	1 a. reddish purple ..	10	10
349	**336**	2 a. cerise	10	10
350	**337**	4 a. orange-brown ..	20	15
351	**336**	14 a. blue	50	25

338. U.N. Emblem and Lotus.

1954 (24 Oct.). *United Nations Day. W* **69** (*sideways*). *P* 13.

352	**338**	2 a. turquoise-green ..	12	10

339. Forest Research Institute.

1954 (11 Dec.). *Fourth World Forestry Congress, Dehra Dun. W* **69.** *P* 14½×14.

353	**339**	2 a. ultramarine	10	10

340. Tractor.

341. Power Loom.

342. Bullock-driven Well.

343. Damodar Valley Dam.

344. Woman Spinning.

345. Woman Weaving with Hand Loom.

346. Bullocks.

348. Chittaranjan Locomotive Works.

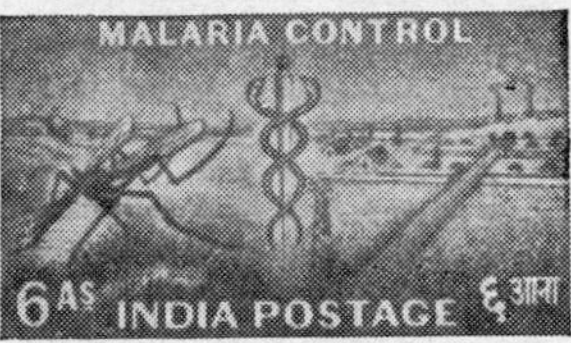

347. " Malaria Control " (Mosquito and Staff of Aesculapius).

349. Marine Drive, Bombay.

350. Hindustan Aircraft Factory, Bangalore.

352. Telephone Engineer.

351. Kashmir Landscape.

353. Cape Comorin.

354. Mt. Kangchenjunga.

355. Rare Earth Factory, Alwaye.

356. Sindri Fertiliser Factory.

357. Steel Plant.

1955 (26 JAN.). *Five Year Plan.* *W* **69** (*sideways on small horiz. designs*). *P* 14×14½ (*small horiz.*) *or* 14½×14 (*others*).

354 **340**	3 p. bright purple	..	5	5
355 **341**	6 p. violet	..	5	5
356 **342**	9 p. orange-brown	..	5	5
357 **343**	1 a. blue-green	..	5	5
358 **344**	2 a. light blue ..	..	5	5
359 **345**	3 a. pale blue-green	..	5	5
360 **346**	4 a. rose-carmine	..	10	5
361 **347**	6 a. yellow-brown	..	10	5
362 **348**	8 a. blue	..	12	5
363 **349**	10 a. turquoise-green	..	25	12
364 **350**	12 a. bright blue	..	25	5
365 **351**	14 a. bright green	..	20	12
366 **352**	1 r. deep dull green	..	50	10
367 **353**	1 r. 2 a. grey ..	..	60	40
368 **354**	1 r. 8 a. reddish purple		75	50
369 **355**	2 r. cerise ..	..	60	20
370 **356**	5 r. brown ..	..	2·50	50
371 **357**	10 r. orange ..	..	4·50	1·00
354/71	.. .. *Set of* 18		9·00	2·75

For stamps as Nos. 366, 369/71 but W **374** see Nos. 413/6.

358. Bodhi Tree.

359. Round Parasol and Bodhi Tree.

(Des. C. R. Pakrashi (2 a.), R. D'Silva (14 a.).)

1956 (24 MAY). *Buddha Jayanti.* *W* **69** (*sideways on* 14 *a.*). *P* 13×13½ (2 *a.*) *or* 13½×13 (14 *a.*).

372 **358**	2 a. sepia	.. ..	10	10
373 **359**	14 a. vermilion ..	..	50	50

360. Lokmanya Bal Gangadhar Tilak.

361. Map of India.

1956 (23 JULY). *Birth Centenary of Tilak* (*journalist*). *W* **69.** *P* 13×13½.

374 **360**	2 a. chestnut	.. ..	5	5

Currency changed. 100 n(aye) p(aise) = 1 rupee.

1957 (1 APR.)–**58.** *W* **69** (*sideways*). *P* 14×14½.

375 **361**	1 n.p. blue-green	..	5	5
376 "	2 n.p. light brown	..	5	5
377 "	3 n.p. deep brown	..	5	5
378 "	5 n.p. bright green	..	5	5
379 "	6 n.p. grey ..	..	5	5
379*a* "	8 n.p. light blue-green (7.5.58) ..	..	15	8
380 "	10 n.p. deep dull green ..		5	5
381 "	13 n.p. bright carmine-red		5	5
381*a* "	15 n.p. violet (16.1.58) ..		10	5
382 "	20 n.p. blue ..	..	10	5
383 "	25 n.p. ultramarine	..	10	5
384 "	50 n.p. orange ..	..	20	5
385 "	75 n.p. reddish purple ..		35	12
385*a* "	90 n.p. brt. pur. (16.1.58)		45	15
375/85*a*	.. .. *Set of* 14		1·25	55

The 8, 15 and 90 n.p. have their value expressed as " nP ".

For similar stamps but W **374** see Nos. 399/412

362. The Rani of Jhansi.

363. Shrine.

1957 (15 AUG.). *Indian Mutiny Centenary.* *W* **69.** *P* 14½×14 (15 *n.p.*) *or* 13×13½ (90 *n.p.*).

386 **362**	15 n.p. brown	.. ..	15	5
387 **363**	90 n.p. reddish purple	..	60	25

364. Henri Dunant and Conference Emblem.

1957 (28 OCT.). 19*th International Red Cross Conference, New Delhi.* *W* **69** (*sideways*). *P* 13½×13.

388 **364**	15 n.p. deep grey & carm.	8	5

365. " Nutrition ".

366. " Education ". (*Horiz.*)
367. " Recreation ". (*Vert.*)

1957 (14 Nov.). *National Children's Day.* *W* **69** (*sideways on* 90 *n.p.*). *P* 14×13½ (90 *n.p.*) *or* 13½×14 (*others*).

389	**365**	8 n.p. reddish purple ..	8	5
390	**366**	15 n.p. turquoise-green ..	8	5
391	**367**	90 n.p. orange-brown ..	25	15

368. Bombay University.

369. Calcutta University.

370. Madras University. (*As T* **369.**)

1957 (31 Dec.). *Centenary of Indian Universities.* *W* **69** (*sideways on T* **368**). *P* 14×14½ (No. 392) *or* 13½×14 (*others*).

392	**368**	10 n.p. violet	8	8
393	**369**	10 n.p. grey	8	8
394	**370**	10 n.p. light brown ..	8	8

371. J. N. Tata (founder) and Steel Plant.

1958 (1 Mar.). *50th Anniv. of Steel Industry.* *W* **69.** *P* 14½×14.

395	**371**	15 n.p. orange-red ..	8	5

372. Dr. D. K. Karve.

1958 (18 Apr.). *Centenary of Birth of Karve* (*educationalist*). *W* **69** (*sideways*). *P* 14.

396	**372**	15 n.p. orange-brown ..	8	5

373. " Wapiti " and " Hunter " Aircraft.

1958 (30 Apr.). *Silver Jubilee of Indian Air Force.* *W* **69.** *P* 14½×14.

397	**373**	15 n.p. blue	8	8
398	,,	90 n.p. ultramarine ..	40	25

374. Asokan Capital.

1958–63. *As Nos.* 366, 369/71 *and* 375/85*a but* *W* **374.**

399	**361**	1 n.p. blue-green ..	5	5
		a. Imperf. (pair) ..	50·00	
400	,,	2 n.p. light brown ..	5	5
401	,,	3 n.p. deep brown ..	5	5
402	,,	5 n.p. bright green ..	5	5
403	,,	6 n.p. grey	5	5
404	,,	8 n.p. light blue-green ..	5	5
405	,,	10 n.p. deep dull green ..	5	5
406	,,	13 n.p. bright carmine red	5	5
407	,,	15 n.p. violet	5	5
408	,,	20 n.p. blue	5	5
409	,,	25 n.p. ultramarine ..	8	5
410	,,	50 n.p. orange	8	5
411	,,	75 n.p. reddish purple ..	15	5
412	,,	90 n.p. bright purple ..	20	5
413	**352**	1 r. deep dull green ..	20	5
414	**355**	2 r. cerise	75	15
415	**356**	5 r. brown	1·50	40
416	**357**	10 r. orange	3·00	1·50
399/416		.. .. *Set of* 18	4·50	2·00

Dates of issue:—1958, 3, 8 n.p.; 27th Oct., 2, 5, 10, 20, 25 n.p. 1959 50 n.p., 75 n.p., 1 r. to 10 r. 1960, 1 n.p., 90 n.p.; Oct., 15 n.p. 1963, 6 n.p., 13 n.p.

The 5, 10, 15, 20, 25 and 50 n.p. with serial numbers on the back are coil stamps prepared from sheets for experimenting with coil machines. In the event the machines were not purchased and the stamps were sold over the counter.

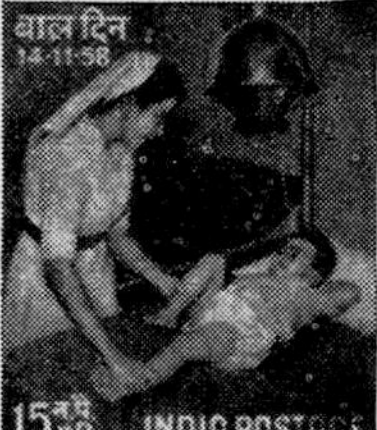

375. Bipin Chandra Pal. **376.** Nurse with Child Patient.

1958 (7 Nov.). *Birth Centenary of Pal* (*patriot*). *W* **374.** *P* 14×13½.

418	**375**	15 n.p. deep dull green ..	5	5

1958 (14 Nov.). *National Children's Day.* *W* **374.** *P* 14×13½.

419	**376**	15 n.p. violet	5	5

377. Jagadis Chandra Bose.

1958 (30 Nov.). *Centenary of Birth of Bo* (*botanist*). *W* **374.** *P* 14×13½.

420	**377**	15 n.p. dp. turq.-green ..		5

378. Exhibition Gate.

1958 (30 Dec.). *India* 1958 *Exhibition, Ne Delhi.* *W* **374** (*sideways*). *P* 14½×14.

421	**378**	15 n.p. reddish purple ..		5

379. Sir Jamsetjee Jejeebhoy.

1959 (15 Apr.). *Death Centenary of Jejeebh* (*philanthropist*). *W* **374.** *P* 14×13½.

422	**379**	15 n.p. brown		5

380. " The Triumph of Labour " (after Chowdhury).

1959 (15 June). *40th Anniv. of Internation Labour Organization.* *W* **374** (*sideways* *P* 14½×14.

423	**380**	15 n.p. dull green ..		5

381. Boys awaiting admission to Children's Home. **383.** Thiruvalluvar (poet

382. " Agriculture ".

1959 (14 Nov.). *National Children's Day. W* **374.** *P* 14×14½.
424 **381** 15 n.p. deep dull green .. 5 5
a. Imperf. (pair) .. £150

1959 (30 Dec.). *First World Agriculture Fair, New Delhi. W* **374.** *P* 13½×13.
425 **382** 15 n.p. grey 5 5

1960 (15 Feb.). *Thiruvalluvar Commemoration. W* **374.** *P* 14×13½.
426 **383** 15 n.p. reddish purple .. 5 5

384. Yaksha pleading with the Cloud (from the " Meghaduta ").

385. Shakuntala writing a letter to Dushyanta (from the " Shakuntala ").

1960 (22 June). *Kalidasa (poet) Commemoration W* **374.** *P* 13.
427 **384** 15 n.p. grey 8 8
428 **385** 1 r. 3 n.p. pale yellow and brown .. 25 25

386. S. Bharati (poet). **387.** Dr. M. Visvesvaraya.

1960 (11 Sept.). *Subramania Bharati Commemoration. W* **374.** *P* 14×13½.
429 **386** 15 n.p. blue 5 5

1960 (15 Sept.). *Centenary of Birth of Dr. M. Visvesvaraya (engineer). W* **374.** *P* 13×13½.
430 **387** 15 n.p. brn. & brt. carm. 5 5

388. " Children's Health ".

1960 (14 Nov.). *Children's Day. W* **374.** *P* 13½×13.
431 **388** 15 n.p. deep dull green .. 5 5

389. Children greeting U.N. Emblem.

1960 (11 Dec.). *U.N.I.C.E.F. Day. W* **374.** *P* 13½×13.
432 **389** 15 n.p. orange brown and olive-brown .. 5 5

390. Tyagaraja (Indian Saint).

1961 (6 Jan.). *Tyagaraja Commemoration. W* **374.** *P* 14×13½.
433 **390** 15 n.p. greenish blue .. 5 5

391. " First Aerial Post " cancellation.

392. " Air India " Boeing 707 jetliner and Humber-Sommer plane.

393. H. Pecquet flying Humber-Sommer plane, and " Aerial Post " cancellation. (*As T* **392**)

1961 (18 Feb.). *50th Anniv. of First Official Air-mail Flight, Allahabad-Naini. W* **374.** *P* 14 (5 *n.p.*) *or* 13×13½ (*others*).
434 **391** 5 n.p. olive-drab .. 10 10
435 **392** 15 n.p. dp. green & grey 15 15
436 **393** 1 r. purple and grey .. 75 50

394. Shivaji on horseback. **395.** Motilal Nehru. (politician).

1961 (17 Apr.). *Shivaji Commemoration. W* **374.** *P* 13×13½.
437 **394** 15 n.p. brown and green 5 5

1961 (6 May). *Birth Centenary of Pandit Motilal Nehru. W* **374.** *P* 14.
438 **395** 15 n.p. olive-brown and brown-orange .. 5 5

396. Tagore (poet).

1961 (7 May). *Birth Centenary of Rabindranath Tagore. W* **374.** *P* 13×13½.
439 **396** 15 n.p. yellow-orange and blue-green .. 10 12

397. All India Radio Emblem and Transmitting Aerials.

1961 (8 June). *Silver Jubilee of All India Radio. W* **374.** *P* 13½×13.
440 **397** 15 n.p. ultramarine .. 5 5

398. P. Chandra Ray. **399.** V. N. Bhatkande.

1961 (2 Aug.). *Birth Centenary of Ray (scientist). W* **374.** *P* 14×13½.
441 **398** 15 n.p. grey 5 5

1961 (1 Sept.). *Birth Centenary of Bhatkande (musician). W* **374.** *P* 13×13½.
442 **399** 15 n.p. olive-brown .. 5 5

400. Child at Lathe. **401.** Fair Emblem and Main Gate.

1961 (14 Nov.). *Children's Day. W* **374.** *P* 14×13½.
443 **400** 15 n.p. brown 5 5

1961 (14 Nov.). *Indian Industries Fair, New Delhi. W* **374.** *P* 14×14½.
444 **401** 15 n.p. blue and carmine 5 5

402. Indian Forest. **403.** Pitalkhora: Yaksha.

404. Kalibangan Seal.

1961 (21 Nov.). *Centenary of Scientific Forestry. W* **374.** *P* 13×13½.
445 **402** 15 n.p. green and brown 5 5

1961 (14 Dec.). *Centenary of Indian Archaeological Survey. W* **374.** *P* 14×13½ (15 *n.p.*) *or* 13½×14 (90 *n.p.*).
446 **403** 15 n.p. orange-brown .. 8 8
447 **404** 90 n.p. yellow-olive and light brown .. 25 20

405. M. M. Malaviya. **406.** Gauhati Refinery.

1961 (24 Dec.). *Birth Centenary of Malaviya (President of National Congress). W* **374.** *P* 14×13½.
448 **405** 15 n.p. deep slate .. 5 5

1962 (1 Jan.). *Inauguration of Gauhati Oil Refinery. W* **374.** *P* 13×13½.
449 **406** 15 n.p. blue 5 5

407. Bhikaiji Cama. **408.** Panchayati at work and Parliament Building.

1962 (26 Jan.). *Birth Centenary of Bhikaiji Cama (revolutionary). W* **374.** *P* 14.
450 **407** 15 n.p. reddish purple .. 5 5

1962 (26 Jan.). *Panchayati Raj Commemoration W* **374.** *P* 13×13½.
451 **408** 15 n.p. bright purple .. 5 5

409. D. Saraswati (religious educator). **410.** G. S. Vidhyarthi (patriot).

1962 (4 Mar.). *Saraswati Commemoration. W* **374.** *P* 14.
452 **409** 15 n.p. orange-brown .. 5 5

1962 (25 Mar.). *Vidhyarthi Commemoration. W* **374.** *P* 14×13½.
453 **410** 15 n.p. red-brown .. 5 8

411. Malaria Eradication Emblem. **412.** Dr. R. Prasad (former President of India).

1962 (7 Apr.). *Malaria Eradication. W* 37 *P* 13×13½.
454 **411** 15 n.p. yellow and claret 5

1962 (13 May). *Dr. Rajendra Prasad Commemoration. W* **374.** *P* 13.
455 **412** 15 n.p. brt. pur. (*shades*) 5

413. Calcutta High Court.

414. Madras High Court.
415. Bombay High Court.

1962. *Centenary of Indian High Courts. W* 37 *P* 14.
456 **413** 15 n.p. dull green (1 July) 5
457 **414** 15 n.p. red-brown (6 Aug.) 5
458 **415** 15 n.p. slate (14 Aug.) .. 5

416. Ramabai Ranade.

1962 (15 Aug.). *Birth Centenary of Ramab Ranade (social reformer). W* **374.** *P* 14×13
459 **416** 15 n.p. orange-brown .. 5

417. Indian One-horned Rhinoceros.

1962 (1 Oct.). *Wild Life Week. W* **374.** *P* 13½×1
460 **417** 15 n.p. red-brown & deep turquoise.. .. 5

NSCRIPTIONS. From No. 461 onwards all lesigns are inscribed " BHARAT " in Devanagri, in .ddition to " INDIA " in English.

418. " Passing the Flag to Youth ".

.962 (14 Nov.). *Children's Day.* *W* **374.** *P* 13½ × 13.
.61 **418** 15 n.p. orange-red and turquoise-green .. 5 5

419. Human Eye within Lotus Blossom.

.962 (3 Dec.). *19th International Ophthalmology Congress, New Delhi.* *W* **374.** *P* 13½ × 13.
.62 **419** 15 n.p. deep olive-brown 5 5

420. S. Ramanujan. **421.** S. Vivekananda.

.962 (22 Dec.). *75th Anniv. of Birth of Ramanujan (mathematician).* *W* **374** *P* 13½ × 14.
.63 **420** 15 n.p. deep olive-brown 5 5

963 (17 Jan.). *Birth Centenary of Vivekananda (philosopher).* *W* **374.** *P* 14 × 14½.
64 **421** 15 n.p. orange-brown and yellow-olive .. 5 5

Re.1

═══

(422)

963 (2 Feb.). *No.* 428 *surch. with T* **422.**
65 **385** 1 r. on 1 r. 3 n.p. pale yellow and brown .. 15 10

423. Hands reaching for F.A.O. Emblem.

1963 (21 Mar.). *Freedom from Hunger.* *W* **374.** *P* 13.
466 **423** 15 n.p. grey-blue 5 5

424. Henri Dunant (founder) and Centenary Emblem.

1963 (8 May). *Red Cross Centenary.* *W* **374.** *P* 13.
467 **424** 15 n.p. red and grey .. 8 5
a. Red (cross) omitted .. £900

425. Artillery and Helicopter.

426. Sentry and Parachutists.

1963 (15 Aug.). *Defence Campaign.* *W* **374.** *P* 14.
468 **425** 15 n.p. grey-green .. 8 8
469 **426** 1 r. red-brown .. 25 20

427. D. Naoroji (patriot).

1963 (4 Sept.). *Dadabhoy Naoroji Commemoration.* *W* **374.** *P* 13.
470 **427** 15 n.p. grey 5 5

428. Mrs. Annie Besant (patriot and theosophist, born 1847). (Stamp wrongly dated " 1837 ").

1963 (1 Oct.). *Mrs. Annie Besant Commemoration.* *W* **374.** *P* 13½ × 14.
471 **428** 15 n.p. turquoise-green .. 5 5

429. Gaur.

430. Himalayan Panda.

431. Indian Elephant. (*As T* **430.**)

432. Tiger.

433. Indian Lion. (*As T* **432.**)

1963 (7 Oct.). *Wild Life Preservation.* *W* **374.** *P* 13½ × 14 (10 *n.p.*) *or* 13 (*others*).

472	**429**	10 n.p. black & yell.-orge	15	10
473	**430**	15 n.p. orge.-brn. & green	10	10
474	**431**	30 n.p. slate & yell.-ochre	20	10
475	**432**	50 n.p. orange and deep grey-green ..	30	10
476	**433**	1 r. lt. brown and blue	60	25
472/6		.. .. *Set of* 5	1·25	50

434. " School Meals ".

1963 (14 Nov.). *Children's Day.* W **374.** *P* 14×13½.
477 **434** 15 n.p. bistre-brown .. 5 5

435. Eleanor Roosevelt at Spinning-wheel.

1963 (10 Dec.). *15th Anniv. of Declaration of Human Rights.* W **374.** *P* 13½×13.
478 **435** 15 n.p. reddish purple .. 5 5

436. Dipalakshmi (bronze).

1964 (4 Jan.). *26th International Orientalists Congress, New Delhi.* W **374.** *P* 13×13½.
479 **436** 15 n.p. deep ultramarine 5 5

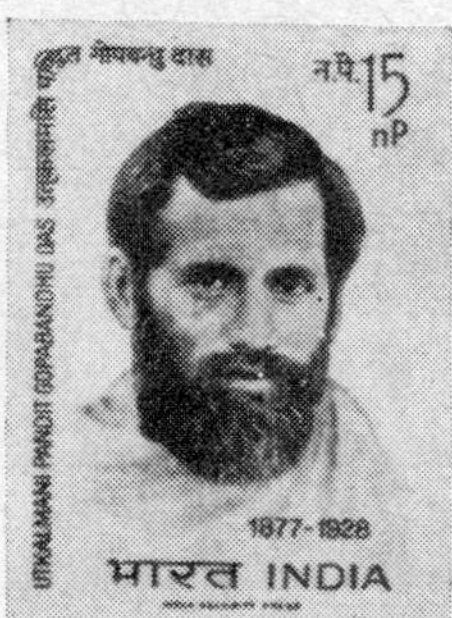

437. Gopabandhu Das (patriot and social reformer).

1964 (4 Jan.). *Gopabandhu Das Commemoration.* W **374.** *P* 13×13½.
480 **437** 15 n.p. deep dull purple.. 5 5

438. Purandaradasa.

1964 (14 Jan.). *400th Anniv. of Death of Purandaradasa (musician).* W **374.** *P* 13×13½.
481 **438** 15 n.p. light brown .. 5 5

439. S. C. Bose and I.N.A. Badge.

440. Bose and Indian National Army.

1964 (23 Jan.). *67th Anniv. of Birth of Subhas Chandra Bose (nationalist).* W **374.** *P* 13.
482 **439** 15 n.p. yellow-bistre .. 8 8
483 **440** 55 n.p. black, orange and orange-red .. 20 25

441. Sarojini Naidu. **442.** Kasturba Gandhi.

1964 (13 Feb.). *85th Anniv. of Birth of Mrs. Sarojini Naidu (patriot).* W **374.** *P* 14.
484 **441** 15 n.p. deep grey-green and purple .. 5 5

1964 (22 Feb.). *20th Anniv. of Death of Kasturba Gandhi.* W **374.** *P* 14×13½.
485 **442** 15 n.p. orange-brown .. 5 8

443. Dr. W. M. Haffkine (immunologist).

1964 (16 Mar.). *Haffkine Commemoratio*
W **374.** *P* 13.
486 **443** 15 n.p. dp. purple-brown/*buff* 5

(Value expressed as paisa instead of naye paise

444. Jawaharlal Nehru (statesman).

1964 (12 June). *Nehru Mourning Issue.* N *wmk.* *P* 13½×13.
487 **444** 15 p. deep slate 5

445. Sir A. Mookerjee.

1964 (29 June). *Birth Centenary of Sir Asutos Mookerjee (education reformer).* W **374.** *P* 13½×13.
488 **445** 15 p. bistre-brown and yellow-olive .. 5

446. Sri Aurobindo.

1964 (15 Aug.). *92nd Birth Anniv. of Sr Aurobindo (religious leader).* W **37**
P 13×13½.
489 **446** 15 p. dull purple 5

447. Raja R. Roy (social reformer).

1964 (27 Sept.). *Raja Rammohun Roy Commemoration. W* **374.** *P* 13½ × 13½.
490 **447** 15 n.p. brown 5 8

448. I.S.O. Emblem and Globe.

1964 (9 Nov.). *Sixth International Organization for Standardization General Assembly, Bombay. No wmk. P* 13 × 13½.
491 **448** 15 p. carmine 5 8

449. Jawaharlal Nehru (medallion). **450.** St. Thomas (after statue, Ortona Cathedral, Italy).

1964 (14 Nov.). *Children's Day. No wmk. P* 14 × 13½.
492 **449** 15 p. slate.. .. .. 5 8

1964 (2 Dec.). *St. Thomas Commemoration. No wmk. P* 14 × 13½.
493 **450** 15 p. reddish purple .. 5 5

No. 493 was issued on the occasion of Pope Paul's visit to India.

451. Globe.

1964 (14 Dec.). *22nd International Geological Congress. W* **374.** *P* 14 × 13½.
494 **451** 15 p. blue-green 5 5

453. J. Tata (industrialist).

1965 (7 Jan.). *Jamsetji Tata Commemoration. No wmk. P* 13½ × 13.
495 **452** 15 p. dull purple & orange 5 5

453. Lala Lajpat Rai.

1965 (28 Jan.). *Birth Centenary of Lala Lajpat Rai (patriot). No wmk. P* 13 × 13½.
496 **453** 15 p. light brown.. .. 5 5

454. Globe and Congress Emblem.

1965 (8 Feb.). *20th International Chamber of Commerce Congress, New Delhi. No wmk. P* 13½ × 13.
497 **454** 15 p. grey-green & carm. 5 5

455. Freighter *Jalausha* and Visakhapatnam.

1965 (5 Apr.). *National Maritime Day. W* **374** *(sideways). P* 14½ × 14.
498 **455** 15 p. blue.. .. .. 5 5

456. Abraham Lincoln.

1965 (15 Apr.). *Death Centenary of Abraham Lincoln. W* **374.** *P* 13.
499 **456** 15 p. brown & yell.-ochre 5 8

457. I.T.U. Emblem and Symbols.

1965 (17 May). *I.T.U. Centenary. W* **374** *(sideways). P* 14½ × 14.
500 **457** 15 p. reddish purple .. 8 8

458. "Everlasting Flame".

1965 (27 May). *First Anniv. of Nehru's Death. W* **374.** *P* 13.
501 **458** 15 p. carmine and blue .. 5 8

459. I.C.Y. Emblem.

1965 (26 June). *International Co-operation Year. No wmk. P* 13½ × 13.
502 **459** 15 p. deep olive and yellow-brown 5 5

460. Climbers on Summit.

1965 (15 Aug.). *Indian Mount Everest Expedition. No wmk. P* 13.
503 **460** 15 p. deep reddish purple 5 5

461. Bidri Vase.

462. Brass Lamp.

462*a*. Coffee Berries.

463 "Family Planning".

464. Konarak Elephant.

465. Chital (spotted deer).

466. Electric Locomotive.

467. Plucking Tea.

468. Folland "Gnat" Fighter.

469. Indian Dolls.

470. Calcutta G.P.O.

471. Mangoes.

472. Somnath Temple.

473. Hampi Chariot (sculpture).

474. Medieval Sculpture.

475. Dal Lake, Kashmir.

476. Bhakra Dam, Punjab.

477. Atomic Reactor, Trombay.

1965–76. (*a*) *W* **374** (*sideways on* 2 *p.*, 3 *p.*, 5 *p.*, 6 *p.*, 8 *p.*, 30 *p.*, 50 *p.*, 60 *p.*, 2 *r.*, 5 *r.*, 10 *r.*). *P* 14 × 14½ (4 *p.*, 10 *p.*, 15 *p.*, 20 *p.*, 40 *p.*, 70 *p.*, 1 *r.*). *or* 14½ × 14 (*others*).

504 **461** 2 p. red-brown (16.10.67) 5 5
505 **462** 3 p. brn.-olive (16.10.67) 5 5
505*a* **462*a*** 4 p. lake-brown (*shades*) (15.5.68) 5 5
506 **463** 5 p. cerise (16.10.67) .. 5 5
a. Imperf. (pair) .. £200
507 **464** 6 p. grey-black (1.7.66) 5 5
508 **465** 8 p. red-brown (15.3.67) 5 5
509 **466** 10 p. new blue (1.7.66) .. 5 5
510 **467** 15 p. bronze-grn. (15.8.65) 5 5
511 **468** 20 p. purple (16.10.67) .. 5 5
512 **469** 30 p. sepia (15.3.67) .. 5 5
513 **470** 40 p. maroon (2.10.68) .. 8 5
514 **471** 50 p. blue-green (15.3.67) 5 5
515 **472** 60 p. deep grey (16.10.67) 5 5
516 **473** 70 p. chalky blue (15.3.67) 8 5
517 **474** 1 r. red-brown and plum (1.7.66) 10 5
518 **475** 2 r. new blue and deep slate-violet (15.3.67) 20 8
519 **476** 5 r. deep slate-violet and brown (15.3.67) .. 50 15
520 **477** 10 r. black and bronze-green (14.11.65) .. 1·00 65
504/20 .. .. *Set of* 18 2·25 1·10

(*b*) *Wmk. Large Star and* "INDIA GOVT" *in sheet.* *P* 14½ × 14.

521 **463** 5 p. cerise (1975) .. 5 5

(*c*) *No wmk.* *P* 14½ × 14.

521*a* **463** 5 p. cerise (1976) .. 5 5

Crude postal forgeries exist of No. 511, without watermark and rough perf. 15.

479. G. B. Pant (statesman).

480. V. Patel.

1965 (10 SEPT.). *Govind Ballabh Pant Commemoration.* *W* **374.** *P* 13.

522 **479** 15 p. brown & dp. green 5 5

1965 (31 OCT.). *90th Birth Anniv. of Vallabhbhai Patel* (*statesman*). *W* **374.** *P* 14 × 13½.

523 **480** 15 p. blackish brown .. 5 5

481. C. Das.

482. Vidyapati (poet).

1965 (5 NOV.). *95th Birth Anniv. of Chittaranjan Das* (*lawyer and patriot*). *W* **374.** *P* 13.

524 **481** 15 p. yellow-brown .. 5 8

1965 (17 NOV.). *Vidyapati Commemoration.* *W* **374.** *P* 14 × 14½.

525 **482** 15 p. yellow-brown .. 5 5

483. Sikandra, Agra.

1966 (24 JAN.). *Pacific Area Travel Association Conference, New Delhi.* *No wmk.* *P* 13½ × 14.

526 **483** 15 p. slate 5 5

484. Soldier, Fighters and Warship.

1966 (26 JAN.). *Indian Armed Forces.* *No wmk.* *P* 14.

527 **484** 15 p. violet 5 8

485. Lal Bahadur Shastri (statesman). **486.** Kambar (poet).

1966 (26 Jan.). *Shastri Mourning Issue. No wmk. P* 13×13½.
528 **485** 15 p. black 5 5

1966 (5 Apr.). *Kambar Commemoration. P* 14×14½.
529 **486** 15 p. grey-green 5 8

487. B. R. Ambedkar. **488.** Kunwar Singh (patriot).

1966 (14 Apr.). *75th Birth Anniv. of Dr. B. R. Ambedkar (lawyer and reformer). P* 14×13½.
530 **487** 15 p. purple-brown .. 5 8

1966 (23 Apr.). *Kunwar Singh Commemoration. P* 14×13½.
531 **488** 15 p. chestnut 5 8

489. G. K. Gokhale.

1966 (9 May). *Birth Centenary of G. K. Gokhale (patriot). P* 13½×13.
532 **489** 15 p. brown-purple & pale yellow 5 5

490. Acharya Dvivedi (writer).

1966 (15 May). *Dvivedi Commemoration. P* 13½×14.
533 **490** 15 p. drab.. .. .. 5 5

491. Maharaja Ranjit Singh (warrior).

1966 (28 June). *Maharaja Ranjit Singh Commemoration. P* 14×13½.
534 **491** 15 p. purple 5 8

492. Homi Bhabha (scientist) and Nuclear Reactor.

1966 (4 Aug.). *Homi Bhabha Commemoration. P* 14½×14.
535 **492** 15 p. dull purple 8 8

493. A. K. Azad (scholar).

1966 (11 Nov.). *Abul Kalam Azad Commemoration. P* 13½×14.
536 **493** 15 p. chalky blue.. .. 5 5

494. S. R. Tirtha.

1966 (11 Nov.). *60th Death Anniv. of Swami Rama Tirtha (social reformer). P* 13×13½.
537 **494** 15 p. turquoise-blue .. 5 8

495. Infant and Dove Emblem.

1966 (14 Nov.). *Children's Day. P* 13×13½.
538 **495** 15 p. bright purple .. 8 8

496. Allahabad High Court.

1966 (25 Nov.). *Centenary of Allahabad High Court. P* 14½×14.
539 **496** 15 p. dull purple.. .. 8 8

497. Indian Family.

1966 (12 Dec.). *Family Planning. P* 13.
540 **497** 15 p. brown 5 8

498. Hockey Game.

1966 (31 Dec.). *India's Hockey Victory in Fifth Asian Games. P* 13.
541 **498** 15 p. new blue 8 8

499. "Jai Kisan".

1967 (11 Jan.). *First Anniv. of Shastri's Death. P* 13½×14.
542 **499** 15 p. yellow-green .. 5 5

500. Voter and Polling Booth. **501.** Guru Dwara Shrine, Patna.

1967 (13 Jan.). *Indian General Election. P* 13½×14.
543 **500** 15 p. red-brown 5 5

1967 (17 Jan.). *300th Birth Anniv. (in 1966) of Guru Gobind Singh (National leader).* *P* 14×13½.
544 **501** 15 p. bluish violet .. 5 5

502. Taj Mahal.

1967 (19 Mar.). *International Tourist Year.* *P* 14½×14.
545 **502** 15 p. bistre-brn. & orange 5 8

503. Nandalal Bose and "Garuda".

1967 (16 Apr.). *First Death Anniv. of Nandalal Bose (painter).* *P* 14×13½.
546 **503** 15 p. bistre-brown .. 5 5

504. Survey Emblem and Activities.

1967 (1 May). *Survey of India Bicentenary.* *P* 13½×13.
547 **504** 15 p. reddish lilac .. 5 8

505. Basaveswara.

1967 (11 May). *800th Death Anniv. of Basaveswara (reformer and statesman).* *P* 13½×14.
548 **505** 15 p. orange-red 5 5

506. Narsinha Mehta (poet).

507. Maharana Pratap (warrior).

1967 (30 May). *Narsinha Mehta Commemoration.* *P* 14×13½.
549 **506** 15 p. blackish brown .. 5 8

1967 (11 June). *Maharana Pratap Commemoration.* *P* 14×14½.
550 **507** 15 p. red-brown 5 8

508. Narayana Guru (reformer).

509. President Radhakrishnan.

1967 (21 Aug.). *Narayana Guru Commemoration.* *P* 14.
551 **508** 15 p. brown 5 8

1967 (5 Sept.). *Radhakrishnan Commemoration.* *P* 13.
552 **509** 15 p. claret 5 8

510. Martyrs' Memorial, Patna.

1967 (1 Oct.). *25th Anniv. of "Quit India" Movement.* *P* 14½×14.
553 **510** 15 p. lake 8 8

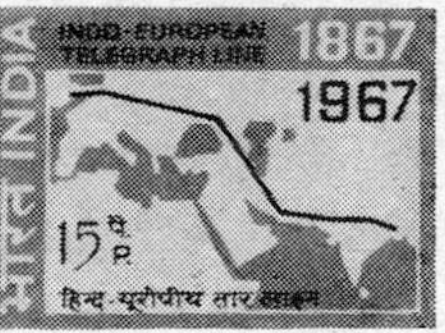

511. Route Map.

1967 (9 Nov.). *Centenary of Indo-European Telegraph Service.* *P* 13½×14.
554 **511** 15 p. black and light blue 5 8

512. Wrestling.

1967 (12 Nov.). *World Wrestling Championships.* *P* 13½×14.
555 **512** 15 p. purple and light orange-brown .. 5 8

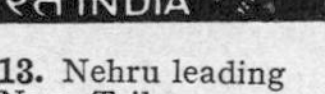

513. Nehru leading Naga Tribesmen.

514. Rashbehari Basu (nationalist).

1967 (1 Dec.). *"Nehru and Nagaland".* *P* 13×13½.
556 **513** 15 p. ultramarine .. 5 8

1967 (26 Dec.). *Rashbehari Basu Commemoration.* *P* 14.
557 **514** 15 p. maroon 5 8

515. Bugle, Badge and Scout Salute.

1967 (27 Dec.). *Diamond Jubilee of Scout Movement.* *P* 14½×14.
558 **515** 15 p. chestnut 5 5

516. Men Embracing Universe.

1968 (1 Jan.). *Human Rights Year.* *P* 13.
559 **516** 15 p. bronze-green .. 5 5

517. Globe and Book of Tamil.

1968 (3 Jan.). *International Conference-Seminar of Tamil Studies, Madras.* *P* 13.
560 **517** 15 p. reddish lilac .. 5 5

518. U.N. Emblem and Transport.

968 (1 Feb.). *United Nations Conference on Trade and Development.* P 14½ × 14.
61 **518** 15 p. turquoise-blue .. 5 5

519. Quill and Bow Symbol.

968 (20 Feb.). *Amrita Bazar Patrika (Newspaper) Centenary.* P 13½ × 14.
62 **519** 15 p. sepia & orge.-yellow 5 8

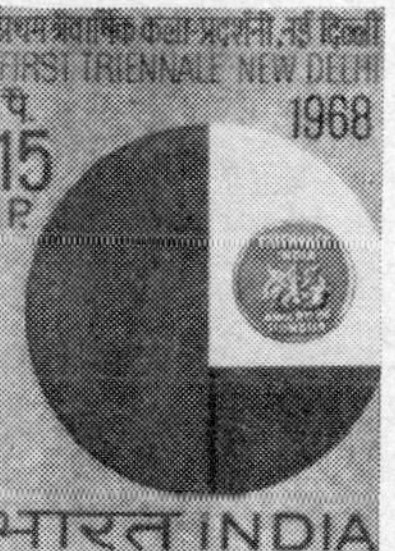

520. Maxim Gorky. **521.** Emblem and Medal.

968 (28 Mar.). *Birth Centenary of Maxim Gorky.* P 13½.
63 **520** 15 p. plum 5 8

968 (31 Mar.). *First Triennale, New Delhi.* P 13.
64 **521** 15 p. orange, Royal blue and light blue .. 5 5
a. Orange omitted .. £600

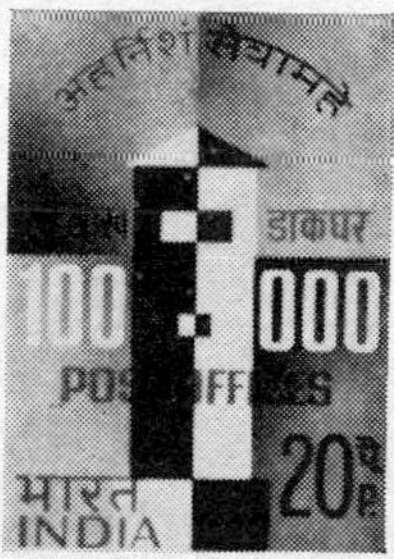

522. Letter-box and " 100,000 ".

(Des. C. R. Pakrashi.)

968 (1 July). *Opening of 100,000th Indian Post Office.* P 13.
65 **522** 20 p. red, blue and black 5 8

23. Stalks of Wheat, Agricultural Institute and Production Graph.

968 (17 July). *Wheat Revolution.* P 13.
66 **523** 20 p. bluish green and orange-brown .. 5 5

524. Gaganendranath Tagore.

(Des. from self-portrait.)

1968 (17 Sept.). *30th Death Anniv. of Gaganendranath Tagore (painter).* P 13.
567 **524** 20 p. brown-pur. & ochre 5 8

525. Lakshminath Bezbaruah.

1968 (5 Oct.). *Birth Centenary of Lakshminath Bezbaruah (writer).* P 13½ × 14.
568 **525** 20 p. blackish brown .. 5 8

526. Athlete's Legs and Olympic Rings.

1968 (12 Oct.). *Olympic Games, Mexico.* P 14½ × 14.
569 **526** 20 p. brown and grey .. 8 5
570 ,, 1 r. sepia & brown-olive 25 20

527. Bhagat Singh and Followers.

1968 (19 Oct.). *61st Birth Anniv. of Bhagat Singh (revolutionary).* P 13.
571 **527** 20 p. yellow-brown .. 5 8

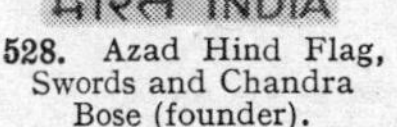

528. Azad Hind Flag, Swords and Chandra Bose (founder). **529.** Sister Nivedita.

1968 (21 Oct.). *25th Anniv. of Azad Hind Government.* P 14 × 14½.
572 **528** 20 p. deep blue 5 8

1968 (27 Oct.). *Birth Centenary of Sister Nivedita.* P 14 × 14½.
573 **529** 20 p. deep bluish green .. 5 8

530. Marie Curie and Radium Treatment.

1968 (6 Nov.). *Birth Centenary of Marie Curie.* P 14½ × 14.
574 **530** 20 p. slate-lilac .. 5 8

531. Map of the World.

1968 (1 Dec.). *21st International Geographical Congress.* P 13.
575 **531** 20 p. new blue 5 8

532. Cochin Synagogue.

1968 (15 Dec.). *400th Anniv. of Cochin Synagogue.* P 13.
576 **532** 20 p. blue and carmine .. 5 8

533. I.N.S. *Nilgiri*.

1968 (15 DEC.). *Navy Day. P* 13.
577 **533** 20 p. grey-blue 5 8

534. Blue Magpie.

535. Woodpecker. (*Horiz.*)
536. Babbler. (*Vert.*)
537. Sunbird. (*Horiz.*)

1968 (31 DEC.). *Birds. P* 14 × 14½ (1 *r.*) *or* 14½ × 14 (*others*).
578 **534** 20 p. multicoloured .. 8 8
579 **535** 50 p. scarlet, black and turquoise-green .. 10 10
580 **536** 1 r. deep blue, yellow-brown and pale blue 20 15
581 **537** 2 r. multicoloured .. 40 40

538. Bankim Chandra Chatterjee.

539. Dr. Bhagavan Das.

1969 (1 JAN.). *130th Birth Anniv. of Bankim Chandra Chatterjee* (*writer*). *P* 13½.
582 **538** 20 p. ultramarine .. 5 8

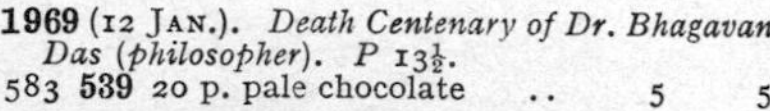

1969 (12 JAN.). *Death Centenary of Dr. Bhagavan Das* (*philosopher*). *P* 13½.
583 **539** 20 p. pale chocolate .. 5 5

540. Dr. Martin Luther King.

1969 (25 JAN.). *Martin Luther King Commemoration. P* 13½.
584 **540** 20 p. deep olive brown .. 5 8

541. Mirza Ghalib and Letter Seal.

1969 (17 FEB.). *Death Centenary of Mirza Ghalib* (*poet*). *P* 14½ × 14.
585 **541** 20 p. sepia, brown-red and flesh 5 5

542. Osmania University.

1969 (15 MAR.). *50th Anniv. of Osmania University. P* 14½ × 14.
586 **542** 20 p. olive-green .. 5 8

543. Rafi Ahmed Kidwai.

1969 (1 APR.). *20th Anniv. of "ALL-UP" Air Mail Scheme. P* 13.
587 **543** 20 p. deep blue 5 8

544. ILO Badge and Emblem.

1969 (11 APR.). *50th Anniv. of International Labour Organisation. P* 14½ × 14.
588 **544** 20 p. chestnut 5 8

545. Memorial, and Hands dropping Flowers.

1969 (13 APR.). *50th Anniv. of Jallianwala Bagh Massacre. P* 14 × 13½.
589 **545** 20 p. rose-carmine .. 5 5

546. Shri Nageswara Rao (patriot).

1969 (1 MAY). *Kasinadhuni Nageswara Rao Pantulu Commemoration. P* 13½ × 14.
590 **546** 20 p. brown 5

547. Ardaseer Cursetjee Wadia, and Ships.

1969 (27 MAY). *Ardaseer Cursetjee Wadia* (*ship building engineer*). *P* 14½ × 14.
591 **547** 20 p. turquoise-green .. 5

548. Serampore College.

1969 (7 JUNE). *150th Anniv. of Serampore College. P* 13½.
592 **548** 20 p. plum 5

549. Dr. Zakir Husain.

1969 (11 JUNE). *President Dr. Zakir Husain* (*patriot*) *Commemoration. P* 13.
593 **549** 20 p. sepia 5

550. Laxmanrao Kirloskar.

1969 (20 JUNE). *Birth Centenary of Laxmanrao Kirloskar* (*agriculturalist*). *P* 13.
594 **550** 20 p. grey-black 5 8

551. Gandhi and his wife.

552. Gandhi's Head and Shoulders.

553. Gandhi walking (woodcut).

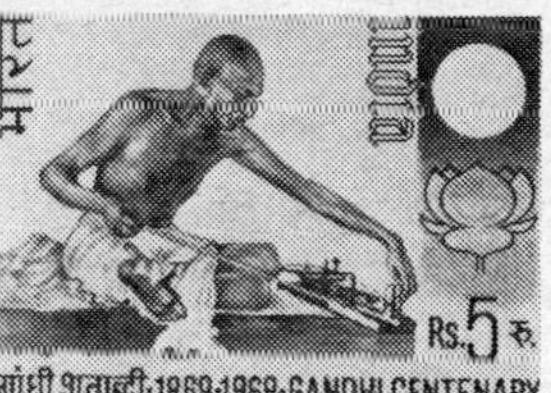

554. Gandhi with Charkha.

Des. Suraj Sadan (20 p.), P. B. Chitnis (75 p.), Indian Security Press (1 r.) and C. R. Pakrashi (5 r.).)

969 (2 Oct.). *Birth Centenary of Mahatma Gandhi. P* 13½ × 14 (20 *p.*), 14 × 14½ (1 *r.*) *or* 13 (*others*).

95 **551** 20 p. blackish brown .. 8 8
96 **552** 75 p. cinnamon and drab 15 15
97 **553** 1 r. blue.. .. .. 25 25
98 **554** 5 r. greyish brown and red-orange .. .. 1·00 85

555. Oil Tanker and I.M.C.O. Emblem.

969 (14 Oct.). 10*th Anniv. of Inter-Governmental Maritime Consultative Organization. P* 13.

99 **555** 20 p. violet-blue 5 8

56. Outline of Parliament Building and Globe.

1969 (30 Oct.). 57*th Inter-Parliamentary Conference, New Delhi. P* 14½ × 14.

600 **556** 20 p. new blue 5 8

557. Man walking beside Space Module on Moon.

558. " Shri Nankana Sahib Gurudwara ".

1969 (19 Nov.). *First Man on the Moon. P* 14 × 14½.

601 **557** 20 p. olive-brown .. 5 8

1969 (23 Nov.). 500*th Birth Anniv. of Guru Nanak. P* 13½.

602 **558** 20 p. slate-violet .. 5 8

559. Tiger's Head and Hands holding Globe.

1969 (24 Nov.). *International Union for the Conservation of Nature and Natural Resources Conference, New Delhi. P* 14½ × 14.

603 **559** 20 p. orange-brown and bronze-green .. 5 8

560. Sadhu Vaswani.

561. Thakkar Bapa.

1969 (25 Nov.). 90*th Birth Anniv. of Sadhu Vaswani* (*Educationist*). *P* 14 × 14½.

604 **560** 20 p. grey 5 5

1969 (29 Nov.). *Birth Centenary of Thakkar Bapa* (*humanitarian*). *P* 13½.

605 **561** 20 p. chocolate 5 5

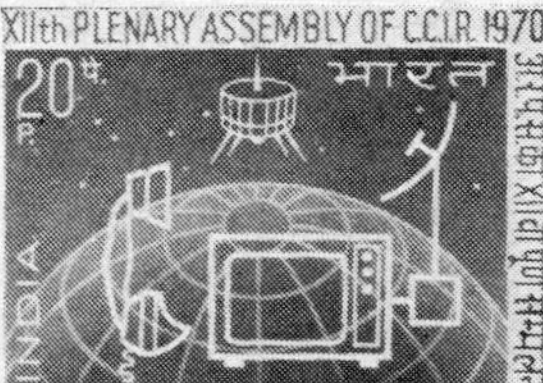

562. Satellite, Television, Telephone and Globe.

1970 (21 Jan.). 12*th Plenary Assembly of International Radio Consultative Committee. P* 13.

606 **562** 20 p. Prussian blue .. 5 5

563. Thiru Annadurai.

1970 (3 Feb.). *First Death Anniv. of Thiru Annadurai* (*statesman*). *P* 13.

607 **563** 20 p. reddish purple and Royal blue .. 5 8

564. M. N. Kishore and Printing Press.

1970 (19 Feb.). *Munshi Newal Kishore* (*publisher*) *Commemoration. P* 13.

608 **564** 20 p. lake 5 8

565. Nalanda College.

1970 (27 Mar.). *Centenary of Nalanda College. P* 14½ × 14.

609 **565** 20 p. brown 5 8

566. Swami Shraddhanand (social reformer).

1970 (30 Mar.). *Swami Shraddhanand Commemoration. P* 14 × 13½.

610 **566** 20 p. yellow-brown .. 5 5

567. Lenin.

1970 (22 APR.). *Birth Centenary of Lenin. P* 13.
611 **567** 20 p. orange-brn. & sepia 5 5

568. New U.P.U. H.Q. Building.

1970 (20 MAY). *New U.P.U. Headquarters Building. P* 13.
612 **568** 20 p. emerald, grey & blk. 5 8

569. Sher Shah Suri (15th-century Ruler).

1970 (22 MAY). *Sher Shah Suri Commemoration. P* 13.
613 **569** 20 p. deep bluish green .. 5 8

570. V. D. Savarkar (patriot) and Cellular Jail.

1970 (28 MAY). *V. D. Savarkar Commemoration. P* 13.
614 **570** 20 p. orange-brown .. 5 8

571. "UN" and Globe.

1970 (26 JUNE). *25th Anniv. of United Nations. P* 13.
615 **571** 20 p. light new blue .. 5 5

572. Symbol and workers.

1970 (18 AUG.). *Asian Productivity Year. P* $14\frac{1}{2} \times 14$.
616 **572** 20 p. violet 5 5

573. Dr. Montessori and I.E.Y. Emblem.

1970 (31 AUG.). *Birth Centenary of Dr. Maria Montessori (educationist). P* 13.
617 **573** 20 p. dull purple .. 5 5

574. J. N. Mukherjee (revolutionary) and Horse.

1970 (9 SEPT.). *Jatindra Nath Mukherjee Commemoration. P* $14\frac{1}{2} \times 14$.
618 **574** 20 p. chocolate 5 8

575. V. S. Srinivasa Sastri.

1970 (22 SEPT.). *Srinivasa Sastri (educationist). P* $13 \times 13\frac{1}{2}$.
619 **575** 20 p. yellow and brown-purple 5 5

576. I. C. Vidyasagar.

1970 (26 SEPT.). *150th Birth Anniv. of I. C Vidyasagar (educationist). P* 13.
620 **576** 20 p. brown and purple.. 5

577. Maharishi Valmiki.

1970 (14 OCT.). *Maharishi Valmiki (Holy Poet) P* 13.
621 **577** 20 p. purple 5

578. Calcutta Port.

1970 (17 OCT.). *Centenary of Calcutta Por Trust. P* $13\frac{1}{2} \times 13$.
622 **578** 20 p. greenish blue .. 5

579. University Building.

1970 (29 OCT.) *50th Anniv. of Jamia Milli Islamia University. P* $14\frac{1}{2} \times 14$.
623 **579** 20 p. yellow-green .. 5

580. Jamnalal Bajaj.

1970 (4 NOV.). *Jamnalal Bajaj (patriot). W* **374** *P* $13\frac{1}{2} \times 13$.
624 **580** 20 p. olive-grey 5

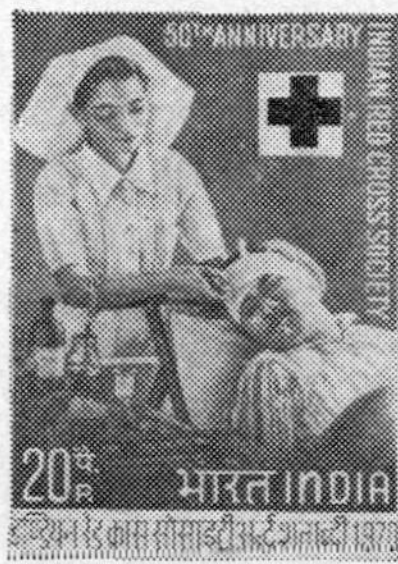

581. Nurse and Patient.

70 (5 Nov.). *50th Anniv. of Indian Red Cross. W* **374** *(sideways). P* 13 × 13½.
5 **581** 20 p. red and greenish blue 5 5

582. Sant Namdeo.

70 (9 Nov.). *700th Birth Anniv. of Sant (Saint) Namdeo. W* **374**. *P* 13.
6 **582** 20 p. orange 5 5

583. Beethoven.

70 (16 Dec.). *Birth Bicentenary of Beethoven. P* 13.
7 **583** 20 p. orange & greyish blk. 5 5

584. Children examining Stamps.

70 (23 Dec.). *Indian National Philatelic Exhibition. T* **584** *and similar horiz. design. P* 13.
8 20 p. orange & myrtle-green 8 8
9 1 r. orange-brown and pale yellow-brown 20 20

Design:—1 r. Gandhi commemorative through agnifier.

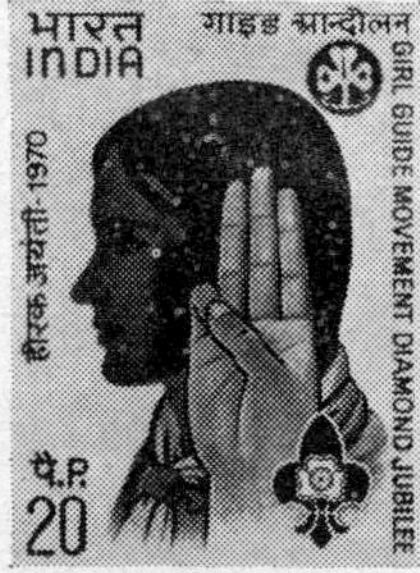

585. Girl Guide.

70 (27 Dec.). *Diamond Jubilee of Girl Guide Movement. P* 13.
o **585** 20 p. maroon 5 5

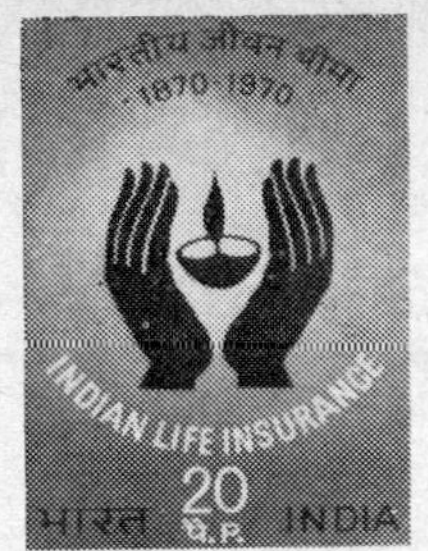

586. Hands and Lamp (Emblem).

1971 (11 Jan.). *Indian Life Insurance. P* 13.
631 **586** 20 p. sepia and crimson .. 5 5

587. Vidyapith Building.

1971 (10 Feb.). *Golden Jubilee of Kashi Vidyapith. P* 14½ × 14.
632 **587** 20 p. blackish brown .. 5 5

588. Saint Ravidas.

1971 (10 Feb.). *Guru Ravidas (15th-cent. Saint). P* 13.
633 **588** 20 p. lake 5 5

589. C. F. Andrews.

1971 (12 Feb.). *Birth Centenary of Deenabandhu C. F. Andrews (philosopher). P* 13 × 13½.
634 **589** 20 p. chestnut 5 5

MINIMUM PRICE

The minimum price quoted is 5p which represents a handling charge rather than a basis for valuing common stamps. For further notes about prices see introductory pages.

590. Acharya Narendra Deo (reformer).

1971 (19 Feb.). *15th Death Anniv. of Acharya Narendra Deo. P* 13.
635 **590** 20 p. dull green 5 5

591. Crowd and "100".

1971 (10 Mar.). *Census Centenary. P* 13.
636 **591** 20 p. brown and blue .. 5 5

592. Sri Ramana Maharishi (mystic).

1971 (14 Apr.). *21st Death Anniv. of Ramana Maharishi. P* 13½.
637 **592** 20 p. orange and sepia .. 5 5

593. Raja Ravi Varma and "Damayanti and the Swan".

1971 (29 Apr.). *65th Death Anniv. of Ravi Varma (artist). P* 13.
638 **593** 20 p. green 5 5

594. Dadasaheb Phalke (cinematographer) and Camera.

1971 (30 Apr.). *Birth Centenary of Dadasaheb Phalke.* P 13½ × 13.
639 **594** 20 p. dark maroon .. 5 5

595. "Abhisarika" (Abanindranath Tagore). **596.** Swami Virjanand (Vedic scholar).

1971 (7 Aug.). *Abanindranath Tagore Commemoration.* P 14 × 14½.
640 **595** 20 p. grey, buff-yellow and blackish brown .. 5 5

1971 (14 Sept.). *Swami Virjanand Commemoration.* P 13½.
641 **596** 20 p. chestnut 5 5

597. Cyrus the Great and Procession.

1971 (12 Oct.). *2500th Anniv. of Charter of Cyrus the Great.* P 13.
642 **597** 20 p. blackish brown .. 5 5

598. Globe and Money Box.

1971 (31 Oct.). *World Thrift Day.* P 14½ × 14.
643 **598** 20 p. blue-grey 5 5

599. Ajanta Caves Painting. **600.** Women at Work.

1971 (4 Nov.). *25th Anniv. of Unesco.* P 13.
644 **599** 20 p. red-brown 5 5

(Des. from painting by Geeta Gupta.)

1971 (14 Nov.). *Children's Day.* P 14 × 14½.
645 **600** 20 p. scarlet 5 5

शरणार्थी सहायता REFUGEE RELIEF
(601)

Refugee Relief
(602)

शरणार्थी सहायता REFUGEE RELIEF
(603)

REFUGEE RELIEF
(604)

REFUGEE RELIEF
(605)

Refugee Relief
(606)

607. Refugees.

1971. *Obligatory Tax. Refugee Relief.*
(*a*) *Provisional issues. No.* 506 *variously optd.*
(i) *For all India, optd. at Nasik.*
646 **601** 5 p. cerise (15 Nov.) .. 5 5
a. Opt. double .. ..

(ii) *For various areas.*
647 **602** 5 p. Bangalore (15 Nov.) 15 15
a. Opt. double, one inverted
648 **603** 5 p. Jaipur 50
649 **604** 5 p. Rajasthan 50
a. Error. "RELIEF REFUGEE"
650 **605** 5 p. New Delhi 50
a. Opt. inverted .. ..
650*b* **606** 5 p. Goa 50
(*b*) *Definitive issue.* W **374.** P 14 × 14½.
651 **607** 5 p. carmine 5 5

As from 15 Nov. 1971, the Indian Government levied a 5 p. surcharge on all mail, except postcards and newspapers, for the relief of refugees from the former East Pakistan.

As supplies of the provisional overprint could not be sent to all Indian post offices in time, local postmasters were authorised to make their own overprints. Most of these were applied by rubber stamps and so we do not list them. Those listed have typographed overprints and No. 649 also has a rubber handstamp in native language. Some of the above overprints were also used in areas other than those where they were produced.

608. C. V. Raman (scientist) and Jewel.

1971 (21 Nov.). *Dr. C. V. Raman Commemoration.* P 13.
652 **608** 20 p. orange & dark brn. 5 5

609. Visva Bharati Building and Rabindranath Tagore (pioneer).

1971 (24 Dec.). *Golden Jubilee of Visva Bharati.* P 14½ × 14.
653 **609** 20 p. sepia & yellow-brn. 5 5

610. Cricketers.

1971 (30 Dec.). *Indian Cricket Victories.* P 14½ × 14.
654 **610** 20 p. green, myrtle-green and sage-green .. 5

611. Map and Satellite.

1972 (26 Feb.). *Arvi Satellite Earth Station.* P 13½.
655 **611** 20 p. plum 5

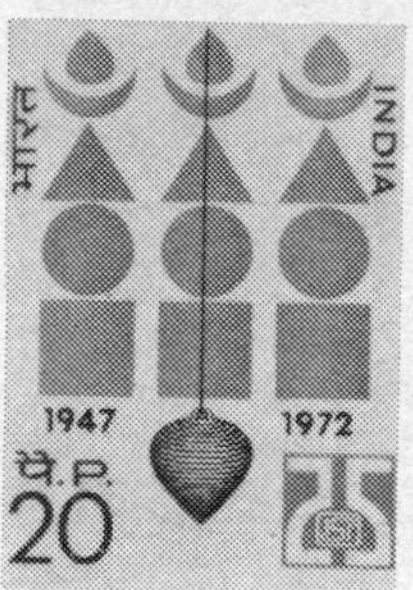

612. Elemental Symbols and plumb-line.

1972 (29 May). *Silver Jubilee of Indian Standards Institution.* P 13.
656 **612** 20 p. turquoise-grey and black 5

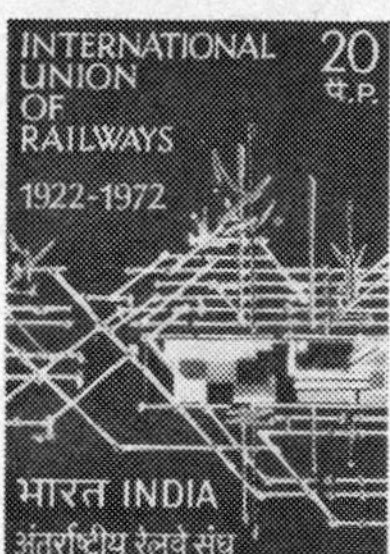

613. Signal-box panel.

1972 (30 June). *50th Anniv. of International Railways Union.* P 13.
657 **613** 20 p. multicoloured .. 5

614. Hockey-player.

72 (10 Aug.). *Olympic Games, Munich. T* **614** *and similar horiz. design. P* 13.
8 20 p. deep bluish violet .. 5 5
9 1 r. 45, light turquoise-grn., and brown-lake .. 20 20
Design:—1 r. 45, Various sports.

615. Symbol of Sri Aurobindo.

72 (15 Aug.). *Birth Centenary of Sri Aurobindo. P* 13½.
o **615** 20 p. yellow and new blue 5 5

.6. Celebrating Independence Day in front of Parliament.

72 (15 Aug.). *25th Anniversary of Independence (1st issue). P* 13.
1 **616** 20 p. multicoloured .. 5 5
See also Nos. 673/4.

617. Inter-Services Crest.

72 (15 Aug.). *Defence Services Commemoration. P* 13.
2 **617** 20 p. multicoloured .. 5 5

618. V. O. Chidambaram Pillai (lawyer and politician) and Ship.

1972 (5 Sept.). *Birth Centenary of V. O. Chidambaram Pillai. P* 13.
663 **618** 20 p. new blue and purple-brown 5 5

619. Bhai Vir Singh.

1972 (16 Oct.). *Birth Centenary of Bhai Vir Singh (Poet and Saint). P* 13.
664 **619** 20 p. plum 5 5

620. T. Prakasam.

1972 (16 Oct.). *Birth Centenary of T. Prakasam (lawyer). P* 13.
665 **620** 20 p. brown 5 5

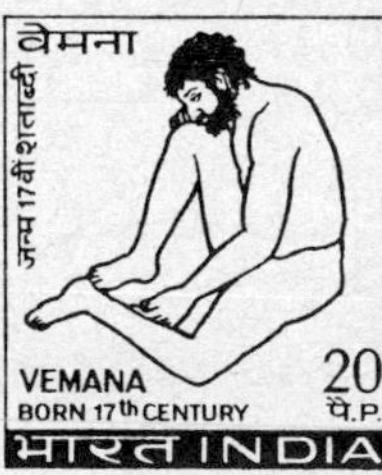

621. Vemana. **622.** Bertrand Russell.

1972 (16 Oct.). *300th Birth Anniv. of Vemana (poet). W* **374**. *P* 13½×14.
666 **621** 20 p. black 5 5

1972 (16 Oct.). *Birth Centenary of Bertrand Russell (philosopher). P* 13½×14.
667 **622** 1 r. 45, black 20 20

623. Symbol of "Asia '72"

1972 (3 Nov.). *"Asia '72" (Third Asian International Trade Fair). T* **623** *and similar vert. design. W* **374**. *P* 13.
668 **623** 20 p. black and orange .. 5 5
669 - 1 r. 45, orange and slate-black 20 20

Design:—1 r. 45, Hand of Buddha.

624. V. A. Sarabhai and Rocket.

1972 (30 Dec.). *First Death Anniv. of Vikram A. Sarabhai (scientist). P* 13.
670 **624** 20 p. brown & myrtle-grn. 5 5

625. Flag of U.S.S.R. and Kremlin Tower.

1972 (30 Dec.). *50th Anniv. of U.S.S.R. P* 13.
671 **625** 20 p. light yellow and red 5 5

626. Exhibition Symbol.

1973 (8 Jan.). *"Indipex '73" Stamp Exhibition (1st issue). P* 13.
672 **626** 1 r. 45, light mauve, gold and black 25 25
See also Nos. 701/**MS**704

627. "Democracy".

1973 (26 JAN.). *25th Anniv. of Independence (2nd issue). T* **627** *and similar multicoloured design. P* 13 (20 *p.*) *or* $14\frac{1}{2} \times 14$ (1 *r.* 45).

673 20 p. Type **627** 5 5
674 1 r. 45, "Gnat" fighters over India Gate 20 20

No. 674 is horizontal, 38 × 20 mm.

628. Sri Ramakrishna Paramahamsa (religious leader).

1973 (18 FEB.). *Sri Ramakrishna Paramahamsa Commemoration. P* 13.

675 **628** 20 p. light brown .. 5 5

629. Postal Corps Emblem.

1973 (1 MAR.). *First Anniv. of Army Postal Service Corps. P* 13.

676 **629** 20 p. deep ultram. & verm. 5 5

630. Flag and Map of Bangladesh.

1973 (10 APR.). *"Jai Bangla" (Inauguration of First Bangladesh Parliament). P* 13.

677 **630** 20 p. multicoloured .. 5 5

631. Kumaran Asan.

1973 (12 APR.). *Birth Centenary of Kumaran Asan (writer and poet). P* 13.

678 **631** 20 p. sepia 5 5

632. Flag and Flames.

(Des. C. R. Parakshi.)

1973 (13 APR.). *Homage to Martyrs for Independence. P* 13.

679 **632** 20 p. multicoloured .. 5 5

633. Dr. B. R. Ambedkar (social thinker and agitator).

(Des. Shri Charanjitlal.)

1973 (14 APR.). *Ambedkar Commemoration. P* 13.

680 **633** 20 p. bronze green and deep purple .. 5 5

634. "Radha-Kishangarh" (Nihal Chand).

1973 (5 MAY). *Indian Miniature Paintin[gs]. T* **634** *and similar vert. designs. Multicolour[ed]. P* 13.

681 20 p. Type **634** 8
682 50 p. "Dance Duet" (Aurangzeb's period) .. 10
683 1 r. "Lovers on a Camel" (Nasir-ud-din) .. 20
684 2 r. "Chained Elephant" (Zain-al-Abidin) .. 35

635. The Himalayas.

1973 (15 MAY). *15th Anniv. of Indian Mo[un]taineering Foundation. P* 13.

685 **635** 20 p. blue 5

636. Tail of Boeing "747".

(Des. Air-India Art Studios from photograph [by] Jehangir Gazdar.)

1973 (8 JUNE). *25th Anniv. of Air-India's Int[er]national Services. P* 13.

686 **636** 1 r. 45, indigo and carmine-red .. 20

637. Cross, Church of St. Thomas' Mou[nt], Madras.

973 (3 JULY). *19th Death Centenary of St. Thomas.* *P* 13.
87 **637** 20 p. blue-grey and agate 5 5

38. Michael Madhusudan Dutt (poet—Death Centenary).

973 (21 JULY). *Centenaries.* *T* **638** *and similar horiz. designs.* *P* 13.
88 20 p. sage-grn. & orge.-brn. 5 5
a. Orange-brown omitted ..
89 30 p. red-brown 5 5
90 50 p. deep brown 5 8
91 1 r. dull violet & orge.-verm. 12 15

Designs:—30 p. V. D. Paluskar (musician—Birth Centenary); 50 p. Dr. Hansen (Centenary of iscovery of leprosy bacillus); 1 r. Nicolaus opernicus (astronomer—Fifth Birth Centenary).

639. A. O. Hume.

973 (31 JULY). *A. O. Hume Commemoration.* *P* 13.
92 **639** 20 p. grey 5 5

640. Gandhi and Nehru.

(Des. C. R. Pakrashi from photograph.)

973 (15 AUG.). *Gandhi and Nehru Commemoration.* *P* 13.
93 **640** 20 p. multicoloured .. 5 5

641. R. C. Dutt.

1973 (27 SEPT.). *R. C. Dutt Commemoration.* *P* 13.
694 **641** 20 p. brown 5 5

642. K. S. Ranjitsinhji.

1973 (27 SEPT.). *K. S. Ranjitsinhji Commemoration.* *P* 13.
695 **642** 30 p. myrtle-green .. 5 5

643. Vithalbhai Patel (nationalist).

1973 (27 SEPT.). *Vithalbhai Patel Commemoration.* *P* 13.
696 **643** 50 p. light red-brown .. 5 8

644. President's Bodyguard.

1973 (30 SEPT.). *200th Anniv. of President's Bodyguard.* *P* 13.
697 **644** 20 p. multicoloured .. 5 5

645. Interpol Emblem.

1973 (9 OCT.). *50th Anniv. of Interpol.* *P* 13.
698 **645** 20 p. brown 5 5

646. Syed Ahmad Khan (social reformer).

1973 (17 OCT.). *Syed Ahmad Khan Commemoration.* *P* 13.
699 **646** 20 p. sepia 5 5

647. "Children at Play" (detail, Bela Raval).

1973 (14 NOV.). *Children's Day.* *P* 13.
700 **647** 20 p. mult. 5 5

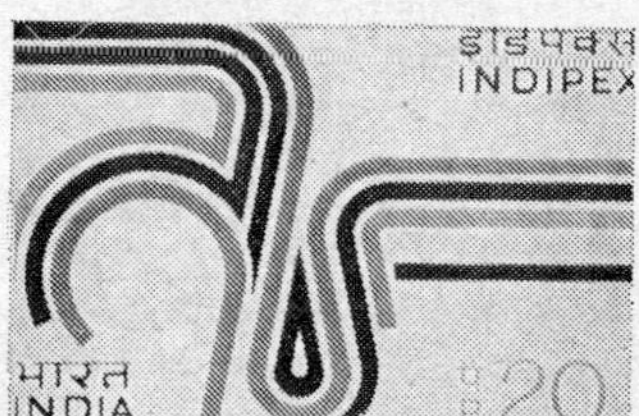

648. Indipex Emblem.
(*Illustration reduced. Actual size* 54 × 36 *mm.*)

1973 (14 NOV.). *"Indipex '73" Philatelic Exhibition, New Delhi (2nd issue).* *T* **648** *and similar multicoloured designs.* *P* 13½ × 13 (*2 r.*) *or* 13 × 13½ (*others*).
701 20 p. Type **648** 5 5
702 1 r. Ceremonial elephant and 1½ a. stamp of 1947 (*vert.*) 12 15
703 2 r. Peacock (*vert.*) 25 30
MS704 127 × 127 mm. Nos. 672 and 701/3. Imperf. 50 55

HAVE YOU READ THE NOTES AT THE BEGINNING OF THIS CATALOGUE?

These often provide answers to the enquiries we receive.

649. Emblem of National Cadet Corps.

1973 (25 Nov.). *Silver Jubilee of National Cadet Corps. P* 13.
705 **649** 20 p. multicoloured .. 5 5

650. Chakravarti Rajagopalachari (statesman).

1973 (25 Dec.). *C. Rajagopalachari Commemoration. P* 13.
706 **650** 20 p. olive-brown .. 5 5

651. "Sun" Mask.

1974 (15 Apr.). *Indian Masks. T* **651** *and similar multicoloured designs. P* 13.
707 20 p. Type **651** 5 5
708 50 p. "Moon" mask 8 8
709 1 r. "Narasimha" 15 15
710 2 r. "Ravana" (*horiz.*) .. 30 30
MS711 109 × 135 mm. Nos. 707/10 45 50

652. Chhatrapati.

1974 (2 June). *300th Anniv. of Coronation of Chhatrapati Shri Shivaji Maharaj (patriot and ruler). P* 13.
712 **652** 25 p. multicoloured .. 5 5

653. Maithili Sharan Gupta (poet).

1974 (3 July). *Indian Personalities (1st series). T* **653** *and similar vert. designs. P* 13.
713 25 p. chestnut (T **653**) .. 5 5
714 25 p. deep brown 5 5
715 25 p. sepia 5 5

Portraits:—No. 714, Jainarain Vyas (politician and journalist); No. 715, Utkal Gourab Madhusudan Das (social reformer).

654. Kandukuri Veeresalingam (reformer).

1974 (15 July). *Indian Personalities (2nd series). T* **654** *and similar vert. designs. P* 13.
716 25 p. lake-brown 5 5
717 50 p. dull purple 5 8
718 1 r. chestnut-brown 12 15

Portraits:—50 p. Tipu Sultan (patriot); 1 r. Max Mueller (Sanskrit scholar).

655. Kamala Nehru.

(Des. Shri Charanjit Lal.)

1974 (1 Aug.). *Kamala Nehru Commemoration. P* 14½ × 14.
719 **655** 25 p. multicoloured .. 5 5

656. W.P.Y. Emblem.

1974 (14 Aug.). *World Population Yea*
P 13½.
720 **656** 25 p. maroon and buff .. 5

657. Chital.

658. President Giri.

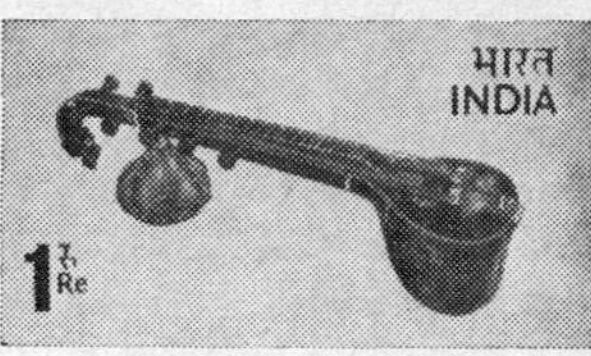

657*a*. Sitar.

1974–75. *Various designs as T* **657**/*a*.

(i) *Values expressed with "p" or "Re*
W **374** *(sideways). P* 14½ × 14.
721 15 p. brownish black (1.10.74) 5
722 25 p. sepia (20.8.74) 5
a. Imperf. (pair) .. ..
723 1 r. red-brn. & blk (1.10.74) 12

(ii) *Values expressed in numerals only. W 3*
(sideways on 15 p., 1 r. and 2 r.). P 14 × 1
(20 and 50 p.) or 14½ × 14 *(others)*.
728 15 p. blackish brown (15.7.75) 5
729 20 p. deep dull green (15.7.75) 5
733 50 p. deep violet (15.7.75) .. 5
736 1 r. red-brown & grey-blk. (15.7.75) 10
737 2 r. violet and grey-black (15.7.75) 20
721/37 *Set of* 8 60

Designs as T **657**: *Vert.*—15 p. Tiger. *Horiz.*-
20 p. Handicrafts toy; 50 p. Crane in flight.
T **657***a*:—2 r. Himalayas.

The numbering of the above issues is pr
visional.

(Des. Shri Charanjit Lal.)

1974 (24 Aug.) *Giri Commemoration. P* 13.
739 **658** 25 p. multicoloured .. 5

659. U.P.U. Emblem.

(Des. C. R. Pakrashi (25 p.), A. Ramachandran (1 r.), Jyoti Bhatt (2 r.).)

1974 (3 Oct.). *Centenary of Universal Postal Union. T* **659** *and similar designs. P* 13.

740 25 p. violet-blue, Royal blue and black 5 5
741 1 r. multicoloured 12 12
742 2 r. multicoloured 25 25
MS743 108 × 108 mm. Nos. 740/2 45 50

Design: *Horiz.*—1 r. Birds and nest, "Madhubani" style. *Vert.*—2 r. Arrows around globe.

660. Woman Flute-player (sculpture).

(Des. Benoy Sarkar.)

1974 (9 Oct.). *Mathura Museum. T* **660** *and similar vert. design. P* 13½.

744 25 p. chestnut and black (T **660**) 5 5
745 25 p. chestnut and black .. 5 5

Design:—No. 745, Vidyadhara with garland. Nos. 744/5 were printed together within the sheet, horizontally *se-tenant*.

661. Nicholas Roerich (medallion by H. Dropsy).

1974 (9 Oct.). *Birth Centenary of Professor Roerich. P* 13.

746 **661** 1 r. deep blue-green and greenish yellow .. 12 15

662. Pavapuri Temple.

(Des. Benoy Sarkar.)

1974 (13 Nov.). *2,500th Anniv. of Bhagwan Mahavira's attainment of Nirvana. P* 13.

747 **662** 25 p. indigo 5 5

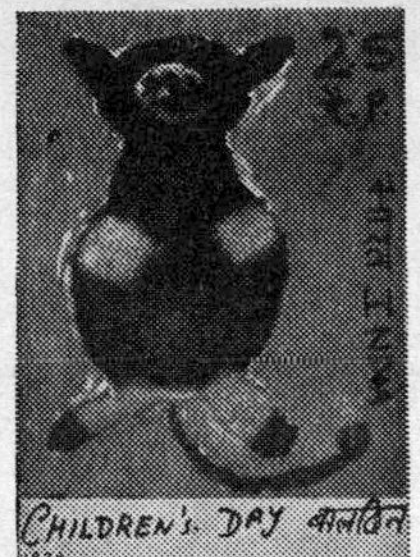

663. "Cat" (Rajesh Bhatia).

1974 (14 Nov.). *Children's Day. P* 13.

748 **663** 25 p. multicoloured .. 5 5

664. Indian Dancers.

(Des. from painting by Amita Shah.)

1974 (14 Nov.). *25th Anniv. of UNICEF in India. P* 14½ × 14.

749 **664** 25 p. multicoloured .. 5 5
a. Black (name, value and background) omitted ..

665. Territorial Army Badge.

(Des. Shri Benoy Sarkar.)

1974 (16 Nov.). *25th Anniv. of Indian Territorial Army. P* 13.

750 **665** 25 p. black, bright yellow and emerald .. 5 5

666. Krishna as Gopal Bal with Cows (Rajasthan painting on cloth).

1974 (2 Dec.). *19th International Dairy Congress New Delhi. P* 13½.

751 **666** 25 p. brown-purple and brown-ochre .. 5 5

667. Symbols and Child's Face.

(Des. Shri Benoy Sarkar.)

1974 (8 Dec.). *Help for Retarded Children. P* 13.

752 **667** 25 p. red-orange and black 5 5

668. Marconi.

1974 (12 Dec.). *Birth Centenary of Guglielmo Marconi (radio pioneer). P* 13.

753 **668** 2 r. deep slate 20 25

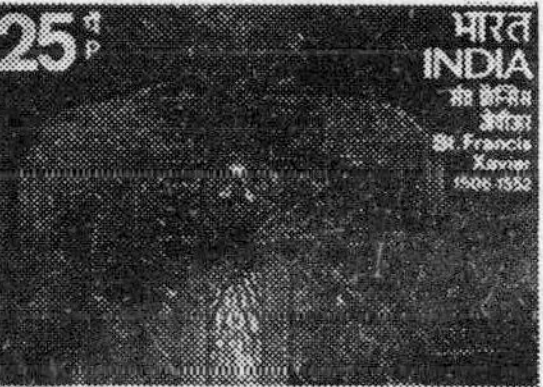

669. St. Francis Xavier's Shrine.

1974 (24 Dec.). *St. Francis Xavier Celebration. P* 13.

754 **669** 25 p. multicoloured .. 5 5

670. Saraswati (Deity of Language and Learning).

1975 (10 Jan.). *World Hindi Convention, Nagpur. P* 14 × 14½.

755 **670** 25 p. slate and carmine-red .. 5 5

For similar stamp see No. 761.

671. Parliament House, New Delhi.

1975 (26 Jan.). *25th Anniv. of Republic.* *P* 13.
756 **671** 25 p. grey-black, silver and azure 5 5

672. Table-tennis Bat.

1975 (6 Feb.). *World Table-tennis Championships, Calcutta.* *P* 13.
757 **672** 25 p. black, vermilion and yellow-olive .. 5 5

673. " Equality, Development and Peace ".

(Des. Shyama Sarabhai.)

1975 (16 Feb.). *International Women's Year.* *P* 13.
758 **673** 25 p. multicoloured .. 5 5

674. Stylised Cannon.

(Des. Benoy Sarkar.)

1975 (8 Apr.). *Bicentenary of Indian Army Ordnance Corps.* *P* 13.
759 **674** 25 p. multicoloured .. 5 5

675. Arya Samaj Emblem.

1975 (11 Apr.). *Centenary of Arya Samaj Movement.* *P* 13.
760 **675** 25 p. light red-orange and brownish black .. 5 5

676. Saraswati.

1975 (12 Apr.). *World Telugu Language Conference, Hyderabad.* *P* 14×14½.
761 **676** 25 p. black and deep bluish green .. 5 5

677. Satellite " Aryabhata ".

1975 (20 Apr.). *Launch of First Indian Satellite.* *P* 13.
762 **677** 25 p. light blue, deep indigo & dull pur. 5 5

678. Indian Pitta.

(Des. J. P. Irani.)

1975 (28 Apr.). *Indian Birds.* T **678** *and similar multicoloured designs.* *P* 13.

763	25 p. Type **678**	5	5
764	50 p. Black-headed Oriole ..	5	5
765	1 r. Western Tragopan (*vert.*)	10	12
766	2 r. Monal Pheasant (*vert.*)	20	25

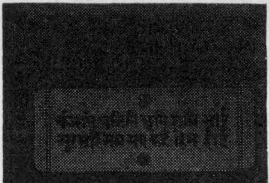

679. " Ramcharitmanas " (poem by Goswam Tulsidas).

(Des. R. K. Joshi.)

1975 (24 May). *Ramcharitmanas Commemora tion.* *P* 13.
767 **679** 25 p. black, orange-yell., and vermilion .. 5

680. Young Women within Y.W.C.A. Badge. **681.** " The Creation "

(Des. Benoy Sarkar.)

1975 (20 June). *Centenary of Indian Y.W.C.A* *P* 13.
768 **680** 25 p. multicoloured .. 5

1975 (28 June). *500th Birth Anniv. of Mich elangelo.* T **681** *and similar multicoloure designs.* *P* 14×13½.

769	50 p. } " Creation of the Sun,	5
770	50 p. } Moon and Planets "	5
771	50 p. } " Creation of Man "	5
772	50 p. } ..	5

T **681** illustrates No. 769. Nos. 770 and 77 are horizontal designs, size 49×34 mm.

Nos. 769/72 were printed in *se-tenant* blocks o four within the sheet, forming two composit designs in horizontal pairs.

682. Commission Emblem.

1975 (28 July). *25th Anniv. of Internationa Commission on Irrigation and Drainage* *P* 13½.
773 **682** 25 p. multicoloured .. 5

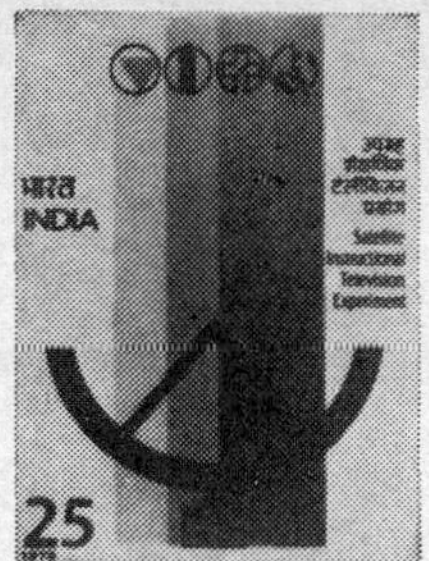

683. Stylised Ground Antenna.

(Des. Benoy Sarkar.)

975 (1 Aug.). *Satellite Instructional Television Experiment.* P 13.
74 **683** 25 p. multicoloured .. 5 5

684. St. Arunagirinathar.

975 (14 Aug.). 600*th Birth Anniv. of St. Arunagirinathar.* P $13\frac{1}{2}$.
75 **684** 50 p. dull pur. & slate-blk. 5 5

685. Commemorative Text.

975 (26 Aug.). *Namibia Day.* P $13\frac{1}{2}$.
76 **685** 25 p. grey-blk. & rose-red 5 5

686. Mir Anees (poet). **687.** Memorial Temple to Ahilyabai Holkar (ruler).

1975 (4 Sept.). *Indian Celebrities.* P $13\frac{1}{2}$ (*No.* 777) *or* 13 (*No.* 778).
77 **686** 25 p. blackish green .. 5 5
78 **687** 25 p. chestnut 5 5

688. Bharata Natyam.

1975 (20 Oct.). *Indian Dances.* T **688** *and similar vert. designs. Multicoloured.* P 13.

779	25 p. Type **688**	5	5
780	50 p. Orissi	5	5
781	75 p. Kathak	8	10
782	1 r. Kathakali	10	12
783	1 r. 50, Kuchipudi	15	20
784	2 r. Manipuri	20	25
779/84	.. .. *Set of* 6	55	65

689. Ameer Khusrau.

1975 (24 Oct.). 650*th Death Anniv. of Ameer Khusrau (poet).* P 13.
785 **689** 50 p. reddish brown and buff 5 5

690. V. K. Krishna Menon.

1975 (24 Oct.). *First Death Anniv. of V. K. Krishna Menon (statesman).* P $13 \times 13\frac{1}{2}$.
786 **690** 25 p. olive 5 5

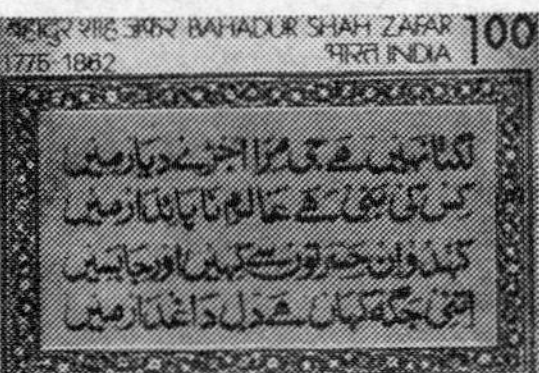

691. Text of Poem.

(Des. R. K. Joshi.)

1975 (24 Oct.). *Birth Bicentenary of Bahadur Shah Zafar.* P $13\frac{1}{2} \times 13$.
787 **691** 1 r. black, stone and yell.-brown 10 10

692. Sansadiya Soudha, New Delhi.

1975 (28 Oct.). *21st Commonwealth Parliamentary Conference, New Delhi.* P $14\frac{1}{2} \times 14$.
788 **692** 2 r. olive 20 20

693. V. Patel.

1975 (31 Oct.). *Birth Centenary of Vallabhbhai Patel (statesman).* P $13 \times 13\frac{1}{2}$.
789 **693** 25 p. slate-green .. 5 5

694. N. C. Bardoloi.

1975 (3 Nov.). *Birth Centenary of Nabin Chandra Bardoloi (politician).* P $13 \times 13\frac{1}{2}$.
790 **694** 25 p. reddish brown .. 5 5

695. "Cow" (drawing by Sanjay Nathubhai Patel).

1975 (14 Nov.). *Children's Day.* P $13\frac{1}{2} \times 13$.
791 **695** 25 p. multicoloured .. 5 5

696. Printing Works, Nasik Road.

1975 (13 Dec.). 50*th Anniv. of the India Security Press.* P 13.
792 **696** 25 p. multicoloured .. 5 5

697. Gurdwara Sisganj (site of martyrdom).

1975 (16 Dec.). *Tercentenary of the Martyrdom of Guru Tegh Bahadur. P* 13.
793 **697** 25 p. multicoloured .. 5 5

698. Theosophical Society Emblem.

1975 (20 Dec.). *Centenary of the Theosophical Society. P* **13**.
794 **698** 25 p. multicoloured .. 5 5

699. Weather Cock.

(Des. Benoy Sarkar.)

1975 (24 Dec.). *Centenary of the Indian Meteorological Department. P* 13 × 13½.
795 **699** 25 p. multicoloured .. 5 5

700. Early Mail Cart.

(Des. Benoy Sarkar.)

1975 (25 Dec.). *"Inpex 75" National Philatelic Exhibition, Calcutta. T* **700** *and similar vert. design. P* 13.
796 **700** 25 p. black and lake-brn. 5 5
797 – 2 r. grey-brown, brown-purple and black .. 20 20
Design:—2 r. Indian Bishop Mark, 1775.

701. L. N. Mishra (politician).

1976 (3 Jan.). *1st Anniv. of Mishra's Death. P* 13.
798 **701** 25 p. olive-sepia .. 5 5

702. Tiger.

1976 (24 Jan.). *Birth Centenary of Jim Corbett (naturalist). P* 13.
799 **702** 25 p. multicoloured .. 5 5
No. 799 is known pre-released on 2nd Dec.

703. Painted Storks.

(Des. Charanjit Lal.)

1976 (10 Feb.). *Keoladeo Ghana Bird Sanctuary, Bharatpur. P* 13.
800 **703** 25 p. multicoloured .. 5 5

704. Vijayanta Tank.

1976 (4 Mar.). *Bicentenary of 16th Light Cavalry Regt. P* 13.
801 **704** 25 p. multicoloured .. 5 5

705. Alexander Graham Bell. **706.** Muthuswami Dikshitar.

1976 (10 Mar.). *Alexander Graham Bell Commemoration. P* 13.
802 **705** 25 p grey-black and yellow-ochre 5

1976 (18 Mar.). *Birth Bicentenary of Dikshita (composer). P* 13½.
803 **706** 25 p. purple 5

707. Eye and Red Cross.

(Des. Benoy Sarkar.)

1976 (7 Apr.). *World Health Day. Preventio of Blindness. P* 13.
804 **707** 25 p. reddish brown and dull vermilion .. 5

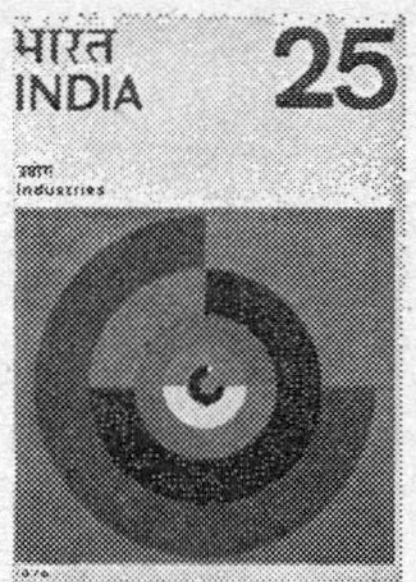

708. "Industries".

(Des. Benoy Sarkar.)

1976 (30 Apr.). *Industrial Development. P* 1
805 **708** 25 p. multicoloured .. 5

709. Diesel Locomotive, 1963.

1976 (15 May). *Locomotives. T* **709** *and simila horiz. designs. Multicoloured. P* 14½ × 14.
806 25 p. Type **709** 5
807 50 p. Steam loco, 1895 .. 5
808 1 r. Steam loco, 1963 .. 10
809 2 r. Steam loco, 1853 .. 20

710. Nehru.

76. *T* **710** *and similar vert. design.* *W* **374.** *P* 13½.
o 25 p. dull violet (27.5.76) .. 5 5
1 25 p. red-brown (2.10.76) .. 5 5

Design: No. 811, Gandhi.

711. " Spirit of 1776 " (Willard).

76 (29 May). *Bicentenary of American Revolution.* *P* 13.
2 **711** 2 r. 80, multicoloured .. 30 35

712. K. Kamaraj (politician).

76 (15 July). *Kamaraj Commemoration.* *P* 13.
3 **712** 25 p. sepia 5 5

713. " Shooting ".

(Des. Gopi Gajwani (25 p., 1 r.), Sukumar Shankar (1 r. 50), India Security Press (2 r. 80).)

1976 (17 July). *Olympic Games, Montreal.* *T* **713** *and similar vert. designs.* *P* 13.
814 25 p. deep violet & vermilion 5 5
815 1 r. multicoloured 10 12
816 1 r. 50, dp. mve. & grey-blk. 15 20
817 2 r. 80, multicoloured .. 30 35

Designs:—1 r. Shot-put; 1 r. 50, Hockey; 2 r. 80, Sprinting.

714. Subhadra Kumari Chauhan (poetess).

1976 (6 Aug.). *S. K. Chauhan Commemoration.* *P* 13.
818 **714** 25 p. grey-blue 5 5

715. Param Chakra Medal.

(Des. Benoy Sarkar.)

1976 (15 Aug.). *Param Vir Chakra Commemoration.* *P* 13.
819 **715** 25 p. multicoloured .. 5 5
No. 819 is known pre-released on 28 January.

716. University Building, Bombay.

1976 (3 Sept.). *50th Anniv. of Shreemati Nathibai Damodar Thackersey Women's University.* *P* 13½.
820 **716** 25 p. bluish violet .. 5 5

717. Bharatendu Harishchandra (poet).

1976 (9 Sept.). *Harishchandra Commemoration.* *P* 13.
821 **717** 25 p. agate 5 5

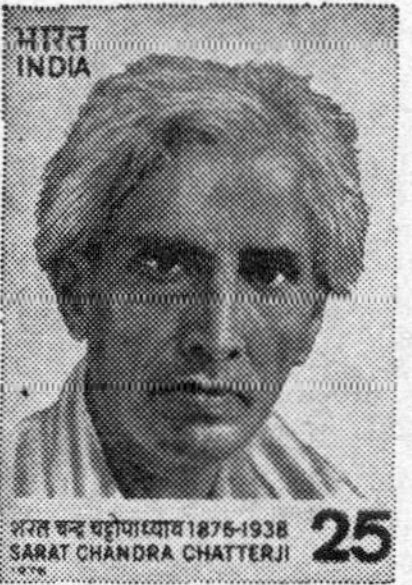

718. S. C. Chatterji (writer).

719. Planned Family.

1976 (15 Sept.). *Birth Centenary of S. C. Chatterji.* *P* 13.
822 **718** 25 p. grey-black 5 5

(Des. A. K. Nagar.)

1976 (22 Sept.). *Family Planning.* *P* 14×14½.
823 **719** 25 p. multicoloured .. 5 5

720. Maharaja Agrasen and Coins.

1976 (24 Sept.). *Maharaja Agrasen.* *P* 13.
824 **720** 25 p. red-brown 5 5

MINIMUM PRICE

The minimum price quoted is 5p which represents a handling charge rather than a basis for valuing common stamps. For further notes about prices see introductory pages.

OFFICIAL STAMPS.

Stamps overprinted "POSTAL SERVICE" or "P. I. N." were not used as postage stamps, and are therefore omitted.

Service.
(O 1)

(Optd. by the Military Orphanage Press, Calcutta.)

1866 (1 Aug.). *Optd. locally with Type* O **1**. *P* 14.

A. *No wmk.*

No.	Type	Description	Unused	Used
O 1	**11**	½ a. blue	—	9·00
O 2	,,	½ a. pale blue	—	9·00
		a. Opt. inverted		
O 3	**11**	1 a. brown	—	9·00
O 4	,,	1 a. deep brown	—	9·00
O 5	,,	8 a. carmine	1·50	4·00

B. *Wmk. Elephant's Head, T* **13**.

No.	Type	Description	Unused	Used
O 6	**11**	½ a. blue	15·00	3·00
O 7	,,	½ a. pale blue	15·00	4·00
		a. Opt. inverted		
		b. No dot on "i" (No. 50 on pane)		
		c. No stop (No. 77 on pane)	—	50·00
O 8	,,	1 a. brown	15·00	4·00
O 9	,,	1 a. deep brown	15·00	4·00
		a. No dot on "i"		
		b. No stop		
O10	,,	2 a. orange	11·00	5·00
O11	,,	2 a. yellow	12·00	5·00
		a. Opt. inverted		
		b. Imperf.		
O12	,,	4 a. green	7·50	6·50
		a. Opt. inverted	48·00	42·00
O13	**17**	4 a. green (Die I)	32·00	18·00

A variety with wide and more open capital "S" occurs six times in sheets of all values. Price four times the normal.

Reprints exist of Nos. O6, O8 and O13; the latter is Die II instead of Die I.

1872 (Jan.). *Optd. with Type* O **1**, *at Calcutta. Wmk. Elephant's Head, T* **13**. *P* 14.

No.	Type	Description	Unused	Used
O14	**12**	8 p. purple	2·50	4·00
		a. No dot on "i"	35·00	
		b. No stop	35·00	17·00

Reprints of the overprint have been made, in a different setting, on the 8 pies, purple, no watermark.

O 2

O 6

O 3

O 4

(No. O15 surch. at Calcutta, others optd. at Madras.)

1866. *Fiscal stamps surch. or optd.*

(*a*) *Surch. as in Type* O **2**. *Thick blue glazed paper. Imperf.* × *perf.* 14.

No.	Type	Description	Unused	Used
O15	O **2**	2 a. purple	£130	48·00

(*b*) *Optd.* "SERVICE POSTAGE" *in two lines as in Types* O **3/4** *and similar type. Imperf.* × *perf.* 14.

No.	Type	Description	Unused	Used
O16	–	2 a. purple (G.)	£130	50·00
O17	O **3**	4 a. purple (G.)	£350	£225
O18	O **4**	8 a. purple (G.)	£1100	£600

(*c*) *Optd.* "SERVICE POSTAGE" *in semi-circle. Wmk. Large Crown. P* 15½ × 15.

No.	Type	Description	Unused	Used
O19	O **6**	½ a. mauve/*lilac* (G.)	60·00	15·00
		a. Opt. double	£400	

So-called reprints of Nos. O15 to O18 are known, but in these the surcharge differs entirely in the spacing, etc., of the words; they are more properly described as Government imitations. The imitations of No. O15 have surcharge in *black* or in *green*. No. O19 exists with reprinted overprint which has a full stop after "POSTAGE.".

PRINTERS. The following stamps up to No. O108 were overprinted by De La Rue and thereafter Official stamps were printed or overprinted by the Security Printing Press at Nasik.

Service.
(O 7)

1867–73. *Optd. with Type* O **7**. *Wmk. Elephant's Head, T* **13**. *P* 14.

No.	Type	Description	Unused	Used
O20	**11**	½ a. blue (Die I)	1·00	8
O21	,,	½ a. pale blue (Die I)	85	10
O22	,,	½ a. blue (Die II)	15·00	5·00
O23	,,	1 a. brown	1·40	8
O24	,,	1 a. deep brown	1·10	8
O25	,,	1 a. chocolate	1·40	15
O26	,,	2 a. yellow	70	30
O27	,,	2 a. orange	40	8
O28	**17**	4 a. pale green (Die I)	25	10
O29	,,	4 a. green (Die I)	15	8
O30	**11**	8 a. rose (Die II)	25	8
O30*a*	,,	8 a. pale rose (Die II)	40	12
		Prepared for use, but not issued.		
O30*b*	**18**	6 a. 8 p. slate	10·00	

On H. M. S.
(O 8)

On H. M. S.
(O 9)

1874–82. *Optd. with Type* O **8**.

No.	Type	Description	Unused	Used
O31	**11**	½ a. blue (Die II)	35	8
O32	,,	1 a. brown	35	8
O33	,,	2 a. yellow	2·50	1·25
O33*a*	,,	2 a. orange	2·00	1·00
O34	**17**	4 a. green (Die I)	70	20
O35	**11**	8 a. rose (Die II)	75	75
		Optd. in blue-black.		
O36	**11**	½ a. blue (Die II)	25·00	5·00
O37	,,	1 a. brown	40·00	8·00

1883–99. *Wmk. Star, T* **34**. *P* 14. *Optd. with Type* O **9**.

No.	Type	Description	Unused	Used
O37*a*	**40**	3 p. aniline carmine	5	5
O38	**23**	½ a. deep blue-green	10	5
		a. Opt. double	—	20·00
O39	,,	½ a. blue-green	5	5
O40	**25**	1 a. brown-purple	5	5
		a. Opt. inverted	15·00	22·00
		b. Opt. double	—	30·00
O41	,,	1 a. plum	5	5
O42	**27**	2 a. pale blue	35	5
O43	,,	2 a. blue	5	5
O44	**29**	4 a. olive-green	12	5
O44*a*	,,	4 a. slate-green	20	5
O45	**31**	8 a. dull mauve	70	12
O46	,,	8 a. magenta	30	5
O47	**37**	1 r. green and rose	60	20
O48	,,	1 r. green and carmine	65	25
O37*a*/O48		*Set of* 7	1·10	35

1900. *Colours changed. Optd. with Type* O **9**.

No.	Type	Description	Unused	Used
O49	**23**	½ a. pale yellow-green	12	
O49*a*	,,	½ a. yellow-green	12	
O50	**25**	1 a. carmine	5	
		a. Opt. inverted	—	30·0
		b. Opt. double	—	35·0
O51	**26**	2 a. pale violet	50	
O52	,,	2 a. mauve	95	

1902–5. *Stamps of King Edward VII optd. wi[th] Type* O **9**.

No.	Type	Description	Unused	Used
O54	**41**	3 p. grey	20	
O55	,,	3 p. slate-grey (1905)	5	
O56	**42**	½ a. green	20	
O57	**43**	1 a. carmine	5	
O58	**44**	2 a. violet	30	
O59	,,	2 a. mauve	5	
O60	**47**	4 a. olive	15	
O61	,,	4 a. pale olive	15	
O62	**48**	6 a. olive-bistre	15	
O63	**49**	8 a. mauve	30	
O64	,,	8 a. magenta	35	
O65	**51**	1 r. green & carmine ('05)	30	
O54/O65		*Set of* 8	1·10	

1906. *New types. Optd. with Type* O **9**.

No.	Type	Description	Unused	Used
O66	**53**	½ a. green	5	
O67	**54**	1 a. carmine	5	

On SERVICE
(O 10) (14 mm.)

H. S.
M.
(O 9*a*)

SERVICE
(O 11) (21½ mm.)

1909. *Optd. with Type* O **9*a***.

No.	Type	Description	Unused	Used
O68	**52**	2 r. carmine & yell.-brn.	95	
O68*a*	,,	2 r. rose-red & yell.-brn.	70	
O69	,,	5 r. ultramarine & violet	2·00	
O70	,,	10 r. green and carmine	3·00	1·
O70*a*	,,	10 r. green and scarlet	5·50	2·
O71	**52**	15 r. blue & olive-brown	5·00	5·
O72	,,	25 r. brownish orge. & bl.	8·00	9·
O68/O72		*Set of* 5	17·00	15·

1912. *Stamps of King George V (wmk. Sin[gle] Star, T* **34**) *optd. with Type* O **10** *or* O [11] *(rupee values).*

No.	Type	Description	Unused	Used
O73	**55**	3 p. grey	5	
O74	,,	3 p. slate-grey	5	
O75	,,	3 p. blue-slate	5	
O76	**56**	½ a. yellow-green	5	
		a. Overprint double	10·00	
O77	,,	½ a. pale blue-green	5	
O80	**57**	1 a. rose-carmine	5	
O81	,,	1 a. carmine	5	
O82	,,	1 a. aniline carmine	5	
		a. Overprint double	—	22·
O83	**59**	2 a. mauve	5	
O84	,,	2 a. purple	5	
O85	**63**	4 a. deep olive	15	
O86	,,	4 a. olive-green	12	
O87	**64**	6 a. yellow-bistre	45	
O88	,,	6 a. deep bistre-brown	80	
O89	**65**	8 a. purple	50	
O89*a*	,,	8 a. mauve	30	
O90	,,	8 a. bright aniline mauve	1·50	
O91	**67**	1 r. red-brn. & blue-grn.	40	
O92	,,	2 r. rose-carm. & brown	70	
O93	,,	5 r. ultram. and violet	2·00	
O94	,,	10 r. green and scarlet	5·00	3·
O95	,,	15 r. blue and olive	7·00	7·
O96	,,	25 r. orange and blue	11·00	12·
O73/O96		*Set of* 13	25·00	22·

NINE

PIES
(O 12)

921. *No.* O80 *surch. with Type* O **12.**

)97	**57**	9 p. on 1 a. rose-carmine..	5	5

922. *No.* 197 *optd. with Type* O **10.**

)98	**57**	1 a. chocolate	5	5

ONE RUPEE

ONE RUPEE

(O **13**) (O **14**)

925. *Official stamps surcharged.*

(*a*) *Issue of* 1909, *as Type* O **13.**

)99	**52**	1 r. on 15 r. blue & olive	70	40
)100	,,	1 r. on 25 r. chest. & bl.	4·00	4·00
)101	,,	2 r. on 10 r. grn. & scar.	80	70
)101*a*	,,	2 r. on 10 r. grn. & carm.	20·00	20·00

(*b*) *Issue of* 1912, *with Type* O **14.**

)102	**67**	1 r. on 15 r. blue & olive	3·00	3·00
)103	,,	1 r. on 25 r. orange & blue	95	50
		a. Surch. inverted ..	60·00	

Error. Issue of 1912, *as Type* O **13.**

)104	**67**	2 r. on 10 r. grn. & scar.	£100	

ONE ANNA

SERVICE

ONE ANNA

(O **15**) (O **16**)

926. *No.* O62 *surch. with Type* O **15.**

)105	**48**	1 a. on 6 a. olive-bistre..	12	12

926. *Postage stamps of* 1911–22 (*wmk. Single Star*), *surch. as Type* O **16.**

)106	**58**	1 a. on 1½ a. choc. (A) ..	5	5
)107	,,	1 a. on 1½ a. choc. (B) ..	12	5
		a. Error. On 1 a. choc. (197)	40·00	
)108	**61**	1 a. on 2½ a. ultram. ..	20	25

The surcharge on No. O108 has no bars at top.

SERVICE SERVICE

(O **17**) (13½ mm.) (O **18**) (19½ mm.)

926–31. *Stamps of King George V* (*wmk. Multiple Star, T* **69**) *optd. with Types* O **17** *or* O **18** (*rupee values*).

)109	**55**	3 p. slate (1.10.29) ..	5	5
)110	**56**	½ a. green ('31).. ..	5	5
)111	**57**	1 a. chocolate	5	5
)112	**70**	2 a. purple	5	5
)113	**71**	4 a. sage-green	5	5
)115	**65**	8 a. reddish purple ..	20	5
)116	**66**	12 a. claret ..	15	5
)117	**67**	1 r. chocolate & grn. ('30)	50	5
)118	,,	2 r. carmine & orge. ('30)	1·00	45
)120	,,	10 r. green & scarlet ('31)	8·50	3·00
)109/O120		.. .. *Set of* 10	9·50	3·25

930. *As No.* O111, *but optd. as Type* O **10** (14 *mm.*).

)125	**57**	1 a. chocolate	3·50	1·00

932–36. *Stamps of King George V* (*wmk. Mult. Star, T* **69**) *optd. with Type* O **17.**

)126	**79**	½ a. green ('35) ..	5	5
)127	**80**	9 p. deep green ..	5	5
)127*a*	**81**	1 a. chocolate ('36) ..	5	5
)128	**82**	1¼ a. mauve ..	5	5
)129	**70**	2 a. vermilion	30	5
)130	**59**	2 a. vermilion ('35) ..	5	20
)130*a*	,,	2 a. vermilion (*small die*) ('36)	12	5
O131	**61**	2½ a. orange (22.4.32) ..	5	5
O132	**63**	4 a. sage-green ('35) ..	20	5
O133	**64**	6 a. bistre ('36)	45	50
O126/O133		.. .. *Set of* 8	80	60

1937–39. *Stamps of King George VI optd. as Types* O **17** *or* O **18** (*rupee values*).

O135	**91**	½ a. red-brown ('38) ..	5	5
O136	,,	9 p. green ('37) ..	35	5
O137	,,	1 a. carmine ('37) ..	5	5
O138	**100**	1 r. grey & red-brn. (5.38)	25	5
O139	,,	2 r. purple & brn. (5.38)	60	25
O140	,,	5 r. green & blue (10.38)	1·25	60
O141	,,	10 r. pur. & claret ('39)	2·00	1·10
O135/O141		.. .. *Set of* 7	4·00	1·90

SERVICE 1A

(O **19**)

INDIA POSTAGE 3 PS 3 PS SERVICE

(O **20**)

1939 (May). *Stamp of King George V, surch. with Type* O **19.**

O142	**82**	1 a. on 1¼ a. mauve ..	5	5

1939 (1 June)–**42.** *Typo. W* **69.** *P* 14.

O143	O **20**	3 p. slate	5	5
O144	,,	½ a. red-brown ..	5	5
O144*a*	,,	½ a. purple ('42) ..	5	5
O145	,,	9 p. green	5	5
O146	,,	1 a. carmine	5	5
O146*a*	,,	1 a. 3 p. bistre ('41) ..	5	5
O146*b*	,,	1½ a. dull violet ('42) ..	5	5
O147	,,	2 a. vermilion ..	5	5
O148	,,	2½ a. bright violet ..	5	5
O149	,,	4 a. brown	5	5
O150	,,	8 a. slate-violet ..	5	5
O143/O150		.. .. *Set of* 11	30	15

1948 (Aug.). *First Anniv. Indian Independence. Mahatma Gandhi postage stamps optd.* "SERVICE", *as Type* O **17.**

O150*a*	**305**	1½ a. brown	10·00	10·00
O150*b*	,,	3½ a. violet	95·00	£100
O150*c*	,,	12 a. grey-green ..	£225	
O150*d*	**306**	10 r. purple-brn. & lake	£750	

SERVICE POSTAGE 3 PS INDIA

SERVICE POSTAGE 1 Re INDIA

O **21.** Asokan Capital. O **22.**

1950–51. *Typo.* (O **21**) *or litho.* (O **22**). *W* **69.** *P*14.

O151	O **21**	3 p. slate-violet ..	5	5
O152	,,	6 p. purple-brown ..	5	5
O153	,,	9 p. green ..	5	5
O154	,,	1 a. turquoise.. ..	5	5
O155	,,	2 a. carmine	5	5
O156	,,	3 a. red-orange ..	15	5
O157	,,	4 a. lake ..	25	5
O158	,,	4 a. ultramarine ..	20	5
O159	,,	6 a. bright violet ..	25	5
O160	,,	8 a. red-brown ..	20	5
O161	O **22**	1 r. violet ..	30	5
O162	,,	2 r. rose-carmine ..	50	15
O163	,,	5 r. bluish-green ..	1·50	75
O164	,,	10 r. reddish brown ..	2·00	1·10
O151/O164		.. .. *Set of* 14	5·00	2·25

Dates of issue: 2.1.50, rupee values; 1.7.50, other values, except 4 a. ultramarine (1.10.51).

1957 (1 Apr.)–**58.** *Value in naye paise. Typo.* (*t.*) *or litho.* (*l.*) *W* **69.** *P* 14.

O165	O **21**	1 n.p. slate (*l.*) ..	5	5
		a. Slate-black (*l.*) ..	5	5
		b. Greenish slate (*t.*) ..	5	5
O166	,,	2 n.p. blackish violet (*t.*)	5	5
O167	,,	3 n.p. chocolate (*t.*) ..	5	5
O168	,,	5 n.p. green (*l.*) ..	5	5
		a. Deep emerald (*t.*) ..	5	5
O169	,,	6 n.p. turquoise-blue (*t.*)	5	5
O170	,,	13 n.p. scarlet (*t.*) ..	5	5
O171	,,	15 n.p. reddish violet (*l.*) (–.6.58) ..	5	5
		a. Reddish violet (*t.*)	35	30
O172	,,	20 n.p. red (*l.*) ..	5	5
		a. Vermilion (*t.*) ..	5	5
O173	,,	25 n.p. violet-blue (*l.*)..	5	5
		a. Ultramarine (*t.*) ..	5	5
O174	,,	50 n.p. red-brown (*l.*)	20	15
		a. Reddish brown (*t.*)	20	15
O165/O174		.. *Set of* 10	55	50

1958–71. *As Nos.* O165/74*a and* O161/4 *but W* **374** (*upright*). *Litho.* (*l*) *or typo.* (*t*). *P* 14.

O175	O **21**	1 n.p. slate-black (*t*) (–.1.59) ..	5	5
O176	,,	2 n.p. blackish violet (*t*) (–.1.59) ..	5	5
O177	,,	3 n.p. chocolate (*t*) (–.11.58) ..	5	5
O178	,,	5 n.p. deep emerald (*t*) (–.11.58) ..	5	5
O179	,,	6 n.p. turquoise-blue (*t*) (–.5.59) ..	5	5
O180	,,	10 n.p. deep grey-green (*l*) ('63) ..	15	10
		a. Deep grey-green (*t*) ('66?) ..	8	5
O181	,,	13 n.p. scarlet (*t*) ('63)	8	5
O182	,,	15 n.p. deep violet (*t*) (–.11.58) ..	8	5
		a. Light reddish violet (*t*) ('61) ..	8	5
O183	,,	20 n.p. vermilion (*t*) (–.5.59) ..	8	5
		a. Red (*t*) ('66?) ..	8	5
O184	,,	25 n.p. ultramarine (*t*) (–.7.59) ..	8	5
O185	,,	50 n.p. reddish brown (*t*) (–.6.59) ..	10	5
		a. Chestnut (*l*) ('66?)	8	5
O186	O **22**	1 r. reddish violet (*l*) (–.2.59) ..	10	5
O187	,,	2 r. rose-carmine (*l*) ('60)	20	8
		a. Wmk. sideways. *Pale rose-carmine* (*l*) ('69?) ..	15	8
O188	,,	5 r. slate-green (*l*) (–.7.59) ..	50	20
		a. Wmk. sideways. *Deep grey-green* (*l*) ('69?) ..	40	20
O189	,,	10 r. brown-lake (*l*) (–.7.59) ..	95	45
		a. Wmk. sideways (*l*) ('71) ..	85	40
O175/189*a*		.. .. *Set of* 15	1·60	95

शरणार्थी सहायता REFUGEE RELIEF

O **23** (O **24**) O **25**

1967 (20 Mar.). *Photo. W* **374** (*sideways*). *P* 15×14.

O190	O **23**	1 r. dull pur. (*shades*)..	10	5

1967 (15 Nov.)–**74(?).** *Wmk. Large Star and* "INDIA GOVT" *in sheet. Photo. P* 15×14. *No gum.*

O191	O **23**	2 p. violet ..	5	5
O192	,,	3 p. chocolate ..	5	5
O193	,,	5 p. green (*shades*) ..	5	5
O194	,,	6 p. turquoise-blue ..	5	5
O195	,,	10 p. myr.-grn. (*shades*)	5	5
O196	,,	15 p. plum	5	5
O197	,,	20 p. red	5	5
O198	,,	25 p. carm.-red (1974?)	5	5
O199	,,	30 p. ultramarine ..	5	5
O200	,,	50 p. chestnut ..	5	8
O191/200		.. .. *Set of* 10	20	25

1971. *Obligatory Tax. Refugee Relief.*
(a) Provisional issue. No. O193 *optd. with Type* O **24.**

O200	O **23**	5 p. yellowish green .. *(shades)*	5	5
		a. Wmk. sideways* ..		

(b) Issue for Bangalore. No. O193 *optd. with T* **602.**

O201	O **23**	5 p. yellowish green ..	15	15

(c) Definitive issue. Wmk. Large Star and INDIA GOVT. *in sheet**. *Litho. P* 15 × 14. *No gum.*

O202	O **25**	5 p. yellowish green ..	5	5
		a. Wmk. sideways ..		
		b. *Yellow-green* (*wmk. upright*)		

*The upright wmk. has the point of star upright and it stands on two points. Sideways wmk. has star pointing to left.

The surcharge on mail for the relief of refugees from the former East Pakistan referred to in the note after No. 651 also applied to official mail. The cost of the stamps used by each Government Department was charged against its budget and the additional charge for refugee stamps meant that each Department had to spend less to keep within its budget.

CHINA EXPEDITIONARY FORCE.

C. E. F.

(C)

Contemporary stamps of India overprinted with Type C, *in black.*

1900. *Stamps of Queen Victoria.*

C 1	**40**	3 p. carmine	5	5
C 2	**23**	½ a. green	5	5
C 3	**25**	1 a. brown-purple ..	12	15
C 4	**27**	2 a. ultramarine	30	50
C 5	**36**	2½ a. green	35	50
C 6	**28**	3 a. orange	1·00	1·75
C 7	**29**	4 a. olive-green	50	70
C 8	**31**	8 a. magenta ..	50	75
C 9	**32**	12 a. purple/*red*	75	90
C10	**37**	1 r. green and carmine ..	1·25	1·25
C1/10		.. .. *Set of* 10	4·50	6·00
		Prepared, but not issued.		
C10*a*	**26**	1 a. 6 p. sepia	15·00	

1904 (27 Feb.).

C11	**25**	1 a. carmine	1·75	1·25

1904. *Stamps of King Edward VII.*

C12	**41**	3 p. grey	20	30
		a. *Slate-grey*	40	40
C13	**43**	1 a. carmine	45	50
C14	**44**	2 a. pale violet ..	60	40
C15	**45**	2½ a. ultramarine ..	50	85
C16	**46**	3 a. orange-brown ..	55	85
C17	**47**	4 a. olive-green	1·00	1·25
C18	**49**	8 a. magenta	1·00	1·25
		a. *Mauve*		
C19	**50**	12 a. purple/*red*	1·50	2·50
C20	**51**	1 r. green and carmine ..	1·25	2·00
C12/20		.. .. *Set of* 9	6·00	9·00

1909. "POSTAGE & REVENUE."

C21	**53**	½ a. green (No. 149) ..	40	40
C22	**54**	1 a. carmine (No. 150) ..	25	20

1913–21. *Stamps of King George V. Wmk. Star.*

C23	**55**	3 p. slate-grey (1913) ..	15	30
C24	**56**	½ a. green	20	30
C25	**57**	1 a. aniline-carmine ..	30	60
C26	**58**	1½ a. chocolate (Type A) ..	65	1·50
C27	**59**	2 a. mauve	75	1·75
C28	**61**	2½ a. bright blue	1·00	1·75
C29	**62**	3 a. orange-brown ..	1·50	2·25
C30	**63**	4 a. olive-green	2·00	3·50
C32	**65**	8 a. mauve	2·00	3·50
C33	**66**	12 a. claret	2·00	3·50
C34	**67**	1 r. red-brn. & blue-grn.	7·00	9·00
C23/C34		.. .. *Set of* 11	16·00	25·00

INDIAN EXPEDITIONARY FORCES 1914-22.

I. E. F.

(E)

1914. *Stamps of India (King George V) optd. with Type E.*

E 1	**55**	3 p. slate-grey ..	5	5
		a. No stop after "F" ..	4·00	3·00
		b. No stop after "E" ..	5·00	4·50
		c. Overprint double ..	6·00	5·00
E 2	**56**	½ a. yellow-green ..	5	5
		a. No stop after "F" ..	5·00	5·00
E 3	**57**	1 a. aniline carmine ..	5	5
		a. No stop after "F" ..	6·00	5·00
E 4	,,	1 a. carmine	15	15
E 5	**59**	2 a. mauve	5	5
		a. No stop after "F" ..	10·00	10·00
		b. No stop after "E" ..	10·00	10·00
E 6	**61**	2½ a. ultramarine ..	10	20
		a. No stop after "F" ..	10·00	11·00
E 7	**62**	3 a. orange-brown ..	10	12
		a. No stop after "F" ..	11·00	14·00
E 8	**63**	4 a. olive-green ..	12	20
		a. No stop after "F" ..	12·00	12·00
E 9	**65**	8 a. purple	20	20
		a. No stop after "F" ..	14·00	14·00
E10	,,	8 a. mauve	1·25	2·00
E11	**66**	12 a. dull claret ..	1·25	1·75
		a. No stop after "F" ..	16·00	17·00
E12	,,	12 a. claret	75	2·50
E13	**67**	1 r. red-brn. & blue-grn.	1·25	2·50
E1/E13		.. .. *Set of* 10	2·75	4·75

INDIAN CUSTODIAN FORCES IN KOREA.

भारतीय
संरक्षा कटक
कोरिया

(K 1)

1953. *Stamps of India optd. with Type* K **1.**

K 1	**307**	3 p. slate-violet ..	5	5
K 2	**308**	6 p. purple-brown ..	5	5
K 3	**309**	9 p. yellow-green ..	8	8
K 4	**328**	1 a. turquoise	10	12
K 5	**311**	2 a. carmine	15	20
K 6	**313**	2½ a. lake	20	20
K 7	**312**	3 a. brown-orange ..	25	25
K 8	**314**	4 a. bright blue ..	35	50
K 9	**315**	6 a. violet	50	80
K10	**316**	8 a. turquoise-green ..	1·00	1·25
K11	**317**	12 a. dull blue	1·00	1·75
K12	**318**	1 r. dull violet & green	2·00	3·50
K1/K12		.. .. *Set of* 12	5·00	4·50

INDIAN U.N. FORCE IN CONGO.

U.N. FORCE
(INDIA)
CONGO

(U 1)

1962 (15 Jan.). *Stamps of India optd. with Type* U **1.** *W* **69** (*sideways*) (13 *n.p.*) *or W* **374** (*others*).

U1	**361**	1 n.p. blue-green ..	5	5
U2	,,	2 n.p. light brown ..	5	5
U3	,,	5 n.p. bright green ..	8	8
U4	,,	8 n.p. light blue-green ..	10	12
U5	,,	13 n.p. bright carmine-red	15	40
U6	,,	50 n.p. orange	20	75
U1/U6		.. .. *Set of* 6	50	1·25

INDIAN U.N. FORCE IN GAZA (PALESTINE).

UNEF

(Z 1)

1965 (15 Jan.). *No.* 492 *of India optd. with Type* Z **1.**

Z1	**449**	15 p. slate (C.)	10	10

INTERNATIONAL COMMISSION IN INDO-CHINA.

अन्तर्राष्ट्रीय आयोग कम्बोज	अन्तर्राष्ट्रीय आयोग लाओस	अन्तर्राष्ट्रीय आयोग वियत नाम
(N 1)	(N 2)	(N 3)

1954 (1 Dec.). *Stamps of India. W* **69.**

(a) Optd. as Type N **1,** *for use in Cambodia.*

N 1	**307**	3 p. slate-violet ..	5	5
N 2	**328**	1 a. turquoise	5	5
N 3	**311**	2 a. carmine	12	25
N 4	**316**	8 a. turquoise-green ..	50	1·00
N 5	**317**	12 a. dull blue	75	1·50

(b) Optd. as Type N **2,** *for use in Laos.*

N 6	**307**	3 p. slate-violet ..	5	5
N 7	**328**	1 a. turquoise	5	8
N 8	**311**	2 a. carmine	12	25
N 9	**316**	8 a. turquoise-green ..	50	1·00
N10	**317**	12 a. dull blue	75	1·50

(c) Optd. as Type N **3,** *for use in Vietnam.*

N11	**307**	3 p. slate-violet ..	5	5
N12	**328**	1 a. turquoise	5	8
N13	**311**	2 a. carmine	12	25
N14	**316**	8 a. turquoise-green ..	50	1·00
N15	**317**	12 a. dull blue	75	1·50
N1/N15		.. .. *Set of* 15	3·50	6·00

1957 (1 Apr.). *Stamps of India. W* **69** (*sideways*).

(a) Optd. as Type N **1** *for use in Cambodia.*

N16	**361**	2 n.p. light brown ..	5	5
N17	,,	6 n.p. grey	5	10
N18	,,	13 n.p. bright carmine-red	5	20
N19	,,	50 n.p. orange	15	75
N20	,,	75 n.p. reddish purple ..	25	1·25

(b) Optd. as Type N **2** *for use in Laos.*

N21	**361**	2 n.p. light brown ..	5	5
N22	,,	6 n.p. grey	5	10
N23	,,	13 n.p. bright carmine-red	5	20
N24	,,	50 n.p. orange	15	75
N25	,,	75 n.p. reddish purple ..	25	1·25

(c) Optd. as Type N **3** *for use in Vietnam.*

N26	**361**	2 n.p. light brown ..	5	5
N27	,,	6 n.p. grey	5	10
N28	,,	13 n.p. bright carmine-red	5	20
N29	,	50 n.p. orange	15	75
N30	,,	75 n.p. reddish purple ..	25	1·25
N16/N30		.. .. *Set of* 15	1·25	6·50

1962–65. *Stamps of India. W* **374.**

(a) Optd. as Type N **1** *for use in Cambodia.*

N32	**361**	2 n.p. light brown ..	40	90

(b) Optd. as Type N **2,** *for use in Laos.*

N38	**361**	2 n.p. light brown ..	40	90
N39	,,	3 n.p. dp. brown (1.8.63)	15	3[illegible]
N40	,,	5 n.p. brt. green (1.8.63)	10	2[illegible]
N41	,,	50 n.p. orange ('65) ..	25	6[illegible]
N42	,,	75 n.p. reddish pur. ('65)	40	9[illegible]

(c) Optd. as Type N **3,** *for use in Vietnam.*

N43	**361**	1 n.p. blue-green ..	20	4[illegible]
N44	,,	2 n.p. light brown ..	40	9[illegible]
N45	,,	3 n.p. deep brown ('63?)	15	3[illegible]
N46	,,	5 n.p. bright green ('63)	10	2[illegible]
N47	,,	50 n.p. orange ('65) ..	25	6[illegible]
N48	,,	75 n.p. reddish pur. ('65)	40	9[illegible]
N32/N48		.. .. *Set of* 12	3·00	7·0[illegible]

ICC (N 4)   ICC (N 5)

1965 (15 Jan.). *No. 492 of India optd. with Type* N **4** *for use in Laos and Viet-Nam.*

N49	**449**	15 p. slate (C.)	20	35

1968 (2 Oct.). *Nos. 504, etc. of India optd. as Type* N **5**, *in red, for use in Laos and Viet-Nam.*

N50	**461**	2 p. red-brown ..	10	15
N51	**462**	3 p. brown-olive ..	10	15
N52	**463**	5 p. cerise	10	15
N53	**466**	10 p. new blue	10	15
N54	**467**	15 p. bronze-green ..	10	15
N55	**472**	60 p. deep grey	15	30
N56	**474**	1 r. red-brown & plum	25	50
N57	**475**	2 r. new blue and deep slate-violet ..	50	1·00
N50/N57		.. .. *Set of* 8	75	1·50

INDIAN NATIONAL ARMY.

The following are stated to have been used in he Japanese-occupied areas of India during the rive on Imphal. Issued by the Indian National Army.

Typo. No gum. Perf. 11½ or imperf. 1 p. violet, 1 p. maroon, 1 a. green.

JAPANESE OCCUPATION OF THE ANDAMAN AND NICOBAR ISLANDS.

The Andaman Islands in the Bay of Bengal were occupied on the 23rd March 1942 and the Nicobar Islands in July 1942. Civil administration was resumed in October 1945.

The following Indian stamps were surcharged with large figures preceded by a decimal point:—

Postage stamps—.3 on ½ a. (No. 248), .5 on 1 a. (No. 250), .10 on 2 a. (No. 236*b*), .30 on 6 a. (No. 274).

Official stamps—.10 on 1 a. 3 p. (No. O146*b*), 20 on 3 p. (No. O143) from booklet panes 20 in red on 3 p. (No. O143).

INDIAN CONVENTION STATES.

These states were in convention status with British India and their stamps were valid throughout British Indian territory.

Stamps of Chamba, Gwalior, Jind, Nabha and Patiala ceased to be valid for postage on January 1st, 1951, when they were replaced by those of the Republic of India, valid from April 1st, 1950.

Stamps of India overprinted.

In the Queen Victoria issues we omit varieties due to broken type, including the numerous small "A" varieties which may have come about through damaged type. We do, however, list the small "G" in "GWALIOR" as this was definitely the result of the use of type of the wrong size.

Variations in the length of the words due to unequal spacing when setting are also omitted.

CHAMBA.

CHAMBA
STATE
(1)

1886–95. *Queen Victoria. Optd. with T* **1**.
1 **23** ½ a. blue-green 5 5
a. Error. "CHMABA" .. 20·00
b. "8TATE" .. 35·00
2 **25** 1 a. brown-purple 5 5
a. Error. "CHMABA" .. 35·00
b. Error. "8TATE" .. 40·00
3 ,, 1 a. plum 5 12
4 **26** 1½ a. sepia (1895) 35 60
5 **27** 2 a. dull blue 12 12
a. "CHAMBA" double ..
b. Error. "CHMABA" .. 75·00
c. Error "8TATE" .. 55·00
6 ,, 2 a. ultramarine 25 30
7 **36** 2½ a. green (1895) .. .. 2·25 2·00
8 **28** 3 a. orange (1887) 80 90
a. Error. "CHMABA" .. £250
9 ,, 3 a. brown-orange .. 20 20
10 **29** 4 a. olive-green 20 30
a. Error. "CHMABA" .. £200
b. Error. "8TATE" .. £150
11 ,, 4 a. slate-green 30 25
12 **21** 6 a. olive-bistre (1890) .. 40 55
13 ,, 6 a. bistre-brown 60 60
14 **31** 8 a. dull mauve (1887) .. 60 80
a. Error. "CHMABA" .. £250
15 ,, 8 a. magenta 30 60
16 **32** 12 a. purple/*red* (1890) .. 50 65
a. Error. "CHMABA" .. £350
b. Error. "SLATE" .. £500
17 **33** 1 r. slate (1887) .. .. 3·50 6·00
a. Error. "CHMABA" .. £500
18 **37** 1 r. green & carm. (1895) .. 50 70
19 **38** 2 r. carm. & yell.-brn. ('95) 8·00
20 ,, 3 r. brown & green (1895) 10·00
21 ,, 5 r. ultram. & violet (1895) 11·00
a. Opt. double, one albino
1/21 .. .. .. *Set of* 15 32·00

1900–4. *Colours changed.*
22 **40** 3 p. carmine 5 5
23 ,, 3 p. grey (1904) 8 5
a. Opt. inverted .. 18·00
24 **23** ½ a. pale yellow-green (1902) 5 5
25 ,, ½ a. yellow-green 5 8
26 **25** 1 a. carmine (1902) .. 5 5
27 **27** 2 a. pale violet (1903) .. 1·25 1·50

1903–5. *King Edward VII. Optd. with T* **1**.
28 **41** 3 p. pale grey 5 5
29 ,, 3 p. slate-grey (1905) .. 5 5
30 **42** ½ a. green 5 5
31 **43** 1 a. carmine 5 5
32 **44** 2 a. pale violet (1904) .. 12 12
33 ,, 2 a. mauve 10 10
34 **46** 3 a. orange-brown (1905) .. 30 25
35 **47** 4 a. olive-green (1904) .. 40 35
36 **48** 6 a. olive-bistre (1905) .. 50 65
37 **49** 8 a. dull mauve (1904) .. 50 55
38 ,, 8 a. magenta 60 65
39 **50** 12 a. purple/*red* (1905) .. 60 65
40 **51** 1 r. green & carmine (1904) 80 90
28/40 .. .. *Set of* 10 3·75 4·00

1907. *Nos. 149/50 of India optd. with T* **1**.
41 **53** ½ a. green 5 5
42 **54** 1 a. carmine 10 12

1913. *King George V optd. with T* **1**.
43 **55** 3 p. slate-grey 5 5
44 **56** ½ a. green 5 5
45 **57** 1 a. rose-carmine 5 5
46 ,, 1 a. aniline carmine .. 5 5
47 **59** 2 a. mauve 5 8
48 **62** 3 a. orange-brown .. 12 25
49 **63** 4 a. olive 25 25
50 **64** 6 a. olive-bistre 25 25
51 **65** 8 a. purple 30 40
52 **66** 12 a. dull claret 60 80
53 **67** 1 r. brown and green .. 90 1·25
43/53 .. .. *Set of* 10 2·75 3·25

CHAMBA
(2)

1921. *No. 192 of India optd. with T* **2**.
54 **57** 9 p. on 1 a. rose-carmine .. 40 50

1922–27. *Optd. with T* **1**. *New values, etc.*
55 **57** 1 a. chocolate 5 5
56 **58** 1½ a. chocolate (Type A) .. 4·50 5·00
57 ,, 1½ a. chocolate (Type B) .. 10 12
58 ,, 1½ a. rose-carm. (Type B) ('27) 30 35
59 **61** 2½ a. ultramarine 30 35
60 ,, 2½ a. orange (1927) 30 35
61 **62** 3 a. ultramarine 50 65

CHAMBA STATE **(3)** **CHAMBA STATE** **(4)**

1927–37. *King George V (Nasik printing, wmk. Mult. Star). Optd. at Nasik with T* **3** *or* **4** *(1 r.).*
62 **55** 3 p. slate ('28) 5 5
63 **56** ½ a. green ('28) 5 5
64 **80** 9 p. deep green ('32) .. 5 5
65 **57** 1 a. chocolate 5 5
66 **82** 1¼ a. mauve 5 5
67 **58** 1½ a. rose-carm. (B) ('32) .. 5 5
68 **70** 2 a. purple ('28) 12 12
69 **61** 2½ a. orange ('32) 25 25
70 **62** 3 a. bright blue ('28) .. 30 30
71 **71** 4 a. sage-green ('28) .. 25 30
72 **64** 6 a. bistre ('37) .. .. 22·00
73 **65** 8 a. reddish purple ('28) .. 35 40
74 **66** 12 a. claret ('28) 50 90
75 **67** 1 r. chocolate & green ('28) 80 90
62/75 *(excl. 72)* .. *Set of* 13 2·50 3·00

1935–36. *New types and colours. Optd. with T* **3**.
76 **79** ½ a. green 5 5
77 **81** 1 a. chocolate 5 5
78 **59** 2 a. vermilion (No. 236*a*) 8 8
79 ,, 2 a. vermilion (*small die*, No. 236*b*) .. .. 6·00
80 **62** 3 a. carmine 30 30
81 **63** 4 a. sage-green ('36) .. 35 35

CHAMBA STATE
(5)

CHAMBA **(6)** **CHAMBA** **(7)**

1938. *King George VI. Optd. with T* **3** *(3 p. to 1 a), T* **5** *(2 a. to 12 a.) or T* **4** *(rupee values).*
82 **91** 3 p. slate 8 10
83 ,, ½ a. red-brown 12 30
84 ,, 9 p. green 30 30
85 ,, 1 a. carmine 8 12
86 **92** 2 a. vermilion 25 35
87 **93** 2½ a. bright violet 30 35
88 **94** 3 a. yellow-green .. .. 1·10 1·2
89 **95** 3½ a. bright blue 30 5
90 **96** 4 a. brown 30 5
91 **97** 6 a. turquoise-green .. 2·50 4·0
92 **98** 8 a. slate-violet .. .. 50 1·2
93 **99** 12 a. lake .. .. .. 1·10 1·7
94 **100** 1 r. grey and red-brown .. 2·50 3·0
95 ,, 2 r. purple and brown .. 3·75 5·2
96 ,, 5 r. green and blue .. 7·00 8·0
97 ,, 10 r. purple and claret .. 17·00 20·0
98 ,, 15 r. brown and green .. 28·00 36·0
99 ,, 25 r. slate-violet & purple 40·00 50·0
82/99 .. .. *Set of* 18 90·00 £12

1943–48. *Optd. with T* **6** *(to 12 a.),* "CHAMBA" *only, as in T* **5** *(14 a.) or T* **7** *(rupee values).*

(a) Stamps of 1937.
100 **91** ½ a. red-brown 50 4
101 ,, 1 a. carmine 60 5
102 **100** 1 r. grey and red-brown 4·00 4·5
103 ,, 2 r. purple and brown 4·00 5·5
104 ,, 5 r. green and blue .. 16·00 17·0
105 ,, 10 r. purple and claret .. 25·00 26·0
106 ,, 15 r. brown and green .. 26·00 29·0
107 ,, 25 r. slate-violet & purple 40·00 45·0
100/107 .. .. *Set of* 8 £100 £12

(b) Stamps of 1940–43.
108 **100a** 3 p. slate 8
109 ,, ½ a. purple 8
110 ,, 9 p. green 8
111 ,, 1 a. carmine 8
112 **101** 1½ a. dull violet .. 8
113 ,, 2 a. vermilion 8 2
114 ,, 3 a. bright violet .. 10 2
115 ,, 3½ a. bright blue 10 3
116 **102** 4 a. brown 10 3
117 ,, 6 a. turquoise-green .. 30 6
118 ,, 8 a. slate-violet .. 50 1·2
119 ,, 12 a. lake .. .. 65 1·2
120 **103** 14 a. purple ('48) .. 2·25 4·0
108/120 .. .. *Set of* 13 4·00 7·0

OFFICIAL STAMPS.

SERVICE

CHAMBA
STATE
(O 1)

1886–98. *Queen Victoria. Optd. with Type* O **1**
O 1 **23** ½ a. blue-green 5
a. Error. "CHMABA" .. 15·00
b. Error. "SERV CE" .. — 18·0
c. Error. "8TATE" .. 27·00
O 2 **25** 1 a. brown-purple .. 5
a. Error. "CHMABA" .. 22·00
b. Error. "SERV CE" .. 35·00
c. Error. "8TATE" .. 40·00
O 3 ,, 1 a. plum 5
a. "SERVICE" double .. 16·00 7·5
O 4 **27** 2 a. dull blue 10 1
a. Error. "CHMABA" .. 90·00
O 5 ,, 2 a. ultramarine (1887) .. 5
O 6 **28** 3 a. orange (1890) .. 65 7
a. Error. "CHMABA" .. £110
O 7 ,, 3 a. brown-orange .. 45 5
O 8 **29** 4 a. olive-green 8
a. Error. "CHMABA" .. 95·00
b. Error. "SERV CE" .. £110
c. Error. "8TATE" .. 65·00
O 9 ,, 4 a. slate-green 25 3
O10 **21** 6 a. olive-bistre (1890) .. 30 3
O11 ,, 6 a. bistre-brown .. 90 1·0
O12 **31** 8 a. dull mauve (1887) .. 30 4
a. Error. "CHMABA" .. £225
O13 ,, 8 a. magenta 35 5
O14 **32** 12 a. purple/*red* (1890) .. 1·75 2·7
a. Error. "CHMABA" .. £225
O15 **33** 1 r. slate (1890) .. .. 3·50 3·5
a. Error. "CHMABA" .. £275
O16 **37** 1 r. green and carmine (1898) .. .. 1·10 1·2
O1/16 .. .. *Set of* 10 6·50 7·5

1902–4. *Colours changed.*
O17 **40** 3 p. grey (1904) 5
O18 **23** ½ a. pale yellow-green .. 5
O19 ,, ½ a. yellow-green 5
O20 **25** 1 a. carmine 8
O21 **27** 1 a. pale violet (1903) .. 50 8

1903-5. *King Edward VII. Optd. as Type* O **1.**

O22	**41**	3 p. pale grey	10	5
O23	,,	3 p. slate-green (1905) ..	5	5
O24	**42**	½ a. yellow-green	5	5
O25	**43**	1 a. carmine	5	5
O26	**44**	1 a. pale violet (1904) ..	25	12
O27	,,	2 a. mauve	5	5
O28	**47**	4 a. olive-green (1905) ..	25	25
O29	**49**	8 a. dull mauve (1905) ..	40	45
O30	,,	8 a. magenta	40	45
O31	**51**	1 r. green & carmine (1905)	40	45
O22/O31		.. .. *Set of* 7	1·75	1·75

The 2 a. mauve King Edward VII, overprinted "On H.M.S.", was discovered in Calcutta, but was not sent to Chamba, and is an unissued variety. (*Price un. £5*)

1907. *Nos.* 149/50 *of India, optd. with Type* O **1.**

O32	**53**	½ a. green	8	5
		a. Opt. inverted	£200	
O33	**54**	1 a. carmine	30	25

The error, No. O32*a* was due to an inverted cliché which was corrected after a few sheets had been printed.

1913-14. *King George V Official stamps (wmk. Single Star) optd. with T* **1.**

O34	**55**	3 p. slate-grey	5	5
O35	,,	3 p. grey	5	5
O36	**56**	½ a. yellow-green	5	5
O37	,,	½ a. pale blue-green ..	5	5
O38	**57**	1 a. aniline carmine ..	5	5
O39	,,	1 a. rose-carmine	5	5
O40	**59**	2 a. mauve (1914) ..	8	12
O41	**63**	4 a. olive	25	30
O42	**65**	8 a. purple	40	45
O43	**67**	1 r. brown & green ('14)..	50	55
O34/O43		.. .. *Set of* 7	1·25	1·50

1914. *King George V. Optd. with Type* O **1.**

O44	**59**	2 a. mauve	2·00	3·00
O45	**63**	4 a. olive	4·50	5·50

1921. *No.* O97 *of India optd. with T* **2** *at top.*

O46	**57**	9 p. on 1 a. rose-carmine	8	25

1925. *As* 1913-14. *New colour.*

O47	**57**	1 a. chocolate	5	5

CHAMBA STATE SERVICE (O 2) — CHAMBA STATE SERVICE (O 3)

1927-39. *King George V (Nasik printing, wmk. Mult. Star), optd. as Nasik with Type* O **2** *or* O **3** *(rupee values).*

O48	**55**	3 p. slate	5	5
O49	**56**	½ a. green	5	5
O50	**80**	9 p. deep green	5	5
O51	**57**	1 a. chocolate	5	5
O52	**82**	1¼ a. mauve	5	5
O53	**70**	2 a. purple	8	10
O54	**71**	4 a. sage-green	5	5
O55	**65**	8 a. reddish purple ..	10	30
O56	**66**	12 a. claret	40	45
O57	**67**	1 r. chocolate and green	50	55
O58	,,	2 r. carmine & orge. ('39)	4·00	
O59	,,	5 r. ultram. & pur. ('39)	6·00	
O60	,,	10 r. green & scarlet ('39)	7·00	
O48/O60		.. .. *Set of* 13	15·00	

1935-39. *New Types and colours. Optd. with Type* O **2.**

O61	**79**	½ a. green	5	5
O62	**81**	1 a. chocolate	5	5
O63	**59**	2 a. vermilion	5	5
O64	,,	2 a. verm. (*small die*) ('39)	5	5
O65	**63**	4 a. sage-green ('36) ..	5	10

1938-40. *King George VI. Optd. with Type* O **2** *or* O **3** *(rupee values).*

O66	**91**	9 p. green	25	30
O67	,,	1 a. carmine	12	25
O68	**100**	1 r. grey & red-brn. ('40?)	£110	£110
O69	,,	2 r. pur. & brown ('40)	2·50	3·00
O70	,,	5 r. green and blue ('40)	4·50	5·50
O71	,,	10 r. pur. & claret ('40)	9·00	10·00
O66/O71		.. .. *Set of* 6	£120	£120

CHAMBA SERVICE (O 4)

1941-43. (*a*) *Official stamps optd. with T* **6.**

O72	O **20**	3 p. slate	8	5
O73	,,	½ a. red-brown ..	30	12
O74	,,	½ a. purple	25	8
O75	,,	9 p. green	8	5
O76	,,	1 a. carmine	8	8
O77	,,	1 a. 3 p. bistre ..	2·50	1·25
O78	,,	1½ a. dull violet ..	10	25
O79	,,	2 a. vermilion.. ..	12	25
O80	,,	2½ a. bright violet ..	35	35
O81	,,	4 a. brown	40	60
O82	,,	8 a. slate-violet ..	80	90

(*b*) *Postage stamps optd. with Type* O **4.**

O83	**100**	1 r. grey and red-brown	2·00	3·00
O84	,,	2 r. purple and brown..	2·25	3·00
O85	,,	5 r. green and blue ..	4·50	7·00
O86	,,	10 r. purple and claret ..	8·00	9·00
O72/O86		.. .. *Set of* 14	16·00	22·00

FARIDKOT.

For earlier issues, see under INDIAN FEUDATORY STATES.

FARIDKOT STATE (1)

1887 (1 JAN.)**-1900.** *Queen Victoria. Optd. with T* **1.**

1	**23**	½ a. deep green	5	5
2	**25**	1 a. brown-purple	10	25
3	,,	1 a. plum	30	40
4	**27**	2 a. blue	50	50
5	,,	2 a. deep blue	45	50
6	**28**	3 a. orange..	40	50
7	,,	3 a. brown-orange ..	45	50
8	**29**	4 a. olive-green	45	50
		a. Error "ARIDKOT" ..	50·00	
9	,,	4 a. slate-green	50	65
10	**21**	6 a. olive-bistre	1·10	1·10
		a. Error. "ARIDKOT" ..	50·00	
11	,,	6 a. bistre-brown	65	70
12	**31**	8 a. dull mauve	1·10	1·10
		a. Error. "ARIDKOT" ..	60·00	
13	,,	8 a. magenta	1·10	1·25
14	**32**	12 a. purple/*red* (1900) ..	4·00	4·00
15	**33**	1 r. slate	4·00	4·00
		a. Error. "ARIDKOT" ..	£275	
16	**37**	1 r. green & carm. (1893)	4·00	4·00
1/16		.. .. *Set of* 10	16·00	16·00

The ½ a., 1 a., 2 a., 3 a., 4 a., 8 a. and 1 r. are known with broken "O" (looking like a "C") in "FARIDKOT".

1900. *Optd. with T* **1.**

17	**40**	3 p. carmine	15	30

OFFICIAL STAMPS.

SERVICE

FARIDKOT STATE (O 1)

1886-96. *Queen Victoria. Optd. with Type* O **1.**

O 1	**23**	½ a. deep green	5	10
		a. Error. "SERV CE" ..	24·00	
O 2	**25**	1 a. brown-purple ..	25	30
O 3	,,	1 a. plum	30	15
		a. Error. "SERV CE" ..	33·00	
O 4	**27**	2 a. dull blue	50	50
		a. Error. "SERV CE" ..	45·00	
O 5	,,	2 a. deep blue	40	50
O 6	**28**	3 a. orange	40	80
O 7	,,	3 a. brown-orange ..	40	65
O 8	**29**	4 a. olive-green	50	65
		a. Error. "SERV CE" ..	45·00	
O 9	,,	4 a. slate-green	65	80
O10	**21**	6 a. olive-bistre	4·00	3·50
		a. Error. "ARIDKOT" ..	55·00	
		b. Error. "SERVIC" ..	45·00	
O11	,,	6 a. bistre-brown ..	1·25	1·50
O12	**31**	8 a. dull mauve	60	75
		a. Error. "SERV CE" ..	60·00	
O13	,,	8 a. magenta	1·10	1·25
O14	**33**	1 r. slate	4·00	5·00
O15	**37**	1 r. green & carm. (1896)	6·50	8·00
O1/O15		.. .. *Set of* 9	11·00	15·00

The ½ a., 1 a., 2 a., 3 a., 4 a. and 8 a. are known with the broken "O".

This State ceased to use overprinted stamps after March 31, 1901.

GWALIOR.

गवालियर

GWALIOR (1) — GWALIOR गवालियर (2)

1885-96. *Queen Victoria.*

A. *Optd. with T* **1.**

(*a*) *Space between two lines of overprint* 13 *mm. Hindi inscription* 13 *to* 14 *mm. long.* (May 1885.)

1	**23**	½ a. blue-green	4·00	4·00
2	**25**	1 a. brown-purple	4·00	4·00
3	**27**	2 a. dull blue..	5·00	4·00

A variety exists of the ½ a. in which the space between the two lines of overprint is only 9½ mm. but this is probably from a proof sheet.

(*b*) *Space between two lines of overprint* 15 *mm. on* 6 *a. and* 16 *to* 17 *mm. on other values.* (June 1885.)

(I) *Hindi inscription* 13 *to* 14 *mm. long.*

(II) *Hindi inscription* 15 *to* 15½ *mm. long.*

			I.		II.	
4	**23**	½ a. blue-green	5·00	—	—	3·00
5	**25**	1 a. brown-pur.	5·00	—	5·00	—
6	**26**	1½ a. sepia ..	5·00	—	6·00	—
7	**27**	2 a. dull blue..	5·00	—	6·00	—
8	**17**	4 a. green ..	5·00	—	8·00	—
9	**21**	6 a. olive-bistre	8·00	—	8·00	—
10	**31**	8 a. dull mauve	8·00	—	8·00	—
11	**33**	1 r. slate ..	8·00	—	9·00	—
4/11		.. *Set of* 8	45·00			

These two overprints are both found on the same sheet in the proportion of three of the former to one of the latter.

B. *Optd. with T* **2.**

(I) *Hindi inscription* 13 *to* 14 *mm. long.*

(II) *Hindi inscription* 15 *to* 15½ *mm. long.*

(*a*) *In red.* (Sept. 1885.)

			I.		II.	
12	**23**	½ a. blue-green	8	10	10	10
13	**27**	2 a. dull blue ..	1·25	1·25	3·50	3·50
14	**17**	4 a. green ..	3·00	3·50	6·00	6·00
15	**33**	1 r. slate ..	3·50	3·50	5·00	5·00

Reprints have been made of Nos. 12 to 15, but the majority of the specimens have the word "REPRINT" overprinted upon them.

(*b*) *In black.* (1885-96.)

16	**23**	½ a. bl.-grn. ('89)	5	5	5	5
		a. Opt. double	—	—	22·00	—
		b. Error. "GWALICR"	†		21·00	—
		c. Small "G"	†		24·00	24·00
17	**24**	9 p. carm. ('91)	5·00	5·00	5·00	4·50
18	**25**	1 a. brn.-purple	8	5	5	5
19	,,	1 a. plum ..	—	—	5	5
		a. Small "G"	†		26·00	26·00
20	**26**	1½ a. sepia ..	5	5	5	5
21	**27**	2 a. dull blue..	35	30	15	5
22	,,	2 a. deep blue	40	40	25	8
		a. Small "G"	†		32·00	32·00
23	**36**	2½ a. yell.grn. ('96)	†		40	80
		a. Error. "GWALICR"	†		65·00	—
24	**28**	3 a. orange ..	35	35	60	50
25	,,	3 a. brn.-orge.	40	35	10	8
		a. Small "G"	†		45·00	—
26	**29**	4 a. ol.-grn. ('89)	50	40	30	30
27	,,	4 a. slate-green	70	40	30	12
		a. Small "G"	†		45·00	—
28	**21**	6 a. olive-bistre ..	40	50	50	40
29	,,	6 a. bistre-brn.	10	10	30	40
30	**31**	8 a. dull mauve	50	60	30	25
31	,,	8 a. magenta ..	—	—	90	90
32	**32**	12 a. pur./*red* ('91)	1·25	1·25	30	10
		a. Pair, with and without opt.	†		—	—

33 **33** 1 r. slate ('89) 5·00 30 30
34 **37** 1 r. green and carm. ('96) † 80 90
a. Error. "GWALICR" † 65·00 —
35 **38** 2 r. carmine & yell.brn. ('96) † 4·50 4·00
a. Small "G" † 55·00 —
36 „ 3 r. brown and green ('96) † 8·00 5·00
a. Small "G" † 65·00 —
37 „ 5 r. ultram. & violet ('96) † 8·00 5·00
a. Small "G" † 65·00 —
16/37 .. *Set of* 16 22·00 20·00

The ½ a., 1 a., 2 a. and 3 a. exist with space between "1" and "o" of "GWALIOR".

1899–1908. *Optd. with T* **2** (II).

38 **40** 3 p. carmine 5 5
a. Opt. inverted .. .. 26·00 26·00
b. Small "G" .. .. 40·00
39 „ 3 p. grey (1904) .. .. 1·25
a. Small "G" .. 40·00
40 **23** ½ a. pale yellow-grn. (1901) 5 5
41 **25** 1 a. carmine (1901) .. 5 5
42 **27** 2 a. pale violet (1901) .. 12 5
43 **36** 2½ a. ultramarine (1903) .. 8 10
38/43 .. .. *Set of* 6 1·25

"GWALIOR" 13 *mm. long. Opt. spaced* 2¾ *mm.* (1908).

44 **38** 3 r. brown and green .. 12·00
45 „ 5 r. ultramarine and violet 13·00

1903–08. *King Edward VII. Optd. as T* **2**.

I. "GWALIOR" 14 *mm. long. Overprint spaced* 1¾ *mm.*

II. "GWALIOR" 13 *mm. long. Overprint spaced* 2¾ *mm.*

			I.		II.	
46	**41**	3 p. pale grey	5	5	5	5
		a. Slate-grey	5	5	5	5
48	**42**	½ a. green ..	5	5	†	
49	**43**	1 a. carmine	5	5	12	10
50	**44**	2 a. pale violet	8	8	†	
		a. Mauve	8	5	5	5
52	**45**	2½ a. ultram.	1·75	—	12	25
53	**46**	3 a. orange-brn.	10	10	8	5
54	**47**	4 a. olive-grn.	25	25	5	5
		a. Slate-green	30	30	†	
56	**48**	6 a. olive-bistre	30	30	25	25
57	**49**	8 a. dull mauve	35	35	40	40
		a. Magenta	25	12	40	40
59	**50**	12 a. purple/*red*	25	30	25	30
60	**51**	1 r. grn. & carm.	35	40	55	30
61	**52**	2 r. carm. & yell.-brn.	12·00	12·00	3·50	3·50
62	„	3 r. brn. & grn.	†		6·50	6·50
		a. Red-brown & grn.	†		6·50	8·00
63	„	5 r. ultram. & vio.	†		5·50	5·50
46/63		.. .. *Set of* 14			15·00	15·00

Dates of issue: Opt. I—1904, Nos. 50, 53; 1905, Nos. 46, 52, 54, 57, 59, 60; 1906, No. 56; Others 1903. Opt. II—1908.

1907. *Nos.* 149 *and* 150 *of India optd. as T* **2**. "GWALIOR" 14 *mm. long. Overprint spaced* 1¾ *mm.*

64 **53** ½ a. green 5 5

"GWALIOR" 13 *mm. long. Opt. spaced* 2¾ *mm.*

65 **53** ½ a. green 5 5
66 **54** 1 a. carmine 5 5

1912–14. *King George V. Optd. as T* **2**.

67 **55** 3 pies, slate-grey 5 5
68 **56** ½ a. green 5 5
a. Opt. inverted ..
69 **57** 1 a. aniline carmine .. 5 5
a. Opt. double .. .. 16·00
70 **59** 2 a. mauve 5 5
71 **62** 3 a. orange-brown .. 5 5
72 **63** 4 a. olive (1913) .. 5 5
73 **64** 6 a. olive-bistre .. 25 5
74 **65** 8 a. purple (1913) .. 10 5
75 **66** 12 a. dull claret (1914) .. 30 12
76 **67** 1 r. brown and green .. 25 25
a. Opt. double, one albino .. 45·00
77 „ 2 r. carm.-rose & brown 1·00 50
a. Opt. double, one albino ..
78 „ 5 r. ultramarine and violet 2·00 2·00
a. Opt. double, one albino ..
67/78 .. .. *Set of* 12 3·25 3·00

GWALIOR

(**3**)

1922. *No.* 192 *of India optd. with T* **3**.

79 **57** 9 p. on 1 a. rose-carmine .. 5 5

1923–7. *Optd. T* **2**. *New colours and values.*

80 **57** 1 a. chocolate ('23) .. 5 5
81 **58** 1½ a. chocolate (B) ('25) .. 10 12
82 „ 1½ a. rose-carm. (B) ('27) .. 5 5
83 **61** 2½ a. ultramarine ('25) .. 25 25
84 „ 2½ a. orange ('27) .. 8 5
85 **62** 3 a. ultramarine ('24) .. 8 5

GWALIOR गवालियर (**4**)

GWALIOR गवालियर (**5**)

1928–36. *King George V (Nasik printing, wmk. Mult. Star), optd. as Nasik with T* **4** *or* **5** *(rupee values).*

86 **55** 3 p. slate ('32) .. 5 5
87 **56** ½ a. green ('30) .. 5 5
88 **80** 9 p. deep green ('33) .. 5 5
89 **57** 1 a. chocolate .. 5 5
90 **82** 1¼ a. mauve ('36) .. 5 5
91 **70** 2 a. purple .. 5 5
92 **62** 3 a. bright blue .. 12 5
93 **71** 4 a. sage-green .. 25 5
94 **65** 8 a. reddish purple .. 30 10
95 **66** 12 a. claret .. 35 35
96 **67** 1 r. chocolate and green .. 65 65
97 „ 2 r. carmine and orange .. 1·25 1·25
98 „ 5 r. ultram. & purple ('29) 5·50 5·50
99 „ 10 r. green and scarlet ('30) 11·00 11·00
100 „ 15 r. blue and olive ('30) .. 13·00 13·00
101 „ 25 r. orange and blue ('30) 21·00 21·00
86/101 .. .. *Set of* 16 45·00 45·00

1936. *New types and colours. Optd. with T* **4**.

102 **79** ½ a. green .. 5 5
103 **81** 1 a. chocolate .. 5 5
104 **59** 2 a. vermilion .. 5 5

1938–49. *King George VI. Optd. with T* **4** *or* **5** *(rupee values).*

105 **91** 3 p. slate ('40) .. 30 10
106 „ ½ a. red-brown .. 30 10
107 „ 9 p. green ('40) .. 8·00 6·00
108 „ 1 a. carmine .. 25 10
109 **94** 3 a. yellow-green ('39) .. 30 25
110 **96** 4 a. brown .. 3·00 3·00
111 **97** 6 a. turquoise-green ('39) 40 40
112 **100** 1 r. grey & red.-brn. ('45) 65 80
113 „ 2 r. purple & brown ('49) 2·75 2·75
114 „ 5 r. green and blue ('49) 8·00 8·00
115 „ 10 r. purple & claret ('49) 11·00 11·00
116 „ 15 r. brown & green ('49) 21·00 22·00
117 „ 25 r. slate-vio. & pur. ('49) 26·00 28·00
105/117 .. .. *Set of* 13 70·00 70·00

1944–8. *King George VI. Optd. with T* **4**.

118 **100a** 3 p. slate .. 8 8
119 „ ½ a. purple .. 8 8
120 „ 9 p. green .. 8 8
121 „ 1 a. carmine .. 8 8
a. Opt. double, .. 16·00 16·00
122 **101** 1½ a. dull violet .. 8 8
123 „ 2 a. vermilion .. 8 8
124 „ 3 a. bright violet .. 20 15
125 **102** 4 a. brown .. 12 25
126 „ 6 a. turquoise-grn. ('48) 1·50 1·50
127 „ 8 a. slate-violet ('45) .. 1·50 1·50
128 „ 12 a. lake ('45) .. 1·50 1·50
118/128 .. .. *Set of* 11 4·50 5·00

GWALIOR
गवालियर

(**6**)

1949. *King George VI. Optd. with T* **6** *at the Gwalior Govt. Ptg. Wks.*

129 **100a** 3 p. slate .. 30 30
130 „ ½ a. purple .. 30 30
131 „ 1 a. carmine .. 40 40
132 **101** 2 a. vermilion .. 65 65
133 „ 3 a. bright violet .. 2·00 2·00
134 **102** 4 a. brown .. 1·50 1·75
135 „ 6 a. turquoise-green .. 7·00 7·00
136 „ 8 a. slate-violet .. 11·00 11·00
137 „ 12 a. lake .. 26·00 26·00
129/137 .. .. *Set of* 9 45·00 45·00

OFFICIAL STAMPS.

गवालियर

सरविस

(O 1)

1895–96. *Queen Victoria. Optd. with Type* O **1**.

O 1 **23** ½ a. blue-green .. 5 5
a. Hindi characters trans. .. 7·00 7·00
b. 4th Hindi char. omitted .. — 8·00
c. Opt. double .. — 35·00
O 2 **25** 1 a. brown-purple .. 8 5
O 3 „ 1 a. plum .. 5 5
a. Hindi characters trans. .. 7·00 8·00
b. 4th Hindi char. omitted .. — 10·00
O 4 **27** 2 a. dull blue .. 12 5
O 5 „ 2 a. deep blue .. 5 5
a. Hindi characters trans. .. 11·00
b. 4th Hindi char. omitted .. 20·00 20·00
O 6 **29** 4 a. olive-green .. 30 30
a. Hindi characters trans. .. 40·00
b. 4th Hindi char. omitted .. — 40·00
O 7 „ 4 a. slate-green .. 15 12
O 8 **31** 8 a. dull mauve .. 50 50
O 9 „ 8 a. magenta .. 35 20
a. Hindi characters trans. .. £150
b. 4th Hindi char. omitted ..
O10 **37** 1 r. green & carm. (1896) 55 60
a. Hindi characters trans. .. £300
O1/O10 *Set of* 6 1·00 1·00

In the errors listed above it is the last two Hindi characters that are transposed, so that the word reads "Sersiv".

1901–4. *Colours changed.*

O23 **40** 3 p. carmine (1902) .. 5 5
O24 „ 3 p. grey (1904) .. 10 8
O25 **23** ½ a. pale yellow-green .. 5 5
O26 „ ½ a. yellow-green .. 5 5
O27 **25** 1 a. carmine .. 15 5
O28 **27** 2 a. pale violet (1903) .. 10 15
O23/O28 *Set of* 5 40 30

1903–5. *King Edward VII. Optd. as Type* O **1**.

Overprint spaced 10 *mm.*

O29 **41** 3 p. pale grey .. 5 5
a. Slate-grey (1905) .. 5 5
O31 **42** ½ a. green .. 5 5
O32 **43** 1 a. carmine .. 5 5
O33 **44** 2 a. pale violet (1905) .. 8 5
a. Mauve .. 8 5
O35 **47** 4 a. olive-green (1905) .. 45 35
O36 **49** 8 a. dull mauve (1905) .. 30 20
a. Magenta .. 25 25
O38 **51** 1 r. green & carm. (1905) 35 25
O29/O38 .. .. *Set of* 7 1·40 1·25

Overprint spaced 8 *mm.*

O39 **41** 3 p. pale grey .. 15 5
a. Slate-grey .. 15 5
O41 **42** ½ a. green .. 8 5
O42 **43** 1 a. carmine .. 5 5
O43 **44** 2 a. mauve .. 15 5
O44 **47** 4 a. olive-green .. 50 30
O45 **49** 8 a. dull mauve .. 1·00 50
O46 **51** 1 r. green and carmine .. 1·00 1·00
O39/O46 .. .. *Set of* 7 2·50 1·75

1907. *Nos.* 149 *and* 150 *of India optd. as Type* O **1**.

Overprint spaced 10 *mm.*

O47 **53** ½ a. green .. 5 5
O48 **54** 1 a. carmine .. 5 5

Overprint spaced 8 *mm.*

O49 **53** ½ a. green .. 5 5
O50 **54** 1 a. carmine .. 5·00 2·00

1913–23. *King George V. Optd. with Type* O **1**.

O51 **55** 3 p. slate-grey .. 5 5
O52 **56** ½ a. green .. 5 5
O53 **57** 1 a. rose-carmine .. 5
a. Aniline carmine .. 5 5
ab. Opt. double .. 25·00
O54 „ 1 a. chocolate (1923) .. 5 5
O55 **59** 2 a. mauve .. 5 5
O56 **63** 4 a. olive .. 5 5
O57 **65** 8 a. purple .. 8 5
O58 **67** 1 r. brown and green .. 35 15
O51/O58 .. *Set of* 8 55 25

1922. *No.* O97 *of India optd. with T* **3**.
O59 **57** 9 p. on 1 a. rose-carmine . . 5 5

गवालियर

सरविस

(O 2)

1927–35. *King George V (Nasik printing, wmk. Mult. Star), optd. at Nasik as Type* O **1** *(but top line measures* 13 *mm. instead of* 14 *mm.) or with Type* O **2** *(rupee values).*
O61 **55** 3 p. slate 5 5
O62 **56** ½ a. green 5 5
O63 **80** 9 p. deep green (1935) 5 5
O64 **57** 1 a. chocolate 5 5
O65 **82** 1¼ a. mauve (1933) . . 5 5
O66 **70** 2 a. purple 5 5
O67 **71** 4 a. sage-green 5 5
O68 **65** 8 a. reddish purple (1928) 15 5
O69 **67** 1 r. chocolate and green 20 5
O70 „ 2 r. car. & orge. ('35) 55 65
O71 „ 5 r. ultram. & pur. ('32) 3·00 3·00
O72 „ 10 r. green & scarlet ('32) 4·00 5·00
O61/O72 . . . . *Set of* 12 7·00 8·50

1936–37. *New types. Optd. as Type* O **1** *(*13 *mm.).*
O73 **79** ½ a. green 5 5
O74 **81** 1 a. chocolate 5 5
O75 **59** 2 a. vermilion 5 5
O76 „ 2 a. vermilion *(small die)* 5 5
O77 **63** 4 a. sage-green (1937) . . 5 5

1938. *King George VI. Optd. as Type* O**1** *(*13 *mm.).*
O78 **91** ½ a. red-brown 40 10
O79 „ 1 a. carmine 40 10

गवालियर

(O 3)

1A——1A

(O 4)

1940–43. *Official stamps optd. with Type* O **3**.
O80 O **20** 3 p. slate 15 15
O81 „ ½ a. red-brown . . 65 40
O82 „ ½ a. purple 15 15
O83 „ 9 p. green 15 15
O84 „ 1 a. carmine 15 15
O85 „ 1 a. 3 p. bistre . . 30 30
O86 „ 1½ a. dull violet . . 20 15
O87 „ 2 a. vermilion . . 20 20
O88 „ 4 a. brown 15 30
O89 „ 8 a. slate-violet . . 40 45
O80/O89 . . . . *Set of* 10 2·25 2·25

1942. *Stamp of* 1932 *(King George V) optd. with Type* O **1** *and surch. with Type* O **4**.
O90 **82** 1 a. on 1¼ a. mauve . . 1·25 40

1944–48. *King George VI. Optd. with Type* O **2**.
O91 **100** 1 r. grey and red-brown 25 35
O92 „ 2 r. purple and brown . . 2·00 1·00
O93 „ 5 r. green and blue . . 6·00 6·00
O94 „ 10 r. purple & claret ('48) 9·00 10·00

JIND.

For earlier issues, see under INDIAN FEUDATORY STATES.

JHIND STATE

(1)

1885. *Queen Victoria. Optd. with T* **1**.
1 **23** ½ a. blue-green 25 20
a. Opt. inverted . . . . 18·00 18·00
2 **25** 1 a. brown-purple . . . . 1·25 1·25
a. Opt. inverted . . . . — 25·00
3 **27** 2 a. dull blue . . . . 1·00 1·00
a. Opt. inverted . . . . 35·00
4 **17** 4 a. green (Die I) . . 3·50 3·50
5 **31** 8 a. dull mauve . . . . 18·00
a. Opt. inverted £200
6 **33** 1 r. slate . . . . 18·00
a. Opt. inverted £200

All six values exist with reprinted overprint. In these, words "JHIND" and "STATE" are 8 and 9 mm. in length respectively, whereas in the originals the words are 9 and 9½ mm.

JEEND STATE (2) JHIND STATE (3) JIND STATE (4)

1885. *Optd. with T* **2**.
7 **23** ½ a. blue-green (R.) . . 6·00
8 **25** 1 a. brown-purple . . . . 6·00
9 **27** 2 a. dull blue (R.) . . 6·00
10 **17** 4 a. green (Die I) (R.) 6·00
11 **31** 8 a. dull mauve . . . . 7·00
12 **33** 1 r. slate (R.) . . . . 8·00
7/12 . . . . *Set of* 6 35·00

1886. *Optd. with T* **3**, *in red.*
13 **23** ½ a. blue-green . . . . 2·00
a. "JEIND" for "JHIND" 20·00
14 **27** 2 a. dull blue . . . . 2·50
a. "JEIND" for "JHIND" 25·00
15 **17** 4 a. green (Die I) . . 4·00
a. Opt. Double, one albino . .
16 **33** 1 r. slate . . . . 5·00
a. "JEIND" for "JHIND" £175

1886–98. *Optd. with T* **3**.
17 **23** ½ a. blue-green (1888) 5 5
a. Opt. inverted . . 65·00
18 **25** 1 a. brown-purple . . 5 5
a. "JEIND" for "JHIND" . . 65·00
19 „ 1 a. plum 10 10
20 **26** 1½ a. sepia (1897) . . 15 15
21 **27** 2 a. dull blue (1891) . . 10 10
22 „ 2 a. ultramarine . . 12 10
23 **28** 3 a. brown-orange . . 8 12
24 **29** 4 a. olive-green (1891) 15 15
25 „ 4 a. slate-green . . 15 15
26 **21** 6 a. olive-bistre (1891) 35 50
27 „ 6 a. bistre-brown . . 25 45
28 **31** 8 a. dull mauve . . 30 50
a. "JEIND" for "JHIND" £150
29 „ 8 a. magenta 35 45
30 **32** 12 a. purple/*red* (1897) 25 35
31 **33** 1 r. slate (1891) . . 1·50 1·50
32 **37** 1 r. green & carm. (1898) 2·00 2·00
33 **38** 2 r. carm. & yell.-brn. ('97) 18·00
34 „ 3 r. brown and green . . 20·00
35 „ 5 r. ultram. & vio. ('97) 25·00
17/35 . . . . *Set of* 14 60·00

Varieties exist in which the word "JHIND" measures 10½ mm. and 9¾ mm. instead of 10 mm. Such varieties are to be found on Nos. 17, 18, 21, 24, 28 and 31.

1900–4. *Colours changed.*
36 **40** 3 p. carmine 5 5
37 „ 3 p. grey (1904) . . 5 5
38 **23** ½ a. pale yellow-grn. (1902) 8 12
39 „ ½ a. yellow-green . . 40 45
40 **25** 1 a. carmine (1902) . . 8 12

1903–9. *King Edward VII. Optd. with T* **3**.
41 **41** 3 p. pale grey 5 5
42 „ 3 p. slate-grey (1905) 5 5
43 **42** ½ a. green 5 5
44 **43** 1 a. carmine 5 5
45 **44** 2 a. pale violet . . 8 8
46 „ 2 a. mauve (1906) . . 12 10
47 **45** 2½ a. ultramarine (1909) 8 12
48 **46** 3 a. orange-brown . . 5 5
a. Opt. double . . 35·00
49 **47** 4 a. olive-green . . 12 15
50 „ 4 a. slate-green . . 15 20
51 **48** 6 a. bistre (1905) . . 15 20
52 **49** 8 a. dull mauve . . 15 20
53 „ 8 a. magenta . . 15 20
54 **50** 12 a. purple/*red* (1905) 30 35
55 **51** 1 r. green & carmine (1905) 30 40
41/55 . . . . *Set of* 11 1·25 1·50

1907–9. *Nos.* 149/50 *of India optd. with T* **3**.
56 **53** ½ a. green 5 5
57 **54** 1 a. carmine (1909) . . 5 5

1913. *King George V. Optd. with T* **3**.
58 **55** 3 pies, slate-grey . . 5 5
59 **56** ½ a. green 5 5
60 **57** 1 a. aniline carmine . . 5 5
61 **59** 2 a. mauve 10 15
62 **62** 3 a. orange-brown . . 40 60
63 **64** 6 a. olive-bistre . . 75 1·00
58/63 . . . . *Set of* 6 1·25 1·60

1914–27. *King George V. Optd. with T* **4**.
64 **55** 3 pies, slate-grey . . 5 5
65 **56** ½ a. green 5 5
66 **57** 1 a. aniline carmine . . 5 5
67 **58** 1½ a. choc. (Type A) (1922) 15 20
68 „ 1½ a. choc. (Type B) (1924) 15 20
69 **59** 2 a. mauve 5 5
70 **61** 2½ a. ultramarine (1922) . . 15 30
71 **62** 3 a. orange-brown . . 8 15
72 **63** 4 a. olive 10 15
73 **64** 6 a. olive-bistre . . 15 15
74 **65** 8 a. purple 15 20
75 **66** 12 a. dull claret . . 15 20
76 **67** 1 r. brown and green . . 40 50
a. Opt. double, one albino . .
77 „ 2 r. carmine & yell.-brown 1·75 2·25
78 „ 5 r. ultramarine and violet 8·00 8·00
64/78 . . *Set of* 15 8·50 10·00

1922. *No.* 192 *of India optd.* "JIND" *in block capitals.*
79 **57** 9 p. on 1 a. rose-carmine . . 1·00 1·25

1924–27. *Optd. with T* **4**. *New colours.*
80 **57** 1 a. chocolate 5 5
81 **58** 1½ a. rose-carmine (Type B) 5 10
82 **61** 2½ a. orange 5 10
83 **62** 3 a. bright blue . . 15 15

JIND STATE (5) JIND STATE (6)

1927–37. *King George V (Nasik printing, wmk. Mult. Star), optd. at Nasik with T* **5** *or* **6** *(rupee values).*
84 **55** 3 pies, slate 5 5
85 **56** ½ a. green 5 5
86 **80** 9 p. deep green . . 5 5
87 **57** 1 a. chocolate 5 5
88 **82** 1¼ a. mauve 5 5
89 **58** 1½ a. rose-carm. (Type B) 5 5
90 **70** 2 a. purple 5 5
91 **61** 2½ a. orange 5 8
92 **62** 3 a. bright blue . . 10 12
93 **83** 3½ a. ultramarine ('37) . . 5 5
94 **71** 4 a. sage-green . . 5 8
95 **64** 6 a. bistre ('37) . . 10 8
96 **65** 8 a. reddish purple . . 20 20
97 **66** 12 a. claret 35 40
98 **67** 1 r. chocolate and green 35 50
99 „ 2 r. carmine and orange . . 1·75 2·75
100 „ 5 r. ultramarine & purple 5·00 5·50
101 „ 10 r. green and carmine . . 9·00 10·00
102 „ 15 r. blue and olive 15·00 20·00
103 „ 25 r. orange and blue . . 22·00 25·00
84/103 . . . . *Set of* 20 50·00 60·00

1934. *New types and colours. Optd. with T* **5**.
104 **79** ½ a. green 5 5
105 **81** 1 a. chocolate 5 5
106 **59** 2 a. vermilion 5 5
107 **62** 3 a. carmine 5 5
108 **63** 4 a. sage-green 5 5

1937–38. *King George VI. Optd. with T* **5** *or T* **6** *(rupee values).*
109 **91** 3 p. slate 8 5
110 „ ½ a. red-brown . . 8 12
111 „ 9 p. green (23.8.37) 10 12
112 „ 1 a. carmine (23.8.37) . . 8 5
113 **92** 2 a. vermilion 8 10
114 **93** 2½ a. bright violet . . 8 12
115 **94** 3 a. yellow-green . . 8 12
116 **95** 3½ a. bright blue . . 10 15
117 **96** 4 a. brown 10 15
118 **97** 6 a. turquoise-green . . 15 20
119 **98** 8 a. slate-violet . . 15 20
120 **99** 12 a. lake 40 70
121 **100** 1 r. grey and red-brown 85 1·00
122 „ 2 r. purple and brown . . 1·25 1·75
123 „ 5 r. green and blue . . 5·00 5·00
124 „ 10 r. purple and claret . . 9·00 10·00
125 „ 15 r. brown and green . . 30·00 32·00
126 „ 25 r. slate-violet & purple 35·00 40·00
109/126 . . . . *Set of* 18 75·00 80·00

JIND

(7)

1942–43. *King George VI. Optd. with T* **7**.
(a) Stamps of 1937.
127 **91** 3 p. slate 80 80
128 „ ½ a. red-brown . . 70 70
129 „ 9 p. green 90 90
130 „ 1 a. carmine 80 80

131 **100** 1 r. grey and red-brown 1·25 1·50
132 ,, 2 r. purple and brown .. 2·00 3·00
133 ,, 5 r. green and blue .. 5·00 7·00
134 ,, 10 r. purple and claret .. 11·00 12·00
135 ,, 15 r. brown and green .. 16·00 18·00
136 ,, 25 r. slate-vio. and purple 22·00 25·00
127/136 .. .. *Set of* 10 60·00 65·00

(*b*) *Stamps of* 1940–43.
137 **100a** 3 p. slate 8 8
138 ,, ½ a. purple 8 8
139 ,, 9 p. green 8 10
140 ,, 1 a. carmine 8 10
141 **101** 1 a. 3 p. bistre 8 15
142 ,, 1½ a. dull violet 20 20
143 ,, 2 a. vermilion 8 8
144 ,, 3 a. bright violet .. 15 15
145 ,, 3½ a. bright blue 15 20
146 **102** 4 a. brown 8 20
147 ,, 6 a. turquoise-green .. 10 30
148 ,, 8 a. slate-violet 35 40
149 ,, 12 a. lake 50 60
137/149 .. .. *Set of* 13 1·50 2·25

OFFICIAL STAMPS.

SERVICE

JHIND STATE SERVICE
(O 15)

JHIND STATE
(O 16)

1885. *Queen Victoria. Optd. with Type* O **15.**
O1 **23** ½ a. blue-green 5 5
O2 **25** 1 a. brown-purple 5 5
O3 **27** 2 a. dull blue .. .. 6·00 6·00

Optd. as Type O **15**, *but* " JHIND STATE " *inverted.*
O4 **23** ½ a. blue-green .. .. 12·00 9·00
O5 **25** 1 a. brown-purple .. .. 3·50 3·50
O6 **27** 2 a. dull blue .. .. 60·00

The three values have had the overprint reprinted in the same way as the ordinary stamps of 1885. See note after No. 6.

1885. *Optd. with T* **2** *and* " SERVICE ".
O7 **23** ½ a. blue-green (R.) .. 8·00
O8 **25** 1 a. brown-purple .. .. 8·00
O9 **27** 2 a. dull blue (R.) .. .. 10·00

1886. *Optd. with Type* O **16**, *in red.*
O10 **23** ½ a. blue-green .. .. 3·00
a. Error. " ERVICE " ..
b. Error. " JEIND " .. 30·00
O11 **27** 2 a. dull blue .. .. 6·00
a. Error. " ERVICE " ..
b. Error. " JEIND " .. 40·00

1886–97. *Optd. with Type* O **16.**
O12 **23** ½ a. blue-green (1888) .. 5 5
O13 **25** 1 a. brown-purple .. 2·00
a. Error. " ERVICE " ..
b. Error. " JEIND " .. 35·00
O14 ,, 1 a. plum 8 5
O15 **27** 2 a. dull blue (1893) .. 10 5
O16 ,, 2 a. ultramarine 8 5
O17 **29** 4 a. olive-green (1892) .. 15 8
O18 ,, 4 a. slate-green 25 20
O19 **31** 8 a. dull mauve (1892) .. 45 60
O20 ,, 8 a. magenta .. .. 75 1·25
O21 **37** 1 r. grn. & carmine (1897) 1·25 1·50
O12/O21 .. .. *Set of* 6 2·00 2·00

Varieties mentioned in note after No. 35 exist on Nos. O12, O15, O17 and O20.

Varieties with " SERVICE " measuring 11½ mm. are to be found in the case of Nos. O12, O16, O18, O20 and O21.

1902. *Colour changed.*
O22 **23** ½ a. yellow-green 5 5

1903–6. *King Edward VII. Optd. with Type* O **16.**
O23 **41** 3 p. pale grey 10 5
O24 ,, 3 p. slate-grey (1906) .. 5 5
O25 **42** ½ a. green 15 5
a. Error "HIND" .. — 45·00
O26 **43** 1 a. carmine 20 5
a. Error "HIND" .. — 45·00
O27 **44** 2 a. pale violet 12 5
O28 ,, 2 a. mauve 5 5
O29 **47** 4 a. olive-green 15 10
O30 **49** 8 a. dull mauve 50 30
O31 ,, 8 a. magenta .. .. 1·25 75
O32 **51** 1 r. green & carmine (1906) 1·25 80
O23/O32 .. .. *Set of* 7 2·50 1·50

1907. *Nos.* 149/50 *of India optd. with Type* O **16.**
O33 **53** ½ a. green 5 5
O34 **54** 1 a. carmine 5 5

1914–27. *King George V. Official stamps of India optd. with T* **4.**
O35 **55** 3 p. slate-grey 5 5
O36 **56** ½ a. green 5 5
O37 **57** 1 a. aniline carmine .. 5 5
O38 ,, 1 a. pale rose-carmine .. 5 5
O39 **59** 2 a. mauve 5 5
O40 **63** 4 a. olive 5 5
O41 **64** 6 a. yellow-bistre 12 15
O42 **65** 8 a. purple 5 8
O43 **67** 1 r. brown and green .. 50 20
O44 ,, 2 r. carmine & yellow-brn. 1·50 2·00
O45 ,, 5 r. ultramarine & violet 6·00 7·00
O35/O45 .. .. *Set of* 10 7·00 9·00

1924. *As* 1914–27. *New colour.*
O46 **57** 1 a. chocolate 5 5

JIND STATE SERVICE
(O 17)

JIND STATE SERVICE
(O 18)

1927–37. *King George V (Nasik printing, wmk. Mult. Star), optd. with Types* O **17** *or* O **18** *(rupee values).*
O47 **55** 3 p. slate 5 5
O48 **56** ½ a. green 5 5
O49 **80** 9 p. deep green 5 5
O50 **57** 1 a. chocolate 5 5
O51 **82** 1¼ a. mauve 5 5
O52 **70** 2 a. purple 8 5
O53 **61** 2½ a. orange ('37) 5 5
O54 **71** 4 a. sage-green 5 5
O55 **64** 6 a. bistre ('37) 12 10
O56 **65** 8 a. reddish purple .. 10 15
O57 **66** 12 a. claret 15 25
O58 **67** 1 r. chocolate and green 30 50
O59 ,, 2 r. carmine and orange 75 1·00
O60 ,, 5 r. ultram. and purple 2·50 2·50
O61 ,, 10 r. green and carmine 4·50 5·00
O47/O61 .. .. *Set of* 15 8·00 9·00

1934. *Optd. with Type* O **17.**
O62 **79** ½ a. green 5 5
O63 **81** 1 a. chocolate 5 5
O64 **59** 2 a. vermilion 5 5
O65 **63** 4 a. sage-green 5 5

1937–42 (?). *King George VI. Optd. with Types* O **17** *or* O **18** *(rupee values).*
O66 **91** ½ a. red-brown (1942?) 50 8
O67 ,, 9 p. green 15 8
O68 ,, 1 a. carmine 12 8
O69 **100** 1 r. grey & red-brn. ('40) 1·50 1·25
O70 ,, 2 r. purple & brown ('40) 3·00 3·00
O71 ,, 5 r. green and blue ('40) 7·00 7·00
O72 ,, 10 r. purple & claret ('40) 9·00 9·00
O66/O72 .. .. *Set of* 7 20·00 18·00

JIND SERVICE
(O 19)

1940–43? (*a*) *Official stamps optd. with T* **7.**
O73 O **20** 3 p. slate 8 8
O74 ,, ½ a. red-brown .. .. 1·00 60
O75 ,, ½ a. purple ('43?) .. 8 8
O76 ,, 9 p. green 8 8
O77 ,, 1 a. carmine 8 8
O78 ,, 1½ a. dull violet 20 15
O79 ,, 2 a. vermilion 8 8
O80 ,, 2½ a. bright violet .. 8 8
O81 ,, 4 a. brown 25 25
O82 ,, 8 a. slate-violet .. 40 40

(*b*) *Postage stamps optd. with Type* O **19.**
O83 **100** 1 r. grey and red-brown 1·25 1·25
O84 ,, 2 r. purple and brown .. 2·00 2·00
O85 ,, 5 r. green and blue .. 4·00 6·00
O86 ,, 10 r. purple and claret .. 10·00 10·00
O73/O86 .. .. *Set of* 14 15·00 18·00

NABHA.

NABHA STATE
(1)

NABHA STATE
(2)

1885 (MAY). *Queen Victoria. Optd. with T* **1.**
1 **23** ½ a. blue-green 20 20
2 **25** 1 a. brown-purple .. .. 3·00 3·50
3 **27** 2 a. dull blue .. .. .. 3·00 2·75
4 **17** 4 a. green .. .. .. 6·00
5 **31** 8 a. dull mauve .. .. 22·00
6 **33** 1 r. slate .. .. .. 24·00
1/6 .. .. .. *Set of* 6 50·00

All six values have had the overprint reprinted. On the reprints the words " NABHA " and " STATE " both measure 9¼ mm. in length, whereas on the originals these words measure 11 and 10 mm. respectively. The varieties with overprint double come from the reprints.

1885–1900. *Optd. with T* **2.**

(*a*) *In red.* (Nov. 1885.)
10 **23** ½ a. blue-green 8 8
11 **27** 2 a. dull blue 20 25
12 **17** 4 a. green .. .. .. 4·00 4·00
13 **33** 1 r. slate .. .. .. 7·00 7·00

(*b*) *In black.* (1887–97.)
14 **23** ½ a. blue-green 5 5
15 **24** 9 p. carmine (1892) .. 15 15
16 **25** 1 a. brown-purple 12 5
17 ,, 1 a. plum 5 5
18 **26** 1½ a. sepia (1891) 8 10
a. "ABHA" for "NABHA" 40·00
19 **27** 2 a. dull blue 12 8
20 ,, 2 a. ultramarine 12 8
21 **28** 3 a. orange (1889) 45 45
22 ,, 3 a. brown-orange .. 12 10
23 **29** 4 a. olive-green 12 8
24 ,, 4 a. slate-green 20 20
25 **21** 6 a. olive-bistre (1889) .. 40 40
26 ,, 6 a. bistre-brown 45 55
27 **31** 8 a. dull mauve 30 30
28 **32** 12 a. purple/*red* (1889) .. 35 35
29 **33** 1 r. slate .. .. .. 1·25 1·25
30 **37** 1 r. green & carmine ('93) 50 50
a. " N BHA " for " NABHA "
31 **38** 2 r. carm. & yell.-brn. ('97) 10·00 12·00
32 ,, 3 r. brown & green (1897) 15·00 18·00
33 ,, 5 r. ultram. & vio. (1897) 18·00 20·00
14/33 .. .. *Set of* 15 35·00 40·00

Nos. 10, 11, 12, 13, and 27 have had the overprint reprinted, but in nearly every case the reprints have had the word " SPECIMEN " overprinted upon them.

New value. In black. (Nov. 1900.)
36 **40** 3 p. carmine 5 5

1903–10. *King Edward VII. Optd. with T* **2.**
37 **41** 3 p. pale grey 5 5
37*a* ,, 3 p. slate-grey (1906) .. 5 5
38 **42** ½ a. green 5 5
a. Error. " NABH " .. 30·00
39 **43** 1 a. carmine 10 10
40 **44** 2 a. pale violet 15 15
40*a* ,, 2 a. mauve 10 10
40*b* **45** 2½ a. ultramarine (1910) .. 9·00
41 **46** 3 a. orange-brown .. 10 5
42 **47** 4 a. olive-green 12 12
43 **48** 6 a. olive-bistre 20 30
44 **49** 8 a. dull mauve 25 30
44*a* ,, 8 a. magenta 30 40
45 **50** 12 a. purple/*red* 40 45
46 **51** 1 r. green and carmine .. 40 45
37/46 .. .. *Set of* 10 1·60 1·75

1907. *Nos.* 149/50 *of India optd. with T* **2.**
47 **53** ½ a. green 5 5
48 **54** 1 a. carmine 12 12

1913. *King George V. Optd. with T* **2.**
49 **55** 3 p. slate 5 5
50 **56** ½ a. green 5 5
51 **57** 1 a. aniline carmine .. 5 5
52 **59** 2 a. mauve 5 5
53 **62** 3 a. orange-brown .. 8 8
54 **63** 4 a. olive 8 8
55 **64** 6 a. olive-bistre 8 10
56 **65** 8 a. purple 12 15
57 **66** 12 a. dull claret 20 20
58 **67** 1 r. brown and green .. 20 20
a. Opt. double, one albino ..
49/58 .. .. *Set of* 10 90 95

1924. *As* 1913. *New Colour.*
59 **57** 1 a. chocolate 5 5

NABHA STATE (3) — NABHA STATE (4)

1928–37. *King George V (Nasik printing, wmk. Mult. Star), optd. as T* **3** *or* **4** *(rupee values).*

50 **55** 3 p. slate ('32) 5 5
51 **56** ½ a. green 5 5
51a **80** 9 p. deep green ('37) .. 5 5
52 **57** 1 a. chocolate 5 5
53 **82** 1¼ a. mauve ('37) 5 5
54 **70** 2 a. purple ('32) 5 5
55 **61** 1½ a. orange ('32) 5 5
56 **62** 3 a. bright blue ('30) .. 8 8
57 **71** 4 a. sage-green ('32) .. 8 12
71 **67** 2 r. carm. & orange ('32) 1·50 2·00
72 „ 5 r. ultram. & purple ('32) 2·50 3·00
50/72 .. .. *Set of* 11 4·00 5·00

1936–37. *New types and colours. Optd. as T* **3.**

73 **79** ½ a. green 5 5
74 **81** 1 a. chocolate 5 5
75 **62** 3 a. carmine ('37) 5 5
76 **63** 4 a. sage-green ('37) .. 5 8

NABHA STATE (5) — NABHA (6)

1938–39. *King George VI. Optd. as T* **3** *(3 p. to 1 a.), T* **5** *(2 a. to 12 a.) or T* **4** *(rupee values).*

77 **91** 3 p. slate 80 30
78 „ ½ a. red-brown 15 20
79 „ 9 p. green .. .. .. 3·00 3·00
80 „ 1 a. carmine 8 8
81 **92** 2 a. vermilion 8 10
82 **93** 2½ a. bright violet .. 12 20
83 **94** 3 a. yellow-green .. 15 25
84 **95** 3½ a. bright blue 20 30
85 **96** 4 a. brown 10 25
86 **97** 6 a. turquoise-green .. 30 60
87 **98** 8 a. slate-violet 25 60
88 **99** 12 a. lake .. .. .. 60 1·00
89 **100** 1 r. grey and red-brown .. 90 1·00
90 „ 2 r. purple and brown .. 1·75 2·25
91 „ 5 r. green and blue .. 6·00 7·00
92 „ 10 r. purple & claret ('39) 12·00 15·00
93 „ 15 r. brown & green ('39) 25·00 30·00
94 „ 25 r. slate-vio. & pur. ('39) 32·00 35·00
77/94 .. .. *Set of* 18 75·00 85·00

1942–45. *King George VI. Optd. with T* **6.**

(a) Stamps of 1937.

95 **91** 3 p. slate .. .. 3·00 60
96 „ ½ a. red-brown .. 7·00 4·00
97 „ 9 p. green .. .. 3·00 75
98 „ 1 a. carmine .. .. 2·00 75

(b) Stamps of 1940–43.

105 **100a** 3 p. slate 8 8
106 „ ½ a. purple 8 8
107 „ 9 p. green 8 8
108 „ 1 a. carmine 8 8
109 **101** 1 a. 3 p. bistre 8 8
110 „ 1½ a. dull violet 8 8
111 „ 2 a. vermilion 8 8
112 „ 3 a. bright violet .. 15 25
113 „ 3½ a. bright blue .. 15 25
114 **102** 4 a. brown 20 25
115 „ 6 a. turquoise-green .. 25 40
116 „ 8 a. slate-violet .. 20 40
117 „ 12 a. lake 50 85
105/117 .. .. *Set of* 13 1·50 2·50

OFFICIAL STAMPS.

NABHA STATE SERVICE (O 8) — SERVICE NABHA STATE (O 9)

1885 (May). *Queen Victoria. Optd. with Type* O **8.**

O1 **23** ½ a. blue-green 15 15
O2 **25** 1 a. brown-purple 5 5
O3 **27** 2 a. dull blue .. .. 10·00 10·00

The three values have had the overprint reprinted in the same way as the ordinary stamps of 1885.

1885–97. *Optd. with Type* O **9.**

(a) In red. (Nov. 1885.)

O4 **23** ½ a. blue-green 25 35
O5 **27** 2 a. deep blue 15 15

(b) In black. (1888–97.)

O 6 **23** ½ a. blue-green 5 5
a. "SERVICE." with stop 8·00 50
b. "S ATE" for "STATE"
O 7 **25** 1 a. brown-purple (1892) 8 5
O 8 „ 1 a. plum 10 5
a. "SERVICE." with stop 1·25 70
b. "NABHA STATE" double .. .. 35·00
O 9 **27** 2 a. dull blue 10 12
O10 „ 2 a. ultramarine 15 15
O11 **28** 3 a. orange (1891) .. 45 50
O12 „ 3 a. brown-orange .. 45 55
O13 **29** 4 a. olive-green 15 15
O14 „ 4 a. slate-green 20 15
O15 **21** 6 a. olive-bistre (1889) .. 35 45
O16 „ 6 a. bistre-grown .. 18·00
O17 **31** 8 a. dull mauve (1889) .. 25 30
O18 **32** 12 a. purple/*red* (1889) .. 2·50 2·50
O19 **33** 1 r. slate (1889) .. .. 4·00 5·00
O20 **37** 1 r. green & carm. ('97) 3·00 4·00
O6/O20 .. .. *Set of* 10 10·00 12·00

Nos. O4, O5 and O7 exist with reprinted overprint, but in nearly every case the stamps bear the words "SPECIMEN."

1903–06. *King Edward VII. Optd. with Type* O **9.**

O24 **41** 3 pies, pale grey (1906) .. 20 20
O25 „ 3 pies, slate-grey (1906) .. 12 12
O26 **42** ½ a. green 5 5
O27 **43** 1 a. carmine 5 5
O28 **44** 2 a. pale violet 15 15
O29 „ 2 a. mauve 10 10
O30 **47** 4 a. olive-green 15 12
O32 **49** 8 a. dull mauve 20 25
O33 „ 8 a. magenta 25 30
O34 **51** 1 r. green and carmine .. 30 50
O24/O34 .. .. *Set of* 7 1·40 1·60

1907. *Nos.* 149/50 *of India optd. with Type* O **9.**

O35 **53** 4 a. green 5 5
O36 **54** 1 a. carmine 8 10

1913. *King George V. Optd. with Type* O **9.**

O37 **63** 4 a. olive .. .. 4·00
O38 **67** 1 r. brown and green .. 15·00

1913. *Official stamps of India optd. with T* **2.**

O39 **55** 3 pies, slate-grey .. 5 10
O39a „ 3 pies, bluish slate .. 5 10
O40 **56** ½ a. green 5 5
O41 **57** 1 a. aniline carmine .. 5 5
O42 **59** 2 a. mauve 8 8
O43 **63** 4 a. olive 10 12
O44 **65** 8 a. dull mauve 20 20
O46 **67** 1 r. brown and green .. 25 30
O39/O46 .. .. *Set of* 7 75 90

NABHA STATE SERVICE (O 10) — NABHA SERVICE (O 11)

1932–45. *King George V (Nasik printing, wmk. Mult. Star), optd. at Nasik with Type* O **10.**

O47 **55** 3 p. slate 5 5
O50 **81** 1 a. chocolate ('35) .. 5 5
O50a **63** 4 a. sage-green ('45) .. 15 8
O51 **65** 8 a. reddish purple ('37) 35 50

1938. *King George VI. Optd. as Type* O **10.**

O54 **91** 9 p. green 30 50
O55 „ 1 a. carmine 15 20

1943–44. *(a) Official stamps optd. with T* **6.**

O56 O **20** 3 p. slate 8 8
O57 „ ½ a. red-brown .. 12 12
O57a „ ½ a. purple ('44) .. 8 8
O58 „ 9 p. green 8 8
O59 „ 1 a. carmine 8 10
O61 „ 1½ a. dull violet .. 10 15
O62 „ 2 a. vermilion .. 10 15
O64 „ 4 a. brown 25 30
O65 „ 8 a. slate-violet .. 40 60

(b) Postage stamps optd. with Type O **11.**

O66 **100** 1 r. grey and red-brown 75 1·00
O67 „ 2 r. purple and brown .. 2·50 3·00
O68 „ 5 r. green and blue .. 7·00 7·00
O56/O68 .. .. *Set of* 11 10·00 11·00

PATIALA.

PUTTIALLA STATE (1) — PUTTIALLA STATE (2) — PATIALA STATE (3)

1884. *Queen Victoria. Optd. with T* **1**, *in red.*

1 **23** ½ a. blue-green 20 20
a. Opt. double .. .. 30·00 30·00
2 **25** 1 a. brown-purple .. .. 3·00 2·50
a. Opt. double .. ..
b. Optd. in red and in black .. 30·00
3 **27** 2 a. dull blue .. .. 1·00 1·25
4 **17** 4 a. green .. .. 1·25 1·00
5 **31** 8 a. dull mauve .. .. 25·00 26·00
a. Opt. inverted .. ..
b. Optd. in red and in black .. 8·00
6 **33** 1 r. slate .. .. 12·00 12·00
1/6 .. .. *Set of* 6 36·00 36·00

1885. *Optd. with T* **2.** *(a) In red.*

7 **23** ½ a. blue-green 12 12
a. Error. "AUTTIALLA" .. 3·00
b. Error. "STATE" only ..
8 **27** 2 a. dull blue 15 12
a. Error. "AUTTIALLA" 3·00
9 **17** 4 a. green 25 25
a. Opt. in red and in black .. 25·00
10 **33** 1 r. slate 70 90
a. Error. "AUTTIALLA" .. 25·00

(b) In black.

11 **25** 1 a. brown-purple 5 5
a. Opt. in red and in black .. 50
b. Error. "AUTTIALLA" 8·00
ba. Error. Opt. in red and in black .. .. 30·00 30·00
12 **31** 8 a. dull mauve 20 30
a. Error. "AUTTIALLA" .. 26·00
7/12 .. .. *Set of* 6 1·40 1·50

The ½, 2, and 4 a. (T **29**), and 1 r. (all overprinted in black), are proofs.

All six values exist with reprinted overprints, and the error "AUTTIALLA STAT." has been reprinted in complete sheets on all values and in addition in black on the ½, 2, 4 a., and 1 r. Nearly all these however, are found with the word "REPRINT" overprinted upon them.

The error "PUTTILLA" formerly catalogued is considered doubtful.

1891–96. *Optd. with T* **3.**

13 **23** ½ a. blue-green 5 5
14 **24** 9 p. carmine 10 12
15 **25** 1 a. brown-purple 8 5
16 „ 1 a. plum 12 5
a. Error. "PATIALA" omitted .. .. .. 25·00 25·00
17 **26** 1½ a. sepia 8 10
18 **27** 2 a. dull blue (1896) .. 15 8
19 „ 2 a. ultramarine .. 15 5
20 **28** 3 a. brown-orange .. 8 10
21 **29** 4 a. olive-green (1896) .. 15 15
a. Error. "PATIALA" omitted .. .. .. 30·00 30·00
22 „ 4 a. slate-green 5 5
23 **21** 6 a. bistre-brown 12 8
24 „ 6 a. olive-bistre .. 35
25 **31** 8 a. dull mauve .. ..
26 „ 8 a. magenta (1896) .. 20 20
27 **32** 12 a. purple/*red* 30 25
28 **37** 1 r. green & carmine ('96) 1·25 1·25
29 **38** 2 r. carm. & yell.-brn. ('95) 12·00
30 „ 3 r. brown & green (1895) 18·00
31 „ 5 r. ultram. & violet ('95) 25·00
13/31 .. .. *Set of* 14 45·00

1899–1902. *Colours changed and new value. Optd. with T* **3.**

32 **40** 3 p. carmine (1899) .. 5 5
33 **23** ½ a. pale yellow-green .. 5 5
34 **25** 1 a. carmine 5 5

1903–06. *King Edward VII. Optd. with T* **3.**

35 **41** 3 p. pale grey 5 5
36 „ 3 p. slate-grey (1906) .. 5 5
37 **42** ½ a. green 5 5
38 **43** 1 a. carmine 5 5
39 **44** 2 a. pale violet 5 5
40 **46** 3 a. orange-brown .. 5 5
41 **47** 4 a. olive-green (1905) .. 12 5
42 **48** 6 a. olive-bistre (1905) .. 15 12
43 **49** 8 a. dull mauve (1906) .. 20 15
44 **50** 12 a. purple/*red* (1906) .. 30 35
45 **51** 1 r. green & carmine ('05) 35 40
35/45 .. .. *Set of* 10 1·10 1·10

1912. *Nos.* 149/60 *of India optd. with T* **3**.
46 **53** ½ a. green 5 5
47 **54** 1 a. carmine 5 5

1912–26. *King George V. Optd. with T* **3**.
48 **55** 3 p. slate-grey 5 5
49 **56** ½ a. green 5 5
50 **57** 1 a. aniline carmine .. 5 5
51 **58** 1½ a. chocolate (Type A) ('22) 15 20
52 **59** 2 a. mauve 5 5
53 **62** 3 a. orange-brown .. 12 8
54 **63** 4 a. olive 10 5
55 **64** 6 a. yellow-brown .. 20 20
a. *Yellow-bistre* 40 40
56 **65** 8 a. purple 20 20
57 **66** 12 a. dull claret 20 20
58 **67** 1 r. brown and green .. 75 75
59 ,, 2 r. carm. & yell.-brn. ('26) 1·75 1·75
60 ,, 5 r. ultram. & violet ('26) 4·00 4·50

1923–6. *As* 1912–26. *New colours.*
61 **57** 1 a. chocolate 5 5
62 **62** 3 a. ultramarine ('26) .. 10 15
48/62 .. .. *Set of* 15 7·00 8·00

PATIALA STATE (4) PATIALA STATE (5)

1928–34. *King George V (Nasik printing, wmk. Mult. Star) optd. at Nasik with T* **4** *or* **5** *(rupee values).*
63 **55** 3 p. slate ('32) 5 5
64 **56** ½ a. green 5 5
65 **80** 9 p. deep green ('34) .. 5 5
66 **57** 1 a. chocolate 5 5
67 **82** 1¼ a. mauve ('33) 5 5
68 **70** 2 a. purple 5 5
69 **61** 2½ a. orange ('34) .. 5 5
70 **62** 3 a. bright blue ('29) .. 5 5
71 **71** 4 a. sage-green 20 15
72 **65** 8 a. reddish purple ('33) .. 20 20
73 **67** 1 r. chocolate & green ('33) 50 50
74 ,, 2 r. carmine and orange .. 1·00 1·25
63/74 .. .. *Set of* 12 1·75 2·00

The 9 p. exists printed both by offset-lithography and typography.

1935–7. *Optd. with T* **4**.
75 **79** ½ a. blue-green ('37) .. 5 5
76 **81** 1 a. chocolate ('36) .. 5 5
77 **59** 2 a. verm. (No. 236*a*) ('36) 5 5
78 **62** 3 a. carmine 5 10
79 **63** 4 a. sage-green 8 12

PATIALA STATE (6) PATIALA (7) PATIALA (8)

1937–8. *King George VI. Optd. with T* **4** *(3 p. to 1 a.), T* **6** *(2 a. to 12 a.), or T* **5** *(rupee values).*
80 **91** 3 p. slate .. .. .. 5·00 4·00
81 ,, ½ a. red-brown 30 15
82 ,, 9 p. green ('37) .. 25 20
83 ,, 1 a. carmine ('37) .. 10 10
84 **92** 2 a. vermilion 15 15
85 **93** 2½ a. bright violet .. 15 30
86 **94** 3 a. yellow-green .. 15 30
87 **95** 3½ a. bright blue 30 50
88 **96** 4 a. brown 30 50
89 **97** 6 a. turquoise-green .. 30 75
90 **98** 8 a. slate-violet 40 75
91 **99** 12 a. lake .. .. .. 1·00 1·50
92 **100** 1 r. grey and red-brown 4·00 4·00
93 ,, 2 r. purple and brown .. 4·00 4·00
94 ,, 5 r. green and blue .. 6·00 6·00
95 ,, 10 r. purple and claret .. 11·00 12·00
96 ,, 15 r. brown and green .. 20·00 20·00
97 ,, 25 r. slate-violet & purple 25·00 30·00
80/97 .. .. *Set of* 18 70·00 75·00

1943–7. *King George VI. Optd. with T* **7** *or* **8** *(rupee value).*

(*a*) *Stamps of* 1937.
98 **91** 3 p. slate 80 30
99 ,, ½ a. red-brown 80 30
100 ,, 9 p. green .. .. 2·50 50
101 ,, 1 a. carmine .. .. 1·00 50
102 **100** 1 r. grey & red-brn. ('47) 75 60
98/102 .. .. *Set of* 5 5·00 2·00

(*b*) *Stamps of* 1940–43.
103 **100*a*** 3 p. slate 8 8
104 ,, ½ a. purple 8 8
105 ,, 9 p. green 8 8
a. Opt. omitted (vert. pr. with normal) £750
106 ,, 1 a. carmine 8 8
107 **101** 1 a. 3 p. bistre 15 20
108 **101** 1½ a. violet 8 8
109 ,, 2 a. vermilion 8 8
110 ,, 3 a. bright violet .. 12 15
111 ,, 3½ a. bright blue .. 15 30
112 **102** 4 a. brown 8 25
113 ,, 6 a. turquoise-green .. 10 25
114 ,, 8 a. slate-violet .. 20 30
115 ,, 12 a. lake 30 50
103/115 .. .. *Set of* 13 1·00 1·90

OFFICIAL STAMPS.

PUTTIALLA SERVICE STATE (O 1) SERVICE PUTTIALLA STATE (O 2) SERVICE PUTTIALLA STATE (O 3)

1884. *Queen Victoria. Optd. with Type* O **1**, "SERVICE" *in black, the rest in red.*
O1 **23** ½ a. blue-green 25 5
O2 **25** 1 a. brown-purple 5 5
a. Red opt. inverted .. 22·00 15·00
b. Red opt. double .. .. — 18·00
c. "SERVICE" double .. 22·00 22·00
d. "SERVICE" inverted .. — 80·00
O3 **27** 2 a. dull blue .. .. 18·00 3·00

1885–90. (*a*) *Optd. with Type* O **2**, "SERVICE" *in black, the rest in red.*
O4 **23** ½ a. blue-green 5 5
a. "SERVICE" double .. — 15·00
b. "AUTTIALLA" for "PUTTIALLA" .. 6·00 80

(*b*) *Optd. with Type* O **2**, *all in black.*
O5 **25** 1 a. brown-purple 5 5
a. "SERVICE" double .. 40·00 40·00
b. Opt. double, one inverted.. — 70·00
c. "AUTTIALLA" for "PUTTIALLA" .. 20·00

(*c*) *Optd. with Type* O **3**.
O6 **23** ½ a. blue-green (Bk.) ('90) 5 5
O7 **27** 2 a. dull blue (R.) 5 5
a. Opt. double, one inverted.. 25·00
b. "PUTTILLA" for "PUTTIALLA"

There are reprints of Nos. O4, O5 and O7. The first has the word "SERVICE" in the large type in *red* instead of the small type in *black*, and the second has the word in the large type in *black* in place of the small type. The 2 a. with Type O **3**, in *black*, is a proof. The ½ a. "AUTTIALLA" has also been reprinted, but nearly all the above have been overprinted "REPRINT". No. O7b is probably from an essay sheet.

SERVICE PATIALA STATE (O 4)

1891–1900. *Optd. with Type* O **4**, *in black.*
O 8 **23** ½ a. blue-green (1895) .. 5 5
a. "SERVICE" inverted .. 18·00
b. "I" of "SERVICE" omitted .. .. 30·00
O 9 **25** 1 a. plum (1900) .. 8 5
a. "SERVICE" inverted .. 18·00
O10 **27** 2 a. dull blue (1898) .. 15 10
a. *Deep blue* 15 20
b. "SERVICE" inverted 18·00
O12 **28** 3 a. brown-orange .. 5 5
a. "I" of "SERVICE" omitted .. ..
O13 **29** 4 a. olive-green .. 5 5
a. *Slate-green* 5 5
b. "I" of "SERVICE" omitted .. ..
O15 **21** 6 a. bistre-brown .. 10 10
O16 **31** 8 a. dull mauve 10 10
a. *Magenta* (1898) 10 15
b. "I" of "SERVICE" omitted .. ..
O18 **32** 12 a. purple/*red* 15 15
a. "I" of "SERVICE" omitted .. ..
O19 **33** 1 r. slate 20 15
a. "I" of "SERVICE" omitted .. ..
O8/O19 .. .. *Set of* 9 80 70

The errors with "SERVICE" inverted are genuine, but it is believed they were never issued.

Varieties are known in which the letters of the word "SERVICE" are irregularly spaced, making the length about 11½ mm. instead of the usual 10½ mm.

1902–03. *Colour changed and new type.*
O20 **40** 1 a. carmine 5 5
O21 **37** 1 r. green & carmine ('03) 3·00 4·00

1903–10. *King Edward VII. Optd. with Type* O **4**.
O22 **41** 3 p. pale grey 5 5
a. *Slate-grey* (1909) .. 5 5
O24 **42** ½ a. green 5 5
O25 **43** 1 a. carmine 5 5
O26 **44** 2 a. pale violet (1905) .. 5 5
a. *Mauve* 5 5
O28 **46** 3 a. orange-brown .. 35 50
O29 **47** 4 a. olive-green (1905) 8 10
O30 **49** 8 a. dull mauve 10 10
a. *Magenta* (1910) .. 10 12
O32 **51** 1 r. green & carm. ('06) 20 20
O22/O32 .. .. *Set of* 8 75 90

1907. *Nos* 149/50 *of India optd. with Type* O **4**.
O33 **53** ½ a. green 5 5
O34 **54** 1 a. carmine 5 5

1913–26. *King George V. Official stamps of India optd. with T* **3**.
O35 **55** 3 p. slate-grey 5 5
a. *Bluish slate* (1926) .. 5 5
O36 **56** ½ a. green 5 5
O37 **57** 1 a. carmine 5 5
O38 ,, 1 a. brown (1925) .. 10 5
O39 **59** 2 a. mauve 8 5
O40 **63** 4 a. olive 10 10
O41 **64** 6 a. yellow-bistre (1926) 12 15
O42 **65** 8 a. purple 20 12
O43 **67** 1 r. brown and green .. 40 60
O44 ,, 2 r. carm. & yell.-brn. ('26) 1·25 2·25
O45 ,, 5 r. ultram. & violet ('26) 3·00 4·00
O35/O45 .. .. *Set of* 11 4·25 6·25

PATIALA STATE SERVICE (O 5) PATIALA STATE SERVICE (O 6)

1927–36. *King George V (Nasik printing, wmk. Mult. Star), optd. at Nasik with Type* O **5** *or Type* O **6**) *(rupee values).*
O47 **55** 3 p. slate 5 5
a. Blue opt. 8 8
O48 **56** ½ a. green ('32) 5 5
O49 **57** 1 a. chocolate 5 5
O50 **82** 1¼ a. mauve ('32) 5 5
O51 **70** 2 a. purple 8 10
O52 ,, 2 a. vermilion ('33) .. 8 10
O53 **61** 2½ a. orange ('33) .. 10 10
O54 **71** 4 a. sage-green ('35) .. 10 10
O55 **65** 8 a. reddish purple ('29) 30 30
O56 **67** 1 r. choc. & grn. ('29) 50 30
O57 ,, 2 r. carm. & orge. ('36) 1·00 1·25
O47/O57 .. .. *Set of* 11 2·25 2·25

1935–9. *New types. Optd. with Type* O **5**.
O58 **79** ½ a. green ('36) 5 5
O59 **81** 1 a. chocolate ('36) .. 5 5
O60 **59** 2 a. vermilion 5 5
O61 ,, 2 a. verm. (*small die*) ('39) 5 5
O62 **63** 4 a. sage-green ('36) .. 5 5

1938–43. *King George VI. Optd. with Types* O **5** *or* O **6** *(rupee values).*
O63 **91** ½ a. red-brown ('39) .. 40 15
O64 ,, 9 p. green ('43) .. .. 6·00 7·00
O65 ,, 1 a. carmine 50 15
O66 **100** 1 r. grey & red-brn. ('39) 80 80
O67 ,, 2 r. purple & brown ('39) 3·00 3·00
O68 ,, 5 r. green and blue ('39) 5·00 5·00
O63/O68 .. .. *Set of* 6 14·00 15·00

(O 7) (O 8)

1939–40. *Stamp of* 1932 *(King George V).*
(*a*) *Optd. with Types* O **5** *and* O **7**.
O69 **82** 1 a. on 1¼ a. mauve .. 25 25
(*b*) *Optd. with T* **4** *and* O **8**.
O70 **82** 1 a. on 1¼ a. mauve ('40) 15 15

"SERVICE" measures 9¼ mm. on No. O69 but only 8¾ mm. on O70.

PATIALA SERVICE
(O 9)

1940–45. (a) *Official stamps optd. with T* **7.**

No.	Type	Description	Unused	Used
O71	O 20	3 p. slate ('41)	8	8
O72	,,	½ a. red-brown ..	8	8
O73	,,	½ a. purple ('44)	8	8
O74	,,	9 p. green	8	8
O75	,,	1 a. carmine	8	8
O76	,,	1 a. 3 p. bistre ..	10	8
O77	,,	1½ a. dull violet ..	8	8
O78	,,	2 a. vermilion ('41) ..	10	10
O79	,,	2½ a. bright violet ('41)	15	12
O80	,,	4 a. brown ('45) ..	15	20
O81	,,	8 a. slate-violet ('45) ..	30	40
		(b) *Postage stamps optd. with Type* O **9.**		
O82	**100**	1 r. grey and red-brown	60	70
O83	,,	2 r. purple and brown	1·50	2·50
O84	,,	5 r. green and blue ('45)	3·50	4·50
O71/84		.. .. *Set of* 14	5·00	7·00

INDIAN FEUDATORY STATES.

These stamps were only valid for use within their respective states.

Postage stamps of the Indian States, current at that date, were replaced by those of the Republic of India on April 1, 1950.

Unless otherwise stated, all became obsolete on May 1, 1950 (with the exception of the "Anchal" stamps of Travancore-Cochin, which remained current until July 1, 1951).

ALWAR.

1 (1 a.)

1877. *Litho. Rouletted.*

No.	Type	Description	Unused	Used
1	**1**	¼ a. grey-blue	40	20
		a. Ultramarine	45	15
		b. Imperf. between (pr.) ..	—	12·00
		c. Bright greenish blue	12·00	5·00
2	,,	1 a. brown	45	35
		a. Imperf. between (pr.) ..	25·00	25·00
		b. Red-brown	50	45
		c. Chocolate	7·00	5·00

1899–1901. *Redrawn.* P 12.

(a) *Wide margins between stamps.*

No.	Type	Description	Unused	Used
3	**1**	¼ a. slate-blue	2·00	1·00
		a. Imperf. between (horiz. pair) ..	£100	£100
		b. Imperf. between (vert. pair) ..	£100	
4	,,	¼ a. emerald-green	£250	
		(b) *Narrower margins* (1901).		
5	**1**	¼ a. emerald-green	1·50	75
		a. Imperf. between (horiz. pair) ..	60·00	
		b. Imperf. between (vert. pair) ..	60·00	
		c. Imperf. horiz. (vert. pair) ..	60·00	
		d. Imperf. (pair)	60·00	
		e. Pale yellow-green	3·00	1·00
		ea. Imperf. (pair)	60·00	

In the redrawn type only the bottom outer frameline is thick, whereas in the original 1877 issue the left-hand frameline is also thick, as shown in Type **1**.

The stamps of Alwar became obsolete in the latter part of 1922.

HAVE YOU READ THE NOTES AT THE BEGINNING OF THIS CATALOGUE?

These often provide answers to the enquiries we receive.

BAHAWALPUR.

See under **PAKISTAN.**

BAMRA.

1 (¼ a.) 2 (½ a.) 3 (1 a.)

4 (2 a.) 5 (4 a.) 6 (8 a.)

(Typo. Jagannata Ballabh Press, Deogarh.)

1888. *Imperf.*

No.	Type	Description	Unused	Used
1	**1**	¼ a. black/*yellow*	15·00	
		a. "g" inverted	£650	
		b. Last native character inverted	£800	
2	**2**	½ a. black/*rose*	14·00	
		a. "g" inverted	£650	
3	**3**	1 a. black/*blue*	14·00	
		a. "g" inverted	£650	
4	**4**	2 a. black/*green*	12·00	
		a. "a" omitted	£650	
5	**5**	4 a. black/*yellow*	12·00	
		a. "a" omitted	£650	
6	**6**	8 a. black/*rose*	12·00	
		a. "a" omitted	£650	

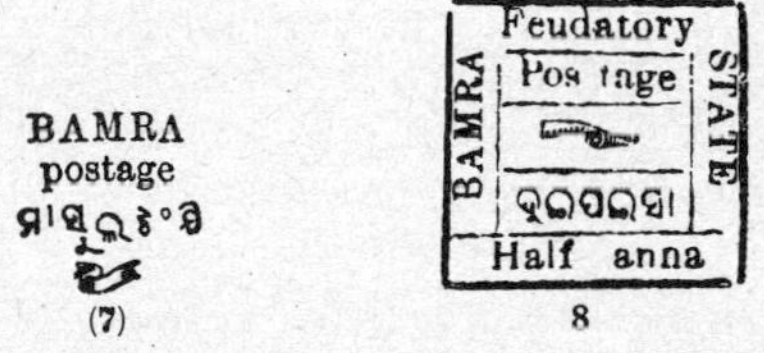

(7) 8

With last native character as in illustration.

No.	Type	Description	Unused	Used
7	**7**	¼ a. black/*yellow*	£600	

These stamps were all printed from the same plate of 96 stamps, 12×8, but for some values only part of the plate was used. We thus have 96 varieties of the ½, 4 and 8 a., 72 of the 1 a., 80 of the 2 a. and not less than 88 of the ¼ a.

One stamp in each sheet has the scroll ornament inverted.

There are two forms of the third native character. In the first five horizontal rows it is as in T **1** and in the last three rows as in T **4**.

These stamps have been reprinted: the ¼ a. and ½ a. in blocks of 8 varieties and all the values in blocks of 20 varieties. T **1** has the fourth character, in the native inscription, in the form which distinguishes the reprints.

1890 (July)–**93.** *Black on coloured paper.*

A. "Postage" *with capital* "P".

No.	Type	Description	Unused	Used
8	**8**	¼ a. on *mauve*	15	20
		a. "Eeudatory"	5·00	6·00
		b. "Quatrer"	5·00	6·00
		c. Inverted "e" in "Postage"	5·00	6·00
9	,,	¼ a. on *bright rose* (1891)	30	20
10	,,	¼ a. on *magenta* (1893) ..	15	25
		a. First "a" in "anna" inverted	9·00	9·00
		b. "AMRA" inverted ..	15·00	15·00
		c. "M" and 2nd "A" of "BAMRA" inverted ..	15·00	15·00
11	,,	½ a. on *blue-green* ..	30	30
		a. "Eeudatory" ..	8·00	9·00
12	,,	½ a. on *green* (1891) ..	35	30
13	**8**	1 a. on *yellow*	75	65
		a. "Eeudatory"	15·00	15·00
14	,,	1 a. on *orange*	12·00	12·00
		a. "annas" for "anna" ..	35·00	35·00
15	,,	2 a. on *mauve*	3·00	3·00
		a. "Eeudatory"	22·00	22·00
16	,,	2 a. on *rose-red* ..	70	70
17	,,	2 a. on *bright rose* ..	80	80
18	,,	4 a. on *mauve*	15·00	15·00
		a. "Eeudatory" ..	50·00	50·00
19	,,	4 a. on *rose-red* ..	1·50	1·50
		a. "Eeudatory" ..	18·00	18·00
		b. "BAMBA" ..	25·00	25·00
20	,,	4 a. on *bright rose* ..	1·00	1·00
21	,,	8 a. on *mauve*	8·00	8·00
		a. "Foudatory" and "Postage"	35·00	35·00
		b. "BAMBA"	40·00	40·00
22	,,	8 a. on *rose-red* ..	2·50	2·00
23	,,	8 a. on *bright rose* ..	2·50	2·00
24	,,	1 r. on *mauve*	15·00	15·00
		a. "Eeudatory" ..	50·00	50·00
		b. "BAMBA" ..	50·00	50·00
		c. "Postage" ..	50·00	50·00
25	,,	1 r. on *bright rose* ..	10·00	10·00
		a. Small "r" in "rupee" ..	70·00	70·00

The native characters are found in one group, or divided into two groups.

B. "postage" *with small* "p" (1891–93).

No.	Type	Description	Unused	Used
26	**8**	¼ a. on *bright rose* (1891) ..	35	25
27	,,	¼ a. on *magenta* (1893) ..	15	20
28	,,	½ a. on *blue-green*	30	45
		a. First "a" in "anna" inverted	4·00	4·50
29	,,	½ a. on *green* (1893) ..	35	45
		a. First "a" in "anna" inverted	4·50	4·50
30	,,	1 a. on *yellow*	45	60
31	,,	1 a. on *orange*	15·00	13·00
32	,,	2 a. on *rose-red* ..	40	50
33	,,	2 a. on *bright rose* ..	45	50
34	,,	4 a. on *rose-red* (1891)	75	1·00
35	,,	4 a. on *bright rose* ..	1·25	1·25
36	,,	8 a. on *mauve* (1891)	7·00	7·00
37	,,	8 a. on *rose-red* ..	1·50	1·50
38	,,	8 a. on *bright rose* ..	2·50	2·50
39	,,	1 r. on *mauve* (1891) ..	13·00	13·00
40	,,	1 r. on *bright rose* ..	12·00	12·00
		a. Small "r" in "rupee" ..	75·00	75·00
		b. Ditto and native characters in the order of 2, 3, 1, 4, 5 ..	£750	£750

There are 10 settings of Type **8.** The first setting (of 20 varieties) has capital "P" throughout. The remaining settings (of 16 varieties) have capital "P" and small "p" mixed.

There are 4 sizes of the central ornament, which represents an elephant's trunk holding a stick:—(*a*) 4 mm. long; (*b*) 5 mm.; (*c*) 6½ mm.; (*d*) 11 mm. These ornaments are also found inverted.

Ornaments (*a*) are found in all settings; (*b*) in all settings from the 3rd to the 10th; (*c*) in the 1st and 2nd settings; and (*d*) only in the 1st setting.

The native characters are found in one or two groups, as before.

The characters are in two groups in the values from 1 a. upwards, in all settings from the third to the tenth.

The stamps of Bamra have been obsolete since 1894.

BARWANI.

PROCESS. All Barwani stamps are typographed.

1. Rana Ranjitsingh.

1921. *Clear impression. Medium wove paper. Pin-perf. 7 all round.*

No.	Type	Description	Unused	Used
1	**1**	¼ a. deep blue-green	24·00	28·00
2	,,	½ a. dull blue	26·00	32·00

The first ¼ a. stamp of Barwani was variously chronicled in India, on issue, as "deep blue-green", "deep blue" and "blue-grey". We did not chronicle the ¼ a. deep blue-green until January, 1925, and it became what has formerly been our No. 12, but erroneously listed as on laid paper. From the evidence of flaws, etc., this ¼ a. may well be the first issue but we are not absolutely satisfied and should be glad to receive any further evidence, either for or against. The only ¼ a. blue-grey which we have seen is that now listed as No. 16*a* but we have no reason to believe that this was the first issue.

Whatever the period of issue, the two stamps listed above are obviously of the same group as, paper, perforation and impression are similar.

1921. *Blurred impression. Soft wove paper. Pin-perf. 7 on* two *or* three *sides.*

No.	Type	Description	Unused	Used
3	**1**	¼ a. green	5·50	6·00
4	,,	½ a. blue (to pale)	6·50	6·50

NOTE. As the small sheets of Barwani stamps were often not perforated all round, many of the earlier stamps are perforated on two or three sides only. Owing to the elementary method of printing, the colours vary greatly in depth, even within a single sheet.

1921–22. *Blurred impression. Pin-perf. 7.*

(*a*) *Glazed paper.*

No.	Type	Description	Unused	Used
5	**1**	¼ a. dull ultramarine	20·00	

(*b*) *Thickish wove paper.*

No.	Type	Description	Unused	Used
6	**1**	¼ a. blue (pale to deep) ..	2·00	
7	,,	½ a. green	6·00	

Nos. 6 and 7 are sometimes perforated all round.

(*c*) *Vertically laid white paper. Imperf.*

No.	Type	Description	Unused	Used
8	**1**	¼ a. green (pale to bright) ..	3·25	
9	,,	½ a. green (pale to deep) ..	1·60	
		a. Perf. 11 at top or bottom only	1·60	
		b. On toned (vert. laid) ..	1·90	
		ba. Perf. 11 at top or bottom only	1·90	

It is suggested that No. 8 may be an error due to printing from the wrong plate.

2. Rana Ranjitsingh. 3.

1922–31. *Perf.* 11. (*a*) *Thick glazed paper.*

No.	Type	Description	Unused	Used
10	**2**	1 a. vermilion	65	2·00
		a. Imperf. between (pr.) ..	26·00	
11	,,	1 a. rose-carmine (1931) ..	1·50	
12	,,	2 a. purple	80	
		a. Doubly printed	24·00	
		b. Imperf. between (pr.) ..	26·00	
		c. *Violet*	3·25	

No. 11 is perforated all round.

(*b*) *Thin smooth unglazed wove paper.*

No.	Type	Description	Unused	Used
13	**1**	½ a. green (bright to deep) ..	65	
		a. Imperf. between (pr.) ..	20·00	
14	**2**	1 a. vermilion	£275	

(*c*) *Thick toned wove paper.*

No.	Type	Description	Unused	Used
15	**2**	2 a. purple	4·50	5·50

1922 (?) *Thin wove paper. Pin-perf.* 8½.

No.	Type	Description	Unused	Used
16	**1**	¼ a. greyish ultramarine ..	65	
		aa. Imperf. (pair)	11·00	
		a. *Blue-grey/toned*	65	
		b. Imperf. between (vert. pr.) ..	11·00	

1923–26. *Various papers and perfs.*

No.	Type	Description	Unused	Used
17	**1**	¼ a. black/*toned* (wove, pin-perf. 7) ('23)	11·00	12·00
18	,,	¼ a. rose (horiz. laid, p. 12) ('23)	50	45
		a. Imperf. between (pr.) ..	20·00	
		b. Pin-perf. 7..	9·00	
		c. Perf. compound of 12 and 6..	9·00	
19	,,	½ a. blue (vert. laid, p. 11) ('26)	50	55

The colours of Nos. 18 and 19 vary considerably. Both are perforated all round and have a papermaker's wmk. in the sheet.

1927. *Very defective impression. Thin, hard wove paper. Perf. 7 all round.*

No.	Type	Description	Unused	Used
20	**1**	¼ a. milky blue	3·75	
21	,,	½ a. bright yellow-green ..	4·00	
		a. Imperf. between (horiz. pr.)	32·00	

In these two stamps the portrait is nearly invisible.

1927–31. (*a*) *Thick wove paper. Sewing machine perf.* 6.

No.	Type	Description	Unused	Used
22	**3**	4 a. yellow-brown	11·00	
		a. Pin-perf. 7..	13·00	

(*b*) *Thin wove paper. Sewing machine perf.* 7.

No.	Type	Description	Unused	Used
23	**3**	4 a. orange-brown	8·00	

(*c*) *Glazed paper. P* 11 *all round.*

No.	Type	Description	Unused	Used
24	**3**	4 a. salmon (to orange) ..	8·00	
		a. Imperf. between (horiz. pr.)	65·00	

1928. *Thick glazed paper. Pin-perf.* 7, *all round.*

No.	Type	Description	Unused	Used
25	**1**	¼ a. deep bright blue ..	1·00	
26	,,	½ a. bright yellow-green ..	1·00	

1928 (Nov.). *Thick glazed paper. P* 11 (*rough*).

No.	Type	Description	Unused	Used
27	**1**	¼ a. ultramarine	50	
		a. Tête-bêche (horiz. pr.) ..	5·50	
28	,,	½ a. apple-green	80	
		a. Tête-bêche (vert. pr.) ..	5·50	

No. 27 was printed in sheets of 8 (4×2) with the two centre pairs *tête-bêche* while No. 28, in similar sheets, had the two horizontal rows *tête-bêche*.

1929 (Jan.). *Thick glazed paper. P* 11 (*clean-cut*) *all round.*

No.	Type	Description	Unused	Used
29	**1**	¼ a. deep blue	40	45
		a. Imperf. between (pr.) ..	11·00	
30	,,	½ a. turquoise-green (to deep blue-green)	40	45
		a. Imperf. between (pr.) ..	11·00	

GUM. Nos. 1 to 30 are ungummed. The following stamps have gum.

4. Rana Devi Singh. 5.

1932–48.

A. *Close setting* (2 *mm.*). *P* 11, 12 *or compound.*
B. *Wide setting* (3–4 *mm.*). *P* 11.

No.	Type	Description	A. Unused	A. Used	B. Unused	B. Used
31	**4**	¼ a. slate ..	80	1·25	40	80
32	,,	½ a. blue-green ..	80	1·25	45	65
33	,,	1 a. brown ..	80	1·25	90	1·25
		a. *Choc.* P 8½ ('48)	†		2·75	—
34	,,	2 a. purple ..	1·25	—	—	—
		a. *Reddish purple*	†		4·00	—
35	,,	4 a. olive-green ..	2·75	4·00	4·00	—

The measurements given in the heading indicate the horizontal spacing between impressions. There are eight settings of this interesting issue: four "Close" where the over-all stamp dimensions from centre to centre of perfs. vary in width from 21½ to 23 mm. and in height from 25 to 27½ mm.; and four "Wide", width 23–23½ mm. and height 29–30 mm.

1935–48. *P* 11. A. *Close setting* (3–4½ *mm.*) B. *Wide setting* (7–10 *mm.*).

No.	Type	Description	A. Unused	A. Used	B. Unused	B. Used
36	**1**	¼ a. black ..	65	—	1·00	1·2
37	,,	½ a. blue-green ('38?) ..	3·25	—	†	
		a. *Dp. yell.-grn.* ..	1·90	—	1·25	1·6
38	**2**	1 a. brn. (*shades*)	1·00	1·25	1·90	—
		a. Perf. 8½ (5 mm.) ('48) ..	†		1·90	—
39	,,	2 a. bright purple ('47?) ..	†		12·00	16·0
40	,,	2 a. rose-carmine ('48) ..	†		5·50	—
41	**3**	4 a. sage-green ..	5·50	5·50	3·25	—
		a. *Pale sage-grn.* ..	†		2·10	3·0

There was one "Close" setting (over-all stam size 25×29 mm.) and four "Wide" setting with over-all sizes 26½–31½×31–36½ mm. Ther was also one "Medium" setting (26½×31 mm. but this was confined to the 1 a. perf. 8½, No 38a.

1938. *P* 11.

No.	Type	Description	Unused	Used
42	**5**	1 a. brown	4·00	

The stamps of Barwani became obsolete o July 1st, 1948.

BHOPAL.

The correct English inscription on thes stamps is "H.H. NAWAB SHAH JAHAN BEGAM" In the case of Nos. 22 and 23 the normal stamp are spelt "BEGAN" and specimens with "BEGAM" are "errors".

As the stamps were printed from lithographi stones on which each unit was drawn separatel by hand, numerous errors of spelling occurred These are constant on all sheets and are listed Some of our illustrations inadvertently includ errors of spelling.

EMBOSSING. Types **1/3** and **6** to **12***a* al have the centre Urdu inscriptions embossed Almost all varieties can be found with th embossing inverted or sideways, as well a upright.

The various basic types were often in con current use but for greater convenience th following list is arranged according to type instead of being in strict chronological order.

Nawab Shah Jahan Begam, 1868–1901.

1 (¼ a.)

1876. *Litho.* (*a*) *Double frame,* 20 *varieties of eac value.*

No.	Type	Description	Unused	Used
1	**1**	¼ a. black	£100	£10
		a. "BFGAM"	£650	£65
		b. "BEGAN"	£650	£65
		c. "EGAM"	£650	£65
2	,,	½ a. red	5·50	5·5
		a. "BFGAM"	32·00	32·0
		b. "BEGAN"	32·00	32·0
		c. "EGAM"	32·00	32·0

2 (½ a.)

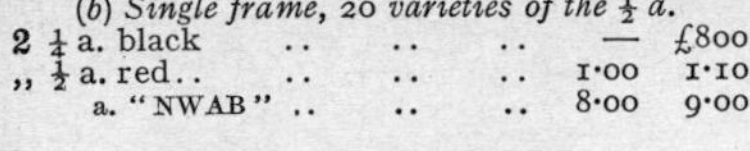

(b) Single frame, 20 varieties of the ½ a.

3 **2** ¼ a. black .. .. .. — £800
4 ,, ½ a. red.. .. .. .. 1·00 1·10
a. "NWAB" .. .. .. 8·00 9·00

3 (¼ a.)

3a (¼ a.)

1878 (JAN.). *All lettered* "EEGAM" *for* "BEGAM".

(a) Plate 1 (20 varieties). Frame lines extend horiz. and vert. between stamps throughout sheet.

5 **3** ¼ a. black 20 25

(b) Plate 2 (20 varieties). Frame lines normal.

5a **3a** ¼ a. black 20 25

Apart from the frame line differences between Types **3** and **3a** the stamps can also be distinguished by the differences in the value tablets, notably the thin vertical line in the centre in Type **3a** compared with the slightly diagonal and heavier line in Type **3**.

4 (¼ a.)

5 (½ a.)

1878 (JUNE?)–**79.** *Value in parenthesis; 32 varieties. Imperf.*

6 **4** ¼ a. green (1879) .. .. 2·75 3·25
7 ,, ¼ a. green (*perf.*) (1879) .. 2·75 3·25
8 **5** ½ a. red .. .. 1·00 1·00
a. "JAHN" .. .. .. 6·50
b. "NWAB" .. .. .. 6·50
c. "EEGAM" .. .. .. 6·50
9 ,, ½ a. brown .. .. .. 8·00 9·00
a. "JAHN" .. .. .. 45·00
b. "NWAB" .. .. .. 45·00
c. "EEGAM" .. .. .. 45·00

1880. *T* **5** *redrawn; value not in parenthesis; 32 varieties of each value.*

(a) Imperf.

10 ¼ a. blue-green 90
a. "NAWA" .. .. .. 6·50
b. "CHAH" .. .. .. 6·50
c. "JABAN" .. .. .. 11·00
11 ½ a. brown-red.. .. .. 1·25 1·25

(b) Perf.

12 ¼ a. blue-green 65
a. "NAWA" .. .. .. 2·75
b. "CHAH" .. .. .. 2·75
c. "JABAN" .. .. .. 7·00
13 ½ a. brown-red 65

1884. *T* **5** *again redrawn; 32 varieties, some with value in parenthesis, others not. Perf.*

14 ¼ a. greenish blue .. .. 1·00
a. "ANAWAB" .. .. 11·00

In this plate there is a slanting dash under and to left of the letters "JA" of "JAHAN," instead of a character like a large comma, as on all previous varieties of this design.

1895. *T* **5** *again redrawn. 8 varieties. Laid paper.*

15 ¼ a. red (*imperf.*) 50 55
16 ¼ a. red (*perf.*) .. .. .. — 16·00

In these cases where the same design has been redrawn several times, and each time in a number of varieties of type, it is not easy to distinguish the various issues. Nos. 6 and 7 may be distinguished from Nos. 10 and 12 by the presence or absence of the parentheses marks (); 8, 9 and 11 differ principally in colour; 8 and 15 are very much alike, but differ in the value as well as in paper.

6 (1 a.)

1881. *24 varieties of each value. Imperf.*

17 **6** ¼ a. black 25 65
a. "NWAB" .. .. 1·90
18 ,, ½ a. red 50 90
a. "NWAB" .. .. .. 2·75
19 ,, 1 a. brown 50 90
a. "NWAB" .. .. .. 2·75
20 ,, 2 a. blue .. .. .. 65 1·25
a. "NWAB" .. .. .. 2·75
21 ,, 4 a. buff .. .. .. 1·90 1·90
a. "NWAB" .. .. .. 6·50

In this issue all values were produced from the same drawing, and therefore show exactly the same varieties of type. The value at foot in this and all the following issues is given to only one form.

7 (½ a.)

1886. *Similar to T* **6** *but normally lettered* "BEGAN"; *larger lettering; 32 varieties.*

(a) Imperf.

22 **7** ½ a. pale red 40 50
a. "BEGAM" .. .. 3·25
b. "NWAB" .. .. 3·25

(b) Perf.

23 **7** ½ a. pale red .. .. 13·00
a. "BEGAM" .. ..
b. "NWAB" .. ..

8 (4 a.)

1886. *T* **8.** *T* **6** *redrawn; 24 varieties. The* "M" *of* "BEGAM" *is an inverted* "W". *The width of the stamps is rather greater than the height. (a) Wove paper. Imperf.*

24 **8** 4 a. yellow .. .. 4·00
a. "EEGAM" .. .. 26·00

(b) Laid paper.

25 **8** 4 a. yellow (*imperf.*) .. 1·25
a. "EEGAM" .. .. 9·00 9·00
26 ,, 4 a. yellow (*perf.*) .. 1·00
a. "EEGAM" .. .. 8·00 8·00

1889. *T* **6** *again redrawn; 32 varieties, lettered* "BEGAN."

27 ¼ a. black (*perf.*) 40 50
a. "EEGAN" .. .. 3·25 4·00
28 ¼ a. black (*imperf.*) 65 65
a. "EEGAN" .. .. 4·50 5·50

9 (¼ a.)

1889–90. *T* **9.** *T* **6** *again redrawn; 24 varieties of each value, all with* "M" *like an inverted* "W". *Wove paper. Imperf.*

29 **9** ¼ a. black 25 40
30 ,, 1 a. brown 40 50
a. "EEGAM" .. .. 2·75 3·25
b. "BBGAM" .. .. 2·75 3·25
31 ,, 2 a. bluc 45 45
a. "BBEGAM" .. .. 4·00 4·00
b. "NAWAH" .. .. 4·00 4·00
32 ,, 4 a. orange-yellow 40 80

Perf.

33 **9** ¼ a. black 40 40
34 ,, 1 a. brown 45 55
a. "EEGAM" .. .. 3·25 4·00
b. "BBGAM" .. .. 3·25 4·00
35 ,, 2 a. blue 40 50
a. "BBEGAM" .. .. 10·00 4·00
b. "NAWAH" .. .. 10·00 4·00
36 ,, 4 a. orange-yellow 65 90

Nos. 32 and 36 are nearly square, in many cases rather larger in height than in width.

1891. *As last, but 32 varieties.*

37 **9** ¼ a. red (*imperf.*) 45 45
38 ,, ½ a. red (*perf.*) 45 45

1894–98. *T* **6** *again redrawn; 24 varieties, almost all showing a character inside the octagon below, as in T* **9.** *Wove paper.*

39 1 a. deep brown (*imperf.*) .. 50 65
a. Red-brown .. .. .. 8·00
b. Printed both sides .. ..
41 1 a. deep brown (*perf.*) .. 90 90

10 (1 a.)

As Nos. 39/41, but printed from a fresh transfer (?), showing the lines blurred and shaky. Wove paper. Imperf. (1898).

42 **10** 1 a. purple-brown .. .. 90 1·25
a. "NAWAH" .. 5·50 6·50
43 ,, 1 a. purple-brown/*buff* .. 65 80
a. "NAWAH" .. 5·25 4·00
b. Printed on both sides ..

The above are known without embossing.

11 (¼ a.)

1895. 8 *varieties, lettered* "EEGAM". *White laid paper.*

44 **11** ¼ a. black (*imperf.*) 65 65
45 „ ¼ a. black (*perf.*) 80 80
a. "NAW B" £400 £400
b. "A" inserted £200 £200

On the perf. stamp the second "A" in "NAWAB" was missing on No. 8 in the setting. This letter was later inserted varying progressively from small to large.

12 (½ a.)

1895. *Narrow label at bottom; 8 varieties, lettered* "W W" *for* "H. H." *Laid paper.*

46 **12** ½ a. black (*imperf.*) 40 40

12a

1895. 8 *varieties. Laid paper.*

47 **12a** ½ a. red (*imperf.*) .. 50 50

No. 47 is a combination of Types **1** and **6**, having the double outer frame to the octagon and the value in one form only.

13 (¼ a.)

14 (¼ a.)

1884. 32 *varieties. Perf.*

48 **13** ½ a. blue-green .. .. 22·00 22·00
a. "JAN" £120
b. "BEGM" £225
c. "NWAB" £225
d. "SHAHAN" £225
e. "JAHA" £225
f. "JN" £225

1895. *T* **14**, *double-lined frame round each stamp; 6 varieties lettered* "JAN.". *Laid paper.*

49 **14** ¼ a. bright green (*imperf.*) .. 65 80

15 (½ a.)

16 (¼ a.)

1884. 32 *varieties of each value. Laid paper.*

50 **15** ¼ a. blue-green (*imperf.*) .. 9·00 9·00
a. "NWAB" .. .. 26·00
b. "SAH" .. .. .. 26·00
c. "NAWA" and "JANAN" £130
51 „ ¼ a. blue-green (*perf.*) .. 15
a. "NWAB" 50
b. "SAH" 50
c. "NAWA" and "JANAN" 2·75
52 „ ½ a. black (*imperf.*) 20 20
a. "NWAB" .. .. 1·00
b. "SAH" .. .. .. 1·00
c. "NAWA" and "JANAN" 4·00
53 „ ½ a. black (*perf.*) 15
a. "NWAB" 65
b. "SAH" 65
c. "NAWA" and "JANAN" 1·50

The ¼ a. of this issue is in *blue-green*, or *greenish blue*. Both values were printed from the same stone, the value alone being altered. There are therefore the same varieties of each. These are the only stamps of this design on laid paper.

1886. *T* **15** *redrawn;* 32 *varieties of each value. Wove paper.*

54 ¼ a. green (*imperf.*) 10 10
a. "NAWA" 75
b. "NWAB" 75
c. "NWABA" 75
d. "NAWAA" 75
e. "BEGAAM" and "NWABA" 80
55 ¼ a. green (*perf.*) 10 12
a. "NAWA" 75
b. "NWAB" 75
c. "NWABA" 75
d. "NAWAA" 75
e. "BEGAAM" and "NWABA" 80
56 ½ a. red (*imperf.*) 20 20
a. "SAH" 75
b. "NAWABA" 75

The ¼ a. varies from *yellow-green* to *deep green*.

In Nos. 54 and 55 the "N" of "NAWAB" and "JAHAN" is reversed except in positions 10, 13 and 15.

1888. *T* **15** *again redrawn;* 32 *varieties, letters in upper angles smaller.* "N" *of* "NAWAB" *correct. Wove paper.*

57 ¼ a. deep green (*imperf.*) .. 12 20
a. "SAH" .. .. .. 1·00
b. "NAWA" .. .. .. 1·00
58 ¼ a. deep green (*perf.*) .. 20 20
a. "SAH" .. .. .. 1·50
b. "NAWA" .. .. .. 1·50

Nos. 50 to 58 have the dash under the letters "JA." as in No. 14.

1891. *T* **15** *again redrawn;* 32 *varieties, lettered* "NWAB." *Wove paper.* (*a*) *Imperf.*

59 ½ a. red 20 30
a. "SAH" .. .. .. 2·00

(*b*) *P* 3 *to* 4½, *or about* 7.

60 ½ a. red 35 35
a. "SAH" .. .. .. 4·00

Nos. 59 and 60 have the comma under "JA".

1894. *T* **15** *again redrawn; letters in corners larger than in* 1888, *value in very small characters;* 32 *varieties, all with* "G" *in left-hand lower corner. Wove paper.*

61 ¼ a. green (*imperf.*) 12 12
a. "NAWAH" .. .. 3·00
b. Value in brackets .. .. 3·00
62 ¼ a. green (*perf.*) 20 20
a. "NAWAH" .. .. 3·00
b. Value in brackets .. .. 3·00

Nos. 61 and 62 have neither the dash nor the comma under "JA".

1896. *T* **16**; *oval narrower, stops after* "H.H." *space after* "NAWAB". *The line down the centre is under the first* "H" *of* "SHAH" *or between* "HA" *instead of being under the second* "H" *or between* "AH". *Wove paper. Imperf.*

63 **16** ¼ a. bright green 8 8
a. "SHAN" 40
64 „ ¼ a. pale green 10 10
a. "SHAN" 80
65 „ ¼ a. black 10 10
a. "SHAN" 80

1899. *T* **15.** *Printed apparently from a transfer from the stone of* 1891; *the first* "A" *of* "NAWAB" *always absent. Numerous defective and malformed letters. Wove paper. Imperf.*

66 ½ a. black (NWAB) 12 45
a. "NWASBAHJANNI" .. 2·75 4·00
b. "SBAH" .. .. .. 2·00 4·00
c. "SBAN" .. .. .. 2·75 4·00
d. "NWIB" .. .. .. 2·75 4·00
e. "BEIAM" .. .. .. 2·50 4·00
f. "SHH" .. .. .. 2·75 4·00
g. "SBAH" and "BBGAM" .. 2·75 4·00
h. "BBGAM" .. .. 2·75 4·00

17 (8 a.)

18 (¼ a.)

1890. *T* **17**; 10 *varieties. Single-line frame to each stamp.* (*a*) *Wove paper.*

67 **17** 8 a. slate-green (*imperf.*) .. 6·50 6·50
a. "HAH" .. .. .. 12·00
b. "JABAN" .. .. 12·00
68 „ 8 a. slate-green (*perf.*) .. 6·50 6·50
a. "HAH" .. .. .. 12·00
b. "JABAN" .. .. 12·00

(*b*) *Thin laid paper.*

69 **17** 8 a. green-black (*imperf.*) .. 6·50 6·50
a. "HAH" .. .. .. 12·00
b. "JABAN" .. .. 12·00
70 „ 8 a. green-black (*perf.*) .. 6·50 6·50
a. "HAH" .. .. .. 12·00
b. "JABAN" .. .. 12·00

1893. *T* **17** *redrawn. No frame to each stamp, but a frame to the sheet.* 10 *varieties.* (*a*) *Wove paper.*

71 8 a. green-black (*imperf.*) .. 6·50 6·50
72 8 a. green-black (*perf.*) .. 6·50 6·50

(*b*) *Thin laid paper. Imperf.*

73 8 a. green-black .. .. 12·00 12·00

1898. *Defective transfer from the stone of* 1893. *Lettering irregular. Wove paper. Imperf.*

74 8 a. green-black .. .. 5·50 5·50
a. Reversed "E" in "BEGAM" 12·00
75 8 a. black .. .. .. 5·50 5·50
a. Reversed "E" in "BEGAM" 12·00

1896–1901. *Wove paper.* 32 *varieties. Imperf.*

76 **18** ¼ a. black 30 30

Printed from a fresh transfer (?), lines shaky. (1899).

77 **18** ¼ a. black 80 80

The same, on thick wove paper (1901).

78 **18** ¼ a. black .. .. .. 26·00 26·00

Nawab Sultan Jahan Begam, 1901–1926.

19 (¼ a.)

20

902. T 19. *With the octagonal embossed device of the previous issues.* 16 *varieties of* ½ a., 8 *varieties of each of the other values. Thin, yellowish wove paper. Imperf.*

) 19 ¼ a. rose 75 75
) ,, ½ a. rose-red 75 75
(,, ½ a. black .. .. .. 1·00 90
a. Printed both sides .. £150
,, 1 a. brown .. .. .. 1·00 90
,, 1 a. red-brown .. .. 1·00 90
,, 2 a. blue .. .. .. 2·75 2·75
,, 4 a. orange .. .. .. 13·00 14·00
,, 4 a. yellow .. .. .. 11·00 11·00
,, 8 a. lilac .. .. .. 13·00 14·00
,, 1 r. rose .. .. .. 20·00 24·00

903. *With a circular embossed device.* 32 *varieties (two plates) of* ¼ a., 8 *fresh varieties of* ½ a. *and* 2 a., 4 a., 8 a., *and* 1 r., *as before.*

A. *Wove paper.* B. *Laid paper.*

		A.		B.	
19 ¼ a. rose-red ..	12	12	30	—
,, ½ a. red	20	30	12	—
,, ½ a. black ..	12	20	35	40
,, 1 a. brown ..	45	—		†
,, 1 a. red-brown ..	45	—	—	—
,, 2 a. blue ..	80	80	—	—
,, 4 a. orange ..		†	13·00	13·00
,, 4 a. yellow ..	11·00	11·00	—	—
,, 8 a. lilac ..	12·00	12·00	—	—
,, 1 r. rose	13·00	13·00	—	—

o. 71 *optd. with initial of the new Begum in red.*
8 a. green-black .. .. 12·00 12·00
a. Opt. inverted .. .. 26·00 26·00

Some of the previous stamps remained on sale nd probably in use) after the issue of the series 1902, and some of these were afterwards put on le with the new form of embossing; fresh ates were made of some of the old designs, in nitation of the earlier issues, and impressions om these were also sold with the new embossed evice. We no longer list these doubtful items.

(Recess. Perkins, Bacon & Co.)

908. *P* 13½.
o 20 1 a. green 65 10
a. Printed both sides .. 55·00
b. Imperf. (pair) .. ..

The ordinary postage stamps of Bhopal ecame obsolete on July 1, 1908.

OFFICIAL STAMPS.

SERVICE

(O 1)

SERVICE (O 2)

SERVICE (O 3)

RINTERS. 1908 issue recess-ptd. and optd. y Perkins, Bacon & Co. Type O 4 and subequent types and opts., ptd. at Indian Govt. tg. Wks., Nasik.

908 (1 JULY). *As T* **20**, *but inscribed* " H.H. BEGUM'S SERVICE " *at left. No wmk. P* 13 *to* 14. *Overprinted (a) with Type* O **1**.
o1 ½ a. yellow-green 65 8
a. Pair, one without overprint .. 32·00
b. Opt. double, one inverted .. 32·00
ba. Do. Imperf. (pair) .. .. 32·00
c. Opt. inverted .. .. 32·00
d. Imperf. between (horiz. pair) 80·00

302 1 a. carmine-red 65 8
a. Opt. inverted .. .. 20·00 20·00
b. Imperf. (pair) .. .. 32·00
c. *Red* 65 5
303 2 a. ultramarine .. .. 2·75 5
a. Imperf. (pair) .. .. 26·00 26·00
304 4 a. brown .. .. .. 5·50 5

(*b*) *With Type* O **2**.
305 ½ a. yellow-green 60 5
306 1 a. carmine-red .. .. 2·00 50
307 2 a. ultramarine .. .. 2·00 10
a. Opt. inverted .. .. 13·00
308 4 a. brown .. .. 13·00 10
a. Opt. inverted .. .. 13·00 13·00
b. Opt. double .. .. 32·00
c. Imperf. (pair) .. .. 40·00
d. Imperf. (pr.) and opt. inverted 40·00

The two overprints differ in the shape of the letters, noticeably in the " R ".

O 4

1930 (1 JULY)**–31.** *Type* O **4** (25½ × 30½ *mm.*) *optd. with Type* O **3**. *Litho. P* 14.
309 O 4 ½ a. sage-green (1931) .. 30 8
310 ,, 1 a. carmine-red .. 40 5
311 ,, 2 a. ultramarine .. 45 5
312 ,, 4 a. chocolate .. 65 10

The ½ a., 2 a., and 4 a. are inscribed " POSTAGE " at left.

1932–33. *As Type* O 4 (21 × 25 *mm.*), *but inscr.* " POSTAGE " *at left. Optd. with Type* O **1**. *Litho.*
(*a*) " BHOPAL STATE " *at right. P* 13.
313 ¼ a. orange 65 5
a. Perf. 11½ .. .. 1·00 5
b. Perf. 14 .. .. 4·00 5
c. Perf. 13½ .. .. 3·00 1·75
ca. Pair, one without opt. .. 20·00

(*b*) " BHOPAL GOVT." *at right. P* 13½.
314 ½ a. yellow-green 8 5
315 1 a. carmine-red 10 5
316 2 a. ultramarine 35 30
317 4 a. chocolate 50 45
a. Perf. 14 .. .. .. 6·50 45

¼A (O 5)

THREE PIES (O 6)

ONE ANNA (O 7)

1935–36. *Nos.* 314, 316 *and* 317 *surch. as Types* O 5 *to* O 7.
318 O 5 ¼ a. on ½ a. yell.-grn. (R.) 2·75 1·50
a. Surch. inverted .. 32·00
319 O 6 3 p. on ½ a. yell.-grn. (R.) 12 5
a. " THEEE PIES " .. 11·00 11·00
b. " THRFE " for " THREE " 11·00 11·00
c. Surch. inverted .. 20·00 20·00
320 O 5 ¼ a. on 2 a. ultram. (R.) .. 2·75 80
a. Surch. inverted .. .. 16·00 13·00
321 O 6 3 p. on 2 a. ultram. (R.) .. 30 30
a. Surch. inverted .. 20·00 20·00
b. " THEEE PIES " .. 11·00 11·00
ba. Do. Surch. inverted .. £100 £100
c. " THRFE for " THREE " 11·00 11·00
ca. Do. Surch. inverted .. £100 £100
322 O 5 ¼ a. on 4 a. chocolate (R.) 26·00 11·00
a. Perf. 14 .. ..
323 ,, ¼ a. on 4 a. chocolate (Bk.) (25.5.36) 6·50 5·00
a. Perf. 14 .. ..

324 O 6 3 p. on 4 a. chocolate (R.) 12·00 6·00
a. " THEEE PIES " .. 60·00 60·00
b. " THRER " for " THREE " 60·00 60·00
c. " THRFE " for " THREE " 60·00 60·00
d. Perf. 14 .. ..
325 ,, 3 p. on 4 a. chocolate (Bk.) (25.5.36) .. .. 1·00 65
a. " THRER " for " THREE " 20·00 20·00
b. " FHREE " for " THREE " 20·00 20·00
c. " PISE " for " PIES " .. 40·00 40·00
d. " PIFS " for " PIES " .. 24·00 24·00
e. Perf. 14 .. ..
326 O 7 1 a. on ½ a. yell.-grn. (V.) 20 20
a. Surch. inverted .. 16·00 16·00
b. First " N " in " ANNA " inverted .. .. 5·50 5·50
ba. Do. Surch. inverted .. 55·00 55·00
327 ,, 1 a. on 2 a. ultram. (R.) 20 12
a. Surch inverted .. 20·00 20·00
b. First " N " in " ANNA " inverted 5·50 5·50
ba. Do. Surch. inverted .. 35·00 35·00
c. " ANNO " £250 £250
327*d* ,, 1 a. on 2 a. ultram. (V.) 16·00 16·00
da. Surch. inverted .. 45·00 45·00
db. First " N " in " ANNA " inverted .. 65·00 65·00
dc. Do. Surch. inverted .. £100 £100
328 ,, 1 a. on 2 a. ultramarine (Bk.) (25.5.36) .. 35 12
329 ,, 1 a. on 4 a. chocolate (B.) 25 10
a. First " N " in " ANNA " inverted .. .. 5·50 5·50
b. Perf. 14 .. ..

Nos. 318 to 325 are arranged in composite sheets of 100 (10 × 10). The two upper horizontal rows of each value are surcharged as Type O **5** and the next five rows as Type O **6**. The remaining three rows are also surcharged as Type O **6** but in a slightly narrower setting.

The surcharge on No. 323 differs from Type O **5** in the shape of the figures and letter.

O 8

1935–39. *As Type* O **8**.
(*a*) *Litho. Inscr.* " BHOPAL GOVT. POSTAGE ". *Optd.* " SERVICE " (13½ *mm.*). *P* 13½.
330 1 a. 3 p. blue and claret .. 10 8

(*b*) *Typo. Inscr.* " BHOPAL STATE POSTAGE ". *Optd.* " SERVICE " (11 *mm.*). *P* 12.
331 1 a. 6 p. blue and claret ('37) 10 10
a. Imperf. between (pair) .. 28·00 28·00
b. Opt. omitted .. .. 28·00 28·00
c. Opt. double, one inverted .. 32·00 32·00
d. Imperf. (pair) .. .. 26·00 26·00
e. Blue printing double .. 16·00 16·00
332 1 a. 6 p. claret ('39) .. 10 10
a. Imperf. between (pair) .. 26·00 26·00
b. Opt. omitted .. .. 28·00 28·00
c. Opt. double, one inverted .. 28·00 28·00
d. Opt. double .. .. 28·00 28·00

O 9

1936 (JULY)–**1938.** *Optd.* " SERVICE ". *Typo. P* 12.

333 O **9** ¼ a. orange (Br.) 10 8
a. Imperf. betwn. (vert. pr.) 26·00 26·00
b. Opt. inverted .. .. 26·00 26·00
c. Black opt. .. .. 6·50 6·50
ca. Do. Opt. inverted .. 40·00 40·00
334 ,, ¼ a. yellow (Br.) (1938) .. 5 5
335 ,, 1 a. scarlet 5 5
a. Imperf. between (horiz. pair) .. .. 16·00 16·00
b. Imperf. between (vert. pair) .. .. 24·00 24·00
c. Imperf. between (block of four) .. .. 45·00 45·00

O **10.** The Moti Mahal.

1936–49. *As Type* O **10** (*various palaces*). *Typo. P* 12.

(*a*) *Optd.* " SERVICE " (13½ *mm.*).
336 ½ a. purple-brn. & yell.-grn. 8 5
a. Imperf. between (vert. pair) .. — 16·00
ab. Imperf. between (horiz. pair) .. — 18·00
b. Opt. double .. .. 20·00 16·00
c. Frame double .. .. 6·50 5·00
d. *Purple-brown & green* ('38) .. 8 5

(*b*) *Optd.* " SERVICE " (11 *mm.*).
337 2 a. brown and blue (1937) .. 8 8
a. Imperf. between (pair) .. 16·00 17·00
b. Opt. inverted .. .. 20·00 20·00
c. Pair, one without opt. .. 35·00
d. As c but opt. inverted ..
338 2 a. green and violet (1938) .. 30 5
a. Imperf. between (vert. pair) .. 13·00 13·00
b. Imp. betwn. (vert. strip of 3) .. 35·00 20·00
c. Frame double .. 24·00 20·00
339 4 a. blue and brown (1937) .. 35 35
a. Imperf. between (pair) .. 26·00 24·00
b. Opt. omitted .. .. 26·00 24·00
c. Opt. double .. .. 26·00 24·00
d. *Blue & reddish brown* (1938).. 40 30
da. Opt. omitted .. .. — 20·00
340 8 a. bright purple & blue ('38) 50 40
a. Imperf. between (pair) .. 40·00 40·00
b. Opt. omitted .. .. 26·00 26·00
c. Opt. double .. .. 26·00 26·00
d. Imperf. between (horiz. pair) and opt. omitted .. .. — 45·00
341 1 r. blue and reddish pur. (Br.) (1938) 80 40
a. Opt. in black (1944) .. 6·50 5·00
ab. *Light blue & bright purple* .. 12·00 12·00

(*c*) *Optd.* " SERVICE " (11½ *mm.*) *with serifs.*
342 1 r. dull blue and bright purple (Bk.) (1949) .. 13·00 13·00
a. " SREVICE " for " SERVICE " 32·00 32·00
b. " SERVICE " omitted

(*d*) *Optd.* " SERVICE " (13½ *mm.*) *with serifs.*
343 8 a. bright purple & blue ('49) 18·00 18·00
a. " SERAICE " for " SERVICE " .. .. 65·00 80·00
b. Fig. " 1 " for " I " in " SERVICE " .. .. 55·00 65·00

The ½ a. is inscr. " BHOPAL GOVT." below the arms, other values have " BHOPAL STATE ".

Designs:—(37½ × 22½ mm.) 2 a. The Moti Masjid; 4 a. Taj Mahal and Be-Nazir Palaces. (39 × 24 mm.) —8a. Ahmadabad Palace. (45½ × 27½ mm.)—1 r. Rait Ghat.

O **11.** Tiger.

1940. *As Type* O **11** (*animals*). *Typo. P* 12.
344 ¼ a. bright blue 45 10
345 1 a. bright purple (Chital) .. 1·25 20

1941. *As Type* O **8** *but coloured centre inscr.* " SERVICE "; *bottom frame inscr.* " BHOPAL STATE POSTAGE ". *Typo. P* 12.
346 1 a. 3 p. emerald-green .. 10 5
a. Imperf. between (pair) .. 60·00 60·00

O **13.** The Moti Mahal.

1944–47. *As Type* O **13** (*various palaces*). *Typo. P* 12 *or imperf.*
347 ½ a. green 20 20
a. Imperf. (pair) .. .. 13·00 13·00
b. Imperf. between (vert. pair) 16·00 16·00
c. Doubly printed .. .. 16·00 16·00
348 2 a. violet 30 30
a. Imperf. (pair) .. .. 13·00 13·00
b. Imperf. between (pair) (*shades*) 32·00 32·00
c. *Bright purple* ('46) 30 30
ca. Doubly printed .. .. 16·00 16·00
d. *Mauve* ('47) .. .. 1·00 75
e. Error. Chocolate .. ..
349 4 a. chocolate 40 30
a. Imperf. (pair) .. .. 16·00 16·00
b. Imperf. between (horiz. pair) .. 21·00 21·00

Design inscr. " BHOPAL STATE ":—2 a. The Moti Masjid; 4 a. Be-Nazir Palaces.

SERVICE

O **14.** Arms of Bhopal.

2 As. (O **15**)

2 As. (O **16**)

1945–49. *Typo. P* 12.
350 O **14** 3 p. bright blue .. 5 5
a. Imperf. between (pair) .. 13·00 13·00
b. Stamp doubly printed .. 12·00 12·00
351 ,, 9 p. chestnut (*shades*) .. 1·00 50
a. Imperf. (pair) .. 13·00 13·00
b. *Orange-brown* .. .. 12·00 12·00
352 ,, 1 a. purple 10 5
a. Imp. horiz. (vert. pair)
b. *Violet* .. .. .. 1·00 25
353 ,, 1½ a. claret 25 25
a. Imperf. between (pair) .. 16·00 16·00
354 ,, 3 a. yellow 12 20
a. Imperf. pair .. .. 13·00 13·00
b. Imperf. horiz. (vert. pair) .. .. 20·00 26·00
c. Imperf. vert. (horiz. pr.)
d. *Orange-brown* ('49) .. 6·50
355 ,, 6 a. carmine .. .. 2·75 2·75
a. Imperf. (pair) .. .. — 17·00
b. Imperf. horiz. (vert. pr.) .. 20·00 20·00
c. Imperf. vert. (horiz. pr.) 20·00 20·00

1949 (JULY). *Surch. with Type* O **15.** *P* 12.
356 O **14** 2 a. on 1½ a. claret .. 20 35
a. Stop omitted .. .. 4·50 4·50
b. Imperf. (pair) .. .. 40·00 40·00
ba. Stop omitted (pair) .. 5·00 5·00

1949 (?). *Surch. with Type* O **16.** *Imperf. or P* 12.
357 O **14** 2 a. on 1½ a. claret .. 80·00 55·00

There are three types of the figure " 2 " in the surcharge.

BHOR.

1

2

1879. *Very thick to thin native paper. Imper*
1 **1** ½ a. carmine (*shades*) 80 9
2 **2** 1 a. carmine (*shades*) 80 9

3. Pant Sachiv Shankarro Chimnaji.

1901. *Typo. Wove paper. Imperf.*
3 **3** ½ a. red .. .. 2·00 11·

BIJAWAR.

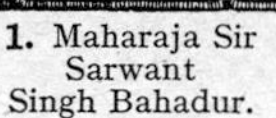

1. Maharaja Sir Sarwant Singh Bahadur.

2. Maharaja Sir Sarwant Singh Bahadur.

(Typo. in Bombay.)

1935–36. (*a*) *P* 11 (1.7.35).
1 **1** 3 p. brown 20 2
a. Imperf. (pair) .. .. 4·50
b. Imp. between (vert. pair) .. 20·00
2 ,, 6 p. carmine 20 2
a. Imp. bet. (vert. or hor. pair) .. 20·00
3 ,, 9 p. violet 20 2
a. Imp. bet. (vert. or hor. pair) .. 20·00
4 ,, 1 a. blue 25 4
a. Imp. bet. (vert. or hor. pair) .. 20·00
b. Imp. vert. (hor. strip 3) .. 45·00
5 ,, 2 a. deep green 40 5
a. Imp. bet. (vert. or hor. pair) .. 9·00

(*b*) *Roul.* 7 (1936).
6 **1** 3 p. brown 20 3
a. Printed on gummed side .. 13·00
7 ,, 6 p. carmine 30 5
8 ,, 9 p. violet 50 6
9 ,, 1 a. blue .. .. .. 90 1·2
10 ,, 2 a. deep green .. .. 1·00 1·2

1937 (MAY). *Typo. P* 9.

11 **2** 4 a. orange .. .. .. 65 1·10
a. Imp. between (vert. pair) .. 55·00
b. Imperf. (pair) £125
12 ,, 6 a. lemon .. .. .. 1·00 1·25
a. Imp. between (vert. pair) .. 55·00
b. Imperf. (pair) £125
13 ,, 8 a. emerald-green .. .. 1·25 1·40
a. Imperf. (pair) £125
14 ,, 12 a. greenish blue .. .. 1·50 2·00
a. Imperf. (pair) £125
15 ,, 1 r. bright violet .. .. 5·50 6·50
a. "1 Rs" for "1 R" .. 16·00 18·00
b. Imperf. (pair) £125
ba. "1 Rs" for "1 R" .. £300

BUNDI.

In Nos. 1 to 17 characters denoting the value are below the dagger, except in Nos. 2*a*, 11 and 17.

All Bundi stamps until 1914, are imperf.

1

1894 (MAY). *Each stamp with a distinct frame and the stamps not connected by the framing lines. Laid or wove paper.*

1 **1** ½ a. slate-grey £800 £800
a. Last two letters of value below the rest .. .. ..

2. (Block of four stamps.)

1894 (DEC.). *Stamps joined together, with no space between them. Thin wove paper.*

2 **2** ½ a. slate-grey .. .. .. 4·00 4·00
a. Value at top, name below .. 65·00 65·00
b. Right upper ornament omitted £150 £150
c. Last two letters of value below the rest £200 £200

3

1896 (Nov.). *Dagger shorter, lines thicker. Stamps separate. Laid paper.*

3 **3** ½ a. slate-grey 65 90
a. Last two letters of value below the rest .. .. .. 80·00 80·00

4. (1 anna)

5. (2 annas)

6. (2 annas)

1897–1900. *No shading in centre of blade of dagger. The stamps have spaces between them, but are connected by the framing lines, both vertically and horizontally. Laid paper.*

1. *Blade of dagger comparatively narrow, and either triangular, as in T* **4** *and* **6**, *or with the left-hand corner not touching the bar behind it, as in T* **5** (1897–98).

4 **4** 1 a. brick-red .. .. 3·00 3·00
5 **5** 1 a. brick-red .. .. 3·25 3·00
6 ,, 2 a. yellowish green .. .. 3·25 3·25
7 **6** 2 a. emerald-green .. .. 4·00 3·25
8 **5** 4 a. green .. .. 6·50 5·00
9 ,, 8 a. brick-red .. .. 11·00 7·00
10 ,, 1 r. yellow/*blue* .. .. 16·00 13·00

7

2. *Blade varying in shape, but as a rule not touching the bar; value above and name below the dagger, instead of the reverse* (Jan., 1898).

11 **7** 4 a. emerald-green .. .. 3·00
a. Yellow-green .. .. 3·25

8. (½ anna)

9. (8 annas)

3. *Blade wider and (except on the ½ a.) almost diamond shaped; it nearly always touches the bar* (1898–1900).

12 **8** ½ a. slate-grey (5.2.98) .. 30 20
13 **9** 1 a. brick-red (7.98) .. 50 20
14 ,, 2 a. pale green (9.11.98) .. 1·00 80
a. First two characters of value (=two) omitted .. .. 65·00 65·00
15 ,, 8 a. brick-red (7.98) .. 1·90 1·90
16 ,, 1 r. yellow/*blue* (7.98) .. 3·25 3·25
a. On wove paper .. .. 4·00 5·00

10

1898 (9 Nov.).

4. *Inscriptions as on No.* 11; *point of dagger to left.*

17 **10** 4 a. green .. .. .. 2·00 2·50
a. Yellow-green .. .. 2·00 2·50

All the above stamps are lithographed in larger sheets, containing as many varieties of type as there are stamps in the sheets.

11. Maharao Raja Sir Raghubir Singh.

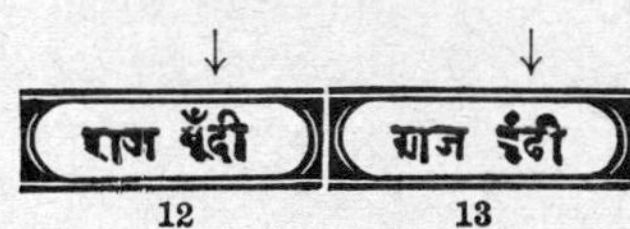

12 13

Top tablet. 1st character of 2nd group differs.

14 16

Top tablet. 1st character of 2nd group changed again. Loop at bottom of character in T **14** is sometimes attached.
Bottom tablet. In T **16** first character of 2nd group changed.

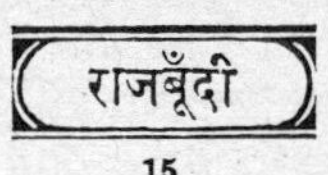

15

Top tablet. As T **14** but run together as one group.

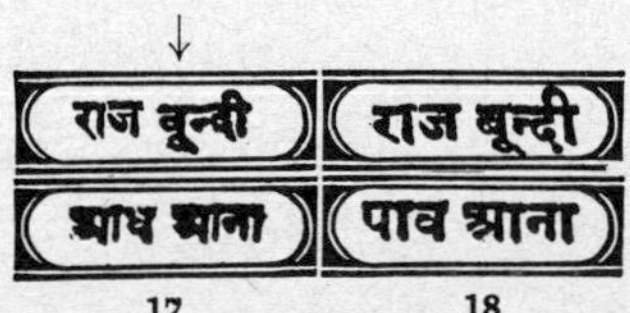

17 18

Top tablet. T **17** is as T **16** but 2nd group has four characters.
T **18** is as T **17** but both tablets have larger characters.

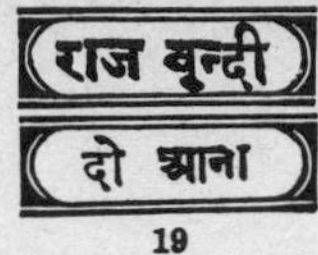

19

As **T 18** but bottom tablet has smaller characters.

The denominations may be identified from the following illustrations. The ½ a., 3 a. and rupee values can be easily distinguished by their colours.

Bottom tablets:—

½ a. 1 a. 2 a. 2½ a. 4 a. 6 a. 8 a. 10 a. 12 a.

1914–41. *T* **11**. *Typo. Ungummed paper except Nos.* 73/78.

(i). ***Rouletted in colour.***

A. *Top tablet as T* **12**.

No.	Description	Unused	Used
18	½ a. black	80	
19	1 a. deep red	45	
20	2 a. emerald	45	
	a. Deep green (coarse ptg.) ..	50	80
21	2½ a. olive-yellow (*shades*) ..	1·25	1·60
22	3 a. brown	1·60	
23	4 a. yellow-green	8·00	
24	6 a. ultramarine	5·50	
25	1 r. violet	8·00	

B. *Top tablet as T* **13**.

No.	Description	Unused	Used
26	¼ a. indigo (*shades*)	25	35
	a. Ultramarine	35	
27	½ a. black	35	35
28	1 a. vermilion	45	
	a. Carmine	45	50
	b. Brown-red	50	
29	2 a. emerald-green (*shades*) ..	50	
30	2½ a. olive-yellow (*shades*) ..	80	1·00
31	3 a. brown	40	
32	4 a. yellow-green	1·25	1·60
	a. Pelure paper (laid) ..		
	b. Error. Pale olive-yellow ..		
33	6 a. ultramarine	3·25	
	a. Indigo	3·25	
34	8 a. orange-brown	3·25	
	a. Pelure paper (laid)		
35	10 a. deep olive	8·00	
36	12 a. blue-green	9·00	
36*a*	1 r. violet	5·50	
	b. Pelure paper (laid)		

C. *Tablets as T* **14**.

No.	Description	Unused	Used
37	¼ a. indigo	30	45
	a. Deep blue	25	
	b. Ultramarine	80	80
38	½ a. black	25	35
39	1 a. red-brown	45	50
	a. Deep red	70	80
40	2 a. emerald	70	80
	a. Sage-green	85	
41	4 a. yellow-green	1·60	3·25
	a. Pale green	1·90	4·00
	b. Error. Pale olive-yellow ..		
42	8 a. orange	3·00	3·00
43	10 a. deep to pale olive ..	3·00	4·00
44	12 a. blue-green	3·00	4·00
45	1 r. lilac	5·50	6·00
46	2 r. brown and black ..	14·00	
	a. Red-brown and black	14·00	
47	3 r. blue and brown	26·00	28·00
48	4 r. green and red	80·00	
49	5 r. red and green	80·00	

D. *Top tablet as T* **15**.

No.	Description	Unused	Used
50	2½ a. buff	3·25	3·25
	a. Chestnut	4·00	4·50
51	3 a. brown (*shades*)	4·50	4·50
	a. Semi-circle and dot omitted from 4th character	9·00	
52	10 a. olive	8·00	
	a. 4th character turned to left instead of downwards ..	11·00	
53	12 a. grey-green	12·00	
	a. 4th character turned to left instead of downwards ..	20·00	

E. *Tablets as T* **16**. (*a*) *Medium wove paper.*

No.	Description	Unused	Used
54	¼ a. deep blue	80	80
	a. Error. Black	6·50	4·75
55	½ a. black	1·60	2·75
56	1 a. dull red	3·25	2·25
	a. Deep red	3·25	
57	3 a. brown (*shades*)	6·50	5·00
58	4 a. olive-green	21·00	16·00
	a. Bright apple-green		
	b. Error. Pale olive-yellow ..		

(*b*) *Very thick wove paper.*

No.	Description	Unused	Used
59	¼ a. indigo	3·25	3·25
60	½ a. black	4·50	
61	1 a. scarlet	3·25	3·25

(*c*) *Medium horizontally laid paper.*

No.	Description	Unused	Used
62	¼ a. indigo (*shades*)	3·25	2·25
63	1 a. red	3·25	3·25

F. *Tablets as T* **17**. *Medium wove paper* (*except* 1 a.).

No.	Description	Unused	Used
64	½ a. black	3·25	3·25
	a. vert. laid paper	40·00	32·00
	b. Horiz. laid paper	45·00	45·00
65	1 a. red (*horiz. laid paper*) ..	45·00	26·00
66	4 a. green	60·00	60·00
	a. Horiz. laid paper	13·00	6·50

G. *Tablets as T* **18**.

No.	Description	Unused	Used
67	¼ a. ultramarine	80	1·25
68	½ a. black	55·00	32·00
69	1 a. scarlet (*shades*)	2·25	2·25
70	4 a. green	8·00	8·00
71	4 r. green and red	45·00	
72	5 r. red and green	50·00	

(ii). *P* 11. *Tablets as T* **18**.

No.	Description	Unused	Used
73	¼ a. ultramarine	13·00	13·00
	a. Turquoise-blue	80	1·60
74	½ a. black	11·00	11·00
75	1 a. scarlet	70·00	45·00
	a. Carmine	5·00	8·00
76	2 a. green	11·00	

H. *Tablets as T* **19**.

No.	Description	Unused	Used
77	½ a. black	55·00	55·00
78	2 a. green	20·00	20·00

20

1941–45. *Typo. P* 11.

No.	Type	Description	Unused	Used
79	**20**	3 p. bright blue	8	20
80	,,	6 p. dark blue	20	30
81	,,	1 a. orange-red	30	40
82	,,	2 a. chestnut	2·00	2·00
		a. Deep brown (*no gum*) ('45) ..	3·25	3·25
83	,,	4 a. bright green	3·00	3·00
84	,,	8 a. dull green	5·00	5·50
85	,,	1 r. deep blue	8·00	

21. Maharao Rajah Bahadur Singh.

22 Bundi.

1947. *Typo. P* 11.

No.	Type	Description	Unused	Used
86	**21**	¼ a. blue-green	10	1·00
87	,,	½ a. violet	10	1·75
88	,,	1 a. yellow-green	30	2·25
89	–	2 a. vermilion	50	
90	–	4 a. orange	65	
91	**22**	8 a. ultramarine	1·25	
92	,,	1 r. chocolate	3·25	

On the 2 and 4 a. the Rajah is in Indian dress.

OFFICIAL STAMPS.

बूंदी BUNDI BUNDI

सरविस SERVICE SERVICE

(O 1) (O 2) (O 3)

1918–41. *T* **11** *handstamped as Types* O **1/3**. *Ungummed paper except Nos.* O 47/52.

A. *Optd. with Type* O **1**. B. *Optd. with Type* O **2**. C. *Optd. with Type* O **3**.

(i) ***Rouletted in colour.***

A. *Top tablet as T* **12**.

No.	Description	A.		B.		C.	
O 1	2 a. emerald	1·25	—		†		†
	a. Deep green (coarse ptg.) ..	2·25	—	4·00	—	13·00	—
	b. Red opt.	2·50	—	3·50	—		†

No.	Description	A.		B.		C.	
O 2	2½ a. olive-yellow (*shades*) ..	1·00	1·50	2·25	3·25	16·00	—
	a. Red opt...	2·25	—	7·00	—	†	
O 3	3 a. brown	1·60	2·25	3·25	—	†	
	a. Green opt.	3·25	—	†		†	
O 4	6 a. ultramarine	4·00	—	6·50	—	16·00	—
	a. Red opt...	11·00	—	13·00	—	16·00	—
O 5	1 r. violet	8·00	—	9·00	—	†	
	B. *Top tablet as T* **13.**						
O 6	½ a. indigo	40	40	40	—	—	—
	a. Red opt...	40	40	50	—	3·25	4·50
O 7	½ a. black	1·25	—	80	—	2·00	—
	a. Red opt...	1·25	—	3·25	—	8·00	—
O 8	1 a. vermilion	85	—	1·10	—	4·00	—
	a. Carmine	50	—	1·25	—	†	
	b. Brown-red	†		2·00	—	†	
O 9	2 a. emerald-green (*shades*)	1·60	—	4·50	—	†	
O10	4 a. yellow-green	3·25	—	6·00	—	†	
O10*a*	4 a. pale olive-yellow ..	—	—	—	—	†	
O11	6 a. ultramarine	3·25	—	†		†	
	a. Indigo	3·25	—	4·50	—	†	
	b. Red opt...	3·25	—	4·50	—	†	
O12	8 a. orange-brown	7·00	—	13·00	—	20·00	—
O13	10 a. deep olive	7·00	—	13·00	—	20·00	—
	a. Red opt...	13·00	—	20·00	—	24·00	—
O14	12 a. blue-green	13·00	13·00	11·00	—	†	
	a. Red opt...	†		†		24·00	—
	C. *Tablets as T* **14.**						
O15	½ a. deep blue	—	—	80	—	3·25	—
	a. Red opt...	60	—	1·60	—	†	
	b. Green opt.	90	—	2·00	—	†	
	c. Ultramarine	8·00	—	8·00	—	24·00	—
	d. Do. Red opt.	13·00	—	13·00	—	32·00	—
O16	½ a. black	1·25	—	1·50	—	4·00	—
	a. Red opt...	40	—	3·25	—	8·00	8·00
	b. Green opt.	90	—	†		†	
O17	1 a. red-brown	50	—	†		†	
	a. Deep red	1·10	—	1·10	—	4·00	—
O18	2 a. emerald	2·00	—	2·25	—	†	
	a. Red opt...	†		8·00	—	†	
	b. Sage-green	2·25	—	3·50	—	8·00	13·00
O19	4 a. yellow-green	4·00	—	7·00	—	†	
	a. Pale green	4·75	—	7·00	—	†	
O19*b*	4 a. pale olive-yellow ..	—	—	—	—	†	
O20	8 a. orange	7·00	—	11·00	—	16·00	—
O21	10 a. deep to pale olive ..	7·00	—	11·00	—	16·00	—
	a. Red opt...	8·00	—	16·00	—	24·00	—
O22	12 a. blue-green	7·00	7·00	8·00	—	†	
	a. Red opt...	†		†		24·00	—
O23	1 r. lilac	20·00	—	†		†	
O24	2 r. brown and black ..	45·00	—	45·00	—	†	
	a. Red-brown and black ..	40·00	40·00	40·00	—	†	
	b. Red opt...	†		55·00	—	†	
O25	3 r. blue and brown ..	55·00	—	55·00	—	†	
	a. Red opt.	55·00	—	†		†	
O26	4 r. green and red	£110		£125	—	†	
O27	5 r. red and green	£110	—	£125	—	†	
	D. *Top tablet as T* **15.**						
O28	2½ a. buff	4·50	—	6·50	—	†	
	a. Chestnut	6·00	—	†		†	
	b. Red opt...	13·00	—	†		†	
O29	3 a. brown (*shades*) ..	4·50	—	8·00	—	†	
	a. Semi-circle and dot omitted from 4th character ..	11·00	—	†		†	
	b. Red opt.	†		16·00	—	†	
O30	10 a. olive	8·00	—	11·00	—	16·00	—
	a. 4th character turned to left instead of downwards	16·00	—	24·00	—	†	
	b. Red opt...	11·00	—	†		†	
O31	12 a. grey-green	9·00	—	14·00	—	18·00	—
	a. 4th character turned to left instead of downwards	18·00	—	32·00	—	†	
	b. Red opt...	16·00	—	18·00	—	†	
	E. *Tablets as T* **16.** (*a*) *Medium wove paper.*						
O32	½ a. deep blue	†		1·60	—	†	
	a. Red opt...	4·00	—	1·25	—	†	
	b. Error. Black	8·00	—	8·00	—	†	
	c. Do. Red opt.	8·00	—	8·00	—	†	
O33	½ a. black	8·00	—	8·00	—	†	
	a. Red opt...	8·00	—	8·00	—	†	
O34	1 a. deep red	8·00	—	8·00	—	16·00	—
O35	3 a. brown (*shades*) ..	13·00	—	16·00	—	32·00	—
	a. Red opt...	24·00	—	32·00	—	†	
	(*b*) *Very thick wove paper.*						
O36	½ a. indigo	5·50	—	8·00	—	†	
	a. Red opt...	5·50	—	8·00	—	†	
	b. Green opt.	5·50	—	†		†	
O37	½ a. black	8·00	—	8·00	—	†	
O38	1 a. scarlet	4·50	—	5·50	—	†	
	(*c*) *Medium horizontally laid paper.*						
O39	½ a. indigo (*shades*) ..	3·25	—	4·50	—	†	
	a. Red opt...	3·25	—	3·25	—	8·00	—
O40	1 a. red	6·00	—	6·00	—	†	
	a. Red opt...	16·00	—	16·00	—	†	
	F. *Tablets as T* **17.** *Medium wove paper* (*except* 4 *a.*).						
O41	½ a. black	28·00	—	35·00	—	†	
	a. Vert. laid paper	35·00	—	40·00	—	†	
	b. Do. Red opt.	35·00	—	40·00	—	†	
	c. Horiz. laid paper (R.) ..	40·00	—	40·00	—	†	
O42	4 a. grn. (*horiz. laid paper*)	24·00	—	†		†	
	a. Red opt...	32·00	—	†		†	
	G. *Tablets as T* **18.**						
O43	½ a. ultramarine	35·00	—	65·00	—	†	
	a. Red opt...	35·00	—	35·00	—	†	
O44	½ a. black	90·00	—	90·00	—	†	
	a. Red opt...	90·00	—	†		90·00	—
O45	1 a. scarlet	40·00	—	40·00	—	80·00	—
O46	4 a. green	45·00	—	45·00	—	80·00	—
	a. Red opt...	65·00	—	†		90·00	—
	(ii) *P* 11. *Tablets as T* **18.**						
O47	½ a. ultramarine	24·00	32·00	24·00	—	32·00	—
	a. Red opt...	32·00	—	32·00	—	†	
	b. Turquoise-blue	24·00	—	35·00	—	32·00	—
	c. Do. Red opt.	40·00	—	†		†	
O48	½ a. black	24·00	—	32·00	32·00	45·00	—
	a. Red opt...	32·00	—	45·00	—	32·00	—
O49	1 a. scarlet	55·00	55·00	65·00	65·00	65·00	—
	a. Carmine	40·00	—	32·00	—	32·00	—
O50	2 a. green	24·00	—	32·00	—	13·00	—
	H. *Tablets as T* **19.**						
O51	½ a. black	24·00	—	32·00	—	45·00	—
O52	2 a. green	32·00	—	35·00	—	†	

Until 1941 it was the general practice to carry official mail free but some of the above undoubtedly exist postally used.

1941. *Nos.* 79 *to* 85 *optd.* "SERVICE".

No.	Type	Description		
O53	**20**	3 p. bright blue (R.) ..	40	45
O54	,,	6 p. dark blue (R.) ..	65	80
O55	,,	1 a. orange-red	1·50	1·50
O56	,,	2 a. brown	2·25	3·00
O57	,,	4 a. bright green	7·00	6·00
O58	,,	8 a. dull green	9·00	11·00
O59	,,	1 r. deep blue (R.) ..	12·00	13·00

For later issues, see RAJASTHAN.

BUSSAHIR (BASHAHR).

1

2

3

4

5

6

7

8

(9)

The initials are those of the Tika Raghunath Singh, son of the then Raja, who was the organiser and former director of the State Post Office.

1895 (20 JUNE). *Laid paper. Optd. with T* **9** *in pale greenish blue* (B.), *rose* (R.), *mauve* (M.) *or lake* (L.).

(*a*) *Imperf.*

No.	Type	Description	Unused	Used
1	**1**	¼ a. pink (M.) (1.9.95)	8·00	
2	**2**	½ a. grey (R.M.)	4·00	
3	**3**	1 a. vermilion (M.)	4·00	
4	**4**	2 a. orange-yellow (R.M.L.)	4·00	28·00
5	**5**	4 a. slate-violet (R.M.L.)	5·50	
		a. Without monogram	21·00	
6	**6**	8 a. red-brown (B.M.)	5·50	6·00
		a. Without monogram	21·00	
		b. Thick paper	21·00	
7	**7**	12 a. green (L.)	5·50	
8	**8**	1 r. ultramarine (R.M.L.)	5·50	
		a. Without monogram	12·00	

(*b*) *Perf. with a sewing machine; gauge and size of holes varying between 7 and 11½.*

No.	Type	Description	Unused	Used
9	**1**	¼ a. pink (B.M.)	8·50	9·50
		a. Without monogram	13·00	
10	**2**	½ a. grey (R.)	6·00	
11	**3**	1 a. vermilion (M.)	6·00	
12	**4**	2 a. orange-yellow (B.M.)	6·50	28·00
13	**5**	4 a. slate-violet (B.R.M.)	8·00	30·00
		a. Without monogram	17·00	
14	**6**	8 a. red-brown (B.R.M.)	6·50	30·00
		a. Without monogram	17·00	
15	**7**	12 a. green (R.M.L.)	6·50	
		a. Without monogram	13·00	
16	**8**	1 r. ultramarine (R.M.)	6·00	
		a. Without monogram	13·00	

1899. *As* 1895, *but pin-perf. or rouletted.*

No.	Type	Description	Unused	Used
17	**3**	1 a. vermilion (M.)	12·00	26·00
18	**4**	2 a. orange-yellow (M.L.)	8·50	22·00
		a. Without monogram	13·00	
19	**5**	4 a. slate-violet (B.R.M.L.)	7·00	
20	**7**	12 a. green (R.)	13·00	
21	**8**	1 r. ultramarine (R.)	13·00	

Nos. 1 to 21 were in sheets of 24. They seem to have been overprinted and perforated as required. Those first issued for use were perforated, but they were subsequently supplied imperf., both to collectors and for use. Nos. 17 to 21 were some of the last supplies. No rule seems to have been observed as to the colour of the overprinted monogram; pale blue, rose and mauve were used from the first. The pale blue varies to greenish blue or blue-green, and appears quite green on the yellow stamps. The lake is possibly a mixture of the mauve and the rose—it is a quite distinct colour and apparently later than the others. Specimens without overprint are either remainders left in the Treasury or copies that have escaped accidentally; they have been found sticking to the backs of others that bore the overprint.

Varieties may also be found doubly overprinted, in two different colours.

10

11

12

T **11.** Lines of shading above and at bottom left and right of shield.

T **12.** White dots above shield and ornaments in bottom corners.

13

14

15

16

(Printed at the Bussahir Press by Maulavi Karam Bakhsh.)

Wove paper. Optd. with monogram "R.S.", *T* **9**, *in colours as* 1895 *issue.*

1896–98. *Printed* (*singly?*) *from plates or dies line-engraved. Imperf., pin perf. or rouletted.*

No.	Type	Description	Unused	Used
22	**10**	¼ a. deep violet (R.)	—	32·00
23	**11**	½ a. grey-blue (*shades*) (R.)	65·00	32·00

1900–01. *Lithographed in sheets of various sizes.*

(*a*) *Imperf.*

No.	Type	Description	Unused	Used
24	**10**	¼ a. slate-violet (B.R.M.L.)	1·00	
25	**11**	½ a. blue (*shades*) (R.M.)	1·00	7·00
		a. Without monogram		
26	**13**	1 a. olive (*shades*) (R.M.L.)	4·50	7·00

(*b*) *Pin-perf. or rouletted.*

No.	Type	Description	Unused	Used
27	**10**	¼ a. slate-violet (R.M.L.)	1·50	4·00
28	**11**	½ a. blue (shades) (R.M.L.)	4·50	7·00
29	**13**	1 a. olive (*shades*) (R.M.L.)	4·50	
30	**14**	2 a. orange-yellow (B.)	26·00	28·00

The ¼ a. and ½ a. are in sheets of 24, the 1 a. and 2 a. in blocks of 4.

¼ a., 1 a. colours changed; ½ a. redrawn type; 2 a. with dash before "STATE" *and characters in lower left label; 4 a. new value.*

(*a*) *Imperf.*

No.	Type	Description	Unused	Used
31	**10**	¼ a. vermilion (B.M.)	65	
		a. Without monogram		
31*b*	**12**	½ a. blue (M.)	1·00	
32	**13**	1 a. vermilion (B.M.)	1·00	
33	**15**	2 a. ochre (M.) (9.'00)	2·75	
34	„	2 a. yellow (M.) (11.'00)	2·75	
35	„	2 a. orange (B.M.) ('01)	2·75	
36	**16**	4 a. claret (B.R.M.)	6·00	20·00
		a. Without monogram	7·00	

(*b*) *Pin-perf. or rouletted.*

No.	Type	Description	Unused	Used
37	**10**	¼ a. vermilion (B.M.)	65	
37*a*	**12**	½ a. blue (M.)	65	
38	**13**	1 a. vermilion (B.M.)	65	1·50
39	„	1 a. brown-red (3.'01)	—	15·00
40	**15**	2 a. ochre (B.M.) (9.'00)	4·00	
41	„	2 a. yell. (B.R.M.) (11.'00)	2·75	3·50
42	„	2 a. orange (B.M.) ('01)	2·75	3·50
43	**16**	4 a. claret (B.R.M.)	8·00	

The ¼ a., ½ a. and 1 a. are in sheets of 24; the 2 a. in sheets of 50 differing throughout in the dash and the characters added at lower left; the 4 a. in sheets of 28.

(17)

The stamps formerly catalogued with large overprint "R.N.S." (T **17**) are now believed never to have been issued for use.

Remainders are also found with overprint "P.S.", the initials of Padam Singh who succeeded Raghunath Singh in the direction of the Post Office, and with the original monogram "R.S." in a damaged state, giving it the appearance of a double-lined "R."

The stamps of Bussahir have been obsolete since March 31, 1901. Numerous remainders were sold after this date, and all values were later reprinted in the colours of the originals, or in fancy colours, from the original stones, or from new ones. Printings were also made from new types, similar to those of the second issue of the 8 a., 12 a., and 1 r., values, in sheets of 8.

Reprints are frequently found on laid paper.

Collectors are warned against obliterated copies bearing the Rampur postmark with date "19 MA 1900." Many thousand remainders and reprints were thus obliterated for export after the closing of the State Post Office.

CHARKHARI.

1

¼ ½ 1 2 4

¼ ½ 1 2 4

The top row shows the figures of value used in the stamps of 1894–97, and the bottom row those for the 1905–7 issue. In the 4 a. the figure slopes slightly to the right in the first issue, and to the left in the second.

1894. *Imperf.*

No.	Type	Description	Unused	Used
1	**1**	½ anna, rose	£650	£650
2	„	1 annas, dull green	£650	
3	„	2 annas, dull green	£650	
4	„	4 annas, dull green	£650	

1897. *Inscr.* "ANNA". *Imperf.*

No.	Type	Description	Unused	Used
5	1	¼ a. magenta	1·25	1·25
		a. Purple	65	65
		b. Violet	65	65
6	,,	½ a. purple	80	1·25
		a. Violet	1·50	1·50
7	,,	1 a. blue-green	1·50	1·50
		a. Turquoise-blue	2·00	2·00
		b. Indigo	2·00	2·00
8	,,	2 a. blue-green	3·00	3·00
		a. Turquoise-blue	3·00	3·00
		b. Indigo	3·00	3·00
9	,,	4 a. blue-green	3·00	4·00
		a. Turquoise-blue	3·00	4·00
		b. Indigo	6·00	7·00

Minor varieties may be found with the first "A" in "ANNA" not printed.

All values are known on various coloured papers, but these are proofs or trial impressions.

1905–7. *Numerals changed as illustrated above.*

No.	Type	Description	Unused	Used
10	1	¼ a. violet	2·75	
11	,,	½ a. violet	3·25	
12	,,	1 a. green	4·50	
13	,,	2 a. green	6·00	
14	,,	4 a. green	7·00	

2

Die I

Die II

Die I. Characters and "INDIA" small.
Die II. Characters and "INDIA" larger.

The above illustrations are of the ½ a. stamps. In the 1 p. and 1 a. Die II the bottom stroke of the first character sometimes extends to the first "I" of "INDIA" (they vary in the sheets); the 2 a. Die II has 5½ mm. between stamps instead of 3½ mm. and the stroke is short instead of long.

1909–19. *Litho. Wove paper.* P 11.

(*a*) *Die* I (1909–11)

No.	Type	Description	Unused	Used
15	2	1 p. chestnut	13·00	13·00
16	,,	1 p. turquoise-blue	15	25
		a. Imperf. between (horiz. pair)	75·00	
		b. Greenish blue (1911)	20	25
17	,,	½ a. rose-red	40	
18	,,	1 a. yellow-olive (*shades*)	45	
19	,,	2 a. blue	1·00	
20	,,	4 a. deep green	1·25	
21	,,	8 a. brick-red	1·25	
22	,,	1 r. pale chestnut	3·00	

(*b*) *Die* II (1912–19)

No.	Type	Description	Unused	Used
23	2	1 p. pale chestnut	85	4·00
		a. Orange-brown	1·25	7·00
24	,,	1 p. turquoise-blue	30	30
		a. Greenish blue		
25	,,	½ a. vermilion	35	
		a. Imperf. (pair)	£120	
26	,,	1 a. yellow-olive (1919)	40	
		a. Sage-green	6·00	6·00
26*b*	,,	2 a. grey-blue	4·00	

See also Nos. 31/44.

3

"JI" below Swords. Right sword overlaps left. Double frame lines.

4

"JI" below Swords. Left sword overlaps right. Single frame line.

1912–17. *Handstamped. Imperf.*

No.	Type	Description	Unused	Used
27	3	1 p. violet	7·00	4·00
		a. Dull purple	7·00	4·00
28	4	1 p. violet (1917)	3·25	3·25
		a. Dull purple	3·25	3·25

5 (*actual size* 63 × 25 *mm.*).

1922. *Handstamped.* (*a*) *Wove paper. Imperf.*

No.	Type	Description	Unused	Used
29	5	1 a. violet	8·00	8·00
		a. Dull purple	9·00	9·00

(*b*) *Laid paper.* P 11.

No.	Type	Description	Unused	Used
30	5	1 a. violet	13·00	16·00

1930–43. *Typo. Imperf.*

No.	Type	Description	Unused	Used
31	2	1 p. deep blue	8	1·25
		a. Vert. pair, top ptd. inverted on back, bottom normal upright	20·00	
32	,,	1 p. dull *to* light green (*pelure*) ('43)	6·00	7·00
33	,,	1 p. violet (1943)	2·75	
		a. Tête-bêche (pair)	9·00	
34	,,	½ a. deep olive	12	
35	,,	½ a. red-brown (1940)	25	2·00
		a. Tête-bêche (pair)	2·00	
36	,,	½ a. black (*pelure*) (1943)	11·00	8·00
37	,,	½ a. red (1943)	4·00	6·00
		a. Tête-bêche (pair)	12·00	
38	,,	½ a. grey-brown	40·00	55·00
39	,,	1 a. green	25	1·50
40	,,	1 a. chocolate (1940)	20	1·50
		a. Tête-bêche (pair)		
41	,,	1 a. red (1940)	16·00	24·00
42	,,	2 a. light blue	35	2·00
		a. Tête-bêche (pair)	2·00	
43	,,	2 a. greenish grey (1943)	11·00	18·00
		a. Tête-bêche (pair)	25·00	
44	,,	4 a. carmine	3·00	6·00
		a. Tête-bêche (pair)	10·00	

6. Imlia Palace.

½ As.
(7)

1931 (25 JUNE). *T* **6** *and similar designs. Typo.* P 11 *or* 12.

No.	Description	Unused	Used
45	½ a. blue-green	5	5
	a. Imperf. between (horiz. pair)	6·00	6·00
46	1 a. blackish brown	5	5
	a. Imperf. btwn. (horiz. or vert. pr.)	4·00	4·00
47	2 a. violet	5	5
	a. Imperf. between (horiz. pr.)		
48	4 a. olive-green	5	5
49	8 a. magenta	5	5
	a. Imperf. btwn. (hor. or vert. pr.)	6·00	6·00
50	1 r. green and rose	12	10
	a. Imperf. between (vert. pair)	7·00	7·00
51	2 r. red and brown	30	10
	a. Imperf. horiz. (vert. pair)	7·00	7·00
52	3 r. chocolate and blue-green	45	10
	a. Imperf. between (horiz. pair)	6·00	6·00
53	5 r. turquoise and purple	65	25
	a. Imperf. between (horiz. pair)	9·00	9·00

Designs:—½ a. The Lake; 2 a. Industrial School; 4 a. Bird's-eye view of City; 8 a. The Fort; 1 r. Guest House. 2 r. Palace Gate; 3 r. Temples at Rainpur; 5 r. Goverdhan Temple.

This issue was the subject of speculative manipulation, large stocks being thrown on the market cancelled to order at very low prices and unused at less than face value. Numerous errors, probably produced clandestinely, exist. The issue was an authorized one but was eventually withdrawn by the State authorities.

1940. *Nos.* 21/2 *surch. as T* **7.**

No.	Type	Description	Unused	Used
54	2	½ a. on 8 a. brick-red	7·00	7·00
		a. No space between "½" and "As."	8·00	11·00
		b. Surch. inverted	65·00	
		c. "1" of "½" inverted	65·00	
55	,,	1 a. on 1 r. chestnut	13·00	16·00
		a. Surch. inverted	80·00	
56	,,	"1 ANNA" on 1 r. chestnut	£130	

COCHIN.

(6 puttans = 5 annas. 12 pies = 1 anna; 16 annas = 1 rupee.)

1

2

(Dies eng. P. Orr & Sons, Madras; typo. Cochin Govt., Ernakulam.)

1892 (1 APRIL). *No wmk., or wmk. large Umbrella in the sheet.* P 12.

No.	Type	Description	Unused	Used
1	1	½ put. buff	1·00	50
		a. Orange-buff	1·00	50
		b. Yellow	1·50	65
		c. Imperf. (pair)	40·00	40·00
2	,,	1 put. purple	1·25	80
		a. Error. Deep violet (colour of 2 p.)	35·00	
3	2	2 put. deep violet	50	50

1896 (END). *Similar to T* **1**, *but much larger.* P 12. (*a*) *Wmk. Arms and inscription in sheet.*

No.	Description	Unused	Used
4	1 put. violet	7·00	7·00

(*b*) *Wmk. Conch Shell to each stamp.*

No.	Description	Unused	Used
5	1 put. deep violet	6·00	5·00

This stamp was originally printed for provisional use as a fiscal; afterwards it was authorized for postal use.

On laid paper.

No.	Type	Description	Unused	Used
6	1	½ put. orange-buff	£110	40·00
		a. Orange	—	40·00
		b. Yellow	—	40·00

1897. *Wmk. a small Umbrella on each stamp.* P 12.

No.	Type	Description	Unused	Used
7	1	½ put. buff	1·00	65
		a. Orange	65	65
		ab. *Orange.* Imperf. (pair)		
		b. Yellow	65	65
8	,,	1 put. purple	80	65
		a. Deep violet (colour of 2 p.)	1·25	80
9	2	2 put. deep violet	1·60	1·25
		a. Imperf. (pair)	13·00	13·00

The paper watermarked with a small umbrella is more transparent than that of the previous issue. The wmk. is not easy to distinguish.

3

4

5

6

1898. *Thin yellowish paper. Wmk. small Umbrella on each stamp. P* 12.

No.	Type	Description	Unused	Used
11	3	3 pies, blue	55	30
12	4	½ put. green	1·00	20
13	5	1 put. pink	65	30
		a. Tête-bêche (pair) ..	£650	£650
		b. Laid paper	—	£650
		ba. Laid paper. Tête-bêche (pair)	—	£1700
		c. Red	65	12
		d. Carmine-red	80	12
14	6	2 put. deep violet	1·50	1·00
		a. Imperf. between (vert. pair)	21·00	21·00

1903. *Thick white paper. Wmk. small Umbrella on each stamp. P* 12.

No.	Type	Description	Unused	Used
16	3	3 pies, blue	10	5
17	4	½ put. green	25	5
		a. Stamp sideways (in pair) ..	£225	£225
18	5	1 put. pink	50	8
		a. Tête-bêche (pair) ..	£700	£700
19	6	2 put. deep violet	65	12
		a. Double impression ..	—	32·00

2 (7) 2 (7a)

1909. *T* 3 (*paper and perf. of* 1903), *surch. with T* 7.

No.	Type	Description	Unused	Used
22	3	2 on 3 pies, rosy mauve ..	12	12
		a. Surch. T 7 inverted ..	24·00	24·00
		b. Surch. T 7a	32·00	32·00
		c. Stamps tête-bêche ..	26·00	26·00
		d. Stamps and surchs. tête-bêche		

Varieties a, c and d were caused by the inversion of one stamp (No. 7) in the plate and the consequent inversion of the corresponding surcharge to correct the error.

8. Raja Sir Sri Rama Varma I. 8a

(Recess. Perkins, Bacon & Co.)

1911–23. *Currency in pies and annas. W* 8*a. P* 14.

No.	Type	Description	Unused	Used
26	8	2 p. brown	10	5
		a. Imperf. (pair)	—	13·00
27	,,	3 p. blue	8	5
		a. Perf. 14 × 12½	8·00	6·00
28	8	4 p. green	45	5
28a	,,	4 p. apple-green	1·25	20
29	,,	9 p. carmine	65	5
		a. Wmk. sideways		
30	,,	1 a. brown-orange ..	65	5
31	,,	1½ a. purple	2·00	10
32	,,	2 a. grey	4·00	20
33	,,	3 a. vermilion	20·00	9·00

9. Maharaja Sir Sri Rama Varma II. 10.

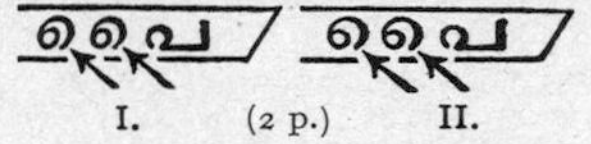

I. (2 p.) II.

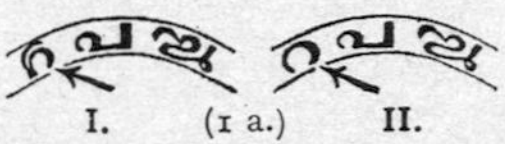

I. (1 a.) II.

(Recess. Perkins, Bacon & Co.)

1918–22. *W* 8*a. P* 13½ *or* 14.

No.	Type	Description	Unused	Used
35	10	2 p. brown (Die I) ..	2·00	5
		a. Imperf. (pair)		
		b. Die II	30	5
36	,,	4 p. green (1919)	55	5
37	,,	6 p. red-brown (1922) ..	40	5
38	,,	8 p. sepia (1922)	80	5
39	,,	9 p. carmine	3·25	8
40	,,	10 p. blue (1922)	60	5
41	9	1 a. orange (Die I) ..	2·75	5
		a. Die II	45	5
42	10	1½ a. purple (1921) ..	1·25	5
43	,,	2 a. grey	2·25	10
44	,,	2¼ a. yellow-green (1922) ..	2·10	30
45	,,	3 a. vermilion	7·00	30

2 2 2

Two pies (11) Two pies (12) Two pies (13)

2 2

Two Pies (14) Two Pies (15)

1922–29. *T* 8 (*P* 14), *surch with T* 11/15.

No.	Type	Description	Unused	Used
46	11	2 p. on 3 p. blue	12	5
		a. Surch. double	21·00	—
47	12	2 p. on 3 p. blue	65	5
		a. Capital "P" in "Pies" ..	7·00	6·00
		b. Surch. double	16·00	
		c. As a. Surcharge double ..		
48	13	2 p. on 3 p. blue (6.24) ..	25	5
		a. Capital "P" in "Pies" ..	7·00	6·00
		b. Perf. 14 × 12½ ..	7·00	6·00
		c. As a. Perf. 14 × 12½ ..	20·00	20·00
49	14	2 p. on 3 p. blue ('29) ..	12	8
		a. Surch, double	65·00	65·00
		b. Surch with Type 15 ..	20·00	20·00
		c. As b. Surch. double ..	£130	£130

There are four settings of these overprints. The first (July, 1922) consisted of 39 stamps with Type **11**, and 9 with Type **12**, and in Type **11** the centre of the "2" is above the "o" of "Two". In the second setting (May, 1924) there were 36 of Type **11** and 12 of Type **12**, and the centre of the figure is above the space between "Two" and "Pies". The third setting (June, 1924) consists of stamps with Type **13** only.

The fourth setting (1929) was also in sheets of 48, No. 49b being the first stamp in the fourth row.

ONE ANNA ഒരു അണ

ANCHAL & REVENUE (16)

Three Pies 3 (17)

1928. *Surch. with T* **16**.

No.	Type	Description	Unused	Used
50	10	1 a. on 2¼ a. yellow-green ..	3·25	6·00
		a. "REVENUF" for "REVENUE"	18·00	18·00
		b. Surch. double	55·00	55·00

1932–33. *Surch. as T* **17**. *W* **8***a*. *P* 14.

No.	Type	Description	Unused	Used
51	10	3 p. on 4 p. green	55	12
52	,,	3 p. on 8 p. sepia	55	8
53	,,	9 p. on 10 p. blue	80	20

18. Maharaja Sir Sri Rama Varma III.

(Recess. Perkins, Bacon & Co.)

1933–38. *T* **18** (*but frame and inscription of* 1 *a. as T* **9**). *W* **8***a*. *P* 13 × 13½.

No.	Type	Description	Unused	Used
54	18	2 p. brown ('36)	35	5
55	,,	4 p. green	45	5
56	,,	6 p. red-brown	50	5
57	–	1 a. brown-orange ..	50	5
58	18	1 a. 8 p. carmine ..	2·00	45
59	,,	2 a. grey ('38)	1·00	5
60	,,	2¼ a. yellow-green ..	1·00	5
61	,,	3 a. vermilion ('38) ..	2·00	10
62	,,	3 a. 4 p. violet	65	5
63	,,	6 a. 8 p. sepia	1·10	45
64	,,	10 a. blue	2·00	55

For stamps in this design, but lithographed, see Nos. 67–71.

1934. *Surcharged as T* **14**. *W* **8***a*. *P* 14.

No.	Type	Description	Unused	Used
65	10	6 p. on 8 p. sepia (R.) ..	65	25
66	,,	6 p. on 10 p. blue (R.) ..	1·60	30

(Lithographed in India.)

1938. *W* **8***a*. (I) *P* 11 *or* (II) *P* 13 × 13½.

No.	Type	Description	I. Unused	I. Used	II. Unused	II. Used
67	18	2 p. brown ..	55	5	2·75	10
68	,,	4 p. green ..	55	5	2·75	5
69	,,	6 p. red-brown	1·25	5	—	—
70	,,	1 a. brown-orge.	7·00	7·50	7·50	13·00
71	,,	2¼ a. sage-green	4·50	10	3·00	30

ANCHAL (19) THREE PIES (20)

SURCHARGED

ANCHAL

ONE ANNA
THREE PIES
(21)

NINE PIES
(22)

ANCHAL

ANCHAL

NINE PIES
(23)

SURCHARGED
NINE PIES
(24)

ANCHAL
(25)

1939–44. *T* **18** *variously optd. or surch.*

I. *Recess-printed stamps. Nos.* 57/8.

No.	Description		
72	3 p. on 1 a. 8 p. carmine (*T* **20**)	13·00	11·00
73	3 p. on 1 a. 8 p. carmine (*T* **21**)	1·50	40
74	6 p. on 1 a. 8 p. carmine (*T* **20**)	65	25
75	1 a. brown-orange (*T* **19**) ..	1·00	5
76	1 a. 3 p. on 1a. 8 p. car. (*T* **21**)	65	8

II. *Lithographed stamps, Nos.* 68 *and* 70.

I. *P* 11. II. *P* 13 × 13½.

No.	Description	I.		II.	
77	3 p. on 4 p. (*T* **21**)*	4·00	20	6·00	40
	a. Spaced 19¼ mm.	—	—	—	—
78	6 p. on 1 a. (*T* **22**)	25·00	8·00	†	
79	6 p. on 1 a. (*T* **23**)	28·00	20·00	6·50	4·00
80	9 p. on 1 a. (*T* **22**)	8·00	8·00	†	
81	9 p. on 1 a. (*T* **23**)	†		20·00	7·00
82	9 p. on 1 a. (*T* **24**)	†		4·00	8
83	1 a. (*T* **19**) ..	7·00	5	8·00	7·00
	a. Double print	—	—	†	
84	1 a. (*T* **25**) ..	4·00	1·25	2·75	25

*No. 77 has the surcharge spaced 20 mm. apart.

26. Maharaja Sri Kerala Varma I.

(**27**) *The actual measurement of this wmk. is* 6¼ × 3⅝ in.

1943. *Frame of* 1 *a. inscr.* "ANCHAL & REVENUE" *Litho.* I. *P* 11. II. *P* 13 × 13½. (*a*) *W* **8***a*.

No.	Type	Description	I.		II.	
85	**26**	2 p. grey-brown	—	—	20	5
		aa. Double print	†		—	40·00
85*a*	,,	4 p. green ..	†		32·00	26·00
85*b*	,,	1 a. brn.-orange	†		32·00	20·00

(*b*) *W* **27**.

No.	Type	Description	I.		II.	
86	**26**	2 p. grey-brown	—	—	1·25	5
87	,,	4 p. green ..	2·00	30	7·00	2·75
88	,,	6 p. red-brown ..	6·00	65	55	5
		a. Double print	16·00	16·00	†	
89	,,	9 p. ultramarine	1·60	30	†	
90	,,	1 a. brn.-orange	13·00	9·00	16·00	7·00
91	,,	2¼ a. yellow-grn.	7·00	3·25	1·25	5

Part of W **27** appears on many stamps in each sheet, while others are entirely without wmk.

1944. *T* **26** *variously optd. or surch.* I. *P* 11. II. *P* 13 × 13½. (*a*) *W* **8***a*.

No.	Description	I.		II.	
92	3 p. on 4 p. (*T* **21**)*	†		16·00	2·00
	aa. Spaced 19 mm.	†		—	—
92*a*	9 p. on 1 a. (*T* **23**)	†		3·00	45
92*b*	9 p. on 1 a. (*T* **24**)	†		10	5
92*c*	1 a. 3 p. on 1 a. (*T* **21**) ..	†		—	—

(*b*) *W* **27**.

No.	Description	I.		II.	
93	2 p. on 6 p. (*T* **20**)	30	5	20	5
94	3 p. on 4 p. (*T* **20**)	45	5	†	
95	3 p. on 4 p. (*T* **21**)*	†		30	5
	a. Spaced 19 mm.	†		2·75	1·00
96	3 p. on 6 p. (*T* **20**)	40	10	10	5
97	4 p. on 6 p. (*T* **20**)	†		40	8

*No. 92 has the surcharge spaced 21 mm. apart and No. 95 20½ mm. apart.

28. Maharaja Sri Ravi Varma. **29.**

I

II

1944–48. *Litho.* *W* **27**. *No gum.*

(*a*) *Type* I. *P* 11.

No.	Type	Description		
98	**28**	9 p. ultramarine (1944) ..	3·00	80

(*b*) *Type* II. *P* 13.

No.	Type	Description		
98*a*	**28**	9 p. ultramarine (1946)	80	8
99	,,	1 a. 3 p. magenta (1948)	4·00	8
100	,,	1 a. 9 p. ultram. (*shades*) ('48)	6·00	45

Nos. 98*a* and 99 are also known perf. 13 × 13½.

1946–48. *Frame of* 1 *a. inscr.* "ANCHAL & REVENUE". *Litho.* *W* **27**. *P* 13.

No.	Type	Description		
101	**29**	2 p. chocolate	20	5
		a. Imperf. horiz. (vert. pr.) ..	£160	£160
		b. Double print	40·00	40·00
		c. Perf. 11	7·00	65
		d. Perf. 11 × 13	40·00	11·00
102	,,	3 p. carmine	1·50	5
103	,,	4 p. grey-green	—	3·50
		a. Double print	—	65·00
104	,,	6 p. red-brown (1947) ..	2·75	10
		a. Perf. 11	22·00	5
105	,,	9 p. ultramarine	1·25	5
		a. Imperf. between (horiz. pair)	£250	
106	,,	1 a. orange (1948)	2·75	1·00
		a. Perf. 11	90·00	
107	,,	2 a. black	6·00	5
		a. Perf. 11	24·00	20
108	,,	3 a. vermilion	6·00	20
		a. Double print	21·00	6·00

30. Maharaja Sri Kerala Varma II.

1948–50. *Litho.* *W* **27**. *P* 11.

No.	Type	Description		
109	**30**	2 p. grey-brown	1·00	5
		a. Imp. between (horiz. pair)	£160	£160
110	,,	3 p. carmine	65	5
		a. Imp. between (vert. pair)	£160	£160
111	,,	4 p. green	1·00	5
		a. Imp. between (horiz. pair)	£200	£200
112	,,	6 p. chestnut	1·00	5
		a. Im between (horiz. pair)	£200	£200
113	,,	9 p. p. ultramarine	65	5
114	,,	2 a. black	5·50	5
115	,,	3 a. orange-red	6·50	5
		a. Imp. between (horiz. pair)	£350	£350
116	,,	3 a. 4 p. violet (1950) ..	15·00	20·00

31. Chinese Nets.

32. Dutch Palace.

1949. *Litho.* *W* **27**. *P* 10½.

No.	Type	Description		
117	**31**	2 a. black	25	30
		a. Imperf. vert. (horiz. pr.)	£225	
118	**32**	2¼ a. green	25	30
		a. Imperf. vert. (horiz. pr.)	£225	

SIX PIES

ആറു പൈ
(33)

1949. *Surch. as T* **33**.

(i) *On* 1944–48 *issue.* *P* 13.

No.	Type	Description		
119	**28**	6 p. on 1 a. 3 p. magenta	40	5
120	,,	1 a. on 1 a. 9 p. ultram. (R.)	1·00	5

(ii) *On* 1946–48 *issue.*

No.	Type	Description		
121	**29**	3 p. on 9 p. ultramarine ..	3·25	1·25
122	,,	6 p. on 1 a. 3 p. magenta ..	30	5
		a. Surch. double		
123	,,	1 a. on 1 a. 9 p. ultram. (R.)	2·25	5
		a. Surch. in black		
		b. Black surch. with smaller native characters 7½ mm. instead of 10 mm. long ..		

(iii) *On* 1948–50 *issue.*

No.	Type	Description		
124	**30**	3 p. on 9 p. ultramarine ..	4·00	4·00
		a. Larger native characters 20 mm. instead of 16½ mm. long	65	10
		b. Surch. double		
125	,,	3 p. on 9 p. ultram. (R.) ..	90	10
126	,,	6 p. on 9 p. ultram. (R.) ..	1·25	45

Nos. 122/3 were not issued without surcharge.

1949. *Surch. as T* **20**. *W* **27**. *P* 13.

No.	Type	Description		
127	**29**	6 p. on 1 a. orange ..	22·00	22·00
128	,,	9 p. on 1 a. orange ..	16·00	16·00

For later issues, see Travancore-Cochin.

OFFICIAL STAMPS.

On C G S — ON C G S

(O 1) (O 2. Small "ON".)

1913. *Optd. with Type* O **1** (3 *p.*) *or* O **2** (*others*).

O 1 **8** 3 p. blue (R.) .. .. 11·00 5
  a. Black opt. .. ..
O 2 „ 4 p. green (*wmk. sideways*) 2·75 5
  a. Opt. inverted .. .. — 75·00
O 3 „ 9 p. carmine .. .. 7·00 5
  a. Wmk. sideways .. ..
O 4 „ 1½ a. purple .. .. 8·00 5
  a. Opt. double .. .. 75·00
O 5 „ 2 a. grey .. .. 7·00 5
O 6 „ 3 a. vermilion .. .. 7·00 8
O 7 „ 6 a. violet .. .. 7·00 1·25
O 8 „ 12 a. ultramarine .. .. 9·00 2·75
O 9 „ 1½ r. deep green .. .. 9·00 9·00

ON C G S — 8 Eight pies

(O 3. "G" without serif.) (O 4. 27½ mm. high.)

1919–33. *Optd. as Type* O **3**.

O10 **10** 4 p. green .. .. 2·00 5
  a. Opt. double .. .. 75·00
O11 „ 6 p. red-brown (1922) .. 2·00 5
  a. Opt. double .. .. 75·00
O12 „ 8 p. sepia .. .. 1·75 5
O13 „ 9 p. carmine .. .. 2·25 5
O14 „ 10 p. blue .. .. 3·00 5
O15 „ 1½ a. purple (1921) .. 2·75 5
O16 „ 2 a. grey .. .. 3·00 5
O17 „ 2¼ a. yellow-green .. 2·75 5
  a. Opt. double £110 £110
O18 „ 3 a. vermilion .. .. 6·00 25
  a. Opt. inverted .. .. — £110
O19 „ 6 a. violet (1924) .. 7·00 40
O19*a* „ 12 a. ultramarine (1929) 8·00 1·50
O19*b* „ 1½ r. deep green (1933) .. 9·00

1923. *T* **8** *and* **10** *surch. with Type* O **4**.

O20 8 p. on 9 p. carm. (No. O3) 35·00 5
  a. "Pies" for "pies" .. — 7·00
O21 8 p. on 9 p. carm. (No. O13) 35·00 5
  a. "Pies" for "pies" — 6·00
  b. Surch. double

Varieties with smaller "i" or "t" in "Eight" and small "i" in "Pies" are also known.

1925 (Apr.). *T* **10** *surch. as Type* O **4**.

O22 10 p. on 9 p. carm. (No. O 13) 35·00 5
  a. Surch. inverted .. ..
  b. Surch. double .. ..
  c. Surch. 25 mm. high .. — 40

1929. *T* **8** *surch. as Type* O **4**.

O23 10 p. on 9 p. carm. (No. O3) .. 55·00 4·50
  a. "Pies" for "pies" .. £160 75·00
  b. Surch. double ..

ON C G S — ON C G S

(O 5. Straight back to "C".) (O 6. Circular "O"; "N" without serifs.)

1931. *Optd. with Type* O **5**.

O24 **10** 4 p. green .. .. 11·00 1·10
O25 „ 6 p. red-brown .. .. 3·50 5
O26 „ 8 p. sepia .. .. .. 3·50 5
O27 „ 10 p. blue .. .. .. 3·50 5
O28 „ 2 a. grey .. .. .. 4·00 5
O29 „ 3 a. vermilion .. .. 4·50 10
O30 „ 6 a. violet .. .. 26·00 2·75

1933. *Nos.* O26/7 *surch. as T* **14**, *in red.*

O32 **10** 6 p. on 8 p. sepia 80 10
O33 „ 6 p. on 10 p. blue .. .. 2·75 5

Inverted "S" is known on Nos. O25/9 and O32/3.

1933–44. *Recess-printed stamps of* 1933–38 *optd.*

(*a*) *With Type* O **5**.

O34 **18** 4 p. green 40 5
O35 „ 6 p. red-brown 55 5
O36 „ 1 a. brown-orange .. 3·25 5
O37 „ 1 a. 8 p. carmine .. 2·00 5
O38 „ 2 a. grey .. .. 3·25 5
O39 „ 2¼ a. yellow-green .. 2·00 5
O40 „ 3 a. vermilion .. .. 6·00 5
O41 „ 3 a. 4 p. violet .. 2·25 5
O42 „ 6 a. 8 p. sepia .. 2·25 8
O43 „ 10 a. blue .. .. .. 2·75 10

(*b*) *With Type* O **6** (*typo.*).

O44 **18** 1 a. brown-orange .. 45·00 5
O45 „ 2 a. grey-black .. .. 11·00 8
O46 „ 3 a. vermilion .. .. 2·75 10

ON C G S — ON C G S

(O 7. Curved back to "C".) (O 8)

ON C G S — ON C G S — ON C G S

(O 9. Circular "O"; "N" with serifs.) (O 10. Oval "O".) (O 11)

1938–44. *Lithographed stamps of* 1938, *W* **8***a*, *optd.*

(*a*) *With Type* O **7** *or* O **8** (1 *a.*).

I. *P* 11. II. *P* 13×13½.

O47 **18** 4 p. green .. 2·25 30 4·00 65
  a. Inverted "S" — — †
O48 „ 6 p. red-brown 1·25 5 †
  a. Inverted "S" — — †
O49 „ 1 a. brn.-orge. 45·00 1·10 †
O50 „ 2 a. grey-black 1·25 5 †
  a. Inverted "S" — — †

(*b*) *With Type* O **9** (*litho.*) *or* O **10** (6 *p.*).

O51 **18** 6 p. red-brown † 30 5
O52 „ 1 a. brn.-orge. 1·00 5 †
O53 „ 3 a. vermilion.. 2·00 5 †

(*c*) *With Type* O **11**.

O53*a* **18** 6 p. red-brown £200 £100 †

1943. *Unissued stamps optd. with Type* O **10**. *Litho. W* **27**.

I. *P* 11. II. *P* 13×13½.

O54 **18** 4 p. green .. 26·00 7·50 12 8
O55 „ 6 p. red-brown 35·00 7·00 13·00 65
O56 „ 1 a. brn.-orge. 11·00 65 65 85
O56*a* „ 2 a. grey-black 28·00 8 †
  ab. Opt. omitted — — †
O56*b* „ 2¼ a. sage-green 45·00 7·00 †
O56*c* „ 3 a. vermilion 8·00 2·25 †

1943. *Official stamps variously surch.* **20** *or* **21**.

(i) *On* 1½ *a. purple, of* 1919–33.

O57 **10** 9 p. on 1½ a. (*T* **20**) .. 32·00 65

(ii) *On recess-printed* 1 *a.* 8 *p. carmine of* 1933–44 (*opt. with Type* O **5**).

O58 3 p. on 1 a. 8 p. (*T* **21**) .. 10 5
O59 9 p. on 1 a. 8 p. (*T* **20**) .. 18·00 4·00
O60 1 a. 9 p. on 1 a. 8 p. (*T* **20**) 50 5
O61 1 a. 9 p. on 1 a. 8 p. (*T* **21**) 50 10

(iii) *On lithographed stamps of* 1938–44. *T* **18**.

(*a*) *W* **8***a*.

I. *P* 11. II. *P* 13×13½.

O62 3 p. on 4 p. (*T* O **7** & **20**) .. † 1·25 10
  a. Surch. double — 50·00
O63 3 p. on 4 p. (*T* O **7** & **21**)* .. † 30·00 11·00
  a. Spaced 19¼ mm. † — —
O64 3 p. on 1 a. (*T* O **9** & **20**) .. 55 5 †
O65 9 p. on 1 a. (*T* O **9** & **20**) .. 16·00 30 †
O66 1 a. 3 p. on 1 a. (*T* O **9** & **21**)* 20·00 11·00 †
  a. Spaced 17 mm. 65·00 32·00 †

(*b*) *W* **27**.

O67 3 p. on 4 p. (*T* O **10** & **20**) .. † 32·00 32·00
O67*a* 3 p. on 1 a. (*T* O **10** & **20**) 13·00 9·00 24·00 11·00

*No. O63 has the surcharge spaced 20 mm. apart and No. O66 19 mm. apart.

1944. *Optd. with Type* O **10**, *W* **27**.

I. *P* 11. II. *P* 13×13½.

O68 **26** 4 p. green .. 11·00 40 55 5
O69 „ 6 p. red-brn. 5 5 5 8
  a. Opt. double — — 13·00 13·00
  b. Stamp doubly printed. .. — — †
O70 „ 1 a. brn.-orge. † £275 20·00
O71 „ 2 a. black .. † 5 5
O72 „ 2¼ a. yell.-grn. † 80 8
  a. Optd. both sides .. † — —
O73 „ 3 a. vermilion 65 20 1·10 12

1944. *Optd. with Type* O **10** *and variously surch. as Types* **20** *and* **21**. *W* **27**.

I. II.

O74 **26** 3 p. on 4 p. (*T* **20**) .. 2·75 20 30 5
  a. Stamp doubly printed .. 16·00 16·00 †
  b. Optd. Type O 10 on both sides — — †
O75 „ 3 p. on 4 p. (*T* **21**)* .. 55·00 20·00 1·75 30
  a. Spaced 19 mm. — — †
O76 „ 3 p. on 1 a. (*T* **20**) .. † 1·25 5
O77 „ 9 p. on 6 p. (*T* **20**) † 1·25 5
O78 „ 9 p. on 6 p. (*T* **21**)* † 10 5
O79 „ 1 a. 3 p. on 1 a. (*T* **20**) † 1·25 5
O80 „ 1 a. 3 p. on 1 a. (*T* **21** spaced 19 mm.) † 1·00 5
  a. T 21 spaced 17 mm. † 4·00 8

*No. O75I has the surcharge spaced 21 mm. apart. No. O75I is known with surcharge spaced 20 mm. and 19½ mm. and No. O78 exists spaced 19½ mm. and 19 mm.

1946–47. *Stamps of* 1944–48 *optd. with Type* O **10**. *Type* II. *P* 13.

O81 **28** 9 p. ultramarine 15 5
  a. Stamp printed both sides .. 30·00 30·00
O82 „ 1 a. 3 p. magenta (1947) .. 15 5
  a. Opt. double .. .. 11·00 8·00
O83 „ 1 a. 9 p. ultramarine (1947) 15 10

1948. *Stamps of* 1946–48 *and unissued values optd. with Type* O **2**. *P* 13.

O84 **29** 3 p. carmine 5 5
O85 „ 4 p. grey-green .. .. 8·00 3·00
O86 „ 6 p. red-brown 20 5
O87 „ 9 p. ultramarine 65 5
O88 „ 1 a. 3 p. magenta .. 35 5
O89 „ 1 a. 9 p. ultramarine .. 25 20
O90 „ 2 a. black 20 5
O91 „ 2¼ a. yellow-green .. 65 20

1949. *Stamps of* 1948–50 *and unissued values optd. with Type* O **8**.

O92 **30** 3 p. carmine 10 5
O93 „ 4 p. green 10 5
  a. Imperf. between (pair) .. £225 £225
  b. Optd. on reverse .. 13·00 13·00
O94 „ 6 p. chestnut 10 5
  a. Imp. between (vert. pair)
O95 „ 9 p. ultramarine 20 5
O96 „ 2 a. black 30 5
O97 „ 2¼ a. yellow-green .. 65 5
O98 „ 3 a. orange-red 65 5
O99 „ 3 a. 4 p. violet .. .. 2·75 2·00

Nos. O92/9 exist with "C" for "G" in the overprint which occurs once on the sheet. Also Nos. O92/8, O103/4 and O104b exist with a flat back to "G" which occurs twice on the sheet.

1949. *Official stamps surch. as T* **33.**

(i) *On 1944 issue.*

O100 **28** 1 a. on 1 a. 9 p. ult. (R.) 35 5

(ii) *On 1948 issue.*

O101 **29** 1 a. on 1 a. 9 p. ult. (R.) 1·50 75

(iii) *On 1949 issue.*

O103 **30** 6 p. on 3 p. carmine 12 5
- a. Imp. between (vert. pair) £225 £225
- b. Surch. double £150 £150
- c. "C" for "G" in opt... 2·00 2·00

O104 „ 9 p. on 4 p. green (18 *mm. long*) 25 8
- a. Imp. between (hor. pair)
- b. Larger native characters, 22 mm. long 20 20
- ba. Ditto. Imp. between (horiz. pair) £175 £175
- c. "C" for "G" in opt. 3·00 3·00
- ca. Ditto. Larger native characters, 22 mm. long

1949. *Stamp of 1949 optd.* "SERVICE".

O105 **30** 3 p. on 9 p. (No. 124a) 30 12

DHAR.

1

2

1897–1900. *Type-set. With oval handstamp Imperf.*

1 **1** ½ pice, black/*red* 15 15
- a. Handstamp omitted .. 18·00
- b. Characters transposed (A) .. 4·50
- c. Characters transposed (B) .. 6·00
- d. Line below upper inscription 45·00 45·00
- e. Five characters at bottom left instead of four 20

2 „ ½ a. black/*orange* (1900) .. 30 40
- a. Handstamp omitted .. 22·00

3 „ ½ a. black/*magenta* 30 30
- a. Line below upper inscription 40·00 40·00

4 „ 1 a. black/*green* 80 80
- a. Line below upper inscription 40·00 40·00
- b. Printed both sides £450

5 „ 2 a. black/*yellow* (1900) .. 4·50 6·00
- a. Ornament of top right corner transposed with one in top frame .. .. .. 40·00 50·00
- *b. Black/buff* .. .. 7·00 8·00
- ba. Do. With var. a .. 55·00 60·00

In (A) the three characters forming the second word in the lower inscription are transposed (2), (3), (1); in (B) they are transposed (3), (2), (1).

Beware of forgeries of Nos. 1d, 3a and 4a.

1898–1900. *Typo. P 11 to 12.*

6 **2** ½ a. carmine 40 40
- a. Imperf. .. .. ..
- *b. Deep rose* 40

7 „ 1 a. claret 40

8 „ 1 a. reddish violet .. .. 1·00
- a. Imperf. between (pair) .. 40·00
- b. Imperf. (pair) .. ..

9 „ 2 a. deep green .. .. 1·50

The stamps of Dhar have been obsolete since 31st March, 1901.

DUTTIA (DATIA).

1 (4 a.) Ganesh.

2 (½ a.)

1893. *Imperf.*

1 **1** ½ a. black/*orange* £800
2 „ ½ a. black/*blue-green* £800
3 **2** 1 a. red £800
4 **1** 2 a. black/*yellow* £800
5 „ 4 a. black/*rose* £800

Stamps of Type **1** come with or without the handstamp as shown in Type **2** (same value in either state).

1897(?). *Imperf.*

6 **2** ½ a. black/*green* .. .. 6·00
- a. Value in one group .. .. 7·00
- b. Do. Tête-bêche (horiz. pair) .. 70·00

7 „ 1 a. black/*white* .. .. 6·00
- a. Tête-bêche (vert. pair) .. 45·00
- b. Laid paper .. .. 4·00

8 „ 2 a. black/*yellow* .. .. 7·00
9 „ 2 a. black/*lemon* .. .. 8·00
10 „ 4 a. black/*rose* .. .. 7·00
- a. Tête-bêche (horiz. pair) .. 70·00

3 (½ a.)

4 (¼ a.)

Name spelt "DATIA."

12 **3** ½ a. black/*green* .. .. 16·00
13 „ 1 a. black/*white* .. .. 17·00
14 „ 2 a. black/*yellow* .. .. 22·00
15 „ 4 a. black/*rose* .. .. 22·00

1899–1906. (*a*) *Rouletted in colour or in black, horizontally and at end of rows.*

16 **4** ¼ a. vermilion 25
- *a. Rose-red* 30
- *b. Pale rose* 35
- *c. Lake* 35
- *d. Carmine* 70
- *e. Brownish red* 70
- ea. Tête-bêche (pair) .. £1200

17 „ ½ a. black/*blue-green* .. 35
- *a. On deep green* 40
- *b. On yellow-green (pelure)* .. 35
- *c. On dull green* (1906) .. 50

18 „ 1 a. black/*white* 40
19 „ 2 a. black/*lemon-yellow* .. 60
- *a. On orange-yellow* 70
- *b. On buff-yellow* 60
- *c. On pale yellow* (1906) .. 60

20 „ 4 a. black/*deep rose* 60
- a. Tête-bêche (pair) .. ..

(*b*) *Rouletted in black between horizontal rows, but imperf. at top and bottom and at ends of rows.*

21 **4** 1 a. black/*white* .. .. 1·50

1904–5. *Without rouletting.*

22 **4** ¼ a. red 60
23 „ ½ a. black/*green* .. .. 2·00
24 „ 1 a. black (1905) 80

1911. *P 13½. Stamps very wide apart.*

25 **4** ¼ a. carmine 70
- a. Imperf. horiz. (vert. pr.) .. 35·00
- b. Stamps closer together .. 1·25
- c. As b. Imp. vert. (horiz. pr.).. 30·00

1912(?). *Printed close together. Coloured roulette × imperf.*

26 **4** ½ a. black/*green* .. .. 2·00

Printed wide apart. P 13½ × *coloured roulette.*

27 **4** ¼ a. carmine 60

P 13½ × *imperf.*

28 **4** ½ a. black/*dull green* .. 1·25

1916. *Colours changed. Imperf.*

29 **4** ¼ a. deep blue .. .. 60 1·50
30 „ ½ a. green .. .. 1·25 3·00
31 „ 1 a. purple .. .. .. 1·50
- a. Tête-bêche (pair) .. .. 8·00

32 „ 2 a. brown .. .. .. 3·00
33 „ 2 a. lilac .. .. .. 3·50
34 „ 4 a. Venetian red (date?) 7·00

1918. *Colours changed. Imperf.*

35 **4** ½ a. blue 35
36 „ 1 a. pink 40

P 11½.

37 **4** ¼ a. black .. .. .. 1·50

1920. *Rouletted.*

38 **4** ¼ a. blue 45 60
- a. Roul. × perf. 7 .. .. 4·50 7·00

39 „ ½ a. pink 60 75
- a. Roul. × perf. 7 .. .. 6·00

1920(?). *Rough perf. about 7.*

40 **4** ½ a. dull red .. .. .. 2·00 2·00

All the stamps of Duttia were impressed with a circular handstamp (as a rule in *blue*) before issue.

This handstamp is an impression of the seal of Maharaja Sir Bhawani Singh, and has a figure of "Ganesh" in centre, surrounded by an inscription in Devanagari.

FARIDKOT.

N **1** (1 folus)

N **2** (1 paisa)

1879–86. *Rough, handstamped impressions. Imperf.*

(*a*) *Native thick laid paper.*

N1 N **1** 1 f. ultramarine .. .. 12·00 15·00
N2 N **2** 1 p. ultramarine .. .. 15·00 20·00

(*b*) *Ordinary laid paper.*

N3 N **1** 1 f. ultramarine .. .. 6·00 7·00
N4 N **2** 1 p. ultramarine .. .. 12·00 18·00

(*c*) *Wove paper, thick to thinnish.*

N5 N **1** 1 f. ultramarine 40 60
- a. Tête-bêche (pair) .. 12·00

N6 N **2** 1 p. ultramarine 50 70

(*d*) *Thin wove whity brown paper.*

N7 N **2** 1 p. ultramarine .. .. 4·00 6·00

N 3

Wove paper. Imperf.

N8 N **3** 1 p. ultramarine 75
- a. Tête-bêche (pair) .. 12·00

It is doubtful whether stamps of Type N **3** were ever used for postage.

Impressions of these types in various colours, the ½ a. labels, and the later printings from re-engraved dies, were never in circulation at all.

Faridkot became a convention state and from 1887 used the Indian stamps overprinted which are listed under the Convention States.

MINIMUM PRICE

The minimum price quoted is 5p which represents a handling charge rather than a basis for valuing common stamps. For further notes about prices see introductory pages.

HYDERABAD.

(DECCAN.)

1

2

(Eng. Mr. Rapkin. Plates by Nissen & Parker London. Recess.)

1869. *P* 11½.

1	**1**	1 a. olive-green	5·00	4·00
		a. Imperf. between (pair)	45·00	40·00
		b. Imperf. (pair)	35·00	35·00

Reprints in the colour of the issue, and also in fancy colours, were made in 1880 on white wove paper, perforated 12½.

1871 (JAN.). *Locally engraved; 240 varieties of each value; wove paper. Recess. P* 11½.

2	**2**	½ a. brown	3·00	3·00
3	,,	2 a. sage-green	12·00	9·00

Stamps exist showing traces of lines in the paper, but they do not appear to be printed on true laid paper.

Reprints of both values were made in 1880 on white wove paper, perforated 12½: the ½ a. in grey-brown, yellow-brown, sea-green and dull blue, and the 2 a. in bright green and in blue-green.

3

A Normal. 2 a. B Variety.

In A the coloured lines surrounding each of the four labels join a coloured circle round their inner edge, in B this circle is missing.

C 3 a. D

C. Normal.
D. Character ʌ omitted.

(Recess. Bradbury, Wilkinson & Co.)

1871–1909. (*a*) *Rough perf.* 11½.

4	**3**	½ a. red-brown	8·00	8·00
5	,,	1 a. purple-brown	18·00	18·00
6	,,	2 a. green (A)	40·00	
7	,,	3 a. ochre-brown	12·00	15·00
8	,,	4 a. slate	20·00	20·00
9	,,	8 a. deep brown		
10	,,	12 a. dull blue	40·00	40·00

(*b*) *Pin-perf.*

11	**3**	½ a. red-brown	30·00	30·00
		a. Orange	30·00	30·00
		b. Orange-brown	30·00	30·00
		e. Error. Magenta	18·00	7·00
12	,,	1 a. drab	60·00	25·00
		a. Grey-black	40·00	25·00
		b. Black	40·00	25·00
12*c*	,,	2 a. green (A)	40·00	25·00
12*d*	,,	3 a. chestnut	45·00	30·00

(*c*) *P* 12½.

13	**3**	½ a. orange-brown	5	5
		a. Imperf. vert. (horiz. pair)	22·00	22·00
		b. Brick-red	5	5
		ba. Imperf. vert. (horiz. pair)	22·00	22·00
		bb. Doubly printed	18·00	18·00
		c. Rose-red	5	5
		d. Error. Magenta	12·00	5·00
14	,,	1 a. purple-brown	35	40
		a. Doubly printed	24·00	24·00
		b. Drab	5	5
		ba. Imperf. (pair)	—	15·00
		bb. Doubly printed	24·00	24·00
		c. Grey-black	10	5
		d. Black (1909)	10	5
		da. Doubly printed	24·00	24·00
		db. Imperf. vert. (horiz. pair)	24·00	24·00
		dc. Imperf. horiz. (vert. pair)	24·00	24·00
15	,,	2 a. green (A)	8	5
		a. Deep green (A)	8	5
		b. Blue-green (A)	10	5
		ba. Blue-green (B)	18·00	18·00
		c. Pale green (A)	10	5
		ca. Pale green (B)	18·00	18·00
		d. Sage-green (A) (1909)	10	5
		da. Sage-green (B)	—	18·00
16	,,	3 a. ochre-brown (C)	15	10
		a. Chestnut (C)	15	10
		aa. Character omitted (D)	30·00	25·00
17	,,	4 a. slate	30	20
		a. Imperf. vert. (horiz. pair)	30·00	30·00
		b. Greenish grey	30	15
		c. Olive-green	1·10	1·00
18	,,	8 a. deep brown	70	45
		a. Imperf. vert. (horiz. pair)		
19	,,	12 a. pale ultramarine	1·25	1·00
		a. Grey-green	90	70

(4) 5

(Eng. Khusrat Ullah, Hyderabad.)

1900. *Surch. with T* **4.** *P* 12½.

20	**3**	¼ a. on ½ a. orange-brown	75	35
		a. Surch. inverted	10·00	7·00

1902. *P* 12½.

21	**5**	¼ a. deep blue	1·25	70
		a. Pale blue	1·25	70

6

7

(Recess. Allan G. Wyon, London.)

1905. *Wmk. T* **7.** *P* 12½.

22	**6**	¼ a. dull blue	75	5
		a. Imperf. (pair)	14·00	10·00
		b. Dull ultramarine	1·50	5
		ba. Perf. 11 × 12½	8·00	8·00
		c. Pale blue-green	75	5
23	,,	½ a. orange	1·50	12
		a. Perf. 11		
		b. Vermilion	1·50	12
		ba. Imperf. (pair)	12·00	10·00
		c. Yellow	15·00	10·00

1908–11. *W* **7.** *Various perfs., also compound.*
A. *Perf.* 12½. B. *Perf.* 11½, 12. C. *Perf.* 11. D. *Perf.* 13½.

			A.		B.		C.		D.	
24	**6**	¼ a. grey	15	5	35	5	2·00	1·00		
		a. Imp. betwn. (horiz. pr.)	16·00	16·00	†		†		†	
25	,,	½ a. green	25	5	40	5	†		2·00	1·00
		a. Pale green	25	5	40	5	†		†	
		b. Blue-green	3·00	50	†		†		†	
26	,,	1 a. carmine	3·00	5	15	5	3·50	1·25	†	
		a. Double impression. P 12½×11	—	—	†		†		†	
27	,,	2 a. lilac	12	5	40	5	50	5	25	5
		a. Imperf. between (pair)	†		†		†		10·00	10·00
		b. Rose-lilac	†		†		†		50	5
28	,,	3 a. brown-orange (1909)	25	5	60	8	25	8	12	5
29	,,	4 a. olive-green (1909)	15	5	2·50	10	3·00	50	10	5
		a. Imp. betwn. (pr.)	†		†		10·00	10·00	†	
30	,,	8 a. purple (1911)	1·50	12	3·00	60	50	10	20	5
31	,,	12 a. blue-green (1911)	1·50	50	1·25	1·25	—	—	35	12

1912. *New plates eng. by Bradbury, Wilkinson & Co. Perfs. as before, or compound.*

			A.		B.		C.		D.	
32	**6**	¼ a. grey-black	10	5	12	5	25	5	5	5
		a. Imp. betwn. (pr.)	25·00	25·00	†		†		†	
33	,,	¼ a. lilac (*shades*)	†		†		†		5	5
		a. Imp. horiz. (vert. pr.)	†		†		†		—	—
34	,,	½ a. deep green	15	5	25	5	1·50	5	1·50	1·50
		a. Imp. betwn. (pr.)	†		†		—	—	16·00	16·00
		b. Imperf. (pair)	6·00	6·00	†		†		†	

8. Symbols.

In Wyon's ¼ a. stamp the fraction of value is closer to the end of the label than in the B. W. issue. In the Wyon ¼ a. and ½ a. the value in English and the label below are further apart than in the B.W.

Wyon's ¼ a. measures 19½ × 20 mm. and the ½ a. 19½ × 20½ mm.; both stamps from the Bradbury plates measure 19¾ × 21½ mm.

9

1915. *Inscr.* "Post & Receipt". *Various perfs. as above, and compound.*

		A.		B.	C.		D.	
35 8	½ a. green	50	5	†	25	5	25	5
	a. Imperf. between (pair)	15·00	15·00	†	15·00	15·00		†
	b. Imperf. (pair)	15·00	15·00	†		†		†
	c. Emerald-green	†		†		†	6·00	1·00
36 ,,	1 a. carmine	1·00	5	†	25	5	25	5
	a. Imp. between (pr.)	16·00	16·00	†		†		†
	b. Imperf. (pair)	15·00	15·00	†		†		†
	c. Perf. 12½×11	—	—	†		†		†
	d. Scarlet	8·00	8·00	†	2·00	1·50	50	10
	da. Imp. between (pr.)	†		†			16·00	16·00

For ½ a. claret, see No. 58.

1927 (1 Feb.). *W* 7. *P* 13½.

37 9	1 r. yellow	2·50	5·00

10. (4 pies.) **11.** (8 pies.)

1930 (6 May). *Surch. as T* **10** *and* **11**. *W* **7**. *P* 13½.

38 6	4 p. on ¼ a. grey-black (R.)	12·00	3·00
	a. Perf. 11	—	50·00
	b. Perf. 12½	10·00	3·00
39 ,,	4 p. on ¼ a. purple (R.)	5	5
	a. Imperf. between (pair)	£125	£125
	b. Perf. 11	£150	£150
	c. Black surch.	£150	£150
40 8	8 p. on ½ a. green (R.)	5	5
	a. Imp. between (horiz. pr.)	35·00	30·00
	b. Perf. 11	40·00	35·00
	c. Perf. 12½		

12. Symbols.

13. The Char Minar.

14. Bidar College.

(Recess. Mint, Hyderabad.)

1931 (12 Nov.)–**47**. *T* **12** *to* **14** (*and similar types*). *W* **7**. *Wove paper*. *P* 13½.

41 12	4 p. black	5	5
	a. Laid paper (1947)	2·50	2·00
	b. Imperf. (pair)	22·00	
42 ,,	8 p. green	5	5
	a. Imperf. between (vert. pr.)	£300	£300
	b. Imperf (pair)	20·00	
	c. Laid paper (1947)	2·50	2·00
43 13	1 a. brown (*shades*)	8	5
44 –	2 a. violet (*shades*)	15	5
	a. Imperf. (pair)		
45 –	4 a. ultramarine	35	5
	a. Imperf. (pair)		
46 –	8 a. orange	75	15
	a. Yellow-orange (1944)	15·00	10·00
47 14	12 a. scarlet	1·25	2·00
48 –	1 r. yellow	1·75	1·75

Designs (*as T* **14**): *Horiz.*—2 a. High Court of Justice; 4 a. Osman Sagar Reservoir. *Vert.*—8 a. Entrance to Ajanta Caves; 1 r. Victory Tower, Daulatabad.

Nos. 41a and 42c have a large sheet watermark "NIZAM'S GOVERNMENT" and arms, but this does not appear on all stamps.

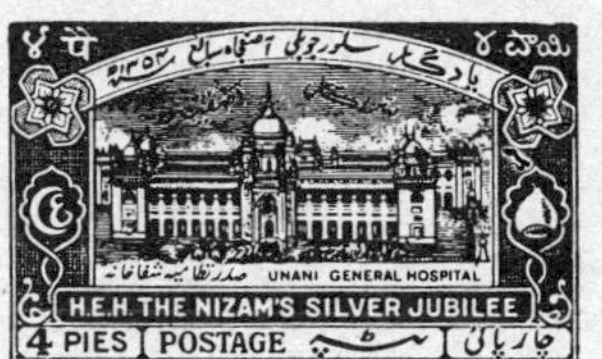

15. Unani General Hospital.

(Offset. Indian Govt. Ptg. Wks., Nasik.)

1937 (13 Feb.). *Various horiz. designs as T* **15**, *inscr.* "H.E.H. THE NIZAM'S SILVER JUBILEE". *P* 14.

49	4 p. slate and violet	8	5
50	8 p. slate and brown	8	5
51	1 a. slate and orange-yellow	10	5
52	2 a. slate and green	40	25

Designs:—8 p. Osmania General Hospital; 1 a. Osmania University; 2 a. Osmania Jubilee Hall.

16. Family Reunion.

1946. *Victory. Typo. Wove paper. P* 13½.

53 16	1 a. blue	5	5
	a. Imp. between (vert. pr.)	£300	
	b. Laid paper	15	15

No. 53 exists with faint wmk. of native characters on each stamp and without wmk.

No. 53b has a large sheet wmk. reading "HYDERABAD GOVERNMENT", in circular frame, but parts of this do not appear on all stamps.

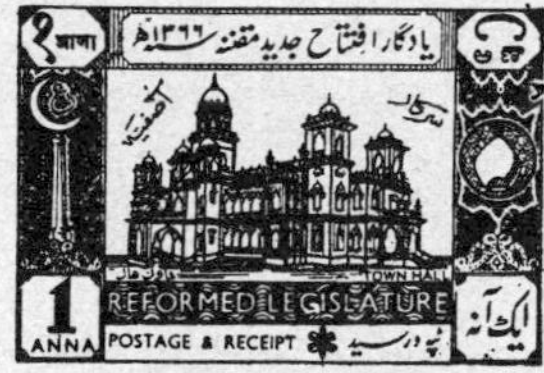

17. Town Hall.

(Litho. Government Press.)

1947 (17 Feb.). *Reformed Legislature. P* 13½.

54 17	1 a. black	5	5
	a. Imperf. between (pair)	£400	£400

18. Power House, Hyderabad.

1947–49. *As T* **18** (*inscr.* "H. E. H. THE NIZAM'S GOVT. POSTAGE"). *Typo. W* **7**. *P* 13½.

55	1 a. 4 p. green	25	5
56	3 a. greenish blue	25	5
	a. Bluish green	25	5
57	6 a. sepia	1·25	75
	a. Red-brown ('49)	12·00	8·00
	ab. Imperf. (pair)	22·00	

Designs:—3 a. Kaktyai Arch, Warangal Fort; 6a. Golkunda Fort.

1947. *As* 1915 *issue but colour changed. P* 13½.

58 8	½ a. claret	15	10
	a. Imperf. between (horizontal pr.)	£125	£125

1948. *As T* **12** ("POSTAGE" *at foot*). *Recess. W* **7**. *P* 13½.

59	6 p. claret	35	20

1949. *T* **12** ("POSTAGE" *at top*). *Litho. W* **7**. *P* 13½.

60 12	2 p. bistre-brown	60	10
	a. Imperf. between (hor. pr.)	£250	£250
	b. Imperf. (pair)	£250	£250

OFFICIAL STAMPS.

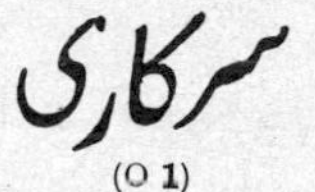

(O 1)

1873–1909. *Optd. as Type* O **1**.
A. In red. B. In black.

		A.		B.	
O1 1	1 a. olive-green	—	6·00	—	—
O2 2	½ a. brown	—	7·00	—	6·00
O3 ,,	2 a. sage-green	—	10·00	—	7·00

Varieties of Type O **1** occur.

Imitations of these overprints on genuine stamps and on reprints are found horizontally or vertically in various shades of red, in magenta and in black.

T **3** *optd. as Type* O **1**.
A. In red. B. In black.
(*a*) *Rough perf.* 11½.

		A.		B.	
O4	½ a. red-brown	—	—	—	—
O5	1 a. purple-brown	—	—	—	—
O6	2 a. green	—	—	—	—
O7	4 a. slate	—	—	—	—
O8	8 a. deep brown	—	—	—	—

(*b*) *P* 12½.

		A.		B.	
O9	½ a. red-brown	1·25	1·25	60	30
	a. Opt. inverted	†		—	—
O10	½ a. orge.-brn. ('09)	†		—	30
	a. Opt. inverted	†		—	—
O11	1 a. pur.-brn.	1·50	1·25	—	35
O12	1 a. drab	1·25		30	30
	a. Opt. inverted	†		—	—
O13	1 a. black ('09)	†		10	5
O14	2 a. grn. (to dp.)	1·50	—	30	—
	a. Opt. inverted	†		—	—
O15	2 a. sage-grn. (A) (1909)	†		—	8
	a. Type B	†		—	4·50
O16	3 a. ochre-brn.	—	—	30	25
O17	4 a. slate	3·25	1·25	75	60
O18	4 a. grnish. grey	†		1·50	—
O19	8 a. deep brown	3·00	—	3·00	1·75
	a. Imperf. btn. (pr.)	8·00	—	†	
O20	12 a. blue	3·50	—	2·00	—

The use of Official Stamps (Serkari) was discontinued in 1878, but was resumed in 1909, when the current stamps were optd. with the old dies.

1909–11. *T* **6** *optd. as Type* O **1.** A. *Perf.* 12½. B. *Perf.* 11½, 12. C. *Perf.* 11.

No.	Description	A.		B.		C.	
O21	½ a. orange	50	25	†		†	
	a. Vermilion	50	5	†		†	
	b. Opt. inverted	15·00	15·00	†		†	
O22	½ a. green (W.)	75	5	75	10	—	—
	a. Pale green (W.)	75	5	75	10	—	—
	b. Opt. inverted	†		8·00	4·00	†	
	c. Imperf. between (pair)	15·00	15·00	†		†	
O23	1 a. carmine	1·25	5	1·00	15	—	1·00
	a. Opt. double	5·00	—	†		†	
	b. Perf. 12½×11	—	—	†		†	
O24	2 a. lilac	1·00	5	75	10	—	—
O25	3 a. brown-orange	80	5	1·50	10	—	—
	a. Opt. inverted	12·00	12·00	†		†	
O26	4 a. olive-green (1911)	50	12	50	12	—	—
O27	8 a. purple (1911)	50	12	50	15	†	
O28	12 a. blue-green (1911)	50	12	50	15	—	—
	a. Perf. 12×12½	†		—	—	†	
	b. Imperf. between (horiz. pair)	†		—	—	†	

The Wyon and Bradbury, Wilkinson stamps are distinguished above and below by the use of the letters (W.) and (B.W.) respectively.

سرکاری

(O 2)

1911–12. *T* **6** *optd. with Type* O **2.** *Various perfs., also compound.*
A. *Perf.* 12½. B. *Perf.* 11½, 12. C. *Perf.* 11. D. *Perf.* 13½.

No.	Description	A.		B.		C.		D.	
O29	¼ a. grey (W.)	1·00	12	8·00	5	8·00	6·00	—	—
O30	¼ a. grey-black (B.W.)	5	5	12	5	5	5	12	5
	a. Opt. inverted	—	—	—	—	†		†	
	b. Pair, one without opt.	—	—	—	—	†		†	
O31	¼ a. lilac (*shades*) (B.W.)	†		†		—	—	10	15
	a. Imperf. horiz. (vert. pr.)	†		†		†		15·00	13·00
O32	½ a. pale green (W.)	1·00	5	—	5	†		—	—
O33	½ a. deep green (B.W.)	10	5	—	5	5	5	10	5
	a. Opt. inverted	8·00	5·00	†		10·00	6·00	†	
	b. Imperf. between (pair)	†		†		15·00	15·00	15·00	8·00
	c. Perf. 11×12½	15·00	15·00	†		†		†	
O34	1 a. carmine	10	5	50	5	5	5	—	—
	a. Opt. inverted	—	3·00	†		†		†	
	b. Perf. 11×12½	15·00	15·00	†		†		†	
O35	2 a. lilac	15	5	50	5	8	5	12	5
	a. Imperf. between (horiz. pr.)	†		†		†		22·00	22·00
	b. Rose-lilac	†		†		†		1·00	5
O36	3 a. brown-orange	25	5	—	8	65	10	3·50	8
	a. Opt. inverted	—	12·00	†		15·00	12·00	15·00	12·00
O37	4 a. olive-green	35	5	25	5	25	5	25	5
	a. Opt. inverted	18·00	12·00	—	—	†		13·00	8·00
O38	8 a. purple	65	8	—	—	75	10	35	5
O39	12 a. blue-green	90	12	—	—	1·00	25	50	12

1917–20. *T* **8** *optd. with Type* O **2.** *Various perfs. as above, also compound.*

No.	Description	A.		B.		C.		D.	
O40	½ a. green	—	—	†		25	5	12	5
	a. Opt. inverted	†		†		—	5·00	—	4·50
	b. Pair, one without opt.	†		†		—	—	†	
	c. Imperf. between (pair)	†		†		†		18·00	14·00
	d. Perf. 11×13½ or 13½×11	†		†		†		14·00	14·00
O41	1 a. carmine	—	—	†		25	5	12	5
	a. Opt. inverted	†		†		—	1·00	†	
	b. Opt. double	†		†		†		20·00	20·00
	c. Imperf. between (vert. pr.)	†		†		†		25·00	25·00
	d. Scarlet (1920)	†		†		†		25	5
	da. Stamp doubly printed	†		†		†		20·00	20·00
	db. Imperf. between (pair)	†		†		†		25·00	25·00

1930–34. *T* **6** *and* **8** *optd. as Type* O **2** *and surch. at top of stamp, in red,* as *T* **10** *or* **11.**

No.	Description		
O42	4 p. on ¼ a. grey-black (O30) ('34)	20·00	8·00
	a. Red surch. superimposed on Type O 2		
	b. Type O 2 superimposed on red surch.		
O43	4 p. on ¼ a. lilac (O31)	15	5
	a. Red surch. superimposed on Type O 2	9·00	7·00
	ab. Type O 2 superimposed on red surch.	9·00	7·00
	b. Imp. between (horiz. pair)	35·00	25·00
	c. Imperf. horiz. (vert. pair)	35·00	25·00
	d. Imp. horiz. (vert. strip of 3)		
	e. Red surch. double		
	f. Black opt. double		
O44	8 p. on ½ a. green (O40)	20	5
	a. Red surch. superimposed on Type O 2	8·00	5
	b. Type O 2 superimposed on red surch.	8·00	5
	c. Imp. between (pair)	35·00	20·00
	d. Red surch. double	15·00	10·00
	e. Stamp doubly printed		
O45	8 p. on ½ a. green (O33)	45·00	20·00
	a. Red surch. superimposed on Type O 2		

Normal copies of Nos. O42/4 have the red surcharge above the official overprint, Type O **2.**

1934–44. *Nos.* 41/8 *optd. with Type* O **2.**

No.	Description		
O46	4 p. black	5	5
	a. Imperf. (pair)	18·00	
	b. Imp. between (pair)	£300	£300
O47	8 p. green	5	5
	a. Opt. inverted	80·00	80·00
	b. Imp. between (pair)	£300	£300
	c. Opt. double	70·00	50·00
O48	1 a. brown	5	5
	a. Imp. between (pair)	£175	£175
O49	2 a. violet	10	5
	a. Imp. between (pair)	£300	£300
O50	4 a. ultramarine	40	8
O51	8 a. orange (1935)	1·25	25
	a. Yellow-orange (1944)	—	18·00
O52	12 a. scarlet (1935)	1·00	30
O53	1 r. yellow (1935)	1·50	70

1947. *No.* 58 *optd. with Type* O **2.**

No.	Description		
O54	**8** ½ a. claret	75	20
	a. Pair, one without opt.		

1949. *No.* 60 *optd. with Type* O **2.**

No.	Description		
O55	**12** 2 p. bistre-brown	75	2

1950. *No.* 59 *optd. with Type* O **2.**

No.	Description		
O56	6 p. claret	90	5

IDAR.

1. Maharaja Shri Himatsinhji. **2.**

(Typo. M.N. Kothari & Sons, Bombay.)

1939 (21 FEB.). *P* 11. (*a*) *White panels.*

No.	Type	Description	
1	**1**	½ a. emerald	1·50
		aa. Imperf. between (pair)	
		a. Yellow-green	
		b. As a. Thick paper	
		(*b*) *Coloured panels.*	
2	**1**	½ a. green (*shades*)	1·75

In No. 2 the whole design is composed of half-tone dots. In No. 1 the dots are confined to the oval portrait.

(Typo. P. G. Mehta & Co., Himmatnagar

1944 (21 OCT.). *P* 12.

No.	Type	Description	
3	**2**	½ a. blue-green	25
		a. Yellow-green	50
		b. Imperf. between (pair)	8·00
4	,,	1 a. violet	12
		a. Imperf. (pair)	75·00
5	,,	2 a. blue	30
		a. Imperf. between (v. or h. pair)	20·00
6	,,	4 a. vermillion	1·25

Nos. 1 to 6 are from booklet panes of 4 stamps producing single stamps with one or two adjacent sides imperf.

The 4 a. in violet is believed to be a colour trial.

INDORE.

(HOLKAR.)

1. Maharaja Tukoji Rao II Holkar XI.

(Litho. Waterlow & Sons.)

1886. *P* 15. (*a*) *Thick white paper.*

No.	Type	Description		
1	**1**	½ a. bright mauve	2·00	2·0
		(*b*) *Thin white or yellowish paper.*		
2	**1**	½ a. pale mauve	70	8
		a. Dull mauve	80	9

2. Type I.

2a. Type II.

NOTE. In addition to the difference in the top-line character (marked by arrow), the two Types can be distinguished by the difference in the angles of the 6-pointed stars and the appearance of the lettering. In Type I the top characters are smaller and more cramped than the bottom; in Type II both are in the same style and similarly spaced.

1889. *Imperf.*

3 **2** ½ a. black/*pink* .. .. 1·00 1·00
4 **2a** ½ a. black/*pink* 75 75

3. Maharaja Shivaji Rao Holkar XII.

(Recess. Waterlow.)

1889–92. *Medium wove paper.* P 14 to 15.

5 **3** ¼ a. orange (9.2.92) 8 8
a. Imperf. between (pair) .. 35·00 35·00
b. Very thick wove paper .. 30 15
c. *Yellow* 10 8
6 ,, ½ a. dull violet 50 35
a. *Brown-purple* 10 8
b. Imperf. between (pair) .. 25·00 25·00
7 ,, 1 a. green (7.2.92) 35 25
a. Imperf. between (pair) .. 35·00 35·00
8 ,, 2 a. vermilion (7.2.92) 75 40
a. Very thick wove paper .. 2·00 2·00

4. Maharaja Tukoji Rao III Holkar XIII. 5.

(Recess. Perkins, Bacon & Co.)

1904. P 13½, 14.

9 **4** ¼ a. orange 5 5
10 **5** ½ a. lake 75 5
a. *Brown-lake (shades)* .. 2·00 25
b. Imperf. (pair) .. .. 8·00
11 ,, 1 a. green .. .. .. 1·25 5
a. Imperf. (pair) .. .. 70·00
12 ,, 2 a. brown .. .. .. 2·50 20
a. Imperf. (pair) .. .. 75·00
13 ,, 3 a. violet .. .. .. 3·00 30
14 ,, 4 a. ultramarine .. .. 3·50 30
a. *Dull blue* .. .. .. 3·50 30

(6)

7. Maharaja Yeshwant Rao II Holkar XIV.

1905. *No. 6a surch.* "QUARTER ANNA" *in Devanagari, as T* **6**.

15 **3** ¼ a. on ½ a. brown-purple .. 50 75

NOTE. From 1st March 1908 the use of Indore stamps was restricted to official mail.

(Recess. Perkins, Bacon & Co.)

1928–38. *P* 13½ (¼, ½, 1 *a.*, 2 *a. sepia and* 8 *a. slate-grey*), 13 (1¼ *a.*) *or* 14 (*others*).

16 **7** ¼ a. orange.. .. .. 10 5
a. Perf. 14 .. .. ..
17 ,, ½ a. claret 10 5
a. Perf. 14 .. .. ..
18 ,, 1 a. green 10 5
19 ,, 1¼ a. green (1933) 15 5
a. Perf. 14 .. ..
20 ,, 2 a. sepia .. .. .. 1·25 50
21 ,, 2 a. bluish green (1936) .. 50 45
a. Imperf. (pair) .. .. 15·00 18·00
22 ,, 3 a. deep violet .. .. 1·25 50
a. Imperf. (pair) .. .. 15·00 18·00
23 ,, 3 a. Prussian blue (date?) 14·00
24 ,, 3½ a. violet (1934) .. .. 1·75 1·50
a. Imperf. (pair) .. .. 16·00 16·00
25 ,, 4 a. ultramarine .. .. 1·75 1·00
26 ,, 4 a. yellow-brown (1938) .. 3·00 1·00
a. Imperf. (pair) .. .. 16·00 18·00
27 ,, 8 a. slate-grey .. .. 3·00 3·00
28 ,, 8 a. red-orange (1938) .. 4·00 4·00
29 ,, 12 a. carmine (1934) .. 7·00 7·00

As T **7**, *but larger* (23 × 28 *mm.*). *P* 14.

30 **7** 1 r. black and light blue .. 7·00 7·00
31 ,, 2 r. black and carmine .. 10·00 10·00
32 ,, 5 r. black and brown-orange 12·00 14·00

(8)

9

1940 (1 Aug.). *Surch. in words as T* **8**.

33 **7** ¼ a. on 5 r. blk. & brn.-orge... 35 12
a. Surch. double (Bk. + G.) .. — 35·00
34 ,, ½ a. on 2 r. black & carm. .. 60 15
35 ,, 1 a. on 1¼ a. green (*p* 13) .. 60 15
a. Perf. 14 .. .. .. 4·00 2·00
b. Surch. inverted. Perf. 14 .. 40·00

(Typo. "*Times of India*" Press, Bombay.)

1941–47. *P* 11.

36 **9** ¼ a. red-orange 15 5
37 ,, ½ a. claret 20 5
38 ,, 1 a. green 20 8
39 ,, 1¼ a. yellow-green 30 20
a. Imperf. (pair) .. .. 70·00
40 ,, 2 a. turquoise-blue .. .. 6·00 2·50
41 ,, 4 a. yellow-brown (1947) .. 9·00 8·00

Larger size (23 × 28 *mm.*).

42 ,, 2 r. black and carmine ('43).. 9·00 9·00
43 ,, 5 r. black & yell.-orge. ('43).. 10·00 11·00

OFFICIAL STAMPS.

SERVICE (S 1) **SERVICE** (S 2)

1904–6. *Optd. with Type* S **1**.

S1 **4** ¼ a. orange (1906) 5 5
S2 **5** ½ a. lake 5 5
a. Opt. inverted .. .. 8·00
b. Opt. double .. .. 7·00
c. Imperf. (pair) .. .. 12·00
d. *Brown-lake* 5 5
da. Opt. inverted .. .. 7·00
S3 ,, 1 a. green 5 5
S4 ,, 2 a. brown (1905) 15 10
a. Pair, one without opt. .. £175
S5 ,, 3 a. violet (1906) .. .. 1·25 60
a. Imperf. (pair) .. .. 40·00
S6 ,, 4 a. ultramarine (1905) .. 1·50 75

Optd. with Type S **2**.

S7 **5** ½ a. lake 5 5

Types S **1** and S **2** differ chiefly in the shape of the letter "R."

JAIPUR.

1. Chariot of the Sun God, Surya. 2.

½ a. 36 varieties (2 plates). Pl. I stamps 2½ mm. apart horizontally; Pl. II stamps 4½ mm. apart.
1 a. and 2 a. 12 varieties.

1904. *Value at sides in small letters and characters. Roughly perf.* 14.

1 **1** ½ a. pale blue (Pl. I) .. .. 8·00 10·00
a. *Ultramarine* .. .. 1·50 1·50
b. Imperf, *ultramarine* ..
2 ,, ½ a. grey blue (Pl. II) .. — £125
a. Imperf. £175 £175
3 ,, 1 a. dull red 60 65
a. *Scarlet* .. .. .. 1·25
4 ,, 2 a. pale green .. .. 1·25 1·25
a. *Emerald-green* .. .. 1·75

Value in larger letters and characters. 24 varieties on one plate. Roughly perf. 14.

5 **2** ½ a. pale blue .. .. 1·50 1·50
a. *Deep blue* .. .. 1·50 1·50
b. *Ultramarine* .. .. 1·50 1·50
c. Imperf. £160

3. Chariot of the Sun God, Surya.

(Recess. Perkins, Bacon & Co.)

1904. P 12.

6 **3** ½ a. blue .. .. .. 1·50 1·10
a. Perf. 12½ .. .. .. 2·00 2·00
b. Perf. comp. of 12 and 12½ .. 8·00 8·00
7 ,, 1 a. brown-red .. .. 15·00 15·00
a. Perf. 12½ .. .. .. 22·00 22·00
b. Perf. comp. of 12 and 12½ .. 90·00 90·00
c. *Carmine* .. .. .. 1·00 75
ca. Imperf. between (vert. pair) .. 40·00
cb. Perf. comp. of 12 and 12½ .. 6·00 6·00
8 ,, 2 a. deep green .. .. 3·50 3·00
a. Perf. 12½ .. .. .. 9·00 7·00
b. Perf. comp. of 12 and 12½ .. 20·00 20·00

1905–8. P 13½.

9 **3** ¼ a. olive-yellow (1906) .. 8 8
10 ,, ½ a. blue 12 8
a. *Indigo* 15 15
11 ,, 1 a. brown-red (1906) .. 2·25 2·25
a. *Bright red* (1908) .. 25 15

No.	Type	Description	Unused	Used
12	3	2 a. deep green	75	50
13	,,	4 a. chestnut	1·40	1·40
14	,,	8 a. bright violet	1·75	1·75
15	,,	1 r. yellow	3·00	3·00
		a. Orange-yellow	3·50	3·50
		b. Yellow-ochre	3·50	3·50

4. Chariot of the Sun God, Surya.

(5)

(Typo. Jail Press, Jaipur.)

1911. *Thin wove paper. Imperf. Six varieties of each value.*

No.	Type	Description	Unused	Used
16	4	¼ a. green	80	75
		a. Doubly printed		
		b. "¼" inv. at rt. upper corner	80	
		c. No stop after "STATE"	80	
17	,,	¼ a. greenish yellow	15	15
		a. "¼" inv. in rt. upper corner	75	
		b. No stop after "STATE"	75	
18	,,	½ a. ultramarine	15	15
		a. Doubly printed	1·00	
		b. No stop after "STATE"	50	
		c. Large "J" in "JAIPUR"	50	
		d. "⅓" for "½" at lower left	1·50	
19	,,	½ a. grey-blue	15	15
		a. No stop after "STATE"	40	
		b. Large "J" in "JAIPUR"	1·00	
		c. "⅓" for "½" at lower left	1·75	
20	,,	1 a. rose-red	15	15
21	,,	2 a. greyish green	3·00	2·50
		a. Deep green	3·00	2·50

One sheet of the ¼ a. is known in blue.

(Typo. Jail Press, Jaipur.)

1913–18. *Paper-maker's wmk.* "DORLING & CO. LONDON" *in sheet. P* 11.

No.	Type	Description	Unused	Used
22	3	¼ a. pale olive-yellow	5	5
		a. Imperf. betwn. (horiz. pair)	40·00	40·00
23	,,	¼ a. olive	5	5
		a. Imperf. between (vert. or horiz. pair)	40·00	40·00
		b. Doubly printed		
24	,,	½ a. bistre	5	5
25	,,	½ a. pale ultramarine	5	5
		a. Imperf. between (pair)	40·00	40·00
		b. Blue	5	5
26	,,	1 a. carmine (1918)	8	8
		a. Imperf. between (vert. pair)	40·00	40·00
27	,,	1 a. rose-red	1·00	
28	,,	1 a. scarlet	12	
		a. Imperf. between (vert. pr.)	40·00	40·00
29	,,	2 a. green (1918)	40	15
30	,,	4 a. chocolate	40	
31	,,	4 a. pale brown	40	
		a. Imperf. betwn. (horiz. pr.)	50·00	

1926. *Surch. with T* **5**.

No.	Type	Description	Unused	Used
32	3	3 a. on 8 a. bright violet (R.)	50	80
		a. Surch. inverted	75·00	75·00
33	,,	3 a. on 1 r. yellow (R.)	50	50
		a. Surch. inverted	75·00	75·00
		b. Orange-yellow		
		c. Yellow-ochre		

1928. *As* 1913–18. *Wmk.* "OVERLAND BANK" *in sheet. P* 12.

No.	Type	Description	Unused	Used
34	3	½ a. ultramarine	4·00	
35	,,	1 a. rose-red	5·00	
36	,,	1 a. scarlet	5·00	
37	,,	2 a. green	20·00	
38	,,	8 a. bright violet	20·00	
39	,,	1 r. orange-vermilion	35·00	

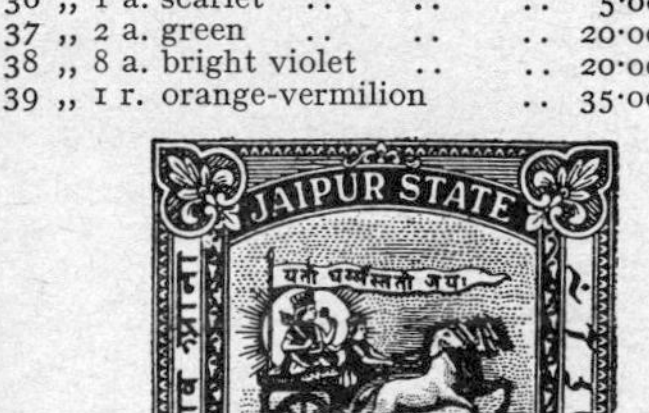

6. Chariot of the Sun God, Surya.

7. Maharaja Sir Man Singh Bahadur.

8. Sowar in Armour.

(Litho. Security Printing Press, Nasik.)

1931 (14 MAR.). *Investiture of Maharaja. T* **6/8** *and similar designs. No wmk. P* 14.

No.	Description	Unused	Used
40	¼ a. black and deep lake	5	5
41	½ a. black and violet	10	5
42	1 a. black and blue	1·00	30
43	2 a. black and buff	1·25	35
44	2½ a. black and carmine	7·00	4·00
45	3 a. black and myrtle	7·00	4·00
46	4 a. black and olive-green	5·00	4·00
47	6 a. black and deep blue	5·00	4·00
48	8 a. black and chocolate	7·00	6·00
49	1 r. black and pale olive	7·00	6·00
50	2 r. black and yellow-green	8·00	10·00
51	5 r. black and purple	11·00	12·00

Designs: *Vert.*—1 a. Elephant and state banner; 2½ a. Dancing peacock; 8 a. Sireh-Deorhi Gate. *Horiz.*—3 a. Bullock carriage; 4 a. Elephant carriage; 6 a. Albert Museum; 1 r. Chandra Mahal; 2 r. Amber Palace; 5 r. Maharajas Jai Singh and Sir Man Singh.

Eighteen of these sets were issued for presentation purposes with a special surcharge "INVESTITURE—MARCH 14, 1931" in red.

10. Maharaja Sir Man Singh Bahadur.

One Rupee

(11)

पाव आना

(12)

(Offset-litho. Security Printing Press, Nasik.)

1932–46. *P* 14. (*a*) *Inscr.* "POSTAGE & REVENUE")

No.	Type	Description	Unused	Used
52	10	1 a. black and blue	5	5
53	,,	2 a. black and buff	5	5
54	,,	4 a. black and grey-green	10	10
55	,,	8 a. black and chocolate	35	40
56	,,	1 r. black and yellow-bistre	5·00	5·00
57	,,	2 r. black and yellow-green	18·00	18·00

(*b*) *Inscr.* "POSTAGE".

No.	Type	Description	Unused	Used
58	7	¼ a. black and brown-lake	5	5
59	,,	¾ a. black & brn.-red ('43?)	5	5
60	,,	1 a. black and blue ('43?)	8	8
61	,,	2 a. black and buff ('43?)	10	10
62	7	2½ a. black and carmine	10	10
63	,,	3 a. black and green	12	12
64	,,	4 a. black & grey-grn. ('43?)	20	20
65	,,	6 a. black and deep blue	70	60
		a. Black and pale blue (1946)	1·25	1·00
66	,,	8 a. black & chocolate ('46)	75	75
67	,,	1 r. black & yell.-bistre ('46)	4·00	3·00

1936. *Nos.* 57 *and* 51 *surch. with T* **11**.

No.	Type	Description	Unused	Used
68	10	1 r. on 2 r. black and yellow-green (R.)	1·00	1·00
69	–	1 r. on 5 r. black and purple	1·00	1·00

1938 (DEC.). *No.* 41 *surch.* "QUARTER ANNA" *in Devanagari, T* **12**.

No.	Type	Description	Unused	Used
70	7	¼ a. on ½ a. black & violet (R.)	1·00	1·00

13. Maharaja and Amber Palace.

(Recess. D.L.R.)

1947 (DEC.)–**48.** *Silver Jubilee of Maharaja's Accession to Throne. Various designs as T* **13**. *P* 13½ × 14.

No.	Description	Unused	Used
71	¼ a. red-brown & green (5.48)	5	5
72	½ a. green and violet	5	5
73	¾ a. black and lake (5.48)	5	5
74	1 a. red-brown & ultramarine	15	15
75	2 a. violet and scarlet	10	15
76	3 a. green and black (5.48)	12	25
77	4 a. ultramarine and brown	25	40
78	8 a. vermilion and brown	35	65
79	1 r. purple and green (5.48)	75	1·00

Designs:—¼ a. Palace Gate; ¾ a. Map of Jaipur; 1 a. Observatory; 2 a. Wind Palace; 3 a. Coat of Arms; 4 a. Amber Fort Gate; 8 a. Chariot of the Sun; 1 r. Maharaja's portrait between State flags.

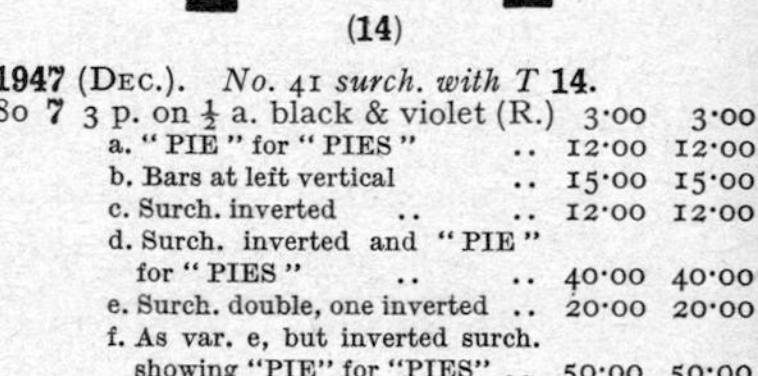

(14)

1947 (DEC.). *No.* 41 *surch. with T* **14**.

No.	Type	Description	Unused	Used
80	7	3 p. on ½ a. black & violet (R.)	3·00	3·00
		a. "PIE" for "PIES"	12·00	12·00
		b. Bars at left vertical	15·00	15·00
		c. Surch. inverted	12·00	12·00
		d. Surch. inverted and "PIE" for "PIES"	40·00	40·00
		e. Surch. double, one inverted	20·00	20·00
		f. As var. e, but inverted surch. showing "PIE" for "PIES"	50·00	50·00

OFFICIAL STAMPS.

SERVICE (O 1)

SERVICE (O 2)

1929–30. *T* **3** *typographed. P* 11, 12, *or compound. Wmk.* "OVERLAND BANK" (¼ *a.*, ½ *a.*, 1 *a. and* 2 *a.*) *or* "DORLING & CO. LONDON" (4 *a.*, 8 *a. and* 1 *r.*). (*a*) *Optd. with Type* O **1**.

No.	Description	Unused	Used
O 1	¼ a. olive	5	5
	a. Bistre	5	5
O 2	½ a. pale ultramarine (Bk.)	5	5
	a. Imperf. between (horiz. pair)	10·00	10·00
	b. Opt. inverted	35·00	35·00
	c. Opt. double (R. and Bk.)	35·00	35·00
O 3	½ a. pale ultram. (R.) ('30)	5	5
	a. Imp. between. (horiz. pair)		
O 3c	1 a. rose-red		
	d. Imperf. between (horiz. pair)	20·00	20·00
O 4	1 a. scarlet	10	5
	a. Opt. inverted	20·00	20·00
O 5	2 a. green	20	20
	a. Imperf. between (vert. pr.)	20·00	20·00
	b. Imperf. between (horiz. pr.)	25·00	25·00

6	4 a. pale brown		1·00	1·25
	a. Chocolate		1·00	1·25
7	8 a. bright violet (R.) ..		10·00	10·00
8	1 r. orange-vermilion ..		18·00	15·00

(*b*) *Optd. with Type* O **2**.

9	½ a. ultramarine (Bk.) ..	28·00	5
	a. Imperf. between (horiz. pr.)	70·00	40·00
10	½ a. ultramarine (R.) ..	45·00	5
	a. Imperf. between (vert. pr.)	£100	40·00
11	8 a. bright violet	65·00	65·00
12	1 r. orange-vermilion ..	65·00	65·00

आध आना (O **3**) SERVICE (O **4**)

32. *No.* O5 *surch. with Type* O **3**.

13 **3**	½ a. on 2 a. green	50·00	10

31–7. *Nos.* 41/3 *and* 46 *optd. at Nasik with Type* O **4**, *in red.*

14 **7**	½ a. black and violet ..	5	5
15 **8**	1 a. black and blue ..	75·00	5
16 ,,	2 a. black and buff ('36) ..	20	12
17 **6**	4 a. blk. & olive-grn. ('37)	40	15

32–7. *Nos.* 52/6 *optd. at Nasik with Type* O **4**, *in red.*

18 **10**	1 a. black and blue ..	5	5
	a. Black and dull blue ..	5	5
19 ,,	2 a. black and buff ..	15	5
20 ,,	4 a. blk. & grey-grn. ('37)	1·75	1·00
21 ,,	8 a. black and chocolate ..	45	50
22 ,,	1 r. black & yellow-bistre	1·75	1·00

32–46. *Stamps of* 1932–46, *inscr.* "POSTAGE". (*a*) *Optd. at Nasik with Type* O **4**, *in red.*

23 **7**	¼ a. blk. & brn.-lake ('36)	10	5
24 ,,	¾ a. black & brn.-red ('44)	10	5
25 ,,	1 a. black and blue ('41?)	20	20
26 ,,	2 a. black and buff	25	25
27 ,,	2½ a. black & carmine ('46)	35	40
28 ,,	4 a. blk. & grey-grn. ('46)	50	30
29 ,,	8 a. black and choc. ('46)	75	75
30 ,,	1 r. black and yellow-bistre (date?) ..	85·00	

(*b*) *Optd. locally as Type* O **2** (16 *mm. long*), *in black.*

31 **7**	¼ a. black & red-brn. ('36)	18·00	15·00

9 PIES

= = (O **5**)

47. *No.* O25 *surch. with Type* O **5**, *in red.*

32 **7**	9 p. on 1 a. black and blue	10	5

47 (DEC.). *No.* O14 *surch. as T.* **14**, *but* "3 PIES" *placed higher.*

33 **7**	3 p. on ½ a. blk. & vio. (R.)	2·00	2·00
	a. Surch. double, one inverted	18·00	18·00
	b. "PIE" for "PIES" ..	75·00	75·00
	c. Surch. inverted	£300	£300

49. *No.* O14 *surch.* "THREE-QUARTER ANNA" *in Devanagari, as T* **12**, *but with two bars on each side.*

34 **7**	¾ a. on ½ a. blk. & vio. (R.)	1·50	1·50
	a. Surch. double	£300	£300

There are three different types of surcharge in the setting of 30, which vary in one or other of the Hindi characters.

For later issues, see RAJASTHAN.

JAMMU AND KASHMIR.

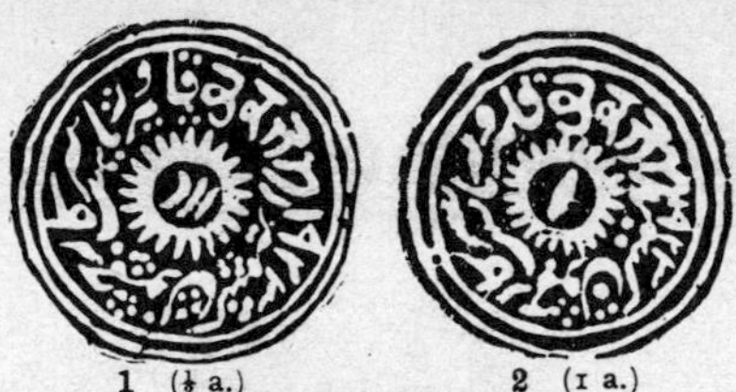

1 (½ a.) **2** (1 a.)

3 (4 a.)

Characters denoting the value (on the circular stamps only) are approximately as shown in the central circle of the stamps illustrated above.

Opinions are still divided as to whether *T* **2** and *T* **3** are given their correct face values above. The character in the centre of *T* **3** does represent 4 annas, whereas that in *T* **2** is meaningless, in this notation. On the other hand other evidence suggests that *T* **3** was the stamp used for 1 anna.

THE CIRCULAR STAMPS. (Types **1** to **3**.)

A. *Handstamped in water colours.*

1866 (MAR.)–**67.** *Native paper, thick to thin, usually having the appearance of laid paper and tinted grey or brown. For Jammu and Kashmir.*

		Cut □		*Cut* O	
1	½ a. grey-black ..	18·00	10·00	5·00	1·25
2	1 a. grey-black ..	30·00	—	6·50	—
3	4 a. grey-black ..	50·00	—	8·00	8·00
4	4 a. royal blue ..	£100	60·00	—	6·00
4*a*	½ a. ultramarine ..	—	—	†	
5	1 a. ultramarine ..	80·00	30·00	15·00	8·00
6	4 a. ultramarine ..	40·00	11·00	—	3·50
7	1 a. indigo ('67) ..	£450	£110	—	40·00

1869–72. *Reissued for use in Jammu only.*

8	½ a. red	8·00	—	2·50	—
9	1 a. red	4·00	7·00	1·25	—
10	4 a. red	12·00	—	4·00	—
11	½ a. orange-red ..	15·00	—	6·00	—
12	1 a. orange-red ..	6·00	—	3·50	—
13	4 a. orange-red ..	15·00	—	5·00	—
13*a*	1 a. carmine-red ..				
13*b*	1 a. orange ('72) ..				

1869–76. *Special Printings.*

14	½ a. deep black ..	3·00	—	50	—
15	1 a. deep black ..	15·00	—	4·00	—
16	4 a. deep black ..	20·00	—	5·00	—
17	½ a. bright blue ..	9·00	—	1·75	—
18	1 a. bright blue ..	9·00	—	1·50	—
19	4 a. bright blue ..	8·00	—	1·25	—
20	½ a. emerald-green	11·00	—	1·25	—
21	1 a. emerald-green	14·00	—	1·75	—
22	4 a. emerald-green	14·00	—	2·00	—
23*a*	½ a. yellow ..	40·00	—	5·00	—
24	1 a. yellow ..	40·00	—	5·00	—
25	4 a. yellow ..	40·00	—	5·00	—
25*a*	1 a. deep blue-black ('76) ..	80·00	45·00	—	—

These special printings were available for use, but little used.

B. *Handstamped in oil colours. Heavy blurred prints.*

1877–78. (*a*) *Native paper.*

26	½ a. red	3·50	4·00	1·25	1·75
27	1 a. red	30·00	£120	7·00	—
28	4 a. red	3·50	—	1·25	—
29	½ a. black	3·00	5·50	80	1·75
32	½ a. slate-blue ..	10·00	—	3·50	—
34	4 a. slate-blue ..	3·00	—	45	—
35	½ a. sage-green ..	35·00	—	5·50	—
36	1 a. sage-green ..	35·00	—	5·50	—
37	4 a. sage-green ..	35·00	—	4·00	—

(*b*) *European laid paper, medium to thick.*

38	½ a. red	—	55·00	—	15·00
39	1 a. red	20·00	—	4·50	—
41	½ a. black ..	2·50	6·00	40	1·75
44	½ a. slate-blue ..	2·50	—	50	—
45	1 a. slate-blue ..	75·00	—	—	—
46	4 a. slate-blue ..	7·00	—	1·25	—
47	1 a. sage-green ..	£400	—	£120	—
48	½ a. yellow ..	45·00	—	5·00	—

(*c*) *Thick yellowish wove paper.*

49	½ a. red ('78) ..	—	£110	—	50·00

Forgeries exist of the ½ a. and 1 a. in types which were at one time supposed to be authentic.

Reprints and imitations (of which some of each were found in the official remainder stock), exist in a great variety of fancy colours, both on native paper, usually thinner and smoother than that of the originals, and on various thin European *wove* papers, on which the originals were never printed.

The imitations, which do not agree in type with the above illustrations, are also to be found on *laid* paper.

All the reprints, etc. are in oil colours or printer's ink. The originals in oil colour are usually blurred, particularly when on native paper. The reprints, etc. are usually clear.

(**3***a*)

1877. *Provisional. Seal obliterator of Jammu handstamped in red water colour on pieces of native paper, and used as a ½ anna stamp.*

50 **3***a*	(½ a.) rose-red	—	60·00

THE RECTANGULAR STAMPS

I. FOR JAMMU.

½ a. ½ a.

1 a. **4** ½ a.

T **4** to **11** have a star at the top of the oval band; the characters denoting the value are in the upper part of the inner oval. All are dated 1923, corresponding with A.D. 1866.

T **4.** *Printed in blocks of four, three varieties of ½ anna and one of 1 anna.*

1867. *In water colour on native paper.*

52	½ a. grey-black	30·00	15·00
53	1 a. grey-black	£175	85·00
54	½ a. indigo	15·00	10·00
55	1 a. indigo	20·00	15·00
56	½ a. deep ultramarine ..	15·00	12·00
57	1 a. deep ultramarine ..	25·00	16·00
58	½ a. deep violet-blue ..	15·00	10·00
59	1 a. deep violet-blue ..	35·00	22·00

1868–77. *In water colour on native paper.*

60	½ a. red (*shades*)	1·50	1·50
61	1 a. red (*shades*)	3·00	3·00
62	½ a. orange-red	25·00	6·00
63	1 a. orange-red	18·00	6·00
64	½ a. orange	22·00	20·00
65	1 a. orange		

1874–6. *Special printings; in water colour on native paper.*

66	½ a. bright blue	40·00	20·00
67	1 a. bright blue	18·00	20·00
68	½ a. emerald-green	£175	£110
69	1 a. emerald-green	£175	£110
69*a*	½ a. jet-black	20·00	28·00
69*b*	1 a. jet-black	£110	£110

1877. *In oil colour.* (*a*) *Native paper.*

70	½ a. red	4·00	3·00
71	1 a. red	7·00	6·00
72	½ a. brown-red	—	10·00
73	1 a. brown-red	—	40·00
74	½ a. black	—	85·00
75	1 a. black	—	£130
76	½ a. deep blue-black	—	£160
77	1 a. deep blue-black	—	£1000
	(*b*) *Laid paper* (*medium or thick*).		
78	½ a. red	—	70·00
	(*c*) *Thick wove paper.*		
79	½ a. red	—	80·00
80	1 a. red		
	(*d*) *Thin laid, bâtonné paper.*		
84	½ a. red	—	£250
85	1 a. red	—	£900

The circular and rectangular stamps listed under the heading "Special Printings" did not supersede those in *red*, which was the normal colour for Jammu down to 1878. It is not known for what reason other colours were used during that period, but these stamps were printed in 1874 or 1875 and were certainly put into use. The rectangular stamps were again printed in *black* (jet-black, as against the greyish black of the 1867 printings) at that time, and impressions of the two periods can also be distinguished by the obliterations, which until 1868 were in *magenta* and after that in *black*.

There are reprints of these, in *oil* colour, *brown-red* and *bright blue*, on native paper; they are very clearly printed, which is not the case with the originals in *oil* colour.

II. For KASHMIR.

5

1866 (Sept.(?)). *Printed from a single die. Native laid paper.*

86	**5**	½ a. black	£350	£110

Forgeries of this stamp are commonly met with, copied from an illustration in *Le Timbre-Poste*.

6 (½ a.)

7 (1 a.)

1866. *Native laid paper.*

87	**6**	½ a. black	£300	45·00
88	**7**	1 a. black	£600	75·00

Printed in sheets of 25 (5×5), the four top rows being ½ a. and the bottom row 1 a.

8 (¼ a.)

9 (2 a.)

10 (4 a.)

11 (8 a.)

1867. *Native laid paper.*

90	**8**	¼ a. black	15	15
91	**6**	½ a. ultramarine	40	12
92	,,	½ a. violet-blue	50	25
93	**7**	1 a. ultramarine	£1100	£450
94	,,	1 a. orange	2·50	1·25
95	,,	1 a. brown-orange ..	1·50	1·25
96	,,	1 a. orange-vermilion ..	2·00	1·25
97	**9**	2 a. yellow	2·00	1·50
98	,,	2 a. buff	2·00	1·50
99	**10**	4 a. green	4·00	3·00
		a. Tête-bêche (pair) ..		
100	,,	4 a. sage-green	15·00	7·00
100*a*	,,	4 a. myrtle-green	£160	£160
101	**11**	8 a. red	4·00	4·00
		a. Tête-bêche (pair) ..		

Of the above, the ¼ a., 1 a., and 2 a. were printed in strips of five varieties, the ½ a. in a block of twenty varieties, and the 4 a. and 8 a. from single dies. Varieties at one time catalogued upon European papers were apparently never put into circulation, though some of them were printed while these stamps were still in use.

Nos. 86 to 101 are in *water* colour.

III. For JAMMU AND KASHMIR.

In the following issues there are 15 varieties on the sheets of the ⅛ a., ¼ a., and ½ a.; 20 varieties of the 1 a. and 2 a. and 8 varieties of the 4 a. and 8 a. The value is in the lower part of the central oval.

12 (⅛ a.)

13 (½ a.)

14 (1 a.)

15 (2 a.)

16 (4 a.)

17 (8 a.)

1878–79. *Provisional printings.*

1\. *Ordinary white laid paper, of varying thickness*

(*a*) *Rough perf.* 10 *to* 12 (i) *or* 13 *to* 16 (ii).

101*b*	**12**	⅛ a. red (i)		
102	**13**	½ a. red (i)	70	4
103	**14**	1 a. red (ii)	£200	
104	**13**	½ a. slate-violet (i) ..	15·00	15·0
104*a*	**14**	1 a. violet (ii)		

(*b*) *Imperf.*

105	**13**	½ a. slate-violet (*shades*) ..	7·00	7·0
106	**14**	1 a. slate-purple	7·00	7·0
107	,,	1 a. mauve	7·00	7·0
108	**15**	2 a. violet	8·00	8·0
109	,,	2 a. bright mauve ..	8·00	8·0
110	,,	2 a. slate-blue	8·00	8·0
111	,,	2 a. dull blue	12·00	12·0
112	**12**	⅛ a. red	6·00	6·0
113	**13**	½ a. red	3·00	3·0
114	**14**	1 a. red	3·00	2·5
115	**15**	2 a. red	12·00	10·0
116	**16**	4 a. red	12·00	10·0

2\. *Medium wove paper.*

(*a*) *Rough perf.* 10 *to* 12.

117	**13**	½ a. red	—	8·0

(*b*) *Imperf.*

117*b*	**12**	⅛ a. red		
118	**13**	½ a. red	2·50	2·5
119	**14**	1 a. red	2·50	2·5
120	**15**	2 a. red	7·00	2·5

3\. *Thick wove paper. Imperf.*

121	**13**	½ a. red	5·00	
122	**14**	1 a. red	7·00	2·5
123	**15**	2 a. red	2·50	2·5

1879. *Definitive issue. Thin wove paper, fin to coarse.*

(*a*) *Rough perf.* 10 *to* 12.

124	**13**	½ a. red	10·00	8·0

(*b*) *Imperf.*

125	**12**	⅛ a. red	25	2
126	**13**	½ a. red	20	2
127	**14**	1 a. red	25	3
		a. Bisected (½ a.) (on cover)	—	£85
128	**15**	2 a. red	40	4
129	**16**	4 a. red	50	6
130	**17**	8 a. red	60	8

1880 (March). *Provisional printing in wate colour on thin bâtonné paper. Imperf.*

130*a*	**12**	⅛ a. ultramarine	£110	70·0

1881–83. *As Nos.* 124 *to* 130. *Colour changed*

(*a*) *Rough perf.* 10 *to* 12.

130*b*	**13**	½ a. orange		

(*b*) *Imperf.*

131	**12**	⅛ a. orange	3·00	1·5
132	**13**	½ a. orange	8·00	6·0
133	**14**	1 a. orange	6·00	1·5
		a. Bisected (½ a.) (on cover)	—	£85
134	**15**	2 a. orange	6·00	2·0
135	**16**	4 a. orange	8·00	
136	**17**	8 a. orange	12·00	

No. 127a was used at Leh in April, 1883 an No. 133a was used there later.

Nos. 125–130 and 132–136 were re-issue between 1890 and 1894 and used concurrentl with the stamps which follow. Such re-issue can be identified by the "three-circle" can cellations, introduced in December, 1890.

18 (⅛ a.)

1883–94. *New colours. Thin wove papers, toned, coarse to fine, or fine white* (1889). *Imperf.*

No.	Type	Description	Unused	Used
138	**18**	⅛ a. yellow-brown	5	5
139	,,	⅛ a. yellow	5	5
140	**12**	¼ a. sepia	10	5
141	,,	¼ a. brown	5	5
		a. Double impression	£400	
142	,,	¼ a. pale brown	5	5
		a. Error. ¼ a. green	12·00	
143	**13**	½ a. dull blue	1·75	
144	,,	½ a. bright blue	18·00	
145	,,	½ a. vermilion	25	8
146	,,	½ a. rose	25	5
147	,,	½ a. orange-red	20	5
148	**14**	1 a. greenish grey	8	8
149	,,	1 a. bright green	12	15
		a. Double impression		
150	,,	1 a. dull green	8	8
151		1 a. blue-green	15	
152	**15**	2 a. red/*yellow*	15	10
153	,,	2 a. red/*yellow-green*	20	25
154	,,	2 a. red/*deep green*	50	50
155	**16**	4 a. deep green	70	70
156	,,	4 a. green	70	70
157	,,	4 a. pale green	80	80
158	,,	4 a. sage-green	70	
159	**17**	8 a. pale blue	2·00	2·00
159*a*	,,	8 a. deep blue	3·00	3·00
160	,,	8 a. bright blue	3·00	3·00
161	,,	8 a. indigo-blue	4·00	4·00
161*a*	,,	8 a. slate-lilac	5·00	5·00

Well-executed forgeries of the ½ a. to 8 a. have come from India, mostly postmarked; they may be detected by the type, which does not agree with any variety on the genuine sheets, and also, in the low values, by the margins being filled in with colour, all but a thin white frame round the stamp. The forgeries of the 8 a. are in sheets of eight like the originals.

Other forgeries of nearly all values also exist, showing all varieties of type. All values are on thin, coarse wove paper.

In February, 1890, a forgery, in watercolour, of the ½ a. orange, appeared, and many have been found genuinely used. (*Price* £1.)

Nos. 143 and 144 were never issued.

1887–94. *Thin creamy laid paper. Imperf.*

No.	Type	Description	Unused	Used
162	**18**	⅛ a. yellow	6·00	6·00
163	**12**	¼ a. brown	4·50	3·00
164	**13**	½ a. brown-red (Mar. '87)	—	12·00
165	,,	½ a. orange-red	3·00	2·00
166	**14**	1 a. grey-green	45·00	40·00

Printed in water colour.

No.	Type	Description	Unused	Used
168	**17**	8 a. blue	60·00	60·00

19

T **19** represents a ½ a. stamp, which exists in sheets of twelve varieties, in *red* and *black*, on thin wove and laid papers, also in *red* on native paper, but which does not appear ever to have been issued for use. It was first seen in 1886.

The ½ a. *brown*, and the 4 a. *green*, exist on ordinary white laid paper; the ½ a. *red* on native paper; the ½ a. in *bright green*, on thin white wove (this may be an error in the colour of the ½ a.); and the 8 a. in *lilac* on thin white wove. None of these are known to have been in use.

OFFICIAL STAMPS.

1878. 1. *Ordinary white laid paper.*

(*a*) *Rough perf.* 10 *to* 12.

No.	Type	Description	Unused	Used
O1	**13**	½ a. black		

(*b*) *Imperf.*

No.	Type	Description	Unused	Used
O2	**13**	½ a. black	50	50
O3	**14**	1 a. black	75	75
O4	**15**	2 a. black	1·10	1·50

2. *Medium wove paper. Imperf.*

No.	Type	Description	Unused	Used
O5	**14**	1 a. black		

1880–94. *Thin wove papers, toned, coarse to fine, or fine white* (1889). *Imperf.*

No.	Type	Description	Unused	Used
O 6	**12**	¼ a. black	5	5
		a. Double print	£120	
O 7	**13**	½ a. black	5	5
O 8	**14**	1 a. black	5	5
O 9	**15**	2 a. black	8	5
O10	**16**	4 a. black	10	10
O11	**17**	8 a. black	12	12

1887–94. *Thin creamy laid paper. Imperf.*

No.	Type	Description	Unused	Used
O12	**12**	¼ a. black	75	75
O13	**13**	½ a. black	75	75
O14	**14**	1 a. black	50	
O15	**15**	2 a. black	15·00	
O16	**16**	4 a. black	8·00	4·00
O17	**17**	8 a. black	8·00	4·00

1889. *Stout white wove paper. Imperf.*

No.	Type	Description	Unused	Used
O18	**12**	¼ a. black		

The stamps of Kashmir have been obsolete since Nov. 1, 1894.

JASDAN.

1. Sun.

(Typo. L. V. Indap & Co., Bombay.)

1942–47(?). *Stamps from booklet panes. Various perfs.*

No.	Type	Description	Unused	Used
1	**1**	1 a. myrtle-grn. (*p.* 10½ × *imp.*)	2·00	
2	,,	1 a. lt. green. (*p.* 10½ × *imp.*)	30	
3	,,	1 a. pale yell.-grn. (*p.* 8½ × *imp.*)	30	
4	,,	1 a. dull yellow-green (*p.* 10)	30	
5	,,	1 a. bluish green (*p.* 9)	2·00	

Nos. 1/3 were issued in panes of four with the stamps imperforate on one or two sides; Nos. 4/5 were in panes of eight perforated all round.

A 1 a. rose with the arms of Jasdan in the centre is a fiscal stamp.

Jasdan was merged with the United State of Kathiawar on 15 February 1948 and renamed the United State of Saurashtra and later issues are listed under Soruth.

JHALAWAR.

(Figure of an Apsara, "RHEMBA", a dancing nymph of the Hindu Paradise.)

1 (1 paisa) **2** (¼ anna)

1887–90. *Laid paper.*

No.	Type	Description	Unused	Used
1	**1**	1 p. yellow-green	75	1·00
		a. Blue-green	1·25	1·50
2	**2**	¼ a. green (*shades*)	35	50

The stamps formerly listed as on wove paper are from sheets on laid paper, with the laid lines almost invisible.

The stamps of Jhalawar have been obsolete since Nov. 1, 1900.

JIND.

J **1** (½ a.)

J **2** (1 a.)

J **3** (2 a.)

J **4** (4 a.)

J **5** (8 a.)

(*The letter " R " on stamp is the initial of Raghbir Singh, at one time Rajah.*)

(Litho. Jind State Rajah's Press, Sungroor.)

1874. *Thin yellowish paper. Imperf.*

No.	Type	Description	Unused	Used
J 1	J **1**	½ a. blue	2·50	1·25
		a. No frame to value. (Retouched all over)	80·00	70·00
J 2	J **2**	1 a. rosy mauve	4·00	3·50
J 3	J **3**	2 a. yellow	50	1·50
J 4	,,	2 a. brown-buff	6·00	3·00
J 5	J **4**	4 a. green	10·00	3·00
J 6	J **5**	8 a. dull purple	45·00	18·00
J 6*a*	,,	8 a. bluish violet	45·00	18·00
J 7	,,	8 a. slate-blue	45·00	18·00

1876. *Bluish laid card-paper. Imperf.*

No.	Type	Description	Unused	Used
J 8	J **1**	½ a. blue	12	60
J 9	J **2**	1 a. purple	25	80
J10	J **3**	2 a. brown	30	1·50
J11	J **4**	4 a. green	50	1·50
J11*a*	J **5**	8 a. bluish violet	4·00	4·50
J12	,,	8 a. slate-blue	3·00	4·50
J13	,,	8 a. steel-blue	6·00	7·00

1885. *Bluish laid card-paper.* P 12.

No.	Type	Description	Unused	Used
J14	J **1**	½ a. blue	1·00	2·00

The 2 a. brown-buff is also known perf. 12 but this may be a private or trial perforation.

J **6** (½ a.)

J **7** (½ a.)

J **8** (1 a.)

J **9** (2 a.)

J 10 (4 a.)

J 11 (8 a.)

(Litho. Jind State Rajah's Press, Sungroor.)

1882–85. *Types* J **6** *to* J **11.** *25 varieties of each value.* A. *Imperf.* (1882–4). B. *P* 12 (1885).

(*a*) *Thin yellowish wove paper.*

		A.		B.	
J15	¼ a. buff (*shades*)	12	20	12	25
J16	¼ a. red-brown ..	12	20	35	—
	a. Doubly printed	12·00	—	†	
J17	½ a. lemon ..	30	30	20	20
J18	½ a. buff ..	40	35	20	20
J19	½ a. brown-buff	40	35	30	35
J20	1 a. brn. (*shades*)	40	35	35	50
J21	2 a. blue.. ..	40	50	45	70
J22	2 a. deep blue ..	40	50	50	70
J23	4 a. sage-green ..	40	50	70	75
J24	4 a. blue-green ..	50	70	1·00	—
	a. Imperf. (betw. pr.)		†	60·00	—
J25	8 a. red	1·50	1·00	2·50	—

(*b*) *Various thick laid papers.*

J26	¼ a. brown-buff..	1·25	—	4·50	—
J27	½ a. lemon ..	2·00	—	6·00	3·50
J27*a*	½ a. brown-buff..	—	—		†
J28	1 a. brown ..	1·25	—	1·50	—
J29	2 a. blue.. ..	—	—	7·00	—
J30	8 a. red	3·00	3·00	2·50	1·50

(*c*) *Thick white wove paper.*

J31	¼ a. brown-buff..	4·00	—		†
J32	½ a. brown-buff..	7·00	—		†
J33	1 a. brown ..	2·00	—	—	—
J34	8 a. red	2·00	2·00	3·00	—

The perforated stamps ceased to be used for postal purposes in July, 1885, but are said to have been used later as fiscals. Other varieties exist, but they must either be fiscals or reprints, and it is not quite certain that all of those listed above were issued as early as 1885.

Jind became a convention state and from 1885 used the Indian stamps overprinted which are listed under the Convention States.

KISHANGARH.

1

1899. (*a*) *Wove paper.*

1	**1**	1 a. green (*imperf.*)	9·00	12·00
2	,,	1 a. green (*pin-perf.*) ..	15·00	

1900. *Thin white wove paper. Imperf.*

3	**1**	1 a. blue	80·00

2 (¼ a.)

3 (½ a.)

4 (1 a.)

5 (2 a.)
Maharaja Sardul Singh.

6 (4 a.)

7 (1 r.)

8 (2 r.)

9 (5 r.)

1899–1901. *Thin white wove paper.*

(*a*) *Imperf.*

4	**2**	¼ a. green	15·00	
5	,,	¼ a. carmine	30	
		a. Rose-pink	12	
6	,,	¼ a. magenta..	3·00	3·00
		a. Doubly printed	45·00	45·00
7	**3**	½ a. lilac	7·00	7·00
8	,,	½ a. red	7·00	4·00
9	,,	½ a. green	8·00	8·00
10	,,	½ a. pale yellow-olive ..	8·00	8·00
		a. Bistre-brown	8·00	8·00
11	,,	½ a. slate-blue	40	50
		a. Pair, one stamp sideways ..	£450	
		b. Deep blue	40	50
		c. Light blue	30	35
12	**4**	1 a. mauve	30·00	30·00
		a. Laid paper		
13	,,	1 a. slate	75	60
		a. Laid paper	15·00	
14	,,	1 a. brown-lilac	70	50
		a. Laid paper	15·00	
15	**5**	2 a. dull orange	2·50	2·50
		a. Laid paper	20·00	20·00
16	**6**	4 a. chocolate	50	
		a. Lake-brown	1·00	1·00
		b. Chestnut	1·00	1·00
		c. Laid paper (*shades*) ..	15·00	12·00
17	**7**	1 r. brown-lilac	13·00	
18	,,	1 r. dull green	6·00	
19	**8**	2 r. brown-red	18·00	
		a. Laid paper	30·00	
20	**9**	5 r. mauve	12·00	
		a. Laid paper	35·00	

(*b*) *Pin-perf.* 12½ *or* 14.

21	**2**	¼ a. green	3·00	7·00
		a. Imperf. between (pair) ..	35·00	35·00
22	,,	¼ a. carmine	10	20
		a. Rose-pink	15	
		b. Rose		
23	,,	¼ a. magenta	12·00	12·00
		a. Bright purple		
		ab. Doubly printed		

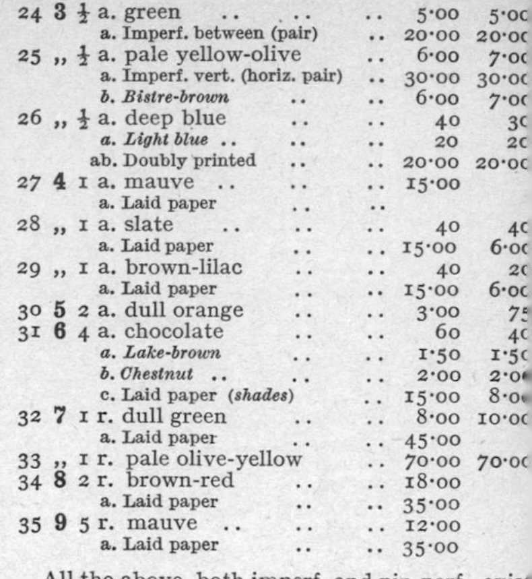

24	**3**	½ a. green	5·00	5·00
		a. Imperf. between (pair) ..	20·00	20·00
25	,,	½ a. pale yellow-olive ..	6·00	7·00
		a. Imperf. vert. (horiz. pair) ..	30·00	30·00
		b. Bistre-brown	6·00	7·00
26	,,	½ a. deep blue	40	30
		a. Light blue	20	20
		ab. Doubly printed	20·00	20·00
27	**4**	1 a. mauve	15·00	
		a. Laid paper		
28	,,	1 a. slate	40	40
		a. Laid paper	15·00	6·00
29	,,	1 a. brown-lilac	40	20
		a. Laid paper	15·00	6·00
30	**5**	2 a. dull orange	3·00	75
31	**6**	4 a. chocolate	60	40
		a. Lake-brown	1·50	1·50
		b. Chestnut	2·00	2·00
		c. Laid paper (*shades*) ..	15·00	8·00
32	**7**	1 r. dull green	8·00	10·00
		a. Laid paper	45·00	
33	,,	1 r. pale olive-yellow ..	70·00	70·00
34	**8**	2 r. brown-red	18·00	
		a. Laid paper	35·00	
35	**9**	5 r. mauve	12·00	
		a. Laid paper	35·00	

All the above, both imperf. and pin-perf., exist in vertical *tête-bêche* pairs imperf. between from the centre of the sheet.

10 (¼ a.)

10*a* (1 r.)

1901. *Toned wove paper. Pin-perf.*

36	**10**	¼ a. dull pink	7·00	7·00
37	**4**	1 a. violet	11·00	11·00
38	**10*a***	1 r. dull green	10·00	10·00

These were printed from plates: Nos. 36 and 37 in sheets of 24, No. 38 in sheets of 16. All the others, except Nos. 1, 2, and 3, were printed singly on paper with spaces ruled in pencil.

The 1 a. (No. 37) differs from T **4** in having an inscription in native characters below the words "ONE ANNA".

11 (½ a.)

12. Maharaja Sardul Singh.

1903. *Thick white wove glazed paper. Imperf.*

39	**11**	½ a. pink	3·00	3·00
		a. Printed both sides ..	£400	£400
40	**12**	2 a. dull yellow	2·25	2·50

12*a* (8 a.)

1904. *Thin paper. Pin-perf.*

41 **12a.** 8 a. grey .. .. 3·00
 a. Tête-bêche (pair) .. 10·00
 b. Doubly printed .. 30·00 30·00

13. Maharaja Madan Singh. **14.**

(*T* **13.** Recess. Perkins Bacon & Co.)

1904–5. *P* 12½ *(all) and P* 13½ *(¼ a. to 4 a.).*

42 **13** ¼ a. carmine 15 15
43 ,, ½ a. chestnut 15 15
44 ,, 1 a. blue 25 15
45 ,, 2 a. orange-yellow .. .. 3·50 2·50
46 ,, 4 a. brown .. .. .. 3·00 2·00
47 ,, 8 a. violet (1905) .. .. 3·00 3·00
48 ,, 1 r. green .. .. .. 4·00 4·00
49 ,, 2 r. olive-yellow .. .. 5·00 7·00
50 ,, 5 r. purple-brown .. .. 9·00 12·00

The 1 a. in brown is a colour trial.

1912. *Printed from half-tone blocks. No ornaments to left and right of value in English; large ornaments on either side of value in Hindi, Small stop after* "STATE".

(*a*) *Thin wove paper. Rouletted.*

51 **14** 2 a. deep violet ("TWO ANNA") .. .. 1·50
 a. Tête-bêche (pair) .. .. 3·00
 b. Imperf. (pair) .. .. 35·00

No. 51 is printed in four rows, each inverted in respect to that above and below it.

(*b*) ***Thick white chalk-surfaced paper. Rouletted in colour.*** **(*Medallion only in half-tone.*)**

52 **14** ¼ a. ultramarine .. .. 6·00 7·00

1913. *No ornaments on either side of value in English. Small ornaments in bottom label. With stop after* "STATE". *Thick white chalk-surfaced paper. Rouletted.*

53 **14** 2 a. pur. ("TWO ANNAS") 2·00 4·50

15

2 TWO ANNAS 2
No. 60 Small figures.

2 TWO ANNAS 2
No. 60b Large figures.

पाव ग्रना
No. 59e
This occurs on R.3/3 on one setting only.

(Typo. Diamond Soap Works, Kishangarh.)

1913 (Aug.). *Thick surfaced paper. Half-tone centre. Type-set inscriptions. Rouletted. Inscr.* "KISHANGARH".

59 **15** ¼ a. pale blue 10 12
 a. Imperf. (pair) .. .. 2·50
 b. Roul. × imperf. (horiz. pr.) .. 7·00
 c. Error. "OUARTER" .. 2·50
 ca. As last, imperf. (pair) 12·00
 cb. As last, roul. × imperf. ..
 d. Error. "KISHANGAHR" 3·00
 da. As last, imperf. (pair) .. 12·00
 db. As last, roul. × imperf. ..
 e. Error. Character omitted .. 5·00 5·00
 ea. As last, imperf. (pair) ..
60 ,, 2 a. purple (A) .. .. 6·00 6·00
 a. Error. "KISHANGAHR" 35·00 35·00
 b. Large figures "2" (B) .. 30·00 30·00

1913–16. *Stamps printed far apart, horizontally and vertically, otherwise as No. 53, except as noted below.*

63 **14** ¼ a. blue 10 10
64 ,, ½ a. green ('15) 10 10
 a. Printed both sides .. 40·00
 b. Emerald-green ('16) .. 1·00
65 ,, 1 a. red 60 50
 a. Without stop* 60 50
66 ,, 2 a. purple ("TWO ANNAS") ('15) .. .. .. 2·50 2·50
67 ,, 4 a. bright blue .. .. 4·00 4·00
68 ,, 8 a. brown .. .. .. 4·00 5·00
69 ,, 1 r. mauve .. .. .. 7·00 8·00
70 ,, 2 r. deep green .. .. 10·00 12·00
71 ,, 5 r. brown .. .. .. 14·00 16·00

*For this issue, ornaments were added on either side of the English value (except in the ¼ a.) and the inscription in the right label was without stop, except in the case of No. 65.

In Nos. 70 and 71 the value is expressed as "RUPIES" instead of "RUPEES".

FISCAL STAMPS. Most of Nos. 63/71 exist in other colours but they are fiscal stamps.

16. Maharaja Yagyanarain Singhji. **17.**

1928–36. *Thick surfaced paper. Typo. Pin-perf.*

72 **16** ¼ a. light blue 20 25
73 ,, ½ a. yellow-green 20 25
 a. Deep green 25 30
 ab. Imperf. (pair) .. .. 12·00 12·00
 ac. Imp. bet. (vert. or hor. pair) 12·00 12·00
74 **17** 1 a. carmine 40 40
 a. Imperf. (pair) .. .. 12·00 12·00
75 ,, 2 a. purple .. .. 1·75 2·00
75a ,, 2 a. magenta ('36) .. 2·00 2·00
76 **16** 4 a. chestnut 70 80
 a. Imperf. (pair) .. ..
77 ,, 8 a. violet .. .. 2·50 2·50
78 ,, 1 r. light green .. .. 5·00 6·00
79 ,, 2 r. lemon-yellow ('29) 10·00 11·00
80 ,, 5 r. claret ('29) .. .. 14·00 15·00
 a. Imperf. (pair) .. .. 40·00

The 4 a. to 5 r. are slightly larger than, but otherwise similar to, the ¼ a. and ½ a. The 8 a. has a dotted background covering the whole design.

1945–7. *As last, but thick, soft, unsurfaced paper. Poor impression. Typo. Pin-perf.*

81 **16** ¼ a. pale dull blue 40 50
 a. Imperf. (pair) .. .. 15·00
82 ,, ¼ a. greenish blue ('47) .. 50 70
 a. Imperf. (pair) .. .. 15·00
83 ,, ½ a. deep green 50 70
 a. Imperf. (pair) .. .. 15·00
 b. Imp. bet. (vert. or hor. pair) 15·00 14·00
84 ,, ½ a. yellow-green ('47) .. 70 70
 a. Imperf. (pair) .. .. 15·00 12·00
 b. Imperf. bet. (vert. or hor. pair) 15·00 12·00
85 **17** 1 a. carmine-red .. .. 1·00 60
 a. Imperf. (pair) .. .. 15·00 14·00
 b. Imp. bet. (vert. or horiz. pair) 15·00 14·00
86 ,, 2 a. bright magenta .. 3·00 2·50
 a. Imperf. (pair) .. .. 15·00
87 ,, 2 a. maroon .. ..
 a. Imperf. (pair) .. .. 15·00 12·00
 b. Imp. bet. (vert. or hor. pair) 15·00 12·00
88 **16** 4 a. brown .. .. 13·00 12·00
89 ,, 8 a. violet .. .. 13·00 12·00
90 ,, 1 r. green .. .. 25·00 20·00
91 ,, 5 r. claret .. .. 50·00 50·00

OFFICIAL STAMPS.

ON
K S
D

(O 1)

1918. *Handstamped with Type* O **1.**

(i) *Stamps of* 1899–1901. (*a*) *Imperf.*

O 1 **4** 1 a. slate .. .. — 35
O 2 **6** 4 a. chocolate .. .. — 3·25

(*b*) *Pin perf.*

O 2b **2** ¼ a. green .. ..
O 3 ,, ¼ a. pink 10 12
O 4 **3** ½ a. blue .. ..
O 5 **4** 1 a. brown-lilac .. 60
O 6 ,, 1 a. slate .. ..
O 7 ,, 1 a. violet (No. 37) .. 80
O 8 **5** 2 a. dull orange ..
O 9 **6** 4 a. chocolate .. .. 8·00 8·00
O10 **7** 1 r. dark green .. .. 18·00 18·00
O11 **8** 2 r. red-brown .. .. 28·00 28·00
O12 **9** 5 r. magenta .. .. 40·00 40·00

(ii) *Stamps of* 1903 *and* 1904.

O13 **12** 2 a. yellow .. .. 9·00 9·00
O13a **12a** 8 a. grey .. .. 10·00 10·00

(iii) *Stamps of* 1904–5.

O14 **13** ¼ a. carmine .. .. 7·00 7·00
O15 ,, ½ a. chestnut 30 10
O16 ,, 1 a. blue .. .. 4·00 3·00
O17 ,, 2 a. orange-yellow ..
O18 ,, 4 a. brown .. .. 7·00 7·00
O19 ,, 8 a. violet .. .. 18·00 18·00
O20 ,, 1 r. green .. .. 60·00 60·00
O21 ,, 5 r. purple-brown ..

(iv) *Stamps of* 1913–16.

O22 **14** ¼ a. blue 30 30
O23 ,, ½ a. green 45 50
O24 ,, 1 a. carmine 45 50
O25 ,, 2 a. purple .. .. 1·60 1·00
O26 ,, 4 a. bright blue .. 9·00 9·00
O27 ,, 8 a. brown .. .. 12·00 12·00
O28 ,, 1 r. lilac .. .. 20·00 20·00
O29 ,, 2 r. deep green .. ..
O30 ,, 5 r. brown .. ..

(v) *Stamps of* 1913.

O31 **15** ¼ a. pale blue .. .. 3·50
O32 ,, 2 a. purple .. .. 6·00

All the above have been reported with overprint inverted, and many with overprint in red and in all sorts of fancy positions. Some irregularities took place at the sale of these latter, and it is doubtful if the varieties should be listed.

For later issues, see RAJASTHAN.

LAS BELA.

1

(Litho. Thacker & Co., Bombay.)

Black impression. Pin-perf.

1897–98. *Thick paper.*

1 **1** ½ a. on *white* .. .. .. 3·00 2·50

1898–1900.

2 **1** ½ a. on *greyish blue* (1898) .. 2·00 2·00

3 „ ½ a. on *greenish grey* (1899) .. 2·00 2·00

a. "BFLA" for "BELA" .. 12·00

4 „ ½ a. on *thin white surfaced paper* (1899) .. 6·00

5 „ ½ a. on *slate* (1900) .. ..

a. Imperf. between (pair) .. 14·00

2

1901–2.

6 **1** ½ a. on *pale grey* .. 3·00 4·00

a. "BFLA" for "BELA" .. 12·00

7 „ ½ a. on *pale green* (1902) .. 3·50 4·00

8 **2** 1 a. on *orange* .. 4·00 5·00

There are at least 14 settings of the above ½ a. stamps, the sheets varying from 16 to 30 stamps.

1904. *Stamps printed wider apart.*

11 **1** ½ a. on *pale blue* .. 3·50 4·00

a. Imperf. between (pair) .. 20·00

12 „ ½ a. on *pale green* .. 3·50 4·00

There are three plates of the above two stamps, each consisting of 18 varieties.

All the coloured papers of the ½ a. show coloured fibres, to a greater or less extent, like what are termed "*granite*" papers.

The stamps of Las Bela have been obsolete since March 1907.

MORVI.

1. Maharaja Sir Lakhdirji Waghji. **2.**

1931 (1 April). *Typo. P* 12.

(*a*) *Printed in blocks of four. Stamps* 10 *mm. apart. Perf. on two or three sides.*

1 **1** 3 p. deep red .. 3·00 4·00

2 „ ½ a. blue .. 5·00 6·00

3 „ 2 a. yellow-brown .. 22·00

(*b*) *Printed in two blocks of four. Stamps* 5½ *mm. apart. Perf. on four sides.*

4 **1** 3 p. bright scarlet .. 50 75

a. Error. Dull blue .. 2·00

b. Ditto. Double print .. 35·00

5 „ ½ a. dull blue .. 1·00 1·50

6 „ 1 a. brown-red .. 1·50 2·00

7 „ 2 a. yellow-brown .. 2·50 3·50

1932–33. *Horizontal background lines wider apart and portrait smaller than in T* **1**. *Typo. P* 11.

8 **2** 3 p. carmine-rose (*shades*) .. 15 60

9 „ 6 p. green .. 25 70

a. Emerald-green .. 35 70

10 „ 1 a. ultramarine (to deep) .. 75 1·50

11 „ 2 a. bright violet ('33) .. 4·00 6·00

a. Imperf. between (vert. pr.) .. £100

3. Maharaja Sir Lakhdirji Waghji.

1934. *Typo. London ptg. P* 14.

12 **3** 3 p. carmine .. 30 60

13 „ 6 p. emerald-green .. 35 70

14 „ 1 a. purple brown .. 60 1·00

15 „ 2 a. bright violet .. 75 1·50

1935–48. *Typo. Morvi Press ptg. Rough perf.* 11.

16 **3** 3 p. scarlet (*shades*) .. 15 30

a. Imperf. between (horiz. pair) 75·00

17 „ 6 p. grey-green .. 25 60

a. Emerald-green .. 1·00

18 „ 1 a. brown .. 4·00 5·00

a. Pale yellow-brown .. 5·00 7·00

b. Chocolate .. 4·00 5·00

19 „ 2 a. dull violet (to deep) .. 2·00 5·00

Nos. 17*a*, 18*a* and 18*b* were issued between 1944 and 1948.

Morvi was incorporated in the Union of Saurashtra on 15 February 1948. For later issues see under SORUTH.

NANDGAON.

1

1892 (Feb.).

1 **1** ½ a. blue .. 75 14·00

a. Dull blue .. 1·25

2 „ 2 a. rose .. 6·00 30·00

Collectors are warned against copies of T **1** with faked postmarks. Genuinely used they are very rare.

(2)

3 (2 a.)

("M.B.D."=Rajah Machant Balram Das.)

1893–94. *Optd. with T* **2** *in purple or grey.*

(i) *Printed wide apart on the sheet, no wavy lines between stamps.*

3 **3** 2 a. red .. 8·00

Without overprint.

4 **3** ½ a. green .. 8·00

5 „ 2 a. red .. 2·00

(ii) *Printed closer together, wavy lines between stamps.*

6 **3** ½ a. green .. 30 40

a. Sage-green .. 50

7 „ 1 a. rose (*laid paper*) .. 6·00 7·00

8 „ 1 a. rose (*wove paper*) .. 1·25 1·50

9 „ 2 a. dull carmine .. 1·25 1·50

Without overprint.

10 **3** ½ a. green .. 5·00 6·00

11 „ 1 a. rose (*laid paper*) .. 45·00

12 „ 1 a. rose (*wove paper*) .. 9·00 9·00

It has been stated that no stamps were regularly issued for postal use without the "control" mark, T **2**, but it is very doubtful if this is correct. The overprint probably indicates official use.

The 1 a. exists in *ultramarine* and in *brown*, but these appear to be reprints.

The stamps of Nandgaon have been obsolete since July, 1895.

NAWANAGAR.

1 (1 docra).

1877. *Laid paper.* (*a*) *Imperf.*

1 **1** 1 doc. blue (*shades*) .. 25 5·00

a. Tête-bêche (pr.) .. £450

(*b*) *Perf.* 12½ (*line*) *or* 11 (*harrow*).

2 **1** 1 doc. slate-blue .. 18·00 25·00

a. Tête-bêche (pr.) (*p.* 11) .. £600

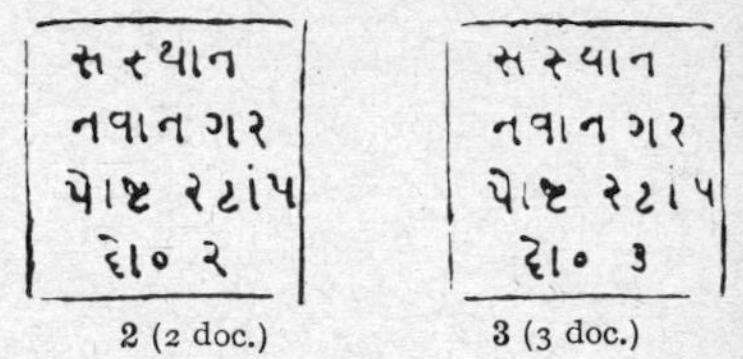

2 (2 doc.) **3** (3 doc.)

1877. *T* **2** *and* **3**. *Black impression. Wove paper Thick horizontal and vertical frame lines.*

A. *Stamp* 14½–15 *mm. wide.*

B. *Stamp* 16 *mm. wide.*

C. *Stamp* 19 *mm. wide.*

		A.	B.	C.
2*b*	1 doc. *deep mauve* ..	45·00	40·00	35·00
2*c*	2 doc. *green*	†	†	50·00
2*d*	3 doc. *yellow*	†	†	75·00

Prices are for used. These stamps are not known unused.

1880. *As last, but thin frame lines, as illustrated.*

D. *Stamp* 15 *to* 18 *mm. wide.*

E. *Stamp* 14 *mm. wide.*

		D.		E.	
3	1 doc. *deep mauve*	40	1·50	†	
	a. On rose ..	30	—	35	65
4	1 doc. *magenta* ..	†		15	—
5	2 doc. *yellow-green*	60	3·00	60	1·50
	a. On blue-green ..	70	—	1·50	—
6	3 doc. *orange-yellow*	1·25	—	†	
	a. On yellow ..	2·50	5·00	1·50	2·50
	ab. On yell. Laid pp.	20·00	—	16·00	—

Error on sheet of one setting of the 3 *docra.*

7	2 doc. *yellow* ..	£140	—	†

There are several different settings of each value of this series.

4 (1 docra).

1893. *P* 12. (*a*) *Thick paper.*

8	**4**	1 doc. black	50	
		a. Imperf.	20·00	
9	,,	3 doc. orange	1·50	
		(*b*) *Thick laid paper.*		
10	**4**	1 doc. black		
		(*c*) *Thin wove paper.*		
11	**4**	1 doc. black to grey	12	15
		a. Imperf. between (pair)	60·00	
		b. Imperf.	20·00	
12	,,	2 doc. green	25	35
		a. Imperf.	20·00	
13	,,	3 doc. orange-yellow	30	
		a. Imperf. between (pair)	60·00	
		b. Orange	35	50
		ba. Imperf.	12·00	
		(*d*) *Thin, soft wove paper.*		
14	**4**	1 doc. black		
15	,,	2 doc. deep green	2·50	
16	,,	3 doc. brown-orange	3·00	

The stamps of this state went out of use at the end of 1895.

NEPAL.

Nepal being an independent state, its stamps will be found listed in Vol. 3 of the Stanley Gibbons Foreign Overseas Catalogue.

ORCHHA.

A set of four stamps, ½ a. red, 1 a. violet, 2 a. yellow and 4 a. deep blue-green, perforated, and in a design roughly similar to T **2**, was prepared in 1897 with State authority but not put into use.

1

2

(T **1/2** litho. Shri Pratap Prabhakar.)

1913. *Background to arms unshaded. Very blurred impression. Wove paper. Imperf.*

1	**1**	½ a. green	8·00	
2	,,	1 a. red	9·00	

1914–17. *Background shaded with short horizontal lines. Clearer impression. Wove paper. Imperf.*

3	**2**	¼ a. bright ultramarine	50	60
		a. Grey-blue	12	20
		b. Deep blue	30	60
4	,,	½ a. green	20	30
5	,,	1 a. scarlet	70	80
		a. Orange-red	1·50	2·00
6	,,	2 a. red-brown (1916)	2·50	2·50
7	,,	4 a. ochre (1917)	4·00	5·00
		a. Yellow-orange	4·00	6·00

There are two sizes of T **2** in the setting, one being the same as T **1** and the other as illustrated.

3. H.H. The Maharaja of Orchha. **4.**

(Offset-litho. Indian Govt. Ptg. Wks., Nasik.)

1939–42? *P* 13½×14 (*T* **3**) *or* 14×13½ (*T* **4**).

8	**3**	¼ a. chocolate	10	
9	,,	½ a. yellow-green	10	
10	,,	¾ a. bright blue	10	
11	,,	1 a. scarlet	20	
12	,,	1¼ a. blue	20	
13	,,	1½ a. mauve	30	
14	,,	2 a. vermilion	30	
15	,,	2½ a. turquoise-green	40	
16	,,	3 a. slate-violet	60	
17	,,	4 a. slate	70	
18	,,	8 a. magenta	1·50	
19	**4**	1 r. grey-green	2·50	
20	,,	2 r. bright violet	8·00	
21	,,	5 r. yellow-orange	20·00	
22	,,	10 r. turquoise-green ('42)	30·00	

A series of 21 values, from ¼ a. to 25 r., bi-coloured and with a portrait of the Ruler in European dress, was introduced in 1935, but owing to lack of proper State control was offered in large quantities to dealers and collectors at less than face value. Eventually the authorities withdrew the issue and exchanged supplies for stamps of the 1939 issue. Though some of the values have been seen with what appears to be genuine postmarks, the circumstances of this issue were such that we feel we are serving the best interests of philately by continuing not to list it.

POONCH.

The stamps of Poonch are all *imperf.*, and printed in water-colours.

1

2

1876. *T* **1** (22×21 *mm.*). *Yellowish white, wove paper.*

1		6 p. red	—	35·00

1877. *As T* **1** (19×17 *mm.*). *Same paper.*

1*a*		½ a. red	£1600	£600

1879. *T* **2** (21×19 *mm.*). *Same paper.*

2		½ a. red	—	£250

3 (½ a.)

4 (1 a.)

5 (2 a.) **6** (4 a.)

1880. *Yellowish white, wove paper.*

3	**3**	½ a. red	7·00	4·50
4	**4**	1 a. red	7·00	5·00
5	**5**	2 a. red	8·00	7·00
6	**6**	4 a. red	9·00	

1884. *Toned wove bâtonné paper.*

7	**3**	½ a. red	1·50	1·50
8	**4**	1 a. red	1·75	
9	**5**	2 a. red	3·00	3·00
10	**6**	4 a. red	3·50	

These are sometimes found gummed.

7. (1 pice)

1884–87. *Various papers.*

		(*a*) *White laid bâtonné or ribbed bâtonné.*		
11	**7**	1 p. red	3·00	3·00
12	**3**	½ a. red	25	30
13	**4**	1 a. red	30	
14	**5**	2 a. red	40	45
15	**6**	4 a. red	1·25	
		(*b*) *Thick white laid paper.*		
22	**7**	1 p. red	70	
23	**3**	½ a. red	2·50	
24	**4**	1 a. red	3·50	
25	**5**	2 a. red	6·00	
26	**6**	4 a. red	7·00	
		(*c*) *Yellow wove bâtonné.*		
27	**7**	1 p. red	1·00	1·00
		a. Normal and sideways *se-tenant*		
28	**3**	½ a. red	1·00	1·00
29	**4**	1 a. red	2·50	
30	**5**	2 a. red	1·00	1·50
31	**6**	4 a. red	75	60
		(*d*) *Orange-buff wove bâtonné.*		
32	**7**	1 p. red	15	15
		a. Normal and sideways *se-tenant*	5·00	
33	**3**	½ a. red	3·00	
34	**5**	2 a. red	4·00	
35	**6**	4 a. red	2·50	
		(*e*) *Yellow laid paper.*		
36	**7**	1 p. red	35	30
37	**3**	½ a. red	1·00	
38	**4**	1 a. red	2·00	
39	**5**	2 a. red	2·50	2·50
40	**6**	4 a. red	3·50	
		(*f*) *Yellow laid bâtonné.*		
41	**7**	1 p. red	3·00	1·50
		(*g*) *Buff laid or ribbed bâtonné paper thicker than* (*d*).		
42	**4**	1 a. red	6·00	
43	**6**	4 a. red	7·00	
		(*h*) *Blue-green laid paper* (1887).		
44	**3**	½ a. red	2·00	
45	**4**	1 a. red	1·75	1·50
46	**5**	2 a. red	1·75	
47	**6**	4 a. red	2·00	
		(*i*) *Yellow-green laid paper.*		
48	**3**	½ a. red		
		(*j*) *Blue-green wove bâtonné.*		
49	**7**	1 p. red	6·00	7·00
50	**4**	1 a. red	15	25
		(*k*) *Lavender wove bâtonné.*		
51	**4**	1 a. red	7·00	
52	**5**	2 a. red	15	30
		(*l*) *Various coloured papers.*		
53	**7**	1 p. red/*grey-blue laid*	1·50	1·75
54	,,	1 p. red/*lilac laid*	14·00	14·00
55	,,	1 p. red/*blue wove bâtonné*	15	20
		a. Normal and sideways *se-tenant*		

1888. *Printed in aniline rose on various papers.*

56	**7**	1 p. on *blue wove bâtonné*	80	
57	,,	1 p. on *buff laid*	1·75	
58	**3**	½ a. on *white laid*	3·00	
59	**4**	1 a. on *green laid*	4·00	3·50
60	,,	1 a. on *green wove bâtonné*	1·25	1·00
61	**5**	2 a. on *lavender wove bâtonné*	1·25	90
62	**6**	4 a. on *yellow laid*	3·00	3·00

OFFICIAL STAMPS.

1888. (*a*) *White laid bâtonné paper.*

O 1	**7**	1 p. black	10	15
		a. Normal and sideways *se-tenant*		
O 2	**3**	½ a. black	15	25
O 3	**4**	1 a. black	20	
O 4	**5**	2 a. black	25	30
O 5	**6**	4 a. black	50	50
		White toned wove bâtonné paper.		
O 6	**7**	1 p. black	40	
O 7	**3**	½ a. black	90	90
O 8	**4**	1 a. black	2·50	2·50
O 9	**5**	2 a. black	1·75	1·50
O10	**6**	4 a. black	2·50	

The stamps of Poonch have been obsolete since 1894.

RAJASTHAN.

Rajasthan was formed in 1948 from a number of States in Rajputana; these included Bundi, Jaipur and Kishangarh, whose posts continued to function more or less separately until ordered by the Indian Government to close, on April 1st, 1950.

BUNDI.

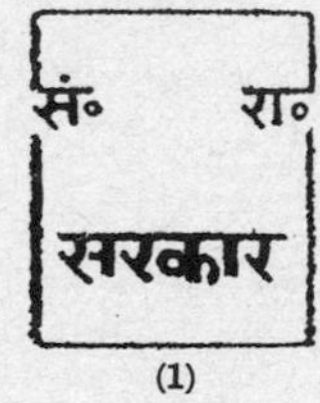

(1)

1949. *Nos. 86/92 of Bundi.* (*a*) *Handstamped with T* **1**.

A. *In black.* B. *In violet.* C. *In blue.*

		A.	B.	C.
1	¼ a. blue-green	20	50	7·00
	a. Pair, one without opt. ..	20·00	†	†
	b. Opt. sideways	†	20·00	†
	c. Opt. double	†	—	†
2	½ a. violet	30	30	3·00
	a. Pair, one without opt. ..	†	30·00	†
	b. Opt. sideways	†	25·00	†
	c. Opt. inverted	†	30·00	†
	d. Opt. double	†	30·00	†
3	1 a. yellow-green ..	30	3·00	3·00
	a. Pair, one without opt. ..	†	30·00	†
	b. Opt. inverted ..	†	25·00	†
4	2 a. vermilion	2·50	7·00	—
5	4 a. orange	4·00	1·50	7·00
	a. Opt. inverted	†	20·00	†
	b. Opt. sideways ..	†	20·00	†
6	8 a. ultramarine	70	70	4·00
	a. Opt. inverted	20·00	20·00	†
	b. Opt. double	†	20·00	†
	c. Opt. sideways ..	†	20·00	†
	d. Opt. double and invtd.	†	30·00	†
7	1 r. chocolate	—	—	12·00
	a. Opt. inverted	†	†	—

The above prices are for unused, used stamps being worth about three times the unused prices.

(*b*) *Machine-printed as T* **1** *in black.*

8	¼ a. blue-green		
9	½ a. violet		
10	1 a. yellow-green		
11	2 a. vermilion	60	3·50
	a. Opt. inverted	15·00	
12	4 a. orange	40	3·50
	a. Opt. double	15·00	
13	8 a. ultramarine	12·00	
	a. Opt. inverted	35·00	
14	1 r. chocolate	2·50	

JAIPUR.

राजस्थान

RAJASTHAN

(2)

1949. *T* **7** *of Jaipur optd. with T* **2**.

15	¼ a. black and brown-lake (No. 58) (B.)	50	1·50
16	½ a. blk. & vio. (No. 41) (R.) ..	60	1·50
17	¾ a. black and brown-red (No. 59) (Blue-blk.)	60	1·50
	a. Opt. in pale blue	4·00	5·00
18	1 a. black & blue (No. 60) (R.)	1·00	1·50
19	2 a. black & buff (No. 61) (R.)	1·00	2·25
20	2½ a. blk. & carm. (No. 62) (B.)	1·00	4·00
21	3 a. blk. & green (No. 63) (R.)	1·10	4·00
22	4 a. black and grey-green (No. 64) (R.)	1·50	6·00
23	6 a. black and pale blue (No. 65*a*) (R.)	1·50	6·00
24	8 a. blk. & choc. (No. 66) (R.)	4·50	7·00
25	1 r. black and yellow-bistre (No. 67) (R.)	6·00	20·00

KISHANGARH.

1949. *Various stamps of Kishangarh handstamped with T* **1** *(Bundi) in red.*

(*a*) *On stamps of* 1899–1901.

26		¼ a. pink (No. 5*a*) (B.) ..		
27		½ a. deep blue (No. 26) ..	12·00	
28		1 a. lilac (No. 29)	8·00	
29		1 a. brn.-lilac (No. 29*b*) ..	8·00	
		a. Opt. inverted	30·00	
		b. Imperf. (pair)		
30		4 a. chocolate (No. 31) ..	13·00	
31		1 r. dull green (No. 32) ..		
31*a*		2 r. brown-red (No. 34) ..		
32		5 r. mauve (No. 35) ..		

(*b*) *On stamps of* 1904–05.

33	**13**	½ a. chestnut	8·00	
33*a*	,,	1 a. blue		
34	,,	4 a. brown	10·00	
		a. Blue handstamp ..	40·00	
35	**12*a***	8 a. grey	18·00	
36	**13**	8 a. violet	9·00	
37	,,	1 r. green	13·00	
38	,,	2 r. olive-yellow	13·00	
39	,,	5 r. purple-brown	13·00	
		a. Blue handstamp		

(*c*) *On stamps of* 1912–16.

40	**14**	½ a. green (No. 64) ..	4·00	4·00
41	,,	1 a. red	4·00	5·00
42	,,	2 a. deep violet (No. 51) ..	4·00	
43	,,	2 a. purple (No. 66) ..	65	2·25
44	,,	4 a. bright blue	9·00	
45	,,	8 a. brown	2·50	
46	,,	1 r. mauve	7·00	
		a. Opt. inverted		
47	,,	2 r. deep green	7·00	
		a. Opt. inverted		
48	,,	5 r. brown	20·00	

(*d*) *On stamps of* 1928–36.

49	**16**	½ a. yellow-green	5·00	
50	,,	4 a. chestnut	7·00	
		a. Opt. inverted	26·00	
51	,,	8 a. violet	7·00	
52	,,	1 r. light green	13·00	
53	,,	2 r. lemon-yellow	13·00	
54	,,	5 r. claret	13·00	

(*e*) *On stamps of* 1945–47.

55	**16**	¼ a. pale dull blue ..	10·00	10·00
		a. Opt. inverted	32·00	
56	,,	¼ a. greenish blue	11·00	11·00
		a. Opt. inverted	40·00	
57	,,	½ a. deep green	4·00	4·00
		a. Opt. inverted	22·00	
58	**17**	1 a. carmine-red	5·50	6·50
59	,,	2 a. bright magenta ..	6·50	
60	,,	2 a. maroon (Imperf.) ..	6·50	5·50
61	**16**	4 a. brown	35	1·00
62	,,	8 a. violet	4·00	
63	,,	1 r. green	4·00	
64	,,	2 r. yellow	25·00	
65	,,	5 r. red-brown	25·00	

Nos. 64/5 were not issued without the Rajasthan overprint.

RAJPIPLA.

1 (1 pice)

2 (2 a.)

3 (4 a.)

1880. *P* 11 (1 *p.*) *or* 12½.

1	**1**	1 p. blue	40	1·25
2	**2**	2 a. green	3·25	4·00
		a. Imperf. between (pair) ..	£225	£225
3	**3**	4 a. red	2·50	3·00

These stamps became obsolete in 1886.

SIRMOOR (SIRMUR).

1 (1 pice)

2

1879–80. *P* 11½.

1	**1**	1 p. pale green	2·75	
2	,,	1 p. blue (on *laid* paper) ..	2·25	24·00
		a. Imperf. between (pair) ..	65·00	65·00
		b. Imperf. (pair)	65·00	65·00

(Printed at Calcutta.)

1892. *Thick wove paper.* *P* 11½.

3	**2**	1 p. yellow-green	30	35
		a. Imperf. between (pair) ..	15·00	
		b. Deep green	20	30
		ba. Imperf. between (pair) ..	20·00	11·00
4	,,	1 p. blue	30	30
		a. Imperf. between (pair) ..	16·00	
		b. Imperf. (pair)	35·00	

These were originally made as *reprints*, about 1891, to supply collectors, but there being very little demand for them they were put into use. The design was copied (including the perforations!) from an illustration in a dealer's catalogue.

3. Raja Sir Shamsher Parkash.

There were seven printings of the 3 and 6 pies, six of the 1 anna, and four of the 2 annas, the last being used optd. for official use (Nos. 99/102), all in sheets of seventy, made up of groups of transfers showing two or more minor varieties. There are two distinct varieties of the 3 p. and 6 p., as shown in Types A and B, C and D. Of these B and D are the types of the **sixth** printing of those values, and A and C those of **all** the other printings.

A

B

C

D

A and C have large white dots evenly placed between the ends of the upper and lower inscriptions; B has small white dots, and less space between the ends of the inscriptions; D has large spaces, and large white dots *not* in the centres of the spaces, especially at the left side.

The last printing of each value is only known with the Waterlow overprint, T **18**.

Roman figures denote printings.

(Litho. Waterlow & Sons.)

1885–96. *P* 14 *to* 15.

5 **3** 3 p. chocolate (A), I, IV .. 20 5
6 ,, 3 p. brown (B), VI .. 10 5
7 ,, 3 p. orange (A), II, III, IV, V 20 10
8 ,, 3 p. orange (B), VI 10 5
a. Imperf. £200
9 ,, 6 p. blue-green (C), I .. 65 40
10 ,, 6 p. bright green (C), III .. 6·00 6·00
11 ,, 6 p. green (C), II, IV .. 40 25
12 ,, 6 p. deep green (C), V .. 10 10
13 ,, 6 p. yellowish green (D), VI 25 25
14 ,, 1 a. bright blue, I 40 40
15 ,, 1 a. dull blue, III .. .. 2·25 2·25
16 ,, 1 a. steel-blue, IV .. .. 4·50 4·50
17 ,, 1 a. grey-blue, V 30 35
18 ,, 1 a. slate-blue, VI 50 55
19 ,, 2 a. pink, I .. .. 2·75 2·75
20 ,, 2 a. carmine, V .. .. 2·25 2·25
21 ,, 2 a. rose-red, VI .. .. 2·25 2·25

3 p. orange Printings III and IV are rare, being worth at least six times the value of other printings.

4

5. Raja Sir Surendar Bikram Parkash.

(Recess. Waterlow & Sons.)

1895–99. *P* 12 *to* 15 *and compounds.*

22 **4** 3 p. orange-brown 65 40
23 ,, 6 p. green 65 40
24 ,, 1 a. blue 65 40
25 ,, 2 a. rose 80 80
26 ,, 3 a. yellow-green .. .. 1·50 2·25
27 ,, 4 a. deep green .. .. 1·50 2·25
28 ,, 8 a. deep blue .. .. 1·75 2·75
29 ,, 1 r. vermilion .. .. 2·00 4·00

(Recess. Waterlow & Sons.)

1899. *P* 13 *to* 15.

30 **5** 3 a. yellow-green .. .. 1·00 2·75
31 ,, 4 a. deep green .. .. 1·50 4·00
32 ,, 8 a. deep blue .. .. 2·00 4·00
33 ,, 1 r. vermilion .. .. 4·00 5·00

OFFICIAL STAMPS

NOTE.—*The varieties occurring in the machine-printed* " On S.S.S." *overprints may, of course, also be found in the inverted and double overprints, and many of them are known thus.*

I. MACHINE-PRINTED.

On
S. S.
S.
(11)

1890. *Optd. with T* **11.**

(*a*) *In black.*

50 **3** 6 p. green .. .. 65·00 65·00
a. Stop before first " S " ..
51 ,, 2 a. rose-red .. .. 13·00 15·00
a. Stop before first " S " .. 60·00

(*b*) *In red.*

52 **3** 6 p. green .. .. 1·25 55
a. Stop before first " S " 20·00
53 ,, 1 a. blue .. .. .. 3·00 1·75
a. Stop before first " S " .. 40·00

(*c*) *Doubly optd. in red and in black.*

53*b* 6 p. green £450
c. Stop before first " S " (R.) ..

On On
S. S. S. S.
S. S.
(12) (13)

1891. *Optd. with T* **12.**

(*a*) *In black.*

54 **3** 3 p. orange 65
a. Opt. inverted .. .. 13·00 13·00
55 ,, 6 p. green 90 90
a. Opt. double .. .. 25·00
b. No stop after lower " S " .. 11·00 11·00
c. Raised stop before lower " S " 11·00 11·00
56 ,, 1 a. blue .. .. ..
57 ,, 2 a. rose-red .. .. 7·00

(*b*) *In red.*

58 **3** 6 p. green .. .. .. 7·00 4·00
a. Opt. inverted .. .. — 24·00
b. Opt. double .. .. — 20·00
59 ,, 1 a. blue .. .. .. 7·00 15·00
a. Opt. inverted .. .. 65·00 —
b. Opt. double .. .. 65·00 65·00
c. No stop after lower " S " .. 18·00 18·00

1892–97. *Optd. with T* **13.**

(*a*) *In black.*

60 **3** 3 p. orange 20 20
a. Opt. inverted .. ..
b. First " S " inverted and stop raised .. .. 8·00 9·00
c. No stop after lower " S " .. 7·00 7·00
d. Raised stop after second " S " 7·00 7·00
61 ,, 6 p. green 25 35
a. First " S " inverted and stop raised .. .. 5·50 4·00
b. Raised stop after second " S " 5·50 4·00
62 ,, 1 a. blue .. .. .. 3·25 4·00
a. Opt. double .. .. 32·00 32·00
b. First " S " inverted and stop raised .. .. 8·00 8·00
c. No stop after lower " S " .. 8·00 8·00
d. Raised stop after second " S " 8·00 8·00
63 ,, 2 a. rose-red .. .. 5·50 5·50
a. Opt. inverted .. .. 32·00 32·00
b. First " S " inverted and stop raised .. .. 20·00 20·00
c. No stop after lower " S " .. 20·00 20·00
d. Raised stop after second " S " 20·00 20·00

(*b*) *In red.*

64 **3** 6 p. green 50 40
a. Opt. inverted .. .. 8·00 8·00
b. First " S " inverted and stop raised .. .. 5·50 5·50
65 ,, 1 a. blue .. .. .. 3·25 65
a. Opt. inverted .. .. 11·00 11·00
b. Opt. double .. .. 16·00 16·00
c. First " S " inverted and stop raised .. .. 8·00 8·00
d. No stop after lower " S " .. 8·00 8·00

(*c*) *Doubly overprinted in black and red.*

65*e* **3** 6 p. green .. .. ..

There are six settings of this overprint. The inverted "S" occurs in the 2nd and 5th settings, and the missing stop in the 2nd setting of all values except the 6 p. In the 5th setting occurs the raised stop after 2nd "S".

On On
S. S. S. S.
S. S.
(14) (15)

1896. *Optd. as T* **14.**

66 **3** 3 p. orange .. .. 2·75 1·25
a. Comma after first " S " .. 13·00 13·00
b. Opt. inverted .. ..
67 ,, 6 p. green .. .. 1·25 50
a. Comma after first " S " .. — 13·00
b. Comma after lower " S " .. — 13·00
c. " S " at right inverted .. 10·00 8·00
68 **3** 1 a. blue .. .. .. 2·75 1·00
a. Comma after first " S " .. 20·00 10·00
b. Comma after lower " S " .. 20·00 10·00
69 ,, 2 a. carmine .. .. 8·00 8·00
a. Comma after first " S " .. 55·00 55·00

There are four settings of this overprint. (1) 23 mm. high, includes the comma after lower " S "; (2) 25 mm. high, with variety, comma after first " S "; (3) and (4) 25 mm. high, with no important varieties.

1898 (Nov.). *Optd. with T* **15.**

70 **3** 6 p. green .. .. .. 8·00 1·50
a. Small " S " at right .. 25·00
b. Comma after lower " S " .. 25·00
c. Lower " S " inverted and stop raised .. .. .. 25·00
71 ,, 1 a. blue .. .. .. 10·00 2·25
a. Small " S " at right. .. 32·00
b. Small " S " without stop .. 32·00

There are two settings of this overprint. Nos. 70a and 71a/b occur in the first setting, and Nos. 70b/c in the second setting.

On On
S S S. S.
S S.
(16) (17)

1899. *Optd. as T* **16** (*but with stop after each* " S ").

72 **3** 3 p. orange .. .. .. — 1·75
73 ,, 6 p. green .. .. .. — 1·25

1900. *Optd. as T* **17.**

74 **3** 3 p. orange .. .. .. — 2·50
a. Raised stop after lower " S " — 11·00
75 ,, 6 p. green .. .. .. — 2·00
a. Raised stop after lower " S " — 11·00
b. Comma after first " S " — 11·00
76 ,, 1 a. blue .. .. .. — 2·75
a. Raised stop after lower " S " — 13·00
77 ,, 2 a. carmine .. .. — 11·00
a. Raised stop after lower " S " — 25·00

There are two settings of this overprint: (1) 22 mm. high, with raised stop variety; (2) 23 mm. high, with " comma " variety in the 6 pies.

On On
S. S. S S
S. S
(18) (19)

(Optd. by Waterlow & Sons.)

1900. *Optd. with T* **18.**

78 **3** 3 p. orange 50 40
79 ,, 6 p. green 20 20
80 ,, 1 a. blue 20 20
81 ,, 2 a. carmine .. .. 1·50 1·50

II. HANDSTAMPED. The words " On " and each letter " S " struck separately.

1894. *Handstamped with T* **19.** (*a*) *In black.*

82 **3** 3 p. orange .. .. .. 1·50 1·50
a. " On " sideways .. .. 32·00
83 ,, 6 p. green .. .. .. 2·75 2·75
a. " On " only .. .. 32·00
84 ,, 1 a. blue .. .. .. 2·75 2·75
85 ,, 2 a. rose-red .. .. 5·50 5·50
a. " On " only .. .. 32·00
b. " On " sideways .. .. 45·00

(*b*) *In red.*

86 **3** 6 p. green .. .. .. 4·00

1896. *Handstamped with letters similar to those of T* **13,** *with stops, but irregular.*

87 **3** 3 p. orange .. .. .. 32·00
88 ,, 6 p. green .. .. .. 32·00
a. " On " omitted .. .. 55·00
89 ,, 2 a. rose-red .. .. .. 32·00

1896. *Handstamped with letters similar to those of T* **14**, *with stops, but irregular.*

90 **3** 3 p. orange .. .. .. 4·00 4·00
a. "On" Double .. .. .. 40·00
91 „ 6 p. green .. .. .. — 5·50
92 „ 1 a. blue .. .. .. — 6·50
93 „ 2 a. rose-red .. .. .. — 7·00

In No. 90a the second "On" is over the lower "S".

ON on S S S S S S
(20) (21)

1896. *Handstamped with T* **20**.

94 **3** 3 p. orange .. .. .. 16·00 16·00
95 „ 2 a. rose-red .. .. .. 20·00 20·00

Handstamped with T **21**.

96 **3** 3 p. orange .. .. .. 32·00 32·00
97 „ 6 p. green .. .. ..
98 „ 1 a. blue .. .. .. 32·00

On On S S S S S S
(22) (23)

***Handstamped with T* 22.**

99 **3** 3 p. orange .. .. ..
100 „ 6 p. green .. .. ..
101 „ 1 a. blue .. .. ..

Handstamped with T **23**.

102 **3** 3 p. orange .. .. .. 6·50 6·50
103 „ 6 p. green .. .. .. 8·00 8·00
a. "On" only .. .. .. 30·00
104 „ 1 a. blue .. .. .. 8·00 8·00
a. "On" only .. .. .. 30·00
105 „ 2 a. rose-red .. .. .. 11·00 11·00

Mixed overprints.

(a) *Handstamped "On" as in T* **19**, *and press-printed opt. T* **13** *complete.*

106 **3** 6 p. green .. .. ..

(b) *Handstamped opt. as T* **14**, *and press-printed overprint T* **13**, *complete.*

107 **3** 6 p. green .. .. ..

Various other types of these handstamps are known to exist, but in the absence of evidence of their authenticity we do not list them. It is stated that stamps of T 4 were never officially overprinted.

The stamps of Sirmoor have been obsolete since 31 March, 1902.

SORUTH.

The name "Soruth" (or "Sorath") was used for all the territory later known as Kathiawar (but referred to also as "Saurashtra"). Strictly speaking the name should have been applied only to a portion of Kathiawar including the state of Junagadh. As collectors have known these issues under the heading of "Soruth" for so long, we retain the name.

The currency was 40 docras = 1 koree but early stamps are inscribed in "annas of a koree", one "anna" being a sixteenth of a koree.

A. JUNAGADH.

1
(= "Saurashtra Post 1864–65")

1864 (Nov.). *Handstamped in water-colour. Imperf.*

1 **1** (1a.) black/*azure* (laid) .. 65·00 6·50
2 „ (1a.) black/*grey* (laid) .. 65·00 6·50
3 „ (1a.) black/*azure* (wove) .. — 8·00
4 „ (1a.) black/*cream* (wove) .. — 8·00

2 (1 a.) 3 (1 a.)

4 (4 a.) 5 (4 a.)

(Type-set at Nitiprakash Ptg. Press.)

1866–68. *T* **2** *to* **5** *(two characters, Devanagri and Gujerati respectively for "1" and "4" as shown in the illustrations). Imperf.*

A. *Inscriptions in Gujerati characters.*

5 1 a. black/*yellowish* (wove) ..

B. *Inscriptions in Devanagri characters (as in the illustrations.)*

I. *Accents over first letters and top and bottom lines. Wove paper.*

6 1 a. red/*green* .. .. .. — £400
7 1 a. red/*blue* .. .. .. — £400
8 1 a. black/*pink* .. .. 28·00 16·00
9 2 a. black/*yellow* (1868) .. — £400

II. *Accents over second letters in top and bottom lines.*

(a) *Wove paper.*

10 **2** 1 a. black/*pink* .. .. 28·00 16·00

(b) *Laid paper.*

11 **2** 1 a. black/*azure* .. .. 9·00 4·00
12 **3** 1 a. black/*azure* .. .. 10·00 5·50
13 „ 1 a. red/*white* .. .. 6·50 6·50
14 **4** 4 a. black/*white* .. .. 35·00 40·00
15 **5** 4 a. black/*white* .. .. 45·00 45·00

Official imitations, consisting of 1 a. carmine-red on white wove and white laid, 1 a. black on blue wove, 4 a. black on white wove, 4 a. black on blue wove, 4 a. red on white laid—all imperforate; 1 a. carmine-red on white laid, 1 a. black on blue wove, 4 a. black on white laid and blue wove—all perforated 12, were made in 1890. Entire sheets of originals have 20 stamps, the imitations only 4 or 16.

6

7

(Dies eng. John Dickinson & Sons, London. Typo. Nitiprakash Ptg. Press, later becoming the Junagadh State Press.)

1869. *Imperf.*

(a) *Medium laid paper, lines wide apart.*
(b) *Thick laid paper, lines wide apart.*
(c) *Thick laid paper, lines close together.*

16 **6** 1 a. green (*a*) 15 15
17 „ 1 a. green (*b*) 10 15
18 „ 1 a. green (*c*) 15 15
a. Printed both sides .. .. 65·00
19 **7** 4 a. vermilion (*a*) 50 60
20 „ 4 a. vermilion/*toned* (*b*) .. 50 60
a. Printed both sides .. .. 65·00
21 „ 4 a. scarlet/*bluish* (*b*) .. 50 60

1886. *P* 12. (*a*) *Wove paper.*

22 **6** 1 a. green 40 40
a. Imperf. (pair) .. .. 4·00 4·00
b. Error. 1 a. blue £250 £250
23 **7** 4 a. red 50 55
a. Imperf. (pair) .. .. 6·00 6·00

(*b*) *Toned laid paper.*

24 **6** 1 a. green 10 1
25 „ 1 a. emerald-green 25 3
a. Error. 1 a. blue £250 £25
26 **7** 4 a. red 30 3
27 „ 4 a. carmine 35 4

(*c*) *Bluish white laid paper.*

28 **6** 1 a. green 45 4
a. Imperf. between (pair) .. 22·00 22·0
29 „ 4 a. scarlet .. .. .. 1·00 1·5

There is a very wide range of colours in bot values. The laid paper is found both vertical an horizontal.

The 1 a. was first issued in sheets of 15 varieties and afterwards in sheets of 20; the 4 a. is i horizontal strips of 5 varieties.

Indian currency.

Three pies. ત્રણ પાઇ. (8)
One anna. એક આનો. (8*a*)

1913. *Surch. in Indian currency with T* **8** *or* **8***a* *P* 12.

(*a*) *On yellowish wove paper.*

34 **6** 3 p. on 1 a. emerald .. 8
a. Imperf. (pair) .. ..

(*b*) *On white wove paper.*

35 **6** 3 p. on 1 a. emerald .. 8
a. Imperf. between (pair) .. 22·00 22·0
b. Surch. inverted .. .. 10·00 10·0
36 **7** 1 a. on 4 a. carmine .. 65 6
a. Imperf. (pair) .. ..
b. Surch. both sides £120
c. Capital "A" in "Anna" .. 3·00

(*c*) *On white laid paper.*

37 **6** 3 p. on 1 a. emerald ..
a. Imperf. (pair) .. .. — 16·0
38 **7** 1 a. on 4 a. red .. .. 2·25 2·2
a. Capital "A" in "Anna" .. 10·00 8·0
b. Surch. inverted .. .. 90·00
c. Surch. double .. .. 90·00
d. Surch. double, one inverted .. 90·00

(*d*) *On toned wove paper.*

39 **7** 1 a. on 4 a. red 45 4
a. Imperf. (pair) .. ..
b. Capital "A" in "Anna" .. 3·00
c. Surch. inverted .. .. 90·00
d. Imperf. between (horiz. pair)

(Dies eng. Thaker & Co., Bombay. Typ Junagadh State Press.)

1914 (1 Sept.). *New plates. Wove paper. P* 1

40 **7** 3 p. bright green 20 2
a. Imperf. (pair) 30 3
41 **6** 1 a. red 20 3
a. Imperf. (pair) .. .. 1·50 1·5
b. Imperf. between (pair) .. £100
c. Laid paper .. .. 1·00 1·0

9 Nawab Sir Mahabatkhanji III. 10

(Typo. Junagadh State Press.)

1923 (1 Sept.). *Blurred impression. Laid pape Pin-perf.* 12.

42 **9** 1 a. red .. .. .. 1·75 1·7

Sheets of 16 stamps (8 × 2).

ત્રણ પાઇ (11) ત્રણ પાઈ (12)

1923 (1 Sept.). *Surch. with T* **11**.

43 **9** 3 p. on 1 a. red 65 6
a. Surch. with T 12.. .. 1·00 1·0

Four stamps in the setting have surch. T 1 i.e. with top of last character curved to right.

1924 (JAN.). *Clear impression. Wove paper. Pin-perf.* 12, *small holes.*

44 **10** 3 p. mauve .. 30 30
45 **9** 1 a. red 50 75
a. Imperf. (pair) .. .. 10·00 10·00

The 1 a. is from new and clearer clichés. Sheets of 16 stamps (4×4).

1928–29. *P* 12, *large holes.*

46 **10** 3 p. mauve (*laid paper*) .. 10 10
a. Imperf. (pair) .. .. 1·25 1·25
b. Imperf. betwn. (horiz. pair) 1·25 1·25
c. Wove paper .. .. 1·25 1·25
47 **9** 1 a. red (*wove paper*) .. 2·50 2·50

No. 47 is as No. 45 except for perf. The laid paper shows wmk. State Arms in sheet. Both values are in sheets of 16 (4×4) or (3 p. only) in sheets of two panes of 16.

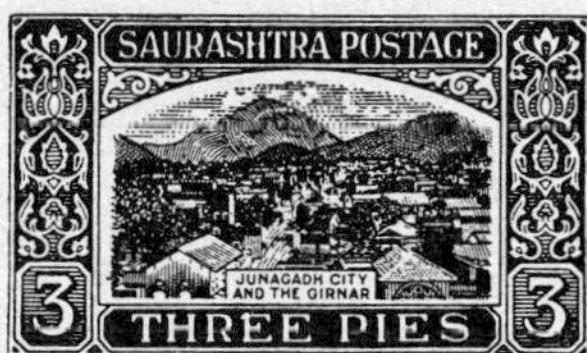

13. Junagadh City.

14. Gir Lion.

15. Nawab Sir Mahabatkhanji III.

16. Kathi Horse.

(Litho. at Nasik.)

1929 (1 OCT.). *P* 14. *Inscr.* "POSTAGE".

49 **13** 3 p. black and blackish green 30 10
50 **14** ½ a. black and deep blue .. 2·25 5
51 **15** 1 a. black and carmine .. 1·25 50
52 **16** 2 a. black and dull orange .. 3·75 70
a. *Grey and dull yellow* .. 15·00 10
53 **13** 3 a. black and carmine .. 75 15
54 **14** 4 a. black and purple .. 6·00 12
55 **16** 8 a. black and yellow-green 7·00 25
56 **15** 1 r. black and pale blue .. 3·00 1·25

1936. *As T* **15**, *but inscr.* "POSTAGE AND REVENUE". *P* 14.

57 **15** 1 a. black and carmine .. 50 60

OFFICIAL STAMPS.

SARKARI (O 1) **SARKARI** (O 2)

1929 (1 OCT.). *Optd. with Type* O **1**, *in vermilion, at Nasik.*

O1 **13** 3 p. black & blackish green 5 5
a. Red opt. .. ..
O2 **14** ½ a. black and deep blue 15 5
a. Red opt. .. ..
O3 **15** 1 a. black & carm. (No. 51) 10 8
a. Red opt. .. ..
O4 **16** 2 a. black and dull orange 1·25 10
a. *Grey and dull yellow* .. 3·00 30
b. Red opt... ..
O5 **13** 3 a. black and carmine .. 10 10
a. Red opt. .. ..
O6 **14** 4 a. black and purple 50 8
O7 **16** 8 a. black and yellow-green 75 15
O8 **15** 1 r. black and pale blue .. 1·00 1·00

1932. *Optd. with Type* O **2**, *in red, at Junagadh State Press.*

O 9 **13** 3 a. black and carmine .. 7·00 5·00
O10 **14** 4 a. black and purple .. 12·00 6·00
O11 **16** 8 a. black & yellow-green 15·00 8·00
O12 **15** 1 r. black and pale blue .. 15·00 10·00

1938. *No.* 57 *optd. with Type* O **1**, *in vermilion.*

O13 **15** 1 a. black and carmine .. 75 20
a. Brown-red opt. .. ..

The state became part of the Indian Union on 9 November 1947.

B. UNITED STATE OF SAURASHTRA.

Under the new Constitution of India the United State of Saurashtra was formed on 15 February 1948, comprising 201 states and principalities of Kathiawar, including Jasdan and Morvi and the former stamp-issuing units of Nawanagar and Wadhwan. Junagadh held a referendum and did not join the new state until 20 January 1949. However, it is believed that the following issues were in use only in Junagadh.

The following issues were surcharged at the Junagadh State Press.

POSTAGE & REVENUE

ONE ANNA
(17)

Postage & Revenue

ONE ANNA

(18)

1949. *Stamps of* 1929 *surch.*

(*a*) *With T* **17** *in red.*

58 **14** 1 a. on ½ a. black & dp. blue 2·50 60
a. Surch. double .. 45·00 45·00
b. "AFNA" for "ANNA" and inverted "N" in "REVENUE" .. £150
c. Cap. first "A" in "ANNA" 80·00 75·00

(*b*) *With T* **18** *in green.*

59 **16** 1 a. on 2 a. grey & dull yell. 2·50 50

A number of other varieties occur on No. 58, including: small "V" in "REVENUE" (No. 8); small "N" in "REVENUE" (Nos. 9, 13 and 14); large first "A" in "ANNA" (No. 10); small "E" in "POSTAGE" (No. 12); thick "A" in "POSTAGE" (No. 19); inverted "N" in "REVENUE" and small second "A" in "ANNA" (No. 25); small "O" in "ONE" (No. 26); small "V" and "U" in "REVENUE" (No. 28); small "N" in "ONE" (No. 37).

In No. 59 no stop after "ANNA" is known on Nos. 4, 17, 25, 34 and 38 and small "N" in "ONE" on Nos. 9, 11, 26 and 31.

19

1949 (OCT.). *Court Fee stamps of Bhavnagar state optd.* "SAURASHTRA" *and further optd.* "U.S.S. REVENUE & POSTAGE" *as in T* **19**, *in black. Typo. P* 11.

60 **19** 1 a. purple .. .. .. 1·00 70
a. "POSTAGE" omitted .. 50·00 50·00
b. Opt. double .. 50·00 50·00

Minor varieties include small "S" in "POSTAGE" (Nos. 9 and 49); small "N" in "REVENUE" (Nos. 15 and 55); small "U" in "REVENUE" (Nos. 18 and 58); small "V" in "REVENUE" (Nos. 24, 37, 64 and 77); and small "O" in "POSTAGE" (Nos. 31 and 71).

Various missing stop varieties also occur.

POSTAGE & REVENUE
ONE ANNA
(20)

1950 (MAR.). *Stamp of* 1929 *surch. with T* **20**.

61 **13** 1 a. on 3 p. black and blackish green .. .. 5·00 5·00
a. "P" of "POSTAGE" omitted .. .. 50·00 50·00
b. "O" of "ONE" omitted.. 50·00 50·00

Other minor varieties include small "S" in "POSTAGE" and small "V" in "REVENUE" (Nos. 14 and 26); small "V" in "REVENUE" (No. 11); and "P" in "POSTAGE" omitted.

OFFICIAL STAMPS.

1948–49. *Nos.* O4/O7 *surch.* "ONE ANNA" (2¼ *mm. high*).

O14 **16** 1 a. on 2 a. grey and dull yellow (B.) (8.48) .. 70·00 10·00
O15 **13** 1 a. on 3 a. black and carmine (11.48) .. 70·00 10·00
O16 **14** 1 a. on 4 a. black and purple (1.49) .. .. 70·00 10·00
a. "ANNE" for "ANNA" £700 £100
b. "ANNN" for "ANNA" £700 £100
O17 **16** 1 a. on 8 a. black and yellow-green (1.49) .. 70·00 10·00
a. "ANNE" for "ANNA" £700 £100
b. "ANNN" for "ANNA" £700 £100

Numerous minor varieties of fount occur in this surcharge.

1948 (NOV.). *Handstamped* "ONE ANNA" (4 *mm. high*).

O18 **15** 1 a. on 1 r. (No. O8) .. 25·00 8·00
O19 „ 1 a. on 1 r. (No. O12) .. 30·00 10·00

A used copy of No. O12 is known overprinted as on Nos. O14/17 in black which may have come from a proof sheet.

1949 (JAN.). *Postage stamps optd. with Type* O **2**, *in red.*

O20 **13** 3 p. black & blackish green 70·00 3·00
O21 **14** ½ a. black and deep blue.. 70·00 3·00
O22 **16** 1 a. on 2 a. grey and dull yellow (No. 59) .. 12·00 7·00

Various wrong fount letters occur in the above surcharges.

Various stamps exist with "Sarkari" in manuscript.

The United State of Saurashtra was integrated with the Indian Postal Service on 1 May 1950 after which Indian stamps were used.

TRAVANCORE.

(16 Cash = 1 Chuckram; 28 Chuckrams = 1 Rupee.)

"Anchel" or "Anchal" = Post Office Department.

PRINTERS. All stamps of Travancore were printed by the State Printing Press, Trivandrum, *unless otherwise stated.*

PRINTING METHODS. The dies were engraved on brass from which electrotypes were made and locked together in a forme for printing the stamps. As individual electrotypes became worn they were replaced by new ones and their positions in the forme were sometimes changed. This makes it difficult to plate the early issues. From 1901 plates were made which are characterised by a frame (or "Jubilee" line) round the margins of the sheets.

Up to the 6 cash of 1910 the dies were engraved by Dharmalingham Asari.

SHADES. We list only the main groups of shades but there are many others in view of the large number of printings and sometimes shade variation is noticeable within the same sheet.

Type **1**. There are small differences in the design in other values.

1. Conch or Chank Shell.

1888 (16 Oct.). *Laid paper. P* 12.

No.	Type	Description	Unused	Used
1	**1**	1 ch. ultramarine (*shades*)	1·25	1·25
2	,,	2 ch. red	3·00	3·00
3	,,	4 ch. green	9·00	9·00

The paper bears a large sheet watermark showing a large conch shell surmounted by "GOVERNMENT" in large outline letters, in an arch with "OF TRAVANCORE" at foot in a straight line. Many stamps in the sheet are without watermark.

These stamps on laid paper in abnormal colours are proofs.

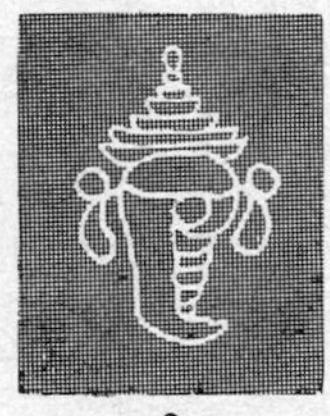

2

A B C

Three forms of watermark Type **2**.

WATERMARKS AND PAPERS.

Type A appeared upright on early printings of the 1, 2 and 4 ch. values on odd-sized sheets which did not fit the number of shells. Later it was always sideways with 15 mm. between the shells on standard-sized sheets of 84 (14 × 6) containing 60 shells (10 × 6). It therefore never appears centred on the stamps and it occurs on hand-made papers only.

Type B is similar in shape but can easily be distinguished as it is invariably upright, with 11 mm. between the shells, and is well centred on the stamps. It also occurs only on hand-made papers. It was introduced in 1904 and from 1915, when Type A was brought back into use, it was employed concurrently until 1925.

Type C is quite different in shape and always occurs upright on machine-made papers. There are two versions. The first, in use from 1925 to 1939, has 84 shells 11 mm. apart and is always well centred. The second, introduced in 1929 and believed not to have been used after 1930, has 60 shells (12 × 5) 15 mm. apart and is invariably badly centred and some stamps in the sheet have no watermark. We do not distinguish between these two in the lists, but stamps known to exist in the second version are indicated in footnotes. The machine-made paper is generally smoother and of more even texture.

NO WATERMARK VARIETIES. Some of these were formerly listed but we have now decided to omit them as they do not occur in full sheets. They arise in the following circumstances: (*a*) on sheets with wmk. A; (*b*) on sheets with the wide-spaced form of wmk. C; and (*c*) on late printings of the pictorial issues of 1939–46. They are best collected in pairs, with and without watermark.

DATES OF ISSUE. In the absence of more definite information the dates quoted usually refer to the first reported date of new printings on different watermarks but many were not noted at the time and the dates of these are indicated by a query. Dated postmarks on single stamps are difficult to find.

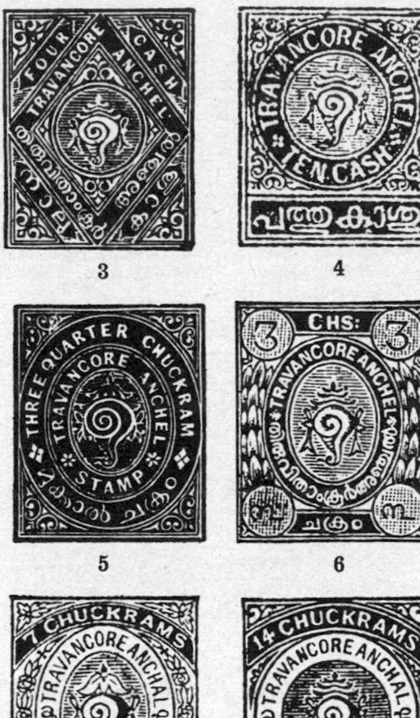

3 4 5 6 7 8

1889–1904. *Wove paper. Wmk.* A (*upright or sideways*). *P* 12 (*sometimes rough*).

No.	Type	Description	Unused	Used
4	**3**	½ ch. slate-lilac (1894)	30	10
		a. Doubly printed	—	35·00
		b. *Reddish lilac*	25	5
		ba. Imperf. between (vert. pair)	40·00	40·00
		bb. Doubly printed	—	35·00
		c. *Purple* (1899)	15	5
		ca. Doubly printed	—	35·00
		d. *Dull purple* (1904)	15	5
5	**5**	¾ ch. black (14.3.01)	15	5
6	**1**	1 ch. ultramarine	45	10
		a. Tête-bêche (pair)	£1200	
		b. Doubly printed	—	75·00
		c. *Pale ultramarine* (1892)	1·00	10
		d. *Violet-blue* (1901)	1·25	20
7	,,	2 ch. salmon (1890)	1·00	15
		a. *Rose* (1891)	1·00	10
		ab. Imperf. (pair)	75·00	
		b. *Pale pink* (1899)	1·00	15
		ba. Imperf. between (vert. pair)	60·00	60·00
		bb. Doubly printed	60·00	60·00
		c. *Red* (1904)	75	10
		ca. Imperf. between (horiz. pair)	35·00	35·00
8	,,	4 ch. green	75	30
		a. *Yellow-green* (1901)	1·00	30
		b. *Dull green* (1904)	1·50	30
		ba. Doubly printed	—	65·00

Nos. 6, 6*c*, 7 and 8 occur with the watermark upright and sideways. No. 7*a* is known only with the watermark upright. The remainder exist only with the watermark sideways.

The sheet sizes were as follows:—

½ ch. 56 (14 × 4) except for No. 4*d* which was 84 (14 × 6) with border.

¾ ch. 84 (14 × 6) with border.

1 ch. No. 6, 80 (10 × 8) and later 84 (14 × 6) with border; No. 6*c*, 96 (16 × 6); No. 6*d*, 84 (14 × 6) with border.

2 ch. No. 7, 80 (10 × 8); No. 7*a*, 70 (10 × 7); Nos. 7*b*, 7*c*, 60 (10 × 6).

4 ch. No. 8, 60 (10 × 6); Nos. 8*a*/*b*, 84 (14 × 6) with border.

After 1904 all stamps in Types **3** to **8** were in standard-sized sheets of 84 (14 × 6) with border.

For later printings watermarked Type A, see Nos. 23/30.

1904–21? *Wmk.* B, *upright* (*centred*). *P* 12, *sometimes rough.*

No.	Type	Description	Unused	Used
9	**3**	4 ca. pink (11.08)	10	5
		a. Imperf. between (vert. pair)	40·00	40·00
10	**1**	6 ca. chestnut (2.10)	15	5
11	,,	½ ch. reddish lilac	10	5
		a. *Reddish violet*	10	5
		b. *Lilac*	10	5
		c. "CHUCRRAM"	2·00	1·50
12	**4**	10 ca. pink (1921?)	—	2·00
13	**5**	¾ ch. black	10	5
14	**1**	1 ch. indigo	20	5
		a. *Deep blue* (1911)	50	15
		b. *Grey-blue* (1912)	20	5
15	,,	1¼ ch. claret (*shades*) (12.19)	15	8
		a. Imperf. between (horiz. pr.)	40·00	40·00
16	,,	2 ch. salmon	5·00	1·00
		a. *Red*	30	5
17	**6**	3 ch. violet (11.3.11)	40	5
		a. Imperf. between (vert. pair)	35·00	35·00
		b. Imperf. betwn. (vert. strip 3)	75·00	60·00
18	**1**	4 ch. dull green	1·00	50
		a. *Slate-green*	80	25
19	**7**	7 ch. claret (1916)	1·00	30
20	**8**	14 ch. orange-yellow (1916)	1·50	50
		a. Imperf. vert. (hor. strip 3)	70·00	70·00

(9)

1 C

(10)

1906. *Surch. as T* **9**. *Wmk.* B.

No.	Type	Description	Unused	Used
21	**1**	¼ on ½ ch. reddish lilac	8	5
		a. *Reddish violet*	8	5
		b. *Lilac*	8	5
		c. "CHUCRRAM"	2·00	2·00
		d. Surch. inverted	12·00	10·00
22	,,	⅜ on ½ ch. reddish lilac	15	5
		a. *Reddish violet*	8	5
		b. *Lilac*	8	5
		c. "CHUCRRAM"	2·00	2·00
		d. Surch. inverted	18·00	18·00
		e. Surch. double		

1915–21. *Reversion to wmk.* A (*sideways*). *P* 12 (*sometimes rough*).

No.	Type	Description	Unused	Used
23	**3**	4 ca. pink (1915)	1·00	10
24	**4**	5 ca. olive-bistre (30.10.21)	15	8
		a. Imperf. between (horiz. pair)	20·00	20·00
		b. Imperf. betwn. (hor. strip 3)	50·00	50·00

25 **1** 6 ca. orange-brown (date?) .. 40 10
26 ,, ½ ch. reddish violet (date?) 20 10
a. "CHUCRRAM" .. 3·00 2·00
b. Imperf. between (horiz. pair) 45·00 45·00
27 **4** 10 ca. pink (30.10.21) .. 15 5
28 **1** 1 ch. grey-blue (date?) .. 75 10
a. Deep blue 75 10
29 ,, 1¼ ch. claret (12.19) 75 10
30 **6** 3 ch. reddish lilac (date?) .. 1·00 25

1921 (MAR.). *Surch. as T* **10**. *Wmk.* A.
31 **3** 1 c. on 4 ca. pink 10 10
a. Surch. inverted .. .. 7·00 4·00
32 **1** 5 c. on 1 ch. grey-blue (R.) .. 10 10
a. Deep blue 10 10
b. Stamp printed both sides ..
c. Imperf. between (vert. pair) .. — 35·00
d. Surch. inverted .. .. 7·00 4·00
e. Surch. double .. .. 10·00 6·00
f. On wmk. B. *Deep blue* .. 2·00 2·00

1925–39. *Wmk.* C. *Machine-made paper. P* 12.
33 **4** 5 ca. olive-bistre (1926) .. 1·00 50
a. Imperf. between (horiz. pair) 15·00 15·00
34 ,, 5 ca. chocolate (1930) .. 50 20
a. Imperf. between (horiz. pair) 18·00 18·00
b. Imperf. between (vert. pair) 18·00 18·00
35 **1** 6 ca. brown-red (date?) .. 50 8
a. Imperf. between (horiz. pair) 12·00 12·00
b. Imperf. between (vert. pair) 16·00 16·00
c. Printed both sides .. 35·00 35·00
d. Perf. 12½ .. .. 2·00 50
e. Perf. comp. of 12 and 12½ .. 7·00 3·00
f. Perf. 12½×11 .. .. — 10·00
36 ,, ½ ch. reddish violet (date?) 2·00 1·00
37 **4** 10 ca. pink (1926) 50 8
a. Imperf. between (horiz. pair) 15·00 15·00
b. Imperf. between (vert. pair) 10·00 10·00
38 **5** ¾ ch. black (1932) 75 20
39 ,, ¾ ch. mauve (16.11.32) .. 15 5
a. Perf. 12½ .. .. 2·00 50
b. Perf. comp. of 12 and 12½ .. 5·00 3·00
40 ,, ¾ ch. reddish violet (1939) .. 15 8
a. Perf. 12½ .. .. 2·00 50
b. Perf. comp. of 12 and 12½ .. 4·00 1·50
c. Perf. 11 .. .. .. — 7·00
d. Perf. comp. of 12 and 11 .. — 7·00
41 **1** 1 ch. slate-blue (date?) .. 25 8
a. Indigo 50 10
b. Imperf. between (horiz. pair) 40·00 40·00
c. Imperf. between (vert. pair) 40·00 40·00
d. Perf. 12½ .. .. 2·00 50
42 ,, 1½ ch. rose (1932) 20 8
a. Imperf. betwn. (hor. strip 3) 35·00 35·00
b. Perf. 12½ .. .. 4·00 1·50
43 ,, 2 ch. carmine-red (date?) .. 1·50 20
44 **6** 3 ch. violet (1926) 50 10
a. Imperf. between (vert. pair) 35·00 35·00
b. Perf. 12½ .. .. 6·00 4·00
c. Perf. comp. of 12 and 12½ 6·00 4·00
45 **1** 4 ch. grey-green (date?) .. 1·00 25
46 **7** 7 ch. claret (1925) .. .. 1·25 50
a. Carmine-red (date?) .. 35·00 35·00
b. Brown-purple (1932) .. 2·00 75
ba. Perf. 12½ .. .. .. 8·00 5·00
bb. Perf. comp. of 12 and 12½ .. 8·00 5·00

It is believed that the 12½ perforation and the perf. 12 and 12½ compound were introduced in 1937 and that the 11 perforation came later, probably in 1939.

The 5 ca. chocolate, 6 ca., 10 ca. and 3 ch. also exist on the wide-spaced watermark (60 shells to the sheet of 84).

11. Sri Padmanabha Shrine.

12. State Chariot.

13. Maharaja Sir Bala Rama Varma.

1 c (**14**) **1 C** (**15**)

(Des. M. R. Madhawan Unnithan. Plates by Calcutta Chromotype Co. Typo. State Printing Press, Trivandrum.)

1931 (6 Nov.). *Coronation. Cream or white paper. Wmk.* C. *P* 11½, 12.
47 **11** 6 ca. black and green .. 15 15
a. Imperf. betwn. (horiz. pair) £200
48 **12** 10 ca. black and ultramarine 15 15
49 **13** 3 ch. black and purple .. 20 20

1932 (14 JAN.). (i) *Surch as T* **14**.
(*a*) *Wmk.* A (*sideways*).
50 **1** 1 c. on 1¼ ch. claret 8 8
a. Imperf. between (horiz. pair) 35·00 35·00
b. Surch. inverted .. .. 3·00 4·00
c. Surch. double .. .. 12·00 12·00
d. Pair, one without surch. .. 40·00 40·00
e. "c" omitted .. .. 25·00 25·00
51 ,, 2 c. on 1¼ ch. claret .. 8 8
a. Surch. inverted .. .. 3·00 4·00
b. Surch. double .. .. 12·00 12·00
c. Surch. treble, one inverted .. 45·00 45·00
d. Pair, one without surch. .. 45·00 45·00
e. "2" omitted .. .. 25·00 25·00
f. "c" omitted .. .. 20·00 20·00
(*b*) *Wmk.* B (*upright*).
52 **1** 1 c. on 1¼ ch. claret 75 75
a. Surch. inverted .. .. 10·00 10·00
b. Surch. double .. .. 12·00 12·00
53 ,, 2 c. on 1¼ ch. claret .. 75 75
a. Imperf. between (horiz. pair) .. 35·00 35·00
(*c*) *Wmk.* C.
54 **1** 1 c. on 1¼ ch. claret .. .. 1·50 1·00
a. Surch. inverted .. .. 10·00 10·00
55 ,, 2 c. on 1¼ ch. claret .. .. 1·50 1·00
(ii) *Surch. as T* **10**. *Wmk.* B.
56 **1** 2 c. on 1¼ ch. claret .. .. 3·00 3·00

1932 (MAR.?). *Surch. as T* **15**. *Wmk.* C.
57 **4** 1 c. on 5 ca. chocolate .. 10 10
a. Imperf. between (horiz. pair) .. 50·00 50·00
b. Surch. inverted .. .. 6·00 7·50
c. Surch. inverted on back only .. 15·00 15·00
d. Pair, one without surch. .. 30·00 30·00
e. "1" omitted .. .. 15·00 15·00
58 ,, 1 c. on 5 ca. slate-purple .. 10 10
a. "1" inverted .. .. 25·00 25·00
59 ,, 2 c. on 10 ca. pink 10 10
a. Imperf. between (horiz. pair) .. 40·00 40·00
b. Surch. inverted .. .. 4·00 5·00
c. Surch. double .. .. 10·00 12·00
d. Surch. double, one inverted .. 20·00 20·00
e. Surch. double, both inverted .. 13·00 13·00
No. 58 was not issued without the surcharge.

16. Maharaja Sir Bala Rama Varma and Subramania Shrine.

(Typo. Travancore Mint.)

1937 (29 MAR.). *Temple Entry Proclamation. T* **16** *and similar horiz. designs. Wmk.* C. *P* 12.
60 6 ca. carmine 10 10
a. Imperf. between (hor. strip 3) £150
b. Perf. 12½ 20 20
61 12 ca. bright blue 12 12
a. Perf. 12½ 20 20
ab. Imperf. between (vert. pair) .. £100
62 1½ ch. yellow-green 20 20
a. Imperf. between (vert. pair) .. £100
b. Perf. 12½ .. .. .. 1·00 50
63 3 ch. violet 30 20
a. Perf. 12½ 50 30

Designs: Maharaja's portrait and temples—12 ca. Sri Padmanabha; 1½ ch. Mahadeva; 3 ch. Kanyakumari.

COMPOUND PERFS. This term covers stamps perf. compound of 12½ and 11, 12 and 11 or 12 and 12½, and where two or more combinations exist the prices are for the commonest. In some instances where a stamp exists only with all round perf. 11 and 12½, compounds of 12 and 12½ or 12 and 11 may be found.

17. Lake Ashtamudi.

18. Maharaja Sir Bala Rama Varma.

(Typo. Travancore Mint.)

1939 (9 Nov.). *Maharaja's 27th Birthday. T* **17/18** *and similar designs. Wmk.* C. *P* 12½.
64 1 ch. yellow-green 8 8
a. Imperf. between (horiz. pair) .. 3·00 3·00
b. Perf. 11 .. .. .. 40 15
ba. Imperf. between (vert. pair) .. 4·00 4·00
bb. Imperf. between (vert. strip 3) 7·00 7·00
c. Perf. 12 .. .. .. 50 20
ca. Imperf. between (horiz. pair) .. 4·00 4·00
cb. Imperf. between (vert. pair) .. 4·00 4·00
d. Compound perf. .. .. 1·00 75
da. Imperf. between (vert. pair) .. 7·50 7·50
65 1½ ch. scarlet 20 15
a. Doubly printed .. .. 8·00 8·00
b. Imperf. between (horiz. pair) .. 5·00 5·00
c. Imperf. between (vert. pair) .. 5·00 5·00
d. Perf. 11 .. .. .. 2·00 2·00
da. Imperf. horiz. (vert. pair) .. 8·00 8·00
e. Perf. 12 .. .. .. 2·00 1·50
f. Perf. 13½ .. .. .. 8·00 8·00
g. Compound perf. .. .. 2·00 1·50
66 2 ch. orange 10 10
a. Perf. 11 .. .. .. 1·00 20
b. Perf. 12 .. .. .. 2·00 1·50
c. Compound perf. .. .. 2·00 1·50
67 3 ch. brown 10 8
a. Doubly printed .. .. 7·00 7·00
b. Imperf. between (horiz. pair) .. 5·00 5·00
c. Perf. 11 .. .. .. 75 25
ca. Doubly printed .. .. 8·00 8·00
d. Perf. 12 .. .. .. 1·00 50
da. Imperf. between (vert. pair) .. 5·00 5·00
e. Compound perf. .. .. 2·00 1·00
68 4 ch. red 25 25
a. Perf. 11 .. .. .. 1·00 30
b. Perf. 12 .. .. .. 1·00 30
c. Compound perf. .. .. 7·00 7·00

69 7 ch. pale blue 45 45
a. Perf. 11 .. .. .. 3·00 1·50
ab. Blue .. .. .. 3·00 1·50
b. Compound perf. .. .. 6·00 4·00
70 14 ch. turquoise-green .. .. 1·00 1·00
a. Perf. 11 .. .. .. 2·00 2·00

Designs: *Vert. as T* **18**—1½ ch., 3 ch. Portraits of Maharaja in different frames. *Horiz. as T* **17**—4 ch. Sri Padmanabha Shrine; 7 ch. Cape Comorin; 14 ch. Pachipari Reservoir.

19. Maharaja and Aruvikara Falls.

1941 (20 Oct.). *Maharaja's 29th Birthday. T* **19** *and similar horiz. design. Wmk.* C. *P* 12½.
71 6 ca. blackish violet 8 5
a. Perf. 11 .. .. .. 30 8
ab. Imperf. between (vert. pair) .. 5·00 5·00
ac. Imperf. horiz. (vert. pair) .. 5·00 5·00
b. Perf. 12 .. .. .. 75 50
ba. Imperf. between (horiz. pair) .. 4·00 4·00
bb. Imperf. between (vert. pair) .. 5·00 5·00
bc. Imperf. between (vert. strip 3) .. 5·00 5·00
c. Compound perf. 40 30
72 ¾ ch. brown 8 5
a. Perf. 11 .. .. .. 30 8
ab. Imperf. between (horiz. pair) .. 6·00 6·00
ac. Imperf. between (vert. pair) .. 5·00 5·00
ad. Imperf. between (vert. strip 3) .. 5·00 5·00
b. Perf. 12 .. .. .. 1·50 1·50
c. Compound perf. .. .. 1·25 75

Design:—¾ ch. Maharaja and Marchanda Varma Bridge, Alwaye.

2 CASH

(**20**)

1943 (17 Sept.). *Nos.* 65, 71 (*colour changed*) *and* 72 *surch. as T* **20**. *P* 12½.
73 2 ca. on 1½ ch. scarlet 8 8
a. Imperf. between (vert. pair) .. 10·00 10·00
b. "2" omitted .. .. .. 12·00 12·00
c. "CA" omitted .. .. 40·00 40·00
d. "ASH" omitted .. .. 40·00 40·00
e. Perf. 11 .. .. .. 8 8
ea. "CA" omitted .. .. 40·00 40·00
f. Compound perf. 60 40
fa. Imperf. between (vert. pair) .. 12·00 12·00
fb. "2" omitted .. .. 14·00 14·00
74 4 ca. on ¾ ch. brown 20 8
a. Perf. 11 .. .. .. 20 8
b. Compound perf. 75 60
75 8 ca. on 6 ca. scarlet 20 8
a. Perf. 11 .. .. .. 30 8
ab. Imperf. between (horiz. pair) .. 12·00 12·00
b. Perf. 12 .. .. .. — 5·00
c. Compound perf. .. .. 1·50 1·50

21. Maharaja Sir Bala Rama Varma.

SPECIAL

(**22**)

1946 (24 Oct.). *Maharaja's 34th Birthday. Wmk.* C. *P* 12½.
76 **21** 8 ca. carmine .. .. 2·00 1·00
a. Perf. 11 .. .. .. 50 50
b. Perf. 12 .. .. .. 3·00 1·50
ba. Imperf. betwn. (horiz. pair) 12·00 12·00
bb. Imperf. betwn. (hor. strip 3) 18·00 18·00

1946. *No.* O103 *revalidated for ordinary postage with opt. T* **22**, *in orange. P* 12½.
77 **19** 6 ca. blackish violet .. 3·00 1·00
a. Perf. 11 .. .. 6·00 3·00
b. Compound perf. .. .. 3·00 1·00

OFFICIAL STAMPS.

GUM. Soon after 1911 the Official stamps were issued without gum. Thus only the initial printings of the 1, 2, 3 and 4 ch. values were gummed.

PRINTINGS. Sometimes special printings of postage stamps were made specifically for overprinting for Official use, thus accounting for Official stamps appearing with watermarks or in shades not listed in the postage issues.

On S S (O 1)   On S S (O 2)

Rounded "O".

1911 (16 Aug.)–**26**. *Contemporary stamps optd. with Type* O **1** (13 *mm. wide*). *P* 12, *sometimes rough.*

(*a*) *Wmk.* B (*upright*) (16.8.11–21).
O 1 **3** 4 ca. pink (1916) 10 8
a. Opt. inverted .. .. 9·00 9·00
b. Opt. double .. .. 12·00 7·00
c. "S S" inverted .. 1·50 1·00
d. Imperf. (pair) .. .. 20·00 20·00
O 2 **1** 6 ca. chestnut (date?) .. 3·00 3·00
O 3 ,, ½ ch. reddish lilac (R.) (1919) 50 25
a. "CHUCRRAM" .. 4·00 3·00
O 4 **4** 10 ca. pink (1921) .. .. 3·00 1·00
a. "O" inverted .. .. 10·00 5·00
b. Left "S" inverted .. 10·00 5·00
c. Right "S" inverted .. 10·00 5·00
O 5 **1** 1 ch. grey-blue (R.) .. 20 5
a. Imperf. betwn. (vert. pair) 35·00 35·00
b. Opt. inverted .. .. 5·00 3·00
c. Opt. double .. .. 25·00 20·00
d. "nO" for "On" .. 30·00 30·00
e. "O" inverted .. .. 1·50 50
f. Left "S" inverted .. 1·50 50
g. Right "S" inverted .. 1·50 50
O 6 ,, 2 ch. red 20 5
a. Opt. inverted .. .. 5·00 5·00
b. "O" inverted .. .. 2·00 50
c. Left "S" inverted .. 2·00 50
d. Right "S" inverted .. 2·00 50
O 7 ,, 2 ch. red (B.) (date?) .. — 15·00
O 8 **6** 3 ch. violet 20 5
a. Imperf. betwn. (vert. pair) 30·00 30·00
b. Imperf. vert. (hor. strip 4) 40·00
c. Opt. inverted .. .. 5·00 5·00
d. Opt. double .. .. 25·00 25·00
e. Right "S" inverted .. 2·50 60
f. Right "S" omitted .. 20·00 20·00
g. Left "S" omitted .. 20·00 20·00
O 9 ,, 3 ch. violet (B.) (date?) .. 15·00 10·00
O10 **1** 4 ch. slate-green 40 5
a. Imperf. between (pair) .. 10·00 10·00
b. Opt. inverted .. .. 7·00 7·00
c. Opt. double .. .. 24·00 24·00
d. "O" inverted .. .. 4·00 1·50
e. Left "S" inverted .. 4·00 1·50
f. Right "S" inverted .. 4·00 1·50
g. Left "S" omitted .. 15·00 15·00
O11 ,, 4 ch. slate-green (B.) (1921) 15·00 7·00
a. "O" inverted .. .. 50·00 20·00
b. Left "S" inverted .. 50·00 20·00
c. Right "S" inverted .. 50·00 20·00

(*b*) *Wmk.* A (*sideways*) (1919–25).
O12 **3** 4 ca. pink 50 10
a. Imperf. (pair) .. .. 40·00 40·00
b. Opt. inverted .. .. 10·00 7·00
c. "O" inverted .. .. 3·00 1·00
d. Left "S" inverted .. 3·00 1·00
e. Right "S" inverted .. 3·00 1·00
O13 ,, 4 ca. pink (B.) (1921) .. 6·00 1·00
a. "O" inverted .. .. — 6·00
O14 **4** 5 ca. olive-bistre (1921) .. 15 8
a. Opt. inverted .. .. 6·00 5·00
b. "O" inverted .. .. 1·25 75
c. Left "S" inverted .. 1·25 75
d. Right "S" inverted .. 1·25 75
O15 **1** 6 ca. orange-brown (1921) 10
a. Imperf. between (vert. pr) 35·00 35·0
b. Opt. inverted .. .. 5·00 5·0
c. Opt. double .. .. 8·00 8·0
d. "O" inverted .. .. 1·25 5
e. Left "S" inverted .. 1·25 5
f. Right "S" inverted .. 1·25 5
O16 ,, 6 ca. orange-brown (B.) (1921) .. .. 5·00 1·5
a. Opt. inverted .. .. 35·00 35·0
b. "O" inverted .. .. 20·00 8·0
c. Left "S" inverted .. 20·00 8·0
d. Right "S" inverted .. 20·00 8·0
O17 ,, ½ ch. reddish violet (R.) (date?) 10
a. *Reddish lilac* (date?) .. 10
b. Imperf. betwn. (horiz. pr.) 30·00 30·0
c. Imperf. betwn. (vert. pair) 25·00 25·0
d. Stamp doubly printed .. 25·00 25·0
e. Opt inverted .. .. 5·00 2·0
f. Opt. double, both inverted 30·00 30·0
g. "CHUCRRAM" .. .. 2·50 1·5
h. "On" omitted .. .. — 30·0
O18 **4** 10 ca. pink (3.21) 15
a. *Scarlet* (1925?) .. .. — 2·0
b. Opt. inverted .. .. 10·00 6·0
c. Opt. double .. .. 15·00 10·0
d. "O" inverted .. .. 1·25 7
e. Left "S" inverted .. 1·25 7
f. Right "S" inverted .. 1·25 7
O19 ,, 10 ca. pink (B.) (date?) .. 10·00 4·0
a. Opt. inverted .. .. — 25·0
b. "O" inverted .. .. — 15·0
O20 **1** 1 ch. grey-blue (R.) (date?) 1·00 5
a. *Deep blue* .. .. 1·00 5
b. "O" inverted .. .. 8·00 4·0
c. Left "S" inverted .. 1·00 3
O21 ,, 1¼ ch. claret (12.19) .. 25 1
a. Stamp doubly printed .. — 25·0
b. Opt. inverted .. .. 6·00 5·0
c. Opt. double .. .. 18·00 18·0
d. "O" inverted .. .. 2·50 1·0
e. Left "S" inverted .. 2·50 1·0
f. Right "S" inverted .. 2·50 1·0
O22 ,, 1¼ ch. claret (B.) (1921) .. 10·00 6·0
a. "O" inverted .. .. 35·00 25·0
b. Left "S" inverted .. 35·00 25·0
c. Right "S" inverted .. 35·00 25·0

(*c*) *Wmk.* C (1925–26).
O23 **4** 5 ca. olive-bistre (1926) .. 15
a. Imperf. betwn. (horiz. pr.) 30·00 30·0
b. Opt. inverted .. .. 7·00 7·0
c. "O" inverted .. .. 1·25 7
d. Left "S" inverted .. 1·25 7
e. Right "S" inverted .. 1·25 7
O24 ,, 10 ca. pink (1926) 20 1
a. Imperf. betwn. (vert. pr.) 35·00 35·0
b. Opt. inverted .. .. 12·00 12·0
c. "O" inverted .. .. 2·00 1·0
d. Left "S" inverted .. 2·00 1·0
e. Right "S" inverted .. 2·00 1·0
O25 **1** 1¼ ch. claret (1926) .. 75 3
a. "O" inverted .. .. 5·00 2·0
b. Left "S" inverted .. 5·00 2·0
c. Right "S" inverted .. 5·00 2·0
O26 **7** 7 ch. claret .. .. 1·00 2
a. "O" inverted .. .. 6·00 1·5
b. Left "S" inverted .. 6·00 1·5
c. Right "S" inverted .. 6·00 1·5
O27 **8** 14 ch. orange-yellow .. 1·00 3
a. "O" inverted .. .. 6·00 2·0
b. Left "S" inverted .. 6·00 2·0
c. Right "S" inverted .. 6·00 2·0

1926–30. *Contemporary stamps optd. with Type* O **2** (16½ *mm. wide*). *Wmk.* C. *P* 12.
O28 **4** 5 ca. olive-bistre 75 3
a. Right "S" inverted .. 5·00 2·0
O29 ,, 5 ca. chocolate (1930) .. 10 1
a. Imperf. betwn. (vert. pr.) — 50·0
b. Opt. inverted .. .. 10·00 10·0
c. "O" inverted .. .. 1·00 1·0
d. Left "S" inverted .. 1·00 1·0
O30 **1** 6 ca. brown-red (date?) .. 75 5
a. "O" inverted .. .. 5·00 3·0
b. Left "S" inverted .. 5·00 3·0
O31 **4** 10 ca. pink 15 8
a. Imperf. betwn. (horiz. pr.) 12·00 12·0
b. Imperf. between (vert. pr.) 12·00 12·0
c. Imperf. vert. (hor. strip 3) 20·00 20·0
d. Opt. inverted .. .. 6·00 6·0
e. "Ou" for "On" .. .. 15·00 15·0
f. "O" inverted .. .. 1·25 75
g. Left "S" inverted .. 1·25 75
h. Right "S" inverted .. 1·25 75
i. Left "S" omitted .. 12·00 12·00

32 1 1¼ ch. claret (*shades*) .. 1·00 20
a. Imperf. betwn. (horiz. pr.) 25·00
b. Imperf. betwn. (vert. pr.) 25·00
c. Opt. inverted .. .. 10·00 10·00
d. "O" inverted .. .. 6·00 1·50
e. Left "S" inverted .. 6·00 1·50
f. Right "S" inverted .. 6·00 1·50
g. Left "S" omitted .. 25·00 25·00
h. Right "S" omitted .. 25·00 25·00

33 6 3 ch. violet .. .. .. 2·50 50
a. Opt. inverted .. .. 40·00 30·00
b. "O" inverted .. .. 15·00 10·00
c. "O" omitted .. .. 25·00 20·00
d. "Ou" for "On" .. 40·00 40·00

34 7 7 ch. claret (date?) .. 8·00 1·00
35 8 14 ch. orange-yellow .. 3·00 50
a. Imperf. between (vert. pr.) 30·00
b. "O" inverted .. .. 15·00 4·00

The 5 ca. olive-bistre, 3 ch. and 7 ch. exist only with the normal watermark spaced 11 mm.; the ca. chocolate and 14 ch. exist only with the wide 15 mm. spacing; the 6 ca., 10 ca. and 1¼ ch. exist in both forms.

On On On

S S S S S S

(O 3) (O 4) (O 5)

Italic "S S".

1930. *Wmk.* C. *P* 12.

(*a*) *Optd. with Type* O **3.**

36 4 10 ca. pink .. .. .. 5·00 3·00
37 1 1¼ ch. carmine-rose .. 1·00 50

(*b*) *Optd. with Type* O **4.**

38 5 ¾ ch. black (R.) 20 5
a. Left "S" omitted .. 10·00
b. Right "S" omitted .. 10·00

(*c*) *Optd. with Type* O **5.**

39 5 ¾ ch. black (R.) 15 5
a. Opt. inverted .. .. 25·00 25·00
b. "n" omitted .. .. 15·00 15·00

40 1 4 ch. slate-green (R.) .. 5·00 2·00

On On On

S S S S S S

(O 6) (O 7) (O 8)

Oval "O".

1930–39 (?) *Contemporary stamps overprinted. P* 12.

(*a*) *With Type* O **6** (16 *mm. high*).

(i) *Wmk.* A.

41 3 4 ca. pink .. .. .. 3·00 3·50
a. Large right "S" as Type O 2 .. .. .. 20·00 20·00

(ii) *Wmk.* B.

42 3 4 ca. pink .. .. .. 4·00 5·00
a. Large right "S" as Type O 2 .. .. .. 20·00 20·00

(iii) *Wmk.* C.

43 1 6 ca. brown-red (1932) .. 15 8
a. Opt. inverted .. .. 10·00 10·00
b. Opt. double .. .. 15·00 15·00
c. "O" inverted .. .. 5·00 3·00

44 4 10 ca. pink .. .. 1·00 50
45 5 ¾ ch. mauve (1933) .. 15 8
a. Imperf. betwn. (horiz. pr.) 15·00 15·00
b. Imperf. between (horiz. strip 3) .. .. 25·00 25·00
c. Imperf. betwn. (vert. pair) 15·00 15·00
d. Perf. 12½ .. .. 1·00 25
e. Perf. comp. of 12 and 12½ 2·00 50

46 1 1¼ ch. carmine-rose .. 5·00 1·50
a. Opt. double .. .. 25·00 15·00
b. Large right "S" as Type O 2 .. .. .. 25·00 15·00

47 ,, 4 ch. grey-green .. .. 1·00 50

O48 1 4 ch. grey-green (R.) (27.10.30) 50 10
a. Imperf. betwn. (horiz. pr.) 20·00 20·00
b. Opt. double .. .. 12·00 12·00
c. "O" inverted .. .. 8·00 5·00
d. Large right "S" as Type O 2 .. .. .. 8·00 5·00

O49 8 14 ch. orange-yellow (1931) 2·00 50
a. Imperf. betwn. (vert. pr.) 15·00 15·00

For the 1¼ ch. and 3 ch., and for Nos. O43 and O48/9 but perf. 12½, see Nos. O66/70 (new setting combining Types O **6** and O **8**).

(*b*) *With Type* O **7** (14 *mm. high*). *Wmk.* C.

O50 3 4 ca. pink .. .. .. 3·00 3·00
a. "O" inverted .. .. 20·00 20·00

O51 4 5 ca. chocolate (1932) .. 10·00 10·00
a. Opt. inverted .. .. 40·00 40·00

O52 1 6 ca. brown-red 10 5
a. Imperf. betwn. (vert. pr.) 30·00 30·00
b. Opt. inverted .. .. 20·00 20·00
c. Opt. double .. .. 15·00 15·00
d. "nO" for "On" .. 20·00 20·00
e. Right "S" inverted .. 3·00 2·00
f. Left "S" omitted .. 10·00 10·00
g. Large "n" as Type O 5 .. 10·00 6·00
h. Large italic left "S" as Type O 5 .. .. 10·00 6·00
i. Perf. 12½ .. .. — 2·00

O53 ,, ½ ch. reddish violet (1932) 15 10
a. "CHUCRRAM" .. 3·00 2·00
b. "Ou" for "On" .. 10·00 10·00
c. Left "S" omitted .. 14·00 14·00

O54 ,, ½ ch. reddish violet (R.) (1935) 10 8
a. "CHUCRRAM" .. 2·00 2·00

O55 4 10 ca. pink (date?) .. 75 30
a. Imperf. betwn. (horiz. pr.) 7·00 7·00
b. Imperf. betwn. (vert. pr.) 7·00 7·00
c. "O" inverted .. 5·00 3·50
d. Right "S" inverted .. 5·00 3·50

O56 5 ¾ ch. mauve (1933?) .. 15 5
a. "Ou" for "On" .. 12·00 12·00
b. "O" inverted .. 2·00 2·00
c. Perf. comp. of 12 and 12½ 5·00 3·00

O57 1 1 ch. deep blue (R.) (1935) 50 10
a. Slate-blue 50 10
b. Imperf. betwn. (horiz. pr.) 15·00 15·00
c. Imperf. betwn. (vert. pr.) 15·00 15·00
d. Perf. 12½ .. .. — 1·00
e. Perf. comp. of 12 and 12½ — 1·50

O58 ,, 1¼ ch. claret 75 30
O59 ,, 1½ ch. rose (1933) 25 10
a. Imperf. betwn. (vert. pr.) 15·00 15·00
b. Opt. double .. .. 12·00 12·00
c. "O" inverted .. .. 2·50 1·50
d. "O" and "n" inverted .. 6·00 5·00
e. Large "n" as Type O 5 .. 7·00 6·00
f. Large italic left "S" as Type O 5 .. .. 7·00 6·00
g. Perf. 12½ .. .. — 2·00
h. Perf. comp. of 12 and 12½ — 3·00

O60 6 3 ch. reddish violet (1933) 75 30
a. "O" inverted .. 5·00 4·00

O61 ,, 3 ch. violet (R.) (1934) .. 40 10
a. Imperf. betwn. (horiz. pr.) 15·00 15·00
b. Imperf. betwn. (vert. pr.) 15·00 15·00
c. Opt. inverted .. 12·00 12·00
d. "O" inverted .. .. 3·00 2·00
e. Perf. 12½ .. .. — 1·00
f. Perf. comp. of 12 and 12½ — 1·50

O62 1 4 ch. grey-green (1934) .. — 10·00
O63 ,, 4 ch. grey-green (R.) (1935?) 50 10
a. "Ou" for "On" .. 15·00 15·00

O64 7 7 ch. claret (*shades*) .. 75 15
a. Imperf. betwn. (vert. pr.) 15·00 15·00
b. Left "S" inverted .. 10·00 4·00
c. Perf. 12½ .. .. — 2·00
d. Perf. comp. of 12 and 12½ — 3·00
da. Imperf. betwn. (vert. pr.) 20·00 20·00
db. Imperf. betwn. (vert. strip 3) .. .. .. 25·00 25·00

O65 8 14 ch. orange (1933) .. 1·00 30
a. Imperf. betwn. (horiz. pr.) 15·00 15·00
b. Imperf. betwn. (vert. pr.) 15·00 15·00
c. Opt. inverted .. .. 15·00 15·00

(*c*) *New setting combining Type* O **8** (18 *mm. high*) *in top row with Type* O **6** (16 *mm. high*) *for remainder. Wmk.* C (dates?).

A. *Type* O **8.** B. *Type* O **6.**

		A		B	
O66 1 6 ca. brown-red		2·00	1·00	†	
a. Perf. 12½ ..		2·00	1·00	50	20
ab. Imp. betwn. (vert. pair)		†		15·00	15·00
O67 ,, 1½ ch. rose ..		3·00	1·50	75	25
a. Perf. 12½ ..		3·00	1·25	75	25
ab. "O" invtd.		†		3·00	1·00
O68 6 3 ch. violet (R.)		5·00	2·00	1·00	40
a. Perf. 12½ ..		5·00	2·00	1·00	40
b. P. comp. 12 and 12½ ..		8·00	3·00	2·00	1·00
O69 1 4 ch. grey-grn. (R.) ..		8·00	4·00	†	
a. Perf. 12½ ..		8·00	4·00	2·00	1·00
ab. Imp. betwn. (hor. pair)		†		30·00	30·00
O70 8 14 ch. orange-yellow ..		5·00	3·00	†	
a. Perf. 12½ ..		5·00	3·00	1·50	50

Nos. O66B and O69/70B naturally exist but are not distinguishable from Nos. O43 and O48/9.

Nos. O66/70A/B in vertical *se-tenant* pairs are very scarce.

As with the postage issues it is believed that the 12½ and compound perforations were issued between 1937 and 1939.

1 ch

8 c 1 ch

(O 9) Wrong fount "1 c"

1932. *Official stamps surch. as T* **14** *or with Type* O **9.** *P* 12.

(*a*) *With opt. Type* O **1.**

(i) *Wmk.* A.

O71 4 6 c. on 5 ca. olive-bistre .. 2·00 1·00
a. "O" inverted .. .. 10·00 5·00
b. Left "S" inverted .. 10·00 5·00
c. Right "S" inverted .. 10·00 5·00

(ii) *Wmk.* C.

O72 4 6 c. on 5 ca. olive-bistre .. 1·00 50
a. "O" inverted .. .. 6·00 3·00
b. Left "S" inverted .. 6·00 3·00
c. Right "S" inverted .. 6·00 3·00

O73 ,, 12 c. on 10 ca. pink .. 4·00 4·00

(*b*) *With opt. Type* O **2.** *Wmk.* C.

O74 4 6 c. on 5 ca. olive-bistre .. 75 25
a. Opt. and surch. inverted .. 10·00 10·00
b. Left "S" inverted .. 5·00 2·00
c. Right "S" inverted .. 5·00 2·00

O75 ,, 6 c. on 5 ca. chocolate .. 8 8
a. Surch. inverted .. 6·00 6·00
b. Surch. double .. 25·00 25·00
c. Surch. double, one inverted 25·00 25·00
d. "O" inverted .. 1·00 1·00
e. Left "S" inverted .. 1·00 1·00

O76 ,, 12 c. on 10 ca. pink .. 8 8
a. Opt. inverted .. 4·00 4·00
b. Surch. inverted .. 4·00 4·00
c. Opt. and surch. inverted .. 6·00 6·00
d. Pair, one without surch. .. £100
e. "O" inverted .. 1·00 1·00
f. Left "S" inverted .. 1·00 1·00
g. "Ou" for "On" .. 15·00 15·00
h. "12" and "c" close .. 10·00 10·00
i. "c" omitted .. 12·00 12·00

O77 1 1 ch. 8 c. on 1¼ ch. claret .. 15 10
a. Surch. inverted .. 18·00 18·00
b. "O" inverted .. 1·50 1·00
c. Left "S" inverted .. 1·50 1·00
d. Right "S" inverted .. 1·50 1·00
e. Wrong fount "1 c" .. 4·00 4·00

(*c*) *With opt. Type* O **3.** *Wmk.* C.

O78 4 12 c. on 10 ca. pink .. — 25·00
O79 1 1 ch. 8 c. on 1¼ ch. carmine-rose .. .. 10·00 7·00
a. "n" omitted .. .. 60·00
b. Wrong fount "1 c" .. 40·00 30·00

(*d*) *With opt. Type* O **6.** *Wmk.* C.

O80 **4** 12 c. on 10 ca. pink .. 2·00 1·00
a. "12" and "c" close .. 15·00 10·00

O81 **1** 1 ch. 8 c. on 1¼ ch. carmine-rose .. .. 8·00 4·00
a. Wrong fount "1 c" .. 30·00 20·00

(*e*) *With opt. Type* O **7.** *Wmk.* C.

O82 **4** 6 c. on 5 ca. chocolate .. 10 10
a. Opt. inverted .. .. 12·00 12·00
b. Surch. inverted .. .. 8·00 8·00
c. Right "S" omitted .. 12·00 12·00
d. Two quads for right "S" £300

O83 „ 12 c. on 10 ca. pink .. 10 10
a. Opt. inverted .. .. 5·00 5·00
b. Surch. inverted .. .. 4·00 4·00
c. Opt. and surch. inverted .. 12·00 12·00
d. Opt. double .. .. 14·00 14·00
e. "O" inverted .. .. 2·00 2·00
f. Right "S" inverted .. 2·00 2·00
g. "On" omitted .. .. 10·00 10·00
h. "n" omitted .. .. 10·00 10·00
i. "c" omitted .. .. 10·00 10·00
j. "12" and "c" close .. 4·00 4·00

O84 **1** 1 ch. 8 c. on 1¼ ch. claret .. 25 15
a. Imperf. betwn. (vert. pr.) 25·00 25·00
b. Opt. omitted .. .. 20·00 20·00
c. Surch. inverted .. .. 10·00 10·00
d. Surch. double .. .. 14·00 14·00
e. "O" inverted .. .. 2·50 1·50
f. Wrong fount "1 c" .. 6·00 5·00

SERVICE (O **10**) 13 mm.

SERVICE (O **11**) 13½ mm.

1939–41. *Nos.* 35 *and* 40 *with type-set opt., Type* O **10.** *P* 12½.

O85 **1** 6 ca. brown-red (1941) .. 50 8
a. Perf. 11 .. .. 50 8
b. Perf. 12 .. .. 50 8
c. Compound perf. .. 1·00 50

O86 **5** ¾ ch. reddish violet .. 4·00 1·00
a. Perf. 12 .. .. 1·00 15
b. Compound perf. .. 6·00 4·00

1939 (9 Nov.). *Maharaja's 27th Birthday Nos,* 64/70 *with type-set opt., Type* O **10.** *P.* 12½.

O87 1 ch. yellow-green 10 8
O88 1½ ch. scarlet 15 10
a. "SESVICE" .. .. 8·00 8·00
b. Perf. 12 .. .. 1·25 1·00
c. Compound perf. .. 1·00 50
O89 2 ch. orange 15 15
a. "SESVICE" .. 10·00 10·00
b. Compound perf. .. 3·50 3·50
O90 3 ch. brown 10 8
a. "SESVICE" .. 7·00 7·00
b. Perf. 12 .. .. 30 20
c. Compound perf. .. 1·50 1·00
O91 4 ch. red 25 20
O92 7 ch. pale blue 50 40
O93 14 ch. turquoise-green .. 1·00 75

1940 (?)**–45.** *Nos.* 40*a and* 42*b optd. with Type* O **11.** *P* 12½.

O94 **5** ¾ ch. reddish violet .. 1·50 10
a. Imperf. betwn. (vert. pr.) 20·00 16·00
b. Perf. 11 .. .. 1·50 10
c. Perf. 12 .. .. 1·00 8
d. Compound perf. .. 3·00 75

O95 **1** 1½ ch. rose (1945) .. 2·50 2·50
a. Perf. 12 .. .. 50 40
b. Compound perf. .. 5·00 5·00

1942 (?). *Nos.* 64/70 *optd. with Type* O **11.** *P* 12½.

O 96 1 ch. yellow-green 10 5
a. Imperf. betwn. (vert. pr.) 8·00 8·00
b. Opt. inverted .. .. 9·00 8·00
c. Opt. double .. .. 11·00 11·00
d. Perf. 11 .. .. 15 5
da. Imperf. betwn. (vert. pr.) 8·00 8·00
db. Opt. double .. .. 7·00 7·00
e. Perf. 12 .. .. 40 25
ea. Imperf. betwn. (vert. pr.) 9·00 9·00
eb. Stamp doubly printed .. 15·00 15·00
ec. Opt. inverted .. .. 10·00 10·00
ed. Opt. double .. .. 11·00 11·00
f. Compound perf. 75 50

O 97 1½ ch. scarlet 15 10
a. Imperf. betwn. (horiz. pr.) 15·00 15·00
b. Perf. 11 .. .. .. 30 15
ba. Imperf. betwn. (vert. pr.) 12·00 12·00
bb. Imperf. between (vert. strip 3) .. .. .. 15·00 15·00
c. Perf. 12 .. .. .. 50 25
ca. Imperf. between (vert. strip 3) .. .. .. 20·00 20·00
d. Compound perf. 50 25
e. Imperf. (pair) .. .. 12·00

O 98 2 ch. orange 40 20
a. Perf. 11 .. .. .. 1·00 30
b. Perf. 12 .. .. .. 3·00 3·00
ba. Imperf. betwn. (vert. pr.) 12·00 12·00
c. Compound perf. .. .. 4·00 4·00

O 99 3 ch. brown 20 8
a. Perf. 11 .. .. .. 40 15
b. Perf. 12 .. .. .. 60 20
ba. Imperf. betwn. (vert. pr.) 12·00 12·00
c. Compound perf. .. .. 2·00 1·00

O100 4 ch. red 30 20
a. Perf. 11 .. .. .. 60 25
b. Perf. 12 .. .. .. 1·00 60
c. Compound perf. .. .. 4·00 4·00

O101 7 ch. pale blue 50 25
a. Perf. 11 .. .. .. 75 50
b. Perf. 12 .. .. .. 3·00 2·00
c. Compound perf. .. .. 5·00 2·00
d. *Blue* (p. 11) .. .. 1·00 50
da. Perf. 12 .. .. .. 2·00 1·00
db. Compound perf. .. .. 5·00 2·00

O102 14 ch. turquoise-green .. 1·00 50
a. Perf. 11 .. .. .. 2·00 1·00
b. Perf. 12 .. .. .. 3·00 1·50
c. Compound perf. .. .. 5·00 2·00

1942. *Maharaja's 29th Birthday. Nos.* 71/2 *optd. with Type* O **11.** *P* 12½.

O103 6 ca. blackish violet .. 15 8
a. Perf. 11 .. .. .. 50 15
b. Perf. 12 .. .. .. 1·50 75
c. Compound perf. .. .. 1·00 50

O104 ¾ ch. brown 15 8
a. Imperf. betwn. (vert. pr.) — 12·00
b. Perf. 11 .. .. .. 50 15
c. Perf. 12 .. .. .. 1·00 60
d. Compound perf. .. .. 1·00 60

SERVICE
8 CASH
(O **12**)

1943. *Surch. with Type* O **12.** *P* 12½.

O105 **19** 8 ca. on 6 ca. scarlet .. 15 8
a. Perf. 11 .. .. 25 8
ab. Surch. inverted .. — 30·00
b. Compound perf. .. 1·00 80

1945. *Nos.* 73/4 *optd. with Type* O **11.** *P* 12½.

O106 2 ca. on 1½ ch. scarlet .. 8 8
a. Perf. 11 .. .. .. 8 8
ab. Pair, one without surch. .. 30·00 30·00
b. Compound perf. 50 50
ba. "2" omitted .. .. 12·00 12·00

O107 4 ca. on ¾ ch. brown 20 8
a. Perf. 11 .. .. .. 30 8
b. Compound perf. 75 50

1947. *Maharaja's 34th Birthday. Optd. with Type* O **11.** *P* 11.

O108 **21** 8 ca. carmine 75 50
a. Imperf. betwn. (horiz. pr.) 18·00 18·00
b. Opt. double .. .. — 30·00
c. Perf. 12½ .. .. 2·00 75
ca. Stamp doubly printed .. 20·00 16·00
d. Perf. 12 .. .. 2·50 75
da. Stamp doubly printed .. 15·00 15·00

For later issues see TRAVANCORE-COCHIN.

TRAVANCORE-COCHIN.

On 1 July 1949 the United State of Travanco[r]
and Cochin was formed ("U.S.T.C.") and th[e]
name was changed to Travancore-Cochi[n]
("T.C.") on 1 April 1950.

NO WATERMARK VARIETIES. These we[re]
formerly listed but we have now decided to om[it]
them as they do not occur in full sheets. The[y]
are best collected in pairs, with and withou[t]
watermarks.

COMPOUND PERFS. The notes above Typ[e]
17 of Travancore also apply here.

ONE ANNA
ഒരണ
(1)

2p. on 6 ca.

രണ്ടു പൈസ
Normal

രണ്ടു രപൈസ
Variety: 1st character of 2nd group as 1st character of 1st group

1949 (1 July). *Stamps of Travancore surch. i[n] "*PIES*" or "*ANNAS*" as T* **1.** *P* 12½.

1 **19** 2 p. on 6 ca. blackish vio. (R.) 12
a. Surch. inverted .. .. 7·00 7·0[0]
b. Character error .. .. 15·00 15·0[0]
c. Perf. 11 .. .. .. 20 1[0]
ca. Imperf. between (vert. pair) .. 6·00 6·0[0]
cb. Pair, one without surch. .. 12·00 12·0[0]
cc. Character error .. .. 10·00 10·0[0]
d. Perf. 12 5
da. Imperf. between (horiz. pair) .. 4·00 4·0[0]
db. Imperf. between (vert. pair) .. 3·00 3·0[0]
dc. Surch. inverted .. .. 7·00 7·0[0]
dd. Character error .. .. 18·00 18·0[0]
e. Perf. 14 .. .. .. — £10[0]
f. Imperf. (pair) .. .. 6·00 6·0[0]

2 **21** 4 p. on 8 ca. carmine 12
a. Surch. inverted .. .. 8·00 8·0[0]
b. "S" inverted .. .. 14·00 14·0[0]
c. Perf. 11 .. .. .. 15 [8]
ca. Imperf. between (vert. pair) .. 8·00 8·0[0]
cb. Surch. inverted .. .. 8·00 8·0[0]
cc. Pair, one without surch. .. 15·00 15·0[0]
cd. "FOUP" for "FOUR" .. 16·00 16·0[0]
ce. "S" inverted .. .. 14·00 14·0[0]
d. Perf. 12 .. .. .. 20 2[0]
da. Imperf. between (vert. pair) .. 6·00 6·0[0]
db. Pair, one without surch. .. 15·00 15·0[0]
dc. "FOUP" for "FOUR" .. 16·00 16·0[0]
dd. "S" inverted .. .. 15·00 15·0[0]
e. Imperf. (pair) .. .. 20·00 20·0[0]

3 **17** ½ a. on 1 ch. yellow-green .. 20 1[5]
a. "NANA" for "ANNA" .. 16·00 16·0[0]
b. Inverted "H" in "HALF" .. 20·00 20·0[0]
c. Perf. 11 .. .. .. 15 1[0]
ca. Imperf. between (vert. pair) .. 6·00 6·0[0]
cb. Surch. inverted .. .. 5·00 5·0[0]
cc. "NANA" for "ANNA" .. 16·00 16·0[0]
cd. Inverted "H" in "HALF" .. 20·00 20·0[0]
d. Perf. 12 .. .. .. 8 5
da. Imperf. between (horiz. pair) .. 4·00 4·0[0]
db. Imperf. between (vert. pair) .. 3·00 3·0[0]
dc. Surch. inverted .. .. 3·50 3·5[0]
dd. "NANA" for "ANNA" .. 15·00 15·0[0]
e. Perf. 14 .. .. .. — £10[0]
f. Imperf. (pair) .. .. 6·00 6·0[0]

4 **18** 1 a. on 2 ch. orange 20 15
a. Perf. 11 .. .. .. 10 8
b. Perf. 12 .. .. .. 20 15
ba. Imperf. between (horiz. pair) .. 2·50 2·50
bb. Imperf. between (vert. pair) .. 2·50 2·50
c. Perf. 13½ .. .. .. 8·00 2·00
d. Imperf. (pair) .. .. 6·00 6·00

5 – 2 a. on 4 ch. red (68) 20 15
a. Surch. inverted .. .. 20·00 20·00
b. Perf. 11 .. .. .. 20 15
c. Perf. 12 .. .. .. 40 40
d. Compound perf. .. .. 3·00 3·00
e. Imperf. (pair) .. .. 10·00 10·00

18 3 a. on 7 ch. pale blue (69) ..	2·00	1·00
a. Perf. 11	2·00	1·00
ab. *Blue*	5·00	2·00
b. Perf. 12	2·50	1·50
c. Compound perf.	5·00	4·00
ca. *Blue*	10·00	10·00
– 6 a. on 14 ch. turq-grn. (70) ..	1·25	50
a. Accent omitted from native surch.	16·00	16·00
b. Perf. 11	2·00	1·50
ba. Accent omitted from native surch.	20·00	20·00
c. Perf. 12	2·00	2·00
ca. Accent omitted from native surch.	20·00	20·00
d. Imperf. (pair)	15·00	15·00

There are two settings of the ½ a. surcharge. n one the first native character is under the econd downstroke of the "H" and in the other is under the first downstroke of the "A" of HALF". They occur on stamps perf. 12½, 11 nd 12 equally commonly and also on the Official tamps.

U. S. T. C. (2) **T.-C.** (3)

949. *No.* 106 *of Cochin optd. with* T **2**.

29 1 a. orange	3·00	5·00
a. No stop after "S"	30·00	
b. Raised stop after "T" ..	30·00	

950 (1 APR.). *No.* 106 *of Cochin optd. with* T **3**.

29 1 a. orange	2·00	4·00
a. No stop after "T"	30·00	
b. Opt. inverted	£150	
ba. No stop after "T"	£1000	

The no stop variety occurs on No. 5 in the sheet nd again on No. 8 in conjunction with a short yphen.

SIX PIES (4)

950 (1 APR.). *No.* 9 *surch. as* T **4**.

29 6 p. on 1 a. orange	50	1·00
a. No stop after "T" ..	12·00	
b. Error. Surch. on No. 8 ..	25·00	
ba. No stop after "S" ..	£250	
bb. Raised stop after "T" ..	£250	
,, 9 p. on 1 a. orange	50	1·00
a. No stop after "T" ..	12·00	
b. Error. Surch. on No. 8 ..	60·00	
ba. No stop after "S" ..	£350	
bb. No raised stop after "T" ..	£350	

5. Conch or Chank Shell.

6. Palm Trees.

950. *Litho.* W **69** *of India.* P 14.

5 2 p. rose-carmine	25	75
6 4 p. ultramarine	40	1·00

OFFICIAL STAMPS.

SERVICE (O 1) **SERVICE** (O 2)

1949–51. *Stamps of Travancore surch. with value as* T **1** *and optd* "SERVICE". *No gum.* P 12½.

(a) *With Type* O **1**.

(i) *Wmk.* C *of Travancore.*

O 1 **19** 2 p. on 6 ca. blackish violet (R.)	5	5
a. Imperf. between (vert. pr.)	10·00	10·00
b. Character error	8·00	8·00
b. Perf. 11	5	5
ca. Imperf. between (vert. pr.)	12·00	12·00
cb. Character error	8·00	8·00
d. Perf. 12	35	35
da. Imperf. between (horiz. pr.)	4·00	4·00
db. Imperf. between (vert. pr.)	4·00	4·00
dc. Character error	12·00	12·00
e. Imperf. (pair)	5·00	5·00
O 2 **21** 4 p. on 8 ca. carmine ..	15	10
a. "FOUP" for "FOUR" ..	12·00	12·00
b. Perf. 11	15	10
ba. "FOUP" for "FOUR" ..	13·00	13·00
c. Perf. 12	15	10
ca. "FOUP" for "FOUR" ..	12·00	12·00
d. Compound perf.	10·00	10·00
O 3 **17** ½ a. on 1 ch. yellow-green	5	5
a. Pair, one without surch. ..	15·00	15·00
b. Surch. inverted	7·00	7·00
c. "NANA" for "ANNA" ..	12·00	12·00
d. Perf. 11..	10	8
da. Pair, one without surch. ..	12·00	12·00
db. Surch. inverted	7·00	7·00
da. "NANA" for "ANNA" ..	12·00	12·00
e. Perf. 12....	1·00	50
ea. "NANA" for "ANNA" ..	20·00	20·00
O 4 **18** 1 a. on 2 ch. orange ..	3·50	2·50
a. Surch. inverted	£100	
b. Perf. 11	3·50	3·00
O 5 – 2 a. on 4 ch. red (68) ..	40	20
a. Pair, one without surch. ..	20·00	
b. Perf. 11	50	30
ba. Imperf. between (vert. pr.)	20·00	20·00
c. Perf. 12	40	20
d. Imperf. (pair)	8·00	8·00
O 6 – 3 a. on 7 ch. pale blue (69)	40	35
a. Imperf. between (vert. pr.)	5·00	5·00
b. *Blue*	75	50
c. Perf. 11	75	40
ca. *Blue*	75	50
d. Perf. 12	75	40
da. Imperf. between (horiz. pr.)	5·00	5·00
db. Imperf. between (vert. pr.)	4·00	4·00
dc. Block of four imp. between (horiz. and vert.)	4·00	4·00
d. *Blue*	75	40
e. Imperf. (pair)	8·00	8·00
O 7 – 6 a. on 14 ch. turquoise-green (70)	1·00	75
a. Imperf. between (vert. pr.)	6·00	6·00
b. Perf. 11	1·00	50
c. Perf. 12	2·50	1·50
ca. Imperf. between (horiz. pr.)	9·00	9·00
cb. Imperf. between (vert. pr.)	12·00	12·00
d. Imperf. (pair)	10·00	10·00

(ii) W **27** *of Cochin.*

O 8 **19** 2 p. on 6 ca. blackish violet (R.)	5	5
a. Type O 1 double	10·00	
b. Perf. 11	10	5
c. Perf. 12	15	15
O 9 – 2 a. on 4 ch. red (68) ..	12	10
a. Perf. 11	20	10
b. Compound perf.	10·00	10·00

(b) *With Type* O **2**.

(i) *Wmk.* C *of Travancore*

O10 **21** 4 p. on 8 ca. carmine ..	5	5
a. "FOUP" for "FOUR" ..	15·00	15·00
b. Perf. 11	5	5
ba. Imperf. between (horiz. pr.)	2·50	2·50
bb. Imperf. between (vert. pr.)	2·50	2·50
bc. "FOUP" for "FOUR" ..	15·00	15·00
c. Perf. 12	12	10
ca. Imperf. between (horiz. pr.)	1·25	1·25
cb. Imperf. between (vert. pr.)	1·25	1·25
cc. Block of four imp. betwn. (horiz. and vert.) ..	2·00	2·00
cd. "FOUP" for "FOUR" ..	12·00	12·00
d. Perf. 13½	1·50	1·50
e. Compound perf.	10·00	10·00
f. Imperf. (pair)	6·00	6·00
O11 **17** ½ a. on 1 ch. yellow-green	5	5
a. "AANA" for "ANNA" ..	10·00	10·00
b. Perf. 11	5	5
ba. Imperf. between (horiz. pr.)	2·00	2·00
bb. Imperf. between (vert. pr.)	2·00	2·00
bc. Block of four imp. between (horiz. and vert.)	5·50	5·50
bd. "AANA" for "ANNA" ..	10·00	10·00
c. Perf. 12	5	5
ca. Imperf. between (horiz. pr.)	3·50	3·50
cb. Imperf. between (vert. pr.)	3·50	3·50
cc. "AANA" for "ANNA" ..	10·00	10·00
d. Compound perf.	2·50	2·50
e. Imperf. (pair)	4·00	4·00
O12 **18** 1 a. on 2 ch. orange ..	12	12
a. Imperf. between (vert. pair)	4·00	4·00
b. Perf. 11	35	35
ba. Imperf. between (horiz. pr.)	3·00	3·00
bb. Imperf. between (vert. pr.)	3·00	3·00
c. Perf. 12	12	12
ca. Imperf. between (horiz. pr.)	2·50	2·50
cb. Imperf. between (vert. pr.)	2·00	2·00
cc. Block of four imp. between (horiz. and vert.)	3·50	3·50
d. Compound perf.	1·50	1·50
e. Imperf. (pair)	10·00	10·00
O13 – 2 a. on 4 ch. red (68) ..	50	50
a. Perf. 11	75	75
b. Perf. 12	1·50	75
ba. Imperf. between (vert. pr.)	20·00	20·00
c. Compound perf.	3·50	3·50
O14 – 3 a. on 7 ch. pale blue (69)	60	50
a. "S" inverted in "SERVICE"	17·00	17·00
b. First "E" inverted ..	20·00	20·00
c. "C" inverted	20·00	20·00
d. Second "E" inverted ..	20·00	20·00
e. Perf. 11	75	50
ea. "S" inverted in "SERVICE"	17·00	17·00
f. Perf. 12	60	50
fa. "S" inverted in "SERVICE"	17·00	17·00
g. Compound perf.	15·00	15·00
h. Imperf. (pair)	18·00	18·00
O15 – 6 a. on 14 ch. turq.-grn. (70)	75	40
a. Accent omitted from native surch.	9·00	7·00
b. "S" inverted in "SERVICE"	20·00	20·00
c. Perf. 11	2·00	1·25
ca. Accent omitted from native surch.	15·00	12·00
cb. "S" inverted in "SERVICE"	25·00	25·00
d. Perf. 12	3·00	75
da. Accent omitted from native surch.	16·00	12·00
db. "S" inverted in "SERVICE"	20·00	20·00
e. Compound perf.	15·00	15·00

(ii) W **27** *of Cochin.*

O16 **17** ½ a. on 1 ch. yellow-green	5	5
a. Perf. 11	5	5
b. Perf. 12	5·00	5·00
c. Compound perf.	3·00	3·00
O17 **18** 1 a. on 2 ch. orange ..	20	15
a. Perf. 11	50	30
b. Perf. 12	—	2·00
c. Perf. 13½	2·50	1·50
d. Compound perf.	3·00	3·00

Nos. O2, O10, O12 and O17 have the value at top in English and at bottom in native characters with "SERVICE" in between. All others have "SERVICE" below the surcharge.

Type O **2** was overprinted at one operation with the surcharges.

WADHWAN.

1

1888. *Thin toned wove paper.*

(*a*) *Irregular perf.* 12½ (*small holes*).

1 **1** ½ pice, black (II) .. .. 3·00
 a. Imperf between (pair) .. ..

(*b*) *P* 12½ (*large holes*).

2 **1** ½ pice, black (I, III) .. .. 2·50

Medium toned wove paper.

3 **1** ½ pice, black (III) (*p.* 12½) .. 1·75
4 ,, ½ pice, black (V) (*p.* 12) .. 1·00

1892 (?). *Thick wove paper. P* 12.

5 **1** ½ pice, black/*toned* (VI, VII) .. 1·00
6 ,, ½ pice, black/*white* (IV) .. 1·00

The stamps were lithographed from seven stones (as indicated by Roman figures), in sheets of from 20 to 42 units, distinguishable by flaws.

Genuinely used copies are rare, but stamps cancelled-to-order are fairly common.

IONIAN ISLANDS.

For GREAT BRITAIN stamp used in Ionian Islands with "PAID AT CORFU" obliteration see index to Great Britain Stamps Used Abroad list.

1

(Recess. Perkins, Bacon & Co.)

1859 (15 May). *Imperf.*

1 **1** (½d.) orange (no wmk.) .. 24·00 £140
2 ,, (1d.) blue (wmk. "**2**") .. 6·00 55·00
3 ,, (2d.) carmine (wmk. "**1**") .. 5·50 55·00

On the 30th May, 1864, the islands were ceded to Greece, and these stamps became obsolete.

Great care should be exercised in buying used stamps, on or off cover, as forged postmarks are plentiful.

IRAQ.

All issues will be found listed in Vol. 2 of the Stanley Gibbons Foreign Overseas Catalogue.

IRELAND (REPUBLIC).

All the issues of Ireland are listed together here, in this section of the Gibbons Catalogue, purely as a matter of convenience to collectors.

I. PROVISIONAL GOVERNMENT.

16 January—6 December 1922.

Stamps of Great Britain overprinted.
T **104/8**, *W* **100**; *T* **109**, *W* **110**.

Rialtas Sealadaċ na hÉireann 1922
(1)

Rialtas Sealadaċ na hÉireann **1922.**
(2)

Rialtas Sealadaċ na hÉireann 1922
(3)

("Provisional Government of Ireland, 1922".)

1922 (17 Feb.). *T* **104** *to* **108** (*W* **100**) *and* **109** *of Great Britain overprinted in black.*

(*a*) *With T* **1**, *by Dollard Printing House, Ltd. Optd. in black.**

1 **105** ½d. green 12 12
 a. Opt. inverted £150 £170
2 **104** 1d. scarlet 12 12
 a. Opt. inverted .. .. 70·00 £120
3 ,, 1d. carmine-red 25 15
4 ,, 2½d. bright blue 45 65
5 **106** 3d. bluish violet .. .. 1·00 60
6 ,, 4d. grey-green .. .. 1·10 1·50
7 **107** 5d. yellow-brown .. 1·75 2·25
8 **108** 9d. agate .. .. 4·00 4·00
9 ,, 10d. turquoise-blue .. 3·00 4·50
1/9 .. .. .. *Set of* 8 11·00 13·00

*All values except 2½d. and 4d. are known with greyish black overprint, but are not easy to distinguish.

The ½d. with red overprint is a trial or proof printing. (*Price* £45.)

Bogus inverted T **1** overprints exist on the 2d., 4d., 9d. and 1s. values.

(*b*) *With T* **2**, *by Alex Thom & Co., Ltd.*

10 **105** 1½d. red-brown 35 35
 a. Error. "PENCF" .. £200 £140
12 **106** 2d. orange (Die I) .. 1·00 15
 a. Opt. inverted .. .. 70·00 85·00
13 ,, 2d. orange (Die II) .. 1·10 15
 a. Opt. inverted £100 £130
14 **107** 6d. reddish purple, **C** .. 2·50 1·25
15 **108** 1s. bistre-brown .. 4·50 2·50

Varieties occur throughout the T **2** overprint in the relative positions of the lines of the overprint, the "R" of "Rialtas" being over either the "Se" or "S" of "Sealadac" or intermediately.

(*c*) *With T* **3**.

17 **109** 2s. 6d. chocolate-brown .. 12·00 15·00
18 ,, 2s. 6d. sepia-brown .. 12·00 15·00
19 ,, 5s. rose-red .. .. 16·00 22·00
21 ,, 10s. dull grey-blue .. .. 42·00 55·00

1922 (1 April–July). *Optd. by Dollard with T* **1**, *in red or carmine.*

22 **104** 2½d. bright blue (R.) .. 65 90
23 **106** 4d. grey-green (R.) .. 2·75 3·00
24 ,, 4d. grey-green (C.) (July) 9·50 11·00
25 **108** 9d. agate (R.) .. .. 4·00 4·00
25*a* ,, 9d. agate (C.) (July) .. 15·00 16·00

1922 (19 June–Aug.). *Optd. as T* **2**, *in black, by Harrison & Sons, for use in horiz. and vert. coils.*

26 **105** ½d. green .. .. .. 65 1·50
27 **104** 1d. scarlet 40 65
28 **105** 1½d. red-brown (21.6) .. 2·25 4·00
29 **106** 2d. bright orange (Die I) 4·00 5·50
29*a* ,, 2d. bt. orge. (Die II) (Aug.) 4·50 7·00

The Harrison overprint measures 15 × 17 mm. (maximum) against the 14½ × 16 mm. of *T* **2** (Thom printing) and is much bolder black than the latter, while the individual letters are taller, the "i" of "Rialtas" being specially outstanding.

The "R" of "Rialtas" is always over the "Se" of "Sealadac".

1922. *Optd. by Thom.*

(*a*) *As T* **2**, *but bolder, in dull to shiny blue-black or red* (June-Nov.).

30 **105** ½d. green .. .. .. 40 4(
31 **104** 1d. scarlet 15 1
 a. "Q" for "O" (No. 357ab) £450 £45
 b. Reversed "Q" for "O" (No. 357ac) .. .. £150 £12(
32 **105** 1½d. red-brown .. .. 2·75 1·0
33 **106** 2d. orange (Die I) .. 5·00 3.
34 ,, 2d. orange (Die II) .. 40 1
35 **104** 2½d. blue (R.) .. .. 2·25 3·0
36 **106** 3d. violet 45 5
37 ,, 4d. grey-green (R.) .. 1·25 1·2
38 **107** 5d. yellow-brown .. 1·50 2·7
39 ,, 6d. reddish purple, **C** .. 1·50 1·1
40 **108** 9d. agate (R.) .. .. 2·25 3·0
41 ,, 9d. olive-green (R.) .. 2·25 3·0
42 ,, 10d. turquoise-blue .. 4·50 5·5
43 ,, 1s. bistre-brown .. 4·50 4·5
30/43 .. .. *Set of* 14 27·00 24·0

Both 2d. stamps exist with the overprin inverted but there remains some doubt as t whether they were issued.

These Thom printings are distinguishable fron the Harrison printings by the size of the over print, and from the previous Thom printings b the intensity and colour of the overprint, th latter being best seen when the stamp is looke through with a strong light behind it.

(*b*) *As with T* **3**, *but bolder, in shiny blue-black* (Oct.-Dec.).

44 **109** 2s. 6d. chocolate-brown .. 55·00 65·0
45 ,, 5s. rose-red .. .. 65·00 70·0
46 ,, 10s. dull grey-blue .. £350 £40

The above differ from Nos. 17/21 not only i the bolder impression and colour of the in but the "h" and "é" of "héireann" are close together

Rialtas Sealadaċ na hÉireann **1922.**
(4)

Saorstát Éireann **1922**
("Irish Free State 1922".
(**5.** Wide date.)

The overprint T **4** measures 15¾ × 16 mm (maximum).

1922 (21 Nov.–Dec.). *Optd. by Thom with T* (*wider setting*) *in shiny blue-black.*

47 **105** ½d. green 20 2
 a. Opt. in jet-black .. — 20·0
48 **104** 1d. scarlet 40 4
49 **105** 1½d. red-brown (4 Dec.) .. 85 9
50 **106** 2d. orange (Die II) .. 3·25 3·2
51 **108** 1s. olive-bistre (4 Dec.) .. 9·50 9·0

II. IRISH FREE STATE

6 December 1922—29 December 1937.

1922 (Dec.)–**23.** (*a*) *Optd. by Thom with T* **5**, *i dull to shiny blue-black or red.*

52 **105** ½d. green 10 1
 a. No accent in "Saorstat" £350 £35
 b. Accent inserted by hand .. 35·00 32·0
53 **104** 1d. scarlet 10 1
 aa. No accent in "Saorstat" £2000
 a. No accent and final "t" missing £850 £90
 b. Accent inserted by hand .. 50·00 55·0
 c. Accent and "t" inserted 70·00 90·0
 d. Reversed "Q" for "O" (No. 357ac) £160 £16
54 **105** 1½d. red-brown 40 6
55 **106** 2d. orange (Die II) .. 40 5
56 **104** 2½d. brt. blue (R.) (6.1.23) 55 7
 a. No accent .. .. 55·00 75·0
57 **106** 3d. bluish violet (6.1.23) 1·00 1·4
 a. No accent .. .. 80·00 90·0
58 ,, 4d. grey-grn. (R.) (16.1.23) 80 1·0
 a. No accent .. .. 70·00 80·0
59 **107** 5d. yellow-brown .. 1·00 1·4
60 ,, 6d. reddish purple, **C** .. 80 8
 a. Accent inserted by hand .. £325 £30
61 **108** 9d. olive-green (R.) .. 95 1·4
 a. No accent £100 £11
62 ,, 10d. turquoise-blue .. 5·50 7·0
63 ,, 1s. bistre-brown .. 4·00 4·0
 a. No accent £1800
 b. Accent inserted by hand .. £325 £30

4 **109** 2s. 6d. chocolate-brown 10·00 15·00
a. Major Re-entry .. £300
b. No accent £130 £130
c. Accent reversed .. £180 £140
5 ,, 5s. rose-red .. 18·00 28·00
a. No accent £180 £180
b. Accent reversed .. £225 £150
6 ,, 10s. dull grey-blue .. 45·00 55·00
a. No accent £900
b. Accent reversed .. £1000
2/66 .. .. *Set of* 15 80·00 £110

The accents inserted by hand are in dull black. ʼhe reversed accents are grave (thus " à ") innstead of acute (" á "). A variety with " S " of ' Saorstat " directly over " é " of " éireann", nstead of to left, may be found in all values xcept the 2½d. and 4d. In the 2s. 6d., 5s. and os. it is very slightly to the left in the " S " over ' é " variety, bringing the " á " of " Saorstat " irectly above the last " n " of " éireann ".

b) Optd. with T **5**, *in dull or shiny blue-black, by Harrison, for use in horiz. or vert. coils* (7.3.23).
7 ½d. green 40 70
a. Long " 1 " in " 1922 " .. 4·00 5·00
8 1d. scarlet .. .. .. 90 1·10
a. Long " 1 " in " 1922 " .. 18·00 22·00
9 1½d. red-brown .. .. .. 2·75 4·00
a. Long " 1 " in " 1922 " .. 28·00 35·00
o 2d. orange (Die II) 70 80
a. Long " 1 " in " 1922 " .. 5·00 6·50

In the Harrison overprint the characters are ather bolder than those of the Thom overprint, nd the foot of the " 1 " of " 1922 " is usually ounded instead of square. The long " 1 " in ' 1922 " has a serif at foot. The second " e " f " éireann " appears to be slightly raised.

PRINTERS. The following and all subsequent ssues to No. 148 were printed at the Govt. ʼrinting Works, Dublin, *unless otherwise stated.*

6. " Sword of Light ".

7. Map of Ireland.

8. Arms of Ireland.

9. Celtic Cross.

10

Des. J. J. O'Reilly, T **6**; J. Ingram, T **7**; Miss M. Girling, T **8**; and Miss L. Williams, T **9**. Typo. Plates made by Royal Mint, London.)

922 (6 Dec.)–**35.** *W* **10.** *P* 15×14.
1 **6** ½d. bright green (20.4.23) .. 20 8
a. Imperf. × perf. 14, wmk. sideways (11.34) .. .. 8·50 8·00
2 **7** 1d. carmine (23.2.23) .. 8 8
a. P 15 × imp. (single perf.) ('33) 20·00 22·00
c. P 15 × imperf. (7.34) .. 7·00 5·50
d. Booklet pane. Three stamps plus three printed labels ..
3 ,, 1½d. claret (2.2.23) .. .. 1·00 8
4 ,, 2d. grey-green (6.12.22) .. 8 8
a. Imperf. × perf. 14, wmk. sideways (11.34) .. .. 15·00 9·00
b. Perf. 15 × imperf. (1935) .. £3000 £400

75 **8** 2½d. red-brown (7.9.23) .. 1·75 75
76 **9** 3d. ultramarine (16.3.23) .. 70 15
77 **8** 4d. slate-blue (28.9.23) .. 1·25 50
78 **6** 5d. deep violet (11.5.23) .. 5·00 2·50
79 ,, 6d. claret (21.12.23) .. 1·60 80
80 **8** 9d. deep violet (26.10.23) .. 7·00 3·50
81 **9** 10d. brown (11.5.23) .. 5·00 4·50
82 **6** 1s. light blue (15.6.23) .. 15·00 2·75
71/82 .. .. *Set of* 12 35·00 14·00

No. 72*a* is imperf. vertically except for a single perf. at each top corner. It was issued for use in automatic machines.

See also Nos. 111/22 and 227/8.

SAORSTÁT
ÉIREANN
1922

11. Narrow Date.)

12. Daniel O'Connell.

1925 (Aug.)–**28.** *T* **109** *of Great Britain (Bradbury, Wilkinson printing) optd. at the Government Printing Works, Dublin.*

(*a*) *With T* **11** *in black or grey-black* (25.8.25).
83 2s. 6d. chocolate-brown .. 15·00 16·00
a. Wide and narrow date (pr.) ('27) 45·00
84 5s. rose-red .. .. 15·00 22·00
a. Wide and narrow date (pr.) ('27) 70·00
85 10s. dull grey-blue .. .. 30·00 50·00
a. Wide and narrow date (pr.) ('27) £200

The varieties with wide and narrow date *se-tenant* are from what is known as the " composite setting," in which some stamps showed the wide date, as T **5**, while in others the figures were close together, as in T **11**.

Single specimens of this printing with wide date may be distinguished from Nos. 64 to 66 by the colour of the ink, which is black or grey-black in the composite setting and blue-black in the Thom printing.

The type of the " composite " overprint usually shows distinct signs of wear.

(*b*) *As T* **5** (*wide date*) *in black* (1927–28).
86 2s. 6d. chocolate-brn. (9.12.27) 11·00 11·00
a. Circumflex accent over " a " .. 60·00 70·00
b. No accent over " a " .. .. 85·00 90·00
87 5s. rose-red (2.28) .. .. 18·00 18·00
a. Circumflex accent over " a " .. 85·00 90·00
88 10s. dull grey-blue (15.2.28) .. 40·00 35·00
a. Circumflex accent over " a " .. £170

This printing can be distinguished from the Thom overprints in dull black, by the clear, heavy impression (in deep black) which often shows in relief on the back of the stamp.

The accent varieties all occur on row 9 No. 2. In the upper pane (all values) it appears as a circumflex but tilted to the right. In the lower pane of the 2s. 6d. the accent was first partially missing and then completely missing on some sheets, but there is also an offset impression on the reverse.

(Des. Leo Whelan. Typo.)

1929 (22 June). *Catholic Emancipation Centenary. W* **10.** *P* 15×14.
89 **12** 2d. grey-green 25 12
90 ,, 3d. blue .. .. .. 1·50 1·10
91 ,, 9d. bright violet .. .. 1·75 1·25

13. Shannon Barrage.

(Des. E. L. Lawrenson. Typo.)

1930 (15 Oct.). *Completion of Shannon Hydro-Electric Scheme. W* **10.** *P* 15×14.
92 **13** 2d. agate 40 25

14. Reaper.

15. The Cross of Cong.

(T **14** and **15** des. G. Atkinson. Typo.)

1931 (12 June). *200th Anniv. of the Royal Dublin Society. W* **10.** *P* 15×14.
93 **14** 2d. blue 55 25

1932 (12 May). *International Eucharistic Congress. W* **10.** *P* 15×14.
94 **15** 2d. grey-green 40 15
95 ,, 3d. blue .. .. .. 1·75 2·00

16. Adoration of the Cross.

17. Hurler.

(T **16** to **19** des. R. J. King. Typo.)

1933 (18 Sept.). " *Holy Year.*" *W* **10.** *P* 15×14.
96 **16** 2d. grey-green 30 12
97 ,, 3d. blue .. .. .. 1·50 1·10

1934 (27 July). *Golden Jubilee of the Gaelic Athletic Association. W* **10.** *P* 15×14.
98 **17** 2d. green 60 20

1935 (Mar.-July). *T* **109** *of Great Britain (Waterlow printings) optd. as T* **5** (*wide date*), *at the Government Printing Works, Dublin.*
99 **109** 2s. 6d. chocolate (No. 450) 11·00 12·00
a. Flat accent on " a " .. 80·00 80·00
100 ,, 5s. brt. rose-red (No. 451) 30·00 28·00
a. Flat accent on " a " .. 85·00 85·00
101 ,, 10s. indigo (No. 452) .. £130 £130
a. Flat accent on " a " .. £225 £225

The accent varieties on Nos. 86/8 all developed into a " flat " accent consisting of a straight line sloping up to the right only very slightly, combined with damage to top of " a " and nick in top of " t ".

18. St. Patrick.

1937 (8 Sept.). *W* **10.** *P* 14×15.
102 **18** 2s. 6d. emerald-green .. 17·00 18·00
103 ,, 5s. maroon .. .. 20·00 22·00
104 ,, 10s. deep blue .. .. 15·00 18·00

See also Nos. 123/5.

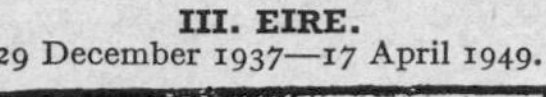

III. EIRE.

29 December 1937—17 April 1949.

19. Ireland and New Constitution.

1937 (29 Dec.). *Constitution Day.* *W* **10.** *P*15×14.

105 **19** 2d. claret 40 30
106 ,, 3d. blue .. .. 1·10 1·25

For similar stamps see Nos. 176/7.

20. Father Mathew.

(Des. Sean Keating. Typo.)

1938 (1 July). *Centenary of Temperance Crusade.* *W* **10.** *P* 15×14.

107 **20** 2d. black 45 35
108 ,, 3d. blue .. .. .. 2·75 3·00

21. George Washington, American Eagle and Irish Harp.

(Des. G. Atkinson. Typo.)

1939 (1 Mar.). *150th Anniv. of U.S. Constitution and Installation of First U.S. President.* *W* **10.** *P* 15×14.

109 **21** 2d. scarlet 40 50
110 ,, 3d. blue .. .. .. 3·25 3·75

22

1941
I gCUIMHNE
AISÉIRGHE
1916

(**23.** *Trans.* "In memory of the rising of 1916".)

SIZE OF WATERMARK. T **22** can be found in various sizes from about 8 to 10 mm. high. This is due to the use of two different dandy rolls supplied by different firms and to the effects of paper shrinkage and other factors such as pressure and machine speed.

1940–68. *Typo.* *W* **22.** *P* 15×14 *or* 14×15 (2*s.* 6*d.* *to* 10*s.*).

111 **6** ½d. bright green (24.11.40) 1·75 25
112 **7** 1d. carmine (26.10.40) .. 5 5
a. From coils. P 14×Imperf. (Sept. '40) .. .. 9·00 9·00
b. From coils. P 15×Imperf. ('46) .. .. .. 5·00 4·00
c. Booklet pane. Three stamps plus three printed labels .. 45·00
113 ,, 1½d. claret (1.40) .. 2·50 20
114 ,, 2d. grey-green (1.40) .. 5 5
115 **8** 2½d. red-brown (3.41) 1·75 20
116 **9** 3d. blue (12.40) .. 25 12
117 **8** 4d. slate-blue (*shades*) (12.40) 15 8
118 **6** 5d. dp. vio. (*shades*) (7.40) 20 8
119 **6** 6d. claret ('42) 30 12
aa. Chalky paper ('67) .. 15 12
119*a* ,, 8d. scarlet (12.9.49) .. 30 30
120 **8** 9d. deep violet (7.40) .. 30 30
121 **9** 10d. brown (7.40) .. 35 30
121*a* ,, 11d. rose (12.9.49) .. 40 50
122 **6** 1s. light blue (6.40) .. 16·00 5·00
123 **18** 2s. 6d. emer.-grn. (10.2.43) 3·50 35
a. Chalky paper ('68?) .. 1·25 60
124 ,, 5s. maroon (15.12.42) .. 5·50 60
a. Chalky paper ('68?) .. 2·00 90
125 ,, 10s. deep blue (7.45) .. 10·00 2·50
a. Chalky paper (*shades*) ('68) 3·00 2·00
111/125 .. .. *Set of* 17 26·00 10·00

There is a wide range of shades and also variation in paper used in this issue.

See also Nos. 227/8.

1941 (12 Apr.). *25th Anniv. of Easter Rising (1916). Provisional issue. T* **7** *and* **9** (2*d. in new colour*), *optd. with T* **23.**

126 **7** 2d. orange (G.) 45 25
127 **9** 3d. blue (V.) .. .. 6·50 4·00

24. Volunteer and G.P.O., Dublin.

(Des. Victor Brown. Typo.)

1941 (27 Oct.). *25th Anniv. of Easter Rising (1916). Definitive issue.* *W* **22.** *P* 15×14.

128 **24** 2½d. blue-black 55 15

25. Dr. Douglas Hyde.

26. Sir William Rowan Hamilton.

(Des. Sean O'Sullivan. Typo.)

1943 (31 July). *50th Anniv. of Founding of Gaelic League.* *W* **22.** *P* 15×14.

129 **25** ½d. green 25 20
130 ,, 2½d. claret 50 35

(Des. Sean O'Sullivan from a bust by Hogan. Typo.)

1943 (13 Nov.). *Centenary of Announcement of Discovery of Quaternions.* *W* **22.** *P* 15×14.

131 **26** ½d. green .. .. .. 1·25 25
132 ,, 2½d. brown .. .. 1·25 35

27. Bro. Michael O'Clery.

(Des. R. J. King. Typo.)

1944 (30 June). *Tercentenary of Death of Michael O'Clery. (Commemorating the "Annals of the Four Masters").* *W* **22.** (*sideways*). *P* 14×15.

133 **27** ½d. emerald-green .. 12 10
134 ,, 1s. red-brown 30 12

Although issued as commemoratives these two stamps were kept in use as part of the current issue, replacing Nos. 111 and 122.

28. Edmund Ignatius Rice.

29. "Youth Sowing Seeds of Freedom".

(Des. Sean O'Sullivan. Typo.)

1944 (29 Aug.). *Death Centenary of Edmun[d] Rice (founder of Irish Christian Brothers)* *W* **22.** *P* 15×14.

135 **28** 2½d. slate .. .. .. 40 1[…]

(Des. R. J. King. Typo.)

1945 (15 Sept.). *Centenary of Death of Thoma[s] Davis (Founder of Young Ireland Movement)* *W* **22.** *P* 15×14.

136 **29** 2½d. blue .. .. .. 35 2[…]
137 ,, 6d. claret .. .. .. 1·25 1·7[…]

30. "Country and Homestead".

(Des. R. J. King. Typo.)

1946 (16 Sept.). *Birth Centenaries of Davitt an[d] Parnell (Land Reformers).* *W* **22.** *P* 15×14

138 **30** 2½d. scarlet .. .. 35 2[…]
139 ,, 3d. blue .. .. .. 1·25 1·4[…]

31. Angel Victor over Rock of Cashel.

32. Over Lough Derg.

33. Over Croagh Patrick.

34. Over Glendalough.

)es. R. J. King. Recess. Waterlow until 1961, then De La Rue.)

948 (7 Apr.)–**65.** *Air.* *W* **22.** *P* 15 (1s. 5*d.*) *or* 15 × 14 (*others*).
40 **31** 1d. chocolate (4.4.49) .. 85 60
41 **32** 3d. blue .. .. 1·60 1·25
42 **33** 6d. magenta 15 8
42*a* **32** 8d. lake-brown (13.12.54) 15 25
43 **34** 1s. green (4.4.49) .. 20 25
43*a* **31** 1s. 3d. red-orge. (13.12.54) 30 40
43*b* „ 1s. 5d. dp. ultram. (1.4.65) 25 35
40/143*b* .. .. *Set of* 7 3·00 2·75

35. Theobald Wolfe Tone.

(Des. K. Uhlemann. Typo.)

948 (19 Nov.). 150*th Anniv. of Insurrection.* *W* **22.** *P* 15 × 14.
44 **35** 2½d. reddish purple .. 50 35
45 „ 3d. violet .. .. .. 2·00 2·25

IV. REPUBLIC OF IRELAND.

18 April 1949.

36. Leinster House and Arms of Provinces.

(Des. Muriel Brandt. Typo.)

949 (21 Nov.). *International Recognition of Republic.* *W* **22.** *P* 15 × 14.
46 **36** 2½d. reddish brown .. 25 20
47 „ 3d. bright blue .. .. 1·25 1·10

37. J. C. Mangan.

38. Statue of St. Peter.

(Des. R. J. King. Typo.)

949 (5 Dec.). 100*th Anniv. of Death of James Clarence Mangan* (*poet*). *W* **22.** *P* 15 × 14.
48 **37** 1d. green .. .. .. 1·25 35

(Recess. Waterlow & Sons.)

950 (11 Sept.). *Holy Year.* *W* **22.** *P* 12½.
49 **38** 2½d. violet 30 35
50 „ 3d. blue .. .. .. 3·00 3·25
51 „ 9d. brown .. .. .. 3·25 3·50

PRINTERS. Nos. 152 to 200 were recess-printed by De La Rue & Co., Dublin, *unless otherwise stated.*

39. Thomas Moore.

40. Irish Harp.

1952 (10 Nov.). *Centenary of Death of Moore* (*poet*). *W* **22.** *P* 13.
152 **39** 2½d. reddish purple .. 15 20
153 „ 3½d. deep olive-green .. 1·50 1·25

(Des. F. O'Ryan. Typo. Govt. Printing Works, Dublin.)

1953 (9 Feb.). "*An Tostal*" (*Ireland at Home*) *Festival.* *W* **22** (*sideways*). *P* 14 × 15.
154 **40** 2½d. emerald-green .. 30 35
155 „ 1s. 4d. blue .. .. 4·50 4·00

41. Robert Emmet.

42. Madonna and Child (Della Robbia).

1953 (21 Sept.). 150*th Anniv. of Death of Emmet* (*patriot*). *W* **22.** *P* 13.
156 **41** 3d. deep bluish green .. 50 50
157 „ 1s. 3d. carmine .. .. 6·00 5·00

1954 (24 May). *Marian Year.* *W* **22.** *P* 15.
158 **42** 3d. blue 65 15
159 „ 5d. myrtle-green .. .. 3·50 4·00

43. Cardinal Newman (first Rector).

44. Statue of Commodore Barry.

(Des. L. Whelan. Typo. Govt. Printing Works, Dublin.)

1954 (19 July). *Centenary of Founding of Catholic University of Ireland.* *W* **22.** *P* 15 × 14.
160 **43** 2d. bright purple 60 30
161 „ 1s. 3d. blue .. .. 4·50 3·50

1956 (16 Sept.). *Barry Commemoration.* *W* **22.** *P* 15.
162 **44** 3d. slate-lilac 20 20
163 „ 1s. 3d. deep blue .. .. 4·00 2·50

45. John Redmond.

46. Thomas O'Crohan.

1957 (11 June). *Birth Centenary of John Redmond* (*politician*). *W* **22.** *P* 14 × 15.
164 **45** 3d. deep blue 20 25
165 „ 1s. 3d. brown-purple .. 3·75 3·50

1957 (1 July). *Birth Centenary of Thomas O'Crohan* (*author*). *W* **22.** *P* 14 × 15.
166 **46** 2d. maroon 65 20
167 „ 5d. violet .. .. .. 3·00 2·50

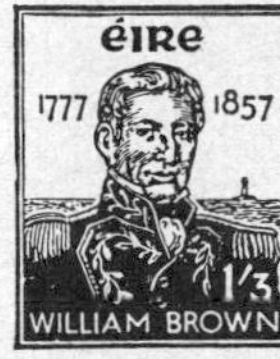

47. Admiral Brown.

48. Father Wadding (painting by Ribera).

(Des. S. O'Sullivan. Typo. Govt. Printing Works, Dublin.)

1957 (23 Sept.). *Death Centenary of Admiral William Brown.* *W* **22.** *P* 15 × 14.
168 **47** 3d. blue 40 40
169 „ 1s. 3d. carmine .. .. 6·00 6·00

1957 (25 Nov.). 300*th Anniv. of Death of Father Luke Wadding* (*theologian*). *W* **22.** *P* 15.
170 **48** 3d. deep blue 30 25
171 „ 1s. 3d. lake .. .. 4·00 3·50

49. Tom Clarke.

50. Mother Mary Aikenhead.

1958 (28 July). *Birth Centenary of Thomas J.* ("*Tom*") *Clarke* (*patriot*). *W* **22.** *P* 15.
172 **49** 3d. deep green 20 20
173 „ 1s. 3d. red-brown .. .. 3·50 3·25

(Recess. Imprimerie Belge de Securité, Brussels, subsidiary of Waterlow & Sons.)

1958 (20 Oct.). *Death Centenary of Mother Mary Aikenhead* (*foundress of Irish Sisters of Charity*). *W* **22.** *P* 15 × 14.
174 **50** 3d. Prussian blue 40 25
175 „ 1s. 3d. rose-carmine .. 4·00 3·50

(Typo. Govt. Printing Works, Dublin.)

1958 (29 Dec.). 21*st Anniv. of the Irish Constitution.* *W* **22.** *P* 15 × 14.
176 **19** 3d. brown 25 20
177 „ 5d. emerald-green .. 2·00 2·25

51. Arthur Guinness.

1959 (20 July). *Bicentenary of Guinness Brewery. W* **22.** *P* 15.
178 **51** 3d. brown-purple 30 25
179 ,, 1s. 3d. blue .. .. 3·50 3·75

52. "The Flight of the Holy Family".

(Des. K. Uhlemann.)

1960 (20 June). *World Refugee Year. W* **22.** *P* 15.
180 **52** 3d. purple 10 8
181 ,, 1s. 3d. sepia .. .. 1·10 1·25

53. Conference Emblem.

(Des. P. Rahikainen.)

1960 (19 Sept.). *Europa. W* **22.** *P* 15.
182 **53** 6d. light brown .. .. 1·25 1·50
183 ,, 1s. 3d. violet .. .. 4·50 4·50

54. Dublin Airport, De Havilland "Dragon" and Boeing "720" jet aircraft.

(Des. J. Flanagan and D. R. Lowther.)

1961 (26 June). *25th Anniv. of Aer Lingus. W* **22.** *P* 15.
184 **54** 6d. blue 75 75
185 ,, 1s. 3d. green .. .. .. 1·25 1·25

55. St. Patrick.

(Recess. B.W.)

1961 (25 Sept.). *Fifteenth Death Centenary of St. Patrick. W* **22.** *P* 14½.
186 **55** 3d. blue 25 15
187 ,, 8d. purple .. .. .. 80 1·00
188 ,, 1s. 3d. green .. .. .. 90 1·10

56. J. O'Donovan and E. O'Curry.

(Recess. Bradbury, Wilkinson.)

1962 (26 Mar.). *Death Centenaries of O'Donovan and O'Curry (scholars). W* **22.** *P* 15.
189 **53** 3d. carmine 25 20
190 ,, 1s. 3d. purple .. .. 1·10 1·25

57. Europa "Tree".

(Des. Lex Weyer.)

1962 (17 Sept.). *Europa. W* **22.** *P* 15.
191 **57** 6d. carmine-red 30 30
192 ,, 1s. 3d. turquoise 60 65

58. Campaign Emblem.

(Des. K. Uhlemann.)

1963 (21 Mar.). *Freedom from Hunger. W* **22.** *P* 15.
193 **58** 4d. deep violet 12 12
194 ,, 1s. 3d. scarlet 65 75

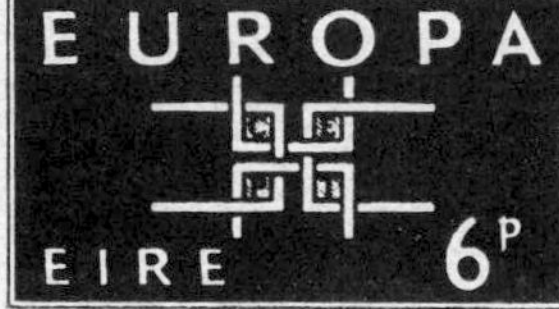

59. "Co-operation".

(Des. A. Holm.)

1963 (16 Sept.). *Europa. W* **22.** *P* 15.
195 **59** 6d. carmine 50 40
196 ,, 1s. 3d. blue .. .. 1·40 1·50

60. Centenary Emblem.

(Des. P. Wildbur. Photo. Harrison & Sons.)

1963 (2 Dec.). *Centenary of Red Cross. W* **22.** *P* 14½ × 14.
197 **60** 4d. red and grey 10 5
198 ,, 1s. 3d. red, grey & lt. emer. 45 45

61. Wolfe Tone.

(Des. P. Wildbur.)

1964 (13 Apr.). *Bicentenary of Birth of Wolfe Tone (revolutionary). W* **22.** *P* 15.
199 **61** 4d. black 40 20
200 ,, 1s. 3d. ultramarine .. 1·75 2·00

62. Irish Pavilion at Fair.

(Photo. Harrison & Sons.)

1964 (20 July). *New York World's Fair. W* **22.** *P* 14½ × 14.
201 **62** 5d. blue-grey, brown, violet and yellow-olive .. 40 2(
202 ,, 1s. 5d. blue-grey, brown, turq.-blue & lt. yell.-grn. 1·75 2·0(

63. Europa "Flower". **65.** W. B. Yeats (poet)

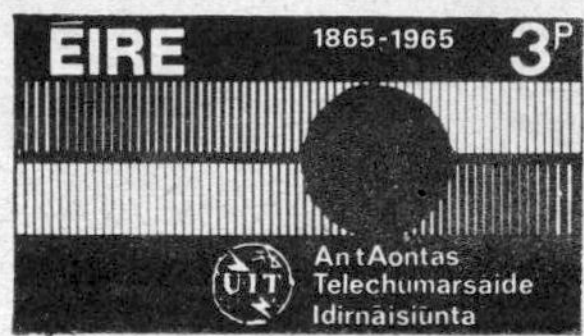

64. "Waves of Communication".

(Des. G. Bétemps. Photo. Harrison.)

1964 (14 Sept.). *Europa. W* **22** *(sideways). P* 14 × 14½.
203 **63** 8d. olive-green and blue .. 40 35
204 ,, 1s. 5d. red-brown & orange 90 8(

(Des. P. Wildbur. Photo. Harrison.)

1965 (17 May). *I.T.U. Centenary. W* **22.** *P* 14½ × 14.
205 **64** 3d. blue and green 35 25
206 ,, 8d. black and green .. 60 60

PRINTERS. Nos. 207 onwards were photogravure-printed by the Stamping Branch of the Revenue Commissioners, Dublin *unless otherwise stated.*

(Des. R. Kyne, from drawing by S. O'Sullivan.)

1965 (14 June). *Yeats' Birth Centenary. W* **22** *(sideways). P* 15.
207 **65** 5d. black, orange-brown and deep green 60 12
208 ,, 1s. 5d. blk., grey-grn. & brn. 1·25 1·50

66. I.C.Y. Emblem.

1965 (16 Aug.). *International Co-operation Year. W* **22.** *P* 15.
209 **66** 3d. ultram. and new blue 60 25
210 ,, 10d. deep brown & brown 1·50 2·00

67. Europa " Sprig ".

(Des. H. Karlsson.)

965 (27 Sept.). *Europa.* **W 22.** *P* 15.

11	**67**	8d. black and brown-red ..	35	30
12	,,	1s. 5d. purple and light turquoise-blue	90	85

68. James Connolly.

Designs as T **68**:—
69. Thomas J. Clarke.
70. P. H. Pearse.

71. " Marching to Freedom ".

72. Eamonn Ceannt.
73. Sean MacDiarmada.
74. Thomas MacDonagh.
75. Joseph Plunkett.

Des. E. Delaney (No. 216), R. Kyne, after portraits by Sean O'Sullivan (others).)

966 (12 Apr.). *50th Anniv. of Easter Rising.* **W 22.** *P* 15.

213	**68**	3d. black and greenish blue	25	20
214	**69**	3d. black and bronze-green	25	20
215	**70**	5d. black and yellow-olive	25	20
216	**71**	5d. blk., orge. & bl.-green	25	20
217	**72**	7d. black & lt. orge.-brown	55	55
218	**73**	7d. black and blue-green ..	55	55
219	**74**	1s. 5d. black and turquoise	55	50
220	**75**	1s. 5d. black & brt. green	55	50
213/20		.. .. *Set of* 8	3·00	2·50
213/20		*Set of four se-tenant pairs*	4·50	7·00

The two designs in each denomination were issued together in sheets with each pair of designs arranged in horizontal *se-tenant* rows.

76. R. Casement.

77. Europa " Ship ".

(Des. R. Kyne.)

1966 (3 Aug.). *50th Death Anniv. of Roger Casement (patriot).* **W 22** (*sideways*). *P* 15.

221	**76**	5d. black	20	8
222	,,	1s. red-brown	40	35

(Des. R. Kyne, after G. and J. Bender.)

1966 (26 Sept.). *Europa.* **W 22** (*sideways*). *P* 15.

223	**77**	7d. emerald and orange ..	25	25
224	,,	1s. 5d. emerald & light grey	45	40

78. Interior of Abbey (from lithograph).

1966 (8 Nov.). *750th Anniv. of Ballintubber Abbey.* **W 22.** *P* 15.

225	**78**	5d. red-brown	12	10
226	,,	1s. black	40	40

1966–67. *As Nos.* 116, 118 *but photo. Smaller design* (17×21 *mm.*). *Chalk-surfaced paper.* **W 22.** *P* 15.

227	**9**	3d. blue (1.8.67)	40	30
228	**6**	5d. bright violet (1.12.66) ..	45	35

No. 228 was only issued in booklets at first but was released in sheets on 1.4.68 in a slightly brighter shade. In the sheet stamps the lines of shading are more regular.

79. Cogwheels.

(Des. O. Bonnevalle.)

1967 (2 May). *Europa.* **W 22** (*sideways*). *P* 15.

229	**79**	7d. light emerald, gold and pale cream	20	20
230	,,	1s. 5d. carmine-red, gold and pale cream ..	50	40

80. Maple Leaves.

(Des. P. Hickey.)

1967 (28 Aug.). *Canadian Centennial.* **W 22.** *P* 15.

231	**80**	5d. multicoloured ..	20	15
232	,,	1s. 5d. multicoloured ..	40	40

81. Rock of Cashel (from **photo by Edwin** Smith).

1967 (25 Sept.). *International Tourist Year.* **W 22** (*inverted*). *P* 15.

233	**81**	7d. sepia	20	20
234	,,	10d. slate-blue	35	40

82. 1 c. Fenian Stamp Essay.

83. 24 c. Fenian Stamp Essay.

1967 (23 Oct.). *Centenary of Fenian Rising.* **W 22** (*sideways*). *P* 15.

235	**82**	5d. black and light green	12	8
236	**83**	1s. black and light pink ..	30	30

84. Jonathan Swift.

85. Gulliver and Lilliputians.

(Des. M. Byrne.)

1967 (30 Nov.). *300th Birth Anniv. of Jonathan Swift.* **W 22** (*sideways*). *P* 15.

237	**84**	3d. black and olive-grey ..	12	8
238	**85**	1s. 5d. blackish brown and pale blue	30	30

86. Europa " Key ".

(Des. H. Schwarzenbach and M. Biggs.)

1968 (29 Apr.). *Europa.* **W 22.** *P* 15.

239	**86**	7d. brown-red, gold & brn.	15	15
240	,,	1s. 5d. new blue, gold and brown	25	30

87. St. Mary's Cathedral, Limerick.

(Des. from photo. by J. J. Bambury. Recess. B.W.)

1968 (26 Aug.). *800th Anniv. of St. Mary's Cathedral, Limerick.* **W 22.** *P* 15.

241	**87**	5d. Prussian blue ..	12	8
242	,,	10d. yellow-green ..	25	25

88. Countess Markievicz.

1968 (23 SEPT.). *Birth Centenary of Countess Markievicz (patriot). W* **22.** *P* 15.

243 **88** 3d. black 10 8
244 ,, 1s. 5d. deep blue and blue 30 30

89. James Connolly.

1968 (23 SEPT.). *Birth Centenary of James Connolly (patriot). W* **22** *(sideways). P* 15.

245 **89** 6d. deep brown & chocolate 12 12
246 ,, 1s. blackish green, apple-green and myrtle-green 25 25

90. Stylised Dog (brooch) **91.** Stag.

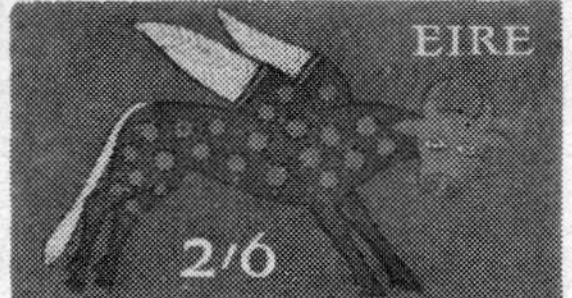

92. Winged Ox (Symbol of St. Luke).

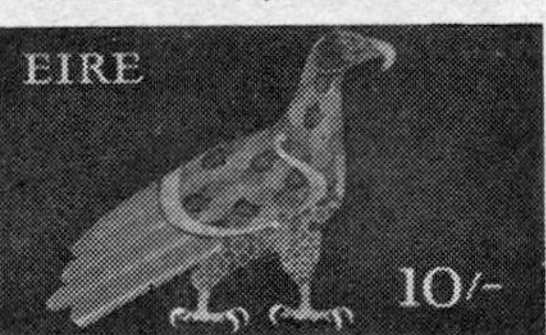

93. Eagle (Symbol of St. John The Evangelist).

(Des. H. Gerl.)

1968–70. *Pence values expressed with* " p ". *W* 22 *(sideways on T* **90/91**). *P* 15.

247 **90** ½d. red-orange (9.6.69) .. 10 12
248 ,, 1d. pale yell.-grn. (9.6.69) 5 5
a. Coil stamp. P 14×15 (8.70?) 45 80
249 ,, 2d. light ochre (14.6.68) 5 5
a. Coil stamp. P 14×15 (8.70?) 45 80
250 ,, 3d. blue (9.6.69) .. 12 5
a. Coil stamp. P 14×15 (8.70?) 45 80
251 ,, 4d. deep brn.-red (31.3.69) 12 10
252 ,, 5d. myrtle-green (31.3.69) 20 25
253 ,, 6d. bistre-brown (24.2.69) 20 12
254 **91** 7d. brown & yell. (9.6.69) 20 30
255 ,, 8d. chocolate and orange-brown (14.6.68) .. 30 45
256 ,, 9d. slate-blue and olive-green (24.2.69) 30 25
257 ,, 10d. chocolate and bluish violet (31.3.69) .. 30 35
258 ,, 1s. chocolate and red-brown (31.3.69) .. 40 25
259 **91** 1s. 9d. black and lt. turq.-blue (24.2.69) .. 55 60
260 **92** 2s. 6d. mult. (14.6.68) .. 1·00 50
261 ,, 5s. mult. (24.2.69) .. 2·50 90
262 **93** 10s. mult. (14.6.68) .. 5·00 2·00
247/62 .. .. *Set of* 16 10·00 5·50

The 1d., 2d., 3d., 5d., 9d., 1s. and 2s. 6d. exist with PVA gum as well as gum arabic. The coil stamps exist on PVA only, and the rest on gum arabic only.

See also Nos. 287/301 and 340 etc.

94. Human Rights Emblem.

1968 (4 NOV.). *Human Rights Year. W* **22** *(sideways). P* 15.

263 **94** 5d. yellow, gold and black 10 10
264 ,, 7d. yellow, gold and red .. 25 25

95. Dail Eireann Assembly.

(Des. M. Byrne.)

1969 (21 JAN.). *50th Anniv. of Dail Eireann (First National Parliament). W* **22** *(sideways). P* 15×14½.

265 **95** 6d. myrtle-green .. 8 8
266 ,, 9d. Prussian blue 25 25

96. Colonnade.

(Des. L. Gasbarra and G. Belli; adapted Myra Maguire.)

1969 (28 APR.). *Europa. W* **22.** *P* 15.

267 **96** 9d. grey, ochre & ultram. 15 15
268 ,, 1s. 9d. grey, gold & scarlet 35 35

97. Quadruple I.L.O. Emblems.

(Des. K. C. Däbczewski.)

1969 (14 JULY). *50th Anniv. of International Labour Organization. W* **22** *(sideways). P* 15.

269 **97** 6d. black and grey .. 12 10
270 ,, 9d. black and yellow .. 20 20

98. Evie Hone Window, Eton Chapel.

(Des. R. Kyne.)

1969 (1 SEPT.). *Contemporary Irish Art* (1st *issue*). *W* **22** *(sideways). P* 15×14½.

271 **98** 1s. multicoloured 30 35

See also Nos. 280, 306, 317, 329, 341, 362, 375 and 398.

99. Mahatma Gandhi.

1969 (2 OCT.). *Birth Centenary of Mahatma Gandhi. W* **22.** *P* 15.

272 **99** 6d. black and green .. 12 10
273 ,, 1s. 9d. black and yellow .. 40 40

100. Symbolic Bird in Tree.

(Des. D. Harrington.)

1970 (23 FEB.). *European Conservation Year. W* **22.** *P* 15.

274 **100** 6d. bistre and black .. 12 12
275 ,, 9d. slate-violet & black 30 25

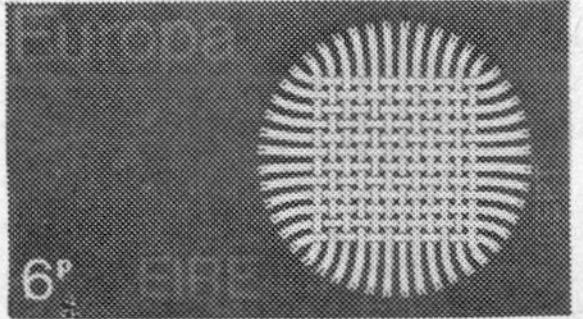

101. " Flaming Sun ".

(Des. L. le Brocquy.)

.970 (4 MAY). *Europa*. W 22. P 15.

:76	**101**	6d. bright violet and silver	12	10
:77	„	9d. brown and silver ..	20	20
:78	„	1s. 9d. deep olive-grey & silver	30	30

102. "Sailing Boats" (by Peter Monamy).

(Des. P. Wildbur and P. Scott.)

.970 (13 JULY). *250th Anniv. of Royal Cork Yacht Club*. W 22. P 15.

:79	**102**	4d. multicoloured ..	12	12

103. "Madonna of Eire" (Mainie Jellett).

104. Thomas MacCurtain.

105. Terence MacSwiney.

.970 (1 SEPT.). *Contemporary Irish Art (2nd issue)*. W 22 (*sideways*). P 15.

:80	**103**	1s. multicoloured ..	30	25

(Des. P. Wildbur.)

.970 (26 OCT.). *50th Death Anniversaries of Irish Patriots*. W 22 (*sideways*). P 15.

:81	**104**	9d. black, bluish violet & greyish black ..	35	35
:82	**105**	9d. black, bluish violet & greyish black ..	35	35
:83	**104**	2s. 9d. black, new blue and greyish black ..	1·00	1·00
:84	**105**	2s. 9d. black, new blue and greyish black ..	1·00	1·00
		Set of two se-tenant pairs ..	3·00	3·50

Nos. 281/2 and 283/4 were printed in *se-tenant* pairs throughout the sheet.

106. Kevin Barry.

(Des. P. Wildbur.)

.970 (2 NOV.). *50th Death Anniv. of Kevin Barry (patriot)*. W 22 (*inverted*). P 15.

85	**106**	6d. olive-green	15	12
86	„	1s. 2d. Royal blue ..	30	30

106a. Stylized Dog (Brooch).

Two types of 10 p.:
I. Outline and markings of the ox in lilac.
II. Outline and markings in brown.

1971 (15 FEB.)-**75**. *Decimal Currency. Designs as Nos. 247/62 but with "p" omitted as in T* **106a**. W 22 (*sideways on 10, 12, 20 and 50 p.*). P 15.

287	**106a**	½ p. bright green ..	5	5
		a. Wmk. sideways ..	12	12
288	„	1 p. blue	25	12
		a. Coil stamp. P 14×14½	12	12
		b. Coil strip. 288a *se-tenant* with 289a and 291a	40	45
		c. Wmk. sideways ..	12	12
		d. Booklet pane. No. 288c ×5 plus one *se-tenant* label (11.3.74) ..	70	
289	„	1½ p. lake-brown ..	12	12
		a. Coil stamp. P 14×14½	12	12
		b. Coil strip. 289a *se-tenant* with 291a, 294a and 290a (2.72) ..	60	
		c. Coil strip (289a×2 *se-tenant* with 290a and 295b) (29.1.74) ..	60	
290	„	2 p. myrtle-green ..	12	8
		a. Coil stamp. P 14×14½ (2.72)	12	12
		b. Wmk sideways (27.1.75)	12	12
		c. Booklet pane. No. 290b ×5 plus one *se-tenant* label (27.1.75) ..	70	
291	„	2½ p. sepia	12	8
		a. Coil stamp. P 14×14½	12	12
		b. Wmk. sideways ..	12	12
292	„	3 p. cinnamon ..	12	12
293	„	3½ p. orange-brown ..	12	25
294	„	4 p. pale bluish violet	12	12
		a. Coil stamp. P 14×14½ (2.72)	12	12
295	**91**	5 p. brown. & yell.-olive	40	20
295a	**106a**	5 p. bright yellow-green (29.1.74) ..	45	20
		b. Coil stamp. P 14×14½	15	20
		c. Wmk. sideways (11.3.74)	20	20
		d. Booklet pane. No. 295c×5 plus one *se-tenant* label (11.3.74)	1·50	
296	**91**	6 p. blackish brn. & slate	85	25
296a	„	7 p. indigo & olive-green (29.1.74)	2·50	30
297	„	7½ p. choc. & reddish lilac	25	20
298	„	9 p. black & turq.-grn.	40	25
299	**92**	10 p. multicoloured (I) ..	45	25
299a	„	10 p. multicoloured (II)	25	25
299b	„	12 p. multicoloured (29.1.74)	30	30
300	„	20 p. multicoloured ..	1·25	45
301	**93**	50 p. multicoloured ..	2·50	1·10
287/301		.. .. *Set of* 18	9·50	4·00

The ½, 1, 2, 2½ p. and 5 p. (No. 295a) with watermark sideways all come from stamp booklets and exist with one or two sides imperforate.

See also Nos. 340 etc.

107. "Europa Chain".

(Des. H. Haflidason; adapted P. Wildbur.)

1971 (3 MAY). *Europa*. W 22 (*sideways*). P 15.

302	**107**	4 p. sepia and olive-yellow	12	15
303	„	6 p. black and new blue ..	25	25

108. J. M. Synge.

109. "An Island Man" (Jack B. Yeats).

(Des. R. Kyne from a portrait by Jack B. Yeats.)

1971 (19 JULY). *Birth Centenary of J. M. Synge (playwright)*. W 22. P 15.

304	**108**	4 p. multicoloured ..	12	12
305	„	10 p. multicoloured ..	40	40

(Des. P. Wildbur.)

1971 (30 AUG.). *Contemporary Irish Art (3rd issue). Birth Centenary of J. B. Yeats (artist)*. W 22. P 15.

306	**109**	6 p. multicoloured ..	30	30

110. Racial Harmony Symbol.

111. "Madonna and Child" (statue by J. Hughes).

(Des. P. Wildbur. Litho. Harrison.)

1971 (18 OCT.). *Racial Equality Year*. *No Wmk.* P 14×14½.

307	**110**	4 p. red	12	12
308	„	10 p. black	40	40

(Des. R. Kyne.)

1971 (15 NOV.). *Christmas*. W 22. P 15.

309	**111**	2½ p. black, gold and deep bluish green ..	12	12
310	„	6 p. blk., gold & ultram.	40	40

112. Heart.

(Des. L. le Brocquy.)

1972 (7 APR.). *World Health Day*. W 22 (*sideways*). P 15.

311	**112**	2½p. gold and brown ..	25	12
312	„	12p. silver and grey ..	50	45

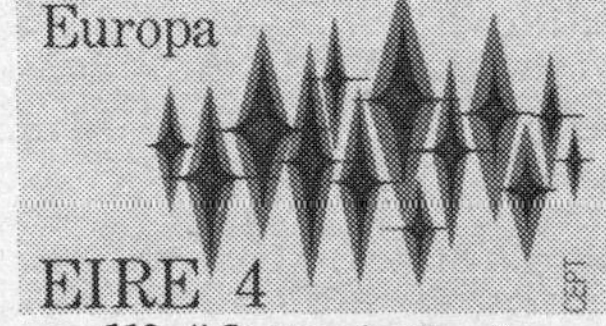

113. "Communications".

(Des. P. Huovinen and P. Wildbur.)

1972 (1 May). *Europa. W* **22** *(sideways). P* 15.
313 **113** 4p. orange, black and silver 25 12
314 ,, 6p. blue, black and silver 50 45

114. Dove and Moon. **116.** " Horseman " (Carved Slab).

115. " Black Lake " (Gerard Dillon).

(Des. P. Scott.)

1972 (1 June). *The Patriot Dead,* 1922–23. *W* **22.** *P* 15.
315 **114** 4p. grey-blue, light orge., and deep blue .. 15 15
316 ,, 6p. deep yellow-green, lemon and deep dull green 30 30

(Des. P. Wildbur.)

1972 (10 July). *Contemporary Irish Art* (4th *issue*). *W* **22** *(sideways). P* 15.
317 **115** 3p. multicoloured .. 20 15

(Des. P. Scott.)

1972 (28 Aug.). *50th Anniv. of Olympic Council of Ireland. W* **22.** *P* 15.
318 **116** 3p. bright yellow, black and gold 12 8
319 ,, 6p. salmon, black and gold 30 30

WATERMARK. All issues from here onwards are on unwatermarked paper.

117. Madonna and Child (from Book of Kells). **118.** 2d. Stamp of 1922.

(Des. P. Scott.)

1972 (16 Oct.). *Christmas. P* 15.
320 **117** $2\frac{1}{2}$p. multicoloured *(shades)* 12 8
321 ,, 4p. multicoloured .. 30 25
322 ,, 12p. multicoloured .. 50 50

(Des. Stamping Branch of the Revenue Commissioners, Dublin.)

1972 (6 Dec.). *50th Anniv. of the First Irish Postage Stamp. P* 15.
323 **118** 6p. light grey and grey-green 25 25
MS324 72×104 mm. No. 323×4 .. 2·00 2·00

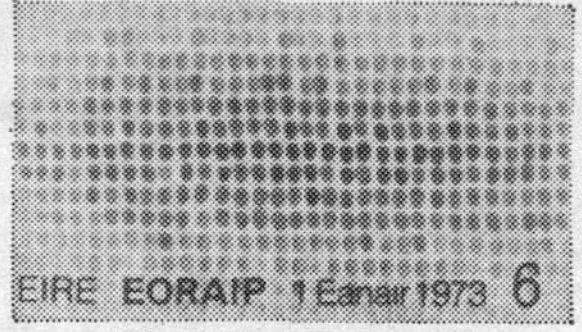

119. Celtic Head Motif.

(Des. L. le Brocquy.)

1973 (1 Jan.). *Entry into European Communities. P* 15.
325 **119** 6p. multicoloured.. .. 30 25
326 ,, 12p. multicoloured.. .. 45 45

120. Europa " Posthorn ".

(Des. Leif Friman; adapted R. Kyne.)

1973 (30 Apr.). *Europa. P* 15.
327 **120** 4p. bright blue 12 12
328 ,, 6p. black 30 30

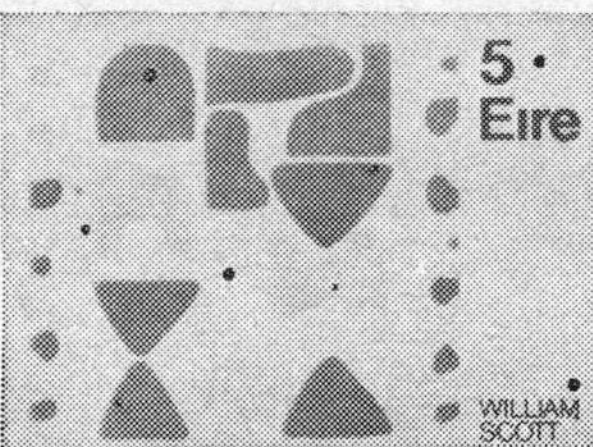

121. " Berlin Blues I " (W. Scott).

(Adapted by R. Scott.)

1973 (9 Aug.). *Contemporary Irish Art* (5th *issue*). *P* 15×$14\frac{1}{2}$.
329 **121** 5p. ultramarine and grey-black 25 25

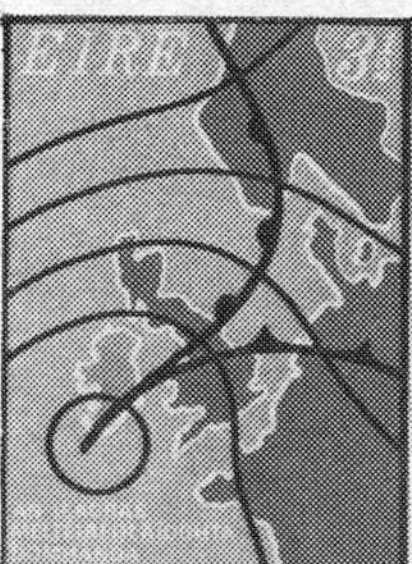

122. Weather Map.

(Des. R. Ballagh.)

1973 (4 Sept.). *I.M.O./W.M.O. Centenary. P* $14\frac{1}{2}$×15.
330 **122** $3\frac{1}{2}$p. multicoloured .. 12 12
331 ,, 12p. multicoloured .. 50 50

123. Tractor ploughing.

(Des. P. Scott.)

1973 (5 Oct.). *World Ploughing Championship. Wellington Bridge. P* 15×$14\frac{1}{2}$.
332 **123** 5p. multicoloured .. 15 1
333 ,, 7p. multicoloured .. 20 2

124. " Flight into Egypt " (Jan de Cock).

(Des. D. Kiely.)

1973 (1 Nov.). *Christmas. P* 15.
334 **124** $3\frac{1}{2}$p. multicoloured .. 12 1
335 ,, 12p. multicoloured .. 40 4

125. Daunt Island Lightship and Ballycotton Lifeboat, 1936.

(Des. M. Byrne from painting by B. Gribble.)

1974 (28 Mar.). *150th Anniv. of Royal National Lifeboat Institution. P* 15×$14\frac{1}{2}$.
336 **125** 5p. multicoloured .. 15 1

126. "Edmund Burke" (Statue by J. H. Foley).

(Des. P. Wildbur.)

1974 (29 Apr.). *Europa. P* $14\frac{1}{2}$×15.
337 **126** 5p. black & pale vio.-bl. 15 1
338 ,, 7p. black and light emer. 20 2

974-76. *As Nos. 287 etc., but no wmk.* P 15.

40	**106a**	1p. blue (2.75) ..	5	5
41	,,	2 p. myrtle-green (4.76)	5	5
42	,,	3p. cinnamon (2.75) ..	8	10
43	,,	3½p. orange-brn. (10.74)	12	12
44	,,	5p. brt. yell.-grn. (8.74)	12	12
45	**91**	6p. blackish brown and slate (10.74) ..	20	20
46	**106a**	6p. slate (17.6.75) ..	20	15
47	**91**	7p. indigo and olive-green (9.74) ..	20	15
48	**106a**	7p. deep yellow-green (17.6.75)	12	15
49	**91**	8p. deep brown & deep orge.-brn. (17.6.75)	20	20
50	**106a**	8 p. chestnut (14.7.76)	15	15
51	**91**	9 p. black and turq.-green (12.74) ..	25	25
52	**106a**	9 p. grnsh. slte. (14.7.76)	15	20
53	**92**	10 p. mult. (II) (12.74) ..	25	20
54	**91**	10 p. black and violet-blue (14.7.76) ..	20	20
55	,,	11 p. black and rose-carmine (14.7.76) ..	20	25
56	**92**	15 p. multicoloured (6.74)	40	30
57	,,	20p. multicoloured (6.74)	50	45
58	**93**	50p. multicoloured (12.74)	1·25	95
59	,,	£1 mult. (17.6.75)	2·25	2·00
40/59		.. .. *Set of* 20	4·75	4·25

27. "Oliver Goldsmith" (Statue by J. H. Foley).

(Des. P. Wildbur.)

974 (24 June). *Death Bicentenary of Oliver Goldsmith (writer).* P 14½×15.

60	**127**	3½p. black & olive-yellow	12	12
61	,,	12p. black and bright yellowish-green ..	35	30

128. "Kitchen Table" (Norah McGuiness).

Design adapted by Norah McGuiness. Photo. Harrison.)

974 (19 Aug.). *Contemporary Irish Art (6th issue).* P 14×14½.

62	**128**	5p. multicoloured ..	15	15

129. Rugby Players.

(Design adapted from Irish Press photograph. Eng. C. Slania. Recess (3½p.) or recess and photo. (12p.). Harrison.)

1974 (9 Sept.). *Centenary of Irish Rugby Football Union.* P 14½×14.

363	**129**	3½p. greenish black (*shades*)	12	12
364	,,	12p. multicoloured ..	30	35

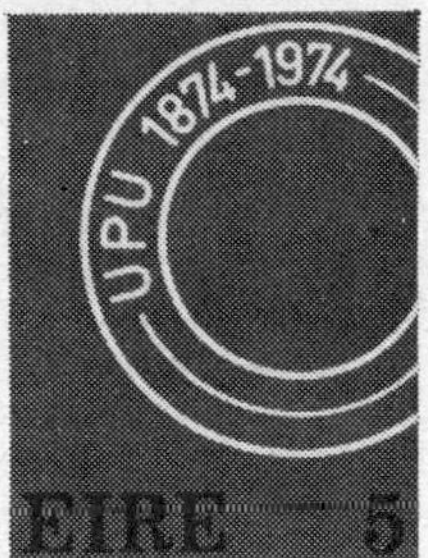

130. U.P.U. "Postmark".

(Des. R. Ballagh.)

1974 (9 Oct.). *Centenary of Universal Postal Union.* P 14½×15.

365	**130**	5p. light yellowish-green and black	12	15
366	,,	7p. lt. ultram. and black	20	20

131. "Madonna and Child" (Bellini).

(Des. P. Wilbur.)

1974 (14 Nov.). *Christmas.* P 14½×15.

367	**131**	5p. multicoloured ..	10	12
368	,,	15p. multicoloured ..	35	40

132. " Peace ".

(Des. Alexandra Wejchert.)

1975 (24 Mar.). *International Women's Year.* P 14½×15.

369	**132**	8p. bright reddish purple and ultramarine ..	25	25
370	,,	15p. ultram. & brt. grn.	40	40

133. " Castletown Hunt " (R. Healy).

(Des. R. Kyne.)

1975 (28 Apr.). *Europa.* P 15×14½.

371	**133**	7p. grey-black	20	20
372	,,	9p. dull blue-green ..	25	25

134. Putting.

(Des. from photographs by J. McManus.)

1975 (26 June). *Ninth European Amateur Golf Team Championship, Killarney.* P 15×14½.

373	**134**	6p. multicoloured (*shades*)	15	15
374	–	9p. multicoloured (*shades*)	25	25

The 9p. is similar to T **134** but shows a different view of the putting green.

135. " Bird of Prey " (sculpture by Oisin Kelly).

(Design adapted by the artist.)

1975 (28 June). *Contemporary Irish Art (7th issue).* P 15×14½.

375	**135**	15p. yellow-brown ..	40	40

136. Nano Nagle (founder) and Waifs.

(Des. Kilkenny Design Workshops.)

1975 (1 Sept.). *Bicentenary of Presentation Order of Nuns.* P 14½×15.

376	**136**	5p. black and pale blue ..	12	12
377	,,	7p. black and light stone	20	20

137. Tower of St. Anne's Church, Shandon.

(Des. P. Scott.)

1975 (6 Oct.). *European Architectural Heritage Year. T* **137** *and similar vert. design. P* 12½.

378	**137**	5p. blackish brown ..	12	12
379	,,	6p. multicoloured ..	15	15
380	–	7p. steel-blue	20	20
381	–	9p. multicoloured ..	25	25

Design:—Nos. 380/1, Interior of Holycross Abbey, Co. Tipperary.

138. St. Oliver Plunkett (commemorative medal by Imogen Stuart).

139. " Madonna and Child " (Fra Filippo Lippi).

(Design adapted by the artist. Recess. Harrison.)

1975 (13 Oct.). *Canonisation of Oliver Plunkett. P* 14×14½.

382	**138**	7p. black	20	20
383	,,	15p. chestnut	40	40

(Des. P. Wildbur.)

1975 (13 Nov.). *Christmas. P* 15.

384	**139**	5p. multicoloured ..	12	12
385	,,	7p. multicoloured ..	20	20
386	,,	10p. multicoloured ..	25	25

140. James Larkin (from a drawing by Sean O'Sullivan).

(Des. P. Wilbur.)

1976 (21 Jan.). *Birth Centenary of James Larkin (Trade Union leader). P* 14½×15.

387	**140**	7p. deep bluish green & pale grey	20	20
388	,,	11p. sepia and yell.-ochre	25	25

141. Alexander Graham Bell.

(Des R. Ballagh.)

1976 (10 Mar.). *Telephone Centenary. P* 14½×15.

389	**141**	9p. multicoloured ..	20	20
390	,,	15p. multicoloured ..	30	35

142. 1847 Benjamin Franklin Essay.

(Des. L. le Brocquy, adapted P. Wildbur (7p., 8p.); P. Wildbur (others). Litho. Irish Security Printing Ltd.)

1976 (17 May). *Bicentenary of American Revolution. T* **142** *and similar horiz. designs. P* 14½×14.

391	7p. ultram., lt. red and silver	15	15
	a. Silver (inscr.) omitted ..	†	—
392	8p. ultram., lt. red and silver	15	20
393	9p. vio.-bl., orange, and silver	20	20
394	15p. light rose-red, grey-bl. and silver	30	35
	a. Silver (face-value and inscr.) omitted		
MS395	95×75 mm. Nos. 391/4	80	
	a. Silver omitted		

Designs:—7p. Thirteen stars; 8p. Fifty stars; 9 and 15p. Type **142**.

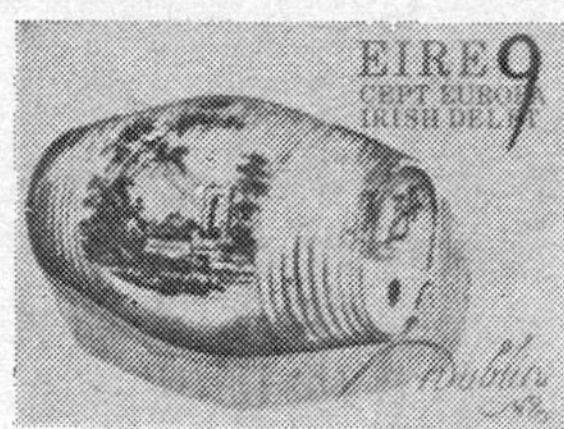

143. Spirit Barrel.

(Des. P. Hickey.)

1976 (1 July). *Europa. Irish Delft. T* **143** *and similar horiz. design. Multicoloured. P* 15×14.

396	9p. Type **143**	20	20
397	11p. Dish	25	25

144. "The Lobster Pots, West of Ireland" (Pa Henry).

(Des. R. McGrath.)

1976 (30 Aug.). *Contemporary Irish Art* (8 *issue*). *P* 15.

398	**144**	15p. multicoloured ..	30	3

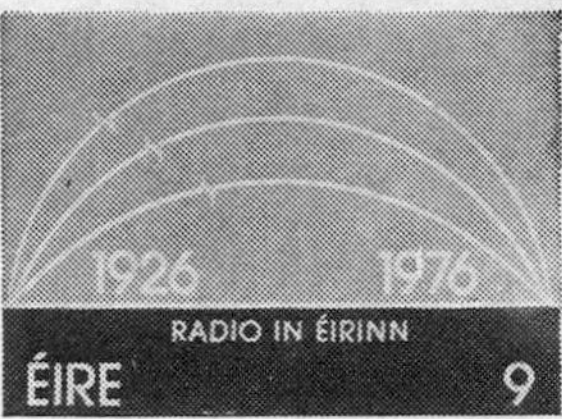

145. Radio Waves.

(Des. G. Shepherd and A. O'Donnell. Lith De La Rue Smurfit Ltd.)

1976 (5 Oct.). *50th Anniv. of Irish Broadcastir Service. T* **145** *and similar vert. desig P* 14½×14 (9*p*.) *or* 14×14½ (11*p*.).

399	9p. light new blue and bottle-green	20	2
400	11p. agate, orange-red and light new blue	25	2

Design:—11p. Transmitter, radio waves ar globe.

146. " The Nativity " (Lorenzo Monaco).

(Des. R. McGrath.)

1976 (11 Nov.). *Christmas. P* 15×14½.

401	**146**	7p. multicoloured ..	15	1
402	,,	9p. multicoloured ..	20	2
403	,,	15p. multicoloured ..	30	3

Stanley Gibbons the complete philatelists

Gibbons stay-at-home services
The collector can make use of virtually all the Stanley Gibbons facilities without ever coming to London! Apart from the catalogues, albums and accessories which he can get from us by mail-order, the stay-at-home collector can use Stanley Gibbons Approval and New Issue services to build up his collection.

The Approvals Service offers the collector the opportunity to browse at leisure through a specially chosen selection of Great Britain or British Commonwealth stamps in the quiet of his own home with his album close at hand.

The New Issues Service provides the collector with a sure and comprehensive service designed to keep his stamp collection right up-to-date.

We also buy stamps
Our buyers search the world for stamps to maintain our stocks against the enormous demands of collectors. Every day individuals walk in casually to offer us their stamps, and collections are posted to us for sale, or for valuation for insurance or probate. If we do buy, immediate cash payment is given no matter what the figure. Please write in the first instance, giving general particulars, before sending stamps or asking our valuer to make a visit.

Rare stamps
We retain a large 'bank' of rare and elusive philatelic material at Romano House. Serious collectors have their wants recorded on our Specialist Register, or send us lists of their 'rare stamp' wants. Investment advice and assistance in building up valuable collections is given here, and collectors appreciate the luxurious, quiet atmosphere of the viewing rooms.

Auctions
The auction is the culmination of many weeks of expert cataloguing and organisation, and of the dissemination well in advance to enquirers throughout the world of fine, illustrated catalogues. Thanks to these catalogues, much of the bidding is by post, but the auction itself is always an occasion of excitement for collectors present.

'The Shop' itself
If you do come to London, 'the Shop' at 391 Strand is the Philatelist's Mecca, with the latest and most complete range of albums, catalogues and accessories; the sales counters for new issues and for a wide selection of stamps of most countries. There's always an interesting window display on some topical aspect of philately. And there's always a welcome for stamp collectors, new and old.

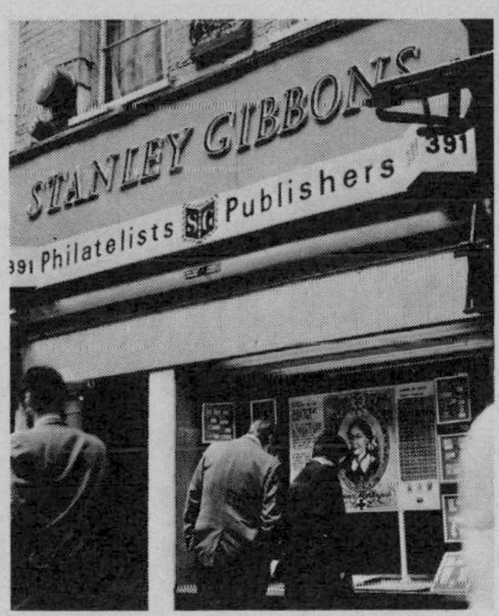

Stamp Publications
Stanley Gibbons Stamp Catalogues (the first was in 1865) are the world's most authoritative and best-known reference guides. They are supported by *Stamp Monthly* the popular Gibbons magazine with its record circulation, fully detailed Catalogue Supplement, regular Stamp Market, Great Britain and Through the Magnifying Glass features and articles on all stamp topics. And there are Gibbons albums and accessories which cater for all the needs of the enthusiast no matter how long he collects. Some of these are shown on the following pages.

Want to know more?
This is only an introduction to the complete service offered by Stanley Gibbons to the collector. If you'd like detailed information about any of the services mentioned here just fill in the coupon and send it off today.

One-Country and G.B. albums

The Popular albums of the Stanley Gibbons One-Country range contain fully illustrated pages, finely printed in black on pure white cartridge size 276 x 222 mm. ($10\frac{7}{8}$ x $8\frac{3}{4}$ in.).
Each album is loose-leaf enabling easy insertion of the supplements which are normally issued annually.

3140 The G.B. One-Country Album is ideal for a straightforward collection and is complete from 1840 to the end of 1976. The G.B. is bound in a luxury padded four-ring maroon P.V.C. binder with Great Britain blocked in gold on the spine. **£6·42**

3264 The Channel Islands One-Country Album is housed in an elegant gold blocked padded 22-ring maroon P.V.C. binder. The pages have spaces for all Jersey and Guernsey issues from 1941 to the end of 1976. **£6·36**

3276 The Isle of Man One-Country Album is designed to house the 1958–1971 Regionals and the issues of the Independent Postal Administration from 1973 to the end of 1976. The Coat of Arms of the Isle of Man is gold blocked on the front of the padded 22-ring maroon P.V.C. binder. **£4·56**

313 Australia One-Country Album £6·19
316 Canada One-Country Album £6·55
3114 New Zealand One-Country Album £6·55

These One-Country Albums are ideal for forming a straightforward and attractive collection. Each album is bound in a luxury padded four-ring maroon P.V.C. binder with the respective national emblem gold blocked on the front cover. Each complete to the end of 1976.

The Windsor G.B. Album is a printed loose-leaf album for the postage, postage due and official stamps of Great Britain from 1840 to the end of 1976. There is also a section for the Channel Islands excluding the independent issues. Each page is printed on quality cartridge paper, size 283 x 248 mm. ($11\frac{1}{8}$ x $9\frac{3}{4}$ in.), and has spaces for stamps on one side only, the other, showing a detailed illustrated catalogue. Includes separate spaces for the plate numbers of the Victorian issues.

This album is supplied complete in a spring-back binder in a choice of two styles.
323 Popular Edition in a choice of red or green. **£7·02**
325 De luxe Presentation Edition in black-padded binder with slip-in box. **£10·80**
The 'Windsor' keeps up-to-date by means of supplements which are normally issued annually.

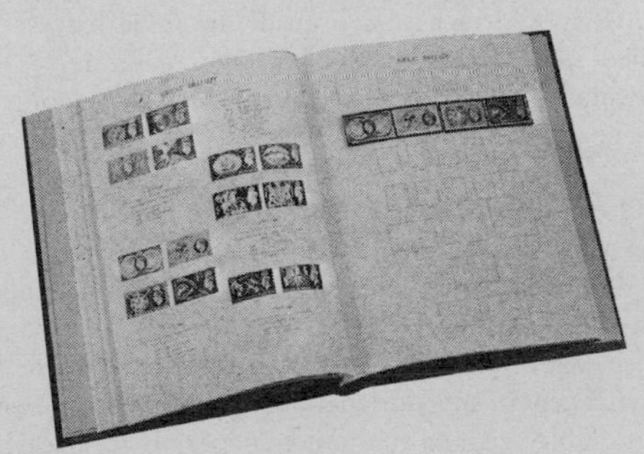

Stanley Gibbons Publications the right way for stamp collectors

Blank Loose-leaf Albums

Our Blank Loose-Leaf Album range provides a choice of spring-back, ring-fitting or peg-fitting albums. Extra binders and packets of extra leaves for loose-leaf albums are available.

386 The Senator Standard spring-back album is bound in a choice of three colours, red, green or black, and is complete with 100 white leaves finely printed in feint grey quadrille, size 282 x 251 mm. ($11\frac{1}{8}$ x $9\frac{7}{8}$ in.). **£5·65**

3834 The Devon has a strong, elegant, large capacity peg-fitting binder and contains 250 fine quality white cartridge quadrille-ruled leaves, size 264 x 248 mm. ($10\frac{3}{8}$ x $9\frac{3}{4}$ in.). Binder available in a choice of four colours – maroon, green, black or blue. **£7·56**

The Exeter has a handsome, fine quality, peg-fitting binder in a choice of red, blue or green. The album includes 40 double linen-hinged leaves, size 264 x 248 mm. ($10\frac{3}{8}$ x $9\frac{3}{4}$ in.), of fine white cartridge, ruled in feint grey quadrille with centre and side markings to aid arrangement, available with or without transparent interleaving attached.

3830 Album complete with 40 double linen-hinged leaves. **£9·42**

3832 Album complete with 40 double linen-hinged transparent faced leaves. **£9·99**

331 The Tower is a modern style spring-back album. The binder is available in a choice of red, green or black, is blocked in gold and contains 100 feint grey quadrille-ruled leaves of white cartridge, size 282 x 251 mm. ($11\frac{1}{8}$ x $9\frac{7}{8}$ in.). **£5·49**

The Ring 22 is Gibbons quality loose-leaf multi-ring fitting album. The padded P.V.C. binder, available in a choice of three colours, olive-green, maroon or dark blue, contains 50 feint quadrille-ruled leaves of black or white cartridge, size 276 x 216 mm. ($10\frac{7}{8}$ x $8\frac{1}{2}$ in.), available with or without transparent inter-leaving attached. The 22-ring proved patent fitting opens at a touch and enables leaves to lie absolutely flat.

3842 Album complete with 50 white transparent faced leaves. **£5·93**

3845 Album complete with 50 black transparent faced leaves. **£5·93**

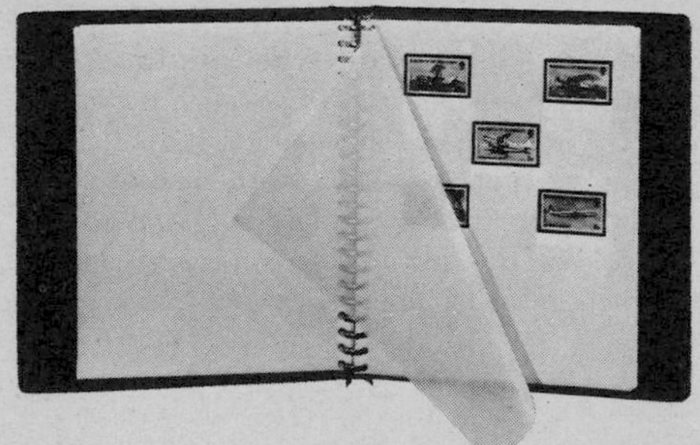

Stanley Gibbons Publications

Cover Albums and Stockbooks

The Cover Albums in the Stanley Gibbons range are especially for the protection and display of first day covers and entires. Extra binders and extra pockets are available.

354 **The Pioneer Cover Album** has a quick release, spring-arch fitting in a strong P.V.C. binder. Bound in red, green or black, the Pioneer contains 50 clear polythene pockets, size 127 x 229 mm. (5 x 9 in.), which will each hold two covers. **£2·87**

356 **The Thames Cover Album** consists of a black P.V.C. ring-fitting binder, gold-blocked on the spine, holding 20 double – and 5 single-sided polythene pockets, size 267 x 229 mm. ($10\frac{1}{2}$ x 9 in.), which will hold over 90 covers. **£3·62**

3515 **The Classic One Luxury Cover Album** has an attractive rich deep red P.V.C. padded binder blocked in gold and contains 20 semi-rigid crystal clear pockets, size 130 x 227 mm. ($5\frac{1}{8}$ x $8\frac{15}{16}$ in.), and these are held in a quick release, spring-arch fitting incorporating a special locking device. Each pocket will hold two covers. **£3·08**

3517 **The Classic Two Luxury Cover Album** is exactly the same quality as above but contains 20 semi-rigid crystal clear pockets, size 140 x 281 mm. ($5\frac{1}{2}$ x $11\frac{1}{16}$ in.). This larger version has been specially designed to hold those long awkward covers and entires. Each pocket will hold two covers. **£3·92**

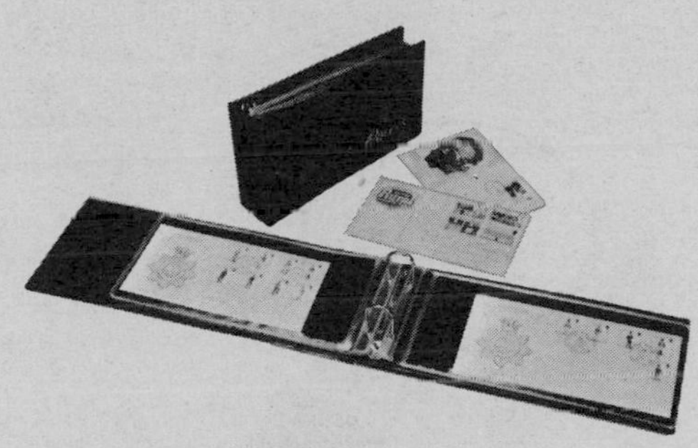

Stockbooks

The seven fastbound stockbooks in the Stanley Gibbons range provide a selection of varying capacities and styles of binding. Each has white leaves with glassine strips and is interleaved with transparent paper.

Item No.	Size mm.	Size in.	No. of Pages	No. of Strips	Cover Description	Price
2625	190 x 133	$7\frac{1}{2}$ x $5\frac{1}{4}$	8	48	Bright four-colour stamp design	95p
2650	298 x 222	$11\frac{3}{4}$ x $8\frac{3}{4}$	8	80		£1·45
2649	197 x 140	$7\frac{3}{4}$ x $5\frac{1}{2}$	12	72	Attractive single-colour binding, gold blocked	£1·65
2651	229 x 178	9 x 7	16	112		£2·30
2652	305 x 229	12 x 9	16	160		£3·40
2653	305 x 229	12 x 9	32	320		£5·60
2631	229 x 178	9 x 7	32	224		£3·85

the right way for stamp collectors

Accessories

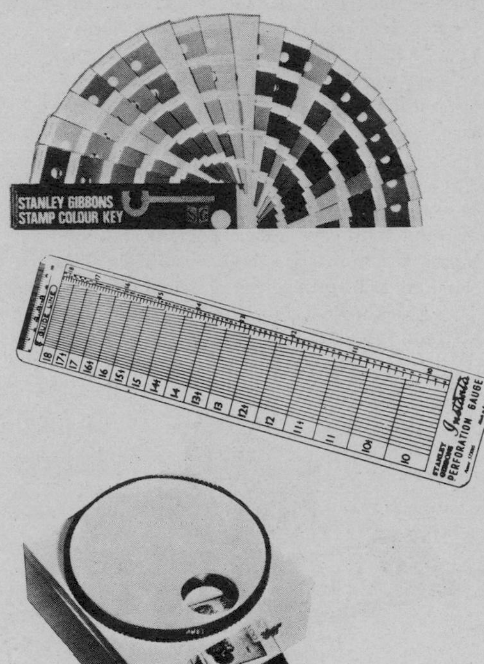

2570 The Philatector
The Philatector is a scientifically designed instrument which will assist in the detection of water marks on postage stamps, without the use of dyes, sprays, benzine or other fluids. Stamps are held in slides and illuminated through colour filters to help you with identification. No risk of damage to stamps. No fluids. No smell. Batteries included. **£6·95**

2534 The Instanta Perforation Gauge
The finest, most accurate and most practicable of perforation gauges. Indicates a definite and unmistakable gauge for every stamp. For the average collector, gives Gibbons Catalogue Standard Descriptions, and for the Specialist requiring great accuracy, gives decimal readings. Is very quick and simple to use. Printed on strong transparent material. **80p**

Tweezers
The finest specially made philatelic tweezers. Continental superb finish $4\frac{3}{4}$ in. long. Gold plated.
255 Medium ends, **£1·30**
256 Broad ends, **£1·30**

2530 Stamp Colour Key
The 200 colour shades open in a fan for matching with loose, on cover or album mounted stamps. Authoritative, compact, comprehensive and easy to use it enables specialised collectors to match shades with great accuracy. **£1·35**

2551 StanGib Folded Stamp Hinges
Extra peelable in packets of 1,000. **32p**

Magnifying Glasses
Excellent for the close examination of small and rare items. In strong metal and glass. Choice of lenses available.
2573 89 mm. ($3\frac{1}{2}$ in. lens). **£2·68**
2574 102 mm. (4 in. lens). **£3·37**
2575 63 mm. ($2\frac{1}{2}$ in. lens) on flexible stand. **£4·15**

2740 Philatelic Terms Illustrated
Compiled by Russell Bennett and James Watson describes and illustrates in colour and black and white all the principal printing methods, paper, types of stamps, etc. that a collector needs to know. The dictionary of philately contains 192 pages and 92 full colour plates. **£1·50**

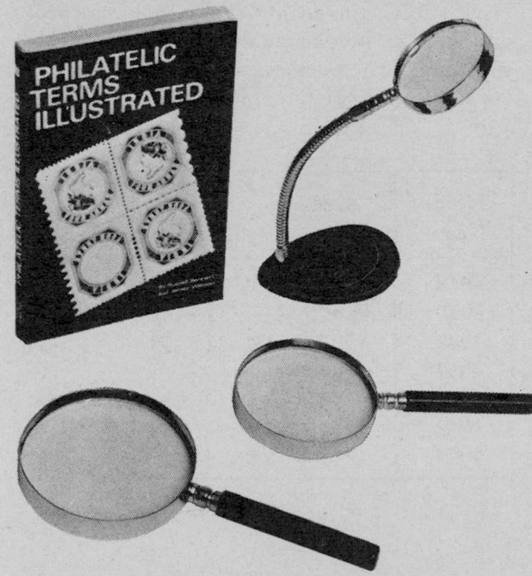

Stanley Gibbons Publications

Hawid and Showgard Mounts

Protective Mounts for unhinged album display of mint or used stamps. These are crystal clear mounts with *black* backgrounds to display stamps – especially mint – to their best advantage and to ensure maximum protection.
Choice of either *Hawid Mounts* which are open on three sides and *Showgard Mounts* which are a protective pocket open on two sides only.

Both *Hawid* and *Showgard* are available in cut-style and in strip form. The cut-style are precisely sized for many popular issues. The strip form is used for in-between stamp sizes. Simply select the correct height size for the stamp, insert it, and cut the basic strip to the desired width. The stamp clings safely inside, without the need of any hinge and with its surface fully protected. The Protective Mount is then placed in the album – it is already gummed on the back. Album leaves can be turned over and the stamp remains safe in its mount.
Complete range of *Hawid* and *Showgard Mounts* and accessories is given below.

Hawid Mounts — Order Form

HAWID strips are 210 mm. (8¼ in.) long. All mm. sizes in the list refer to the size of the stamp. The mount is 4 mm. larger giving a frame of 2 mm. each side.

Cut to size. Blue packets of 50 price 30p			Quantity	£ p
Ref. No.	**Size mm.**	**Description/Usage**		
6014	21 x 24	G.B. Definitives		
6017	41 x 24	Commems. Horizontal		
6030	44 x 27	High Values. 1955–1963		
6101	41 x 30	Paintings, etc.		
6052	30 x 35	High Values. Machin		
6060	24 x 41	Commems. Vertical		
6062	30 x 41	Commems. 1970 onwards		
Strips. Yellow packets of 25 price 75p				
Ref. No.	**Height mm.**	**Description/Usage**		
1024	24	Definitives, Commems.		
1026	26	U.S.A. Canada Commems.		
1027	27	1955–1963 High Values		
1029	29	Jersey – Guernsey		
1030	30	Paintings, etc.		
1031	31	Jersey High Values		
1033	33	Misc. Foreign Issues		
Strips. Green packets of 25 price 95p				
1036	36	G.B. Machin High Values		
1039	39	Various Foreign Issues		
1041	41	G.B. Commems., etc.		
1044	44	Various Foreign Issues		
1048	48	Blocks of Four G.B. Issues		
1055	55	Blocks of Four		
Block sizes. Yellow packets of 10 price 75p				
A 'd' indicates that the mount is sealed both at the top and at the bottom				
Ref. No.	**Size mm.**	**Description/Usage**		
1066	210 x 66d	Suitable for Various Blocks, Miniature Sheets, Postcards, F.D.Cs.		
1070	210 x 70d			
1105	148 x 105d			
1120	160 x 120d			
1170	210 x 170d			
GB Pack				
GB–1	Tray with all seven cut to size packets – 45 mounts per packet £2·25			
Specials				
1000	Mixed packet containing strips of various size 75p			
25601	Cutter and Rule £1·30			
25603	Special Adhesive for Remounting 30p			
			TOTAL £	

Showgard Mounts — Order Form

The ref. no. is also the stamp size. For example, ref. no. 24 is for a stamp which measures 24 mm. high. The strips are 210 mm. (8¼in.) long.

Ref. No.	**Description/Usage**	Quantity	£ p
Strips 70p per packet of 22			
21	G.B. Dues; Canada 1967 Defs.		
24	G.B. Defs; Commems. to 1970		
26	Canada, U.S. Commems. also I.O.M. Defs.		
27	G.B. Castles High Values		
29	Guernsey, Jersey, Commems.		
30	G.B. Horiz. Commems.		
31	Jersey High Values, G.B. Cottages		
33	Misc. Foreign, G.B. 1882 £5		
Strips 70p per packet of 15			
36	G.B. Machin High Values		
39	Misc. Foreign, G.B. 1929 P.U.C.		
41	G.B. Vert Commems, G.B. Gutter Pairs		
44	Misc. Foreign, U.S. Hatteras Scene		
48	G.B. Defs., blocks of four		
55	Misc. blocks of four		
Strips 70p per packet of 10			
60	G.B. Commems., blocks of four		
70	Machin High Values, blocks of four		
Cut style 30p per packet of 45 mounts			
21/24	G.B. Defs. (Low Values)		
41/24	G.B. Horiz. Commems. to 1970		
44/27	G.B. Castles High Values		
41/30	G.B. Horiz. Commems., U.P.U., Sailing		
30/35	G.B. Machin High Values		
24/41	G.B. Vert. Commems. to 1970		
30/41	G.B. Vert. Commems., Christmas 1970		
Jet Set			
UK–1	Tray with all seven cut-style packets – 40 mounts per packet £2·25		
Block sizes			
148/105	Block size (pack of 10) 80p		
190/115	Block size (pack of 10) 80p		
Specials			
MPK	Assortment of 20 sizes 80p		
705	Selection Cards (box of 100) £4·50		
604	Orthomatic Cutter (guillotine type) £7·50		
		TOTAL £	

DO NOT FORGET TO INCLUDE YOUR NAME AND ADDRESS OVERLEAF

the right way for stamp collectors

Order Form

Order today on our itemised order form to ensure a speedy delivery of your goods.

Item No.	Description (Album Name, colour preference, etc)	Quantity Required	Price £ p
—	Hawid Mounts (detailed overleaf)	—	
—	Showgard Mounts (detailed overleaf)	—	
3140	G.B. One-Country Album		
3264	Channel Islands One-Country Album		
3276	Isle of Man One-Country Album		
313	Australia One-Country Album		
316	Canada One-Country Album		
3114	New Zealand One-Country Album		
323	Windsor G.B. Album (Popular)* R G		
325	Windsor G.B. Album (De-Luxe)		
386	Senator Standard Album* R G B		
3834	Devon Album* M G B BL		
3830	Exeter Album* – unfaced R G BL		
3832	Exeter Album* – faced R G BL		
331	Tower Album* R G B		
3842	Ring 22 – white leaves* M G BL		
3845	Ring 22 – black leaves* M G BL		
354	Pioneer Cover Album* R G B		
356	Thames Cover Album		
3515	Classic – One Cover Album		
3517	Classic – Two Cover Album		
2625	190 x 133 mm. Stockbook		
2649	197 x 140 mm. Stockbook		
2650	298 x 222 mm. Stockbook		
2651	229 x 178 mm. Stockbook		
2652	305 x 229 mm. Stockbook		
2653	305 x 229 mm. Stockbook		
2631	229 x 178 mm. Stockbook		
2570	Philatector		
2534	Instanta Perforation Gauge		
255	Tweezers – medium ends		
256	Tweezers – broad ends		
2530	Colour Key		
2551	StanGib Folded Hinges		
2573	89 mm. (3½″) Magnifying Glass		
2574	102 mm. (4″) Magnifying Glass		
2575	63 mm. (2½″) Magnifying Glass – on flexible stand		
2740	Philatelic Terms Illustrated		
	Add for Postage and Packing (see opposite)		
	I enclose cheque/P.O. for £		

*These albums are available in Maroon (M), Red (R), Green (G), Black (B) or Blue (BL). Please indicate colour preference by encircling the appropriate letter. All prices quoted and contents of albums and other specifications are subject to alteration without prior notice.

To: Stanley Gibbons Publications Limited
391 Strand, London WC2R 0LX
Telephone: 01-836 8444

Please send me (Tick here)

- your New Issues Service brochure ☐
- further details of your Approval Service ☐
- your Specialist and Rare Stamp Department brochure ☐
- your brochure detailing the Auction Services ☐
- your current lists of stamp offers ☐
- your full colour Publications brochure ☐
- STAMP MONTHLY subscription details ☐

Holders of the following credit cards – Barclaycard, Access, Canadian Chargex, Bank Americard or American Express – may pay simply by quoting your personal number and indicating the type of card held:

Type of Card....................................

Card No...

Signature.......................................

Remittances are also acceptable by Giro. Our number is 586 6006.

Postage and Packing Charges:
Add 15p for Accessories
Add 25p for Handbooks and Protective Mounts.
Add 50p for Albums and Stockbooks.

Name ....

Address ....

....

....

....

Post Code:..

1978

Cut here

POSTAGE DUE STAMPS.

From 1922 to 1925 Great Britain postage due stamps in both script and block watermarks were used without overprint.

D 1

(Des. Ruby McConnell. Typo. Govt. Printing Works, Dublin.)

1925 (20 Feb.). *W* **10.** *P* 14×15.

D1	D 1	½d. emerald-green ..	4·00	5·00
D2	,,	1d. carmine	3·00	2·25
		a. Wmk. sideways ..	25·00	11·00
D3	,,	2d. deep green	5·00	4·00
		a. Wmk. sideways ..	14·00	7·00
D4	,,	6d. plum	1·50	1·50

1940–70. *W* **22.** *P* 14×15.

D 5	D 1	½d. emerald-green ('42)	4·50	6·00
D 6	,,	1d. carmine ('41) ..	40	50
D 7	,,	1½d. vermilion ('53) ..	50	90
D 8	,,	2d. deep green ('40) ..	40	50
D 9	,,,	3d. blue (10.11.52) ..	50	60
D10	,,	5d. blue-violet (3.3.43) ..	50	60
D11	,,	6d. plum (21.3.60) ..	1·10	60
		a. Wmk. sideways ('68) ..	55	70
D12	,,	8d. orange (30.10.62) ..	2·25	2·50
D13	,,	10d. brt. purple (27.1.65)	2·00	3·00
D14	,,	1s. apple-green (10.2.69)	5·00	5·00
		a. Wmk. sideways ('70) ..	20·00	20·00
D5/14		.. .. *Set of* 10	15·00	18·00

1971 (15 Feb.). *As Nos.* D5/14, *but with values in decimal currency and colours changed.* *W* **22.** *P* 14×15.

D15	D 1	1 p. sepia	5	5
		a. Wmk. sideways ..		
D16	,,	1½ p. light emerald ..	5	5
D17	,,	3 p. stone	10	12
D18	,,	4 p. orange	12	12
D19	,,	5 p. greenish blue ..	12	12
D20	,,	7 p. bright yellow ..	20	20
D21	,,	8 p. scarlet	20	20
D15/21		.. .. *Set of* 7	75	80

CONTROL LETTERS.

PRICES are for mint single copies, except where pairs, etc., are mentioned. Pairs, strips, or blocks, with control, can be supplied at the prices quoted plus the catalogue price of the extra stamps. The control appears below the second stamp, bottom row, except for the 1d. value, where it is beneath the eleventh stamp.

MARGINS. There are two varieties of control, one in which the vertical perforation does not cross the margin of the sheet on which the control appears ("margin imperf.") and the other in which it does ("margin perf."). We price these varieties separately, the price columns being headed I (= Imperf.) and P (= Perf.) respectively. Partially perf. margins are regarded as imperf. * Indicates that the particular variety of margin is not known with the control indicated. A dash (—) means "exists but price cannot be quoted".

I. = Margin imperf. P. = Margin perf.

I. *Dollard printings.* (*a*) *In black.*

			I.	P.
C. 1	Q 21,	10d.	*	19·00
C. 2	R 21,	½d.	9·00	50
C. 3	,,	4d.	45·00	*
C. 4	S 21,	½d.	2·25	2·75
C. 5	,,	1d.	1·25	13·00
C. 6	,,	2½d.	11·00	2·50
C. 7	,,	3d.	14·00	4·50
C. 8	,,	4d.	4·50	50·00
C. 9	,,	5d.	8·50	7·00
C. 10	,,	9d.	6·50	14·00
C. 11	,,	10d.	18·00	10·00
C. 12	S 22,	½d.	1·25	1·25
C. 13	,,	1d.	45	55
C. 13*a*	,,	2½d.	—	*
C. 14	,,	3d.	3·50	11·00
C. 15	S 22,	4d.	—	9·00
C. 16	,,	5d.	5·50	*
C. 16*a*	,,	9d.	*	60·00
C. 16*b*	,,	10d.	*	9·00
C. 17	T 22,	1d.	28·00	15·00

(*b*) *In red or carmine* (C.).

C. 18	R 21,	4d.	6·50	60·00
C. 19	S 21,	2½d.	7·50	60·00
C. 20	,,	4d.	20·00	*
C. 21	,,	9d.	48·00	8·00
C. 22	S 22,	2½d.	5·00	3·00
C. 23	,,	4d.	16·00	18·00
C. 24	,,	4d. (C.)	27·00	65·00
C. 25	,,	9d.	60·00	15·00
C. 25*a*	,,	9d. (C.)	—	75·00

II. *Thom printings.* *T* **2.** *In black.*

C. 26	Q 20,	1½d.	3·00	3·00
C. 27	Q 21,	1½d.	3·50	3·00
C. 28	R 21,	1s.	11·00	22·00
C. 29	S 21,	2d. (Die I) ..	1·50	2·00
C. 30	,,	6d.	3·00	*
C. 31	,,	1s.	12·00	30·00
C. 32	S 22,	2d. (Die I) ..	1·50	2·00
C. 33	,,	2d. (Die II) ..	2·50	1·50
C. 34	,,	1s.	9·00	12·00
C. 35	T 22,	1½d.	60·00	30·00
C. 36	,,	2d. (Die I) ..	10·00	—
C. 37	,,	2d. (Die II) ..	22·00	*
C. 38	,,	6d.	4·50	*

III. *Thom printings, as T* **2** *but bolder.*
(*a*) *In red.*

C. 39	S 22,	4d.	*	55·00
C. 40	,,	9d. agate	8·00	55·00
C. 41	T 22,	2½d.	12·00	7·50
C. 42	,,	4d.	2·25	4·00
C. 43	,,	9d. olive-green ..	7·50	8·50

(*b*) *In dull to shiny blue-black.*

C. 44	S 22,	1d.	5·00	4·50
C. 45	,,	2d. (Die I) ..	12·00	15·00
C. 46	,,	2d. (Die II) ..	3·00	4·50
C. 48	,,	10d.	18·00	23·00
C. 49	,,	1s.	18·00	12·00
C. 50	T 22,	½d.	2·25	2·00
C. 51	,,	1d.	75	75
C. 52	,,	1½d.	3·00	7·50
C. 53	,,	2d. (Die I) ..	15·00	15·00
C. 54	,,	2d. (Die II) ..	2·25	1·50
C. 55	,,	3d.	4·00	1·75
C. 56	,,	5d.	4·50	*
C. 57	,,	6d.	4·50	*
C. 57*a*	,,	10d.	70·00	70·00
C. 58	,,	1s.	7·50	7·50
C. 59	U 22,	6d.	4·50	*

IV. *Thom printings.* *T* **4** (*wide setting*) *in shiny blue-black.*

C. 60	T 22,	1d.	9·00	*
C. 61	,,	1½d.	1·75	2·50
C. 62	,,	2d. (Die II) ..	60·00	26·00
C. 63	,,	1s.	18·00	27·00
C. 64	U 22,	½d.	75	75
C. 65	,,	1d.	6·00	2·25

V. "SAORSTAT" *overprint.*

In dull to shiny blue-black or red (R.).

C. 66	T 22,	½d.	40	40
C. 67	,,	1d.	25	25
C. 68	,,	1½d.	60·00	3·00
C. 69	,,	2d. (Die II) ..	6·00	3·00
C. 70	,,	2½d. (R.)	2·50	22·00
C. 71	,,	4d. (R.)	*	65·00
C. 72	,,	5d.	2·50	2·00
C. 73	,,	9d. (R.)	2·50	3·00
C. 74	,,	10d.	65·00	11·00
C. 75	,,	1s.	11·00	*
C. 76	U 22,	6d.	1·25	*
C. 77	,,	½d.	25	25
C. 78	,,	1d.	35	35
C. 79	,,	1½d.	1·50	2·00
C. 80	,,	3d.	1·50	2·00
C. 81	,,	4d. (R.)	1·50	
C. 82	,,	1s.	11·00	9·00
C. 83	U 23,	½d.	40	25
C. 84	,,	1d.	45·00	7·50
C. 85	,,	2½d. (R.)	3·00	3·50
C. 86	,,	4d. (R.)	2·25	*
C. 87	,,	5d.	2·25	*
C. 88	,,	9d. (R.)	3·00	3·00
C. 89	,,	1s.	7·50	7·50
C. 90	V 23	6d.	1·50	—
C. 91	,,	4d. (R.)	*	2·75
C. 92	W 23,	6d.	2·25	*

Only one specimen of C. 90 with perf. margin is known.

Note.—The Harrison printings (Nos. 26/29*a* and 67/70), being issued in coils only, are not found with control attached.

JAMAICA.

For GREAT BRITAIN stamps used in Jamaica with "A **01**" or "A **27**" to "A **78**" obliterations, see index to Great Britain Stamps used Abroad list.

I. CROWN COLONY.

PRINTERS.—Until 1923, all the stamps of Jamaica were typographed by De La Rue & Co. *unless otherwise stated.*

The official dates of issue are given, where known, but where definite information is not available the dates are those of earliest known use, etc.

CONDITION. *Mint or fine used specimens of stamps with the pineapple watermark are rarely met with and are worth considerably more than our prices which are for stamps in average condition. Inferior specimens can be supplied at much lower prices.*

1 2 3 4 5 6

7

A

1860 (23 Nov.)–**63.** *W* **7.** *P* 14.

1	1	1d. pale blue	22·00	5·00
		a. Pale greenish blue	23·00	7·00
		b. Blue	20·00	4·00
		c. Deep blue	26·00	9·50
		d. Bisected (½d. 11.61) (on cover)	—	£200

2 **2** 2d. rose .. .. .. 50·00 12·00
a. Deep rose .. .. .. 35·00 12·00
3 **3** 3d. green (10.9.63) .. .. 35·00 10·00
4 **4** 4d. brown-orange .. .. 60·00 10·00
a. Red-orange .. .. 60·00 6·50
5 **5** 6d. dull lilac .. .. .. 55·00 6·50
a. Grey-purple .. .. 70·00 11·00
b. Deep purple .. .. £200 14·00
6 **6** 1s. yellow-brown .. .. 90·00 10·00
a. Purple-brown .. .. £120 10·00
b. Dull brown .. .. 65·00 11·00
c. "$" for "S" in "SHILLING" (A) £450 £250

The diagonal bisection of the 1d. was authorized by a P.O. notice dated 20 Nov., 1861. Specimens are only of value when on original envelope or wrapper. The authority was withdrawn as from 1 Dec., 1872. Fakes are frequently met with. Other bisections were unauthorized.

The so-called "dollar variety" of the 1s. occurs once in each sheet of stamps in all shades and in later colours, etc., on the second stamp in the second row of the left upper pane. The prices quoted above are for the dull brown shade, the prices for the other shades being proportionate to their normal value.

All values except the 3d. are known imperf., mint only.

There are two types of watermark in the 3d. and 1s., one being short and squat and the other elongated.

8

9

10

1870–83. *Wmk. Crown CC.* (*a*) *P* 14.
7 **8** ½d. claret (29.10.72) .. .. 3·50 1·00
a. Deep claret (1883) .. .. 3·50 1·00
8 **1** 1d. blue (20.8.73) .. .. 10·00 45
a. Deep blue .. .. 12·00 45
9 **2** 2d. rose (4.70) .. .. 12·00 15
a. Deep rose .. .. 27·00 25
10 **3** 3d. green (1.3.70) .. .. 35·00 1·40
11 **4** 4d. brown-orange (1872) .. 40·00 2·00
a. Red-orange .. .. 80·00 1·25
12 **5** 6d. mauve (10.3.71) .. .. 14·00 2·00
13 **6** 1s. dullbrn.(todeep)(23.2.73) 10·00 3·50
a. "$" for "S" in "SHILLING" (A) £350 £250

(*b*) *P* 12½.
14 **9** 2s. Venetian red (27.8.75) .. 12·00 5·50
15 **10** 5s. lilac (27.8.75) .. .. 28·00 26·00
7/15 .. .. *Set of* 9 £150 35·00

The ½d., 1d., 4d., 2s. and 5s. are known imperforate.

1883–97. *Wmk. Crown CA.* *P* 14.
16 **8** ½d. yellow-green (1885) .. 65 12
a. Green 20 10
17 **1** 1d. blue (1884) .. .. 30·00 1·75
18 ,, 1d. rose (to deep) (3.3.85) .. 8·50 55
a. Carmine .. .. .. 4·00 40
19 **2** 2d. rose (to deep) (17.3.84) .. 40·00 1·60
20 ,, 2d. grey (1885) .. .. 16·00 25
a. Slate .. .. .. 8·00 15
21 **3** 3d. sage-green (1886) .. 2·25 30
a. Pale olive-green .. .. 1·10 50
22 **4** 4d. red-orange* (9.3.83) .. 85·00 4·00
a. Red-brown (shades) .. 1·00 12
23 **5** 6d. deep yellow (4.10.90) .. 4·00 3·50
a. Orange-yellow .. .. 4·00 2·00
24 **6** 1s. brown (to deep) (3.97) 4·00 2·50
a. "$" for "S" in "SHILLING" (A) £300 £150
b. Chocolate .. .. .. 6·50 5·50
25 **9** 2s. Venetian red (1897) .. 14·00 7·00
26 **10** 5s. lilac (1897) .. .. 18·00 18·00
16/26 .. .. *Set of* 11 £110 30·00
16, 18, 20, 21, 22, and 23 Optd. "Specimen" .. *Set of* 6 50·00

* No. 22 is the same colour as No. 11*a*.

The 1d. carmine, 2d. slate, and 2s. are known imperf. All values to the 6d. inclusive are known perf. 12. These are proofs.

11

TWO PENCE
HALF-PENNY
(12)

1889–91. *Value tablet in second colour.* *Wmk. Crown CA.* *P* 14.
27 **11** 1d. purple & mve. (8.3.89) 60 10
28 ,, 2d. green (8.3.89) .. .. 4·00 1·25
a. Deep green (brown gum) .. 1·40 1·40
29 ,, 2½d. dull pur. & blue (25.2.91) 2·00 40
27/29 Optd. "Specimen" *Set of* 3 35·00

A very wide range of shades may be found in the 1d. The head-plate was printed in many shades of purple, and the duty-plate in various shades of mauve and purple and also in carmine, etc. The variations in the other values are not so numerous nor so pronounced.

(Surcharged by C. Vendryes, Kingston.)

1890 (4 (?) June). *No. 22a surch. with T* **12**.
30 **4** 2½d. on 4d. red-brown .. 7·00 4·50
a. Spacing between lines of surch. 1½ mm. .. .. 9·50 8·00
b. Surch. double .. .. 90·00 75·00
c. "PFNNY" for "PENNY" 25·00 20·00
d. "PFNNK" ("F" for "E" and broken "K" for "Y") 45·00 35·00

This provisional was issued pending receipt of No. 29 which is listed above for convenience of reference.

Three settings exist. (1) Ten varieties arranged in a single vertical row and repeated six times in the pane. (2) Twelve varieties, in two horizontal rows of six, repeated five times, alternate rows show 1 and 1½ mm. spacing between lines of surcharge. (3) Three varieties, arranged horizontally and repeated twenty times. All these settings can be reconstructed by examination of the spacing and relative position of the words of the surcharge and of the broken letters, etc., which are numerous.

A variety reading "PFNNK", with the "K" unbroken, is a forgery.

Varieties c. and d. may be found in the double surcharge.

Surcharges misplaced either horizontally or vertically are met with, the normal position being central at the foot of the stamp with "HALF-PENNY" covering the old value.

13. Llandovery Falls, Jamaica (photo. by Dr. J. Johnston).

(Recess. De La Rue.)

1900–1. *Wmk. Crown CC (sideways).* *P* 14.
31 **13** 1d. red (1.5.00) 35 15
32 ,, 1d. slate-blk. & red (25.9.01) 1·00 15
a. Blued paper .. .. 35·00 35·00
b. Imperf. between (pair) .. £1500
31/32 Optd. "Specimen" *Set of* 2 50·00

Many shades exist of both centre and frame c the bi-coloured 1d. which was, of course, printe from two plates and the design shows minc differences from that of the 1d. red which wa printed from a single plate.

14. Arms of Jamaica.

(Typo. D.L.R.)

1903–4. *Wmk. Crown CA.* *P* 14.
33 **14** ½d. grey & dull grn. (16.11.03) 65 1
a. "SER.ET" for "SERVIET" 12·00 11·0
34 ,, 1d. grey & carmine (24.2.04) 90 1
a. "SER.ET" for "SERVIET" 10·00 9·0
35 ,, 2½d. grey & ultram. (16.11.03) 1·10 5
a. "SER.ET" for "SERVIET" 17·00 15·0
36 ,, 5d. grey and yellow (1.3.04) 8·50 9·5
a. "SER.ET" for "SERVIET" £300
33/36 Optd. "Specimen" *Set of* 4 30·00

The "SER.ET" variety occurs once in eac sheet of stamps on the second stamp in th fourth row of the left upper pane.

The centres of the above and later bi-coloure stamps in the Arms type vary in colour from gre to grey-black.

15

16

Arms type redrawn.

1905–11. *Wmk. Mult. Crown CA.* *P* 14.

(*a*) *Arms types.*
37 **14** ½d. grey and dull green, C (24.11.05) .. . 40 1
a. "SER.ET" for "SERVIET" .. .. .. 9·00 9·0
38 **15** ½d. yellow-grn., O (8.11.06) 80 2
a. Dull green 35 1
b. Deep green 40 1
39 **14** 1d. grey and carmine, C (20.11.05) .. .. 3·25 1
40 **16** 1d. carmine, O (1.10.06) .. 40 1
41 **14** 2½d. grey & ultramarine, C (12.11.07) .. .. 1·10 6
42 ,, 2½d. pale ultram., O (21.9.10) 1·60 7
a. Deep ultramarine, O .. 1·50 7
43 ,, 5d. grey & orange-yellow, C (24.4.07) .. .. 7·50 9·0
a. "SER.ET" for "SERVIET" £300 £30
44 ,, 6d. dull & bright purple, C (18.8.11) .. .. 4·00 5·0
45 ,, 5s. grey and violet, C (Nov. '05) .. .. 16·00 15·0
37/45 .. .. *Set of* 9 32·00 28·0
38, 40, 42, 44, 45 Optd. "Specimen" *Set of* 5 35·00

See note above *re* grey centres.

(*b*) *Queen Victoria types.*
46 **3** 3d. olive-green, O (15.5.05) .. 1·10 2
a. Sage-green. O (1907) .. 2·00 2
47 ,, 3d. purple/*yellow*, O (10.3.10) 1·60 1·4
a. Pale purple/yellow, C (11.7.10) 80 5
48 **4** 4d. red-brown, O (6.6.08) .. 13·00 12·0
49 ,, 4d. black/*yellow*, C (21.9.10) 4·50 8·5
50 ,, 4d. red/yellow, O (3.10.11) .. 1·00 2·0
51 **5** 6d. dull orange, O (27.6.06) 6·50 7·0
a. Golden yellow, O (Sept., '09) 6·50 7·0

: 5 6d. lilac, O (19.11.09) .. 6·50 6·00
a. *Purple*, C (July, '10) .. 4·00 4·50
3 6 1s. brown, O (Nov. '06) .. 5·50 5·00
a. *Deep brown*, O .. .. 8·50 4·00
b. "$" for "S" in "SHILLING" (A).. .. .. £350 £350
4 ,, 1s. black/*green*, C (21.9.10) .. 2·75 5·00
a. "$" for "S" in "SHILLING" (A) £350 £350
5 9 2s. Venetian red, O (Nov. '08) 26·00 24·00
5 ,, 2s. purple/*blue*, C (21.9.10) .. 5·00 4·50
5/56 .. .. *Set of* 11 65·00 65·00
7, 49, 50, 52, 54, 56 Optd. "Specimen" *Set of* 6 40·00

17

18

(T **17/18** typo. De La Rue.)

911 (3 Feb.). *Wmk. Mult. Crown CA.* *P* 14.
7 **17** 2d. grey, O (Optd. S. £9) .. 1·10 2·75

912–20. *Wmk. Mult. Crown CA.* *P* 14.
3 **18** 1d. carmine-red, O (5.12.12) 15 8
a. *Scarlet*, O (1916) 20 10
9 ,, 1½d. brn.-orge., O (13.7.16) 65 15
a. *Yellow-orange*, O .. .. 2·50 55
b. Wmk. sideways .. ..
0 ,, 2d. grey, O (2.8.12) .. 55 1·10
a. *Slate-grey*, O 55 90
1 ,, 2½d. blue, O (13.2.13) .. 55 20
a. *Deep bright blue*, O .. 60 25
2 ,, 3d. purple/*yellow*, C (6.3.12) 55 40
a. *White back*, C (2.4.13) .. 55 40
b. *On lemon*, C (25.9.16) (Optd. S. £10) .. .. .. 1·60 55
3 ,, 4d. blk. & red/*yell.*, C (4.4.13) 95 55
a. *White back*, C (7.5.14) .. 75 1·60
b. *On lemon*, C (1916) (Optd. S. £10) .. .. .. 6·50 5·50
c. *On pale yellow*, C (1919) .. 9·00 5·50
4 ,, 6d. dull and bright purple, C (14.11.12) .. .. 2·50 2·25
a. *Dull purple and bright mauve*, C (1915).. .. .. 80 75
b. *Dull purple and bright magenta*, C (1920) .. 85 55
5 ,, 1s. black/*green*, C (2.8.12) 1·50 1·25
a. *White back*, C (4.1.15) .. 1·10 2·25
b. *On blue-green, olive back*, C ('20) .. .. .. 2·75 2·25
6 ,, 2s. pur. & bright blue/*blue*, C (10.1.19) .. .. 4·00 5·00
7 ,, 5s. green & red/*yellow*, C (5.9.19) .. .. 14·00 17·00
a. *On pale yellow*, C.. .. 18·00 20·00
b. *On orange-buff*, C.. .. 22·00 22·00
8/67 .. .. *Set of* 10 21·00 23·00
8/67 Optd. "Specimen" *Set of* 10 50·00

For the ½d. in this design and the 6d. with cript wmk. see Nos. 107 and 90.

The paper of No. 67 is a bright yellow and the um rough and dull. No. 67*a* is on practically he normal creamy "pale yellow" paper, and the um is smooth and shiny. The paper of No. 67*b* pproaches the "coffee" colour of the true orange-buff", and the colours of both head and rame are paler, the latter being of a carmine one.

VAR STAMP. (19) WAR STAMP. (20) WAR STAMP. (21)

(T **19/21** optd. locally.)

916 (1 April–Sept.). *Optd. with T* **19.**
8 **15** ½d. yellow-green 10 20
a. No stop after "STAMP" .. 3·50 4·50
b. Opt. double .. .. 20·00 19·00
c. Opt. inverted .. .. 16·00 16·00
d. *Blue-green* 20 20
da. No stop after "STAMP" .. 1·75 1·75

69 **18** 3d. purple/*yell.* (white back) 1·00 1·10
a. *On lemon* (6.16) .. .. 80 1·10
aa. No stop after "STAMP" .. 5·00 5·50
b. *On pale yellow* (9.16) .. 80 95

Minor varieties: ½d. (i) Small "P"; (ii) Space between "W" and "A"; (iii) "WARISTAMP" (raised quad between words); (iv) Two stops after "STAMP". 3d. "WARISTAMP".

Note.—The above and succeeding stamps with "WAR STAMP" overprint were issued for payment of a special war tax on letters and post-cards or on parcels. Ordinary unoverprinted stamps could also be used for this purpose.

1916 (Sept.–Dec.). *Optd. with T* **20.**
70 **15** ½d. blue-green (*shades*) (2.10.16) 12 15
a. No stop after "STAMP" 2·75 2·50
b. Opt. omitted (in pair) .. 70·00 60·00
c. "R" inserted by hand .. 70·00 60·00
71 **18** 1½d. orange (1.9.16) .. 12 12
aa. Wmk. sideways .. .. — £150
a. No stop after "STAMP" 2·00 1·75
b. "S" in "STAMP" omitd. 14·00 12·00
c. "S" inserted by hand .. 60·00
d. "R" in "WAR" omitted 70·00 60·00
e. "R" inserted by hand .. 65·00 60·00
f. Inverted "d" for "P" .. 45·00 38·00
72 ,, 3d. purple/*lemon* (2.10.16) 30 70
aa. Opt. inverted .. .. 95·00
a. No stop after "STAMP" 6·00 5·00
b. "S" in "STAMP" omitd. 50·00 48·00
c. "S" inserted by hand .. 48·00 45·00
d. "S" inserted inverted .. 65·00 50·00
e. *On yellow* (12.16) .. 2·50 4·00
ea. "S" in "STAMP" omitd. 65·00 50·00
eb. "S" inserted by hand .. 65·00 50·00
ec. "S" inserted inverted .. 70·00 55·00

Minor varieties, such as raised quads, small stop, double stop, spaced letters and letters of different sizes, also exist in this overprint.

1917 (March). *Optd. with T* **21.**
73 **15** ½d. blue-green (*shades*) (25.3.17) 12 15
a. No stop after "STAMP" 3·00 2·75
b. Stop inserted and "P" impressed a second time .. 65·00
c. Optd. on back only .. 20·00
d. Opt. inverted .. .. 4·00 3·50
74 **18** 1½d. orange (3.3.17) .. 8 8
aa. Wmk. sideways .. .. — £200
a. No stop after "STAMP".. 2·75 2·50
b. Stop inserted and "P" impressed a second time .. 65·00
c. Opt. double .. .. 24·00 25·00
d. Opt. inverted .. .. 25·00 24·00
75 ,, 3d. purple/*yellow* (3.3.17).. 20 25
a. No stop after "STAMP".. 3·50 3·50
b. Stop inserted and "P" impressed a second time .. 60·00
c. Opt. inverted .. .. 50·00
d. Opt. sideways (reading up) 70·00

There are numerous minor varieties in this overprint.

WAR STAMP

(22)

(Optd. by De La Rue & Co.)

1919 (4 Oct.). *Optd. with T* **22.**
76 **15** ½d. green (R.) 8 8
77 **18** 3d. purple/*yellow* (R.) .. 60 75
a. *Pale purple/buff* (R.) .. 15 45
b. *Deep purple/buff* (R.) .. 1·60 1·60
76/7 Optd. "Specimen" *Set of* 2 25·00

We list the most distinct variations in the 3d. The buff tone of the paper varies considerably in depth.

23. Jamaica Exhibition, 1891.

24. Arawak Woman Preparing Cassava.

26. King's House, Spanish Town.

25. War Contingent embarking.

Re-entry. No. 80a.

The greater part of the design is re-entered, the hull showing in very solid colour and the people appear very blurred. There are also minor re-entries on stamps above (R. 7/4 and 6/4).

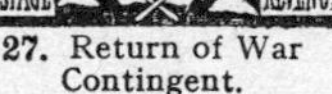
27. Return of War Contingent.

INVERTED NORMAL

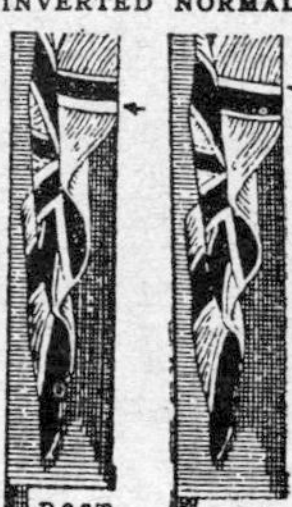
A B

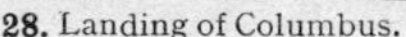
28. Landing of Columbus.

29. Cathedral, Spanish Town.

30. Statue of Queen Victoria, Kingston. **31.** Admiral Rodney Memorial.

32. Sir Charles Metcalfe Monument. **33.** Jamaican scenery.

34

(Typo. (½d., 1d.), recess (others). D.L.R.)

1919–21. *Wmk. Mult. Crown CA* (*sideways on* 1*d.*, 1½*d. and* 10*s.*). *P* 14.

78	**23**	½d. green and olive-green, **C** (12.11.20)	15	15
79	**24**	1d. car. & orge., **C** (3.10.21)	80	25
80	**25**	1½d. green (*shades*) (4.7.19)	20	12
		a. Major re-entry (R. 8/4) ..		
81	**26**	2d. indigo & grn. (18.2.21)	55	70
82	**27**	2½d. dp. bl. & bl. (A) (18.2.21)	4·50	2·00
		a. Blue-black and deep blue (A)	80	85
83	**28**	3d. myrtle-grn. & bl. (8.4.21)	45	20
84	**29**	4d. brn. & dp. grn. (21.2.21)	1·25	1·90
85	**30**	1s. orange-yellow and red-orange (10.12.20) ..	2·50	3·00
		a. Frame inverted	£4000	£2750
86	**31**	2s. lt. bl. & brn. (10.12.20)	12·00	5·00
87	**32**	3s. violet-blue and orange (10.12.20)	11·00	15·00
88	**33**	5s. bl. & yell.-orge. (15.4.21)	22·00	22·00
		a. Blue and pale dull orange ..	20·00	18·00
89	**34**	10s. myrtle-green (6.5.20) ..	28·00	35·00
78/89		.. .. *Set of* 12	70·00	75·00
78/89 Optd.		"Specimen" *Set of* 12	85·00	

The 2½d. of the above series showed the Union Jack at left, incorrectly, as indicated in illustration A. In the issue on paper with Script wmk. the design was corrected (Illustration B).

A 6d. stamp illustrating the abolition of slavery was prepared and sent out in April, 1921, but for political reasons was not issued and the stock was destroyed. Copies overprinted "Specimen" are known on both the Mult. CA and Script CA papers, and are worth £250 each. Price without "Specimen" on Script CA £2750.

1921 (21 Oct.). *Wmk. Mult. Script CA.* *P* 14.

90	**18**	6d. dull purple and bright magenta, **C** (Optd. S. £10)	6·00	2·75

For ½d. value, see No. 107.

35. "POSTAGE & REVENUE" added.

36. Port Royal in 1853.

(Printing as before; the 6d. recess-printed.)

1921–29. *Wmk. Mult. Script CA* (*sideways on* 1*d. and* 1½*d.*). *P* 14.

91	**23**	½d. green & olive-green, **C** (5.2.22)	20	20
		a. Green and deep olive-grn., **C**	12	12
92	**35**	1d. carmine and orange, **C** (5.12.22)	45	12
93	**25**	1½d. grn. (*shades*) (2.2.21)	25	12
94	**26**	2d. indigo & grn. (4.11.21)	95	25
		a. Indigo and grey-green ('25)	1·50	25
95	**27**	2½d. deep blue and blue (B) (4.11.21)	1·50	25
		a. Dull blue and blue (B) ..	1·75	25
96	**28**	3d. myrtle-green and blue (6.3.22)	75	20
		a. Green and pale blue ..	25	12
97	**29**	4d. brn. & dp. grn. (5.12.21)	40	15
		a. Chocolate and dull green ..	25	12
98	**36**	6d. black & blue (5.12.22)	8·00	1·75
		a. Grey and dull blue ..	8·00	1·25
99	**30**	1s. orange and red-orange (4.11.21)	1·40	40
		a. Orange-yell. and brn.-orange	1·00	20
100	**31**	2s. light blue and brown (5.2.22)	1·40	75
101	**32**	3s. violet-blue and orange (23.8.21)	7·00	7·50
102	**33**	5s. blue and yellow-brown (8.11.23)	10·00	11·00
		a. Blue and pale dull orange	20·00	18·00
		b. Blue and yellow-orange ('27)	11·00	10·00
		c. Blue & pale bistre-brn. ('29)	11·00	10·00
103	**34**	10s. myrtle-green (Mar. (?) '22)	18·00	22·00
91/103		.. .. *Set of* 13	45·00	38·00
91/103 Optd.		"Specimen" *Set of* 13	80·00	

The frame of No. 102*a* is the same colour as that of No. 88*a*.

The designs of all values of the pictorial series, with the exception of the 5s. and 10s. (which originated with the Governor, Sir Leslie Probyn), were selected by Mr. F. C. Cundall, F.S.A. The 1d. and 5s. were drawn by Miss Cundall, the 3d. by Mrs. Cundall, and the 10s. by De La Rue & Co. The 6d. is from a lithograph. The other designs are from photographs, the frames of all being the work of Miss Cundall and Miss Wood.

37

38

39

(Centres from photos by Miss V. F. Taylor Frames des. F. C. Cundall, F.S.A., and drawr by Miss Cundall. Recess. B.W.)

1923 (1 Nov.). *Child Welfare.* *Wmk. Mult Script CA.* *P* 12.

104	**37**	½d.+½d. black and green	80	1·1c
105	**38**	1d.+½d. black and scarlet	5·00	6·0c
106	**39**	2½d.+½d. black and blue ..	11·00	12·0c
104/6 Optd.		"Specimen" *Set of* 3	65·00	

Sold at a premium of ½d. for the Child Welfar League, these stamps were on sale annually fron 1 November to 31 January, until 31 January 1927, when their sale ceased, the remainder being destroyed on 21 February, 1927.

Labels bearing a red cross and an aeroplane with or without the inscription "JAMAICA" o "JAMAICA Half penny" were sold by th Jamaica Patriotic Stamp League in aid o various war-time funds. Their use on corre spondence was not forbidden and they ar frequently found postmarked, but they per formed no postal function.

1927 (Nov.). *Wmk. Mult. Script CA.* *P* 14

107	**18**	½d. green, **O** (Optd. S. £14)	12	1:

40

41

42

Die I Die II

(Recess. D.L.R.)

929–32. *Wmk. Mult. Script CA.* *P* 14.

No.	Type	Description		Unused	Used
08	**40**	1d. scarlet (Die I)	..	25	12
		a. Die II (1932) ..	..	12	12
09	**41**	1½d. chocolate ..	..	20	20
10	**42**	9d. maroon ..	..	3·00	2·25
08/10		Perf. " Specimen "	*Set of* 3	22·00	

In Die I the shading below JAMAICA is formed f thickened parallel lines, and in Die II of iagonal cross-hatching.

43. Coco Palms at Columbus Cove.

44. Wag Water River, St. Andrew.

45. Priestman's River, Portland.

(Dies eng. & recess. Waterlow.)

932. *Wmk. Mult. Script CA (sideways on 2d. and 2½d.).* *P* 12½.

No.	Type	Description	Unused	Used
11	**43**	2d. black and green ..	1·50	55
		a. Imperf. between (vert. pair)	£700	
12	**44**	2½d. greenish blue & ultram.	1·10	1·40
		a. Imperf. between (vert. pair)	£700	
13	**45**	6d. grey-black and purple	2·50	2·00
11/13		Perf. " Specimen " *Set of* 3	20·00	

935 (6 May). *Silver Jubilee. As Nos.* 91/4 *of Antigua, but ptd. by B.W.* *P* 11 × 12.

No.	Description		Unused	Used
14	1d. deep blue and scarlet	..	12	12
15	1½d. ultramarine & grey-black		15	20
	a. Extra flagstaff ..	..	18·00	20·00
16	6d. green and indigo ..	..	1·50	2·00
	a. Extra flagstaff ..	..	32·00	35·00
17	1s. slate and purple ..	..	1·75	2·25
	a. Extra flagstaff ..	..	60·00	70·00
14/17	Perf. " Specimen "	*Set of* 4	18·00	

For illustration of " extra flagstaff " variety ee Bechuanaland.

937 (12 May). *Coronation. As Nos.* 13/5 *of Aden.*

No.	Description		Unused	Used
18	1d. scarlet	..	12	12
19	1½d. grey-black ..	..	20	15
20	2½d. bright blue ..	..	45	25
18/20	Perf. " Specimen "	*Set of* 3	12·00	

6. King George VI.

47. Coco Palms at Columbus Cove.

48. Bananas.

49. Citrus Grove.

50. Kingston Harbour.

51. Sugar Industry.

52. Bamboo Walk.

53. King George VI.

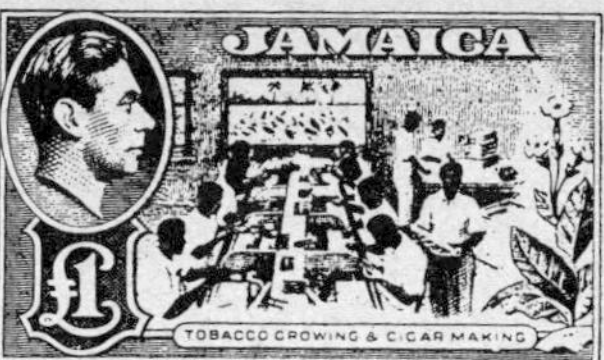

53a. Tobacco Growing and Cigar Making.

(Recess. De La Rue & Co. (T **46**, 5s. and 10s.), Waterlow & Sons (others).)

1938–52. *T* **46** *to* **53***a and as T* **33**, **44** *and* **45** *but with inset portrait of King George VI, as in T* **47**. *Wmk. Mult. Script CA.* *P* 13½ × 14 (*½d.*, *1d.*, *1½d.*), 14 (*5s.*, *10s.*) *or* 12½ (*others*).

No.	Type	Description		Unused	Used
121	**46**	½d. blue-green (10.10.38)		5	5
		a. Wmk. sideways	..	†	£800
121*b*	,,	½d. orange (25.10.51)	..	10	10
122	,,	1d. scarlet (10.10.38)	..	5	5
122*a*	,,	1d. blue-green (25.10.51)		20	12
123	,,	1½d. brown (10.10.38)	..	5	5
124	**47**	2d. grey and green	..	5	5
		a. Perf. 13 × 13½ ..	..	5	5
		b. Perf. 12½ × 13 ('51)	..	15	12
125	**44**	2½d. greenish blue & ultram.		80	95
126	**48**	3d. ultramarine & green ..		10	5
126*a*	,,	3d. greenish blue and ultramarine (15.8.49)		35	15
126*b*	,,	3d. green & scar. (1.7.52)		20	12
127	**49**	4d. brown and green	..	12	12
128	**45**	6d. grey and purple	..	15	12
		a. Perf. 13½ × 13 (10.10.50) ..		12	12
129	**50**	9d. lake	..	25	20
130	**51**	1s. green & purple-brown		30	20
131	**52**	2s. blue and chocolate ..		95	40
132	**33**	5s. slate-blue & yellow-orange ..	..	2·25	1·50
		a. Perf. 13 (24.10.49)	..	3·25	3·25
		ab. Bl. & orge. (10.10.50)	..	1·75	1·75
133	**53**	10s. myrtle-green	..	4·00	3·50
		aa. Perf. 13 (10.10.50) ..		4·50	4·50
133*a*	**53***a*	£1 choc. & violet (15.8.49)		12·00	13·00
121/133*a*		.. ..	*Set of* 18	19·00	18·00
121/33		Perf. " Specimen "	*Set of* 13	40·00	

The 5s. is known line perf. exactly 14 all round instead of the normal comb perf. which measures 13.8 × 13.7.

II. SELF-GOVERNMENT.

54. Courthouse, Falmouth.

55. King Charles II and King George VI.

56. Institute of Jamaica. **57.** "Labour and Learning".

58. House of Assembly.

59. Scroll, Flag and King George VI.

(Recess. Waterlow.)

1945 (20 Aug.)–**1946**. *New Constitution. Wmk. Mult. Script CA. P* 12½.

134 **54** 1½d. sepia 12 12
a. Perf. 12½×13 (1946) .. 25 15
135 **55** 2d. green 45 30
a. Perf. 12½×13 (1945) .. 12 20
136 **56** 3d. ultramarine 12 12
a. Perf. 13 (1946) 40 40
137 **58** 4½d. slate 12 15
a. Perf. 13 (1946) 40 40
138 **57** 2s. red-brown 70 70
139 **59** 5s. indigo .. .. .. 85 1·75
140 **56** 10s. green .. .. .. 2·25 4·00
134/140 .. .. *Set of 7* 3·75 6·00
134/40 Perf. "Specimen" *Set of 7* 60·00

1946 (14 Oct.). *Victory. As Nos.* 28/9 *of Aden. P* 13½×14.

141 1½d. purple-brown 8 8
a. Perf. 13½ 8 8
142 3d. blue 15 20
a. Perf. 13½ 25 30
141/2 Perf. "Specimen" *Set of 2* 14·00

1948 (1 Dec.). *Royal Silver Wedding. As Nos.* 30/1 *of Aden.*

143 1½d. red-brown 12 12
144 £1 scarlet .. .. .. 11·00 14·00

1949 (10 Oct.). *75th Anniv. of Universal Postal Union. As Nos.* 114/7 *of Antigua.*

145 1½d. red-brown 12 12
146 2d. deep blue-green 15 25
147 3d. deep blue 30 40
148 6d. purple 45 45

1951 (16 Feb.). *Inauguration of B.W.I. University College. As Nos.* 118/9 *of Antigua.*

149 2d. black and red-brown 12 12
150 6d. grey-black and purple .. 30 25

60. Scout Badge and Map of Caribbean.

61. Scout Badge and Map of Jamaica.

(Litho. Bradbury, Wilkinson & Co.)

1952 (5 Mar.). *First Caribbean Scout Jamboree. Wmk. Mult. Script CA. P* 13½×13 (*2d.*) *or* 13×13½ (*6d.*)

151 **60** 2d. blue, apple-grn. & black 12 12
152 **61** 6d. yellow-green, carmine-red and black 35 45

1953 (2 June). *Coronation. As No.* 47 *of Aden.*

153 2d. black & dp. yellow-green 8 8

62. Coco Palms at Columbus Cove.

(Recess. Waterlow & Sons, Ltd.)

1953 (25 Nov.). *Royal Visit. Wmk. Mult. Script CA. P* 12½×13.

154 **62** 2d. grey-black and green .. 8 8

63. Man-o'-War at Port Royal.

64. Old Montego Bay.

65. Old Kingston.

66. Proclamation of Abolition of Slavery, 183

(Recess. De La Rue & Co.)

1955 (10 May). *Tercentenary Issue. Wmk. Mu Script CA. P* 12½.

155 **63** 2d. black and olive-green 8
156 **64** 2½d. black & deep brt. blue 20 2
157 **65** 3d. black and claret .. 20 2
158 **66** 6d. black and carmine-red 30 3

67. Palms.

68. Sugar Cane.

69. Pineapple.

70. Bananas.

71. Mahoe.

72. Breadfruit.

73. Ackee.

74. Doctor Bird.

75. Blue Mountain Peak.

76. Royal Botanic Gardens, Hope.

77. Rafting on the Rio Grande.

78. Fort Charles.

79. Arms of Jamaica.

80. Arms of Jamaica.

Recess. Bradbury, Wilkinson (T **79/80**), De La Rue (others).)

956. *Wmk. Mult. Script CA. P* 13 (*½d. to 6d.*), 13½(*8d. to 2s.*) *or* 11½ (*3s. to £1*).

59	**67**	½d. blk. & dp. orange-red	5	5
60	**68**	1d. black and emerald ..	5	5
61	**69**	2d. black & carmine-red	5	5
62	**70**	2½d. blk. & dp. bright blue	8	8
63	**71**	3d. emerald & red-brown	8	10
64	**72**	4d. bronze-green and blue	10	10
165	**73**	5d. scarlet & bronze-green	12	12
166	**74**	6d. black & deep rose-red	12	10
167	**75**	8d. ultram. & red-orange	15	10
168	**76**	1s. yellow-green and blue	20	10
169	**77**	1s. 6d. ultramarine and reddish purple ..	40	15
170	**78**	2s. blue and bronze-green (*shades*)	1·10	65
171	**79**	3s. black and blue ..	90	50
172	,,	5s. black & carmine-red	1·50	75
173	**80**	10s. black and blue-green	3·00	4·00
174	,,	£1 black and purple ..	5·50	4·00
159/174		.. .. *Set of* 16	11·00	9·50

Dates of issue:—1 May, ½d., 1d.; 2 Aug., 2d., 2½d., 3s.; 15 Aug., 5s., 10s., £1; 3 Sept., 6d.; 15 Nov., 8d., 1s., 1s. 6d., 2s.; 17 Dec., 3d., 4d., 5d.

1958 (22 Apr.). *Inauguration of British Caribbean Federation. As Nos.* 135/7 *of Antigua.*

175	2d. deep green	8	5
176	5d. blue	15	15
177	6d. scarlet	20	20

81. *Britannia* flying over 1860 Packet-steamer.

82. Postal Mule-cart and Motor-van.

83. 1s. stamps of 1860 and 1956.

(Recess. Waterlow & Sons.)

1960 (4 Jan.). *Stamp Centenary. W* w.**12**. *P* 13×13½ (*1s.*) *or* 13½×14 (*others*).

178	**81**	2d. blue and reddish purple	10	5
179	**82**	6d. carmine & olive-green	25	25
180	**83**	1s. red-brown, yellow-green and blue	35	35

III. INDEPENDENT.

1 9 6 2 INDEPENDENCE (84)	1 9 6 2 INDEPENDENCE 1962 (85)

1962 (8 Aug.)–**63**. *Independence.* (*a*) *Optd. with T* **85** (*3d. to 2s*) *or as T* **84** (*others*). *Wmk. Mult. Script CA.*

181	**67**	½d. blk. & dp. orange-red	5	5
182	**68**	1d. black and emerald ..	5	5
183	**70**	2½d. blk. & dp. bright blue	10	5
184	**71**	3d. emerald & red-brown	10	10
185	**73**	5d. scarlet & bronze-green	12	12
186	**74**	6d. black and dp. rose-red	12	10
187	**75**	8d. ultram and red-orange (*opt. at upper left*) ..	15	12
		a. Opt. at lower left (17.9.63?)	25	25
188	**76**	1s. yellow-green and blue	20	15
189	**78**	2s. blue and bronze-green (*shades*)	55	45
190	**79**	3s. black and blue ..	1·25	1·25
191	**80**	10s. black and blue-green	3·50	3·50
192	,,	£1 black and purple ..	5·50	5·50
181/92		.. .. *Set of* 12	10·00	10·00

86. Military Bugler and Map.

87. Gordon House and Banner.

88. Map, Factories and Fruit.

(Des. V. Whiteley. Photo. De La Rue.)

(*b*) *W* w.**12**. *P* 13.

193	**86**	2d. carmine, black, yellow and deep green ..	5	5
194	,,	4d. carm., blk., yell. & blue	8	5
195	**87**	1s. 6d. black and red ..	35	40
196	**88**	5s. bluish violet, yellow, green and light blue	95	1·10

89. Weightlifting, Boxing, Football and Cycling.

90. Diving, Sailing, Swimming and Water Polo.

91. Pole-vault, Javelin, Discus, Relay-racing and Hurdles.

92. Arms of Kingston and Athlete.

T **89/91** include the Seal of Kingston.

(Photo. Harrison & Sons.)

1962 (11 Aug.). *Ninth Central American and Caribbean Games, Kingston. W* w.**12**. *P* 14½×14.

197	**89**	1d. sepia and carmine-red	5	5
198	**90**	6d. sepia and greenish blue	12	10
199	**91**	8d. sepia and bistre ..	20	20
200	**92**	2s. sepia, yell., red & blue	50	55

An imperf. miniature sheet exists, but this was never available at face value or at any post office.

93. Farmer and Crops.

(Litho. D.L.R.)

1963 (4 June). *Freedom from Hunger.* P 12½.

201	**93**	1d. multicoloured	8	8
202	,,	8d. multicoloured	35	35

1963 (4 Sept.). *Red Cross Centenary. As Nos.* 147/8 *of Antigua.*

203	2d. red and black	5	5
204	1s. 6d. red and blue	30	30

1963-64. *As Nos.* 181, *etc., but wmk.* w.**12**.

205	**67**	½d. black & deep orange-red (3.12.63*) ..	5	5
206	**68**	1d. black & emer. (3.4.64)	5	5
207	**70**	2½d. black and deep bright blue (3.4.64)	10	8
208	**71**	3d. emerald & red-brown (17.12.63*)	15	12
209	**73**	5d. scarlet and bronze-green (3.4.64)	25	40
210	**75**	8d. ultramarine and red-orange (3.4.64) ..	40	50
211	**76**	1s. yellow-green and blue (21.12.63*)	70	75
212	**77**	2s. deep blue and deep bronze-green (3.4.64)	1·25	1·50
213	**79**	3s. black and blue (5.2.64)	2·00	2·50
205/13		.. .. *Set of* 9	4·50	5·50

The overprint on the 8d., 1s. and 2s. is at lower left, the others are as before.

* These are the earliest known dates recorded in Jamaica.

94. Carole Joan Crawford ("Miss World 1963").

(Photo. D.L.R.)

1964 (14 Feb.–25 May). "*Miss World* 1963" *Commemoration.* P 13.

214	**94**	3d. multicoloured ..	8	5
215	,,	1s. multicoloured ..	15	15
216	,,	1s. 6d. multicoloured ..	30	30
MS216*a*		153 × 101 mm. Nos. 214/6. Imperf. (25.5.64)	70	70

MINIMUM PRICE

The minimum price quoted is 5p which represents a handling charge rather than a basis for valuing common stamps. For further notes about prices see introductory pages.

95. Lignum Vitae.

96. Ackee.

97. Blue Mahoe.

98. Land Shells.

99. National Flag over Jamaica.

100. *Murex antillarum.*

101. *Papilio homerus.*

102. Doctor Bird.

103. Gypsum Industry.

104. National Stadium.

105. Palisadoes International Airport.

106. Bauxite Mining.

107. Blue Marlin (sport fishing).

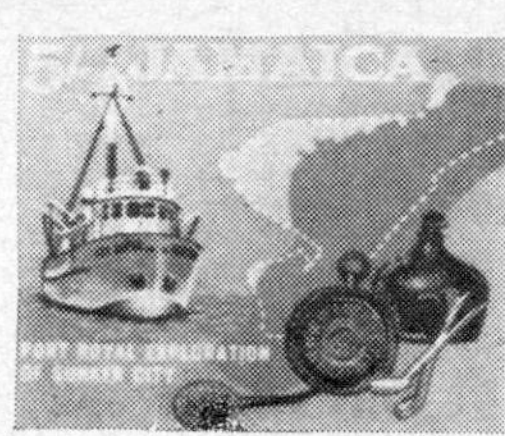

108. Exploration of Sunken City, Port Royal.

109. Arms of Jamaica.

110. Queen Elizabeth II and National Flag.

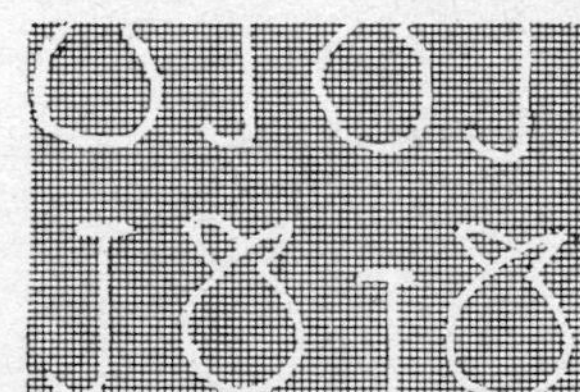

111. Multiple " J " and Pineapple.

(Des. V. Whiteley. Photo. Harrison.)

1964 (4 May). *W* **111**. *P* 14½ (1*d*., 2*d*., 2½*d*., 6*d*., 8*d*.), 14 × 14½ (1½*d*., 3*d*., 4*d*., 10*s*.), 14½ × 14 (9*d*., 1*s*., 3*s*., 5*s*., £1) *or* 13½ × 14½ (1*s*. 6*d*., 2*s*.).

217	**95**	1d. violet-blue, deep grn. and light brown ..	5	5
218	**96**	1½d. multicoloured ..	5	5
219	**97**	2d. red, yell. & grey-grn.	5	5
220	**98**	2½d. multicoloured ..	5	5
221	**99**	3d. yellow, blk. & emer.	5	5
222	**100**	4d. ochre and violet ..	8	5
223	**101**	6d. multicoloured ..	8	8
224	**102**	8d. multicoloured (*shades*)	12	10
225	**103**	9d. blue & yellow-bistre	20	10
226	**104**	1s. black & light brown	20	12
		a. Light brown omitted ..	£100	
		b. Black omitted ..	£250	
227	**105**	1s. 6d. blk., lt. bl. & buff	30	20
228	**106**	2s. red-brn., blk. & lt. bl.	40	25
229	**107**	3s. blue and dull green ..	60	55
		a. Perf. 13½ × 14½	65	70
230	**108**	5s. black, ochre and blue	90	55
231	**109**	10s. multicoloured ..	2·00	1·50
		a. Blue ("JAMAICA", etc.) omitted	£150	
232	**110**	£1 multicoloured ..	4·00	2·50
217/32		.. .. *Set of* 16	8·00	5·50

112. Scout Belt.

113. Globe, Scout Hat and Scarf.

114. Scout Badge and Alligator.

Reduced size illustration. Actual size 61½ × 30½ *mm.*).

(Photo. Harrison.)

1964 (27 Aug.). *Sixth Inter-American Scout Conference, Kingston. W* **111**. *P* 14 (1*s*.) *or* 14½ × 14 (*others*).

233	**112**	3d. red, black and pink	5	5
234	**113**	8d. brt. blue, olive & blk.	20	20
235	**114**	1s. gold, dp. blue & lt. bl.	30	35

115. Gordon House, Kingston.

116. Headquarters House, Kingston.

117. House of Assembly, Spanish Town.

(Des. V. Whiteley. Photo. Harrison.)

1964 (16 Nov.). *Tenth Commonwealth Parliamentary Conference, Kingston. W* **111**. *P* 14½ × 14.

236	**115**	3d. black and yellow-green	5	5
237	**116**	6d. black & carmine-red	10	10
238	**117**	1s. 6d. black & brt. blue	30	30

118. Eleanor Roosevelt.

(Des. V. Whiteley. Photo. Harrison.)

1964 (10 Dec.). *16th Anniv. of Declaration of Human Rights. W* **111**. *P* 14½ × 14.

239	**118**	1s. black, red & lt. green	20	20

119. Guides Emblem on Map.

120. Guide Emblems.

(*Illustration reduced. Actual size* 61½ × 30½ *mm.*)

(Photo. Harrison.)

1965 (17 May). *Golden Jubilee of Jamaica Girl Guides Association. W* **111** (*sideways on* 3*d*.). *P* 14 × 14½ (3*d*.) *or* 14 (1*s*.).

240	**119**	3d. yellow, green and light blue	5	5
241	**120**	1s. yellow, black and apple-green	20	25

121. Uniform Cap.

122. Flag-bearer and Drummer.

(Photo. Harrison.)

1965 (23 Aug.). *Salvation Army Centenary. W* **111**. *P* 14 × 14½ (3*d*.) *or* 14½ × 14 (1*s*. 6*d*.).

242	**121**	3d. multicoloured ..	5	5
243	**122**	1s. 6d. multicoloured ..	25	25

123. Paul Bogle, William Gordon and Morant Bay Court House.

(Photo. Enschedé.)

1965 (29 Dec.). *Centenary of Morant Bay Rebellion. No wmk. P* 14 × 13.

244	**123**	3d. light brown, ultramarine and black ..	5	5
245	,,	1s. 6d. light brown, yellow-green and black ..	25	25
246	,,	3s. lt. brown, rose & black	40	45

124. Abeng-blower, "Telstar", Morse Key and I.T.U. Emblem.

ROYAL VISIT
MARCH 1966

(**125**)

(Photo. Harrison.)

1965 (29 Dec.). *I.T.U. Centenary. W* **111**. *P* 14 × 14½.

247	**124**	1s. black, grey-blue & red	15	15

1966 (3 Mar.). *Royal Visit. Nos.* 221, 223, 226/7 *optd. with T* **125**.

248	**99**	3d. yellow, blk. & emer.	5	5
249	**101**	6d. multicoloured ..	8	8
250	**104**	1s. black and light brown	15	15
251	**105**	1s. 6d. blk., lt. bl. & buff	25	30

126. Sir Winston Churchill.

(Des. Jennifer Toombs. Photo. Harrison.)

1966 (18 April). *Churchill Commemoration. W* **111.** *P* 14.
252 **126** 6d. black and olive-green 15 15
253 ,, 1s. bistre-brown and deep violet-blue 25 25

127. Statue of Athlete and Flags.
128. Racing Cyclists.
129. Stadium, Kingston.
130. Games Emblem.

(Des. V. Whiteley. Photo. Harrison.)

1966 (4 Aug.). *Eighth British Empire and Commonwealth Games. W* **111.** *P* 14½×14.
254 **127** 3d. multicoloured .. 5 5
255 **128** 6d. multicoloured .. 10 10
256 **129** 1s. multicoloured .. 25 25
257 **130** 3s. bright gold and deep blue (*shades*) .. 65 65
MS258 128×103 mm. Nos. 254/7. Imperf. .. .. .. 1·00 1·00

No. **MS**258 has been seen with the whole printing inverted except for the brown background.

131. Bolivar's Statue and Flags of Jamaica and Venezuela.

(Des. and photo. Harrison.)

1966 (5 Dec.). *150th Anniv. of "Jamaica Letter". W* **111.** *P* 14×15.
259 **131** 8d. multicoloured .. 12 12

132. Jamaican Pavilion.

(Des. V. Whiteley. Photo. Harrison.)

1967 (28 Apr.). *World Fair, Montreal. W* **111.** *P* 14½.
260 **132** 6d. multicoloured .. 10 10
261 ,, 1s. multicoloured .. 20 20

133. Sir Donald Sangster (Prime Minister).

(Des. and photo. Enschedé.)

1967 (28 Aug.). *Sangster Memorial Issue. P* 13½.
262 **133** 3d. multicoloured .. 5 5
263 ,, 1s. 6d. multicoloured .. 25 25

134. Traffic Duty.

135. Personnel of the Force.

(*Illustration reduced. Actual size* 56½×20½ *mm.*)

136. Badge and Constables of 1867 and 1967.

(Des. V. Whiteley. Photo. Enschedé.)

1967 (28 Nov.). *Centenary of the Constabulary Force. W* **111.** *P* 13½×14.
264 **134** 3d. multicoloured .. 10 10
a. Wmk. sideways .. 10 10
265 **135** 1s. multicoloured .. 20 20
266 **136** 1s. 6d. multicoloured .. 25 25

1968 (8 Feb.). *M.C.C's West Indies Tour. As T* **84/6** *of Guyana, but inscr.* "JAMAICA". *Multicoloured. W* **111** (*sideways*). *P* 14. *Gum Arabic or PVA gum.*
267 6d. Wicket-keeping 12 15
268 6d. Batting 12 15
269 6d. Bowling 12 15

Nos. 267/9 were issued in small sheets of 9 comprising three *se-tenant* strips of each design.
Strips of three designs 35 45
Complete sheets of nine stamps 1·25 1·50

137. Sir Alexander and Lady Bustamante.

(Photo. Harrison.)

1968 (23 May). *Labour Day. W* **111.** *P* 14.
270 **137** 3d. rose and black .. 5
271 ,, 1s. olive and black .. 15

138. Human Rights Emblem over Map of Jamaica.

139. Hands cupping Human Rights Emblem. (*Vert.*)

140. Jamaican holding "Human Rights". (*Horiz.*)

(Photo. Harrison.)

1968 (3 Dec.). *Human Rights Year. W* **11** *P* 14.
272 **138** 3d. multicoloured .. 5
a. Gold (flame) omitted .. 55·00
273 **139** 1s. multicoloured .. 15
274 **140** 3s. multicoloured .. 40
a. Gold (flame) omitted .. 45·00

Three designs, showing 3d. Bowls of Grai 1s. Abacus, 3s. Hands in Prayer, were prepare but not issued.

141. ILO Emblem.

(Des. V. Whiteley. Litho. Format Internationa

1969 (23 May). *50th Anniv. of Internation Labour Organization. P* 14.
275 **141** 6d. orange-yellow and blackish brown .. 10
276 ,, 3s. bright emerald and blackish brown .. 45

142. Nurse, and Children being weighed and measured.

143. Malaria Eradication. (*Horiz.*)

144. Trainee Nurse. (*Vert.*)

(Des. and photo. Harrison.)

969 (30 May). *20th Anniv. of W.H.O.* *W* **111.** *P* 14.
77 **142** 6d. grey, brown & orange 8 8
78 **143** 1s. black, sepia & bl.-grn. 15 15
79 **144** 3s. grey-black, brown & pale bright blue .. 50 50

(New currency. 100 cents=1 dollar.)

C-DAY
8th September
1969
1c
(**145**)

969 (8 Sept.). *Decimal currency. Nos.* 217, 219, 221/3 *and* 225/32 *surch. as T* **145.** *Sterling values unobliterated except* 1 *c. to* 4 *c. and* 8 *c.*
80 **95** 1 c. on 1d. viol-bl., deep green & light brown 5 5
81 **97** 2 c. on 2d. red, yellow and grey-green .. 5 5
82 **99** 3 c. on 3d. yellow, black and emerald .. 5 5
83 **100** 4 c. on 4d. ochre & violet 5 5
84 **101** 5 c. on 6d. multicoloured 8 8
85 **103** 8 c. on 9d. blue and yellow bistre 12 12
86 **104** 10 c. on 1s. black and light brown 15 12
87 **105** 15 c. on 1s. 6d. black, light blue and buff 20 30
88 **106** 20 c. on 2s. red-brown, black and light blue 30 25
89 **107** 30 c. on 3s. blue and dull green 40 35
90 **108** 50 c. on 5s. black, ochre and blue 75 70
91 **109** $1 on 10s. mult. .. 1·50 1·50
92 **110** $2 on £1 multicoloured 3·00 3·00
80/92 .. .. *Set of* 13 6·00 5·50

No. 281 exists with PVA gum as well as gum arabic.

146. "The Adoration of the Kings" (detail) (Foppa).

147. "Madonna, Child and St. John" (Raphael).

148. "The Adoration of the Kings" (detail) (Dosso Dossi).

(Des. J. E. Cooter. Litho. De La Rue.)

969 (25 Oct.). *Christmas.* *W* **111.** *P* 13.
93 **146** 2 c. multicoloured .. 5 5
94 **147** 5 c. multicoloured .. 8 8
95 **148** 8 c. multicoloured .. 15 15

149. Half Penny, 1869.

150. One Penny, 1869.

(Des. G. Drummond. Litho. Perkins Bacon.)

1969 (27 Oct.). *Centenary of First Jamaican Coins.* *W* **111.** *P* 12½.
269 **149** 3 c. silver, black, & mve. 1·10
a. Wmk. sideways .. 5 5
297 **150** 15 c. silver, blk. & lt. emer. 20 20

151. George William Gordon.
156. "Christ Appearing to St. Peter" (Carracci).
152. Sir Alexander Bustamante.
157. "Christ Crucified" (Antonello).
153. Norman Manley.
154. Marcus Garvey.
158. Easter Lily.
155. Paul Bogle.

(Des. G. L. Vasarhelyi. Litho. Enschedé.)

1970 (11 Mar.). *National Heroes. Multicoloured; background colours given.* *P* 12×12½.
298 **151** 1 c. bluish lilac 5 5
299 **152** 3 c. light blue 5 5
300 **153** 5 c. grey 8 8
301 **154** 10 c. pale rose 15 15
302 **155** 15 c. pale green 25 25
299/302 .. .. *Set of* 5 50 50

(Des. G. Drummond. Photo. Enschedé.)

1970 (23 Mar.). *Easter. Centres multicoloured: frame colours given.* *W* **111.** *P* 12×12½.
303 **156** 3 c. cerise 5 5
304 **157** 10 c. olive-green 20 20
305 **158** 20 c. grey 30 30

2c ■
(**159**)

160. Lignum Vitae.

1970 (16 July). *No.* 219 *surch. with T* **159.**
306 **97** 2 c. on 2d. red, yellow and grey-green 8 8

1970. *Decimal Currency. Designs as T* **95** *etc., but inscr. in decimal currency as T* **160.** *W* **111** *(sideways on* 2 *c.,* 4 *c.,* 15 *c.,* 20 *c., and* $1*). P* 14½ (1 *c.,* 5 *c.*) 14×14½ (4 *c.,* $1), 13½×14½ (15 *c.,* 20 *c.*) *or* 14½×14 (*others.*)
307 **160** 1 c. violet-blue, dp. green and light brown 5 5
308 **97** 2 c. red, yellow and grey-green 5 5
309 **99** 3 c. yellow, black and emerald 5 5
310 **100** 4 c. ochre and violet .. 5 5
311 **101** 5 c. multicoloured .. 8 5
312 **103** 8 c. blue & yellow-bistre 12 10
a. Wmk. sideways .. 30 30
313 **104** 10 c. black & light brown 15 12
314 **105** 15 c. black, light blue and buff 20 30
315 **106** 20 c. red-brown, black and light blue 30 25
316 **107** 30 c. blue and dull green 40 35
317 **108** 50 c. black, ochre and blue 75 70
318 **109** $1 multicoloured .. 1·50 1·50
319 **110** $2 multicoloured .. 3·00 3·00
307/19 .. .. *Set of* 13 6·00 5·50

Dates of issue:—7 Sept., 1 c. to 10 c.; 2 Nov., others.

161. Cable Ship *Dacia*.

162. Bright's Cable Gear aboard *Dacia*.
163. Morse Key and Chart.

(Des. G. Drummond. Litho. J.W.)

1970 (12 Oct.). *Centenary of Telegraph Service.* *W* **111** (*sideways*). *P* 14½×14.
320 **161** 3 c. yellow, red and black 5 5
321 **162** 10 c. black and turquoise 20 20
322 **163** 50 c. multicoloured .. 75 75

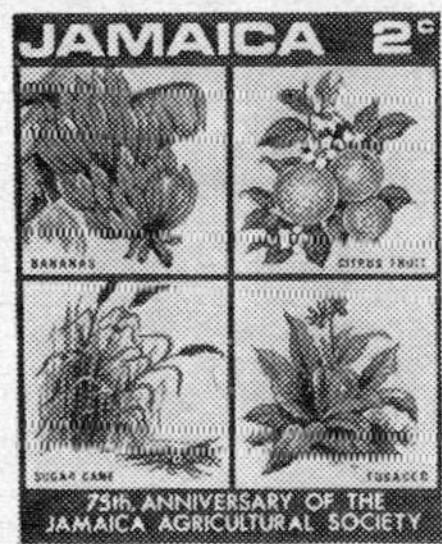

164. Bananas, Citrus, Sugar-Cane and Tobacco.

(Des. G. Drummond. Litho. Questa.)

1970 (2 Nov.). *75th Anniv. of Jamaican Agricultural Society.* *W* **111.** *P* 14.
323 **164** 2 c. multicoloured .. 5 5
324 ,, 10 c. multicoloured .. 15 20

165. "The Projector" (1845).

166. Engine "54" (1944).
167. Engine "102" (1967).

(Des. V. Whiteley. Litho. Format.)

1970 (21 Nov.). *125th Anniv. of Jamaican Railways.* *W* **111** (*sideways*). *P* 13½.
325 **165** 3 c. multicoloured .. 10 10
326 **166** 15 c. multicoloured .. 30 30
327 **167** 50 c. multicoloured .. 70 70

168. Church of St. Jago de la Vega.

(Des. R. Granger Barrett. Litho. J.W.)

1971 (22 FEB.). *Centenary of the disestablishment of the Church of England in Jamaica. T* **168** *and similar vert. design. W* **111.** *P* 14½.

328	**168**	3 c. multicoloured ..	5	5
329	,,	10 c. multicoloured ..	12	12
330	,,	20 c. multicoloured ..	30	30
331	–	30 c. multicoloured ..	40	40

Design:—30 c. Emblem of Church of England in Jamaica.

169. Henry Morgan and Ships.

(Des. J. W. Litho. Questa.)

1971 (10 MAY). *Pirates and Buccaneers. T* **169** *and similar horiz. designs. Multicoloured. W* **111** *(sideways). P* 14.

332	3 c. Type **169**	10	10
333	15 c. Mary Read, Anne Bonny and trial pamphlet ..	25	25
334	30 c. Pirate schooner attacking merchantman ..	50	50

170. 1s. Stamp of 1919 with Frame Inverted.

(Des. Jennifer Toombs. Litho. J.W.)

1971 (30 OCT.). *Tercentenary of Post Office Establishment. T* **170** *and similar designs. W* **111** *(sideways, except* 50 *c.). P* 13½.

335	3 c. black and lake	8	8
336	5 c. grey-blk. & bright green	8	10
337	8 c. black and violet ..	12	15
338	10 c. brown, black & indigo	15	15
339	20 c. multicoloured	25	30
340	50 c. ochre, black and slate ..	70	70
335/40	.. .. *Set of* 6	1·25	1·25

Designs: *Horiz.*—3 c. Dummer packet letter, 1705; 5 c. Pre-stamp inland letter, 1793; 8 c. Harbour St. P.O., Kingston, 1820; 10 c. Modern stamp and cancellation; 20 c. British stamps used in Jamaica, 1859.

171. Satellite and Dish Aerial.

(Des. Cable & Wireless Ltd. Litho. J.W.)

1972 (17 FEB.). *Opening of Jamaican Earth Satellite Station. W* **111.** *P* 14×13½.

341	**171**	3 c. multicoloured ..	5	5
342	,,	15 c. multicoloured ..	20	20
343	,,	50 c. multicoloured ..	60	65

172. Causeway, Kingston Harbour.

173. Air Jamaica Hostess and Aircraft.

(Des. J. W. Ltd. Litho. Format.)

1972. *Multicoloured designs as T* **172** *(*1 *to* 6 *c.) or T* **173** *(*8 *c. to* $2*). W* **111** *(sideways on horiz. designs). P* 14½×14 *(*1 *and* 2 *c.),* 14×14½ *(*3 *to* 6 *c.) or* 13½ *(*8 *c. to* $2*).*

344	1 c. Pimento	5	5
345	2 c. Red Ginger	5	5
346	3 c. Bauxite Industry ..	5	5
347	4 c. Type **172**	5	5
348	5 c. Oil Refinery	5	5
349	6 c. Senate Building, University of the West Indies	5	8
350	8 c. National Stadium ..	8	10
351	9 c. Devon House	10	10
352	10 c. Type **173**	10	12
353	15 c. Old Iron Bridge, Spanish Town	15	20
354	20 c. College of Arts, Science and Technology	20	25
355	30 c. Dunn's River Falls ..	30	35
356	50 c. River rafting	55	65
357	$1 Jamaica House	1·10	1·25
358	$2 Kings House	2·10	2·25
344/58	.. .. *Set of* 15	4·25	4·75

The 1, 2, 15 and 30 c. are vert. designs, and the remainder are horiz.

Dates of issue: 17.4.72, 4 c., 10 c.; 5.6.7 1, 2, 3, 5 to 9, 50 c.; 2.10.72, 15, 20, 30 c., $1, $

TENTH
ANNIVERSARY
INDEPENDENCE
1962-1972
(174)

175. Arms of Kingston.

1972 (8 AUG.). *Tenth Anniv. of Independenc Nos.* 346, 352 *and* 356 *optd. as T* **174.**

359	3 c. Bauxite Industry ..	5	
360	10 c. Type **173**	15	
361	50 c. River rafting	60	

(Des. R. Granger Barrett. Litho. J.W.)

1972 (4 DEC.). *Centenary of Kingston as Capita W* **111** *(sideways on* 50 *c.). P* 13½×14 *(*5 *ar* 30 *c.). or* 14×13½ *(*50 *c.).*

362	**175**	5 c. multicoloured ..	8	
363	,,	30 c. multicoloured ..	40	
364	–	50 c. multicoloured ..	60	

The 50 c. is as T **175,** but horiz.

176. Mongoose on Map.

(Des. R. Granger Barrett. Litho. Questa

1973 (9 APR.). *Centenary of Introduction of t. Mongoose. T* **176** *and similar horiz. design W* **111** *(sideways). P* 14×14½.

365	8 c. light apple-grn., yellow-green and black	12	
366	40 c. light cobalt, light blue and black	50	
367	60 c. salmon-pink, brownish salmon and black ..	80	
MS368	165×95 mm. Nos. 365/7	3·50	3·5

Designs:—40 c. Mongoose and rat; 60 Mongoose and chicken.

177. *Euphorbia punicea.*

(Des. Sylvia Goaman. Litho. Questa.)

973 (9 JULY). *Flora. T* **177** *and similar diamond-shaped designs. Multicoloured. W* **111**. *P* 14.

69	1 c. Type **177**	5	5
70	6 c. *Hylocereus triangularis* ..	8	8
71	9 c. *Columnea argentea* ..	10	10
72	15 c. *Portlandia grandiflora* ..	20	20
73	30 c. *Samyda pubescens* ..	35	35
74	50 c. *Cordia sebestena* ..	60	60
69/74	.. .. *Set of* 6	1·25	1·25

178. *Broughtonia sanguinea.*

(Des. Sylvia Goaman. Litho. B.W.)

973 (8 OCT.). *Orchids. T* **178** *and similar multicoloured designs. W* **111** *(sideways on* 5 *c.,* $1, **MS**379). *P* 14 × 13½ (5 *c.,* $1) *or* 13½ × 14 *(others).*

75	5 c. Type **178**	5	5
76	10 c. *Arpophyllum jamaicense* *(vert.)*	12	12
77	20 c. *Oncidium pulchellum* *(vert.)*	25	25
78	$1 *Brassia maculata* ..	1·10	1·10
MS379	161 × 95 mm. Nos. 375/8. P 12	1·75	1·75

179. *Mary*, 1808–15.

(Des. J. E. Cooter. Litho. J.W.)

974 (8 APR.). *Mail Packet Boats. T* **179** *and similar horiz. designs. Multicoloured. W* **111** *(sideways on Nos.* 380/3, *upright on* **MS**384). *P* 13½ (5 *c.,* 50 *c.) or* 14 *(others).*

80	5 c. Type **179**	5	5
	a. Perf. 14	7·00	1·25
81	10 c. *Queensbury*, 1814–27 ..	15	15
82	15 c. *Sheldrake*, 1829–34 ..	25	25
83	50 c. *Thames*, 1842	60	60
MS384	133 × 159 mm. Nos. 380/4. P 13½ *(sold at* 90 *c.)*	1·25	1·25

180. "Journeys".

(Des. R. Granger Barrett. Litho. Questa.)

1974 (1 AUG.). *National Dance Theatre Company. T* **180** *and similar vert. designs showing dance-works. Multicoloured. W* **111**. *P* 13½.

385	5 c. Type **180**	5	5
386	10 c. "Jamaican Promenade"	12	12
387	30 c. "Jamaican Promenade"	30	35
388	50 c. "Misa Criolla"	50	55
MS389	161 × 102 mm. Nos. 385/8	1·00	1·00

181. U.P.U. Emblem and Globe.

(Des. V. Whiteley. Litho. J.W.)

1974 (9 OCT.). *Centenary of Universal Postal Union. W* **111** *(sideways). P* 14.

390	**181**	5 c. multicoloured ..	5	5
391	„	9 c. multicoloured ..	10	10
392	„	50 c. multicoloured ..	50	55

182. Senate Building and Sir Hugh Wooding.

(Des. R. Granger Barrett. Litho. Questa).

1975 (13 JAN.). *25th Anniv. of University of West Indies. T* **182** *and similar horiz. design. Multicoloured. W* **111** *(sideways). P* 14.

393	5 c. Type **182**	5	5
394	10 c. University Chapel and H.R.H. Princess Alice ..	12	12
395	30 c. Type **182**	30	35
396	50 c. As 10 c.	50	55

183. Commonwealth Symbol.

(Des. C. Abbott. Litho. Questa.)

1975 (29 APR.). *Heads of Commonwealth Conference. T* **183** *and similar square designs. Multicoloured. W* **111**. *P* 13½.

397	5 c. Type **183**	5	5
398	10 c. Jamaican coat-of-arms ..	12	12
399	30 c. Dove of Peace	30	35
400	50 c. Jamaican flag	50	55

184. Jamaican Kite Swallowtail.

(Des. J. E. Cooter. Litho. Questa.)

1975 (25 AUG.). *Butterflies. T* **184** *and similar vert. designs. Multicoloured. W* **111**. *P* 14.

401	10 c. Type **184**	12	12
402	20 c. Jamaican Swallowtail ..	20	25
403	25 c. Thersites Swallowtail ..	25	30
404	30 c. Homerus Swallowtail ..	30	35
MS405	134 × 179 mm. Nos. 401/4 *(sold at* 95 *c.)*	1·10	

185. Koo Koo or Actor Boy.

(Des. C. Abbott. Litho. J.W.)

1975 (3 NOV.). *Christmas. T* **185** *and similar vert. designs showing Belisario prints of "John Canoe" (Christmas) Festival* (1*st series*). *Multicoloured. W* **111**. *P* 14.

406	8 c. Type **185**	8	10
407	10 c. Red Set-girls	12	12
408	20 c. French Set-girls	25	25
409	50 c. Jaw-bone or House John Canoe	50	60
MS410	138 × 141 mm. Nos. 406/9. P 13½ *(sold at* $1)	1·00	1·10

See also Nos. 421/**MS**424.

186. Bordone Map, 1528.

(Des. L. Curtis. Litho. Questa.)

1976 (12 MAR.). *16th Century Maps of Jamaica. T* **186** *and similar horiz. designs. W* **111** *(sideways). P* 13½.

411	**186**	10 c. brown, light stone & light vermilion ..	10	10
412	–	20 c. multicoloured ..	20	20
413	–	30 c. multicoloured ..	30	35
414	–	50 c. multicoloured ..	50	55

Designs:—20 c. Porcacchi map, 1576; 30 c. DeBry map, 1594; 50 c. Langenes map, 1598.

187. Olympic Rings.

(Des. V. Whiteley Studio. Litho. Walsall.)

1976 (14 JUNE). *Olympic Games, Montreal. W* **111** *(sideways). P* 13½.
415 **187** 10 c. multicoloured .. 12 15
416 ,, 20 c. multicoloured .. 25 30
417 ,, 25 c. multicoloured .. 30 35
418 ,, 50 c. multicoloured .. 60 70

1976 (9 AUG.). *West Indian Victory in World Cricket Cup. As Nos.* 559/60 *of Barbados.*
419 15 c. Map of the Caribbean .. 20 25
420 15 c. Prudential Cup 20 25

(Des. C. Abbott. Litho. J.W.)

1976 (8 NOV.). *Christmas. Belisario Prints (2nd series). Multicoloured designs as T* **185.** *W* **111.** *P* 13½.
421 10 c. Queen of the set-girls .. 12 15
422 20 c. Band of the Jaw-bone John-Canoe 25 30
423 50 c. Koo Koo (actor-boy) .. 60 70
MS424 110×140 mm. Nos. 421/3. P 14×14½ *(sold at* 90 c.*)* .. .. 1·10

POSTAL FISCALS.

Revenue stamps were authorized for postal use by Post Office notice of 12 *October,* 1887.

CONDITION. The note at the beginning also applies to Nos. F1/6.

F 1

(Typo. D.L.R.)

1865–71 (Issued). *P* 14.
(a) Wmk. Pineapple (T **7**).
F1 **F 1** 1d. rose (1865) .. .. 23·00 30·00
a. Imperf. £100
(b) Wmk. Crown CC.
F2 **F 1** 1d. rose (1868) .. .. 11·00 13·00
(c) Wmk. CA over Crown (Type w. **7** *sideways, covering two stamps).*
F3 **F 1** 1d. rose (1870 or 1871) 2·50 2·50
a. Imperf. .. ..

F 2

F 3

(Typo. D.L.R.)

1855–74 (Issued). *Glazed paper. P* 14.
(a) No wmk.
F4 **F 2** 1½d. blue/*blue* (1857) .. 9·00 12·00
a. Imperf. (1855) .. ..
b. Blue on white .. .. 12·00 15·00
F5 ,, 3d. purple/*blue* (1857) .. 9·00 12·00
a. Imperf. (1855) .. ..
b. Purple on lilac (1857) .. 11·00 13·00
ba. Imperf. (1855) .. ..
c. Purple on white (1857) .. 9·00 12·00
(b) Wmk. Crown CC.
F6 **F 2** 3d. purple/*lilac* (1874) .. 90 1·10

All the above stamps *imperf.* are exceedingly rare postally used.

1858 (1 JAN.) (Issued). *No wmk. P* 15½×15.
F7 **F 3** 1s. rose/*bluish* .. .. 12·00 13·00
F8 ,, 5s. lilac/*bluish* .. 50·00 65·00
F9 ,, 10s. green/*bluish* .. 50·00 65·00

Telegraph stamps were also used postally, but no authority was given for such use.

OFFICIAL STAMPS.

OFFICIAL (O 1)   OFFICIAL (O 2)

(Optd. by C. Vendryes, Kingston.)

1890 (1 APRIL). *No.* 16 *optd. with Type* O **1.**
(a) " OFFICIAL " 17 to 17½ mm. long.
O1 **8** ½d. green 55 45
a. " O " omitted .. .. 80·00
b. One " I " omitted .. ..
c. Both " I "s omitted .. 80·00 80·00
d. " L " omitted .. .. — £100
e. Opt. inverted .. .. 11·00 12·00
f. Opt. double .. .. 11·00 12·00
g. Opt. double, one inverted .. 65·00 65·00
h. Opt. double, one vertical .. £140
j. Pair, overprints tête-bêche ..
(b) " OFFICIAL " 15 to 16 mm. long.
O2 **8** ½d. green .. .. .. 3·00 3·00
a. Opt. double .. .. 80·00

There were four (or possibly five) settings of this overprint, all but one being of the longer type. There are numerous minor varieties, due to broken type, etc. (*e.g.* a broken " E " used for " F ").

Stamps with the 17–17½ mm. opt. were reissued in 1894 during a temporary shortage of No. O3.

(Optd. by D.L.R.)

1890–1. *Optd. with Type* O **2.** *Wmk. Crown CA. P* 14.
O3 **8** ½d. green (1891) 25 12
O4 **11** 1d. rose (1.4.90) 35 12
O5 ,, 2d. grey (1.4.90) 50 20
O3/5 Optd. " Specimen " *Set of* 3 25·00

JORDAN.

(Formerly **TRANSJORDAN**)

All issues will be found listed in Vol. 2 of th Stanley Gibbons Foreign Overseas Catalogue.

KENYA.

I. INDEPENDENT.

46. Cattle Ranching. **47.** Wood-carving.

48. National Assembly.

(Des. V. Whiteley. Photo. Harrison.)

1963 (12 DEC.). *Independence. T* **46/8** *an similar designs. P* 14×15 *(small designs)* 14½ *(others).*
207 5 c. brown, deep blue, green and bistre .. 5
208 10 c. brown 5
209 15 c. magenta 5
210 20 c. black & yellow-green 5
211 30 c. black and yellow .. 5
212 40 c. brown and light blue 5
213 50 c. crimson, blk. & grn. 8
214 65 c. dp. turq.-grn. & yell. 10 1
215 1s. multicoloured .. 12 1
216 1s. 30, brown, black and yellow-green 25 1
217 2s. multicoloured .. 40 2
218 5s. brn., ult. & yell.-grn. 1·00 4
219 10s. brown and deep blue 2·50 1·2
220 20s. black and rose .. 5·00 3·7
207/20 .. .. *Set of* 14 8·50 5·5

Designs: *As T* **46/7**—15 c. Heavy industry 20 c. Timber industry; 30 c. Jomo Kenyatta an Mt. Kenya; 40 c. Fishing industry; 50 c. Keny flag; 65 c. Pyrethrum industry. *As T* **48**– 1s. 30, Tourism (Treetop Hotel); 2s. Coffee in dustry; 5s. Tea industry; 10s. Mombasa Por 20s. Royal College, Nairobi.

II. REPUBLIC.

49. Cockerel.

(Des. M. Goaman. Photo. J. Enschedé.)

1964 (12 DEC.). *Inauguration of Republic. T* **49** *and similar vert. designs. Multicoloured. P* 13×12½.

21	15 c. Type **49**	5	5
22	30 c. Pres. Kenyatta	10	8
23	50 c. Lion	15	20
24	1s. 30, Hartlaub's Touraco ..	45	75
25	2s. 50, Nandi flame	1·10	1·75
21/5	.. .. *Set of* 5	1·75	2·50

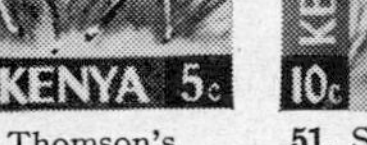

50. Thomson's Gazelle. **51.** Sable Antelope.

52. Greater Kudu.

(Des. Mrs. R. M. Fennessy. Photo. Harrison.)

1966 (12 DEC.)–**71.** *Various designs as T* **50/2.** *Chalk-surfaced paper. P* 14×14½ (5 *c. to* 70 *c.) or* 14½ *(others).*

26	5 c. orge., blk. and sepia	5	5
27	10 c. black & apple-green	5	5
	a. Glazed, ordinary paper (13.7.71)	5	5
28	15 c. black and orange ..	5	5
	a. Glazed, ordinary paper (13.7.71)	5	5
29	20 c. ochre, black and blue	5	5
	a. Glazed ordinary paper (22.1.71)	5	5
230	30 c. Prussian blue, blue & black	5	5
231	40 c. black & yellow-brown	5	5
	a. Glazed, ordinary paper (19.2.71)	5	5
232	50 c. black and red-orange	8	5
	a. Glazed, ordinary paper (19.2.71)	8	5
233	65 c. black and light green	12	10
233*a*	70 c. blk. & claret (15.9.69)	12	12
	b. Glazed, ordinary paper (19.2.71)	12	12
234	1s. olive-brown, black & slate-blue	15	8
	a. Glazed ordinary paper (22.1.71)	15	15
235	1s. 30, indigo, light olive-green and black ..	20	12
235*a*	1s. 50, black, orange-brn. and dull sage-green (15.9.69)	20	35
	b. Glazed ordinary paper (22.1.71)	25	35
236	2s. 50, yellow, black and olive-brown	35	35
	a. Glazed ordinary paper (22.1.71)	35	35
237	5s. yellow, black & emer.	85	60
	a. Glazed ordinary paper (22.1.71)	85	60
238	10s. yellow-ochre, black & red-brown	1·75	1·50
239	20s. yellow-ochre, yellow-orange, black & gold	3·50	2·75
226/39	.. .. *Set of* 16	6·75	5·50
227a/37a	.. .. *Set of* 10	1·75	1·50

Designs: *As T* **50/1**—15 c. Ant bear; 20 c. Bush-baby; 30 c. Wart-hog; 40 c. Zebra; 50 c. Buffalo; 65 c. Rhinoceros; 70 c. Ostrich. *As T* **52**—1s. 30, Elephant; 1s. 50, Bat-eared fox; 2s. 50, Cheetah; 5s. Vervet monkey; 10s. Pangolin; 20s. Lion.

On chalk-surfaced paper, all values except 30 c., 50 c. and 2s. 50 exist with PVA gum as well as gum arabic but the 70 c. and 1s. 50 exist with PVA gum only. The stamps on glazed, ordinary paper exist with PVA gum only.

53. Rose Dawn. **54.** Rock Shell.

50 c. A. Inscr. "*Janthina globosa*".
B. Inscr. "*Janthina janthina*".
70 c. C. Inscr. "*Nautilus pompileus*".
D. Inscr. "*Nautilus pompilius*".

(Des. Mrs. R. Fennessy. Photo. Harrison.)

1971 (15 DEC.)–**74.** *T* **53/4** *and similar vert. designs showing seashells. Multicoloured.*

(*a*) *Size as T* **53.** *P* 14½×14.

240	5 c. Type **53**	5	5
241	10 c. Bishop's Cap (*shades*) ..	5	5
242	15 c. Strawberry Shell ..	5	5
243	20 c. Black Prince	5	5
244	30 c. Mermaid's Ear	5	5
245	40 c. Top Shell	5	5
246	50 c. Violet Shell (A)	5	5
247	50 c. Violet Shell (B) (21.1.74)	5	5
248	60 c. Cameo	5	8
249	70 c. Pearly Nautilus (C) ..	8	8
250	70 c. Pearly Nautilus (D) (21.1.74)	8	10

(*b*) *Size as T* **54.** *P* 14.

251	1s. Type **54** (*shades*) ..	10	12
252	1s. 50, Triton ..	15	20
253	2s. 50, Neptune's Trumpet	25	30
254	5s. Turban Shell (*shades*) ..	50	60
255	10s. Cloth of Gold	1·00	1·10
256	20s. Spider Shell (*shades*) ..	2·10	2·25
240/56	.. .. *Set of* 17	4·50	4·75

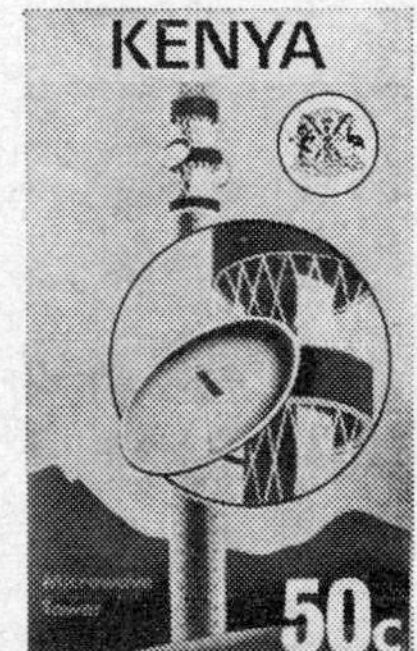

= 2/-

(55) **56.** Microwave Tower.

1975 (17 NOV.). *Nos.* 252/3 *and* 256 *surch. as T* **55.**

257	2s. on 1s. 50, Triton ..	25	30
258	3s. on 2s. 50, Neptune's Trumpet	10·00	10·00
259	40s. on 20s. Spider Shell ..	5·00	5·25

The surcharge on No. 259 does not have a dot beneath the stroke following the face value.

For commemorative stamps, issued between 1964 and 1976, inscribed "UGANDA KENYA TANGANYIKA & ZANZIBAR" (or "TANZANIA UGANDA KENYA") see under EAST AFRICA.

(Des. H. Nickelsen. Litho. Format.)

1976 (15 APR.). *Telecommunications Development. T* **56** *and similar multicoloured designs. P* 14½.

260	50 c. Type **56**	5	8
261	1s. Cordless switchboard (*horiz.*)	12	15
262	2s. Telephones	25	30
263	3s. Message Switching Centre (*horiz.*)	35	40
MS264	120×120 mm. Nos. 260/3. Imperf.	80	

57. Akii Bua, Ugandan Hurdler.

(Des. Beryl Moore. Litho. Format.)

1976 (5 JULY). *Olympic Games, Montreal. T* **57** *and similar horiz. designs. Multicoloured. P* 14½.

265	50 c. Type **57**	5	8
266	1s. Filbert Bayi, Tanzanian runner	12	15
267	2s. Steve Muchoki, Kenyan boxer	25	30
268	3s. Olympic flame and East African flags	35	40
MS269	129×154 mm. Nos. 265/8. P 13	80	

58. Tanzania-Zambia Railway.

(Des. Hameed Moghul. Litho. Format.)

1976 (4 OCT.). *Railway Transport. T* **58** *and similar horiz. designs. Multicoloured. P* 14½.

270	50 c. Type **58**	5	8
271	1s. Nile Bridge, Uganda ..	12	15
272	2s. Nakuru Station, Kenya	25	30
273	3s. Class A locomotive, 1896	35	40
MS274	154×103 mm. Nos. 270/3. P 13	80	

POSTAGE DUE STAMPS.

The Postage Due stamps of Kenya, Uganda and Tanganyika were used in Kenya until 2nd January, 1967.

D 3

(Litho. De La Rue.)

1967 (3 Jan.)–**70.** *Chalk-surfaced paper. P* 14×13½.

D13	D 3	5 c. red	5	5
		a. Perf. 14. *Brownish red*, O (16.12.69) ..	5	5
D14	„	10 c. green	5	5
		a. Perf. 14. O (16.12.69)	5	5
D15	„	20 c. blue	5	5
		a. Perf. 14. *Deep blue*, O (16.12.69)	5	5
D16	„	30 c. brown	5	5
		a. Perf. 14. *Light red-brown*, O (16.12.69) ..	5	5
D17	„	40 c. bright purple ..	12	12
		a. Perf. 14. *Pale bright purple*, O (16.12.69) ..	12	12
D18	„	1s. orange	20	20
		a. Perf. 14. *Yellow-orange*, O (18.2.70)	20	20
D13/18		.. .. *Set of* 6	45	45
D13a/18a		.. .. *Set of* 6	45	45

1971–73. *As Nos.* D14 *etc., but P* 14×15.

(*a*) *Chalk-surfaced paper* (13.7.71).

D19	D 3	10 c. green	5	5
D20	„	20 c. deep dull blue ..	5	5
D21	„	30 c. red-brown ..	5	5
D22	„	1 s. yellow-orange ..	20	20

(*b*) *Glazed, ordinary paper* (20.2.73).

D23	D 3	5 c. red	5	5
D24	„	10 c. dull yellow-green ..	5	5
D25	„	20 c. deep blue	5	5
D27	„	40 c. bright purple ..	12	12
D28	„	1s. bright orange ..	20	20
D19/28		.. .. *Set of* 9	70	70

1973 (12 Dec.). *Glazed, ordinary paper. P* 15.

D29	D 3	5 c. scarlet	5	5
D30	„	10 c. emerald	5	5
D31	„	20 c. deep blue	5	5
D32	„	30 c. red-brown	5	5
D33	„	40 c. bright mauve ..	5	5
D34	„	1 s. bright orange ..	10	12
D29/34		.. .. *Set of* 6	20	20

OFFICIAL STAMPS.

Intended for use on official correspondence of the Kenya Government only but there is no evidence that they were so used.

OFFICIAL

(O 4)

(15 c., 30 c. opt. typo.; others in photogravure.)

1964 (1 Oct.). *Optd. with Type* O **4.**

O21	**46**	5 c. brown, deep blue, green and bistre ..	5
O22	**47**	10 c. brown	5
O23	**48**	15 c. magenta	8
O24	**49**	20 c. black & yellow-green	10
O25	**50**	30 c. black and yellow ..	15
O26	**62**	50 c. crimson, black & grn.	20
O21/26		.. .. *Set of* 6	50

KENYA, UGANDA AND TANGANYIKA.

For earlier issues see British East Africa and Uganda.

For the issues of the Mandated Territory of Tanganyika and the war-time issues that preceded them, see Tanganyika.

PRINTERS. All the stamps issued between 1903 and 1927 were typographed by De La Rue & Co.

USED HIGH VALUES. Beware of cleaned fiscally cancelled copies with faked postmarks.

I. EAST AFRICA AND UGANDA.

1

2

1903–4. P 14. (a) *Wmk. Crown CA.*

1	1	½ a. green	85	85
2	,,	1 a. grey and red	80	45
3	,,	2 a. dull and bright purple	2·25	2·50
4	,,	2½ a. blue	6·50	6·00
5	,,	3 a. brown-purple & green	5·00	6·00
6	,,	4 a. grey-green and black..	6·00	6·00
7	,,	5 a. grey & orange-brown	12·00	13·00
8	,,	8 a. grey and pale blue	12·00	12·00
		(b) *Wmk. Crown CC.*		
9	2	1 r. green, OC	6·50	7·50
10	,,	2 r. dull & bright purple, O	12·00	13·00
11	,,	3 r. grey-green & black, O	14·00	15·00
12	,,	4 r. grey & emer.-green, O	18·00	19·00
13	,,	5 r. grey and red, O	18·00	20·00
14	,,	10 r. grey and ultram, OC..	60·00	50·00
15	,,	20 r. grey & stone, O (Optd. S. £50)..	£250	£200
16	,,	50 r. grey & red-brown, O (Optd. S. £100) ..	£500	£500
1/13		.. .. *Set of* 13	£100	£110
1/14		Optd. "Specimen" *Set of* 14	70·00	

1904–07. *Wmk. Mult. Crown CA.* P 14.

17	1	½ a. grey-green, OC ..	30	30
18	,,	1 a. grey and red, OC ..	50	40
19	,,	2 a. dull & brt. purple, OC	1·90	1·90
20	,,	2½ a. blue, O	3·75	4·00
21	,,	2½ a. ultram. & blue, O ..	3·00	3·50
22	,,	3 a. brown-pur. & grn., OC	2·25	3·00
23	,,	4 a. grey-grn. & blk., OC..	3·00	3·75
24	,,	5 a. grey & orge.-brn., OC	4·00	4·50
25	,,	8 a. grey & pale blue, OC	4·50	5·00
26	2	1 r. green, C (1907) ..	7·50	7·50
27	,,	2 r. dull and bright purple, C (1906)	12·00	11·00
28	,,	3 r. grey-grn. & blk., C ('07)	15·00	15·00
29	,,	4 r. grey & em.-grn., C ('07)	15·00	20·00
30	,,	5 r. grey and red, C ('07) ..	19·00	20·00
31	,,	10 r. grey & ultram., C ('07)	70·00	65·00
32	,,	20 r. grey and stone, C ('07)	£160	£190
33	,,	50 r. grey & red-brn., C ('07)	£650	£600
17/30		.. .. *Set of* 13	85·00	90·00

Currency changed (100 cents = 1 rupee).

1907–08. *Wmk. Mult. Crown CA.* P 14.

34	1	1 c. brown, O (1908) ..	20	30
35	,,	3 c. grey-green, O.. ..	20	30
		a. Blue-green, O	15	45
36	,,	6 c. red, O..	70	25
37	,,	10 c. lilac and pale olive, C	2·50	2·50
38	,,	12 c. dull & bright purple, C	2·50	2·00
39	,,	15 c. bright blue, O.. ..	2·50	3·00
40	,,	25 c. grey-green & black, C	3·00	4·00
41	,,	50 c. grey-green and orange-brown, C	3·75	4·50
42	,,	75 c. grey & pale bl., C ('08)	5·00	7·00
34/42		.. .. *Set of* 9	18·00	22·00
34/42		Optd. "Specimen" *Set of* 9	48·00	

Original

Redrawn

1910. *T* 1 *redrawn. Printed from a single plate. Wmk. Mult. Crown CA.* P 14.

43		6 c. red, O	1·60	25

In the redrawn type a fine white line has been cut around the value tablets and above the name tablet separating the latter from the leaves above, East Africa and Uganda is in shorter and thicker letters and Protectorates in taller letters than in No. 36.

3

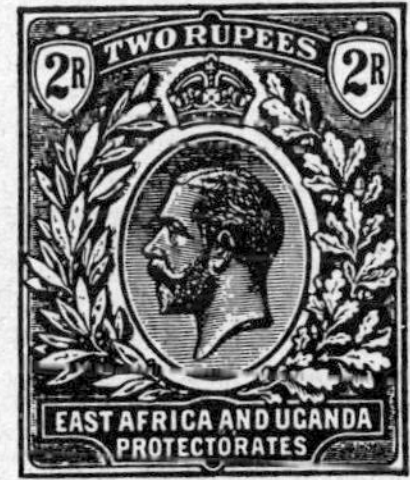

4

1912–22. *Wmk. Mult. Crown CA.* P 14.

44	3	1 c. black, O	25	20
45	,,	3 c. green, O	50	20
		a. Deep blue-green, O (1917) ..	60	20
46	,,	6 c. red, O	25	25
		a. Scarlet, O (1917)	1·00	25
47	,,	10 c. yellow-orange, O	2·00	25
		a. Orange, O (1921) ..	1·75	25
48	,,	12 c. slate-grey, O ..	1·00	90
49	,,	15 c. bright blue, O ..	1·00	60
50	,,	25 c. black & red/*yellow*, C	80	55
		a. White back (Optd. S. £7) ..	80	90
		b. On lemon (1916) (Optd. S. £7)	4·00	3·25
		c. On orange-buff (1921) ..	7·00	1·60
		d. On pale yellow (1921) ..	4·00	1·50
51	,,	50 c. black and lilac, C	1·50	1·10
52	,,	75 c. black/*green*, C ..	2·00	2·50
		a. White back (Optd. S. £7) ..	1·75	3·00
		b. On blue-green, olive back (Optd. S. £7)	4·50	3·00
		c. On emerald, olive back ..	22·00	23·00
		d. On emerald back	4·00	3·50
53	4	1 r. black/*green*, C ..	3·00	2·75
		a. On emerald back ..	4·00	4·00
54	,,	2 r. red and black/*blue*, C	8·00	8·00
55	,,	3 r. violet and green, C ..	8·00	9·00
56	,,	4 r. red & green/*yellow*, C	14·00	14·00
		a. On pale yellow	15·00	15·00
57	,,	5 r. blue and dull purple, C	15·00	15·00
58	,,	10 r. red and green/*green*, C	20·00	25·00
59	,,	20 r. black & purple/*red*, C	£100	90·00
60	,,	20 r. purple & bl./*bl.*, C ('18)	£100	90·00
61	,,	50 r. carmine & green, C O (Optd. S. £80)	£350	£350
		a. Dull rose-red and dull greyish green, O	£350	£350
62	,,	100 r. purple and black/*red*, C (Optd. S. £250) ..	£1100	£700
63	,,	500 r. green and red/*green*, C (Optd. S. £650) ..	£5000	
44/58		.. .. *Set of* 15	70·00	75·00
44/60		Optd. "Specimen" *Set of* 17	£130	

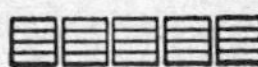

4
cents
(5)

1919. *T* 3 *surch. locally with T* 5.

64		4 c. on 6 c. scarlet (*shades*) ..	12	20
		a. Bars omitted..	10·00	14·00
		b. Surch. double	32·00	38·00
		c. Surch. inverted	28·00	35·00
		d. Pair, one without surch. ..	70·00	£100
64 H/S		"Specimen"	16·00	

1921–22. *Wmk. Mult. Script CA.* P 14.

65	3	1 c. black, O	40	25
66	,,	3 c. green, O	60	60
		a. Blue-green, O	1·40	70
67	,,	6 c. carmine-red, O ..	1·00	55
68	,,	10 c. orange, O	85	25
69	,,	12 c. slate-grey, O ..	2·75	6·00
70	,,	15 c. bright blue, O ..	2·00	2·00
71	,,	50 c. black & dull purple, C	6·00	6·00
72	4	2 r. red and black/*blue*, C	14·00	14·00
73	,,	3 r. violet and green, C ..	16·00	16·00
74	,,	5 r. blue and dull purple, C	25·00	27·00
75	,,	50 r. carmine and green, C (Optd. S. £130) ..	£700	£750
65/74		.. .. *Set of* 10	60·00	65·00
65/74		Optd. "Specimen" *Set of* 10	65·00	

II. KENYA AND UGANDA.

Currency changed (100 cents = 1 shilling).

6

7

1922–27. *Wmk. Script CA.* P 14.

(a) *Wmk. upright. Ordinary paper.*

76	6	1 c. pale brown	20	25
		a. Deep brown (1923) ..	45	45
77	,,	5 c. dull violet	45	20
		a. Bright violet	45	45
78	,,	5 c. green (1927) ..	45	12
79	,,	10 c. green	45	20
80	,,	10 c. black (1927) ..	20	12
81	,,	12 c. jet-black	2·75	3·75
		a. Grey-black	95	2·25
82	,,	15 c. rose-carmine ..	40	20
83	,,	20 c. dull orange-yellow ..	1·10	20
		a. Bright orange	80	12
84	,,	30 c. ultramarine	45	20
85	,,	50 c. grey	80	20
86	,,	75 c. olive	1·75	2·75
		(b) Wmk. sideways. *Chalky* **paper.**		
87	7	1s. green	2·00	85
88	,,	2s. dull purple	2·75	2·00
89	,,	2s. 50 c. brown (1925) ..	10·00	20·00
90	,,	3s. brownish grey ..	6·00	5·00
		a. Jet-black	9·00	9·00
91	,,	4s. grey (1925) ..	14·00	20·00
92	,,	5s. carmine-red	11·00	11·00
93	,,	7s. 50 c. orange-yell. ('25) ..	20·00	35·00
94	,,	10s. bright blue	23·00	23·00
95	,,	£1 black and orange ..	75·00	75·00
96	,,	£2 green and purple (1925) (S. £70)	£350	
97	,,	£3 purple and yellow (1925) (S. £80)	£500	
98	,,	£4 black & magenta (1925) (S. £140)	£850	
99	,,	£5 black & blue (S. £150)	£900	
100	,,	£10 black & green (S. £180)	£2500	
101	,,	£20 red and green (1925) (S. £250)	£4500	
102	,,	£25 black and red (S. £250)	£4500	
103	,,	£50 black & brown (S. £350)	£9000	
104	,,	£75 purple and grey (1925) (S. £350)	£13000	
105	,,	£100 red and black ('25) (S. £400)	£16000	
76/95		.. .. *Set of* 20	£160	£180
76/95		Optd. "Specimen" *Set of* 20	£150	

Specimen copies of Nos. 96/105 are all overprinted.

III. KENYA, UGANDA AND TANGANYIKA.

8. Kavirondo Cranes.

9. Dhow on Lake Victoria.

10. East African Lion.

11. Kilimanjaro.

12. Jinja Bridge by Ripon Falls.

13. Mt. Kenya.

14. Lake Naivasha.

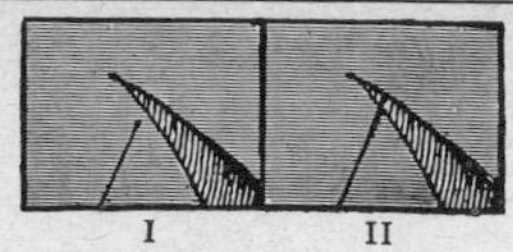

I II

(Des. 1 c., 20 c., 10s., R. C. Luck. 10 c., £1, A. Ross. 15 c., 2s., G. Gill Holmes. 30 c., 5s., R. N. Ambasana. 65 c., L. R. Cutts. T **10** typo., remainder recess. De La Rue & Co.)

1935 (1 May)–**1936.** *Wmk. Mult. Script CA. P* 12 × 13 (**10**), 14 (**9** *and* **14**) and 13 (*remainder*).

No.	Type	Description	Unused	Used
110	**8**	1 c. black and red-brown	10	10
111	**9**	5 c. black and green (I) ..	10	10
		a. Perf. 13 × 12 (I) ..	55·00	20·00
		b. Rope joined to sail (II) (perf. 14)	60	25
		c. Rope joined to sail (II) (perf. 13 × 12)	80·00	15·00
112	**10**	10 c. black and yellow, C	55	10
113	**11**	15 c. black and scarlet ..	40	10
114	**8**	20 c. black and orange ..	12	10
115	**12**	30 c. black and blue ..	25	50
116	**9**	50 c. brt. purple & blk. (I)	55	45
117	**13**	65 c. black and brown ..	65	70
118	**14**	1s. black and green ..	70	55
		a. Perf. 13 × 12 (1936) ..	£200	17·00
119	**11**	2s. lake and purple ..	3·00	4·00
120	**14**	3s. blue and black ..	4·00	5·00
		a. Perf. 13 × 12	£350	
121	**12**	5s. black and carmine ..	8·00	8·00
122	**8**	10s. purple and blue ..	18·00	17·00
123	**10**	£1 black and red, C ..	38·00	35·00
110/123		.. .. *Set of* 14	65·00	65·00
110/23		Perf. "Specimen" *Set of* 14	50·00	

1935 (6 May). *Silver Jubilee. As T* **13** *of Antigua. Recess. D.L.R. & Co. Wmk. Mult. Script CA. P* 13½ × 14.

No.	Description	Unused	Used
124	20 c. light blue & olive-green	10	8
125	30 c. brown and deep blue ..	55	40
126	65 c. green and indigo ..	1·40	1·40
127	1s. slate and purple ..	1·50	1·50
124/7	Perf. "Specimen" *Set of* 4	15·00	

1937 (12 May). *Coronation. As T* **2** *of Aden. Recess. D.L.R. & Co. Wmk. Mult. Script CA. P* 14.

No.	Description	Unused	Used
128	5 c. green	8	8
129	20 c. orange	8	8
130	30 c. bright blue	15	25
128/30	Perf. "Specimen" *Set of* 3	11·00	

15. Dhow on Lake Victoria.

10c
KENYA
TANGANYIKA
UGANDA
(**16**)

Retouch on 1 c. (Pl. 2, R. 9/6)

Retouch on 10 c. and 1s. (Pl. 7B, R. 5/10 and 6/7)

With dot.

Dot removed.

In the 50 c., on Frame-plate 3, the dot was removed by retouching on all but five stamps (R.5/2, 6/1, 7/2, 7/4 and 9/1). In addition, other stamps show traces of the dot where the retouching was not completely effective.

(T **10** typo., others recess. D.L.R.)

1938–54. *As T* **8** *to* **14** (*but with portrait of King George VI in place of King George V, as in T* **15**). *Wmk. Mult. Script CA.*

(*In this issue, to aid identification, the perforations are indicated to the nearest quarter.*)

No.	Type	Description	Unused	Used
131	**8**	1 c. blk. & red-brn. (*p.* 13¼)	10	20
		a. Perf. 13¼ × 13¾. *Black and chocolate-brown* (1942) ..	8	12
		ab. Retouched value tablet ..	6·00	4·50
		ac. *Blk. & dp. choc.-brn.* ('46)	8	12
		ad. Do. Retouched tablet ..	3·00	2·25
		ae. *Blk. & red-brown* (26.9.51)	8	12
132	**15**	5 c. black and green (II) (*p.* 13 × 11¾)	8	10
133	,,	5 c. reddish brn. & orange (*p.* 13 × 11¾) (1.6.49)	15	25
		a. Perf. 13 × 12½ (14.6.50) ..	10	25
134	**14**	10 c. red-brown & orange (*p.* 13 × 11¾)	8	10
		a. Perf. 14 (1941)	7·50	50
135	,,	10 c. black and green (*p.* 13 × 11¾) 1.6.49) ..	8	12
		a. Mountain retouch ..	5·50	5·50
		b. Perf. 13 × 12½ (14.6.50) ..	8	12
136	,,	10 c. brown and grey (*p.* 13 × 12½) (1.4.52)	8	12
137	**11**	15 c. blk. & rose-red (*p.* 13¼)	15	10
		a. Perf. 13¾ × 13¼ (2.43) ..	20	25
138	,,	15 c. black and green (*p.* 13¾ × 13¼) (1.4.52)	10	25
139	**8**	20 c. black & orge. (*p.* 13¼)	50	20
		a. Perf. 14 (1941)	2·00	80
		b. Perf. 13¼ × 13¾ (1.6.42) ..	10	10
		ba. *Deep black & dp. orange* (8.51)	10	10
140	**15**	25 c. black and carmine-red (*p.* 13 × 12½) (1.4.52)	30	65
141	**12**	30 c. black and dull violet-blue (*p.* 13¼)	1·25	25
		a. Perf. 14 (1941)	13·00	2·50
		b. Perf. 13¼ × 13¾ (9.42) ..	10	10
142	,,	30 c. dull purple & brown (*p.* 13¼ × 13¾) (1.4.52)	10	10
143	**8**	40 c. black and blue (*p.* 13¼ × 13¾) (1.4.52)	15	15
144	**15**	50 c. purple and black (II) (*p.* 13 × 11¾)	15	10
		a. Rope not joined to sail (I)	50·00	32·00
		b. *Dull claret & black* (29.7.47)	10	10
		c. *Brown-purple & blk.* (4.48)	10	10
		d. *Reddish purple and black* (28.4.49)	10	10
		e. Do. Perf. 13 × 12½ (10.49)	10	10
		ea. Dot removed (14.6.50)	1·25	1·00
		eb. Do. in pair with normal	65·00	32·00
145	**14**	1s. black and yellowish brown (*p.* 13 × 11¾) ..	20	10
		a. *Black and brown* (9.42) ..	40	20
		ab. Mountain retouch (7.49) ..	13·00	6·50
		b. Perf. 13 × 12½ (10.49) ..	30	12
		ba. *Dp. blk. & brn.* (*clearer impression*) (14.6.50) ..	25	10
146	**11**	2s. lake-brown and brown-purple (*p.* 13¼) ..	3·25	85
		a. Perf. 14 (1941)	5·00	2·50
		b. Perf. 13¾ × 13¼ (24.2.44) ..	40	25
147	**14**	3s. dull ultramarine and black (*p.* 13 × 11¾) ..	1·00	65
		a. *Deep violet-blue & black* (29.7.47)	1·25	80
		b. Do. Perf. 13 × 12½ (14.6.50)	1·00	80
148	**12**	5s. black & carm. (*p.* 13¼)	7·00	2·00
		a. Perf. 14 (1941)	3·25	1·25
		b. Perf. 13¼ × 13¾ (24.2.44) ..	85	40
149	**8**	10s. purple and blue (*p.* 13¼)	7·50	4·00
		a. Perf. 14. *Reddish purple & blue* (1941)	6·00	5·50
		b. Perf. 13¼ × 13¾ (24.2.44) ..	2·00	1·25
150	**10**	£1 black and red, (*p.* 11¾ × 13), C ..	30·00	16·00
		a. Perf. 14, C (1941) ..	4·50	4·00
		ab. Ordinary paper (24.2.44)	4·00	3·50
		b. Perf. 12½, C (21.1.54) ..	4·50	5·00
131/150b		(*cheapest*) *Set of* 20	9·00	7·00
131/150		Perf. "Specimen" *Set of* 13	32·00	

Dates of original issue:—11.4.38, 5 c.; 2.5.38, 1 c. to 10s.; and 12.10.38, £1. Others as indicated above.

Stamps perf. 14, together with Nos. 131a, 137a, 139b, 141b, 146b, 148b and 149b, are known as "Blitz perfs.", the differences in perforation being the result of air raid damage to the De La Rue works in which the perforators normally used were destroyed.

1941 (1 July)–**42.** *Pictorial Stamps of South Africa variously surch. as T* **16.** *Inscr. alternately in English and Afrikaans.*

		Un. pair	*Used pair*
151	5 c. on 1d. grey & carm. (56)	30	40
152	10 c. on 3d. ultram. (No. 59)	30	40
153	20 c. on 6d. green and vermilion (No. 61*a*) ..	25	40
154	70 c. on 1s. brown and chalky blue (No. 62) (20.4.42) ..	25	40
151/4	Handstamped "Specimen" *Set of 4 pairs*	55·00	

1946 (11 Nov.). *Victory. As Nos.* 28/9 *of Aden.*

		Un.	*Used*
155	20 c. red-orange	15	10
156	30 c. blue	8	8
155/6	Perf. "Specimen" *Set of 2*	13·00	

1948 (1 Dec.). *Royal Silver Wedding. As Nos.* 30/1 *of Aden.*

157	20 c. orange	12	12
158	£1 scarlet	9·50	12·00

1949 (10 Oct.). *75th Anniv. of Universal Postal Union. As Nos.* 114/17 *of Antigua.*

159	20 c. red-orange	12	12
160	30 c. deep blue	12	20
161	50 c. grey	20	15
162	1s. red-brown	40	45

17. Lake Naivasha.

(Recess. De La Rue & Co.)

1952 (1 Feb.). *Visit of Princess Elizabeth and Duke of Edinburgh. Wmk. Mult. Script CA. P* 13×12½.

163	**17**	10 c. black and green ..	8	12
164	,,	1s. black and brown ..	55	80

1953 (2 June). *Coronation. As No.* 47 *of Aden.*

165 20 c. black and red-orange .. 8 8

1954 (28 Apr.). *Royal Visit. As No.* 171 *but inscr.* "ROYAL VISIT 1954" *below portrait.*

166 30 c. black & dp. ultramarine 8 8

18. Owen Falls Dam. **19.** Giraffe.

20. Lion. (*Vert.*)

21. Kilimanjaro. (*Horiz.*)

22. Elephants. (*Horiz.*)

23. Royal Lodge, Sagana.

24. Queen Elizabeth II.

(Des. O. C. Meronti (T **18, 20**), G. Gill Holmes (T **19**), H. Grieme (T **22**), R. McLellan Sim (T **23**), De La Rue (others). Recess. De La Rue.)

1954 (1 June)–**59.** *Wmk. Mult. Script. CA. P* 13 (£1); *others,* 12½×13 (*vert.*) *or* 13×12½ (*horiz.*).

167	**18**	5 c. black & deep brown	5	8
		a. Vignette inverted ..	—	£8000
168	**19**	10 c. carmine-red ..	5	5
169	**22**	15 c. black and light blue (28.3.58)	10	5
		a. Redrawn. Stop below "c" of "15 c." (29.4.59)	10	5
170	**20**	20 c. black and orange ..	8	5
		a. Imperf. (pair)	£300	
171	**18**	30 c. black & dp. ultram.	5	5
172	**20**	40 c. bistre-brn. (28.3.58)	8	8
173	**19**	50 c. reddish purple (*shades*)	10	5
174	**21**	65 c. bluish green & brown-purple (1.12.55) ..	30	25
175	**20**	1s. black and claret ..	15	5
176	**22**	1s. 30, orange and deep lilac (1.12.55) ..	20	5
177	**21**	2s. black & green (*shades*)	40	12
178	**22**	5s. black and orange ..	1·00	40
179	**23**	10s. blk. & deep ultram.	2·25	95
180	**24**	£1 brown-red and black (*shades*)	5·50	4·00
167/180		.. .. *Set of* 14	9·00	5·50

Only one used copy of No. 167a is known.

25. Map of E. Africa showing Lakes.

(Recess. Waterlow.)

1958 (30 July). *Centenary of Discovery of Lakes Tanganyika and Victoria by Burton and Speke. W* w.**12.** *P* 12½.

181	**25**	40 c. blue and deep green ..	15	20
182	,,	1s. 30 c. green and violet	30	55

26. Sisal. **27.** Cotton.

28. Coffee. **29.** Gnu.
30. Ostrich. **31.** Thomson's Gazelle.
32. Manta Ray. **33.** Zebra.
34. Cheetah.

(*T* **28/34** *are as T* **26.**)

35. Mt. Kenya and Giant Plants.

36. Murchison Falls and Hippopotamus.
37. Mt. Kilimanjaro and Giraffe.
38. Candelabra Tree and Rhinoceros.
39. Crater Lake and Mountains of the Moon.
40. Ngorongoro Crater and Buffalo.

(*T* **36/40** *are as T* **35.**)

41. Queen Elizabeth II.

(Des. M. Goaman. Photo. (5 c. to 65 c.), recess (others). D.L.R.)

1960 (1 Oct.). *W* w.**12.** *P* 15×14 (5 *c. to* 65 *c.*), 13 (20*s.*) *or* 14 (*others*).

183	**26**	5 c. Prussian blue ..	5	5
184	**27**	10 c. yellow-green	5	5
185	**28**	15 c. dull purple ..	5	5
186	**29**	20 c. magenta	5	5
187	**30**	25 c. bronze-green ..	8	5
188	**31**	30 c. vermilion	8	5
189	**32**	40 c. greenish blue ..	8	5
190	**33**	50 c. slate-violet	10	5
191	**34**	65 c. yellow-olive	25	25
192	**35**	1s. deep reddish violet and reddish purple ..	20	5
193	**36**	1s. 30, chocolate and brown-red	25	8
194	**37**	2s. deep grey-blue and greenish blue ..	30	10
195	**38**	2s. 50, olive-green and deep bluish green ..	45	45
196	**39**	5s. rose-red and purple ..	80	35
197	**40**	10s. blackish green and olive-green	2·00	1·00
198	**41**	20s. violet-blue and lake ..	5·00	3·25
183/198		.. .. *Set of* 16	8·50	5·00

The 10 c. and 50 c. exist in coils with the designs slightly shorter in height, a wider horizontal gutter every eleven stamps and, in the case of the 10 c. only, printed with a coarser 200 screen instead of the normal 250. (*Price* 10 *c.* 5*p. un.*) Plate 2 of 30 c. shows coarser 200 screen. (*Price* 10*p. un.*)

42. Land Tillage.

43. African with Corncob.

(Des. V. Whiteley. Photo. Harrison.)

1963 (21 MAR.). *Freedom from Hunger. P* 14½.

199	**42**	15 c. blue and yellow-olive	5	5
200	**43**	30 c. red-brown & yellow	12	10
201	**42**	50 c. blue & orange-brown	15	12
202	**43**	1s. 30, red-brn. & lt. blue	30	30

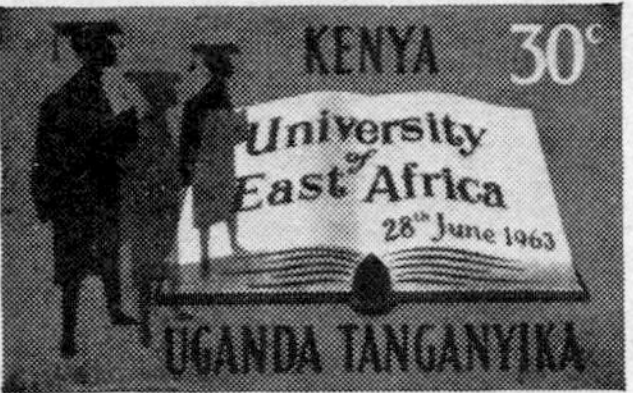

44. Scholars and Open Book.

(Photo. Harrison.)

1963 (28 JUNE). *Founding of East African University. P* 14½.

203	**44**	30 c. lake, violet, black and greenish blue ..	8	8
204	,,	1s. 30, lake, blue, red and light yellow-brown ..	20	20

45. Red Cross Emblem.

(Des. V. Whiteley. Photo. Harrison.)

1963 (2 SEPT.). *Centenary of Red Cross. P* 14½.

205	**45**	30 c. red and blue	5	8
206	,,	50 c. red and yellow-brown	15	15

OFFICIAL STAMPS.

For use on official correspondence of the Tanganyika Government.

OFFICIAL

(O 1)

1959 (1 JULY). *Optd. as Type* O **1**.

O 1	**18**	5 c. black & deep brown	5	5
O 2	**19**	10 c. carmine-red ..	5	5
O 3	**22**	15 c. black and light blue (No. 169a)	5	5
O 4	**20**	20 c. black and orange ..	5	5
		a. Opt. double ..	—	£120
O 5	**18**	30 c. black & deep ultram.	5	5
O 6	**19**	50 c. reddish purple ..	8	5
O 7	**20**	1s. black and claret ..	12	10
O 8	**22**	1s. 30, orge. & dp. lilac	25	30
O 9	**21**	2s. black & bronze-green	30	40
O10	**22**	5s. black and orange ..	80	80
O11	**23**	10s. black & dp. ultram.	2·00	2·25
O12	**24**	£1 brown-red and black	4·50	4·50
O1/12		.. .. *Set of* 12	7·50	7·50

The 30 c. and 1s. exist with overprint double, but with the two impressions almost coincident.

OFFICIAL (O 2) **OFFICIAL** (O 3)

1960 (18 OCT.). *Optd. with Type* O **2** *(cents values) or* O **3**.

O13	**26**	5 c. Prussian blue ..	5	5
O14	**27**	10 c. yellow-green ..	5	5
O15	**28**	15 c. dull purple ..	5	5
O16	**29**	20 c. magenta	5	5
O17	**31**	30 c. vermilion	5	5
O18	**33**	50 c. slate-violet ..	8	8
O19	**35**	1s. deep reddish violet and reddish purple..	15	25
O20	**39**	5s. rose-red and purple	75	1·00
O13/20		.. .. *Set of* 8	1·00	1·50

POSTAGE DUE STAMPS.

D 1

D 2

(Typo. Waterlow & Sons, Ltd.)

1928–33. *Wmk. Mult. Script CA. P* 15 × 14.

D1	**D 1**	5 c. violet	15	30
D2	,,	10 c. vermilion	20	35
D3	,,	20 c. yellow-green ..	25	45
D4	,,	30 c. brown (1931) ..	60	85
D5	,,	40 c. dull blue	1·10	1·75
D6	,,	1s. grey-green ('33) ..	4·00	5·50
D1/6		.. .. *Set of* 6	5·50	8·00
D1/6 Optd./Perf. "Specimen" *Set of* 6			40·00	

(Typo. De La Rue & Co.)

1935 (1 MAY)–**60.** *Wmk. Mult. Script CA. P* 14.

D 7	**D 2**	5 c. violet	8	10
D 8	,,	10 c. scarlet	8	10
D 9	,,	20 c. green	12	10
D10	,,	30 c. brown	25	15
		a. Bistre-brown (19.7.60) ..	25	10
D11	,,	40 c. ultramarine ..	25	12
D12	,,	1s. grey	40	20
D7/12		.. .. *Set of* 6	1·00	60
D7/12 Perf. "Specimen" *Set of* 6			25·00	

The Postage and Official stamps of Kenya, Uganda and Tanganyika were withdrawn on 11th December 1963 and the Postage Due stamps on 2nd January 1967. Separate issues are listed under KENYA, TANGANYIKA and UGANDA respectively and joint commemorative issues are listed under EAST AFRICA.

KUWAIT.

An independent Arab Shaikhdom, with an Indian postal administration from 1915, at first using unoverprinted Indian stamps. A British postal administration operated from 1st April 1948 to 31st January 1959.

KUWAIT (1) **KUWAIT** (2)

1923 (1 APR.)–**1924.** *Stamps of India (King George V), optd. with T* **1** *or* **2** *(rupee values, 15½ mm.) Star wmk. P.* 14.

1	**56**	½ a. green	25	50
		a. Opt. double		
		b. Vert. pair, one without opt.		
2	**57**	1 a. chocolate	25	40
3	**58**	1½ a. chocolate (A) ..	25	45
4	**59**	2 a. mauve..	25	30
5	**61**	2 a. 6 p. ultramarine ..	65	1·75
6	**62**	3 a. orange-brown ..	1·25	3·00
		a. Opt. inverted ..	11·00	
7	,,	3 a. ultramarine (1924) ..	2·00	40
8	**63**	4 a. olive-green	2·00	3·00
9	**64**	6 a. yellow-bistre	2·50	3·00
10	**65**	8 a. purple	3·00	3·25
11	**66**	12 a. claret	4·00	4·00
12	**67**	1 r. brown and green ..	4·50	2·00
13	,,	2 r. carmine & yellow-brn.	12·00	12·00
14	,,	5 r. ultramarine and violet	20·00	22·00
15	,,	10 r. green and scarlet ..	35·00	42·00
1/15		.. .. *Set of* 15	80·00	90·00

Ordinary and Service stamps with overprint "KOWEIT" were prepared for use but were not issued. These are rare.

KUWAIT (3) **KUWAIT** (4)

1929–37. *Stamps of India (King George V, Nasik printing), optd. with T* **3** *or* **4** *(rupee values). Mult. Star wmk. P* 14.

16	**56**	½ a. green	12	30
16*a*	**79**	½ a. green ('34)	1·10	30
17	**57**	1 a. chocolate	2·00	30
17*a*	**81**	1 a. chocolate ('34) ..	80	30
18	**70**	2 a. purple	25	30
19	,,	2 a. vermilion	7·50	7·00
19*a*	**59**	2 a. vermilion ('34) ..	3·00	1·50
19*b*	,,	2 a. verm. *(small die)* ('37)	35	30
20	**62**	3 a. bright blue	2·25	50
21	,,	3 a. carmine	2·25	2·25
22	**71**	4 a. sage-green	7·50	7·50
22*a*	**63**	4 a. sage-green ('34) ..	1·50	1·50
22*b*	**64**	6 a. bistre ('37)	1·50	2·00
23	**65**	8 a. reddish purple ..	3·00	3·00
24	**66**	12 a. claret	4·00	4·00
25	**67**	1 r. chocolate and green	2·25	2·25
26	,,	2 r. carmine and orange..	5·50	5·50
27	,,	5 r. ultram. & pur. ('37)	15·00	16·00
28	,,	10 r. green & scarlet ('34)	28·00	30·00
29	,,	15 r. blue and olive (37) ..	48·00	50·00
16/29		.. .. *Set of* 20	£120	£120

1933 (FEB.)–**34.** *Air. Stamps of India optd. as T* **2** *(16½ mm.).*

31	**72**	2 a. deep blue-green ..	1·60	2·25
32	,,	3 a. blue	50	40
		a. Stamp doubly printed ..		
33	,,	4 a. drab	35·00	40·00
34	,,	6 a. bistre (2.34)	1·60	1·75

1939. *Stamps of India (King George VI), optd. with T* **3** *or* **4** *(rupee values).*

36	**91**	½ a. red-brown	25	25
38	,,	1 a. carmine	25	25
39	**92**	2 a. vermilion	35	35
41	**94**	3 a. yellow-green	50	55
43	**96**	4 a. brown	65	1·40
44	**97**	6 a. turquoise-green ..	75	1·75
45	**98**	8 a. slate-violet	1·40	2·00
46	**99**	12 a. lake	1·75	2·75
47	**100**	1 r. grey and red-brown	75	75
48	,,	2 r. purple and brown ..	1·50	1·75
49	,,	5 r. green and blue ..	4·50	4·00
50	,,	10 r. purple and claret ..	11·00	11·00
		a. Opt. double ..	70·00	80·00
51	,,	15 r. brown and green ..	15·00	17·00
36/51		.. .. *Set of* 13	35·00	40·00

1945. *Stamps of India (King George VI on white background) optd. with T* **3**.

52	**100***a*	3 p. slate	15	20
53	,,	½ a. purple	15	20
54	,,	9 p. green	15	30
55	,,	1 a. carmine	15	25
56	**101**	1½ a. dull violet	15	25
57	,,	2 a. vermilion	15	25
58	,,	3 a. bright violet	15	25
59	,,	3½ a. bright blue	15	25
60	**102**	4 a. brown	15	50
60*a*	,,	6 a. turquoise-green ..	2·25	2·50
61	,,	8 a. slate-violet	30	40
62	,,	12 a. lake	35	75
63	**103**	14 a. purple	2·00	3·00
52/63		.. .. *Set of* 13	5·50	8·00

KUWAIT
1 ANNA (5)

KUWAIT
5 RUPEES (6)

NOTE. From 1948 onwards, for stamps with similar surcharges, but without name of country, see British Postal Agencies in Eastern Arabia.

1948 (1 APR.)–**1949.** *Stamps of Great Britain (K.G. VI), surch. as T* **5** *or* **6** *(rupee values).*

64	**128**	½ a. on ½d. pale green ..	8	12
65	,,	1 a. on 1d. pale scarlet ..	8	12
66	,,	1½ a. on 1½d. pale red-brn.	8	12
67	,,	2 a. on 2d. pale orange ..	8	15
68	,,	2½ a. on 2½d. light ultram.	8	25

69 **128** 3 a. on 3d. pale violet .. 8 15
a. Pair, one albino .. £850 £550
70 **129** 6 a. on 6d. purple .. 12 12
71 **130** 1 r. on 1s. bistre-brown .. 25 25
72 **131** 2 r. on 2s. 6d yell.-grn. 80 1·00
73 ,, 5 r. on 5s. red .. .. 1·75 2·00
73*a* **132** 10 r. on 10s. ultram. (4.7.49) 8·50 6·50
64/73*a* .. .. *Set of* 11 11·00 10·00

KUWAIT
$2\frac{1}{2}$
ANNAS
(7)

KUWAIT
15
RUPEES
(8)

1948. *Royal Silver Wedding. Nos.* 493/4 *of Great Britain surch. with T* **7** *or* **8.**
74 **137** $2\frac{1}{2}$ a. on $2\frac{1}{2}$d. ultramarine 10 10
75 **138** 15 r. on £1 blue .. .. 6·50 9·00

1948. *Olympic Games. Nos.* 495/8 *of Great Britain surch. as T* **7**, *but in one line* (6 *a.*) *or two lines* (*others*).
76 **139** $2\frac{1}{2}$ a. on $2\frac{1}{2}$d. ultramarine 12 15
77 **140** 3 a. on 3d. violet .. 15 25
78 **141** 6 a. on 6d. bright purple 35 40
79 **142** 1 r. on 1s. brown .. 50 60

1949 (10 Oct.). *75th Anniv. of U.P.U. Nos.* 499/502 *of Great Britain surch.* "KUWAIT" *and new values.*
80 **143** $2\frac{1}{2}$ a. on $2\frac{1}{2}$d. ultramarine 15 25
81 **144** 3 a. on 3d. violet .. 25 25
82 **145** 6 a. on 6d. bright purple 35 55
83 **146** 1 r. on 1s. brown .. 60 65

KUWAIT 2 RUPEES
(8*a*)
"2" level with "RUPEES". "KUWAIT" sharp.

KUWAIT 2 RUPEES
(8*b*)
"2" raised. "KUWAIT" worn.

1950–55. *Nos.* 503/11 *of Great Britain surch. as T* **5** *or* **8a** (*rupee values*).
84 **128** $\frac{1}{2}$ a. on $\frac{1}{2}$d. pale orange .. 5 10
85 ,, 1 a. on 1d. light ultram. 5 10
86 ,, $1\frac{1}{2}$ a. on $1\frac{1}{2}$d. pale green .. 8 10
87 ,, 2 a. on 2d. pale red-brown 8 10
88 ,, $2\frac{1}{2}$ a. on $2\frac{1}{2}$d. pale scarlet .. 15 10
89 **129** 4 a. on 4d. light ultram. 10 10
90 **147** 2 r. on 2s. 6d. yellow-grn. 1·25 1·00
a. Surch. with Type 8*b* ('55) 30·00 12·00
91 **148** 5 r. on 5s. red .. 1·75 2·25
92 **149** 10 r. on 10s. ultramarine .. 3·00 2·50
84/92 .. .. *Set of* 9 6·00 5·75

Dates of issue:—2.10.50, 4 a.; 3.5.51, others.
Two used copies are known of No. 92 with surch. spaced 10 mm. apart instead of 9 mm.

1952–54. *Stamps of Great Britain (Queen Elizabeth II). Wmk. Tudor Crown surch. as T* **5.**
93 **154** $\frac{1}{2}$ a. on $\frac{1}{2}$d. orange-red .. 5 5
94 ,, 1 a. on 1d. ultramarine 5 5
95 ,, $1\frac{1}{2}$ a. on $1\frac{1}{2}$d. green .. 5 5
96 ,, 2 a. on 2d. red-brown .. 5 5
97 **155** $2\frac{1}{2}$ a. on $2\frac{1}{2}$d. carmine-red 5 5
98 ,, 3 a. on 3d. deep lilac (B.) 5 5
99 **156** 4 a. on 4d. ultramarine 8 10
100 **157** 6 a. on 6d. reddish pur. 10 8
101 **160** 12 a. on 1s. 3d. green 25 25
102 **159** 1 r. on 1s. 6d. grey-blue 25 25
93/102 .. .. *Set of* 10 75 90

Dates of issue:—10.12.52, $1\frac{1}{2}$ a., $2\frac{1}{2}$ a.; 31.8.53, $\frac{1}{2}$ a., 1 a., 2 a.; 2.11.53, 4 a., 12 a., 1 r.; 18.1.54, 3 a., 6 a.

1953 (3 June). *Coronation. Stamps of Great Britain surch.* "KUWAIT" *and new values.*
103 **161** $2\frac{1}{2}$ a. on $2\frac{1}{2}$d. carmine-red 25 25
104 **162** 4 a. on 4d. ultramarine .. 35 35
105 **163** 12 a. on 1s. 3d. deep yellow-green 85 85
106 **164** 1 r. on 1s. 6d. deep grey-blue 95 95

KUWAIT 2 RUPEES I
KUWAIT 2 RUPEES II
(9)

KUWAIT 5 RUPEES I
KUWAIT 5 RUPEES II
(10)

KUWAIT 10 RUPEES I
KUWAIT 10 RUPEES II
(11)

Type I (**9/11**). Type-set overprints. Bold (generally thicker) letters with sharp corners and straight edges. Bars close together and usually slightly longer than in Type II.

Type II (**9/11**). Plate-printed overprints. Thinner letters, rounder corners and rough edges. Bars wider apart.

1955–57. *Nos.* 536/8 *of Great Britain surch.*

		I. (23.9.55)		II. (10.10.57)	
107 **166**	2 r. on 2s. 6d. blk.-brn.	55	90	10·00	2·50
108 **167**	5 r. on 5s. rose-red	1·25	1·75	20·00	3·00
109 **168**	10 r. on 10s. ultram.	2·50	2·50	40·00	15·00

1956. *Stamps of Great Britain (Queen Elizabeth II), Wmk. St. Edward's Crown, surch.* "KUWAIT" *and new value.*
110 **154** $\frac{1}{2}$ a. on $\frac{1}{2}$d. orange-red .. 5 5
111 ,, 1 a. on 1d. ultramarine 5 5
112 ,, $1\frac{1}{2}$ a. on $1\frac{1}{2}$d. green .. 5 5
113 ,, 2 a. on 2d. red-brown .. 5 5
114 **155** $2\frac{1}{2}$ a. on $2\frac{1}{2}$d. carmine-red 5 5
116 **156** 4 a. on 4d. ultramarine 45 45
117 **157** 6 a. on 6d. reddish pur. 8 8
118 **160** 12 a. on 1s. 3d. green .. 75 75
119 **159** 1 r. on 1s. 6d. grey-blue 25 25
110/19 .. .. *Set of* 9 1·40 1·40

Currency changed. 100 n(aye) p(aise) = 1 rupee.

KUWAIT NP 1 NP
(12)

KUWAIT NP 3 NP
(13)

KUWAIT 75 NP
(14)

1957 (1 June)–**58.** *Stamps of Great Britain (Queen Elizabeth II).* W **165**, *St. Edward's Crown, surch. as T* **12** (1, 15, 25, 40, 50 *n.p.*), **14** (75 *n.p.*) *or* **13** (*others*).
120 **157** 1 n.p. on 5d. brown .. 5 5
121 **154** 3 n.p. on $\frac{1}{2}$d. orange-red 5 5
122 ,, 6 n.p. on 1d. ultramarine 5 5
123 ,, 9 n.p. on $1\frac{1}{2}$d. green .. 5 5
124 ,, 12 n.p. on 2d. lt. red-brn. 5 5
125 **155** 15 n.p. on $2\frac{1}{2}$d. carmine-red (Type I) .. 12 12
a. Type II (-.11.58) .. 14·00 10·00
126 ,, 20 n.p. on 3d. dp. lilac (B.) 12 5
127 **156** 25 n.p. on 4d. ultramarine 12 30
128 **157** 40 n.p. on 6d. reddish pur. 20 15
129 **158** 50 n.p. on 9d. bronze-grn. 35 60
130 **160** 75 n.p. on 1s. 3d. green .. 35 50
120/30 .. .. *Set of* 11 1·25 1·75

15. Shaikh Abdullah as-Salim as-Sabah.

16. Dhow.

17. Oil-Drilling Rig.

18. Single-masted Dhow.

(Recess. De La Rue.)

1959 (1 Feb.). *Various designs as T* **15/18.** *P* $12\frac{1}{2}$ (*Nos.* 131/6), $13\frac{1}{2}\times13$ (137/9) *or* $14\times13\frac{1}{2}$ (140/3).
131 **15** 5 n.p. bluish green .. 8 5
132 ,, 10 n.p. rose-red (*shades*) .. 8 5
133 ,, 15 n.p. brown 8 5
134 ,, 20 n.p. slate-violet .. 8 5
135 ,, 25 n.p. orange-red (*shades*) 8 5
136 ,, 40 n.p. maroon 50 30
137 **16** 40 n.p. blue 10 5
138 – 50 n.p. scarlet 10 5
139 – 75 n.p. bronze-green .. 20 12
140 **17** 1 r. brown-purple .. 20 12
141 **18** 2 r. light blue & brown 50 35
142 – 5 r. blue-green .. .. 1·00 75
143 – 10 r. deep lilac .. 5·00 3·00
131/43 .. .. *Set of* 13 7·50 4·25

Designs: *As T* **16**—50 n.p. Oil pipelines; 75 n.p. Power Station. *As T* **18**—5 r. Kuwait Mosque; 10 r. Main Square, Kuwait Town.

Nos. 131, 132 and 136 were issued on February 1st, 1958, but were valid only for internal use in Kuwait prior to February 1st, 1959.

19. Shaikh Abdullah and Flag.

(Recess. De La Rue.)

1960 (25 Feb.). *Tenth Anniv. of Shaikh's Accession. P* 14.
144 **19** 40 n.p. scarlet & olive-grn. 20 20
145 ,, 60 n.p. scarlet and deep ultramarine 25 25

Currency changed. 1,000 fils = 1 dinar.

20. Shaikh Abdullah.

21. "Viscount" Airliner over South Pier, Mina al Ahmadi.

22. Shuwaikh Secondary School.

23. Wara Hill.

(Recess. D.L.R.)

1961 (1 Apr.–8 May). *New designs T* **20/23**, *and old designs T* **16** (*now larger*, 32 × 22 *mm.*), *T* **18**, *No.* 142, *inscr. in new currency. P* 12½ (*T* **20**), 13½ (*T* **22**) *or* 14 × 13½ (*others*).

No.	Type	Description	Unused	Used
146	20	1 f. bluish green	5	5
147	,,	2 f. brown-red	5	5
148	,,	4 f. brown	5	5
149	,,	5 f. slate-violet	5	5
150	,,	8 f. orange-red	5	5
151	,,	15 f. maroon	5	5
152	–	20 f. blue-green	5	5
153	21	25 f. blue	8	5
154	18	30 f. light blue and brown	8	8
155	22	35 f. black and red (8.5.61)	8	8
156	16	40 f. blue	10	8
157	23	45 f. chocolate	15	8
158	18	75 f. sepia & emerald-green (27.4.61)	25	20
159	22	90 f. brown & deep ultramarine (27.4.61) ..	20	15
160	21	100 f. carmine-red ..	30	25
161	16	250 f. bronze-green ..	3·00	1·50
162	23	1 d. red-orange	7·00	1·75
163	–	3 d. red	13·00	13·00
146/63		.. .. *Set of* 18	22·00	17·00

The 20 f. and 3 d. are as No. 142 and show the Kuwait Mosque.

Later stamp issues will be found in Vol. 3 of the Stanley Gibbons Foreign Overseas Catalogue.

OFFICIAL STAMPS.

KUWAIT SERVICE (O 1)

KUWAIT SERVICE (O 2)

1923–24. *Stamps of India* (*King George V*), *optd. with Types* O **1** *or* O **2** (*rupee values*, 15½–16 *mm*). *Star wmk. P* 14.

No.	Type	Description	Unused	Used
O 1	56	½ a. green	15	55
O 2	57	1 a. chocolate	20	55
O 3	58	1½ a. chocolate (A) ..	45	1·10
O 4	59	2 a. mauve	45	1·10
O 5	61	2 a. 6p. ultramarine ..	90	1·60
O 6	62	3 a. orange-brown ..	1·25	2·75
O 7	,,	3 a. ultramarine (1924) ..	55	1·60
O 8	63	4 a. olive-green ..	95	2·75
O 9	65	8 a. purple	1·10	2·75
O10	67	1 r. brown and green ..	1·90	5·00
O11	,,	2 r. carmine & yell.-brn.	2·75	8·00
O12	,,	5 r. ultramarine & violet	7·00	16·00
O13	,,	10 r. green and scarlet ..	13·00	30·00
O14	,,	15 r. blue and olive ..	18·00	42·00
O1/O14		.. .. *Set of* 14	45·00	£100

1929–33. *Stamps of India* (*Nasik printing*) *optd. as Types* O **1** (*spaced* 10 *mm.*) *or* O **2** (14½ *mm. between* × 19–20 *mm. wide*). *Mult. Star wmk. P* 14.

No.	Type	Description	Unused	Used
O16	57	1 a. chocolate	15	45
O17	70	2 a. purple	2·75	2·75
O19	62	3 a. blue	30	40
O20	71	4 a. sage-green	1·10	1·25
O21	65	8 a. reddish purple ..	65	1·60
O22	66	12 a. claret	2·00	2·75
O23	67	1 r. chocolate and green	1·60	6·00
O24	,,	2 r. carmine and orange	2·25	13·00
O25	,,	5 r. ultramarine & purple	4·50	21·00
O26	,,	10 r. green and scarlet ..	9·00	42·00
O27	,,	15 r. blue and olive ..	18·00	55·00
O16/O27		.. .. *Set of* 10	38·00	£130

LABUAN.

CROWN COLONY.

1

(Recess. De La Rue & Co.)

1879 (May). *Wmk. CA over Crown, sideways. P* 14.

No.	Type	Description	Unused	Used
1	1	2 c. blue-green	£160	£150
2	,,	6 c. orange-brown	35·00	32·00
3	,,	12 c. carmine	£140	£110
4	,,	16 c. blue	10·00	11·00

This watermark is always found sideways, and extends over two stamps, a single specimen showing only a portion of the Crown or the letters CA, which latter are tall and far apart. This paper was chiefly used for long fiscal stamps.

1880 (Jan.)–**82.** *Wmk. Crown CC. P* 14.

No.	Type	Description	Unused	Used
5	1	2 c. yellow-green	2·50	3·00
6	,,	6 c. orange-brown	11·00	11·00
7	,,	8 c. carmine (4.82) ..	11·00	11·00
8	,,	10 c. brown	10·00	11·00
9	,,	12 c. carmine	25·00	25·00
10	,,	16 c. blue (1881)	10·00	12·00
5/10		.. .. *Set of* 6	60·00	60·00

8 ▬ (2) 8 ∞ (3) Eight Cents (4) Eight Cents (5)

1880 (Aug.). *No.* 9 *surch. with numerals in centre, in black, and the original value obliterated, as T* **2**, *in red or black.*

No.	Description	Unused	Used
11	8 c. on 12 c. carmine ..	£120	£110
	a. "8" inverted	£120	£110
	b. "12" not obliterated ..	£130	£120
	c. As b. with "8" inverted ..		

No. 4 *surch. with two upright figures and No.* 9 *surch. with numeral in centre, and another across the original value as T* **3**.

No.	Description	Unused	Used
12	6 c. on 16 c. blue (R.) ..	£130	£120
	a. With one "6" only ..		
13	8 c. on 12 c. carmine		
	a. Both "8's" upright ..		
	b. Upright "8" inverted ..	£120	£110

1881 (Mar.). *No.* 9 *surch. as T* **4**.

No.	Description	Unused	Used
14	8 c. on 12 c. carmine ..	28·00	28·00

1881 (June). *No.* 9 *surch. as T* **5**.

No.	Description	Unused	Used
15	8 c. on 12 c. carmine	10·00	10·00
	a. Surch. double	55·00	
	b. Surch. inverted	£140	
	c. Error "Eighr"	£650	

The error "Eighr" was No. 6 in the first printing, but this was soon corrected.

1883. *Wmk. Crown CA. P* 14.

No.	Type	Description	Unused	Used
17	1	2 c. green	2·25	2·50
		a. Imperf. between (horiz. pr.)	£180	
18	,,	8 c. carmine	18·00	12·00
19	,,	10 c. yellow-brown ..	5·00	5·50
20	,,	16 c. blue	9·00	10·00
21	,,	40 c. amber	3·00	4·00

(6) (7) (8)

1883 (May). *No.* 10 *surch.* "*One Dollar A.S.H.*" *by hand, as T* **6**.

No.	Description	Unused	Used
22	1 $1 on 16 c. blue (R.) ..	£400	

The initials are those of the postmaster, Mr. A. S. Hamilton.

1885 (June). *Nos.* 18 *and* 10 *handstamped as T* **7**.

No.	Type	Description	Unused	Used
23	1	2 c. on 8 c. carmine	11·00	
24	,,	2 c. on 16 c. blue	£130	£120

1885 (June). *No.* 20 *Surch as T* **8**.

No.	Type	Description	Unused	Used
25	1	2 c. on 16 c. blue	14·00	15·00
		a. Surch. double		

2 Cents (9) 6 Cents (10)

1885 (Sept.). *No.* 18 *handstamped diag. as T* **9**.

No.	Type	Description	Unused	Used
26	1	2 c. on 8 c. carmine	6·50	7·50

1885–86. *Wmk. Crown CA. P* 14.

No.	Type	Description	Unused	Used
30	1	2 c. rose-red (9.85)	50	70
		a. Pale rose-red (5.86) ..	50	70
31	,,	8 c. deep violet (9.85) ..	2·75	2·50
		a. Mauve (5.86) ..	2·50	2·50
32	,,	10 c. sepia (5.86) ..	1·10	2·25
33	,,	16 c. grey (5.86)	10·00	8·00
30/33		Optd. "Specimen" *Set of* 4	40·00	

Issues of British North Borneo Company.

From Jan. 1st, 1890, while remaining a Crown Colony, the administration of Labuan was transferred to the British North Borneo Co., which issued the following stamps.

1891 (Aug.). *T* **1** *surch. as T* **10**. *P* 14.

No.	Description	Unused	Used
34	6 c. on 8 c. deep violet (No. 31)	5·00	5·00
	a. Surch. inverted	8·00	8·00
	b. Surch. double	35·00	
	c. Surch. double, one inverted ..	60·00	
	d. "Cents" omitted	60·00	60·00
	e. Imperf. between (horiz. pair) ..		
35	6 c. on 8 c. mauve (No. 31a)	1·00	1·10
	a. Surch. inverted	6·00	6·00
	b. Surch. double, one inverted ..		
	c. Surch. double, both inverted ..	60·00	
	d. "6" omitted	50·00	
	e. Pair, one without surcharge ..	60·00	60·00
	f. Inverted. "Cents" omitted ..	60·00	
	g. Pair, one without surch., one surch. inverted	75·00	
36	6 c. on 8 c. mauve (R.) (No. 31a)	60·00	32·00
	a. Surch. inverted ..	60·00	32·00
37	6 c. on 16 c. blue (No. 4) ..	£400	£350
	a. Surch. inverted	£600	£450
38	6 c. on 40 c. amber (No. 21) ..	£400	£450
	a. Surch. inverted	£600	£550

(Recess. D.L.R.)

1892–93. *No wmk. P* 14.

No.	Type	Description	Unused	Used
39	1	2 c. rose-lake	35	40
40	,,	6 c. bright green	70	65
41	,,	8 c. violet	65	70
		a. Pale violet (1893) ..	70	70
43	,,	10 c. brown	65	65
		a. Sepia-brown (1893) ..	50	70
45	,,	12 c. bright blue	65	70
46	,,	16 c. grey	80	70
47	,,	40 c. ochre	2·75	2·50
		a. Brown-buff (1893) ..	3·75	3·75
39/47		.. .. *Set of* 7	6·00	6·00

The 6 c., 12 c., 16 c., and 40 c. are in sheets of 10, as are all the earlier issues. The other values are in sheets of 30.

Two Cents (11)
Six Cents (12)

1892 (Dec.). *Nos. 47 and 46 surch. locally as T* **11** *or* **12**.
49 **1** 2 c. on 40 c. ochre (13 Dec.) 14·00 12·00
a. Surch. inverted 35·00
50 „ 6 c. on 16 c. grey (20 Dec.) 20·00 18·00
a. Surch. inverted 40·00 32·00

There are 10 types of each of these surcharges.

(Litho. De La Rue.)

1894 (April). *No wmk. P* 14.
51 **1** 2 c. carmine-pink 50 50
52 „ 6 c. bright green 1·10 80
a. Imperf. between (horiz. pr.) £200
53 „ 8 c. bright mauve 2·00 1·00
54 „ 10 c. brown 2·25 1·00
55 „ 12 c. pale blue 2·50 1·75
56 „ 16 c. grey 2·75 1·25
57 „ 40 c. orange-buff 4·00 2·50
51/57 *Set of* 7 13·00 8·00
51/57 H/S "Specimen" *Set of* 7 40·00

Collectors are warned against forgeries of this issue.

CANCELLED TO ORDER. The used prices quoted are for stamps postally used. However, Nos. 51/79, 83/101, 116*a*/26 and D1/9 exist cancelled to order and are worth 10p. each, except for errors and those quoted.

PERFORATION. There are a number of small variations in the perforation of the Waterlow issues of 1894 to 1905 which we believe to be due to irregularity of the pins rather than different perforators.

In the following lists, stamps perf. 12, 12½, 13 or compound are described as perf. 12–13 and stamps perf. 13½, 14 or compound are described as perf. 13½–14 and those perf. 14½, 15 or compound are listed as perf. 14½–15. In addition the 13½–14 perforation exists compound with 14½–15 and with 12–13, whilst perf. 16 comes from a separate perforator.

13

LABUAN (14)
40 CENTS (14)

1894 (May)–**96**. *T* **24/32** *of North Borneo (colours changed), with* "LABUAN" *engraved on vignette plate as in T* **13**. *P* 14½–15.

(*a*) *Name and central part of design in black.*
62 **24** 1 c. grey-mauve 40 50
a. Imperf. between (vert. pair) 75·00 45·00
b. Perf. 13½–14 50
c. Perf. 13½–14, comp. 14–15
d. Perf. 13½–14, comp. 12–13
63 **25** 2 c. blue 50 50
a. Imperf. (pair) 75·00
b. Perf. 13½–14 40 50
c. Perf. 13½–14, comp. 14–15
d. Perf. 13½–14, comp. 12–13
64 **26** 3 c. ochre 50
a. Perf. 13½–14 50 60
b. Perf. 13½–14, comp. 14–15
c. Perf. 13½–14, comp. 12–13
65 **27** 5 c. green 70 1·40
a. Perf. 13½–14 70 65
b. Perf. 13½–14, comp. 12–13 70
67 **28** 6 c. brown-lake 75 65
a. Imperf. (pair) (*canc.*) † 65·00
b. Perf. 13½–14 (canc. 55p.)
c. Perf. 13½–14, comp. 14–15 (canc. 45p.)
d. Perf. 13½–14, comp. 12–13
68 **29** 8 c. rose-red 1·75 2·00
a. Perf. 13½–14 1·75 2·00
69 **29** 8 c. pink (1896) 55 1·25
a. Perf. 13½–14 1·40
70 **30** 12 c. orange-vermilion 2·00 2·50
a. Perf. 13½–14 (*canc.* £1)
b. Perf. 12½–13
71 **31** 18 c. olive-brown 2·00 2·50
a. Perf. 13½–14 2·50
72 „ 18 c. olive-bistre (1896) 2·50 2·00
a. Perf. 13½–14 2·50 2·50
b. Perf. 13½–14, comp. 12–13

(*b*) *Name and central part in blue.*
73 **32** 24 c. pale mauve 2·00 2·50
a. Perf. 13½–14 2·00 2·50
74 „ 24 c. dull lilac (1896) 2·00
a. Perf. 13½–14 2·00
62/74 Optd. "Specimen" *Set of* 9 50·00

1895 (June). *No. 83 of North Borneo* ($1 *inscr.* "STATE OF NORTH BORNEO") *surch. as T* **14**.
75 **32c** 4 c. on $1 scarlet 40 50
76 „ 10 c. on $1 scarlet 50 65
77 „ 20 c. on $1 scarlet 1·25 90
78 „ 30 c. on $1 scarlet 1·00 1·00
79 „ 40 c. on $1 scarlet 1·40 1·10
75/79 Optd. "Specimen" *Set of* 5 40·00

LABUAN (15)
1846 JUBILEE 1896 (16)

T **32a** *to* **32c** *of North Borneo (as Nos.* 81 *to* 83, *but colours changed) optd. with T* **15**.
80 25 c. green 4·00 4·00
a. Opt. omitted (*canc.* 65p.) 2·00
b. Imperf. Opt. omitted 8·00
c. Imperf. (pair). Stamps ptd. double, one inverted
81 50 c. maroon 5·00 5·00
a. Opt. omitted (*canc.* 65p.) 3·00
b. Imperf. Opt. omitted 8·00
c. Imperf. (pair). Stamps ptd. both sides
82 $1 blue 5·50 4·00
a. Opt. omitted (*canc.* 65p.) 3·00
b. Imperf. Opt. omitted 8·00
80/82 Optd. "Specimen" *Set of* 3 22·00

1896 (24 Sept.). *Jubilee of Cession of Labuan to Gt. Britain. Nos.* 62 *to* 68, *optd. with T* **16**. *P* 14½–15.
83 1 c. black and grey-mauve 1·25 3·25
a. Error. "JEBILEE" — 40·00
b. Opt. double 20·00 20·00
c. Opt. in orange 20·00 20·00
d. Perf. 13½–14 1·25
e. Perf. 13½–14, comp. 12–13 1·25 1·40
84 2 c. black and blue 1·50 1·75
a. Imperf. horiz. (vert. pair) 40·00
b. Error. "JEBILEE" 90·00
c. Perf. 13½–14 1·50 1·75
d. Perf. 13½–14, comp. 14½–15
e. Perf. 13½–14, comp. 12–13
85 3 c. black and ochre 2·00 2·50
a. Error. "JEBILEE" — £200
b. Opt. double 20·00 11·00
c. Opt. treble £200
d. Perf. 13½–14 3·50 3·50
e. Perf. 13½–14, comp. 14½–15
86 5 c. black and green 2·50 2·50
a. Opt. double 18·00 18·00
b. Perf. 13½–14 2·50 2·50
c. Perf. 13½–14, comp. 12–13
87 6 c. black and brown-lake 2·25 2·25
a. Opt. double 30·00 30·00
b. Perf. 13½–14, comp. 14½–15
88 8 c. black and pink 2·50 2·50
a. Perf. 13½–14 2·50 2·50
b. Perf. 13½–14, comp. 14½–15
83/88 *Set of* 6 11·00 13·00
83/88 Optd. "Specimen" *Set of* 6 55·00

No. 84b is known in a vertical strip of 3 imperf. horizontally except at the base of the bottom stamp.

1897 (Apr.)–**1901**. *T* **34/45** *of North Borneo (colours changed), optd.* "LABUAN" *as in T* **13**. *Name and central part in black (24 c. in blue). P* 13½–14.
89 **34** 1 c. greyish purple (*p.* 14½–15) 85 85
a. Perf. 13½–14, comp. 14½–15
b. Brown (1901) 85 85
ba. Perf. 13½–14
bb. Perf. 16 85 85
90 **35** 2 c. blue 1·25 65
a. Imperf. between (pair)
b. Perf. 14½–15
c. Perf. 13½–14, comp. 12–13 1·75
d. Perf. 16
91 **36** 3 c. ochre 1·10 1·25
a. Imperf. between (pair)
b. Perf. 14½–15 1·10 1·25
c. Perf. 13½–14, comp. 12–13
92 **38** 5 c. green
a. Perf. 14½–15 1·60 2·00
b. Perf. 13½–14, comp. 12–13
93 **39** 6 c. brown-lake 1·10 2·00
a. Imperf. between (pair)
b. Perf. 14½–15 85 2·00
c. Perf. 13½–14, comp. 12–13 (canc. £1·50)
94 **40** 8 c. rose-red
a. Perf. 14½–15 1·25 80
b. Perf. 13½–14, comp. 12–13 (canc. £1·25)
c. Vermilion
ca. Perf. 16 (canc. £1·50)
95 **42** 12 c. vermilion 2·75 3·00
a. Perf. 14½–15
96 **44** 18 c. olive-bistre 1·40 1·75
a. Imperf. between (pair)
b. Perf. 16
97 **45** 24 c. grey-lilac 1·60 2·00
a. Perf. 14½–15
89/97 Optd. "Specimen" *Set of* 9 55·00

The 12, 18, and 24 c. above were errors; in the 12 c., "LABUAN" is over the value at the top; the 18 c. has "POSTAL REVENUE" instead of "POSTAGE AND REVENUE", and the 24 c. is without "POSTAGE AND REVENUE".

1897 (Oct.–Dec.). *Types of North Borneo (colours changed), optd.* "LABUAN" *as in T* **13**. *P* 13½–14.
98 **42** 12 c. black & verm. (Dec.) (*canc.* 90*p*)
a. Perf. 14½–15 2·75 2·75
b. Perf. 13½–14, comp. 14½–15
c. Perf. 16
99 **46** 18 c. black and olive-bistre
a. Perf. 14½–15 6·50 6·50
b. Perf. 16 (canc. £4·25)
100 **47** 24 c. blue & lilac brown 2·50 3·75
a. Perf. 14½–15 2·50 3·75
b. Perf. 13½–14, comp. 12–13
c. Perf. 16
d. Blue and ochre (*p.* 14½)
98, 100 Optd. "Specimen" *Set of* 2 20·00

In the 12 c. "LABUAN" is now correctly placed at foot of stamp. The 18 c. and 24 c. have the inscriptions on the stamps corrected, but the 18 c. still has "LABUAN" *over* the value at foot, and was further corrected as follows.

As No. 99, *but* "LABUAN" *at top.*
101 **46** 18 c. black & olive-bistre (Dec.) (Optd. S. £11) 2·50 2·50
a. Perf. 14½–15 2·50 2·50
b. Perf. 13½–14, comp. 12–13 1·40 1·40
c. Perf. 12–13

4 CENTS (17)
18

1899. *Surch. with T* **17**. (*a*) *P* 14½–15.
102 **38** 4 c. on 5 c. (No. 92a) 2·25 4·00
103 **39** 4 c. on 6 c. (No. 93b) 2·25 4·00
a. Perf. 13½–14 5·00
104 **40** 4 c. on 8 c. (No. 94a)
a. Perf. 13½–14 2·25 4·00
b. Perf. 13½–14, comp. 12–13 5·00
c. Perf. 12–13
105 **42** 4 c. on 12 c. (No. 98a) 2·25 4·00
a. Perf. 13½–14 5·00
b. Perf. 16
106 **46** 4 c. on 18 c. (No. 101a) 2·25 4·00
a. Surch. double 65·00 55·00
107 **47** 4 c. on 24 c. (No. 100a) 2·25 4·00
a. Perf. 13½–14 2·25
b. Perf. 13½–14, comp. 12–13 — 1·60
c. Perf. 16 4·50

(*b*) *P* 14.

108 **32a** 4 c. on 25 c. (No. 80) .. 2·25 2·75
109 **32b** 4 c. on 50 c. (No. 81) .. 2·25 3·25
110 **32c** 4 c. on $1 (No. 82) .. 2·25 3·25
102/110 Optd. "Specimen" *Set of* 9 55·00

The 1 c., 2 c. and 3 c. values of this set were also surcharged "4 CENTS" but were not issued. They exist overprinted "Specimen" (*price £65 the set of three*).

1899–1901. *Types of North Borneo, optd.* "LABUAN" *as in T* **13.** *P* 13½–14.

111 **35** 2 c. black and green (1900) 80 1·40
a. Perf. 13½–14, comp. 12–13
112 **37** 4 c. black and yellow-brown 1·25
a. Imperf. between (pair) .. 42·00
b. Perf. 13½–14, comp. 12–13
113 „ 4 c. black and carm. (1900) 1·10 55
a. Perf. 14½–15 .. .. 1·10 55
b. Perf. 13½–14, comp. 12–13 1·25 80
114 **38** 5 c. black and pale blue (1900) .. .. .. 1·75 2·25
a. Perf. 13½–14, comp. 12–13
115 **41** 10 c. brown and slate-lilac (*p.* 14½–15) (1901) .. 2·25
116 **43** 16 c. green & chestnut ('01) 2·75
a. Perf. 13½–14, comp. 12–13 2·75 2·75
b. Perf. 12–13 .. ..
111/116 Optd. "Specimen" *Set of* 6 45·00

(Recess. Waterlow & Sons.)

1902 (SEPT.)**–03.** *P* 13½–14.

116*c* **18** 1 c. black & pur. (10.03) 40 40
d. Perf. 14½–15 .. ..
117 „ 2 c. black and green .. 40 25
a. Perf. 14½–15 .. ..
117*b* „ 3 c. black & sepia (10.03) 45 30
118 „ 4 c. black and carmine .. 35 25
119 „ 8 c. black and vermilion 25 35
a. Perf. 14½–15 .. ..
120 „ 10 c. brown & slate-blue 35 45
a. Imp. betwn. (pair) (*canc.*) † 48·00
b. Perf. 14½–15 .. ..
121 „ 12 c. black and yellow .. 50 50
a. Perf. 16 .. ..
122 „ 16 c. green and brown .. 35 40
123 „ 18 c. black & pale brown 35 75
124 „ 25 c. green & greenish bl. 35 80
a. Perf. 14½–15..
125 „ 50 c. dull purple & lilac 1·00 1·75
a. Perf. 13½–14, comp. 12–13
126 „ $1 claret and orange .. 60 3·00

Error of colour.

126*a* **18** 25 c. black and greenish blue (*canc.*) .. .. † 18·00
116*c*/126 .. .. *Set of* 12 4·00 7·00
116*c*/26 Optd. "Specimen" *Set of* 12 60·00

The 10 c., 50 c. and $1 normally exist perf. 14 and the 12 c. perf. 13½ but the remainder exist in both perforations.

1904 (DEC.). *Issues of* 1895 *and* 1897–8 *surch. with T* **19.** (*a*) *P* 14½–15.

127 **38** 4 c. on 5 c. (No. 92a) .. 2·00
128 **39** 4 c. on 6 c. (No. 93b) .. 2·00
129 **40** 4 c. on 8 c. (No. 94a) .. 2·00
130 **42** 4 c. on 12 c. (No. 98a) .. 2·00
a. Perf. 16 .. .. 3·00
131 **46** 4 c. on 18 c. (No. 101) (*p.* 13½–14) .. .. 2·00 2·50
a. Perf. 13½–14, comp. 12–13 2·75
132 **47** 4 c. on 24 c. (No. 100a) .. 2·00
a. Perf. 13½–14 .. .. 2·00
b. Perf. 13½–14, comp. 12–13 2·75

(*b*) *P* 14.

133 **32a** 4 c. on 25 c. (No. 80) .. 2·00
134 **32b** 4 c. on 50 c. (No. 81) .. 2·00
a. Surch. double .. .. 42·00
b. Surch. triple .. ..
135 **32c** 4 c. on $1 (No. 82) .. 2·00

4 cents
(19)

LABUAN
(20)

LABUAN
(21)

1905 (FEB.–NOV.). *Nos.* 81, 83 (*in Labuan colour*), *and* 84/6 *of North Borneo optd. locally with T* **20** (25 c., $2) *or* **21** *others*).

136 **32a** 25 c. indigo .. .. £125 85·00
137 **32c** $1 blue .. .. † 70·00
138 **32d** $2 dull green £700 £225
139 **14** $5 bright purple .. £700 £225
140 **15** $10 brown (Nov.) .. † £500

Dangerous forgeries exist.
The overprint on No. 138 is 12 mm. long.
No. 137 in said to have been issued in 189 .

POSTAGE DUE STAMPS.

POSTAGE DUE
(D 1)

1901. *Optd. with Type* D **1**, *vertically. P* 13½–14.

D1 **35** 2 c. black and green (111) 1·25 30
a. Opt. double .. .. 28·00
b. Perf. 13½–14, comp. 12–13
D2 **36** 3 c. black and ochre (91) 1·00
a. Perf. 13½–14, comp. 12–13
D3 **37** 4 c. black & carmine (113) 1·25
a. Opt. double (*canc.*) .. — 20·00
b. Perf. 14½–15 .. .. 1·25
D4 **38** 5 c. black & pale blue (114) (*canc.* £1·10) .. .. 1·10
a. Perf. 14½–15 .. .. 1·10
D5 **39** 6 c. black & brn.-lake (93) 1·40
a. Perf. 14½–15 .. ..
b. Perf. 16 .. .. ..
D6 **40** 8 c. black & verm. (94*c*) 2·00
a. Frame inverted (*canc.*) .. — £300
b. Perf. 14½–15 .. .. 1·25
c. Perf. 16 .. .. ..
d. *Black and rose-red* (94) ..
da. Perf. 14½–15 (canc. £4)
db. Perf. 13½–14, comp. 12–13
D7 **42** 12 c. black and verm. (98) (*canc.* £4) .. .. 4·00 6·00
a. Perf. 14½–15 .. ..
D8 **46** 18 c. blk. & olive-bis. (101) (*p.* 14½–15) .. .. 1·10
D9 **47** 24 c. bl. & lilac-brn. (100) 2·00
a. Perf. 14½–15 .. ..
ab. *Blue and ochre* .. ..
b. Perf. 16 .. .. 1·10
D1/9b .. .. *Set of* 9 7·50 8·00

By letters Patent dated 30 October, 1906, Labuan was incorporated with Straits Settlements and ceased issuing its own stamps. In 1946 it became part of the Colony of North Borneo.

LAGOS.

PRINTERS. All the stamps of Lagos were typographed by De La Rue & Co.

1
Type 1.

1874 (10 JUNE)**–75.** *Wmk. Crown CC. P* 12½.

The colour of the words of value (the second colour given below) frequently differs from that of the body of the stamp.

1 1d. lilac-mauve .. .. .. 18·00 10·00
2 2d. blue .. .. .. 16·00 9·00
3 3d. red-brown (3.75) .. .. 30·00 12·00
4 3d. red-brn & chestnut .. 28·00 12·00
5 4d. carmine .. .. 20·00 12·00
6 6d. blue-green .. .. 25·00 6·00
8 1s. orange (value 15½ mm.) (3.75) 70·00 40·00
9 1s. orange (value 16½ mm.) .. 65·00 20·00
1/9 .. .. .. *Set of* 6 £150 60·00

1876. *Wmk. Crown CC. P* 14.

10 1d. lilac-mauve .. .. 12·00 3·50
11 2d. blue .. .. .. 12·00 4·25
12 3d. red-brown .. .. 28·00 7·00
13 3d. chestnut .. .. 28·00 10·00
14 4d. carmine .. .. 33·00 3·50
a. Wmk sideways .. .. £200 40·00
15 6d. green .. .. .. 16·00 5·00
16 1s. orange (value 16½ mm. long) £100 20·00
10/16 .. .. *Set of* 6 £180 38·00

1882 (JUNE). *Wmk. Crown CA. P* 14.

17 1d. lilac-mauve .. .. 5·00 3·50
18 2d. blue .. .. .. 25·00 3·00
19 3d. chestnut .. .. .. 4·00 3·00
20 4d. carmine .. .. .. 22·00 3·50
17/20 .. .. *Set of* 4 50·00 11·00

1884 (DEC.)**–86.** *New values and colours. Wmk. Crown CA. P* 14.

21 ½d. dull green (2.86) 15 15
22 1d. rose-carmine 25 20
23 2d. grey .. .. .. 7·00 2·75
24 4d. pale violet .. .. 11·00 4·00
25 6d. olive-green .. .. 3·00 4·00
26 1s. orange (3.85) .. .. 3·00 4·50
27 2s. 6d. olive-black (10.86) .. £140 £120
28 5s. blue (10.86) £300 £140
29 10s. purple-brown (10.86) .. £650 £400
21/29 .. .. *Set of* 9 £1000 £600
27/29 Optd. "Specimen" *Set of* 3 £200

We would warn collectors against clever forgeries of No. 27 to 29 on genuinely watermarked paper.

2½ PENNY A.

2½ PENNY B.

1887 (MAR.)**–1902.** *Wmk. Crown CA. P* 14.

30 **1** 2d. dull mauve and blue .. 50 45
31 „ 2½d. ultramarine (A) (12.90) 45 50
a. Larger letters of value (B) 6·00 5·00
b. *Blue* .. .. .. 20·00 12·00
32 „ 3d. dull mve. & chest. (4.91) 1·10 1·40
33 „ 4d. dull mauve & black .. 1·00 1·25
34 „ 5d. dull mauve & grn (2.94) 1·10 4·50
35 „ 6d. dull mauve & mauve .. 3·00 3·00
a. *Dull mauve & carmine* (10.02) 2·75 3·50
36 „ 7½d. dull mve. & carm. (2.94) 1·40 4·50
37 „ 10d. dull mve. & yell. (2.94) 1·75 4·50
38 „ 1s. yellow-green & black .. 2·00 4·50
a. *Blue-green and black* 2·75 5·00
39 „ 2s. 6d. green and carmine 8·00 9·00
40 „ 5s. green and blue .. 10·00 15·00
41 „ 10s. green and brown .. 16·00 20·00
30/41 .. .. *Set of* 13 35·00 55·00
30/41 Optd. "Specimen" *Set of* 13 80·00

HALF PENNY
(2)

(3)

1893 (AUG.). *No.* 33 *surch. with T* **2.**

42 **1** ½d. on 4d. dull mauve & blk. 1·00 1·10
a. Surch. double .. .. 16·00 16·00
b. Surch. treble .. .. 20·00
c. Error. ½d. on 2d. (No. 30) £4000 £4000

There were four settings of this surcharge, a scarce setting in which "HALF PENNY" is 16½ mm. and three others in which the length is 16 mm. Of No. 42c, one copy is known unused and one used.

1904 (22 JAN.–NOV.). *Wmk. Crown CA. P* 14.

44 **3** ½d. dull green and green .. 1·00 1·40
45 „ 1d. purple and black/*red* .. 35 20
46 „ 2d. dull purple and blue .. 2·75 5·50
47 „ 2½d. dull pur. & blue/*blue* (B) 70 1·40
a. Smaller letters of value as A 2·00 3·00
48 „ 3d. dull purple and brown .. 85 2·50
49 „ 6d. dull purple and mauve .. 8·00 5·00
50 „ 1s. green and black .. 8·00 6·50
51 „ 2s. 6d. green and carmine .. 40·00 55·00
52 „ 5s. green and blue .. 40·00 35·00
53 „ 10s. green and brown (Nov.) £140 £140
44/53 .. .. *Set of* 10 £200 £225
44/53 Optd. "Specimen" *Set of* 10 70·00

1904–05. *Wmk. Mult. Crown CA. P* 14.

54 **3** ½d. dull green & green, OC (30.10.04) 20 35
55 „ 1d. purple and black/*red* OC (22.10.04) 12 15
56 „ 2d. dull purple and blue, OC (2.05) 55 65
57 „ 2½d. dull purple and blue/*blue*, (B), C (13.10.05) .. 1·00 1·60
a. Smaller letters of value as A 15·00 18·00

58 3 3d. dull purple and brown, OC (27.4.05) 60 85
59 ,, 6d. dull purple and mauve, OC (31.10.05) .. .. 1·10 1·10
60 ,, 1s. green and black, OC (31.10.05) .. .. 1·75 1·50
61 ,, 2s. 6d. grn. & carm., OC 6·00 7·00
62 ,, 5s. grn. & bl., OC (3.12.05) 7·00 8·00
63 ,, 10s. grn. & brn. OC (3.12.05) 18·00 20·00
54/63 .. .. *Set of* 10 32·00 35·00

By an Order in Council dated 16 February, 1906, the administration of the Southern Nigerian Protectorate was amalgamated with that of the Colony of Lagos, and became the Colony and Protectorate of Southern Nigeria (*q.v.*).

LEEWARD ISLANDS.

Issues superseding the earlier issues, or in concurrent use with the later issues (from 1903), of Antigua, Dominica (*to* 31 Dec., 1939), Montserrat, Nevis, St. Christopher, St. Kitts-Nevis, and Virgin Islands.

PRINTERS. All the stamps of Leeward Islands were typographed by De La Rue & Co., *except where otherwise stated.*

1

2

1890. *Name and value in second colour. Wmk. Crown CA. P* 14.
1 1 ½d. dull mauve and green .. 25 15
2 ,, 1d. dull mauve and rose 45 15
3 ,, 2½d. dull mauve and blue .. 1·25 35
4 ,, 4d. dull mauve and orange 2·50 2·50
5 ,, 6d. dull mauve and brown .. 2·50 2·75
6 ,, 7d. dull mauve and slate .. 1·75 2·50
7 2 1s. green and carmine .. 10·00 10·00
8 ,, 5s. green and blue .. .. 50·00 60·00
1/8 .. .. *Set of* 8 60·00 70·00
1/8 Optd. "Specimen" *Set of* 8 60·00
The colours of this issue are fugitive.

(3)

One Penny
(4)

One Penny
(5)

1897. *Queen Victoria's Diamond Jubilee. Handstamped with T* 3.
9 1 ½d. dull mauve and green .. 3·00 4·00
a. Opt. double £150
10 ,, 1d. dull mauve and rose .. 3·00 4·50
a. Opt. double £150
b. Opt. triple £1000
11 ,, 2½d. dull mauve and blue .. 4·00 4·50
a. Opt. double £150
12 ,, 4d. dull mauve and orange 10·00 12·00
a. Opt. double £160
13 ,, 6d. dull mauve and brown .. 18·00 20·00
a. Opt. double £350
14 ,, 7d. dull mauve and slate .. 18·00 20·00
a. Opt. double £350
15 2 1s. green and carmine .. 70·00 85·00
a. Opt. double £600
16 ,, 5s. green and blue £350 £350
a. Opt. double £2000
9/16 .. .. *Set of* 8 £450 £450
Beware of forgeries.

1902. *Nos.* 4/6 *surch.*
17 4 1d. on 4d. dull mauve & orge. 85 2·00
a. Pair, one with tall narrow "O" in "One" .. .. 9·00 10·00
b. Surch. double .. ..
18 ,, 1d. on 6d. dull mauve & brn. 55 2·00
a. Pair, one with tall narrow "O" in "One" .. .. .. 12·00 14·00
19 5 1d. on 7d. dull mauve & slate 85 2·00

6

7

8

1902. *Wmk. Crown CA. P* 14.
20 6 ½d. dull purple and green .. 35 45
21 ,, 1d. dull purple and carmine 55 20
22 7 2d. dull purple and ochre .. 1·25 1·25
23 6 2½d. dull purple & ultram... 1·40 1·40
a. Wide "A" in "LEEWARD"
24 7 3d. dull purple and black .. 1·25 1·75
25 6 6d. dull purple and brown 1·40 4·00
26 8 1s. green and carmine .. 4·50 4·50
27 7 2s. 6d. green and black .. 11·00 13·00
28 8 5s. green and blue .. 18·00 23·00
20/28 .. .. *Set of* 9 35·00 45·00
20/8 Optd. "Specimen" *Set of* 9 55·00

1905–8. *Wmk. Mult. Crown CA. P* 14.
29 6 ½d. dull pur. & grn., OC ('06) 20 25
30 ,, 1d. dull pur. & car., C ('06) 60 25
31 7 2d. dull pur. & ochre, C ('08) 1·60 4·00
32 6 2½d. dull pur. & ultram., C ('06) .. .. .. 6·00 6·50
a. Wide "A" in "LEEWARD"
33 7 3d. dull pur. & black, OC 2·75 4·50
34 6 6d. dull pur. & brn., C ('08) 6·00 8·50
35 8 1s. green & carmine, C ('08) 10·00 13·00
29/35 .. .. *Set of* 7 25·00 35·00

1907–11. *Wmk. Mult. Crown CA. P* 14.
36 7 ¼d. brown, O (4.7.09) .. 12 30
37 6 ½d. dull green, O 25 15
38 ,, 1d. bright red, O 40 15
a. Rose-carmine .. .. 4·00 25
39 7 2d. grey, O (1911) .. .. 65 2·00
40 6 2½d. bright blue, O .. .. 75 1·60
a. Wide "A" in "LEEWARD"
41 7 3d. pur./*yellow*, C (1910) .. 95 1·90
42 6 6d. dull & brt. pur., C ('11) 1·00 2·00
43 8 1s. black/*green*, C (1911) .. 3·50 5·50
44 7 2s. 6d. blk. & red/*bl.*, C ('11) 11·00 15·00
45 8 5s. grn. & red/*yell.*, C ('11) 24·00 26·00
36/45 .. .. *Set of* 10 38·00 50·00
36/45 Optd. "Specimen" *Set of* 10 55·00

10

11

12

13

1912–22. *Wmk. Mult. Crown CA. P* 14.
46 10 ¼d. brown, O 20 12
a. Pale brown 20 20
47 11 ½d. yellow-grn., O (2.13) 30 25
a. Deep green 30 25
48 ,, 1d. carmine-red, O 40 15
a. Bright scarlet (1915) .. 40 15
49 10 2d. slate-grey, O (2.13) .. 40 80
50 11 2½d. bright blue, O .. 2·50 2·25
a. Deep bright blue .. 1·75 1·00
51 10 3d. purple/*yellow*, C (2.13) 40 1·10
a. White back (Optd. S. £11) (11.13) .. .. 9·50 11·00
b. On lemon (1916) .. .. 1·10 2·00
c. On orange-buff .. .. 80 1·40
d. On pale yellow (1919) .. 7·00 9·50
52 ,, 4d. black and red/*pale yellow*, C (Die II) ('22) 65 1·50
53 11 6d. dull & brt. pur., C (2.13) 65 1·50
54 12 1s. black/*green*, C (2.13) 2·75 2·25
a. White back (Optd. S. £11) (11.13) .. .. 8·00 10·00
b. On blue-green, olive back ('14) (Optd. S. £11) .. .. 1·10 2·25
55 10 2s. purple & blue/*blue*, C (Die II) (1922) 2·75 4·00
56 ,, 2s. 6d. blk. & red/*blue*, C (2.13) .. .. 9·00 8·50
57 12 5s. green & red/*yellow*, C (1915) .. .. 10·00 11·00
a. White back (Opdt. S. £11) (11.13) .. .. 11·00 12·00
b. On lemon (1916) .. .. 5·00 7·50
c. On orange-buff (1920?) ..
46/57 .. .. *Set of* 12 21·00 26·00
46/57 Optd. "Specimen" *Set of* 12 65·00

1921–32. *Wmk. Mult. Script. CA, except* £1 (*Mult. Crown CA*). *P* 14.

(*a*) *Die* II (1921–29.)
58 10 ¼d. brown, O (1.4.22) .. 12 20
59 11 ½d. blue-green, O ('21) .. 12 20
60 ,, 1d. carmine-red, O ('21) .. 15 12
61 ,, 1d. bright violet, O (8.22) 15 15
62 ,, 1d. bright scarlet, O ('29) 10 10
63 10 1½d. carmine-red, O (1926) 15 40
64 ,, 1½d. red-brown, O (1929) .. 12 10
65 ,, 2d. slate-grey, O (6.22) .. 25 40
66 11 2½d. orange-yellow, O (7.23) 4·00 8·00
67 ,, 2½d. bright blue, O (1927) 40 40
68 10 3d. lt. ultram., O (7.23) .. 3·50 4·00
a. Deep ultramarine .. .. 7·00 9·00
69 ,, 3d. purple/*yellow*, C (1927) 45 1·25
70 ,, 4d. black & red/*pale yellow* C (1924) .. .. 50 1·75
71 ,, 5d. dull purple and olive-green, C (1.4.22) .. 40 95
72 11 6d. dull and bright purple, C (1923) .. .. 3·00 5·00
73 12 1s. black/*emerald*, C ('23) 1·10 2·75
74 10 2s. pur. & bl./*blue*, C (1.4.22) .. .. 10·00 12·00
a. Red-purple and blue/blue, C (1926) .. .. 4·00 6·00
75 ,, 2s. 6d. black and red/*blue*, C (1923) .. .. 5·00 9·00
76 ,, 3s. bright green and violet, C (1.4.22) .. .. 7·00 10·00
77 ,, 4s. black & red, C (1.4.22) 8·00 12·00
78 12 5s. green & red/*pale yellow*, C (1923) .. .. 18·00 22·00
79 13 10s. grn. & red/*grn.*, C ('28) 30·00 35·00
80 ,, £1 pur. & blk./*red*, C ('28) 60·00 80·00
58/80 .. .. *Set of* 22 £130 £180
58/80 Optd./Perf. "Specimen" *Set of* 22 £140

(*b*) *Reversion to Die* I (*Plate* 23) (1931–32).
81 10 ¼d. brown, O 20 30
82 11 ½d. blue-green, O ('31) .. 20 90
83 ,, 1d. bright scarlet, O .. 15 15
84 10 1½d. red-brown, O 45 60
85 11 2½d. bright blue, O .. 1·00 1·25
86 ,, 6d. dull & bright purple, C 2·75 4·00
87 12 1s. black/*emerald*, C .. 9·50 12·00
81/87 .. .. *Set of* 7 13·00 18·00

1935 (6 May). *Silver Jubilee. As Nos.* 91/4 *of Antigua but printed by Waterlow. P* 11 × 12.
88 1d. deep blue and scarlet .. 15 15
89 1½d. ultramarine and grey .. 25 45
90 2½d. brown and deep blue .. 95 1·25
91 1s. slate and purple .. 2·75 4·00
88/91 Perf. "Specimen" *Set of* 4 17·00

1937 (12 May). *Coronation. As Nos.* 13/15 *of Aden. P* 14.

92	1d. scarlet	15	15
93	1½d. buff	15	15
94	2½d. bright blue	25	25
92/4	Perf. "Specimen" *Set of* 3	12·00	

14

15

(Die A)

(Die B)

In Die B the figure "1" has a broader top and more projecting serif.

1938 (25 Nov.)–**51.** *T* **14** (*and similar type, but with shaded value tablet,* ½*d.,* 1*d.,* 2½*d.,* 6*d.*) *and* **15** (10*s.,* £1). *P* 14.

(*a*) *Wmk. Mult. Script. CA.*

95	¼d. brown, O	15	15
	a. Deep brown, C ('49) ..	15	15
96	½d. blue-green	15	15
97	½d. slate-grey, C ('49) ..	15	15
98	1d. scarlet (Die A)	70	70
99	1d. scar. (*shades*) (Die B) ('40)	15	15
	a. Carmine ('42)	35	1·25
100	1d. blue-green, C ('49) ..	15	15
101	1½d. red-brown	15	15
102	1½d. orange & black, C ('49)	15	15
103	2d. slate-grey	15	15
104	2d. scarlet, C ('49)	40	40
105	2½d. bright blue	15	15
106	2½d. black & purple, C ('49)	30	25
107	3d. orange, C	3·00	80
	a. Pale orange, O	30	30
108	3d. bright blue, C ('49) ..	25	15
109	6d. dull and brt. purple, C O	15	15
110	1s. black/*emerald,* C O ..	55	55
	a. Grey & black/emerald, O ('42)	3·50	2·75
	b. Black & grey/emerald, O ('42)	10·00	3·50
111	2s. reddish purple and blue/*blue,* C O	1·25	1·00
	a. Deep pur. & blue/blue, O ('47)	90	1·00
112	5s. green & red/*yellow,* C O	1·75	2·00
113	10s. green & red/*green,* C O	4·50	5·00

(*b*) *Wmk. Mult. Crown CA.*

114	£1 brn.-purple & blk./*red,* C	35·00	30·00
	a. Purple & blk./carm., C ('41)	6·00	10·00
	b. Brn.-pur. & blk./sal., C ('43)	5·50	9·00
	c. *Perf.* 13. *Violet and black/scarlet,* C (13.12.51) ..	4·50	7·50
	ac. Wmk. sideways, p. 13 ..	£400	
95/114*c*	.. .. *Set of* 19	13·00	17·00
95/114	Perf. "Specimen" *Set of* 13	48·00	

1946 (1 Nov.). *Victory. As Nos.* 28/9 *of Aden.*

115	1½d. brown	8	8
116	3d. red-orange	8	8
115/16	Perf. "Specimen" *Set of* 2	14·00	

1949 (2 Jan.). *Royal Silver Wedding. As Nos.* 30/1 *of Aden.*

117	2½d. ultramarine	8	8
118	5s. green	2·75	3·50

1949 (10 Oct.). *75th Anniv. of Universal Postal Union. As Nos.* 114/7 *of Antigua.*

119	2½d. blue-black	12	12
120	3d. deep blue	20	25
121	6d. magenta	40	40
122	1s. blue green	55	55

1951 (16 Feb.). *Inauguration of B.W.I. University College. As Nos.* 118/9 *of Antigua.*

123	3 c. orange and black ..	10	10
124	12 c. rose-carmine & reddish violet	25	25

1953 (2 June). *Coronation. As No.* 47 *of Aden.*

125	3 c. black and green.. ..	20	30

16. Queen Elizabeth II. **17.**

1954 (22 Feb.). *Chalk-surfaced paper. Wmk. Mult. Script CA. P* 14 (*T* **16**) *or* (*T* **17**).

126	**16**	½ c. brown	5	5
127	"	1 c. grey	5	5
128	"	2 c. green	5	5
129	"	3 c. yellow-orge. & black	5	5
130	"	4 c. rose-red	5	5
131	"	5 c. black & brown-purple	5	5
132	"	6 c. yellow-orange ..	5	5
133	"	8 c. ultramarine	8	8
134	"	12 c. dull & reddish purple	12	12
135	"	24 c. black and green ..	25	30
136	"	48 c. dull purple & ultram.	60	60
137	"	60 c. brown and green ..	70	80
138	"	$1.20, yell.-grn & rose-red	1·00	1·10
139	**17**	$2.40, bluish green & red	2·00	2·50
140	"	$4.80, brn.-purple & blk.	3·50	4·00
126/140		.. .. *Set of* 15	8·00	9·00

The 3 c., 4 c., 6 c., 8 c., 24 c., 48 c., 60 c. and $1.20 have their value tablets unshaded.

The stamps of Leeward Islands were withdrawn and invalidated on 1st July, 1956.

LESOTHO.

(Formerly Basutoland.)

INDEPENDENT.

31. Moshoeshoe I and Moshoeshoe II.

(Des. and photo. Harrison & Sons.)

1966 (4 Oct.). *Independence. P* 12½×13.

106	**31**	2½ c. light brown, black & red	5	5
107	"	5 c. light brown, black & new blue	8	8
108	"	10 c. light brown, black & emerald	20	20
109	"	20 c. light brown, black & bright purple ..	30	35

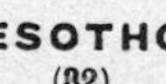

(**32**)

33. "Education, Culture and Science".

1966 (1 Nov.). *Stamps of Basutoland optd. as T* **32.** A, *Nos.* 69/71 *and* 73/9 (*Script CA wmk.*) B, *Nos.* 84, 86, 88, 90, 92 *and unissued* 1 r (*wmk.* w.**12**).

				A.		B.	
110	**8**	½c.	..	5	5		†
111	**9**	1 c.	..	5	5	5	
112	**10**	2 c.	..	5	5		†
113	**26**	2½ c.	..		†	8	
114	**12**	3½ c.	..	5	5		†
115	**13**	5 c.	..	12	12	12	1
116	**14**	10 c.	..	20	25		†
117	**15**	12½ c.	..	45	45	20	4
118	**16**	25 c.	..	40	45		†
119	**17**	50 c.	..	80	1·25	75	1·2
120	**18**	1 r.	..	2·25	2·50	1·50	2·5
		a. Error. "LSEOTHO"		50·00	—	30·00	—
		b. Opt. double		60·00	—		†
110A/120A		*Set of* 10		4·00	4·75		
111B/120B		*Set of* 6				2·50	4·0

(Des. V. Whiteley. Litho. De La Rue.)

1966 (1 Dec.). *20th Anniv. of U.N.E.S.C.O. P* 14½×14.

121	**33**	2½ c. orange-yellow and emerald-green ..	5	
122	"	5 c. light green & olive ..	8	
123	"	12½ c. light blue and red ..	15	2
124	"	25 c. red-orange and deep greenish blue ..	35	4

34. Maize.

35. Cattle.
36. Aloes.
37. Basotho Hat.
38. Merino Sheep ("Wool").
39. Basotho Pony.
40. Wheat.
41. Angora Goat ("Mohair").
42. Maletsunyane Falls.
43. Diamonds.
44. Arms of Lesotho.

(*T* **35/44** *are as T* **34.**

45. Moshoeshoe II.

(Des. and photo. Harrison.)

1967 (1 Apr.). *No Wmk. P* 14½×13½ (2 *r.*) *o* 13½×14½ (*others*).

125	**34**	½ c. bluish green and light bluish violet ..	5	
126	**35**	1 c. sepia and rose-red ..	5	
127	**36**	2 c. orange-yellow and light green	5	
128	**37**	2½ c. black and ochre ..	8	
129	**38**	3½ c. chalky blue & yell.	8	
130	**39**	5 c. bistre and new blue	10	1
131	**40**	10 c. yellow-brown and bluish grey ..	15	1
132	**41**	12½ c. black & red-orange	20	3
133	**42**	25 c. blk. & bright blue	50	5
134	**43**	50 c. blk., new bl. & turq.	1·00	1·2
135	**44**	1 r. multicoloured ..	1·60	1·6
136	**45**	2 r. black, gold & mag.	3·50	4·5
125/36		.. .. *Set of* 12	6·50	7·5

See also Nos. 147/59 and 191/203.

46. Students and University.

(Des. V. Whiteley. Photo. Harrison.)

1967 (7 Apr.). *First Conferment of University Degrees. P* 14×14½.

137 **46** 1 c. sepia, ultramarine & light yellow-orange 5 5

138 ,, 2½ c. sepia, ultramarine & light greenish blue .. 5 5

139 ,, 12½ c. sepia, ultram. & rose 15 20

140 ,, 25 c. sepia, ultramarine and light violet .. 30 35

47. Statue of Moshoeshoe I.

48. National Flag.

49. Crocodile (national emblem).

(Des. and photo. Harrison.)

1967 (4 Oct.). *First Anniv. of Independence. P* 14½×14.

141 **47** 2½ c. black & lt. yell.-grn. 5 5

142 **48** 12½ c. multicoloured .. 20 20

143 **49** 25 c. blk., grn. & lt. ochre 30 30

50. Lord Baden-Powell and Scout Saluting.

(Des. V. Whiteley. Photo. Harrison.)

1967 (1 Nov.). *60th Anniv. of Scout Movement. P* 14×14½.

144 **50** 15 c. multicoloured .. 20 25

51. W.H.O. Emblem and World Map.

52. Nurse and Child.

(Des. G. L. Vasarhelyi. Photo. Harrison.)

1968 (7 Apr.). *20th Anniv. of World Health Organization. P* 14×14½.

145 **51** 2½ c. blue, gold and carmine-red 5 5
a. Gold (emblem) omitted

146 **52** 25 c. multicoloured .. 30 35

53. Basuto Hat.

54. Sorghum.

1968–69. *As Nos.* 125/36, *but wmk.* **53** (*sideways on* 2 *r.*) *and new value.*

147 **34** ½ c. bluish green & light bluish violet (*shades*) (26.11.68) .. 5 5

148 **35** 1 c. sepia and rose-red (26.11.68) 5 5

149 **36** 2 c. orge.-yell. & lt. grn. (*shades*) (26.11.68).. 5 5

150 **37** 2½ c. black and ochre (*shades*) (21.10.68).. 8 8

151 **54** 3 c. chocolate, green and yellow-brn. (1.8.68) 10 10

152 **38** 3½ c. chalky blue and yellow (26.11.68) 10 12

153 **39** 5 c. bistre and new blue (22.7.68) 12 15

154 **40** 10 c. yellow-brown & pale bluish grey (26.11.68) 20 25

155 **41** 12½ c. black & red-orange (30.9.69) 25 35

156 **42** 25 c. black and bright blue (30.9.69) .. 50 60

157 **43** 50 c. black, new blue and turquoise (30.9.69) 1·00 1·25

158 **44** 1 r. mult. (26.11.68) .. 2·00 2·25

159 **45** 2 r. black, gold and magenta (30.9.69) .. 4·00 4·50

147/59 .. .. *Set of* 13 8·00 9·00

55. Running Hunters.

56. Baboons. (*Horiz.*)

57. Javelin Thrower. (*Vert.*)

58. Archers. (*Horiz.*)

59. Blue Cranes. (*Vert.*)

60. Eland. (*Horiz.*)

61. Hunting Scene. (*Horiz.*)

(Des. Jennifer Toombs. Photo. Harrison.)

1968 (1 Nov.). *Rock Paintings. W* **53** (*sideways on* 5 *c.*, 15 *c.*). *P* 14×14½ (5 *c.*, 15 *c.*) *or* 14½×14 (*others*).

160 **55** 3 c. yell.-brn., light blue-grn. & blackish green 5 8

161 **56** 3½ c. greenish yellow, yell.-olive and sepia .. 8 8

162 **57** 5 c. Venetian red, yellow-ochre & blackish brn. 10 10

163 **58** 10 c. yell., rose & dp. mar. 15 15

164 **59** 15 c. light buff, pale olive-yell. & blackish brn. 25 25

165 **60** 20 c. yellow-grn., greenish yell. & blackish brown 35 35

166 **61** 25 c. yell., orge.-brn. & blk. 40 40

160/6 .. .. *Set of* 7 1·25 1·25

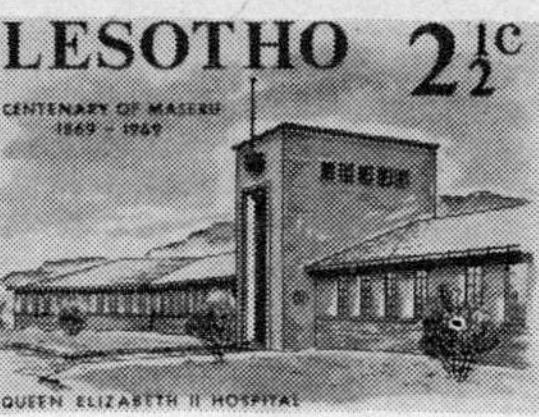

62. Queen Elizabeth II Hospital.

63. Lesotho Radio Station.

64. Leabua Jonathan Airport.

65. Royal Palace.

(Des. C. R. Househam and G. Drummond. Litho. Perkins Bacon Ltd.)

1969 (11 Mar.). *Centenary of Maseru (capital). W* **53** (*sideways*). *P* 14×13½.

167 **62** 2½ c. multicoloured .. 5 5

168 **63** 10 c. multicoloured .. 15 15

169 **64** 12½ c. multicoloured .. 20 25

170 **65** 25 c. multicoloured .. 35 35

66. Rally Car passing Basuto Tribesman.

67. Rally Car on Mountain Road.

68. Chequered Flags and " Roof of Africa " Plateau.

69. Map of Rally Route and Independence Trophy.

(Des. P. Wheeler. Photo. Harrison.)

1969 (26 Sept.). *" Roof of Africa " Car Rally. W* 53. *P* 14.

171 **66** 2½ c. yell., mauve & plum 5 5

172 **67** 12½ c. cobalt, greenish yellow and olive-grey.. 20 25

173 **68** 15 c. blue, black & mauve 20 25

174 **69** 20 c. black, red & yellow 30 35

70. Dinosaur Footprints at Moyeni. (60×23 *mm.*).

71. Gryponyx and Footprints.

72. Plateosauravus and Footprints.

73. Tritylodon and Footprints.

74. Massospondylus and Footprints.
T **72/4** *are as T* **71.**

(Des. Jennifer Toombs. Photo. Harrison.)

1970 (5 Jan.). *Prehistoric Reptiles' Footprints. W* **53** (*sideways*). *P* 14×14½ (3 *c.*) *or* 14½×14 (*others*).

175 **70** 3 c. pale brown, yellow-brown and sepia .. 5 5

176 **71** 5 c. dull purple, pink and sepia 10 10

177 **72** 10 c. pale yellow, black, and sepia 20 20

178 **73** 15 c. ol.-yell., blk. & sepia 30 30

179 **74** 25 c. cobalt and black .. 50 50

175/9 .. .. *Set of* 5 1·00 1·00

75. Moshoeshoe I, when a Young Man.

76. Moshoeshoe I, when an Old Man.

(Des. G. L. Vasarhelyi. Litho. De La Rue.)

1970 (11 Mar.). *Death Centenary of Chief Moshoeshoe I. W* **53.** *P* 13½.

180	**75**	2½ c. pale green & magenta	5	5
181	**76**	25 c. pale blue & chestnut	40	40

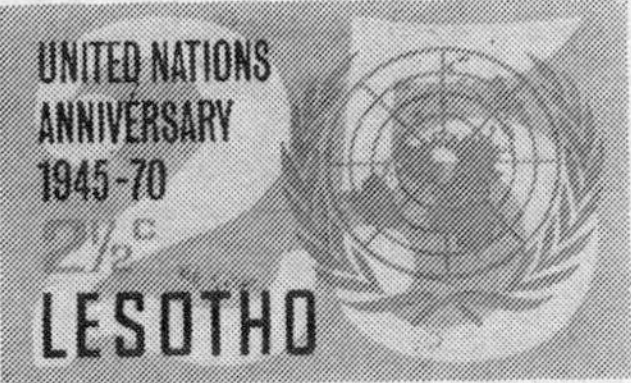

77. U.N. Emblem and "25".

(Des. V. Whiteley. Litho. Questa.)

1970 (26 June). *25th Anniv. of United Nations. T* **77** *and similar horiz. designs. W* **53** *(sideways). P* 14½×14.

182	2½ c. light pink, light blue and maroon	5	5
183	10 c. multicoloured ..	15	15
184	12½ c. brn.-red, cobalt & drab	20	20
185	25 c. multicoloured ..	40	40

Designs:—10 c. U.N. Building; 12½ c. "People of the World"; 25 c. Symbolic dove.

78. Gift Shop, Maseru.

(Des. G. Drummond. Litho. Questa.)

1970 (27 Oct.). *Tourism. T* **78** *and similar horiz. designs. Multicoloured. W* **53** *(sideways). P* 14.

186	2½ c. Type **78**	8	8
187	5 c. Trout fishing	10	10
188	10 c. Pony trekking ..	20	20
189	12½ c. Skiing, Maluti Mts. ..	25	25
190	20 c. Holiday inn, Maseru ..	40	40
186/90	.. .. *Set of* 5	90	90

79. Maize.

(Des. Harrison & Sons. Litho. Questa.)

1971 (4 Jan.–1 Apr.). *As Nos.* 147/58 *but in new format omitting portrait of Moshoeshoe II, as in T* **79.** 4 *c. and* 2 *r. in new designs. W* **53** *(sideways except* 2 *r.). P* 14.

191	**79**	½ c. blue-green, and light bluish violet ..	5	5
192	**35**	1 c. brown & orange-red	5	5
193	**36**	2 c. yellow and green ..	5	5
194	**37**	2½ c. black, olive-green and yellow-ochre ..	5	5
195	**54**	3 c. brown, green and yellow-ochre ..	5	5
196	**38**	3½ c. indigo and yellow ..	5	5
196*a*	–	4 c. mult. (1.4.71) ..	8	8
197	**39**	5 c. yellow-brown and pale blue	8	8
198	**40**	10 c. orange-brown and grey-blue	12	15
199	**41**	12½ c. chocolate and yellow-orange	15	20
200	**42**	25 c. slate and pale bright blue	30	35
201	**43**	50 c. black, pale blue and turquoise-green ..	60	70
202	**44**	1 r. multicoloured ..	1·25	1·40
203	–	2 r. yellow-brown and ultramarine ..	2·25	2·50
191/203		.. .. *Set of* 14	4·50	5·00

Designs: *Horiz.*—4 c. National flag. *Vert.*—2 r. Statue of Moshoeshoe I.

80. Lämmergeier.

(Des. R. Granger Barrett. Litho. J.W.)

1971 (1 Mar.). *Birds. T* **80** *and similar vert. designs. Multicoloured. W* **53.** *P* 14.

204	2½ c. Type **80**	10	10
205	5 c. Bald Ibis	10	10
206	10 c. Orange-breasted Rock Jumper	20	20
207	12½ c. Blue Korhaan	25	25
208	15 c. Painted Snipe	30	30
209	20 c. Golden-breasted Bunting	40	40
210	25 c. Ground Woodpecker ..	50	55
204/10	.. .. *Set of* 7	1·75	1·75

81. Lionel Collett Dam.

(Des. G. Drummond. Litho. J.W.)

1971 (15 July). *Soil Conservation. T* **81** *an[d] similar horiz. designs. Multicoloured. W* **5[3]** *(sideways). P* 14.

211	4 c. Type **81**	8	
212	10 c. Contour ridges	15	1
213	15 c. Earth dams	25	2
214	25 c. Beaver dams	40	4

82. Diamond Mining.

(Des. J. Waddington Ltd. Litho. Questa.)

1971 (4 Oct.). *Development. T* **82** *and simila[r] horiz. designs. Multicoloured. W* **53** *(side-ways). P* 14.

215	4 c. Type **82**	8	
216	10 c. Pottery	20	2
217	15 c. Weaving	30	3
218	20 c. Construction	40	4

83. Mail Cart.

(Des. D. B. Picton-Phillips. Litho. Questa.)

1972 (3 Jan.). *Post Office Centenary. T* **83** *an[d] similar designs. W* **53** *(sideways on* 5, 10 *an[d]* 20 *c.). P* 14×13½ (15 *c.) or* 13½×14 *(others).*

219	5 c. pale pink and black ..	10	1
220	10 c. multicoloured	25	2
221	15 c. pale drab, light blue and black	35	3
222	20 c. multicoloured	45	4

Designs: *Horiz.*—10 c. Postal bus; 20 c. Maseru P.O. *Vert.*—15 c. Cape of Good Hope 4[d] stamp of 1876.

84. Sprinting.

(Des. J. W. Ltd. Litho. Questa.)

1972 (1 Sept.). *Olympic Games, Munich. T* **8[4]** *and similar vert. designs. Multicoloure[d]. W* **53.** *P* 14.

223	4 c. Type **84**	5	
224	10 c. Shot putting	20	2
225	15 c. Hurdling	30	3
226	25 c. Long-jumping	50	5

85. "Adoration of the Shepherds" (Matthias Stomer).

(Des. and litho. J.W.)

1972 (1 Dec.). *Christmas.* *W* **53** (*sideways*). *P* 14.

227 **85** 4 c. multicoloured .. 8 8
228 „ 10 c. multicoloured .. 20 20
229 „ 25 c. multicoloured .. 50 50

86. W.H.O. Emblem.

(Des. J. E. Cooter. Litho. Questa.)

1973 (7 Apr.). *25th Anniv. of W.H.O.* *W* **53.** *P* 13½.

230 **86** 20 c. greenish blue & yell. 35 35

O.A.U.
10th Anniversary
Freedom in Unity

(**87**)

1973 (25 May). *Tenth Anniv. of O.A.U. Nos. 194 and 196a/8 optd. with T* **87** *by Lesotho Govt. Printers.*

231 **37** 2½ c. black, olive-green and yellow-ochre 5 5
232 – 4 c. multicoloured .. 5 5
233 **39** 5 c. yellow-brn. & pale blue 10 10
234 **40** 10 c. orange-brn. & grey-blue 20 20

88. Basuto Hat and W.F.P. Emblem.

(Des. locally; adapted J. E. Cooter. Litho. Format.)

1973 (1 June). *Tenth Anniv. of World Food Programme. T* **88** *and similar horiz. designs. Multicoloured. W* **53** (*sideways*). *P* 13½.

235 4 c. Type **88** 10 10
236 15 c. School feeding 25 25
237 20 c. Infant feeding 30 30
a. Imperf. (pair) .. ..
238 25 c. " Food for Work " .. 40 40

89. Mountain Beauty.

(Des. A. McLeod; artwork G. Drummond. Litho. Questa.)

1973 (3 Sept.). *Butterflies. T* **89** *and similar horiz. designs. Multicoloured. W* **53** (*sideways*). *P* 14.

239 4 c. Type **89** 8 8
240 5 c. Christmas Butterfly .. 8 8
241 10 c. Painted Lady 15 15
242 15 c. Yellow Pansy 25 25
243 20 c. Blue Pansy 25 30
244 25 c. African Monarch .. 35 35
245 30 c. Orange Tip 45 50
239/45 .. .. *Set of* 7 1·40 1·50

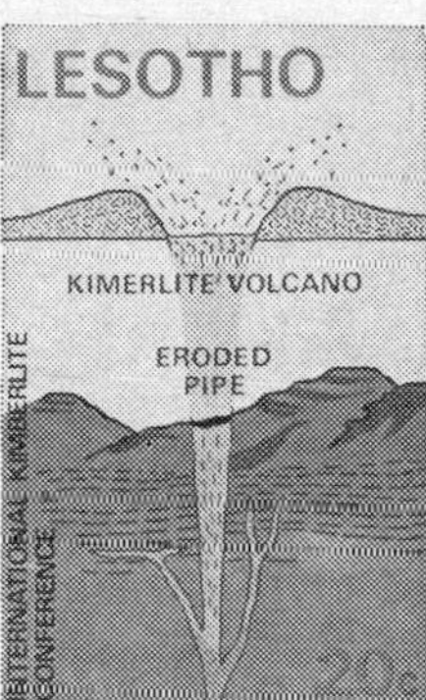

90. Kimberlite Volcano.

(Des. PAD Studio. Litho. Questa.)

1973 (1 Oct.). *International Kimberlite Conference. T* **90** *and similar multicoloured designs. W* **53** (*sideways on* 10 *and* 15 *c.*). *P* 13½.

246 10 c. Map of diamond-mines (*horiz.*) 15 15
247 15 c. Kimberlite-diamond rock (*horiz.*) 20 20
248 20 c. Type **90** 25 30
249 30 c. Diamond prospecting .. 40 45

Type **90** is incorrectly inscribed "KIMERLITE VOLCANO".

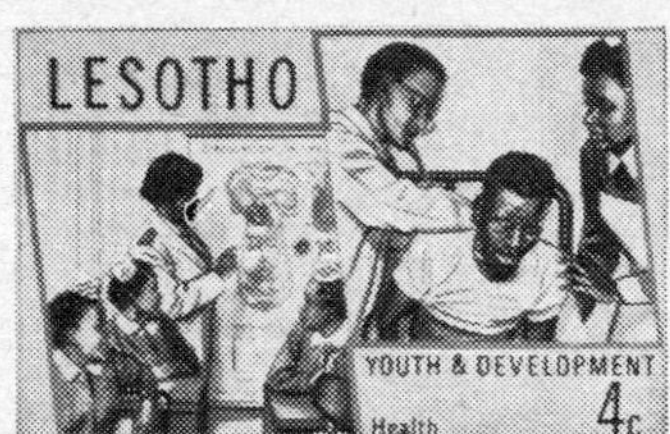

91. " Health ".

(Des. R. Granger Barrett. Litho. Questa.)

1974 (18 Feb.). *Youth and Development. T* **91** *and similar horiz. designs. Multicoloured. W* **53** (*sideways*). *P* 13½.

250 4 c. Type **91** 8 8
251 10 c. " Education " 12 15
252 20 c. " Agriculture " 25 30
253 25 c. " Industry " 30 35
254 30 c. " Service " 40 45
250/4 .. .. *Set of* 5 1·00 1·10

92. Open Book and Wreath.

(Des. PAD Studio. Litho. Questa.)

1974 (7 Apr.). *Tenth Anniv. of U.B.L.S. T* **92** *and similar vert. designs. Multicoloured. W* **53.** *P* 14.

255 10 c. Type **92** 12 15
256 15 c. Flags, mortar-board and scroll 20 25
257 20 c. Map of Africa 25 30
258 25 c. King Moshoeshoe II capping a graduate .. 30 35

93. Senqunyane River Bridge, Marakabei.

(Des. J. E. Cooter. Litho. Questa.)

1974 (26 June). *Rivers and Bridges. T* **93** *and similar horiz. designs. Multicoloured. W* **53** (*sideways*). *P* 14½.

259 4 c. Type **93** 8 8
260 5 c. Tsoelike River and bridge 8 8
261 10 c. Makhaleng River Bridge 12 15
262 15 c. Seaka Bridge, Orange/Senqu River 20 20
263 20 c. Masianokeng Bridge, Phuthiatsana River .. 25 30
264 25 c. Mahobong Bridge, Hlotse River 30 35
259/64 .. .. *Set of* 6 85 95

94. U.P.U. Emblem.

(Des. R. Granger Barrett. Litho. Enschedé.)

1974 (6 Sept.). *Centenary of Universal Postal Union. T* **94** *and similar horiz. designs. W* **53** (*sideways*). *P* 13½ × 13.

265 4 c. light emerald and black .. 8 8
266 10 c. orange, greenish yellow and black 12 15
267 15 c. multicoloured 20 20
268 20 c. multicoloured 25 30

Designs:—10 c. Map of air-mail routes; 15 c. Post Office H.Q., Maseru; 20 c. Horseman taking rural mail.

95. Siege of Thaba-Bosiu.

(Des. Jennifer Toombs. Litho. Enschedé.)

1974 (25 Nov.). *150th Anniv. of Siege of Thaba-Bosiu. T* **95** *and similar multicoloured designs. W* **53** *(sideways on 4 and 5 c.). P* $12\frac{1}{2}\times 12$ *(4 and 5 c.) or* $12\times 12\frac{1}{2}$ *(others).*

269	4 c. Type **95**	8	8
270	5 c. The wreath-laying ..	8	8
271	10 c. Moshoeshoe I (*vert.*) ..	12	15
272	20 c. Makoanyane, the warrior (*vert.*)	25	30

96. Mamokhorong.

(Des. PAD Studio. Litho. Questa.)

1975 (25 Jan.). *Basotho Musical Instruments. T* **96** *and similar horiz. designs. Multicoloured. W* **53** *(sideways). P* 14.

273	4 c. Type **96**	8	8
274	10 c. Lesiba	12	15
275	15 c. Setolotolo	20	20
276	20 c. Meropa	25	30
MS277	108 × 92 mm. Nos. 273/6	65	70

97. Horseman in Rock Archway.

(Des. J. E. Cooter. Litho. Questa.)

1975 (15 Apr.). *Sehlabathebe National Park. T* **97** *and similar horiz. designs. Multicoloured. W* **53** *(sideways). P* 14.

278	4 c. Type **97**	8	8
279	5 c. Mountain view through arch	8	8
280	15 c. Antelope by stream ..	20	20
281	20 c. Mountains and lake ..	25	30
282	25 c. Tourists by waterfall ..	30	35
278/82	.. .. *Set of* 5	75	85

98. Morena Moshoeshoe I.

(Des. G. L. Vasarhelyi. Litho. Questa.)

1975 (10 Sept.). *Leaders of Lesotho. T* **98** *and similar vert. designs. W* **53**. *P* 14.

283	3 c. black and light blue ..	5	5
284	4 c. black and light mauve ..	8	8
285	5 c. black and pink	8	8
286	6 c. black and lt. grey-brn.	8	8
287	10 c. black and light claret ..	12	15
288	15 c. black and lt. orange-red	20	20
289	20 c. black and dull green ..	25	25
290	25 c. black and azure	30	30
283/90	.. .. *Set of* 8	1·00	1·10

Designs:—4 c. King Moshoeshoe II; 5 c. Morena Letsie I; 6 c. Morena Lerotholi; 10 c. Morena Letsie II; 15 c. Morena Griffith; 20 c. Morena Seeiso Griffith Lerotholi; 25 c. Mofumahali Mantsebo Seeiso, O.B.E.

The 25 c. also commemorates International Women's Year.

99. Mokhibo Dance.

(Des. PAD Studio. Litho. Questa.)

1975 (17 Dec.). *Traditional Dances. T* **99** *and similar horiz. designs. Multicoloured. W* **53** *(sideways). P* $14\times 14\frac{1}{2}$.

291	4 c. Type **99**	5	5
292	10 c. Ndlamo	12	15
293	15 c. Baleseli	20	25
294	20 c. Mohobelo	25	25
MS295	111 × 100 mm. Nos. 291/94	65	65

100. Enrolment.

(Des. Leslie Curtis. Litho. Questa.)

1976 (20 Feb.). *25th Anniv. of the Lesotho Red Cross. T* **100** *and similar horiz. designs. Multicoloured. W* **53** *(sideways). P* 14.

296	4 c. Type **100**	5	5
297	10 c. Medical aid	12	15
298	15 c. Rural service	20	25
299	25 c. Relief supplies	30	30

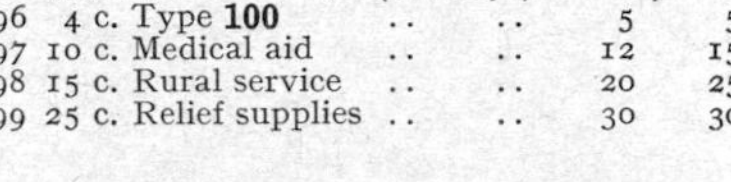

101. Tapestry.

(Des. V. Whiteley Studio. Litho. Format.)

1976 (2 June). *Various multicoloured designs as T* **101**. *W* **53** *(upright on* 1 r.*, sideways on others). P* 14.

300	2 c. Type **101**	5	5
301	3 c. Mosotho horseman ..	5	5
302	4 c. Map of Lesotho	5	5
303	5 c. Lesotho brown diamond	5	5
304	10 c. Lesotho Bank	12	12
305	15 c. Lesotho and O.A.U. flags	20	20
306	25 c. Sehlabathebe National Park	30	35
307	40 c. Pottery	50	55
308	50 c. Pre-historic Rock art	60	70
309	1 r. King Moshoeshoe II (*vert.*)	1·25	1·40
300/309	.. .. *Set of* 10	2·75	3·00

102. Football.

(Des. P. B. Powell. Litho. Questa.)

1976 (9 Aug.). *Olympic Games, Montreal. T* **102** *and similar vert. designs. Multicoloured. W* **53**. *P* 14.

310	4 c. Type **102**	5	5
311	10 c. Weightlifting	12	15
312	15 c. Boxing	20	20
313	25 c. Throwing the discus ..	30	35

See *Addenda*.

POSTAGE DUE STAMPS.

1966 (1 Nov.). *Nos. D9/10 of Basutoland optd. as T* **32** *but smaller.*

D11	D **2**	1 c. carmine	15	25
		a. Error. "LSEOTHO"..	20·00	
D12	,,	5 c. deep reddish violet..	25	35
		a. Error. "LSEOTHO" ..	40·00	

No. D11 exists with the overprint centred near the foot of the stamp (just above "POSTAGE DUE"). It is believed that this comes from a proof sheet which was issued in the normal way. It contains the "LSEOTHO" error, which only occurred in the first printing.

D 1

(Litho. Bradbury, Wilkinson & Co.)

1967 (18 Apr.). *No wmk. P* $13\frac{1}{2}$.

D13	D **1**	1 c. blue	5	5
D14	,,	2 c. brown-rose	5	5
D15	,,	5 c. emerald	5	8

1976 (30 Nov.). *W* **53** *(sideways). P* $13\frac{1}{2}$.

D17	D **1**	2 c. rose-red	5	5
D18	,,	5 c. emerald	5	8

LONG ISLAND.

(AEGEAN SEA)

1916 (7TH TO 26TH MAY). *Turkish fiscal Stamps optd. " G.R.I., POSTAGE ", and new value. No wmk. P 12.*

1 ½d. on 20 pa. green & buff (C). £650 £1600
2 1d. on 10 pa. carmine & buff £650
3 2½d. on 1 pi. violet & buff (Mag.) £800

Quantities issued: ½d., 25; 1d., 25; 2½d., 20.

1

1916 (7–26 MAY). *Type-written in various colours or carbons and each stamp initialled by the Civil Administrator. Imperf.*

(a) *On pale green paper ruled with horiz. grey lines. No wmk. Sheets of 16, initialled in red ink.*

4 1 ½d. black £160
a. " 7 " for " & " .. ..
5 „ ½d. blue £160
6 „ ½d. mauve £180
a. " G.R.I." twice .. ..

Quantities issued, 140 in all.

(b) *On thin horiz. laid paper, wmkd. " SILVER LINEN " in sheet in double-lined capitals. Sheets of 20. Initialled in red ink.*

7 1 ½d. black .. .. .. 42·00
a. " postage " for " Postage " £160
8 „ ½d. blue .. .. .. 70·00
9 „ ½d. mauve .. .. .. 55·00
a. " 7 " for " & " £150
10 „ 1d. black .. .. .. 48·00
a. " 7 " for " & " and " RVEVUE " £150
11 „ 1d. blue .. .. .. 45·00
a. " ONR " for " ONE " .. £120
b. " postage " for " Postage " £120
12 „ 1d. mauve .. .. .. 70·00 70·00
a. " ONR " for " ONE " .. £180
b. " Postegg " for " Postage " £150
13 „ 1d. red .. .. .. 40·00 48·00
a. " 7 " for " & " £150
b. " ONR " for " ONE " .. £150
14 „ 2½d. black .. .. .. 70·00
15 „ 2½d. blue .. .. .. 80·00 90·00
16 „ 2½d. mauve .. .. .. 80·00
17 „ 6d. black £150
19 „ 6d. mauve .. .. .. 55·00 65·00
20 „ 1s. black .. .. .. 45·00
a. " ISLANA " for " ISLAND " £150
b. " Postge " for " Postage " .. £225
c. " Rebeuue " for " Revenue "
21 „ 1s. blue .. .. .. 40·00
22 „ 1s. mauve .. .. .. 40·00
a. " ISLANA " for " ISLAND " £150
b. " Rebenue " for " Revenue " £225

Quantities issued (all colours): ½d., 280; 1d., 1178; 2½d., 80; 6d., 100; 1s., 532.

(c) *On thin wove paper. No wmk. Sheets of 24. Initialled in pencil.*

23 1 ½d. black .. .. .. 55·00
24 „ ½d. mauve £110
25 „ 1d. black .. .. .. 55·00 60·00
26 „ 1d. red £140 £120
27 „ 2d. black .. .. .. 60·00
a. " ISTAD " for " ISLAND " £425
b. 1d. in sheet of 2d. .. ..
28 1 2d. mauve .. .. .. 55·00
b. 1d. in sheet of 2d. £300
29 „ 2½d. black .. .. .. 45·00
30 „ 2½d. mauve £120 £110
31 „ 6d. black .. .. .. 55·00
a. " Rvenne " for " Revenue " £150
b. 2d. in sheet of 6d., also " ISLND " for " ISLAND " .. £300
32 „ 6d. blue .. .. .. 60·00
b. 2d. in sheet of 6d., also " ISLND " for " ISLAND " £300

Quantities issued (all colours): ½d., 144; 1d., 144; 2d., 288; 2½d., 144; 6d. 244.

MADAGASCAR.

BRITISH CONSULAR MAIL.

USED STAMPS. Postmarks are not usually found on these issues. Cancellations usually take the form of a manuscript line or cross in crayon, ink or pencil or as five parallel horizontal bars in black or red, approximately 15 mm. long.

1

(*Illustration reduced. Actual size 38×63 mm.*)

1884 (MAR.). *Rouletted vertically in colour. With circular handstamp, " BRITISH VICE CONSULATE ANTANANARIVO " in black.*

(a) *Inscribed " LETTER ".*

1 1 6d. magenta .. .. .. 65·00 70·00
a. Handstamp in violet .. £120 £130
2 „ 1s. magenta .. .. .. 42·00 45·00
3 „ 1s. 6d. magenta .. .. 42·00 45·00
4 „ 2s. magenta £120 £130

(b) *Inscribed " POSTAL PACKET ".*

5 1 1d. magenta (1 oz.) .. .. 32·00 42·00
a. Without handstamp .. £250 £275
6 „ 2d. magenta (2 oz.) .. .. 42·00 42·00
7 „ 3d. magenta (3 oz.) .. .. 32·00 42·00
8 „ 4d. magenta (1 oz.) .. ..
a. Handstamp in violet .. £120 £110
b. Without handstamp .. £300 £300
c. Altered by pen to " 4 oz." .. £120 £130

Several of the values are known with the handstamp inverted and also double printed.

1886. *No. 2 with " SHILLING " erased and " PENNY " written above in red ink, and the same stamp with " 1 oz." altered in red to " 4½d." and the Vice-Consul's initials, " W.C.P.", added.*

9 1 1d. on 1s. magenta .. ..
10 „ 4½d. on 1s. magenta .. ..

1886. *Colour changed.*

11 1 6d. rose-red .. .. .. 50·00 50·00

As T 1, but handstamp reading " British Consular Mail—ANTANANARIVO."

12 4d. magenta (Bk.) £275 £275
13 4d. magenta (V.) £300 £300

Nos. 1 to 13 were printed in horizontal strips of four, two with the full stops normal and two with one of the full stops appearing as a small circle. This " hollow stop " appears after the " B " in the 1d., 4d., 6d. and 2s. and after the " M " in the 2d., 3d., 1s. and 1s. 6d.

2

(*Illustration reduced. Actual size 45×68 mm.*)

1886. *Rouletted vertically in colour.*

(a) *With period after " POSTAGE " and value.*

A. *Handstamp in black.* B. *In violet.*

			A.		B.	
14	2	1d. rose	16·00	16·00	30·00	30·00
15	„	1½d. rose	45·00	45·00	75·00	80·00
16	„	2d. rose	16·00	16·00	30·00	30·00
17	„	3d. rose	45·00	45·00	30·00	30·00
18	„	4½d. rose	45·00	45·00	32·00	32·00
19	„	8d. rose	65·00	65·00	80·00	85·00
20	„	9d. rose	—	—	£150	£150

(b) *Without period after " POSTAGE " and value. Handstamp in violet.*

21 2 1d. rose £150 £150
22 „ 1½d. rose £180 £180
23 „ 3d. rose £225 £225
24 „ 4½d. rose £110 £120
25 „ 6d. rose £110 £120

(c) *Period after value. " POSTAGE " measures 24½ mm. in place of 29½ mm. Handstamp in violet.*

26 2 4d. rose .. .. .. 50·00 55·00
27 „ 8d. rose £110 £110
28 „ 1s. 6d. rose £300 £325
29 „ 2s. rose £250 £250
a. Handstamp in black ..

1886. *As T 2, but handstamped reading " BRITISH CONSULAR MAIL, ANTANANARIVO ". Rouletted vertically in colour.*

(a) *With period after " POSTAGE " and the value.*

A. *Handstamp in black.* B. *In violet.*

		A.		B.	
30	1d. rose	11·00	12·00		†
31	1½d. rose	11·00	12·00		†
32	2d. rose	12·00	12·00		†
33	3d. rose	12·00	12·00		†
34	4½d. rose	12·00	12·00		†
35	8d. rose	12·00	14·00	£180	£180
36	9d. rose	12·00	14·00	30·00	30·00
	a. Without handstamp	£250	£250		

C. *Handstamp in red.*

37 3d. rose .. .. .. — £375
38 4½d. rose .. .. .. — £325

(b) *Without period after " POSTAGE " and the value.*

A. *Handstamp in black.* B. *In violet.*

		A.		B.	
39	1d. rose	11·00	11·00	12·00	12·00
	a. Without handstamp	90·00	90·00		
40	1½d. rose	11·00	11·00	12·00	12·00
	a. Without handstamp	90·00	90·00		
41	2d. rose	11·00	11·00	12·00	12·00
42	3d. rose	11·00	11·00	12·00	12·00
	a. Without handstamp	£200	£200		
43	4½d. rose	12·00	12·00	15·00	15·00
	a. Without handstamp	£225	£225		
44	6d. rose	12·00	12·00	25·00	25·00
	a. Without handstamp	£250	£250		

(c) *Period after value. " POSTAGE " 24½ mm. long in place of 29½ mm.*

A. *Handstamp in black.* B. *In violet.*

		A.		B.	
45	4d. rose	12·00	12·00	25·00	25·00
	a. Without handstamp	£150	£150		
46	8d. rose	38·00	38·00	40·00	40·00
	a. Without handstamp	£180	£180		
47	1s. rose	23·00	23·00	90·00	90·00
	a. Without handstamp	£180	£180		

48 1s. 6d. rose .. 50·00 50·00 £150 £150
 a. Without handstamp £275 £275
49 2s. rose .. .. 75·00 75·00 £150 £150
 a. Without handstamp £275 £275

These stamps were suppressed in 1887.

BRITISH INLAND MAIL.

USED STAMPS. Postmarks are found on the following issues.

4

5. Malagasy Runners.

1895 (Jan.). *Type-set at Antananarivo. Rouletted in black.*

(a) Thick laid paper.

50 **4** 4d. black .. .. .. 7·50 6·00
 a. "FUOR" for "FOUR" .. — £140

(b) Wove paper.

51 **4** 1d. blue-grey .. .. 7·50 6·00
52 ,, 6d. pale yellow .. .. 7·50 7·50
53 ,, 8d. salmon .. .. .. 7·50 7·50
54 ,, 1s. fawn .. .. .. 13·00 7·50
55 ,, 2s. bright rose .. .. 13·00 9·00
 a. Italic "2" at left .. .. 38·00 32·00
56 ,, 4s. grey .. .. .. 15·00 7·50

There are six types of each value, printed in groups repeated four times on each sheet; the upper and lower groups are *tête-bêche*.

(Litho. John Haddon & Co., London.)

1895 (Mar.). *The inscription in the lower label varies for each value. P* 12.

57 **5** 2d. blue .. .. .. 2·10
 a. Imperf. between (pair) .. £170
58 ,, 4d. rose .. .. .. 2·10
 a. Imperf. between (pair) .. £140
59 ,, 6d. green .. .. .. 2·10
 a. Imperf. between (pair) .. £170
60 ,, 1s. slate-blue.. .. .. 3·00
 a. Imperf. between (pair) .. £180
61 ,, 2s. chocolate .. .. 3·25
 a. Imperf. between (pair) .. £180
62 ,, 4s. bright purple .. .. 5·00
 a. Imperf. between (pair) ..

This post was suppressed when the French entered Antananarivo at the end of September 1895.

MALAWI

(Formerly Nyasaland.)

INDEPENDENT.

44. Independence Monument.

45. Rising Sun.
46. National Flag.
47. Coat-of-Arms.

The portrait is of Dr. Hastings Banda (Prime Minister).

(Des. M. Goaman. Photo. Harrison.)

1964 (6 July). *Independence. P* 14½.

211 **44** 3d. yell.-olive & dp. sepia 5 5
212 **45** 6d. red, gold, blue, carmine and lake 10 10
213 **46** 1s. 3d. red, green, black and bluish violet .. 20 20
214 **47** 2s. 6d. multicoloured .. 35 40

48. Tung Tree.

(Des. V. Whiteley. Photo. Harrison.)

1964 (6 July)–**65.** *As Nos.* 199/210 *of Nyasaland but inscr.* "MALAWI", *and new value and design* (9*d.*). *No wmk. P* 14½.

215 – ½d. reddish violet .. 5 5
216 – 1d. black and green .. 5 5
217 – 2d. light red-brown .. 5 5
218 – 3d. red-brown, yellow-green and bistre-brown .. 8 8
219 – 4d. black and orange-yell. 10 10
220 – 6d. bluish violet, yellow-green and light blue .. 15 15
221 **48** 9d. bistre-brn., grn. & yell. 25 25
222 – 1s. brown, turquoise-blue and pale yellow .. 30 30
223 – 1s. 3d. bronze-green and chestnut 40 45
224 – 2s. 6d. brown and blue .. 60 1·00
225 – 5s. blue, grn., yell. & sep. 1·40 1·60
225*a* – 5s. blue, green, yellow and sepia (1.6.65) .. 95 1·00
226 – 10s. grn., orge.-brn. & blk. 1·75 2·00
227 – £1 deep reddish purple and yellow .. .. 3·50 4·00
215/27 .. .. *Set of* 14 8·50 10·00

No. **225*a*** is inscribed "LAKE MALAWI" instead of "LAKE NYASA".

See also Nos. 252/62.

49. Christmas Star and Globe.

(Des. V. Whiteley. Photo. Harrison.)

1964 (1 Dec.). *Christmas. P* 14½.

228 **49** 3d. blue-green and gold .. 5 5
229 ,, 6d. magenta and gold .. 12 12
230 ,, 1s. 3d. reddish vio. & gold 25 25
231 ,, 2s. 6d. blue and gold .. 45 45
MS231*a* 83 × 126 mm. Nos. 228/31. Imperf. .. .. .. 1·60 1·50

50. Coins.

(Des. V. Whiteley. Photo. J. Enschedé & Sons.)

1965 (1 Mar.). *Malawi's First Coinage. Coins in black and silver. P* 13½.

232 **50** 3d. green 5 5
233 ,, 9d. magenta 12 12
234 ,, 1s. 6d. purple 20 20
235 ,, 3s. blue 40 40
MS235*a* 126 × 104 mm. Nos. 232/5. Imperf. 80 85

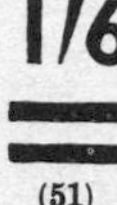

(51)

1965 (14 June). *Nos.* 223/4 *surch. as T* **51**.

236 1s. 6d. on 1s. 3d. bronze-green and chestnut .. 20 25
237 3s. on 2s. 6d. brown and blue 35 40

On No. 237 "3/–" occurs below the bars.

52. Chilembwe leading Rebels.

(Des. M. Goaman. Photo. Harrison.)

1965 (20 Aug.). *50th Anniv. of* 1915 *Rising. P* 14 × 14½.

238 **52** 3d. violet & lt. olive-green 5 5
239 ,, 9d. olive-brn. & red-orge. 12 12
240 ,, 1s. 6d. red-brn. & grey-bl. 25 25
241 ,, 3s. turq.-grn. & slate-blue 40 40
MS241*a* 127 × 83 mm. Nos. 238/41 1·60 1·50

53. "Learning and Scholarship".

(Des. H. E. Baxter. Photo. Harrison.)

1965 (6 Oct.). *Opening of Malawi University. P* 14½.

242 **53** 3d. black and emerald .. 5 5
243 ,, 9d. black and magenta .. 12 15
244 ,, 1s. 6d. blk. & reddish violet 25 25
245 ,, 3s. black and blue .. 40 40
MS246 127 × 84 mm. Nos. 242/5.. 1·60 1·50

54. *Papilio ophidicephalus mkuwadzi.*

(Des. V. Whiteley. Photo. Enschedé.)

1966 (15 Feb.). *Malawi Butterflies. T* **54** *and similar horiz. designs. Multicoloured. P* 13½.

No.	Description	Unused	Used
247	4d. Type **54**	5	5
248	9d. *Papilio magdae*	12	12
249	1s. 6d. *Epamera handmani* ..	25	25
250	3s. *Amauris crawshayi* ..	40	45
MS251	130×100 mm. Nos. 247/50	2·00	1·50

55. Cockerels.

56. Burley Tobacco.

57. *Cyrestis camillus sublineatus* (butterfly).

(New values des. V. Whiteley (1s. 6d.), M. Goaman (£2). Photo. Harrison.)

1966–67. *As Nos.* 215 *etc. but W* **55** *(sideways on* ½*d.,* 2*d.), and new values and designs* (1*s.* 6*d.,* £2). *P* 14½.

No.	Type	Description	Unused	Used
252	–	½d. reddish violet (1.4.66)	5	5
253	–	1d. black & grn. (1.4.66)	5	5
254	–	2d. lt. red-brown (16.5.67)	5	5
255	–	3d. red-brn., yell.-green & bistre-brown (27.6.67)	5	5
256	–	6d. bluish vio., yell.-grn. & light blue (16.5.67)	10	10
257	**48**	9d. bistre-brown, green and yellow (16.5.67)	15	15
258	–	1s. brown, turq.-blue and pale yellow (1.4.66) ..	20	20
259	**56**	1s. 6d. chocolate and yellow-green (15.11.66) ..	25	25
260	–	5s. blue, green, yellow and sepia (16.5.67) ..	85	85
261	–	10s. green, orange-brown and black (16.5.67) ..	2·25	2·25
262	**57**	£2 black, orange-yellow, pale yellow and slate-violet (7.9.66) ..	7·00	8·00
252/62		.. .. *Set of* 11	10·00	11·00

No. 260 is inscribed "LAKE MALAWI".

The 2d. exists with both PVA gum and gum arabic.

58. British Central Africa 6d. Stamp of 1891.

(Des. V. Whiteley. Photo. Harrison.)

1966 (4 May). *75th Anniv. of Postal Services. W* **55.** *P* 14½.

No.	Type	Description	Unused	Used
263	**58**	4d. grey-blue and yellow-green	5	5
264	,,	9d. grey-blue and claret ..	12	12
265	,,	1s. 6d. grey-blue and red-dish lilac	25	25
266	,,	3s. grey-blue and new blue	45	45
MS267		83×127 mm. Nos. 263/6 (10.6.66)	1·60	1·50

REPUBLIC.

59. President Banda.

(Des. M. Goaman. Photo. Harrison.)

1966 (6 July). *Republic Day. W* **55**. *P* 14×14½.

No.	Type	Description	Unused	Used
268	**59**	4d. brown, silver & emerald	5	5
269	,,	9d. brown, silver & magenta	12	12
270	,,	1s. 6d. brown, silver & vio.	20	20
271	,,	3s. brown, silver & blue ..	40	40
MS272		83×127 mm. Nos. 268/71	95	95

60. Bethlehem.

(Des. and photo. Harrison.)

1966 (12 Oct.). *Christmas. W* **55.** *P* 14½.

No.	Type	Description	Unused	Used
273	**60**	4d. myrtle-green & gold ..	8	8
274	,,	9d. brown-purple & gold ..	20	20
275	,,	1s. 6d. orange-red & gold	30	25
276	,,	3s. blue and gold	60	55

61. *Ilala I.*

(Des. Mrs. H. Breggar. Photo. Harrison.)

1967 (4 Jan.). *Lake Malawi Steamers. T* **61** *and similar horiz. designs. W* **55.** *P* 14½.

No.	Description	Unused	Used
277	4d. black, yellow & bright grn.	8	8
278	9d. black, yellow & magenta	12	12
279	1s. 6d, black, red and violet	25	25
280	3s. black, red and bright blue	45	45

Designs:—9d. *Dove*; 1s. 6d. *Chauncy Maples* (wrongly inscr. "Chauncey"); 3s. *Guendolen.*

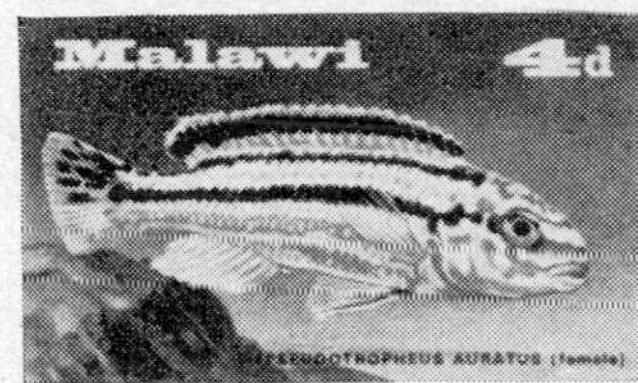

62. Turquoise-gold Chichlid.

(Des. R. Granger Barrett. Photo. Enschedé.)

1967 (3 May). *Lake Malawi Chichlids. T* **62** *and similar horiz. designs. Multicoloured. W* **55** *(sideways). P* 12½×12.

No.	Description	Unused	Used
281	4d. Type **62**	8	8
282	9d. Red Finned chichlid ..	15	15
283	1s. 6d. Zebra chichlid ..	25	25
284	3s. Golden chichlid	50	50
	a. Imperf. (pair)	85·00	

63. Rising Sun and Gearwheel.

(Des. Jennifer Toombs. Litho. De La Rue.)

1967 (5 July). *Industrial Development. P* 13½×13.

No.	Type	Description	Unused	Used
285	**63**	4d. black and emerald ..	5	5
286	,,	9d. black and carmine ..	10	10
287	,,	1s. 6d. black and reddish violet	20	20
288	,,	3s. black and bright blue ..	35	35
MS289		134×108 mm. Nos. 285/8	80	80

64. Mary and Joseph beside Crib.

(Des. Jennifer Toombs. Photo. Harrison.)

1967 (21 Nov.). *Christmas.* *W* **55.** *P* 14×14½.

No.	Type	Description	Unused	Used
290	**64**	4d. Royal blue & turq.-grn.	8	8
291	,,	9d. Royal blue & light red	15	15
292	,,	1s. 6d. Royal blue & yell.	25	25
293	,,	3s. Royal blue and new blue	50	50
MS294		114×100 mm. Nos. 290/3. W **55** (sideways). *P* 14×13½ (1.12.67)	1·75	1·75

65. *Calotropis procera.*

(Des. G. Drummond. Litho. De La Rue.)

1968 (24 Apr.). *Wild Flowers.* *T* **65** *and similar horiz. designs. Multicoloured.* *W* **55** *(sideways).* *P* 13½×13.

No.	Description	Unused	Used
295	4d. Type **65**	5	5
296	9d. *Borreria dibrachiata* ..	15	15
297	1s. 6d. *Hibiscus rhodanthus* ..	25	25
298	3s. *Bidens pinnatipartita* ..	50	50
MS299	135×91 mm. Nos. 295/8	1·50	1·50

66. Saddleback Steam Engine, "Thistle No. 1".

(Des. R. Granger Barrett. Photo. Harrison.)

1968 (24 July). *Malawi Locomotives.* T **66** *and similar horiz. designs.* *W* **55.** *P* 14×14½.

No.	Description	Unused	Used
300	4d. grey-green, slate-blue and red	8	8
301	9d. red, slate-blue and myrtle-green	20	20
302	1s. 6d. multicoloured ..	30	30
303	3s. multicoloured	60	60
MS304	120×88 mm. Nos. 300/3. P 14½	1·75	1·75

Designs:—9d. "G" class steam engine; 1s. 6d. Diesel electric locomotive, "Zambesi"; 3s. Diesel rail car.

67. "The Nativity" (Piero della Francesca).

(Des. and photo. Harrison.)

1968 (6 Nov.). *Christmas. Paintings.* *T* **67** *and similar horiz. designs. Multicoloured.* *W* **55** *(sideways on 4d.).* *P* 14×14½.

No.	Description	Unused	Used
305	4d. Type **67**	8	8
306	9d. "The Adoration of the Shepherds" (Murillo) ..	15	15
307	1s. 6d. "The Adoration of the Shepherds" (Reni) ..	25	25
308	3s. "Nativity, with God the Father and Holy Ghost" (Pittoni)	50	50
MS309	115×101 mm. Nos. 305/8. P 14×13½	1·25	1·25

68. Scarlet-chested Sunbird. **69.** Lilian's Lovebird.

70. Carmine Bee-eater.

(Des. V. Whiteley. Photo. Harrison.)

1968 (13 Nov.). *Birds.* *T* **68/70** *and similar designs. Multicoloured.* *W* **55** *(sideways on 1d. to 4d. and 3s. to £1).* *P* 14½.

No.	Description	Unused	Used
310	1d. Type **68**	5	5
311	2d. Violet-backed Starling ..	5	5
312	3d. White-browed Robin ..	5	5
313	4d. Red-billed Firefinch ..	8	8
	a. Red omitted		
314	6d. Type **69**	8	10
315	9d. Yellow Bishop	10	12
316	1s. Type **70**	15	20
317	1s. 6d. Grey-headed Bush Shrike	35	35
318	2s. Paradise Whydah ..	40	40
319	3s. Paradise Flycatcher ..	50	60
320	5s. Bateleur	75	75
321	10s. Saddlebill	1·60	2·25
322	£1 Purple Heron	2·75	3·00
323	£2 Livingstone's Loerie ..	7·00	10·00
310/323	.. .. *Set of* 14	12·00	16·00

Sizes:—2d. to 4d. as T **68**; 9d. as T **69**; 1s. 6d., 2s., £2 as T **70**; 3s. to £1 as T **70** but vertical.

71. I.L.O. Emblem.

(Des. G. Drummond. Photo., emblem die-stamped. Harrison.)

1969 (5 Feb.). *50th Anniv. of the International Labour Organization.* *W* **55** *(sideways on No.* **MS**328). *P* 14.

No.	Type	Description	Unused	Used
324	**71**	4d. gold and myrtle-green	5	5
325	,,	9d. gold and chocolate ..	12	12
326	,,	1s. 6d. gold & blackish brn.	20	20
327	,,	3s. gold and indigo ..	35	35
MS328		127×89 mm. Nos. 324/7 ..	1·25	1·25

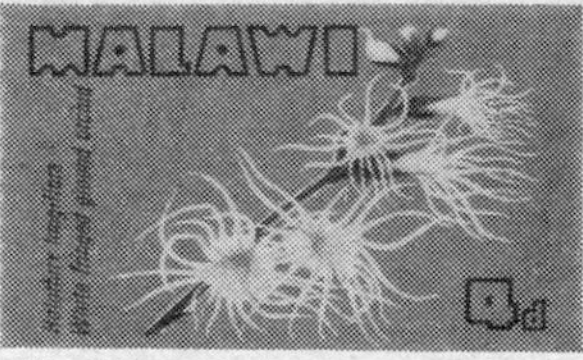

72. White-fringed Ground Orchid.

(Des. J. Waddington Ltd. Litho. Bradbury, Wilkinson.)

1969 (9 July). *Orchids of Malawi.* *T* **72** *and similar horiz. designs. Multicoloured.* *W* **55.** *P* 13½×13.

No.	Description	Unused	Used
329	4d. Type **72**	5	5
330	9d. Red Ground orchid ..	15	15
331	1s. 6d. Leopard Tree orchid	25	25
332	3s. Blue Ground orchid ..	50	50
MS333	118×86 mm. Nos. 329/32	1·00	1·00

73. African Development Bank Emblem.

(Des. G. L. Vasarhelyi. Litho. De La Rue.)

1969 (10 Sept.). *Fifth Anniv. of African Development Bank.* *W* **55.** *P* 14.

No.	Type	Description	Unused	Used
334	**73**	4d. yellow, yellow-ochre and chocolate ..	5	5
335	,,	9d. yellow, yellow-ochre and myrtle-green ..	10	10
336	,,	1s. 6d. yellow, yellow-ochre & blackish brn.	20	20
337	,,	3s. yellow, yellow-ochre and indigo	40	40
MS338		102×137 mm. Nos. 334/7	75	1·00

74. Dove over Bethlehem.

(Des. Jennifer Toombs. Photo. Harrison.)

1969 (5 Nov.). *Christmas.* *W* **55.** *P* 14½×14.

No.	Type	Description	Unused	Used
339	**74**	2d. black and olive-yellow	5	5
340	,,	4d. black and deep turq.	8	8
341	,,	9d. black and scarlet ..	15	15
342	,,	1s. 6d. black and deep bluish violet	25	25
343	,,	3s. black and ultramarine	50	50
MS344		130×71 mm. Nos. 339/43	1·00	1·00
339/43		.. .. *Set of* 5	75	75

75. Elegant Grasshopper.

(Des. V. Whiteley. Litho. Format International).

1970 (4 Feb.). *Insects of Malawi.* *T* **75** *and similar vert. designs. Multicoloured.* *W* **55.** *P* 14.

345	4d. Type **75**	5	5
346	9d. Beam Blister beetle ..	15	15
347	1s. 6d. Pumpkin ladybird ..	25	25
348	3s. Praying mantis	50	50
MS349	86×137 mm. Nos. 345/8	75	1·00

Rand Easter Show
1970

(76)

1970 (18 Mar.). *Rand Easter Show.* *No.* 317 *optd. with T* **76.**

350	1s. 6d. multicoloured ..	25	30

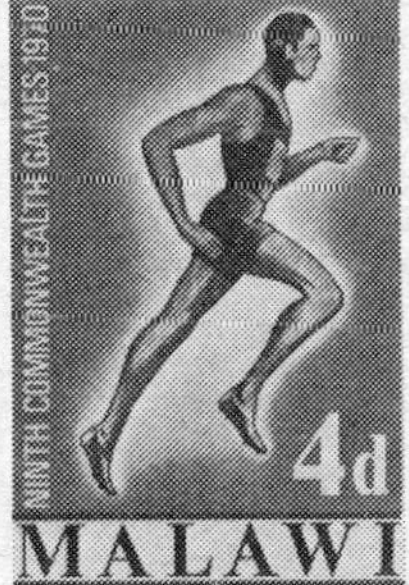

77. Runner.

(Des. J. E. Cooter. Litho. B.W.)

1970 (3 June). *Ninth British Commonwealth Games, Edinburgh.* *W* **55.** *P* 13.

351	**77**	4d. Royal blue & blue-green	5	5
352	,,	9d. Royal blue & carmine	15	15
353	,,	1s. 6d. Royal blue and dull yellow	25	25
354	,,	3s. Royal blue & new blue	50	50
MS355		146×96 mm. Nos. 351/4	75	85

(New Currency. 100 tambalas = 1 kwacha.)

10t
(78)

79. *Aegocera trimenii.*

1970 (2 Sept.). *Decimal Currency. Nos.* 316 *and* 318 *surch. as T* **78.**

356	10 t. on 1s. multicoloured ..	12	12
357	20 t. on 2s. multicoloured ..	25	25

(Des. R. Granger Barrett. Litho. B.W.)

1970 (30 Sept.). *Moths.* *T* **79** *and similar horiz. designs. Multicoloured.* *W* **55.** *P* 11×11½.

358	4d. Type **79**	5	5
359	9d. *Epiphora bauhiniae* ..	15	15
360	1s. 6s. *Parasa karschi* ..	25	25
361	3s. *Teracotona euprepia* ..	50	50
MS362	112×92 mm. Nos. 358/61	1·00	1·00

80. Mother and Child.

(Des. Brother W. Meyer. Litho. J.W.)

1970 (4 Nov.). *Christmas.* *W* **55** *(sideways). P* 14.

363	**80**	2d. black and light yellow	5	5
364	,,	4d. black and emerald	8	8
365	,,	9d. black and orange-red..	15	15
366	,,	1s. 6d. black & light purple	25	25
367	,,	2s. black and blue ..	50	50
MS368		166×100 mm. Nos. 362/7	90	90
363/8		.. .. *Set of* 5	85	85

30t
Special
United
Kingdom
Delivery
Service
(81)

1971 (8 Feb.). *No.* 319 *surch. with T* **81.**

369	30 t. on 3s. multicoloured ..	40	2·00

No. 369 was issued for use on letters carried by an emergency airmail service from Malawi to Great Britain during the British postal strike. The fee of 30 t. was to cover the charge for delivery by a private service, and ordinary stamps to pay the normal airmail fee had to be affixed as well.

The strike ended on 8 March, when private delivery services were withdrawn.

82. Decimal Coinage and Cockerel.

(Des. V. Whiteley. Litho. Format.)

1971 (15 Feb.).*Decimal Coinage.* *W* **55** *(sideways). P* 14.

370	**82**	3 t. multicoloured ..	5	5
371	,,	8 t. multicoloured ..	10	10
372	,,	15 t. multicoloured ..	20	20
373	,,	30 t. multicoloured ..	35	35
MS374		140×101 mm. Nos. 370/73	80	80

83. Greater Kudu. **84.** Eland.

(Des. and litho. J. Waddington Ltd.)

1971 (15 Feb.)–**74**. *Decimal Currency. Antelopes. Vert. designs as T* **83** *(1 t. to 8 t.), or T* **84** *(others). Multicoloured P* 13½×14 *(1 t to 8 t.) or* 14½ *(others).* *W* **55** *(sideways on 1 t. to 8 t.).*

375	1 t. Type **83**	5	5
	a. Coil stamp. P 14½×14 ..	5	5
	b. Perf. 14† (12.11.74) ..	5	5
376	2 t. Nyala	5	5
377	3 t. Reed Buck	5	5
	a. Perf. 14† (12.11.74) ..	5	5
378	5 t. Puku	8	8
	a. Perf. 14† (12.11.74) ..	8	8
379	8 t. Impala	10	12
380	10 t. Type **84** *(shades)* ..	15	12
381	15 t. Klipspringer	20	20
382	20 t. Livingstone's Suni ..	25	25
383	30 t. Roan Antelope ..	35	40
384	50 t. Waterbuck	60	65
385	1 k. Bushbuck	1·10	1·25
386	2 k. Red Duiker	2·25	2·40
387	4 k. Grey Duiker*	4·50	4·50
375/87	.. .. *Set of* 13	9·00	9·00

* No. 387 is incorrectly inscr. " Gray Duiker ".

† These actually gauge 14.2×14 instead of 13.7×14 and are line-perforated; in blocks they can easily be distinguished as in alternate rows across the sheet the horizontal perfs. have two holes where they cross the vertical perfs.; the watermark is also sideways inverted.

85. " Christ on the Cross " (Dürer).

86. " The Resurrection " (Dürer).

(Des. G. Drummond from " The Small Passion" by Dürer. Litho. Questa.)

1971 (7 Apr.). *Easter.* *W* **55.** *P* 13½.

388	**85**	3 t. black and green ..	5	5
389	**86**	3 t. black and green ..	5	5
390	**85**	8 t. black and orange-red	12	12
391	**86**	8 t. black and orange-red	12	12
392	**85**	15 t. black and violet ..	25	25
393	**86**	15 t. black and violet ..	25	25
394	**85**	30 t. black and bright blue	45	45
395	**86**	30 t. black and bright blue	45	45
388/95		.. .. *Set of* 8	1·50	1·50
MS396		Two sheets each 95×145 mm. with Nos. 388/95 in blocks of 4, one Type **85** and the other Type **86** *Per pair*	2·00	2·00

Each value has *T* **85/6** printed *se-tenant* throughout the sheet.

87. *Holarrhena febrifuga.*

(Des. G. Drummond. Litho. J.W.)

1971 (14 July). *Flowering Shrubs and Trees. T* **87** *and similar vert. designs. Multicoloured. W* **55.** *P* 14.

397 3 t. Type **87** 5 5
398 8 t. *Brachystegia spiciformis* 12 12
399 15 t. *Securidaca longepedunculata* 25 25
400 30 t. *Pterocarpus rotundifolius* 45 45
MS401 102 × 135 mm. Nos. 397/400 85 85

88. Drum Major.

(Des. J. W. Ltd. Litho. Questa.)

1971 (5 Oct.). *50th Anniv. of Malawi Police Force. W* **55.** *P* 14 × 14½.

402 **88** 30 t. multicoloured .. 40 45

89. " Madonna and Child " (William Dyce).

(Des. J. E. Cooter. Litho. Format.)

1971 (10 Nov.). *Christmas. T* **89** *and similar vert. designs. Multicoloured. W* **55.** *P* 14½.

403 3 t. Type **89** 8 8
404 8 t. " The Holy Family " (M. Shongauer) .. 12 12
405 15 t. " The Holy Family with St. John " (Raphael) .. 25 25
406 30 t. " The Holy Family " (Bronzino) 45 45
MS407 101 × 139 mm. Nos. 403/6 1·00 1·00

90. Vickers " Viscount ".

(Des. R. Granger-Barrett. Litho. Questa.)

1972 (9 Feb.). *Air. Malawi Aircraft. T* **90** *and similar horiz. designs. Multicoloured. W* **55** *(sideways). P* 13½.

408 3 t. Type **90** 5 5
409 8 t. Hawker Siddeley " 748 " 12 12
410 15 t. Britten-Norman " Islander " 25 25
411 30 t. B.A.C. " One-Eleven " 45 50
MS412 143 × 94 mm. Nos. 408/11 1·25 1·25

91. Figures (Chencherere Hill).

(Des. R. Granger Barrett. Litho. Format.)

1972 (10 May). *Rock Paintings. T* **91** *and similar horiz. designs. W* **55** *(sideways). P* 13½.

413 3 t. apple-green, grey-green and black 5 5
414 8 t. red, grey and black .. 12 12
415 15 t. multicoloured 25 25
416 30 t. multicoloured 45 45
MS417 121 × 97 mm. Nos. 413/16. P 15 .. .. 1·00 1·00

Designs:—8 t. Lizard and cat (Chencherere Hill); 15 t. Schematics (Diwa Hill); 30 t. Sun through rain (Mikolongwe Hill).

92. Boxing.

(Des. locally. Litho. Harrison.)

1972 (9 Aug.). *Olympic Games, Munich. W* **55** *(sideways). P* 14 × 14½.

418 **92** 3 t. multicoloured .. 5 5
419 ,, 8 t. multicoloured .. 12 12
420 ,, 15 t. multicoloured .. 25 25
421 ,, 30 t. multicoloured .. 45 45
MS422 110 × 92 mm. Nos. 418/21. *P* 14 × 13½. 85 85

93. Arms of Malawi.

(Des. G. Drummond. Litho. Questa.)

1972 (20 Oct.). *Parliamentary Conference. W* **55.** *P* 13½.

423 **93** 15 t. multicoloured .. 20 20

94. " Adoration of the Kings " (Orcagna).

(Des. V. Whiteley. Litho. Questa.)

1972 (8 Nov.). *Christmas. T* **94** *and similar vert. designs. Multicoloured. W* **55.** *P* 14½ × 14.

424 3 t. Type **94** 5 5
425 8 t. " Madonna and Child Enthroned " (Florentine School) 12 12
426 15 t. " Virgin and Child " (Crivelli) 25 25
427 30 t. " St. Anne with the Virgin and Child " (Bruges) 45 45
MS428 95 × 121 mm. Nos. 424/7 1·00 1·00

Inscr. "MALAŴI".

All issues from No. 429 onwards have a circumflex accent over the "W", to give the correct pronunciation of "Malavi".

95. *Charaxes bohemani.*

(Des. PAD Studio. Litho. Questa.)

1973 (7 Feb.–5 Apr.). *Butterflies. T* **95** *and similar horiz. designs. Multicoloured. W* **55** *(sideways). P* 13½ × 14.

429 3 t. Type **95** 5 5
430 8 t. *Uranothauma crawshayi* 12 12

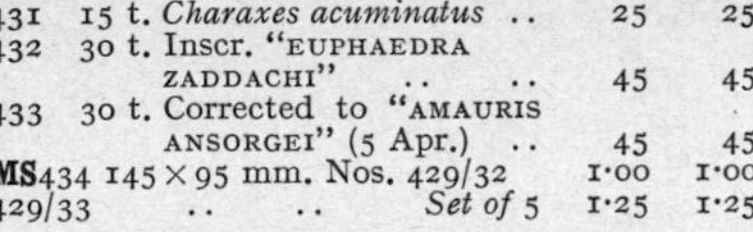

431 15 t. *Charaxes acuminatus* .. 25 25
432 30 t. Inscr. "EUPHAEDRA ZADDACHI" 45 45
433 30 t. Corrected to "AMAURIS ANSORGEI" (5 Apr.) .. 45 45
MS434 145 × 95 mm. Nos. 429/32 1·00 1·00
429/33 .. .. *Set of* 5 1·25 1·25

96. Livingstone and Map.

(Des. J.W. Ltd. Litho. Format.)

1973 (1 MAY). *Death Centenary of David Livingstone* (*1st issue*). *W* **55** (*sideways*). *P* 13½ × 14.

435 **96** 3 t. multicoloured .. 5 5
436 „ 8 t. multicoloured .. 12 12
437 „ 15 t. multicoloured .. 25 25
438 „ 30 t. multicoloured .. 45 45
MS439 144 × 95 mm. Nos. 435/8 .. 90 90

See also Nos. 450/**MS**451.

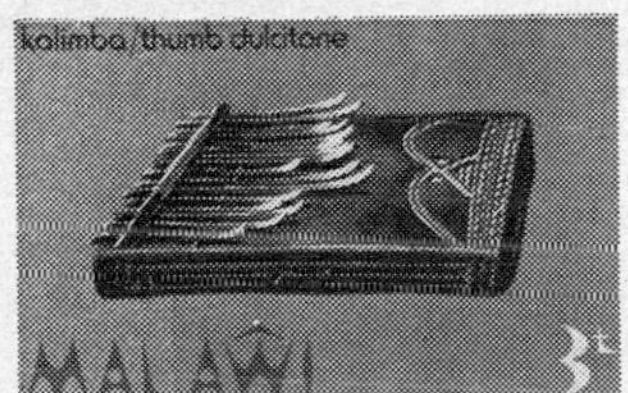

97. Thumb Dulcitone.

(Des. Jennifer Toombs. Litho. Questa.)

1973 (8 AUG.). *Musical Instruments. T* **97** *and similar multicoloured designs. W* **55** (*sideways on* 8, 15 *t. and* **MS**444). *P* 14.

440 3 t. Type **97** 5 5
441 8 t. Hand zither (*vert.*) .. 12 12
442 15 t. Hand drum (*vert.*) .. 25 25
443 30 t. One-stringed fiddle .. 45 45
MS444 120 × 103 mm. Nos. 440/3 .. 90 90

98. The Magi.

(Des. J.W. Ltd. Litho. Format.)

1973 (7 Nov.). *Christmas. W* **55** (*sideways*). *P* 13½.

445 **98** 3 t. greenish blue, deep lilac and dull ultram. 5 5
446 „ 8 t. salmon-red, bluish lilac and red-brown .. 12 12
447 „ 15 t. reddish mauve, greenish blue and deep mauve 25 25
448 „ 30 t. orange-yellow, bluish lilac and light lake-brown 45 45
MS449 165 × 114 mm. Nos. 445/8 90 90

99. Stained-glass Window, Livingstonia Mission.

(Des. PAD Studio. Litho. Questa.)

1973 (12 DEC.). *Death Centenary of David Livingstone* (*2nd issue*). *W* **55** (*sideways*). *P* 13½.

450 **99** 50 t. multicoloured .. 75 75
MS451 71 × 77 mm. No. 450 .. 1·00 1·00

100. Largemouth Black Bass.

(Des. Sylvia Goaman. Litho. Questa.)

1974 (20 FEB.). *35th Anniv. of Malawi Angling Society. T* **100** *and similar horiz. designs. Multicoloured. W* **55** (*sideways*). *P* 14.

452 3 t. Type **100** 5 5
453 8 t. Rainbow Trout .. 12 12
454 15 t. Large Salmon 25 25
455 30 t. Tiger Fish 45 45
MS456 169 × 93 mm. Nos. 452/5 90 90

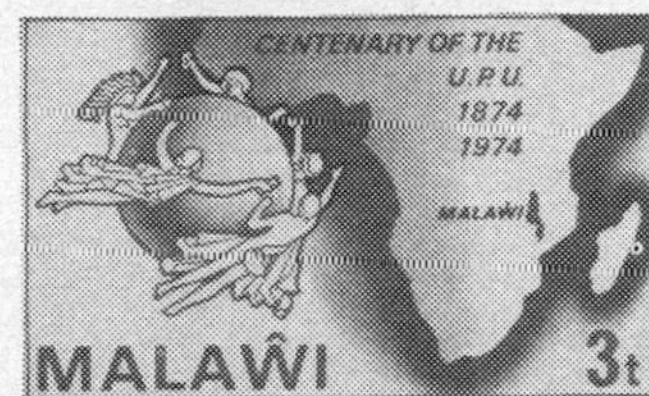

101. U.P.U. Monument and Map of Africa.

(Des. J. E. Cooter. Litho. J.W.)

1974 (24 APR.). *Centenary of Universal Postal Union. W* **55** (*sideways*). *P* 13½ (*Nos.* 460/**MS**461) *or* 14½ × 14 (*others*).

457 **101** 3 t. green and ochre .. 5 5
458 „ 8 t. red and ochre .. 12 12
459 „ 15 t. violet and ochre .. 25 25
460 „ 30 t. indigo and ochre .. 45 45
MS461 115 × 146 mm. Nos. 457/60 90 90

102. Capital Hill, Lilongwe.

(Des. PAD Studio. Litho. Questa.)

1974 (3 JULY). *Tenth Anniv. of Independence. W* **55** (*sideways*). *P* 14.

462 **102** 3 t. multicoloured .. 5 5
463 „ 8 t. multicoloured .. 10 12
464 „ 15 t. multicoloured .. 20 20
465 „ 30 t. multicoloured .. 35 35
MS466 120 × 86 mm. Nos. 462/5 75 80

103. "Madonna of the Meadow" (Bellini).

(Des. Jennifer Toombs. Litho. Enschedé.)

1974 (4 DEC.). *Christmas. T* **103** *and similar horiz. designs. Multicoloured. W* **55** (*sideways*). *P* 13 × 13½.

467 3 t. Type **103** 5 5
468 8 t. "The Holy Family with Sts. John and Elizabeth" (Jordaens) 10 12
469 15 t. "The Nativity" (Peter de Grebber) 20 20
470 30 t. "Adoration of the Shepherds" (Lorenzo di Credi) 35 40
MS471 163 × 107 mm. Nos. 467/70 75 80

104. Arms of Malawi.

(Des. and litho. Harrison.)

1975 (1 FEB.). *Coil stamp. W* **55.** *P* 14½ × 14.

472 **104** 1 t. deep blue 5 5

105. African Snipe. **106.** Spurwing Goose.

(Des. J.W. Ltd. Litho. Questa.)

1975 (19 FEB.). *Birds. T* **105/6** *and similar multicoloured designs. W* **55** *sideways on horiz. designs* (2, 3, 8, 50 *t.*, 1 *k.*, 4 *k.*). *White, ordinary paper.*

(*a*) *Size as T* **105.** *P* 13½ × 14 (1, 5 *t.*) *or* 14 × 13½ (*others*).

473 1 t. Type **105** 5 5
474 2 t. Double-banded Sandgrouse 5 5
475 3 t. Blue Quail 5 5
476 5 t. Red-necked Francolin .. 5 5
477 8 t. Harlequin Quail .. 10 12

(*b*) *Size as T* **106.** *P* 14.

478 10 t. Type **106** 12 15
479 15 t. Stanley Bustard .. 20 25
480 20 t. Knob-billed Duck .. 20 25
481 30 t. Crowned Guineafowl .. 30 35
482 50 t. Pigmy Goose 55 65
483 1 k. Garganey .. .. 1·00 1·10
484 2 k. White-faced Tree Duck 2·50 2·75
485 4 k. Green Pigeon .. .. 4·25 4·50
473/85 .. .. *Set of* 13 8·50 9·50

See also Nos. 503/12.

107. M.V. *Mpasa.*

(Des. R. Granger Barrett. Litho. J.W.)

1975 (12 Mar.). *Ships of Lake Malawi. T* **107** *and similar horiz. designs. Multicoloured. W* **55** *(sideways). P* 13½.

486 3 t. Type **107** 5 5
487 8 t. M.V. *Ilala II* 10 12
488 15 t. M.V. *Chauncy Maples* .. 20 20
489 30 t. M.V. *Nkwazi* 35 40
MS490 105 × 142 mm. Nos. 486/9. *P* 14 .. .. 75 80

108. *Habenaria splendens.*

(Des. Sylvia Goaman. Litho. Questa.)

1975 (6 June). *Malawi Orchids. T* **108** *and similar vert. designs. Multicoloured. W* **55**. *P* 14.

491 3 t. Type **108** 5 5
492 10 t. *Eulophia cucullata* .. 12 15
493 20 t. *Disa welwitischii* .. 20 25
494 40 t. *Angraecum conchiferum* .. 40 45
MS495 127 × 111 mm. Nos. 491/4 90 1·00

109. Bush Baby.

10th ACP
Ministerial
Conference
1975

(**110**)

(Des. R. Granger Barrett. Litho. Walsall.)

1975 (3 Sept.). *Malawi Animals. T* **109** *and similar vert. designs. Multicoloured. W* **55** *(inverted). P* 14.

496 3 t. Type **109** 5 5
497 10 t. Leopard 12 15
498 20 t. Roan Antelope 25 30
499 40 t. Burchell's Zebra .. 45 50
MS500 88 × 130 mm. Nos. 496/9. W **55** (sideways) .. .. .. 90 1·00

1975 (1 Oct.). *As Nos.* 473 *etc., but no wmk. Toned, chalk-surfaced paper.*

503 3 t. Blue Quail 5 5
506 10 t. Type **106** 10 12
507 15 t. Stanley Bustard .. 15 20
512 2 k. White-faced Tree Duck 2·10 2·25

Nos. 501/13 have been reserved for this issue.

1975 (9 Dec.). *Tenth Africa, Caribbean and Pacific Ministerial Conference. No.* 482 *optd. with T* **110**.

514 50 t. Pigmy Goose 55 65

111. "A Castle with the Adoration of the Magi".

(Des. PAD Studio. Litho. J.W.)

1975 (12 Dec.). *Christmas. T* **111** *and similar horiz. designs showing religious medallions. Multicoloured. W* **55** *(sideways). P* 13 × 13½.

515 3 t. Type **111** 5 5
516 10 t. "The Nativity" .. 10 12
517 20 t. "The Adoration of the Magi" 20 25
518 40 t. "The Angel appearing to the Shepherds" 45 50
MS519 98 × 168 mm. Nos. 515/18. P 14 85

112. Alexander Graham Bell.

(Des. C. Abbott. Litho. Questa.)

1976 (24 Mar.). *Centenary of the Telephone. W* **55**. *P* 14.

520 **112** 3 t. black and dull green 5 5
521 ,, 10 t. black and magenta 10 12
522 ,, 20 t. black and light red-dish violet .. 20 25
523 ,, 40 t. black & bright blue 45 50
MS524 137 × 114 mm. Nos. 520/3 85

113. President Banda.

(Des. PAD Studio. Litho. J.W.)

1976 (2 July). *Tenth Anniv. of the Republic. Multicoloured; frame colour given. W* **55**. *P* 13.

525 **113** 3 t. green 5 5
526 ,, 10 t. magenta 12 15
527 ,, 20 t. new blue 25 30
528 ,, 40 t. dull ultramarine .. 50 55
MS529 102 × 112 mm. Nos. 524/8. P 13½ .. .. 1·00

114. Bagnall Shunter.

(Des. G. Drummond. Litho. Questa.)

1976 (1 Oct.). *Malawi Locomotives. T* **114** *and similar horiz. designs. Multicoloured. W* **55** *(sideways). P* 14½ × 14.

530 3 t. Type **114** 5 5
531 10 t. Shire Class loco 12 15
532 20 t. Nippon Sharyo loco .. 25 30
533 40 t. Hunslet shunter 50 55
MS534 130 × 118 mm. Nos. 530/3 85

**Blantyre
Mission
Centenary
1876-1976**

(**115**)

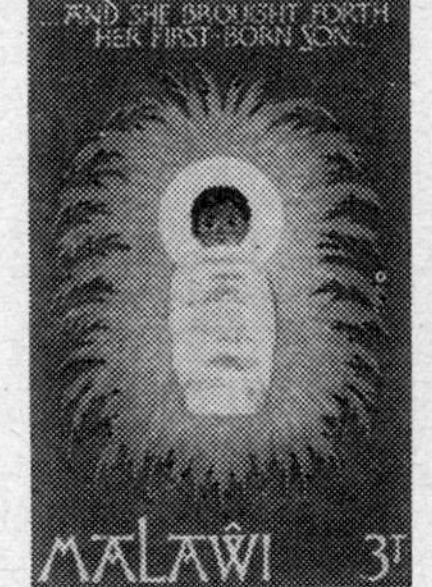

116. Child on Bed of Straw.

1976 (22 Oct.). *Centenary of Blantyre Mission. Nos.* 507 *and* 481 *optd. with T* **115**.

535 15 t. Stanley Bustard .. 20 25
536 30 t. Crowned Guinea Fowl .. 35 40

(Des. Jennifer Toombs. Litho. Walsall.)

1976 (6 Dec.). *Christmas. W* **55**. *P* 14.

537 **116** 3 t. multicoloured .. 5 5
538 ,, 10 t. multicoloured .. 12 15
539 ,, 20 t. multicoloured .. 25 30
540 ,, 40 t. multicoloured .. 50 55

POSTAGE DUE STAMPS.

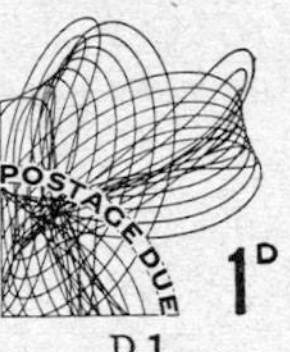

D 1

(Litho. Bradbury, Wilkinson.)

1967 (1 Sept.). *W* **55**. *P* 11½.

D 6 **D 1** 1d. carmine 5 8
D 7 ,, 2d. sepia 5 8
D 8 ,, 4d. reddish violet .. 8 12
D 9 ,, 6d. blue 10 15
D10 ,, 8d. emerald 12 20
D11 ,, 1s. black 20 30
D6/11 .. .. *Set of* 6 40 60

1971 (15 Feb.). *As Nos.* D6/11 *but values tambalas. W* **55**. *P* 11½.

D12 **D 1** 2 t. greenish drab .. 5 5
D13 ,, 4 t. deep mauve .. 5 5
D14 ,, 6 t. Royal blue 8 8
D15 ,, 8 t. dull green 8 10
D16 ,, 10 t. blackish brown .. 10 12
D12/16 .. .. *Set of* 5 30 35

(Litho. Walsall Security Ptrs. Ltd.)

1975 (15 Sept.). *Design redrawn, with circumflex accent over* "W" *of* "MALAWI". *W* **55** *(sideways). P* 14.

D17 **D 1** 2 t. bistre-brown .. 5 5

MALAYA.

Under this heading we list for convenience of reference the various component stamp issuing units of the FEDERATION OF MALAYA.

On 16th September, 1963, this Federation became part of MALAYSIA, which also incorporates NORTH BORNEO (SABAH), SARAWAK and SINGAPORE, until the latter became an independent state on 9th August, 1965.

We retain under MALAYA the issues of Johore, Kedah, Kelantan, Malacca, Negri Sembilan, Pahang, Penang, Perak, Perlis, Selangor and Trengganu, as they still use their own stamps.

There were no separate issues for Negri Sembilan, Pahang, Perak and Selangor between 1900 and 1935, during which time the general issues of the Federated Malay States were in use. In 1935 the formation of the Malayan Postal Union resulted in the reappearance of distinctive sets. Sungei Ujong ceased issuing stamps in 1895 when it was merged in Negri Sembilan.

PRINTERS. All Malayan postage stamps were typographed by De La Rue & Co., *unless otherwise stated.*

FEDERATED MALAY STATES

These issues were for use in the states of Negri Sembilan, Pahang, Perak and Selangor whose individual stamps they replaced.

FEDERATED MALAY STATES (1)

FEDERATED MALAY STATES (2)

1900. *Optd. with T* **1** (*cent values*) *or* **2** (*dollar values*).

(*a*) *Stamps of* Negri Sembilan (*T* **3**).

No.	Description	Unused	Used
1	1 c. dull purple and green	80	1·10
2	2 c. dull purple and brown	6·50	6·50
3	3 c. dull purple and black	1·10	1·25
4	5 c. dull purple & olive yellow	8·00	10·00
5	10 c. dull purple and orange	80	3·00
6	20 c. green and olive	8·00	10·00
7	25 c. green and carmine	18·00	20·00
8	50 c. green and black	9·00	11·00
1/8	*Set of* 8	48·00	55·00
1/8	Optd. "Specimen" *Set of* 8	45·00	

(*b*) *Stamps of* Perak (*T* **31** *and* **32**).

No.	Description	Unused	Used
9	5 c. dull purple & olive-yellow	5·00	7·00
10	10 c. dull purple and orange	8·00	10·00
	a. Bar omitted	90·00	
11	$1 green and pale green	14·00	16·00
12	$2 green and carmine	13·00	16·00
13	$5 green and ultramarine	50·00	45·00
14	$25 grn. & orge. (Optd. S. £110)	£1400	
11/13	Optd. "Specimen" *Set of* 3	25·00	

3

1900–1. *Perf.* 14. *T* **3.** *Wmk. Crown CA, sideways* (1901).

No.	Description	Unused	Used
15	1 c. black and green	12	15
	a. Grey and green	20	15
	b. Grey-brown and green	75	12
16	3 c. black and brown	65	15
	a. Grey and brown	50	12
	b. Grey-brown and brown	20	12
17	4 c. black and carmine	80	30
	a. Grey and carmine	1·60	30
	b. Grey-brown and carmine	1·60	20
18	5 c. green & carmine/*yellow*	85	1·00
19	8 c. black and ultramarine	4·50	80
	a. Grey and ultramarine	4·50	80
	b. Grey-brown & ultramarine	4·50	75
20	10 c. black and claret	4·00	65
	a. Grey and claret	3·25	30
	b. Black and purple	6·00	40
	c. Grey and purple	2·50	30
	d. Grey-brown and purple	4·00	40
21	20 c. mauve and black	5·00	75
22	50 c. black and orange-brown	11·00	7·00
	a. Grey and orange-brown	10·00	5·50
	b. Grey-brown & orange-brown	12·00	4·50
15/22	*Set of* 8	22·00	7·00
15/22	Optd. "Specimen" *Set of* 8	50·00	

Later printings in 1903–4 show the two upper lines of shading in the background at the corner nearest to the "S" of "STATE" blurred and running into one another, whereas in earlier printings these lines are distinct. Two plates were used for printing the central design of T **3**. In Plate 1 the lines of background are regular throughout, but in Plate 2 they are lighter around the head and back of the tiger. The 5 c. was the only value with single wmk. to be printed from Plate 2. Stamps with multiple wmk. were printed for a short time from Plate 1, and show the two blurred lines of background near "S" of "STATE," but the majority of these stamps were printed from Plate 2 and later plates.

T **4**, *Wmk. Crown CC* (1900).

No.	Description	Unused	Used
23	$1 green and pale green	15·00	13·00
24	$2 green and carmine	18·00	14·00
25	$5 green & brt. ultramarine	30·00	27·00
	a. Green and pale ultramarine	32·00	30·00
26	$25 grn. & orge. (Optd. S. £100)	£400	£225
23/5	Optd. "Specimen" *Set of* 3	32·00	

4

Two dies for 1 *c. green and* 4 *c. scarlet.*

Die I. "Head" and duty plates. Thick frame line below "MALAY" and in the 1 c. the "c" is thin whilst in the 4 c. it is thick.

Die II. Single working plate. Thin frame line below "MALAY" and in the 1 c. the "c" is thicker whilst in the 4 c. it is thinner.

1904–22. *T* **3** *and* **4** (*dollar values*). *Wmk. Mult. Crown CA* (*sideways in T* **3**). *Ordinary paper except where otherwise indicated. P* 14.

No.	Description	Unused	Used
27	1 c. grey & green (10.10.04)	5·00	1·25
	a. Grey-brown and green	1·00	40
28	1 c. green (Die I) (8.7.06)	20	15
29	1 c. green (Die II)	30	15
	a. Yellow-green	1·25	12
	b. Blue-green	2·00	12
30	1 c. deep brown (21.1.19)	1·00	50
31	2 c. green (18.2.19)	15	25
32	3 c. grey & brown, O (10.04)	2·75	55
	a. Grey-brown and brown, OC (12.05)	1·00	12
33	3 c. brown (11.7.06)	30	12
34	3 c. carmine (2.2.09)	55	12
	a. Scarlet (1.17)	85	12
35	3 c. grey (29.10.18)	50	15
36	4 c. grey & scar., O (10.10.04)	2·00	30
	a. Grey and rose, C	65	25
	b. Grey-brown and scarlet, O	1·00	20
	c. Black and scarlet, O	2·50	25
	d. Black and rose, O	1·00	15
	e. Black & deep rose (aniline), O (1909)	—	50
	f. Jet-black and rose, O (1914)	1·00	25
37	4 c. scarlet (Die I) (11.2.19)	40	20
38	4 c. scarlet (Die II) (15.4.19)	30	12
	a. Wmk. upright (2.22)		
39	5 c. green and carmine/*yellow,* CO (5.06)	1·10	40
	a. Dp. green & carm./yellow, O	45	50
	b. On orange-buff, O (1921)	75	15
	c. On pale yellow (4.22)	30	15
40	6 c. orange (11.2.19)	90	40
41	8 c. grey & ultram., O (3.05)	2·50	2·00
	a. Grey-brown and ultram., OC (12.05)	2·00	1·00
	b. Wmk. upright, O (4.07)	2·00	1·00
42	8 c. ultramarine (8.3.10)	2·25	45
	a. Deep blue (1918)	2·25	50
43	10 c. grey-brown & claret OC (10.10.04)	1·00	15
	a. Black and claret, O	40	12
	b. Grey-brown and purple, O (1905)	2·00	20
	c. Black and purple, O	1·10	25
	d. Jet-black & brt. pur., O (1914)	1·40	15
44	10 c. deep blue (3.6.19)	1·40	40
	a. Bright blue	1·60	40
	b. Wmk. upright (inverted)		
45	20 c. mauve & black, OC (3.05)	40	15
46	35 c. scarlet/*pale yell.* (25.8.22)	4·00	2·75
47	50 c. grey and orange, O (3.05)	3·25	55
	a. Grey-brown & orange-brown, OC (1906)	3·00	70
	b. Grey and orange-brown, C	3·25	60
	c. Black and orange-brown, C	4·50	65
	d. Jet-black & orge.-brn., C (1914)	4·50	55
48	$1 grey-grn. & grn., C (11.07)	7·00	5·50
	a. Green and pale green	7·00	5·50
49	$2 green & carm., C (12.07)	14·00	10·00
50	$5 green and blue, C (1.08)	26·00	20·00
51	$25 green & orange, C (8.10) (Optd. S. £26)	£225	£150
27/49	*Set of* 22	38·00	21·00
28, 30/1, 33/5, 37, 40, 42, 44, 46	Optd. "Specimen" *Set of* 11	75·00	

Nos. 29/*b*, 30, 31, 33, 34/*a* and 35 were printed from single working plates and all the rest from double plates.

1922–34. *Wmk. Mult. Script CA* (*sideways in T* **3**). *P* 14.

No.	Type	Description	Unused	Used
52	**3**	1 c. deep brown, O (1.8.22)	70	55
53	,,	1 c. black, O (12.6.23)	20	15
54	,,	2 c. brown, O (5.8.25)	60	55
55	,,	2 c. green, O (15.6.26)	15	12
56	,,	3 c. grey, O (27.12.22)	1·25	90
57	,,	3 c. green, O (22.1.24)	2·00	80
58	,,	3 c. brown, O (31.5.27)	15	15
59	,,	4 c. carmine-red, O (Die II) (27.11.23)	40	15
60	,,	4 c. orange, O (9.11.26)	12	12
		a. No watermark	40·00	
61	,,	5 c. mauve/*pale yellow,* O (17.3.22)	15	20
62	,,	5 c. brown, O (1.3.32)	30	12
63	,,	6 c. orange, O (2.5.22)	20	20
64	,,	6 c. scarlet, O (9.11.26)	20	15
65	,,	10 c. bright blue, O (23.10.23)	35	30
66	,,	10 c. blk. & bl., O (18.1.24*)	40	40
67	,,	10 c. purple/*pale yellow,* C (14.7.31)	2·50	40
68	,,	12 c. ultramarine, O (12.9.22)	65	15
69	,,	20 c. dull purple and black, OC (3.4.23)	1·40	15
70	,,	25 c. purple & bright magenta, C (3.9.29)	95	40
71	,,	30 c. purple & orange-yellow, C (3.9.29)	1·75	35
72	,,	35 c. scarlet/pale yellow, O (6.11.28)	3·00	2·00
73	,,	35 c. scar. & pur., C (29.9.31)	4·50	3·50
74	,,	50 c. blk. & orge., C (24.4.24)	2·25	30
		a. Black and orange-brown	2·00	20
75	,,	50 c. black/*green,* C (16.6.31)	3·00	80
76	**4**	$1 p. grn. & grn., C (2.2.26)	6·50	3·50
		a. Grey-green and emerald, C (5.10.26)	4·00	3·00
77	**3**	$1 blk. & red/*bl.,* C (10.3.31)	6·00	80
78	**4**	$2 grn. & carm., C (17.8.26)	4·50	5·50
79	**3**	$2 green and red/*yellow,* C (6.2.34)	10·00	8·00

80 **4** $5 green & blue, C (24.2.25) 24·00 18·00
81 **3** $5 grn. & red/*grn.*, C (7.34) 45·00 22·00
82 **4** $25 green and orange, C (14.2.28) (Optd. S. £22) £200 £110
52/80 .. .. *Set of* 30 70·00 45·00
52/81 Optd./Perf. "Specimen" *Set of* 30 £120

Nos. 52, 56 and 59 were printed from single working plates and the rest from double plates.

* No. 66 was released in London by the Crown Agents some months earlier but this is the official date of issue in the States.

The 5 c. in mauve on white Script paper is the result of soaking early printings of No. 61 in water.

POSTAGE DUE STAMPS.

D 1

(Typo. Waterlow.)

1924 (1 Dec.)–**26.** *Wmk. Mult. Script CA (sideways). P* 15×14.

D1 **D 1** 1 c. violet 50 12
D2 „ 2 c. black 12 15
D3 „ 4 c. green (4.26) 65 60
D4 „ 8 c. red 65 80
D5 „ 10 c. orange 80 85
D6 „ 12 c. blue .. .. .. 1·25 1·25
D1/6 .. .. *Set of* 6 3·50 3·50
D1/6 Optd. "Specimen" *Set of* 6 35·00

JOHORE.

A state of the Federation of Malaya.

1876 (July). *T* 5 *of Straits optd. with Crescent and Star. Wmk. Crown CC.*

1 2 c. brown £700 £450
a. Opt. double .. .. ..

From Sept. 1878 to Aug. 1884 no overprinted stamps were supplied by Singapore to Johore.

1884–91. *T* 5 *of Straits Settlements optd. Wmk. Crown CA. P* 14.

JOHORE (1) JOHORE. (2) JOHORE (3)

(i) *Believed optd. locally* (1884–85).

2 **1** 2 c. rose (June '84) £110
3 **2** 2 c. rose (March'85) .. .. 15·00 18·00
a. Short lower bar to "E" ..
4 **3** 2 c. rose (1885) .. ..

JOHORE (4) Var. (*a*) JOHORE (5)

Type **4**: (*a*) "H" and "E" wide; (*b*) "H" wide, "E" narrow.

(ii) *Optd. at Singapore.*

(*a*) *Spelt* "JOHORE" (1884–86).

5 **4** 2 c. rose (*a*) Opt. 16 mm. long) (Aug. '84) .. .. .. 65·00 40·00
a. Opt. double .. .. ..
b. Opt. 16¾ mm. long .. .. 60·00 40·00
ba. Opt. double .. .. — £110
6 „ 2 c. rose (*b*) (Opt. 16 mm. long) (Aug. '84) .. .. 65·00 40·00
a. Opt. double .. ..
7 **5** 2 c. rose (Apr. '86) .. .. 6·50

Nos. 5, 6, and 5b make up a triplet setting.

JOHOR (6) Var. (*c*) JOHOR (7) JOHOR (8)

JOHOR (9) JOHOR (10) JOHOR (11)

Type **6**: (*c*) All letters narrow; (*d*) "H" wide.

(*b*) *Spelt* "JOHOR" (1884–91).

8 **6** 2 c. rose (*c*) (Aug. '84) .. 2·50 2·75
9 **7** 2 c. rose (Oct. '84) .. .. 1·75 1·75
a. Thin narrow "J" .. 8·00 8·00
10 **8** 2 c. rose (Jan. '85) .. .. 6·00 6·00
11 **6** 2 c. rose (*d*) (Feb. '85) .. 6·00 6·00
12 **9** 2 c. rose (Apr. '86) .. .. 4·50 5·00
13 **7** 2 c. rose (with stop) ('88) .. 6·00 6·50
a. Thin narrow "J" ..
14 „ 2 c. bright rose (1890) .. 5·00 5·00
a. Thin narrow "J" .. 19·00 19·00
15 **10** 2 c. bright rose (Sept. '90) .. 1·50 1·90
a. Large wide "J" .. ..
16 **11** 2 c. deep rose (1891) .. £110

There are several triplet settings of No. 8, the word varying from 12 to 15 mm. No. 11 (wide "H") occurs in the first unit of one setting with two units of No. 8.

Two CENTS (12) Two CENTS (13)

Two CENTS (14) *Two* CENTS (15)

1891 (May). *T* 7 *of Straits Settlements optd. with name as T* 7 *and surch. as T* 12 *to* 15.

17 **12** 2 c. on 24 c. green .. 6·50 7·00
18 **13** 2 c. on 24 c. green .. .. 4·50 5·00
19 **14** 2 c. on 24 c. green .. .. 8·00 8·50
20 **15** 2 c. on 24 c. green .. .. 6·00 6·50
a. Error. "CENST" (T 15) .. 55·00 50·00

16. Sultan Aboubakar.

3 cents. (17)

KEMAHKOTAAN (18)

1891 (16 Nov.)–**94.** *No wmk. P* 14.

21 **16** 1 c. dull pur. & mve. (7.94) 20 25
22 „ 2 c. dull purple and yellow 25 50
23 „ 3 c. dull pur. & carm. (7.94) 40 25
24 „ 4 c. dull purple and black 1·50 75
25 „ 5 c. dull purple and green .. 3·00 3·00
26 „ 6 c. dull purple and blue .. 3·00 3·25
27 „ $1 green and carmine 6·00 7·50
21/27 .. .. *Set of* 7 13·00 14·00

1894 (March). *Surch. with T* 17.

28 **16** 3 c. on 4 c. dull pur. & blk. 40 25
a. No stop .. .. 6·00 6·00
29 „ 3 c. on 5 c. dull pur. & grn. 45 65
a. No stop .. .. 6·00 6·00
30 „ 3 c. on 6 c. dull pur. & blue 45 50
a. No stop .. .. 6·00 6·00
31 „ 3 c. on $1 green & carmine 3·00 3·50
a. No stop .. .. 12·00 12·00

1896 (March). *Coronation of Sultan. Optd. with T* 18.

32 **16** 1 c. dull purple and mauve 30 45
a. Error. "KETAHKOTAAN" 1·10 1·50
33 „ 2 c. dull purple and yellow 20 35
a. Error. "KETAHKOTAAN" 1·25 1·25
34 „ 3 c. dull purple and carmine 45 60
a. Error. "KETAHKOTAAN" 1·25 2·00
35 „ 4 c. dull purple and black .. 60 70
a. Error. "KETAHKOTAAN" 75 1·25
36 „ 5 c. dull purple and green .. 1·50 1·75
a. Error. "KETAHKOTAAN" 1·50 1·75
37 „ 6 c. dull purple and blue .. 80 1·00
a. Error. "KETAHKOTAAN" 1·25 1·40
38 „ $1 green and carmine 9·00 10·00
a. Error. "KETAHKOTAAN" 11·00 12·00
32/38 .. .. *Set of* 7 11·00 13·00

19. Sultan Ibrahim. 20.

21

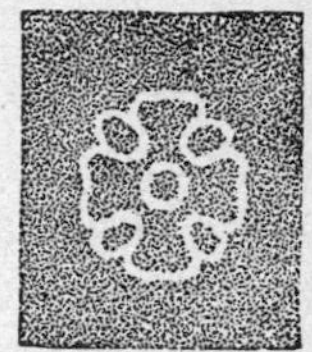
22

1896 (26 Aug.)–**1899.** *W* **22.** *P* 14.

39 **19** 1 c. green 45 12
40 „ 2 c. green and blue .. 20 12
41 „ 3 c. green and purple .. 50 12
42 „ 4 c. green and carmine .. 25 12
43 „ 4 c. yellow and red (1899) 40 20
44 „ 5 c. green and brown .. 45 35
45 „ 6 c. green and yellow .. 50 55
46 **20** 10 c. green and black .. 3·50 4·50
47 „ 25 c. green and mauve .. 4·00 4·50
48 „ 50 c. green and carmine .. 6·00 6·50
49 **19** $1 dull purple & green .. 5·50 5·50
50 **21** $2 dull purple & carmine 7·00 7·00
51 „ $3 dull purple & blue .. 9·00 9·00
52 „ $4 dull purple & brown .. 10·00 11·00
53 „ $5 dull purple & yellow 17·00 15·00
39/53 .. *Set of* 15 60·00 60·00

Nos. 46 to 53 were issued in 1898.

3 cents. (23) 10 cents. (24)

1903 (April). *Surch. with T* 23 *or* 24.

54 **19** 3 c. on 4 c. yellow and red 30 40
a. Original value uncancelled 1·10 1·40
55 „ 10 c. on 4 c. green & carmine 90 1·40
a. Tall "1" in "10" .. 12·00 12·00
b. Original value uncancelled .. 7·00 7·00
ba. As b with tall "1" in "10" 85·00

The bars on these stamps were ruled by hand with pen and ink.

50 Cents. (25) One Dollar (26)

1903 (Oct.). *Surch. with T* 25 *or* 26.

56 **21** 50 c. on $3 dull pur. & blue 5·00 8·00
57 „ $1 on $2 dull pur. & carm. 13·00 14·00
a. Variety. "e" of "One" inverted £200

10 CENTS. (27)

1904. *Surch. as* T **27.**

No.	Type	Description	Unused	Used
58	**19**	10 c. on 4 c. yell. & red (Apr.)	9·00	8·00
		a. Surcharge double	£350	
59	,,	10 c. on 4 c. grn. & car. (Aug.)	3·50	3·50
60	**21**	50 c. on $5 dull purple and yellow (May)	13·00	14·00

28

29

30. Sultan Sir Ibrahim.

3 CENTS.

(**31**)

1904 (Sept.). W **22.** P 14.

No.	Type	Description	Unused	Used
61	**28**	1 c. dull pur. & grn., OC	10	12
62	,,	2 c. dull pur. & orge., OC	35	35
63	,,	3 c. dull pur. & olive-blk., O	30	20
64	,,	4 c. dull pur. & carmine, O	90	45
65	,,	5 c. dull pur. & sage-grn., O	40	1·00
66	**30**	8 c. dull purple & blue, O	90	90
67	**29**	10 c. dull pur. & black, OC	1·25	1·75
68	,,	25 c. dull pur. & grn., O	1·25	1·75
69	,,	50 c. dull purple and red, O	1·40	2·00
70	**28**	$1 green and mauve, O	6·00	6·00
71	**30**	$2 green and carmine, O	6·50	6·00
72	,,	$3 green and blue, O	7·00	7·50
73	,,	$4 green and brown, O	8·50	10·00
74	,,	$5 green and orange, O	13·00	10·00
75	**29**	$10 green and black, O	18·00	14·00
76	,,	$50 green and ultram., O	£100	£120
77	,,	$100 green and scarlet, O	£250	£250
61/75		*Set of* 15	60·00	55·00

1910 (Dec.)–**19.** *Wmk. Mult. Rosettes* (*vertical*). P 14.

No.	Type	Description	Unused	Used
78	**28**	1 c. dull purple & green, C	12	10
79	,,	2 c. dull pur. & orange, C	25	15
80	,,	3 c. dull pur. & olive-blk., C	65	20
		a. Wmk. horizontal (1910)	90	45
81	,,	4 c. dull pur. & carmine, C	35	15
		a. Wmk. horizontal (1910)	1·10	65
82	,,	5 c. dull pur. & sage-grn., C	40	15
83	**30**	8 c. dull purple & blue, C	1·10	1·10
84	**29**	10 c. dull purple & black, C	1·25	60
		a. Wmk. horizontal (1911)	3·00	1·60
85	,,	25 c. dull purple & green, C	90	1·50
86	,,	50 c. dull pur. & red, C ('19)	7·00	6·50
87	**28**	$1 grn. & mve., C (1918)	12·00	11·00
78/87		*Set of* 10	22·00	19·00

Nos. 78 to 85 were issued in 1912.

1912 (March). *No.* 66 *surch. with* T **31**

No.	Type	Description	Unused	Used
88		3 c. on 8 c. dull pur. & blue, O	90	90
		a. "T" of "CENTS" omitted	£100	

1918–21. *Chalk-surfaced paper. Wmk. Mult. Crown CA.* P 14.

No.	Type	Description	Unused	Used
89	**28**	2 c. dull pur. & grn. (1919)	15	15
90	,,	2 c. pur. & orange (1921)	15	15
91	,,	4 c. dull purple and red	20	12
92	,,	5 c. dull purple and sage-green (1920)	40	45
93	**29**	10 c. dull purple and blue	60	60
94	,,	21 c. dull pur. & orge. (1919)	90	1·00
95	,,	25 c. dull pur. & grn. (1920)	2·00	2·00
96	,,	50 c. dull pur. & red (1920)	1·75	2·00
97	**28**	$1 green and mauve	3·25	3·50
98	**30**	$2 green and carmine	6·00	7·00
99	,,	$3 green and blue	11·00	10·00
100	,,	$4 green and brown	9·00	8·50
101	,,	$5 green and orange	14·00	14·00
102	**29**	$10 green and black	27·00	24·00
89/102		*Set of* 14	70·00	65·00
89/102		Optd. "Specimen" *Set of* 14	75·00	

1922–40. *Chalk-surfaced paper. Wmk. Mult. Script CA.* P 14.

No.	Type	Description	Unused	Used
103	**28**	1 c. dull purple and black	12	10
104	,,	2 c. purple & sepia (1924)	50	45
105	,,	2 c. green (1928)	15	15
106	,,	3 c. green (1925)	70	75
107	,,	3 c. purple & sepia (1928)	40	35
108	,,	4 c. pur. & carmine (1924)	40	10
109	,,	5 c. dull pur. & sage-grn.	15	10
110		6 c. dull purple and claret	15	12
111	**29**	10 c. dull purple and blue	2·50	2·00
112	,,	10 c. dull pur. & yell. (1922)	15	12
113	**28**	12 c. dull purple and blue	90	35
114	,,	12 c. ultramarine (1940)	4·00	3·50
115	**29**	21 c. dull pur. & orge. (28)	1·50	1·00
116	,,	25 c. dull purple & myrtle	50	40
117	**30**	30 c. dull pur. & orge. ('36)	50	50
118	,,	40 c. dull pur. & brn. ('36)	70	1·00
119	**29**	50 c. dull purple and red	60	40
120	**28**	$1 green and mauve	1·25	50
121	**30**	$2 grn. & carmine (1923)	2·50	1·10
122	,,	$3 green and blue (1925)	7·00	7·50
123	,,	$4 green & brown (1926)	8·00	8·50
124	,,	$5 green and orange	10·00	7·50
125	**29**	$10 green & black (1924)	30·00	24·00
126	,,	$50 grn.& ultram. (S. £70)	£250	
127	,,	$100 grn. & scarlet (S. £130)	£750	
128	**30**	$500 blue&red('26)(S.£300)	£8000	
103/125		*Set of* 23	65·00	55·00
103/25		Optd./Perf. "Specimen" *Set of* 23	£110	

Specimen copies of Nos. 126/8 are all overprinted.

32. Sultan Sir Ibrahim and Sultana.

(Recess. Waterlow & Sons.)

1935 (15 May). *Wmk. Mult. Script CA.* (*sideways*). P 12½.

No.	Type	Description	Unused	Used
129	**32**	8 c. bright violet & slate	40	35
129		Perf. "Specimen"	16·00	

33. Sultan Sir Ibrahim. **34.**

(Recess. De La Rue & Co.)

1940 (Feb.). *Wmk. Mult. Script CA.* P 13½.

No.	Type	Description	Unused	Used
130	**33**	8 c. black and pale blue	30	25
130		Perf. "Specimen"	14·00	

1948 (1 Dec.). *Royal Silver Wedding. As Nos.* 30/1 *of Aden.*

No.	Type	Description	Unused	Used
131		10 c. violet	10	10
132		$5 green	5·50	6·50

1949 (2 May)–**1955.** *Wmk. Mult. Script CA. Chalk-surfaced paper.* P 17½ × 18.

No.	Type	Description	Unused	Used
133	**34**	1 c. black	10	10
134	,,	2 c. orange	10	10
		a. Orange-yellow (22.1.52)	12	12
135	,,	3 c. green (*shades*)	15	12
136	,,	4 c. brown	10	10
136*a*	,,	5 c. bright purple (1.9.52)	10	10
137	,,	6 c. grey	15	15
		a. Pale grey (22.1.52)	15	15
		ac. Error. St. Ed. Crown W9b	£100	
138	,,	8 c. scarlet	25	35
138*a*	,,	8 c. green (1.9.52)	15	20
139	,,	10 c. magenta	12	10
		aa. Imperf. (pair)	£250	
139*a*	,,	12 c. scarlet (1.9.52)	20	30
140	**34**	15 c. ultramarine	40	20
141	,,	20 c. black and green	30	15
141*a*	,,	20 c. bright blue (1.9.52)	20	15
142	,,	25 c. purple and orange	20	15
142*a*	,,	30 c. scarlet & pur. (5.9.55)	55	35
142*b*	,,	35 c. scarlet & pur. (1.9.52)	50	45
143	,,	40 c. red and purple	60	70
144	,,	50 c. black and blue	40	12
145	,,	$1 blue and purple	70	50
146	,,	$2 green and scarlet	2·25	1·10
147	,,	$5 green and brown	3·50	2·50
133/147		*Set of* 21	10·00	7·00

1949 (10 Oct.). *75th Anniv. of U.P.U. As Nos.* 114/7 *of Antigua.*

No.	Type	Description	Unused	Used
148		10 c. purple	10	12
149		15 c. deep blue	12	20
150		25 c. orange	30	35
151		50 c. blue-black	50	55

1953 (2 June). *Coronation. As No.* 47 *of Aden.*

No.	Type	Description	Unused	Used
152		10 c. black and reddish purple	8	8

35. Sultan Sir Ibrahim.

(Recess. D.L.R.)

1955 (1 Nov.). *Diamond Jubilee of Sultan. Wmk. Mult. Script CA.* P 14.

No.	Type	Description	Unused	Used
153	**35**	10 c. carmine-red	8	8

36. Sultan Sir Ismail and Johore Coat-of-Arms.

(Photo. Courvoisier.)

1960 (10 Feb.). *Coronation of Sultan. No wmk.* P 11½.

No.	Type	Description	Unused	Used
154	**36**	10 c. multicoloured	8	8

1960. *As* T **10/19** *of Kedah, but with portrait of Sultan Ismail.* **$1** *P* 13½, *others. P* 12½ × 13 (*vert.*) *or* 13 × 12½ (*horiz.*).

No.	Type	Description	Unused	Used
155		1 c. black (7.10.60)	10	12
156		2 c. orange-red (7.10.60)	10	10
157		4 c. sepia (19.8.60)	10	10
158		5 c. carmine-lake (7.10.60)	10	10
159		8 c. myrtle-green (9.12.60)	10	12
160		10 c. deep maroon (10.6.60)	10	10
161		20 c. blue (9.12.60)	10	10
162		50 c. blk. & brt. blue (19.8.60)	25	10
163		$1 ultram. & reddish pur. (9.12.60)	45	35
164		$2 bronze-green and scar. (9.12.60)	90	90
165		$5 brown and bronze-green (7.10.60)	2·25	1·75
155/65		*Set of* 11	4·00	3·50

In No. 161 there are only two figures in the boat, the steersman being missing. In the 20 c. value for all the other States there are three figures.

The 6, 12, 25 and 30 c. values used in Johore were Nos. 1/4 of Malayan Federation.

37. *Vanda hookeriana.*

38. *Arundina graminifolia.*

39. *Paphiopedilum niveum.*

40. *Spathoglottis plicata.*

41. *Arachnis flos-aeris.*

42. *Rhyncostylis retusa.*

43. *Phalaenopsis violacea.*
(Inset portrait of Sultan Ismail.)

(Des. A. Fraser-Brunner. Photo. Harrison.)

1965 (15 Nov.). *W* w.**13** (*upright*). *P* 14½.

166 **37** 1 c. multicoloured .. 5 5
a. Black omitted (orchid's name and part of flower)
167 **38** 2 c. multicoloured .. 5 5
168 **39** 5 c. multicoloured .. 5 5
169 **40** 6 c. multicoloured .. 5 5
170 **41** 10 c. multicoloured .. 5 5
171 **42** 15 c. multicoloured .. 5 5
172 **43** 20 c. multicoloured .. 8 8
a. Bright purple (blooms) omitted .. .. 20·00
166/172 .. .. *Set of* 7 30 30

The 2 c. to 15 c. exist with both PVA gum and gum arabic.

The 2 c. with black (name of state) omitted is listed under Sarawak No. 213a as there is some evidence that a sheet was issued there; if it also exists from any of the other states it would, of course, be identical.

The higher values used in Johore were Nos. 20/27 of Malaysia.

1970. *As No.* 166 *and* 170 *but W* w.**13** (*sideways*).

173 **37** 1 c. mult. (20.11.70) .. 5 5
174 **41** 10 c. mult. (27.5.70) .. 10 10

44. Malayan Jezebel.
(Inset portrait of Sultan Ismail.)

(Des. V. Whiteley. Litho. B.W.)

1971 (1 Feb.). *Butterflies. T* **44** *and similar horiz. designs. Multicoloured. No Wmk. P* 13½×13.

175 1 c. Type **44** 5 5
176 2 c. Black-veined Tiger .. 5 5
177 5 c. Clipper Butterfly .. 5 5
178 6 c. Lime Butterfly .. 5 5
179 10 c. Great Orange Tip .. 5 5
180 15 c. Blue Pansy Butterfly .. 5 5
181 20 c. Wanderer 8 8
175/81 .. .. *Set of* 7 20 20

The higher values used with this issue are Nos. 64/71 of Malaysia.

POSTAGE DUE STAMPS.

D 1

(Typo. Waterlow.)

1938 (1 Jan.). *Wmk. Mult. Script CA. P* 12½.

D1 **D 1** 1 c. carmine 60 80
D2 ,, 4 c. green .. .. 1·00 1·25
D3 ,, 8 c. orange .. .. 1·50 1·75
D4 ,, 10 c. brown .. .. 1·75 2·00
D5 ,, 12 c. purple .. .. 3·00 4·50
D1/5 .. .. *Set of* 5 7·00 9·50
D1/5 Perf. "Specimen" *Set of* 5 25·00

KEDAH.

A State of the Federation of Malaya.

1. Sheaf of rice.

2. Malay ploughing.

3. Council Chamber.

(Recess. De La Rue.)

1912 (July). *Wmk. Mult. Crown CA. P* 14.

1 **1** 1 c. black and green .. 12 1
2 ,, 3 c. black and red .. 30 2
3 ,, 4 c. rose and grey .. .. 1·00 1
4 ,, 5 c. green and chestnut .. 80 8
5 ,, 8 c. black and ultramarine 35 6
6 **2** 10 c. blue and sepia .. 65 4
7 ,, 20 c. black and green .. 1·00 1·2
8 ,, 30 c. black and rose .. 1·00 1·6
9 ,, 40 c. black and purple .. 1·75 2·5
10 ,, 50 c. brown and blue .. 2·00 2·7
11 **3** $1 black and red/*yellow* .. 3·00 4·0
12 ,, $2 green and brown .. 4·00 5·0
13 ,, $3 black and blue/*blue* .. 12·00 14·0
14 ,, $5 black and red .. 20·00 22·0
1/14 .. .. *Set of* 14 45·00 50·0
1/14 Optd. "Specimen" *Set of* 14 65·00

(i) Printed from separate plates for frame an centre, with dotted shading extending close t the central sheaf.

(ii) Printed from single plate, with white spac around sheaf (as shown in T **1**).

1919–21. *New colours and values. Wmk. Mul Crown CA. P* 14.

15 **1** 1 c. brown (i) 15 2
18 ,, 2 c. green (ii) 12 1
19 ,, 3 c. deep purple (i) .. 30 4
20 ,, 4 c. rose (i) 50 1
21 ,, 4 c. red (ii) 12 1
22 **2** 21 c. purple .. .. .. 2·50 3·0
23 ,, 25 c. blue and purple ('21) .. 1·00 1·7
15/23 Optd. "Specimen" *Set of* 6 38·00

ONE

DOLLAR

(4)

MALAYA-
BORNEO
EXHIBITION.

(5)

(Surch. by Ribeiro & Co., Penang.)

1919. *Surch. as T* **4.**

24 **3** 50 c. on $2 green and brown 15·00 16·0
a. "C" of "CENTS" inserted by hand £225 £22
25 ,, $1 on $3 black & blue/*blue* 9·00 11·0

In 1919 1 c., 3 c. and 4 c. (both purple an scarlet) stamps of Straits Settlements wer authorized for use in Kedah during a temporar shortage of Kedah stamps. Stamps so used ca be identified by the postmark.

1921–24. *Wmk. Mult. Script CA. P* 14.

26 **1** 1 c. brown (ii) 15 1
27 ,, 2 c. dull green (ii) (Die I)* 10 2
28 ,, 3 c. deep purple (ii) .. 50 5
29 ,, 4 c. deep carmine (ii) .. 55 1
30 **2** 10 c. blue and sepia .. 45 5
31 ,, 20 c. black & yellow-green .. 80 9
32 ,, 21 c. mauve and purple .. 1·25 2·0
33 ,, 25 c. blue and purple .. 90 1·0
34 ,, 30 c. black and rose .. 1·25 8
35 ,, 40 c. black and purple .. 1·25 1·4
36 ,, 50 c. brown and grey-blue .. 70 8
37 **3** $1 black & red/*yellow* .. 2·50 2·0
38 ,, $2 myrtle and brown .. 7·00 8·0
39 ,, $3 black and blue/*blue* .. 11·00 13·0
40 ,, $5 black and deep carmine 20·00 20·0
26/40 .. .. *Set of* 15 45·00 45·0
26/40 Optd. "Specimen" *Set of* 15 70·00

*For 2 c., Die II, see No. 69.

.922. *Optd as T* **5.**

I. " BORNEO " 14 *mm. long.*

(*a*) *Wmk. Mult. Crown CA.*

1 **1** 2 c. green (ii) .. .. 1·25 1·75
2 **2** 21 c. mauve and purple .. 4·50 6·00
3 ,, 25 c. blue and purple .. 6·50 7·50
a. Overprint inverted .. £300
4 ,, 50 c. brown and grey-blue .. 6·00 9·50

(*b*) *Wmk. Mult. Script CA.*

5 **1** 1 c. brown (ii) .. .. 90 1·25
6 ,, 3 c. purple (ii) .. .. 1·00 1·75
7 ,, 4 c. deep carmine (ii) .. 1·25 2·75
8 **2** 10 c. blue and sepia .. 2·00 3·00
1/48 .. .. *Set of* 8 21·00 30·00

There are setting variations in the size and shape of the letters, stop raised, stop omitted, etc., etc.

II. " BORNEO " 15–15½ *mm. long.* *Wmk. Mult. Crown CA.*

9 **2** 21 c. mauve and purple .. 4·50 11·00
0 ,, 25 c. blue and purple .. 7·00
1 ,, 50 c. brown and grey-blue .. 13·00

1922–36. *New colours, etc. Wmk. Mult. Script CA. P* 14.

2 **1** 1 c. black (ii) (Die I)* .. 10 10
3 ,, 3 c. green (ii) 30 25
4 ,, 4 c. violet (ii) (1926) .. 45 12
5 ,, 5 c. yellow (ii) 25 12
6 ,, 6 c. carmine (ii) (1926) .. 12 25
7 ,, 8 c. grey-black (Oct. '36) .. 2·50 12
8 **2** 12 c. black & indigo (1926) .. 1·25 2·25
9 ,, 35 c. purple (1926) .. .. 3·25 6·00
2/59 .. .. *Set of* 8 7·50 8·50
2/9 Optd./Perf. " Specimen " *Set of* 8 38·00

*For 1 c., Die II, see No. 68*a*.

6. Sultan Abdul Hamid Halimshah.

(Recess. Waterlow & Sons.)

1937 (30 JUNE). *Wmk. Mult. Script CA. P* 12½.

0 **6** 10 c. ultramarine and sepia .. 30 10
1 ,, 12 c. black and violet .. 2·50 2·50
2 ,, 25 c. ultramarine and purple 75 75
3 ,, 30 c. green and scarlet .. 95 1·10
4 ,, 40 c. black and purple .. 30 1·25
5 ,, 50 c. brown and blue .. 30 1·00
6 ,, $1 black and green .. 80 1·00
7 ,, $2 green and brown .. 13·00 9·00
8 ,, $5 black and scarlet .. 3·50 5·50
0/68 .. .. *Set of* 9 20·00 20·00
0/8 Perf. " Specimen " *Set of* 9 38·00

I. II. I. II.

1938–40. *As Nos.* 52 *and* 27, *but figures redrawn, as Dies* II.

8*a* **1** 1 c. black .. .. .. 7·00 4·50
9 ,, 2 c. bright green ('40) .. 22·00 1·10

1 c. Die II. Figures " 1 " have square-cut corners instead of rounded, and larger top serif. Larger " C ". Line perf.

2 c. Die II. Figures " 2 " have circular instead of oval drops and the letters " c " are thin and all instead of thick and rounded. Size of design: 19½ × 23 mm. instead of about 18½ × 22½ mm. Line perf.

948 (1 DEC.). *Royal Silver Wedding. As Nos.* 30/1 *of Aden, but inscr.* " MALAYA KEDAH ".

0 10 c. violet 12 15
1 $5 carmine .. .. .. 6·00 8·00

1949 (10 OCT.). *75th Anniv. of U.P.U. As Nos.* 114/7 *of Antigua, but inscr.* " MALAYA KEDAH ".

72 10 c. purple 10 12
73 15 c. deep blue 12 25
74 25 c. orange 30 40
75 50 c. blue-black 55 70

7. Sheaf of Rice.

8. Sultan Tengku Badlishah.

1950 (1 JUNE)–**55.** *Wmk. Mult. Script CA. Chalk-surfaced paper. P* 17½ × 18.

76 **7** 1 c. black 5 5
77 ,, 2 c. orange 5 5
78 ,, 3 c. green 15 15
79 ,, 4 c. brown 5 5
79*a* ,, 5 c. brt. pur. (*shades*) (1.9.52) 5 5
80 ,, 6 c. grey 10 10
81 ,, 8 c. scarlet 20 35
81*a* ,, 8 c. green (*shades*) (1.9.52) 25 15
82 ,, 10 c. magenta 20 15
82*a* ,, 12 c. scarlet (1.9.52) .. 12 12
83 ,, 15 c. ultramarine 30 20
84 ,, 20 c. black and green .. 30 35
84*a* ,, 20 c. bright blue (1.9.52) .. 30 25
85 **8** 25 c. purple and orange .. 20 10
85*a* ,, 30 c. scar. & purple (5.9.55) 30 25
85*b* ,, 35 c. scar. & purple (1.9.52) 35 40
86 ,, 40 c. red and purple .. 30 85
87 ,, 50 c. black and blue .. 30 12
88 ,, $1 blue and purple .. 60 40
89 ,, $2 green and scarlet .. 2·25 2·75
90 ,, $5 green and brown .. 3·75 5·00
76/90 .. .. *Set of* 21 9·00 11·00

1953 (2 JUNE). *Coronation. As No.* 47 *of Aden.*

91 10 c. black & reddish purple .. 5 5

9. Copra.

10. Pineapples.

11. Ricefield.

12. Masjid Alwi Mosque, Kangar.

13. East Coast Railway.

14. Tiger.

15. Fishing Craft. **16.** Aborigines with Blowpipes.

17. Government Offices.

18. Bersilat.

19. Weaving.

(Recess. De La Rue.)

1957. *Inset portrait of Sultan Tengku Badlishah W* w.**12.** *P* 13×12½ (1 *c. to* 8 *c.*), 12½×13 (10 *c.*, 20 *c.*,) 12½ (50 *c.*, $2, $5) *or* 13½ ($1).

92 **9** 1 c. black 5 10
93 **10** 2 c. orange-red 5 10
94 **11** 4 c. sepia 5 12
95 **12** 5 c. carmine-lake 5 12
96 **13** 8 c. myrtle-green .. 10 25
97 **14** 10 c. deep brown 10 12
98 **15** 20 c. blue 12 12
99 **16** 50 c. black and blue .. 30 25
100 **17** $1 ultramarine and reddish purple .. .. 60 1·25
101 **18** $2 bronze-grn. & scarlet 1·75 1·75
102 **19** $5 brown & bronze-grn. 2·75 3·75
92/102 .. .. *Set of* 11 5·50 6·50

Dates of issue:—26.6.57, 20 c., $5; 25.7.57; 2 c., 50 c., $1; 4.8.57, 10 c.; 21.8.57, others.

The 6, 12, 25 and 30 c. values used in Kedah were Nos. 1/4 of Malayan Federation.

20. Sultan Tengku Abdul.

(Photo. Harrison.)

1959 (20 Feb.). *Installation of the Sultan. W* w.**12.** *P* 14×14½.

103 **20** 10 c. yellow, red, brown and bright blue .. 5 5

21. Sultan Tengku Abdul.

1959 (1 July)–**62.** *As Nos.* 92/102 *but with inset portrait of Sultan Tengku Abdul as in T* **21.**

104 **21** 1 c. black 5 5
105 **10** 2 c. orange-red 5 5
106 **11** 4 c. sepia 5 5
107 **12** 5 c. carmine-lake .. 5 5
108 **13** 8 c. myrtle-green .. 5 8
109 **14** 10 c. deep brown .. 5 5
109*a* ,, 10 c. dp. maroon (19.12.61) 5 5
110 **15** 20 c. blue 8 5
111 **16** 50 c. black and blue (*p.* 12½) 30 20
  a. Perf. 12½×13 (14.6.60) .. 25 15
112 **17** $1 ultramarine & reddish purple .. 40 35
113 **18** $2 bronze-grn. & scarlet 80 1·75
114 **19** $5 brown & bronze-grn. (*p.* 12½) .. .. 2·25 2·25
  a. Perf. 13×12½ (26.11.62) 2·00 1·75
104/14 . .. *Set of* 12 3·50 4·00

22. *Vanda hookeriana.*

1965 (15 Nov.). *As Nos.* 166/72 *of Johore but with inset portrait of Sultan Tengku Abdul as in T* **22.** *W* w.**13** (*upright*).

115 1 c. multicoloured 5 5
  a. Black omitted (orchid's name and part of flower) .. 30·00
116 2 c. multicoloured 5 5
117 5 c. multicoloured 5 5
  a. Black (country name and head) omitted .. .. 40·00
118 6 c. multicoloured 5 5
119 10 c. multicoloured 5 5
120 15 c. multicoloured 8 5
121 20 c. multicoloured 8 8
  a. Bright pur. (blooms) omitted
115/21 .. .. *Set of* 7 30 30

The 1 c. to 15 c. exist with PVA gum as well as gum arabic.

The 6 c. value exists with black (country name) omitted and is listed under Sarawak where it was issued.

The higher values used in Kedah were Nos. 20/27 of Malaysia.

1970 (27 May). *As Nos.* 115 *and* 119 *but W* w.**13** (*sideways*).

122 **22** 1 c. multicoloured .. 5 5
123 – 10 c. multicoloured .. 8 8

23. Black-veined Tiger.

1971 (1 Feb.). *As Nos.* 175/81 *of Johore but with portrait of Sultan Tengku Abdul as in T* **23.**

124 1 c. multicoloured 5 5
125 2 c. multicoloured 5 5
126 5 c. multicoloured 5 5
127 6 c. multicoloured 5 5
128 10 c. multicoloured 5 5
129 15 c. multicoloured 5 5
130 20 c. multicoloured 8 8
124/30 .. .. *Set of* 7 20 20

The higher values used with this issue are Nos. 64/71 of Malaysia.

KELANTAN.

A State of the Federation of Malaya.

1

MALAYA

BORNEO

EXHIBITION

(**2**)

1911 (Jan.) *Wmk Mult. Crown CA. P* 14.

1 **1** 1 c. yellow-green, O .. 30 10
  a. Blue-green, O 20 12
2 ,, 3 c. red, O 20 8
3 ,, 4 c. black and red, O .. 20 8
4 **1** 5 c. green & red/*yellow*, O 35 1[illegible]
5 ,, 8 c. ultramarine, O .. 90 4[illegible]
6 ,, 10 c. black and mauve, O .. 1·00 1[illegible]
7 ,, 30 c. dull purple and red, C 1·25 1[illegible]
  a. Purple and carmine, C .. 3·50 2·2[illegible]
8 ,, 50 c. black and orange, C .. 1·25 1·1[illegible]
9 ,, $1 green and emerald, C .. 6·50 7·0[illegible]
10 ,, $2 green and carmine, C .. 75 2·0[illegible]
11 ,, $5 green and blue, C .. 3·75 4·0[illegible]
12 ,, $25 green and orange, C .. 15·00 17·0[illegible]
1/12 .. .. *Set of* 12 28·00 29·0[illegible]
1/12 Optd. "Specimen" *Set of* 12 60·00

1915. *Colours changed. Wmk. Mult. Crown CA. P* 14.

13 **1** $1 green & brown, C (Optd. S. £14) .. .. 6·00 1·5[illegible]

1921–28. *Wmk. Mult. Script. CA. P* 14.

14 **1** 1 c. dull green, C .. 80 3[illegible]
15 ,, 1 c. black, O (1923) .. 30 2[illegible]
16 ,, 2 c. brown, O (1922) .. 90 1·0[illegible]
16*a* ,, 2 c. green, O (1926) .. 30 2[illegible]
16*b* ,, 3 c. brown, O (1927) .. 40 6[illegible]
17 ,, 4 c. black & red, O (1922) 12 1[illegible]
18 ,, 5 c. green and red/*pale yellow*, O ('22) .. 20 1[illegible]
19 ,, 6 c. claret, O (1922) .. 75 9[illegible]
19*a* ,, 6 c. scarlet, O (1928) .. 1·50 1·7[illegible]
20 ,, 10 c. black and mauve, O 60 2[illegible]
21 ,, 30 c. pur. & carm., C (1926) 75 1·1[illegible]
22 ,, 50 c. black & orange, C ('25) 1·25 1·5[illegible]
23 ,, $1 green & brown, C ('24) 5·00 6·0[illegible]
14/23 .. .. *Set of* 13 12·00 13·0[illegible]
14/23 Optd. "Specimen" *Set of* 13 60·00

For the 4 c., 5 c. and 6 c. surcharged, see issue under "Japanese Occupation".

1922 (Mar.). *Optd. with T* **2.**

(*a*) *Wmk. Mult. Crown CA.*

30 **1** 4 c. black and red .. 1·00 2·5[illegible]
31 ,, 5 c. green & red/*pale yellow* 1·25 2·5[illegible]
32 ,, 30 c. dull purple and red .. 1·50 3·7[illegible]
33 ,, 50 c. black and orange .. 2·50 4·7[illegible]
34 ,, $1 green and brown .. 6·00 8·0[illegible]
35 ,, $2 green and carmine .. 10·00 15·0[illegible]
36 ,, $5 green and blue.. .. 35·00 40·0[illegible]

(*b*) *Wmk. Mult. Script CA.*

37 **1** 1 c. green .. .. .. 90 2·0[illegible]
38 ,, 10 c. black and mauve .. 1·75 4·0[illegible]
30/38 .. .. *Set of* 9 55·00 75·0[illegible]

3. Sultan Ismail. **4.**

(Recess. D.L.R.)

1928–33. *Wmk. Mult. Script CA.*

39 **3** $1 blue (*p.* 12) (Perf. S. £10) 3·50 6·5[illegible]
39*a* ,, $1 blue (*p.* 14) ('33) .. 10·00 13·0[illegible]

(Recess. B.W.)

1937–40. *Wmk. Mult. Script CA. P* 12.

40 **4** 1 c. grey-olive and yellow 15 1[illegible]
41 ,, 2 c. green 15
42 ,, 4 c. scarlet .. .. .. 40 2[illegible]
43 ,, 5 c. red-brown .. .. 45 1[illegible]
44 ,, 6 c. lake .. .. .. 1·00 3[illegible]
45 ,, 8 c. grey-olive .. .. 55 2[illegible]
46 ,, 10 c. purple .. .. .. 1·00 5[illegible]
47 ,, 12 c. blue .. .. .. 50 8[illegible]
48 ,, 25 c. vermilion and violet .. 1·10 1·0[illegible]
49 ,, 30 c. violet and scarlet .. 3·00 3·0[illegible]
50 ,, 40 c. orange and blue-green 2·00 2·0[illegible]
51 ,, 50 c. grey-olive and orange 3·50 3·5[illegible]
52 ,, $1 violet and blue-green .. 1·75 2·5[illegible]
53 ,, $2 red-brown and scarlet 30·00 30·0[illegible]
54 ,, $5 vermilion and lake .. 45·00 48·0[illegible]
40/54 .. .. *Set of* 15 80·00 85·0[illegible]
40/54 Perf. "Specimen" *Set of* 15 65·00

Dates of issue: 10.37, 6, 10, 30, 50 c., $1; .40, $2, $5; 7.37, others.

For above issue surcharged see issues under Japanese Occupation ".

948 (1 Dec.). *Royal Silver Wedding. As Nos. 30/1 of Aden.*
5 10 c. violet 10 12
6 $5 carmine .. .. .. 4·50 7·50

949 (10 Oct.). *75th Anniv. of Universal Postal Union. As Nos. 114/17 of Antigua.*
7 10 c. purple 15 25
8 15 c. deep blue 25 40
9 25 c. orange 40 60
0 50 c. blue-black .. .. 60 1·00

5. Sultan Tengku Ibrahim.

951 (11 July)–**55**. *Chalk-surfaced paper. Wmk. Mult. Script. CA. P* $17\frac{1}{2}\times18$.
1 **5** 1 c. black 5 8
2 ,, 2 c. orange (*shades*) .. 5 5
3 ,, 3 c. green 15 20
4 ,, 4 c. brown 5 5
5 ,, 5 c. brt. pur. (*shades*) (1.9.52) 5 5
6 ,, 6 c. grey 8 10
7 ,, 8 c. scarlet 20 25
8 ,, 8 c. green (1.9.52) 15 15
9 ,, 10 c. magenta 10 5
0 ,, 12 c. scarlet (1.9.52) .. 15 20
1 ,, 15 c. ultramarine 20 25
2 ,, 20 c. black and green .. 40 35
3 ,, 20 c. bright blue (1.9.52) .. 30 25
4 ,, 25 c. purple and orange .. 30 25
5 ,, 30 c. scar. & purple (5.9.55) 40 50
6 ,, 35 c. scar. & purple (1.9.52) 50 70
7 ,, 40 c. red and purple .. .. 60 1·10
8 ,, 50 c. black and blue .. 35 40
9 ,, $1 blue and purple .. 75 75
0 ,, $2 green and scarlet .. 1·50 3·25
1 ,, $5 green & brown (*shades*) 4·00 7·50
1/81 .. .. *Set of* 21 9·00 15·00

953 (2 June). *Coronation. As No. 47 of Aden.*
2 10 c. black and reddish purple 8 5

957–63. *As Nos. 92/102 of Kedah but with inset portrait of Sultan Tengku Ibrahim.*
3 **9** 1 c. black 5 5
4 **10** 2 c. orange-red 5 5
a. *Red-orange* (17.11.59) .. 5 5
5 **11** 4 c. sepia 5 5
6 **12** 5 c. carmine-lake .. 5 5
7 **13** 8 c. myrtle-green .. 10 10
8 **14** 10 c. deep brown 8 5
9 ,, 10 c. deep maroon (19.4.61) 8 15
0 **15** 20 c. blue 12 12
1 **16** 50 c. black and blue (*p.* $12\frac{1}{2}$) 30 25
a. Perf. $12\frac{1}{2}\times13$ (28.6.60) .. 30 25
2 **17** $1 ultramarine and reddish purple 60 50
3 **18** $2 bronze-green and scarlet (*p.* $12\frac{1}{2}$) .. .. 1·40 2·00
a. Perf. $13\times12\frac{1}{2}$ (9.4.63) .. 1·25 2·00
4 **19** $5 brown & bronze-green (*p.* $12\frac{1}{2}$) .. .. 3·00 3·00
a. Perf. $13\times12\frac{1}{2}$ (13.8.63) .. 2·50 2·75
3/94 .. .. *Set of* 12 4·75 6·00

Dates of issue:—26.6.57, 20 c., $5; 25.7.57, c., 50 c., $1; 4.8.57, 10 c.; 21.8.57, others.

6. Sultan Yahya Petra and Crest of Kelantan.

(Photo. Harrison.)

1961 (17 July). *Installation of the Sultan. W* w.**12.** *P* 15×14.
95 **6** 10 c. multicoloured 8 8

7. Sultan Yahya Petra.

(Recess. De La Rue & Co.)

1961–62. *As Nos. 92/8 of Kedah but with inset portrait of Sultan Yahya Petra as in T* **7.** *W* w. **13.** *P* $12\frac{1}{2}\times13$ (*vert.*) *or* $13\times12\frac{1}{2}$ (*horiz.*).
96 1 c. black (1.3.62) 5 5
97 2 c. orange-red (1.3.62) .. 5 5
98 4 c. sepia (1.3.62) 5 5
99 5 c. carmine-lake (1.3.62) .. 5 5
100 8 c. myrtle-grn.(*shades*)(1.3.62) 5 8
101 10 c. deep maroon (2.12.61) .. 5 5
102 20 c. blue (1.3.62) 10 10
96/102 .. .. *Set of* 7 30 30

The 6, 12, 25 and 30 c. values used in Kelantan were Nos. 1/4 of Malayan Federation.

8. *Vanda hookeriana.*

1965 (15 Nov.). *As Nos. 166/72 of Johore but with inset portraits of Sultan Yahya Petra as in T* **8.** *W* w. **13.** (*upright*).
103 1 c. multicoloured 5 5
a. Magenta omitted .. ..
104 2 c. multicoloured 5 5
105 5 c. multicoloured 5 5
106 6 c. multicoloured 5 5
107 10 c. multicoloured 8 5
108 15 c. multicoloured 5 5
109 20 c. multicoloured 8 8
103/109 .. .. *Set of* 7 30 30

The 5 c. and 10 c. exist with PVA gum as well as gum arabic.

The higher values used in Kelantan were Nos. 20/27 of Malaysia.

1970 (20 Nov.). *As Nos.* 103 *and* 107 *but W* w.**13** (*sideways*).
110 **8** 1 c. multicoloured 5 5
111 – 10 c. multicoloured 8 8

9. Clipper Butterfly.

1971 (1 Feb.). *As Nos. 175/81 of Johore but with portrait of Sultan Yahya Petra and arms, as in T* **9.**
112 1 c. multicoloured 5 5
113 2 c. multicoloured 5 5
114 5 c. multicoloured 5 5
115 6 c. multicoloured 5 5
116 10 c. multicoloured 5 5
117 15 c. multicoloured 5 5
118 20 c. multicoloured 8 8
112/118 .. .. *Set of* 7 20 20

The higher values used with this issue are Nos. 64/71 of Malaysia.

MALACCA.

A former British Settlement, now part of the Federation of Malaya.

1948 (1 Dec.). *Royal Silver Wedding. As Nos. 30/1 of Aden, but inscr.* " MALAYA MALACCA ".
1 10 c. violet 10 12
2 $5 brown .. .. .. 7·50 8·50

1949 (1 Mar.)–**52.** *As T* **58** *of Straits Settlements, but inscr.* " MALACCA " *at foot. Wmk. Mult. Script CA. Chalk-surfaced paper. P* $17\frac{1}{2}\times18$.
3 1 c. black 10 20
4 2 c. orange 10 20
5 3 c. green 12 35
6 4 c. brown 10 15
6a 5 c. bright purple (1.9.52) .. 10 30
7 6 c. grey 10 30
8 8 c. scarlet 25 35
8a 8 c. green (1.9.52) 15 40
9 10 c. purple 12 25
9a 12 c. scarlet (1.9.52) 20 50
10 15 c. ultramarine 30 30
11 20 c. black and green 25 50
11a 20 c. bright blue (1.9.52) .. 40 45
12 25 c. purple and orange .. 20 35
12a 35 c. scarlet & purple (1.9.52) 20 60
13 40 c. red and purple .. .. 55 1·10
14 50 c. black and blue 40 45
15 $1 blue and purple .. .. 90 1·10
16 $2 green and scarlet .. .. 1·50 2·00
17 $5 green and brown .. .. 2·50 3·50
3/17 .. .. *Set of* 20 7·50 12·00

1949 (10 Oct.). *75th Anniv. of U.P.U. As Nos. 114/17 of Antigua.*
18 10 c. purple 10 15
19 15 c. deep blue 10 15
20 25 c. orange 30 40
21 50 c. blue-black 40 55

1953 (2 June). *Coronation. As No. 47 of Aden.*
22 10 c. black and reddish purple 10 10

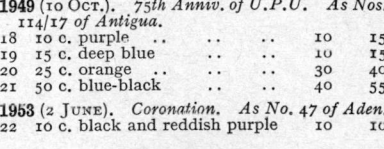

1. Queen Elizabeth II.

1954–5. *Chalk-surfaced paper. Wmk. Mult. Script CA. P* $17\frac{1}{2}\times18$.
23 **1** 1 c. black 5 10
24 ,, 2 c. yellow-orange 5 10
25 ,, 4 c. brown (*shades*) .. 8 10
26 ,, 5 c. bright purple 8 10
27 ,, 6 c. grey 10 12
28 ,, 8 c. green 15 15
29 ,, 10 c. brown-purple (*shades*) .. 12 5
30 ,, 12 c. rose-red 15 20
31 ,, 20 c. bright blue 25 30
32 ,, 25 c. brn.-purple & yell.-orge. 30 15
33 ,, 30 c. rose-red & brown-purple 40 25
34 ,, 35 c. rose-red & brown-purple 50 35
35 ,, 50 c. black and bright blue .. 50 30
36 ,, $1 brt. blue & brn.-purple 90 90
37 ,, $2 emerald and scarlet .. 2·25 3·50
38 ,, $5 emerald and brown .. 6·50 6·50
23/38 .. .. *Set of* 16 11·00 12·00

Dates of issue: 9.6.54, 4 and 6 c.; 1.7.54, 10 c.; 12.7.54, 5 c.; 8.9.54, 35 c., $1; 5.1.55, 8, 12, 20, 50 c.; 27.4.55, 1, 2, 25 c., $2, $5; 5.9.55, 30 c.

1957. *As Nos. 92/102 of Kedah but with inset portrait of Queen Elizabeth II.*

39 **9** 1 c. black 5 5
40 **10** 2 c. orange-red 5 5
41 **11** 4 c. sepia 5 5
42 **12** 5 c. carmine-lake 5 5
43 **13** 8 c. myrtle-green 10 15
44 **14** 10 c. deep brown 10 5
45 **15** 20 c. blue 20 10
46 **16** 50 c. black and blue 30 15
47 **17** $1 ultramarine and reddish purple .. .. 60 1·40
48 **18** $2 bronze-green & scarlet 1·50 2·50
49 **19** $5 brown & bronze-green 3·00 5·00
39/49 .. .. *Set of* 11 5·50 8·50

Dates of issue:—26.6.57, 20 c., $5; 25.7.57, 2 c., 50 c., $1; 4.8.57, 10 c.; 21.8.57, others.

The 6, 12, 25 and 30 c. values used in Malacca were Nos. 1/4 of Malayan Federation.

2. Copra.

(Recess. D.L.R.)

1960 (15 Mar.)–**62.** *As Nos. 39/49, but with inset picture of Melaka tree and Pelandok (mouse deer) as in T* **2.** *W* w.**12.** *P* 13×12½ (1 *c. to* 8 *c.*, $2, $5), 12½×13 (10 *c. to* 50 *c.*) *or* 13½ ($1).

50 1 c. black 5 5
51 2 c. orange-red 5 5
52 4 c. sepia 5 5
53 5 c. carmine-lake 5 5
54 8 c. myrtle-green 8 10
55 10 c. deep maroon 5 5
56 20 c. blue 8 8
57 50 c. black and blue 25 20
  a. Black & ultramarine (9.1.62) 20 15
58 $1 ultram. & reddish purple 40 40
59 $2 bronze-green & scarlet .. 1·00 85
60 $5 brown and bronze-green 2·00 1·40
50/60 .. .. *Set of* 11 3·50 2·75

3. *Vanda hookeriana.*

1965 (15 Nov.). *As Nos. 166/72 of Johore but with Arms of Malacca inset and inscr.* " MELAKA " *as in T* **3.** *W* w.**13.** (*upright*)

61 1 c. multicoloured 5 5
62 2 c. multicoloured 5 5
63 5 c. multicoloured 5 5
64 6 c. multicoloured 5 5
65 10 c. multicoloured 5 5
66 15 c. multicoloured 8 5
67 20 c. multicoloured (*shades*) .. 10 8
61/7 .. .. *Set of* 7 35 30

The 5 c., 6 c., 10 c. and 20 c. exist with PVA gum as well as gum arabic.

The higher values used in Malacca were Nos. 20/27 of Malaysia.

1970. *As Nos. 61 and 65 but W* w.**13** (*sideways*).

68 **3** 1 c. mult. (27.5.70) .. 5 5
69 – 10 c. mult. (20.11.70) .. 15 15

4. Lime Butterfly.

1971 (1 Feb.). *As Nos. 175/81 of Johore but with arms of Malacca and inscr.* " melaka ", *as in T* **4.**

70 1 c. multicoloured 5 5
71 2 c. multicoloured 5 5
72 5 c. multicoloured 5 5
73 6 c. multicoloured 5 5
74 10 c. multicoloured 5 5
75 15 c. multicoloured 5 5
76 20 c. multicoloured 8 8
70/76 .. .. *Set of* 7 20 20

The higher values used with this issue are Nos. 64/71 of Malaysia.

MALAYA (BRITISH MILITARY ADMINISTRATION).

For use throughout all Malay States and in Singapore. From 1948 this general issue was gradually replaced by individual issues for each state.

BMA
MALAYA
(1)

1945–48. *T* **58** *of Straits Settlements optd. with T* **1.** *Values* 1 *c. to* 15 *c. from Die I (double-plate printing) or Die II (single-plate printing). Wmk. Mult. Script CA. P* 14 *or* 15×14 (No. 11).

1 1 c. black, C O (I) (R.) .. 8 5
2 2 c. orange, O C (II) .. 8 5
3 2 c. orange, O (I) ('46) .. 25 45
4 3 c. yellow-green, O (II) .. 15 5
  a. Blue-green OC (II) ('47) .. 12 5
5 5 c. brown, C (II) 8 5
6 6 c. grey, O C (II) 8 5
7 8 c. scarlet, O (II) 8 5
8 10 c. slate-purple, C (I) .. 8 5
  a. Purple, OC (I) ('45) 8 10
  b. Magenta, C (I) ('48) 12 10
9 10 c. purple, C (II) ('48) .. 8 5
10 12 c. brt. ultramarine, C (I) .. 25 50
11 15 c. brt. ultramarine, O (II) .. 55 1·60
12 15 c. brt. ultram. OC (II) (R.) 8 10
  a. Blue, OC (II) (R.) ('47) .. 2·50 40
13 25 c. dull purple & scarlet, OC 8 5
14 50 c. black/*emerald*, CO (I) (R.) ('46) 10 10
15 $1 black and red, O .. 30 8
16 $2 green and scarlet, O .. 55 20
17 $5 green and red/*emerald*, C 12·00 15·00
18 $5 purple and orange, O .. 1·75 45
1/18 .. .. *Set of* 15 14·00 15·00
1/11, 13/16, 18 Perf. " Specimen " *Set of* 14 75·00

The 8 c. grey with " B M A " opt. was prepared but not officially issued.

Nos. 3 and 9 do not exist without the overprint.

Nos. 1, 2, 6, 7, 8*a* and 13 exist also on thin, rough ordinary paper.

No. 8*a* with reddish purple medallion and dull purple frame is from a printing with the head in fugitive ink which discolours with moisture.

MALAYAN FEDERATION.

Comprising the Settlements of Malacca and Penang and all the Malay States.

We list below the stamps intended for use throughout the Federation. See notes at the beginning of Malaya.

1. Tapping Rubber.

2. Federation Coat-of-Arms.

3. Tin Dredge.

4. Map of the Federation.

(Centre recess, frame litho. (6 c., 25 c.); cent litho, frame recess (12 c.); recess (30 c. De La Rue & Co.)

1957 (5 May)–**61.** *W* w.**12.**

1 **1** 6 c. dp. blue, red, yellow and grey-blue (*shades*) (*p.* 13) 5
2 **2** 12 c. red, yellow, blue, black and scarlet (*p.* 13) .. 5
3 **3** 25 c. maroon, red, yellow and dull gr'nish blue (*p.* 13) 12
4 **4** 30 c. orange-red and lake (*p.* 13×12½) 25 1
  a. Perf. 13. *Orange-red & deep lake* (*shades*) (20.6.61) .. 15

5. Chief Minister Tengku Abdul Rahman and Populace greeting Independence.

(Des. A. B. Saman. Recess. Waterlow.)

1957 (31 Aug.). *Independence Day. Wm Mult. Script CA. P* 12½.

5 **5** 10 c. bistre-brown 8

6. United Nations Emblem.

7. United Nations Emblem.

(Recess. De La Rue & Co., Ltd.)

958 (5 Mar.). *U.N. Economic Commission for Asia and Far East Conference, Kuala Lumpur. W* w.**12**. *P* 13½ (12 *c.*) *or* 12½ (30 *c.*).
6 12 c. carmine-red 12 12
7 30 c. maroon 15 12

8. Merdeka Stadium, Kuala Lumpur.

The Yang di Pertuan Agong (Abdul Rahman).

(Photo. Harrison.)

958 (31 Aug.). *First Anniv. of Independence. W* w.**12**. *P* 13½×14½ (10 *c.*) *or* 14½×13½ (30 *c.*).
8 10 c. green, yellow, red & blue 5 5
9 30 c. red, yellow, violet-blue and green 12 10

0. ' ' Human Rights ".

12. Mace and Malayan Peoples.

11. Malayan with Torch of Freedom.

(Des. J. P. Hendroff. Litho. (10 c.), photo. (30 c.). D.L.R.)

1958 (10 Dec.). *Tenth Anniv. of Declaration of Human Rights.* (*a*) *W* w.**12**. *P* 12½×13.
10 **10** 10 c. blue, blk., carm. & orge. 5 5
(*b*) *Wmk. Mult. Script CA. P* 13×12½.
11 **11** 30 c. deep green 15 12

(Photo. J. Enschedé & Sons, Haarlem.)

1959 (12 Sept.). *Inauguration of Parliament. No wmk. P* 13×14.
12 **12** 4 c. rose-red 5 5
13 ,, 10 c. violet 5 5
14 ,, 25 c. yellow-green 10 8

13

14

(Recess. D.L.R.)

1960 (7 Apr.). *World Refugee Year. W* w.**12**. *P* 13½ (12 *c.*) *or* 12½×13 (30 *c.*).
15 **13** 12 c. purple 15 20
16 **14** 30 c. deep green 15 15

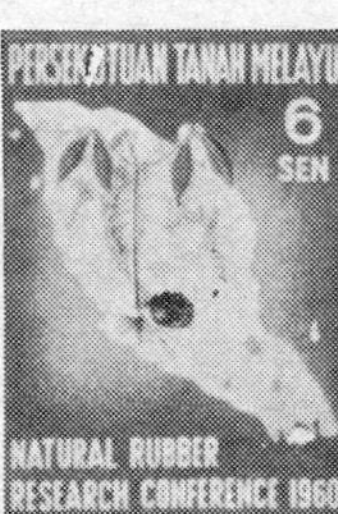

15. Seedling Rubber Tree and Map.

16. The Yang di-Pertuan Agong (Syed Putra).

(Photo. Japanese Govt. Ptg. Wks.)

1960 (19 Sept.). *Natural Rubber Research Conference and 15th International Rubber Study Group Meeting, Kuala Lumpur. T* **15** *and similar vert. design. No wmk. P* 13.
17 6 c. yellow-green, black, orange and red-brown .. 5 5
18 30 c. yellow-green, black, orange and bright blue 12 12

No. 18 is inscribed " INTERNATIONAL RUBBER STUDY GROUP 15TH MEETING KUALA LUMPUR " at foot.

(Photo. Harrison.)

1961 (4 Jan.). *Installation of Yang di-Pertuan Agong, Tuanku Syed Putra. W* w.**12**. *P* 14×14½.
19 **16** 10 c. black and blue .. 5 5

17. Colombo Plan Emblem.

18. Malaria Eradication Emblem.

(Photo. Japanese Govt. Ptg. Works.)

1961 (30 Oct.). *Colombo Plan Conference, Kuala Lumpur. P* 13.
20 **17** 12 c. black and magenta .. 5 8
21 ,, 25 c. black & apple-green .. 10 8
22 ,, 30 c. black & turq.-blue .. 15 10

(Photo. Harrison.)

1962 (7 Apr.). *Malaria Eradication. W* w.**13**. *P* 14×14½.
23 **18** 25 c. orange-brown.. .. 8 5
24 ,, 30 c. deep lilac 10 10
25 ,, 50 c. ultramarine 20 25

19. Palmyra Palm Leaf.

(Photo. Harrison.)

1962 (21 July). *National Language Month. W* w.**13**. *P* 13½.
26 **19** 10 c. lt. brn. & dp. redsh. vio. 5 5
27 ,, 20 c. lt. brn. & dp. bl'sh grn. 8 5
28 ,, 50 c. lt. brown and magenta 25 25

20. " Shadows of the Future ".

(Photo. J. Enschedé & Sons.)

1962 (1 Oct.). *Introduction of Free Primary Education. W* w.**13**. *P* 13½.
29 **20** 10 c. bright purple 5 5
30 ,, 25 c. ochre 10 10
31 ,, 30 c. emerald 20 20

21. Harvester and Fisherman.

(Photo. Courvoisier.)

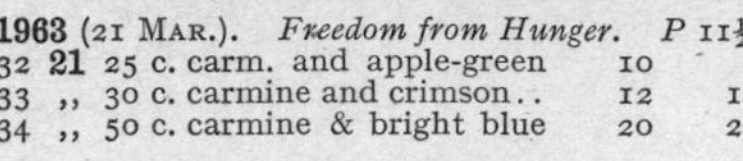

1963 (21 Mar.). *Freedom from Hunger.* P 11½.
32 **21** 25 c. carm. and apple-green .. 10 8
33 ,, 30 c. carmine and crimson .. 12 10
34 ,, 50 c. carmine & bright blue 20 20

22. Dam and Pylon.

(Photo. Harrison.)

1963 (26 June). *Cameron Highlands Hydro-Electric Scheme. Wmk.* w.**13.** P 14.
35 **22** 20 c. green & reddish violet 8 8
36 ,, 30 c. blue-green & ultram. 12 12

The definitive general issue for Malaysia and the low value sets for the individual states superseded the stamps of the Malayan Federation on 15th November, 1965.

MALAYAN POSTAL UNION.

POSTAGE DUE STAMPS.

D 1

10

cents

(D 2)

(Typo. Waterlow until 1961, then De La Rue.)

1936–38. *Wmk. Mult. Script CA.* P 15×14.
D 1 **D 1** 1 c. slate-purple (1938) 15 30
D 2 ,, 4 c. green 35 30
D 3 ,, 8 c. scarlet 65 80
D 4 ,, 10 c. yellow-orange .. 40 12
D 5 ,, 12 c. pale ultramarine .. 70 1·25
D 6 ,, 50 c. black (1.38) .. 1·00 1·25
D1/6 .. .. *Set of* 6 3·00 3·50
D1/6 Perf. "Specimen" *Set of* 6 30·00

For use in Negri Sembilan, Pahang, Perak, Selangor and Straits Settlements including Singapore.

1945–49. *New values and colours. Wmk. Mult. Script CA.* P 15×14.
D 7 **D 1** 1 c. purple 35 40
D 8 ,, 3 c. green .. .. 1·00 1·25
D 9 ,, 5 c. scarlet .. .. 1·40 1·75
D10 ,, 8 c. yellow-orange ('49) (Perf. S. £30) .. 3·50 3·50
D11 ,, 9 c. yellow-orange .. 6·00 6·00
D12 ,, 15 c. pale ultramarine .. 9·00 8·00
D13 ,, 20 c. bl. ('48) (Perf. S. £18) 2·00 2·50
D7/13 .. .. *Set of* 7 21·00 21·00

1951 (8 Aug.)–**62.** *Wmk. Mult. Script CA.* P 14.
D14 **D 1** 1 c. violet (21.8.52) .. 8 10
D15 ,, 2 c. dp.slate-bl. (16.11.53) 8 10
a. Perf. 12½ (15.11.60) .. 10 15
b. P. 12½. Chalky paper (10.7.62) 8 20
ba. Do. Imp. betwn. (vt. pr.)
D16 ,, 3 c. deep green (21.8.52) 40 50
D17 ,, 4 c. sepia (16.11.53) .. 10 12
a. Perf. 12½ (15.11.60) .. 10 20
b. P. 12½ *Bistre-brown.* Chalky paper (10.7.62) 8 20
D18 ,, 5 c. vermilion 50 75
D19 ,, 8 c. yellow-orange .. 15 20
D20 ,, 12 c. brt. purple (1.2.54) 20 25
a. P. 12½. Chalky paper (10.7.62) 15 50
D21 **D 1** 20 c. blue 40 50
a. P 12½. *Deep blue* (10.12.57) 25 40
b. P 12½. *Deep blue.* Chalky paper (15.10.63) .. 50 1·00
D14/21 .. .. *Set of* 8 1·50 2·25

Nos. D7 to D21b were for use in the Federation and Singapore, and from 1963 throughout Malaysia.

1964 (14 Apr.)–**65.** *Chalk-surfaced paper. Wmk.* w.**12** (*sideways on* 1 c.). P 12½.
D22 **D 1** 1 c. maroon 5 10
a. P. 12. Wmk. upright (4.5.65) 5 10
D23 ,, 2 c. deep slate-blue .. 8 10
a. Perf. 12 (9.3.65) .. 5 12
D24 ,, 4 c. bistre-brown .. 12 15
a. Perf. 12 (9.3.65) .. 5 15
D25 ,, 8 c. yellow-orge. (*p.* 12) (4.5.65) 15 30
D27 ,, 12 c. bright purple .. 25 35
a. Perf. 12 (4.5.65) .. 12 40
D28 ,, 20 c. deep blue 45 50
a. Perf. 12 (4.5.65) .. 20 50
D22/8 .. .. *Set of* 6 55 1·25

1965 (Jan.). *As No.* D19 *surch. locally with Type* D **2.**
D29 **D 1** 10 c. on 8 c. yellow-orge. 12 20

First supplies of this stamp differed from No. D19 in that they had been climatically affected but later a fresh printing of No. D19 was surcharged.

1967? *Unsurfaced paper. Wmk.* w.**12.** P 15×14.
D30 **D 1** 50 c. black .. ..

Nos. D22/9 were for use throughout Malaysia and Singapore. They were superseded on 15th August 1966 by the postage dues inscribed "MALAYSIA", but continued in use for Singapore until 31st January, 1968 when they were replaced by Singapore Postage Dues.

NEGRI SEMBILAN.

A State of the Federation of Malaya.

Negri
Sembilan
(1)

1891 (Aug?). T **5** *of Straits (wmk. Crown CA) optd. with* T **1.**
1 2 c. rose .. .. 90 1·10

2

3

1891–94. *Wmk. Crown CA.* P 14.
2 **2** 1 c. green (1893) 90 45
3 ,, 2 c. rose .. .. .. 1·25 1·25
4 ,, 5 c. blue (1894) .. .. 3·25 3·25
2/4 Optd. "Specimen" *Set of* 3 25·00

1896–99. *Wmk. Crown CA.* P 14.
5 **3** 1 c. dull purp. & green (1899) 90 1·00
6 ,, 2 c. dull purple and brown 3·50 3·00
7 ,, 3 c. dull purple and carmine 90 40
8 ,, 5 c. dull purp. & orge.-yell. 1·00 1·75
9 ,, 8 c. dull purple and ultram. 3·25 3·25
10 ,, 10 c. dull purple and orange 4·50 4·00
11 ,, 15 c. green and violet .. 5·00 3·75
12 ,, 20 c. green and olive .. 7·00 7·00
13 ,, 25 c. green and carmine .. 8·50 8·50
14 ,, 50 c. green and black .. 12·00 12·00
5/14 .. .. *Set of* 10 42·00 40·00
5/14 Optd. "Specimen" *Set of* 10 45·00

Four cents.
(4)

Four cents.
(5)

1898 (Dec.)–**1899.** (*a*) *Surch. as* T **4.**
15 **3** 1 c. on 15 c. green & violet 17·00 20·0
a. Inverted stop .. .. 55·00 60·0
16 **2** 4 c. on 1 c. green .. 55 1·0
17 **3** 4 c. on 3 c. dull pur. & carm. 1·25 1·4
a. Surcharge omitted (in pair with normal) .. £180 £18
b. Surcharge double .. .. £110 90·0
c. Surcharge inverted ..
d. "cents" repeated at left .. 32·00 32·0
e. "Four" repeated at right .. 32·00 32·0
f. Without bar .. £110
g. Bar double .. .. † £15
18 **2** 4 c. on 5 c. blue .. .. 50 1·0

On Nos. 15 and 17 the bar is at the top of th stamp.

(*b*) *Surch. as* T **5.**
19 **3** 4 c. on 8 c. dull purple and ultramarine (G.) (12.98) 1·00 1·1
a. Pair, one without surch. .. £225 £19
b. Surch. double £150
c. Surch. double (G. + R.) .. £200 £20
20 ,, 4 c. on 8 c. dull purple and ultramarine (Bk.) .. 65·00 65·0

6. Arms of Negri Sembilan. **7.**

1935–41. *Chalk-surfaced or ordinary paper* (O *Wmk. Mult. Script CA.* P 14.
21 **6** 1 c. black 25 1
22 ,, 2 c. green 35 1
23 ,, 2 c. orange 30 6
24 ,, 3 c. green 25 4
25 ,, 4 c. orange 15 1
26 ,, 5 c. brown 20 1
27 ,, 6 c. scarlet .. .. 1·00 1·0
a. Stop omitted at right (R. 10/9) 8·00 6·0
28 ,, 6 c. grey, O .. .. 60 3·0
a. Stop omitted at right (R. 10/9) 8·00 6·0
29 ,, 8 c. grey 50 1
30 ,, 10 c. dull purple .. 20 1
31 ,, 12 c. bright ultramarine .. 50 3
32 ,, 15 c. ultramarine, O .. 1·00 2·5
33 ,, 25 c. dull purple & scarlet 40 5
34 ,, 30 c. dull purple & orange 1·00 1·1
35 ,, 40 c. scarlet and dull purple 50 1·2
36 ,, 50 c. black/*emerald* 1·50 6
37 ,, $1 black and red/*blue* 75 9
38 ,, $2 green and scarlet 7·50 5·5
39 ,, $5 green & red/*emerald* .. 5·00 6·0
21/39 .. .. *Set of* 19 20·00 22·0
21/39 Perf. "Specimen" *Set of* 19 60·00

An 8 c. scarlet was issued but only with op during Japanese Occupation of Malaya. Unove printed specimens result from leakages.

Dates of issue:—2.12.35, 4 c., 8 c., 40 c 5.12.35, 5 c.; 1.1.36, 1 c., 2 c. grn., 10 c., 12 c 30 c.; 1.2.36, 50 c.; 1.4.36, 25 c., $1; 16.5.3 $2, $5; 1.1.37, 6 c. scar.; 21.8.41, 3 c.; 1.10.4 15 c.; 11.12.41, 2 c. orge; 18.12.41, 6 c. grey.

1948 (1 Dec.). *Royal Silver Wedding. As No* 30/1 *of Aden.*
40 10 c. violet 8
41 $5 green .. .. .. 5·00 6·0

1949 (1 Apr.)–**55.** *Chalk-surfaced paper. Wmk Mult. Script CA.* P 17½×18.
42 **7** 1 c. black 5
43 ,, 2 c. orange 5
44 ,, 3 c. green 8 2
45 ,, 4 c. brown 5
46 ,, 5 c. brt. pur. (*shades*) (1.9.52) 5 1
47 ,, 6 c. grey (*shades*) 5
48 ,, 8 c. scarlet 15 3
49 ,, 8 c. green (1.9.52) 8 2
50 ,, 10 c. purple 8 1
51 ,, 12 c. scarlet (1.9.52) .. 10 2
52 ,, 15 c. ultramarine 30 1
53 ,, 20 c. black and green .. 20 4
54 ,, 20 c. bright blue (1.9.52) .. 20 1
55 ,, 25 c. purple and orange .. 15 1
56 ,, 30 c. scar. & purple (5.9.55) 30 3

57 **7** 35 c. scar. & purple (1.9.52) 30 35
58 ,, 40 c. red and purple 30 75
59 ,, 50 c. black and blue 30 25
60 ,, $1 blue and purple .. 50 35
61 ,, $2 green and scarlet .. 1·50 55
62 ,, $5 green and brown .. 3·50 2·00
42/62 .. .. *Set of* 21 7·50 5·75

1949 (10 Oct.). *75th Anniv. of U.P.U. As Nos. 114/7 of Antigua.*
63 10 c. purple 10 10
64 15 c. deep blue 15 25
65 25 c. orange 30 35
66 50 c. blue-black 40 45

1953 (2 June). *Coronation. As No. 47 of Aden.*
67 10 c. black and reddish purple 8 8

1957–63. *As Nos. 92/102 of Kedah but with inset Arms of Negri Sembilan.*
68 **9** 1 c. black 5 5
69 **10** 2 c. orange-red 5 5
70 **11** 4 c. sepia 5 5
71 **12** 5 c. carmine-lake 5 5
72 **13** 8 c. myrtle-green 10 10
73 **14** 10 c. deep brown 5 5
74 ,, 10 c. deep maroon (10.1.61) 5 5
75 **15** 20 c. blue 10 8
76 **16** 50 c. black and blue (*p.* 12½) 30 15
a. Perf. 12½×13 (19.7.60) .. 25 20
77 **17** $1 ultram. & reddish pur. 55 45
78 **18** $2 brnz-grn. & scar. (*p.* 12½) 1·40 1·75
a. Perf. 13×12½ (15.1.63) .. 1·00 1·40
79 **19** $5 brn. & brz.-grn. (*p.* 12½) 3·00 2·00
a. Perf. 13×12½ (6.3.62) .. 2·75 1·75
b. P 13×12½. *Brown & yellow-olive* (13.11.62) 3·50 2·50
68/79 .. .. *Set of* 12 4·75 3·75

Dates of issue:—26.6.57, 20 c., $5; 25.7.57, 2 c., 50 c., $1; 4.8.57, 10 c.; 21.8.57, others.

The 6, 12, 25 and 30 c. values used in Negri Sembilan were Nos. 1/4 of Malayan Federation.

8. Tuanku Munawir.

(Photo. Enschedé & Sons.)

1961 (17 Apr.). *Installation of Tuanku Munawir as Yang di-Pertuan Besar of Negri Sembilan. No wmk. P* 14×13.
80 **8** 10 c. multicoloured .. 8 8

9. *Vanda hookeriana.*

1965 (15 Nov.). *As Nos. 166/72 of Johore but with Arms of Negri Sembilan inset and inscr.* "NEGERI SEMBILAN" *as in T* **9.** *W* w.**13** (*upright*).
81 1 c. multicoloured 5 5
82 2 c. multicoloured 5 5
83 5 c. multicoloured 5 5
84 6 c. multicoloured 5 5
85 10 c. multicoloured 5 5
86 15 c. multicoloured 5 5
87 20 c. multicoloured (*shades*) .. 8 8
81/87 .. .. *Set of* 7 30 30

The 2 c., 6 c., 15 c. and 20 c. exist with PVA gum as well as gum arabic.

The higher values used in Negri Sembilan were Nos. 20/27 of Malaysia.

See also No. 90.

10. Negri Sembilan Crest and Tuanku Ja'afar.

(Des. Z. Noor. Photo. Govt. Ptg. Bureau, Japan.)

1968 (8 Apr.). *Installation of Tuanku Ja'afar as Yang di-Pertuan Besar of Negri Sembilan. P* 13.
88 **10** 15 c. multicoloured .. 8 10
89 ,, 50 c. multicoloured .. 30 40

1970 (27 May.). *As No. 81 but with W* w.**13** (*sideways*).
90 **9** 1 c. multicoloured 12 12

11. Great Orange Tip.

1971 (1 Feb.). *As Nos. 175/81 of Johore but with Arms of Negri Sembilan and inscr. "negri sembilan", as in T* **11.**
91 1 c. multicoloured 5 5
92 2 c. multicoloured 5 5
93 5 c. multicoloured 5 5
94 6 c. multicoloured 5 5
95 10 c. multicoloured 5 5
96 15 c. multicoloured 8 8
97 20 c. multicoloured 8 8
91/97 .. .. *Set of* 7 25 25

The higher values used with this issue are Nos. 64/71 of Malaysia.

PAHANG.

A State of the Federation of Malaya.

1889–90. *T* **5, 6, 19** *and* **7** *of Straits (wmk. Crown CA) optd. or surch.*

PAHANG (A) PAHANG (B)

1889 (Jan.).
1 A 2 c. rose .. .. 10·00 10·00
2 ,, 8 c. orange £225 £225
3 ,, 10 c. slate .. .. 70·00 70·00

The 8 c. and 10 c. were overprinted in triplet form.

1889.
4 B 2 c. rose .. .. .. 1·75 2·00
a. Antique letters .. 65·00

The letters of the overprint on No. 4*a* are thinner and appear broader than those on No. 4.

PAHANG (C) PAHANG (D)

1890.
5 C 2 c. rose £225 £200
6 D 2 c. rose .. .. 10·00 7·00

1891. *Optd. as No. 6 and surch. with new value with bar through old value.*
7 Two CENTS on 24 c. green .. 50·00

No. 7 has the word "Two" as in No. 8 and "CENTS" as in No. 10, but in roman capitals.

PAHANG Two CENTS (E) PAHANG *Two* CENTS (F) PAHANG *Two* CENTS (G)

1891.
8 E 2 c. on 24 c. green .. .. 10·00 11·00
9 F 2 c. on 24 c. green .. .. 10·00 11·00
10 G 2 c. on 24 c. green .. .. 10·00 11·00

1 2

1891–95. *Wmk. Crown CA. P* 14.
11 **1** 1 c. green (1895) .. .. 90 1·00
12 ,, 2 c. rose 45 45
13 ,, 5 c. blue (1893) .. .. 1·10 1·75
11/13 Opt. "Specimen" *Set of* 3 25·00

1895–99. *Wmk. Crown CA. P* 14.
14 **2** 3 c. dull purple & carmine 55 40
15 ,, 4 c. dull pur. & car,. (1899) 75 65
16 ,, 5 c. dull pur. & olive-yellow 3·25 3·50
14/16 Optd. "Specimen" *Set of* 3 25·00

1897 (Aug.). *No.* 13 *divided diagonally, top half surch.* "3 c." *in MS., bottom half surch.* "2 c." *and* "5" *struck out in MS., both halves being initialled* "J.F.O." *in MS.*
17 **2** c. on half of 5 c. blue (R.) .. £110 90·00
a. Surch. in black .. .. — £300
b. Divided horiz. Surch. in red .. — 75·00
18 3 c. on half 5 c. blue (R.) .. £110 80·00
a. Surch. in black £350 £300
b. Divided horiz. Surch. in red .. — 75·00

The initials stand for John Fortescue Owen, District Treasurer at Kuala Lipis, where the provisionals were made.

Pahang. (3) Pahang. (4)

1898. *T* **31** *of Perak optd. with T* **3.**
19 10 c. dull purple and orange .. 5·00 6·00
20 25 c. green and carmine .. 7·00 8·00
21 50 c. green and black .. .. 15·00 13·00
22 50 c. dull pur. & greenish blk. 23·00 19·00

Nos. 72 and 75 of Perak, optd. with T **4.**
23 $1 green and pale green .. 20·00 20·00
24 $5 green and ultramarine .. 60·00 60·00

Pahang Four cents (5) Four cents. (6)

1898. *T* **31** *of Perak surch. with T* **5.**
25 4 c. on 8 c. dull pur. & ultram. 1·50 2·00
a. Surch. inverted £200 £150
b. Surch. double .. .. 90·00

T **5** *on plain paper (no stamp), but issued for postage.*
26 4 c. black .. .. .. — 90·00
27 5 c. black .. .. .. 75·00

1899. *No. 16 surch. with T* **6.**
28 4 c. on 5 c. dull purple and olive-yellow .. .. 4·00 4·00

7. Sultan Sir Abu Bakar.

8. Sultan Sir Abu Bakar.

1935–41. *Chalk-surfaced or ordinary paper* (O). *Wmk. Mult. Script. CA. P* 14.

29 **7** 1 c. black 10 20
30 ,, 2 c. green 25 20
31 ,, 3 c. green, OC 20 35
32 ,, 4 c. orange 10 20
33 ,, 5 c. brown 30 12
34 ,, 6 c. scarlet .. .. .. 1·00 1·00
35 ,, 8 c. grey 40 10
36 ,, 8 c. scarlet (11.12.41) .. 35 2·00
37 ,, 10 c. dull purple 15 12
38 ,, 12 c. bright ultramarine .. 75 85
39 ,, 15 c. ultramarine, O .. 60 2·25
40 ,, 25 c. dull purple and scarlet 75 60
41 ,, 30 c. dull purple and orange 45 75
42 ,, 40 c. scarlet and dull purple 50 1·10
43 ,, 50 c. black/*emerald* .. .. 1·75 80
44 ,, $1 black and red/*blue* .. 1·25 2·00
45 ,, $2 green and scarlet .. 8·00 8·00
46 ,, $5 green and red/*emerald* 4·00 8·00
29/46 .. .. *Set of* 18 20·00 26·00
29/46 Perf. "Specimen" *Set of* 18 60·00

A 2 c. orange and a 6 c. grey were prepared but not officially issued.

Dates of issue as for Negri Sembilan.

1948 (1 Dec.). *Royal Silver Wedding. As Nos.* 30/1 *of Aden.*

47 10 c. violet 8 10
48 $5 green .. .. .. 6·00 8·00

1949 (10 Oct.). *75th Anniv. of Universal Postal Union. As Nos.* 114/7 *of Antigua.*

49 10 c. purple 8 12
50 15 c. deep blue 10 20
51 25 c. orange 25 35
52 50 c. blue-black 40 55

1950 (1 June)–**55.** *Wmk. Mult. Script CA. Chalk-surfaced paper. P* 17½×18.

53 **8** 1 c. black 5 5
54 ,, 2 c. orange 5 5
55 ,, 3 c. green 20 15
56 ,, 4 c. brown (*shades*) .. 5 5
57 ,, 5 c. brt. pur. (*shades*) (1.9.52) 8 5
58 ,, 6 c. grey 8 10
59 ,, 8 c. scarlet 12 20
60 ,, 8 c. green (1.9.52) 12 20
61 ,, 10 c. magenta 5 5
62 ,, 12 c. scarlet (1.9.52) .. 15 25
63 ,, 15 c. ultramarine 15 20
64 ,, 20 c. black and green .. 20 40
65 ,, 20 c. bright blue (*shades*) (1.9.52) 25 25
66 ,, 25 c. purple and orange .. 20 12
67 ,, 30 c. scarlet and brown-purple (*shades*) (5.9.55) .. 35 30
68 ,, 35 c. scar. & purple (1.9.52) 40 45
69 ,, 40 c. red and purple 40 70
70 ,, 50 c. black and blue 30 20
71 ,, $1 blue and purple .. 70 70
72 ,, $2 green and scarlet .. 1·75 4·00
73 ,, $5 green & brn. (*shades*) 4·50 5·50
53/73 .. .. *Set of* 21 9·00 12·00

1953 (2 June). *Coronation. As No.* 47 *of Aden.*

74 10 c. black and reddish purple 5 5

1957–62. *As Nos.* 92/102 *of Kedah but with inset portrait of Sultan Sir Abu Bakar.*

75 **9** 1 c. black 5 5
76 **10** 2 c. orange-red 5 5
77 **11** 4 c. sepia 5 5
78 **12** 5 c. carmine-lake 5 5
79 **13** 8 c. myrtle-green 8 15
80 **14** 10 c. deep brown 5 5
81 ,, 10 c. dp. maroon (21.2.61) 5 5
82 **15** 20 c. blue 8 8
83 **16** 50 c. black and blue (*p.* 12½) 35 25
a. Perf. 12½×13 (17.5.60) .. 25 20
84 **17** $1 ultram. & reddish pur. 45 35
85 **18** $2 brz.-grn. & scar. (*p.* 12½) 85 1·00
a. Perf. 13×12½ (13.11.62) .. 80 1·00
86 **19** $5 brn. & brz.-grn. (*p.* 12½) 3·00 3·00
a. Perf. 13×12½ (17.5.60) .. 3·50 3·00
b. P 13×12½. *Brown and yellow-olive* (23.10.62) .. .. 4·25 3·50
75/86 .. .. *Set of* 12 4·50 4·50

The 6, 12, 25 and 30 c. values used in Pahang were Nos. 1/4 of Malayan Federation.

9. *Vanda hookeriana.*

1965 (15 Nov.). *As Nos.* 166/72 *of Johore but with inset portrait of Sultan Sir Abu Bakar as in T* **9.** *W* w.**13** (*upright*).

87 1 c. multicoloured 5 5
88 2 c. multicoloured 5 5
89 5 c. multicoloured 5 5
90 6 c. multicoloured 5 5
91 10 c. multicoloured 5 5
92 15 c. multicoloured 8 8
93 20 c. multicoloured 8 8
87/93 .. .. *Set of* 7 30 30

The 2 c., 5 c. and 6 c. exist with PVA gum as well as gum arabic.

The higher values used in Pahang were Nos. 20/27 of Malaysia.

1970 (27 May). *As Nos.* 87 *and* 91 *but W* w.**13** (*sideways*).

94 **9** 1 c. multicoloured 5 5
95 – 10 c. multicoloured 15 15

10. Blue Pansy Butterfly.

1971 (1 Feb.). *As Nos.* 175/81 *of Johore but with portrait of Sultan Sir Abu Bakar and arms, as in T* **10.**

96 1 c. multicoloured 5 5
97 2 c. multicoloured 5 5
98 5 c. multicoloured 5 5
99 6 c. multicoloured 5 5
100 10 c. multicoloured 5 5
101 15 c. multicoloured 8 8
102 20 c. multicoloured 8 8
96/102 .. .. *Set of* 7 25 25

The higher values used with this issue are Nos. 64/71 of Malaysia.

11. Sultan Haji Ahmad Shah.

(Des. Union Advertising, Kuala Lumpur. Litho. Harrison.)

1975 (8 May). *Installation of the Sultan. P* 14×14½.

103 **11** 10 c. slate-green, light lilac and gold 5 5
104 ,, 15 c. greenish black, yellow and deep green .. 8 8
105 ,, 50 c. black, light violet-blue & greenish blk. 20 20

PENANG.

A former British Settlement, now part of the Federation of Malaya.

1948 (1 Dec.). *Royal Silver Wedding. As Nos.* 30/1 *of Aden.*

1 10 c. violet 5 8
2 $5 brown .. .. .. 6·00 8·0

1949 (21 Feb.)–**52.** *As T* **58** *of Straits Settlements, but inscr.* "PENANG" *at foot. Wmk Mult. Script CA. Chalk-surfaced paper P* 17½×18.

3 1 c. black 5 5
4 2 c. orange 5 5
5 3 c. green 8 8
6 4 c. brown 5 5
7 5 c. bright purple (1.9.52) .. 8 1
8 6 c. grey 5
9 8 c. scarlet 15 3
10 8 c. green (1.9.52) 10 3
11 10 c. purple 5
12 12 c. scarlet (1.9.52) 12 2
13 15 c. ultramarine 12 1
14 20 c. black and green 20 2
15 20 c. bright blue (1.9.52) .. 15 1
16 25 c. purple and orange .. 12 1
17 35 c. scarlet & purple (1.9.52) . 25 3
18 40 c. red and purple 25 8
19 50 c. black and blue 25 1
20 $1 blue and purple .. 60 2
21 $2 green and scarlet .. 1·00 4
22 $5 green and brown .. 3·00 1·2
3/22 .. .. *Set of* 20 6·00 4·5

1949 (10 Oct). *75th Anniv. of U.P.U. As Nos* 114/7 *of Antigua.*

23 10 c. purple 5
24 15 c. deep blue 8 2
25 25 c. orange 25 3
26 50 c. blue-black 40 6

1953 (2 June). *Coronation. As No.* 47 *of Aden*

27 10 c. black and reddish purple 8

1954–55. *As T* **1** *of Malacca* (*Queen Elizabeth II, but inscr.* "PENANG" *at foot. Chalk-surfaced paper. Wmk. Mult. Script CA. P* 17½×18.

28 1 c. black 5
29 2 c. yellow-orange 5
30 4 c. brown (*shades*) 8
31 5 c. bright purple (*shades*) .. 5
32 6 c. grey 12 1
33 8 c. green 12 1
34 10 c. brown-purple 8
35 12 c. rose-red 12 1
36 20 c. bright blue 25 1
37 25 c. brn.-purple & yell.-orange 30 1
38 30 c. rose-red & brown-purple 35 2
39 35 c. rose-red & brown-purple 45 3
40 50 c. black and bright blue .. 45 1
41 $1 brt. blue & brown-purple 65 3
42 $2 emerald and scarlet .. 1·40 8
43 $5 emerald and brown .. 5·50 2·5
28/43 .. .. *Set of* 16 9·00 4·7

Dates of issue: 1954—9 June, 6 c.; 1 Sept. 4 c., 10 c., 20 c.; 8 Sept., 2 c., 35 c.; 1 Oct., 5 c. $1, $2; 1 Dec., 25 c., 50 c. 1955—5 Jan., 1 c. 8 c., 12 c., $5; 5 Sept., 30 c.

1957. *As Nos.* 92/102 *of Kedah, but with inse portrait of Queen Elizabeth II.*

44 **9** 1 c. black 5
45 **10** 2 c. orange-red 5
46 **11** 4 c. sepia 5
47 **12** 5 c. carmine-lake 5
48 **13** 8 c. myrtle-green 8
49 **14** 10 c. deep brown 5
50 **15** 20 c. blue 15
51 **16** 50 c. black and blue .. 25 1
52 **17** $1 ultram. & reddish pur. 60 3
53 **18** $2 bronze-green & scarlet 1·50 1·5
54 **19** $5 brown & bronze-green 3·00 1·7
44/54 .. .. *Set of* 11 5·00 3·7

Dates of issue:—26.6.57, 20 c., $5; 25.7.57 2 c., 50 c., $1; 4.8.57, 10 c.; 21.8.57, others.

The note after No. 86 of Pahang also applie here.

1. Copra.

(Recess. De La Rue.)

1960 (15 MAR.). *As Nos. 44/54 but with inset Arms of Penang as in T* **1**. *W* w.**12**. *P* 13×12½ (1 *c. to* 8 *c.*, $2, $5), 12½×13 (10 *c. to* 50 *c.*) *or* 13½ ($1).

55 1 c. black 5 8
56 2 c. orange-red 5 8
57 4 c. sepia 5 5
58 5 c. carmine-lake 5 5
59 8 c. myrtle-green 5 8
60 10 c. deep maroon 5 5
61 20 c. blue 8 5
62 50 c. black and blue 20 5
63 $1 ultram. & reddish purple 40 20
64 $2 bronze-green and scarlet 80 55
65 $5 brown and bronze-green 2·25 1·00
55/65 .. .. *Set of* 11 3·50 1·75

2. *Vanda hookeriana.*

1965 (15 NOV.). *As Nos.* 166/72 *of Johore but with Arms of Penang inset and inscr.* "PULAU PINANG" *as in T* **2**. *W* w.**13** (*upright*).

66 1 c. multicoloured 5 5
67 2 c. multicoloured 5 5
68 5 c. multicoloured 5 5
a. Blue (background and inscr.) omitted .. .. .. 40·00
69 6 c. multicoloured 5 5
70 10 c. multicoloured (*shades*) .. 5 5
71 15 c. multicoloured 8 5
a. Green (value and leaves) omitted .. .. .. 40·00
72 20 c. multicoloured 8 8
66/72 .. .. *Set of* 7 35 30

The 2 c., 5 c., 6 c., 10 c. and 20 c. exist with PVA gum as well as gum arabic.

The higher values used in Penang were Nos. 20/27 of Malaysia.

1970. *As Nos.* 66 *and* 70 *but W* w.**13** (*sideways*).

73 **2** 1 c. mult. (27.5.70) .. 5 5
74 – 10 c. mult. (20.11.70) .. 10 10

3. Wanderer.

1971 (1 FEB.). *As Nos.* 175/81 *of Johore but with arms of Penang and inscr.* "pulau pinang", *as in T* **3**.

75 1 c. multicoloured 5 5
76 2 c. multicoloured 5 5
77 5 c. multicoloured 5 5
78 6 c. multicoloured 5 5
79 10 c. multicoloured 5 5
80 15 c. multicoloured 8 5
81 20 c. multicoloured 8 5
75/81 .. .. *Set of* 7 25 20

The higher values used with this issue are Nos. 64/71 of Malaysia.

PERAK.

A State of the Federation of Malaya.

1878. *T* **5** *of Straits Settlements optd. with Crescent, Star and* "P" *in an oval. Wmk. Crown CC.*

1 2 c. brown £250 £170

PERAK (1) Variety (*f*).
PERAK (2)

1880–81. *T* **5** *of Straits, Wmk. Crown CC, optd. as T* **1**.
Varieties. (*a*) *All letters wide.* (*b*) *All letters wide, but close together.* (*c*) "R" *narrow.* (*d*) "R" *and* "A" *narrow.* (*e*) "P" *and* "K" *wide.* (*f*) *All letters narrow.* (*g*) *All letters narrow, but close together.*

2 **1** 2 c. brown (*a*) .. .. — 35·00
3 „ 2 c. brown (*b*) .. .. — 32·00
4 „ 2 c. brown (*c*) .. .. 13·00 14·00
5 „ 2 c. brown (*d*) .. .. 13·00 14·00
6 „ 2 c. brown (*e*) .. .. 30·00 27·00
7 „ 2 c. brown (*f*) .. .. 13·00 14·00
8 „ 2 c. brown (*g*) .. .. 35·00 32·00

Variety (*a*) is a single unit setting (1880). Triplet settings are as follows:—1880 (*b*)+(*b*)+(*b*); 1881 (*d*)+(*c*)+(*c*); 1881 (*c*)+(*c*)+(*e*). Variety (*g*) (1880) may be either a single unit or a triplet setting. Variety (*f*) (1881) is probably a triplet setting.

1881. *Same type and wmk., optd. with T* **2**.

9 **2** 2 c. brown .. .. .. 3·50 3·75

1882–83. *Same type optd. as T* **1**, *Wmk. Crown CA.*
Varieties. (*h*) "E" *wide* (*k*) "A" *wide.*

10 **1** 2 c brown (*f*) .. .. 3·00 3·25
a. Opt. double .. ..
11 „ 2 c. rose (*f*) .. .. .. 2·25 2·50
12 „ 2 c. rose (*h*) .. .. .. 2·25 2·50
a. Opt. double .. ..
13 „ 2 c. rose (*k*) .. .. .. 2·40 2·40

Triplet settings are as follows:—1882, 2 c. brown (*f*)+(*f*)+(*f*). 1883, 2 c. rose (*f*)+(*k*)+(*h*); (*h*)+(*f*)+(*f*); (*h*)+(*f*)+(*k*).

2 CENTS PERAK (3)
2 CENTS PERAK (3*a*)

Same type surch. or optd. Wmk. Crown CA.

1883 (JULY). *Surch. vertically upwards.*
(*a*) "E" *of* "PERAK" *wide* (1¾ *mm.*).

14 **3** 2 c. on 4 c. rose .. .. 60·00 45·00

(*b*) *All letters narrow* ("E" 1½ *mm. wide*).

15 **3** 2 c. on 4 c. rose .. .. 50·00 40·00

Setting composed of two separate triplets, one for "2 CENTS" and one for "PERAK", the latter composed of two units of No. 15 and one of No. 14. This setting was employed on the lower nine rows of the sheet.

(*c*) *Unified surch.* ("2 CENTS" *spaced* 19¾×3¼ *mm. and* "PERAK" *set closer*).

15*a* **3*a*** 2 c. on 4 c. rose .. ..
ab. On Straits No. 12 (wmk. Crown CC) .. ..

It is believed that T **3*a*** was used only in the top row of the sheet.

PERAK (4)
PERAK (5)
PERAK (6)
PERAK (7)
1 CENT (7*a*)

1884–90.

16 **4** 2 c. rose ("E" wide) .. 45 55
a. "PERAK" double .. — £120
b. "PERAK" inverted .. 55·00
17 „ 2 c. rose ("E" narrow) .. 3·00 4·00
a. "PERAK" inverted .. 65·00 60·00

Triplet settings occur of:—1884. Nos. 17+16+16; Nos. 16+16+16. There is a setting of 30 (3×10) (1888) which contained two units of No. 17, also several settings of 60 (6×10) (1888–90) one of which contained three units of No. 17.

The variety "PERAK" inverted occurs in a triple setting and also in one setting of 60.

1886.

18 **5** 2 c. rose 30 50
a. Error. "FERAK" .. 35·00 35·00
19 **6** 2 c. rose 45 90
a. Opt. double .. ..
20 **7** 2 c. rose .. .. .. 8·00 9·00

No. 18a is usually found with the "F" altered in ink to "P".

Nos. 19 and 20 are each triplet settings.

1886? *No.* 16 *surch. with T* **7*a***.

20*a* **5** 1 c. on 2 c. rose .. ..

ONE CENT PERAK (8)
1 CENT PERAK (9)

1886. *Surch vertically. No stop.*

21 **8** 1 c. on 2 c. rose .. .. 85·00

As last, but stop after "PERAK".

22 1 c. on 2 c. rose .. .. 5·00 5·00
a. Surch. double .. ..
23 1 c. on 2 c. (letters "N" wide) .. .. .. 5·00 5·00

A triplet setting composed of Nos. 22+23+22.

1886.

24 **9** 1 c. on 2 c. rose .. .. 6·00 6·50
a. Surch. double .. ..

A triplet setting.

One CENT PERAK (10)
ONE CENT PERAK (11)

1886.

25 **10** 1 c. on 2 c. rose 45 55
a. Error. "One" inverted .. £150
b. Surch. double .. £150

A triplet setting. The error occurred in the third unit on part of the printing only.

1887. *Surch. vertically.*

26 **11** 1 c. on 2 c. rose (B.) .. 3·75 4·00
27 „ 1 c. on 2 c. rose (Bk.) .. £160 £160

I CENT PERAK (12)
1 CENT PERAK (13)

1886.

28 **12** 1 c. on 2 c. rose .. .. 55·00 55·00

The figure "I" in *T* **12** is a small roman character. A triplet setting.

1897.

29 **13** 1 c. on 2 c. rose £150

One CENT PERAK (14)
PERAK ONE CENT. (15)
One CENT PERAK (16)

1887–90.

30 **14** 1 c. on 2 c. rose 25 40
a. Surch. double .. ..

The first printings were in triplet form. Another printing was in a setting of 30 (3×10). In later printings it formed the upper five rows of settings of 60.

1889. *As No.* 30, *but with seriffed italic* "K".

31 1 c. on 2 c. rose .. .. 11·00

1889. *Surch. as T* **14**, *but* "CENT" *in roman* (*upright*) *letters as in T* **17**.

32 1 c. on 2 c. rose .. .. 85·00 85·00

1889.

33 **15** 1 c. on 2 c. rose .. .. 11·00 10·00
34 **16** 1 c. on 2 c. rose .. .. 9·00 9·50

One CENT PERAK (17)
One CENT PERAK (18)
One CENT PERAK. (19)

1889–90.

35 **17** 1 c. on 2 c. rose .. .. 2·50 2·75
a. Error. "PREAK" .. 60·00 60·00
36 **18** 1 c. on 2 c. rose .. .. 1·60 1·60
37 **19** 1 c. on 2 c. rose .. .. 1·60 1·60

PERAK

PERAK ONE CENT (20) One CENT PERAK (21) PERAK (22)

1890.

38 **20** 1 c. on 2 c. rose .. .. — 35·00
39 **21** 1 c. on 2 c. rose .. .. 3·00 2·50

1891.

40 **22** 2 c. rose .. .. .. 2·75 3·75

1891. *Optd.* " PERAK " *only, in bold roman letters* $2\frac{3}{4}$ *mm. high and* 13 *mm. long.*

41 2 c. rose .. .. ..

PERAK One CENT (23) PERAK Two CENTS (24) PERAK One CENT (25)

PERAK One CENT (26) PERAK One CENT (27) PERAK One CENT (28)

PERAK One CENT (29)

1891. *Variously surch. with bar through original value.*

42 **23** 1 c. on 2 c. rose 35 40
 a. Narrow " O " in " One " .. 2·00 2·25
 b. Without bar .. .. 35·00
 c. No bar and narrow " O " ..
43 **25** 1 c. on 2 c. rose .. .. 85 1·00
 a. Without bar £100
44 **26** 1 c. on 2 c. rose 25 40
 a. Without bar .. .. 60·00
45 **27** 1 c. on 2 c. rose .. .. 85 1·10
 a. Without bar £100
46 **23** 1 c. on 6 c. lilac .. .. 4·00 4·00
47 **26** 1 c. on 6 c. lilac .. .. 5·50 6·00
48 **27** 1 c. on 6 c. lilac .. .. 5·50 6·00
49 **28** 1 c. on 6 c. lilac .. .. 5·50 6·00
50 **29** 1 c. on 6 c. lilac .. .. 7·00 7·00
51 **24** 2 c. on 24 c. green .. .. 1·60 1·60
52 **26** 2 c. on 24 c. green .. .. 4·00 4·00
53 **27** 2 c. on 24 c. green .. .. 4·50 4·50
54 **28** 2 c. on 24 c. green .. .. 6·00 6·00
55 **29** 2 c. on 24 c. green .. .. 4·75 4·75

30

3 CENTS (30*a*)

1892 (1 JAN.)–**95.** *Wmk. Crown CA. P* 14.

57 **30** 1 c. green 35 12
58 ,, 2 c. rose 50 25
59 ,, 2 c. orange (9.9.95) 15 80
60 ,, 5 c. blue 45 80
57/60 Optd. " Specimen " *Set of* 4 32·00

1895 (18 APR.). *Surch. with T* **30a.**

61 **30** 3 c. on 5 c. rose (Optd. S. £11) 25 50

31

32

1895–99. *P* 14. (*a*) *T* **31.** *Wmk. Crown CA.*

62 1 c. dull purple and green .. 20 25
63 2 c. dull purple and brown .. 35 20
64 3 c. dull purple and carmine .. 60 15
65 4 c. dull purple & carm. (1899) 90 1·10
66 5 c. dull purple & olive-yellow 85 35
67 8 c. dull purple and ultram. .. 2·00 40
68 10 c. dull purple and orange .. 2·00 55
69 25 c. green and carmine .. 11·00 4·00
70 50 c. dull pur. & greenish black 8·00 5·00
71 50 c. green and black (1899) .. 14·00 9·00

(*b*) *T* **32.** *Wmk. Crown CC.*

72 $1 green and pale green .. 18·00 13·00
73 $2 green and carmine .. 25·00 19·00
74 $3 green and ochre .. .. 23·00 17·00
75 $5 green and ultramarine .. 80·00 38·00
76 $25 green and orange (S. £40) £450 £150
62/72 .. .. *Set of* 11 55·00 30·00
62/75 Optd. " Specimen " *Set of* 14 75·00

One Cent. (33) ONE CENT. (34)

Three Cent. (35) Three Cent. (36)

1900. *Stamps of* 1895–99 *surch.*

77 **33** 1 c. on 2 c. dull pur. & brn. 15 20
 a. Antique " e " in " One " .. 9·00
 b. Antique " e " in " Cent " .. 8·00
78 **34** 1 c. on 4 c. dull pur. & carm. 15 30
79 **33** 1 c. on 5 c. dull purple and olive-yellow 20 40
 a. Antique " e " in " One " .. 9·00
 b. Antique " e " in " Cent " .. 8·00 5·00
80 **35** 3 c. on 8 c. dull pur. & ult. 50 70
 a. Antique " e " in " Cent " .. 10·00
 b. No stop after " Cent " .. 12·00
 c. Surch. double .. .. 32·00
81 ,, 3 c. on 50 c. green & black 40 70
 a. Antique " e " in " Cent " .. 13·00
 b. No stop after " Cent " .. 12·00
82 **36** 3 c. on $1 grn. & pale grn. 7·50 8·50
 a. Small " t " in " Cent " .. 26·00 26·00
 b. Surch. double .. ..
83 ,, 3 c. on $2 green & carmine 4·25 6·00
77/83 .. .. *Set of* 7 12·00 15·00

37. Sultan Iskandar. **38.**

1935–37. *Chalk-surfaced paper. Wmk. Mult. Script CA. P* 14.

84 **37** 1 c. black 12 8
85 ,, 2 c. green 8 8
86 ,, 4 c. orange 15 8
87 ,, 5 c. brown 8 8
88 ,, 6 c. scarlet 70 70
89 ,, 8 c. grey 30 12
90 ,, 10 c. dull purple 8 8
91 ,, 12 c. bright ultramarine .. 40 60
92 ,, 25 c. dull purple and scarlet 35 35
93 ,, 30 c. dull purple & orange 50 75
94 ,, 40 c. scarlet and dull purple 1·10 1·40
95 ,, 50 c. black/*emerald* .. 1·10 80
96 ,, $1 black and red/*blue* .. 1·00 90
97 ,, $2 green and scarlet .. 3·00 2·50
98 ,, $5 green & red/*emerald* .. 8·00 6·00
84/98 .. .. *Set of* 15 15·00 13·00
84/98 Perf. " Specimen " *Set of* 15 45·00

Dates of issue as for Negri Sembilan.

1938–41. *Chalk-surfaced or ordinary paper* (O). *Wmk. Mult. Script CA. P* 14.

99 **38** 1 c. black 15 10
100 ,, 2 c. green 35 12
101 ,, 2 c. orange, OC 15 40
102 ,, 3 c. green, OC 15 30
103 ,, 4 c. orange 30 10
104 ,, 5 c. brown 8 8
105 ,, 6 c. scarlet .. .. 2·00 10
106 ,, 8 c. grey 35 8
107 ,, 8 c. scarlet .. .. 55 1·40
108 ,, 10 c. dull purple 50 10
109 ,, 12 c. bright ultramarine .. 90 90
110 ,, 15 c. bright ultram., O .. 70 3·00
111 ,, 25 c. dull pur. and scarlet 2·50 90
112 ,, 30 c. dull purple & orange 35 70
113 ,, 40 c. scarlet & dull purple 1·25 90
114 ,, 50 c. black/*emerald* .. 55 60
115 ,, $1 black and red/*blue* .. 5·00 4·00
116 ,, $2 green and scarlet .. 10·00 9·00
117 ,, $5 green & red/*emerald* 22·00 24·00
99/117 .. .. *Set of* 19 42·00 42·00
99/117 Perf. " Specimen " *Set of* 19 60·00

Dates of issue:—2.5.38, 40 c.; 17.10.38, 10 c., 12 c., 30 c. and 50 c.; 1.12.38, 8 c. grey; 13.1.39, 2 c. green; 1.2.39, 5 c.; –.4.39, 1 c.; –.5.39, 4 c.; –.–.39, 6 c. and 25 c.; –.–.40, $1; –.9.40, $2; –.1.41, $5; 30.10.41, 2 c. orge; –.–.41, 3 c., 8 c. scarlet and 15 c.

1948 (1 DEC.). *Royal Silver Wedding. As Nos.* 30/1 *of Aden.*

118 10 c. violet 5 8
119 $5 green .. .. .. 5·00 7·00

1949 (10 OCT.). *75th Anniv. of Universal Postal Union. As Nos.* 114/7 *of Antigua.*

120 10 c. purple 5 5
121 15 c. deep blue 8 15
122 25 c. orange 25 35
123 50 c. blue-black 50 60

39. Sultan Yussuf 'Izzuddin Shah.

1950 (17 AUG.)–**55.** *Chalk-surfaced paper. Wmk Mult. Script CA. P* $17\frac{1}{2}\times18$.

124 **39** 1 c. black 5 5
125 ,, 2 c. orange 5 5
126 ,, 3 c. green (*shades*) .. 20 10
127 ,, 4 c. brown (*shades*) .. 5 5
128 ,, 5 c. brt. purple (*shades*) (1.9.52) 5 5
129 ,, 6 c. grey 5 5
130 ,, 8 c. scarlet 12 20
131 ,, 8 c. green (1.9.52) .. 15 20
132 ,, 10 c. purple (*shades*) .. 8 5
133 ,, 12 c. scarlet (1.9.52) .. 15 20
134 ,, 15 c. ultramarine 20 10
135 ,, 20 c. black and green .. 20 10
136 ,, 20 c. bright blue (1.9.52) .. 20 10
137 ,, 25 c. purple and orange .. 12 8
138 ,, 30 c. scarlet & pur. (5.9.55) 30 20
139 ,, 35 c. scarlet & pur. (1.9.52) 25 25
140 ,, 40 c. red and purple .. 40 40
141 ,, 50 c. black and blue .. 25 8
142 ,, $1 blue and purple .. 70 35
143 ,, $2 green and scarlet .. 1·50 70
144 ,, $5 green and brown .. 3·50 2·50
124/44 .. .. *Set of* 21 8·00 5·00

1953 (2 JUNE). *Coronation. As No.* 47 *of Aden.*

145 10 c. black & reddish purple 8 5

1957–61. *As Nos.* 92/102 *of Kedah but with inset portrait of Sultan Yussuf 'Izzuddin Shah.*

146 1 c. black 5 5
147 2 c. orange-red 5 5
 a. *Red-orange* (16.12.59) .. 5 5
148 4 c. sepia 5 5
149 5 c. carmine-lake 5 5
150 8 c. myrtle-green 8 8
151 10 c. deep brown 5 5
152 10 c. deep maroon 5 5
153 20 c. blue 8 5
154 50 c. black and blue (*p.* $12\frac{1}{2}$) 20 8
 a. Perf. $12\frac{1}{2}\times13$ (24.5.60) .. 25 10

155 $1 ultramarine and reddish purple 40 15
156 $2 brz.-grn. & scar. (p. 12½) 85 65
a. Perf. 13 × 12½ (21.2.61) .. 80 45
157 $5 brn. & brz.-grn. (p. 12½) 2·25 1·25
a. Perf. 13 × 12½ (24.5.60) .. 2·00 1·00
146/57 .. .. Set of 12 3·50 1·75

Dates of issue:—26.6.57, 20 c., $5; 25.7.57, 2 c., 50 c., $1; 4.8.57, 10 c. brown; 21.2.61, 10 c. maroon; 21.8.57, others.

The 6, 12, 25 and 30 c. values used in Perak were Nos. 1/4 of Malayan Federation.

40. Sultan Idris Shah.

(Photo. Harrison.)

1963 (26 Oct.). *Installation of the Sultan of Perak.* W w. **13**. *P* 14½.
158 **40** 10 c. red, black, blue & yell. 5 5

41. *Vanda hookeriana.*

1965 (15 Nov.). *As Nos. 166/72 of Johore but with inset portrait of Sultan Idris as in T* **41**. *W* w.**13** (*upright*).

159	1 c. multicoloured	5	5
160	2 c. multicoloured	5	5
161	5 c. multicoloured (*shades*)	5	5
162	6 c. multicoloured	5	5
163	10 c. multicoloured	5	5
164	15 c. multicoloured	5	5
	a. Magenta (background) omitted	40·00	
	b. Black (country name and head) omitted	50·00	
165	20 c. multicoloured	8	8
	a. Bright purple (blooms) omitted		
159/65	.. .. Set of 7	30	30

No. 164b comes from a horizontal strip of three, the centre stamp having the black completely omitted. The two outer stamps show the colour partly omitted.

The 2 c. to 15 c. exist with PVA gum as well as gum arabic.

The higher values used in Perak were Nos. 20/27 of Malaysia.

1970. *As Nos.* 159 *and* 163 *but W* w.**13** (*sideways*).
166 **41** 1 c. mult. (27.5.70) .. 5 5
167 – 10 c. mult. (20.11.70) .. 10 10

42. Malayan Jezebel.

1971 (1 Feb.). *As Nos. 175/81 of Johore but with portrait of Sultan Idris and arms, as in T* **42**.

168	1 c. multicoloured	5	5
169	2 c. multicoloured	5	5
170	5 c. multicoloured	5	5
171	6 c. multicoloured	5	5
172	10 c. multicoloured	5	5
173	15 c. multicoloured	8	5
174	20 c. multicoloured	8	8
168/74	.. .. Set of 7	25	20

The higher values used with this issue are Nos. 64/71 of Malaysia.

OFFICIAL STAMPS.

P.G.S. (O 1)   Service. (O 2)

1889 (1 Nov.). *Stamps of Straits Settlements optd. with Type* O **1**.

O1	2 cents, CA, rose	1·10	1·10
	a. Overprint double	£300	£300
	b. No stop after "S"	9·00	
	c. Wide space between "G" & "S"	10·00	
O2	4 cents, CA, brown	2·00	3·00
	a. No stop after "S"	18·00	
	b. Wide space between "G" & "S"	15·00	
O3	6 cents, CA, lilac	6·00	8·00
	a. Wide space between "G" & "S"	18·00	
O4	8 cents, CA, orange	6·50	8·50
	a. Wide space between "G" & "S"	18·00	
O5	10 cents, CA, slate	10·00	10·00
	a. Wide space between "G" & "S"	25·00	25·00
O6	12 cents, CC, blue	20·00	
	a. Wide space between "G" & "S"	60·00	
O7	12 cents, CA, brown-purple ..	30·00	
	a. Wide space between "G" & "S"	60·00	
O8	24 cents, CC, green	70·00	
	a. Wide space between "G" & "S"	£150	
O9	24 cents, CA, green	20·00	
	a. Wide space between "G" & "S"	60·00	

1894 (1 June) *No. 60 optd. with Type* O **2**.
O10 5 c. blue .. .. 2·50 35
a. Overprint inverted .. .. 32·00 32·00

1897. *No. 66 optd. with Type* O **2**.
O11 5 c. dull purple & olive-yell. 50 12
a. Overprint double .. .. 25·00 25·00

PERLIS.

A State of the Federation of Malaya.

1948 (1 Dec.). *Royal Silver Wedding. As Nos. 30/1 of Aden, but inscr.* "MALAYA PERLIS".
1 10 c. violet 5 8
2 $5 brown .. .. .. 5·00 7·00

1949 (10 Oct.). *75th Anniv. of U.P.U. As Nos. 114/7 of Antigua, but inscr.* "MALAYA PERLIS".

3	10 c. purple	8	20
4	15 c. deep blue	10	30
5	25 c. orange	25	40
6	50 c. blue-black	40	55

1. Raja Syed Putra.

1951 (26 Mar.)–**55**. *Chalk-surfaced paper. Wmk. Mult. Script. CA. P* 17½ × 18.

7	**1**	1 c. black	5	8
8	,,	2 c. orange	5	8
9	,,	3 c. green	35	40
10	,,	4 c. brown	5	8
11	,,	5 c. bright purple (1.9.52) ..	5	5
12	,,	6 c. grey	5	8
13	,,	8 c. scarlet	25	30
14	,,	8 c. green (1.9.52)	30	35
15	,,	10 c. purple	10	5
16	,,	12 c. scarlet (1.9.52)	10	25
17	,,	15 c. ultramarine	45	55
18	,,	20 c. black and green ..	60	60
19	,,	20 c. bright blue (1.9.52) ..	25	25
20	,,	25 c. purple and orange ..	25	25
21	,,	30 c. scarlet & purple (5.9.55)	40	45
22	,,	35 c. scarlet & purple (1.9.52)	40	50
23	,,	40 c. red and purple	55	65
24	,,	50 c. black and blue	35	35
25	,,	$1 blue and purple	1·25	1·75
26	,,	$2 green and scarlet	1·75	2·75
27	,,	$5 green and brown	4·00	6·00
7/27		.. .. Set of 21	10·00	14·00

1953 (2 June). *Coronation. As No. 47 of Aden.*
28 10 c. black and reddish purple 15 15

1957–62. *As Nos. 92/102 of Kedah but with inset portrait of Raja Syed Putra.*

29	**9**	1 c. black	5	5
30	**10**	2 c. orange-red	5	5
31	**11**	4 c. sepia	5	5
32	**12**	5 c. carmine-lake	5	5
33	**13**	8 c. myrtle-green	8	15
34	**14**	10 c. deep brown	8	8
35	,,	10 c. deep maroon (14.3.61)	5	5
36	**15**	20 c. blue	8	8
37	**16**	50 c. black and blue (p. 12½)	25	35
		a. Perf. 12½ × 13 (8.5.62) ..	20	20
38	**17**	$1 ultram. & reddish pur.	50	65
39	**18**	$2 bronze-green & scarlet	95	95
40	**19**	$5 brown & bronze-green	2·25	2·25
29/40		.. .. Set of 12	3·75	4·25

Dates of issue:—26.6.57, 20 c., $5; 25.7.57, 2 c., 50 c., $1; 4.8.57, 10 c.; 21.8.57, others.

The 6, 12, 25 and 30 c. values used in Perlis were Nos. 1/4 of Malayan Federation.

2. *Vanda hookeriana.*

1965 (15 Nov.). *As Nos. 166/72 of Johore but with inset portrait of Tunku Bendahara Abu Bakar as in T* **2**.

41	1 c. multicoloured	5	5
42	2 c. multicoloured	5	5
43	5 c. multicoloured	5	5
44	6 c. multicoloured	5	5
45	10 c. multicoloured	5	5
46	15 c. multicoloured	8	8
47	20 c. multicoloured	8	10
41/7	.. .. Set of 7	35	35

The 6 c. exists with PVA gum as well as gum arabic.

The higher values used in Perlis were Nos. 20/27 of Malaysia.

3. Black-veined Tiger.

1971 (1 Feb.). *As Nos. 175/81 of Johore but with portrait of Sultan Syed Putra and Arms, as in T* **3**.

48	1 c. multicoloured	5	5
49	2 c. multicoloured	5	5
50	5 c. multicoloured	5	5
51	6 c. multicoloured	5	5
52	10 c. multicoloured	5	5
53	15 c. multicoloured	8	8
54	20 c. multicoloured	8	8
48/54	.. .. Set of 7	25	25

The higher values used with this issue are Nos. 64/71 of Malaysia.

4. Raja Syed Putra.

(Des. Citizen Studio & Engravers, Kuala Lumpur. Litho. Enschedé.)

1971 (28 Mar.). *25th Anniv. of Installation of Raja Syed Putra. P* 13½×13.

55 **4** 10 c. multicoloured 5 5
56 ,, 15 c. multicoloured 8 8
57 ,, 50 c. multicoloured 20 20

SELANGOR.

A State of the Federation of Malaya.

SELANGOR
(1)

1881–82. *T* **5** *of Straits, wmk. Crown CC, optd. as T* **1.**
Varieties. (a) *All letters narrow.* (b) " S " *wide.* (c) " S ", " E ", " A ", *and* " N " *wide.* (d) " SELAN " *wide.* (e) " SEL " *and* " N " *wide.* (f) " EL " *wide.* (g) " E " *wide.* (s) " N " *wide.*

1 **1** 2 c. brown (a) .. .. .. 5·50 6·00
a. " S " inverted .. .. 26·00
2 ,, 2 c. brown (b) .. .. .. 6·50 7·50
3 ,, 2 c. brown (c) .. .. .. 14·00
4 ,, 2 c. brown (d) .. .. .. 14·00
5 ,, 2 c. brown (e) .. .. .. 14·00
6 ,, 2 c. brown (s) .. .. .. — 60·00

Overprinted in triplets composed of: 1881. (a)+(b)+(a); 1881. (b)+(a)+(a); 1882. (c)+(e)+(d). The setting containing (s) (1881) is not known.

1882. *Same type, wmk. Crown CA, optd. with capital* " S ".
7 2 c. brown .. .. .. — £300

1882–83. *T* **5** *of Straits, wmk. Crown CA. optd. as T* **1.**
Varieties. (i) " SEL ", " N ", *and* " G " *wide.* (j). " E " *and* " ANG " *wide.* (k) " ELANG " *wide.* (l) " SE " *and* " N " *wide.* (m) " S " *and* " N " *wide.* (n) " S " *and* " A " *wide.* (o) " S " *and* " L " *wide.*

8 **1** 2 c. brown (a) .. .. — 10·00
9 ,, 2 c. brown (b) .. .. 11·00 11·00
10 ,, 2 c. brown (f) .. .. — 16·00
11 ,, 2 c. brown (g) .. .. 14·00 14·00
12 ,, 2 c. brown (i) .. .. 14·00 14·00
13 ,, 2 c. brown (j) .. .. 14·00 14·00
14 ,, 2 c. brown (k) .. .. 14·00 14·00
15 ,, 2 c. brown (l) .. .. 9·00 9·00
16 ,, 2 c. brown (m) .. .. 9·00 9·00
17 ,, 2 c. brown (n) .. .. — 24·00
18 ,, 2 c. brown (o) .. .. — 75·00

Triplets are known of: 1882. (i)+(j)+(k); 1883. (n)+(g)+(f); 1883. (l)+(b)+(m). 1882. (b)+(a)+(?) are known in a pair; 1883. (o) is the first unit of a triplet but the second and third units are not yet known.

1883–85. *Wmk. Crown CA.*
Varieties. (p) " E " *and* " A " *wide.* (q) " A " *wide.* (r) " L " *wide.* (s) " N " *wide.* (t) *all letters wide.* (u) " A " *narrow.* (v) " L " *narrow.*

19 **1** 2 c. rose (b) .. .. .. 6·50 7·00
20 ,, 2 c. rose (f) .. .. .. 5·50 5·50
21 ,, 2 c. rose (g) .. .. .. 5·50 6·00
22 ,, 2 c. rose (o) .. .. .. 7·00 7·00
23 ,, 2 c. rose (p) .. .. .. 6·50 7·00
24 ,, 2 c. rose (q) .. .. .. 8·00 7·50
25 ,, 2 c. rose (r) .. .. .. 9·00 8·00
26 ,, 2 c. rose (s) .. .. .. 7·00 7·00
27 ,, 2 c. rose (t) .. .. .. 8·00 7·50
28 ,, 2 c. rose (u) .. .. .. 6·00 7·00
29 ,, 2 c. rose (v) .. .. .. 6·00 6·00

Triplets are known of: 1883. (o)+(g)+(g); 1884. (s)+(s)+(f); 1884. (b)+(p)+(f); 1885. (v)+(u)+(v). The settings containing (1884) (q) and (r) and (1885) (t) are not known.

The 2 c. with all letters narrow, formerly listed, does not exist. Specimens with the wide " A " or wide " L " may be mistaken for this variety where these letters are defective, but may be detected by the spacing.

T5 of Straits, wmk. Crown CA, optd. " SELANGOR ", *in various types.*

SELANGOR (2) SELANGOR (3) Selangor (4)

1885.
30 **2** 2 c. rose .. .. .. 1·00 1·10
a. Opt. double .. ..
31 **3** 2 c. rose (Oct.) .. .. 1·40 1·75
32 **4** 2 c. rose .. .. .. 75·00 90·00

SELANGOR (5) SELANGOR. (6)

1886 (May).
33 **5** 2 c. rose .. .. .. 3·00 3·00
34 **6** 2 c. rose (with stop) (8.87) .. 1·75 2·00
35 ,, 2 c. rose (without stop) (1887) 1·25 1·25

SELANGOR (7) SELANGOR (8)

SELANGOR (9)

1889. *Optd. vertically.*
36 **7** 2 c. rose .. .. .. 30·00 8·00
37 **8** 2 c. rose (Feb.) .. .. 12·00 10·00
38 **9** 2 c. rose (Feb.) .. .. 3·25 2·00
Opt. similar to T **8**, *but diagonal.*
39 2 c. rose £150
Opt. as T **9** *but horizontal.*
40 2 c. rose £350

1890. *Optd. with T* **6** *vertically. No stop.*
41 2 c. deep rose .. .. 3·00

SELANGOR (10) SELANGOR (11)

1890.
42 **10** 2 c. rose .. .. .. 10·00 1·00
43 **11** 2 c. deep rose (1891) .. 40·00 30·00

SELANGOR Two CENTS (12) SELANGOR Two CENTS (13)

SELANGOR Two CENTS (14) SELANGOR Two CENTS (15) SELANGOR Two CENTS (16)

1891. *T* **7** *of Straits, surch. horizontally, with bar obliterating old value.*
44 **12** 2 c. on 24 c. green .. .. 10·00 10·00
45 **13** 2 c. on 24 c. green .. 10·00
a. Error. " SELANGCR " ..
46 **14** 2 c. on 24 c. green .. .. 10·00
47 **15** 2 c. on 24 c. green .. .. 10·00
48 **16** 2 c. on 24 c. green .. .. 2·00

The error, No. 45a occurs in the first printing only and is No. 45 on the pane.

17

3 CENTS
(17a)

1891–95. *Wmk. Crown CA. P* 14.
49 **17** 1 c. green 45 20
50 ,, 2 c. rose 45 25
51 ,, 2 c. orange (1895) 35 25
52 ,, 5 c. blue .. .. .. 1·00 65
49/52 Optd. " Specimen " *Set of* 4 32·00

1894. *Surch. with T* **17a.**
53 **17** 3 c. on 5 c. rose (Optd. S. £10) 25 20

18

19

1895–98. *Wmk. Crown CA or Crown CC (dolla values). P* 14.
54 **18** 3 c. dull purple & carmine . 75 1
55 ,, 5 c. dull pur. & olive-yell. 20 1
56 ,, 8 c. dull pur. and ultram. 7·00 2·2
57 ,, 10 c. dull purple and orange 1·10 1
58 ,, 25 c. green and carmine .. 9·00 7·0
59 ,, 50 c. green and black .. 28·00 10·0
60 ,, 50 c. dull pur. & grnsh blk. 5·50 4·0
61 **19** $1 green & yellow-green 9·00 6·5
62 ,, $2 green and carmine .. 18·00 12·0
63 ,, $3 green and ochre .. 38·00 16·0
64 ,, $5 green and blue .. 18·00 16·0
65 ,, $10 green & purple (S. £30) 80·00 50·0
66 ,, $25 green & orange (S. £55) £200
54/62 .. .. *Set of* 9 70·00 38·0
54/64 Optd. " Specimen " *Set of* 11 55·00

One cent. (20) Three cents. (21)

1900. *Nos.* 55 *and* 59 *surch. with T* **20** *or* **21**
66a **18** 1 c. on 5 c. dull purple and olive-yellow .. .. 6·00 7·0
66b ,, 1 c. on 50 c. green & black 45 1·2
c. " cent " repeated at left .. £150
67 ,, 3 c. on 50 c. green and black 1·75 1·7
a. Antique " t " in " cents " 14·00 14·0

22. Mosque at Palace, Klang.

23. Sultan Suleiman.

1935–41. *Chalk-surfaced or ordinary paper* (O) *Wmk. Mult. Script CA. P* 14 *or* 14×14½ (*No* 70).
68 **22** 1 c. black 12
69 ,, 2 c. green 8
70 ,, 2 c. orange, OC (21.8.41) 8 3
a. Perf. 14, O (Sept. '41) .. 3·00 1·0
71 ,, 3 c. green, OC 10 3
72 ,, 4 c. orange 8
73 ,, 5 c. brown 8
74 ,, 6 c. scarlet 35 1
75 ,, 8 c. grey 20 1
76 ,, 10 c. dull purple 20
77 ,, 12 c. bright ultramarine .. 1·00 1
78 ,, 15 c. brt. ultramarine, O .. 90 2·0
79 ,, 25 c. dull purple & scarlet .. 65 6
80 ,, 30 c. dull purple & orange .. 90 9
81 ,, 40 c. scarlet and dull purple 1·00 9
82 ,, 50 c. black/*emerald* .. 90 5
83 **23** $1 black and rose/*blue* .. 2·00 5
84 ,, $2 green and scarlet .. 6·00 3·2
85 ,, $5 green & red/*emerald* .. 13·00 8·0
68/85 .. .. *Set of* 18 25·00 16·0
68/85 Perf. " Specimen " *Set of* 18 50·00

Dates of issue as for Negri Sembilan, excep Nos. 70/*a*.

An 8 c. scarlet was issued but only with overprint during the Japanese Occupation of Malaya. Unoverprinted specimens result from leakages.

24. Sultan Hisamud-din Alam Shah. **25.**

1941. *Wmk. Mult. Script CA. P* 14.
86 **24** $1 blk. & red/*bl.*, C (15.4.41) 1·50 2·25
87 ,, $2 grn. & scarlet, C (7.7.41) 4·50 6·00
86/7 Perf. "Specimen" *Set of* 2 20·00

A $5 green and red on emerald, T **24**, was issued overprinted during the Japanese occupation of Malaya. Unoverprinted specimens are known, but were not issued thus.

1948 (1 Dec.). *Royal Silver Wedding. As Nos.* 30/1 *of Aden.*
88 10 c. violet 5 5
89 $5 green .. .. .. 5·00 8·00

1949 (12 Sept.)–**55.** *Chalk-surfaced paper. Wmk. Mult. Script CA. P* 17½ × 18.
90 **25** 1 c. black 5 10
91 ,, 2 c. orange 5 10
92 ,, 3 c. green 5 15
93 ,, 4 c. brown 5 5
94 ,, 5 c. bt. pur. (*shades*)(1.9.52) 5 8
95 ,, 6 c. grey 10 8
96 ,, 8 c. scarlet 15 25
97 ,, 8 c. green (1.9.52) .. 12 30
98 ,, 10 c. purple 8 5
99 ,, 12 c. scarlet (1.9.52) .. 20 25
100 ,, 15 c. ultramarine .. 20 10
101 ,, 20 c. black and green .. 35 25
102 ,, 20 c. bright blue (1.9.52) .. 35 20
103 ,, 25 c. purple and orange .. 25 5
104 ,, 30 c. scar. & purple (5.9.55) 40 20
105 ,, 35 c. scar. & purple (1.9.52) 40 35
106 ,, 40 c. scarlet and purple .. 45 55
107 ,, 50 c. black and blue .. 40 12
108 ,, $1 blue and purple .. 50 15
109 ,, $2 green and scarlet .. 1·50 35
110 ,, $5 green and brown .. 3·00 70
90/110 .. .. *Set of* 21 8·00 4·00

1949 (10 Oct.). *75th Anniv. of Universal Postal Union. As Nos.* 114/17 *of Antigua, but inscr.* "MALAYA SELANGOR".
111 10 c. purple 8 8
112 15 c. deep blue 8 20
113 25 c. orange 20 30
114 50 c. blue-black 45 50

1953 (2 June). *Coronation. As No.* 47 *of Aden.*
115 10 c. black & reddish purple 5 5

1957–61. *As Nos.* 92/102 *of Kedah but with inset portrait of Sultan Hisamud-din Alam Shah.*
116 1 c. black 5 5
117 2 c. orange-red (*shades*) .. 5 5
118 4 c. sepia 5 5
119 5 c. carmine-lake .. 5 5
120 8 c. myrtle-green .. 5 5
121 10 c. deep brown .. 5 5
122 10 c. deep maroon (9.5.61) .. 5 5
123 20 c. blue 12 8
124 50 c. black and blue (*p.* 12½) 25 12
a. Perf. 12½ × 13 (10.5.60) .. 25 10
125 $1 ultram. & reddish purple 40 15
126 $2 brz.-grn. & scar. (*p.* 12½) 80 70
a. Perf. 13 × 12½ (6.12.60) .. 70 50
127 $5 brn. & brz.-grn. (*p.* 12½) 2·00 1·25
a. Perf. 13 × 12½ (10.5.60) .. 2·00 80
116/27a .. .. *Set of* 12 3·50 1·75

Dates of issue:—26.6.57, 20 c., $5; 25.7.57, 2 c., 50 c., $1; 4.8.57, 10 c.; 21.8.57, others.

The 6, 12, 25 and 30 c. values used in Selangor were Nos. 1/4 of Malayan Federation.

26. Sultan Salahuddin Abdul Aziz Shah.

(Photo. Harrison.)

1961 (28 June). *Installation of the Sultan. W* w.**12.** *P* 15 × 14.
128 **26** 10 c. multicoloured .. 8 5
a. Black ptg. misplaced .. 85·00

No. 128a is "The Double-headed Sultan" error, from one sheet where the majority of the stamps showed considerable black printing misplacement.

27. Sultan Salahuddin Abdul Aziz Shah.

1961–62. *As Nos.* 92/8 *of Kedah but with inset portrait of Sultan Salahuddin Abdul Aziz as in T* **27.** *W* w. **13.** *P* 12½ × 13 (*vert.*) *or* 13 × 12½ (*horiz.*).
129 1 c. black (1.3.62) 5 8
130 2 c. orange-red (1.3.62) .. 5 8
131 4 c. sepia (1.3.62) 5 5
132 5 c. carmine-lake (1.3.62) .. 5 5
133 8 c. myrtle-green (1.3.62) 8 8
134 10 c. deep maroon (1.11.61) .. 8 5
135 20 c. blue (1.3.62) 8 8
129/35 .. .. *Set of* 7 35 30

28. *Vanda hookeriana.*

1965 (15 Nov.). *As Nos.* 166/72 *of Johore but with inset portrait of Sultan Salahuddin Abdul Aziz Shah as in T* **28.**
136 1 c. multicoloured 5 5
a. Magenta omitted .. ..
137 2 c. multicoloured 5 5
138 5 c. multicoloured 5 5
139 6 c. multicoloured 5 5
140 10 c. multicoloured 5 5
141 15 c. multicoloured 5 5
142 20 c. multicoloured 8 8
136/42 .. .. *Set of* 7 30 30

The 2 c. to 20 c. values exist with PVA gum as well as gum arabic.

The higher values used in Selangor were Nos. 20/27 of Malaysia.

1970 (20 Nov.). *As Nos.* 136 *etc. but W* w.**13** (*sideways*).
143 **28** 1 c. multicoloured .. 8 8
144 – 10 c. multicoloured .. 10 10
145 – 20 c. multicoloured .. 15 15

29. Clipper Butterfly.

1971 (1 Feb.). *As Nos.* 175/81 *of Johore but with portrait of Sultan Salahuddin Abdul Aziz Shah and Arms, as in T* **29.**
146 1 c. multicoloured 5 5
147 2 c. multicoloured 5 5
148 5 c. multicoloured 5 5
149 6 c. multicoloured 5 5
150 10 c. multicoloured 5 5
151 15 c. multicoloured 5 5
152 20 c. multicoloured 8 8
146/52 .. .. *Set of* 7 20 20

The higher values used with this issue are Nos. 64/71 of Malaysia.

STRAITS SETTLEMENTS.

Former Crown Colony comprising Singapore, Penang (with Province Wellesley and (until 1934) The Dindings), Malacca, Labuan, Cocos or Keeling Islands and Christmas Island.

THREE-HALF-CENTS (1) 32 CENTS (2)

1867 (1 Sept.). *Stamps of India surch. as T* **1** *or* **2** (24 *c.*, 32 *c.*). *Wmk. Elephant's Head. P* 14.
1 **11** 1½ c. on ½ a. blue (Die I) (R.) 14·00 19·00
2 ,, 2 c. on 1 a. brown (R.) .. 16·00 16·00
3 ,, 3 c. on 1 a. brown (B.) .. 18·00 18·00
4 ,, 4 c. on 1 a. brown (Bk.) .. 27·00 21·00
5 ,, 6 c. on 2 a. yellow (P.) .. 50·00 30·00
6 ,, 8 c. on 2 a. yellow (G.) .. 27·00 13·00
7 **17** 12 c. on 4 a. green (R.) .. 65·00 30·00
a. Surch. double £275
8 **11** 24 c. on 8 a. rose (Die II) (B.) 42·00 17·00
9 ,, 32 c. on 2 a. yellow (Bk.) .. 35·00 17·00
1/9 Optd. "Specimen" *Set of* 9 £1200

The 32 c. was re-issued for postal use in 1884.

No. 7a is only known unused.

Used examples of these stamps are very rarely seen without disfiguring firm's "chops". Stamps without "chop" are worth a premium over the prices quoted.

1869 (?). *No.* 1 *with* "THREE HALF" *deleted and* "2" *written above, in black manuscript.*
10 2 on 1½ c. on ½ a. blue .. £500 £450

This stamp has been known from very early days and was apparently used in the Straits Settlements, but nothing is known of its history.

5

6

7

8

9

1867 (Dec.)–**72.** *Wmk. Crown CC. P* 14.
Ornaments in corners differ for each value.

11 **5** 2 c. brown (6.68) .. .. 1·00 70
a. *Yellow-brown* .. .. 1·50 80
b. *Deep brown* .. .. 5·50 3·00
12 ,, 4 c. rose (7.68) .. .. 1·50 1·10
a. *Deep rose* .. .. 3·00 1·40
13 ,, 6 c. dull lilac (1.68) .. .. 5·50 4·25
a. *Bright lilac* .. .. 5·50 4·25
14 **6** 8 c. orange-yellow .. .. 8·00 2·50
a. *Orange* .. .. 8·00 3·25
15 ,, 12 c. blue .. .. .. 7·50 2·00
a. *Ultramarine* .. .. 7·50 3·50
16 **7** 24 c. blue-green .. .. 8·00 2·00
a. *Yellow-green* .. .. 10·00 5·50
17 **8** 30 c. claret (12.72) .. .. 10·00 3·00
18 **9** 32 c. pale red .. .. 25·00 9·00
19 ,, 96 c. grey .. .. .. 25·00 8·00
a. Perf. 12½ (6.71) .. .. 90·00 30·00

Stamps of 1867–71, surcharged.

Five Cents. (10) Seven Cents. (11)

1879 (May). *With T* **10** *and* **11.**
20 **6** 5 c. on 8 c. orange .. .. 11·00 11·00
a. No stop after "Cents" .. 45·00 45·00
b. "F i" spaced .. 55·00 55·00
21 **9** 7 c. on 32 c. pale red .. .. 11·00 11·00
a. No stop after "Cents" .. 60·00 60·00

10 cents. (12)

10 (*a*) 10 (*b*) 10 (*c*) 10 (*d*)
10 (*e*) 10 (*f*) 10 (*g*) 10 (*h*)
10 (*i*) 10 (*j*) 10 (*jj*) 10 (*k*) 10 (*l*)

(*a*) "1" thin curved serif and thin foot; "0" narrow.
(*b*) "1" thick curved serif and thick foot; "0" broad. Both numerals heavy.
(*c*) "1" as (*a*); "0" as (*b*).
(*d*) "1" as (*a*) but thicker; "0" as (*a*).
(*e*) As (*a*) but sides of "0" thicker.
(*f*) "1" as (*d*); "0" as (*e*).
(*g*) As (*a*) but "0" narrower.
(*h*) "1" thin, curved serif and thick foot; "0" as (*g*).
(*i*) "1" as (*b*); "0" as (*a*).
(*j*) "1" as (*d*); "0" as (*g*) but raised.
(*jj*) "1" as (*a*) but shorter, and with shorter serif and thicker foot; "0" as (*g*) but level with "1".
(*k*) "1" as (*jj*); "0" as (*d*).
(*l*) "1" straight serif; "0" as (*d*).

1880 (Mar). *With T* **12** (*ten varieties of figures* "10").
22 10 c. on 30 c. claret (*a*) .. 23·00 11·00
23 10 c. on 30 c. claret (*b*) .. 23·00 11·00
24 10 c. on 30 c. claret (*c*) .. 55·00 28·00
25 10 c. on 30 c. claret (*d*) .. 55·00 35·00
26 10 c. on 30 c. claret (*e*) .. £150 75·00
27 10 c. on 30 c. claret (*f*) .. £150 75·00
28 10 c. on 30 c. claret (*g*) .. 85·00 75·00
29 10 c. on 30 c. claret (*h*) .. £150 75·00
30 10 c. on 30 c. claret (*i*) .. £150 75·00
31 10 c. on 30 c. claret (*j*) .. £160 85·00
32 10 c. on 30 c. claret (*jj*) .. £160 85·00
No. 23 is known with large stop after "cents" and also with stop low.

1880 (April). *As T* **12** *but without "cents."* (*eight varieties of figures* "10".)
33 10 on 30 c. claret (*a*) .. .. 14·00 12·00
34 10 on 30 c. claret (*b*) .. .. 14·00 12·00
35 10 on 30 c. claret (*c*) .. .. 55·00 30·00
36 10 on 30 c. claret (*g*) .. .. £170 85·00
37 10 on 30 c. claret (*i*) £225 £150
38 10 on 30 c. claret (*k*) £250 £150
39 10 on 30 c. claret (*l*) £250 £150
40 10 on 30 c. claret (*m*) .. ..
Variety (*m*) has the "1" as (*b*) and the "0" as (*g*).

5 cents. (13) 5 cents. (14) 5 cents. (15)

1880 (Aug.). *With T* **13** *to* **15.**
41 **13** 5 c. on 8 c. orange .. .. 12·00 13·00
42 **14** 5 c. on 8 c. orange .. .. 12·00 13·00
43 **15** 5 c. on 8 c. orange .. .. 40·00 40·00
In this setting, the first four rows of the pane have surcharge T **13**; the next five, T **14**; and the last, T **15**.

10 cents. (16) 5 cents. (17)

1880–81. *With T* **16.**
44 10 c. on 6 c. lilac (11.81) .. 6·00 4·50
45 10 c. on 12 c. ultram. (1.81) .. 8·00 7·00
a. *Blue* .. .. .. 6·00 5·50
46 10 c. on 30 c. claret (12.80) .. 25·00 10·00
A second printing of the 10 c. on 6 c. has the surcharge heavier and the "10" usually more to the left or right of "cents."

1882 (Jan.). *With T* **17.**
47 5 c. on 4 c. rose .. .. 60·00 40·00

STRAITS SETTLEMENTS POSTAGE FIVE CENTS
18

STRAITS SETTLEMENTS POSTAGE TEN CENTS
19

TWO CENTS
(20)

1882 (Jan.). *Wmk. Crown CC. P* 14.
48 **18** 5 c. purple-brown .. 10·00 8·00
49 **19** 10 c. slate (Optd. S. £11) .. 15·00 7·00

1882. *Wmk. Crown CA. P* 14.
50 **5** 2 c. brown (Aug.) .. 13·00 3·50
51 ,, 4 c. rose (April) .. .. 12·00 3·00
52 **6** 8 c. orange (Sept.) .. 1·00 25
53 **19** 10 c. slate (Oct.) 75 25

1883 (April). *Nos.* 52 *and* 18 *surch. with T* **20.**
(*a*) "CENTS" in narrow letters.
(*b*) Wide "E".
(*c*) Wide "EN" and "S".
(*d*) Wide "N".
(*e*) Wide "S".
(*f*) Wide "E" and "S".
54 **6** 2 c. on 8 c. orange (*a*) .. 11·00 10·00
a. Surch. double £200 £160
55 ,, 2 c. on 8 c. orange (*c*) .. 18·00 18·00
56 ,, 2 c. on 8 c. orange (*d*) .. 9·00 9·00
57 ,, 2 c. on 8 c. orange (*e*) .. 10·00 9·00
58 ,, 2 c. on 8 c. orange (*f*) .. 10·00 9·00
59 **9** 2 c. on 32 c. pale red (*b*) .. 40·00 22·00
a. Surch. double .. ..
60 ,, 2 c. on 32 c. pale red (*e*) .. 40·00 22·00
Nos. 54/60 were surcharged in triplets as follows:—
2 *c. on* 8 *c.* (*e*)+(*f*)+(*d*) with (*a*) as a single unit for the top row only. Also (*a*)+(*a*)+(*a*) with (*c*) as the single unit.
2 *c. on* 32 *c.* (*e*)+(*b*)+(*e*) with (*b*) as the single unit.

2 Cents. (21) 4 Cents (22) 8 Cents (23)

1883 (July). *Nos.* 51 *and* 15 *surch. with T* **21**
61 2 c. on 4 c. rose (*CA*) .. .. 5·00 6·0
a. "s" of "Cents" inverted .. £150 £11
62 2 c. on 12 c. blue (*CC*) .. 25·00 19·0
a. "s" of "Cents" inverted .. £190

1883 (July)–**91.** *Wmk. Crown CA. P* 14.
63 **5** 2 c. pale rose .. .. 1·75 5
a. *Bright rose* 15 1
64 ,, 4 c. pale brown .. .. 1·00 4
a. *Deep brown* .. .. 3·00 1·2
65 **18** 5 c. blue (8.83) 40 2
66 **5** 6 c. lilac (11.84) .. .. 4·50 3·0
a. *Violet* 80 7
67 **6** 12 c. dull purple .. .. 2·00 1·5
68 **7** 24 c. yellow-green (2.84) .. 8·00 8
a. *Blue-green* .. .. 1·10 9
69 **8** 30 c. claret (9.91) .. .. 2·00 1·5
70 **9** 32 c. orange-verm. (1.87) .. 2·25 1·0
71 ,, 96 c. olive-grey (8.88) .. 10·00 7·5
63*a*/71 .. .. *Set of* 9 18·00 12·0
63/65, 67 Optd. "Specimen" ..
Set of 4 30·0

1884 (Feb.–Aug.). *Surch. with T* **22** *or* **23.**
72 **18** 4 c. on 5 c. blue (Aug.) .. £250 £27
73 ,, 4 c. on 5 c. blue (R.) (Aug.) 15·00 15·0
74 **6** 8 c. on 12 c. blue (*CC*) (Feb.) 30·00 20·0
75 ,, 8 c. on 12 c. dull pur. (Aug.) 30·00 20·0
No. 75 is known with "s" of "Cents" low

1884 (Aug.). *Surch. with T* **20.**
76 **18** 2 c. on 5 c. blue (*a*) .. 10·00 12·0
77 ,, 2 c. on 5 c. blue (*b*) .. 10·00 12·0
78 ,, 2 c. on 5 c. blue (*c*) .. 10·00 12·0
a. Pair, with and without surch. .. .. ..
b. Surch. double .. ..
Nos. 76/8 were surcharged in a triplet com posed of (*c*)+(*a*)+(*b*).
In Type (*a*) the letters "TS" are below th line of the word.

8 (24) 3 CENTS (25) THREE CENTS (26)

1884 (Sept.). *Nos.* 73 *and* 75 *surch. with larg numeral, as T* **24,** *in addition, in red.*
79 **18** "4" on 4 c. in *red* on 5 c. blue — £200
80 **6** "8" on 8 c. in *black* on 12 c. dull purple .. .. 25·00 28·0
a. T 24 double £450
81 ,, "8" on 8 c. in *blue* on 12 c. dull purple £500
No. 80 is known with "s" of "Cents" low

1885. *No.* 65 *and T* **9** *in new colour, wmk Crown CA, surch. with T* **25** *and* **26.**
82 **25** 3 c. on 5 c. blue (Sept.) .. 13·00 13·0
a. Surch. double £200
83 **26** 3 c. on 32 c. pale magenta (Dec.) (Optd. S. £12) .. 70 1·1
a. *Deep magenta* 60 6

3 cents (27) 2 Cents. (28)

1886 (April). *No.* 48 *surch. with T* **27.**
84 **18** 3 c. on 5 c. purple-brown .. 27·00 27·0

1887 (July). *No.* 65 *surch. with T* **28.**
85 **18** 2 c. on 5 c. blue .. .. 4·00 5·0
a. "C" of "Cents" omitted — £25
b. Surch. double £120
Nos. 82, 84 and 85 were surcharged in triple settings.

10 CENTS (29) THIRTY CENTS (30)

891 (Nov.). *Nos.* 68 *and* 70 *surch. with T* **29** *and* **30.**
6 **7** 10 c. on 24 c. yellow-green .. 55 55
a. Narrow "0" in "10" .. 4·00 4·50
7 **9** 30 c. on 32 c. orange-verm... 1·75 2·00
The "R" of "THIRTY" and "N" of "CENTS" re found wide or narrow and in all possible ombinations.

ONE
CENT
(31)

ONE CENT
(32)

892. *Stamps of* 1882–91 (*wmk. Crown CA*) *surch. with T* **31.**
8 1 c. on 2 c. rose (March) .. 25 35
9 1 c. on 4 c. brown (April) .. 70 60
a. Surch. double .. .. 80·00
o 1 c. on 6 c. lilac (Feb.) .. 40 45
a. Surch. double, one inverted .. 90·00 80·00
1 1 c. on 8 c. orange (Jan.) .. 25 45
2 1 c. on 12 c. dull purple (Mar.) 1·25 3·00
8/92 .. .. *Set of* 5 2·50 4·25
The following varieties may be found in **31**:—(1) narrow "N" on "ONE" and "CENT"; 2) wide "N" in "ONE" and "CENT"; (3) narrow N" in "ONE", wide "N" in "CENT"; 4) wide "N" in "ONE", narrow "N" in CENT"; (5) narrow "O" in "ONE"; (6) ntique "E" in "CENT".

892–94. *Colours changed. Wmk. Crown CA. P* 14. *Surch. with T* **32** *and* **26.**
3 **6** 1 c. on 8 c. green (Mar. '92) 12 30
4 **9** 3 c. on 32 c. carmine-rose (June, 1894) 25 40
a. Error. Surch. omitted .. £350
3/94 Optd. "Specimen" *Set of* 2 25·00

33

34

892–99. *Wmk. Crown CA. P* 14.
95 **33** 1 c. green (9.92) 15 15
96 ,, 3 c. carmine-rose (2.95) .. 50 25
97 ,, 3 c. brown (3.99) 50 15
a. Yellow-brown 60 25
98 **5** 4 c. deep carmine (7.99) .. 65 25
99 **18** 5 c. brown (6.94) 55 35
00 ,, 5 c. magenta (7.99) .. 80 50
01 **6** 8 c. ultramarine (6.94) .. 55 20
a. Bright blue 80 25
02 ,, 12 c. brown-purple (3.94) .. 2·00 1·75
03 **33** 25 c. pur.-brn. & grn. (3.92) 2·40 1·10
a. Dull purple and green .. 2·00 90
04 ,, 50 c. olive-green & carmine (3.92) .. .. 3·50 1·10
05 **34** $5 orange & carm. (10.98) 70·00 70·00
9/105 .. .. *Set of* 11 75·00 75·00
9/101, 103/5 Optd. "Specimen" *Set of* 10 55·00

4
cents.
(35)

FOUR CENTS
(36)

898 (26 Dec.). *T* **18** *and* **6** *surch. with T* **35.**
06 4 c. on 5 c. brown (No. 99) .. 40 60
07 4 c. on 5 c. blue (No. 65) .. 40 60
a. Surch. double
08 4 c. on 8 c. ultram. (No. 101) 40 75
a. Surch. double £110 £120
b. Bright blue (No. 101*a*) .. 55 40
Nos. 107 and 108*b* exist with stop spaced 1½ nm. from the "S".

1899 (Mar.). *T* **18** (*wmk. Crown CA. P* 14), *surch. with T* **36.**
109 4 c. on 5 c. carm. (Optd. S. £10) 12 8
a. Error. Surch. omitted .. £1200
No. 109a is only known unused.

37

38

1902. *Wmk. Crown CA. P* 14.
110 **37** 1 c. grey-green 8 15
a. Pale green 70 15
111 ,, 3 c. dull purple & orange 15 20
112 ,, 4 c. purple/*red* 75 25
113 **38** 5 c. dull purple 75 20
114 ,, 8 c. purple/*blue* .. .. 1·10 25
115 ,, 10 c. purple & black/*yell.* 1·40 40
116 **37** 25 c. dull purple and green 1·75 90
117 **38** 30 c. grey and carmine .. 2·50 1·75
118 **37** 50 c. deep green & carmine 2·50 1·75
a. Dull green and carmine .. 4·50 4·00
119 **38** $1 dull green and black 8·00 5·00
120 **37** $2 dull purple & black .. 11·00 9·00
121 **38** $5 dull grn. & brn.-orge. 30·00 12·00
122 **37** $100 purple & green/*yellow* (Optd. S. £150) .. £1500
110/121 .. .. *Set of* 12 55·00 30·00
110/21 Optd. "Specimen" *Set of* 12 65·00

39

40

41

42

1903–4. *Wmk. Crown CA. P* 14.
123 **39** 1 c. grey-green 15 25
124 **40** 3 c. dull purple 80 50
125 **41** 4 c. purple/*red* 35 15
126 **42** 8 c. purple/*blue* .. .. 1·75 65
123/6 Optd. "Specimen" *Set of* 4 30·00

1904–6. *Wmk. Multiple Crown CA. P* 14.
127 **39** 1 c. deep green, OC .. 15 8
128 **40** 3 c. dull purple, OC .. 10 15
a. Plum, O .. 65 20
129 **41** 4 c. purple/*red,* OC .. 35 10
130 **38** 5 c. dull purple, OC ('06) 50 80
131 **42** 8 c. purple/*blue,* OC .. 1·75 15
132 **38** 10 c. pur. & blk./*yell.,* OC 75 15
133 **37** 25 c. dull pur. & grn., OC 1·60 90
134 **38** 30 c. grey & carmine, OC 2·00 1·00
135 **37** 50 c. dull grn. & car., OC 2·50 1·75
136 **38** $1 dull grn. & black, OC 5·00 2·00
137 **37** $2 dull pur. & blk., C .. 15·00 10·00
138 **38** $5 dull green and brown-orange, OC .. 20·00 12·00
139 **37** $25 grey-green and black, C (Optd. S. £65) .. £400
140 " $100 pur. & grn./*yell.,* C £2000
127/138 .. .. Set of 12 45·00 26·00

STRAITS
SETTLEMENTS.
(43)

Straits Settlements.
(44)

STRAITS
SETTLEMENTS.

FOUR CENTS.
(45)

1907. *T* **18** *of Labuan* (*Nos.* 116*c, etc.*) *optd. with T* **43** *or* **44** (10 *c.*), *or surch. with T* **45**, *in brownish red or black* (Bk.). *P* 13½.
141 1 c. black & pur. (*p.* 14½–15) 5·50 7·00
142 2 c. black & grn. (*p.* 14 × 13½) 15·00 15·00
a. Perf. 14½–15 .. ..
143 3 c. black and sepia .. 3·25 4·25
144 4 c. on 12 c. black & yellow .. 45 90
a. No stop after "CENTS" .. 16·00
b. Perf. 14×13½
ba. No stop after "CENTS" ..
145 4 c. on 16 c. grn. & brn. (Bk.) 45 1·00
a. "STRAITS SETTLEMENTS" double (Br.-R.+Bk.) .. 80·00 80·00
b. Do., Invert. pair with normal
146 4 c. on 18 c. blk. & pale brown 40 80
a. No stop after "CENTS" .. 17·00
b. "FOUR CENTS." and bar double £550
c. "FOUR CENTS." and bar 1½ mm. below normal position (pr. with normal) .. .. 30·00
147 8 c. black and vermilion .. 40 1·10
148 10 c. brown and slate .. 80 1·10
a. No stop after "SETTLEMENTS" .. .. .. 17·00
149 25 c. green and greenish blue 90 2·50
a. Perf. 14½–15 .. ..
150 50 c. dull purple and lilac .. 2·50 4·00
151 $1 claret and orange .. 8·50 8·50
a. Perf. 14½–15 .. ..
141/51 .. .. *Set of* 11 35·00 42·00
No. 146c only occurred in a few sheets of the first printing.
The 2 c. also exists perf. 14 all round and is rare.

46

47

1906–11. *Wmk. Mult. Crown CA. P* 14.
152 **39** 1 c. blue-green, O (1910) 20 15
153 **40** 3 c. red, O (1908) .. 10 10
154 **41** 4 c. red, O (1907) .. 10 20
155 ,, 4 c. dull purple, OC ('08) 10 10
156 ,, 4 c. claret, O (1911) .. 35 45
157 **38** 5 c. orange, O (1909) .. 1·00 20
158 **42** 8 c. blue, O (1906) .. 25 15
159 **38** 10 c. purple/*yell.,* OC ('08) 35 10
160 **47** 21 c. dull purple & claret, C (11.10) .. .. 1·50 3·25
161 **37** 25 c. dull & brt. pur., C ('09) 1·50 1·00
162 **38** 30 c. pur. and orange-yell., C ('09) .. .. 1·60 50
163 **47** 45 c. black/*green,* C (11.10) 1·25 2·00
164 **37** 50 c. black/*green,* C ('10) .. 1·10 70
165 **38** $1 blk. & red/*bl.,* C ('11) 2·50 1·25
166 **37** $2 green & red/*yellow,* C ('09) .. .. 5·00 4·00
167 **38** $5 green and red/*green,* C ('10) .. .. 15·00 11·00
168 **46** $25 purple and blue/*blue,* C ('11) (Optd. S. £60) £250 90·00
169 ,, $500 purple and orange, C ('10) (Optd. S. £400) £15000
152/167 .. .. *Set of* 16 29·00 22·00
153/167 Optd. "Specimen" *Set of* 15 60·00
Beware of dangerous forgeries of No. 169.

48

49

50

51

52

53

54

RED CROSS

2c.

(55)

1912–23. $25, $100 *and* $500 *as T* **46**, *but with head of King George V. Wmk. Mult. Crown CA. P* 14.

193 **48** 1 c. green, O (9.12) .. 20 15
a. Pale green (1.14) .. 20 15
b. Blue-green (1917) .. 15 15
194 ,, 1 c. black, O (2.19) .. 10 15
195 **52** 2 c. green, O (10.19) .. 10 15
196 **49** 3 c. red, O (2.13) .. 35 15
a. Scarlet (2.17) .. 10 10
197 **50** 4 c. dull purple, C (3.13) .. 35 15
a. Wmk. sideways ..
198 ,, 4 c. rose-scarlet, O (2.19) 35 15
a. Carmine .. 30 15
199 **51** 5 c. orange, O (8.12) .. 30 15
a. Yellow-orange .. 55 15
200 **52** 6 c. dull claret, O (3.20) .. 65 35
a. Deep claret .. 1·75 90
201 ,, 8 c. ultramarine, O (3.13) 20 15
202 **51** 10 c. purple/*yellow*, C (8.12) 35 15
a. White back (9.13) (Optd. S. £8) .. 25 20
b. On lemon (1916) (Optd. S. £12) .. 3·00 50
203 ,, 10 c. dp. brt. blue, O (2.19) 1·25 20
a. Bright blue .. 70 20
204 **53** 21 c. dull & bright purple, C (11.13) .. 90 1·25
205 **54** 25 c. dull purple & mauve, C (7.14) .. 90 75
206 ,, 25 c. dull purple & violet, C (1919) .. 2·50 65
207 **51** 30 c. dull purple & orange, C (12.14) .. 80 65
208 **53** 45 c. black/*green*, C (*white back*) (12.14) .. 90 1·40
a. On blue-green, olive back (7.18) (Optd. S. £8) .. 90 1·10
b. On emerald back (6.22) .. 90 1·50
209 **54** 50 c. black/*green*, C (7.14) .. 2·00 90
a. On bl.-grn., olive back ('18) 2·10 90
b. On emerald back (10.21) .. 2·75 90
c. On emerald back (Die II) (3.23) (Optd. S. £8) .. 1·00 80
210 **51** $1 black and red/*blue*, C (10.14) .. 2·75 1·50
211 **54** $2 green & red/*yellow*, C (7.15) .. 3·50 2·50
a. White back (7.14) (Optd. S. £8) .. 2·25 1·50
b. On orange-buff (1920) .. 5·00 4·50
c. On pale yellow (1921) .. 6·50
212 **51** $5 green & red/*green*, C (4.15) .. 12·00 4·00
a. White back, OC (11.13) (Optd. S. £8) .. 11·00 4·25
b. On bl.-grn., olive back ('18) 11·00 3·25
c. On emerald back (6.21) .. 17·00 9·00
d. Die II (1923) (Optd. S. £13) 10·00 5·00
213 – $25 purple and blue/*blue*, C (Optd. S. £40) .. £300 £100
214 – $100 carmine & black/*blue*, C (Optd. S. £100) .. £1000
215 – $500 purple & orange-brn., C (8.12) (Optd. S. £200) £8000
193/212 .. .. *Set of* 20 24·00 13·00
193/212 Optd. "Specimen" *Set of* 19 £120

The 6 c. is similar to T **52**, but the head is in a beaded oval as in T **53**. The 2 c., 6 c. (and 12 c. below) have figures of value on a circular ground while in the 8 c. this is of oval shape.

1917 (May). *Surch. with T* **55**.

216 **49** 2 c on 3 c. scarlet .. 60 1·60
a. No stop .. 15·00
217 **50** 2 c. on 4 c. dull purple .. 60 1·60
a. No stop .. 20·00 20·00

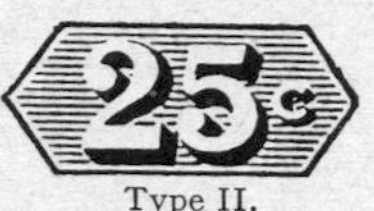

Type I. Type II.

Two types of duty plate in the 25 c. In Type II the solid shading forming the back of the figure 2 extends to the top of the curve; the upturned end of the foot of the 2 is short; two background lines above figure 5; c close to 5; STRAITS SETTLEMENTS in taller letters.

1921–33. *Wmk. Mult. Script CA. P* 14.

218 **48** 1 c. black, O (3.22) .. 8 8
219 **52** 2 c. green, O (5.21) .. 8 8
220 ,, 2 c. brown, O (12.25) .. 60 55
221 **49** 3 c. green, O (9.23) .. 35 25
222 **50** 4 c. carm.-red, O (10.21) 60 15
223 ,, 4 c. brt. violet, O (8.24) .. 10 8
224 ,, 4 c. orange, O (8.29) .. 10 8
225 **51** 5 c. orange, O (Die II) (5.21) .. 15 12
a. Die I (12.22) .. 25 12
226 ,, 5 c. brn., O (Die II) (2.32) 25 8
a. Die I (1933) .. 15 8
227 **52** 6 c. dull claret, O (10.22) 25 12
228 ,, 6 c. rose-pink, O (2.25) .. 3·00 1·25
229 ,, 6 c. scarlet, O (1.27) .. 55 12
230 **51** 10 c. brt. blue, O (Die I) (3.21) .. 55 12
231 ,, 10 c. purple/*yellow*, C (Die I) (6.25) .. 1·00 85
a. Die II. *On pale yellow* (11.26) .. 45 8
b. Die I. *On pale yellow* ('33) 35 12
232 **52** 12 c. bright blue, O (1.22) 40 8
233 **53** 21 c. dull & bright purple, C (2.23) .. 3·00 3·50
234 **54** 25 c. dull purple & mauve, C (Die I, Type I) (2.23) 4·00 2·75
a. Die II. Type I (9.23) .. 3·50 1·25
b. Die II. Type II (1927) .. 1·50 35
235 **51** 30 c. dull purple & orange, C (Die I) (5.21) .. 3·75 3·25
a. Die II (1923) .. 75 15
236 **53** 35 c. dull purple & orange-yellow, C (8.22) .. 3·00 1·25
a. Dull purple and orange .. 1·25 1·25
237 ,, 35 c. scar. & pur., C (4.31) 2·25 1·60
238 **54** 50 c. black/*emer.*, C (9.25) 75 20
239 **51** $1 black and red/*blue*, C (6.22) .. 1·75 25
240 **54** $2 green & red/*pale yell.*, C (5.15) .. 3·25 2·00
240*a* **51** $5 green & red/*green*, C (8.26) .. 10·00 5·00
240*b* – $25 purple & blue/*blue*, C (5.23) (Optd. S. £40) £170 45·00
240*c* – $100 carmine & black/*blue*, C (5.23) (Optd. S. £90) £900
240*d* – $500 purple & orange-brn., C (4.23) (Optd. S. £80) £6000
218/240*a* .. .. *Set of* 24 28·00 16·0[illegible]
218/240*a* (*excl.* 229) Optd./Perf. "Specimen" .. *Set of* 23 £120

Nos. 240*b*/*d* are as Type **46**, but with portra[it] of George V.

An 8 c. in carmine was prepared but not issue[d] (Optd. "Specimen" £45).

The paper of No. 231b is the normal *pa[le] yellow* at the back, but with a bright yello[w] surface. No. 231 is on paper of a *pale lemo[n]* tint and the impression is smudgy.

MALAYA-
BORNEO
EXHIBITION.

(56)

1922. *T* **48** *and* **50** *to* **54**, *overprinted with T* **5[6]**

(*a*) *Wmk. Mult. Crown CA.*

241 2 c. green .. .. .. 3·25 3·2[illegible]
242 4 c. scarlet .. .. .. 1·25 1·5[illegible]
243 5 c. orange .. .. .. 2·00 2·2[illegible]
244 8 c. ultramarine .. .. 75 9[illegible]
245 25 c. dull pur. & mve. (No. 202) 1·75 2·0[illegible]
246 45 c. black/*blue-grn.* (olive back) 1·25 2·1[illegible]
247 $1 black and red/*blue* .. 25·00 28·0[illegible]
248 $2 green and red/*orange-buff* 7·00 9·0[illegible]
a. On pale yellow .. .. 14·00 17·0[illegible]
249 $5 green and red/*blue-green* (olive back) .. .. 35·00 40·0[illegible]

(*b*) *Wmk. Mult. Script CA.*

250 1 c. black .. .. .. 20 3[illegible]
251 2 c. green .. .. .. 75 1·0[illegible]
252 4 c. carmine-red .. .. 85 1·4[illegible]
253 5 c. orange (Die II) .. 1·25 1·7[illegible]
254 10 c. bright blue (Die I) .. 1·25 2·0[illegible]
255 $1 black & red/*blue* (Die II) 6·50 9·0[illegible]
241/255 .. .. *Set of* 11 50·00 65·0[illegible]

The following varieties may be found in mos[t] values: (a) Small second "A" in "MALAYA." (b) No stop. (c) No hyphen. (d) Oval las[t] "O" in "BORNEO." (e) "EXH.BITION."

1935 (6 May). *Silver Jubilee. As Nos.* 91/4 *[of] Antigua but ptd. by W'low & Sons. P* 11 × 12.

256 5 c. ultramarine and grey .. 10 1[illegible]
257 8 c. green and indigo .. 35 3[illegible]
258 12 c. brown and deep blue .. 35 4[illegible]
259 25 c. slate and purple .. 75 7[illegible]
256/9 Perf. "Specimen" *Set of* 4 16·00

57

58

1936–37. *Chalk-surfaced paper. Wmk. Mul[t.] Script CA. P* 14.

260 **57** 1 c. black (1.1.37) .. 5
261 ,, 2 c. green 8
262 ,, 4 c. orange 10
263 ,, 5 c. brown 10
264 ,, 6 c. scarlet 12
265 ,, 8 c. grey 20 1
266 ,, 10 c. dull purple .. 40 1
267 ,, 12 c. bright ultramarine .. 1·60 4
268 ,, 25 c. dull purple & scarlet 60 1
269 ,, 30 c. dull purple & orange 75 2
270 ,, 40 c. scarlet & dull purple 90 6
271 ,, 50 c. black/*emerald* .. 1·10 5
272 ,, $1 black and red/*blue* .. 1·75 9
273 ,, $2 green and scarlet .. 6·00 4·0[illegible]
274 ,, $5 green & red/*emerald* (1.1.37) .. .. 13·00 7·5[illegible]
260/274 .. .. *Set of* 15 24·00 13·0[illegible]
260/74 Perf. "Specimen" *Set of* 15 40·00

1937 (12 May). *Coronation. As Nos.* 13/15 *o[f] Aden. P* 14.

275 4 c. orange 5
276 8 c. grey-black 8
277 12 c. bright blue .. .. 15 1[illegible]
275/7 Perf. "Specimen" *Set of* 3 10·00

937–41. *Chalk surfaced or ordinary paper* (O). *Wmk. Mult. Script CA. P* 14 *or* 15 × 14 (15 *c.*).

(*a*) *Die I* (*printed at two operations*).

78	**58**	1 c. black	8	8
79	„	2 c. green	8	8
80	„	4 c. orange	30	10
81	„	5 c. brown	20	10
82	„	6 c. scarlet	30	8
83	„	8 c. grey	50	8
84	„	10 c. dull purple	35	8
85	„	12 c. ultramarine	45	8
86	„	25 c. dull purple & scarlet	2·50	20
87	„	30 c. dull purple & orange	1·25	40
88	„	40 c. scarlet & dull purple	1·25	65
89	„	50 c. black/*emerald*	50	15
90	„	$1 black and red/*blue*	80	20
91	„	$2 green and scarlet	3·50	1·10
92	„	$5 green & red/*emerald*	5·50	2·00

(*b*) *Die II* (*printed at one operation*).

93	**58**	2 c. green	50	10
94	„	2 c. orange	15	20
95	„	3 c. green, O	20	25
96	„	4 c. orange	1·75	12
97	„	5 c. brown	55	8
98	„	15 c. ultramarine, O	75	1·00
78/298		*Set of* 18	17·00	6·00
78/92, 294/5, 298		Perf. "Specimen" *Set of* 18	60·00	

Dates of issue:—

	Nos.		Nos.		Nos.
8.11.37	284	1.1.38	278	29.10.38	296
19.11.37	281	1.1.38	280	28.12.38	293
1.12.37	287	10.1.38	282	18.2.39	297
6.12.37	279	10.1.38	285	5.9.41	295
11.12.37	286	26.1.38	283	6.10.41	294
20.12.37	288	26.1.38	289/92	6.10.41	298

Die I. Lines of background outside central val touch the oval and the foliage of the palm ree is usually joined to the oval frame. The ownward-pointing palm frond, opposite the King's eye, has two points.

Die II. Lines of background are separated rom the oval by a white line and the foliage of he palm trees does not touch the outer frame. he palm frond has only one point.

The 6 c. grey, 8 c. scarlet and $5 purple and range were issued only with the BMA overprint, ut the 8 c. without opt. is known although in his state it was never issued.

The above issues ceased with the Japanese ccupation in 1942. After World War II, stamps f MALAYA (BRITISH MILITARY ADMINISTRATION) vere issued.

POSTAGE DUE STAMPS.

D 1

924–26. *Wmk. Mult. Script CA. P* 14.

D1	**D 1**	1 c. violet	50	15
D2	„	2 c. black	40	12
D3	„	4 c. green ('26)	40	35
D4	„	8 c. scarlet	60	20
D5	„	10 c. orange	60	25
D6	„	12 c. bright blue	1·10	20
D1/6		*Set of* 6	3·25	1·10
D1/6		Optd. "Specimen" *Set of* 6	45·00	

For later issues of Postage Due stamps, see MALAYAN POSTAL UNION.

MINIMUM PRICE

The minimum price quoted is 5p which epresents a handling charge rather than a basis for valuing common stamps. For further notes about prices see introductory pages.

SUNGEI UJONG.

Incorporated in Negri Sembilan in 1895. Now part of the Federation of Malaya.

(1)

SUNGEI UJONG (2) SUNGEI UJONG (3)

T 5 *of Straits Settlements, wmk. Crown CC.*

1878. *Optd. with T* **1**.

1	**1**	2 c. brown	£450	£450

The 2 c. brown, Wmk. Crown CC, optd. with letters "S. U." is a trial, not an issued stamp.

1881–82. *Optd. as T* **2**. *Varieties.* (*a*) "S" *wide.* (*b*) *All letters narrow.* (*c*) *Letters* "N" *wide.* (*d*) "N," "E" *of* "SUNGEI," *and* "U," "NG" *of* "UJONG" *wide.* (*e*) "G," "J" *and* "O" *narrow,* (*f*) "G E" *and* "J O" *narrow.* (*h*) "S" *and* "E" *wide.* (*i*) "N" *of* "UJONG" *wide.*

2	**2**	2 c. brown (*a*)	10·00	
		a. "S" inverted	£120	
3	„	2 c. brown (*b*)	10·00	
4	„	2 c. brown (*d*)	11·00	
5	„	2 c. brown (*e*)	11·00	
6	„	2 c. brown (*f*)	11·00	
7	„	4 c. rose (*a*)	£110	
8	„	4 c. rose (*b*)	£100	
9	„	4 c. rose (*h*)		

On the 2 c. brown, the word "SUNGEI" was printed as a triplet and "UJONG" as a single unit. Triplets are known of: 1881. (*a*)+(*b*)+(*b*) 1881. (*d*)+(*e*)+(*f*).

On the 4 c. rose, "SUNGEI" and "UJONG" were printed as separate triplets. 1882. (*b*)+(*a*)+(*b*) for "SUNGEI" *and* (*b*)+(*b*)+(*b*) for "UJONG". The setting of (*h*) is not known.

1881. *Optd. as T* **3**.

10	**3**	2 c. brown (*a*)	50·00	
11	„	2 c. brown (*b*)	12·00	
12	„	2 c. brown (*c*)	90·00	90·00
13	„	2 c. brown (*i*)	£140	

In the above settings, "SUNGEI" was printed as a triplet and "UJONG" as a single unit. A known triplet consists of: 1881. (*b*)+(*b*)+(*a*). Varieties (*i*) and (*c*) form the first and third units of another setting. A third setting appears to consist of three units of (*b*).

Wmk. Crown CA.

1882. *Optd. with letters* "S.U." (*with stops*).

14	2 c. brown	20·00	
15	4 c. rose	£275	£400

1882. "SU" *without stops.*

16	2 c. brown	16·00	20·00

1882–84. *Optd. with T* **2**. *Variety.* (*k*) "E" *wide.*

17	**2**	2 c. brown (*a*)	45·00	32·00
18	„	2 c. brown (*b*)	40·00	30·00
19	„	2 c. rose (*a*)	10·00	10·00
20	„	2 c. rose (*b*)	10·00	10·00
21	„	2 c. rose (*h*)	10·00	10·00
22	„	2 c. rose (*i*)	10·00	10·00
		a. "UJONG" double		
23	„	2 c. rose (*k*)	8·00	8·50
24	„	8 c. orange (*a*)	£150	90·00
25	„	8 c. orange (*b*)	£150	90·00
26	„	10 c. slate (*a*)	50·00	50·00
27	„	10 c. slate (*b*)	50·00	50·00

On all the above "SUNGEI" and "UJONG" were printed as separate triplets. The 2 c. brown and the 8 c. and 10 c. were overprinted with the same triplets as were used for the 4 c. rose, CC. The "SUNGEI" triplet of this was: 1882. (*b*)+(*a*)+(*b*).

The 2 c. rose was overprinted in two settings of: 1884. (*b*)+(*a*)+(*h*) *and* (*h*)+(*k*)+(*i*).

Optd. with T **3**.

28	**3**	10 c. slate (*b*)	—	50·00

SUNGEI UJONG (4) SUNGEI UJONG (5) Sungei Ujong (6)

1883. *Optd. with T* **4**, *with stop after* "UJONG".

29	**4**	2 c. brown (*b*)	7·00	
30	„	2 c. brown (*h*)	6·50	
31	„	2 c. brown (*i*)	6·50	
31*a*	„	8 c. orange (*b*)		

1884. *Optd. with T* **4**, *without stop.*

32	**4**	2 c. rose (*b*)	6·50	7·00
33	„	2 c. rose (*h*)	6·50	7·00
34	„	2 c. rose (*k*)	6·50	7·00
35	„	4 c. brown (*b*)	22·00	22·00
36	„	4 c. brown (*h*)	20·00	
37	„	4 c. brown (*k*)	20·00	

"SUNGEI" and "UJONG" were printed as separate triplets on Nos. 29 to 37. The triplets on the 2 c brown were: (*b*)+(*h*)+(*i*) and on the 2 c. rose and 4 c. brown (*h*)+(*k*)+(*b*).

1885–90. *Overprinted with name in various types.*

1885.

38	**5**	2 c. rose (without stop)	3·75	
39	**6**	2 c. rose	4·50	5·00
		a. Opt. double	65·00	60·00

SUNGEI UJONG (7) SUNGEI UJONG (8)

SUNGEI UJONG (9) SUNGEI UJONG (10)

1886–87.

40	**7**	2 c. rose	7·50	8·50
41	**8**	2 c. rose	6·50	7·00
		a. Opt. double		
42	**9**	2 c. rose (*long* "J")	7·50	8·50
		a. Opt. double		
43	**10**	2 c. rose (1887)	3·00	4·00

1889. *As T* **5**, *but stop after* "UJONG".

44	2 c. rose	6·50	7·00
	a. Error. "UNJOG"	£225	£250

SUNGEI UJONG (11) SUNGEI UJONG (12)

1889–90.

45	**11**	2 c. rose	1·75	2·50
46	**12**	2 c. rose (1890)	4·50	4·50

No. 45 exists with narrow "E" (only 2 mm. wide) which occurs in two positions on two of the three settings.

No. 46 has two varieties in the setting—antique "G" in "SUNGEI" and antique "G" in "UJONG".

SUNGEI UJONG Two CENTS (13) SUNGEI UJONG *Two* CENTS (14)

SUNGEI UJONG *Two* CENTS (15)

1891. *T* **7** *of Straits, surch.*

47	**13**	2 c. on 24 c. green	20·00	20·00
48	**14**	2 c. on 24 c. green	30·00	
49	**15**	2 c. on 24 c. green	15·00	15·00
50	–	2 c. on 24 c. green*	35·00	

No. 49 has the antique "G" varieties as on No. 46.

*On No. 50 the word "TWO" is a in *T* **13** and the word "CENTS" smaller (9 instead of 10 mm.).

16

17

1891–94. *Wmk. Crown CA. P 14.*

51	16	2 c. rose	1·50	1·25
52	,,	2 c. orange (1894)	60	1·00
53	,,	5 c. blue (1893)	65	1·10
51/3		Optd. "Specimen" *Set of* 3	27·00	

3 CENTS
(18)

1894. *Surch. as T* **18.**

54	16	1 c. on 5 c. green	35	30
55	,,	3 c. on 5 c. rose	35	40

1895. *Wmk. Crown CA. P 14.*

56	17	3 c. dull purple and carmine	40	35
54/6		Optd. "Specimen" *Set of* 3	18·00	

In 1895 Sungei Ujong was incorporated with Negri Sembilan.

TRENGGANU.

A State of the Federation of Malaya.

1. Sultan Zain ul ab din. **2.**

1910–19. *T* **1** *and* **2** *($5 and $25). Wmk. Mult. Crown CA. P 14.*

1	1	1 c. blue-green, O ..	30	35
		a. Green, O..	40	30
2	,,	2 c. brown & purple, C ('15)	40	35
3	,,	3 c. carmine-red, O ..	60	40
4	,,	4 c. orange, O	80	85
5	,,	4 c. red-brn. & grn., C ('15)	75	1·00
5*a*	,,	4 c. carmine-red, O ('19)	30	40
6	,,	5 c. grey, O	55	65
7	,,	5 c. grey & brown, C ('15)	90	60
8	,,	8 c. ultramarine, O ..	65	1·00
9	,,	10 c. purple/*yellow* ..	1·00	1·25
		a. On pale yellow	70	75
10	,,	10 c. grn. & red/*yell.*, O ('15)	55	90
11	,,	20 c. dull & brt. purple, C	1·10	1·40
12	,,	25 c. grn. & dull pur., C ('15)	1·25	1·60
13	,,	30 c. dull pur. & blk., C ('15)	1·25	1·60
14	,,	50 c. black/*green*, C ..	1·60	2·00
15	,,	$1 black & carm./*blue*, C	3·00	3·75
16	,,	$3 grn. & red/*green*, C ('15)	15·00	16·00
17	2	$5 grn. & dull purple, C	30·00	35·00
18	,,	$25 rose-carmine & green, C (Optd. S. £50)	£300	
1/17		.. .. *Set of* 18	55·00	60·00
1/17		Optd. "Specimen" *Set of* 18	£100	

RED CROSS

2c.
(3)

1917 (Oct.). *Surch. with T* **3.**

19	1	2 c. on 3 c. carmine-red ..	25	55
		a. Comma after "2 c." ..	1·00	
		b. "SS" in "CROSS" inverted	50·00	50·00
		c. "CSOSS" for "CROSS" ..	8·00	
		d. "2" in thick block type ..	3·00	3·50
		e. Surch. inverted	£110	
		f. Surch. omitted (pair) ..	£150	£150
20	1	2 c. on 4 c. orange	40	60
		a. Comma after "2 c". ..	3·25	
		b. "SS" in "CROSS" inverted	£120	
		c. "CSOSS" for "CROSS" ..	30·00	
21	,,	2 c. on 8 c. ultramarine ..	40	1·25
		a. Comma after "2 c". ..	3·25	
		b. "SS" in "CROSS" inverted	£120	
		c. "CSOSS" for "CROSS" ..	25·00	
		d. "RED CROSS" double ..		

1918. *Colour changed.*

22	1	2 c. on 4 c. red-brown & grn.	70	1·40
		a. Surch. omitted in pair ..	£100	

During a temporary shortage in 1921, 2 c., 4 c. and 6 c. stamps of the Straits Settlements were authorized for use in Trengganu.

4. Sultan Suleiman. **5.**

1921. *Chalk surfaced paper. P 14. (a) Wmk. Mult. Crown CA.*

23	4	$1 purple and blue/*blue* ..	3·00	4·00
24	,,	$3 green & red/*emerald* ..	11·00	14·00
25	5	$5 green & red/*pale yellow*	18·00	22·00
		(b) Wmk. Mult. Script CA.		
26	4	2 c. green	15	8
27	,,	4 c. carmine-red	25	10
28	,,	5 c. grey and deep brown ..	1·10	50
29	,,	10 c. bright blue	1·10	10
30	,,	20 c. dull purple & orange ..	1·10	60
31	,,	25 c. green and deep purple	1·00	65
32	,,	30 c. dull purple and black..	1·40	60
33	,,	50 c. green and brt. carmine	1·25	55
34	5	$25 purple and blue (S. £40)	£250	£150
35	,,	$50 green & yellow (S. £80)	£550	£550
36	,,	$100 green & scarlet (S. £140)	£1800	
23/33		.. .. *Set of* 11	35·00	40·00
23/33		Optd. "Specimen" *Set of* 11	70·00	

1922. *Optd.* "MALAYA-BORNEO EXHIBITION" *as T* **56** *of Straits Settlements.*

37	4	2 c. green	30	1·00
38	,,	4 c. carmine-red	90	1·25
39	1	5 c. grey and brown ..	1·10	1·40
40	,,	10 c. green and red/*yellow* ..	90	1·40
41	,,	20 c. dull and bright purple	60	2·00
42	,,	25 c. green and dull purple..	60	2·00
43	,,	30 c. dull purple and black..	80	2·00
44	,,	50 c. black/*green*	90	2·25
45	,,	$1 black and carmine/*blue*	3·00	5·00
46	,,	$3 green and red/*green* ..	25·00	28·00
47	2	$5 green and dull purple..	45·00	50·00
37/47		.. .. *Set of* 11	70·00	90·00

Minor varieties of this overprint exist as in Straits Settlements (*q.v.*).

1924–38. *New values, etc. Chalk-surfaced paper. Wmk. Mult. Script CA. P 14.*

48	4	1 c. black ('26)	15	10
49	,,	3 c. green ('26)	25	30
50	,,	3 c. brown ('38)	75	1·10
51	,,	5 c. purple/*yellow* ('26) ..	45	35
52	,,	6 c. orange ('24)	1·50	25
53	,,	8 c. grey ('38)	90	40
54	,,	12 c. bright ultramarine ('26)	1·10	1·40
55	,,	35 c. carmine/*yellow* ('26) ..	1·50	2·75
56	,,	$1 purple & blue/*blue* ('29)	5·00	2·50
57	,,	$3 green & red/*green* ('26)	11·00	13·00
58	,,	$5 green & red-*yellow* ('38)	40·00	60·00
48/58		.. .. *Set of* 11	55·00	70·00
48/58		Optd./Perf. "Specimen" *Set of* 11	70·00	

The 2 c. yellow, 6 c. grey, 8 c. red and 15 c. blue were issued, but only with opt. during the Japanese occupation of Malaya. Unoverprinted specimens are due to leakages.

2 CENTS
(6)

1941 (1 May). *Nos. 31 and 29 surch. as T* **6.**

59	4	2 c. on 5 c. purple/*yellow* ..	1·00	1·25
60	,,	8 c. on 10 c. bright blue ..	1·50	2·00

1948 (1 Dec.). *Royal Silver Wedding. As No 30/1 of Aden.*

61	10 c. violet	5	
62	$5 carmine	6·00	7·o

1949 (10 Oct.). *75th Anniv. of Universal Post Union. As Nos. 114/7 of Antigua.*

63	10 c. purple	12	1
64	15 c. deep blue	20	3
65	25 c. orange	30	5
66	50 c. blue-black	45	5

7. Sultan Ismail.

1949 (27 Dec.)–**55.** *Chalk-surfaced paper. Wmk Mult. Script CA. P* $17\frac{1}{2} \times 18$.

67	7	1 c. black	5	
68	,	2 c. orange	5	
69	,,	3 c. green	10	2
70	,,	4 c. brown	5	
71	,,	5 c. bright purple (1.9.52) ..	8	
72	,,	6 c. grey	12	1
73	,,	8 c. scarlet	12	2
74	,,	8 c. green (*shades*) (1.9.52)..	20	2
75	,,	10 c. purple	12	1
76	,,	12 c. scarlet (1.9.52).. ..	15	2
77	,,	15 c. ultramarine	15	1
78	,,	20 c. black and green ..	25	3
79	,,	20 c. bright blue (1.9.52) ..	15	1
80	,,	25 c. purple and orange ..	15	2
81	,,	30 c. scarlet & purple (5.9.55)	30	3
82	,,	35 c. scarlet & purple (1.9.52)	35	4
83	,,	40 c. red and purple.. ..	60	8
84	,,	50 c. black and blue.. ..	25	3
85	,,	$1 blue and purple ..	60	6
86	,,	$2 green and scarlet ..	1·75	2·5
87	,,	$5 green and brown ..	5·50	10·c
67/87		.. .. *Set of* 21	10·00	15·o

1953 (2 June). *Coronation. As No. 47 of Ader*

88	10 c. black and reddish purple	12	1

1957–63. *As Nos. 92/102 of Kedah, but with ins portrait of Sultan Ismail.*

89	1 c. black	5	
90	2 c. orange-red	5	
	a. Red-orange (21.2.61) ..	5	
91	4 c. sepia	5	
92	5 c. carmine-lake	8	
93	8 c. myrtle-green	12	1
94	10 c. deep brown	5	
94*a*	10 c. deep maroon (21.2.61) ..	5	
95	20 c. blue	10	1
96	50 c. black and blue (*p.* $12\frac{1}{2}$)..	30	3
	a. Perf. $12\frac{1}{2} \times 13$ (17.5.60) ..	40	4
	ab. Black and ultram. (20.3.62) ..	25	2
97	$1 ultram. & reddish purple	50	7
98	$2 bronze-green and scarlet	1·25	1·5
99	$5 brown and bronze-green	2·50	2·5
	a. Perf. $13 \times 12\frac{1}{2}$ (13.8.63) ..	2·25	2·2
89/99a	.. .. *Set of* 12	4·50	5·o

Dates of issue: 26.6.57, 20 c., $5; **25.7.5** 2 c., 50 c., $1; **4.8.57. 10 c.; 21.8.57,** others.

The 6, 12, 25 and 30 c. values used in Trenggan were Nos. 1/4 of Malayan Federation.

8. *Vanda hookeriana.*

1965 (15 Nov.). *As Nos. 166/72 of Johore but wit inset portrait of Sultan Ismail Nasiruddin Sha as in T* **8.**

100	1 c. multicoloured	5	
101	2 c. multicoloured	5	
102	5 c. multicoloured	5	
103	6 c. multicoloured	5	

4 10 c. multicoloured 5 5
5 15 c. multicoloured 8 8
6 20 c. multicoloured 8 8
a. Bright purple (blooms) omitted 20·00
o/6 .. .. *Set of* 7 30 30

The 5 c. value exists with PVA gum as well gum arabic.

No. 101a, formerly listed here, is now listed as arawak No. 213a.

The higher values used in Trengganu were os. 20/27 of Malaysia.

9. Sultan of Trengganu.

es. Enche Nik Zainal Abidin. Photo. Harrison.)

970 (16 Dec.). *25th Anniv. of Installation of H.R.H. Tuanku Ismail Nasiruddin Shah as Sultan of Trengganu. P* $14\frac{1}{2} \times 13\frac{1}{2}$.
07 **9** 10 c. multicoloured .. 5 5
08 „ 15 c. multicoloured .. 8 8
09 „ 50 c. multicoloured .. 25 25

10. Lime Butterfly.

971 (1 Feb.). *As Nos. 175/81 of Johore but with portrait of Sultan Ismail Nasiruddin Shah and Arms, as in T* **10**
10 1 c. multicoloured 5 5
11 2 c. multicoloured 5 5
12 5 c. multicoloured 5 5
13 6 c. multicoloured 5 5
14 10 c. multicoloured 5 5
15 15 c. multicoloured 8 8
16 20 c. multicoloured 8 8
10/16 .. .. *Set of* 7 25 25

The higher values used with this issue are os. 64/71 of Malaysia.

POSTAGE DUE STAMPS.

D 1

937 (10 Aug.). *Wmk. Mult. Script CA. P* 14.
1 D **1** 1 c. scarlet .. .. 40 1·00
2 „ 4 c. green .. .. 40 1·00
3 „ 8 c. yellow .. .. 2·50 5·00
4 „ 10 c. brown .. .. 3·75 9·00
1/4 Perf. "Specimen" *Set of* 4 25·00

JAPANESE OCCUPATION.

I. MALAYA.

For convenience we have included in one list the stamps of various States which could be used throughout Malaya and those which were issued and used in one State or district only; the latter being indicated by footnotes.

Collectors are warned against forgeries of the various overprints, particularly on the scarcer stamps.

The stamps listed below were all valid for postal use. A number of others overprinted with Types **2** or **4** were subsequently made available by favour and are known as "request stamps". Although they had postal validity they were not on sale to the public.

"Seal of Post Office of Malayan Military Dept."
(**1**)

(Handstamped at Singapore.)

1942 (16 Mar.). *Stamps of Straits Settlements optd. with T* **1**, *in red.*
J1 **58** 1 c. black .. .. .. 3·50 4·00
J2 „ 2 c. orange.. .. .. 4·00 4·50
J3 „ 3 c. green .. .. .. 11·00 14·00
J4 „ 8 c. grey .. .. .. 4·50 4·50
J5 „ 15 c. ultramarine .. .. 4·50 4·00

The overprint Type **1** has a double-lined frame, although the two lines are not always apparent, as in the illustration. Three chops were used, differing slightly in the shape of the characters, but forgeries also exist. It is distinguishable from Type **2** by its extra width, measuring approximately 14 mm. against $12\frac{1}{2}$ mm.

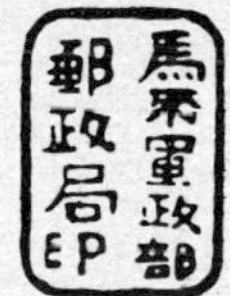

(**2**) (Upright)

(Handstamped at Singapore and Kuala Lumpur.)

1942 (3 Apr.). *Stamps optd. with T* **2**.
(a) On Straits Settlements.
J 6 **58** 1 c. black (R.) 75 75
a. Black opt. .. .. 20·00 20·00
b. Violet opt. .. .. 25·00 25·00
J 7 „ 2 c. green (V.) £200 £200
J 8 „ 2 c. orange (R.) 80 80
a. Black opt. .. .. 9·00 11·00
b. Violet opt. .. .. 9·00 11·00
c. Brown opt. .. .. 30·00 38·00
J 9 „ 3 c. green (R.) 90 85
a. Black opt. .. .. 25·00 25·00
b. Violet opt. .. .. 26·00 26·00
J10 „ 5 c. brown (R.) .. .. 2·75 3·50
a. Black opt. .. .. 32·00 32·00
J12 „ 8 c. grey (R.) .. .. 1·00 85
a. Black opt. .. .. 23·00 23·00
J13 „ 10 c. dull purple (R.) .. 3·75 5·00
a. Brown opt. .. .. 85·00 85·00
J14 „ 12 c. ultramarine (R.) .. 12·00 14·00
J15 „ 15 c. ultramarine (R.) .. 1·50 1·25
a. Violet opt. .. .. 32·00 32·00
J17 „ 30 c. dull pur. & orge. (R.) £140 £170
J18 „ 40 c. scar. & dull pur. (R.) 12·00 14·00
a. Brown opt. .. .. 32·00 26·00
J19 „ 50 c. black/*emerald* (R.) .. 8·00 8·50
J20 „ $1 black & red/*blue* (R.) 12·00 13·00
J21 „ $2 green & scarlet (R.) 18·00 20·00
J22 „ $5 green & red/*emer.*(R.) 23·00 26·00

(b) On Negri Sembilan.
J23 **6** 1 c. black (R.) .. .. 5·50 6·50
a. Violet opt. .. .. 5·50 5·50
b. Brown opt. .. .. 4·50 5·00
c. Black opt. .. .. 5·50 9·00
J24 **6** 2 c. orange (R.) .. .. 3·00 4·00
a. Violet opt. .. .. 8·50 7·00
b. Black opt. .. .. 6·00 7·00
c. Brown opt. .. .. 6·50 7·00
J25 „ 3 c. green (R.) .. .. 4·50 5·00
a. Violet opt. .. .. 8·50 8·50
b. Violet opt. (sideways) .. 38·00 38·00
c. Brown opt. .. .. 8·00 9·00
J27 „ 5 c. brown .. .. 4·50 5·50
a. Brown opt. .. .. 4·00 4·50
b. Red opt. .. .. 2·50 3·00
c. Violet opt. .. .. 8·00 8·00
J29 „ 6 c. grey .. .. .. 20·00 22·00
a. Brown opt. .. .. 65·00 65·00
J31 „ 8 c. scarlet .. .. 6·50 11·00
J32 „ 10 c. dull purple .. .. 12·00 14·00
a. Red opt. .. .. 8·50 9·00
b. Brown opt. .. .. 20·00 20·00
J32*c* „ 12 c. bright ultram. (Br.) 70·00 70·00
J33 „ 15 c. ultramarine (R.) .. 4·00 3·50
a. Violet opt. .. .. 8·00 8·50
J34 „ 25 c. dull purple & scarlet 9·00 9·00
a. Red opt. .. .. 17·00 20·00
b. Brown opt. .. .. 32·00 38·00
J35 „ 30 c. dull purple & orange 23·00 27·00
a. Brown opt. .. .. 70·00 75·00
J36 „ 40 c. scarlet and dull purple 60·00 65·00
a. Brown opt. £120 £130
J37 „ 50 c. black/*emerald* .. 24·00 28·00
J38 „ $1 black and red/*blue* 13·00 16·00
a. Red opt. .. .. 25·00 27·00
b. Brown opt. .. .. 55·00 55·00
J39 „ $5 green and red/*emerald* 55·00 65·00
a. Red opt. .. .. 55·00 65·00

(c) On Pahang.
J40 **7** 1 c. black .. .. .. 8·00 9·00
a. Red opt. .. .. 8·00 9·00
b. Violet opt. .. .. 27·00 32·00
c. Brown opt. .. .. 23·00 23·00
J41 „ 3 c. green .. .. .. 12·00 16·00
a. Red opt. .. .. 65·00 80·00
b. Violet opt. .. .. 85·00 85·00
J42 „ 5 c. brown .. .. 2·75 2·40
a. Red opt. .. .. 17·00 20·00
b. Brown opt. .. .. 26·00 26·00
c. Violet opt. .. .. 45·00 45·00
J44 8 c. grey .. .. .. 20·00 20·00
J45 „ 8 c. scarlet .. .. 5·00 2·50
a. Red opt .. .. 12·00 14·00
b. Violet opt. .. .. 12·00 14·00
c. Brown opt. .. .. 16·00 18·00
J46 „ 10 c. dull purple .. .. 8·00 9·00
a. Red opt. .. .. 12·00 15·00
b. Brown opt. .. .. 40·00 45·00
J47 „ 12 c. bright ultramarine .. £180 £180
a. Red opt. £325 £325
J48 „ 15c. ultramarine .. .. 13·00 13·00
a. red opt. .. .. 20·00 20·00
a. Violet opt. .. .. 65·00 65·00
c. Brown opt. .. .. 38·00 38·00
J49 „ 25 c. dull purple & scarlet .. 8·00 9·00
J50 „ 30 c. dull purple and orange 6·50 7·50
a. Red opt. .. .. 38·00 55·00
J51 „ 40 c. scarlet & dull purple .. 5·00 6·50
a. Brown opt. .. .. 32·00 35·00
b. Red opt. .. .. 8·00 8·00
J52 „ 50 c. black/*emerald* .. 35·00 45·00
a. Red opt. .. .. 65·00 65·00
J53 „ $1 black and red/*blue* (R.) 18·00 18·00
a. Black opt. .. .. 32·00 32·00
b. Brown opt. .. .. 65·00 65·00
J54 „ $5 green & red/*emerald* 80·00 85·00
a. Red opt. .. .. 85·00 90·00

(d) On Perak.
J55 **38** 1 c. black .. .. 6·00 6·50
a. Violet opt. .. .. 13·00 14·00
b. Brown opt. .. .. 17·00 18·00
J57 „ 2 c. orange .. .. 4·00 4·50
a. Violet opt. .. .. 13·00 14·00
b. Red opt. .. .. 6·00 6·00
c. Brown opt. .. .. 12·00 12·00
J58 „ 3 c. green .. .. 7·00 8·00
a. Violet opt. .. .. 32·00 35·00
b. Brown opt. .. .. 30·00 30·00
c. Red opt. .. .. 30·00 30·00
J59 „ 5 c. brown .. .. 2·00 2·00
a. Brown opt. .. .. 6·00 6·50
b. Violet opt. .. .. 18·00 22·00
c. Red opt. .. .. 18·00 22·00
J61 „ 8 c. grey .. .. 8·00 8·50
a. Red opt. .. .. 38·00 40·00
b. Brown opt. .. .. 38·00 40·00
J62 „ 8 c. scarlet .. .. 4·00 12·00
a. Violet opt. .. .. 38·00

No.	Type	Description	Un.	Used
J63	**38**	10 c. dull purple	4·00	8·00
		a. Red opt.	18·00	20·00
J64	,,	12 c. bright ultramarine ..	20·00	22·00
J65	,,	15 c. ultramarine	6·50	8·50
		a. Red opt.	12·00	12·00
		b. Violet opt.	27·00	27·00
		c. Brown opt.	23·00	23·00
J66	,,	25 c. dull purple and scarlet	4·00	5·50
J67	,,	30 c. dull purple & orange	7·50	9·50
		a. Brown opt.	24·00	26·00
		b. Red opt.	12·00	12·00
J68	,,	40 c. scarlet & dull purple	42·00	45·00
		a. Brown opt.	75·00	75·00
J69	,,	50 c. black/*emerald* ..	5·50	8·00
		a. Red opt.	9·00	9·50
		b. Brown opt.	19·00	19·00
J70	,,	$1 black and red/*blue*	42·00	50·00
		a. Brown opt.	85·00	
J71	,,	$2 green and scarlet ..	£150	£150
J72	,,	$5 green & red/*emerald*	£120	
		a. Brown opt.	£200	

(*e*) *On Selangor.*

No.	Type	Description	Un.	Used
J73	**22**	1 c. black, S	2·50	2·50
		a. Red opt., SU ..	4·00	4·50
		b. Violet opt., SU ..	8·00	9·00
J74	,,	2 c. green, U	75·00	75·00
		a. Violet opt., U ..	£130	£130
J75	,,	2 c. orange (*p.* 14×15), S	8·00	9·00
		a. Red opt., U ..	19·00	21·00
		b. Violet opt., U ..	30·00	23·00
		c. Brown opt., S ..	8·00	9·00
J76	,,	2 c. orange (*p.* 14), S ..	10·00	12·00
		a. Red opt., U ..	21·00	24·00
		b. Violet opt., U ..	45·00	45·00
J77	,,	3 c. green, SU	4·00	5·00
		a. Red opt., SU ..	4·00	5·00
		b. Violet opt., S ..	12·00	14·00
		c. Brown opt., SU ..	2·50	2·50
J78	,,	5 c. brown, S	1·75	1·60
		a. Red opt., S ..	4·00	4·50
		b. Violet opt., SU ..	6·00	7·00
		c. Brown opt., SU ..	10·00	10·00
J79	,,	6 c. scarlet, S	30·00	32·00
		a. Red opt., S ..	38·00	38·00
		b. Brown opt., S ..	55·00	
J80	,,	8 c. grey, S	4·00	4·50
		a. Red opt., SU ..	6·00	7·00
		b. Violet opt., U ..	8·00	9·00
		c. Brown opt., S ..	12·00	8·00
J81	,,	10 c. dull purple, S ..	4·00	5·00
		a. Red opt., S ..	10·00	10·00
		b. Brown opt., S ..	8·00	6·00
J82	,,	12 c. brt. ultramarine, S ..	8·50	9·00
		a. Red opt., S ..	16·00	17·00
		b. Brown opt., S ..	17·00	17·00
J83	,,	15 c. ultramarine, S ..	4·00	4·50
		a. Red opt., SU ..	8·00	9·00
		b. Violet opt., U ..	26·00	26·00
		c. Brown opt., S ..	8·00	9·00
J84	,,	25 c. dull pur. & scar., S	20·00	21·00
		a. Red opt., S ..	17·00	18·00
J85	,,	30 c. dull pur. & orge., S	5·50	7·00
		a. Brown opt., S ..	23·00	23·00
J86	,,	40 c. scarlet & dull pur., S	10·00	11·00
		a. Brown opt., S ..	26·00	24·00
J87	,,	50 c. black/*emerald*, S ..	10·00	11·00
		a. Red opt., S ..	15·00	16·00
		b. Brown opt., S ..	16·00	17·00
J88	**24**	$1 black and red/*blue*	9·00	9·00
		a. Red opt.	20·00	22·00
J89	,,	$2 green and scarlet ..	10·00	11·00
		a. Red opt.	30·00	35·00
J91	,,	$5 green & red/*emerald*	15·00	15·00

On T **22** the overprint is normally sideways (with "top" to either right or left), but on T **24** it is always upright.

S = Sideways
U = Upright
SU = Sideways or upright (our prices being for the cheaper).

(*f*) *On Trengganu* (*all Script wmk.*).

No.	Type	Description	Un.	Used
J92	**4**	1 c. black	20·00	22·00
		a. Red opt.	27·00	30·00
		b. Brown opt.	45·00	45·00
J93	,,	2 c. green	30·00	35·00
		a. Red opt.	35·00	40·00
		b. Brown opt.	50·00	50·00
J94	,,	2 c. on 5 c. (No. 59)	20·00	20·00
		a. Red opt.	12·00	12·00
J95	,,	3 c. brown	21·00	20·00
		a. Brown opt.	60·00	60·00
J96	,,	4 c. carmine-red ..	38·00	30·00
J97	,,	5 c. purple/*yellow* ..	3·50	4·00
		a. Red opt.	5·50	
J98	**4**	6 c. orange	4·00	6·00
		a. Red opt.	6·50	
		b. Brown opt.	26·00	26·00
J99	,,	8 c. grey	4·50	4·50
		a. Brown to red opt. ..	9·00	
J100	,,	8 c. on 10 c. (No. 60) ..	4·00	7·50
		a. Red opt.	8·50	
J101	,,	10 c. bright blue	4·50	7·00
		a. Red opt.	8·50	
		b. Brown opt.	30·00	30·00
J102	,,	12 c. bright ultramarine ..	4·00	5·50
		a. Red opt.	8·50	
J103	,,	20 c. dull purple & orange	4·50	6·00
		a. Red opt.	6·50	
J104	,,	25 c. green & deep purple	4·50	6·00
		a. Red opt.	6·50	
		b. Brown opt.	20·00	20·00
J105	,,	30 c. dull purple & black ..	4·50	6·00
		a. Red opt.	6·50	
J106	,,	35 c. carmine/*yellow* ..	4·50	6·00
		a. Red opt.	6·50	
J107	,,	50 c. green & brt. carmine	14·00	16·00
J108	,,	$1 purple and blue/*blue*	£225	£225
J109	,,	$3 green and red/*green*	13·00	14·00
		a. Red opt.	14·00	
J110	**5**	$5 green & red/*yellow* ..	30·00	32·00
J111	,,	$25 purple and blue ..	£110	
		a. Red opt.	£225	
J112	,,	$50 green and yellow ..	£225	
J113	,,	$100 green and scarlet ..	£150	

Nos. J92/113 were issued in Trengganu only.

軍政部
マラッカ州
政廳之印

(3. "Seal of the Government Office of the Malacca Military Dept." (approx. size).)

1942 (23 Apr.). *Stamps of Straits Settlements handstamped as T* **3**, *in red, each impression covering four stamps.*

No.	Type	Description	Single Un.	Single Used
J114	**58**	1 c. black	11·00	12·00
J115	,,	2 c. orange	11·00	12·00
J116	,,	3 c. green	11·00	12·00
J117	,,	5 c. brown	22·00	26·00
J118	,,	8 c. grey	30·00	26·00
J119	,,	10 c. dull purple	12·00	14·00
J120	,,	12 c. ultramarine ..	20·00	20·00
J121	,,	15 c. ultramarine ..	17·00	17·00
J123	,,	40 c. scarlet & dull pur.	32·00	35·00
J124	,,	50 c. black/*emerald* ..	80·00	80·00
J125	,,	$1 black and red/*blue*	90·00	£100

Nos. J114 to J125 were issued in Malacca only. Blocks of 4 are worth from about six times the single prices.

DAI NIPPON 2602 MALAYA
(4)

DAI NIPPON 2602 MALAYA 2 Cents
(5)

SELANGOR EXHIBITION DAI NIPPON 2602 MALAYA
(6)

1942. *Optd. with T* **4.**

(*a*) *On Straits Settlements.*

No.	Type	Description	Un.	Used
J128	**58**	2 c. orange	30	30
		a. Opt. inverted	3·50	4·00
		b. Opt. double, one inverted	12·00	15·00
J129	,,	3 c. green	12·00	13·00
J130	,,	8 c. grey	90	90
		a. Opt. inverted	6·50	8·50
J131	,,	15 c. blue	2·50	2·25

(*b*) *On Negri Sembilan.*

No.	Type	Description	Un.	Used
J132	**6**	1 c. black	25	25
		a. Opt. inverted	4·50	6·00
		b. Opt double, one inverted	12·00	14·00
J133	,,	2 c. orange	25	25
J134	,,	3 c. green	25	35
J135	,,	5 c. brown	30	40
J136	,,	6 c. grey	55	60
		a. Opt. inverted	—	£160
J137	,,	8 c. scarlet	90	80
J138	**6**	10 c. dull purple	2·25	2·0
J139	,,	15 c. ultramarine	2·00	2·2
J140	,,	25 c. dull purple & scarlet	90	2·2
J141	,,	30 c. dull purple & orange	1·10	2·0
J142	,,	$1 black and red/*blue* ..	30·00	38·0

(*c*) *On Pahang.*

No.	Type	Description	Un.	Used
J143	**7**	1 c. black	20	2
J144	,,	5 c. brown	40	5
J145	,,	8 c. scarlet	7·00	2
J146	,,	10 c. dull purple	4·50	2·5
J147	,,	12 c. bright ultramarine ..	45	7
J148	,,	25 c. dull purple & scarlet	1·75	2·5
J149	,,	30 c. dull purple & orange	45	8

(*d*) *On Perak.*

No.	Type	Description	Un.	Used
J151	**38**	2 c. orange	30	3
		a. Opt. inverted	7·00	8·5
J152	,,	3 c. green	25	3
		a. Opt. inverted	4·50	6·0
J154	,,	8 c. scarlet	40	2
		a. Opt. inverted	3·25	3·5
		b. Opt. double, one inverted	40·00	42·0
		c. Opt. omitted, (pair with normal)	75·00	
J155	,,	10 c. dull purple	2·50	3·2
J156	,,	15 c. ultramarine ..	1·25	1·1
J158	,,	50 c. black/*emerald* ..	1·10	1·5
J159	,,	$1 black and red/*blue*	50·00	60·0
J160	,,	$5 green & red/*emerald*	12·00	13·0
		a. Opt. inverted ..	70·00	80·0

(*e*) *On Selangor.*

No.	Type	Description	Un.	Used
J162	**22**	3 c. green	25	3
J165	,,	12 c. bright ultramarine	55	9
J166	,,	15 c. ultramarine ..	1·75	1·2
J168	,,	40 c. scarlet & dull purple	1·25	1·6
J170	,,	$2 green and scarlet ..	6·00	7·0

On T **22** the overprint is sideways, with "top to left or right.

(*f*) *On Trengganu* (*all Script wmk.*).

No.	Type	Description	Un.	Used
J172	**4**	1 c. black	2·50	2·5
J173	,,	2 c. green	40·00	42·0
J174	,,	2 c. on 5 c. (No. 59) ..	2·50	2·5
J175	,,	3 c. brown	3·50	5·5
J176	,,	4 c. carmine-red ..	2·50	3·5
J177	,,	5 c. purple/*yellow* ..	2·50	2·5
J178	,,	6 c. orange	2·50	3·5
J179	,,	8 c. grey	12·00	7·5
J180	,,	8 c. on 10 c. (No. 60) ..	2·00	2·5
J181	,,	12 c. bright ultramarine ..	1·90	3·2
J182	,,	20 c. dull purple & orange	2·50	4·0
J183	,,	25 c. green & dp. purple ..	2·50	5·0
J184	,,	30 c. dull purple & black ..	2·50	5·0
J185	,,	$3 green and red/*green*	12·00	17·0

Nos. J172/85 were issued in Trengganu only

1942. *No.* 104 *of Perak surch. with T* **5.**

No.	Type	Description	Un.	Used
J186	**38**	2 c. on 5 c. brown ..	80	3

1942 (3 Nov.). *Agri-horticultural Exhibitio Nos.* 294 *and* 283 *of Straits Settlements opt. with T* **6.**

No.	Type	Description	Un.	Used
J187	**58**	2 c. orange	2·50	2·5
		a. "C" for "G" in "SELANGOR" ..	30·00	35·0
		b. Opt. inverted	£100	£10
J188		8 c. grey	1·60	1·6
		a. "C" for "G" in "SELANGOR" ..	30·00	35·0
		b. Opt. inverted	£100	£10

Nos. J187/8 were only issued in Selangor.

DAI NIPPON 2602
(7)

DAI NIPPON 2602
(8)

1942 (13 May). *Stamps of Kedah* (*Script wmk optd.*

(*a*) *With T* **7.**

No.	Type	Description	Un.	Used
J189	**1**	1 c. black (R.)	60	8
J190	,,	2 c. bright green (R.) ..	4·50	5·5
J191	,,	4 c. violet (R.)	45	5
J192	,,	5 c. yellow (R.)	45	4
		a. Black opt.	40·00	40·0
J193	,,	6 c. carmine	45	8
J194	,,	8 c. grey-black (R.) ..	80	6

(*b*) *With T* **8.**

No.	Type	Description	Un.	Used
J195	**6**	10 c. ultram. & sepia (R.)	90	9
J196	,,	12 c. black and violet (R.)	3·00	5·5
J197	,,	25 c. ultram. & pur. (R.)	1·60	1·6
		a. Black opt.	40·00	45·0
J198	,,	30 c. green and scarlet (R.)	13·00	14·0
J199	,,	40 c. black & purple (R.)	4·50	6·0
J200	,,	50 c. brown and blue (R.)	5·00	7·5
J201	,,	$1 black and green (R.)	22·00	22·0
		a. Opt. inverted	70·00	70·0
J202	,,	$2 green and brown (R.)	30·00	30·0

ɪ203 6 $5 black & scarlet (R.) 12·00 12·00
a. Black opt. .. .. 75·00 80·00

Nos. J189 to J203a were issued in Kedah only.

奥川 (8a) kugawa Seal. (8b) Ochibury Seal. 亮印奥川 (8c) Okugawa-Ryo Seal.

942 (30 Mar.). *Straits Settlements stamps optd.*
(a) As T **8a** *(three forms of this seal).*

203b 58 1 c. black .. .. 2·00 2·00
203c ,, 2 c. orange .. .. 4·50 4·50
203d ,, 3 c. green .. .. 4·00 4·50
203e ,, 5 c. brown .. .. 4·00 4·50
203f ,, 8 c. grey .. .. 4·50 4·50
203g ,, 10 c. dull purple .. .. 4·50 4·50
203h ,, 12 c. ultramarine .. .. 4·50 6·00
203i ,, 15 c. ultramarine .. .. 6·00 6·00
203j ,, 40 c. scarlet & dull pur. 12·00 12·00
203k ,, 50 c. black/*emerald* .. 13·00 13·00
203l ,, $1 black and red/*blue* 20·00 20·00
203m ,, $2 green and scarlet .. 35·00 40·00
203n ,, $5 green & red/*emerald* £120 £140

(b) With T **8b**.

203o 58 1 c. black .. .. 8·50 9·00
203p ,, 2 c. orange .. .. 9·00 10·00
203q ,, 3 c. green .. .. 8·00 9·00
203r ,, 5 c. brown .. .. 60·00 60·00
203s ,, 8 c. grey .. .. 6·50 7·00
203t ,, 10 c. dull purple .. .. 6·50 9·00
203u ,, 12 c. ultramarine .. .. 6·50 9·00
203v ,, 15 c. ultramarine .. .. 6·50 9·00

Nos. J203b/v were issued only in Penang.

We have seen the 2 c. orange and 3 c. green verprinted with T **8c** supported by Expert ommittee certificates and the 1 c. is also re-orted to exist. These are believed to be evenue stamps that may have done postal duty ithout authorisation.

AI NIPPON 2602 PENANG (9)

DAI NIPPON YUBIN 2 Cents ("Japanese Postal Service.") (10)

942 (15 Apr.). *Straits Settlements stamps optd. with T* **9**.

204 58 1 c. black (R.) 40 45
a. Opt. inverted .. .. 20·00 20·00
205 ,, 2 c. orange 60 70
a. "PE" for "PENANG" 10·00 11·00
b. Opt. inverted .. 20·00
c. Opt. double .. ..
206 ,, 3 c. green (R.) 40 45
207 ,, 5 c. brown (R.) 40 50
a. "N PPON" .. .. 20·00
b. Opt. double .. ..
208 ,, 8 c. grey (R.) 90 80
a. "N PPON" .. .. 7·50 9·00
b. Opt. double, one invtd. 20·00
209 ,, 10 c. dull purple (R.) .. 90 90
a. Opt. double .. .. 32·00
210 ,, 12 c. ultramarine (R.) .. 90 95
a. "N PPON" .. .. 45·00
b. Opt. double .. .. 32·00
211 ,, 15 c. ultramarine (R.) .. 90 90
a. "N PPON" .. .. 20·00
b. Opt. inverted .. .. 55·00
c. Opt. double .. .. 55·00
212 ,, 40 c. scarlet & dull pur. 1·10 1·25
213 ,, 50 c. black/*emerald* (R.) 2·25 2·40
214 ,, $1 black & red/*blue* .. 3·00 4·00
215 ,, $2 green and scarlet .. 7·50 8·50
216 ,, $5 green & red/*emerald* 65·00 70·00

Nos. J204/16 were issued in Penang and Vellesley Province only.

942 (Dec.). *Perak stamps surch. or optd. only, as in T* **10**.

217 38 1 c. black .. .. 70 1·10
a. Opt. inverted .. .. 8·50 9·50
218 ,, 2 c. on 5 c. brown 80 65
a. "DAI NIPPON YUBIN" inverted .. .. 6·50 8·00
b. Do and "2 Cents" omitted .. .. 12·00 18·00

J219 38 8 c. scarlet .. .. 1·00 70
a. Opt. inverted .. .. 6·50 7·50

In December 1942 contemporary Japanese 3, 5, 8 and 25 c. stamps were issued without overprint in Singapore and the 1, 2, 4, 6, 7, 10, 30 and 50 c. and $1 values were issued in February 1943.

大日本郵便 (11)

Error. 2nd character sideways → 大日本郵便 (13)

大日本郵便 ("Japanese Postal Service.") (12)

6cts. (14) 6 cts. (15) 2 Cents (16)

6 cts. (17) $1.00 (18)

1943–45. *Stamps of the various Malayan territories optd. with T* **11** *or* **12** *(so-called "Kanji" characters), in black or red, some stamps surch. in addition as T* **14** *to* **18**.

(a) On Straits Settlements (opt. T **11**).

J221 58 8 c. grey (Bk.) 20 20
a. Opt. inverted .. .. 10·00 10·00
b. Red opt. 30 30
J222 ,, 12 c. ultramarine 30 80
J223 ,, 40 c. scarlet & dull purple 40 65

(b) On Negri Sembilan (opt. T **11**).

J224 6 1 c. black 12 25
a. Opt. inverted .. .. 4·50 6·00
b. Error. T 13 .. .. 6·00 6·00
ba. T 13 inverted £120
J225 ,, 2 c. on 5 c. brown (T **14**) 15 15
J226 ,, 6 c. on 5 c. brown (T **15**) 20 20
J227 ,, 25 c. dull purple & scarlet 60 70

(c) On Pahang (opt. T **11**).

J228 7 6 c. on 5 c. brown (T **14**) 30 40
J229 , 6 c. on 5 c. brown (T **15**) 60 70

(d) On Perak (opt. T **11**).

J230 38 1 c. black 20 25
a. Error. T 13 .. .. 30·00 32·00
J232 ,, 2 c. on 5 c. brown (T **14**) 30 30
a. Opt. & surch. inverted .. 9·00 12·00
b. Opt. only inverted .. 9·00 12·00
c. Error. T 13 .. .. 11·00 12·00
J233 ,, 2 c. on 5 c. brown (T **16**) 30 30
a. Opt. & surch. inverted .. 9·00 12·00
b. Surch. only inverted .. 9·00 12·00
c. Error. T 13 .. .. 8·00 9·00
ca. Opt. & surch. inverted .. £200
cb. Surch. only inverted .. £180
J235 ,, 5 c. brown 30 25
a. Opt. inverted .. .. 12·00 14·00
b. Error. T 13 .. .. 65·00 £120
J237 ,, 8 c. scarlet 40 35
a. Opt. inverted .. .. 8·00 9·00
b. Error. T 13 .. .. 16·00 22·00
ba. T 13 inverted £180
J238 ,, 10 c. dull purple 45 35
J239 ,, 30 c. dull purple & orange 90 1·10
J240 ,, 50 c. black/*emerald* .. 2·00 2·25
J241 ,, $5 green & red/*emerald* 16·00 18·00

(e) On Selangor.

(i) *Opt. T* **11** *placed horizontally either way on T* **22** *and vertically on T* **24**.

J242 22 1 c. black 35 35
J243 ,, 3 c. green 25 30
a. Error. T 13 .. .. 6·50 8·00
J244 ,, 12 c. bright ultramarine 30 65
a. Error. T 13 .. .. 6·50 9·00
J245 ,, 15 c. ultramarine .. 1·60 1·60
a. Error. T 13 .. .. 9·00 11·00
J246 24 $1 black and red/*blue* 1·75 2·00
a. Error. T 13 .. .. 80·00 £100
b. Opt. inverted .. .. 80·00 £100
J247 ,, $2 green and scarlet 5·50 6·00
J248 ,, $5 green & red/*emerald* 8·00 9·00
a. Opt. inverted .. .. 80·00 90·00

(ii) *Opt. T* **12**.

J249 22 1 c. black (R.) 15 20
J250 ,, 2 c. on 5 c. brn. (T **15**) (R.) 12 30
J251 ,, 3 c. on 5 c. brown (T **15**) 12 30
a. "s" in "cts." inverted 12·00 17·00
b. Comma after "cts." .. 12·00 17·00
J252 ,, 5 c. brown (R.) 15 25
J253 ,, 6 c. on 5 c. brown (T **15**) 10 25
J254 ,, 6 c. on 5 c. brown (T **17**) 10 12
a. "6" inverted .. £120
J255 ,, 15 c. ultramarine .. 2·50 2·50
J256 ,, $1.00 on 10 c. dull purple (T **18**) 12 60
J257 ,, $1.50 on 30 c. dull purple & orange (T **18**) .. 12 60

(f) On Trengganu (opt. T **11**).

J258 4 1 c. black .. .. .. 2·00 6·00
J259 ,, 2 c. green .. .. .. 2·00 7·50
J260 ,, 2 c. on 5 c. purple/*yellow* (No. 59) .. .. 2·00 6·00
J261 ,, 5 c. purple/*yellow* .. 2·00 6·00
J262 ,, 6 c. orange .. .. 3·00 7·00
J263 ,, 8 c. grey .. .. .. 12·00 16·00
J264 ,, 8 c. on 10 c. bright blue (No. 60) .. .. 6·00 11·00
J265 ,, 10 c. bright blue .. .. 22·00 38·00
J266 ,, 12 c. bright ultramarine .. 4·00 9·00
J267 ,, 20 c. dull pur. & orange 4·00 9·00
J268 ,, 25 c. green & dp. purple 4·00 10·00
J269 ,, 30 c. dull purple & black 4·00 10·00
J270 ,, 35 c. carmine/*yellow* .. 4·00 10·00

Nos. J258/70 were issued in Trengganu only.

大日本 マライ郵便 50セント (18a)

大日本 マライ郵便 1ドル (18b)

大日本 マライ郵便 1½ドル (18c)

1944 (16 Dec.). *Stamps intended for use on Red Cross letters. Surch. with T* **18a/c**.

(a) On Straits Settlements.

J270a 58 50 c. on 50 c. black/*emer.* 3·00 6·00
J270b ,, $1 on $1 blk. & red/*bl.* 4·50 8·50
J270c ,, $1.50 on $2 grn. & scar. 8·00 17·00

(b) On Johore.

J270d 29 50 c. on 50 c. dull purple and red .. .. 3·00 6·00
J270e ,, $1.50 on $2 green and carmine .. .. 2·25 5·00

(c) On Selangor.

J270f 24 $1 on $1 blk. & red/*bl.* 2·25 5·50
J270g ,, $1.50 on $2 grn. & scar. 3·00 6·00

No. J270a/g were issued in Singapore but were withdrawn after one day, probably because supplies of Nos. J256/7 were received and issued on the 18th December.

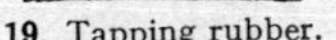

19. Tapping rubber.

20. Fruit.

21. Tin-dredger.

22. War Memorial.

23. Huts.

24. Japanese shrine, Singapore.

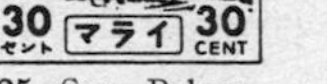

25. Sago Palms.

26. Straits of Johore.

27. Malay Mosque, Kuala Lumpur.

(Printed by offset-litho in Batavia.)

1943. *P* 12½.

J271	**19**	1 c. grey-green (1 Oct.)	10	10
J272	**20**	2 c. pale emer. (1 June)	10	10
J273	**19**	3 c. drab (1 Oct.) ..	10	10
J274	**21**	4 c. carm.-rose (29 Apr.)	10	10
J275	**22**	8 c. dull blue (29 Apr.) ..	10	10
J276	**23**	10 c. brown-pur. (1 Oct.)	10	10
J277	**24**	15 c. violet (1 Oct.) ..	15	12
J278	**25**	30 c. olive-green (1 Oct.)	15	15
J279	**26**	50 c. blue (1 Oct.) ..	30	30
J280	**27**	70 c. blue (1 Oct.) ..	3·00	2·50
J271/80		.. .. *Set of* 10	3·75	3·25

28. Ploughman.

29. Rice-planting.

1943 (1 SEPT.). *Savings Campaign. Litho. P* 12½.

J281	**28**	8 c. violet	3·00	75
J282	,,	15 c. scarlet	1·75	80

(Des. Hon Chin. Litho.)

1944 (15 FEB.). *"Re-birth" of Malaya. P* 12½.

J283	**29**	8 c. rose-red	1·40	1·00
J284	,,	15 c. magenta	1·40	1·00

POSTAGE DUE STAMPS.

Postage Due stamps of the various Malayan territories overprinted.

1942 (3 APR.). *Handstamped with T* **2** *in black*

(a) On Malayan Postal Union.

JD1	D **1**	1 c. slate-purple ..	3·00	3·50
		a. Red opt.	6·00	7·00
		b. Brown opt.	12·00	14·00
JD2	,,	3 c. green	3·25	4·00
		a. Red opt.	10·00	16·00
JD3	,,	4 c. green	3·25	1·60
		a. Red opt.	8·50	9·00
		b. Brown opt.	16·00	18·00
JD4	D **1**	8 c. scarlet	4·50	5·50
		a. Red opt.	12·00	12·00
		b. Brown opt.	16·00	16·00
JD5	,,	10 c. yellow-orange ..	4·50	5·50
		a. Red opt.	4·50	5·50
		b. Brown opt.	8·00	9·00
JD6	,,	12 c. ultramarine ..	5·00	5·50
		a. Red opt.	8·50	9·00
JD7	,,	50 c. black	8·50	9·00
		a. Red opt.	18·00	20·00

(b) On Johore.

JD 8	D **1**	1 c. carmine (R). ..	12·00	
		a. Black opt.	12·00	
JD 9	,,	4 c. green (R.) ..	12·00	
		a. Black opt.	16·00	
JD10	,,	8 c. orange (R.) ..	20·00	
		a. Black opt.	12·00	
JD11	,,	10 c. brown (R.) ..	6·00	
		a. Black opt.	5·50	
JD12	,,	12 c. purple (R.) ..	8·00	
		a. Black opt.	8·00	

The above were issued only in Johore.

(c) On Trengganu.

JD13	,,	1 c. scarlet	10·00	13·00
JD14	,,	4 c. green	12·00	10·00
		a. Red opt.	10·00	12·00
JD15	,,	8 c. yellow	6·50	10·00
JD16	,,	10 c. brown	6·50	10·00

Nos. JD13/16 were issued in Trengganu only.

1942 (23 APR.). *Handstamped on Malayan Postal Union with T* **3**, *in red, each impression covering four stamps.*

JD17	D **1**	1 c. slate-purple ..	16·00	16·00
JD18	,,	4 c. green	24·00	26·00
JD19	,,	8 c. scarlet	£200	£170
JD20	,,	10 c. yellow-orange ..	32·00	32·00
JD21	,,	12 c. ultramarine ..	40·00	45·00
JD22	,,	50 c. black	£200	£250

Nos. JD17/22 were issued in Malacca only. Prices quoted are for single stamps. Blocks of four are worth about six times the price of a single stamp.

1942. *Optd. on Malayan Postal Union with T* **4**, *in black.*

JD23	D **1**	1 c. slate-purple ..	40	45
JD24	,,	3 c. green	1·00	1·10
JD25	,,	4 c. green	1·25	1·10
JD26	,,	8 c. scarlet	1·75	2·00
JD27	,,	10 c. yellow-orange ..	1·00	1·10
JD28	,,	12 c. ultramarine ..	1·00	1·10

1943–45. *Optd. with T* **11.**

(a) On Malayan Postal Union.

JD29	D **1**	1 c. slate-purple ..	20	45
JD30	,,	3 c. green	20	55
JD31	,,	4 c. green	8·00	10·00
JD32	,,	5 c. scarlet	25	85
JD33	,,	9 c. yellow-orange ..	40	90
		a. Opt. inverted ..	12·00	12·00
JD34	,,	10 c. yellow-orange ..	40	1·10
		a. Opt. inverted ..	18·00	18·00
JD35	,,	12 c. ultramarine ..	40	1·25
JD36	,,	15 c. ultramarine ..	40	1·25

(b) On Johore.

JD37	D **1**	1 c. carmine	40	1·40
		a. Error. Optd. with T 13	8·00	12·00
JD38	,,	4 c. green	40	1·40
		a. Error. Optd. with T 13	8·00	12·00
JD39	,,	8 c. orange	1·00	3·00
		a. Error. Optd. with T 13	12·00	14·00
JD40	,,	10 c. brown	85	3·50
		a. Error. Optd. with T 13	12·00	14·00
JD41	,,	12 c. purple	85	3·50
		a. Error. Optd. with T 13	12·00	14·00

Nos. JD37/41 were used only in Johore. Postage stamps of Johore optd. with Type **4** were authorized for use for revenue purposes only.

II. KELANTAN.

40 CENTS
(JK 1)

$1.00
(JK 2)

Sunagawa Seal.

Handa Seal.

1942 (JUNE). *Kelantan stamps surch. as Ty[pe] JK* **1** *or JK* **2** *(dollar values).*

(a) With Sunagawa Seal in red.

JK 1	**4**	1 c. on 50 c. grey-olive and orange ..	32·00	35·[…]
JK 2	,,	2 c. on 40 c. orange and blue-green	24·00	30·[…]
JK 3	,,	4 c. on 30 c. vio. & scar.	65·00	70·[…]
JK 4	,,	5 c. on 12 c. blue (R.) ..	18·00	22·[…]
JK 5	,,	6 c. on 25 c. verm. & vio.	22·00	30·[…]
JK 6	,,	8 c. on 5 c. red-brn. (R.)	30·00	32·[…]
JK 7	,,	10 c. on 6 c. lake	17·00	20·[…]
JK 8	,,	12 c. on 8 c. grey-olive (R.)	12·00	16·[…]
JK 9	,,	25 c. on 10 c. purple (R.)	£120	£1[…]
JK10	,,	30 c. on 4 c. scarlet ..	£130	£1[…]
JK11	,,	40 c. on 2 c. green (R.) ..	13·00	18·[…]
JK12	,,	50 c. on 1 c. grey-olive and yellow	65·00	70·[…]
JK13	**1**	$1 on 4 c. black and red (R., bars Bk.)	16·00	18·[…]
JK14	,,	$2 on 5 c. green and red/*yellow* (R.)	16·00	17·[…]
JK15	,,	$5 on 6 c. scarlet ..	16·00	18·[…]

(b) With Handa Seal in red.

JK16		12 c. on 8 c. grey-olive (R.)	25·00	30·[…]

1 Cents

(JK 3)

1942. *Kelantan stamps surcharged as Type* JK [3]

(a) With Sunagawa Seal in red.

JK17	**4**	1 c. on 50 c. grey-olive and orange	20·00	20·[…]
JK18	,,	2 c. on 40 c. orange and blue-green	20·00	20·[…]
JK19	,,	5 c. on 12 c. blue (R.) ..	13·00	14·[…]
JK20	,,	8 c. on 5 c. red-brn. (R.)	13·00	13·[…]
JK21	,,	10 c. on 6 c. lake	13·00	14·[…]
JK22	,,	12 c. on 8 c. grey-ol. (R.)	13·00	16·[…]
JK23	,,	30 c. on 4 c. scarlet ..	£130	£1[…]
JK24	,,	40 c. on 2 c. green (R.) ..	13·00	17·[…]
JK25	,,	50 c. on 1 c. grey-olive & yellow	60·00	65·[…]

(b) With Handa Seal in red.

JK26	**4**	1 c. on 50 c. grey-olive & orange	20·00	26·[…]
JK27	,,	2 c. on 40 c. orange and blue-green	20·00	26·[…]
JK28	,,	8 c. on 5 c. red-brown ..	20·00	26·[…]
JK29	,,	10 c. on 6 c. lake ..	21·00	24·[…]

The above stamps all exist with error "Cente[s]" for "Cents" (No. 41 on sheet). They are wort[h] about five times the prices for the normal stamp[s].

All the above were overprinted with th[e] personal Seals of Sunagawa, the Governor or [of] Handa, the Assistant Governor, to indicate tha[t] these were Japanese stamps. Some of these als[o] exist without the seals and come from remainde[r] stocks sent to Singapore and Kuala Lumpur afte[r] Kelantan was ceded to Thailand.

THAI OCCUPATION.

Stamps issued for use in the four Mala[y] States of Kedah, Kelantan, Perlis and Trenggan[u] ceded by Japan to Thailand on 19th October, 194[3] and restored to British rule on the defeat of th[e] Japanese.

I. KELANTAN.

TK 1

(Ptd. at Khota Baru.)

1943 (15 Nov.). *Surch. with value and inscr. in black. No gum. P 11.*

TK1 TK **1** 1 c. violet .. .. 10·00 12·00
TK2 ,, 2 c. violet .. .. 10·00 12·00
a. Violet omitted .. 50·00
TK3 ,, 4 c. violet .. .. 10·00 12·00
a. Violet omitted ..
TK4 ,, 8 c. violet .. .. 10·00 12·00
a. Violet omitted .. 30·00
TK5 ,, 10 c. violet .. .. 10·00 15·00

The above bear sheet watermarks in the form of double-lined "STANDARD" with curved "CROWN" above and "AGENTS" below which occur four times in the sheet.

These stamps but with centres printed in red were for fiscal use.

II. MALAYA.

TM **1.** War Memorial.

(Litho. Survey Dept.)

1943 (Dec.). *Thick opaque, or thin semi-transparent paper. Gummed or ungummed. P $12\frac{1}{2}$ or $12\frac{1}{2} \times 11$.*

TM1 TM **1** 1 c. yellow .. .. 75 1·25
TM2 ,, 2 c. red-brown 55 65
a. Imperf. (pair) .. 35·00
TM3 ,, 3 c. green .. .. 1·25 2·00
TM4 ,, 4 c. purple .. .. 70 1·10
TM5 ,, 8 c. carmine 55 70
TM6 ,, 15 c. blue .. .. 75 1·25

III. TRENGGANU.

TRENGGANU
(TT 1)

(Overprinted at Trengganu Survey Office.)

1944 (1 Oct.). *Various stamps optd. with Type* TT **1.**

(i) *On Trengganu stamp optd. with T* **2.**

TT 1 **4** 8 c. grey (J99) .. .. 12·00 7·00

(ii) *On stamps optd. with T* **4.**

(*a*) *Pahang.*

TT 2 **7** 12 c. brt. ultram. (J147) 12·00 7·00

(*b*) *Trengganu.*

TT 3 **4** 2 c. on 5 c. (J174)* .. 12·00 12·00
TT 4 ,, 8 c. on 10 c. (J180) (inverted) .. .. 7·00 7·00
TT 5 ,, 12 c. brt. ultram. (J181) (inverted) .. .. 7·00 7·00

* This is spelt "TRENGANU" with one "G".

(iii) *On stamps optd. with T* **11.**

(*a*) *Straits Settlements.*

TT 6 **58** 12 c. ultramarine (J222) 12·00 12·00
TT 7 ,, 40 c. scarlet & dull purple (J223) .. .. 12·00 12·00

(*b*) *On Perak.*

TT 8 **38** 30 c. dull purple & orange (J239) .. .. 20·00 12·00

(*c*) *On Selangor.*

TT 9 **22** 3 c. green (J243) .. 7·00 7·00
TT10 ,, 12 c. bright ultramarine (J244) (L. to R.) .. 5·00 5·00
TT11 ,, 12 c. bright ultramarine (J244) (R. to L.) .. 4·00 4·00
a. Error. T 13.. .. 95·00 95·00

(iv) *On Selangor stamps optd. with T* **12.**

TT12 **22** 2 c. on 5 c. (J250) .. 12·00 12·00
TT13 ,, 3 c. on 5 c. (J251) .. 12·00 12·00

(v) *On pictorials of 1943 (Nos. J271 etc.).*

TT14 **19** 1 c. grey-green .. .. 10·00 12·00
TT15 **20** 2 c. pale emerald .. 10·00 6·00
TT16 **19** 3 c. drab .. .. 12·00 12·00
TT17 **21** 4 c. carmine-rose .. 12·00 12·00
TT18 **22** 8 c. dull blue .. .. 20·00 20·00
TT19 **23** 10 c. brown-purple ..
TT20 **24** 15 c. violet .. .. 12·00 9·00
TT21 **25** 30 c. olive-green .. 12·00 7·00
TT22 **26** 50 c. blue .. .. 20·00 20·00
TT23 **27** 70 c. blue .. .. 35·00 35·00

(vi) *On Savings Campaign stamps (Nos. J281/2).*

TT24 **28** 8 c. violet .. .. 25·00 25·00
TT25 ,, 15 c. scarlet .. .. 25·00 25·00

(vii) *On stamps of Japan.*

TT26 – 5 s. claret (No. 396) .. 14·00 20·00
TT27 – 25 s. brown and chocolate (No. 329) .. 7·00 4·00
TT28 – 30 s. blue-green (No. 330) 14·00 10·00

(viii) *On Trengganu Postage Due stamp optd. with T* **2.**

TT29 D **1** 1 c. scarlet (JD13) .. 65·00 65·00

MALAYSIA.

General issues intended for use throughout the new Federation. See notes at the beginning of MALAYA.

STATES OF MALAYSIA. Stamps inscribed with the names of the states in addition to "MALAYSIA" are listed as follows :—

Inscr.	Where listed
"JOHOR"	Malaya (Johore)
"MELAKA"	,, (Malacca)
"NEGERI SEMBILAN"	,, (Negri Sembilan)
"PULAU PINANG"	,, (Penang)

Others inscribed "KEDAH", "KELANTAN", "PAHANG", "PERAK", "PERLIS", "SELANGOR" and "TRENGGANU" are listed after Malaya under these names, whilst "SABAH" and "SARAWAK" are listed alphabetically under "S".

1. Federation Map.

(Photo. Harrison & Sons.)

1963 (16 Sept.). *Inauguration of Federation. W* w.**13.** *P $14\frac{1}{2}$.*

1 **1** 10 c. yellow & bluish violet .. 8 8
a. Yellow omitted .. ..
2 ,, 12 c. yellow & deep green .. 12 12
3 ,, 50 c. yellow & chocolate .. 25 25

2. Bouquet of Orchids.

(Photo. J. Enschedé & Sons.)

1963 (3 Oct.). *Fourth World Orchid Conference, Singapore. No wmk. P 13 × 14.*

4 **2** 6 c. multicoloured 8 8
5 ,, 25 c. multicoloured 25 20

The stamp commemorating the Installation of the Sultan of Perak which was formerly listed here is now listed under Perak, No. 158.

4. Parliament House, Kuala Lumpur.

(Des. V. Whiteley. Photo. Harrison.)

1963 (4 Nov.). *Ninth Commonwealth Parliamentary Conference, Kuala Lumpur. W* w.**13** *(inverted). P $13\frac{1}{2}$.*

7 **4** 20 c. deep magenta and gold .. 8 8
8 ,, 30 c. deep green and gold .. 12 10

5. "Flame of Freedom" and Emblems of Goodwill, Health and Charity.

(Photo. Harrison.)

1964 (10 Oct.). *Eleanor Roosevelt Commemoration. W* w.**13.** *P $14\frac{1}{2} \times 13\frac{1}{2}$.*

9 **5** 25 c. black, red and greenish blue 10 8
10 ,, 30 c. black, red & dp. lilac 15 15
11 ,, 50 c. black, red and ochre-yellow 25 25

6. Microwave Tower and I.T.U. Emblem.

(Photo. Courvoisier.)

1965 (17 May). *I.T.U. Centenary. P $11\frac{1}{2}$.*

12 **6** 2 c. multicoloured 5 5
13 ,, 25 c. multicoloured 12 12
14 ,, 50 c. multicoloured 25 25

7. National Mosque.

(Photo. Harrison.)

1965 (27 Aug.). *Opening of National Mosque, Kuala Lumpur. W* w.**13.** *P $14 \times 14\frac{1}{2}$.*

15 **7** 6 c. carmine 5 5
16 ,, 15 c. red-brown 8 8
17 ,, 20 c. deep bluish green .. 10 10

8. Air Terminal.

(Photo. Harrison.)

1965 (30 Aug.). *Opening of International Airport, Kuala Lumpur.* W w.**13**. P 14½ × 14.

18 **8** 15 c. black, yellow-green and new blue 5 5
19 ,, 30 c. black, yellow-green and magenta 15 20

9. Crested Green Wood Partridge.

10. Blue-backed Fairy Bluebird.

11. Black-naped Oriole.

12. Rhinoceros Hornbill.

13. Barred Ground Dove.

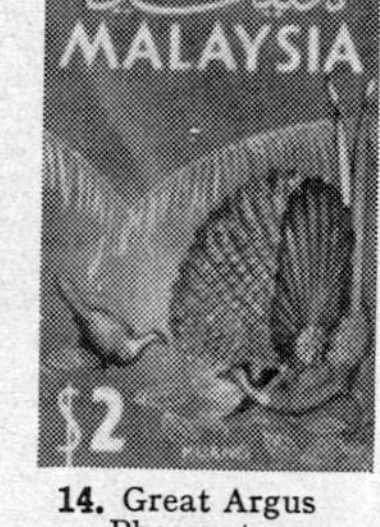

14. Great Argus Pheasant.

15. Paradise Flycatcher.

16. Banded Pitta.

(Des. A. Fraser-Brunner. Photo. Harrison.)

1965 (9 Sept.). W w.**13**. P 14½.

20 **9** 25 c. multicoloured 10 8
21 **10** 30 c. multicoloured 12 10
a. Blue omitted .. .. 40·00
22 **11** 50 c. multicoloured 25 12
23 **12** 75 c. multicoloured 30 15
24 **13** $1 multicoloured 50 20
25 **14** $2 multicoloured .. .. 1·00 25
26 **15** $5 multicoloured .. .. 2·50 75
27 **16** $10 multicoloured .. .. 4·00 2·00
20/7 .. .. *Set of* 8 8·00 3·25

All values except the 75 c. and $10 exist with PVA gum as well as gum arabic.

17. Sepak Raga (ball-game) and Football.

18. Running.

19. Diving.

(Des. E. A. F. Anthony. Litho. Japanese Govt. Ptg. Wks.)

1965 (14 Dec.). *Third South East Asian Peninsular Games.* P 13 × 13½.

28 **17** 25 c. black and olive-green 10 8
29 **18** 30 c. black and brt. purple 12 12
30 **19** 50 c. black and light blue.. 30 25

20. National Monument.

(Photo. Harrison.)

1966 (8 Feb.). *National Monument, Kuala Lumpur.* W w.**13**. P 13½.

31 **20** 10 c. multicoloured.. .. 5 5
32 ,, 20 c. multicoloured.. .. 12 12

21. The Yang di-Petuan Agong (Ismail Nasiruddin Shah).

(Photo. Japanese Govt. Ptg. Wks.)

1966 (11 Apr.). *Installation of Yang di-Pertuan Agong, Tuanku Ismail Nasiruddin Shah.* P 13½.

33 **21** 15 c. black and light yellow 5
34 ,, 50 c. black & greenish blue 25

22. School Building.

(Photo. De La Rue.)

1966 (21 Oct.). *150th Anniv. of Penang Free School.* W w.**13** (*sideways*). P 13.

35 **22** 20 c. multicoloured .. 8
36 ,, 50 c. multicoloured .. 30

The 50 c. is also inscr. "ULANG TAHUN KE-150" at foot and bears a shield at bottom left corner.

23. "Agriculture".

(Des. E. Ng Peng Nam. Photo. Japanese Govt. Ptg. Wks.)

1966 (1 Dec.). *First Malaysia Plan.* T **23** *and similar horiz. designs. Multicoloured.* P 13½.

37 15 c. Type **23** 10 8
38 15 c. "Rural Health" 10 8
39 15 c. "Communications" .. 10 8
40 15 c. "Education" 10 8
41 15 c. "Irrigation" 10 8
37/41 .. .. .. *Set of* 5 45 35

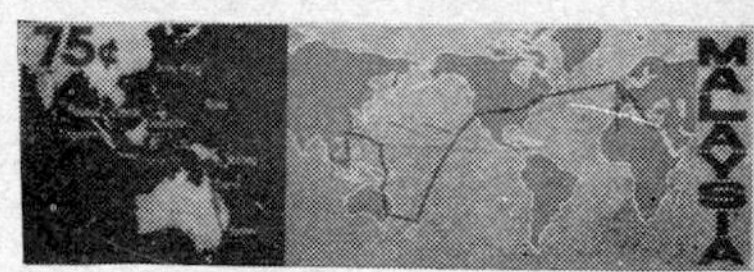

28. Cable Route Maps.

(*Reduced size illustration. Actual size* 68 × 22 *mm.*)

(Des. Ng Peng Nam. Photo. Japanese Govt. Ptg. Wks., Tokio.)

1967 (30 Mar.). *Completion of Malaysia–Hong Kong Link of SEACOM Telephone Cable.* P 13½.

42 **28** 30 c. multicoloured 10 10
43 75 c. multicoloured 40 40

29. Hibiscus and Rulers.

(Photo. Harrison.)

67 (31 Aug.). *Tenth Anniv. of Independence.* *W* w.**13**. *P* 14½.
29 15 c. multicoloured .. 5 5
,, 50 c. multicoloured .. 25 20

30. Mace and Shield.

es. Enche Ng Peng Nam. Photo. Harrison.)

67 (8 Sept.). *Centenary of Sarawak Council.* *W* w.**13**. *P* 14½.
30 15 c. multicoloured .. 5 5
,, 50 c. multicoloured .. 25 25

. Straits Settlements 8 c. Stamp of 1867 and Malaysian 25 c. Stamp.

. Straits Settlements 24 c. Stamp of 1867 and Malaysian 30 c. Stamp.

. Straits Settlements 32 c. Stamp of 1867 and Malaysian 50 c. Stamp.

es. Enche Ng Peng Nam. Photo. Japanese Govt. Ptg. Works.)

67 (2 Dec.). *Stamp Centenary.* *P* 11½.
31 25 c. multicoloured .. 10 8
32 30 c. multicoloured .. 12 12
33 50 c. multicoloured .. 25 25

Nos. 48/50 were each issued in sheets of 50, ranged *tête-bêche.*

34. Tapping Rubber, and Molecular Unit.

. Tapping Rubber, and Export Consignment.

36. Tapping Rubber, and Aircraft Tyres.

(Litho. Bradbury, Wilkinson.)

68 (29 Aug.). *Natural Rubber Conference, Kuala Lumpur.* *W* w.**13**. *P* 12.
34 25 c. multicoloured .. 10 8
35 30 c. multicoloured .. 15 15
36 50 c. multicoloured .. 30 30

. Mexican Sombrero and Blanket with Olympic Rings.

38. Olympic Rings and Mexican Embroidery.

(Litho. Bradbury, Wilkinson.)

1968 (12 Oct.). *Olympic Games, Mexico.* *W* w.**13**. *P* 12 × 11½.
54 **37** 30 c. multicoloured .. 15 15
55 **38** 75 c. multicoloured .. 45 45

39. Tunku Abdul Rahman **40.** against background of Pandanus Weave.

41. Tunku Abdul Rahman with Pandanus Pattern. (*Horiz.*).

(Photo. Japanese Govt. Ptg. Wks.)

1969 (8 Feb.). *Solidarity Week.* *P* 13½.
56 **39** 15 c. multicoloured .. 5 5
57 **40** 20 c. multicoloured .. 15 15
58 **41** 50 c. multicoloured .. 35 35

42. Peasant Girl with Sheaves of Paddy.

(Des. Enche Hoessein Anas. Photo. Harrison.)

1969 (8 Dec.). *National Rice Year.* *W* w.**13**. *P* 13½.
59 **42** 15 c. multicoloured .. 5 5
60 ,, 75 c. multicoloured .. 40 40

43. Satellite tracking Aerial.

44. " Intelsat III " in Orbit.

(Photo. Enschedé.)

1970 (6 Apr.). *Satellite Earth Station.* *W* w.**13**. *P* 14 × 13 (15 *c.*) *or* 13½ × 13 (30 *c.*).
61 **43** 15 c. multicoloured .. 5 5
62 **44** 30 c. multicoloured* .. 25 20
63 ,, 30 c. multicoloured* .. 25 20

No. 61 was issued in the sheets, **horizontally** *tête-bêche.*

* Nos. 62/3 are of the same design, differing only in the lettering colours (No. 62 white; No. 63 gold).

45. Blue-banded King Crow Butterfly. **46.** Emblem.

(Des. V. Whiteley. Litho. B.W.)

1970. *Butterflies.* *T* **45** *and similar vert. designs. Multicoloured.* *P* 13 × 13½.
64 25 c. Type **45** 10 5
65 30 c. Saturn 12 5
66 50 c. Common Nawab .. 20 5
67 75 c. Great Mormon 30 10
68 $1 Orange Albatross .. 40 12
69 $2 Raja Brooke's Birdwing 75 25
70 $5 Centaur Oak Bird .. 2·00 65
71 $10 Royal Assyrian .. .. 3·75 2·00
64/71 .. .. *Set of* 8 6·50 3·00

Dates of issue:—31 Aug., 25 c. to 75 c.; 16 Nov., others.

(Litho. Harrison.)

1970 (7 Sept.). *50th Anniv. of International Labour Organization.* *P* 14 × 13½.
72 **46** 30 c. grey and new blue .. 12 10
73 ,, 75 c. pink and new blue .. 40 40

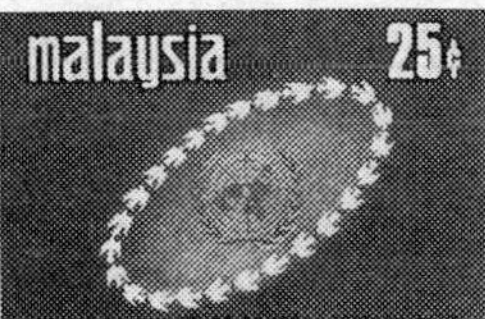

47. U.N. Emblem encircled by Doves.

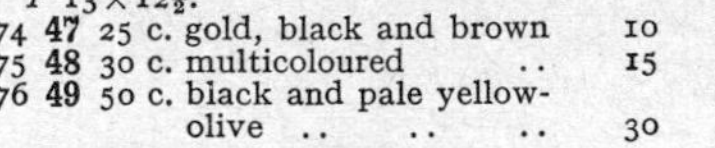

48. Line of Doves and U.N. Emblem.

49. Doves looping U.N. Emblem.

(Des. Enche Ng Peng Nam. Litho. D.L.R.)

1970 (24 Oct.). *25th Anniv. of United Nations.* *P* 13 × 12½.
74 **47** 25 c. gold, black and brown 10 10
75 **48** 30 c. multicoloured .. 15 15
76 **49** 50 c. black and pale yellow-olive 30 30

50. The Yang di-Pertuan Agong.

(Des. Union Art Corporation, Kuala Lumpur. Photo. Harrison.)

1971 (20 Feb.). *Installation of Yang di-Pertuan Agong (Paramount Ruler of Malaysia). P* 14½ × 14.

77 **50** 10 c. black, gold and lemon .. 5 5
a. Gold (value and inscr.) omitted .. .. .. 50·00
78 ,, 15 c. blk., gold & brt. mauve 10 10
79 ,, 50 c. blk., gold & new blue 25 20

51. Bank Negara Complex.

(Photo. Harrison.)

1971 (15 May). *Opening of Bank Negara Building. P* 13½ *(and around design)*.

80 **51** 25 c. black and silver .. 10 10
81 ,, 50 c. black and gold .. 30 30

52. Aerial view of Parliament Buildings.

(*Illustration reduced. Actual size* 59 × 33 *mm.*)

(Des. Union Art Corp., Kuala Lumpur. Litho. Harrison.)

1971 (13 Sept.). *17th Commonwealth Parliamentary Association Conference, Kuala Lumpur. T* **52** *and similar multicoloured design. P* 13½ (25 *c.*) *or* 12½ × 13 (75 *c.*).

82 25 c. Type **52** 15 15
83 75 c. Ground view of Parliament Buildings 40 40

The 75 c. is a horizontal design, size 73 × 23½ mm.

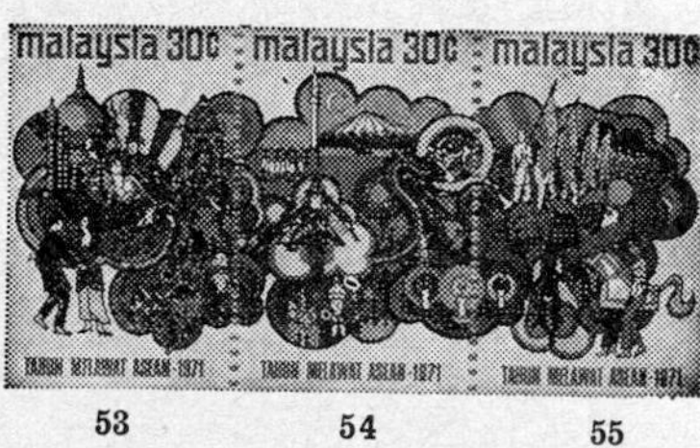

53 54 55

(The above is a reduced size illustration of the three stamps, the actual size being 63½ × 32 mm. Together they form a composite design of a Malaysian Carnival, and were issued horizontally *se-tenant* within sheets of 90.)

(Des. locally. Litho. Harrison.)

1971 (18 Sept.). *Visit ASEAN* Year. P* 14½.

84 **53** 30 c. multicoloured .. 20 20
85 **54** 30 c. multicoloured .. 20 20
86 **55** 30 c. multicoloured .. 20 20
84/86 Strip of 3 60

* ASEAN = Association of South East Asian Nations.

56. Trees, Elephant and Tiger.

(Des. from children's drawings. Litho. Harrison.)

1971 (2 Oct.). *25th Anniv. of UNICEF. T* **56** *and similar multicoloured designs. P* 12½.

87 15 c. Type **56** 10 8
88 15 c. Cat and kittens 10 8
89 15 c. Sun, flower and bird (*vert.*, 22 × 29 mm.) .. 10 8
90 15 c. Monkey, elephant and lion in jungle 10 8
91 15 c. Spider and butterflies .. 10 8
Strip of 5 .. .. 40 40

Nos. 87/91 were issued in horizontal *se-tenant* strips of 5 throughout the sheet.

57. Athletics.

(Des. Union Art Corp., Kuala Lumpur. Litho. B.W.)

1971 (11 Dec.). *Sixth S.E.A.P.* Games, Kuala Lumpur. T* **57** *and similar horiz. designs. Multicoloured. P* 14½ × 14.

92 25 c. Type **57** 10 12
93 30 c. Sepak Raga players .. 12 12
94 50 c. Hockey 40 40

* S.E.A.P. = South East Asian Peninsular.

58 59 60

(The above is a reduced size illustration of the three stamps, the actual size being 65 × 36 mm. Together they form a composite design of a Map and Tourist Attractions, and were issued horizontally *se-tenant* within sheets of 90.)

(Des. locally. Litho. Harrison.)

1972 (31 Jan.). *Pacific Area Tourist Association Conference. P* 14 × 14½.

95 **58** 30 c. multicoloured .. 20 15
96 **59** 30 c. multicoloured .. 20 15
97 **60** 30 c. multicoloured .. 20 15
Strip of 3 60

61. Kuala Lumpur City Hall.

(*Reduced size illustration. Actual size* 54 × 33 *mm*

(Des. from colour transparencies. Litho. Harrison.)

1972 (1 Feb.). *City Status for Kuala Lumpu T* **61** *and similar horiz. design. Multicoloure P* 14½ × 14.

98 25 c. Type **61** 10
99 50 c. City Hall in floodlights .. 30

62. SOCSO Emblem. **64.** Fireworks, Nation Flag and Flower.

63. W.H.O. Emblem.

(Des. B.W. Litho. Harrison.)

1973 (2 July). *Social Security Organisati P* 13½.

100 **62** 10 c. multicoloured .. 5
101 ,, 15 c. multicoloured .. 5
102 ,, 50 c. multicoloured .. 20

(Des. Union Advertising, Kuala Lumpur. Litho. B.W.)

1973 (1 Aug.). *25th Anniv. of W.H.O. P* 1
103 **63** 30 c. multicoloured .. 15
104 – 75 c. multicoloured .. 35

The 75 c. is similar to T **63**, but vertical.

(Des. Clover Associates, Kuala Lumpur. Lith Harrison.)

1973 (31 Aug.). *Tenth Anniv. of Malaysi P* 13½.

105 **64** 10 c. multicoloured .. 5
106 ,, 15 c. multicoloured .. 5
107 ,, 50 c. multicoloured .. 20

65. Emblems of Interpol and Royal Malaysian Police.

es. Union Advertising, Kuala Lumpur. Litho. Harrison.)

73 (15 Sept.). *50th Anniv. of Interpol. T* **65** *and similar vert. design. Multicoloured. P* 13½.

8 25 c. Type **65** 12 12
9 75 c. Emblems within " 50 " 35 35

66. Aeroplane and M.A.S. Emblem.

es. Art Dept., Malaysia Airline System. Litho. Harrison.)

73 (1 Oct.). *Foundation of Malaysia Airline System. P* 14½.

o **66** 15 c. multicoloured .. 5 5
1 ,, 30 c. multicoloured .. 15 15
2 ,, 50 c. multicoloured .. 25 25

67. Kuala Lumpur.

es. Malaysian Advertising Services. Litho. B.W.)

74 (1 Feb.). *Establishment of Kuala Lumpur as Federal Territory. P* 12½ × 13.

3 **67** 25 c. multicoloured .. 12 12
4 ,, 50 c. multicoloured .. 25 25

68. Development Projects.

es. Malaysian Advertising Services. Litho. Rosenbaum Bros., Vienna.)

74 (25 Apr.). *Seventh Annual Meeting of Asian Development Bank's Board of Governors, Kuala Lumpur. P* 13½.

5 **68** 30 c. multicoloured .. 15 15
6 ,, 75 c. multicoloured .. 35 35

69. Scout Badge and Map.

Des. Malaysian Advertising Services. Litho. Harrison.)

74 (1 Aug.). *Malaysian Scout Jamboree. T* **69** *and similar multicoloured designs. P* 13 × 13½ (15 *c.*) *or* 14 × 13½ (*others*).

7 10 c. Type **69** 5 5
8 15 c. Scouts saluting and flags (46 × 24 *mm.*) .. 5 5
9 50 c. Scout badge 25 25

70. Coat-of-arms and Power Installations.

(Des. Malaysian Advertising Services. Litho. Harrison.)

1974 (1 Sept.). *25th Anniv. of National Electricity Board. T* **70** *and similar multicoloured design. P* 14 (30 *c.*) *or* 14 × 14½ (75 *c.*).

120 30 c. Type **70** 15 15
121 75 c. National Electricity Board Building (37 × 27 *mm.*) .. 35 35

71. U.P.U. and Post Office Emblems within "100".

(Des. Clover Associates. Litho. Harrison.)

1974 (9 Oct.). *Centenary of Universal Postal Union. P* 14½ × 14.

122 **71** 25 c. dull yel.-grn., bt. yel. & lt. rose-car. .. 12 12
123 ,, 30 c. lt. new blue, brt. yel. & lt. rose-car... .. 15 15
124 ,, 75 c. brnsh. or., brt. yell. & lt. rose-car... .. 35 35

72. Gravel Pump in Tin Mine.

(Des. Malaysian Advertising Services. Litho. D.L.R.)

1974 (31 Oct.). *Fourth World Tin Conference, Kuala Lumpur. T* **72** *and similar horiz. designs. Multicoloured. P* 13½.

125 15 c. Type **72** 5 5
126 20 c. Open-cast mine 10 10
127 50 c. Dredge within "ingot" .. 25 25

73. Hockey-players, World Cup and Federation Emblem.

(Des. Malaysian Advertising Services. Litho. Harrison.)

1975 (1 Mar.). *Third World Cup Hockey Championships. P* 13½ × 13.

128 **73** 30 c. multicoloured .. 12 12
129 ,, 75 c. multicoloured .. 30 30

74. Congress Emblem.

(Des. Malaysian Advertising Services. Litho. Harrison.)

1975 (1 May). *25th Anniv. of Malaysian Trade Union Congress. P* 14 × 14½.

130 **74** 20 c. multicoloured .. 8 8
131 ,, 25 c. multicoloured .. 10 10
132 ,, 30 c. multicoloured .. 12 12

75. Emblem of M.K.P.W. (Malayan Women's Organisation).

(Des. Malaysian Advertising Services. Litho. Harrison.)

1975 (25 Aug.). *International Women's Year. P* 14.

133 **75** 10 c. multicoloured .. 5 5
134 ,, 15 c. multicoloured .. 8 5
135 ,, 50 c. multicoloured .. 20 20

76. Ubudiah Mosque, Kuala Kangsar.

(Des. Malaysian Advertising Services. Litho. Harrison.)

1975 (22 Sept.). *Koran Reading Competition. T* **76** *and similar horiz. designs. Multicoloured. P* 14.

136 15 c. Type **76** 8 5
137 15 c. Zahir Mosque, Alor Star 8 5
138 15 c. National Mosque, Kuala Lumpur 8 5
139 15 c. Sultan Abu Bakar Mosque, Johore Bahru .. 8 5
140 15 c. Kuching State Mosque, Sarawak 8 5
136/40 .. .. *Set of* 5 30 25

The above were printed together, horizontally *se-tenant* throughout the sheet.

77. Plantation and Emblem.

(Des. E. Sulaiman bin Haji Hassan and E. Hoh Lian Yong. Litho. Harrison.)

1975 (22 Oct.). *50th Anniv. of Malaysian Rubber Research Institute. T* **77** *and similar horiz. designs. Multicoloured. P* $14 \times 14\frac{1}{2}$.

141	10 c. Type **77**	5	5
142	30 c. Latex cup and emblem ..	12	12
143	75 c. Natural rubber in test-tubes	30	39

78. Scrub Typhus.

79. The Yang di-Pertuan Agong.

(Des. Lap Loy Fong (25 c.), Lee Eng Kee (others). Litho. Harrison.)

1976 (6 Feb.). *75th Anniv. of the Institute of Medical Research. T* **78** *and similar vert. designs. Multicoloured. P* 14.

144	20 c. Type **78**	8	8
145	25 c. Malaria diagnosis ..	8	10
146	\$1 Beri-beri	35	40

(Des. Union Advertising. Photo. Harrison.)

1976 (28 Feb.). *Installation of H.M. The Yang di-Pertuan Agong. T* **79** *and similar vert. designs. P* $14\frac{1}{2} \times 13\frac{1}{2}$.

147	**79**	10 c. black, bistre & yell.	5	5
148	,,	15 c. black, bistre and brt. mauve	5	5
149	,,	50 c. black, bistre & ultram.	15	20

80. State Council Complex.

(Des. Encik Rahman. Litho. Harrison.)

1976 (17 Aug.). *Opening of the State Council Complex and Administrative Building, Sarawak. P* $12\frac{1}{2}$.

150	**80**	15 c. grey-green and light yellow	8	8
151	,,	20 c. grey-green and light bright mauve ..	8	10
152	,,	50 c. grey-green and pale blue	20	25

81. E.P.F. Building.

(Litho. Harrison.)

1976 (18 Oct.). *25th Anniv. of Employees' Provident Fund. T* **81** *and similar multicoloured designs. P* $14\frac{1}{2}$ *(25 c.) or* $13\frac{1}{2} \times 14\frac{1}{2}$ *(others)*.

153	10 c. Type **81**	5	8
154	25 c. E.P.F. emblems (27 × 27 *mm.*)	12	12
155	50 c. E.P.F. Building at night	20	25

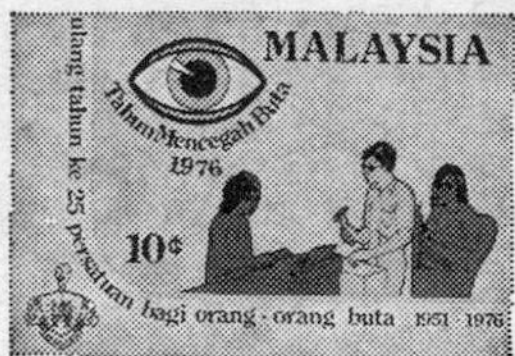

82. Blind People at Work.

(Des. Malayan Association for the Blind, Messrs. Advertising Sales Promotion Sdn. Bhd. and Hexxon Grafic Sdn. Bhd. Litho. Harrison.)

1976 (20 Nov.). *25th Anniv. of Malayan Association for the Blind. T* **82** *and similar horiz. design. Multicoloured. P* $13\frac{1}{2} \times 14\frac{1}{2}$.

156	10 c. Type **82**	5	8
157	75 c. Blind man and shadow ..	35	40

83. Independence Celebrations, 1957.

(Des. Hexxon Grafic Sdn. Bhd. Photo. Harrison.)

1977 (14 Jan.). *First Death Anniversary of Tun Abdul Razak (Prime Minister). T* **83** *and similar horiz. designs. Sepia and gold. P* 14.

158	15 c. Type **83**	8	8
159	15 c. "Education"	8	8
160	15 c. Tun Razak and map ("Development")	8	8
161	15 c. "Rukunegara" (National Philosophy)	8	8
162	15 c. ASEAN meeting	8	8
158/62	.. .. .. *Set of* 5	35	35

The above were printed together, horizontally *se-tenant* throughout the sheet.

POSTAGE DUE STAMPS.

Until 15th August 1966 the postage due stan of Malayan Postal Union were in use throu out Malaysia.

D 1

(Litho. Harrison.)

1966 (15 Aug.)–**71**. *Ordinary paper. W* w *(upright). P* $14\frac{1}{2} \times 14$.

D1	**D 1**	1 c. rose	5
D2	,,	2 c. indigo	5
D3	,,	4 c. apple-green	5
D4	,,	8 c. blue-green	8
		a. Bright blue-green, C (1.6.71)	8
D5	,,	10 c. bright blue	8
		a. Chalky paper (1.6.71) ..	8
D6	,,	12 c. reddish violet ..	5
D7	,,	20 c. red-brown	10
		a. Brown-purple (shades), C (22.4.69)	10
D8	,,	50 c. brownish bistre ..	30
		a. Olive-bistre, C (1.6.71) ..	40
D1/8		.. .. *Set of* 8	60

1972 (23 May). *Glazed paper. W* **w.13** *(si ways). P* $14\frac{1}{2} \times 14$.

D12	**D 1**	8 c. turquoise-green ..	5
D13	,,	10 c. dull ultramarine ..	5
D15	,,	20 c. pale chocolate ..	8
D16	,,	50 c. pale olive-bistre ..	20

MALDIVE ISLANDS.

MALDIVES

(1)

906. *Stamps of Ceylon optd. with T* **1.** *Wmk. Mult. Crown CA. P* 14.
44 2 c. orange-brown, O .. 6·00 8·00
45 3 c. green, O .. .. 8·00 10·00
,, 4 c. orange & ultram., O .. 20·00 35·00
46 5 c. dull purple, C .. .. 3·50 4·00
48 15 c. blue, O.. .. .. 30·00 38·00
,, 25 c. bistre, O .. .. 32·00 38·00
/6 .. .. *Set of* 6 90·00 £120

2. Minaret, Juma Mosque, Malé.

3

(Recess. D.L.R.)

909 (May). *T* **2** (18½ × 22½ *mm.*). *W* **3.** *P* 14.
7 **2** 2 c. orange-brown 75 25
8 ,, 3 c. deep myrtle 25 25
9 ,, 5 c. purple 25 20
o ,, 10 c. carmine.. .. .. 45 35

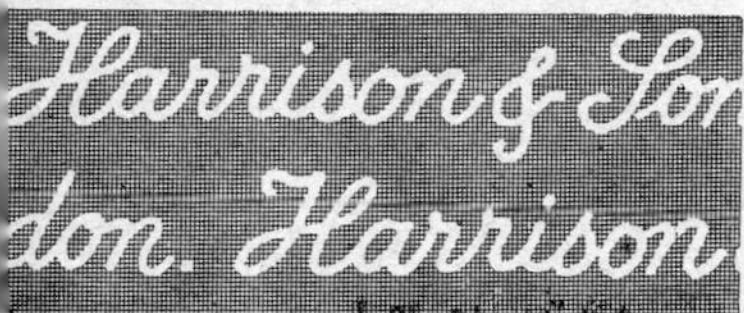

4

(Photo. Harrison.)

933. *T* **2** *redrawn (reduced to* 18 × 21½ *mm.). W* **4.** *P* 15 × 14.
1 **2** 2 c. grey 40 35
2 ,, 3 c. red-brown 35 50
3 ,, 5 c. claret (*vert. wmk.*) .. 3·25 3·75
4 ,, 5 c. mauve (*horiz. wmk.*) .. 1·40 2·00
5 ,, 6 c. scarlet 60 60
6 ,, 10 c. green 30 30
7 ,, 15 c. black 55 60
8 ,, 25 c. brown 75 75
9 ,, 50 c. purple 80 80
0 ,, 1 r. deep blue .. .. 1·40 1·25
1/20 .. .. *Set of* 10 9·00 10·00
All values exist with both vert. and horiz. mks.

(Currency changed. 100 larees = 1 rupee.)

5. Palm Tree and Boat.

(Recess. B.W.)

950 (24 Dec.). *P* 13.
1 **5** 2 l. olive-green 35 45
2 ,, 3 l. blue 80 70
3 ,, 5 l. emerald-green 90 80
4 ,, 6 l. red-brown 25 25
5 ,, 10 l. scarlet 25 25
6 ,, 15 l. orange 30 35
7 ,, 25 l. purple 35 40
8 ,, 50 l. violet 50 50
9 ,, 1 r. chocolate .. .. 2·50 2·75
1/29 .. .. *Set of* 9 5·00 5·50

7. Fish.

8. Native Products.

(Recess. Bradbury, Wilkinson & Co.)

1952. *P* 13.
30 **7** 3 l. blue 25 30
31 **8** 5 l. emerald 12 20
The Maldive Islands became a republic on 1 Jan., 1953, but reverted to a sultanate in 1954.

9. Malé Harbour.

10. Fort and Building.

(Recess. B.W.)

1956 (Feb.). *P* 13½ (*T* **9**) *or* 11½ × 11 (*T* **10**).
32 **9** 2 l. purple 5 5
33 ,, 3 l. slate 5 5
34 ,, 5 l. red-brown 5 5
35 ,, 6 l. blackish violet 5 5
36 ,, 10 l. emerald 5 5
37 ,, 15 l. chocolate 5 8
38 ,, 25 l. rose-red 5 5
39 ,, 50 l. orange 10 15
40 **10** 1 r. bluish green 25 25
41 ,, 5 r. blue 80 90
42 ,, 10 r. magenta .. .. 1·75 2·00
32/42 .. .. *Set of* 11 2·75 3·25

11. Cycling.

12. Basketball.

(Des. C. Bottiau. Recess and typo. B.W.)

1960 (20 Aug.). *Olympic Games. P* 11½ × 11 (*T* **11**) *or* 11 × 11½ (*T* **12**).
43 **11** 2 l. purple and green .. 5 5
44 ,, 3 l. greenish slate & purple 5 5
45 ,, 5 l. red-brown & ultram... 5 5
46 ,, 10 l. emerald-grn. & brown 5 5
47 ,, 15 l. sepia and blue .. 5 8
48 **12** 25 l. rose-red and olive .. 10 10
49 ,, 50 l. orange and violet .. 20 20
50 ,, 1 r. emerald and purple .. 30 35
43/50 .. .. *Set of* 8 75 75

13. Tomb of Sultan.

14. Custom House.

15. Cowrie Shells.

16. Old Royal Palace.

17. Road to Juma Mosque, Malé.

18. Council House.

19. New Government Secretariat.

20. Prime Minister's Office.

21. Old Ruler's Tomb.

22. Old Ruler's Tomb (distant view).

23. Maldivian Port.

(Recess. B.W.)

1960 (15 Oct.). *P* 11½×11.

51	**13**	2 l. purple	5	5
52	**14**	3 l. emerald-green	5	5
53	**15**	5 l. orange-brown	5	5
54	**16**	6 l. bright blue	5	5
55	**17**	10 l. carmine	5	5
56	**18**	15 l. sepia	5	5
57	**19**	25 l. deep violet	5	5
58	**20**	50 l. slate-grey	8	8
59	**21**	1 r. orange	15	15
60	**22**	5 r. deep ultramarine ..	75	85
61	**23**	10 r. grey-green	1·50	1·75
51/61		.. .. *Set of* 11	2·25	2·50

Higher values were also issued, intended mainly for fiscal use.

24. " Care of Refugees ".

(Recess. B.W.)

1960 (15 Oct.). *World Refugee Year. P* 11½×11.

62	**24**	2 l. dp. vio., orge. and grn.	5	5
63	,,	3 l. brown, green and red	5	5
64	,,	5 l. dp. grn., sepia and red	5	5
65	,,	10 l. bluish green, reddish violet and red ..	5	5
66	,,	15 l. reddish violet, grey-green and red ..	5	5
67	,,	25 l. blue, red-brown and bronze-green	8	8
68	,,	50 l. yellow-olive, rose-red and blue	10	10
69	,,	1 r. carmine, slate and vio.	20	45
62/9		.. .. *Set of* 8	40	50

25. Coconuts.

26. Map of Malé.

(Photo. Harrison.)

1961 (20 Apr.). *P* 14×14½ (*Nos.* 70/74) *or* 14½×14 (*others*).

70	**25**	2 l. yell.-brown & dp. green	5	5
71	,,	3 l. yellow-brn. & brt. blue	5	5
72	,,	5 l. yellow-brn. & magenta	5	5
73	,,	10 l. yell.-brn. & red-orange	5	5
74	,,	15 l. yellow-brown & black	5	5
75	,,	25 l. multicoloured	8	8
76	,,	50 l. multicoloured	10	10
77	,,	1 r. multicoloured	20	15
70/7		.. .. *Set of* 8	40	50

27. 5 c. stamp of 1906.

28. 3 c. stamp of 1906 and Post Horn.

29. 2 c. stamp of 1906 and Olive Sprig.

(Des. M. Shamir. Photo. Harrison.)

1961 (9 Sept.). 55*th Anniv. of First Maldivia*[n] *Stamp. P* 14½×14.

78	**27**	2 l. brown-purple, ultramarine and light green	5	
79	,,	3 l. brown-purple, ultramarine and light green	5	
80	,,	5 l. brown-purple, ultramarine and light green	5	
81	,,	6 l. brown-purple, ultramarine and light green	5	
82	**28**	10 l. grn., claret & maroon	5	
83	,,	15 l. grn., claret & maroon	5	
84	,,	20 l. grn., claret & maroon	8	
85	**29**	25 l. claret, green and black	8	
86	,,	50 l. claret, green and black	15	2
87	,,	1 r. claret, green and black	30	
78/87		.. .. *Set of* 10	55	
MS87*a*		114×88 mm. No. 87 (block of four). Imperf.	75	1·0

30. Malaria Eradication Emblem.

(Recess. B.W.)

1962 (7 Apr.). *Malaria Eradication. P* 13½×1[3]

88	**30**	2 l. chestnut	5	
89	,,	3 l. emerald	5	
90	,,	5 l. turquoise-blue ..	5	
91	,,	10 l. red	5	
92	,,	15 l. deep purple-brown ..	5	
93	,,	25 l. deep blue	8	1
94	,,	50 l. deep green	12	1
95	,,	1 r. purple	25	3
88/95		.. .. *Set of* 8	40	5

31. Children of Europe and America.

32. Children of Middle East and Far East.

(Des. C. Bottiau. Photo. Harrison.)

1962 (9 Sept.). 15*th Anniv. of U.N.I.C.E.*[F.] *P* 14½×14.

96	**31**	2 l. multicoloured ..	5	
97	,,	6 l. multicoloured ..	5	
98	,,	10 l. multicoloured ..	5	
99	,,	15 l. multicoloured ..	5	
100	**32**	25 l. multicoloured ..	5	
101	,,	50 l. multicoloured ..	10	1
102	,,	1 r. multicoloured ..	20	2
103	,,	5 r. multicoloured ..	70	7
96/103		.. .. *Set of* 8	90	9

33. Sultan Mohamed Farid Didi.

(Photo. Harrison.)

962 (29 Nov.). *Ninth Anniv. of Enthronement of Sultan.* T **33**. P 14×14½.

No.	Description	Unused	Used
04	3 l. orange-brn. & blsh. grn.	5	5
05	5 l. orange-brown & indigo	5	5
06	10 l. orange-brown and blue	5	5
07	20 l. orge.-brown & olive-grn.	8	10
08	50 l. orge.-brn. & dp. magenta	10	15
09	1 r. orge.-brown & slate-lilac	20	30
04/9	.. .. *Set of* 6	35	45

34. Angel Fish.
35. Moorish Idol (fish).
36. Soldier Fish.
37. Surgeon Fish.
38. Butterfly Fish.

(Des. R. Hegeman. Photo. Enschedé.)

963 (2 Feb.). *Tropical Fish.* P 13½.

No.	Type	Description	Unused	Used
10	**34**	2 l. multicoloured ..	5	5
11	,,	3 l. multicoloured ..	5	5
12	,,	5 l. multicoloured ..	5	5
13	**35**	10 l. multicoloured ..	5	5
14	,,	25 l. multicoloured ..	8	8
15	**36**	50 l. multicoloured ..	10	10
16	**37**	1 r. multicoloured ..	20	20
17	**38**	5 r. multicoloured ..	75	75
10/17		.. .. *Set of* 8	1·00	1·00

39. Fishes in Net.

40. Handful of Grain.

(Photo. State Ptg. Wks., Vienna.)

1963 (21 Mar.). *Freedom from Hunger.* P 12.

No.	Type	Description	Unused	Used
118	**39**	2 l. brown & dp. blsh. grn.	5	5
119	**40**	5 l. brown and orange-red	5	5
120	**39**	7 l. brown and turquoise	5	5
121	**40**	10 l. brown and blue ..	5	5
122	**39**	25 l. brown and brown-red	8	8
123	**40**	50 l. brown and violet ..	15	15
124	**39**	1 r. brown & dp. magenta	25	30
118/24		.. .. *Set of* 7	40	45

41. Centenary Emblem.

(Photo. Harrison.)

1963 (Oct.). *Centenary of Red Cross.* P 14×14½.

No.	Type	Description	Unused	Used
125	**41**	2 l. red and deep purple ..	5	5
126	,,	15 l. red & dp. bluish grn.	5	5
127	,,	50 l. red and deep brown ..	8	8
128	,,	1 r. red and indigo ..	15	15
129	,,	4 r. red & dp. brown-olive	45	45
125/9		.. .. *Set of* 5	60	70

42. Maldivian Scout Badge.

(Photo. Enschedé.)

1964. *World Scout Jamboree, Marathon* (1963). P 13½.

No.	Type	Description	Unused	Used
130	**42**	2 l. green and violet ..	5	5
131	,,	3 l. green and bistre-brn.	5	5
132	,,	25 l. green and blue ..	8	10
133	,,	1 r. green and crimson ..	25	40

43. Mosque, Malé.

(Recess. Bradbury, Wilkinson & Co.)

1964 (10 Aug.). "*Maldives Embrace Islam*". W w.**12**. P 11½.

No.	Type	Description	Unused	Used
134	**43**	2 l. purple	5	5
135	,,	3 l. emerald-green ..	5	5
136	,,	10 l. carmine	5	5
137	,,	40 l. deep dull purple ..	8	8
138	,,	60 l. blue	15	15
139	,,	85 l. orange-brown ..	15	15
134/9		.. .. *Set of* 6	30	30

44. Putting the Shot.
45. Running.

(Litho. Enschedé.)

1964 (Oct.). *Olympic Games, Tokio.* W w.**12**. P 14×13½.

No.	Type	Description	Unused	Used
140	**44**	2 l. dp. mar. & turq.-blue	5	5
141	,,	3 l. crimson and chestnut	5	5
142	,,	5 l. bronze-green and deep green	5	5
143	,,	10 l. slate-violet and reddish purple	5	5
144	**45**	15 l. sepia & yellow-brown	5	5
145	,,	25 l. indigo and deep blue	8	10
146	,,	50 l. deep olive-green and yellow-olive ..	15	20
147	,,	1 r. deep maroon and olive-grey ..	30	35
140/7		.. .. *Set of* 8	40	45
MS147*a*		126×140 mm. Nos. 145/7. Imperf.	60	75

46. Telecommunications Satellite.

(Des. M. Shamir. Photo. Harrison.)

1965 (1 July). *International Quiet Sun Years.* P 14½.

No.	Type	Description	Unused	Used
148	**46**	5 l. blue	5	5
149	,,	10 l. brown	5	5
150	,,	25 l. green	10	10
151	,,	1 r. deep magenta ..	35	35

On 26th July, 1965, Maldive Islands became independent and left the British Commonwealth. Later issues will be found in Vol. 3 of the Stanley Gibbons Foreign Overseas Catalogue.

MALTA.

For GREAT BRITAIN stamps used in Malta with "M" or "A 25" obliterations, see index to Great Britain Used Abroad list.

I. CROWN COLONY.

PRINTERS. Nos. 1–156. Printed by De La Rue; typographed except where otherwise stated.

1

The unused prices for Nos. 1/15a are for stamps without full gum. Well centred copies with full original gum are worth 50% more.

Type **1.**

1860 (Dec.)–**63.** *No wmk. P* 14.

(i) *Blued paper.* (1 Dec., 1860.)
1 ½d. buff (optd. S. £350) £500 £300
a. Imperf. £4000

(ii) *White paper.* (Nov., 1861–63.)
2 ½d. pale buff £350 £120
3 ½d. brown-orange £300 £120
4 ½d. buff (1863) £300 £120

The impression of Nos. 2 and 4 is clear, No. 3 being the blurred and muddy printing. In Nos. 3 and 4, and also No. 5, specks of carmine can be detected with a magnifying glass, and the inks are always muddy. Specimens also exist in which parts of the design are pure rose due to defective mixing of the ink.

1863–67. *Wmk. Crown CC. P* 14.
5 ½d. buff (June, 1863) .. .. 35·00 20·00
6 ½d. bright orange (Dec., 1864) 50·00 30·00
7 ½d. brown-red (1867) .. £100 30·00

Specimens of No. 5 exist on thin, surfaced paper, and others, reissued in 1865 and 1866, are on unsurfaced paper. The ink of No. 6 is mineral and, unlike No. 12, does not stain the paper. Most specimens are on thin, surfaced paper. Some shades of No. 7 may be described as chestnut. The ink of No. 7 is never muddy but clear, although sometimes in excess, and this distinguishes it from No. 5, with the deep shades of which it might otherwise be confused.

1868–71. *Wmk. Crown CC. P* 12½ *rough* (*No.* 8) *or clean-cut* (*No.* 9).
8 ½d. buff-brown (1868) .. 30·00 25·00
a. Imperf. between (vert. pair) ..
9 ½d. yellow-orange (May, 1871) 75·00 70·00

1870–78. *Wmk. Crown CC. P* 14.
10 ½d. dull orange (April, 1870) .. 45·00 25·00
11 ½d. orange-buff (May, 1872) .. 45·00 25·00
12 ½d. golden yell. (aniline) (1874) £120 £110
13 ½d. yellow-buff (Sept., 1875) .. 35·00 30·00
14 ½d. pale buff (Mar., 1878) .. 35·00 20·00

1878 (July). *Wmk. Crown CC. P* 14 × 12½.
15 ½d. yellow-buff .. .. 50·00 30·00
a. Perf. 12½ × 14 .. ..

1880–81. *Wmk. Crown CC. P* 14.
16 ½d. bright orange-yellow (4.80) 25·00 18·00
17 ½d. yellow (Apr., 1881) .. 25·00 18·00

1882 (April)–**84.** *Wmk. Crown CA. P* 14.
18 ½d. orange-yellow .. .. 11·00 15·00
19 ½d. red-orange (1884) .. 11·00 15·00

2

3

4

5

1885 (1 Jan.). *Wmk. Crown CA. P* 14.
20 **1** ½d. green 75 40
21 **2** 1d. rose .. .. .. 12·00 11·00
22 ,, 1d. carmine 80 75
23 **3** 2d. grey 65 80
24 **4** 2½d. dull blue .. .. 7·50 55
25 ,, 2½d. bright blue .. .. 7·50 55
26 ,, 2½d. ultramarine .. .. 6·00 80
27 **3** 4d. brown .. .. .. 3·00 3·50
a. Imperf. (pair) ('93) .. £2250 £2000
28 ,, 1s. violet .. .. .. 13·00 10·00
29 ,, 1s. pale violet .. .. 20·00 10·00
20/29 .. .. *Set of* 6 22·00 14·00
20/28 Optd. "Specimen" *Set of* 6 £170

1886 (1 Jan.). *Wmk. Crown CC. P* 14.
30 **5** 5s. rose (Optd. S. £85) .. 35·00 30·00

6. Harbour of Valletta.

7. Gozo Fishing Boat.

8. Ancient Maltese Galley.

9. Emblematic figure of Malta.

10. Shipwreck of St. Paul.

(T **6/10** recess.)

1899 (4 Feb.)–**1901.** *P* 14.

(*a*) *Wmk. Crown CA* (*sideways on ¼d. and 5d.*)
31 **6** ¼d. brown (1.1.01) .. 70
a. *Red-brown* 70
32 **7** 4½d. sepia .. .. .. 5·50 4·
33 **8** 5d. vermilion .. .. 9·00 9·

(*b*) *Wmk Crown CC.*
34 **9** 2s. 6d. olive-grey .. .. 13·00 12·
35 **10** 10s. blue-black .. .. 35·00 32·
31/35 Optd. "Specimen" *Set of* 5 80·00

One
Penny
(11)

12

1902 (4 July). *Nos.* 24 *and* 25 *surch. locally Govt. Ptg. Office with T* **11.**
36 1d. on 2½d. dull blue (Optd. S. £22) 35
a. Surch. double £1000 £8
b. Error. "One Pnney" .. 9·00 11·
ba. Surch. double, with error "One Pnney" .. ..
37 1d. on 2½d. bright blue .. 35
a. Error. "One Pnney" .. 9·00 11·

(Des. Emil Fuchs.)

1903–4. *Wmk. Crown CA. P* 14.
38 **12** ½d. green 85
39 ,, 1d. black and red .. 1·25
40 ,, 2d. purple and grey .. 4·00 3·
41 ,, 2½d. maroon and blue .. 5·50 1·
42 ,, 3d. grey and purple .. 1·00
43 ,, 4d. black and brown (1904) 10·00 7·
44 ,, 1s. grey and violet .. 6·50 4·
38/44 .. .. *Set of* 7 27·00 15·
38/44 Optd. "Specimen" *Set of* 7 65·00

1904–14. *Wmk. Mult. Crown CA* (*sideways* o
¼d.). *P* 14.
45 **6** ¼d. red-brown (10.10.05) 55
a. *Deep brown* (1910) .. 40
47 **12** ½d. green (6.11.04) .. 1·00
a. *Deep green* (1909) .. 85
48 ,, 1d. black & red (24.4.05) 1·10
49 ,, 1d. red (1907) 70
50 ,, 2d. purple & grey (22.2.05) 2·50
51 ,, 2d. grey (1911) 90
52 ,, 2½d. maroon & blue (8.10.04) 1·40
53 ,, 2½d. bright blue (1911) .. 1·40
54 ,, 4d. black & brown (1.4.06) 4·25 4·
55 ,, 4d. black & red/*yell.* ('11) 2·00 1·
57 **7** 4½d. brown (27.2.05) .. 6·50 4·5
58 ,, 4½d. orange (1912) .. 3·00 2·5
59 **8** 5d. vermilion (20.2.05) .. 5·00 2·5
60 ,, 5d. pale sage-green (1909) 2·25 2·7
a. *Deep sage-green*, C (1914) .. 5·50 5·5
61 **12** 1s. grey & violet (20.12.04) 9·00 2·2
62 ,, 1s. black/*green* (1911) .. 3·00 3·0
63 ,, 5s. green & red/*yell.*, C ('11) 40·00 40·0
45/63 .. .. *Set of* 17 80·00 60·0
45/63 (1907/11 *colours*) Optd. "Specimen" .. *Set of* 10 95·00

13

14

15

WAR TAX
(16)

1914–22. *Wmk. Mult. Crown CA.* *P* 14.

69	**13**	¼d. brown, O (2.1.14) ..	25	20
		a. Deep brown (1919) ..	20	20
71	,,	½d. green, O (21.1.14) ..	60	20
		aa. Wmk. sideways		
		a. Deep green (1919) ..	25	20
73	,,	1d. carm.-red, O (15.4.14)	55	20
		a. Scarlet (1915)	85	30
75	,,	2d. grey, O (12.8.14) ..	3·50	2·25
		a. Deep slate (1919) ..	5·50	5·00
77	,,	2½d. brt. blue, O (11.3.14)	35	30
78	**14**	3d. purple/*yellow*, C (1920)	4·00	4·00
		a. On orange-buff	5·50	6·00
79	**6**	4d. black, C (21.8.15) ..	6·00	5·50
		a. Grey-black (1916)	10·00	5·50
80	**13**	6d. dull & bright pur., C, (10.3.14)	4·00	4·00
		a. Dull purple & magenta ('19)	4·00	4·50
81	**14**	1s. black/*green*, C (1915)	5·50	5·00
		aa. Wmk. sideways ..	£400	
		a. White back (Optd. S. £5)	4·50	5·00
		b. On blue-green, olive back ..	5·00	5·00
		c. On emerald surface (1921) ..	5·00	5·00
		d. On emerald back (1922) ..	5·50	5·00
86	**15**	2s. pur. & brt. blue/*blue*, C (15.4.14)	20·00	18·00
		a. Dull pur. & blue/blue ('21)	20·00	18·00
87	**9**	2s. 6d. olive-green, O ('19)	23·00	25·00
		a. Olive-grey (1920) ..	23·00	25·00
88	,,	5s. green and red/*yellow*, C (21.3.17)	38·00	40·00
69/88		.. .. *Set of* 12	90·00	95·00
69/88		(*excl.* 87) Optd. "Specimen" *Set of* 11	£110	

The design of Nos. 79/*a* differs in various details from that of Type **6**.

We have only seen one copy of No. 71aa; it is in used condition.

A 3d. purple on yellow on white back, T **14**, was prepared for use but not issued. It exists overprinted "Specimen", *price* £40.

1917–18. *Optd. with T* **16**.

92	**13**	½d. deep green (17.12.17*) ..	25	20
93	**12**	3d. grey and purple (5.3.18*)	1·75	2·50
92/3		Optd. "Specimen" *Set of* 2	70·00	

*These are the earliest known dates of use. The ½d. is believed to have been issued on 15 December 1917.

17

18

(T **17** recess.)

1919. *Wmk. Mult. Crown CA.* *P* 14.

96	**17**	10s. black (Optd. S. £400) ..	£1100	£1000

1921–22. *Wmk. Mult. Script CA.* *P* 14.

97	**13**	¼d. brown, O	20	35
98	,,	½d. green, O	70	65
99	,,	1d. scarlet, O	25	25
100	**18**	2d. grey, O (1921) ..	2·00	60
101	**13**	2½d. bright blue, O ..	1·40	1·75
102	,,	6d. dull & brt. purple, C	7·50	9·00
103	**15**	2s. purple & blue/*blue*, C	50·00	60·00
104	**17**	10s. black, O	£250	£300
97/104		.. .. *Set of* 8	£275	£350
97/104		Optd. "Specimen" *Set of* 8	£130	

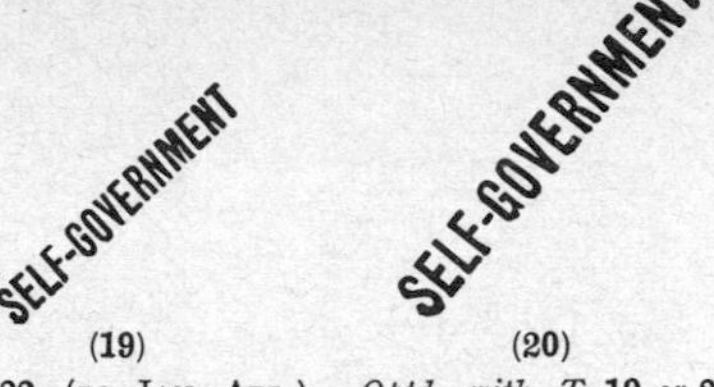

(19) (20)

1922 (12 Jan.–Apr.). *Optd. with T* **19** *or* **20** (*large stamps*), *at Govt. Printing Office, Valletta.*

(*a*) *Wmk. Crown CC.*

105	**10**	10s. blue-black, O (R.) ..	£110	£100

(*b*) *Wmk. Mult. Crown CA.*

106	**13**	½d. green, O	20	15
107	,,	2½d. bright blue, O ..	95	1·25
108	**14**	3d. purple/*orange-buff*, C	70	1·75
109	**13**	6d. dull & bright pur., C	85	1·75
110	**14**	1s. black/*emerald*, C ..	1·40	1·50
111	**15**	2s. dull purple and blue/*blue*, C (R.)	90·00	£100
112	**9**	2s. 6d. olive-grey, O ..	12·00	13·00
113	**15**	5s. green & red/*yellow*, C	20·00	25·00
106/113		.. .. *Set of* 8	£110	£130

(*c*) *Wmk. Mult. Script CA.*

114	**13**	¼d. brown, O	10	20
115	,,	½d. green, O	30	30
116	,,	1d. scarlet, O	20	20
117	**18**	2d. grey, O	45	60
118	**13**	2½d. bright blue, O ..	40	60
119	,,	6d. dull & bright purple, C	1·10	1·90
120	**15**	2s. dull purple and blue/*blue*, C (R.)	16·00	18·00
121	**17**	10s. black, O (R.) (19.1.22)	60·00	70·00
114/121		.. .. *Set of* 8	70·00	80·00

One Farthing
(21)

1922 (15 Apr.). *No.* 100 *surch. with T* **21**, *at Govt. Printing Office, Valletta.*

122	**18**	¼d. on 2d. grey	10	10

22

23

(Des. C. Dingli (T **22**) and G. Vella (**23**).)

1922 (1 Aug.)–**26**. *Wmk. Mult. Script CA, (sideways on T* **22**, *except No.* 140). *P* 14.

(*a*) *Typo. Chalk-surfaced paper.*

123	**22**	¼d. brown (22.8.22) ..	25	25
		a. Chocolate-brown	25	20
124	,,	½d. green	20	12
125	,,	1d. orange and purple ..	35	40
126	,,	1d. bright violet (28.4.24)	35	30
127	,,	1½d. brown-red (1.10.23) ..	40	15
128	,,	2d. bistre-brn. & turquoise (28.8.22)	25	20
129	,,	2½d. ultramarine (16.2.26) ..	55	1·00
130	,,	3d. cobalt (28.8.22) ..	90	1·00
		a. Bright ultramarine ..	80	90
131	,,	3d. black/*yellow* (16.2.26) ..	70	95
132	,,	4d. yell. & brt. blue (8.22)	70	1·00
133	,,	6d. olive-green and violet	80	1·00
134	**23**	1s. indigo and sepia ..	1·75	1·75
135	,,	2s. brown and blue ..	4·00	4·50
136	,,	2s. 6d. bright mag. & black (28.8.22)	5·50	6·00
137	,,	5s. orange-yellow & bright ultramarine (28.8.22) ..	7·00	7·00
138	,,	10s. slate-grey and brown (28.8.22)	16·00	18·00

(*b*) *Recess.*

139	**22**	£1 blk. & carm.-red (28.8.22)	60·00	70·00
140	,,	£1 blk. & brt. carm. (14.5.25)	60·00	70·00
123/140		.. .. *Set of* 17	90·00	£100
123/39		Optd. "Specimen" *Set of* 17	£200	

No. 139 has the watermark sideways and No. 140 has it upright.

Two pence halfpenny
(24)

POSTAGE
(25)

1925. *Surch. with T* **24**, *at Govt. Printing Office, Valletta.*

141	**22**	2½d. on 3d. cobalt (3 Dec.)	45	45
142	,,	2½d. on 3d. brt. ult. (9 Dec.)	40	45

1926 (1 April). *Optd. with T* **25**, *at Govt. Printing Office, Valletta.*

143	**22**	¼d. brown	15	25
144	,,	½d. green	15	20
145	,,	1d. bright violet	15	40
146	,,	1½d. brown-red	35	35
147	,,	2d. bistre-brown & turq.	30	40
148	,,	2½d. ultramarine	40	35
149	,,	3d. black/*yellow*	45	70
		a. Opt. inverted	£200	£225
150	,,	4d. yellow & bright blue	1·00	2·25
151	,,	6d. olive-green and violet	95	60
152	**23**	1s. indigo and sepia ..	2·75	4·00
153	,,	2s. brown and blue ..	18·00	20·00
154	,,	2s. 6d. brt. mag. & blk. ..	9·00	9·50
155	,,	5s. orge-yell. & brt. ultra.	5·50	8·50
156	,,	10s. slate-grey and brown	10·00	13·00
143/156		.. .. *Set of* 14	45·00	55·00

26

27. Valletta Harbour.

28. St. Publius.

29. Mdina (Notabile).

30

31. Neptune.

32. Ruins at Mnajdra.

33. St. Paul.

(T **26** typo., others recess. Waterlow.)

1926–27. *T* **26** *(P* 15 × 14*) and* **27** *to* **33** *(P* 12½*). Inscr.* "POSTAGE". *Wmk. Mult. Script CA.*

157	**26**	¼d. brown	15	12
158	,,	½d. yellow-green ..	20	12
159	,,	1d. rose-red (1927) ..	15	20
160	,,	1½d. chestnut	30	15
161	,,	2d. greenish grey (1927)	1·10	1·25
162	,,	2½d. blue (1927)	85	25
162*a*	,,	3d. violet (1927) ..	85	1·10
163	,,	4d. black and red ..	2·00	2·25
164	,,	4½d. lavender and ochre ..	2·00	2·00
165	,,	6d. violet and scarlet ..	2·00	2·00
166	**27**	1s. black	2·00	2·25
167	**28**	1s. 6d. black and green ..	5·00	5·00
168	**29**	2s. black and purple ..	6·00	7·00
169	**30**	2s. 6d. black & vermilion	7·00	7·00
170	**31**	3s. black and blue ..	7·00	7·50
171	**32**	5s. black and green ..	12·00	14·00
172	**33**	10s. black & carm. (9.2.27)	35·00	40·00
157/172		.. .. *Set of* 17	80·00	85·00
157/72 Optd. "Specimen"		*Set of* 17	£170	

AIR MAIL. (**34**)

POSTAGE AND REVENUE (**35**)

POSTAGE AND REVENUE. (**36**)

1928 (1 APR.). *Air. Optd. with T* **34.**

173	**26**	6d. violet and scarlet ..	5·50	6·50

1928 (1 OCT.–DEC.). *T* **26** *to* **33** *optd.*

174	**35**	¼d. brown..	12	10
175	,,	½d. yellow-green ..	10	10
176	,,	1d. rose-red	10	35
177	,,	1d. chestnut (5.12.28) ..	35	8
178	,,	1½d. chestnut	15	25
179	,,	1½d. rose-red (5.12.28)	40	12
180	,,	2d. greenish grey ..	1·40	1·60
181	,,	2½d. blue	40	15
182	,,	3d. violet	70	40
183	,,	4d. black and red ..	70	1·10
184	,,	4½d. lavender and ochre ..	1·25	1·10
185	,,	6d. violet and scarlet ..	1·50	1·60
186	**36**	1s. black (R.)	1·25	1·25
187	,,	1s. 6d. black & green (R.)	5·00	6·00
188	,,	2s. black & purple (R.)	6·00	5·50
189	,,	2s. 6d. black & verm. (R.)	8·00	9·00
190	,,	3s. black and blue (R.)..	8·00	8·50
191	,,	5s. black and green (R.)	17·00	22·00
192	,,	10s. black and carmine (R.)	32·00	38·00
74/192		.. .. *Set of* 19	80·00	90·00
74/92 Optd. "Specimen"		*Set of* 19	£200	

1930 (20 OCT.). *As Nos.* 157/172, *but inscr.* "POSTAGE (&) REVENUE".

193	¼d. brown	8	8
194	½d. yellow-green	15	8
195	1d. chestnut	12	8
196	1½d. rose-red	20	8
197	2d. greenish grey	40	55
198	2½d. blue	40	15
199	3d. violet	50	40
200	4d. black and red	70	1·40
201	4½d. lavender and ochre ..	90	1·40
202	6d. violet and scarlet ..	1·00	1·50
203	1s. black	2·50	3·50
204	1s. 6d. black and green ..	5·00	5·50
205	2s. black and purple ..	5·50	7·00
206	2s. 6d. black and vermilion	8·00	9·00
207	3s. black and blue	10·00	13·00
208	5s. black and green ..	14·00	16·00
209	10s. black and carmine ..	40·00	45·00
193/209	.. .. *Set of* 17	80·00	95·00
193/209 Perf. "Specimen"	*Set of* 17	90·00	

1935 (6 MAY). *Silver Jubilee. As Nos.* 91/4 *of Antigua, but printed by B.W. P* 11 × 12.

210	½d. black and green ..	12	12
	a. Extra flagstaff	15·00	
211	2½d. brown and deep blue ..	60	70
	a. Extra flagstaff	45·00	
212	6d. light blue and olive-green	3·50	4·00
	a. Extra flagstaff	45·00	
213	1s. slate and purple ..	7·50	8·50
	a. Extra flagstaff	£110	
210/13 Perf. "Specimen"	*Set of* 4	25·00	

For illustration of the "extra flagstaff" variety see Bechuanaland.

1937 (12 MAY). *Coronation. As Nos.* 13/15 *of Aden. P* 14.

214	½d. green	8	8
215	1½d. scarlet	8	10
	a. Brown-lake	£170	£170
216	2½d. bright blue	35	40
214/16 Perf. "Specimen"	*Set of* 3	18·00	

37. Grand Harbour, Valletta.

38. H.M.S. *St. Angelo.*

39. Verdala Palace.

41. Victoria and Citadel, Gozo.

40. Hypogeum, Hal Saflieni.

42. De l'Isle Adam entering Mdina.

43. St. John's Co-Cathedral.

44. Ruins at Mnajdra.

45. Statue of Manoel de Vilhena.

47. St. Publius.

46. Maltese Girl wearing Faldetta.

48. Mdina Cathedral.

50. Palace Square, Valletta.

49. Statue of Neptune.

51. St. Paul.

(Recess. Waterlow.)

1938 (17 FEB.*)–**43.** *Wmk. Mult. Script CA (sideways on No.* 217*). P* 12½.

217	**37**	¼d. brown	8	8
218	**38**	½d. green	12	8
218*a*	,,	½d. red-brown (8.3.43) ..	8	8
219	**39**	1d. red-brown	25	8
219*a*	,,	1d. green (8.3.43) ..	12	8
220	**40**	1½d. scarlet	8	8
220*a*	,,	1½d. slate-black (8.3.43)	8	8
221	**41**	2d. slate-black	20	30
221*a*	,,	2d. scarlet (8.3.43) ..	8	8
222	**42**	2½d. greyish blue ..	20	30
222*a*	,,	2½d. dull violet (8.3.43)	12	8
223	**43**	3d. dull violet	15	40
223*a*	**43**	3d. blue (8.3.43) ..	8	8
224	**44**	4½d. olive-grn. & yell.-brn.	30	20
225	**45**	6d. olive-green & scarlet	25	20
226	**46**	1s. black	50	50
227	**47**	1s. 6d. black & olive-grn.	1·25	1·75
228	**48**	2s. green and deep blue	1·25	1·75
229	**49**	2s. 6d. black and scarlet	2·25	2·00
230	**50**	5s. black and green ..	4·00	4·50
231	**51**	10s. black and carmine ..	8·50	8·00
217/231		.. .. *Set of* 21	18·00	18·00
217/31 Perf. "Specimen"		*Set of* 21	£120	

* This is the local date of issue but the stamps were released in London on 15 February.

1946 (3 Dec.). *Victory. As Nos. 28/9 of Aden, but inscr.* "MALTA" *between Maltese Cross and George Cross.*

232 1d. green 8 8
233 3d. blue 15 15
232/3 Perf. "Specimen" *Set of* 2 19·00

II. SELF-GOVERNMENT.

(52)

(Optd. by Waterlow.)

1948 (25 Nov.)–**53.** *New Constitution. As Nos.* 217/231 *but optd. as T* **52**; *reading up on* ½*d. and* 5*s., down on other values, and smaller on* ¼*d. value.*

234 **37** ¼d. brown 8 8
235 **38** ½d. red-brown 8 8
236 **39** 1d. green 8 8
236*a* ,, 1d. grey (R.) (8.1.53) .. 8 8
237 **40** 1½d. blue-black (R.) .. 8 8
237*a* ,, 1½d. green (8.1.53) .. 8 8
b. Opt. omitted .. .. — £2250
238 **41** 2d. scarlet 8 8
238*a* ,, 2d. yellow-ochre (8.1.53) 8 8
239 **42** 2½d. dull violet (R.) .. 8 8
239*a* ,, 2½d. scarlet-vermilion (8.1.53) 25 25
240 **43** 3d. blue (R.) 12 8
240*a* ,, 3d. dull violet (R.) (8.1.53) 12 8
241 **44** 4½d. olive-green & yellow-brown 40 50
241*a* ,, 4½d. olive-green and deep ultram. (R.) (8.1.53) 25 25
242 **45** 6d. olive-green & scarlet 12 12
243 **46** 1s. black 50 50
244 **47** 1s. 6d. blk. & ol.-green 1·10 1·10
245 **48** 2s. green & deep blue (R.) 1·25 1·25
246 **49** 2s. 6d. black and scarlet 3·00 3·00
247 **50** 5s. black and green (R.) 4·50 4·50
248 **51** 10s. black and carmine .. 10·00 10·00
234/248 .. .. *Set of* 21 20·00 20·00

1949 (4 Jan.). *Royal Silver Wedding. As Nos.* 30/1 *of Aden, but inscr.* "MALTA" *between Maltese Cross and George Cross* (*recess* £1).

249 1d. green 8 8
250 £1 indigo .. .. .. 16·00 19·00

1949 (10 Oct.). *75th Anniv. of Universal Postal Union. As Nos.* 114/7 *of Antigua, but inscr.* "MALTA" (*recess*).

251 2½d. violet 12 15
252 3d. deep blue.. .. .. 30 30
253 6d. carmine-red 75 55
254 1s. blue-black .. .. 1·25 1·40

53. Queen Elizabeth II when Princess.

54. Virgin Mary Bestowing Scapular.

(T **53**/4. Recess. Bradbury, Wilkinson.)

1950 (1 Dec.). *Visits of Princess Elizabeth to Malta. Wmk. Mult. Script CA. P* 12 × 11½.

255 **53** 1d. green 8 8
256 ,, 3d. blue 25 25
257 ,, 1s. black 70 75

1951 (12 July). *Seventh Centenary of the Scapular. Wmk. Mult. Script CA. P* 12 × 11½.

258 **54** 1d. green 8 8
259 ,, 3d. violet 12 20
260 ,, 1s. black 85 90

55. St. John's Co-Cathedral.

56. Altar-piece. Collegiate Parish Church, Cospicua.

1953 (3 June). *Coronation, As No.* 47 *of Aden.*

261 ,, 1½d. black & deep yellow-grn. 15 12

(Recess. Waterlow.)

1954 (3 May). *Royal Visit. Wmk. Mult. Script CA. P* 12½.

262 **55** 3d. violet 15 12

(Photo. Harrison.)

1954 (8 Sept.). *Centenary of Dogma of the Immaculate Conception. Wmk. Mult. Script CA. Chalk-surfaced paper. P* 14½ × 14.

263 **56** 1½d. emerald 5 5
264 ,, 3d. bright blue 15 10
265 ,, 1s. grey-black 60 60

57. Monument of the Great Siege, 1565.

58. Wignacourt Aqueduct Horsetrough.

59. Victory Church.

60. War Memorial.

62. Auberge de Castle.

61. Mosta Dome.

63. The King's Scroll.

65. Neolithic Temples at Tarxien.

64. Roosevelt's Scroll.

66. Vedette.

67. Mdina Gate.

68. "Les Gavroches" (Statue).

69. Monument of Christ the King.

70. Grand Master Cottoner's Monument.

71. Grand Master Perellos's Monument.

72. St. Paul.

73. Baptism of Christ.

(Recess. Waterlow (2s. 6d. to £1). Bradbury Wilkinson (others).)

1956 (23 Jan.)–**57.** *Wmk. Mult. Script CA. P* 14 × 13½ (*2s. 6d. to £1*), 11½ (*others*).

266	**57**	¼d. violet	5	5
267	**58**	½d. orange	5	5
268	**59**	1d. black (9.2.56) ..	5	5
269	**60**	1½d. bluish green (9.2.56)	10	8
270	**61**	2d. brown (*shades*) (9.2.56)	8	8
271	**62**	2½d. orange-brown ..	12	10
272	**63**	3d. rose-red (22.3.56) ..	12	8
273	**64**	4½d. deep blue	20	20
274	**65**	6d. indigo (9.2.56) ..	20	12
275	**66**	8d. bistre-brown	30	30
276	**67**	1s. deep reddish violet ..	35	35
277	**68**	1s. 6d. deep turq.-green ..	90	45
278	**69**	2s. olive-green	1·10	70
279	**70**	2s. 6d. chestnut (22.3.56)	2·25	1·75
280	**71**	5s. green (11.10.56) ..	4·00	3·00
281	**72**	10s. carm.-red (19.11.56) ..	16·00	12·00
282	**73**	£1 yellow-brown (5.1.57)	26·00	22·00
266/282		.. .. *Set of* 17	48·00	38·00

See also Nos. 314/5.

74. "Defence of Malta". **76.** Bombed Buildings.

75. Searchlights over Malta.

(Des. E. V. Cremona. Photo. Harrison.)

1957 (15 Apr.). *George Cross Commemoration. Cross in silver. Wmk. Mult. Script CA. P* 14½ × 14 (*3d.*) *or* 14 × 14½ (*others*).

283	**74**	1½d. deep dull green ..	10	10
284	**75**	3d. vermilion	15	15
285	**76**	1s. reddish brown ..	35	45

77. " Design ".

78. " Construction ". (*Vert.*)

79. Technical School, Paola. (*Horiz.*)

(Des. E. V. Cremona. Photo. Harrison.)

1958 (15 Feb.). *Technical Education in Malta. W* **w.12.** *P* 14 × 14½ (*3d.*) *or* 14½ × 14 (*others*).

286	**77**	1½d. black and deep green	10	10
287	**78**	3d. black, scarlet and grey	12	12
288	**79**	1s. grey, brt. pur. & black	45	50

80. Bombed-out Family.

81. Sea Raid on Grand Harbour, Valletta.

82. Searchlight Crew.

(Photo. Harrison & Sons.)

1958 (15 Apr.). *George Cross Commemoration. Cross in first colour, outlined in silver. W* **w.12.** *P* 14 × 14½ (*3d.*) *or* 14½ × 14 (*others*).

289	**80**	1½d. blue-green and black	12	12
290	**81**	3d. red and black ..	12	12
291	**82**	1s. reddish violet & black	45	50

83. Air Raid Casualties.

85. Maltese under Bombardment.

84. " For Gallantry ".

(Photo. Harrison & Sons.)

1959 (15 Apr.). *George Cross Commemoration. W* **w.12.** *P* 14½ × 14 (*3d.*) *or* 14 × 14½ (*others*).

292	**83**	1½d. grey-grn., blk. & gold	10	10
293	**84**	3d. red'ish vio., blk. & gold	12	12
294	**85**	1s. blue-grey, blk. & gold	50	5[illegible]

86. Shipwreck of St. Paul (after Palombi).

87. Consecration of St. Publius, First Bishop of Malta. (*Vert.*)

88. Departure of St. Paul (after Palombi). (*Vert.*)

89. Statue of St. Paul, Rabat, Malta.

0. Angel with the *Acts of the Apostles*. (*As T* **89**.)
1. St. Paul with the *Second Epistle to the Corinthians*. (*As T* **89**.)

(Photo. Harrison.)

960 (9 Feb.). *19th Centenary of the Shipwreck of St. Paul.* W **w.12.** P 13 (1½d., 3d., 6d.) *or* 14×14½ (*others*).

95	**86**	1½d. blue, gold & yell.-brn.	12	12
		a. Gold (dates and crosses) omitted	80·00	
96	**87**	3d. brt. pur., gold & blue	20	12
97	**88**	6d. carm., gold & pale grey	35	30
98	**89**	8d. black and gold ..	60	60
99	**90**	1s. maroon and gold ..	75	75
00	**91**	2s. 6d. blue, deep bluish green and gold ..	4·00	3·50
		a. Gold omitted		
95/300		.. .. *Set of* 6	5·50	4·75

92. Stamp of 1860.

(Centre litho; frame recess. Waterlow.)

960 (1 Dec.). *Stamp Centenary.* W **w.12.** P 13½.

01	**92**	1½d. buff, pale blue and green (*shades*) ..	10	8
02	,,	3d. buff, pale blue and deep carmine ..	15	15
03	,,	6d. buff, pale blue and ultramarine	45	50

93. George Cross.

94. George Cross.

95. George Cross.

(Photo. Harrison.)

961 (15 Apr.). *George Cross Commemoration.* W **w.12.** P 15×14.

04	**93**	1½d. black, cream & bistre	15	15
05	**94**	3d. olive-brown & green-ish blue	15	12
06	**95**	1s. olive-green, lilac and deep reddish violet ..	1·00	1·00

96. " Madonna Damascena ".

97. Great Siege Monument.

98. Grand Master La Valette.

99. Assault on Fort St. Elmo.

(Photo. Harrison & Sons.)

1962 (7 Sept.). *Great Siege Commemoration.* W **w.12.** P 13×12.

307	**96**	2d. bright blue	10	10
308	**97**	3d. red	10	10
309	**98**	6d. bronze-green	30	25
310	**99**	1s. brown-purple	85	85

1963 (4 June). *Freedom from Hunger. As No.* 76 *of Aden.*

311		1s. 6d. sepia	3·50	2·50

1963 (2 Sept.). *Red Cross Centenary. As No.* 147/8 *of Antigua.*

312		2d. red and black	15	12
313		1s. 6d. red and blue	3·25	3·00

1963 (15 Oct.)–**64.** *As Nos.* 268 *and* 270, *but wmk.* **w.12.**

314	**59**	1d. black	20	25
315	**61**	2d. deep brown (11.7.64*)	35	45

* This is the earliest known date recorded in Malta.

100. Bruce, Zammit and Microscope.

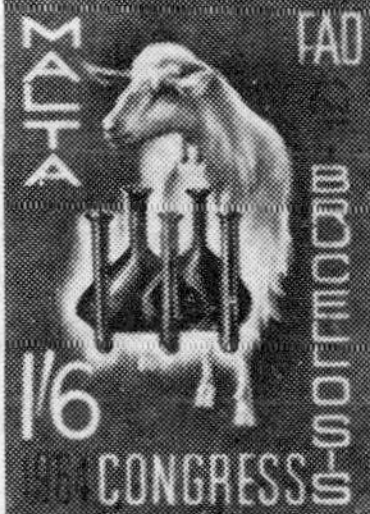

101. Goat and Laboratory Equipment.

(Des. E. V. Cremona. Photo. Harrison.)

1964 (14 April). *Anti-Brucellosis Congress.* W **w.12.** P 14.

316	**100**	2d. light brown, black and bluish green	8	8
		a. Black omitted	90·00	
317	**101**	1s. 6d. black and maroon	1·00	1·00

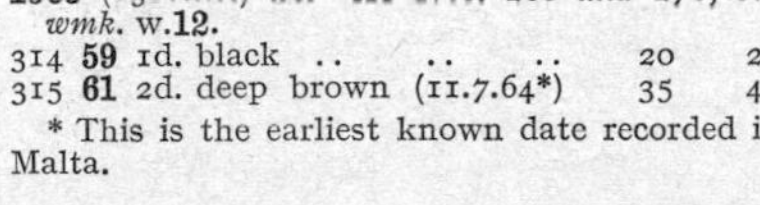

102. " Tending the Sick ".

103. St. Luke and Hospital.

104. Sacra Infermeria, Valletta.

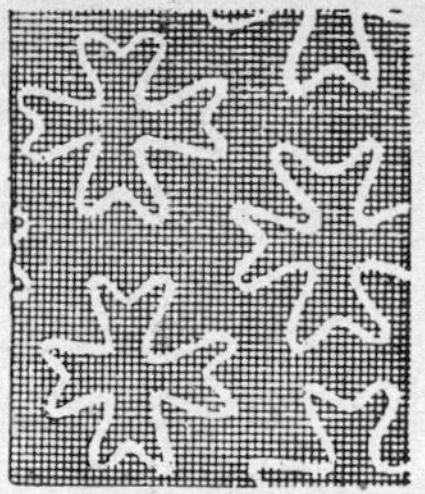

In this illustration the points of the crosses meet in a vertical line. When the watermark is sideways they meet in a horizontal line.

105. Maltese Cross (*Upright*).

(Des. E. V. Cremona. Photo. Harrison.)

1964 (5 Sept.). *First European Catholic Doctors' Congress, Vienna.* W **105** (*sideways*). P 13½×11½.

318	**102**	2d. red, black, gold and grey-blue	12	10
319	**103**	6d. red, black, gold and bistre	35	40
320	**104**	1s. 6d. red, black, gold and reddish violet ..	1·00	1·40

III. INDEPENDENCE.

106. Dove and British Crown.

107. Dove's and Pope's Tiara.

108. Dove and U.N. Emblem.

(Des. E. V. Cremona. Photo. Harrison.)

1964 (21 Sept.). *Independence.* W **105.** P 14½×13½.

321	**106**	2d. olive-brown, red and gold	15	12
322	**107**	3d. brown purple, red and gold	25	15
323	**108**	6d. slate, red and gold ..	90	45
324	**106**	1s. blue, red and gold ..	2·00	1·00
325	**107**	1s. 6d. indigo, red & gold	5·00	3·00
326	**108**	2s. 6d. deep violet-blue, red and gold ..	8·00	5·00
321/6		.. .. *Set of* 6	15·00	9·00

109. " The Nativity ".

(Des. E. V. Cremona. Photo. De La Rue.)

1964 (3 Nov.). *Christmas.* W **105** (*sideways*). P 13×13½.

327	**109**	2d. bright purple & gold	15	12
328	,,	4d. bright blue and gold	35	30
329	,,	8d. deep bluish green and gold	1·40	1·25

110. Neolithic Era.

111. Punic Era.

112. Roman Era.

113. Proto Christian Era.

114. Saracenic Era.

115. Siculo Norman Era.

116. Knights of Malta.

117. Maltese Navy.

117a. Fortifications.

118. French Occupation.

119. British Rule.

119a. Naval Arsenal.

120. Maltese Corps of the British Army.

121. International Eucharistic Congress, 1913.

122. Self-Government, 1921.

123. Gozo Civic Council.

124. State of Malta.

125. Independence, 1964.

126. HAFMED (Allied Forces, Mediterranean

127. The Maltese Islands (map).

128. Patron Saints.

(Des. E. V. Cremona. Photo. Harrison.)

1965 (7 Jan.)–**71.** *Chalk-surfaced paper.* *W* **10**
P 14×14½ (*vert.*) *or* 14½ (*horiz.*).

330	**110**	½d. multicoloured ..	5	
		a. "½d" (white) printed twice†		
331	**111**	1d. multicoloured ..	5	
		a. Gold (ancient lettering) omitted	40·00	
332	**112**	1½d. multicoloured ..	8	
333	**113**	2d. multicoloured ..	8	
334	**114**	2½d. multicoloured ..	8	
		a. Orange omitted* ..	40·00	
335	**115**	3d. multicoloured ..	8	
		a. Gold (windows) omitted	40·00	
		b. "MALTA" (silver) omitted	30·00	
		c. Imperf. (pair).. ..	£300	
336	**116**	4d. multicoloured ..	8	
		a. "KNIGHTS OF MALTA" (silver) omitted ..	35·00	
337	**117**	4½d. multicoloured ..	10	1
337*a*	**117*a***	5d. mult. (1.8.70) ..	15	1
		b. "FORTIFICATIONS" (gold) omitted ..	35·00	
338	**118**	6d. multicoloured ..	10	1
		a. "MALTA" omitted ..	35·00	
339	**119**	8d. multicoloured ..	12	1
		a. Gold (centre) omitted ..	35·00	
		b. Gold (frame) omitted ..	35·00	
339*c*	**119*a***	10d. mult. (1.8.70) ..	30	3
		d. Glazed paper (9.8.71)..	40	4
340	**120**	1s. multicoloured ..	40	4
		a. Gold (framework) omitted	35·00	

341 **121** 1s. 3d. multicoloured .. 1·00 1·00
a. Gold (centre) omitted .. 40·00
b. Gold (framework) omitted
342 **122** 1s. 6d. multicoloured .. 70 70
a. Head omitted .. £160
b. Gold (centre) omitted .. 40·00
c. Gold (frame) omitted 40·00
343 **123** 2s. multicoloured .. 50 50
a. Gold (centre) omitted ..
b. Gold (framework) omitted 30·00
344 **124** 2s. 6d. multicoloured .. 90 90
345 **125** 3s. multicoloured .. 1·10 1·10
a. Gold (framework) omitted 30·00
346 **126** 5s. multicoloured .. 1·40 1·40
a. Gold (framework) omitted 35·00
347 **127** 10s. multicoloured .. 2·25 2·50
a. Gold (centre) omitted .. 45·00
348 **128** £1 multicoloured .. 4·00 4·50
330/48 .. .. *Set of* 21 12·00 13·00

*The effect of this is to leave the Saracenic pattern as a pink colour.

† Second impression is $6\frac{1}{2}$ mm. lower; stamps with almost co-incidental double impression are common.

The $\frac{1}{2}$d. and 1d. had white printing plates. Two silver plates were used on the 4d., one for "KNIGHTS OF MALTA" and the other for "MALTA". Two gold plates were used for the 8d. to 10s., one for the framework and the other for the gold in the central part of the designs.

The $\frac{1}{2}$d. to 4d., 1s. and 1s. 6d. to 5s. values exist with PVA gum as well as gum arabic and the 5d. and 10d. have PVA gum only.

129. Dante.

(Des. E. V. Cremona. Photo. Govt. Ptg. Wks., Rome.)

1965 (7 JULY). *700th Anniv. of Dante's Birth. P* 14.
349 **129** 2d. indigo 8 10
350 ,, 6d. bronze-green .. 30 20
351 ,, 2s. chocolate 80 80

130. Turkish Camp.
131. Battle Scene. (*Square.*)

132. Turkish Armada.

134. Grand Master J. de La Valette's Arms.

133. Arrival of Relief Force. (*Square.*)
135. "Allegory of Victory" (from mural by M. Pret). (*Square.*)
136. Victory Medal. (*Square.*)

(Des. E. V. Cremona. Photo. Harrison.)

1965 (1 SEPT.). *400th Anniv. of Great Siege. W* **105** (*sideways*). *P* 13 (*6d.*, *1s.*) *or* $14\frac{1}{2} \times 14$ (*others*).
352 **130** 2d. olive-grn., red & blk. 10 10
353 **131** 3d. olive-green, red, black and light drab .. 15 12
354 **132** 6d. multicoloured .. 40 30
a. Gold (framework and dates) omitted .. ..
355 **133** 8d. red, gold, ind. & blue 50 45
356 **134** 1s. red, gold and deep grey-blue 95 90
357 **135** 1s. 6d. ochre, red & blk. 1·00 1·10
358 **136** 2s. 6d. sepia, black, red and yellow-olive .. 3·25 3·00
352/8 .. .. *Set of* 7 6·00 5·00

137. "The Three Kings".

(Des. E. V. Cremona. Photo. Enschedé.)

1965 (7 OCT.). *Christmas. W* **105** (*sideways*). *P* $11 \times 11\frac{1}{2}$.
359 **137** 1d. slate-purple and red 5 5
360 ,, 4d. slate-purple and blue 80 80
361 ,, 1s. 3d. slate-purple and bright purple .. 1·00 70

138. Sir Winston Churchill.

139. Sir Winston Churchill and George Cross.

(Des. E. V. Cremona. Photo. Harrison.)

1966 (24 JAN.). *Churchill Commemoration. W* **105** (*sideways*). *P* $14\frac{1}{2} \times 14$.
362 **138** 2d. black, red and gold .. 5 5
363 **139** 3d. bronze-green, yellow-olive and gold .. 10 10
364 **138** 1s. maroon, red and gold 35 40
365 **139** 1s. 6d. chalky blue, violet-blue and gold .. 55 55

140. Grand Master La Valette.
141. Pope Pius V.
142. Map of Valletta.
143. Francesco Laparelli (architect).
144. Girolamo Cassar (architect).

(Des. E V. Cremona. Photo. State Ptg. Wks., Vienna.)

1966 (28 MAR.). *400th Anniv. of Valletta. W* **105** (*sideways*). *P* 12.
366 **140** 2d. multicoloured .. 5 5
367 **141** 3d. multicoloured .. 5 5
368 **142** 6d. multicoloured .. 20 20
369 **143** 1s. multicoloured .. 30 30
370 **144** 2s. 6d. multicoloured .. 65 70
366/70 .. .. *Set of* 5 1·10 1·10

145. Pres. Kennedy and Memorial.

(Des. E. V. Cremona. Photo. Harrison.)

1966 (28 MAY). *President Kennedy Commemoration. W* **105** (*sideways*). *P* 15×14.
371 **145** 3d. olive, gold and black 8 8
a. Gold inscr. omitted ..
372 ,, 1s. 6d. Prussian blue, gold and black 35 40

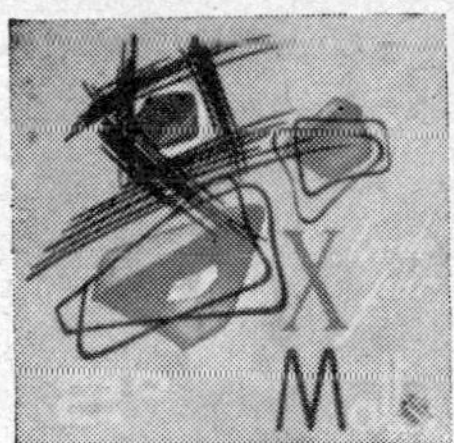

146 "Trade".

(Des. E. V. Cremona. Photo. De La Rue.)

1966 (16 JUNE). *Tenth Malta Trade Fair. W* **105** (*sideways*). *P* $13\frac{1}{2}$.
373 **146** 2d. multicoloured .. 8 8
374 ,, 8d. multicoloured .. 30 30
375 ,, 2s. 6d. multicoloured .. 90 90

147. "The Child in the Manger".

148. George Cross.

(Des. E. V. Cremona. Photo. De La Rue.)

1966 (7 OCT.). *Christmas. W* **105.** *P* $13\frac{1}{2}$.
376 **147** 1d. black, gold, turq.-blue and slate-purple .. 5 5
377 ,, 4d. black, gold, ultram. & slate-purple 8 8
378 ,, 1s. 3d. black, gold, bright purple & slate-purple 25 30
a. Gold omitted .. ..

(Des. E. V. Cremona. Photo. Harrison.)

1967 (1 Mar.). *25th Anniv. of George Cross Award to Malta.* W **105** (*sideways*). P 14½ × 14.

379 **148** 2d. multicoloured .. 5 5
380 ,, 4d. multicoloured .. 10 10
381 ,, 3s. multicoloured .. 40 40

149. Crucifixion of St. Peter.

150. Open Bible and Episcopal Emblems.

151. Beheading of St. Paul. (*Square.*)

(Des. E. V. Cremona. Photo. Harrison.)

1967 (28 June). *1,900th Anniv. of Martyrdom of Saints Peter and Paul.* W **105** (*sideways*). P 13½ × 14½ (8*d*.) *or* 14½ (*others*).

382 **149** 2d. chestnut, orange and black 5 5
383 **150** 8d. yellow-olive, gold and black 15 15
384 **151** 3s. blue, lt. blue & black 45 50

152. " St. Catherine of Siena ".

153. " St. Thomas of Villanova ".

154. " Baptism of Christ " (detail).

155. " St. John the Baptist " (from " Baptism of Christ ").

(Des. E. V. Cremona. Photo. J. Enschedé & Sons.)

1967 (1 Aug.). *300th Death Anniv. of Melchior Gafa (sculptor).* W **105** (*sideways*). P 13½ × 13.

385 **152** 2d. multicoloured .. 5 5
386 **153** 4d. multicoloured .. 8 8
387 **154** 1s. 6d. multicoloured .. 25 25
388 **155** 2s. 6d. multicoloured .. 40 45

156. Temple Ruins, Tarxien.

157. Façade of Palazzo Falzon, Notabile.

158. Parish Church, Birkirkara.

159. Portal, Auberge de Castille.

(Des. E. V. Cremona. Photo. Harrison.)

1967 (12 Sept.). *15th International Historical Architecture Congress, Valletta.* W **105.** P 15 × 14½.

389 **156** 2d. multicoloured .. 5 5
390 **157** 6d. multicoloured .. 12 12
391 **158** 1s. multicoloured .. 25 25
392 **159** 3s. multicoloured .. 45 45

160. " Angels ".

161. " Crib ".

162. " Angels ".

(Des. E. V. Cremona. Photo. De La Rue.)

1967 (20 Oct.). *Christmas.* W **105** (*sideways*). P 14.

393 **160** 1d. multicoloured .. 5 5
a. In triptych with Nos. 394/5 .. .. .. 40 40
b. White stars (red omitted) 40·00
394 **161** 8d. multicoloured .. 10 10
395 **162** 1s. 4d. multicoloured .. 25 25

Nos. 393/5 were issued in sheets of 60 of each value (arranged *tête-bêche*), and also in sheets containing the three values *se-tenant*, thus forming a triptych of the Nativity.

163. Queen Elizabeth II and Arms of Malta.

164. Queen in Robes of Order of St. Michael and St. George. (*Vert.*)

165. Queen and Outline of Malta. (*Horiz.*)

(Des. E. V. Cremona. Photo. Harrison.)

1967 (13 Nov.). *Royal Visit.* W **105** (*sideways on 2d., 3s.*). P 14 × 15 (4*d*.) *or* 15 × 14 (*others*).

396 **163** 2d. multicoloured 5 5
397 **164** 4d. black, brown-purple and gold 12 15
398 **165** 3s. multicoloured .. 40 45

166. Human Rights Emblem and People.

167. Human Rights Emblem and People.

168. Human Rights Emblem and People. (*Reverse of T* **166.**)

(Des. E. V. Cremona. Photo. Harrison.)

1968 (2 May). *Human Rights Year.* W **105.** P 12½ (6*d*.) *or* 14½ (*others*).

399 **166** 2d. multicoloured .. 5 5
400 **167** 6d. multicoloured .. 12 12
401 **168** 2s. multicoloured .. 40 40

169. Fair " Products ".

(Des. E. V. Cremona. Photo. Harrison.)

1968 (1 June). *Malta International Trade Fair.* W **105** (*sideways*). P 14½ × 14.

402 **169** 4d. multicoloured .. 5 5
403 ,, 8d. multicoloured .. 12 15
404 ,, 3s. multicoloured .. 45 50

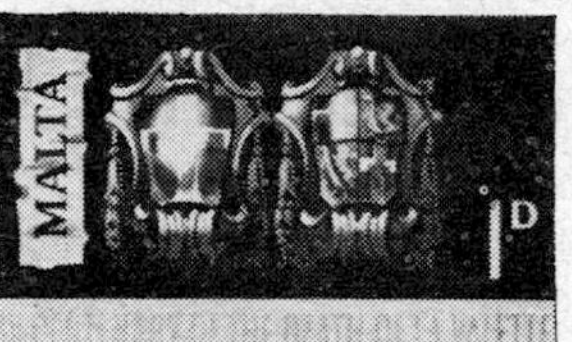

170. Arms of the Order of St. John and La Valette.

172. La Valette's Tomb.

171. La Valette.

173. Angels and Scroll bearing Date of Death.

(Des. E. V. Cremona. Photo. Govt. Printer, Israel.)

1968 (1 Aug.). *Fourth Death Centenary of Grand Master La Valette.* *W* **105** (*upright, 1s. 6d.; sideways, others*). *P* 13×14 (*1d., 1s. 6d.*) *or* 14×13 (*others*).

405	**170**	1d. multicoloured ..	5	5
406	**171**	8d. multicoloured ..	12	12
407	**172**	1s. 6d. multicoloured ..	25	25
408	**173**	2s. 6d. multicoloured ..	40	40

174. Star of Bethlehem and Angel waking Shepherds.

175. Mary and Joseph with Shepherd watching over Cradle.

176. Three Wise Men and Star of Bethlehem.

(Des. E. V. Cremona. Photo. Harrison.)

1968 (3 Oct.). *Christmas.* *W* **105** (*sideways*). *P* 14½×14.

409	**174**	1d. multicoloured ..	5	5
410	**175**	8d. multicoloured ..	12	15
411	**176**	1s. 4d. multicoloured ..	25	30

The shortest side at top and the long side at the bottom both gauge 14½, the other three sides are 14. Nos. 409/11 were issued in sheets of 60 arranged in ten strips of six, alternately upright and inverted.

177. Agriculture.

178. F.A.O. Emblem and Coin.

179. "Agriculture" sowing Seeds.

(Des. E. V. Cremona. Photo. Enschedé.)

1968 (21 Oct.). *Sixth Food and Agricultural Organization Regional Conference for Europe.* *W* **105** (*sideways*). *P* 12½×12.

412	**177**	4s. multicoloured ..	5	5
413	**178**	1s. multicoloured ..	20	20
414	**179**	2s. 6d. multicoloured ..	60	60

180. Mahatma Gandhi.

(Des. E. V. Cremona. Photo. Enschedé.)

1969 (24 Mar.). *Birth Centenary of Mahatma Gandhi.* *W* **105.** *P* 12×12½.

415	**180**	1s. 6d. blackish brown, black and gold ..	30	30

181. I.L.O. Emblem.

(Des. E. V. Cremona. Photo. Harrison.)

1969 (26 May). *50th Anniv. of International Labour Organization.* *W* **105** (*sideways*). *P* 13½×14½.

416	**181**	2d. indigo, gold and turq.	5	5
417	,,	6d. sepia, gold & chestnut	15	12

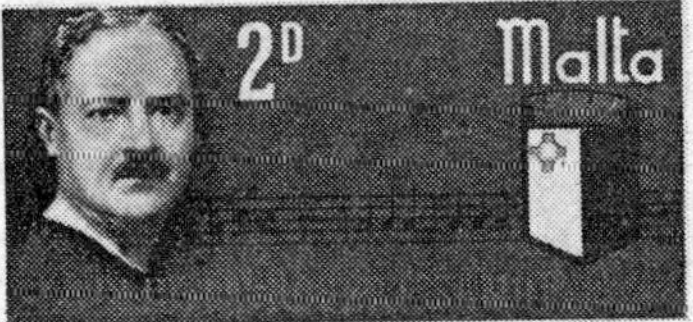

182. Robert Samut.

(Des. E. V. Cremona. Photo. De La Rue.)

1969 (26 July). *Birth Centenary of Robert Samut (composer of Maltese National Anthem).* *W* **105** (*sideways*). *P* 13.

418	**182**	2d. multicoloured ..	12	12

183. Dove of Peace, U.N. Emblem and Sea-Bed.

(Des. E. V. Cremona. Photo. De La Rue.)

1969 (26 July.) *United Nations Resolution on Oceanic Resources.* *W* **105** (*sideways*). *P* 13.

419	**183**	5d. multicoloured ..	12	12

184. "Swallows" returning to Malta.

(Des. E. V. Cremona. Photo. De La Rue.)

1969 (26 July). *Maltese Migrants' Convention.* *W* **105** (*sideways*). *P* 13.

420	**184**	10d. black, gold and yellow-olive	25	25

185. University Arms and Grand Master de Fonseca (founder).

(Des. E. V. Cremona. Photo. De La Rue.)

1969 (26 July). *Bicentenary of University of Malta.* *W* **105** (*sideways*). *P* 13.

421	**185**	2s. multicoloured ..	35	40

186. 1919 War Monument.

187. Flag of Malta and Birds.

Designs as T **187**:—

188. "Tourism". (*Vert.*)

189. U.N. and Council of Europe Emblems. (*Vert.*)

190. "Trade and Industry". (*Vert.*)

(Des. E. V. Cremona. Photo. Enschedé.)

1969 (20 Sept.). *Fifth Anniv. of Independence.* *W* **105** (*upright on 5d., sideways others*). *P* 13×12½ (*2d.*), 12×12½ (*5d.*) *or* 12½×12 (*others*).

422	**186**	2d. multicoloured ..	8	8
423	**187**	5d. black, red and gold ..	8	8
424	**188**	10d. black, turquoise-blue and gold	15	15
425	**189**	1s. 6d. multicoloured ..	50	50
426	**190**	2s. 6d. black, olive-brown and gold	55	55
422/6		.. .. *Set of* 5	1·10	1·10

191. Peasants playing Tambourine and Bagpipes.

192. Angels playing Trumpet and Harp.

193. Choir Boys Singing.

(Des. E. V. Cremona. Litho. De La Rue.)

1969 (8 Nov.). *Christmas. Children's Welfare Fund.* *W* **105** *(sideways).* *P* 12½.

427	**191**	1d.+1d. multicoloured ..	8	8
		a. In triptych with Nos. 428/9	60	60
428	**192**	5d.+1d. multicoloured ..	12	12
429	**193**	1s. 6d.+3d. multicoloured	40	40

Nos. 427/9 were issued in sheets of 60 of each value, and also in sheets containing the three values *se-tenant*, thus forming the triptych No. 427a.

194. "The Beheading of St. John" (Caravaggio) *(Illustration reduced. Actual size* 56×30¼ *mm.)*

195. " St. John the Baptist " (Mattia Preti). *(As T* **194**, *but* 45×31¾ *mm.)*

196. Interior of St. John's Co-Cathedral, Valletta, *(As T* **194**, *but* 39×39 *mm.)*

197. " Allegory of the Order " (Mattia Preti). *(As T* **195**.)

198. " St. Jerome " (Caravaggio). *(As T* **194**.)

199. Articles from the Order of St. John in Malta. *(As T* **194**, *but* 63×21 *mm.)*

200. " The Blessed Gerard receiving Godfrey de Bouillon " (A. de Favray). *(As T* **194**, *but* 45×34½ *mm.)*

201. Cape and Stolone (16th-cent.). *(As T* **199**.)

(Des. E. V. Cremona. Photo. Enschedé.)

1970 (21 Mar.). *13th Council of Europe Art Exhibition.* *W* **105** *(upright, 10d., 2s.; sideways, others).* *P* 14×13 *(1d., 8d.),* 12 *(10d., 2s.) or* 13×13½ *(others).*

430	**194**	1d. multicoloured ..	5	5
431	**195**	2d. multicoloured ..	8	8
432	**196**	5d. multicoloured ..	10	10
433	**197**	6d. multicoloured ..	12	12
434	**198**	8d. multicoloured ..	25	25
435	**199**	10d. multicoloured ..	25	25
436	**200**	1s. 6d. multicoloured ..	40	40
437	**201**	2s. multicoloured ..	50	50
430/37		.. .. *Set of* 8	1·60	1·60

202. Artist's Impression of Fujiyama.

(Des. E. V. Cremona. Photo. D.L.R.)

1970 (29 May). *World Fair, Osaka.* *W* **105** *(sideways).* *P* 15.

438	**202**	2d. multicoloured ..	5	5
439	,,	5d. multicoloured ..	12	12
440	,,	3s. multicoloured ..	50	50

203. " Peace and Justice ".

204. Carol-Singers, Church and Star.

205. Church, Star and Angels with Infant.

206. Church, Star and Nativity Scene.

(Des. J. Casha. Litho. Harrison.)

1970 (30 Sept.). *25th Anniv. of United Nations.* *W* **105**. *P* 14×14½.

441	**203**	2d. multicoloured ..	5	5
442	,,	5d. multicoloured ..	12	12
443	,,	2s. 6d. multicoloured ..	45	45

(Des. E. V. Cremona. Photo. Govt. Printer, Israel.)

1970 (7 Nov.). *Christmas.* *W* **105** *(sideways).* *P* 14×13.

444	**204**	1d.+½d. multicoloured	5	5
445	**205**	10d.+2d. multicoloured	25	25
446	**206**	1s. 6d.+3d. mult. ..	45	45

207. Books and Quill.

208. Dun Karm, Books Pens and Lamp.

(Des. H. Alden (1s. 6d.), A. Agius (2s.). Litho. D.L.R.)

1971 (20 Mar.). *Literary Anniversaries. Death Bicentenary* (1970) *of De Soldanis (historian)* (1s. 6d.) *and Birth Centenary of Dun Karm (poet)* (2s.). *W* **105** *(sideways).* *P* 13×13½.

447	**207**	1s. 6d. multicoloured ..	25	25
448	**208**	2s. multicoloured ..	30	30

209. Europa " Chain ".

(Des. H. Haflidason; adapted E. V. Cremona. Litho. Harrison.)

1971 (3 May). *Europa.* *W* **105** *(sideways).* *P* 13½×14½.

449	**209**	2d. orge., blk. & yell.-olive	5	5
450	,,	5d. orge., blk. & vermilion	10	10
451	,,	1s. 6d. orge., blk. & slate	45	45

210. " St. Joseph and Angels " (G. Cali).

(Des. E. V. Cremona. Litho. D.L.R.)

1971 (24 July). *Centenary of Proclamation of St Joseph as Patron Saint of Catholic Church, and 50th Anniv. of the Coronation of the Statue of " Our Lady of Victories ".* *T* **210** *and similar horiz. design. Multicoloured.* *W* **105** *(sideways).* *P* 13×13½.

452	2d. Type **210**	5	5
453	5d. Statue of " Our Lady of Victories " and Galley ..	8	8
454	10d. Type **210**	25	25
455	1s. 6d. As 5d.	40	45

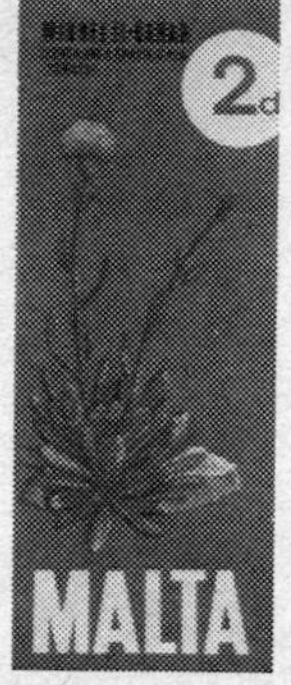

211. *Centaurea spathulata.*

(Des. Reno Psaila. Litho. Harrison.)

1971 (18 Sept.). *National Plant and Bird of Malta.* *T* **211** *and similar horiz. design. Multicoloured.* *W* **105** *(sideways on 5d. and 10d.).* *P* 14½×14.

456	2d. Type **211**	5	5
457	5d. *Monticola solitarius* (thrush)	8	8
458	10d. As 5d.	25	25
459	1s. 6d. Type **211**	45	45

212. Angel.

(Illustration reduced. Actual size 59×21 *mm.)*

(Des. E. V. Cremona. Litho. Format.)

1971 (8 Nov.). *Christmas.* *T* **212** *and similar horiz. designs. Multicoloured.* *W* **105** *(sideways).* *P* 13½×14.

460	1d.+½d. Type **212** ..	5	5
461	10d.+2d. Mary and the Child Jesus	25	25
462	1s. 6d.+3d. Joseph lying awake	45	50
MS463	131×113 mm. Nos. 460/2. P 15	80	90

213. Heart and W.H.O. Emblem.

(Des. A. Agius. Litho. Format.)

1972 (20 Mar.). *World Health Day.* *W* **105**. *P* 13½×14.

464	**213**	2d. multicoloured ..	5	5
465	,,	10d. multicoloured ..	12	12
466	,,	2s. 6d. multicoloured ..	45	45

(New currency. 10 mils = 1 cent; 100 cents = 1 Maltese pound.)

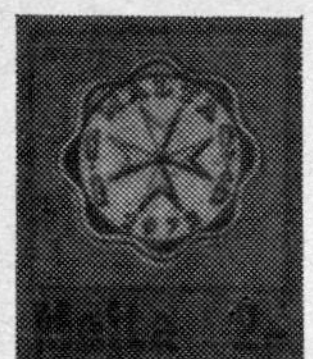

= 1c3

214. Maltese Cross. (215)

(Des. G. M. Pace. Litho. Format.)

1972 (16 May). *Decimal Currency. T* **214** *and similar vert. designs showing decimal coins. Multicoloured. W* **105**. *P* 14 (2 *m.*, 3 *m.*, 2 *c.*), 14½ × 14 (5 *m.*, 1 *c.*, 5 *c.*) *or* 13½ (10 *c.*, 50 *c.*).

467 2 m. Type **214** 5 5
468 3 m. Bee on honeycomb 5 5
469 5 m. Earthen lampstand 5 5
470 1 c. George Cross 5 5
471 2 c. Classical head .. 8 8
472 5 c. Ritual altar 20 20
473 10 c. Grandmaster's galley 45 45
474 50 c. Great Siege Monument 1·75 1·75
467/74 .. .. *Set of* 8 2·40 2·40

Sizes:—2 m., 3 m. and 2 c. as T **214**; 5 m., 1 c. and 5 c. 22 × 27 mm.; 10 c. and 50 c. 27 × 35 mm.

1972 (30 Sept.). *Nos.* 337*a*, 339 *and* 341 *surch. as T* **215**, *by Govt. Printing Works, Valletta.*

475 **117***a* 1 c. 3 on 5d. mult. .. 8 8
476 **119** 3 c. on 8d. multicoloured 10 10
a. Surch. inverted .. 50·00
477 **121** 5 c. on 1s. 3d. mult. 30 30
a. Surch. double .. 50·00
b. Surch. inverted ..
c. Gold (centre) omitted ..

PRINTERS. All stamps from No. 478 onwards were printed in lithography by Printex Ltd., Malta.

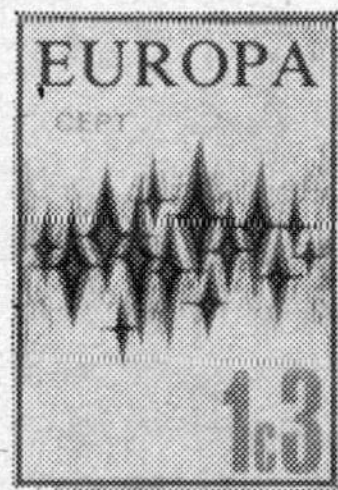

216. " Communications ".

(Des. Huovinen; adapted G. M. Pace.)

1972 (11 Nov.). *Europa. W* **105** (*sideways*). *P* 13.

478 **216** 1 c. 3, multicoloured .. 5 5
479 „ 3 c. multicoloured .. 8 8
480 „ 5 c. multicoloured .. 15 15
481 „ 7 c. 5, multicoloured .. 35 35

217. Angel.

(*Illustration reduced. Actual size* 58 × 22 *mm.*)

(Des. E.V. Cremona.)

1972 (9 Dec.). *Christmas. T* **217** *and similar horiz. designs. W* **105** (*sideways*). *P* 13½.

482 8 m. + 2 m. dull sepia, brownish grey and gold 8 8
483 3 c. + 1 c. plum, lavender and gold 15 15
484 7 c. 5 + 1 c. 5, indigo, azure and gold 30 30
MS485 137 × 113 mm. Nos. 482/4 60 60

Designs:—No. 483, Angel with tambourine; No. 484, Singing angel.

See also Nos. 507/10.

218. Archaeology.

(Des. E. V. Cremona.)

1973 (31 Mar.)–**76**. *T* **218** *and similar designs. Multicoloured. W* **105** (*sideways*). *P* 13½ × 14 (*Nos.* 500/*a*) *or* 13½ (*others*).

486 2 m. Type **218** 5 5
487 4 m. History 5 5
a. Gold (inscr. and decoration) omitted .. ..
488 5 m. Folklore 5 5
489 8 m. Industry 5 5
490 1 c. Fishing industry .. 5 5
491 1 c. 3, Pottery 5 5
492 2 c. Agriculture 5 5
493 3 c. Sport 8 10
494 4 c. Yacht Marina .. 10 10
495 5 c. Fiesta 10 12
496 7 c. 5, Regatta 15 20
497 10 c. Voluntary service .. 20 25
498 50 c. Education .. .. 1·00 1·25
499 £1 Religion .. .. 2·10 2·25
500 £2 Coat-of-arms (*horiz.*) .. 4·75 5·00
500*a* £2 National Emblem (*horiz.*) (28.1.76) .. 4·25 4·50
486/500*a* .. .. *Set of* 16 12·00 13·00

Nos. 500/*a* are larger, 32 × 27 mm.

219. Europa " Posthorn ".

(Des. L. F. Anisdahl; adapted G. M. Pace.)

1973 (2 June). *Europa. W* **105**. *P* 14.

501 **219** 3 c. multicoloured .. 8 8
502 „ 5 c. multicoloured .. 15 15
503 „ 7 c. 5, multicoloured .. 25 25

220. Emblem, and Woman holding Corn.

(Des. H. D. Alden.)

1973 (6 Oct.). *Anniversaries. T* **220** *and similar vert. designs showing emblem and allegorical figures. W* **105** (*sideways*). *P* 13½.

504 1 c. 3, multicoloured .. 5 5
505 7 c. 5, multicoloured .. 25 25
506 10 c. multicoloured 35 35

Anniversaries:—1 c. 3, Tenth Anniv. of World Food Programme; 7 c. 5, 25th Anniv. of W.H.O.; 10 c. 25th Anniv. of Universal Declaration of Human Rights.

(Des. E. V. Cremona.)

1973 (10 Nov.). *Christmas. Horiz. designs as T* **217**. *Multicoloured. W* **105** (*sideways*). *P* 13½.

507 8 m. + 2 m. Angels and organ pipes 5 5
508 3 c. + 1 c. Madonna and Child 25 25
509 7 c. 5 + 1 c. 5, Buildings and Star 30 35
MS510 137 × 112 mm. Nos. 507/9 65 70

221. Girolamo Cassar (architect).

(Des. E. V. Cremona.)

1974 (12 Jan.). *Prominent Maltese. T* **221** *and similar vert. designs. W* **105**. *P* 14.

511 1 c. 3, dull myrtle-green, dull grey-green and gold .. 5 5
512 3 c. dp. turq., grey-bl. & gold 10 10
513 5 c. dull sepia, deep sage-green and gold 12 15
514 7 c. 5, slate-blue, lt. sage-blue and gold 20 25
515 10 c. purple, dull purple & gold 30 35
511/15 .. .. *Set of* 5 70 80

Designs:—3 c. Guiseppe Barth (ophthalmologist); 5 c. Nicolo' Isouard (composer); 7 c. 5, John Borg (botanist); 10 c. Antonio Sciortino (sculptor).

222. "Air Malta" Emblem.

(Des. E. V. Cremona.)

1974 (30 Mar.). *Air. T* **222** *and similar horiz. design. Multicoloured. W* **105** (*sideways*). *P* 13½.

516 3 c. Type **222** 5 8
517 4 c. Boeing " 707 " 8 10
518 5 c. Type **222** 10 12
519 7 c. 5, As 4 c. 15 20
520 20 c. Type **222** 40 45
521 25 c. As 4 c. 50 60
522 35 c. Type **222** 75 80
516/22 .. .. *Set of* 7 1·75 2·25

223. Prehistoric Sculpture.

(Des. E. V. Cremona.)

1974 (13 July). *Europa. T* **223** *and similar designs. W* **105** (*sideways on Nos.* 523 *and* 525). *P* 13½.

523 1 c. 3, dull purple, grey-black and gold 5 5
524 3 c. lt. bistre-brown, grey-black and gold 8 8
525 5 c. purple, grey-black and gold 12 15
526 7 c. 5, sepia, grey-black and gold 25 25

Designs: *Vert.*—3 c. Old Cathedral Door, Mdina; 7 c. 5, "Vetlina" (sculpture by A. Sciortino). *Horiz.*—5 c. Silver Monstrance.

224. Heinrich von Stephan (founder) and Land Transport.

(Des. S. and G. Sullivan.)

1974 (20 Sept.). *Centenary of Universal Postal Union. T* **224** *and similar horiz. designs. W* **105**. *P* 13½×14.

527 1 c. 3, blue-green, light violet-blue and yellow-orange .. 5 5
528 5 c. brown, dull vermilion and yellow-green .. 15 15
529 7 c. 5, deep dull blue, light vio.-bl. and yellow-green 20 20
530 50 c. purple, dull vermilion and yellow-orange .. .. 1·10 1·25
MS531 126×91 mm. Nos. 527/30 1·60 1·75

Designs (each containing portrait as T **224**):—5 c. S.S. *Washington* and modern liner; 7 c. 5, Balloon and Boeing "747", 50 c. U.P.U. Buildings, 1874 and 1974.

225. Decorative Star and Nativity Scene.

(Des. E. V. Cremona.)

1974 (22 Nov.). *Christmas. T* **225** *and similar vert. designs, each with decorative star. Multi-coloured. W* **105** *(sideways). P* 14.

532 8 m. + 2 m. Type **225** .. 5 5
533 3 c. + 1 c. "Shepherds" .. 10 10
534 5 c. + 1 c. "Shepherds with gifts" 15 15
535 7 c. 5 + 1 c. 5, "The Magi" .. 25 25

IV. REPUBLIC.

226. Swearing-in of Prime Minister.

(Des. E. V. Cremona.)

1975 (31 Mar.). *Inauguration of Republic. T* **226** *and similar horiz. designs. W* **105** *(sideways). P* 14.

536 1 c. 3, multicoloured 5 5
537 5 c. rose-red and grey-black 12 12
538 25 c. multicoloured 60 65

Designs:—5 c. National flag; 25 c. Minister of Justice, President and Prime Minister.

227. Mother and Child ("Family Life").

(Des. D. Friggieri.)

1975 (30 May). *International Women's Year T* **227** *and similar horiz. design. W* **105**. *P* 13½×14.

539 **227** 1 c. 3, lt. violet and gold 5 5
540 – 3 c. light blue and gold .. 8 8
541 **227** 5 c. dull ol.-sepia & gold 12 12
542 – 20 c. chestnut and gold .. 45 50

Design:—3 c., 20 c. Office secretary ("Public Life").

228. "Allegory of Malta" (Francesco de Mura).

(Des. E. V. Cremona.)

1975 (15 July). *Europa. T* **228** *and similar horiz. designs. Multicoloured. W* **105**. *P* 14×13½.

543 5 c. Type **228** 12 15
544 15 c. "Judith and Holofernes" (Valentin de Boulogne) .. 35 40

The 15 c. is a smaller design than the 5 c. (47×23 mm.), though the perforated area is the same.

229. Plan of Ggantija Temple.

(Des. R. England.)

1975 (16 Sept.). *European Architectural Heritage Year. T* **229** *and similar horiz. designs. W* **105** *(sideways). P* 13½.

545 1 c. 3, brownish black and light orange-red 5 5
546 3 c. dull purple, lt. orge.-red and blackish brown .. 8 10
547 5 c. blackish brown and light orange-red 12 15
548 25 c. dull grey-olive, light orge.-red and brownish black .. 60 70

Designs:—3 c. Mdina skyline; 5 c. View of Victoria, Gozo; 25 c. Silhouette of Fort St. Angelo.

230. Farm Animals. **231.** "The Right to Work".

(Des. E. V. Cremona.)

1975 (4 Nov.). *Christmas. T* **230** *and similar multicoloured designs. P* 13½.

549 8 m. + 2 m. Type **230** 5 5
a. In triptych with Nos. 550/1 35
550 3 c. + 1 c. Nativity scene (50×23 mm.) 8 10
551 7 c. 5 + 1 c. 5, Approach of the Magi 20 20

Nos. 549/51 were issued in sheets of 50 of each value, and also in sheets containing the three values horizontally *se-tenant*, thus forming the triptych No. 549a which is a composite design of "The Nativity" by Maestro Alberto.

(Des. A. de Giovanni.)

1975 (12 Dec.). *First Anniv. of Republic. T* **231** *and similar vert. designs. W* **105**. *P* 14.

552 1 c. 3, multicoloured .. 5 5
553 5 c. multicoloured 10 12
554 25 c. deep rose, light steel-blue and black 50 60

Designs:—5 c. "Safeguarding the Environment"; 25 c. National Flag.

232. "Festa Tar-Rahal".

(Des. M. Camilleri.)

1976 (26 Feb.). *Maltese Folklore. T* **232** *an similar multicoloured designs. W* **105** *(side ways on 5 c. and 7 c.5). P* 14.

555 1 c. 3, Type **232** 5
556 5 c. "L-Imnarja" (*horiz.*) 12 1
557 7 c. 5, "Il-Karnival" (*horiz.*) 20 2
558 10 c. "Il-Gimgha L-Kbira" 25 3

233. Waterpolo.

(Des. H. Alden.)

1976 (28 Apr.). *Olympic Games, Montrea. T* **233** *and similar horiz. designs. Multicoloure W* **105**. *P* 13½×14.

559 1 c. 7, Type **233** 5
560 5 c. Sailing 12 1
561 30 c. Athletics 70 7

234. Lace-making.

(Des. F. Portelli.)

1976 (8 July). *Europa. T* **234** *and simila horiz. design. Multicoloured. W* **105** *(sideways P* 13½×14.

562 7 c. Type **234** 15 2
563 15 c. Stone carving 35 4

235. Nicola Cotoner.

(Des. E. V. Cremona.)

1976 (14 Sept.). *300th Anniv. of School o Anatomy and Surgery. T* **235** *and simila horiz. designs. Multicoloured. W* **105** *(side ways). P* 13½.

564 2 c. Type **235** 5
565 5 c. Arm 12 1
566 7 c. Giuseppe Zammit .. 15 2
567 11 c. Sacra Infermeria .. 25 3

236. St. John the Baptist and St. Michael.

(Des. E. V. Cremona.)

1976 (23 Nov.). *Christmas. Designs showing portions of "Madonna and Saints" by Domenico di Michelino. Multicoloured. W* **105** *(sideways on No. 571). P 13½×14 (No. 571) or 13½ (others).*

No.	Description	Unused	Used
568	1 c. + 5 m. Type **236**	5	5
569	5 c. + 1 c. Madonna and Child	15	20
570	7 c. + 1 c. 5, St. Christopher and St. Nicholas	20	25
571	10 c. + 2 c. Complete painting (32×27 *mm.*)	30	35

POSTAGE DUE STAMPS.

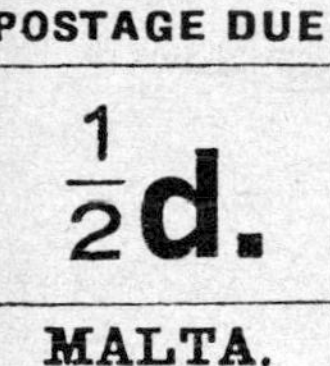

D 1

D 2

1925. *Type-set by Govt. Printing Office, Valletta. Imperf.*

No.	Type	Description	Unused	Used
D 1	D 1	½d. black	20	35
D 2	„	1d. black	30	70
D 3	„	1½d. black	50	80
D 4	„	2d. black	60	80
D 5	„	2½d. black	70	80
		a. "2" of "½" omitted	£130	£130
D 6	„	3d. black/*grey*	80	1·25
D 7	„	4d. black/*buff*	90	1·25
D 8	„	6d. black/*buff*	1·25	1·75
D 9	„	1s. black/*buff*	2·50	3·00
D10	„	1s. 6d. black/*buff*	4·00	6·00
D1/10		*Set of* 10	11·00	15·00

All the above may be had in *tête-bêche* pairs from the junction of the panes, price about four times that of a single stamp. Dangerous forgeries of No. D5a are in circulation.

(Typo. Bradbury, Wilkinson.)

1925. *Wmk. Mult. Script CA (sideways). P* 12.

No.	Type	Description	Unused	Used
D11	D 2	½d. green	10	10
D12	„	1d. violet	15	15
D13	„	1½d. brown	15	15
D14	„	2d. grey	3·00	3·00
D15	„	2½d. orange	20	15
D16	„	3d. blue	40	40
D17	„	4d. olive-green	5·50	6·00
D18	„	6d. purple	30	30
D19	„	1s. black	45	45
D20	„	1s. 6d. carmine	80	80
D11/20		*Set of* 10	10·00	10·00
D11/20		Optd. "Specimen" *Set of* 10	50·00	

1953 (5 Nov.)–**57.** *Chalk-surfaced paper. Wmk. Mult. Script CA (sideways). P* 12.

No.	Type	Description	Unused	Used
D21	D 2	½d. emerald	5	5
D22	„	1d. purple (*shades*)	5	5
D23	„	1½d. yellow-brown	12	12
D24	D 2	2d. grey-brown (*shades*) (20.3.57)	5·00	5·00
D25	„	3d. deep slate-blue	25	25
D26	„	4d. yellow-olive	80	80
D21/6		*Set of* 6	5·50	5·50

1966 (Oct.). *As No.* D24, *but wmk.* w.**12** *(sideways).*

No.	Type	Description	Unused	Used
D27	D 2	2d. grey-brown	4·00	4·00

1967–70. *Ordinary paper. W* **105** *(sideways).*

No.	Type	Description	Unused	Used
		(*a*) *P* 12, *line* (9.11.67).		
D28	D 2	½d. emerald	5	5
D29	„	1d. purple	5	5
D30	„	2d. blackish brown	10	10
D31	„	4d. yellow-olive	75·00	75·00
		(*b*) *P* 12½, *comb* (30.5.68–70).		
D32	D 2	½d. emerald	5	5
D33	„	1d. purple	5	5
D34	„	1½d. yellow-brown	8	8
		a. Orange-brown (23.10.70)	8	8
D35	„	2d. blackish brown	12	12
		a. Brownish blk. (23.10.70)	12	12
D36	„	2½d. yellow-orange	12	12
D37	„	3d. deep slate-blue	12	12
D38	„	4d. yellow-olive	20	20
D39	„	6d. purple	30	30
D40	„	1s. black	40	40
D41	„	1s. 6d. carmine	60	60
D32/41		*Set of* 10	1·75	1·75

The above are the local release dates. In the 12½ perforation the London release dates were 21st May for the ½d. to 4d. and 4th June for the 6d. to 1s. 6d.

Nos. D34a and D35a are on glazed paper.

D 3. Maltese Lace.

(Des. G. M. Pace. Litho. Printex Ltd., Malta.)

1973 (28 Apr.). *W* **105**. *P* 13×13½.

No.	Type	Description	Unused	Used
D42	D 3	2 m. grey-brown and reddish brown	5	5
D43	„	3 m. dull orange and Indian red	5	5
D44	„	5 m. rose and bright scarlet	5	5
D45	„	1 c. turq. and bottle green	5	5
D46	„	2 c. slate and black	5	5
D47	„	3 c. lt. yell.-brown. & red-brown	8	10
D48	„	5 c. dull blue & Royal blue	12	15
D49	„	10 c. reddish lilac and plum	25	30
D42/9		*Set of* 8	60	70

MAURITIUS.

I. CROWN COLONY.

1 ("POST OFFICE")

2 ("POST PAID")

(Engraved on copper by J. O. Barnard.)

1847 (21 Sept.). *Head of Queen on groundwork of diagonal and perpendicular lines. Imperf.*

No.	Type	Description	Unused	Used
1	**1**	1d. orange-red	£250000	£85000
2	„	2d. deep blue	£150000	£85000

NOTE.—*Our prices for early Mauritius are for stamps in very fine condition. Exceptional copies are worth more, poorer copies considerably less.*

1848 (May). *T* **2**. 12 *varieties on the sheet. Imperf.*

A. *Earliest impressions. Design deep, sharp and clear. Diagonal lines predominate. Thick paper.*

No.	Description	Unused	Used
3	1d. orange-vermilion/*yellowish*	£16000	£10000
4	2d. indigo-blue/*grey to bluish*	£18000	£10000
	a. "PENOE" for "PENCE"	£28000	£17000
5	2d. deep blue/*grey to bluish*	£20000	£10000
	a. "PENOE" for "PENCE"	—	£20000

B. *Early impressions. Design sharp and clear but some lines slightly weakened. Paper not so thick, grey to yellowish white or bluish.*

No.	Description	Unused	Used
6	1d. vermilion	£8500	£4000
7	1d. orange-vermilion	£9000	£4000
8	2d. blue	£12000	£4500
	a. "PENOE" for "PENCE"	£14000	£7500
9	2d. deep blue	£15000	£5000

C. *Intermediate impressions. White patches appear where design has worn. Paper yellowish white, grey or bluish, of poorish quality.*

No.	Description	Unused	Used
10	1d. bright vermilion	£6000	£1600
11	1d. dull vermilion	£6000	£1600
12	1d. red	£6000	£1500
13	2d. deep blue	£5500	£1600
14	2d. blue	£3750	£1600
	a. "PENOE" for "PENCE" (*shades*) *from*	£7500	£3000
15	2d. light blue	£3750	£1600

D. *Worn impressions. Much of design worn away but some diagonal lines distinct. Paper yellowish, grey or bluish, of poorish quality.*

No.	Description	Unused	Used
16	1d. red/*yellowish or grey*	£1000	£250
17	1d. red-brn./*yellowish or grey*	£1000	£250
18	1d. red/*bluish*	£650	£225
19	1d. red-brown/*bluish*	£600	£225
20	2d. blue (*shades*)/*yellowish or grey*	£1000	£450
	a. "PENOE" for "PENCE" *from*	—	£700
21	2d. grey-blue/*yellowish or grey*	£1200	£450
22	2d. blue (*shades*) *bluish*	£1000	£400
	a. Doubly printed		

E. *Latest impressions. Almost none of design showing except part of Queen's head and frame. Paper yellowish, grey or bluish, of poorish quality.*

23 1d. red £550 £200
24 1d. red-brown £600 £200
25 2d. grey-blue/*bluish* £600 £250
a. "PENOE" for "PENCE" .. £1000 £550

The stamp lettered "PENOE" is No. 7 on the sheet.

3

(Engraved on copper by J. Lapirot.)

1859 (MARCH). 12 *varieties on the sheet. Imperf. Early impressions.*

26 **3** 2d. deep blue £2750 £1400
27 ,, 2d. blue £2000 £1300

1859 (AUG.). *Intermediate prints. Lines of background, etc., partly worn away.*

28 **3** 2d. blue £1500 £500

1859 (OCT.). *Impressions from worn plate; bluish paper.*

29 **3** 2d. blue £600 £275

4 5

(The plate of 1848 re-engraved by R. Sherwin.)

1859 (OCT.). *Bluish paper. Imperf.*

30 **4** 2d. deep blue £17000 £2500

Autotype illustrations in deep blue, on stout white wove paper faced with blue, were taken in 1877 from a sheet reprinted in black from the original plate.

(Lithographed in the colony by L. A. Dardenne.)

1859 (DEC.). *White laid paper. Imperf.*

31 **5** 1d. deep red £1500 £650
31*a* ,, 1d. red £1200 £500
32 ,, 1d. dull vermilion .. £850 £450
33 ,, 2d. slate-blue £1500 £525
33*a* ,, 2d. blue £700 £300
34 ,, 2d. pale blue £675 £250

Retouched varieties

34*a* **5** 2d. blue, heavy retouch on neck .. .. .. — £700
34*b* ,, 2d. blue, slight retouches (several varieties) .. — £400

6

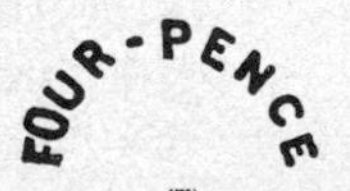

(7)

(Recess. Perkins Bacon & Co.)

1854 (8 APRIL). *Surch. with T* **7**. *Imperf.*

35 **6** 4d. green £350 £200

1858–62. *No value expressed. Imperf.*

36 **6** (4d.) green £200 £125
37 ,, (6d.) vermilion .. .. 10·00 15·00
38 ,, (9d.) dull magenta £200 £125

Prepared for use, but not issued.

39 **6** (No value), red-brown (1859) 2·00
40 ,, (No value), blue (1858) .. 1·75

Remainders of these were overprinted "L.P.E. 1890" in *red*, perforated at the London Philatelic Exhibition and sold as souvenirs.

No. 38 *reissued as* 1d.; *stamps obliterated* "B 53" *were so used.*

41 **6** (1d.) dull magenta (11.62) .. — 80·00

8

(Recess. Perkins Bacon & Co.)

1859. *Imperf.*

42 **8** 6d. blue .. .. .. £200 20·00
43 ,, 1s. vermilion .. .. £800 28·00

1861. *Colours corrected. Imperf.*

44 **8** 6d. dull purple-slate .. 12·00 12·00
45 ,, 1s. yellow-green .. .. £100 40·00

1862. *Intermediate perf.* 14 *to* 16.

46 **8** 6d. slate .. .. .. 10·00 10·00
a. Imperf. between (pair) .. £350
47 ,, 1s. deep green £550 £140

9 10

(Typo. D.L.R.)

1860–3. *No wmk. P* 14.

48 **9** 1d. purple-brown .. .. 20·00 6·00
49 ,, 2d. blue .. .. .. 25·00 9·00
50 ,, 4d. rose .. .. .. 25·00 6·00
51 ,, 6d. green (1862) .. .. 90·00 25·00
52 ,, 6d. slate (1863) .. .. 28·00 18·00
53 ,, 9d. dull purple (Optd. S. £28) 20·00 12·00
54 ,, 1s. buff (1862) .. .. 40·00 16·00
55 ,, 1s. green (1863) .. .. 90·00 42·00

1863–72. *Wmk. Crown CC. P* 14.

56 **9** 1d. purple-brown (1870) .. 6·00 2·50
57 ,, 1d. brown .. .. .. 8·00 2·75
58 ,, 1d. bistre .. .. .. 10·00 2·75
59 ,, 2d. pale blue .. .. 10·00 2·50
60 ,, 2d. bright blue .. .. 9·00 2·50
61 ,, 3d. deep red .. .. 15·00 8·00
61*a* ,, 3d. dull red .. .. 10·00 4·00
62 ,, 4d. rose .. .. .. 10·00 2·50
63 ,, 6d. dull violet (1864) .. 13·00 8·00
64 ,, 6d. yellow-green (1865) .. 15·00 6·00
65 ,, 6d. blue-green .. .. 13·00 2·50
66 ,, 9d. yellow-green (1872) .. 27·00 17·00
67 **10** 10d. maroon (1872) .. .. 18·00 6·00
68 **9** 1s. yellow .. .. .. 22·00 5·50
69 ,, 1s. orange .. .. .. 22·00 5·50
70 ,, 1s. blue (1870) .. .. 25·00 7·00
71 ,, 5s. rosy mauve .. .. 25·00 10·00
72 ,, 5s. bright mauve (1865) .. 42·00 9·00

Variety. Imperf. (pair).

73 **9** 2d. blue £500 £500

½ d — HALF PENNY (11)

HALF PENNY (12)

Prepared for use, but not issued. No. 53 *surch. with T***11**.

74 **9** ½d. on 9d. dull purple (R.) (Optd. S. £22) £150
a. Error. "PRNNY" .. ..
75 ,, ½d. on 9d. dull purple (Bk.) £200

1876. *Nos.* 53 *and* 67 *surch. with T* **12**.

76 **9** ½d. on 9d. dull purple .. 2·25 2·75
a. Surch inverted .. .. 90·00
b. Surch. double .. ..
77 **10** ½d. on 10d. maroon .. 1·50 3·50

HALF PENNY (13)

One Penny (14)

One Shilling (15)

1877. *T* **9** *and* **10**, *wmk. Crown CC, surch. with T* **13/5**. *P* 14.

79 ½d. on 10d. rose (Apr.) .. 4·00 5·00
80 1d. on 4d. rose-carmine (6 Dec.) 5·00 5·00
81 1s. on 5s. rosy mauve (6 Dec.) 38·00 22·00
82 1s. on 5s. bright mauve (6 Dec.) 50·00 32·00

2 CENTS (16)

2 RS. 50 C. (17)

1878 (3 JAN.). *T* **10** *(with lower label blank) surch. with T* **16**. *Wmk. Crown CC. P* 14.

83 2 c. dull rose .. .. .. 2·00 2·25

1878. *Surch. as T* **16** *or* **17**. *Wmk. Crown CC. P* 14.

84 **9** 4 c. on 1d. bistre .. .. 3·50 2·25
85 ,, 8 c. on 2d. blue .. .. 4·00 1·00
86 ,, 13 c. on 3d. orange-red .. 2·50 3·00
87 ,, 17 c. on 4d. rose .. .. 12·00 1·40
88 ,, 25 c. on 6d. slate-blue .. 14·00 2·75
89 ,, 38 c. on 9d. pale violet .. 7·00 4·00
90 ,, 50 c. on 1s. green .. .. 7·00 2·00
91 ,, 2 r. 50 c. on 5s. brt. mauve 7·00 3·75
84/91 .. .. *Set of* 8 50·00 18·00

18

19

20

21

22

23

24

25

26

(Typo. D.L.R.)

1879–80. *Wmk. Crown CC. P* 14.
92 **18** 2 c. Venetian red .. 7·00 5·00
93 **19** 4 c. orange (1879) .. 7·00 2·00
94 **20** 8 c. blue .. .. .. 5·00 1·10
95 **21** 13 c. slate .. .. .. 28·00 14·00
96 **22** 17 c. rose .. .. .. 7·00 2·50
97 **23** 25 c. olive-yellow (1879) .. 18·00 4·50
98 **24** 38 c. bright purple .. 30·00 25·00
99 **25** 50 c. green .. .. .. 1·40 1·10
100 **26** 2 r. 50 c., brown-purple .. 8·50 7·00
92/100 .. .. *Set of* 9 £100 55·00

1882–83. *Wmk. Crown CA. P* 14.
101 **18** 2 c. Venetian red .. 2·00 2·00
102 **19** 4 c. orange .. .. 7·00 1·75
103 **23** 25 c. olive-yellow (1883) .. 1·75 1·00

16 CENTS (27)

SIXTEEN CENTS (28)

(*a*) Surcharge 14 mm. long and $3\frac{1}{2}$ high.
(*b*) Surcharge 15 mm. long and $3\frac{1}{2}$ high.
(*c*) Surcharge 15 mm. long and $2\frac{1}{2}$ high.

1883 (26 Feb.). *No.* 96 *surch. as T* **27**.
104 **22** 16 c. on 17 c. rose (*a*) .. 7·00 6·50
a. Surch. double .. ..
105 „ 16 c. on 17 c. rose (*b*) .. 8·50 6·50
106 „ 16 c. on 17 c. rose (*c*) .. 16·00 13·00

1883 (14 July). *Wmk. Crown CA. Surch. with T* **28**. *P* 14.
107 **22** 16 c. on 17 c. rose .. 4·00 1·75

2 CENTS (29)

30

2 CENTS (31)

1885 (11 May). *No.* 98 *surch. with T* **29**.
108 **24** 2 c. on 38 c. bright purple 13·00 11·00
a. Without bar .. .. — 20·00
b. Surch. inverted .. .. 80·00 80·00
c. Surch. double £110

(Typo. D.L.R.)

1885–91. *Wmk. Crown CA. P* 14.
110 **18** 2 c. green 40 30
111 **19** 4 c. carmine 25 15
112 **20** 8 c. blue (1891) 65 80
113 **30** 16 c. chestnut 65 40
114 **25** 50 c. orange (1887) .. 6·50 4·00
110/114 .. .. *Set of* 5 8·50 5·00
110/114 *excl.* 112 optd. "Specimen" *Set of* 4 28·00

1887 (6 July). *No.* 95 *surch. with T* **31**.
115 **21** 2 c. on 13 c. slate (R.) .. 6·00 6·00
a. Surch. inverted .. 16·00 16·00
b. Surch. double .. — 75·00
c. Surch. double, one on back of stamp £100

TWO CENTS (32)

TWO CENTS (33)

1891 (Sept.). *Various stamps surcharged.*
117 **32** 2 c. on 4 c. (No. 111) 40 30
a. Surch. inverted .. 25·00
b. Surch. double .. .. 30·00 28·00
c. Surch. double, one inverted 30·00 30·00
118 „ 2 c. on 17 c. (No. 96) .. 6·50 8·50
a. Surch. inverted .. 45·00
b. Surch. double .. .. 75·00 75·00
119 **33** 2 c. on 38 c. (No. 89) .. 1·10 2·25
a. Surch. inverted .. 42·00
b. Surch. double .. .. 75·00 75·00
c. Surch. double, one inverted 18·00
120 **32** 2 c. on 38 c. (No. 98) .. 2·25 2·75
a. Surch. inverted .. 75·00
b. Surch. double .. 22·00
c. Surch. double, one inverted 22·00

Minor varieties are also known with portions of the surcharge missing, due to defective printing.

ONE CENT (34)

ONE CENT (35)

1893 (1 Jan.). *Surch. with T* **34/5**. *Wmk. Crown CA. P* 14.
123 **18** 1 c. on 2 c. pale violet (Optd. S. £12) .. 15 40
124 **30** 1 c. on 16 c. chestnut .. 25 60

1893–4. *Wmk. Crown CA. P* 14.
125 **18** 1 c. pale violet 15 40
126 **30** 15 c. chestnut 30 40
127 „ 15 c. blue .. .. .. 1·25 40
125/127 Optd. "Specimen" *Set of* 3 22·00

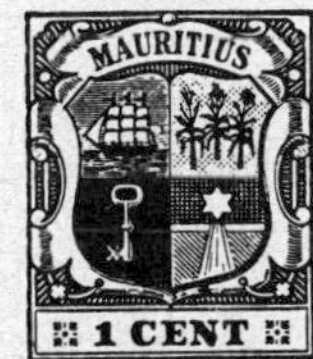

36

(Typo. D.L.R.)

1895–9. *Wmk. Crown CA. P* 14.
128 **36** 1 c. dull pur. & ultram. 15 20
129 „ 2 c. dull pur. & orange 65 20
130 „ 3 c. dull pur. & dp. pur. 50 50
131 „ 4 c. dull pur. & emerald 55 35
131*a* „ 6 c. green and rose-red 1·00 55
132 „ 18 c. green & ultramarine 2·25 2·25
128/132 .. .. *Set of* 6 4·50 3·50
128/132 Optd. "Specimen" *Set of* 6 42·00

37

(Typo. D.L.R.)

1898 (23 May). *Jubilee issue. Wmk. CA over Crown, sideways. P* 14.
133 **37** 36 c. orange and ultramarine (Optd. S. £25) 6·00 6·00

6 CENTS (38)

15 CENTS (39)

1899. *Nos.* 132/3 *surcharged.*
134 **38** 6 c. on 18 c. grn. & ult. (R.) 15 15
a. Surch. inverted .. 45·00 40·00
135 **39** 15 c. on 36 c. or. & ult. (B.) 1·60 1·10
a. Bar of surch. omitted .. 42·00

The space between "6" and "cents" varies from $2\frac{1}{2}$ to 4 mm.

40. Admiral Mahé de Labourdonnais, Governor of Mauritius, 1735–46.

(Recess. D.L.R.)

1899 (Dec.). *Bicentenary of Birth of Labourdonnais. Wmk. Crown CC. P* 14.
136 **40** 15 c. ultram. (Optd. S. £28) 4·50 1·60

4 Cents (41)

12 CENTS (42)

1900. *No.* 113 *surch. with T* **41**.
137 **30** 4 c. on 16 c. chestnut .. 40 40

1900. *Wmk. Crown CA. P* 14.
138 **36** 1 c. grey and black .. 45 25
139 „ 2 c. dull and bright purple 12 12
140 „ 4 c. pur. & carm./*yellow* 35 35
141 „ 15 c. green and orange .. 1·60 2·50
138/141 Optd. "Specimen" *Set of* 4 25·00

1902. *No.* 132 *surch. with T* **42**.
142 **36** 12 c. on 18 c. grn. & ultram. 1·10 3·00

The bar cancelling the original value seems in some cases to be one thick bar and in others two thin ones.

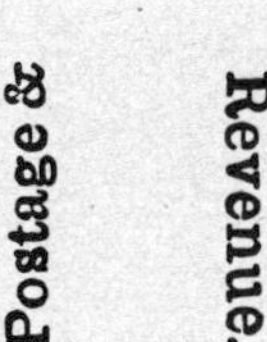

(43)

44

1902. *Various stamps optd. with T* **43**.
143 4 c. pur. & car./*yell.* (No. 140) 25 15
144 6 c. green & red (No. 131a) 55 90
145 15 c. green & orange (No. 141) 35 45
146 25 c. olive-yellow (No. 103) .. 65 1·25
147 50 c. green (No. 99) .. .. 1·60 80
148 2 r. 50 c. brn.-pur. (No. 100) 12·00 14·00
143/148 .. .. *Set of* 6 14·00 16·00

1902. *No.* 133 *surch. as T* **42**, *but with longer bar.*
149 **37** 12 c. on 36 c. orge. & ultram. 1·00 1·25
a. Surch. inverted .. 85·00 75·00

The note below No. 142 also applies to No. 149.

(Typo. D.L.R.)

1902–5. *T* **36** *and* **44** (*rupee values*). *Wmk. Crown CC* (1 *r.*) *or Crown CA* (*others*), *sideways on* 2 *r.* 50 *and* 5 *r. P* 14.
150 3 c. green and carmine/*yellow* 40 40
151 4 c. grey-green and violet .. 45 75

152 4 c. black and carmine/*blue* 60 8
153 5 c. dull & bright purple/*buff* 1·60 7·00
154 5 c. dull purple & black/*buff* 65 75
155 6 c. purple and carmine/*red* .. 25 15
156 8 c. green and black/*buff* .. 65 1·60
157 12 c. grey-black and carmine 75 85
158 15 c. black and blue/*blue* ('05) 3·75 2·00
159 25 c. green & carmine/*grn.* OC 1·60 3·50
160 50 c. dull grn. & deep grn./*yell.* 2·25 4·50
161 1 r. grey-black and carmine 9·00 7·50
162 2 r. 50, green & black/*blue* 9·00 10·00
163 5 r. purple and carmine/*red* 24·00 26·00
150/163 .. .. *Set of* 14 50·00 60·00
150/163 Optd. "Specimen" Set of 14 75·00

1904–7. *T* **36** *and* **44** (1 *r.*). *Wmk. Mult. Crown CA. P* 14.
164 1 c. grey and black, C (1907) 85 70
165 2 c. dull & brt. pur., OC ('05) 65 12
166 3 c. green & carmine/*yell.*, C 3·00 1·40
167 4 c. black & carm./*blue*, OC 65 8
168 6 c. purple & carm./*red*, OC 25 8
171 15 c. black & blue/*blue*, C ('07) 1·60 65
174 50 c. grn. & dp. grn./*yellow*, C 75 1·60
175 1 r. grey-blk. & car., C ('07) 7·50 7·00
164/175 .. .. *Set of* 8 14·00 10·00

46

47

(Typo. D.L.R.)

1910. *Wmk. Mult. Crown CA. P* 14.
181 **46** 1 c. black, O 8 8
182 „ 2 c. brown, O 20 12
183 „ 3 c. green, O 20 30
184 „ 4 c. pale yellow-green and carmine, O 35 8
185 **47** 5 c. grey and carmine, O 40 80
186 **46** 6 c. carmine-red, O .. 25 15
a. pale red .. .. 1·10 15
187 „ 8 c. orange, O .. .. 40 1·00
188 **47** 12 c. greyish slate, O .. 25 50
189 **46** 15 c. blue, O 40 12
190 **47** 25 c. black & red/*yellow*, C 2·25 3·50
191 „ 50 c. dull pur. & black, C 1·75 3·25
192 „ 1 r. black/*green*, C .. 3·00 3·25
193 „ 2 r. 50, blk. & red/*blue*, C 8·50 10·00
194 „ 5 r. green & red/*yellow*, C 18·00 20·00
195 „ 10 r. green & red/*green*, C 55·00 60·00
181/195 .. .. *Set of* 15 80·00 95·00
181/195 Optd. "Specimen" *Set of* 15 70·00

In Nos. 188, 190 and 195, the value labels are as in T **49**.

48

49

(Typo. D.L.R.)

1913–23. *T* **48** *and* **49** (12 *c.*, 25 *c.*, *and* 10 *r.*). *Wmk. Mult. Crown CA. P* 14.
196 5 c. grey & carm., O (1915) 75 75
197 5 c. slate-grey & carmine, O 2·00 2·00
198 12 c. greyish slate, O (1915) .. 25 50
199 25 c. black & red/*yell.*, C ('13) 55 85
a. White back (1916) .. .. 1·60 1·90
b. On orange-buff .. .. 9·00 9·00
c. On pale yellow (Die I) .. 7·50 7·00
d. On pale yellow (Die II)(Opt.S.£11) 75 1·75
200 50 c. dull pur. & blk., C (Die I) 7·00 9·00
201 1 r. black/*blue-green*, C (*olive back*) (1917) .. .. 1·00 1·90
a. On emerald surface .. 2·50 5·50
b. On emer. back (Die II)(Opt.S.£13) 1·60 2·50
202 2 r. 50, black & red/*blue*, C 4·00 6·50
203 5 r. green and red/*orge.-buff*, C 16·00 18·00
a. On pale yellow (Die I) .. 16·00 18·00
b. On pale yellow (Die II) .. 26·00 27·00
204 10 r. green and red/*green*, C 16·00 20·00
a. On blue-green, olive back .. £225
b. On emerald surface .. 16·00 20·00
c. On emerald back (Die I) .. 16·00 20·00
d. On emerald back (Die II) (Opt. S £11) .. .. 15·00 20·00
196/204 .. .. *Set of* 8 45·00 50·00
196/204 Optd. "Specimen" (Die I) *Set of* 8 50·00

A

B

Two types of duty plate in the 12 c. In Type B the letters of "MAURITIUS" are larger; the extremities of the downstroke and the tail of the "2" are pointed, instead of square, and the "c" is larger.

1921–34. *Wmk. Mult. Script CA. P* 14. (*a*) *T* **46.**
205 1 c. black, O 12 25
206 2 c. brown, O 15 8
207 4 c. pale olive-grn. & car., O 80 1·00
208 4 c. green, O 30 8
209 6 c. carmine, O .. .. .. 2·00 2·50
210 6 c. bright mauve, O 25 25
210*a* 8 c. orange, O .. .. .. 1·10 1·40
211 10 c. grey, O .. .. .. 1·50 2·00
212 12 c. carmine-red, O 30 65
213 15 c. blue, O .. .. .. 3·75 70
214 20 c. blue, O .. .. .. 1·40 80
205/214 .. .. *Set of* 11 10·00 8·50
205/214 Optd. "Specimen" *Set of* 11 55·00

(*b*) *T* **48** *and* **49.**
215 5 c. grey & carm., O (Die II) 8 8
215*a* 5 c. grey & carm., O (Die I) ('32) 55 12
216 12 c. grey, O (1921) (A) 45 95
216*a* 12 c. pale grey, O ('28) (A) (Optd. S. £9) 15 8
216*b* 12 c. grey, O ('34) (B) (Optd. S. £9) 15 20
217 12 c. carmine-red, O ('22) .. 25 1·10
218 25 c. black and red/*pale yellow*, C (Die II) .. 15 25
218*a* 25 c. black and red/*pale yellow*, C (Die I) ('32) .. 55 2·00
219 50 c. dull purple & black, C (Die II) .. .. 2·00 1·40
220 1 r. blk./*emer.*, C (Die II) .. 55 55
220*a* 1 r. blk./*emer.*, C (Die I)('32) 4·00 4·50
221 2 r. 50 c. blk. & red/*blue*, C 4·00 1·00
222 5 r. green & red/*yellow*, C .. 12·00 16·00
223 10 r. grn. & red/*emer.*, C ('28) 20·00 22·00
215/223 .. .. *Set of* 9 35·00 38·00
215/23 Optd. "Specimen" *Set of* 9 45·00

1924. *T* **44**, *but Arms similar to T* **46.** *Wmk. Mult. Script CA. P* 14.
224 50 r. dull purple & green, C £275 £300
224 Optd. "Specimen" .. .. 55·00

(50)

51

1925. *T* **46** *surch. as T* **50.**
225 3 c. on 4 c. green 70 70
226 10 c. on 12 c. carmine-red .. 25 15
227 15 c. on 20 c. blue 30 35
225/7 Optd. "Specimen" *Set of* 3 35·00

1926. *Wmk. Mult. Script CA. P* 14.
228 **46** 2 c. purple/*yellow*, O .. 10 20
229 „ 3 c. green, O 30 45
230 „ 4 c. brown, O 15 45
231 „ 10 c. carmine-red, O .. 25 45
232 „ 12 c. grey, O 45 75
233 „ 15 c. cobalt, O 40 25
234 „ 20 c. purple, O .. .. 1·60 1·90
228/234 .. .. *Set of* 7 2·75 4·00
228/234 Optd. "Specimen" *Set of* 7 42·00

1926–34. *As T* **49** (*King*). *Wmk. Mult. Script CA. P* 14.
235 1 c. black, O 8 20
236 2 c. brown, O 8 8
237 3 c. green, O 20 35
238 4 c. sage-green and carmine, O (Die II) ('27) .. 35 30
238*a* 4 c. sage-green and carmine, O (Die I) ('32) .. .. 1·00 2·25
238*b* 4 c. green, O (Die I) ('33) .. 25 70
239 6 c. sepia, O ('28) 15 70
240 8 c. orange, O 25 70
241 10 c. carmine-red, O (Die II) 20 15
241*a* 10 c. car.-red, O (Die I) ('32) 12 55
242 15 c. Prussian blue, O ('28) 55 55
243 20 c. purple, O ('27) 30 90
244 20 c. Prussian blue, O (Die I) ('33) .. .. .. 1·40 1·60
244*a* 20 c. Prussian blue, O (Die II) ('34) .. .. .. 1·60 1·00
235/244 .. .. *Set of* 11 3·50 5·00
235/244 (*excl.* 238*a*, 241*a*) Optd./Perf. "Specimen" *Set of* 11 48·00

1935 (6 May). *Silver Jubilee. As Nos.* 91/4 *of Antigua.*
245 5 c. ultramarine and grey .. 8 8
246 12 c. green and indigo .. 40 25
247 20 c. brown and deep blue .. 1·10 90
248 1 r. slate and purple .. 13·00 13·00
245/8 Perf. "Specimen" *Set of* 4 17·00

1937 (12 May). *Coronation. As Nos.* 13/5 *of Aden.*
249 5 c. violet 8 8
250 12 c. scarlet 8 8
251 20 c. bright blue 8 8
249/251 Perf. "Specimen" *Set of* 3 11·00

(Typo. De La Rue.)

1938–49. *T* **51** *and similar types. Wmk. Mult. Script CA. P* 14.
252 2 c. olive-grey (9.3.38) .. 8 8
a. Perf. 15×14 (1942) 12 15
253 3 c. reddish purple and scarlet (27.10.38) 8 8
a. Reddish lilac and red (4.43) .. 8 8
254 4 c. dull green (26.2.38) .. 8 10
a. Deep dull green (4.43) .. 8 10
255 5 c. slate-lilac (23.2.38) .. 12 8
a. Pale lilac (*shades*) (4.43) .. 8 8
b. Perf. 15×14 (1942) .. .. 1·75 45
256 10 c. rose-red (9.3.38) .. 10 12
a. Deep reddish rose (*shades*) (4.43) 8 8
b. Perf. 15×14. *Pale reddish rose* (1942) .. .. .. 1·60 1·25
257 12 c. salmon (*shades*) (26.2.38) 8 8
a. Perf. 15×14 (1942) .. .. 4·00 2·25
258 20 c. blue (26.2.38) 8 8
259 25 c. brown-purple, CO (2.3.38) 8 8
260 1 r. grey-brown, CO (2.3.38) 30 30
a. Drab, C (4.49) 30 30
261 2 r. 50, pale violet, CO (2.3.38) .. .. .. 1·00 1·25
a. Slate-violet, C (4.48) .. 6·00 6·00
262 5 r. olive-green, CO (2.3.38) 3·25 3·00
a. Sage-green, O (4.43) .. .. 4·00 3·50
263 10 r. reddish purple (*shades*), CO (2.3.38) .. .. 4·50 5·50
252/263 .. .. *Set of* 12 9·00 9·50
252/263 Perf. "Specimen" *Set of* 12 27·00

The stamps perf. 15×14 were printed by Bradbury, Wilkinson from De La Rue plates and issued only in the colony in 1942. De La Rue printings of the 2 c. to 20 c. in 1943–45 were on thin, whiter paper. 1943–45 printings of the 25 c. to 10 r. were on unsurfaced paper.

1946 (20 Nov.). *Victory. As Nos.* 28/9 *of Aden.*
264 5 c. lilac 8 8
265 20 c. blue 8 8
264/5 Perf. "Specimen" *Set of* 2 14·00

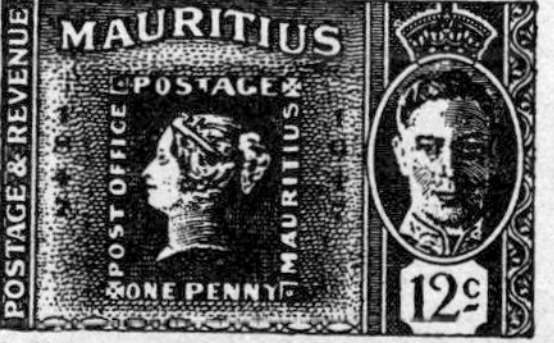

52. 1d. "Post Office" Mauritius and King George VI.

(Recess. Bradbury, Wilkinson.)

1948 (22 MAR.). *Centenary of First British Colonial Postage Stamp. P* 11½ × 11.
266 **52** 5 c. orange & magenta .. 8 8
267 ,, 12 c. orange and green .. 8 8
268 – 20 c. blue and light blue .. 8 8
269 – 1 r. blue and red-brown .. 20 20
266/9 Perf. "Specimen" *Set of* 4 40·00
Design:—20 c., 1 r. As T **52** but showing 2d. "Post Office" Mauritius.

1948 (25 OCT.). *Royal Silver Wedding. As Nos.* 30/1 *of Aden.*
270 5 c. violet 8 8
271 10 r. magenta .. .. 4·50 6·50

1949 (10 OCT.). *75th Anniv. of U.P.U. As Nos.* 114/7 *of Antigua.*
272 12 c. carmine.. .. .. 20 35
273 20 c. deep blue 20 35
274 35 c. purple 30 45
275 1 r. sepia 40 50

53. Sugar Factory.

54. Grand Port.

55. Aloe Plant.

56. Tamarind Falls.

57. Rempart Mountain.

58. Transporting Cane.

59. Dodo and Map.

60. Legend of Paul and Virginie. (*inscr.* "VIRGINIA").

61. Labourdonnais Statue.

62. Government House.

63. Pieter Both Mountain.

64. Mauritius Deer.

65. Port Louis.

66. Beach Scene.

67. Arms of Mauritius.

(Photo. Harrison.)

1950 (1 JULY). *Wmk. Mult. Script CA. Chalk-surfaced paper. P* 13½ × 14½ (*horiz.*), 14½ × 13½ (*vert.*).
276 **53** 1 c. bright purple .. 12 15
277 **54** 2 c. rose-carmine.. .. 15 8
278 **55** 3 c. yellow-green.. .. 25 25
279 **56** 4 c. green 15 8
280 **57** 5 c. blue 12 8
281 **58** 10 c. scarlet 25 25
282 **59** 12 c. olive-green 15 20
283 **60** 20 c. ultramarine 15 15
284 **61** 25 c. brown purple .. 20 25
285 **62** 35 c. violet 12 20
286 **63** 50 c. emerald-green .. 20 25
287 **64** 1 r. sepia 95 65
288 **65** 2 r. 50, orange .. .. 1·00 1·60
289 **66** 5 r. red-brown .. .. 1·60 3·25
290 **67** 10 r. dull blue .. .. 4·50 4·50
276/290 .. .. *Set of* 15 9·00 11·00

1953 (2 JUNE). *Coronation. As No.* 47 *of Aden.*
291 10 c. black and emerald .. 12 10

68. Tamarind Falls.

69. Historical Museum, Mahebourg.

(Photo. Harrison & Sons, Ltd.)

1953 (3 NOV.)–**54.** *As T* **53/67**, *but with portrait of Queen Elizabeth II in place of King George VI, as in T* **68/9**. *Wmk. Mult. Script CA. Chalk-surfaced paper. P* 13½ × 14½ (*horiz.*) *or* 14½ × 13½ (*vert.*).
293 **54** 2 c. bright carmine (1.6.54) 5 5
294 **55** 3 c. yellow-green. (1.6.54) 5 5
295 **53** 4 c. bright purple .. 5 5
296 **57** 5 c. Prussian blue (1.6.54) 8 8
297 **68** 10 c. bluish green (*shades*) 12 10
298 **69** 15 c. scarlet 12 10
299 **61** 20 c. brown-purple .. 12 10
300 **60** 25 c. bright blue (*shades*).. 15 10
301 **62** 35 c. reddish violet (1.6.54) 20 12
302 **63** 50 c. bright green 20 15

302a 59 60 c. deep green (*shades*) (2.8.54) 35 30
303 **64** 1 r. sepia (*shades*) .. 30 25
304 **65** 2 r. 50, orange (1.6.54) .. 1·10 1·10
305 **66** 5 r. red-brown (*shades*) (1.6.54) .. .. 2·50 2·25
306 **67** 10 r. dp. grey-blue (1.6.54) 3·00 2·50
293/306 .. .. *Set of* 15 7·00 6·00

70. Queen Elizabeth II and King George III (after Lawrence).

(Litho. Enschedé.)

1961 (11 Jan.). *150th Anniv. of British Post Office in Mauritius.* *W* w.**12**. *P* $13\frac{1}{2}\times14$.
307 **70** 10 c. black and brown-red 12 12
308 ,, 20 c. ultram. and light blue 20 20
309 ,, 35 c. black and yellow .. 30 30
310 ,, 1 r. deep maroon & green 65 65

1963 (4 June). *Freedom from Hunger. As No. 76 of Aden.*
311 60 c. reddish violet 35 35

1963 (2 Sept.). *Red Cross Centenary. As Nos. 147/8 of Antigua.*
312 10 c. red and black 10 10
313 60 c. red and blue 40 40

1963 (12 Nov.)–**64.** *As Nos. 297, 302a and 304 but wmk.* w. **12**.
314 **68** 10 c. bluish green (*shades*) ('64) 15 12
315 **59** 60 c. bronze-green (28.5.64) 35 40
316 **65** 2 r. 50, orange .. .. 1·25 1·40

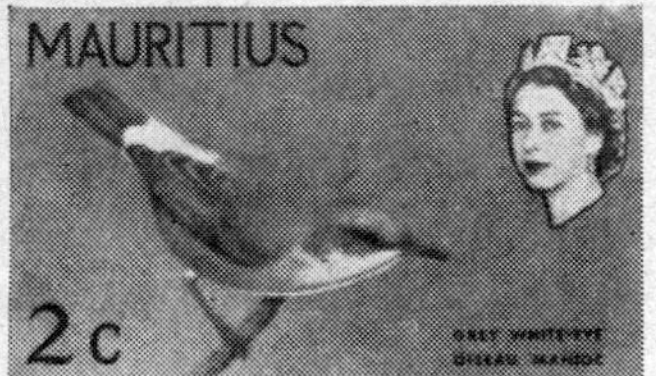

71. Grey White-eye.

72. Rodrigues Fody.
73. Olive White-eye.
74. Paradise Flycatcher.
75. Mauritius Fody.
76. Parakeet.
77. Cuckoo-shrike.
78. Kestrel.
79. Pink Pigeon.
80. Bulbul.
81. Dutch Pigeon (extinct).
82. Mauritius Dodo (extinct).
83. Rodrigues Solitaire (extinct).
84. Red Rail (extinct).
85. Broad-billed Parrot (extinct).

(Des. D. M. Reid-Henry. Photo. Harrison.)

1965 (16 Mar.). *W* w.**12** (*upright*). *Multi-coloured; background colours given.* *P* $14\frac{1}{2}\times14$.
317 **71** 2 c. lemon 5 5
318 **72** 3 c. brown 5 5
319 **73** 4 c. light reddish purple 5 5
a. Mauve-pink omitted* .. 25·00
320 **74** 5 c. grey-brown 5 5
321 **75** 10 c. light grey-green .. 5 8
322 **76** 15 c. pale grey .. 8 8
323 **77** 20 c. light yellow-bistre .. 10 10
324 **78** 25 c. bluish grey 10 10
325 **79** 35 c. greyish blue .. 15 10
326 **80** 50 c. light yellow-buff .. 15 12
327 **81** 60 c. light greenish yellow 20 20
328 **82** 1 r. light yellow-olive .. 40 40
329 **83** 2 r. 50, pale stone .. 95 95
330 **84** 5 r. pale grey-blue .. 1·75 1·75
331 **85** 10 r. pale bluish green .. 4·00 4·00
317/31 .. .. *Set of* 15 7·00 7·00

* In the 4 c. the background is printed in two colours and in No. 319a the background colour is similar to that of the 5 c.

The 50 c. and 2 r. 50 exist with PVA gum as well as gum arabic.

See also Nos. 340/1 and 370/5.

1965 (17 May). *I.T.U. Centenary. As Nos. 166/7 of Antigua.*
332 10 c. red-orange & apple-grn. 10 10
333 60 c. yellow and bluish violet 30 30

1965 (25 Oct.). *International Co-operation Year. As Nos. 168/9 of Antigua.*
334 10 c. reddish purple and turquoise-green 5 5
335 60 c. deep bluish green and lavender 30 30

1966 (24 Jan.). *Churchill Commemoration. As Nos. 170/3 of Antigua.*
336 2 c. new blue 5 5
337 10 c. deep green 5 5
338 60 c. brown 30 30
339 1 r. bluish violet 60 60

1966–67. *As Nos. 320, 325 but wmk.* w.**12** *sideways.*
340 **74** 5 c. grey-brown ('66) .. 10 10
341 **79** 35 c. greyish blue (27.6.67) 25 25

1966 (1 Dec.). *20th Anniv. of U.N.E.S.C.O. As Nos. 196/8 of Antigua.*
342 5 c. slate-violet, red, yellow and orange 5 5
343 10 c. orange-yellow, violet & deep olive 10 10
344 60 c. black, bright purple and orange 30 35

II. SELF GOVERNMENT.

86. Red-tailed Tropic Bird.

87. Rodrigues Brush-warbler.
88. Rodrigues Parakeet (extinct).
89. Mauritius Swiftlet.

(Des. D. M. Reid Henry. Photo. Harrison.)

1967 (1 Sept.). *Self Government.* *W* w.**12.** *P* $14\frac{1}{2}$.
345 **86** 2 c. multicoloured .. 5 5
346 **87** 10 c. multicoloured .. 10 10
347 **88** 60 c. multicoloured .. 25 25
348 **89** 1 r. multicoloured .. 35 40

SELF GOVERNMENT 1967
(90)

1967 (1 Dec.). *Self Government. T* **71/85** *optd. with T* **90.** *W* w.**12** (*sideways on* 5 c., 10 c. *and* 35 c.). *P* $14\times14\frac{1}{2}$.
349 **71** 2 c. multicoloured .. 5 5
350 **72** 3 c. multicoloured .. 5 5
351 **73** 4 c. multicoloured .. 5 5
352 **74** 5 c. multicoloured .. 5 5
353 **75** 10 c. multicoloured .. 8 5
354 **76** 15 c. multicoloured .. 8 8
355 **77** 20 c. multicoloured .. 12 10
356 **78** 25 c. multicoloured .. 12 12
357 **79** 35 c. multicoloured .. 15 12
358 **80** 50 c. multicoloured .. 20 20
359 **81** 60 c. multicoloured .. 25 25
360 **82** 1 r. multicoloured .. 40 35
361 **83** 2 r. 50, multicoloured .. 1·10 1·40
362 **84** 5 r. multicoloured .. 2·00 2·25
363 **85** 10 r. multicoloured .. 4·00 4·50
349/63 .. .. *Set of* 15 8·00 9·00

III. INDEPENDENCE.

91. Flag of Mauritius.

92. Arms and Dodo Emblem.

(Litho. De La Rue.)

1968 (12 Mar.). *Independence.* *P* $13\frac{1}{2}\times13$.
364 **91** 2 c. multicoloured .. 5 5
365 **92** 3 c. multicoloured .. 8 8
366 **91** 15 c. multicoloured .. 10 10
367 **92** 20 c. multicoloured .. 12 12
368 **91** 60 c. multicoloured .. 25 25
369 **92** 1 r. multicoloured .. 35 35
364/9 .. .. *Set of* 6 80 80

1968 (12 July). *As Nos.* 317/8, 322/3 *and* 327/8 *but background colours changed as below.*
370 **71** 2 c. olive-yellow 8 8
a. Black printing double ..
371 **72** 3 c. cobalt 8 8
372 **76** 15 c. cinnamon 10 10
373 **77** 20 c. buff 12 12
374 **81** 60 c. rose 30 30
375 **82** 1 r. reddish purple .. 55 55
370/5 .. .. *Set of* 6 1·10 1·10

93. Dominique rescues Paul and Virginie.

94. Paul and Virginie Crossing the River.

95. Visit of Labourdonnais to Madame de la Tour. (*Horiz.*)

96. Meeting of Paul and Virginie in Confidence. (*Vert.*)

97. Departure of Virginie for Europe. (*Horiz.*)

98. Bernardin de St. Pierre. (*Vert.*)

(Des. V. Whiteley, from prints. Litho. Format International.)

1968 (2 Dec.). *Bicentenary of Bernardin de St. Pierre's Visit to Mauritius. P* 13½.

376	**93**	2 c. multicoloured ..	5	5
377	**94**	15 c. multicoloured ..	8	8
378	**95**	50 c. multicoloured ..	15	15
379	**96**	60 c. multicoloured ..	25	25
380	**97**	1 r. multicoloured ..	45	45
381	**98**	2 r. 50, multicoloured ..	1·00	1·00
376/81		.. .. *Set of* 6	1·75	1·75

99. Batardé.

100. Red Reef Crab.

101. Episcopal Mitre.

102. Bourse.

103. Starfish.

104. Sea Urchin.

105. Fiddler Crab.

106. Spiny Shrimp.

107. Single Harp Shells, and Double Harp Shell.

108. Argonaute.

109. Nudibranch.

110. Violet and Orange Spider Shells.

111. Blue Marlin.

112. *Conus clytospira.*

113. Dolphin.

114. Spiny Lobster.

115. Sacré Chien Rouge.

116. Croissant Queue Jaune.

(Des. J. Vinson (3 c., 20 c., 1 r.), R. Granger Barrett (others). Photo. Harrison.)

1969 (12 Mar.)–**73.** *W* w.**12** (*sideways on* 2, 3, 4, 5, 10, 15, 60 *and* 75 *c.*). *Chalk-surfaced paper, P* 14.

382	**99**	2 c. multicoloured ..	5	5
383	**100**	3 c. multicoloured ..	5	5
384	**101**	4 c. multicoloured ..	5	5
385	**102**	5 c. multicoloured ..	10	10
386	**103**	10 c. scarlet, blk. & flesh	10	10
387	**104**	15 c. ochre, blk. & cobalt	5	5
388	**105**	20 c. multicoloured ..	10	10
		a. Glazed, ordinary paper (20.2.73)	10	10
389	**106**	25 c. red, black and pale apple-green ..	12	12
		a. Glazed ordinary paper (22.1.71)	10	10
390	**107**	30 c. multicoloured ..	10	10
		a. Glazed, ordinary paper (20.2.73)	10	10
391	**108**	35 c. multicoloured ..	12	12
		a. Glazed ordinary paper (3.2.71)	10	10
392	**109**	40 c. multicoloured ..	10	10
		a. Glazed, ordinary paper (20.2.73)	10	10
393	**110**	50 c. multicoloured ..	15	15
		a. Glazed ordinary paper (22.1.71)	12	12
394	**111**	60 c. blk., rose & ultram.	20	15
395	**112**	75 c. multicoloured ..	25	25
396	**113**	1 r. multicoloured ..	30	30
		a. Glazed ordinary paper (22.1.71)	25	25
397	**114**	2 r. 50, multicoloured ..	1·00	1·00
		a. Glazed, ordinary paper (20.2.73)	60	60
398	**115**	5 r. multicoloured ..	1·60	1·60
		a. Glazed ordinary paper (22.1.71)	1·10	1·10
399	**116**	10 r. multicoloured	3·00	3·00
382/99		.. .. *Set of* 18	6·50	6·50
388a/398a		.. .. *Set of* 9	2·25	2·25

See also Nos. 437/54.

117. Gandhi as Law Student.

118. Gandhi as Stretcher-bearer during Zulu Revolt.

119. Gandhi as Satyagrahi in South Africa.

120. Gandhi at No. 10 Downing Street, London.

121. Gandhi in Mauritius, 1901.

122. Gandhi, the "Apostle of Truth and Non-Violence".

(Des. J. Waddington Ltd. Litho. Format International.)

1969 (1 July). *Birth Centenary of Mahatma Gandhi. W* w.**12.** *P* 13½.

400	**117**	2 c. multicoloured ..	5	5
401	**118**	15 c. multicoloured ..	10	10
402	**119**	50 c. multicoloured ..	20	20
403	**120**	60 c. multicoloured ..	25	25
404	**121**	1 r. multicoloured ..	40	40
405	**122**	2 r. 50, mult. ..	85	85
MS406		153×153 mm. Nos. 400/5 ..	2·00	2·00
400/5		.. .. *Set of* 6	1·60	1·60

123. Three-roller Vertical Mill.

124. Frangourinier Cane-crusher (18th-cent.).

125. Beau Rivage Factory, 1867.

126. Mon Désert-Alma Factory, 1969.

127. Dr. Charles Telfair. (*Vert.*)

(Des. V. Whiteley. Photo. Enschedé.)

1969 (22 Dec.).* *150th Anniv. of Telfair's Improvements to the Sugar Industry. W* w.**12** (*sideways on 2 c. to 1 r.*). *P* 11½×11 (*2 r. 50*) *or* 11×11½ (*others.*)

407	**123**	2 c. multicoloured ..	5	5
408	**124**	15 c. multicoloured ..	8	8
409	**125**	60 c. multicoloured ..	20	20
410	**126**	1 r. multicoloured ..	25	25
411	**127**	2 r. 50, multicoloured ..	60	65
MS412		159×88 mm. Nos. 407/11† *W* w.**12** (*sideways*). *P* 11×11½*	1·25	1·25
407/411		.. .. *Set of* 5	1·10	1·10

* This was the local release date but the Crown Agents issued the stamps on 15th December.

† In the miniature sheet the 2 r. 50 is perf. 11 at the top and imperf. on the other three sides.

EXPO '70' OSAKA

(128)

1970 (7 Apr.). *World Fair, Osaka. Nos.* 394 *and* 396 *optd. with T* **128** *by Harrison & Sons.*

413	**111**	60 c. black, rose & ultram.	20	20
414	**113**	1 r. multicoloured ..	30	35

129. Morne Plage, Mountain and Lufthansa Airliner.

130. Airliner and Map. (*Vert.*)

(Des. H. Rose. Litho. G. Gehringer, Kaiserslautern, Germany.)

1970 (2 May). *Inauguration of Lufthansa Flight, Mauritius-Frankfurt. P* 14.

415	**129**	25 c. multicoloured ..	10	10
416	**130**	50 c. multicoloured ..	15	20

131. Lenin as a Student.

132. Lenin as Founder of U.S.S.R. (*Vert.*).

(Photo. State Ptg. Works, Moscow.)

1970 (15 May). *Birth Centenary of Lenin. P* 12×11½.

417	**131**	15 c. blackish grn. & silver	8	8
418	**132**	75 c. blackish brn. & gold	30	40

133. 2d. "Post Office" Mauritius and original Post Office.

134. G.P.O. Building (built 1870).

135. Mail Coach (*c.* 1870).

136. Port Louis Harbour (1970).

137. Arrival of Pierre A. de Suffren (1783).

(Des. and litho. De La Rue.)

1970 (15 Oct.). *Port Louis, Old and New. W* w.**12** *(sideways). P* 14.

No.	Type	Description		
419	**133**	5 c. multicoloured ..	5	5
420	**134**	15 c. multicoloured ..	8	8
421	**135**	50 c. multicoloured ..	15	15
422	**136**	75 c. multicoloured ..	25	25
423	**137**	2 r. 50, multicoloured ..	70	80
MS424		165 × 95 mm. Nos. 419/23	1·25	1·40
419/23		.. .. *Set of* 5	1·10	1·25

138. U.N. Emblem and Symbols.

(Des. Jennifer Toombs. Litho. Format.)

1970 (24 Oct.). *25th Anniv. of United Nations. W* w.**12** *(sideways). P* 14½.

No.	Type	Description		
425	**138**	10 c. multicoloured ..	5	5
426	„	60 c. multicoloured ..	20	25

139. Rainbow over Waterfall.

(Des. R. Granger-Barrett from local ideas (20 c.), R. Granger-Barrett from local ideas and adapted by N. Mossae (others). Litho. Format.)

1971 (12 Apr.). *Tourism. T* **139** *and similar horiz. designs. Multicoloured. W* w.**12** *(sideways). P* 14.

No.	Description		
427	10 c. Type **139**	5	5
428	15 c. Trois Mamelles Mountains	8	8
429	60 c. Beach scene	15	15
430	2 r. 50, Marine life	65	65

Nos. 427/30 are inscribed on the reverse with details of tourist attractions in Mauritius.

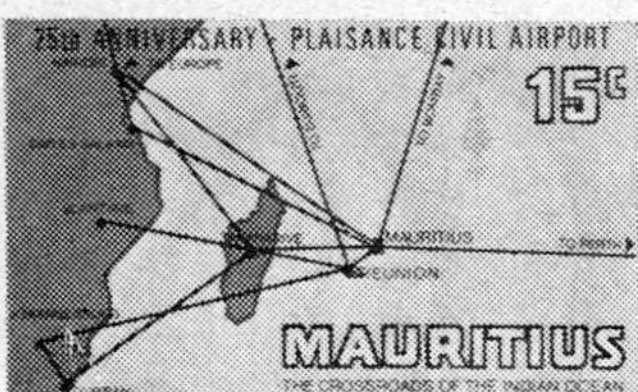

140. " Crossroads " of Indian Ocean.

(Des. R. Granger-Barrett (60 c.) or V. Whiteley (others). Litho. Harrison.)

1971 (23 Oct.). *25th Anniv. of Plaisance Airport. T* **140** *and similar horiz. designs. Multicoloured. W* w.**12** *(sideways on* 15 *c.). P* 14.

No.	Description		
431	15 c. Type **140**	5	5
432	60 c. " Boeing 707 " and Terminal Buildings ..	15	15
433	1 r. Air Hostesses on gangway	25	25
434	2 r. 50, The " Roland Garros " (plane), Choisy Airfield, 1937 ..	80	80

141. Princess Margaret Orthopaedic Centre.

(Des. and litho. Harrison.)

1971 (2 Nov.). *Third Commonwealth Medical Conference. T* **141** *and similar horiz. design. Multicoloured. W* w.**12**. *P* 14 × 13½.

No.	Description		
435	10 c. Type **141**	5	5
436	75 c. Operation Theatre in National Hospital ..	15	15

1972–74. *As Nos.* 382/99 *but W* w.**12** *upright* (2, 3, 4, 5, 10, 15, 60, 75 *c.*) *or sideways* (*others*).

A. *Glazed, ordinary paper.*
B. *Chalk-surfaced paper.*

No.	Type	Description	A.		B.	
437	**99**	2 c. mult.	5	5	5	5
438	**100**	3 c. mult.	5	5	5	5
439	**101**	4 c. mult.	†		5	5
440	**102**	5 c. mult.	5	5	5	5
441	**103**	10 c. scar., blk. & flesh	5	5	5	5
442	**104**	15 c. ochre, blk. & cobalt	5	5	5	5
443	**105**	20 c. mult.	†		5	5
444	**106**	25 c. red, blk. & apple-grn.	†		5	5
445	**107**	30 c. mult.	†		5	5
446	**108**	35 c. mult.	†		5	5
447	**109**	40 c. mult.	†		5	8
448	**110**	50 c. mult.	†		8	10
449	**111**	60 c. blk., rose & ultram.	10	12	8	10
450	**112**	75 c. mult.	12	12	10	12
451	**113**	1 r. mult.	†		15	20
452	**114**	2 r. 50, mult.	†		35	40
453	**115**	5 r. mult.	†		85	95
454	**116**	10 r. mult.	†		1·75	2·00
437/450A		*Set of* 7	35	40		
437/454B		*Set of* 18			3·50	4·00

Dates of issue:

Glazed paper—10.1.72, 5 c., 10 c.; 20.2.73, 2 c., 3 c., 15 c., 60 c., 75 c.

Chalk-surfaced paper—8.11.73, 10 c., 20 c., 30 c., 35 c., 40 c., 75 c., 1 r., 10 r.; 12.12.73, 25 c., 50 c., 2 r. 50, 5 r.; 25.2.74, 5 c., 15 c., 60 c.; 13.6.74, 2 c., 3 c., 4 c.

See also Nos. 478, etc.

142. Queen Elizabeth and Prince Philip.

(Des. and photo. Harrison.)

1972 (24 Mar.). *Royal Visit. T* **142** *and similar multicoloured design. W* w.**12**. *P* 14.

No.	Description		
455	15 c. Type **142**	10	10
456	2 r. 50, Queen Elizabeth (*vert.*)	80	80

143. Theatre Façade.

(Des. and litho. Harrison.)

1972 (26 June). *150th Anniversary of Port Louis Theatre T* **143** *and similar horiz. design. Multicoloured. W* w.**12**. *P* 14.

No.	Description		
457	10 c. Type **143**	5	5
458	1 r. Theatre Auditorium ..	25	25

144. Pirate Dhow.

(Des. and litho. Harrison.)

1972 (17 Nov.). *Pirates and Privateers. T* **144** *and similar multicoloured designs. W* w.**12** *(sideways on* 60 *c. and* 1 *r.). P* 14½ × 14 *(60 c., 1 r.) or* 14 × 14½ *(others).*

No.	Description		
459	15 c. Type **144**	5	5
460	60 c. Treasure chest (*vert.*) ..	15	15
461	1 r. Lememe and *L'Hirondelle* (*vert.*) ..	25	25
462	2 r. 50, Robert Surcouf ..	75	75

145. Mauritius University.

(Des. and litho. Harrison.)

1973 (10 Apr.). *Fifth Anniv. of Independence. T* **145** *and similar horiz. designs. Multicoloured. W* w.**12** *(sideways). P* 14.

No.	Description		
463	15 c. Type **145**	5	5
464	60 c. Tea Development ..	15	15
465	1 r. Bank of Mauritius ..	25	25

146. Map and Hands.

(Des. and litho. Harrison.)

1973 (25 Apr.). *O.C.A.M.* Conference. T* **146** *and similar multicoloured design. W* w.**12** *(sideways on* 10 *c.). P* 14½ × 14 (10 *c.*) *or* 14 × 14½ (2 *r.* 50).

No.	Description		
466	10 c. O.C.A.M. emblem (*horiz.*)	5	5
467	2 r. 50, Type **146**	60	60

*O.C.A.M. = Organisation Commune Africaine Malgache et Mauricienne.

147. W.H.O. Emblem.

(Des. and litho. Harrison.)

1973 (20 Nov.). *25th Anniv. of W.H.O.* *W* w.**12**. *P* 14.
468 **147** 1 r. multicoloured 25 25
a. Wmk. sideways 25 25

148. Meteorological Station, Vacoas.

(Des. and litho. Harrison.)

1973 (27 Nov.). *I.M.O./W.M.O. Centenary.* *W* w.**12** (*sideways*). *P* 14.
469 **148** 75 c. multicoloured .. 20 20

149. Capture of the *Kent*.

(Des. and litho. Harrison.)

1974 (21 Mar.). *Birth Bicent. of Robert Surcouf (privateer).* *W* w.**12** (*sideways*). *P* 14.
470 **149** 60 c. multicoloured .. 20 20

150. P. Commerson (naturalist).

(Des. and litho. Harrison.)

1974 (18 Apr.). *Death Bicent. of Philibert Commerson* (1973). *W* w.**12**. *P* 14½.
471 **150** 2 r. 50, multicoloured .. 55 60

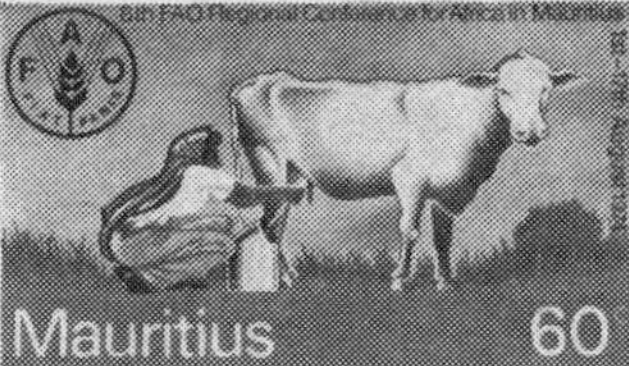

151. Cow being Milked.

(Des. and litho. Harrison.)

1974 (23 Oct.). *Eighth F.A.O. Regional Conference for Africa, Mauritius.* *W* w.**12** (*sideways*). *P* 14.
472 **151** 60 c. multicoloured .. 15 15

152. Mail Train.

(Des. and litho. Harrison.)

1974 (4 Dec.). *Centenary of Universal Postal Union.* *T* **152** *and similar horiz. design. Multicoloured.* *W* w.**12**. *P* 14.
473 15 c. Type **152** 5 5
474 1 r. New G.P.O., Port Louis 20 25

1975 (21 Jan.)–**76**. *As Nos.* 385, *etc. but* *W* w.**14** (*sideways on* 5 *and* 15 *c.*). *Chalk-surfaced paper.*
478 **102** 5 c. mult. (19.3.75) 5 5
480 **104** 15 c. ochre, black & cobalt 5 5
481 **105** 20 c. mult. (19.3.76) .. 5 5
482 **106** 25 c. red, black and apple-green (19.3.75) .. 5 5
483 **107** 30 c. multicoloured .. 5 5
484 **108** 35 c. mult. (19.3.76) .. 5 5
485 **109** 40 c. mult. (19.3.76) .. 5 5
486 **110** 50 c. mult. (19.3.76) .. 8 8
489 **113** 1 r. mult. (19.3.76) .. 12 15
491 **115** 5 r. multicoloured .. 65 75
492 **116** 10 r. multicoloured .. 1·25 1·50
478/92 .. .. *Set of* 11 2·25 2·50

153. " Cottage Life " (F. Leroy).

(Des. and litho. Harrison.)

1975 (6 Mar.). *Aspects of Mauritian Life.* *T* **153** *and similar multicoloured designs showing paintings.* *W* w.**14** (*sideways on* 15 *c.*, 60 *c. and* 2 *r.* 50). *P* 14.
493 15 c. Type **153** 5 5
494 60 c. " Milk Seller " (A. Richard) (*vert.*) .. 12 12
a. Brown and stone (ornaments and frame) double ..
495 1 r. " Entrance of Port Louis Market " (Thuillier) .. 20 25
496 2 r. 50, " Washerwomen " (Max Boullé) (*vert.*) .. 50 55

154. Mace across Map.

(Des. Harrison. Litho. Questa.)

1975 (21 Nov.). *French-speaking Parliamentary Assemblies Conference, Port Louis.* *W* w.**14** (*sideways*). *P* 14.
497 **154** 75 c. multicoloured .. 15 15

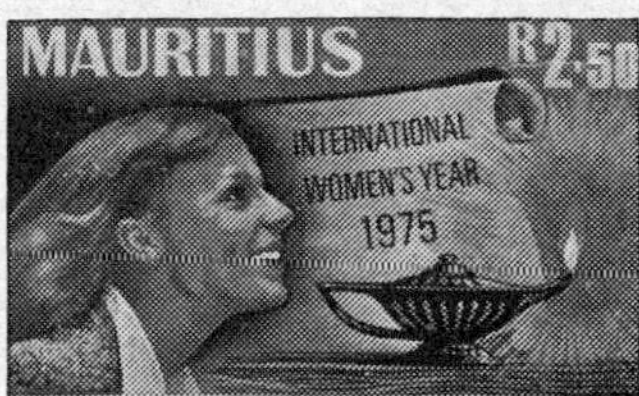

155. Woman with Lamp (" The Light of the World ").

(Des. Harrison. Litho. Questa.)

1975 (5 Dec.). *International Women's Year.* *W* w.**14** (*sideways*). *P* 14½.
498 **155** 2 r. 50, multicoloured .. 45 50

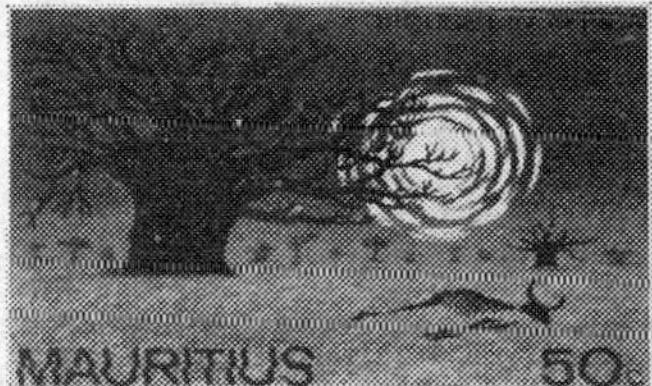

156. Parched Landscape.

(Des. Harrison (50 c.), J.W. Ltd. (60 c.). Litho. Questa.)

1976 (26 Feb.). *Drought in Africa.* *T* **156** *and similar design. Multicoloured.* *W* w.**14** (*sideways on* 50 *c.*). *P* 14.
499 50 c. Type **156** 10 10
500 60 c. Map of Africa and carcass (*vert.*) 12 12

157. *Pierre Loti*, 1953–70.

(Des. J.W. Ltd. Litho. Questa.)

1976 (2 July). *Mail Carriers to Mauritius.* *T* **157** *and similar horiz. designs. Multicoloured.* *W* w.**14** (*sideways*). *P* 14½ × 14.
501 10 c. Type **157** 5 5
502 15 c. *Secunder*, 1907 .. .. 5 5
503 50 c. *Hindoostan*, 1842 .. 8 10
504 60 c. *St. Geran*, 1740 .. .. 10 10
505 2 r. 50, *Maën*, 1638 .. .. 40 45
501/5 .. .. *Set of* 5 55 65
MS506 115 × 138 mm. Nos. 501/5 65

158. "The Flame of Hindi carried across the Seas".

(Des. J.W. Ltd. Litho. Questa.)

1976 (28 Aug.). *Second World Hindi Convention. T* **158** *and similar horiz. design. Multicoloured. W* w.**14** *(sideways). P* 14.

507	10 c. Type **158**	5	5
508	75 c. Type **158**	10	12
509	1 r. 20, Hindi script	20	25

159. Conference Logo and Map of Mauritius.

(Des. J.W. Ltd. Litho. Questa.)

1976 (22 Sept.). *22nd Commonwealth Parliamentary Association Conference. T* **159** *and similar vert. design. Multicoloured. W* w.**14.** *P* 14.

510	1 r. Type **159**	15	20
511	2 r. 50, Conference logo . .	40	45

160. King Priest and Breastplate.

(Des. J.W. Ltd. Litho. Walsall.)

1976 (15 Dec.). *Moenjodaro Excavations, Pakistan. T* **160** *and similar vert. designs. Multicoloured. W* w.**14.** *P* 14.

512	60 c. Type **160**	10	10
513	1 r. House with well and goblet	15	20
514	2 r. 50, Terracotta figurine and necklace	40	45

161. Sega Scene.

(Des. BG Studio. Litho. J.W.)

1977 (20 Jan.). *Second World Black and African Festival of Arts and Culture, Nigeria. W* w.**14** *(sideways). P* 13.

515 **161**	1 r. multicoloured . .	15	20

EXPRESS DELIVERY STAMPS.

EXPRESS DELIVERY 15c. (E 1)

EXPRESS DELIVERY (INLAND) 15c. (E 2)

EXPRESS DELIVERY (INLAND) 15 c. (E 3)

EXPRESS DELIVERY (INLAND) 15 c (E 4)

Type E **2**. "(INLAND)" was inserted at a second printing on stamps already surcharged with Type E **1** (No. E1).

Type E **3**. New setting made at one printing. More space above and below "(INLAND)".

Type E **4**. New setting with smaller "15 c" and no stop.

1903–04. *No.* 136 *surch. in red.*

E1 E **1**	15 c. on 15 c. ultramarine	2·25	3·00
E2 E **2**	15 c. on 15 c. ultramarine	3·00	3·50
	a. "A" inverted	45·00	50·00
E3 E **3**	15 c. on 15 c. ultramarine	1·60	65
	a. Surch. inverted . .	—	30·00
	b. Surch. double, both inverted		
	c. Imperf. between (vert. pr.)		
E4 E **4**	15 c. on 15 c. ultram. ('04)	28·00	28·00
	a. Surch. inverted . .		
	b. Surch. double		
	c. Surch. double, both invtd.		
	d. "c" omitted		

(FOREIGN) EXPRESS DELIVERY 18 CENTS (E 5)

1904. *T* **44** *(without value in label), wmk. Crown CC, surch. with Type* E **5.** *P* 14.

E5	18 c. green	1·50	2·00
	a. Note of exclamation "!" for "I" in "FOREIGN" . .	60·00	

1904. *T* **44** *surch. with Type* E **3.**

E6	15 c. grey-green (R.)	85	95
	a. Surch. inverted	38·00	38·00
	b. Surch. double		
	c. Surch. double, one "LNIAND"	38·00	38·00

POSTAGE DUE STAMPS.

D 1

(Typo. Waterlow & Sons, Ltd.)

1933–54. *Wmk. Mult. Script CA. P* 15 × 14.

D1 D **1**	2 c. black	8	5
D2 ,,	4 c. violet	5	5
D3 ,,	6 c. scarlet	5	8
D4 ,,	10 c. green	5	8
D5 ,,	20 c. bright blue . .	15	15
D6 ,,	50 c. dp. magenta (1.3.54)	30	30
D7 ,,	1 r. orange (1.3.54) . .	15	20
D1/7	. . . . *Set of* 7	70	80
D1/5	Perf. "Specimen" *Set of* 5	15·00	

(Typo. De La Rue.)

1966–69. *Chalk-surfaced paper. Wmk.* w.**12.** *P* 15 × 14.

D 8 D **1**	2 c. black (11.7.67) . .	5	5
D 9 ,,	4 c. slate-lilac (7.1.69) . .	5	5
D10 ,,	6 c. red-orange (7.1.69)	5	5
D11 ,,	10 c. yell.-grn. (16.2.67)	5	5
D12 ,,	20 c. blue (*shades*) (3.1.66)	5	5
D13 ,,	50 c. deep magenta (*shades*) (7.1.69)	8	8
D8/13	. . . . *Set of* 6	20	25

FISCALS USED FOR POSTAGE.

INLAND REVENUE (F 1)

INLAND REVENUE (F 2)

1889. *T* **19**, *wmk. Crown CA, optd. P* 14.

R1 F **1**	4 c. carmine	1·40	2·50
R2 F **2**	4 c. lilac	2·00	3·00

F 3

(Typo. D.L.R.)

1896–98. *Wmk. Crown CA. P* 14.

R3 F **3**	4 c. dull purple	4·00	
R4 ,,	4 c. green (1898)	4·00	

MONTSERRAT.

For GREAT BRITAIN stamps used in Montserrat with "A 08" obliteration, see index to Great Britain Stamps Used Abroad list.

1

MONTSERRAT
(2)

(T 1. Recess. D.L.R.)

1876 (Sept.). *Stamps of Antigua optd. with T 2. Wmk. Crown CC. P 14.*

1 1 1d. red .. .. 9·00 11·00
a. Bisected (½d.) (on cover) .. — £600
b. Inverted "S" £500 £500
2 ,, 6d. green .. .. .. 20·00 16·00
a. Bisect (used as 2½d.) (on cover)
b. Inverted "S" £1000 £900
3 ,, 6d. blue-green £450
a. Inverted "S" .. ..

No. 1 was bisected and used for a ½d. in 1883. This bisected stamp is found surcharged with a small "½" in *black* and also in *red*; both were unofficial and they did not emanate from the Montserrat P.O. The 6d. in blue-green is only known unused.

3 (Die I.)

(T 3. Typo. D.L.R.)

1880 (Jan.). *Wmk. Crown CC. P 14.*

4 3 2½d. red-brown .. .. £100 70·00
5 ,, 4d. blue .. .. .. 55·00 40·00

1884–85. *Wmk. Crown CA. P 14.*

6 3 ½d. dull green .. .. 1·25 1·75
7 1 1d. red .. .. .. 4·00 8·50
a. Inverted "S" £500 £500
b. Rose-red .. .. .. 6·00 7·00
ba. Bisected vert. (½d.) (on cover) — £600
9 3 2½d. red-brown .. .. 50·00 40·00
10 ,, 2½d. ultramarine .. .. 5·50 6·00
11 ,, 4d. blue £1000 £140
12 ,, 4d. mauve .. .. 4·50 4·50
10, 12 Optd. "Specimen" *Set of 2* 18·00

1884 (May). *Wmk. Crown CA. P 12.*

13 1 1d. red .. .. .. 22·00 20·00
a. Inverted "S" £1000 £800
b. Bisected (½d.) (on cover) .. — £500

The stamps for Montserrat were temporarily superseded by the general issue for Leeward Islands in 1890, but the following issues were in concurrent use with the stamps inscribed "LEEWARD ISLANDS" until July 1st 1956, when Leeward Islands stamps were withdrawn and invalidated.

4. Device of the Colony. 5

(Typo. D.L.R.)

1903. (a) *Wmk. Crown CA. P 14.*

14 4 ½d. grey-green and green .. 70 1·75
15 ,, 1d. grey-black and red .. 55 55
16 ,, 2d. grey and brown .. 3·25 5·00
17 ,, 2½d. grey and blue .. .. 2·75 4·00
18 ,, 3d. dull orange and deep pur. 5·00 6·50
19 ,, 6d. dull purple and olive .. 6·50 9·00
20 ,, 1s. green and bright purple 8·00 10·00
21 ,, 2s. green and brown-orange 11·00 14·00
22 ,, 2s. 6d. green and black .. 17·00 22·00

(b) *Wmk. Crown CC. P 14.*

23 5 5s. black and scarlet .. 70·00 85·00
14/23 .. .. *Set of 10* £110 £140
14/23 Optd. "Specimen" *Set of 10* 90·00

1903–8. *Wmk. Mult. Crown CA. P 14.*

24 4 ½d. grey-green & green, OC 30 45
25 ,, 1d. grey-blk. & red, C ('08) 4·50 5·50
26 ,, 2d. grey and brown, OC .. 75 1·25
27 ,, 2½d. grey and blue, C ('05).. 1·10 2·50
28 ,, 3d. dull orge. & dp. pur., OC 1·50 1·75
29 ,, 6d. dull purple & olive, OC 2·00 3·50
30 ,, 1s. grn. & brt. pur., C ('08) 4·50 5·50
31 ,, 2s. green & orange, C ('08) 14·00 19·00
32 ,, 2s. 6d. grn. & black, C ('08) 20·00 22·00
33 5 5s. black and red, C ('07) .. 60·00 75·00
24/33 .. .. *Set of 10* £100 £120

1908–13. *Wmk. Mult. Crown CA. P 14.*

35 4 ½d. deep green, O 45 60
36 ,, 1d. rose-red, O 85 25
38 ,, 2d. greyish slate, O .. 1·25 2·50
39 ,, 2½d. blue, O .. .. 1·75 2·50
40 ,, 3d. purple/*yellow*, C .. 1·10 2·50
a. White back (1913) (Optd. S. £6) .. .. .. 2·00 3·25
43 ,, 6d. dull and deep purple, C 4·50 7·00
a. Dull and bright purple .. 4·50 6·00
44 ,, 1s. black/*green*, C .. 4·50 6·00
45 ,, 2s. pur. & brt. blue/*blue*, C 14·00 16·00
46 ,, 2s. 6d. black & red/*blue*, C 16·00 19·00
47 5 5s. red and green/*yellow*, C 35·00 40·00
35/47 .. .. *Set of 10* 75·00 90·00
35/47 Optd. "Specimen" *Set of 10* 80·00

7

8

WAR STAMP
(9)

(T 7/8 typo. D.L.R.)

1914. *Wmk. Mult. Crown CA. P 14.*

48 7 5s. red and green/*yellow*, C 55·00 75·00
48 Optd. "Specimen" .. .. 40·00

1916–23. *Wmk. Mult. Crown CA. P 14.*

49 8 ½d. green, O 15 25
50 ,, 1d. scarlet, O 30 40
a. Carmine-red .. .. 1·50 1·10
51 ,, 2d. grey, O .. .. 95 1·75
52 ,, 2½d. bright blue, O .. .. 1·75 2·25
53 ,, 3d. purple/*yellow*, C .. 1·10 2·25
a. On pale yellow (Optd. S. £8).. 1·60 2·25
54 ,, 4d. grey-black and red/*pale yellow*, C (1923) 3·50 5·00
55 ,, 6d. dull and deep purple, C 2·25 4·50
56 ,, 1s. blk./*blue-grn.*, C (*olive back*) .. .. .. 3·00 4·50
57 ,, 2s. purple and blue/*blue*, C 7·50 10·00
58 ,, 2s. 6d. black & red/*blue*, C 16·00 17·00
59 ,, 5s. green and red/*yellow*, C 22·00 28·00
44/59 .. .. *Set of 11* 55·00 70·00
49/59 Optd. "Specimen" *Set of 11* 65·00

1917 (Oct.)–**18.** *No. 49 optd. with T 9.*

60 8 ½d. green (R.) 12 25
61 ,, ½d. green (Bk.) (1918) .. 20 30
a. Deep green 20 30

1919. *T 8. Special printing in orange. Value and "war stamp" as T 9 inserted in black at one printing.*

62 1½d. black and orange .. 12 30
60/2 Optd. "Specimen" *Set of 3* 35·00

1922–9. *Wmk. Mult. Script CA. P 14.*

63 8 ½d. brown, O 20 40
64 ,, ½d. green, O 15 20
65 ,, 1d. bright violet, O .. 25 25
66 ,, 1d. carmine, O (1929) .. 65 65
67 ,, 1½d. orange-yellow, O .. 1·75 2·50
68 ,, 1½d. carmine, O 25 60
69 ,, 1½d. red-brown, O (1929) .. 30 60
70 ,, 2d. grey, O 65 90
71 ,, 2½d. deep bright blue, O .. 1·90 2·75
a. Pale bright blue ('26) (Optd. S. £10) 70 90
72 ,, 2½d. orange-yellow, O (1923) 1·50 2·25
73 ,, 3d. dull blue, O (1923) .. 65 1·40
74 ,, 3d. purple/*yellow*, C (1927) 90 2·00
75 ,, 4d. black & red/*pale yell.*, C 65 1·25
76 ,, 5d. dull purple and olive, C 2·75 5·00
77 ,, 6d. pale and bright purple, C 90 2·25
78 ,, 1s. black/*emerald*, C .. 3·50 5·00
79 ,, 2s. purple and blue/*blue*, C 3·00 5·00
80 ,, 2s. 6d. black and red/*blue*, C 11·00 13·00
81 ,, 3s. green and violet, C .. 9·00 11·00
82 ,, 4s. black and scarlet, C .. 11·00 14·00
83 ,, 5s. grn. & red/*pale yellow*, C 16·00 20·00
63/83 .. .. *Set of 21* 60·00 80·00
63/83 Optd./Perf. "Specimen" *Set of 21* £150

10. Plymouth.

(Recess. D.L.R.)

1932 (18 April). *Tercentenary. Wmk. Mult. Script CA. P 14.*

84 10 ½d. green 60 80
85 ,, 1d. scarlet 60 90
86 ,, 1½d. red-brown .. .. 1·00 1·75
87 ,, 2d. grey .. .. .. 1·10 2·00
88 ,, 2½d. ultramarine .. .. 1·25 3·00
89 ,, 3d. orange .. .. .. 2·25 3·50
90 ,, 6d. violet .. .. .. 4·50 6·50
91 ,, 1s. olive-brown .. .. 11·00 14·00
92 ,, 2s. 6d. purple .. .. 38·00 45·00
93 ,, 5s. chocolate .. .. 60·00 70·00
84/93 .. .. *Set of 10* £110 £130
84/93 Perf. "Specimen" *Set of 10* 90·00

1935 (6 May). *Silver Jubilee. As Nos. 91/4 of Antigua, but printed by W'low & Sons. P 11 × 12.*

94 1d. deep blue and scarlet .. 45 25
95 1½d. ultramarine and grey .. 25 60
96 2½d. brown and deep blue .. 1·40 2·25
97 1s. slate and purple .. .. 5·50 6·00
94/7 Perf. "Specimen" *Set of 4* 20·00

1937 (12 May). *Coronation. As Nos. 13/15 of Aden. P 14.*

98 1d. scarlet 10 20
99 1½d. yellow-brown 10 20
100 2½d. bright blue 15 25
98/100 Perf. "Specimen" *Set of 3* 14·00

11. Carr's Bay.

12. Sea Island Cotton.

13. Botanic Station.

(Recess. D.L.R.)

1938 (2 Aug.)–**48.** *Wmk. Mult. Script CA.*

101 **11** ½d. blue-green (*p.* 13) .. 12 12
a. Perf. 14 ('42) 8 15
102 **12** 1d. carmine (*p.* 13) .. 12 12
a. Perf. 14 ('43) 12 12
103 „ 1½d. purple (*p.* 13) .. 1·60 60
a. Perf. 14 ('42) 8 8
104 **13** 2d. orange (*p.* 13) .. 1·25 65
a. Perf. 14 ('42) 12 12
105 **12** 2½d. ultramarine (*p.* 13) 12 25
a. Perf. 14. ('43) 8 8
106 **11** 3d. brown (*p.* 13) .. 30 25
a. Perf. 14. *Red-brown* ('42) 12 20
ab. *Deep brown* ('43) .. 1·25 1·75
107 **13** 6d. violet (*p.* 13) .. 55 45
a. Perf. 14 ('43) 20 15
108 **11** 1s. lake (*p.* 13) .. .. 1·60 1·00
a. Perf. 14 ('42) .. 40 45
109 **13** 2s. 6d. slate-blue (*p.* 13) 1·10 1·00
a. Perf. 14 ('43) .. 1·25 2·50
110 **11** 5s. rose-carmine (*p.* 13) 4·00 4·50
a. Perf. 14 ('42) .. 1·40 1·75
111 **13** 10s. pale blue (*p.* 12) ('48) 4·00 5·50
112 **11** £1 black (*p.* 12) ('48) .. 9·50 11·00
101/112 .. .. *Set of* 12 16·00 18·00
101/12 Perf. " Specimen " *Set of* 12 75·00

1946 (1 Nov.). *Victory. As Nos.* 28/9 *of Aden.*
113 1½d. purple 8 8
114 3d. chocolate 8 8
113/14 Perf. " Specimen " *Set of* 2 17·00

1949 (3 Jan.). *Royal Silver Wedding. As Nos.* 30/1 *of Aden.*
115 2½d. ultramarine 8 8
116 5s. carmine .. .. .. 2·75 4·00

1949 (10 Oct.). *75th Anniv. of Universal Postal Union. As Nos.* 114/7 *of Antigua.*
117 2½d. ultramarine 15 25
118 3d. brown 20 35
119 6d. purple 55 60
120 1s. purple 75 90
(New Currency. 100 cents = 1 dollar.)

1951 (16 Feb.). *Inauguration of B.W.I. University College. As Nos.* 118/9 *of Antigua.*
121 3 c. black and purple .. 15 15
122 12 c. black and violet .. 30 30

14. Government House.

15. Sea Island Cotton: Cultivation.

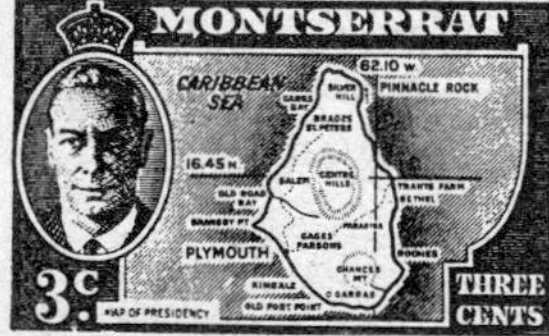

16. Map of Presidency.

17. Picking Tomatoes.

18. Badge of Presidency.

19. Sea Island Cotton: Ginning.

20. St. Anthony's Church.

21. Government House.

(Recess. B.W.)

1951 (17 Sept.). *Wmk. Mult. Script. CA. P* 11½ × 11.
123 **14** 1 c. black 15 15
124 **15** 2 c. green 12 15
125 **16** 3 c. orange-brown .. 15 15
126 **17** 4 c. carmine 15 15
127 **20** 5 c. reddish violet .. 15 20
128 **18** 6 c. olive-brown 20 40
129 **19** 8 c. deep blue 30 30
130 **20** 12 c. blue and chocolate .. 40 45
131 **17** 24 c. carmine & yellow-grn. 80 95
132 **19** 60 c. black and carmine .. 90 1·40
133 **15** $1.20, yellow-grn. & blue 3·25 3·50
134 **21** $2.40, black and green .. 3·25 4·00
135 **18** $4.80, black and purple .. 6·00 7·50
123/135 .. .. *Set of* 13 14·00 18·00

In the 5 c. the portrait is on the left and in the 24 c. it is on the right.

1953 (2 June). *Coronation. As No.* 47 *of Aden.*
136 2 c. black and deep green .. 15 25

22. Government House.

Types **16** and **18.** I. inscr. " PRESIDENCY ". II. inscr. " COLONY ".

(Recess. B.W.)

1953–58. *As T* **14/21**, *but with portrait of Queen Elizabeth II as in T* **22**. *Wmk. Mult. Script CA. P* 11½ × 11.
136*a* **16** ½ c. deep violet (I) .. 5 5
136*b* „ ½ c. deep violet (II) .. 5 8
137 **22** 1 c. black 5 5
138 **15** 2 c. green 5 5
139 **16** 3 c. orange-brown (I) .. 8 10
139*a* „ 3 c. orange-brown (II) .. 8 10
140 **17** 4 c. carmine-red .. 8 8
141 **20** 5 c. reddish lilac .. 8 8
142 **18** 6 c. dp. bistre-brown (I) 12 12
142*a* „ 6 c. deep bistre-brown (II) (*shades*) .. 15 15
143 **19** 8 c. deep bright blue .. 12 12
144 **20** 12 c. blue and red-brown 12 12
145 **17** 24 c. carm.-red and green 20 25
145*a* **15** 48 c. yellow-olive & purple 45 50
146 **19** 60 c. black and carmine .. 70 70
147 **15** $1·20, grn. & greenish bl. 1·50 1·75
148 **21** $2.40, blk. & bluish grn. 2·50 3·00
149 **18** $4.80, blk. & dp. pur. (I) 9·00 11·00
149*a* „ $4.80, blk. & dp. pur. (II) 6·00 8·00
136*b*/149*a* .. .. *Set of* 15 11·00 13·00

Dates of issue: 1953—15 Oct., 1 c., 2 c., 3 c. (I). 1955—1 June, 4 c., 5 c., 6 c. (I), 8 c., 12 c., 24 c., 60 c., $1.20, $2.40, $4.80 (I). 1956—3 July, ½ c. (I). 1957—15 Oct., 48 c. 1958—1 Sept., ½ c. (II), 3 c. (II), 6 c. (II), $4.80 (II).

In the 5 c. the portrait is on the left and in the 24 c. it is on the right.

1958 (22 Apr.). *Inauguration of British Caribbean Federation. As Nos.* 135/7 *of Antigua.*
150 3 c. deep green 12 12
151 6 c. blue 20 20
152 12 c. scarlet 30 30

1963 (8 July). *Freedom from Hunger. As No.* 76 *of Aden.*
153 12 c. reddish violet 40 40

1963 (2 Sept.). *Red Cross Centenary. As Nos.* 147/8 *of Antigua.*
154 4 c. red and black 12 12
155 12 c. red and blue 45 50

1964 (23 April). *400th Birth Anniv. of William Shakespeare. As No.* 164 *of Antigua.*
156 12 c. indigo 40 40

1964 (29 Oct.). *As No.* 138 *but wmk.* w.**12**.
157 **15** 2 c. green 15 20

1965 (17 May). *I.T.U. Centenary. As Nos.* 166/7 *of Antigua.*
158 4 c. vermilion and violet .. 12 12
159 48 c. light emerald & carmine 60 65

23. Pineapple. **24.** Avocado.

(Des. S. Goaman. Photo. Harrison.)

1965 (16 Aug.). *T* **23/4** *and similar vert. designs showing vegetables, fruit or plants. Multi-coloured. W* w.**12** (*upright*). *P* 15 × 14.
160 1 c. Type **23** 5 5
161 2 c. Type **24** 5 5
162 3 c. Soursop 5 5
163 4 c. Pepper 5 5
164 5 c. Mango 5 5
165 6 c. Tomato 5 5
166 8 c. Guava 8 8
167 10 c. Ochro 10 10
168 12 c. Lime 12 12
169 20 c. Orange 20 20
170 24 c. Banana 20 25
171 42 c. Onion 65 65
172 48 c. Cabbage 70 70
173 60 c. Pawpaw 80 90

:74 $1.20, Pumpkin .. .. 1·25 1·40
75 $2.40, Sweet potato .. 2·00 2·00
76 $4.80, Egg plant .. .. 4·00 4·00
60/76 .. .. *Set of* 17 9·50 9·50
See also Nos. 213/22.

965 (25 Oct.). *International Co-operation Year. As Nos. 168/9 of Antigua.*
77 2 c. reddish purple and turquoise-green 5 5
78 2 c. deep bluish green and lavender 25 25

966 (26 Jan.). *Churchill Commemoration. As Nos. 170/3 of Antigua.*
79 1 c. new blue 5 5
80 2 c. deep green 5 5
81 24 c. brown 35 35
82 42 c. bluish violet 60 70

966 (4 Feb.). *Royal Visit. As Nos. 174/5 of Antigua.*
83 14 c. black and ultramarine .. 20 20
84 24 c. black and megenta .. 30 35

966 (20 Sept.). *Inauguration of W.H.O. Headquarters, Geneva. As Nos. 178/9 of Antigua.*
85 12 c. black, yellow-green and light blue 15 20
86 60 c. black, light purple and yellow-brown .. 55 65

966 (1 Dec.). *20th Anniv. of U.N.E.S.C.O. As Nos. 196/8 of Antigua.*
87 4 c. slate-violet, red, yellow and orange 8 8
88 60 c. orange-yellow, violet and deep olive 50 60
89 $1.80, black, bright purple and orange .. .. 2·00 2·25

25. Yachting.

(Des. and photo. Harrison.)

967 (29 Dec.). *International Tourist Year. T* **25** *and similar designs.* W w.**12** (*sideways on* 15 c.). P 14.
90 5 c. multicoloured 5 5
91 15 c. multicoloured 12 12
92 16 c. multicoloured 15 15
93 24 c. multicoloured 30 30

Designs: *Vert.*—15 c. Waterfall near Chance Iountain. *Horiz.*—16 c. "Fishing, skin diving nd swimming"; 24 c. Playing golf.

$1.00
(26)

968 (6 May). *Nos. 168, 170, 172 and 174/6 surch. as T* **26.** *W* w.**12** (*upright*).
94 15 c. on 12 c. Lime 12 15
95 25 c. on 24 c. Banana .. 25 25
96 50 c. on 48 c. Cabbage .. 35 40
97 $1 on $1.20, Pumpkin .. 70 80
98 $2.50 on $2.40, Sweet potato 1·75 2·00
99 $5 on $4.80, Egg plant .. 3·50 4·50
94/9 .. .. *Set of* 6 6·00 7·50
See also Nos. 219, etc.

27. Sprinting.

28. Weightlifting. (*Horiz.*)
29. Gymnastics. (*Horiz.*)

30. Sprinting, and Aztec Pillars.

(Des. G. L. Vasarhelyi. Photo. Harrison.)

1968 (31 July). *Olympic Games, Mexico.* W w.**12** (*sideways on* $1). P 14.
200 **27** 15 c. deep claret, emerald and gold 10 10
201 **28** 25 c. blue, orange and gold 15 15
202 **29** 50 c. green, red and gold .. 35 40
203 **30** $1 multicoloured .. 70 75

31. Alexander Hamilton.

(Des. and Photo. Harrison.)

1968 (2 Dec.). *Human Rights Year. T* **31** *and similar horiz. designs. Multicoloured.* W w.**12.** P 14×14½.
204 5 c. Type **31** 5 5
205 15 c. Albert T. Marryshow .. 10 10
206 25 c. William Wilberforce .. 15 20
207 50 c. Dag Hammarskjöld .. 30 45
208 $1 Dr. Martin Luther King 60 1·00
204/8 .. *Set of* 5 85 1·25

Although first day covers were postmarked 2 December, those stamps were not put on sale in Montserrat until 6 December.

32. "The Two Trinities" (Murillo). **33.** "The Adoration of the Kings" (detail, Botticelli).

(Des. and photo. Harrison.)

1968 (16 Dec.). *Christmas.* W w.**12** (*sideways*). P 14½×14.
209 **32** 5 c. multicoloured .. 5 5
210 **33** 15 c. multicoloured .. 15 15
211 **32** 25 c. multicoloured .. 25 25
212 **33** 50 c. multicoloured .. 40 45

1969–70. *As Nos. 160/4, 167, 169 and 194/6 but wmk.* w.**12** *sideways.*
213 1 c. Type **23** (24.6.69) .. 5 5
214 2 c. Type **24** (23.4.70) .. 5 8
215 3 c. Soursop (24.6.69) .. 8 8
216 4 c. Pepper (24.6.69) .. 8 8
217 5 c. Mango (23.4.70) .. 10 10
218 10 c. Ochro (24.6.69) .. 20 25
219 15 c. on 12 c. Lime (24.6.69) 30 35
220 20 c. Orange (17.3.69) .. 40 40
221 25 c. on 24 c. Banana (24.6.69) 40 55
222 50 c. on 48 c. Cabbage (24.6.69) 75 1·25
213/22 .. .. *Set of* 10 2·00 2·75

The 1 c., 3 c., 4 c., 10 c., 15 c. and 20 c. exist with PVA gum as well as gum arabic, but the 2 c. and 5 c. exist with PVA gum only.

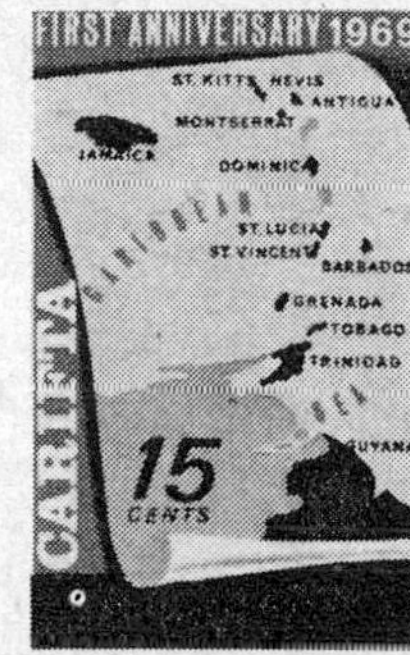

34. Map showing " CARIFTA " Countries.

35. " Strength in Unity ".

(Des. J. E. Cooter. Photo. Harrison.)

1969 (27 May). *First Anniv. of CARIFTA (Caribbean Free Trade Area).* W w.**12** (*sideways on T* **34**). P 14.
223 **34** 15 c. multicoloured .. 12 12
224 ,, 20 c. multicoloured .. 15 15
225 **35** 35 c. multicoloured .. 25 25
226 ,, 50 c. multicoloured .. 40 40

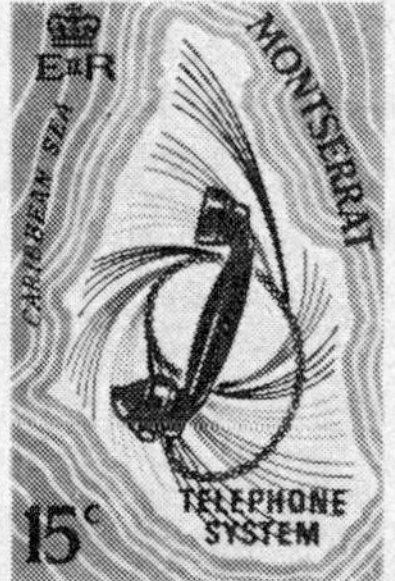

36. Telephone Receiver and Outline of Island.

37. School Symbols and Outline of Island.

38. "HS 748" Aircraft and Outline of Island.

39. Electricity Pylon and Outline of Island.

(Des. R. Reid adapted by V. Whiteley. Litho. Perkins, Bacon.)

1969 (29 July). *Development Projects.* W w.**12.** P 13½.
227 **36** 15 c. multicoloured .. 12 12
228 **37** 25 c. multicoloured .. 20 20
229 **38** 50 c. multicoloured .. 35 35
230 **39** $1 multicoloured .. 60 60

40. Dolphin.

(Des. Harrison. Photo. Enschedé.)

1969 (1 Nov.). *Game Fish. T* **40** *and similar horiz. designs. Multicoloured. P* 13×13½.

231	5 c. Type **40**	5	5
232	15 c. Atlantic sailfish ..	15	15
233	25 c. Blackfin tuna	25	25
234	40 c. Spanish mackerel ..	40	40

41. King Caspar before the Virgin and Child (detail) (stained glass window).

42. " Nativity " (Leonard Limosin).

(Des. J. E. Cooter. Litho. De La Rue.)

1969 (10 Dec.). *Christmas. Paintings multicoloured; frame colours given. W* w.**12** (*sideways on* 50 *c.*). *P* 13.

235	**41**	15 c. black, gold and violet	12	12
236	„	25 c. black and vermilion	25	25
237	**42**	50 c. black, ultramarine and yellow-orange ..	40	45

43. " Red Cross Sale ".

(Des. and litho. J.W.)

1970 (13 Apr.). *Centenary of British Red Cross. T* **43** *and similar horiz. designs. Multicoloured. W* w.**12** (*sideways*). *P* 14½×14.

238	3 c. Type **43**	5	5
239	4 c. School for deaf children	8	8
240	15 c. Transport services for disabled	15	15
241	20 c. Workshop	20	20

44. Red-Footed Booby.

(Des. V. Whiteley. Photo. Harrison.)

1970 (2 July)–**74.** *Birds. T* **44** *and similar multicoloured designs. W* w.**12** (*sideways on vert. designs and upright on horiz. designs*). *P* 14×14½ (*horiz.*) *or* 14½×14 (*vert.*).

A. *Chalk-surfaced paper* (2.7.70).

B. *Glazed, ordinary paper* (30.10.74, $10; 22.1.71, others).

		A.		B.	
242	1 c. Type **44** ..	5	5	†	
243	2 c. Killy Hawk	10	10	5	5
244	3 c. Frigate Bird	5	5	†	
245	4 c. White Egret	8	8	†	
246	5 c. Brown Pelican	8	8	5	5
247	10 c. Bananaquit	12	15	12	12
248	15 c. Ani	20	25	15	15
249	20 c. Tropic Bird	15	15	15	20
250	25 c. Montserrat Oriole ..	30	30	20	20
251	50 c. Green throated Carib ..	35	40	25	30
252	$1 Antillean Crested Hummingbird ..	70	75	40	45
253	$2.50, Little Blue Heron ..	1·60	1·75	1·00	1·10
254	$5 Purple throated Carib	2·50	3·00	2·25	2·50
254*a*	$10 Forest Thrush	†		4·50	5·00
242A/54A	*Set of* 13	5·50	6·50		
243B/54*a*B	*Set of* 11			8·50	9·50

The 1 c., 15 c., 20 c., 25 c., $1, $5 and $10 are horizontal, and the remainder are vertical designs.

See also Nos. 295, etc.

45. " Madonna and Child with Animals " (Dürer).

(Des. G. Drummond. Litho. D.L.R.)

1970 (1 Oct.).* *Christmas. T* **45** *and similar multicoloured design. W* w.**12**. *P* 13½×14.

255	5 c. Type **45**	5	5
256	15 c. " The Adoration of the Shepherds " (Domenichino)	12	12
257	20 c. Type **45**	15	15
258	$1 As 15 c.	65	65

* This was the local date of issue but the stamps were released by the Crown Agents on 21st September.

46. War Memorial.

(Des. V. Whiteley. Litho. J.W.)

1970 (30 Nov.). *Tourism. T* **46** *and similar horiz. designs. Multicoloured. W* w.12 (*sideways*). *P* 14½×14.

259	5 c. Type **46**	5	5
260	15 c. Plymouth from Fort St. George	12	12
261	25 c. Carrs Bay	20	20
262	50 c. Golf Fairway	40	40
MS263	135×109 mm. Nos. 259/62	65	65

47. Girl Guide and Badge.

(Des. V. Whiteley. Litho. Questa.)

1970 (31 Dec.). *Diamond Jubilee of Montserrat Girl Guides. T* **47** *and simliar vert. designs. Multicoloured. W* w.**12**. *P* 14.

264	10 c. Type **47**	8	[illegible]
265	15 c. Brownie and Badge ..	12	[illegible]
266	25 c. As 15 c.	25	[illegible]
267	40 c. Type **47**	35	[illegible]

48. " Descent from the Cross " (Van Hemessen).

(Des. J.W. Photo. Enschedé.)

1971 (22 Mar.). *Easter. T* **48** *and similar vert. design. Multicoloured. W* w.**12**. *P* 13½.

268	5 c. Type **48**	5	[illegible]
269	15 c. " Noli me tangere " (Orcagna)	12	[illegible]
270	20 c. Type **48**	20	[illegible]
271	40 c. As 15 c.	30	[illegible]

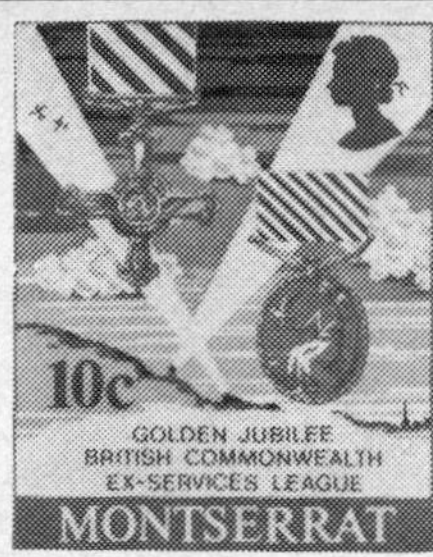

49. D.F.C. and D.F.M. in Searchlights.

(Des. Col. A Maynard Litho. Questa.)

1971 (8 JULY). *Golden Jubilee of Commonwealth Ex-Services League. T* **49** *and similar vert. designs. Multicoloured. W* w.**12**. *P* 14.

272	10 c. Type **49**	8	8
273	20 c. M.C., M.M. and jungle patrol	20	20
274	40 c. D.S.C., D.S.M. and submarine action	30	30
275	$1 V.C. and soldier attacking bunker	65	65

50. " The Nativity with Saints " (Romanino).

(Des. G. Drummond. Litho. Questa.)

1971 (16 SEPT.). *Christmas. T* **50** *and similar vert. design. Multicoloured. W* w.**12**. *P* 14 × 13½.

276	5 c. Type **50**	5	5
277	15 c. " Choir of Angels " (Simon Marmion) ..	10	10
278	20 c. Type **50**	15	15
279	$1 As 15 c	70	75

51. Piper " Apache ".

(Des. and litho. J.W.)

1971 (16 DEC.). *14th Anniv. of Inauguration of L.I.A.T. (Leeward Islands Air Transport). T* **51** *and similar horiz. designs. Multicoloured. W* w.**12** *(sideways). P* 13½.

280	5 c. Type **51**	5	5
281	10 c. Beech " Twin Bonanza "	8	8
282	15 c. De Havilland " Heron "	15	20
283	20 c. Britten Norman " Islander "	15	20
284	40 c. De Havilland " Twin Otter "	30	35
285	75 c. Hawker Siddeley " 748 "	70	75
280/5	.. .. *Set of* 6	1·25	1·40
MS286	203 × 102 mm. Nos. 280/5	1·50	1·75

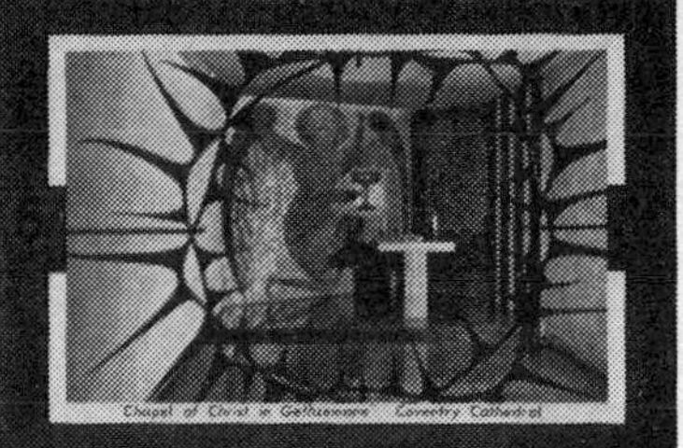

52. " Chapel of Christ in Gethsemane ", Coventry Cathedral.

(Des. G. Drummond. Litho. A. & M.)

1972 (9 MAR.). *Easter. T* **52** *and similar horiz. design. Multicoloured. W* w.**12**. *P.* 13.

287	5 c. Type **52**	5	5
288	10 c. " The Agony in the Garden " (Bellini) ..	8	8
289	20 c. Type **52**	15	15
290	75 c. As 10 c.	60	65

53. Lizard.

(Des. G. Drummond. Litho. Questa.)

1972 (20 JULY). *Reptiles. T* **53** *and similar multicoloured designs. W* w.**12** *(sideways on* 40 *c. and* $1*). P* 14½.

291	15 c. Type **53**	10	10
292	20 c. Mountain Chicken (frog)	12	12
293	40 c. Iguana (*horiz.*)	25	30
294	$1 Tortoise (*horiz.*) ..	50	50

1972–74. *As No.* 242 *etc., but W* w.**12**, *sideways on horiz. designs* (1, 15, 20, 25 *c.*) *and upright on vert. designs (others). Glazed, ordinary paper.*

295	1 c. Type **44**	8	5
	a. Chalk-surfaced paper ..	5	5
296	2 c. Killy Hawk	8	5
	a. Chalk-surfaced paper ..	5	5
297	3 c. Frigate Bird	5	5
298	4 c. White Egret (*chalky*) ..	5	5
299	5 c. brown Pelican	8	5
	a. Chalk-surfaced paper ..	5	5
300	15 c. Ani	12	12
	a. Chalk-surfaced paper ..	8	8
301	20 c. Tropic Bird (*chalky paper*)	15	15
302	25 c. Montserrat Oriole (*chalky*)	15	15
295/302	.. .. *Set of* 8	50	55

Dates of issue:—21.7.72, 1, 2, 3 c. (Nos. 295/7); 8.3.73, 5, 15 c. (Nos. 299, 300); 2.10.73, 15 c. (No. 300a), 20 c.; 4.2.74, 1 c. (No. 295a), 2 c. (No. 296a), 4 c. (No. 298), 5 c. (No. 299a); 17.5.74, 25 c.

54. " Madonna della Seggiola " (Raphael).

(Des. J. E. Cooter. Litho. Format.)

1972 (18 OCT). *Christmas. T* **54** *and similar horiz. designs. Multicoloured. W* w.**12**. *P* 13½.

303	10 c. Type **54**	8	8
304	35 c. " Virgin and Child " (Fungai)	20	20
305	50 c. " Madonna del Magnificat " (Botticelli) ..	35	35
306	$1 " Virgin and Child with St. John " (Botticelli) ..	65	65

55. Lime, Tomatoes and Pawpaw.

(Des. (from photographs by D. Groves) and photo. Harrison.)

1972 (20 NOV.). *Royal Silver Wedding. Multicoloured; background colour given. W* w.**12**. *P* 14 × 14½.

307	**55** 35 c. rose	20	25
308	,, $1 bright blue	60	65

56. *Passiflora herbertiana.*

(Des. J. E. Cooter. Litho. Walsall Security Printers Ltd.)

1973 (9 APR.). *Easter. T* **56** *and similar vert. designs showing passion-flowers. Multicoloured. W* w.**12**. *P* 13½.

309	20 c. Type **56**	12	12
310	35 c. *P. vitifolia*	20	20
311	75 c. *P. amabilis*	65	65
312	$1 *P. alata-caerulea* ..	75	75

Nos. 309/12 are inscribed on the reverse with information about the passion-flower.

57. Montserrat Monastery, Spain.

(Des. J. E. Cooter. Litho. Format.)

1973 (9 JULY). *480th Anniv. of Columbus's Discovery of Montserrat. T* **57** *and similar horiz. designs. Multicoloured. W* w.**12**. *P* 13½.

313	10 c. Type **57**	8	8

314 35 c. Columbus sighting Montserrat 20 20
315 60 c. Columbus's ship off Montserrat 45 50
316 $1 Colony badge and map of voyage 70 75
MS317 126×134 mm. Nos. 313/16 2·00 2·00

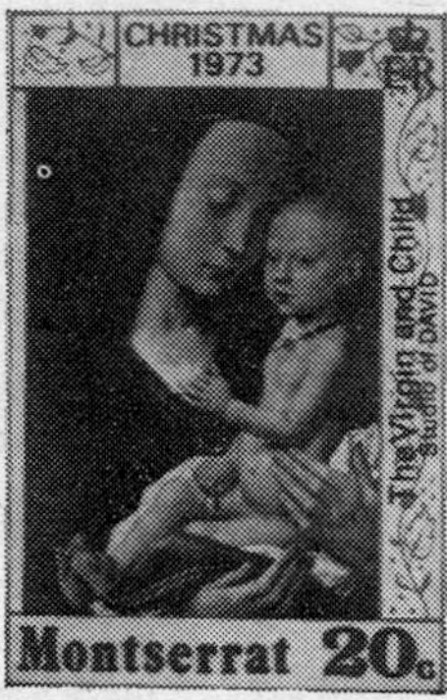

58. "Virgin and Child" (School of Gerard David).

(Des. J. E. Cooter. Litho. Questa.)

1973 (22 Oct.). *Christmas. T* **58** *and similar vert. designs. Multicoloured. W* w.**12** *(sideways). P* 13½.

318 20 c. Type **58** 12 12
319 35 c. "The Holy Family with St. John" (Jordaens) .. 20 20
320 50 c. "Virgin and Child" (Bellini) 40 40
321 90 c. "Virgin and Child" (Dolci) 70 75

1973 (14 Nov.). *Royal Wedding. As Nos.* 165/6 *of Anguilla. Centre multicoloured. W* w.**12** *(sideways). P* 13½.

322 35 c. sage-green 20 20
323 $1 violet-blue 45 50

59. Steel Band.

(Des. J.W. Ltd. Litho. Questa.)

1974 (8 Apr.). *25th Anniv. of University of West Indies. T* **59** *and similar designs. Multicoloured. W* w.**12** *(sideways on* 20 c., $1 *and* **MS**333).

324 20 c. Type **59** 12 12
325 35 c. Masqueraders (*vert.*) 20 20
326 60 c. Student weaving (*vert.*) .. 40 45
327 $1 University Centre, Montserrat 60 65
MS328 130×89 mm. Nos. 324/7 1·75 2·00

60. Hands with Letters.

(Des. P. B. Powell. Litho. Walsall Security Ptrs.)

1974 (3 July). *Centenary of Universal Postal Union. T* **60** *and similar horiz. design. W* w.**12**. *P* 14½×14.

329 **60** 1 c. multicoloured .. 5 5
330 – 2 c. light rose-red, orange-vermilion and black .. 5 5
331 **60** 3 c. multicoloured .. 5 5
332 – 5 c. light yellow-orange, reddish orge. & blk. 8 8
333 **60** 50 c. multicoloured .. 25 30
334 – $1 pale blue, turquoise-blue and black .. 55 60
329/34 .. .. *Set of* 6 85 90

Design:—2 c., 5 c., $1 Figures from U.P.U. Monument.

02¢

(61)

1974 (2 Oct.). *Various stamps surch. as T* **61**.

335 2 c. on $1 (No. 252B) .. 1·25 1·25
336 5 c. on 50 c. (No. 333) .. 1·50 1·50
337 10 c. on 60 c. (No. 326) .. 2·50 3·00
338 20 c. on $1 (No. 252B) .. 2·00 2·25
339 35 c. on $1 (No. 334) .. .. 2·00 2·25
335/9 .. .. *Set of* 5 8·50 10·00

62. Churchill and Houses of Parliament.

(Des. R. Granger Barrett. Litho. D.L.R.)

1974 (30 Nov.). *Birth Centenary of Sir Winston Churchill. T* **62** *and similar vert. design. Multicoloured. No wmk. P* 13×13½.

340 35 c. Type **62** 20 20
341 70 c. Churchill and Blenheim Palace 35 40
MS342 81×85 mm. Nos. 340/1 65 70

63. Carib "Carbet".

(Des. C. Abbott. Litho. Walsall Security Ptrs., Ltd.)

1975 (3 Mar.). *Carib Artefacts. T* **63** *and similar horiz. designs.*

(*a*) *W* w. **12** *(sideways). From sheets. P* 14.

343 5 c. lake-brown, yell. & blk. 5 5
344 20 c. blk., lake-brown & yell. 12 12
345 35 c. black, yell. & lake-brown 20 20
346 70 c. yellow, lake-brown & blk. 35 40

(*b*) *No wmk. Self-adhesive with advertisements on the reverse. From booklets. Rouletted.*

347 5 c. lake-brown, yell. & blk. 5 5
a. Booklet pane. Nos. 347/50 *se-tenant* 65
348 20 c. black, lk.-brown & yell. 12 12
a. Booklet pane. No. 348×3 and No. 349×3 65
349 35 c. black, yellow & lk.-brown 20 2
350 70 c. yellow, lk.-brown & blk. 40 4
343/50 .. .. *Set of* 8 1·25 1·2

Designs:—20 c. "Caracoli"; 35 c. Club o mace; 70 c. Canoe.

64. One-Bitt Coin.

(Des. J. E. Cooter. Litho. Questa.)

1975 (1 Sept.). *Local Coinage,* 1785–1801 *T* **64** *and similar diamond-shaped designs W* w.**14** *(sideways). P* 13½.

351 5 c. black, lt. violet-blue and silver 5
352 10 c. black, salmon and silver 8
353 35 c. black, light blue-grn. and silver 20 2
354 $2 black, bright rose & silver 80 9
MS355 142×142 mm. Nos. 351/4 1·25 1·4

Designs:—10 c. Eighth dollar; 35 c. Quarte dollar; $2 One dollar.

65. 1d. and 6d. Stamps of 1876.

(Des. J. Cooter. Litho. J.W.)

1976 (5 Jan.). *Centenary of First Montserra Postage Stamp. T* **65** *and similar horiz designs. W* w.**12** *(sideways). P* 13.

356 5 c. deep carmine, yellowish green and black 5
357 10 c. light yellow-ochre, scarlet and black 5
358 40 c. multicoloured 15 1
359 55 c. deep mauve, yellowish green and black 20 2
360 70 c. multicoloured 25 2
361 $1.10, yellowish green, bright blue and grey-black .. 40 4
356/61 .. .. *Set of* 6 1·00 1·1
MS362 170×159 mm. Nos. 356/61. P 13½ .. .. .. 1·25

Designs:—10 c. G.P.O. and bisected 1d stamp; 40 c. Bisects on cover; 55 c. G.B. 6d. use in Montserrat and local 6d. of 1876; 70 c. Stamp for 2½d. rate, 1876, $1.10 Packet boat *Antelop* and 6d. stamp.

66. " The Trinity ".

2¢

(67)

(Des. J. E. Cooter. Litho. Questa.)

1976 (5 Apr.). *Easter. Unissued stamps prepared for Easter* 1975 *with values and date obliterated by black bars. T* **66** *and similar vert. designs showing paintings by Orcagna. Multicoloured. W* w.**14**. *P* 13½.

363	15 c. on 5 c. Type **66**	5	8
364	40 c. on 35 c. " The Resurrection "	15	20
365	55 c. on 70 c. " The Ascension "	25	30
366	$1.10, on $1 " Pentecost " ..	50	55
MS367	160 × 143 mm. Nos. 363/6	1·00	
	a. Surch. omitted		

The above were printed for Easter 1975 and have the date obliterated and the face-value altered. For No. 363 the "1" was added to the original 5 c. to make 15 c.

1976 (12 Apr.). *Nos.* 244A, 246A *and* 247A *surch. as T* **67**.

368	2 c. on 5 c. Brown pelican ..	5	5
369	30 c. on 10 c. Bananaquit ..	12	15
370	45 c. on 3 c. Frigate bird ..	20	25

68. White Frangipani.

(Des. J. E. Cooter. Litho. Questa.)

1976 (5 July). *Various horiz. designs showing Flowering Trees as T* **68**. *Multicoloured. W* w.**14** (*sideways*). *P* 13½.

371	1 c. Type **68**	5	5
372	2 c. Cannon-ball Tree ..	5	5
373	3 c. Lignum vitae	5	5
374	5 c. Malay apple	5	5
375	10 c. Jacaranda	5	5
376	15 c. Orchid Tree	5	5
377	20 c. Manjak	8	8
378	25 c. Tamarind	10	10
379	40 c. Flame of the Forest ..	15	15
380	55 c. Pink Cassia	20	20
381	70 c. Long John	25	30
382	$1 Saman	35	40
383	$2.50, Immortelle	90	1·00
384	$5 Yellow Poui	1·75	2·00
385	$10 Flamboyant	3·50	4·00
371/85	.. .. *Set of* 15	6·50	7·50

69. Mary and Joseph.

(Des. L. D. Curtis. Litho. Format.)

1976 (4 Oct.). *Christmas. T* **69** *and similar vert. designs. Multicoloured. W* w.**14**. *P* 14.

386	15 c. Type **69**	5	8
387	20 c. The Shepherds	8	10
388	55 c. Mary and Jesus	20	25
389	$1.10, The Magi	45	50
MS390	95 × 135 mm. Nos. 386/9	80	

70. Hudson River Review, 1976.

(Des. and litho. J.W.)

1976 (13 Dec.). *Bicentenary of American Revolution. T* **70** *and similar vert. designs. Multicoloured. W* w.**14**. *P* 13.

391	15 c. Type **70**	5	8
392	40 c. } The *Raleigh* attacking ..	15	20
393	75 c. } H.M.S. *Druid*, 1777* ..	30	35
394	$1.25, Hudson River Review	50	55
MS395	95 × 145 mm. Nos. 395/8. P 13½	1·10	

*The date is wrongly given on the stamps as "1776".

Nos. 392/3 and 391 and 394 were printed in horizontal *se-tenant* pairs throughout the sheet, each pair forming a composite design.

71. The Crowning.

(Des. G. L. Vasarhelyi. Litho. J.W.)

1977 (7 Feb.). *Silver Jubilee. T* **71** *and similar horiz. designs. Multicoloured. W* w.**14** (*sideways*). *P* 13.

396	30 c. Royal Visit, 1966 ..	12	15
397	45 c. Cannons firing salute ..	20	20
398	$1 Type **71**	40	45

OFFICIAL STAMPS

O H.M.S. (O 1) **O.H.M.S.** (O 2)

1976 (12 Apr.). *Various stamps, some already surcharged, optd. locally with Type* O **1**.

O1	5 c. multicoloured (No. 246A)
O2	10 c. multicoloured (No. 247A)
O3	30 c. on 10 c. mult. (No. 369)
O4	45 c. on 3 c. mult. (No. 370)
O5	$5 multicoloured (No. 254A)
O6	$10 multicoloured (No. 254*a*B)

These stamps were issued for use on mail from the Montserrat Philatelic Bureau. They were not available for sale in either unused or used condition.

1976 (1 Oct.). *Nos.* 374/8, 380/2 *and* 384 *optd. with Type* O **2**.

O 7	5 c. Malay Apple	†	5
O 8	10 c. Jacaranda	†	5
O 9	15 c. Orchid Tree	†	5
O10	20 c. Manjak	†	8
O11	25 c. Tamarind	†	10
O12	55 c. Pink Cassia	†	25
O13	70 c. Long John	†	30
O14	$1 Saman	†	40
O15	$5 Yellow Poui	†	2·00
O7/15	.. .. *Set of* 9	†	3·00

Nos. O7/15 were not available in an unused condition, and were sold to the public cancelled-to-order.

MOROCCO AGENCIES.
(BRITISH POST OFFICES.)

I. "GIBRALTAR" PERIOD

FOR USE AT ALL BRITISH POST OFFICES IN MOROCCO.

Until 1907 all British Post Offices in Morocco were under the control of the Gibraltar P.O.

Morocco Agencies (1) Morocco Agencies (2)

1898. *T* **7** *of Gibraltar optd.*

1. *Locally (at "Gibraltar Chronicle" office). Type* **1** *(wide "M" and ear of "g" projecting upwards), in black.*

1 5 c. green 15 12
2 10 c. carmine 15 10
 a. Opt. double. £150
 b. Bisected (5 c.) (on cover) .. — £300
3 20 c. olive-green 65 70
 a. Opt. double. .. £100
 b. Olive-green and brown .. 65 40
4 25 c. ultramarine 30 25
5 40 c. orange-brown 80 85
 a. Blue opt. .. .. .. 8·00 8·00
6 50 c. bright lilac .. .. 4·00 6·00
 a. Blue opt. .. .. .. 2·25 2·75
7 1 p. bistre and ultramarine .. 2·50 4·50
 a. Blue opt. .. .. .. 30·00 32·00
8 2 p. black and carmine .. 1·50 4·50
1/8 .. .. *Set of* 8 7·50 12·00

The *blue* overprint can be easily distinguished by looking through the stamp in front of a strong light.

OVERPRINT VARIETY: "A" for "A". Prices for un.; used 20% higher. 5 c. £6; 10 c. £90; 20 c. (No. 3 or 3b), £7; 25 c. £32; 40 c. £50; 50 c. £75; 1 p. £50; 2 p. £75.

This variety occurred in the first setting, No. 36 of right-hand pane. Numerous other minor varieties exist.

Morocco (3)

II. *London opt., in black. T* **2** *(narrow "M" and ear of "g" horizontal).*

9 5 c. green 8 8
10 10 c. carmine 12 8
11 20 c. olive-green 30 25
12 25 c. ultramarine 90 30
13 40 c. orange-brown .. .. 2·50 2·25
14 50 c. bright lilac .. .. 1·75 1·10
15 1 p. bistre and ultramarine .. 4·00 4·50
16 2 p. black and carmine .. 5·50 6·00
9/16 .. .. *Set of* 8 13·00 13·00
9/16 Optd. "Specimen" *Set of* 8 55·00

OVERPRINT VARIETIES: Prices for un.; used 10% higher.

(A). Broad top to "M" (T **3**). No. 39 of left-hand pane. 5 c. £1·50; 10 c. £1·50; 20 c. £4; 25 c. £4; 40 c. £20; 50 c. £25; 1 p. £30; 2 p. £90.

(B). Hyphen between "n" and "c" of "Agencies". No. 17 of right-hand pane.

5 c. £1·50; 10 c. £1·50; 20 c. £4; 25 c. £4; 40 c. £20; 50 c. £25; 1 p. £30; 2 p. £90.

1903–5. *As T* **8** *of Gibraltar, but with value in Spanish currency, optd. with T* **2**. *Wmk. Crown CA. P* 14.

17 5 c. grey-green & grn. (1.03) 85 20
18 10 c. dull purple/*red* (8.03) .. 85 25
19 20 c. grey-green & carm. (9.04) 1·50 4·50
20 25 c. pur. & blk./*blue* (1.7.03) 40 20
21 50 c. purple & violet (3.7.05) 22·00 26·00
22 1 p. black & carm. (19.11.05) 20·00 22·00
23 2 p. black & blue (19.11.05) 24·00 22·00
17/23 .. .. *Set of* 7 65·00 70·00
17/23 Optd. "Specimen" *Set of* 7 55·00

OVERPRINT VARIETIES: Prices for un.; used 10% higher.

(A). As T **3**.

5 c. £6; 10 c. £6; 20 c. £10; 25 c. £9; 50 c. £90; 1 p. £75; 2 p. £95.

(B). Hyphen between "n" and "c".

5 c. £6; 10 c. £6; 20 c. £10; 25 c. £9; 50 c. £90; 1 p. £75; 2 p. £95.

1905–6. *As Nos.* 17/23, *but wmk. Mult. Crown CA.*

24 5 c. grey-green & green, OC 20 15
25 10 c. dull purple/*red*, OC .. 30 12
26 20 c. grey-grn. & car., O ('06) 85 2·25
27 25 c. pur. & blk./*blue*, C ('06) 9·00 3·50
28 50 c. purple & violet, C ('06) 3·50 3·00
29 1 p. black and carmine, C .. 12·00 14·00
30 2 p. black and blue, C .. 9·00 8·00
24/30 .. .. *Set of* 7 32·00 28·00

OVERPRINT VARIETIES: Prices for un.; used 10% higher.

(A). As T **3**.

5 c. £5; 10 c. £6; 20 c. £22; 25 c. £3; 50 c. £55; 1 p. £70; 2 p. £95.

(B). Hyphen between "n" and "c".

5 c. £75.

NOTE. In 1907 control of the post offices was assumed by the H.M. Postmaster-General.

ALL THE FOLLOWING ISSUES ARE OVERPRINTED ON GREAT BRITAIN.

II. BRITISH CURRENCY.

Stamps overprinted "MOROCCO AGENCIES" only were primarily intended for use on parcels (and, later, air-mail correspondence), and were on sale at British P.Os. throughout Morocco including Tangier, until 1937.

PRICES. Our prices for used stamps with these overprints are for specimens used in Morocco. These stamps could be used in the United Kingdom, with official sanction, from the summer of 1950 onwards, and with U.K. postmarks are worth about 25 per cent. less.

MOROCCO AGENCIES (4) MOROCCO AGENCIES (5)

1907–13. *King Edward VII optd. as T* **4** *or* **5** *(2s. 6d.). (a) De La Rue printings.*

31 ½d. pale yellowish green, O .. 20 45
32 1d. scarlet, O 70 75
33 2d. grey-green and carmine, C 70 1·40
34 4d. green & choc.-brown, C .. 5·50 1·25
35 4d. orange, O (1912) .. .. 1·00 1·10
36 6d. dull purple, C .. .. 2·00 1·00
37 1s. dull green & carmine, C .. 4·50 3·00
38 2s. 6d. pale dull purple, C .. 28·00 26·00
39 2s. 6d. dull purple, C .. .. 28·00 26·00
31/39 .. .. *Set of* 8 40·00 32·00
37/8 H/S "Specimen" *Set of* 2 35·00

(b) Later printings (1913).

40 4d. bright orange, O (No. 286) 3·25 4·50
41 2s. 6d. dull pur., O (No. 315) 30·00 30·00

MOROCCO AGENCIES (6)

1914–31. *King George V. (i) Optd. with T* **4**. *W* **100**.

42 **105** ½d. green 12 20
43 **104** 1d. scarlet 12 10
44 **105** 1½d. red-brown (1921) .. 70 80
45 **106** 2d. orange (Die I) .. 45 25
46 ,, 3d. bluish violet (1921) .. 80 30
47 ,, 4d. grey-green (1921) .. 90 40
48 **107** 6d. reddish pur., C (1921) 2·25 2·25
49 **108** 1s. bistre-brown (1917) .. 4·50 75
 a. Triple opt. (two albino) 80·00

(ii) *Optd. with T* **6**.

(a) Waterlow printing.

50 **109** 2s. 6d. sepia-brown (1914) 20·00 16·00
 a. Re-entry £250 £225
 b. Opt. double, one albino ..

(b) De La Rue printings.

51 **109** 2s. 6d. yellow-brown (1917) 20·00 15·00
 a. Opt. double (1917) .. £300 £250
52 ,, 2s. 6d. grey-brown .. 18·00 18·00

(c) Bradbury Wilkinson printings.

53 **109** 2s. 6d. chocolate-brown .. 26·00 10·00
 a. Opt. double, one albino* .. £180
54 ,, 5s. rose-red (1931) .. 22·00 24·00
42/54 .. .. *Set of* 10 45·00 35·00
49/50, 54 H/S "Specimen" *Set of* 3 30·00

* The albino overprint is quite clear, with the "MOROCCO" appearing just below "AGENCIES" of the normal overprint and a little to the right as seen from the back; however, this occurs with a second faint albino impression just below the normal overprint.

MOROCCO AGENCIES (7) S (A) MOROCCO AGENCIES (8) S (B)

(A) Opt. 14 mm. long; ends of "s" cut off diagonally.

(B) Opt. 15½ mm. long; ends of "s" cut off horizontally.

1925–36. *King George V, optd. with T* **7** (A) *or T* **8** (B). *W* **111**.

			A		B	
55	**105**	½d. green ..	40	20	25	35
56	,,	1½d. chest. ('31)	3·75	4·50	†	
57	**106**	2d. orange ..	90	70	†	
58	**104**	2½d. blue ..	1·10	60	30·00	16·00
59	**106**	4d. grey-green (1.36) ..	†		2·50	6·00
60	**107**	6d. pur., O ('31)	1·10	1·40	45	50
61	**108**	1s. bistre-brn.	3·75	2·50	16·00	11·00
55/61 (*cheapest*) *Set of* 7			11·00	12·00		
61A H/S "Specimen"			17·00			

1935 (8 MAY). *Silver Jubilee stamps. Optd. "*MOROCCO AGENCIES*" only, as in T* **17**.

62 **123** ½d. green (B.) 20 35
63 ,, 1d. scarlet (B.) 35 80
64 ,, 1½d. red-brown (B.) .. 1·00 1·90
65 ,, 2½d. blue (R.) .. .. 1·40 1·75

1935–37. *King George V. (a) Harrison photo. ptgs. optd. with T* **8**.

66 **119** 1d. scarlet ('35) 20 20
67 **118** 1½d. red-brown ('36) .. 70 1·60
68 **120** 2d. orange (11.5.36) .. 15 12
69 **119** 2½d. ultramarine (11.2.36) 90 85
70 **120** 3d. violet (2.3.36) .. 15 10
71 ,, 4d. dp. grey-grn. (19.5.36) 20 12
72 **122** 1s. bistre-brown ('36) .. 60 45

(b) Waterlow re-engraved ptg. optd. with T **6**.

73 **109** 2s. 6d. choc.-brn. (No. 450) 9·00 10·00
74 ,, 5s. bright rose-red (No. 451) (2.3.37) .. .. 9·00 12·00
66/74 .. .. *Set of* 9 18·00 22·00
72/3 H/S "Specimen" *Set of* 2 30·00

1936. *King Edward VIII, optd. "*MOROCCO AGENCIES*" only, as in T* **18**.

A. MOROCCO 14¼ mm. long.

B. MOROCCO 15¼ mm. long.

			A		B	
75	**124**	1d. scarlet ..	10	10	45	80
76	,,	2½d. brt. blue..	12	12	45	70

In 1937 unoverprinted Great Britain stamps replaced overprinted "MOROCCO AGENCIES" issues as stocks became exhausted. In 1949 overprinted issues reappeared and were in use at Tetuan (Spanish Zone), the only remaining British P.O. apart from that at Tangier.

MOROCCO AGENCIES (9) MOROCCO AGENCIES (10)

1949. (16 AUG.). *King George VI, optd. with T* **9** *or* **10** *(2s. 6d., 5s.).*

77 **128** ½d. pale green 8 20
78 ,, 1d. pale scarlet 8 20
79 ,, 1½d. pale red-brown .. 10 30
80 ,, 2d. pale orange 10 30
81 ,, 2½d. light ultramarine .. 10 30
82 ,, 3d. pale violet 10 20
83 **129** 4d. grey-green 12 20
84 ,, 5d. brown 20 40
85 ,, 6d. purple 15 40
86 **130** 7d. emerald-green .. 20 45
87 ,, 8d. bright carmine .. 20 45
88 ,, 9d. deep olive-green .. 20 55
89 ,, 10d. turquoise-blue .. 25 60
90 ,, 11d. plum 70 75
91 ,, 1s. bistre-brown .. 35 70
92 **131** 2s. 6d. yellow-green .. 3·25 4·00
93 ,, 5s. red .. .. .. 7·50 7·50
77/93 .. .. *Set of* 17 12·00 16·00

1951 (3 May). *King George VI* (*Nos.* 503/7, 509/10), *optd. with T* **9** *or* **10** (*2s. 6d., 5s.*).
94 **128** ½d. pale orange 8 12
95 „ 1d. light ultramarine .. 8 12
96 „ 1½d. pale green 10 20
97 „ 2d. pale red-brown .. 10 25
98 „ 2½d. pale scarlet 10 35
99 **147** 2s. 6d. yellow-green .. 2·00 2·75
100 **148** 5s. red .. .. .. 3·00 5·00
94/100 .. .. *Set of* 7 5·00 8·00

1952–55. *Queen Elizabeth II* (*Tudor Crown wmk.*), *optd. with T* **9**.
101 **154** ½d. orange-red (31.8.53) 5 5
102 „ 1d. ultramarine (31.8.53) 5 5
103 „ 1½d. green (5.12.52) .. 5 5
104 „ 2d. red-brown (31.8.53) 10 10
105 **155** 2½d. carmine-red (5.12.52) 10 12
106 **156** 4d. ultramarine (1.3.55) 20 35
107 **157** 5d. brown (6.7.53) .. 30 40
108 „ 6d. reddish pur. (1.3.55) 35 45
109 **158** 8d. magenta (6.7.53) .. 60 90
110 **159** 1s. bistre-brown (6.7.53) 30 50
101/110 .. .. *Set of* 10 1·75 2·50

1956 (10 Sept.). *Queen Elizabeth II* (*St. Edward's Crown wmk.*), *optd. with T* **9**.
111 **155** 2½d. carmine-red (No. 544) 50 60

Stamps overprinted "MOROCCO AGENCIES" were withdrawn from sale on December 31st 1956.

III. SPANISH CURRENCY.

Stamps surcharged in Spanish currency were sold at British P.Os. throughout Morocco until the establishment of the French Zone and the Tangier International Zone, when their use was confined to the Spanish Zone.

MOROCCO AGENCIES
5 CENTIMOS
(11)

MOROCCO AGENCIES
6 PESETAS
(12)

1907–13. *King Edward VII, surch. as T* **11** (*5 c. to 1 p.*) *or* **12** (*3 p. to 12 p.*). (*a*) *De La Rue printings.*
112 5 c. on ½d. pale yellowish green, O 10 8
113 10 c. on 1d. scarlet, O .. 10 10
114 15 c. on 1½d. purple & grn., C 20 12
a. "1" of "15" omitted .. £550
115 20 c. on 2d. grey-green and carmine, C 25 10
116 25 c. on 2½d. ultramarine, O 45 10
117 40 c. on 4d. green and chocolate-brown, C .. .. 70 1·75
118 40 c. on 4d. orange, O (1910) 25 40
119 50 c. on 5d. purple and ultramarine, C 95 30
120 1 p. on 10d. pur. & carm., C 2·00 2·75
a. No cross on crown .. ..
121 3 p. on 2s. 6d. pale dull purple, C .. .. .. 8·50 8·50
122 6 p. on 5s. carmine, O .. 20·00 22·00
123 12 p. on 10s. ultramarine, O 30·00 26·00
112/123 .. .. *Set of* 12 55·00 55·00
123 H/S "Specimen" .. .. 18·00

(*b*) *Harrison printing.*
124 25 c. on 2½d. bright blue (No. 283) ('12) .. .. 4·00 4·50

(*c*) *Somerset House printing.*
125 12 p. on 10s. bright blue (No. 319) ('13) .. .. 50·00 55·00

1912. *King George V, surch. as T* **11**.
126 5 c. on ½d. green (No. 339) 45 8
127 10 c. on 1d. scarlet (No. 342) 60 8
a. No cross on crown .. .. 22·00 14·00

MOROCCO AGENCIES
3
CENTIMOS
(13)

MOROCCO AGENCIES
10
CENTIMOS
(14)

MOROCCO AGENCIES
15 CENTIMOS
(15)

MOROCCO AGENCIES
6 PESETAS
(16)

1914–26. *King George V.* (i) *Surch. as T* **11** (*5 c.*), **13** (*3 c. and 40 c.*)*, **15** (*15 c.*) *and* **14** (*remainder*). *W* **100**.
128 **105** 3 c. on ½d. green ('17) .. 10 75
129 „ 5 c. on ½d. green .. 25 8
130 **104** 10 c. on 1d. scarlet .. 12 8
131 **105** 15 c. on 1½d. red-brn. ('15) 12 8
132 **106** 20 c. on 2d. orange (Die I) 20 40
a. Surch. double, one albino
133 **104** 25 c. on 2½d. blue (*shades*) 20 10
134 **100** 40 c. on 4d. grey grn. ('17) 1·60 2·25
135 **108** 1 p. on 10d. turq.-blue.. 65 1·10

* The surcharge on Nos. 134, 148 and 158 is as T **13** for the value and T **15** for "MOROCCO AGENCIES".

(ii) *Surch as T* **16**. *Waterlow printings.*
136 **109** 6 p. on 5s. rose-carmine 17·00 19·00
a. Surch. double, one albino 75·00
b. Surch. treble, one albino
137 „ 6 p. on 5s. pale rose-carm. 75·00
a. Surch. double, one albino
138 „ 12 p. on 10s. indigo-blue (R.) .. .. .. 42·00 50·00
a. Surch. double, one albino £250
136 & 138 H/S "Specimen" *Set of* 2 38·00

De La Rue printings.
139 **109** 3 p. on 2s. 6d. grey-brn. ('18) .. .. .. 16·00 18·00
140 „ 3 p. on 2s. 6d. yell.-brn. 16·00 20·00
141 „ 12 p. on 10s. blue (R.) .. 26·00 28·00

Bradbury Wilkinson printings.
142 **109** 3 p. on 2s. 6d. choc.-brn. ('26) .. .. 10·00 12·00
128/142 .. .. *Set of* 11 50·00 60·00

1925–31. *King George V, surch. as T* **11, 13, 14** *or* **15**. *W* **111**.
143 **105** 5 c. on ½d. green ('31) .. 12 55
144 **104** 10 c. on 1d. scarlet ('29) 1·40 3·25
145 **105** 15 c. on 1½d. red-brown.. 4·50 4·00
146 **106** 20 c. on 2d. orange ('31) 1·00 1·25
a. Surch. double, one albino .. ..
147 **104** 25 c. on 2½d. blue .. 25 40
148 **106** 40 c. on 4d. grey-grn. ('30) 25 25
143/148 .. .. *Set of* 6 7·00 9·00

MOROCCO AGENCIES
10 CENTIMOS
(17)

1935 (8 May). *Silver Jubilee, surch. as T* **17**.
149 **123** 5 c. on ½d. green (B.) .. 12 25
150 „ 10 c. on 1d. scarlet (B.) .. 1·00 1·25
a. Pair, one with "CENTIMES".. £350
151 „ 15 c. on 1½d. red-brn. (B.) 25 1·25
152 „ 25 c. on 2½d. blue (R.) .. 2·00 1·50

Beware of forgeries of the error, No. 150*a*.

1935–37. *King George V, surch. as T* **11, 13, 14** *or* **15**.
153 **118** 5 c. on ½d. green (17.6.36) 10 25
154 **119** 10 c. on 1d. scarlet 20 40
155 **118** 15 c. on 1½d. red-brown.. 2·00 1·40
156 **120** 20 c. on 2d. orange ('36).. 20 25
157 **119** 25 c. on 2½d. ultram. ('36) 80 95
158 **120** 40 c. on 4d. deep grey-green (18.5.37) .. 12 40
159 **122** 1 p. on 10d. turquoise-blue (21.4.37) .. 12 15
153/159 .. .. *Set of* 7 3·00 3·25

MOROCCO 10 AGENCIES
CENTIMOS
(18)

1936. *King Edward VIII, surch. as T* **18.**
A. "MOROCCO" 14¼ mm. long.
B. "MOROCCO" 15¼ mm. long.

			A		B	
160	**124**	5 c. on ½d. green	8	8	†	
161	„	10 c. on 1d. scar.	8	10	15	20
162	„	15 c. on 1½d. red-brown	10	10	†	
163	„	25 c. on 2½d. brt. blue ..	12	10	†	

MOROCCO AGENCIES
15 CENTIMOS
(19)

1937 (13 May). *Coronation, surch. as T* **19.**
164 **126** 15 c. on 1½d. maroon (B.) 8 8

MOROCCO AGENCIES
10
CENTIMOS
(20)

MOROCCO AGENCIES
10
CENTIMOS
(21)

1937–52. *King George VI, surch. as T* **20.**
165 **128** 5 c. on ½d. green (B.) .. 8 8
166 „ 10 c. on 1d. scarlet 8 10
167 „ 15 c. on 1½d. red-brn. (B.) 8 10
168 „ 25 c. on 2½d. ultramarine 8 10
169 **129** 40 c. on 4d. grey-green .. 35 35
170 **130** 70 c. on 7d. emerald-green 15 25
171 „ 1 p. on 10d. turq.-blue.. 15 40
165/171 .. .. *Set of* 7 85 1·25

Dates of issue:—June '37, 5 c., 10 c. 25 c.; 4 Aug. '37, 15 c.; Sept. '40, 40 c., 70 c.; 16 June '52, 1 p.

1940 (6 May). *Centenary of First Adhesive Postage Stamps, surch. as T* **21.**
172 **134** 5 c. on ½d. green (B.) .. 8 15
173 „ 10 c. on 1d. scarlet .. 8 15
174 „ 15 c. on 1½d. red-brn. (B.) 10 35
175 „ 25 c. on 2½d. ultramarine 12 25

25
CENTIMOS
MOROCCO AGENCIES
(22)

45 PESETAS
MOROCCO AGENCIES
(23)

1948 (26 Apr.). *Silver Wedding, surch. with T* **22** *or* **23**.
176 **137** 25 c. on 2½d. ultramarine 8 8
177 **138** 45 p. on £1 blue .. .. 6·00 9·50

1948 (29 July). *Olympic Games, variously surch. as T* **22**.
178 **139** 25 c. on 2½d. ultramarine 8 15
179 **140** 30 c. on 3d. violet .. 8 15
180 **141** 60 c. on 6d. bright purple 10 15
181 **142** 1 p. 20 c. on 1s. brown .. 25 45
a. Surch. double .. £150

1951 (3 May)–**52**. *King George VI, surch. as T* **20**.
182 **128** 5 c. on ½d. pale orange .. 8 15
183 „ 10 c. on 1d. light ultram. 8 15
184 „ 15 c. on 1½d. pale green .. 8 15
185 „ 25 c. on 2½d. pale scarlet 15 15
186 **129** 40 c. on 4d. light ultramarine (26.5.52) .. 10 30

1954–55. *Queen Elizabeth II (Tudor Crown wmk.), surch. as T* **20**.
187 **154** 5 c. on ½d. orange-red (1.9.54) 5 10
188 „ 10 c. on 1d. ultram. (1.3.55) 8 10

1956. *Queen Elizabeth II (St. Edward's Crown wmk.), surch. as T* **20**.
189 **154** 5 c. on ½d. orge.-red (June) 10 10
190 **156** 40 c. on 4d. ult. (15 Aug.) 20 40

Stamps surcharged in Spanish currency were withdrawn from sale on December 31st, 1956.

IV. FRENCH CURRENCY.

Stamps surcharged in French currency were sold at British P.Os. in the French Zone.

MOROCCO AGENCIES 25 CENTIMES (24) MOROCCO AGENCIES 1 FRANC (25)

1917–24. *King George V, surch. as T* **24** *or* **25** *(1 f.). W* **100**.
191 **105** 3 c. on ½d. green (R.) .. 5 45
192 „ 5 c. on ½d. green .. 5 5
193 **104** 10 c. on 1d. scarlet .. 12 15
194 **105** 15 c. on 1½d. red-brown .. 65 10
195 **104** 25 c. on 2½d. blue .. 12 8
196 **106** 40 c. on 4d. slate-green .. 50 20
197 **107** 50 c. on 5d. yell.-brn. ('23) 65 65
198 **108** 75 c. on 9d. olive-grn. ('24) 30 40
199 „ 1 f. on 10d. turq.-blue .. 50 50
a. Opt. double, one albino 30·00
191/199 .. .. *Set of* 9 2·50 2·25

1924–32. *King George V, surch. as T* **25**, *but closer vertical spacing.*
200 **109** 3 f. on 2s. 6d. choc.-brn. 5·00 2·25
a. Major re-entry .. £150 £160
b. Reddish brown .. 9·50 2·50
201 „ 6 f. on 5s. rose-red ('32) 17·00 14·00
200/1 H/S "Specimen" *Set of* 2 30·00

1925–34. *King George V, surch. as T* **24** *or* **25** *(1 f.). W* **111**.
202 **105** 5 c. on ½d. green .. 10 30
203 **104** 10 c. on 1d. scarlet .. 8 10
204 **105** 15 c. on 1½d. red-brown 65 65
205 **104** 25 c. on 2½d. blue .. 10 10
206 **106** 40 c. on 4d. grey-green .. 35 20
207 **107** 50 c. on 5d. yellow-brown 35 10
208 **108** 75 c. on 9d. olive-green .. 70 10
209 „ 90 c. on 9d. olive-green .. 45 80
210 „ 1 f. on 10d. turquoise-bl. 25 12
211 „ 1 f. 50 on 1s. bistre-brn. (H/S S. £12) .. 65 1·10
202/211 .. .. *Set of* 10 3·25 3·00

1935 (8 May). *Silver Jubilee, surch. as T* **17**, *but in French currency.*
212 **123** 5 c. on ½d. green (B.) .. 8 8
213 „ 10 c. on 1d. scarlet (B.) .. 55 80
214 „ 15 c. on 1½d. red-brn. (B.) 12 25
215 „ 25 c. on 2½d. blue (R.) .. 20 20

1935–37. *King George V, surch. as T* **24** *or* **25** *(1 f.).*
216 **118** 5 c. on ½d. green .. 8 8
217 **119** 10 c. on 1d. scar. (2.3.36) 8 8
218 **118** 15 c. on 1½d. red-brown .. 15 15
219 **119** 25 c. on 2½d. ultram. ('36) 10 10
220 **120** 40 c. on 4d. deep grey-green (2.12.36) .. 10 10
221 **121** 50 c. on 5d. yell.-brn. ('36) 10 10
222 **122** 90 c. on 9d. deep olive-green (17.2.37) .. 20 20
223 „ 1 f. on 10d. turquoise-blue (17.2.37) .. 12 12
224 „ 1 f. 50 on 1s. bistre-brn. (20.7.37) (Optd. S. £11) 20 20

1935–36. *King George V (Waterlow re-engraved ptgs.), surch. as T* **25**, *but closer vertical spacing.*
225 **109** 3 f. on 2s. 6d. chocolate-brown (No. 450) .. 3·75 4·00
226 „ 6 f. on 5s. bright rose-red (No. 451) (17.6.36) .. 11·00 13·00
216/226 .. .. *Set of* 11 14·00 17·00
225/6 H/S "Specimen" *Set of* 2 30·00

1936. *King Edward VIII, surch. as T* **18**, *but in French currency.*
227 **124** 5 c. on ½d. green .. 8 8
a. Bar through "POSTAGE" .. .. 50·00
228 „ 15 c. on 1½d. red-brown .. 12 8

1937 (13 May). *Coronation, surch. as T* **19**, *but in French currency.*
229 **126** 15 c. on 1½d. maroon (B.) 8 8

1937 (June). *King George VI, surch. as T* **20**, *but in French currency.*
230 **128** 5 c. on ½d. green (B.) .. 8 10

Stamps surcharged in French currency were withdrawn from sale on 8th January, 1938.

V. TANGIER INTERNATIONAL ZONE.

This Zone was established in 1914 and the first specially overprinted stamps issued in 1927.

PRICES. Our note re U.K. usage (at beginning of Section II) also applies to "TANGIER" optd. stamps.

TANGIER (26)

1927. *King George V, optd. with T* **26**. *W* **111**.
231 **105** ½d. green 35 8
a. Opt. double, one albino
232 **104** 1d. scarlet 25 8
a. Inverted "Q" for "O" (R. 20/3) .. ..
233 **105** 1½d. chestnut .. .. 1·25 75
234 **106** 2d. orange 45 10
231/234 Optd. "Specimen" *Set of* 4 65·00

1934–35. *King George V, optd. with T* **26**.
235 **118** ½d. green 40 25
236 **119** 1d. scarlet 80 25
237 **118** 1½d. red-brown 15 10

TANGIER TANGIER (27)

1935 (8 May). *Silver Jubilee, optd. with T* **27**.
238 **123** ½d. green (B.) 25 30
239 „ 1d. scarlet 65 70
240 „ 1½d. red-brown (B.) .. 20 20

1936. *King Edward VIII, optd. with T* **26**.
241 **124** ½d. green 8 8
242 „ 1d. scarlet 8 8
243 „ 1½d. red-brown 8 8

TANGIER TANGIER (28)

1937 (13 May). *Coronation, optd. with T* **28**.
244 **126** 1½d. maroon (B.) .. 8 8

TANGIER (29)

1937. *King George VI, optd. with T* **29**.
245 **128** ½d. green (B.) (June) .. 8 12
246 „ 1d. scarlet (June) .. 8 12
247 „ 1½d. red-brn. (B.) (4 Aug.) 8 15

TANGIER (30) TANGIER (31)

1940 (6 May). *Centenary of First Adhesive Postage Stamps, optd. with T* **30**.
248 **134** ½d. green (B.) 8 10
249 „ 1d. scarlet 10 15
250 „ 1½d. red-brown (B.) .. 20 30

1944. *King George VI, optd. with T* **29**.
251 **128** ½d. pale green (B.) .. 8 12
252 „ 1d. pale scarlet 25 30

1946 (11 June). *Victory, optd. as T* **31**.
253 **135** 2½d. ultramarine .. 15 8
254 **136** 3d. violet 15 10

The opt. on No. 254 is smaller (23 × 2½ mm.).

1948 (26 Apr.). *Royal Silver Wedding, optd. with T* **30**.
255 **137** 2½d. ultramarine 8 8
a. Opt. omitted (in vert. pr. with stamp optd. at top) £400
256 **138** £1 blue .. .. 6·00 9·00

No. 255a comes from a sheet in which the overprint is misplaced downwards resulting in the complete absence of the opt. from the six stamps of the top row. On the rest of the sheet the opt. falls at the top of each stamp instead of at the foot.

1948 (29 July). *Olympic Games, optd. with T* **30**.
257 **139** 2½d. ultramarine 8 8
258 **140** 3d. violet 8 8
259 **141** 6d. bright purple .. 10 10
260 **142** 1s. brown 15 15

1949 (1 Jan). *King George VI, optd. with T* **29**.
261 **128** 2d. pale orange 8 15
262 „ 2½d. light ultramarine .. 8 15
263 „ 3d. pale violet 8 15
264 **129** 4d. grey-green 25 25
265 „ 5d. brown 20 40
266 „ 6d. purple 10 20
267 **130** 7d. emerald-green 12 30
268 „ 8d. bright carmine .. 20 40
269 „ 9d. deep olive-green .. 12 40
270 „ 10d. turquoise-blue .. 15 40
271 „ 11d. plum 20 45
272 „ 1s. bistre-brown .. 20 40
273 **131** 2s. 6d. yellow-green .. 1·50 2·00
274 „ 5s. red .. .. 4·00 5·50
275 **132** 10s. ultramarine .. .. 7·50 9·00
261/275 .. .. *Set of* 15 13·00 18·00

1949 (10 Oct.). *75th Anniv. of U.P.U., optd. with T* **30**.
276 **143** 2½d. ultramarine 8 15
277 **144** 3d. violet 10 20
278 **145** 6d. bright purple .. 12 30
279 **146** 1s. brown 20 40

1950–51. *King George VI, optd. with T* **29** *or* **30** *(shilling values).*
280 **128** ½d. pale orange .. 8 10
281 „ 1d. light ultramarine .. 8 10
282 „ 1½d. pale green 8 20
283 „ 2d. pale red-brown .. 10 30
284 „ 2½d. pale scarlet 10 15
285 **129** 4d. light ultramarine .. 20 30
286 **147** 2s. 6d. yellow-green .. 65 75
287 **148** 5s. red .. .. 1·10 1·50
288 **149** 10s. ultramarine .. .. 3·50 5·50
280/288 .. .. *Set of* 9 5·50 8·00

Dates of issue:—2.10.50, 4d.; 3.5.51, others.

1952–54. *Queen Elizabeth II (Tudor Crown wmk.), optd. with T* **29**.
289 **154** ½d. orange-red (31.8.53) 5 5
290 „ 1d. ultramarine (31.8.53) 5 5
291 „ 1½d. green (5.12.52) 5 5
292 „ 2d. red-brown (31.8.53) 5 5
293 **155** 2½d. carm.-red (5.12.52) .. 8 5
294 „ 3d. dp. lilac (B.) (18.1.54) 5 8
295 **156** 4d. ultramarine (2.11.53) 12 12

296	157	5d. brown (6.7.53) ..	30	60
297	„	6d. reddish pur. (18.1.54)	12	10
298	„	7d. bright green (18.1.54)	30	60
299	158	8d. magenta (6.7.53) ..	30	60
300	„	9d. bronze-green (8.2.54)	25	25
301	„	10d. Prussian bl. (8.2.54)	40	60
302	„	11d. brown-purple (8.2.54)	40	60
303	159	1s. bistre-brown (6.7.53)	20	20
304	160	1s. 3d. green (2.11.53) ..	25	30
305	159	1s. 6d. grey-bl. (2.11.53)	30	30
289/305		.. .. *Set of* 17	3·00	4·00

1953 (3 June). *Coronation, optd. with T* **30**.

306	161	2½d. carmine-red	20	25
307	162	4d. ultramarine	40	70
308	163	1s. 3d. dp. yellow-green	90	1·40
309	164	1s. 6d. deep grey-blue ..	1·00	1·60

1955 (23 Sept.). *Queen Elizabeth II, optd. with T* **30**.

310	166	2s. 6d. black-brown ..	1·00	1·50
311	167	5s. rose-red	2·50	2·75
312	168	10s. ultramarine	5·00	6·00

1956. *Queen Elizabeth II (St. Edward's Crown wmk.), optd. with T* **29**.

313	154	½d. orge.-red (21 March)	5	5
314	„	1d. ultram. (13 April) ..	8	8
315	„	1½d. green (22 Oct.)	20	25
316	„	2d. red-brown (25 July)	25	30
317	„	2d. lt. red-brn. (10 Dec.)	15	25
318	155	2½d. carm.-red (19 Dec.)	25	25
319	„	3d. dp. lilac (B.) (22 Oct.)	25	25
320	156	4d. ultramarine (25 June)	25	30
321	157	6d. reddish pur. (22 Oct.)	25	25
322	160	1s. 3d. green (26 Nov.) ..	40	65
313/22		.. .. *Set of* 10	1·90	2·40

1857-1957 **1857-1957 TANGIER**

TANGIER

(32) (33)

1957 (1 Apr.). *Centenary of British Post Office in Tangier.* (a) *Nos.* 540/2 *and* 543b/56 *optd. as T* **32** *or* **33** (7d.).

323	154	½d. orange-red	5	5
324	„	1d. ultramarine	5	5
325	„	1½d. green	5	5
326	„	2d. light red-brown ..	5	5
327	155	2½d. carmine-red	5	5
328	„	3d. deep lilac (B.) ..	5	5
329	156	4d. ultramarine	8	8
330	157	5d. brown	10	12
331	„	6d. reddish purple ..	12	12
332	„	7d. bright green ..	20	20
333	158	8d. magenta	20	20
334	„	9d. bronze-geen	20	20
		a. "TANGIER" omitted	£1400	
335	„	10d. Prussian blue ..	20	20
336	„	11d. brown-purple ..	25	25
337	159	1s. bistre-brown ..	20	20
338	160	1s. 3d. green ..	25	25
339	159	1s. 6d. grey-blue ..	30	30
		(b) *Nos.* 536/8 *optd. as T* **32**.		
340	166	2s. 6d. black-brown ..	75	1·50
		a. Hyphen omitted ..	50·00	
		b. Hyphen inserted ..	25·00	
341	167	5s. rose-red	1·00	2·00
		a. Hyphen omitted ..	50·00	
		b. Hyphen inserted ..	4·50	
342	168	10s. ultramarine ..	2·50	4·00
		a. Hyphen omitted ..	55·00	
		b. Hyphen inserted ..	5·00	
323/42		.. .. *Set of* 20	6·00	9·00

Nos. 340a/b, 341a/b and 342 a/b occur on stamp No. 34 in the sheet of 40 (4×10). They are best collected in marginal blocks of four from the bottom left corner of the sheet. Specialists recognise two forms of No. 340b; one where the hyphen on stamp No. 34 was inserted separately to correct the error, No. 340a; the other from a later printing where a new and corrected overprinting plate was used. (*Price* £6 *un.*)

All stamps overprinted "TANGIER" were withdrawn from sale on April 30th, 1957.

MOSUL.

BRITISH OCCUPATION.

POSTAGE

I.E.F. 'D'

1 Anna **4** **4**

(1) I (*normal*). II (*small*).

(*a*) Central design shows large "toughra" or sign-manual of El Ghazi 7 mm. high.

(*b*) Smaller "toughra" of Sultan Rechad 5½ mm. high.

1919 (Feb.). *Turkish Fiscal stamps surch. as T* **1**. *P* 11½ (½ *a.*), 12 (1 *a.*) *or* 12½ (*others*).

1	½ a. on 1 pi. green and red ..	70	70
2	1 a. on 20 pa. black/*red* (*a*) ..	70	70
3	1 a. on 20 pa. black/*red* (*b*) ..	2·00	1·50
	a. Imperf. between (pair) ..	£100	
4	2½ a. on 1 pi. mauve & yell. (*b*)	80	80
	a. No bar to fraction	10·00	10·00
5	3 a. on 20 pa. green (*a*) ..	80	80
6	3 a. on 20 pa. grn. & orge. (*b*)	7·00	8·00
7	4 a. on 1 pi. dark violet (*a*) (I)	1·50	1·50
	a. "4" omitted ..	£500	
	b. Small "4" (II)	2·00	2·00
8	8 a. on 10 pa. lake (*a*) ..	2·00	2·00
	a. Surch. inverted	£120	£120
	b. Surch. double	£120	£120
	c. No comma after "D" ..	10·00	
	d. Inverted. No comma after "D"		
	e. Error. 8 a. on 1 pi. dark violet	£500	

MUSCAT.

An independent Arab Sultanate in Eastern Arabia with an Indian postal administration from 1864 using unoverprinted Indian stamps.

The following issues were on sale only in Muscat Town.

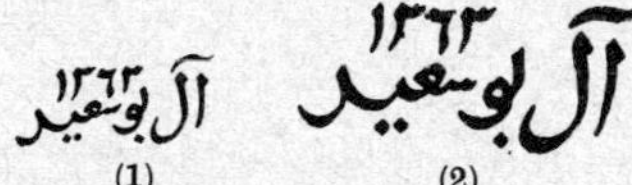

(1) (2)

1944 (20 Nov.). *Bicentenary of Al-Busaid Dynasty. Stamps of India optd.* ("AL BUSAID 1363" *in Arabic script*) *as T* **1** *or* **2** (*rupee values*).

1	100*a*	3 p. slate	8	10
2	„	½ a. purple	8	10
3	„	9 p. green	8	10
4	„	1 a. carmine	8	10
5	101	1½ a. dull violet	8	10
		a. Opt. double ..	85·00	
6	„	2 a. vermilion	8	10
7	„	3 a. bright violet ..	8	12
8	„	3½ a. bright blue	8	12
9	102	4 a. brown	8	12
10	„	6 a. turquoise-green ..	10	20
11	„	8 a. slate-violet	15	35
12	„	12 a. lake	20	40
13	103	14 a. purple	30	45
14	100	1 r. grey and red-brown	35	80
15	„	2 r. purple and brown ..	55	1·75
1/15		.. .. *Set of* 15	2·00	4·50

OFFICIAL STAMPS.

1944 (20 Nov.). *Bicentenary of Al-Busaid Dynasty. Official stamps of India optd. as T* **1** *or* **2** (1 *r.*).

O 1	O 20	3 p. slate	8	12
O 2	„	½ a. purple	8	12
O 3	„	9 p. green	8	12
O 4	„	1 a. carmine	8	12
O 5	„	1½ a. dull violet	8	12
O 6	„	2 a. vermilion	8	12
O 7	„	2½ a. bright violet ..	8	12
O 8	„	4 a. brown	8	20
O 9	„	8 a. slate-violet ..	12	35
O10	100	1 r. grey and red-brown (No. O138) ..	25	90
O1/O10		.. .. *Set of* 10	80	2·00

From December 1947 there was a Pakistani postal administration and stamps of Pakistan were used until 31st March 1948. The subsequent British administration operated from 1st April 1948 to 29th April 1966 when the stamps of the British Postal Agencies in Eastern Arabia were used (*q.v.*).

Later issues for this area will be found listed under Oman in Volume 3 of the Stanley Gibbons Foreign Overseas Catalogue.

NAGALAND.

Labels inscribed "NAGALAND" with currency in cents and chaplees are considered to be propaganda labels.

NATAL.

1

2

3

4 5

(Embossed in plain relief on coloured wove paper.)

1857 (26 May, *the* 1d. *in* **1858**). *Imperf.*

1	1	1d. rose	—	£650
2	„	1d. buff	—	£350
3	„	1d. blue	—	£450
4	2	3d. rose	—	£150
		a. Tête-bêche (pair)		
5	3	6d. green	—	£450
6	4	9d. blue	—	£3000
7	5	1s. buff	—	£2000

All the above have been reprinted more than once, and the early reprints of some values cannot always be distinguished with certainty from originals.

Stamps on surface-coloured paper, *P* 12½, are fiscals.

NOTE.—*The value of the above stamps depends on their dimensions, and the clearness of the embossing, but our prices are for fine used.*

6

7

(Recess. Perkins, Bacon & Co.)

1859–60. *No wmk. P* 14.
9 **6** 1d. rose-red .. .. .. 40·00 30·00
10 ,, 3d. blue .. .. .. 30·00 14·00

1861. *No wmk. Intermediate perf.* 14 *to* 16.
11 **6** 3d. blue .. .. .. 65·00 25·00

1862. *No wmk. Rough perf.* 14 *to* 16.
12 **6** 3d. blue .. .. .. 28·00 10·00
a. Imperf. between (pair) .. £450
b. Imperf. (pair) .. .. — £450
13 ,, 6d. grey .. .. .. 45·00 16·00

1862. *Wmk. Small Star. Rough. perf.* 14 *to* 16.
15 **6** 1d. rose-red .. .. .. 35·00 18·00

The 1d. and 3d. wmk. Star, *imperf.*, are proofs, and are therefore not included. The 3d. wmk. Star, *perforated*, is believed to exist only with forged watermark.

(Recess. D.L.R.)

1863. *Thick paper. No wmk. P* 13.
18 **6** 1d. lake .. .. .. 25·00 10·00
19 ,, 1d. carmine-red .. .. .. 25·00 7·00

1864. *Wmk. Crown CC. P* 12½.
20 **6** 1d. brown-red .. .. .. 40·00 12·00
21 ,, 1d. rose .. .. .. 30·00 10·00
22 ,, 1d. bright red .. .. .. 30·00 10·00
23 ,, 6d. lilac .. .. .. 20·00 6·00
24 ,, 6d. violet .. .. .. 14·00 10·00

(Typo. De La Rue.)

1867 (April). *Wmk. Crown CC. P* 14.
25 **7** 1s. green .. .. .. 40·00 10·00

1869 (23 Aug.). *Optd. horiz. in Natal. No wmk.* (3*d.*), *wmk. Crown CC* (*others*). *P* 14 *or* 14–16 (3*d.*), 12½ (1*d.*, 6*d.*) *or* 14 (1*s.*).

POSTAGE *Tall capitals.*

26 **6** 1d. rose .. .. .. 85·00 20·00
27 ,, 1d. bright red .. .. .. 90·00 20·00
28 ,, 3d. blue (No. 10) .. ..
28*a* ,, 3d. blue (No. 11) .. .. £130 80·00
28*b* ,, 3d. blue (No. 12) .. .. 90·00 22·00
29 ,, 6d. lilac .. .. .. — 18·00
30 ,, 6d. violet .. .. .. £120 18·00
31 **7** 1s. green .. .. .. — £400

Postage. 12¾ *mm. long.*

32 **6** 1d. rose .. .. .. 90·00 22·00
33 ,, 1d. bright red .. .. .. 90·00 22·00
a. Opt. double .. .. — £200
34 , 3d. blue (No. 10) .. .. — 85·00
34*a* ,, 3d. blue (No. 11) .. .. £130 65·00
34*b* ,, 3d. blue (No. 12) .. .. £120 22·00
35 ,, 6d. lilac .. .. .. £100 18·00
36 ,, 6d. violet .. .. .. 90·00 18·00
37 **7** 1s. green .. .. .. — £150

Postage. 13¾ *mm. long.*

38 **6** 1d. rose .. .. .. £140 40·00
39 ,, 1d. bright red .. .. .. — 40·00
40 ,, 3d. blue (No. 10) .. ..
40*a* ,, 3d. blue (No. 11) .. ..
40*b* ,, 3d. blue (No. 12) .. .. £325 90·00
41 ,, 6d. lilac .. .. .. — 40·00
42 ,, 6d. violet .. .. .. £275 40·00
43 **7** 1s. green .. .. .. — £550

Postage. 14½ *to* 15½ *mm. long.*

44 **6** 1d. rose .. .. .. £140 75·00
45 ,, 1d. bright red .. .. .. £150 70·00
46 ,, 3d. blue (No. 10) .. ..
46*a* ,, 3d. blue (No. 11) .. .. — 80·00
46*b* ,, 3d. blue (No. 12) .. .. — 80·00
47 ,, 6d. lilac .. .. .. — 24·00
48 ,, 6d. violet .. .. .. £325 25·00
49 **7** 1s. green .. .. .. — £550

POSTAGE. *With a stop.*

50 **6** 1d. rose .. .. .. 22·00 10·00
51 ,, 1d. bright red .. .. .. 42·00 10·00
52 ,, 3d. blue (No. 10) .. .. 65·00 15·00
53 ,, 3d. blue (No. 11) .. .. 30·00 14·00
54 ,, 3d. blue (No. 12) .. .. 50·00 12·00
a. Opt. double .. .. — £225
54*b* ,, 6d. lilac .. .. .. 30·00 14·00
55 ,, 6d. violet .. .. .. 28·00 14·00
56 **7** 1s. green .. .. .. 30·00 14·00

All values exist with this overprint at top or bottom of stamp.

POSTAGE
(8)

1870. *No.* 25 *optd. with T* **8**.
57 **7** 1s. green (C.) £1200
58 ,, 1s. green (Bk.) £650 £400
a. Opt. double £1100 £425
59 ,, 1s. green (G.) .. .. .. 11·00 4·00

For No. 57 but printed in orange, see No. 108.

POSTAGE POSTAGE
(9)
POSTAGE
(10)
POSTAGE POSTAGE
(11)

1870–73. *Optd. with T* **9**. *Wmk. Crown CC. P* 12½.
60 **6** 1d. bright red .. .. .. 20·00 7·00
61 ,, 3d. bright blue (R.) .. .. 22·00 7·50
62 ,, 6d. mauve .. .. .. 40·00 13·00

1873 (July). *Optd. up centre of stamp with T* **10**. *Wmk. Crown CC. P* 14.
63 **7** 1s. purple-brown .. .. 22·00 4·25

1874 (July). *No.* 21 *optd. with T* **11**.
65 **7** 1d. rose .. .. .. 35·00 7·00
a. Opt. double .. ..

12

13

14

15

16

(Typo. De La Rue).

1874–78. *Wmk. Crown CC. P* 14.
66 **12** 1d. dull rose .. .. 4·00 50
67 ,, 1d. bright rose .. .. 3·75 45
68 **13** 3d. blue .. .. .. 7·00 5·00
a. Perf. 14×12½ £450 £375
69 **14** 4d. brown (1878) .. .. 12·00 4·50
a. Perf. 12½ .. .. .. 75·00 22·00
70 **15** 6d. lilac .. .. .. 6·50 2·50
71 **16** 5s. maroon .. .. .. 30·00 7·50
a. Perf. 15½×15 .. .. 28·00 22·00
72 ,, 5s. rose .. .. .. 20·00 5·50
73 ,, 5s. carmine (H/S S. £30) .. 18·00 6·50

The 5s. stamps normally have wmk. sideways.

POSTAGE
(17)

POSTAGE
(18)

1875. *Wmk. Crown CC. P* 14 (1*s.*) *or* 12½ (*others*).

(*a*) *Optd. with T* **17**.
76 **6** 1d. rose .. .. .. 24·00 11·00
a. Opt. double £200 £180
77 ,, 1d. bright red .. .. 22·00 20·00

(*b*) *Optd. with T* **18** (14½ *mm. long, without stop*).
81 **6** 1d. rose .. .. .. 11·00 11·00
a. Opt. inverted £300 £150
82 ,, 1d. yellow .. .. .. 12·00 13·00
83 ,, 6d. violet .. .. .. 10·00 2·00
a. Opt. double .. .. — £225
b. Opt. inverted £275 £120
84 **7** 1s. green .. .. .. 12·00 2·25
a. Opt. double .. .. — £125

·POSTAGE

½
HALF
(19)

(21)

There are several varieties of this surcharge, of which T **19** is an example. They may be divided as follows:

(*a*) "½" 4½ mm. high, "2" has straight foot.
(*b*) As last but "½" is 4 mm. high.
(*c*) As last but "2" has curled foot.
(*d*) "½" 3½ mm. high, "2" has straight foot.
(*e*) As last but "2" has curled foot.
(*f*) As last but "2" smaller.

As the "½" and "HALF" were overprinted separately, they vary in relative position, and are frequently overlapping.

1877 (13 Feb.). *No.* 66 *surch. as T* **19**.
85 **12** ½d. on 1d. rose (*a*) .. .. 6·00 22·00
a. "½" double .. ..
86 ,, ½d. on 1d. rose (*b*) .. .. 24·00
87 ,, ½d. on 1d. rose (*c*) .. .. 20·00
88 ,, ½d. on 1d. rose (*d*) .. .. 11·00
89 ,, ½d. on 1d. rose (*e*) .. .. 12·00
90 ,, ½d. on 1d. rose (*f*) .. .. 12·00

1877–79. *T* **6** (*wmk. Crown CC, P* 12½) *surch. as T* **21**.
91 ½d. on 1d. yellow .. .. 3·25 3·75
a. Surch. inverted .. .. 85·00 85·00
b. Surch. double .. .. 85·00 85·00
c. Surch. omitted (lower stamp, vertical pair).. .. .. £400 £375
d. "POSTAGE" omitted (in pair with normal).. .. .. £450
e. "S" of "POSTAGE" omitted 70·00 70·00
f. "T" of "POSTAGE" omitted 70·00

92 1d. on 6d. violet .. .. 5·50 1·40
a. "S" of "POSTAGE" omitted £100
93 1d. on 6d. rose .. .. 12·00 5·50
a. Surch. inverted .. .. — 70·00
b. Surch. double .. .. — 85·00
c. Surch. double, one inverted .. £100 £100
d. Surch. four times .. .. £140 70·00
e. "S" of "POSTAGE" omitted £100

No. 93c is known with one surcharge showing variety "s" of "POSTAGE" omitted.

Other minor varieties exist in these surcharges.

23

ONE HALF-PENNY.

(24)

(Typo. D.L.R.)

1880 (13 Oct.). *Wmk. Crown CC. P* 14.
96 **23** ½d. blue-green 70 85
a. Imperf. between (vert. pair)

1882–89. *Wmk. Crown CA. P* 14.
97 **23** ½d. blue-green .. .. 12·00 5·00
a. Dull green 12 12
99 **12** 1d. rose (*shades*) 12 12
a. Carmine 85 15
100 **13** 3d. blue .. .. .. 12·00 5·00
101 ,, 3d. grey (1889) 12 12
102 **14** 4d. brown 50 30
103 **15** 6d. mauve 60 40
97a, 99a, 101/3 H/S "Specimen" *Set of* 5 £100

1885 (26 Jan.). *No.* 99 *surch. with T* **24**.
104 **12** ½d. on 1d. rose .. .. 4·00 3·50

TWO PENCE

(25)

NATAL POSTAGE TWO PENCE

26

TWOPENCE HALFPENNY

(27)

1886. *Surch. locally with T* **25**.
105 **13** 2d. on 3d. grey .. .. 5·00 3·50

(Typo. De La Rue.)

1887–89. *Wmk. Crown CA. P* 14.
106 **26** 2d. olive-green Die I* (Optd. S. £22) .. .. .. 5·00 30
107 ,, 2d. olive-green, Die II 40 30

* The differences between Dies I and II are shown in the Introduction.

1888. *Optd. with T* **8**, *by De La Rue.*
108 **7** 1s. orange (C.) (H/S S. £22) 50 30
a. Opt. double .. ..

1890. *Surch. locally with T* **27**.
109 **14** 2½d. on 4d. brown (H/S S. £40) .. .. 2·00 1·50
a. "TWOPENGE" .. 20·00 20·00
b. "HALFPENN" .. — 60·00
c. Surch. double .. .. 90·00 60·00
d. Surch. inverted .. .. 95·00 90·00

28

POSTAGE. Half-Penny

(29)

(Typo. De La Rue.)

1891 (June). *Wmk. Crown CA. P* 14.
113 **28** 2½d. bright blue (H/S S. £22) 35 35

POSTAGE.

Varieties of long-tailed letters.

1895. (12 Mar.). *No.* 24 *surch. with T* **29** *in carmine.*
114 ½d. on 6d. violet (H/S S. £20) 35 40
a. "Ealf-Penny" .. .. 6·50
b. "Half-Penny" .. .. 5·00
c. No stop after "POSTAGE" .. 5·50
d. Long "P" 80
e. Long "T" 80
f. Long "A" 80
g. Long "P" and "T" .. 90
h. Long "P" and "A" .. 80 1·10
i. Long "T" and "A" .. 80 1·10
k. Long "P", "T" and "A" 90
l. Surcharge double, one vertical 90·00
la. Surcharge double, "Ealf-Penny"
lb. Surcharge double, "Half-Penny"

No. 114 is known with surcharge double and widely spaced, but the second surcharge is extremely faint.

No. 114k is known without stop and also with comma instead of a stop after "POSTAGE".

HALF

(30)

1895 (18 Mar.). *No.* 99 *surch. with T* **30**.
125 HALF on 1d. rose (*shades*) (H/S S. £25) 35 40
a. Surch. double £110 £120
b. "H" with longer left limb .. 8·00

No. 125b occurs on the second, fourth, sixth etc., stamps of the first vertical row of the right-hand pane. It was very soon corrected.

In some printings what appears to be a broken "E" (with the top limb removed) was used instead of "L" in "HALF" on the last stamp in the sheet. (*Price* £12)

31

(Typo. De La Rue.)

1902–3. *Inscr.* "POSTAGE REVENUE". *Wmk. Crown CA. P* 14.
127 **31** ½d. blue-green 8 8
128 ,, 1d. carmine 8 8
129 ,, 1½d. green and black .. 12 20
130 ,, 2d. red and olive-green .. 40 20
131 ,, 2½d. bright blue 45 45
132 ,, 3d. purple and grey .. 40 12
133 ,, 4d. carmine and cinnamon 55 65
134 ,, 5d. black and orange .. 85 65
135 ,, 6d. green & brown-purple 90 40
136 ,, 1s. carmine and pale blue 1·25 45
137 ,, 2s. green and bright violet 5·50 4·50
138 ,, 2s. 6d. purple .. .. 7·00 6·00
139 ,, 4s. deep rose and maize .. 11·00 7·50
127/139 .. .. *Set of* 13 26·00 19·00
127/39 Optd. "Specimen" *Set of* 13 85·00

32

(Typo. D.L.R.)

1902–3. *Wmk. Crown CC. P* 14.
140 **32** 5s. dull blue and rose .. 8·50 3·50
141 ,, 10s. dp. rose & chocolate .. 22·00 6·00
142 ,, £1 black and bright blue 65·00 22·00
143 ,, £1 10s. grn. & vio. (Optd. S. £50) .. .. £150 40·00
144 ,, £5 mauve & blk. (Optd. S. £75) £850 £110
145 ,, £10 green & orge. (Optd. S. £225) £5000
145a ,, £20 red & green (Optd. S. £350) £11000
140/2 Optd. "Specimen" *Set of* 3 75·00

USED HIGH VALUES. Collectors are warned against fiscally used high value Natal stamps with penmarks cleaned off and forged postmarks added.

1904–8. *Wmk. Mult. Crown CA. P* 14.
146 **31** ½d. blue-green 8 8
147 ,, 1d. rose-carmine 8 8
148 ,, 1d. deep carmine 20 8
149 ,, 2d. red and olive-green .. 25 15
152 ,, 4d. carmine and cinnamon 65 40
153 ,, 5d. black & orange (1908) 1·25 1·25
155 ,, 1s. carmine and pale blue 9·00 2·75
156 ,, 2s. dull grn. & brt. violet 9·00 7·00
157 ,, 2s. 6d. purple .. .. 9·50 6·00
162 **32** £1 10s. brown-orange and deep purple, C (1908) (Optd. S. £150) .. £850
146/157 .. .. *Set of* 9 27·00 16·00

1908–9. *Inscr.* "POSTAGE POSTAGE". *Wmk. Mult. Crown CA. P* 14.
165 **31** 6d. dull and bright purple 1·25 85
166 ,, 1s. black/*green* .. 2·25 90
167 ,, 2s. pur. and brt. blue/*blue* 5·50 2·50
168 ,, 2s. 6d. black and red/*blue* 7·00 2·50
169 **32** 5s. green and red/*yellow* 14·00 6·50
170 ,, 10s. green and red/*green* .. 30·00 20·00
171 ,, £1 purple and black/*red* £130 70·00
165/170 .. .. *Set of* 6 55·00 30·00
165/71 Optd. "Specimen" *Set of* 7 £140

FISCALS USED FOR POSTAGE.

1869. *Embossed on coloured wove, surfaced paper. P* 12½.
F1 **1** 1d. yellow .. .. .. 13·00 26·00

1873 (July). *Wmk. Crown CC. P* 14.
F2 **7** 1s. purple-brown .. .. 7·00 13·00

1875. *Wmk. Crown CC. P* 12½.
F3 **6** 1d. yellow .. .. .. 2·00 7·00
F4 ,, 6d. rose .. .. .. 4·50 10·00

F 1

(Typo. D.L.R.)

1903. *Wmk. Crown CA. P* 14.
F5 **F 1** 5s. dull mauve & carmine 30·00 45·00
F6 ,, £1 green .. .. .. 35·00 45·00
F7 ,, £1 10s. dull mauve & blue 80·00 £100
F8 ,, £5 green and red .. £200 £225
F9 ,, £10 green and blue .. £500 £400

OFFICIAL STAMPS.

OFFICIAL

(O 1)

1904. *T* **31**, *wmk. Mult. Crown CA, optd. with Type* O **1**. *P* 14.
O1 ½d. blue-green 90 12
O2 1d. carmine 20 12
O3 2d. red and olive-green .. 2·50 2·25
O4 3d. purple and grey .. .. 1·00 1·40
O5 6d. green and brown-purple .. 5·00 4·00
O6 1s. carmine and pale blue .. 7·50 17·00

The use of stamps overprinted as above was discontinued after 30 May, 1907. Stamps perforated with the letters "N.G.R." were for use on Government Railways.

Natal now uses the stamps of South Africa.

NAURU.

I. BRITISH MANDATE.

NAURU (1) NAURU (2)

1916 (Oct.)–**23**. *Stamps of Great Britain (1912–22) overprinted.*

(*a*) *With T* **1** (12½ *mm. long*) *at foot.*

No.	Type	Description	Unused	Used
1	**105**	½d. green	12	20
		a. "NAUP.U"	80·00	
		b. Double opt., one albino	40·00	
2	**104**	1d. scarlet	15	30
		a. "NAUP.U"	80·00	
		b. Double opt., one albino	40·00	
3	**105**	1½d. red-brown (1923)	11·00	12·00
4	**106**	2d. orange (Die I)	20	40
		a. "NAUP.U"	80·00	
		b. Double opt., one albino	40·00	
5	,,	2d. orange (Die II) (1923)	18·00	18·00
6	**104**	2½d. blue	55	65
		a. "NAUP.U"	80·00	
		b. Double opt., one albino	40·00	
7	**106**	3d. bluish violet	75	85
		a. "NAUP.U"	80·00	
		b. Double opt., one albino	40·00	
8	,,	4d. slate-green	85	1·40
		a. "NAUP.U"	90·00	
		b. Double opt., one albino	45·00	
9	**107**	5d. yellow-brown	1·25	1·75
		a. "NAUP.U"	£120	
		b. Double opt., one albino	45·00	
10	,,	6d. purple, C	1·50	2·00
		a. "NAUP.U"	£120	
		b. Double opt., one albino	45·00	
11	**108**	9d. agate	2·00	2·50
		a. Double opt., one albino	70·00	
12	,,	1s. bis.-brn. (H/S S. £22)	2·50	3·00
		a. Double opt., one albino		
1/12		*Set of* 11	18·00	23·00

(*b*) *With T* **2** (13½ *mm. long*) *at centre* (1923).

No.	Type	Description	Unused	Used
13	**105**	½d. green	3·50	6·00
14	**104**	1d. scarlet	3·50	6·00
15	**105**	1½d. red-brown	3·50	6·00
		a. Double opt., one albino		
16	**106**	2d. orange (Die II)	7·50	15·00

There is a constant variety consisting of short left stroke to "N" which occurs on Nos. 1, 2, 4 (£9 *each*); 3 (£35); 5 (£35); 6, 7 (£12 *each*); 8, 9, 10 (£16 *each*); 11, 12 (£16 *each*). All unused prices.

NAURU
(3)

T **109** *optd. with T* **3**. *Waterlow printing.*

No.	Description	Unused	Used
17	5s. rose-carmine	£450	£550
18	10s. ind.-bl. (R.) (H/S S. £120)	£700	£800
	a. Double opt. one albino	£1000	

De La Rue printing

No.	Description	Unused	Used
19	2s. 6d. deep brown	£200	£250
	a. Double opt., one albino	£700	
	b. Treble opt., two albinos	£800	
20	2s. 6d. yellow-brown	25·00	32·00
	a. Re-entry		
21	2s. 6d. brown	26·00	35·00
22	5s. bright carmine (*shades*)	26·00	35·00
	a. Treble opt., two albinos	£350	
23	10s. pale blue (R.)	75·00	85·00
23*a*	10s. deep bright blue (R.)	£170	£180
19, 20, 22	H/S "Specimen" *Set of* 3	£150	

Bradbury, Wilkinson printing (1919).

No.	Description	Unused	Used
24	2s. 6d. chocolate-brown	22·00	25·00
	a. Major re-entry		
	b. Double opt., one albino	£100	
25	2s. 6d. pale brown	15·00	22·00
	a. Double opt., one albino	80·00	

II. AUSTRALIAN MANDATE.

PRINTERS. See note at beginning of Australia.

4

(Des. R. A. Harrison. Eng. T. S. Harrison. Recess. Note Printing Branch of the Treasury, Melbourne and from 1926 by the Commonwealth Bank of Australia.)

1924–48. *T* **4**. *No wmk. P* 11.

I. Rough surfaced, greyish paper (1924–34).
II. Shiny surfaced, white paper (1937–47).

No.	Description	I. Unused	I. Used	II. Unused	II. Used
26	½d. chestnut	60	1·25	2·50	3·00
	a. Perf. 14 ('47)	†		60	1·00
27	1d. green	60	1·40	1·25	1·60
28	1½d. scarlet	80	1·25	40	80
29	2d. orange	80	1·40	30	70
30	2½d. slate-blue	2·00	2·50	†	
30*a*	2½d. grnsh. bl. ('34)	2·00	2·75	†	
30*b*	2½d. dull blue	†		50	1·10
	ba. Imp. between (pair) ('48)	†		£1200	£1200
31	3d. pale blue	1·00	1·75	†	
31*a*	3d. greenish grey	†		50	1·00
32	4d. olive-green	1·60	2·00	1·00	1·25
33	5d. brown	1·60	1·75	60	90
34	6d. dull violet	2·50	3·00	90	1·40
35	9d. olive-brown	3·00	4·00	2·50	3·50
36	1s. brown-lake	3·50	4·00	2·00	2·50
37	2s. 6d. grey-green	8·00	9·00	8·00	9·00
38	5s. claret	25·00	27·00	22·00	25·00
39	10s. yellow	30·00	35·00	28·00	30·00
26I/39I	*Set of* 14	75·00	90·00	†	
26II/39II	*Set of* 15	†		65·00	75·00

HIS MAJESTY'S JUBILEE.

1910 - 1935
(5)

1935 (12 July). *Silver Jubilee. T* **4** (*surfaced paper*) *optd. with T* **5**.

No.	Description	Unused	Used
40	1½d. scarlet	15	25
41	2d. orange	30	45
42	2½d. dull blue	1·00	80
43	1s. brown-lake	2·00	1·75

6

(Recess. John Ash, Melbourne.)

1937 (10 May). *Coronation. P* 11.

No.	Type	Description	Unused	Used
44	**6**	1½d. scarlet	8	8
45	,,	2d. orange	8	10
46	,,	2½d. blue	8	10
47	,,	1s. purple	20	20

7. Nauruan Netting Fish.

8. Anibare Bay.

9. Loading Phosphate from Cantilever.

10. Frigate Bird.

11. Nauruan Canoe.

12. "Domaneab" (Meeting-house).

13. Palm Trees. **15.** Map of Nauru.

14. Buada Lagoon.

(Recess. Note Printing Branch, Commonwealth Bank, Melbourne, and from 1960 by Note Ptg. Branch, Reserve Bank of Australia, Melbourne.)

1954 (6 Feb.)–**61**. *Toned paper. P* 13½ × 14½ (*horiz.*) *or* 14½ × 13½ (*vert.*).

No.	Type	Description	Unused	Used
48	**7**	½d. deep violet	5	5
		a. Violet (8.5.61)	5	5

9	**8**	1d. bluish green	10	10
		a. Emerald-green (shades) (8.5.61)	10	12
0	**9**	3½d. scarlet	12	12
		a. Vermilion (1958).. ..		
1	**10**	4d. grey-blue	20	20
		a. Deep blue (1958).. ..		
2	**11**	6d. orange	25	25
3	**12**	9d. claret	40	35
4	**13**	1s. deep purple	50	40
5	**14**	2s. 6d. deep green ..	1·25	1·00
6	**15**	5s. magenta	2·75	2·00
8*a*/56		.. .. *Set of* 9	5·00	4·00

Nos. 48*a*, 49*a*, 50*a* and 51*a* are on white paper.

16. Micronesian Pigeon.

17. Poison Nut.

18. "Iyo" (*calophyllum*).

19. Black Lizard.

20. Capparis.

21. White Tern.

22. Coral Pinnacles.

23. Reed Warbler.

(Recess (10d., 2s. 3d.) or photo (others). Note Ptg. Branch, Reserve Bank of Australia, Melbourne.)

1963–65. *P* 13½ (*2d., 3d., 1s. 3d., 3s. 3d.*).

57	**16**	2d. black, blue, red-brown & orange-yell. (3.5.65)	8	8
58	**17**	3d. multicoloured (16.4.64)	10	10
59	**18**	5d. multicoloured, *p.* 13½ × 13 (22.4.63) ..	20	20
60	**19**	8d. black and green, *p.* 13 × 13½ (1.7.63) ..	30	30
61	**20**	10d. black, *p.* 14½ × 13½ (16.4.64)	50	40
62	**21**	1s. 3d. blue, black and yellow-green (3.5.65) ..	75	70
63	**22**	2s. 3d. ultramarine, *p.* 15 × 14½ (16.4.64) ..	1·50	90
64	**23**	3s. 3d. multicoloured (3.5.65)	2·25	1·50
57/64		.. .. *Set of* 8	5·00	3·75

1965 (14 APR.). *50th Anniv. of Gallipoli Landing. As T* **181** *of Australia, but slightly larger* (22 × 34½ *mm.*). *Photo.*

65	5d. sepia, black and emerald ..	30	30

(100 cents = $1 Australian.)

24. Anibare Bay. **25.** "Iyo" (*calophyllum*).

Recess (1, 2, 3, 5, 8, 10, 25c. and $1) or photo. (others).)

1966 (14 FEB.—25 MAY). *Decimal Currency. Various stamps with values in cents and dollars as T* **24/5** *and some colours changed. Recess printed stamps on helecon paper.*

66	**24**	1 c. deep blue	5	5
67	**7**	2 c. brown-purple (25 May)	5	5
68	**9**	3 c. bluish green (25 May)	8	8
69	**25**	4 c. multicoloured ..	8	8
70	**13**	5 c. deep ultram. (25 May)	10	10
71	**19**	7 c. black and chestnut ..	12	12
72	**20**	8 c. olive-green	15	15
73	**10**	10 c. red	20	20
74	**21**	15 c. blue, black and yellow-green (25 May) ..	50	50
75	**22**	25 c. deep brown (25 May)	60	60
76	**17**	30 c. multicoloured ..	75	85
77	**23**	35 c. multicoloured (25 May)	1·00	1·25
78	**16**	50 c. multicoloured ..	1·50	1·50
79	**15**	$1 magenta	3·00	3·00
66/79		.. .. *Set of* 14	7·00	7·50

The 25 c. is as T **22** but larger, 27½ × 24½ mm.

III. REPUBLIC.

Nauru became independent on 31st January 1968 and was later admitted into special membership of the British Commonwealth.

REPUBLIC
OF
NAURU

(**26**)

1968 (31 JAN.–15 MAY). *Nos. 66/79 optd. with T* **26.**

80	**24**	1 c. deep blue (R.) ..	5	5
81	**7**	2 c. brown-purple ..	5	5
82	**9**	3 c. bluish green	8	8
83	**25**	4 c. multicoloured (15.5.68)	8	8
84	**13**	5 c. deep ultramarine (R.)	10	10
85	**19**	7 c. black and chestnut (R.) (15.5.68)	12	12
86	**20**	8 c. olive-green (R.) ..	15	15
87	**10**	10 c. red	20	20
88	**21**	15 c. blue, blk. & yell.-grn.	2·50	1·25
89	**22**	25 c. deep brown (R.) ..	45	50
90	**17**	30 c. multicoloured (15.5.68)	50	65
91	**23**	35 c. multicoloured (15.5.68)	90	1·25
92	**16**	50 c. multicoloured ..	1·40	1·75
93	**15**	$1 magenta	3·00	3·25
80/93		.. .. *Set of* 14	8·50	8·50

27. " Towards the Sunrise ".

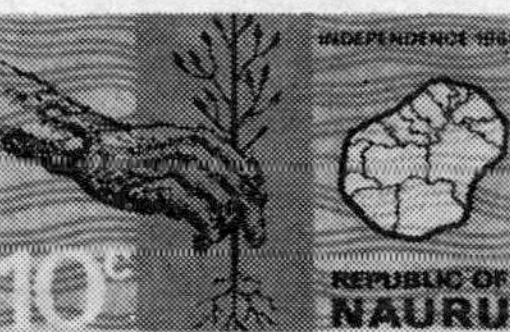

28. Planting Seedling, and Map.

(Des. H. Fallu (5 c.), Note Ptg. Branch (10 c.). Photo. Note Ptg. Branch, Reserve Bank of Australia, Melbourne.)

1968 (11 SEPT.). *Independence. P* 13½.

94	**27**	5 c. black, slate-lilac, orange-yellow & yellow-green	15	20
95	**28**	10 c. black, yellow-green and new blue	25	30

29. Flag of Independent Nauru.

(Des. J. Mason. Photo. Note Ptg. Branch, Reserve Bank of Australia, Melbourne.)

1969 (31 JAN.). *P* 13 × 13½.

96	**29**	15 c. yellow, orange and Royal blue	30	35

This is a definitive issue which was put on sale on the first anniversary of Independence.

30. Island, " C " and Stars.

(Des. R. Brooks. Litho. Format.)

1972 (7 FEB.). *25th Anniv. of South Pacific Commission. P* 14½ × 14.

97	**30**	25 c. multicoloured ..	55	60

Independence 1968-1973

(31)

1973 (31 JAN.). *Fifth Anniv. of Independence. No.* 96 *optd. with T* **31** *in gold.*
98 **29** 15 c. yellow, orange and Royal blue 75 75

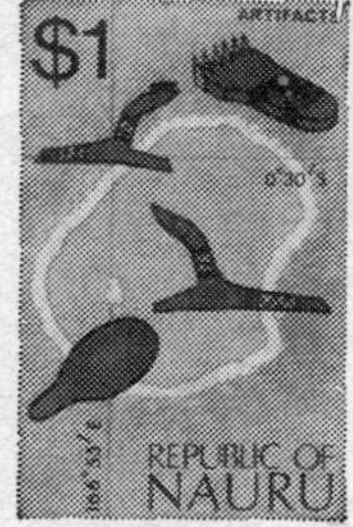

32. Denea. **33.** Artefacts and Map.

(Des. locally; adapted G. L. Vasarhelyi. Litho. Format.)

1973. *Various multicoloured designs as T* **32** (1 *to* 5 *c.*) *or T* **33** (*others*). *P* 14 (1 *to* 5 *c.*), 14½ × 14 (7, 8, 10, 30, 50 *c.*) *or* 14 × 14½ (*others*).
99 1 c. Ekwenababae 5 5
100 2 c. Kauwe Iud 5 5
101 3 c. Rimone 5 5
102 4 c. Type **32** 5 5
103 5 c. Erekogo 5 5
104 7 c. Ikimago (fish) 8 8
105 8 c. Catching flying-fish .. 8 10
106 10 c. Itsibweb (ball game) .. 10 12
107 15 c. Nauruan wrestling .. 12 15
108 20 c. Snaring Frigate Birds .. 20 25
109 25 c. Nauruan girl 25 30
110 30 c. Catching Noddy Birds .. 30 35
111 50 c. Frigate Birds 50 60
112 $1 Type **33** .. .. .. 1·00 1·10
99/112 .. .. *Set of* 14 2·50 2·75

The 1 to 5 c. show flowers, and the 7, 8, 10, 30 and 50 c. are horiz. designs.

Dates of issue:—28.3.73, 1 to 5 c. and $1 (this is the local date of issue; the Crown Agents put the stamps on sale on 21 March); 23.5.73, 8 to 20 c.; 25.7.73, remainder.

34. Co-op Store.

(Des. G. L. Vasarhelyi. Litho. Format.)

1973 (20 DEC.). *50th Anniv. of Nauru Co-operative Society. T* **34** *and similar multicoloured designs. P* 14 × 14½ (50 c.) *or* 14½ × 14 (*others*).
113 5 c. Type **34** 10 10
114 25 c. Timothy Detudamo (founder) 45 45
115 50 c. N.C.S. trademark (*vert.*) 85 90

35. Phosphate Mining.

(Des. G. L. Vasarhelyi (7 c. from original by R. Mason; 10 c. from original by K. Depaune). Litho. Format.)

1974 (21 MAY). *175th Anniv. of First Contact with the Outside World. T* **35** *and similar horiz. designs. Multicoloured. P* 13 × 13½ (7, 35, 50 *c.*) *or* 13½ × 13 (*others*).
116 7 c. M.V. *Eigamoiya* 12 12
117 10 c. Type **29** 20 20
118 15 c. Fokker Friendship "Nauru Chief" 30 30
119 25 c. Nauruan chief in early times 40 40
120 35 c. Capt. Fearn and the *Hunter* 55 55
121 50 c. The *Hunter* off Nauru .. 90 90
116/121 .. .. *Set of* 6 2·25 2·25

The 7, 35 and 50 c. are larger, 70 × 22 mm.

36. Map of Nauru.

(Des. G. L. Vasarhelyi. Litho. Format.)

1974 (23 JULY). *Centenary of Universal Postal Union. T* **36** *and similar multicoloured designs. P* 13½ × 14 (5 *c.*), 13 × 13½ ($1) *or* 13½ × 13 (*others*).
122 5 c. Type **36** 10 10
123 8 c. Nauru Post Office .. 12 12
124 20 c. Nauruan postman .. 35 35
125 $1 U.P.U. Building and Nauruan flag .. .. 1·50 1·60
MS126 157 × 105 mm. Nos. 122/5. Imperf. .. .. 2·25

The 8 and 20 c. are horiz. (33 × 21 mm.), and the $1 is vert. (21 × 33 mm.).

37. Rev. P. A. Delaporte.

(Des. J.W. Ltd. Litho. Format.)

1974 (10 DEC.). *Christmas and 75th Anniv. of Rev. Delaporte's Arrival. P* 14½.
127 **37** 15 c. multicoloured .. 20 25
128 „ 20 c. multicoloured .. 35 40

38. Map of Nauru, Lump of Phosphate Rock and Albert Ellis.

(Des. S. and M. Goaman. Litho. Format.)

1975 (23 JULY). *Phosphate Mining Anniversaries. T* **38** *and similar horiz. designs. Multicoloured. P* 14½ × 14.
129 5 c. Type **38** 10 10
130 7 c. Coolies and mine .. 12 12
131 15 c. Electric railway, barges and ship 25 25
132 25 c. Modern ore extraction .. 35 40

Anniversaries:—5 c. 75th Anniv. of discovery; 7 c. 70th Anniv. of Mining Agreement; 15 c. 55th Anniv. of British Phosphate Commissioners; 25 c. 5th Anniv. of Nauru Phosphate Corporation.

39. Micronesian Outrigger.

(Des. M. and S. Goaman. Litho. Format.)

1975 (1 SEPT.). *South Pacific Commission Conference, Nauru* (1*st series*). *T* **39** *and similar horiz. designs. Multicoloured. P* 13½ × 14.
133 20 c. Type **39** 25 3
134 20 c. Polynesian double-hull .. 25 3
135 20 c. Melanesian outrigger .. 25 3
136 20 c. Polynesian outrigger .. 25 3

Nos. 133/6 were printed in *se-tenant* blocks of four throughout the sheet.

40. New Civic Centre.

(Des. M. and S. Goaman. Litho. Format.)

1975 (29 SEPT.). *South Pacific Commission Conference. Nauru* (2*nd series*). *T* **40** *and simila horiz. design. Multicoloured. P* 14.
137 30 c. Type **40** 40 4
138 50 c. Domaneab (meeting-house) 70 7

41. " Our Lady " (Yaren Church).

(Des. S. and M. Goaman. Litho. Format.)

1975 (7 NOV.). *Christmas. T* **41** *and simila vert. design showing stained-glass windo Multicoloured. P* 14½ × 14.
139 5 c. Type **41** 8
140 7 c. " Suffer little children . . ." (Orro Church) 10 1
141 15 c. As 7 c. 25 2
142 25 c. Type **41** 35 4

42. Flowers floating towards Nauru.

(Des. S. and M. Goaman. Litho. Format.)

1976 (31 Jan.*). *30th Anniv. of the Return from Truk. T* **42** *and similar horiz. designs. Multicoloured. P* 14½.

No.	Value	Design	Unused	Used
143	10 c.	Type **42**	15	15
144	14 c.	Nauru encircled by garland	20	20
145	25 c.	Reed warbler and maps	35	35
146	40 c.	Return of the islanders ..	50	55

* This is the local date of issue; the Crown Agents released the stamps one day earlier.

43. 3d. and 9d. Stamps of 1916.

(Des. M. and S. Goaman. Litho. Format.)

1976 (6 May). *60th Anniv. of Nauruan Stamps. T* **43** *and similar horiz. designs. Multicoloured. P* 13½.

No.	Value	Design	Unused	Used
147	10 c.	Type **43**	12	15
148	15 c.	6d. and 1s. stamps ..	20	25
149	25 c.	2s. 6d. stamp	35	40
150	50 c.	5s. "Specimen" stamp	65	75

Nos. 147/8 show stamps with errors: the 3d. "Short N" and the 6d. "P" for "R".

44. *Pandanus Mei* and Nauruan Ship.

(Des. M. & S. Goaman. Litho. Format.)

1976 (26 July). *South Pacific Forum, Nauru. T* **44** *and similar horiz. designs. Multicoloured. P* 13½.

No.	Value	Design	Unused	Used
151	10 c.	Type **44**	15	15
152	20 c.	*Tournefortia argentea* and Nauruan aircraft ..	30	35
153	30 c.	*Thespesia populnea* and Nauru Tracking Station	40	45
154	40 c.	*Cordia subcordata* and produce	55	65

45. Nauruan Choir.

(Des. G. L. Vasarhelyi. Litho. Format.)

1976 (17 Nov.). *Christmas. T* **45** *and similar vert. designs. Multicoloured. P* 13½.

No.	Value	Design	Unused	Used
155	15 c.	Type **45**	20	20
156	15 c.	Nauruan choir	20	20
157	20 c.	Angel in white dress ..	25	30
158	20 c.	Angel in red dress ..	25	30

Nos. 155/6 and 157/8 were printed horizontally *se-tenant* throughout the sheet, both forming composite designs.

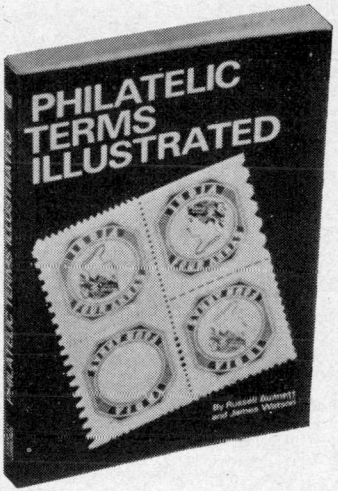

NEVIS.

For GREAT BRITAIN stamps used in Nevis with "A 09" obliteration, see index to Great Britain Stamps Used Abroad list.

1

2

3

4

The designs on the stamps refer to a medicinal spring on the island.

(Recess. Nissen & Parker, London.)

1861. *P* 13. (*a*) *Blued paper.*

1 **1** 1d. dull rose .. .. .. 55·00 38·00
2 **2** 4d. rose .. .. .. £200 55·00
3 **3** 6d. grey-lilac .. .. .. £170 80·00
4 **4** 1s. green .. .. .. £275 65·00

(*b*) *Greyish paper.*

5 **1** 1d. dull lake .. .. .. 11·00 11·00
6 **2** 4d. rose .. .. .. 25·00 21·00
7 **3** 6d. grey .. .. .. 21·00 15·00
8 **4** 1s. green .. .. .. 55·00 21·00

1866. *White paper.* *P* 15.

9 **1** 1d. pale-red .. .. .. 10·00 11·00
10 „ 1d. deep red .. .. .. 10·00 11·00
11 **2** 4d. orange .. .. .. 38·00 10·00
12 „ 4d. deep orange .. .. 38·00 10·00
13 **4** 1s. blue-green .. .. 55·00 14·00
14 „ 1s. yellow-green .. .. £350 40·00
a. Laid paper £4500 £1400
b. No. 9 on sheet with crossed lines on hill £750 £140
c. Ditto. On laid paper .. ..

(Lithographed by transfer from the engraved plates. Nissen & Parker. London.)

1876. *P* 15.

15 **1** 1d. pale rose-red .. .. 4·50 5·50
a. Imperf. (pair) .. .. 80·00
16 „ 1d. deep rose-red .. .. 5·00 6·00
17 „ 1d. vermilion-red .. .. 5·50 6·00
a. Bisected (on cover) .. .. — £250
18 **2** 4d. orange-yellow .. .. 55·00 10·00
a. Imperf. between (vert. pair) .. £1200
19 **3** 6d. grey .. .. .. 55·00 50·00
20 **4** 1s. pale green .. .. 15·00 30·00
a. Imperf. .. .. ..
b. Imperf. between (strip of three) £1100
c. No. 9 on sheet with crossed lines on hill .. .. .. 85·00
21 „ 1s. deep green .. .. 15·00 35·00

With one exception, resulting from a stone which was not retouched, No. 9 on the sheet of the 1s. *deep* green, has not the distinct "crossed lines on hill" of Nos. 14b and 20c, but traces of the lines are visible.

RETOUCHES.
1d. *Lithograph.*

i. No. 1 on sheet. Top of hill over kneeling figure redrawn by five thick lines and eight small slanting lines .. .. .. 65·00 70·00
ii. No. 1 on sheet. Another retouch. Three series of short vertical strokes behind the kneeling figure 65·00 70·00
iii. No. 3 on sheet. Right upper corner star and border below star retouched 65·00 70·00
iv. No. 9 on sheet. Retouch in same position as on No. 3 but differing in detail .. 65·00 70·00
v. No. 12 on sheet. Dress of standing figure retouched by a number of horizontal and vertical lines .. 70·00 75·00

1878. *Litho.* *P* 11½.

22 **1** 1d. vermilion-red .. .. 7·50 15·00
a. Bisected (on cover) .. .. — £250
b. Imperf. (pair) .. .. 70·00
c. Imperf. between (pair) ..

5 (Die I)

NEVIS. ½d.
(6)

(Typo. D.L.R.)

1879–80. *Wmk. Crown CC.* *P* 14.

23 **5** 1d. lilac-mauve (1880) .. 11·00 10·00
a. Bisected (½d.) (on cover) .. — £140
24 „ 2½d. red-brown .. 35·00 32·00

1882–90. *Wmk. Crown CA.* *P* 14.

25 **5** ½d. dull green (1883) .. 1·75 2·00
26 „ 1d. lilac-mauve .. .. 25·00 10·00
a. Bisected (½d.) on cover .. — £140
27 „ 1d. carmine (1884) .. .. 1·40 1·75
a. Dull rose .. .. 5·00 4·50
28 „ 2½d. red-brown .. .. 35·00 28·00
29 „ 2½d. ultramarine (1884) .. 2·10 2·10
30 „ 4d. blue .. .. £110 25·00
31 „ 4d. grey (1884) .. .. 2·10 2·10
32 „ 6d. green (1883) £130 £130
33 „ 6d. chestnut (1888) .. 10·00 15·00
34 „ 1s. pale violet (1890) .. 35·00 85·00
33, 34 Optd. "Specimen" *Set of* 2 45·00

1883. *No.* 26 *bisected vertically and surch. with T* **6**.

35 ½d. on half 1d. lilac-mauve (V.) £100 14·00
a. Surch. double .. .. — £100
b. Surch. on half "REVENUE" stamp No. F6 .. .. — £225
36 ½d. on half 1d., lilac-mauve .. 85·00 14·00
a. Surch. double .. .. — £100
b. Whole stamp with surch. on right half only .. .. ..
c. Surch. on half "REVENUE" stamp No. F6 .. .. — £225

FISCALS USED FOR POSTAGE.

Revenue (F 1) REVENUE (F 2)

1882. *Stamps of* 1876 *optd. with Type* F **1**.

F1 1d. bright red .. .. .. 7·00
F2 1d. rose .. .. .. 7·00 3·00
F3 4d. orange .. .. .. 10·00
F4 6d. grey .. .. .. 17·00
F5 1s. green .. .. .. 28·00

Nos. 26, 30 *and* 32 *optd. with Type* F **2**.

F6 1d. lilac-mauve .. .. 4·50 5·00
F7 4d. blue .. .. .. 3·50 5·50
F8 6d. green .. .. .. 3·50 6·00

The retouches listed for the 1d. *lithograph* also occur on No. F1. (*Price from* £55.)

For later issues *see* ST. KITTS-NEVIS.

NEW BRUNSWICK.

1. Royal Crown and Heraldic Flowers of the United Kingdom.

(Recess. Perkins, Bacon & Co.)

1851 (SEPT.). *Blue paper.* *Imperf.*

1 **1** 3d. bright red £1000 £200
2 „ 3d. dull red £1500 £200
a. Bisected (1½d.) (on cover) .. — £1500
2*b* „ 6d. mustard-yellow .. .. — £1600
3 „ 6d. yellow £3000 £750
4 „ 6d. olive-yellow £2500 £700
a. Bisected (3d.) (on cover) .. — £2000
b. Quartered (1½d.) (on cover) .. — £10000
5 „ 1s. reddish mauve £8000 £3000
6 „ 1s. dull mauve £7500 £2500
a. Bisected (6d.) (on cover) .. — £20000
b. Quartered (3d.) (on cover) .. — £20000

Reprints of all three values were made in 1890 on thin, hard, white paper. The 3d. is bright orange, the 6d. and 1s. violet-black.

Nos. 2a and 4b were to make up the 7½d. rate.

2

3

3*a*. Charles Connell.

4

Mathematically aligned images continue:

5

6

7. King Edward VII when Prince of Wales

(Recess. American Bank Note Co.)

1860 (15 MAY)–**1863.** *No wmk.* *P* 12.

7 **2** 1 c. brown-purple .. .. 11·00 10·00
8 „ 1 c. purple .. .. 6·00 8·00
9 „ 1 c. dull claret .. .. 6·00 8·00
a. Imperf. between (horiz. pr.) £250
10 **3** 2 c. orange (1863) .. .. 6·00 8·00
11 „ 2 c. orange-yellow .. 6·00 8·00
12 „ 2 c. deep orange .. .. 6·00 8·00
a. Imperf. between (vert. pair) £250
13 **3*a*** 5 c. brown £1100
14 **4** 5 c. yellow-green .. .. 6·00 6·50
15 „ 5 c. deep green .. .. 6·00 6·50
16 „ 5 c. sap-green .. .. £110 20·00
17 **5** 10 c. red .. .. .. 10·00 11·00
a. Bisected (5 c.) (on cover) (1860) .. .. .. — £325
18 **6** 12½ c. indigo .. .. .. 15·00 16·00
19 **7** 17 c. black .. .. .. 10·00 14·00

In March, 1868, issues of the Dominion of Canada replaced those of New Brunswick.

Beware of forged cancellations.

NEWFOUNDLAND.

1

2

3

4

5

Royal Crown and heraldic flowers of the United Kingdom.

(Recess. Perkins, Bacon & Co.)

857 (1 Jan.). *No wmk. Thick paper. Imperf.*

1	**1**	1d. brown-purple ..	.. 20·00	55·00
		a. Bisected (½d.) on cover ..	†	£4000
2	**2**	2d. scarlet-vermilion	.. £7500	£3500
3	**3**	3d. yellowish green..	.. £140	£200
4	**4**	4d. scarlet-vermilion	.. £2500	£1600
		a. Bisected (2d.) (on cover) ..		
5	**1**	5d. brown-purple ..	.. 70·00	£140
6	**4**	6d. scarlet-vermilion	.. £6000	£1500
7	**5**	6½d. scarlet-vermilion	.. £1200	£1500
8	**4**	8d. scarlet-vermilion	.. £110	£150
		a. Bisected (4d.) (on cover) ..	†	£1500
9	**2**	1s. scarlet-vermilion	.. £9000	£2500
		a. Bisected (6d.) (on cover) ..	†	£6000

The 6d. and 8d. differ from the 4d. in many de-ails, as does also the 1s. from the 2d.

860. *Medium paper. Imperf.*

0	**2**	2d. orange-vermilion	.. £110	£150
1	**3**	3d. green *to* deep green*	.. 12·00	45·00
2	**4**	4d. orange-vermilion	.. £1000	£500
		a. Bisected (2d.) (on cover) ..	—	£4500
3	**1**	5d. Venetian red ..	.. 11·00	45·00
4	**4**	6d. orange-vermilion	.. £1400	£600
5	**2**	1s. orange-vermilion	.. £15000	£6000
		a. Bisected (6d.) (on cover) ..		

*No. 11 includes stamps from the November 861 printing which are very difficult to distin-uish.

The 1s. on horizontally or vertically *laid* paper now considered to be a proof.

ISECTS. Collectors are warned against buying sected stamps of these issues without a reliable uarantee.

861. *New colours. Imperf.*

(*a*) *1st printing. Soft paper* (July)

6	**2**	2d. deep rose-lake ..	.. 80·00	£275
7	**4**	4d. deep rose-lake ..	25·00	£100
		a. Bisected (2d.) (on cover) ..		
8	,,	6d. deep rose-lake ..	.. 25·00	£100
		a. Bisected (3d.) (on cover) ..		
9	**5**	6½d. deep rose-lake ..	.. £150	£350
0	**2**	1s. deep rose-lake ..	.. £150	£350
		a. Bisected (6d.) (on cover) ..	—	£8000

(*b*) *2nd printing. Hard paper* (Nov).

1	**1**	1d. chocolate-brown	.. 25·00	80·00
		a. Red-brown	.. £1800	
2	**2**	2d. pale rose-lake ..	.. 40·00	£180
3	**4**	4d. pale rose-lake ..	.. 4·50	40·00
24	**1**	5d. chocolate-brown	.. 15·00	£140
		a. Red-brown	.. 11·00	80·00
24*b*	**4**	6d. pale rose-lake ..	.. 4·50	50·00
24*c*	**5**	6½d. pale rose-lake ..	.. 15·00	£180
24*d*	**4**	8d. pale rose-lake ..	.. 15·00	£200
24*e*	**2**	1s. pale rose-lake ..	.. 7·00	90·00

Stamps of the second printing of the pale rose-lake shades have a more transparent look due to the paper being generally thinner, but paper thickness alone is not a sure test for distinguishing the printings.

Stamps of this issue may be found with part of the paper-maker's watermark "STACEY WISE 1858".

Beware of buying used specimens of the stamps which are worth much less in unused condition, as many unused stamps have been provided with faked postmarks. A guarantee should be obtained.

6. Codfish.

7. Seal on ice-floe.

8. Prince Consort.

9. Queen Victoria.

10

11. Queen Victoria.

(Recess. American Bank Note Co., New York.)

1865 (Nov.)–**70.** *P 12.* (*a*) *Thin yellowish paper.*

25	**6**	2 c. yellowish green ..	75·00	13·00
		a. Bisected (1 c.) (on cover)..	†	£2000
26	**7**	5 c. brown	.. £300	90·00
		a. Bisected (2½ c.) (on cover)..		
27	**8**	10 c. black	.. £110	30·00
		a. Bisected (5 c.) (on cover)..	†	£1700
28	**9**	12 c. red-brown ..	.. £160	90·00
		a. Bisected (6 c.) (on cover)..		
29	**10**	13 c. orange-yellow..	.. 35·00	30·00
30	**11**	24 c. blue	.. 15·00	12·00

(*b*) *Medium white paper.*

31	**6**	2 c. bluish green (to deep)	32·00	12·00
32	**8**	10 c. black	.. 50·00	15·00
33	**9**	12 c. chestnut ..	.. 15·00	11·00
33*a*	**11**	24 c. blue	.. £225	£100

12. King Edward VII when Prince of Wales.

I.

(Recess. National Bank Note Co., New York.)

1868. *P 12.*

34	**12**	1 c. dull purple (I) ..	.. 15·00	18·00

14. Queen Victoria.

II.

In Type II the white oval frame line is unbroken by the scroll containing the words "ONE CENT", the letters "N.F." are smaller and closer to the scroll, and there are other minor differences.

(Recess. American Bank Note Co., New York.)

1868-73. *P 12.*

35	**12**	1 c. brown-purple (II) ('71)	20·00	15·00
36	**14**	3 c. vermilion (1870) ..	£120	55·00
37	,,	3 c. blue (1873) ..	.. 70·00	7·00
38	**7**	5 c. black	.. 80·00	35·00
39	**14**	6 c. rose (1870) ..	.. 5·00	4·50

1876-79. *Rouletted.*

40	**12**	1 c. lake-purple (II) (1877)	28·00	15·00
41	**6**	2 c. bluish green (1879)	.. 75·00	50·00
42	**14**	3 c. blue (1877) ..	.. 75·00	4·50
43	**7**	5 c. blue (1876) ..	.. 90·00	5·50
		a. Imperf. (pair) ..	..	

15. King Edward VII when Prince of Wales.

16. Codfish.

17

18. Seal on Ice-floe.

(Recess. British-American Bank Note Co., Montreal.)

1880. *P* 12.

44	**15**	1 c. dull grey-brown	5·50	4·00
		a. Dull brown	4·50	3·75
		b. Red-brown	7·50	5·00
46	**16**	2 c. yellow-green	11·00	4·00
47	**17**	3 c. pale dull blue	11·00	3·50
		a. Bright blue	24·00	1·50
48	**18**	5 c. pale dull blue	75·00	4·00

19. Newfoundland Dog.

20. Atlantic Brigantine.

(Recess. British-American Bank Note Co., Montreal.)

1887. *New colours and values.* *P* 12.

49	**19**	½ c. rose-red	2·00	2·00
50	**15**	1 c. blue-green	1·40	80
		a. Green	1·25	80
		b. Yellow-green	1·60	1·25
51	**16**	2 c. orange-vermilion ..	2·00	1·60
52	**17**	3 c. deep brown	4·00	1·60
53	**18**	5 c. deep blue	20·00	1·75
54	**20**	10 c. black	11·00	10·00
49/54		.. .. *Set of* 6	35·00	15·00

For reissues of 1880/87 stamps in similar colours, see Nos. 62/65*a*.

21. Queen Victoria.

(Recess. British-American Bank Note Co., Ottawa.)

1890. *P* 12.

55	**21**	3 c. deep slate	4·00	15
		a. Imperf. (pair)		
56	,,	3 c. slate-grey (to grey) ..	5·50	15
		a. Imperf. between (pair) ..	£350	
57	,,	3 c. slate-violet	4·00	90
58	,,	3 c. grey-lilac	4·00	12
58*a*	,,	3 c. brown-grey	4·00	2·00
58*b*	,,	3 c. purple-grey	4·00	1·40

There is a very wide range of shades in this stamp, and those given only cover the main groups.

Stamps on pink paper are from a consignment recovered from the sea and which were affected by the salt water.

(Recess. British-American Bank Note Co., Montreal.)

1894. *Changes of colour.* *P* 12.

59	**19**	½ c. black	1·40	1·40
59*a*	**18**	5 c. bright blue	4·00	2·00
60	**14**	6 c. crimson-lake	4·00	4·00
61	**9**	12 c. deep brown	8·00	10·00

The 6 c. is printed from the old American Bank Note Company's plates.

1896–97. *Reissues.* *P* 12.

62	**19**	½ c. orange-vermilion ..	15·00	18·00
63	**15**	1 c. deep green	1·50	1·00
63*a*	,,	1 c. deep brown	7·00	5·00
64	**16**	2 c. green	6·00	5·00
65	**17**	3 c. deep blue	6·00	4·00
65*a*	,,	3 c. chocolate-brown ..	9·00	8·00
62/65*a*		.. .. *Set of* 6	40·00	38·00

The above were *reissued* for postal purposes. The colours were generally brighter than those of the original stamps.

22. Queen Victoria.

23. Jean Cabot.

24. Cape Bonavista.

25. Caribou-hunting.

26. Mining.

27. Logging.

28. Fishing.

29. Cabot's ship.

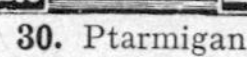

30. Ptarmigan.

31. Group of Seals.

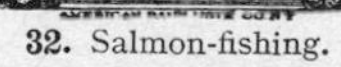

32. Salmon-fishing.

33. Seal of the Colony.

34. Iceberg off St. John's.

35. Henry VII.

(Recess. American Bank Note Co.)

1897 (24 JUNE). *400th Anniv. of Discovery o Newfoundland and 60th year of Queen Victoria' reign.* *P* 12.

66	**22**	1 c. green	1·00	1·0
67	**23**	2 c. bright rose	1·00	1·0
		a. Bisected (1 c.) on cover ..	†	£12
68	**24**	3 c. bright blue	1·25	7.
		a. Bisected (1½ c.) on cover ..	†	£10
69	**25**	4 c. olive-green	1·75	1·7
70	**26**	5 c. violet	2·00	1·7
71	**27**	6 c. red-brown	1·75	1·7
		a. Bisected (3 c.) on cover ..	†	£10
72	**28**	8 c. orange	5·00	3·2
73	**29**	10 c. sepia	6·00	3·2
74	**30**	12 c. deep blue	8·00	3·2
75	**31**	15 c. bright scarlet ..	7·50	3·5
76	**32**	24 c. dull violet-blue ..	5·50	4·5
77	**33**	30 c. slate-blue	11·00	7·5
78	**34**	35 c. red	17·00	16·0
79	**35**	60 c. black	5·50	5·5
66/79		.. .. *Set of* 14	65·00	50·0

The 60 c. surcharged "TWO—2—CENTS" i three lines is an essay made in December, 1918

ONE CENT

(36)

ONE CENT

(37)

ONE CENT

(38)

1897 (OCT.). *T* **21** *surch. with T* **36** *to* **38.**

80	**36**	1 c. on 3 c. grey-purple ..	5·00	5·0
		a. Double surch., one diagonal	£600	
		b. Surch. in red	£600	
		c. Surch. in red and black ..	£550	
		d. Vert pr., one without lower bar and "ONE CENT" ..	£1800	
81	**37**	1 c. on 3 c. grey-purple ..	25·00	25·0
		a. Surch. in red	£1500	
		b. Surch. in red and black ..	£1700	
82	**38**	1 c. on 3 c. grey-purple ..	£120	£12
		a. Surch. in red	£2000	
		b. Surch. double in red ..	£2500	
		c. Surch. in red and black ..	£2250	

This surcharge is known on stamps of variou shades.

Dangerous forgeries exist of the errors.

39. Prince Edward, later Duke of Windsor.

40. Queen Victoria.

41. King Edward VII when Prince of Wales.

43. Queen Mary when Duchess of York.

42. Queen Alexandra when Princess of Wales.

44. King George V when Duke of York.

(Recess. American Bank Note Co.)

897–1918. *P* 12.

3	**39**	½ c. olive (8.97)	1·10	1·10
		a. Imperf. (pair)	£100	
4	**40**	1 c. carmine (12.97) ..	1·10	1·10
5	,,	1 c. blue-green (6.98) ..	1·10	12
		a. Yellow-green	1·10	12
		b. Imperf. between (pair) ..	75·00	
5	**41**	2 c. orange (12.97)	1·00	1·00
7	,,	2 c. scarlet (6.98)	1·75	20
		a. Imperf. (pair)	£100	
		b. Imperf. between (pair) ..		
3	**42**	3 c. orange (6.98)	1·40	25
		a. Imperf. between (pair) ..	£110	
		b. Imperf. (pair)	£110	
		c. Red-orange/bluish (6.18) ..	4·00	1·25
9	**43**	4 c. violet (10.01)	4·00	1·25
		a. Imperf. (pair)	£100	
0	**44**	5 c. blue (6.99)	4·25	1·00
3/90		.. .. *Set of* 8	14·00	5·50

No. 88*c* was an emergency war-time printing made by the American Bank Note Co. from the old plate, pending receipt of the then current 3 c. from England.

45. Map of Newfoundland.

(Recess. American Bank Note Co.)

908 (Sept.). *P* 12.

45	2 c. lake	5·00	40

46. King James I.

47. Arms of Colonisation Co.

48. John Guy.

49. Guy's ship.

50. Cupids.

51. Sir Francis Bacon.

52. View of Mosquito.

53. Logging Camp.

54. Paper mills.

55. King Edward VII.

56. King George V.

(Litho. Whitehead, Morris & Co., Ltd.)

1910 (15 Aug.). (*a*) *P* 12.

95	**46**	1 c. green	75	60
		a. "NFWFOUNDLAND"	30·00	35·00
		b. Imperf.between(horiz.pr.)	£140	£150
96	**47**	2 c. rose-carmine ..	1·25	40
97	**48**	3 c. olive	3·50	4·00
98	**49**	4 c. violet	4·00	4·00
99	**50**	5 c. bright blue	3·25	3·00
100	**51**	6 c. claret (A)	17·00	17·00
100*a*	,,	6 c. claret (B)	7·00	7·00
101	**52**	8 c. bistre-brown ..	12·00	13·00
102	**53**	9 c. olive-green	12·00	13·00
103	**54**	10 c. purple-slate ..	15·00	15·00
104	**55**	12 c. pale red-brown ..	15·00	15·00
		a. Imperf. (pair)	£200	
105	**56**	15 c. black	13·00	13·00
95/105		.. .. *Set of* 11	80·00	80·00

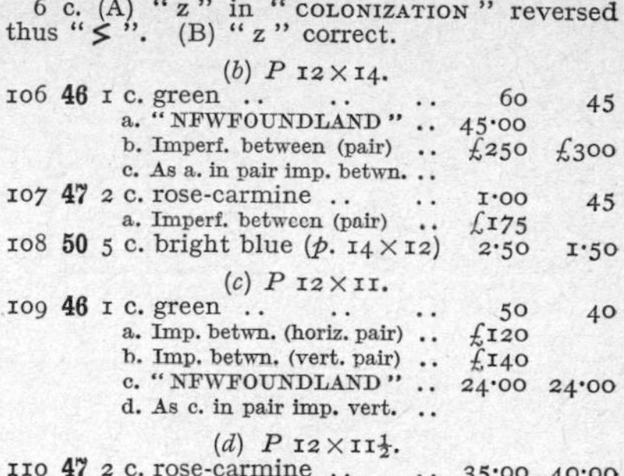

6 c. (A) "z" in "COLONIZATION" reversed thus "ƨ". (B) "z" correct.

(*b*) *P* 12×14.

106	**46**	1 c. green	60	45
		a. "NFWFOUNDLAND" ..	45·00	
		b. Imperf. between (pair) ..	£250	£300
		c. As a. in pair imp. betwn. ..		
107	**47**	2 c. rose-carmine	1·00	45
		a. Imperf. between (pair) ..	£175	
108	**50**	5 c. bright blue (*p.* 14×12)	2·50	1·50

(*c*) *P* 12×11.

109	**46**	1 c. green	50	40
		a. Imp. betwn. (horiz. pair) ..	£120	
		b. Imp. betwn. (vert. pair) ..	£140	
		c. "NFWFOUNDLAND" ..	24·00	24·00
		d. As c. in pair imp. vert. ..		

(*d*) *P* 12×11½.

110	**47**	2 c. rose-carmine	35·00	40·00

(Dies. eng. Macdonald & Sons. Recess. A. Alexander & Sons, Ltd.)

1911 (Feb.). *Types as* **51** *to* **56**, *but recess printed. P* 14.

111	6 c. claret (B)	5·50	5·50
112	8 c. yellow-brown	14·00	14·00
	a. Imperf. between (horiz. pair) ..	£200	
	b. Imperf. (pair)	£150	
113	9 c. sage-green	12·00	13·00
	a. Imperf. between (horiz. pair) ..	£150	
114	10 c. purple-black	25·00	25·00
	a. Imperf. between (horiz. pair) ..	£150	
	b. Imperf. (pair)	£130	
115	12 c. red-brown ..	17·00	17·00
116	15 c. slate-green ..	17·00	17·00
111/6	.. .. *Set of* 6	80·00	80·00

The 9 c. exists with paper-maker's wmk.

57. Queen Mary.

58. King George V

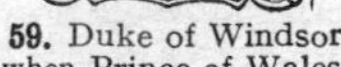
59. Duke of Windsor when Prince of Wales.

60. King George VI when Prince Albert.

61. Princess Mary, late Princess Royal.

62. Prince Henry, Duke of Gloucester.

63. Prince George, late Duke of Kent.

64. Prince John.

65. Queen Alexandra.

66. Duke of Connaught.

67. Seal of Newfoundland.

(1 c. to 5 c., 10 c. eng. and recess D.L.R.; others eng. Macdonald & Co., recess G. Alexander & Sons.)

1911 (19 June)–**16**. *Coronation.* *P* 13½×14 *(comb)* (1 *c. to* 5 *c.*, 10 *c.*) *or* 14 *(line)* *(others).*

117 **57** 1 c. yellow-green .. .. 1·00 12
a. Blue-green (1915) .. 55 12
118 **58** 2 c. carmine 55 12
a. Rose-red (blurred impression). Perf. 14 (1916) .. 1·60 25
119 **59** 3 c. red-brown .. .. 6·00 6·00
120 **60** 4 c. purple .. .. 6·00 6·00
121 **61** 5 c. ultramarine .. .. 3·00 1·00
122 **62** 6 c. slate-grey .. .. 8·00 8·00
123 **63** 8 c. greenish blue .. 22·00 22·00
a. Aniline blue .. .. 20·00 20·00
124 **64** 9 c. violet-blue .. .. 6·00 6·00
125 **65** 10 c. deep green .. .. 8·00 8·00
126 **66** 12 c. plum .. .. 8·00 8·00
127 **67** 15 c. lake .. .. 7·00 7·00
117/127 .. .. *Set of* 11 65·00 65·00

The 2 c. rose-red, No. 118*a*, is a poor war-time printing by Alexander & Sons.

68. Caribou.

Each value bears with "Trail of the Caribou" the name of a different action: 1 c. Suvla Bay; 3 c. Gueudecourt; 4 c. Beaumont Hamel; 6 c. Monchy; 10 c. Steenbeck; 15 c. Langemarck; 24 c. Cambrai; 36 c. Combles. 2 c., 5 c., 8 c., and 12 c. inscribed "Royal Naval Reserve-Ubique."

(Des. J. H. Noonan. Recess. D.L.R.)

1919 (2 Jan.). *Newfoundland Contingent,* 1914–1918. *P* 14.

130 **68** 1 c. green (*a*) (*b*) 50 15
131 „ 2 c. scarlet (*a*) (*b*) 60 20
a. Carmine-red (b) 80 30
132 „ 3 c. brown (*a*) (*b*) 60 12
a. Red-brown (b) 60 12
133 „ 4 c. mauve (*a*) 75 45
a. Purple (b) 75 45
134 „ 5 c. ultramarine (*a*) (*b*) .. 1·10 45
135 „ 6 c. slate-grey (*a*) .. 5·00 5·00
136 „ 8 c. bright magenta (*a*) .. 4·50 4·50
137 „ 10 c. deep grey-green (*a*) 3·00 1·50
138 „ 12 c. orange (*a*) .. .. 12·00 10·00
139 „ 15 c. indigo (*a*) .. .. 6·00 6·00
a. Prussian blue (a) .. 75·00 60·00
140 „ 24 c. bistre-brown (*a*) .. 9·00 9·00
141 „ 36 c. sage-green (*a*) .. 6·00 6·00
130/141 .. .. *Set of* 12 45·00 40·00

Perforations. Two perforating heads were used: (*a*) comb 14×13·9; (*b*) line 14·1×14·1.

FIRST TRANS-ATLANTIC AIR POST April, 1919.
(69)

Trans-Atlantic AIR POST, 1919. ONE DOLLAR
(70)

1919 (12 Apr.). *Air. Optd. with T* **69**, *by Robinson & Co. Ltd., at the offices of the "Daily News".*

142 **68** 3 c. brown £6500 £6000

These stamps franked correspondence carried by Mr. Hawker on his Atlantic flight. 18 were damaged and destroyed, 95 used on letters, 11 given as presentation copies, and the remaining 76 were sold in aid of the Marine Disasters Fund.

1919 (April). *Optd. in MS.* "Aerial Atlantic Mail. J.A.R."

142*a* **68** 3 c. brown .. .. —£15000

This provisional was made by the Postmaster Mr. J. A. Robinson, for use on correspondence intended to be carried on the abortive Morgan-Raynham Trans-Atlantic flight. The mail was eventually delivered by sea.

1919 (9 June). *Air. Surch. with T* **70** *by J. W. Withers at the offices of the "Royal Gazette".*

143 **31** $1 on 15 c. bright scarlet .. 60·00 60·00
a. No comma after "AIR POST" .. .. .. 90·00 £100
b. As Var. a and no stop after "1919" £130 £130
c. As Var. a and "A" of "AIR" under "a" of "Trans" £130 £130

These stamps were issued for use on the mail carried on the first successful flight across the Atlantic by Alcock and Brown, and on other projected Trans-Atlantic flights (Alcock flown cover, *Price* £500).

THREE CENTS
(71)

A. Bars of surch. 10½ mm. apart.
B. Bars 13½ mm. apart.

1920 (Sept.). *Surch. as T* **71**, *by J. W. Withers.* (2 *c. with only one bar, at top of stamp.*)

144 **33** 2 c. on 3 c. slate-blue .. 2·25 2·25
a. Surch. inverted £200
145 **31** 3 c. on 15 c. brt. scar. (A) 30·00 30·00
a. Surch. inverted £275
146 „ 3 c. on 15 c. brt. scar. (B) 2·50 2·50
147 **34** 3 c. on 35 c. red .. .. 2·50 2·50
a. Surch. inverted .. ..
b. Lower bar omitted .. 60·00 65·00
c. "THREE" omitted .. £550

Our prices for Nos. 147b and 147c are for stamps with lower bar of "THREE" entirely missing. The bar may be found in all stages of incompleteness and stamps showing broken bar are not of much value.

On the other hand, stamps showing either only the top or bottom of the letters "THREE" are scarce, though not as rare as No. 147c.

The 6 c. T **27**, surcharged "THREE CENTS," in red or black, is an essay. (*Price* £130). The 2 c. on 30 c. with red surcharge is a colour trial (*Price* £130).

AIR MAIL to Halifax, N.S. 1921.
(72)

1921 (16 Nov.). *Air. T* **34** *optd. with T* **72**.

I. 2¾ *mm. between* "AIR" *and* "MAIL".

148 35 c. red (I) .. .. .. 60·00 45·0
a. No stop after "1921" .. 50·00 40·0
b. No stop and first "1" of "1921" below "f" of "Halifax" .. .. 90·00 80·0
c. As No. 148, inverted .. £1500
d. As 148a, inverted £1300
e. As No. 148b, inverted .. £3000

II. 1½ *mm. between* "AIR" *and* "MAIL".

148*f* 35 c. red (II) .. .. .. 65·00 50·0
g. No stop after "1921" .. .. 75·00 65·0
h. No stop and first "1" of "1921" below "f" of "Halifax" .. .. 90·00 80·0
i. As 148f, inverted £1600
k. As No. 148g, inverted .. £2000
l. As No. 148h, inverted .. £3000

73. Twin Hills, Tor's Cove.

74. South-West Arm Trinity.

75. Statue of the Fighting Newfoundlander, St. John's.

76. Humber River.

77. Coast at Trinity.

78. Upper Steadie Humber River.

79. Quidi Vidi, near St. John's.

80. Caribou crossin Lake.

81. Humber River Cañon.

82. Shell Bird Islan

83. Mount Moriah, Bay of Islands.

84. Humber River near Little Rapids

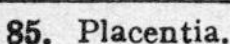

85. Placentia.

86. Topsail Falls.

(Recess. D.L.R.)

1923 (9 JULY)–26. *P* 14 (*comb or line*).

149	**73**	1 c. green	65	12
		a. Booklet pane of 8 (1926)	£130	
150	**74**	2 c. carmine	65	12
		a. Imperf. (pair)	£100	
		b. Booklet pane of 8 (1926)	70·00	
151	**75**	3 c. brown	65	10
152	**76**	4 c. deep purple	75	55
153	**77**	5 c. ultramarine	1·50	65
154	**78**	6 c. slate	1·50	1·50
155	**79**	8 c. purple	1·40	1·40
156	**80**	9 c. slate-green	7·50	7·50
157	**81**	10 c. violet	1·75	85
		a. Purple	1·75	1·00
158	**82**	11 c. sage-green	2·25	2·25
159	**83**	12 c. lake	2·75	2·75
160	**84**	15 c. Prussian blue	4·00	4·00
161	**85**	20 c. chestnut (28.4.24)	3·50	3·50
162	**86**	24 c. sepia (22.4.24)	18·00	19·00
149/162		*Set of* 14	42·00	40·00

Perforations. Three perforating heads were used: comb 13.8 × 14 (all values); line 13.7 and 14, and combinations of these two (for all except 6, 8, 9 and 11 c.).

Air Mail
DE PINEDO
1927

(**87**)

1927 (18 MAY). *Air. T* **35** *optd. with T* **87**, *by Robinson & Co., Ltd.*

163 60 c. black (R.) £10000 £5000

For the mail carried by De Pinedo to Europe 300 stamps were overprinted, 230 used in correspondence, 66 presented to De Pinedo, Government Officials, etc., and 4 damaged and destroyed. Stamps without overprint were also used.

88. Newfoundland and Labrador.

89. S.S. *Caribou.*

90. King George V and Queen Mary.

91. Duke of Windsor when Prince of Wales.

92. Express Train.

93. Hotel, St. John's.

94. Heart's Content.

95. Cabot Tower St. John's.

96. War Memorial, St. John's.

97. G.P.O., St. John's.

98. Trans-Atlantic flight.

99. Colonial Building St. John's.

100. Grand Falls, Labrador.

(Recess. De La Rue.)

1928 (3 JAN.)–29. *"Publicity" issue. P* 13 *to* 14.

164	**88**	1 c. deep green (*a*)	45	20
165	**89**	2 c. carmine (*b*)	65	20
166	**90**	3 c. brown (*b*) (*c*)	75	20
167	**91**	4 c. mauve (*b*)	1·25	1·25
		a. Rose-purple ('29)	6·00	5·00
168	**92**	5 c. slate-grey (*b*) (*c*)	1·75	1·40
169	**93**	6 c. ultramarine (*b*) (*c*)	1·50	1·50
170	**94**	8 c. red-brown (*c*)	2·50	2·50
171	**95**	9 c. deep green (*c*)	2·75	2·75
172	**96**	10 c. deep violet (*b*) (*c*)	2·25	1·50
173	**97**	12 c. carmine-lake (*c*)	1·75	1·75
174	**95**	14 c. brown-purple (*b*) (*c*)	2·50	2·50
175	**98**	15 c. deep blue (*c*)	2·75	2·75
176	**99**	20 c. grey-black (*b*) (*c*)	1·75	1·75
177	**97**	28 c. deep green (*c*)	6·50	6·50
178	**100**	30 c. sepia (*c*)	2·50	3·00
164/178		*Set of* 15	27·00	26·00

See also Nos. 180/90 and 198/208.

Perforations. Three perforating heads were used: (*a*) comb 14 × 13.9; (*b*) comb 13.5 × 12.75; (*c*) line 13.7 to 14 or compound.

THREE
CENTS

(**101**)

(Surch. by Messrs. D. R. Thistle, St. John's.)

1929 (23 AUG.). *Surch. with T* **101**.

179	**78**	3 c. on 6 c. slate (R.)	1·10	1·10
		a. Surch. inverted	£170	
		b. Surch. in black	£325	

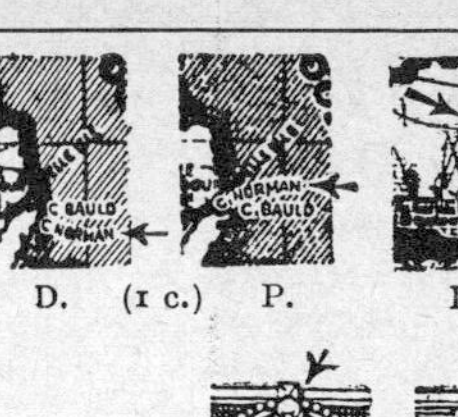

D. (1 c.) P. D. (2 c.) P.

D. (3 c.) P.

D. (4 c.) P.

D. (5 c.) P.

D. (6 c.) P.

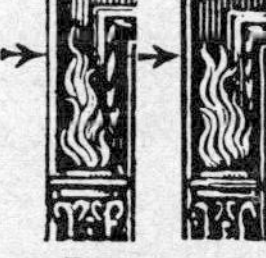

D. (10 c.) P.

D. (15 c.) P.

D. (20 c.) P.

D. "De La Rue" printing.

P. "Perkins, Bacon" printing.

1929–31. *"Perkins, Bacon" printing. Former types re-engraved. No wmk. P* 13½ *to* 14.

180	**88**	1 c. green (*a*) (*d*) (26.9.29)	75	20
		a. Imperf. between (pair)	65·00	
		b. Imperf. (pair)	65·00	
181	**89**	2 c. scarlet (*b*) (*d*) (10.8.29)	70	12
		a. Imperf. (pair)	45·00	
182	**90**	3 c. red-brown (*c*) (10.8.29)	80	12
		a. Imperf. (pair)	55·00	
183	**91**	4 c. reddish purple (*c*) (26.8.29)	1·10	35
		a. Imperf. (pair)	55·00	
184	**92**	5 c. deep grey-green (*c*) (14.9.29)	1·10	40
185	**93**	6 c. ultram. (*b*) (*d*) (8.11.29)	3·75	3·75
188	**96**	10 c. violet (*c*) (5.10.29)	1·75	90
189	**98**	15 c. blue (*c*) (Jan. '30)	10·00	10·00
190	**99**	20 c. black (*d*) (1.1.31)	14·00	7·00
180/190		*Set of* 9	30·00	20·00

Perforations. Four perforating heads were used: (*a*) comb 14 × 13.9; (*b*) comb 13.6 × 13.5; (*c*) comb 13.6 × 13.8; (*d*) line 13.7 to 14 or compound.

Trans-Atlantic
AIR MAIL
By B. M.
"Columbia"
September
1930
Fifty Cents
(**102**)

1930 (25 Sept.). *Air.* *T* **68** *surch. with T* **102** *by Messrs. D. R. Thistle.*
191 50 c. on 36 c. sage-green .. £2000 £2250

103. Aeroplane and Dog-team.

104.
Vickers-Vimy Biplane and early Sailing Packet.

105. Routes of historic Transatlantic Flights.

106

(Des A. B. Perlin. Recess. Perkins, Bacon.)

1931. *Air. T* **103** *to* **105.** *P* 14.
(*a*) *Without wmk.* (2.1.31).
192 15 c. chocolate .. .. 1·75 2·00
a. Imperf. between (horiz. or vert. pair) £250
b. Imperf. (pair) £275
193 50 c. green .. .. 5·00 6·00
a. Imperf. between (horiz. or vert. pair) £250 £225
b. Imperf. (pair) £275
194 $1 deep blue .. .. 16·00 16·00
a. Imperf. between (horiz. or vert. pair) £300
b. Imperf. (pair) £275

(*b*) *Wmk. T* **106**, *sideways* (13.3.31).
195 15 c. chocolate .. .. 1·75 2·00
a. Pair, with and without wmk. 12·00
b. Imperf. between (horiz. or vert. pair) £250
ba. Do., one without wmk. (vert. pair) .. ..
c. Imperf. (pair) £150
d. Wmk. Cross (pair) .. .. 35·00
196 50 c. green .. .. 8·00 10·00
a. Imperf. between (horiz. or vert. pair) £250
b. Imperf. (pair) £250
c. Pair, with and without wmk.
197 $1 deep blue .. .. 23·00 25·00
a. Imperf. between (horiz. or vert. pair) £450
b. Imperf. horiz. (vert. pair) .. £275
c. Pair, with and without wmk.
d. Imperf. (pair) £175

"WITH AND WITHOUT WMK." PAIRS listed in the issues from No. 195a onwards must have one stamp *completely* without any trace of watermark.

1931. "*Perkins, Bacon*" *printing* (*re-engraved types*). *W* **106**. *P* 13½ *to* 14.
198 **88** 1 c. green .. .. 1·25 30
a. Imperf. betwn. (horiz. pr.) £400
199 **89** 2 c. scarlet .. .. 1·40 35
200 **90** 3 c. red-brown .. .. 1·40 20
201 **91** 4 c. reddish purple .. 2·25 70
202 **92** 5 c. deep grey-green .. 3·00 3·00
203 **93** 6 c. ultramarine (25.3.31) 6·50 6·50
204 **94** 8 c. chestnut (1.4.31) .. 6·50 6·50
205 **96** 10 c. violet .. .. 3·00 3·00
206 **98** 15 c. blue .. .. .. 10·00 10·00
207 **99** 20 c. black .. .. 14·00 4·50
208 **100** 30 c. sepia .. .. 8·00 8·00
198/208 .. .. *Set of* 11 50·00 40·00

Perforations. Two perforating heads were used: comb 13.4 × 13.4 for 1 c.; comb 13.6 × 13.8 for other values.

107. Codfish.

108. King George V.

109. Queen Mary.

110. Duke of Windsor when Prince of Wales.

111. Caribou.

112. Queen Elizabeth II when Princess.

113. Salmon.

114. Newfoundland Dog.

115. Seal.

116. Cape Race.

117. Sealing Fleet.

118. Fishing Fleet.

(Recess. Perkins, Bacon.)

1932 (1 Jan). *W* **106**. *P* 13½ (*comb*).
209 **107** 1 c. green 60 20
a. Imperf. (pair) .. .. 50·00
b. Perf. 13 (line) .. .. 16·00 18·00
ba. Imp. betwn. (vert. pr.) .. 60·00
c. Booklet pane of 4 (P 13) 20·00
210 **108** 2 c. carmine 50 15
a. Imperf. (pair) .. .. 50·00
b. Perf. 13 (line) .. .. 16·00 18·00
c. Perf. 14 (line). Small holes
d. Booklet pane of 4 (P 13½) 7·00
e. Booklet pane of 4 (P 13) 10·00
211 **109** 3 c. orange-brown .. 35 15
b. Perf. 13 (line) 16·00
c. Perf. 14 (line). Small holes 20·00
ca. Imp. betwn. (vert. pr.) .. 50·00
d. Booklet pane of 4 (P 13½) 15·00
e. Booklet pane of 4 (P 13) 25·00
f. Booklet pane of 4 (P 14) 15·00
212 **110** 4 c. bright violet .. 1·60 50
213 **111** 5 c. maroon .. .. 2·25 50
a. Imperf. (pair) £100
214 **112** 6 c. light blue .. .. 4·50 4·50

215 **113** 10 c. black-brown .. 50 20
a. Imperf. (pair) .. .. 48·00
216 **114** 14 c. black 90 90
a. Imperf. (pair) .. .. 70·00
217 **115** 15 c. claret 90 90
a. Imperf. (pair) .. .. 80·00
b. Perf. 14 (line) .. .. 4·00 6·50
218 **116** 20 c. green .. .. 1·00 45
a. Imperf. (pair) .. .. 70·00
b. Perf. 14 (line) .. .. 18·00
219 **117** 25 c. slate.. .. .. 1·00 85
a. Imperf. (pair) .. .. 75·00
b. Perf. 14 (line) .. .. 6·00 6·00
ba. Imp. betwn. (vert. pr.) .. £120
220 **118** 30 c. ultramarine .. 7·00 7·50
a. Imperf. (pair) £180
b. Imp. between (vert. pr.) £225
c. Perf. 14 (line) £100
209/220 .. .. *Set of* 12 19·00 15·00
For similar stamps perf. 12½ see Nos. 276/289.

TRANS-ATLANTIC
WEST TO EAST
Per Dornier DO-X
May, 1932.
One Dollar and Fifty Cents

(119)

1932 (19 May). *Air. Surch. as T* **119**, *by Messrs. D. R. Thistle. W* **106**. *P* 14.
221 **105** $1.50 on $1 deep blue (R.) £130 £130
a. Surch. inverted.. .. £3000

120. Queen Mother, when Duchess of York.

121. Paper Mills.

122. Bell Island.

(Recess. Perkins Bacon.)

1932–38. *Wmk. T* **106** (*sideways on vert. designs*). *P* 13½ (*comb.*).
222 **107** 1 c. grey.. .. .. 15 10
a. Imperf. (pair).. .. 40·00
b. Perf. 14 (line).. .. 5·00
c. P 14 (line). Small holes 12·00
d. Pr. with & without wmk.
e. Booklet pane of 4 (P 13½) 14·00
f. Booklet pane of 4 (P 14) 14·00
223 **108** 2 c. green 35 10
a. Imperf. (pair).. .. 48·00
b. Perf. 14 (line).. .. 5·00
ba. Imp. betwn. (horiz. pair) £120
c. P 14 (line). Small holes 8·50
d. Pr. with & without wmk. 15·00
e. Booklet pane of 4 (P 13½) 5·50
f. Booklet pane of 4 (P 14) 5·50
224 **110** 4 c. carmine 25 10
a. Imperf. (pair).. .. 35·00
b. Perf. 14 (line).. .. 2·50
ba. Imp. btwn. (hor. or vert. pr.) 60·00
225 **111** 5 c. violet (Die I) .. 2·50 15
a. Imperf. (pair).. .. 48·00
b. P 14 (line). Small holes 15·00
c. Die II 40 10
ca. Imperf. (pair).. .. 75·00
cb. Perf. 14 (line) .. .. 12·00
cc. Imp. betwn. (horiz. pair) 85·00
cd. Pr. with & without wmk.
226 **120** 7 c. red-brown.. .. 50 60
b. Perf. 14 (line).. ..
ba. Imp. btwn. (horiz. pair) £200
c. Imperf. (pair).. .. 75·00
227 **121** 8 c. brownish red .. 55 45
a. Imperf. (pair).. .. 35·00
228 **122** 24 c. bright blue .. 1·25 1·25
aa. Imperf. (pair).. .. 80·00
ab. Doubly printed .. £500
228*a* **118** 48 c. red-brown (1.1.38) 2·50 1·50
b. Imperf. (pair).. .. 30·00
222/228*a* .. .. *Set of* 8 5·50 3·75

No. 223. Two dies exist of the 2 c. Die I was used for No. 210 and both dies for No. 223. The differences, though numerous, are very slight.

No. 225. There are also two dies of the 5 c., Die I only being used for No. 213 and both dies for the violet stamp. In Die II the antler pointing to the "T" of "POSTAGE" is taller than the one pointing to the "S" and the individual hairs on the underside of the caribou's tail are distinct.

For similar stamps perf. 12½ see Nos. 276/289.

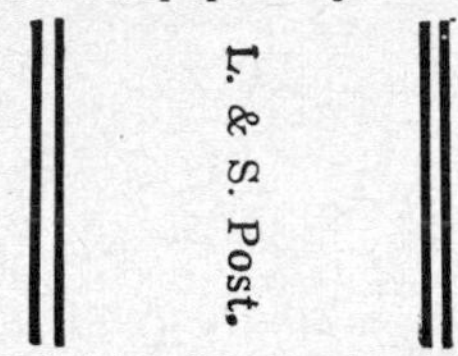

(**123**) "L. & S."—Land and Sea.

1933 (9 Feb.). *Optd. with T* **123** *for ordinary postal use, by Messrs. D. R. Thistle. W* **106** *sideways. P* 14.
229 **103** 15 c. chocolate .. .. 2·75 3·50
a. Pair, one without wmk. 9·00
b. Opt. reading up .. £450
c. Vt. pr., one without surch. £750

124. Put to Flight.

125. Land of Hearts Delight.

126. Spotting the Herd.

127. News from Home.

128. Labrador.

(Des. J. Scott. Recess. Perkins, Bacon.)

1933 (31 May). *Air. W* **106**. *P* 14 (*a*) *or* 11½ (*b*).
230 **124** 5 c. red-brown (*a*) .. 4·00 4·00
a. Imperf. (pair) .. £110
b. Imp. between (horiz. or vert. pair) .. £1000
231 **125** 10 c. orange-yellow (*b*) .. 4·50 5·00
a. Imperf. (pair) .. £100
232 **126** 30 c. light blue (*a*) .. 9·00 10·00
a. Imperf. (pair) .. £180
233 **127** 60 c. green (*b*) .. .. 15·00 16·00
a. Imperf. (pair) .. £180
234 **128** 75 c. yellow-brown (*a*) .. 16·00 17·00
a. Imperf. (pair) .. £140
b. Imp. between (horiz. or vert. pair) £1000
230/234 .. .. *Set of* 5 42·00 48·00

1933
GEN. BALBO
FLIGHT.
$4.50
(**129**)

(Surch. by Robinson & Co., St. John's.)

1933 (24 July). *Air. Balbo Transatlantic Mass Formation Flight. Surch. with T* **129**. *W* **106**. *P* 14.
235 **128** $4.50 on 75 c. yellow-brn. £170 £170
a. Surch. inverted .. £3000
b. Surch. on 10 c. (No. 231).. £12000

No. 235a. When this error was discovered the stamps were ordered to be officially destroyed but in fact four copies which had been torn were recovered and skilfully repaired and the price quoted is for one of these. In addition there exist four unrepaired examples which, of course, are worth considerably more.

130. Sir Humphrey Gilbert.

131. Compton Castle, Devon.

132. Gilbert Coat-of-Arms.

133. Eton College.

134. Anchor Token.

135. Gilbert commissioned by Elizabeth.

136. Fleet leaving Plymouth, 1583.

137. Arrival at St. John's.

138. Annexation, 5th August, 1583.

139. Royal Arms.

140. Gilbert in the *Squirrel*.

141. Map of Newfoundland.

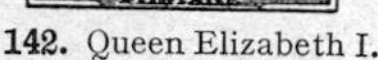

142. Queen Elizabeth I.

143. Gilbert's Statue at Truro.

(Recess. Perkins, Bacon.)

1933 (3 Aug.). *350th Anniv. of the Annexation by Sir Humphrey Gilbert.* W **106.** P $13\frac{1}{2}$ (*comb.*)*

236	**130**	1 c. slate..	50	30
		a. Imperf. (pair)	25·00	
237	**131**	2 c. green	50	30
		a. Imperf. (pair).. ..	35·00	
		b. Doubly printed ..	£300	
238	**132**	3 c. chestnut	75	45
239	**133**	4 c. carmine	75	30
		a. Imperf. (pair).. ..	25·00	
240	**134**	5 c. violet	90	45
241	**135**	7 c. greenish blue ..	4·00	4·00
		a. Perf. 14	8·00	10·00
242	**136**	8 c. vermilion	4·00	4·00
		a. Brownish red.. ..	£250	
		b. Bisected (4 c.) (on cover)	†	£120
243	**137**	9 c. ultramarine ..	3·25	3·25
		a. Imperf. (pair).. ..	80·00	
		b. Perf. 14	5·00	6·00
244	**138**	10 c. brown-lake	3·00	1·75
		a. Imperf. (pair) ..	£150	
		b. Perf. 14	10·00	10·00
245	**139**	14 c. grey-black	6·50	6·50
		a. Perf. 14	9·00	9·00
246	**140**	15 c. claret	8·00	8·00
247	**141**	20 c. grey-green	4·00	4·50
		a. Perf. 14	6·00	7·00
248	**142**	24 c. maroon	9·00	9·00
		a. Imperf. (pair)	60·00	
		b. Perf. 14	12·00	14·00
249	**143**	32 c. olive-black	10·00	10·00
		a. Perf. 14	15·00	16·00
236/249		.. .. *Set of* 14	50·00	55·00

* *Perforations.* Two perforating heads were used: comb. 13·4 × 13·4 for all values; line 13·8 (listed above as 14) for a second printing of some values.

1935 (6 May). *Silver Jubilee. As Nos.* 91/4 *of Antigua, but ptd. by B. W. & Co.* P 11 × 12.

250	4 c. rosine	40	20
251	5 c. bright violet	45	35
252	7 c. blue	80	60
253	24 c. olive-green	1·75	1·50
250/253	Perf. "Specimen" *Set of* 4	35·00	

1937 (12 May). *Coronation Issue. As Nos.* 13/15 *of Aden but name and value uncoloured on coloured background and ptd. by B. W. & Co.* P 11 × 11½.

254	2 c. green	15	12
255	4 c. carmine	20	12
256	5 c. purple	35	25
254/256	Perf. "Specimen" *Set of* 3	25·00	

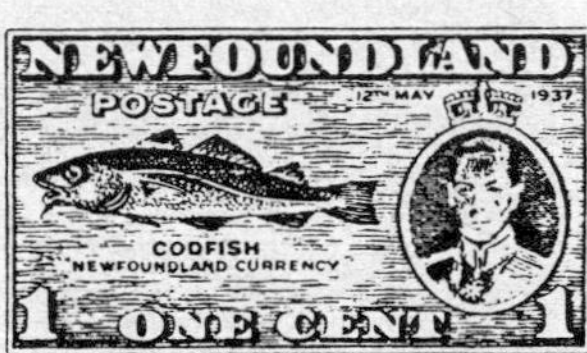

144. Codfish.

145. Map of Newfoundland.

146. Caribou.

147. Corner Brook Paper Mills.

148. Salmon.

149. Newfoundland Dog.

150. Northern Seal.

151. Cape Race.

152. Bell Island.

153. Sealing Fleet.

154. The Banks Fishing Fleet.

Die. I. Die II.

No. 258. In Die II the shading of the King's face is heavier and dots have been added down the ridge of the nose. The top frame line is thicker and more uniform.

(Recess. Perkins, Bacon.)

1937 (12 MAY). *Additional Coronation Issue. T* **144** *to* **154.** *W* **106.** A. *P* 14 *or* 13½ (*line*). B. *P* 13 (*comb.*)

		A.		B.	
257	1 c. grey ..	20	10	6·00	7·00
	a. Pair with & without wmk.	7·00		—	—
258	3 c. orge.-brn. (I)	30	15	35	20
	a. Pair with & without wmk.	18·00		†	
	b. Die I Imp. btwn. (horiz. or vert. pr.)	£180		†	
	c. Die II	30	20	30	25
	d. Die II. Imp. btwn. (horiz. or vert .pr.)	£240		†	
	e. Die II. Pr. with & without wmk.	—	—		
259	7 c. brt. ultram.	35	35	30·00	
	a. Pair with & without wmk.	—	—	†	
260	8 c. scarlet ..	55	55	1·10	1·10
	a. Pair with & without wmk.	11·00		†	
	b. Imperf. btwn. (horiz. or vert. pr.)	£275		†	
	c. Imperf. (pair)	90·00			
261	10 c. deep olive	75	75	2·00	1·50
	a. Pair with & without wmk.	20·00		†	
262	14 c. black ..	1·00	1·00	—	£550
	a. Pair with & without wmk.	13·00		†	
263	15 c. claret ..	1·25	1·25	1·50	1·50
	a. Pair with & without wmk.	13·00		—	—
	b. Imperf. between (vert. pr.)	£140		†	
264	20 c. green ..	1·00	1·00	1·25	1·25
	a. Pair with & without wmk.	35·00		†	
	b. Imperf. between (vert. pair)	£250		†	
265	24 c. light blue	1·25	1·25	1·50	1·75
	a. Pair with & without wmk.	35·00		†	
	b. Imp. between (vert. pair)	£275		†	
266	25 c. slate ..	1·10	1·10	4·00	4·00
	a. Pair with & without wmk.	18·00		†	
267	48 c. slate-purple	1·50	1·50	7·00	7·00
	a. Pair with & without wmk.	35·00		†	
	b. Imp. between (vert. pair)	£275		†	
257/267	*Set of* 11	8·00	8·00		

See note after No. 197 re the watermark varieties.

The line perforation "A" was produced by two machines measuring respectively 13.7 and 14.1. The comb perforation "B" measures 13.3 × 13.2.

155. King George VI. **156.** Queen Mother.

157. Queen Elizabeth II as Princess. **158.** Queen Mary.

(Recess. Perkins, Bacon.)

1938 (12 MAY). *W* **106** (*sideways*). *P* 13½ (*comb.*).

268	**155**	2 c. green	1·00	12
		a. Pair, with and without wmk.	70·00	
		b. Imperf. (pair)	35·00	
269	**156**	3 c. carmine	1·00	12
		a. Perf. 14 (*line*)	£100	40·00
		b. Pr. with and without wmk.	90·00	
		c. Imperf. (pair) ..	30·00	
270	**157**	4 c. light blue	1·10	12
		a. Pr., with and without wmk.	40·00	
		b. Imperf. (pair) ..	35·00	
271	**158**	7 c. deep ultramarine ..	70	70
		a. Imperf. (pair)	35·00	

For similar designs, perf. 12½, see Nos. 277/281.

159. King George VI and Queen Elizabeth.

(Recess. B.W.)

1939 (17 JUNE). *Royal Visit. No wmk. P* 13½.

272	**159**	5 c. deep ultramarine ..	50	50

2

CENTS

(**160**)

1939 (20 NOV.). *No. 272 surch. as T* **160,** *at St. John's.*

273	**159**	2 c. on 5 c. dp. ultram.(Br.)	75	75
274	,,	4 c. on 5 c. dp. ultram.(C.)	50	50

161. Grenfell on the *Strathcona* (after painting by Gribble).

(Recess. Canadian Bank Note Co.)

1941 (1 DEC.). *Sir Wilfred Grenfell's Labrador Mission. P* 12.

275	**161**	5 c. blue	25	20

(Recess. Waterlow.)

1941–44. *W* **106** (*sideways on vert. designs*). *P* 12½.

276	**107**	1 c. grey	8	8
277	**155**	2 c. green	10	5
278	**156**	3 c. carmine	12	5
		a. Pair, with and without wmk.	25·00	
279	**157**	4 c. blue	30	5
		a. Pair, with and without wmk.	45·00	
280	**111**	5 c. violet (Die I) ..	30	8
		a. Pair, with and without wmk.		
281	**158**	7 c. deep ultramarine ..	45	45
		a. Pair, with and without wmk.	45·00	
282	**121**	8 c. rose-red	45	30
		a. Pair, with and without wmk.	45·00	
283	**113**	10 c. black-brown ..	50	30
284	**114**	14 c. black	75	75
285	**115**	15 c. claret	75	75
286	**116**	20 c. green	75	60
287	**122**	24 c. blue	1·25	1·00
288	**117**	25 c. slate	1·25	1·00
289	**118**	48 c. red-brown ('44) ..	1·50	1·00
276/289		.. .. *Set of* 14	7·50	5·50

Nos. 277/8 are redrawn versions of T **155/6.** No. 280. For Die I see note relating to No. 225.

162. Memorial University College.

(Recess. Canadian Bank Note Co.)

1943 (2 JAN.). *P* 12.

290	**162**	30 c. carmine	1·00	75

163. St. John's.

(Recess. Canadian Bank Note Co.)

1943 (1 JUNE). *Air. P* 12.

291	**163**	7 c. ultramarine	25	20

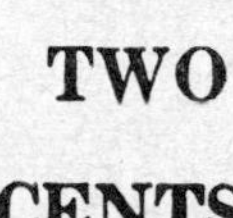

(**164**)

165. Queen Elizabeth II when Princess.

1946 (23 MAR.). *Surch. locally with T* **164.**

292	**162**	2 c. on 30 c. carmine ..	20	25

(Recess. Waterlow.)

1947 (21 APR.). *Princess Elizabeth's 21st Birthday. W* **106** (*sideways*). *P* 12½.

293	**165**	4 c. light blue	20	12

166. Cabot off Cape Bonavista.

(Recess. Waterlow.)

1947 (23 June). *450th Anniv. of Cabot's Discovery of Newfoundland. W* **106** *(sideways). P* 12½.
294 **166** 5 c. mauve 20 20
a. Imperf. between (horiz. pair) £300

POSTAGE DUE STAMPS.

D 1

(Litho. John Dickinson & Co., Ltd.)

1939 (1 May)–**49**. *P* 10.
D1 **D 1** 1 c. green 60 60
a. Perf. 11 ('49) .. .. 1·00
D2 ,, 2 c. vermilion .. .. 1·25 1·25
a. Perf. 11 × 9 ('46) .. 1·60 1·60
D3 ,, 3 c. ultramarine .. .. 1·25 1·25
a. Perf. 11 × 9 ('49) .. 2·50 2·50
b. Perf. 9 .. .. ..
D4 ,, 4 c. orange .. .. 2·25 2·25
a. Perf. 11 × 9 (May '48) .. 2·50 2·50
D5 ,, 5 c. brown .. .. 1·00 1·00
D6 ,, 10 c. violet .. .. 1·00 1·00
a. Perf. 11 (W 106) ('49) .. 2·50
ab. As last, imp. btwn. (vert. pr.) £130

On 1 April, 1949, Newfoundland joined the Confederation of Canada whose stamps it now uses.

NEW GUINEA.
(FORMERLY NEW BRITAIN.)
STAMPS OF GERMAN NEW GUINEA.

G.R.I. 2d. (1) G.R.I. 1s. (2)

Measurements are taken from the bottom of the "R" to the top of the "d" in the low values, or to the top of the figure of value in the large stamps.

Stamps of 1900, *German Colonial issue (no wmk.), surcharged as T* **1** *or* **2** *(mark values).*

First Printing.

1914 (17 Oct.). "G.R.I." *and value 6 mm. apart.*
1 1d. on 3 pf. brown .. .. 15·00 15·00
2 1d. on 5 pf. green .. .. 6·00 6·00
3 2d. on 10 pf. carmine .. .. 9·00 9·00
4 2d. on 20 pf. ultramarine .. 9·00 9·00
a. "2d." doubly printed without the "G.R.I." £200
5 2½d. on 10 pf. carmine .. .. 20·00 20·00
6 2½d. on 20 pf. ultramarine .. 25·00 25·00
7 3d. on 25 pf. black & red/*yell.* 40·00 40·00
8 3d. on 30 pf. blk. & oran./*buff* 50·00 50·00
9 4d. on 40 pf. black & carmine 70·00 70·00
a. Surch. double £300 £300
b. Surch. inverted £300
10 5d. on 50 pf. black & pur./*buff* £130 £130
11 8d. on 80 pf. blk. & carm./*rose* £200 £200
a. No stop .. .. ..

"G.R.I." *and value* 3½ *to* 4 *mm. apart.*
12 1s. on 1 m. carmine .. £350 £350
13 2s. on 2 m. blue .. £375 £375
14 3s. on 3 m. violet-black .. £400 £400
15 5s. on 5 m. carmine and black £1000 £1000
a. No stop after "I" .. ..
b. No stops after "R" and "I" .. £1100

Second Printing.

1914 (16 Dec.). "G.R.I." *and value 5 mm. apart.*
16 1d. on 3 pf. brown .. .. 12·00 12·00
a. Figure "1" omitted .. .. — £100
b. Surch. double .. .. 70·00
c. Surch. inverted .. .. 75·00
17 1d. on 5 pf. green .. .. 4·00 4·00
a. "d" inverted £200 £150
b. No stops after "G R I" .. 40·00 35·00
c. Surch. double £120
d. Small "I" .. .. 7·00 7·00
e. "1d." double .. .. 60·00
f. "G.I.R." for "G.R.I." .. £600
18 2d. on 10 pf. carmine .. .. 8·00 8·00
a. Surch. double £140
b. Surch. double, one inverted .. £350 £350
c. Error. Surcharged "G.I.R. 3d." £1600
d. Stop before instead of after "G" £500
e. Error. "1d." for "2d." and stop before "G" £450 £400
19 2d. on 20 pf. ultramarine .. 10·00 10·00
a. "R" inverted £450 £450
b. Surch. double £300
c. Surch. double, one inverted .. £400 £400
d. Error. Surch. "G.R.I. 1d." .. £800 £800
20 2½d. on 10 pf. carmine .. 25·00 25·00
21 2½d. on 20 pf. ultramarine .. £400 £350
a. Surch. double, one inverted ..
22 3d. on 25 pf. black & red/*yellow* 35·00 35·00
a. "G.I.R." for "G.R.I." .. £400
23 3d. on 30 pf. blk. & orge./*buff* 40·00 40·00
a. "d" inverted .. .. — £225
b. Surch. double £300
c. Surch. double, one inverted .. £400
d. Error. "1d." for "3d." .. £1000
24 4d. on 40 pf. black & carmine 30·00 30·00
a. Surch. double, one inverted .. £375
25 5d. on 50 pf. black & pur./*buff* 60·00 60·00
a. Figure "5" omitted £200
b. Surch. double £200
c. Surch. double, one inverted .. £200
d. "G.I.R." for "G.R.I." ..
26 8d. on 80 pf. blk. & carm./*rose* £150 £150
a. Surch. double, one inverted .. £550 £550
b. Surch. double £550 £550
c. Surch. triple £550 £550

"G.R.I." *and value* 5½ *mm. apart.*
27 1s. on 1 m. carmine £400 £400
28 2s. on 2 m. blue £400 £400
a. Surch. double
29 3s. on 3 m. violet-black .. £600 £600
30 5s. on 5 m. carm. and black .. £1400 £1400

There appears to be also a third printing of most of the low values with 7½ mm. between "G.R.I." and top of the "d".

1915. *Nos.* 18 *and* 19 *further surch. as in T* **5**.
31 "1" on 2d. on 10 pf. ..
32 "1" on 2d. on 20 pf. ..

R G.R.I. 1. Rabaul (Deutsch Neuguinea) № 570

3

1915. *Registration Labels as T* **3**, *surch. and used for postage.*

3d. black and red/*buff*.

Inscr. "(Deutsch Neuguinea)" *spelt in various ways as indicated.*

I. *With name of town in sans-serif letters.*
33 Rabaul "(Deutsch Neuguinea)" 40·00 45·00
a. "G.R.I. 3d." double £200 £150
b. No bracket before "Deutsch" .. 90·00 90·00
c. No stop after "I" .. ..
d. "(Deutsch-Neuguinea)" .. 45·00 45·00
34 Deulon "(Deutsch Neuguinea)" £800
35 Friedrich-Wilhelmshafen "(Deutsch Neuguinea)" .. 40·00 45·00
a. No stop after "d" .. .. 60·00
36 Herbetshöhe "(Deutsch Neuguinea)" .. .. 60·00 60·00
a. "(Deutsch Neu-Guinea)" .. 75·00 75·00
b. No stop after "d" £100
37 Käwieng "(Deutsch-Neuguinea)" 40·00 45·0
a. "(Deutsch Neu-Guinea)" .. 50·00 55·0
b. Without brackets .. .. 40·00 40·0
c. As b, without stop after "d" .. 75·00
d. As b, with "G.R.I. 3d." double £150
38 Kieta "(Deutsch-Neuguinea)" 90·00 90·0
a. No bracket before "Deutsch" .. £130 £130
b. No stop after "d" £130
39 Manus "(Deutsch Neuguinea)" 60·00 70·0
a. "G.R.I. 3d." double £200
40 Stephansort "(Deutsch Neu-Guinea)" .. .. — £400
a. No stop after "d" .. .. — £450

II. *With name of town in letters with serifs.*
41 Friedrich-Wilhelmshafen "(Deutsch-Neuguinea)" .. 40·00 50·0
a. "(Deutsch Neuguinea)" .. 75·00 75·0
42 Käwieng "(Deutsch Neuguinea)" 40·00 50·0
a. No stop after "d" .. .. 75·00
43 Manus "(Deutsch-Neuguinea)" £200
a. No stop after "I" £300

SERVICE STAMPS.

O. S. G.R.I. 1d. (4)

Special Printing.

1914 (Oct.). "G.R.I." *and value* 3½ *mm. apart. Optd. as T* **4**.
48 1d. on 3 pf. brown .. .. 4·00 4·0
49 1d. on 5 pf. green .. .. 15·00 15·0

II. STAMPS OF MARSHALL ISLANDS.

1914 (16 Dec.). *Stamps of German Colonial issue surch. as T* **1** *and* **2** *(mark values).*

"G.R.I." *and value 5 mm. apart.*
50 1d. on 3 pf. brown .. .. 12·00 12·0
a. "1" with straight serif .. 30·00 30·0
b. Surch. inverted £300
51 1d. on 5 pf. green .. .. 14·00 14·0
a. No stop after "d" .. ..
b. "1" and "d" wider apart .. £120
52 2d. on 10 pf. carmine .. .. 4·00 4·00
a. No stop after "G" £140
b. Surch. double £250
c. Surch. double, one inverted .. £250
53 2d. on 20 pf. ultramarine .. 5·00 5·0
a. No stop after "d" .. .. 14·00
b. Surch. double £150
c. Surch. double, one inverted .. £300
54 3d. on 25 pf. black and red/*yell.* £120 £120
a. No stop after "d" £200 £200
b. Surch. double £350 £350
c. Surch. double, one inverted ..
55 3d. on 30 pf. blk. & orge./*buff* £120 £120
a. No stop after "d" £200
56 4d. on 40 pf. black & carmine 25·00 25·0
a. No stop after "d" .. .. 60·00 60·0
b. Surch. inverted £300
57 5d. on 50 pf. blk. & purple/*buff* 40·00 40·00
a. "5" only for "5d." £150
58 8d. on 80 pf. blk. & carm./*rose* £160 £160
59 1s. on 1 m. carmine £400 £400
a. No stop after "I" £550
b. Surch. double .. ..
60 2s. on 2 m. blue £275 £275
a. Surch. double, one inverted .. — £700
b. Large "S" after "2" .. ..
61 3s. on 3 m. violet-black .. £700 £800
a. Surch. double .. ..
b. No stop after "I" £800
62 5s. on 5 m. carmine & black £1500 £1600
a. Surch. double, one inverted .. £2000 £2000

G.R.I. 1d. (5)

1915. *Nos.* 52 *and* 53 *further surch. as in T* **5**.
63 "1" on 2d. on 10 pf. carmine 50·00 55·00
64 "1" on 2d. on 20 pf. ultram... £900 £500

III. AUSTRALIAN STAMPS OVERPRINTED.

N. W. PACIFIC SLANDS. 6 (*a*)   N. W. PACIFIC ISLANDS. (*b*)   N. W. PACIFIC ISLANDS. (*c*)

7 (5)

8 (2)

9 (6)

The Type numbers shown in brackets are the equivalent Type numbers of Australia.

1915–16. *Stamps of Australia optd. in black as T* **6** (*a*), (*b*) *or* (*c*).

(i) *W* **7.** *P* 14 (4 Jan.–15 March, 1915).

55 **5a** ½d. green 50 60
56 ,, ½d. bright green 50 60
57 ,, 1d. pale rose (Die I) (4.1) .. 50 70
58 ,, 1d. dull-red (Die I) .. 90 1·00
59 ,, 1d. carmine-red (Die I) .. 90 1·00
a. Substituted cliché.. .. — £200
59*b* ,, 1d. carmine-red (Die II) .. 50·00
c. Substituted cliché.. .. £300
70 ,, 4d. yellow-orange .. .. 1·50 1·90
a. Line through "FOURPENCE" .. .. 40·00 45·00
71 ,, 4d. yellow .. .. .. 80·00 85·00
72 ,, 5d. brown .. .. .. 2·25 2·50

(ii) *W* **8.** *P* 12 (4 Jan. 1915 March, 1916).

73 **1** 2d. grey (Die I) .. .. 1·10 1·60
74 ,, 2½d. indigo (4.1.15) .. .. 1·10 1·60
76 ,, 3d. yellow-olive (Die I) .. 2·25 4·50
a. Die II .. .. .. 65·00 75·00
ab. In pair with Die I.. .. £100 £110
77 ,, 3d. greenish olive (Die I) .. 60·00 80·00
a. Die II £350
ab. In pair with Die I.. .. £425
8 ,, 6d. ultramarine .. .. 4·50 5·50
a. Retouched "E" £1200
79 ,, 9d. violet .. .. .. 6·00 9·00
1 ,, 1s. green .. .. .. 8·00 10·00
3 ,, 5s. grey and yellow (3.16) £180 £170
4 ,, 10s. grey and pink (12.15).. 35·00 45·00
5 ,, £1 brown and ultramarine (12.15) £170 £160

(iii) *W* **7.** *P* 12 (Oct.-July, 1916).

6 **1** 2d. grey (Die I) .. .. 1·10 1·25
7 ,, 2½d. indigo (7.16) £1000 £900
8 ,, 6d. ultramarine .. .. 2·50 2·75
9 ,, 9d. violet (12.15) .. .. 2·50 2·75
0 ,, 1s. emerald (12.15) .. 3·00 4·00
1 ,, 2s. brown (12.15) .. .. 25·00 27·00
2 ,, 5s. grey and yellow (12.15) 25·00 27·00

(iv) *W* **9.** *P* 12 (Dec. 1915–Aug. 1916).

4 **1** 2d. grey (Die I) .. .. 1·50 1·75
a. Die II .. .. .. 3·00 3·50
ab. In pair with Die I .. .. 40·00
6 ,, 3d. yellow-olive (Die I) .. 2·00 3·00
a. Die II .. .. .. 20·00 15·00
ab. In pair with Die I .. .. 35·00
7 ,, 2s. brown (8.16) .. .. 7·50 8·00
9 ,, £1 brown and ultramarine.. (8.16) £160 £170

Dates for Nos. 67 and 74 are issue dates. All other dates are those of despatch. Nos. 65/6. 68/73, 76/81 were despatched on 15 March 1915.

SETTINGS. The overprint T **6** shows three main varieties differing in the letters "S" of "ISLANDS". (*a*) Both "SS" normal. (*b*) First "S" with small head and large tail and second "S" normal. (*c*) Both "SS" with small head and large tail.

It has been established, by the study of minor variations, that there are actually six settings of the overprint, including that represented by T **11**, but the following are the different arrangements of the letters "S", taking these above into account.

A. Horizontal rows 1' and 2 all Type (*a*) Row 3 all Type (*b*). Rows 4 and 5 all Type (*c*).

B. (½d. green, only). As A, except that the types in the bottom row run (*c*) (*c*) (*c*) (*c*) (*c*) (*b*) (*c*),

C. As A, but bottom row now shows types (*a*) (*c*) (*c*) (*c*) (*b*) (*c*).

Horizontal strips and pairs showing varieties (*a*) and (*c*), or (*b*) and (*c*) *se-tenant* are scarce.

The earliest printing of the 1d. and 2½d. values was made on sheets with margin attached on two sides, the later printings being on sheets from which the margins had been removed. In this printing the vertical distances between the overprints are less than in later printings, so that in the lower horizontal rows of the sheet the overprint is near the top of the stamp.

The settings used on King George stamps and on the Kangaroo type are similar, but the latter stamps being smaller the overprints are closer together in the vertical rows.

PURPLE OVERPRINTS. We no longer differentiate between purple and black overprints in the above series. In our opinion the two colours are nowadays insufficiently distinct to warrant separation.

PRICES. The prices quoted for Nos. 65 to 101 apply to stamps with opts., Types **6** (*a*) or **6** (*c*). Stamps with opt. Type **6** (*b*) are worth double. Vertical strips of three, showing (*a*), (*b*) and (*c*), can be supplied if in stock, at about five times the prices quoted for singles.

One Penny (10)   N. W. PACIFIC ISLANDS. (11)

1918 (23 MAY). *Nos.* 72 *and* 81 *surch. locally with T* **10.**

100 1d. on 5d. brown .. .. 35·00 30·00
101 1d. on 1s. green .. .. 35·00 30·00

Types **6** (*a*), (*b*), (*c*) oc cur on these stamps also.

1918–23. *Stamps of Australia, optd. with T* **11** ("P" *of* "PACIFIC" *over space between* "I" *and* "S" *of* "ISLANDS").

(i) *T* **5***a* (*King*). *W* **7.** *P* 14.

102 ½d. green 40 60
103 1d. carmine-red (Die I) .. 80 60
a. Substituted cliché £200
b. Rosine. Rough paper, locally gummed (perfd. "O S") .. — 45·00
103*c* 1d. carmine-red (Die II) .. 60·00 20·00
d. Substituted cliché £200
e. Rosine. Rough paper, locally gummed (perfd. "O S") ..
104 4d. yellow-orange (1919) .. 4·00 5·00
a. Line through "FOURPENCE".. .. .. £200
105 5d. brown (1919) .. .. 2·00 4·00

(ii) *T* **1** (*Kangaroo*). *W* **9.** *P* 12.

106 2d. grey (Die I) (1919) .. 2·00 3·00
a. Die II .. .. .. 4·50 4·50
107 2½d. indigo (1919) .. .. 4·00 4·50
a. "1" of "½" omitted .. £850 £800
108 2½d. blue (1920) .. .. 2·00 3·25
109 3d. greenish olive (Die I) (1919) 3·00 4·00
a. Die II .. .. .. 10·00 11·00
ab. In pair with Die I .. .. 70·00
b. Light olive (Die II) ('23) .. 2·00 2·25
110 6d. ultramarine (1919) .. 3·00 4·00
111 6d. greyish ultram. (1922) .. 11·00 12·00
112 9d. violet (1919) .. .. 4·50 8·00
113 1s. emerald .. .. .. 4·50 6·50
114 1s. pale blue-green .. .. 5·00 7·00
115 2s. brown (1919) .. .. 8·00 9·00
116 5s. grey and yellow (1919) .. 14·00 15·00
117 10s. grey and bright pink ('19) 45·00 50·00
118 £1 brown and ultram. ('22) £160

(iii) *T* **5***a*. *W* **6***a of Australia.* (*Mult. Crown* "A"). *P* 14.

119 ½d. green (1919) 20 50

Type **11***b* differs from Type **6** (*a*) in the position of the "P" of "PACIFIC", which is further to the left in Type **11***b*.

1921–22. *T* **5***a of Australia. W* **7.** *Colour changes and new value. Optd. with T* **11.**

120 1d. bright violet (1922) .. 90 1·75
121 2d. orange .. .. .. 3·00 3·25
122 2d. scarlet (1922) .. .. 1·50 5·00
123 4d. violet (1922) .. .. 9·00 10·00
a. "FOURPENCE" in thinner letters £170
124 4d. ultramarine (1922) .. 6·00 7·50
a. "FOURPENCE" in thinner letters £170

IV. TERRITORY OF NEW GUINEA.

PRINTERS. See note at the beginning of Australia.

12. Native Village.

(Des. R. A. Harrison. Eng. T. S. Harrison. Recess. Note Printing Branch, Commonwealth Bank of Australia, Melbourne, from 1926 Note Ptg. Branch, Reserve Bank of Australia, Melbourne.)

1925–28. *P* 11.

125 **12** ½d. orange .. .. .. 30 1·00
126 ,, 1d. green .. .. .. 35 1·00
126*a* ,, 1½d. orange-verm. (1926) .. 1·00 1·00
127 ,, 2d. claret .. .. .. 1·25 1·50
128 ,, 3d. blue .. .. .. 2·00 1·75
129 ,, 4d. olive-green .. .. 3·00 3·50
130 ,, 6d. dull yellow-brown .. 3·50 5·50
a. Olive-bistre (1927) .. .. 3·50 5·50
b. Pale yellow-bistre (1928) .. 4·00 6·00
131 9d. dull purple (to violet).. 5·00 6·50
132 ,, 1s. dull blue-green .. .. 5·00 6·00
133 ,, 2s. brown-lake .. .. 7·00 9·00
134 ,, 5s. olive-bistre .. .. 12·00 13·00
135 ,, 10s. dull rose .. .. 22·00 25·00
136 ,, £1 dull olive-green .. 40·00 45·00
125/136 .. .. *Set of* 13 95·00 £110

(13)

14. Bird of Paradise. (Dates either side of value.)

1931 (8 JUNE). *Air. Optd. with T* **13.** *P* 11.

137 **12** ½d. orange 20 40
138 ,, 1d. green 30 50
139 ,, 1½d. orange-vermilion .. 60 1·40
140 ,, 2d. claret .. .. .. 70 2·50
141 ,, 3d. blue .. .. .. 1·10 1·50
142 ,, 4d. olive-green .. .. 1·50 2·00
143 ,, 6d. pale yellow-bistre .. 1·60 2·50
144 ,, 9d. violet .. .. .. 1·75 4·25

145	12	1s. dull blue-green	3·00	4·50
146	,,	2s. brown-lake	5·50	6·00
147	,,	5s. olive-bistre	11·00	12·00
148	,,	10s. bright pink	28·00	30·00
149	,,	£1 olive-grey	50·00	60·00
137/149		Set of 13	95·00	£110

AIR MAIL

(15)

(Recess. John Ash, Melbourne.)

1931 (2 Aug.). *Tenth Anniv. of Australian Administration. T* **14** *(with dates). P* 11.

150	14	1d. green	20	25
151	,,	1½d. vermilion	1·75	1·75
152	,,	2d. claret	75	65
153	,,	3d. blue	90	90
154	,,	4d. olive-green	2·00	2·50
155	,,	5d. deep blue-green	2·25	2·50
156	,,	6d. bistre-brown	2·25	2·75
157	,,	9d. violet	2·50	3·50
158	,,	1s. pale blue-green	2·75	3·75
159	,,	2s. brown-lake	5·00	5·50
160	,,	5s. olive-brown	10·00	11·00
161	,,	10s. bright pink	35·00	40·00
162	,,	£1 olive-grey	60·00	70·00
150/162		Set of 13	£110	£130

1931 (2 Aug.). *Air. Optd. with T* **15.**

163	14	½d. orange	20	30
164	,,	1d. green	45	50
165	,,	1½d. vermilion	75	75
166	,,	2d. claret	80	80
167	,,	3d. blue	1·00	1·00
168	,,	4d. olive-green	1·10	1·50
169	,,	5d. deep blue-green	1·50	2·00
170	,,	6d. bistre-brown	3·00	3·50
171	,,	9d. violet	2·75	4·00
172	,,	1s. pale blue-green	3·00	4·00
173	,,	2s. dull lake	5·00	7·00
174	,,	5s. olive-brown	9·00	12·00
175	,,	10s. bright pink	40·00	40·00
176	,,	£1 olive-grey	60·00	60·00
163/176		Set of 14	£110	£120

1932 (30 June)–**1934.** *T* **14** *(redrawn without dates). P* 11.

177	1d. green	20	20
178	1½d. claret	35	60
179	2d. vermilion	30	35
179*a*	2½d. green (14.9.34)	1·50	3·00
180	3d. blue	50	60
180*a*	3½d. aniline carmine (14.9.34)	2·75	2·75
181	4d. olive-green	60	70
182	5d. deep blue-green	70	70
183	6d. bistre-brown	70	1·00
184	9d. violet	3·00	4·50
185	1s. blue-green	1·75	3·25
186	2s. dull lake	3·00	4·00
187	5s. olive	9·00	10·00
188	10s. pink	35·00	35·00
189	£1 olive-grey	40·00	35·00
177/189	Set of 15	90·00	90·00

1932 (30 June)–**34.** *Air. T* **14** *(redrawn without dates), optd. with T* **15.** *P* 11.

190	½d. orange	20	20
191	1d. green	20	25
192	1½d. claret	35	50
193	2d. vermilion	60	50
193*a*	2½d. green (14.9.34)	1·00	85
194	3d. blue	70	45
194*a*	3½d. aniline carmine (14.9.34)	1·50	1·10
195	4d. olive-green	1·00	1·00
196	5d. deep blue-green	1·50	2·00
197	6d. bistre-brown	1·10	2·25
198	9d. violet	2·00	2·50
199	1s. pale blue-green	2·00	2·00
200	2s. dull lake	3·00	3·50
201	5s. olive-brown	9·00	10·00
202	10s. pink	30·00	28·00
203	£1 olive-grey	35·00	20·00
190/203	Set of 16	80·00	70·00

Two sheets were reported of the ½d. without overprint but it is believed they were not issued.

16. Bulolo Goldfields.

(Recess. John Ash.)

1935 (1 May). *Air. P* 11.

204	16	£2 bright violet	80·00	65·00
205	,,	£5 emerald-green	£250	£200

HIS MAJESTY'S JUBILEE. 1910 — 1935

(17)

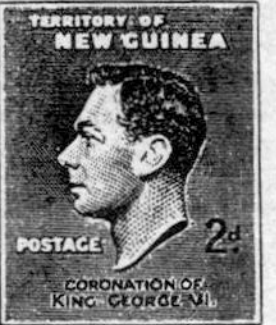

18

1935 (27 June). *Silver Jubilee. As Nos.* 177 *and* 179, *but shiny paper. Optd. with T* **17.**

206	1d. green	45	45
207	2d. vermilion	75	90

(Recess. John Ash, Melbourne.)

1937 (18 May). *Coronation. P* 11.

208	18	2d. scarlet	12	15
209	,,	3d. blue	12	15
210	,,	5d. green	15	20
		a. Re-entry (design completely duplicated)	15·00	15·00
211	,,	1s. purple	25	35

(Recess. John Ash, Melbourne.)

1939 (1 Mar.). *Air. Inscr.* "AIR MAIL POSTAGE" *at foot. P* 11.

212	16	½d. orange	80	40
213	,,	1d. green	20	35
214	,,	1½d. claret	50	1·00
215	,,	2d. vermilion	1·00	1·10
216	,,	3d. blue	1·50	1·60
217	,,	4d. yellow-olive	1·25	1·60
218	,,	5d. deep green	80	1·00
219	,,	6d. bistre-brown	1·60	2·25
220	,,	9d. violet	2·25	3·25
221	,,	1s. pale blue-green	2·75	3·25
222	,,	2s. dull lake	10·00	11·00
223	,,	5s. olive-brown	17·00	19·00
224	,,	10s. pink	45·00	45·00
225	,,	£1 olive-green	38·00	40·00
212/225		Set of 14	£110	£120

OFFICIAL STAMPS.

Australian stamps perforated "O S" exist with overprint Type **11** for use in New Guinea. We do not list such varieties but can supply when in stock.

O S (O 1) **O S** (O 2)

1925–31. *Optd. with Type* O **1.** *P* 11.

O1	12	1d. green	40	1·00
O2	,,	1½d. orange-vermilion ('31)	1·50	2·00
O3	,,	2d. claret	65	90
O4	,,	3d. blue	85	1·10
O5	,,	4d. olive-green	1·00	1·40
O6	,,	6d. olive-bistre	2·25	4·50
		a. Pale yellow-bistre ('31)	2·25	4·50
O7	,,	9d. violet	2·25	5·00
O8	,,	1s. dull blue-green	2·00	5·00
O9	,,	2s. brown-lake	7·00	12·00
O1/O9		Set of 9	16·00	30·00

1931 (2 Aug.). *Optd. with Type* O **2.** *P* 11.

O10	14	1d. green	45	1·00
O11	,,	1½d. vermilion	75	1·10
O12	,,	2d. claret	70	1·10
O13	,,	3d. blue	80	1·25
O14	,,	4d. olive-green	80	1·75
O15	14	5d. deep blue-green	1·10	2·50
O16	,,	6d. bistre-brown	2·00	3·75
O17	,,	9d. violet	2·00	3·75
O18	,,	1s. pale blue-green	3·50	5·00
O19	,,	2s. brown-lake	6·00	9·00
O20	,,	5s. olive-brown	23·00	30·00
O10/O20		Set of 11	38·00	55·00

1932 (30 June)–**34.** *T* **14** *(redrawn without dates), optd. with Type* O **2.** *P* 11.

O21	1d. green	20	60
O22	1½d. claret	55	75
O23	2d. vermilion	55	75
O24	2½d. green (14.9.34)	90	1·10
O25	3d. blue	1·25	1·50
O26	3½d. aniline carmine (14.9.34)	1·25	1·75
O27	4d. olive-green	1·25	1·50
O28	5d. deep blue-green	1·25	1·75
O29	6d. bistre-brown	1·75	3·00
O30	9d. violet	3·00	4·00
O31	1s. pale blue-green	4·50	5·50
O32	2s. dull lake	9·00	11·00
O33	5s. olive-brown	28·00	30·00
O21/O33	Set of 13	48·00	55·00

Civil Administration in New Guinea was suspended in 1942. On resumption, after the Japanese defeat in 1945, Australian stamps were used until the appearance of the issue for the combined territories of Papua & New Guinea (*q.v.*).

NEW HEBRIDES.

ANGLO-FRENCH CONDOMINIUM.

From the 1880s stamps of New Caledonia and New South Wales were used.

NEW HEBRIDES. CONDOMINIUM. (1) NEW HEBRIDES CONDOMINIUM (2)

1908 (29 Oct.). *T* **23** *and* **24** *of Fiji optd. with T* **1** *by Govt. Printing Establishment, Suva. On the bicoloured stamps the word* "FIJI" *obliterated by a bar in the colour of the word. P* 14.

(*a*) *Wmk. Multiple Crown CA.*

1	½d. green and grey-green, O	20	75
2	1d. red, O	30	75
	a. Opt. omitted (in vert. pr. with normal)	£3000	
3	1s. green and carmine, C	8·00	10·00

(*b*) *Wmk. Crown CA.*

4	½d. green and grey-green	14·00	14·00
5	2d. dull pur. and orange	60	75
6	2½d. dull pur. and blue/*blue*	60	75
7	5d. dull pur. and green	2·25	2·75
8	6d. dull pur. and carmine	2·25	2·75
9	1s. green and carmine	75·00	80·00
1/9	Set of 9	90·00	£100

1910 (15 Dec.). *Types as last. Wmk. Multiple Crown CA. P* 14. *Optd. with T* **2** *by De La Rue.*

10	½d. green, O	1·40	1·75
11	1d. red, O	1·75	2·00
12	2d. grey, O	40	90
13	2½d. bright blue, O	50	1·25
14	5d. dull pur. & olive-grn., C	65	1·50
15	6d. dull and deep purple, C	1·00	1·40
16	1s. black/*green*, C (R.)	1·00	1·75
10/16	Set of 7	6·00	9·50
10/16 Optd. "Specimen"	Set of 7	£100	

3. Weapons and Idols.

(Des. J. Giraud. Recess. D.L.R.)

911 (25 July). *Wmk. Mult. Crown CA. P* 14.
3 **3** ½d. green 45 45
) ,, 1d. red 60 90
) ,, 2d. grey .. .. 1·00 1·00
c ,, 2½d. ultramarine .. .. .. 65 1·00
4 ,, 5d. sage-green .. .. .. 80 1·00
5 ,, 6d. purple .. .. 1·10 1·10
5 ,, 1s. black/*green* .. .. .. 1·40 2·00
7 ,, 2s. purple/*blue* .. .. .. 5·00 6·00
3 ,, 5s. green/*yellow* .. .. .. 10·00 11·00
3/28 .. .. *Set of* 9 19·00 22·00
3/28 Optd. "Specimen" *Set of* 9 60·00

1d.

(4)

920 (June)–**21**. *Surch. with T* **4** *at Govt. Printing Establishment, Suva.*
) **3** 1d. on 5d. sage-grn. (10.3.21) 6·00 7·00
a. Surch. inverted. £250
: ,, 1d. on 1s. black/*green* .. 1·50 4·00
: ,, 1d. on 2s. purple/*blue* .. 1·50 4·00
; ,, 1d. on 5s. green/*yellow* .. 1·50 4·00

amps of French issue with similar surcharge.
(a) *Wmk. Mult. Crown CA.*
3 2d. on 40 c. red/*yellow* .. 1·50 4·00
) *Wmk. "RF" in sheet (some stamps without wmk.).*
,, 2d. on 40 c. red/*yellow* .. £140 £150

921 (Sept.–Oct.). *Wmk. Mult. Script CA. P* 14.
3 1d. scarlet .. .. 90 1·25
,, 2d. slate-grey .. .. .. 1·75 2·75
,, 6d. purple .. .. 3·50 4·00
/9 Optd. "Specimen" *Set of* 3 22·00

24 (1 May). *Surch. as T* **4**, *at Suva.*
3 1d. on ½d. green (No. 18) .. 70 3·00
,, 3d. on 1d. scarlet (No. 36) .. 1·50 3·00
,, 5d. on 2½d. ultram. (No. 21) 3·00 4·00
a. Surch. inverted £275

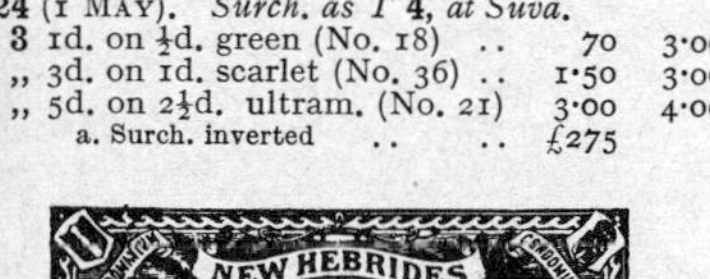

5

(Recess. D.L.R.)

25 (June). *Wmk. Mult. Script CA. P* 14.
5 ½d. (5 c.) black 25 45
,, 1d. (10 c.) green 40 55
,, 2d. (20 c.) slate-grey .. 40 55
,, 2½d. (25 c.) brown 55 70
,, 5d. (50 c.) ultramarine .. 80 80
,, 6d. (60 c.) purple .. .. 1·25 1·75
,, 1s. (1.25 fr.) black/*emerald* 1·50 1·75
,, 2s. (2.50 fr.) purple/*blue* .. 2·75 3·50
,, 5s. (6·25 fr.) green/*yellow* .. 5·00 6·00
/51 .. .. *Set of* 9 11·00 14·00
/51 Optd. "Specimen" *Set of* 9 60·00

6. Lopevi Is. and Copra Canoe.

(Des. J. Kerhor. Recess. B.W.)

8 (1 June). *Gold Currency. Wmk. Mult. Script CA. P* 12.
6 5 c. blue-green 40 45
,, 10 c. orange 65 55
,, 15 c. bright violet 65 65
55 **6** 20 c. scarlet .. .. .. 75 1·00
56 ,, 25 c. reddish brown .. .. 75 1·00
57 ,, 30 c. blue .. .. .. 90 1·00
58 ,, 40 c. grey-olive .. .. 1·10 1·25
59 ,, 50 c. purple .. .. .. 1·10 80
60 ,, 1 f. red/*green* .. .. 3·25 3·25
61 ,, 2 f. blue/*green* .. .. 4·50 4·50
62 ,, 5 f. red/*yellow* .. .. 10·00 10·00
63 ,, 10 f. violet/*blue* .. .. 18·00 18·00
52/63 .. .. *Set of* 12 38·00 38·00
52/63 Perf. "Specimen" *Set of* 12 60·00

(Recess. Waterlow.)

1949 (10 Oct.). *75th Anniv. of Universal Postal Union. As T* **21** *of Antigua, but inscribed* "NEW HEBRIDES". *Wmk. Mult. Script CA. P* 13½–14.
64 10 c. red-orange 15 20
65 15 c. violet 20 20
66 30 c. ultramarine 30 40
67 50 c. purple 50 55

7. Outrigger Sailing Canoe.

8. Native carving.
9. Two Natives outside Hut.

(Recess. Waterlow.)

1953 (30 Apr.). *Wmk. Mult. Script CA. P* 12½.
68 **7** 5 c. green 5 5
69 ,, 10 c. scarlet 5 5
70 ,, 15 c. yellow-ochre 5 8
71 ,, 20 c. ultramarine 8 10
72 **8** 25 c. olive 10 12
73 ,, 30 c. brown 15 15
74 ,, 40 c. blackish brown .. 15 20
75 ,, 50 c. violet 20 20
76 **9** 1 f. orange 40 45
77 ,, 2 f. reddish purple .. .. 90 1·00
78 ,, 5 f. scarlet .. .. .. 2·25 2·50
68/78 .. .. *Set of* 11 4·00 4·50

1953 (2 June). *Coronation. As No.* 47 *of Aden.*
79 10 c. black and carmine .. 45 60

10. Quirós' Caravel and Map.

11. "Marianne", "Talking Drum" and "Britannia".

(Photo. Harrison.)

1956 (20 Oct.). *50th Anniv. of Condominium. Wmk. Mult. Script CA. P* 14½ × 14.
80 **10** 5 c. emerald 8 8
81 ,, 10 c. scarlet 10 12
82 **11** 20 c. deep bright blue .. 15 20
83 ,, 50 c. deep lilac 40 55

12. Port Vila: Iririki Islet.

13. River Scene and Spear Fisherman.

14. Woman drinking from Coconut. (*As T* **13**.)

(Des. H. Cheffer (T **12**), P. Gandon (others). Recess. Waterlow.)

1957 (3 Sept.). *Wmk. Mult. Script CA. P* 13½.
84 **12** 5 c. green 5 5
85 ,, 10 c. scarlet 5 5
86 ,, 15 c. yellow-ochre 8 8
87 ,, 20 c. ultramarine 10 10
88 **13** 25 c. olive 12 12
89 ,, 30 c. brown 15 15
90 ,, 40 c. sepia 30 30
91 ,, 50 c. violet 30 30
92 **14** 1 f. orange 55 55
93 ,, 2 f. mauve .. .. .. 1·25 1·25
94 ,, 5 f. black .. .. .. 2·50 2·50
84/94 .. .. *Set of* 11 4·50 4·50

1963 (2 Sept.). *Freedom from Hunger. As No.* 76 *of Aden.*
95 60 c. green 35 40

15. Red Cross Emblem.

(Des. V. Whiteley. Litho. Bradbury, Wilkinson.

1963 (2 Sept.). *Red Cross Centenary. W* **w.12**. *P* 13½.
96 **15** 15 c. red and black 15 20
97 ,, 45 c. red and blue 45 60

16. Exporting Manganese, Forari.

17. Cocoa Beans.

18. Copra.

19. Fishing from Palikulo Point.

20. Picasso Fish.

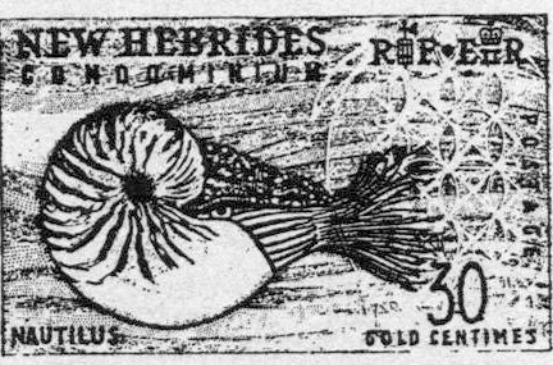

21. Nautilus Shell.

22. Stingfish.

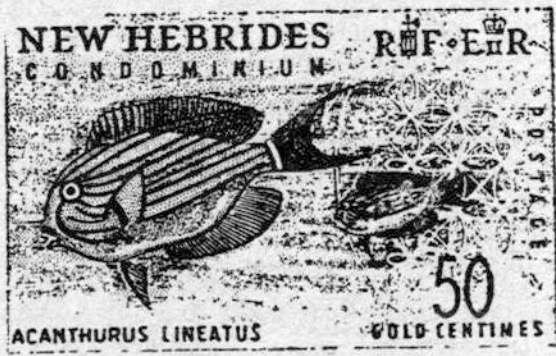

23. Blue Lined Surgeon.

24. Cardinal Honey-eater.

25. Buff-bellied Flycatcher.

26. Thicket Warbler.

27. White-collared Kingfisher.

(Des. V. Whiteley, from drawings by J. White (10 c., 20 c.), K. Penny (40 c.), C. Robin (3 f.), Photo. Harrison. Des. C. Robin (5 c., 1 f.), J. White (15 c.), G. L. Vasarhelyi (25 c., 5 f.), Larkins, Turrell and Thoma (30 c., 50 c., 2 f.). Recess. Govt. Printing Works, Paris.)

1963 (25 Nov.)–72. *W* w.**12** (10 *c.*, 20 *c.*, 40 *c.*, 3 *f.*) *or no wmk.* (*others*). *P* 14 (3 *f.*), 12½ (10 *c.*, 20 *c.*, 40 *c.*) *or* 13 (*others*).

98	**16**	5 c.	lake, purple-brown & greenish blue (15.8.66)	5	5
			*a. Lake and greenish blue** (29.2.72)		
99	**17**	10 c.	light brown, buff and emerald (16.8.65) ..	5	5
100	**18**	15 c.	yellow-bistre, red-brown and deep violet	8	8
101	**19**	20 c.	black, olive-green and greenish blue (16.8.65)	8	10
102	**20**	25 c.	reddish violet, orange-brn. & crim. (15.8.66)	10	10
103	**21**	30 c.	chestnut, bistre and violet	25	25
104	**22**	40 c.	vermilion and deep blue (16.8.65) ..	30	30
105	**23**	50 c.	green, yellow and greenish blue ..	40	40
106	**24**	1 f.	red, black and deep bluish green (15.8.66)	60	60
107	**25**	2 f.	black, brown-purple and yellow-olive ..	1·25	1·25
108	**26**	3 f.	deep violet, orange-brown, emerald and black (16.8.65) ..	2·00	2·00
109	**27**	5 f.	blue, deep blue and black (24.1.67) ..	3·50	3·50
98/109			.. .. *Set of* 12	7·50	7·50

*In No. 98*a* the globe is printed in the same colour as the centre instead of purple-brown.

See also No. 129.

28. I.T.U. Emblem.

(Des. M. Goaman. Litho. Enschedé.)

1965 (17 May). *I.T.U. Centenary. W* w.**12**. *P* 11×11½.

110	**28**	15 c.	scarlet and drab ..	15	15
111	,,	60 c.	blue and light red ..	45	45

29. I.C.Y. Emblem.

(Des. V. Whiteley. Litho. Harrison.)

1965 (24 Oct.). *International Co-operation Yea*
W w.**12**. *P* 14½.

112	**29**	5 c.	reddish purple and turquoise-green ..	5	
113	,,	55 c.	deep bluish green and lavender	40	4

30. Sir Winston Churchill and St. Paul
Cathedral in Wartime.

(Des. Jennifer Toombs. Photo. Harrison.)

1966 (24 Jan.). *Churchill Commemoratio*
W w.**12**. *P* 14.

114	**30**	5 c.	black, cerise, gold and new blue	5	
115	,,	15 c.	black, cerise, gold and deep green	12	
116	,,	25 c.	black, cerise, gold and brown	25	
117	,,	30 c.	black, cerise, gold and bluish violet ..	30	

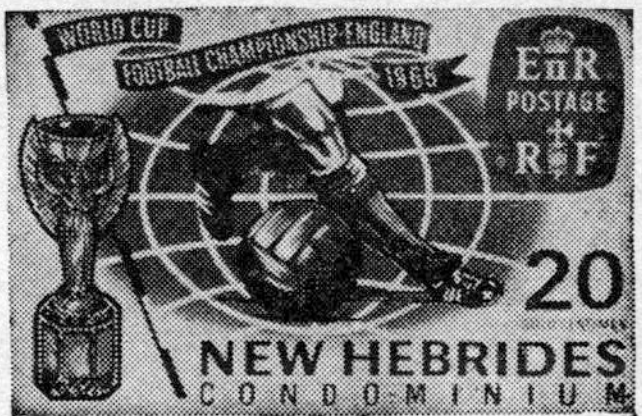

31. Footballer's Legs, Ball and Jules Rimet Cu

(Des. V. Whiteley. Litho. Harrison.)

1966 (1 July). *World Cup Football Champio ships. W* w.**12** (*sideways*). *P* 14.

118	**31**	20 c.	violet, yellow-green, lake & yellow-brown	10	
119	,,	40 c.	chocolate, blue-green, lake & yellow-brown	20	

32. W.H.O. Building.

(Des. M. Goaman. Litho. Harrison.)

1966 (20 Sept.). *Inauguration of W.H.O. Hea quarters, Geneva. W* w.**12** (*sideways*). *P* 1

120	**32**	25 c.	black, yellow-green & light blue	12	
121	,,	60 c.	black, light purple & yellow-brown ..	30	

33. " Education ".

34. " Science ".
35. " Culture ".

(Des. Jennifer Toombs. Litho. Harrison.)

1966 (1 Dec.). *20th Anniv. of U.N.E.S.C.O. W* w.**12** (*sideways*). *P* 14.

122 **33** 15 c. slate-violet, red, yell. and orange 10 10
123 **34** 30 c. orange-yellow, violet and deep olive .. 20 25
124 **35** 45 c. black, bright purple and orange 30 30

36. The Coast Watchers.

The above illustration is reduced. Actual size $55\frac{1}{2}\times41$ *mm.*)

37. Map of War Zone, U.S. Marine and Australian Soldier.
38. H.M.A.S. *Canberra.*
39. " Flying Fortress ".

(Des. R. Granger Barrett. Photo. Enschedé.)

1967 (26 Sept.). *25th Anniv. of the Pacific War. W* w.**12.** *P* 14 × 13.

125 **36** 15 c. multicoloured .. 10 10
126 **37** 25 c. multicoloured .. 15 15
127 **38** 60 c. multicoloured .. 40 40
128 **39** 1 f. multicoloured .. 65 65

1967 (5 Dec.). *New value with W* w.**12** *sideways.*

129 **22** 60 c. verm. and dp. blue .. 25 30

40. Globe and Hemispheres.

41. Ships *La Boudeuse* and *L'Etoile*, and Map.
42. Bougainville, Ship's Figure-head and Bougainvillea Flowers.

(Des. and eng. J. Combet. Recess. Govt. Printing Works, Paris.)

1968 (23 May). *Bicentenary of Bougainville's World Voyage. P* 13.

130 **40** 15 c. emerald, slate-violet and red 10 10
131 **41** 25 c. deep olive, maroon and ultramarine .. 15 15
132 **42** 60 c. bistre-brown, brown-purple & myrtle-green 25 30

43. " Concorde " and Vapour Trails.

44. " Concorde " in Flight.

(Des. S. W. Moss (25 c.), R. Granger Barrett (60 c.). Litho. De La Rue.)

1968 (9 Oct.). *Anglo-French " Concorde " Project. W* w.**12** (*sideways*). *P* 14.

133 **43** 25 c. light blue, orange-red and deep violet-blue 20 20
134 **44** 60 c. red, black and bright blue 35 35

45. Kauri Pine.

(Des. V. Whiteley. Litho. Format International.)

1969 (30 June). *Timber Industry. W* w.**12.** *P* $14\frac{1}{2}$.

135 **45** 20 c. multicoloured (*shades*) 20 20

No. 135 was issued in small sheets of 9 (3 × 3) printed on a simulated wood-grain background and with a decorative border showing various stages of the local timber industry. There is a wide range of shades on the printing. (*Price* £2.)

46. Cyphers, Flags and Relay Runner receiving Baton.

47. Cyphers, Flags and Relay Runner passing Baton.

(Des. C. Haley. Photo. Delrieu.)

1969 (13 Aug.). *Third South Pacific Games, Port Moresby. P* $12\frac{1}{2}$.

136 **46** 25 c. multicoloured .. 15 15
137 **47** 1 f. multicoloured .. 50 65

48. Diver on Platform.

49. Diver Jumping.
50. Diver at end of Fall.

(Des. V. Whiteley. Litho. Perkins, Bacon.)

1969 (15 Oct.). *Pentecost Island Land Divers. W* w.**12** (*sideways*). *P* $12\frac{1}{2}$.

138 **48** 15 c. multicoloured .. 10 10
139 **49** 25 c. multicoloured .. 15 15
140 **50** 1 f. multicoloured .. 50 50

51. U.P.U. Emblem and New Headquarters Building.

(Des. and eng. J. Gauthier. Recess. Govt. Ptg. Wks., Paris.)

1970 (20 May). *Inauguration of New U.P.U. Headquarters Building. P* 13.

141 **51** 1 f. 05, slate, red-orange and bright purple .. 45 50

52. General de Gaulle.

35
(**53**)

(Des. V. Whiteley. Photo. Govt. Ptg. Wks. Paris.)

1970 (20 July). *30th Anniv. of New Hebrides' Declaration for the Free French Government. P* 13.

142 **52** 65 c. multicoloured .. 25 30
143 „ 1 f. 10, multicoloured .. 60 65

1970 (15 Oct.). *As No.* 101, *but W* w.**12** (*sideways*) *and surch. with T* **53.**

144 **19** 35 c. on 20 c. black, olive-green & greenish blue 25 30

54. " The Virgin and Child " (Bellini).

(Des. V. Whiteley. Litho. Harrison.)

1970 (30 Nov.). *Christmas. T* **54** *and similar vert. design. Multicoloured. W* w.**12** *(sideways). P* 14½×14.

145 15 c. Type **54** 10 10
146 50 c. " The Virgin and Child " (Cima) 25 30

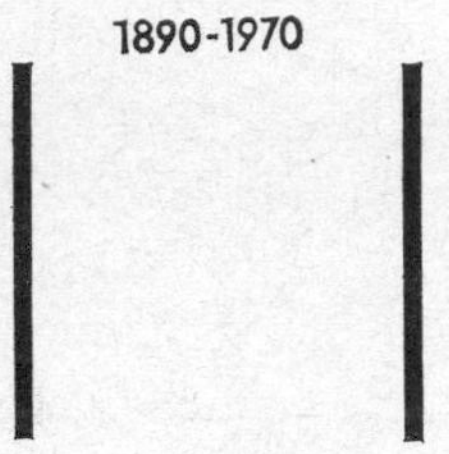

(55)

1971 (19 Jan.). *Death of General Charles de Gaulle. Nos.* 142/3 *optd. with T* **55**, *vertical bars in black, inscriptions in gold.*

147 **52** 65 c. multicoloured 40 40
148 ,, 1 f. 10, multicoloured 60 60

56. Football.

(Des. G. Bétemps. Photo. Delrieu.)

1971 (13 July). *Fourth South Pacific Games, Papeete, French Polynesia. T* **56** *and similar multicoloured design. P* 12½.

149 20 c. Type **56** 10 12
150 65 c. Basketball (*vert.*) 35 35

MINIMUM PRICE

The minimum price quoted is 5p which represents a handling charge rather than a basis for valuing common stamps. For further notes about prices see introductory pages.

57. Kauri Pine, Cone and Arms of Royal Society.

(Des. P. B. Powell. Litho. Harrison.)

1971 (7 Sept.). *Royal Society Expedition to New Hebrides*, 1971. *W* w.**12** (*sideways*). *P* 14½×14.

151 **57** 65 c. multicoloured 30 35

58. " The Adoration of the Shepherds " (detail, Louis Le Nain).

(Des. G. Drummond. Litho. Questa.)

1971 (23 Nov.). *Christmas. T* **58** *and similar vert. design. Multicoloured. W* w.**12**. *P* 14×13½.

152 25 c. Type **58** 15 15
153 50 c. " The Adoration of the Shepherds " (detail, Tintoretto) 40 40

59. " Drover " Mk. III.

(Des. M. Goaman. Photo. Delrieu.)

1972 (29 Feb.). *Aircraft. T* **59** *and similar horiz. designs. Multicoloured. P* 13.

154 20 c. Type **59** 10 12
155 25 c. " Sandringham " flying-boat 15 15
156 30 c. D.H. " Dragon Rapide " 20 20
157 65 c. " Caravelle " 35 35

60. Ceremonial Headdress.

(Des. Ballais (bird designs), Pierrette Lambe (others). Photo. Govt. Printing Works, Paris

1972 (24 July). *T* **60** *and similar vert. design Multicoloured. P* 12½×13.

158 5 c. Type **60** 5
159 10 c. Baker's pigeon 5
160 15 c. Gong and carving .. 5
161 20 c. Royal parrot-finch .. 8
162 25 c. *Cribraria fischeri* (shell) 10
163 30 c. *Oliva rubrolabiata* (shell) 12
164 35 c. Chestnut-bellied Kingfisher 12
165 65 c. *Strombus plicatus* (shell) 25
166 1 f. Gong and carving .. 35
167 2 f. Green Palm Lorikeet .. 65
168 3 f. Ceremonial headdress .. 1·00 1·
169 5 f. Green Snail Shell .. 1·75 2·
158/69 .. .. *Set of* 12 4·00 4·

61. " Adoration of the Magi " (Spranger).

(Des. G. Drummond. Litho. J.W.)

1972 (25 Sept.). *Christmas. T* **61** *and simil vert. design. Multicoloured. W* w.**12**. *P* 1

170 25 c. Type **61** 15
171 70 c. " The Virgin and Child " (Provoost) 40

62. Royal and French Ciphers.

(Des. (from photographs by D. Groves) an photo. Harrison.)

1972 (20 Nov.). *Royal Silver Wedding. Mult coloured; background colour given. W* w.1 *P* 14×14½.

172 **62** 35 c. violet-black 20 2
173 ,, 65 c. yellow-olive 40 4

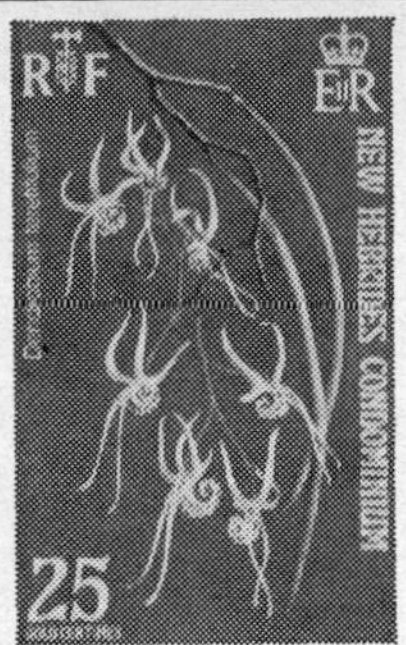

63. *Dendrobium teretifolium.*

(Des. Jennifer Toombs. Litho. Questa.)

1973 (26 Feb.). *Orchids. T* **63** *and similar vert. designs. Multicoloured. W* w.**12** (*sideways*). *P* 14×14½.

174	25 c. Type **63**	10	10
175	30 c. *Ephemerantha comata*	15	15
176	35 c. *Spathoglottis petri* ..	15	15
177	65 c. *Dendrobium mohlianum*	30	30

64. New Wharf at Vila.

(Des. PAD Studio. Litho. Questa.)

1973 (14 May). *New Wharf at Vila. P* 14×14½ (25 *c.*) *or* 14½×14 (70 *c.*).

178	**64**	25 c. multicoloured ..	12	12
179	–	70 c. multicoloured ..	35	40

The 70 c. is as T **64**, but in a horizontal format.

65. Wild Horses.

(Des. Pierrette Lambert. Photo. Govt. Printing Works, Paris.)

1973 (13 Aug.). *Tanna Island. T* **65** *and similar horiz. design. Multicoloured. P* 13×12½.

180	35 c. Type **65**	15	15
181	70 c. Yasur Volcano	35	40

66. Mother and Child.

(Des. Mr. Moutouh (35 c.), Mr. Tatin d'Avesnières (70 c.); adapted PAD Studio. Litho. Questa.)

1973 (19 Nov.). *Christmas. T* **66** *and similar vert. design. Multicoloured. W* w.**12** (*sideways*). *P* 13½.

182	35 c. Type **66**	15	15
183	70 c. Lagoon scene	35	40

67. Pacific Dove.

(Des. J. & H. Bregulla. Photo. Govt. Printing Works, Paris.)

1974 (11 Feb.). *Wild Life. T* **67** *and similar horiz. designs. Multicoloured. P* 13×12½.

184	25 c. Type **67**	10	10
185	35 c. Night Swallowtail (butterfly)	15	15
186	70 c. Green Sea Turtle ..	35	40
187	1 f. 15, Flying Fox	45	50

ROYAL VISIT 1974

(68)

1974 (11 Feb.). *Royal Visit of Queen Elizabeth II. Nos.* 164 *and* 167 *optd. with T* **68**.

188	35 c. Chestnut-bellied Kingfisher (R.)	15	15
189	2 f. Green Palm Lorikeet ..	95	1·00

69. Old Post Office.

(Des. O. Ballais. Photo. Govt. Printing Works, Paris.)

1974 (6 May). *Inauguration of New Post Office, Vila. T* **69** *and similar triangular design. Multicoloured. P* 12.

190	35 c. Type **69**	15	15
191	70 c. New Post Office	35	40

The above were printed together, in *tête-bêche* pairs throughout the sheet.

70. Capt. Cook and Map.

(Des. J. E. Cooter. Litho. J.W.)

1974 (1 Aug.). *Bicentenary of Discovery. T* **70** *and similar horiz. designs. Multicoloured. W* w.**12** (*sideways on* 1 *f.* 15). *P* 11 (1 *f.* 15) *or* 13 (*others*).

192	35 c. Type **70**	15	15
193	35 c. William Wales and beach landing	15	15
194	35 c. William Hodges and island scene	15	15
195	1 f. 15, Capt. Cook, map and H.M.S. *Resolution* (59×34 *mm.*)	45	45

The 35 c. values were printed together, horizontally *se-tenant* within the sheet, and form a composite design of the landing scene.

71. U.P.U. Emblem and Letters.

(Des. P. Lambert. Photo. Govt. Printing Works, Paris.)

1974 (9 Oct.). *Centenary of Universal Postal Union. P* 13×12½.

196	**71**	70 c. multicoloured ..	30	30

72. "Adoration of the Magi" (Velazquez).

(Des. J. E. Cooter. Litho. Questa.)

1974 (14 Nov.). *Christmas. T* **72** *and similar horiz. design. Multicoloured. W* w.**12** (*sideways on* 70 *c.*). *P* 13½.

197	35 c. Type **72**	15	15
198	70 c. "The Nativity" (Gerard van Honthorst)	30	30

73. Charolais Bull.

(Des. and eng. J. Pheulpin. Recess. Govt. Printing Works, Paris.)

1975 (29 Apr.). *P* 13 × 12½.
199 **73** 10 f. bistre-brown, green and dull ultramarine 3·50 3·75

74. Canoeing.

(Des. J. E. Cooter. Litho. Questa.)

1975 (5 Aug.). *World Scout Jamboree, Norway. T* **74** *and similar vert. designs. Multicoloured. P* 13½.

200 25 c. Type **74** 10 12
201 35 c. Preparing meal 15 15
202 1 f. Map-reading 35 40
203 5 f. Fishing .. .. .. 1·90 2·10

75. " Pitti Madonna " (Michelangelo).

(Des. PAD Studio. Litho. Harrison.)

1975 (11 Nov.). *Christmas. Michelangelo's Sculptures. T* **75** *and similar vert. designs. Multicoloured. W* w.**12** (*sideways*). *P* 14.

204 35 c. Type **75** 15 15
205 70 c. " Bruges Madonna " .. 30 35
206 2 f. 50, " Taddei Madonna " 1·00 1·10

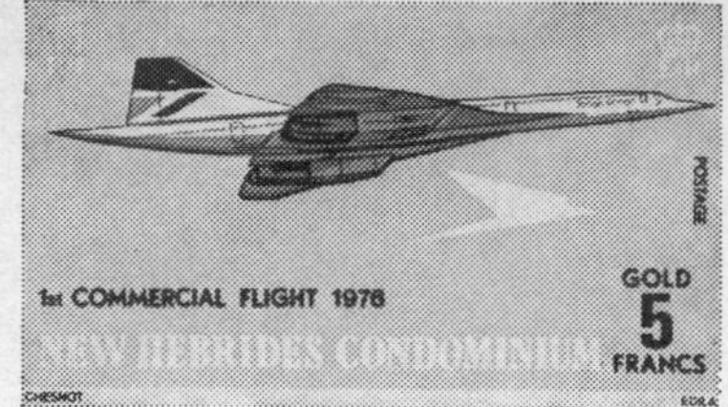

76. " Concorde ".

(Des. J. B. F. Chesnot. Typo. EDILA.)

1976 (30 Jan.). *First Commercial Flight of "Concorde". P* 13.
207 **76** 5 f. multicoloured .. 2·00 2·25

77. Telephones of 1876 and 1976.

(Des. J. Gauthier. Photo. Delrieu.)

1976 (31 Mar.). *Telephone Centenary. T* **77** *and similar vert. designs. Multicoloured. P* 13.

208 25 c. Type **77** 10 12
209 70 c. Alexander Graham Bell 30 35
210 1 f. 15, Satellite and Nouméa Earth Station 50 55

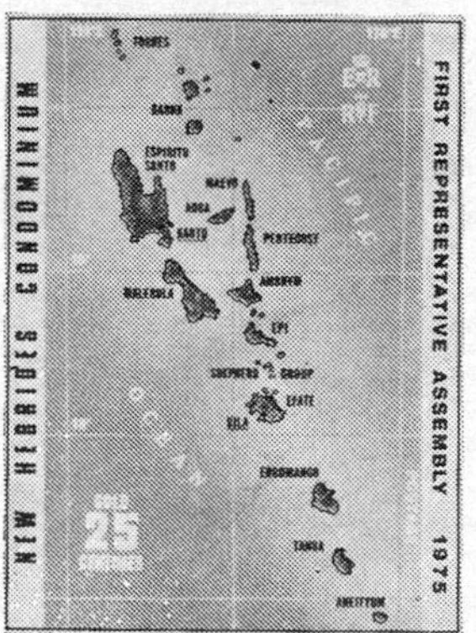

78. Map of the Islands.

(Des. Odette Baillais. Photo. Govt. Printing Works, Paris.)

1976 (29 June). *Constitutional Changes. T* **78** *and similar multicoloured designs. P* 13 (25 *c.*) *or* 13 × 12½ (*others*).

211 25 c. Type **78** 10 12
212 1 f. View of Santo 40 45
213 2 f. View of Vila 80 90

Nos. 212/13 are horiz. designs, 36 × 26 mm.

79. " The Flight into Egypt " (Lusitano).

(Des. J. E. Cooter. Litho. Walsall.)

1976 (8 Nov.). *Christmas. T* **79** *and simi vert. designs. Multicoloured. W* w.
P 13½.

214 35 c. Type **79** 15
215 70 c. " Adoration of the Shepherds " 30
216 2 f. 50, " Adoration of the Magi " .. .. .. 1·00 1·

Nos. 215/16 show retables by the Master Santos-o-Novo.

POSTAGE DUE STAMPS.

POSTAGE DUE (D 1) **POSTAGE DUE** (D 2)

1925 (June). *Optd. with Type* D **1**, *by D.L.R.*

D1 **5** 1d. (10 c.) green .. .. —
D2 „ 2d. (20 c.) slate-grey .. —
D3 „ 3d. (30 c.) red .. — 1
D4 „ 5d. (50 c.) ultramarine .. — 1·
D5 „ 10d. (1 f.) carmine/*blue* .. — 1·
D1/5 .. .. *Set of* 5 50·00 4·

1938 (1 June). *Optd. with Type* D **2**, *by B.*

D 6 **6** 5 c. blue-green .. .. 90 1·
D 7 „ 10 c. orange .. .. 1·00 1·
D 8 „ 20 c. scarlet .. .. 1·40 2·
D 9 „ 40 c. grey-olive .. .. 2·00 3·
D10 „ 1 f. red/*green* .. .. 5·50 7·
D6/10 .. .. *Set of* 5 10·00 13·
D6/10 Perf. " Specimen " *Set of* 5 40·00

POSTAGE DUE (D 3)

1953 (30 Apr.). *Optd. with Type* D **3**, *by Waterlo*

D11 **7** 5 c. green 8
D12 „ 10 c. scarlet 10
D13 „ 20 c. ultramarine 20
D14 **8** 40 c. blackish brown .. 35
D15 **9** 1 f. orange 50
D11/15 .. .. *Set of* 5 1·00 1·

1957 (3 Sept.). *Optd. with Type* D **3**, *Waterlow.*

D16 **12** 5 c. green 5
D17 „ 10 c. scarlet 5
D18 „ 20 c. ultramarine 12
D19 **13** 40 c. sepia 35
D20 **14** 1 f. orange 75
D16/20 .. .. *Set of* 5 1·00 1·

EW REPUBLIC, SOUTH AFRICA.

(The territory of this ephemeral State was part Zululand, but was subsequently annexed to the uth African Republic, as a new district, named ijheid. In January, 1903, the territory was nexed to the Colony of Natal.)

1

nted with a rubber handstamp on paper bought in Europe and sent out ready gummed and perforated.

36 (Jan.)–1887. *T* 1. *Various dates indicating late of printing. P* 11½. (*a*) *Yellow paper.*

1d. black 9 JAN 86 .. ..
1d. violet .. .. .. 2·25 2·25
9 JAN 86 2·75 2·75 | 6 SEP 86 2·75
3 JAN 86 9·00 | 13 OCT 86 2·75 2·25
7 MAR 86 | 3 NOV 86
7 MAR 86 | 13 NOV 86
4 APR 86 | 24 NOV 86 3·50
4 APR 86 | 4 JAN 87
4 MAY 86 | 17 JAN 87
0 AUG 86 2·25 2·25 |

2d. violet .. .. .. 2·25 2·25
a. "d" omitted (13 OCT 86) ..
9 JAN 86 4·00 4·00 | 13 OCT 86 2·75 2·75
3 JAN 86 3·50 3·50 | 24 NOV 86 2·75 2·75
4 MAY 86 | 4 JAN 87
0 AUG 86 3·00 | 17 JAN 87
6 SEP 86 2·25 2·25 |

3d. violet .. .. .. 6·00 6·00
a. "d" omitted (13 OCT 86) ..
3 JAN 86 | 13 OCT 86 6·00 6·00
0 AUG 86 6·00 | 24 NOV 86 7·50 7·50
6 SEP 86 9·00 | 17 JAN 87

4d. violet .. .. .. 8·00
0 AUG 86 12·00 | 13 OCT 86 8·00
6 SEP 86 10·00

6d. violet .. .. .. 7·50 7·50
a. Double impression (30 AUG 86) ..
1 MAY 86 | 6 SEP 86 7·50
2 JUL 86 | 13 OCT 86 7·50 7·50
0 AUG 86 7·50

9d. violet .. .. .. 7·50
3 JAN 86 | 6 SEP 86 7·50
0 AUG 86 12·00 | 13 OCT 86 8·00

1s. violet .. .. .. 16·00
0 AUG 86 16·00 | 13 OCT 86 18·00
6 SEP 86 24·00

6/s. violet 13 OCT 86 ..
1/6 violet .. .. .. 16·00
0 AUG 86 16·00 | 13 OCT 86 38·00
6 SEP 86 18·00 | 26 NOV 86

1s. 6d. violet 6 SEP 86 ..
1s. 6d. violet 13 OCT 86 .. 23·00
2s. violet .. .. .. 9·00
0 AUG 86 24·00 | 13 OCT 86 9·00
6 SEP 86 25·00

2/6 violet .. .. .. 38·00
3 JAN 86 | 6 SEP 86 38·00
9 AUG 86 | 13 OCT 86 42·00
0 AUG 86

2s. 6d. violet .. .. ..
a. Double impression (7 MAR 86) ..
0 FEB 86 | 19 AUG 86
7 MAR 86

4s. violet 17 JAN 87 .. ..
5s. violet .. .. .. 7·00 7·00
a. "5" of "5s." omitted (7 MAR 86)
JAN 86 7·00 7·00 | 6 SEP 86
7 MAR 86 — 23·00 | 13 OCT 86 11·00
4 MAY 86

18 5/6 violet .. .. .. 6·00
20 FEB 86 | 7 MAR 86 6·00
19 5s. 6d. violet .. .. .. 45·00
20 FEB 86 | 7 MAR 86 45·00
20 7/6 violet .. .. .. 45·00
a. Double impression (24 MAY 86) ..
3 JAN 86 | 24 MAY 86 45·00
21 7s. 6d. violet .. .. .. — 24·00
24 MAY 86 | 6 SEP 86
22 10s. violet .. .. .. — 24·00
6 SEP 86 | 24 NOV 86
13 OCT 86 — 24·00 |
23 10s. 6. violet .. .. .. 12·00
a. Double impression (JAN 86) ..
JAN 86 | 13 OCT 86 12·00
23*a* 10s. 6d. violet 7 JAN 86 ..
24 13s. violet .. .. ..
24 NOV 86 | 4 JAN 87
25 £1 violet .. .. .. 30·00
13 JAN 86 | 13 OCT 86 30·00
6 SEP 86 |
26 30s. violet .. .. .. 24·00
13 JAN 86 | 24 NOV 86 24·00

(*b*) *Blue granite paper.*

27 1d. violet .. .. .. 3·00 3·00
a. "d" omitted (24 NOV 86) .. 90·00
JAN 20 86 | 30 JUN 86
20 JAN 86 | JUN 30 86 3·75 3·75
24 JAN 86 4·50 | 6 OCT 86
21 MAY 86 | 24 NOV 86 9·00 4·50
24 MAY 86 3·00 3·00 | 4 JAN 87 3·00 3·50
26 MAY 86 27·00 | 17 JAN 87
28 2d. violet .. .. .. 3·00 3·00
a. "d" omitted (24 NOV 86) ..
b. Double impression (20 JAN 87) ..
24 JAN 86 7·00 | 13 OCT 86 3·00 3·00
7 MAR 86 | 24 NOV 86 4·50
24 APR 86 | 4 JAN 87 4·00 3·00
24 MAY 86 3·50 3·50 | 20 JAN 87
30 AUG 86 3·00 3·00 |
29 3d. violet 13 OCT 86 .. .. 3·50 3·75
30 4d. violet .. .. .. 3·00 3·75
24 MAY 86 | 24 NOV 86 3·50 3·75
13 OCT 86 7·00 7·00 |
31 6d. violet .. .. .. 5·00 5·00
a. "6" of "6d." omitted (24 MAY 86)
24 MAY 86 | 24 NOV 86 5·00 5·00
6 SEP 86 5·00 5·00 |
32 9d. violet .. .. ..
6 SEP 86 | 24 NOV 86
33 1s. violet .. .. .. 7·00 7·00
7 MAR 86 | 2 JUL 86
29 APR 86 | 6 SEP 86 16·00
21 MAY 86 7·00 7·00 | 13 OCT 86 7·00
24 MAY 86 | 24 NOV 86 11·00 11·00
34 1s. 6d. violet .. .. ..
2 JUL 86 | 6 SEP 86
35 1/6 violet .. .. .. 38·00
a. Double impression (13 OCT 86) ..
13 OCT 86 38·00 | 24 NOV 86
36 2s. violet .. .. .. 27·00
a. Double impression (24 MAY 86) ..
21 MAY 86 | 13 OCT 86 27·00
24 MAY 86 | 24 NOV 86
37 2s. 6d. violet 19 AUG 86 .. 35·00
38 2/6 violet .. .. .. 45·00
19 AUG 86 45·00 | 6 SEP 86
39 4s. violet 17 JAN 87 .. ..
40 5s. 6d. violet 13 JAN 86 ..
41 5/6 violet .. .. ..
13 JAN 86 | 13 JAN 87
42 7/6 violet .. .. ..
13 JAN 86 | 13 JAN 87
43 10s. violet .. .. ..
JAN 86 | 2 JUL 86
13 JAN 86 |
44 10s. 6d. violet .. .. .. — 30·00
a. "d" omitted (2 JUL 86) ..
b. Double impression (13 JAN 86) ..
7 JAN 86 | 2 JUL 86
13 JAN 86 — 30·00 | 6 SEP 86
45 10s. 6. violet 2 JUL 86 ..
46 12s. violet 13 JAN 86 .. .. 80·00
47 13s. violet 17 JAN 87 .. .. 80·00
48 £1 violet 13 JAN 86 .. .. 60·00
a. Double impression .. ..
49 30s. violet .. .. .. 60·00
13 JAN 86 60·00 | 17 JAN 87 60·00

Varieties. Stamps printed tête-bêche (pairs).

50 2s. (on *yellow*), 6 SEP 86 .. £120
51 30s. (on *yellow*), 24 NOV 86 ..
52 3d. (on *blue*), 13 OCT 86 .. 80·00
53 1s. (on *blue*), 21 MAY 86 .. £100
54 1s. 6d. (on *blue*), 6 SEP 86 .. £120
55 10s. (on *blue*), 2 JUL 86 .. £130

T 1, *with Arms embossed. P* 11½.

The motto on the embossed Arms is "EENDRAGT REGTVAARDIGHEID EN LIEFDE" (Union, Justice and Charity).

(*a*) *Yellow paper.*

56 1d. violet .. .. .. 3·00 3·50
20 JAN 86 | JUL 7 86
10 FEB 86 | 4 AUG 86 14·00
17 MAR 86 12·00 | 13 SEP 86 12·00
14 APR 86 6·00 | 6 OCT 86 6·00 4·50
26 MAY 86 | 3 NOV 86 3·00 3·50
28 MAY 86 | 2 DEC 86 3·00 3·50
JUN 30 86 3·50 3·75 |
57 2d. violet .. .. .. 3·00 3·50
2 DEC 86 3·00 3·50 | 20 JAN 87
58 4d. violet .. .. .. 4·50 5·50
2 DEC 86 24·00 | DEC 86 4·50 5·50
59 6d. violet .. .. .. 11·00
2 DEC 86 12·00 | DEC 86 11·00

Varieties. Arms inverted.

60 1d. violet .. .. .. 6·00 6·00
20 JAN 86 12·00 | JUL 7 86 24·00 24·00
JAN 20 86 | 13 SEP 86 12·00
10 FEB 86 12·00 | 3 NOV 86 6·00 6·00
14 APR 86 30·00 | 2 DEC 86 42·00
26 MAY 86 24·00 | JAN 20 87
JUN 30 86 6·00 6·00 |
61 2d. violet .. .. .. 5·50 6·00
24 NOV 86 | 20 JAN 87
2 DEC 86 5·50 6·00 |
62 4d. violet DEC 86 .. .. 24·00 14·00

(*b*) *Blue granite paper.*

63 1d. violet .. .. .. 3·50 3·75
20 JAN 86 24·00 | JUL 7 86 3·00 3·75
JAN 20 86 | 4 AUG 86
10 FEB 86 | 13 SEP 86 23·00
17 MAR 86 24·00 | 6 OCT 86 11·00 4·50
14 APR 86 11·00 | 3 NOV 86 3·50
26 MAY 86 | 2 DEC 86 3·50
JUN 30 86 11·00 9·00 |
64 2d. violet .. .. .. 3·50 3·75
30 AUG 86 11·00 | 4 JAN 87 11·00
2 DEC 86 3·50 2·50 | 20 JAN 87 11·00

Varieties. Arms inverted.

65 1d. violet .. .. .. 9·00 9·00
10 FEB 86 9·00 | JUL 7 86 14·00 9·00
17 MAR 86 23·00 | 6 OCT 86 23·00
26 MAR 86 32·00 | 3 NOV 86 9·00 9·00
23 MAY 86 24·00 | 2 DEC 86 11·00
26 MAY 86 12·00 12·00 |
66 2d. violet .. .. .. 12·00
30 AUG 86 | 20 JAN 87 24·00
2 DEC 86 12·00 |

Varieties. Arms embossed tête-bêche (pairs).

67 1d. (on *yellow*), 3 NOV 86 .. 27·00 27·00
68 1d. (on *yellow*), JUN 30 86 .. 60·00 60·00
69 1d. (on *blue*), 3 NOV 86 ..
70 2d. (on *blue*), 2 DEC 86 ..
71 4d. (on *yellow*), DEC 86 .. 60·00

1887 (Feb.–Mar.). *As T* 1, *but without date. With embossed Arms.*

(*a*) *Blue granite paper.*

72 1d. violet .. .. .. 3·50 3·50
a. Imperf. between (pair) ..
b. Stamps tête-bêche (pair) .. 75·00
c. Arms tête-bêche (pair) ..
d. Arms inverted .. .. 5·50 5·50
e. Arms omitted .. .. 27·00 27·00
73 2d. violet .. .. .. 2·00 2·00
a. Stamps tête-bêche (pair) .. 75·00
b. Arms inverted .. .. 5·50 5·50
c. Arms omitted .. .. — 24·00
74 3d. violet .. .. .. 3·00 3·00
a. Stamps tête-bêche (pair) .. 90·00
b. Arms tête-bêche (pair) ..
c. Arms inverted .. .. 12·00 12·00
75 4d. violet .. .. .. 3·00 3·00
a. Stamps tête-bêche (pair) .. 75·00
b. Arms tête-bêche (pair) .. 70·00
c. Arms inverted .. .. 23·00
76 6d. violet .. .. .. 3·00 3·00
a. Arms inverted .. .. 23·00
77 1/6 violet .. .. .. 3·00 3·00
a. Arms inverted .. ..

(*b*) *Yellow paper* (March, 1887).

78 2d. violet (*arms omitted*) .. 3·00
79 3d. violet .. .. .. 3·00 3·00
a. Imperf. between (pair) ..
b. Stamps tête-bêche (pair) .. 75·00 75·00
c. Arms tête-bêche (pair) ..
d. Arms inverted .. .. 6·00 6·00
da. Double impression .. ..
80 4d. violet .. .. .. 3·00 3·00
a. Arms inverted .. .. 3·50 3·50

81 6d. violet .. .. .. 2·10 2·10
a. Arms tête-bêche (pair) .. 75·00
b. Arms inverted .. .. 11·00 11·00
c. Arms omitted .. ..
ca. Double impression .. ..
82 9d. violet .. .. .. 2·40 2·40
83 1s. violet .. .. .. 2·40 2·40
a. Arms inverted .. .. 18·00
84 1/6 violet .. .. .. 3·00 3·00
85 2s. violet .. .. .. 5·50 4·50
a. Arms inverted .. .. — 15·00
b. Arms omitted .. .. 3·00
86 2/6 violet .. .. .. 6·00 6·00
a. Arms inverted .. .. 7·50 7·50
87 3s. violet .. .. .. 11·00 11·00
a. Arms inverted .. .. 12·00 12·00
88 4s. violet .. .. .. 3·00 3·00
a. Arms omitted (4s.) .. ..
b. Arms omitted (4/-) .. ..
89 5s. violet .. .. .. 3·00 3·00
a. Imperf. between (pair) ..
b. Arms inverted .. .. — 23·00
90 5/6 violet .. .. .. 3·00 3·00
91 7/6 violet .. .. .. 4·00 4·50
a. Arms tête-bêche (pair) ..
b. Arms inverted .. ..
92 10s. violet .. .. .. 3·00 3·00
a. Imperf. between (pair) ..
b. Arms tête-bêche (pair) .. 30·00
c. Arms inverted .. .. 6·00
d. Arms omitted .. .. — 12·00
93 10/6 violet .. .. .. 4·50 4·50
a. Imperf. between (pair) ..
b. Arms inverted .. ..
94 £1 violet .. .. .. 12·00 12·00
a. Stamps tête-bêche (pair) .. 90·00 90·00
b. Arms inverted .. .. 14·00
95 30s. violet .. .. .. 23·00

NEW SOUTH WALES.

1

2

(Engraved by Robert Clayton, Sydney.)

1850 (1 Jan.). *T* **1**. *Plate I. No clouds.*

(*a*) *Soft yellowish paper.*

1 1d. crimson-lake £1500 £275
2 1d. carmine £1400 £250
3 1d. reddish rose £1300 £225
4 1d. brownish red £1400 £250

(*b*) *Hard bluish paper.*

5 1d. pale red £1300 £225
6 1d. dull lake £1300 £225

1850 (Aug.). *T* **2**. *Plate I, re-engraved by H. C. Jervis, commonly termed Plate II. With clouds.*

(*a*) *Hard toned yellowish paper.*

7 1d. vermilion £700 £150
8 1d. dull carmine £600 £150
a. No trees on hill (No. 7) .. £900 £180
b. Hill unshaded (No. 8) £900 £180
c. Without clouds (No. 15) .. £900 £180

(*b*) *Hard greyish or bluish paper.*

9 1d. crimson-lake £750 £180
10 1d. gooseberry-red £1000 £250
11 1d. dull carmine £600 £150
12 1d. brownish red £600 £150
a. No trees on hill (No. 7) .. £750 £180
b. Hill unshaded (No. 8) £750 £180
c. Without clouds (No. 15) .. £750 £180

(*c*) *Laid paper.*

13 1d. carmine £1200 £225
14 1d. vermilion £1400 £250
a. No trees on hill (No. 7) .. — £300
b. Hill unshaded (No. 8) .. .. — £300
c. Without clouds (No. 15) .. — £300

The varieties quoted with the letters "a", "b", "c" of course exist in each shade; the prices quoted are for the commonest shade, and the same applies to the following portions of this list.

The numbers given in brackets throughout indicate position on sheet.

3

4

A (Pl. I).

Illustrations A, B, C, and D are sketches of the lower part of the inner circular frame, showing the characteristic variations of each plate.

(Engraved by John Carmichael.)

1850 (1 Jan.). *Plate I. Vertical-lined background. T* **3**. (*a*) *Early impressions, full details of clouds, etc.*

15 2d. greyish blue £1500 £225
16 2d. deep blue .. .. .. — £275
a. Double lines on bale (No. 19) .. — £300

Intermediate impressions.

16*b* 2d. greyish blue £900 £150
16*c* 2d. deep blue £900 £150

T **4**. (*b*) *Later impressions, clouds, etc., mostly gone.*

17 2d. blue .. .. £550 60·00
18 2d. dull blue .. .. .. £400 60·00

1850 (end Jan.). *Stamps in the lower row partially retouched.*

19 2d. blue £750 £120
20 2d. greyish blue £700 £100

An interesting variety occurs on positions 9, 10, 11 and 19 in all five plates. It consists of ten loops of the engine-turning on each side of the design instead of the normal nine loops.

5

B (Pl. II)

(Plate entirely re-engraved by H. C. Jervis.)

1850 (Apr.). *T* **5**. *Plate II. Horizontal-lined background. Bale on left side supporting the seated figure, dated. Dot in centre of the star in each corner.*

(*a*) *Early impressions.*

21 2d. indigo £1200 £160
22 2d. lilac-blue .. .. .. — £300
23 2d. grey-blue £1200 £140
24 2d. bright blue £1200 £140
a. Fan as in Pl. III, but with shading outside (No. 1) .. .. — £150
b. Fan as in Pl. III, but without shading, and inner circle intersects the fan (No. 2) .. .. — £150
c. Pick and shovel omitted (No. 10) — £150
d. "CREVIT" omitted (No. 13) — £150
e. No whip (Nos. 4, 8, and 20) .. — £130

(*b*) *Worn impressions.*

25 2d. dull blue .. .. .. £375 70·00
26 2d. Prussian blue .. .. £450 90·00
a. Fan as in Pl. III, but with shading outside (No. 1) .. .. — £110
b. Fan as in Pl. III, but without shading, and inner circle intersects the fan (No. 2) .. .. — £110
c. Pick and shovel omitted (No. 10) — £110
d. "CREVIT" omitted (No. 13) — £110
e. No whip (Nos. 4, 8, and 20) .. — 90·00

1850 (Aug.). *Bottom row retouched with dots ar dashes in lower spandrels.*

27 2d. Prussian blue £750 £1
28 2d. dull blue .. .. .. £600 75·
a. No whip (No. 20) .. .. — £1
b. "CREVIT" omitted (No. 13) — £1

C (Pl. III).

(Plate re-engraved a second time by H. C. Jervis

1850 (Sept.). *Plate III. Bale not dated ar single-lined, except Nos. 7, 10 and 12, which a double-lined. No dots in stars.*

29 2d. ultramarine .. .. £600 90·
30 2d. deep blue .. .. .. £550 90·
a. No whip (Nos. 15 and 19) .. — £1
b. Fan with 6 segments (No. 20) — £1
c. Double lines on bale (No. 7, 10, and 12) .. .. .. — £1

(Plate re-engraved a third time by H. C. Jervis

1851 (Jan.). *Plate IV. Double-line bale, a circle in centre of each star.*

(*a*) *Hard bluish grey wove paper.*

31 2d. ultramarine .. .. £750 90·
32 2d. Prussian blue .. .. £600 75·
33 2d. bright blue .. .. .. £650 80·
a. Hill not shaded (No. 12) .. — 90·
b. Fan with 6 segments (No. 20) .. — 90·
c. No clouds (No. 22) .. .. — 90·
d. Retouch (No. 13) .. .. — 90·
e. No waves (Nos. 9 and 17) .. — 80·

(*b*) *Stout yellowish vertically laid paper.*

34 2d. ultramarine .. .. £650 90·
35 2d. Prussian blue .. .. £750 80·
a. Hill not shaded (No. 12) .. — £1
b. Fan with 6 segments (No. 20) .. — £1
c. No clouds (No. 22) .. .. — £1
d. Retouch (No. 13) .. .. — £1
e. No waves (Nos. 9 and 17) .. — 90·

6

D (Pl. V).

(Plate re-engraved a fourth time by H. C. Jervis

1851 (Apr.). *T* **6**. *Plate V. Pearl in fan.*

(*a*) *Hard greyish wove paper.*

36 2d. ultramarine .. .. £600 75·
37 2d. dull blue .. .. .. £550 75·
a. Pick and shovel omitted (No. 17) — 90·
b. Fan with 6 segments (No. 20) .. — 90·

(*b*) *Stout yellowish vertically laid paper.*

38 2d. dull ultramarine £1100 £1
a. Pick and shovel omitted (No. 17) — £1
b. Fan with 6 segments (No. 20) .. — £2

7

8

(Engraved by H. C. Jervis.)

1850. *T* **7**.

(*a*) *Soft yellowish wove paper.*

39 3d. yellow-green £650 £1
40 3d. myrtle-green £1800 £6
41 3d. emerald-green £800 £1
a. No whip (Nos. 18 and 19) .. — £14
b. "SIGIIIUM" for "SIGILLUM" (No. 23) .. .. — £15

(b) Bluish to grey wove paper.

2 3d. yellow-green .. .. £600 90·00
3 3d. emerald-green .. .. £600 90·00
b. No whip (Nos. 18 and 19) .. — £110
c. "SIGIIIUM" for "SIGILLUM" (No. 23) .. .. — £140

(c) Yellowish to bluish laid paper.

3d 3d. bright green £1500 £150
3e 3d. yellowish green £1500 £150
f. No whip (Nos. 18 and 19) .. — £160
g. "SIGIIIUM" for "SIGILLUM" (No. 23) .. .. — £180

Des. A. W. Manning from sketch by W. T. Levinge; engraved on steel by John Carmichael, Sydney.)

851 (18 Dec.). *T* **8**. *Imperf.*

(a) Thick yellowish wove paper.

4 1d. carmine £500 £120
a. No leaves right of "SOUTH" — £150
b. Two leaves right of "SOUTH" — £150
c. "WALE" .. .. .. — £160

852. *(b) Bluish medium wove paper.*

5 1d. carmine .. .. .. £275 55·00
6 1d. scarlet .. .. .. £300 55·00
7 1d. vermilion .. .. .. £275 55·00
8 1d. brick-red .. .. .. £275 55·00
a. No leaves right of "SOUTH" (Nos. 7 and 8) .. .. — 75·00
b. Two leaves right of "SOUTH" (No. 15) .. .. .. — 90·00
c. "WALE" (No. 9) .. .. — 90·00

852 (?). *(c) Thick vertically laid bluish paper.*

9 1d. orange-brown £900 £160
1d. claret £900 £160
a. No leaves right of "SOUTH" — £180
b. Two leaves right of "SOUTH" — £180
c. "WALE" .. .. .. — £200

(Engraved on steel by John Carmichael.)

851 (24 July). *T* **8**. *Plate I. Imperf.*

(a) Thick yellowish wove paper.

2d. ultramarine .. .. £150 30·00

(b) Fine impressions, blue to greyish medium paper.

2 2d. ultramarine .. .. £150 15·00
3 2d. chalky blue .. .. £140 15·00
4 2d. dark blue .. .. .. £140 15·00
5 2d. greyish blue .. .. £140 15·00

(c) Worn plate, blue to greyish medium paper.

6 2d. ultramarine .. .. 90·00 15·00
7 2d. Prussian blue .. .. 70·00 15·00

(d) Worn plate, blue wove medium paper.

8 2d. ultramarine .. .. 75·00 15·00
9 2d. Prussian blue .. .. 70·00 15·00

9

(Plate II engraved by H. C. Jervis.)

853 (Oct.). *T* **9**. *Plate II. Stars in corners. Imperf.*

(a) Bluish medium to thick wove paper.

2d. deep ultramarine .. .. £300 45·00
2d. indigo .. .. .. £350 38·00
a. "WAEES" (No. 23).. .. — 60·00

(b) Worn plate, hard blue wove paper.

2d. deep Prussian blue .. £300 38·00
a. "WAEES" (No. 23).. .. — 55·00

855 (Sept.). *Plate III, being Plate I re-engraved by H. C. Jervis. Background of crossed lines. Imperf.*

(a) Medium bluish wove paper.

2d. Prussian blue .. .. £120 18·00
a. "WALES" covered with wavy lines (No. 3) .. .. .. — 28·00

(b) Stout white wove paper.

2d. Prussian blue .. .. £110 18·00
a. "WALES" covered with wavy lines (No. 3) .. .. .. — 38·00

(Engraved by John Carmichael.)

1852 (3 Dec.). *T* **8**. *Imperf.*

(a) Medium greyish blue wove paper.

65 3d. deep green.. .. .. £500 70·00
66 3d. green .. .. .. £375 55·00
67 3d. dull yellow-green .. .. £350 42·00
a. "WAEES" (No. 37).. .. — 75·00

(b) Thick blue wove paper.

69 3d. emerald-green .. .. £375 80·00
71 3d. blue-green .. .. .. £375 80·00
a. "WAEES" (No. 37).. .. — £120

(Apr.). *As T* **8**. *Fine background. Imperf.*

(a) Medium white wove paper.

72 6d. vandyke-brown .. .. — £225
a. "WALLS" (No. 8) .. .. — £300

(b) Medium bluish grey wove paper.

73 6d. vandyke-brown .. .. £450 80·00
74 6d. yellow-brown .. .. £500 90·00
75 6d. chocolate-brown .. .. £450 75·00
76 6d. grey-brown .. .. £400 75·00
a. "WALLS" (No. 8) .. .. — £110

1853 (June). *Plate I re-engraved by H. C. Jervis. Coarse background. Imperf.*

77 6d. brown .. .. .. £550 90·00
78 6d. grey-brown .. .. £450 80·00

(Engraved by H. C. Jervis.)

1853 (May). *Medium bluish paper. Imperf.*

79 8d. dull yellow £750 £200
80 8d. orange-yellow £750 £200
81 8d. orange £900 £225
a. No bow at back of head (No. 9) — £250
b. No leaves right of "SOUTH" (No. 21) .. .. .. — £250
c. No lines in spandrel (Nos. 12, 22, and 32) .. .. .. — £225

10

NOTE.—All watermarked stamps from No. 82 to No. 172 have double-lined figures, as T **10**.

1854 (Feb.). *T* **8**. *Wmk.* "**1**", *T* **10**. *Imperf. Yellowish wove paper.*

82 1d. red-orange .. .. 38·00 7·50
83 1d. orange-vermilion .. .. 38·00 7·50
a. No leaves right of "SOUTH" (Nos. 7 and 21) .. .. 48·00 15·00
b. Two leaves right of "SOUTH" (No. 15) .. .. .. 90·00 38·00
c. "WALE" (No. 9) .. .. 90·00 38·00

1854 (Jan.). *Plate III. Wmk.* "**2**". *Imperf.*

84 2d. ultramarine .. .. 27·00 3·75
85 2d. Prussian blue .. .. 27·00 3·75
86 2d. chalky blue .. .. 27·00 3·75
a. "WALES" partly covered .. 80·00 11·00

1854 (Mar.). *Wmk.* "**3**". *Imperf.*

87 3d. yellow-green) .. .. 38·00 12·00
a. "WAEES" (No. 37).. .. — 27·00
b. Error. Wmk. "2" .. .. — £900

13

14

(Engraved by John Carmichael.)

1856 (1 Jan.). *For Registered Letters. T* **13**. *No wmk. Imperf. Soft medium yellowish paper.*

88 (6d.) vermilion & Prussian blue £150 45·00
a. Frame printed on back .. £900 £450
89 (6d.) salmon and indigo .. £225 60·00
90 (6d.) orange and Prussian blue £225 65·00
91 (6d.) orange and indigo .. £225 60·00

1859 (Apr.). *Hard medium bluish wove paper, with manufacturer's wmk. in sans-serif, double-lined capitals across sheet and only showing portions of letters on a few stamps in a sheet.*

(a) Imperf.

92 (6d.) orange and Prussian blue £160 38·00
92*a* (6d.) verm. and Prussian blne £225 65·00

1860 (Feb). *(b) P* 12.

93 (6d.) orange and Prussian blue 90·00 12·00
94 (6d.) orange and indigo .. 75·00 12·00

Coarse yellowish wove paper having the manufacturer's wmk. in Roman capitals.

(a) P 12.

95 (6d.) rose-red & Prussian bluc 60·00 11·00
96 (6d.) rose-red and indigo .. 75·00 18·00
97 (6d.) salmon and indigo ..

1862. *(b) P* 13.

98 (6d.) rose-red & Prussian-blue 55·00 13·00

1863 (May). *Yellowish wove paper. Wmk.* "**6**". *P* 13.

99 (6d.) rose-red & Prussian blue 23·00 5·50
100 (6d.) rose-red and indigo .. 27·00 7·50
101 (6d.) rose-red and pale blue.. 14·00 4·50
a. Double impression of frame ..

(T **14/21** and **24** printed in the Colony from plates engraved by Messrs. Perkins, Bacon & Co.)

Two plates of the 2d. and 6d. were used. On Plate II of the 2d. the stamps are wider apart and more regularly spaced than on Plate I.

1856 (6 Apr.). *Wmk.* "**1**" *Imperf.*

102 **14** 1d. orange-vermilion .. 27·00 7·00
a. Error. wmk. "2"
103 „ 1d. carmine vermilion .. 27·00 7·00
104 „ 1d. orange-red .. .. 23·00 7·00
a. Printed on both sides .. — £375

1856 (7 Jan.). *Plate I. Wmk.* "**2**". *Imperf.*

105 **14** 2d. light ultramarine .. 27·00 3·00
106 „ 2d. Prussian blue . .. 27·00 3·50
107 „ 2d. dull blue .. .. 27·00 2·75
108 „ 2d. cobalt-blue .. .. 38·00 5·50
a. Error, wmk. "1" ..
b. Error, wmk. "5" .. £120 6·00
c. Error, wmk. "8" ..

1858. *Plate I, retouched.*

109 **14** 2d. dull blue .. .. £450 65·00

1859 (Aug.). *Lithographic transfer of Plate I.*

110 **14** 2d. pale cobalt-blue .. — £150
a. Retouched .. .. — £750

1860 (Jan.). *Plate II. Recess. Stamps printed wider apart.*

110*b* **14** 2d. blue .. .. .. 90·00 7·50

1856 (10 Oct.). *Wmk.* "**3**". *Imperf.*

111 **14** 3d. yellow-green .. .. £200 38·00
112 „ 3d. bluish-green .. .. £225 38·00
113 „ 3d. dull green .. .. £225 45·00
a. Error, wmk. "2" .. — £900

In the 3d. the value is in block letters on a white ground.

15 17

19

21

(6d. and 1s. des. E. H. Corbould after sketches by T. W. Levinge.)

1855 (1 Dec.). *Wmk.* "**5**". *Imperf.*
114 **15** 5d. dull green £250 £200

1854 (Feb.). *Wmk.* "**6**". *Imperf.*
115 **17** 6d. deep slate .. .. £150 11·00
116 ,, 6d. greenish grey .. .. £110 11·00
117 ,, 6d. slate-green .. .. £110 11·00
a. Printed both sides ..
118 ,, 6d. bluish grey .. .. £120 14·00
119 ,, 6d. fawn .. .. .. £120 20·00
120 ,, 6d. grey .. .. .. £120 12·00
121 ,, 6d. olive-grey .. .. £120 12·00
122 ,, 6d. greyish brown .. .. £120 12·00

1859 (15 Aug.). *Error. Wmk.* "**8**".
123 **17** 6d. fawn .. .. .. £450 32·00
124 ,, 6d. greyish brown .. .. £450 38·00

1855 (1 Dec.). *Wmk.* "**8**". *Imperf.*
125 **19** 8d. golden yellow £1800 £450
126 ,, 8d. dull yellow-orange .. £1700 £450

1854 (Feb.). *Wmk.* "**12**". *Imperf.*
127 **21** 1s. rosy vermilion .. £160 18·00
128 ,, 1s. pale red .. .. £160 18·00
129 ,, 1s. brownish red .. .. £160 18·00

1857 (20 June). *Error. Wmk.* "**8**".
130 **21** 1s. rosy-vermilion .. £650 65·00

1860 (Feb.)–**63**. *Wmk. double-lined figure of value. P* 12.
131 **14** 1d. orange-red .. .. 35·00 3·75
a. Imperf. between (pair) ..
b. Double impression ..
132 ,, 1d. scarlet .. .. .. 23·00 3·75
133 ,, 2d. cobalt-blue (Pl. I) .. £140 23·00
a. Retouched .. — £550
134 ,, 2d. greenish blue (Pl. II) .. 27·00 3·75
136 ,, 2d. Prussian blue (Pl. II) .. 30·00 3·75
a. Error. Wmk. "1" .. — £900
b. Retouched (*shades*) .. — £110
137 ,, 2d. Prussian blue (Pl. I) (3.61) .. .. 38·00 4·50
138 ,, 2d. dull blue (Pl. I) .. 32·00 3·75
139 ,, 3d. yellow-green (1860) .. £375 23·00
140 ,, 3d. blue-green .. .. £120 11·00
141 **15** 5d. dull green (1863) .. 35·00 15·00
142 ,, 5d. yellowish green (1863) 35·00 15·00
143 **17** 6d. grey-brown .. .. 65·00 9·00
144 ,, 6d. olive-brown .. .. 65·00 9·00
145 ,, 6d. greenish grey .. .. £150 14·00
146 ,, 6d. fawn .. .. .. 60·00 7·50
147 ,, 6d. mauve .. .. .. 80·00 9·00
148 ,, 6d. violet .. .. .. 60·00 4·50
a. Imperf. between (pair) ..
149 **19** 8d. lemon-yellow .. .. — £375
150 ,, 8d. orange .. .. .. £550 90·00
151 ,, 8d. red-orange .. .. £550 90·00
152 **21** 1s. brownish red .. .. £110 15·00
153 ,, 1s. rose-carmine .. .. £110 15·00
a. Imperf. between (pair) ..

No. 133 was made by perforating a small remaining stock of No. 108. Nos. 137/8 were printed from the original plate after its return from London, where it had been repaired.

1862–72. *Wmk. double-lined figure of value. P* 13.
154 **14** 1d. scarlet (1862) .. 15·00 3·00
155 ,, 1d. dull red .. .. 15·00 3·00
156 ,, 3d. blue-green (Dec., '62) 14·00 3·75
157 ,, 3d. yellow-green .. .. 15·00 3·00
158 ,, 3d. dull green .. .. 6·50 2·75
a. Wmk. "6", yellow-green (July, '72) .. .. 15·00 3·75
b. Wmk. "6", dark green .. 16·00 5·00
160 **15** 5d. bluish green .. .. 14·00 4·00
161 ,, 5d. bright yellow-green .. 15·00 7·00
162 ,, 5d. sea-green .. .. 15·00 4·50
162*a* ,, 5d. dark bluish green .. 10·00 5·50
163 **17** 6d. reddish purple (Pl. I, July, '62) .. .. 12·00 2·00
164 ,, 6d. mauve .. .. 12·00 2·00
165 ,, 6d. purple (Pl. II, 1864) .. 11·00 1·50
a. Error, wmk. "5" (7.66) 55·00 9·00
b. Error, wmk. "12" (12.66) 38·00 6·00
166 ,, 6d. violet .. .. .. 11·00 2·00
167 ,, 6d. aniline mauve .. £225 30·00
167*a* **19** 8d. red-orange .. .. 18·00 11·00
167*b* ,, 8d. yellow-orange .. 18·00 9·00
167*c* ,, 8d. bright yellow .. 18·00 9·00
168 **21** 1s. rose-carmine .. .. 15·00 2·75
169 ,, 1s. carmine .. .. 15·00 3·00
170 ,, 1s. crimson lake .. .. 15·00 3·00
Perf. compound 12 × 13.
171 **14** 1d. scarlet .. .. — £375
172 ,, 2d. dull blue .. .. £450 90·00

23

1864 (June). *T* **14**. *W* **23**. *P* 13.
173 1d. pale red .. .. .. 6·00 5·00

24 25

(Des. E. H. Corbould, R.I.)

1861–88. *T* **24**. *W* **25**. *Various perfs.*
174 5s. dull violet, *perf.* 12 ('61) .. £450 £120
a. Perf. 13 ('61) .. .. 65·00 12·00
175 5s. royal purple, *perf.* 13 ('72) 90·00 18·00
176 5s. deep rose-lilac, *p.* 13 ('75) 38·00 12·00
177 5s. deep purple, *perf.* 13 ('80) 55·00 16·00
a. Perf. 10 (1882) .. .. 55·00 18·00
178 5s. rose-lilac, *perf.* 10 ('83) .. 45·00 16·00
179 5s. purple, *perf.* 12 ('85) .. — 18·00
a. Perf. 10 × 12 (1885) .. .. — 45·00
180 5s. reddish purple, *p.* 10 ('86) 45·00 16·00
a. Perf. 12 × 10 (1887) .. 90·00 18·00
181 5s. rose-lilac, *perf.* 11 ('88) .. — 45·00

This value was replaced by Nos. 274, etc. in 1888 but reissued in 1897, *see* Nos. 297*c*/f.

26 28

29

A. Printed by Messrs. De La Rue & Co., and perf. at Somerset House, London.

1862–65. *Surfaced paper. P* 14.
(i) *W* **23**.
186 **26** 1d. dull red (Pl. I.4.64) .. 30·00 9·00
(ii) *No wmk.*
187 **26** 1d. dull red (Pl. II, 1.65) .. 23·00 9·00
188 **28** 2d. pale blue (3.62) .. 23·00 9·00

B. Printed from the De La Rue plates in the Colony.

1862 (12 Apr.). *Wmk. double lined* "**2**". *P* 13.
189 **28** 2d. blue .. .. .. 15·00 2·75
a. Perf. 12 .. .. .. 45·00 4·50
b. Perf. 12 × 13 .. .. £160

1864–65. *W* **23**. *P* 13.
190 **26** 1d. dark red-brown (Pl. I) 27·00 3·75
191 ,, 1d. brownish red (Pl. II) .. 5·50 60
192 **26** 1d. brick-red (Plate II) .. 5·50 6
a. Highly surfaced paper (1865) 65·00
194 **28** 2d. pale blue .. .. 38·00 1·5

Plates I and II were made from the same die they can only be distinguished by the colour or b the marginal inscription.

1865–66. *Thin wove paper. No wmk. P* 1
195 **26** 1d. brick-red .. .. 35·00 3·7
196 ,, 1d. brownish red .. .. 35·00 3·7
197 **28** 2d. pale blue .. .. 14·00 1·2

1863–69. *W* **29**. *P* 13.
198 **26** 1d. pale red (3.69) .. 27·00 2·7
199 **28** 2d. pale blue .. .. 1·50 2
a. Perf. 12 .. .. ..
200 ,, 2d. cobalt-blue .. .. 1·50 2
201 ,, 2d. Prussian blue .. .. 6·00 1·1

1862 (Sept.). *Wmk. double-lined* "**5**". *P* 1
202 **28** 2d. dull blue .. .. 35·00 5·5

32 34

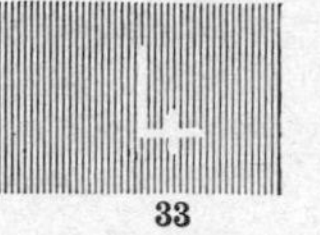

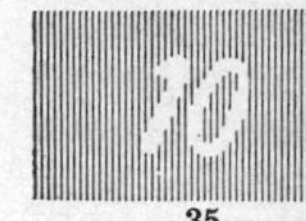

33 35

1867 (Sept.)–**93**. *W* **33** *and* **35**.
203 **32** 4d. red-brown, *perf.* 13 .. 5·50 7
204 ,, 4d. pale red-brn., *perf.* 13 5·50 7
205 **34** 10d. lilac, *perf.* 13 .. .. 1·50 1·1
a. Imperf. between (pair) .. £120
206 ,, 10d. lilac, *perf.* 11 (1893) .. 2·00 1·1
a. Perf. 10 .. .. 3·00 1·5
b. Perf. 10 and 11, compound 4·50 2·7
c. Perf. 12 × 11 .. .. 35·00 6·0

36 37

38

NINEPENCE
(39)

From 1871 to 1903 the 9d. is formed from th 10d. by a *black* surch. (T **39**), 15 mm. long o Nos. 219 to 220h, and 13½ mm. long on sub sequent issues.

1871–84. *W* **36**.
207 **26** 1d. dull red, *perf.* 13 (8.71) 75
a. Imperf. vert. (horiz. pr.) ..
208 ,, 1d. salmon, *perf.* 13 .. 75 1
a. Perf. 10 .. .. .. 85·00 3·5
b. Perf. 13 × 10 .. .. 3·50 1
c. *Scarlet.* Perf. 10 .. .. — 75·0
209 **28** 2d. Pruss.-bl., *p.*13 (11.71) 75
a. Perf. 11 × 12, comb .. 85·00 18·0
b. Imperf. vert. (horiz. pair) ..
210 ,, 2d. pale blue, *perf.* 13 .. 65
aa. "TWO PENCE" double impression at right ..
a. Perf. 10 .. .. .. 85·00 6·0
b. Perf. 13 × 10 80
c. Surfaced paper, perf. 13 ..

11 **14** 3d. yell.-green. (3.74), *p.* 13 .. 4·50 65
- a. Perf. 10 .. .. .. 18·00 1·50
- b. Perf. 11 .. .. .. 65·00 50·00
- c. Perf. 12 .. .. .. — 75·00
- d. Perf. 10×12 .. .. 65·00 15·00
- e. Perf. 12×11 .. .. 45·00 15·00

12 ,, 3d. bright green, *perf.* 10 .. 45·00 3·00
- a. Perf. 10×13 .. .. 38·00 3·75

13 **32** 4d. pale red-brown (8.77), *perf.* 13 .. .. 8·00 2·00

14 ,, 4d. red-brown, *perf.* 13 .. 8·00 2·00
- a. Perf. 10 .. .. .. 75·00 14·00
- b. Perf. 13×10 .. .. 20·00 90

15 **15** 5d. bluish green (8.84), *p.* 10 3·50 2·00
- a. Perf. 12 .. .. .. 80·00 42·00
- b. Perf. 13×10 .. ..
- c. Perf. 10×12 .. .. 5·00 2·00

16 **37** 6d. brt. mauve (1.72), *p.* 13 1·50 5
- a. Imperf. between (horiz. pair) — £150

17 ,, 6d. pale lilac, *perf.* 13 .. 3·75 5
- a. Perf. 10 .. .. .. 80·00 3·50
- b. Perf. 13×10 .. .. 9·00 60
- c. Imperf. between (horiz. pair) Perf. 13×10 .. .. — £150

18 **19** 8d. yellow (3.77), *p.* 13 .. 5·50 90
- a. Perf. 10 .. .. .. 80·00 3·50
- b. Perf. 13×10 .. .. 65·00 3·00

19 **34** 9d. on 10d. pale red-brown (8.71), *perf.* 13 .. .. 4·50 90

20 ,, 9d. on 10d. red-brn., *p.* 13 4·50 2·00
- a. Perf. 10 .. .. .. 2·00 90
- b. Perf. 12 .. .. .. 2·00 90
- c. Perf. 11 .. .. .. 7·00 2·00
- d. Perf. 10×12 .. .. 90·00 70·00
- e. Perf. 10×11 .. .. 9·00 2·75
- f. Perf. 12×11 .. .. 3·00 1·50
- g. Perf. 11×12, comb. .. 3·00 1·50
- h. In black and blue, perf. 11 45·00

21 **38** 1s. black (4.76), *perf.* 13 .. 7·00 35
- a. Perf. 10 .. .. .. 80·00 3·75
- b. Perf. 10×13 .. .. 38·00 1·00
- c. Perf. 11 .. .. ..
- d. Imperf. between (horiz. pair) — £200

Collectors should note that the classification of perforations is that adopted by the Royal Philatelic Society, London. "Perf. 12" denotes the perforation formerly called "11½, 12" and "perf. 13" that formerly called "12½, 13".

40

882–93. *W* **40.**

22 **26** 1d. salmon, *perf.* 10 .. 1·40 10
- a. Perf. 13 .. .. ..
- b. Perf. 10×13 .. .. 9·00 90

23 ,, 1d. orange *to* scarlet, *p.* 13
- a. Perf. 10 .. .. .. 1·25 5
- ab. Imperf. between (horiz. pair)
- b. Perf. 10×13 .. .. 45·00 2·00
- c. Perf. 10×12 .. .. 90·00 23·00
- d. Perf. 10×11 .. .. £150 38·00
- e. Perf. 12×11 .. .. — 38·00
- f. Perf. 11×12, comb .. 8 5
- h. Perf. 11 .. .. .. — 45·00

24 **28** 2d. pale blue, *p.* 13 .. £150 38·00
- a. Perf. 10 .. .. .. 1·50 5
- b. Perf. 13×10 .. .. 23·00 90

25 ,, 2d. Prussian blue, *perf.* 10 3·50 5
- a. Perf. 13×10 .. .. 23·00 75
- b. Perf. 12 .. .. .. — 75·00
- c. Perf. 11 .. .. .. — 42·00
- d. Perf. 12×11 .. .. — 42·00
- e. Perf. 12×10 .. .. 80·00 23·00
- f. Perf. 10×11 .. .. £160 38·00
- g. Perf. 11×12, comb .. 30 8

26 **14** 3d. yell.-grn. (1886), *p.* 10 60 8
- a. Perf. 10×12 .. .. 55·00 4·00
- b. Perf. 11 .. .. .. 60 8
- c. Perf. 12×11 .. .. 60 8
- d. Perf. 12 .. .. .. 1·50 10
- e. Imperf. between (horiz. pair) 38·00
- f. Imperf. (pair) .. .. 38·00

227 **14** 3d. bluish green, *perf.* 10 .. 75 8
- a. Perf. 11 .. .. .. 75 8
- b. Perf. 10×11 .. .. 3·75 35
- c. Perf. 12×11 .. .. 75 25
- d. Perf. 12×10 .. .. 23·00 90

228 ,, 3d. emerald-grn. ('93), *p.* 10 14·00 2·00
- a. Perf. 10×11 .. .. 14·00 75
- b. Perf. 12×10 .. .. 23·00 2·00

229 **32** 4d. red-brown, *p.* 10 .. 1·50 35
- a. Perf. 10×12 .. .. — 48·00
- b. Perf. 11×12. comb. .. 6·50 25

230 ,, 4d. dark brown *perf.* 10 7·00 75
- a. Perf. 12 .. .. .. — 15·00
- b. Perf. 10×12 .. .. — 40·00
- c. Perf. 11×12, comb. .. 2·75 20

231 **15** 5d. dull grn. (1891), *perf.* 10 2·75 30
- a. Perf. 11×10 .. .. 8·00 75
- b. Perf. 12×10 .. .. 23·00 90

232 ,, 5d. bright green, *perf.* 10 8·00 1·10
- a. Perf. 11 .. .. .. — 1·10
- b. Perf. 10×11 .. .. 9·00 1·50
- c. Perf. 12×10 .. .. 45·00 2·00

233 ,, 5d. blue-green, *perf.* 10 .. 2·25 50
- a. Perf. 12 .. .. .. 3·00 50
- b. Perf. 11 .. .. .. 1·50 30
- c. Perf. 10×11 .. .. 7·50 75
- d. Perf. 11×12 or 12×11 .. 1·25 25
- e. Imperf. (pair) .. .. 60·00

234 **37** 6d. pale lilac, *p.* 10 .. 1·50 8
- a. Perf. 10×13 or 13×10 .. — 80·00
- b. Perf. 10×12 .. .. 4·00 35

235 ,, 6d. mauve, *perf.* 10 .. 2·00 8
- a. Perf. 12 .. .. .. 27·00 75
- b. Perf. 11 .. .. .. 27·00 2·00
- c. Perf. 10×12 .. .. 3·00 20
- d. Perf. 11×12 .. .. 3·00 30
- e. Perf. 10×11 .. .. 9·00 12
- f. Imperf. between (horiz. pair) Perf. 12×10 .. .. — £200

236 **19** 8d. yellow (1883), *perf.* 10 9·00 80
- a. Perf. 12 .. .. .. 27·00 4·00
- b. Perf. 11 .. .. .. 9·00 1·10
- c. Perf. 10×12 .. .. 16·00 3·00

237 **38** 1s. black, *perf.* 10 .. 4·50 20
- a. Perf. 11 .. .. .. 38·00 2·25
- b. Perf. 10×12 .. ..
- c. Perf. 10×13 .. .. — 3·00
- d. Perf. 11×12, comb .. 2·75 20

41

1886–87. *W* **41.**

238 **26** 1d. scarlet, *perf.* 10 .. 2·75 1·10
- a. Perf. 11×12, comb .. 80 30

239 **28** 2d. deep blue, *perf.* 10 .. 14·00 2·00
- a. Perf. 11×12, comb .. 2·00 45
- b. Imperf. .. .. ..

1891 (JULY). *Wmk.* "10" *as T* **35.** *P* 10.

240 **14** 3d. green .. .. 3·00 2·00

241 ,, 3d. dark green 45 20

42

NOTE. The spacing between the Crown and "NSW" is 1 mm. in T **42**, as against 2 mm. in T **40**.

1903–8. *W* **42.**

241*a* **14** 3d. yellow-green, *perf.* 11 80 8
- b. Perf. 12 .. .. .. 45 8
- c. Perf. 11×12 .. .. 45 8

242 ,, 3d. dull green, *perf.* 12 .. 4·50 35
- a. Perf. 11×12 .. .. 90 8

243 **15** 5d. dark blue-green, *p.* 11×12 .. .. 45 8
- a. Perf. 11 .. .. .. 2·75 8
- b. Perf. 12 .. .. .. 4·50 90
- c. Imperf. (pair) .. ..

43

1885–86. *T* **43.** *W* **41.**

(i) *Overprinted* "POSTAGE", *in black.*

244 5s. green and lilac, *perf.* 13 ..
- a. Perf. 10 .. .. ..
- b. Perf. 12×10 .. .. 27·00 12·00

245 10s. claret and lilac, *perf.* 13 ..
- a. Perf. 12 .. .. .. 90·00 45·00

246 £1 claret and lilac, *perf.* 13 .. — £300
- a. Perf. 12 .. .. .. £150 80·00

(ii) *Overprinted in blue.*

247 10s. claret and mauve, *perf.* 10 £150 38·00
- a. Perf. 12 .. .. .. 27·00 15·00
- b. Perf. 12×11 .. .. 65·00

248 £1 claret and rose-lilac, *perf.* 12×10 .. .. .. £275

44

Overprinted "POSTAGE" *in blue.*

1894. *T* **43.** *W* **44.**

249 10s. claret and mauve, *p.* 10 .. 60·00 12·00

249*a* 10s. claret and violet, *p.* 12 .. 18·00 9·00
- b. Perf. 11 .. .. .. 15·00 9·00
- c. Perf. 12×11 .. .. 16·00 9·00

250 10s. aniline crimson and violet, *perf.* 12×11 .. .. 23·00 11·00
- a. Perf. 12 .. .. .. 27·00 15·00

250*b* £1 claret & violet, *p.* 12×11

1903–04. *T* **43.** *optd.* "POSTAGE" *in blue. Chalk-surfaced paper. W* **44.**

250*c* 10s. aniline crimson & violet, *perf.* 12×11

251 10s. rosine & vio., *p.* 12 ('04) 18·00 9·00
- a. Perf. 11 .. .. .. 23·00 9·00
- b. Perf. 12×11 .. .. 23·00 9·00

252 10s. clar. & vio., *p.* 12×11('04) 38·00 9·00

45. View of Sydney.

46. Emu.

47. Captain Cook.

48. Queen Victoria and Arms of Colony.

49. Lyre bird.

50. Kangaroo.

1888–99. *W* **40.**

No.	Type	Description	Unused	Used
253	**45**	1d. lilac, *perf.* 11×12	30	5
		a. Perf. 12×11½	4·50	45
		b. Perf. 12	45	5
		c. Imperf. (pair)		
254	,,	1d. mauve, *perf.* 11×12	25	5
		a. Perf. 12×11½	1·10	5
		b. Perf. 12	65	5
		c. Imperf. between (pair), perf. 11×12		
255	**46**	2d. Pruss.-bl., *p.* 11×12	25	5
		a. Perf. 12×11½	2·00	5
		b. Perf. 12	1·10	5
		c. Imperf. (pair)	38·00	
		d. Imperf. between (horiz. pair), perf. 11×12 ..	£110	
256	,,	2d. chalky-bl., *p.* 11×12	25	5
		a. Perf. 12×11½		
		b. Perf. 12	75	5
257	**47**	4d. pur.-brn., *p.* 11×12 ..	60	5
		a. Perf. 12×11½	7·00	1·50
		b. Perf. 12	6·00	35
		c. Perf. 11	£110	38·00
258	,,	4d. red-brown, *p.* 11×12	90	5
		a. Perf. 12×11½	2·75	5
		b. Perf. 12	3·00	5
259	,,	4d. orge.-brn., *p.* 12×11½	3·00	5
260	,,	4d. yell.-brn., *p.* 12×11½	2·25	25
261	**48**	6d. carmine, *p.* 11×12 ..	90	5
		a. Perf. 12×11½	4·00	15
		b. Perf. 12	1·50	10
262	,,	6d. emerald-green, *perf.* 11×12 (1898) ..	5·00	1·10
		a. Perf. 12×11½	5·00	1·10
		b. Perf. 12	2·75	1·10
262*c*	,,	6d. orge.-yell., *p.* 11×12 (1899)	1·25	30
		d. Perf. 12×11½	90	25
		e. Perf. 12	4·50	45
263	,,	6d. yellow, *perf.* 12×11½	1·50	20
264	**49**	8d. lilac rose, *p.* 11×12 ..	1·50	20
		a. Perf. 12×11½	12·00	2·75
		b. Perf. 12	1·50	35
265	,,	8d. magenta, *p.* 11×12 ..	23·00	2·00
		a. Perf. 12×11½	1·10	35
		b. Perf. 12	75	45
266	**34**	9d. on 10d. red-brn. *perf.* 11×12 (1897) ..	1·50	60
		a. Perf. 12	2·00	1·00
		b. Perf. 11	2·00	1·10
		c. Double surcharge, perf. 11	38·00	35·00
268	,,	10d. violet, *p.* 11×12 (1897)	1·25	90
		a. Perf. 12×11½	90	60
		b. Perf. 12	2·75	1·25
		c. Perf. 11	2·75	1·25
269	**50**	1s. maroon *perf.* 11×12 (1889)	1·10	8
		a. Perf. 12×11½	2·25	8
		b. Perf. 12	4·00	8
270	,,	1s. vio.-brn., *p.* 11×12 ..	1·50	8
		a. Perf. 12×11½	9·00	25
		b. Perf. 12	9·00	8
		c. Imperf. (pair)	£200	

All these perforations, with the exception of perf. 11, are from comb machines.

1888. *W* **41.** *P* 11×12 *comb.*

No.	Type	Description	Unused	Used
271	**45**	1d. lilac	2·00	
272	,,	1d. mauve	1·50	5
273	**46**	2d. Prussian blue	14·00	90

51. Map of Australia.

52. Capt. Arthur Phillip, first Governor and Lord Carrington, Governor in 1888.

1888–89. *W* **25.** *P* 10.

No.	Type	Description	Unused	Used
274	**51**	5s. deep purple	38·00	18·00
275	,,	5s. deep violet	30·00	15·00
276	**52**	20s. cobalt blue	60·00	45·00
274 & 276		Optd. "Specimen" *Set of 2*	70·00	

53

1890. *W* **53.**

No.	Type	Description	Unused	Used
277	**51**	5s. lilac, *perf.* 10	18·00	7·50
		a. Perf. 11	32·00	15·00
		aa. Imperf. between (horiz. pair)		
		b. Perf. 12	70·00	14·00
		c. Perf. 10×11 or 11×10 ..	40·00	7·00
278	,,	5s. mauve, *perf.* 10 ..	32·00	9·00
		a. Perf. 11	30·00	12·00

54

55. Allegorical figure of Australia.

1890. *W* **54.**

No.	Type	Description	Unused	Used
279	**52**	20s. cobalt-blue, *perf.* 10 ..	45·00	23·00
		a. Perf. 11	60·00	15·00
		b. Perf. 11×10		
280	,,	20s. ultramarine, *perf.* 11	45·00	14·00
		a. Perf. 12	75·00	27·00
		b. Perf. 11×12 or 12×11 ..	45·00	14·00

1890 (22 Dec.). *W* **40.**

No.	Type	Description	Unused	Used
281	**55**	2½d. ultramarine, *p.* 11×12 *comb*	30	8
		a. Perf. 12×11½ comb ..	18·00	
		b. Perf. 12, comb	2·75	8

Halfpenny (56)

SEVEN-PENCE
HALFPENNY (57)

1891 (5 Jan.). *Surch. as T* **56** *and* **57.** *W* **40.**

No.	Type	Description	Unused	Used
282	**26**	½d. on 1d. grey, *perf.* 11×12 *comb*	30	25
		a. Surch. omitted ..		
		b. Surch. double ..		
283	**37**	7½d. on 6d. brown, *p.* 10	80	30
		a. Perf. 11	80	30
		b. Perf. 12	1·10	75
		c. Perf. 11×12	90	60
		d. Perf. 10×12	1·10	60
284	**38**	12½d. on 1s. red, *perf.* 10 ..	1·10	90
		a. Perf. 11	1·10	75
		b. Perf. 11×12, comb ..	1·00	60
		c. Perf. 12×11½, comb ..	75	60
		d. Perf. 12, comb	1·50	60

58

Die I.

1892 (21 Mar.)–**1899.** *T* **58.** *Die I. Narro*
"H" *in* "HALF". *W* **40.**

No.	Description	Unused	Used
285	½d. grey, *perf.* 10	6·00	2
	a. Perf. 11	42·00	2·0
	b. Perf. 10×12	38·00	3·0
	c. Perf. 11×12	30	
	d. Perf. 12	35	
286	½d. slate, *perf.* 11×12 (1897)	30	
	a. Perf. 12×11½	30	
	b. Perf. 12	30	
	c. Imperf. between (horiz. pair) perf. 11×12	£110	
287	½d. bluish grn., *p.* 11×12 ('99)	70	
	a. Perf. 12×11½	30	
	b. Perf. 12	35	

The perforations 11×12, 12×11½, 12, are fror comb machines.

58*a*

(*Illustration reduced. Actual size* 47×38 *mm.*)

58*b*

(*Illustration reduced. Actual size* 38×46 *mm.*)

(Des. Charles Taylor. Typo. Govt. Printin Office, Sydney)

1897. *Charity. T* **58*a*** *and* **58*b***. *Wmk. T* **4(**
P 12×11 (1*d.*) *or* 11 (2½d.).

No.	Description	Unused	Used
287*c*	1d. (1s.) grn. & brn. (22.6) ..	15·00	11·0
287*d*	2½d. (2s. 6d.), gold, carmine and blue (28.6) ..	55·00	60·0
287*c/d*	Optd. "Specimen" *Set of 2*	80·00	

These stamps, sold at 1s. and 2s. 6d. respec tively, paid postage of 1d. and 2½d. only, th difference being given to a Consumptives' Hom

59

60

61

Dies of the 1d.

Die I.

Die II.

1d. Die I.—The first pearl on the crown on the ·ft side is merged into the arch, the shading nder the fleur-de-lis is indistinct, the "s" of "WALES" is open.

Die II.—The first pearl is circular, the vertical hading under the fleur-de-lis clear, the "s" of WALES" not so open.

Dies of the 2½d.

Die I.

Die II.

2½d. Die I.—There are 12 radiating lines in ıe star on the Queen's breast.

Die II.—There are 16 radiating lines in the tar and the eye is nearly full of colour.

897–99. *W* **40.**

No.	Type	Description	Unused	Used
88	**59**	1d. carm. (Die I), *p.* 11×12	60	8
		a. Perf. 12×11½	70	8
89	,,	1d. scar. (Die I), *p.* 11×12	60	8
		a. Perf. 12×11½	1·50	20
		b. Perf. 12	1·50	25
		ba. Imp. horiz. (vert. pair)		
90	,,	1d. rose-carmine (Die II), *perf.* 11×12	50	8
		a. Perf. 12×11½	35	8
		b. Perf. 12	35	8
		c. Imperf. between (pair)	£120	
91	,,	1d. salmon-red (Die II), *perf.* 12×11½	45	8
		a. Perf. 12	90	15
92	**60**	2d. deep dull blue, *perf.* 11×12	30	8
		a. Perf. 12×11½	30	8
		b. Perf. 12	1·50	8
93	,,	2d. cobalt-bl. *perf.* 11×12	90	8
		a. Perf. 12×11½	60	8
		b. Perf. 12	90	8
94	,,	2d. ultram., *perf.* 11×12	60	8
		a. Perf. 12×11½	35	8
		b. Perf. 12	35	8
		c. Imperf. between (pair)		
95	**61**	2½d. pur. (Die I), *p.* 12×11	1·10	25
		a. Perf. 11½×12	2·25	12
		b. Perf. 11	2·00	60
96	,,	2½d. deep violet (Die II), *perf.* 12×11	90	5
		a. Perf. 11½×12	2·00	30
		b. Perf. 12	80	30
97	,,	2½d. Pruss. blue, *p.* 12×11	2·00	
		a. Perf. 11½×12	90	5
		b. Perf. 12	75	12

The perforations 11×12, 12×11½, and 12 are om comb machines, the perforation 11 is from single-line machine.

897. *Reissue of T* **24.** *W* **25.** *P* 11.

No.	Type	Description	Unused	Used
97c		5s. reddish purple (*shades*)	14·00	5·50
		d. Perf. 12	18·00	9·00
		e. Perf. 11×12 or 12×11	14·00	7·50
		f. Perf. 11×imperf. between (pr.)	£1400	

1899 (Oct.). *Chalk-surfaced paper.* *W* **40.** *P* 12×11½ *or* 11½×12 (2½*d.*), *comb.*

No.	Type	Description	Unused	Used
298	**58**	½d. blue-green (Die I)	12	8
		a. Imperf. (pair)	18·00	11·00
299	**59**	1d. carmine (Die II)	25	8
		a. Imperf. horiz. (vert. pr.)		
300	,,	1d. scarlet (Die II)	25	8
301	,,	1d. salmon-red (Die II)	25	8
		a. Imperf. (pair)	12·00	15·00
302	**60**	2d. cobalt-blue	25	8
		a. Imperf. (pair)	12·00	
303	**61**	2½d. Pruss. blue (Die II)	25	8
		a. Imperf. (pair)	16·00	
303*b*	**47**	4d. red-brown	50	8
		c. Imperf. (pair)	75·00	
304	,,	4d. orange-brown	50	8
305	**48**	6d. deep orange	65	8
		a. Imperf. (pair)	45·00	
306	,,	6d. orange-yellow	60	8
307	,,	6d. emerald-green	7·50	30
		a. Imperf. (pair)	55·00	
308	**49**	8d. magenta	1·10	30
309	**34**	9d. on 10d. dull brown	90	30
		a. Surcharge double	38·00	25·00
		b. Without surcharge	38·00	
310	,,	10d. violet	1·25	50
311	**50**	1s. maroon	75	8
312	,,	1s. purple-brown	75	35
		a. Imperf. (pair)	55·00	

62. Lyre bird.

63

1902. *Chalk-surfaced paper.* *W* **42.** *P* 12×11½ *or* 11½×12 (2½*d.*), *comb.*

No.	Type	Description	Unused	Used
313	**58**	½d. blue-green, (Die I)	1·10	8
		a. Perf. 12×11	1·10	
314	**59**	1d. carmine (Die II)	25	8
315	**60**	2d. cobalt-blue	25	8
316	**61**	2½d. dark blue (Die II)	30	8
317	**47**	4d. orange-brown	3·75	8
318	**48**	6d. yellow-orange	3·00	8
319	,,	6d. orange	1·50	8
320	,,	6d. orange-buff	1·50	8
321	**49**	8d. magenta	1·60	10
322	**34**	9d. on 10d. brnish. orge.	75	60
323	,,	10d. violet	4·50	75
324	**50**	1s. maroon	1·25	8
325	,,	1s. purple-brown	1·90	8
326	**62**	2s. 6d. grn. (Optd. S. £15)	9·00	60

1903. *Wmk. double-lined V over Crown, Type* w. **10.**

No.	Type	Description	Unused	Used
327	**63**	9d. brown & ultramarine, *perf.* 12¼×12½, *comb.* (Optd. S. £15)	3·00	60
328	,,	9d. brown & deep blue, *perf.* 12¼×12½, *comb.*	3·00	60
329	,,	9d. brown & blue, *perf.* 11	£160	90·00

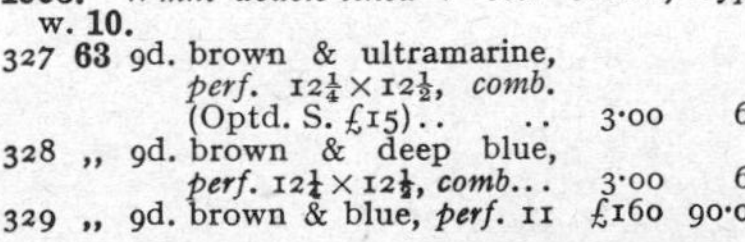

Die II. Broad "H" in "HALF".

66

1905–10. *Chalk-surfaced paper.* *W* **66.** *P* 12×11½ *or* 11½×12 (2½*d.*) *comb, unless otherwise stated.*

No.	Type	Description	Unused	Used
330	**58**	½d. blue-green (Die I)	45	8
		a. Perf. 11½×11		
331	,,	½d. blue-green (Die II)	25	8
		a. Perf. 11½×11	45	
332	**59**	1d. rose-carm. (Die II)	25	8
		a. Perf. 11½×11	65	
333	**60**	2d. deep ultramarine	25	8
		b. Perf. 11½×11	35	
333*d*	,,	2d. milky blue (1910)	25	8
		e. Perf. 11	23·00	
334	**61**	2½d. Prussian blue (Die II)	35	8
335	**47**	4d. orange-brown	60	8
336	,,	4d. red-brown	1·10	8
337	**48**	6d. dull yellow	1·10	20
		a. Perf. 11½×11	4·50	
338	,,	6d. orange-yellow	1·10	8
		a. Perf. 11×11½	7·50	
339	,,	6d. deep orange	45	8
		a. Perf. 11	70·00	
339*b*	,,	6d. orange-buff	70	8
		c. Perf. 11½×11	1·90	1·00
340	**49**	8d. magenta	1·50	25
341	,,	8d. lilac-rose	1·50	45
342	**34**	10d. violet	1·60	60
		a. Perf. 11½×11	1·50	45
		b. Perf. 11	1·50	35
343	**50**	1s. maroon	75	8
344	,,	1s. purple-brown (1908)	1·00	8
345	**62**	2s. 6d. blue-green	9·00	65
		a. Perf. 11½×11	1·50	35
		b. Perf. 11	3·00	75

67

1905 (Dec.). *Chalk-surfaced paper.* *W* **67.** *P* 11.

No.	Type	Description	Unused	Used
346	**52**	20s. cobalt-blue	38·00	12·00
		a. Perf. 12	38·00	12·00
		b. Perf. 11×12 or 12×11	38·00	12·00

1906. *Wmk. double-lined* "A" *and Crown, T* w.**11.** *P* 12×12½, *comb.*

No.	Type	Description	Unused	Used
347	**63**	9d. brown and ultram.	50	35
		a. Perf. 11	14·00	14·00
348	,,	9d. yell.-brn. & ultram.	50	15

1907 (July). *Wmk.* *T* w. **11.** *P* 12×11½ *or* 11½×12 (2½*d.*), *comb, unless otherwise stated.*

No.	Type	Description	Unused	Used
349	**58**	½d. blue-green (Die I)	70	8
351	**59**	1d. dull rose (Die II)	45	8
352	**60**	2d. cobalt-blue	35	8
353	**61**	2½d. Pruss. blue (Die II)	11·00	
354	**47**	4d. orange-brown	1·10	50
355	**48**	6d. orange-buff	3·00	70
356	,,	6d. dull yellow	1·90	60
357	**49**	8d. magenta	1·25	60
358	**34**	10d. violet, *perf.* 11	4·50	
359	**50**	1s. purple-brown	2·75	75
		a. Perf. 11		
360	**62**	2s. blue-green	9·00	3·00

OFFICIAL STAMPS.

Various stamps overprinted.

O S

(O 1)

The space between the letters is normally 7 mm. as illustrated, except on the 5d. and 8d. (11–11½ mm.), 5s. (12 mm.) and 20s. (14 mm.). Later printings of the 3d., *W* **40**, are 5½ mm., and these are listed. Varieties in the settings are known on the 1d. (8 and 8½ mm.), 2d. (8½ mm.) and 3d. (9 mm.).

Varities of Type O **1** exist with "O" sideways.

Overprinted with Type O **1.**

1879. *Wmk. double-lined* "6". *P* 13.

No.	Type	Description	Unused	Used
O1	**14**	3d. dull green	—	80·00

1879 (Oct.)–**85.** *W* **36.** *P* 13.

No.	Type	Description	Unused	Used
O2	**26**	1d. salmon	1·50	35
		a. Perf. 10 (5.81)	60·00	7·50
		b. Perf. 13×10 (1881)	4·00	90
O3	**28**	2d. blue	2·00	35
		a. Perf. 10 (7.81)	70·00	10·00
		b. Perf. 13×10 (1881)	4·50	75
		c. Perf. 10×13 (1881)	11·00	2·00
		d. Perf. 11×12 (11.84?)	—	70·00
O4	**14**	3d. dull green (R.) (12.79)	—	55·00
O5	,,	3d. dull green (3.80)	75·00	14·00
		a. Perf. 10 (1881)		
		b. Yell.-grn., perf. 10 (10.81)	45·00	7·50
		c. Do. Perf. 13×10 (1881)	45·00	7·50
		d. Do. Perf. 12 (4.85)		
		e. Do. Perf. 12×10 (4.85)		

O 6 **32** 4d. red brown .. .. 45·00 2·25
a. Perf. 10 (1881) .. .. — 55·00
b. Perf. 13×10 (1881) .. ..
c. Perf. 10×13 (1881) .. .. 70·00 3·50
O 7 **15** 5d. green, *perf.* 10 (8.84) 1·60 2·00
O 8 **37** 6d. pale lilac .. .. 70·00 1·50
a. Perf. 10 (1881) .. .. — 14·00
b. Perf. 13×10 (1881) .. ..
O 9 **19** 8d. yellow (R.) (12.79) .. — 45·00
O10 „ 8d. yellow (1880) .. — 2·00
a. Perf. 10 (1881) .. .. 70·00 27·00
O11 **34** 9d. on 10d. brown, *p.* 10 ('94) .. .. .. 55·00
O12 **38** 1s. black (R.) .. .. 55·00 2·00
a. Perf. 10 (1881) .. .. — 4·00
b. Perf. 13×10 (1881) .. .. — 2·25
c. Perf. 10×13 (1881) .. .. — 14·00

Other stamps are known with red overprint but their status is in doubt.

1880–88. *Wmk.* **"5/-"**, *T* **25.**

(*a*) *Perf.* 13.

O13 **24** 5s. deep purple (15.2.80) £100 23·00
a. Royal purple .. .. — £110
b. Deep rose-lilac .. .. — £110

(*b*) *Perf.* 10.

O14 **24** 5s. deep purple (9.82) .. £120 70·00
b. Rose-lilac (1883) .. .. 70·00 38·00

(*c*) *Perf.* 10×12.

O15 **24** 5s. purple (10.86) ..

(*d*) *Perf.* 12×10.

O16 **24** 5s. reddish purple (1886) 75·00 38·00

(*e*) *Perf.* 12.

O17 **24** 5s. purple .. .. — 55·00

(*f*) *Perf.* 11.

O18 **24** 5s. rose-lilac (1888) .. 23·00 23·00

1882–85. *W* **40.** *P* 10.

O19 **26** 1d. salmon .. .. 1·50 25
a. Perf. 13×10 .. .. — 55·00
O20 „ 1d. orange *to* scarlet .. 75 8
a. Perf. 10×13 .. .. — 55·00
b. Perf. 11×12, comb (1.84) 8 8
c. Perf. 10×12 (4.85) .. — 42·00
d. Perf. 12×11 (12.85) ..
O21 **28** 2d. blue 12 8
a. Perf. 13×10 .. ..
b. Perf. 10×13 .. .. 70·00 27·00
c. Perf. 11×12, comb (1.84) 8 8
d. Do. Opt. double ..
e. Perf. 12×11 (12.85) ..
O22 **14** 3d. yellow-green (*7 mm.*) 25 8
a. Perf. 12 (4.85) .. .. 45·00 30·00
b. Perf. 12×10 (4.85) .. ..
O23 „ 3d. bluish green (*7 mm.*) 30 10
a. Perf. 12 (4.85) .. .. 45·00 30·00
b. Perf. 12×10 (4.85) .. ..
c. Perf. 10×11 (12.85) .. ..
O24 „ 3d. yellow-green (*5½ mm.*) 25 8
a. Perf. 12×10 or 10×12 (4.85) 30 25
b. Perf. 10×11 or 11×10 (12.85) .. .. ..
O25 „ 3d. bluish green (*5½ mm.*) 25 15
a. Perf. 12×10 or 10×12 (4.85) 35 60
c. Perf. 10×11 or 11×10 (12.85) 25 25
O26 **32** 4d. red-brown .. .. 8·00 50
a. Perf. 11×12, comb (1.84) 15 15
b. Perf. 10×12 (4.85) .. — 23·00
O27 „ 4d. dark brown .. .. 2·25 25
a. Perf. 11×12, comb (1.84) 8 8
b. Perf. 12 (4.85) .. .. 70·00 55·00
c. Perf. 10×12 (4.85) .. 70·00 32·00
O28 **15** 5d. dull green 8 8
a. Perf. 12×10 (4.85) ..
O29 „ 5d. blue-green 25 25
a. Perf. 12 (4.85) .. .. 30·00
b. Perf. 10×11 .. .. 30 30
O30 **37** 6d. pale lilac 30 25
a. Perf. 11 (12.85) 90 12
O31 „ 6d. mauve 25 25
a. Perf. 12 (4.85) .. .. — 18·00
b. Perf. 12×10 (4.85) .. 12 8
c. Perf. 10×12 (4.85) .. 23·00 15·00
d. Perf. 11×10 (12.85) .. 35 25
e. Perf. 12×11 (12.85) .. 15·00 5·50
O32 **19** 8d. yellow 35 30
a. Perf. 12 (4.85) .. .. 45·00 15·00
b. Perf 12×10 or 10×12 (4.85) 10 8
d. Perf. 11 (12.85) 90 45
e. Do. Opt. double .. ..

O33 **38** 1s. black (R.) 12 8
a. Perf. 10×13 .. .. — 15·00
b. Perf. 11×12, comb (1.84).. 12 8
c. Do. Opt. double .. ..

1886–87. *W* **41.** *P* 10.

O34 **26** 1d. scarlet .. .. 5·50 90
O35 **28** 2d. deep blue .. ..
a. Perf. 11×12 .. ..

O S (O 2) **O S** (O 3)

1887–89. *Nos.* 247/8 *overprinted in black.*

(*a*) *With Type* O **1.**

O36 **43** 10s. claret & mauve, *p.* 12 — 55·00

(*b*) *With Type* O **2.** (April 1889).

O37 **43** 10s. claret & mauve, *p.* 12 75·00 45·00
a. Perf. 10 .. .. £375 £225

(*c*) *With Type* O **3.** (Jan., 1887).

O38 **43** £1 claret & rose-lilac *p.* 12×10 .. .. £350
a. Opt. double .. ..

1888–89. *Optd. as Type* O **1,** *P* 11×12.

(i) *W* **40.**

O39 **45** 1d. mauve (5.88) 8 8
a. Perf. 12 .. .. .. 8 8
O40 „ 1d. lilac 8 8
a. Perf. 12 .. .. .. 8 8
O41 **46** 2d. Prussian blue (9.88) .. 8 8
a. Perf. 12.. .. .. 8 8
O42 **47** 4d. purple-brown (10.88) 12 8
a. Perf. 12.. .. .. 90 8
b. Perf. 11
O43 „ 4d. red-brown 8 8
a. Perf. 12 .. .. 75 8
O44 **48** 6d. carmine (12.88) .. 8 8
a. Perf. 12 .. .. .. 75 8
O45 **49** 8d. lilac-rose (3.89) .. 12 8
a. Perf. 12.. .. .. — 1·50
O46 **50** 1s. maroon (3.89) .. 25 8
a. Perf. 12.. .. .. 45 8
O47 „ 1s. purple-brown.. .. 25 8
a. Perf. 12.. .. .. 30 8
b. Opt. double .. ..

(ii) *W* **41** (1889).

O48 **45** 1d. mauve .. ..
O49 **46** 2d. blue .. .. ..

1888–89. *Optd. as Type* O **1.** *W* **25.** *P* 10.

O50 **51** 5s. deep purple (R.) (4.89) £180 £180
O51 **52** 20s. cobalt-blue (11.88) .. £375

1890–91. *Optd. as Type* O **1.** *W* **53** (5*s.*) *or* **54** (20*s.*). *P* 10.

O52 **51** 5s. lilac (2.90) .. .. 11·00 9·00
a. Mauve .. .. .. 15·00 11·00
b. Dull lilac. Perf. 12 ..
O53 **52** 20s. cobalt-blue (3.91) .. £375

1891 (JAN.)–**92.** *Nos.* 281/5 *optd. as Type* O **1.** *W* **40.** *P* 11×12.

O54 **55** 2½d. ultramarine .. 8 8
O55 **26** ½d. on 1d. grey .. 1·50 1·50
O56 **37** 7½d. on 6d. brown, *p.* 10 35 1·50
O57 **38** 12½d. on 1s. red .. 45 1·50
O58 **58** ½d. grey (5.92) 8 8
a. Perf. 10 .. .. 25 75
b. Perf. 12 .. .. 10 8
c. Perf. 12×11½ 90

1894 (30 JUNE). *Optd. as Type* O **1.** *Wmk.* **"10"**, *T* **35.**

O59 **34** 10d. lilac .. .. .. 23·00 27·00
a. Perf. 10×11 .. .. 38·00 55·00

POSTAGE DUE STAMPS.

D 1

1891 (1 JAN.)–**1892.** *W* **40.** *P* 10.

D 1 D **1** ½d. green.. .. .. 15 8
D 2 „ 1d. green.. .. .. 15 8
a. Perf. 11 .. .. 15 8
b. Perf. 12 .. .. 2·50 65
c. Perf. 12×10 .. .. — 25
d. Perf. 10×11 .. .. 75 8
e. Perf. 11×12 or 12×11 .. 15 8
D 3 „ 2d. green.. .. .. 15 8
a. Perf. 11 .. .. 15 8
b. Perf. 12 .. ..
c. Perf. 12×10 .. .. 2·50 90
d. Perf. 10×11 .. .. 75 15
e. Perf. 11×12 or 12×11 .. 15 8
D 4 „ 3d. green.. .. .. 30 12
a. Perf. 10×11 .. .. 30 12
D 5 „ 4d. green.. .. .. 50 20
a. Perf. 11 .. .. 8 8
b. Perf. 10×11 .. .. 20 8
D 6 „ 6d. green.. .. .. 35 15
D 7 „ 8d. green.. .. .. 35 12
D 8 „ 5s. green.. .. .. 3·75 75
a. Perf. 11 .. .. 18·00 15·00
b. Perf. 11×12 .. ..
D 9 „ 10s. green.. .. .. 18·00
a. Perf. 12×10 .. .. 7·50
D10 „ 20s. green.. .. .. 30·00 2·00
a. Perf. 12 .. .. 30·00
b. Perf. 12×10 .. .. 6·50 4·00
D1/10 Optd. "Specimen" *Set of* 10 £100

1900. *Chalk-surfaced paper.* *W* **40.** *P* 11.

D11 D **1** ½d. emerald-green ..
D12 „ 1d. emerald-green .. 25 20
a. Perf. 12 .. .. 1·60 1·00
b. Perf. 11×12 or 12×11 .. 8 8
D13 „ 2d. emerald-green .. 25 25
a. Perf. 12 .. ..
b. Perf. 11×12 or 12×11.. 12 8
D14 „ 3d. emer.-grn. *p.* 11×12 or 12×11 .. .. 12 8
D15 „ 4d. emerald-green .. 25 15

New South Wales now uses stamps of Australia.

NEW ZEALAND.

1

(Eng. by Humphrys. Recess. Perkins, Bacon.)

Type **1.**

1855 (18 JULY). *Wmk. Large Star, T* w.1. *Imperf.*

1 1d. dull carmine (*white p.*) .. £5000 £3000
2 2d. dull blue (*blued p.*).. .. £2750 £275
3 1s. pale yellow-green (*blued p.*) £5000 £1100
a. Bisected (6d.) (on cover) .. — £5000

The 2d. and 1s. on white paper formerly listed are now known to be stamps printed on blued paper which have had the bluing washed out.

(Printed by J. Richardson, Auckland, N.Z.)

1855 (Nov.). *First printing. Wmk. Large Star White paper. Imperf.*

3*b* 1d. orange .. .. ..

1855 (Nov.). *No wmk. Blue paper. Imperf.*

4 1d. red £1500 £300
5 2d. blue £750 £100
a. Without value .. ..
6 1s. green £3000 £700
a. Bisected (6d.) (on cover) .. — £3500

These stamps on blue paper may occasionally be found wmkd. double-lined letters, being portions of the paper-maker's name.

1857 (Jan.). *Wmk. Large Star. White paper similar to the issue of July,* 1855.

No.	Description	Unused	Used
7	1d. dull orange	—	£5000

This stamp is in the precise shade of the 1d. of the 1858 printing by Richardson on *no wmk.* white paper. An unsevered pair is known with Dunedin cancellation on a cover bearing arrival postmark of Auckland dated "19.1.1857".

1858–62. *Hard or soft white paper. No wmk.*

(*a*) *Imperf.*

No.	Description	Unused	Used
8	1d. dull orange (1858) ..	£200	£100
8*a*	2d. deep ultram. (1858) ..	£425	£200
9	2d. pale blue	£200	70·00
10	2d. blue	£200	70·00
11	2d. dull deep blue	—	70·00
12	6d. bistre-brown (Aug. '59) ..	£550	£170
13	6d. brown	£250	£100
14	6d. pale brown	£250	£100
15	6d. chestnut	£500	£150
16	1s. dull emerald-green ..	£2000	£300
17	1s. blue-green	£2000	£350

(*b*) *Pin-roulette, about* 10.

No.	Description	Unused	Used
18	1d. dull orange	—	£550
19	2d. blue	—	£500
20	6d. brown	—	£550
21	1s. blue-green	—	£1200

(*c*) *Serrated perf. about* 16 *or* 18.

No.	Description	Unused	Used
22	1d. dull orange	—	£550
23	2d. blue	—	£500
24	6d. brown	—	£500
25	6d. chestnut	—	£1000
26	1s. blue-green	—	£1000

(*d*) *Rouletted* 7.

No.	Description	Unused	Used
27	1d. dull orange	£900	£650
28	2d. blue	£1100	£550
29	6d. brown	£650	£500
	a. Imperf. between (pair) ..	£2250	£1800
30	1s. dull emerald-green ..	£1100	£850
31	1s. blue-green	£1300	£850

(*e*) *P* 13 *at Dunedin* (1862).

No.	Description	Unused	Used
31*a*	1d. dull orange	—	£800
31*b*	2d. pale blue	£900	£700
32	6d pale brown		

Other forms of separation, in addition to those shown above, are known, both on the stamps of this issue and on those of 1862. Some of the varieties are extremely rare, only single copies being known.

The 2d. in a distinctive deep bright blue on white paper wmkd. Large Star is believed by experts to have been printed by Richardson in 1861 or 1862. This also exists doubly printed and with serrated perf.

(Printed by John Davies at the G.P.O., Auckland, N.Z.)

1862 (Feb.). *Wmk. Large Star.* (*a*) *Imperf.*

No.	Description	Unused	Used
33	1d. orange-vermilion	70·00	50·00
34	1d. vermilion	75·00	50·00
35	1d. carmine-vermilion ..	80·00	60·00
36	2d. deep blue (Plate I) ..	70·00	30·00
37	2d. slate-blue (Plate I) ..	£350	75·00
37*a*	2d. milky blue (Pl. I, worn) ..		
38	2d. pale blue (Pl. I, worn) ..	50·00	35·00
39	2d. blue (*to* deep) (Pl. I, very worn)	60·00	35·00
40	3d. brown-lilac	70·00	50·00
41	6d. black-brown	£150	40·00
42	6d. brown	£150	40·00
43	6d. red-brown	75·00	35·00
44	1s. green	£150	75·00
45	1s. yellow-green	£150	70·00
46	1s. deep green	£160	70·00

Nos. 37*a*/38 show some signs of wear on right of Queen's head and shades of No. 39 show moderate to advanced states of wear.

1862 (June). (*b*) *Rouletted* 7.

No.	Description	Unused	Used
47	1d. orange-vermilion	£650	£150
48	1d. vermilion	£450	£150
48*a*	1d. carmine-vermilion ..		
49	2d. deep blue	£350	£120
50	2d. slate-blue	£550	£200
51	2d. pale blue	£325	£150
52	3d. brown-lilac	£350	£150
53	6d. black-brown	£400	£120
54	6d. brown	£350	£100
55	6d. red-brown	£350	£100
56	1s. green	£350	£150
57	1s. yellow-green	£600	£150
58	1s. deep green	£600	£200

1862 (Aug.). (*c*) *Serrated perf.* 14 *or* 16.

No.	Description	Unused	Used
59	1d. orange-vermilion	—	£300
60	2d. deep blue	—	£250
	a. Imperf. between (pair) ..	£850	£850
61	2d. slate-blue		
62	3d. brown-lilac	—	£450
63	6d. black-brown	—	£500
64	6d. brown	—	£500
65	1s. yellow-green	—	£600

1862 (Aug.). (*d*) *Pin-perf.* 10.

No.	Description	Unused	Used
66	2d. deep blue	—	£550
67	6d. black-brown	—	£550

The dates put to above varieties are the earliest that have been met with.

1862. *Wmk. Large Star. P* 13 (*at Dunedin*).

No.	Description	Unused	Used
68	1d. orange-vermilion	£130	50·00
69	1d. carmine-vermilion ..	£130	50·00
70	2d. deep blue (Plate I) ..	70·00	20·00
71	2d. slate-blue (Plate I) ..	—	£250
72	2d. blue (Plate I)	60·00	20·00
72*a*	2d. milky blue		
73	2d. pale blue (Plate I) ..	60·00	20·00
74	3d. brown-lilac	£130	40·00
75	6d. black-brown	£130	35·00
	a. Imperf. between (horiz. pair) ..		
76	6d. brown	95·00	25·00
77	6d. red-brown	85·00	20·00
78	1s. dull green	80·00	50·00
79	1s. deep green	£100	50·00
80	1s. yellow-green	£100	50·00

See also Nos. 110/125 and the note that follows these.

1862. *Pelure paper. No wmk.* (*a*) *Imperf.*

No.	Description	Unused	Used
81	1d. orange-vermilion	£900	£450
82	2d. ultramarine	£650	£200
83	2d. pale ultramarine	£650	£200
84	3d. lilac	£6000	
85	6d. black-brown	£180	85·00
86	1s. deep green	£900	£200

The 3d. is known only unused.

(*b*) *Rouletted* 7.

No.	Description	Unused	Used
87	1d. orange-vermilion ..		£850
88	6d. black-brown	£400	£150
89	1s. deep green	£800	£300

(*c*) *P* 13.

No.	Description	Unused	Used
90	1d. orange-vermilion	£2000	£900
91	2d. ultramarine	£850	£200
92	2d. pale ultramarine	£850	£200
93	6d. black-brown	£600	£120
94	1s. deep green	£1500	£300

(*d*) *Serrated perf.* 15.

No.	Description	Unused	Used
95	6d. black-brown	—	£850

1863 (early). *Hard or soft white paper. No wmk.* (*a*) *Imperf.*

No.	Description	Unused	Used
96	2d. dull deep blue (*shades*) ..	£400	£150

(*b*) *P* 13.

No.	Description	Unused	Used
96*a*	2d. dull deep blue (*shades*) ..	£350	85·00

These stamps show slight beginnings of wear of the printing plate in the background to right of the Queen's ear, as one looks at the stamps. By the early part of 1864, the wear of the plate had spread, more or less, all over the background of the circle containing the head. The major portion of the stamps of this printing appears to have been consigned to Dunedin and to have been there perforated 13.

NZ

2

1864. *Wmk.* "N Z", *T* **2.** (*a*) *Imperf.*

No.	Description	Unused	Used
97	1d. carmine-vermilion ..	£170	70·00
98	2d. pale blue (Plate I worn)	£200	70·00
99	6d. red-brown	£650	£170
100	1s. green	£200	95·00

(*b*) *Rouletted* 7.

No.	Description	Unused	Used
101	1d. carmine-vermilion ..	£900	£550
102	2d. pale blue (Plate I worn)	£300	£200
103	6d. red-brown	£800	£650
104	1s. green	£550	£180

(*c*) *P* 13 (*at Dunedin*).

No.	Description	Unused	Used
104*a*	1d. carmine-vermilion ..	£1400	£1000
105	2d. pale blue (Plate I worn)	£150	60·00
106	1s. green	£300	£150
	a. Imperf. between (horiz. pair)	£1200	

(*d*) *P* 12½ (*at Auckland*).

No.	Description	Unused	Used
106*b*	1d. carmine-vermilion ..	£1000	£650
107	2d. pale blue (Plate I worn)	65·00	25·00
108	6d. red-brown	65·00	15·00
109	1s. yellow-green	—	£750

1864–67. *Wmk. Large Star. P* 12½ (*at Auckland*).

No.	Description	Unused	Used
110	1d. carmine-vermilion (1864)	30·00	10·00
111	1d. pale orange-vermilion ..	30·00	10·00
	a. Imperf. (pair)	£350	£200
112	1d. orange	65·00	20·00
113	2d. p. blue (Pl. I worn) (1864)	30·00	10·00
114	2d. dp. blue (Pl. II) (1866)	30·00	10·00
	a. Imperf. between (pair) ..	—	£450
115	2d. blue (Plate II)	30·00	10·00
	a. Retouched (Plate II) (1867) ..	40·00	10·00
	c. Imperf. (pair) (Plate II) ..	£300	£300
	d. Retouched. Imperf. (pair) ..	£350	£350
116	3d. brown-lilac (1864) ..	£220	£140
117	3d. lilac	25·00	10·00
	a. Imperf. (pair)	£300	£200
118	3d. deep mauve	85·00	25·00
	a. Imperf. (pair)	£400	£200
119	4d. deep rose (1865) ..	£150	75·00
120	4d. yellow (1865)	30·00	20·00
121	4d. orange	£400	£350
122	6d. red-brown (1864) ..	30·00	10·00
122*a*	6d. brown	30·00	10·00
	b. Imperf. (pair)	£200	£200
123	1s. deep green (1864) ..	£120	60·00
124	1s. green	80·00	30·00
125	1s. yellow-green	35·00	25·00

The above issue is sometimes difficult to distinguish from Nos. 68/80 because the vertical perforations usually gauge 12¾ and sometimes a full 13. However stamps of this issue invariably gauge 12½ horizontally, whereas the 1862 stamps measure a full 13.

The 1d., 2d. and 6d. were officially reprinted imperforate, without gum, in 1884 for presentation purposes. They can be distinguished from the errors listed by their shades which are pale orange, dull blue and dull chocolate-brown respectively, and by the worn state of the plates from which they were printed.

1871. *Wmk. Large Star.* (*a*) *P* 10.

No.	Description	Unused	Used
126	1d. brown	£100	30·00

(*b*) *P* 12½×10.

No.	Description	Unused	Used
127	1d. deep brown	—	£200

(*c*) *P* 10×12½.

No.	Description	Unused	Used
128	1d. brown	30·00	10·00
	a. Perf. 12½ comp. 10 (1 side) ..	—	25·00
129	2d. deep blue (Plate II) ..	—	£1300
	a. Perf. 10*		
130	2d. vermilion	30·00	10·00
	a. Retouched	30·00	10·00
	b. Perf. 12½ comp. 10 (1 side) ..	—	35·00
	c. Perf. 10*		
131	6d. deep blue	£280	£140
	a. *Blue*	£230	90·00
	b. Imperf. between (vert. pair) ..	—	£900
	c. Perf. 12½ comp. 10 (1 side) ..	£130	60·00

(*d*) *P* 12½.

No.	Description	Unused	Used
132	1d. red-brown	30·00	10·00
	a. *Brown* (*shades, worn plate*) ..	30·00	10·00
	b. Imperf. horiz. (vert. pair) ..	—	£400
133	2d. orange	20·00	10·00
	a. Retouched	30·00	15·00
134	2d. vermilion	30·00	10·00
	a. Retouched	50·00	25·00
135	6d. blue	30·00	10·00
136	6d. pale blue	20·00	10·00

In or about 1872 both 1d. and 2d. stamps were printed on some paper having a wmk. of script letters "W.T. & Co." (=Wiggins Teape & Co.) in the sheet, and other paper with the name "T. H. Saunders" in double-lined caps in the sheet; portions of these letters are occasionally found on stamps.

* Only one used copy each of Nos. 129a and 130c have been reported.

1872. *No wmk. P* 12½.

No.	Description	Unused	Used
137	1d. brown	75·00	20·00
138	2d. vermilion	20·00	10·00
	a. Retouched	50·00	20·00
139	4d. orange-yellow	50·00	£100

1872. *Wmk.* "N Z", *T* **2.** *P* 12½.

No.	Description	Unused	Used
140	1d. brown	£2250	£700
141	2d. vermilion	80·00	30·00
	a. Retouched	£120	50·00

1872. *Wmk. Lozenges, with* "INVICTA" *in double-lined capitals four times in the sheet. P* 12½.

No.	Description	Unused	Used
142	2d. vermilion	£700	£250
	a. Retouched	£1000	£300

3

4

(Des. John Davies. Die eng. on wood in Melbourne. Printed from electrotypes at Govt. Ptg. Office, Wellington.)

1873 (1 Jan.). (*a*) *Wmk.* "NZ", *T* **2**.

143	**3**	½d. pale dull rose (*p.* 10) ..	12·00	4·50
144	,,	½d. pale dull rose (*p.* 12½) ..	30·00	12·00
145	,,	½d. p. dull rose (*p* 12½ × 10)	22·00	10·00
		(*b*) *No wmk.*		
146	**3**	½d. pale dull rose (*p.* 10) ..	14·00	6·00
147	,,	½d. pale dull rose (*p.* 12½) ..	30·00	14·00
148	,,	½d. p. dull rose (*p.* 12½ × 10)	25·00	12·00

As the paper used for Nos. 143/5 was originally intended for fiscal stamps which were more than twice as large, about one-third of the impressions fall on portions of the sheet showing no watermark, giving rise to varieties Nos. 146/8. In later printings of No. 151 a few stamps in each sheet are without watermark. These can be distinguished from No. 147 by the shade.

1875 (Jan.). *Wmk. Star. T* **4**.

149	**3**	½d. pale dull rose (*P.* 12½) ..	1·25	25
		a. Imperf. between (pair) ..	60·00	40·00
150	,,	½d. dull pale rose (*p. nearly* 12)	20·00	1·50

1892 (June). *Wmk.* "*N Z and Star*", *T* **12*b***. *P* 12½.

151	**3**	½d. bright rose (*shades*) ..	50	10
		a. No wmk.	80	60

5

6

7

8

9

10

11

12

12*a* 6 mm.

12*b* 7 mm.

12*c* 4 mm.

(T **5/10** eng. De La Rue. T **11** and **12** des., eng. & plates by Bock & Cousins, Wellington. Typo. Govt. Ptg. Office, Wellington.)

1874 (1 Jan.). *W* **12*a***.

		A. *White paper.* (*a*) *P* 12½.		
152	**5**	1d. lilac	8·00	85
		a. Imperf.	85·00	
153	**6**	2d. rose	8·00	50
154	**7**	3d. brown	15·00	10·00
155	**8**	4d. maroon	40·00	10·00
156	**9**	6d. blue	35·00	5·00
157	**10**	1s. green	£160	10·00
		(*b*) *Perf. nearly* 12.		
158	**6**	2d. rose	£100	40·00
		(*c*) *Perf. compound of* 12½ *and* 10.		
159	**5**	1d. lilac	30·00	10·00
160	**6**	2d. rose	60·00	15·00
161	**7**	3d. brown	30·00	15·00
162	**8**	4d. maroon	60·00	20·00
163	**9**	6d. blue	40·00	10·00
164	**10**	1s. green	£160	20·00
		(*d*) *Perf. nearly* 12 × 12½.		
164*a*	**5**	1d. lilac	90·00	45·00
165	**6**	2d. rose	90·00	45·00
		B. *Blued paper.* (*a*) *P* 12½.		
166	**5**	1d. lilac	15·00	7·50
167	**6**	2d. rose	20·00	7·00
168	**7**	3d. brown	20·00	12·00
169	**8**	4d. maroon	60·00	20·00
170	**9**	6d. blue	45·00	10·00
171	**10**	1s. green	£160	60·00
		(*b*) *Perf. compound of* 12½ *and* 10.		
172	**5**	1d. lilac	35·00	10·00
173	**6**	2d. rose	95·00	25·00
174	**7**	3d. brown	25·00	12·00
175	**8**	4d. maroon	65·00	25·00
176	**9**	6d. blue	60·00	20·00
177	**10**	1s. green	£160	60·00

1875. *Wmk. Large Star, Type* w.1. *P* 12½.

178	**5**	1d. deep lilac	80·00	15·00
179	**6**	2d. rose	30·00	2·50

1878. *W* **12*a***. *P* 12 × 11½ (*comb*).

180	**5**	1d. mauve-lilac	6·00	50
181	**6**	2d. rose	5·00	50
182	**8**	4d. maroon	20·00	8·00
183	**9**	6d. blue	10·00	5·00
184	**10**	1s. green	20·00	8·00
185	**11**	2s. deep rose	£120	£120
186	**12**	5s. grey	£140	£140

This perforation is made by a horizontal "comb" machine, giving a gauge of 12 horizontally and about 11¾ vertically. Single specimens can be found apparently gauging 11½ all round or 12 all round, but these are all from the same machine. The perforation described above as "nearly 12" was from a single-line machine.

13

14

15

16

17

18

19

20

21

22

Description of Watermarks.

W **12*a***. 6 mm. between "N Z" and star; broa irregular star; comparatively wide "N' "N Z" 11½ mm. wide.

W **12*b***. 7 mm. between "N Z" and sta narrower star; narrow "N"; "N Z 10 mm. wide.

W **12*c***. 4 mm. between "N Z" and sta narrow star; wide "N"; "N Z 11½ mm. wide.

Description of Papers.

1882–88. Smooth paper with horizontal mesl *W* **12*a***.

1888–98. Smooth paper with vertical mesl *W* **12*b***.

1890–91. Smooth paper with vertical mesl *W* **12*c***.

1898. Thin yellowish toned, coarse paper wit clear vertical mesh. *W* **12*b***. Pe 11 only.

In 1899–1900 stamps appeared on medium t thick white coarse paper but we do not differe tiate these (except where identifiable by shad as they are more difficult to distinguish.

Description of Dies.

1d.

Die 1.

Die 2.

Die 3.

1882. Die 1. Background shading complete and heavy.

1886. Die 2. Background lines thinner. Two lines of shading weak or missing left of Queen's forehead.

1889. Die 3. Shading on head reduced; ornament in crown left of chignon clearer, with unshaded "arrow" more prominent.

2d.

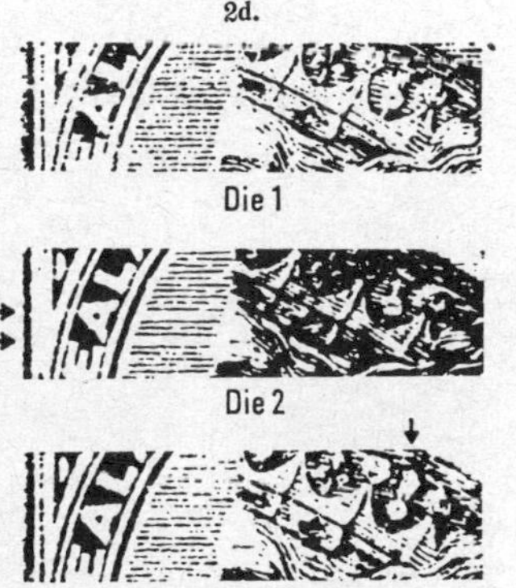

Die 1

Die 2

Die 3

1882. Die 1. Background shading complete and heavy.

1886. Die 2. Weak line of shading left of forehead and missing shading lines below "TA".

1889. Die 3. As Die 2 but with comma-like white notch in hair below "&".

6d.

Die 1

Die 2

1882. Die 1. Shading heavy. Top of head merges into shading.

1892. Die 2. Background lines thinner. Shading on head more regular with clear line of demarcation between head and background shading.

(Des. F. W. Sears (½d.), A. E. Cousins (2½d.), A. W. Jones (5d.); others adapted from 1874 issue by W. H. Norris. Dies eng. A. E. Cousins (½d.), W. R. Bock and A. E. Cousins (remainder). Typo. Govt. Ptg. Office.)

1882–1900. *Inscr.* "POSTAGE & REVENUE".

A. *W* **12***a*. *Paper with horiz. mesh* (1.4.82–86).

(*a*) *P* 12×11½.

187 **14** 1d. rose to rose-red (Die 1) .. .. 9·00 2·00
- a. Imperf. (pair) .. .. 30·00
- b. Imperf. btwn. (vert. pair)
- c. Die 2. *Pale rose to carmine-rose* (1886) .. .. 9·00 2·00

188 **15** 2d. lilac to lilac-purple (Die 1) .. .. 12·00 2·00
- a. Imperf. (pair) .. .. 50·00
- b. Imperf. btwn. (vert. pair) 65·00
- c. Die 2. *Lilac* (1886) .. 9·00 2·00

189 **17** 3d. yellow (1884) .. 9·00 1·25
190 **18** 4d. blue-green .. .. 9·00 2·00
191 **20** 6d. brown (Die 1) .. 9·00 2·00
192 **21** 8d. blue .. .. .. 10·00 6·00
193 **22** 1s. red-brown .. .. 18·00 6·00

(*b*) *P* 12½ (1884?).

193*a* **14** 1d. rose to rose-red (Die 1) .. .. 60·00 30·00

B. *W* **12***b*. *Paper with vert. mesh* (1888–95).

(*a*) *P* 12×11½ (1888–95).

194 **13** ½d. black (1.4.95) .. 3·50 10·00
195 **14** 1d. rose to rosine (Die 2) 6·50 1·75
- a. Die 3. *Rose to carmine* (1889) .. .. .. 6·50 1·75

196 **15** 2d. lilac (Die 2) .. .. 8·50 1·75
- a. Die 3. *Lilac to purple* (1889) .. .. .. 8·50 1·75

197 **16** 2½d. pale blue (1891) .. 3·50 1·50
- a. *Ultram.* (green adverts.) (1893) .. .. ..

198 **17** 3d. yellow .. .. 6·50 1·25
199 **18** 4d. green to bluish green 9·00 1·75
200 **19** 5d. olive-black (1.2.91) .. 6·00 2·25
- a. Imperf. (pair) .. .. 60·00

201 **20** 6d. brown (Die 1) .. 8·50 1·75
- a. Die 2 (1892) .. .. — 14·00

202 **21** 8d. blue .. .. .. 15·00 10·00
203 **22** 1s. red-brown .. .. 15·00 4·50

(*b*) *Perf. compound of* 12 *and* 12½ (1888–91).

204 **14** 1d. rose (Die 2) .. .. 60·00 30·00
- a. Die 3 (1889) .. ..

(*c*) *P* 12½ (1888–89).

205 **14** 1d. rose (Die 3) (1889) .. 45·00 30·00
206 **15** 2d. lilac (Die 2) .. ..
- a. Die 3. *Deep lilac* (1889) .. 30·00 18·00

207 **16** 2½d. blue (1891) .. .. 45·00 25·00

(*d*) *Mixed perfs.* 12×11½ *and* 12½ (1891–93).

207*a* **14** 1d. rose (Die 3) .. ..
207*b* **15** 2d. lilac (Die 3) .. ..
207*c* **18** 4d. green .. .. ..
207*d* **19** 5d. olive-black .. ..
207*e* **20** 6d. brown (Die 1) ..
- ea. Die 2 .. .. ..

C. *W* **12***c*. *Paper with vert. mesh* (1890).

(*a*) *P* 12×11½.

208 **14** 1d. rose (Die 3) .. .. 10·00 1·75
209 **15** 2d. purple (Die 3) .. 6·50 1·75
210 **16** 2½d. ultram. (*usually green adverts.*) (27.12) .. 6·50 1·75
211 **17** 3d. yellow .. .. 8·50 1·25
- a. *Lemon-yellow* .. .. 8·50 1·25

212 **20** 6d. brown (Die 1) .. 15·00 10·00
213 **22** 1s. deep red-brown .. 15·00 4·50

(*b*) *P* 12½.

214 **14** 1d. rose (Die 3) .. .. 45·00 30·00
215 **15** 2d. purple (Die 3) .. 60·00 30·00
216 **16** 2½d. ultramarine .. .. 60·00 30·00

(*c*) *Perf. compound of* 12 *and* 12½.

216*a* **20** 6d. brown (Die 1) .. 45·00 45·00

D. *Continuation of W* **12***b*. *Paper with vert. mesh* (1891–1900).

(*a*) *Perf. compound of* 10 *and* 12½ (1891–94).

216*b* **14** 1d. rose (Die 3) .. .. 30·00 25·00
216*c* **15** 2d. lilac (Die 3) .. .. 45·00 18·00
216*d* **16** 2½d. blue (1893) .. .. 35·00 18·00
216*e* **17** 3d. yellow .. .. 45·00 30·00
216*f* **18** 4d. green .. .. 45·00 40·00
216*g* **19** 5d. olive-black (1894) .. 45·00 45·00
216*h* **20** 6d. brown (Die 1) .. 60·00 60·00
- i. Die 2 (1892) .. .. 45·00 45·00

216*j* **22** 1s. red-brown .. .. 45·00 45·00

(*b*) *P* 10 (1891–95).

217 **13** ½d. black (1895) .. 55 10
218 **14** 1d. rose (Die 3) .. .. 1·00 10
- a. *Carmine* .. .. 1·50 65
- b. Imperf. (pair) .. .. 60·00 60·00
- c. Imperf. between (pair) .. 45·00
- d. Imperf. horiz. (vert. pr.) 45·00
- e. Mixed perfs. 10 and 12½ .. 45·00 35·00

219 **15** 2d. lilac (Die 3) .. .. 1·75 10
- a. *Purple* .. .. 1·75 10
- b. Imperf. between (pair) .. 45·00
- c. Mixed perfs. 10 and 12½ .. 20·00 18·00

220 **16** 2½d. blue (1892) .. .. 3·25 1·50
- a. *Ultramarine* .. .. 3·25 1·50
- b. Mixed perfs. 10 and 12½ .. 45·00 20·00

221 **17** 3d. pale orange-yellow .. 3·75 1·00
- a. *Orange* .. .. 3·75 1·00
- b. *Lemon-yellow* .. .. 6·50 1·00
- c. Mixed perfs. 10 and 12½ .. — 45·00

222 **18** 4d. green (1892) .. .. 8·50 2·00
- a. *Blue-green* (usually purple adverts.) .. .. 8·50 2·00
- b. Mixed perfs. 10 and 12½ .. 75·00 45·00

223 **19** 5d. olive-black (1893) .. 5·00 2·00
224 **20** 6d. brown (Die 1) .. 20·00 3·25
- a. Mixed perfs. 10 and 12½ ..
- b. Die 2 (1892) .. .. 7·00 1·75
- ba. *Black-brown* .. .. 7·00 1·75
- c. Imperf. (pair) .. .. 75·00
- d. Mixed perfs. 10 and 12½ ..

225 **21** 8d. blue (*adverts. only*) .. 13·00 10·00
226 **22** 1s. red-brown .. .. 10·00 4·50
- a. Imperf. between (pair) .. 30·00
- b. Mixed perfs. 10 and 12½ .. 60·00 45·00

(*c*) *Perf. compound of* 11 *and* 10 (1895).

226*c* **13** ½d. black .. .. .. 1·00 10
226*d* **14** 1d. rose (Die 3) .. .. 1·00 10
226*e* **20** 6d. brown (Die 2) .. 7·00 1·50

(*d*) *Perf. compound of* 10 *and* 11 (1895–97).

227 **13** ½d. black (1896) .. .. 1·00 10
- a. Mixed perfs. 10 and 11 .. 14·00 7·00

228 **14** 1d. rose (Die 3) .. .. 1·00 10
- a. Mixed perfs. 10 and 11 .. 30·00 15·00

229 **15** 2d. purple (Die 3) .. 2·00 10
- a. Mixed perfs. 10 and 11 .. 18·00 14·00

230 **16** 2½d. blue (1896) .. .. 4·50 1·75
- a. *Ultramarine* .. .. 4·50 1·75
- b. Mixed perfs. 10 and 11 ..

231 **17** 3d. lemon-yellow (1896) 3·75 1·00
232 **18** 4d. pale green (1896) .. 10·00 2·00
- a. Mixed perfs. 10 and 11 ..

233 **19** 5d. olive-black (1897) .. 5·00 2·25
234 **20** 6d. deep brown (Die 2) (1896) .. .. 8·00 1·50
- a. Mixed perfs. 10 and 11 ..

235 **22** 1s. red-brown (1896) .. 10·00 4·50
- a. Mixed perfs. 10 and 11 .. — 25·00

(*e*) *P* 11 (1895–1900).

236 **13** ½d. black (1897) 65 10
- a. Thin coarse toned paper (1898) .. .. .. 1·00 25
- b. Do. Wmk. sideways .. — 30·00

237 **14** 1d. rose (Die 3) .. .. 1·00 10
- a. *Deep carmine* .. .. 1·25 10
- b. Imperf. between (pair) .. 75·00
- c. *Dp. carmine/thin coarse toned* (1898) .. .. 2·00 10
- d. Do. Wmk. sideways .. — 45·00

No.	Type	Description	Unused	Used
238	**15**	2d. mauve (Die 3)	2·00	10
		a. Purple	2·00	10
		b. Dp. purple/thin coarse toned (1898)	2·50	15
		c. Do. Wmk. sideways	—	75·00
239	**16**	2½d. blue (1897)	3·00	1·50
		a. Thin coarse toned paper (1898)	4·75	2·25
240	**17**	3d. pale yellow (1897)	5·00	1·50
		a. Pale dull yellow/thin coarse toned (1898)	5·00	1·50
		b. Orange (1899)	4·00	1·25
		c. Dull orange-yellow (1900)	6·50	1·25
241	**18**	4d. yellowish green	3·75	2·00
		a. Bluish green (1897)	3·75	2·00
242	**19**	5d. olive-black/*thin coarse toned* (1899)	5·50	2·00
243	**20**	6d. brown (Die 2) (1897)	8·00	1·50
		a. Black-brown	8·00	1·50
		b. Brown/thin coarse toned (1898)	10·00	2·00
244	**21**	8d. blue (1898)	10·00	5·50
245	**22**	1s. red-brown (1897)	10·00	5·00

Only the more prominent shades have been included.

Stamps perf. compound of 11 and 12½ exist but we do not list them as there is some doubt as to whether they are genuine.

In 1893 stamps were issued with commercial advertisements on the back. They are known on Nos. 195/200, 201a, 203, 205, 206a, 207b, 216b/g and 216i/j (most), 218/23 and 224b/226b (most).

For the ½d. and 2d. with double-lined watermark, see Nos. 292/3.

23. Mount Cook or Aorangi.

24. Lake Taupo and Mount Ruapehu.

25. Pembroke Peak, Milford Sound.

28. Sacred Huia birds.

26. Lake Wakatipu and Mount Earnslaw, inscribed "WAKITIPU".

29. White Terrace, Rotomahana.

27. Lake Wakatipu and Mount Earnslaw, inscribed "WAKATIPU".

31. Apteryx or Kiwi.

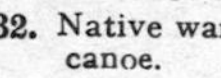

32. Native war canoe.

33. Pink Terrace, Rotomahana.

34. Kea and Kaka, or hawk-billed parrot.

30. Otira Gorge and Mount Ruapehu.

35. Milford Sound.

36. Mount Cook.

(Recess. Waterlow.)

1898 (5 Apr.). *No wmk. P* 12 *to* 14, 14, 15, *and* 16.

No.	Type	Description	Unused	Used
246	**23**	½d. purple-brown	50	12
		a. Imperf. between (pair)	£140	£120
247	,,	½d. purple-slate	40	12
248	,,	½d. purple-black	95	60
249	**24**	1d. blue & yellow-brown	15	15
		a. Imperf. between (pair)	£110	95·00
		b. Imperf. vert. (horiz. pair)	85·00	75·00
		c. Imperf. horiz. (vert. pair)	85·00	75·00
250	,,	1d. blue and brown	95	65
		a. Imperf. between (pair)		
251	**25**	2d. lake	1·75	12
		a. Imperf. vert. (horiz. pair)	£100	95·00
252	,,	2d. rosy lake	1·75	12
		a. Imperf. between (pair)	£100	£100
		b. Imperf. vert. (horiz. pair)	£100	£100
253	**26**	2½d. sky-bl. ("WAKITIPU")	1·00	2·75
254	,,	2½d. blue ("WAKITIPU")	1·00	2·75
255	**27**	2½d. blue ("WAKATIPU")	1·50	50
256	,,	2½d. dp. bl. ("WAKATIPU")	1·75	65
257	**28**	3d. yellow-brown	1·75	70
258	**29**	4d. bright rose	1·40	2·10
259	,,	4d. lake-rose	2·50	3·00
260	,,	4d. dull rose	1·40	2·10
261	**30**	5d. sepia	10·00	15·0
262	**30**	5d. purple-brown	3·00	2·0
263	**31**	6d. green	6·00	6·0
264	,,	6d. grass-green	8·00	8·5
265	**32**	8d. indigo	3·75	2·2
266	,,	8d. Prussian blue	3·75	2·2
267	**33**	9d. purple	3·50	3·5
268	**34**	1s. vermilion	4·50	2·2
269	,,	1s. dull red	4·50	2·2
		a. Imperf. between (pair)	£200	£13
270	**35**	2s. grey-green	14·00	14·0
		a. Imperf. between (vert. pair)	£125	£12
271	**36**	5s. vermilion	40·00	40·0
246/271		*Set of* 13	80·00	75·0

1899. *Printed by the Govt. Printer at Wellingto[n]. Pirie paper. No wmk. P* 11.

No.	Type	Description	Unused	Used
272	**27**	2½d. blue	1·25	5
		a. Imperf. between (pair)	75·00	65·0
		b. Imperf. horiz. (vert. pair)	75·00	65·0
273	,,	2½d. deep blue	1·25	5
274	**28**	3d. yellow-brown	1·25	3
		a. Imperf. between (pair)	60·00	50·0
		b. Imperf. vert. (horiz. pair)	60·00	50·0
275	,,	3d. deep brown	1·25	3
		a. Imperf. between (pair)		
276	**30**	5d. purple-brown	2·25	9
277	,,	5d. deep purple-brown	2·25	9
		a. Imperf. between (pair)	95·00	80·
278	**31**	6d. yellow-green	5·00	6·5
279	,,	6d. deep green	5·00	6·5
280	**32**	8d. indigo	1·75	1·7
281	,,	8d. Prussian blue	1·75	1·7
282	**33**	9d. deep purple	3·00	3·0
283	,,	9d. rosy purple	2·50	2·5
284	**34**	1s. red	4·00	1·0
285	,,	1s. dull orange-red	3·00	5
286	,,	1s. dull brown-red	3·50	1·2
287	,,	1s. bright red	4·50	1·0
288	**35**	2s. blue-green	8·50	6·5
289	,,	2s. grey-green	8·50	6·5
290	**36**	5s. vermilion	35·00	35·0
291	,,	5s. carmine-red	40·00	40·0
272/291		*Set of* 9	60·00	55·0

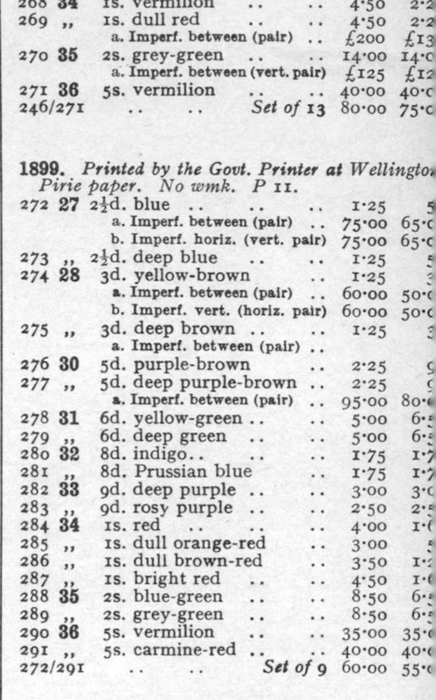

36*a*

1900. *Pirie paper. Wmk. double-lined* "N Z *and Star, T* **36*a***, *sideways. P* 11.

No.	Type	Description	Unused	Used
292	**13**	½d. black (Apr.)	35	
293	**15**	2d. bright purple (18 Apr.)	70	

37. White Terrace, Rotomahana.

38*a*.

38. Commemorative of the New Zealand contingent in the South African War.

(Recess. Govt. Ptg. Office, Wellington. T 38 des. J. Nairn.)

1900–1. *W 36a. P 11.*

No.	Type	Description	Unused	Used
294	23	½d. deep green	75	8
294a	,,	½d. green	60	8
		b. Imperf. between (pair)	75·00	60·00
295	,,	½d. yellow-green	60	8
296	,,	½d. pale yellow-green	75	50
297	37	1d. lake	1·75	60
298	,,	1d. crimson	60	8
299	,,	1d. rose-red	60	8
		a. Imperf. between (pair)	75·00	60·00
		b. Imperf. vert. (horiz. pair)	75·00	60·00
299c	38	1½d. khaki*	75·00	60·00
300	,,	1½d. brown	6·00	7·50
		a. Imperf. vert. (horiz. pair)	75·00	
		b. Imperf. (pair)	90·00	
301	,,	1½d. chestnut	95	70
		a. Imperf. vert. (horiz. pair)		
		b. Imperf. horiz. (vert. pair)		
302	,,	1½d. pale chestnut	1·40	85
		a. Imperf. (pair)		
303	38a	2d. dull violet	45	15
		a. Imperf. between (pair)	90·00	80·00
304	,,	2d. mauve	65	30
305	,,	2d. purple	65	15
		a. Imperf. between (pair)	80·00	

The above ½d. stamps are slightly smaller than those of the previous printing. A new plate was made to print 240 stamps instead of 120 as previously, and to make these fit the watermarked paper the border design was redrawn and contracted, the centre vignette remaining as before. The stamp varies in shade from *very deep green* to *pale yellow-green*. The 2d. stamp is also from a new and smaller plate.

* No 299c is the rare first printing.

39. Lake Taupo and Mount Ruapehu.

40

1900. *No wmk. P 11.*

No.	Type	Description	Unused	Used
307	39	4d. indigo and brown	1·25	60
308	,,	4d. bright blue & chestnut	1·25	60
309	,,	4d. deep blue & bistre-brn.	1·25	60
310	31	6d. pale rose	2·00	60
		a. Imperf. vert. (horiz. pair)	75·00	
311	,,	6d. rose-red	2·00	75
		a. Doubly printed	£100	
		b. Imperf. between (pair)	75·00	75·00
		c. Imperf. vert. (horiz. pair)	40·00	
312	,,	6d. scarlet	6·00	3·00
		a. Imperf. vert. (horiz. pair)	75·00	

(Des. Guido Bach. Recess. Waterlow.)

1901 (1 Jan.). *Universal Penny Postage. No wmk. P 12 to 16.*

No.	Type	Description	Unused	Used
313	40	1d. carmine	3·00	2·00

(Recess. Govt. Ptg. Office, Wellington.)

1901 (Feb.). (i) *Pirie paper, thick and soft. W* **36a.**

(a) *P 11.*

No.	Type	Description	Unused	Used
314	40	1d. carmine-lake	5·00	4·00
315	,,	1d. deep carmine	50	12
		a. Imperf. between (pair)	75·00	
316	,,	1d. carmine	50	12
		a. Imperf. between (pair)	75·00	

(b) *P 14.*

No.	Type	Description	Unused	Used
317	23	½d. green	1·00	35
318	40	1d. carmine	5·00	75
		a. Imperf. between (pair)	75·00	

(c) *Perf. compound of 11 and 14.*

No.	Type	Description	Unused	Used
319	23	½d. green	2·75	50
320	,,	½d. deep green	3·00	50
321	40	1d. carmine	95·00	35·00

(d) *P 11 and 14 mixed.**

No.	Type	Description	Unused	Used
322	23	½d. green	9·00	6·00
323	40	1d. carmine	75·00	35·00

* The term " mixed " is applied to stamps from sheets which were at first perforated 14, or 14 and 11 compound, and either incompletely or defectively perforated. These sheets were patched on the back with strips of paper, and re-perforated 11 in those parts where the original perforation was defective.

1901 (Dec.). (ii). *Basted Mills, thin hard paper. W 36a.* (a) *P 11.*

No.	Type	Description	Unused	Used
324	23	½d. green	10·00	10·00
325	40	1d. carmine	10·00	10·00

(b) *Perf. 14.*

No.	Type	Description	Unused	Used
326	23	½d. green	4·00	1·50
		a. Imperf. between (pair)	75·00	
327	40	1d. carmine	3·00	40
		a. Imperf. between (pair)	75·00	

(c) *Perf. compound of 11 and 14.*

No.	Type	Description	Unused	Used
328	23	½d. green	3·00	3·00
329	,,	½d. deep green	3·00	3·00
330	40	1d. carmine	1·90	40

(d) *Mixed perfs.*

No.	Type	Description	Unused	Used
331	23	½d. green	30·00	30·00
332	40	1d. carmine	25·00	25·00

1902 (Jan.). (iii) *Cowan, thin hard paper. No wmk.*

(a) *P 11.*

No.	Type	Description	Unused	Used
333	23	½d. green	30·00	30·00

(b) *P 14.*

No.	Type	Description	Unused	Used
334	23	½d. green	1·00	35
335	40	1d. carmine	2·00	35

(c) *Perf. compound of 11 and 14.*

No.	Type	Description	Unused	Used
336	23	½d. green	35·00	35·00
337	40	1d. carmine	35·00	30·00

(d) *Mixed perfs.*

No.	Type	Description	Unused	Used
338	23	½d. green	35·00	35·00
339	40	1d. carmine	40·00	40·00

41. " Single " Wmk.

1902 (Apr.). (iv) *Cowan, thin hard paper. Wmk. single-lined " N Z " and Star, T* **41.**

(a) *P 11.*

No.	Type	Description	Unused	Used
340	23	½d. green	8·00	8·00
341	40	1d. carmine	£180	£180

(b) *P 14.*

No.	Type	Description	Unused	Used
341a	23	½d. yellow-green	60	12
341b	,,	½d. pale yellow-green	60	25
342	,,	½d. green	30	15
		a. Imperf. between (pair)	75·00	
343	,,	½d. deep green	75	15
		a. Imperf. between (pair)	75·00	
344	40	1d. carmine	35	8
		a. Imperf. between (pair)	75·00	
345	,,	1d. pale carmine	20	8
		a. Imperf. between (pair)	75·00	
345b	,,	1d. deep carmine*	8·00	2·00

(c) *Perf. compound of 11 and 14.*

No.	Type	Description	Unused	Used
346	23	½d. green	2·00	4·00
347	,,	½d. deep green	3·00	4·00
348	40	1d. carmine	35·00	25·00
348a	,,	1d. deep carmine*	£140	£150

(d) *Mixed perfs.*

No.	Type	Description	Unused	Used
349	23	½d. green	3·00	4·00
350	,,	½d. deep green	4·00	5·00
351	40	1d. carmine	5·00	4·00
351a	,,	1d. pale carmine	5·00	4·00
351b	,,	1d. deep carmine*	£100	£120

* Nos. 345b, 348a and 351b were printed from a plate made by Waterlow & Sons, known as the " Reserve " plate. The stamps do not show evidence of wearing and the area surrounding the upper part of the figure is more deeply shaded.

1902–9. *W* **41** *(sideways on 3d., 5d., 6d., 8d., 1s. and 5s.).*

(a) *P 11 (1902–7).*

No.	Type	Description	Unused	Used
352	27	2½d. blue	1·50	1·00
353	,,	2½d. deep blue (1905)	1·50	1·00
354	28	3d. yellow-brown	1·00	20
355	,,	3d. bistre-brown	1·00	12
356	,,	3d. pale bistre	1·50	40
357	39	4d. deep blue and deep brown/*bluish*	2·00	3·00
		a. Imperf. vert. (horiz. pair)	75·00	60·00
358	30	5d. red-brown	4·00	1·40
359	,,	5d. deep brown (1904)	4·00	85
360	,,	5d. sepia (1906)	5·00	2·75
361	31	6d. rose	3·00	60
362	,,	6d. rose-red	1·25	60
		a. Wmk. upright	75·00	40·00
363	,,	6d. rose-carmine	2·25	60
		a. Imperf. vert. (horiz. pair)	75·00	75·00
		b. Imperf. horiz. (vert. pair)		
364	,,	6d. brt. carm.-pink ('05)	8·00	1·25
365	,,	6d. scarlet	8·00	3·00
366	32	8d. blue	2·00	1·25
367	,,	8d. steel-blue (1904)	2·00	1·25
		a. Imperf. vert. (horiz. pair)	75·00	75·00
		b. Imperf. horiz. (vert. pair)	75·00	75·00
368	33	9d. purple	2·75	2·00
369	34	1s. brown-red	3·75	60
370	,,	1s. bright red	3·75	65
371	,,	1s. orange-red	2·75	50
372	,,	1s. orange-brown	3·75	55
373	35	2s. green	8·50	8·50
374	,,	2s. blue-green (1907)	8·50	8·50
375	36	5s. deep red	35·00	35·00
		a. Wmk. upright	35·00	35·00
376	,,	5s. vermilion (1906)	35·00	35·00
		aa. Wmk. upright	35·00	35·00

Variety. Paper as that used for Nos. 187, *etc. W* **12b** (1903?).

No.	Type	Description	Unused	Used
376a	34	1s. orange-red	—	£180

Variety. Laid paper. No wmk. **(Mar., 1903).**

No.	Type	Description	Unused	Used
377	35	2s. green	25·00	18·00

(b) *P 14 (1903–9).*

No.	Type	Description	Unused	Used
378	38	1½d. chestnut (1907)	70	2·00
379	38a	2d. grey-purple (1903)	45	8
380	,,	2d. purple	45	8
		a. Imperf. vert. (horiz. pair	65·00	65·00
		b. Imperf. horiz. (vert. pair	65·00	65·00
381	,,	2d. bright reddish purple	60	20
382	27	2½d. blue (1907)	85	30
383	,,	2½d. deep blue	85	30
384	28	3d. bistre-brown	1·25	35
		a. Imperf. vert. (horiz. pair)	75·00	50·00
385	,,	3d. bistre (1906)	1·25	35
386	,,	3d. pale yellow-bistre	2·75	1·25
387	39	4d. deep blue and deep brown/*bluish* (1903)	1·40	1·40
		a. Imperf. vert. (horiz. pair)	60·00	50·00
		b. Imperf. horiz. (vert. pair)	60·00	50·00
		c. Centre inverted	†	£5000
388	,,	4d. blue and chestnut/*bluish* (1906)	1·40	55
389	,,	4d. blue and ochre-brown/*bluish* (1909)	1·40	50
390	30	5d. black-brown	5·00	3·00
391	,,	5d. red-brown (1906)	4·00	2·00
392	31	6d. brt. carm.-pink ('06)	5·00	85
		a. Imperf. vert. (horiz. pair)	75·00	50·00
393	,,	6d. rose-carmine	5·00	1·25
394	32	8d. steel-blue (1907)	1·75	95
395	33	9d. purple (1906)	2·50	2·50
396	34	1s. orange-brown	4·00	80
397	,,	1s. orange-red	3·00	70
398	,,	1s. pale red (1907)	4·50	2·25
399	35	2s. green	8·50	8·50
400	,,	2s. blue-green (1907)	10·00	8·50
401	36	5s. deep red	35·00	35·00
		a. Wmk. upright	40·00	40·00
402	,,	5s. dull red	35·00	35·00
		aa. Wmk. upright	40·00	40·00

(c) *Perf. compound of 11 and 14.*

No.	Type	Description	Unused	Used
402a	38	1½d. chestnut	75·00	75·00
403	38a	2d. purple (1903)	30·00	30·00
403a	28	3d. bistre-brown	75·00	75·00
403b	39	4d. blue & yell.-brn	75·00	75·00
403c	30	5d. red-brown	£100	£100
404	31	6d. rose-carmine (1907)	30·00	30·00
404a	32	8d. steel-blue	£100	£100
404b	33	9d. purple	£175	£140
404c	36	5s. deep red	£175	£175

(d) *Mixed perfs.*

No.	Type	Description	Unused	Used
405	38	1½d. chestnut	75·00	75·00
406	38a	2d. purple	20·00	15·00
407	28	3d. bistre-brown	£100	£100
408	39	4d. blue and chestnut/*bluish* ('04)	60·00	60·00
409	,,	4d. bl. & yell.-brn./*bluish*	60·00	60·00
409a	30	5d. red-brown	£100	£100
410	31	6d. rose-carmine	35·00	35·00
411	,,	6d. bright carmine-pink	35·00	35·00
412	32	8d. steel-blue	£100	£100
413	33	9d. purple	£175	£140
413a	35	2s. blue-green	£140	£140
414	36	5s. vermilion	£175	£175

Two sizes of paper were used for the above stamps, viz.:—

(1) A sheet containing 240 wmks., with a space of 9 mm. between each.

(2) A sheet containing 120 wmks., with a space of 24 mm. between each vertical row.

Size (1) was used for the ½d., 1d., 2d., and 4d., and size (2) for 2½d., 5d., 9d., and 2s. The paper in each case exactly fitted the plates, and had the watermark in register, though in the case of the 4d., the plate of which contained only 80 stamps, the paper was cut up to print it. The 3d., 6d., 8d., and 1s. were printed on variety (1), but with watermark sideways: by reason of this, specimens from the margins of the sheets show parts of the words "NEW ZEALAND POSTAGE" in large letters, and some copies have no watermark at all. For the 1½d. and 5s. stamps variety (1) was also used, but two watermarks appear on each stamp. The 6d. also exists on paper with the words "LISBON SUPERFINE" wmkd. once in the sheet; the paper was obtained from Parsons Bros., an American firm with a branch at Auckland. (*Price £1 un. or us.*)

1904. *Printed from new "dot" plates.* *W* **41.**

(a) P 14.

415 **40** 1d. rose-carmine .. 25 8
415*a* ,, 1d. pale carmine .. 25 8

(b) Perf. compound of 11 and 14.

416 **40** 1d. rose-carmine .. 45·00 45·00

(c) Mixed perfs.

417 **40** 1d. rose-carmine .. 5·00 24·00
417*a* ,, 1d. pale carmine .. 5·00 24·00

The above new plates have a minute dot between the stamps in the horizontal rows, but it is frequently cut out by the perforations. However, they can be further distinguished by the notes below.

A special plate was introduced in 1902 to print booklet panes and also had the minute dot, but a special characteristic of the booklet plate was that the pearl in the top left-hand corner was large.

In 1906 fresh printings were made from four new plates, two of which, marked in the margin "W1" and "W2", were supplied by Waterlow Bros. and Layton, and the other two, marked "R1" and "R2", by W. R. Royle & Son. The intention was to note which pair of plates wore the best and produced the best results. They can be distinguished as follows:—

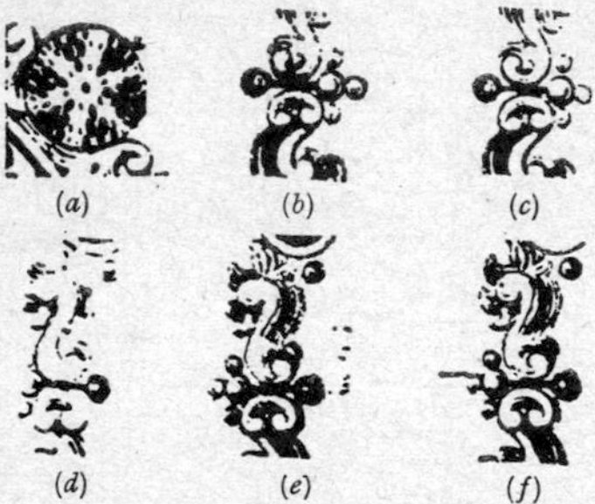

(*a*) (*b*) (*c*)

(*d*) (*e*) (*f*)

(*a*) Four o'clock flaw in rosette at top right corner. Occurs in all these plates but not in the original Waterlow plates.

(*b*) Pearl at right strong.

(*c*) Pearl at right weak.

(*d*) Dot at left and S-shaped ornament unshaded.

(*e*) S-shaped ornament with one line of shading within.

(*f*) As (*e*) but with line from left pearl to edge of stamp.

"Dot" plates comprise (*a*) and (*d*).
Waterlow plates comprise (*a*), (*b*) and (*e*).
Royle plates comprise (*a*), (*c*) and (*e*) and the line in (*f*) on many stamps but not all.

1906. *W* **41.** A. *Printed from new plates by Waterlow.*

(a) P 14.

418 **40** 1d. deep rose-carmine .. 2·00 15
aa. Imperf. between (pair) .. 75·00
418*a* ,, 1d. aniline carmine .. 2·00 20
ab. Imperf. between (pair) .. 75·00
418*b* ,, 1d. rose-carmine .. 2·00 20

(b) P 11.

418*c* **40** 1d. aniline carmine .. 80·00 80·00

(c) Perf. compound of 11 and 14.

419 **40** 1d. rose-carmine .. £100 £100

(d) Mixed perfs.

419*a* **40** 1d. deep rose-carmine .. £100 £100

B. *Printed from new plates by Royle.*

(a) P 14.

419*b* **40** 1d. rose-carmine .. 25 8
c. Imperf. btwn. (vert. pr.) 75·00 75·00
419*d* ,, 1d. bright rose-carmine 3·00 15

(b) P 11.

419*e* **40** 1d. bright rose-carmine 75·00 75·00

(c) Perf. compound of 11 and 14.

419*f* **40** 1d. rose-carmine .. 30·00 30·00

(d) Mixed perfs.

419*g* **40** 1d. rose-carmine .. 35·00 35·00

(e) P 14 × 14½ (comb) (May).

419*h* **40** 1d. bright rose-carmine 10·00 6·00
419*i* ,, 1d. rose-carmine .. 10·00 6·00

Nos. 419*h*/*i* are known both with and without the small dot.

See also No. 441.

1905–6. *Stamps supplied to penny-in-the-slot machines.* *W* **41.**
(i) "*Dot*" *plates of* 1904. (ii) *Waterlow* "*reserve*" *plate of* 1902.

(*a*) *Imperf. top and bottom; zigzag roulette* 9½ *on one or both sides, two large holes at sides.*

420 **40** 1d. rose-carmine (i) .. 30·00
420*a* ,, 1d. deep carmine (ii) .. 30·00

(*b*) *As last but rouletted* 14½.

420*b* **40** 1d. rose-carmine (i) .. 35·00
420*c* ,, 1d. deep carmine (ii) ..

(*c*) *Imperf. all round, two large holes each side.*

421 **40** 1d. rose-carmine (i) .. 50·00
421*a* ,, 1d. deep carmine (ii) .. 40·00

(*d*) *Imperf. all round.*

422 **40** 1d. deep carmine (ii) .. 30·00

(*e*) *Imperf. all round. Two small indentations on back of stamp.*

422*a* **40** 1d. deep carmine (ii) .. 30·00 30·00

(*f*) *Imperf. all round; two small pin-holes in stamp.*

422*b* **40** 1d. deep carmine (ii) .. 30·00 30·00

No. 421 *only* exists from strips of Nos. 420 or 420*b* (resulting from the use of successive coins) which have been separated by scissors. Similarly strips of Nos. 420*a* and 420*c* can produce single copies of No. 421*a* but this also exists in singles from a different machine.

Most used copies of Nos. 420/2 are forgeries and they should only be collected on cover.

42. Maori Canoe, *Te Arawa.*

43. Maori Art.
44. Landing of Cook.
45. Annexation of New Zealand.

(Des. L. J. Steele. Eng. W. R. Bock. Typo. Govt. Ptg. Office.)

1906 (1–17 Nov.). *New Zealand Exhibition Christchurch.* *W* **41.** *P* 14.

424 **42** ½d. emerald-green .. 15·00 15·00
425 **43** 1d. vermilion .. .. 15·00 12·00
a. Claret £1500
426 **44** 3d. brown and blue .. 50·00 55·00
427 **45** 6d. pink & olive-grn. (17.11) 90·00 95·00

The 1d. in claret was the original printing, which was considered unsatisfactory. One sheet was issued at the Exhibition P.O.

46

47 (T **28** reduced).

48 (T **31** reduced).

49 (T **34** reduced).

(New plates (except 4d.), supplied by Perkin Bacon. Recess (T **46** typo.) by Govt. Printe Wellington.)

1907–8. *Wmk. single-lined* "N Z" *and Star, T* 4

(a) P 14.

428 **23** ½d. green 95 3
429 ,, ½d. yellow-green 95 2
429*a* ,, ½d. deep yellow-green .. 95 2
430 **47** 3d. brown (1907) .. 3·50 3·0
431 **48** 6d. carmine-pink (1907) .. 3·50 6
432 ,, 6d. red .. .. .. 4·00 2·0

(*b*) *p* 14 × 13, 13½ (*comb*).

433 **23** ½d. green (1907) .. .. 1·00 5
434 ,, ½d. yellow-green 50 1
435 **47** 3d. brown .. .. 3·50 3·0
436 ,, 3d. yellow-brown .. 3·75 3·0
437 **39** 4d. blue & yell.-brn./*bluish* 2·75 2·5
438 **48** 6d. pink .. .. .. 28·00 10·0
439 **49** 1s. orange-red (1907) .. 12·00 5·5

(*c*) *P* 14 × 15 (*comb*).

440 **23** ½d. yellow-green (1907) .. 40 1
441 **46** 1d. carmine 75 1
442 **47** 3d. brown .. .. 3·50 3·0
443 ,, 3d. yellow-brown .. 4·00 3·5
445 **48** 6d. carmine-pink .. 2·75 6
446 **49** 1s. orange-red .. .. 10·00 5·0
447 ,, 1s. deep orange-brown .. 40·00 –

Error. Imperf. (pair).

448 **23** ½d. green .. .. .. 30·00

The ½d. stamps of this 1907–8 issue have minute dot in the margin between the stamp where not removed by the perforation. (See no after No. 417*a*).

Stamps of T **47**, **48** and **49** also have a sma dot as described in note after No. 417*a*.

Stamps T **46** are typographed but the desig also differs from T **40**. The rosettes in the upp corners are altered and the lines on the glob diagonal instead of vertical. The paper chalk-surfaced.

50

51

(Eng. Perkins, Bacon & Co. Typo. in Ne Zealand.)

1909 (8 Nov.). *Chalk-surfaced "De La Rue paper. Toned gum.* *W* **41.** *P* 14 × 15, *com*

449 **50** ½d. yellow-green 20 1
aa. Deep green 25 1
a. Imperf. (pair) .. .. 55·00
b. Booklet pane. Five stamps plus one label printed with star .. .. ..
450 **51** 1d. carmine 15 1
a. Imperf. (pair) .. .. 75·00

½d. and 1d. stamps with blurred and heav appearance are from booklets.

See also Nos. 520, etc.

52

AUCKLAND EXHIBITION, 1913.

(59)

(Eng. W. R. Royle & Son, London, and recess-printed in New Zealand.)

1909 (9 Nov.)–**13.** *T* **52** *(and similar types). W* **41.**

(a) P 14×14½, *comb machine.*

452	2d. mauve	3·00	65
453	2d. deep mauve	3·00	70
454	3d. chestnut	2·25	20
455	4d. orange-red	2·25	2·25
456	4d. orange-yellow (1912)	2·25	1·00
457	5d. brown (1910)	2·25	20
458	5d. red-brown	2·50	20
459	6d. carmine (1910)	4·50	12
460	6d. deep carmine (29.10.13)	4·50	12
461	8d. indigo-blue	2·25	20
461*a*	8d. deep bright blue	2·25	35
462	1s. vermilion (1910)	12·00	2·00
452/462	*Set of* 7	30·00	5·00

(b) P 14, *line machine.**

463	3d. chestnut (1910)	6·00	75
464	4d. orange (1910)	1·75	2·25
465	5d. brown	3·00	1·50
466	5d. red-brown (15.9.11)	3·00	1·50
467	6d. carmine	5·00	2·00
469	1s. vermilion	12·00	2·00

*In addition to showing the usual characteristics of a line perforation, these stamps may be distinguished by their vertical perforation which measures 13.8. Nos. 452 to 462 generally measure vertically 14 to 14.3. An exception is 13.8 one vertical side but 14 the other.

See also No. 478 with sideways wmk.

1913. *Auckland Exhibition. T* **50, 51** *and* **52** *optd. with T* **59.**

470	½d. green	20·00	20·00
471	1d. carmine	20·00	20·00
472	3d. chestnut (*perf.* 14×14½)	75·00	75·00
473	6d. carmine (*perf.* 14×14½)	£110	£110

These overprinted stamps were only available for letters in New Zealand and to Australia.

1915–16. *T* **52** *(and similar types). W* **41.** *P* 14×13½.

474	3d. chestnut	8·00	10·00
	a. Vert. pr., p. 14×13½ & 14×14½	30·00	30·00
475	5d. red-brown (1916)	3·00	35
	a. Vert. pr., p. 14×13½ & 14×14½	10·00	10·00
476	6d. carmine	8·00	8·00
	a. Vert. pr., p. 14×13½ & 14×14½	30·00	30·00
477	8d. indigo-blue (3.16)	4·00	1·50
	a. Vert. pr., p. 14×13½ & 14×14½	15·00	15·00
477*b*	8d. deep bright blue (1916)	4·00	35
	c. Vert. pr., p. 14×13½ & 14×14½	15·00	15·00
474/477*b*	*Set of* 5	25·00	16·00

All four values exist in complete sheets perf. 14×14½ and the 3d. and 6d. also in full sheets perf. 14×13½. The 3d., 5d. and 6d. also exist in two combinations: *(a)* five top rows perf. 14×13½ with five bottom rows perf. 14×14½ and *(b)* four top rows perf. 14×13½ with six bottom rows perf. 14×14½. The 8d. exists also as *(b)*.

On paper with widely spaced wmk. as used for 2½d. *of pictorial issue and wmk. sideways (see note after* No. 414). *P* 14, *line.*

478	8d. indigo-blue (8.16)	1·75	2·00
	a. No wmk.	15·00	15·00

No. 478a must show no trace of the wmk.

60

(Des. H. Linley Richardson, R.B.A.; plates made in London by Perkins, Bacon & Co. and stamps recess-printed in New Zealand.)

1915 (30 July)–**29.** *W* **41.** *P* 14×14½, *comb. (See notes below.)*

479	**60** 1½d. grey-slate	30	20
	a. Perf. 14×13½	30	20
	b. Vert. pair 479/9a	8·00	10·00
480	,, 2d. bright violet	1·25	2·00
	a. Perf. 14×13½	1·25	2·00
	b. Vert. pair, 480/80a	8·00	10·00
481	**60** 2d. yellow (15.1.16)	75	1·50
	a. Perf. 14×13½	75	1·50
	b. Vert. pair, 481/1a	4·75	6·00
482	,, 2½d. blue	1·50	65
	a. Perf. 14×13½	65	50
	b. Vert. pair, 482/2a	8·00	10·00
483	,, 3d. chocolate	2·25	12
	a. Perf. 14×13½	2·25	12
	b. Vert. pair, 483/3a	9·00	12·00
484	,, 4d. yellow	65	5·50
	a. Perf. 14×13½	65	5·50
	b. Vert. pair, 484/4a	6·00	20·00
485	,, 4d. bright violet (7.4.16)	2·00	12
	a. Perf. 14×13½	2·00	12
	b. Imperf. (pair)	£450	
	c. Vert. pair, 485/5a	9·00	12·00
486	,, 4½d. deep green	4·50	2·75
	a. Perf. 14×13½	4·50	2·75
	b. Vert. pair, 486/6a	15·00	18·00
487	,, 5d. light blue (4.22)	5·50	4·00
	a. Perf. 14×13½	2·25	40
	b. Imperf. (pair)	50·00	
488	,, 5d. pale ultramarine	5·50	2·25
	a. Perf. 14×13½	3·00	65
	b. Vert. pair, 488/8a (1929)	15·00	18·00
489	,, 6d. carmine	2·00	35
	a. Perf. 14×13½	2·00	12
	b. Vert. pair, 489/9a (1916)	20·00	25·00
	c. Imperf. three sides (pair)	£450	
	d. Carmine-lake, P 14×13½	50·00	35·00
490	,, 7½d. red-brown	1·75	1·95
	a. Perf. 14×13½	1·75	1·95
	b. Vert. pair, 490/0a (10.20)	15·00	25·00
491	,, 8d. indigo-blue (19.4.21)	1·75	2·25
	a. Perf. 14×13½	1·75	2·25
	b. Vert. pair, 491/1a	7·50	8·50
492	,, 8d. red-brown (*p.* 14×13½) (2.22)	2·00	40
493	,, 9d. sage-green	3·00	1·00
	a. Perf. 14×13½	2·00	50
	b. Vert. pair, 493/3a	20·00	25·00
	c. Imperf. three sides (pair)	£500	
	d. Imperf. (pair)	£500	
	e. Yellowish olive. P 14×13½ (12.25)	8·00	2·75
494	,, 1s. vermilion (1916)	3·75	12
	a. Perf. 14×13½	4·50	30
	b. Imperf. (pair)	£450	
	c. Vert. pair 494/4a	25·00	25·00
495	,, 1s. pale orange-red	4·50	2·00
	a. Imperf. (pair)	£170	
	b. Orange-brown	£140	75·00
479/495	*Set of* 15	30·00	18·00

The 1½d., 2½d., 4½d. and 7½d. have value tablets as shown in T **60.** In the other values, the tablets are shortened, and the ornamental border at each side of the crown correspondingly extended.

The perfs. 14×14½ and 14×13½ may both be found on the same sheet in all the above values from 1½d. to 1s. and vertical pairs from the 4th and 5th horizontal rows would show both perforations *se-tenant*, except for the 4d. (both colours) and 5d. values where the *se-tenant* pairs are from the 5th and 6th horizontal rows (see Note after No. 477*c*).

Sheets of the 1½d., 2½d., 4d. yellow, 4d. violet, 4½d., 6d., 7½d., 9d. and 1s. are known perf. 14×13½ throughout, while sheets of the 4d. violet and 1s. are known perf. 14×14½ throughout.

Any stamps with the wmk. with perforations measuring 14×14 or nearly must be classed as 14×14½, this being an irregularity of the comb machine, and not a product of the 14-line machine.

1916 (Mar.–Aug.). *T* **60.** *On paper of pictorial issue, as* No. 478 *(wmk. sideways on* 2d., 3d., 6d.).

496	1½d. grey-slate (*p.* 14×14½) (Mar.)	20	20
	a. No wmk.	50	45
497	1½d. grey-slate (*p.* 14×13½)	15	20
	a. No wmk.	40	40
	b. Vert. pair, 496/497	8·00	10·00
	c. As last. No wmk.	12·00	15·00
498	2d. yellow (*p.* 14) (June)	1·00	2·00
	a. No wmk.	4·50	8·00
499	3d. chocolate (*p.* 14) (June)	40	35
	a. No wmk.	5·00	5·00
500	6d. carmine (*p.* 14) (Aug.)	1·75	2·25
	a. No wmk.	7·00	8·00

The "no wmk." varieties must show no trace of the wmk.

60*a*

60*b*

(Die eng. W. R. Bock, Wellington. Typo. in N.Z. from plates made locally.)

1916 (April). *W* **41.** *P* 14×15.

501	**60*a*** 1½d. grey-black	1·00	12
502	,, 1½d. black	1·25	12

Nos. 501 and 502 differ from No. 505 in many respects. The shading of the portrait is *diagonal* in the former and *horizontal* in the latter.

1915–19. *T* **60*b***, *typo. from steel plates by Perkins, Bacon & Co. Chalk-surfaced "De La Rue" paper. Toned gum. W* **41.** *P* 14×15.

503	½d. green (30.7.15)	40	12
504	½d. yellow-green	1·60	45
	a. Very thick, hard, highly surfaced paper, white gum (12.15)	4·00	5·00
505	1½d. slate (5.9.16)	50	12
506	1½d. orange-brown (9.18)	35	12
507	2d. yellow (9.16)	30	12
508	2d. pale yellow	1·00	12
509	3d. chocolate (5.19)	1·25	20
503/509	*Set of* 5	3·25	55

The first note after No. 495*b* also applies to *T* **60*b***.

See also Nos. 519, etc.

WAR STAMP
(61)

1915 (24 Sept.). *Optd. with T* **61.** *P* 14×15.

510	**60*b*** ½d. green	10	8

62

63

66

64

65

67

(Plates by Perkins, Bacon; Waterlow and De La Rue. Typo. D.L.R.)

1920 (27 JAN.). *Victory.* **W 41.** *P* 14.

511 **62** ½d. green 20 15
  a. Pale yellow-green .. 3·00 3·00
512 **63** 1d. carmine-red 25 12
  a. Bright carmine 45 20
513 **64** 1½d. brown-orange .. 20 15
514 **65** 3d. chocolate .. .. 5·50 5·00
515 **66** 6d. violet .. .. .. 10·00 8·00
516 **67** 1s. orange-red .. .. 20·00 22·00
511/516 .. .. *Set of* 6 35·00 35·00

The above stamps were placed on sale in London in November, 1919.

2d. **2d.**

TWOPENCE

(**68**)

69

1922 (MAR.). *Surch. with T* **68.**

517 **62** 2d. on ½d. green (R.) .. 30 20

(Des. and eng. W. R. Bock. Typo. at Wellington.)

1923. *Restoration of Penny Postage. Chalky paper. Yellowish gum.* **W 41.** *P* 14×15.

518 **69** 1d. carmine 8 8

"De La Rue" paper is chalk-surfaced and has a smooth finish. The watermark is as illustrated. The gum is toned and strongly resistant to soaking.

"Jones" paper is chalk-surfaced and has a coarser texture, is poorly surfaced and the ink tends to peal. The outline of the watermark commonly shows on the surface of the stamp. The ink is colourless or only slightly toned and washes off readily. Introduced in 1924.

"Cowan" paper is chalk-surfaced and is white and opaque. The watermark is usually smaller than in the "Jones" paper and is often barely visible. Introduced in 1925.

"Wiggins, Teape" paper is chalk-surfaced and is thin and hard. It has a vertical mesh with a narrow watermark, whereas the other papers have a horizontal mesh and a wider watermark. Introduced in 1926.

1924–25. **W 41.** *P* 14×15.

(*a*) *"Jones" chalky paper, white gum.*

519 **60*b*** ½d. green 75 35
520 **51** 1d. deep carmine 30 8
  a. *Pale carmine.* Unsurfaced paper .. .. .. 70·00
521 **69** 1d. carmine 85 8
522 **60*b*** 2d. dull yellow .. .. 1·00 1·00
523 ,, 3d. deep chocolate .. 3·50 1·00

Only one half-sheet of No. 520a is known, due to faulty manufacture.

(*b*) *Medium, unsurfaced paper, toned gum.*

524 **51** 1d. rose-carmine (4.25) .. 1·00 15·00

(*c*) *Medium to thick chalky paper, toned gum. Wmk. sideways.*

526 **51** 1d. bright carmine(4.25) 15 65
  a. No wmk. .. .. 1·25 1·25
  b. Imperf. (pair) .. ..

Many stamps in the sheet of No. 526 are without watermark, while others show portions of "NEW ZEALAND POSTAGE" in double-lined capitals.

1925. *No wmk. but bluish* "N Z" *and Star lithographed on back.* *P* 14×15.

527 **60*b*** ½d. apple-green 20 15
  a. "N Z" and Star almost colourless .. .. 3·50
528 **51** 1d. rose-carmine 30 15
  a. "N Z" and Star in black 4·00
  b. "N Z" and Star colourless 18·00 15·00
529 **60*b*** 2d. yellow .. .. 1·00 3·25

1925–30. *As* 1924–5, *but "Cowan" thick, opaque chalky paper, white gum.* **W 41.**

530 **60*b*** ½d. green (*p.* 14×15) .. 15 12
  a. Perf. 14 .. .. 20 12
531 **51** 1d. dp. carm. (*p.* 14×15) (8.25) 40 12
  a. Imperf. (pair) .. .. 15·00 18·00
532 **60*b*** 1½d. orge.-brn. (*p.* 14) ('30) 2·00 1·50
  a. Perf. 14×15 .. .. 15·00 15·00
533 ,, 2d. yellow (*p.* 14×15) .. 95 12
  a. Perf. 14 ('30) 95 12
534 ,, 3d. chocolate (*p.* 14×15) 1·25 12
  a. Perf. 14 ('30) .. .. 2·25 70
530/534 .. .. *Set of* 5 4·00 2·00

"Cowan" unsurfaced paper (4.25).

535 **69** 1d. carm.-pink (*p.* 14×15) 2·75 1·40

This is a medium soft paper similar to that on which the line-engraved stamps of **T 60** were printed, with very shiny gum.

1926 (JUNE)–30. *"Wiggins Teape" thin, hard, chalk-surfaced paper.* **W 41.**

535*a* **51** 1d. rose-carm. (*p.* 14×15) 1·00 40
535*b* **60*b*** 1½d. orange-brown (*perf.* 14) ('30) .. .. 12·00 12·00
535*c* ,, 2d. yellow (*p.* 14×15) .. 1·25 95
  d. Perf. 14 (July 1927). .. 95 95

70

(Des. H. Linley Richardson. Eng. and typo. Govt. Ptg. Office, Wellington.)

1925 (17 NOV.). *Dunedin Exhibition. Thick "Cowan" chalky paper.* **W 41.** *P* 14×15.

536 **70** ½d. yellow-green/*green* .. 2·00 2·50
537 ,, 1d. carmine/*rose* .. 2·00 2·50
538 ,, 4d. mauve/*pale mauve* .. 35·00 40·00
  a. "POSTAGF" at right .. 60·00 70·00

71

72

(Des. H. L. Richardson; plates by Waterlow Typo. Wellington.)

1926–27. *Chalky paper.* **W 41.** *P* 14.

(*a*) *"Cowan paper".*

539 **71** 1d. rose-carmine (12.11.26) 10
  a. Perf. 14×15 (11.27) .. 10
  b. Imperf. (pair) .. .. 20·00

(*b*) *"Jones" paper* (12.7.26).

540 **72** 2s. deep blue .. .. 20·00 10·0
541 ,, 3s. mauve .. .. .. 30·00 30·0

(*c*) *"Cowan" paper.*

542 **72** 2s. light blue (5.27) .. 18·00 4·0
543 ,, 3s. pale mauve (9.27) .. 28·00 28·0

The 1d. value exists in a range of colour including scarlet and deep carmine to magent but we have insufficient evidence to show tha these were issued thus. There are also severa shades of the issued stamp.

73. Nurse.

74. Smiling Boy.

(Typo. Govt. Printing Office, Wellington.)

1929–30. *Anti-Tuberculosis Fund.* **T 73** (*an similar type*). **W 41.** *P* 14.

(*a*) *Inscribed* "HELP STAMP OUT TUBERCULOSIS"

544 1d.+1d. scarlet (11.12.29) .. 4·00 4·0

(*b*) *Inscribed* "HELP PROMOTE HEALTH".

545 1d.+1d. scarlet (29.10.30) .. 12·00 12·0

For the "Arms" types and surcharges on the formerly listed here, see under Postal Fisca stamps.

(Des. L. C. Mitchell. Dies and plates, Perkins Bacon. Typo. Govt. Ptg. Office, Wellington

1931 (31 OCT.). *Health Stamps.* **W 41** *P* 14½×14.

546 **74** 1d.+1d. scarlet .. .. 45·00 45·0
547 ,, 2d.+1d. blue .. .. 45·00 45·0

75. New Zealand Lake Scenery.

Des. L. C. Mitchell. Typo. Govt. Ptg. Office.)

931 (11 Nov.). *Air.* W **41.** P 14×14½.
48 **75** 3d. chocolate .. .. 8·00 8·00
a. Perf. 14×15 .. 30·00 40·00
49 ,, 4d. blackish purple .. 8·00 8·00
50 ,, 7d. brown-orange .. 10·00 10·00

FIVE PENCE
(76)

931 (18 Dec.). *Air. Surch. with T* **76.**
51 **75** 5d. on 3d. green (R.) .. 4·50 4·00

77. Hygeia, oddess of Health.

78. The Path to Health.

Des. R. E. Tripe and W. J. Cooch. Eng. H. T. Peat. Recess. Govt. Printing Office, Wellington.)

932 (18 Nov.). *Health Stamp.* W **41.** P 14.
52 **77** 1d.+1d. carmine .. 12·00 12·00

Des. J. Berry. Eng. H. T. Peat. Recess. Govt. Printing Office, Wellington.)

33 (8 Nov.). *Health Stamp.* W **41.** P 14.
3 **78** 1d.+1d. carmine .. 6·00 6·00

TRANS-TASMAN AIR MAIL "FAITH IN AUSTRALIA."
(79)

34 (Feb.). *Air. T* **75** *in new colour optd. with T* **79.** W **41.** P 14×14½.
4 **75** 7d. light blue (B.) .. 7·50 8·50

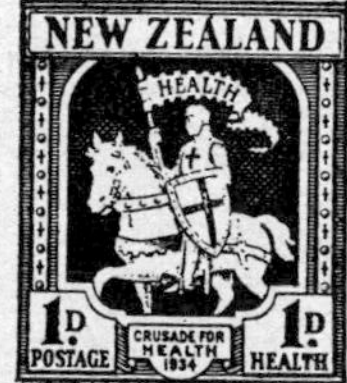

80. Crusader.

(Des. J. Berry. Recess. D.L.R.)

34 (26 Oct.). *Health Stamp.* W **41.** P 14×13½.
5 **80** 1d.+1d. carmine .. 4·00 5·00

81. Pied fantail.

82. Kiwi.

83. Maori woman.

84. Maori carved house.

85. Mt. Cook.

86. Maori girl.

87. Mitre Peak.

88. Swordfish.

89. Harvesting.

90. Tuatara lizard.

91. Maori panel.

92. Tui.

93. Capt. Cook at Poverty Bay.

94. Mt. Egmont.

Die I Die II

(Des. J. Fitzgerald (½d., 4d.), C. H. and R. J. G. Collins (1d.), M. Matthews (1½d.), H. W. Young (2d.), L. C. Mitchell (2½d., 3d., 8d., 1s., 3s.), W. J. Cooch and R. E. Tripe (5d.). T. I. Archer (6d.), I. F. Calder (9d.) and I. H. Jenkins (2s.). Litho. Waterlow (9d.). Recess. D.L.R. (remainder).)

1935 (1 May). W **41.**
556 **81** ½d. brt. green, *p.* 14×13½ 8 8
557 **82** 1d. scar. (Die I), *p.* 14×13½ 8 8
a. Perf. 13½×14 .. .. 5·50 4·00
b. Die II, *p.* 14×13½ .. 50 35
558 **83** 1½d. red-brown, *p.* 14×13½ 35 30
a. Perf. 13½×14 .. .. 35 30
559 **84** 2d. orange, *p.* 14×13½ .. 15 8
560 **85** 2½d. chocolate and slate, *p.* 13–14×13½ .. 40 45
a. Perf. 13½×14 .. 40 45
561 **86** 3d. brown, *p.* 14×13½ .. 1·25 30
562 **87** 4d. black and sepia, *p.* 14 30 8
563 **88** 5d. ultram., *p.* 13–14×13½ 2·50 50
a. Perf. 13½×14 .. 3·00 30
564 **89** 6d. scarlet, *p.* 13½×14 .. 50 15
565 **90** 8d chocolate, *p.* 14×13½ 50 40
566 **91** 9d. scarlet and black, *p.* 14×14½ .. 50 35
567 **92** 1s. deep green, *p.* 14×13½ 2·00 30
568 **93** 2s. ol.-grn., *p.* 13–14×13½ 2·50 65
a. Perf. 13½×14 .. 4·00 85
569 **94** 3s. choc. & yellow-brown, *p.* 13–14×13½ .. 4·00 3·00
a. Perf. 13½×14 .. .. 4·00 3·00
556/569 .. .. *Set of* 14 13·00 6·00

In the 2½d., 5d., 2s. and 3s. perf. 13–14×13½ the horizontal perforations of each stamp are in two sizes, one half of each horizontal side measuring 13 and the other 14.

See also Nos. 577/90 and 626/7.

95. Bell Block Aerodrome.

(Des. J. Berry. Eng. Stamp Printing Office, Melbourne. Recess. Govt. Printing Office, Wellington.)

1935 (4 May). *Air.* *W* **41.** *P* 14.

570	**95**	1d. carmine	30	30
571	,,	3d. violet	1·50	1·25
572	,,	6d. blue	1·50	1·25

96. King George V and Queen Mary.

(Frame by J. Berry. Recess. B.W.)

1935 (7 May). *Silver Jubilee.* *W* **41.** *P* 11 × 11½.

573	**96**	½d. green	8	8
574	,,	1d. carmine	8	8
575	,,	6d. red-orange	10·00	12·00

97. " The Key to Health ".

(Des. S. Hall. Recess. J. Ash, Melbourne.)

1935 (30 Sept.). *Health Stamp.* *W* **41.** *P* 11.

576	**97**	1d. + 1d. scarlet	1·50	1·50

98. " Multiple Wmk."

In T **41** the wmk. units are in vertical columns widely spaced and the sheet margins are unwatermarked or wmkd. " NEW ZEALAND POSTAGE " in large letters.

In T **98** the wmk. units are arranged alternately in horizontal rows closely spaced and are continued into the sheet margins.

(Litho. Govt. Ptg. Office, Wellington (9d.). Recess. Waterlow or D.L.R. (others).)

1936–43. *W* **98.**

577	**81**	½d. bright grn., *p.* 14 × 13½	8	8
578	**82**	1d. scarlet (Die II), *p.* 14 × 13½	8	8
579	**83**	1½d. red-brn., *p.* 14 × 13½	35	30
580	**84**	2d. orange, *p.* 14 × 13½	8	8
		a. Perf. 12½† (6.41)	15	8
		c. Perf. 14 (6.41)	40	30
		d. Perf. 14×15 (6.41)	60	30
581	**85**	2½d. chocolate and slate, *p.* 13–14 × 13½	40	45
		a. Perf. 14	35	45
		b. Perf. 14×13½ ('42)	45	65
582	**86**	3d. brown, *p.* 14 × 13½	1·25	8
583	**87**	4d. blk. & sep., *p.* 14 × 13½	10	8
		a. Perf. 12½* ('41)	35	10
		b. Perf. 14, line ('41)	4·00	3·00
		c. Perf. 14×14½ comb. (–.7.42)	10	8
584	**88**	5d. ultram., *p.* 13–14 × 13½	2·75	20
		a. Perf. 12½*† (7.41, '42)	2·75	20
		b. Perf. 14×13½ ('42)	2·75	20
585	**89**	6d. scarlet, *p.* 13½ × 14	35	8
		a. Perf. 12½* ('41)	20	8
		b. Perf. 14½×14 ('42)	15	8
586	**90**	8d. chocolate, *p.* 14 × 13½ (*wmk. s.*)	1·50	40
		aa. Wmk. upright ('39)	35	8
		a. Perf. 12½* (*wmk. sideways*) ('41)	35	15
		b. Perf. 14×14½ (*wmk. sideways*) ('43)	40	10
587	**91**	9d. red & grey, *p.* 14 × 15 (*wmk. sideways*)	1·25	25
		a. Red and grey-black, p. 14×14½ (1.3.38)	1·25	15
588	**92**	1s. deep green, *p.* 14 × 13½	65	8
		a. Perf. 12½* (11.41)	1·65	75
589	**93**	2s. olive-green, *p.* 13–14 × 13½	2·50	50
		a. Perf. 13½×14 ('38)	18·00	1·00
		b. Perf. 12½*† ('41, '42)	2·25	20
		c. Perf. 14×13½ ('42)	1·50	25
590	**94**	3s. chocolate and yellow-brown, *p.* 13–14 × 13½	2·75	75
		a. Perf. 12½* ('41)	5·00	2·00
		b. Perf. 14×13½ ('42)	2·00	35
577/590		*Set of* 14	13·00	2·75

*† Stamps indicated with an asterisk were printed and perforated by Waterlow; those having a dagger were printed by D.L.R. and perforated by Waterlow. No. 580d was printed by D.L.R. and perforated by Harrison and No. 583b was printed by Waterlow and perforated by D.L.R. These are all known as " Blitz perfs." because De La Rue were unable to maintain supplies after their works were damaged by enemy action. All the rest, except the 9d., were printed and perforated by D.L.R.

1d. and 2d. Perf. 14 × 13½ varies in the sheet and is sometimes nearer 13½. 2d. perf. 14 × 15 is sometimes nearer 14 × 14½.

2½d., 5d., 2s. and 3s. In perf. 13–14 × 13½ one half the length of each horizontal perforation measures 13 and the other 14. In perf. 14 × 13½ the horizontal perforation is regular.

4d. No. 583b is line-perf. measuring 14 exactly and has a blackish sepia frame. No. 583c is a comb-perf. measuring 14 × 14.3 or 14 × 14.2 and the frame is a warmer shade.

2s. No. 589a is comb-perf. and measures 13.5 × 13.75.

For 9d. typographed, see Nos. 630/1.

99. N.Z. Soldier at Anzac Cove.

(Des. L. C. Mitchell. Recess. John Ash, Melbourne.)

1936 (27 Apr.). *Charity. 21st Anniv. of "Anzac" Landing at Gallipoli.* *W* **41.** *P* 11.

591	**99**	½d. + ½d. green	25	25
592	,,	1d. + 1d. scarlet	25	25

100. Wool. **101.** Butter. **102.** Sheep. **103.** Apples. **104.** Exports.

(Des. L. C. Mitchell. Recess. J. Ash, Melbourne

1936 (1 Oct.). *Congress of British Empi Chambers of Commerce, Wellington. N.Z Industries Issue.* *W* **41.** *P* 11½.

593	**100**	½d. emerald-green	8	
594	**101**	1d. scarlet	8	
595	**102**	2½d. blue	1·00	1·1
596	**103**	4d. violet	1·10	1·4
597	**104**	6d. red-brown	1·00	1·0
593/597		*Set of* 5	2·75	3·2

105. Health Camp.

(Des. J. Berry. Recess. J. Ash, Melbourne

1936 (2 Nov.). *Health Stamp.* *W* **41.** *P* 1

598	**105**	1d. + 1d. scarlet	80	8

106. King George VI and Queen Elizabeth.

(Recess. Bradbury, Wilkinson & Co.)

1937 (13 May). *Coronation.* *W* **98.** *P* 14 × 13

599	**106**	1d. carmine	8	
600	,,	2½d. Prussian blue	12	
601	,,	6d. red-orange	30	

107. Rock-climbing.

(Des. G. Bull and J. Berry. Recess. J. As

1937 (1 Oct.). *Health Stamp.* *W* **41.** *P* 11.

602	**107**	1d. + 1d. scarlet	1·40	1·4

108. King George VI. **108*a*.**

(Des. W. J. Cooch. Recess. B.W.)

1938–44. *W* **98.** *P* 14 × 13½.

603	**108**	½d. green (1.3.38)	15	
604	,,	½d. brn.-orge. (10.7.41)	5	
605	,,	1d. scarlet (1.7.38)	30	
606	,,	1d. green (21.7.41)	5	
607	**108*a***	1½d. pur.-brn. (26.7.38)	90	
608	,,	1½d. scarlet (1.2.44)	5	
609	,,	3d. blue (26.9.41)	8	
603/609		*Set of* 7	1·40	

For other values see Nos. 680/89.

09. Children playing. 110. Beach Ball.

(Des. J. Berry. Recess. Bradbury, Wilkinson & Co.)

938 (1 Oct.). *Health Stamp. W* **98.** *P* 14×13½.
10 **109** 1d+1d. scarlet .. .. 1·10 1·00

Des. S. Hall. Recess. Note Printing Branch 'ommonwealth Bank of Australia, Melbourne.)

939 (16 Oct.). *Health Stamps. Surcharged with new value. W* **41.** *P* 11.
11 **110** 1d. on ½d.+½d. green .. 75 1·00
12 ,, 2d. on 1d.+1d. scarlet .. 1·00 1·25

111. Arrival of the Maoris, 1350.

12. *Endeavour*, Chart of N.Z., and Capt. Cook.

113. British Monarchs.

114. Tasman with his Ship and Chart.

15. Signing Treaty of Waitangi, 1840. **118.** H.M.S. *Britomar* at Akaroa, 1840.

116. Landing of Immigrants, 1840.

117. Road, rail, sea and air transport.

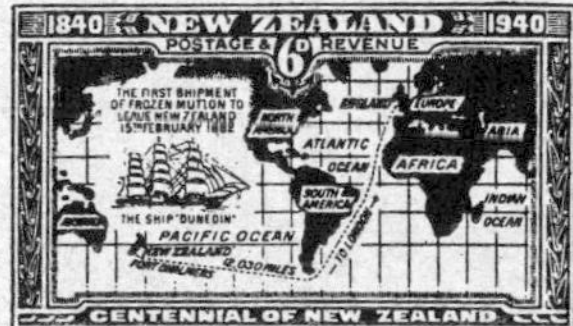

119. *Dunedin* and "frozen mutton route" to London.

120. Maori Council.

121. Gold Mining in 1861 and 1940.

122. Giant Kauri tree.

(Des. L. C. Mitchell (½d., 3d., 4d.); J. Berry (others). Recess. Bradbury, Wilkinson.)

1940 (2 Jan.–8 Mar. (8*d.*)). *Centenary of Proclamation of British Sovereignty. W* **98.** *P* 14×13½ (2½*d.*), 13½×14 (5*d.*) *or* 13½ (*others*).
613 **111** ½d. blue-green 5 5
614 **112** 1d. chocolate & scarlet 8 5
615 **113** 1½d. light blue and mauve 25 15
616 **114** 2d. blue-green & choc. 10 5
617 **115** 2½d. blue-green and blue 15 25
618 **116** 3d. purple and carmine 75 15
619 **117** 4d. chocolate and lake.. 70 25
620 **118** 5d. pale blue and brown 80 80
621 **119** 6d. emer.-green & violet 70 20
622 **120** 7d. black and red .. 1·50 2·50
623 ,, 8d. black and red .. 75 45
624 **121** 9d. olive-grn. & orange 1·60 1·25
625 **122** 1s. sage-grn. & dp. green 4·00 1·00
613/625 .. .. *Set of* 13 10·00 6·00

1940 (1 Oct.). *Health. As T* **110**, *but without extra surcharge. W* **41.** *P* 11.
626 **110** 1d.+½d. blue-green .. 80 1·00
627 ,, 2d.+1d. brown-orange .. 1·10 1·40

1D 1D

■ ■ 2D 1941

(**123**) Inserted "2". (**124**)

1941. *Surch. as T* **123.**
628 **108** 1d. on ½d. green (1.5.41) 8 5
629 **108a** 2d. on 1½d. purple-brown (–.4.41) 8 5
a. Inserted "2" £180 £140

The surcharge on No. 629 has only one figure, at top left, and there is only one square to obliterate the original value at bottom right.

The variety "Inserted 2" occurs on the 10th stamp, 10th row. It is identified by the presence of remnants of the damaged "2", and by the spacing of "2" and "D" which is variable and different from the normal.

(Typo. Govt. Printing Office, Wellington.)

1941. *As T* **91**, *but smaller* (17½×20½ *mm.*). *P* 14×15. (*a*) *W* **41.**
630 **91** 9d. scarlet & blk. (–.5.41).. 5·00 60
(*b*) *W* **98.**
631 **91** 9d. scarlet & blk. (29.9.41) 70 20

1941 (4 Oct.). *Health Stamps. Nos.* 626/7, *optd. with T* **124.**
632 **110** 1d.+½d. blue-green .. 35 45
633 ,, 2d.+1d. brown-orange .. 50 55

125. Boy and Girl on Swing.

(Des. S. Hall. Recess. Note Printing Branch. Commonwealth Bank of Australia, Melbourne.)

1942 (1 Oct.). *Health Stamps. W* **41.** *P* 11.
634 **125** 1d.+½d. blue-green .. 25 30
635 ,, 2d.+1d. orange-red .. 30 40

126. Princess Margaret.

127. Queen Elizabeth II as Princess.

(Des. J. Berry. Recess. B.W.)

1943 (1 Oct.). *Health Stamps.* *W* **98.** *P* 12.
636 **126** 1d. + ½d. green 8 8
a. Imperf. between (vert. pair) £1500
637 **127** 2d. + 1d. red-brown .. 8 10
a. Imperf. between (vert. pair) £1700

For "Arms" types watermarked Type **98** formerly listed here see under Postal Fiscal stamps.

(128)

1944 (1 May). *No.* 615 *surch. with T* **128.**
662 10d. on 1½d. lt. blue & mauve 15 15

129. Queen Elizabeth II as Princess and Princess Margaret.

(Recess. Bradbury, Wilkinson.)

1944 (9 Oct.). *Health Stamps.* *W* **98.** *P* 13½.
663 **129** 1d.+½d. green 5 5
664 „ 2d.+1d. blue 8 8

130. Statue of Peter Pan, Kensington Gardens.

(Des. J. Berry. Recess. Bradbury, Wilkinson.)

1945 (1 Oct.). *Health Stamps.* *W* **98.** *P* 13½.
665 **130** 1d.+½d. green and buff.. 5 5
666 „ 2d.+1d. carmine and buff 8 8

131. Lake Matheson.

132. King George VI and Parliament House, Wellington.

133. St. Paul's Cathedral.

134. The Royal Family.

135. R.N.Z.A.F. Badge and Aeroplanes.

136. Army Badge, Tank and Plough.

137. Navy Badge, War and Trading Ships.

138. N.Z. Coat-of-Arms, Foundry and Farm.

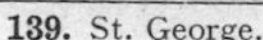

139. St. George.

141. National Memorial Campanile.

140. Southern Alps and Franz Josef Glacier.

(Des. J. Berry. Photo. Harrison (1½d. and 1s.). Recess. Bradbury, Wilkinson (1d. and 2d.) and Waterlow (others).)

1946 (1 Apr.). *Peace issue.* *W* **98** (*sideways on 1½d.*). *P* 13 (*1d., 2d.*), 14 × 14½ (*1½d., 1s.*), 13 (*others*).
667 **131** ½d. green and brown .. 5
668 **132** 1d. green 5
669 **133** 1½d. scarlet 5
670 **134** 2d. purple 5
671 **135** 3d. ultramarine and grey 8
672 **136** 4d. bronze-grn. and orge. 10 1
673 **137** 5d. green & ultramarine 12 1
674 **138** 6d. choc. and vermilion 12 1
675 **139** 8d. black and carmine.. 15 1
676 **140** 9d. blue and black .. 25 2
677 **141** 1s. grey-black 30 3
667/677 .. .. *Set of* 11 1·10 1·1

142. Soldier Helping Child over Stile.

(Des. J. Berry. Recess. Waterlow & Sons.)

1946 (24 Oct.). *Health Stamps.* *W* **98.** *P* 13½
678 **142** 1d.+½d. green & orange-brown.. 5
a. Yellow-green and orge.-brn. 2·00 2·0
679 „ 2d.+1d. chocolate and orange-brown .. 8

MINIMUM PRICE

The minimum price quoted is 5p which represents a handling charge rather than a basis for valuing common stamps. For further notes about prices see introductory pages.

144. King George VI.

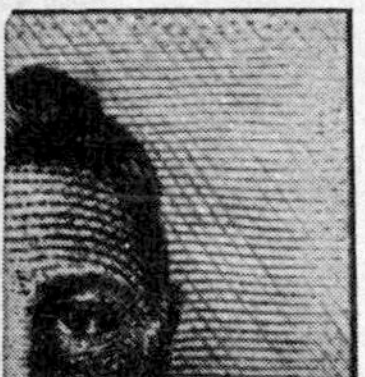

Plate 1.

Plate 2.

(Des. W. J. Cooch. Recess. T **108a**, B.W.; T **144**, D.L.R.)

1947–52. *W* **98** (*sideways on "shilling" values*).

(*a*) *P* 14×13½.

No.	Type	Description	Unused	Used
680	**108a**	½d. orange	5	5
681	,,	4d. bright purple ..	8	5
682	,,	5d. slate	35	8
683	,,	6d. carmine	15	5
684	,,	8d. violet	35	10
685	,,	9d. purple-brown ..	35	8
680/685		.. *Set of* 6	1·10	25

(*b*) *P* 14.

No.	Type	Description	Unused	Used
686	**144**	1s. red-brn.&carm.(Pl.1)	30	15
		a. Wmk. upright (Pl. 1) ..	35	12
		b. Wmk. upright (Pl. 2) ..	25	8
687	,,	1s. 3d. red-brown & blue (Pl. 2)	40	8
		a. Wmk. upright (14.1.52)	40	20
688	,,	2s. brn.-orge.&grn.(Pl.1)	55	15
		a. Wmk. upright (Pl. 1) ..	60	25
689	,,	3s. red-brn.& grey (Pl. 2)	1·00	30

In head-plate 2 the diagonal lines of the background have been strengthened and result in the upper corners and sides appearing more deeply shaded.

145. Statue of Eros.

(Des. J. Berry. Recess. Waterlow.)

1947 (1 Oct.). *Health Stamps.* *W* **98** (*sideways*). *P* 13½.

No.	Type	Description	Unused	Used
690	**145**	1d.+½d. green	5	5
691	,,	2d.+1d. carmine ..	8	8

146. Port Chalmers, 1848.

147. Cromwell, Otago.

148. First Church, Dunedin.

149. University of Otago.

(Des. J. Berry. Recess. B.W.)

1948 (23 Feb.). *Centennial of Otago.* *W* **98** (*sideways on 3d.*). *P* 13½.

No.	Type	Description	Unused	Used
692	**146**	1d. blue and green ..	5	5
693	**147**	2d. green and brown ..	5	5
694	**148**	3d. purple	8	8
695	**149**	6d. black and rose ..	15	20

150. Boy Sunbathing and Children Playing.

(Des. E. Linzell. Recess. B.W.)

1948 (1 Oct.). *Health Stamps.* *W* **98.** *P* 13½.

No.	Type	Description	Unused	Used
696	**150**	1d.+½d. blue and green ..	5	5
697	,,	2d.+1d. purple and scar.	8	8

151. Nurse and Child.

1½d.

POSTAGE

(152)

(Des. J. Berry. Photo. Harrison.)

1949 (3 Oct.). *Health Stamps.* *W* **98.** *P* 14×14½.

No.	Type	Description	Unused	Used
698	**151**	1d.+½d. green	5	5
699	,,	2d.+1d. ultramarine ..	8	8
		a. No stop below "D" of "1 D."	6·00	7·00

1950 (28 July). *As Type* F **6**, *but without value, surch. with* T **152.** *W* **98.** *Chalk-surfaced paper.* *P* 14.

No.	Type	Description	Unused	Used
700	F **6**	1½d. carmine	8	5

Originally issued with the watermark inverted, this later appeared with it upright.

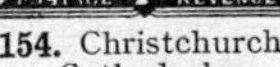

153. Queen Elizabeth II and Prince Charles.

(Des. J. Berry and R. S. Phillips. Photo. Harrison.)

1950 (2 Oct.). *Health Stamps.* *W* **98.** *P* 14×14½.

No.	Type	Description	Unused	Used
701	**153**	1d.+½d. green	5	5
702	,,	2d.+1d. plum	8	8

154. Christchurch Cathedral.

156. John Robert Godley.

155. Cairn on Lyttleton Hills.

157. Canterbury University College.

158. Aerial View of Timaru.

(Des. L. C. Mitchell (2d.), J. A. Johnstone (3d). and J. Berry (others). Recess. B.W.)

1950 (20 Nov.). *Centennial of Canterbury, N.Z. W* **98** *(sideways on 1d. and 3d.). P* 13½.

703	**154**	1d. green and blue ..	5	5
704	**155**	2d. carmine and orange	5	5
705	**156**	3d. dark blue and blue ..	8	5
706	**157**	6d. brown and blue ..	15	20
707	**158**	1s. reddish pur. and blue	35	30
703/707		.. .. *Set of* 5	60	55

159. " Takapuna " class Yachts.

(Des. J. Berry & R. S. Phillips. Recess. B.W.)

1951 (1 Nov.). *Health Stamps. W* **98.** *P* 13½.

708	**159**	1½d.+½d. scarlet & yellow	5	5
709	,,	2d.+1d. dp. grn. & yellow	5	5

160. Princess Anne. **161.** Prince Charles.

(From photographs by Marcus Adams. Photo. Harrison.)

1952 (1 Oct.). *Health Stamps. W* **98.** *P* 14×14½.

710	**160**	1½d.+½d. carmine-red ..	12	10
711	**161**	2d.+1d. brown ..	12	10

3D

(**162**)

1952–53. *Nos.* 604 *and* 606 *surch. as T* **162.**

712	**108**	1d. on ½d. brown-orange (11.9.53)	8	10
713	,,	3d. on 1d. grn. (12.12.52*)	8	10

*Earliest known date used.

163. Buckingham Palace.

164. Queen Elizabeth II. **166.** Westminster Abbey.

165. Coronation State Coach.

167. St. Edward's Crown and Royal Sceptre.

(Des. L. C. Mitchell (1s. 6d.), J. Berry (others). Recess. D.L.R. (2d., 4d.), Waterlow (1s. 6d.). Photo. Harrison (3d., 8d.).)

1953 (25 May). *Coronation. W* **98.** *P* 13. *(2d., 4d),* 13½ *(1s. 6d.) or* 14×14½ *(3d., 8d).*

714	**163**	2d. deep bright blue ..	5	5
715	**164**	3d. brown	10	8
716	**165**	4d. carmine	20	25
717	**166**	8d. slate-grey	35	50
718	**167**	1s. 6d. purple & ultram.	60	70
714/8		.. .. *Set of* 5	1·10	1·40

168. Girl Guides. **169.** Boy Scouts.

(Des. J. Berry. Photo. Harrison.)

1953 (7 Oct.). *Health. W* **98.** *P* 14×14½.

719	**168**	1½d.+½d. blue	8	5
720	**169**	2d.+1d. dp. yellow-grn.	8	5

No. 720 exists imperf. three sides.

170. Queen Elizabeth II.

171. Queen Elizabeth II and Duke of Edinburgh.

(Des. L. C. Mitchell. Recess. Waterlow & Sons.)

1953 (9 Dec.). *Royal Visit. W* **98.** *P* 13×14 *(3d.) or* 13½ *(4d.).*

721	**170**	3d. dull purple	8	5
722	**171**	4d. deep ultramarine ..	12	15

172

173. Queen Elizabeth II. **174.**

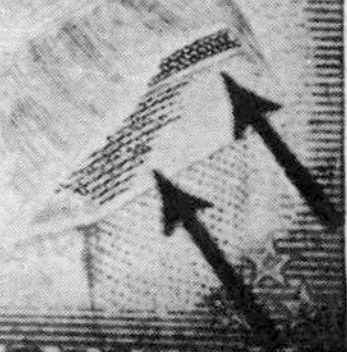

Die I. Die II.

(Des. L. C. Mitchell (T **172/3**), J. Berry (T **174**). Recess. D.L.R. (T **173**). B.W. (others).)

1953–8. *W* **98.** *P* 14×13½ *(T* **172**), 14 *(T* **173**) *or* 13½ *(T* **174**).

723	**172**	½d. slate-black	5	5
724	,,	1d. orange	5	5
725	,,	1½d. brown-lake ..	10	5
726	,,	2d. bluish green ..	8	5
727	,,	3d. vermilion ..	8	5
728	,,	4d. blue	12	5
729	,,	6d. purple	35	8
730	,,	8d. carmine	30	15
731	**173**	9d. brown & brt. green	30	10
732	,,	1s. black & carmine-red (Die I)	25	10
		a. Die II (1958)	40·00	10·00
733	,,	1s. 6d. blk. & brt. blue	50	12
733*a*	,,	1s. 9d. black and red-orange	90	20
733*b*	**174**	2s. 6d. brown	10·00	4·00
734	,,	3s. bluish green ..	3·50	60
735	,,	5s. carmine	3·50	1·25
736	,,	10s. deep ultramarine ..	12·00	6·00
723/36		.. .. *Set of* 16	29·00	12·00

Dates of issue:—15.12.53. 1½d.; 1.7.57. 1s. 9d., 2s. 6d.; 1.3.54, others.

1s. Dies I and II. The two dies of the Queen's portrait differ in the shading on the sleeve at right. The long lines running upwards from left to right are strong in Die I and weaker in Die II. In the upper part of the shading the fine cross-hatching is visible in Die I only between the middle two of the four long lines, but in Die II it extends clearly across all four lines.

In the lower part of the shading the strength of the long lines in Die I makes the cross-hatching appear subdued, whereas in Die II the weaker long lines make the cross-hatching more prominent.

Centre plates 1A, 1B and 2B are Die I; 3A and 3B are Die II.

For stamps as T **172** but with larger figures of value see Nos. 745/51.

1958 NEW PAPER. A new white opaque paper first came into use in August 1958 and was used for later printings of Nos. 733*a*, 745, 747/9, O159, O161, O163/4, O166 and L54. It is slightly thicker than the paper previously used, but obviously different in colour (white, against cream) and opacity (the previous paper being *relatively* transparent).

175. Young Climber and Mts. Aspiring and Everest.

(Des. J. Berry. Recess; vignette litho. Bradbury, Wilkinson.)

1954 (4 Oct.). *Health Stamps.* W **98.** P 13½.

737	**175**	1½d.+½d. sepia and deep violet	10	10
738	,,	2d.+1d. sepia and blue-black	10	10

176. Maori Mail-carrier. **177.** Queen Elizabeth II.

178. Douglas " DC 3 " Airliner.

(Des. R. M. Conly (2d.), J. Berry (3d.), A. G. Mitchell (4d.). Recess. D.L.R.)

1955 (18 July). *Centenary of First New Zealand Postage Stamps.* W **98.** P 14 (2*d.*), 14×14½ (3*d.*) *or* 13 (4*d.*).

739	**176**	2d. sepia and deep green	8	5
740	**177**	3d. brown-red	10	5
741	**178**	4d. black and bright blue	20	20

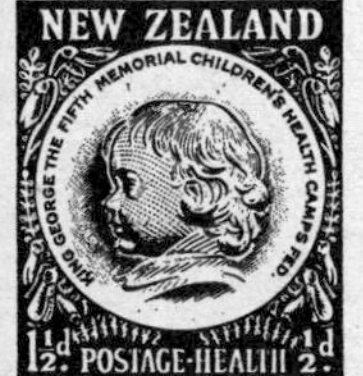

179. Children's Health Camps, Federation Emblem. **180**

(Des. E. M. Taylor. Recess. B.W.)

1955 (3 Oct.). *Health Stamps.* W **98** (*sideways*). P 13½×13.

742	**179**	1½d.+½d. sepia & orange-brown	10	10
743	,,	2d.+1d. red-brn. & grn.	12	12
744	,,	3d.+1d. sepia and deep rose-red	15	15
		a. Centre omitted ..	£2000	

1955–59. *As Nos.* 724/30 *but larger figures of value and stars omitted from lower right corner.*

745	**180**	1d. orange (12.7.56) ..	5	5
746	,,	1½d. brown-lake (1.12.55)	15	10
747	,,	2d. bluish green (19.3.56)	5	5
748	,,	3d. vermilion (1.5.56) ..	15	10
749	,,	4d. blue (3.2.58)	15	8
750	,,	6d. purple (20.10.55)	20	5
751	,,	8d. chestnut (1.12.59) ..	1·75	1·50
745/51		.. .. *Set of* 7	2·00	1·80

See note *re* white opaque paper after No. 736. No. 751 exists only on white paper.

181. " The Whalers of Foveaux Strait ".

182. " Farming ".

183. *Notornis.*

(Des. E. R. Leeming (2d.), L. C. Mitchell (3d.), M. R. Smith (8d.). Recess. D.L.R.)

1956 (Jan.). *Southland Centennial.* W **98.** P 13½×13 (8*d.*) *or* 13×12½ (*others*).

752	**181**	2d. deep blue-green ..	5	5
753	**182**	3d. sepia	8	8
754	**183**	8d. slate-violet & rose-red	40	40

184. Children Picking Apples.

(Des. L. C. Mitchell, after photo by J. F. Louden. Recess. B.W.)

1956 (24 Sept.). *Health Stamps.* W **98.** P 13×13½.

755	**184**	1½d.+½d. purple-brown ..	10	10
		a. Blackish brown ..	1·25	1·50
756	,,	2d.+1d. blue-green ..	12	10
757	,,	3d.+1d. claret	15	10

185. New Zealand Lamb and Map. **187.** Sir Truby King.

186. Lamb, *Dunedin* and Modern Ship.

(Des. M. Goaman. Photo. Harrison.)

1957 (15 Feb.). *75th Anniv. of First Export of N.Z. Lamb.* W **98** (*sideways on* 4*d.*). P 14×14½ (4*d.*) *or* 14½×14 (8*d.*).

758	**185**	4d. blue	25	25
759	**186**	8d. deep orange-red ..	50	50

(Des. M. R. Smith. Recess. B.W.)

1957 (14 May). *50th Anniv. of Plunket Society.* W **98.** P 13.

760	**187**	3d. bright carmine-red ..	8	5

188. Life-savers in Action.

189. Children on Seashore.

(Des. L. Cutten (2d.), L. C. Mitchell (3d.). Recess. Waterlow.)

1957 (25 Sept.). *Health Stamps.* W **98** (*sideways*). P 13½.

761	**188**	2d.+1d. black & emerald	10	10
		a. Wmk. upright	30	40
762	**189**	3d.+1d. ultram. & rose-red	10	10
		a. Wmk. upright	30	40
MS762*b*		Two sheets each 112×96 mm. with Nos. 761 and 762 in blocks of 6 (2×3). *Per pair*	2·00	2·00
MS762*c*		As last but with Nos. 761a and 762a. *Per pair*	4·00	4·50

Nos. 761a and 762a only exist from No. **MS**762*c*.

2d

●

(190)

1958 (15 Jan.). *No. 746 surch. as T* **190.**

763 **180** 2d. on 1½d. brown-lake .. 8 5
a. Smaller dot in surch. .. 8 5
b. Error. Surch. on No. 725 30·00 25·00

Diameter of dot on No. 763 is 4¼ mm.; on No. 763a 3¾ mm.

191. Girls' Life Brigade Cadet. **192.** Boys' Brigade Bugler.

(Des. J. Berry. Photo. Harrison & Sons.)

1958 (20 Aug.). *Health Stamps. W* **98.** *P* 14×14½.

764 **191** 2d.+1d. green 10 10
765 **192** 3d.+1d. blue 10 10
MS765*a* Two sheets each 104×124 mm. with Nos. 764/5 in blocks of 6 (3×2). *Per pair* 2·00 2·00

(Recess. Commonwealth Bank of Australia Note Ptg. Branch.)

1958 (27 Aug.). *30th Anniv. of First Air Crossing of the Tasman Sea. As T* **120** *of Australia, but inscr.* "NEW ZEALAND". *W* **98** *(sideways). P* 14×14½.

766 6d. deep ultramarine .. 30 25

193. Seal of Nelson.

(Des. M. J. Macdonald. Recess. B.W.)

1958 (29 Sept.). *Centenary of City of Nelson. W* **98.** *P* 13½×13.

767 **193** 3d. carmine 8 5

194. "Pania" Statue, Napier. **196.** Maori sheep-shearer.

195. Gannets on Cape Kidnappers.

(Des. M. R. Smith (2d.), J. Berry (3d.), L. C. Mitchell (8d.). Photo. Harrison.)

1958 (3 Nov.). *Centenary of Hawke's Bay Province. W* **98** *(sideways on 3d.). P* 14½×14 *(3d.) or* 13½×14½ *(others).*

768 **194** 2d. yellow-green 8 5
769 **195** 3d. blue 8 5
770 **196** 8d. red-brown 70 70

197. "Kiwi" Jamboree Badge.

(Des. Mrs. S. M. Collins. Recess. Bradbury, Wilkinson.)

1959 (5 Jan.). *Pan-Pacific Scout Jamboree, Auckland. W* **98.** *P* 13½×13.

771 **197** 3d. sepia and carmine .. 10 5

198. Careening H.M. Bark *Endeavour* at Ship Cove.

199. Shipping Wool, Wairau Bar, 1857.
200. Salt Industry, Grassmere.

(Des. G. R. Bull and G. R. Smith. Photo. Harrison.)

1959 (2 Mar.). *Centenary of Marlborough Province. W* **98** *(sideways) P* 14½×14.

772 **198** 2d. green 10 10
773 **199** 3d. deep blue 8 5
774 **200** 8d. light brown 65 65

201. Red Cross Flag.

(Photo. Harrison.)

1959 (3 June). *Red Cross Commemoration. W* **98** *(sideways). P* 14½×14.

775 **201** 3d.+1d. red & ultram. .. 15 10
a. Red Cross omitted .. £500

202. Tete (Grey Teal). **203.** Poaka (Pied Stilt).

(Des. Display Section, G.P.O. Photo. Harrison.)

1959 (16 Sept.). *Health Stamps. W* **98** *(sideways). P* 14×14½.

776 **202** 2d.+1d. greenish yellow, olive and rose-red .. 10 10
777 **203** 3d.+ 1d. black, pink and light blue 15 12
a. Pink ptg. omitted .. 75·00
b. Pink ptg. shifted to left (at least 2¼ mm.) .. .. 12·00
MS777*c* Two sheets each 95×109 mm. with Nos. 776/7 in blocks of 6 (3×2). *Per pair* 2·00 2·00

204. "The Explorer". **205.** "The Gold Digger".

206. "The Pioneer Woman".

(Des. G. R. Bull and G. R. Smith. Photo. Harrison.)

1960 (16 May). *Centenary of Westland Province. W* **98.** *P* 14×14½.

778 **204** 2d. deep dull green .. 10 8
779 **205** 3d. orange-red 10 8
780 **206** 8d. grey-black 65 65

207. Manuka (Tea Tree). **208.** Karaka.

209. Kowhai Ngutu-kaka (Kaka Beak). **209***a*. Titoki.

210. Kowhai. **211.** Puarangi (Hibiscus).

211a. Matua Tikumu (Mountain Daisy).

212. Pikiarero (Clematis).

212a. Koromiko.

213. Rata.

214. National Flag.

216. Trout.

217. Tiki.

215. Timber Industry.

218. Aerial Top Dressing.

219. Taniwha (Maori Rock Drawing).

220. Butter Making.

221. Tongariro National Park and Château.

221a. Tongariro National Park and Château.

222. Sutherland Falls.

224. Pohutu Geyser.

223. Tasman Glacier.

(Des. Harrison & Sons (½d.), G. F. Fuller (1d., 3d., 6d.), A. G. Mitchell (2d., 4d., 5d., 8d., 3s., 10s., £1), P.O. Public Relations Division (7d.), P.O. Publicity Section (9d.), J. Berry (1s., 1s. 6d.), R. E. Barwick (1s. 3d.), J. C. Boyd (1s. 9d.), D. F. Kee (2s.), L. C. Mitchell (2s. 6d., 5s.). Photo. De La Rue & Co. (½d., 1d., 2d., 3d., 4d., 6d., 8d.) or Harrison & Sons (others).)

1960 (11 July)–**66.** *Ordinary or chalk-surfaced paper* (C). *W* **98** (*sideways on* 2½d., 5d., 1s. 3d., 1s. 6d., 2s. 6d., 3s. *and* 10s.). *P* 14×15 (1s. 3d., 1s. 6d., 2s., 5s., £1) *or* 15×14 (*others*).

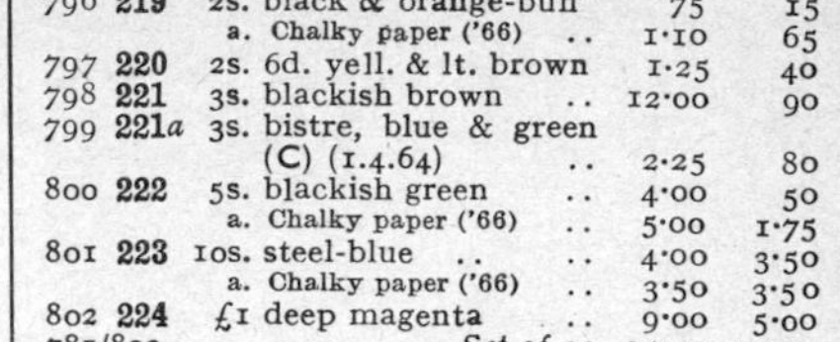

No.	Type	Description	Unused	Used
781	**207**	½d. grey, green & cerise (1.9.60)	5	5
782	**208**	1d. orange, green, lake and brown (1.9.60) ..	5	5
		a. Coil. Perf. 14½×13. Wmk. sideways (11.63) ..	35	35
		b. Chalky paper ('65?) ..	8	5
783	**209**	2d. carmine, black, yellow and green ..	5	5
784	**209a**	2½d. red, yellow, black & green (C) (1.11.61) ..	5	5
785	**210**	3d. yell., grn., yell.-brn. & dp. greenish blue (1.9.60)	10	8
		a. Coil. Perf. 14½×13. Wmk. sideways (3.10.63) ..	50	50
		b. Chalky paper ('65?) ..	15	10
786	**211**	4d. purple, buff, yellow-green & light blue ..	10	8
		a. Chalky paper ('65?) ..	70·00	5·00
787	**211a**	5d. yell., dp. grn., blk. & violet (C) (14.5.62) ..	20	10
788	**212**	6d. lilac, green & deep bluish green (1.9.60)	25	10
		a. No wmk.	6·00	5·00
		b. Chalky paper ('66?) ..	25	25
788c	**212a**	7d. red, green, yellow & pale red (C) (16.3.66)	35	35
789	**213**	8d rose-red yellow green and grey (1.9.60) ..	30	10
790	**214**	9d. red & ultram. (1.9.60)	30	10
791	**215**	1s. brown & deep green	30	10
792	**216**	1s. 3d. carmine sepia & bright blue (*shades*)	65	15
793	**217**	1s. 6d. olive-green and orange-brown ..	65	15
794	**218**	1s. 9d. bistre-brown ..	3·00	45
795	,,	1s. 9d. orge.-red, bl., grn. & yell. (C) (4.11.63)	60	25
796	**219**	2s. black & orange-buff	75	15
		a. Chalky paper ('66) ..	1·10	65
797	**220**	2s. 6d. yell. & lt. brown	1·25	40
798	**221**	3s. blackish brown ..	12·00	90
799	**221a**	3s. bistre, blue & green (C) (1.4.64) ..	2·25	80
800	**222**	5s. blackish green ..	4·00	50
		a. Chalky paper ('66) ..	5·00	1·75
801	**223**	10s. steel-blue	4·00	3·50
		a. Chalky paper ('66) ..	3·50	3·50
802	**224**	£1 deep magenta ..	9·00	5·00
781/802		.. .. *Set of* 23	35·00	12·00

"MISSING COLOURS" (in the above issue are known in the following:—½d. (green and grey), 1d. (orange), 2d. (black and yellow), 2½d. red, yellow, green and red and green on same stamp), 3d. (yellow, green and brown), 4d. (purple, buff and yellow-green), 5d. (yellow), 6d. (lilac and green), 9d. (red), 1s. 3d. (carmine), and 2s. 6d. (yellow).

Nos. 782a and 785a were replaced by coils with upright watermark perf. 15×14, in 1966.

Chalky paper. The chalk-surfaced paper is not only whiter but also thicker, making the watermark difficult to see.

225. Kotare (Kingfisher).

226. Kereru (Wood Pigeon).

(Des. Display Section, G.P.O. Recess. Bradbury, Wilkinson.)

1960 (10 Aug.). *Health Stamps.* *W* **98.** *P* 13½.

No.	Type	Description	Unused	Used
803	**225**	2d.+1d. sepia & turq.-blue	15	10
		a. Perf. 11½×11 ..	30	30
804	**226**	3d.+1d. dp. purple-brown and orange ..	15	12
		a. Perf. 11½×11 ..	30	30
MS804b		Two sheets each 95×107 mm. with Nos. 803a and 804a in blocks of 6 (3×2) *Per pair*	3·00	3·50

227. "The Adoration of the Shepherds" (after Rembrandt).

(Photo. Harrison & Sons.)

1960 (1 Nov.). *Christmas Issue.* *W* **98.** *P* 12.

No.	Type	Description	Unused	Used
805	**227**	2d. red & dp. brn./*cream*	1·00	20
		a. Red omitted	£250	

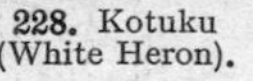

228. Kotuku (White Heron). **229.** Karearea (Bush Hawk).

(Des. Display Section, G.P.O. Recess. B.W.)

1961 (2 Aug.). *Health Stamps.* *W* **98.** *P* 13½.
806 **228** 2d. + 1d. black and purple 15 10
807 **229** 3d. + 1d. deep sepia and yellow-green 15 10
MS807*a* Two sheets each 97×121 mm. with Nos. 806/7 in blocks of 6 (3×2) *Per pair* 2·50 2·50

2½d 2½d

(230) (231)

1961 (1 Sept.). *No.* 748 *surch. with T* **230** (*wide setting*).
808 **180** 2½d. on 3d. vermilion .. 5 5
a. Narrow setting (T 231) .. 8 8
b. Pair, wide and narrow .. 5·50 5·00

The difference in the settings is in the overall width of the new value, caused by two different spacings between the " 2 ", " ½ " and " d ".

232. " Adoration of the Magi " (Dürer).

(Photo. Harrison.)

1961 (16 Oct.). *Christmas.* *W* **98** (*sideways*). *P* 14½×14.
809 **232** 2½d. multicoloured .. 65 20

233. Morse Key and Port Hills, Lyttleton.

234. Modern Teleprinter.

(Des. A. G. Mitchell (3d.), L. C. Mitchell (8d.). Photo. Harrison & Sons.)

1962 (1 June). *Telegraph Centenary.* *W* **98** (*sideways*). *P* 14½×14.
810 **233** 3d. sepia and bluish green 8 5
a. Green omitted £200
811 **234** 8d. black and brown-red 65 65
a. Imperf. (pair) £375
b. Black omitted £120

No. 811a comes from a sheet with the two top rows imperforate and the third row imperforate on three sides.

235. Kakariki (Parakeet). **236.** Tieke (Saddleback).

(Des. Display Section, G.P.O. Photo. De La Rue.)

1962 (3 Oct.). *Health.* *W* **98.** *P* 15×14.
812 **235** 2½d.+1d. multicoloured 15 10
a. Orange ptg. omitted ..
813 **236** 3d.+1d. multicoloured 20 12
a. Orange ptg. omitted .. £300
MS813*b* Two sheets each 96×101 mm. with Nos. 812/3 in blocks of 6 (3×2) *Per pair* 2·75 3·00

237. " Madonna in Prayer " (after Sassoferrato).

(Photo. Harrison & Sons.)

1962 (15 Oct.). *Christmas.* *W* **98.** *P* 14½×14.
814 **237** 2½d. multicoloured .. 50 12

238. Prince Andrew. **239.**

(Design after photographs by Studio Lisa, London. Recess. De La Rue.)

1963 (7 Aug.). *Health Stamps.* *W* **98.** *P* 14.
815 **238** 2½d.+1d. ultram. (*shades*) 15 10
816 **239** 3d.+1d. carmine .. 20 15
MS816*a* Two sheets each 93×100 mm. with Nos. 815/6 in blocks of 6 (3×2) .. .. *per pair* 2·00 2·50

240. " The Holy Family " (Titian).

(Photo. Harrison.)

1963 (14 Oct.). *Christmas.* *W* **98** (*sideways*). *P* 12½.
817 **240** 2½d. multicoloured .. 15 10
a. Imperf. (pair).. .. £120

241. Steam Locomotive " Pilgrim " and " DG " Diesel Electric Loco.

242. Diesel Express and Mt. Ruapehu.

(Des. Commercial Art Section, N.Z. Railways Photo. De La Rue.)

1963 (25 Nov.). *Railway Centenary.* *W* **98** (*sideways*). *P* 14.
818 **241** 3d. multicoloured .. 12 10
a. Blue (sky) omitted .. £100
819 **242** 1s. 9d. multicoloured .. 1·00 1·00
a. Red (value) omitted .. £275

1963 (3 Dec.). *Opening of COMPAC (Trans Pacific Telephone Cable). As T* **174** *of Australia but inscr.* " NEW ZEALAND ". *No wmk.* *P* 13½
820 8d. red, blue, black & yellow 70 70

243. Road Map and Car Steering-wheel.

(Des. L. C. Mitchell. Photo. Harrison.)

1964 (1 May). *Road Safety Campaign.* *W* **98** *P* 15×14.
821 **243** 3d. blk., ochre-yell. & bl. 10 8

244. Tarapunga (gull).

245. Korora (penguin).

(Des. Display Section G.P.O., after Miss T. Kelly. Photo. Harrison.)

1964 (5 Aug.). *Health Stamps.* W **98** *P* 14½.
822 **244** 2½d.+1d. multicoloured 15 10
823 **245** 3d.+1d. multicoloured 20 12
MS823*a* Two sheets each 171×84 mm. with Nos. 822/3 in blocks of 8 (4×2) *Per pair* 4·00 4·50

246. Rev. S. Marsden taking first Christian service at Rangihoua Bay, 1814.

(Des. L. C. Mitchell. Photo. Harrison.)

1964 (12 Oct.). *Christmas.* W **98** (*sideways*). *P* 14×13½.
824 **246** 2½d. multicoloured .. 20 12

7D

POSTAGE

(247)

1964 (14 Dec.). *As Type* F **6**, *but without value, surch. with T* **247**. W **98**. *Unsurfaced paper. P* 14×13½.
825 F **6** 7d. carmine-red 15 25

248. Anzac Cove.

249. Anzac Cove and Poppy.

(Des. R. M. Conly. Photo. Harrison.)

1965 (14 Apr.). *50th Anniv. of Gallipoli Landing.* W **98.** *P* 12½.
826 **248** 4d. yellow-brown .. 15 15
827 **249** 5d. green and red .. 35 35

250. I.T.U. Emblem and Symbols.

(Photo. Harrison.)

1965 (17 May). *I.T.U. Centenary.* W **98.** *P* 14½×14.
828 **250** 9d. blue & pale chocolate 25 25

(From photograph by Karsh. Photo. Note Ptg. Branch, Reserve Bank of Australia.)

1965 (24 May). *Churchill Commemoration. As T* **186** *of Australia but inscr.* " NEW ZEALAND ". *P* 13½
829 7d. black, pale grey and light blue.. .. .. 25 25

251. Wellington Provincial Council Building.

(Des. from painting by L. B. Temple (1867). Photo. Harrison.)

1965 (26 July). *Centenary of Government in Wellington.* W **98** (*sideways*). *P* 14½×14.
830 **251** 4d. multicoloured .. 8 5

252. Kaka.

253. Piwakawaka (fantail), (after Miss T. Kelly).

(Des. Display Section, G.P.O. Photo. Harrison.)

1965 (4 Aug.). *Health Stamps.* W **98.** *P* 14×14½.
831 **252** 3d.+1d. multicoloured .. 12 15
832 **253** 4d.+1d. multicoloured .. 15 12
a. Green (" POSTAGE HEALTH " and on leaves) omitted .. ..
MS832*b* Two sheets each 100×109 mm. with Nos. 831/2 in blocks of 6 (3×2) *Per pair* 3·00 3·50

254. I.C.Y. Emblem.

(Litho. De La Rue.)

1965 (28 Sept.). *International Co-operation Year.* W **98** (*sideways*). *P* 14.
833 **254** 4d. carmine-red and light yellow-olive . . 8 5

255. " The Two Trinities ", after Murillo.

(Photo. Harrison.)

1965 (11 Oct.). *Christmas.* W **98.** *P* 13½×14.
834 **255** 3d. multicoloured .. 20 12

256. Arms of New Zealand.

257. Parliament House, Wellington, and Badge.
258. Wellington from Mt. Victoria.

(Des. Display Section, G.P.O. Photo. De La Rue.)

1965 (30 Nov.). *11th Commonwealth Parliamentary Conference. P* 14.
835 **256** 4d. multicoloured .. 20 15
a. Blue (incl. value) omitted £325
836 **257** 9d. multicoloured .. 30 20
837 **258** 2s. multicoloured .. 1·25 1·10

259. " Progress " Arrowhead.

260. Bellbird.

261. Weka (rail).

(Des. Display Section, G.P.O. Photo. Harrison.)

1966 (5 Jan.). *Fourth National Scout Jamboree, Trentham.* W **98.** *P* 14×15.
838 **259** 4d. gold & myrtle-green 10 5
a. Gold (arrowhead) omitted £225

(Des. Display Section, G.P.O. Photo. Harrison.)

1966 (3 Aug.). *Health Stamps.* W **98** (*sideways*). *P* 14×14½.
839 **260** 3d.+1d. multicoloured .. 10 12
840 **261** 4d.+1d. multicoloured .. 15 12
a. Deep brown (values and date) omitted £200
MS841 Two sheets each 107×91 mm. Nos. 839/40 in blocks of 6 (3×2) *Per pair* 2·00 2·00

In No. 840*a* besides the value, " 1966 " and " Weka " are also omitted and the bird, etc. appears as light brown.

262. " The Virgin with Child " (after Maratta).

(Photo. Harrison.)

1966 (3 Oct.). *Christmas.* W **98** (*sideways*). *P* 14½.
842 **262** 3d. multicoloured .. 12 12

263. Queen Victoria and Queen Elizabeth II.

264. Half-sovereign of 1867 and Commemorative Dollar Coin.

(Des. Display Section, G.P.O. Photo. Harrison.)

1967 (3 Feb.). *Centenary of New Zealand Post Office Savings Bank.* W **98** *(sideways on* 4d.*).* *P* 14 × 14½.

843	**263**	4d. black, gold & maroon	12	5
844	**264**	9d. gold, silver, black, light blue and deep green ..	25	25

(New currency. 100 cents = 1 dollar.)

265. Manuka (Tea Tree).

266. Pohutu Geyser.

1967 (10 July)–**70.** *Decimal Currency. Designs as earlier issues, but with values inscr. in decimal currency as T* **265/6**. *Chalky paper.* W **98** *(sideways on* 8, 10, 20, 50 *c. and* $2*).* *P* 13½ × 14 (½ *c. to* 3 *c.,* 5 *c. and* 7 *c.*), 14½ × 14 (4 *c.,* 6 *c.,* 8 *c.,* 10 *c.,* 25 *c.,* 30 *c. and* $1) *or* 14 × 14½ (15 *c.,* 20 *c.,* 50 *c. and* $2).

845	**265**	½ c. pale blue, yellow-green and cerise ..	5	5
846	**208**	1 c. yellow, carmine, green & light brown	5	5
		a. Booklet pane. Five stamps plus one printed label..	40	
847	**209**	2 c. carmine, black, yellow and green ..	5	5
848	**210**	2½ c. yell., grn., yell.-brn. & dp. bluish green	8	5
		a. Deep bluish green omitted*	£300	
		b. Imperf. (pair)†	75·00	
849	**211**	3 c. purple, buff, yell.-grn. & lt. grnish. bl.	8	5
850	**211a**	4 c. yellow, deep green, black and violet ..	10	5
851	**212**	5 c. lilac, yellow-olive and bluish green ..	12	5
852	**212a**	6 c. red, green, yellow and light pink ..	12	8
853	**213**	7 c. rose-red, yellow, green and grey ..	15	8
854	**214**	8 c. red & ultramarine	15	8
855	**215**	10 c. brown & dp. green	55	40
856	**217**	15 c. olive green and orange-brown ..	60	75
857	**219**	20 c. black and buff ..	50	10
858	**220**	25 c. yellow & lt. brown	1·50	1·25
859	**221a**	30 c. olive-yellow, green and greenish blue	80	45
		a. No wmk. ('70) ..	80	50

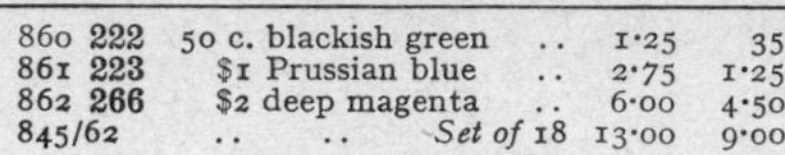

860	**222**	50 c. blackish green ..	1·25	35
861	**223**	$1 Prussian blue ..	2·75	1·25
862	**266**	$2 deep magenta ..	6·00	4·50
845/62		.. .. *Set of* 18	13·00	9·00

* This occurred on one horizontal row of ten, affecting the background colour so that the value is also missing. In the row above and the row below, the colour was partially omitted. The price is for a vertical strip.

† This comes from a sheet of which the six right-hand vertical rows were completely imperforate and the top, bottom and left-hand margins had been removed.

The 4 c., 30 c. and 50 c. exist with PVA gum as well as gum arabic. No. 859a exists with PVA gum only.

For $4 to $10 in the " Arms " type, see under Postal Fiscal stamps.

See also Nos. 870, etc.

268. Running with Ball.

269. Positioning for place-kick. (*Horiz.*)

(Des. L. C. Mitchell. Photo. Harrison.)

1967 (2 Aug.). *Health Stamps. Rugby Football.* W **98** *(sideways on* 2½ *c.).* *P* 14½ × 14 (2½ *c.*) *or* 14 × 14½ (3 *c.*).

867	**268**	2½ c. + 1 c. multicoloured	10	10
868	**269**	3 c. + 1 c. multicoloured	12	10
MS869		Two sheets: 76 × 130 mm. (2½ c.) and 130 × 76 mm. (3 c.). Nos. 867/8 in blocks of six. *Per pair*	2·00	2·00

270. Trawler and Catch.

271. Brown Trout.

277. Fox Glacier, Westland National Park.

272. Apples and Orchard.

273. Forest and Timber.

274. Sheep and the " Woolmark ".

275. Consignments of Beef and Herd of Cattle

276. Dairy Farm, Mt. Egmont and Butter Consignment.

(Des. Display Section, G.P.O. (7, 8, 10, 18, 20, 25 c. and 28 c. from photo), R. M. Conly (7½ c.). Litho. Bradbury, Wilkinson (7, 8, 18, 20 c.) or photo. De La Rue (7½ c.) and Harrison (10, 25, 28 c.). Others (15 c., $2) as before.)

1967–69. *New values and designs or old designs in new colours. Chalky paper (except* 7, 8, 18, 20 *c.). No wmk.* (7, 8, 20 *c.*) *or* W **98** *(sideways on* 7½, 10, 15, 25 *c., upright on* 18 *c.,* 28 *c.,* $2.). *P* 13½ (7, 7½ *c.*), 13 × 13½ (8, 18, 20 *c.*), 14½ × 14 (10, 25 *c.*) *or* 14 × 14½ (15 *c.,* 28 *c.,* $2).

870	**270**	7 c. mult. (3.12.69) ..	35	25
871	**271**	7½ c. mult.* (29.8.67) ..	30	30
		a. Wmk. upright (10.68)	30	30
872	**272**	8 c. mult. (8.7.69) ..	30	25
873	**273**	10 c. mult. (2.4.68) ..	30	12
874	**217**	15 c. apple-green, myrtle-green and carmine† (19.3.68)	50	30
875	**274**	18 c. mult. (8.7.69) ..	45	35
876	**275**	20 c. mult. (8.7.69) ..	50	35
877	**276**	25 c. mult. (10.12.68) ..	80	45
878	**277**	28 c. mult. (30.7.68) ..	60	30
879	**266**	$2 black, ochre and pale blue (10.12.68) ..	5·00	5·00
870/79		.. .. *Set of* 10	8·50	7·00

* No. 871 was originally issued to commemorate the introduction of the brown trout into New Zealand.

† No. 874 is slightly larger than No. 856, measuring 21 × 25 mm. and the inscriptions and numerals differ in size.

278. "The Adoration of the Shepherds" (Poussin).

(Photo. Harrison.)

1967 (3 Oct.). *Christmas.* *W* **98** (*sideways*). *P* 13½ × 14.
880 **278** 2½ c. multicoloured .. 12 10

279. Mount Aspiring, Aurora Australis and Southern Cross.

280. Sir James Hector (founder).

(Des. J. Berry. Litho. De La Rue.)

1967 (10 Oct.). *Centenary of the Royal Society of New Zealand.* *W* **98** (*sideways on* 4 *c.*). *P* 14 (4 *c.*) *or* 13 × 14 (8 *c.*).
881 **279** 4 c. multicoloured .. 12 12
882 **280** 8 c. multicoloured .. 25 25

281. Open Bible.

(Des. Display Section, G.P.O. Litho. De La Rue.)

1968 (23 Apr.). *Centenary of Maori Bible.* *W* **98.** *P* 13½.
883 **281** 3 c. multicoloured .. 8 8
a. Gold (inscr. etc.) omitted

282. Soldiers and Tank.

283. Airmen, "Canberra" and "Kittyhawk" Aircraft.

284. Sailors and Warships.

(Des. L. C. Mitchell. Litho. De La Rue.)

1968 (7 May). *New Zealand Armed Forces.* *W* **98** (*sideways*). *P* 14 × 13½.
884 **282** 4 c. multicoloured .. 10 5
885 **283** 10 c. multicoloured .. 40 35
886 **284** 28 c. multicoloured .. 1·00 80

285. Boy breasting Tape, and Olympic Rings.

286. Girl swimming and Olympic Rings.

(Des. L. C. Mitchell. Photo. Harrison.)

1968 (7 Aug.). *Health Stamps.* *P* 14½ × 14.
887 **285** 2½ c.+1 c. multicoloured 12 12
888 **286** 3 c.+1 c. multicoloured 15 12
MS889 Two sheets each 145 × 95 mm. Nos. 887/8 in blocks of six. .. .. *Per pair* 2·00 2·00

287. Placing Votes in Ballot Box.

288. Human Rights Emblem.

(Des. J. Berry. Photo. Japanese Govt. Ptg. Bureau, Tokyo.)

1968 (19 Sept.). *75th Anniv. of Universal Suffrage in New Zealand.* *P* 13.
890 **287** 3 c. ochre olive-green and light blue .. 10 8

(Photo. Japanese Govt. Ptg. Bureau, Tokyo.)

1968 (19 Sept.). *Human Rights Year.* *P* 13.
891 **288** 10 c. scarlet, yellow and deep green 30 30

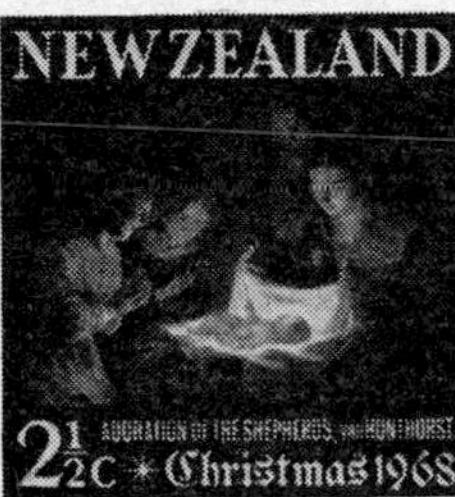

289. "Adoration of the Shepherds" (G. van Honthorst).

(Photo. Harrison.)

1968 (1 Oct.). *Christmas.* *W* **98** (*sideways*). *P* 14 × 14½.
892 **289** 2½ c. multicoloured .. 8 8

290. I.L.O. Emblem.

(Photo. Harrison.)

1969 (11 Feb.). *50th Anniv. of International Labour Organization.* *W* **98** (*sideways*). *P* 14½ × 14.
893 **290** 7 c. black & carmine-red 25 25

291. Supreme Court Building, Auckland.

292 Law Society's Coat-of-Arms.

293. "Justice" (from Memorial Window in University of Canterbury, Christchurch).

(Des. R. M. Conly. Litho. Bradbury, Wilkinson.)

1969 (8 Apr.). *Centenary of New Zealand Law Society.* *P* 13½ × 13 (3 *c.*) *or* 13 × 13½ (*others*).
894 **291** 3 c. mult. (*shades*) .. 8 8
895 **292** 10 c. multicoloured .. 30 30
896 **293** 18 c. mult. (*shades*) .. 75 60

294. Otago University. (*Vert.*)

295. Student being conferred with Degree.

(Des. R. M. Conly. Litho. Bradbury, Wilkinson.)

1969 (3 June). *Centenary of Otago University.* *P* 13 × 13½ (3 *c.*) *or* 13½ × 13 (10 *c.*).
897 **294** 3 c. multicoloured .. 8 8
898 **295** 10 c. multicoloured .. 35 30

296. Boys playing Cricket.

297. Girls playing Cricket. (*Horiz.*)

HAVE YOU READ THE NOTES AT THE BEGINNING OF THIS CATALOGUE?

These often provide answers to the enquiries we receive.

298. Dr. Elizabeth Gunn (founder of First Children's Health Camp).

(Des. R. M. Conly (4 c.); L. C. Mitchell (others). Litho. Bradbury, Wilkinson.)

1969 (6 Aug.). *Health Stamps.* *P* $12\frac{1}{2} \times 13$ (*No.* 901) *or* $13 \times 12\frac{1}{2}$ (*others*).

899	**296**	$2\frac{1}{2}$ c.+1 c. multicoloured	10	10
900	**297**	3 c.+1 c. multicoloured	15	15
901	**298**	4 c.+1 c. brown and ultramarine	20	20
MS902		Two sheets each 144×84 mm. Nos. 899/900 in blocks of six .. .. *Pair*	2·00	2·00

299. Oldest existing House in New Zealand, and Old Stone Mission Store, Kerikeri.

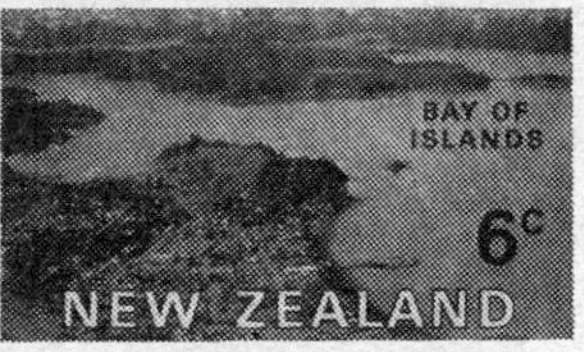

300. View of Bay of Islands.

(Litho. D.L.R.)

1969 (18 Aug.). *Early European Settlement in New Zealand, and* 150*th Anniv. of Kerikeri.* *W* **98** (*sideways*). *P* $13 \times 13\frac{1}{2}$.

903	**299**	4 c. multicoloured ..	30	30
904	**300**	6 c. multicoloured ..	50	50

301. "The Nativity" (Federico Fiori).

(Photo. Harrison.)

1969 (1 Oct.). *Christmas.* *P* 13×14. A. *W* **98.** B. *No wmk.*

			A.		B. ('69).	
905	**301**	$2\frac{1}{2}$ c. mult. ..	10	8	10	8

302. Captain Cook. Transit of Venus and "Octant".

303. Sir Joseph Banks (naturalist) and Outline of the *Endeavour*.

304. Dr. Daniel Solander (botanist) and his Plant.

305. Queen Elizabeth II and Cook's Chart, 1769.

(Des. Miss E. Mayo. Photo; portraits embossed. Harrison.)

1969 (9 Oct.). *Bicentenary of Captain Cook's Landing in New Zealand.* *P* $14\frac{1}{2} \times 14$.

906	**302**	4 c. black, cerise & blue	12	12
907	**303**	6 c. slate-green, purple-brown and black ..	20	20
908	**304**	18 c. purple-brown, slate-green and black ..	55	55
909	**305**	28 c. cerise, black & blue	85	85
MS910		109×90 mm. Nos. 906/9 ..	3·75	3·75

306. Girl, Wheat Field and C.O.R.S.O. Emblem.

307. Mother feeding her Child, Dairy Herd and C.O.R.S.O. Emblem.

(Des. L. C. Mitchell. Photo. Japanese Govt Printing Bureau, Tokyo.)

1969 (18 Nov.). 25*th Anniv. of C.O.R.S.O* (*Council of Organizations for Relief Service* [illegible] *Overseas*). *P* 13.

911	**306**	7 c. multicoloured ..	25	2[illegible]
912	**307**	8 c. multicoloured ..	30	3[illegible]

308. "Cardigan Bay" (champion trotter).

(Des. L. C. Mitchell. Photo. Courvoisier.)

1970 (28 Jan.). *Return of "Cardigan Bay"* [illegible] *New Zealand.* *P* $11\frac{1}{2}$.

913	**308**	10 c. multicoloured ..	30	3[illegible]

309. Red Admiral Butterfly.

310. Queen Elizabeth II and New Zealand Coat-of-Arms.

(Des. Miss E. Hunter ($\frac{1}{2}$ c., 1 c., 2 c., 18 c., 20 c. Miss E. Mayo ($2\frac{1}{2}$ c. to 7 c.), D. B. Stevenso[illegible] ($7\frac{1}{2}$ c., 8 c.), M. Cleverley (10 c., 15 c., 25 c 30 c., $1, $2), M. V. Askew (23 c., 50 c. Photo. Harrison ($\frac{1}{2}$ c. to 20 c.), Ensched[illegible] (23 c., 50 c.), B.W. (25 c., 30 c.), Courvoisi[illegible] ($1, $2).

1970–76. *Various designs as T* **309/10.** *W* 9[illegible] (*sideways on* 10, 15 *and* 20 *c.*) *or No Wm*[illegible] (23 *c. to* $2).

(*a*) *Size as T* **309.** *P* $13\frac{1}{2} \times 13$.

914	$\frac{1}{2}$ c. multicoloured	5	
915	1 c. multicoloured	5	
	a. Wmk. sideways (booklets) ..	10	1[illegible]
	b. Booklet pane. No. 915a×3 with three *se-tenant* printed labels	45	
916	2 c. multicoloured	5	
917	$2\frac{1}{2}$ c. multicoloured	5	
918	3 c. black, brown & orange	10	
	a. Wmk. sideways (booklets)	10	1[illegible]
919	4 c. multicoloured	10	
	a. Wmk. sideways (booklets) ..	10	1[illegible]
920	5 c. multicoloured	12	1[illegible]
921	6 c. blackish green, yellow-green and carmine ..	15	[illegible]
922	7 c. multicoloured	15	[illegible]
923	$7\frac{1}{2}$ c. multicoloured	25	2[illegible]
924	8 c. multicoloured	15	[illegible]

(*b*) *Size as T* **310.** *Various Perfs.*

925	10 c. mult. (*p.* $14\frac{1}{2} \times 14$) ..	20	[illegible]
926	15 c. black, flesh and pale brown (*p.* 14×13) ..	20	[illegible]
927	18 c. chestnut, black and apple-green (*p.* 13×14)	25	2[illegible]
928	20 c. black and yellow-brown (*p.* 14×13)	30	1[illegible]
929	23 c. mult. (*p.* $13\frac{1}{2} \times 12\frac{1}{2}$) ..	25	2[illegible]

930 25 c. mult. ($p.$ 13 × 13½) .. 30 25
a. Perf. 14 × 13½ (1976) .. 25 30
931 30 c. mult. ($p.$ 13 × 13½) .. 35 25
a. Perf. 14 × 13½ (1976) .. 30 35
932 50 c. mult. ($p.$ 13½ × 12½) .. 50 30
933 $1 multicoloured ($p.$ 11½) .. 95 70
934 $2 multicoloured ($p.$ 11½) .. 1·90 1·25
914/34 .. .. *Set of* 21 5·50 4·00

Designs: *Vert.*—½ c. Glade Copper Butterfly; 1 c. Type **309**; 2 c. Tussock Butterfly; 2½ c. Magpie Moth; 3 c. Lichen Moth; 4 c. Puriri Moth; 5 c. Scarlet Parrot Fish; 6 c. Sea Horses; 7 c. Leather Jacket (fish); 7½ c. Garfish; 8 c. John Dory (fish); 18 c. Maori Club; 25 c. Hauraki Gulf Maritime Park; 30 c. Mt. Cook National Park. *Horiz.*—10 c. Type **310**; 15 c. Maori fish hook; 20 c. Maori tattoo pattern; 23 c. Egmont National Park; 50 c. Abel Tasman National Park; $1 Geothermal Power; $2 Agricultural Technology.

Although issued as a definitive, No. 925 was put on sale on the occasion of the Royal Visit to New Zealand.

Dates of issue:—12.3.70, 10 c.; 2.9.70, ½ c. to 4 c. (except Nos. 915a/b, 918a, 919a); 4.11.70, 5 c. to 8 c.; 20.1.71, 15 c. to 20 c.; 14.4.71, $1, $2; 6.7.71, Nos. 915a/b, 918a, 919a; 1.9.71, 25, 30 and 50 c.; 1.12.71, 23 c.

See also Nos. 1008, etc.

311. Geyser Restaurant.

(Des. M. Cleverley. Photo. Japanese Govt. Printing Bureau, Tokyo.)

1970 (8 Apr.). *World Fair, Osaka. T* **311** *and similar horiz. designs. Multicoloured. P* 13.
935 7 c. Type **311** 30 30
936 8 c. New Zealand Pavilion .. 30 30
937 18 c. Bush Walk 50 50

312. U.N. H.Q. Building.

Des. R. M. Conly (3 c.), L. C. Mitchell (10 c.). Litho. D.L.R.)

1970 (24 June). *25th Anniv. of United Nations. T* **312** *and similar vert. design. P* 13½.
938 3 c. multicoloured 8 5
939 10 c. scarlet and yellow .. 30 25

Design:—10 c. Tractor on Horizon.

313. Soccer.

(Des. L. C. Mitchell. Litho. D.L.R.)

1970 (5 Aug.). *Health. T* **313** *and similar multicoloured design. P* 13½.
940 2½ c. + 1 c. Netball (*vert.*) .. 12 10
941 3 c. + 1 c. Type **313** .. 15 12
MS942 Two Sheets: 102 × 125 mm. (2½ c.) and 125 × 102 mm. (3 c.). Nos. 940/1 in blocks of six *Per Pair* 2·00 2·00

314. " Adoration of the Child " (Correggio).

315. Stained Glass Window, Invercargill Presbyterian Church.

(Litho. D.L.R.)

1970 (1 Oct.). *Christmas. T* **314/5** *and similar design. P* 12½.
943 2½ c. multicoloured 5 5
944 3 c. multicoloured 10 10
a. Green (Inscr. and value) omitted .. .. .. 80·00
945 10 c. black, orange and silver 30 30

Design: *Horiz.*—10 c. Tower of Roman Catholic Church, Sockburn.

316. Chatham Islands Lily.

(Des. Miss E. Mayo. Photo. Japanese Govt. Printing Bureau, Tokyo.)

1970 (2 Dec.). *Chatham Islands. T* **316** *and similar horiz. design. Multicoloured. P* 13.
946 1 c. Type **316** 5 5
947 2 c. Mollymawk (bird) .. 8 8

317. Country Women's Institute Emblem.

(Des. L. C. Mitchell. Photo. Japanese Govt. Ptg. Bureau, Tokyo.)

1971 (10 Feb.). *50th Anniversaries of Country Women's Institutes and Rotary International in New Zealand. T* **317** *and similar horiz. design. Multicoloured. P* 13.
948 4 c. Type **317** 12 12
949 10 c. Rotary emblem and map of New Zealand .. 30 30

318. Racing Yacht.

(Des. J. Berry (5 c.), G. F. Fuller (8 c.). Litho. B.W.)

1971 (3 Mar.). *One Ton Cup Racing Trophy. T* **318** *and similar horiz. design. Multicoloured. P* 13½ × 13.
950 5 c. Type **318** 15 15
951 8 c. One Ton Cup 30 30

319. Civic Arms of Palmerston North.

(Des. R. M. Conly. Photo. Japanese Govt. Ptg. Bureau, Tokyo.)

1971 (12 May). *City Centenaries. T* **319** *and similar horiz. designs. Multicoloured. P* 13.
952 3 c. Type **319** 5 5
953 4 c. Arms of Auckland .. 8 8
954 5 c. Arms of Invercargill .. 12 12

320. Antarctica on Globe.

(Des. Eileen Mayo. Photo. Japanese Govt. Ptg. Bureau, Tokyo.)

1971 (9 June). *Tenth Anniv. of Antarctic Treaty. P* 13.
955 **320** 6 c. multicoloured .. 20 20

321. Child on Swing.

(Des. Eileen Mayo. Photo. Japanese Govt. Ptg. Bureau, Tokyo.)

1971 (9 June). *25th Anniv. of UNICEF. P* 13.
956 **321** 7 c. multicoloured .. 20 20

4c **4c** **4c**

(**322**) (**322*a***) (**322*b***)

T **322**. Photo, showing screening dots; thin bars, wide apart.
T **322*a***. Typo, without screening dots; thick bars, closer together.
T **322*b***. Typo; bars similar to T **322**.

1971–74. *No. 917 surcharged.*

(*a*) *In photogravure, by Harrison* (23.6.71*).

957 **322** 4 c. on 2½c. multicoloured 10 8

(*b*) *Typographically, by Harrison* (8.71).

957*a* **322***a* 4 c. on 2½ c. multicoloured 10 8
ab. Albino surch. .. ..

(*c*) *Typographically, locally* (6.74).

957*b* **322***b* 4 c. on 2½ c. multicoloured 10 8

* This is the earliest known dated postmark.

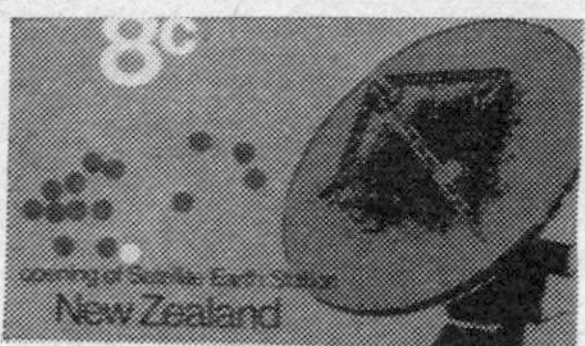

323. Satellite-tracking Aerial.

(Des. M. Cleverley. Photo. Courvoisier.)

1971 (14 July). *Opening of Satellite Earth Station. T* **323** *and similar horiz. design. P* 11½.

958 8 c. blk., drab-grey & verm. 20 20
959 10 c. black, turquoise-green and pale bluish violet.. 30 30

Design:—10 c. Satellite.

324. Girls playing Hockey.

(Des. L. C. Mitchell. Litho. Harrison.)

1971 (4 Aug.). *Health. T* **324** *and similar horiz. designs. Multicoloured. W* **98** (*sideways on* 5 *c.*). *P* 13½×13.

960 3 c.+1 c. Type **324** 10 12
961 4 c.+1 c. Boys playing hockey 12 15
962 5 c.+1 c. Dental Health .. 20 20
MS963 Two sheets each 122×96 mm. Nos. 960/1 in blocks of six *Per pair* 1·50 1·50

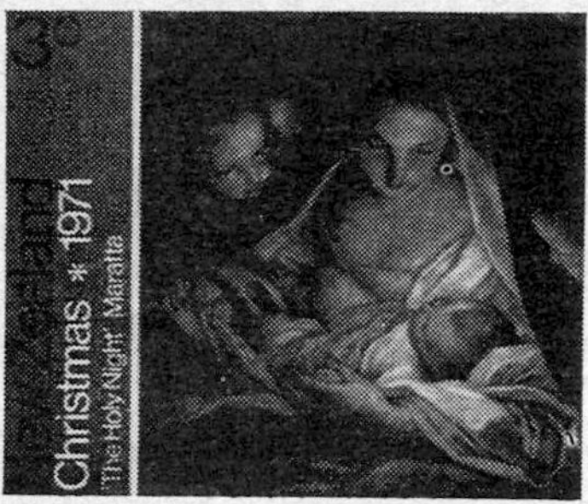

325. "Holy Night" (Maratta).

(Des. Enid Hunter (10 c.) or D. A. Hatcher (others). Photo. Harrison.)

1971 (6 Oct.). *Christmas. T* **325** *and similar vert. designs. Multicoloured. P* 13×13½.

964 3 c. Type **325** 5 5
965 4 c. Stained-glass window .. 8 5
966 10 c. "The Three Kings" .. 30 30

Nos. 965/6 are smaller, size 21½×38 mm.

326. "Tiffany" Rose.

(Des. A. G. Mitchell. Photo. Courvoisier.)

1971 (3 Nov.). *First World Rose Convention, Hamilton. T* **326** *and similar vert. designs showing roses. Multicoloured. P* 11½.

967 2 c. Type **326** 10 10
968 5 c. "Peace" 25 25
969 8 c. "Chrysler Imperial" .. 40 40

327. Lord Rutherford and Alpha Particles.

(Des. M. Cleverley. Litho. B.W.)

1971 (1 Dec.). *Birth Centenary of Lord Rutherford* (*scientist*). *T* **327** *and similar horiz. design. Multicoloured. P* 13½×13.

970 1 c. Type **327** 5 5
971 7 c. Lord Rutherford and formula 25 25

328. Benz (1895).

(Des. A. G. Mitchell. Litho. B.W.)

1972 (2 Feb.). *International Vintage Car Rally. T* **328** *and similar horiz. designs. Multicoloured. P* 14.

972 3 c. Type **328** 12 12
973 4 c. Oldsmobile (1904) .. 25 25
974 5 c. Ford "Model T" (1914) 25 25
975 6 c. Cadillac Service car (1915) 30 30
976 8 c. Chrysler (1924) .. 35 35
977 10 c. Austin "7" (1923) .. 45 45
972/7 .. .. *Set of* 6 1·60 1·60

329. Coat-of-Arms of Wanganui.

330. Black Scree Cotula.

(Des. M. Cleverley. Litho. Harrison.)

1972 (5 Apr.). *Anniversaries. T* **329** *and similar designs. P* 13×13½ (3, 5 *and* 8 *c.*) *or* 13½×1 (*others*).

978 3 c. multicoloured 5
979 4 c. red-orange, brown-bistre and black 5
980 5 c. multicoloured 8
981 8 c. multicoloured 15 1
982 10 c. multicoloured 45 4
978/82 .. .. *Set of* 5 70 7

Designs and Events: *Vert.*—3 c. Type 32 (100th Anniv. of Wanganui Council govt.); 5 c De Havilland "Dominie" and Boeing "737" (25th Anniv. National Airways Corp.); 8 c. French frigate and Maori palisade (Bicent. of landing by Marion du Fresne). *Horiz.*—4 c. Postal Union symbol (Tenth Anniv. of Asian-Oceanic Posta Union); 10 c. Stone cairn (150th Anniv. of New Zealand Methodist Church).

(Des. Miss E. Mayo. Litho. Harrison.)

1972 (7 June). *Alpine Plants. T* **330** *an similar vert. designs. Multicoloured. P* 13½

983 4 c. Type **330** 5
984 6 c. North Island Eidelweiss 12 1
985 8 c. Haast's Buttercup .. 20 2
986 10 c. Brown Mountain Daisy 45 4

331. Boy playing Tennis.

332. "Virgin and Child" (Murillo).

(Des. L. C. Mitchell. Litho. Harrison.)

1972 (2 Aug.). *Health. T* **331** *and similar ver design. P* 13×13½.

987 3 c. +1 c. lt. grey & chestnut 12 1
988 4 c. +1 c. light red-brown, grey and lemon 12 1
MS989 Two sheets each 107×123 mm. Nos. 987/8 in blocks of six *Per Pair* 1·25 1·2

Design: No. 988, Girl playing tennis.

(Des. D. A. Hatcher. Photo. Courvoisier.)

1972 (4 Oct.). *Christmas. T* **332** *and simila vert. designs. Multicoloured. P* 11½.

990 3 c. Type **332** 5
991 5 c. Stained-glass window St. John's Church, Levin .. 8
992 10 c. Pohutukawa flower .. 20 2

333. Lake Waikaremoana.

(Des. D. A. Hatcher. Photo. Courvoisier.)

1972 (6 Dec.). *Lake Scenes. T* **333** *and simila vert. designs. Multicoloured. P* 11½.

993 6 c. Type **333** 20 2
994 8 c. Lake Hayes 30 3
995 18 c. Lake Wakatipu 80 8
996 23 c. Lake Rotomahana .. 1·00 1·0

334. Old Pollen Street.

(Des. Miss V. Jepsen (3c.), B. Langford (others). Litho. Harrison.)

1973 (7 Feb.). *Commemorations. T* 334 *and similar horiz. designs. Multicoloured* (*except* 8 *c.*). *P* 13½×13.

997 3 c. Type **334** 5 5
998 4 c. Coal-mining and pasture 5 5
999 5 c. Cloister 8 8
1000 6 c. Forest, birds and lake .. 10 10
1001 8 c. Rowers (light grey, indigo and gold) 15 15
1002 10 c. Graph and people .. 20 20
997/1002 .. .. *Set of* 6 60 60

Events:—3 c. Centennial of Thames Borough; 4 c. Centennial of Westport Borough; 5 c. Centennial of Canterbury University; 6 c. 50th Anniv. of Royal Forest and Bird Protection Society; 8 c. Success of N.Z. Rowers in 1972 Olympics; 10 c. 25th Anniv. of E.C.A.F.E.

335. Class "W" Locomotive.

(Des. R. M. Conly. Litho. Harrison.)

1973 (4 Apr.). *New Zealand Steam Locomotives. T* **335** *and similar horiz. designs. Multicoloured. P* 14×14½.

1003 3 c. Type **335** 10 10
1004 4 c. Class "X" 10 10
1005 5 c. Class "Ab" 12 12
1006 10 c. Class "Ja" 40 40

1973–76. *As Nos.* 914 *etc., but no wmk.*

1008 1 c. multicoloured (7.9.73) .. 5 5
 a. Booklet pane. No. 1008×3 with three *se-tenant* printed labels (1974) 25
1009 2 c. multicoloured (6.73?) .. 5 5
1010 3 c. black, light brown and orange (1974) 5 5
1011 4 c. multicoloured (7.9.73) .. 5 5
1012 5 c. multicoloured (1973) .. 8 8
1013 6 c. blackish grn., yell.-grn. and rose-carmine (7.9.73) 8 8
1014 7 c. multicoloured (1974) .. 10 10
1015 8 c. multicoloured (1974) .. 12 10
1017 10 c. mult., *p.* 13½×13 (6.73?) 10 10
 a. Silver (Arms) omitted £180
1018 15 c. blk., flesh & pale brn., *p.* 13½×13 (1976) .. 15 15
1019 18 c. chestnut, black and apple-green (1974) .. 20 15
1020 20 c. blk. & yell.-brn. (1974) 20 15
1008/20 .. .. *Set of* 12 1·10 90

336. "Maori Woman and Child". **337.** Prince Edward.

(Des. and photo. Courvoisier.)

1973 (6 June). *Paintings by Frances Hodgkins. T* **336** *and similar vert. designs. Multicoloured. P* 11½.

1027 5 c. Type **336** 10 10
1028 8 c. "The Hill Top" .. 15 15
1029 10 c. "Barn in Picardy" 20 20
1030 18 c. "Self Portrait Still Life" 35 35

(Des. and litho. Harrison.)

1973 (1 Aug.). *Health. P* 13×13½.

1031 337 3 c. + 1 c. dull yellowish green & reddish brown .. 8 8
1032 " 4 c.+1 c. rose-red and blackish brown .. 10 8

MS1033 Two sheets each 96×121 mm. with Nos. 1031/2 in blocks of 6 (3×2) .. .. *Per pair* 1·50 1·50

338. "Tempi Madonna" (Raphael). **339.** Mitre Peak.

(Des. A. Mitchell. Photo. Enschedé.)

1973 (3 Oct.). *Christmas. T* **338** *and similar vert. designs. Multicoloured. P* 12½×13½.

1034 3 c. Type **338** 5 5
1035 5 c. "Three Kings" (St. Theresa's Church, Auckland) 10 10
1036 10 c. Family entering church 25 25

(Des. D. A. Hatcher. Photo. Enschedé.)

1973 (5 Dec.). *Mountain Scenery. T* **339** *and similar multicoloured designs. P* 13×13½ (6, 8 *c.*) *or* 13½×13 (*others*).

1037 6 c. Type **339** 12 12
1038 8 c. Mt. Ngauruhoe .. 20 20
1039 18 c. Mt. Sefton (*horiz.*) .. 40 40
1040 23 c. Burnett Range (*horiz.*) 50 50

340. Hurdling. **341.** Queen Elizabeth II.

(Des. M. Cleverley. Litho. Harrison.)

1974 (9 Jan.). *Tenth British Commonwealth Games, Christchurch. T* **340** *and similar vert. designs.* 5 *c. black and violet-blue, others multicoloured. P* 13×14.

1041 4 c. Type **340** 8 8
1042 5 c. Ball-player 8 8
1043 10 c. Cycling 15 15
1044 18 c. Rifle-shooting .. 40 40
1045 23 c. Bowls 40 40
1041/5 .. .. *Set of* 5 1·00 1·00

No. 1042 does not show the Games emblem, and commemorates the Fourth Paraplegic Games, held at Dunedin.

(Des. D. A. Hatcher and A. Mitchell. Litho. Harrison.)

1974 (5 Feb.). *New Zealand Day. Sheet* 131×74 *mm. T* **341** *and similar horiz. designs, size* 37×20 *mm. Multicoloured. P* 13.

MS1046 4 c. (×5) Treaty House, Waitangi; signing Waitangi Treaty; Type **341**; Parliament Buildings Extensions; Children in Class 40 40

342. "Spirit of Napier" Fountain. **344.** Children, Cat and Dog.

343. Boeing Seaplane, 1919

(Des. Miss V. Jepson. Photo. Courvoisier.)

1974 (3 Apr.). *Centenaries of Napier and U.P.U. T* **342** *and similar vert. designs. Multicoloured. P* 11½.

1047 4 c. Type **342** 5 5
1048 5 c. Clock Tower, Berne .. 10 10
1049 8 c. U.P.U. Monument, Berne 15 15

(Des. R. M. Conly. Litho. Harrison.)

1974 (5 June). *History of New Zealand Airmail Transport. T* **343** *and similar horiz. designs. Multicoloured. P* 14×13.

1050 3 c. Type **343** 5 5
1051 4 c. Lockheed "Electra", 1937 .. .. .. 8 8
1052 5 c. Bristol Freighter, 1958 8 8
1053 23 c. Empire "S 30" flying-boat, 1940 .. .. 40 40

(Des. B. Langford. Litho. Harrison.)

1974 (7 Aug.). *Health. P* 13×13½.

1054 **344** 3 c. +1 c. multicoloured 8 5
1055 – 4 c. +1 c. multicoloured 8 8
1056 – 5 c. +1 c. multicoloured 10 8

MS1057 145×123 mm. No. 1055 in block of ten 80 80

Nos. 1055/6 are as T **344**, showing children and pets.

345. "L'Adoration des Mages" (Konrad Witz).

(Des. Eileen Mayo. Photo. Courvoisier.)

1974 (2 Oct.). *Christmas. T* **345** *and similar horiz. designs. Multicoloured. P* 11½.

1058 3 c. Type **345** 5 5
1059 5 c. Stained-glass window, Old St. Pauls Church, Wellington 10 10
1060 10 c. Madonna Lily 20 20

346. Great Barrier Island.

(Des. D. A. Hatcher. Photo. Enschedé.)

1974 (4 DEC.). *Off-shore Islands. T* **346** *and similar horiz. designs. Multicoloured. P* 13½ × 13.

1061 6 c. Type **346** 8 8
1062 8 c. Stewart Island .. 10 10
1063 18 c. White Island 25 25
1064 23 c. The Brothers 30 30

347. Crippled Child.

(Des. Miss V. Jepson (3 c., 5 c.), A. Mitchell (10 c., 18 c.). Litho. Harrison.)

1975 (5 FEB.). *Anniversaries and Events. T* **347** *and similar horiz. designs. Multicoloured. P* 13½.

1065 3 c. Type **347** 8 8
1066 5 c. Farming family .. 10 10
1067 10 c. I.W.Y. symbols .. 20 20
1068 18 c. Medical School Building, Otago University .. 30 30

Commemorations:—3 c. 40th Anniv. of N.Z. Crippled Children Society; 5 c. 50th Anniv. of Women's Division, Federated Farmers of N.Z.; 10 c. International Women's Year; 18 c. Centenary of Otago Medical School.

348. Scow *Lake Erie.*

(Des. R. M. Conly. Litho. Harrison.)

1975 (2 APR.). *Historic Sailing Ships. T* **348** *and similar horiz. designs. P* 13½ × 13.

1069 4 c. black and red 5 5
1070 5 c. black and turq.-blue 10 10
1071 8 c. black and yellow .. 12 12
1072 10 c. black and olive-yellow 15 15
1073 18 c. black and light brown .. 25 30
1074 23 c. black and slate-lilac .. 30 35
1069/74 .. .. *Set of* 6 85 90

Ships:—5 c. Schooner *Herald*; 8 c. Brigantine *New Zealander*; 10 c. Topsail schooner *Jessie Kelly*; 18 c. Barque *Tory*; 23 c. Full-rigged clipper *Rangitiki.*

349. Lake Sumner Forest Park.

(Des. and photo. Enschedé.)

1975 (4 JUNE). *Forest Park Scenes. T* **349** *and similar horiz. designs. Multicoloured. P* 13.

1075 6 c. Type **349** 8 8
1076 8 c. North-west Nelson .. 10 10
1077 18 c. Kaweka 25 25
1078 23 c. Coromandel 25 25

350. Girl feeding Lamb.

(Des. Mrs. M. Chapman. Litho. Harrison.)

1975 (6 AUG.). *Health. T* **350** *and similar horiz. designs. Multicoloured. P* 13½ × 13.

1079 3 c. + 1 c. Type **350** .. 5 5
1080 4 c. + 1 c. Boy with hen and chicks 5 5
1081 5 c. + 1 c. Boy with duck and duckling 8 8
MS1082 123 × 146 mm. No. 1080 in block of 10 .. .. .. 60 60

351. " Virgin and Child "
(Zanobi Machiavelli).

(Des. Enid Hunter. Photo. Harrison.)

1975 (1 OCT.). *Christmas. T* **351** *and similar horiz. designs. Multicoloured. P* 13 × 13½ (3 *c.*) *or* 13½ × 13 (*others*).

1083 3 c. Type **351** 5 5
a. Red omitted*
1084 5 c. Stained-glass window, Greendale Church .. 5 5
1085 10 c. " I saw three ships . . ." (carol) 12 12

* This occurred in the last two vertical rows of the sheet with the red partially omitted on the previous row.

352. " Sterling Silver". **353.** Maripi (knife).

(Des. A. Mitchell. Photo. Harrison (1 to 9 c.), Courvoisier (others).)

1975 (26 NOV.)–**76.** *Various multicoloured designs as T* **352/3.**

(*a*) *Garden Roses as T* **352.** *P* 14 × 14½ (6, 7 *and* 8 *c.*) *or* 14 × 13½ (*others*).

1086 1 c. Type **352** 5 5
1087 2 c. " Lilli Marlene " .. 5 5
1088 3 c. " Queen Elizabeth " .. 5 5
1089 4 c. " Super Star " 5 5
1090 5 c. " Diamond Jubilee " .. 5 5
1091 6 c. " Cresset " 5 8
a. Perf. 14 × 13½ (1976) .. 5 5
1092 7 c. " Michele Meilland " .. 8 8
a. Perf. 14 × 13½ (1976) .. 8 8
1093 8 c. " Josephine Bruce " .. 8 10
a. Perf. 14 × 13½ (1976) .. 8 8
1094 9 c. " Iceberg " 8 10

(*b*) *Maori Artefacts as T* **353.** *P* 11½ (24.11.76).

1095 11 c. Type **353** 10 10
1096 12 c. Putorino (flute) .. 12 12
1097 13 c. Wahaika (club) .. 12 15
1098 14 c. Kotiate (club) 15 15
1086/98 .. .. *Set of* 13 75 85

Nos. 1099/1109 have been reserved for further additions to this definitive set.

354. Family and League of Mothers Badge.

(Des. A. P. Derrick. Litho. J.W.)

1976 (4 FEB.). *Anniversaries and Metrification. T* **354** *and similar horiz. designs. Multicoloured. P* 13½ × 14.

1110 6 c. Type **354** 5
1111 7 c. Weight, temperature, linear measure and capacity 5
1112 8 c. Ship, mountain and New Plymouth 8
1113 10 c. Two women shaking hands and Y.W.C.A. badge 8 1
1114 25 c. Map of the world showing cable links .. 20 2
1110/14 .. *Set of* 5 40 4

Anniversaries:—6 c. League of Mothers, 50th Anniv. 7 c. Metrication; 8 c. Centenary of New Plymouth; 10 c. 50th Anniv. of New Zealand Y.W.C.A.; 25 c. Centenary of link with International Telecommunications Network.

355. Gig.

(Des. G. F. Fuller. Litho. Harrison.)

1976 (7 APR.). *Vintage Farm Transport. T* **355** *and similar horiz. designs. Multicoloured. P* 13½ × 13.

1115 6 c. Type **355** 5
1116 7 c. Thorneycroft lorry .. 8
1117 8 c. Scandi wagon 8 1
1118 9 c. Traction engine .. 10 1
1119 10 c. Wool wagon 10 1
1120 25 c. Cart 25 3
1115/20 .. .. *Set of* 6 60 7

356. Purakaunui Falls.

(Des. and photo. Courvoisier.)

976 (2 June). *Waterfalls. T* **356** *and similar vert. designs. Multicoloured. P* 11½.

121	10 c. Type **356**	10	12
122	14 c. Marakopa Falls	15	15
123	15 c Bridal Veil Falls	15	15
124	16 c. Papakorito Falls	15	20

357. Boy and Pony. **358.** " Nativity " (Spanish carving).

(Des. Margaret Chapman. Litho. Harrison.)

976 (4 Aug.). *Health. T* **357** *and similar vert. designs. Multicoloured. P* 13 × 13½.

125	7 c. + 1 c. Type **357**	8	10
126	8 c. + 1 c. Girl and calf	10	10
127	10 c. + 1 c. Girls and bird	10	12
IS1128	96 × 121 mm. Nos. 1125/7 × 2		60

Des. Margaret Chapman (18 c.), D. A. Hatcher (others). Photo. Harrison.)

976 (6 Oct.). *Christmas. T* **358** *and similar horiz. designs. Multicoloured. P* 14 × 14½ (7 *c.*) *or* 14½ × 14 (*others*).

129	7 c. Type **358**	8	8
130	11 c. " Resurrection " (stained-glass window, Auckland)	10	12
131	18 c. Angels	20	25

EXPRESS DELIVERY STAMPS.

E 1

903. *Value in first colour. W* **41.** *P* 11.

1	E **1**	6d. red and violet	6·00	4·50

926–36. *Thick, white, opaque chalk-surfaced " Cowan " paper. W* **41.** (*a*) *P* 14 × 14½.

2	E **1**	6d. vermilion & brt. violet	3·50	4·50

(*b*) *P* 14 × 15 (1936).

3	E **1**	6d. carmine & brt. violet	6·00	7·00

937–39. *Thin, hard, chalk-surfaced " Wiggins, Teape " paper.* (*a*) *P* 14 × 14½.

4	E **1**	6d. carmine & brt. violet	3·50	4·50

(*b*) *P* 14 × 15 (1939).

5	E **1**	6d. vermilion & brt. violet	8·00	11·00

E **2.** Express Mail Delivery Van.

Des. J. Berry. Eng. Stamp Ptg. Office, Melbourne. Recess. Govt. Ptg. Office, Wellington.)

939 (16 Aug.). *W* **41.** *P* 14.

6	E **2**	6d. violet	75	75

POSTAGE DUE STAMPS.

D 1

(I)

(II)

3D. 5D.

(*a*) Large " D " (*b*) Small " D "

(Typo. Govt. Printing Office, Wellington.)

1899 (Dec.). *W* **12***b*. *Coarse paper. P* 11.

Type I. *Circle of* 14 *ornaments,* 17 *dots over " N.Z.", " N.Z." large.* (*a*) *Large " D ".*

D1	D **1**	½d. carmine and green	1·00	2·50
		a. No stop after " D "	12·00	15·00
D2	„	8d. carmine and green	12·00	15·00
D3	„	1s. carmine and green	12·00	15·00
D4	„	2s. carmine and green	25·00	30·00

To avoid further subdivision the 1s. and 2s. are placed with the *pence* values, although the two types of " D " do not apply to the higher values.

(*b*) *Small " D ".*

D6	D **1**	5d. carmine and green	5·00	5·00
D7	„	6d. carmine and green	6·50	6·50
D8	„	10d. carmine and green	12·00	40·00

Type II. *Circle of* 13 *ornaments,* 15 *dots over " N.Z.", " N.Z." small.* (*a*) *Large " D ".*

D 9	D **1**	½d. vermilion and green	30	1·00
		a. No stop after " D "	15·00	15·00
D10	„	1d. vermilion and green	1·75	15
D11	„	2d. vermilion and green	10·00	1·50
D12	„	3d. vermilion and green	3·00	75

(*b*) *Small " D ".*

D14	D **1**	1d. vermilion and green	2·00	40
D15	„	2d. vermilion and green	4·00	1·00
D16	„	4d. vermilion and green	10·00	4·00

D **2**

D **3**

(Des. W. R. Bock. Typo. Govt. Printing Office.)

1902 (28 Feb.). *No wmk. P* 11.

D17	D **2**	½d. red and deep green	30	35

1904–10. *" Cowan " unsurfaced paper. W* **41** (*sideways*). (*a*) *P* 11.

D18	D **2**	½d. red and green ('04)	30	30
		a. Imperf. between (pair)	50·00	
D19	„	1d. red & green (5.12.05)	2·00	1·50
D20	„	2d. red & green (5.4.06)	40·00	35·00

(*b*) *P* 14.

D21	D **2**	1d. carmine & green ('06)	2·00	20
		a. Rose-pink and green ('10)	1·00	10
D22	„	2d. carmine & green ('06)	1·25	1·00
		a. Rose-pink and green ('10)	1·00	25

1913. *" De La Rue " chalky paper. Toned gum. W* **41.** *P* 14 × 15.

D23	D **2**	½d. carmine and green	40	30
D24	„	1d. carmine and green	1·00	10
D25	„	2d. carmine and green	1·50	30

1924 (Nov.). *" Jones " chalky paper. White gum. W* **41.** *P* 14 × 15.

D26	D **2**	½d. carmine and green	4·00	4·00

1925 (July). *No. wmk., but bluish " N Z " and Star lithographed on back. P* 14 × 15.

D27	D **2**	½d. carmine and green	30	2·50
D28	„	2d. carmine and green	1·00	2·50

1925 (Nov.)–**29.** *" Cowan " thick, opaque chalky paper. W* **41.** (*a*) *P* 14 × 15.

D29	D **2**	½d. carmine & grn. (12.27)	25	30
D30	„	1d. carmine and green	1·00	12
D31	„	2d. carmine and green	2·00	50
D32	„	3d. carmine & grn. ('28?)	5·00	4·50

(*b*) *P* 14.

D33	D **2**	½d. carm. & grn. (10.28)	85	1·25
D34	„	1d. rose and pale yellow-green (6.28)	1·00	12
D35	„	2d. carm. & grn. (10.29)	1·50	40
D36	„	3d. carmine & grn. (5.28)	5·00	4·00

1937–38. *" Wiggins, Teape " thin, hard chalky paper. W* **41.** *P* 14 × 15.

D37	D **2**	½d. carmine & yell.-grn. (2.38)	40	2·00
D38	„	1d. carmine & yell.-grn. (1.37)	85	10
D39	„	2d. carmine & yell.-grn. (6.37)	1·50	55
D40	„	3d. carmine & yell.-grn. (11.37)	5·00	5·00

(Des. J. Berry. Typo. Govt. Printing Office, Wellington.)

1939–49. *P* 15 × 14.

(*a*) *W* **41** *sideways* (16.8.39.).

D41	D **3**	½d. turquoise-green	25	25
D42	„	1d. carmine	20	8
D43	„	2d. bright blue	1·50	20
D44	„	3d. orange-brown	3·00	1·50

(*b*) *W* **98** *sideways.*

D45	D **3**	1d. carmine (4.49)	20	8·00
D46	„	2d. bright blue (12.46)	40	1·50
D47	„	3d. orange-brown (6.45)	2·50	50
		a. Wmk. upright (1943)	4·00	4·00

OFFICIAL STAMPS.

1892–1906. *Contemporary issues handstamped " O.P.S.O." diagonally.*

(*a*) *Stamp of* 1873 *type. W* **12***b*. *P* 12½.

O 1	**3**	½d. rose (V.)	—	30·00

(*b*) *Stamps of* 1882–97. *W* **12***b*. *In rose or magenta.*

O 2	**13**	½d. black (*p.* 10)	—	15·00
		a. Violet opt.	—	18·00
O 3	„	½d. black (*p.* 10 × 11)	—	15·00
O 4	**14**	1d. rose (*p.* 12 × 11½)	—	15·00
O 5	„	1d. rose (*p.* 11)	—	15·00
O 6	**15**	2d. purple (*p.* 11)	—	15·00
O 7	„	2d. mauve-lilac (*p.* 10)	—	15·00
		a. Violet opt.		
O 8	**16**	2½d. blue (*p.* 11)	—	15·00
O 9	„	2½d. ultramarine (*p.* 10)	—	15·00
O10	„	2½d. ultram. (*p.* 10 × 11)	—	15·00
O11	**19**	5d. olive-blk. (*p.* 12 × 11½)	—	18·00
O12	**20**	6d. brown (*p.* 12 × 11½)	—	25·00

(*c*) *Stamps of* 1898–1906. *P* 11.

In violet.

(i) *No wmk.*

O13	**23**	½d. green (*p.* 14) (No. 334)	—	15·00
O14	**26**	2½d. blue (*p.* 12–16)	—	25·00
O15	**27**	2½d. blue	—	18·00
O16	**39**	4d. indigo and brown	—	20·00
O17	**30**	5d. purple-brown	—	20·00
		a. Green opt.	—	20·00
O18	**32**	8d. indigo	—	25·00

(ii) *W* **36***a*.

O19	**40**	1d. carmine	—	15·00

(iii) *W* **41** (*sideways on* 3*d.,* 1*s.*).

O20	**40**	1d. carm. (*p.* 14) (No. 344)	—	15·00
		a. Green opt.	—	15·00
O21	**27**	2½d. blue	—	20·00
O22	**28**	3d. yellow-brown	—	20·00
O23	**34**	1s. orange-red	—	45·00
O24	**35**	2s. green	—	45·00

The letters signify " On Public Service Only," and stamps so overprinted were used by the Post Office Department on official correspondence between the department and places abroad.

OFFICIAL.

(O 3)

1907–08. *Stamps of 1902–7 optd. with Type* O **3** *(vertically upwards). W* **41** *(sideways on 3d., 6d., 1s., 5s. and £1.). P 14.*

O59 **23** ½d. yellow-green 20 8
O60 **40** 1d. carmine (Waterlow) .. 50 20
a. Perf. compound of 11 & 14 55·00 50·00
b. Mixed perfs. .. .. 55·00 50·00
O60c „ 1d. carmine (Royle) .. 20 8
d. Perf. compound of 11 & 14 30·00 30·00
e. Mixed perfs. .. .. 30·00 30·00
O61 **38a** 2d. purple 20 8
O62 „ 2d. bright purple 20 8
a. Mixed perfs. .. .. 25·00 25·00
O63 **28** 3d. bistre-brown 85 20
O64 **31** 6d. pink .. .. .. 5·00 2·00
a. Imperf. vert. (horiz. pair) 75·00
b. Mixed perfs. .. .. 40·00 40·00
O65 **34** 1s. red .. .. .. 5·00 1·75
O66 **35** 2s. blue-green .. .. 10·00 4·00
a. Imperf. between (pair) .. £110
b. Imperf. vert. (horiz. pair)
O67 **36** 5s. deep red .. .. 30·00 20·00
a. Wmk. upright .. .. 40·00 30·00
O68 F **4** £1 rose-pink (F89) ('08) 25·00 25·00
O59/O68 .. .. *Set of* 9 75·00 45·00

1908. *Optd. as Type* O **3**. *W* **41**.

O69 **23** ½d. green (*p*. 14×15) .. 50 20
O70 **46** 1d. carmine (*p*. 14×15) .. 2·00 20
O71 **48** 6d. pink (*p*. 14×15) .. 4·00 2·00
O72 „ 6d. pink (*p*. 14×13, 13½) 6·00 3·00

1910–15. *Optd. as Type* O **3**. *W* **41**. *P* 14×15.

O73 **50** ½d. yellow-green 75 8
O74 **51** 1d. carmine 20 8

T **52** *(and similar types), optd. as Type* O **3**. *W* **41**. *P* 14×14½.

O76 3d. chestnut (1915) 85 30
a. Perf. 14×13½ (1915) .. 15·00 15·00
b. Vert. pair, O76/6a .. 35·00 40·00
O77 6d. carmine .. .. 1·00 80
O78 6d. deep carmine .. .. 1·00 80
O79 1s. vermilion .. .. 6·00 5·00

1913–25. *Postal Fiscal stamps optd. with Type* O **3**.

(i) *Chalk-surfaced "De La Rue" paper.*

(*a*) *P* 14 (1913–14).

O80 F **4** 2s. blue (30.9.14) .. 3·00 1·25
O81 „ 5s. yellow-green (13.6.13) 7·50 3·75
O82 „ £1 rose-carmine (1913) 25·00 18·00

(*b*) *P* 14½×14, *comb* (1915).

O83 F **4** 2s. deep blue (Aug.) .. 3·00 1·25
a. No stop after "OFFICIAL" .. .. 10·00 10·00
O84 „ 5s. yellow-green (Jan.) .. 7·50 3·75
a. No stop after "OFFICIAL" .. .. 15·00 15·00

(ii) *Thick, white, opaque chalk-surfaced "Cowan" paper. P* 14½×14 (1925).

O85 F **4** 2s. blue .. .. 8·50 8·50
a. No stop after "OFFICIAL" .. .. 15·00 15·00

The overprint on these last and on No. O69 is from a new set of type, giving a rather sharper impression than Type O **3**, but otherwise resembling it closely.

Various stamps overprinted as Type O **3**. *W* **41** *(except No.* O105).

1915–19. *T* **60***a*/*b*. *P* 14×15.

O86 **60b** ½d. green (12.10.15) .. 10 8
O87 **60a** 1½d. grey-black (6.16) .. 10 8
O88 **60b** 1½d. slate (12.16) .. 20 8
O89 „ 1½d. orange-brown (4.19) 20 20
O90 „ 2d. yellow (4.17) .. 15 8
O91 „ 3d. chocolate (11.19) .. 1·25 10
O86/O91 .. .. *Set of* 6 1·90 50

See also Nos. O102, etc.

1916 (May). *T* **52**. *P* 14×14½.

O92 **52** 8d. indigo-blue (R.) .. 1·00 1·25
a. Perf. 14×13½ .. 1·00 1·25
b. Vert. pair, O92/2a .. 5·00 6·00

1916–27. *T* **60**. *P* 14×14½.

O93 **60** 3d. chocolate (5.16) .. 65 30
a. Perf. 14×13½ 75 40
b. Vert. pair, O93/3a .. 10·00 15·00
O94 „ 4d. red-violet (*p*. 14×13½) (4.25) .. .. 4·00 35
a. Perf. 14×14½. *Violet* (4.27) 5·00 35
O95 „ 6d. carmine (6.16) .. 50 10
a. Perf. 14×13½ .. 20 10
b. Vert. pair, O95/5a .. 10·00 15·00
O96 „ 8d. red-brown (*p*. 14×13½) (8.22) .. .. 50·00 40·00
O97 „ 9d. sage-green (*p*. 14×13½) (4.25) .. .. 3·00 4·00
O98 „ 1s. vermilion (9.16) .. 3·00 1·50
a. Perf. 14×13½ .. 10·00 6·50
b. Vert. pair, O98/8a .. 25·00 28·00
O99 „ 1s. pale orange-red .. 3·00 1·50
O93/O99 .. .. *Set of* 7 60·00 45·00

1916 (July). *On pictorial issue paper. Wmk. sideways. P* 14.

O100 **60** 3d. chocolate 75 75
a. No wmk. .. .. 3·50 3·50

1924–34. *T* **51** *and* **60***b*. *P* 14×15.

(*a*) *"Jones" chalky paper. White gum.*

O102 **60b** ½d. green 45 20
O103 **51** 1d. deep carmine ('25) .. 1·25 35
O104 **60b** 3d. deep chocolate .. 3·00 75

(*b*) *No wmk. Bluish "N Z" and Star lithographed on back.*

O105 **51** 1d. carmine-pink, ('25) .. 55 35

(*c*) *"Cowan" thick, opaque, chalky paper. White gum.*

O106 **60b** ½d. green ('25) .. 8 8
a. Perf. 14 ('29) .. 20 8
b. No stop after "OFFICIAL" (Perf. 14) 2·00 2·00
O107 **51** 1d. deep carmine .. 40 30
O108 **60b** 1½d. orge.-brown (*p*. 14) ('29) .. .. 45 1·00
a. No stop after "OFFICIAL" .. 3·25 4·00
b. Perf. 14×15 ('34) .. 1·25 1·00
O109 „ 2d. yellow (*p*. 14) ('31) 30 15
a. No stop after "OFFICIAL" .. 3·50 3·50
O110 „ 3d. chocolate ('25) .. 1·10 12
a. No stop after "OFFICIAL" .. 4·50 3·00
b. Perf. 14 ('30) .. 1·50 40
c. Ditto. no stop after "OFFICIAL" .. 5·50 4·00
O106/O110 .. .. *Set of* 5 2·25 1·50

1927–33. *T* **71**/**2** *and as Type* F **6**. *P* 14.

O111 **71** 1d. rose-carmine .. 20 8
a. No stop after "OFFICIAL" .. 2·00 2·00
b. Perf. 14×15 .. .. 20 8
O112 **72** 2s. light blue (No. 542) (2.28) .. .. 15·00 15·00
O113 F **6** 5s. green (1933) .. 80·00 80·00

Official (O 4) **Official** (O 5)

1936–61. *Pictorial issue optd. horiz. or vert.* (2s.) *with Type* O **4**.

(*a*) *W* **41** *(Single "N Z" and Star).*

O115 **82** 1d. scarlet (Die I) (*p*. 14×13½) .. 10 8
a. Perf. 13½×14 .. 8·50 7·50
O116 **83** 1½d. red-brn. (*p*. 13½×14) 40 40
a. Perf. 14×13½
O118 **92** 1s. dp. grn. (*p*. 14×13½) 1·25 2·00
O119 F **6** 5s. green (*p*. 14) .. 7·00 5·00

The watermark of O119 is almost invisible Only 4 copies of O116a exist.

(*b*) *W* **98** *(Mult. "N Z" and Star).*

O120 **81** ½d. brt. grn., *p*. 14×13½ 15 1
O121 **82** 1d. scarlet (Die II), *p*. 14×13½ .. 10 8
O122 **83** 1½d. red-brn., *p*. 14×13½ 30 4
O123 **84** 2d. orge., p. 14×13½ .. 8 8
a. Perf. 12½ ('42) .. 10·00 6·0
c. Perf. 14 ('42) .. 35 3
O124 **85** 2½d. chocolate and slate, *p*. 13–14×13½ .. 75 1·5
a. Perf. 14 ('38) .. 75 1·7
O125 **86** 3d. brown, *p*. 14×13½ 3·50 2
O126 **87** 4d. black and sepia, *p*. 14×13½ .. 50 20
a. Perf. 14 (Aug., '41) .. 35 2
b. Perf. 12½ ('41) .. 50 2
c. Perf. 14×14½ (-.10.42) 35 20
O127 **89** 6d. scarlet, *p*. 13½×14 40 20
a. Perf. 12½ ('41) .. 40 20
b. Perf. 14½×14 (-.7.42) 40 2
O128 **90** 8d. chocolate, *p*. 12½, (*wmk. sideways*) .. 50 6
a. Perf. 14×14½ (*wmk. sideways*) ('45) .. 75 6
b. Perf. 14×13½ .. † —
O129 **91** 9d. red and grey-black (G.) (No. 587*a*), *p*. 14×14½ .. 3·00 3·5
O130 „ 9d. scar. & black (Bk.) (No. 627), *p*. 14×15 2·00 2·7
O131 **92** 1s. dp. grn., *p*.14×13½ 60 2
a. Perf. 12½ ('42) .. 60 2
O132 **93** 2s. olive-green *p*. 13–14×13½ .. 4·25 1·7
a. Perf. 12½ ('42) .. 4·25 1·2
b. Perf. 13½×14 ('39) .. 11·00 1·5
c. Perf. 14×13½ ('44) .. 4·25 1·2
O133 F **6** 5s. grn., C, *p*. 14 (3.43) 4·00 2·5
a. Perf. 14×13½. *Yellow-green*, O (10.61) .. 3·25 3·2
O120/O133 .. .. *Set of* 14 18·00 13·0

The opt. on No. O127a was sometimes applie at the top of the stamp, instead of always at th bottom, as on No. O127.

Dates of first issue: 1936—July, No. O122 Aug., No. O126; Nov., No. O121. 1937—Feb. No. O131; May, No. O132; July, No. O120 Dec., No. O127. 1938—Jan., No. O123; 1 Mar. Nos. O125 and O129; 26 July, No. O124; Dec. No. O119. 1942—No. O128. 1943—Nos. O13 and O133.

See notes on perforations after No. 590b.

1938–51. *Nos.* 603 *etc., optd. with Type* O **4**.

O134 **108** ½d. green (1.3.38) .. 10
O135 „ ½d. brn.-orange ('46) 8
O136 „ 1d. scarlet (1.7.38) .. 8
O137 „ 1d. green (10.7.41) .. 8
O138 **108a** 1½d. pur.-brn. (26.7.38) 1·25 5
O139 „ 1½d. scarlet (2.4.51) .. 8
O140 „ 3d. blue (16.10.41) .. 8
O134/O140 .. .. *Set of* 7 1·40 7

1940 (2 Jan.–8 Mar. (8d.)). *Centennial. No.* 613, *etc., optd. with Type* O **5**.

O141 ½d. blue-green (R.) .. 8
a. "ff" joined, as Type O 4 .. 6·00 5·0
O142 1d. chocolate & scarlet (Bk.) 8
a. "ff" joined, as Type O 4 .. 6·00 5·0
O143 1½d. light blue & mve. (Bk.) 15 1
O144 2d. blue-grn. & choc. (Bk.) 20
a. "ff" joined, as Type O 4 .. 6·00 5·0
O145 2½d. blue-grn. & ultram. (Bk.) 8 2
a. "ff" joined, as Type O 4 .. 6·00 5·0
O146 3d. purple & carmine (R.) .. 60 2
a. "ff" joined, as Type O 4 .. 6·00 5·0
O147 4d. chocolate & lake (Bk.) .. 75 4
a. "ff" joined, as Type O 4 .. 6·00 5·0
O148 6d. emerald-grn. & vio. (Bk.) 1·00 5
a. "ff" joined, as Type O 4 .. 6·00 5·0
O149 8d. black and red (Bk.) .. 1·00 1·1
a. "ff" joined, as Type O 4 .. 6·00 5·0
O150 9d. olive-grn. & verm. (Bk.) 85 7
O151 1s. sage-grn. & dp. grn. (Bk.) 4·50 7
O141/O151 .. .. *Set of* 11 8·75 4·0

1947–49. *Nos.* 680, *etc., optd. with Type* O **4**.

O152 **108a** 2d. orange 8
O153 „ 4d. bright purple .. 20 1
O154 „ 6d. carmine 40 2
O155 „ 8d. violet 60 2
O156 „ 9d. purple-brown .. 1·50 1·5

O157 **144** 1s. red-brown & carm. (*wmk. upright*) (Pl. 1) 1·50 40
a. Wmk. sideways (Pl. 1) ('49) 1·50 40
b. Wmk. upright (Pl. 2) 2·25 1·00
O158 „ 2s. brown-orge. & grn. (*wmk. sideways*) (Pl. 1) .. .. 2·00 75
a. Wmk. upright (Pl. 1) .. 2·00 75
O152/O158 .. .. *Set of 7* 6·00 3·00

O 6. Queen Elizabeth II.

6d

(**O 7**)

(Des. J. Berry. Recess. Bradbury, Wilkinson.)

1954 (1 Mar.)–**63.** *W* **98.** *P* 14×13½.
O159 **O 6** 1d. orange 12 8
O160 „ 1½d. brown-lake .. 25 40
O161 „ 2d. bluish green .. 30 10
O162 „ 2½d. olive (1.3.63) .. 40 30
O163 „ 3d. vermilion 12 8
O164 „ 4d. blue 25 10
a. Ptd. on gummed side 55·00
O165 „ 9d. carmine 40 25
O166 „ 1s. purple 40 15
O167 „ 3s. slate (1.3.63) . 8·00 10·00
O159/O167 .. .. *Set of 9* 9·00 10·00

See note *re* white opaque paper after No. 736. Nos. O162 and O167 exist only on white paper.

1959 (1 Oct.). *No.* O160 *surch. with Type* O **7.**
O168 **O 6** 6d. on 1½d. brown-lake 25 25

1961 (1 Sept.). *No.* O161 *surch. as Type* O **7.**
O169 **O 6** 2½d. on 2d. bluish green 30 30

Owing to the greater use of franking machines by Government Departments, the use of official stamps was discontinued on 31st March, 1965, but they remained on sale at the G.P.O. until 31st December, 1965.

PROVISIONALS ISSUED AT REEFTON AND USED BY THE POLICE DEPARTMENT.

1907 (Jan.). *Current stamps of* 1906, *overwritten* "Official," *in red ink, and marked* "Greymouth—paid—3" *inside a circular postmark-stamp. P* 14.
P1 **23** ½d. green .. .. .. 40·00 80·00
P2 **40** 1d. carmine .. .. .. 40·00 80·00
P3 **38***a* 2d. purple .. .. .. 50·00 80·00
P4 **28** 3d. bistre .. .. .. 50·00 80·00
P5 **31** 6d. pink .. .. .. 60·00 80·00
P6 **34** 1s. orange-red .. .. 80·00 £110
P7 **35** 2s. green .. .. .. — £400

LIFE INSURANCE DEPARTMENT.

L 1. Lighthouse. **L 2.**

(Des. W. B. Hudson and J. F. Rogers; eng. A. E. Cousins. Typo. Govt. Printing Office, Wellington.)

1891–98. A. *W* **12***c.*

P 12×11½ (2.1.91).
L 1 **L 1** ½d. bright purple .. 5·00 75
L 2 „ 1d. blue .. .. 5·00 75
a. Wmk. Type 12*b* .. 18·00 1·50
L 3 „ 2d. brown-red .. 12·00 75
a. Wmk. Type 12*b* .. 18·00 75
L 4 „ 3d. deep brown .. .. 18·00 5·00
L 5 „ 6d. green .. .. 25·00 9·00
L 6 „ 1s. rose .. .. 40·00 18·00

B. *W* **12***b* (1893–98).
(*a*) *P* 10 (1893)
L 7 **L 1** ½d. bright purple .. 4·00 75
L 8 „ 1d. blue .. .. 4·00 30
L 9 „ 2d. lake .. .. 4·00 85
(*b*) *Perf. compound of* 11 *and* 10 (1896).
L 9*a* **L 1** ½d. bright purple .. 8·50 3·00
L 9*b* „ 1d. blue .. .. 5·00 1·25
(*c*) *Perf. compound of* 10 *and* 11 (1897).
L10 **L 1** ½d. bright purple ..
L11 „ 1d. blue ..
(*d*) *Mixed perfs.* 10 *and* 11 (1897).
L12 **L 1** 2d. brown-red .. .. 45·00 45·00
(*e*) *P* 11 (1897–98).
L13 **L 1** ½d. bright purple .. 2·00 30
a. Thin coarse toned paper (1898) .. .. 4·00 85
L14 „ 1d. blue .. .. 4·00 10
a. Thin coarse toned paper (1898) .. .. 4·00 10
L15 „ 2d. brown-red .. 4·00 85
a. *Chocolate* .. .. 20·00 5·00
b. Thin coarse toned paper (1898) .. .. 5·00 1·10

1902–04. *W* **41** (*sideways*). (*a*) *P* 11.
L16 **L 1** ½d. bright purple (1903) 2·50 45
L17 „ 1d. blue (1902) .. 4·00 25
L18 „ 2d. brown-red (1904) .. 4·25 1·00
(*b*) *Perf. compound of* 11 *and* 14.
L19 **L 1** ½d. bright purple (1903)
L20 „ 1d. blue (1904) .. 8·50 95

Nos. L16/17 and L20 are known without watermark from the margins of the sheet.

1905–6. *Redrawn, with* "V.R." *omitted. W* **41** (*sideways*). (*a*) *P* 11.
L21 **L 2** 2d. brown-red (12.05) .. 65·00 8·50
(*b*) *P* 14.
L22 **L 2** 1d. blue (1906) .. .. 8·50 2·25
(*c*) *Perf. compound of* 11 *and* 14.
L23 **L 2** 1d. blue (1906) .. .. 25·00 25·00
a. Mixed perfs. .. ..

1913 (2 Jan.)–**37.** *New values and colours. W* **41.**
(*a*) *P* 14×15.
L24 **L 2** ½d. green 40 30
a. *Yellow-green* (1925) 40 30
L25 „ 1d. carmine .. 1·10 20
a. *Carmine-pink* (1925) .. 3·50 30
b. *Scarlet* (3.37) .. 40 20
L26 „ 1½d. black (1917) .. 4·00 2·00
L27 „ 1½d. chestnut-brown ('19) 20 40
L28 „ 2d. bright purple .. 5·00 3·00
L29 „ 2d. yellow (1920) .. 1·00 75
L30 „ 3d. yellow-brown .. 6·00 6·00
L31 „ 6d. carmine-pink .. 4·00 3·00
(*b*) *P* 14.
L32 **L 2** ½d. yellow-green (1926) 30 10
L33 „ 1d. scarlet (1931) .. 1·00 30
L34 „ 2d. yellow (1937) .. 85 85
L35 „ 3d. brown-lake (1931) .. 5·00 5·00
L36 „ 6d. pink (1925) .. 4·00 4·00

In the 1½d. the word "postage" is in both the side-labels instead of at left only.

1944–47. *W* **98.** *P* 14×15.
L37 **L 2** ½d. yellow-green (7.47) .. 65 65
L38 „ 1d. scarlet (6.44) .. 30 15
L39 „ 2d. yellow (1946) .. 50 1·00
L40 „ 3d. brown-lake (10.46) .. 2·50 2·50
L41 „ 6d. pink (7.47) .. 4·00 3·25

L 3. Castlepoint Lighthouse.

L 4. Taiaroa Lighthouse.

L 5. Cape Palliser Lighthouse.

L 6. Cape Campbell Lighthouse.

L 7. Eddystone Lighthouse.

L 9. The Brothers Lighthouse.

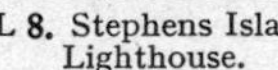

L 8. Stephens Island Lighthouse.

L 10. Cape Brett Lighthouse.

(Des. J. Berry. Recess. Bradbury, Wilkinson & Co.)

1947 (1 Aug.)–**65.** *W* **98** (*sideways on* 1*d.*, 2*d.*, 2½*d.*). *P* 13½.
L42 **L 3** ½d. grey-grn. & orge.-red 90 80
L43 **L 4** 1d. olive-grn. & pale bl. 10 8
L44 **L 5** 2d. dark bl. & grey-blk. 15 15
L45 **L 6** 2½d. black and bright blue (*whiter paper*) (4.11.63) 85 85
L46 **L 7** 3d. mauve & pale blue 20 20
L47 **L 8** 4d. brown & yell.-orge. 30 25
a. Wmk. sideways (13.10.65) 40 20
L48 **L 9** 6d. chocolate and blue 40 40
L49 **L 10** 1s. red-brown and blue 40 40
L42/49 .. .. *Set of* 8 3·00 3·00

2c

10c

(**L 11.**) (**L 12.**)

1967 (10 July)–**68.** *Decimal currency. Stamps of* 1947–65, *surch. as Type* **L 12** *or* **L 11** (2 *c.*).
L50 **L 4** 1 c. on 1d. (No. L43) .. 10 10
a. Wmk. upright (*whiter paper*) (10.5.68) .. 10 10
L51 **L 6** 2 c. on 2½d. (No. L45) 70 70

L52	L 7	2½ c. on 3d. (No. L46) ..	70	70
		a. Wmk. sideways (*whiter paper*) (4.68?) ..	20	20
L53	L 8	3 c. on 4d. (No. L47a)	35	35
L54	L 9	5 c. on 6d. (No. L48) ..	70	70
L55	L 10	10 c. on 1s. (No. L49) ..	70	70
		a. Wmk. sideways (*whiter paper*)	45	45
L50/55a		.. .. *Set of* 6	2·50	2·50

See note *re* white opaque paper below No. 736. No. L54 exists on both ordinary and whiter paper.

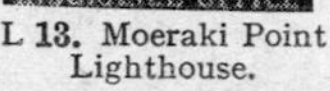

L 13. Moeraki Point Lighthouse.

L 15. Baring Head Lighthouse.

L 14. Puysegur Point Lighthouse.

(Des. J. Berry. Litho. B.W.)

1969 (27 MAR.)–**76**. *Types* L **13/15** *and similar designs. No wmk. P* 14 (8, 10 *c.*) *or* 13½ (*others*).

L56	½ c. greenish yellow, red and deep blue	1·25	1·25
L57	2½ c. ultramarine, green and pale buff	5	5
L58	3 c. reddish brown and yellow	5	5
L59	4 c. light new blue, yellowish green and apple-green ..	5	5
L60	8 c. multicoloured (17.11.76)	8	8
L61	10 c. multicoloured (17.11.76)	10	10
L62	15 c. blk., lt. yellow & ultram.	15	15
L56/62	.. .. *Set of* 7	1·50	1·50

Designs: *Horiz.*—4 c. Cape Egmont Lighthouse; *Vert.*—8 c. East Cape; 10 c. Farewell Spit; 15 c. Dog Island Lighthouse.

MINIMUM PRICE

The minimum price quoted is 5p which represents a handling charge rather than a basis for valuing common stamps. For further notes about prices see introductory pages.

POSTAL FISCAL STAMPS.

As from 1st April 1882 fiscal stamps were authorised for postal use and conversely postage stamps became valid for fiscal use. Stamps in the designs of 1867 with "STAMP DUTY" above the Queen's head were withdrawn and although some passed through the mail quite legitimately they were mainly "philatelic" and we no longer list them. The issue which was specifically authorised in 1882 was the one which had originally been put on sale for fiscal use in 1880.

Although all fiscal stamps were legally valid for postage only values between 2s. and £1 were stocked at ordinary post offices. Other values could only be obtained by request from the G.P.O., Wellington or from offices of the Stamp Duties Department. Later the Arms types above £1 could also be obtained from the head post offices in Auckland, Christchurch, Dunedin and also a branch post office at Christchurch North where there was a local demand for them.

It seems sensible to list under Postal Fiscals the Queen Victoria stamps up to the £1 value and the Arms types up to the £5 because by 1931 the higher values were genuinely needed for postal purposes. Even the £10 was occasionally used on insured airmail parcels.

Although 2s. and 5s. values were included in the 1898 pictorial issue, it was the general practice for the Postal Department to limit the postage issues to 1s. until 1926 when the 2s. and 3s. appeared. These were then dropped from the fiscal issues and when in turn the 5s. and 10s. were introduced in 1953 and the £1 in 1960 no further printings of these values occurred in the fiscal series.

FORGED POSTMARKS. Our prices are for stamps with genuine postal cancellations. Beware of forged postmarks on stamps from which fiscal cancellations have been cleaned off.

Many small post offices acted as agents for government departments and it was the practice to use ordinary postal date-stamps on stamps used fiscally, so that when they are removed from documents they are indistinguishable from postally used specimens unless impressed with the embossed seal of the Stamp Duties Department.

Date-stamps very similar to postal date-stamps were sometimes supplied to offices of the Stamp Duties Department and it is not clear when this practice ceased. Prior to the Arms types the only sure proof of the postal use of off-cover fiscal stamps is when they bear a distinctive duplex, registered or parcel post cancellation, but beware of forgeries of the first two.

F 1

(Die eng. W. R. Bock and A. E. Cousins. Typo. Govt. Ptg. Office.)

1882 (FEB.). *W* **12***a*. *P* 12×11½.

F1	F 1	1d. lilac	10·00	30·00
F2	,,	1d. blue	4·50	1·25

The 1d. fiscal was specifically authorised for postal use in February 1882 owing to a shortage of the 1d. Type **5** and pending the introduction of the 1d. Type **14** on 1st April.

The 1d. lilac fiscal had been replaced by the 1d. blue in 1878 but postally used copies with 1882 duplex postmarks are known although most postally used examples are dated from 1890 and these must have been philatelic.

F 2

F 3

(Dies eng. W. R. Bock and A. E. Cousins. Typo. Govt. Ptg. Office.)

1882 (Early). *W* **12***a*. *P* 12×11½.

F3 F **2** 1s. grey-green .. ..
F4 F **3** 1s. grey-green and red ..

Copies of these are known postally used in 1882 and although not specifically authorised for postal use it is believed that their use was permitted where there was a shortage of the 1s. postage stamp.

The 2s. value Type F **3** formerly listed is not known with 1882–83 postal date-stamps.

Wmk. Type F 5. The balance of the paper employed for the 1867 issue was used for early printings of Type F **4** introduced in 1880 before changing over to the "N Z" and Star watermark. The values we list with this watermark are known with 1882–83 postal date-stamps. Others have later dates and are considered to be philatelic, but should they be found with 1882–83 postal dates we would be prepared to add them to the list.

In the following list the 4d., 6d., 8d. and 1s. are known with early 1882 postal date-stamps and, like Nos. F3/4, it is assumed that they were used to meet a temporary shortage of postage stamps.

F 4

F 5

The 12s. 6d. value has the head in an oval (as Type **10**), and the 15s. and £1 values have it in a broken circle (as Type **7**).

(Dies eng. W. R. Bock. Typo. Govt. Ptg. Office.)

1882 (1 Apr.). *Type* F **4** *and similar types. "De La Rue" paper.*

A. *W* **12***a* (6 *mm.*).

(*a*) *P* 12 (1882).

No.	Description	Unused	Used
F 5	4d. orange-red (*Wmk. Type* F **5**)		
F 6	6d. lake-brown		
F 7	8d. green (*Wmk. Type* F **5**)		
F 8	1s. pink		
F 9	2s. blue	6·00	75
F10	2s. 6d. grey-brown	6·00	75
	a. Wmk. Type F 5		
F11	3s. mauve	8·50	1·25
F12	4s. brown-rose	12·00	2·00
F13	5s. green	18·00	1·25
	a. *Yellow-green*	18·00	1·25
F14	6s. rose	18·00	2·25
F15	7s. ultramarine	20·00	3·50
F16	7s. 6d. bronze-grey	20·00	4·50
F17	8s. deep blue	20·00	4·00
F18	9s. orange	25·00	4·00
F19	10s. brown-red	25·00	3·50
	a. Wmk. Type F 5		
F20	15s. green	25·00	4·00
F21	£1 rose-pink	40·00	12·00

(*b*) *P* 12½ (1886).

No.	Description	Unused	Used
F22	2s. blue	6·00	75
F23	2s. 6d. grey-brown	6·00	75
F24	3s. mauve	8·50	1·25
F25	4s. purple-claret	13·00	2·25
	a. *Brown-rose*	12·00	2·00
F26	5s. green	18·00	1·00
	a. *Yellow-green*	18·00	1·00
F27	6s. rose	18·00	2·25
F28	7s. ultramarine	20·00	3·50
F29	8s. deep blue	20·00	4·00
F30	9s. orange	25·00	4·00
F31	10s. brown-red	25·00	3·50
F32	15s. green	25·00	4·00
F33	£1 rose-pink	40·00	12·00

B. *W* **12***b* (7 *mm.*). *P* 12½ (1888).

No.	Description	Unused	Used
F34	2s. blue	6·00	75
F35	2s. 6d. grey-brown	6·00	75
F36	3s. mauve	8·50	1·25
F37	4s. brown-rose	12·00	2·00
	a. *Brown-red*	12·00	2·00
F38	5s. green	18·00	1·25
	a. *Yellow-green*	18·00	1·25
F39	6s. rose	18·00	2·25
F40	7s. ultramarine	20·00	3·50
F41	7s. 6d. bronze-grey	20·00	5·00
F42	8s. deep blue	20·00	4·00
F43	9s. orange	25·00	4·00
F44	10s. brown-red	25·00	3·50
	a. *Maroon*	25·00	3·50
F45	£1 pink	40·00	12·00

C. *W* **12***c* (4 *mm.*). *P* 12½ (1890).

No.	Description	Unused	Used
F46	2s. blue	12·00	3·00
F47	3s. mauve	18·00	3·00
F48	4s. brown-red	18·00	4·00
F49	5s. green	20·00	2·50
F50	6s. rose	25·00	2·50
F51	7s. ultramarine	30·00	6·50
F52	8s. deep blue	25·00	4·00
F53	9s. orange	25·00	4·00
F54	10s. brown-red	25·00	4·00
F55	15s. green	45·00	8·50

D. *Continuation of W* **12***b*. *P* 11 (1895–1901).

No.	Description	Unused	Used
F56	2s. blue	4·00	1·50
F57	2s. 6d. grey-brown	4·00	75
	a. Inscr. "COUNTERPART" (1901)*	18·00	
F58	3s. mauve	8·50	1·00
F59	4s. brown-red	10·00	2·25
F60	5s. yellow-green	10·00	1·00
F61	6s. rose	12·00	2·25
F62	7s. pale blue	20·00	3·50
F63	7s. 6d. bronze-grey	20·00	4·50
F64	8s. deep blue	20·00	4·00
F65	9s. orange	25·00	4·00
F66	10s. brown-red	20·00	3·25
	a. *Maroon*	20·00	3·25
F67	15s. green	25·00	4·00
F68	£1 rose-pink	40·00	12·00

* The plate, normally printed in yellow and inscribed "COUNTERPART" just above the bottom value panel, was for use on the counterparts of documents but was issued in error in the colour of the normal fiscal stamp and accepted for use.

E. *W* **41** (*sideways*).

(i) *Unsurfaced "Cowan" paper.*

(*a*) *P* 11 (1903).

No.	Description	Unused	Used
F69	2s. 6d. grey-brown	4·00	75
F70	3s. mauve	8·50	1·00
F71	4s. orange-red	10·00	2·25
F72	6s. rose	12·00	2·25
F73	7s. pale blue	20·00	3·50
F74	8s. deep blue	20·00	4·00
F75	10s. brown-red	25·00	4·00
	a. *Maroon*	25·00	4·00
F76	15s. green	25·00	4·00
F77	£1 rose-pink	40·00	12·00

(*b*) *P* 14 (1906).

No.	Description	Unused	Used
F78	2s. 6d. grey-brown	4·00	75
F79	3s. mauve	8·50	1·00
F80	4s. orange-red	10·00	1·25
F81	5s. yellow-green	10·00	2·00
F82	6s. rose	12·00	2·25
F83	7s. pale blue	20·00	3·50
F84	7s. 6d. bronze-grey	20·00	5·00
F85	8s. deep blue	20·00	4·00
F86	9s. orange	25·00	4·00
F87	10s. maroon	20·00	3·25
F88	15s. green	25·00	4·00
F89	£1 rose-pink	40·00	12·00

(*c*) *P* 14½×14, *comb* (*clean-cut*) (1907).

No.	Description	Unused	Used
F90	2s. blue	3·00	75
F91	2s. 6d. grey-brown	4·00	75
F92	3s. mauve	8·50	1·00
F93	4s. orange-red	6·50	1·25
F94	6s. rose	12·00	2·25
F95	10s. maroon	20·00	3·25
F96	15s. green	25·00	4·00
F97	£1 rose-pink	40·00	12·00

(ii) *Chalk surfaced "De La Rue" paper.*

(*a*) *P* 14 (1913).

No.	Description	Unused	Used
F 98	2s. blue	3·00	75
F 99	2s. 6d. grey-brown	4·00	1·00
F100	3s. purple	8·50	1·00
F101	4s. orange-red	6·50	1·00
F102	5s. yellow-green	6·50	1·25
F103	6s. rose	12·00	2·25
F104	7s. pale blue	18·00	2·50
F105	7s. 6d. bronze-grey	20·00	4·50
F106	8s. dark blue	15·00	2·25
F107	9s. orange	25·00	4·00
F108	10s. maroon	20·00	3·25
F109	15s. green	25·00	4·00
F110	£1 rose-carmine	40·00	12·00

(*b*) *P* 14½×14, *comb* (1913–21).

No.	Description	Unused	Used
F111	2s. deep blue	3·00	75
F112	2s. 6d. grey-brown	4·00	1·00
F113	3s. purple	8·50	1·00
F114	4s. orange-red	6·50	1·25
F115	5s. yellow-green	6·50	1·25
F116	6s. rose	10·00	2·25
F117	7s. pale blue	18·00	2·50
F118	8s. dark blue	15·00	2·25
F119	9s. orange	20·00	4·00
F120	10s. maroon	20·00	3·00
F121	12s. 6d. deep plum (1921)	45·00	
F122	15s. green	25·00	3·00
F123	£1 rose-carmine	40·00	12·00

The "De La Rue" paper has a smooth finish and has toned gum which is strongly resistant to soaking.

(iii) *Chalk-surfaced "Jones" paper.*
P 14½×14, *comb* (1924).

No.	Description	Unused	Used
F124	2s. deep blue	3·00	75
F125	2s. 6d. deep grey-brown	4·00	1·00
F126	3s. purple	8·50	1·00
F127	5s. yellow-green	6·50	1·25
F128	10s. brown-red	20·00	3·25
F129	12s. 6d. deep purple	45·00	
F130	15s. green	25·00	5·00

The "Jones" paper has a coarser texture, is poorly surfaced and the ink tends to peal. The outline of the watermark commonly shows on the surface of the stamp. The gum is colourless or only slightly toned and washes off readily.

(iv) *Thick, opaque, chalk-surfaced "Cowan" paper.*
P 14½×14, *comb* (1925–30).

No.	Description	Unused	Used
F131	2s. blue	3·00	75
F132	2s. 6d. deep grey-brown	4·00	75
F133	3s. mauve	18·00	1·00
F134	4s. orange-red	6·50	1·25
F135	5s. yellow-green	6·50	1·25
F136	6s. rose	12·00	2·25
F137	7s. pale blue	18·00	2·50
F138	8s. dark blue	15·00	2·25
	a. Error Blue (as 2s.) (1930)		
F139	10s. brown-red	20·00	3·00
F140	12s. 6d. blackish purple	45·00	
F141	15s. green	25·00	3·00
F142	£1 rose-pink	40·00	12·00

The "Cowan" paper is white and opaque and the watermark, which is usually smaller than in the "Jones" paper, is often barely visible.

(v) *Thin, hard, chalk-surfaced "Wiggins, Teape" paper.*
P 14½×14, *comb* (1926).

No.	Description	Unused	Used
F143	4s. orange-red	8·50	1·00
F144	£1 rose-pink	40·00	18·00

The "Wiggins, Teape" paper has a vertical mesh with narrow watermark, whereas other chalk-surfaced papers with this perforation have a horizontal mesh and wider watermark.

F 6

35/-
(F 7)

(Des. H. L. Richardson. Typo. Govt. Ptg. Office.)

1931–40. *As Type* **F 6** *(various frames).* **W 41.** *P* 14.

(i) *Thick, opaque, chalk-surfaced "Cowan" paper, with horizontal mesh* (1931–35).

F145 1s. 3d. lemon (4.31) .. 1·50 1·50
F146 1s. 3d. orange-yellow .. 3·00 2·00
F147 2s. 6d. deep brown .. 2·50 1·00
F148 4s. red .. .. .. 3·50 1·00
F149 5s. green .. .. .. 6·00 2·25
F150 6s. carmine-rose .. .. 6·00 2·00
F151 7s. blue .. .. .. 10·00 2·50
F152 7s. 6d. olive-grey .. .. 12·00 12·00
F153 8s. slate-violet .. .. 7·00 2·50
F154 9s. brown-orange .. .. 10·00 6·00
F155 10s. carmine-lake .. .. 8·00 2·50
F156 12s. 6d. deep plum (9.35) .. 40·00 32·00
F157 15s. sage-green .. .. 18·00 5·00
F158 £1 pink .. .. .. 18·00 8·00
F159 25s. greenish blue .. .. 70·00 50·00
F160 30s. brown (1935) .. .. 60·00 42·00
F161 35s. orange-yellow £500 £500
F162 £2 bright purple .. .. £130 25·00
F163 £2 10s. red .. .. .. 90·00 80·00
F164 £3 green .. .. .. 90·00 35·00
F165 £3 10s. rose (1935) .. £400 £275
F166 £4 light blue (1935) .. £100 35·00
F167 £4 10s. dp. olive-grey (1935) £225 £225
F168 £5 indigo-blue .. .. £175 50·00

(ii) *Thin, hard "Wiggins, Teape" paper with vertical mesh* (1936–40).

(*a*) *Chalk-surfaced* (1936–39).

F169 1s. 3d. pale orange-yellow .. 1·60 25
F170 2s. 6d. dull brown .. .. 3·75 75
F171 4s. pale red-brown .. .. 5·00 75
F172 5s. green .. .. .. 8·00 2·00
F173 6s. carmine-rose .. .. 8·00 3·25
F174 7s. pale blue .. .. 10·00 5·00
F175 8s. slate-violet .. .. 20·00 12·00
F176 9s. brown-orange .. .. 12·00 6·50
F177 10s. pale carmine-lake .. 12·00 2·25
F178 15s. sage-green .. .. 25·00 10·00
F179 £1 pink .. .. .. 20·00 10·00
F180 30s. brown (1.39) .. .. 70·00 55·00
F181 35s. orange-yellow £500 £500
F182 £2 bright purple (1937) .. £140 28·00
F183 £3 green (1937) .. .. £100 35·00
F184 £5 indigo-blue (1937) .. £180 45·00

(*b*) *Unsurfaced* (1940).

F185 7s. 6d. olive-grey .. .. 20·00 12·00

Not all values listed above were stocked at ordinary post offices as some of them were primarily required for fiscal purposes but all were valid for postage.

1939. *No.* F161 *surch. with Type* F **7**.

F186 35/- on 35s. orange-yellow .. 30·00 30·00

Because the 35s. orange-yellow could so easily be confused with the 1s. 3d. in the same colour it was surcharged.

1940 (JUNE). *New values surch. as Type* F **7**. **W 41.** *"Wiggins, Teape" chalk-surfaced paper. P* 14.

F187 3/6 on 3s. 6d. grey-green .. 3·50 1·60
F188 5/6 on 5s. 6d. lilac .. .. 7·00 4·00
F189 11/- on 11s. yellow .. .. 20·00 10·00
F190 22/- on 22s. scarlet .. .. 42·00 35·00

These values were primarily needed for fiscal use.

1940–58. *As Types* **F 6** *(various frames).* **W 98.**

(i) *P* 14. *"Wiggins, Teape" chalk-surfaced paper with vertical mesh* (1940–56).

F191 1s. 3d. orange-yellow .. 1·40 25
F192 1s. 3d. yellow and black (*wmk. inverted*) (14.6.55) 1·50 25
a. Wmk. upright (9.9.55) .. 15·00 12·00
b. Error. Yellow and blue. Wmk. inverted (7.56) .. 5·00 5·00
F193 2s. 6d. deep brown .. .. 1·00 20
F194 4s. red-brown .. .. 2·00 35
F195 5s. green .. .. .. 3·00 60
F196 6s. carmine-rose .. .. 5·00 1·75
F197 7s. pale blue .. .. 5·00 2·25
F198 7s. 6d. olive-grey (*wmk. inverted*) (21.12.50) .. 10·00 10·00
F199 8s. slate-violet .. .. 5·00 2·00
F200 9s. brown-orange (1.46) .. 5·00 2·75
F201 10s. carmine-lake .. .. 5·00 1·25
F202 15s. sage-green .. .. 6·00 4·00
F203 £1 pink .. .. .. 8·00 3·00
F204 25s greenish blue (1946) .. 60·00 60·00
F205 30s. brown (1946) .. .. 60·00 60·00
F206 £2 bright purple (1946) .. 15·00 5·00
F207 £2 10s. red (*wmk. inverted*) (9.8.51) .. .. .. 80·00 80·00
F208 £3 green (1946) .. .. 25·00 15·00
F209 £3 10s. rose (11.48) .. £350 £275
F210 £4 light blue (*wmk. inverted*) (12.2.52) .. .. 35·00 18·00
F211 £5 indigo-blue .. .. 60·00 40·00

THREE SHILLINGS I.

THREE SHILLINGS II.

3s. 6d.

Type I. Broad seriffed capitals.

Type II. Taller capitals, without serifs.

Surcharged.

F212 3/6 on 3s. 6d. grey-green (I) (1942) .. .. .. 3·00 2·00
F213 3/6 on 3s. 6d. grey-green (II) (6.53) .. .. .. 15·00 15·00
F214 5/6 on 5s. 6d. lilac (1944) .. 6·00 3·00
F215 11/- on 11s. yellow (1942) .. 18·00 10·00
F216 22/- on 22s. scarlet (1945) .. 40·00 35·00

(ii) *P* 14 × 13½. *"Wiggins, Teape" unsurfaced paper with horizontal mesh* (1956–58).

F217 1s. 3d. yellow & blk. (11.56) 1·00 20
F218 £1 pink (20.10.58) .. .. 20·00 8·50

No. F192b had the inscription printed in blue in error but as many as 378,000 were printed.

From about 1949–53 inferior paper had to be used and for technical reasons it was necessary to feed the paper into the machine in a certain way which resulted in whole printings with the watermark inverted for most values. These are fully listed in the *Elizabethan Specialised Catalogue.* In the above list the prices are for the cheapest form.

F 8

1967 (10 JULY). *Decimal currency.* **W 98** *(sideways). Unsurfaced paper. P* 14.

F219 F **8** $4 deep reddish violet 5·00 5·00
F220 ,, $6 emerald .. .. 7·50 7·50
F221 ,, $8 light greenish blue .. 10·00 10·00
F222 ,, $10 deep ultramarine .. 12·00 12·00

The original printings were line perf. on paper with the sideways watermark inverted ("N Z" to right of star when viewed from the front). From 1968 the stamps were comb perforated with the sideways watermark normal. The prices quoted are for the current printings. Both are listed in the *Elizabethan Specialised Catalogue.*

ANTARCTIC EXPEDITIONS.

KING EDWARD VII LAND.

1908. *Shackleton Expedition.* T **40** *of New Zealand (p.* 14), *optd.* "King Edward VII Land" *in two lines, reading up.*

A1 1d. rose-carmine (No. 419*b* Royle) (G.) .. .. £180 15·00
a. Opt. double .. .. .. — £550
A1*b* 1d. rose-carmine (No. 418*b* Waterlow) (G.) £350 £200

A single used copy has been reported on the "dot" plate, No. 415.

VICTORIA LAND.

1911. *Scott Expedition. Stamps of New Zealand optd.* "VICTORIA LAND." *in two lines.*

A32 **50** ½d. green £250 £200
A **51** 1d. carmine .. .. .. 20·00 20·00
a. No stop after "LAND" .. £325 £375

These issues were made under authority of the New Zealand Postal Department and, while not strictly necessary, they actually franked correspondence to New Zealand. They were sold to the public at a premium.

NEW ZEALAND DEPENDENCIES

The British islands of Aitutaki, Niue and Penrhyn were annexed by New Zealand on 11 June 1901.

AITUTAKI.

Stamps of New Zealand overprinted or surcharged.

AITUTAKI. (1)

Ava Pene. 2 (½d.)

Tai Pene. 3 (1d.)

Rua Pene Ma Te Ava. 4 (2½d.)

Toru Pene. 5 (3d.)

Ono Pene. 6 (6d.)

Tai Tiringi. 7 (1s.)

1903 (JUNE)–**11.** 1902 *issue surch. with* T **1** *at top, and* T **2** *to* **7** *at foot.* **W 41.**

(*a*) *P* 14.

1 **23** ½d. green (R.) .. .. 1·25 2·25
2 **40** 1d. carmine (B.) .. .. 1·60 2·75
3 **27** 2½d. deep blue (R.) (9.11) .. 1·60 3·25
a. "Ava" without stop .. 35·00 38·00

(*b*) *P* 11.

4 **27** 2½d. blue (R.) .. .. 2·00 3·00
5 **28** 3d. yellow-brown (B.) .. 1·50 4·50
6 **31** 6d. rose-red (B.) .. .. 3·75 9·00
7 **34** 1s. bright red (B.) .. 21·00 24·00
a. "Tiringi" without stop .. 70·00 80·00
8 ,, 1s. orange-red (B.) .. 20·00 24·00
a. "Tiringi" without stop .. 80·00 90·00
b. *Orange-brown* .. 32·00 30·00
c. Do. "Tiringi" without stop £110 £120

With the exception of No. 3, the above were issued in Auckland on 12 June and in Aitutaki on 29 June 1903.

AITUTAKI.

Ono Pene.

(8)

1911–16. ½*d. and* 1*d. surch. as on Nos.* 1/2, 6*d. and* 1*s. as* T **8**.

9 **50** ½d. green (R.) (9.11) .. 30 80
10 **51** 1d. carmine (B.) (2.13) .. 45 1·25
11 **52** 6d. carm. (B.) (*p.* 14 × 14½) (23.5.16) .. .. 11·00 21·00
12 ,, 1s. verm. (B.) (*p.* 14 × 14½) (9.14) .. .. 21·00 26·00

1916–17. *King George V stamps surch. as* T **8**. *P* 14 × 14½.

13 **60** 6d. carmine (B.) (6.6.16) .. 3·00 6·00
a. Perf. 14 × 13½ .. .. 7·50 13·00
b. Vert. pair, 13/3a .. .. 20·00 24·00
14 ,, 1s. vermilion (B.) (3.17) .. 13·00 18·00
a. Perf. 14 × 13½ .. .. 12·00 21·00
b. Vert. pair, 14/4a .. .. 27·00 42·00
c. "Tai" without dot .. 60·00 70·00
d. "Tiringi" no dot on second "i" 70·00 75·00
e. "Tiringi" no dot on third "i" 90·00 £100

1917–18. *K.G.V stamps optd.* "AITUTAKI", *only, as in T* **8.** *W* **41.** *P* 14×14½.

15 **60** 2½d. deep blue (R.) (12.18) 45 1·25
 a. Perf. 14×13½ .. .. 60 1·25
 b. Vert. pair, 15/5a .. .. 15·00 20·00
16 „ 3d. chocolate (B.) (1.18) .. 75 2·25
 a. Perf. 14×13½ .. .. 1·00 2·25
 b. Vert. pair, 16/6a .. .. 14·00 18·00
17 „ 6d. carmine (B.) (11.17) .. 1·25 2·25
 a. Perf. 14×13½ .. .. 2·50 5·00
 b. Vert. pair, 17/7a .. .. 15·00 20·00
18 „ 1s. vermilion(B.) (11.17) .. 2·25 4·50
 a. Perf. 14×13½ .. .. 3·75 5·50
 b. Vert. pair, 18/8a .. .. 17·00 23·00

1917–20. *Optd.* "AITUTAKI" *as in T* **8.** *Typo.* *W* **41.** *P* 14×15.

19 **60b** ½d. green (R.) (2.20) .. 30 60
20 **51** 1d. carmine (B.) (5.20) .. 45 80
21 **60b** 1½d. slate (R.) (11.17) .. 60 1·50
22 „ 1½d. orge.-brn. (R.) (2.19) 60 1·50
23 „ 3d. chocolate (B.) (6.19) .. 1·00 2·50
19/23 .. .. *Set of* 5 2·75 7·00

(Des. and recess. Perkins, Bacon & Co.)

1920 (23 Aug.). *As Types of Cook Islands, but inscr.* "AITUTAKI". *No wmk.* *P* 14.

24 **10** ½d. black and deep green .. 75 90
25 **11** 1d. black and dull carmine 45 90
26 **12** 1½d. black and sepia .. 60 1·10
27 **13** 3d. black and deep blue .. 75 1·50
28 **14** 6d. red-brown and slate .. 1·50 3·25
29 **15** 1s. black and purple .. 2·25 4·50
24/29 .. .. *Set of* 6 6·00 14·00

(Recess. Govt. Printing Office, Wellington.)

1924–27. *As Types of Cook Islands, but inscr.* "AITUTAKI". *W* **41.** *P* 14.

30 **10** ½d. black and green (5.27) 45 90
31 **11** 1d. blk. & dp. carm. (10.24) 35 90
32 **16** 2½d. black & dull blue (10.27) 2·00 3·00

Cook Islands stamps superseded those of Aitutaki on 15 March, 1932. Separate issues were resumed in 1972 (see after Cook Islands).

NIUE.

NIUE

(1)

Stamps of New Zealand overprinted.

1902 (4 Jan.). *Handstamped with T* **1**, *in green or bluish green. Waterlow paper. Wmk. double-lined* "N Z" *and Star, T* **36a.** *P* 11.

1 **40** 1d. carmine £140 £140

A few overprints were made with a *greenish violet* ink. These occurred only in the first vertical row and part of the second row of the first sheet overprinted owing to violet ink having been applied to the pad.

NIUE.
½ PENI.
(2)

NIUE.
TAHA PENI.
3 (1d.)

NIUE.
2½ PENI.
(4)

1902 (4 Apr.). *Type-set surcharges. T* **2, 3,** *and* **4.**

(i) *Waterlow paper. No wmk.* *P* 11.

2 **27** 2½d. blue (R.) .. .. 45 1·10
 a. No stop after "PENI" .. 7·00 8·00

(ii) *Basted Mills paper. Wmk. double-lined* "N Z" *and Star, T* **36a.** (a) *Perf.* 14.

3 **23** ½d. green (R.) 30 75
 a. Spaced "U" and "E" .. 1·50 2·25
 b. Surch. inverted .. .. 60·00 70·00
4 **40** 1d. carmine (B.) .. .. 1·50 3·00
 a. Spaced "U" and "E" .. 5·00 6·00
 b. No stop after "PENI" .. 23·00 24·00
 c. Vars. a. and b. on same stamp 30·00 35·00

(b) *P* 11 *and* 14 *compound.*

5 **40** 1d. carmine (B.) 30 75
 a. Spaced "U" and "E" .. 1·50 2·00
 b. No stop after "PENI" .. 3·75 5·00
 c. Vars. a. and b. on same stamp 18·00 21·00

(c) *Mixed perfs.*

6 **23** ½d. green (R.) .. .. 60·00
7 **40** 1d. carmine (B.) .. .. 75·00

1902 (2 May). *Type-set surcharges, T* **2, 3.** *Cowan paper. Wmk. single-lined* "N Z" *and Star, T* **41.** (a) *P* 14.

8 **23** ½d. green (R.) 25 40
 a. Spaced "U" and "E" .. 1·10 1·75
9 **40** 1d. carmine (B.) 20 30
 a. Surcharge double £150
 b. Spaced "U" and "E" .. 4·50 5·00
 c. No stop after "PENI" .. 4·00 6·00
 d. Vars. b. and c. on same stamp 10·00 12·00

(b) *Perf.* 11 *and* 14 *compound.*

10 **23** ½d. green (R.) .. ..

(c) *Mixed perfs.*

11 **23** ½d. green (R.) .. .. 90·00
12 **40** 1d. carmine (B.) .. .. 60·00
 a. Spaced "U" and "E" ..

NIUE.
(5)

Tolu e Pene.
6 (3d.)

Ono e Pene.
7 (6d.)

Taha e Sileni.
8 (1s.)

1903 (28 Feb.). *Optd. with name at top, T* **5,** *and values at foot, T* **6/8,** *in blue.* *W* **41.** *P* 11.

13 **28** 3d. yellow-brown .. .. 1·10 2·00
14 **31** 6d. rose-red .. .. 45 3·00
15 **34** 1s. brown-red (*Error* "Tahae" joined) .. £250
16 " 1s. bright red .. .. 3·00 4·50
 a. Orange-red. .. .. 6·00 10·00

NIUE.
½ PENI.
(9)

NIUE.
(10)

1911 (30 Nov.). *½d. surch. with T* **9,** *others optd. at top as T* **5** *and values at foot as T* **7, 8.** *W* **41.** *P* 14×14½.

17 **50** ½d. green (C.) 25 30
18 **52** 6d. carmine (B.) .. .. 2·00 2·75
19 „ 1s. vermilion (B.) .. .. 3·75 7·00

1915 (Sept.). *Surch. as T* **4.** *W* **41.** *P* 14.

20 **27** 2½d. deep blue (C.) .. 75 1·75

1917 (Aug.). *1d. surch. as T* **3**, *3d. optd. as T* **5** *with value as T* **6.** *W* **41.**

21 **51** 1d. carmine (*p.* 14×15) (Br.) 70 1·75
 a. No stop after "Peni" .. 35·00
22 **60** 3d. choc. (*p.* 14×14½) (B.) 24·00 30·00
 a No stop after "Pene" .. £140
 b. Perf. 14×13½ .. .. 32·00 42·00
 c. Vert. pair, 22/2b .. .. 60·00

1917–21. *Optd. with T* **10.** *W* **41.**

(a) *P* 14×15.

23 **60b** ½d. green (R.) (2.20) .. 15 20
24 **51** 1d. carmine (B.) (10.17) 20 45
25 **60b** 1½d. slate (R.) (11.17) .. 40 75
26 „ 1½d. orange-brown (R.) (2.19) 30 70
27 „ 3d. chocolate (B.) (6.19) 40 75

(b) *P* 14×14½.

28 **60** 2½d. dp. blue (R.) (10.20) 40 75
 a. Perf. 14×13½ 55 75
 b. Vert. pair, 28/8a .. .. 6·50 9·00
29 „ 3d. chocolate (B.) (10.17) 75 80
 a. Perf. 14×13½ .. .. 80 1·50
 b. Vert. pair, 29/a .. .. 11·00 13·00
30 „ 6d. carmine (B.) (8.21) .. 1·25 2·00
 a. Perf. 14×13½ .. .. 1·50 2·50
 b. Vert. pair, 30/a .. .. 11·00 13·00
31 „ 1s. vermilion (B.) (10.18) 1·50 2·50
 a. Perf. 14×13½ .. .. 2·00 2·50
 b. Vert. pair, 31/a .. .. 11·00 13·00
23/31 .. .. *Set of* 9 5·00 8·00

1918–29. *Postal Fiscal stamps as Type* F **4** *of New Zealand optd. with T* **10.** *W* **41** (*sideways*).

(i) *Chalk-surfaced* "*De La Rue*" *paper.*

(a) *P* 14.

32 5s. yellow-green (R.) (7.18) .. 45·00 55·00

(b) *P* 14½×14, *comb.*

33 2s. deep blue (R.) (9.18) .. 10·00 15·00
34 2s. 6d. grey-brown (R.) (2.23) 10·00 15·00
35 5s. yellow-green (R.) (10.18) .. 12·00 18·00
36 10s. maroon (B.) (2.23) .. 50·00 60·00
37 £1 rose-carmine (B.) (2.23) .. 95·00 £110

(b) *Thick, opaque, white chalk-surfaced* "*Cowan*" *paper.* *P* 14½×14.

37a 5s. yellow-green (R.) (10.29) 12·00 18·00
37b 10s. brown-red (B.) (2.27) .. 50·00 60·00
37c £1 rose-pink (B.) (2.28) .. 95·00 £110

(Des., eng. and ptd. by Perkins, Bacon & Co.)

1920 (23 Aug.). *As T* **10** *to* **15** *of Cook Is., but inscr.* "NIUE". *No wmk.* *P* 14.

38 ½d. black and green 20 35
39 1d. black and dull carmine .. 35 70
40 1½d. black and red 30 70
41 3d. black and blue 45 75
42 6d. red-brown and green .. 75 1·50
43 1s. black and sepia .. .. 1·50 2·50
38/43 .. .. *Set of* 6 3·00 6·00

1925–27. *Pictorial stamps as* 1920 *and new values as T* **16/17** *of Cook Islands, but inscr.* "NIUE". *W* **41.** *P* 14.

44 ½d. black and green ('27) .. 20 35
45 1d. black & dp. carmine ('25) 20 45
46 2½d. black and blue (10.27) .. 45 90
47 4d. black and violet (10.27) .. 75 1·25

1927–28. *Admiral type of New Zealand optd. as T* **10.** *W* **41.** *P* 14. (a) "*Jones*" *paper.*

48 **72** 2s. deep blue (2.27) (R.) .. 6·00 11·00

(b) "*Cowan*" *paper.*

49 **72** 2s. light blue (R.) (2.28) .. 4·50 7·00

1931 (Apr.). *No.* 40 *surch. as T* **18** *of Cook Is.*

50 2d. on 1½d. black and red .. 35 45

1931 (12 Nov.). *Postal Fiscal stamps as Type* F **6** *of New Zealand optd. as T* **10.** *W* **41.** *Thick, opaque, chalk-surfaced* "*Cowan*" *paper.* *P* 14.

51 2s. 6d. deep brown (B.) .. 7·00 9·00
52 5s. green (R.) .. .. .. 12·00 18·00
53 10s. carmine-lake (B.) .. .. 25·00 30·00
54 £1 pink (B.) .. .. .. 40·00 45·00

See also Nos. 79/82 for different type of overprint.

(Des. L. C. Mitchell. Recess. Perkins, Bacon & Co.)

1932 (16 Mar.). *As T* **19** *to* **25** *of Cook Is., but frames include* "NIUE" *as well as* "COOK ISLANDS." *No wmk.* *P* 13.

55 ½d. black and emerald .. 20 30
 a. Perf. 14×13 .. .. 27·00
56 1d. black and deep lake .. 10 10
57 2d. black and red-brown .. 20 35
58 2½d. black and slate-blue .. 1·00 1·50
59 4d. black and greenish blue .. 1·75 2·00
 a. Perf. 14 .. .. 1·75 1·50
60 6d. black & orange-vermilion 80 1·50
61 1s. black and purple (*p.* 14) .. 1·75 2·10
55/61 .. .. *Set of* 7 7·00 8·50

(Recess-printed from Perkins, Bacon's plates at Govt. Ptg. Office, Wellington, N.Z.)

1932–36. *Pictorial types as* 1932, *but W* **41.** *P* 14.

62 ½d. black and emerald .. 10 12
63 1d. black and deep lake .. 10 10
64 2d. black & yell.-brn. (1.4.36) 10 10
65 2½d. black and slate-blue .. 10 20
66 4d. black and greenish blue .. 20 20
67 6d. black and red-orge. (1.4.36) 35 25
68 1s. black and purple (1.4.36) .. 1·00 1·50
62/68 .. .. *Set of* 7 1·75 2·50

See also Nos. 89/97.

1935 (7 May). *Silver Jubilee. Designs as Nos.* 63, 65 *and* 67 *(colours changed) optd. as T* **26** *of Cook Is. (wider vertical spacing on 6d.).* *W* **41.** *P* 14.

69 1d. red-brown and lake .. 20 35
a. Narrow "K" in "KING" .. 1·25 4·50
b. Narrow "B" in "JUBILEE" 1·25 4·50
70 2½d. dull and deep blue (R.) .. 75 1·25
a. Narrow first "E" in "GEORGE" .. 2·25 4·50
b. Imperf. between (vert. pair) .. £190
71 6d. green and orange .. 2·00 2·75
a. Narrow "N" in "KING" .. 7·50 12·00

For illustrations of varieties, see Cook Islands.

NIUE (13) NIUE. (14)

1937 (13 May). *Coronation Issue. Nos.* 599 *to* 601 *of New Zealand optd. with T* **13.**

72 1d. carmine 8 8
73 2½d. Prussian blue 8 8
74 6d. red-orange 15 25

1938 (2 May). *As T* **29** *to* **31** *of Cook Is., but frames inscr.* "NIUE COOK ISLANDS". *W* **41.** *P* 14.

75 1s. black and violet .. 60 60
76 2s. black and red-brown .. 80 80
77 3s. light blue & emerald-green 1·25 1·25

1940 (2 Sept.). *As T* **32** *of Cook Islands, but additionally inscr.* "NIUE". *W* **98.** *P* 13½ × 14.

78 3d. on 1½d. black and purple 10 10

1941–67. *Postal Fiscal stamps as Type* F **6** *of New Zealand with thin opt., T* **14.** *P* 14.

(i) *Thin, hard, chalk-surfaced "Wiggins, Teape" paper with vertical mesh* (1941–43).

(*a*) *W* **41.**

79 2s. 6d. deep brown (B.) (4.41) 5·00 6·00
80 5s. green (R.) (4.41) .. .. 35·00 40·00
81 10s. pale carm.-lake (B.) (6.42) 30·00 35·00
82 £1 pink (B.) (2.43?) .. .. 38·00 40·00

(*b*) *W* **98** (1944–45).

83 2s. 6d. deep brown (B.) (3.45) 1·10 1·25
84 5s. green (R.) (11.44) .. .. 1·25 1·60
85 10s. carmine-lake (B.) (11.45) .. 4·00 5·00
86 £1 pink (B.) (6.42) .. .. 7·00 8·00

(ii) *Unsurfaced "Wiggins, Teape" paper with horizontal mesh.* *W* **98** (1957–67).

87 2s. 6d. deep brown (*p.* 14 × 13½) (1.11.57) .. .. 65 1·00
88 5s. pale yellowish green (*Wmk. sideways*) (6.67) .. 18·00 20·00

Nos. 83/5 were later printed with the watermark inverted for technical reasons and the prices quoted are for the cheapest form. They are fully listed in the *Elizabethan Specialised Catalogue.*

No. 88 came from a late printing made to fill demands from Wellington, but no supplies were sent to Niue. It exists in both line and comb perf.

1944–46. *As T* **19** *to* **24** *and* **29** *to* **31** *of Cook Is. but additionally inscr.* "NIUE". *W* **98** *(sideways on ½d., 1d., 1s. and 2s.).*

89 ½d. black and emerald .. 8 8
90 1d. black and deep lake .. 8 8
91 2d. black and red-brown .. 8 8
92 2½d. black and slate-blue ('46) 10 10
93 4d. black and greenish blue .. 10 15
94 6d. black and red-orange .. 20 20
95 1s. black and violet .. 35 50
96 2s. black & red-brown ('45) 70 75
97 3s. light blue and emerald-green ('45) .. .. 1·00 1·10
89/97 .. .. *Set of* 9 2·40 2·75

1946 (1 June). *Peace. Stamps of New Zealand optd. as T* **14**, *but without stop (twice, reading up and down on 2d.).*

98 **132** 1d. green (Bk.) 5 5
99 **134** 2d. purple (B.) 8 8
100 **138** 6d. choc. and verm. (Bk.) 8 10
a. Opt. double, one albino ..
101 **139** 8d. black and carmine (B.) 10 12

Nos. 102/112 are no longer used.

15. Map of Niue.

16. Capt. Cook's *Resolution.*

17. Alofi Landing.

18. Native Hut.

19. Arch at Hikutavake.

20. Alofi Bay.

21. Spearing Fish.

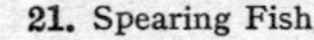

22. Cave, Makefu.

23. Bananas.

24. Matapa Chasm.

(Des. J. Berry. Recess. Bradbury, Wilkinson.)

1950 (3 July). *W* **98** *of New Zealand (sideways inverted on 1d., 2d., 3d., 4d., 6d. and 1s.).* *P* 13½ × 14 *(horiz.),* 14 × 13½ *(vert.).*

113 **15** ½d. orange and blue .. 5 5
114 **16** 1d. brown and blue-green 5 5
115 **17** 2d. black and carmine .. 8 8
116 **18** 3d. blue and violet-blue .. 8 8
117 **19** 4d. olive-grn. and pur.-brn. 10 10
118 **20** 6d. green & brown-orange 15 15
119 **21** 9d. orange and brown .. 25 25
120 **22** 1s. purple and black .. 30 30
121 **23** 2s. brn.-orge. & dull green 70 80
122 **24** 3s. blue and black .. 90 1·00
113/22 .. .. *Set of* 10 2·25 2·50

1953 (25 May). *Coronation. As Nos,* 715 *and* 717 *of New Zealand, but inscr.* "NIUE".

123 **164** 3d. brown 10 10
124 **166** 6d. slate-grey 15 20

(New currency. 100 cents = 1 dollar.)

1c

(25)

26

1967 (10 July). *Decimal currency.* (*a*) *Nos* 113/22 *surch. as T* **25.**

125 **15** ½ c. on ½d. 5
126 **16** 1 c. on 1d. 5
127 **17** 2 c. on 2d. 5
128 **18** 2½ c. on 3d. 5
129 **19** 3 c. on 4d. 8
130 **20** 5 c. on 6d. 12 1
131 **21** 8 c. on 9d. 15 1
132 **22** 10 c. on 1s. 20 2
133 **23** 20 c. on 2s. 50 6
134 **24** 30 c. on 3s. 65 7
125/34 .. .. *Set of* 10 1·75 1·9

(*b*) *Arms type of New Zealand without value, surch as in T* **26.** *W* **98** *of New Zealand (sideways)* *P* 14.

135 **26** 25 c. deep yellow-brown .. 45 5
a. Rough perf. 11 .. 5·50 5·5
136 „ 50 c. pale yellowish green 1·00 1·0
a. Rough perf. 11 .. 5·50 5·5
137 „ $1 magenta .. .. 2·00 2·0
a. Rough perf. 11 .. 6·50 6·5
138 „ $2 light pink .. .. 4·00 4·0
a. Rough perf. 11 .. 10·00 10·0

All values in perf. 14 exist in both line an comb perf. The perf. 11 stamps resulted fro an emergency measure in the course of printin

1967 (3 Oct.). *Christmas. As T* **278** *of Ne Zealand, but inscr.* "NIUE".

139 2½ c. multicoloured 10 1

1969 (1 Oct.). *Christmas. As T* **301** *of Ne Zealand, but inscr.* "NIUE". *W* **98** *of Ne Zealand.* *P* 13½ × 14½.

140 2½ c. multicoloured 10

27. "Pua".

28. "Golden Shower"
29. Flamboyant.
30. Frangipani.
31. Niue Crocus.
32. Hibiscus.
33. "Passion Fruit".
34. "Kampui".

35. Queen Elizabeth II (after Anthony Buckley

36. Tapeu Orchid.

(Des. Mrs. K. W. Billings. Litho. Enschedé

1969 (27 Nov.). *Flowers. Multicoloured; fram colours given.* *P* 12½ × 13½.

141 **27** ½ c. myrtle-green 5
142 **28** 1 c. orange-red 5
143 **29** 2 c. blackish olive 5
144 **30** 2½ c. yellow-brown 5
145 **31** 3 c. greenish blue 5
146 **32** 5 c. red 8
147 **33** 8 c. violet 10
148 **34** 10 c. yellow 15
149 **35** 20 c. steel-blue 30
150 **36** 30 c. bronze-green 40 4
141/150 .. .. *Set of* 10 1·10 1·

37. Kalahimu.

(Des. G. F. Fuller. Photo. Enschedé.)

1970 (19 Aug.). *Indigenous Edible Crabs. T* **37** *and similar horiz. designs. Multicoloured. P* 13½×12½.

151 3 c. Type **37** 5 5
152 5 c. Kalavi 12 10
153 30 c. Unga 45 45

1970 (1 Oct.). *Christmas. As T* **314** *of New Zealand, but inscr.* " NIUE ".

154 2½ c. multicoloured .. 10 15

38. Native Canoe and Aircraft over Jungle.

(Des. L. C. Mitchell. Litho. B.W.)

1970 (9 Dec.). *Opening of Niue Airport. T* **38** *and similar horiz. designs. Multicoloured. P* 13½.

155 3 c. Type **38** 5 5
156 5 c Ship, and Aircraft over Harbour 12 12
157 8 c. Aircraft over Airport .. 20 20

39. Polynesian Triller.

(Des. A. G. Mitchell. Litho. B.W.)

1971 (23 June). *Birds. T* **39** *and similar horiz. designs. Multicoloured. P* 13½.

158 5 c. Type **39** 10 10
159 10 c. Crimson Crowned Fruit-dove 20 20
160 20 c. Blue Crowned Lory .. 40 40

1971 (6 Oct.). *Christmas. As T* **325** *of New Zealand, but inscr.* " Niue ".

161 3 c. multicoloured 10 10

40. Niuean Boy.

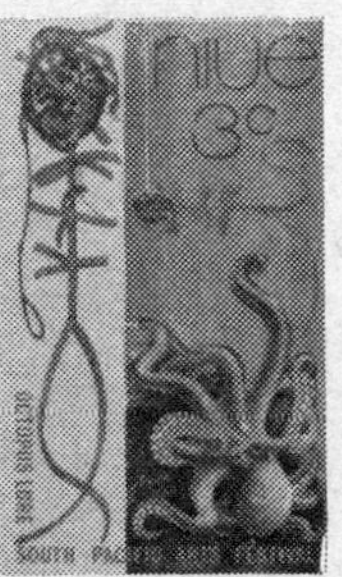

41. Octopus Lure.

(Des. L. C. Mitchell. Litho. Harrison.)

1971 (17 Nov.). *Niuean Portraits. T* **40** *and similar vert. designs. Multicoloured. P* 13×14.

162 4 c. Type **40** 5 5
163 6 c. Girl with garland .. 10 10
164 9 c. Man 15 15
165 14 c. Woman with garland .. 25 25

(Des. A. G. Mitchell. Litho. B.W.)

1972 (3 May). *South Pacific Arts Festival, Fiji. T* **41** *and similar multicoloured designs. P* 13½.

166 3 c. Type **28** 5 5
167 5 c. War weapons 8 8
168 10 c. Sika throwing (*horiz.*) .. 15 15
169 25 c. Vivi dance (*horiz.*) .. 40 40

42. Alofi Wharf.

(Des. A. G. Mitchell. Litho. Questa.)

1972 (6 Sept.). *25th Anniversary of South Pacific Commission. T* **42** *and similar horiz. designs. Multicoloured. P* 14.

170 4 c. Type **42** 8 8
171 5 c. Medical Services .. 10 10
172 6 c. Schoolchildren .. 12 12
173 18 c. Dairy cattle 35 35

1972 (4 Oct.). *Christmas. As T* **332** *of New Zealand but inscr.* " NIUE ".

174 3 c. multicoloured 10 10

43. Kokio.

(Des. G. F. Fuller. Litho. Harrison.)

1973 (27 June). *Fishes. T* **43** *and similar horiz. designs. Multicoloured. P* 14×13½.

175 8 c. Type **43** 15 15
176 10 c. Loi 20 20
177 15 c. Malau 30 30
178 20 c. Palu 35 35

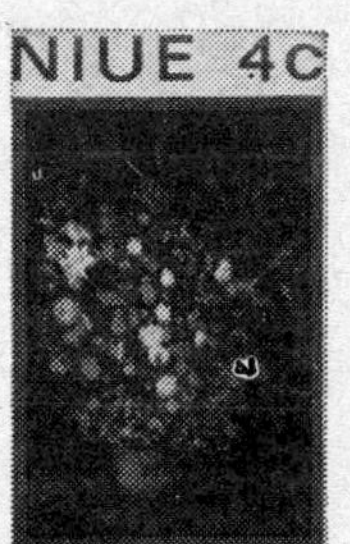

44. Flowers (Jan Brueghel).

(Des. and litho. Enschedé.)

1973 (21 Nov.). *Christmas. T* **44** *and similar vert. designs showing flower studies by the artists listed. Multicoloured. P* 14×13½.

179 4 c. Type **44** 10 10
180 5 c. Bollongier 10 10
181 10 c. Ruysch 25 25

45. Capt. Cook and Bowsprit.

(Des. A. Mitchell. Litho. Questa.)

1974 (20 June). *Bicentenary of Capt. Cook's Visit. T* **45** *and similar horiz. designs each showing Cook's portrait. Multicoloured. P* 13½×14.

182 2 c. Type **32** 5 5
183 3 c. Niue landing place .. 8 8
184 8 c. Map of Niue 15 15
185 20 c. Ensign of 1774 and Administration Building .. 35 35

SELF-GOVERNMENT.

46. King Fataaiki.

(Des. A. Mitchell. Litho. Questa.)

1974 (19 Oct.). *Self-Government. T* **46** *and similar multicoloured designs. P* 14×13½ *(4 and 8 c.) or* 13½×14 *(others).*

186 4 c. Type **46** 5 5
187 8 c. Annexation Ceremony, 1900 .. .. .. 12 15
188 10 c. Legislative Assembly Chambers (*horiz.*) .. 15 20
189 20 c. Village meeting (*horiz.*) .. 30 35

47. Decorated Bicycles.

(Des. B. C. Strong. Litho. D.L.R.)

1974 (13 Nov.). *Christmas. T* **47** *and similar vert. designs. P* 12½

190 3 c. multicoloured 5 5
191 10 c. multicoloured 20 20
192 20 c. dull red-brown, slate and black 30 35

Designs:—10 c. Decorated motorcycles; 20 c. Motor transport to church.

48. Children going to Church.

(Des. Enid Hunter. Litho. Questa.)

1975 (29 Oct.). *Christmas. T* **48** *and similar horiz. designs. Multicoloured. P* 14.

193	4 c. Type **48**	5	5
194	5 c. Child with balloons on bicycle	8	8
195	10 c. Balloons and gifts on tree	15	15

49. Hotel Buildings.

(Des. B. C. Strong. Litho. Harrison.)

1975 (19 Nov.). *Opening of Tourist Hotel. T* **49** *and similar horiz. design. Multicoloured. P* 13½×13.

196	8 c. Type **49**	8	10
197	20 c. Ground-plan and buildings	20	25

50. Preparing Ground for Taro.

(Des. A. Mitchell. Litho. Questa.)

1976 (3 Mar.). *T* **50** *and similar horiz. designs showing food gathering. Multicoloured. P* 13½×14.

198	1 c. Type **50**	5	5
199	2 c. Planting taro	5	5
200	3 c. Banana gathering ..	5	5
201	4 c. Harvesting taro	5	5
202	5 c. Gathering shell fish ..	5	5
203	10 c. Reef fishing	10	10
204	20 c. Luku gathering	20	20
205	50 c. Canoe fishing	50	55
206	$1 Coconut husking ..	95	1·10
207	$2 Uga gathering	1·90	2·25
198/207	.. .. *Set of* 10	3·25	3·75

51. Water.

(Des. A. Mitchell. Litho. Questa.)

1976 (7 July). *Utilities. T* **51** *and similar vert. designs. Multicoloured. P* 14.

208	10 c. Type **51**	10	12
209	15 c. Power	15	20
210	20 c. Telecommunications ..	20	25

52. Christmas Tree, Alofi.

(Des. A. Mitchell. Litho. Questa.)

1976 (15 Sept.). *Christmas. T* **52** *and similar horiz. design. Multicoloured. P* 14.

211	9 c. Type **52**	10	10
212	15 c. Church Service, Avatele	15	20

PENRHYN ISLAND.

Stamps of New Zealand overprinted or surcharged

PENRHYN ISLAND.
½ PENI.
(1)

PENRHYN ISLAND.
TAI PENI.
2 (1d.)

PENRHYN ISLAND.
2½ PENI.
(3)

1902 (5 May). 1902 *issue surch. with T* **1, 2** *and* **3.**

(1) *Waterlow paper. No wmk. P* 11.

1	**27**	2½d. blue (R.)	35	7
		a. "½" and "P" spaced ..	3·75	5·5

(2) *Basted Mills paper. Wmk. double-lined "N Z" and Star. T* **36a**. (*a*) *P* 11.

3	**40**	1d. carmine (Br.)	21·00	23·0

(*b*) *P* 14.

4	**23**	½d. green (R.)	35	5
		a. No stop after "ISLAND"	28·00	30·0
5	**40**	1d. carmine (Br.)	60	1·0
		a. *Pale carmine*	60	1·0

(*c*) *P* 11×14.

7	**40**	1d. carmine (Br.)	24·00	28·0

(*d*) *Mixed perfs.*

8	**40**	1d. carmine (Br.)	55·00	

(3) *Cowan paper. Wmk. single-lined "N Z" and Star, T* **41**. (*a*) *P* 14.

9	**23**	½d. green (R.)	25	3
		a. No stop after "ISLAND"	21·00	24·0
10	**40**	1d. carmine (B.)	25	3
		a. No stop after "ISLAND"	13·00	17·0

(*b*) *P* 11×14.

11	**40**	1d. carmine (B.)		

(*c*) *Mixed perfs.*

12	**23**	½d. green (R.)	45·00	50·0
13	**40**	1d. carmine (B.)	24·00	32·0

PENRHYN ISLAND.
(4)

Toru Pene.
5 (3d.)

Ono Pene.
6 (6d.)

Tahi Silingi.
7 (1s.)

1903 (28 Feb.). 1902 *issue surch. with name at top, T* **4**, *and values at foot, T* **5/7**. *W* **41** *P* 11.

14	**28**	3d. yellow-brown (B.) ..	2·00	3·0
15	**31**	6d. rose-red (B.)	4·50	6·0
16	**34**	1s. brown-red (B.)	10·00	14·0
17	,,	1s. bright red (B.)	10·00	14·0
18	,,	1s. orange-red (B.)	12·00	17·0

1914–15. *Surch. with T* **1** (*½d.*) *or optd. with T at top and surch. with T* **6/7** *at foot.*

19	**50**	½d. yellow-green (C.) (5.14)	35	6
		a. No stop after "ISLAND" ..	12·00	15·0
		b. No stop after "PENI" ..	23·00	27·0
20	,,	½d. yellow-green (V.) (1.1	20	3
		a. No stop after "ISLAND"	6·00	7·0
		b. No stop after "PENI" ..	12·00	15·0
22	**52**	6d. carmine (B.) (8.14) ..	12·00	15·0
23	,,	1s. vermilion (B.) (8.14) ..	15·00	23·0

1917–20. *K.G. V stamps optd. with name only T* **4**. *P* 14×14½.

24	2½d. blue (R.) (10.20)	45	7
	a. No stop after "ISLAND" ..	18·00	23·0
	b. Perf. 14×13½	75	1·1
	c. Vert. pair, 24/4b	12·00	15·0
25	3d. chocolate (B.) (6.18) ..	3·00	4·5
	a. Perf. 14×13½	3·25	6·0
	b. Vert. pair 25/5a	17·00	20·0
26	6d. carmine (B.) (1.18) ..	2·00	3·0
	a. No stop after "ISLAND" ..	27·00	35·0
	b. Perf. 14×13½	2·00	3·0
	c. Vert. pair, 26/6b	14·00	18·0
27	1s. vermilion (B.) (12.17) ..	4·50	6·0
	a. No stop after "ISLAND" ..	27·00	32·0
	b. Perf. 14×13½	5·50	6·0
	c. Vert. pair, 27/7b	27·00	30·0

1917–20. *Optd. as T* **4**. *Typo. W* **41**. *P* 14×15.

28	**60b**	½d. green (R.) (2.20) ..	20	35
		a. No stop after "ISLAND"	6·00	8·50
		b. Narrow spacing..	..	
29	„	1½d. slate (R) (11.17) ..	75	1·10
		a. Narrow spacing..	..	
30	„	1½d. orange-brn. (R.) (2.19)	25	50
		a. Narrow spacing..	..	
31	„	3d. chocolate (B.) (6.19)..	60	1·00
		a. Narrow spacing..	..	

The overprint was applied in a setting of 30 (6×5) in which Nos. 22 to 24 had "PENRHYN ISLANDS." spaced approximately ½ mm. apart instead of 1¼ mm.

(Recess. Perkins Bacon & Co., Ltd.)

1920 (23 Aug.). *As Types of Cook Islands but inscr.* "PENRHYN". *No wmk. P* 14.

32	**10**	½d. black and emerald ..	25	35
		a. Imperf. between (vert. pr.)	£190	
33	**11**	1d. black and deep red ..	45	75
34	**12**	1½d. black and deep violet	60	1·00
35	**13**	3d. black and red	75	1·10
36	**14**	6d. red-brown and sepia ..	1·10	2·50
37	**15**	1s. black and slate-blue ..	2·25	4·50
32/37		.. .. *Set of* 6	5·00	9·00

(Recess. Govt. Printing Office, Wellington.)

1927–29. *As Types of Cook Islands, but inscr.* "PENRHYN". *W* **41**. *P* 14.

38	**10**	½d. black and green (5.29)	30	70
39	**11**	1d. blk. & dp. carm. (14.3.28)	50	75
40	**16**	2½d. red-brn. & dull bl. (10.27)	80	2·50

Cook Islands stamps superseded those of Penrhyn Islands on 15th March, 1932. Separate issues were resumed in 1973 (see after COOK ISLANDS).

For stamps of New Zealand overprinted "**RAROTONGA**" see Cook Islands and for stamps overprinted "**SAMOA**" see list under that heading.

ROSS DEPENDENCY.

This comprises a sector of the Antarctic continent and a number of islands. It was claimed by Great Britain on 30 July 1923 and soon afterward put under the jurisdiction of New Zealand.

1. H.M.S. *Erebus*.

2. Shackleton and Scott.

3. Map of Ross Dependency and New Zealand.

4. Queen Elizabeth II.

(Des. E. M. Taylor (3d.), L. C. Mitchell (4d.) R. Smith (8d.), J. Berry (1s. 6d.). Recess D.L.R.)

1957 (11 Jan.). *W* **98** *of New Zealand (Mult. NZ and Star). P* 13 (1s. 6d.) *or* 14 (*others*).

1	**1**	3d. indigo	15	20
2	**2**	4d. carmine-red	25	30
3	**3**	8d. bright carmine-red and ultramarine (*shades*) ..	35	40
4	**4**	1s. 6d. slate-purple	80	90

(New currency. 100 cents = 1 dollar.)

5. H.M.S. *Erebus*.

1967 (10 July). *Decimal currency. As Nos.* 1/4 *but with values inscr. in decimal currency as T* **5**. *Chalky paper (except* 15 c.). *W* **98** *of New Zealand (sideways on* 7 c.). *P* 13 (15 c.) *or* 14 (*others*).

5	**5**	2 c. indigo (*shades*)	12	15
6	**2**	3 c. carmine-red	20	25
7	**3**	7 c. bright carmine-red and ultramarine	30	30
8	**4**	15 c. slate-purple	65	70

6. Skua.

7. Scott Base.

(Des. M. Cleverley. Litho. B.W.)

1972 (18 Jan.). *Various horiz. designs as T* **6/7**. *P* 14½×14 (10 c., 18 c.) *or* 13 (*others*).

9	3 c. black, brownish grey and pale blue	5	5
10	4 c. black, Royal blue & vio.	5	8
11	5 c. black, brownish grey and rose-lilac	5	10
12	8 c. black, yellow-brown and brownish grey	8	15
13	10 c. black, turquoise-green & slate-green	10	20
14	18 c. black, vio. & bright vio.	20	30
9/14	.. .. *Set of* 6	50	75

Designs: *Size as T* **6**—4 c. "Hercules" aeroplane at Williams Field; 5 c. Shackleton's Hut; 8 c. Supply ship H.M.N.Z.S. *Endeavour*. *Size as T* **7**—18 c. Tabular ice floe.

TOKELAU ISLANDS.

Formerly known as the Union Islands, and administered as part of the Gilbert & Ellice Islands Colony, they were transferred to New Zealand on 4 Nov. 1925 and then administered by Western Samoa. The islands were finally incorporated in New Zealand on 1 Jan. 1949 and became a dependency. The name Tokelau was adopted on 7 May 1946.

1. Atafu Village and Map.

2. Nukunonu Hut and Map.

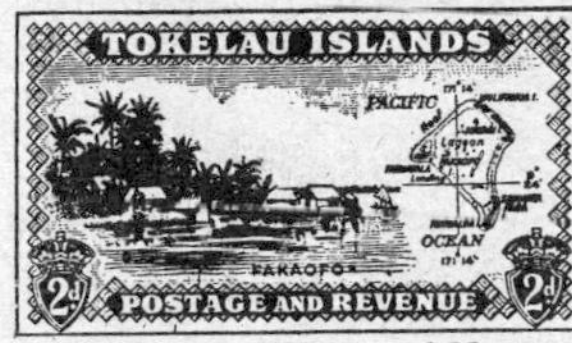

3. Fakaofo Village and Map.

(Des. J. Berry from photographs by T. T. C. Humphrey. Recess. Bradbury, Wilkinson.)

1948 (22 June). *Wmk. T* **98** *of New Zealand (Mult. N Z and Star). P* 13½.

1	**1**	½d. red-brown and purple ..	8	15
2	**2**	1d. chestnut and green ..	12	15
3	**3**	2d. green and ultramarine ..	15	25

1953 (15 June*). *Coronation. As No.* 715 *of New Zealand, but inscr.* "TOKELAU ISLANDS".

4	**164**	3d. brown	85	1·50

* This is the date of issue in Tokelau Islands but the stamps were released in New Zealand on 25th May.

ONE SHILLING

(4)

6D TOKELAU ISLANDS

(5)

1956 (27 Mar.). *No.* 1 *surch. with T* **4**.

5	**1**	1s. on ½d. red-brown & purple	60	1·40

1966 (8 Nov.). *Stamps of New Zealand, as T* **73a**, *but without value, surch. as T* **5**. *W* **98** *of New Zealand. P* 14.

6	**73a**	6d. light blue	15	20
7	„	8d. light emerald	35	40
8	„	2s. light pink	60	70

(New currency. 100 cents = 1 dollar (New Zealand).)

1c

(6)

1967 (10 July). *Decimal currency.* (*a*) *Nos.* 1/3 *surch. in decimal currency as T* **6**.

9	**2**	1 c. on 1d.	5	5
10	**3**	2 c. on 2d.	5	5
11	**1**	10 c. on ½d.	20	20

5c TOKELAU ISLANDS

(7)

(b) *Stamps of New Zealand, as T* **73a**, *but without value, surch. as T* **7**. *W* **98** *of New Zealand (sideways). P* 14 *(line or comb).*

12	**73a**	3 c. reddish lilac	5	8
13	,,	5 c. light blue	10	10
14	,,	7 c. light emerald ..	10	12
15		20 c. light pink	50	50

8. British Protectorate (1877).

9. Annexed to Gilbert and Ellice Islands (1916).

10. New Zealand Administration (1925).

11. New Zealand Territory (1948).

(Des. Tokelau Islands Administration. Litho. B.W.)

1969 (8 Aug.). *History of Tokelau Islands. W* **98** *of New Zealand. P* 13 × 12½.

16	**8**	5 c. ultram., yell. & black	10	10
17	**9**	10 c. verm., yellow & black	15	15
18	**10**	15 c. green, yellow & black	25	25
19	**11**	20 c. yell-brn., yell. & black	35	35

1969 (1 Oct.). *Christmas. As T* **301** *of New Zealand, but inscr.* "TOKELAU ISLANDS". *W* **98** *of New Zealand. P* 13½ × 14½.

20	**301**	2 c. multicoloured ..	10	15

1970 (1 Oct.). *Christmas. As T* **314** *of New Zealand, but inscr.* "TOKELAU ISLANDS". *P* 12½.

21	**314**	2 c. multicoloured ..	10	15

12. H.M.S. *Dolphin*, 1765. **13.** Fan.

(Des. D. B. Stevenson. Litho. B.W.)

1970 (9 Dec.). *Discovery of the Tokelau Islands T* **12** *and similar multicoloured designs. P* 13½.

22	5 c. Type **12**	10	10
23	10 c. H.M.S. *Pandora*, 1791 (*vert.*)	20	20
24	25 c. *General Jackson*, 1835 (*horiz.*)	45	45

(Des. Enid Hunter. Litho. Harrison.)

1971 (20 Oct.). *Various horiz. designs as T* **13** *showing handicrafts. Multicoloured. P* 14.

25	1 c. Type **13**	5	5
26	2 c. Hand-bag	5	5
27	3 c. Basket	5	5
28	5 c. Hand-bag	5	5
29	10 c. Shopping-bag	10	12
30	15 c. Fishing box	15	20
31	20 c. Canoe	20	25
32	25 c. Fishing hooks	25	30
25/32	.. .. *Set of* 8	80	90

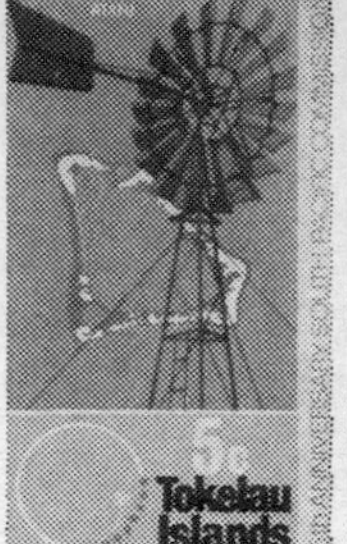

14. Windmill Pump. **15.** Horny Coral.

(Des. A. G. Mitchell. Litho. Questa.)

1972 (6 Sept.). *25th Anniversary of South Pacific Commission. T* **14** *and similar vert. designs. Multicoloured. P* 14 × 13½.

33	5 c. Type **14**	10	10
34	10 c. Community well ..	20	20
35	15 c. Pest eradication ..	30	30
36	20 c. Flags of member nations	40	40

In No. 35 "PACIFIC" is spelt "PACFIC".

(Des. Eileen Mayo. Litho. B.W.)

1973 (12 Sept.). *Coral. T* **15** *and similar vert. designs. Multicoloured. P* 13.

37	3 c. Type **15**	5	5
38	5 c. Soft Coral	10	10
39	15 c. Mushroom Coral	30	30
40	25 c. Staghorn Coral	50	50

16. Hump-back Cowrie.

(Des. G. F. Fuller. Litho. Questa.)

1974 (13 Nov.). *"Shells of the Coral Reef". T* **16** *and similar horiz. designs. Multicoloured. P* 14.

41	3 c. Type **16**	5	5
42	5 c. Tiger Cowrie	8	8
43	15 c. Mole Cowrie	25	25
44	25 c. Eyed Cowrie	35	40

17. Moorish Idol.

(Des. Eileen Mayo. Litho. Questa.)

1975 (19 Nov.). *Fishes. T* **17** *and similar vert. designs. Multicoloured. P* 14.

45	5 c. Type **17**	5	5
46	10 c. Long-nosed Butterfly-fish	8	10
47	15 c. Lined Butterfly-fish ..	15	20
48	25 c. Red Fire-fish	25	30

18. Canoe Making.

(Des. Faraimo Paulo. Litho. Questa.)

1976 (27 Oct.). *T* **18** *and similar multicoloure designs showing local life. P* 14 × 13½ (9 *to* $1) *or* 13½ × 14 *(others).*

49	1 c. Type **18**	5	
50	2 c. Reef fishing	5	
51	3 c. Weaving preparation ..	5	
52	5 c. Umu (kitchen)	5	
53	9 c. Carving	8	1
54	20 c. Husking coconuts ..	20	2
55	50 c. Wash day	50	5
56	$1 Meal time	1·00	1·1
49/56	.. .. *Set of* 8	1·60	1·8

Nos. 53/6 are vertical designs.

NIGER COAST PROTECTORATE.

For GREAT BRITAIN stamps used in Niger Coast, see index to Great Britain Stamps Used Abroad list.

I. OIL RIVERS PROTECTORATE.

Constituted on 5 June 1885 by the Berlin Conference.

OIL RIVERS

(1)

(2)

1892 (JULY). *Stamps of Great Britain optd. by D.L.R. with T* **1**.

71 ½d. vermilion .. .. 1·50 1·90
57 1d. lilac .. .. .. 1·50 1·90
a. Opt. reversed "OIL RIVERS" at top .. £850
b. Bisected (½d.) (on cover) .. † £550
73 2d. green and carmine .. 2·25 2·25
a. Bisected (1d.) (on cover) ..
74 2½d. purple/*blue* .. .. 1·75 1·90
78 5d. dull purple and blue .. 2·25 2·50
82 1s. green .. .. .. 11·00 11·00
/6 .. .. *Set of* 6 18·00 19·00
/6 H/S "Specimen" *Set of* 6 £100

Control letters. ½d. E, K, L, M.
1d. L, N, O, P, Q.

Nos. 2 to 6 surcharged locally.

1893 (3 SEPT.). *As T* **2**.

7 ½d. on half of 1d. (R.) .. 32·00 32·00
aa. Unsevered pair £120 £110
a. Surch. inverted and dividing line reversed (unsevered pair) .. — £950
b. Surch. reversed (dividing line running from left to right) ..
c. Straight top to "1" in "½" .. 55·00 55·00
d. "½" omitted .. ..
e. Surch. double (in pr. with normal)
8 ½d. on half of 1d. (V.) .. £850 £850
a. Surch. double (pair) £2000

Nos. 7 and 8 exist *se-tenant. Price* £1000 *used.*

HALF
PENNY.

(3)

HALF
PENNY.

(4)

1893 (DEC.). *With T* **3**.

9 ½d. on 2d. (V.) .. .. 60·00 60·00
a. Surch. inverted .. ..
b. Surch. diagonal (up) ..
c. Surch. vertical (up or down) .. £250
10 ½d. on 2½d. (Verm.) £1300
a. Surch. carmine .. £2200

With T **4**.

11 ½d. on 2½d. (G.) .. .. 60·00 60·00
a. Surch. double £450
b. Surch. diagonally inverted .. £325
12 ½d. on 2½d. (Verm.) .. .. 70·00 70·00
13 ½d. on 2½d. (C.) .. .. 60·00 60·00
a. Surch. omitted (in pr.) ..
14 ½d. on 2½d. (B.) .. .. 90·00 90·00
15 ½d. on 2½d. (Bk.) £450
a. Surch. inverted .. ..
b. Surch. diagonal inverted (up or down) £450
16 ½d. on 2½d. (B.-Bk.) £325

In T **3** "HALF" measures 9½ mm. and "PENNY" 12½ mm. with space 1½ mm. between the words. Bar 14½ mm. ending below the stop. The "F" is nearly always defective.

In T **4** "HALF" is 8½ mm., "PENNY" 12½ mm., spacing 2½ mm., and bar 16 mm., extending beyond the stop.

HALF
PENN.Y

HALF
PENNY

5. (Stop after "N") **6.** (No stop after "N").

With T **5**.

17 ½d. on 2½d. (Verm.) .. .. 70·00 70·00
a. Surch. double.. .. .. — £250
b. Surch. vertical (up) .. ..

With T **6**.

18 ½d. on 2d. (V.) .. .. .. £120 80·00
19 ½d. on 2½d. (Verm.) .. .. 38·00 35·00
a. Surch. inverted £240
b. Surch double.. .. .. — £230
c. Surch. diagonal (up or down) .. £230
d. Surch. omitted (in strip of 3) .. £1000
e. Surch. vertical (up or down) .. £170
f. Surch. diagonal, inverted (up or down) £375

In T **5** the "P" and "Y" are raised, and the space between the words is about 4 mm. Bar is short, approx. 13½ mm. T **6** is similar but without the stop after "N".

Half
Penny

(7)

Half
Penny

(8)

With T **7**.

20 ½d. on 2d. (V.) .. .. .. 38·00 38·00
a. Surch. double .. .. — £1200
b. Surch. vertical (up or down) .. £230
c. Surch. diagonal (up or down) .. £240
d. Surch. diagonal (inverted) ..
21 ½d. on 2½d. (Verm.) .. .. 38·00 34·00
a. Surch. double £800
b. Surch. vertical (up or down) .. £240
c. Surch. inverted £325
d. Surch. diagonal (up or down) .. £240
e. Surch. diagonal, inverted (up) .. £650
22 ½d. on 2½d. (B.) £850 £750
23 ½d. on 2½d. (C.) .. ..
24 ½d. on 2½d. (V.) £375

With T **8**.

25 ½d. on 2½d. (Verm.) .. .. 48·00 50·00
a. Surch. diagonal (up) .. ..
26 ½d. on 2½d. (B.) .. ..
27 ½d. on 2½d. (G.) .. .. 42·00 42·00
28 ½d. on 2½d. (C.) .. ..

In T **7** the "a" and "e" are narrow and have a short upward terminal hook. The "l" has a very small hook. The letters "nny" have curved serifs, and the distance between the words is 5½ mm.

In T **8** the "a" and "e" are wider. The "l" has a wider hook. The letters "nny" have straight serifs, and the distance between the words is 4½ mm.

HALF
PENNY.

(9)

HALF
PENNY

(10)

With T **9**.

29 ½d. on 2d. (V.) .. .. .. 48·00 55·00
30 ½d. on 2d. (B.) £140 £130
a. Surch. double .. ..
31 ½d. on 2½d. (Verm.) £110 £110
a. Surch. double .. .. ..
32 ½d. on 2½d. (B.) .. .. 65·00 65·00
33 ½d. on 2½d. (G.) .. .. 65·00 65·00
a. Surch. double (G.) £230
b. Surch. double (G. + Verm.) ..
34 ½d. on 2½d. (V.) £650

With T **10**.

35 ½d. on 2½d. (G.) .. .. 85·00 85·00
36 ½d. on 2½d. (Verm.) £850

One
Shilling

(11)

5/-

(12)

With T **11**.

37 1s. on 2d. (V.) .. .. 70·00 70·00
a. Surch inverted £400
b. Surch, vertical (up or down) .. £400
c. Surch diagonal (up or down) .. £400
d. Surch. diagonal, inverted (up or down) £500
38 1s. on 2d. (Verm.) .. .. 70·00 80·00
a. Surch. inverted .. ..
b. Surch. diagonal (up or down) .. £850
c. Surch, vertical (up or down) .. £850
39 1s. on 2d. (Bk.) £1600
a. Surch. inverted .. ..
b. Surch, vertical (up or down) .. £2000

There are two main types of the "One Shilling" surcharge:—

Type A. The "O" is over the "hi" of "Shilling" and the downstrokes of the "n" in "One", if extended, would meet the "ll" of "Shilling". The "g" is always raised. Type A is known in all three colours.

Type B. The "O" is over the first "i" of "Shilling" and the downstrokes of the "n" would meet the "li" of "Shilling". Type B is known in violet and vermilion.

There is a third, minor type of the black surcharge, but the differences are very slight.

Various types of the surcharges on Nos. 9 to 39 were printed on the same sheet, and different types in different colours may be found *se-tenant.* These are of great rarity.

As T **12**.

40 5s. on 2d. (V.) £2400 £2500
a. Surch. inverted .. ..
b. Surch. vertical (up or down) .. £2400 £2500
c. Surch. diagonal (down) .. £2700
41 10s. on 5d. (Verm.) £2400 £2500
a. Surch. inverted £2400
b. Surch. ivertical (up or down) .. £2000
c. Surch. diagonal (down) ..
42 20s. on 1s. (V.) £20000
a. Surch. inverted £40000
43 20s. on 1s. (Verm.) £30000
44 20s. on 1s. (Bk.).. .. ..

II. NIGER COAST PROTECTORATE.

This change of name took effect on 12 May 1893.

13

14

(Des. G. D. Drummond. Recess. Waterlow.)

1893 (Nov. (?)). *T* **13** *(with* "OIL RIVERS" *obliterated and* "NIGER COAST" *in top margin). Various frames. No wmk. Thick and thin papers. P* 14, 15, *and* 12 *to* 15 *in various combinations.*

45 ½d. vermilion .. .. .. 1·00 1·25
46 1d. pale blue .. .. .. 1·25 1·50
a. Bisected, and half used for ½d. ..
b. *Dull blue* .. .. .. 1·25 1·40
ba. Do. Bisected (½d.) (on cover) .. † £120
47 2d. green .. .. .. 3·00 3·50
a. Imperf. between (pair) .. — £800
b. Bisected (1d.) (on cover) .. † £230
48 2½d. carmine-lake .. .. 1·00 1·25
49 5d. grey-lilac .. .. .. 1·25 2·00
a. *Lilac* .. .. 1·75 3·50
50 1s. black .. .. .. 4·00 4·00
45/50 .. .. *Set of* 6 10·00 12·00

All values exist perf. 14 and perf. 15. There were three printings of each value, in June, 1893, Jan., 1894 and March, 1894.

(Recess. Waterlow.)

1894 (May). *T* **14** *(various frames). No wmk. P* 14, 15, 16 *and* 12 *to* 15 *in various combinations.*

51 ½d. yellow-green 50 60
a. *Dark green* 60 80
52 1d. orange-vermilion .. .. 1·75 2·25
a. *Vermilion* .. .. .. 70 1·10
b. Bisected diagonally (½d.) (on cover) .. .. — £120
53 2d. lake 70 80
a. Bisected diagonally (1d.) (on cover) .. ..
54 2½d. blue .. .. .. £140 1·00
a. *Pale blue* 90 80
55 5d. purple .. .. .. 90 1·10
a. *Deep violet* .. .. .. 1·40 1·50
56 1s. black .. .. .. 1·50 2·25
51/56 .. .. *Set of* 6 6·00 7·00

All values exist perf. 15 and all except the 5d., perf. 14. The 1d. is known perf. 16.

½ (15) 1 (16) ONE = = HALF PENNY (17)

1894. *Provisionals. Issued at Opobo.*

(a) Nos. 46b and 46 bisected vertically and surch. with T **15**. (May–June.)

57 "½" on half of 1d. dull blue (R.) (May) .. .. .. £140 50·00
a. Surch. inverted (in strip of 3 with normals) £1100
58 "½" on half of 1d. pale blue (R.) (June) .. .. .. £180 50·00
a. Surch. tête-bêche (pair) ..
b. Surcharge inverted £450

(b) No. 3 bisected vertically and surch. with T **16** *(12 mm. high).* (June–Oct.)

59 "1" on half of 2d. (Verm.) .. 90·00 70·00
a. Surch. double £200 £180
b. Surch. inverted .. .. — £180

Smaller "1" (4¾ mm. high).

60 "1" on half of 2d. (C.) .. .. — £450

Smaller "1" (3¾ mm. high).

61 "1" on half of 2d. (C.) ..

Nos. 60 and 61 exist *se-tenant*. *(Price* £8000 *used.)*

(c) No. 52a bisected, surch. with T **15**. (Aug.–Sept.)

62 ½ on half of 1d. vermilion (Bk.) £200 70·00
63 ½ on half of 1d. vermilion (V.) £200 60·00
64 ½ on half of 1d. vermilion (B.) £200 50·00
a. "½" double .. .. ..

The stamp is found divided down the middle and also diagonally.

1894 (10 Aug.). *Issued at Old Calabar.*

No. 54 *surch. with T* **17** *and two bars through value at foot.*

65 ½d. on 2½d. blue .. .. 50·00 38·00
a. Surch. double £250 £240
b. "OIE" for "ONE" £230 £180
c. Do. Surch. double .. .. — £325

There are eight types in the setting of T **17**.

(Recess. Waterlow.)

1897 (Mar.)–**98**. *As T* **14** *(various frames). Wmk. Crown CA. P* 14, 15 *and* 12 *to* 16 *in various combinations.*

66 ½d. green 20 20
a. *Sage-green* 25 70
67 1d. orange vermilion 40 50
a. *Vermilion* 50 50
b. Imperf. between (pr.) .. ..
68 2d. lake 50 50
69 2½d. slate-blue .. .. .. 60 1·10
a. *Deep bright blue* 60 70
70 5d. red-violet .. .. .. 1·90 4·50
a. *Purple* .. .. .. 1·75 4·50
71 6d. yellow-brown (June, 1898) 2·25 1·60
72 1s. black .. .. .. 2·25 2·75
73 2s. 6d. olive-bistre .. .. 6·00 9·00
74 10s. deep violet (June, 1898) .. 26·00 30·00
a. *Bright violet* (June, 1898) .. 28·00 30·00
66/74 .. .. *Set of* 9 36·00 45·00
71, 73/4 Optd. "Specimen" *Set of* 3 35·00

All values exist perf. 14 and all except the 5d. perf. 15, the latter perf. being the scarcer except in the 6d.

Owing to a temporary shortage in Southern Nigeria, the above issue was again put into use during 1902, all stamps being perf. 14, probably from the last printing made.

On 28th December, 1899, the territory occupied by the Royal Niger Company was taken over by the Imperial Government, and with Lagos and the Niger Coast Protectorate was divided into two Administrations, Northern and Southern Nigeria, later merged in Nigeria.

NIGERIA.

(Comprising the Combined Territories of Northern and Southern Nigeria and Lagos.)

I. CROWN COLONY.

1

2

(Typo. D.L.R.)

1914–27. *Wmk. Mult. Crown CA. Ordinary paper (½d. to 2½d.) or chalk-surfaced paper (others). P* 14.

A. **1914** (1 June)–**21**. *Die I.*

1 1 ½d. green 15 15
2 ,, 1d. carmine-red 15 12
a. *Scarlet* (6.17) 40 12
3 ,, 2d. grey 70 40
a. *Slate-grey* (1918) 85 45
4 ,, 2½d. bright blue 55 30
a. *Dull blue* (1915) .. ..
5 2 3d. purple/*yellow* (*white back*) 60 1·10
a. *On yellow* (*lemon back*) (8.15) 1·25 60
b. *On deep yellow* (*yellow back, thick paper*) (1915) .. 2·50 1·40
c. *On pale yellow* (*orange-buff back*) (12.20) .. .. 1·40 85
d. *On pale yellow* (*pale yellow back*) (1921) .. .. 1·60 55
6 ,, 4d. black and red/*yellow* (*white back*) .. .. 65 1·25
a. *On yellow* (*lemon back* (8.15) 1·25 1·40
b. *On deep yellow* (*yellow back, thick paper*) (1915) .. 1·60 1·60
c. *On pale yellow* (*orange-buff back*) (1921) .. .. 1·10 1·40
d. *On pale yellow* (*pale yellow back*) (1921) .. .. 2·50 3·50
7 ,, 6d. dull & brt. pur. (*shades*) 1·00 1·00

8 1 1s. black/*pale blue-green* (*white back*) .. .. 85 1·
a. *On yellow-green* (*white back*)
b. *On pale blue-green* (*yellow-green back*) (1915) .. .. 1·75 1·
c. *On pale blue-green* (*blue-green back*) (1915) .. .. 1·10 1·
d. *On pale blue-green* (*pale olive back*) (1918) .. .. 3·00 2·
e. *On emerald-green* (*pale olive back*) (12.20) .. .. 2·75 2·
f. *On emerald-green* (*emerald-green back*) (1921) .. .. 90 2·
9 ,, 2s. 6d. black and red/*blue* .. 2·50 3·
10 2 5s. green and red/*yellow* (*white back*) .. .. 4·00 5·
a. *On yellow* (*lemon back*) (8.15) 6·50 6·
b. *On deep yellow* (*yellow back, thick paper*) (1915) .. 6·00 6·
c. *On yellow* (*orange-buff back*) ('21) .. .. .. 6·00 6·
d. *On pale yellow* (*pale yellow back*) (1921) .. .. 7·50 7·
11 1 10s. green and red/*blue-green* (*white back*) .. .. 15·00 15·
a. *On blue-green* (*blue-green back*) (8.15) .. .. .. 15·00 15·
b. *On blue-green* (*pale olive back*) (1918) £350 £3
c. *On emerald green* (*pale olive back*) (12.20) .. .. 25·00 22·
d. *On emerald-green* (*emerald-back*) (1921) .. .. 15·00 13·
12 2 £1 deep purple & black/*red* 48·00 50·

B. **1927** (19 Jan.). *Change to Die II.*

13 2 £1 purple and black/*red* .. 55·00 60·
1/12 .. .. *Set of* 12 65·00 70·
5/6, 8, 10/11 Optd. "Specimen" (white backs) *Set of* 5 50·00
1/12 12 values optd. "Specimen" (coloured backs) *Set of* 12 90·00

1921–32. *Wmk. Mult. Script CA. Ordina paper (½d. to 3d.) or chalk-surfaced pap (others). P* 14.

A. **1921–6.** *The basic issue. Die I for the ½ 1d., 2d., 2½d., 3d. and 6d., Die II remainder.*

15 1 ½d. green (1921) 15
16 ,, 1d. rose-carmine (1921) .. 12
17 ,, 2d. grey (5.21) .. .. 1·10
18 ,, 2½d. bright blue (5.21) .. 40
19 2 3d. bright violet (1.24) .. 1·25 1·
20 ,, 4d. black and red/*pale yellow* (10.23) 30
21 ,, 6d. dull & brt. pur. (5.21) 1·25 1·
22 1 1s. black/*emerald* (7.24) .. 75
23 ,, 2s. 6d. black and red/*blue* (8.25) .. .. .. 3·50 4·
24 2 5s. grn. & red/*yellow* (10.26) 6·50 6·
25 1 10s. green & red/*grn.* (4.26) 16·00 18·
15/25 .. .. *Set of* 11 28·00 29·
15/25 Optd. "Specimen" *Set of* 11 75·00

B. **1924–5.** *Change to Die II.*

25*a* 1 ½d. green (5.25) 10
25*b* ,, 1d. rose-carmine (5.25) .. 10
25*c* ,, 2d. grey (1924) 40
25*d* 2 3d. bright violet (5.25) .. 1·10 1·
25*e* ,, 6d. dull & brt. pur. (7.24) .. 55
25*a*/25*e* .. .. *Set of* 5 2·00 2·

C. **1927–31.** *New value and colours change Die II.*

26 2 1½d. orange (1.4.31) .. 35
27 1 2d. chestnut (1.10.27) .. 75
28 ,, 2d. chocolate (1.7.28) .. 15
29 2 3d. bright blue (1.4.31) .. 1·10
26/7, 29 Optd./Perf. "Specimen" *Set of* 3 26·00

D. **1932** (Mar.–Aug.). *Reappearance of Die (Key Plate 23).*

29*a* 1 2d. chocolate (Mar.) .. 1·10
29*b* 2 4d. black and red/*pale yellow* .. .. .. 6·00 4·
29*c* 1 2s. 6d. black and red/*blue* 5·50 4·
29*d* 2 5s. green and red/*yellow* .. 14·00 16·
29*e* 1 10s. green and red/*green* .. 35·00 35·
29*a*/29*e* .. .. *Set of* 5 55·00 55·

1935 (6 May). *Silver Jubilee. As Nos.* 91/4 *Antigua but ptd. by Waterlow. P* 11×12.

30 1½d. ultramarine and grey .. 15
31 2d. green and indigo 20
32 3d. brown and deep blue .. 40
33 1s. slate and purple .. .. 1·40 1·7
30/3 Perf. "Specimen" *Set of* 4 16·00

3. Apapa Wharf.

7. Fishing Village.

4. Cocoa. (*As T* **3.**)
5. Tin Dredger. (*As T* **3.**)
6. Timber Industry. (*As T* **3.**)
8. Cotton Ginnery. (*As T* **7.**)
9. Habe Minaret. (*As T* **7.**)
10. Fulani Cattle. (*As T* **7.**)

11. Victoria-Buea Road.

12. Oil Palms. (*Horiz.*)
13. R. Niger at Jebba. (*Horiz.*)
14. Canoe Pulling. (*Horiz.*)

(Recess. D.L.R.)

936 (1 FEB.). *Wmk. Mult. Script CA.*
(*a*) *P* 11½ × 13.

4 **3** ½d. green 15 12
5 **4** 1d. carmine 15 12
6 **5** 1½d. brown 20 12
a. Perf. 12½ × 13½ .. .. 7·50 40
7 **6** 2d. black 45 25
8 **7** 3d. blue 60 50
a. Perf. 12½ × 13½ .. .. 20·00 7·50
9 **8** 4d. red-brown 80 80
0 **9** 6d. dull violet 75 55
1 **10** 1s. sage-green .. .. 2·75 2·50

(*b*) *P* 14

2 **11** 2s. 6d. black & ultram. .. 3·50 4·50
3 **12** 5s. black and olive-green 7·00 7·50
4 **13** 10s. black and grey .. 18·00 20·00
5 **14** £1 black and orange .. 35·00 35·00
4/45 .. .. *Set of* 12 65·00 65·00
4/45 Perf. "Specimen" *Set of* 12 45·00

937 (12 MAY). *Coronation. As Nos.* 13/15 *of Aden, but printed by B. W. & Co. P* 11 × 11½.

6 1d. carmine 8 8
7 1½d. brown 10 10
8 3d. blue 15 20
6/8 Perf. "Specimen" *Set of* 3 13·00

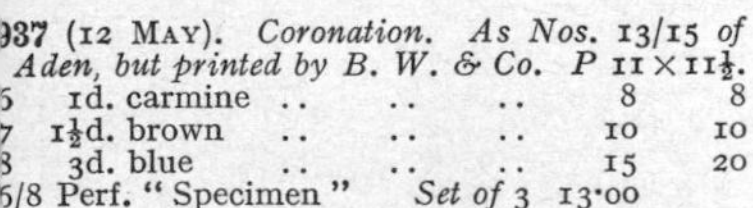

15. King George VI.

16. Victoria-Buea Road.

17. R. Niger at Jebba. (*Horiz.*)

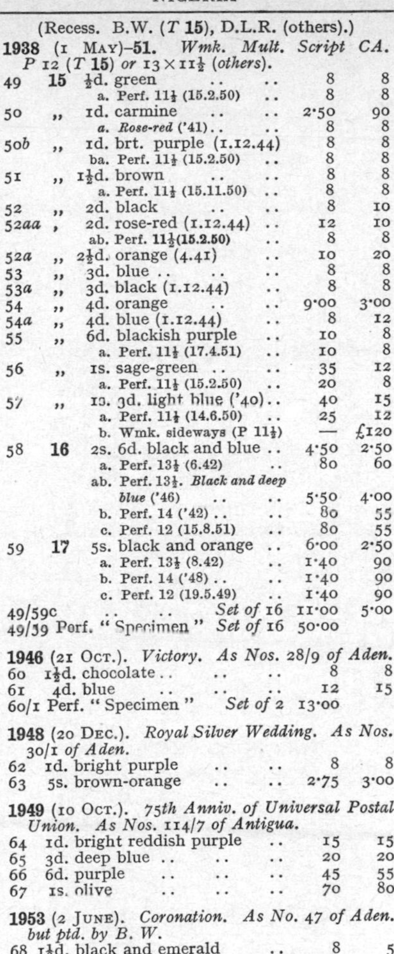

(Recess. B.W. (*T* **15**), D.L.R. (others).)

1938 (1 MAY)–**51.** *Wmk. Mult. Script CA. P* 12 (*T* **15**) *or* 13 × 11½ (*others*).

49 **15** ½d. green 8 8
a. Perf. 11½ (15.2.50) .. 8 8
50 ,, 1d. carmine .. .. 2·50 90
a. *Rose-red* ('41) 8 8
50*b* ,, 1d. brt. purple (1.12.44) 8 8
ba. Perf. 11½ (15.2.50) .. 8 8
51 ,, 1½d. brown 8 8
a. Perf. 11½ (15.11.50) .. 8 8
52 ,, 2d. black 8 10
52*aa* ,, 2d. rose-red (1.12.44) .. 12 10
ab. Perf. 11½ (15.2.50) .. 8 8
52*a* ,, 2½d. orange (4.41) .. 10 20
53 ,, 3d. blue 8 8
53*a* ,, 3d. black (1.12.44) .. 8 8
54 ,, 4d. orange .. .. 9·00 3·00
54*a* ,, 4d. blue (1.12.44) .. 8 12
55 ,, 6d. blackish purple .. 10 8
a. Perf. 11½ (17.4.51) .. 10 8
56 ,, 1s. sage-green 35 12
a. Perf. 11½ (15.2.50) .. 20 8
57 ,, 1s. 3d. light blue ('40) .. 40 15
a. Perf. 11½ (14.6.50) .. 25 12
b. Wmk. sideways (P 11½) — £120
58 **16** 2s. 6d. black and blue .. 4·50 2·50
a. Perf. 13½ (6.42) .. 80 60
ab. Perf. 13½. *Black and deep blue* ('46) .. .. 5·50 4·00
b. Perf. 14 ('42) 80 55
c. Perf. 12 (15.8.51) .. 80 55
59 **17** 5s. black and orange .. 6·00 2·50
a. Perf. 13½ (8.42) .. 1·40 90
b. Perf. 14 ('48) .. .. 1·40 90
c. Perf. 12 (19.5.49) .. 1·40 90
49/59c .. .. *Set of* 16 11·00 5·00
49/59 Perf. "Specimen" *Set of* 16 50·00

1946 (21 OCT.). *Victory. As Nos.* 28/9 *of Aden.*

60 1½d. chocolate 8 8
61 4d. blue 12 15
60/1 Perf. "Specimen" *Set of* 2 13·00

1948 (20 DEC.). *Royal Silver Wedding. As Nos.* 30/1 *of Aden.*

62 1d. bright purple 8 8
63 5s. brown-orange .. .. 2·75 3·00

1949 (10 OCT.). *75th Anniv. of Universal Postal Union. As Nos.* 114/7 *of Antigua.*

64 1d. bright reddish purple .. 15 15
65 3d. deep blue 20 20
66 6d. purple 45 55
67 1s. olive 70 80

1953 (2 JUNE). *Coronation. As No.* 47 *of Aden. but ptd. by B. W.*

68 1½d. black and emerald .. 8 5

18. Old Manilla Currency.

19. Bornu Horsemen.

20. "Groundnuts".

21. "Tin".

Type A.

Gap in row of dots.

Type B.

Unbroken row of dots.

Nos. 72*a*/*d*. The original cylinder used was Type A (July '56); later Type B (Sept. '57). The above illustrations will help classification, but two stamps per sheet of 60 of Type A show faint dots. However, one of these has the "2d." re-entry which does not exist in Type B sheets, and shades are distinctive.

Nos. 72*b* and 72*d* were released in Colony only.

22. Jebba Bridge and R. Niger.

23. "Cocoa".

24. Ife Bronze.

25. "Timber".

26. Victoria Harbour.

27. "Palm-oil".

28. "Hides and Skins".

29. New and Old Lagos.

(Des. M. Fievet. Recess. Waterlow.)

1953 (1 Sept.)–**57.** *Wmk. Mult. Script CA. P* 14.

69	**18**	½d. black and orange ..	5	5
70	**19**	1d. black & bronze-green	5	5
71	**20**	1½d. blue-green	8	8
72	**21**	2d. black & ochre (*shades*)	8	5
72*a*	,,	2d. slate-violet (Type A) (23.7.56)	30	30
		b. *Slate-blue* (*shades*) (Type A) (*Col.*)	60	10
		c. *Bluish grey* (Type B) (25.9.57)	45	15
		d. *Grey* (*shades*) (Type B) (*Col.*)	8	5
73	**22**	3d. black & purple (*shades*)	8	5
		b. Imperf. (pair)		
74	**23**	4d. black and blue	8	5
75	**24**	6d. orge.-brn. & blk. (*shades*)	10	8
76	**25**	1s. black and maroon ..	20	10
77	**26**	2s. 6d. blk. & grn. (*shades*)	50	15
78	**27**	5s. black and red-orange ..	85	40
79	**28**	10s. black and red-brown ..	2·00	75
80	**29**	£1 black and violet ..	5·00	2·50
69/80		.. .. *Set of* 13	8·50	4·00

Nos. 72*a*/*d* and Nos. 70 and 73 (from September 1958), printed on rotary machines by subsidiary company, Imprimerie Belge de Securité, in Belgium.

ROYAL VISIT
1956
(30)

1956 (28 Jan.). *Royal Visit. No.* 72 *optd. with T* **30.**

81	**21**	2d. black and ochre	8	5
		a. Opt. inverted		

31. Victoria Harbour.

(Recess. Waterlow & Sons, Ltd.)

1958 (1 Dec.). *Centenary of Victoria. W* w.**12.** *P* 13½ × 14.

82	**31**	3d. black and purple ..	8	5

32. Lugard Hall.

33. Kano Mosque.

(Recess. Waterlow.)

1959 (14 Mar.). *Attainment of Self-Government, Northern Region of Nigeria. W* w.**12.** *P* 13½ (3*d.*) *or* 13½ × 14 (1*s.*).

83	**32**	3d. black and purple ..	8	5
84	**33**	1s. black and green ..	25	25

II. INDEPENDENT FEDERATION.

34

35. Legislative Building.

36. African paddling Canoe.

37. Federal Supreme Court.

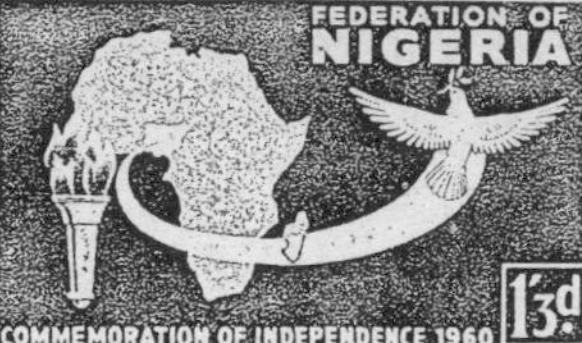

38. Dove, Torch and Map.

(Des. R. D. Baxter (6d.), R. Crawford (3d.) L. J. Wittington (1d.), J. White (1s. 3d.) Photo. Waterlow & Sons.)

1960 (1 Oct.). *Independence. W* **34.** *P* 13 (1*s.* 3*d.*) *or* 14 (*others*).

85	**35**	1d. black and scarlet ..	5	
86	**36**	3d. black and greenish blue	10	1
87	**37**	6d. green and red-brown ..	12	1
88	**38**	1s. 3d. brt. blue and yellow	25	2

39. Groundnuts.

40. Coal Mining.

41. Adult Education.

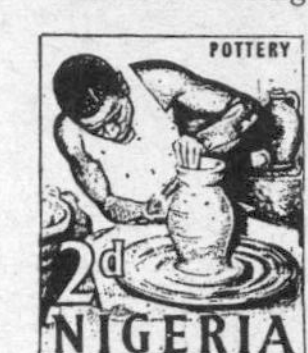

42. Pottery.

43. Oyo Carver.

44. Weaving.

45. Benin Mask.

46. Hornbill.

47. Camel Train.

48. Central Bank.

49. Nigeria Museum.

50. Kano Airport.

51. Lagos Railway Station.

961 1 Jan.). *W* **34.** *P* 15×14 (*½d. to 1s. 3d.*) *or* 14½ (*others*).

89	**39**	½d. emerald	5	5
90	**40**	1d. reddish violet ..	5	5
91	**41**	1½d. carmine-red	8	10
92	**42**	2d. deep blue	5	5
93	**43**	3d. deep green	5	5
94	**44**	4d. blue	8	5
95	**45**	6d. yellow and black ..	8	5
		a. Yellow omitted	—	£150
96	**46**	1s. yellow-green	15	5
7	**47**	1s. 3d. orange	25	8
8	**48**	2s. 6d. black and yellow	40	12
9	**49**	5s. black and emerald ..	1·00	25
0	**50**	10s. black and ultramarine	2·25	75
1	**51**	£1 black & carmine-red	4·50	2·50
/101		.. .. *Set of* 13	8·50	3·50

RINTERS. The above and all following issues No. 206 were printed in photogravure by arrison & Sons, *except where otherwise stated.*

52. Globe and Railway Locomotive.

53. Globe and Mail-van.
54. Globe and Aircraft.
55. Globe and Ship.

(Des. M. Goaman.)

961 (25 July). *Admission of Nigeria into U.P.U.* *W* **34.** *P* 14½.

2	**52**	1d, red-orange and blue ..	5	5
3	**53**	3d. olive-yellow and black	8	8
4	**54**	1s. 3d. blue and carmine-red	20	15
5	**55**	2s. 6d. deep green and blue	35	35

56. Coat-of-Arms.

57. Natural Resources Map. (*Horiz.*)

58. Nigerian Eagle. (*Horiz.*)

59. Eagles in Flight. (*Horiz.*)

60. Nigerians and Flag. (*Horiz.*)

(Des. S. Bodd (3d.), R. Hopeman (4d.), C. Adesina (6d.), M. Shamir (1s. 6d.), B. Enweonwu (2s. 6d.).)

1961 (1 Oct.). *First Anniv. of Independence.* *W* **34.** *P* 14½.

106	**56**	3d. multicoloured ..	5	5
107	**57**	4d. yell.-grn. & yellow-orge.	10	12
108	**58**	6d. emerald-green ..	10	10
109	**59**	1s. 3d. grey, emer. & blue	20	20
110	**60**	2s. 6d. green & grey-blue	35	35
106/110		.. .. *Set of* 5	70	70

A used copy of No. 106 has been seen with both the silver (large " Y " appearing grey) and the yellow (appearing white) omitted.

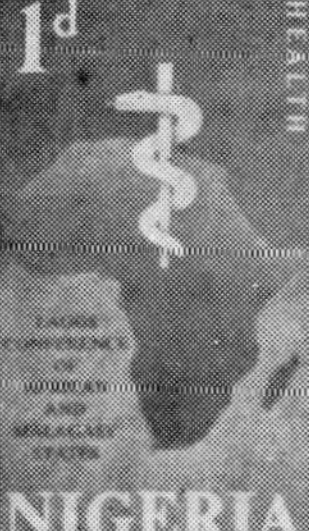

61. " Health ".

62. " Culture ".

63. " Commerce ".

64. " Communications ".

65. " Co-operation ".

(Des. M. Shamir.)

1962 (25 Jan.). *Lagos Conference of African and Malagasy States.* *W* **34.** *P* 14×14½.

111	**61**	1d. yellow-bistre	5	5
112	**62**	3d. deep reddish purple ..	8	8
113	**63**	6d. deep green	10	10
114	**64**	1s. brown	15	15
115	**65**	1s. 3d. blue	20	20
111/115		.. .. *Set of* 5	50	50

66. Malaria Eradication Emblem and Parasites.

67. Insecticide-spraying.

68. Aerial Spraying.

69. Mother, Child and Microscope.

1962 (7 Apr.). *Malaria Eradication.* *W* **34.** *P* 14½.

116	**66**	3d. green and orange-red	5	5
117	**67**	6d. blue and bright purple	10	10
118	**68**	1s. 3d. mag. & violet-blue	20	20
119	**69**	2s. 6d. blue and yell.-brn.	30	35

70. National Monument.

71. Benin Bronze.

(Des. Sandor Bodo (3d.), Ben Enwonwu (5s.).

1962 (1 Oct.). *Second Anniv. of Independence.* *W* **34.** *P* 14½×14 (*3d.*) *or* 14×14½ (*5s.*).

120	**70**	3d. emerald and blue ..	5	5
		a. Emerald omitted		
121	**71**	5s. red, emerald & violet	65	75

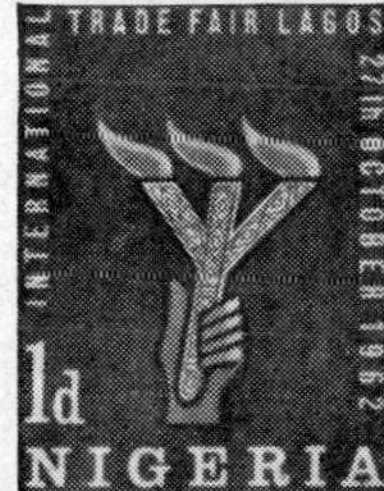

72. Fair Emblem.

73. " Cogwheels of Industry ".

74. " Cornucopia of Commerce ". (*Horiz.*)
75. Oilwells and Tanker. (*Horiz.*)

(Des. M. Goaman (1d., 2s. 6d.), J. O. Gbagbeolu and M. Goaman (6d.), R. Hegeman (1s.).)

1962 (27 Oct.). *International Trade Fair, Lagos.* *W* **34.** *P* 14½.

122	**72**	1d. olive-brown & orge.-red	5	5
123	**73**	6d. carmine-red and black	8	8
124	**74**	1s. orange-brown & black	15	15
125	**75**	2s. 6d. ultram. and yellow	35	35

76. " Arrival of Delegates ".

78. Mace as Palm Tree.

77. National Hall. (*Horiz.*)

(Des. S. Akosile (2½d.), M. Goaman (others).)

1962 (5 Nov.). *Eighth Commonwealth Parliamentary Conference, Lagos. W* **34**. *P* 14½.

126 **76** 2½d. greenish blue .. 8 8
127 **77** 4d. indigo and rose-red .. 8 8
128 **78** 1s. 3d. sepia and lemon .. 20 20

79. Herdsman. (*Vert.*)

80. Tractor and Maize.

(Des. M. Goaman.)

1963 (21 Mar.). *Freedom from Hunger. W* **34**. *P* 14.

129 **79** 3d. olive-green 5 5
130 **80** 6d. magenta 12 12

81. Mercury Capsule and Kano Tracking Station.

82. Satellite and Lagos Harbour.

(Des. R. Hegeman.)

1963 (21 June). *"Peaceful Use of Outer Space". W* **34**. *P* 14½ × 14.

131 **81** 6d. blue and yellow-green 8 8
132 **82** 1s. 3d. black and blue-grn. 25 25

83. Scouts Shaking Hands.

(*Illustration reduced: actual size* 60 × 30 *mm.*)

84. Campfire.

(Des. S. Apostolou (3d.), G. Okiki (1s.).)

1963 (1 Aug.). *11th World Scout Jamboree Marathon. W* **34**. *P* 14.

133 **83** 3d. red and bronze-green .. 5 5
134 **84** 1s. black and red .. 25 25
MS134*a* 93 × 95 mm. Nos. 133/4 50 50

85. Emblem and First Aid Team.

86. Emblem and " Hospital Services ".

87. Patient (" Medical Services ") and Emblem.

(Des. M. Goaman.)

1963 (1 Sept.). *Red Cross Centenary. W* **34**. *P* 14½.

135 **85** 3d. red & dp. ultramarine 5 5
136 **86** 6d. red and deep green .. 8 8
137 **87** 1s. 3d. red & deep sepia .. 20 20
MS137*a* 102 × 102 mm. No. 137 (block of four) 75 75

88. President Azikiwe and State House.

The buildings on the 1s. 3d. and the 2s. 6d. are the Federal Supreme Court and the Parliament Building, respectively.

(Des. M. Shamir. Photo. Govt. Printer, Israel.)

1963 (1 Oct.). *Republic Day. P* 14 × 13.

138 **88** 3d. yell.-olive & grey-grn. 5 5
139 – 1s. 3d. yell.-brn. & sepia .. 20 20
a. Yellow-brn. (portrait) omitted
140 – 2s. 6d. turquoise-blue and deep violet-blue .. 35 35

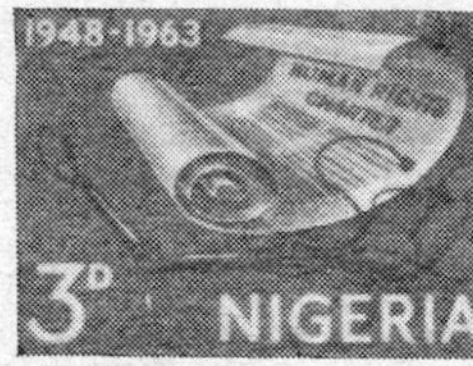

89. Charter and Broken Whip.

90. " Freedom of Worship ".

91. " Freedom from Want ". (*Vert.*)

92. " Freedom of Speech ". (*Vert.*)

(Des S. Apostolou (3d.), Mrs. F. P. Effiong (others). Photo. D.L.R.)

1963 (10 Dec.). *15th Anniv. of Declaration of Human Rights. W* **34**. *P* 13.

141 **89** 3d. vermilion 5 5
142 **90** 6d. blue-green 8 8
143 **91** 1s. 3d. ultramarine .. 20 20
144 **92** 2s. 6d. bright purple .. 35 35

93. Queen Nefertari.

94. Rameses II.

(Des. M. Shamir.)

1964 (8 Mar.). *Nubian Monuments Preservation W* **34**. *P* 14½.

145 **93** 6d. yellow-olive & emerald 8 8
146 **94** 2s. 6d. brown, deep olive and emerald 35 35

95. President Kennedy.

96. President Kennedy and Flags.

97. President Kennedy (U.S. Coin Head) and Flags.

(Des. M. Shamir (1s. 3d.), M. Goaman (2s. 6d.) Mr. Bottiau (5s.). Photo. Govt. Printer Israel (1s. 3d.); litho. Lewin-Epstein, Bat Yam, Israel (others).)

1964 (27 Aug.). *President Kennedy Memorial Issue. P* 13 × 14 (*1s. 3d.*) *or* 14 (*others*).

147 **95** 1s. 3d. light violet & black 20 20
148 **96** 2s. 6d. black, red, blue and green 45 45
149 **97** 5s. black, deep blue, red and green 85 85
MS149*a* 154 × 135 mm. No. 149 (block of four) Imperf. .. .. 3·50 3·50

98. President Azikiwe.

99. Herbert Macaulay.

100. King Jaja of Opobo. (*As T* **99**.)

Des. S. Apostolou (3d.), W. H. Irvine (others) Photo. Govt. Printer, Israel (3d.); Harrison (others).)

964 (1 Oct.). *First Anniv. of Republic. P* 14×13 (3*d.*) *or* 14½ (*others*).

50 **98** 3d. red-brown 5 5
51 **99** 1s. 3d. green 20 20
52 **100** 2s. 6d. deep grey-green .. 35 35

101. Boxing Gloves.

102. High-jumping. (*Horiz.*)
103. Running. (*vert.*)

104. Hurdling.

Illustration of T **104** *is reduced: actual size* 60×30 *mm.*)

Des. A. Adalade (3d.), S. Medahunsi (6d.), M. Shamir (1s. 3d.), M. Goaman (2s. 6d.).)

964 (10 Oct.). *Olympic Games, Tokyo. W* **34**. *P* 14 (2*s.* 6*d.*) *or* 14½ (*others*).

53 **101** 3d. sepia and olive-green 5 5
54 **102** 6d. emerald and indigo .. 8 8
55 **103** 1s. 3d. sepia & yell.-olive 20 20
56 **104** 2s. 6d. sepia & chestnut .. 35 35
IS156*a* 102×102 mm. No. 156 (block of four). Imperf. .. 1·50 1·50

106. Scout Badge on Shield.

107. Scout Badges.

108. Chief Scout and Nigerian Scout.

05. Scouts on Hill top.

Des. S. Apostolou (1d., 1s. 3d.), H. N. G. Cowhan and Eagle Scout N. A. Lasisi (3d.), W. H. Irvine (6d.).)

965 (1 Jan.). *50th Anniv. of Nigerian Scout Movement. P* 14×14½.

57 **105** 1d. brown 5 5
58 **106** 3d. red, black & emerald 8 8
59 **107** 6d. red, sepia, and yellow-green 10 10
60 **108** 1s. 3d. bistre-brown, greenish yellow and black-green 25 25
IS160*a* 76×104 mm. No. 160 (block of four). Imperf. .. 1·00 1·00

109. " Telstar ".

110. Solar Satellite.

(Des. M. Shamir. Photo. Govt. Printer, Israel.)

1965 (1 Apr.). *International Quiet Sun Years. P* 14×13.

161 **109** 6d. reddish violet and turquoise-blue .. 10 10
162 **110** 1s. 3d. green & redd. lilac 30 30

111. Native Tom-tom and Modern Telephone.

112. Microwave Aerial. (*Vert.*)
113. Telecommunications Satellite and Part of Globe. (*Horiz.*)

(Des. C. Botham (5s.), H. N. G. Cowham (others). Photo. Enschedé.)

1965 (2 Aug.). *I.T.U. Centenary. P* 11½×11 (1*s.* 3*d.*) *or* 11×11½ (*others*).

163 **111** 3d. black, carmine and yellow-brown .. 5 5
164 **112** 1s. 3d. black, blue-green and chalky blue .. 20 20
165 **113** 5s. black, carmine, blue & bright greenish blue 75 75

114. I.C.Y. Emblem and Diesel Locomotive.

115. Students and Lagos Teaching Hospital.
116. Kainji (Niger) Dam.

(Des. W. H. Irvine. Photo. D.L.R.)

1965 (1 Sept.). *International Co-operation Year. W* **34**. *P* 14×15.

166 **114** 3d. green, red and orange 5 5
167 **115** 1s. blk., brt. blue & lemon 15 15
168 **116** 2s. 6d. green, bright blue and yellow 60 60

117. Carved Frieze.

118. Stone Images at Ikom. (*Vert.*)
119. Tada Bronze. (*Vert.*)

(Des. S. Apostolou (3d.), W. H. Irvine (others). Photo. De La Rue.)

1965 (1 Oct.). *2nd Anniv. of Republic. P* 14×15 (3*d.*) *or* 15×14 (*others*).

169 **117** 3d. blk., red & orge.-yell. 5 5
170 **118** 1s. 3d. red-brown, deep green & lt. ultramarine 15 15
171 **119** 5s. brown, blackish brown and light green .. 1·00 1·00

120. Lion and Cubs.

126. Saddle-billed Stork.

121. Elephants.

122. Splendid Sunbird.

123. Weavers.

124. Cheetah.

125. Leopards.

127. Grey Parrots.

128. Kingfishers.

129. Crowned Cranes.

130. Kobs.

131. Giraffes.

132. Hippopotamus.

133. Buffalo.

(Des. M. Fievet. Photo. Harrison (1d., 2d., 3d., 4d. (No. 177a), 9d.) or Delrieu (others).)

1965 (1 Nov.)–**66.** *Without printers' imprint Chalk-surfaced paper* (*1d., 2d., 3d., 4d., 9d.*) *P* 12×12½ (*½d., 6d.*), 12½×12 (*1½d., 4d.*) 14×13½ (*1d., 2d., 3d., 9d.*) *or* 12½ (*others*).

172	**120**	½d. mult. (1.11.65) ..	5	5
173	**121**	1d. mult. (1.11.65) ..	5	5
174	**122**	1½d. mult. (2.5.66) ..	5	5
175	**123**	2d. mult. (1.4.66) ..	5	5
176	**124**	3d. mult. (17.10.66) ..	5	5
177	**125**	4d. mult. (2.5.66) ..	20	5
		a. Perf. 14×13½ ('66) ..	5	5
178	**126**	6d. mult. (2.5.66) ..	12	5
179	**127**	9d. Prussian blue and orange-red (17.10.66)	15	10
180	**128**	1s. mult. (2.5.66) ..	20	5
181	**129**	1s. 3d. mult. (2.5.66) ..	20	15
182	**130**	2s. 6d. orange-brown, buff and brn. (2.5.66)	45	30
183	**131**	5s. chestnut, light yellow and brown (2.5.66) ..	1·00	60
		a. Pale chestnut, yellow and brown-purple ('66) ..	1·00	60
184	**132**	10s. mult. (2.5.66) ..	2·00	1·40
185	**133**	£1 mult. (2.5.66) ..	4·00	2·25
172/85		.. .. *Set of* 14	7·50	4·75

The 2d. and 3d. exist with PVA gum as well as gum arabic.

See also Nos. 220, etc.

The 1d., 3d., 4d. (No. 177a), 1s. 3d., 2s. 6d., 5s. and £1 values exist overprinted "F.G.N." (Federal Government of Nigeria) twice in black. They were prepared in 1968 at the request of one of the State Governments for use as official stamps but the scheme was abandoned and meter machines were used instead. Some stamps held at Lagos Post Office were sold over the counter in error and passed through the post. The 3d., 4d. and 2s. 6d. exist used on official mail. The Director of Posts then decided to put limited supplies on sale "in order not to create an artificial scarcity" but they had no postal validity.

COMMONWEALTH
P. M. MEETING
11. JAN. 1966

(134)

1966 (11 Jan.). *Commonwealth Prime Ministers' Meeting, Lagos. No. 98 optd. with T* **134** *by the Nigerian Security Printing and Minting Co., Lagos, in red.*

186	**48**	2s. 6d. black and yellow ..	30	35

135. Y.W.C.A. Emblem and H.Q., Lagos.

(Des. S. B. Ajayi. Litho. Nigerian Security Printing & Minting Co. Ltd.)

1966 (1 Sept.). *Nigerian Y.W.C.A's. Diamond Jubilee. P* 14.

187	**135**	4d. yellow-orge., ultram., orge.-brn. & yell.-grn.	5	5
188	,,	9d. yellow-orge., ultram., brown and turq.-green	15	15

136. Dove and Flag. (*Vert.*)

137. Telephone Handset and Linesman.

138. Niger Bridge. (*Horiz.*)

(Des. S. B. Ajayi (4d.), N. Lasisi (1s. 6d.), B. Enweonwu (2s. 6d.).)

1966 (1 Oct.). *Third Anniv. of Republic. W* **34.** *P* 14½×14.

189	**136**	4d. green	5	5
190	**137**	1s. 6d. black, brown and reddish violet ..	25	25
191	**138**	2s. 6d. indigo, blue, yellow and green	40	4

139. "Education, Science and Culture".

(Des. V. Whiteley from sketch by Babajide Salisu.)

1966 (4 Nov.). *20th Anniv. of U.N.E.S.C.O W* **34** (*sideways*). *P* 14½×14.

192	**139**	4d. black, lake & orange-yellow	5	[illegible]
193	,,	1s. 6d. black, lake & turquoise-green	25	2
194	,,	2s. 6d. black, lake & rose-pink	40	4

140. Children drinking.

141. Tending Patient. (*Vert.*)

142. Tending Casualties, and Badge. (*Horiz.*)

(Des. V. Whiteley, after M. O. Afamefuna (4d.) I. U. Anawanti (1s. 6d.) and S. Adeyem (2s. 6d.).)

1966 (1 Dec.). *Nigerian Red Cross. W* **34** *P* 14×14½ (*1s. 6d.*) *or* 14½×14 (*others*).

195	**140**	4d.+1d. black, reddish violet and red ..	10	1
196	**141**	1s. 6d.+3d. mult. ..	35	3
197	**142**	2s. 6d.+3d. mult. ..	50	5

143. Surveying.

144. Water Gauge on Dam. (*Vert.*)

(Des. M. Goaman.)

1967 (1 Feb.). *International Hydrological Decade W* **34.** *P* 14½×14 (*4d.*) *or* 14×14½ (*2s. 6d.*)

198	**143**	4d. multicoloured ..	5	
199	**144**	2s. 6d. multicoloured ..	45	4

145. Globe and Weather Satellite.

146. Passing Storm and Sun.

(Des. M. Shamir (4d.), S. Bodo (1s. 6d.).)

1967 (23 Mar.). *World Meteorological Day* W **34**. *P* 14½ × 14.
200 **145** 4d. magenta and blue .. 5 5
201 **146** 1s. 6d. black, yell. & blue 30 30

147. Eyo Masquerades.

148. Crowd watching Acrobat. (*Horiz.*)

149. Stilt Dancer. (*Vert.*)

Des. G. A. Okiki (4d.), A. B. Saka Lawal (1s. 6d.), S. Bodo (2s. 6d.). Photo. Enschedé.)

967 (1 Oct.). *4th Anniv. of Republic. P* 11½ × 11 (*2s. 6d.*) *or* 11 × 11½ (*others*).
202 **147** 4d. multicoloured .. 5 5
203 **148** 1s. 6d. multicoloured .. 45 45
204 **149** 2s. 6d. multicoloured .. 45 60

150. Tending Sick Animal.

(Des. G. Drummond.)

967 (1 Dec.). *Rinderpest Eradication Campaign. P* 14½ × 14.
05 **150** 4d. multicoloured .. 5 5
06 „ 1s. 6d. multicoloured .. 45 45

RINTERS AND PROCESS. The following ssues were printed in photogravure by the Iigerian Security Printing and Minting Co., Ltd., *nless otherwise stated.*

151. Smallpox Vaccination.

152. African and Mosquito.

(Des. J. Owei. Litho.)

968 (7 Apr.). *20th Anniv. of World Health Organization. P* 14.
07 **151** 4d. magenta and black .. 5 5
08 **152** 1s. 6d. orge., lemon & blk. 30 30

153. Chained Hands and Outline of Nigeria.

154. Nigerian Flag and Human Rights Emblem. (*Vert.*)

(Des. Jennifer Toombs.)

1968 (1 July). *Human Rights Year. P* 14.
209 **153** 4d. greenish blue, black and yellow 5 5
210 **154** 1s. 6d. myrtle-green, orange-red and black 30 30

155. Hand grasping at Doves of Freedom.

(Des. G. L. Vasarhelyi.)

1968 (1 Oct.). *4th Anniv. of Federal Republic. P* 13½ × 14.
211 **155** 4d. multicoloured .. 5 5
212 „ 1s. 6d. multicoloured .. 30 30

156. Map of Nigeria and Olympic Rings.

157. Nigerian Athletes, Flag and Olympic Rings.

(Des. J. Owei.)

1968 (14 Oct.). *Olympic Games, Mexico. P* 14.
213 **156** 4d. blk., grn. & scarlet 5 5
214 **157** 1s. 6d. multicoloured .. 30 30

158. G.P.O., Lagos.

(Des. De La Rue Staff Artists.)

1969 (11 Apr.). *Inauguration of Philatelic Service. P* 14.
215 **158** 4d. black and green .. 5 5
216 „ 1s. 6d. black and blue .. 40 40

159. Yakubu Gowon and Victoria Zakari.

Des. Adapted from photo by Jackie Phillips. Litho.)

1969 (20 Sept.). *Wedding of General Gowon. P* 13 × 13½.
217 **159** 4d. chocolate & emerald 5 5
218 , 1s. 6d. black and emerald 30 30

1969–72. *As No. 173, etc., but printed by Nigerian Security Printing and Minting Co. Ltd. With printer's imprint* "N.S.P. & M. CO. LTD." *P* 13½ (*6d.*) *or P* 13 × 13½ (*others*).
220 **121** 1d. multicoloured .. 5 5
222 **123** 2d. multicoloured .. 5 5
a. Smaller imprint* (22.6.71) 65 25
223 **124** 3d. multicoloured (7.71) .. 5 5
a. Larger imprint*(22.10.71) 1·50 25
224 **125** 4d. multicoloured .. 8 5
a. Smaller imprint† .. ..
225 **126** 6d. multicoloured ('71) .. 10 8
226 **127** 9d. Prussian blue and orange-red ('70) .. 15 10
227 **128** 1s. multicoloured (8.71) .. 20 12
228 **129** 1s. 3d. multicoloured ('71) 25 15
229 **130** 2s. 6d. multicoloured ('72) 45 35
230 **131** 5s. multicoloured ('72) .. 1·00 75
220/30 .. .. *Set of* 10 2·00 1·60

* On No. 222a the designer's name measures 4¾ mm. On No. 223a the imprints measure 9 and 8½ mm. respectively. The normal imprints on Nos. 222/3 both measure 5½ mm.

The dates given for Nos. 222a and 223a are for the earliest known used copies.

† No. 224 has the left-hand imprint 6 mm. long and the right-hand 5½ mm. On No. 224a the imprints are 5½ mm. and 4½ mm. respectively. The width of the design is also ½ mm. smaller.

As Nos. 222 and 224, but redrawn, and printed by Enschedé. No printer's imprint; designer's name at right. P 14½ × 13.
231 **123** 2d. multicoloured (9.70) 3·00 85
232 **125** 4d. multicoloured (3.71) 2·00 75

In the 2d. the face value is white instead of yellow, and in the 4d. the white lettering and value are larger.

160. Bank Emblem and "5th Anniversary". **161.** Bank Emblem and Rays.

(Des. J. Owei (4d.), B. Salisu (1s. 6d.). Litho.)

1969 (18 Oct.). *Fifth Anniv. of African Development Bank. P* 14.
233 **160** 4d. orange, black & blue 5 5
234 **161** 1s. 6d. lemon, blk. & plum 30 30

162. I.L.O Emblem.

163. World Map and I.L.O. Emblem.

(Des. David West.)

1969 (15 Nov.). *50th Anniv. of International Labour Organisation. P* 14.
235 **162** 4d. black and bright red-dish violet 5 5
236 **163** 1s. 6d. emerald and black 30 40

164. Olumo Rock.

165. Traditional Musicians. (*Vert.*)
166. Assob Falls. (*Vert.*)

(Des. Austin Onwudimegwu.)

1969 (30 Dec.). *International Year of African Tourism.* P 14.
237 **164** 4d. multicoloured .. 5 5
238 **165** 1s. blk. & bright emerald 15 15
239 **166** 1s. 6d. multicoloured .. 25 25

167. Symbolic Tree.

169. Scroll.

168. U.P.U. H.Q. Building.

(Des. E. Emokpae (4d., 1s., 2s.), B. Onobrakpeya (1s. 6d.). Photo. Enschedé.)

1970 (28 May). "*Stamp of Destiny*"; *End of Civil War.* T **167** *and similar designs.* P 11 × 11½ (2s.) *or* 11½ × 11 (*others.*)
240 4d. gold, new blue and black 5 5
241 1s. multicoloured 20 20
242 1s. 6d. yellow-green & black 30 30
243 2s. multicoloured 40 40

Designs: *Vert.*—1s. Symbolic Wheel; 1s. 6d. United Nigerians supporting Map. *Horiz.*—2s. Symbolic Torch.

(Des. A. Onwudimegwu.)

1970 (29 June). *New U.P.U. Headquarters Building.* P 14.
244 **168** 4d. reddish violet and greenish yellow .. 5 5
245 ,, 1s. 6d. light greenish blue and deep blue .. 30 30

(Des. A. Onwudimegwu.)

1970 (1 Sept.). *25th Anniv. of United Nations.* T **169** *and similar vert. design.* P 14.
246 4d. orange-brown, buff and black 5 5
247 1s. 6d. steel-blue, cinnamon and gold 30 30

Design:—1s. 6d. U.N. Building.

170. Oil Rig.

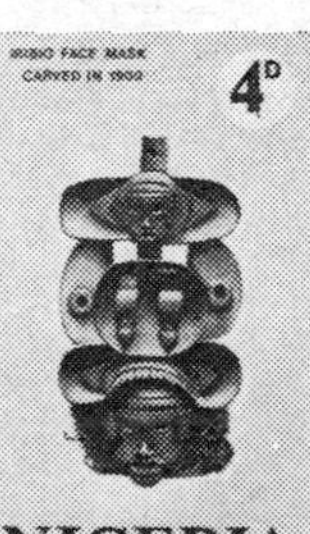

172. Ibibio Face Mask.

171. Children and Globe.

(Des. E. Emokpae. Litho. Enschedé.)

1970 (30 Sept.). *Tenth Anniv. of Independence.* T **170** *and similar vert. designs. Multicoloured.* P 13½ × 13.
248 2d. Type **170** 5 5
249 4d. University Graduate .. 5 8
250 6d. Durbar Horsemen .. 10 10
251 9d. Servicemen raising Flag 15 15
252 1s. Footballer 20 20
253 1s. 6d. Parliament Building 30 30
254 2s. Kainji Dam 40 40
255 2s. 6d. Agricultural Produce 50 50
248/55 .. .. *Set of* 8 1·50 1·50

(Des. E. O. Emokpae and A. Onwudimegwu. Photo. Enschedé.)

1971 (21 Mar.). *Racial Equality Year.* T **171** *and similar multicoloured designs.* P 13 × 13½ (*4d., 2s.*) *or* 13½ × 13 (*others*).
256 4d. Type **171** 5 5
257 1s. Black and white men uprooting "Racism" (*vert.*) 15 15
258 1s. 6d. The world in black and white (*vert.*) 25 25
259 2s. Black and white men united 40 40

(Des. A. Onwudimegwu.)

1971 (30 Sept.). *Antiquities of Nigeria.* T **172** *and similar vert. designs.* P 13½ × 14.
260 4d. black and pale blue .. 5 5
261 1s. 3d. blackish brn. & ochre 20 20
262 1s. 9d. emerald, sepia and olive-yellow 30 30

Designs:—1s. 3d. Benin bronze; 1s. 9d. Ife bronze.

173. Children and Symbol.

174. Mast and Dish Aerial.

(Des. E. Emokpae.)

1971 (11 Dec.). *25th Anniv. of UNICEF.* T **173** *and similar vert. designs, each incorporating the the UNICEF symbol.* P 13½ × 14.
263 4d. multicoloured 5 5
264 1s. 3d. yellow-orange, orange-red and carmine-lake .. 20 20
265 1s. 9d. pale greenish blue and deep greenish blue .. 30 30

Designs:—1s. 3d. Mother and child; 1s. 9d. Mother carrying child.

(Des. A. Onwudimegwu.)

1971 (30 Dec.). *Opening of Nigerian Earth Satellite Station.* T **174** *and similar horiz. designs.* P 14.
266 **174** 4d. multicoloured .. 5 5
267 – 1s. 3d. green, blue & blk. 20 20
268 – 1s. 9d. brn., orange & blk. 30 30
269 – 3s. mauve, blk. & mag. 50 50

Designs:—267/9, as T **174**, but showing different views of the Satellite Station.

The 4d. has been seen on a cover from Ilorin, postmarked 23.12.71.

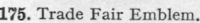

175. Trade Fair Emblem.

177. Nok Style Terracotta Head.

176. Traffic.

(Des. E. Emokpae (4d.), A. Onwudimegwu (others). Litho. D.L.R.)

1972 (23 Feb.). *All-Africa Trade Fair.* T **175** *and similar designs.* P 13.
270 4d. multicoloured 5 5
271 1s. 3d. deep lilac, lemon and gold 20 2
272 1s. 9d. yellow-orange, orange-yellow and black .. 30 3

Designs: *Horiz.*—1s. 3d. Map of Africa with pointers to Nairobi. *Vert.*—1s. 9d. Africa on globe.

(Des. A. Onwudimegwu (4d., 3s.), E. Emokpa (1s. 3d.), J. Owei (1s. 9d.). Litho. D.L.R.)

1972 (23 June). *Change to Driving on the Right* T **176** *and similar horiz. designs. Multicoloured (except 4d.).* P 13.
273 4d. Type **176** (yellow-orange, deep chestnut and black) 5
274 1s. 3d. Roundabout 20 2
275 1s. 9d. Highway 30 3
276 3s. Road junction 50 5

(Des. G. Okiki (1s. 3d.), A. Aiyegbusi (others) Litho. D.L.R.)

1972 (1 Sept.). *All-Nigeria Arts Festival.* T **17** *and similar multicoloured designs.* P 13.
277 4d. Type **177** 5
278 1s. 3d. Bronze pot from Igbo-Ukwu 25 2
279 1s. 9d. Bone harpoon (*horiz.*) 35 3

(New currency. 100 kobo = 1 naira.)

178. Hides and Skins.

(Des. E. Emokpae (8, 25, 30, 50 k., 1 n.), A Onwudimegwu (others).)

1973–74. T **178** *and similar designs.* P 14.
(*a*) *Photo. Left-hand imprint* 5¼ *mm. long* (2 Jan.–2 Apr.).
280 1 k. multicoloured (deep green foliage) 5
*a. Light emerald foliage** (2.4.73) 5
281 2 k. multicoloured 5

282 5 k. multicoloured (emerald hills) 25 20
a. Bright yellow-green hills (2.4.73)* 12 8
283 10 k. multicoloured 20 12
284 12 k. black, pale emerald and deep cobalt 50 50
285 18 k. multicoloured 75 75
286 20 k. multicoloured .. .. 1·00 1·00
287 30 k. multicoloured .. .. 1·00 1·00
288 50 k. multicoloured (black background and figure) 1·25 90
a. Deep chocolate background and figure (2.4.73)* 80 45
289 1 n. multicoloured .. .. 3·00 3·00
280/9 .. .. *Set of* 10 6·50 6·25

(*b*) *Litho. Left-hand imprint* 6 *mm. long* (2 Apr. 1973–74).
290 1 k. multicoloured (8.73) .. 5 5
291 2 k. multicoloured (2.7.74) ** 5 5
292 3 k. multicoloured 5 5
293 5 k. multicoloured (*shades*) (2.74) 8 5
294 7 k. multicoloured 10 5
295 8 k. multicoloured 12 8
296 10 k. multicoloured (8.73) .. 15 10
297 12 k. black, green and cobalt (*shades*) 20 12
298 15 k. multicoloured 25 15
299 18 k. multicoloured 30 15
300 20 k. multicoloured 30 20
301 25 k. multicoloured 40 25
302 30 k. multicoloured 45 30
303 35 k. multicoloured 55 35
305 1 n. multicoloured (*shades*) .. 1·50 1·10
306 2 n. multicoloured (*shades*) .. 3·00 2·25
290/306 .. .. *Set of* 16 6·50 5·00

Designs: *Horiz.*—2 k. Natural gas tanks; 3 k. Cement works; 5 k. Cattle ranching; 7 k. Timber mill; 8 k. Oil refinery; 10 k. Leopards, Yankari Game Reserve; 12 k. New Civil Building; 15 k. Sugar-cane harvesting; 20 k. Vaccine production; 25 k. modern wharf; 35 k. Textile machinery; 1 n. Eko Bridge; 2 n. Teaching Hospital, Lagos. *Vert.*—18 k. Palm oil production; 30 k. Argungu Fishing Festival; 50 k. Pottery.

*On Nos. 280*a*, 282*a* and 288*a* other colours also differ, but the shades can best be identified by the distinctive features noted.

† Although First Day Covers of Nos. 280/9 were dated 1 January the stamps were not placed on sale until the 2nd.

** This is the earliest known postmark date. No. 291 was not released by the Crown Agents in London until 11 September 1975.

Differences between printings:

1 k. In photogravure printings the stretched hide at left is in brownish black; on the litho. stamps this hide is brown and yellow.

2 k. On the litho. stamp the line of division between the black and pale blue colours of the gas tanks is a regular curve; on the photogravure printing it is horizontal and irregular. The litho. stamp also has a wider mauve border at top.

5 k. The litho. printing differs from the photogravure (Nos. 282/*a*) in having brown on the herdsman, instead of black.

10 k. The litho. version has much less black on the leopards and tree trunk. It also shows black details at the left-hand end of the trunk, which do not appear on the photogravure version.

12 k. No. 284 is much darker than the litho. version, especially within the building and amongst the trees at right.

18 k. The lithographed printing shows two oil-drums in the foreground which are not present on the photogravure stamp.

20 k. The lithographed printing includes a brown plate not present on the photogravure version. This affects the colour of the chemist and apparatus.

30 k. No. 287 is much darker, with greater use of black in the design.

1 n. On the photogravure stamp the traffic is shown driving on the left. For the litho. version the traffic is corrected to show it driving on the right.

PROCESS. From No. 307 onwards all stamps were lithographed by the Nigerian Security Printing and Minting Co. Ltd.

179. Athlete.

1973 (8 Jan.). *Second All-African Games, Lagos. T* **179** *and similar multicoloured designs* (*except* 5 *k.*). *P* 13.
307 5 k. Type **179** (light lilac, light greenish blue and black) 8 8
308 12 k. Football 20 20
309 18 k. Table-tennis 30 30
310 25 k. National Stadium (*vert.*) 40 40

180. All-Africa House, Addis Ababa.

1973 (25 May.). *Tenth Anniv. of O.A.U. T* **180** *and similar vert. designs. Multicoloured. P* 14.
311 5 k. Type **180** 10 10
312 18 k. O.A.U. flag 30 30
313 30 k. O.A.U. emblem and symbolic flight of ten stairs 45 45

181. Dr. Hansen.

(Des. A. Onwudimegwu.)

1973 (30 July). *Centenary of Discovery of Leprosy Bacillus. P* 14.
314 **181** 5 k. + 2 k. light red-brown, flesh & black 15 15

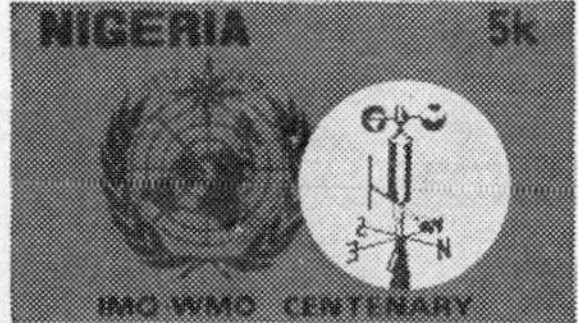

182. W.M.O. Emblem and Weather-vane.

(Des. O. I. Oshiga.)

1973 (4 Sept.). *I.M.O./W.M.O. Centenary. P* 14.
315 **182** 5 k. multicoloured .. 10 10
316 „ 30 k. multicoloured .. 45 45

183. University Complex.

(Des. A. Onwudimegwu (5, 18 k.), C. Okechukwu (12 k.), O. I. Oshiga (30 k.).)

1973 (17 Nov.). *25th Anniv. of Ibadan University. T* **183** *and similar multicoloured designs. P* 13½ × 14 (12*k.*) *or* 14 × 13½ (*others*).
317 5 k. Type **183** 10 10
318 12 k. Students' population growth (*vert.*) 20 20
319 18 k. Tower and students .. 30 30
320 30 k. Teaching Hospital .. 45 45

184. Lagos 1d. Stamp of 1874.

(Des. A. Onwudimegwu (30 k.), S. Eluare (others).)

1974 (10 June). *Stamp Centenary. T* **184** *and similar horiz. designs. P* 14 × 13½.
321 5 k. light emerald, yellow-orange and black .. 10 10
322 12 k. multicoloured 20 20
323 18 k. light yellowish green, mauve and black .. 30 30
324 30 k. multicoloured 45 45

Designs:—5 k. Graph of mail traffic growth; 12 k. Northern Nigeria £25 stamp of 1904; 30 k. Forms of mail transport.

185. U.P.U. Emblem on Globe.

(Des. S. Eluare (5 k.), A. Onwudimegwu (18 k.), O. I. Oshiga (30 k.).)

1974 (9 Oct.). *Centenary of Universal Postal Union. T* **185** *and similar horiz. designs. P* 14.
325 5 k. light greenish blue, yellow-orange and black .. 10 10
326 18 k. multicoloured 30 30
327 30 k. bistre-brown, light greenish blue and black .. 45 45

Designs:—18 k. World transport map; 30 k. U.P.U. emblem and letters.

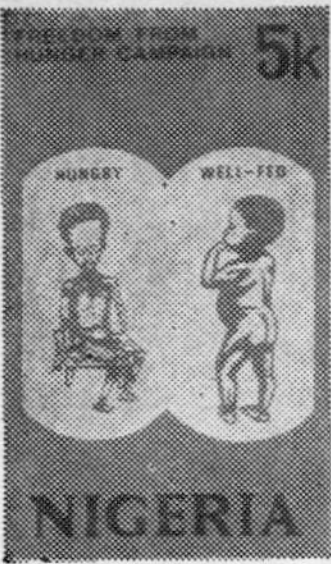

186. Starving and Well-fed Children.

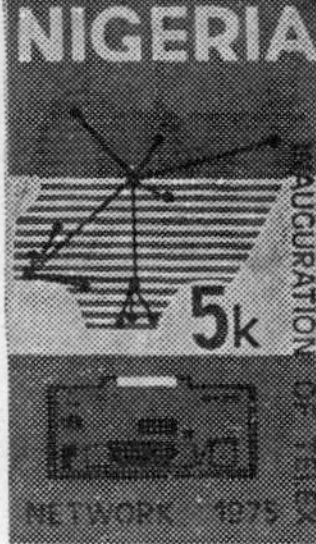

187. Telex Network and Teleprinter.

(Des. A. Onwudimegwu (12 k.), Sam Eluare (others).)

1974 (25 Nov.). *Freedom from Hunger Campaign.* T **186** *and similar designs.* P 14.

328	5 k. apple-green, buff and grey-black	8	8
329	12 k. multicoloured	20	20
330	30 k. multicoloured	45	45

Designs: *Horiz.*—12 k. Poultry battery. *Vert.*—30 k. Water-hoist.

(Des. S. Eluare.)

1975 (3 July). *Inauguration of Telex Network.* T **187** *and similar vert. designs.* P 13½ × 14.

331	5 k. black, yellow-orange and light olive-green	5	8
332	12 k. black, lemon and orange-brown	15	20
333	18 k. multicoloured	25	30
334	30 k. multicoloured	40	45

Nos. 332/4 are as T **187** but have the motifs arranged differently.

188. Queen Amina of Zaria.

(Des. A. Onwudimegwu.)

1975 (18 Aug.). *International Women's Year.* P 14.

335	**188**	5 k. deep olive, light yellow and azure ..	5	8
336	,,	18 k. purple, pale blue and light mauve ..	25	30
337	,,	30 k. multicoloured ..	40	45

189

190. Alexander Graham Bell.

(Des. A. Onwudimegwu.)

1976 (10 Mar.). *Telephone Centenary.* T **190** *and similar designs.* W **189** (*inverted on 18 k., sideways on others*). P 13½.

338	5 k. multicoloured	8	10
339	18 k. multicoloured	30	35
340	25 k. royal blue, pale blue and blackish brown	40	45

Designs: *Horiz.*—18 k. Gong and modern telephone system. *Vert.*—25 k. Telephones, 1876 and 1976.

191. Child Writing.

(Des. A. Onwudimegwu (5 k.), S. Eluare (18 k.), N. Lasisi (25 k.).)

1976 (20 Sept.). *Launching of Universal Primary Education.* T **191** *and similar designs.* W **189** (*sideways on 18 and 25 k.*). P 14.

341	5 k. lemon, light violet and bright mauve	8	10
342	18 k. multicoloured	30	35
343	25 k. multicoloured	45	50

Designs: *Vert.*—18 k. Children entering school; 25 k. Children in class.

192. Festival Emblem.

(Des. O. Oshiga (5 k., 30 k.), A. Onwudimegwu (10 k., 12 k.), Nojim Lasisi (18 k.).)

1976–77. *Second World Black and African Festival of Arts and Culture, Nigeria.* T **192** *and similar horiz. designs.* W **189** (*inverted on 5 and 10 k.*). P 14.

344	5 k. gold & blackish brown (1.11.76)	8	10
345	10 k. light red-brown, light yellow and blk. (15.1.77)	20	20
346	12 k. blk., yell. & crimson (15.1.77)	20	25
347	18 k. chrome-yellow, lt. brown and black (1.11.76) ..	30	35
348	30 k. magenta & blk. (15.1.77)	55	65
344/8	.. .. *Set of* 5	1·25	1·40

Designs:—10 k. National Arts Theatre; 12 k. African hair-styles; 18 k. Musical instruments; 30 k. " Nigerian arts and crafts ".

POSTAGE DUE STAMPS.

D 1

(Litho. Bradbury, Wilkinson.)

1959 (4 Jan.). *Wmk. Mult. Script CA.* P 14½ × 1[4]

D1	**D 1**	1d. red-orange	5	
D2	,,	2d. red-orange	5	
D3	,,	3d. red-orange	5	
D4	,,	6d. red-orange	10	
D5	,,	1s. grey-black	20	
D1/D5		.. .. *Set of* 5	40	

1961 (1 Aug.). W **34.** P 14½ × 14.

D 6	**D 1**	1d. red	5	
D 7	,,	2d. light blue	5	
D 8	,,	3d. emerald	5	
D 9	,,	6d. yellow	8	
D10	,,	1s. blue (*shades*) ..	15	
D6/D10		.. .. *Set of* 5	35	

(Typo. Nigerian Security Printing & Mintin[g] Co.)

1973 (3 May). *New Currency. No wm[k.]* P 12½ × 13½.

D11	**D 1**	2 k. red	5	
D12	,,	3 k. blue	5	
D13	,,	5 k. orge.-yell. (*shades*)	8	
D14	,,	10 k. lt. apple-grn. (*shades*)	15	

BIAFRA.

The following stamps were issued by Biaf[ra] (the Eastern Region of Nigeria) during the ci[vil] war with the Federal Government, 1967–70.

They were in regular use within Biafra fro[m] the time when supplies of Nigerian stamps we[re] exhausted; and towards the end of the confli[ct] they began to be used on external mail carried [by] air via Libreville.

1. Map of Republic.

2. Arms, Flag an[d] Date of Independen[ce]

3. Mother and Child.

(Typo. and litho. Mint, Lisbon.)

1968 (5 Feb.). *Independence.* P 12½.

1	**1**	2d. multicoloured	5
2	**2**	4d. multicoloured	10
3	**3**	1s. multicoloured	20

(4)

1968. *Stamps of Nigeria optd. as T* **4** (*without* "SOVEREIGN" *on* 10s.).

No.	Type	Description	Unused	Used
4	**120**	½d. mult. (No. 172) ..	30	25
5	**121**	1d. mult. (No. 173) ..	40	30
6	**122**	1½d. mult. (No. 174) ..	50	40
7	**123**	2d. mult. (No. 175) ..	2·00	2·00
8	**125**	4d. mult. (No. 177a) ..	2·00	2·00
9	**126**	6d. mult. (No. 178) ..	55	70
10	**127**	9d. Prussian blue and orange-red (No. 179)	60	85
11	**128**	1s. multicoloured (Bk.+R.) (No. 180) ..	25·00	25·00
12	**129**	1s. 3d. multicoloured (Bk.+R.) (No. 181) ..	18·00	20·00
13	**130**	2s. 6d. orange-brown, buff and brown (Bk.+R.) (No. 182)	1·00	1·25
		a. Red opt. omitted ..		
14	**131**	5s. chest., lt. yell. & brn. (Bk.+R.) (No. 183) ..	1·25	2·50
		a. Red opt. omitted ..		
		b. *Pale chestnut, yell. & brn.-purple* (No. 183*a*) ..	1·50	2·50
15	**132**	10s. mult. (No. 184) ..	5·00	6·00
16	**133**	£1 multicoloured (Bk.+R.) (No. 185) ..	6·00	6·50
		a. Black ("SOVEREIGN BIAFRA") omitted ..	£100	
/16		.. .. *Set of* 13	55·00	60·00

+5/-

BIAFRA - FRANCE
FRIENDSHIP 1968

SOVEREIGN
BIAFRA

(**4***a*)

1968. *Nos. 172/3 of Nigeria surch. with premium as T* **4***a*.

No.	Type	Description	Unused	Used
6*b*	**120**	½d. + 5s. multicoloured ..	70	
		ba. Surch. double		
		bb. Surch. double, one inverted		
6*c*	**121**	1d. + £1 multicoloured ..	1·75	
		ca. Surch. double		
		cb. Surch. double, one inverted		

5. Weapon Maintenance.

6. Victim of Atrocity.

Nurse and Refugees.

8. Biafran Arms and Banknote.

9. Orphaned Child.

+6D
HELP
BIAFRAN
CHILDREN
(**10**)

(Litho. Mint, Lisbon.)

1968. *First Anniv. of Independence.* P 12½.

No.	Type	Description	Unused	Used
17	**5**	4d. multicoloured	8	8
18	**6**	1s. multicoloured	12	20
19	**7**	2s. 6d. multicoloured ..	25	50
20	**8**	5s. multicoloured ..	45	80
21	**9**	10s. multicoloured ..	85	1·75
17/21		.. .. *Set of* 5	1·50	3·00

1968 (30 MAY). *Nos. 17/21 surch. as T* **10**.

No.	Type	Description	Unused	Used
22	**5**	4d.+2d. multicoloured ..	8	10
		a. Surch. inverted	38·00	
23	**6**	1s.+6d. multicoloured ..	20	25
24	**7**	2s. 6d.+1s. multicoloured	35	50
25	**8**	5s.+2s. 6d. multicoloured	75	1·25
26	**9**	10s.+2s. 6d. multicoloured	1·25	2·00
		a. Surch. double	38·00	
22/26		.. .. *Set of* 5	2·40	3·75

11. *Papilio dardanus* (butterfly) and *Lankesteria barteri* (plant).

12. *Papilio antimachus* and *Ipomoea involucrata.*

13. *Papilio zalmoxis* and *Haemanthus cinnabarinus.*

14. *Papilio hesperus* and *Clerodendrum splendens.*

1968 (2 SEPT.). *Butterflies and Plants. Litho.* P 14.

No.	Type	Description	Unused	Used
27	**11**	4d. multicoloured	8	8
28	**12**	1s. 6d. multicoloured ..	20	25
29	**13**	2s. 6d. multicoloured ..	35	45
30	**14**	5s. multicoloured	65	85

MEXICO OLYMPICS
1968
(**15**)

1968. *Olympic Games, Mexico. Nos.* 27/30 *optd. with T* **15**.

No.	Type	Description	Unused	Used
31	**11**	4d. multicoloured	8	8
32	**12**	1s. 6d. multicoloured ..	20	25
		a. Opt. inverted		
33	**13**	2s. 6d. multicoloured ..	35	45
34	**14**	5s. multicoloured	65	85

16. Child in Chains and Globe.

1969 (30 MAY). *Second Anniv. of Independence. Multicoloured; frame colours given. Litho.* P 13×13½.

No.	Type	Description	Unused	Used
35	**16**	2d. yellow-orange	5	5
36	,,	4d. red-orange	8	10
		a. Green (wreath) and orange (Sun) omitted		
37	,,	1s. new blue	12	20
38	,,	2s. 6d. emerald	35	60

A miniature sheet with a face value of 10s. was also released.

17. Papal Arms.

18. Arms of the Vatican.

19. St. Peter's Basilica, Vatican.

20. Statue of St. Peter.

T **17/20** each include Pope Paul VI and map of Africa.

1969 (25 SEPT.). *Visit of Pope Paul to Africa. Multicoloured; background colours given.* P 13×13½.

No.	Type	Description	Unused	Used
39	**17**	4d. yellowish orange ..	8	8
40	**18**	6d. deep new blue	8	12
41	**19**	9d. blue-green	12	20
42	**20**	3s. magenta	45	65

A miniature sheet with a face value of 10s. was also released.

The 3s. is known with the background in brown-red or brown.

Biafra was overrun by Federal troops on 10 January, 1970 and surrender took place on 15 January.

On 17 December the French Agency released a Christmas issue consisting of Nos. 39/42 overprinted "CHRISTMAS 1969 PEACE ON EARTH AND GOODWILL TO ALL MEN" together with the miniature sheet overprinted "CHRISTMAS 1969" and surcharged £1. Later Nos. 35/38 were released overprinted in red "SAVE BIAFRA 9TH JAN 1970" with a premium of 8d., 1s. 4d., 4s., and 10s. respectively together with the miniature sheet with a premium of £1. We have no evidence that these issues were actually put on sale in Biafra before the collapse, but it has been reported that the 4d. Christmas issue and 2d.+8d. Save Biafra exist genuinely used before capitulation.

Nos. 40/41 have been seen surcharged "+10/– HUMAN RIGHTS" and the United Nations emblem but it is doubtful if they were issued.

NORFOLK ISLAND.

AUSTRALIAN ADMINISTRATION.

PRINTERS. Nos. 1 to 42 were printed at the Note Printing Branch, Reserve Bank of Australia (until 14 Jan. 1960, known as the Note Printing Branch, Commonwealth Bank) by recess. See note at the beginning of Australia *re* imprints.

1. Ball Bay.

Note. Stamps of T **1**, perf. 11, or in different colours, perf. 11, are in the same category as those mentioned in AUSTRALIA after No. 221.

1947 (10 JUNE)–**59.** *P* 14.

No.	Type	Description	Unused	Used
1	**1**	½d. orange	8	8
2	,,	1d. bright violet	10	8
3	,,	1½d. emerald-green	15	15
4	,,	2d. reddish violet	20	20
5	,,	2½d. scarlet	25	25
6	,,	3d. chestnut	30	30
6*a*	,,	3d. emerald-green (6.7.59)	1·75	1·75
7	,,	4d. claret	35	35
8	,,	5½d. indigo	40	40
9	,,	6d. purple-brown	50	50
10	,,	9d. magenta	75	75
11	,,	1s. grey-green	90	90
12	,,	2s. yellow-bistre	3·25	2·50
12*a*	,,	2s. deep blue (6.7.59) ..	8·00	8·00
1/12*a*		.. .. *Set of* 14	16·00	15·00

The ½d., 1d., 1½d. and 2d. were printed on white paper from November, 1956.

2. Warder's Tower.

3. Airfield.

4. First Governor's Residence.

5. Barracks Entrance.

6. Salt House.

7. Bloody Bridge.

1953 (10 JUNE). *P* 14½×15 (*vert.*) *or* 15×14½ (*horiz.*).

No.	Type	Description	Unused	Used
13	**2**	3½d. brown-lake	60	70
14	**3**	6½d. deep green	1·10	1·00
15	**4**	7½d. deep blue	1·60	1·40
16	**5**	8½d. chocolate	2·00	1·75
17	**6**	10d. reddish violet	1·50	1·25
18	**7**	5s. sepia	13·00	10·00
13/18		.. .. *Set of* 6	18·00	15·00

See also No. 30 and 35.

8. Norfolk Island Seal and Pitcairners Landing.

1956 (8 JUNE). *Centenary of Landing of Pitcairn Islanders on Norfolk Island. P* 15×14½.

No.	Type	Description	Unused	Used
19	**8**	3d. deep bluish green ..	25	30
20	,,	2s. violet (*shades*)	3·00	3·00

Alternate stamps of the 2s. value were printed from a different die which is distinguishable by a dot in the bottom right corner.

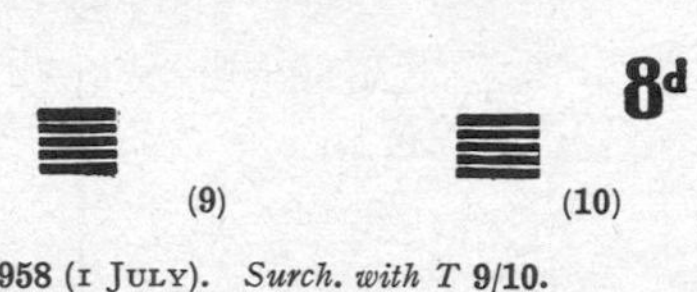

(9) (10)

1958 (1 JULY). *Surch. with T* **9/10**.

No.	Type	Description	Unused	Used
21	**4**	7d. on 7½d. deep blue ..	1·25	1·25
22	**5**	8d. on 8½d. chocolate ..	1·40	1·40

NORFOLK ISLAND

(11)

1959 (7 DEC.). 150*th Anniv. of Australian Post Office. No.* 331 *of Australia surch. with T* **11**.

No.	Type	Description	Unused	Used
23	**143**	5d. on 4d. slate (R.) ..	80	90

12. *Hibiscus insularis.*

13. *Lagunaria patersonii.*

14. White Tern.

16. Red Hibiscus.

15. Lantana.

17. Queen Elizabeth II and Cereus.

18. Fringed Hibiscus.

19. Providence Petre

20. Passion-flower.

21. Rose Apple.

22. Red-tailed Tropic Bird.

(Design recess; centre typo. (T **21**).)

1960–62. *P* 14½ *or* 14½×14 (10*s*.).

No.	Type	Description	Unused	Used
24	**12**	1d. bluish green (23.5.60)	5	
25	**13**	2d. rose and myrtle-green (23.5.60)	8	
26	**14**	3d. green (1.5.61)	15	
27	**15**	5d. bright purple (20.6.60)	35	
28	**16**	8d. red (20.6.60) ..	55	
29	**17**	9d. ultramarine (23.5.60) ..	55	
30	**6**	10d. brown & reddish violet (27.2.61)	60	
31	**18**	1s. 1d. carm.-red (16.10.61)	35	
32	**19**	2s. sepia (1.5.61) ..	1·10	
33	**20**	2s. 5d. deep violet (5.2.62)	80	
34	**21**	2s. 8d. cinnamon & deep grn. (9.4.62)	1·00	1·
35	**7**	5s. sepia & deep green (27.2.61)	2·50	2·
36	**22**	10s. emerald-green (14.8.61)	12·00	12·
24/36		.. .. *Set of* 13	18·00	17·

Nos. 30 and 35 are redrawn.

(23)

(24) (25)

1960. *As Nos.* 13/5 *but colours changed, sur with T* **23/5**.

No.	Type	Description	Unused	Used
37	**2**	1s. 1d. on 3½d. deep ultramarine (26.9.60)	2·50	2·
38	**3**	2s. 5d. on 6½d. bluish green (26.9.60)	3·00	3·
39	**4**	2s. 8d. on 7½d. sepia (29.8.60)	4·50	4·

26. Queen Elizabeth II and Map.

960 (24 Oct.). *Introduction of Local Government. P* 14.
26 2s. 8d. reddish purple .. 8·00 10·00

960 (21 Nov.). *Christmas. As No.* 338 *of Australia.*
5d. bright purple .. .. 4·50 5·00

961 (20 Nov.). *Christmas. As No.* 341 *of Australia.*
5d. slate-blue .. .. 1·25 1·50

RINTERS. All the following issues were rinted in photogravure by Harrison and Sons xcept issues which are in the same designs as ustralia, *and where otherwise stated.*

27. "Tweed Trousers" (*Atypichthys latus*).

28. "Trumpeter".

29. "Po'ov".

30. "Dreamfish".

31. "Hapoeka".

32. "Ophie" (*carangidae*).

962–63. *P* 14½ × 14.

27	6d. sepia, yellow and deep bluish green (16.7.62) ..	25	25
28	11d. red-orange, brown and blue (25.2.63)	50	50
29	1s. blue, pink and yellow-olive (17.9.62)	55	55
30	1s. 3d. blue, red-brown and green (15.7.63) ..	65	65
31	1s. 6d. sepia, violet and light blue (6.5.63)	90	90
32	2s. 3d. deep blue, red and greenish yellow (23.9.63)	1·25	1·25
/8	.. .. *Set of* 6	3·00	2·75

962 (19 Nov.). *Christmas. As No.* 345 *of Australia.*
5d. ultramarine 60 75

963 (11 Nov.). *Christmas. As No.* 361 *of Australia.*
5d. red 60 75

33. Overlooking Kingston.

37. Norfolk Pine.

34. Kingston.

35. The Arches (Kingston).

36. Slaughter Bay.

964 (24 Feb.–28 Sept.). *P* 14½ × 14.

33	5d. multicoloured ..	20	20
34	8d. multicoloured ..	30	30
35	9d. multicoloured (11.5) ..	35	35
36	10d. multicoloured (28.9) ..	40	40

(Photo. Note Ptg. Branch, Reserve Bank of Australia, Melbourne.)

1964 (1 July). *50th Anniv. of Norfolk Island as Australian Territory. P* 13½.

55	**37**	5d. black, red and orange	30	30
56	„	8d. black, red & grey-green	40	40

1964 (9 Nov.). *Christmas. As No.* 372 *of Australia.*
57 5d. green, blue, buff and violet 85 1·00

1965 (14 Apr.). *50th Anniv. of Gallipoli Landing. As T* **184** *of Australia, but slightly larger* (22 × 34½ *mm.*). *Photo.*
58 5d. sepia, black and emerald .. 25 25

1965 (25 Oct.). *Christmas. Helecon paper. As No.* 381 *of Australia.*
59 5d. multicoloured 35 30

(New currency. 100 cents = $1 Australian.)

38. *Hibiscus insularis.*

1966 (14 Feb.). *Decimal currency. Various stamps surch. in black on silver tablets, which vary slightly in size, obliterating old value as in T* **38**. *Surch. typo.*

60	**38**	1 c. on 1d. bluish grn. (*value tablet* 4 × 5 *mm.*) ..	8	8
		a. Value tablet larger, 5½ × 5½ mm.	20	25
61	**13**	2 c. on 2d. rose and myrtle-green	8	8
62	**14**	3 c. on 3d. green ..	8	8
63	**15**	4 c. on 5d. bright purple ..	10	10
64	**16**	5 c. on 8d. red	12	12
65	**6**	10 c. on 10d. brown and red-dish violet	20	20
66	**18**	15 c. on 1s. 1d. carmine-red	40	35
67	**19**	20 c. on 2s. sepia	50	40
68	**20**	25 c. on 2s. 5d. deep violet	50	50
69	**21**	30 c. on 2s. 8d. cinnamon and deep green ..	60	60
70	**7**	50 c. on 5s. sepia & dp. grn.	1·00	1·25
71	**22**	$1 on 10s. emer.-grn. (*value tablet* 7 × 6½ *mm.*) ..	3·00	3·50
		a. Value tablet smaller, 6½ × 4 mm.	2·75	2·75
60/71a		.. .. *Set of* 14	6·00	6·00

39. Headstone Bridge.

40. Cemetery Road.

1966 (27 June). *P* 14½ × 14.

72	**39**	7 c. multicoloured	25	25
73	**40**	9 c. multicoloured	30	30

41. St. Barnabas' Chapel (exterior).

42. St. Barnabas' Chapel (exterior).

1966 (23 Aug.). *Centenary of Melanesian Mission. P* 14 × 14½.

74	**41**	4 c. multicoloured ..	15	15
75	**42**	25 c. multicoloured ..	50	50

43. Star over Philip Island.

(Des. B. W. G. McCoy.)

1966 (24 Oct.). *Christmas. P* 14½.
76 **43** 4 c. multicoloured 12 12

44. H.M.S. *Resolution*, 1774.

45. *La Boussole* and *L'Astrolabe*, 1788.

46. H.M. Brig *Supply*, 1788.

47. H.M.S. *Sirius*, 1790.

48. *The Norfolk*, 1798.

49. H.M. Survey Cutter *Mermaid*, 1825.

50. *Lady Franklin*, 1853.

51. *The Morayshire*, 1856.

52. *Southern Cross*, 1866.

53. *The Pitcairn*, 1891.

54. Norfolk Whaleboat, 1895.

55. H.M.C.S. *Iris*, 1907.

56. *The Resolution*, 1926.

57. S.S. *Morinda*, 1931.

1967 (17 Apr.)–**68**. *P* 14 × 14½.

77	**44**	1 c. multicoloured ..	5	5
78	**45**	2 c. multicoloured ..	5	5
79	**46**	3 c. multicoloured ..	5	5
80	**47**	4 c. multicoloured ..	8	8
81	**48**	5 c. multicoloured (14.8.67)	8	10
82	**49**	7 c. multicoloured (14.8.67)	12	12
83	**50**	9 c. multicoloured (14.8.67)	20	20
84	**51**	10 c. multicoloured (14.8.67)	20	20
85	**52**	15 c. multicoloured (18.3.68)	35	35
86	**53**	20 c. multicoloured (18.3.68)	50	50
87	**54**	25 c. multicoloured (18.3.68)	65	65
88	**55**	30 c. multicoloured (18.6.68)	1·00	1·00
89	**56**	50 c. multicoloured (18.6.68)	1·25	1·25
90	**57**	$1 multicoloured (18.6.68)	2·75	2·75
77/90		.. .. *Set of* 14	6·50	6·50

1967 (7 June). *50th Anniv. of Lions International. As No.* 411 *of Australia but colours changed.*
91 4 c. black, bluish green and olive-yellow 40 40

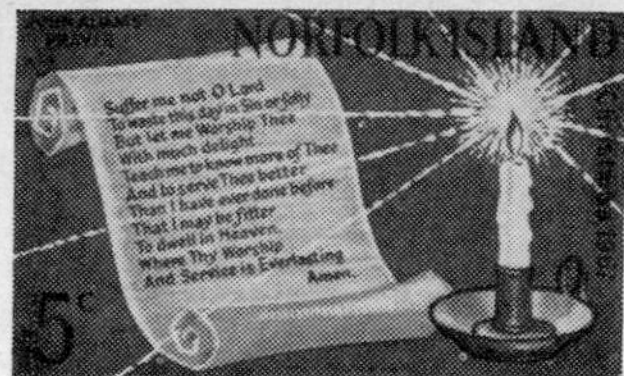

58. John Adam's Prayer and Candle.

(Des. B. G. W. McCoy.)

1967 (16 Oct.). *Christmas. P* 14.
92 **58** 5 c. black, light yellow-olive and red 15 15

1968 (5 Aug.)–**71**. *Coil Stamps. As T* **199** *of Australia.*
93 3 c. blk., lt. brn. & vermilion 5 5
94 4 c. blk., lt. brn. & blue-grn. 5 5
95 5 c. blk., lt. brn. & dp violet 5 8
95*a* 6 c. black, light brown and lake-brown (25.8.71) .. 8 10

59. "Skymaster" and "Lancastrian" Aircraft.

1968 (25 Sept.). *21st Anniv. of QANTAS Air Service, Sydney-Norfolk Island. P* 14.
96 **59** 5 c. bluish black, carmine-red and light blue .. 15 15
97 ,, 7 c. blackish brown, carmine-red and turquoise .. 20 20

60. Bethlehem Star and Flowers.

1968 (24 Oct.). *Christmas. P* 14×14½.
98 **60** 5 c. multicoloured 15 15

61. Captain Cook, Quadrant and Chart of Pacific Ocean.

(Des. V. Whiteley from sketch by J. G. Cowan.)

1969 (3 June). *Bicentenary of Observation of the transit of Venus across the Sun, by Captain Cook, from Tahiti. P* 14.
99 **61** 10 c. multicoloured .. 30 30

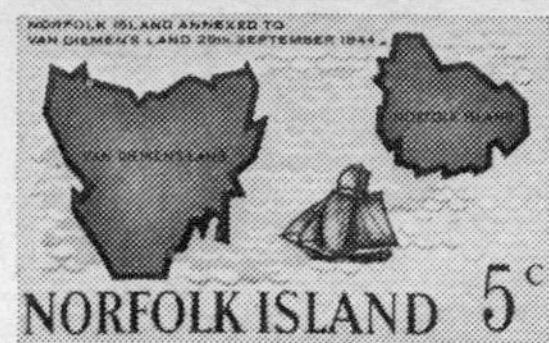

62. Van Diemen's Land, Norfolk Island and Sailing Ship.

(Des. Mrs. A. Bathie and Mrs. M. J. McCoy.)

1969 (29 Sept.). *125th Anniv. of the Annexation of Norfolk Island to Van Diemen's Land. P* 14×14½.
100 **62** 5 c. multicoloured .. 12 12
101 ,, 30 c. multicoloured .. 60 60

63. "The Nativity" (carved mother-of-pearl plaque).

1969 (27 Oct.). *Christmas. P* 14½×14.
102 **63** 5 c. multicoloured .. 15 20

64. Norfolk Island Fly-eater.

(Des. G. Mathews.)

1970–71. *Birds. T* **64** *and similar multicoloured designs. Chalk-surfaced paper. P* 14.
103 1 c. Norfolk Island Robins (22.7.70) 5 5
104 2 c. Norfolk Island Thick-head (24.2.71) 5 5
105 3 c. Type **64** (25.2.70) .. 8 8
106 4 c. Long-tailed Cuckoos (25.2.70) 8 8
107 5 c. Norfolk Island Green Parrot (24.2.71) .. 10 10
108 7 c. Norfolk Island Cater-pillar-catchers (22.7.70) 12 15
109 9 c. Grey-headed Blackbird (25.2.70) 15 20
110 10 c. Norfolk Island Owl (22.7.70) 20 20
111 15 c. Norfolk Island Pigeon (24.2.71) 30 30
112 20 c. White-breasted White-eye (16.6.71) 35 40
113 25 c. Philip Island Parrots (22.7.70) 45 50
a. Error. Glazed, ordinary paper 45·00
114 30 c. Norfolk Island Fantail (16.6.71) 60 65
115 45 c. Norfolk Island Starlings (25.2.70) .. .. 1·00 1·00
116 50 c. Red Parrot (24.2.71) .. 1·25 1·25
117 $1 Norfolk Island King-fisher (16.6.71) .. .. 2·50 2·50
103/117 .. .. *Set of* 15 6·50 6·50

Nos. 105, 106, 109, 112, 114, 115 and 117 are horizontal, and the remainder vertical designs.

65. Capt. Cook and Map of Australia.

(Des. R. Bates.)

1970 (29 Apr.). *Bicentenary of Captain Coo Discovery of Australia's East Coast. T* **65** *a similar horiz. design. Multicoloured. P* 1
118 5 c. Type **65** 12
119 10 c. H.M.S. *Endeavour* and Aborigine 20

66. First Christmas Service, 1788.

(Des. R. Bates.)

1970 (15 Oct.). *Christmas. P* 14.
120 **66** 5 c. multicoloured .. 15

67. Bishop Patteson, and Martyrdom of St. Stephen.

(Des. R. Bates.)

1971 (20 Sept.). *Death Centenary of Bish Patteson. T* **67** *and similar horiz. desig Multicoloured. P* 14×14½.
121 6 c. Type **67** 15
122 6 c. Bible, Martyrdom of St. Stephen and knotted palm-frond 15
123 10 c. Bishop Patteson and stained-glass 25
124 10 c. Cross and Bishop's Arms 25

Nos. 121/2 and 123/4 were printed in *se-ten* pairs throughout the sheet.

68. Rose Window, St. Barnabas Chapel.

(Des. G. Hitch. Photo. Heraclio Fournier, Spain.)

1971 (25 Oct.). *Christmas.* P 14 × 13½.

125	**68**	6 c. multicoloured ..	15	15

69. Map and Flag.

1972 (7 Feb.). *25th Anniv. of South Pacific Commission.* P 14 × 14½.

126	**69**	7 c. multicoloured ..	40	40

70. Stained-glass Window All Saints, Norfolk Is.). **71.** Cross and Pines. (Stained-glass Window, All Saints Church).

(Des. Mrs. M. McCoy.)

1972 (16 Oct.). *Christmas.* P 14.

127	**70**	7 c. multicoloured ..	15	15

1972 (20 Nov.). *Centenary of First Pitcairner-built Church.* P 14.

128	**71**	12 c. multicoloured ..	25	25

72. *Resolution* in the Antarctic.

1973 (17 Jan.). *Bicentenary of Capt. Cook's Crossing the Antarctic Circle.* P 14.

129	**72**	35 c. multicoloured ..	65	70

73. Child and Christmas Tree.

(Des. B. W. McCoy (T **73**), R. Westwood (35 c.).)

1973 (22 Oct.). *Christmas.* T **73** *and similar vert. designs. Multicoloured.* P 14.

130	7 c. Type **73**	15	15
131	12 c. Type **73**	25	25
132	35 c. Fir trees and star ..	65	70

74. Protestant Clergyman's Quarters.

1973–75. *Historic Buildings. Type* **74** *and similar horiz. designs. Multicoloured.* P 14 × 14½.

133	1 c. Type **74** (*a*)	5	5
134	2 c. Royal Engineer's Office (*b*)	5	5
135	3 c. Double Quarters for Free Overseers (*d*)	5	5
136	4 c. Guard House (*c*)	5	5
137	5 c. Entrance to Pentagonal Gaol (*a*)	8	10
138	7 c. Pentagonal Gaol (*b*) ..	10	10
139	8 c. Prisoners' Barracks (*d*) ..	10	10
140	10 c. Officers' Quarters, New Military Barracks (*a*) ..	15	15
141	12 c. New Military Barracks (*b*)	15	15
142	14 c. Beach Stores (*c*)	20	20
143	15 c. The Magazine (*d*) ..	20	20
144	20 c. Entrance, Old Military Barracks (*c*)	25	25
145	25 c. Old Military Barracks (*d*)	30	35
146	30 c. Old Stores (Crankmill) (*b*)	35	40
147	50 c. Commissariat Stores (*a*)	60	65
148	$1 Government House (*c*) ..	1·40	1·60
133/48	.. .. *Set of* 16	3·75	4·00

Dates of issue: (*a*) 19.11.73; (*b*) 1.5.74; (*c*) 12.7.74; (*d*) 19.2.75.

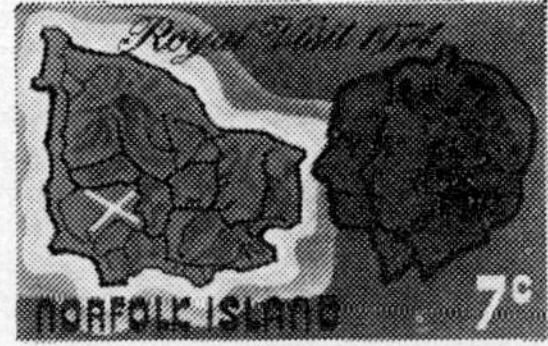

75. Royal Couple and Map.

1974 (8 Feb.). *Royal Visit.* P 14 × 14½.

149	**75**	7 c. multicoloured ..	20	20
150	,,	25 c. multicoloured ..	70	70

76. Chichester's "Madame Elijah".

(Des. B. McCoy. Litho. State Bank Note Printing Works, Helsinki.)

1974 (28 Mar.). *First Aircraft Landing on Norfolk Island.* P 14.

151	**76**	14 c. multicoloured ..	55	55

77. "Captain Cook" (Engraving by J. Basire).

(Litho. Questa.)

1974 (8 Oct.). *Bicentenary of Discovery.* T **77** *and similar vert. designs. Multicoloured.* P 14.

152	7 c. Type **77**	12	12
153	10 c. "*Resolution*" (H. Roberts)	20	20
154	14 c. Norfolk Island Pine ..	25	25
155	25 c. "Norfolk Island flax" (G. Raper)	40	40

78. Nativity Scene (Pearl-shell Pew Carving).

1974 (18 Oct.). *Christmas.* P 14½.

156	**78**	7 c. multicoloured ..	15	15
157	,,	30 c. multicoloured ..	50	55

79. Norfolk Pine.

(Manufactured by Walsall Security Ptrs. Ltd.)

1974 (16 Dec.). *Centenary of Universal Postal Union. T* **79** *and similar "island"-shaped designs. Multicoloured. Imperf. (backing-paper roul.* 20). *Self-adhesive.*

158 10 c. Type **79** 60 75
159 15 c. Offshore islands .. 75 1·00
160 35 c. Island birds .. .. 2·00 2·25
161 40 c. Pacific map .. .. 2·50 2·75
MS162 106×101 mm. Map of Norfolk Is. cut-to-shape with reduced-size replicas of Nos. 158/61 .. .. 5·00 6·00

80. H.M. Survey Cutter *Mermaid.*

(Manufactured by Walsall Security Ptrs. Ltd.)

1975 (18 Aug.). 150*th Anniv. of Second Settlement. T* **80** *and similar "island"-shaped design. Multicoloured. Imperf. (backing-paper roul.* 20). *Self-adhesive.*

163 10 c. Type **80** 15 15
164 35 c. Kingston, 1835 (from painting by T. Seller) .. 50 50

81. Star on Norfolk Island Pine. **82.** Memorial Cross.

(Des. Harrison.)

1975 (6 Oct.). *Christmas. P* 14.

165 **81** 10 c. multicoloured .. 15 20
166 ,, 15 c. multicoloured .. 25 30
167 ,, 35 c. multicoloured .. 50 55

(Des. Harrison.)

1975 (24 Nov.). *Centenary of St. Barnabas Chapel. T* **82** *and similar horiz. design. Multicoloured. P* 14.

168 30 c. Type **82** 40 45
169 60 c. Laying foundation stone and Chapel in 1975 .. 80 90

83. Launching of *Resolution.*

(Des. Harrison.)

1975 (1 Dec.). 50*th Anniv. of Launching of the "Resolution". T* **83** *and similar horiz. design. Multicoloured. P* 14.

170 25 c. Type **83** 35 40
171 45 c. *Resolution* at sea .. 60 65

84. Whaleship *Charles W. Morgan.*

(Des. Harrison.)

1976 (5 July). *Bicentenary of American Revolution. T* **84** *and similar horiz. designs. Multicoloured. P* 14.

172 18 c. Type **84** 25 25
173 25 c. Thanksgiving Service .. 35 40
174 40 c. "Flying Fortress" over Norfolk Is. 55 60
175 45 c. Californian Quail .. 60 70

85. Sea Bird and Sun.

1976 (4 Oct.). *Christmas. P* 14.

176 **85** 18 c. multicoloured .. 25 30
177 ,, 25 c. multicoloured .. 35 40
178 ,, 45 c. multicoloured .. 65 70

86. *Bassaris itea.*

(Des. B. Hargreaves. Photo. Harrison.)

1976–77. *Butterflies and Moths. T* **86** *and simil horiz. designs. Multicoloured. P* 14.

179 1 c. Type **86** 5
180 2 c. *Utetheisa pulchelloides vaga* 5
183 5 c. *Leucania loreyimima* .. 5
184 10 c. *Hypolimnas bolina nerina* 10
185 15 c. *Pyrrhorachis pyrrhogona subcrenulata* 15
186 16 c. *Austrocarea iocephala millsi* 15
187 17 c. *Pseudocoremia christiani* 20
188 18 c. *Cleora idiocrossa* 20
189 19 c. *Simplicia caeneusalis buffetti* 20
190 20 c. *Austrocidaria ralstonae* .. 20
191 30 c. *Hippotion scrofa* .. 30
192 40 c. *Papilio ilioneus ilioneus* 45
193 50 c. *Tiracola plagiata* .. 55
194 $1 *Precis villida calybe* .. 1·00 1·
179/94 .. .. *Set of* 14 3·25 3·

Dates of issue: 1, 5, 10, 16, 18 c., $1 17.11.7 2, 15, 30, 50 c. 22.2.77; 17, 19, 20, 40 c. 10.5.7

NORTH BORNEO.

BRITISH NORTH BORNEO COMPANY ADMINISTRATION.

PRINTERS. The stamps of this country up 1894 were designed by T. Macdonald and hographed by Blades, East and Blades, ondon.

1

8 Cents.

(2)

EIGHT CENTS

(3)

383. *P* 12.

1	2 c. red-brown	2·25	3·50

The figure "2" varies in size.

383. *No.* 1 *surch. as T* **2** *or* **3**.

2	8 c. on 2 c. red-brown	70·00	55·00
3	8 c. on 2 c. red-brown	55·00	23·00
	a. Surch. double		

Type **2** was handstamped and stamps without op are generally forgeries. Type **3** was a setting 50 (10 × 5) providing ten varieties; it normally s a stop which sometimes failed to print.

> **NOTE.**—Prices are separately indicated (in a third price column, in brackets, or by notes below certain issues) for remainders of the stamps of North Borneo cancelled with black bars, where these exist. The issues since 1923 have not been thus cancelled.
>
> It should be noted, however, that a postmark of this form was in use for postal purposes up to this period, and was used at one or two of the smaller post-offices until 1949. A small oval with five bars was used temporarily to mark railway mail during 1947–49.

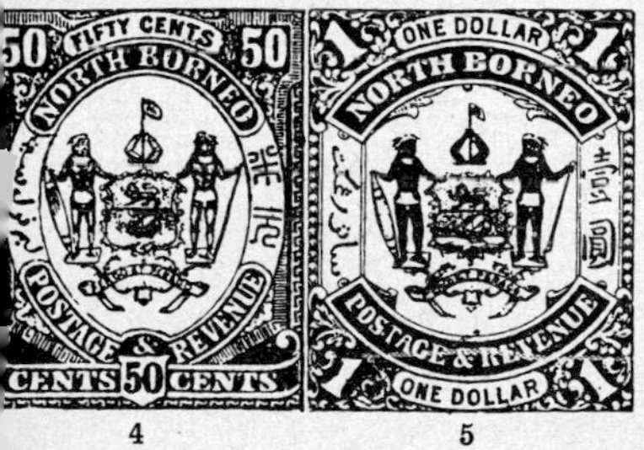

4 5

383. *P* 14.

4	50 c. violet	12·00	—	3·00
	a. Error. "FIFTY" ..	45·00	—	25·00
5	$1 scarlet	11·00	—	2·50

383. *P* 12.

1	4 c. pink	2·50	5·00
	a. Imperf. (horiz. pair) ..	†	—
,,	8 c. pale green	3·50	3·50

86. *P* 14.

1	½ c. magenta	5·50	11·00
,,	1 c. orange	15·00	23·00
	a. Imperf. (pair)	45·00	
,,	2 c. brown	1·75	1·75
	a. Imperf. between (pair) ..	30·00	
,,	4 c. pink	2·25	5·00
,,	8 c. green	2·25	5·00
	a. Imperf. between (pair) ..		
,,	10 c. blue	2·40	3·50
	a. Imperf. (pair)	30·00	
13	.. .. *Set of* 6 *un.*	26·00	45·00

and
evenue

(6)

3
CENTS

(7)

3
CENTS

(8)

1886. *Nos.* 8 *and* 13 *optd. with T* **6**.

14	½ c. magenta	7·50	14·00
15	10 c. blue	18·00	23·00

1886. *T* **1** *surch. with T* **7** *or* **8**. (*a*) *P* 12.

16	**7**	3 c. on 4 c. pink	18·00	45·00
		a. "3" T 7, "CENTS" T 8 ..		
17	**8**	3 c. on 4 c. pink	£550	
18	**7**	5 c. on 8 c. green	70·00	75·00

(*b*) *P* 14.

19	**7**	3 c. on 4 c. pink	7·00	18·00
20	**8**	3 c. on 4 c. pink	45·00	
21	**7**	5 c. on 8 c. green	11·00	21·00
		a. Surch. inverted	£190	

9

10 11

12 13

1886-87. *P* 14.

21*b*	**9**	½ c. magenta	1·60	
22	,,	½ c. rose	75	1·10
		a. Imperf. (pair)	3·00	
23	,,	1 c. orange-yellow ..	1·10	1·50
		a. Imperf. between (pair) ..		
		b. Imperf. (pair)	3·00	
24	,,	1 c. orange	40	70
		a. Imperf. (pair)	2·10	
25	,,	2 c. brown	55	75
		a. Imperf. (pair)	2·10	
26	,,	4 c. pink	40	80
		a. Imperf. (pair)	2·10	
		b. Imperf. between (pair) ..		
27	,,	8 c. green	70	1·00
		a. Imperf. (pair)	3·00	
28	,,	10 c. blue	1·25	2·25
		a. Imperf. between (pair) ..		
		b. Imperf. (pair)	3·00	
29	**10**	25 c. indigo (c. £3) ..	12·00	
		a. Imperf. between (pair) ..		
		b. Imperf. (pair) (c. £4) ..	18·00	
30	**11**	50 c. violet (c. £3·50) ..	12·00	
		a. Imperf. (pair) (c. £3) ..	12·00	
31	**12**	$1 scarlet (c. £3) ..	30·00	
		a. Imperf. (pair) (c. £3) ..	15·00	
32	**13**	$2 sage-green (c. £6) ..	37·00	
		a. Imperf. (pair) (c. £5) ..	18·00	
21*b*/32		.. .. *Set of* 10	85·00	

Error on sheet of 4 *c.*

33	**9**	1 c. pink (strip of 3 with error in centre) ..	15·00	30·00
		a. Imperf. between (pair) ..		
		b. Imperf. (in strip as No. 33) ..	£550	

(*b*) *P* 12.

34	**9**	½ c. magenta	23·00	37·00
35	,,	1 c. orange	12·00	17·00

14

15

1889. *P* 14.

36	**14**	$5 bright purple ..	15·00	18·00	2·25
		a. Imperf. (pair) ..	11·00	—	6·00
37	**15**	$10 brown ..	24·00	36·00	3·50
		a. Imperf. (pair) ..	30·00	—	7·50
		b. "DOLLAPS" for "DOLLARS" ..	£200	—	£100
		ba. Ditto. Imperf. (pr.) ..	£350	—	£225

16

1888-92. *P* 14.

38	**16**	½ c. magenta ..	1·00	1·00	—
		a. Imperf. between (horiz. pair)			
		b. Rose	12	25	12
39	,,	1 c. orange ..	12	20	12
		a. Imperf. vert. (horiz. pair)			
40	,,	2 c. brown	1·10	70	12
		a. Imp. betwn. (horiz. pr.)			
		b. Lake-brown ..	25	30	12
41	,,	3 c. violet	45	45	12
42	,,	4 c. rose-pink ..	45	45	12
		a. Imperf. between (pr.)			
43	,,	5 c. slate	45	45	12
		a. Imperf. between (pr.)			
44	,,	6 c. lake (1892) ..	70	75	15
45	,,	8 c. blue-green ..	70	75	15
		a. Yellow-green ..	1·50	1·50	15
46	,,	10 c. blue	70	75	20
		a. Dull blue ..	85	70	20
38/46		.. *Set of* 9	5·00	5·25	

This set also exists imperf. (*Price* £1·50 *per pair unused;* £1·25 *cancelled.*)

17 18

19 20

1888. *T* **17** *to* **20** (**10** *to* **13** *redrawn*). *P* 14.

47 **17** 25 c. indigo .. .. 3·50 11·00 20
a. Imperf. (pair) .. 20·00 — 1·00
48 **18** 50 c. violet .. .. 7·00 14·00 20
a. Imperf. (pair) .. 20·00 — 1·00
49 **19** $1 scarlet .. 7·00 14·00 20
a. Imperf. (pair) .. 20·00 — 1·00
50 **20** $2 dull green .. 10·00 17·00 45
a. Imperf. (pair) .. 24·00 — 1·25

The new 25 c. has the inscription "BRITISH NORTH BORNEO" in taller capitals. In the 50 c. the "o" of the numerals "50" in the two upper corners is square-shaped at the top and bottom instead of being oval. The 1 dollar has 14 pearls instead of 13 at each side, and on the 2 dollars the word "BRITISH" measures 10½ to 11 mm. in length in place of 12 mm.

Two Cents. (21) **6 cents.** (22) **1 cent.** (23)

1890. *Surch. as T* **21**, *in red.*

51 **17** 2 c. on 25 c. indigo .. .. 7·50 6·00
a. Surch. inverted .. .. 55·00 55·00
52 ,, 8 c. on 25 c. indigo .. .. 11·00 10·00

1891–92. *Surch. with T* **22**.

54 **9** 6 c. on 8 c. green (1892) .. £1200 £1100
a. Large "s" in "cents." .. £1900
55 **16** 6 c. on 8 c. yellow-green .. 2·25 2·25
a. Surch. inverted .. .. 35·00
b. "cents." for "cents." .. 60·00
c. "cetns." for "cents." .. 60·00 60·00
d. Large. "s" in "cents." .. 10·00 12·00
56 **9** 6 c. on 10 c. blue .. .. 7·00 3·50
a. Surch. inverted .. .. 20·00
b. Surch. double £130
c. Surch. treble .. .. 45·00
d. Large "s" in "cents." .. 12·00 12·00
57 **16** 6 c. on 10 c. blue .. .. 8·00 6·00
a. Large "s" in "cents." .. 21·00 21·00

1892. *Surch. as T* **23** ("Cents." *with capital* "C" *as in T* **21** *on No.* 65), *in red.*

63 **16** 1 c. on 4 c. rose-pink .. 3·75 2·25
a. Surch. double .. ..
b. Surch. on back and on front — 75·00
64 ,, 1 c. on 5 c. slate .. .. 1·25 90
65 **17** 8 c. on 25 c. indigo .. .. 15·00 15·00

24. Dyak Chief.

25. Sambar Stag (*Cervus unicolor*).

26. Sago Palm.

27. Argus Pheasant.

28. Arms of the Company.

29. Malay Dhow.

30. Crocodile.

31. Mount Kinabalu.

32. Arms of the Company with Supporters.

PERFORATION. There are a number of small variations in the perforation of the Waterlow issues of 1894 to 1922 which we believe to be due to irregularity of the pins rather than different perforators.

In the following lists, stamps perf. 12, 12½, 1 or compound are described as perf. 12–13 an stamps perf. 13½, 14 or compound are describe as perf. 13½–14 and those perf. 14½, 15 or com pound are listed as perf. 14½–15. In addition th 13½–14 perforation exists compound with 14½–1 and with 12–13, whilst perf. 15½–16 comes fror a separate perforator.

(Recess. Waterlow & Sons.)

1894. *P* 14½–15.

66 **24** 1 c. black & olive-bistre .. 55 7
a. Imperf. between (pair) ..
b. Perf. 13½–14 .. .. 55 8
c. Perf. 13½–14, comp. 14½–15
d. Perf. 13½–14, comp. 12–13 .. 1·60 2·1
e. Perf. 12–13 .. ..
67 ,, 1 c. black & bistre-brown 40 7
a. Perf. 13½–14 .. 55
b. Perf. 13½–14, comp. 12–13 1·60 2·5
68 **25** 2 c. black & rose-lake .. 1·25 1·5
a. Imperf. between (pair) .. 75·00
b. Perf. 13½–14 .. .. 5·00
69 ,, 2 c. black and lake .. 1·25 1·5
a. Perf. 13½–14 .. .. 4·25 7·0
b. Perf. 13½–14 comp. 12–13 .. 1·50
c. Imperf. between (pair) ..
70 **26** 3 c. olive-grn. & mauve .. 90 1·5
a. Imperf. between (pair) .. 90·00
b. Perf. 13½–14 .. ..
71 ,, 3 c. ol.-grn. and vio. (*p.* 14) 1·50 2·5
72 **27** 5 c. black & vermilion .. 1·60 3·0
a. Imperf. between (pair) .. 90·00
b. Perf. 13½–14 .. .. 5·25 9·
c. Perf. 13½–14, comp. 12–13 — 8·
d. Perf. 13½–14, comp. 14½–15
e. Perf. 12–13 .. ..
73 **28** 6 c. black & bistre-brown 5·00 7·
a. Perf. 13½–14 .. .. 1·50 2·
b. Perf. 13½–14, comp. 12–13 — 5·
c. Perf. 13½–14, comp. 14½–15
d. Imperf. between (pair) ..
74 **29** 8 c. black & dull purple .. 90 2·
a. Imp. between. (vert. pr.) .. 90·00
b. Perf. 13½–14 .. .. 1·50 2·
ba. Imperf. betwn. (vert. pr.) 90·00
d. Perf. 13½–14, comp. 12–13
75 **30** 12 c. black and blue .. 8·50 9·
a. Perf. 13½–14 .. .. 8·50 9·
76 ,, 12 c. black and ultramarine 8·50 9·
a. Perf. 13½–14 .. .. 5·00
b. Imperf. between (pair) ..
78 **31** 18 c. black & deep green .. 3·00 4·
a. Perf. 13½–14 .. .. 3·75 5·
79 **32** 24 c. blue and rose-lake .. 4·50 5·
a. Imperf. between (pair) .. 90·00
b. Perf. 13½–14 .. .. 4·50 5·
c. Perf. 13½–14, comp. 14½–15
66/79 .. .. *Set of* 9 24·00 32·

NOTE.—The prices in the used column a for postally used stamps with circular postmar Stamps cancelled with bars can be supplied about one-third of these prices.

32*a*

32*b*

32*c*

32*d*

(Ptd. by Blades, East & Blades.)

32a to 32d, and T **14** *and* **15**, *but inscribed* "THE STATE OF NORTH BORNEO". *P* 14.

ɪ	25 c. indigo	4·25	5·50	30
	a. Imperf. (pair)..	—	—	1·00
	b. Imperf. between (pair)	£150		
	c. Ptd. double, one invtd.	†	†	—
2	50 c. deep slate-purple ..	4·25	5·50	30
	a. Imperf. (pair) ..	—	—	1·00
	b. Chalky blue			
3	$1 scarlet	3·00	4·50	40
	a. Perf. 14×11 ..	21·00		
	b. Imperf. (pair) ..	5·50	—	2·10
	c. Ptd. both sides ..	5·50	—	—
4	$2 dull green	5·00	8·50	40
	a. Imperf. (pair) ..	—	—	1·75
5	$5 bright purple ..	30·00	40·00	3·50
	a. Imperf. (pair) ..	—	—	5·00
	b. Dull purple	15·00	20·00	1·60
6	$10 brown	30·00	37·00	2·10
	a. Imperf. (pair) ..	—	—	4·50
ɪ/86..	.. *Set of* 6	70·00	£100	—
ɪ/86	Optd. "Specimen" *Set of* 6	50·00		

For Nos. 81 to 83 in other colours, see Labuan oa, 81*a* and 82*a*.

4

CENTS

3. (4 c. has $3\frac{1}{2}$ mm. between lines of surcharge.)

895 (June). *No.* 83 *surch. as T* **33**.

7	4 cents on $1 scarlet ..	1·10	1·25	40
	a. Surch. double ..	50·00		
8	10 cents on $1 scarlet..	1·50	1·50	40
9	20 cents on $1 scarlet..	1·60	1·60	40
o	30 cents on $1 scarlet..	2·00	2·00	40
ɪ	40 cents on $1 scarlet..	2·25	2·25	50
7/91	„ „ *Set of* 5	7·50	7·50	—
7/91	Optd. "Specimen" *Set of* 5	23·00		

For 4 c. on $1 with wider spacing see No. 121.

34

35

36

37. Orang-Utan.

38

39

40

41. Bruang or honey-bear.

42

43. Borneo railway train.

44

45

(Recess. Waterlow & Sons.)

1897–1902. *T* **34** *to* **45**. *New frames.* *P* $13\frac{1}{2}$–14.

92	1 c. black and bistre-brown	1·25	1·10
	aa. Perf. 16		
	a. Perf. $14\frac{1}{2}$–15	1·35	1·25
	b. Perf. $13\frac{1}{2}$–14, comp. 12–13 ..	5·00	
	e. Imperf. between (pair) ..		
93	1 c. black and ochre ..	3·75	3·00
	a. Perf. $14\frac{1}{2}$–15	1·50	1·50
	b. Perf. $13\frac{1}{2}$–14, comp. 12–13 ..		
94	2 c. black and lake ..	2·10	1·00
	a. Perf. $14\frac{1}{2}$–15	2·10	1·00
	b. Perf. $13\frac{1}{2}$–14, comp. 12–13 ..	—	2·10
95	2 c. black and green ..	2·10	1·10
	a. Perf. $14\frac{1}{2}$–15		2·00
	b. Perf. $13\frac{1}{2}$–14, comp. 12–13..	5·50	2·50
	c. Imperf. between (pair) ..		
96	3 c. green and rosy mauve	2·10	2·10
	a. Perf. $14\frac{1}{2}$–15	3·50	3·50
	b. Perf. $13\frac{1}{2}$–14, comp. 12–13 ..	4·50	4·50
97	3 c. green & dull mauve (*p.* $14\frac{1}{2}$–15)	1·10	1·10
98	4 c. black and green (1900)	1·25	
	a. Perf. $13\frac{1}{2}$–14, comp 12–13		
99	4 c. black & carmine (1900)	1·25	1·25
	a. Perf. 16	—	3·50
	a. Perf. $14\frac{1}{2}$–15	3·50	1·25
	c. Perf. $13\frac{1}{2}$–14, comp. 12–13 ..	1·50	3·00
100	5 c. blk. & orange-vermilion	1·60	1·25
	a Perf. $14\frac{1}{2}$–15	2·50	1·00
	b. Perf. $13\frac{1}{2}$–14, comp. 12–13	2·50	1·60
101	6 c. black and bistre-brown	3·00	1·25
	a. Perf. $14\frac{1}{2}$–15	1·60	1·25
102	8 c. black & brown-purple	2·50	
	a. Perf. 16	7·50	2·10
	b. Perf. $14\frac{1}{2}$–15	1·50	1·25
	c. Imperf. between (vert. pair)		
103	8 c. black and brown ..	1·25	
	a. Perf. $14\frac{1}{2}$–15	3·00	
104	10 c. brn. & slate-lilac (1902)	5·00	4·00
	a. Imperf. between (vert. pair) ..		
105	10 c. brn. & slate-bl. (1902)	7·50	6·00
106	12 c. black and dull blue ..	7·50	6·00
	a. Imperf. between (pair) ..		
	b. Perf. $14\frac{1}{2}$–15	7·50	6·00
	c. Perf. $13\frac{1}{2}$–14, comp. 12–13 ..	13·00	8·50
107	16 c. green & chestnut (1902)	4·50	12·00
	a. Perf. $14\frac{1}{2}$–15	7·50	17·00
108	18 c. black & green (*perf.* 16)	2·10	2·10
	a. Imperf. betwn. (pair) (*canc.*)	—	18·00
109	24 c. blue and lake	2·50	5·50
	a. Perf. $13\frac{1}{2}$–14, comp. 12–13	6·00	5·50
92/109 (*excl.* 98) ..	*Set of* 13	30·00	28·00
92/109 (*excl.* 93, 97, 105) Optd. "Specimen" ..	*Set of* 14	15·00	

In the above the 18 c. has "POSTAL REVENUE" instead of "POSTAGE AND REVENUE" and the 24 c. has those words omitted. These stamps were replaced by others with corrected inscriptions; see Nos. 110 and 111.

NOTE.—Stamps cancelled to order can be supplied at about one-third the prices quoted above for postally used specimens, except in the case of some of the scarcer perforation varieties.

46

47

1897. *Corrected inscriptions.* *P* $13\frac{1}{2}$–14.

110	**46**	18 c. black and green ..	5·00	4·00
		a. Perf. $14\frac{1}{2}$–15	6·00	4·00
		b. Perf. $13\frac{1}{2}$–14, comp. 12–13		
111	**47**	24 c. blue and lake ..	7·00	6·00
		a. Perf. 16	7·50	7·50
		b. Perf. $14\frac{1}{2}$–15	6·00	
		c. Perf. $13\frac{1}{2}$–14, comp. 12–13		
110/111		Optd. "Specimen" *Set of* 2	15·00	

NOTE.—Price note after No. 109 applies here.

BRITISH

4

CENTS **PROTECTORATE.**

48. ($4\frac{1}{2}$ mm. between lines of surcharge.) (**49**)

1899. *Surch. with T* **48.** (*a*) *P* 14½–15.

112 4 c. on 5 c. (No. 100a) .. ..
  a. Perf. 13½–14 .. .. 2·50 2·50
  b. Perf. 13½–14, comp. 12–13 .. 7·50 5·00
113 4 c. on 6 c. (No. 101a) .. 5·00 5·00
  a. Perf. 13½–14 .. .. 2·50 3·50
114 4 c. on 8 c. (No. 102b) .. 3·50 2·50
115 4 c. on 12 c. (No. 106b) .. 3·50 3·50
  a. Imperf. between (pair) .. 75·00
  b. Perf. 13½–14 .. ..
116 4 c. on 18 c. (No. 110a) .. 3·50 3·50
  a. Perf. 13½–14 .. ..
117 4 c. on 24 c. (No. 111b) .. 3·00 3·00
  a. Perf. 16 .. .. .. 8·00 9·00
  b. Perf. 13½–14 .. .. 4·50
  c. Perf. 13½–14, comp. 12–13 .. 4·50
  d. Perf. 12–13 .. .. 3·00 3·00

(*b*) *P* 14.

118 4 c. on 25 c. indigo (No. 81) 2·50 3·50
  a. Imperf. between (pair) .. £190
119 4 c. on 50 c. deep slate-purple (No. 82) .. .. .. 3·50 3·50
  a. Chalky blue .. 7·50
121 4 c. on $1 scarlet (No. 83) .. 2·50 2·50
122 4 c. on $2 dull green. (No. 84) 3·50 5·00
123 4 c. on $5 brt. pur. (No. 85) 17·00 20·00
  a. Dull purple .. 8·50 11·00
124 4 c. on $10 brown (No. 86) .. 8·50 11·00
112/124 .. .. *Set of* 12 45·00 45·00
112/124 Optd. "Specimen" *Set of* 12 60·00

No. 121 differs only from No. 87 in having the "4" and "cents" wider apart.

The 1 c., 2 c. and 3 c. values of this set were also surcharged "4 CENTS" but were not issued. They exist overprinted "Specimen" (*price* £50 *the set of three*).

1900 (?). *Surch. as T* **48** *but* 8½ *mm. between lines of surcharge.* *P* 14.

125 4 c. on $5 (No. 85) .. .. 5·00 4·50
126 4 c. on $10 (No. 86) .. .. 4·50 4·50

1901–5. *Optd. as T* **49.** (*a*) *P* 13½–14.

127 1 c. (No. 92) (R.) 80 70
  a. Perf. 14½–15 .. .. 70 75
128 2 c. (No. 95) (R.) .. .. 1·00 80
  a. Perf. 16 .. .. .. 70 80
  b. Perf. 14½–15 .. .. 90 75
129 3 c. (No. 96) 50 80
  a. Perf. 14½–15 .. .. 2·00 70
  b. Perf. 13½–14, Comp. 14½–15 5·00
130 4 c. (No. 99) (G.) .. .. 1·60 70
  a. Perf. 14½–15 .. .. 1·10 70
131 5 c. (No. 100) (G.) .. .. — 80
  a. Perf. 14½–15 .. .. 1·25 75
132 6 c. (No. 101) (R.) .. 4·50 4·50
  a. No stop after "Protectorate" 17·00 17·00
  b. Perf. 16 .. .. 1·00 1·00
133 8 c. (No. 102) (B.) .. 1·25 1·25
  a. No stop after "Protectorate" 1·50 3·25
  b. Perf. 13½–14, comp. 12–13 .. 5·00 1·60
134 10 c. (No. 104) (R.) .. 3·50 1·60
  a. Perf. 14½–15 .. .. 4·50 2·10
  c. Perf. 13½–14. No stop after "Protectorate" .. .. 26·00
  d. Overprint double .. 60·00
135 12 c. (No. 106) (R.) .. 6·00 3·75
136 16 c. (No. 107) .. .. 3·00 2·10
  a. Perf. 14½–15 .. .. 3·00 2·50
  b. Perf. 13½–14, comp. 12–13 .. 5·00 2·50
137 18 c. (No. 110) (R.) .. 2·50 2·75
  a. No stop after "Protectorate"
  b. Perf. 13½–14, Comp. 12–13
138 24 c. (No. 111) .. .. 4·50 4·50
  a. Perf. 14½–15 .. .. 6·00 6·00
  b. Imperf. between (pair) ..

(*b*) *P* 14.

139 25 c. (No. 81) (R.) (c. 8p.) .. 1·50 3·50
  a. No stop after "Protectorate" 21·00
  b. Overprints tête-bêche (pair) £225
  c. Overprint inverted.. .. £110
140 50 c. (No. 82) (R.) (c. 10p) .. 1·75 3·50
  a. No stop after "Protectorate" 11·00 12·00
  b. Chalky blue .. ..
141 $1 (No. 83) (R.) .. .. 6·00 8·00
142 $1 (No. 83) (1903) (c. 75p) 5·00 6·50
  a. Imperf. between (vert. pr.) £110
  b. Opt. double .. ..
143 $2 (No. 84) (R.) ('05) (c. £1) 10·00 12·00
  a. Opt. double £225
144 $5 (No. 85*b*) (R.) (c. £1·10) 20·00 23·00
145 $10 (No. 86) (R.) (c. £1·75) 28·00 28·00
  a. Opt. inverted £300
127/145 .. .. *Set of* 18 85·00 90·00
127/140 Optd. "Specimen" *Set of* 14 75·00

There was more than one setting of the overprint for some of the values. Full sheets of the 6 c. and 8 c. are known, without stop throughout.

NOTE.—Nos. 127/38 cancelled to order can be supplied at about one-third of the prices quoted for postally used specimens. Prices for Nos. 139/45, cancelled, are given in brackets.

4

cents

(**50**)

1904–5. *Surch. locally with T* **50.** (*a*) *P* 14½–15.

146 4 c. on 5 c. (No. 100a) .. 3·50 3·75
147 4 c. on 6 c. (No. 101a) .. 1·50 2·00
  a. Surch. inverted .. .. 60·00
148 4 c. on 8 c. (No. 102b) .. 4·25 5·00
  a. Surch. inverted .. .. 60·00
149 4 c. on 12 c. (No. 106b) .. 4·50 5·00
  a. Perf. 13½–14 .. .. 5·00 4·25
  b. Perf. 13½–14, comp. 12-13 ..
150 4 c. on 18 c. (No. 110a) .. 5·50 5·50
  a. Perf. 13½–14.. .. ..
151 4 c. on 24 c. (No. 111b) .. 5·50 5·50
  a. Perf. 16 .. .. 3·75 5·00
  b. Perf. 13½–14 .. .. 5·00 5·50
  c. Perf. 12–13 .. ..

(*b*) *P* 14.

152 4 c. on 25 c. (No. 81) .. 2·10 3·50
153 4 c. on 50 c. (No. 82) .. 2·10 4·00
154 4 c. on $1 (No. 83) .. .. 3·75 5·00
155 4 c. on $2 (No. 84) .. .. 5·00 5·50
156 4 c. on $5 (No. 85) .. .. 5·50 6·50
157 4 c. on $10 (No. 86).. .. 5·50 6·50
  a. Surch. inverted £300
146/157 .. .. *Set of* 12 45·00 50·00

51. Tapir.

52. Traveller's-tree.

53. Railway at Jesselton.

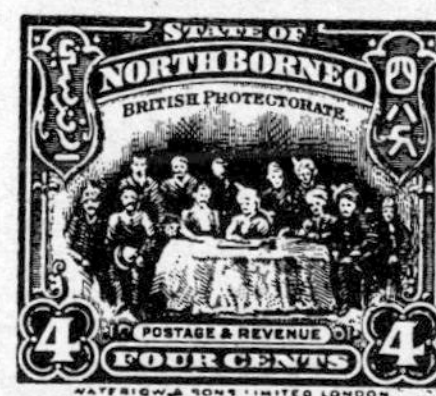

54. The Sultan of Sulu, his staff and W. C. Cowie, first Chairman of the Company.

55. Asiatic Elephant.

56. Rhinoceros.

57. Ploughing with Buffalo.

58. Wild Boar.

59. Great Black Cockatoo.

60. Hornbill.

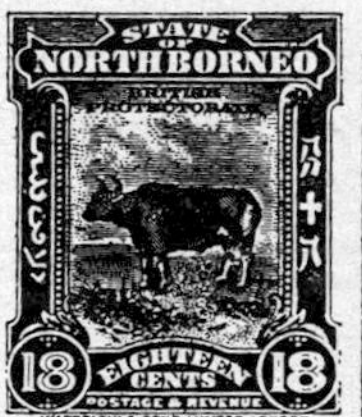

61. Wild Bull.

62. Cassowary.

(Recess. Waterlow & Sons, Ltd.)

1909 (JULY)–**1922.** *Centres in black.* *P* 13½–14

158 **51** 1 c. chocolate-brown 1·00 30 1
  a. Perf. 14½–15 .. 2·00 1·25 —
159 ,, 1 c. brown .. .. 1·25 40 —
  a. Perf. 14½–15 .. 2·10 75 1
160 **52** 2 c. green 70 25 1
  a. Imperf. between (pair)
  b. Perf. 14½–15 .. 90 30 —
161 **53** 3 c. lake 70 40 1
162 ,, 3 c. rose-lake .. 90 25 1
  a. Perf. 14½–15 .. — — 3
163 ,, 3 c. green (1922) .. 2·25 40 —
164 **54** 4 c. scarlet 90 30 1
  b. Perf. 14½–15 .. 2·25 75 2
165 **55** 5 c. yellow-brown .. 2·10 60 1
  a. Perf. 14½–15 ..
166 ,, 5 c. dark brown .. 2·00 60 —
167 **56** 6 c. olive-green .. 2·00 60 1
  a. Perf. 14½–15 .. 6·00 1·50 4
168 ,, 6 c. apple-green .. 3·75 75 —
169 **57** 8 c. lake .. .. 1·25 60 1
  a. Perf. 14½–15 ..
170 **58** 10 c. greyish blue .. 5·00 1·00 1
  a. Perf. 14½–15 .. 5·00 3·00 —
171 ,, 10 c. blue .. .. 5·00 1·00 —
172 ,, 10 c. turquoise-blue .. 4·50 1·00 —
  a. Perf. 14½–15 .. 5·50 1·25 —

173 **59** 12 c. deep blue .. 4·00 80 25
a. Perf. 14½–15 ..
173*b* ,, 12 c. deep bright blue
174 **60** 16 c. brown-lake .. 4·50 1·60 55
175 **61** 18 c. blue-green .. 5·50 3·75 70
176 **62** 24 c. mauve .. 6·50 1·50 40
158/176 .. *Set of* 13 32·00 11·00 —
158/176 Optd. "Specimen" *Set of* 13 65·00

For this issue perf. 12½ see Nos. 277, etc.

20

CENTS

(63)

1909 (Aug.). *T* **61** *surch. with T* **63**. *P* 13½–14.
177 20 c. on 18 c. blue-green (R.) (Optd. S. £9) .. 1·50 70 25
a. Perf. 14½–15 45·00 17·00 —

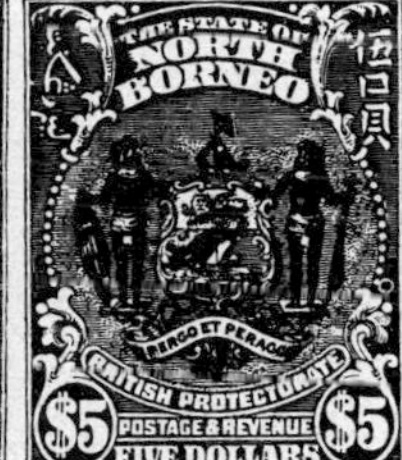

64 65

(Recess Waterlow.)

1911. *P* 13½–14.
178 **64** 25 c. black & yellow-green 1·60 1·10
a. Perf. 14½–15 .. .. 3·50
b. Imperf. (pair) .. .. 9·00
178*c* ,, 25 c. black and blue-green
179 ,, 50 c. black and steel-blue 2·50 1·60
a. Perf. 14½–15 .. 5·50 4·00
b. Imperf. (pair) .. 15·00
c. Imperf. between (pair) ..
180 ,, $1 black & chestnut .. 4·50 2·10
a. Perf. 14½–15 .. .. 8·50 4·00
b. Imperf. (pair) .. .. 12·00
181 ,, $2 black & lilac .. 8·50 3·50
182 **65** $5 black & lake .. 20·00 13·00
b. Imperf. (pair) .. .. 20·00
183 ,, $10 black & brick-red .. 37·00 27·00
a. Imperf. (pair) .. .. 20·00
178/183 .. .. *Set of* 6 65·00 45·00
178/183 Optd. "Specimen" *Set of* 6 40·00

BRITISH PROTECTORATE (66)   2 cents (67)   (68)

1912. *Nos.* 85 *and* 86 *optd. with T* **66**.
184 $5 brt. pur. (R.) (c. £2·50) .. £190
185 $10 brown (R.) (c. £2·50) .. £250

1916. *Stamps of* 1909–22 *surch. as T* **67**. *P* 13½–14.
186 2 c. on 3 c. black & rose-lake 1·60 1·50
a. "s" inverted .. 15·00 14·00
187 4 c. on 6 c. blk. & olive-grn. (R.) 1·60 1·60
a. "s" inverted .. .. 26·00 26·00
b. "s" inserted by hand .. — 70·00
c. Perf. 14½–15 .. ..
188 10 c. on 12 c. black and deep blue (R.) .. .. 2·50 3·00
a. "s" inverted .. .. 26·00 26·00
186/188 Optd. "Specimen" *Set of* 3 25·00

1916 (May). *Stamps of* 1909–11 *optd. with T* **68**. *P* 13½–14. *Centres in black,* (a) *Cross in vermilion.*
189 **51** 1 c. brown .. .. 3·50 7·50
190 **52** 2 c. green .. .. 12·00 20·00
a. Perf. 14½–15 .. .. 15·00 23·00
191 **53** 3 c. rose-lake .. .. 8·50 12·00
192 **54** 4 c. scarlet .. .. 3·50 7·00
a. Perf. 14½–15 .. .. — 37·00
193 **55** 5 c. yellow-brown .. 7·50 14·00
194 **56** 6 c. apple-green .. 12·00 20·00
195 **57** 8 c. lake .. .. .. 7·00 14·00
196 **58** 10 c. blue .. .. .. 14·00 25·00
197 **59** 12 c. deep blue .. .. 15·00 25·00
198 **60** 16 c. brown-lake .. .. 15·00 25·00
199 **61** 20 c. on 18 c. blue-green 14·00 24·00
200 **62** 24 c. dull mauve .. .. 21·00 32·00
201 **64** 25 c. green (*p.* 14½–15) .. 70·00 £140
189/201 .. .. *Set of* 13 £180 £350
(b) *Cross in carmine.*
202 **51** 1 c. brown .. .. 6·00 11·00
203 **52** 2 c. green .. .. 10·00 7·50
204 **53** 3 c. rose-lake .. .. 7·00 12·00
205 **55** 5 c. yellow-brown .. 7·00 14·00
206 **56** 6 c. apple-green .. 6·00 12·00
207 **57** 8 c. lake .. .. .. 6·00 12·00
208 **58** 10 c. blue .. .. .. 7·00 17·00
209 **59** 12 c. deep blue .. .. 14·00 27·00
210 **60** 16 c. brown-lake .. .. 15·00 30·00
211 **61** 20 c. on 18 c. blue-green .. 20·00 37·00
212 **62** 24 c. dull mauve .. .. 24·00 48·00
213 **64** 25 c. green (*p.* 14½–15) .. £120 £225
202/213 .. .. *Set of* 12 £220 £400

RED CROSS

TWO CENTS (69)   FOUR CENTS (70)

1918. *Stamps of* 1909–11 *surch. as T* **69**. *P* 13½–14.
A. *Lines of surcharge* 9 *mm. apart.*
214 **51** 1 c. brown .. .. 70 2·50
a. Imperf. between (pair) .. £110
215 **52** 2 c. green .. .. 50 1·50
a. Imperf. between (pair) .. £120
216 **53** 3 c. rose-red .. .. 1·25 3·00
a. Imperf. between (pair) .. £120
b. Perf. 14½–15 .. .. 7·00 13·00
217 ,, 3 c. dull rose-carmine .. 45·00
a. Perf. 14½–15 .. .. 50·00
218 **54** 4 c. scarlet .. .. 50 1·50
a. Surch. inverted.. .. 60·00
219 **55** 5 c. deep brown .. 1·60 3·50
220 ,, 5 c. pale brown .. 1·50 5·00
221 **56** 6 c. olive-green .. 1·60 6·50
a. Perf. 14½–15 .. .. 50·00
221*b* ,, 6 c. apple-green ..
c. Perf. 14½–15 .. ..
222 **57** 8 c. lake .. .. 1·50 2·75
a. Inverted figure "3" for "C" in "CENTS" .. ..
223 **58** 10 c. blue .. .. 1·60 5·00
224 **59** 12 c. deep bright blue .. 1·60 5·50
a. Surch. inverted.. .. 70·00
225 **60** 16 c. brown-lake .. .. 2·10 6·50
226 **62** 24 c. mauve .. .. 2·75 6·50
B. *Lines of surch.* 13–14 *mm. apart.*
227 **52** 2 c. green .. .. 14·00 21·00
228 **56** 6 c. olive-green .. 70·00 £120
229 **64** 25 c. green .. .. 5·50 12·00
230 ,, 50 c. steel-blue .. .. 5·50 12·00
231 ,, $1 chestnut .. .. 14·00 20·00
232 ,, $2 lilac .. .. 20·00 37·00
233 **65** $5 lake £140 £225
234 ,, $10 brick-red £140 £225
214/234 .. .. *Set of* 17 £300 £525

The above stamps were dispatched from London in three consignments, of which two were lost through enemy action at sea.

These stamps were sold at a premium of 2 c. per stamp, which went to the Red Cross Society.

1918. *Stamps of* 1909–11 *surch. with T* **70**, *in red.* *P* 13½–14.
235 **51** 1 c. chocolate .. 50 1·25
a. Imperf. between (horiz. pr.)
236 **52** 2 c. green .. .. 70 1·50
237 **53** 3 c. rose-lake .. .. 50 1·10
238 **54** 4 c. scarlet .. .. 50 1·60
239 **55** 5 c. brown .. .. 85 2·10
240 **56** 6 c. apple-green .. 90 3·00
a. Imperf. between (pair) .. £180
241 **57** 8 c. lake .. .. 1·10 2·75
242 **58** 10 c. turquoise-blue .. 1·60 5·00
242*a* ,, 10 c. greenish blue .. 2·10 5·00
243 **59** 12 c. deep blue .. .. 2·00 3·50
244 **60** 16 c. brown-lake .. .. 2·00 5·00
245 **62** 24 c. mauve .. .. 2·75 6·50
246 **64** 25 c. yellow-green.. .. 3·00 7·50
247 ,, 25 c. blue-green .. .. 7·00 18·00
248 ,, 50 c. steel-blue .. .. 5·50 10·00
a. Perf. 14½–15 .. .. 21·00
249 ,, $1 chestnut .. .. 7·00 14·00
a. Perf. 14½–15 .. ..
250 ,, $2 lilac .. .. 13·00 27·00
251 **65** $5 lake .. .. 90·00 £150
252 ,, $10 brick-red .. .. 90·00 £150
235/252 .. *Set of* 17 £200 £350

Nos. 235/52 were sold at face, plus 4 c. on each stamp for Red Cross Funds.

MALAYA-BORNEO EXHIBITION 1922. (71)

1922. *Stamps of* 1909–22 *optd. as T* **71**. *P* 13½–14.
253 **51** 1 c. brown (R.) .. .. 1·10 3·25
a. Error "BORHEO" .. 70·00
b. Error "BORNEQ" .. 60·00 70·00
c. Stop after "EXHBN." .. 5·00
d. Perf. 14½–15 .. .. 1·60 4·00
da. Error. "BORHEO" .. 70·00
db. Error. "BORNEQ" ..
dc. Raised stop after "1922." 26·00
dd. Errors "EXHIBITICN." with stop.. .. .. £160
de. Error. "MILAYA" ..
df. Stop after "EXHBN." .. 7·00
253*e* ,, 1 c. brown (B.) (*p.* 14½–15) £150
f. Pair, with and without opt. £250
g. Raised stop after "1922." £160
h. Error "BORHEO" .. £275
i. Error "BORNEQ" .. £275
j. Error "EXHIBITIOH" .. £275
k. Errors "EXHIBITICN." with stop.. .. .. £350
l. Error. "MILAYA" ..
254 ,, 1 c. orange-brown (R.) .. 1·60 5·00
255 **52** 2 c. green (R.) .. .. 50 2·40
a. Stop after "EXHBN." .. 2·40
256 **53** 3 c. rose-lake (B.) .. 1·00 2·40
a. Stop after "EXHBN." .. 3·50
257 **54** 4 c. scarlet (B.) .. 75 2·10
a. Stop after "EXHBN." .. 2·40
b. Perf. 14½–15 .. ..
258 **55** 5 c. orange-brown (B.) .. 1·25 3·50
a. Imperf. between (pair) £130 £140
b. Stop after "EXHBN." .. 2·75
c. Opt. double £250
d. Opt. double (with stop) .. £300
259 ,, 5 c. chestnut (B.) .. 2·10 5·50
260 **56** 6 c. apple-green (R.) .. 1·10 3·50
a. Stop after "EXHBN." .. 2·75
b. Opt. double £240
261 **57** 8 c. dull rose (B.) .. 1·50 4·00
262 ,, 8 c. deep rose-lake (B.) .. 1·50 4·00
a. Stop after "EXHBN." .. 3·50
263 **58** 10 c. turquoise-blue (R.) .. 1·50 5·00
a. Perf. 14½–15 .. .. 5·00
b. Stop after "EXHBN." .. 4·00
264 ,, 10 c. greenish blue (R.) .. 1·50 4·00
a. Stop after "EXHBN." .. 5·00
265 **59** 12 c. deep blue (R.) .. 1·60 5·00
a. Stop after "EXHBN." .. 5·00
266 ,, 12 c. deep bright blue (R.) 7·00
a. Stop after "EXHBN." .. 17·00
267 **60** 16 c. brown-lake (B.) .. 1·10 5·00
a. Stop after "EXHBN." .. 5·00
b. Opt. in red £350
268 **61** 20 c. on 18 c. blue-green (B.) 2·10 6·50
a. Stop after "EXHBN." .. 11·00
269 ,, 20 c. on 18 c. blue-grn. (R.) 15·00 32·00
a. Stop after "EXHBN." .. 24·00 48·00
270 **62** 24 c. mauve (R.) .. .. 1·60 5·00
a. Stop after "EXHBN." .. 5·50
271 ,, 24 c. lilac (R.) .. .. 2·75 5·00
a. Stop after "EXHBN." .. 5·50
272 ,, 24 c. reddish lilac (R.) .. 4·50 10·00
a. Stop after "EXHBN." .. 10·00
273 **64** 25 c. blue-green (R.) .. 2·25 5·00
a. Stop after "EXHBN." .. 5·50

274	64	25 c. yellow-green (R.) ..	2·75	8·00
		a. Stop after "EXHBN." ..	8·00	
		b. Opt. double	£150	
		c. Perf. 14½–15	5·00	16·00
		ca. Stop after "EXHBN." ..	45·00	
		cb. Opt. double	£150	
275	,,	50 c. steel-blue (R.) ..	2·10	6·50
		a. Stop after "EXHBN."	11·00	
		b. Perf. 14½–15	10·00	
		ba. Stop after "EXHBN."	20·00	
253/275		.. .. *Set of* 14	18·00	55·00
253/75		Optd. "Specimen" *Set of* 14	£125	

THREE

CENTS

(72)

1923. *T* 54 *surch. with T* 72.

276		3 c. on 4 c. black and scarlet	75	1·00
		a. Surch. double		
276		Optd. "Specimen"	18·00	

1925–28. *As* 1909–22, *but perf.* 12½. *Centres in black. Colour changed* (2 *c.*).

277	51	1 c. chocolate-brown	35	30
		a. Imperf. betwn. (horiz. pr.)	75·00	
278	52	2 c. claret	35	30
279	53	3 c. green ('25)	1·25	1·00
280	54	4 c. scarlet	65	15
		a. Imperf. between (vert. pr.)	65·00	
		b. Imperf. betwn. (horiz. pr.)	80·00	
281	55	5 c. yellow-brown ..	1·00	60
282	56	6 c. olive-green	1·00	45
283	57	8 c. carmine	1·00	30
		a. Imperf. between (vert. pr.)	65·00	
284	58	10 c. turquoise-blue ..	1·00	30
		a. Imperf. betwn. (horiz. pr.)	80·00	
285	59	12 c. deep blue	1·00	65
286	60	16 c. red-brown	1·25	1·50
287	61	20 c. on 18 c. blue-grn. (R.)	1·50	1·25
288	62	24 c. violet	3·75	3·00
289	64	25 c. green	2·25	1·25
290	,,	50 c. steel-blue	2·75	2·75
291	,,	$1 chestnut	6·00	5·50
292	,,	$2 mauve	9·00	11·00
293	65	$5 lake ('28)	27·00	27·00
294	,,	$10 orange-red ('28) ..	45·00	45·00
277/294		.. .. *Set of* 18	95·00	95·00

73. Head of a Murut. 74. Orang-Utan.

75. Dyak Warrior. (*Vert.*)

76. Mount Kinabalu.

77. Clouded Leopard. (*Horiz.*)

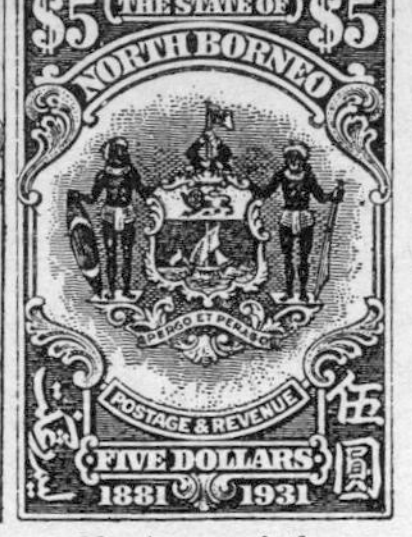

78. Arms of the Company. 80. Arms of the Company.

79. Arms of the Company. (*Horiz.*)

(Recess. Waterlow & Sons.)

1931 (1 JAN.). *Fiftieth Anniv. of British North Borneo Company. P* 12½.

295	73	3 c. black and blue-green	1·50	1·00
296	74	6 c. black and orange ..	5·50	1·75
297	75	10 c. black and scarlet ..	3·75	3·25
298	76	12 c. black and ultram. ..	2·50	3·25
299	77	25 c. black and violet ..	11·00	13·00
300	78	$1 black & yellow-green	13·00	14·00
301	79	$2 black and chestnut ..	16·00	18·00
302	80	$5 black and purple ..	35·00	45·00
295/302		.. .. *Set of* 8	80·00	90·00
295/302		Optd. "Specimen" *Set of* 8	80·00	

81. Buffalo Transport.

82. Great Black Cockatoo. 83. Native.

84. Proboscis-Monkey. 85. Mounted Bajaus.

86. Eastern Archipelago.

87. Orang-Utan. 89. Dyak.

88. Murut with Blow-pipe.

90. River Scene.

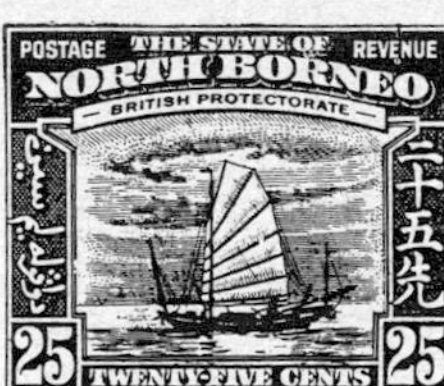

91. Native Boat.

92. Mt. Kinabalu.

93. Arms of the Company. 94.

95. Arms of the Company.

(Recess. Waterlow.)

939 (1 Jan.). *P* 12½.

03	**81**	1 c. green and red-brown	15	20
04	**82**	2 c. purple & greenish blue	15	15
05	**83**	3 c. slate-blue and green	15	20
06	**84**	4 c. bronze-green & violet	35	35
07	**85**	6 c. deep blue and claret	15	25
08	**86**	8 c. scarlet	15	25
09	**87**	10 c. violet & bronze-green	2·00	1·25
10	**88**	12 c. green and royal blue	30	1·00
		a. Green and blue		
11	**89**	15 c. blue-green and brown	1·00	1·00
12	**90**	20 c. violet and slate-blue	1·25	1·25
13	**91**	25 c. green and chocolate	1·25	1·50
14	**92**	50 c. chocolate and violet	1·50	1·60
15	**93**	$1 brown and carmine..	2·40	4·00
16	**94**	$2 violet and olive-green	11·00	14·00
17	**95**	$5 indigo and pale blue	27·00	27·00
03/317		.. .. *Set of* 15	45·00	50·00
03/17		Perf. "Specimen" *Set of* 15	45·00	

WAR TAX (96)

WAR TAX (97)

941 (24 Feb.). *Nos.* 303/4 *optd. with T* **96/7.**

18	**81**	1 c. green and red-brown	8	12
19	**82**	2 c. purple & greenish blue	30	35

I. BRITISH MILITARY ADMINISTRATION.

BMA (98)

(99)

945 (17 Dec.). *Nos.* 303/17 *optd. with T* **98.**

20	**81**	1 c. green and red-brown	30	25
21	**82**	2 c. purple & greenish blue	30	25
22	**83**	3 c. slate-blue and green	20	20
23	**84**	4 c. bronze-green & violet	2·40	2·40
24	**85**	6 c. deep blue and claret	25	30
25	**86**	8 c. scarlet	45	75
26	**87**	10 c. violet & bronze-green	75	90
27	**88**	12 c. green and blue ..	45	60
28	**89**	15 c. blue-green and brown	45	60
29	**90**	20 c. violet and slate-blue	60	70
30	**91**	25 c. green and chocolate..	1·00	90
31	**92**	50 c. chocolate and violet	1·25	1·60
32	**93**	$1 brown and carmine..	6·00	6·00
33	**94**	$2 violet and olive-green	6·00	7·00
		a. Opt. double	£450	
34	**95**	$5 indigo and pale blue	6·00	8·00
20/334		.. .. *Set of* 15	24·00	28·00

These stamps and the similarly overprinted tamps of Sarawak were obtainable at all post ffices throughout British Borneo (Brunei, abuan, North Borneo and Sarawak), for use n local and overseas mail.

III. CROWN COLONY.

947. *Nos.* 303 *to* 317 *optd. with T* **99** *and bars obliterating words* "THE STATE OF" *and* "BRITISH PROTECTORATE".

35	**81**	1 c. green and red-brown	15	15
36	**82**	2 c. purple & greenish blue	15	20
37	**83**	3 c. slate-blue & green (R.)	15	20
38	**84**	4 c. bronze-green & violet	8	8
39	**85**	6 c. deep blue & claret (R.)	15	20
40	**86**	8 c. scarlet	8	12
41	**87**	10 c. violet and bronze-green	15	12
42	**88**	12 c. green and royal blue	15	20
43	**89**	15 c. blue-green and brown	15	15
44	**90**	20 c. violet and slate-blue	15	25
45	**91**	25 c. green and chocolate..	15	20
46	**92**	50 c. chocolate and violet	25	35
347	**93**	$1 brown and carmine..	35	45
348	**94**	$2 violet and olive-green	1·10	2·00
349	**95**	$5 indigo & pale bl. (R.)	3·50	5·00
335/349		.. .. *Set of* 15	6·00	8·50
335/349		Perf. "Specimen" *Set of* 15	65·00	

Dates of issue:—1.9.47, 4 c. and 8 c.; 15.12.47, 1 c. and 10 c.; 22.12.47, other values.

1948 (1 Nov.). *Royal Silver Wedding. As Nos.* 30/1 *of Aden.*

350	8 c. scarlet	12	15
351	$10 mauve	6·00	9·00

1949 (10 Oct.). *75th Anniv. of Universal Postal Union. As Nos.* 114/7 *of Antigua.*

352	8 c. carmine..	20	15
353	10 c. brown	20	25
354	30 c. orange-brown	60	70
355	55 c. blue	80	1·00

100. Mount Kinabalu.

101. Native Musical Instrument.

102. Coconut Grove.

103. Hemp Drying.

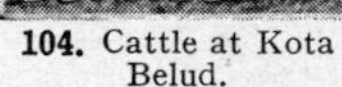

104. Cattle at Kota Belud.

109. Suluk Craft, Lahad Datu.

105. Map.

106. Logging.

107. Native Prahu, Sandakan.

108. Bajau Chief.

110. Clock Tower, Jesselton.

111. Bajau Horsemen.

112. Murut with Blowpipe.

113. Net-Fishing.

114. Arms of North Borneo.

(Photo. Harrison.)

1950 (1 July)–**52.** *Wmk. Mult. Script CA. Chalk-surfaced paper. P* 13½×14½ (*horiz.*), 14½×13½ (*vert.*).

356	**100**	1 c. red-brown	8	10
357	**101**	2 c. blue	8	8
358	**102**	3 c. green	8	10
359	**103**	4 c. bright purple ..	8	12
360	**104**	5 c. violet	20	12
361	**105**	8 c. scarlet	15	15
362	**106**	10 c. maroon	12	15
363	**107**	15 c. ultramarine ..	20	15
364	**108**	20 c. brown	30	25
365	**109**	30 c. olive-brown ..	35	20
366	**110**	50 c. rose-car. (JESSLETON)	40	80
366*a*	,,	50 c. rose-car. (JESSELTON) (1.5.52)	40	80
367	**111**	$1 red-orange ..	70	90
368	**112**	$2 grey-green ..	1·40	2·00
369	**113**	$5 emerald-green ..	3·25	5·50
370	**114**	$10 dull blue	6·50	8·00
356/370		.. .. *Set of* 15	13·00	18·00

1953 (3 June). *Coronation. As No.* 47 *of Aden.*

371	10 c. black and bright scarlet	20	30

115. Logging.

(Photo. Harrison.)

1954–57. *Types of* 1950 (*but with portrait of Queen Elizabeth II in place of King George VI as in T* **115**). *Chalk-surfaced paper. Wmk. Mult. Script CA. P* 14½×13½ (*vert.*) *or* 13½×14½ (*horiz.*).

372	**100**	1 c. red-brown	5	5
373	**101**	2 c. blue	5	5
374	**102**	3 c. green (*shades*)	5	5
375	**103**	4 c. bright purple ..	8	8
376	**104**	5 c. reddish violet ..	8	8
377	**105**	8 c. scarlet	8	8
378	**115**	10 c. maroon	10	10
379	**107**	15 c. bright blue	20	15
380	**108**	20 c. brown	20	15
381	**109**	30 c. olive-brown ..	20	15
382	**110**	50 c. rose-carmine (Jesselton) (*shades*) ..	25	25
383	**111**	$1 red-orange	55	50
384	**112**	$2 deep green (*shades*)	1·50	1·50
385	**113**	$5 emerald-green ..	4·50	4·50
386	**114**	$10 deep blue	7·50	7·50
372/86		.. .. *Set of* 15	13·00	12·00

Plate 2 of the 30 c., released 10 Aug. 1960, had a finer, 250 screen, instead of the previous 200 (*price* £1·40 *un.*).

Dates of issue:—1.3.54, 10 c.; 1.7.54, 5 c.; 3.8.54, 20 c., 30 c.; 1.10.54, 1 c., 8 c.; 1.4.55, $1; 16.5.55, 4 c., 15 c.; 1.10.55, $2; 10.2.56, 50 c.; 1.6.56, 2 c.; 1.2.57, 3 c., $5, $10.

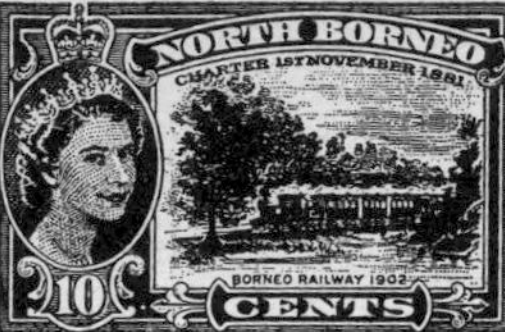

116. Borneo Railway, 1902.

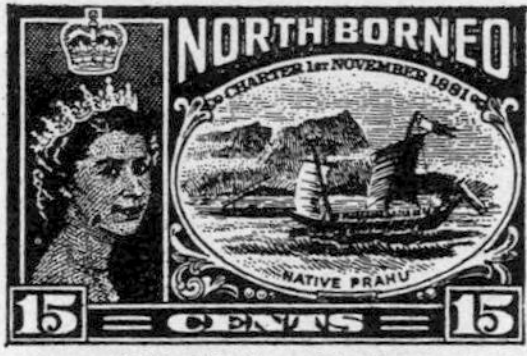

117. Native Prahu.

118. Mount Kinabalu.

119. Arms of Chartered Company.

(Recess. Waterlow & Sons.)

1956 (1 Nov.). *75th Anniv. of British North Borneo Co. Wmk. Mult. Script CA. P* 13×13½ (*horiz.*) *or* 13½×13 (*vert.*).

387	**116**	10 c. black & rose-carm.	12	15
388	**117**	15 c. black and red-brown	25	30
389	**118**	35 c. black & bluish grn.	40	45
390	**119**	$1 black and slate ..	1·00	1·25

120. Sambar Stag.

121. Honey Bear.
122. Clouded Leopard.
123. Dusun Woman with Gong.
124. Map of Borneo.
125. Tembadau (Wild Bull).
126. Butterfly Orchid.
127. Sumatran Rhinoceros.
128. Murut with Blow-pipe.
129. Mount Kinabalu.
130. Dunsun and Buffalo Transport.
131. Bajau Horsemen.

(*T* **121/31** *are horiz. as T* **120.**)

132. Orang-utan.

Vert. designs as T **132**:–

133. Hornbill.
134. Crested Wood Partridge.
135. Arms of North Borneo.

(Des. Chong Yun Fatt. Recess. Waterlow (unt 1962), then D.L.R.)

1961 (1 Feb.). *W* w.**12.** *P* 13.

391	**120**	1 c. emerald & brn.-red	5	
392	**121**	4 c. bronze-grn. & orge.	5	
393	**122**	5 c. sepia and violet ..	8	
394	**123**	6 c. black and blue-green	10	1
395	**124**	10 c. green and red ..	12	1
396	**125**	12 c. brown & grey-green	15	1
397	**126**	20 c. blue-grn. & ultram.	20	1
398	**127**	25 c. grey-black & scarlet	25	3
399	**128**	30 c. sepia and olive ..	25	2
400	**129**	35 c. slate-bl. & red-brn.	30	3
401	**130**	50 c. emerald & yell.-brn.	30	3
402	**131**	75 c. grey-bl. & brt. pur.	50	3
403	**132**	$1 brown & yellow-grn.	65	5
404	**133**	$2 brown and slate ..	1·50	1·0
405	**134**	$5 emerald and maroon	4·50	3·5
406	**135**	$10 carmine and blue ..	5·50	6·0
391/406		.. .. *Set of* 16	13·00	12·0

1963 (4 June). *Freedom from Hunger. As N 76 of Aden.*

407	12 c. ultramarine	20	2

POSTAL FISCALS.

Three Cents. Revenue

(F **1**)
(Raised stop.)

Ten Cents. Revenue

(F **2**)

1886. *Regular issues surch. as Type* F **1** *or* F

F1	**1**	3 c. on 4 c. pink (No. 6) ..	5·50	9·0
		a. Raised stop after "Cents."		
F2	,,	5 c. on 8 c. green (No. 7) ..	5·50	9·0
		a. Raised stop after "Cents."		
F3	**4**	10 c. on 50 c. violet (No. 4) ..	8·00	13·0
		a. Surch. double		
		b. No stop after "Cents." and stop after "Revenue" ..		

POSTAGE DUE STAMPS.

NOTE.—Postage Due stamps cancelled to orde can be supplied at about one-third of the price quoted for postally used specimens. The issue since 1923 have not been thus cancelled.

POSTAGE DUE

(D **1**)

1895. *Stamps of* 1894 *optd. with Type* D *P* 14½–15.

A. *Vertically* (*reading upwards*).

D 1	**25**	2 c. black and rose-lake	2·25	4·5
		a. Opt. reading downwards		
D 2	,,	2 c. black and lake ..	1·50	2·0
		a. Perf. 13½–14		
D 3	**26**	3 c. olive-green & mauve	1·25	2·0
D 3*a*	,,	3 c. olive-green & violet		
D 4	**27**	5 c. black and vermilion	2·00	4·0
		a. Stop after "DUE." ..	7·50	
		b. Perf. 13½-14	—	7·5
		c. Perf. 13½-14, comp. 12–13	—	7·5
D 5	**28**	6 c. black & bistre-brown	2·00	4·0
		a. Perf. 13½-14	1·25	2·7
		b. Perf. 12–13		
		c. Opt. reading downwards		
D 6	**31**	18 c. black and deep green	4·00	7·5
		a. Opt. reading downwards	30·00	42·0
D3/4 & D6		Optd. "Specimen" *Set of* 3	30·00	

B. *Horizontally.*
D 7 **29** 8 c. black and dull purple 2·25 4·50
a. Opt. double .. ..
b. Perf. 13½–14 .. ..
ba. Opt. inverted .. .. — 26·00
c. Perf. 13½–14, comp. 12–13
D 8 **30** 12 c. black and blue .. — 4·50
a. Opt. double .. ..
b. Perf. 13½–14 .. .. 2·25 4·50
D 9 ,, 12 c. black & ultramarine (*p.* 13½–14) .. 5·50
D10 **31** 18 c. black and deep green 3·50 7·50
a. Opt. inverted .. .. 35·00 55·00
b. Perf. 13½–14 .. .. 4·50 7·00
D11 **32** 24 c. blue and rose-lake .. — 7·50
a. Perf. 13½–14 .. .. 4·00
b. Perf. 13½–14, comp. 14½–15
D8 & D11 Optd. "Specimen" *Set of* 2 15·00

1897. *Stamps of* 1897 *optd. with Type* D **1.** *P* 14½–15.

A. *Vertically.*
D12 2 c. black and lake .. .. 1·10 1·50
a. Perf. 13½-14 .. .. 2·25

B. *Horizontally.*
D13 2 c. black and lake .. .. 2·00 3·00
D14 8 c. black and brown-purple 2·00 3·00
a. Stop after "DUE." .. .. 3·75 5·50
D12 & D14 Optd. "Specimen" *Set of* 2 15·00

1901. *Issue of* 1897–1902 *optd. with Type* D **1.** *P* 13½–14.

A. *Vertically.*
D15 2 c. black and green .. 1·25 1·50
a. Perf. 13½–14, comp. 12–13 .. — 3·00
b. Perf. 16 .. .. ..
c. Perf. 12–13 .. ..
D16 3 c. green and rosy mauve .. 1·25 1·50
a. Stop after "DUE." .. 3·00 3·75
b. Perf. 14½–15 .. .. 75 1·00
c. Perf. 13½–14, comp. 14½–15 ..
d. Opt. double .. ..
e. Opt. double. Stop after "DUE." 23·00
D17 3 c. green and dull mauve (*p.* 14½–15) .. .. 1·25 1·50
a. Stop after "DUE." .. .. 3·00 3·75
b. Opt. double. Stop after "DUE."
D18 4 c. black and carmine .. 1·00 1·25
D19 5 c. black & orange-verm. .. 1·10 1·50
a. Perf. 14½–15 .. .. — 2·40
b. Stop after "DUE." .. .. 5·00
D20 6 c. black and bistre-brown — 1·10 (Optd. "Specimen" S. £15)
a. Perf. 14½–15 .. .. 75 1·00
b. Perf. 13½–14, comp. 12–13 ..
D20*c* 8 c. black and brown-pur. (*p.* 16) .. .. ..
D21 8 c. black and brown ..
a. Perf. 14½–15 .. .. 80 1·00
D22 12 c. black and dull blue .. 2·40 3·00
a. Perf. 14½–15 .. ..
D23 18 c. black & green (No. 108)
D24 18 c. black & green (No. 110) 2·40 2·40
a. Perf. 13½–14, comp. 12–13 .. 2·40 2·50
D25 24 c. blue and lake (No. 109) — 1·60
D26 24 c. blue and lake (*p.* 14½–15) (No. 111b) .. .. 2·40 3·00

B. *Horizontally*
D27 2 c. black and green .. 3·75
D28 8 c. blk. & brown (*p.* 14½–15) 4·50
a. Stop after "DUE." ..

1902–5. *Stamps of* 1901–5 *optd.* "British Protectorate," *further optd. with Type* D **1.** *P* 13½–14.

A. *Vertically* (1902)
D29 2 c. black & green (*perf.* 16) — 35·00
D30 3 c. green & rosy mauve .. 21·00 18·00
D31 5 c. black and orange-verm. (*p.* 14½–15) .. .. 26·00 18·00
D32 8 c. black and brown .. 26·00 23·00
D33 24 c. blue and lake .. .. — 16·00

B. *Horizontally, at top of stamp* (1904–5).
D34 2 c. black & green (*p.* 14½–15) 35·00 13·00
a. Perf. 16 .. .. .. 20·00 18·00
D35 4 c. black and carmine .. 24·00 4·00

C. *Horizontally, at centre of stamp* (1904–5).
D35*a* 1 c. black and bistre-brown
b. Perf. 14½–15 .. ..
D36 2 c. black and green .. 50 25
a. Perf. 14½–15 .. .. 16·00 13·00
D37 3 c. olive-grn. & rosy mauve 50 35
a. Perf. 14½–15 .. .. 21·00 3·75
D38 4 c. black and carmine .. 1·10 65
a. Overprint double .. .. 20·00
b. Perf. 14½–15 .. .. 75 90
D39 5 c. black & orge.-vermilion 75 50
a. Perf. 14½–15 .. .. 2·00 2·10
D40 6 c. black and bistre-brown 1·60 80
a. Overprint inverted .. .. — 21·00
b. No stop after "PROTECTORATE" .. ..
c. Perf. 16 .. .. .. 3·50 3·50
D41 8 c. black and brown .. 2·00 1·10
a. No stop after "PROTECTORATE" .. .. 8·00 4·50
D42 10 c. brown and slate-lilac .. 3·50 2·00
a. No stop after "PROTECTORATE" .. ..
D42*b* 10 c. brown and slate-blue .. 4·00 2·75
D43 12 c. black and blue .. 1·60 2·75
D44 16 c. green and chestnut .. 2·00 1·60
D45 18 c. black and green .. 1·50 1·50
a. Opt. double .. .. — 16·00
D46 24 c. blue and lake .. .. 2·10 4·50
a. Opt. double .. .. — 16·00

D. *Horizontally. Optd. locally, with stop after* "DUE." (1904–5).
D47 1 c. black & bistre-brown .. 1·60 5·50
a. With raised stop after "DUE." 2·00

*No. D35*a*/b are usually found cancelled to order suggesting that they came from remainder stocks which were not issued, but we have also seen two unused copies.

1920–31. *Stamps of* 1909–22, *optd. with Type* D **1.** *P* 13½-14.

A. *Horizontally at top of stamp.*
D48 4 c. black and scarlet (1920) 4·50 2·00

B. *Horizontally towards foot of stamp.*
D49 2 c. black and green .. 1·00 1·25
a. Perf. 14½–15 90
D50 3 c. black and green .. 45 50
D51 4 c. black and scarlet .. 50 45
D52 5 c. black and yellow-brown 75 50
D53 6 c. black and olive-green .. 1·50 1·60
D54 8 c. black and rose-lake .. 50 45
D55 10 c. black & turquoise-blue 1·50 1·60
a. Perf. 14½–15 .. .. 10·00
D56 12 c. black and deep blue .. 2·00 2·75
D56*a* 16 c. black and brown-lake .. 2·75 3·75
b. Black and red-brown .. .. 6·00
D49 & D56*a* Optd. "Specimen" *Set of* 2 15·00

Nos. D51/3 also exist with the overprint towards the centre of the stamp.

1926–31. *As* 1920–31, *but perf.* 12½.
D57 2 c. black and claret .. 25 45
D58 3 c. black and green .. 25 45
D59 4 c. black and scarlet .. 30 45
D60 5 c. black and yellow-brown 1·00 1·25
D61 6 c. black and olive-green .. 90 1·00
D62 8 c. black and carmine .. 90 1·25
D63 10 c. black & turqoise-blue 1·25 2·10
D64 12 c. black and deep blue .. 2·00 2·40
D65 16 c. black & red-brown ('31) 2·25 3·00

Nos. D49/65 exist with two types of opt.; A. Thick letters; pointed beard to "G". B. Thinner letters; "G" with square end to beard and "D" more open. No. D56*a* is Type B and D56*b*, Type A.

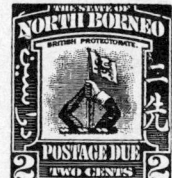

D **2.** Crest of the Company.

(Recess. Waterlow.)

1939 (1 Jan.). *P* 12½.
D66 D **2** 2 c. brown .. .. 65 5·50
D67 ,, 4 c. scarlet .. .. 80 8·00
D68 ,, 6 c. violet .. .. 1·00 11·00
D69 ,, 8 c. green .. .. 1·60 14·00
D70 ,, 10 c. blue .. .. .. 2·25 15·00
D66/70 .. .. *Set of* 5 6·00 48·00
D66/70 Perf. "Specimen" *Set of* 5 35·00

The stamps of North Borneo were withdrawn on 30 June 1964. For later issues see Sabah.

JAPANESE OCCUPATION OF NORTH BORNEO.

The stamps listed under this heading were valid for use throughout British Borneo (i.e. in Brunei, Labuan, North Borneo and Sarawak).

1942 (June). *Stamps of N. Borneo optd. in one line as T* **1** *of Jap. Occupation of Brunei.*
J 1 **81** 1 c. green and red-brown 24·00 35·00
J 2 **82** 2 c. purple & greenish blue 18·00 30·00
J 3 **83** 3 c. slate-blue and green 18·00 30·00
J 4 **84** 4 c. bronze-grn. & violet 11·00 21·00
J 5 **85** 6 c. deep blue and claret 18·00 30·00
J 6 **86** 8 c. scarlet .. .. 18·00 30·00
J 7 **87** 10 c. violet & bronze-green 18·00 30·00
J 8 **88** 12 c. green and bright blue 27·00 55·00
J 9 **89** 15 c. blue-green and brown 27·00 55·00
J10 **90** 20 c. violet and slate-blue 27·00 55·00
J11 **91** 25 c. green and chocolate 27·00 55·00
J12 **92** 50 c. chocolate and violet 50·00 60·00
J13 **93** $1 brown and carmine .. 32·00 75·00
J14 **94** $2 violet and olive-green 60·00 £110
J15 **95** $5 indigo and pale blue 80·00 £150

Nos. 318 *and* 319 ("WAR TAX") *of N. Borneo optd. in one line, as last.*
J16 **81** 1 c. green and red-brown 27·00 18·00
J17 **82** 2 c. purple & greenish blue 32·00 18·00

1. Mt. Kinabalu.

2. Borneo Scene.

(Litho. G. Kolff, Batavia.)

1943 (29 Apr.). *P* 12½.
J18 **1** 4 c. red .. .. .. 5·50 6·00
J19 **2** 8 c. blue .. .. .. 5·50 6·00

大日本
帝國郵便
北ボルネオ
(**3**)

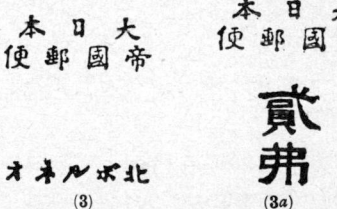

大日本
帝國郵便
貳弗
(**3*a***)

("Imperial Japanese Postal Service North Borneo.")

1944 (30 Sept.). *Stamps of N. Borneo optd. as T* **3.**
J20 **81** 1 c. green and red-brown 50 75
J21 **82** 2 c. purple & grn'ish blue 50 75
J22 **83** 3 c. slate-blue and green 50 80
J23 **84** 4 c. bronze-grn. and violet 60 80
J24 **85** 6 c. deep blue and claret 75 80
J25 **86** 8 c. scarlet .. .. 1·25 1·00
J26 **87** 10 c. violet & bronze-green 80 1·00
J27 **88** 12 c. green and bright blue 60 1·00
J28 **89** 15 c. blue-green and brown 1·00 1·25
J29 **90** 20 c. violet and slate-blue 3·00 3·00
J30 **91** 25 c. green and chocolate .. 2·75 3·75
J31 **92** 50 c. chocolate and violet .. 6·00 7·50
J32 **93** $1 brown and carmine .. 11·00 12·00

The spacing between the second and third lines of the overprint is 12 mm. on the horizontal stamps, and 15 mm. on the upright.

1944. *No.* J7 *with T* **3** *opt. in addition.*
J32*a* **87** 10 c. violet & bronze-grn. 25·00

The 2 c., 3 c., 8 c., 12 c. and 15 c. stamps of the 1942 issue are also known with Type **3** opt.

1945. *No.* J1 *surch. with T* **3*a*.**
J33 **81** $2 on 1 c. green & red-brn. £240 £300

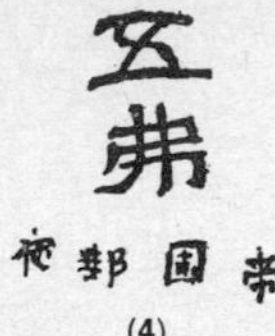

(4)

1945 (?). *North Borneo No.* 315 *surch. with T* **4.**
J34 **93** $5 on $1 brown & carmine £375 £375

5. Girl War-worker.

オネルボ北

6. (" North Borneo.")

1945. *Contemporary stamps of Japan as T* **5** *(various subjects) optd. with T* **6.**
J35 1 s. red-brown (No. 391) .. 25 30
J36 2 s. scarlet (No. 318) .. 25 30
J37 3 s. emerald-green (No. 319) 30 30
J38 4 s. yellow-green (No. 395) 30 30
J39 5 s. claret (No. 396) .. 45 50
J40 6 s. orange (No. 322) .. 50 75
J41 8 s. violet (No. 324) .. 50 75
J42 10 s. carm. & pink (No. 399) 60 75
J43 15 s. blue (No. 401) 60 75
J44 20 s. blue-slate (No. 328) .. 16·00 21·00
J45 25 s. brn. & choc. (No. 329) 12·00 14·00
J46 30 s. turquoise-blue (No. 330) 42·00 32·00
J47 50 s. olive & bistre (No. 331) 11·00 15·00
J48 1 y. red-brn. & choc. (No. 332) 11·00 15·00

Designs:—2 s. General Nogi; 3 s. Hydro-electric Works; 4 s. Hyuga Monument and Mt. Fuji; 5 s. Admiral Togo; 6 s. Garambi Lighthouse, Formosa; 8 s. Meiji Shrine; 10 s. Palms and map of S.E. Asia; 15 s. Airman; 20 s. Mt. Fuji and cherry blossoms; 25 s. Horyu Temple; 30 s. Torii, Itsukushima Shrine at Miyajima; 50 s. Kinkaku Temple; 1 y. Great Buddha, Kamakura.

NORTHERN NIGERIA.

PRINTERS. All issues were typographed by De La Rue & Co.

1

2

1900 (Mar.). *Wmk. Crown CA. P* 14.
1 **1** ½d. dull mauve and green .. 30 35
2 ,, 1d. dull mauve and carmine 80 75
3 ,, 2d. dull mauve and yellow .. 1·50 2·00
4 ,, 2½d. dull mauve and ultram. 3·50 3·50
5 **2** 5d. dull mauve and chestnut 5·00 5·50
6 ,, 6d. dull mauve and violet .. 5·00 5·50
7 **1** 1s. green and black .. .. 7·00 7·00
8 ,, 2s. 6d. green & ultramarine 35·00
9 ,, 10s. green and brown .. £100
1/9 .. .. *Set of* 9 £140
1/9 Optd. " Specimen " *Set of* 9 60·00

3

4

1902 (1 July). *Wmk. Crown CA. P* 14.
10 **3** ½d. dull purple and green .. 15 25
11 ,, 1d. dull purple and carmine 30 20
12 ,, 2d. dull purple and yellow 55 80
13 ,, 2½d. dull purple and ultram. 35 55
14 **4** 5d. dull purple & chestnut 90 2·00
15 ,, 6d. dull purple and violet .. 3·00 3·00
16 **3** 1s. green and black .. 2·25 2·25
17 ,, 2s. 6d. green and ultram. .. 4·50 6·50
18 ,, 10s. green and brown .. 25·00 25·00
10/18 .. .. *Set of* 9 35·00 38·00
10/18 Optd. " Specimen " *Set of* 9 65·00

1904 (April). *Wmk. Multiple Crown CA. P* 14.
19 **4** £25 green and carmine, O .. £14000

1905 (Aug.-Oct.). *Wmk. Mult. Crown CA. P* 14.
20 **3** ½d. dull purple & green, OC 20 25
21 ,, 1d. dull purple & carm., OC 30 15
22 ,, 2d. dull purple & yell., OC 50 75
23 ,, 2½d. dull purple & ultram., O 1·50 2·00
24 **4** 5d. dull pur. & chest., OC 3·00 4·00
25 ,, 6d. dull pur. & violet, OC 2·50 3·00
26 **3** 1s. green and black, OC .. 4·50 5·50
27 ,, 2s. 6d. green & ultram., OC 5·50 6·00
20/27 .. .. *Set of* 8 16·00 19·00

1910–11. *Wmk. Mult. Crown CA. P* 14.
28 **3** ½d. green, O (4.10) 8 8
29 ,, 1d. carmine, O (1.10) .. 10 8
30 ,, 2d. grey, O (10.11) 60 90
31 ,, 2½d. blue, O (10.10) 55 90
32 **4** 3d. purple/*yellow*, C (9.11) 45 30
34 ,, 5d. dull purple and olive-green, C (2.11) .. 90 1·25
35 ,, 6d. dull purple and purple, C (11.10) .. .. 1·00 1·60
a. Dull & brt. pur., (1911) .. 60 1·10
36 **3** 1s. black/*green*, C (11.10) .. 90 80
37 ,, 2s. 6d. black and red/*blue*, C (3.11) .. 6·50 4·00
38 **4** 5s. green and red/*yellow*, C (9.11) .. .. .. 12·00 11·00
39 **3** 10s. green and red/*green*, C (3.11) .. .. .. 20·00 20·00
28/39 .. .. *Set of* 11 38·00 38·00
28/39 Optd. " Specimen " *Set of* 11 60·00

5

6

1912. *Wmk. Mult. Crown CA. P* 14.
40 **5** ½d. deep green, O 12 12
41 ,, 1d. red, O 12 8
42 ,, 2d. grey, O 40 65
43 **6** 3d. purple/*yellow*, C .. 35 45
44 ,, 4d. black and red/*yellow*, C 30 30
45 ,, 5d. dull pur. & olive-grn., C 50 65
46 ,, 6d. dull & bright purple, C 60 90
47 ,, 9d. dull purple and carm., C 65 1·10
48 **5** 1s. black/*green*, C 85 85
49 ,, 2s. 6d. black & red/*blue*, C 4·00 4·00
50 **6** 5s. green and red/*yellow*, C 9·50 10·00
51 **5** 10s. green and red/*green*, C 14·00 15·00
52 **6** £1 purple and black/*red*, C 40·00 30·00
40/52 .. .. *Set of* 13 65·00 60·00
40/52 Optd. " Specimen " *Set of* 13 75·00

Since 1 January, 1914, Northern Nigeria has formed part of Nigeria.

NORTHERN RHODESIA.

1

2

(Eng. W. G. Fairweather. Recess. Waterlow.

1925 (1 April)–**29.** *Wmk. Mult. Script CA P* 12½.
1 **1** ½d. green 8
2 ,, 1d. brown 8
3 ,, 1½d. carmine-red 8
4 ,, 2d. yellow-brown 20 1
5 ,, 3d. ultramarine 55 3
6 ,, 4d. violet 65 3
7 ,, 6d. slate-grey 70 2
8 ,, 8d. rose-purple .. .. 3·50 5·5
9 ,, 10d. olive-green .. .. 3·50 5·5
10 **2** 1s. yellow-brown and black 1·50 6
11 ,, 2s. brown and ultramarine 5·00 6·0
12 ,, 2s. 6d. black and green .. 4·00 3·5
13 ,, 3s. violet and blue ('29) .. 7·00 5·5
14 ,, 5s. slate-grey and violet .. 7·00 5·5
15 ,, 7s. 6d. rose-purple & black 30·00 35·0
16 ,, 10s. green and black .. 16·00 16·0
17 ,, 20s. carmine-red & rose-pur. 60·00 65·0
1/17 .. .. *Set of* 17 £120 £13
1/17 Optd. Perf. " Specimen " *Set of* 17 £350

1935 (6 May). *Silver Jubilee. As Nos.* 91/4 *Antigua. P* 13½ × 14.
18 1d. light blue and olive-green 15 2
19 2d. green and indigo 40 4
20 3d. brown and deep blue .. 1·00 1·1
21 6d. slate and purple .. .. 1·40 1·5
a. Frame printed double, one albino .. .. ..
18/21 Perf. " Specimen " *Set of* 4 16·00

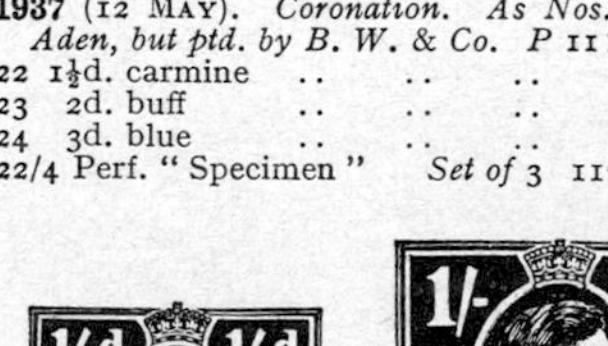

1937 (12 May). *Coronation. As Nos.* 13/15 *Aden, but ptd. by B. W. & Co. P* 11 × 11½.
22 1½d. carmine 8
23 2d. buff 15 1
24 3d. blue 25 3
22/4 Perf. " Specimen " *Set of* 3 11·00

3

4

(Recess. Waterlow.)

1938 (1 Mar.)–**52.** *Wmk. Mult. Script CA. P* 12
25 **3** ½d. green 8
26 ,, ½d. chocolate (15.11.51) .. 15
a. Perf. 12½ × 14 (10.12.52) .. 15
27 ,, 1d. brown 8
a. Chocolate ('48) 12
28 ,, 1d. green (15.11.51) .. 30
29 ,, 1½d. carmine-red .. .. 1·10
a. Imperf. between (horiz. pair) £3500
30 ,, 1½d. yellow-brown (10.1.41) 8
31 ,, 2d. yellow-brown .. .. 9·00 1·5
32 ,, 2d. carmine-red (10.1.41) .. 15 1
33 ,, 2d. purple (1.12.51) .. 15
34 ,, 3d. ultramarine 15
35 ,, 3d. scarlet (1.12.51) .. 25
36 ,, 4d. dull violet 20
37 ,, 4½d. blue (5.5.52) .. .. 80 1·1
38 ,, 6d. grey 25
39 ,, 9d. violet (5.5.52) .. .. 1·00 1·4

40 **4** 1s. yellow-brown and black 45 12
41 ,, 2s. 6d. black and green .. 1·10 85
42 ,, 3s. violet and blue .. 1·10 90
43 ,, 5s. grey and dull violet .. 2·00 2·25
44 ,, 10s. green and black .. 3·00 3·50
45 ,, 20s. carm.-red and rose-pur. 7·00 8·00
25/45 .. .. *Set of* 21 26·00 20·00
25/45 Perf. "Specimen" *Set of* 15 55·00

1946 (26 Nov.). *Victory. As Nos.* 28/9 *of Aden. P* 13½×14.
46 1½d. red-orange 8 8
a. Perf. 13½ 25 30
47 2d. carmine 10 10
46/7 Perf. "Specimen" *Set of* 2 14·00

1948 (1 Dec.). *Royal Silver Wedding. As Nos.* 30/1 *of Aden, but inscr.* "NORTHERN RHODESIA" (*recess* 20s.).
48 1½d. orange 8 8
49 20s. brown-lake .. .. 6·00 9·00

1949 (10 Oct.). *75th Anniv. of U.P.U. As Nos.* 114/7 *of Antigua.*
50 2d. carmine 15 15
51 3d. deep blue 20 25
52 6d. grey 40 40
53 1s. red-orange 75 75

5. Cecil Rhodes and Victoria Falls.

(Recess. De La Rue.)

1953 (30 May). *Centenary of Birth of Cecil Rhodes. Wmk. Mult. Script CA. P* 12×11½.
54 **5** ½d. brown 10 10
55 ,, 1d. green 10 10
56 ,, 2d. mauve 10 10
57 ,, 4½d. blue 50 90
58 ,, 1s. orange and black .. 60 90
54/58 .. .. *Set of* 5 1·25 1·90

6. Arms of the Rhodesias and Nyasaland.

(Recess. Waterlow.)

1953 (30 May). *Rhodes Centenary Exhibition. Wmk. Mult. Script CA. P* 14×13½.
59 6d. violet 25 30

1953 (2 June). *Coronation. As Nos.* 47 *of Aden.*
60 1½d. black and yellow-orange.. 10 12

7

8

(Recess. Waterlow.)

1953 (15 Sept.). *Wmk. Mult. Script CA. P* 12½×14 (*pence values*) *or* 12½×13½ (*shilling values*).
61 **7** ½d. deep brown 5 5
62 ,, 1d. bluish green 5 5
63 ,, 1½d. orange-brown 8 8
64 ,, 2d. reddish purple 8 5
65 ,, 3d. scarlet 8 8
66 ,, 4d. slate-lilac 10 10
67 ,, 4½d. deep blue 20 25
68 ,, 6d. grey-black 15 12
69 ,, 9d. violet 25 35
70 **8** 1s. orange-brown and black 25 20
71 ,, 2s. 6d. black and green .. 75 1·00
72 ,, 5s. grey and dull purple .. 1·50 3·00
73 ,, 10s. green and black .. 4·00 6·00
74 ,, 20s. rose-red and rose-purple 11·00 13·00
61/74 .. .. *Set of* 14 17·00 22·00

For issues from 1954 to 1963, see Rhodesia and Nyasaland.

9. Arms. **10.**

(Photo. Harrison & Sons.)

1963 (10 Dec.). *Arms black, gold and blue; portrait and inscriptions black; background colours below. P* 14½ (*T* **9**) *or* 13½×13 (*T* **10**).
75 **9** ½d. bright violet 5 5
a. Value omitted .. .. 35·00
76 ,, 1d. light blue 5 5
a. Value omitted .. .. 8·00
77 ,, 2d. brown 5 5
78 ,, 3d. yellow 5 5
a. Value omitted .. .. 38·00
79 ,, 4d. green 10 10
a. Value omitted .. .. 45·00
80 ,, 6d. light olive-green .. 10 10
a. Value omitted .. .. 45·00
81 ,, 9d. yellow-brown 12 15
a. Value omitted .. .. 60·00
82 ,, 1s. slate-purple 15 15
83 ,, 1s. 3d. bright purple .. 40 20
84 **10** 2s. orange 30 35
85 ,, 2s. 6d. lake-brown.. .. 40 50
86 ,, 5s. magenta .. .. 1·25 2·00
87 ,, 10s. mauve .. .. .. 2·00 3·00
88 ,, 20s. blue .. .. .. 4·50 8·00
a. Value omitted £350
75/88 .. .. *Set of* 14 8·50 13·00

POSTAGE DUE STAMPS.

D 1

D 2

(Typo. De La Rue & Co.)

1929–52. *Wmk. Mult. Script CA. P* 14.
D1 **D 1** 1d. grey-black 50 30
a. *Black*. Chalky paper (22.1.52) 30 30
b. Error. St. Edward's Crown, W9b, C .. .. .. 12·00
D2 ,, 2d. grey-black 40 40
D3 ,, 3d. grey-black 50 50
aa. *Black*. Chalky paper (22.1.52) 25 35
a. Error. Crown missing, W9a, C .. .. .. 16·00
b. Error. St. Edward's Crown, W9b, C .. .. .. 12·00
D4 ,, 4d. grey-black 70 80
D1/4 Perf. "Specimen" *Set of* 4 20·00

(Des. D. Smith. Litho. Govt. Ptr., Lusaka.)

1963 (10 Dec.). *P* 12½.
D 5 **D 2** 1d. orange 10 12
D 6 ,, 2d. deep blue 12 15
D 7 ,, 3d. lake 15 25
D 8 ,, 4d. ultramarine 20 30
D 9 ,, 6d. purple 30 45
D10 ,, 1s. light emerald .. 60 1·00
a. Imperf. (vert. pair) ..
b. Block of four imperf. horiz. and imp. betwn. vert. ..
D5/10 .. .. *Set of* 6 1·25 2·00

In all values the stamps in the right-hand vertical row of the sheet are imperforate on the right.

The stamps of Northern Rhodesia were withdrawn on 23 October 1964 when the territory attained independence. For later issues see Zambia.

NORTH-WEST PACIFIC ISLANDS.

See NEW GUINEA.

NOVA SCOTIA.

1

2

Crown and Heraldic Flowers of United Kingdom and Mayflower of Nova Scotia.

(Recess. Perkins, Bacon & Co.)

1851 (1 Sept.)–**57.** *Bluish paper. Imperf.*
1 **1** 1d. red-brown (12.5.53) .. £1500 £300
a. Bisected (½d.) (on cover) .. £30000
2 **2** 3d. deep blue £1000 £250
a. Bisected (1½d.) (on cover) .. — £1700
3 ,, 3d. bright blue (1857) .. .. £600 95·00
a. Bisected (1½d.) (on cover) .. — £1700
4 ,, 3d. pale blue (1857) £550 £100
a. Bisected (1½d.) (on cover) .. — £1700
5 ,, 6d. yellow-green £2500 £325
a. Bisected (3d.) (on cover) .. — £2500
6 ,, 6d. deep green (1857) £4500 £600
a. Bisected (3d.) (on cover) .. — £3500
b. Quartered (1½d.) (on cover) .. — £20000
7 ,, 1s. cold violet £12000 £5000
a. Bisected (6d.) (on cover) .. — £25000
b. Quartered (3d.) (on cover) .. — £35000
7c ,, 1s. deep purple (1851) .. £10000 £4000
d. Watermarked £12000 £5500
8 ,, 1s. purple (1856) £9000 £2250
a. Bisected (6d.) (on cover) .. — £20000

The watermark on No. 7d consists of the whole or part of a letter from the name "P. H. Saunders" (the papermakers).

The stamps formerly catalogued on almost white paper are probably some from which the bluish paper has been discharged.

Reprints of all four values were made in 1890 on thin, hard, white paper. The 1d. is brown, the 3d. blue, the 6d. deep green, and the 1s. violet-black.

The 3d. bisects are only found used on cover to make up the 7½d. rate.

3

4

5

(Recess. American Bank Note Co., New York.)

1860–63. *P* 12.

(a) Yellowish paper.

No.	Type	Description	Unused	Used
9	**3**	1 c. jet black	1·50	5·00
		a. Bisected (½ c.) (on cover) ..		£5000
10	,,	1 c. grey-black	1·50	5·00
11	,,	2 c. grey-purple	5·00	6·00
11*a*	,,	2 c. purple	8·00	6·00
12	,,	5 c. blue	70·00	7·00
13	,,	5 c. deep blue	70·00	7·00
14	**4**	8½ c. deep green	1·50	
15	,,	8½ c. yellow-green	1·40	
16	,,	10 c. scarlet	6·00	7·00
17	**5**	12½ c. black	9·00	5·50
17*a*	,,	12½ c. greyish black ..	—	5·50

(b) White paper.

No.	Type	Description	Unused	Used
18	**3**	1 c. black	1·50	5·00
		a. Imperf. between (horiz. pair)	60·00	
19	,,	1 c. grey	1·50	5·00
20	,,	2 c. dull purple	2·00	6·00
21	,,	2 c. purple	2·10	6·00
22	,,	2 c. grey-purple	2·00	6·00
		a. Bisected (1 c.) (on cover)	—	£2000
23	,,	2 c. slate-purple	2·00	5·50
24	,,	5 c. blue	70·00	7·00
25	,,	5 c. deep blue	70·00	7·00
26	**4**	8½ c. deep green	7·00	9·00
27	,,	10 c. scarlet	2·00	7·00
28	,,	10 c. vermilion	2·25	7·00
		a. Bisected (5 c.) (on cover) ..	—	£500
29	**5**	12½ c. black	9·00	7·00

Since 1868 Nova Scotia has used stamps of the Dominion of Canada.

NYASALAND PROTECTORATE.

I. BRITISH CENTRAL AFRICA PROTECTORATE.

B.C.A.

(1)

1891 (April)–**1895.** *Stamps of Rhodesia optd. as T* **1**. *P* 14, 14½.

No.	Type	Description	Unused	Used
1	**1**	1d. black	75	75
2	**4**	2d. sea-green and vermilion	60	1·50
		a. Bisected (1d.) (on cover) ..	—	£450
3	,,	4d. reddish chestnut & blk.	75	1·50
4	**1**	6d. ultramarine	12·00	8·00
5	,,	6d. deep blue	2·50	2·50
6	**4**	8d. rose-lake & ultramarine	3·50	7·50
6*a*	,,	8d. red and ultramarine ..	6·00	9·00
7	**1**	1s. grey-brown	4·00	3·75
8	,,	2s. vermilion	7·50	8·00
9	,,	2s. 6d. grey-purple ..	11·00	11·00
9*a*	,,	2s. 6d. lilac..	9·00	9·00
10	**4**	3s. brown and green ('95)	11·00	11·00
11	,,	4s. grey-blk. & ver. (2.93)	15·00	15·00
12	**1**	5s. orange-yellow	15·00	22·00
13	,,	10s. deep green	25·00	40·00
14	**2**	£1 deep blue	£150	£200
15	**2**	£2 rose-red	£240	
16	,,	£5 sage-green	£500	
17	,,	£10 brown	£1200	
1/14		.. .. *Set of* 13	£225	£300

The overprint varies on values up to 10s. Sets may be made with *thin* or *thick* letters.

B.C.A.
FOUR
SHILLINGS.
(2)

ONE PENNY.
(3)

1892–93. *Stamps of Rhodesia surch. as T* **2**.

No.	Type	Description	Unused	Used
18	**4**	3s. on 4s. grey-blk. & verm.	75·00	75·00
19	**1**	4s. on 5s. orange-yellow ..	23·00	23·00

The 4s. was issued in Aug., 1892, the 3s. in Oct., 1893.

1895. *No.* 2 *surch. at Cape Town with T* **3**.

No.	Type	Description	Unused	Used
20	**4**	1d. on 2d. sea-grn. & verm.	4·50	8·50
		a. Surch. double	£600	£700

Specimens are known with double surcharge, without stop after "PENNY". These are from a trial printing made at Blantyre, but it is believed that they were not issued to the public. (*Price* £200 *un.*)

5 Arms of the Protectorate. 6

(Litho. De La Rue & Co.)

1895. *No wmk. P* 14.

No.	Type	Description	Unused	Used
21	**5**	1d. black	1·25	1·60
22	,,	2d. black and green ..	3·50	3·75
23	,,	4d. black and reddish buff	5·50	5·50
24	,,	6d. black and blue ..	7·00	4·00
25	,,	1s. black and rose	8·00	7·00
26	**6**	2s. 6d. black & brt. mag.	45·00	27·00
27	,,	3s. black and yellow ..	38·00	12·00
28	,,	5s. black and olive ..	45·00	27·00
29	,,	£1 black & yellow-orange	£425	£150
30	,,	£10 black and orange-verm. (Optd. S. £100) ..	£1500	
31	,,	£25 black and blue-green (Optd. S. £250) ..	£2750	£1800
21/28		.. .. *Set of* 8	£140	75·00
21/29		Optd. "Specimen" *Set of* 9	£125	

1896 (Feb.). *Wmk. Crown CA* (*T* **5**) *or CC* (*T* **6**), *P* 14.

No.	Type	Description	Unused	Used
32	**5**	1d. black	1·60	2·00
33	,,	2d. black and green ..	3·50	3·00
34	,,	4d. black & orange-brown	4·00	4·00
35	,,	6d. black and blue ..	3·50	2·75
36	,,	1s. black and rose	5·50	5·50
37	**6**	2s. 6d. black and magenta	27·00	27·00
38	,,	3s. black and yellow ..	16·00	11·00
39	,,	5s. black and olive ..	30·00	27·00
40	,,	£1 black and blue	£500	£275
41	,,	£10 black & orge. (Optd. S. £75)	£2000	£900
42	,,	£25 black & grn. (Optd. S. £150)	£4000	
32/39		.. .. *Set of* 8	75·00	60·00
32/40		Optd. "Specimen" *Set of* 9	£125	

7

8

1897 (Aug.). *T* **7** (*wmk. Crown CA*) *and* **8** (*wmk Crown CC*). *P* 14.

No.	Type	Description	Unused	Used
43	**7**	1d. black & ultramarine ..	60	3
44	,,	2d. black & yellow ..	35	6
45	,,	4d. black and carmine ..	2·10	2·1
46	,,	6d. black & green ..	3·50	3·0
47	,,	1s. black & dull purple ..	2·10	3·0
48	**8**	2s. 6d. blk. & ultramarine	12·00	11·0
49	,,	3s. black & sea-green ..	80·00	80·0
50	,,	4s. black & carmine ..	16·00	16·0
50*a*	,,	10s. black & olive-green ..	35·00	42·0
51	,,	£1 black & dull purple ..	£120	80·0
52	,,	£10 black and yellow (Optd. S. £85)	£1800	£90
43/51		.. .. *Set of* 10	£240	£20
43/51		Optd. "Specimen" *Set of* 10	55·00	

ONE

PENNY

(9)

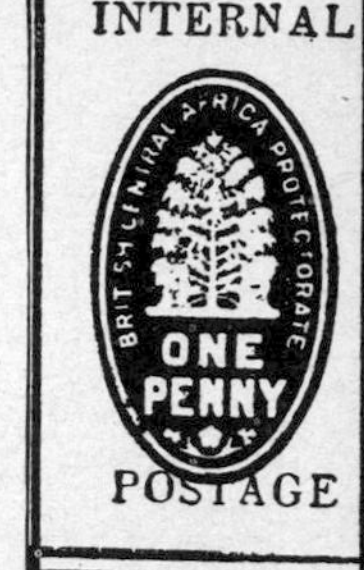

10

1898. *No.* 49 *surch. with T* **9**, *in red.*

No.	Type	Description	Unused	Used
53	**8**	1d. on 3s. black & sea-green ..	3·75	4·0
		a. Error "PNNEY"	£450	
		b. Error "PENN"	£225	
		c. Double surch.	£225	£20

1898 (11 Mar.). *T* **10**. *Imperf.*

Setting I. *The vertical frame lines of the stamp cross the space between the two rows of the shee*

(i) *With the initials* "J.G." *or* "J.T.G." *on th back in black ink.*

No.	Description	Unused	Used
54	1d. vermilion and grey-blue ..	—	£16
	a. Without the initials	£450	
	b. Without the initials and centre inverted	£2250	

(ii) *With a control number and letter, letters, o printed in plain relief at the back.*

No.	Description	Unused	Used
55	1d. vermilion and grey-blue ..	—	21·0

Setting II. *The vertical frame lines do not cros the space between the rows except at the extrem ends of the sheet.*

As No. 55.

No.	Description	Unused	Used
55*b*	1d. vermilion and pale ultram.	—	7·0
	c. Control on face	—	£120
	d. Centre omitted (vert. pr. with normal)	£1700	
56	1d. vermilion and deep ultram.	—	7·0
	a. Without Control at back ..	£250	18·0
	b. Control doubly impressed ..		

1898 (June). *T* **10**. *Setting* II. *P* 12.

No.	Description	Unused	Used
57	1d. vermilion & pale ultram.	£225	3·5
57*a*	1d. vermilion & deep ultram.	—	3·0
	b. Without Control at back ..	£250	12·0
	c. Two diff. Controls on back ..	—	£15

The two different settings of these stamps ar each in 30 types, issued without gum.

1901. *Wmk. Crown CA. P* 14.

No.	Type	Description	Unused	Used
57*d*	**7**	1d. dull pur. & carmine-rose	45	6
57*e*	,,	4d. dull pur. & olive-green ..	2·40	2·7
58	,,	6d. dull purple & brown ..	3·75	4·0
57*d*/58		Optd. "Specimen" *Set of* 3	40·00	

11

12

(Typo. De La Rue.)

.903–4. *T* **11** (*Wmk. Crown CA*) *and* **12** (*Wmk. Crown CC*). *P* 14.

59 **11** 1d. grey and carmine .. 80 20
50 ,, 2d. dull & bright purple .. 2·00 90
51 ,, 4d. grey-green and black .. 2·40 2·40
52 ,, 6d. grey & reddish buff .. 2·40 2·40
52*a* ,, 1s. grey and blue .. 2·40 3·50
53 **12** 2s. 6d. grey-green & green 9·00 9·00
54 ,, 4s. dull & bright purple .. 15·00 15·00
55 ,, 10s. grey-green and black .. 27·00 35·00
56 ,, £1 grey and carmine .. 90·00 80·00
57 ,, £10 grey & bl. (Optd. S. £150) £1500 £1200
59/66 .. .. *Set of* 9 £150 £120
59/66 Optd. "Specimen" *Set of* 9 £100

.907. *T* **11.** *Wmk. Mult. Crown CA. P* 14.

58 1d. grey and carmine, C .. 60 50
59 2d. dull and bright purple, C £6000
70 4d. grey-green and black, C .. £6000
71 6d. grey and reddish buff, C .. 12·00 14·00

.I. NYASALAND PROTECTORATE.

The change of name took effect on 6 July, 1907.

13

14

(Typo. De La Rue.)

.908 (22 July). *Wmk. Crown CA. P* 14.

.a **13** 1s. black/*green*, C .. .. 1·00 1·50

Wmk. Mult. Crown CA. P 14.

73 **13** ½d. green, O 12 30
74 ,, 1d. carmine, O 8 12
75 ,, 3d. purple/*yellow*, C .. 90 1·10
76 ,, 4d. black and red/*yellow*, C 90 1·50
77 ,, 6d. dull pur. & brt. pur., C 1·50 2·00
78 **14** 2s. 6d. black & red/*blue*, C 9·00 11·00
79 ,, 4s. carmine and black, C 11·00 13·00
80 ,, 10s. green and red/*green*, C 30·00 45·00
81 ,, £1 purple and black/*red*, C £120 £140
82 ,, £10 purple & ultramarine, C (Optd. S. £120) .. £2750
72/81 .. .. *Set of* 10 £150 £190
72/81 Optd. "Specimen" *Set of* 10 £110

15

16

(Typo. De La Rue.)

913 (1 Apr.)–**1918.** *T* **15** *and* **16** (*2s. 6d., etc.*). *Wmk. Mult. Crown CA. P* 14.

83 ½d. green, O 25 20
84 ½d. blue-green, O (1918) .. 30 20
85 1d. carmine-red, O .. 40 20
86 1d. scarlet, O (1916) .. 25 20
87 2d. grey, O (1916) 80 30
88 2d. slate, O .. .. .. 1·50 30
89 2½d. bright blue, O 45 50
90 3d. purple/*yellow*, C (1914) .. 90 1·00
a. On pale yellow .. .. 1·25 1·25
91 4d. black & red/*yell.* C, (*shades*) 1·10 1·10
a. On pale yellow .. .. 1·60 1·60
92 6d. dull & bright purple, C .. 1·00 1·10
92*a* 6d. dull pur. & brt. violet, C 2·75 3·00
93 1s. black/*green*, C .. .. 2·00 1·60
a. On blue-green, olive back .. 1·00 1·10
b. On emerald back .. .. 1·10 1·25
94 2s. 6d. black & red/*blue*, C 3·75 4·50

95 4s. carmine and black, C .. 4·50 5·00
96 10s. green & red/*green*, C .. 16·00 20·00
97 10s. pale grn. & red/*green*, C 20·00 20·00
98 £1 purple & black/*red*, C .. 35·00 30·00
99 £10 purple and blue, C (Optd. S. £90) £1100 £675
83/98 .. .. *Set of* 12 60·00 60·00
83/98 Optd. "Specimen" *Set of* 12 90·00

For stamps optd. "N.F." see TANGANYIKA.

1921–30. *T* **15** *and* **16** (*2s., etc.*). *Wmk. Mult. Script CA. P* 14.

100 ½d. green, O 20 12
101 1d. carmine, O 20 15
102 1½d. orange, O .. .. 5·50 5·50
103 2d. grey, O 35 30
105 3d. purple/*pale yellow*, C .. 1·00 80
106 4d. black & red/*yellow*, C .. 75 90
107 6d. dull & bright purple, C 1·10 1·25
108 1s. black/*emerald*, C ('30) 3·00 2·75
109 2s. purple and blue/*blue*, C 5·50 6·00
110 2s. 6d. blk. & red/*blue*, C ('24) 6·00 7·00
111 4s. carmine and black, C 4·50 4·00
112 5s. green & red/*yellow*, C ('29) 14·00 15·00
113 10s. green and red/*green*, C 35·00 35·00
100/113 .. .. *Set of* 13 70·00 75·00
100/13 Optd./Perf. "Specimen" *Set of* 13 60·00

17. King George V and Symbol of the Protectorate.

(Des. Major H. E. Green. Recess Waterlow.)

1934 (June)–**35.** *Wmk. Mult. Script CA. P* 12½.

114 **17** ½d. green 15 15
115 ,, 1d. brown 25 20
116 ,, 1½d. carmine 45 45
117 ,, 2d. pale grey 35 35
118 ,, 3d. blue 65 60
119 ,, 4d. brt. magenta (20.5.35) 1·00 1·00
120 ,, 6d. violet 80 80
121 ,, 9d. olive-bistre (20.5.35) 1·50 3·00
122 ,, 1s. black and orange .. 1·50 2·75
114/122 .. .. *Set of* 9 6·00 9·00
114/22 Perf. "Specimen" *Set of* 9 30·00

1935 (6 May). *Silver Jubilee. As Nos.* 91/4 *of Antigua but ptd. by W'low & Sons. P* 11×12.

123 1d. ultramarine and grey .. 20 20
124 2d. green and indigo .. 60 60
125 3d. brown and deep blue .. 1·60 2·00
126 1s. slate and purple .. 3·50 4·00
123/6 Perf. "Specimen" *Set of* 4 15·00

1937 (12 May). *Coronation. As Nos.* 13/15 *of Aden, but ptd. by B. W. & Co. P* 11×11½.

127 ½d. green 8 8
128 1d. brown 8 8
129 2d. grey-black 20 25
127/9 Perf. "Specimen" *Set of* 3 10·00

18. Symbol of the Protectorate.

19

(T **18** recess, Waterlow; T **19** typo, D.L.R.)

1938 (1 Jan.)–**42.** *P* 12½ (*T* **18**) *or* 14 (*T* **19**).

(*a*) *Wmk. Mult. Script CA.*

130 **18** ½d. green 25 10
130*a* ,, ½d. brown ('42) .. 8 8
131 ,, 1d. brown 25 10
131*a* ,, 1d. green ('42) .. 8 8
132 ,, 1½d. carmine 50 60
132*a* ,, 1½d. grey ('42) .. 15 20
133 ,, 2d. grey 50 25
133*a* ,, 2d. carmine ('42) .. 10 10
134 ,, 3d. blue 8 8
135 ,, 4d. bright magenta .. 15 35
136 ,, 6d. violet 15 25
137 ,, 9d. olive-bistre .. 25 80
138 ,, 1s. black and orange .. 30 40
139 **19** 2s. purple & blue/*blue*, C 70 1·00
140 ,, 2s. 6d. black & red/*blue*, C 55 1·00
141 ,, 5s. pale grn. & red/*yell.*, C 4·50 7·00
a. Green and red/pale yell., O 8·00 11·00
142 ,, 10s. green & red/*green*, C O 4·00 4·50

(*b*) *Wmk. Mult. Crown CA.*

143 **19** £1 purple & black/*red*, C 6·00 8·00
130/143 .. .. *Set of* 18 17·00 23·00
130/43 Perf. "Specimen" *Set of* 18 90·00

No. 141*a* has a yellow surfacing often applied in horizontal lines giving the appearance of laid paper.

20. Lake Nyasa.

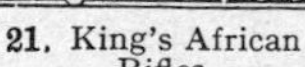

21. King's African Rifles.

24. Fishing Village.

22. Tea Estate.

23. Map of Nyasaland.

25. Tobacco.

26. Badge of Nyasaland.

(Recess. Bradbury, Wilkinson.)

1945 (1 SEPT.). *Wmk. Mult. Script CA (sideways on horiz. designs). P* 12.

144	**20**	½d. black and chocolate..	8	8
145	**21**	1d. black and emerald ..	8	8
146	**22**	1½d. black and grey-green	8	10
147	**23**	2d. black and scarlet ..	10	8
148	**24**	3d. black and light blue..	10	8
149	**25**	4d. black and claret ..	12	25
150	**22**	6d. black and violet ..	15	8
151	**20**	9d. black and olive ..	20	50
152	**23**	1s. indigo and deep green	25	12
153	**24**	2s. emerald and maroon..	70	90
154	**25**	2s. 6d. emerald and blue	90	1·10
155	**26**	5s. purple and blue ..	1·40	1·60
156	**23**	10s. claret and emerald ..	2·50	3·50
157	**26**	20s. scarlet and black ..	5·50	7·00
144/157		.. .. *Set of* 14	11·00	14·00
144/57		Perf. "Specimen" *Set of* 14	75·00	

1946 (16 DEC.). *Victory. As Nos.* 28/9 *of Aden.*

158	1d. green	8	8
159	2d. red-orange	8	8
158/9	Perf. "Specimen" *Set of* 2	14·00	

27. Symbol of the Protectorate.

(Recess. Bradbury, Wilkinson.)

1947 (20 OCT.). *Wmk. Mult. Script. CA. P* 12.

160 **27**	1d. red-brn. and yell.-grn.	8	8
160	Perf. "Specimen"	16·00	

1948 (15 DEC.). *Royal Silver Wedding. As Nos.* 30/1 *of Aden.*

161	1d. green	8	8
162	10s. mauve	4·00	5·50

1949 (21 NOV.). *75th Anniv. of U.P.U. As Nos.* 114/7 *of Antigua.*

163	1d. blue-green	12	15
164	3d. greenish blue	25	30
165	6d. purple	35	45
166	1s. ultramarine	55	60

28. Arms in 1891 and 1951.

(Recess. Bradbury, Wilkinson.)

1951 (15 MAY). *Diamond Jubilee of Protectorate. Wmk. Mult. Script CA. P* 11 × 12.

167	**28**	2d. black and scarlet ..	12	15
168	,,	3d. black and turq.-blue..	12	20
169	,,	6d. black abd violet ..	25	40
170	,,	5s. black and indigo ..	2·00	2·50

1953 (30 MAY). *Rhodes Centenary Exhibition. As No.* 59 *of Northern Rhodesia.*

171	6d. violet	30	40

1953 (2 JUNE). *Coronation. As No.* 47 *of Aden, but ptd. by B. W. & Co.*

172	2d. black and brown-orange	10	12

29. Grading Cotton.

(Recess. Bradbury, Wilkinson.)

1953 (1 SEPT.)–**54.** *As T* **20** *and* **22/7**, *but with portrait of Queen Elizabeth II, as in T* **29**. *Wmk. Mult. Script CA. P* 12.

173	**20**	½d. black and chocolate..	8	5
		a. Perf. 12 × 12½ (8.3.54) ..	5	5
174	**27**	1d. brown & bright green	5	5
175	**22**	1½d. blk. & dp. grey-green	8	25
176	**23**	2d. blk. & yellow-orange	5	5
		a. Perf. 12 × 12½ (8.3.54) ..	8	8
177	**29**	2½d. green and black ..	10	10
178	**25**	3d. black and scarlet ..	12	12
179	**24**	4½d. black and light blue..	25	30
180	**22**	6d. black and violet ..	20	25
		a. Perf. 12 × 12½ (8.3.54) ..	20	25
181	**20**	9d. black and deep olive	30	40
182	**23**	1s. deep blue & slate-grn.	25	30
183	**24**	2s. deep grn. & brown-red	70	1·25
184	**25**	2s. 6d. deep emerald and deep blue	85	1·50
185	**26**	5s. purple & Prussian blue	1·75	3·50
186	**23**	10s. carm. & deep emerald	5·00	6·00
187	**26**	20s. red and black ..	8·00	12·00
173/87		.. .. *Set of* 15	16·00	23·00

Stamps perf. 12 × 12½ come from sheets comb-perforated 11.8 × 12.25. They were also issued in coils of 480 stamps made up from sheets.

For issues between 1954 and 1963, see RHODESIA AND NYASALAND.

30

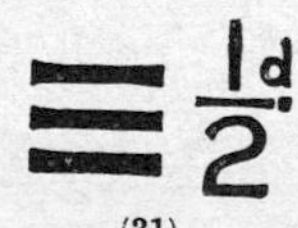

(31)

(Recess. B.W.)

1963 (1 NOV.). *T* **30.** *Revenue stamps optd* "POSTAGE", *or additionally surch. as T* **31.** *P* 12.

188	½d. on 1d. greenish blue ..	5	
189	1d. green	5	
190	2d. scarlet	8	1
191	3d. blue	10	1
192	6d. brown-purple	20	2
193	9d. on 1s. cerise	25	3
194	1s. purple	25	3
195	2s. 6d. black	55	6
196	5s. chocolate	90	1·2
197	10s. yellow-olive (*shades*) ..	3·00	3·0
198	£1 deep violet	5·00	8·0
188/198	.. .. *Set of* 11	9·50	12·0

32. Mother and Child. **33.** Chambo (fish).

34. Zebu Bull.
35. Groundnuts.
36. Fishing.
(*T* **34/6** *are as T* **32/3.**)

37. Tea Industry.

38. Timber.
39. Turkish Tobacco Industry.
40. Cotton Industry.
41. Monkey Bay, Lake Nyasa.
42. Forestry—Afzelia.
(*T* **38/42** *are as T* **37.**)

43. Nyala.

(Des. V. Whiteley. Photo. Harrison.)

1964 (1 JAN.). *P* 14½.

199	**32**	½d. reddish violet ..	5	
200	**33**	1d. black and green ..	10	
201	**34**	2d. light red-brown ..	12	
202	**35**	3d. red-brown, yellow-green and bistre-brown	12	
203	**36**	4d. indigo & orange-yell.	12	
204	**37**	6d. purple, yellow-green and light blue ..	15	
205	**38**	1s. brown, turquoise-blue and pale yellow ..	30	
206	**39**	1s. 3d. bronze-grn. & chest.	30	
207	**40**	2s. 6d. brown and blue..	65	
208	**41**	5s. blue, grn., yell. & blk.	1·25	1·
209	**42**	10s. grn., orge.-brn. & blk.	3·00	3·
210	**43**	£1 dp. redsh. pur. & yell.	5·00	6·
199/210		.. .. *Set of* 12	10·00	12·

POSTAGE DUE STAMPS.

(Typo. D.L.R.)

1950 (1 July). *As Type* D 1 *of Gold Coast, but inscr.* "NYASALAND". *Wmk. Mult. Script CA.* P 14.

D1 1d. scarlet 15 30
D2 2d. ultramarine 30 60
D3 3d. green 45 90
D4 4d. purple .. .. .. 60 1·25
D5 6d. yellow-orange .. .. 90 2·00
D1/D5 .. .. *Set of* 5 2·25 4·50

The stamps of Nyasaland were withdrawn on 5 July 1964 when the territory attained independence. For later issues see MALAWI.

ORANGE FREE STATE.

(CALLED ORANGE RIVER COLONY, 1900–1910.)

I. INDEPENDENT REPUBLIC.

NOTE. All stamps are perf. 14.

1

(Typo. De La Rue & Co.)

1868 (1 Jan.)–**1890.**

1 1 1d. pale brown .. .. 1·00 20
2 „ 1d. red-brown .. .. 1·00 20
3 „ 1d. deep brown .. .. 1·10 20
4 „ 6d. pale rose (1868) .. .. 2·25 1·50
5 „ 6d. rose (1871) .. .. 2·00 1·50
6 „ 6d. rose-carmine (1877) .. 4·50 5·50
7 „ 6d. bright carmine (1890) .. 1·50 1·10
8 „ 1s. orange-buff .. .. 4·00 2·25
a. Double Print £700
9 „ 1s. orange-yellow .. .. 1·50 1·00
3 & 6 Optd. "Specimen" *Set of* 2 50·00

4 (a) 4 (b) 4 (c) 4 (d)

1877. *No. 6 surcharged as above.*

10 4 on 6d. rose-carmine (*a*) .. 18·00 11·00
11 4 on 6d. rose-carmine (*b*) .. £120 38·00
12 4 on 6d. rose-carmine (*c*) .. 14·00 7·00
13 4 on 6d. rose-carmine (*d*) .. 14·00 7·00

Varieties. (i.) *Surcharge inverted.*

14 4 on 6d. rose-carmine (*a*) .. — £120
15 4 on 6d. rose-carmine (*b*) .. — £120
16 4 on 6d. rose-carmine (*c*) .. — 55·00
17 4 on 6d. rose-carmine (*d*) .. — 60·00

(ii.) *Surcharge double, one inverted.*

17*a* 4 on 6d. rose-carmine (*a* and *c*) — £160
17*b* 4 on 6d. rose-carmine (*b* and *d*) — £160

1878 (July). *T* 1.

18 4d. pale blue .. .. .. 2·75 1·00
19 4d. ultramarine .. .. .. 2·75 1·50
20 5s. green .. .. .. 4·00 3·75

1d. (a) 1d. (b) 1d. (c)

1d. (d) 1d. (e)

1881 (June). *No.* 20 *surch. as above, with a heavy black bar cancelling the old value.* (*a*) *Small* "1" *and* "d." (*b*) *Sloping serif.* (*c*) *Same size as* (*b*), *but* "1" *with straight horizontal serif.* (*d*) *Taller* "1" *with horizontal serif.* (*e*) *Same size as* (*d*) *but with sloping serif and thin line at foot.*

21 1d. on 5s. green (*a*) .. .. 7·50 3·00
22 1d. on 5s. green (*b*) .. .. 4·00 3·50
23 1d. on 5s. green (*c*) .. .. 11·00 5·50
24 1d. on5s. green (*d*) .. .. 4·00 3·50
25 1d. on 5s. green (*e*) .. .. 32·00

There are two varieties of No. 24—one with an antique "d." the other with a Roman "d.".

Varieties. (i) *Surcharge inverted.*

27 1d. on 5s. green (*b*) .. .. — £150
28 1d. on 5s. green (*c*) .. .. — £160
29 1d. on 5s. green (*d*) £120 £120
30 1d. on 5s. green (*e*) .. .. — £160

(ii). *Surcharge double.*

32 1d. on 5s. green (*b*) .. .. — £150
33 1d. on 5s. green (*c*) .. ..
34 1d. on 5s. green (*d*) .. .. — £150
35 1d. on 5s. green (*e*) .. ..

No. 21 was the first printing in one type only. Nos. 22 to 25 constitute the second printing about a year later, and are all found on the same sheet; and as certain varieties are known with surcharge inverted and double, all probably exist.

Owing to defective printing, specimens may be found with the obliterating bar at the top of the stamps and others without the bar.

½d

1882 (Aug.). *No.* 20, *surch.* "½d" *as above and with a thin black line cancelling old value.*

36 ½d. on 5s. green .. .. 1·00 1·10
a. Surch. double .. .. £100 90·00
b. Surch. inverted .. ..
c. Surch. double, both inverted ..

3d (a) 3d (b) 3d (c)

3d (d) 3d (e)

1882. *No.* 19 *surch. as above with thin black line cancelling value.*

38 3d. on 4d. ultramarine (*a*) .. 11·00 8·00
a. Surch double .. .. — £150
39 3d. on 4d. ultramarine (*b*) .. 7·50 7·00
a. Surch. double .. .. — £150
40 3d. on 4d. ultramarine (*c*) .. 7·50 7·00
a. Surch. double .. .. — £150
41 3d. on 4d. ultramarine (*d*) .. 10·00 7·00
a. Surch. double .. .. — £140
42 3d. on 4d. ultramarine (*e*) .. 38·00 21·00
a. Surch. double .. .. — £150

1883–84.

48 1 ½d. chestnut 35 25
49 „ 2d. pale mauve 65 25
50 „ 2d. bright mauve 65 25
51 „ 3d. ultramarine .. .. 1·00 80

For 1d. purple, see No. 68.

2d (a) 2d (b)

1888 (Sept.–Oct.). *No.* 51 *surch. as above.*

(*a*) *Wide* "2". (*b*) *Narrow* "2".

52 2d. on 3d. ultram. (*a*) (Sept.) .. 3·75 3·00
a. Surch. inverted .. .. — £110
53 2d. on 3d. ultramarine (*b*) .. 2·25 1·00
a. Surch. inverted .. .. — £110

A variety exists having "2" with a curly tail.

1d (a) 1d (b) Id (c)

1890 (Dec.)–**1891** (Mar.). *Nos.* 51 *and* 19 *surch. as above.*

54 1d. on 3d. ultramarine (*a*) .. 45 45
a. Surch. double .. .. 24·00
b. Surch. double (*a*) & (*b*) .. 32·00
c. "1" and "d" wide apart .. 42·00 38·00
55 1d. on 3d. ultramarine (*b*) .. 2·00 1·50
a. Surch. double .. .. 32·00
57 1d. on 4d. ultramarine (*a*) .. 4·50 1·50
a. Surch. double .. .. 32·00 30·00
b. Surch. double (*a*) & (*b*) ..
58 1d. on 4d. ultramarine (*b*) .. 16·00 14·00
a. Surch. double .. .. 55·00
59 1d. on 4d. ultramarine (*c*) .. £110 90·00

The settings of the 1d. on 3d. and on 4d. are not identical. The variety (*c*) does not exist on the 3d.

2½d.

1892 (Oct.). *No.* 51 *surch. as above.*

67 2½d. on 3d. ultramarine .. 50 30
a. No stop after "d" .. .. 7·50

1894 (Sept.). *Colour changed.*

68 1 1d. purple 20 20

½d (a) ½d (b) ½d (c)

½d (d) ½d (e) ½d (f) ½d (g)

Types (*a*) and (*e*) differ from types (*b*) and (*f*) respectively, in the serifs of the "1", but owing to faulty overprinting this distinction is not always clearly to be seen.

1896 (Sept.). *No.* 51 *surch. as above.*

69 ½d. on 3d. ultramarine (*a*) .. 50 65
70 ½d. on 3d. ultramarine (*b*) .. 1·40 1·50
71 ½d. on 3d. ultramarine (*c*) .. 1·50 1·50
72 ½d. on 3d. ultramarine (*d*) .. 1·50 1·50
73 ½d. on 3d. ultramarine (*e*) .. 1·40 1·50
74 ½d. on 3d. ultramarine (*f*) .. 1·25 1·25
75 ½d. on 3d. ultramarine (*g*) .. 75 1·00

Variety. Surcharge double.

76 ½d. on 3d. ultramarine .. 4·50 4·50

The double surcharges are often different types, but are always type (*g*), or in combination with type (*g*).

Halve
Penny.

1896. *No.* 51 *surch. as above.*

77 ½d. on 3d. ultramarine .. 20 20

Varieties. (i.) *Errors in setting.*

78 ½d. on 3d. (no stop) .. 3·75 3·75
79 ½d. on 3d. ("Peuny") .. 4·50 4·50
80 ½d. on 3d. (no bar) .. 1·60 1·50
80*a* ½d. on 3d. (no bar or stop) ..
80*b* ½d. on 3d. (no bar and "Peuny")

(ii.) *Surch. inverted.*

81 ½d. on 3d. .. .. .. 10·00
81*a* ½d. on 3d. (no stop) .. ..
81*b* ½d. on 3d. ("Peuny") .. ..

(iii.) *Surch. double, one inverted.*

81*c* ½d. on 3d. (Nos. 77 and 81) .. 55·00 55·00
81*d* ½d. on 3d. (Nos. 77 and 81*a*) .. £140
81*e* ½d. on 3d. (Nos. 77 and 81*b*) .. £150
81*f* ½d. on 3d. (Nos. 81 and 78) ..
82 ½d. on 3d. (Nos. 81 and 79) .. — £150

Nos. 69 to 75 also exist surcharged as last but they are considered not to have been issued with authority.

2½

1897 (1 Jan.). *No.* 51 *surch. as above.*

(*a*) *As in illustration.*

(*b*) *With Roman* "1" *and antique* "2" *in fraction.*

83 2½ on 3d. ultramarine (*a*) .. 50 50
83*a* 2½ on 3d. ultramarine (*b*) .. 32·00 27·00

1897.

84 1 ½d. yellow (March) 20 20
85 „ ½d. orange 20 20
87 „ 1s. brown (Aug.) .. .. 1·50 1·00

The 6d. blue was prepared for use in the Orange Free State, but had not been brought into use when the stamps were seized in Bloemfontein. A few have been seen without the "V.R.I." overprint, but they were not authorized or available for postage. (*Price* £15.)

II. BRITISH OCCUPATION.

V. R. I.

4d

31. (Level stops.)

(Surch. by Messrs. Curling, Bloemfontein.)

1900. *T* **1** *surch. as T* **31/33** (2½ *on* 3*d. optd.* "V.R.I." *only*).

(*a*) *First printings surch. as T* **31** *with stops level* (March).

101 ½d. orange 40 20
a. No stop after "V" .. 5·50 5·50
b. No stop after "I" .. 45·00 45·00
c. "½" omitted .. .. 45·00 45·00
d. "I" omitted .. ..
e. "V.R.I." omitted .. 50·00
f. Value omitted .. .. 28·00
g. Small "½" .. .. 14·00 14·00
h. Surch. double .. .. 15·00
102 1d. purple 20 20
a. Error. Brown .. .. 50·00 48·00
b. No stop after "V" .. 4·00 4·00
c. No stop after "R" .. 50·00
d. No stop after "I" ..
e. "1" omitted .. .. 38·00
f. "I" omitted .. .. 14·00 14·00
g. "I" and stop after "R" omitted .. .. .. 14·00 14·00
h. "V.R.I." omitted .. 60·00
i. "d" omitted .. .. 80·00
j. Value omitted .. .. 32·00
k. Inverted stop after "R" .. 60·00
l. Wider space between "1" and "d" .. .. .. 42·00 42·00
m. "V" and "R" close .. 50·00
n. Pair, one without surch. .. 75·00
103 2d. bright mauve 20 20
a. No stop after "V" .. 3·75 3·75
b. No stop after "R" .. £140
c. No stop after "I" ..
d. "V.R.I." omitted .. 70·00
104 2½ on 3d. ultramarine (*a*) .. 1·50 1·40
a. No stop after "V" .. 20·00 20·00
105 2½ on 3d. ultramarine (*b*) .. 45·00 45·00
106 3d. ultramarine 20 20
a. No stop after "V" .. 3·75 3·75
b. Pair, one without surch. ..
107 4d. ultramarine .. .. 1·25 1·10
a. No stop after "V" .. 14·00 14·00
108 6d. bright carmine .. .. 16·00 15·00
a. No stop after "V" .. 80·00 80·00
b. "6" omitted .. .. 80·00 80·00
109 6d. blue 60 50
a. No stop after "V" .. 7·50 7·50
b. "6" omitted .. .. 12·00 12·00
c. "V.R.I." omitted ..
110 1s. brown 60 60
a. Error. Orange-yellow .. — £140
b. No stop after "V" .. 7·50 7·50
c. "1" omitted .. .. 30·00 30·00
d. "1" omitted and spaced stop after "s" .. .. 30·00
e. "V.R.I." omitted .. 45·00 38·00
f. Value omitted .. .. — 45·00
g. Raised stop after "s" .. 3·75 3·75
h. Wider space between "1" and "s" .. .. .. 45·00
111 5s. green .. .. .. 6·00 5·50
a. No stop after "V" .. 75·00 70·00
b. "5" omitted £225
c. Inverted stop after "R" .. £120
d. Wider space between "5" and "s" .. .. .. 38·00 38·00

All values are found with a rectangular stop instead of an oval stop after "R". Misplaced surcharges (upwards or sideways) also occur.

V. R. I. **V. R. I.**

½d (32) (Raised stops.) **½d** (33)

Thin "V" Thick "V"

(*b*) *Subsequent printings.* (i) *Surch. as T* **32**.

112 ½d. orange 20 20
a. Raised and level stops mixed 60 70
b. Pair, one with level stops .. 2·75 3·50
c. No stop after "V" .. 75 75
d. No stop after "I" .. .. 7·50 7·50
e. "V" omitted .. .. 80·00
f. Small "½" .. .. 3·75 4·00
g. As a, and small "½" .. 3·75 4·00
h. As b, and small "½"
i. Space between "V" and "R"
113 1d. purple 20 20
a. Raised and level stops mixed 45 50
b. Pair, one with level stops .. 5·50 5·50
c. No stop after "V" .. 1·50 1·50
d. No stop after "R" .. 3·75 3·75
e. No stop after "I" .. .. 3·75 4·00
f. No stops after "V" and "I" £140
g. Surch. inverted .. .. 75·00
h. Surch. double .. .. 23·00 20·00
i. Pair, one without surch. ..
j. Short figure "1" .. ..
k. Space between "V" and "R" 23·00 27·00
l. Space between "R" and "I" 27·00
m. Space between "1" and "d" 48·00
114 2d. bright mauve 20 20
a. Raised and level stops mixed 2·00 2·00
b. Pair, one with level stops .. 2·25 2·25
c. Surch. inverted .. .. 48·00
d. "I" raised .. ..
115 2½ on 3d. ultramarine (*a*) .. 48·00 45·00
a. Raised and level stops mixed
116 2½ on 3d. ultramarine (*b*) .. £350
117 3d. ultramarine 20 20
a. Raised and level stops mixed 2·00 2·00
b. Pair, one with level stops .. 3·75 3·75
c. No stop after "V" .. 45·00
d. No stop after "R" ..
e. "I" omitted .. .. 75·00
f. Surch. double .. .. 90·00
g. Surch. double, one diag. .. 90·00
h. Do., diag. surch. with mixed stops .. .. ..
118 4d. ultramarine 60 50
a. Raised and level stops mixed 2·00
b. Pair, one with level stops .. 5·00 5·00
119 6d. bright carmine .. .. 11·00 9·00
a. Raised and level stops mixed 48·00 50·00
b. Pair, one with level stops 50·00
120 6d. blue 35 20
a. Raised and level stops mixed 2·25 2·25
b. Pair, one with level stops .. 5·50 5·50
c. No stop after "V" ..
121 1s. brown 35 45
a. Error. Orange-yellow .. £110
b. Raised and level stops mixed 3·75
c. Pair, one with level stops .. 5·50 5·50
d. No stop after "V" .. ..
e. No stop after "R" .. ..
f. "s" omitted .. .. 30·00
122 5s. green (Optd. S. £15) .. 1·50 1·10
a. Raised and level stops mixed 75·00 75·00
b. Pair, one with level stops .. £250
c. Short top to "5" .. .. 18·00 18·00

(ii) *Surch. as T* **33**.

123 ½d. orange 20 20
124 1d. purple 20 20
a. Inverted "1" for "I" .. 3·75 3·75
b. No stops after "R" and "I" 27·00 27·00
c. No stop after "R" .. .. 11·00 11·00
d. Surch. double .. .. — 60·00
125 2d. bright mauve 20 20
a. Inverted "1" for "I" .. 5·50 5·00
126 2½ on 3d. ultramarine (*a*) .. £190
127 2½ on 3d. ultramarine (*b*) ..
128 3d. ultramarine 45 50
a. Inverted "1" for "I" .. 27·00 15·00
129 6d. bright carmine £140
130 6d. blue .. .. .. 1·25 1·50
131 1s. brown .. .. .. 1·50 1·60
132 5s. green .. .. .. 2·00 2·00

Stamps with thick "V" occur in certain positions in *later* settings of the type with stops above the line (T **32**). *Earlier* settings with stops above the line have all stamps with thin "V".

Some confusion was caused by the listing of certain varieties as though they occurred on stamps with thick "V", whereas they occur in panes of the thick "V" settings, but on stamps showing the normal thin "V".

All varieties which occur on stamps with thin "V" are shown under that heading, whether they occur in panes of the thick "V" settings or not.

As small blocks of unsurcharged Free State stamps could be handed in for surcharging, varieties thus occur which are not found in the complete settings.

III. BRITISH COLONY.

ORANGE RIVER COLONY.
(34)

1900–2. *Cape of Good Hope stamps (wmk. Cabled Anchor. P* 14) *optd. with T* **34**.

133 **17** ½d. green (Oct. 1900) .. 15 12
a. No stop .. .. 4·50 4·50
b. Opt. double £160
134 ,, 1d. carmine (July, 1902) .. 25 25
a. No stop .. .. 5·50 5·50
135 **15** 2½d. ultram. (Aug., 1900) 25 25
a. No stop .. .. 11·00 11·00

In the ½d. and 2½d., the "no stop" after "COLONY" variety was the first stamp in the left lower pane. In the 1d. it is the twelfth stamp in the right lower pane on which the stop was present at the beginning of the printing but became damaged and soon failed to print.

E. R. I.

4d (35) **6d** (36) **One Shilling** * (37)

1902 (Feb.). *Surch. with T* **35**.

136 4d. on 6d. blue (No. 120) (R.) 25 25
a. No stop after "R" .. .. 9·00 9·00
b. No stop after "I" .. ..
c. Thick "V" .. .. 1·10 1·50
d. Thick "V" and inverted "1" for "I" .. .. .. 2·25 2·25

1902 (Aug.). *Surch. with T* **36**.

137 **1** 6d. blue 75 75
a. Surch. double, one inverted .. £150
b. Wide space between "6" and "d" .. .. .. 20·00 20·00

1902 (Oct.). *Surch. with T* **37**.

138 **1** 1s. on 5s. green (O.) .. 1·60 2·00
a. Thick "V" .. .. 3·50 3·75
b. Short top to "5" .. .. 24·00 24·00
c. Surch. double .. ..

38. King Edward VII, Springbok and Gnu.

(Typo. D.L.R.)

1903–4. *Wmk. Crown CA.* *P* 14.

139 **38** ½d. yellow-green 20 1
140 ,, 1d. scarlet 15 1
141 ,, 2d. brown 65 6
142 ,, 2½d. bright blue 30 3
143 ,, 3d. mauve 50 3
144 ,, 4d. scarlet and sage-green 1·25 1·1
a. "IOSTAGE" for "POSTAGE" £200 £15
145 ,, 6d. scarlet and mauve .. 90 4
146 ,, 1s. scarlet and bistre .. 2·75 8
147 ,, 5s. blue and brown (1904) 14·00 7·0
139/147 .. .. .. *Set of* 9 20·00 9·0
139/147 Optd. "Specimen" *Set of* 9 60·00

Several of the above values are found with th overprint "C.S.A.R.", in black, for use by th Central South African Railways.

1905–9. *Wmk. Mult. Crown CA.* *P* 14.

148 **38** ½d. yellow-green (1907) .. 15 1
149 ,, 1d. scarlet 15 1
150 ,, 4d. scarlet and sage-green 1·00 4
a. "IOSTAGE" for "POSTAGE" .. .. .. 55·00 48·0
151 ,, 1s. scarlet and bistre ('09) 8·00 1·5

POSTCARD STAMPS.

Postage stamps of Type **1** (tree), of several lenominations, surcharged or unsurcharged, overprinted with Arms similar to above illustration, and in some cases surcharged in addition, were for use on postcards, the overprinting being done after the stamps were affixed to the cards.

FISCAL STAMPS USED FOR POSTAGE.

The following were issued in 1878 (Nos. F1 and F3 in 1882) and were authorised for postal use between 1882 and 1886.

F 1

F 2

(Typo. D.L.R.)

1882–86. *P* 14.

1	F 1	6d. pearl-grey	30	1·40
2	,,	6d. purple-brown ..	—	1·40
3	F 2	1s. purple-brown ..	50	2·75
4	,,	1s. pearl-grey	—	5·50
5	,,	1s. 6d. blue	90	50
6	,,	2s. magenta	90	50
7	,,	3s. chestnut	1·40	5·50
8	,,	4s. grey		
9	,,	5s. rose	1·40	
10	,,	6s. green	—	5·50
11	,,	7s. violet		
12	,,	10s. orange	3·00	
13	,,	£1 purple	4·50	
14	,,	£2 red-brown	2·75	
14*a*	,,	£4 carmine		
15	,,	£5 green	7·50	2·75

The 8s. yellow was prepared but we have no evidence of its use postally without surcharge Type F **3**.

ZES PENCE.

(F **3**)

1886. *Surch. with Type* F **3**.

16	F **2**	6d. on 4s. grey		
17	,,	6d. on 8s. yellow ..	18·00	

Postage stamps overprinted for use as Telegraph stamps and used postally are omitted as it is impossible to say with certainty which stamps were genuinely used for postal purposes.

Stamps of SOUTH AFRICA are now in use.

PAKISTAN.

I. DOMINION.

PAKISTAN (1) **PAKISTAN** (2)

1947. *Stamps of India, optd. by offset-litho. at Nasik, as T* **1** (*3 p. to 12 a.*) *or* **2** (*14 a. and rupee values*).

1	**100***a*	3 p. slate	5	5
2	,,	½ a. purple	5	5
3	,,	9 p. green	5	5
4	,,	1 a. carmine	5	5
5	**101**	1½ a. dull violet	5	5
6	,,	2 a. vermilion	5	5
7	,,	3 a. bright violet ..	5	5
8	,,	3½ a. bright blue	10	20
9	**102**	4 a. brown	5	5
10	,,	6 a. turquoise-green ..	12	10
11	,,	8 a. slate-violet	12	5
12	,,	12 a. lake	20	8
13	**103**	14 a. purple	25	25
14	**100**	1 r. grey and red-brown	25	20
		a. Overprint omitted in pair with normal ..	£160	
		b. Overprint inverted ..	48·00	
15	,,	2 r. purple and brown ..	50	30
16	,,	5 r. green and blue ..	85	50
17	,,	10 r. purple and claret ..	2·00	1·10
18	,	15 r. brown and green ..	3·50	2·75
19	,,	25 r. slate-violet & purple	5·50	5·00
1/19		.. .. *Set of* 19	12·00	10·00

Numerous provisional "PAKISTAN" overprints, both hand-stamped and machine-printed, in various sizes and colours, on Postage and Official stamps, also exist.

These were made under authority of Provincial Governments, District Head Postmasters or Local Postmasters and are of considerable philatelic interest.

The 1 a. 3 p. (India No. 269) exists only as a local issue (*price*, Peshawar opt., 25 *p. un.*; 50 *p. us.*).

3. Constituent Assembly Building, Karachi.

4. Karachi Airport Entrance.

5. Gateway to Lahore Fort.

6. Crescent and Stars.

(Des. A. R. Chughtai (1 r.). Recess. D.L.R.)

1948 (9 July). *Independence. P* 13½×14 *or* 11½ (1 *r.*).

20	**3**	1½ a. ultramarine	5	5
21	**4**	2½ a. green	5	5
22	**5**	3 a. purple-brown	5	5
23	**6**	1 r. scarlet	15	15
		a. Perf. 14×13½	2·00	2·00

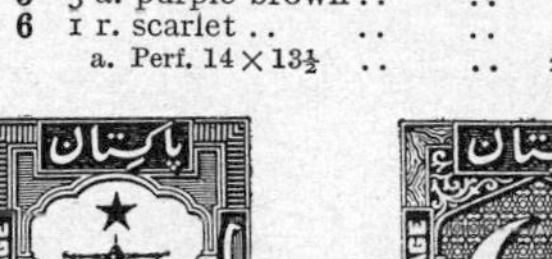

7. Scales of Justice. **8.** Star and Crescent.

9. Lloyds Barrage. **11.** Karachi Port Trust.

10. Karachi Airport.

12. Salimullah Hostel, Dacca University.

13. Khyber Pass.

(Recess. Pakistan Security Ptg. Corp., Ltd., Karachi (P 13 and 13½), D.L.R. (others).)

1948 (14 Aug.)–**56**?

24	**7**	3 p. red (*p.* 12½) ..	5	5
		a. Perf. 13½ ('54?) ..	5	5
25	,,	6 p. violet (*p.* 12½)	5	5
		a. Perf. 13½ ('54?) ..	5	5
26	,,	9 p. green (*p.* 12½)	5	5
		a. Perf. 13½ ('54?) ..	8	5
27	**8**	1 a. blue (*p.* 12½) ..	5	5
28	,,	1½ a. grey-green (*p.* 12½) ..	5	5
29	,,	2 a. red (*p.* 12½) ..	5	5
30	**9**	2½ a. green (*p.* 14×13½)	5	5
31	**10**	3 a. green (*p.* 13½×14)	5	5
32	**9**	3½ a. brt. blue (*p.* 14×13½)	12	10
33	,,	4 a. reddish brown (*p.* 12½)	10	10
34	**11**	6 a. blue (*p.* 14×13½)	5	5
35	,,	8 a. black (*p.* 12½)	8	5
36	**10**	10 a. scarlet (*p.* 13½×14) ..	12	12
37	**11**	12 a. scarlet (*p.* 14×13½) ..	10	10
38	**12**	1 r. ultram. (*p.* 13½×14) ..	20	10
		a. Perf. 13½ ('54) ..	60	30
39	,,	2 r. chocolate (*p.* 13½×14)	40	15
		a. Perf. 13½ ('54?) ..	1·00	50
40	,,	5 r. carmine (*p.* 13½×14)	1·25	20
		a. Perf. 13½ (7.53) ..	1·25	40
41	**13**	10 r. magenta (*p.* 14×13½)	2·50	2·25
		a. Perf. 12 ..	3·50	70
		b. Perf. 13 ('51) ..	4·00	80
42	,,	15 r. blue-green (*p.* 12)	2·50	85
		a. Perf. 14×13½ ..	4·00	4·00
		b. Perf. 13 ('56?) ..	4·00	4·50
43	,,	25 r. violet (*p.* 14×13½)	4·00	4·50
		a. Perf. 12 ..	5·50	2·00
		b. Perf. 13 ('54) ..	6·00	3·00
24/43		.. *Set of* 20	11·00	4·25

For 25 r. with W **98**, see No. 210.

14

(Recess. D.L.R.)

1949 (11 Sept.). *First Death Anniv. of Mahomed Ali Jinnah.* T **14** *and similar type. P* 13½×14.

44	**14**	1½ a. brown ..	20	20
45	,,	3 a. green ..	20	20
46	–	10 a. black ..	85	85

Design:—10 a. Inscription reads "QUAID-I-AZAM/MOHAMMAD ALI JINNAH" etc.

15. Star and Crescent.

16. Karachi Airport.

(Recess. Pakistan Security Ptg. Corp. (P 13½), D.L.R. (others).)

1949–53? *Redrawn. Crescent moon with points to left as T* **15/16.**

47	**15**	1 a. blue (*p.* 12½) ..	5	5
		a. Perf. 13½ ('53?) ..	5	5
48	,,	1½ a. grey-green (*p.* 12½) ..	5	5
		a. Perf. 13½ ('52?) ..	5	5
49	,,	2 a. red (*p.* 12½) ..	5	5
		a. Perf. 13½ ('53?) ..	5	5
50	**16**	3 a. green (*p.* 13½×14) ..	10	8
51	**11**	6 a. blue (*p.* 14×13½) ..	20	5
52	,,	8 a. black (*p.* 12½) ..	20	5
53	**16**	10 a. scarlet (*p.* 13½×14) ..	20	20
54	**11**	12 a. scarlet (*p.* 14×13½) ..	30	15
47/54		.. .. *Set of* 8	85	40

17. Pottery.

I.   II.

18. Aeroplane and Hour-glass.

19. Saracenic Leaf Pattern.

20. Archway and Lamp.

(Des. A. R. Chughtai. Recess. De La Rue, later printings, Pakistan Security Ptg. Corp.)

1951 (14 Aug.)–**56.** *Fourth Anniv. of Independence. P* 13.

55	**17**	2½ a. carmine	5	5
56	**18**	3 a. purple	5	5
57	**17**	3½ a. blue (I)	20	20
57*a*	,,	3½ a. blue (II) (Dec. '56) ..	12	12
58	**19**	4 a. green	8	5
59	,,	6 a. brown-orange ..	8	5
60	**20**	8 a. sepia	10	5
61	,,	10 a. violet	10	8
62	**18**	12 a. slate	15	5
55/62		.. .. *Set of* 9	75	50

The above and the stamps issued on the 14th August 1954, 1955 and 1956, are basically definitive issues, although issued on the Anniversary date of Independence.

21. "Scinde Dawk" stamp and Ancient and Modern Transport.

(Recess. D.L.R.)

1952 (14 Aug.). *Centenary of "Scinde Dawk" Issue of India. P* 13.

63	**21**	3 a. deep olive/*yellow-olive*	25	25
64	,,	12 a. deep brown/*salmon* ..	50	50

PRINTERS. All issues up to No. 219 were recess-printed by the Pakistan Security Printing Corporation, *unless otherwise stated.*

22. Kaghan Valley.

23. Mountains, Gilgit.

24. Badshahi Mosque, Lahore. (*As T* **23.**)

25. Mausoleum of Emperor Jehangir, Lahore (*As T* **22.**)

26. Tea Plantation, East Pakistan.

27. Cotton Plants, West Pakistan. (*As T* **26.**)

28. Jute Fields and River, East Pakistan. (*As T* **26.**)

1954 (14 Aug.). *Seventh Anniv. of Independence P* 13½ (14 *a.*, 1 *r.*, 2 *r.*) *or* 13 (*others*).

65	**22**	6 p. reddish violet ..	5	5
66	**23**	9 p. blue	5	15
67	**24**	1 a. carmine	5	5
68	**25**	1½ a. red	5	5
69	**26**	14 a. deep green	20	10
70	**27**	1 r. green	25	8
71	**28**	2 r. red-orange	40	15
65/71		.. .. *Set of* 7	90	55

29. View of K 2.

1954 (25 DEC.). *Conquest of K 2 (Mount Godwin-Austen). P* 13.
72 **29** 2 a. deep violet 12 10

30. Karnaphuli Paper Mill, Type I (Arabic fraction on left). Type II (Arabic fraction on right).

31. Textile Mill, West Pakistan.
32. Jute Mill, East Pakistan.
33. Main Sui Gas Plant.

1955 (14 AUG.)–**56.** *Eighth Anniv. of Independence. P* 13.
73 **30** 2½ a. scarlet (I) 15 15
73*a* ,, 2½ a. scarlet (II) (12.56) .. 10 10
74 **31** 6 a. deep ultramarine .. 10 5
75 **32** 8 a. deep reddish violet .. 12 5
76 **33** 12 a. carmine and orange .. 20 8
73/6 .. .. *Set of* 5 60 35

TENTH
ANNIVERSARY
UNITED NATIONS

24.10.55.

(34)

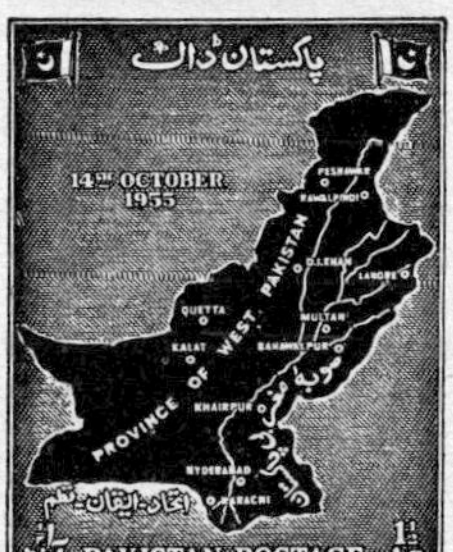

35. Map of West Pakistan.

1955 (24 OCT.). *Tenth Anniv. of United Nations. Nos.* 68 *and* 76 *optd. with T* **34.**
77 **25** 1½ a. red (B.) 75 75
78 **33** 12 a. carmine & orange (B.) 60 60
A second setting of T **34** exists in which "UNITED NATIONS" is 1 mm. further to the left.

1955 (7 DEC.). *West Pakistan Unity. P* 13½.
79 **35** 1½ a. myrtle-green 8 8
80 ,, 2 a. sepia 10 10
81 ,, 12 a. deep rose-red .. 30 30

II. REPUBLIC.

36. Constituent Assembly Building, Karachi.

(Litho. De La Rue.)

1956 (23 MAR.). *Republic Day. P* 13.
82 **36** 2 a. myrtle-green 5 5

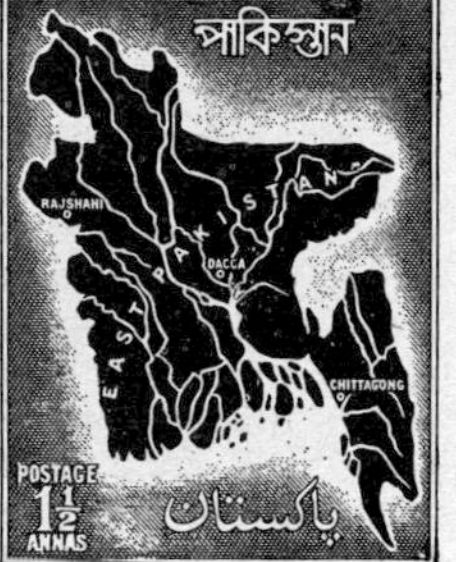

37 **38.** Map of East Pakistan.

1956 (14 AUG.). *Ninth Anniv. of Independence. P* 13½.
83 **37** 2 a. scarlet 5 5

1956 (15 OCT.). *First Session of National Assembly of Pakistan at Dacca. P* 13½.
84 **38** 1½ a. myrtle-green 5 5
85 ,, 2 a. sepia 10 10
86 ,, 12 a. deep rose-red .. 30 30

39. Karnaphuli Paper Mill, East Bengal.

40. Pottery.

41. Orange Tree.

1957 (23 MAR.). *First Anniv. of Republic. P* 13.
87 **39** 2½ a. scarlet 5 5
88 **40** 3½ a. blue 5 5
89 **41** 10 r. myrt.-grn. & yell.-orge. 1·75 75

The above and No. 95 are primarily definitive issues, although issued on the Anniversary of Republic Day.
For 10 r. with W **98**, see No. 208.

42. Pakistani Flag.

(Litho. De La Rue.)

1957 (10 MAY). *Centenary of Struggle for Independence (Indian Mutiny). P* 13.
90 **42** 1½ a. bronze-green 5 5
91 ,, 12 a. light blue 20 20

43. Pakistani Industries.

(Litho. D.L.R.)

1957 (14 AUG.). *Tenth Anniv. of Independence. P* 13½ × 14.
92 **43** 1½ a. ultramarine 5 5
93 ,, 4 a. orange-red 12 12
94 ,, 12 a. mauve 25 30

44. Coconut Tree.

1958 (23 MAR.). *Second Anniv. of Republic. P* 13.
95 **44** 15 r. red & dp. reddish pur. 2·25 1·50
This is a definitive issue, see note below No. 89.

45

(Photo. Harrison & Sons.)

1958 (21 APR.). *20th Anniv. of Death of Muhammad Iqbal (poet). P* 14½ × 14.
96 **45** 1½ a. yellow-olive & black .. 5 5
97 ,, 2 a. orange-brown & black 5 5
98 ,, 14 a. turquoise-blue & black 30 35

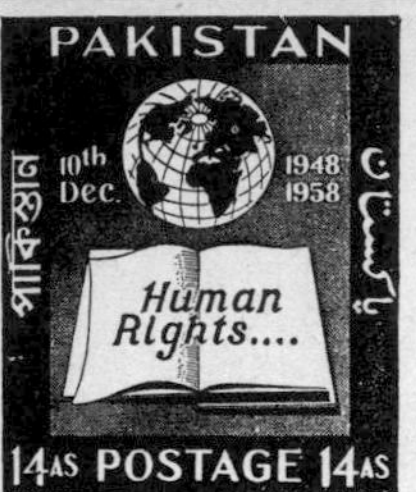

46. U.N. Charter and Globe.

PAKISTAN
BOY SCOUT
2nd NATIONAL
JAMBOREE

CHITTAGONG
Dec. 58—Jan. 59

(47)

1958 (10 Dec.). *Tenth Anniv. of Declaration of Human Rights. P* 13.

99	**46**	1½ a. turquoise-blue ..	5	5
100	,,	14 a. sepia	25	25

1958 (28 Dec.). *Second Pakistan Boy Scouts National Jamboree, Chittagong. Nos.* 65 *and* 75 *optd. with T* **47**.

101	**22**	6 p. reddish violet	5	5
102	**32**	8 a. deep reddish violet ..	30	30

REVOLUTION
DAY
Oct. 27, 1959

(48)

49. "Centenary of An Idea".

1959 (27 Oct.). *Revolution Day. No* 74 *optd. with Type* **48** *in red.*

103	**31**	6 a. deep ultramarine ..	12	12

1959 (19 Nov.). *Red Cross Commemoration. P* 13. *Recess; cross typo.*

104	**49**	2 a. red and green ..	5	5
105	,,	10 a. red and deep blue ..	20	25

50. Armed Forces Badge.

(Litho. De La Rue.)

1960 (10 Jan.). *Armed Forces Day. P* 13½ × 13.

106	**50**	2 a. red, ultram. & bl.-grn.	5	5
107	,,	14 a. red and bright blue ..	20	20

51. Map of Pakistan.

1960 (23 Mar.). *P* 13 × 13½.

108	**51**	6 p. deep purple	5	5
109	,,	2 a. brown-red	5	5
110	,,	8 a. deep green	10	8
111	,,	1 r. blue	20	20

52. Uprooted Tree.

1960 (7 Apr.). *World Refugee Year. P* 13.

112	**52**	2 a. rose-carmine ..	5	5
113	,,	10 a. green	15	20

53. Punjab Agricultural College.

54. College Arms.

1960 (10 Oct.). *Golden Jubilee of Punjab Agricultural College, Lyallpur. P* 12½ × 14.

114	**53**	2 a. slate-blue & carm.-red	5	5
115	**54**	8 a. bluish green and reddish violet	20	20

55. "Land Reforms, Rehabilitation and Reconstruction".

(Des. M. H. Hanjra. Photo. De La Rue.)

1960 (27 Oct.). *Revolution Day. P* 13 × 13½.

116	**55**	2 a. green, pink & brown	5	5
		a. Green and pink omitted	12·00	
117	,,	14 a. grn., yell. & ultram.	25	25

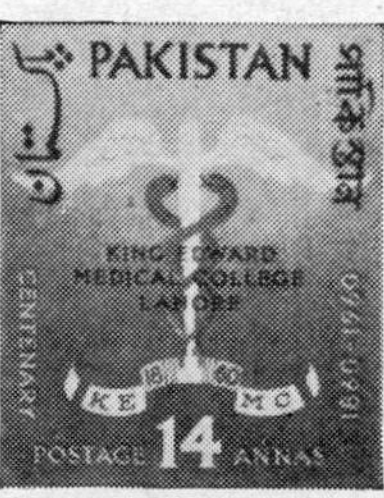

56. Caduceus.

(Photo. De La Rue.)

1960 (16 Nov.). *Centenary of King Edwar Medical College, Lahore. P* 13.

118	**56**	2 a. yellow, blk. & blue	5	5
119	,,	14 a. emer., blk. & carmine	25	25

57. "Economic Co-operation".

1960 (5 Dec.). *International Chamber of Commerc C.A.F.E.A. Meeting, Karachi. P* 13.

120	**57**	14 a. orange-red	25	25

58. Zam-Zama Gun, Lahore ("Kim's Gun," after Rudyard Kipling).

(Centre typo., background recess. Pakistan Security Ptg. Corp.)

1960 (24 Dec.). *Third Pakistan Boy Scout National Jamboree, Lahore. P* 12½ × 14.

121	**58**	2 a. carmine, yellow & deep bluish green	10	

Currency changed. 100 paisa = 1 rupee.

I PAISA

(59)

(Surch. by Pakistan Security Ptg. Corp. (Nos 123/4, 126) or by The Times Press, Karach (others).)

1961 (1 Jan.). *Surch. as T* **59**.

122	**25**	1 p. on 1½ a. red	5	
123	**7**	2 p. on 3 p. red (*p.* 13½)	5	
124	**51**	3 p. on 6 p. dp. purple	5	
		a. "PASIA" for "PAISA"	3·50	
125	**24**	7 p. on 1 a. carmine ..	12	1
126	**51**	13 p. on 2 a. brown-red ..	15	1
		a. "PAIS" for "PAISA"	3·50	
127	**37**	13 p. on 2 a. scarlet ..	15	1
122/7		.. .. *Set of* 6	50	4

No. 122. Two settings were used, the first wit figure "1" 2½ mm. tall and the second 3 mm

On the 1 p. with tall "1" and the 13 p (No. 127), the space between the figures of valu and "P" of "PAISA" varies between 1½ mm and 3 mm.

See also Nos. 262/4.

ERRORS. In the above issue and the corresponding official stamps we have listed errors in th stamps surcharged by the Pakistan Securit Printing Corp. but have not included the ver large number of errors which occurred in th stamps surcharged by the less experienced Time Press. This was a very hurried job and there wa no time to carry out the usual checks. It is als known that some errors were not issued to th public but came on the market by other mean

NOTE. Stamps in the old currency were als *handstamped* with new currency equivalents an issued in various districts but these local issue are outside the scope of this catalogue.

60. Khyber Pass.

61. Shalimar Gardens, Lahore.

62. Chota Sona Masjid (gateway).

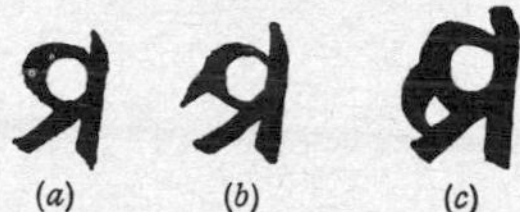

Types (a) and (b) show the first letter in the top right-hand inscription; (*a*) wrongly engraved, "SH" (*b*) corrected to "P".

On Nos. 131/2 and 134 the corrections were made individually on the plate, so that each stamp in the sheet may be slightly different.

Type (c) refers to No. 133a only.

1961–63. *No wmk. P* 13 (*T* **62**) *or* 14 (*others*).

(*a*) *Inscribed* "SHAKISTAN" *in Bengali.*

128	**60**	1 p. violet (1.1.61) ..	5	5
129	,,	2 p. rose-red (1.1.61) ..	5	5
130	,,	5 p. ultramarine (23.3.61)	5	5

(*b*) *Inscribed* "PAKISTAN" *in Bengali.*

131	**60**	1 p. violet..	5	5
132	,,	2 p. rose-red	5	5
133	,,	3 p. reddish pur. (27.10.61)	5	5
		a. Re-engraved. First letter of Bengali inscription as Type (c) ('63).. ..	5	5
134	,,	5 p. ultramarine	5	5
135	,,	7 p. emerald (23.3.61) ..	5	5
136	**61**	10 p. brown (14.8.61) ..	5	5
137	,,	13 p. slate-violet (14.8.61)	8	5
138	,,	25 p. deep blue (1.1.62) ..	8	5
139	,,	40 p. deep purple (1.1.62)	10	8
140	,,	50 p. deep bluish green (1.1.62)	15	8
141	,,	75 p. carmine-red (23.3.62)	30	8
142	,,	90 p. yellow-green (1.1.62)	30	8
143	**62**	1 r. vermilion (7.1.63) ..	25	10
144	,,	1 r. 25, reddish violet (27.10.61)	35	15
144*a*	,,	2 r. orange (7.1.63) ..	50	20
144*b*	,,	5 r. green (7.1.63) ..	1·25	40
128/144*b*		.. .. *Set of* 19	3·25	1·10

See also Nos. 170/81 and 204/7.

LAHORE STAMP
EXHIBITION
1961

(**63**)

1961 (12 FEB.). *Lahore Stamp Exhibition. Optd. with T* **63.**

145	**51**	8 a. deep green (R.) ..	15	15

64. Warsak Dam and Power Station.

1961 (1 JULY). *Completion of Warsak Hydro-Electric Project. P* 12½ × 14.

146	**64**	40 p. black and blue ..	10	10

65. Narcissus.

1961 (2 OCT.). *Child Welfare Week. P* 14.

147	**65**	13 p. turquoise-blue ..	8	8
148	,,	90 p. bright purple ..	20	20

66. Ten Roses.

1961 (4 NOV.). *Co-operative Day. P* 13.

149	**66**	13 p. rose-red & dp. green	5	5
150	,,	90 p. rose-red and blue ..	20	20

67. Police Crest and "Traffic Control".

(Photo. De La Rue.)

1961 (30 NOV.). *Police Centenary. P* 13.

151	**67**	13 p. silver, black & blue	5	5
152	,,	40 p. silver, black & red ..	15	15

RAILWAY CENTENARY 1861-1961

68. Locomotive "Eagle" of 1861.

69. Diesel Locomotive and Tracks forming "1961".

(Des. M. Thoma. Photo. De La Rue.)

1961 (31 DEC.). *Railway Centenary. P* 14.

153	**68**	13 p. green, blk. & yellow	5	5
154	**69**	50 p. yellow, black & grn.	20	25

FIRST JET FLIGHT
KARACHI-DACCA
13
Paisa

(**70**)

1962 (6 FEB.). *First Karachi-Dacca Jet Flight. No.* 87 *surch. with T* **70.**

155	**39**	13 p. on 2½ a. scarlet (R.) ..	8	8

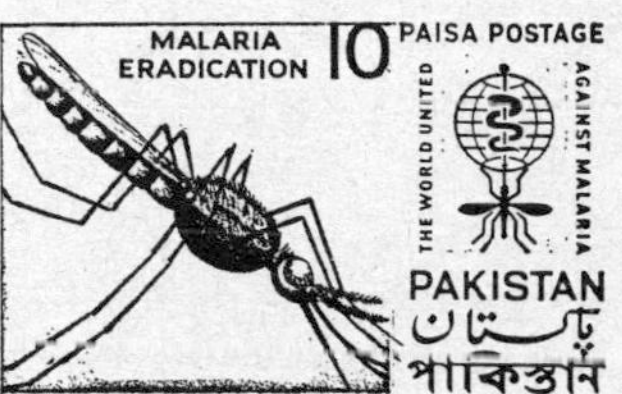

71. Mosquito.

72. Mosquito Pierced by Blade.

(Photo. D.L.R.)

1962 (7 APR.). *Malaria Eradication. P* 14.

156	**71**	10 p. black, yellow, red ..	5	5
157	**72**	13 p. blk., grnsh. yell. & red	8	5

73. Pakistan Map and Jasmine.

(Photo. Courvoisier.)

1962 (8 JUNE). *New Constitution. P* 12.

158	**73**	40 p. yellow-green, bluish green and grey ..	15	15

74. Football.

75. Hockey.

76. Squash.

77. Cricket.

1962 (14 AUG.). *Sports. P* 12½ × 14.

159	**74**	7 p. black and blue ..	5	5
160	**75**	13 p. black and green ..	5	5
161	**76**	25 p. black and purple ..	10	10
162	**77**	40 p. black & orange-brown	15	15

78. Marble Fruit Dish and Bahawalpuri Clay Flask.

79. Sports Equipment.
80. Camel-skin Lamp and Brassware.
81. Wooden Powderbowl and Basket-work.
82. Inlaid Cigarette-box and Brassware.

1962. (10 Nov.). *Small Industries.* P 13.

163	**78**	7 p. brown-lake	5	5
164	**79**	13 p. deep green	10	8
165	**80**	25 p. reddish violet ..	10	10
166	**81**	40 p. yellow-green ..	15	15
167	**82**	50 p. deep red	20	20
163/7		.. .. *Set of* 5	45	45

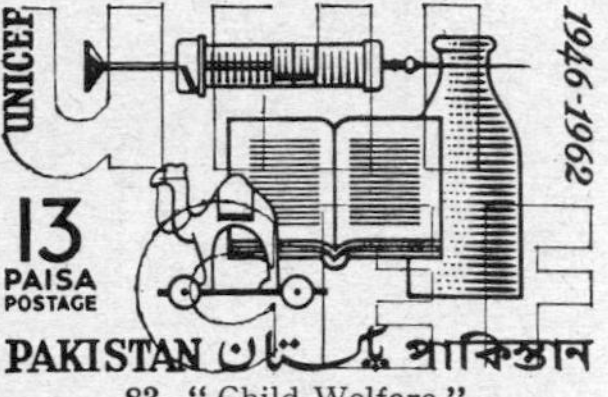

83. "Child Welfare".

(Des. M. Thoma. Photo. D.L.R.)

1962 (11 Dec.). *16th Anniv. of U.N.I.C.E.F.* P 14.

168	**83**	13 p. blk., lt. bl. & maroon	5	5
169	,,	40 p. blk., yell. & turq.-bl.	12	12

Nos. 170, etc. Nos. 131/42.

1962–70. *As T* **60/1** *but with redrawn Bengal inscription at top right. No wmk.*

170	**60**	1 p. violet ('63)	5	5
171	,,	2 p. rose-red ('64) ..	5	5
172	,,	3 p. reddish purple ('70)	5	5
173	,,	5 p. ultramarine ('63) ..	5	5
174	,,	7 p. emerald ('64) ..	5	5
175	**61**	10 p. brown ('63)	5	5
176	,,	13 p. slate-violet	5	5
176*a*	,,	15 p. brt. purple (1.1.65)	5	5
176*b*	,,	20 p. myrtle-grn. (26.1.70)	5	5
177	,,	25 p. deep blue ('63) ..	5	5
178	,,	40 p. deep purple ('64) ..	5	5
		a. Imperf. (pair)		
179	,,	50 p. dp. bluish green ('64)	5	5
180	,,	75 p. carmine-red ('64) ..	5	5
181	,,	90 p. yellow-green ('64) ..	8	5
170/81		.. .. *Set of* 14	45	45

Other values are known imperforate but we are not satisfied as to their status.

U.N.FORCE W.IRIAN

(84)

1963 (15 Feb.). *Pakistan U.N. Force in West Irian. No.* 176 *optd. with T* **84**.

182	**61**	13 p. slate-violet (R.) ..	8	5

85. "Dancing" Horse, Camel and Bull.

(Des. S. Jahangir. Photo. Courvoisier.)

1963 (13 Mar.). *National Horse and Cattle Show.* P $11\frac{1}{2}$.

183	**85**	13 p. blue, sepia and cerise	8	5

86. Wheat and Tractor.

87. Rice.

1963 (21 Mar.). *Freedom from Hunger.* P $12\frac{1}{2} \times 14$.

184	**86**	13 p. orange-brown ..	5	5
185	**87**	50 p. bistre-brown ..	15	12

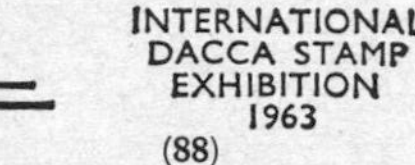

(88)

1963 (23 Mar.). *2nd International Stamp Exhibition, Dacca. Surch. with T* **88**.

186	**51**	13 p. on 2 a. brown-red ..	10	10

89. Centenary Emblem.

1963 (25 June). *Centenary of Red Cross. Recess; cross typo.* P 13.

187	**89**	40 p. red and deep olive ..	12	10

90. Paharpur.

91. Moenjodaro. (*Vert.*)
92. Taxila. (*Horiz.*)
93. Mainamati. (*Horiz.*)

1963 (16 Sept.). *Archaeological Series.* P $14 \times 12\frac{1}{2}$ (13 *p.*) *or* $12\frac{1}{2} \times 15$ (*others*).

188	**90**	7 p. ultramarine	5	5
189	**91**	13 p. sepia	10	10
190	**92**	40 p. carmine	15	15
191	**93**	50 p. deep reddish violet ..	20	20

100 YEARS OF P.W.D.
OCTOBER, 1963

13

(94)

1963 (7 Oct.). *Centenary of Public Works Department. No.* 133 *surch. with T* **94**.

192	**60**	13 p. on 3 p. reddish purp.	8	5

95. Ataturk's Mausoleum.

1963 (10 Nov.). *25th Death Anniv. of Kemal Atatürk.* P $13\frac{1}{2}$.

193	**95**	50 p. red	20	20

96. Globe and U.N.E.S.C.O. Emblem.

(Photo. De La Rue.)

1963 (10 Dec.). *15th Anniv. of Declaration of Human Rights.* P 14.

194	**96**	50 p. brown, red & ultram.	12	8

97. Thermal Power Installations.

1963 (25 Dec.). *Completion of Multan Thermal Power Station.* P $12\frac{1}{2} \times 14$.

195	**97**	13 p. ultramarine	5	5

98. Multiple Star and Crescent.

1963–75? *As Nos.* 43*b*, 89 *and* 143/44*b*, *but W* **98**.

204	**62**	1 r. vermilion	8	5
205	,,	1 r. 25, reddish vio. ('64)	10	10
		a. *Purple* (1975?)	10	10
206	,,	2 r. orange ('64)	15	10
		a. Imperf. (pair)		
207	,,	5 r. green ('64)	40	25
208	**41**	10 r. myrtle-green and yellow-orange ('68)	85	45
		a. Wmk. sideways ..		
210	**13**	25 r. violet ('68)	2·10	1·00
204/210		.. *Set of* 6	3·25	1·75

Other values exist imperforate but we are not satisfied as to their status.

99. Temple of Thot, Queen Nefertari and Maids.

100. Temple of Abu Simbel.

1964 (30 Mar.). *Nubian Monuments Preservation.* P 13×13½.
211 **99** 13 p. turq.-blue and red 5 5
212 **100** 50 p. brt. purple & black 20 20

101. " Unisphere " and Pakistan Pavilion.

102. Pakistan Pavilion on " Unisphere " (*Vert.*).

1964 (22 Apr.). *New York World's Fair.* P 12½×14 (13 *p.*) *or* 14×12½ (1 *r.* 25).
213 **101** 13 p. ultramarine .. 5 5
214 **102** 1 r. 25, ultramarine and red-orange 40 40

103. Shah Abdul Latif's Mausoleum.

1964 (25 June). *Bicentenary of Death of Shah Abdul Latif of Bhit.* P 13½×13.
215 **103** 50 p. bright blue and carmine-lake 20 20

104. Mausoleum of Quaid-i-Azam.

MINIMUM PRICE

The minimum price quoted is 5p which represents a handling charge rather than a basis for valuing common stamps. For further notes about prices see introductory pages.

105. Mausoleum.

1964 (11 Sept.). *16th Death Anniv. of Mahomed Ali Jinnah (Quaid-i-Azam).* P 13½ (15 *p.*) *or* 13 (50 *p.*).
216 **104** 15 p. emerald-green .. 5 5
217 **105** 50 p. bronze-green .. 20 20

106. Bengali and Urdu Alphabets.

1964 (5 Oct.). *Universal Children Day.* P 13.
218 **106** 15 p. brown 5 8

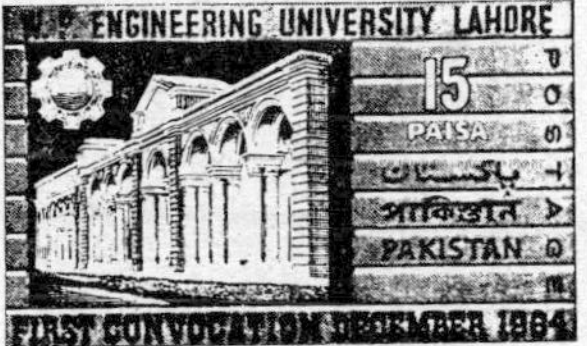

107. University Building.

1964 (21 Dec.). *First Convocation of the West Pakistan University of Engineering and Technology, Lahore.* P 12½×14.
219 **107** 15 p. chestnut 5 8

PROCESS. All the following issues were lithographed by the Pakistan Security Printing Corporation, *unless otherwise stated.*

108. " Help the Blind ".

(Des. A. Chughtai.)

1965 (28 Feb.). *Blind Welfare.* P 13.
220 **108** 15 p. ultram. and yellow 5 8

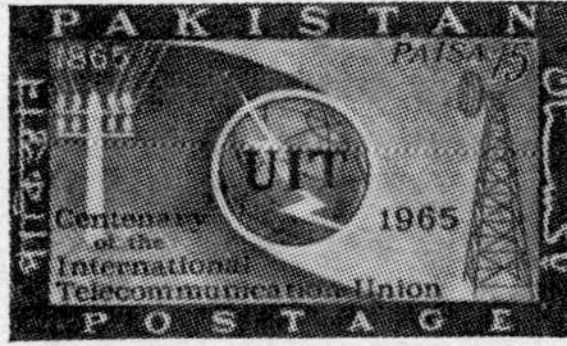

109. I.T.U. Emblem and Symbols.

1965 (17 May). *I.T.U. Centenary. Recess.* P 12½×14.
221 **109** 15 p. reddish purple .. 5 5

110. I.C.Y. Emblem.

1965 (26 June). *International Co-operation year.* P 13×13½.
222 **110** 15 p. black and light blue 5 5
223 „ 50 p. green and yellow .. 20 20

111. " Co-operation ".

112. Globe and Flags of Turkey, Iran and Pakistan.

1965 (11 July). *First Anniv. of Regional Development Co-operation Pact.* P 13½×13 (15 *p.*) *or* 13 (50 *p.*).
224 **111** 15 p. multicoloured .. 5 5
225 **112** 50 p. multicoloured .. 15 15

113. Soldier and Tanks.

114. Naval Officer and Destroyer.

115. Airman and " F-104 " Starfighters.

1965 (25 Dec.). *Pakistan Armed Forces.* P 13½×13.
226 **113** 7 p. bistre-brown, cinnamon, red & lt. blue 5 5
227 **114** 15 p. orange-brown, blackish brown, blue and light blue 5 5
228 **115** 50 p. black, orange-brown, ochre and light blue 20 20

116. Army, Navy and Air Force Crests.

1966 (13 FEB.). *Armed Forces Day. P* 13½ × 13.
229 **116** 15 p. royal blue, dull green, bright blue and buff 12 5

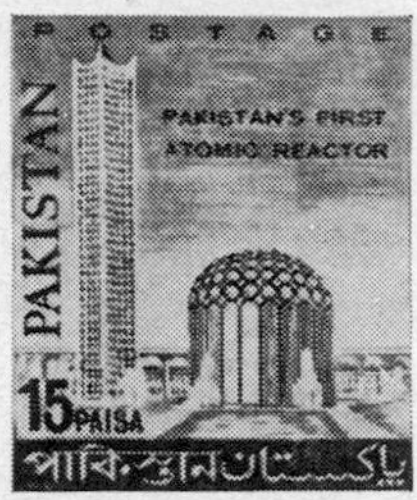

117. Atomic Reactor, Islamabad.

1966 (30 APR.). *Inauguration of Pakistan's First Atomic Reactor. Recess. P* 13.
230 **117** 15 p. black 5 5

118. Bank Crest.

1966 (25 AUG.). *Silver Jubilee of Habib Bank. P* 12½ × 14.
231 **118** 15 p. blue-green, yellow-orange and sepia .. 5 5

119. Children.

1966 (3 OCT.). *"Universal Children's Day". P* 13½.
232 **119** 15 p. black, red and pale yellow 5 5

120. U.N.E.S.C.O. Emblem.

1966 (24 NOV.). *20th Anniv. of U.N.E.S.C.O. P* 14.
233 **120** 15 p. multicoloured .. 8 8

121. Flag, Secretariat Building and President Ayub.

(*Reduced size illustration. Actual size* 57 × 27 *mm.*)

1966 (29 NOV.). *Islamabad* (*new capital*). *P* 13.
234 **121** 15 p. deep bluish green, chestnut, light blue and bistre-brown .. 5 5
235 ,, 50 p. deep bluish green, chestnut, light blue and black 12 12

122. Avicenna.

1966 (3 DEC.). *Foundation of Health and Tibbi Research Institute. P* 13 × 13½.
236 **122** 15 p. dull green & salmon 5 5

123. Mohamed Ali Jinnah.

125. Emblem of Pakistan T. B. Association.

124. Tourist Year Emblem.

1966 (25 DEC.). *90th Birth. Anniv. of Mahomed Ali Jinnah. T* **123** *and similar design bearing same portrait but in different frame. Litho. and recess. P* 13.
237 **123** 15 p. black, orange and greenish blue .. 5 5
238 – 50 p. black, purple and ultramarine .. 20 20

1967 (1 JAN.). *International Tourist Year. P* 13½ × 13.
239 **124** 15 p. black, light blue and yellow-brown .. 5 8

1967 (10 JAN.). *Tuberculosis Eradication Campaign. P* 13½ × 13.
240 **125** 15 p. red, sepia & chest. 8 5

126. Scout Salute and Badge.

1967 (29 JAN.). *4th National Scout Jamboree. Photo. P* 12½ × 14.
241 **126** 15 p. light orange-brown and maroon .. 10 8

127. "Justice".

1967 (17 FEB.). *Centenary of West Pakistan High Court. P* 13.
242 **127** 15 p. black, slate, light red and slate-blue.. 10 8

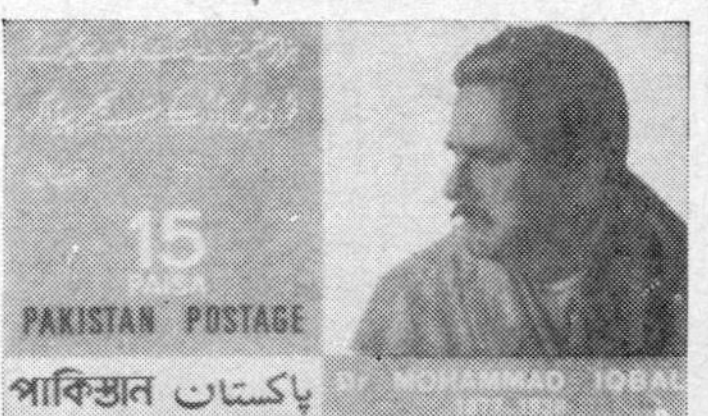

128. Dr. Mohammad Iqbal (philosopher).

1967 (21 APR.). *Iqbal Commemoration. P* 13.
243 **128** 15 p. sepia and light red 5 5
244 ,, 1 r. sepia and deep green 30 30

129. Hilal-i-Isteqlal Flag.

1967 (15 MAY). *Award of Hilal-i-Isteqlal (for Valour) to Lahore, Sialkot, and Sargodha. P* 13.

245 **129** 15 p. bluish green, light red, royal blue and light blue 10 8

130. " 20th Anniversary ".

1967 (14 AUG.). *20th Anniv. of Independence. Photo. P* 13.

246 **130** 15 p. red and deep bluish green 10 5

131. " Rice Exports ".

132. Cotton Plant, Yarn and Textiles.

133. Raw Jute, Bale and Bags. (*As T* **132.**)

1967 (26 SEPT.). *Pakistan Exports. Photo. P* 13 × 13½.

247 **131** 10 p. yellow, deep bluish green and deep blue 5 5
248 **132** 15 p. multicoloured .. 5 5
a. Pale orange (top panel) omitted .. .. 12·00
249 **133** 50 p. multicoloured .. 25 20

134. Clay Toys.

1967 (2 OCT.). *Universal Children's Day. P* 13.

250 **134** 15 p. multicoloured .. 5 5

135. Shah and Empress of Iran and Gulistan Palace, Teheran.

1967 (26 OCT.). *Coronation of Shah Mohammed Riza Pahlavi and Empress Farah of Iran. Recess and litho. P* 13.

251 **135** 50 p. purple, blue and light yellow-ochre .. 20 20

136. " Each For All — All for Each ".

1967 (4 NOV.). *Co-operative Day. P* 13.

252 **136** 15 p. multicoloured .. 5 5

137. Mangla Dam.

1967 (23 NOV.). *Indus Basin Project. P* 13.

253 **137** 15 p. multicoloured .. 5 8

138. Crab Pierced by Sword.

1967 (26 DEC.). *The Fight Against Cancer. P* 13.

254 **138** 15 p. red and black .. 5 5

139. Human Rights Emblem.

1968 (31 JAN.). *Human Rights Year. Photo. P* 14 × 13.

255 **139** 15 p. red and deep turquoise-blue .. 5 5
256 ,, 50 p. red, yellow and silver-grey 20 20

140. Agricultural University, Mymensingo.

1968 (28 MAR.). *First Convocation of East Pakistan Agricultural University. Photo. P* 13½ × 13.

257 **140** 15 p. multicoloured .. 5 8

141. W.H.O. Emblem.

1968 (7 APR.). *20th Anniv. of World Health Organization. Photo. P* 14 × 13.

258 **141** 15 p. green & orange-red 5 5
259 ,, 50 p. red-orange & indigo 20 20

142. Kazi Nazrul Islam (poet, composer and patriot).

1968 (25 JUNE). *Nazrul Islam Commemoration. Recess and litho. P* 13.

260 **142** 15 p. sepia and pale yellow 5 5
261 ,, 50 p. sepia & pale rose-red 20 20

4 PAISA
(143)

1968. *Nos.* 56, 74 *and* 61 *surch. as* T **143.**
262 **18** 4 p. on 3 a. purple .. 5 5
253 **31** 4 p. on 6 a. deep ultramarine (R.) (Aug.) .. 5 5
264 **20** 60 p. on 10 a. violet (R.) 30 35
a. Surch. in black .. 35 40

144. Children running with Hoops.

1968 (7 Oct.). *Universal Children's Day.* P 13.
265 **144** 15 p. multicoloured .. 5 5

145. " National Assembly ".

146. Industry and Agriculture.
147. Army, Navy and Air Force.
148. Minaret and Atomic Reactor Plant.

1968 (27 Oct.). *"A Decade of Development".* P 13.
266 **145** 10 p. multicoloured .. 5 5
267 **146** 15 p. multicoloured .. 5 5
268 **147** 50 p. multicoloured .. 20 20
269 **148** 60 p. light blue, dull purple and vermilion .. 25 25

149. Chittagong Steel Mill.

1969 (7 Jan.). *Pakistan's First Steel Mill, Chittagong.* P 13.
270 **149** 15 p. grey, light blue and pale yellow-olive .. 8 5

150. " Family ".

1969 (14 Jan.). *Family Planning.* P $13\frac{1}{2} \times 13$.
271 **150** 15 p. bright purple and pale greenish blue .. 8 5

151. Olympic Gold Medal and Hockey Player.

1969 (30 Jan.). *Olympic Hockey Champions. Photo.* P $13\frac{1}{2}$.
272 **151** 15 p. black, gold, deep green and pale blue 5 5
273 ,, 1 r. black, gold, deep green and flesh-pink 30 30

152. Mirza Ghalib and Lines of Verse.

1969 (15 Feb.). *Death Centenary of Mirza Ghalib (poet).* P 13.
274 **152** 15 p. multicoloured .. 5 5
275 ,, 50 p. multicoloured .. 20 20

The lines of verse on No. 275 are different from those in T **152.**

153. Dacca Railway Station.

1969 (27 Apr.). *First Anniv. of New Dacca Railway Station.* P 13.
276 **153** 15 p. multicoloured .. 10 5

154. I.L.O. Emblem and "1919–1969".

1969 (15 May). *50th Anniv. of International Labour Organisation.* P. $13\frac{1}{2}$.
277 **154** 15 p. buff, and bluish grn. 5 5
278 ,, 50 p. cinnamon and cerise 30 20

155. Mughal Miniature (Pakistan).

156. Safavi Miniature (Iran).
157. Ottoman Miniature (Turkey).

1969 (21 July). *Fifth Anniv. of Regiona[l] Co-operation for Development.* P 13.
279 **155** 20 p. multicoloured .. 5
280 **156** 50 p. multicoloured .. 12
281 **157** 1 r. multicoloured .. 25

158. Eastern Refinery, Chittagong.

1969 (14 Sept.). *First Oil Refinery in Eas[t] Pakistan. Photo.* P $13\frac{1}{2} \times 13$.
282 **158** 20 p. multicoloured .. 10

159. Children playing Outside " School ".

1969 (6 Oct.). *Universal Children's Day. Phot[o].* P 13.
283 **159** 20 p. multicoloured .. 8

160. Japanese Doll and P.I.A. Air Routes.

1969 (1 Nov.). *Inauguration of P.I.A. Pearl Route, Dacca–Tokyo.* P $13\frac{1}{2}\times13$.

284 **160** 20 p. multicoloured .. 5 5
a. Yellow and pink omitted 15·00
285 „ 50 p. multicoloured .. 15 20
a. Yellow and pink omitted 15·00

161. " Reflection of Light " Diagram.

1969 (4 Nov.). *Millenary Commemorative of Ibn-al-Haitham (physicist). Photo.* P 13.

286 **161** 20 p. black, lemon and light blue 8 8

162. Vickers " Vimy " and Karachi Airport.

1969 (2 Dec.). *50th Anniv. of First England–Australia Flight. Photo.* P $13\frac{1}{2}\times13$.

287 **162** 50 p. multicoloured .. 15 15

163. Flags, Sun Tower and Expo Site Plan.

1970 (15 Mar.). *World Fair, Osaka.* P 13.

288 **163** 50 p. multicoloured .. 20 20

164. New U.P.U. H.Q. Building.

1970 (20 May). *New U.P.U. Headquarters Building.* P $13\frac{1}{2}\times13$.

289 **164** 20 p. multicoloured .. 5 5
290 „ 50 p. multicoloured .. 25 15

The above in a miniature sheet, additionally inscr. " U.P.U. Day 9th Oct, 1971 ", were put on sale on that date in very limited numbers. It is understood that the rest of the printing was not issued to the public.

165. U.N. H.Q. Building.

166. U.N. Emblem.

1970 (26 June). *25th Anniv. of United Nations.* P $13\times13\frac{1}{2}$.

291 **165** 20 p. multicoloured .. 5 5
292 **166** 50 p. multicoloured .. 20 15

167. I.E.Y. Emblem, Book and Pen.

1970 (6 July). *International Education Year.* P 13.

293 **167** 20 p. multicoloured .. 5 5
294 „ 50 p. multicoloured .. 10 10

168. Saiful Malook Lake (Pakistan).

169. Seeyo-Se-Pol Bridge, Esfahan (Iran).
170. View from Fethiye (Turkey).

1970 (31 July). *Sixth Anniv. of Regional Co-operation for Development.* P 13.

295 **168** 20 p. multicoloured .. 5 5
296 **169** 50 p. multicoloured .. 10 10
297 **170** 1 r. multicoloured .. 20 20

171. Asian Productivity Symbol.

1970 (18 Aug.). *Asian Productivity Year. Photo.* P $12\frac{1}{2}\times14$.

298 **171** 50 p. multicoloured .. 12 15

172. Dr. Maria Montessori.

1970 (31 Aug.). *Birth Centenary of Dr. Maria Montessori (educationist).* P 13.

299 **172** 20 p. multicoloured .. 5 5
300 „ 50 p. multicoloured .. 15 15

173. Tractor and Fertilizer Factory.

1970 (12 Sept.). *Tenth Near East F.A.O. Regional Conference, Islamabad.* P 13.

301 **173** 20 p. bright green, and orange-brown .. 5 5

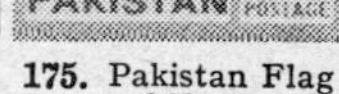

174. Children and Open Book.

175. Pakistan Flag and Text.

1970 (5 Oct.). *Universal Children's Day. Photo.* P 13.

302 **174** 20 p. multicoloured .. 5 5

1970 (7 Dec.). *General Elections for National Assembly. P* 13½×13.

303 **175** 20 p. green & bluish violet 5 5

1970 (17 Dec.). *General Elections for Provincial Assembly. As No.* 303, *but inscr.* "PROVINCIAL ASSEMBLIES 17TH DEC., 1970".

304 **175** 20 p. green & pale mag. 5 5

176. Conference Crest and burning Al-Aqsa Mosque.

(*Illustration reduced. Actual size* 55×33 *mm.*)

1970 (26 Dec.). *Conference of Islamic Foreign Ministers. Karachi. P* 13.

305 **176** 20 p. multicoloured .. 5 5

177. Coastal Embankments.

1971 (25 Feb.). *Coastal Embankments in East Pakistan Project. P* 13.

306 **177** 20 p. multicoloured .. 5 5

178. Emblem and United Peoples of the World.

1971 (21 Mar.). *Racial Equality Year. P* 13.

307 **178** 20 p. multicoloured .. 5 5

308 ,, 50 p. multicoloured .. 12 12

179. Maple Leaf Cement Factory, Daudkhel.

1971 (1 July). *20th Anniv. of Colombo Plan. P* 13.

309 **179** 20 p. brown, black and reddish violet .. 5 5

180. Chaharbagh School (Iran).

1971 (21 July). *Seventh Anniv. of Regional Co-operation for development. T* **180** *and similar horiz. designs. Multicoloured. P* 13.

310 10 p. Selimiye Mosque (Turkey) 5 5

311 20 p. Badshahi Mosque (Lahore) 5 5

312 50 p. Type **180** 15 12

181. Electric Locomotive and Boy with Toy Train.

(*Illustration reduced. Actual size* 56×26 *mm.*)

1971 (4 Oct.). *Universal Children's Day. P* 13.

313 **181** 20 p. multicoloured .. 5 5

182. Horseman and Symbols.

1971 (15 Oct.). *2500th Anniv. of Persian Monarchy. P* 13.

314 **182** 10 p. multicoloured .. 5 5

315 ,, 20 p. multicoloured .. 5 5

316 ,, 50 p. multicoloured .. 15 15

The above exist in a miniature sheet, but only a very limited quantity was put on sale. It is understood that the rest of the printing was not issued to the public.

183. Hockey-player and Trophy.

1971 (24 Oct.). *World Cup Hockey Tournament. P* 13.

317 **183** 20 p. multicoloured .. 5 5

184. Great Bath, Moenjodaro.

1971 (4 Nov.). *25th Anniv. of UNESCO and Campaign to save the Moenjodaro Excavations. P* 13.

318 **184** 20 p. multicoloured .. 5 5

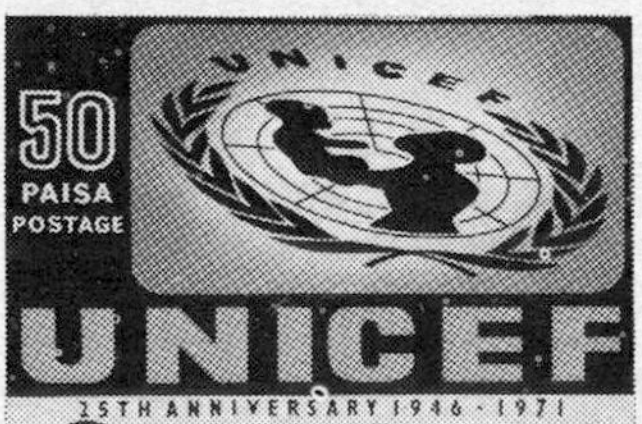

185. UNICEF Symbol.

1971 (11 Dec.). *25th Anniv. of UNICEF. P* 13.

319 **185** 50 p. multicoloured .. 15 15

186. King Hussein and Jordanian Flag.

1971 (25 Dec.). *50th Anniv. of Hashemite Kingdom of Jordan. P* 13.

320 **186** 20 p. multicoloured .. 5 5

187. Badge of Hockey Federation and Trophy.

1971 (31 Dec.). *Hockey Championships Victory. P 13.*
321 **187** 20 p. multicoloured .. 5 5

188. Reading Class.

1972 (15 Jan.). *International Book Year. P 13½.*
322 **188** 20 p. multicoloured .. 5 5

III. INDEPENDENT OF THE BRITISH COMMONWEALTH.

30th January, 1972.

For the convenience of collectors we continue to list later issues in this volume.

189. View of Venice.

1972 (7 Feb.). *U.N.E.S.C.O. Campaign to Save Venice. P 13.*
323 **189** 20 p. multicoloured .. 5 5

190. ECAFE Emblem and Discs.

1972 (28 Mar.). *25th Anniv. of ECAFE (Economic Commission for Asia and the Far East). P 13.*
324 **190** 20 p. multicoloured .. 5 5

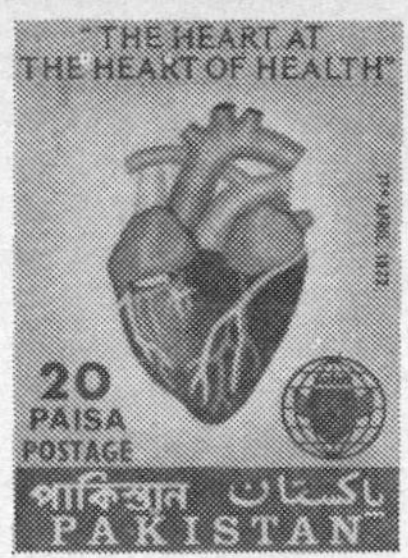

191. Human Heart.

1972 (7 Apr.). *World Health Day. P 13×13½.*
325 **191** 20 p. multicoloured .. 5 5

192. " Only One Earth ".

1972 (5 June). *U.N. Conference on the Human Environment, Stockholm. P 13×13½.*
326 **192** 20 p. multicoloured .. 5 5

193. " Fisherman " (Cevat Dereli).

1972 (31 July). *Eighth Anniv. of Regional Co-operation for Development. T* **193** *and similar vert. designs. Multicoloured. P 13.*
327 10 p. Type **193** 5 5
328 20 p. " Iranian Woman " (Behzad) 5 5
329 50 p. " Will and Power " (A. R. Chughtai) .. 10 12

194. Mahomed Ali Jinnah and Tower.

195. Donating Blood.

1972 (14 Aug.). *25th Anniv. of Independence. T* **194** *and similar horiz. designs. Multicoloured. P 13 (10 and 60 p.) or 14×12½ (20 p.).*
330 10 p. Type **194** 5 5
331 20 p. " Land Reform " .. 5 5
332 20 p. " Labour Reform " .. 5 5
333 20 p. " Education Policy " .. 5 5
334 20 p. " Health Policy " .. 5 5
335 60 p. State Bank Building .. 8 10
330/5 .. .. *Set of* 6 30 30

The 60 p. is 46×28 mm.; Nos. 331/4 are 74×23½ mm., and were printed *se-tenant* throughout the sheet.

1972 (6 Sept.). *National Blood Transfusion Service. P 13½×12½.*
336 **195** 20 p. multicoloured .. 5 5

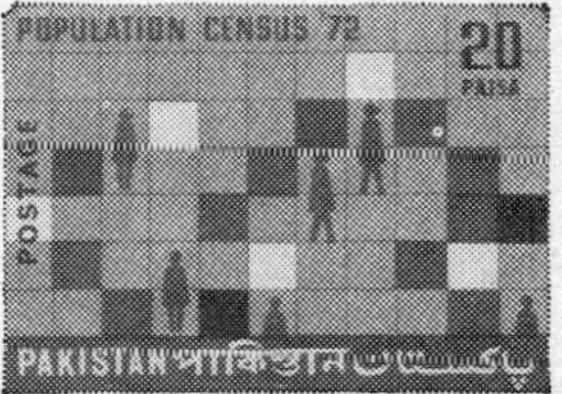

196. People and Squares.

1972 (16 Sept.). *Centenary of Population Census. P 13½.*
337 **196** 20 p. multicoloured .. 5 5

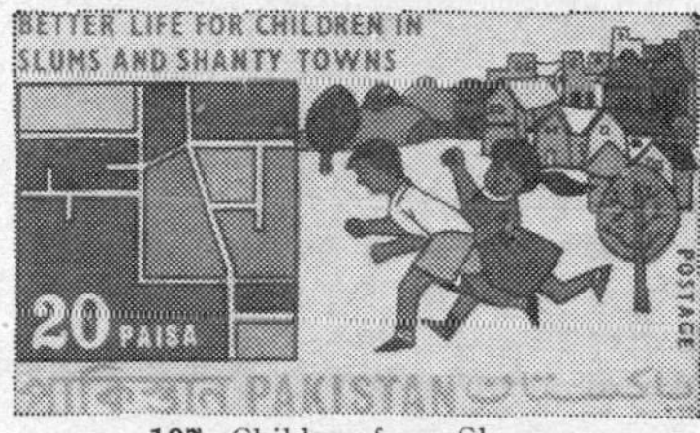

197. Children from Slums.

1972 (2 Oct.). *Universal Children's Day. P 13.*
338 **197** 20 p. multicoloured .. 5 5

198. People and Open Book.

1972 (23 Oct.). *Education Week. P 13.*
339 **198** 20 p. multicoloured .. 5 5

199. Nuclear Power Plant.

1972 (28 Nov.). *Inauguration of Karachi Nuclear Power Plant. P 13.*
340 **199** 20 p. multicoloured .. 5 5

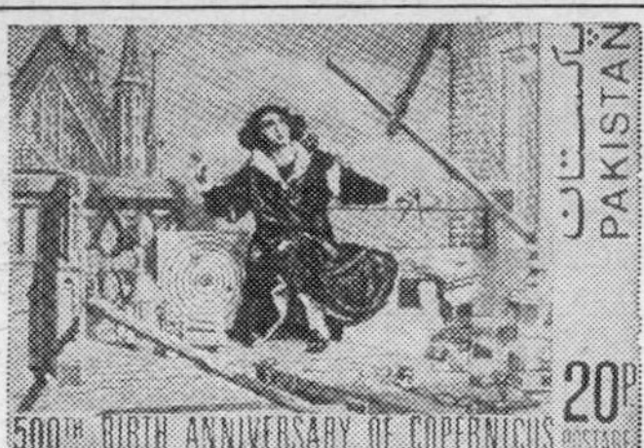

200. Copernicus in Observatory.

1973 (2 Feb.). *500th Birth Anniv. of Nicholas Copernicus (astronomer).* *P* 13.
341 **200** 20 p. multicoloured .. 5 5

201. Moenjodaro Excavations.

1973 (23 Feb.). *50th Anniv. of Moenjodaro Excavations.* *P* 13×13½.
342 **201** 20 p. multicoloured .. 5 5

202. Elements of Meteorology.

1973 (23 Mar.). *I.M.O./W.M.O. Centenary.* *P* 13.
343 **202** 20 p. multicoloured .. 5 5

203. Prisoners-of-war.

1973 (18 Apr.). *Prisoners-of-war in India.* *P* 13.
344 **203** 1 r. 25, multicoloured .. 15 20

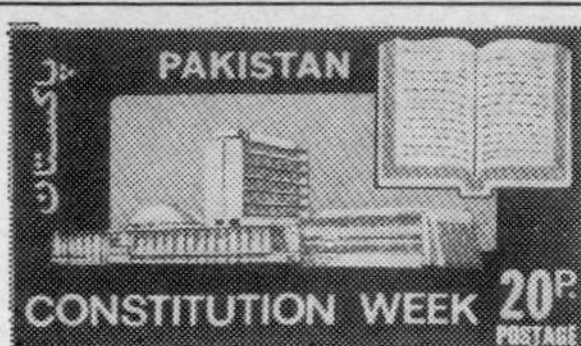

204. National Assembly Building and Constitution Book.

1973 (21 Apr.). *Constitution Week.* *P* 12½×13½.
345 **204** 20 p. multicoloured .. 5 5

205. Badge and State Bank Building.

1973 (1 July). *25th Anniv. of Pakistan State Bank.* *P* 13.
346 **205** 20 p. multicoloured .. 5 5
347 „ 1 r. multicoloured .. 12 15

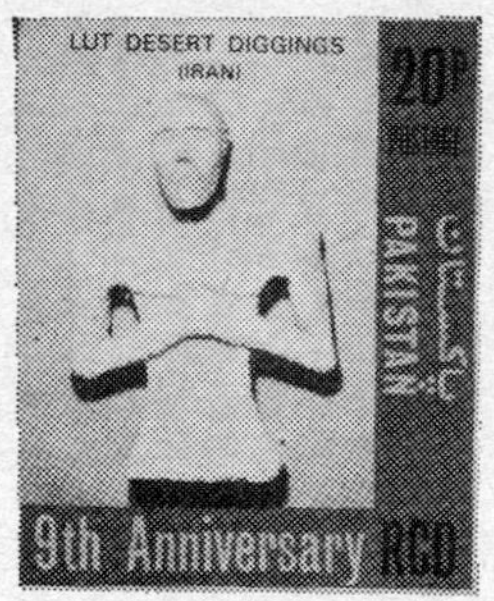

206. Lut Desert Excavations (Iran).

1973 (21 July). *9th Anniv. of Regional Co-operation for Development.* *T* **206** *and similar vert. designs. Multicoloured.* *P* 13×13½.
348 20 p. Type **206** 5 5
349 60 p. Main Street, Moenjodaro (Pakistan) 8 8
350 1 r. 25, Mausoleum of Antiochus I (Turkey) .. 12 15

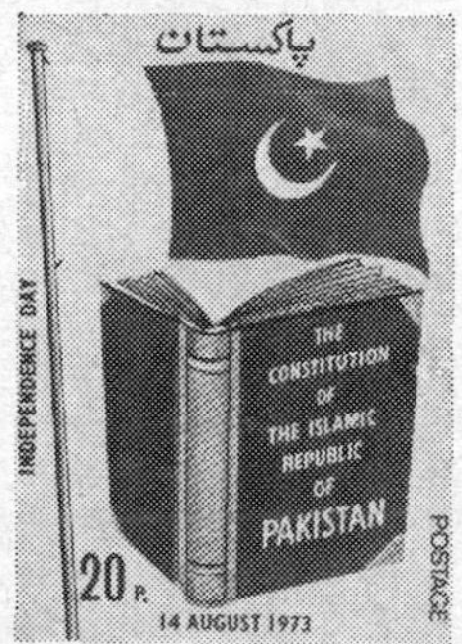

207. Constitution Book and Flag.

1973 (14 Aug.). *Independence Day and Enforcement of the Constitution.* *P* 13.
351 **207** 20 p. multicoloured .. 5 5

208. Mahomed Ali Jinnah (Quaid-i-Azam).

1973 (11 Sept.). *25th Death Anniv. of Mahomed Ali Jinnah.* *P* 13.
352 **208** 20 p. light emerald, pale yellow and black 5

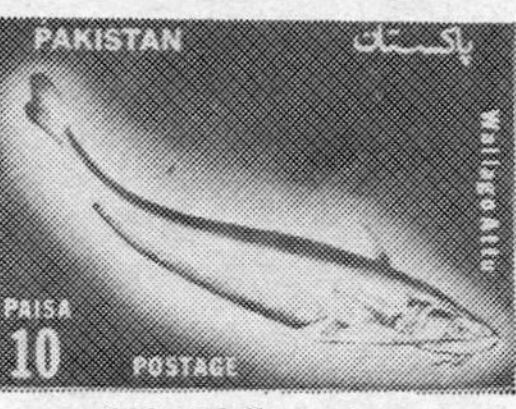

209. *Wallago attu.*

1973 (24 Sept.). *Fishes.* *T* **209** *and simila horiz. designs. Multicoloured.* *P* 13½.
353 10 p. Type **209** 5
354 20 p. *Labeo rohita* 5
355 60 p. *Tilapia mossambica* .. 15 1
356 1 r. *Catla catla* 20 2

Nos. 353/6 were printed within one shee horizontally *se-tenant*.

210. Children's Education.

1973 (1 Oct.). *Universal Children's Day.* *P* 1
357 **210** 20 p. multicoloured .. 5

211. Harvesting.

1973 (15 Oct.). *Tenth Anniv. of World Foo Programme.* *P* 13.
358 **211** 20 p. multicoloured .. 5

212. Ankara and Kemal Atatürk.

1973 (29 Oct.). *50th Anniv. of Turkish Republic. P* 13.
359 **212** 50 p. multicoloured .. 8 8

213. Boy Scout.

214. "Basic Necessities".

1973 (11 Nov.). *National Silver Jubilee, Scout Jamboree. P* 13.
360 **213** 20 p. multicoloured .. 5 5

1973 (16 Nov.). *25th Anniv. of Declaration of Human Rights. P* 13.
361 **214** 20 p. multicoloured .. 5 5

215. Al-Biruni and Nandana Hill.

1973 (26 Nov.). *Al-Biruni Millennium Congress. P* 13.
362 **215** 20 p. multicoloured .. 5 5
363 „ 1 r. 25, multicoloured 12 15

216. Dr. Hansen, Microscope and Bacillus.

1973 (29 Dec.). *Centenary of Hansen's Discovery of Leprosy Bacillus. P* 13.
364 **216** 20 p. multicoloured .. 5 5

217. Family and Emblem.

1974 (1 Jan.). *World Population Year. P* 13.
365 **217** 20 p. multicoloured .. 5 5
366 „ 1 r. 25, multicoloured 12 15

218. Conference Emblem.

1974 (22 Feb.). *Islamic Summit Conference, Lahore. T* **218** *and similar design. P* 14 × 12½ (20 *p.*) *or* 13 (65 *p.*).
367 20 p. Type **218** 5 5
368 65 p. Emblem on "Sun" (*horiz.*, 42 × 30 *mm.*) 8 8
MS369 102 × 102 mm. Nos. 367/8. Imperf. 30 30

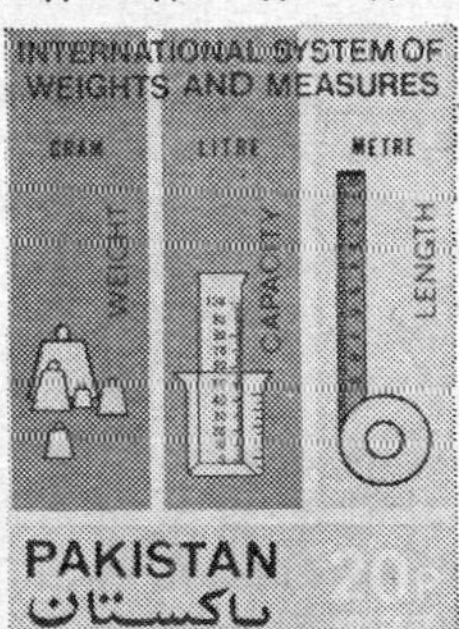

219. Units of Weight and Measurement.

1974 (1 July). *Adoption of International Weights and Measures System. P* 13.
370 **219** 20 p. multicoloured .. 5 5

220. "Chand Chauthai" Carpet, Pakistan.

1974 (21 July). *Tenth Anniv. of Regional Co-operation for Development. Vert. designs as T* **220** *showing carpets from member countries. Multicoloured. P* 13.
371 20 p. Type **220** 5 5
372 60 p. Persian carpet, 16th-century 8 8
373 1 r. Anatolian carpet, 15th-century 12 15

221. Hands protecting Sapling.

1974 (9 Aug.). *Tree Planting Day. P* 13.
374 **221** 20 p. multicoloured .. 5 5

222. Torch and Map.

1974 (26 Aug.). *Namibia Day. P* 13.
375 **222** 60 p. multicoloured .. 5 5

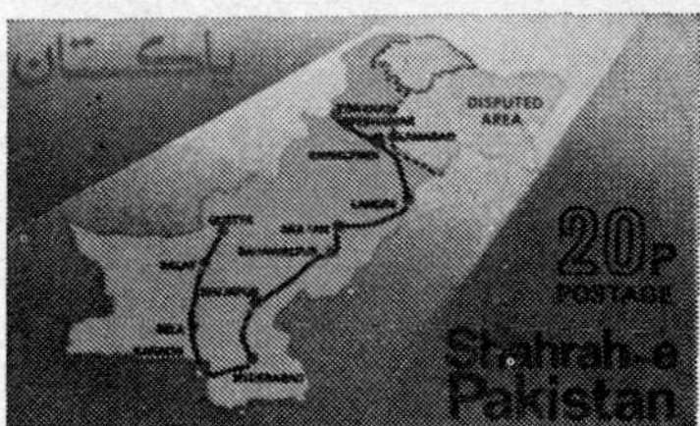

223. Highway Map.

1974 (23 Sept.). *Shahrah-e-Pakistan* (*Pakistan Highway*). *P* 13.
376 **223** 20 p. multicoloured .. 8 8

224. Boy at Desk.

1974 (7 Oct.). *Universal Children's Day.* P 13.
377 **224** 20 p. multicoloured .. 5 5

225. U.P.U. Emblem. **226.** Liaquat Ali Khan.

1974 (9 Oct.). *Centenary of Universal Postal Union. T* **225** *and similar vert. design. Multicoloured.* P 13 × 13½ (20 *p.*) *or* 13 (2 *r.* 25).
378 20 p. Type **225** 5 5
379 2 r. 25, U.P.U. emblem, aeroplane and mail-wagon (30 × 41 *mm.*) 25 30
MS380 100 × 101 mm. Nos. 378/9. Imperf. 25 25

1974 (16 Oct.). *Liaquat Ali Khan (First Prime Minister of Pakistan).* P 13 × 13½.
381 **226** 20 p. black and light verm. 5 5

227. Dr. Mohammad Iqbal (poet and philosopher).

1974 (9 Nov.). *Birth Centenary of Dr. Iqbal (1977) (1st issue).* P 13.
382 **227** 20 p. multicoloured .. 5 5
See also Nos. 399 and 433.

228. Dr. Schweitzer and River Scene.

1975 (14 Jan.). *Birth Centenary of Dr. Albert Schweitzer.* P 13.
383 **228** 2 r. 25, multicoloured .. 25 30

229. Tourism Year Symbol.

1975 (15 Jan.). *South East Asia Tourism Year.* P 13.
384 **229** 2 r. 25, multicoloured .. 25 25

230. Assembly Hall, Flags and Prime Minister Bhutto.

(Des. A. Salahuddin.)

1975 (22 Feb.). *First Anniv. of Islamic Summit Conference, Lahore.* P 13.
385 **230** 20 p. multicoloured .. 5 5
386 ,, 1 r. multicoloured .. 12 12

231. " Scientific Research ".

(Des. A. Salahuddin (20 p.), M. Ahmad (2 r. 25).)

1975 (15 June). *International Women's Year. T* **231** *and similar horiz. design. Multicoloured.* P 13.
387 20 p. Type **231** 5 5
388 2 r. 25, Girl teaching woman (" Adult Education ") .. 25 30

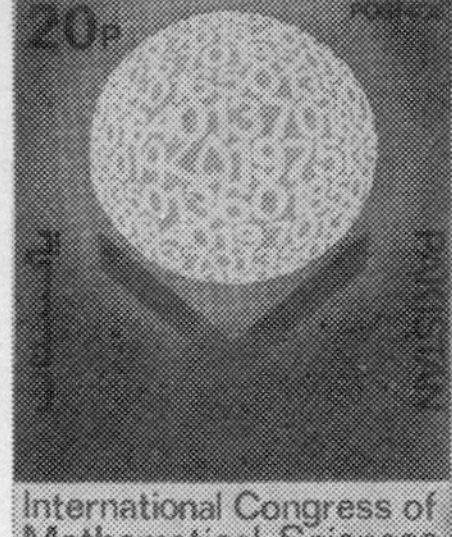

232. " Globe " and Algebraic Symbol.

1975 (14 July). *International Congress of Mathematical Sciences, Karachi.* P 13.
389 **232** 20 p. multicoloured .. 5 5

233. Pakistani Camel-skin Vase.

(Des. Ilyas Ahmed Gilani.)

1975 (21 July). *Eleventh Anniv. of Regional Co-operation for Development. T* **233** *and similar multicoloured designs.* P 13.
390 20 p. Type **233** 5 5
391 60 p. Iranian tile (*horiz.*) .. 5 8
392 1 r. 25, Turkish porcelain vase 12 15

234. Sapling and Dead Trees.

1975 (9 Aug.). *Tree Planting Day.* P 13 × 13½
393 **234** 20 p. multicoloured .. 5 5

235. Black Partridge.

(Des. A. Salahuddin.)

1975 (30 SEPT.). *Wildlife Protection* (1st series). *P* 13.
394 **235** 20 p. multicoloured .. 5 5
395 ,, 2 r. 25, multicoloured .. 25 30
See also Nos. 400/1, 411/12 and 417/18.

"**236.** Today's Girls".

1975 (6 OCT.). *Universal Children's Day.* *P* 13.
396 **236** 20 p. multicoloured .. 5 5

237. Hazrat Amir Khusrau, Sitar and Tabla. (*Illustration reduced. Actual size* 74 × 23 *mm.*)

(Des. A. Salahuddin.)

1975 (24 OCT.). *700th Birth Anniv. of Hazrat Amir Khusrau* (*poet and musician*). *P* 13½ × 12½.
397 **237** 20 p. multicoloured .. 5 5
398 ,, 2 r. 25, multicoloured .. 25 30

238. Dr. Mohammad Iqbal.

(Des. A. Salahuddin.)

1975 (9 Nov.). *Birth Centenary of Dr. Iqbal* (1977) (*2nd issue*). *P* 13.
399 **238** 20 p. multicoloured .. 5 5

239. Urial (wild sheep.)

(Des. Munawar Ahmed.)

1975 (31 DEC.). *Wildlife Protection* (*2nd series*). *P* 13.
400 **239** 20 p. multicoloured .. 5 5
401 ,, 3 r. multicoloured .. 25 30

240. Moenjodaro Remains.

(Des. A. Salahuddin.)

1976 (29 FEB.). "*Save Moenjodaro*" (1*st series*). *T* **240** *and similar vert. designs. Multicoloured. P* 13.
402 10 p. Type **240** 5 5
403 20 p. Remains (*different*) .. 5 5
404 65 p. The Citadel 5 5
405 3 r. Well inside a house .. 30 35
406 4 r. The "Great Bath" .. 40 45
402/6 .. .. *Set of* 5 70 80

Nos. 402/6 were printed horizontally *se-tenant* within the sheet, the five stamps forming a composite design of the excavations.

See also Nos. 414 and 430.

241. Dome and Minaret of Rauza-e-Mubarak.

(Des. A. Ghani. Photo.)

1976 (3 MAR.). *International Congress on Seerat.* *P* 13 × 13½.
407 **241** 20 p. multicoloured .. 5 5
408 ,, 3 r. multicoloured .. 30 35

242. Alexander Graham Bell and Telephone Dial. (*Illustration reduced. Actual size* 57 × 27 *mm.*)

(Des. M. M. Saeed. Photo.)

1976 (10 MAR.). *Telephone Centenary.* *P* 13.
409 **242** 3 r. multicoloured .. 30 35

243. College Arms within "Sun".

(Des. A. Salahuddin.)

1976 (15 MAR.). *Centenary of National College of Arts, Lahore.* *P* 13.
410 **243** 20 p. multicoloured .. 5 5

244. Peacock.

(Des. A. Salahuddin.)

1976 (31 MAR.). *Wildlife Protection* (*3rd series*). *P* 13.
411 **244** 20 p. multicoloured .. 5 5
412 ,, 3 r. multicoloured .. 30 35

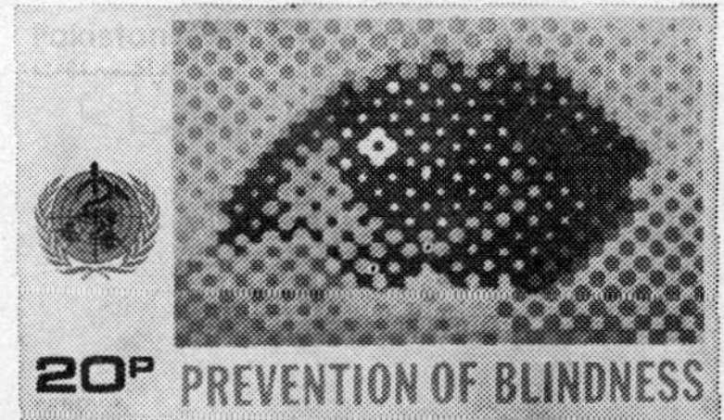

245. Human Eye.

(Des. M. M. Saeed.)

1976 (7 APR.). *Prevention of Blindness.* *P* 13.
413 **245** 20 p. multicoloured .. 5 5

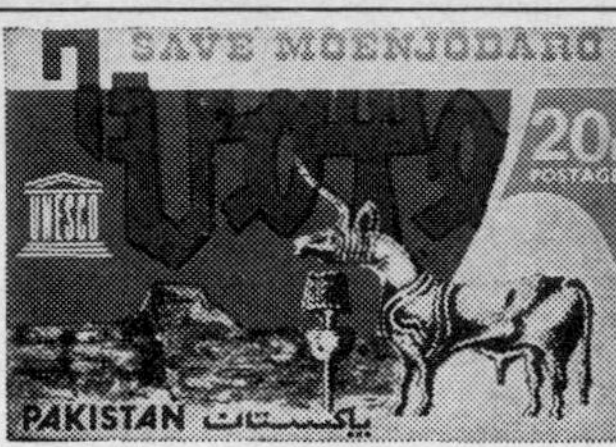

246. Unicorn and Ruins.

(Des. I. A. Gilani.)

1976 (31 May). *" Save Moenjodaro " (2nd series). P 13.*

414	**246**	20 p. multicoloured ..	5	5

247. Jefferson Memorial.

(Des. I. A. Gilani (90 p.), A. Salahuddin (4 r.).)

1976 (4 July). *Bicentenary of American Revolution. T* **247** *and similar horiz. design. Multicoloured. P 13 (90 p.) or 13½ (4 r.).*

415	90 p. Type **247**	8	10
416	4 r. " Declaration of Independence " (47×36 *mm.*)	40	45

248. Ibex.

(Des. M. Ahmed.)

1976 (12 July). *Wildlife Protection (4th series). P 13.*

417	**248**	20 p. multicoloured ..	5	5
418	,,	3 r. multicoloured ..	30	35

249. Mahomed Ali Jinnah.

(Des. A. Salahuddin.)

1976 (21 July). *Twelfth Anniv. of Regional Co-operation for Development. T* **249** *and similar diamond-shaped designs. Multicoloured. P 14.*

419	20 p. Type **249**	5	5
420	65 p. Reza Shah the Great ..	5	8
421	90 p. Kemal Atatürk	8	8

Nos. 419/21 were printed vertically *se-tenant* throughout the sheet.

250. Urdu Text. **251.** Mahomed Ali Jinnah and Wazir Mansion.

1976 (14 Aug.). *Birth Centenary of Mahomed Ali Jinnah. P 13.*

(*a*) *Type* **250**.

422	5 p. black, new blue & yellow	5	5
423	10 p. black, yellow & magenta	5	5
424	15 p. black and violet-blue ..	5	5
425	1 r. black, yellow & new blue	10	12

(*b*) *Multicoloured designs as T* **251**, *different buildings in the background.*

426	20 p. Type **251**	5	5
427	40 p. Sind Madressah	5	5
428	50 p. Minar Qarardad-e-Pakistan	5	8
429	3 r. Mausoleum	30	35
422/9	.. .. *Set of* 8	50	60

Nos. 422/9 were printed in *se-tenant* blocks of 8 throughout the sheet.

252. Dancing-girl, Ruins and King Priest. (*For illustration see Addenda.*)

(Des. A. Salahuddin.)

1976 (31 Aug.). *" Save Moenjodaro " (3rd series). P 14.*

430	**252**	65 p. multicoloured ..	8	8

253. U.N. Racial Discrimination Emblem.

(Des. A. Salahuddin.)

1976 (15 Sept.). *U.N. Decade to Combat Racial Discrimination. P 12½×13½.*

431	**253**	65 p. multicoloured ..	8	8

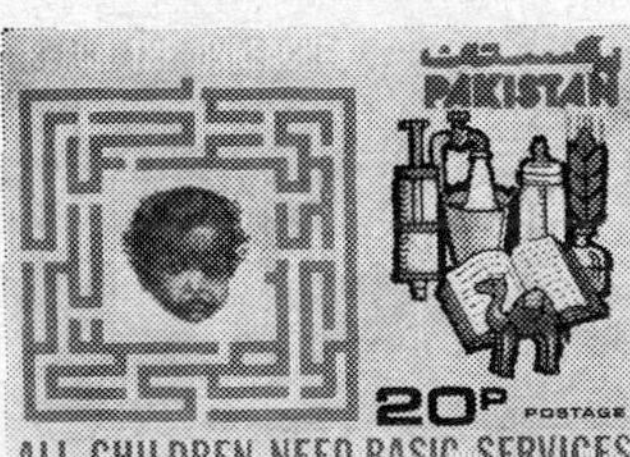

254. Child in Maze and Basic Services.

(Des. M. Ahmad.)

1976 (4 Oct.). *Universal Children's Day. P 13.*

432	**254**	20 p. multicoloured ..	5	5

255. Verse from " Allama Iqbal ".

(Des. M. A. Javed.)

1976 (9 Nov.). *Birth Centenary of Dr. Iqba (1977) (3rd issue). P 13.*

433	**255**	20 p. multicoloured ..	5	5

256. Mahomed Ali Jinnah giving Scout Salute

(Des. I. A. Gilani.)

1976 (20 Nov.). *Quaid-i-Azam Centenary Jamboree. P 13½.*

434	**256**	20 p. multicoloured ..	5	5

OFFICIAL STAMPS.

PAKISTAN

(O 1)

1947. *Official stamps of India, Nos.* O143/50, *optd as Type* O **1** *and Nos.* O138/41 *optd. as T by offset-litho, at Nasik.*

O 1	O **20**	3 p. slate	5	5
O 2	,,	½ a. purple	5	5
O 3	,,	9 p. green	5	5
O 4	,,	1 a. carmine	5	5
O 5	,,	1½ a. dull violet	5	5
O 6	,,	2 a. vermilion	5	5
O 7	,,	2½ a. bright violet ..	5	5
O 8	,,	4 a. brown	8	[illegible]
O 9	,,	8 a. slate-violet ..	12	1
O10	**100**	1 r. grey and red-brown	15	1
O11	,,	2 r. purple and brown	30	2
O12	,,	5 r. green and blue ..	95	9
O13	,,	10 r. purple and claret ..	1·75	1·6
O1/O13		.. .. *Set of* 13	3·00	3·0

See note after No. 19. The 1 a. 3 p. (India No. O146*a*) exists only as a local issue (*price* Peshawar opt., 50*p. un.*, 60*p. us.*).

SERVICE (O 2) **SERVICE** (O 3) **SERVICE** (O 4)

NOTE. Apart from a slight difference in size, Types O **2** and O **3** can easily be distin guished by the difference in the shape of th " c ". Type O **4** is taller and thinner in appear ance.

PRINTERS. Type O 2 was overprinted by D La Rue and Types O **3** and O **4** by the Pakista Security Ptg. Corp.

1948 (14 Aug.)–**54?** *Optd. with Type* O **2.**

No.	Type	Description	Unused	Used
O14	**7**	3 p. red (No. 24)	5	5
O15	,,	6 p. violet (No. 25 (R.)	5	5
O16	,,	9 p. green (No. 26) (R.) ..	5	5
O17	**8**	1 a. blue (No. 27) (R.) ..	5	5
O18	,,	1½ a. grey-grn. (No. 28) (R.)	5	5
O19	,,	2 a. red (No. 29) ..	5	5
O20	**10**	3 a. green (No. 31) ..	5	5
O21	**9**	4 a. reddish brn. (No. 33)	5	5
O22	**11**	8 a. black (No. 35) (R.) ..	10	5
O23	**12**	1 r. ultramarine (No. 38)	15	8
O24	,,	2 r. chocolate (No. 39) ..	25	15
O25	,,	5 r. carmine (No. 40) ..	60	40
O26	**13**	10 r. magenta (No. 41) ..	1·50	90
		a. Perf. 12 (10.10.51) ..	2·25	1·00
		b. Perf. 13 ('54?)	2·00	1·50
O14/O26		.. .. *Set of* 13	2·60	1·60

1949. *Optd. with Type* O **2.**

No.	Type	Description	Unused	Used
O27		1 a. blue (No. 47) (R.) ..	5	5
O28		1½ a. grey-grn. (No. 48) (R.)	5	5
		a. Opt. inverted	—	18·00
O29		2 a. red (No. 49)	5	5
		a. Opt. omitted (in pair with normal)		
O30		3 a. green (No. 50) ..	5	5
O31		8 a. black (No. 52) (R.) ..	12	10
O27/O31		.. .. *Set of* 5	15	10

1951 (14 Aug.). *4th Anniv. of Independence. As Nos.* 56, 58 *and* 60, *but inscr.* "SERVICE" *instead of* "PAKISTAN POSTAGE".

No.	Type	Description	Unused	Used
O32	**18**	3 a. purple	5	8
O33	**19**	4 a. green	8	8
O34	**20**	8 a. sepia	10	8

1953. *Optd. with Type* O **3.**

No.	Type	Description	Unused	Used
O35		3 p. red (No. 24a)	5	5
O36		6 p. violet (No. 25a) (R.) ..	5	5
O37		9 p. green (No. 26a) (R.) ..	5	5
O38		1 a. blue (No. 47a) (R.) ..	5	5
O39		1½ a. grey-grn. (No. 48a) (R.)	5	5
O40		2 a. red (No. 49a) ('53?) ..	5	5
O41		1 r. ultramarine (No. 38a)	30	15
O42		2 r. chocolate (No. 39a) ..	75	45
O43		5 r. carmine (No. 40a) ..	1·00	50
O44		10 r. mag. (No. 41b) (date?)	2·00	1·50
O35/O44		.. .. *Set of* 10	3·25	2·25

1954 (14 Aug.). *Seventh Anniv. of Independence issue, optd. with Type* O **3.**

No.	Type	Description	Unused	Used
O45	**22**	6 p. reddish violet (R.)	5	5
O46	**23**	9 p. blue (R.)	5	5
O47	**24**	1 a. carmine	5	5
O48	**25**	1½ a. red	5	5
O49	**26**	14 a. deep green (R.) ..	15	15
O50	**27**	1 r. green (R.)	30	20
O51	**28**	2 r. red-orange	60	40
O45/O51		.. .. *Set of* 7	1·00	75

1955 (14 Aug.). *Eighth Anniv. of Independence issue, optd. with Type* O **3.**

No.	Type	Description	Unused	Used
O52	**32**	8 a. dp. reddish violet (R.)	15	20

1957 (Jan.)–**59.** *Seventh Anniv. of Independence issue, optd. with Type* O **4.**

No.	Type	Description	Unused	Used
O53	**22**	6 p. reddish violet (R.)	5	5
		a. Opt. inverted		
O54	**23**	9 p. blue (R.) (1.59) ..	5	5
		a. Opt. inverted		
O55	**24**	1 a. carmine	5	5
		a. Opt. inverted		
O56	**25**	1½ a. red	5	5
		a. Opt. double		
O57	**26**	14 a. dp. green (R.) (2.59)	20	8
O58	**27**	1 r. green (R.) (4.58) ..	30	20
O59	**28**	2 r. red-orange (4.58)	60	40
O53/O59		.. .. *Set of* 7	1·10	75

1958 (Jan.)–**61.** *Optd. with Type* O **4.**

No.	Type	Description	Unused	Used
O60	**7**	3 p. red (No. 24a) ..	5	5
O61	**12**	5 r. carm. (No. 40a) (7.59)	1·00	75
O62	**41**	10 r. myrtle-green & yell.-orge. (No. 89) (R.) ('61)	85	85

1958 (Jan.)–**61.** *Eighth Anniv. of Independence issue, optd. with Type* O **4.**

No.	Type	Description	Unused	Used
O63	**31**	6 a. dp. ultram. (R.) (4.61)	15	15
O64	**32**	8 a. deep reddish violet (R.)	12	12

1959 (Aug.). *Ninth Anniv. of Independence issue, optd. with Type* O **4.**

No.	Type	Description	Unused	Used
O65	**37**	2 a. scarlet	8	8

1961 (Apr.). *Nos.* 110/111 *optd. with Type* O **4.**

No.	Type	Description	Unused	Used
O66	**51**	8 a. deep green	12	12
O67	,,	1 r. blue	20	20
		a. Opt. inverted	6·00	

NEW CURRENCY. In addition to the local *handstamped* surcharges mentioned in the note above No. 122, the following *typographed* surcharges were made at the Treasury at Mastung and issued in the Baluchi province of Kalat: 6 p. on 1 a. (No. O55), 9 p. on 1½ a. (No. O56) and 13 p. on 2 a. (No. O65). They differ in that the surcharges are smaller and "PAISA" is expressed as "Paisa". Being locals they are outside the scope of this catalogue.

1961. *Optd. with Type* O **4.**

No.	Type	Description	Unused	Used
O68		1 p. on 1½ a. (No. 122) ..	5	5
		a. Optd. with Type O 3 ..	60	75
O69		2 p. on 3 p. (No. 123) (1.1.61)	5	5
		a. Surch. double		
		b. Optd. with Type O 3 ..	1·25	1·25
O70		3 p. on 6 p. (No. 124) ..	5	5
O71		7 p. on 1 a. (No. 125) ..	5	5
		a. Optd. with Type O 3 ..	1·50	1·50
O72		13 p. on 2 a. (No. 126) ..	5	5
O73		13 p. on 2 a. (No. 127) ..	5	5
O68/O73		.. .. *Set of* 6	15	15

No. O68 exists with small and large "1" (see note below Nos. 122/7, etc.).

ERRORS. See note after No. 127.

SERVICE

(O **5**)

1961–63. *Nos.* 128/44*b* *optd. with Type* O **4** (*rupee values*) *or* O **5** (*others*).

(*a*) *Inscribed* "SHAKISTAN".

No.	Type	Description	Unused	Used
O74		1 p. violet (R.) (1.1.61) ..	5	5
O75		2 p. rose-red (R.) (12.1.61)	5	5
O76		5 p. ultram. (R.) (23.3.61)	5	5

(*b*) *Inscribed* "PAKISTAN".

No.	Type	Description	Unused	Used
O77		1 p. violet (R.)	5	5
O78		2 p. rose-red (R.)	5	5
O79		3 p. reddish purple (R.) (27.10.61)	5	5
O80		5 p. ultramarine (R.) ..	5	5
O81		7 p. emerald (R.) (23.3.61)	5	5
O82		10 p. brown (R.)	5	5
		a. Opt. inverted		
O83		13 p. slate-vio. (R.) (14.2.61)	5	5
O85		40 p. deep purple (R.) (1.1.62)	8	5
O86		50 p. deep bluish green (R.) (1.1.62) ..	15	8
O87		75 p. carm.-red (R.) (23.3.62)	20	12
O88		1 r. vermilion (7.1.63) ..	30	12
O89		2 r. orange (7.1.63) ..	50	30
O90		5 r. green (R.) (7.1.63) ..	1·25	75
O74/O90		.. .. *Set of* 16	2·50	1·75

1963–72. *Nos.* 170, *etc., optd. with Type* O **5**, *in red.*

No.	Type	Description	Unused	Used
O 91		1 p. violet	5	5
O 92		2 p. rose-red ('65) ..	5	5
		a. Opt. inverted		
O 93		3 p. reddish purple ('67) ..	5	5
		a. Opt. double		
O 94		5 p. ultramarine	5	5
O 95		7 p. emerald (date?) ..	5	5
O 96		10 p. brown ('65)	5	5
		a. Opt. inverted		
O 97		13 p. slate-violet	5	5
O 98		15 p. brt. purple (1.1.65) ..	5	5
O 99		20 p. myrtle-grn. (26.1.70)	5	5
O100		40 p. deep purple ('72?) ..	5	5
O101		50 p. dp. bluish green ('65)	5	5
O102		75 p. carmine-red (date ?)	5	5
O91/O102		.. .. *Set of* 12	25	20

1968–(?). *Nos.* 204, 206 *and* 207 *optd. with Type* O **4.**

No.	Type	Description	Unused	Used
O103	**62**	1 r. vermilion	8	8
		a. Opt. inverted		
O104	,,	2 r. orange (date ?) ..	15	12
O105	,,	5 r. green (R.) (date ?) ..	40	30

BAHAWALPUR.

PRINTERS. All the following issues were recess-printed by De La Rue & Co.

The stamps of Bahawalpur only had validity for use within the state. For external mail Pakistan stamps were used.

1. Amir Muhammad Bahawal Khan I Abbasi.

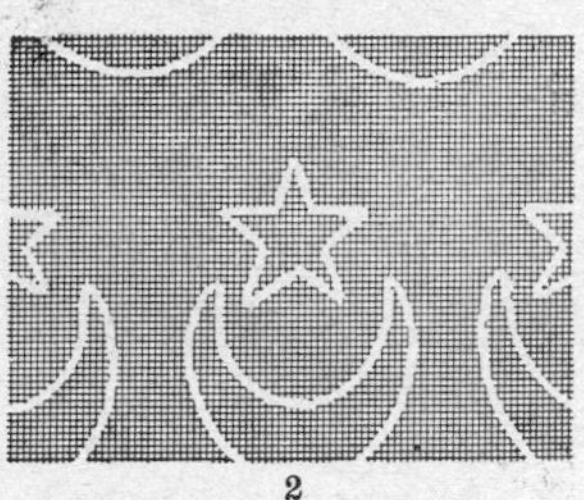

2

1948. *Bicentenary Commemoration.* *W* **2** (*sideways*). *P* 12½ × 11½.

1	**1**	½ a. black and carmine	..	10

3. H.H. the Ameer of Bahawalpur.

4. The Tombs of the Ameers.

5. Mosque in Sadiq-Garh.

6. Fort Derawar, from the Lake.

7. Nur-Mahal Palace.

8. The Palace, Sadiq-Garh.

9. H.H. the Ameer of Bahawalpur.

10. Three Generations of Rulers; H.H. the Ameer in centre.

1948 (1 Apr.). *W* **2** (*sideways on vert. designs*) *P* 12½ (*T* **3**), 11½ × 12½ (*T* **4**, **6**, **7** *and* **8**) 12½ × 11½ (*T* **5** *and* **9**) *or* 13½ × 14 (*T* **10**).

2	**3**	3 p. black and blue	..	5
3	,,	½ a. black and claret	..	5
4	,,	9 p. black and green	..	5
5	,,	1 a. black and carmine	..	5
6	,,	1½ a. black and violet	..	5
7	**4**	2 a. green and carmine	..	5
8	**5**	4 a. orange and brown	..	5
9	**6**	6 a. violet and blue	..	5
10	**7**	8 a. carmine and violet	..	8
11	**8**	12 a. green and carmine	..	10
12	**9**	1 r. violet and brown	..	12
13	,,	2 r. green and claret	..	25
14	,,	5 r. black and violet	..	60
15	**10**	10 r. scarlet and black	..	1·00

11. H.H. The Ameer of Bahawalpur an Mahomed Ali Jinnah.

1948 (3 Oct.). *First Anniv. of Union o Bahawalpur with Pakistan.* *W* **2**. *P* 13.

16	**11**	1½ a. carmine and blue-green	5

12. Soldiers of 1848 and 1948.

1948 (15 Oct.). *Multan Campaign Centenary* *W* **2**. *P* 11½.

17	**12**	1½ a. black and lake	..	10

1948. *As Nos.* 12/15, *but colours changed.*

18	**9**	1 r. deep green & orange	..	8
19	,,	2 r. black and carmine	..	15
20	,,	5 r. chocolate and ultram.		30
21	**10**	10 r. red-brown and green	..	50

13. Irrigation.

14. Wheat.
15. Cotton.
16. Sahiwal Bull.

1949 (3 Mar.). *Silver Jubilee of Accession of H.H. the Ameer of Bahawalpur.* W **2**. P 14.

22 **13** 3 p. black and ultramarine 5
23 **14** ½ a. black and brn.-orange 5
24 **15** 9 p. black and green .. 5
25 **16** 1 a. black and carmine .. 5

17. U.P.U. Monument, Berne.

1949 (10 Oct.). *75th Anniv. of Universal Postal Union.* W **2**. P 13.

26 **17** 9 p. black and green .. 5
a. Perf. 17½×17 5
27 ,, 1 a. black and magenta .. 5
a. Perf. 17½×17 5
28 ,, 1½ a. black and orange .. 5
a. Perf. 17½×17 5
29 ,, 2½ a. black and blue .. 5
a. Perf. 17½×17 5

OFFICIAL STAMPS.

O 1. Panjnad Weir.

O 2. Camel and Calf.

O 3. Blackbuck Antelope.

O 4. Pelicans.

O 5. Juma Masjid Palace, Fort Derawar.

O 6. Temple at Pattan Munara.

1945 (1 Jan.). *Various horizontal pictorial designs, with red Arabic opt.* W **2**. P 14.

O1 O **1** ½ a. black and green .. 8 15
O2 O **2** 1 a. black and carmine .. 15 25
O3 O **3** 2 a. black and violet .. 15
O4 O **4** 4 a. black and olive-green 20
O5 O **5** 8 a. black and brown .. 20
O6 O **6** 1 r. black and orange .. 25

Stamps without overprint must be regarded as being ordinary revenue stamps, unless found *se-tenant* with overprinted stamps.

O 7. Baggage Camels.

1945 (10 Mar.). *Red Arabic opt. No wmk.* P 14.

O7 O **7** 1 a. black and brown .. 10·00 10·00

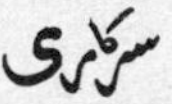

(O 8)

1945 (Mar.–June). *Surch. as Type* O **8** *(at Security Printing Press, Nasik) instead of red Arabic opt. No wmk.* P 14.

O11 O **5** ½ a. on 8 a. blk. & purple 60 45
O12 O **6** 1½ a. on 1 r. blk. & orge. 1·25 1·00
O13 O **1** 1½ a. on 2 r. black and blue (1 June) .. 2·00 1·75

SERVICE

(O 9)

1945. *Optd. with Type* O **9** *(by D.L.R.) instead of red Arabic opt. No wmk.* P 14.

O14 O **1** ½ a. black and carmine.. 10 10
O15 O **2** 1 a. black and carmine.. 15 20
O16 O **3** 2 a. black and orange .. 20 25

O 10. H.H. the Ameer of Bahawalpur.

1945. P 14.

O17 O **10** 3 p. black and blue .. 5 5
O18 ,, 1½ a. black and violet.. 5 5

O 11. Allied Banners.

(Des. E. Meronti. Recess. Background litho.)

1946 (May). *Victory.* P 14.

O19 O **11** 1½ a. green and grey 15 20

1948. *Nos.* 2, 5, 7, 8 *and* 18/21 *optd. as Nos.* O1/6.

O20 **3** 3 p. black and blue (R.) 5
O21 ,, 1 a. black & carm. (Bk.) 5
O22 **4** 2 a. green & carm. (Bk.) 5
O23 **5** 4 a. orange & brn. (Bk.) 5
O24 **9** 1 r. dp. grn. & orge. (R.) 8
O25 ,, 2 r. blk. & carmine (R.) 12
O26 ,, 5 r. choc. & ultram. (R.) 25
O27 **10** 10 r. red-brn. & grn. (R.) 50

1949 (10 Oct.). *75th Anniv. of Universal Postal Union. Nos.* 26/9 *optd. as Nos.* O1/6.

O28 **17** 9 p. black and green .. 5
a. Perf. 17½×17.. .. 5
O29 ,, 1 a. black and magenta.. 5
a. Perf. 17½×17.. .. 5
O30 ,, 1½ a. black and orange .. 5
a. Perf. 17½×17.. .. 5
O31 ,, 2½ a. black and blue .. 5
a. Perf. 17½×17.. .. 5

Since 1949 only Pakistan stamps have been used in Bahawalpur for both internal and external mail.

LAS BELA.

The stamps for Las Bela, formerly listed here, will now be found under Indian Feudatory States since it was part of India at the time when the stamps were issued.

PALESTINE.

BRITISH MILITARY OCCUPATION:

Valid also for use in Transjordan, Cilicia, Northern Egypt and Syria.

1 (2)

"E.E.F." = Egyptian Expeditionary Force.

(Litho. Typographical Dept., Survey of Egypt, Giza, Cairo.)

1918 (10 Feb.). *Wmk. Royal Cypher in column* (*T* **100** *of Great Britain*). *Ungummed. Roul.* 20.

No.	Type	Description	Unused	Used
1	**1**	1 p. indigo (Optd. S. £325) ..	£165	£130
		a. Deep blue	£150	£120
		b. Blue	£165	£130

Control. A 18. (Prices, corner block of 4: No. 1, £775. No. 1*a*, £700. No. 1*b*, £775.)

1918 (16 Feb.). *As last* (*ungummed*), *surch. with T* **2**.

No.	Type	Description	Unused	Used
2	**1**	5 m. on 1 p. cobalt-blue (Optd. S. £350)	85·00	£500
		a. Error. "MILLILMES" (No. 10 in sheet)	£1700	

Control. B 18 A. (Corner block, £675.)

1918 (5 Mar.). *As No.* 1 *but colour changed. With gum.*

No.	Type	Description	Unused	Used
3	**1**	1 p. ultramarine	1·10	1·10

Control. C 18. (Corner block, £45.)

1918 (5 Mar. *and* 13 May). *No.* 3 *surch. with T* **2**.

No.	Type	Description	Unused	Used
4	**1**	5 m. on 1 p. ultramarine ..	3·00	2·50
		a. Error. Arabic surch. wholly or partly missing (No. 11 in sheet)	£325	

Controls. C 18 B (Mar.). (Corner block, £575.)
D 18 C (May). (Corner block, £125.)

3

(Typo. Stamping Dept, Board of Inland Revenue Somerset House, London.)

1918 (16 July–27 Dec.). *Wmk. Royal Cypher in column. P* 15 × 14.

No.	Type	Description	Unused	Used
5	**3**	1 m. sepia	8	8
		a. Deep brown	12	12
6	,,	2 m. blue-green	10	10
		a. Deep green	15	15
7	,,	3 m. yellow-brown (17 Dec.)	15	15
		a. Chestnut	4·25	3·25
8	,,	4 m. scarlet	15	15
9	,,	5 m. yellow-orange (25 Sept.)	15	12
		a. Orange	25	20
10	**3**	1 p. deep indigo (9 Nov.) ..	15	5
11	,,	2 p. pale olive	25	25
		a. Olive	30	30
12	,,	5 p. purple	50	65
13	,,	9 p. ochre (17. Dec.) ..	95	1·60
14	,,	10 p. ultramarine (17 Dec.)	85	1·50
15	,,	20 p. pale grey (27 Dec.) ..	2·75	5·00
		a. Slate-grey	5·50	8·00
5/15		.. .. *Set of* 11	5·50	9·00

There are two sizes of the design of this issue:
19 × 23 *mm.* 1, 2, and 4 m., and 2 and 5 p.
18 × 21½ *mm.* 3 and 5 m., and 1, 9, 10 and 20 p.

There are numerous minor plate varieties in this issue, such as stops omitted in "E.E.F.", malformed Arabic characters, etc.

Originally issued by the Military Authorities for use of the civil population in occupied enemy territories (including at one time or another, a large part of Asia Minor), these stamps were used in Palestine until superseded by the following issue. They were demonetised on 1 May, 1922.

CIVIL ADMINISTRATION UNDER BRITISH HIGH COMMISSIONER.

(1 July, 1920.)

فلسطين PALESTINE פלשתינה א״י
(4)

فلسطين PALESTINE פלשתינה א״י
(5)

(Optd. at Greek Orthodox Convent, Jerusalem.)

1920 (1 Sept.). *Optd. with T* **4**. (*Arabic* 8 *mm. long.*) (*a*) *P* 15 × 14.

No.	Type	Description	Unused	Used
16	**3**	1 m. sepia	45	55
17	,,	2 m. blue-green	3·50	1·50
18	,,	3 m. chestnut	1·10	1·10
		a. Opt. inverted	£275	£350
19	,,	4 m. scarlet	50	65
20	,,	5 m. yellow-orange.. ..	2·75	1·25
21	,,	1 p. deep indigo (Sil.) ..	40	25
22	,,	2 p. deep olive	60	75
23	,,	5 p. deep purple	3·25	5·50
24	,,	9 p. ochre	3·75	9·00
25	,,	10 p. ultramarine	4·50	8·00
26	,,	20 p. pale grey	7·50	16·00
		(*b*) *P* 14.		
27	**3**	2 m. blue-green	60	70
28	,,	3 m. chestnut	16·00	20·00
29	,,	5 m. orange	60	40
16/29		(*cheapest*) .. *Set of* 11	21·00	38·00

Two settings of T **4** are known to specialists, the first being used for all values perf. 15 × 14 except the 1 p. and the second for all values in both perfs.

Apart from minor varieties due to broken type, there are three major errors which are rare in some values. These are (*a*) two Hebrew characters at left transposed (all values of first setting only); (*b*) diamond-shaped dot over the Arabic "t" making the word read "Faleszin" for "Falestin" (2 p. to 20 p. of first setting and 1 m. and 3 m. perf. 15 × 14 and 5 m. perf. 14 of second setting); (*c*) "B" for final "E" of "PALESTINE" (2 p. to 20 p. of first setting and all values of second setting except 3 m. perf. 14).

Faulty registration of the overprint in this issue has resulted in numerous misplaced overprints, either vertically or horizontally, which are not of great importance with the exception of Nos. 21 and 29 which exist with the overprint out of sequence, i.e. Hebrew/Arabic/English or English/Arabic/Hebrew or English/Hebrew only. Also all values are known with Arabic/English only.

1920 (22 Sept.)–**1921** (21 June). *Optd. with T* **5***. (*Arabic* 10 *mm. long.*)

No.	Type	Description	Unused	Used
		(*a*) *P* 15 × 14.		
30	**3**	1 m. sepia	25	35
		a. Opt. inverted	£250	†
31	,,	2 m. blue-green	90	1·25
32	,,	3 m. yellow-brown	25	35
33	,,	4 m. scarlet	35	50
34	,,	5 m. yellow-orange	90	35
35	,,	1 p. deep indigo (Silver) ..	£300	2·50
36	,,	2 p. olive	25·00	10·00
37	,,	5 p. deep purple	10·00	3·75
		(*b*) *P* 14.		
38	**3**	1 m. sepia	£350	£475
39	,,	2 m. blue-green	95	1·10
40	,,	4 m. scarlet	24·00	35·00
41	,,	5 m. orange	60·00	7·50
		a. Yellow-orange	65	40
42	,,	1 p. deep indigo (Silver)	10·00	55
43	,,	5 p. purple	£125	£280
30/43		(*cheapest*) .. *Set of* 8	38·00	14·00

* In this setting the Arabic and Hebrew characters are badly worn and blunted, the Arabic "s" and "t" are joined (i.e. there is no break in the position indicated by the arrow in our illustration); the letters of "PALESTINE" are often irregular or broken; and the space between the two groups of Hebrew characters varies from 1 mm. to over 1¾ mm. (*For clear, sharp overprint, see Nos.* 47/59.)

Dates of issue: 22.9.20, 5 m.; 27.12.20, 1 to 4 m.; 21.6.21, 1 to 5 p.

The dates of issue given are irrespective of the perforations, i.e. one or both perfs could have been issued on the dates shown.

Nos. 31 and 39 exist with any one line of the overprint both partly and almost completely missing.

فلسطين PALESTINE פלשתינה א״י
(6)

Differences:—
T **5**. 20 mm. vert. and 7 mm. between English and Hebrew.
T **6**. 19 mm. and 6 mm. respectively.

1920 (6 Dec.). *Optd. with T* **6**. (*a*) *P* 15 × 14.

No.	Type	Description	Unused	Used
44	**3**	3 m. yellow-brown ..	18·00	20·00
44*a*	,,	5 m. yellow-orange ..	—	£5500
		(*b*) *P* 14.		
45	**3**	1 m. sepia	13·00	17·00
46	,,	5 m. orange	£350	18·00

1921 (29 May–4 Aug.). *Optd. as T* **5**†.

No.	Type	Description	Unused	Used
		(*a*) *P* 15 × 14.		
47	**3**	1 m. sepia	1·50	1·00
48	,,	2 m. blue-green	3·50	2·00
49	,,	3 m. yellow-brown ..	7·50	1·40
		a. "PALESTINE" omitted	£1250	
50	,,	4 m. scarlet	7·50	1·50
51	,,	5 m. yellow-orange.. ..	8·00	65
52	,,	1 p. deep indigo (Silver) ..	8·00	40
53	,,	2 p. olive	11·00	3·50
54	,,	5 p. purple	12·00	5·00
55	,,	9 p. ochre	15·00	70·00
56	,,	10 p. ultramarine	15·00	7·50
57	,,	20 p. pale grey	30·00	26·00
47/57		.. .. *Set of* 11	£100	£100
		(*b*) *P* 14.		
58	**3**	1 m. sepia	—	£1200
59	,,	20 p. pale grey	£6000	£2000

† In this setting the Arabic and Hebrew characters are sharp and pointed as in T **6**; there is usually a break between the Arabic "s" and "t" though this is sometimes filled with ink; and the whole overprint is much clearer. The space between the two groups of Hebrew characters is always 1¾ mm. (*cf. note below* No. 43).

Dates of issue: 29 May, 5 m.; 23 June, 1 to 4 m.; July, 1 p.; 4 Aug., 2 p. to 20 p.

فلسطين	فلسطين
PALESTINE	PALESTINE
פלשתינה א"י	פלשתינה א"י
(7)	(8)

(Opt. by Stamping Dept., Board of Inland Revenue, Somerset House, London.)

1921 (Sept.–Oct.). *Optd. with* T **7** ("PALESTINE" *in sans-serif letters*). *Wmk. Royal Cypher in column.* P 15×14.

No.	Type	Description	Unused	Used
60	**3**	1 m. sepia	15	12
61	,,	2 m. blue-green	15	15
62	,,	3 m. yellow-brown	15	10
63	,,	4 m. scarlet	25	25
64	,,	5 m. yellow-orange	25	10
65	,,	1 p. bright turquoise-blue	35	10
66	,,	2 p. olive	55	25
67	,,	5 p. deep purple	2·00	2·75
68	,,	9 p. ochre	5·00	6·00
69	,,	10 p. ultramarine	7·00	£200
70	,,	20 p. pale grey	24·00	£450
60/70		*Set of* 11	35·00	

(Printed and optd. by Waterlow & Sons from new plates.)

1922 (Sept.–Nov.). T **3** (*redrawn*), *optd. with* T **8**. *Wmk. Mult. Script CA.* (*a*) P 14.

No.	Type	Description	Unused	Used
71	**3**	1 m. sepia	10	5
		a. Deep brown	15	5
		b. Opt. inverted	—	£5250
		c. Opt. double	£150	£240
72	,,	2 m. yellow	15	8
		a. Orange-yellow	55	20
73	,,	3 m. greenish blue	20	5
74	,,	4 m. carmine-pink	15	10
		a. Very thin paper	32·00	45·00
75	,,	5 m. orange	20	5
76	,,	6 m. blue-green	35	15
77	,,	7 m. yellow-brown	45	15
78	,,	8 m. scarlet	35	12
79	,,	1 p. grey	45	10
80	,,	13 m. ultramarine	40	8
81	,,	2 p. olive	55	15
		a. Opt. inverted	£225	£250
		b. Ochre	55·00	4·00
82	,,	5 p. deep purple	2·50	60
82*a*	,,	9 p. ochre	£500	£150
83	,,	10 p. light blue	12·00	2·50
		a. "E.F.F." for "E.E.F." in bottom panel	£350	£325
84	,,	20 p. bright violet	80·00	55·00
		(*b*) P 15×14.		
86	**3**	5 p. deep purple	16·00	2·00
87	,,	9 p. ochre	6·00	4·50
88	,,	10 p. light blue	4·50	1·25
		a. "E.F.F." for "E.E.F." in bottom panel	£300	£275
89	,,	20 p. bright violet	6·00	4·00
71/89		(*cheapest*) *Set of* 15	20·00	10·00
71/89		Optd. "Specimen" *Set of* 15	£200	

In this issue the design of all denominations is the same size, viz. 18 mm.×21½ mm. Varieties may be found with one or other of the stops between "E.E.F." missing.

BRITISH MANDATE TO THE LEAGUE OF NATIONS.
23 September, 1923.

9. Rachel's Tomb.

10. Dome of the Rock.

11. Citadel, Jerusalem.

12. Sea of Galilee.

(Des. F. Taylor. Typo. Harrison & Sons.)

1927–45. *Wmk. Mult. Script CA.* P 13½×14½ (2 *m. to* 20 *m.*) *or* 14.

No.	Type	Description	Unused	Used
90	**9**	2 m. greenish blue	5	5
91	,,	3 m. yellow-green	5	5
92	**10**	4 m. rose-pink	75	30
93	**11**	5 m. orange	5	5
		a. From coils. P14½×14 ('36)	1·10	1·90
		b. Yellow (12.44)	8	8
		c. Yellow. From coils. Perf. 14½×14 ('45)	2·00	2·00
94	**10**	6 m. pale green	90	55
		a. Deep green	8	8
95	**11**	7 m. scarlet	90	25
96	**10**	8 m. yellow-brown	2·40	1·50
97	**9**	10 m. slate	8	5
		a. Grey. From coils. Perf. 14½×14 (11.38)	1·50	1·75
		b. Grey ('44)	5	5
98	**10**	13 m. ultramarine	1·00	15
99	**11**	20 m. dull olive-green	12	5
		a. Bright olive-green (12.44)	8	5
100	**12**	50 m. deep dull purple	30	10
		a. Bright purple (12.44)	30	10
101	,,	90 m. bistre	11·00	10·00
102	,,	100 m. turquoise-blue	40	8
103	,,	200 m. deep violet	2·50	1·00
		a. Bright violet (1928)	5·00	3·00
		b. Blackish violet (12.44)	60	40
90/103 *b*		*Set of* 14	16·00	12·00
90/103 H/S "Specimen"		*Set of* 14	£200	

Three sets may be made of the above issue; one on thin paper, one on thicker paper with a ribbed appearance, and another on thick white paper without ribbing.

2 m. stamps in the grey colour of the 10 m. exist as also 50 m. stamps in blue, but it has not been established whether they were issued.

Dates of issue:—1.6.27, 3 and 13 m; 14.8.27, others.

1932 (1 June)–**44.** *New values and colours. Wmk. Mult. Script CA.* P 13½×14½ (4 *m. to* 15 *m.*) *or* 14.

No.	Type	Description	Unused	Used
104	**10**	4 m. purple (1.11.32)	5	5
105	**11**	7 m. deep violet	5	5
106	**10**	8 m. scarlet	5	5
107	,,	13 m. bistre (1.8.32)	10	5
108	,,	15 m. ultramarine (1.8.32)	20	5
		a. Grey-blue (12.44)	10	5
		b. Greenish blue	10	5
109	**12**	250 m. brown (15.1.42)	45	50
110	,,	500 m. scarlet (15.1.42)	1·00	90
111	,,	£P1 black (15.1.42)	1·50	90
104/111		*Set of* 8	3·00	2·00
104/11 Perf. "Specimen"		*Set of* 8	£275	

POSTAL FISCALS.

Type-set stamps inscribed "O.P.D.A."(= Ottoman Public Dept. Administration) or "H.J.Z." (Hejaz Railway); British 1d. stamps (No. 336); and Palestine stamps overprinted with one or other of the above groups of letters, or with the word "Devair", with or without surcharge of new value, are fiscal stamps. They are known used as postage stamps, alone, or with other stamps to make up the correct rates, and were passed by the postal authorities, although they were not definitely authorised for postal use.

POSTAGE DUE STAMPS.

D 1

(Typo. Greek Orthodox Convent, Jerusalem.)

1923 (1 Apr.). P 11.

No.	Type	Description	Unused	Used
D1	**D 1**	1 m. yellow-brown	7·00	8·00
		a. Imperf. (pair)	£375	
		b. Imperf. btwn. (horiz. pr.)	£550	
D2	,,	2 m. blue-green	3·75	3·75
		a. Imperf. (pair)	£375	
D3	,,	4 m. scarlet	4·00	4·00
D4	,,	8 m. mauve	2·00	2·00
		a. Imperf. (pair)	£120	
		b. Imperf. btwn. (horiz. pr.)	—	£1500
D5	,,	13 m. steel blue	2·25	2·00
		a. Imperf. btwn. (horiz. pr.)	£550	
D1/5		*Set of* 5	15·00	15·00

Perfectly centred and perforated stamps of this issue are worth considerably more than the above prices, which are for average specimens.

D 2 (MILLIEME). D 3 (MIL).

(Types D **2/3**. Typo. D.L.R.)

1924 (1 Dec.). *Wmk. Mult. Script CA.* P 14.

No.	Type	Description	Unused	Used
D 6	**D 2**	1 m. deep brown	45	60
D 7	,,	2 m. yellow	50	60
D 8	,,	4 m. green	55	60
D 9	,,	8 m. scarlet	70	40
D10	,,	13 m. ultramarine	1·25	1·25
D11	,,	5 p. violet	2·25	90
D6/11		*Set of* 6	5·00	3·00
D6/11 Optd. "Specimen"		*Set of* 6	£160	

1928 (1 Feb.)–**45.** *Wmk. Mult. Script CA.* P 14.

No.	Type	Description	Unused	Used
D12	**D 3**	1 m. brown	12	12
		a. Perf. 15×14 (1945)	4·50	6·50
D13	,,	2 m. yellow	15	20
D14	,,	4 m. green	20	20
		a. Perf. 15×14 (1945)	4·00	5·00
D15	,,	6 m. orange-brn. (10.33)	45	45
D16	,,	8 m. carmine	30	25
D17	,,	10 m. pale grey	30	25
D18	,,	13 m. ultramarine	45	50
D19	,,	20 m. pale olive-green	60	45
D20	,,	50 m. violet	60	50
D12/20		*Set of* 9	2·75	2·50
D12/20 Optd./Perf. "Specimen"		*Set of* 9	£160	

The British Mandate terminated on 14 May, 1948. Later issues of stamps and occupation issues will be found listed under Gaza, Israel and Jordan in Vol. 2 of the Stanley Gibbons Foreign Overseas Catalogue.

PAPUA.
(BRITISH NEW GUINEA.)

1. Lakatoi (Native Canoe) with Hanuabada Village in Background.

2. (Horizontal.)

(Recess. D.L.R.)

1901–5. *T* **1.** *Wmk. Mult. Rosettes, T* **2.** *P* 14.

I. *Thick paper. Wmk. horizontal.*

1	½d. black and yellow-green ..	2·00	2·75
2	1d. black and carmine ..	1·25	1·90
3	2d. black and violet	2·25	2·25
4	2½d. black and ultramarine ..	4·00	5·50
5	4d. black and sepia	9·00	9·00
6	6d. black and myrtle-green ..	7·00	9·00
7	1s. black and orange ..	18·00	20·00
8	2s. 6d. black and brown ..	£200	£190

II. *Thick paper. Wmk. vertical.*

9	½d. black and yellow-green ..	1·25	1·40
10	1d. black and carmine ..	1·25	1·25
11	2d. black and violet	1·25	1·40
12	2½d. black and ultramarine ..	3·50	5·50
13	4d. black and sepia ..	12·00	14·00
14	6d. black and myrtle-green ..	14·00	17·00
14*a*	1s. black and orange ..	14·00	20·00
14*b*	2s. 6d. black and brown ..	£250	£275

III. *Thin paper. Wmk. horizontal.*

14*c*	½d. black and yellow-green ..	30·00	30·00
14*d*	2½d. black and ultramarine ..	35·00	32·00
14*e*	2½d. black and dull blue ..	35·00	32·00

IV. *Thin paper. Wmk. vertical.*

15	½d. black and yellow-green ..	2·75	3·50
16	1d. black and carmine ..	12·00	12·00
17	2d. black and violet ..	10·00	5·50
18	2½d. black and ultramarine ..	40·00	35·00
18*a*	2½d. black and dull blue ..	40·00	38·00
19	4d. black and sepia ..	24·00	28·00
20	6d. black and myrtle-green ..	75·00	80·00
21	1s. black and orange ..	75·00	80·00
22	2s. 6d. black and brown ..	£180	£190
1/22	.. .. *Set of* 8	£200	£225

The 20th stamp in sheets of the ½d., 2d., and 2½d. shows a variety known as "white leaves", while stamp No. 27 of the 2d. and 2½d. and No. 28 of the ½d. and 1s. show what is known as the "unshaded leaves" variety.

MINIMUM PRICE

The minimum price quoted is 5p which represents a handling charge rather than a basis for valuing common stamps. For further notes about prices see introductory pages.

Papua. (3) **Papua.** (4)

1906–7. *T* **1** *optd. P* 14. A. *With T* **3** (*large opt.*), *at Port Moresby* (8 Nov., 1906).

I. *Thick paper. Wmk. horizontal.*

23	4d. black and sepia	55·00	55·00
24	6d. black and myrtle-green ..	7·00	9·00
25	1s. black and orange ..	5·50	7·00
26	2s. 6d. black and brown ..	35·00	38·00

II. *Thick paper. Wmk. vertical.*

27	2½d. black and ultramarine ..	2·25	4·00
28	4d. black and sepia	48·00	48·00
29	6d. black and myrtle-green ..	7·00	9·00
29*a*	1s. black and orange ..	65·00	65·00
29*b*	2s. 6d. black and brown ..	£350	£400

III. *Thin paper. Wmk. vertical.*

30	½d. black and yellow-green ..	2·25	2·75
31	1d. black and carmine ..	3·25	2·75
32	2d. black and violet	1·50	1·90
23/32 (cheapest)	.. *Set of* 8	95·00	£100

B. *With T* **4** (*small opt.*), *at Brisbane* (May–June 1907).

I. *Thick paper. Wmk. horizontal.*

34	½d. black and yellow-green ..	9·00	14·00
35	2½d. black and dull blue ..	18·00	20·00
36	1s. black and orange ..	16·00	20·00
37	2s. 6d. black and brown ..	12·00	14·00
	a. Opt. reading downwards ..	£250	
	b. Opt. double reading downwards	£600	
	c. Opt. double (horiz.)	—	£250
	d. Opt. triple (horiz.)	—	£225

II. *Thick paper. Wmk. vertical.*

38	2½d. black and ultramarine ..	2·00	2·50
	a. Opt. double		
38*b*	1s. black and orange ..	14·00	16·00
38*c*	2s. 6d. black and brown ..	£350	£450

III. *Thin paper. Wmk. horizontal.*

38*d*	½d. black and yellow-green ..	20·00	20·00
39	2½d. black and ultramarine ..	4·00	7·00
	a. Opt. double		
39*b*	2½d. black and dull blue ..	18·00	20·00

IV. *Thin paper. Wmk. vertical.*

40	½d. black and yellow-green ..	1·25	1·60
	a. Opt. double	£400	
41	1d. black and carmine ..	1·40	1·90
	a. Opt. reading upwards (pair)	£130	£130
42	2d. black and violet ..	1·10	70
42*a*	2½d. black and ultramarine ..		
43	4d. black and sepia	7·50	9·00
44	6d. black and myrtle-green ..	6·50	9·00
	a. Opt. double	£350	£400
45	1s. black and orange ..	9·50	11·00
	a. Opt. double		
46	2s. 6d. black and brown ..	7·00	9·50
34/46 (cheapest) ..	*Set of* 8	32·00	40·00

In the setting of this overprint Nos. 10, 16, and 21 have the "p" of "Papua" with a defective foot or inverted "d" for "p", and in No. 17 the "pua" of "Papua" is a shade lower than the first "a".

PRINTERS. All the following issues were printed at Melbourne. See notes at beginning of Australia.

5. Large "PAPUA".

B

C

Three types of the 2s. 6d.:—

A. Thin top to "2" and small ball. Thin "6" and small ball. Thick uneven stroke.

B. Thick top to "2" and large, badly shaped ball. Thick "6" and uneven ball. Thick uneven line.

C. Thin top to "2" and large, well shaped ball. Thin "6" and large ball. Very thick stroke, nearly even.

Type A is not illustrated as the stamp is distinguishable by perf. and watermark.

The litho. stones were prepared from the engraved plates of the 1901 issue, value for value except the 2s. 6d. as the original plate for this was mislaid. No. 48 containing Type A was prepared from the original 6d. plate with the value inserted on the stone and later a fresh stone was prepared from the 1d. plate and this contained Types B and C mixed. Finally, the original plate of the 2s. 6d. was found and a third stone was prepared from this, and these were issued in 1911. This, however, is not listed as there is no overall distinguishing feature and the only means of identification is by plating the minor flaws.

6. Small "PAPUA".

Litho. Government Printing Office, Melbourne, from transfers from original engraved plates.

1907–10. *T* **5/6.** *Wmk. Crown over A, Type* w.**11.**

A. *Large* "PAPUA".

(*a*) *Wmk. upright. P* 11.

47	**5**	½d. blk. & yellow-grn. (11.07)	55	85

(*b*) *Wmk. sideways. P* 11.

48	**5**	2s. 6d. black and chocolate (A) (12.07)	12·00	14·00

B. *Small* "PAPUA".

I. *Wmk. upright.*

(*a*) *P* 11 (1907–8).

49	**6**	1d. black and rose (6.08) ..	1·00	1·25
50	,,	2d. black & purple (10.08)	1·25	1·50
51	,,	2½d. blk. & brt. ultram. (7.08)	3·75	6·50
		a. Black and pale ultramarine..	1·25	2·00
52	,,	4d. black and sepia (11.07)	1·25	1·40
53	,,	6d. blk. & myrtle-grn. (4.08)	3·25	4·50
54	,,	1s. black and orange (10.08)	3·25	4·50

(*b*) *P* 12½ (1907–9).

55	**6**	2d. black & purple (10.08)	1·40	1·50
56	,,	2½d. blk. & brt. ultram. (7.08)	5·50	11·00
		a. Error. Wmk. sideways ..	12·00	14·00
		b. Black and pale ultramarine	3·75	7·00
57	,,	4d. black and sepia (11.07)	2·25	2·25
58	,,	1s. black and orange (1.09)	13·00	17·00

II. *Wmk. sideways.*

(*a*) *P* 11 (1909–10).

59	**6**	½d. blk. & yell.-grn. (12.09)	1·10	1·40
		a. Black and deep green ('10) ..	9·00	10·00
60	,,	1d. black & carmine (1.10)	3·00	2·75
61	,,	2d. black and purple (2.10)	1·40	1·00
62	,,	2½d. black & dull bl. (1.10)	1·40	1·75
63	,,	4d. black and sepia (1.10) ..	1·50	1·75
64	,,	6d. blk. & myrtle-grn. (12.09)	4·50	3·00
65	,,	1s. black and orange (3.10)	9·00	11·00

(*b*) *P* 12½ (1909–10).

66	**6**	½d. blk. & yell.-grn. (12.09)	40	90
		a. Black and deep green ('10) ..	9·50	11·00
67	,,	1d. black & carmine (12.09)	2·25	1·40
68	,,	2d. black and purple (1.10)	1·10	75
69	,,	2½d. black & dull blue (1.10)	2·75	3·50
70	,,	6d. blk. & myrtle-grn. (12.09)	£325	£300
71	,,	1s. black and orange (3.10)	4·00	5·50

(*c*) *Perf. compound of* 11 *and* 12½.

72	**6**	½d. black and yellow-green ..		
73	,,	2d. black and purple	£160	
74	,,	4d. black and sepia		

Litho. at Commonwealth Stamp Printing Office, Melbourne, by J. B. Cooke, from new stones made by fresh transfers.

1910. *Large* "PAPUA". *Wmk. upright. P* 12½.
75 5 ½d. black and green (Dec.) .. 1·00 1·00
76 ,, 1d. black & carmine (Sept.) 1·40 95
77 ,, 2d. black and dull purple (*shades*) (Nov.) .. 1·25 1·25
a. "C" for "O" in "POSTAGE" .. .. 15·00 17·00
78 ,, 2½d. black & blue-violet (Oct.) 1·75 2·50
79 ,, 4d. black and sepia (Oct.) .. 1·40 2·75
80 ,, 6d. blk. & myrtle-grn. (Sept.) 2·25 2·50
81 ,, 1s. blk. & dp. orange (Nov.) 4·00 5·00
82 ,, 2s. 6d. black and brown (B) (Sept.) .. .. .. 11·00 14·00
83 ,, 2s. 6d. black and brown (C) (Sept.) .. .. .. 11·00 13·00
75/83 .. .. *Set of* 8 22·00 27·00

A variety showing a white line or "rift" in clouds occurs on stamp No. 23 in Nos. 49/74 and the "white leaves" variety mentioned below No. 22 occurs on the 2d. and 2½d. values in both issues. They are worth about four times the normal price.

8

ONE PENNY
(9)

(Typo. J. B. Cooke.)

1911–15. *Printed in one colour.* W **8**, *sideways.*
(*a*) *P* 12½ (1911–12).
84 6 ½d. yellow-green 35 40
a. *Green* 25 40
85 ,, 1d. rose-pink 65 25
86 ,, 2d. bright mauve 45 55
87 ,, 2½d. bright ultramarine .. 2·00 2·75
a. *Dull ultramarine* .. .. 2·00 2·75
88 ,, 4d. pale olive-green .. 1·50 2·25
89 ,, 6d. orange-brown .. .. 1·40 2·50
90 ,, 1s. yellow .. .. .. 3·25 4·00
91 ,, 2s. 6d. rose-carmine .. 8·50 11·00
84/91 .. .. *Set of* 8 16·00 21·00
(*b*) *P* 14.
92 6 1d. rose-pink (6.15) .. .. 4·50 3·50
a. *Pale scarlet* .. .. 1·75 1·40

(Surch. at Port Moresby.)

1918. *Above issue surch. with T* **9**.
93 5 1d. on ½d. yellow-green .. 40 35
a. *Green* 35 40
94 ,, 1d. on 2d. bright mauve .. 2·50 2·75
95 ,, 1d. on 2½d. ultramarine .. 1·00 1·10
96 ,, 1d. on 4d. pale olive-green .. 1·00 1·40
97 ,, 1d. on 6d. orange-brown .. 3·25 3·25
98 ,, 1d. on 2s. 6d. rose-carmine .. 1·40 2·50
93/98 .. .. *Set of* 6 8·50 10·00

(Typo. J. B. Cooke (1916–18), T. S. Harrison (1918–26), A. J. Mullett (No. 101*a* only) (1926–27), or John Ash (1927–31).)

1916–31. *Printed in two colours.* W **8**, *sideways. P* 14.
99 6 ½d. myrtle & apple-green (*Harrison* and *Ash*) ('19) 15 12
a. *Myrtle & pale olive-grn.* ('27) 12 25
100 ,, 1d. blk. & carm.-red ('16) 55 20
a. *Grey-black and red* (1918) .. 65 12
b. *Intense black and red* (*Harrison*) (1926) 90 40
101 ,, 1½d. pale grey-blue (*shades*) and brown (1925) .. 30 15
a. *Cobalt and light brown* (*Mullett*) (1927) .. .. 2·75 1·40
b. *Brt. blue & brt. brown* (1929) 55 25
c. "POSTACE" at right (all ptgs.) .. .. *From* 8·50 9·00
102 ,, 2d. brown-purple and brown-lake (1919) .. 1·00 55
a. *Deep brn.-pur. & lake* ('31) 5·00 95
b. *Brown-purple & claret* ('31) 1·40 60
103 ,, 2½d. myrtle & ultram. ('19) 1·25 2·75
104 6 3d. black and bright blue-green ('16) 70 70
a. Error. Black and deep greenish Prussian blue* .. 80·00 80·00
b. *Sepia-black and bright blue-green* (*Harrison*) .. .. 7·00 5·00
c. *Black and blue-green* ('27) 70 90
105 ,, 4d. brown & orange ('19) 2·00 2·25
a. *Light brown & orange* ('27) 2·25 4·50
106 ,, 5d. bluish slate and pale brown ('31) .. .. 2·00 2·50
107 ,, 6d. dull & pale pur. ('19) 1·00 1·40
a. *Dull pur. & red-pur.* ('27) 1·60 2·50
b. "POSTACE" at left (all ptgs.) .. .. *From* 14·00
108 ,, 1s. sepia and olive ('19) .. 1·60 2·25
a. *Brown and yellow-olive* ('27) 1·40 2·25
109 ,, 2s. 6d. maroon and pale pink ('19) .. .. 7·00 9·00
a. *Maroon and bright pink* (*shades*) ('27) .. .. 7·00 9·00
110 ,, 5s. blk. & dp. green ('16) 13·00 12·00
111 ,, 10s. green and pale ultramarine ('25) .. .. 42·00 45·00
99/111 .. .. *Set of* 13 65·00 70·00

*Beware of similar shades produced by removal of yellow pigment.

The printers of the various shades can be determined by their dates of issue. The Ash printings are on whiter paper.

For 9d., and 1s. 3d. values, see Nos. 127/8.

AIR MAIL
(10)

(11)

(Optd. by Govt. Printer, Port Moresby.)

1929–30. *Air. T* **6** *optd. with T* **10**.
(*a*) *Cooke printing. Yellowish paper.*
112 3d. black & bright blue-grn. 1·25 1·75
a. Opt. omitted in vert. pair with normal £550
(*b*) *Harrison printing. Yellowish paper.*
113 3d. sepia-black & brt. blue-grn. 17·00 18·00
(*c*) *Ash printing. White paper.*
114 3d. black and blue-green .. 1·00 1·40
a. Opt. omitted in horiz. pair with normal £850
b. Ditto, but vert. pair £750
c. Opt. vertical, on back .. £750
d. Opts. tête-bêche (pair) .. £450

(Optd. by Govt. Printer. Port Moresby.)

1930 (15 Sept.). *Air. T* **6** *optd. with T* **11**, *in carmine.*
(*a*) *Harrison printings. Yellowish paper.*
115 3d. sepia-black and bright blue-green .. .. 75·00
a. Opt. double £500 £550
116 6d. dull and pale purple 3·25 4·00
a. "POSTACE" at left .. 18·00
117 1s. sepia and olive .. 7·00 11·00
a. Opt. inverted £550
(*b*) *Ash printings. White paper.*
118 3d. black and blue-green .. 40 90
119 6d. dull purple and red-purple 2·25 2·75
a. "POSTACE" at left .. 15·00
120 1s. brown and yellow-olive .. 2·75 3·25

5d.

TWO PENCE
(12)

FIVE PENCE
(13)

(Surch. by Govt. Printer, Port Moresby.)

1931 (1 Jan.). *T* **6** *surch. with T* **12**.
(*a*) *Mullett printing.*
121 2d. on 1½d. cobalt & lt. brn. 4·50 5·00
a. "POSTACE" at right .. 20·00
(*b*) *Ash printing.*
122 2d. on 1½d. brt. blue & brt. brn. 90 1·00
a. "POSTACE" at right .. 10·00

(Surch. by Govt. Printer, Port Moresby.)

1931. *T* **6** *surch. as T* **13**.
(*a*) *Cooke printing.*
123 1s. 3d. on 5s. blk. & dp. grn. 1·50 2·00
(*b*) *Harrison printing. Yellowish paper.*
124 9d. on 2s. 6d. maroon and pale pink (Dec.) .. .. 1·40 1·90
(*c*) *Ash printings. White paper.*
125 5d. on 1s. brown and yellow-olive (26.7) .. .. 60 1·00
126 9d. on 2s. 6d. maroon and bright pink .. .. 1·50 2·50

(Typo. J. Ash.)

1932. W **15** *of Australia* (*Mult.* "C of A"). *P* 11.
127 5 9d. lilac and violet .. .. 3·00 3·50
128 ,, 1s. 3d. lilac & p. greenish bl. 5·00 5·00
127/8 Optd. "Specimen" *Set of* 2 £150

15. Motuan Girl.

16. A Chieftain's Son.

17. Tree-Houses.

19. Papuan Dandy.

18. Bird of Paradise.

20. Native Mother and Child.

21. Masked Dancer.

22. Papuan Motherhood.

23. Papuan Shooting Fish.

24. *Dubu*—or Ceremonial Platform.

25. Lakatoi.

26. Papuan Art.

27. Pottery Making.

28. Native Policeman.

29. Lighting a Fire.

30. Delta House.

(Des. F. E. Williams (2s., £1 and frames of other values), E. Whitehouse (2d., 4d., 6d., 1s., and 10s.); remaining centres from photos by Messrs. F. E. Williams and Gibson. Recess. J. Ash (all values) and W. C. G. McCracken (½d., 1d., 2d., 4d.).)

1932 (14 Nov.). *No wmk.* *P* 11.

No.	Type	Description	Unused	Used
130	**15**	½d. black and orange ..	15	25
		a. Black and buff (McCracken)	6·00	6·50
131	**16**	1d. black and green ..	10	10
132	**17**	1½d. black and lake ..	55	1·10
133	**18**	2d. red	1·10	20
134	**19**	3d. black and blue ..	1·25	2·00
135	**20**	4d. olive-green	1·25	1·90
136	**21**	5d. black and slate-green	1·10	1·25
137	**22**	6d. bistre-brown ..	1·75	1·75
138	**23**	9d. black and violet ..	3·50	4·00
139	**24**	1s. dull blue-green ..	2·25	3·75
140	**25**	1s. 3d. black & dull purple	5·00	6·50
141	**26**	2s. black and slate-green	5·00	6·50
142	**27**	2s. 6d. black & rose-mve.	9·00	11·00
143	**28**	5s. black and olive-brown	13·00	13·00
144	**29**	10s. violet	26·00	32·00
145	**30**	£1 black and olive-grey ..	55·00	50·00
130/145		.. .. *Set of* 16	£110	£120

31. Hoisting the Union Jack.

32. Scene on H.M.S. *Nelson*.

(Recess. J. Ash.)

1934 (6 Nov.). *50th Anniv. of Declaration of British Protectorate.* *P* 11.

No.	Type	Description	Unused	Used
146	**31**	1d. green	70	85
147	**32**	2d. scarlet	1·10	1·00
148	**31**	3d. blue	2·75	2·75
149	**32**	5d. purple	5·00	5·50

HIS MAJESTY'S JUBILEE.

1910 1935
(33)

HIS MAJESTY'S
JUBILEE.
1910 — 1935
(34)

1935 (9 July). *Silver Jubilee.* *Optd. with T* **33** *or* **34** (*2d.*).

No.	Type	Description	Unused	Used
150	**16**	1d. black and green ..	25	30
151	**18**	2d. scarlet	40	55
152	**19**	3d. black and blue	1·00	1·40
153	**21**	5d. black and slate-green ..	3·50	4·00

35

(Recess. J. Ash.)

1937 (14 May). *Coronation.* *P* 11.

No.	Type	Description	Unused	Used
154	**35**	1d. green	8	8
155	,,	2d. scarlet	8	8
156	,,	3d. blue	12	10
157	,,	5d. purple	15	15

36. Port Moresby.

(Recess. J. Ash.)

1938 (6 Sept.). *Air.* *50th Anniv. of Declaration of British Possession.* *P* 11.

No.	Type	Description	Unused	Used
158	**36**	2d. rose-red	55	1·1
159	,,	3d. bright blue	1·00	1·4
160	,,	5d. green	1·40	1·7
161	,,	8d. brown-lake	3·00	4·0
162	,,	1s. mauve	6·00	5·5
158/162		.. .. *Set of* 5	11·00	13·0

37. Native Poling Rafts.

(Recess. J. Ash.)

1939 (6 Sept.). *Air.* *P* 11.

No.	Type	Description	Unused	Used
163	**37**	2d. rose-red	70	8
164	,,	3d. bright blue	80	1·1
165	,,	5d. green	1·40	9
166	,,	8d. brown-lake	2·25	2·7
167	,,	1s. mauve	3·50	3·5

(Recess. W. C. G. McCracken.)

1941 (2 Jan.). *Air.* *P* 11½.

No.	Type	Description	Unused	Used
168	**37**	1s. 6d. olive-green	14·00	16·0
163/168		.. .. *Set of* 6	20·00	23·0

OFFICIAL STAMPS.

STAMPS PERFORATED "O S."

We have a number of these in stock with the initials perforated through the stamps. We do not catalogue such varieties, but can send selections to collectors who are interested in them. In most cases the prices are those of used copies of the corresponding number in Catalogue.

O S
(O 1)

(Typo. by T. S. Harrison (1d. and 2s. 6d.) and J. Ash.)

1931 (29 July)–**32**. *T* **6** *optd. with Type* O **1** *W* **8** *or W* **15** *of Australia* (*9d., 1s. 3d.*). *P* 1 *or* 11 (*9d., 1s. 3d.*).

No.	Description	Unused	Used
O 1	½d. myrtle and apple-green ..	35	8

O 2	1d.	grey-black and red ..	35	1·10
		a. Intense black and red ..	20	1·00
O 3	1½d.	brt. blue & brt. brown	75	1·75
		a. **" POSTACE " at right** ..	13·00	13·00
O 4	2d.	brn.-purple and claret	70	1·75
O 5	3d.	black and blue-green ..	70	2·75
O 6	4d.	light brown and orange	95	2·75
O 7	5d.	bluish slate & pale brown	1·50	3·00
O 8	6d.	dull pur. & red-purple ..	2·50	3·50
		a. **" POSTACE " at left** ..	13·00	13·00
O 9	9d.	lilac and violet ('32) ..	5·50	9·00
O10	1s.	brown and yellow-olive	3·50	5·00
O11	1s.	3d. lilac and pale greenish blue ('32)	8·00	12·00
O12	2s.	6d. maroon and pale pink (*Harrison*) ..	8·00	12·00
		a. Maroon and bright pink (Ash)	8·00	12·00
O1/O12		.. .. *Set of* 12	30·00	50·00

Civil Administration, in Papua, was suspended in 1942; on resumption, after the Japanese defeat in 1945, Australian stamps were used until the appearance of the issue of the combined territories of PAPUA & NEW GUINEA (*q.v.*).

PAPUA NEW GUINEA.

The name of the combined territory was changed from " Papua and New Guinea " to " Papua New Guinea " at the beginning of 1972.

I. AUSTRALIAN TRUST TERRITORY

1. Tree Kangaroo.

2. Buka Head-dresses.

3. Native Youth.

4. Bird of Paradise.

5. Native Policeman.

6. Papuan Head-dress.

7. Kiriwina Chief House.

8. Kiriwina Yam House.

9. Copra Making.

10. Lakatoi.

11. Rubber Tapping.

12. Sepik Dancing Masks.

13. Native Shepherd and Flock.

14. Map of Papua and New Guinea.

15. Papuan Shooting Fish.

(Recess. Note Printing Branch, Commonwealth Bank, Melbourne.)

1952 (30 OCT.)–**58.** *P* 14.

1	**1**	½d. emerald	10	8
2	**2**	1d. deep brown	8	5
3	**3**	2d. blue	15	8
4	**4**	2½d. orange	50	40
5	**5**	3d. deep green	25	10
6	**6**	3½d. carmine-red	25	15
6*a*	,,	3½d. black (2.6.58)	2·50	1·25
7	**7**	6½d. dull purple (*shades*) ..	60	20
8	**8**	7½d. blue	4·50	3·00
9	**9**	9d. brown	80	40
10	**10**	1s. yellow-green	70	30
11	**11**	1s. 6d. deep green ..	1·10	45
12	**12**	2s. indigo	1·75	60
13	**13**	2s. 6d. brown-purple ..	1·75	65
14	**14**	10s. blue-black	16·00	6·00
15	**15**	£1 deep brown	24·00	9·00
1/15		.. .. *Set of* 16	50·00	20·00
14/15		Optd. " Specimen " *Set of* 2	28·00	

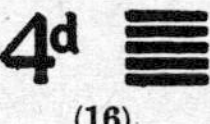

(16)

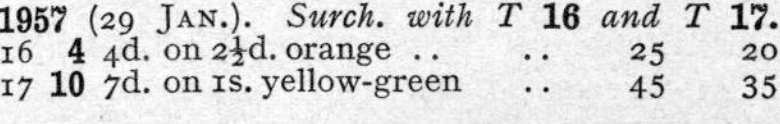

(17)

1957 (29 JAN.). *Surch. with T* **16** *and T* **17.**

16	**4**	4d. on 2½d. orange	25	20
17	**10**	7d. on 1s. yellow-green ..	45	35

18. Cacao Plant.

21. Coffee Beans.

19. Klinki Plymill.

20. Cattle.

(Recess. Note Ptg. Branch, Commonwealth Bank, Melbourne.)

1958 (2 JUNE)–**60.** *New values. P* 14.

18	**18**	4d. vermilion	15	8
19	,,	5d. green (10.11.60) ..	15	8
20	**19**	7d. bronze-green	1·50	45
21	,,	8d. dp. ultramarine (10.11.60)	1·50	1·25
22	**20**	1s. 7d. red-brown	19·00	16·00
23	,,	2s. 5d. vermilion (10.11.60)	2·25	2·25
24	**21**	5s. crimson and olive-green	2·25	1·50
18/24		.. .. *Set of* 7	24·00	19·00

(22) **23.** Council Chamber, Port Moresby.

1959 (1 Dec.). *No. 1 surch. with T* **22.**
25 **1** 5d. on ½d. emerald 25 10

(Photo. Harrison & Sons.)

1961 (10 Apr.). *Reconstitution of Legislative Council. P* 15 × 14.
26 **23** 5d. deep green and yellow .. 80 25
27 ,, 2s. 3d. deep green and light salmon .. .. .. 9·00 9·00

24. Female, Goroka, New Guinea. **25.** Tribal Elder, Tari Papua.

26. Female Dancer. **27.** Male Dancer.

28. Traffic Policeman.

(Des. Pamela M. Prescott. Recess. Note Ptg. Branch, Reserve Bank of Australia, Melbourne.)

1961 (26 July)–**62.** *P* 14½ × 14 (*1d., 3d., 3s.*) *or* 14 × 14½ (*others*).
28 **24** 1d. lake 8 8
29 **25** 3d. indigo 12 10
30 **26** 1s. bronze-green .. .. 2·00 50
31 **27** 2s. maroon 60 50
32 **28** 3s. dp. bluish grn. (5.9.62) 75 60
28/32 .. .. *Set of* 5 3·25 1·50

29. Campaign Emblem.

(Recess. Note Ptg. Branch, Reserve Bank of Australia, Melbourne.)

1962 (7 Apr.). *Malaria Eradication. P* 14.
33 **29** 5d. carm.-red and lt. blue .. 25 20
34 ,, 1s. red and sepia .. 1·25 1·25
35 ,, 2s. black and yellow-green 2·50 2·50

30. Map of South Pacific.

(Des. Pamela M. Prescott. Recess. Note Ptg. Branch, Reserve Bank of Australia, Melbourne.)

1962 (9 July). *Fifth South Pacific Conference, Pago Pago. P* 14½ × 14.
36 **30** 5d. scarlet and light green .. 25 25
37 ,, 1s. 6d. dp. violet & lt. yellow 1·25 1·25
38 ,, 2s. 6d. deep green & lt. blue 2·75 2·75

31. Throwing the Javelin. **32.** High Jump.

33. Runners.

(Des. G. Hamori. Photo. Courvoisier.)

1962 (24 Oct.). *Seventh British Empire and Commonwealth Games, Perth. P* 11½.
39 **31** 5d. brown and light blue .. 40 25
40 **32** 5d. brown and orange .. 40 25
41 **33** 2s. 3d. brown & light green 1·75 1·75

Nos. 39/40 are arranged together *se-tenant* in sheets of 100 (*price for se-tenant pair* £1·25 *un. or us.*).

4. Bird of Paradise. **35.** Golden Opossum.

36. Rabaul.

37. Queen Elizabeth II.

(Des. S. T. Cham (10s.), A. Buckley (photo) (£1). Photo. Harrison (£1), Courvoisier (others).)

1963. *P* 14½ (£1) *or* 11½ *others.*
42 **34** 5d. yellow, chestnut and sepia (27 Mar.) .. 12 12
43 **35** 6d. red, yellow-brown and grey (27 Mar.) 50 75
44 **36** 10s. multicoloured (13 Feb.) 8·00 7·00
45 **37** £1 sepia, gold and blue-green (3 July) .. .. 7·00 6·50
44/5 Optd. "Specimen" *Set of* 2 12·00

1963 (1 May). *Red Cross Centenary. As No.* 351 *of Australia.*
46 5d. red, grey-brown and bluish green 15 20

38. Waterfront, Port Moresby.

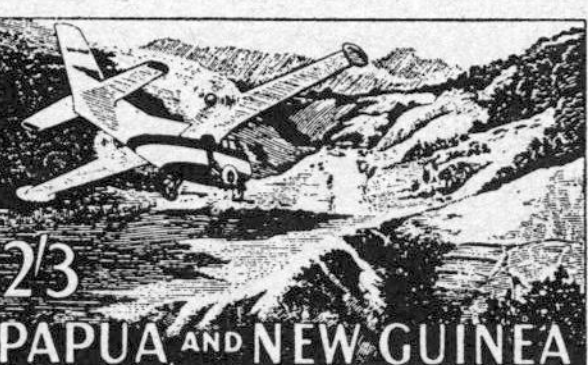

39. Piaggio P-166 Aircraft landing at Tapini.

(Des. J. McMahon (8d.), Pamela M. Prescott (2s. 3d.). Recess. Note Ptg. Branch, Reserve Bank of Australia, Melbourne.)

1963 (8 May). *P* 14 × 13½.
47 **38** 8d. green 25 25
48 **39** 2s. 3d. ultramarine .. 75 75

40. Games Emblem.

(Des. Pamela M. Prescott. Recess. Note Ptg. Branch, Reserve Bank of Australia, Melbourne.)

.963 (14 Aug.). *First South Pacific Games, Suva.* *P* 13½×14½.

.9 **40**	5d. bistre	.. .. ..	35	25
:o ,,	1s. deep green	.. ..	90	90

41. Watam Head.

42. Watam Head (*different*).

43. Bosmun Head.

44. Medina Head.

Des. Pamela M. Prescott. Photo. Courvoisier.)

.964 (5 Feb.). *Native Artifacts.* *P* 11½.

1 **41**	11d. multicoloured ..	..	30	30
2 **42**	2s. 5d. multicoloured	..	60	60
3 **43**	2s. 6d. multicoloured	..	70	70
4 **44**	5s. multicoloured ..	..	1·25	1·25

45. Casting Vote.

(Photo. Courvoisier).

964 (4 Mar.). *Common Roll Elections.* *P* 11½.

5 **45**	5d. brown and drab	..	15	15
6 ,,	2s. 3d. brown and pale blue		80	80

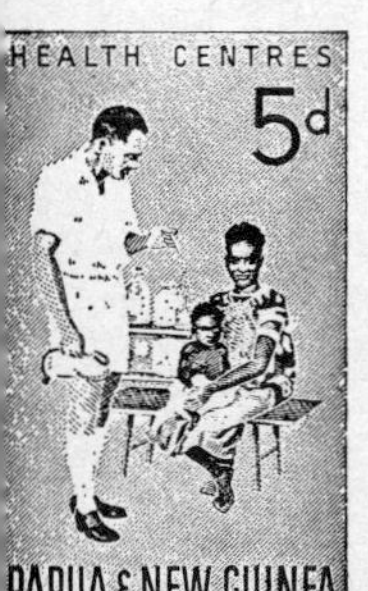

46. " Health Centres ".

47. " School Health ".

48. " Infant, Child and Maternal Health ".

49. " Medical Training ".

(Recess. Note Ptg. Branch, Reserve Bank of Australia, Melbourne.)

1964 (5 Aug.). *Health Services.* *P* 14.

57 **46**	5d. violet	.. .. ..	15	10
58 **47**	8d. bronze-green	.. ..	20	20
59 **48**	1s. blue	.. .. ..	30	30
60 **49**	1s. 2d. brown-red	.. ..	40	40

50. Striped Gardener Bowerbird.

55. Emperor of Germany Bird of Paradise.

51. New Guinea Regent Bowerbird.

52. Blue Bird of Paradise.

53. Lawes' Six-wired Bird of Paradise.

54 Black-billed Sickle-billed Bird of Paradise.

(*T* **51/4** *as T* **50.**)

56. Brown Sickle-billed Bird of Paradise.

57. Lesser Bird of Paradise.

58. Magnificent Bird of Paradise.

59. Twelve-wired Bird of Paradise.

60. Magnificent Rifle Bird.

(*T* **56/60** *as T* **55.**)

(Photo. Courvoisier.)

1964 (28 Oct.)–**65.** *Designs multicoloured; background colours given.* *P* 11½ (1d. *to* 8d.) *or* 12×11½ (*others*).

61 **50**	1d. pale olive-yell. (20.1.65)		10	8
62 **51**	3d. light grey (20.1.65)	..	12	10
63 **52**	5d. pale red (20.1.65)	..	12	10
64 **53**	6d. pale green	.. ..	15	15
65 **54**	8d. lilac	.. .. ..	20	20
66 **55**	1s. salmon ..	.. ..	30	30
67 **56**	2s. light blue (20.1.65)	..	45	45
68 **57**	2s. 3d. lt. green (20.1.65)	..	60	65
69 **58**	3s. pale yellow (20.1.65)	..	80	90
70 **59**	5s. cobalt (20.1.65)	..	1·60	1·60
71 **60**	10s. pale drab	.. ..	3·00	3·25
61/71 ..	.. ..	*Set of* 11	6·50	7·00

61. Canoe Prow.

T **62/4** all show different carved canoe prows.

(Des. Pamela M. Prescott. Photo. Courvoisier.)

1965 (24 Mar.). *Sepik Canoe Prows in Port Moresby Museum.* *P* 11½.

72 **61**	4d. multicoloured ..	..	20	15
73 **62**	1s. 2d. multicoloured	..	80	1·00
74 **63**	1s. 6d. multicoloured	..	45	45
75 **64**	4s. multicoloured ..	..	1·00	1·25

1965 (14 Apr.). *50th Anniv. of Gallipoli Landing. As T* **184** *of Australia, but slightly larger* (22×34½ *mm.*). *Photo.*

76	2s. 3d. sepia, black & emerald	60	60

65. Urban Plan and Native House.

(Des. G. Hamori. Photo. Courvoisier.)

1965 (7 July). *Sixth South Pacific Conference, Lae.* *T* **65** *and similar horiz. design.* *P* 11½.

77	6d. multicoloured	.. ..	12	12
78	1s. multicoloured	.. ..	30	30

No. 78 is similar to T **65** but with the plan on the right and the house on the left. Also " URBANISATION " reads downwards.

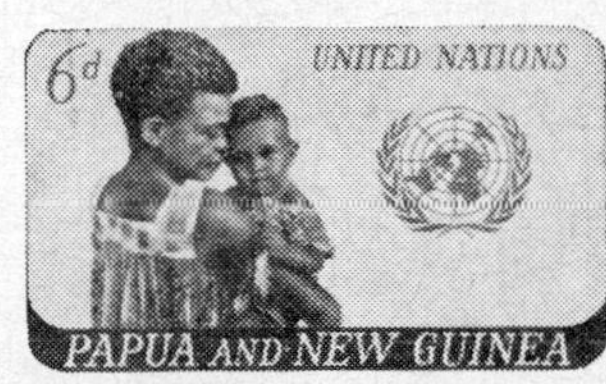

66. Mother and Child.

67. Globe and U.N. Emblem.

68. U.N. Emblem and Globes.

(Photo. Courvoisier.)

1965 (13 Oct.). *20th Anniv. of U.N.O.* *P* 11½.

79 **66**	6d. sepia, blue and pale turquoise-blue	12	12
80 **67**	1s. orange-brown, blue and deep reddish violet ..	25	25
81 **68**	2s. blue, blue-green and light yellow-olive ..	40	40

(New Currency. 100 cents=$1 Australian.)

60. Blue Emperor.

70. White-banded Map Butterfly.

71. Mountain Swallowtail. (*Vert.*)

72. Port Moresby Terinos. (*Vert.*)

73. New Guinea Birdwing.

73a. Blue Crow (butterfly).
74. Euchenor Butterfly.
75. White-spotted Parthenos.
76. Orange Jezebel.
77. New Guinea Emperor.
78. Blue Spotted Leaf-wing
79. Paradise Birdwing.
(*T* **73a/79** *are all horiz. as T* **73.**)

(Photo. Courvoisier.)

1966 (14 Feb.–12 Oct.). *Decimal Currency. P* 11½.

82	**69**	1 c. multicoloured	..	5	5
83	**70**	3 c. multicoloured	..	10	10
84	**71**	4 c. multicoloured	..	12	12
85	**72**	5 c. multicoloured	..	12	10
86	**73**	10 c. multicoloured	..	25	25
86a	**73a**	12 c. multicoloured	(12.10)	60	60
87	**74**	15 c. multicoloured	..	70	70
88	**75**	20 c. multicoloured	..	50	50
89	**76**	25 c. multicoloured	..	70	70
90	**77**	50 c. multicoloured	..	1·25	1·00
91	**78**	$1 multicoloured	..	2·50	2·50
92	**79**	$2 multicoloured	..	4·50	4·75
82/92		.. ..	*Set of* 12	10·00	10·00

80. " Molala Harai ".

81. " Marai ".

82. " Meavea Kivovia ".

83. " Toivita Tapaivita ".

(Des. Rev. H. A. Brown. Photo. Courvoisier.)

1966 (8 June). *Folklore. Elema Art. P* 11½.

93	**80**	2 c. black and carmine ..	5	5
94	**81**	7 c. black, light yellow and light blue	15	15
95	**82**	30 c. black, carmine & apple-green	55	60
96	**83**	60 c. black, carmine & yell.	1·50	1·60

Nos. 93/6 are supplementary values to the decimal currency definitive issue.

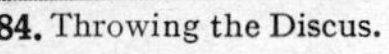

84. Throwing the Discus. **87.** *Mucuna novoguineensis.*

(Photo. Courvoisier.)

1966 (31 Aug.). *South Pacific Games, Nouméa. T* **84** *and similar vert. designs. Multicoloured. P* 11½.

97	5 c. Type **84**	10	10
98	10 c. Football	25	25
99	20 c. Tennis	45	45

(Des. Mrs. D. Pearce. Photo. Courvoisier.)

1966 (7 Dec.). *Flowers. T* **87** *and similar vert. designs. Multicoloured. P* 11½.

100	5 c. Type **87**	15	15
101	10 c. *Tecomanthe dentrophila*	25	25
102	20 c. *Rhododendron macgregoriae*	45	45
103	60 c. *Rhododendron konori* ..	1·25	1·25

91. " Fine Arts ".

(Des. G. Hamori. Photo. Courvoisier.)

1967 (8 Feb.). *Higher Education. T* **91** *and similar horiz. designs. Multicoloured. P* 12½×12.

104	1 c. Type **91**	5	5
105	3 c. " Surveying "	10	10
106	4 c. " Civil Engineering " ..	10	10
107	5 c. " Science "	10	10
108	20 c. " Law "	40	40
104/8	.. .. *Set of* 5	60	60

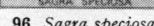

96. *Sagra speciosa.* **100.** Laloki River.

(Des. Pamela M. Prescott. Photo. Courvoisier.)

1967 (12 Apr.). *Fauna Conservation (Beetles). T* **96** *and similar vert. designs. Multicoloured. P* 11½.

109	5 c. Type **96**	10	10
110	10 c. *Eupholus schoenherri* ..	25	25
111	20 c. *Sphingnotus albertisi* ..	40	35
112	25 c. *Cyphogastra albertisi* ..	45	45

(Des. G. Wade. Photo. Courvoisier.)

1967 (28 June). *Laloki River Hydro-Electric Scheme, and " New Industries ". T* **100** *and similar vert. designs. Multicoloured. P* 12½.

113	5 c. Type **100**	10	10
114	10 c. Pyrethrum	25	25
115	20 c. Tea Plant	40	40
116	25 c. Type **100**	50	50

103. Air Attack at Milne Bay.

104. Kokoda Trail. (*Vert.*)
105. The Coast Watchers. (*Horiz.*)
106. Battle of the Coral Sea. (*Horiz.*)

(Des. R. Hodgkinson (2 c.), F. Hodgkinson (5 c.), G. Wade (20 c., 50 c.). Photo. Courvoisier.)

1967 (30 Aug.). *25th Anniv. of the Pacific War. P* 11½.

117	**103**	2 c. multicoloured ..	5	5
118	**104**	5 c. multicoloured ..	10	10
119	**105**	20 c. multicoloured ..	40	35
120	**106**	50 c. multicoloured ..	95	95

107. Fairy Lory.

108. Vulturine Parrot.

109. Dusk-orange Lory.

110. Edward's Fig Parrot.

(Des. T. Walcott. Photo. Courvoisier.)

1967 (29 Nov.). *Christmas. Territory Parrot*[s] *P* 12½.

121	**107**	5 c. multicoloured	..	12	1
122	**108**	7 c. multicoloured	..	20	2
123	**109**	20 c. multicoloured	..	50	5
124	**110**	25 c. multicoloured	..	60	6

111. Chimbu Head-dresses. **114.**

112. Southern Highlands Head-dress. (*Horiz.*)
113. Western Highlands Head-dress. (*Horiz*

(Des. P. Jones. Photo. Courvoisier.)

1968 (21 Feb.). " *National Heritage* ". *P* 12 × 1[2] (5 *c.*, 60 *c.*) *or* 12½ × 12 (*others*).

125	**111**	5 c. multicoloured	..	12	
126	**112**	10 c. multicoloured	..	25	
127	**113**	20 c. multicoloured	..	45	4
128	**114**	60 c. multicoloured	..	1·25	1·2

115. *Hyla thesaurensis.*

(Des. and photo. Courvoisier.)

1968 (24 Apr.). *Fauna Conservation (Frog*[s] *T* **115** *and similar horiz. designs. Multicoloure*[d] *P* 11½.

129	5 c. Type **115**	12	
130	10 c. Hyla iris	25	
131	15 c. *Ceratobatrachus guentheri*	35	
132	20 c. *Nyctimystes narinosa* ..	45	

119. Human Rights Emblem and Papuan Head-dress (abstract).

120. Human Rights in the World (abstract.)

(Des. G. Hamori. Litho. Enschedé.)

968 (26 June). *Human Rights Year. P* 13½ × 12½.

33	**119**	5 c. multicoloured	..	12	12
34	**120**	10 c. multicoloured	..	25	25

121. Leadership (abstract).

122. Leadership of the Community (abstract).

(Des. G. Hamori. Litho. Enschedé.)

968 (26 June). *Universal Suffrage. P* 13½ × 12½.

35	**121**	20 c. multicoloured	..	45	45
36	**122**	25 c. multicoloured	..	60	60

123. Egg Cowry.

124. Laciniated Conch.
125. Lithograph Cone.
126. Marbled Cone.
127. Episcopal Mitre.
128. Red Volute.
129. Areola Bonnet.
130. Scorpion Conch.
131. Fluted Clam.
132. Chocolate Flamed Venus Shell.
133. Giant Murex.
134. Chambered Nautilus.
135. Pacific Triton.
136. Emerald Snail.
(*T* 124/136 *are horiz.*)
137. Glory of the Sea. (*Vert.*)

(Des. P. Jones. Photo. Courvoisier.)

968–69. *Seashells. P* 12 × 12½ ($2), 12½ × 12 (1 *c. to* 20 *c.*) *or* 11½ (*others*).

37	**123**	1 c. mult. (29.1.69)	..	5	5
38	**124**	3 c. mult. (30.10.68)	..	8	8
39	**125**	4 c. mult. (29.1.69)	..	10	10
40	**126**	5 c. mult. (28.8.68)	..	10	10
41	**127**	7 c. mult. (29.1.69)	..	12	15
42	**128**	10 c. mult. (30.10.68)	..	20	20
43	**129**	12 c. mult. (29.1.69)	..	25	25
44	**130**	15 c. mult. (30.10.68)	..	30	30
45	**131**	20 c. mult. (28.8.68)	..	40	40
46	**132**	25 c. mult. (28.8.68)	..	50	50
47	**133**	30 c. mult. (28.8.68)	..	70	75
48	**134**	40 c. mult. (30.10.68)	..	80	80
49	**135**	60 c. mult. (28.8.68)	..	1·25	1·25
50	**136**	$1 mult. (30.10.68)	..	2·25	2·25
51	**137**	$2 mult. (29.1.69)	..	4·00	4·00
37/51		.. .. *Set of* 15		10·00	10·00

The 1, 5, 7, 15, 40, 60 c. and $1 exist with PVA gum as well as gum arabic.

138. Tito Myth. **140.** Luvuapo Myth.

139. Iko Myth. **141.** Miro Myth.

(Des. from native motifs by Rev. H. A. Brown. Litho. Enschedé.)

1969 (9 Apr.). *Folklore. Elema Art. P* 12½ × 13½ × *Roul.* 9 *between se-tenant pairs.*

152	**138**	5 c. black, yellow & red	15	15
153	**139**	5 c. black, yellow & red	15	15
154	**140**	10 c. black, grey and red	30	30
155	**141**	10 c. black, grey and red	30	30

Nos. 152/3 and 154/5 were issued in vertical *se-tenant* pairs, separated by a line of roulette.

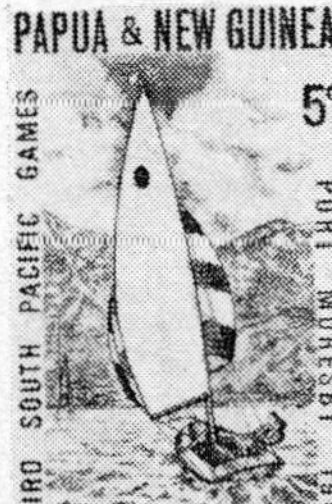

142. " Fireball " class Yacht.

143. Swimming Pool, Boroko. (*Horiz.*)

144. Games Arena, Konedobu. (*Horiz.*)

(Des. J. Fallas. Recess. Note Ptg. Branch, Reserve Bank of Australia.)

1969 (25 June). *Third South Pacific Games, Port Moresby. P* 14 × 14½ (5 *c.*) *or* 14½ × 14 (*others*).

156	**142**	5 c. black	.. ..	12	12
157	**143**	10 c. deep bluish violet	..	25	25
158	**144**	20 c. myrtle-green	..	45	45

145. *Dendrobium ostinoglossum.*

146. *Dendrobium lawesii.*

147. *Dendrobium pseudofrigidum.*

148. *Dendrobium conanthum.*

(Des. P. Jones. Photo. Courvoisier.)

1969 (27 Aug.). *Flora Conservation* (*Orchids*). *P* 11½.

159	**145**	5 c. multicoloured	..	12	12
160	**146**	10 c. multicoloured	..	25	25
161	**147**	20 c. multicoloured	..	40	40
162	**148**	30 c. multicoloured	..	65	65

149. Bird of Paradise.

150. Native Potter.

(Des. G. Hamori. Photo. Note Ptg. Branch, Reserve Bank of Australia.)

1969 (24 Sept.)–**71.** *Coil stamps. Perf.* 15 × *imperf.*

162*a*	**149**	2 c. blue, black and red (1.4.71)	5	5
163	,,	5 c. bright green, brown and red-orange ..	5	8

(Des. G. Hamori. Photo. Courvoisier.)

1969 (24 Sept.). 50*th Anniv. of International Labour Organization. P* 11½.

164	**150**	5 c. multicoloured	..	12	10

151. Tareko.

152. Garamut.

153. Iviliko.

154. Kundu.

(Des. G. Hamori. Photo. Courvoisier.)

1969 (29 Oct.). *Musical Instruments. P* 12½ × 12

165	**151**	5 c. multicoloured ..	12	12
166	**152**	10 c. black, olive-green and pale yellow ..	25	25
167	**153**	25 c. black, yell. & brn.	50	50
168	**154**	30 c. multicoloured ..	65	65

155. Prehistoric Ambun Stone.

156. Masawa Canoe of Kula Cicuit.
157. Torres' Map, 1606.
158. H.M.S. *Basilisk.*

(Des. R. J. Bates. Photo. Courvoisier.)

1970 (11 Feb.). " *National Heritage*". *P* 12½ × 12.

169	**155**	5 c. multicoloured	..	12	12
170	**156**	10 c. multicoloured	..	25	25
171	**157**	25 c. multicoloured	..	50	50
172	**158**	30 c. multicoloured	..	65	65

159. " King of Saxony ".

160. " Little King ".

161. " Augusta Victoria ".

162. " Sickle-crested ".

(Des. T. Walcot. Photo. Courvoisier.)

1970 (13 MAY). *Fauna Conservation (Birds of Paradise). P* 12 × 11½.

173	**159**	5 c. multicoloured ..	12	12
174	**160**	10 c. multicoloured ..	25	25
175	**161**	15 c. multicoloured ..	35	35
176	**162**	25 c. multicoloured ..	55	55

163. DC–6B and Mt. Wilhelm.

164. Lockheed Electra and Mt. Yule.

165. Boeing 727 and Mt. Giluwe.

166. Fokker Friendship and Manam Island.

167. DC–3 and Matupi Volcano.

168. Boeing 707 and Hombrom's Bluff.

(Des. D. Gentleman. Photo. Harrison.)

1970 (8 JULY). *Australian and New Guinea Air Services. P* 14½ × 14.

177	**163**	5 c. multicoloured ..	12	12
178	**164**	5 c. multicoloured ..	12	12
179	**165**	5 c. multicoloured ..	12	12
180	**166**	5 c. multicoloured ..	12	12
181	**167**	25 c. multicoloured ..	55	55
182	**168**	30 c. multicoloured ..	60	65
177/82		.. .. *Set of* 6	1·25	1·25

Nos. 177/80 were issued together *se-tenant* in blocks of four throughout the sheet.

169. N. Miklouho-Maclay (scientist) and Effigy.

(Des. D. Gentleman. Photo. Courvoisier.)

1970 (19 AUG.). *42nd ANZAAS (Australian–New Zealand Association for the Advancement of Science) Congress, Port Moresby. T* **169** *and similar horiz. designs. P* 11½.

183	5 c. multicoloured	12	12
184	10 c. multicoloured	25	25
185	15 c. multicoloured	40	40
186	20 c. multicoloured	50	50

Designs:—10 c. B. Malinowski (anthropologist, and native hut; 15 c. T. Salvadori (ornithologist) and cassowary; 20 c. F. R. R. Schlechter, (botanist) and flower.

170. Wogeo Island Food Bowl.

171. Eastern Highlands Dwelling.

(Des. P. Jones. Photo. Courvoisier.)

1970 (28 OCT.). *Native Artifacts. T* **170** *and similar multicoloured designs. P* 12½ × 12 *(30 c.) or* 12 × 12½ *(others).*

187	5 c. Type **170**	12	12
188	10 c. Lime Pot	25	25
189	15 c. Aibom Sago Storage Pot	35	35
190	30 c. Manus Island Bowl ..	60	60

The 30 c. is a horizontal design.

(Des. G. Wade. Photo. Courvoisier.)

1971 (27 JAN.). *Native Dwellings. T* **171** *and similar vert. designs showing dwellings from the places given. Multicoloured. P* 11½.

191	5 c. Type **171**	12	12
192	7 c. Milne Bay	20	20
193	10 c. Purari Delta	30	30
194	40 c. Sepik	90	90

172. Spotted Cuscus.

174. Bartering fish for vegetables.

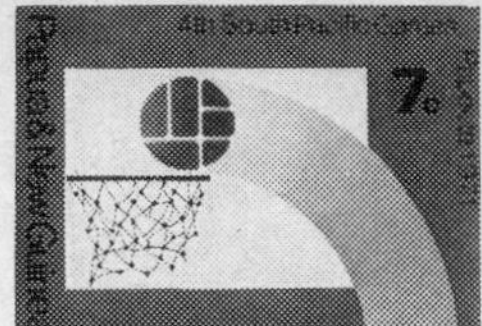

173. " Basketball ".

(Des. R. J. Bates. Photo. Courvoisier.)

1971 (31 MAR.). *Fauna Conservation. T* 17 *and similar multicoloured designs. P* 11½.

195	5 c. Type **172**	12	
196	10 c. Brown and White Striped Possum ..	25	
197	15 c. Feather-tailed Possum	30	
198	25 c. Spiny Ant-Eater ..	50	
199	30 c. Goodfellow's Tree-climbing Kangaroo	65	
195/99	.. .. *Set of* 5	1·60	1·6

The 25 c. and 30 c. are horiz. designs.

(Des. G. Hamori. Litho. D.L.R.)

1971 (9 JUNE). *Fourth South Pacific Game Papeete, Tahiti. T* **173** *and similar hori designs. Multicoloured. P* 13½ × 14.

200	7 c. Type **173**	20	
201	14 c. " Sailing "	35	
202	21 c. " Boxing "	45	
203	28 c. " Athletics "	70	

(Des. G. Wade. Photo. Courvoisier.)

1971 (18 AUG.). *Primary Industries. T* **174** *ar similar vert. designs. Multicoloured. P* 11½.

204	7 c. Type **174**	15	
205	9 c. Man stacking yams ..	25	
206	14 c. Vegetable market ..	30	
207	30 c. Highlanders cultivating garden	70	

175. Sia Dancer.

(Des. Bette Hays. Photo. Courvoisier.)

1971 (27 OCT.). *Native Dancers. T* **175** *ar similar multicoloured designs. P* 11½.

208	7 c. Type **175**	15	
209	9 c. Urasena dancer ..	25	
210	20 c. Siassi Tubuan dancers (*horiz.*)	40	
211	28 c. Sia dancers (*horiz.*) ..	70	

176. Papuan Flag over Australian Flag.

(Des. R. Bates. Photo. Courvoisier.)

1972 (26 JAN.). *Constitutional Developmen T* **176** *and similar horiz. design. P* 12½ × 12

212	**176**	7 c. multicoloured ..	20	
213	–	7 c. multicoloured ..	20	

Design:—No. 213, Crest of Papua New Guinea
d Australian coat-of-arms.

Nos. 212/3 were printed vertically *se-tenant*
thin the sheet.

7. Map of Papua New Guinea and Flag of South Pacific Commission.

(Des. R. Bates. Photo. Courvoisier.)

72 (26 JAN.). *25th Anniv. of South Pacific Commission.* *T* **177** *and similar horiz. design.* *P* 12½×12.

4	**177**	15 c. multicoloured ..	35	35
5	–	15 c. multicoloured ..	35	35

Design:—No. 215, Man's face and flag of the
mmission.

Nos. 214/5 were printed vertically *se-tenant*
thin the sheet.

178. Turtle.

(Des. R. Bates. Photo. Courvoisier.)

72 (15 MAR.). *Fauna Conservation (Reptiles).* *T* **178** *and similar horiz. designs. Multi-coloured.* *P* 11½.

6	7 c. Type **178**	15	15
7	14 c. Rainforest Dragon ..	45	50
8	21 c. Green Python	45	50
9	30 c. Salvador's Monitor ..	55	55

179. Curtiss "Seagull MF6" and Ship.

Des. Major L. G. Halls. Photo. Courvoisier.)

72 (7 JUNE). *50th Anniv. of Aviation.* *T* **179** *and similar horiz. designs. Multicoloured.* *P* 11½.

0	7 c. Type **179**	15	15
1	14 c. De Havilland "37" and native porters ..	45	45
2	20 c. Junkers "G–31" and gold dredge ..	45	45
3	25 c. Junkers "F–13" and mission church ..	50	50

180. New National Flag.

(Des. R. Bates. Photo. Courvoisier.)

1972 (16 AUG.). *National Day.* *T* **180** *and similar vert. designs. Multicoloured.* *P* 11½.

224	7 c. Type **180**	12	12
225	10 c. Native drum	40	40
226	30 c. Blowing the conch-shell	70	70

181. Rev. Copland King.

(Des. G. Wade. Photo. Courvoisier.)

1972 (25 OCT.). *Christmas (Missionaries).* *T* **181** *and similar horiz. designs. Multicoloured.* *P* 11½.

227	7 c. Type **181**	20	20
228	7 c. Rev. Dr. Flierl ..	20	20
229	7 c. Bishop Verjus	20	20
230	7 c. Pastor Ruatoka.. ..	20	20

182. Mt. Tomavatur Station.

(Des. R. Bates. Photo. Courvoisier.)

1973 (24 JAN.). *Completion of Telecommunications Project, 1968–72.* *T* **182** *and similar horiz. designs. Multicoloured.* *P* 12½ *(Nos. 231/4) or* 11½ *(others).*

231	7 c. Type **182**	15	15
232	7 c. Mt. Kerigomma Station	15	15
233	7 c. Sattelburg Station ..	15	15
234	7 c. Wideru Station ..	15	15
235	9 c. Teleprinter	20	20
236	30 c. Network Map ..	60	60
231/6	.. .. *Set of* 6	1·25	1·25

Nos. 231/4 were printed in *se-tenant* blocks of four within the sheet, and Nos. 235/6 are larger, 36×26 mm.

183. Queen Carol's Bird of Paradise.

(Des. W. T. Cooper. Photo. Courvoisier.)

1973 (30 MAR.). *Birds of Paradise.* *T* **183** *and similar vert. designs. Multicoloured.* *P* 11½.

237	7 c. Type **183**	20	20
238	14 c. Decorative	35	35
239	21 c. Ribbon-tailed ..	60	60
240	28 c. Princess Stephanie ..	70	70

Nos. 239/40 are 18×49 mm.

184. Wood Carver.

(Des. R. Bates. Photo. Courvoisier.)

1973–74. *T* **184** *and similar horiz. designs. Multicoloured.* *P* 11½.

241	1 c. Type **184**	5	5
242	3 c. Wig-makers	5	5
243	5 c. Mt. Bagana	8	8
244	6 c. Pig Exchange ..	10	10
245	7 c. Coastal village	10	12
246	8 c. Arawe mother	10	12
247	9 c. Fire dancers	10	12
248	10 c. Tifalmin hunter.. ..	12	15
249	14 c. Crocodile hunters ..	20	20
250	15 c. Mt. Elimbari ..	20	20
251	20 c. Canoe-racing ..	25	30
252	21 c. Making sago ..	25	30
253	25 c. Council House	30	35
254	28 c. Menyamya bowmen ..	35	40
255	30 c. Shark-snaring ..	35	40
256	40 c. Fishing canoes	50	55
257	60 c. Tapa cloth-making ..	75	85
258	$1 Asaro Mudmen	1·75	1·75
259	$2 Enga "Sing Sing" ..	3·00	3·25
241/59	.. .. *Set of* 19	8·00	8·50

Dates of issue:—13.6.73, 1, 7, 9, 15, 25, 40 c.; 22.8.73, 5, 14, 21, 28, 30 c.; 23.1.74, 3, 8, 10, 20, 60 c., $1; 7.8.74, 6 c., $2.

185. Stamps of German New Guinea, 1897.

(Illustration reduced. Actual size 55×31 *mm.)*

(Des. R. Bates. Photo. (1 c.), litho. and recess (6 c.) or litho. (7 c.). State Printing Works, Berlin. Photo. and recess. D.L.R. (9 c.). Recess and typo. Reserve Bank of Australia (25 and 30 c.).)

1973 (24 OCT.). *75th Anniv. of Papua New Guinea Stamps.* *T* **185** *and similar designs. Chalky paper* (25, 30 *c.*). *P* 13½ (1, 6, 7 *c.*), 14×13½ (9 *c.*) *or* 14×14½ (25, 30 *c.*).

260	1 c. multicoloured ..	8	8
261	6 c. indigo, new blue & silver	20	20
262	7 c. multicoloured	25	25
263	9 c. multicoloured	35	35
264	25 c. orange and gold ..	80	90
265	30 c. plum and silver ..	1·00	1·10
260/65	.. .. *Set of* 6	2·40	2·50

Designs: *Horiz.*— *size as T* **185**—6 c. 2 mark stamp of German New Guinea, 1900; 7 c. Surcharged registration label of New Guinea, 1914. 46×35 *mm.*—9 c. Papua 1s. stamp, 1901. 45×38 *mm.*—25 c. ½d. stamp of New Guinea, 1925; 30 c. Papua 10s. stamp, 1932.

II. SELF-GOVERNMENT.

186. Native Carved Heads.

(Des. G. Wade. Photo. Courvoisier.)

1973 (5 DEC.). *Self-Government.* P 11½.

266	**186**	7 c. multicoloured ..	20	20
267	„	10 c. multicoloured ..	35	35

187. Queen Elizabeth II (from photograph by Karsh).

(Des. and photo. Harrison.)

1974 (22 FEB.). *Royal Visit.* P 14×14½.

268	**187**	7 c. multicoloured ..	15	15
269	„	30 c. multicoloured ..	55	60

188. Kokomo (Wreathed Hornbill).

(Des. T. Nolan. Photo. Courvoisier.)

1974 (12 JUNE). *Birds' Heads. T* **188** *and similar multicoloured designs.* P 11½ (10 *c.*) *or* 12 (*others*).

270	7 c. Type **140**	30	30
271	10 c. Muruk (Great Cassowary) (33×49 *mm.*)	50	50
272	30 c. Tarangau (Kapul Eagle)	1·60	1·60

189. *Dendrobium bracteosum.*

(Des. T. Nolan. Photo. Courvoisier.)

1974 (20 NOV.). *Flora Conservation. T* **189** *and similar vert. designs. Multicoloured.* P 11½.

273	7 c. Type **189**	12	12
274	10 c. *D. anosmum*	20	20
275	20 c. *D. smillieae*	35	35
276	30 c. *D. insigne*	45	45

190. Motu Lagatoi.

(Des. G. Wade. Photo. Courvoisier.)

1975 (26 FEB.). *National Heritage—Canoes. T* **190** *and similar horiz. designs. Multicoloured.* P 11½.

277	7 c. Type **190**	12	12
278	10 c. Tami two-master morobe	20	20
279	25 c. Aramia racing canoe ..	40	40
280	30 c. Buka canoe	50	50

(New currency. 100 toea = 1 kina.)

191. 1-toea Coin.

(Des. G. Wade. Photo. Courvoisier.)

1975 (21 APR.). *New Coinage. T* **191** *and similar multicoloured designs.* P 11½.

281	1 t. Type **191**	5	5
282	7 t. New 2 t. and 5 t. coins (*horiz.*—45×26 *mm.*) ..	10	10
283	10 t. New 10 t. coin	15	15
284	20 t. New 20 t. coin	35	35
285	1 k. New 1 k. coin (*size as No.* 282)	1·40	1·60
281/5	.. .. *Set of* 5	1·75	2·00

192. *Ornithoptera alexandrae.*

(Des. R. Bates. Photo. Courvoisier.)

1975 (11 JUNE). *Fauna Conservation (Birdwing Butterflies). T* **192** *and similar vert. designs. Multicoloured.* P 11½.

286	7 t. Type **192**	10	10
287	10 t. *O. victoriae regis*	15	15
288	30 t. *O. allottei*	45	45
289	40 t. *O. chimaera*	60	60

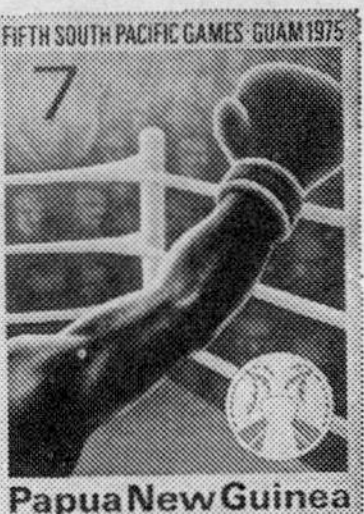

193. Boxing.

(Des. R. Bates. Photo. Courvoisier.)

1975 (2 AUG.). *Fifth South Pacific Games Guam. T* **193** *and similar vert. designs Multicoloured.* P 11½.

290	7 t. Type **193**	10	1
291	20 t. Running	30	3
292	25 t. Basketball	35	3
293	30 t. Swimming	40	4

III. INDEPENDENT.

194. Map and National Flag.

(Des. and photo. Courvoisier.)

1975 (10 SEPT.). *Independence. T* **194** *an similar horiz. design. Multicoloured.* P 11

294	7 t. Type **194**	10	1
295	30 t. Map and National emblem	40	4
MS296	116×58 mm. Nos. 294/5	50	5

195. M.V. *Bulolo.*

(Des. R. Bates. Photo. Courvoisier.)

1976 (21 JAN.). *Ships of the* 1930's. *T* **195** *an similar horiz. designs. Multicoloured.* P 11

297	7 t. Type **195**	10	1
298	15 t. M.V. *Macdhui*	20	2
299	25 t. M.V. *Malaita*	35	3
300	60 t. S.S. *Montoro*	75	8

196. Rorovana Carvings.

(Des. R. Bates. Photo. Courvoisier.)

1976 (17 MAR.). *Bougainville Art. T* **196** *an similar horiz. designs. Multicoloured.* P 11

301	7 t. Type **196**	10	1
302	20 t. Upe hats	25	2
303	25 t. Kapkaps	30	3
304	30 t. Canoe paddles	40	4

197. Rabaul House.

(Des. G. Wade. Photo. Courvoisier.)

1976 (9 June). *Native Dwellings. T* **197** *and similar horiz. designs. Multicoloured. P* 11½.

05	7 t. Type **197**	10	12
06	15 t. Aramia house	20	25
07	30 t. Telefomin house ..	40	45
08	40 t. Tapini house	55	65

198. Landscouts.

(Des. R. Bates. Photo. Courvoisier.)

976 (18 Aug.). *50th Anniversaries of Flight and Scouting in Papua New Guinea. T* **198** *and similar horiz. designs. Multicoloured. P* 11½.

09	7 t. Type **198**	12	15
10	10 t. D.H. floatplane	15	15
11	15 t. Seascouts	20	25
12	60 t. Floatplane on water ..	85	95

99. Father Ross and New Guinea Highlands.

(Des. R. Bates. Photo. Courvoisier.)

976 (28 Oct.). *William Ross Commemoration. P* 11½.

13	**199** 7 t. multicoloured ..	12	15

200. Clouded Rainbow Fish.

(Des. P. Jones. Photo. Courvoisier.)

976 (28 Oct.). *Fauna Conservation (Tropical Fish). T* **200** *and similar horiz. designs. Multicoloured. P* 11½.

14	5 t. Type **200**	8	10
15	15 t. Emperor or Imperial Angel Fish	20	25
16	30 t. Freckled Rock Cod ..	40	45
17	40 t. Threadfin Butterfly Fish	55	65

201. Wasara Headdress.

(Des. R. Bates. Litho. Questa.)

1977 (12 Jan.). *T* **201** *and similar horiz. design. Multicoloured. P* 14.

318	1 k. Type **201**	1·40	1·60
319	2 k. Mekeo headdress	2·75	3·00

POSTAGE DUE STAMPS.

POSTAL CHARGES

6d.

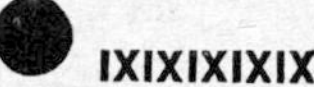

(D 1)

POSTAL CHARGES

3s.

(D 2)

1960 (1 Mar.). *Postage stamps surcharged.*

(a) *With Type* D **1**.

D1 **8** 6d. on 7½d. blue (R.) ..	£250	£250
a. Surch. double	£850	£850

(b) *As Type* D **2**.

D2 **7** 1d. on 6½d. maroon ..	1·50	1·50
D3 **1** 3d. on ½d. emerald (B.) ..	2·00	2·50
a. Surch. double	£160	
D4 **8** 6d. on 7½d. blue (R.) ..	3·00	4·00
a. Surch. double	£160	
D5 **6** 1s. 3d. on 3½d. black (Or.)	6·00	8·00
D6 **4** 3s. on 2½d. orange	10·00	12·00
D2/D6 .. .. *Set of* 5	20·00	25·00

Of No. D1a, only a few copies are known from a sheet used at Goroka.

D 3

(Typo. Note Ptg. Branch, Reserve Bank of Australia, Melbourne.)

1960 (2 June). *W* **14** *of Papua. P* 14.

D 7	D **3**	1d. orange	5	5
D 8	,,	3d. yellow-brown ..	20	20
D 9	,,	6d. blue	25	25
D10	,,	9d. deep red	40	40
D11	,,	1s. light emerald ..	25	25
D12	,,	1s. 3d. violet	60	60
D13	,,	1s. 6d. pale blue ..	60	60
D14	,,	3s. yellow	85	85
D7/D14		.. .. *Set of* 8	2·75	2·75

The use of Postal Charge stamps was discontinued on February 12th, 1966, but they remained on sale at the Philatelic Bureau until August 31st, 1966.

MINIMUM PRICE

The minimum price quoted is 5p which represents a handling charge rather than a basis for valuing common stamps. For further notes about prices see introductory pages.

PITCAIRN ISLANDS.

CROWN COLONY.

1. Cluster of Oranges.

2. Christian on *Bounty* and Pitcairn Island.

3. John Adams and his House.

4. Lt. Bligh and *Bounty*.

5. Pitcairn Islands and Pacific Ocean.

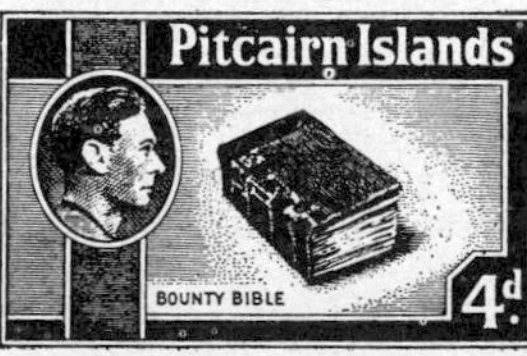

5a. *Bounty* Bible.

6. H.M. Armed Vessel *Bounty*.

6a. School, 1949.

7. Fletcher Christian and Pitcairn Island.

8. Christian on *Bounty* and Pitcairn Coast.

(Recess. B.W. (1d., 3d., 4d., 8d. and 2s. 6d.) and Waterlow (others).)

1940 (15 Oct.)–**51.** *Wmk. Mult. Script CA P* 11½×11 (*1d., 3d., 4d., 8d. and 2s. 6d.*) *o* 12½ (*others*).

1	**1**	½d. orange and green ..	15	2
2	**2**	1d. mauve and magenta ..	15	2
3	**3**	1½d. grey and carmine ..	20	2
4	**4**	2d. green and brown ..	45	6
5	**5**	3d. yellow-green and blue	50	7
5a	**5a**	4d. blk. & emer.-grn. (1.9.51)	3·50	4·5
6	**6**	6d. brown and grey-blue ..	75	9
6a	**6a**	8d. olive-grn. & mag. (1.9.51)	3·50	5·5
7	**7**	1s. violet and grey ..	1·00	1·6
8	**8**	2s. 6d. green and brown ..	2·25	3·0
1/8		.. .. *Set of* 10	11·00	16·0
1/8		(Ex. *a* Nos.) Perf. " Specimen " *Set of* 8	55·00	

1946 (2 Dec.). *Victory. As Nos.* 28/9 *of Aden*

9	2d. brown	15	2
10	3d. blue	45	4
9/10	Perf. "Specimen" *Set of* 2	25·00	

1949 (1 Aug.). *Royal Silver Wedding. As Nos* 30/1 *of Aden.*

11	1½d. scarlet	30	3
12	10s. mauve	16·00	22·0

1949 (10 Oct.). *75th Anniv. of Universal Posta Union. As Nos.* 114/7 *of Antigua.*

13	2½d. red-brown	90	1·1
14	3d. deep blue..	80	1·6
15	6d. deep blue-green	2·25	2·7
16	1s. purple	3·50	4·0

1953 (2 June). *Coronation. As No.* 47 *c Aden, but ptd. by B. W.*

17	4d. black & deep bluish green	2·00	3·0

9. *Cordyline terminalis.*

10. Pitcairn Islands Map.

11. John Adams and *Bounty* Bible.

12. Handicrafts: Bird Model.

13. Bounty Bay.

14. Pitcairn School.

15. Pacific Ocean Map.

16. Inland Scene.

17. Handicrafts: Ship Model.

18. Island Wheelbarrow.

19. Launching New Whaleboat.

(Recess. D.L.R.)

957 (2 July)–**58.** *Wmk. Mult. Script CA. P* 13 × 12½ (*horiz.*) *or* 12½ × 13 (*others*).

8	**9**	½d. grn. & red'sh lilac (*shades*)	8	8
9	**10**	1d. blk. & olive-grn. (*shades*)	15	20
0	**11**	2d. brown & greenish blue	20	25
1	**12**	2½d. dp. brn. & red-orange	35	40
2	**13**	3d. emerald & deep ultram.	35	40
23	**14**	4d. scarlet & dp. ultram. (I)	90	1·00
23*a*	,,	4d. carmine-red and deep ultram. (II) (5.11.58)	50	65
24	**15**	6d. pale buff and indigo	50	65
25	**16**	8d. deep olive-green and carmine-lake	80	1·00
26	**17**	1s. black & yellowish brn.	1·00	1·00
27	**18**	2s. green and red-orange	4·00	4·25
28	**19**	2s. 6d ultramarine & lake (*shades*)	4·50	5·00
18/28		*Set of* 12	12·00	13·00

Nos. 23/*a*. Type I is inscribed "PITCAIRN SCHOOL"; Type II "SCHOOLTEACHER'S HOUSE".

See also No. 33.

20. Pitcairn Island and Simon Young.

21. Norfolk and Pitcairn Islands.

22. Migrant schooner *Mary Ann.*

(Des. H. E. Maud. Photo. Harrison.)

1961 (15 Nov.). *Centenary of Return of Pitcairn Islanders from Norfolk Island. W* w.**12.** *P* 14½ × 13½.

29	**20**	3d. black and yellow	50	60
30	**21**	6d. red-brown and blue	90	1·00
31	**22**	1s. red-orange & blue-grn.	1·75	1·90

1963 (4 June). *Freedom from Hunger. As No.* 76 *of Aden.*

32	2s. 6d. ultramarine	4·00	3·50

1963 (4 Dec.). *As No.* 18 *but wmk.* w.**12.**

33	**9**	½d. green & reddish purple	50	50

1963 (9 Dec.). *Red Cross Centenary. As Nos.* 147/8 *of Antigua.*

34	2d. red and black	25	25
35	2s. 6d. red and blue	3·75	4·00

23. Pitcairn Is. Longboat.

(Des. M. C. Farrar-Bell. Photo. Harrison.)

1964 (5 Aug.). *T* **23** *and similar horiz. designs. Multicoloured. W* w.**12.** *P* 14 × 14½.

36	½d. Type **23**	8	8
37	1d. The *Bounty*	5	5
38	2d. "Out from Bounty Bay"	5	8
39	3d. Frigate Bird	8	8
40	4d. Fairy Tern	8	10
41	6d. Pitcairn Sparrow	10	12
42	8d. Austin Bird	15	20
43	10d. Bosun Birds	25	30
44	1s. Chicken Bird	25	30
45	1s. 6d. Red Breast	35	40
46	2s. 6d. Ghost Bird	70	75
47	4s. Wood Pigeon	1·00	1·25

35. Queen Elizabeth II (after Anthony Buckley).

(Des. M. C. Farrar-Bell. Photo. Harrison.)

1965 (5 Apr.). *W* w.**12.** *P* 14 × 14½.

48	**35**	8s. multicoloured	2·25	2·50
36/48		*Set of* 13	4·75	5·50

1965 (17 May). *I.T.U. Centenary. As Nos.* 166/7 *of Antigua.*

49	1d. mauve and orange-brown	15	15
50	2s. 6d. turquoise-green and bright blue	3·25	3·50

1965 (15 Oct.). *International Co-operation Year. As Nos.* 168/9 *of Antigua.*

51	1d. reddish pur. & turq.-grn.	12	15
52	1s. 6d. dp. bluish grn. & lav.	2·00	2·25

1966 (24 Jan.). *Churchill Commemoration. As Nos.* 170/3 *of Antigua.*

53	2d. new blue	25	20
54	3d. deep green	40	35
55	6d. brown	1·25	90
56	1s. bluish violet	2·25	1·75

1966 (1 Aug.). *World Cup Football Championships. As Nos. 176/7 of Antigua.*

57 4d. violet, yellow-green, lake and yellow-brown 15 20
58 2s. 6d. chocolate, blue-green, lake and yellow-brown .. 1·00 1·10

1966 (20 Sept.). *Inauguration of W.H.O. Headquarters, Geneva. As Nos. 178/9 of Antigua.*

59 8d. black, yellow-grn. & lt. blue 60 60
60 1s. 6d. black, light purple and yellow-brown .. .. 1·25 1·25

1966 (1 Dec.). *20th Anniv. of U.N.E.S.C.O. As Nos. 196/8 of Antigua.*

61 ½d. slate-violet, red, yellow and orange 8 8
62 10d. orange-yellow, violet and deep olive 40 50
63 2s. black, bright purple & orge. 1·00 1·25

36. Mangarevan, *c.* 1325.

(Des. V. Whiteley. Photo. Harrison.)

1967 (1 Mar.). *Bicentenary of Pitcairn Islands' Discovery. T* **36** *and similar horiz. designs. W* w.**12**. *P* 14½.

64 ½d. multicoloured 5 5
65 1d. multicoloured 5 5
66 8d. multicoloured 15 25
67 1s. multicoloured 25 40
68 1s. 6d. multicoloured 40 60
64/8 .. .. .. *Set of* 5 75 1·00

Designs:—1d. P. F. de Quiros and *San Pedro y Pablo*, 1606; 8d. *San Pedro* and *Los Tres Reyes*, 1606; 1s. Carteret and H.M.S. *Swallow*, 1767; 1s. 6d. *Hercules*, 1819.

(New currency. 100 cents = 1 Australian dollar.)

½c

(**41.** *Bounty* Anchor.)

1967 (10 July). *Decimal currency. Nos. 36/48 surch. in decimal currency by die-stamping in gold as T* **41**.

69 ½ c. on ½d. mult. (*shades*) .. 5 5
70 1 c. on 1d. multicoloured .. 5 5
71 2 c. on 2d. multicoloured .. 8 8
72 2½ c. on 3d. multicoloured .. 8 8
73 3 c. on 4d. multicoloured .. 8 10
74 5 c. on 6d. multicoloured .. 10 12
75 10 c. on 8d. multicoloured .. 20 25
76 15 c. on 10d. multicoloured .. 40 50
77 20 c. on 1s. multicoloured .. 50 60
78 25 c. on 1s. 6d. multicoloured .. 60 70
79 30 c. on 2s. 6d. multicoloured .. 75 80
80 40 c. on 4s. multicoloured .. 1·00 1·10
81 45 c. on 8s. multicoloured .. 1·25 1·40
69/81 .. .. *Set of* 13 4·50 5·00

The ½ c. and 1 c. exist with PVA gum as well as gum arabic.

42. Bligh and *Bounty's* Launch.

43. Bligh and Followers Cast Adrift.

44. Bligh's Tomb.

(Des. Jennifer Toombs. Litho. De La Rue.)

1967 (7 Dec.). *150th Death Anniv. of Admiral Bligh. P* 13½ × 13.

82 **42** 1 c. black, ultramarine and pale blue (*shades*) .. 5 5
83 **43** 8 c. blk., yellow & magenta 20 25
84 **44** 20 c. blk., brn. & pale buff 45 50

45. Human Rights Emblem.

(Des. G. Hamori. Litho. De La Rue.)

1968 (4 Mar.). *Human Rights Year. P* 13½ × 13.

85 **45** 1 c. multicoloured .. 5 8
86 ,, 2 c. multicoloured .. 8 12
87 ,, 25 c. multicoloured .. 50 60

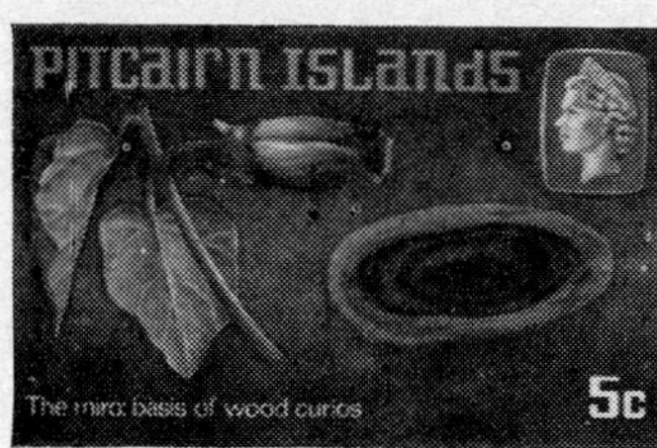

46. Miro Wood and Flower.

47. Flying Fish Model. (*Horiz.*)

48. " Hand " Vases. (*Vert.*)

49. Woven Baskets. (*Vert.*)

(Des. Jennifer Toombs. Photo. Harrison.)

1968 (19 Aug.). *Handicrafts. W* w.**12** (*sideways on vert. designs*). *P* 14 × 13½ (*horiz. designs*) *or* 13½ × 14 (*others*).

88 **46** 5 c. multicoloured .. 10 12
89 **47** 10 c. bronze-green, brown and orange 20 25
90 **48** 15 c. deep bluish violet, chocolate and salmon 30 35
91 **49** 20 c. multicoloured .. 45 50

50. Microscope and Slides.

51. Hypodermic Syringe and Jars of Tablets.

(Des. Jennifer Toombs. Litho. De La Rue.)

1968 (25 Nov.). *20th Anniv. of World Health Organization. W* w.**12** (*sideways*). *P* 14.

92 **50** 2 c. blk., turq.-bl. & ultram. 5 5
93 **51** 20 c. blk., orge. & bright pur. 45 50

52. Pitcairn Island.

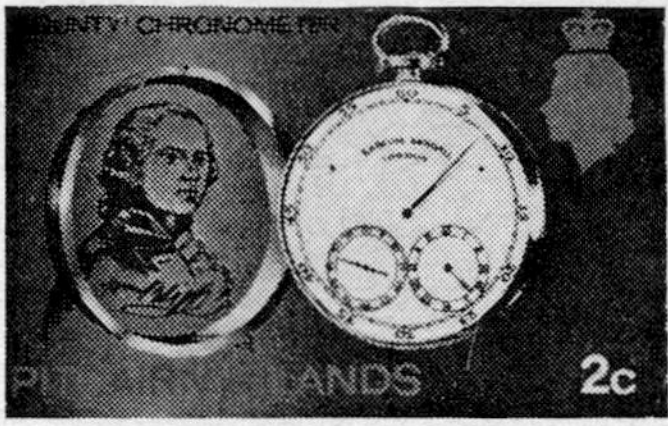

53. Captain Bligh and *Bounty* Chronometer.

54. *Bounty* Anchor.

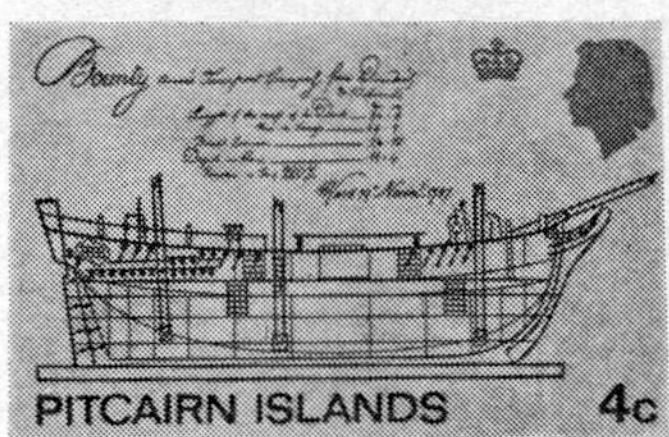

55. Plans and Drawing of *Bounty*.

56. Breadfruit Containers and Plant.

57. Bounty Bay.

58. Pitcairn Longboat.

59. Ship Landing Point.

60. Fletcher Christian's Cave.

61. Thursday October Christian's House.

62. " Flying Fox " Cable System.

63. Radio Station, Taro Ground.

64. *Bounty* Bible.

64a. Pitcairn Coat-of-Arms.

64b. Queen Elizabeth II.

(Des. Jennifer Toombs. Litho. Questa (50 c., $1), D.L.R. (others).)

1969 (17 Sept.)–**75.** *Chalk-surfaced paper. W* w.**12** *(upright on vert. designs, sideways on* $1 *and horiz. designs). P* 14½×14 (50 *c.*), 14 ($1) *or* 13 *(others).*

94	**52**	1 c. multicoloured ..	10	10
		a. Glazed, ordinary paper (9.8.71)	10	12
95	**53**	2 c. multicoloured ..	5	5
96	**54**	3 c. multicoloured ..	5	5
97	**55**	4 c. multicoloured ..	5	5
98	**56**	5 c. multicoloured ..	5	5
99	**57**	6 c. multicoloured ..	5	5
100	**58**	8 c. multicoloured ..	8	8
101	**59**	10 c. multicoloured ..	90	90
		a. Glazed, ordinary paper (9.8 71)	15	20
102	**60**	15 c. multicoloured ..	15	15
		a. Queen's head omitted ..	£200	
103	**61**	20 c. multicoloured ..	20	20
104	**62**	25 c. multicoloured ..	25	25
105	**63**	30 c. multicoloured ..	30	35
106	**64**	40 c. multicoloured ..	35	40
106a	**64a**	50 c. mult. *(glazed, ord. paper)* (2.1.73)	50	55
106b	**64b**	$1 mult. *(glazed, ord. paper)* (21.4.75) ..	95	1·10
94/106b		.. .. *Set of* 15	3·00	3·25

See also No. 133.

65. Lantana.

66. " Indian Shot ".

67. Pulau.

68. Wild Gladiolus.

(Des. Jennifer Toombs. Litho. De La Rue.)

1970 (23 Mar.). *Flowers. W* w.**12.** *P* 14.

107	**65**	1 c. multicoloured ..	5	5
108	**66**	2 c. multicoloured ..	5	8
109	**67**	5 c. multicoloured ..	15	20
110	**68**	25 c. multicoloured ..	95	1·00

69. Auntie and Ann (grouper).

(Des. Jennifer Toombs. Photo. Harrison.)

1970 (12 Oct.). *Fishes. T* **69** *and similar horiz. designs. Multicoloured. W* w.**12.** *P* 14.

111	5 c. Type **69**	12	12
112	10 c. Dream Fish (rudder fish)	25	30
113	15 c. Elwyn's Trousers (wrasse)	35	40
114	20 c. Whistling Daughter (wrasse)	50	55

ROYAL VISIT 1971

(70)

1971 (22 Feb.). *Royal Visit. No.* 101 *optd. with T* **70**, *in silver.*

115	**59**	10 c. multicoloured ..	4·50	4·50

71. Polynesian Rock Carvings.

(Des. Jennifer Toombs. Litho. A. & M.)

1971 (3 May). *Polynesian Pitcairn. T* **71** *and similar multicoloured designs. W* w.**12** *(sideways on* 10 *and* 15 *c.). P* 13½.

116	5 c. Type **71**	10	10
117	10 c. Polynesian artifacts *(horiz.)*	25	30
118	15 c. Polynesian stone fish-hook *(horiz.)* ..	35	40
119	20 c. Polynesian stone deity	50	55

72. Commission Flag.

(Des. Jennifer Toombs. Litho. Questa.)

1972 (4 APR.). *25th Anniv. of South Pacific Commission. T* **72** *and similar horiz. designs. Multicoloured (except* 4 c.). *W* w.**12** *(sideways on* 4 c.). *P* 14.

120 4 c. deep blue, blue-violet and bright yellow (T **72**) 10 10
121 8 c. Young and Elderly (Health) 20 20
122 18 c. Junior School (Education) 35 40
123 20 c. Goods Store (Economy) 40 45

73. Bosun Birds and Longboat.

(Des. (from photographs by D. Groves) and photo. Harrison.)

1972 (20 NOV.). *Royal Silver Wedding. Multicoloured; background colour given. W* w.**12**. *P* 14×14½.

124 **73** 4 c. slate-green 20 20
125 ,, 20 c. bright blue .. .. 1·75 1·50

74. Rose-apple.

(Des. Jennifer Toombs. Litho. J.W.)

1973 (25 JUNE). *Flowers. T* **74** *and similar vert. designs. Multicoloured. W* w.**12** *(sideways). P* 14.

126 4 c. Type **74** 8 8
127 8 c. Mountain-apple .. 20 20
128 15 c. "Lata" 30 30
129 20 c. "Dorcas-flower" .. 40 40
130 35 c. Guava 70 70
126/30 .. .. *Set of* 5 1·25 1·25

1973 (14 NOV.). *Royal Wedding. As Nos.* 165/6 *of Anguilla. Centre multicoloured. W* w.**12** *(sideways). P* 13½.

131 10 c. bright mauve 20 20
132 25 c. emerald 50 60

1974 (4 FEB.). *As No.* 94 *but wmk. upright. Glazed, ordinary paper.*

133 **52** 1 c. multicoloured 5 8

Nos. 134/46 have been reserved for further additions to this issue.

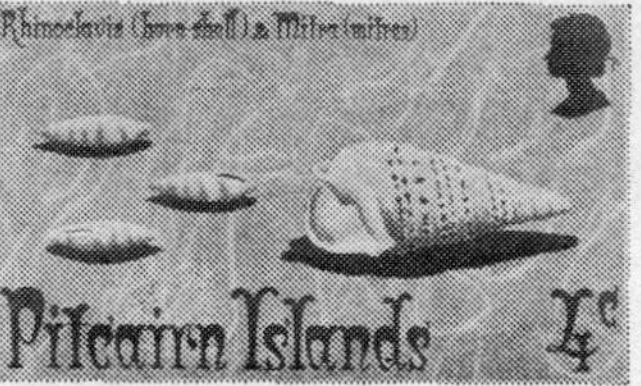

75. Horn-shells and Mitres.

(Des. Jennifer Toombs. Litho. Questa.)

1974 (15 APR.). *Shells. T* **75** *and similar horiz. designs. Multicoloured. W* w.**12**. *P* 14.

147 4 c. Type **75** 8 8
148 10 c. Dove-shell 20 20
149 18 c. Limpet and False Limpet 35 35
150 50 c. Lucine shell .. .. 1·00 1·00
MS151 130×121mm. Nos. 147/50 1·40 1·60

76. Island Post Office.

(Des. Jennifer Toombs. Litho. Questa.)

1974 (22 JULY). *Centenary of Universal Postal Union. T* **76** *and similar horiz. designs. W* w.**12** *(sideways). P* 14.

152 4 c. multicoloured 8 8
153 20 c. bright purple, light cinnamon and black .. 35 40
154 35 c. multicoloured 65 70

Designs:—20 c. Pre-stamp letter, 1922; 35 c. mailship and Pitcairn longboat.

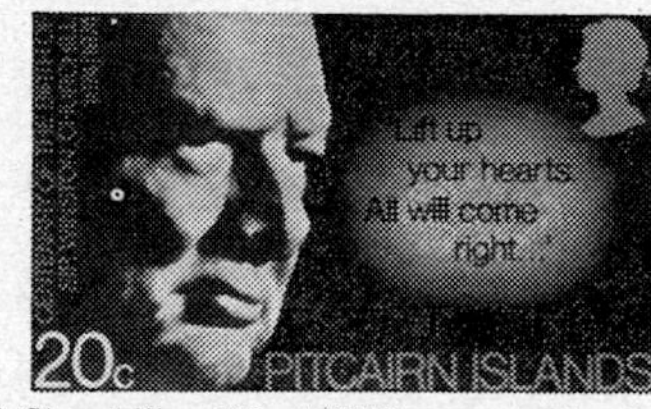

77. Churchill and Text "Lift up your Hearts . . .".

(Des. Jennifer Toombs. Litho. Questa.)

1974 (30 NOV.). *Birth Centenary of Sir Winston Churchill. T* **77** *and similar horiz. design. W* w.**14** *(sideways). P* 14½.

155 20 c. blackish olive, apple-grn. & deep slate .. 35 40
156 35 c. sepia, greenish yell. and deep slate 55 60

Design:—35 c. Text "Give us the tools . . .".

78. H.M.S. *Seringapatam*, 1830.

(Des. Jennifer Toombs. Litho. Walsall.)

1975 (22 JULY). *Mailboats. T* **78** *and similar horiz. designs. Multicoloured. W* w.**14** *(sideways). P* 14.

157 4 c. Type **78** 8 8
158 10 c. The *Pitcairn*, 1890 .. 15 15
159 18 c. R.M.S. *Athenic*, 1904 .. 30 35
160 50 c. S.S. *Gothic*, 1948 .. .. 70 75
MS161 145×110 mm. Nos. 157/60 1·25 1·40

79. Pitcairn Wasp.

(Des. Jennifer Toombs. Litho. Questa.)

1975 (9 NOV.). *Pitcairn Insects. T* **79** *and similar horiz. designs. Multicoloured. W* w.**12** *(sideways). P* 14.

162 4 c. Type **79** 5 5
163 6 c. Grasshopper 10 10
164 10 c. Moths 15 15
165 15 c. Devil's Needle 20 25
166 20 c. Banana Moth 30 35
162/6 .. .. *Set of* 5 70 80

80. Fletcher Christian.

(Des. Jennifer Toombs. Litho. J.W.)

1976 (4 JULY). *Bicentenary of American Revolution. T* **80** *and similar vert. designs. Multicoloured. W* w.**14**. *P* 13½.

167 5 c. Type **80** 8
168 10 c. H.M.S. *Bounty* 12 1
169 30 c. George Washington .. 35 4
170 50 c. *Mayflower* 55 6

81. Chair of Homage.

(Des. Jennifer Toombs. Litho. J.W.)

1977 (6 FEB.). *Silver Jubilee. T* **81** *and similar vert. designs. Multicoloured. W* w.**14**. *P* 13

171 8 c. Prince Philip's visit, 1971 8 1
172 20 c. Type **81** 20 2
173 50 c. Enthronement 55 6

PRINCE EDWARD ISLAND.

1

2

3

4

5

6

(Typo. Charles Whiting, London.)

861 (1 Jan.). *Yellowish toned paper. P* 9.
1 **1** 2d. rose .. .. .. 60·00 40·00
a. Imperf. vert. (horiz. pair) ..
b. Imperf. horiz. (vert. pair) ..
c. Bisected (1d.) (on cover) ..
2 ,, 2d. rose-carmine .. .. 60·00 40·00
3 **2** 3d. blue .. .. .. £150 65·00
a. Bisected (1½d.) (on cover) ..
b. Double print £500
4 **3** 6d. yellow-green .. .. £200 85·00

Rouletted

5 **1** 2d. rose .. .. ..

The 2d. and 3d., perf. 9, were authorised to be bisected and used for half their nominal value.

862. *Yellowish toned paper. P* 11.
6 **4** 1d. brown-orange .. .. 12·00 30·00
7 **6** 9d. bluish lilac (29.3.62) .. 20·00 8·00
8 ,, 9d. dull mauve .. .. 20·00 8·00

863–68. *Yellowish toned paper.* (*a*) *P* 11½–12.
9 **4** 1d. yellow-orange .. .. 4·50 6·00
a. Bisected (½d.) (on cover) .. † £300
b. Imperf. between (horiz. pair) .. £100
0 ,, 1d. orange-buff .. .. 5·00 6·00
1 ,, 1d. yellow .. .. .. 6·00 7·00
2 **1** 2d. rose .. .. .. 3·00 4·50
a. Imperf. vert. (horiz. pair) ..
b. Bisected (1d.) (on cover) .. † £400
3 ,, 2d. deep rose .. .. .. 3·50 5·00
4 **2** 3d. blue .. .. .. 4·50 6·00
a. Imperf. horiz. (vert. pair) ..
b. Bisected (1½d.) (on cover) ..
5 ,, 3d. deep blue .. .. .. 4·50 4·00
6 **5** 4d. black (1867) .. .. 6·00 8·00
a. Imperf. vert. (horiz. pair) ..
b. Bisected (2d.) (on cover) .. † £350
7 **3** 6d. yellow-green (15.12.66) .. 9·00 9·00
a. Bisected (3d.) (on cover) ..
8 ,, 6d. blue-green (1868) .. 9·00 9·00
9 **6** 9d. lilac .. .. .. 8·00 8·00
0 ,, 9d. reddish mauve .. .. 8·00 8·00
a. Imperf. vert. (horiz. pair) .. £125
b. Bisected (4½d.) (on cover) .. † £375

(*b*) *Perf. compound of* 11 *and* 11½–12.
21 **4** 1d. yellow-orange .. .. 65·00 30·00
22 **1** 2d. rose .. .. .. 65·00 30·00
23 **2** 3d. blue .. .. .. 70·00 30·00
24 **5** 4d. black .. .. .. 90·00 80·00
25 **3** 6d. yellow-green .. .. 75·00 80·00
26 **6** 9d. reddish mauve .. .. 80·00 80·00

1870. *Coarse, wove bluish white paper. P* 11½–12.
27 **1** 2d. rose .. .. .. 3·50 4·50
28 ,, 2d. rose-pink .. .. .. 3·00 4·00
a. Variety "TWC" .. .. 20·00
b. Imperf. between (horiz. pair) 50·00
29 **2** 3d. pale blue .. .. .. 3·00 4·50
30 ,, 3d. blue .. .. .. 3·00 4·50
a. Imperf. between (horiz. pair) .. £100
31 **5** 4d. black .. .. .. 1·75 14·00
a. Imperf. between (horiz. pair) 50·00
b. Bisected (2d.) (on cover) .. † £400
c. Perf. compound 11 and 11½–12

7

(Recess. British-American Bank Note Co., Montreal and Ottawa.)

1870 (1 June). *P* 12.
32 **7** 4½d. (3d. stg.), yellow-brown 7·00 14·00
33 ,, 4½d. (3d. stg.), deep brown .. 7·00 14·00

8

9

10

11

12

13

(Typo. Charles Whiting, London.)

1872 (1 Jan.). (*a*) *P* 11½–12.
34 **8** 1 c. orange .. .. .. 85 4·00
35 ,, 1 c. yellow-orange .. .. 80 3·50
36 ,, 1 c. brown-orange .. .. 1·25 4·00
37 **10** 3 c. rose .. .. .. 1·75 3·50
a. Stop between "PRINCE EDWARD" .. .. 8·00 10·00
b. Bisected (1½ c.) (on cover) ..
c. Imperf. horiz. (vert. pair) .. £110

(*b*) *Perf.* 12 *to* 12¼, *large holes.*
38 **9** 2 c. blue .. .. .. 1·25 9·00
a. Bisected (1 c.) (on cover) ..
39 **11** 4 c. yellow-green .. .. 70 7·00
40 ,, 4 c. deep green .. .. 1·25 5·00
a. Bisected (2 c.) (on cover) .. † £600
41 **12** 6 c. black .. .. .. 80 5·50
a. Bisected (3 c.) (on cover) † £300
b. Imperf. between (horiz. pr.) 90·00
c. Imperf. vert. (horiz. pair) ..
42 **13** 12 c. reddish mauve .. 85 11·00

(*c*) *P* 12½–13, *smaller holes.*
43 **8** 1 c. orange .. .. 6·00
44 ,, 1 c. brown-orange .. .. 85 3·25
45 **10** 3 c. rose .. .. .. 4·00 4·00
a. Stop between "PRINCE EDWARD" .. .. 20·00 20·00
45*b* **12** 6 c. black .. .. .. — £110

(*d*) *Perf. compound of* (*a*) *and* (*c*) 11½–12 × 12½–13.
46 **8** 1 c. orange .. .. 15·00 17·00
47 **10** 3 c. rose .. .. 17·00 16·00
a. Stop between "PRINCE EDWARD" .. .. 70·00 75·00

The stamps were withdrawn 1, July, 1873, when the Colony became a Province of the Dominion of Canada.

QATAR.

An independent Arab Shaikhdom, with a British postal administration until May 23rd, 1963. The postal service was introduced in May 1950 (Doha) and February 1956 (Umm Said); the stamps of the British Postal Agencies in Eastern Arabia were at first used.

ALL STAMPS TO 1960 SURCHARGED ON ISSUES OF GREAT BRITAIN

QATAR NP 1 NP (1)

QATAR NP 3 NP (2)

QATAR 75 NP (3)

1957 (1 Apr.)–**59.**

(*a*) *T* **154/60** (*St. Edward's Crown wmk. T* **165**) *surch. as T* **1** *to* **3**.
1 **1** 1 n.p. on 5d. brown .. 5 5
2 **2** 3 n.p. on ½d. orange-red .. 5 5
3 ,, 6 n.p. on 1d. ultramarine .. 5 5
4 ,, 9 n.p. on 1½d. green .. 5 5
5 ,, 12 n.p. on 2d. lt. red-brown 5 5
6 **1** 15 n.p. on 2½d. carm.-red (I) 8 10
7 **2** 20 n.p. on 3d. dp. lilac (B.) .. 5 5
8 **1** 25 n.p. on 4d. ultramarine .. 15 20
9 ,, 40 n.p. on 6d. reddish purple 20 12
a. *Deep claret* (21.7.59) .. 15 20
10 ,, 50 n.p. on 9d. bronze-green .. 15 20
11 **3** 75 n.p. on 1s. 3d. green .. 30 30
12 ,, 1 r. on 1s. 6d. grey-blue 25 25
1/12 .. .. *Set of* 12 1·25 1·25

QATAR 2 RUPEES I

QATAR 2 RUPEES II

(4)

QATAR 5 RUPEES I

QATAR 5 RUPEES

II

(5)

QATAR 10 RUPEES

 I

QATAR 10 RUPEES

 II

(6)

Type I (**4/6**). Type-set overprints. Bold thick letters with sharp corners and straight edges. Bars close together and usually slightly longer than in Type II.

Type II (**4/6**). Plate-printed overprints. Thinner letters, rounded corners and rough edges. Bars wider apart.

(*b*) *Nos.* 536/8 *surch. with T* **4/6**.

			I (1.4.57)		II (18.9.57)	
13	**166**	2 r. on 2s. 6d. blk.-brn.	90	1·60	2·25	2·75
14	**167**	5 r. on 5s. rose-red ..	3·00	3·50	9·00	10·00
15	**168**	10 r. on 10s. ultram.	5·50	6·00	19·00	22·00

QATAR
15 NP

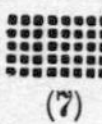

(7)

1957 (1 Aug.). *World Scout Jubilee Jamboree. Nos.* 557/9 *surch. in two lines as T* **7** (15 *n.p.*) *or in three lines* (*others*).

16	15 n.p. on 2½d. carmine-red ..	12	12
17	25 n.p. on 4d. ultramarine ..	20	25
18	75 n.p. on 1s. 3d. green ..	35	40

1960. *Q.E.II* (*Mult. Crowns wmk. T* **179**) *surch. as T* **1** *or* **2**.

20	**2**	3 n.p. on ½d. orange-red ..	25	40
21	,,	6 n.p. on 1d. ultramarine ..	25	50
22	,,	9 n.p. on 1½d. green ..	25	40
23	,,	12 n.p. on 2d. lt. red-brown ..	75	1·25
24	**1**	15 n.p. on 2½d. carm.-red (II)	12	12
25	**2**	20 n.p. on 3d. dp. lilac (B.) ..	15	15
26	**1**	40 n.p. on 6d. deep claret ..	20	20
20/6		.. .. *Set of* 7	1·75	2·50

Dates of issue: 26 Apr., 15 n.p.; 21 June, 6 and 40 n.p.; 28 Sept., 3, 9, 12 and 20 n.p.

8. Shaikh Ahmad bin Ali al Thani.

9. Falcon.

10. Dhow.

11. Oil Derrick.

12. Mosque.

(Des. O. C. Meronti (T **8**), M. Goaman (T **9**) M. C. Farrar-Bell (T **10**), J. Constable and O.C. Meronti (T **11/12**). Photo. Harrison & Sons (T **8/10**). Recess. De La Rue (T **11/12**).)

1961 (2 Sept.). *P* 14½ (5 *n.p.* to 75 *n.p.*) *or* 13 (1 *r.* to 10 *r.*).

27	**8**	5 n.p. carmine	5	10
28	,,	15 n.p. black	5	10
29	,,	20 n.p. reddish purple ..	5	10
30	,,	30 n.p. deep green	8	10
31	**9**	40 n.p. red	8	10
32	,,	50 n.p. sepia	12	20
33	**10**	75 n.p. ultramarine ..	15	25
34	**11**	1 r. scarlet	20	25
35	,,	2 r. ultramarine ..	40	50
36	**12**	5 r. bronze-green ..	1·00	1·25
37	,,	10 r. black	2·00	2·50
27/37		.. .. *Set of* 11	3·50	5·00

The Qatar Post Department took over the postal services on May 23rd 1963. Later stamp issues will be found listed in Vol. 4 of Stanley Gibbons Foreign Overseas Catalogue.

QUEENSLAND.

From 26 January, 1860, to 1 November, 186[0] current stamps of New South Wales were used i[n] Queensland. The stamps so used were the 1d. 2d. and 3d. diademed heads, the large square 6d. 8d. and 1s., and the "registered" stamp. Suc[h] stamps bearing a Queensland postmark may b[e] included in a collection of the stamps of thi[s] country.

1

2. Large Star.

(Dies eng. W. Humphrys. Recess. Perkin[s] Bacon & Co.)

1860 (1 Nov.). *W* **2.** *Imperf.*

1	**1**	1d. carmine-rose	£700	£30
2	,,	2d. blue	£1600	£65
3	,,	6d. green	£1500	£30

1860 (Nov.). *W* **2.** *Clean-cut perf.* 14–15½.

4	**1**	1d. carmine-rose (1.11) ..	£425	95·0
5	,,	2d. blue (1.11)..	£140	32·0
		a. Imperf. between (pair) ..		
6	,,	6d. green (15.11)	£140	22·0

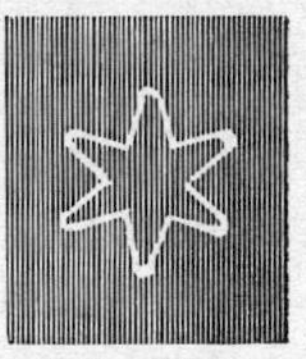

3. Small Star.

1860–61. *W* **3.** *Clean-cut perf.* 14–15½.

7	**1**	2d. blue	£160	32·0
		a. Imperf. between (horiz. pair)	—	£22
8	,,	3d. brown (15.4.61)	85·00	21·0
9	,,	6d. green	£190	21·0
10	,,	1s. violet (15.11.60).. ..	£160	21·0
11	,,	"REGISTERED", olive-yellow (1.61)	£120	24·0
		a. Imperf. between (pair) ..	£800	

The perforation of the 3d. is that known [as] "intermediate between clean-cut and rough"

1861 (July (?)). *W* **3.** *Clean-cut perf.* 14.

12	**1**	1d. carmine-rose	32·00	11·0
13	,,	2d. blue	£110	11·0

1861 (Sept.). *W* **3.** *Rough perf.* 14–15½.

14	**1**	1d. carmine-rose	16·00	11·
15	,,	2d. blue	25·00	8·
		a. Imperf. between (pair) ..		
16	,,	3d. brown	8·00	9·
		a. Imperf. between (pair) ..	£450	
17	,,	6d. deep green	50·00	9·0
18	,,	6d. yellow-green	60·00	9·0
19	,,	1s. violet	£100	25·0
20	,,	"REGISTERED" orge.-yell.	6·00	11·0

(Printed and perforated in Brisbane.)

1862–67. *Thick toned paper. No wmk.*

(*a*) *Rough perf.* 13 (1862–63).

21	**1**	1d. Indian red (16.12.62) ..	£110	15·
22	,,	1d. orange-vermilion (2.63)..	16·00	7·
		a. Imperf. (pair)	—	65·0
		b. Imperf. between (pair) ..		
23	,,	2d. blue (16.12.62)	16·00	6·
24	,,	2d. pale blue	35·00	7·
		a. Imperf. (pair)	—	60·
		b. Imperf. between (horiz. pair)		
25	,,	3d. brown	14·00	9·
26	,,	6d. apple-green (17.4.63) ..	22·00	4·
27	,,	6d. yellow-green	16·00	3·
		a. Imperf. between (horiz. pair)	—	£3

28 1 6d. blue-green .. .. 29·00 8·00
a. Imperf. (pair) .. .. — 85·00
29 ,, 1s. grey (14.7.63) .. .. 26·00 4·25
a. Imperf. between (horiz pair) — £300
b. Imperf. between (vert. pair). .

(*b*) *P* 12½ *square holes × rough perf.* 13 (1867).

30 1 1d. orange-vermilion .. 14·00 6·00
31 ,, 2d. blue .. .. .. 16·00 5·50
32 ,, 3d. brown .. .. .. 16·00 5·50
33 ,, 6d. apple-green .. .. — 6·00
34 ,, 6d. yellow-green .. .. — 6·00
35 ,, 1s. grey .. .. .. 36·00 7·50
a. Imperf. between (horiz. pair)

(*c*) *P* 13 *round holes* (1867).

36 1 1d. orange-vermilion (9.8.67) 14·00 3·50
37 ,, 2d. blue (30.3.67) .. .. 14·00 2·75
38 ,, 2d. pale blue .. .. 45·00
a. Imperf. between (horiz. pr.) — £300
38*b* ,, 3d. brown .. .. .. — £120
39 ,, 6d. apple-green (8.7.67) .. 29·00 3·50
40 ,, 6d. yellow-green .. .. 29·00 3·50

The 1d., 2d. and 6d. are known perf. 12½ square holes × 13 round holes.

1864–65. *W* **3.** (*a*) *Rough perf.* 13.

44 1 1d. orange-vermilion (1.65) .. 16·00 5·50
a. Imperf. between (horiz. pair) £130
45 ,, 2d. pale blue (1.65) .. 16·00 5·50
46 ,, 2d. deep blue .. .. 16·00 5·50
a. Imperf. between (vert. pair). . £275
b. Bisected (1d.) (on cover) .. † £600
47 ,, 6d. yellow-green (1.65) .. 40·00 5·50
48 ,, 6d. deep green .. .. 45·00 6·00
49 ,, "REGISTERED," orange-yell. (21.6.64) .. .. .. 13·00 6·00
a. Double printed £225
b. Imperf. .. .. ..

(*b*) *P* 12½ *square holes × rough perf.* 13.

50 1 1d. orange-vermilion .. 28·00 13·00

1866 (24 JAN.). *Wmk.* "QUEENSLAND/POSTAGE—POSTAGE/STAMPS—STAMPS" *in three lines in script capitals with double wavy lines above and below the wmk. and single wavy lines with projecting sprays between each line of words. There are ornaments* ("*fleurons*") *between* "POSTAGE" "POSTAGE" *and between* "STAMPS" "STAMPS". *Single stamps only show a portion of one or two letters of this wmk. Rough perf.* 13.

51 1 1d. orange-vermilion .. 40·00 5·50
52 ,, 2d. blue .. .. .. 14·00 3·00

1866 (24 SEPT.). *Lithographed on thick paper. No wmk. P* 13, *round holes.*

53 1 4d. slate .. .. .. 40·00 6·00
55 ,, 4d. lilac .. .. .. 13·00 3·00
56 ,, 4d. reddish lilac .. .. 13·00 5·50
57 ,, 5s. bright rose .. .. 50·00 17·00
58 ,, 5s. pale rose .. .. .. 40·00 13·00
a. Imperf. between (vert. pair) — £225

The 4d. is from a transfer taken from the 3d. die, and the 5s. was taken from the 1s. die, the final "s" being added. The alteration in the values was made by hand on the stone, and there are many varieties, such as tall and short letters in "FOUR PENCE", some of the letters of "FOUR" smudged out, and differences in the position of the two words.

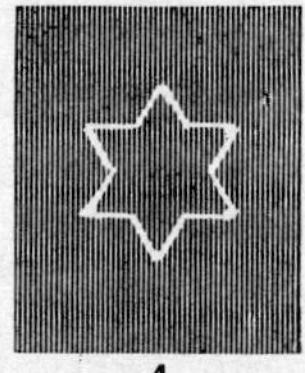

4

1868–74. *Wmk. small truncated Star, T* **4** *on each stamp, and the word* "QUEENSLAND" *in single-lined Roman capitals four times in each sheet.* (*a*) *P* 13.

59 1 1d. orange-vermilion (18.1.71) 14·00 1·10
60 ,, 2d. pale blue .. .. 14·00 1·10
61 ,, 2d. blue (3.4.68) .. .. 11·00 65
62 ,, 2d. bright blue .. .. 14·00 60
63 ,, 2d. greenish blue .. .. 28·00 60
64 ,, 2d. dark blue .. .. 14·00 70
a. Imperf. .. .. ..

65 1 3d. olive-brown (27.2.71) .. 26·00 1·50
66 ,, 3d. greenish brown .. .. 28·00 1·60
67 ,, 3d. brown .. .. .. 26·00 1·60
68 ,, 6d. yellow-green (10.11.71) .. 35·00 2·00
69 ,, 6d. green .. .. .. 35·00 3·00
70 ,, 6d. deep green .. .. 50·00 4·25
71 ,, 1s. dull claret (13.11.72) .. £110 11·00
72 ,, 1s. brownish grey .. .. £110 11·00
73 ,, 1s. mauve (19.2.74) .. .. 65·00 7·50

(*b*) *P* 12 (about Feb., 1874).

74 1 1d. orange-vermilion .. 85·00 9·00
75 ,, 2d. blue .. .. .. — 11·00
76 ,, 3d. greenish brown .. .. — 50·00
77 ,, 3d. brown .. .. .. 85·00 45·00
78 ,, 6d. deep green .. .. £300 13·00
79 ,, 1s. mauve .. .. .. — 13·00

(*c*) *P* 13 × 12.

80 1 1d. orange-vermilion .. — 45·00
81 ,, 2d. blue .. .. .. £300 13·00
82 ,, 3d. brown .. .. ..

Reprints were made in 1895 of all five values on the paper of the regular issue, and perforated 13; the colours are:—1d. orange and orange-brown, 2d. dull blue and bright blue, 3d. deep brown, 6d. yellow-green, 1s. red-violet and dull violet. The "Registered" was also reprinted with these on the same paper, but perforated 12.

5

6

(4d., litho. Other values recess.)

1868–78. *Wmk. Crown and Q, T* **5.**

(*a*) *P* 13 (1868–75).

83 1 1d. orange-verm. (10.11.68) 14·00 1·40
a. Imperf. .. .. ..
84 ,, 1d. pale rose-red (4.11.74) .. 14·00 2·75
85 ,, 1d. deep rose-red .. .. 28·00 2·75
86 ,, 2d. pale blue (4.11.74) .. 17·00 60
87 ,, 2d. deep blue (20.11.68) .. 12·00 1·50
a. Imperf. (pair) .. .. 95·00
b. Imperf. between (vert. pair)
88 1 3d. brown (11.6.75) .. 17·00 4·50
89 ,, 4d. yellow (1.1.75) .. .. £140 11·00
90 ,, 6d. deep green (9.4.69) .. 28·00 2·75
91 ,, 6d. yellow-green .. .. 22·00 2·00
92 ,, 6d. pale apple-green (1.1.75) 40·00 2·75
a. Imperf. .. .. .. 40·00
93 ,, 1s. mauve .. .. .. — 11·00

(*b*) *P* 12 (1876–78).

94 1 1d. deep orange-vermilion .. 12·00 1·10
95 ,, 1d. pale orange-vermilion .. 13·00 1·10
a. Imperf. between (vert. pair)
96 ,, 1d. rose-red .. .. .. 14·00 2·25
97 ,, 1d. flesh .. .. .. 17·00 2·75
98 ,, 2d. pale blue .. .. 32·00 4·00
99 ,, 2d. bright blue .. .. 5·50 35
100 ,, 2d. deep blue .. .. 7·00 45
101 ,, 3d. brown .. .. .. 14·00 2·75
102 ,, 4d. yellow .. .. .. 95·00 4·50
103 ,, 4d. buff .. .. .. 95·00 3·50
104 ,, 6d. deep green .. .. 35·00 2·25
105 ,, 6d. green .. .. .. 32·00 1·25
106 ,, 6d. yellow-green .. .. 36·00 1·40
107 ,, 6d. apple-green .. .. 36·00 2·25
108 ,, 1s. mauve .. .. .. 14·00 2·75
109 ,, 1s. purple .. .. .. 35·00 1·40
a. Imperf. between (pair) ..

(*c*) *P* 13 × 12.

110 1 1d. orange-vermilion .. — 28·00
111 ,, 2d. deep blue .. .. £350 32·00
112 ,, 4d. yellow .. .. ..
113 ,, 6d. deep green .. .. — 42·00

The 1d. and 2d. are known perf. 12½ square holes × 13 round holes.

1879. *No wmk. P* 12.

116 1 6d. pale emerald-green .. 50·00 7·00
a. Imperf. between (horiz. pr.) — £160

Lilac burelé band at back.

117 1 1s. mauve (*fisc.-canc.* £1) .. 33·00 14·00

The *burelé* is usually very indistinct.

Reprints exist of the 1d., 2d., 3d., 6d. and 1s. on thicker paper, Wmk. Type **6a**, and in different shades from the originals.

1881. *Lithographed from transfers from the* 1s. *die. Wmk. Crown and Q, T* **6.** *P* 12.

118 1 2s. pale blue (6 Apr.) .. 12·00 6·00
119 ,, 2s. blue (*fisc.-canc.* 25p.) .. 9·00 6·00
a. Imperf. vert. (horiz. pair). .
120 ,, 2s. deep blue .. .. 14·00 4·25
121 ,, 2s. 6d. dull scarlet (28 Aug.) 17·00 6·00
122 ,, 2s. 6d. bright scarlet (*fisc.-canc.* 25p.) .. .. 12·00
123 ,, 5s. pale yell.-ochre (28 Aug.) 12·00 6·00
124 ,, 5s. yellow-ochre .. .. 12·00 6·00
125 ,, 10s. reddish brown (Mar.) .. 60·00 22·00
a. Imperf. .. .. .. 75·00
126 ,, 10s. bistre-brown .. .. 60·00 22·00
127 ,, 20s. rose (*fisc.-canc.* 50p.) .. 60·00 17·00

Of the 2s. and 20s. stamps there are five types of each, and of the other values ten types of each.

Beware of fiscally used copies that have been cleaned and provided with forged postmarks.

7

DIE I.

DIE II.

Dies I. and II. occur in the same sheet.

DIE I. The whole horizontal inner line of the triangle in the upper right-hand corner merges into the outer white line of the oval above the "L".

DIE II. The same line is short and does not touch the inner oval.

1879–80. *Typo. P* 12.

(*a*) *Wmk. Crown and Q, T* **5.**

128 7 1d. reddish brown (Die I) .. 14·00 1·75
129 ,, 1d. orange-brown (Die I) .. 17·00 1·75
130 ,, 1d. reddish brown (Die II) .. 17·00 1·75
a. Error. "QOEENSLAND"
131 ,, 2d. blue (Die I) .. .. 17·00 1·10
a. Error. "PENGE" .. ..
132 ,, 4d. orange-yellow .. .. 80·00 6·00

(*b*) *No wmk., with lilac burelé band on back.*

133 7 1d. reddish brown (Die I) .. 95·00 12·00
134 ,, 1d. reddish brown (Die II) .. 95·00 21·00
a. Error. "QO" .. .. — £500
135 ,, 2d. blue (Die I) .. .. £110 6·00
a. Error. "PENGE" £1000 £200

(*c*) *Wmk. Crown and Q, T* **6.**

136 7 1d. reddish brown (Die I) .. 1·50 55
a. Imperf. between (pair) .. — 45·00
137 ,, 1d. reddish brown (Die II) 4·25 55
a. Error. "QO" .. .. 26·00
b. Imperf. between (pair) .. — 35·00
138 ,, 1d. dull orange (Die I) 1·50 55
139 ,, 1d. dull orange (Die II) 1·50 55
a. Error. "QO" .. .. 17·00 7·00
140 ,, 1d. scarlet (Die I) .. 1·50 30
141 ,, 1d. scarlet (Die II) .. 2·00 40
a. Error. "QO" .. .. 24·00 9·00
142 ,, 2d. bright blue (Die I) 4·25 30
143 ,, 2d. grey-blue (Die I) 2·25 25
a. Error. "PENGE" .. — 19·00
b. Imperf. between (pair) £110
144 ,, 2d. pale blue (Die II) 4·25 55
a. "TW" joined 3·50 40
145 ,, 2d. deep blue (Die II) 4·25 1·40
a. "TW" joined .. 3·50 15
146 ,, 4d. orange-yellow .. 3·50 55
a. Imperf. between (pair) ..

147 **7** 6d. deep green .. .. 4·25 85
a. Imperf. between (pair) ..
148 ,, 6d. yellow-green .. .. 5·50 85
149 ,, 1s. deep violet .. .. 4·25 1·25
150 ,, 1s. pale lilac .. .. 3·50 2·00

The variety "QO" is No. 48 in the first arrangement, and No. 44 in a later arrangement on the sheets. The "PENGE" error is No. 116 on Plate I.

All these values have been seen imperf, and unused, but we have no evidence that any of them were used in this condition.

The above were printed in sheets of 120, from plates made up of 30 groups of four electrotypes. There are four different types in each group, and two such groups of four are known of the 1d. and 2d., thus giving eight varieties of these two values. There was some resetting of the first plate of the 1d., and there are several plates of the 2d.; the value in the first plate of the latter value is in thinner letters, and in the last plate three types in each group of four have the "TW" of "TWO" joined, the letters of "PENCE" are larger and therefore much closer together, and in one type the "O" of "TWO" is oval, that letter being circular in the other types.

Half-penny

(8)

1880. (21 FEB.). *Surch. with T* **8**, *vert.*
151 **7** ½d. on 1d. (No. 136) (Die I) 14·00 12·00
151*a* ,, ½d. on 1d. (No. 137) (Die II) £140 £110
b. Error "QO" £250 £225

9

10

1882–86. *Recess.* *P* 12.

(*a*) *Thin paper.* *W* **5** *twice sideways.*
152 **9** 2s. bright blue .. .. 12·00 6·00
153 ,, 2s. 6d. vermilion .. .. 14·00 7·00
154 ,, 5s. rose .. .. 12·00 6·50
155 ,, 10s. brown .. .. 17·00 12·00
156 ,, £1 deep green .. .. 35·00 28·00

(*b*) *Thin paper.* *W* **6** *twice sideways.*
157 **9** 2s. 6d. vermilion .. .. 12·00 9·00
158 ,, 5s. rose .. .. 13·00 6·00
159 ,, 10s. brown .. .. 45·00 14·00
160 ,, £1 deep green .. .. 26·00 17·00

(*c*) *Thick paper.* *W* **10.**
161 **9** 2s. bright blue .. .. 17·00 7·00
162 ,, 2s. 6d. vermilion .. .. 9·00 6·50
163 ,, 5s. rose .. .. 9·00 7·00
164 ,, 10s. brown .. .. 12·00 11·00
165 ,, £1 deep green .. .. 26·00 14·00

See also Nos. 270/1.

11

12

In T **12** the shading lines do not extend entirely across, as in T **11**, thus leaving a white line down the front of the throat and point of the bust.

1882–83. *W* **6.** (*a*) *P* 12.
166 **11** 1d. pale vermilion-red .. 70 8
a. Double print .. ..
167 ,, 1d. deep vermilion-red .. 70 5
168 ,, 2d. blue .. .. 1·10 5
a. Imperf. between (horiz. pr.)
169 ,, 4d. pale yellow .. .. 1·75 15
a. "PENGE" for "PENCE" 26·00 11.00
170 ,, 6d. green 85 5
171 ,, 1s. violet .. .. .. 3·50 25
172 ,, 1s. lilac .. .. .. 1·10 25
173 ,, 1s. deep mauve .. .. 1·10 12
174 ,, 1s. pale mauve .. .. 1·25 12

(*b*) *P* 9½ × 12
176 **11** 1d. pale red .. .. 14·00 5·50
177 ,, 2d. blue .. .. 55·00 8·00
178 ,, 1s. mauve .. .. .. 26·00 6·00

The above were printed from plates made up of groups of four electrotypes as previously. In the 1d. the words of value are followed by a full stop. There are four types of the 4d., 6d., and 1s., eight types of the 1d., and twelve types of the 2d.

1887–89. *W* **6.** (*a*) *P* 12.
179 **12** 1d. vermilion-red 60 8
a. Imperf. .. .. .. 6·50 9·00
180 ,, 2d. blue .. .. .. 1·25 8
181 ,, 2s. deep brown .. .. 8·00 7·50
182 ,, 2s. pale brown .. .. 7·50 6·00

(*b*) *P* 9½ × 12.
183 **12** 2d. blue .. .. .. 45·00 6·00

These are from new plates; four types of each value grouped as before. The 1d. is without stop. In all values No. 2 in each group of four has the "L" and "A" of "QUEENSLAND" joined at the foot, and No. 3 of the 2d. has "P" of word "PENCE" with a long downstroke. Varieties are known (*perf.* 12) in which the "P" has been made normal, probably by hand on the plate.

13

14

1890–94. *W* **6.** *P* 12½, 13 (*comb. machine*).
184 **13** ½d. pale green 45 5
185 ,, ½d. deep green 45 5
186 ½d. deep blue-green .. 60 5
187 **12** 1d. vermilion-red 30 5
188 ,, 2d. blue (old plate) .. 80 5
189 ,, 2d. pale blue (old plate) .. 55 5
190 ,, 2d. pale blue (retouched plate) 45 12
191 **14** 2½d. carmine 45 5
192 **12** 3d. brown 45 10
193 **11** 4d. yellow 50 12
a. "PENGE" for "PENCE" 5·00
194 ,, 4d. orange 85 12
a. "PENGE" for "PENCE" 9·00 3·50
195 ,, 4d. lemon .. .. 1·75 15
a. "PENGE" for "PENCE" 12·00
196 ,, 6d. green 85 12
197 **12** 2s. red-brown .. .. 2·75 45
198 ,, 2s. pale brown .. .. 2·75 70

The 1d. vermilion-red is known *imperf.*

This issue is perforated by a new vertical comb machine, gauging about 12¾ × 12¾. The 3d. is from a plate similar to those of the last issue, No. 2 in each group of four types having "L" and "A" joined at the foot. The ½d. and 2½d. are likewise in groups of four types, but the differences are very minute. In the ½d. the watermark is sideways. In the retouched plate of the 2d. the letters "L" and "A" no longer touch in No. 2 of each group and the "P" in No. 3 is normal.

1894–95. A. *Thick paper.* *W* **10.** (*a*) *P* 12½, 13.
202 **12** 1d. vermilion-red 45 5
203 ,, 1d. red-orange 40 5
204 ,, 2d. blue (retouched plate) 25 5

(*b*) *P* 12.
205 **11** 1s. mauve .. .. .. 1·10 70

B. *Unwmkd. paper; with blue burelé band at back.* *P* 12½, 13.
206 **12** 1d. deep vermilion-red .. 8 5

C. *Thin paper.* *Crown and Q faintly impressed.* *P* 12½, 13.
207 **12** 2d. blue (retouched plate) 1·00

15

16

17 18

1895–96. *P* 12½, 13.

A. *W* **6.**
208 **15** ½d. green 8
209 ,, ½d. deep green 8
a. Printed both sides .. 19·00
210 **16** 1d. orange-red 30
211 ,, 1d. pale red 25
212 ,, 2d. blue 25
213 **17** 2½d. carmine 85
214 ,, 2½d. rose .. .. .. 1·10
215 **18** 5d. purple-brown .. 85

P 12.
217 **16** 1d. red .. .. ..
218 ,, 2d. blue .. .. .. —

B. *Thick paper.* *W* **10** (*part only on each stamp*

(*a*) *P* 12½, 13.
219 **15** ½d. green 8
220 ,, ½d. deep green 8

(*b*) *P* 12.
221 **15** ½d. green .. .. .. 3·50
222 ,, ½d. deep green .. .. 3·50

C. *No wmk.; with blue burelé band at back.*

(*a*) *P* 12½, 13.
223 **15** ½d. green 8
a. Without burelé band .. 14·00
224 ,, ½d. deep green 12

(*b*) *P* 12.
225 **15** ½d. green .. .. .. 4·00
a. Without burelé band .. 14·00

Nos. 223*a* and 225*a* are from the margins of th sheet.

D. *Thin paper, with Crown and Q faintly impressed.* *P* 12½, 13.
227 **15** ½d. green 25
228 **16** 1d. orange-red 45

19

1896. *W* **6.** *P* 12½, 13.
229 **19** 1d. vermilion 8

20

21

22

23

24

25

897–1907. *Figures in all corners. W* **6.** *P* 12½, 13.

31	**20**	½d. deep green	25	10
		a. Perf. 12	—	28·00
32	**21**	1d. orange-vermilion ..	12	5
33	,,	1d. vermilion	12	5
34	,,	2d. blue	12	5
35	,,	2d. deep blue	12	5
36	**22**	2½d. rose	1·00	45
37	,,	2½d. purple/*blue*	40	5
38	,,	2½d. brown-purple/*blue*	30	5
39	,,	2½d. slate/*blue*	3·00	85
40	**21**	3d. brown	80	15
41	,,	3d. deep brown	40	8
42	,,	3d. reddish brown (1906)	40	10
43	,,	3d. grey-brown (1907) ..	70	10
44	,,	4d. yellow	55	12
45	,,	4d. yellow-buff	55	12
46	**23**	5d. purple-brown ..	40	8
47	,,	5d. dull brown (1906) ..	80	30
48	,,	5d. black-brown (1907) ..	70	40
49	**21**	6d. green	60	10
50	,,	6d. yellow-green	60	12
51	**24**	1s. pale mauve	1·00	40
52	,,	1s. dull mauve	1·00	40
53	,,	1s. bright mauve ..	1·25	50
54	**25**	2s. turquoise-green ..	2·00	80

The 1d. perf. 12 × 9½, was privately printed.

899. *W* **6.** (*a*) *Zigzag roulette in black.* (*b*) *The same but plain.* (*c*) *Roulette* (*a*) *and also* (*b*). (*d*) *Roulette* (*b*) *and perf.* 12½, 13. (*e*) *Roulette* (*a*) *and perf.* 12½, 13. (*f*) *Compound of* (*a*), (*b*), *and perf.* 12½, 13.

56	**21**	1d. vermilion (*a*)	1·60	1·10
57	,,	1d. vermilion (*b*)	55	30
58	,,	1d. vermilion (*c*)	1·40	
59	,,	1d. vermilion (*d*)	80	60
60	,,	1d. vermilion (*e*)	20·00	
61	,,	1d. vermilion (*f*)	26·00	

26

27

899–1906. *W* **6.** *P* 12½, 13.

62	**26**	½d. deep green	10	5
63	,,	½d. grey-green	10	5
64	,,	½d. pale green (1906) ..	10	5

Stamps of *T* **26** without wmk., are proofs.

1900 *Charity. T* **27** *and horiz. design showing Queen Victoria in medallion inscr.* "PATRIOTIC FUND 1900". *W* **5.** *P* 12.

264*a*		1d. (1s.), claret	32·00	35·00
264*b*		2d. (2s.), violet	55·00	65·00

These stamps, sold at 1s. and 2s. respectively, paid postage of 1d. and 2d. only, the difference being contributed to a Patriotic Fund.

28

QUEENSLAND
(*a*)

QUEENSLAND
(*b*)

Two types of the word "QUEENSLAND".

Dates on T **28** are those of the establishment of the colonies.

(Eng. and typo. in Melbourne, Victoria.)

1903. *Wmk.* w.**10.** *P* 12½.

265	**28**	9d. brown & ultram. (*a*) ..	1·75	45
266	,,	9d. brown & ultram. (*b*) ..	1·75	45

1903. W **6.** *P* 12.

267	**26**	½d. green	25	8
268	**21**	1d. vermilion	80	30
269	,,	2d. blue	—	1·40

1905. *Recess. W* **10.** *P* 12½, 13 (*irregular*).

270	**9**	2s. 6d. vermilion	22·00	12·00
271	,,	£1 deep green	£140	85·00

29

1905–10. *Litho.* A. *W* **6,** *twice sideways.* (*a*) *P* 12 (1905–6).

272	**9**	5s. rose (7.06)	24·00	21·00
273	,,	£1 deep green (7.11.05) ..	42·00	28·00
		(*b*) *P* 12½, 13 (*irregular*).		
274	**9**	£1 deep green (7.06) ..	£110	28·00

B. *W* **29,** *twice sideways. P* 12½, 13 (*irregular*) (1907–10).

275	**9**	2s. 6d. vermilion	14·00	9·00
276	,,	2s. 6d. dull orange (1910)	16·00	11·00
277	,,	5s. rose	14·00	9·00
278	,,	5s. deep rose	14·00	11·00
279	,,	10s. deep brown	17·00	12·00
280	,,	£1 bluish green	35·00	26·00
280*a*	,,	£1 deep green	£100	80·00

30

32

Redrawn types of T **21.**

T **30.** The head is redrawn, the top of the crown is higher and touches the frame, as do also the back of the chignon and the point of the bust. The forehead is filled in with lines of shading, and the figures in the corners appear to have been redrawn also.

T **32.** The forehead is plain (white instead of shaded), and though the top of the crown is made higher, it does not touch the frame; but the point of the bust and the chignon still touch. The figure in the right lower corner does not touch the line below, and has not the battered appearance of that in the first redrawn type. The stamps are very clearly printed, the lines of shading being distinct.

1906 (SEPT.). *W* **6.** *P* 12½, 13.

281	**30**	2d. dull blue (*shades*) ..	80	25

1907–12. *Wmk. Crown and double-lined A, Type* w.**11.** (*a*) *P* 12 × 12½.

282	**28**	9d. brown & ultram. (*a*) ..	5·50	80
283	,,	9d. brown & ultram. (*b*) ..	2·00	55
283*a*	,,	9d. pale brown & blue (*a*) ..		
284	,,	9d. pale brown & blue (*b*) ..	2·00	65
		(*b*) *P* 11 (1912).		
285	**28**	9d. brown and blue (*b*) ..	—	60·00

1907–09. *W* **29.** (*a*) *P* 12½, 13.

286	**26**	½d. deep green	12	5
287	,,	½d. deep blue-green ..	12	5
288	**21**	1d. vermilion	12	5
		a. Variety. Imperf. (pair) ..	45·00	
289	**30**	2d. dull blue	25	5
289*a*	,,	2d. bright blue (3.08) ..	3·00	85
290	**32**	2d. bright blue (4.08) ..	30	5
291	**21**	3d. pale brown (8.08) ..	85	5
292	,,	3d. bistre-brown	70	10
293	,,	4d. yellow	1·40	35
294	,,	4d. grey-black (4.09) ..	40	25
295	**23**	5d. dull brown	60	25
295*a*	,,	5d. sepia (12.09) ..	2·00	55
296	**21**	6d. yellow-green	1·40	25
297	,,	6d. bright green	1·50	55
298	**24**	1s. violet ('08)	1·50	70
299	,,	1s. bright mauve ..	1·75	60
300	**25**	2s. turquoise-green (8·08)	3·00	1·00
		(*b*) *P* 13 × 11 *to* 12½.		
301	**26**	½d. deep green		
302	**21**	1d. vermilion	15	5
303	**32**	2d. blue	40	25
304	**21**	3d. bistre-brown	40	10
305	,,	4d. grey-black	1·25	
306	**23**	5d. dull brown	85	
307	**21**	6d. yellow-green	1·40	
308	**23**	1s. violet	3·50	

The perforation (*b*) is from a machine introduced to help cope with the demands caused by the introduction of penny postage. The three rows at top (or bottom) of the sheet show varieties gauging 13 × 11½, 13 × 11, and 13 × 12 respectively, these are obtainable in strips of three showing the three variations.

1911. *W* **29.** *Perf. irregular compound,* 10½ *to* 12½.

309	**21**	1d. vermilion		

This was from another converted machine, formerly used for perforating Railway stamps. The perforation was very unsatisfactory and only one or two sheets were sold.

POSTAL FISCALS.

Authorised for use from 1 *Jan.,* 1880.

CANCELLATIONS. Beware of stamps which have had pen-cancellations cleaned off and then had faked postmarks applied.

F 1

F 2

1866–68. A. *No. wmk. P* 13.

F 1	**F 1**	1d. blue	4·50	
F 2	,,	6d. deep violet	—	9·00
F 3	,,	1s. blue-green		
F 4	,,	2s. brown	—	13·00
F 5	,,	2s. 6d. dull red ..	—	8·00
F 6	,,	5s. yellow		
F 7	,,	10s. green	16·00	
F 8	,,	20s. rose		
		B. *Wmk. Type* F **2.** *P* 13.		
F 9	**F 1**	1d. blue	1·40	6·50
F10	,,	6d. deep violet	—	8·00
F11	,,	6d. blue		
F12	,,	1s. blue-green	2·25	
F13	,,	2s. brown		
F13*a*	,,	5s. yellow		
F14	,,	10s. green		
F15	,,	20s. rose		

F 3

F 4

1871–2. *P 12 or 13.*

A. *Wmk. Large Crown and Q, as T* **10**.

F16	**F 3**	1d. mauve	1·00	1·00
F17	,,	6d. red-brown	2·00	2·25
F18	,,	1s. green	2·00	2·25
F19	,,	2s. blue	2·25	2·25
F20	,,	2s. 6d. brick-red ..	4·50	4·50
F21	,,	5s. orange-brown ..	6·50	4·50
F22	,,	10s. brown	—	16·00
F23	,,	20s. rose	—	32·00

B. *No wmk. Blue burelé band at back.*

F24	**F 3**	1d. mauve	2·00	
F25	,,	6d. red-brown	2·25	
F26	,,	6d. mauve	4·00	
F27	,,	1s. green	3·00	3·00
F28	,,	2s. blue	4·50	16·00
F29	,,	2s. 6d. vermilion ..		
F30	,,	5s. yellow-brown ..	—	9·00
F31	,,	10s. brown	—	21·00
F32	,,	20s. rose	—	25·00

1878–9.

A. *No wmk. Lilac burelé band at back. P 12.*

F33	**F 4**	1d. violet	—	2·25

B. *Wmk. Crown and Q, T* **5**. *P 12.*

F34	**F 4**	1d. violet	1·00	1·00

F 5

1892. *Wmk. Crown and Q, T* **5**, *sideways. P 12.*

F35	**F 5**	6d. green	8·00	21·00
F36	,,	5s. carmine	16·00	21·00
F37	,,	10s. brown	26·00	

Queensland now uses Australian stamps.

RHODESIA.

I. Issues for the Area formerly covered by the British South Africa Company.

1

2

(Recess. Bradbury, Wilkinson.)

1892 (2 Jan.). *Thin wove paper. P 14, 14½.*

1	**1**	1d. black	3·00	1·50
2	,,	6d. ultramarine	20·00	8·00
3	,,	6d. deep blue	6·00	3·00
4	,,	1s. grey-brown	10·00	7·00
5	,,	2s. vermilion	12·00	9·00
6	,,	2s. 6d. grey-purple	11·00	11·00
7	,,	2s. 6d. lilac	11·00	11·00
8	,,	5s. orange-yellow	20·00	18·00
9	,,	10s. deep green	30·00	35·00
10	**2**	£1 deep blue	80·00	80·00
11	,,	£2 rose-red*	£200	80·00
12	,,	£5 sage-green	£1000	£250
13	,,	£10 brown	£1500	£400
1/10		.. .. *Set of* 10	£180	£170

* For later printing of the £2 see No. 74.

Nos. 3 and 7 came from later printings.

Great caution is needed in buying the high values in either used or unused condition, many stamps offered being revenue stamps cleaned and re-gummed or with forged postmarks.

The following sheet watermarks are known in the issues of 1892 and 1892–94. (1) William Collins, Sons & Co's paper watermarked with the firm's monogram, and "PURE LINEN WOVE BANK" in double-lined capitals. (2) As (1) with "EXTRA STRONG" and "139" added. (3) Paper by Wiggins, Teape & Co., watermarked "W T & Co" in script letters in double-lined wavy border. (4) The same firm's paper, watermarked "1011" in double-lined figures. (5) "WIGGINS TEAPE & CO LONDON" in double-lined block capitals. Many values can also be found on a slightly thicker paper without wmk. but single specimens are not easily distinguishable.

½d.

(3)

1892 (2 Jan.).* *Nos. 2 and 4 surch. as T* **3**.

14	**1**	½d. on 6d. ultramarine ..	40·00	45·00
15	,,	2d. on 6d. ultramarine ..	35·00	60·00
16	,,	4d. on 6d. ultramarine ..	45·00	70·00
17	,,	8d. on 1s grey-brown ..	45·00	70·00

* This, being the date when postal services commenced, is the earliest date when these stamps could have been used, but it has not been established whether supplies arrived in time.

Caution is needed in buying these surcharges as both forged surcharges and forged postmarks exist.

4

5. (Ends of Scrolls behind Legs of Springboks.)

(T4. Centre recess; value typo. Bradbury, Wilkinson.)

1892 (2 Jan.)–**94**. *Thin wove paper (wmks. as note after No. 13). P 14, 14½.*

18	**4**	½d. dull blue and vermilion ..	1·00	1·00
19	,,	½d. deep blue and vermilion	1·00	1·00
20	,,	2d. sea-green and vermilion	1·75	1·00
21	,,	3d. grey-black & green (8.92)	1·75	1·50
22	,,	4d. chestnut and black ..	1·75	1·50
23	,,	8d. rose-lake & ultramarine	1·75	1·75
24	,,	8d. red and ultramarine ..	1·75	1·75
25	,,	3s. brown and green (1894) ..	25·00	30·00
26	,,	4s. grey-black & verm. (1893)	11·00	15·00
18/26		.. .. *Set of* 8	40·00	45·00

(Recess. Perkins, Bacon from the Bradbury, Wilkinson plates.)

1895?. *Thick soft wove paper. P 12½.*

27	**4**	2d. green and red	6·00	2·00
28	,,	4d. yellow-brown and black	6·00	3·00
		a. Imperf. (pair)	£400	

(Centre recess; value typo. Perkins, Bacon.)

1896–97. *Wove paper. P 14.*

(*a*) Die I. Plates 1 and 2.

Small dot to the right of the tail of the right-hand supporter in the coat of arms. Body of lion only partly shaded.

29	**5**	1d. scarlet and emerald ..	1·75	1·0
30	,,	2d. brown and mauve ..	1·75	1·0
31	,,	3d. chocolate & ultramarine	1·00	1·0
32	,,	4d. ultramarine and mauve	1·50	1·75
		a. Imperf. between (pair) ..		
33	,,	6d. mauve and pink	6·00	1·75
34	,,	8d. green and mauve/*buff* ..	1·00	1·0
		a. Imperf. between (pair) ..		
		b. Imperf. (pair)	£450	
35	,,	1s. green and blue	2·50	1·5
36	,,	3s. green and mauve/*blue* ..	10·00	10·0
		a. Imperf. (pair)	£450	
37	,,	4s. orange-red & blue/*green*	9·00	8·0
29/37		.. .. *Set of* 9	25·00	22·0

(*b*) Die II. Plates 3 and 4.

No dot. Body of lion heavily shaded all over.

41	**5**	½d. slate and violet ..	60	1·0
42	,,	1d. scarlet and emerald ..	50	1·0
43	,,	2d. brown and mauve ..	1·25	1·7
44	,,	4d. ultramarine and mauve	11·00	3·0
45	,,	4d. blue and mauve ..	1·00	5
46	,,	6d. mauve and rose ..	1·00	1·0
47	,,	2s. indigo and green/*buff* ..	6·00	1·7
48	,,	2s. 6d. brown & purple/*yell.*	7·00	8·0
49	,,	5s. chestnut and emerald ..	10·00	10·0
50	,,	10s. slate and vermilion/*rose*	22·00	22·0
41/50		.. .. *Set of* 9	45·00	45·0

One Penny

(6)

THREE PENCE.

(7)

1896 (April). *Matabele Rebellion provisionals. Surch. at Bulawayo with T* **6** *and* **7**.

51	**6**	1d. on 3d. (No. 21)	£125	£20
		a. "P" in "Penny" inverted ..	£1500	
52	,,	1d. on 4s. (No. 26)	£110	80·0
		a. "P" in "Penny" inverted ..	£1500	
		b. "y" in "Penny" inverted ..	£1500	
		c. Single bar through original value	£250	£30
53	**7**	3d. on 5s. (No. 8)	70·00	90·0
		a. "R" in "THREE" inverted	£2000	
		b. "T" in "THREE" inverted	£2000	

Nos. 51 and 52 occur in two settings, one wit[h] 9¾ mm. between value and upper bar, the othe[r] with 11 mm. between value and upper bar.

BRITISH SOUTH AFRICA COMPANY.

(8)

9. (Ends of scrolls between legs of springboks.)

1896 (22 May). *Cape of Good Hope stamps opt[d.] by Argus Printing Co., Cape Town, with T [8]. Wmk. Anchor (3d. wmk. Crown CA). P 14.*

58	**6**	½d. grey-black (No. 48*a*) ..	2·00	3·0
59	**17**	1d. rose-red (No. 58) ..	2·00	3·0
60	**6**	2d. deep bistre (No. 50*a*) ..	3·00	2·5
61	,,	3d. pale claret (No. 40) ..	12·00	15·0
62	,,	4d. blue (No. 51)	5·00	5·0
		a. "COMPANY." omitted ..	£2250	
63	**4**	6d. deep purple (No. 52*a*) ..	16·00	18·0
64	**6**	1s. yellow-ochre (No. 65) ..	30·00	40·0
58/64		.. .. *Set of* 7	65·00	75·0

(Recess. Waterlow.)

397. *P* 13½ *to* 16.
5 **9** ½d. grey-black and purple .. 75 1·00
7 ,, 1d. scarlet and emerald .. 1·25 1·50
,, 2d. brown and mauve .. 1·00 1·00
,, 3d. brown-red and slate-blue 1·00 1·00
a. Imperf. between (pair) .. £350
,, 4d. ultramarine and claret .. 1·25 1·10
a. Imperf. between (pair) .. £1200 £1200
,, 6d. dull purple and pink .. 1·25 2·00
,, 8d. green and mauve/*buff* .. 2·25 1·75
a. Imperf. between (pair) .. — £300
3 ,, £1 black & red-brown/*green* £200 £120

Recess. Waterlow, from the Bradbury plate.)

397 (Jan.). *P* 15.
2 £2 rosy red £650 £120

10

11

12

(Recess. Waterlow.

98–1908. *P* 14–14½ *or* 13½ (£20).
10 ½d. dull bluish green .. 30 10
a. Yellow-green (1904) .. 35 10
aa. Imperf. between (pair) .. £175
ab. Imperf. (pair) £175
,, ½d. deep green (*shades*) (1908) 6·00 12
,, 1d. rose (*shades*) .. 30 10
a. Imperf. (pair) £200 £180
b. Imperf. between (pair) .. £180
,, 1d. red (*shades*) (1905) 75 10
a. Imperf. between (pair) .. £100
b. Imperf. (pair) £150
,, 2d. brown 60 10
,, 2½d. dull blue (*shades*) 1·00 15
a. Imperf. between (pair) .. £150 £150
b. Grey-blue (*shades*) (1903) .. 1·50 15
,, 3d. claret .. .. 1·50 1·25
a. Imperf. between (pair) .. £200
,, 4d. olive .. .. 1·25 20
a. Imperf. between (pair) .. £250
,, 6d. reddish purple .. 1·50 1·00
a. Reddish mauve (1902) .. 3·00 3·00
11 1s. bistre .. .. 1·75 1·00
a. Imperf. between (pair) .. £650
b. Deep olive-bistre (1907) .. 50·00
bc. Imperf. (pair) £650
bd. Imperf. between (horiz. pair) £700
c. Bistre-brown (1908) .. 5·00 2·50
d. Brownish yellow (1908) .. 3·00 1·50
,, 2s. 6d. bluish grey (11.06) 4·50 1·75
a. Imperf. between (pair) .. £300 £175
,, 3s. deep violet (1902) .. 2·50 1·50
a. Deep bluish violet (1908) .. 7·00 3·00
,, 5s. brown-orange .. 7·00 3·00
,, 7s. 6d. black (11.01) .. 11·00 11·00
,, 10s. grey-green .. 5·00 4·00
12 £1 greyish red-purple (*p.* 15½) (7.01) .. .. 60·00 12·00
a. Perf. 14. *Blackish pur.* (1902) 60·00 12·00
,, £2 brown (5.08) .. .. 30·00 10·00
,, £5 deep blue (7.01) .. £2000 £1250
,, £10 lilac (7.01) £2000 £1250
a ,, £20 yellow-bistre (1901?) .. £2500
90 .. .. .. *Set of* 14 70·00 25·00
1, 85/6, 88/93 Perf. " Specimen " *Set of* 10 £250

A £100 cherry-red perf. 13½ was prepared but t issued.

13. Victoria Falls.

(Recess. Waterlow.)

1905 (13 July). *Visit of British Association and Opening of Victoria Falls Bridge. P* 13½ *to* 15.
94 **13** 1d. red .. .. .. 1·00 1·00
95 ,, 2½d. deep blue .. .. 2·50 2·50
96 ,, 5d. claret (Perf. S. £15) .. 5·00 7·00
97 ,, 1s. blue-green .. .. 5·00 7·00
a. Imperf. (pair) £2500
b. Imperf. vert. (horiz. pair) £2500
c. Imperf. horiz. (vert. pair) .. £3000
98 ,, 2s. 6d. black .. .. 20·00 25·00
99 ,, 5s. violet .. .. 13·00 15·00
94/99 .. .. *Set of* 6 42·00 50·00
94/9 Perf. " Specimen " *Set of* 6 70·00

RHODESIA.

(14)

1909 (15 Apr.)–**12.** *Optd. as T* **14.** *P* 14–14½.
100 **10** ½d. green to deep green .. 15 10
a. No stop .. .. .. 10·00 7·00
b. Yellow-green (1911) .. 10·00 10·00
101 ,, 1d. carmine-rose .. 15 10
a. No stop .. .. .. 12·00 7·00
b. Imperf. between (pair) .. 90·00
c. Deep carmine-rose .. 15 10
cd. Imperf. between (pair) .. £120
102 ,, 2d. brown 75 50
a. No stop .. .. .. 12·00 10·00
103 ,, 2½d. pale dull blue .. 20 20
a. No stop .. .. .. 7·00 7·00
104 ,, 3d. claret 70 50
a. No stop .. .. .. 20·00 15·00
105 ,, 4d. olive .. .. 1·00 50
a. No stop .. .. .. 15·00 15·00
106 ,, 6d. dull purple .. 2·50 1·50
a. No stop .. .. .. 15·00 12·00
b. Reddish purple .. .. 1·10 50
107 **11** 1s. deep brownish bistre 1·50 50
a. No stop .. .. .. 15·00 10·00
108 ,, 2s. 6d. bluish grey .. 4·50 3·00
a. No stop .. .. .. 15·00 15·00
109 ,, 3s. deep violet .. 4·50 4·50
110 ,, 5s. orange .. .. 7·50 5·00
a. No stop .. .. .. 15·00 15·00
111 ,, 7s. 6d. black .. 10·00 5·00
112 ,, 10s. dull green .. 7·00 7·00
a. No stop .. .. .. 45·00 45·00
113 **12** £1 grey-purple .. .. 30·00 15·00
a. Vertical pair, one without opt. £3500
b. Overprint in violet .. 50·00 50·00
113*c* ,, £2 brown (*bluish paper*) £1600 £100
113*d* ,, £2 rosy brown (*p.* 14½ × 15) (1912) £1600 £100
113*e* ,, £5 deep blue (*bluish paper*) £1600 £750
100/113 .. .. *Set of* 14 40·00 30·00
100/13 Perf. " Specimen " *Set of* 14 £100

In some values the no-stop variety occurs in every stamp in a vertical row of a sheet, in other values only once in a sheet. Other varieties, such as no serif to the right of apex of " A ", no serif to top of " E ", etc., exist in some values.

RHODESIA.
5d

(15)

RHODESIA.
TWO SHILLINGS.

(16)

1909 (April)–**11.** *T* **10** *and* **11** *surch. as T* **15** *and* **16** (2s.), *in black.*
114 5d. on 6d. reddish purple .. 1·75 1·75
a. Surcharge in violet .. .. 10·00
115 5d. on 6d. dull purple .. 2·00 2·00
116 7½d. on 2s. 6d. bluish grey .. 1·50 1·50
a. Surcharge in violet .. .. 3·00 2·50
117 10d. on 3s. deep violet .. 3·50 3·50
a. Surcharge in violet .. .. 1·50 1·50
118 2s. on 5s. orange .. 3·50 3·50
114/18 Perf. " Specimen " *Set of* 4 40·00

In the 7½d. and 10d. surcharges, the bars spaced as in *T* **16**.

17

(Recess. Waterlow.)

1910 (11 Nov.)–**13.** *T* **17.** (*a*) *P* 14.
119 ½d. yellow-green .. .. 1·00 25
a. Imperf. (pair) £1200 £1500
120 ½d. bluish green .. .. 2·50 25
121 ½d. olive-green .. .. 6·00 50
122 ½d. dull green .. .. 18·00 10·00
123 1d. bright carmine .. 1·00 10
a. Imperf. between (pair) .. £3500
124 1d. carmine-lake .. .. 5·00 12
125 1d. rose-red .. .. 1·50 10
126 2d. black and grey .. 5·00 1·75
127 2d. black-pur. & slate-grey 50·00 60·00
128 2d. black and slate-grey .. 5·00 1·75
129 2d. black and slate .. 4·50 1·75
130 2d. black and grey-black .. 5·00 1·75
131 2½d. ultramarine .. .. 6·00 4·00
131*a* 2½d. bright ultramarine .. 4·50 4·00
132 2½d. dull blue .. .. 5·00 4·00
133 2½d. chalky blue .. .. 5·00 4·00
134 3d. purple and ochre .. 4·00 2·00
135 3d. purple and yellow-ochre 5·00 2·00
136 3d. magenta & yellow-ochre 18·00 15·00
137 3d. violet and ochre .. 18·00 15·00
138 4d. greenish black & orange 25·00 18·00
139 4d. brown-purple & orange 18·00 10·00
140 4d. black and orange .. 4·00 4·00
141 5d. purple-brn. & olive-grn. 8·00 7·00
141*a* 5d. purple-brn. & olive-yell. 8·00 7·00
142 5d. pur.-brn. & ochre (*error*) £150 60·00
143 5d. lake-brown and olive .. 30·00 18·00
143*a* 5d. lake-brown and green .. £6000 £1000
144 6d. red-brown and mauve.. 5·00 4·00
145 6d. brown and purple .. 5·00 2·50
145*a* 6d. bright chestnut & mauve £150 15·00
146 8d. black and purple .. £250 50·00
147 8d. dull purple and purple 50·00 15·00
148 8d. greenish black & purple 30·00 12·00
149 10d. scarlet & reddish mauve 10·00 15·00
150 10d. carmine and deep purple 35·00 13·00
151 1s. black and deep blue-grn. 7·00 6·00
152 1s. black & pale blue-green 6·00 3·00
152*a* 1s. purple-black & blue-grn. 75·00 12·00
153 2s. black and ultramarine.. 15·00 12·00
154 2s. black and dull blue .. £100 15·00
154*a* 2s. purple-black & ultram. £1250 £125
155 2s. 6d. black and lake .. 75·00 85·00
155*a* 2s. 6d. black and crimson.. 75·00 85·00
156 2s. 6d. sepia & deep crimson £100 £100
156*a* 2s. 6d. bistre-brn. & crimson £250 £125
157 2s. 6d. black & rose-carmine 80·00 90·00
158 3s. green and violet (*shades*) 25·00 30·00
158*a* 3s. bright green & magenta £250 £150
159 5s. vermilion & deep green 60·00 65·00
160 5s. scarlet & pale yell.-grn. 60·00 65·00
160*a* 5s. crimson and yellow-grn. 60·00 65·00
160*b* 7s. 6d. carmine & pale blue £175 £175
161 7s. 6d. carmine & light blue £175 £175
162 7s. 6d. carmine & brt. blue £225 £225
163 10s. deep myrtle and orange £175 £100
164 10s. blue-green and orange £160 £110
165 £1 carm.-red & bluish black £200 £110
166 £1 rose-scarlet & bluish blk. £250 £110
166*a* £1 crimson and slate-black £350 £200
166*b* £1 scarlet & reddish mauve (*error*) £3000

(b) P 15.

No.	Description	Unused	Used
167	½d. blue-green	80·00	4·50
168	½d. yellow-green	£110	4·50
169	½d. apple-green	£175	6·00
170	1d. carmine	£110	2·50
170*a*	1d. carmine-lake	£140	2·50
170*b*	1d. rose-carmine	£125	2·50
171	2d. black and grey-black ..	£150	6·00
171*a*	2d. black and grey ..	£150	6·00
171*b*	2d. black and slate ..	£150	6·00
172	2½d. ultramarine (*shades*) ..	40·00	15·00
173	3d. purple and yellow-ochre	£400	15·00
173*a*	3d. claret & pale yell.-ochre	£350	15·00
174	4d. black & orange (*shades*)	16·00	15·00
175	5d. lake-brown & olive-green	£250	20·00
176	6d. brown and mauve ..	£300	16·00
177	1s. blk. & blue-grn. (*shades*)	£250	12·00
178	2s. black and dull blue ..	£350	£140
179	£1 red and black	£3500	£1500

(c) P 15 × 14 or 14 × 15.

No.	Description	Unused	Used
179*a*	½d. yellow-green	£1000	£1000
180	3d. purple & ochre	£750	£100
181	4d. black & orange	£150	£150
181*a*	1s. black & blue-green ..	£1500	£750

(d) P 13½.

No.	Description	Unused	Used
182	½d. yellow-green	£100	11·00
182*a*	½d. green	£100	11·00
183	1d. bright carmine	£500	12·00
184	2½d. ultramarine (*shades*) ..	11·00	12·00
185	8d. black & purple (*shades*)	50·00	75·00
185*a*	8d. grey-purple & dull pur.	50·00	60·00
119/185	Optd. "Specimen" perf. 14 except 2½d. and 8d. perf. 13½ .. *Set of* 18	£650	

Plate varieties in T **17** are:—½d., Double dot below "D" in right-hand value tablet (*from* £110 *un.*, £100 *used*); 2d. to £1 excluding 2½d., straight stroke in Queen's right ear known as the "gash in ear" variety (*from* 3 *to* 6 *times normal*).

Stamps from the above and the next issue are known compound perf. with 14 or 15 on one side only or on adjoining sides but we no longer list them.

18

(Recess. Waterlow.)

1913 (1 Sept.)–**22**. *T* **18**. *No wmk.*

(i.) *From single working plates.* (*a*) *P* 14.

No.	Description	Unused	Used
186	½d. blue-green	75	10
	a. Imperf. between (pair) ..	£150	£150
187	½d. deep green	50	10
188	½d. yellow-green	1·00	15
	a. Imperf. between (pair) ..	£150	£150
188*b*	½d. dull green	90	10
189	½d. bright green	1·25	10
190	1d. rose-carmine	30	10
	a. Imperf. between (pair) ..	£150	£150
191	1d. carmine-red (*shades*) ..	1·00	10
	a. Imperf. between (pair) ..	£250	
192	1d. brown-red	60	10
193	1d. red	60	10
194	1d. scarlet	1·50	10
195	1d. rose-red	45	10
196	1d. crimson	£120	6·00
197	1½d. brown-ochre (1919) ..	30	10
	a. Imperf. between (pair) ..	£150	£150
198	1½d. bistre-brown (1917) ..	60	10
	a. Imperf. between (pair) ..	£150	£150
199	1½d. drab-brown (1917) ..	60	10
	a. Imperf. between (pair) ..	£150	
200	2½d. deep blue	1·00	1·25
201	2½d. bright blue	1·00	1·25

(b) P 15.

No.	Description	Unused	Used
202	½d. blue-green	1·25	80
203	½d. green	1·25	80
204	1d. carmine-red	£125	£125
	a. Imperf. between (pair) ..	£700	
204*b*	1d. rose-red	£150	£125
205	1d. brown-red	40	60
206	1½d. bistre-brown (1919) ..	1·75	1·25
206*a*	1½d. drab-brown	1·50	1·10
207	2½d. deep blue	2·50	2·50
208	2½d. bright blue	2·50	2·50

(c) P 14 × 15.

No.	Description	Unused	Used
208*a*	½d. green	£300	50·00

(d) P 15 × 14.

No.	Description	Unused	Used
208*b*	½d. green	£300	50·00
208*c*	1½d. drab-brown		

(e) P 13½.

No.	Description	Unused	Used
208*d*	1d. red (*shades*)	—	£200

Die I Die II Die III

The remaining values were printed from double, i.e. head and duty, plates. There are at least four different head plates made from three different dies, which may be distinguished as follows:—

Die I. The King's left ear is neither shaded nor outlined; no outline to top of cap.

Die II. The ear is shaded all over, but has no outline. The top of the cap has a faint outline.

Die III. The ear is shaded and outlined; a heavy continuous outline round the cap.

(ii.) *Printed from double plates, head Die* I.

(a) P 14.

No.	Description	Unused	Used
209	2d. black and grey	1·50	1·25
210	3d. black and yellow ..	6·00	1·50
211	4d. black and orange-red ..	1·50	1·75
212	5d. black and green ..	1·50	1·75
213	6d. black and mauve ..	25·00	5·00
214	2s. black and brown ..	7·00	6·00

(b) P 15.

No.	Description	Unused	Used
215	3d. black and yellow ..	1·75	1·75
216	4d. black and orange-red ..	25·00	2·50
217	6d. black and mauve ..	1·25	1·00
218	2s. black and brown ..	3·25	4·00

(iii.) *Head Die* II. (*a*) *P* 14.

No.	Description	Unused	Used
219	2d. black and grey	1·50	1·25
220	2d. black and brownish grey	3·00	1·25
221	3d. black and deep yellow ..	3·00	75
222	3d. black and yellow ..	6·00	45
223	3d. black and buff	1·00	50
224	4d. black and orange-red ..	1·75	75
225	4d. black & dp. orange-red	1·25	75
226	5d. black and grey-green ..	1·50	2·00
227	5d. black and bright green ..	1·25	2·00
228	6d. black and mauve ..	2·00	75
229	6d. black and purple ..	3·50	75
230	8d. violet and green ..	3·50	3·00
231	10d. blue and carmine-red ..	2·50	3·00
232	1s. black and greenish blue	3·00	3·00
233	1s. black and turquoise-blue	1·50	1·75
234	2s. black and brown ..	6·50	2·50
235	2s. black and yellow-brown	12·00	5·00
236	2s. 6d. indigo & grey-brown	6·50	2·50
236*a*	2s. 6d. pale blue and brown	9·00	3·00
236*b*	3s. brown and blue ..	8·00	9·00
237	3s. chestnut and bright blue	8·00	9·00
238	5s. blue and yellow-green ..	20·00	8·00
239	5s. blue and blue-green ..	10·00	8·00
240	7s. 6d. blackish purple and slate-black	30·00	32·00
241	10s. crimson and yellow-green	30·00	32·00
242	£1 black and purple ..	£150	£140
243	£1 black and violet ..	£160	£170

(b) P 15.

No.	Description	Unused	Used
244	2d. black and grey	1·00	1·50
245	4d. black & dp. orange-verm.	£175	90·00
246	8d. violet and green ..	50·00	50·00
247	10d. blue and red	2·00	2·50
248	1s. black and greenish blue	2·00	1·25
249	2s. 6d. indigo & grey-brown	6·00	6·00
250	3s. chocolate and blue ..	£180	£125
251	5s. blue and yellow-green ..	15·00	12·00
251*a*	5s. blue and blue-green ..	£125	
252	7s. 6d. blackish purple and slate-black	20·00	25·00
253	10s. red and green	75·00	85·00
254	£1 black and purple ..	£250	£250
254*a*	£1 black and deep purple ..	£250	£250
186/254*a*	Optd. "Specimen" (various Dies and Perfs.) *Set of* 19	£350	

(iv.) *Head Die* III. *Toned paper, yellowish gu*

(a) P 14.

No.	Description	Unused	Used
255	2d. black and brownish grey	2·00	1·
256	2d. black and grey-black ..	60	
	a. Imperf. between (pair) ..	£1100	£12
257	2d. black and grey	75	
258	2d. black and sepia ..	2·00	
259	3d. black and yellow ..	1·25	
260	3d. black and ochre ..	1·25	
261	4d. black and orange-red ..	2·50	
262	4d. black and dull red ..	2·00	1·
263	5d. black and pale green ..	1·10	1·
	a. Imperf. between (pair) ..	£1500	
264	5d. black and green ..	1·25	1·
265	6d. black and reddish mauve	1·50	1·
266	6d. black and dull mauve ..	1·25	1·
	a. Imperf. between (pair) ..		
267	8d. mauve & dull blue-green	5·00	4·
	a. Imperf. vert. (horiz. pair) ..		
268	8d. mauve & greenish blue	5·00	4·
269	10d. indigo and carmine ..	3·00	3·
270	10d. blue and red	2·25	2·
271	1s. black and greenish blue	1·50	1·
272	1s. black & pale blue-green	1·50	1·
272*a*	1s. black and light blue ..	3·50	2·
272*b*	1s. black and green ..	10·00	5·
273	2s. black and brown ..	3·50	3·
	aa. Imperf. between (vert. pair)	—	£35
273*a*	2s. black and yellow-brown	15·00	6·
274	2s. 6d. deep ult. & grey-brn.	6·00	6·
274*a*	2s. 6d. pale blue and pale bistre-brown (*shades*) ..	18·00	7·
274*b*	3s. chestnut and light blue	30·00	8·
275	5s. deep blue & blue-green (*shades*)	12·00	8·
276	5s. blue & pale yellow-green (*shades*)	12·00	8·
276*a*	7s. 6d. maroon & slate-blk.	£175	£2
277	10s. carm.-lake & yell.-green	£100	50·
278	£1 black and bright purple	£110	£1
279	£1 black and deep purple ..	£110	£1
279*a*	£1 black and violet indigo	£110	£1
279*b*	£1 black and deep violet ..	£120	£1

(b) P 15.

No.	Description	Unused	Used
279*c*	2d. black and brownish grey	£1000	£4

Half Penny (19) **Half-Penny.** (20)

1917 (15 Aug.). *No.* 190. *surch. at the Northe Rhodesian Administrative Press, Livingsto with T* **19**, *in violet or violet-black.*

No.	Description	Unused	Used
280	½d. on 1d. rose-carm. (*shades*)	75	1·
	a. Surch. inverted	£1500	£15
	b. Letters "n n" spaced wider	2·00	3·
	c. Letters "n y" spaced wider	1·25	2·

The setting was in two rows of 10 repeat three times in the sheet.

The two colours of the surcharge occur on t same sheet.

1917 (22 Sept.). *No.* 190 *surch. as T* **20** (*n setting with hyphen, and full stop af* "Penny"), *in deep violet.*

No.	Description	Unused	Used
281	½d. on 1d. rose-carm. (*shades*)	40	

1922–24. *T* **18**. *New printings on white pa with clear white gum.*

(i.) *Single working plates.*

(a) P 14.

No.	Description	Unused	Used
282	½d. dull green (1922) ..	1·00	
	a. Imperf. between (pair) ..	£350	
283	½d. deep blue-green (1922)	60	
284	1d. bright rose (1922) ..	75	
285	1d. bright rose-scarlet (1923)	50	
	a. Imperf. between (pair) ..	£350	
286	1d. aniline red (8.24) ..	12·00	1·
287	1½d. brown-ochre (1923) ..	55	
	a. Imperf. between (pair) ..	£300	

(b) P 15.

No.	Description	Unused	Used
288	½d. dull green (1923) ..	4·00	2·
289	1d. bright rose-scarlet (1923)	6·00	6·
290	1½d. brown-ochre (1923) ..	5·00	3·

(ii.) *Double plates. Head Die* III.

(*a*) *P* 14.

1 2d. black & grey-pur. (1922) 75 40
2 2d. black & slate-pur. (1923) 1·00 50
3 3d. black and yellow (1922) 1·75 2·50
4 4d. blk. & oran.-ver. (1922–3) 2·00 1·50
5 6d. jet-black & lilac (1922–3) 75 40
6 8d. mauve and pale blue-green (1922) .. .. 5·00 4·00
7 8d. violet & grey-grn. (1923) 5·00 4·00
8 10d. brt. ultram. & red (1922) 2·50 3·00
9 10d. bright ultramarine and carmine-red (1923) .. 2·50 3·00
0 1s. blk. & dull blue (1922–3) 90 1·00
a. Imperf. between (pair) .. £1250
1 2s. black & brown (1922–3) 3·00 2·50
2 2s. 6d. ultramarine & sepia (1922) .. .. .. 7·00 7·00
3 2s. 6d. violet-blue & grey-brown (1923) .. .. 5·00 4·00
4 3s. red-brown & turquoise-blue (1922) .. .. 7·00 4·00
5 3s. red-brown & grey-blue (1923) .. .. .. 11·00 7·50
6 5s. bright ultramarine and emerald (1922) .. .. 15·00 9·00
7 5s. dp. bl. & brt. grn. (1923) 15·00 9·00
8 7s. 6d. brown-purple and slate (1922) .. .. 32·00 35·00
9 10s. crimson & bright yellow-green (1922) .. .. 35·00 32·00
0 10s. carm. & yell.-grn (1923) 35·00 40·00
1 £1 blk. & dp. magenta (1922) £150 £160
1*a* £1 black & magenta (1923) £150 £160

(*b*) *P* 15 (1923).

2 2d. black and slate-purple.. 10·00
3 4d. black & orange-vermilion 10·00
4 6d. jet-black and lilac .. 10·00
5 8d. violet and grey-green .. 10·00
6 10d. brt. ultram. & carm.-red 15·00
7 1s. black and dull blue .. 15·00
8 2s. black and brown .. 30·00
9 2s. 6d. vio.-blue & grey-brn. 30·00
0 3s. red-brown & grey-blue 35·00
1 5s. deep blue & bright green 40·00
2 £1 black and magenta .. £250

The 1922 printing shows the mesh of the paper ry clearly through the gum. In the 1923 inting the gum is very smooth and the mesh of e paper is not so clearly seen. Where date is ven as "(1922–23)" two printings were made, ich do not differ sufficiently in colour to be ted separately.

Nos. 312/22 were never sent out to Rhodesia t only issued in London. Any used copies uld, therefore, only have been obtained by vour.

In 1924 Rhodesia was divided into NORTHERN d SOUTHERN RHODESIA (*q.v.*) and between 54 and 1964 these were merged in the Central rican Federation (*see* RHODESIA AND NYASA-ND). In 1964 there were again separate issues Northern and Southern Rhodesia but after rthern Rhodesia became independent and s renamed Zambia, Southern Rhodesia was named RHODESIA in October 1964.

ISSUES FOR THE FORMER SOUTHERN RHODESIA

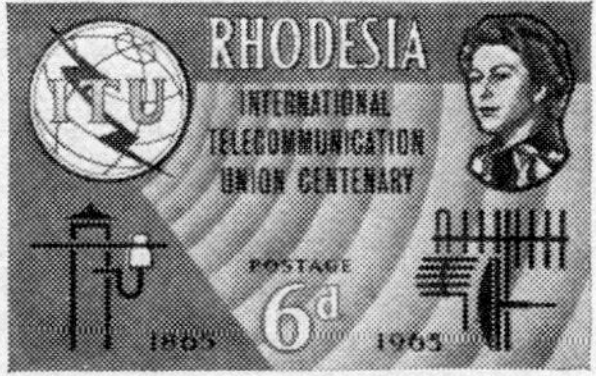

59. "Telecommunications".

(Des. V. Whiteley. Photo. Harrison.)

65 (17 MAY). *I.T.U. Centenary.* *P* 14½.
59 6d. violet & lt. yell.-olive 15 15
,, 1s. 3d. violet and lilac .. 35 35
,, 2s. 6d. violet and lt. brown 55 60

60. Bangala Dam.

61. Irrigation Canal.

62. Cutting Sugar Cane.

(Des. V. Whiteley. Photo. Harrison.)

1965 (19 JULY). *Water Conservation.* *P* 14.
354 **60** 3d. multicoloured .. 10 10
355 **61** 4d. multicoloured .. 12 20
356 **62** 2s. 6d. multicoloured .. 55 65

63. Sir Winston Churchill, Quill, Sword and Houses of Parliament.

(Des. H. Baxter. Photo. Harrison.)

1965 (16 AUG.). *Churchill Commemoration.* *P* 14½.
357 **63** 1s. 3d. black & bright blue 70 80

III. UNILATERAL DECLARATION OF INDEPENDENCE.

Independence was declared by Rhodesia on 11 November 1965 but this was not recognised by the British Government and therefore the stamps subsequently issued are retained in this catalogue.

64. Coat-of-Arms.

(Des. Col. C. R. Dickenson. Litho. Mardon Printers, Salisbury.)

1965 (8 DEC.). "*Independence*". *P* 11.
358 **64** 2s. 6d. multicoloured .. 40 40
a. Imperf. (pair) £250

INDEPENDENCE
11th November
1965

INDEPENDENCE
11th November 1965 = **5/-**

(65) (66)

1966 (17 JAN.). *Nos. 92/105 of Southern Rhodesia optd. with T* **65** *or larger (5s. to £1).*
359 **45** ½d. yellow, yellow-green and light blue .. 5 5
360 **46** 1d. reddish violet and yellow-ochre .. 5 5
361 **47** 2d. yellow & deep violet 5 5
362 **48** 3d. chocolate & pale blue 5 8
363 **49** 4d. yell.-orge. & dp. green 8 8
364 **50** 6d. carmine-red, yellow and deep dull green.. 10 10
365 **51** 9d. red-brown, yellow and olive-green 12 15
a. Opt. double .. .. 75·00
366 **52** 1s. blue-green and ochre 20 20
a. Opt. double .. ..
367 **53** 1s. 3d. red, violet and yellow-green .. 25 25
368 **54** 2s. blue and ochre .. 50 50
369 **55** 2s. 6d. ultram. and verm. 35 45
370 **56** 5s. lt. brown, bistre-yellow and light blue .. 3·50 5·00
a. Opt. double .. .. 90·00
371 **57** 10s. black, yellow-ochre, lt. blue & carmine-red 2·50 3·00
372 **58** £1 brown, yellow-green, buff and salmon-pink 4·50 5·50

No. 357 *surch. with T* **66**.
373 **63** 5s. on 1s. 3d. black and bright blue (R.) .. 12·00 14·00
359/73 .. .. *Set of* 15 22·00 26·00

Owing to the existence of forgeries, No. 370a should only be purchased when accompanied by a certificate of genuineness.

67. Emeralds.

(Des. V. Whiteley. Photo. Harrison.)

1966 (9 FEB.). *As T* **45/51** *and* **53/8** *of Southern Rhodesia, but inscr.* "RHODESIA" *as T* **67**. *Some designs and colours changed.* *P* 14½ (1*d. to* 4*d.*), 13½ × 13 (6*d. to* 2*s.* 6*d.*) *or* 14½ × 14 (5*s. to* £1).
374 **46** 1d. reddish violet and yellow-ochre 5 5
375 **49** 2d. yell.-orge. & dp. grn. 5 5
a. Yellow-orange omitted ..
376 **48** 3d. chocolate & pale blue 8 5
a. Chocolate omitted .. £250
b. Pale blue omitted .. £150
377 **67** 4d. emerald and sepia .. 10 10
378 **50** 6d. carmine-red, yellow and deep dull green.. 10 10
379 **47** 9d. yellow and deep violet 15 15
380 **45** 1s. yellow, yellow-green and light blue .. 15 12
381 **54** 1s. 3d. blue and ochre 30 25
382 **51** 1s. 6d. red-brown, yellow and olive-green .. 35 30
383 **53** 2s. red, violet & yell.-grn. 35 50
384 **55** 2s. 6d. blue, vermilion and turquoise-blue .. 50 50
385 **56** 5s. light brown, bistre-yellow and light blue 85 85
386 **57** 10s. black, yellow-ochre, lt. blue & carmine-red 1·60 1·90
387 **58** £1 brown, yellow-green, buff and salmon-pink 3·50 4·00
374/87 .. *Set of* 14 7·00 8·00

T **45** and **47** are in larger format, as T **50**.

No. 376a occurred in the bottom row of a sheet and No. 376b in the top two rows of a sheet.

For stamps printed by lithography, see Nos. 397/407.

TRADING WITH RHODESIA. The importation of Nos. 358/87 was permitted, after which it became illegal to import any Rhodesian stamps.

For reference purposes we list the stamps which have been issued and prices will be quoted after the resumption of trade with Rhodesia.

PRINTERS. All the following stamps were printed by lithography by Mardon Printers, Salisbury.

68. Zeederberg Coach, *c.* 1895.

(Des. V. Whiteley (Nos. 388/90).)

1966 (2 May). *28th Congress of Southern Africa Philatelic Federation ("Rhopex"). T* **68** *and similar horiz. designs. P* 14½.
388 3d. multicoloured .. ..
389 9d. grey-buff, sepia and grey-green .. .. ..
390 1s. 6d. pale blue and black ..
391 2s. 6d. salmon-pink, pale dull green and black .. ..
MS392 126×84 mm. Nos. 388/91

Designs:—9d. Sir Rowland Hill; 1s. 6d. The Penny Black; 2s. 6d. Rhodesian stamp of 1892 (No. 12).

69. De Havilland "Rapide" (1946).

1966 (1 June). *20th Anniv. of Central African Airways. T* **69** *and similar horiz. designs. P* 14½×14.
393 6d. black, blue, yellow & grn.
394 1s. 3d. blue, yellow-orange, black and green .. ..
395 2s. 6d. black, blue, yellow and green .. ..
396 5s. black and blue .. ..

Aircraft:—1s. 3d. Douglas "D.C.3." (1953); 2s. 6d. Vickers "Viscount" (1956); 5s. Modern jet.

1966–69. *As Nos.* 374/87 *but litho. P* 14½ (1*d. to* 2*s.*) *or* 14½×14 (*others*). *Cream gum* (2*d.*, 1*s.* 3*d.*) *or white gum* (*others*).
397 **46** 1d. reddish violet & yell.-ochre (*shades*) (2.6.66)
398 **49** 2d. orange and green (1.11.67) .. ..
399 **48** 3d. choc.-brown and pale greenish blue (29.1.68)
400 **67** 4d. emerald, bistre-brown and drab (21.9.66) ..
401 **50** 6d. carmine-red, yellow & olive-grey (1.11.66) ..
402 **47** 9d. yellow & light violet (20.11.67) .. ..
403 **51** 1s. 3d. blue and ochre (9.11.66) .. ..
404 **53** 2s. dull red, violet and sage-green (18.7.66) ..
405 **53** 5s. yell.-brn., dp. bistre-yell. & lt. bl. (25.6.66)
406 **57** 10s. blk., buff, light blue & carmine-red (10.8.66)
407 **58** £1 pale brown, yellow-green, brown-ochre & salmon (10.8.66) ..
397/407 .. .. *Set of* 11

In addition to the change in printing process from photogravure to lithography and the difference in perforation in the 6d. to 2s. values (14½ instead of 13½×13) and shade variations, the oval portrait frame is larger (and in some values thicker) in the 1d. to 2s., and in the 1s. 3d. the Queen's head is also larger.

Other values also exist with cream and other gums and these are listed in the *Elizabethan Specialised Catalogue*.

MINIMUM PRICE

The minimum price quoted is 5p which represents a handling charge rather than a basis for valuing common stamps. For further notes about prices see introductory pages.

70. Kudu.

1967–68. *Dual Currency Issue. As Nos.* 376, 380 *and* 382/4 *but value in decimal currency in addition as in T* **70**. *Litho. P* 14½. *White gum* (*No.* 408) *or cream gum* (*others*).
408 **70** 3d./2½ c. choc.-brn. & pale greenish blue (15.3.67)
409 **45** 1s./10 c. yellow, green and greenish blue (1.11.67)
410 **51** 1s. 6d./15 c. red-brn., yell. & yell.-green (11.3.68)
411 **53** 2s./20 c. dull red, violet & sage-green (11.3.68) ..
412 **55** 2s. 6d./25 c. ultram.-blue, vermilion and bright turquoise-blue (9.12.68)
408/12 .. .. *Set of* 5

71. Dr. Jameson (Administrator).

(Des. from painting by F. M. Bennett.)

1967 (17 May). *Famous Rhodesians* (1*st issue*) *and* 50*th Death Anniv. of Dr. Jameson. P* 14½.
413 **71** 1s. 6d. multicoloured ..

See also Nos. 426, 430, 457, 458, 469, 480, 488 and 513.

72. Soapstone Sculpture (Joram Mariga).

1967 (12 July). *Tenth Anniv. of Opening of Rhodes National Gallery. T* **72** *and similar vert. designs. P* 14½×14 (3*d.*, 9*d.*) *or* 14 (*others*).
414 3d. reddish chestnut, yellow-olive and black .. ..
415 9d. light greenish blue, deep olive-brown and black ..
a. Perf. 13½ .. ..
416 1s. 3d. multicoloured ..
417 2s. 6d. multicoloured ..

Designs:—9d. "The Burgher of Calais" (detail, Rodin); 1s. 3d. "Totem" (Roberto Crippa); 2s. 6d. "John the Baptist" (Tosini).

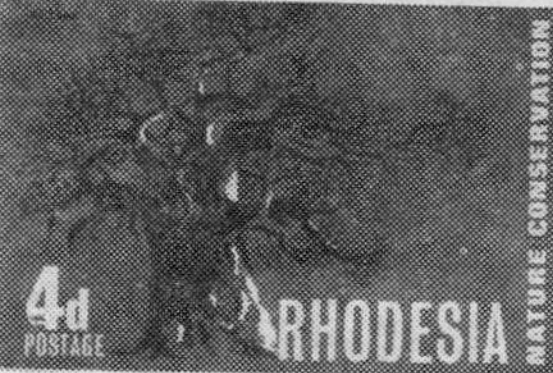

73. Baobab Tree.

1967 (6 Sept.). *Nature Conservation. T and similar designs. P* 14½.
418 4d. light brown and black ..
419 4d. yellow-olive and black ..
420 4d. deep grey and black ..
421 4d. yellow-orange and black

Designs: *Horiz.*—No. 418, Type **73**; No. 4 White Rhino; No. 420, Elephants. *Vert.*—N 421, Wild Gladiolus.

74. Wooden Hand Plough.

(Des. Rose Martin.)

1968 (26 Apr.). 15*th World Ploughing Conte Norton, Rhodesia. T* **74** *and similar hor designs. P* 14½.
422 3d. pale orange, orange-vermilion and lake-brown ..
423 9d. multicoloured .. ..
424 1s. 6d. multicoloured ..
425 2s. 6d. multicoloured ..

Designs:—9d. Early wheel plough; 1s. Steam powered tractor, and ploughs; 2s. Modern tractor, and plough.

75. Alfred Beit (National Benefactor).

(Des. from painting.)

1968 (15 July). *Famous Rhodesians* (2 *issue*). *P* 14½.
426 **75** 1s. 6d. pale orange, black and brown .. ..

76. Raising the Flag, Bulawayo, 1893.

(Des. Rose Martin.)

.968 (4 Nov.). *75th Anniv. of Matabeleland. T* **76** *and similar vert. designs. P* 14½.

.27 3d. pale orange, red-orange and black .. ..
.28 9d. multicoloured .. ..
.29 1s. 6d. pale turquoise-green, dp. emer. & blackish grn.

Designs:—9d. View and coat-of-arms of 3ulawayo; 1s. 6d. Allan Wilson (combatant in he Matabele War).

77. Sir William Henry Milton (Administrator).

(Des. from painting by S. Kendrick.)

.969 (15 Jan.). *Famous Rhodesians (3rd issue). P* 14½.

430 **77** 1s. 6d. multicoloured ..

78. 2 ft. Gauge Locomotive (1899).

(Des. Rose Martin.)

.969 (22 May). *70th Anniv. of Opening of Beira-Salisbury Railway. T* **78** *and similar horiz. designs showing locomotives. Multicoloured. P* 14½.

.31 3d. Type **78** .. .. ..
.32 9d. Steam loco (1904) ..
.33 1s. 6d. Articulated loco (1950)
.34 2s. 6d. Diesel-electric (1955)

79. Low Level Bridge.

(Des. Rose Martin.)

969 (18 Sept.). *Bridges of Rhodesia. T* **79** *and similar horiz. designs. Multicoloured. P* 14½.

.35 3d. Type **79** .. .. ..
.36 9d. Mpudzi bridge .. ..
.37 1s. 6d. Umniati bridge ..
.38 2s. 6d. Birchenough bridge..

(New currency. 100 cents = 1 dollar)

80. Harvesting Wheat.

81. Devil's Cataract, Victoria Falls.

(Des. from colour-transparencies (3, 6 c.), Rose Martin (others).)

1970 (17 Feb.)–**73**. *Decimal Currency. T* **80/1** *and similar horiz. designs. Brown gummed paper. P* 14½.

439 1 c. multicoloured .. ..
440 2 c. multicoloured .. ..
441 2½ c. pale greenish blue, bright blue and black.. ..
441c 3 c. multicoloured (1.1.73)
442 3½ c. multicoloured .. ..
442a 4 c. multicoloured (1.1.73)
443 5 c. multicoloured .. ..
443a 6 c. multicoloured (1.1.73)
443b 7½ c. multicoloured (1.1.73)
444 8 c. multicoloured .. ..
445 10 c. multicoloured .. ..
446 12½ c. multicoloured .. ..
446a 14 c. multicoloured (1.1.73)
447 15 c. multicoloured .. ..
448 20 c. multicoloured .. ..
449 25 c. red-orange, grey & black
450 50 c. turquoise and ultram.
451 $1 ultram, turquoise & blk.
452 $2 multicoloured .. ..

Designs: *Size as T* **80**—2 c. Pouring molten metal; 2½ c. Zimbabwe Ruins; 3 c. Articulated lorry; 3½ c. and 4 c. Statue of Cecil Rhodes; 5 c. Mine headgear; 6 c. Hydrofoil *Seaflight*. *Size as T* **81**—7½ c. As 8 c.; 10 c. Yachting on Lake McIlwaine; 12½ c. Hippo in river; 14 and 15 c. Kariba Dam; 20 c. Irrigation canal. *As T* **80/1** *but larger* (31×26 *mm.*)—25 c. Bateleur eagles; 50 c. Radar antenna and Vickers "Viscount"; $1 "Air Rescue"; $2 Rhodesian flag.

82. Despatch Rider, *c.* 1890.

(Des. Rose Martin.)

1970 (1 July). *Inauguration of Posts and Telecommunications Corporation. T* **82** *and similar horiz. designs. Multicoloured. P* 14½.

453 2½ c. Type **82** .. ..
454 3½ c. Loading mail at Salisbury airport .. ..
455 15 c. Constructing telegraph line, *c.* 1890 .. ..
456 25 c. Telephone and modern telecommunications equipment .. ..

83. Mother Patrick (Dominican Nurse and Teacher).

(Des. Rose Martin from photograph.)

1970 (16 Nov.). *Famous Rhodesians (4th issue). P* 14½.

457 **83** 15 c. multicoloured ..

84. Frederick Courteney Selous (Big-game Hunter, Explorer and Pioneer).

(Des. from painting by L. C. Dickinson.)

1971 (1 Mar.). *Famous Rhodesians (5th issue). P* 14½.

458 **84** 15 c. multicoloured ..

85. African Hoopoe.

86. Porphyritic Granite.

(Des. from photographs by Peter Ginn.)

1971 (1 June). *Birds of Rhodesia. T* **85** *and similar multicoloured designs. P* 14½.

459 2 c. Type **85** .. ..
460 2½ c. Half-collared Kingfisher (*horiz.*) .. .. ..
461 5 c. Golden-breasted Bunting
462 7½ c. Carmine Bee-eater ..
463 8 c. Red-eyed Bulbul ..
464 25 c. Wattled Plover (*horiz.*)

(Des. from photographs by University of Rhodesia and Dept. of Geological Survey.)

1971 (30 Aug.). *"Granite 71" Geological Symposium. T* **86** *and similar vert. designs. Multicoloured. P* 14.

465 2½ c. Type **86** .. ..
466 7½ c. Muscovite mica seen through microscope ..
467 15 c. Granite seen through microscope .. ..
468 25 c. Geological map of Rhodesia .. ..

87. Dr. Robert Moffat (Missionary).

1972 (14 Feb.). *Famous Rhodesians (6th issue). P* 14½.

469 **87** 13 c. multicoloured ..

88. Bird ("Be Airwise").

(Des. C. Lawton.)

1972 (17 July). *"Prevent Pollution". T* **88** *and similar horiz. designs. Multicoloured. P* 14½.

470 2½ c. Type **88** .. .. ..
471 3½ c. Antelope ("Be Countrywise") .. .. ..
472 7 c. Fish ("Be Waterwise")
473 13 c. City ("Be Citywise") ..

1972 (28 Aug.). *"Rhophil '72". Nos.* 439 *and* 441/2 *printed in sheets of four* 66×78 mm.
MS474 1 c. multicoloured ..
MS475 2½ c. pale greenish blue, bright blue and black
MS476 3½ c. multicoloured

89. "The Three Kings".

(Des. Rose Martin.)

1972 (18 Oct.). *Christmas.* P 14.
477 **89** 2 c. multicoloured ..
478 ,, 5 c. multicoloured ..
479 ,, 13 c. multicoloured ..

90. Dr. David Livingstone.

1973 (2 Apr.). *Famous Rhodesians (7th issue).* P 14.
480 **90** 14 c. multicoloured ..

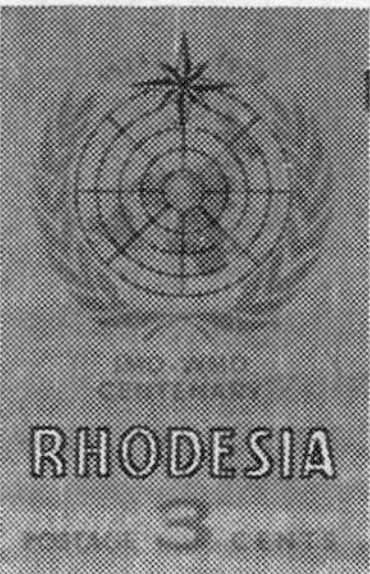

91. W.M.O. Emblem.

(Des. S. J. Ivey.)

1973 (2 July). *I.M.O./W.M.O. Centenary.* P 14.
481 **91** 3 c. multicoloured ..
482 ,, 14 c. multicoloured ..
483 ,, 25 c. multicoloured ..

92. Arms of Rhodesia.

1973 (10 Oct.). *50th Anniv. of Responsible Government.* P 14.
484 **92** 2½ c. multicoloured ..
485 ,, 4 c. multicoloured ..
486 ,, 7½ c. multicoloured ..
487 ,, 14 c. multicoloured ..

93. George Pauling (Construction Engineer).

(Des. P. Birch.)

1974 (15 May). *Famous Rhodesians (8th issue).* P 14.
488 **93** 14 c. multicoloured .. ..

94. Kudu.

95. Thunbergia.

96. Pearl Charaxes.

(Des. J. Huntly.)

1974 (14 Aug.)–**76**. *Various vert. designs as T* **94/8** *Multicoloured.* P 14½ (1 *to* 14 *c.*) *or* 14 (*others*).

(*a*) *Antelopes. Size as T* **94**.
489 1 c. Type **94** .. ..
490 2½ c. Eland ..
491 3 c. Roan Antelope ..
492 4 c. Reedbuck ..
493 5 c. Bushbuck .. ..

(*b*) *Wild Flowers. Size as T* **95**.
494 6 c. Type **95** .. ..
495 7½ c. Flame Lily .. ..
496 8 c. As 7½ c. (1.7.76) ..
497 10 c. Devil Thorn .. ..
498 12 c. Hibiscus (1.7.76) ..
499 12½ c. Pink Sabi Star ..
500 14 c. Wild Pimpernel ..
501 15 c. As 12½ c. (1.7.76) ..
502 16 c. As 14 c. (1.7.76) .. ..

(*c*) *Butterflies. Size as T* **96**.
503 20 c. Type **96** .. ..
504 24 c. Yellow Pansy (1.7.76) ..
505 25 c. As 24 c. .. .. ..
506 50 c. Queen Purple Tip ..
507 $1 Large Striped Swordtail
508 $2 Guinea Fowl Butterfly ..

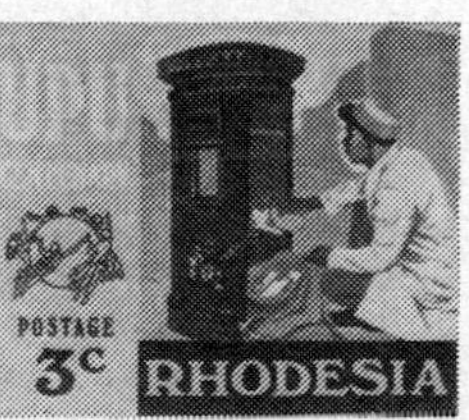

97. Collecting Mail.

(Des. M. C. Chase.)

1974 (20 Nov.). *Centenary of Universal Posta Union. T* **97** *and similar horiz. designs Multicoloured.* P 14.
509 3 c. Type **97** .. ..
510 4 c. Sorting mail .. ..
511 7½ c. Mail delivery .. ..
512 14 c. Weighing parcel ..

98. Thomas Baines (artist).

(Des. from self-portrait.)

1975 (12 Feb.). *Famous Rhodesians (9th issue)* P 14.
513 **98** 14 c. multicoloured ..

99. *Euphorbia confinalis.*

(Des. Nancy Abrey.)

1975 (16 July). *International Succulent Congress Salisbury ("Aloe '75"). T* **99** *and simila vert. designs. Multicoloured.* P 14½.
514 2½ c. Type **99** .. ..
515 3 c. *Aloe excelsa* .. ..
516 4 c. *Hoodia lugardii* .. ..
517 7½ c. *Aloe ortholopha* .. ..
518 14 c. *Aloe musapana* .. ..
519 25 c. *Aloe saponaria* .. ..

100. Prevention of Head Injuries.

(Des. Val Bond.)

1975 (15 Oct.). *Occupational Safety. T* **100** *an similar horiz. designs. Multicoloured.* P 14
520 2½ c. Type **100** .. .. ..
521 4 c. Bandaged hand and gloved hand ..
522 7½ c. Broken glass and eye
523 14 c. Blind man and welder with protective mask ..

101. Telephones, 1876 and 1976. **(102)**

8c

(Des. M. C. Chase.)

.976 (10 Mar.). *Telephone Centenary.* *T* **101** *and similar vert. design.*
:24 3 c. grey-black and pale blue
'25 14 c. brownish black & lt. stone

Design:—14 c. Alexander Graham Bell.

.976 (1 July). *Nos.* 495, 500 *and* 505 *surch. as T* **102.**
26 8 c. on 7½ c. Flame Lily ..
.27 16 c. on 14 c. Wild Pimpernel
'28 24 c. on 25 c. Yellow Pansy ..

103. Roan Antelope.

(Des. N. Pedersen.)

976 (21 July). *Vulnerable Wildlife.* *T* **103** *and similar horiz. designs. Multicoloured. P* 14.
29 4 c. Type **103** .. .. ..
30 6 c. Brown Hyena .. ..
31 8 c. Wild Dog .. ..
32 16 c. Cheetah .. .. ..

104. Msasa.

(Des. Nancy Abrey.)

976 (17 Nov.). *Trees of Rhodesia.* *T* **104** *and similar vert. designs. Multicoloured. P* 14.
33 4 c. Type **104** .. .. ..
34 6 c. Red Mahogany .. ..
35 8 c. Mukwa .. ..
36 16 c. Rhodesian Teak .. ..

POSTAGE DUE STAMPS.

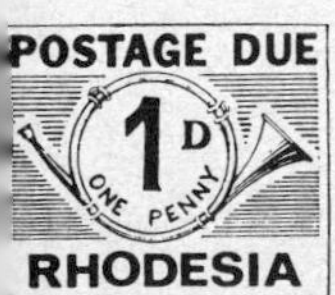

D 2.

D **3.** Zimbabwe Bird (Soapstone Sculpture).

Typo. Printing and Stationery Dept., Salisbury.)

.965 (17 June). *Roul.* 9.
)1 D **2** 1d. orange-red (*roul.* 5) .. 40 45
a. Roul. 9 .. .. .. 10 12
)2 ,, 2d. deep blue 10 10
)3 ,, 4d. green 5 8
)4 ,, 6d. plum 10 15

The 2d. has a stop below the "D".

(Litho. Mardon Printers, Salisbury.)

1966 (15 Dec.). *P* 14½.
D 5 D **3** 1d. red .. .. ..
D 6 ,, 2d. blue .. .. ..
D 7 ,, 4d. pale green .. ..
D 8 ,, 6d. reddish violet ..
D 9 ,, 1s. red-brown .. ..
D10 ,, 2s. black .. ..

1970 (17 Feb.)–**73.** *Decimal Currency. As Type D* **3**, *but larger* (26 × 22½ *mm.*). *P* 14½.
D11 D **3** 1 c. bright green ..
D12 ,, 2 c. ultramarine ..
D13 ,, 5 c. bright reddish violet
D14 ,, 6 c. pale lemon (7.5.73)
D15 ,, 10 c. cerise .. ..

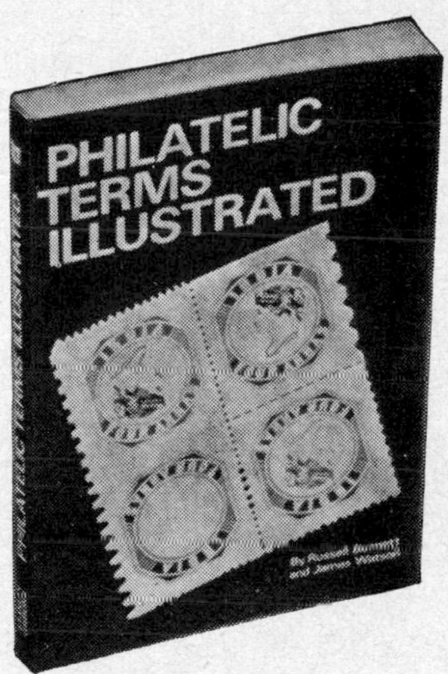

RHODESIA & NYASALAND.

Stamps for the Central African Federation of Northern and Southern Rhodesia and Nyasaland Protectorate.

1

2

3. Queen Elizabeth II.

(Recess. Waterlow and Sons.)

1954 (1 July)–**56.** *P* 13½×14 (*T* **1**), 13½×13 (*T* **2**) *or* 14×13½ (*T* **3**).

1	**1**	½d. red-orange	5	5
		a. Coil stamp. P 12½×14 (6.2.56)	20	25
2	,,	1d. ultramarine	5	5
		a. Coil stamp. P 12½×14 (*shades*) (1.10.55)	30	40
3	,,	2d. bright green	5	5
3*a*	,,	2½d. ochre (15.2.56) ..	12	12
4	,,	3d. carmine-red	10	8
5	,,	4d. red-brown	20	15
6	,,	4½d. blue-green	25	30
7	,,	6d. brt. reddish pur. (*shades*)	30	15
8	,,	9d. violet	35	40
9	,,	1s. grey-black	30	15
10	**2**	1s. 3d. red-orge. & ultram.	30	12
11	,,	2s. dp. blue & yellow-brown	45	35
12	,,	2s. 6d. black and rose-red..	75	65
13	,,	5s. violet and olive-green..	1·50	80
14	**3**	10s. dull blue-green & orge.	4·00	3·00
15	,,	£1 olive-green and lake ..	11·00	5·00
1/15		.. .. *Set of* 16	18·00	10·00

Nos. 1a and 2a printed on rotary machines by subsidiary company, Imprimerie Belge de Securité, in Belgium.

4. Aeroplane over Victoria Falls.

5. Livingstone and Victoria Falls.

(Des. J. E. Hughes (3d.), V. E. Horne (1s.). Recess. Waterlow.)

1955 (15 June). *Centenary of Discovery of Victoria Falls. P* 13½ (3*d.*) *or* 13 (1*s*).

16	**4**	3d. ultramarine and deep turquoise-green	12	12
17	**5**	1s. purple and deep blue ..	50	60

6. Tea picking.

7. V.H.F. Mast.

8. Copper Mining.

9. Fairbridge Memorial.

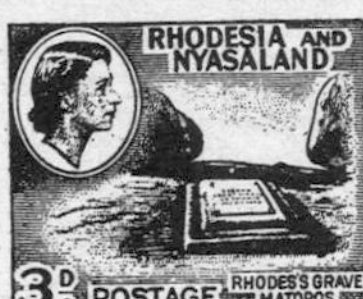

10. Rhodes's Grave.

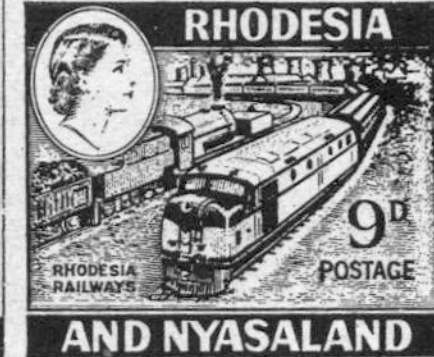

11. Lake Bangweulu.

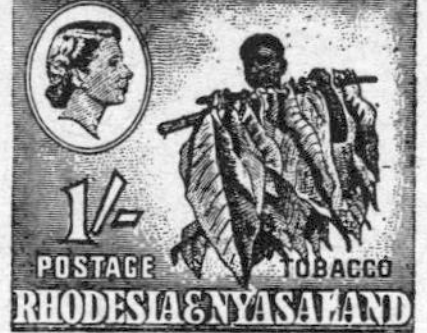

12. Eastern Cataract, Victoria Falls.

12*a*. Rhodesian Railway Trains.

13. Tobacco.

14. Lake Nyasa.

15. Chirundu Bridge.

16. Salisbury Airport.

17. Rhodes Statue.

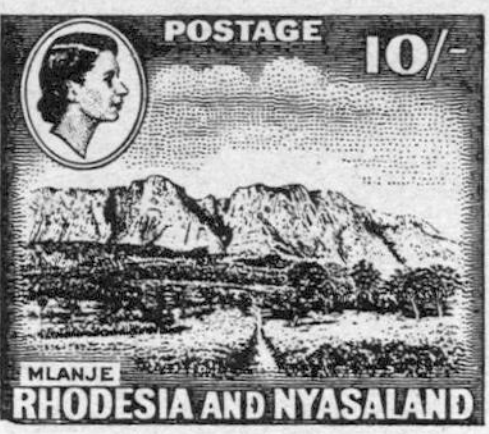

18. Mlanje.

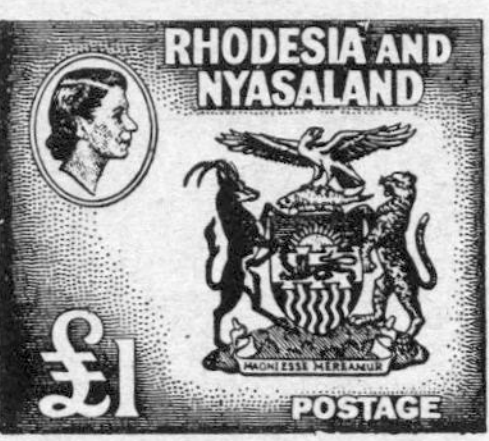

19. Federal Coat-of-Arms.

(Des. M. Kinsella (9d.). Recess. Waterlow (½d., 1d., 2d., 1s.) until 1962, then De La Rue. De La Ru (2½d., 4d., 6d., 9d., 2s., 2s. 6d.) and Bradbury Wilkinson (others).)

1959 (12 Aug.)–**62.** *P* 13½×14 (½*d.*, 1*d.*, 2*d.*), 14 (2½*d.*, 4*d.*, 6*d.*, 9*d.*, 2*s.*, 2*s.* 6*d.*), 14×13½ (3*d.*) 13½×13 (1*s.*), 14 (1*s.* 3*d.*) *or* 11 (*others*).

18	**6**	½d. black & light emerald	5	
		a. Coil stamp. P 12½×14 ..	20	2
19	**7**	1d. carmine-red and black	5	
		a. Coil stamp (*shades*). P 12½×14	25	2
20	**8**	2d. violet & yellow-brown	5	
21	**9**	2½d. purple and grey-blue..	12	2
22	**10**	3d. black and blue ..	8	
		a. Centre omitted		
23	**11**	4d. maroon and olive ..	12	1
24	**12**	6d. ultramarine and deep myrtle-green	15	1
24*a*	**12*a***	9d. orange-brn. & reddish violet (15.5.62) ..	45	6
25	**13**	1s. light green & ultram...	25	1
26	**14**	1s. 3d. emerald & dp. choc.	40	1
27	**15**	2s. grey-green & carmine	60	5
28	**16**	2s. 6d. light blue and yellow-brown	75	5
29	**17**	5s. dp. choc. & yell.-grn.	1·25	1·0
30	**18**	10s. olive-brown & rose-red	2·50	3·5
31	**19**	£1 black and deep violet	5·50	7·0
18/31		.. .. *Set of* 15	11·00	12·0

20. Kariba Gorge 1955.

21. 330kV. Power Lines.

22. Barrage Wall.

23. Barrage and Lake.

24. Interior of Power Station.

25. Barrage Wall and Queen Mother (top left).

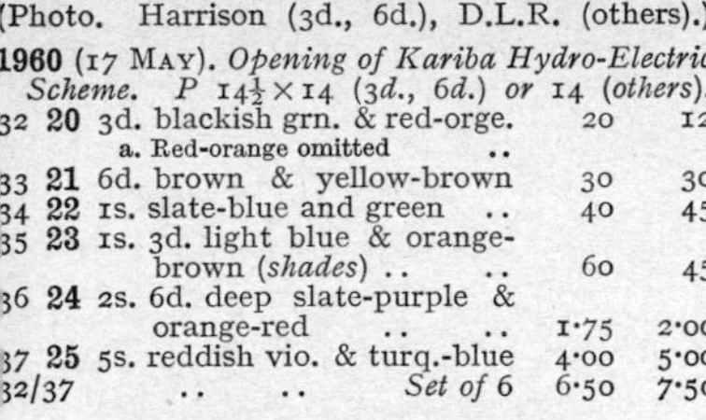

(Photo. Harrison (3d., 6d.), D.L.R. (others).)

1960 (17 MAY). *Opening of Kariba Hydro-Electric Scheme. P* 14½ × 14 (3*d*., 6*d*.) *or* 14 (*others*).

32	**20**	3d. blackish grn. & red-orge.	20	12
		a. Red-orange omitted ..		
33	**21**	6d. brown & yellow-brown	30	30
34	**22**	1s. slate-blue and green ..	40	45
35	**23**	1s. 3d. light blue & orange-brown (*shades*)	60	45
36	**24**	2s. 6d. deep slate-purple & orange-red	1·75	2·00
37	**25**	5s. reddish vio. & turq.-blue	4·00	5·00
32/37		.. .. *Set of* 6	6·50	7·50

26. Miner Drilling.

27. Surface Installations, Nchanga Mine.

(Des. V. Whiteley. Photo. Harrison.)

1961 (8 MAY). *Seventh Commonwealth Mining and Metallurgical Congress. P* 15 × 14.

38	**26**	6d. olive-green & orge.-brn.	25	30
39	**27**	1s. 3d. black and light blue	50	45

28. D.H. "Hercules" on Rhodesian air-strip.

29. Empire "C" Class Flying-boat taking-off from Zambesi.

30. D.H. "Comet" at Salisbury Airport.

(Des. M. Kinsella (6d., 2s. 6d.). Photo. Harrison.)

1962 (6 FEB.). 30*th Anniv. of First London-Rhodesia Airmail Service. P* 14½ × 14.

40	**28**	6d. bronze-grn. & vermilion	20	20
41	**29**	1s. 3d. lt. bl., blk. & yell.	40	45
42	**30**	2s. 6d. rose-red & dp. violet	85	1·00

31. Tobacco Plant.

32. Tobacco Field.

33. Auction Floor.

34. Cured Tobacco.

(Des. V. Whiteley. Photo. Harrison.)

1963 (18 FEB.). *World Tobacco Congress, Salisbury. P* 14 × 14½.

43	**31**	3d. green and olive-brown ..	10	12
44	**32**	6d. green, brown and blue	15	20
45	**33**	1s. 3d. chestnut and indigo	35	35
46	**34**	2s. 6d. yellow and brown ..	80	1·10

35. Red Cross Emblem.

(Photo. Harrison.)

1963 (6 AUG.). *Red Cross Centenary. P* 14½ × 14.

47	**35**	3d. red	10	10

36. African "Round Table" Emblem.

(Des. V. Whiteley. Photo. Harrison.)

1963 (11 SEPT.). *World Council of Young Men's Service Clubs, Salisbury. P* 14½ × 14.

48	**36**	6d. black, gold & yell.-green	20	25
49	,,	1s. 3d. black, gold, yellow-green and lilac	35	45

POSTAGE DUE STAMPS.

The 1d. and 2d. (Nos. 2/3) exist with a rubber-stamped "POSTAGE DUE" cancellation. In the absence of proper labels these values were used as postage dues at the Salisbury G.P.O. but according to the G.P.O. the handstamp was intended as a cancellation and not as an overprint (although "unused" examples of the 1d. are known). Its use was discontinued at the end of August 1959.

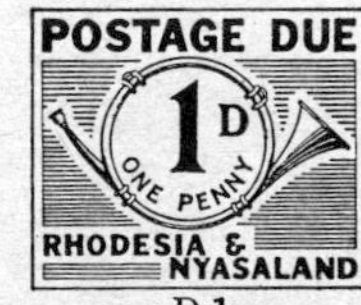

D 1

(Typo. Federal Printing & Stationery Dept., Salisbury.)

1961 (19 APR.). *P* 12½.

D1	**D 1**	1d. vermilion	10	10
		a. Imperf. between (horiz. pr.)	75·00	
D2	,,	2d. deep violet-blue ..	12	20
D3	,,	4d. green	30	50
D4	,,	6d. purple..	30	50

The 2d. has a stop below the "D".

The stamps of the Federation were withdrawn on 19th February, 1964 when all three constituent territories had resumed issuing their own stamps.

SABAH.

(FORMERLY NORTH BORNEO.)

SABAH (136) SABAH (137)

1964 (1 JULY). *Nos.* 391/406 *of North Borneo* (*D.L.R. printings*), *optd. Cents values optd. with T* **136**, *dollar values with T* **137**.

408	**120**	1 c. emerald & brown-red	5	5
409	**121**	4 c. bronze-green & orge.	5	5
410	**122**	5 c. sepia & violet (*shades*)	5	5
411	**123**	6 c. black & blue-green	8	8
412	**124**	10 c. green and red ..	10	8
413	**125**	12 c. brown & grey-green	10	10
414	**126**	20 c. blue-green & ultram.	15	12
415	**127**	25 c. grey-black & scarlet	25	25
416	**128**	30 c. sepia and olive ..	30	20
417	**129**	35 c. slate-blue & red-brn.	40	35
418	**130**	50 c. emer. & yell.-brown	40	35
419	**131**	75 c. grey-blue and bright purple	60	50
420	**132**	$1 brown & yellow-grn.	60	60
421	**133**	$2 brown and slate ..	1·25	1·40
422	**134**	$5 emerald and maroon	3·00	2·50
423	**135**	$10 carmine and blue ..	7·50	9·00
408/23		.. .. *Set of* 16	13·00	14·00

Old stocks bearing Waterlow imprints of the 4 c., 5 c., 20 c. and 35 c. to $10 were used for overprinting, but in addition new printings of all values by De La Rue using the original plates with the De La Rue imprint replacing the Waterlow imprint were specially made for overprinting.

138. *Vanda hookeriana.*

1965 (15 NOV.). *As Nos.* 166/72 *of Johore, but with Arms of Sabah inset as in T* **138**.

424		1 c. multicoloured	5	5
425		2 c. multicoloured	5	5
426		5 c. multicoloured	5	5
427		6 c. multicoloured	8	8
428		10 c. multicoloured	10	10
429		15 c. multicoloured (*shades*) ..	15	12
430		20 c. multicoloured	12	12
424/30		.. .. *Set of* 7	50	50

The 5 c. to 15 c. exist with PVA gum as well as gum arabic.

The higher values used in Sabah were Nos. 20/27 of Malaysia.

1970 (20 NOV.). *As No.* 428, *but W* w.**13** (*sideways*).

431	–	10 c. multicoloured ..	15	20

139. Great Orange Tip.

1971 (1 FEB.). *As Nos.* 175/81 *of Johore but with Arms of Sabah, as in T* **139**.

432		1 c. multicoloured	5	5
433		2 c. multicoloured	5	5
434		5 c. multicoloured	5	5
435		6 c. multicoloured	5	5
436		10 c. multicoloured	5	5
437		15 c. multicoloured	8	8
438		20 c. multicoloured	10	10
432/8		.. .. *Set of* 7	35	35

The higher values used with this issue are Nos. 64/71 of Malaysia.

ST. CHRISTOPHER.

For GREAT BRITAIN stamps used in St. Christopher with "A 12" obliteration, see index to Great Britain Stamps Used Abroad list.

1

(Typo. D.L.R.)

1870 (1 April)–**76**. *Wmk. Crown CC.* (*a*) *P* 12½.
1 **1** 1d. dull rose .. .. 15·00 14·00
a. Wmk. sideways .. .. 80·00 60·00
2 „ 1d. magenta .. .. 11·00 11·00
3 „ 1d. pale magenta .. .. 12·00 11·00
4 „ 6d. green .. .. .. 28·00 7·50
5 „ 6d. yellow-green .. .. 28·00 11·00

(*b*) *P* 14 (1875–6).
6 **1** 1d. magenta .. .. 20·00 6·00
a. Bisected diag. or vert. (½d.) (on cover) .. .. † £300
7 „ 1d. pale magenta .. .. 18·00 5·50
8 „ 6d. green .. .. .. 11·00 6·00
a. Imperf. between (pair) ..
b. Wmk. sideways .. .. 65·00

1879 (Nov.). *New values. Wmk. Crown CC. P* 14.
9 **1** 2½d. red-brown .. .. 50·00 40·00
10 „ 4d. blue .. .. .. 50·00 11·00
a. Wmk. sideways .. ..

1882–90. *Wmk. Crown CA. P* 14.
11 **1** ½d. dull green 60 70
a. Wmk. sideways .. ..
12 „ 1d. dull magenta .. .. £120 32·00
a. Bisected diagonally (½d.) (on cover) .. ..
13 „ 1d. carmine-rose 45 60
a. Bisected (½d.) (on cover) ..
14 „ 2½d. pale red-brown .. 60·00 28·00
15 „ 2½d. deep red-brown .. 65·00 32·00
16 „ 2½d. ultramarine (1884) .. 1·50 1·75
17 „ 4d. blue .. .. .. £150 20·00
18 „ 4d. grey (1884) .. .. 1·10 1·25
19 „ 6d. olive-brown (1890) .. 60·00 60·00
20 „ 1s. mauve (1887) .. .. 60·00 55·00
21 „ 1s. bright mauve .. .. 65·00 60·00
19/20 Optd. "Specimen" *Set of* 2 40·00

Halfpenny (2) FOUR PENCE (3)

1885 (March). *No.* 13 *bisected and No.* 8 *surch. with T* **2** (*diag.*) *and T* **3** *respectively.*
22 ½d. on half of 1d. carmine-rose 9·00 15·00
a. Whole stamp unsevered .. 40·00 48·00
ab. Do., one surch. inverted ..
b. Surch. inverted £140 £110
c. Surch. double .. .. ..
23 4d. on 6d. green 16·00 20·00
a. Full stop after "PENCE" .. 30·00 32·00
b. Surch. double £550

ONE PENNY. (4) 4d. (5)

1886 (June). *No.* 8 *surch. with T* **4** *or* **5**.
24 **1** 1d. on 6d. green .. .. 7·00 12·00
a. Surch. inverted £2000
b. Surch. double .. .. — £450
25 „ 4d. on 6d. green .. .. 20·00 35·00
a. No stop after "d" .. .. 65·00 70·00
b. Surch. double £500 £600

No. 24b is only known penmarked or with violet handstamp.

1887 (May). *Surch. with T* **4**.
26 **1** 1d. on ½d. dull green .. 14·00 15·00

ONE PENNY. (7)

1888 (May). *No.* 16 *surch.*
(*a*) *As T* **4** *but without bar through old value.*
27 **1** 1d. on 2½d. ultramarine .. — £3500
(*b*) *With T* **7**.
28 **1** 1d. on 2½d. ultramarine .. 14·00 18·00
a. Surch. inverted £2750 £1700

The only unused copy known of No. 27 is in the Royal Collection.

The 1d. of Antigua was used provisionally in St. Christopher in 1890, and can be distinguished by the postmark, which is "A 12" in place of "A 02" (*price from* £50 *used*).

REVENUE STAMPS USED FOR POSTAGE.

Saint Christopher (8) SAINT KITTS NEVIS REVENUE (9)

1883. *Nos.* F6 *and* F8 *of Nevis optd. with T* **8**, *in violet. Wmk. Crown CA. P* 14.
R1 1d. lilac-mauve .. .. .. 65·00
R2 6d. green .. .. .. 11·00 14·00

1885. *Optd. with T* **9**. *Wmk. Crown CA. P* 14.
R3 **1** 1d. rose .. .. .. 60 1·75
R4 „ 3d. mauve .. .. .. 1·75 5·00
R5 „ 6d. orange-brown .. .. 80 5·00
R6 „ 1s. olive .. .. .. 65 5·00

Other fiscal stamps with overprints as above also exist, but none of these was ever available for postal purposes.

The stamps for St. Christopher were superseded by the general issue for Leeward Islands on 31st October, 1890.

For later issues see also "St. Kitts-Nevis."

ST. HELENA.

CROWN COLONY.

1

(Recess. Perkins, Bacon & Co.)

Wmk. Large Star, Type w.1.

1856 (Jan.). *Imperf.*
1 **1** 6d. blue .. .. .. £180 70·00

1861 (April (?)). *Clean-cut perf.* 14 to 16.
2 **1** 6d. blue .. .. .. £225 60·00

1864 *Rough perf.* 14 to 16.
2*a* **1** 6d. blue .. .. .. £100 48·00

ONE PENNY (2) FOUR PENCE (3) ONE SHILLING (4) ONE SHILLING (5) ONE PENNY (6) ONE SHILLING (7)

(Printed by De La Rue & Co.)

NOTE :—The issues which follow consist of 6d. stamps, T **1**, printed in various colours and (except in the case of the 6d. values) surcharged with a new value, as T **2** to **7**, *e.g.* stamps described as "1d." are, in fact, 1d. on 6d. stamps, and so on.

The numbers in the Type column below refer to the *types of the lettering* of the surcharge.

The supply of 6d. stamps printed by Messrs Perkins, Bacon & Co. lasted till the year 1873.

Wmk. Crown CC.

1863 (July). *Thin bar approximately the same length as the words. Two varieties of the 1d. Imperf.*
3 **2** 1d. lake (bar 16–17 mm.) .. 35·00 38·0
a. Surch. double £1000 £50
4 „ 1d. lake (bar 18½–19 mm.) 35·00 27·0
a. In vert. pr. with No. 3 .. £300
5 **3** 4d. carm. (bar 15½–16½ mm.) £170 65·0
a. Surch. double £2500 £250

Error. Surcharge omitted.
6 „ 6d. lake (1d.) £4500

1864–83.
A. *Thin bar* (16½ *to* 17 *mm.*) *nearly the same length as the words. P* 12½ (1864–67).
7 **2** 1d. lake .. .. .. 8·00 9·0
8 **3** 3d. purple .. .. .. 18·00 14·0
9 „ 4d. carmine .. .. .. 18·00 12·0
a. Surch. double .. .. — £180
10 **4** 1s. deep yellow-green .. 14·00 8·0
a. Surch. double .. .. — £800

It is believed that no example exists of the 1d. with surcharge double other than the one in the Royal Collection.

B. *Thick bar* (14 *to* 14½ *mm.*) *much shorter than words* (*except in the* 2d. *where it is nearly the same length.*

(*a*) *P* 12½ (1865–68).
12 **2** 1d. lake .. .. .. 14·00 13·0
13 **3** 2d. yellow ('68) .. .. 14·00 17·0
14 „ 3d. purple ('68) .. .. 12·00 12·0
14*a* „ 3d. light purple £1000 £25
15 „ 4d. carmine (*words* 18 *mm.*) 14·00 13·0
16 „ 4d. carmine-rose (*words* 19 *mm.*) .. .. .. 28·00 23·0
17 **5** 1s. deep yellow-green .. 65·00 23·0
18 „ 5s. yellow ('68) .. .. 48·00 48·0
18*a* „ 5s. orange ('68) .. .. 11·00 14·0

Varieties. (i) *Surcharge double.*
18*b* **2** 1d. lake .. .. ..
18*c* **3** 3d. purple .. .. .. — £180
18*d* „ 4d. carmine .. .. .. — £150
18*e* **5** 1s. deep yellow-green .. £3750

(ii) *Surcharged with the long and short surcharges on same stamp.*
18*f* **3** 4d. carmine £3750 £375

(iii) *Imperf.*
18*g* **2** 1d. lake £850
18*h* **3** 2d. yellow £2500
18*i* „ 3d. purple £250
18*j* „ 4d. carmine £2500
18*k* **5** 1s. deep yellow-green .. £5000

(iv) *Surcharge omitted.*
18*l* **1** 6d. carmine-rose (4d.) † ..
18*m* „ 6d. deep yellow-green (1s.)* £3750

(*b*) *P* 14×12½ (1879).
19 **2** 1d. lake .. .. .. 9·00 6·0
20 **3** 2d. yellow .. .. .. 15·00 11·0
21 „ 3d. purple .. .. .. 48·00 17·0
22 „ 4d. carm. (*words* 16½ *mm.*) 18·00 11·0

(*c*) *P* 14 (1883).
23 **2** 1d. lake .. .. .. 9·00 5·0
24 **3** 2d. yellow .. .. .. 11·00 7·5
25 **5** 1s. yellow-green .. .. 8·00 5·0

C. *Words of surcharge same length as bar (17 to 18 mm.), the 1d. in thin, taller type.*

(*a*) *P* 12½ (1871–73).

26 **6** 1d. lake .. .. .. 5·00 5·00
 a. Surch. in blue-black .. £225 £150
27 „ 2d. yellow .. .. 17·00 6·00
 a. Surch. in blue-black .. £1800 £1000
28 **7** 1s. deep green .. .. 55·00 5·00
 a. Surch. in blue-black .. ..

(*b*) *P* 14×12½ (1879).

29 **7** 1s. deep green .. .. 55·00 7·00

† The only known copy of No. 18*l* is in the Royal Collection, although a second badly damaged example may exist.

* No. 18*m* is from a sheet of the 1s. with surcharge misplaced, the fifth row of 12 stamps being thus doubly surcharged and the tenth row without surcharge.

1873–85. *No surcharge. Wmk. Crown CC.*

(*a*) *P* 12½.

30 **1** 6d. dull blue (1873) .. £100 28·00
31 „ 6d. ultramarine (1874) .. 90·00 28·00

(*b*) *P* 14×12½ (1879).

32 **1** 6d. milky blue .. .. 38·00 8·00

(*c*) *P* 14 (March 1885).

33 **1** 6d. milky blue .. .. 26·00 8·00

$2\frac{1}{2}$d

(8)

1884–94. *T* **1**, *surch. similarly to* (B) *above (except 2½d., T* **8**, *and the 1s., in which the bar is nearly the same length as the words). The 6d. as before without surcharge.*

Wmk. Crown CA. P 14.

34 **3** ½d. green (*words 17 mm.*) .. 70 1·00
 a. "N" and "Y" spaced ..
35 „ ½d. emerald (*words 17 mm.*) 2·00 2·25
 a. "N" and "Y" spaced .. £200
 b. Surch. double .. £325
 c. Ditto. "N" and "Y" spaced*
36 **3** ½d. deep green (*words 14½ mm.*) ('94) 65 80
37 **2** 1d. red ('87) .. .. 1·25 1·25
38 „ 1d. pale red ('87) .. .. 1·25 1·25
39 **3** 2d. yellow ('94) .. .. 1·25 1·40
40 **8** 2½d. ultramarine ('93) .. 1·25 2·00
 a. Surch. double £3500
 b. Stamp doubly printed .. £1700
41 **3** 3d. mauve ('87) .. .. 1·25 1·60
 a. Surch. double .. .. — £3750
42 „ 3d. deep violet ('87) .. 1·75 2·25
 a. Surch. double £1800 £1800
43 „ 4d. p. brown (*words 16½ mm.*) ('90) .. .. 3·25 4·50
43*a* „ 4d. sepia (*words 17 mm.*) .. 4·50 3·25
44 – 6d. grey ('88) .. .. 4·50 4·00
45 **7** 1s. yellow-green ('94) .. 4·50 5·00
 a. Surch. double .. ..
41/2, 43, 44 Optd. "Specimen" *Set of* 4 25·00

Examples of the above are sometimes found showing no watermark; these are from the bottom row of the sheet, which has escaped the watermark.

Some are found without bar and others with bar at top of stamp, due to careless overprinting.

Of the 2½d. with double surcharge only six copies exist, and of the 2½d. double printed, one row of 12 stamps existed on one sheet only.

* No. 35c. No. 35a occurs on stamp No. 216 on the sheet. In No. 35c only one of the two surcharges shows the variety.

CANCELLATIONS. Nos. 36–45, both inclusive, and No. 18*a*, have been sold cancelled with a violet diamond-shaped grill with four interior bars extending over two stamps. These cannot be considered as *used* stamps, and they are consequently not priced in the list.

This violet obliteration is easily removed and many of these remainders have been cleaned and offered as unused; some are re-postmarked with a date and name in thin type rather larger than the original, a usual date being "Ap. 4.01."

9

10

(Typo. D.L.R.)

1890–97. *Wmk. Crown CA. P* 14.

Plate I for the 1½d. Plate II for the other values (for difference see Seychelles).

46 **9** ½d. green ('97) .. .. 75 1·00
47 „ 1d. carmine ('96) .. .. 1·40 1·40
48 „ 1½d. red-brown & green ('90) 1·50 1·50
49 „ 2d. orange-yellow ('96) .. 1·60 2·40
50 „ 2½d. ultramarine ('96) .. 2·50 3·00
51 „ 5d. violet ('96) .. .. 5·00 7·00
52 „ 10d. brown ('96) .. .. 7·00 9·00
46/52 .. .. *Set of* 7 18·00 23·00
46/52 Optd. "Specimen" *Set of* 7 55·00

The note below No. 45*a re* violet diamond-shaped grill cancellation also applies to Nos. 46/52.

1902. *Wmk. Crown CA. P* 14.

53 **10** ½d. green (Mar.) 30 50
54 „ 1d. carmine (24 Feb.) .. 80 1·10
53/4 Optd. "Specimen" *Set of* 2 22·00

11. Government House.

12. The Wharf.

13

(Typo. D.L.R.)

1903 (June). *Wmk. Crown CC. P* 14.

55 **11** ½d. brown and grey-green .. 60 90
 a. Bluish paper .. .. 40·00 30·00
56 **12** 1d. black and carmine .. 80 90
 a. Bluish paper .. .. 40·00 30·00
57 **11** 2d. black and sage-green .. 4·00 4·00
 a. Bluish paper .. .. 40·00 30·00
58 **12** 8d. black and brown .. 7·50 8·50
59 **11** 1s. brown and brown-orange 7·00 10·00
60 **12** 2s. black and violet .. 12·00 14·00
55/60 .. .. *Set of* 6 29·00 35·00
55/60 Optd. "Specimen" *Set of* 6 55·00

Unissued 1d. red. optd. "Specimen" £130.

(Typo. D.L.R.)

1908 (May). *P* 14. *Wmk. Mult. Crown CA.*

64 **13** 2½d. blue, O .. .. 80 1·25
66 „ 4d. blk. & red/*yellow*, O C 80 1·40
67 „ 6d. dull & dp. purple, O C 1·25 2·50

Wmk. Crown CA.

71 **13** 10s. green and red/*green*, C £110 £150
64/71 Optd. "Specimen" *Set of* 4 75·00

14

15

(Typo. D.L.R.)

1912–16. *Wmk. Mult. Crown CA. P* 14.

72 **14** ½d. black and green .. 15 25
73 **15** 1d. black and carmine-red 25 45
 a. Black and scarlet (1916) .. 13·00 12·00
74 „ 1½d. black and orange 80 1·40
75 **14** 2d. black and greyish slate 1·00 1·40
76 **15** 2½d. black and bright blue 1·00 1·75
77 **14** 3d. black and purple/*yellow* 1·25 1·75
78 **15** 8d. black and dull purple 4·00 6·00
79 **14** 1s. black and black/*green* 6·00 9·00
80 **15** 2s. black and blue/*blue* .. 11·00 14·00
81 „ 3s. black and violet .. 17·00 20·00
72/81 .. .. *Set of* 10 38·00 50·00
72/81 Optd. "Specimen" *Set of* 10 75·00

No. 73*a* is on thicker paper than 73.

16

17

(Typo. D.L.R.)

1912. *Wmk. Mult. Crown CA. P* 14.

83 **16** 4d. black and red/*yellow*, C 1·40 5·00
84 „ 6d. dull and deep purple, C 1·50 5·00
83/4 Optd. "Specimen" *Set of* 2 22·00

1913. *Wmk. Mult. Crown CA. P* 14.

85 **17** 4d. black and red/*yellow*, O 1·50 2·75
86 „ 6d. dull and deep purple, O 3·50 7·00
85/6 Optd. "Specimen" *Set of* 2 28·00

The split "A" variety illustrated above No. 86 of Gambia also occurs on Nos. 85/6. (*Prices*: 4d. £18, 6d. £30 *un.*)

WAR TAX

ONE PENNY

(18)

WAR TAX

1d.

(19)

1916 (Sept.). *No. 73a on thin paper, surch. with T* **18**.

87 **15** 1d. + 1d. black and scarlet 20 40
 a. Surch. double .. .. — £2000
87 Optd. "Specimen" .. .. 18·00

1919. *No. 73 on thicker paper, surch. with T* **19**.

88 **15** 1d. + 1d. black & carmine-red (*shades*) (Optd. S. £18) .. 15 15

1922 (JAN.). *Printed in one colour. Wmk. Mult. Script CA. P* 14.

89	**15**	1d. green	40	1·40
90	,,	1½d. rose-scarlet	2·75	4·50
91	**14**	3d. bright blue	5·00	7·00
89/91 Optd. "Specimen" *Set of* 3			28·00	

20. Badge of St. Helena.

(Des. T. Bruce. Typo. D.L.R.)

1922 (JUNE)-**36.** *T* **20.** *P* 14.

(*a*) *Wmk. Mult. Crown CA.*

92	4d. grey & blk./*yell.*, C (2.23)	1·25	2·00
93	1s. 6d. grey & grn./*bl.-grn.*, C	6·00	9·00
94	2s. 6d. grey & red/*yellow*, C	9·00	12·00
95	5s. grey and green/*yellow*, C	14·00	17·00
96	£1 grey and purple/*red*, C	£100	£130
92/96	.. .. *Set of* 5	£120	£150
92/6 Optd. "Specimen"	*Set of* 5	£150	

The paper of No. 93 is bluish on the surface with a full green back.

(*b*) *Wmk. Mult. Script. CA.*

97	½d. grey and black, C (2.23)	15	15
98	1d. grey and green, C ..	25	15
99	1½d. rose-red, C (2.23) ..	70	1·00
	a. Carmine-rose (1936) ..	5·50	7·00
	b. Deep carmine-red (1936) ..	45·00	60·00
100	2d. grey and slate, C (2.23)	55	55
101	3d. bright blue, C (2.23) ..	40	70
103	5d. grn. & car./*green*, C ('27)	1·10	1·60
104	6d. grey & bright purple, C	95	1·60
105	8d. grey & brt. vio., C (2.23)	1·75	2·50
106	1s. grey and brown, C ..	1·40	3·00
107	1s. 6d. grey & grn./*grn.* ('27)	5·00	7·50
108	2s. pur. & blue/blue, C ('27)	5·00	7·50
109	2s. 6d. grey & red/*yell.* ('27)	5·00	8·00
110	5s. grey & green/*yellow* ('27)	12·00	16·00
111	7s. 6d. grey & yell.-orge., C	22·00	32·00
112	10s. grey and olive-green, C	35·00	35·00
113	15s. grey and purple/*blue*, C	£250	£350
97/112	.. .. *Set of* 15	85·00	£110
97/113 Optd. "Specimen"	*Set of* 16	£225	

21. Lot and Lot's Wife.

22. The "Plantation".

23. Map of St. Helena.

24. Quay at Jamestown.

25. James Valley.

26. Jamestown.

27. Munden's Promontory.

28. St. Helena.

29. High Knoll.

30. Badge of St. Helena.

(Recess. Bradbury, Wilkinson & Co. Ltd.)

1934 (23 APRIL). *Centenary of British Colonisation. Wmk. Mult. Script CA. P* 12.

114	**21**	½d. black and purple ..	30	4
115	**22**	1d. black and green ..	65	7
116	**23**	1½d. black and scarlet ..	1·10	1·2
117	**24**	2d. black and orange ..	1·40	1·6
118	**25**	3d. black and blue ..	2·50	2·7
119	**26**	6d. black and light blue	4·00	4·5
120	**27**	1s. black and chocolate..	7·50	11·0
121	**28**	2s. 6d. black and lake ..	17·00	22·0
122	**29**	5s. black and chocolate..	26·00	32·0
123	**30**	10s. black and purple ..	70·00	85·0
114/123		.. .. *Set of* 10	£120	£15
114/23 Perf. "Specimen" *Set of* 10			90·00	

1935 (6 MAY). *Silver Jubilee. As Nos.* 91/4 *o Antigua. P* 13½ × 14.

124	1½d. deep blue and carmine	30	4
125	2d. ultramarine and grey ..	60	7
126	6d. green and indigo ..	3·00	3·2
127	1s. slate and purple ..	7·00	7·5
124/7 Perf. "Specimen"	*Set of* 4	17·00	

1937 (19 MAY). *Coronation. As Nos.* 13/15 *o Aden. P* 14.

128	1d. green	10	1
129	2d. orange	25	2
130	3d. bright blue	25	2
128/30 Perf. "Specimen"	*Set of* 3	12·00	

31. Badge of St. Helena.

(Recess. Waterlow.)

1938 (12 MAY)-**44.** *Wmk. Mult. Script CA P* 12½.

131	**31**	½d. violet	10	1
132	,,	1d. green	3·50	3·0
132*a*	,,	1d. yellow-orange (1940)	10	1
133	,,	1½d. scarlet	10	1
134	,,	2d. red-orange	12	1
135	,,	3d. ultramarine.. ..	14·00	7·5
135*a*	,,	3d. grey (1940)	20	2
135*b*	,,	4d. ultramarine (1940) ..	25	3
136	,,	6d. light blue	20	3
136*a*	,,	8d. sage-green (1940) ..	80	1·4
		b. Olive-green (5.40) ..	1·50	2·5
137	,,	1s. sepia	55	7
138	,,	2s. 6d. maroon	1·50	2·0
139	,,	5s. chocolate	2·50	3·0
140	,,	10s. purple	5·00	6·0
131/140		.. .. *Set of* 14	26·00	23·0
131/40 Perf. "Specimen" *Set of* 14			55·00	

1946 (21 OCT.). *Victory. As Nos.* 28/9 *of Aden*

141	2d. red-orange	12	1
142	4d. blue	12	1
141/2 Perf. "Specimen"	*Set of* 2	14·00	

1948 (20 OCT.). *Royal Silver Wedding. As Nos* 30/1 *of Aden.*

143	3d. black	10	1
144	10s. violet-blue	4·00	5·5

1949 (10 OCT.). *75th Anniv. of Universal Posta Union. As Nos.* 114/7 *of Antigua.*

145	3d. carmine	10	2
146	4d. deep blue..	25	3
147	6d. olive	60	7
148	1s. blue-black	95	1·1

1949 (1 NOV.). *Wmk. Mult. Script CA. P* 12½

149	**31**	1d. black and green ..	25	4
150	,,	1½d. black and carmine ..	40	6
151	,,	2d. black and scarlet ..	40	6

1953 (2 JUNE). *Coronation. As No.* 47 *of Aden*

152	3d. black & dp. reddish violet	75	1·0

32. Badge of St. Helena.

33. Flax Plantation. (*Horiz.*)

34. Heart-shaped Waterfall.

Horiz. designs as T **32**:—

35. Lace-making.
36. Drying Flax.
37. Wire Bird.
38. Flagstaff and The Barn.
39. Donkeys carrying Flax.
40. Island Map.
41. The Castle.
42. Cutting Flax.
43. Jamestown.
44. Longwood House.

(Recess. D.L.R.)

1953 (4 Aug.). *Wmk. Mult. Script CA. P* 14.

153	**32**	½d. black & bright green	5	5
154	**33**	1d. black and deep green	5	8
155	**34**	1½d. black & reddish purple (*shades*)	10	10
156	**35**	2d. black and claret ..	15	15
157	**36**	2½d. black and red ..	15	15
158	**37**	3d. black and brown ..	20	20
159	**38**	4d. black and deep blue ..	25	25
160	**39**	6d. black and deep lilac ..	25	30
161	**40**	7d. black and grey-black	35	35
162	**41**	1s. black and carmine ..	60	60
163	**42**	2s. 6d. black and violet ..	2·75	2·75
164	**43**	5s. black and deep brown	4·00	4·50
165	**44**	10s. black & yellow-orange	13·00	13·00
153/65		.. .. *Set of* 13	20·00	20·00

45. Stamp of 1856.

(Recess. De La Rue & Co.)

1956 (3 Jan.). *St. Helena Stamp Centenary. Wmk. Mult. Script CA. P* 11½.

166	**45**	3d. Prussian blue & carm.	25	25
167	,,	4d. Prussian blue and red-dish brown	35	35
168	,,	6d. Prussian blue & deep reddish purple ..	70	70

46. Arms of East India Company.

47. *London* off James Bay.

48. Commemoration Stone.

(Recess. Waterlow & Sons.)

1959 (5 May). *Tercentenary of Settlement. W* w.**12**. *P* 12½ × 13.

169	**46**	3d. black and scarlet ..	25	25
170	**47**	6d. lt. emerald & slate-blue	45	50
171	**48**	1s. black and orange ..	70	80

ST. HELENA
Tristan Relief
9d +

(**49**)

1961 (12 Oct.). *Tristan Relief Fund. Stamps of Tristan da Cunha surch. as T* **49**.

172	**21**	2½ c.+3d. blk. & brn.-red		
173	**24**	5 c.+6d. black and blue		
174	**25**	7½ c.+9d. black & rose-carmine		
175	**26**	10 c.+1s. black & lt. brown		
172/5		.. .. *Set of* 4	£1100	£600

The above stamps were withdrawn from sale on October 19th. 434 complete sets sold.

50. Cunning Fish.

51. Cape Canary.

53. Queen Elizabeth II.

52. Brittle Starfish.

54. Red-wood Flower.

55. " Red Bird " (Weaver).

56. Trumpet Fish.

57. Feather Starfish.

58. Gum-wood Flower.

59. Fairy Tern.

60. Orange Starfish.

61. Night-blooming Cereus.

62. Deep-water Bull's-eye.

63. Queen Elizabeth II with Prince Andrew (after Cecil Beaton).

(Des. V. Whiteley. Photo. Harrison.)

1961 (12 Dec.)–**65.** *W* w.**12.** *P* 11½ × 12 (*horiz.*), 12 × 11½ (*vert.*) *or* 14½ × 14 (£1).

176 **50** 1d. brt. blue, dull violet, yellow and carmine 8 10
 a. Chalky paper (4.5.65) .. 5 5
177 **51** 1½d. yellow, green, black & light drab 5 5
178 **52** 2d. scarlet and grey .. 8 8
179 **53** 3d. light blue, black, pink & deep blue 15 20
 a. Chalky paper (30.11.65).. 12 12
180 **54** 4½d. yellow-green, green, brown and grey .. 12 15
181 **55** 6d. red, sepia and light yellow-olive 20 25
 a. Chalky paper (30.11.65) 15 20
182 **56** 7d. red-brn., blk. & violet 15 20
183 **57** 10d. brown-purple & light blue 25 30
184 **58** 1s. greenish yellow, bluish green and brown .. 25 30
185 **59** 1s. 6d. grey, black and slate-blue 60 70
186 **60** 2s. 6d. red, pale yellow & turquoise, C 60 80
187 **61** 5s. yellow, brown & green 1·50 1·50
188 **62** 10s. orge.-red, blk. & blue 2·50 3·00
189 **63** £1 chocolate & light blue 5·50 8·00
 a. Chalky paper (30.11.65).. 5·00 6·00
176/89*a* .. .. *Set of* 14 10·00 12·00

1963 (4 June). *Freedom from Hunger. As No.* 76 *of Aden.*

190 1s. 6d. ultramarine .. .. 2·50 2·00

1963 (2 Sept.). *Red Cross Centenary. As Nos.* 147/8 *of Antigua.*

191 3d. red and black 30 30
192 1s. 6d. red and blue .. .. 2·75 2·50

FIRST LOCAL POST
4th JANUARY 1965

(64)

1965 (4 Jan.). *First Local Post. Optd. with T* **64.**

193 **50** 1d. bright blue, dull violet, yellow and carmine .. 10 10
194 **53** 3d. light blue, black, pink and deep blue .. 12 12
195 **55** 6d. red, sepia and light yellow-olive 20 20
196 **59** 1s. 6d. grey, black and slate-blue 45 45

1965 (17 May). *I.T.U. Centenary. As Nos.* 166/7 *of Antigua.*

197 3d. blue and grey-brown .. 30 30
198 6d. brt. purple & bluish green 60 60

1965 (15 Oct.). *International Co-operation Year. As Nos.* 168/9 *of Antigua.*

199 1d. reddish pur. & turq.-grn. 12 12
200 6d. dp. bluish green & lav. 80 70

1966 (24 Jan.). *Churchill Commemoration. As Nos.* 170/3 *of Antigua.*

201 1d. new blue 10 10
202 3d. deep green 25 25
203 6d. brown 50 50
204 1s. 6d. bluish violet .. .. 1·60 1·60

1966 (1 July). *World Cup Football Championships. As Nos.* 176/7 *of Antigua.*

205 3d. violet, yellow-green, lake and yellow-brown .. 20 20
206 6d. chocolate, blue-green, lake and yellow-brown. .. 50 50

1966 (20 Sept.). *Inauguration of W.H.O. Headquarters, Geneva. As Nos.* 178/9 *of Antigua.*

207 3d. black, yellow-green & light blue 20 20
208 1s. 6d. black, light purple and yellow-brown .. .. 95 1·00

1966 (1 Dec.). *20th Anniv. of U.N.E.S.C.O. As Nos.* 196/8 *of Antigua.*

209 3d. slate-vio., red, yell. & orge. 25 25
210 6d. orge.-yell., vio. & dp. olive 45 45
211 1s. 6d. blk., brt. pur. & orge. 1·50 1·25

65. Badge of St. Helena.

(Des. W. H. Brown. Photo. Harrison.)

1967 (5 May). *New Constitution. W* w.**12** (*sideways*). *P* 14½ × 14.

212 **65** 1s. multicoloured 35 30
213 ,, 2s. 6d. multicoloured .. 80 70
 a. Red (ribbon, etc.) omitted £150

66. Fire of London.

67. East Indiaman *Charles.*

68. Settlers Landing at Jamestown.

69. Settlers Clearing Scrub.

(Des. M. Goaman. Recess. De La Rue.)

1967 (4 Sept.). *300th Anniv. of Arrival of Settler[s] after Great Fire of London. W* w.**12.** *P* 13.

214 **66** 1d. car.-red & blk. (*shades*) 8
215 **67** 3d. ultramarine and black 15 1[illegible]
216 **68** 6d. slate-violet and black 30 3[illegible]
217 **69** 1s. 6d. olive-green & black 60 6[illegible]

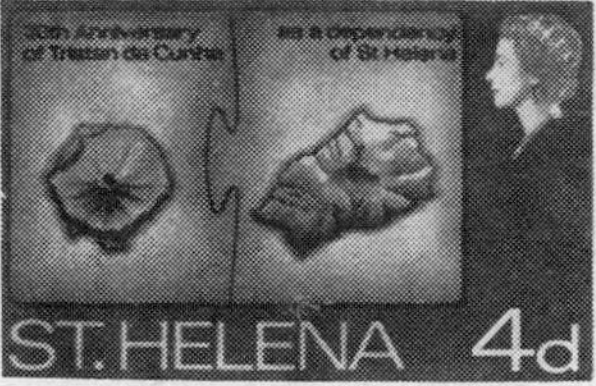

70. Interlocking Maps of Tristan and St. Helena

71. Interlocking Maps of St. Helena and Tristan

(Des. Jennifer Toombs. Photo. Harrison.)

1968 (4 June). *30th Anniv. of Tristan da Cunh[a] as a Dependency of St. Helena. W* w.**12.** *Perf* 14 × 14½.

218 **70** 4d. purple and chocolate .. 10 1[illegible]
219 **71** 8d. olive and brown .. 20 2[illegible]
220 **70** 1s. 9d. ultram. & chocolate 40 4[illegible]
221 **71** 2s. 3d. greenish bl. & brn. 60 6[illegible]

72. Queen Elizabeth and Sir Hudson Lowe.

73. Queen Elizabeth and Sir George Bingham.

(Des. R. Farrar Bell. Litho. De La Rue.)

1968 (4 Sept.). *150th Anniv. of the Abolition o[f] Slavery in St. Helena. W* w.**12** (*sideways*). *P* 13 × 12½.

222 **72** 3d. multicoloured .. .. 12 1[illegible]
223 ,, 9d. multicoloured .. .. 20 2[illegible]
224 **73** 1s. 6d. multicoloured .. 40 4[illegible]
225 ,, 2s. 6d. multicoloured .. 70 6[illegible]

74. Road Construction.

75. Electricity Development.

76. Dental Unit.

77. Pest Control.

78. Flats in Jamestown.

79. Pasture and Livestock Improvement.
80. Schools Broadcasting.
81. Country Cottages.
82. New School Buildings.
83. Reafforestation.
84. Heavy Lift Crane.
85. Lady Field Children's Home.
86. Agricultural Training.
87. New General Hospital.
88. Lifeboat *John Dutton*.

Plants shown in the designs:
½d., 4d., 1s. 6d. Blue gum Eucalyptus
1d., 6d., 2s. 6d. Cabbage-tree
1½d., 8d., 5s. St. Helena Redwood
2d., 10d., 10s. Scrubweed
3d., 1s., £1 Tree-fern

(Des. Mrs. Sylvia Goaman. Litho. Perkins, Bacon.)

1968 (4 Nov.). *W* w.**12** (*sideways*). *P* 13½.

No.	Type			
226	**74**	½d. multicoloured ..	8	8
227	**75**	1d. multicoloured ..	5	5
228	**76**	1½d. multicoloured ..	5	5
229	**77**	2d. multicoloured ..	8	8
230	**78**	3d. multicoloured ..	10	10
231	**79**	4d. multicoloured ..	12	12
232	**80**	6d. multicoloured ..	15	20
233	**81**	8d. multicoloured ..	15	20
234	**82**	10d. multicoloured ..	25	25
235	**83**	1s. multicoloured ..	25	30
236	**84**	1s. 6d. multicoloured ..	35	40
237	**85**	2s. 6d. multicoloured ..	50	60
238	**86**	5s. multicoloured ..	90	1·10
239	**87**	10s. multicoloured ..	1·75	2·00
240	**88**	£1 multicoloured ..	3·50	3·75
226/40		.. .. *Set of* 15	7·50	8·00

See also No. 274 for distinct shade of £1 value.

89. Brig *Perseverance*.

90. R.M.S. *Dane*.
91. S.S. *Llandovery Castle*.
92. R.M.S. *Good Hope Castle*.

(Des. J. Waddington Ltd. Litho. Perkins, Bacon Ltd.)

1969 (19 Apr.). *Mail Communications. W* w.**12** (*sideways*). *P* 13½.

No.	Type			
241	**89**	4d. multicoloured ..	10	10
242	**90**	8d. multicoloured ..	20	20
243	**91**	1s. 9d. multicoloured ..	40	40
244	**92**	2s. 3d. multicoloured ..	60	60

93. W.O. and Drummer of the 53rd Foot, 1815.

94. Officer and Surgeon, 20th Foot, 1816.
95. Drum Major, 66th Foot, 1816, and Royal Artillery Officer, 1920.
96. Private, 91st Foot, and 1832 2nd Corporal, Royal Sappers and Miners.

(Des. Rene North. Litho. Format International.)

1969 (3 Sept.). *Military Uniforms. W* w.**12**. *P* 14.

No.	Type			
245	**93**	6d. multicoloured ..	12	12
246	**94**	8d. multicoloured ..	20	25
247	**95**	1s. 8d. multicoloured ..	45	50
248	**96**	2s. 6d. multicoloured ..	75	80

97. Dickens, Mr. Pickwick and Job Trotter (*Pickwick Papers*).

(Des. Jennifer Toombs. Litho. P.B.)

1970 (9 June). *Death Centenary of Charles Dickens. T* **97** *and similar horiz. designs each incorporating a portrait of Dickens. Multicoloured. Chalk-surfaced paper. W* w.**12** (*sideways*). *P* 13½ × 13.

249		4d. Type **97**	10	10
		a. Shiny unsurfaced paper	10	12
250		8d. Mr. Bumble and Oliver (*Oliver Twist*)	20	20
		a. Shiny unsurfaced paper ..	20	20
251		1s. 6d. Sairey Gamp and Mark Tapley (*Martin Chuzzlewit*)	40	40
		a. Shiny unsurfaced paper ..	40	40
252		2s. 6d. Jo and Mr. Turveydrop (*Bleak House*)	70	70
		a. Shiny unsurfaced paper ..	70	75

Supplies sent to St. Helena were on paper with a dull surface which reacts to the chalky test and with PVA gum. Crown Agents supplies were from a later printing on shiny paper which does not respond to the chalky test and with gum arabic.

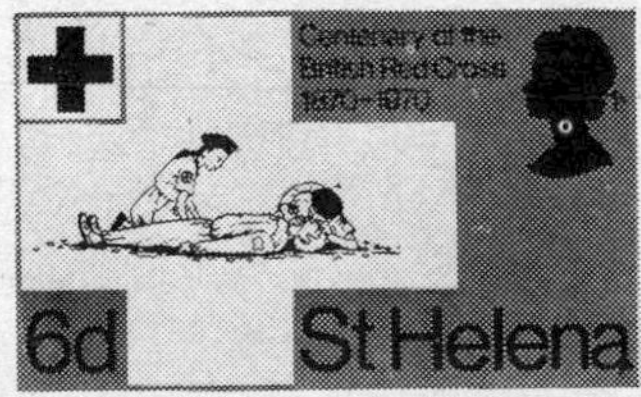

98. " Kiss of Life ".

(Des. Jennifer Toombs. Litho. J.W.)

1970 (15 Sept.). *Centenary of British Red Cross. T* **98** *and similar horiz. designs. W* w.**12** (*sideways*). *P* 14.

253	6d. bistre, vermilion & black	10	10
254	9d. turq.-grn., verm. & black	15	20
255	1s. 9d. pale grey, verm. & blk.	40	40
256	2s. 3d. pale lavender, vermilion and black ..	45	50

Designs:—9d. Nurse with Girl in Wheelchair; 1s. 9d. Nurse bandaging Child's knee; 2s. 3d. Red Cross Emblem.

99. Officer's Shako Plate (20th Foot).

(Des. J. Waddington Ltd. Litho. Questa.)

1970 (2 Nov.). *Military Equipment* (1st *issue*). *T* **99** *and similar vert. designs. Multicoloured. W* w.**12**. *P* 12.

No.			
257	4d. Type **99**	12	12
258	9d. Officer's Breast Plate (66th Foot)	30	35
259	1s. 3d. Officer's Full Dress Shako (91st Foot) ..	45	50
260	2s. 11d. Ensign's Shako (53rd Foot)	1·10	1·25

See also Nos. 281/4, 285/8 and 291/4.

100. Electricity Development.

(Litho. Perkins, Bacon.)

1971 (15 Feb.). *Decimal Currency. Designs as T* **75/88**, *but with values inscr. in decimal currency as in T* **100**. *W* w.**12** (*sideways*). *P* 13½.

No.	Type			
261	**100**	½p multicoloured ..	5	5
262	**76**	1p multicoloured ..	5	5
263	**77**	1½p multicoloured ..	5	5
264	**78**	2p multicoloured ..	8	8
265	**79**	2½p multicoloured ..	8	8
266	**80**	3½p multicoloured ..	10	10
267	**81**	4½p multicoloured ..	12	15
268	**82**	5p multicoloured ..	15	20
269	**83**	7½p multicoloured ..	20	25
270	**84**	10p multicoloured ..	25	30
271	**85**	12½p multicoloured ..	25	30
272	**86**	25p multicoloured ..	50	55
273	**87**	50p multicoloured ..	1·00	1·10
274	**88**	£1 multicoloured ..	2·25	2·50
261/74		.. .. *Set of* 14	4·50	5·00

Although the design of No. 274 in no way differs from that of No. 240, it was reprinted specially for decimalisation, and differs considerably in shade from No. 240, as do others from their counterparts in the 1968 set.

The main differences in No. 274 are in the mountain which is blue rather than pinkish blue and in the sea which is light blue instead of greenish blue.

See also No. 309.

101. St. Helena holding the " True Cross ".

(Des. R. Granger Barrett. Litho. Questa.)

1971 (5 Apr.). *Easter.* *W* w.**12**. *P* 14×14½.
275 **101** 2p. multicoloured .. 10 10
276 „ 5p. multicoloured .. 20 20
277 „ 7½p. multicoloured .. 35 35
278 „ 12½p. multicoloured .. 60 65

102. Napoleon (after painting by David) and Tomb on St. Helena.

(Des. J.W. Ltd. Litho Questa.)

1971 (5 May). *150th Death Anniv. of Napoleon, T* **102** *and similar vert. design. Multicoloured.* *W* w.**12**. *P* 13½.
279 2p. Type **102** 15 15
280 34p. Napoleon at St. Helena (after painting by Delaroche) .. .. 1·25 1·40

(Des. J.W. Ltd. Litho. Questa.)

1971 (10 Nov.). *Military Equipment (2nd issue). Multicoloured designs as T* **99**. *W* w.**12**. *P* 14.
281 1½p. Artillery Private's hanger 8 8
282 4p. Baker rifle and socket bayonet 20 20
283 6p. Infantry Officer's sword 30 30
284 22½p. Baker rifle and sword bayonet .. .. .. 1·00 1·00

(Des. and litho. J.W.)

1972 (19 June). *Military Equipment (3rd issue). Multicoloured designs as T* **99**. *W* w.**12**. *P* 14.
285 2p. multicoloured 8 10
286 5p. reddish lilac, new blue and black 20 20
287 7½p. multicoloured 30 35
288 12½p. pale olive-sepia, brown and black 50 55

Designs:—2p. Royal Sappers and Miners breast-plate, post 1823; 5p. Infantry sergeant's spontoon, *c.* 1830; 7½p. Royal Artillery officer's breast-plate, *c.* 1830; 12½p. English military pistol, *c.* 1800.

103. Wire Bird and White Fairy Tern.

(Des. (from photograph by D. Groves) and photo. Harrison.)

1972 (20 Nov.). *Royal Silver Wedding. Multicoloured; background colour given.* *W* w.**12**. *P* 14×14½.
289 **103** 2p. slate-green 10 15
290 „ 16p. lake-brown (*shades*) 75 85

(Des. J.W. Ltd. Litho. Questa.)

1973 (20 Sept.). *Military Equipment (4th issue). Multicoloured designs as T* **99**. *W* w.**12** *(sideways).* *P* 14.
291 2p. Other Rank's shako, 53rd Foot, 1815 .. .. 8 10
292 5p. Band and Drums sword, 1830 .. .. .. 20 25
293 7½p. Royal Sappers and Miners Officer's hat, 1830 .. 35 35
294 12½p. General's sword, 1831 60 65

1973 (14 Nov.). *Royal Wedding. As Nos.* 165/6 *of Anguilla. Centre multicoloured.* *W* w.**12** *(sideways).* *P* 13½.
295 2p. violet-blue 10 12
296 18p. light emerald 50 55

104. *Westminster* and *Claudine* beached, 1849.

(Des. J.W. Ltd. Litho. Questa.)

1973 (17 Dec.). *Tercentenary of East India Company Charter. T* **104** *and similar horiz. designs. Multicoloured.* *W* w.**12**. *P* 14.
297 1½p. Type **104** 8 8
298 4p. *True Briton*, 1790 .. 15 15
299 6p. *General Goddard* in action, 1795 .. .. .. 20 25
300 22½p. *Kent* burning in the Bay of Biscay, 1825 .. .. 75 80

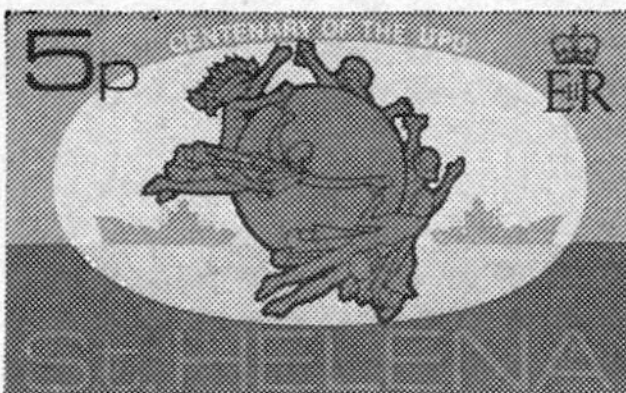

105. U.P.U. Emblem and Ships.

(Des. J.W. Ltd. Litho. Questa.)

1974 (15 Oct.). *Centenary of Universal Postal Union. T* **105** *and similar horiz. design. Multicoloured.* *W* w.**12** *(sideways on* **MS**303). *P* 14.
301 5p. Type **105** 20 20
302 25p. U.P.U. emblem and letters 60 65
MS303 89×84 mm. Nos. 301/2 85 90

106. Churchill in Sailor Suit, and Blenheim Palace.

(Des. Jennifer Toombs. Litho. Questa.)

1974 (30 Nov.). *Birth Centenary of Sir Winston Churchill. T* **106** *and similar horiz. design.* *W* w.**14** *sideways* (Nos. 304/5) *or W* w.**12** *sideways* (**MS**306). *P* 14.
304 5p. multicoloured 15 15
305 25p. black, flesh and reddish purple 55 60
MS306 108×93 mm. Nos. 304/5 70 75

Design:—25 p. Churchill and River Thames.

107. Capt. Cook and H.M.S. *Resolution.*

(Des. J. E. Cooter. Litho. Questa.)

1975 (14 July). *Bicentenary of Capt. Cook's Return to St. Helena. T* **107** *and similar horiz. design. Multicoloured.* *W* w.**14** *(sideways on* 25*p.*). *P* 13½.
307 5p. Type **107** 15 15
308 25p. Capt. Cook and Jamestown 50 55

(Litho. Questa.)

1975 (13 Aug.). *As No.* 264 *but P* 14 *and white paper.* *W* w.**12** *(sideways).*
309 **78** 2p. multicoloured .. 8 8

108. *Mellissia begonifolia* (tree).

(Des. Jennifer Toombs. Litho. J.W.)

975 (20 Oct.). *Centenary of Publication of "St. Helena" by J. C. Melliss.* T **108** *and similar multicoloured designs.* W w.**14** (*sideways on* 12 *and* 25*p.*). P 13.

10	2p. Type **108**	8	8
11	5p. *Mellissius adumbratus* (beetle)	12	15
12	12p. *Aegialitis sanctae-helenae* (bird) (*horiz.*)	25	30
13	25p. *Scorpaenia mellissii* (fish) (*horiz.*)	50	55

109. £1 Note.

(Des. V. Whiteley Studio. Litho. J.W.)

976 (15 Mar.). *First Issue of Currency Notes.* T **109** *and similar horiz. design. Multicoloured.* W w.**12** (*sideways*). P 13½.

14	8p. Type **109**	20	25
15	33p. £5 Note	65	75

110. 1d. Stamp of 1863.

(Des. C. Abbott. Litho. J.W.)

976 (4 May). *Festival of Stamps, London.* T **110** *and similar designs.* W w.**14** (*sideways on* 5 *and* 25*p.*). P 13½.

16	5p. light red-brown, black and light flesh	12	15
17	8p. black, green and pale dull green	20	25
18	25p. multicoloured	50	55

Designs: *Vert.*—8p. 1d. stamp of 1922. *oriz.*—25p. Mail carrier *Good Hope Castle.*

For Miniature Sheet containing No. 318 see scension No. **MS**218.

111. High Knoll, 1806.

(Des. C. Abbott. Litho. Questa.)

976 (14 Sept.–23 Nov.). *Aquatints and Lithographs of St. Helena.* T **111** *and similar horiz. designs. Multicoloured.* W w.**14** (*sideways*). P 13½ (£1, £2) *or* 14 (*others*).

19	1p. Type **111**	5	5
20	3p. The Friar Rock, 1815 ..	5	5
21	5p. The Column Lot, 1815 ..	8	10
22	6p. Sandy Bay Valley, 1809 (23.11)	10	12
23	8p. Scene from Castle Davis, 1815	15	15
324	9p. The Briars, 1815 (23.11) ..	15	20
325	10p. Plantation House, 1821 ..	20	20
326	15p. Longwood House, 1821 (23.11)	25	30
327	18p. St. Paul's Church ..	30	35
328	26p. St. James's Valley, 1815	45	50
329	40p. St. Matthew's Church, 1860	70	80
330	£1 St. Helena, 1815	1·75	2·00
331	£2 Sugar Loaf Hill, 1821 (23.11)	3·50	4·00
319/31	.. .. *Set of* 13	7·00	8·00

The £1 and £2 are larger, 47×34 mm.

112. Duke of Edinburgh paying Homage.

(Des. M. Shamir. Litho. J.W.)

1977 (7 Feb.). *Silver Jubilee.* T **112** *and similar horiz. designs. Multicoloured.* W w.**14** (*sideways*). P 13.

332	8p. Royal visit, 1947	15	20
333	15p. Queen's sceptre with dove	30	35
334	26p. Type **112**	55	65

ST. KITTS-NEVIS.

I. CROWN COLONY.

1 Christopher Columbus.

2 Medicinal Spring.

(Typo. D.L.R.)

1903. *Wmk. Crown CA.* P 14.

1 **1**	½d. dull purp. & deep green	1·40	1·10
2 **2**	1d. grey-black and carmine	1·50	40
3 **1**	2d. dull purple and brown	2·25	5·50
4 „	2½d. grey-black and blue ..	7·50	5·00
5 **2**	3d. deep green and orange ..	3·75	5·50
6 **1**	6d. grey-black & brt. pur.	4·50	5·50
7 „	1s. grey-green and orange	4·50	5·50
8 **2**	2s. deep green & grey-black	9·00	6·50
9 **1**	2s. 6d. grey-black & violet	13·00	17·00
10 **2**	5s. dull purple & sage-grn.	25·00	28·00
1/10	.. .. *Set of* 10	65·00	75·00
1/10 Optd. "Specimen"	*Set of* 10	65·00	

1905–18. *Wmk. Mult. Crown CA.* P 14.

11 **1**	½d. dull pur. & dp. grn., O	2·75	3·25
12 „	½d. grey-green, O (1907) ..	40	60
	a. Dull blue-green, O ..	20	65
13 **2**	1d. grey-black & carm., C	70	70
14 „	1d. carmine, O (1907) ..	85	30
	a. Scarlet, O	40	30
15 **1**	2d. dull pur. & brown, OC	85	1·50
16 „	2½d. grey-black and blue, O	8·00	4·50
17 „	2½d. bright blue, O (1907) ..	75	80
18 **2**	3d. dp. green & orange, OC	1·50	1·75
19 **1**	6d. grey-blk. & dp. vio., O	4·50	7·50
	a. Grey-black and deep purple, C (1908)	3·00	5·50
	b. Grey-black and bright purple, C (1916)	3·00	5·50
20 „	1s. grey-green and orange, OC (1909)	2·25	5·00
21 **2**	5s. dull purple & sage-green, C (11.18)	20·00	25·00
11/21	.. .. *Set of* 11	35·00	45·00
12, 14, 17 Optd. "Specimen"	*Set of* 3	26·00	

WAR TAX (3)

WAR STAMP (3*a*)

1916 (Oct.). *Optd. with* T **3**. *Wmk. Mult. Crown CA.* P 14.

22 **1**	½d. green (Optd. S. £17) ..	12	15
	a. Grey-green	10	15

1918 (Aug.). *Special printing, optd. with* T **3a**. *Wmk. Mult. Crown CA.* P 14.

23 **1**	1½d. orange (Optd. S. £17) ..	12	20

4

5

(Typo. D.L.R.)

1920–22. *Wmk. Mult. Crown CA (sideways). P 14.*

24 **4** ½d. blue-green, O 40 25
25 **5** 1d. carmine, O 35 35
26 **4** 1½d. orange-yellow, O .. 40 70
27 **5** 2d. slate-grey, O .. .. 1·50 2·25
28 **4** 2½d. ultramarine, O .. 70 1·00
29 **5** 3d. purple/*yellow*, C .. 75 1·60
30 **4** 6d. dull pur. & brt. mve., C 1·50 2·75
31 **5** 1s. grey and black/*green*, C 1·10 2·75
32 **4** 2s. dull pur. & blue/*blue*, C 5·50 6·00
33 **5** 2s. 6d. grey and red/*blue*, C 6·00 9·00
34 **4** 5s. grn. & red/*pale yellow*, C 7·50 13·00
35 **5** 10s. green and red/*green*, C 17·00 22·00
36 **4** £1 pur. & blk./*red*, C (1922) 95·00 £130
24/36 .. .. *Set of* 13 £120 £180
24/36 Optd. "Specimen" *Set of* 13 £130

1921–9. *Wmk. Mult. Script CA (sideways). P 14.*

37 **4** ½d. blue-green, O .. 15 20
a. Yellow-green, O .. .. 1·25 75
38 **5** 1d. rose-carmine, O .. 20 25
39 „ 1d. deep violet, O (1922) 75 25
a. Pale violet, O (1929) 20 15
40 **4** 1½d. red, O (1925) .. 60 75
40*a* „ 1½d. red-brown, O (1929) .. 25 30
41 **5** 2d. slate-grey, O (1922) .. 25 30
42 **4** 2½d. pale brt. blue, O ('22) 75 2·50
43 „ 2½d. brown, O (1922) .. 55 1·75
44 „ 2½d. ultramarine, C (1927) 55 1·60
a. Ultramarine, O (1927) .. 1·10 75
45 **5** 3d. dull ultram., O (1922) 55 1·10
45*a* „ 3d. purple/*yellow*, C (1926) 70 1·10
46 **4** 6d. dull & brt. pur., C ('24) 1·10 1·75
46*a* **5** 1s. black/*green*, C (1929).. 3·50 4·50
47 **4** 2s. pur. & blue/*blue*, C ('22) 3·75 5·00
47*a* **5** 2s. 6d. black and red/*blue*, C (1927) .. 6·50 8·50
47*b* **4** 5s. grn. & red/*yell.*, C ('29) 13·00 17·00
37/47*b* .. .. *Set of* 16 30·00 45·00
37/47*b* Optd./Perf. "Specimen" *Set of* 16 £130

No. 38 is overprinted "Specimen". A later printing exists perforated "Specimen". (*Price* £35.)

6. Old Road Bay and Mount Misery.

(Typo. D.L.R.)

1923. *Tercentenary of Colony. Chalk-surfaced paper. P 14. (a) Wmk. Mult. Script CA (sideways).*

48 **6** ½d. black and green .. 90 1·00
49 „ 1d. black and bright violet 90 1·00
50 „ 1½d. black and scarlet .. 1·40 2·00
51 „ 2d. black and slate-grey .. 1·40 2·00
52 „ 2½d. black and brown .. 2·25 3·00
53 „ 3d. black and ultramarine 2·50 4·50
54 „ 6d. black & bright purple 5·00 7·00
55 „ 1s. black and sage-green 7·00 10·00
56 „ 2s. black and blue/*blue* .. 13·00 17·00
57 „ 2s. 6d. black and red/*blue*.. 18·00 20·00
58 „ 10s. black and red/*emerald*.. £130 £225

(*b*) *Wmk. Mult. Crown CA (sideways).*

59 **6** 5s. black & red/*pale yellow* 75·00 £120
60 „ £1 black and purple/*red* .. £450 £650
48/60 .. .. *Set of* 13 £650 £900
48/60 Optd. "Specimen" *Set of* 13 £400

1935 (6 May). *Silver Jubilee. As Nos. 91/4 of Antigua, but ptd. by Waterlow. P 11 × 12.*

61 1d. deep blue and scarlet .. 20 25
62 1½d. ultramarine and grey .. 25 40
63 2½d. brown and deep blue .. 55 90
64 1s. slate and purple .. .. 3·00 4·00
61/4 Perf. "Specimen" *Set of* 4 17·00

1937 (12 May). *Coronation. As Nos. 13/15 of Aden.*

65 1d. scarlet 12 12
66 1½d. buff 12 12
67 2½d. bright blue 15 35
65/7 Perf. "Specimen" *Set of* 3 13·00

Nos. 61/7 are inscribed "ST. CHRISTOPHER AND NEVIS".

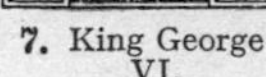

7. King George VI.

8. King George VI and Medicinal Spring.

9. King George VI and Christopher Columbus.

10. King George VI and Anguilla Island.

(Typo; centre litho. (*T* **10**). D.L.R.)

1938 (15 Aug.)–**48.** *Wmk. Mult. Script CA (sideways on T* **8** *and* **9**). *P 14 (T* **7** *and* **10**) *or 13 × 12 (T* **8/9**).

68 **7** ½d. green 8 8
a. Blue-green ('43) 8 10
69 „ 1d. scarlet 15 15
a. Carmine ('43) 8 10
b. Rose-red ('47) 8 10
70 „ 1½d. orange 8 8
71 **8** 2d. scarlet and grey, O 3·75 1·10
aa. Carmine and deep grey, C .. 4·00 3·75
a. P.14. *Scar. &p.grey*, OC ('41) 20 15
ab. P.14. *Scar. & dp. grey*, O ('43) 5·00 2·25
72 **7** 2½d. ultramarine 45 40
a. Bright ultramarine ('43) .. 10 8
73 **8** 3d. dull purple & scar., OC 65 80
a. Perf. 14, CO ('42) 25 25
74 **9** 6d. green & brt. purple, O 70 80
a. P. 14. *Green & purple* C ('42) 7·50 6·00
ab. P. 14. *Green & brt. purple*, OC 40 35
75 **8** 1s. black and green, O .. 90 80
a. Perf. 14, OC ('43).. .. 45 45
76 „ 2s. 6d. black and scarlet, O 4·50 4·50
a. Perf. 14, CO ('42) .. 1·10 2·25
77 **9** 5s. green and scarlet, O .. 9·00 10·00
a. Perf. 14, CO ('42) 2·75 3·00
77*b* **10** 10s. blk. & ultram. (1.9.48) 5·50 7·00
77*c* „ £1 black & brown (1.9.48) 8·00 11·00
68/77*c* .. .. *Set of* 12 17·00 22·00
68/77 Perf. "Specimen" *Set of* 10 32·00

1946 (1 Nov.). *Victory. As Nos. 28/9 of Aden.*

78 1½d. red-orange 8 8
79 3d. carmine 8 8
78/9 Perf. "Specimen" *Set of* 2 14·00

1949 (3 Jan.). *Royal Silver Wedding. As Nos. 30/1 of Aden.*

80 2½d. ultramarine 8
81 5s. carmine .. .. 3·00 4·0

1949 (10 Oct.). *75th Anniv. of Universal Post Union. As Nos. 114/7 of Antigua.*

82 2½d. ultramarine 12 2
83 3d. carmine-red 20 4
84 6d. magenta 55 7
85 1s. blue-green 80 9

ANGUILLA ANGUILLA

TERCENTENARY 1650-1950 (11)

TERCENTENARY 1650—1950 (12)

1950 (10 Nov.). *Tercentenary of British Settlement in Anguilla. T* **7** *optd. as T* **11** *and T* **8/9**, *perf. 13 × 12, optd. as T* **12**.

86 **7** 1d. bright rose-red .. 8
87 „ 1½d. orange 8
a. Error. Crown missing ..
b. Error. St. Edward's Crown ..
88 „ 2½d. bright ultramarine 10
89 **8** 3d. dull purple & scarlet .. 8 1
90 **9** 6d. green & bright purple.. 25 3
91 **8** 1s. black and green (R.) .. 40 4
86/91 .. .. *Set of* 6 85 8

Nos. 87a/b occur on a row in the watermark in which the crowns and letters "CA" alternat

(New Currency. 100 cents = 1 West Indian dollar)

1951 (16 Feb.). *Inauguration of B.W.I. University College. As Nos. 118/9 of Antigua.*

92 3 c. black and yellow-orange 15 2
93 12 c. turquoise-grn. & magenta 25 3

ST. CHRISTOPHER, NEVIS AND ANGUILLA.

II. LEGISLATIVE COUNCIL.

13. Bath House and Spa.

14. Warner Park. (*Horiz.*)

15. Map of the Islands.

16. Brimstone Hill. (*Horiz.*)
17. Nevis from the Sea, North. (*Horiz.*)
18. Pinney's Beach. (*Horiz.*)
19. Sir Thomas Warner's Tomb. (*Vert.*)
20. Old Road Bay. (*Horiz.*)
21. Sea Island Cotton. (*Horiz.*)
22. The Treasury. (*Horiz.*)
23. Salt Pond. (*Horiz.*)
24. Sugar Factory. (*Horiz.*)

(Recess. Waterlow.)

952 (14 JUNE). *Wmk. Mult. Script CA. P* 12½.
94 **13** 1 c. deep green & ochre .. 15 15
95 **14** 2 c. green 20 20
96 **15** 3 c. carmine-red & violet 20 25
97 **16** 4 c. scarlet 25 25
98 **17** 5 c. bright blue & grey .. 25 20
99 **18** 6 c. ultramarine 30 25
00 **19** 12 c. dp. blue & reddish brn 40 30
01 **20** 24 c. black & carmine-red 50 40
02 **21** 48 c. olive & chocolate .. 90 1·25
03 **22** 60 c. ochre & deep green .. 1·10 2·00
04 **23** $1.20 dp. green & ultram. 2·75 2·50
05 **24** $4.80 green & carmine .. 7·00 7·50
4/105 .. .. *Set of* 12 12·00 14·00

953 (2 JUNE). *Coronation. As No.* 47 *of Aden.*
06 2 c. black and bright green .. 12 20

25. Sombrero Lighthouse.

26. Map of Anguilla and Dependencies.

Recess. Waterlow (until 1961), then De La Rue.)

954–57. *Types of* 1952 (*but with portrait of Queen Elizabeth II in place of King George VI as in T* **25/6**). *Wmk. Mult. Script CA. P* 12½.
6*a* **23** ½ c. deep olive 5 5
7 **13** 1 c. deep green and ochre (*shades*) 5 5
8 **14** 2 c. green (*shades*) .. 5 5
9 **15** 3 c. carmine-red & violet (*shades*) 8 8
0 **16** 4 c. scarlet 8 8
1 **17** 5 c. bright blue and grey 10 10
2 **18** 6 c. ultramarine (*shades*) 15 15
2*a* **25** 8 c. grey-black 12 12
3 **19** 12 c. deep blue & red-brn. 12 12
4 **20** 24 c. black & carm.-red .. 25 25
5 **21** 48 c. olive-bistre & choc. 50 60
6 **22** 60 c. ochre & deep green 70 85
7 **23** $1.20, deep green and ultramarine (*shades*) 1·50 2·00
7*a* **26** $2.40, black & red-orange 4·00 5·00
8 **24** $4.80, green and carmine 8·00 10·00
6*a*/18 .. .. *Set of* 15 14·00 18·00

Dates of issue:—1954—1 Mar., 1 c., to 6 c., c. 1 Dec., 24 c. to $1.20, $4.80. 1956—3 July, c. 1957—1 Feb., 8 c., $2.40.

The above stamps, from No. 1 onwards, were concurrent use with the stamps inscribed LEEWARD ISLANDS" until July 1st, 1956, when e general Leeward Islands stamps were ithdrawn.

27. Alexander Hamilton and View of Nevis.

(Des. Miss Eva Wilkin. Recess. Waterlow.)

1957 (11 JAN.). *Bicentenary of Birth of Alexander Hamilton. Wmk. Mult. Script CA. P* 12½.
119 **27** 24 c. green and deep blue .. 35 40

1958 (22 APR.). *Inauguration of British Caribbean Federation. As Nos.* 135/7 *of Antigua.*
120 3 c. deep green 10 12
121 6 c. blue 15 20
122 12 c. scarlet 30 35

III. MINISTERIAL GOVERNMENT.

28. One Penny stamp of 1861.

29. Fourpence stamp of 1861.
30. Sixpence stamp of 1861.
31. One shilling stamp of 1861.

(Recess. Waterlow.)

1961 (15 JULY). *Nevis Stamp Centenary. W* w.**12**. *P* 14.
123 **28** 2 c. red-brown and green 10 12
124 **29** 8 c. red-brown & dp. blue 20 20
125 **30** 12 c. black & carmine-red 30 30
126 **31** 24 c. deep bluish green and red-orange 45 50

1963 (2 SEPT.). *Red Cross Centenary. As Nos.* 147/8 *of Antigua.*
127 3 c. red and black 12 12
128 12 c. red and blue 65 65

32. New Lighthouse, Sombrero.

33. Loading Sugar Cane, St. Kitts.

34. Pall Mall Square, Basseterre. (*Vert.*)
35. Gateway, Brimstone Hill Fort, St. Kitts. (*Vert.*)
36. Nelson's Spring, Nevis. (*Horiz.*)
37. Grammar School, St. Kitts. (*Horiz.*)
38. Crater, Mt. Misery, St. Kitts. (*Horiz.*)
39. Hibiscus. (*Horiz.*)
40. Sea Island Cotton, Nevis. (*Vert.*)
41. Boat-building, Anguilla. (*Horiz.*)
42. White-crowned Pigeon. (*Vert.*)
43. St. George's Church Tower, Basseterre. (*Horiz.*)
44. Alexander Hamilton. (*Vert.*)
45. Map of St. Kitts-Nevis. (*Vert.*)
46. Map of Anguilla. (*Horiz.*)
47. Arms of St. Christopher, Nevis and Anguilla. (*Vert.*)

(Des. V. Whiteley. Photo. Harrison.)

1963 (20 NOV.). *W* w.**12** (*upright*). *P* 14.
129 **32** ½ c. sepia and light blue .. 5 5
130 **33** 1 c. multicoloured .. 5 5
131 **34** 2 c. multicoloured .. 5 5
a. White fountain and Church .. .. 80·00
132 **35** 3 c. multicoloured .. 5 5
133 **36** 4 c. multicoloured .. 5 5
134 **37** 5 c. multicoloured .. 8 8
135 **38** 6 c. multicoloured .. 10 10
136 **39** 10 c. multicoloured .. 10 10
137 **40** 15 c. multicoloured .. 12 12
138 **41** 20 c. multicoloured .. 15 15
139 **42** 25 c. multicoloured (*shades*) 25 20
140 **43** 50 c. multicoloured .. 40 40
141 **44** 60 c. multicoloured .. 40 35
142 **45** $1 greenish yellow & bl. 75 75
143 **46** $2.50 multicoloured .. 2·00 2·75
144 **47** $5 multicoloured .. 4·00 4·00
129/144 .. .. *Set of* 16 7·50 8·00

The 1, 4, 5, 6, 10 and 20 c. values exist with PVA gum as well as gum arabic.
See also Nos. 166, etc.

ARTS
FESTIVAL
ST KITTS
1964
(48)

49. Festival Emblem.

1964 (14 SEPT.). *Arts Festival. Optd. as T* **48**.
145 **35** 3 c. multicoloured .. 8 8
a. Opt. double .. ..
146 **42** 25 c. multicoloured .. 25 30

1965 (17 MAY). *I.T.U. Centenary. As Nos.* 166/7 *of Antigua.*
147 2 c. bistre-yell. & rose-carm. 8 8
148 50 c. turq.-blue & yell.-olive 60 65

1965 (15 OCT.). *International Co-operation Year. As Nos.* 168/9 *of Antigua.*
149 2 c. reddish pur. & turq.-grn. 10 10
150 25 c. dp. bluish green & lav. 30 35

1966 (24 JAN.). *Churchill Commemoration. As Nos.* 170/3 *of Antigua.*
151 ½ c. new blue 5 5
152 3 c. deep green 5 8
153 15 c. brown 25 30
154 25 c. bluish violet 45 50

1966 (4 FEB.). *Royal Visit. As Nos.* 174/5 *of Antigua.*
155 3 c. black and ultramarine .. 5 8
156 25 c. black and magenta .. 30 35

1966 (1 JULY). *World Cup Football Championships. As Nos.* 176/7 *of Antigua.*
157 6 c. violet, yellow-green, lake and yellow-brown .. 5 8
158 25 c. chocolate, blue-grn., lake and yellow-brown .. 30 35

(Photo. Harrison.)

1966 (15 AUG.). *Arts Festival.* *P* 14×14½.
159 **49** 3 c. black, buff, emerald-green and gold .. 5 10
160 ,, 25 c. black, buff, emerald-green and silver .. 25 30

1966 (20 SEPT.). *Inauguration of W.H.O. Headquarters, Geneva. As Nos.* 178/9 *of Antigua.*
161 3 c. black, yellow-green, and light blue 5 8
162 40 c. black, light purple, and yellow-brown 40 45

1966 (1 DEC.). *20th Anniv. of U.N.E.S.C.O. As Nos.* 196/8 *of Antigua.*
163 3 c. slate-violet, red, yellow and orange 5 5
164 6 c. orange-yellow, violet and deep olive 8 8
165 40 c. black, bright purple and orange 45 45

IV. ASSOCIATED STATEHOOD.

(27 Feb. 1967)

1967–69. *As Nos.* 129, *etc. but wmk.* w.**12** (*sideways*).
166 **32** ½ c. sepia & lt. bl. (9.1.69) 5 8
168 **34** 2 c. mult. (27.6.67) .. 8 8
169 **35** 3 c. mult. (16.7.68) .. 10 10
174 **40** 15 c. mult. (16.7.68) .. 25 25
176 **42** 25 c. mult. (16.7.68) .. 35 35
179 **45** $1 greenish yellow and blue (16.7.68) (*shades*) 1·40 1·40
166/79 .. .. *Set of* 6 1·90 2·00

The 2 c. and $1 values exist with PVA gum as well as gum arabic.

50. Government Headquarters, Basseterre.

(Des. V. Whiteley. Photo. Harrison.)

1967 (1 JULY). *Statehood.* *T* **50** *and similar horiz. designs. Multicoloured.* *W* w.**12.** *P* 14½×14.
182 3 c. Type **50** 5 8
183 10 c. National Flag 10 12
184 25 c. Coat-of-Arms 30 35

53. John Wesley and Cross.

54. Charles Wesley and Cross.

55. Thomas Coke and Cross.

(Litho. De La Rue.)

1967 (1 DEC.). *West Indies Methodist Conference.* *P* 13×13½.
185 **53** 3 c. black, cerise and reddish violet 5 5
186 **54** 25 c. black, light greenish blue and blue .. 25 25
187 **55** 40 c. blk., yellow & orange 35 40

56. " Herald " Aircraft over Merchant Ship.

(Des. and litho. De La Rue.)

1968 (30 JULY). *Caribbean Free Trade Area.* *W* w.**12** (*sideways*). *P* 13.
188 **56** 25 c. multicoloured .. 20 25
189 ,, 50 c. multicoloured .. 35 40

57. Dr. Martin Luther King.

(Des. G. L. Vasarhelyi. Litho. Enschedé.)

1968 (30 SEPT.). *Martin Luther King Commemoration.* *W* w.**12.** *P* 12×12½.
190 **57** 50 c. multicoloured .. 40 40

58. " The Mystical Nativity " (Botticelli). **59.** " The Adoration of the Magi " (Rubens).

(Des. and photo. Harrison.)

1968 (27 NOV.). *Christmas.* *W* w.**12** (*sideways*). *P* 14½×14.
191 **58** 12 c. multicoloured .. 12 12
192 **59** 25 c. multicoloured .. 20 25
193 **58** 40 c. multicoloured .. 35 35
194 **59** 50 c. multicoloured .. 40 45

60. Tarpon.

61. Garfish.
62. Horse-eye Jack.
63. Redsnapper.

(Des. G. Drummond. Photo. Harrison.)

1969 (25 FEB.). *Fishes.* *W* w.**12.** *P* 14×14½.
195 **60** 6 c. multicoloured .. 10
196 **61** 12 c. black, turquoise-green and greenish blue .. 12
197 **62** 40 c. multicoloured .. 35
198 **63** 50 c. multicoloured .. 45

64. The Warner Badge and Islands.

65. Sir Thomas Warner's Tomb.
66. Charles I's Commission.

(Des. V. Whiteley. Litho. Format International.)

1969 (1 SEPT.). *Sir Thomas Warner Commemo tion.* *W* w.**12** (*sideways*). *P* 13½×14.
199 **64** 20 c. multicoloured .. 20
200 **65** 25 c. multicoloured .. 25
201 **66** 40 c. multicoloured .. 35

67. "The Adoration of the Kings" (Mostaer

68. " The Adoration of the Kings " (Geertgen

(Des. J. Enschedé & Sons. Litho. Bradbu Wilkinson.)

1969 (17 NOV.). *Christmas.* *W* w.**12** (*sideway* *P* 13½.
202 **67** 10 c. multicoloured .. 10
203 ,, 25 c. multicoloured .. 25
204 **68** 40 c. multicoloured .. 35
205 ,, 50 c. multicoloured .. 40

69. Pirates and Treasure at Frigate Bay. (*Vert.*)
70. English Two-decker Warship, 1650. (*Vert.*)
71. Naval Flags of Colonizing Nations. (*Vert.*)
72. Rapier Hilt (17th-cent.). (*Vert.*)

73. Portuguese Caravels (16th-cent.).

74. Sir Henry Morgan and Fireships, 1669. (*Horiz.*)
75. L'Ollonois and Pirate Carrack (16th-cent.). (*Horiz.*)
76. 17th-Century Smugglers' Ship. (*Horiz.*)
77. " Piece-of-Eight ". (*Vert.*)
78. Cannon (17th-cent.). (*Horiz.*)
79. Humphrey Cole's Astrolabe, 1574. (*Vert.*)
80. Flintlock Pistol (17th-cent.). (*Horiz.*)
81. Dutch Flute (17th-cent.). (*Vert.*)
82. Capt. Bartholomew Roberts and His Crew's Death Sentence. (*Vert.*)
83. Railing Piece (16th-cent.). (*Horiz.*)
84. Drake, Hawkins and Sea Battle. (*Horiz.*)

(Des. and litho. John Waddington Ltd.)

1970 (2 FEB.–8 SEPT.). *W* w.**12** (*upright on vert. designs, sideways on horiz. designs.*). *P* 14.

206	**69**	½ c. black, pale orange and emerald	5	5
207	**70**	1 c. multicoloured ..	5	5
208	**71**	2 c. multicoloured ..	5	5
209	**72**	3 c. multicoloured ..	5	5
210	**73**	4 c. multicoloured ..	5	5
211	**74**	5 c. multicoloured ..	5	5
212	**75**	6 c. multicoloured ..	8	8
213	**76**	10 c. multicoloured ..	10	10
214	**77**	15 c. multicoloured (I) ..	20	20
214*a*	,,	15 c. mult. (II) (8.9.70) ..	15	15
215	**78**	20 c. multicoloured ..	20	20
216	**79**	25 c. multicoloured ..	25	25
217	**80**	50 c. multicoloured ..	35	40
218	**81**	60 c. multicoloured ..	25	30
219	**82**	$1 multicoloured ..	50	55
220	**83**	$2.50, multicoloured ..	90	1·00
221	**84**	$5 multicoloured ..	1·75	1·90
206/221		.. .. *Set of* 17	4·50	5·00

Nos. 214/*a*. Type I, coin inscribed "HISPANIANUM"; Type II, corrected to "HISPANIARUM". No 214*a* also differs considerably in shade from No. 214.

See also Nos. 269/84 and 327 etc.

85. Graveyard Scene (*Great Expectations*).

(Des. Jennifer Toombs. Litho. B.W.)

1970 (1 MAY). *Death Centenary of Charles Dickens. T* **85** *and similar designs. W* w.**12** (*sideways on horiz. designs*). *P* 13.

222	4 c. bistre-brown, gold and deep blue-green	10	10
223	20 c. bistre-brown, gold and reddish-purple	25	25
224	25 c. bistre-brown, gold and olive-green	30	30
225	40 c. bistre-brown, gold and ultramarine	50	50

Designs: *Horiz.*—20 c. Miss Havisham and Pip (*Great Expectations*). *Vert.*—25 c. Dickens' Birthplace; 40 c. Charles Dickens.

86. Local Steel Band.

(Des. V. Whiteley. Litho. Enschedé.)

1970 (1 AUG.). *Festival of Arts. T* **86** *and similar horiz. designs. Multicoloured. W* w.**12** (*sideways*). *P* 13½.

226	20 c. Type **86**	15	15
227	25 c. Local String Band ..	20	20
228	40 c. Scene from *A Midsummer Night's Dream*	35	35

87. 1d. Stamp of 1870 and Post Office, 1970.

(Des. J. E. Cooter. Litho. J.W.)

1970 (14 SEPT.). *Stamp Centenary. T* **87** *and similar horiz. designs. W* w.**12** (*sideways*). *P* 14½.

229	½ c. green and rose	8	8
230	20 c. deep blue, green & rose	20	20
231	25 c. brown-purple, green and rose	25	25
232	50 c. scarlet, green and black	1·00	1·00

Designs:—20 c., 25 c. 1d. and 6d. Stamps of 1870; 50 c. 6d. Stamp of 1870 and Early Postmark.

88. " Adoration of the Shepherds " (detail) (Frans Floris).

(Des. Enschedé. Litho. Format.)

1970 (16 NOV.). *Christmas. T* **88** *and similar vert. design. Multicoloured. W* w.**12**. *P* 14.

233	3 c. Type **88**	5	5
234	20 c. " The Holy Family " (Van Dyck)	20	20
235	25 c. As 20 c.	25	25
236	40 c. Type **88**	35	40

89. Monkey Fiddle.

(Des. Sylvia Goaman. Litho. Format.)

1971 (1 MAR.). *Flowers. T* **89** *and similar horiz. designs. Multicoloured. W* w.**12** (*sideways*). *P* 14½.

237	½ c. Type **89**	5	5
238	20 c. Tropical Mountain Violet	20	20
239	30 c. Trailing Morning Glory	25	25
240	50 c. Fringed Epidendrum ..	40	45

90. Royal Poinciana.

(Des. Enschedé. Litho. J.W.)

1971 (1 JUNE). *Phillipe de Poincy Commemoration. T* **90** *and similar multicoloured designs. W* w.**12** (*sideways on* 20 *and* 30 *c.*). *P* 13½.

241	20 c. Type **90**	20	20
242	30 c. Château de Poincy ..	30	30
243	50 c. De Poincy's badge (*vert.*)	40	40

91. The East Yorks.

(Des. V. Whiteley. Litho. Walsall Security Printers Ltd.)

1971 (1 SEPT.). *Siege of Brimstone Hill,* 1782. *T* **91** *and similar horiz. designs. Multicoloured. W* w.**12** (*sideways*). *P* 14½.

244	½ c. Type **91**	5	5
245	20 c. Royal Artillery ..	20	20
246	30 c. French infantry ..	30	35
247	50 c. The Royal Scots ..	55	60

92. " Crucifixion " (Massys).

(Des. J. E. Cooter. Litho. J.W.)

1972 (1 APR.). *Easter. W* w.**12**. *P* 14 × 13½.

248	**92**	4 c. multicoloured ..	5	5
249	,,	20 c. multicoloured ..	15	20
250	,,	30 c. multicoloured ..	25	30
251	,,	40 c. multicoloured ..	35	40

93. "Virgin and Child" (Bergognone).

(Des. J. E. Cooter. Litho. J.W.)

1972 (2 Oct.). *Christmas. T* **93** *and similar multicoloured designs. W* w.**12** (*sideways on vert. designs*). *P* 14.

252	3 c. Type **93**	5	5
253	20 c. "Adoration of the Kings" (J. Bassano) (*horiz.*)	20	20
254	25 c. "Adoration of the Shepherds" (Domenichino)	25	25
255	40 c. "Virgin and Child" (Fiorenzo)	40	40

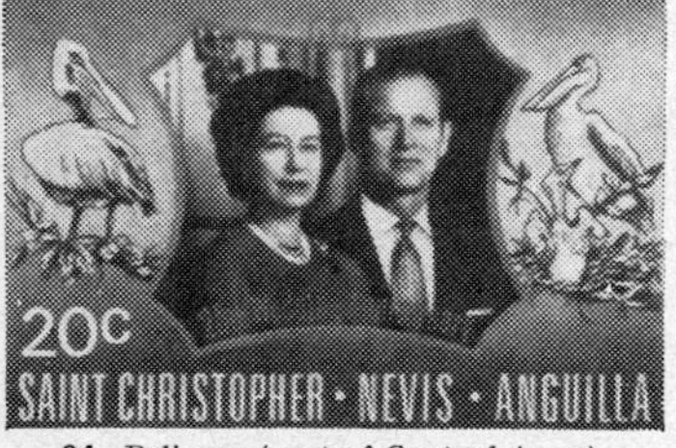

94. Pelicans (part of Coat-of-Arms).

(Des. (from photograph by D. Groves) and photo. Harrison.)

1972 (20 Nov.). *Royal Silver Wedding. Multicoloured; background colour given. W* w.**12.** *P* 14×14½.

256 **94**	20 c. carmine	20	20
257 ,,	25 c. bright blue	25	25

95. Landing on St. Christopher, 1623.

(Des. J.W. Ltd. Litho. Questa.)

1973 (28 Jan.). *350th Anniv. of Sir Thomas Warner's landing on St. Christopher. T* **95** *and similar horiz. designs. Multicoloured. W* w.**12.** *P* 13½.

258	4 c. Type **95**	5	5
259	25 c. Growing tobacco	20	20
260	40 c. Building fort at Old Road	35	40
261	$2.50, Warner's ship ..	1·90	2·00

96. "The Last Supper" (Titian).

(Des. J. E. Cooter. Litho. Walsall Security Printers Ltd.)

1973 (16 Apr.). *Easter. Paintings of "The Last Supper" by the artists listed. Multicoloured. W* w.12 (*sideways on* $2.50). *P* 13½×14 ($2.50) *or* 14×13½ (*others*).

262	4 c. Type **96**	5	5
263	25 c. Ascr. to Roberti ..	20	25
264	$2.50, Juan de Juanes (*horiz.*)	1·75	1·75

VISIT OF
H. R. H. THE PRINCE OF WALES 1973
(97)

1973 (31 May). *Royal Visit. Nos.* 258/61 *optd. with T* **97** *by Questa.*

265	4 c. Type **95**	5	5
266	25 c. Growing tobacco ..	15	15
267	40 c. Building fort at Old Road	25	25
268	$2.50, Warner's ship ..	2·50	2·75

(Des. J.W. Ltd. Litho. Harrison ($10), J.W. (others).)

1973 (12 Sept.)–**74.** *As Nos.* 206 *etc. and new value* ($10), *but W* w.**12** *sideways on vert. designs and upright on horiz. designs.*

269 **69**	½ c. black, pale orange and emerald	5	5
271 **71**	2 c. multicoloured ..	5	5
272 **72**	3 c. multicoloured ..	5	5
274 **74**	5 c. multicoloured ..	5	5
275 **75**	6 c. multicoloured ..	8	8
276 **76**	10 c. multicoloured ..	8	8
277 **77**	15 c. multicoloured (II) ..	8	8
278 **78**	20 c. multicoloured ..	15	15
279 **79**	25 c. multicoloured ..	10	10
280 **80**	50 c. multicoloured ..	20	20
282 **82**	$1 multicoloured ..	35	40
284 –	$10 mult. (16.11.74) ..	3·50	4·00
269/84	.. .. *Set of* 12	4·25	4·75

Design: *Horiz.*—$10 The apprehension of Blackbeard (Edward Teach).

See also Nos. 327 etc.

99. Harbour Scene and 2d. Stamp of 1903.

(Des. V. Whiteley Studio. Litho. Enschedé.)

1973 (1 Oct.). *70th Anniv. of First St. Kitts-Nevis Stamps. T* **99** *and similar horiz. designs. Multicoloured. W* w.**12** (*sideways*). *P* 13×13½.

285	4 c. Type **99**	5	5
286	25 c. Sugar-mill and 1d. stamp of 1903	25	25
287	40 c. Unloading boat and ½d. stamp of 1903	35	40
288	$2.50, Rock-carvings and 3d. stamp of 1903	1·90	2·00
MS289	144×95 mm. Nos. 285/8 ..	2·75	3·00

1973 (14 Nov.). *Royal Wedding. As Nos.* 165/6 *of Anguilla. Centre multicoloured. W* w.**12** (*sideways*). *P* 13½.

290	25 c. light emerald	20	20
291	40 c. brown-ochre	30	30

100. "Virgin and Child" (Murillo).

(Des. J. E. Cooter. Litho. Format.)

1973 (1 Dec.). *Christmas. T* **100** *and similar multicoloured designs showing "The Holy Family" by the artists listed. W* w.**12** (*sideways on* $1). *P* 13½.

292	4 c. Type **100**	5	5
293	40 c. Mengs	30	30
294	60 c. Sassoferrato	40	40
295	$1 Filippino Lippi (*horiz.*)	55	60

101. "Christ Carrying the Cross" (S. del Piombo).

(Des. J. E. Cooter. Litho. D.L.R.)

1974 (8 Apr.). *Easter. T* **101** *and similar multicoloured designs. W* w.**12** (*sideways on* $2.50). *P* 13½.

296	4 c. Type **101**	5	5
297	25 c. "The Crucifixion" (Goya)	20	20
298	40 c. "The Trinity" (Ribera)	30	30
299	$2.50, "The Deposition" (Fra Bartolomeo) (*horiz.*)	1·50	1·75

102. University Centre, St. Kitts.

(Des. G. Drummond. Litho. Questa.)

1974 (1 JUNE). *25th Anniv. of University of West Indies. T* **102** *and similar horiz. design. Multicoloured. W* w.**12** *(sideways). P* 13½.

300 10 c. Type **102** 10 10
301 $1 As Type **102** but showing different buildings .. 55 60
MS302 99×95 mm. Nos. 301/2 65 70

103. Hands reaching for Globe.

(Des. Jennifer Toombs. Litho. Questa.)

1974 (5 AUG.). *Family Planning. T* **103** *and similar designs. W* w.**12** *(sideways on* 25 *c. and* $2.50*). P* 14.

303 4 c. orange-brown, new blue and black 5 5
304 25 c. multicoloured 15 20
305 40 c. multicoloured 25 30
306 $2.50, multicoloured .. 1·40 1·50

Designs: *Horiz.*—25 c. Instruction by nurse; $2.50, Emblem and globe on scales. *Vert.*—40 c. Family group.

104. Churchill as Army Lieutenant.

(Des. PAD Studio. Litho. Questa.)

1974 (30 Nov.). *Birth Centenary of Sir Winston Churchill. T* **104** *and similar vert. designs. Multicoloured. W* w.**12**. *P* 13½.

307 4 c. Type **104** 5 5
308 25 c. Churchill as Prime Minister 15 20
309 40 c. Churchill as Knight of the Garter 25 30
310 60 c. Churchill's statue, London 30 35
MS311 99×148 mm. Nos. 307/10 75 90

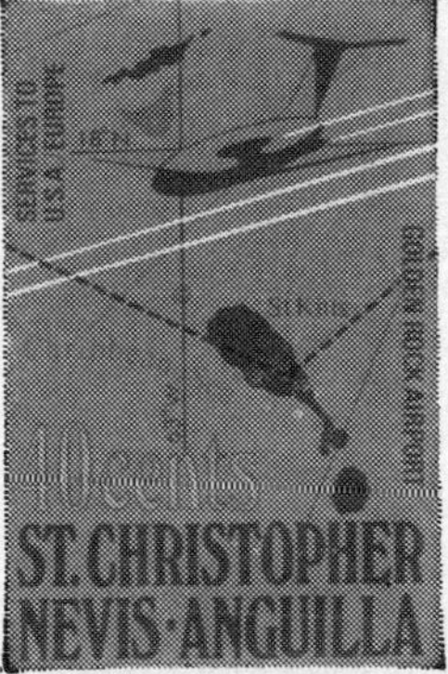

105. Aeroplane and Map.

(Des. J.W. Ltd. Litho. Questa.)

1974 (16 DEC.). *Opening of Golden Rock Airport, St. Kitts. Sheets* 98×148 *mm. W* w.**12**. *P* 13½.

MS312 **105** 40 c. multicoloured .. 25 30
MS313 „ 45 c. multicoloured .. 25 30

106. " The Last Supper " (Doré).

(Des. PAD Studio. Litho. Questa.)

1975 (24 MAR.). *Easter. T* **106** *and similar vert. designs showing paintings by Doré. Multicoloured. W* w.**12**. *P* 14½.

314 4 c. Type **106** 5 5
315 25 c. " Christ Mocked " .. 15 15
316 40 c. " Jesus Falling Beneath the Cross " 20 25
317 $1 " The Erection of the Cross " 45 50

107. E.C.C.A. H.Q. Buildings, Basseterre.

(Des. J. E. Cooter. Litho. Enschedé.)

1975 (2 JUNE*). *Opening of East Caribbean Currency Authority's Headquarters. T* **107** *and similar horiz. designs. W* w.**14** *(sideways). P* 13×13½.

318 12 c. multicoloured 8 8
319 25 c. multicoloured 12 15
320 40 c. light vermilion, silver and grey-black 20 25
321 45 c. multicoloured 25 25

Designs:—25 c. Specimen one-dollar banknote; 40 c. Half-dollar of 1801 and current 4-dollar coin; 45 c. Coins of 1801 and 1960.

* This is the local date of issue; the Crown Agents released the stamps on 28 April.

1975–76. *As Nos.* 206 *etc. but W* w.**14** *(upright on* 3 *and* 15 *c.; sideways on others).*

325 **72** 3 c. multicoloured .. 5 5
326 **73** 4 c. multicoloured .. 5 5
327 **74** 5 c. multicoloured .. 5 5
328 **75** 6 c. multicoloured .. 5 5
329 **76** 10 c. multicoloured .. 5 5
330 **77** 15 c. multicoloured .. 5 8
331 **78** 20 c. multicoloured .. 8 8
334 **81** 60 c. multicoloured .. 20 25
325/34 .. .. *Set of* 8 40 45

Dates of issue: 11.6.75, 5, 6 and 20 c.; 11.6.76, others.

Nos. 322/37 have been allocated to this issue.

108. Evangeline Booth (Salvation Army General).

(Des. Jennifer Toombs. Litho. Questa.)

1975 (15 SEPT.). *International Women's Year. T* **108** *and similar vert. designs. Multicoloured. W* w.**12**. *P* 14.

338 4 c. Type **108** 5 5
339 25 c. Sylvia Pankhurst .. 12 15
340 40 c. Marie Curie 20 25
341 $2·50, Lady Annie Allen (teacher and guider) .. 1·25 1·40

109. Golfer.

(Des. Sue Lawes. Litho. Questa.)

1975 (1 Nov.). *Opening of Frigate Bay Golf Course. W* w.**14** *(sideways). P* 13½.

342 **109** 4 c. black and rose-red 5 5
343 „ 25 c. blk. & greenish yell. 12 15
344 „ 40 c. black and lt. emerald 20 25
345 „ $1 black and new blue .. 40 45

110. " St. Paul " (Sacchi Pier Francesco).

(Des. J.W. Ltd. Litho. Questa.)

1975 (1 Dec.). *Christmas. T* **110** *and similar vert. designs showing details from paintings in the National Gallery, London. Multicoloured. W* w.**14**. *P* 13½.

346	25 c. Type **110**	12	15
347	40 c. " St. James " (Bonifazio di Pitati)	15	20
348	45 c. " St. John " (Mola) ..	20	25
349	$1 " St. Mary " (Raphael) ..	45	50

111. " Crucifixion " (detail).

(Des. J. E. Cooter. Litho. Questa.)

1976 (14 Apr.). *Easter. Stained-glass Windows. T* **111** *and similar vert. designs. Multicoloured. W* w.**14**. *P* 14×13½ (4 *c.*) *or* 14 (*others*).

350	4 c. } " Crucifixion "	5	5
351	4 c. } " Crucifixion " ..	5	5
352	4 c. } " Crucifixion "	5	5
353	25 c. " Last Supper " ..	12	15
354	40 c. " Last Supper " (*different*)	20	25
355	$1 " Baptism of Christ "	40	45
350/5	.. .. *Set of* 6	70	80

Nos. 350/2 were printed horizontally *se-tenant*, together forming a composite design, No. 350 being illustrated.

Nos. 353/5 are smaller, 27×35 mm.

1976 (8 July). *West Indian Victory in World Cricket Cup. As Nos.* 559/60 *of Barbados.*

356	12 c. Map of the Caribbean ..	8	8
357	40 c. Prudential Cup ..	20	20
MS358	95×80 mm. Nos. 356/7 ..	30	30

112. Crispus Attucks and the Boston Massacre.

(Des. J.W. Ltd. Litho. Questa.)

1976 (26 July). *Bicentenary of American Revolution. T* **112** *and similar horiz. designs. Multicoloured. W* w.**14** (*sideways*). *P* 13½.

359	20 c. Type **112**	10	10
360	40 c. Alexander Hamilton and Battle of Yorktown ..	20	20
361	45 c. Jefferson and Declaration of Independence ..	20	20
362	$1 Washington and the Crossing of the Delaware	40	45

113. " The Nativity " (Sforza Book of Hours).

(Des. Jennifer Toombs. Litho. Questa.)

1976 (1 Nov.). *Christmas. T* **113** *and similar vert. designs. Multicoloured. W* w.**14**. *P* 14.

363	20 c. Type **113**	8	10
364	40 c. " Virgin and Child with St. John " (Pintoricchio)	15	20
365	45 c. " Our Lady of Good Children " (Ford Maddox-Brown)	20	20
366	$1 " Little Hands Outstretched to Bless " (M. Tarrant)	40	45

114. Royal Visit, 1966.

(Des. J.W. Ltd. Litho. Questa.)

1977 (7 Feb.). *Silver Jubilee. T* **114** *and similar vert. designs. Multicoloured. W* w.**14**. *P* 13½.

367	50 c. Type **114**	20	25
368	55 c. The Sceptre	25	25
369	$1.50, Bishops paying homage	60	70

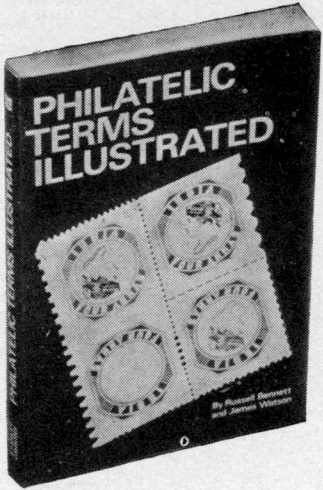

ST. LUCIA.

For GREAT BRITAIN stamps used in St. Lucia with "A 11" obliteration, see index to Great Britain Stamps Used Abroad list.

I. CROWN COLONY.

1

(Recess. Perkins, Bacon & Co.)

1860 (18 Dec.). *Wmk. Small Star, T w.2.* P 14 to 16.
1 **1** (1d.) rose-red .. .. 55·00 45·00
a. Imperf. betwn. (horiz. pr.)
b. Double impression ..
2 ,, (4d.) blue £180 £150
2a ,, (4d.) deep blue .. ..
b. Imperf. between (horiz. pr.)
3 ,, (6d.) green £200 £175
a. Imperf. between (horiz. pr.)
4 ,, (6d.) deep green £200 £175

(Printed by De La Rue.)

1863. *Wmk. Crown CC.* P 12½.
5 **1** (1d.) lake .. .. 25·00 35·00
a. Imperf. £600
6 ,, (1d.) brownish lake .. 35·00 40·00
7 ,, (4d.) indigo .. .. 75·00 80·00
a. Imperf. £400
8 ,, (6d.) emerald-green .. £150 £140

Half penny (2) HALFPENNY (3) 2½ PENCE (4)

Prepared for use, but not issued.

Surch. as T **2**. *Wmk. Crown CC.* P 12½.
9 **1** ½d. on (6d.) emerald-green 20·00
10 ,, 6d. on (4d.) indigo .. £650

1864 (19 Nov.). *Wmk. Crown CC.* (a) P 12½.
11 **1** (1d.) black .. .. 10·00 10·00
a. Intense black .. .. 9·00 9·00
aa. Imperf. (pair) £300
12 ,, (4d.) yellow .. .. 55·00 22·00
a. Imperf. .. ..
b. Lemon-yellow £200
c. Chrome-yellow .. .. 55·00 22·00
d. Olive-yellow .. .. 60·00 30·00
13 ,, (6d.) violet .. .. 30·00 22·00
a. Mauve .. .. 70·00 22·00
aa. Imperf. £250
b. Deep lilac .. .. 40·00 22·00
ba. Imperf. £250
14 ,, (1s.) brown-orange .. 90·00 22·00
a. Imperf. £250
b. Orange .. .. 90·00 22·00
c. Pale orange .. .. 70·00 22·00
ca. Imperf. between horiz. pr.)

(b) P 14.
15 **1** (1d.) black .. .. 9·00 10·00
a. Imperf. between (horiz. pr.)
16 ,, (4d.) yellow .. .. 28·00 15·00
a. Olive-yellow .. .. 32·00 30·00
17 ,, (6d.) mauve .. .. 30·00 18·00
a. Pale lilac .. .. 30·00 15·00
b. Violet .. .. 75·00 30·00
18 ,, (1s.) orange .. .. £100 20·00
a. Deep orange .. .. 75·00 15·00
aa. Imperf. £175

1881 (Sept.). *Surch. with T* **3** *or* **4**. *Wmk. Crown CC.* P 14.
23 **1** ½d. green .. .. .. 18·00 20·00
24 ,, 2½d. brown-red .. .. 10·00 10·00

The 1d. black is known surcharged "1d." in violet ink by hand, but there is no evidence that this was done officially.

1882–84. *Surch. as T* **3**. *Wmk. Crown CA.*

(a) P 14.
25 **1** ½d. green (1882) .. .. 10·00 12·00
26 ,, 1d. black (C.) .. .. 9·00 9·00
a. Bisected (on cover) .. † £550
27 ,, 4d. yellow .. .. 60·00 20·00
28 ,, 6d. violet .. .. 18·00 18·00
29 ,, 1s. orange .. .. £100 75·00

(b) P 12.
30 **1** 4d. yellow .. .. £100 18·00

Deep blue stamps, wmk. Crown CA, perf. 14 or 12, are fiscals from which the overprint "THREE PENCE—REVENUE", or "REVENUE", has been fraudulently removed.

5

(Typo. D.L.R.)

1882–86. *Wmk. Crown CA.* P 14. Die I.
31 **5** ½d. dull green .. .. 1·40 1·40
32 ,, 1d. carmine-rose .. .. 7·00 7·00
33 ,, 2½d. blue .. .. 4·50 1·10
34 ,, 4d. brown (1885) .. .. 6·00 1·40
a. Imperf. £200
35 ,, 6d. lilac (1886) £120 £110
a. Imperf. (pair) £800
36 ,, 1s. orange-brown (1885) .. £110 60·00

Wmk. Crown CA. P 14.

1886–87. Die I.
39 **5** 1d. dull mauve .. .. 1·75 3·25
a. Imperf. (pair) £250
40 ,, 3d. dull mauve and green .. 12·00 9·50
41 ,, 6d. dull mve. & blue (1887) 4·25 6·50
42 ,, 1s. dull mve. & red (1887) 15·00 13·00
39/42 Optd. "Specimen" *Set of* 4 40·00

1891–98. Die II.
43 **5** ½d. dull green 12 15
44 ,, 1d. dull mauve 40 15
45 ,, 2d. ultram. & orange ('98) 1·10 1·10
46 ,, 2½d. ultramarine .. .. 1·00 25
47 ,, 3d. dull mauve and green 2·00 2·25
48 ,, 4d. brown .. .. 1·75 2·00
49 ,, 6d. dull mauve and blue .. 3·00 5·00
50 ,, 1s. dull mauve and red .. 2·25 4·00
51 ,, 5s. dull mauve and orange 11·00 16·00
52 ,, 10s. dull mauve and black .. 23·00 24·00
43/52 .. .. *Set of* 10 40·00 50·00
45, 51, 52 Optd. "Specimen" *Set of* 3 40·00

For description and illustration of differences between Die I and Die II see Introduction.

ONE HALF PENNY (6) ½d (7) ONE PENNY (8)

N Normal "N". N Thick "N".

Three types of T **8**.

I. All letters "N" normal.
II. Thick diagonal stroke in first "N".
III. Thick diagonal stroke in second "N".

1891–92. *Stamps of Die I surch.*
53 **6** ½d. on 3d. dull mve. & green 22·00 22·00
a. Small "A" in "HALF" .. 32·00 32·00
b. Small "O" in "ONE" .. 32·00 32·00
54 **7** ½d. on half 6d. dull mauve and blue .. .. 8·00 8·00
a. No fraction bar .. .. 60·00 60·00
b. Surch. sideways £125
c. Surch. double £150 £160
d. "2" in fraction omitted .. £125
e. Thick "1" with sloping serif 60·00 60·00
f. Surch. triple £225
g. Figure "7" used as fraction bar £100 £100
55 **8** 1d. on 4d. brown (I) (12.91) 3·00 3·00
a. Surch. double .. 65·00
b. Surch. inverted .. — £250
c. Type II .. .. 5·00 5·00
ca. Surch. double .. 65·00
cb. Surch. inverted .. — £250
d. Type III .. .. 6·00 6·00

Stamp of Die II surch.
56 **6** ½d. on 3d. dull mve. & green 18·00 15·00
a. Surch. double £300 £275
b. Surch. inverted £650 £275
c. Small "O" in "ONE" .. 60·00 60·00
d. Small "A" in "HALF" .. 60·00 60·00

9

10

(Typo. De La Rue.)

1902–3. *Wmk. Crown CA.* P 14.
58 **9** ½d. dull purple and green 45 40
59 ,, 1d. dull purple & carmine 55 45
60 ,, 2½d. dull purple & ultram. 4·00 4·50
61 **10** 3d. dull purple and yellow 3·50 4·00
62 ,, 1s. green and black .. 5·00 6·00
58/62 .. .. *Set of* 5 12·00 14·00
58/62 Optd. "Specimen" *Set of* 5 42·00

11. The Pitons.

(Recess. De La Rue.)

1902 (15 Dec.). *400th Anniv. of Discovery by Columbus. Wmk. Crown CC, sideways.* P 14.
63 **11** 2d. green and brown .. 2·75 4·00
63 Optd. "Specimen" .. .. 40·00

This stamp was formerly thought to have been issued on 16 December but it has been seen on a postcard clearly postmarked 15 December.

1904–10. *Wmk. Mult. Crown CA.* P 14.
64 **9** ½d. dull purple & grn., CO 35 40
65 ,, ½d. green, O (1907) 25 15
66 ,, 1d. dull pur. & carm., CO 35 12
67 ,, 1d. carmine, O (1907) .. 35 12
68 ,, 2½d. dull pur. & ultram., CO 1·90 3·00
69 ,, 2½d. blue, O (1907) .. .. 1·50 2·25
70 **10** 3d. dull purple & yellow, O 2·25 4·00
71 ,, 3d. purple/*yellow*, C (1909) 90 2·50
72 ,, 6d. dull purple & violet, CO (1905) .. .. 4·00 5·00
a. Dull & brt. purple, C ('07) 3·50 5·50
73 ,, 6d. dull purple, C (1910) .. 7·00 8·00
74 ,, 1s. green & black, C ('05) 8·00 9·00
75 ,, 1s. black/*green*, C (1909) .. 5·50 7·00
76 ,, 5s. green & carm., O ('05) 15·00 18·00
77 ,, 5s. grn. & red/*yell.*, C ('07) 18·00 22·00
64/77 .. .. *Set of* 13 60·00 75·00
65, 67, 69, 71/3, 75/7 Optd. "Specimen" .. .. *Set of* 9 75·00

12

13

14

15

16

(Typo. De La Rue.)

1912–20. *Wmk. Mult. Crown CA.* P 14.

No.	Type	Description	Unused	Used
78	**12**	½d. deep green, O ..	15	15
		a. *Yellow-green*, O ('16) ..	20	15
79	,,	1d. carmine-red, O ..	1·00	8
		a. *Scarlet*, O (1916) ..	80	8
		b. *Rose-red*, O	70	25
80	**13**	2d. grey, O	1·60	2·50
		a. *Slate-grey*, O (1916) ..	3·50	4·00
81	**12**	2½d. ultramarine, O ..	1·25	1·60
		a. *Bright blue*, O (1918) ..	1·10	1·60
		b. *Deep bright blue*, O ..	3·00	3·00
82	**15**	3d. purple/*yellow*, C ..	65	1·10
		a. *On pale yellow* (Die I) ..	3·25	3·50
		b. *On pale yellow* (Die II) ..	3·25	4·50
83	**14**	4d. black & red/*yellow*, C	85	2·00
		a. *White back* (Optd. S. £8) ..	80	2·00
84	**15**	6d. dull & bright pur., C	1·60	3·25
		a. *Grey-pur. & pur.*, C ('18)	3·25	4·50
85	,,	1s. black/*green*, C ..	2·25	3·25
		a. *On blue-green, olive back* ..	3·00	3·50
86	,,	1s. orge.-brn., C (1920) ..	1·00	2·50
87	**16**	2s. 6d. blk. & red/*blue*, C	8·00	10·00
88	**15**	5s. green & red/*yellow*, C	15·00	18·00
78/88		.. .. *Set of* 11	30·00	42·00
78/88		Optd. "Specimen" *Set of* 11	75·00	

(17)

WAR TAX
(18)

1916 (June). *Optd. locally with T* **17**.

No.	Type	Description	Unused	Used
89	**12**	1d. scarlet	1·60	2·75
		a. Opt. double	£120	£130
		b. *Carmine*	11·00	12·00

1916 (Sept.). *Optd. in London with T* **18**.

No.	Type	Description	Unused	Used
90	**12**	1d. scarlet (Optd. S. £17)	8	8

1921–26. *Wmk. Mult. Script CA.* P 14.

No.	Type	Description	Unused	Used
91	**12**	½d. green, O	12	10
92	,,	1d. rose-carmine, O ..	90	2·50
93	,,	1d. deep brown, O (1922)	20	12
94	**14**	1½d. dull carmine, O (1922)	25	45
95	**13**	2d. slate-grey, O ..	20	15
96	**12**	2½d. bright blue, O ..	95	1·10
97	,,	2½d. orange, O (1925)	4·00	4·50
98	,,	2½d. dull blue, O (1926) ..	1·00	1·10
99	**15**	3d. bright blue, O (1922)	2·50	3·50
		a. *Dull blue*, O (1926) ..	90	1·40
100	,,	3d. purple/*yellow*, C (1926)	40	1·10
		a. *Deep purple/yellow*, C ..	1·40	1·90
101	**14**	4d. blk. & red/*yell.*, C ('24)	55	1·90
102	**15**	6d. grey-pur. & pur., C ..	1·10	2·50
103	,,	1s. orange-brown, C ..	1·40	3·00
104	**16**	2s. 6d. black and red/blue, C (1924)	5·50	9·50
105	**15**	5s. green & red/*pale yell.*, C (1923)	11·00	14·00
91/105		.. .. *Set of* 15	26·00	40·00
91/105		Optd. "Specimen" *Set of* 15	90·00	

1935 (6 May). *Silver Jubilee. As Nos.* 91/4 *of Antigua.* P 13½ × 14.

No.	Description	Unused	Used
109	½d. black and green	15	25
110	2d. ultramarine and grey ..	40	65
111	2½d. brown and deep blue ..	75	1·10
112	1s. slate and purple ..	2·50	3·00
109/12	Perf. "Specimen" *Set of* 4	17·00	

19. Port Castries.

20. Columbus Square, Castries.

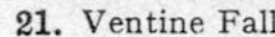
21. Ventine Falls.

23. Inniskilling Monument.

22. Fort Rodney, Pigeon Island.

24. Government House.

25. The Badge of the Colony.

(Recess. De La Rue & Co. Ltd.)

1936 (1 Mar.–Apr.). *Wmk. Mult. Script CA.* P 14 *or* 13 × 12 (1s. *and* 10s.).

No.	Type	Description	Unused	Used
113	**19**	½d. black & bright green	15	12
		a. P. 13 × 12 (8.4.36) ..	12	35
114	**20**	1d. black and brown ..	12	12
		a. P 13 × 12 (8.4.36)	80	80
115	**21**	1½d. black and scarlet ..	15	20
		a. P 12 × 13	4·50	1·40
116	**19**	2d. black and grey ..	15	25
117	**20**	2½d. black and blue ..	25	30
118	**21**	3d. black and dull green	60	70
119	**19**	4d. black and red-brown	40	65
120	**20**	6d. black and orange ..	60	80
121	**22**	1s. black and light blue	80	1·75
122	**23**	2s. 6d. black and ultram.	4·50	5·50
123	**24**	5s. black and violet ..	5·00	7·00
124	**25**	10s. black and carmine ..	18·00	22·00
113/124		.. .. *Set of* 12	27·00	35·00
113/24		Perf. "Specimen" *Set of* 12	48·00	

1937 (12 May). *Coronation Issue. As T* **2** *of Aden, inscr.* "ST. LUCIA". *Recess. B. W. & Co. Wmk. Mult. Script CA.* P 11 × 11½.

No.	Description	Unused	Used
125	1d. violet	8	8
126	1½d. carmine	8	8
127	2½d. blue	8	8
125/27	Perf. "Specimen" *Set of* 3	12·00	

26. King George VI.

31. Device of St. Lucia.

27. Columbus Square.

28. Government House.

29. The Pitons.

30. Loading Bananas.

(Recess. Waterlow (T **26** and **30**), D.L.R. (T **27/8**) and B.W. (T **29** and **31**).)

1938 (22 Sept.)–**48**. *Wmk. Mult. Script CA (sideways on 2s.).*

128 **26** ½d. green (*p*. 14½×14) .. 10 8
  a. Perf. 12½ ('43) .. 8 8
129 ,, 1d. violet (*p*. 14½×14) .. 65 10
  a. Perf. 12½ ('38) .. 8 10
129*b* ,, 1d. scarlet (*p*. 12½) ('47) 10 8
  c. Perf. 14½×14 ('48) .. 10 8
130 ,, 1½d. scarlet (*p*. 14½×14) 10 8
  a. Perf. 12½ ('43) .. 10 15
131 ,, 2d. grey (*p*. 14½×14) .. 8 15
  a. Perf. 12½ ('43) .. 8 8
132 ,, 2½d. ultram. (*p*. 14½×14) 8 8
  a. Perf. 12½ ('43) .. 8 8
132*b* ,, 2½d. violet (*p*. 12½) ('47) .. 8 8
133 ,, 3d. orange (*p*. 14½×14 10 10
  a. Perf. 12½ ('43) .. 10 8
133*b* ,, 3½d. ultram. (*p*. 12½) ('47) 10 10
134 **27** 6d. claret (*p*. 13½) .. 50 50
  a. Carmine-lake (*p*. 13½,) ('45) 1·75 1·10
  aa. Perf. 12. *Claret* ('48) .. 1·10 1·10
134*b* **26** 8d. brown (*p*. 12½) ('46) 30 40
135 **28** 1s. brown (*p*. 13½) .. 55 55
  a. Perf. 12 ('48) .. .. 75 1·10
136 **29** 2s. blue & purple (*p*. 12) 1·10 1·10
136*a* **26** 3s. brt. pur. (*p*. 12½) ('46) 1·90 2·75
137 **30** 5s. blk. & mauve (*p*. 12½) 1·60 2·75
138 **31** 10s. black/*yellow* (*p*. 12) .. 2·75 4·00
141 **26** £1 sepia (*p*. 12½) ('46) .. 8·00 8·50
128/141 .. .. *Set of* 17 16·00 18·00
128/41 Perf. "Specimen" *Set of* 17 95·00

1946 (8 Oct.). *Victory. As Nos.* 28/9 *of Aden.*

142 1d. lilac 8 8
143 3½d. blue 10 8
142/3 Perf. "Specimen" *Set of* 2 14·00

1948 (26 Nov.). *Royal Silver Wedding. As Nos.* 30/1 *of Aden.*

144 1d. scarlet 8 8
145 £1 purple-brown .. .. 6·50 8·00

New Currency. 100 cents = 1 West Indian dollar.

32. King George VI. 33. Device of St. Lucia.

(Recess. Waterlow (**32**). B.W. (**33**).)

1949 (1 Oct.)–**50**. *Value in cents or dollars. Wmk. Mult. Script CA. P* 12½ (1 *c. to* 16 *c.*), 11×11½ *others*).

146 **32** 1 c. green 8 8
  a. Perf. 14 ('49) 25 35
147 **32** 2 c. magenta 8 8
  a. Perf. 14½×14 ('49) .. 50 60
148 ,, 3 c. scarlet 8 10
149 ,, 4 c. grey 8 8
  a. Perf. 14½×14 .. .. — £500
150 ,, 5 c. violet 8 8
151 ,, 6 c. orange 8 8
152 ,, 7 c. ultramarine 8 8
153 ,, 12 c. claret 20 30
  a. Perf. 14½×14 ('50) .. £100 75·00
154 ,, 16 c. brown 20 15
155 **33** 24 c. light blue 25 25
156 ,, 48 c. olive-green 90 80
157 ,, $1.20, purple .. .. 1·10 1·40
158 ,, $2.40, blue-green .. 2·75 3·75
159 ,, $4.80, rose-carmine .. 5·50 6·00
146/159 .. .. *Set of* 14 10·00 12·00

1949 (10 Oct.). *75th Anniv. of Universal Postal Union. As Nos.* 114/7 *of Antigua.*

160 5 c. violet 10 15
161 6 c. orange 10 15
162 12 c. magenta 20 35
163 24 c. blue-green 40 65

1951 (16 Feb.). *Inauguration of B.W.I. University College. As Nos.* 118/9 *of Antigua.*

164 3 c. black and scarlet .. 8 8
165 12 c. black and deep carmine 15 15

34. Phoenix Rising from Burning Buildings.

NEW 1951
CONSTITUTION
(35)

(Flames typo., rest recess. B.W.)

1951 (19 June). *Reconstruction of Castries. Wmk. Mult. Script CA. P* 13½×13.

166 **34** 12 c. red and blue .. 40 45

1951 (25 Sept.). *New Constitution. Optd. with T* **35** *by Waterlow. P* 12½.

167 **32** 2 c. magenta 8 8
168 ,, 4 c. grey 8 8
169 ,, 5 c. violet 10 12
170 ,, 12 c. claret 15 30

1953 (2 June). *Coronation. As No.* 47 *of Aden.*

171 3 c. black and scarlet .. 12 30

36. Queen Elizabeth II. 37. Device of St. Lucia.

(Recess. Waterlow (T **36**) until 1960, then De La Rue. B.W. (T **37**).)

1953–54. *Wmk. Mult. Script CA. P* 14½×14 (*T* **36**) *or* 11×11½ (*T* **37**).

172 **36** 1 c. green 5 5
173 ,, 2 c. magenta 5 5
174 ,, 3 c. red 5 5
175 ,, 4 c. slate 5 5
176 ,, 5 c. violet (*shades*) .. 8 8
177 ,, 6 c. orange (*shades*) .. 10 10
178 ,, 8 c. lake 10 12
179 ,, 10 c. ultramarine (*shades*) 15 20
180 ,, 15 c. red-brown (*shades*) .. 20 20
181 **37** 25 c. deep turquoise-blue 35 35
182 ,, 50 c. deep olive-green .. 85 85
183 ,, $1 bluish green .. 1·50 1·75
184 ,, $2.50 carmine .. 4·50 5·00
172/84 .. .. *Set of* 13 7·00 7·50

Dates of issue:—28.10.53, 2 c.; 7.1.54, 4 c.; 1.4.54, 1 c., 5 c.; 2.9.54, others.

1958 (22 Apr.). *Inauguration of British Caribbean Federation. As Nos.* 135/7 *of Antigua.*

185 3 c. deep green 10 12
186 6 c. blue 15 20
187 12 c. scarlet 30 30

II. MINISTERIAL GOVERNMENT.

38. Columbus's *Santa Maria* off the Pitons.

(Recess. Waterlow.)

1960 (1 Jan.). *New Constitution for the Windward and Leeward Islands. W* w.**12**. *P* 13.

188 **38** 8 c. carmine-red 25 25
189 ,, 10 c. red orange 30 30
190 ,, 25 c. deep blue 45 50

39. Stamp of 1860.

(Recess. Waterlow.)

1960 (18 Dec.). *Stamp Centenary. W* w.**12**. *P* 13½.

191 **39** 5 c. rose-red & ultram. .. 25 25
192 ,, 16 c. dp. blue & yell.-grn. 40 40
193 ,, 25 c. green & carmine-red 55 60

1963 (4 June) *Freedom from Hunger. As No.* 76 *of Aden.*

194 25 c. bluish green 45 45

1963 (2 Sept.). *Red Cross Centenary. As Nos.* 147/8 *of Antingua.*

195 4 c. red and blue 10 10
196 25 c. red and blue 60 65

40. Queen Elizabeth II 41. (after A. C. Davidson-Houston).

42. Fishing Boats.

43. Pigeon Island. (*As T* **42.**)

44. Reduit Beach. (*As T* **42.**)

45. Castries Harbour.

46. The Pitons. (*As T* **45.**)

47. Vigie Beach. **48.** Queen Elizabeth II.

(Des. V. Whiteley. Photo. Harrison.)

1964 (1 Mar.). *W* w.**12**. *P* 14½ (*T* **40**), *others* 14½ × 14 (*vert.*) *or* 14 × 14½ (*horiz.*).

197 **40**	1 c. crimson	.. ..	5	5
198 ,,	2 c. bluish violet	..	5	5
199 ,,	4 c. turq.-green (*shades*)	..	5	5
200 ,,	5 c. Prussian blue	..	8	8
201 ,,	6 c. yellow-brown	..	8	8
202 **41**	8 c. multicoloured	..	10	10
203 ,,	10 c. multicoloured	..	12	12
204 **42**	12 c. multicoloured	..	15	15
205 **43**	15 c. multicoloured	..	20	20
206 **44**	25 c. multicoloured	..	35	30
207 **45**	35 c. blue and buff	..	60	45
208 **46**	50 c. multicoloured	..	65	80
209 **47**	$1 multicoloured	..	1·75	1·75
210 **48**	$2.50 multicoloured	..	3·50	3·00
197/210	.. .. *Set of* 14		6·50	6·00

See also No. 249.

1964 (23 April). *400th Anniv. of Birth of William Shakespeare. As No.* 164 *of Antigua.*

211	10 c. blue-green	.. ..	20	25

1965 (17 May). *I.T.U. Centenary. As Nos.* 166/7 *of Antigua.*

212	2 c. mauve and magenta	..	8	10
213	50 c. lilac and light olive-green		65	70

1965 (25 Oct.). *International Co-operation Year. As Nos.* 168/9 *of Antigua.*

214	1 c. reddish pur. & turq.-grn.		5	5
215	25 c. dp. bluish green & lav.		35	40

1966 (24 Jan.). *Churchill Commemoration. As Nos.* 170/3 *of Antigua.*

216	4 c. new blue	.. ..	8	10
217	6 c. deep green	.. ..	10	10
218	25 c. brown	.. ..	30	35
219	35 c. bluish violet	.. ..	45	50

1966 (4 Feb.). *Royal Visit. As Nos.* 174/5 *of Antigua.*

220	4 c. black and ultramarine	..	8	10
221	25 c. black and magenta	..	35	40

1966 (1 July). *World Cup Football Championships. As Nos.* 176/7 *of Antigua.*

222	4 c. violet, yellow-green, lake and yellow-brown	..	8	10
223	25 c. chocolate, blue-grn., lake and yellow-brown	..	25	30

1966 (20 Sept.). *Inauguration of W.H.O. Headquarters, Geneva. As Nos.* 178/9 *of Antigua.*

224	4 c. black, yellow-green and light blue	.. ..	8	8
225	25 c. black, light purple and yellow-brown	.. ..	35	40

1966 (1 Dec.). *20th Anniv. of U.N.E.S.C.O. As Nos.* 196/8 *of Antigua.*

226	4 c. slate-violet, red, yellow and orange	.. ..	8	8
227	12 c. orange-yellow, violet and deep olive	.. ..	15	15
228	25 c. black, bright purple and orange	.. .. ..	35	40

III. ASSOCIATED STATEHOOD.

STATEHOOD
1st MARCH 1967
(49)

STATEHOOD
1st MARCH 1967
(50)

51. Map of St. Lucia.

(Optd. by Art Printery, Castries from dies supplied by Harrison.)

1967 (7 Mar.). *Statehood.* (*a*) *Postage. Nos.* 198 *and* 200/9 *optd. with T* **49** (2, 5, 6 *c.*) *or T* **50** (*others*) *in red.*

229 **40**	2 c. bluish violet	..	8	8
	a. Horiz. pair, one without opt.			
230 ,,	5 c. Prussian blue	..	8	8
	a. Opt. inverted ..	..	40·00	
231 ,,	6 c. yellow-brown	..	10	10
232 **41**	8 c. multicoloured	..	12	12
233 ,,	10 c. multicoloured	..	15	15
234 **42**	12 c. multicoloured	..	20	20
235 **43**	15 c. multicoloured	..	25	30
236 **44**	25 c. multicoloured	..	40	45
237 **45**	35 c. blue and buff	..	55	60
238 **46**	50 c. multicoloured	..	75	85
239 **47**	$1 multicoloured	..	1·50	1·75
229/39	.. .. *Set of* 11		3·75	4·00

Overprinted 1 c. and $2.50 stamps were prepared for issue but were not put on sale over the post office counter. Later, however, they were accepted for franking.

(Photo. Harrison.)

(*b*) *Air. P* 14½ × 14.

240 **51**	15 c. new blue	.. ..	15	20

52. " Madonna, Child and St. John " (Raphael).

(Des. and photo. Harrison.)

1967 (16 Oct.). *Christmas. W* w.**12** (*sideways*). *P* 14½.

241 **52**	4 c. multicoloured	..	10	10
242 ,,	25 c. multicoloured	..	30	35

53. Batsman and Sir Frederick Clarke (Governor).

(Des. V. Whiteley. Photo. Harrison.)

1968 (8 Mar.). *M.C.C.'s West Indies Tour. W* w.**12** (*sideways*). *P* 14½ × 14.

243 **53**	10 c. multicoloured	..	10	10
244 ,,	35 c. multicoloured	..	30	35

54. " The Crucifixion " (after Raphael). **55.** " Noli me tangere " (detail by Titian).

(Des. and photo. Harrison.)

1968 (25 Mar.). *Easter Commemoration. W* w.**12** (*sideways*). *P* 14 × 14½.

245 **54**	10 c. multicoloured	..	8	8
246 **55**	15 c. multicoloured	..	10	10
247 **54**	25 c. multicoloured	..	20	20
248 **55**	35 c. multicoloured	..	25	25

1968. *As No.* 205 *but W* w.**12** (*sideways*).

249 **43**	15 c. mult. (14.5.68)	..	15	15

56. Dr. Martin Luther King.

(Des. V. Whiteley. Litho. De La Rue.)

1968 (4 July). *Martin Luther King Commemoration. W* w.**12**. *P* 13½ × 14.

250 **56**	25 c. blue, black and flesh		25	25
251 ,,	35 c. vio.-bl., blk. & flesh		30	30

57. " Virgin and Child in Glory " (Murillo).

58. " Virgin and Child " (Murillo).

(Des. and photo. Harrison.)

1968 (17 Oct.). *Christmas.* W w.**12** (*sideways*). P 14½×14.

252	**57**	5 c. multicoloured ..	5	5
253	**58**	10 c. multicoloured ..	10	10
254	**57**	25 c. multicoloured ..	25	25
255	**58**	35 c. multicoloured ..	30	35

59. Humming bird.

60. St. Lucia Parrot.

(Des. V. Whiteley. Litho. Format International.)

1969 (10 Jan.). *Birds.* W w.**12** (*sideways*). P 14.

256	**59**	10 c. multicoloured ..	8	8
257	**60**	15 c. multicoloured ..	12	12
258	**59**	25 c. multicoloured ..	25	25
259	**60**	35 c. multicoloured ..	30	35

61. " Ecce Homo " (Reni).

62. " Resurrection of Christ " (Sodoma).

(Des. and photo. Harrison.)

1969 (20 Mar.). *Easter Commemoration.* W w.**12**. (*sideways*. P 14½×14.

260	**61**	10 c. multicoloured ..	10	10
261	**62**	15 c. multicoloured ..	15	15
262	**61**	25 c. multicoloured ..	25	25
263	**62**	35 c. multicoloured ..	30	30

63. Map Showing " CARIFTA " countries.

64. Handclasp and Names of " CARIFTA " Countries.

(Des. J. E. Cooter. Photo. Harrison.)

1969 (29 May). *First Anniv. of CARIFTA (Caribbean Free Trade Area).* W w.**12**. P 14.

264	**63**	5 c. multicoloured ..	5	5
265	,,	10 c. multicoloured ..	8	8
266	**64**	25 c. multicoloured ..	20	20
267	,,	35 c. multicoloured ..	30	35

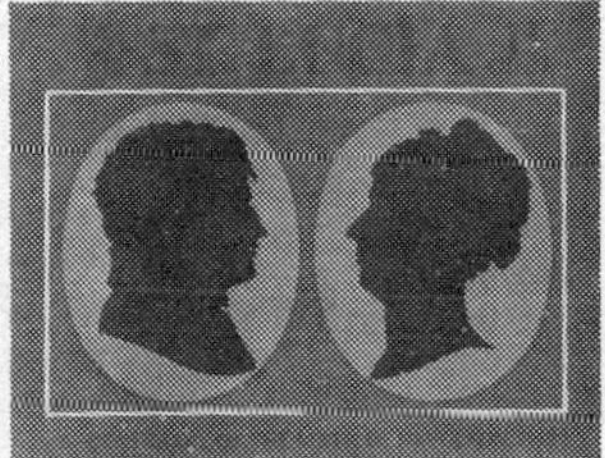

65. Emperor Napoleon and Empress Josephine.

(Des. and litho. Enschedé.)

1969 (22 Sept.). *Birth Bicentenary of Napoleon Bonaparte.* P 14×13.

268	**65**	15 c. multicoloured ..	10	12
269	,,	25 c. multicoloured ..	20	20
270	,,	35 c. multicoloured ..	30	30
271	,,	50 c. multicoloured ..	40	45

66. " Virgin and Child " (Delaroche).

67. " Holy Family " (Rubens).

(Des. J. Waddington Ltd. Photo. Harrison.)

1969 (27 Oct.). *Christmas. Paintings multicoloured; background colours given.* W w.**12** (*sideways*). P 14½×14.

272	**66**	5 c. gold and brt. purple	5	5
273	**67**	10 c. gold & greenish blue	8	8
274	**66**	25 c. gold and crimson ..	25	25
275	**67**	35 c. gold and green ..	30	35

68. House of Assembly.

(Des. J. E. Cooter ($10), Sylvia and M. Goaman) (others). Litho. Questa ($10), Format (others).)

1970 (2 Feb.)–**73**. *T* **68** *and similar designs. Multicoloured.* W w.**12** (*sideways on* 1 *c. to* 35 *c. and* $10). P 14.

276	1 c. Type **68**	5	5
277	2 c. Roman Catholic Cathedral	5	5
278	4 c. The Boulevard, Castries	8	8
279	5 c. Castries Harbour ..	5	5
280	6 c. Sulphur springs ..	5	5
281	10 c. Vigie Airport	8	8
282	12 c. Reduit Beach	8	8
283	15 c. Pigeon Island	10	10
284	25 c. The Pitons and yacht ..	15	15
285	35 c. Marigot Bay	20	20
286	50 c. Diamond Waterfall ..	25	25
287	$1 Flag of St. Lucia ..	40	45
288	$2.50, St. Lucia Coat-of-Arms	1·10	1·25
289	$5 Queen Elizabeth II ..	2·25	2·50
289*a*	$10 Map of St. Lucia .. (3.12.73)	4·50	5·00
276/89*a*	*Set of* 15	8·50	9·50

Nos. 286/9*a* are vertical designs.

See also Nos. 367/8 and 395/8.

70. " The Three Marys at the Tomb" (Hogarth) (*As T* **69.**)

71. " The Ascension " (Hogarth). (*As T* **69** *but larger,* 39×55 *mm.*)

69. " The Sealing of the Tomb " (Hogarth).

(Des. V. Whiteley from the Hogarth Triptych. Litho. Enschedé.)

1970 (7 Mar.). *Easter.* W w.**12** (*sideways*). *Roul.* 9×P 12½.

290	**69**	25 c. multicoloured ..	30	30
291	**70**	35 c. multicoloured ..	40	40
292	**71**	$1 multicoloured ..	1·10	1·25
Strip of three		.. .. ..	1·75	1·90

Nos. 290/2 were issued in sheets of 30 (6×5) containing the Hogarth Triptych spread over all three values of the set. This necessitated a peculiar arrangement with the $1 value (which depicts the centre portion of the triptych) 10 mm. higher than the other values in the *se-tenant* strip.

72. Charles Dickens and Dickensian Characters.

(Des. V. Whiteley. Litho. B.W.)

1970 (8 June). *Death Centenary of Charles Dickens.* W w.**12** (*sideways*). P 14.

293	**72**	1 c. multicoloured ..	5	5
294	,,	25 c. multicoloured ..	25	25
295	,,	35 c. multicoloured ..	30	30
296	,,	50 c. multicoloured ..	40	40

73. Nurse and Emblem.

(Des. R. Granger Barrett. Litho. J.W.)

1970 (18 Aug.). *Centenary of British Red Cross. T* **73** *and similar horiz. design. Multicoloured. W* w.**12** (*sideways*). *P* 14.

297	10 c. Type **73**	8	8
298	15 c. Flags of Great Britain, Red Cross and St. Lucia	10	12
299	25 c. Type **73**	15	20
300	35 c. As 15 c.	25	30

74. " Madonna with the Lilies " (Luca della Robbia).

(Des. Perkins Bacon Ltd. Litho. and embossed. Walsall Security Printers Ltd.)

1970 (16 Nov.). *Christmas. P* 11.

301	**74**	5 c. multicoloured ..	10	10
302	,,	10 c. multicoloured ..	12	12
303	,,	35 c. multicoloured ..	30	35
304	,,	40 c. multicoloured ..	35	40

75. " Christ on the Cross " (Rubens).

(Des. and litho. Enschedé.)

1971 (29 Mar.). *Easter. T* **75** *and similar vert. design. Multicoloured. W* w.**12**. *P* $13\frac{1}{2} \times 13$.

305	10 c. Type **75**	10	10
306	15 c. " Descent from the Cross " (Rubens) ..	12	12
307	35 c. Type **75**	30	30
308	40 c. As 15 c.	30	35

76. Moule à Chique Lighthouse.

(Des. J. Waddington Ltd. Litho. Questa.)

1971 (1 May). *Opening of Beane Field Airport. T* **76** *and similar horiz. designs. Multicoloured. W* w.**12** (*sideways*). *P* $14\frac{1}{2} \times 14$.

309	5 c. Type **76**	8	8
310	25 c. Aircraft landing at Beane Field	25	30

77. Morne Fortune.

78. Morne Fortune, Modern View.

(Des. V. Whiteley. Litho. Questa.)

1971 (10 Aug.). *Old and New Views of St. Lucia. T* **77/8** *and similar horiz. designs. Multicoloured. W* w.**12** (*sideways*). *P* $13\frac{1}{2} \times 13$.

311	5 c.	Type **77**	5	5
312	5 c.	Type **78**	5	5
313	10 c.	} Castries city ..	10	10
314	10 c.	} ..	10	10
315	25 c.	} Pigeon Island ..	20	20
316	25 c.	} ..	20	20
317	50 c.	} View from grounds	40	40
318	50 c.	} of Govt. House ..	40	40
311/18		.. .. *Set of* 8	1·25	1·25

Each value of this issue was printed horizontally and vertically *se-tenant* in two designs showing respectively old and new views of St. Lucia.

79. " Virgin and Child " (Verrocchio).

(Des. J. E. Cooter. Litho. J.W.)

1971 (15 Oct.). *Christmas. T* **79** *and similar vert. designs. Multicoloured. W* w.**12**. *P* 14.

319	5 c. Type **79**	5	5
320	10 c. " Virgin and Child " (Morando)	8	8
321	35 c. " Virgin and Child " (Battista)	30	35
322	40 c. Type **79**	35	40

80. " St. Lucia " (Dolci School) and Coat-of-Arms.

(Des. and litho. Harrison.)

1971 (13 Dec.). *National Day. W* w.**12**. *P* $14 \times 14\frac{1}{2}$.

323	**80**	5 c. multicoloured ..	5	5
324	,,	10 c. multicoloured ..	8	8
325	,,	25 c. multicoloured ..	30	30
326	,,	50 c. multicoloured ..	40	45

81. " The Dead Christ Mourned " (Carracci).

(Des. G. Drummond. Litho. Questa.)

1972 (15 Feb.). *Easter. T* **81** *and similar horiz. design. Multicoloured. W* w.**12**. *P* 14.

327	10 c. Type **81**	8	8
328	25 c. " Angels weeping over the dead Christ " (Guercino)	20	20
329	35 c. Type **81**	25	25
330	50 c. As 25 c.	40	45

82. Science Block and Teachers' College.

(Des. P. B. Powell. Litho. Questa.)

1972 (18 Apr.). *Morne Educational Complex T* **82** *and similar horiz. designs. Multicoloured W* w.**12**. *P* 14.

331	5 c. Type **82**	5	5
332	15 c. University Centre ..	12	12
333	25 c. Secondary School ..	15	20
334	35 c. Technical College ..	30	30

83. Steamship Stamp and Map.

(Des. J. E. Cooter. Litho. Questa.)

1972 (22 June). *Centenary of First Postal Service by St. Lucia Steam Conveyance Co. Ltd.* T **83** *and similar horiz. designs.* W w.**12.** P 14.

335 5 c. multicoloured .. 10 10
336 10 c. ultramarine, mauve and black 15 15
337 35 c. light rose-carmine, pale greenish blue and black 30 30
338 50 c. multicoloured .. 40 40

Designs:—10 c. Steamship stamp and Castries Harbour; 35 c. Steamship stamp and Soufrière; 50 c. Steamship stamps.

84. " The Holy Family " (Sebastiano Ricci).

(Des. J. E. Cooter. Litho. J.W.)

1972 (18 Oct.). *Christmas.* W w.**12** (*sideways*). P 14½.

339 **84** 5 c. multicoloured .. 5 5
340 ,, 10 c. multicoloured .. 8 8
341 ,, 35 c. multicoloured .. 30 30
342 ,, 40 c. multicoloured .. 35 35

85. Arms and St. Lucia Parrot.

(Des. (from photograph by D. Groves) and photo. Harrison.)

1972 (20 Nov.). *Royal Silver Wedding. Multicoloured; background colour given.* W w.**12.** P 14×14½.

343 **85** 15 c. carmine 20 25
344 ,, 35 c. yellow-olive .. 35 40

86. Week-day Headdress. **87.** Coat-of-arms.

(Des. Sylvia Goaman. Litho. A. & M.)

1973 (1 Feb.). *Local Headdresses.* T **86** *and similar vert. designs. Multicoloured.* W w.**12.** P 13.

345 5 c. Type **86** 5 5
346 10 c. Formal style 10 10
347 25 c. Unmarried girl's style 25 25
348 50 c. Ceremonial style .. 40 40

(Des. and litho. Harrison.)

1973–76. *Coil Stamps.* P 14½×14.

A. W w.**12** *upright* (19.4.73).
B. W w.**12** *sideways* (1976).

			A.		B.	
349 **87**	5 c. olive-green		5	5	5	5
350 ,,	10 c. new blue		8	8	5	8
351 ,,	25 c. lake-brown		12	12		†

88. H.M.S. *St. Lucia.*

(Des. R. Granger Barrett. Litho. Questa.)

1973 (24 May). *Old Ships.* T **88** *and similar horiz. designs. Multicoloured.* W w.**12.** P 13½×14.

352 15 c. Type **88** 12 12
353 35 c. H.M.S. *Prince of Wales* 30 30
354 50 c. *Oliph Blossom* 40 40
355 $1 H.M.S. *Rose* 70 75
MS356 122×74 mm. Nos. 352/5 2·00 2·00

89. Plantation and Flower.

(Des. PAD Studio. Litho. Walsall.)

1973 (26 July). *Banana Industry.* T **89** *and similar horiz. designs. Multicoloured.* W w.**12.** P 14.

357 5 c. Type **89** 5 5
358 15 c. Aerial spraying .. 15 15
359 35 c. Boxing plant .. 30 30
360 50 c. Loading a boat .. 40 40

90. " The Virgin with Child " (Maratta).

(Des. J. E. Cooter. Litho. Walsall.)

1973 (17 Oct.). *Christmas.* T **90** *and similar vert. designs. Multicoloured.* W w.**12** (*sideways*). P 13½.

361 5 c. Type **90** 5 5
362 15 c. " Virgin in the Meadow " (Raphael) 12 12
363 35 c. " The Holy Family " (Bronzino) 20 25
364 50 c. " Madonna of the Pear " (Dürer) 35 35

1973 (14 Nov.). *Royal Wedding. As Nos.* 165/6 *of Anguilla. Centre multicoloured.* W w.**12** (*sideways*). P 13½.

365 40 c. grey-green 20 25
366 50 c. rosy lilac.. .. .. 25 30

1974 (15 Mar.). *As Nos.* 277/8 *but wmk. upright.*

367 2 c. Roman Catholic Cathedral 5 5
368 4 c. The Boulevard, Castries .. 8 8

See also Nos. 395/8.

91. "The Betrayal".

(Des. J. E. Cooter. Litho. D.L.R.)

1974 (1 Apr.). *Easter.* T **91** *and similar horiz. designs showing paintings by Ugolino. Multicoloured.* W w.**12** (*sideways on Nos.* 369/72, *upright on* **MS**373). P 13.

369 5 c. Type **91** 5 5
370 35 c. "The Way to Calvary" .. 20 20
371 80 c. "The Deposition" .. 45 50
372 $1 "The Resurrection" 55 60
MS373 180×140 mm. Nos. 369/72 1·40 1·60

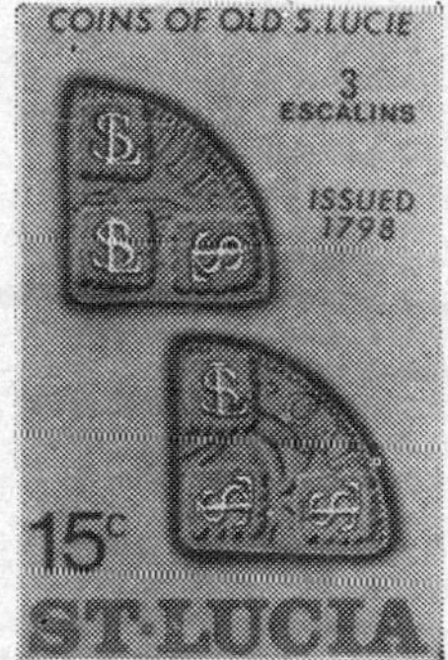

92. 3-Escalins Coins, 1798.

(Des. J. E. Cooter. Litho. Format.)

1974 (20 May). *Coins of Old St. Lucie.* T **92** *and similar vert. designs. Multicoloured.* W w.**12** (*sideways*). P 14×13½.

374 15 c. Type **92** 10 10
375 35 c. 6-escalins coins, 1798 .. 20 20
376 40 c. 2-livres 5-sols coins, 1813 25 25
377 $1 6-livres 15-sols coins, 1813 50 50
MS378 151×115 mm. Nos. 374/7 1·10 1·10

93. Baron de Laborie.

(Des. J.W. Ltd. Litho. Questa.)

1974 (29 Aug.). *Past Governors of St. Lucia. T* **93** *and similar vert. designs. Multicoloured. W* w.**12** *(sideways on Nos.* 379/82, *upright on* **MS**383). *P* 14.

379	5 c. Type **93**	5	5
380	35 c. Sir John Moore	20	20
381	80 c. Sir Dudley Hill	40	45
382	$1 Sir Frederick Clarke ..	45	50
MS383	153×117 mm. Nos. 379/82	1·10	1·25

94. "Virgin and Child" (Andrea del Verrocchio).

(Des. PAD Studio. Litho. D.L.R.)

1974 (18 Nov.). *Christmas. T* **94** *and similar vert. designs. Multicoloured. W* w.**12.** *P* 13×13½.

384	5 c. Type **94**	5	5
385	35 c. "Virgin and Child" (Andrea della Robbia) ..	20	20
386	80 c. "Madonna and Child" (Luca della Robbia) ..	40	45
387	$1 "Virgin and Child" (Rossellino)	45	50
MS388	92×140 mm. Nos. 384/7	1·25	1·40

95. Churchill and Montgomery.

(Des. PAD Studio. Litho. Format.)

1974 (30 Nov.). *Birth Centenary of Sir Winston Churchill. T* **95** *and similar horiz. design. Multicoloured. W* w.**12** *(sideways). P* 14.

389	5 c. Type **95**	5	5
390	$1 Churchill and Truman ..	45	50

96. "The Crucifixion" (Van der Weyden).

(Des. J. E. Cooter. Litho. Questa.)

1975 (27 Mar.). *Easter. T* **96** *and similar vert. designs. Multicoloured. W* w.**12.** *P* 13½.

391	5 c. Type **96**	5	5
392	35 c. "Noli me tangere" (Romano)	15	20
393	80 c. "The Crucifixion" (Gallego)	35	40
394	$1 "Noli me tangere" (Correggio)	45	50

1975 (28 July). *As Nos.* 278 *etc. but W* w.**14** *(sideways).*

395	4 c. The Boulevard, Castries	5	5
396	5 c. Castries Harbour ..	5	5
397	10 c. Vigie Airport	8	8
398	15 c. Pigeon Island	10	10

97. "Nativity" (French Book of Hours).

(Des. J. Cooter. Litho. Questa.)

1975 (12 Dec.). *Christmas. T* **97** *and similar vert. designs. Multicoloured. W* w.**12.** *P* 14½.

399	5 c. Type **97**	5	5
400	10 c. Epiphany scene	8	8
401	10 c. (stained-glass	8	8
402	10 c. window)	8	8
403	40 c. "Nativity" (Hastings Book of Hours) ..	20	25
404	$1 "Virgin and Child" (Bergogne)	40	45
399/404	.. .. *Set of* 6	80	90
MS405	105×109 mm. Nos. 399 and 403/4	70	75

Nos. 400/2 were printed horizontally *se-tenant* within the sheet to form the composite design listed.

98. Naval Vessel *Hanna.*

(Des. J.W. Ltd. Litho. Format.)

1976 (26 Jan.). *Bicentenary of American Revolution. T* **98** *and similar horiz. designs showing ships. Multicoloured. P* 14½.

406	½ c. Type **98**	5	5
407	1 c. Mail Packet *Prince of Orange*	5	5
408	2 c. H.M.S. *Edward*	5	5
409	5 c. Merchantman *Millern*	5	5
410	15 c. Lugger *Surprise*	8	10
411	35 c. H.M.S. *Serapis* ..	15	20
412	50 c. Frigate *Randolph* ..	25	25
413	$1 Frigate *Alliance* ..	40	45
406/13	.. .. *Set of* 8	1·00	1·10
MS414	142×116 mm. Nos. 410/13 P 13	90	95

99. Laughing Gull.

(Des. J.W. Ltd. Litho. Questa.)

1976 (17 May). *T* **99** *and similar vert. designs. Multicoloured. W* w.**12** *(*1 *c.), W* w.**14** *(others). P* 14.

415	1 c. Type **99**	5	5
416	2 c. Little Blue Heron ..	5	5
417	4 c. Belted Kingfisher ..	5	5
418	5 c. St. Lucia Parrot ..	5	5
419	6 c. St. Lucia Oriole	5	5
420	8 c. Trembler	5	5
421	10 c. Sparrow Hawk ..	5	5
422	12 c. Red-billed Tropicbird ..	5	5
423	15 c. Common Gallinule ..	5	5
424	25 c. Brown Noddy	10	10
425	35 c. Sooty Tern	12	15
426	50 c. Osprey	20	20
427	$1 White Breasted Thrasher	35	40
428	$2.50, St. Lucia Black Finch	90	1·00
429	$5 Ramier	1·75	2·00
430	$10 Caribbean Elaenia ..	3·50	4·00
415/30	.. .. *Set of* 16	6·50	7·50

1976 (19 July). *West Indian Victory in World Cricket Cup. As Nos.* 559/60 *of Barbados.*

431	50 c. Caribbean map	20	25
432	$1 Prudential Cup	40	45
MS433	92×79 mm. Nos. 431/2	60	

100. H.M.S. *Ceres.*

(Des. J. E. Cooter. Litho. Walsall.)

1976 (4 Sept.). *Royal Naval Crests. T* **100** *and similar vert. designs. Multicoloured. W* w.**14** *(inverted). P* 14.

434	10 c. Type **100**	5	5
435	20 c. H.M.S. *Pelican*	8	10
436	40 c. H.M.S. *Ganges*	15	20
437	$2 H.M.S. *Ariadne* ..	80	90

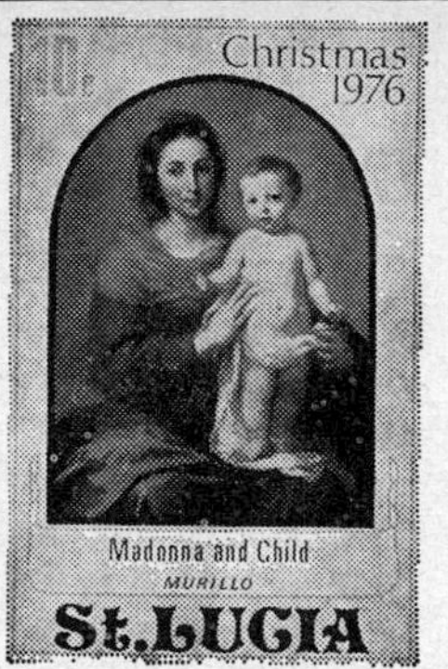

101. " Madonna and Child " (Murillo).

(Des. J. E. Cooter. Litho. Questa.)

976 (15 Nov.). *Christmas. T* **101** *and similar vert. designs. Multicoloured. W* w.**14**. *P* 13½.

38	10 c. Type **101**	5	5
39	20 c. " Virgin and Child " (Costa)	8	10
40	50 c. " Madonna and Child " (Isenbrandt)	20	25
41	$2 " Madonna and Child with St. John " (Murillo) ..	80	90
MS442	105×93 mm. $2.50 T **101**	1·00	1·10

POSTAGE DUE STAMPS.

No. ..4545
ST. LUCIA.
1d.
POSTAGE DUE

D 1

(Type-set. *The Voice* Newspaper, Castries.)

1931. *No wmk. or gum. Rough perf.* 12.

(a) Horizontally laid paper.

D1 D **1**	1d. black/*blue*	40	40
	a. Wide, wrong fount " No."	1·10	1·25

(b) Wove paper.

D2 D **1**	2d. black/*yellow*	60	60
	a. Wide, wrong fount " No."	2·75	2·00
	b. Imperf. between (vert. pr.)	£750	

Nos. D1a and D2a occur in the bottom row of the sheet.

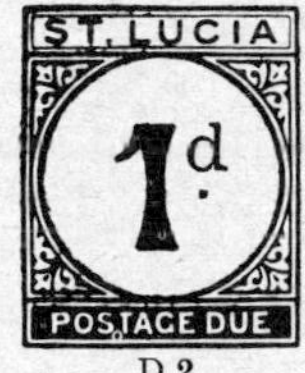

D 2

D 3

(Typo. De La Rue.)

1933–47. *Wmk. Mult. Script CA. P* 14.

D3 D **2**	1d. black	25	25
D4 ,,	2d. black	40	40
D5 ,,	4d. black (28.6.47) ..	40	45
D6 ,,	8d. black (28.6.47) ..	50	55
D3/6	Perf. " Specimen " *Set of* 4	42·00	

1949 (1 Oct.)–**52.** *Value in cents. Wmk. Mult. Script CA. Typo. P* 14.

D 7 D **3**	2 c. black	12	12
	a. Chalky paper (27.11.52)	10	8
	ab. Error. Crown missing, W 9a	16·00	
	ac. Error. St. Edward's Crown, W 9b ..	10·00	
D 8 ,,	4 c. black	20	20
	a. Chalky paper (27.11.52)	12	8
	ab. Error. Crown missing, W 9a	16·00	
	ac. Error. St. Edward's Crown, W 9b ..	12·00	
D 9 ,,	8 c. black	25	30
	a. Chalky paper (27.11.52)	8	8
	ac. Error. St. Edward's Crown, W 9b ...	25·00	
D10 ,,	16 c. black	50	55
	a. Chalky paper (27.11.52)	10	10
	ac. Error. St. Edward's Crown, W 9b ..	18·00	

1965 (9 Mar.). *As Nos.* D7/8 *but wmk.* w.**12**. *Unsurfaced paper. P* 14.

D11 D **3**	2 c. black	8	8
D12 ,,	4 c. black	8	8

POSTAL FISCAL STAMPS.

CANCELLATIONS. Most "used" examples of the Postal Fiscal stamps are with pen cancellations cleaned and forged postmarks applied.

SHILLING STAMP (F 1)

One Penny Stamp (F 2)

1881. *T* 1. *Wmk. Crown CC. P* 14.

(a) Surch. as Type F **1**.

F1	ONE PENNY STAMP, black (C.)	10·00	12·00
	a. Surch inverted	£300	£300
	b. Surch double	£250	£300
F2	FOUR PENNY STAMP, yellow ..	20·00	24·00
	a. Bisected (2d.) (on cover) ..		
F3	SIX PENCE STAMP, mauve ..	35·00	40·00
F4	SHILLING STAMP, orange ..	20·00	24·00
	a. Error. " SHILEING " ..	£250	
	b. Error. " SHILDING " ..	£250	£275

(b) Surch. as Type F **2**.

F 7	One Penny Stamp, black (R.)	10·00	12·00
	a. Surch. double	£300	
F 8	Four Pence Stamp, yellow ..	14·00	16·00
F 9	Six Pence Stamp, mauve ..	14·00	16·00
F10	Shilling Stamp, orange ..	15·00	25·00

HALFPENNY Stamp (F 3)

FOUR PENCE REVENUE (F 4)

(c) Surch. as Type F **3**.

F11	Halfpenny Stamp, green ..	10·00	12·00
	a. " Stamp " double	£160	£175
F12	One Shilling Stamp, orange (*wmk. Crown CA*)	18·00	22·00
	a. " Stamp " double	£160	£200

1882. *T* 1. *Wmk. Crown CA. Surch. as Type* F **4**.

(a) P 14.

F13	1d. black (C.)	5·00	6·00
	a. Imperf. (pair)	£250	
F14	2d. pale blue	2·50	3·50
	a. Imperf. (pair)		
F15	3d. deep blue (C.)	9·00	10·00
F16	4d. yellow	2·50	3·00
F17	6d. mauve	5·50	7·00

(b) P 12.

F18	1d. black (C.)	5·50	7·00
F19	3d. deep blue (C.)	7·00	8·00
F20	1s. orange	7·00	10·00

Revenue (F 5)

REVENUE (F 6)

1883. *Nos.* 25 *and* 26 *optd. at foot with Type* F **5** *locally.*

(a) Word 11 *mm. long.*

F21	1d. black (C.)	4·50	
	a. Opt. inverted		
	b. Opt. double	80·00	£110

(b) Word 13 *mm.*

F22	1d. black (C.)	—	9·00

(c) Word 15½ *mm.*

F23	½d. green	—	10·00
	a. " Revenue " double ..	—	65·00
F24	1d. black (C.)	3·50	4·00
	a. " Revenue " double ..	45·00	
	b. " Revenue " triple ..	80·00	
	c. " Revenue " double, one invtd.	80·00	£100

Nos. 30 *and* 32 *surch. as (c) above.*

F25	1d. rose	—	8·00
F26	4d. yellow	—	11·00

1884. *Optd. with Type* F **6**. *Wmk. Crown CA. P* 14.

F27 **5**	1d. slate (C.)	2·50	3·50
	a. Imperf. (pair)		
F28 ,,	1d. dull mauve (Die I) ..	2·50	3·00

ST. VINCENT.

For GREAT BRITAIN stamps used in St. Vincent with "A 10" obliteration, see index to Great Britain Stamps Used Abroad list.

I. CROWN COLONY.

(T **1**, **3** and **7** recess. Perkins, Bacon & Co.)

1

1861 (8 May). *No wmk.*
(*a*) *Intermediate perf.* 14 *to* 16.
1 **1** 1d. rose-red .. .. .. — £250
a. Imperf. vert. (horiz. pair) .. £400
2 ,, 6d. deep yellow-green .. £2500 £170
(*b*) *Rough perf.* 14 *to* 16.
3 **1** 1d. rose-red .. .. .. 17·00 11·00
a. Imperf. vert. (horiz. pair) .. £225
b. Imperf. (pair) £150

1862 (Sept.). *No wmk. Rough perf.* 14 *to* 16.
4 **1** 6d. deep green.. .. .. 33·00 11·00
a. Imperf. between (horiz. pair) £400
b. Imperf. (pair) £200

1863–68. *No wmk.* (*a*) *P* 11 to 12½.
5 **1** 1d. rose-red (3.63) .. .. 18·00 13·00
6 ,, 4d. deep blue (*shades*) ('66) .. £130 55·00
a. Imperf. between (horiz. pair)
7 ,, 6d. deep green (7.68) .. £100 40·00
8 ,, 1s. slate-grey (8.66) .. £900 £550
(*b*) *P* 14 *to* 16.
9 **1** 1s. slate-grey (*shades*) .. £130 55·00
(*c*) *P* 11 *to* 12½ × 14 *to* 16.
10 **1** 1d. rose-red £1200 £650
11 ,, 1s. slate-grey (*shades*) .. £110 60·00

1869. *Colours changed. No wmk. P* 11 *to* 12½.
12 **1** 4d. yellow .. .. .. £170 80·00
13 ,, 1s. indigo .. .. .. £170 55·00
14 ,, 1s. brown .. .. .. £200 80·00

1871 (Apr.). *Wmk. Small Star, Type* w.**2.** *Rough perf.* 14 *to* 16.
15 **1** 1d. black .. .. .. 20·00 11·00
a. Imperf. between (vert. pair) £2100
16 ,, 6d. deep green .. .. £120 45·00

1872. *Colour changed. W* w.**2.** *P* 11 *to* 12½.
17 **1** 1s. deep rose-red .. .. £325 70·00

1872–75. *W* w.**2.** (*a*) *Perf. about* 15.
18 **1** 1d. black (*shades*) (1872) .. 16·00 8·00
19 ,, 6d. dull bl-grn. (*shades*) (1873) £250 21·00
a. Deep blue-green (1875) .. £300 26·00
(*b*) *P* 11 *to* 12½ × 15.
20 **1** 1s. lilac-rose (1873) £2500 £400

No. 19*a always* has the watermark sideways and Nos. 16 and 19 normally have it upright but are known with it sideways.

1875. *Colour changed. W* w.**2.** *P* 11 to 12½.
21 **1** 1s. claret £260 £110

1876–78. *W* w.**2.** (*a*) *P* 11 *to* 12½ × 15.
22 **1** 1d. black (*shades*) (1876) .. 24·00 6·00
a. Imperf. between. (horiz. pair) — £1200
23 ,, 6d. pale green (1877) .. £180 38·00
24 ,, 1s. vermilion (2.77) .. .. £250 70·00
a. Imperf. vert. (horiz. pair) ..
(*b*) *P* 11 *to* 12½.
25 **1** 4d. deep blue (7.77) .. .. £140 50·00
(*c*) *Perf. about* 15.
26 **1** 6d. pale green (3.77) .. .. — £250
a. Light yellow-green (1878) .. £160 20·00
27 ,, 1s. vermilion (1878?) .. — £2000
a. Imperf. .. .. .. — £950

Nos. 23 and 26 *always* have the watermark sideways but No. 26*a* always has the watermark upright.

d
1
(2)

3

1880 (May). *No.* 19*a divided vertically by a line of perforation gauging* 12, *and surch. locally as T* **2.**
28 **1** 1d. on half 6d. bright blue-green (R) £150 £100
a. Unsevered pair £450 £300

1880 (June). *W* w.**2.** *P* 11 *to* 12½.
29 **1** 1d. olive-green .. .. 35·00 7·00
30 ,, 6d. bright green .. .. £160 40·00
31 ,, 1s. bright vermilion.. .. £200 40·00
a. Imperf. between (horiz. pair)
32 **3** 5s. rose-red £350 £260
a. Imperf. .. .. ..

d ½ (4) — ONE PENNY (5) — 4d (6)

1881. *Nos.* 30/31 *surch. locally. No.* 33 *is divided vert. like No.* 28.
33 **4** ½d. on half 6d. bright green (R.) (1.9) .. .. 70·00 70·00
a. Unsevered pair .. £160 £160
b. Fraction bar omitted (pair with and without bar) .. £2000 £2500
34 **5** 1d. on 6d. bright green (30.11) £160 £120
35 **6** 4d. on 1s. bright verm. (28.11) £450 £325

Three unused single copies of No. 33 are known with the surcharge omitted.

7

1881 (Dec.). *W* w.**2.** *P* 11 *to* 12½.
36 **7** ½d. orange (*shades*) .. .. 4·50 3·50
37 **1** 1d. drab (*shades*) .. .. £350 7·00
38 ,, 4d. bright blue .. .. £500 55·00
a. Imperf. between. (horiz. pair)

Recess. De La Rue from Perkins, Bacon plates.

2½ PENCE (8) — 1d 2½ PENCE (9)

1882 (Nov.)–**83.** *No.* 40 *is surch. with T* **8.** *Wmk Crown CA. P* 14.
39 **1** 1d. drab .. .. .. 7·50 3·5
40 ,, 2½d. on 1d. lake (1883) .. 4·00 2·0
41 ,, 4d. ultramarine .. .. 80·00 18·0
a. Dull ultramarine .. .. £180 80·0

1883–84. *Wmk. Crown CA. P* 12.
42 **7** ½d. green (1884) .. .. 15·00 11·0
43 **1** 4d. ultramarine-blue .. 80·00 9·0
a. Grey-blue .. .. .. £300 80·0
44 ,, 6d. bright green £120 £11
45 ,, 1s. orange-vermilion .. 20·00 20·0

The ½d. orange, 1d. rose-red, 1d. milky blu (without surcharge) and 5s. carmine-lake whic were formerly listed are now considered to b colour trials. They are, however, of grea interest. (*Prices un.* ½d. £700, 1d. red £700 1d. blue £1000, 5s. £1500.)

1885 (Mar.). *No.* 40 *surch. locally as in T* **9.**
46 **1** 1d. on 2½d. on 1d. lake .. 5·00 5·5

Stamps with three cancelling bars instead c two are considered to be proofs.

1885–93. *No.* 49 *is surch. with T* **8.** *Wmk Crown CA. P* 14.
47 **7** ½d. green 45 1
a. Deep green .. .. 1·40 4
48 **1** 1d. rose-red 90 6
a. Rose (1886) .. .. 3·00 1·0
b. Red (1887) 65 2
c. Carmine-red (1889) .. 10·00 2·7
49 ,, 2½d. on 1d. milky blue (1889) 9·00 3·2
50 ,, 4d. red-brown .. .. £130 11·0
51 ,, 4d. purple-brown (1886) .. 9·00 3·0
a. Chocolate (1887) .. .. 8·00 2·2
52 ,, 6d. violet (1888) .. .. 40·00 35·0
53 **3** 5s. lake (1888) .. .. 11·00 11·0
a. Brown-lake (1893) .. 12·00 9·0
49, 50, 52 Optd. "Specimen" *Set of* 3 20·00

2½d. (10) — 5 PENCE (11)

1890. *No.* 51*a surch. with T* **10.**
54 **1** 2½d. on 4d. chocolate .. 20·00 22·0
a. No fraction bar .. .. 70·00 70·0

1890–93. *No.* 55 *is surch. with T* **8.** *Colour changed. Wmk. Crown CA. P* 14.
55 **1** 2½d. on 1d. grey-blue (1890) 5·00 9
a. Blue (1893) 50 2
56 ,, 4d. yellow (1893) (Optd. S. £10) .. .. .. 80 1·4
57 ,, 6d. dull purple (1891) .. 1·10 1·9
58 ,, 1s. orange (1891) .. 3·00 4·5
a. Red-orange (1892) .. 5·00 5·5

1892. *No.* 51*a surch. with T* **11,** *in purple.*
59 **1** 5d. on 4d. chocolate (Optd. "S" £12) .. .. 3·75 4·0

Some letters are known double due to loos type, the best known being the first "E", bu they are not constant.

FIVE PENCE
(12)

1893–94. *Surch. with T* **12.** *Wmk. Crown CA. P* 14.
o 1 5d. on 6d. carmine-lake (Optd. "S" £14) .. .. 3·50 4·50
a. Deep lake (1893) 65 90
b. Lake (1894) .. .. 1·10 1·90
c. Surch. double .. .. — £1700

(Recess. De La Rue.)

1897 (13 July). *New values. Wmk. Crown CA. P* 14.
1 1 2½d. blue .. .. .. 1·10 2·50
2 ,, 5d. sepia .. .. .. 3·50 4·50
1/2 Optd. "Specimen" *Set of* 2 25·00

1897 (6 Oct.). *Surch. as T* **12.** *Wmk. Crown CA. P* 14.
3 1 3d. on 1d. mauve (Optd. "S" £17) .. .. .. 2·75 3·00
a. Red-mauve .. .. .. 3·50 4·50

13

14

(Typo. D.L.R.)

1899. *Wmk. Crown CA. P* 14.
7 13 ½d. dull mauve and green 25 30
8 ,, 1d. dull mauve & carmine 1·25 45
9 ,, 2½d. dull mauve and blue 1·60 3·25
o ,, 3d. dull mauve and olive 2·25 3·25
1 ,, 4d. dull mauve and orange 1·60 4·00
2 ,, 5d. dull mauve and black 3·50 5·50
3 ,, 6d. dull mauve and brown 5·00 7·00
4 14 1s. green and carmine .. 9·00 11·00
5 ,, 5s. green and blue .. 25·00 30·00
7/75 .. .. *Set of* 9 45·00 60·00
7/75 Optd. "Specimen" *Set of* 9 65·00

15

16

(Typo. D.L.R.)

1902. *Wmk. Crown CA. P* 14.
6 15 ½d. dull purple and green 20 25
7 ,, 1d. dull purple & carmine 25 10
8 16 2d. dull purple and black 1·40 1·75
9 15 2½d. dull purple and blue .. 2·25 2·50
o ,, 3d. dull purple and olive.. 3·00 3·00
1 ,, 6d. dull purple and brown 4·00 5·00
2 16 1s. green and carmine .. 7·50 11·00
3 15 2s. green and violet .. 12·00 15·00
4 16 5s. green and blue .. 22·00 25·00
6/84 .. .. *Set of* 9 48·00 60·00
6/84 Optd. "Specimen" *Set of* 9 65·00

1904–11. *Wmk. Mult. Crown CA. P* 14.
5 15 ½d. dull purple and green OC (1905) 15 25
6 ,, 1d. dull purp. & carm., OC 1·25 55
8 ,, 2½d. dull purp. & bl., C ('06) 3·00 4·00
9 ,, 6d. dull purple & brown C (1905) .. .. 5·50 7·00
o 16 1s. grn. & carm., OC ('06) 5·50 7·00
1 15 2s. purple and bright blue/*blue*, C (3.09?) .. 14·00 17·00
2 16 5s. green and red/*yellow*, C (3.09?) .. .. 19·00 22·00
3 ,, £1 purple and black/*red*, C (1911) £170 £225
5/93 .. .. *Set of* 8 £200 £250
1/3 Optd. "Specimen" *Set of* 3 £100

17

18

(Recess. D.L.R.)

1907–08. *Wmk. Mult. Crown CA. P* 14.
94 17 ½d. green (2.7.07) 20 25
95 ,, 1d. carmine (4.07) .. 70 45
96 ,, 2d. orange (5.08) .. .. 1·10 1·90
97 ,, 2½d. blue (8.07) .. .. 3·50 4·00
98 ,, 3d. violet (1.6.07) .. .. 4·50 7·00
94/98 *Set of* 5 9·00 12·00
94/8 Optd. "Specimen" *Set of* 5 42·00

1909. *No dot below* "d". *Wmk. Mult. Crown CA. P* 14.
99 18 1d. carmine (3.09?) .. 45 45
100 ,, 6d. dull purple (16.1.09) .. 4·50 8·00
101 ,, 1s. black/*green* (16.1.09) .. 3·50 4·50
99/101 Optd. "Specimen" *Set of* 3 25·00

1909 (Nov.?)–**11.** *T* **18,** *redrawn* (*dot below* "d", *as in T* **17**). *Wmk. Mult. Crown CA. P* 14.
102 ½d. green (31.10.10) .. 30 35
103 1d. carmine 15 15
104 2d. grey (3.8.11) 80 90
105 2½d. ultramarine (25.7.10) .. 80 1·90
106 3d. purple/*yellow* .. .. 1·10 1·40
107 6d. dull purple .. .. 1·60 3·00
102/107 .. .. *Set of* 6 4·25 7·00
102 and 104/6 Optd. "Specimen" *Set of* 4 32·00

19

ONE

PENNY.
(20)

(Recess. D.L.R.)

1913–17. *Wmk. Mult. Crown CA. P* 14.
108 19 ½d. green 8 10
109 ,, 1d. red 25 12
a. Rose-red 40 12
b. Scarlet (1.17) .. .. 90 1·10
110 ,, 2d. grey .. .. .. 1·90 3·00
a. Slate .. .. .. 90 1·40
111 ,, 2½d. ultramarine .. 40 50
112 ,, 3d. purple/*yellow* .. 70 1·50
a. On lemon .. .. 1·60 2·50
b. On pale yellow .. 1·10 1·90
113 ,, 4d. red/*yellow* .. .. 45 1·10
114 ,, 5d. olive-green .. .. 1·10 4·00
115 ,, 6d. claret .. .. 1·10 1·50
116 ,, 1s. black/*green* .. .. 1·75 2·00
117 ,, 1s. bistre (1914) .. .. 2·50 3·50
118 18 2s. blue and purple .. 4·50 7·00
119 ,, 5s. carmine and myrtle 9·00 11·00
120 ,, £1 mauve and black .. 48·00 60·00
108/120 .. .. *Set of* 13 65·00 85·00
108/20 Optd. "Specimen" *Set of* 13 85·00

Nos. 118/20 are from new centre and frame dies, the motto "PAX ET JUSTITIA" being slightly over 7 mm. long, as against just over 8 mm. in Nos. 99 to 107. Nos. 139/41 are also from the new dies.

1915. *Surch. with T* **20.**
121 19 1d. on 1s. black/*green* (R.) 1·10 4·00
a. "ONE" omitted .. £300
b. "ONE" double .. £300
c. "PENNY" and bar double £275

The spacing between the two words varies from 7¾ mm. to 10 mm.

WAR STAMP.
(21)

WAR STAMP.
(22)

WAR STAMP
(24)

1916 (June). *Optd. locally with T* **21.** *First and second settings; words* 2 *to* 2½ *mm. apart.*
122 19 1d. red 80 90
a. Opt. double .. .. 50·00 50·00
b. Comma for stop .. .. 3·00 3·50

In the first printing every second stamp has the comma for stop. The second printing of this setting has full stops only. These two printings can therefore only be distinguished in blocks or pairs.

Third setting; words only 1½ *mm. apart.*
123 19 1d. red .. .. .. 19·00

Stamps of the first setting are offered as this rare one. Care must be taken to see that the distance between the lines is not over 1½ mm.

Fourth setting; optd. with T **22.** *Words* 3½ *mm. apart.*
124 19 1d. carmine-red 70 90
a. Opt. double .. .. 70·00

1916 (Aug.)–**18.** *T* **19,** *new printing, optd. with T* **24.**
126 1d. carmine-red (Optd. S. £22) 20 20
127 1d. pale rose-red 12 15
128 1d. deep rose-red 10 20
129 1d. pale scarlet (1918) .. 10 20

1921–32. *Wmk. Mult. Script CA. P* 14.
131 19 ½d. green 8 8
132 ,, 1d. carmine 10 10
a. Red 8 8
132*b* ,, 1½d. brown ('32) .. 20 20
133 ,, 2d. grey 12 12
133*a* ,, 2½d. bright blue (1926) .. 25 30
134 ,, 3d. bright blue .. .. 1·40 2·00
135 ,, 3d. purple/*yellow* (1926) 70 90
135*a* ,, 4d. red/*yellow* ('30) .. 90 1·75
136 ,, 5d. sage-green .. 85 1·75
137 ,, 6d. claret (1.11.27) .. 1·10 1·75
138 ,, 1s. bistre-brown .. 1·10 2·00
a. Ochre (1927) .. .. 2·00 3·75
139 18 2s. blue and purple .. 4·50 6·00
140 ,, 5s. carmine and myrtle 9·00 14·00
141 ,, £1 mauve & black ('28) 50·00 65·00
131/141 .. .. *Set of* 14 65·00 90·00
131/41 Optd./Perf. "Specimen" *Set of* 14 70·00

1935 (6 May). *Silver Jubilee. As Nos.* 91/4 *of Antigua but ptd. by Waterlow. P* 11 × 12.
142 1d. deep blue and scarlet 15 20
143 1½d. ultramarine and grey .. 25 30
144 2½d. brown and deep blue .. 80 1·00
145 1s. slate and purple .. 2·00 3·00
142/5 Perf. "Specimen" *Set of* 4 17·00

1937 (12 May). *Coronation. As Nos.* 13/5 *of Aden but ptd. by B.W. P* 11 × 11½.
146 1d. violet 8 8
147 1½d. carmine 10 10
148 2½d. blue 25 25
146/8 Perf. "Specimen" *Set of* 3 12·00

25

26. Young's Island and Fort Duvernette.

27. Kingstown and Fort Charlotte.

28. Bathing Beach at Villa.

29. Victoria Park, Kingstown.

(Recess. Bradbury, Wilkinson.)

1938 (11 Mar.)–**47.** *Wmk. Mult. Script CA. P* 12.

149 **25** ½d. blue and green .. 10 8
150 **26** 1d. blue and lake-brown 8 8
151 **27** 1½d. green and scarlet .. 8 8
152 **25** 2d. green and black .. 40 40
153 **28** 2½d. blue-blk. & blue-grn. 8 8
153*a* **29** 2½d. grn. & pur.-brn. ('47) 8 8
154 **25** 3d. orange and purple .. 10 8
154*a* **28** 3½d. bl.-blk. & bl.-grn. ('47) 25 25
155 **25** 6d. black and lake .. 30 25
156 **29** 1s. purple and green .. 50 30
157 **25** 2s. blue and purple .. 1·10 85
157*a* ,, 2s. 6d. red-brn. & bl. ('47) 1·10 1·90
158 ,, 5s. scarlet & deep green 1·90 2·50
158*a* ,, 10s. violet & brown ('47) 3·50 3·50
159 ,, £1 purple and black .. 7·00 7·00
149/159 .. .. *Set of* 15 15·00 16·00
149/59 Perf. "Specimen" *Set of* 15 75·00

1946 (15 Oct.). *Victory. As Nos.* 28/9 *of Aden.*

160 1½d. carmine 8 8
161 3½d. blue 8 8
160/1 Perf. "Specimen" *Set of* 2 14·00

1948 (30 Nov.). *Royal Silver Wedding. As Nos.* 30/1 *of Aden.*

162 1½d. scarlet 8 8
163 £1 bright purple .. .. 7·00 9·00

New Currency. 100 cents = 1 West Indian dollar·

1949 (26 Mar.)–**52.** *Value in cents and dollars. Wmk. Mult. Script CA. P* 12.

164 **25** 1 c. blue and green .. 8 10
164*a* ,, 1 c. grn. & blk. (10.6.52) 8 10
165 **26** 2 c. blue and lake-brown 8 10
166 **27** 3 c. green and scarlet .. 10 12
166*a* **25** 3 c. orange and purple (10.6.52) 8 10
167 ,, 4 c. green and black .. 8 12
167*a* ,, 4 c. blue & grn. (10.6.52) 8 10
168 **29** 5 c. green & purple-brn. 8 10
169 **25** 6 c. orange and purple.. 10 15
169*a* **27** 6 c. green and scarlet (10.6.52) 8 10
170 **28** 7 c. blue-black and blue-green 15 35
170*a* ,, 10 c. blue-black and blue-green (10.6.52) .. 20 35
171 **25** 12 c. black and lake .. 20 35
172 **29** 24 c. purple and green .. 40 55
173 **25** 48 c. blue and purple .. 80 1·50
174 ,, 60 c. red-brown and blue 90 1·75
175 ,, $1.20, scarlet & dp. green 3·50 4·00
176 ,, $2.40, violet and brown 4·50 4·50
177 ,, $4.80, purple and black 5·50 6·00
164/177 .. .. *Set of* 19 16·00 18·00

1949 (10 Oct.). *75th Anniv. of Universal Postal Union. As Nos.* 114/17 *of Antigua.*

178 5 c. blue 12 12
179 6 c. purple 12 12
180 12 c. magenta 35 35
181 24 c. blue-green 60 70

1951 (16 Feb.). *Inauguration of B.W.I. University College. As Nos.* 118/19 *of Antigua.*

182 3 c. deep green and scarlet 12 8
183 12 c. black and purple .. 15 15

1951 (21 Sept.). *New Constitution. Optd. with T* **34** *of Dominica, by B.W.*

184 **27** 3 c. green and scarlet .. 25 30
185 [illegible] 4 c. green and black .. 25 30
186 [illegible]9 5 c. green & purple-brown 20 30
187 **25** 12 c. black and lake .. 20 35

1953 (2 June). *Coronation. As No.* 47 *of Aden.*

188 4 c. black and green.. .. 25 30

30

31

(Recess. Waterlow (until 1961), then D.L.R.)

1955 (16 Sept.). *Wmk. Mult. Script CA. P* 13½×14 (*T* **30**) *or* 14 (*T* **31**).

189 **30** 1 c. orange (*shades*) .. 5 5
190 ,, 2 c. ultramarine (*shades*) 8 8
191 ,, 3 c. slate 8 8
192 ,, 4 c. brown 10 10
193 ,, 5 c. scarlet 12 15
194 ,, 10 c. reddish violet (*shades*) 20 25
195 ,, 15 c. deep blue 20 20
196 ,, 20 c. green 30 35
197 ,, 25 c. black-brown 50 60
198 **31** 50 c. red-brown (*shades*) .. 80 90
199 ,, $1 myrtle-grn. (*shades*) 2·25 2·75
200 $2.50, dp. blue (*shades*) 5·50 7·00
189/200 .. .. *Set of* 12 9·00 10·00

1958 (22 Apr.). *Inauguration of British Caribbean Federation. As Nos.* 135/7 *of Antigua.*

201 3 c. deep green 10 12
202 6 c. blue 20 20
203 12 c. scarlet 35 35

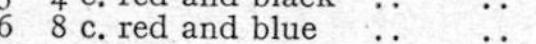

II. MINISTERIAL GOVERNMENT.

1963 (4 June). *Freedom from Hunger. As No.* 76 *of Aden.*

204 8 c. reddish violet 80 65

1963 (2 Sept.). *Red Cross Centenary. As Nos.* 147/8 *of Antigua.*

205 4 c. red and black 35 30
206 8 c. red and blue 85 75

1964–65. *As* 1955 *but wmk.* w.**12.**

(*a*) *P* 12½ (14 Jan.–Feb. 1964).

207 **30** 10 c. deep lilac 35 35
208 ,, 15 c. deep blue 60 60
209 ,, 20 c. green (24.2.64*) .. 3·00 3·00
210 ,, 25 c. black-brown 80 90
211 **31** 50 c. red-brown .. .. 1·25 1·25
207/211 .. .. *Set of* 5 5·50 5·50

(*b*) *P* 13×14 (*T* **30**) *or* 14 (*T* **31**).

212 **30** 1 c. orange (15.12.64) .. 10 10
213 ,, 2 c. blue (15.12.64) .. 12 12
214 ,, 3 c. slate (15.12.64) .. 25 25
215 ,, 5 c. scarlet (15.12.64) .. 20 20
216 ,, 10 c. deep lilac (15.12.64) 25 25
217 ,, 15 c. deep blue (9.11.64) .. 30 35
218 ,, 20 c. green (1964) .. 45 55
219 ,, 25 c. black-brn. (20.10.64) 55 70
220 **31** 50 c. chocolate (18.1.65) .. 2·25 2·50
212/220 .. .. *Set of* 9 4·00 4·50

*This is the earliest known date recorded in St. Vincent although it may have been put on sale on 14.1.64.

32. Scout Badge and Proficiency Badges.

(Des. V. Whiteley. Litho. Harrison.)

1964 (23 Nov.). *50th Anniv. of St. Vincent Bo Scouts Association. W* w.**12.** *P* 14½.

221 **32** 1 c. yell.-grn. & chocolate 5
222 ,, 4 c. blue & brown-purple 10 1
223 ,, 20 c. yellow & black-violet 25 2
224 ,, 50 c. red and bronze-green 60 6

33. Tropical Fruits.

34. Breadfruit and the *Providence.* (*Horiz.*)
35. Doric Temple and Pond. (*Vert.*)
36. Talipot Palm and Doric Temple. (*Vert.*)

(Des. V. Whiteley. Photo. Harrison.)

1965 (23 Mar.). *Botanic Gardens Bicentenary W* w.**12.** *P* 14½×13½ (*horiz.*) *or* 13½×14 (*vert.*).

225 **33** 1 c. multicoloured .. 5
226 **34** 4 c. multicoloured .. 8
227 **35** 25 c. multicoloured .. 30 3
228 **36** 40 c. multicoloured .. 60 5

1965 (17 May). *I.T.U. Centenary. As Nos* 166/7 *of Antigua.*

229 4 c. light blue and light olive-green 10 1
230 48 c. ochre-yellow and orange 80 7

37. Boat-building, Bequia (inscr. "BEQUIA").

MINIMUM PRICE

The minimum price quoted is 5p whic represents a handling charge rather tha a basis for valuing common stamps For further notes about prices se introductory pages.

(Des. M. Goaman. Photo. Harrison.)

1965 (16 Aug.)–**67**. *T* **37** *and similar multi-coloured designs. W* w.**12**. *P* 14½ × 13½ *(horiz. designs) or* 13½ × 14½ *(vert.)*.

231	1 c. Type **37** (" BEOUIA ") ..	5	5
231*a*	1 c. Type **37** (" BEQUIA ") (27.6.67)	10	10
232	2 c. Friendship Beach, Bequia	5	5
233	3 c. Terminal Building, Arnos Vale Airport ..	5	5
234	4 c. Woman with bananas ..	20	20
235	5 c. Crater Lake	8	8
236	6 c. Carib Stone	8	8
237	8 c. Arrowroot	8	8
238	10 c. Owia Salt Pond ..	10	10
239	12 c. Deep water wharf ..	12	12
240	20 c. Sea Island cotton ..	20	20
241	25 c. Map of St. Vincent and islands	25	25
242	50 c. Breadfruit	50	50
243	$1 Baleine Falls	1·00	1·00
244	$2.50, St. Vincent Parrot ..	2·25	2·25
245	$5 Arms of St. Vincent ..	3·75	4·00
231/45	.. .. *Set of* 16	8·00	8·50

The 1, 2, 3, 5, 10 and 12 c. are horizontal designs, and the remainder are vertical.

The 1 c. (No. 231*a*), 2 c., 3 c., 5 c. and 10 c. exist with PVA gum as well as gum arabic.

See also No. 261.

1966 (24 Jan.). *Churchill Commemoration. As Nos.* 170/3 *of Antigua.*

246	1 c. new blue	5	5
247	4 c. deep green	8	8
248	20 c. brown	35	35
249	40 c. bluish violet	65	60

1966 (4 Feb.). *Royal Visit. As Nos.* 174/5 *of Antigua.*

250	4 c. black and ultramarine	8	8
251	25 c. black and magenta ..	60	50

1966 (20 Sept.). *Inauguration of W.H.O. Headquarters, Geneva. As Nos.* 178/9 *of Antigua.*

252	4 c. black, yellow-green and light blue	8	8
253	25 c. black, light purple and yellow-brown	60	55

1966 (1 Dec.). *20th Anniv. of U.N.E.S.C.O. As Nos.* 196/8 *of Antigua.*

254	4 c. slate-violet, red, yellow and orange	8	8
255	8 c. orange-yellow, violet and deep olive	20	20
256	25 c. black, bright purple and orange	55	55

38. Coastal View of Mount Coke Area.

(Des. and photo. Harrison.)

1967 (1 Dec.). *Autonomous Methodist Church. Type* **38** *and similar horiz. designs. Multi-coloured. W* w.**12**. *P* 14 × 14½.

257	2 c. Type **38**	5	5
258	8 c. Kingston Methodist Church	8	8
259	25 c. First Licence to perform marriages ..	20	20
260	35 c. Conference Arms ..	30	30

1968 (20 Feb.). *As No.* 234, *but W* w.**12** *sideways.*

261	4 c. Woman with bananas ..	15	15

The above exists with PVA gum as well as gum arabic.

39. Meteorological Institute.

(Des. G. L. Vasarhelyi. Photo. Harrison.)

1968 (28 May). *World Meteorological Day. W* w.**12**. *P* 14 × 14½.

262	**39**	4 c. multicoloured ..	5	5
263	,,	25 c. multicoloured ..	25	25
264	,,	35 c. multicoloured ..	30	30

40. Dr. Martin Luther King and Cotton Pickers.

(Des. V. Whiteley. Litho. D.L.R.)

1968 (28 Aug.). *Martin Luther King Commemoration. W* w.**12** *(sideways). P* 13.

265	**40**	5 c. multicoloured ..	8	8
266	,,	25 c. multicoloured ..	25	25
267	,,	35 c. multicoloured ..	35	35

3c
19 68
FREEDOM OF ASSEMBLY
FREEDOM OF SPEECH
St.VINCENT

41. Speaker addressing Demonstrators.

42. Scales of Justice and Human Rights Emblem.

(Des. V. Whiteley. Photo. Enschedé.)

1968 (1 Nov.). *Human Rights Year. P* 13 × 14 *(3 c.) or* 14 × 13 *(35 c.).*

268	**41**	3 c. multicoloured ..	5	5
269	**42**	35 c. Royal blue & turq.-bl.	35	30

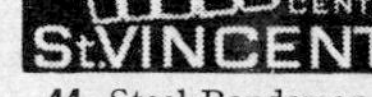

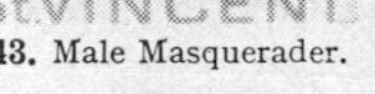

43. Male Masquerader. **44.** Steel Bandsman.

45. Carnival Revellers.

46. Queen of Bands.

(Des. V. Whiteley. Litho. Format International.)

1969 (17 Feb.). *St. Vincent Carnival. P* 14.

270	**43**	1 c. multicoloured ..	5	5
271	**44**	5 c. red & deep chocolate	8	8
272	**45**	8 c. multicoloured ..	12	12
273	**46**	25 c. multicoloured ..	35	35

METHODIST
CONFERENCE
MAY
1969
(47)

1969 (May). *Methodist Conference. Nos.* 257/8, 241 *and* 260 *optd. with T* **47**.

274	2 c. multicoloured	8	8
275	8 c. multicoloured	15	15
276	25 c. multicoloured	40	40
277	35 c. multicoloured	5·00	4·25

48. " Strength in Unity ".

49. Map of " CARIFTA " Countries.

(Des. J. E. Cooter. Litho. De La Rue.)

1969 (1 July). *First Anniv. of CARIFTA (Caribbean Free Trade Area). W* w.**12** *(sideways on T***48***). P* 13.

278 **48** 2 c. blk., pale buff & red 5 5
279 **49** 5 c. multicoloured 5 5
280 **48** 8 c. black, pale buff and pale green 10 10
281 **49** 25 c. multicoloured .. 35 30

50. Flag of St. Vincent.

(Des. V. Whiteley, based on local designs. Photo. Harrison.)

1969 (27 Oct.). *Statehood. T* **50** *and similar horiz. designs. W* w.**12**. *P* 14×14½.

282 4 c. multicoloured 5 5
283 10 c. multicoloured 15 15
284 50 c. grey, black and orange 50 50

Designs:—10 c. Battle scene with insets of Petroglyph and Carib chief Chatoyer; 50 c. Carib House with maces and scales.

51. Green Heron.

(Des. J.W. Ltd. Photo. Harrison.)

1970 (12 Jan.).–**71**. *T* **51** *and similar multi-coloured designs. Chalk-surfaced paper. W* w.**12** *(sideways on 1, 2, 3, 6, 8, 20, 25 c., $1, $2.50 and upright on others.) P* 14.

285 ½ c. House Wren (*vert.*) .. 5 5
286 1 c. Type **51** 10 10
a. Glazed, ordinary paper (9.8.71) 5 5
287 2 c. Bullfinches 5 5
288 3 c. St. Vincent Parrots .. 8 8
289 4 c. Soufrière Bird (*vert.*) .. 8 8
290 5 c. Ramier Pigeon (*vert.*) .. 15 15
a. Glazed, ordinary paper (9.8.71) 10 10
291 6 c. Bannanaquits 12 12
292 8 c. Hummingbird 8 8
293 10 c. Mangrove Cuckoo (*vert.*) 12 12
294 12 c. Black Hawk (*vert.*) .. 15 15
295 20 c. Bare-eyed Thrush .. 20 20
296 25 c. Prince 20 20
297 50 c. Blue Hooded Euphonia 30 35
298 $1 Barn Owl (*vert.*) .. 50 60
299 $2.50, Crested Elaenia (*vert.*) .. .. .. 1·50 1·75
300 $5 Ruddy Quail Dove .. 3·00 3·25
285/300 .. .. *Set of* 16 6·00 6·50

See also Nos. 361/8 and 396/8.

52. " DHC-6 ", Twin Otter.

(Des. R. Granger Barrett. Litho. Enschedé.)

1970 (13 Mar.). *20th Anniv. of Regular Air Services. Type* **52** *and similar horiz. designs. Multi-coloured. W* w.**12** *(sideways). P* 14×13.

301 5 c. Type **52** 8 10
302 8 c. Grumman " Goose " .. 15 15
303 10 c. Hawker Siddeley " HS-748 " 35 35
304 25 c. Douglas " DC-3 " .. 80 80

53. " Children's Nursery ".

(Des. R. Granger Barrett. Photo. Harrison.)

1970 (1 June). *Centenary of British Red Cross. T* **53** *and similar horiz. designs. Multicoloured. W* w.**12**. *P* 14.

305 3 c. Type **53** 5 5
306 5 c. " First Aid " 5 5
307 12 c. " Voluntary Aid Detachment " 20 20
308 25 c. " Blood Transfusion " 35 35

54. Stained-glass Window.

(Des. L. D. Curtis. Litho. J.W.)

1970 (7 Sept.). *150th Anniv. of St. George's Cathedral, Kingstown. T* **54** *and similar multi-coloured designs. W* w.**12** *(sideways on horiz. design.). P* 14.

309 ½ c. Type **54** 5 5
310 5 c. St. George's Cathedral (*horiz.*) 5 5
311 25 c. Tower, St. George's Cathedral (*vert.*) .. 25 25
312 35 c. Interior, St. George's Cathedral (*horiz.*). .. 35 35
313 50 c. Type **54** 50 50
309/13 .. .. *Set of* 5 1·00 1·00

55. " The Adoration of the Shepherds " (Le Nain).

(Des. J. E. Cooter. Litho. Questa.)

1970 (23 Nov.). *Christmas. T* **55** *and similar vert. design. Multicoloured. W* w.**12** *(sideways on 25 c., 50 c.). P* 14.

314 8 c. " The Virgin and Child" (Bellini) 10 8
315 25 c. Type **55** 25 25
316 35 c. As 8 c. 35 35
317 50 c. Type **55** 55 50

56. New Post Office and 6d. Stamp of 1861.

(Des. J. Cooter. Litho. Questa.)

1971 (29 Mar.). *110th Anniv. of First St. Vincent Stamps. T* **56** *and similar horiz. design. Multicoloured. W* w.**12** *(sideways). P* 14.

318 2 c. Type **56** 8 8
319 4 c. 1d. Stamp of 1861 and New Post Office .. 10 10
320 25 c. Type **56** 30 25
321 $1 As 4 c. .. .. .. 1·10 1·10

57. Trust Seal and Wildlife.

(Des. G. Drummond. Litho. J.W.)

1971 (4 Aug.). *St. Vincent's National Trust. T* **57** *and similar horiz. design. Multicoloured. W* w.**12** *(sideways). P* 13½×14.

322 12 c. Type **57** 10 10
323 30 c. Old Cannon, Fort Charlotte 30 30
324 40 c. Type **57** 40 40
325 45 c. As 30 c. 45 45

58. " Madonna appearing to St. Anthony " (Tiepolo).

(Des. J. E. Cooter. Litho. Questa.)

1971 (6 Oct.). *Christmas. T* **58** *and similar horiz. design. Multicoloured. W* w.**12** *(sideways on* 10 *c. and* $ 1*). P* 14½×14 *(*10 *c.,* $1*) or* 14×14½ *(*5 *c.,* 25 *c.).*

No.	Value	Description	Unused	Used
326	5 c.	Type **58**	5	5
327	10 c.	" The Holy Family with Angels " (detail, Pietro da Cortona)	12	12
328	25 c.	Type **58**	30	25
329	$1	As 10 c.	1·25	1·25

59. Careening.

(Des. J. E. Cooter. Litho. J.W.)

1971 (25 Nov.). *The Grenadines of St. Vincent. T* **59** *and similar vert. designs. Multicoloured. W* w.**12**. *P* 13½.

No.	Value	Description	Unused	Used
330	1 c.	Type **59**	5	5
331	5 c.	Seine fishermen	5	5
332	6 c.	Map of the Grenadines	8	8
333	15 c.	Type **59**	20	20
334	20 c.	As 5 c.	25	25
335	50 c.	As 6 c.	70	60
330/5		.. .. *Set of* 6	1·25	1·10
MS336		177×140 mm. Nos. 330/5	2·25	2·25

60. Private, Grenadier Company, 32nd Foot (1764).

(Des. and litho. J.W.)

1972 (14 Feb.). *Military Uniforms. T* **60** *and similar vert. designs. W* w.**12**. *P* 14×13½.

No.	Type	Value	Description	Unused	Used
337	**60**	12 c.	multicoloured ..	15	12
338	–	30 c.	multicoloured ..	35	35
339	–	50 c.	multicoloured ..	65	60

Designs:—30 c. Officer, Battalion Company, 31st Foot (1772); 50 c. Private, Grenadier Company, 6th Foot (1772).

61. Breadnut Fruit.

(Des. P. B. Powell. Litho. Questa.)

1972 (16 May). *Fruit. T* **61** *and similar vert. designs. Multicoloured. W* w.**12** *(sideways). P* 13½.

No.	Value	Description	Unused	Used
340	3 c.	Type **61**	5	5
341	5 c.	Pawpaw	8	5
342	12 c.	Plumrose or Roseapple	20	15
343	25 c.	Mango	40	35

62. Candlestick Cassia.

(Des. Sylvia Goaman. Litho. B.W.)

1972 (31 July). *Flowers. T* **62** *and similar vert. designs. Multicoloured. P* 13½×14.

No.	Value	Description	Unused	Used
344	1 c.	Type **62**	5	5
345	30 c.	Lobster Claw	40	35
346	40 c.	White Trumpet ..	45	45
347	$1	Soufriere tree	1·00	1·00

63. Sir Charles Brisbane and his Coat-of-arms.

(Des. Jennifer Toombs. Litho. J.W.)

1972 (29 Sept.). *Birth Centenary of Sir Charles Brisbane. T* **63** *and similar horiz. designs. W* w.**12** *(sideways). P* 13½.

No.	Value	Description	Unused	Used
348	20 c.	yellow-ochre, gold and red-brown	25	20
349	30 c.	light yellow, light mauve and black ..	35	40
350	$1	multicoloured ..	1·00	75
MS351		171×111 mm. Nos. 348/50 (*sold at* $2)	1·75	1·50

Designs:—30 c. H.M.S. *Arethusa*; $1 H.M.S. *Blake*.

64. Arrowroot and Breadfruit.

(Des. (from photograph by D. Groves) and photo. Harrison.)

1972 (20 Nov.). *Royal Silver Wedding. Multicoloured; background colour given. W* w.**12**. *P* 14×14½.

No.	Type	Value	Description	Unused	Used
352	**64**	30 c.	red-brown	30	25
353	,,	$1	myrtle-green ..	85	75

65. Sighting St. Vincent.

(Des. J. E. Cooter. Litho. Enschedé.

1973 (31 Jan.). *475th Anniv. of Columbus's Third Voyage to the West Indies. T* **65** *and similar triangular designs. Multicoloured. W* w.**12**. *P* 13½.

No.	Value	Description	Unused	Used
354	5 c.	Type **65**	8	8
355	12 c.	Caribs watching Columbus's fleet ..	12	12
356	30 c.	Christopher Columbus	35	35
357	50 c.	*Santa Maria*	60	60

66. " The Last Supper " (French Stained-glass Window).

(Des. J. E. Cooter. Litho. Questa.)

1973 (19 Apr.). *Easter.* T **66** *and similar vert. designs. Multicoloured.* W w.**12** (*sideways*). P 14 × 13½.

358 **66**	15 c. multicoloured ..	12	12
359 –	60 c. multicoloured ..	50	50
360 –	$1 multicoloured ..	90	90
	Strip of three	1·50	1·50

Nos. 358, 360 and 359 were printed, in that order, horizontally *se-tenant* throughout a sheet of 45 stamps, and form a composite design of " The Last Supper ".

1973. *As Nos.* 285 *etc., but* W w.**12** *upright on* 2, 3, 6, 20 *c. and sideways on others. Glazed paper.*

361	2 c. Bullfinches	5	5
362	3 c. St. Vincent Parrots ..	5	5
363	4 c. Soufrière Bird (*vert.*) ..	5	5
364	5 c. Ramier Pigeon (*vert.*) ..	10	10
365	6 c. Bananaquits	8	8
366	10 c. Mangrove Cuckoo (*vert.*)	8	8
367	12 c. Black Hawk (*vert.*) ..	10	10
368	20 c. Bare-eyed Thrush ..	15	15
361/8	.. .. *Set of* 8	55	55

Dates of issue:—13.6.73, 5 c.; 23.11.73, others.

67. William Wilberforce and Poster.

(Des. Jennifer Toombs. Litho. D.L.R.)

1973 (11 July). 140*th Death Anniv. of William Wilberforce.* T **67** *and similar horiz. designs. Multicoloured.* W w.**12**. P 14 × 13½.

369	30 c. Type **67**	30	20
370	40 c. Slaves cutting cane ..	40	30
371	50 c. Wilberforce and medallion	50	40

68. P.P.F. Symbol.

(Des. PAD Studio. Litho. Walsall Security Printers Ltd.)

1973 (3 Oct.). 21*st Anniv. of International Planned Parenthood Federation.* T **68** *and similar vert. design. Multicoloured.* W w.**12** (*sideways*). P 14.

372	12 c. Type **68**	12	10
373	40 c. " IPPF " and symbol	45	45

1973 (14 Nov.). *Royal Wedding. As Nos.* 165/6 *of Anguilla. Centre multicoloured.* W w.**12** (*sideways*). P 13½.

374	50 c. deep blue	30	35
375	70 c. grey green	40	45

69. Administrative Block, Mona.

(Des. PAD Studio. Litho. Questa.)

1973 (13 Dec.). 25*th Anniv. of West Indies University.* T **69** *and similar multicoloured designs.* W w.**12** (*sideways on* $1). P 14.

376	5 c. Type **69**	5	5
377	10 c. University Centre, Kingston	8	8
378	30 c. Aerial view, Mona University	25	25
379	$1 University coat-of-arms (*vert.*)	60	60

30c

(**70**)

1973 (15 Dec.). *Nos.* 297, 292 *and* 298 *surch. in half sheets with* T **70**, *by the Govt. Printer, St. Vincent.*

380	30 c. on 50 c. multicoloured ..	20	20
	a. Surch. double		
	b. Surch. inverted		
381	40 c. on 8 c. multicoloured ..	30	30
382	$10 on $1 multicoloured ..	4·50	4·75
	a. Surch. double	75·00	
	b. Surch. inverted	90·00	
	c. Surch. double, one inverted ..	85·00	

71. "The Descent from the Cross" (Sansovino).

(Des. PAD Studio. Litho. Enschedé.)

1974 (10 Apr.). *Easter.* T **71** *and similar vert. designs showing sculptures. Multicoloured.* W w.**12** (*sideways*). P 14 × 13½.

383	5 c. Type **71**	5	5
384	30 c. "The Deposition" (English, 14th-century) ..	20	25
385	40 c. "Pieta" (Fernandez) ..	20	25
386	$1 "The Resurrection" (French, 16th-century) ..	50	55

72. *Istra.*

(Des. PAD Studio. Litho. Questa.)

1974 (28 June). *Cruise Ships.* T **72** *and similar horiz. designs. Multicoloured.* W w.**12** (*sideways*). P 14.

387	15 c. Type **72**	8	10
388	20 c. *Oceanic*	12	12
389	30 c. *Alexander Pushkin* ..	20	20
390	$1 *Europa*	50	55
MS391	134 × 83 mm. Nos. 387/90	90	1·00

73. U.P.U. Emblem.

(Des. J.W. Ltd. Litho. Questa.)

1974 (25 July). *Centenary of Universal Postal Union.* T **73** *and similar horiz. designs. Multicoloured,* W w.**12**. P 14.

392	5 c. Type **73**	5	5
393	12 c. Globe within posthorn ..	10	10
394	60 c. Map of St. Vincent and hand-cancelling	30	35
395	90 c. Map of the World ..	50	55

74. Royal Tern.

(Des. J.W. Ltd. Litho. Questa.)

1974 (29 Aug.). *Type* **74** *and similar vert. designs. Multicoloured. Glazed paper.* W w.**12** (*sideways on* 40 *c. and* $10). P 14.

396	30 c. Type **74**	12	15
397	40 c. Brown Pelican	15	20
398	$10 Frigatebird	4·00	4·25

75. Scout Badge and Emblems.

(Des. Sylvia Goaman. Litho. Enschedé.)

1974 (9 Oct.). *Diamond Jubilee of Scout Movement in St. Vincent.* W w.**12**. P 13 × 13½.

399 **75**	10 c. multicoloured ..	8	8
400 ,,	25 c. multicoloured ..	20	20
401 ,,	45 c. multicoloured ..	25	25
402 ,,	$1 multicoloured ..	50	55

76. Sir Winston Churchill.

(Des. C. Abbott. Litho. Questa.)

1974 (28 Nov.). *Birth Centenary of Sir Winston Churchill. T* **76** *and similar vert. designs. Multicoloured. W* w.**12**. *P* 14.

403	25 c. Type **76**	20	20
404	35 c. Churchill in military uniform	20	25
405	45 c. Churchill in naval uniform	25	25
406	$1 Churchill in air-force uniform	50	55

77. The Shepherds.

(Des. Jennifer Toombs. Litho. Enschedé.)

1974 (5 Dec.). *Christmas. T* **77** *and similar vert. designs. W* w.**12**. *P* 12 × 12½.

407	**77**	3 c. violet-blue & black	5	5
408	–	3 c. violet-blue & black	5	5
409	–	3 c. violet-blue & black	5	5
410	–	3 c. violet-blue & black	5	5
411	**77**	8 c. apple-green & black	8	8
412	–	35 c. rose and deep maroon	20	25
413	–	45 c. ol.-bistre & brn.-blk.	25	25
414	–	$1 lavender & slate-blk.	50	55
407/14		.. .. *Set of* 8	1·10	1·25

Designs:—Nos. 408, 412 Mary and crib; Nos. 409, 413 Joseph, Ox and ass; Nos. 410, 414 The Magi.

Nos. 407/10 were issued horizontally *se-tenant* within the sheet, together forming a composite design of the Nativity.

78. Faces.

(Des. G. Drummond. Litho. D.L.R.)

1975 (7–27 Feb.). *Kingstown "Carnival '75". T* **78** *and similar horiz. designs. Multicoloured. W* w.**12**. *P* 14 × 13½.

415	1 c. Type **78**	5	5
	a. Booklet pane. No. 415 × 2 plus printed label (27.2)	12	
	b. Booklet pane. Nos. 415, 417 and 419 (27.2)	40	
416	15 c. Pineapple women ..	10	10
	a. Booklet pane Nos. 416, 418 and 420 (27.2)	85	
417	25 c. King of the Bands ..	15	15
418	35 c. Carnival dancers ..	20	20
419	45 c. Queen of the Bands ..	20	25
420	$1.25, "African Splendour"	55	60
415/20	.. .. .. *Set of* 6	1·10	1·25
MS421	146 × 128 mm. Nos. 415/20	1·10	1·25

79. French Angelfish.

$2.50. Type I. Fishing-line joined to fish's mouth.
Type II. Fishing-line omitted.

(Des. G. Drummond. Litho. Questa.)

1975 (10 Apr.)-**76**. *T* **79** *and similar horiz. designs. Multicoloured. W* w.**14** *(sideways). P* 14½.

422	1 c. Type **79**	5	5
423	2 c. Spotfin Butterfly-fish ..	5	5
424	3 c. Horse-eyed Jack ..	5	5
425	4 c. Mackerel	5	5
426	5 c. French Grunt	5	5
427	6 c. Spotted Goatfish ..	5	5
428	8 c. Ballyhoo	5	5
429	10 c. Sperm Whale	5	5
430	12 c. Humpback Whale ..	5	5
431	15 c. Cowfish	5	8
432	15 c. Skipjack (14.10.76) ..	5	5
433	20 c. Queen Angelfish ..	8	8
434	25 c. Princess Parrotfish ..	10	10
435	35 c. Red Hind	12	15
436	45 c. Atlantic Flying Fish ..	15	20
437	50 c. Porkfish	20	20
438	70 c. Albacore (14.10.76) ..	25	30
439	90 c. Pompano (14.10.76) ..	35	35
440	$1 Queen Triggerfish ..	35	40
441	$2.50, Sailfish (I)	1·00	1·10
	a. Type II (12.7.76)	90	1·00
442	$5 Dolphin Fish	1·75	2·00
443	$10 Blue Marlin	3·50	3·75
422/43	.. .. *Set of* 22	7·50	8·00

Some of the above issue exist with different dates in the imprint at the foot of each stamp.

80. Cutting Bananas.

(Des. G. Drummond. Litho. Questa.)

1975 (26 June). *Banana Industry. T* **80** *and similar horiz. designs. Multicoloured. W* w.**12** *(sideways). P* 13½.

447	25 c. Type **80**	12	12
448	35 c. Packaging Station, La Croix	15	15
449	45 c. Cleaning and boxing ..	20	20
450	70 c. Shipping bananas aboard *Geeste Tide*	30	35

81. Snorkel Diving.

(Des. G. Drummond. Litho. Questa.)

1975 (31 July). *Tourism. T* **81** *and similar horiz. designs. Multicoloured. W* w.**14** *(sideways). P* 13½.

451	15 c. Type **81**	8	8
452	20 c. Aquaduct Golf Course ..	10	10
453	35 c. Steel Band at Mariner's Inn	15	15
454	45 c. Sunbathing at Young Island	20	20
455	$1.25, Yachting Marina ..	50	55
451/5	.. .. *Set of* 5	95	1·00

82. George Washington, John Adams, Thomas Jefferson and James Madison.

(Des. G. Drummond. Litho. Questa.)

1975 (11 Sept.). *American Independence Bicentennial. T* **82** *and similar horiz. designs. P* 14.

456	½ c. black and lavender ..	5	5
457	1 c. black and light emerald	5	5
458	1½ c. black and light magenta	5	5
459	5 c. black and brt. yell.-green	5	5
460	10 c. blk. & light violet-blue	8	8
461	25 c. black & dull orge.-yell.	15	15
462	35 c. black & lt. greenish blue	15	15
463	45 c. black and bright rose ..	20	20
464	$1 black and light orange ..	40	45
465	$2 black & lt. yellow-olive	80	90
456/65	.. .. *Set of* 10	1·75	1·90
MS466	179 × 156 mm. Nos. 456/65	1·90	2·00

Presidents:—1 c. Monroe, Quincy Adams, Jackson, van Buren; 1½ c. W. Harrison, Tyler, Polk, Taylor; 5 c. Fillmore, Pierce, Buchanan, Lincoln; 10 c. Andrew Johnson, Grant, Hayes, Garfield; 25 c. Arthur, Cleveland, B. Harrison, McKinley; 35 c. Theodore Roosevelt, Taft, Wilson, Harding; 45 c. Coolidge, Hoover, Franklin Roosevelt, Truman; $1 Eisenhower, Kennedy, Lyndon Johnson, Nixon; $2 Pres. Ford and White House.

83/4. "Shepherds".

(Illustration reduced. Actual size 56 × 56 *mm.)*

(Des. Jennifer Toombs. Litho. Harrison.)

1975 (4 Dec.). *Christmas. T* **83/4** *and similar triangular designs. P* 13½×14. A. *W* w.**12** (*upright*). B. *W* w.**12** (*sideways*).

		A.		B.	
467	3 c. black and magenta	5	5	5	5
468	3 c. black and magenta	5	5	5	5
469	3 c. black and magenta	5	5	5	5
470	3 c. black and magenta	5	5	5	5
471	8 c. black and light greenish blue ..	5	5	5	5
472	8 c. black and light greenish blue ..	5	5	5	5
473	35 c. black and yellow	15	15	15	15
474	35 c. black and yellow	15	15	15	15
475	45 c. blk. & yellow-grn.	20	20	20	20
476	45 c. blk. & yellow-grn.	20	20	20	20
477	$1 blk. & bright lilac	40	45	40	45
478	$1 blk. & bright lilac	40	45	40	45
467/78	.. .. *Set of* 12	1·60	1·75	1·60	1·75

Designs:—No. 467, "Star of Bethlehem; No. 468, "Holy Trinity"; No. 469, As T **83**; No. 470, "Three Kings"; No. 471/2, As No. 467; No. 473/4, As No. 468; No. 475/6, T **83/4**; No. 477/8, As No. 470. The two designs of each denomination (Nos. 471/8) differ in that the longest side is at the top and at the foot respectively as in *T* **83/4**.

Each denomination was printed in sheets of 16, the designs being *se-tenant* and so arranged that the watermark comes upright, inverted, sideways right and sideways left.

85. Carnival Dancers.

(Des. G. Drummond. Litho. Questa.)

1976 (19 Feb.). *Kingstown "Carnival '76". T* **85** *and similar horiz. designs. Multicoloured. W* w.**14** (*sideways.*) *P* 13½.

479	1 c. Type **85**	5	5
	a. Booklet pane. Nos. 479 and 480 plus printed label ..	12	
480	2 c. Humpty-Dumpty people	5	5
	a. Booklet pane. Nos. 480/2 ..	20	
481	5 c. Smiling faces	5	5
482	35 c. Dragon worshippers ..	15	20
	a. Booklet pane. Nos. 482/4 ..	85	
483	45 c. Carnival tableaux ..	20	25
484	$1.25, Bumble-Bee dancers	50	55
479/84	.. .. *Set of* 6	90	1·00

87. Blue-headed Hummingbird and Yellow Hibiscus.

70¢

(**86**)

1976 (8 Apr.). *Nos.* 424 *and* 437 *surch. as T* **86**.

485	70 c. on 3 c. Horse-eyed Jack	30	35
486	90 c. on 50 c. Porkfish ..	40	45

(Des. G. Drummond. Litho. Walsall.)

1976 (20 May). *Hummingbirds and Hibiscuses. T* **87** *and similar vert. designs. Multicoloured. W* w.**14** (*inverted*). *P* 13½.

487	5 c. Type **87**	5	5
488	10 c. Crested Hummingbird and Pink Hibiscus ..	5	5
489	35 c. Purple-throated Carib and White Hibiscus ..	15	15
490	45 c. Blue-headed Hummingbird and Red Hibiscus ..	20	20
491	$1.25, Green-throated Carib and Peach Hibiscus ..	50	60
485/91	.. .. *Set of* 5	80	90

1976 (16 Sept.). *West Indian Victory in World Cricket Cup. As Nos.* 559/60 *of Barbados.*

492	15 c. Map of the Caribbean ..	5	8
493	45 c. Prudential Cup	20	20

88. St. Mary's Church, Kingstown.

(*For illustration see Addenda*).

(Des. G. Drummond. Litho. Questa.)

1976 (18 Nov.). *Christmas. T* **88** *and similar horiz. designs. Multicoloured. W* w.**14** (*sideways*). *P* 14.

494	35 c. Type **88**	15	15
495	45 c. Anglican Church, Georgetown	20	20
496	50 c. Methodist Church, Georgetown	20	25
497	$1·25 St. George's Cathedral, Kingstown	55	65

89. Barrancoid Pot-stand.

(*Horiz.*—41×25 *mm.*)

(Des. G. L. Vasarhelyi. Litho. J.W.)

1976 (16 Dec.). *National Trust. T* **89** *and similar horiz. designs. Multicoloured. W* w.**14** (*sideways*). *P* 13½.

498	5 c. Type **89**	5	5
499	45 c. National Museum ..	20	20
500	70 c. Carib sculpture	30	35
501	$1 Ciboney petroglyph ..	40	45

GRENADINES OF ST. VINCENT

A group of islands south of St. Vincent which include Bequia, Mustique, Canouan and Union.

For stamps inscribed "The Grenadines of St. VINCENT" issued by St. Vincent in 1971, see under St. Vincent Nos. 330/**MS**336.

1973 (14 Nov.). *Royal Wedding. As Nos.* 165/6 *of Anguilla. Centre multicoloured. W* w.**12** (*sideways*). *P* 13½.

1	25 c. light green	12	15
2	$1 ochre	45	45

These stamps exist optd. "SPECIMEN".

GRENADINES
OF
(1)

1974 (24 Apr.). *Stamps of St. Vincent, T* **51** *etc., optd. in litho. with T* **1** *by Harrison & Sons. Glazed paper. W* w.**12** (*sideways on* 4, 5, 10, 12, 50 *c. and* $5).

3	1 c. Green Heron	5	5
4	2 c. Bullfinches	8	8
5	3 c. St. Vincent Parrots ..	12	12
6	4 c. Soufrière Bird	5	5
7	5 c. Ramier Pigeon	5	5
8	6 c. Bananaquits	8	8
9	8 c. Hummingbird	8	8
10	10 c. Mangrove Cuckoo ..	8	8
11	12 c. Black Hawk	10	10
12	20 c. Bare-eyed Thrush ..	15	15
13	25 c. Prince	20	20
14	50 c. Blue Hooded Euphonia ..	30	30
15	$1 Barn Owl	55	60
16	$2.50, Crested Elaenia ..	1·40	1·50
17	$5 Ruddy Quail Dove ..	2·75	3·00
3/17	.. .. .. *Set of* 15	5·50	6·00

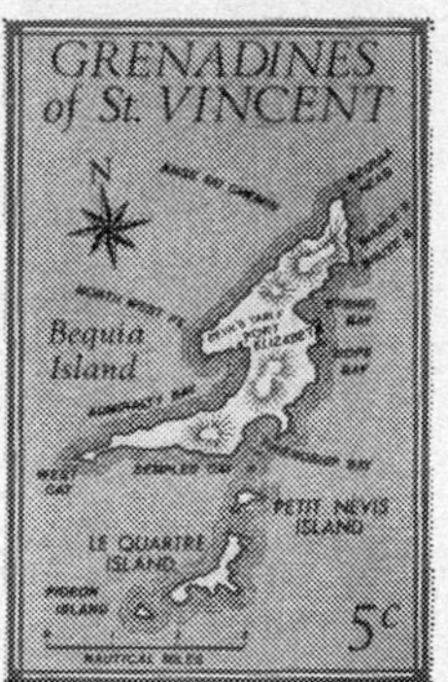

2. Map of Bequia.

(Des. G. Drummond. Litho. Enschedé.)

1974 (9 May). *Maps* (1*st series*). *T* **2** *and similar vert. designs. W* w.**12** (*sideways*). *P* 13×12½.

18	5 c. black, light dull green and deep dull green	5	5
19	15 c. multicoloured	8	10
20	20 c. multicoloured	12	12
21	30 c. black, lt. rose-lilac and lake	15	15
22	40 c. black, lav. & deep ultram.	20	20
23	$1 blk., cobalt & brt. ultram.	45	50
18/23	.. .. *Set of* 6	95	1·00

Maps:—15 c. The Grenadines and Prune Is. (inset); 20 c. Mayreau Is. and Tobago Cays; 30 c. Mustique Is.; 40 c. Union Is.; $1 Canouan Is.

See also Nos. 85/8.

GRENADINES
OF
(3)

1974 (7 June). *Nos.* 361/2 *of St. Vincent optd. in typo. with T* **3** *by Govt. Printer, St. Vincent. Glazed paper. W* w.**12**.

24	2 c. Bullfinches	5	5
25	3 c. St. Vincent Parrots ..	5	5
	a. Chalky paper. Wmk. sideways (No. 288)	8·50	9·50

1974 (25 July). *Centenary of Universal Postal Union. As Nos.* 392/5 *of St. Vincent but colours and face-values changed and inscr.* "Grenadines of St. Vincent".

No.	Value	Design	Unused	Used
26	2 c.	U.P.U. emblem	5	5
27	15 c.	Globe within posthorn ..	10	12
28	40 c.	Map of St. Vincent and hand-cancelling	25	25
29	$1	Map of the world	50	55

4. Boat-building.

(Des. G. Drummond. Litho. Questa.)

1974. *Bequia Island. T* **4** *and similar horiz. designs. Multicoloured. P* 14.

(*a*) *W* w.**12** *sideways* (26.9.74).

No.	Value	Design	Unused	Used
30	5 c.	Type **4**	3·25	2·25
31	30 c.	Careening at Port Elizabeth	20	25
32	35 c.	Admiralty Bay	25	25
33	$1	Fishing boat race	50	55

(*b*) *W* w.**14** *sideways* (12.74).

No.	Value	Design	Unused	Used
34	5 c.	Type **4**	5	5

5. Atlantic Thorny Oyster.

(Des. R. Granger Barrett. Litho. Questa.)

1974 (27 Nov.)–**76**. *Shells and molluscs. T* **5** *and similar horiz. designs. Multicoloured. W* w.**14** (*sideways*). *P* 14.

A. *No imprint.* B. *Imprint at foot.*

			A.		B.	
35	1 c.	Type **5** ..	5	5	†	
36	2 c.	Zigzag Scallop	5	5	†	
37	3 c.	Reticulated Helmet ..	5	5	†	
38	4 c.	Music Volute	5	5	5	5
39	5 c.	Amber Pen Shell	5	5	5	5
40	6 c.	Angular Triton	5	5	5	5
41	8 c.	Flame Helmet	5	5	5	5
42	10 c.	Caribbean Olive	5	5	5	5
43	12 c.	Common Sundial	5	5	†	
44	15 c.	Glory of the Atlantic Cone	5	5	†	
45	20 c.	Flame Auger	8	10	8	8
46	25 c.	King Venus ..	10	10	†	
47	35 c.	Long-spined Star-shell ..	15	15	12	15
48	45 c.	Speckled Tellin	15	20	†	
49	50 c.	Rooster Tail Conch ..	20	25	20	20
50	$1	Green Star Shell	40	45	35	40
51	$2.50,	Incomparable Cone	90	1·00	†	
52	$5	Rough File Clam	1·75	2·00	†	
52*a*	$10	Measled Cowrie	3·50	4·00	†	
35A/52*a*A		*Set of* 19	7·00	8·00		
38B/50B		*Set of* 9			75	85

Dates of issue: 27.11.74, Nos. 35A/52A; 12.7.76, Nos. 52aA and 38B/50B.

1974 (28 Nov.). *Birth Centenary of Sir Winston Churchill. As Nos.* 403/406 *of St. Vincent but colours and face-values changed and inscr.* "GRENADINES OF ST. VINCENT".

No.	Value	Design	Unused	Used
53	5 c.	Type **75**	12	15
54	40 c.	As 35 c.	25	25
55	50 c.	As 45 c.	30	30
56	$1	As $1	50	55

6. Cotton House, Mustique.

(Des. G. Drummond. Litho. Questa.)

1975 (27 Feb.). *Mustique Island. T* **6** *and similar horiz. designs. Multicoloured. W* w.**14** (*sideways*). *P* 14.

No.	Value	Design	Unused	Used
57	5 c.	Type **6**	5	5
58	35 c.	" Blue Waters ", Endeavour Bay ..	15	15
59	45 c.	Endeavour Bay ..	20	20
60	$1	" Les Jolies Eaux ", Gelliceaux Bay ..	45	45

7. Soldier Martinique.

(Des. G. Drummond. Litho. Questa.)

1975 (15 May). *Butterflies. T* **7** *and similar horiz. designs. Multicoloured. W* w.**14** (*sideways*). *P* 14.

No.	Value	Design	Unused	Used
61	3 c.	Type **7**	5	5
62	5 c.	Silver-spotted Flambeau	5	5
63	35 c.	Gold Rim	15	20
64	45 c.	Bright Blue and Donkey's Eye	20	20
65	$1	Biscuit	40	45
61/5		.. .. *Set of* 5	75	85

8. Resort Pavilion.

(Des. G. Drummond. Litho. Harrison.)

1975 (24 July). *Petit St. Vincent. T* **8** *and similar horiz. designs. Multicoloured. W* w.**14** (*sideways*). *P* 14.

No.	Value	Design	Unused	Used
66	5 c.	Type **8**	5	5
67	35 c.	The Harbour	15	20
68	45 c.	The Jetty	20	25
69	$1	Sailing in coral lagoon ..	50	55

9. Ecumenical Church, Mustique.

(Des. G. Drummond. Litho. Questa.)

1975 (20 Nov.). *Christmas. T* **9** *and similar horiz. designs. Multicoloured. W* w.**12** (*sideways*). *P* 14.

No.	Value	Design	Unused	Used
70	5 c.	Type **9**	5	5
71	25 c.	Catholic Church, Union Is.	12	15
72	50 c.	Catholic Church, Bequia	20	25
73	$1	Anglican Church, Bequia	40	45

10. Sunset Scene.

(Des. G. Drummond. Litho. J.W.)

1976 (26 Feb.). *Union Island. T* **10** *and similar horiz. designs. Multicoloured. W* w.**14** (*sideways*). *P* 13½.

No.	Value	Design	Unused	Used
74	5 c.	Type **10**	5	5
75	35 c.	Customs and Post Office, Clifton	15	20
76	45 c.	Anglican Church, Ashton	20	20
77	$1	Mailboat, Clifton Harbour	40	45

11. Staghorn Coral.

(Des. G. Drummond. Litho. Questa.)

1976 (13 May). *Corals. T* **11** *and similar horiz. designs. Multicoloured. W* w.**14** (*sideways*). *P* 14.

No.	Value	Design	Unused	Used
78	5 c.	Type **11**	5	5
79	35 c.	Elkhorn coral	15	15
80	45 c.	Pillar coral	20	20
81	$1	Brain coral	40	45

12. 25 c. Bicentennial Coin.

(Des. J. E. Cooter. Litho. Questa.)

1976 (15 July). *Bicentenary of American Revolution. T* **12** *and similar horiz. designs. W* w.**14** (*sideways*). *P* 13½.

No.	Value	Design	Unused	Used
82	25 c.	silver, black and light violet-blue	12	15
83	50 c.	silver, black and light rose-red	20	25
84	$1	silver, black and mauve ..	40	45

Designs: 50 c. Half-dollar coin; $1 One dollar coin.

(Des. G. Drummond. Litho. Questa.)

1976 (23 SEPT.). *Maps (2nd series). Vert. designs as T* **2**, *showing various islands as detailed below. W* w.**14**. *P* 13½.

A. Bequia D. Mustique
B. Canouan E. Petit St. Vincent
C. Mayreau F. Prune
G. Union.

To indicate individual islands, use the above letters as a suffix to the following catalogue numbers.

85	5 c. black, myrtle-green and pale emerald	5	5
	a. Booklet pane. Nos. 85/6 and 88 plus printed label	25	
	b. Booklet pane. Nos. 85×2 and 86 plus printed label	8	
86	10 c. black, ultramarine and greenish blue	5	5
	a. Booklet pane. Nos. 86×2 and 87 plus printed label.. ..	25	
87	35 c. black, red-brown and brt. rose	15	15
	a. Booklet pane. Nos. 87×2 and 88 plus printed label	45	
88	45 c. black, scar. & yell.-orge.	20	20
85/8	.. *Set of* 4 (*one island*)	35	40
85/8	.. *Set of* 28 (*seven islands*)	2·50	2·75

Nos. 85/7 were only issued in $2.50 stamp booklets.

13. Station Hill School and Post Office.

(*Horiz.*—42 × 26 *mm*.)

(Des. G. Drummond. Litho. Questa.)

1976 (2 DEC.). *Mayreau Island. T* **13** *and similar horiz. designs. Multicoloured. W* w.**14** (*sideways*). *P* 14.

89	5 c. Type **13**	5	5
90	35 c. Church at Old Wall ..	15	15
91	45 c. La Sourciere Anchorage	20	20
92	$1 Saline Bay	40	45

SAMOA.

I. INDEPENDENT.

1

(Des. H. H. Glover. Litho. S. T. Leigh & Co., Sydney, N.S.W.)

1877–80.

A. 1st state: *line above "x" in "EXPRESS" not broken. P 12½* (1 Oct. 1877).

No.	Type	Description	Unused	Used
1	1	1d. ultramarine	15·00	20·00
2	,,	3d. deep scarlet	15·00	20·00
3	,,	6d. bright violet	20·00	22·00
		a. Pale lilac	20·00	22·00

B. 2nd state: *line above "x" broken, and an extra dot to the left of "o", in the row of small pearls over "SAMOA". P 12½* (1878–79).

No.	Type	Description	Unused	Used
4	1	1d. ultramarine	15·00	20·00
5	,,	3d. bright scarlet	15·00	20·00
6	,,	6d. bright violet	15·00	20·00
7	,,	1s. dull yellow	18·00	22·00
		a. Line above "X" not broken	20·00	30·00
		b. Perf. 12 (1879)		
		c. Orange-yellow	20·00	30·00
8	,,	2s. red-brown	32·00	30·00
		a. Chocolate	45·00	60·00
9	,,	5s. green	£140	£150

C. 3rd state: *line above "x" repaired* (1879).

(*a*) *P 12½.*

No.	Type	Description	Unused	Used
10	1	1d. ultramarine	20·00	25·00
11	,,	3d. vermilion	20·00	25·00
12	,,	6d. lilac	20·00	25·00
13	,,	2s. brown	35·00	35·00
		a. Chocolate	35·00	35·00
14	,,	5s. green	£100	£110
		a. Line above "X" not repaired		

(*b*) *P 12.*

No.	Type	Description	Unused	Used
15	1	1d. blue	10·00	10·00
		a. Deep blue	10·00	10·00
		b. Ultramarine	12·00	12·00
16	,,	3d. vermilion	14·00	15·00
		a. Carmine-vermilion	12·00	15·00
17	,,	6d. bright violet	12·00	15·00
		a. Deep violet	12·00	15·00
18	,,	2s. deep brown	25·00	40·00
19	,,	5s. yellow-green	£100	£110
		a. Deep green	£100	£110
		b. Line above "X" not repaired (Nos. 29, 30)		

D. 4th state: *spot of colour under middle stroke of "M". P 12* (1880).

No.	Type	Description	Unused	Used
20	1	9d. orange-brown	15·00	20·00

Originals exist imperf., but are not known used in this state.

On sheets of the 1d., 1st state, at least eight stamps have a stop after "PENNY". In the 2nd state, three stamps have the stop, and in the 3rd state, only one.

In the 1st state, all the stamps, 1d., 3d. and 6d., were in sheets of 20 and also the 1d. in the 3rd state.

All values in the 2nd state and all values except the 1d. in the 3rd state were in sheets of 10.

As sheets of all printings of the originals were imperf. at the outer edges, the only stamps which can have perforations on all four sides are Nos. 1 to 3*a*, 10 and 15 to 15*b*, all other originals being imperf. on one or two sides.

The perf. 12 stamps, which gauge 11.8, are generally very rough but later the machine was repaired and the 1d., 3d. and 6d. are known with clean-cut perforations.

Remainders, in sheets of 21, of the 1d. and 6d., the *2d. rose* (which was never *issued*), and of the 9d., in sheets of 12, and of the 9d., 1s., 2s. and 5s. (probably also in sheets of 12), were found in the Samoan post office when this service closed down. The remainders are rare in complete sheets, but of very little value as singles, compared with the originals.

Reprints of all values, in sheets of 40, were made after the originals had been withdrawn from sale. These are practically worthless.

The majority of both reprints and remainders are in the 4th state as the 9d. with the spot of colour under the middle stroke of the "M", but a few stamps (both remainders and reprints) do not show this, while on some it is very faint.

There are three known types of forgery, one of which is rather dangerous, the others being crude.

II. KINGDOM.

2. Palm Trees.

3. King Malietoa Laupepa.

4a. 6 mm.

4b. 7 mm.

4c. 4 mm.

Description of Watermarks

(These are the same as W **12***a/c* of New Zealand.)

W **4***a*. 6 mm. between "N Z" and star; broad irregular star; comparatively wide "N"; "N Z" 11½ mm. wide.

W **4***b*. 7 mm. between "N Z" and star; narrower star; narrow "N"; "N Z" 10 mm. wide.

W **4***c*. 4 mm. between "N Z" and star; narrow star; wide "N"; "N Z" 11 mm. wide.

(Dies eng. W. R. Bock and A. E. Cousins. Typo. Govt. Ptg. Office, Wellington.)

1886–1900. (i) *W* **4***a*.

(*a*) *P 12½* (Oct.–Nov. 1886).

No.	Type	Description	Unused	Used
21	2	½d. purple-brown	1·00	50
22	,,	1d. yellow-green	1·00	50
23	,,	2d. dull orange	1·00	50
24	,,	4d. blue	1·50	75
25	,,	1s. rose-carmine	5·00	2·50
		a. Bisected (2½d.) (on cover)* ..		
26	,,	2s. 6d. reddish lilac	10·00	5·00

(*b*) *P 12×11½* (July–Nov. 1887).

No.	Type	Description	Unused	Used
27	2	½d. purple-brown	15	10
28	,,	1d. yellow-green	15	10
29	,,	2d. yellow	15	10
30	,,	4d. blue	2·00	50
31	,,	6d. brown-lake	30	15
32	,,	1s. rose-carmine	10·00	4·00
33	,,	2s. 6d. reddish lilac	15·00	7·00

(ii) *W* **4***c*. *P 12×11½* (May 1890).

No.	Type	Description	Unused	Used
34	2	½d. purple-brown	15	10
35	,,	1d. green	15	10
36	,,	2d. brown-orange	15	10
37	,,	4d. blue	1·00	20
38	,,	6d. brown-lake	2·00	40
39	,,	1s. rose-carmine	5·00	60
40	,,	2s. 6d. reddish lilac	20·00	10·00

(iii) *W* **4***b*.

(*a*) *P 12×11½* (1890–92).

No.	Type	Description	Unused	Used
41	2	½d. pale purple-brown	15	10
		a. Blackish purple	10	5
42	,,	1d. myrtle-green (5.90) ..	15	10
		a. Green	10	5
		b. Yellow-green	10	5
43	,,	2d. dull orange (5.90) ..	10	5
44	3	2½d. rose (11.92)	20	10
		a. Pale rose	20	10
45	2	4d. blue	1·00	25
46	,,	6d. brown-lake	1·00	25
47	,,	1s. rose-carmine	5·00	50
48	,,	2s. 6d. slate-lilac	5·00	50

(*b*) *P 12½* (Mar. 1891–92).

No.	Type	Description	Unused	Used
49	2	½d. purple-brown	10·00	5·00
50	,,	1d. green	10·00	5·00
51	,,	2d. orange-yellow	10·00	5·00
52	3	2½d. rose (1.92)	50	15
53	2	4d. blue	50·00	15·00
54	,,	6d. brown-purple	50·00	15·00
55	,,	1s. rose-carmine	£100	25·00
56	,,	2s. 6d. slate-lilac	£200	50·00

(*c*) *P 11* (1895–1900).

No.	Type	Description	Unused	Used
57	2	½d. purple-brown	10	5
		a. Deep purple-brown	10	5
		b. Blackish purple (1900) ..	10	1·00
58	,,	1d. green	10	5
		a. Bluish green (1897) ..	10	5
		b. Deep green (1900) ..	20	1·00
59	,,	2d. pale yellow	3·00	2·50
		a. Orange (1896)	40	10
		b. Bright yellow (1.97) ..	1·00	25
		c. Pale ochre (10.97)	40	10
		d. Dull orange (1900)	50	2·00
60	3	2½d. rose	20	10
		a. Deep rose-carmine (1900) ..	50	1·00
61	2	4d. blue	1·00	1·00
		a. Deep blue (1900)	50	1·00
62	,,	6d. brown-lake	1·00	1·00
		a. Brown-purple (1900) ..	50	1·00
63	,,	1s. rose	1·50	1·00
		a. Dull rose-carmine/toned (5.98)	50	50
		b. Carmine (1900)	50	1·50
64	,,	2s. 6d. purple	2·50	2·50
		a. Reddish lilac (wmk. inverted) (1897)	2·50	2·50
		b. Deep purple/toned (wmk. reversed) (5.98)	1·50	1·50
		ba. Imperf. between (vert. pair)	£200	
		c. Slate-violet	25·00	

*Following a fire on 1 April 1895 which destroyed stocks of all stamps except the 1s. value perf. 12½, this was bisected and used as a 2½d. stamp for overseas letters between April and May 1895, and was cancelled in blue or black. Fresh supplies of the 2½d. did not arrive until July 1895, although other values were available from 23rd May.

Bisects of the 1s. perf. 11 are known on cover cancelled in black in May and June 1895 and were later made to fill a philatelic demand; these are found on piece and are cancelled in black only (*price* £2.50).

The dates given relate to the earliest dates of printing in the various watermarks and perforations and not to issue dates.

The perf. 11 issues (including those later surcharged or overprinted), are very unevenly perforated owing to the large size of the pins. Evenly perforated copies are extremely hard to find.

For the 2½d. black, see Nos. 81/2 and for the ½d. green and 1d. red-brown, see Nos. 88/9.

FIVE PENCE (5)

FIVE PENCE (6)

5d (7)

1893 (Nov.–Dec.). *Handstamped singly, at Apia.*

(*a*) *In two operations.*

No.	Type	Description	Unused	Used
65	5	5d. on 4d. blue (37) ..	10·00	10·00
		a. Bars omitted		
66	,,	5d. on 4d. blue (45) ..	10·00	10·00
67	6	5d. on 4d. blue (37) ..	25·00	25·00
68	,,	5d. on 4d. blue (45) ..	25·00	25·00

(*b*) *In three operations* (Dec.).

69 **7** 5d. on 4d. deep blue (37)(R.) 50 10
 a. Stop after "d" .. ..
 b. Bars omitted .. ..
70 ,, 5d. on 4d. blue (45) (R.) .. 50 10

In Types **5** and **6** the bars obliterating the original value vary in length from 13½ to 16½ mm. and can occur with either the thick bar over the thin one or vice versa.

Double handstamps exist but we do not list them.

No. 69a came from a separate handstamp which applied the "5d." at one operation. Where the "d" was applied separately its position in relation to the "5" naturally varies.

SAMOA POST FIVE 5 PENCE
8

Surcharged 1½d.
(9)

R 3d.
(10)

The "R" in Type **10** indicates use for registration fee.

(Die eng. W. R. Bock and A. E. Cousins. Typo. New Zealand Govt. Ptg. Office.)

1894–1900. *W* **4***b* (*sideways*). (*a*) *P* 11½×12.

71 **8** 5d. dull vermilion (3.94) .. 50 50
 a. Dull red 50 50

(*b*) *P* 11.

72 **8** 5d. dull red (1895) .. .. 1·00 1·00
 a. Deep red (1900) 10 10

1895–1900. *W* **4***b*.

(i) *Handstamped with T* **9** *or* **10**.

(*a*) *P* 12×11½ (26.1.95).

73 **2** 1½d. on 2d. dull orange (B.) .. 1·00 1·00
74 ,, 3d. on 2d. dull orange .. 1·50 1·00

(*b*) *P* 11 (6.95).

75 **2** 1½d. on 2d. orange (B.) .. 50 50
 a. Pair, one without handstamp
 b. On 2d. yellow .. .. 25·00 25·00
76 ,, 3d. on 2d. orange .. .. 1·00 1·00
 a. On 2d. yellow .. .. 25·00 25·00

(ii) *Surch. printed**. *P* 11.

77 **2** 1½d. on 2d. orange-yellow (B.)

(iii) *Handstamped as T* **9** *or* **10**.† *P* 11 (1896).

78 **2** 1½d. on 2d. orange-yellow (B.)
79 ,, 3d. on 2d. orange-yellow .. 1·00 1·25
 a. Imperf. between (vert. pair) 75·00
 b. Pair, one without handstamp

(iv) *Surch. typo. as T* **10**. *P* 11 (Feb. 1900).

80 **2** 3d. on 2d. dp. red-orange (G.)

*It is believed that this was type-set from which clichés were made and set up in a forme and then printed on a hand press. This would account for the clear indentation on the back of the stamp and the variation in the position on the stamps which probably resulted from the clichés becoming loose in the forme.

†In No. 78 the "2" has a serif and the handstamp is in pale greenish blue instead of deep blue. In No. 79 the "R" is slightly narrower. In both instances the stamp is in a different shade.

A special printing in a distinctly different colour was made for No. 80 and the surcharge is in green.

Most of the handstamps exist double.

1896 (Aug.). *Printed in the wrong colour. W* **4***b*.

(*a*) *Perf. compound of* 10 *and* 11.

81 **3** 2½d. black .. .. ..

(*b*) *P* 11.

82 **3** 2½d. black .. .. 75 1·00
 a. Mixed perfs. 10 and 11 ..

Surcharged 2½d.
(11)

PROVISIONAL GOVT.
(12)

1898–99. *W* **4***b*. *P* 11.

(*a*) *Handstamped as T* **11** (10.98).

83 **2** 2½d. on 1s. dull rose-carmine/*toned* .. .. .. 1·50 1·50

(*b*) *Surch. as T* **11** (1899).

84 **2** 2½d. on 1d. bluish green (R.) 30 30
 a. Surch. inverted .. .. — 60·00
85 **2** 2½d. on 1s. dull rose-carmine/*toned* (R.) .. .. 1·00 1·00
 a. Surch. double £100
86 ,, 2½d. on 1s. dull rose-carmine/*toned* (Bk.) .. .. 1·00 1·00
87 ,, 2½d. on 2s. 6d. dp. pur./*toned* 2·00 2·00

The typographed surcharge was applied in a setting of nine, giving seven types differing in the angle and length of the fractional line, the type of stop, etc.

1899. *Colours changed. W* **4***b*. *P* 11.

88 **2** ½d. dull blue-green .. 25 25
 a. Deep green 25 25
89 ,, 1d. deep red-brown .. 25 25

1899–1900. *Provisional Government. New printings optd. with T* **12** (*longer words and shorter letters on* 5*d.*). *W* **4***b*. *P* 11.

90 **2** ½d. dull blue-green (R.) .. 10 10
 a. Yellowish green (1900) .. 10 10
91 ,, 1d. chestnut (B.) 10 10
92 ,, 2d. dull orange (R.) .. 10 10
 a. Orange-yellow (1900) .. 15 15
93 ,, 4d. deep dull blue (R.) .. 30 30
94 **8** 5d. dull vermilion (B.) .. 50 50
 a. Red (1900) 50 50
95 **2** 6d. brown-lake (B.) .. 75 75
96 ,, 1s. rose-carmine (B.) .. 1·50 1·50
97 ,, 2s. 6d. reddish purple (R.) .. 3·00 3·00

The Samoan group of islands was partitioned in 1899: Western Samoa (Upolu, Savaii, Apolima and Manono) to Germany and Eastern Samoa (Tutuila, the Manu'a Is. and Rose Is.) to the United States. German issues of 1900-14 will be found listed in Vol. 4 of the Stanley Gibbons Foreign Overseas Catalogue; there were no U.S. issues.

The German Islands of Samoa surrendered to the New Zealand Expeditionary Force on 29 August, 1914 and were administered by New Zealand until 1962.

III. NEW ZEALAND ADMINISTRATION.

G.R.I. 1d.
(13)

G.R.I. 1 Shillings.
(14)

(Surch. *Samoanische Zeitung*, Apia.)

1914 (3 Sept.). *German Colonial issue* (*ship*) (*no wmk.*) *surch. as T* **13** *or* **14** (*mark values*).

101 ½d. on 3 pf. brown .. .. 4·00 3·00
 a. Surch. double £200
 b. No fraction bar .. .. 15·00 13·00
 c. Comma after "I" £300 £150
 d. "1" to left of "2" in "½" 14·00 13·00
102 ½d. on 5 pf. green .. .. 10·00 5·00
 a. No fraction bar .. .. 20·00 15·00
 c. Comma after "I" .. .. £200 80·00
 d. Surch. double £110 £110
 e. "1" to left of "2" in "½" 18·00 18·00
103 1d. on 10 pf. carmine .. 38·00 15·00
 a. Surch. double £150 £150
104 2½d. on 20 pf. ultramarine .. 13·00 5·50
 a. No fraction bar .. .. 20·00 15·00
 b. "1" to left of "2" in "½" 20·00 14·00
 c. Surch. inverted £250 £250
 d. Comma after "I" £250 £175
 e. Surch. double £225 £225
105 3d. on 25 pf. blk. & red/*yell.* 25·00 15·00
 a. Surch. double £150 £100
 b. Comma after "I" £1800
106 4d. on 30 pf. blk. & orge./*buff* 35·00 22·00
 a. Error. 3d. on 30 pf. .. £1500 £1300
107 5d. on 40 pf. blk. & carmine 35·00 30·00
 a. Error. 4d. on 40 pf. .. £1500 £1300
108 6d. on 50 pf., blk. & pur./*buff* 20·00 10·00
 a. Surch. double £180 £180
 b. Inverted "9" for "6" .. 50·00 38·00
109 9d. on 80 pf., blk. & car./*rose* 75·00 38·00
110 "1 shillings" on 1 m. carm. £900 £900
111 "1 shilling" on 1 m. carm. £3250 £2500
112 2s. on 2 m. blue £850 £800
113 3s. on 3 m. violet-black .. £400 £400
 a. Surch. double £1500 £1700
114 5s. on 5 m.carmine & black £450 £400

The ½d. to 9d. were surcharged in a vertica[l] setting of 10.

No. 108b is distinguishable from 108, as th[e] "d" and the "9" are not in a line, and th[e] upper loop of the "9" turns downwards to th[e] left.

SAMOA.
(15)

1914 (29 Sept.). *Stamps of New Zealand, T* **50**, **51, 52,** *and* **27,** *optd. as T* **15,** *but optd. only* 14 *mm. long on all except* 2½*d. Wmk.* "N Z" *and Star, T* **41.**

115 ½d. yell.-grn. (R.) (*p.* 14×15) 15 2
116 1d. carm. (B.) (*p.* 14×15) .. 15 1
117 2d. mauve (R.) (*p.* 14×14½) 55 6
118 2½d. deep blue (R.) (*p.* 14) .. 90 1·1
119 6d. carm. (B.) (*p.* 14×14½).. 1·10 1·4
 a. Perf. 14×13½ .. .. 7·00 7·5
 b. Vert. pair, 119/9a .. .. 12·00 13·0
120 6d. pale car. (B.) (*p.* 14×14½) 5·00 4·5
121 1s. verm. (B.) (*p.* 14×14½).. 2·75 3·5

1914–24. *Postal Fiscal stamps as Type* F **4** *o[f] New Zealand optd. with T* **15**. *W* **41** (*sideways*). *Chalk-surfaced "De La Rue" paper.*

(*a*) *P* 14 (Nov. 1914–17).

122 2s. blue (R.) (9.17) .. .. 65·00 75·0
123 2s. 6d. grey-brown (B.) (9.17) 3·50 4·0
124 5s. yellow-green (R.) .. 5·50 7·0
125 10s. maroon (B.) .. .. 18·00 20·0
126 £1 rose-carmine (B.) .. 40·00 45·0

(*b*) *P* 14½×14, *comb* (1917-24).

127 2s. deep blue (R.) (3.18) .. 3·50 4·5
128 2s. 6d. grey-brown (B.) (10.24) 45·00 50·0
129 3s. purple (R.) (6.23) .. 4·50 9·0
130 5s. yellow-green (R.) (9.17) 6·00 7·5
131 10s. maroon (B.) (3.18) .. 19·00 24·0
132 £1 rose-carmine (B.) (3.18) 38·00 42·0

We no longer list the £2 value as it is doubtfu[l] if this was used for postal purposes.

See also Nos. 165/166*d*.

1916–19. *King George V stamps of New Zealan[d] optd. as T* **15**, *but* 14 *mm. long.*

(*a*) *T* **60***b*. *Typo. P* 14×15.

134 ½d. yellow-green (R.) .. 12 1
135 1½d. slate (R.) (1917) 15 2
136 1½d. orange-brown (R.) (1919) 15 4
137 2d. yellow (R.) (14.2.18) .. 20 1
138 3d. chocolate (B.) (1919) .. 55 8

(*b*) *T* **60**. *Recess. P* 14×14½, *etc.*

139 2½d. blue (R.) 40 4
 a. Perf. 14×13½ 25 4
 b. Vert. pair 139/9a .. .. 4·00 5·0
140 3d. chocolate (B.) (1917) .. 30 6
 a. Perf. 14×13½ 55 7
 b. Vert pair, 140/40a .. .. 3·50 5·5
141 6d. carmine (B.) (5.5.17) .. 85 1·1
 a. Perf. 14×13½ .. .. 85 1·7
 b. Vert. pair, 141/1a .. .. 4·00 6·0
142 1s. vermilion (B.) .. .. 1·50 4·0
 a. Perf. 14×13½ .. .. 1·10 1·5
 b. Vert. pair, 142/2a .. .. 5·00 8·0

IV. LEAGUE OF NATIONS MANDATE.

(Administered by New Zealand.)

1920 (July). *Victory. T* **62** *to* **67** *of Ne[w] Zealand, optd. as T* **15**, *but* 14 *mm. long.*

143 ½d. green (R.) 20 2
144 1d. carmine (B.) 20 4
145 1½d. brown-orange (R.) .. 55 7
146 3d. chocolate (B.) .. .. 70 1·7
147 6d. violet (R.) .. .. 1·75 2·5
148 1s. orange-red (B.) .. .. 2·75 4·0
143/148 .. .. *Set of* 6 5·50 8·5

16. Native Hut.

SILVER JUBILE[E] OF KING GEORGE V 1910-1935.
(17)

(Eng. Bradbury, Wilkinson. Recess-printed a[t] Wellington, N.Z.)

1921 (23 Dec.). *W* **41** *of New Zealand.*

(*a*) *P* 14×14½.

149 **16** ½d. green 30 4

150 **16** 1d. lake 15 30
151 ,, 1½d. chestnut 20 75
152 ,, 2d. yellow 25 60

(*b*) *P* 14×13½.

153 **16** ½d. green 20 25
154 ,, 1d. lake 12 10
155 ,, 1½d. chestnut .. .. 1·25 1·75
156 ,, 2d. yellow 90 25
157 ,, 2½d. grey-blue 40 75
158 ,, 3d. sepia 70 85
159 ,, 4d. violet 70 90
160 ,, 5d. light blue .. .. 75 1·60
161 ,, 6d. bright carmine .. 1·00 1·60
162 ,, 8d. red-brown .. .. 1·40 2·75
163 ,, 9d. olive-green .. .. 1·40 2·75
164 ,, 1s. vermilion .. .. 2·00 4·00
153/164 .. .. *Set of* 12 10·00 16·00

1925–28. *As Nos.* 127/32, *but thick, opaque, white chalk-surfaced "Cowan" paper.*

165 2s. blue (R.) (12.25) .. .. 75·00 85·00
166 2s. 6d. deep grey-brown (B.) (10.28) .. .. 60·00 75·00
166*a* 3s. mauve (R.) (9.25) .. 40·00 50·00
166*b* 5s. yellow-green (R.) (11.26) 7·50 9·00
ba. Opt. at top of stamp ..
166*c* 10s. brown-red (B.) (12.25) .. 20·00 25·00
166*d* £1 rose-pink (B.) (11.26) .. 50·00 60·00

1926–27. *T* 72 *of New Zealand, optd. with T* **15**, *in red.* (*a*) *"Jones" paper.*

167 2s. deep blue (11.26) .. .. 2·50 4·50
168 3s. mauve (10.26) .. .. 3·50 5·00

(*b*) *"Cowan" paper.*

169 2s. light blue (10.11.27) .. 5·00 7·00
170 3s. pale mauve (10.11.27) .. 15·00 20·00

1932 (AUG.). *Postal Fiscal stamps as Type* F **6** *of New Zealand optd. with T* **15**. *W* **41**. *Thick, opaque, white chalk-surfaced "Cowan" paper. P* 14.

171 2s. 6d. deep brown (B.) .. 10·00 12·00
172 5s. green (R.) .. .. 15·00 20·00
173 10s. carmine-lake (B.) .. 28·00 35·00
174 £1 pink (B.) .. .. 35·00 40·00
175 £2 bright purple (R.) .. £200
176 £5 indigo-blue (R.) £700

The £2 and £5 values were primarily for fiscal use.

1935 (7 MAY). *Silver Jubilee. Optd. with T* **17**. *P* 14×13½.

177 **16** 1d. lake 20 35
a. Perf. 14×14½ .. .. 23·00 32·00
178 ,, 2½d. grey-blue 55 90
179 ,, 6d. bright carmine .. 2·50 3·00

18. Samoan Girl.

19. Apia.

20. River Scene.

21. Chief and Wife.

22. Canoe and House.

23. R. L. Stevenson's home "Vailima".

24. Stevenson's Tomb.

25. Lake Lanuto'o.

26. Falefa Falls.

(Recess. De La Rue & Co.)

1935 (7 AUG.). *W* **41** *of New Zealand* ("N Z" *and Star*). (*a*) *P* 14×13½, (*b*) *P* 13½×14 *or* (*c*) *P* 14.

180 **18** ½d. green (*a*) 12 8
181 **19** 1d. black and carmine (*b*) 12 8
182 **20** 2d. black and orange (*c*) 12 12
a. Perf. 13½×14 .. .. 90 90
183 **21** 2½d. black and blue (*a*) .. 12 8
184 **22** 4d. slate and sepia (*b*) .. 25 15
185 **23** 6d. bright magenta (*b*) .. 25 20
186 **24** 1s. violet and brown (*b*) 50 30
187 **25** 2s. green & pur.-brn. (*a*) 80 65
188 **26** 3s. blue & brown-orge. (*a*) 1·10 1·10
180/188 .. .. *Set of* 9 3·00 2·50

See also Nos. 200/3.

WESTERN
SAMOA.
(27)

1935–42. *Postal Fiscal stamps as Type* F **6** *of New Zealand optd. with T* **27**. *W* **41**. *P* 14.

(*a*) *Thick, opaque chalk-surfaced "Cowan" paper* (7.8.35).

189 2s. 6d. deep brown (B.) .. 3·50 4·50
190 5s. green (B.) .. .. 5·50 7·00
191 10s. carmine-lake (B.) .. 12·00 14·00
192 £1 pink (B.) .. .. .. 25·00 30·00
193 £2 bright purple (R.) .. 65·00 80·00
194 £5 indigo-blue (R.) £150 £180

(*b*) *Thin, hard chalk-surfaced "Wiggins, Teape" paper* (1941–42).

194*a* 5s. green (B.) (6.42) .. 12·00 14·00
194*b* 10s. pale carm-lake (B.) (6.41) 20·00 22·00
194*c* £2 bright purple (R.) (2.42) £100 £120
194*d* £5 indigo-blue (R.) (2.42) .. £150 £180

The £2 and £5 values were primarily for fiscal use.

See also Nos. 207/14.

28. Coastal Scene.

29. Western Samoa.

30. Samoan Dancing Party.

31. Robert Louis Stevenson.

(Des. J. Berry (1d. and 1½d.). L. C. Mitchell (2½d. and 7d.). Recess. Bradbury, Wilkinson & Co.)

1939 (29 AUG.). *25th Anniv. New Zealand Control. W* **98** *of New Zealand. P* 13½× 14 *or* 14×13½ (*7d.*).

195 **28** 1d. olive-green & scarlet 25 30
196 **29** 1½d. lt. blue & red-brown 40 45
197 **30** 2½d. red-brown and blue 1·25 1·40
198 **31** 7d. violet and slate-green 3·00 3·00

32. Samoan Chief.

33. Apia Post Office.

(Recess. B.W.)

1940 (2 SEPT.). *W* **98** *of New Zealand* (*Mult.* "N Z" *and Star*). *P* 14×13½.

199 **32** 3d. on 1½d. brown 8 8
T **32** was not issued without surcharge.

(T **33**. Des. L. C. Mitchell. Recess. B.W.).

1944–49. *W* **98** *of New Zealand* (*Mult.* "N Z" *and Star*) (*sideways on* 2½*d.*) *P* 14 *or* 13½×14 (*5d.*).

200 **18** ½d. green 12 30
202 **20** 2d. black and orange .. 45 45
203 **21** 2½d. black and blue ('48) 70 80
205 **33** 5d. sepia and blue (8.6.49) 25 40

1945–48. *Postal Fiscal stamps as Type* F **6** *of New Zealand optd. with T* **27**. *W* **98**. *Thin, hard, chalk-surfaced "Wiggins, Teape" paper. P* 14.

207 2s. 6d. deep brown (B.) (6.45) 85 2·00
208 5s. green (B.) (5.45) .. 2·00 4·00
209 10s. carmine-lake (B.) (4.46) 6·00 8·00
210 £1 pink (B.) (6.48) .. 20·00 28·00
211 30s. brown (8.48) .. .. 45·00 65·00
212 £2 bright purple (R.) (11.47) 55·00 75·00
213 £3 green (8.48) .. .. 65·00 £100
214 £5 indigo-blue (R.) (1946) .. £140 £200

The £2 to £5 values were mainly used for fiscal purposes. The £5 also exists from a printing in May 1953 with the watermark inverted.

See also Nos. 232/5.

WESTERN
SAMOA
(34)

1946 (1 JUNE). *Peace Issue. Stamps of New Zealand optd. with T* **34** (*reading up and down at sides on 2d.*).

215 **132** 1d. green 8 8
216 **134** 2d. purple (B.) 8 8
217 **138** 6d. chocolate & vermilion 10 15
218 **139** 8d. black & carmine (B.) 10 20

V. UNITED NATIONS TRUST TERRITORY.

(Administered by New Zealand.)

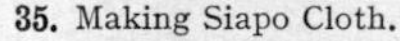
35. Making Siapo Cloth.

37. Seal of Samoa.

36. Native Houses and Flags.

38. Malifa Falls.
(wrongly inscribed " Aleisa Falls ").

39. Manumea (Tooth-billed Pigeon).

40. Bonito Fishing Canoe.

41. Cacao Harvesting.

43. Preparing Copra.

42. Thatching a Native Hut.

44. Samoan Chieftainess.

(Recess. Bradbury, Wilkinson.)

1952 (10 MAR.). *W* **98** *of New Zealand* (*sideways on* 1s. *and* 3s.). *P* 13 ($\frac{1}{2}$*d.*, 2*d.*, 5*d. and* 1s.) *or* 13$\frac{1}{2}$ (*others*).

219	**35**	$\frac{1}{2}$d. claret and orange-brn.	8	8
220	**36**	1d. olive-green and green . .	8	10
221	**37**	2d. carmine-red	10	12
222	**38**	3d. pale ultram. & indigo	12	15
223	**39**	5d. brown and deep green	15	20
224	**40**	6d. pale ultramarine and rose-magenta	20	20
225	**41**	8d. carmine	30	30
226	**42**	1s. sepia and blue . .	35	35
227	**43**	2s. yellow-brown	65	65
228	**44**	3s. choc. and brown-olive	1·40	1·40
219/228		. . . . *Set of* 10	3·00	3·00

1953 (25 MAY). *Coronation. As designs of New Zealand, but inscr.* " WESTERN SAMOA ".

229	**164**	2d. brown	12	12
230	**166**	6d. slate-grey	25	30

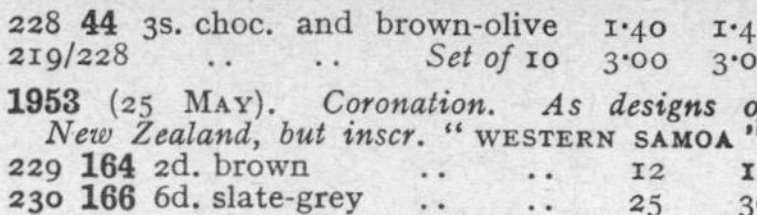

WESTERN

SAMOA

(45)

1955 (14 NOV.). *Postal Fiscal stamps as Type* F **6** *of New Zealand optd. with T* **45**. *W* **98**. *Chalk-surfaced " Wiggins, Teape " paper. P* 14.

232	5s. green (B.)	6·00	9·00
233	10s. carmine-lake (B.) . .	8·00	11·00
234	£1 pink (B.)	13·00	16·00
235	£2 bright purple (R.) . .	35·00	65·00

The £2 value was mainly used for fiscal purposes.

46. Native Houses and Flags.

47. Seal of Samoa.

48. Map of Samoa, and the Mace.

(Recess. B.W.)

1958 (21 MAR.). *Inauguration of Samoan Parliament. W* **98** *of New Zealand* (*sideways*). *P* 13$\frac{1}{2}$×13 (*6d.*) *or* 13$\frac{1}{2}$ (*others*).

236	**46**	4d. cerise	20	20
237	**47**	6d. deep reddish violet . .	25	25
238	**48**	1s. deep ultramarine . .	30	35

VI. INDEPENDENT STATE.

Samoa became independent on January 1st, 1962.

49. Samoan Fine Mat.

55. Samoan Orator.

50. Samoa College.

51. Public Library.

52. Fono House.

53. Map of Samoa.

54. Airport.

56. " Vailima ".

57. Samoan Flag.

58. Samoan Seal.

(Litho. Bradbury, Wilkinson.)

1962 (2 July). *Independence. W* **98** *of New Zealand (sideways on horiz. stamps). P* 13½.

239 **49** 1d. brown & rose-carmine 5 5
240 **50** 2d. brn., green, yell. & red 5 5
241 **51** 3d. brn., blue-green & blue 8 8
242 **52** 4d. mag., yell., bl. & black 12 15
243 **53** 6d. yellow and blue .. 12 15
244 **54** 8d. bluish green, yellow-green and blue .. 20 25
245 **55** 1s. brown and bluish green 25 30
246 **56** 1s. 3d. yellow-green & blue 30 35
247 **57** 2s. 6d. red and ultramarine 55 65
248 **58** 5s. ultram., yell., red & drab 1·40 1·60
239/248 .. .. *Set of* 10 2·75 3·25

See Nos. 257/62

59. Seal and Joint Heads of State.

(Des. L. C. Mitchell. Photo. Harrison.)

1963 (1 Oct.). *First Anniv. of Independence. W* **98** *of New Zealand. P* 14.

49 **59** 1d. deep sepia and green .. 5 5
50 ,, 4d. deep sepia and blue .. 8 10
51 ,, 8d. dp. sepia and rose-pink 15 20
52 ,, 2s. deep sepia and orange 40 45

60. Signing the Treaty.

(Des. L. C. Mitchell. Photo. Enschedé.)

1964 (1 Sept.). *2nd Anniv. of New Zealand-Samoa Treaty of Friendship. P* 13½.

53 **60** 1d. multicoloured .. 5 5
54 ,, 8d. multicoloured .. 12 15
55 ,, 2s. multicoloured .. 30 35
56 ,, 3s. multicoloured .. 40 45

61. Kava Bowl.

1965 (4 Oct.)–**66**? *As Nos.* 239, *etc. but W* **61** *(sideways on horiz. designs).*

57 **49** 1d. brown & rose-carmine 15 20
58 **51** 3d. brown, blue-green and blue (?66) .. .. 6·50 6·50
59 **52** 4d. mag., yell., blue & blk. 12 15
60 **53** 6d. yellow and blue .. 15 20
61 **54** 8d. bluish green, yellow-green and blue .. 20 25
62 **55** 1s. brown & bluish green 25 25
57/262 .. .. *Set of* 6 7·00 7·00

62. Tropic Bird.

63. Flying Fish.

(Des. L. C. Mitchell. Photo. Harrison.)

1965 (29 Dec.). *Air. W* **61** *(sideways). P* 14½.

263 **62** 8d. blk., red-orge. & blue 12 15
264 **63** 2s. black and blue .. 35 35

64. Aerial View of Deep Sea Wharf.

65. Aerial View of Wharf and Bay.

(Des. Tecon. Co. (U.S.A.). Photo. Enschedé.)

1966 (2 Mar.). *Opening of First Deep Sea Wharf, Apia. W* **61** *(sideways). P* 13½.

265 **64** 1d. multicoloured .. 5 5
266 **65** 8d. multicoloured .. 12 15
267 ,, 2s. multicoloured .. 30 35
268 **64** 3s. multicoloured .. 45 45

66. W.H.O. Building.

67. W.H.O. Building on Flag.

(Des. M. Goaman. Photo. De La Rue.)

1966 (4 July). *Inauguration of W.H.O. Headquarters, Geneva. W* **61** *(sideways). P* 14.

269 **66** 3d. yellow-ochre, blue and light slate-lilac .. 5 5
270 **67** 4d. blue, yellow, green and light orange-brown .. 8 8
271 **66** 6d. reddish lilac, emerald and yellow-olive .. 10 12
272 **67** 1s. blue, yellow, green and turquoise-green .. 20 25

HURRICANE RELIEF
6d

(**68**)

1966 (1 Sept.). *Hurricane Relief Fund. No.* 261 *surch. with T* **68** *by Bradbury Wilkinson.*

273 **54** 8d.+6d. bluish green, yell.-green and blue .. 25 25

69. Hon. Tuatagaloa L. S. (Minister of Justice).

70. Hon. F. C. F. Nelson (Minister of Works, Marine and Civil Aviation).

71. Hon. To'omata T. L. (Minister of Lands).

72. Hon. Fa'alava'au G. (Minister of Post Office, Radio and Broadcasting).

(Des. and photo. Harrison.)

1967 (16 Jan.). *Fifth Anniv. of Independence. W* **61** *(sideways). P* 14½×14.

274 **69** 3d. sepia and bluish violet 8 10
275 **70** 8d. sepia and lt. new blue 15 15
276 **71** 2s. sepia and olive .. 30 35
277 **72** 3s. sepia and magenta .. 45 45

73. Samoan Fales (houses), 1890.

74. Fono (Parliament) House, 1967.

(Des. V. Whiteley. Photo. Harrison.)

1967 (16 May). *Centenary of Mulinu'u as Seat of Government. W* **61.** *P* 14½×14.

278 **73** 8d. multicoloured .. 12 15
279 **74** 1s. multicoloured .. 20 25

(New currency. 100 sene or cents=1 tala or dollar.)

75. Wattled Honey-eater.

Designs as T **75**:—

76. Pacific Pigeon.
77. Samoan Starling.
78. Samoan Broadbill.
79. Red-headed Parrot-finch.
80. Purple Swamp-hen
81. Barn Owl.
82. Tooth-billed Pigeon.
83. Island Thrush.
84. Samoan Fantail.

84a. Mao.

84b. Samoan White-eye. (As T **84a**).

(Des. V. Whiteley. Litho. Format International ($2, $4). Photo. Harrison (others).)

1967 (10 July)–**69**. *Decimal currency.* *W* **6.** (*sideways*). *P* 13½ ($2, $4) *or* 14×14½ (*others*).

280	**75**	1 s. multicoloured ..	5	5
281	**76**	2 s. multicoloured ..	5	5
282	**77**	3 s. multicoloured ..	8	8
283	**78**	5 s. multicoloured ..	10	10
284	**79**	7 s. multicoloured ..	12	12
285	**80**	10 s. multicoloured ..	20	20
286	**81**	20 s. multicoloured ..	35	40
287	**82**	25 s. multicoloured ..	40	45
288	**83**	50 s. multicoloured ..	80	85
289	**84**	$1 multicoloured ..	1·75	2·00
289*a*	**84*a***	$2 mult. (14.7.69) ..	3·50	4·00
289*b*	**84*b***	$4 mult. (6.10.69) ..	7·00	7·50
280/89*b*		.. .. *Set of* 12	13·00	14·00

85. Nurse and Child.

(Des. G. L. Vasarhelyi. Photo. De La Rue.)

1967 (27 Nov.). *South Pacific Health Service.* *T* **85** *and similar horiz. designs. Multicoloured. P* 14.

290	3 s. Type **85**	8	8
291	7 s. Leprosarium	12	12
292	20 s. Mobile X-ray Unit ..	30	35
293	25 s. Apia Hospital ..	40	45

89. Thomas Trood.

(Des. M. C. Farrar Bell. Litho. Bradbury, Wilkinson.)

1969 (15 Jan.). *6th Anniv. of Independence.* *T* **89** *and similar portraits. Multicoloured. P* 13½.

294	2 s. Type **89**	5	5
295	7 s. Dr. Wilhelm Solf ..	12	12
296	20 s. J. C. Williams	30	35
297	25 s. Fritz Marquardt ..	40	45

94. Breadfruit.

95. Copra.

96. Bananas.

93. Cocoa.

(Des. Jennifer Toombs. Photo. Enschedé.)

1968 (15 Feb.). *Agricultural Development.* *W* **61.** *P* 13×12½.

298	**93**	3 s. deep red-brown, yellow-green and black	8	8
299	**94**	5 s. myrtle-green, greenish yellow & lt. brown	12	12
300	**95**	10 s. scarlet, blackish brown and olive-yellow ..	20	20
301	**96**	20 s. yellow-bistre, yellow and blackish olive ..	30	35

97. Women Weaving Mats.

(Des. G. L. Vasarhelyi. Photo. Harrison.)

1968 (22 Apr.). *21st Anniv. of the South Pacific Commission.* *T* **97** *and similar horiz. designs. Multicoloured.* *W* **61.** *P* 14½×14.

302	7 s. Type **97**	12	12
303	20 s. Palm Trees and Bay ..	35	35
304	25 s. Sheltered Cove.. ..	40	45

1928-1968
KINGSFORD-SMITH
TRANSPACIFIC FLIGHT
20
SENE
=

(100)

1968 (13 June). *40th Anniv. of Kingsford Smith's Trans-Pacific Flight. No.* 285 *surch. with T* **100.**

305	**80**	20 s. on 10 s. mult. ..	40	45

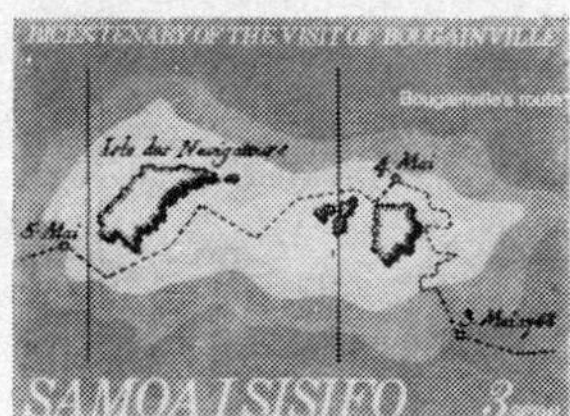

101. Bougainville's Route.

102. Louis de Bougainville.
103. Bougainvillea Flower.
104. Ships *La Boudeuse* and *L'Etoile*.

(Des. Jennifer Toombs. Litho. Bradbury Wilkinson.)

1968 (17 June). *Bicentenary of Bougainville's Visit to Samoa.* *W* **61** (*sideways*). *P* 14.

306	**101**	3 s. new blue and black	8	8
307	**102**	7 s. lt. ochre and black	12	15
308	**103**	20 s. multicoloured ..	35	35
309	**104**	25 s. multicoloured ..	40	45

105. Globe and Human Rights Emblem.

(Des. G. L. Vasarhelyi. Photo. Harrison.)

1968 (26 Aug.). *Human Rights Year.* *W* **61.** *P* 14.

310	**105**	7 s. greenish blue, brown and gold	12	15
311	,,	20 s. orange, green & gold	30	35
312	,,	25 s. violet, green & gold	40	45

106. Dr. Martin Luther King. **107.** Polynesian Versio[n] of Madonna and Child.

(Des. and litho. D.L.R.)

1968 (23 Sept.). *Martin Luther King Com[memoration].* *W* **61.** *P* 14½×14.

313	**106**	7 s. black & olive-green	12	1
314	,,	20 s. black & brt. purple	35	3

(Des. and litho. D.L.R.)

1968 (14 Oct.). *Christmas.* *W* **61.** *P* 14.

315	**107**	1 s. multicoloured ..	5	
316	,,	3 s. multicoloured ..	8	
317	,,	20 s. multicoloured ..	35	3
318	,,	30 s. multicoloured ..	50	5

108. Frangipani—*Plumeria acuminata.*

(Des. J. W. Ltd. Litho. Format.)

1969 (20 Jan.). *Seventh Anniv. of Independen[ce]. Type* **108** *and similar multicoloured design[s]. P* 14½.

319	2 s. Type **108**	5	
320	7 s. Hibiscus (*vert.*).. ..	12	
321	20 s. Red-Ginger (*vert.*) ..	30	
322	30 s. " Moso'oi "	50	

109. R. L. Stevenson and *Treasure Island.*

(Des. Jennifer Toombs. Litho. D.L.R.)

1969 (21 Apr.). *75th Death Anniv. of Rob[ert] Louis Stevenson. Horiz. designs, each showi[ng] portrait as in T* **109.** *Multicoloured.* *W* [**61**] (*sideways*). *P* 14.

323	3 s. Type **109**	8	
324	7 s. *Kidnapped*	15	
325	20 s. *Dr. Jekyll and Mr. Hyde*	35	
326	22 s. *Weir of Hermiston* ..	45	

111. Yachting.

112. Boxing.

110. Weightlifting.

Des. J. Mason. Photo. Note Ptg. Branch, Reserve Bank of Australia.)

969 (21 July). *Third South Pacific Games, Port Moresby.* P 13½.

27	**110**	3 s. black and sage green	8	8
28	**111**	20 s. black and light blue	35	40
29	**112**	22 s. black & dull orange	40	45

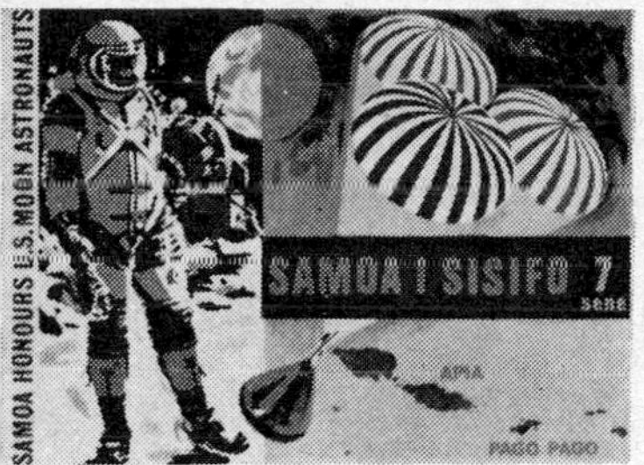

13. U.S. Astronaut on the Moon and the Splashdown near Samoan Islands.

Des. J. Mason. Photo. Note Ptg. Branch, Reserve Bank of Australia.)

969 (24 July). *First Man on the Moon.* P 13½.

30	**113**	7 s. multicoloured ..	15	15
31	„	20 s. multicoloured ..	35	55

114. "Virgin with Child" (Murillo).

Des. and photo. Heraclio Fournier, Spain.)

969 (6 Oct.). *Christmas. Type* **114** *and similar vert. designs. Multicoloured.* P 14.

32	1 s. Type **114**	5	5
33	3 s. "The Holy Family" (El Greco)	8	8
34	20 s. "The Nativity" (El Greco)	35	40
35	30 s. "The Adoration of the Magi" (detail, Velazquez)	50	55
IS336	116×126 mm. Nos. 332/5	1·10	1·25

115. Seventh Day Adventists' Sanatorium, Apia.

116. Rev. Father Violette and Roman Catholic Cathedral, Apia. (*Horiz.*)

117. Mormon Church of Latter Day Saints, Tuasivi-on-Safotulafai. (*Vert.*)

118. John Williams, 1797–1839, and London Missionary Society Church, Sapali'i. (*Horiz.*).

(Des. V. Whiteley. Litho. Format.)

1970 (19 Jan.). *Eighth Anniv. of Independence* W **61** (*sideways on 2, 7 and 22 s.*). P 14.

337	**115**	2 s. yellow-brown, pale slate and black ..	5	5
338	**116**	7 s. violet, buff & black	12	15
339	**117**	20 s. rose, lilac and black	30	35
340	**118**	22 s. olive-green, cinnamon and black ..	35	40

119. Wreck of S.M.S. *Adler*.

(Des. J. Waddington Ltd. Litho. Questa.)

1970 (27 Apr.). *Great Apia Hurricane of* 1889. *T* **119** *and similar horiz. designs. Multicoloured.* W **61** (*sideways*). P 13½.

341	5 s. Type **119**	12	12
342	7 s. U.S.S. *Nipsic*	20	20
343	10 s. H.M.S. *Calliope* ..	30	30
344	20 s. Apia after the Hurricane	60	65

120. Sir Gordon Taylor's "Frigate Bird III".

(Des. R. Honisett. Photo. Note Ptg. Branch, Reserve Bank of Australia.)

1970 (27 July). *Air. Aircraft. T* **120** *and similar horiz. designs. Multicoloured.* P 13½×13.

345	3 s. Type **120**	5	5
346	7 s. Polynesian Airlines "DC–3" ..	15	15
347	20 s. Pan-American "Samoan Clipper"	45	45
348	30 s. Air Samoa Britten-Norman "Islander" ..	65	65

121. Kendal's Chronometer and Cook's Sextant.

(Des. J. Berry. Litho. Questa.)

1970 (14 Sept.). *Cook's Exploration of the Pacific. T* **121** *and similar designs.* W **61** (*sideways on 30 s.*). P 14.

349	1 s. carmine, silver & black	5	5
350	2 s. multicoloured	8	8
351	20 s. black, bright blue and gold	40	40
352	30 s. multicoloured	60	60

Designs: *Vert.*—2 s. Cook's Statue, Whitby; 20 s. Cook's Head. *Horiz.* (83×25 *mm.*)—30 s. Cook, H.M.S. *Endeavour* and Island.

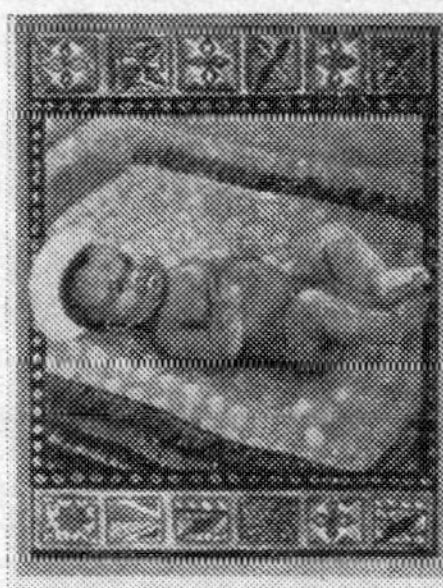

122. "Peace for the World" (F. B. Eccles).

(Des. from paintings. Photo. Heraclio Fournier, Spain.)

1970 (26 Oct.). *Christmas. T* **122** *and similar vert. designs. Multicoloured.* P 13.

353	2 s. Type **122**	5	5
354	3 s. "The Holy Family" (W. E. Jahnke) ..	8	8
355	20 s. "Mother and Child" (F. B. Eccles)	40	40
356	30 s. "Prince of Peace" (Meleane Fe'ao) ..	60	60
MS357	111×158 mm. Nos. 353/6	1·25	1·25

123. Pope Paul VI.

(Des. E. J. Cooter. Litho. Format.)

1970 (29 Nov.). *Visit of Pope Paul to Samoa. W* **61.** *P* 14×14½.

358 **123** 8 s. black and grey-blue 15 15
359 „ 20 s. black and plum .. 40 40

124. Native and Tree.

(Des. G. Drummond from sketches by the American Timber Co. Litho. Questa.)

1971 (1 Feb.). *Timber Industry. T* **124** *and similar multicoloured designs. P* 13½.

360 3 s. Type **124** 8 8
361 8 s. Bulldozer in clearing .. 15 15
362 20 s. Log in sawmill .. 40 40
363 22 s. Floating logs, and harbour 45 45

The 8 s. and 20 s. are horizontal designs.

125. Canoe (fautasi) in Apia Harbour and first stamps of Samoa and U.S.A.

(*Illustration reduced. Actual size* 84×26 *mm.*)

(Des. E. Roberts. Photo. Courvoisier.)

1971 (12 Mar.). *"Interpex" Philatelic Exhibition, New York. Sheet* 138×80 *mm. P* 11½.

MS364 **125** 70 s. multicoloured .. 1·50 1·50

126. Silva Dance.

(Des. and litho. J.W.)

1971 (9 Aug.). *Tourism. T* **126** *and similar horiz. designs. Multicoloured. W* **61** *(sideways). P* 14.

365 5 s. Type **126** 10 10
366 7 s. Samoan cricket .. 12 15
367 8 s. Hideaway Hotel .. 15 15
368 10 s. Aggie Grey and her hotel 20 25

127. " Queen Salamasina".

(Des. Jennifer Toombs from carvings by S. Ortquist. Litho. J.W.)

1971 (20 Sept.). *Myths and Legends of Old Samoa (1st series). T* **127** *and similar vert. designs. Multicoloured. W* **61** *(sideways). P* 14×13½.

369 3 s. Type **127** 8 8
370 8 s. " Lu and his Sacred Hens " 15 15
371 10 s. " God Tagaloa fishes Samoa from the sea " 20 20
372 22 s. " Mount Vaea and the Pool of Tears " .. 45 45

See also Nos. 426/9.

128. " The Virgin and Child " (Bellini).

(Des. J. E. Cooter. Litho. J.W.)

1971 (4 Oct.). *Christmas. T* **128** *and similar design. W* **61.** *P* 14×13½.

373 **128** 2 s. multicoloured .. 5 5
374 „ 3 s. multicoloured .. 8 8
375 – 20 s. multicoloured .. 40 40
376 – 30 s. multicoloured .. 60 60

Design: *Vert.*—20 s., 30 s. " The Virgin and Child with St. Anne and John the Baptist " (Leonardo da Vinci).

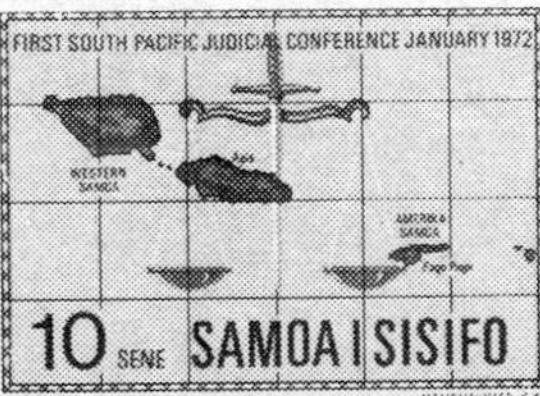

129. Map and Scales of Justice.

(Des. E. W. Roberts. Photo. Courvoisier.)

1972 (10 Jan.). *First South Pacific Judicia[l] Conference. P* 11½×11.

377 **129** 10 s. multicoloured .. 20 2

130. Asau Wharf. Savaii.

(Des. V. Whiteley. Litho. A. & M.)

1972 (10 Jan.). *Tenth Anniv. of Independenc[e]. T* **130** *and similar horiz. designs. Mult[i]coloured. W* **61** *(sideways). P* 13.

378 1 s. Type **130** 5
379 8 s. Parliament Building .. 15 1
380 10 s. Mother's Centre .. 20 2
381 22 s. Vailima Residence and rulers 35 4

131. Flags of Member Countries.

(Des. V. Whiteley. Litho. Questa.)

1972 (17 Mar.). *25th Anniv. of South Paci[fic] Commission. T* **131** *and similar multicolour[ed] designs. W* **61** *(sideways on* 8 *s. and* 10 *s.). P* 14×13½ *(*3 *and* 7 *s.) or* 13½×14 *(others).*

382 3 s. Type **131** .. 8
383 7 s. Flag and Afoafouvale Misimoa (Gen. Sec.) .. 15
384 8 s. H.Q. building, Noumea 15
385 10 s. Flags and area map .. 20

The 8 and 10 s. are horiz. designs.

132. Expedition Ships.

(Des. J. Berry; adapted J. E. Cooter. Lit[h] Questa.)

1972 (14 June). *250th Anniv. of sighting Western Samoa by Jacob Roggeveen. T* **132** *a[nd] similar horiz. designs. Multicoloured. W (sideways, except* 2 *s.). P* 14½.

386 2 s. Type **132** 5
387 8 s. Ships in storm .. 15
388 10 s. Ships passing island .. 20
389 30 s. Route of Voyage (85×25 *mm.*) 50

133. Bull Conch.

(Des. Format ($5) or J.W. (others). Litho. Format ($5), Questa others).)

1972 (18 Oct.)–**75.** *T* **133** *and similar multi-coloured designs. W* **61** *(sideways, on* 1 *s. to* 50 *s.). P* $13\frac{1}{2}$ *($1 to $5) or* $14\frac{1}{2}$ *(others).*

390 1 s. Type **133** 5 5
391 2 s. Rhinocerus Beetle .. 5 5
392 3 s. Skipjack (fish) .. 5 5
393 4 s. Painted Crab .. 5 5
394 5 s. Butterfly Fish 5 8
395 7 s. Samoan Monarch (butterfly) 8 10
396 10 s. Triton Shell 12 12
397 20 s. Jewel Beetle 25 25
398 50 s. Spiny Lobster 60 65
399 $1 Hawkmoth .. .. 1·25 1·40
399*a* $2 Green Turtle (18.6.73) 2·40 2·50
399*b* $4 Black Marlin (27.3.74) 4·75 5·00
399*c* $5 Green Tree Lizard (30.6.75) .. .. 6·50 7·00
390/9*c* .. .. *Set of* 13 15·00 16·00

Nos. 399/*c* are vert., 29 × 45 mm.

134. " The Ascension ".

(Des. PAD Studio from stained-glass windows in Apia. Litho. Harrison.)

1972 (1 Nov.). *Christmas. T* **134** *and similar vert. designs. Multicoloured. W* **61.** *P* $14\times14\frac{1}{2}$.

400 1 s. Type **134** 5 5
401 4 s. " The Blessed Virgin, and Infant Christ " .. 8 8
402 10 s. " St. Andrew blessing Samoan canoe " .. 20 20
403 30 s. " The Good Shepherd " 60 60
MS404 70 × 159 mm. Nos. 400/3 1·00 1·00

135. Erecting a Tent.

(Des. G. Drummond. Litho. Format.)

1973 (29 Jan.). *Boy Scout Movement. T* **135** *and similar horiz. designs. Multicoloured. W* **61** *(sideways). P* 14.

405 2 s. Saluting the flag .. 5 5
406 3 s. First-aid 8 8
407 8 s. Type **135** .. 15 15
408 20 s. Samoan action-song .. 40 40

136. Hawker Siddeley "748".

(Des. E. W. Roberts. Photo. Courvoisier.)

1973 (9 Mar.). *Air. T* **136** *and similar horiz. designs showing aircraft at Faleolo Airport. Multicoloured. P* $11\frac{1}{2}$

409 8 s. Type **136** 10 10
410 10 s. H.S. "748" in flight .. 12 12
411 12 s. H.S. "748" on runway 15 15
412 22 s. B.A.C. 1–11 .. .. 25 30

137. Apia General Hospital.

(Des. C. Abbott. Litho. Questa.)

1973 (20 Aug.). *25th Anniv. of W.H.O. T* **137** *and similar vert. designs. Multicoloured. W* **61.** *P* 14.

413 2 s. Type **137** 5 5
414 8 s. Baby clinic 15 15
415 20 s. Filariasis research .. 35 35
416 22 s. Family welfare .. 35 40

138. Mother and Child, and Map.

(Des. W. E. Jahnke (3 s.), Fiasili Keil (4 s.), E. Coter (others); adapted Jennifer Toombs. Litho. J.W.)

1973 (15 Oct.). *Christmas. T* **138** *and similar vert. designs. Multicoloured. W* **61.** *P* 14.

417 3 s. Type **138** 8 8
418 4 s. Mother and child, and village 10 10
419 10 s. Mother and child, and beach 20 20
420 30 s. Samoan stable 50 55
MS421 144 × 103 mm. Nos. 417/20 95 1·00

139. Boxing.

(Des. G. Drummond. Litho. Questa.)

1974 (24 Jan.). *Commonwealth Games, Christchurch. T* **139** *and similar horiz. designs. Multicoloured. W* **61** *(sideways). P* 14.

422 8 s. Type **139** 15 15
423 10 s. Weightlifting 20 25
424 20 s. Bowls 35 35
425 30 s. Athletics stadium .. 50 55

(Des. Jennifer Toombs from carvings by S. Ortquist. Litho. Questa.)

1974 (13 Aug.). *Myths and Legends of Old Samoa (2nd series). Multicoloured designs as T* **127.** *W* **61.** *P* $14\times13\frac{1}{2}$.

426 2 s. Tigilau and sacred dove 8 8
427 8 s. Pili, his sons and fishing net 15 15
428 20 s. Sina and the origin of the coconut 30 35
429 30 s. The warrior, Nafanua .. 50 55

140. Mail-van at Faleolo Airport.

(Des. E. W. Roberts. Photo. Heraclio-Fournier.)

1974 (4 Sept.). *Centenary of Universal Postal Union. T* **140** *and similar horiz. designs. Multicoloured. P* $13\times12\frac{1}{2}$ *(50 s.) or* 13 *(others).*

430 8 s. Type **140** 15 15
431 20 s. Ship at Apia Wharf .. 30 35
432 22 s. Early Post Office, Apia, and letter 35 40
433 50 s. William Willis and sailing-raft (87 × 29 *mm.*) .. 80 85
MS434 140 × 82 mm. No. 433 .. 85 90

The stamp in **MS**434 has a coloured margin, whereas that of No. 433 is white.

141. "Holy Family" (Sebastiano).

(Des. PAD Studio. Litho. Enschedé.)

1974 (18 Nov.). *Christmas. T* **141** *and similar horiz. designs. Multicoloured. W* **61** *(sideways). P* 13×13½.

No.	Description	Unused	Used
435	3 s. Type **141**	8	8
436	4 s. "Virgin and Child with Saints" (Lotto)	10	10
437	10 s. "Madonna and Child with St. John" (Titian) ..	20	20
438	30 s. "Adoration of the Shepherds" (Rubens)	50	55
MS439	128×87 mm. Nos. 435/8	95	1·00

142. Winged Passion Flower.

(Des. J.W. Ltd. Litho. Questa.)

1975 (15 Jan.). *Tropical Flowers. T* **142** *and similar multicoloured designs. W* **61** *(sideways on 8 and 30 s.). P* 14.

No.	Description	Unused	Used
440	8 s. Type **142**	15	15
441	20 s. Gardenia (*vert.*)	30	35
442	22 s. *Barringtonia samoensis* (*vert.*)	35	40
443	30 s. Malay apple	50	55

143. *Joyita* loading at Apia.

(Des. E. W. Roberts. Photo. Heraclio-Fournier.)

1975 (14 Mar.). "*Interpex* 1975" *Stamp Exhibition, New York, and* "*Joyita Mystery*". *T* **143** *and similar horiz. designs. Multicoloured. P* 13½.

No.	Description	Unused	Used
444	1 s. Type **143**	5	5
445	8 s. *Joyita* sails for Tokelau Is.	15	15
446	20 s. Taking to rafts ..	30	35
447	25 s. *Joyita* abandoned ..	35	40
448	50 s. Discovery of *Joyita* north of Fiji	75	80
444/8	.. .. *Set of* 5	1·40	1·60
MS449	150×100 mm. Nos. 444/8 Imperf.	1·60	1·75

144. "Pate" Drum.

(Des. Iosua To'afa; adapted L. D. Curtis. Litho. Harrison.)

1975 (30 Sept.). *Musical Instruments. T* **144** *and similar vert. designs. Multicoloured. W* **61** *(sideways). P* 14.

No.	Description	Unused	Used
450	8 s. Type **144**	15	15
451	20 s. "Lali" drum	30	35
452	22 s. "Logo" drum	35	40
453	30 s. "Pu" shell horn ..	45	50

145. "Mother and Child" (Meleane Fe'ao).

(Des. local artists; adapted G. L. Vasarhelyi. Litho. Walsall Security Ptrs. Ltd.)

1975 (25 Nov.). *Christmas. T* **145** *and similar vert. designs. Multicoloured. W* **61** *(inverted). P* 14.

No.	Description	Unused	Used
454	3 s. Type **145**	8	8
455	4 s. "The Saviour" (Polataia Tuigamala) ..	8	8
456	10 s. "A Star is Born" (Iosua To'afa) ..	20	20
457	30 s. "Madonna and Child" (Ernesto Coter) ..	45	50
MS458	101×134 mm. Nos. 454/7	85	90

146. "The Boston Massacre, 1770" (Paul Revere.)

(Des. J. Cooter. Litho. Walsall.)

1976 (20 Jan.). *Bicentenary of American Revolution. T* **146** *and similar horiz. designs. Multicoloured. W* **61** *(sideways). P* 13½.

No.	Description	Unused	Used
459	7 s. Type **146**	12	12
460	8 s. "The Declaration of Independence" (Trumbull)	15	15
461	20 s. "The Ship that Sank in Victory, 1779" (Ferris)	30	35
462	22 s. "Pitt addressing the Commons, 1782" (R. A. Hickel)	35	40
463	50 s. "The Battle of Princetown" (Mercer) ..	75	85
459/63	.. .. *Set of* 5	1·50	1·60
MS464	160×125 mm. Nos. 459/63	1·60	1·75

147. Mullet Fishing.

(Des. V. Whiteley Studio. Litho. Harrison.)

1976 (27 Apr.). *Fishing. T* **147** *and similar horiz. designs. Multicoloured. W* **61**. *P* 14

No.	Description	Unused	Used
465	10 s. Type **147**	15	2
466	12 s. Fish traps	20	2
467	22 s. Samoan fishermen ..	35	4
468	50 s. Net fishing	75	8

148. Paul Revere's Ride.

(Des. J. Berry. Photo. Heraclio Fournier.)

1976 (29 May). "*Interphil*" *Stamp Exhibition Sheet* 120×80 *mm. P* 13.

No.	Description	Unused	Used
MS469	**148** $1 gold, blk. & emerald	1·60	1·7

149. Boxing.

(Des. C. Abbott. Litho. Questa.)

1976 (21 June). *Olympic Games, Montreal. T* **149** *and similar horiz. designs. Multicoloured. W* **61** *(sideways). P* 14.

No.	Description	Unused	Used
470	10 s. Type **149**	15	2
471	12 s. Wrestling	20	2
472	22 s. Javelin	35	4
473	50 s. Weightlifting ..	75	8

150. Mary and Joseph going to Bethlehem.

(Des. C. Abbott. Litho. Questa.)

976 (18 Oct.). *Christmas.* T **150** *and similar vert. designs. Multicoloured.* W **61**. P 13½.

74	3 s. Type **150**	5	8
75	5 s. The Shepherds	8	10
76	22 s. The Holy Family ..	30	35
77	50 s. The Magi	65	75
IS478	124×115 mm. Nos. 474/7	1·10	

151. Queen Elizabeth and View of Apia.

(Des. BG Studio. Litho. Questa.)

977 (11 Feb.). *Silver Jubilee and Royal Visit.* T **151** *and similar horiz. designs. Multicoloured.* W **61** (*sideways*). P 13½.

79	12 s. Type **151**	15	20
80	26 s. Presentation of Spurs of Chivalry	35	40
81	32 s. Queen and Royal Yacht *Britannia*	40	45
82	50 s. Queen leaving Abbey ..	65	75

SARAWAK.

Sarawak was placed under British protection in 1888. It was ceded to Great Britain on 1 July, 1946; a Crown Colony until 16 Sept. 1963 when it became a state of the Federation of Malaysia.

Sir James Brooke. 1842–11 June, 1868.
Sir Charles Brooke. 11 June, 1868–17 May, 1917.

1. Sir James Brooke. **2.** Sir Charles Brooke.

The initials in the corners of T **1** and **2** stand for "James (Charles) Brooke, Rajah (of) Sarawak".

(T **1** and **2**. Die eng. Wm. Ridgway. Litho. Maclure, Macdonald & Co., Glasgow.)

1869 (1 MAR.). *P* 11.
1 **1** 3 c. brown/*yellow* .. .. 15·00 50·00

Specimens are known printed from the engraved die in orange-brown on orange surface-coloured paper, and perf. 12. These were submitted to the Sarawak authorities as examples of the stamps and exist both with and without obliterations.

1871 (1 JAN.). *P* 11 (*irregular*).
2 **2** 3 c. brown/*yellow* .. .. 1·00 1·50
a. Stop after "THREE" .. 5·00
b. Imperf. between (vert. pair) .. £100
c. Imperf. between (horiz. pair) .. £100

The "stop" variety, No. 2a, which occurs on stamp No. 97 in the sheet, is of no more philatelic importance than any of the numerous other variations, such as narrow first "A" in "SARAWAK" (No. 17) and "R" with long tail in left lower corner (No. 90), but it has been accepted by collectors for many years, and we therefore retain it. The papermaker's wmk. "L N L" appears once or twice in sheets of No. 2.

Specimens are known, recess-printed, similar to those mentioned in the note after No. 1.

TWO CENTS

Copies of No. 2 surcharged as above were first reported in 1876 but following the discovery of dies for forgeries and faked postmarks in 1892 it was concluded that the issue was bogus, especially as the availability of the 2 c. of 1875 made it unnecessary to issue a provisional. It has now been established that a 2 c. postal rate was introduced from 1 August 1874 for the carriage of newspapers. Moreover one example is known with a stop after "CENTS." and showing other minor differences from the forgery illustrated. This stamp could be genuine and if others come to light we will reconsider listing it.

1875 (1 JAN.). *P* 11½–12.
3 **2** 2 c. mauve/*lilac* (*shades*) .. 1·00 2·00
4 ,, 4 c. red-brown/*yellow* .. 1·25 1·00
a. Imperf. between (vert. pair) £125
5 ,, 6 c. green/*green* .. .. 1·00 1·25
6 ,, 8 c. bright blue/*blue* .. .. 1·50 2·00
7 ,, 12 c. red/*pale rose* .. .. 2·50 2·50
3/7 *Set of* 5 7·00 8·00

Nos. 3, 4, 6 and 7 have the wmk. "L N L" in the sheet, as No. 2. No. 5 is wmkd. "L N T".

All values exist imperf. and can be distinguished from the proofs by shade and impression. Stamps rouletted, pin-perf., or roughly perf. 6½ to 7 are proofs clandestinely perforated.

The 12 c. "laid" paper, formerly listed, is not on a true laid paper, the "laid" effect being accidental and not consistent.

The lithographic stones for Nos. 3 to 7 were made up from strips of five distinct impressions hence there are five types of each value differing mainly in the lettering of the tablets of value. There are flaws on nearly every individual stamp, from which they can be plated.

4. Sir Charles Brooke.

(Typo. D.L.R.)

1888 (10 Nov.)–**1897**. *No wmk.* *P* 14.
8 **4** 1 c. purple & black (6.6.92) 60 75
9 ,, 2 c. purple and carmine .. 1·25 75
a. Purple and rosine (1897) .. 2·00 1·00
10 ,, 3 c. purple and blue (11.88) 60 75
11 ,, 4 c. purple & yell. (10.11.88) 3·50 4·50
12 ,, 5 c. purple & grn. (12.6.91) 2·50 1·50
13 ,, 6 c. purple & brn. (11.11.88) 3·00 4·50
14 ,, 8 c. green and carmine .. 1·25 1·50
a. Green and rosine (1897) .. 3·00 2·50
15 ,, 10 c. green & purple (12.6.93) 5·50 5·00
16 ,, 12 c. green & blue (11.11.88) 1·00 2·25
17 ,, 16 c. green & orge. (28.12.97) 6·00 6·00
18 ,, 25 c. green & brn. (19.11.88) 6·00 6·00
19 ,, 32 c. green & black (28.12.97) 6·00 7·00
20 ,, 50 c. green (26.7.97) .. .. 7·00 8·00
21 ,, $1 green & black (2.11.97) 11·00 12·00
8/21 .. .. *Set of* 14 50·00 55·00

Prepared for use but not issued.
21*a* $2 green and blue £250
21*b* $5 green and violet .. £250
21*c* $10 green and carmine .. £250

On No. 21 the value is in black on an uncoloured ground.

The tablet of value in this and later similar issues is in the second colour given.

One Cent. (5) **one cent.** (6)

2c. (7) **5c** (8) **5c.** (9)

1889 (3 AUG.)–**92**. *T* **4** *surch.* *P* 14.
22 **5** 1 c. on 3 c. (12.1.92) .. .. 11·00 11·00
a. Surch. double .. .. 75·00 75·00
23 **6** 1 c. on 3 c. (Feb., 1892) .. 2·00 3·00
a. No stop after "cent" .. 25·00
24 **7** 2 c. on 8 c. (3.8.89) .. .. 1·50 3·00
a. Surch. double .. .. 75·00
b. Surch. inverted £300
c. Surch. omitted (in pair with normal) £250
25 **8** 5 c. on 12 c. (17.2.91) .. 10·00 11·00
a. No stop after "C" .. 12·00 12·00
b. "C" omitted .. .. 50·00
c. Surch. double £200
d. Surch. double, one vertical .. £350
e. Surch. omitted (in pair with normal) .. .. .
26 **9** 5 c. on 12 c. (17.2.91) .. 20·00 25·00
a. No stop after "C" .. 40·00 40·00
b. "C" omitted .. .. 65·00 65·00
c. Surch. double £200

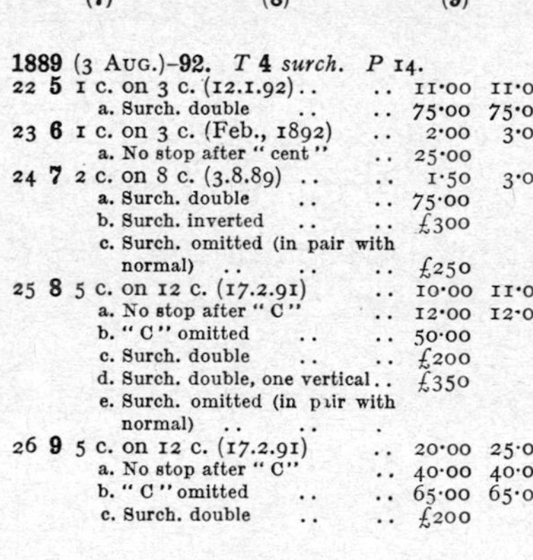

ONE CENT

(10)

1892 (23 MAY). *No. 2 surch. with T* **10**.
27 **2** 1 c. on 3 c. brown/*yellow* .. 50 75
a. Stop after "THREE" .. 5·00 6·00
b. Imperf. between (vert. pair) .. 75·00
c. Surch. double .. .. 55·00

Varieties with part of the surcharge missing are due to gum on the face of the unsurcharged stamps receiving part of the surcharge, which was afterwards washed off.

11 12

13. Sir Charles Brooke. **14.**

(Die eng. Wm. Ridgway. Recess. Perkins, Bacon & Co.)

1895 (1 JAN.–SEPT.). *No wmk.* *P* 11½–12.
28 **11** 2 c. brown-red .. .. 2·50 3·5
a. Imperf. between (vert. pair) 60·00
b. Imperf. between (horiz. pair) 60·00
c. Second ptg. Perf. 12½ (Sept.) 1·50 2·0
ca. Perf. 12½. Imperf. between (horiz. pair) .. .. 70·00
29 **12** 4 c. black .. .. .. 2·00 1·5
a. Imperf. between (horiz. pair) 60·00
30 **13** 6 c. violet .. .. .. 3·00 4·0
31 **14** 8 c. green .. .. .. 4·00 5·0

Stamps of these types, printed in wron colours, are trials and these, when surcharge with values in "pence", are from waste shee that were used by Perkins, Bacon & Co. as tri paper when preparing an issue of stamps fc British South Africa.

4 CENTS.

(15)

1899. *Surch. as T* **15**.
32 **2** 2 c. on 3 c. brn./*yell.* (19.9.99) 75 1·5
a. Stop after "THREE" .. 10·00
b. Imperf. between (vert. pair) .. £100
33 ,, 2 c. on 12 c. red/*pale rose* (29.6.99) .. .. 80 1·2
a. Surch. inverted .. £150 £2c
34 ,, 4 c. on 6 c. green/*green* (R.) (16.11.99) .. .. 7·00 8·c
35 ,, 4 c. on 8 c. bt. blue/*blue* (R.) (29.6.99) .. .. 1·50 2·5

Re "laid paper" varieties previously liste see note after No. 7.

A variety of surcharge with small "s" i "CENTS" may be found in the 2 c. on 12 c. an 4 c. on 8 c. and a raised stop after "CENTS" c the 4 c. on 6 c.

The omission of parts of the surcharge is du to gum on the surface of the stamps (see no after No. 27).

(Typo. D.L.R.)

1899 (10 Nov.)–**1908**. *Inscribed* "POSTAG POSTAGE." *No wmk.* *P* 14.
36 **4** 1 c. grey-blue & rosine (1.1.01) 35
a. Grey-blue and red .. 30
b. Ultramarine and rosine .. 1·25
c. Dull blue and carmine .. 2·00 2·0
37 ,, 2 c. green (16.12.99) .. 20
38 ,, 3 c. dull purple (1.2.08) .. 60
39 ,, 4 c. rose-carmine (10.11.99) 1·00
a. Aniline carmine .. 1·50

40 4 8 c. yellow & blk. (6.12.99) 1·25 1·10
41 ,, 10 c. ultramarine (10.11.99) 1·40 20
42 ,, 12 c. mauve (16.12.99) .. 2·00 1·25
a. *Bright mauve* (1905) 5·00 3·00
43 ,, 16 c. chest. & grn. (16.12.99) 2·00 1·50
44 ,, 20 c. bistre & brt. mve. (4.00) 2·50 3·50
45 ,, 25 c. brn. & blue (16.12.99) 2·50 3·50
46 ,, 50 c. sage-green & carmine (16.12.99) .. .. 6·00 7·00
47 ,, $1 rose-carmine & green (16.12.99) .. .. 11·00 12·00
a. *Rosine and pale green* .. 15·00 15·00
36/47 .. .. *Set of* 12 25·00 25·00

The figures of value in the $1 are in colour on an uncoloured ground.

Prepared for use but not issued.

48 4 5 c. olive-grey and green .. 10·00

16

1902. *Inscribed* "POSTAGE POSTAGE". *W* **16.** *P* 14.
49 4 2 c. green .. .. .. 4·50 1·10

Sir Charles Vyner Brooke.
17 May, 1917–1 July, 1946.

17. Sir Charles Vyner Brooke.

ONE
cent

(**18**)

(Typo. D.L.R.)

1918 (26 MAR.). *No wmk. Chalky paper. P* 14.
50 17 1 c. slate-blue and red .. 12 15
a. *Dull blue and carmine* .. 20 15
51 ,, 2 c. green 30 25
52 ,, 3 c. brown-purple .. 70 80
53 ,, 4 c. rose-carmine .. 70 60
a. *Rose-red* .. 55 90
54 ,, 8 c. yellow and black .. 90 2·00
55 ,, 10 c. blue (*shades*) .. 75 1·60
56 ,, 12 c. purple .. .. 1·00 2·00
57 ,, 16 c. chestnut and green .. 1·40 1·75
58 ,, 20 c. olive & violet (*shades*) 1·00 1·40
59 ,, 25 c. brown & bright blue 1·25 1·75
60 ,, 50 c. olive-green & carmine 1·60 2·00
61 ,, $1 bright rose and green 4·00 5·00
50/61 .. .. *Set of* 12 12·00 18·00
50/61 Optd. "Specimen" *Set of* 12 55·00

On the $1 the figures of value are in colour on an uncoloured ground.

Prepared for use but not issued.

62 17 1 c. slate-blue and slate .. 18·00

1922–23. *New colours and values. No wmk. Chalk-surfaced paper. P* 14.
63 17 2 c. purple (5.3.23) 20 40
64 ,, 3 c. dull green (23.3.22) .. 20 20
65 ,, 4 c. brown-purple (10.4.23) 20 12
66 ,, 5 c. yellow-orange .. 20 40
67 ,, 6 c. claret (1.22) .. 40 50
68 ,, 8 c. bright rose-red .. 70 1·00
69 ,, 10 c. black (1923) .. 80 1·10
70 ,, 12 c. bright blue (12.22) .. 2·50 4·00
a. *Pale dull blue* .. .. 2·00 3·50
71 ,, 30 c. ochre-brown and slate 1·10 2·00
63/71 .. .. *Set of* 9 5·00 8·50

1923 (JAN.). *Surch. as T* **18.**
(*a*) *First printing. Bars* $1\frac{1}{4}$ *mm. apart.*
72 17 1 c. on 10 c. dull blue .. 5·00 6·50
a. "cnet" for "cent" .. 65·00 70·00
73 ,, 2 c. on 12 c. purple 1·60 3·00
a. Thick, narrower "W" in "TWO" .. .. 4·50 6·50
(*b*) *Second printing. Bars* $\frac{3}{4}$ *mm. apart.*
74 17 1 c. on 10 c. blue .. .. 17·00
a. "en" of "cent" scratched out and "ne" overprinted £350
75 ,, 2 c. on 12 c. purple .. 9·00
a. Thick, narrower "W" in "TWO" .. .. 20·00

In the 2 c. on 12 c. the words of the surcharge are about $7\frac{1}{2}$ mm. from the bars.

Variety 74a arose from a native printer "correcting" an already correct surcharge in the second printing in the endeavour exactly to reproduce the "cnet" error of the first printing.

The thick "W" variety occurs on all stamps of the last two horizontal rows of the first printing (12 stamps per sheet), and in the last two vertical rows of the second (20 stamps per sheet).

1928 (APR.)–**29.** *W* **16** (*Multiple*). *Chalk-surfaced paper. P* 14.
76 17 1 c. slate-blue and carmine 25 25
77 ,, 2 c. bright purple .. 25 12
78 ,, 3 c. green 25 45
79 ,, 4 c. brown-purple .. 80 8
80 ,, 5 c. yellow-orange (5.8.29) 50 1·10
81 ,, 6 c. claret 40 20
82 ,, 8 c. bright rose-red .. 90 1·10
83 ,, 10 c. black .. .. .. 60 1·00
84 ,, 12 c. bright blue .. 85 1·00
85 ,, 16 c. chestnut and green .. 85 1·00
86 ,, 20 c. olive-bistre and violet 85 1·00
87 ,, 25 c. brown & bright blue.. 95 1·10
88 ,, 30 c. bistre-brown and slate 2·25 1·40
89 ,, 50 c. olive-green & carmine 1·25 1·60
90 ,, $1 bright rose and green 4·00 4·50
76/90 .. .. *Set of* 15 13·00 14·00
76/90 Optd./Perf. "Specimen" *Set of* 15 65·00

In the $1 the value is as before.

19. Sir Chas. Vyner Brooke.

20

(Recess. Waterlow.)

1932 (1 JAN.). *W* **20.** *P* $12\frac{1}{2}$.
91 19 1 c. indigo 30 15
92 ,, 2 c. green 30 15
93 ,, 3 c. violet.. .. .. 40 15
94 ,, 4 c. red-orange 20 8
95 ,, 5 c. deep lake 40 12
96 ,, 6 c. scarlet .. .. 1·10 2·00
97 ,, 8 c. orange-yellow .. 70 90
98 ,, 10 c. black .. .. 75 1·50
99 ,, 12 c. deep ultramarine .. 80 1·50
100 ,, 15 c. chestnut .. .. 1·10 2·25
101 ,, 20 c. red-orange and violet 1·10 2·00
102 ,, 25 c. oran.-yell. & chestnut 2·00 2·75
103 ,, 30 c. sepia and vermilion 2·00 3·00
104 ,, 50 c. carm.-red & olive-grn. 2·50 3·25
105 ,, $1 green and carmine .. 4·50 6·00
91/105 .. .. *Set of* 15 16·00 24·00
91/105 Perf. "Specimen" *Set of* 15 45·00

21. Sir Charles Vyner Brooke.

BMA

(**22**)

(Recess. B.W.)

1934 (1 MAY)–**41.** *No wmk. P* 12.
106 21 1 c. purple 10 8
107 ,, 2 c. green 8 8
107*a* ,, 2 c. black (1.3.41) .. 30 50
108 ,, 3 c. black 8 8
108*a* ,, 3 c. green (1.3.41) .. 12 25
109 ,, 4 c. bright purple .. 15 8
110 ,, 5 c. violet 8 8
111 ,, 6 c. carmine 10 20
111*a* ,, 6 c. lake-brown (1.3.41) 15 45
112 ,, 8 c. red-brown 8 10
112*a* ,, 8 c. carmine (1.3.41) .. 15 12
113 ,, 10 c. scarlet 35 35
114 ,, 12 c. blue 20 35
114*a* ,, 12 c. orange (1.3.41) .. 20 1·40
115 ,, 15 c. orange .. .. 15 1·00
115*a* ,, 15 c. blue (1.3.41) .. 25 1·25
116 ,, 20 c. olive-grn. & carmine 45 45
117 ,, 25 c. violet and orange .. 20 40
118 ,, 30 c. red-brown & violet.. 40 80
119 ,, 50 c. violet and scarlet .. 80 80
120 ,, $1 scarlet and sepia .. 90 90
121 ,, $2 bt. purple & violet.. 2·00 4·00
122 ,, $3 carmine and green .. 3·00 4·00
123 ,, $4 blue and scarlet .. 4·00 6·00
124 ,, $5 scarlet & red-brown 7·00 9·00
125 ,, $10 black and yellow .. 12·00 14·00
106/125 .. .. *Set of* 26 29·00 42·00
106/25 Perf. "Specimen" *Set of* 26 £110

For the 3 c. green, wmkd. Mult. Script CA, see No. 152a.

1945 (17 DEC.). *British Military Administration. Optd. with T* **22.**
126 21 1 c. purple 8 10
127 ,, 2 c. black (R.) 8 8
128 ,, 3 c. green 8 10
129 ,, 4 c. bright purple .. 8 8
130 ,, 5 c. violet (R.) 15 30
131 ,, 6 c. lake-brown 25 45
132 ,, 8 c. carmine .. .. 1·60 2·25
133 ,, 10 c. scarlet 25 40
134 ,, 12 c. orange 30 90
135 ,, 15 c. blue 30 15
136 ,, 20 c. olive-green & carmine 50 1·00
137 ,, 25 c. violet and orange (R.) 45 1·10
138 ,, 30 c. red-brown and violet 50 1·60
139 ,, 50 c. violet and scarlet .. 45 25
140 ,, $1 scarlet and sepia .. 80 1·10
141 ,, $2 bright pur. & violet .. 2·00 2·50
142 ,, $3 carmine and green .. 2·00 3·25
143 ,, $4 blue and scarlet .. 3·00 3·25
144 ,, $5 scarlet and red-brown 12·00 12·00
145 ,, $10 black and yellow (R.) 14·00 16·00
126/145 .. .. *Set of* 20 35·00 42·00

These stamps, and the similarly overprinted stamps of North Borneo, were obtainable at all post offices throughout British Borneo (Brunei, Labuan, North Borneo and Sarawak), for use on local and overseas mail.

23. Sir James Brooke, Sir Chas. Vyner Brooke and Sir Charles Brooke.

(Recess. B.W.)

1946 (18 MAY). *Centenary Issue. P* 12.
146 23 8 c. lake 10 20
147 ,, 15 c. blue 30 35
148 ,, 50 c. black and scarlet .. 55 90
149 ,, $1 black and sepia .. 2·75 4·00
146/9 Perf. "Specimen" *Set of* 4 32·00

(**24**)

(Opt. typo. B.W.)

1947 (16 Apr.). *Crown Colony Issue. Optd. with* **T 24** *in blue-black or red. Wmk. Mult. Script. CA. P* 12.

150	**21**	1 c. purple	8	8
151	,,	2 c. black (R.)	8	8
152	,,	3 c. green (R.)	8	8
		a. Albino opt.	£450	
153	,,	4 c. bright purple ..	10	10
154	,,	6 c. lake-brown	10	12
155	,,	8 c. carmine	8	8
156	,,	10 c. scarlet	10	10
157	,,	12 c. orange	8	15
158	,,	15 c. blue (R.)	8	12
159	,,	20 c. olive-grn. & carm. (R)	20	30
160	,,	25 c. violet and orange (R.)	15	12
161	,,	50 c. violet and scarlet (R.)	10	12
162	,,	$1 scarlet and sepia ..	40	65
163	,,	$2 bright purple & violet	90	1·10
164	,,	$5 scarlet and red-brown	2·00	2·50
150/164		.. .. *Set of* 15	4·00	5·00
150/64		Perf. "Specimen" *Set of* 15	85·00	

No. 152a shows an uninked impression of T **24**.

1948 (25 Oct.). *Royal Silver Wedding. As Nos.* 30/1 *of Aden.*

165	8 c. scarlet	12	12
166	$5 brown	4·00	6·50

1949 (10 Oct.). *75th Anniv. of Universal Postal Union. As Nos.* 114/117 *of Antigua.*

167	8 c. carmine..	12	15
168	15 c. deep blue	20	25
169	25 c. deep blue-green ..	25	45
170	50 c. violet	75	85

25. Troides Brookiana.

26. Tarsier.

27. Kayan Tomb.

28. Kayan Girl and Boy.

29. Bead work.

30. Dayak Dancer.

31. Scaly Ant Eater.

32. Kenyah Boys.

33. Fire-Making.

34. Kelemantan Rice Barn.

35. Pepper Vines.

36. Iban Woman.

37. Kelabit Smithy.

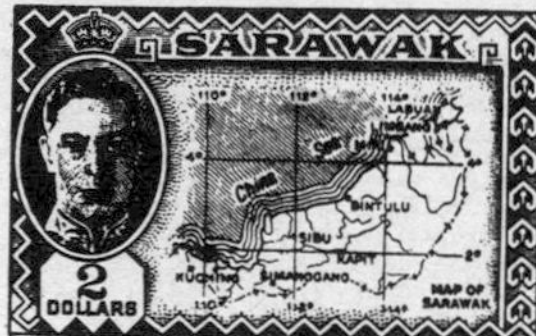

38. Map of Sarawak.

39. Arms of Sarawak.

(Recess; Arms typo. B.W.)

1950 (3 Jan.). *Wmk. Mult. Script CA. P* 11½×1[illegible] (*horiz.*) *or* 11×11½ (*vert.*).

171	**25**	1 c. black	10	[illegible]
172	**26**	2 c. red-orange	12	[illegible]
173	**27**	3 c. green	12	[illegible]
174	**28**	4 c. chocolate	12	[illegible]
175	**29**	6 c. turquoise-blue ..	12	[illegible]
176	**30**	8 c. scarlet	12	[illegible]
177	**31**	10 c. orange	35	[illegible]
178	**32**	12 c. violet..	20	[illegible]
179	**33**	15 c. blue	15	[illegible]
180	**34**	20 c. pur.-brn. & red-orge.	20	[illegible]
181	**35**	25 c. green and scarlet ..	25	[illegible]
182	**36**	50 c. brown and violet ..	35	[illegible]
183	**37**	$1 green and chocolate	60	[illegible]
184	**38**	$2 blue and carmine ..	1·25	[illegible]
185	**39**	$5 blk., yell., red & pur.	3·00	[illegible]
171/185		.. .. *Set of* 15	6·00	[illegible]

40. Map of Sarawak.

(Recess. B.W.)

1952 (1 Feb.). *Wmk. Mult. Script CA P* 11½×11.

186	**40**	10 c. orange	8	[illegible]

1953 (3 June). *Coronation. As No.* 47 *of Aden*

187	10 c. blk. & deep violet-blue	30	[illegible]

41. Logging.

42. Young Orang-Utan.

43. Kayan Dancing.

44. Hornbill.

45. Shield with Spears.

46. Kenyah Ceremonial Carving.

47. Barong Panau.

48. Turtles.

49. Melanau Basket-making.

50. Astana, Kuching.

51. Queen Elizabeth II.

52. Queen Elizabeth II (after Annigoni).

(Des. J. D. Hughes (6 c., 12 c.), G. A. Gundersen (20 c.), K. M. Munnich (25 c.). Recess. Arms typo. ($5). Bradbury, Wilkinson.)

1955–57. *$5 as T* **39** *(but with portrait of Queen Elizabeth II in place of King George VI). Wmk. Mult. Script CA. P* 11 × 11½ (1 *c.,* 2 *c.,* 4 *c.*), 12 × 13 (30 *c.,* 50 *c.,* $1, $2) *or* 11½ × 11 *(others).*

188	**41**	1 c. green	5	5
189	**42**	2 c. red-orange	5	5
190	**43**	4 c. lake-brown (*shades*) ..	5	5
191	**44**	6 c. greenish blue ..	8	8
192	**45**	8 c. rose-red	10	10
193	**46**	10 c. deep green	10	10
194	**47**	12 c. plum	12	12
195	**48**	15 c. ultramarine	20	15
196	**49**	20 c. olive and brown ..	20	12
197	**50**	25 c. sepia and green ..	25	20
198	**51**	30 c. red-brn. & deep lilac	25	10
199	,,	50 c. black and carmine ..	25	20
200	**52**	$1 myrtle-green & orange brown	50	50
201	,,	$2 violet & bronze-green	1·50	1·50
202	**39**	$5 black, yellow, red and deep purple	3·50	3·50
188/202		.. .. *Set of* 15	6·50	6·00

Dates of issue: 1.6.55, 30 c.; 1.10.57, others.

1963 (4 JUNE). *Freedom from Hunger. As No. 76 of Aden.*

203	12 c. sepia	20	25

1964–65. *As* 1955–57 *but wmk.* w.**12.** *Perfs. as before.*

204	**41**	1 c. green (8.9.64)	5	8
205	**42**	2 c. red-orange (17.8.65)	5	10
206	**44**	6 c. greenish blue (8.9.64)	12	25
207	**46**	10 c. deep green (8.9.64) ..	20	40
208	**47**	12 c. plum (8.9.64) ..	25	50
209	**48**	15 c. ultramarine (17.8.65)	35	60
210	**49**	20 c. olive & brn. (9.6.64)	50	90
211	**50**	25 c. deep sepia and bluish green (8.9.64) ..	60	1·25
204/211		.. .. *Set of* 8	1·75	3·50

53. *Vanda hookeriana.*

1965 (15 Nov.). *As Nos.* 166/72 *of Johore but with Arms of Sarawak inset as in T* **53.**

212	1 c. multicoloured	5	5
213	2 c. multicoloured	5	5
	a. Black (country name and shield) omitted		
214	5 c. multicoloured	5	5
215	6 c. multicoloured	5	5
	a. Black (country name and shield) omitted	45·00	
216	10 c. multicoloured (*shades*)	8	5
217	15 c. multicoloured ..	8	10
218	20 c. multicoloured ..	10	10
212/218	.. .. *Set of* 7	35	35

The 1 c., 6 c., 10 c. and 15 c. exist with PVA gum as well as gum arabic.

No. 213a was formerly listed as Trengganu No. 101a but there is evidence that this was issued in Sarawak.

The higher values used in Sarawak were Nos. 20/27 of Malaysia.

54. Blue Pansy Butterfly.

1971 (1 FEB.). *As Nos.* 175/81 *of Johore bu with Arms of Sarawak inset as in T* **54.**

219	1 c. multicoloured	5	5
220	2 c. multicoloured	5	5
221	5 c. multicoloured	5	5
222	6 c. multicoloured	5	5
223	10 c. multicoloured	5	5
224	15 c. multicoloured	8	8
225	20 c. multicoloured	10	10
219/25	.. .. *Set of* 7	30	30

The higher values used in Sarawak are Nos. 64/71 of Malaysia.

JAPANESE OCCUPATION OF SARAWAK.

The stamps listed under this heading were valid for use throughout North Borneo, (i.e. in Brunei, Labuan, North Borneo and Sarawak).

府政國帝本日大

(" Imperial Japanese Government ")

(1)

1942. *Stamps of Sarawak optd. with T* **1** *in violet.*

J 1	**21**	1 c. purple	2·50	3·00
J 2	,,	2 c. green	7·50	9·00
J 3	,,	2 c. black	7·50	9·00
J 4	,,	3 c. black	14·00	16·00
J 5	,,	3 c. green	5·50	6·00
J 6	,,	4 c. bright purple ..	3·00	3·00
J 7	,,	5 c. violet	4·00	5·00
J 8	,,	6 c. carmine	6·00	6·00
J 9	,,	6 c. lake-brown ..	4·50	6·00
J10	,,	8 c. red-brown ..	14·00	16·00
J11	,,	8 c. carmine	16·00	20·00
J12	,,	10 c. scarlet	4·00	4·50
J13	,,	12 c. blue	8·00	9·00
J14	,,	12 c. orange	16·00	20·00
J15	,,	15 c. orange	14·00	16·00
J16	,,	15 c. blue	7·50	9·00
J17	,,	20 c. olive-green and carm.	4·00	5·50
J18	,,	25 c. violet and orange ..	4·00	5·50
J19	,,	30 c. red-brown and violet	4·00	5·50

J20	21	50 c. violet and scarlet ..	6·00	6·00
J21	,,	$1 scarlet and sepia ..	6·50	8·00
J22	,,	$2 bright purple & violet	16·00	20·00
J23	,,	$3 carmine and green ..	60·00	80·00
J24	,,	$4 blue and scarlet ..	20·00	24·00
J25	,,	$5 scarlet & red-brown	16·00	20·00
J26	,,	$10 black and yellow ..	23·00	27·00

The overprint, being handstamped, exists inverted on all values.

Stamps of T **21** optd. with Japanese symbols within an oval frame are revenue stamps, while the same stamps overprinted with three Japanese characters between two vertical double rules, were used as seals.

SEYCHELLES.

I. DEPENDENCY OF MAURITIUS.

PRINTERS. Nos. 1 to 123 were typographed by De La Rue & Co.

1

Die I.

Die II.

In Die I there are lines of shading in the middle compartment of the diadem which are absent from Die II.

1890 (5 April)–**92**. *Wmk. Crown CA. P* 14.

(i) Die I.

1	**1**	2 c. green and carmine ..	65	2·25
2	,,	4 c. carmine and green ..	2·75	3·50
3	,,	8 c. brown-purple and blue	1·00	2·00
4	,,	10 c. ultramarine and brown	1·60	3·25
5	,,	13 c. grey and black ..	1·10	3·25
6	,,	16 c. chestnut and blue ..	1·60	1·60
7	,,	48 c. ochre and green ..	6·00	6·50
8	,,	96 c. mauve and carmine ..	9·50	11·00
1/8		.. .. *Set of* 8	22·00	30·00
1/8		Optd. "Specimen" *Set of* 8	70·00	

(ii) Die II. (1892).

9	**1**	2 c. green and rosine ..	50	55
10	,,	4 c. carmine and green ..	55	55
11	,,	8 c. brn.-pur. & ultramarine	90	1·10
12	,,	10 c. bright ultram. & brown	1·10	1·00
13	,,	13 c. grey and black ..	1·10	1·00
14	,,	16 c. chestnut & ultramarine	4·50	4·00
9/14		.. .. *Set of* 6	8·00	7·50

3
cents
(**2**)

18 CENTS
(**3**)

4

1893 (1 Jan.). *Surch. locally as T* **2**.

15	3 c. on 4 c. (No. 10) ..	35	65
	a. Surch. inverted	£100	£110
	b. Surch. double	£120	
	c. Surch. omitted (in pair with normal)	£1100	
16	12 c. on 16 c. (No. 6)	90	1·00
	a. Surch. inverted	£150	
	b. Surch. double	£700	
17	12 c. on 16 c. (No. 14) ..	1·00	1·10
	a. Surch. double		
18	15 c. on 16 c. (No. 6)	3·50	4·00
	a. Surch. inverted	90·00	90·00
	b. Surch. double	£170	£170
19	15 c. on 16 c. (No. 14) ..	2·25	1·10
	a. Surch. inverted	£180	£180
	b. Surch. double	£275	£180
	c. Surch. treble		
20	45 c. on 48 c. (No. 7)	3·00	2·25
21	90 c. on 96 c. (No. 8)	8·50	9·50
15/21	.. .. *Set of* 7	17·00	18·00

Nos. 15, 16, 18, 19 and 20 exist with "cents" omitted and with "cents" above value and are due to misplacement of the surcharge. No. 17 exists with surcharge omitted in pair with normal due to misplacement sideways.

1893 (Nov.). *New values. Die* II. *Wmk. Crown CA. P* 14.

22	**1**	3 c. dull purple and orange	20	30
23	,,	12 c. sepia and green	50	80
24	,,	15 c. sage-green and lilac ..	1·10	1·10
25	,,	45 c. brown and carmine ..	6·50	7·00
22/25		Optd. "Specimen" *Set of* 4	27·00	

1896 (1 Aug.). *No. 25 surch. as T* **3**.

26	**1**	18 c. on 45 c. brn. & carm.	2·00	2·00
		a. Surch. double	£275	£275
		b. Surch. treble	£200	
27	,,	36 c. on 45 c. brn. & carm.	4·00	6·00
		a. Surch. double	£350	
26/27		H/S "Specimen" *Set of* 2	27·00	

1897–1900. *Colours changed and new values. Die* II. *Wmk. Crown CA. P* 14.

28	**1**	2 c. orange-brn. & grn. ('00)	25	65
29	,,	6 c. carmine (1900)	65	90
30	,,	15 c. ultramarine (1900) ..	2·00	1·75
31	,,	18 c. ultramarine	1·10	1·90
32	,,	36 c. brown and carmine ..	6·00	5·50
33	**4**	75 c. yellow & violet (1900)	9·50	11·00
34	,,	1 r. bright mauve & dp. red	5·50	4·50
35	,,	1 r. 50 c. grey & carm. ('00)	14·00	16·00
36	,,	2 r. 25 c. bright mauve and green (1900)	14·00	16·00
28/36		.. .. *Set of* 9	48·00	50·00
28/36		Optd. "Specimen" *Set of* 9	70·00	

3 cents

(**5**)

6 cents

(**5***a*)

1901. *Nos.* 12, 14, 32 *and* 11 *surch. locally with T* **5** *or* **5a**.

37	3 c. on 10 c. (10.01) ..	55	1·10
	a. Surch. double	£180	
38	3 c. on 16 c. (8.01)	55	1·25
	a. Surch. inverted	£180	£180
	b. Surch. double	£180	
	c. "3 cents" omitted	£180	
39	3 c. on 36 c. (21.6.01) ..	55	1·10
	a. Surch. double	£250	
	b. "3 cents" omitted	£180	£225
40	6 c. on 8 c. (8.01)	55	1·10
	a. Surch. inverted	£180	£180
37/40	H/S "Specimen" *Set of* 4	38·00	

1902 (June). *Surch. locally as T* **5**.

41	**1**	2 c. on 4 c. (No. 10) ..	1·10	2·25
42	**4**	30 c. on 75 c. (No. 33) ..	2·25	5·00
		a. Narrow "0" in "30" ..	8·50	19·00
43	,,	30 c. on 1 r. (No. 34) ..	2·25	5·00
		a. Narrow "0" in "30" ..	8·50	19·00
		b. Surch. double	£180	
44	,,	45 c. on 1 r. (No. 34) ..	3·25	6·50
45	,,	45 c. on 2 r. 25 c. (No. 36) ..	5·00	7·00
		a. Narrow "5" in "45" ..	30·00	40·00
41/45		.. .. *Set of* 5	12·00	24·00
41/45		H/S "Specimen" *Set of* 5	48·00	

6

7

1903 (June). *T* **6** (2 *c. to* 45 *c.*) *and* **7** (*highe values*). *Wmk. Crown CA. P* 14.

46	2 c. chestnut and green .	15	3
47	3 c. dull green	45	5
48	6 c. carmine	30	1
49	12 c. olive-sepia & dull green	75	3
50	15 c. ultramarine	85	1·2
51	18 c. sage-green and carmine	2·00	3·0
52	30 c. violet and dull green ..	2·50	3·0
53	45 c. brown and carmine ..	2·50	3·5
54	75 c. yellow and violet ..	3·25	4·5
55	1 r. 50 c. black and carmine	8·50	8·5
56	2 r. 25 c. purple and green	7·00	8·5
46/56	.. .. *Set of* 11	26·00	30·0
46/56	Optd. "Specimen" *Set of* 11	75·00	

3 cents

(8)

1903. *T* **6** *surch. locally with T* **8**.

57	3 c. on 15 c. ultramarine (3.7)	1·10	1·6
58	3 c. on 18 c. sage-green and carmine (2.9)	3·00	3·5
59	3 c. on 45 c. brown & carmine (21.7)	95	2·5
57/9	H/S "Specimen" *Set of* 3	38·00	

II. CROWN COLONY.

31 August 1903.

1906. *Wmk. Mult. Crown CA. P* 14.

60	**6**	2 c. chestnut and green ..	15	2
61	,,	3 c. dull green	30	2
62	,,	6 c. carmine	25	1
63	,,	12 c. olive-sepia & dull green	95	2
64	,,	15 c. ultramarine	50	1·4
65	,,	18 c. sage-green and carmine	1·00	1·7
66	,,	30 c. violet and dull green ..	2·50	2·5
67	,,	45 c. brown and carmine ..	2·00	3·2
68	**7**	75 c. yellow and violet ..	4·50	5·5
69	,,	1 r. 50 c. black and carmine	6·50	7·0
70	,,	2 r. 25 c. purple and green ..	9·00	10·0
60/70		.. .. *Set of* 11	25·00	29·0

9

10

1912–13. *Wmk. Mult. Crown CA. P* 14.

71	**9**	2 c. chestnut and green ..	12	4
72	,,	3 c. green	15	1
73	,,	6 c. aniline carmine ..	3·75	2·5
		a. Carmine-red	90	
74	,,	12 c. olive-sepia & dull grn.	55	1·6
75	,,	15 c. ultramarine	75	5
76	,,	18 c. sage-green & carmine	45	2·0
77	,,	30 c. violet and green ..	2·25	6
78	,,	45 c. brown and carmine ..	1·00	2·4
79	**10**	75 c. yellow and violet ..	3·25	2·0
80	,,	1 r. 50 c. black & carmine	1·90	1·0
81	,,	2 r. 25 c. rose-pur. & grn.	10·00	10·0
		a. Bright purple and green ..	9·50	4·5
71/81*a*		.. .. *Set of* 11	18·00	14·0
71/81		Optd. "Specimen" *Set of* 11	70·00	

The split "A" variety illustrated above No. 8 of Gambia also occurs on Nos. 71/81. (*Pric about three times normal.*)

The 2 c., 3 c. and 15 c. were issued in Apr 1912, the 6 c. in June 1913 and the remainde in January 1913.

11

12

13

917–22. *Wmk. Mult. Crown CA. P* 14.

2	**11**	2 c. chestnut & green, O	8	20
3	,,	3 c. green, O	8	8
4	**12**	5 c. deep brown, O (1920)	8	30
5	**11**	6 c. carmine, O ..	12	8
		a. Rose, O (1919)	1·25	25
5	,,	12 c. grey, O (1919) ..	20	75
7	,,	15 c. ultramarine, O ..	12	1·00
3	,,	18 c. purple/*yell.*, C (1919)	80	1·60
		a. On orange-buff (1920) ..	3·75	4·50
		b. On pale yell. (Die II) ('22)	1·00	2·75
)	**13**	25 c. blk. & red/*yellow*, C	1·25	1·90
		a. On orange-buff (1920) ..	10·00	12·00
		b. On pale yell. (Die II) ('22)	1·60	1·60
)	**11**	30 c. dull pur. & olive, C	2·00	3·00
:	,,	45 c. dull purple and orange, C (1919)	1·25	2·50
2	**13**	50 c. dull purple and black, C (1920)	1·60	2·50
3	,,	75 c. black/*blue-green*, C (*olive back*)	1·60	2·50
		a. On emer. back (Die II) ('22)	2·25	3·50
4	,,	1 r. dull pur. & red, C ('20)	5·50	6·50
5	,,	1 r. 50 c. reddish purple and blue/*blue*, C ..	7·50	7·50
		a. Blue-purple and blue/blue, C (Die II) (1922)	4·50	7·00
5	,,	2 r. 25 c. yellow-green and violet, C	11·00	12·00
7	,,	5 r. green and blue, C ('20)	16·00	19·00
2/97		.. *Set of* 16	42·00	55·00
2/97		Optd. "Specimen" *Set of* 16	£110	

921–32. *Wmk. Mult. Script CA. P* 14.

8	**11**	2 c. chestnut & green, O	10	12
9	,,	3 c. green, O	10	12
0	,,	3 c. black, O (1922) ..	12	20
1	,,	4 c. green, O (1922) ..	12	20
2	,,	4 c. sage-green & carmine, O (1928)	1·00	2·75
3	**12**	5 c. deep brown, O ..	90	1·10
4	**11**	6 c. carmine, O ..	25	65
5	,,	6 c. deep mauve, O (1922)	8	8
6	**13**	9 c. red, O (1927) ..	45	1·00
7	**11**	12 c. grey, O (Die II) ..	50	25
8	,,	12 c. carmine-red, O (1922)	15	10
9	,,	12 c. grey, O (Die I) (1932)	1·00	1·10
10	,,	15 c. bright blue, O ..	2·00	2·50
11	,,	15 c. yellow, O (1922) ..	45	1·90
12	,,	18 c. pur./*pale yell.*, C ('25)	1·00	2·50
13	**13**	20 c. bright blue, O (1922)	75	1·00
		a. Dull blue, O (1926) ..	1·60	1·00
14	**11**	25 c. black and red/*pale yellow* C (1925) ..	90	2·00
15	,,	30 c. dull purple & olive, C	75	2·00
16	,,	45 c. dull pur. & orange, C	75	2·00
17	**13**	50 c. dull purple & black, C	95	2·00
18	,,	75 c. black/*emerald*, C ('24)	3·50	4·00
19	,,	1 r. dull purple and red, C (Die II)	4·50	5·50
20	,,	1 r. dull purple and red, C (Die I) (1932) ..	4·50	6·50
21	,,	1 r. 50, purple and blue/*blue*, C (1924) ..	4·50	6·50
22	,,	2 r. 25, yellow-green and violet, C	5·50	7·50
23	,,	5 r. yellow-grn. & blue, C	13·00	14·00
3/123		.. .. *Set of* 25	40·00	55·00
3/123		Optd. "Specimen" *Set of* 25	£160	

The 3 c. green and 12 c. grey (Die II) were issued in 1927. "Specimens" of these also exist.

1935 (6 May.). *Silver Jubilee. As Nos.* 91/4 *of Antigua but ptd. by B. W. & Co. P* 11 × 12.

128	6 c. ultramarine & grey-black	8	15
	a. Extra flagstaff	45·00	
129	12 c. green and indigo ..	20	30
	a. Extra flagstaff	£250	
130	20 c. brown and deep blue ..	25	45
	a. Extra flagstaff	45·00	
131	1 r. slate and purple ..	85	1·90
	a. Extra flagstaff	35·00	
128/31	Perf. "Specimen" *Set of* 4	17·00	

For illustration of "extra flagstaff" variety see Bechuanaland.

1937 (12 May). *Coronation. As Nos.* 13/15 *of Aden, but ptd. by B. W. & Co. P* 11 × 11½.

132	6 c. sage-green	8	8
133	12 c. orange	8	10
134	20 c. blue	20	20
132/4	Perf. "Specimen" *Set of* 3	11·00	

14. Coco-de-mer Palm.

15. Giant Tortoise.

16. Fishing Pirogue.

(Photo. Harrison.)

1938 (1 Jan.)–**49**. *Wmk. Mult. Script CA. P* 14½ × 13½ (*vert.*) *or* 13½ × 14½.

135	**14**	2 c. pur.-brn. CO (10.2.38)	8	8
136	**15**	3 c. green, C	50	25
136*a*		3 c. orange, CO (8.8.41)	15	12
137	**16**	6 c. orange, C ..	50	25
137*a*	,,	6 c. greyish grn., C (8.8.41)	25	15
		b. Green, OC (11.42)	8	8
138	**14**	9 c. scarlet, C (10.2.38)	75	1·00
138*a*	,,	9 c. grey-blue, CO (8.8.41)	10	10
		b. Dull blue (19.11.45) ..	25	15
139	**15**	12 c. reddish violet, C ..	2·50	90
139*a*	,,	15 c. brn.-carm., C (8.8.41)	30	25
		b. Brown-red, O (19.11.45)	20	15
139*c*	**14**	18 c. carm.-lake, O (8.8.41)	10	8
		d. Rose-carm. OC (19.11.45)	10	8
140	**16**	20 c. blue, C	2·40	90
140*a*	,,	20 c. brn.-ochre, CO (8.8.41)	8	10
141	**14**	25 c. brown-ochre, C ..	6·50	3·25
142	**15**	30 c. carmine, C (10.2.38)	3·50	3·00
142*a*	,,	30 c. blue, CO (8.8.41) ..	10	10
143	**16**	45 c. choc., CO (10.2.38)	10	12
		a. Purple-brown, OC (11.42)	10	12
144	**14**	50 c. deep reddish violet, CO (10.2.38) ..	12	12
144*a*	,,	50 c. brt. lil., C (13.6.49)	12	12
145	**15**	75 c. slate-blue C (10.2.38)	11·00	11·00
145*a*	,,	75 c. deep slate-lilac, CO (8.8.41)	20	20
146	**16**	1 r. yell.-grn., C (10.2.38)	15·00	13·00
146*a*	,,	1 r. grey-blk, CO (8.8.41)	25	15
147	**14**	1 r. 50, ultm., CO (10.2.38)	50	55
148	**15**	2 r. 25, olive, CO (10.2.38)	55	60
149	**16**	5 r. red, CO (10.2.38) ..	2·00	2·00
135/149		*Set of* 24	45·00	35·00
135/49		Perf. "Specimen" *Set of* 24	£120	

The stamps on ordinary paper appeared in 1942–43.

1946 (23 Sept.). *Victory. As Nos.* 28/9 *of Aden.*

150	9 c. light blue	8	8
151	30 c. deep blue	10	8
150/1	Perf. "Specimen" *Set of* 2	13·00	

1948 (5 Nov.). *Royal Silver Wedding. As Nos.* 30/1 *of Aden.*

152	9 c. ultramarine	8	30
153	5 r. carmine	3·25	4·00

1949 (10 Oct.). *75th Anniv. of Universal Postal Union. As Nos.* 114/7 *of Antigua, but inscr.* "SEYCHELLES" (*recess*).

154	18 c. bright reddish purple ..	8	10
155	50 c. purple	25	25
156	1 r. grey	25	40
157	2 r. 25, olive	1·00	1·00

17. Sail-fish.

18. Map of Indian Ocean.

(Photo. Harrison.)

1952 (3 Mar.). *Various designs as T* **14/16** *but with new portrait and crown as in T* **17/18**. *Chalk-surfaced paper. Wmk. Mult. Script CA. P* 14½ × 13½ (*vert.*) *or* 13½ × 14½ (*horiz.*).

158	**17**	2 c. lilac	8	10
		a. Error. Crown missing ..		
		b. Error. St. Edward's Crown		
159	**15**	3 c. orange	8	10
		a. Error. Crown missing ..		
		b. Error. St. Edward's Crown		
160	**14**	9 c. chalky blue ..	8	10
		a. Error. Crown missing ..		
		b. Error. St. Edward's Crown		
161	**16**	15 c. deep yellow-green ..	8	10
		a. Error. Crown missing ..		
		b. Error. St. Edward's Crown		
162	**18**	18 c. carmine-lake ..	8	10
		a. Error. Crown missing ..		
		b. Error. St. Edward's Crown		
163	**16**	20 c. orange-yellow ..	8	10
		a. Error. Crown missing ..		
		b. Error. St. Edward's Crown		
164	**15**	25 c. vermilion	10	10
		a. Error. Crown missing ..		
		b. Error. St. Edward's Crown		
165	**17**	40 c. ultramarine	12	15
		a. Error. Crown missing ..		
		b. Error. St. Edward's Crown		
166	**16**	45 c. purple-brown ..	12	15
		a. Error. Crown missing ..		
		b. Error. St. Edward's Crown		
167	**14**	50 c. reddish violet ..	12	12
		a. Error. Crown missing ..		
		b. Error. St. Edward's Crown		
168	**18**	1 r. grey-black	25	30
		b. Error. St. Edward's Crown		
169	**14**	1 r. 50, blue	65	90
		b. Error. St. Edward's Crown		
170	**15**	2 r. 25, brown-olive ..	95	1·25
		b. Error. St. Edward's Crown		
171	**18**	5 r. red	2·50	3·00
		b. Error. St. Edward's Crown		
172	**17**	10 r. green	4·50	5·50
158/172		.. .. *Set of* 15	9·00	11·00

See *Introduction* re the watermark errors.

1953 (2 June). *Coronation. As No.* 47 *of Aden.*

173	9 c. black & deep bright blue	20	35

19. Sail-fish.

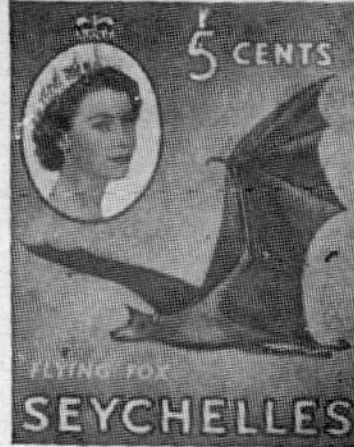

20. " Flying Fox " (fruit bat).

(Photo. Harrison & Sons, Ltd.)

1954 (1 Feb.)–**57.** *As T* **14/18** (*but with portrait of Queen Elizabeth II in place of King George VI., as in T* **19**) *and T* **20.** *Chalk-surfaced paper. Wmk. Mult. Script CA. P* 14½×13½ (*vert.*) *or* 13½×14½ (*horiz.*).

No.	Type			
174	**19**	2 c. lilac	12	12
175	**15**	3 c. orange	15	15
175*a*	**20**	5 c. violet (25.10.57) ..	15	15
176	**14**	9 c. chalky blue ..	15	15
176*a*	,,	10 c. chalky blue (*shades*) (15.9.56)	15	15
177	**16**	15 c. deep yellow-green ..	10	10
178	**18**	18 c. crimson	25	30
179	**16**	20 c. orange-yellow ..	12	15
180	**15**	25 c. vermilion	15	20
180*a*	**18**	35 c. crimson (15.9.56) ..	20	25
181	**19**	40 c. ultramarine ..	30	35
182	**16**	45 c. purple-brown ..	35	35
183	**14**	50 c. reddish violet ..	35	40
183*a*	**16**	70 c. purple-brn. (15.9.56)	35	40
184	**18**	1 r. grey-black	45	60
185	**14**	1 r. 50, blue	70	1·50
186	**15**	2 r. 25, brown-olive ..	1·50	2·00
187	**18**	5 r. red	3·00	4·00
188	**19**	10 r. green	5·50	7·00
174/188		.. .. *Set of* 19	13·00	17·00

21. " La Pierre de Possession ".

═ 5
cents

(22)

(Photo. Harrison.)

1956 (15 Nov.). *200th Anniv. of " La Pierre de Possession ". Wmk. Mult. Script CA. P* 14½×13½.

189	**21**	40 c. ultramarine	25	25
190	,,	1 r. black	50	55

ee ss cc

191 191*a* 191 191*b* 191 191*c*

1957 (16 Sept.). *No.* 182 *surch. with T* **22.**

191	5 c. on 45 c. purple-brown ..	30	35
	a. Italic " e "	5·00	
	b. Italic " s "	5·00	
	c. Italic " c "	3·00	
	d. Thick bars omitted ..	£350	
	e. Surch. double	£150	

23. Mauritius 6d. Stamp with Seychelles " B 64 " Cancellation.

(Recess; cancellation typo. Bradbury, Wilkinson.)

1961. (11 Dec.). *Centenary of First Seychelles Post Office. W* w.**12.** *P* 11½.

193	**23**	10 c. blue, black & purple	12	12
194	,,	35 c. blue, black and myrtle-green ..	20	25
195	,,	2 r. 25, blue, black and orange-brown ..	85	95

24. Black Parrot.

25. Vanilla Vine.

26. Fisherman.

27. Denis Island Lighthouse.

28. Clock Tower, Victoria.

32. Cascade Church.

29. Anse Royale Bay.

30. Government House.

31. Fishing Pirogue.

33. Sail-fish.

34. Coco-de-mer Palm

35. Cinnamon.

36. Copra.

37. Map.

38. Land Settlement.

39. Regina Mundi Convent.

45 CENTS

40. Colony's Badge. (41)

(Des. V. Whiteley (45 c., 75 c.). All photo. Harrison.)

962 (21 Feb.)–68. W w.12 (*upright*). P 13½×14½ (*horiz. designs and* 10 *r.*) *or* 14½×13½ (*others*).

96	24	5 c. multicoloured	5	5
97	25	10 c. multicoloured	5	5
98	26	15 c. multicoloured	5	5
99	27	20 c. multicoloured	5	5
00	28	25 c. multicoloured	8	8
00a	29	30 c. mult. (15.7.68)	10	10
01	,,	35 c. multicoloured	40	40
02	30	40 c. multicoloured	15	15
03	31	45 c. multicoloured (1.8.66)	20	20
04	32	50 c. multicoloured	20	20
05	33	70 c. ultram. & light blue	80	80
06	34	75 c. multicoloured (1.8.66)	25	25
07	35	1 r. multicoloured	30	30
08	36	1 r. 50, multicoloured	60	1·00
09	37	2 r. 25, multicoloured	1·00	1·50
10	38	3 r. 50, multicoloured	1·50	2·50
11	39	5 r. multicoloured	1·75	2·50
12	40	10 r. multicoloured	4·50	6·00
96/212		*Set of* 18	11·00	14·00

The 1 r. exists with PVA gum as well as gum arabic, but the 30 c. exists with PVA gum only.

See also Nos. 233/7.

For stamps of the above issue overprinted "B.I.O.T." see under British Indian Ocean Territory.

963 (4 June). *Freedom from Hunger. As No.* 76 *of Aden.*

13	70 c. reddish violet	40	40

963 (16 Sept.). *Red Cross Centenary. As Nos.* 147/8 *of Antigua.*

14	10 c. red and black	10	10
15	75 c. red and blue	45	45

965 (15 Apr.). *Surch. as T* 41.

16	29	45 c. on 35 c. multicoloured	15	15
17	33	75 c. on 70 c. ultramarine and light blue	25	25

965 (1 June). *I.T.U. Centenary. As Nos.* 166/7 *of Antigua.*

18	5 c. orange and ultramarine	8	8
19	1 r. 50, mauve & apple-green	60	65

965 (25 Oct.). *International Co-operation Year. As Nos.* 168/9 *of Antigua.*

20	5 c. reddish pur. & turq.-grn.	5	5
21	40 c. deep bluish green & lav.	25	30

966 (24 Jan.). *Churchill Commemoration. As Nos.* 170/3 *of Antigua.*

22	5 c. new blue	5	5
23	15 c. deep green	8	8
24	75 c. brown	35	40
25	1 r. 50, bluish violet	65	70

966 (1 July). *World Cup Football Championships. As Nos.* 176/7 *of Antigua.*

26	15 c. violet, yellow-green, lake and yellow-brown	10	10
27	1 r. chocolate, blue-grn., lake and yellow-brown	30	35

966 (20 Sept.). *Inauguration of W.H.O. Headquarters, Geneva. As Nos.* 178/9 *of Antigua.*

28	20 c. black, yellow-green and light blue	8	8
29	50 c. black, light purple and yellow-brown	30	30

966 (1 Dec.). *20th Anniv. of U.N.E.S.C.O. As Nos.* 196/8 *of Antigua.*

30	15 c. slate-violet, red, yellow and orange	8	8

231		1 r. orange-yellow, violet and deep olive	30	40
232		5 r. black, bright purple and orange	1·60	1·75

42. Flying Fox.

UNIVERSAL ADULT SUFFRAGE 1967

(43)

1967–69. *As Nos.* 196 *etc., but wmk.* w.12 (*sideways*), *new values and design.*

233	24	5 c. multicoloured (7.2.67)	8	8
234	25	10 c. multicoloured (4.6.68)	10	10
235	32	50 c. mult. (13.5.69)	20	25
236	42	60 c. red, blue and blackish brown (15.7.68)	25	35
237	33	85 c. ultramarine and light blue (15.7.68)	30	60
233/237		*Set of* 5	75	1·25

The 10 c. exists with PVA gum as well as gum arabic, but the 50 c. to 85 c. exist with PVA gum only.

1967 (18 Sept.). *Universal Adult Suffrage. As Nos.* 198 *and* 206, *but W* w.12 (*sideways*), *and Nos.* 203 *and* 210 (*wmk. upright*), *optd. with T* 43.

238	26	15 c. multicoloured	5	5
239	31	45 c. multicoloured	12	15
240	34	75 c. multicoloured	25	25
241	38	3 r. 50, multicoloured	80	85

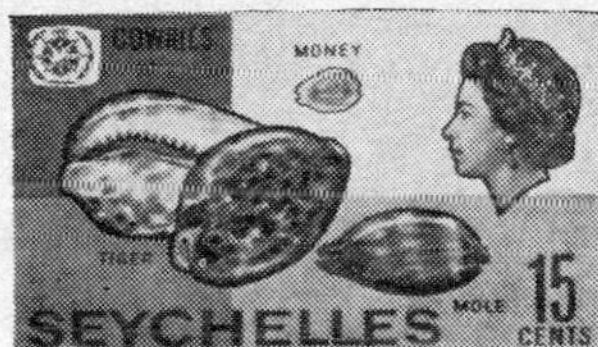

44. Cowrie Shells.

45. Cone Shells.

46. Arthritic Spider Conch.

47. Subulate Auger and Triton Shells.

(Des. V. Whiteley. Photo. Harrison.)

1967 (4 Dec.). *International Tourist Year. W* w.12. *P* 14×13.

242	44	15 c. multicoloured	5	5
243	45	40 c. multicoloured	12	15
244	46	1 r. multicoloured	30	30
245	47	2 r. 25, multicoloured	55	60

= 30

(48)

1968 (16 Apr.). *Nos.* 202/3 *and as No.* 206 *surch. as T* 48 (30 *c.*) *or with* "CENTS" *added, and three bars* (*others*). *W* w.12 (*sideways on No.* 248).

246	30	30 c. on 40 c. multicoloured	8	10
247	31	60 c. on 45 c. multicoloured	15	20
248	34	85 c. on 75 c. multicoloured	25	30

49. Farmer with Wife and Children at Sunset.

(Des. Mrs. Mary Hayward. Litho. Harrison.)

1968 (2 Sept.). *Human Rights Year. W* w.12. *P* 14½×13½.

249	49	20 c. multicoloured	5	8
250	,,	50 c. multicoloured	15	20
251	,,	85 c. multicoloured	25	25
252	,,	2 r. 25, multicoloured	50	55

50. Expedition landing at Anse Possession.

51. Vessels at Anchor. (*Vert.*)

52. Coco-de-Mer and Black Parrot. (*Vert.*)

53. Vessels under Sail. (*Horiz.*)

(Des. Mrs. Mary Hayward. Litho. and die-stamped. Harrison.)

1968 (30 Dec.). *Bicentenary of First Landing on Praslin. W* w.12 (*sideways on* 50 *c.*, 85 *c.*). *P* 14.

253	50	20 c. multicoloured	8	8
254	51	50 c. multicoloured	15	20
255	52	85 c. multicoloured	25	30
256	53	2 r. 25, multicoloured	65	80

LOCAL HANDSTAMP. In March 1969 there was an exceptional demand for 10 c. stamps to frank election communications for the Victoria District Council but a reprint of the current 10 c. stamp which had been ordered did not arrive until 25 March. Authority was given for the use of a handstamp on internal mail between 6th and 25th March. This was a decorated circular 23 mm. handstamp inscribed "SEYCHELLES" at top, "POSTAGE PAID" in lower half and "10 CENTS" between stars across the centre.

54. Apollo Launching.

55. Module leaving Mother-ship for the Moon. (*Horiz.*)

56. Astronauts and Space Module on the Moon. (*Horiz.*)

57. Tracking Station. (*Horiz.*)

58. Moon Craters with Earth on the "Horizon". (*Horiz.*)

(Des. V. Whiteley. Litho. Format International.)

1969 (9 Sept.). *First Man on the Moon. W* w.12 (*sideways on horiz. designs*). *P* 13½.

257	54	5 c. multicoloured	5	5
258	55	20 c. multicoloured	8	8
259	56	50 c. multicoloured	12	15
260	57	85 c. multicoloured	20	25
261	58	2 r. 25, multicoloured	50	55
257/61		*Set of* 5	80	95

59. Picault's Landing, 1742.

60. U.S. Satellite-Tracking Station.

61. *Königsberg I* at Aldabra, 1914.

Design incorrectly shows the vessel *Königsberg II* and date "1915".)

62. Fleet re-fuelling off St. Anne, 1939–45.

63. Exiled Ashanti King Prempeh.

64. Laying Stone of Possession, 1756.

65. Pirates and Treasure.

66. Corsairs attacking Merchantman.

67. Impression of proposed Airport.

68. French Governor capitulating to British Naval Officer, 1794.

69. *Sybille* and *Chiffone* in Battle, 1801.

70. Visit of the Duke of Edinburgh, 1956

71. Chevalier Queau de Quincy.

72. Indian Ocean Chart, 1574.

73. Badge of Seychelles.

(Des. Mrs. M. Hayward. Litho. Enschedé.)

1969 (3 Nov.)–**75.** *W* w.**12** (*sideways*). *Slightly toned paper.* *P* 13×12½.

262	**59**	5 c. multicoloured ..	5	5
263	**60**	10 c. multicoloured ..	8	10
		a. Glazed, whiter paper (8.3.73)	5	5
264	**61**	15 c. multicoloured ..	8	10
		a. Glazed, whiter paper (8.3.73)	5	5
265	**62**	20 c. multicoloured ..	8	10
		a. Glazed, whiter paper (13.6.74)	5	5
266	**63**	25 c. multicoloured ..	8	10
		a. Glazed, whiter paper (8.3.73)	5	5
267	**64**	30 c. multicoloured ..	10	10
268	,,	40 c. mult. (11.12.72) ..	8	10
		a. Glazed, whiter paper (13.6.74)	5	5
269	**65**	50 c. multicoloured ..	10	12
		a. Glazed, whiter paper (13.6.74)	5	5
270	**66**	60 c. multicoloured ..	30	40
271	,,	65 c. mult. (11.12.72) ..	10	12
		a. Glazed, whiter paper (13.8.75)	8	10
272	**67**	85 c. multicoloured ..	40	60
273	,,	95 c. mult. (11.12.72) ..	20	25
		a. Glazed, whiter paper (13.6.74)	12	15
274	**68**	1 r. multicoloured ..	20	25
		a. Glazed, whiter paper (8.3.73)	12	15
275	**69**	1 r. 50, multicoloured ..	30	35
		a. Glazed, whiter paper (8.3.73)	20	25
276	**70**	3 r. 50, multicoloured ..	50	55
		a. Glazed, whiter paper (13.8.75)	45	50
277	**71**	5 r. multicoloured ..	65	70
278	**72**	10 r. multicoloured ..	1·25	1·40
279	**73**	15 r. multicoloured ..	1·90	2·25
262/79		.. .. *Set of* 18	6·00	6·50
263a/76a		.. .. *Set of* 11	1·10	1·25

The stamps on the whiter paper are highly glazed, producing shade variations and are easily distinguishable from the original printings on glazed, slightly toned paper.

74. Sea-gulls, Ship and Island.

75. Flying Fish, Ship and Island.

76. Compass and Chart.

77. Anchor on Sea-bed.

(Des. Aidan Smith adapted by V. Whiteley. Litho. De La Rue.)

1970 (27 Apr.). *Bicentenary of First Settlement, St. Anne Island.* *W* w.**12** (*sideways*). *P* 14.

280	**74**	20 c. multicoloured ..	10	10
281	**75**	50 c. multicoloured ..	15	20
282	**76**	85 c. multicoloured ..	25	30
283	**77**	3 r. 50, multicoloured ..	75	80

78. Girl and Optician's Chart.

(Des. A. Smith. Litho. Questa.)

1970 (4 Aug.). *Centenary of British Red Cross.* *T* **78** *and similar multicoloured designs.* *W* w.**12** (*sideways on horiz. designs.*). *P* 14.

284	20 c. Type **78**	8	8
285	50 c. Baby, Scales and Milk Bottles	15	20
286	85 c. Woman with Child and Umbrella	25	25
287	3 r. 50, Red Cross Local H.Q. Building	70	75

The 85 c. is vertical and the remainder are horizontal designs.

79. Pitcher Plant.

(Des. G. Drummond. Litho. J.W.)

1970 (29 Dec.). *Flowers.* *T* **79** *and similar vert. designs.* *Multicoloured.* *W* w.**12.** *P* 14.

288	20 c. Type **79**	8	8
289	50 c. Wild Vanilla	15	20
290	85 c. Tropic-Bird Orchid ..	25	25
291	3 r. 50, Vare Hibiscus ..	1·00	1·00
MS292	81×133 mm. Nos. 288/91	1·50	1·60

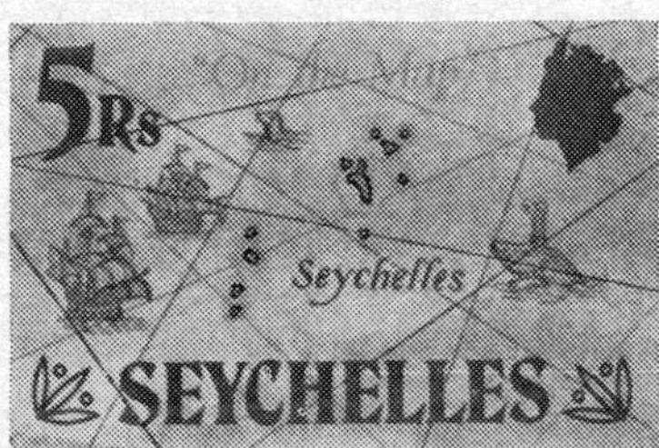

80. Seychelles " On the Map ".

(Des. and litho. J. Waddington Ltd.)

1971 (18 May). " *Putting Seychelles on the Map* ". *Sheet* 152×101 *mm.* *W* w.**12** (*sideways*). *P* 13½.

MS293	**80**	5 r. multicoloured ..	1·40	1·50

81. Piper " Navajo ".

(Des. and litho. J.W.)

1971 (28 June). *Airport Completion.* *T* **81** *a[nd] similar multicoloured designs showing aircra[ft].* *W* w.**12** (*sideways on horiz. designs*). *P* 14×1[...] (5, 20 *and* 60 *c.*) *or* 14×14½ (*others*).

294	5 c. Type **81**	8	
295	20 c. Westland " Wessex " ..	8	
296	50 c. " Catalina " flying-boat (*horiz.*)	15	
297	60 c. Grumman " Albatross "	20	
298	85 c. Short " G " Class flying-boat (*horiz.*)	25	
299	3 r. 50, Vickers Supermarine " Walrus " (*horiz.*) ..	90	
294/9	.. .. *Set of* 6	1·40	1·[...]

82. Santa Claus delivering Gifts (Jean-Clau[de] Waye Hive).

(Des. Jennifer Toombs from drawings by lo[cal] children. Litho. A. & M.)

1971 (12 Oct.). *Christmas.* *T* **82** *and simi[lar] horiz. designs.* *Multicoloured.* *W* w.**12** (*si[de]ways*). *P* 13½.

300	10 c. Type **82**	5	
301	15 c. Santa Claus seated on turtle (Edison Thérésine)	8	
302	3 r. 50, Santa Claus landing on island (Isabelle Tirant)	75	

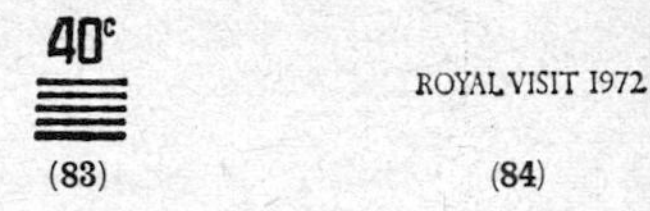

(83) (84)

1971 (21 Dec.). *Nos.* 267, 270 *and* 272 *surch. [in] grey as T* **83.**

303	**64**	40 c. on 30 c. mult. ..	12	
304	**66**	65 c. on 60 c. mult. ..	20	
305	**67**	95 c. on 85 c. mult. ..	25	

1972 (20 Mar.). *Royal Visit.* *Nos.* 265 *and* 2[...] *optd. with T* **84**.

306	**62**	20 c. multicoloured ..	8	
307	**71**	5 r. multicoloured (Gold)	1·00	1·[...]

85. Brush Warbler.

(Des. R. Gillmor. Litho. Questa.)

972 (24 July). *Rare Seychelles Birds. T* **85** *and similar vert. designs. Multicoloured. W* w.**12** *(sideways). P* 13½.

o8	5 c. Type **85**	5	5
o9	20 c. Scops Owl	8	8
10	50 c. Blue Pigeon	12	15
11	65 c. Magpie Robin	20	20
12	95 c. Paradise Flycatcher ..	25	30
13	3 r. 50, Kestrel	75	90
o8/13	.. .. *Set of* 6	1·25	1·40
IS314	144 × 162 mm. Nos. 308/13	1·25	1·40

86. Fireworks Display.

(Des. V. Whiteley. Litho. Questa.)

972 (18 Sept.). *" Festival '72 ". T* **86** *and similar multicoloured designs. W* w.**12** *(sideways on* 10 *and* 25 *c.). P* 14.

15	10 c. Type **86**	5	5
16	15 c. Pirogue race (*horiz.*) ..	5	8
17	25 c. Floats and costumes ..	8	10
18	5 r. Water skiiing (*horiz.*) ..	1·25	1·40

87. Giant Tortoise and Sailfish.

Des. from photograph by D. Groves) and photo. Harrison.)

972 (20 Nov.). *Royal Silver Wedding. Multicoloured; background colour given. W* w.**12**. *P* 14 × 14½.

19	**87**	95 c. turquoise-blue ..	25	30
20	,,	1 r. 50, red-brown ..	35	45

973 (14 Nov.). *Royal Wedding. As Nos.* 165/6 *of Anguilla. Centre multicoloured. W* w.**12** *(sideways). P* 13½.

21	95 c. ochre	25	25
22	1 r. 50, dull deep blue ..	30	30

88. Soldier Fish.

(Des. G. Drummond. Litho. Questa.)

1974 (5 Mar.). *Fishes. T* **88** *and similar horiz. designs. Multicoloured. W* w.**12**. *P* 14½ × 14.

323	20 c. Type **88**	8	8
324	50 c. File Fish	15	15
325	95 c. Butterfly Fish ..	25	30
326	1 r. 50, Gaterin	35	40

89. Globe and Letter.

(Des. Sylvia Goaman. Litho. Enschedé.)

1974 (9 Oct.). *Centenary of Universal Postal Union. T* **89** *and similar horiz. designs. Multicoloured. W* w.**12** *(sideways). P* 12½ × 12.

327	20 c. Type **89**	5	5
328	50 c. Globe and radio beacon ..	12	15
329	95 c. Globe and postmark ..	20	25
330	1 r. 50, Emblems within " UPU "	35	40

90. Sir Winston Churchill.

(Des. G. L. Vasarhelyi. Litho. Questa.)

1974 (30 Nov.). *Birth Centenary of Sir Winston Churchill. T* **90** *and similar horiz. design. Multicoloured. W* w.**12**. *P* 14.

331	95 c. Type **90**	25	25
332	1 r. 50, Profile portrait ..	35	40
MS333	81 × 109 mm. Nos. 331/2	60	

VISIT OF Q.E. II (91)

INTERNAL SELF-GOVERNMENT OCTOBER 1975 (92)

1975 (8 Feb.). *Visit of R.M.S. " Queen Elizabeth II ". Nos.* 265a, 269a, 273a *and* 275a *optd. with T* **91**.

334	**62**	20 c. multicoloured ..	5	5
335	**65**	50 c. multicoloured ..	15	15
336	**67**	95 c. mult. (Sil.) ..	25	25
337	**69**	1 r. 50, multicoloured ..	35	35

1975 (1 Oct.). *Internal Self-Government. Nos.* 265a, 271a, 274a *and* 276a *optd. with T* **92** *in gold, by Enschedé.*

338	**62**	20 c. multicoloured ..	5	5
339	**66**	65 c. multicoloured ..	12	15
340	**68**	1 r. multicoloured ..	15	20
341	**70**	3 r. 50, multicoloured ..	55	65

93. Queen Elizabeth I.

(Des. C. Abbott. Litho. Walsall.)

1975 (15 Dec.). *International Women's Year. T* **93** *and similar vert. designs. Multicoloured. W* w.**14** *(inverted). P* 13½.

342	10 c. Type **93**	5	5
343	15 c. Gladys Aylward ..	5	5
344	20 c. Elizabeth Fry	5	5
345	25 c. Emmeline Pankhurst ..	8	8
346	65 c. Florence Nightingale ..	12	15
347	1 r. Amy Johnson ..	15	20
348	1 r. 50, Joan of Arc ..	25	30
349	3 r. 50, Eleanor Roosevelt	55	65
342/9	.. .. *Set of* 8	1·10	1·25

94. Map of Praslin and Postmark.

(Des. J.W. Ltd. Litho. Questa.)

1976 (30 Mar.). *Rural Posts. T* **94** *and similar vert. designs showing maps and postmarks. Multicoloured. W* w.**14**. *P* 14.

350	20 c. Type **94**	5	5
351	65 c. La Digue	12	15
352	1 r. Mahé with Victoria postmark	15	20
353	1 r. 50, Mahé with Anse Royale postmark ..	25	30
MS354	166 × 127 mm. Nos. 350/3	60	65

III. INDEPENDENT.

29 June 1976.

95. First Landing, 1609.

(Des. G. Drummond. Litho. J.W.)

1976 (29 June). *Independence. T* **95** *and similar vert. designs. Multicoloured. W* w.**12** (*sideways*). *P* 13½.

No.	Description	Unused	Used
355	20 c. Type **95**	5	5
356	25 c. The Possession Stone ..	5	5
357	40 c. First settlers, 1770 ..	8	8
358	75 c. Chevalier Queau de Quincy	12	12
359	1 r. Sir Bickham Sweet-Escott	15	20
360	1 r. 25, Legislative Building	20	25
361	1 r. 50, Seychelles badge ..	25	30
362	3 r. 50, Seychelles flag ..	55	65
355/62	.. .. *Set of* 8	1·25	1·40

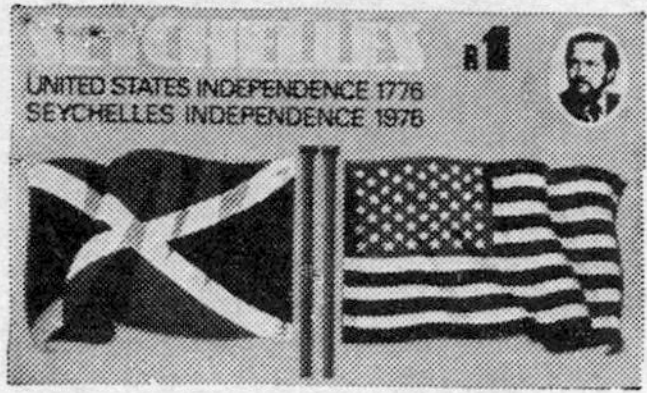

96. Flags of Seychelles and U.S.A.

(Des. and litho. J.W.)

1976 (12 July). *Seychelles Independence and American Independence Bicentenary. T* **96** *and similar horiz. design. Multicoloured. W* w.**12** (*sideways*). *P.* 13½.

No.	Description	Unused	Used
363	1 r. Type **96**	15	20
364	10 r. Statehouses of Seychelles and Philadelphia ..	1·50	1·75

97. Swimming.

(Des. J.W. Ltd. Litho. Questa.)

1976 (26 July). *Olympic Games, Montreal. T* **97** *and similar horiz. designs. W* w.**14** (*sideways*). *P* 14.

No.	Description	Unused	Used
365	20 c. ultram., cobalt & sepia	5	5
366	65 c. bottle-green, apple-grn., and grey-black	10	12
367	1 r. chestnut, blue-green and grey-black	15	20
368	3 r. 50, crimson, rose and grey-black	55	65

Designs:—65 c. Hockey; 1 r. Basketball; 3 r. 50 Football.

98. Seychelles Paradise Flycatcher.

(Des. Mrs. R. M. Fennessy. Litho. Questa.)

1976 (8 Nov.). *Fourth Pan-African Ornithological Congress, Seychelles. T* **98** *and similar multicoloured designs. W* w.**14** (*sideways on Nos.* 370/1). *P* 14.

No.	Description	Unused	Used
369	20 c. Type **98**	5	5
370	1 r. 25, Seychelles Sunbird ..	20	25
371	1 r. 50, Seychelles White-eye	25	30
372	5 r. Seychelles Black Parrot	75	80
MS373	161×109 mm. Nos. 369/72	1·25	

Nos. 370/1 are horizontal designs.

POSTAGE DUE STAMPS.

D 1

(Frame recess, value typo. Bradbury, Wilkinson.)

1951 (1 Mar.). *Wmk. Mult. Script CA. P* 11½.

No.	Type	Description	Unused	Used
D1	D **1**	2 c. scarlet and carmine	15	20
D2	„	3 c. scarlet and green ..	15	20
D3	„	6 c. scarlet and bistre ..	5	5
D4	„	9 c. scarlet and orange ..	5	5
D5	„	15 c. scarlet and violet ..	5	5
D6	„	18 c. scarlet and blue ..	5	5
D7	„	20 c. scarlet and brown ..	5	8
D8	„	30 c. scarlet and claret ..	8	10
D1/D8		.. .. *Set of* 8	55	70

1964 (7 July)–**65.** *As* 1951 *but wmk.* w.**12.**

No.	Type	Description	Unused	Used
D 9	D **1**	2 c. scarlet and carmine	5	5
D10	„	3 c. scar. & grn. (14.9.65)	5	5

MINIMUM PRICE

The minimum price quoted is 5p which represents a handling charge rather than a basis for valuing common stamps. For further notes about prices see introductory pages.

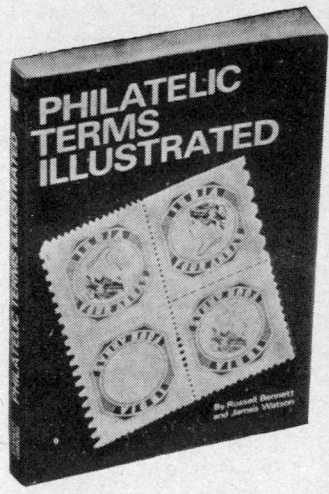

SIERRA LEONE.

I. CROWN COLONY AND PROTECTORATE.

RINTERS. All issues of Sierra Leone until 932 were typographed by De La Rue & Co.

1

2

The 6d. on *blue* paper, *imperf.*, is believed to be nly a proof, and is therefore omitted. (*Price*, 40.)

859 (21 SEPT.). *No wmk. P* 14.
2 **1** 6d. dull purple/*bluish* .. .. 26·00 15·00
3 ,, 6d. grey lilac .. .. 55·00 12·00
4 ,, 6d. dull violet .. .. 50·00 8·00

872. *No wmk. P* 12½.
5 **1** 6d. dull violet/*bluish* .. .. 55·00 15·00
6 ,, 6d. dull violet .. .. £140 80·00

872–73. *Wmk. Crown CC. P* 12½.
(*a*) *Wmk. sideways* (April 1872).
7 **2** 1d. rose-red .. .. 8·00 7·00
8 ,, 3d. buff .. .. .. 20·00 8·00
9 ,, 4d. bluo .. .. .. 26·00 8·00
0 ,, 1s. green .. .. .. 28·00 8·00
(*b*) *Wmk. upright* (Sept., 1873).
1 **2** 1d. rose-red .. .. 8·00 5·50
2 ,, 2d. magenta .. .. 20·00 8·00
3 ,, 3d. saffron-yellow .. .. £140 32·00
4 ,, 4d. blue .. .. .. 35·00 15·00
5 ,, 1s. green .. .. .. 70·00 35·00

876–77. *Wmk. Crown CC. P* 14.
6 **2** ½d. brown .. .. .. 90 1·75
7 ,, 1d. rose-red .. .. .. 4·00 3·50
8 ,, 1½d. lilac (1877) .. .. 3·50 1·75
,, 2d. magenta .. .. 7·00 1·75
,, 3d. buff .. .. .. 6·00 1·75
1 ,, 4d. blue .. .. .. 15·00 2·00
2 ,, 1s. green .. .. .. 9·00 3·25
6/22 .. .. *Set of* 7 40·00 13·00

883 (JUNE–26 SEPT.). *Wmk. Crown CA. P* 14.
3 **2** ½d. brown .. .. .. 5·50 7·00
4 ,, 1d. rose-red (26.9.83) .. 80·00 9·00
,, 2d. magenta .. .. 8·00 1·90
6 ,, 4d. blue .. .. .. £180 7·00

884 (JULY)–**93.** *Wmk. Crown CA. P* 14.
7 **2** ½d. dull green 10 8
,, 1d. carmine 45 12
a. *Rose-carmine* (1885?) .. 9·00 3·00
9 ,, 1½d. pale violet (1893) .. 60 1·25
0 ,, 2d. grey .. .. .. 1·75 80
1 ,, 2½d. ultramarine (1891) .. 1·75 15
2 ,, 3d. yellow (1892) .. .. 80 1·00
3 ,, 4d. brown 80 80
,, 1s. red-brown (1888) .. 3·25 2·00
7/34 .. .. *Set of* 8 8·00 5·50
7/34 excl. 29, 32
Optd. " Specimen " *Set of* 6 70·00

885–96. *Wmk. Crown CC. P* 14.
5 **1** 6d. dull violet (1885) .. 17·00 7·00
a. Bisected (3d.) (on cover) .. † £550
6 ,, 6d. brown-purple (1890) .. 5·50 5·00
a. Paper slightly blued .. 12·00 9·00
7 ,, 6d. purple-lake (1896) .. 2·25 2·75
6 Optd. "Specimen" .. .. 10·00

HALF

PENNY

(3)

893. *Surch. with T* **3.** *P* 14.
(*a*) *Wmk. Crown CC.*
8 **2** ½d. on 1½d. lilac £150 £150
a. Error. " PFNNY ' .. £750 £900
(*b*) *Wmk. Crown CA.*
9 ,, ½d. on 1½d. pale violet .. 1·75 2·00
a. Surch. inverted .. .. 50·00 50·00
c. Error. " PFNNY " .. 20·00 20·00
d. " PFNNY " inverted .. £350

4

5

1896–97. *Wmk. Crown CA. P* 14.
41 **4** ½d. dull mauve & grn. ('97) 15 15
42 ,, 1d. dull mauve & carmine 20 12
43 ,, 1½d. dull mve. & black ('97) 1·10 1·00
44 ,, 2d. dull mauve and orange 90 85
45 ,, 2½d. dull mauve & ultram... 65 40
46 **5** 3d. dull mauve and slate .. 3·00 2·00
47 ,, 4d. dull mauve & carm. ('97) 2·25 3·00
48 ,, 5d. dull mauve & black ('97) 2·25 3·00
49 ,, 6d. dull mauve ('97) .. 3·25 3·25
50 ,, 1s. green and black .. 3·25 3·25
51 ,, 2s. green and ultramarine.. 11·00 9·50
52 ,, 5s. green and carmine .. 22·00 20·00
53 ,, £1 purple/*red* .. .. 70·00 £100
41/53 .. .. *Set of* 13 £110 £130
41/53 Optd. " Specimen " *Set of* 13 £100

6

POSTAGE

AND

REVENUE

(7)

1897 (MAR.). *Wmk. CA over Crown*, w.**7**. *Optd. with T* **7**. *P* 14.
54 **6** 1d. dull purple and green .. 65 75
a. Opt. double £300 £300

2½d.

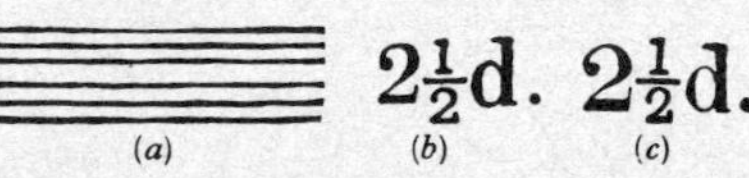

(*a*) (*b*) (*c*)

2½d. 2½d. 2½d.
(*d*) (*e*) (*f*)

T **6** *surch. in addition with* " 2½d." *below T* **7.** *Original value cancelled by* 6 *bars.*
55 2½d. on 3d. dull pur. & grn. (*a*) 3·25 3·25
56 2½d. on 3d. dull pur. & grn. (*c*) 12·00 15·00
57 2½d. on 3d. dull pur. & grn. (*d*) 32·00 38·00
58 2½d. on 3d. dull pur. & grn. (*e*) 55·00 65·00
59 2½d. on 6d. dull pur. & grn. (*a*) 3·25 3·25
60 2½d. on 6d. dull pur. & grn. (*c*) 9·50 12·00
61 2½d. on 6d. dull pur. & grn. (*d*) 24·00 26·00
62 2½d. on 6d. dull pur. & grn. (*e*) 45·00 50·00
Error. Surch. double.
62*a* 2½d. (*a*) and 2½d. (*a*) on 3d.
62*b* 2½d. (*a*) and 2½d. (*c*) on 3d. £900
62*c* 2½d. (*a*) and 2½d. (*d*) on 3d.

The 2½d. on 3d. and 2½d. on 6d. are printed in sheets containing two settings of thirty, of which there are twenty-two of (*a*), five of (*c*), two of (*d*), and one of (*e*).

Two copies are known of No. 62*a*, five of 62*b* (of which two are in the Royal collection), and two of 62*c* (of which one is in the Royal collection). The Royal collection also contains one copy of the 2½d. (*a*) with 2½d. (*e*) on 3d. but this is probably unique.

POSTAGE AND REVENUE

(8)

Similar to last, but optd. with T **8.** *The surcharge* " 2½d. " *is above T* **8**, *and there are only* 5 *bars cancelling original value instead of* 6.
63 2½d. on 1s. dull lilac (*a*) .. 35·00 20·00
64 2½d. on 1s. dull lilac (*b*) .. £350 £300
65 2½d. on 1s. dull lilac (*c*) .. £160 £150
66 2½d. on 1s. dull lilac (*d*) .. £110 £100
66*a* 2½d. on 1s. dull lilac (*f*) .. £350 £300
67 2½d. on 2s. dull lilac (*a*) .. £275 £250
68 2½d. on 2s. dull lilac (*b*) .. £3000
69 2½d. on 2s. dull lilac (*c*) .. £1500
70 2½d. on 2s. dull lilac (*d*) .. £800
71 2½d. on 2s. dull lilac (*f*) .. £3000

9

10

1903. *Wmk. Crown CA. P* 14.
73 **9** ½d. dull purple and green 90 90
74 ,, 1d. dull purple and rosine 15 15
75 ,, 1½d. dull purple and black.. 1·00 1·60
76 ,, 2d. dull pur. & brn.-orange 2·00 3·00
77 ,, 2½d. dull purple & ultram. 2·50 2·25
78 **10** 3d. dull purple and grey .. 2·50 3·00
79 ,, 4d. dull purple and rosine 3·00 3·50
80 ,, 5d. dull purple and black 3·50 3·00
81 ,, 6d. dull purple .. 3·50 3·00
82 ,, 1s. green and black .. 9·00 8·50
83 ,, 2s. green and ultramarine 16·00 15·00
84 ,, 5s. green and carmine .. 22·00 27·00
85 ,, £1 purple/*red* £100 £110
73/85 .. .. *Set of* 13 £150 £160
73/85 Optd. " Specimen " *Set of* 13 £110

1904–5. *T* **9** *and* **10.** *Wmk. Mult. Crown CA. P* 14.
86 ½d. dull pur. & green, C ('04) 1·60 40
87 1d. dull pur. & rosine, OC ('04) 15 12
88 1½d. dull purple and black, C 65 1·50
89 2d. dull pur. & brn.-orge., C 1·00 80
90 2½d. dull purple and ultram., C 1·10 1·25
91 3d. dull purple and grey, C.. 2·25 1·50
92 4d. dull purple and rosine, C 1·00 95
93 5d. dull purple and black, C 2·50 1·60
94 6d. dull purple, C .. .. 90 1·25
95 1s. green and black, C .. 3·25 3·25
96 2s. green and ultramarine, C 6·00 5·50
97 5s. green and carmine, C .. 20·00 18·00
98 £1 purple/*red*, C £100 £110
86/98 .. .. *Set of* 13 £120 £130

1907–10. *Wmk. Mult. Crown CA. P* 14.
99 **9** ½d. green, O (1907) .. 25 15
100 ,, 1d. carmine, O 90 15
a. Red, O (1907) 20 12
101 ,, 1½d. orange, O (1910) .. 15 75
102 ,, 2d. greyish slate, O .. 50 75
103 ,, 2½d. blue, O (1907) .. 45 80
104 **10** 3d. purple/*yellow*, OC .. 1·10 1·10
105 ,, 4d. black & red/*yellow*, C 80 60
106 ,, 5d. purple & ol.-green, C 1·10 1·75
107 ,, 6d. dull & bright pur., C 1·10 1·25
108 ,, 1s. black/*green*, C .. 2·50 2·25
109 ,, 2s. pur. & brt. blue/*blue*, C 8·50 6·00
110 ,, 5s. green & red/*yellow*, C 18·00 20·00
111 ,, £1 purple & black/*red*, C 75·00 90·00
99/111 .. .. *Set of* 13 £100 £110
99/111 Optd. " Specimen " *Set of* 13 90·00

11

12

13

14

1912–16. *Wmk. Mult. Crown CA. P* 14.

No.	Type	Description	Unused	Used
112	11	½d. blue-green, O ..	40	25
		a. Yellow-green	30	25
		b. Deep green	75	40
113	„	1d. carmine-red, O ..	35	8
		a. Scarlet (1916)	30	15
		b. Rose-red	55	10
114	„	1½d. orange, O ..	55	55
		a Orange-yellow	90	60
115	„	2d. greyish slate, O ..	40	8
116	„	2½d. deep blue, O ..	2·50	80
		a. Ultramarine	60	55
117	12	4d. black & red/*yellow*, O	75	1·00
		a. On lemon	2·25	2·50
		b. On pale yellow (Die II) ..	45	1·10
118	„	5d. purple & olive-grn., O	55	1·10
119	„	6d. dull & brt. purple, C	1·25	1·40
120	13	7d. purple and orange, C	65	1·25
121	„	9d. purple and black, C ..	2·25	2·00
122	12	10d. purple and red, C ..	1·00	2·25
		T **14.**		
123		3d. purple/*yellow*, C ..	80	1·10
		a. On pale yellow	1·25	1·40
124		1s. black/*green*, C ..	1·60	1·75
		a. On blue-green, green back ..	1·00	1·40
125		2s. blue and purple/*blue*, C ..	3·25	1·60
126		5s. red and green/*yellow*, C ..	4·50	6·00
127		10s. red and green/*green*, C ..	15·00	18·00
		a. Carmine and blue-green/green	18·00	20·00
		b. Carmine & yellow-grn./green	18·00	18·00
128		£1 black and purple/*red*, C	35·00	38·00
129		£2 blue & dull pur., C (S. £50)	£225	£250
130		£5 orange&green, C (S. £100)	£600	
112/128		.. .. *Set of* 17	60·00	70·00
112/28		Optd. " Specimen " *Set of* 17	£140	

1921–28. *Wmk. Mult. Script CA. P* 14.

No.	Type	Description	Unused	Used
131	11	½d. dull green, O ..	20	8
		a. Bright green	45	20
132	„	1d. brt. vio., O (Die I) ('24)	40	15
		a. Die II (1926)	25	8
133	„	1½d. scarlet, O (1925) ..	30	25
134	„	2d. grey, O (1922) ..	30	8
135	„	2½d. ultramarine, O ..	30	40
136	12	3d. bright blue, O (1922)	25	12
137	„	4d. black and red/*pale yellow*, O ('25)	90	65
138	„	5d. pur. & olive-grn., O	45	55
139	„	6d. grey-purple and bright purple, C	65	55
140	13	7d. purple & orge., C ('28)	90	2·00
141	„	9d. purple & black, C ('22)	1·10	1·60
142	12	10d. purple and red, C ('26)	1·60	2·00
143	14	1s. black/*emerald*, C ('25)	90	1·25
144	„	2s. blue and dull purple/*blue*, C	3·00	2·75
145	„	5s. red & grn./*yell.*, C ('27)	4·50	5·50
146	„	10s. red & grn./*grn.*, C ('27)	16·00	17·00
147	„	£2 blue and dull purple, C (Optd. S. £50) ('23)	£250	£300
148	„	£5 orange and green, C (Optd. S. £100) ('23) ..	£700	
131/146		.. .. *Set of* 16	28·00	32·00
131/46		Optd. "Specimen" *Set of* 16	£100	

15. Rice Field.

16. Palms and Kola Tree.

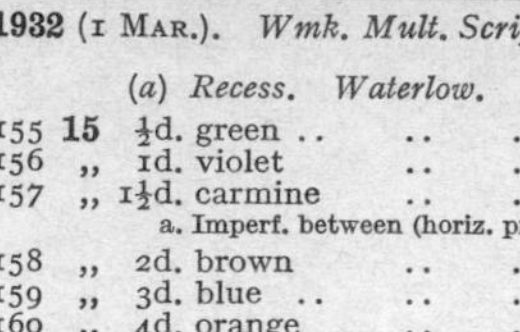

1932 (1 Mar.). *Wmk. Mult. Script CA.*

(*a*) *Recess. Waterlow. P* 12½.

No.	Type	Description	Unused	Used
155	15	½d. green	15	20
156	„	1d. violet	8	8
157	„	1½d. carmine	25	45
		a. Imperf. between (horiz. pr.)		
158	„	2d. brown	25	20
159	„	3d. blue	30	35
160	„	4d. orange	45	55

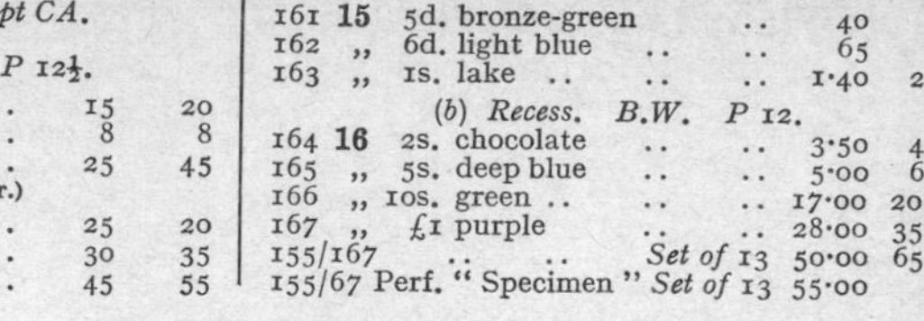

No.	Type	Description	Unused	Used
161	15	5d. bronze-green ..	40	6
162	„	6d. light blue	65	8
163	„	1s. lake	1·40	2·0
		(*b*) *Recess. B.W. P* 12.		
164	16	2s. chocolate	3·50	4·5
165	„	5s. deep blue	5·00	6·0
166	„	10s. green	17·00	20·0
167	„	£1 purple	28·00	35·0
155/167		.. .. *Set of* 13	50·00	65·
155/67		Perf. " Specimen " *Set of* 13	55·00	

17. Arms of Sierra Leone.

18. " Freedom ".

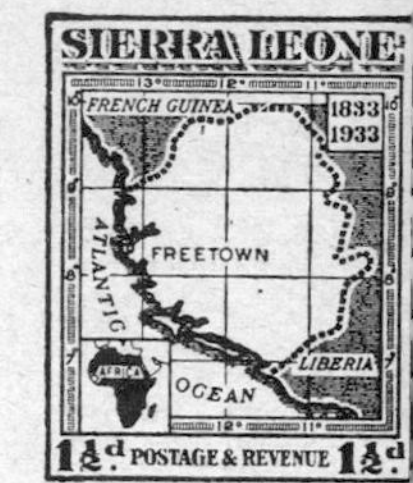

19. Map of Sierra Leone

20. Old Slave Market, Freetown.

22. Government Sanatorium.

21. Native Fruit Seller.

23. Bullam Canoe.

24. Punting near Banana.

25. Government Buildings.

26. Bunce Island.

27. African Elephant.

28. King George V.

29. Freetown Harbour.

(Des. Father F. Welch. Recess. B.W.)

1933 (2 Oct.). *Centenary of Abolition of Slave and of Death of William Wilberforce. Wm Mult. Script CA. P* 12.

No.	Type	Description	Unused	Used
168	17	½d. green	25	4
169	18	1d. black and brown ..	15	
170	19	1½d. chestnut	1·60	2·
171	20	2d. purple	90	1
172	21	3d. blue	70	1·
173	22	4d. brown	2·25	3·
174	23	5d. green and chestnut ..	3·50	5·

75	**24**	6d. black & brown-orange	3·50	4·00
76	**25**	1s. violet	4·00	4·50
77	**26**	2s. brown and light blue	12·00	16·00
78	**27**	5s. black and purple ..	50·00	80·00
79	**28**	10s. black and sage-green	50·00	80·00
80	**29**	£1 violet and orange ..	£225	£300
68/180		.. .. *Set of* 13	£325	£450
68/80		Perf. "Specimen" *Set of* 13	£250	

935 (6 May). *Silver Jubilee. As Nos.* 91/4 *of Antigua, but ptd. by B.W. P* 11×12.

81	1d. ultramarine & grey-black	8	8
	a. Extra flagstaff	8·00	
82	3d. brown and deep blue ..	40	40
	a. Extra flagstaff	9·00	
83	5d. green and indigo ..	65	70
	a. Extra flagstaff	22·00	
84	1s. slate and purple	1·00	1·40
	a. Extra flagstaff	42·00	
81/4	Perf. "Specimen" *Set of* 4	17·00	

For illustration of "extra flagstaff" variety ee Bechuanaland.

937 (12 May). *Coronation. As Nos.* 13/5 *of Aden, but ptd. by B.W. P* 11×11½.

85	1d. orange	15	10
86	2d. purple	15	12
87	3d. bluc	20	25
85/7	Perf. "Specimen" *Set of* 3	11·00	

30. Freetown from the Harbour.

31. Rice Harvesting.

(Recess. Waterlow.)

938 (1 May)–**44.** *Wmk. Mult. Script CA, sideways. P* 12½.

88	**30**	½d. black and blue-green	8	8
89	,,	1d. black and lake ..	8	8
		a. Imperf. between (pair)	—	£550
90	**31**	1½d. scarlet	2·25	15
90*a*	,,	1½d. mauve (1.2.41) ..	8	8
91	,,	2d. mauve	4·50	1·00
91*a*	,,	2d. scarlet (1.2.41) ..	8	8
92	**30**	3d. black & ultramarine	8	8
93	,,	4d. black and red-brown (20.6.38)	20	25
94	**31**	5d. olive-green (20.6.38)	30	75
95	,,	6d. grey (20.6.38) ..	10	8
96	**30**	1s. blk. & ol.-grn. (20.6.38)	20	15
96*a*	**31**	1s. 3d. yellow-orge. ('44)	30	15
97	**30**	2s. blk. & sepia (20.6.38)	45	60
98	**31**	5s. red-brown (20.6.38)	1·10	1·00
99	,,	10s. emerald-grn. (20.6.38)	2·25	2·50
00	**30**	£1 deep blue (20.6.38)	5·00	5·50
88/200		.. .. *Set of* 16	16·00	11·00
88/200		Perf. "Specimen" *Set of* 16	60·00	

946 (1 Oct.). *Victory. As Nos.* 28/9 *of Aden.*

01	1½d. lilac	8	8
02	3d. ultramarine	8	8
01/2	Perf. "Specimen" *Set of* 2	13·00	

948 (1 Dec.). *Royal Silver Wedding. As Nos.* 30/1 *of Aden.*

03	1½d. bright purple	8	8
04	£1 indigo	5·00	6·50

949 (10 Oct.). *75th Anniv. of U.P.U. As Nos.* 114/7 *of Antigua.*

05	1½d. purple	10	12
06	3d. deep blue	12	12
07	6d. grey	30	30
08	1s. olive	55	55

1953 (2 June). *Coronation. As No.* 47 *of Aden but ptd. by B.W.*

209	1½d. black and purple ..	10	10

32. Cape Lighthouse.

33. Queen Elizabeth II Quay. (*Horiz.*)
34. Piassava Workers. (*Horiz.*)

35. Cotton Tree, Freetown.

36. Rice Harvesting.

37. Iron Ore Production, Marampa. (*Horiz.*)
38. Whale Bay, York Village. (*Horiz.*)
39. Bullom Boat. (*Vert.*)
40. Aeroplane and Map. (*Horiz.*)
41. Orugu Bridge. (*Vert.*)
42. Kuranko Chief. (*Vert.*)
43. Law Courts, Freetown. (*Horiz.*)
44. Government House. (*Horiz.*)

(Recess. Waterlow.)

1956 (2 Jan.)–**61.** *Wmk. Mult. Script CA. P* 13½×13 (*horiz.*) *or* 14 (*vert.*).

210	**32**	½d. black and deep lilac ..	5	5
211	**33**	1d. black and olive ..	5	5
212	**34**	1½d. black & ultramarine	5	8
213	**35**	2d. black and brown ..	5	5
214	**36**	3d. black and bright blue	8	5
		a. Perf. 13×13½	1·50	1·25
215	**37**	4d. black and slate-blue ..	8	8
216	**38**	6d. black and violet ..	8	8
217	**39**	1s. black and scarlet ..	12	12
218	**40**	1s. 3d. black and sepia ..	20	20
219	**41**	2s. 6d. black & chestnut	40	35
220	**42**	5s. black and deep green	85	85
221	**43**	10s. black and bright reddish purple	3·00	3·25
		a. Black and purple (19.4.61)	7·00	10·00
222	**44**	£1 black and orange ..	4·50	5·00
210/22		.. .. *Set of* 13	8·50	9·00

II. INDEPENDENT STATE.

45. Palm Fruit Gathering.

47. Bundu Mask.

46. Licensed Diamond Miner.

48. Bishop Crowther and Old Fourah Bay College. (*Vert.*)
49. Sir Milton Margai. (*Horiz.*)
50. Lumley Beach. (*Horiz.*)
51. Forces Bugler. (*Vert.*)

52

(Des. K. Penny (T **45**), Messrs. Thoma, Turrell and Larkins (T **46, 49**), W. G. Rumley (T **47**), J. H. Vandi (T **48**), R. A. Sweet (T **50**). J. White (T **51**). Recess. B.W.)

1961 (27 Apr.). *Independence. W* **52.** *P* 13½.

223	**45**	½d. choc. & dp. bluish grn.	5	5
224	**46**	1d. orange-brown and myrtle-green	5	5
225	**47**	1½d. black and emerald ..	5	8
226	**48**	2d. black and ultramarine	5	5
227	**49**	3d. orange-brown & blue	5	5
228	**50**	4d. turq.-blue and scarlet	5	8
229	**49**	6d. black and purple ..	8	8
230	**45**	1s. chocolate & yell.-orge.	12	12
231	**50**	1s. 3d. turq.-blue & violet	20	20
232	**46**	2s. 6d. dp. green and black	35	40
233	**47**	5s. black and red ..	80	1·00
234	**48**	10s. black and green ..	1·75	2·00
235	**51**	£1 carmine-red & yellow	3·50	4·00
223/235		.. .. *Set of* 13	6·00	7·00

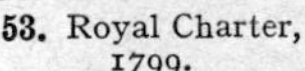

53. Royal Charter, 1799.

54. King's Yard Gate, Freetown, 1817.

55. Old House of Representatives, Freetown, 1924.

56. H.M. Yacht *Britannia* at Freetown.

(Des. C. P. Rang (T **53/4**), F. H. Burgess (T **56**). Recess. B.W.)

1961 (25 Nov.). *Royal Visit.* *W* **52.** *P* 13½.

236	**53**	3d. black and rose-red ..	8	8
237	**54**	4d. black and violet ..	10	10
238	**55**	6d. black & yellow-orange	12	12
239	**56**	1s. 3d. black and blue ..	25	25

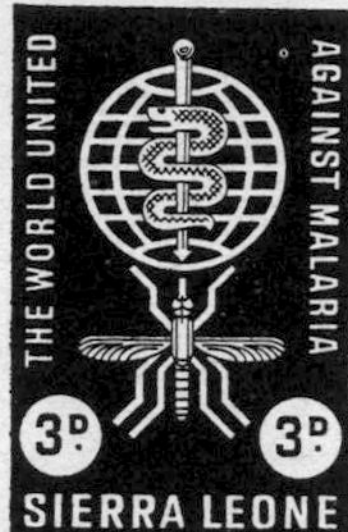

57. Campaign Emblem.

(Recess. B.W.)

1962 (7 Apr.). *Malaria Eradication.* *W* **52.** *P* 11×11½.

240	**57**	3d. carmine-red	8	8
241	,,	1s. 3d. deep green ..	25	25

58. Fireball Lily.

59. Jina-gbo.

60. Stereospermum. (*Vert.*)
61. Black-eyed Susan. (*Horiz.*)
62. Beniseed. (*Vert.*)
63. Blushing Hibiscus. (*Vert.*)
64. Climbing Lily. (*Horiz.*)
65. Beautiful Crinum. (*Vert.*)
66. Blue Bells. (*Horiz.*)
67. Broken Hearts. (*Vert.*)
68. Ra-ponthi. (*Vert.*)
69. Blue Plumbago. (*Vert.*)
70. African Tulip Tree. (*Horiz.*)

(Des. M. Goaman. Photo. Harrison.)

1963 (1 Jan.). *Flowers in natural colours; background colours below.* *W* **52** *(sideways on vert. format).* *P* 14.

242	**58**	½d. bistre-brown	5	5
243	**59**	1d. vermilion	5	5
244	**60**	1½d. emerald-green ..	5	5
245	**61**	2d. olive-yellow	8	8
246	**62**	3d. deep bluish green ..	10	10
247	**63**	4d. violet-blue	12	15
248	**64**	6d. deep greenish blue ..	12	15
249	**65**	1s. light yellow-green ..	20	15
250	**66**	1s. 3d. bronze-green ..	20	25
251	**67**	2s. 6d. dull purple ..	45	45
252	**68**	5s. bluish violet	1·00	1·25
253	**69**	10s. bright purple ..	2·00	1·90
254	**70**	£1 light greenish blue ..	4·50	5·50
242/254		.. .. *Set of* 13	8·00	9·50

71. Threshing Machine and Corn Bins.

72. Girl with Onion Crop.

(Des. V. Whiteley. Recess. B.W.)

1963 (21 Mar.). *Freedom from Hunger.* *W* **52.** *P* 11½×11.

255	**71**	3d. black and yellow-ochre	10	10
256	**72**	1s. 3d. sepia & emer.-green	25	25

2nd Year of Independence 19 Progress 63 Development
3d.
(73)

2nd Year Independence Progress Development 1963
10d.
(74)

(Optd. by Govt. Printer, Freetown.)

1963 (27 Apr.). *Second Anniv. of Independence. Surch. or optd. as T* **73/4.** *(a) Postage.*

257	**32**	3d. on ½d. (No. 210) (R.)	5	5
		a. Small "c" in "INDEPENDENCE"	5·00	5·00
258	**34**	4d. on 1½d. (No. 212) (Br.)	5	8
259	**32**	6d. on ½d. (No. 210) (O.) ..	8	8
		a. Small "c" in "INDEPENDENCE"	7·00	7·00
260	**36**	10d. on 3d. (No. 214) (R.)	15	15
261	,,	1s. 6d. on 3d. (No. 214) (V.)	25	25
262	,,	3s. 6d. on 3d. (No. 214) (Ult.)	50	50
		(b) Air. Additionally optd. "AIR MAIL".		
263	**34**	7d. on 1½d. (No. 212) (C.)	12	12
264	,,	1s. 3d. on 1½d. (No. 212) (R.)	15	20
265	**41**	2s. 6d. (No. 219) (V.) ..	35	35
266	**36**	3s. on 3d. (No. 214) (B.) ..	35	40
267	,,	6s. on 3d. (No. 214) (R.)	70	80
268	**43**	11s. on 10s. (No. 221) (C.)	1·75	2·00
269	**44**	11s. on £1 (No. 222) (C.) ..	£200	£140
257/268		.. .. *Set of* 12	4·00	4·50

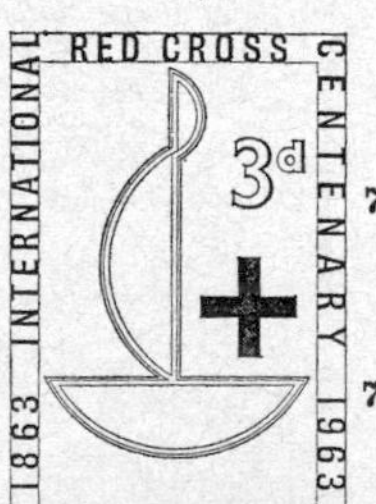

75. Centenary Emblem.

76. Red Cross Emblem.

77. Centenary Emblem.

(Des. M. Goaman. Recess. Bradbury, Wilkinson

1963 (1 Nov.). *Centenary of Red Cross.* *W* **52** *P* 11×11½.

270	**75**	3d. red and violet ..	8	
271	**76**	6d. red and black ..	12	1
272	**77**	1s. 3d. red & dp. blsh. grn.	25	3

1853–1859–1963 Oldest Postal Service Newest G.P.O. in West Africa
1s.
(78)

1853–1859–1963 Oldest Postage Stam Newest G.P.O. in West Africa
AIRMAIL
(79)

(Optd. by Govt. Printer, Freetown.)

1963 (4 Nov.). *Postal Commemorations. Variou stamps optd. or surch.* *(a) Postage.* *As T* **7**

273	**36**	3d. (No. 214) (Mag.) ..	5	
274	**34**	4d. on 1½d. (No. 212) (C.) ..	5	
275	,,	9d. on 1½d. (No. 212) (V.) ..	12	1
276	**50**	1s. on 1s. 3d. (No. 231) (C.)	15	1
277	**32**	1s. 6d. on ½d. (No. 210) (Mag.)	20	2
278	**36**	2s. on 3d. (No. 214) (Br.) ..	25	3
		(b) Air. As T **79.**		
279	**53**	7d. on 3d. (No. 236) (Br.) ..	12	1
280	**56**	1s. 3d. (No. 239) (C.) ..	15	2
281	**50**	2s. 6d. on 4d. (No. 228) ..	40	5
282	**53**	3s. on 3d. (No. 236) (V.) ..	45	6
283	**55**	6s. on 6d. (No. 238) (Ult.)	1·00	1·2
284	**44**	£1 (No. 222) (R.)	4·50	5·5
273/284		.. .. *Set of* 12	6·50	8·0

The events commemorated are: 1853, "Fir Post Office"; 1859, "First Postage Stamps" and 1963, "Newest G.P.O." in West Afric Nos. 273, 278 have the opt. in five lines; No 279, 282 in six lines (incl. "AIRMAIL"). number of errors and varieties exist.

80. Lion Emblem and Map.

(Recess and litho. Walsall Lithographic Co. Ltd

1964 (10 Feb.). *World's Fair, New York. Imper Self-adhesive.* *(a) Postage.* *T* **80.**

285		1d. multicoloured	5	
286		3d. multicoloured	5	
287		4d. multicoloured	5	
288		6d. multicoloured	8	
289		1s. multicoloured	12	1
		a. "POSTAGE 1/-" omitted ..	35·00	
290		2s. multicoloured	20	2
291		5s. multicoloured	50	6
		a. "POSTAGE 5/-" omitted ..	35·00	

81. Globe and Map.

(*b*) *Air.* *T* **81.**

92 7d. multicoloured 8 8
93 9d. multicoloured 10 10
a. "AIR MAIL 9d." omitted ..
94 1s. 3d. multicoloured .. 15 20
a. "AIR MAIL 1/3" omitted .. 35·00
95 2s. 6d. multicoloured .. 20 30
96 3s. 6d. multicoloured .. 40 40
a. "AIR MAIL 3/6" omitted ..
97 6s. multicoloured 60 70
98 11s. multicoloured .. .. 1·25 1·25
a. "AIR MAIL 11/-" omitted 35·00
85/298 .. .. *Set of* 14 3·50 3·75

Nos. 285/98 were issued in sheets of 30 (6×5) n green (postage) or yellow (airmail) backing aper with the emblems of Samuel Jones & Co., td., self-adhesive paper-makers, on the back.

Warning. These and later self-adhesive stamp, hould be kept on their backing paper except ommercially used, which should be retained n cover or piece.

82. Inscription and Map.

(Recess. and litho. Walsall.)

964 (11 May). *President Kennedy Memorial Issue. Imperf. Self-adhesive.*

(*a*) *Postage. Green backing paper.*

99 **82** 1d. multicoloured .. 5 5
00 ,, 3d. multicoloured .. 5 5
01 ,, 4d. multicoloured .. 5 5
02 ,, 6d. multicoloured .. 8 8
03 ,, 1s. multicoloured .. 12 12
04 ,, 2s. multicoloured .. 20 25
05 ,, 5s. multicoloured .. 50 65

83. Pres. Kennedy and Map.

(*b*) *Air. Yellow backing paper.*

06 **83** 7d. multicoloured .. 8 8
07 ,, 9d. multicoloured .. 10 10
08 ,, 1s. 3d. multicoloured .. 15 15
09 ,, 2s. 6d. multicoloured .. 25 30
10 ,, 3s. 6d. multicoloured .. 35 40
11 ,, 6s. multicoloured .. 60 70
12 ,, 11s. multicoloured .. 1·25 1·25
99/312 .. .. *Set of* 14 3·50 3·75

(New currency. 100 cents. = 1 leone.)

AIRMAIL
3c (84) 7c (85) LE 1·00 (86)

1964–66. *Decimal currency. Various stamps surch. locally.* (i) *First issue* (4.8.64).

(*a*) *Postage. As T* **84.**

313 **64** 1 c. on 6d. mult. (R.) .. 5 5
314 **53** 2 c. on 3d. blk. & rose-red 5 5
315 **62** 3 c. on 3d. multicoloured 5 5
a. Surch. inverted
316 **45** 5 c. on ½d. chocolate and dp. bluish green (B.) 8 5
317 **71** 8 c. on 3d. black and yellow-ochre (R.) .. 10 8
318 **66** 10 c. on 1s. 3d. mult. (R.) 10 10
319 **65** 15 c. on 1s. multicoloured 15 15
320 **55** 25 c. on 6d. black and yellow-orange (V.) .. 30 35
321 **46** 50 c. on 2s. 6d. deep green and black (O.) .. 55 60

(*b*) *Air. As T* **85** *or* **86** (*Nos.* 326/7).

322 **72** 7 c. on 1s. 3d. sepia and emerald-green (B.).. 10 10
323 **50** 20 c. on 4d. turquoise-blue and scarlet 25 25
324 **48** 30 c. on 10s. black and green (R.) 35 40
325 **47** 40 c. on 5s. blk. & red (B.) 50 50
326 **83** 1 l. on 1s. 3d. mult. (R.).. 1·25 1·25
327 ,, 2 l. on 11s. multicoloured 2·25 2·50
313/327 .. .. *Set of* 15 5·50 6·00

1c (87) TWO LEONES Le 2·00 (88)

(ii) *Second issue* (20.1.65).
Surch. as T **87** *or* **88** (*Nos.* 332/3).

(*a*) *Postage.*

328 **49** 1 c. on 3d. orge.-brn. & bl 5 5
329 **82** 2 c. on 1d. multicoloured 5 5
330 ,, 4 c. on 3d. multicoloured 8 8
a. Error. 4 c. on 1d. (No. 299) — 10·00
331 **61** 5 c. on 2d. olive-yellow.. 8 8
332 **68** 1 l. on 5s. bluish violet (Gold) .. .. 1·25 1·25
333 **51** 2 l. on £1 carmine-red and yellow (B.) .. .. 2·25 2·25
a. Surch. double (B.+Bk.) .. — 25·00

(*b*) *Air.*

334 **83** 7 c. on 7d. mult. (R.) .. 10 10
335 ,, 60 c. on 9d. multicoloured 75 75
328/335 .. .. *Set of* 8 4·00 4·00

(iii) *Third issue* (4.65).
Surch. in figures (various sizes). (*a*) *Postage.*

336 **47** 1 c. on 1½d. black and emerald (R.) .. 5 5
337 **82** 2 c. on 3d. multicoloured 8 8
338 **80** 2 c. on 4d. multicoloured 8 8
339 **59** 3 c. on 1d. vermilion .. 8 8
340 **48** 3 c. on 2d. black & ultramarine (R.) 5 5
341 **50** 5 c. on 1s. 3d. turquoise-blue and violet (R.) .. 8 8
342 **82** 15 c. on 6d. multicoloured 40 40
343 ,, 15 c. on 1s. mult. (R.) .. 65 65
344 **49** 20 c. on 6d. black and purple (R.) 25 25
345 **64** 25 c. on 6d. deep greenish blue (R.) 30 30
346 **49** 50 c. on 3d. orange-brown and blue (R.) .. 60 60
347 **80** 60 c. on 5s. mult. (V.) .. 1·10 1·10
348 **82** 1 l. on 4d. mult. (R.) .. 1·50 1·50
349 **51** 2 l. on £1 carmine-red & yellow (B.) .. .. 2·75 2·25

(*b*) *Air.*

350 **81** 7 c. on 9d. multicoloured 12 12
336/350 .. .. *Set of* 15 7·00 7·00

2c (89) TWO Leones (90)

(iv) *Fourth issue* (9.11.65).
Surch. as T **89.**

(*a*) *Postage.*

351 **80** 1 c. on 6d. mult. (V.) .. 2·50 3·50
352 ,, 1 c. on 2s. mult. (V.) .. 2·50 3·50
353 **82** 1 c. on 2s. mult. (V.) .. 2·50 3·50
354 ,, 1 c. on 5s. mult. (V.) .. 2·50 3·50

(*b*) *Air.*

355 **81** 2 c. on 1s. 3d. mult. .. 2·50 3·50
356 **83** 2 c. on 1s. 3d. mult. .. 2·50 3·50
357 ,, 2 c. on 3s. 6d. mult. .. 2·50 3·50
358 **81** 3 c. on 7d. multicoloured.. 2·50 3·50
359 **83** 3 c. on 9d. multicoloured.. 2·50 3·50
360 **81** 5 c. on 2s. 6d. mult. .. 2·50 3·50
361 **83** 5 c. on 2s. 6d. mult. .. 2·50 3·50
362 **81** 5 c. on 3s. 6d. mult. .. 2·50 3·50
363 ,, 5 c. on 6s. multicoloured .. 2·50 3·50
364 **83** 5 c. on 6s. multicoloured .. 2·50 3·50
351/364 .. .. *Set of* 14 30·00 40·00

(v) *Fifth issue* (28.1.66).
Air. No. 374 *further surch. with T* **90.**

365 **64** 2 l. on 30 c. on 6d. .. 4·00 3·00

IN MEMORIAM 2c
TWO GREAT LEADERS

SIR MILTON MARGAI 1895-1964 SIR WINSTON CHURCHILL 1874-1965

(**91.** Margai and Churchill.)

1965 (19 May). *Sir Milton Margai and Sir Winston Churchill Commemoration. Flower stamps of* 1963 *surch. as T* **91** *on horiz. designs or with individual portraits on vert. designs as indicated. Multicoloured.* (*a*) *Postage.*

366 **59** 2 c. on 1d. 5 5
367 **62** 3 c. on 3d. Margai .. 5 5
368 **65** 10 c. on 1s. Churchill .. 12 12
369 **66** 20 c. on 1s. 3d. 25 25
370 **63** 50 c. on 4d. Margai .. 65 65
371 **68** 75 c. on 5s. Churchill .. 1·00 1·00

(*b*) *Air. Additionally optd.* "AIR-MAIL".

372 **61** 7 c. on 2d. 8 8
373 **58** 15 c. on ½d. Margai .. 25 25
374 **64** 30 c. on 6d. (O. and W.) 40 40
375 **70** 1 l. on £1 .. .. 1·40 1·50
376 **69** 2 l. on 10s. Churchill .. 3·00 3·25
366/376 .. .. *Set of* 11 6·50 7·00

92. Cola Plant and Nut.

93. Arms of Sierra Leone.

94. Inscription and Necklace.

(Des. M. Meers. Manufactured by the Walsall Lithographic Co., Ltd.)

1965 (Nov.). *Imperf. Self-adhesive.*
A. *Embossed on silver foil, backed with paper bearing advertisements. Emerald, olive-yellow and carmine; denominations in colours given. Postage.*

377 **92** 1 c. emerald 10 10
378 ,, 2 c. carmine 10 10
379 ,, 3 c. olive-yellow 10 10
380 ,, 4 c. silver/*emerald* .. 15 12
381 ,, 5 c. silver/*carmine* .. 15 12

B. *Recess on cream paper backed with paper bearing advertisements.*
(*a*) *Postage.*

382 **93** 20 c. multicoloured .. 35 25
383 ,, 50 c. multicoloured .. 75 60

(*b*) *Air.*

384 **93** 40 c. multicoloured .. 75 60

C. *Foil-backed and photo-litho, with advertisements on white paper backing (see footnote). Air.*

385 **94** 7 c. multicoloured .. 15 12
386 ,, 15 c. multicoloured .. 30 25
377/386 .. .. *Set of* 10 2·75 2·40

The above stamps were issued in single form with attached tabs to remove the backing paper, with the exception of No. 385 which was in sheets of 25 bearing a single large advertisement on the back.

For other stamps in Type **92** see Nos. 421/31 and 435/42.

2c 15c
AIRMAIL
FIVE YEARS FIVE YEARS
INDEPENDENCE INDEPENDENCE
1961-1966 1961-1966
(95) (96)

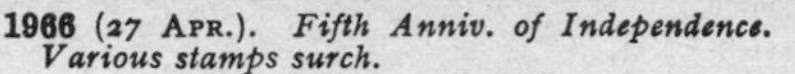

1966 (27 Apr.). *Fifth Anniv. of Independence. Various stamps surch.*
(*a*) *Postage. As T* **95.**

387 **64** 1 c. on 6d. multicoloured 5 5
388 **63** 2 c. on 4d. multicoloured 5 5
389 **34** 3 c. on 1½d. black and ultramarine (B.) .. 5 5
390 **65** 8 c. on 1s. mult. (B.) .. 12 12
391 **67** 10 c. on 2s. 6d. mult. (B.) 15 12
392 **35** 20 c. on 2d. blk. & brn. (B.) 25 25

(*b*) *Air. As T* **96.**

393 **75** 7 c. on 3d. red and violet 10 10
394 **65** 15 c. on 1s. multicoloured 25 20
395 **67** 25 c. on 2s. 6d. mult. .. 35 40
396 **60** 50 c. on 1½d. multicoloured 65 75
397 **63** 1 l. on 4d. multicoloured 1·40 1·50
387/397 .. .. *Set of* 11 3·00 3·25

The inscription on No. 387 is in larger type.

97. Lion's Head.

98. Map of Sierra Leone.

(Des. and embossed. Walsall Security Printers Ltd.)

1966 (12 Nov.). *First Sierra Leone Gold Coinage Commemoration. Circular designs, embossed on gold foil, backed with paper bearing advertisements. Imperf.* (*a*) *Postage.*
(i) ¼ *golde coin. Diameter* 1½ *in.*

398 **97** 2 c. magenta & yell.-orge. 5 5
399 **98** 3 c. emerald & brt. purple 5 5

(ii) ½ *golde coin. Diameter* 2½ *in.*

400 **97** 5 c. verm. & ultramarine 8 8
401 **98** 8 c. turq.-blue and black 12 12

(iii) 1 *golde coin. Diameter* 3¼ *in.*

402 **97** 25 c. violet and emerald .. 35 35
403 **98** 1 l. orange and cerise .. 1·50 1·50

(*b*) *Air.* (i) ¼ *golde coin. Diameter* 1½ *in.*

404 **98** 7 c. red-orange and cerise 10 10
405 **97** 10 c. cerise & greenish blue 15 12

(ii) ½ *golde coin. Diameter* 2⅛ *in.*

406 **98** 15 c. orange and cerise .. 25 25
407 **97** 30 c. bright purple & black 40 45

(iii) 1 *golde coin. Diameter* 3¼ *in.*

408 **98** 50 c. bright green & purple 65 65
409 **97** 2 l. black and emerald .. 3·00 3·00
398/409 .. .. *Set of* 12 6·00 6·00

12½ 17½ =17½
(99) (100) (101)

1967 (2 Dec.). *Decimal Currency Provisionals, Various stamps surch. as T* **99** (*Nos.* 410/3), *T* **100** (*Nos.* 415/7) *or T* **101** (*others*). (*a*) *Postage.*

410 **68** 6½ c. on 75 c. on 5s. (R.) .. 12 12
411 ,, 7½ c. on 75 c. ln 5s. (S.) .. 12 12
412 **63** 9½ c. on 50 c. on 4d. (G.) .. 15 15
413 **66** 12½ c. on 20 c. on 1s. 3d. (V.) 20 20
414 **93** 17½ c. on 50 c. .. .. 1·00 1·00
415 **82** 17½ c. on 1 l. on 4d. (B.) .. 1·00 1·00
416 ,, 18½ c. on 1 l. on 4d. .. 1·00 1·00
417 **80** 18½ c. on 60 c. on 5s. .. 3·50 3·50
418 **93** 25 c. on 50 c. 35 35

(*b*) *Air.*

419 **93** 11½ c. on 40 c. 15 15
420 ,, 25 c. on 40 c. 40 40
410/20 .. .. *Set of* 11 7·00 7·00

102. Eagle.

(*Illustration reduced.*) *Actual size* 70×35 *mm.*

(Manufactured by the Walsall Security Printers Ltd.)

1967 (2 Dec.)–**69.** *Decimal Currency. Imperf. Self-adhesive.* (*a*) *Postage. As T* **92**, *but embossed on white paper, backed with paper bearing advertisements. Background colours given first, and value tablet colours in brackets.*

421 **92** ½ c. carmine-red (carmine/*white*) 8 5
422 ,, 1 c. carm. (carm./*white*) .. 5 5
423 ,, 1½ c. orange-yellow (green/*white*) 5 5
424 ,, 2 c. carmine-red (green/*white*) 10 8
425 ,, 2½ c. apple-green (yellow/*white*) 8 8
426 ,, 3 c. carmine-red (white/*carmine*) 8 8
427 ,, 3½ c. reddish purple (white/*green*) 10 10
428 ,, 4 c. carmine-red (white/*green*) 10 10
429 ,, 4½ c. dull grn. (grn./*white*) 12 12
430 ,, 5 c. carmine (yell./*white*) 10 10
431 ,, 5½ c. brown-red (green/*white*) 12 12

(*b*) *Air. T* **102** *embossed on black paper, backed with paper bearing advertisements; or,* (*No.* 433), *as T* **93**, *recess on cream paper, also with advertisements.*

432 **102** 9½ c. red and gold/*black* .. 15 15
432*a* ,, 9½ c. blue and gold/*black* (10.9.69) 20 20
433 **93** 10 c. mult. (red frame) .. 20 20
433*a* ,, 10 c. mult. (black frame) (10.9.69) 20 20
434 **102** 15 c. green and gold/*black* 30 30
434*a* ,, 15 c. red and gold/*black* (10.9.69) 30 30
421/34*a* .. .. *Set of* 17 2·00 2·00

The ½, 1½, 2, 2½, 3, 3½ and 5 c. also exist without advertisements.

The footnote below Nos. 377/86 also applies here.

Although only released for collectors on 2nd December, the 5 c. was known to be in use locally in February and the 3 c. in March. The 1 c. and 2 c. were also released locally some months earlier.

See also Nos. 538/44.

1968. *No advertisements on back, and colours in value tablet reversed. Background colours given first, and value tablet colours in brackets.*

435 **92** ½ c. carmine-red (white/*green*) 5 5
436 ,, 1 c. carm. (white/*carmine*) 5 5
437 ,, 2 c. carm. (white/*green*) .. 30 30
438 ,, 2½ c. apple-green (white/*yellow*) 60 60

39 **92** 3 c. carmine-red (carmine/*white*) 15 15

On Nos. 435 and 438, the figure "½" is larger han in Nos. 421 and 425.

It is believed that the ½ c. was released in ebruary, the 2½ c. in April and the others in 1arch.

The 1 c. also exists with advertisements on he backing paper.

The footnote below Nos. 377/86 also applies ere.

968–69. *No advertisements on back, colours changed and new value (7 c.). Background colours given first, and value tablet colours in brackets.*

(*a*) *Postage.*

40 **92** 2 c. pink (white/*brown-lake*) 15 15
41 „ 2½ c. deep bluish green (white/*orange*) .. 15 15
42 „ 3½ c. olive-yellow (blue/*white*) 15 15

(*b*) *Air.*

42*a* **92** 7 c. yellow (carmine/*white*) (10.9.69) .. 15 15
35/42*a* *Set of* 9 1·50 1·50

On Nos. 441/2 the fraction "½" is larger than n Nos. 425 and 427.

It is believed that the 3½ c. was released in 1arch 1968 and the 2 and 2½ c. in May 1968.

The 2 c. also exists with advertisements on he backing paper.

The footnote below Nos. 377/86 also applies ere.

103. Outline Map of Africa.

(Litho. Walsall Security Printers Ltd.)

968 (25 Sept.). *Human Rights Year. Each value comes in six types, showing different territories in yellow, as below, Imperf. Self-adhesive.*

A. Portuguese Guinea.
B. South Africa.
C. Mozambique.
D. Rhodesia.
E. South West Africa.
F. Angola.

To indicate yellow territory use above letters s suffix to the following catalogue numbers.

(*a*) *Postage.*

Each Territory.

43 **103** ½ c. multicoloured .. 8 8
44 „ 2 c. multicoloured .. 8 8
45 „ 2½ c. multicoloured .. 8 8
46 „ 3½ c. multicoloured .. 8 8
47 „ 10 c. multicoloured .. 15 15
48 „ 11½ c. multicoloured .. 20 20
49 „ 15 c. multicoloured .. 25 25

(*b*) *Air.*

50 **103** 7½ c. multicoloured .. 12 12
51 „ 9½ c. multicoloured .. 20 20
52 „ 14½ c. multicoloured .. 25 25
53 „ 18½ c. multicoloured .. 30 30
54 „ 25 c. multicoloured .. 40 40
55 „ 1 l. multicoloured .. 2·25 2·25
56 „ 2 l. multicoloured .. 6·00 6·00
43/56 Each territory *Set of* 14 9·50 9·50
43/56 Six territories *Set of* 84 50·00 50·00

Nos. 443/56 were issued in sheets of 30 (6×5) n backing paper depicting diamonds or the oat-of-arms on the reverse. The six types ccur once in each horizontal row.

MEXICO 1968 OLYMPIC PARTICIPATION

POSTAGE

* 6½

(**104**)

1968 (30 Nov.). *Mexico Olympics Participation.* (*a*) *Postage. No.* 383 *surch. or optd.* (*No.* 461) *as T* **104.**

457 **93** 6½ c. on 50 c. mult. .. 10 10
458 „ 17½ c. on 50 c. mult. .. 25 25
459 „ 22½ c. on 50 c. mult. .. 35 35
460 „ 28½ c. on 50 c. mult. .. 40 50
461 „ 50 c. multicoloured .. 70 85

(*b*) *Air. No.* 384 *surch. or optd.* (*No.* 466) *as T* **104,** *in red.*

462 **93** 6½ c. on 40 c. mult. .. 10 10
463 „ 17½ c. on 40 c. mult. .. 25 25
464 „ 22½ c. on 40 c. mult. .. 35 35
465 „ 28½ c. on 40 c. mult. .. 40 45
466 „ 40 c. multicoloured .. 60 75
457/66 .. .. *Set of* 10 3·00 3·50

105. Old Type **1.**

111. Old Type **94.**

(Litho. Walsall Security Printers Ltd.)

1969 (1 Mar.). *Fifth Anniv. of World's First Self-adhesive Postage Stamps. Reproductions of earlier issues. Multicoloured. Imperf. Self-adhesive.* (*a*) *Postage. Vert. designs.*

467 1 c. Type **105** 5 5
468 2 c. Type **92** 5 5
469 3½ c. Type **51** 5 5
470 5 c. Type **93** 8 10
471 12½ c. No. 204 .. .. 20 25
472 1 l. Type **14** .. .. 1·60 1·75

(*b*) *Air. Horiz. designs.*

473 7½ c. Type **111** 12 15
474 9½ c. Type **102** 15 20
475 20 c. Type **81** 30 35
476 30 c. Type **83** 45 50
477 50 c. Type **29** 75 85
478 2 l. No. 269 .. .. 4·25 4·50
467/478 .. .. *Set of* 12 7·00 8·00

Nos. 467 and 473 were issued with tabs as note under Nos. 377/86 and No. 474 exists with tabs and also in the normal version on backing paper.

All values are on white backing paper with advertisements printed on the reverse.

117. Ore-Ship, Globe and Flags of Sierra Leone and Japan.

118. Ore-Ship, Map of Europe and Africa and Flags of Sierra Leone and Netherlands.

The 3½ c., 9½ c., 2 l. and 10 c., 50 c., 1 l. are as T **118** but show respectively the flags of Great Britain and West Germany instead of the Netherlands.

(Litho. Walsall Security Printers Ltd.)

1969 (10 July). *Pepel Port Improvements. Imperf. Self-adhesive, backed with paper bearing advertisements.* (*a*) *Postage.*

479 **117** 1 c. multicoloured .. 5 5
480 **118** 2 c. multicoloured .. 5 5
481 – 3½ c. multicoloured .. 8 8
482 – 10 c. multicoloured .. 12 12
483 **118** 18½ c. multicoloured .. 25 25
484 – 50 c. multicoloured .. 65 65

(*b*) *Air.*

485 **117** 7½ c. multicoloured .. 10 10
486 – 9½ c. multicoloured .. 15 15
487 **117** 15 c. multicoloured .. 25 25
488 **118** 25 c. multicoloured .. 35 35
489 – 1 l. multicoloured .. 1·25 1·25
490 – 2 l. multicoloured .. 2·50 2·50
479/90 .. .. *Set of* 12 5·00 5·00

119. African Development Bank Emblem.

(Litho. and embossed. Walsall Security Printers Ltd.)

1969 (10 Sept.). *Fifth Anniv. of African Development Bank. Self-adhesive, backed with paper bearing advertisements. Imperf.*

(a) Postage.

491	**119**	3½ c. deep green, gold and blue	15	15

(b) Air.

492	**119**	9½ c. bluish violet, gold and apple-green ..	35	35

120. Boy Scouts Emblem in " Diamond ".

(Litho. Walsall Security Printers Ltd.)

1969 (6 Dec.). *Boy Scouts Diamond Jubilee. T* **120** *and similar design. Imperf. Self-adhesive, backed with paper bearing advertisements.*

(a) Postage.

493	**120**	1 c. multicoloured ..	5	5
494	,,	2 c. multicoloured ..	5	5
495	,,	3½ c. multicoloured ..	8	8
496	,,	4½ c. multicoloured ..	10	10
497	,,	5 c. multicoloured ..	12	12
498	,,	75 c. multicoloured ..	3·50	3·00

(b) Air.

499	–	7½ c. multicoloured ..	20	20
500	–	9½ c. multicoloured ..	25	25
501	–	15 c. multicoloured ..	35	30
502	–	22 c. multicoloured ..	70	70
503	–	55 c. multicoloured ..	2·25	2·00
504	–	3 l. multicoloured ..	15·00	11·00
493/504	..	.. *Set of* 12	20·00	16·00

Design: *Octagonal Shape* (65 × 51 *mm.*)—Nos. 499/504 Scout Saluting, Baden-Powell and Badge.

(121)

1970 (28 Mar.). *Air. No.* 443 *surch. as T* **121.**

			Each Territory	
505	**103**	7½ c. on ½ c. mult. (G.) ..	12	12
506	,,	9½ c. on ½ c. mult. (P.) ..	15	15
507	,,	15 c. on ½ c. mult. (B.) ..	25	25
508	,,	28 c. on ½ c. mult. (G.) ..	35	45
509	,,	40 c. on ½ c. mult. (B.) ..	75	1·00
510	,,	2 l. on ½ c. mult. (Sil.) ..	3·00	3·50
505/10		*Each Territory Set of* 6	4·25	5·00
505/10		*Six Territories Set of* 36	25·00	28·00

122. Expo Symbol and Maps of Sierra Leone and Japan.

(Litho. Walsall Security Printers Ltd.)

1970 (22 June). *World Fair, Osaka. T* **122** *and similar design. Imperf. Self-adhesive, backed with paper bearing advertisements. (a) Postage.*

511	**122**	2 c. multicoloured ..	5	5
512	,,	3½ c. multicoloured ..	5	5
513	,,	10 c. multicoloured ..	12	12
514	,,	12½ c. multicoloured ..	15	15
515	,,	20 c. multicoloured ..	25	25
516	,,	45 c. multicoloured ..	60	75

(b) Air.

517	–	7½ c. multicoloured ..	10	10
518	–	9½ c. multicoloured ..	12	12
519	–	15 c. multicoloured ..	20	20
520	–	25 c. multicoloured ..	40	50
521	–	50 c. multicoloured ..	75	1·00
522	–	3 l. multicoloured ..	4·50	5·00
511/22	..	.. *Set of* 12	6·50	7·50

Design: *Chrysanthemum shape* (43 × 42 *mm.*)—Nos. 517/22 Maps of Sierra Leone and Japan.

123. Diamond.

124. Palm Nut.

(Litho. & embossed. Walsall Security Printers Ltd.)

1970 (3 Oct.). *Imperf. Self-adhesive, backed with paper bearing advertisements.*

523	**123**	1 c. multicoloured ..	5	5
524	,,	1½ c. multicoloured ..	5	5
525	,,	2 c. multicoloured ..	5	5
526	,,	2½ c. multicoloured ..	5	5
527	,,	3 c. multicoloured ..	5	5
528	,,	3½ c. multicoloured ..	8	8
529	,,	4 c. multicoloured ..	8	8
530	,,	5 c. multicoloured ..	8	8
531	**124**	6 c. multicoloured ..	8	8
532	,,	7 c. multicoloured ..	10	1
533	,,	8½ c. multicoloured ..	12	1
534	,,	9 c. multicoloured ..	12	1
535	,,	10 c. multicoloured ..	12	1
536	,,	11½ c. multicoloured ..	15	2
537	,,	18½ c. multicoloured ..	25	3

1970 (3 Oct.). *Air. As T* **102,** *but embossed on white paper. Backed with paper bearing advertisements.*

538	**102**	7½ c. gold and red ..	10	1
539	,,	9½ c. rose & bright green	15	2
540	,,	15 c. pink & greenish blue	20	2
541	,,	25 c. gold and purple ..	35	4
542	,,	50 c. bright green & orge.	75	8
543	,,	1 l. Royal blue & silver	1·50	1·7
544	,,	2 l. ultramarine & gold	3·00	4·0
523/44	..	.. *Set of* 22	6·50	7·5

126. " Jewellery Box " and Sewa Diadem.

(Illustration reduced. Actual size 61 × 68 *mm.)*

(Litho. and embossed. Walsall Security Printers Ltd.)

1970 (30 Dec.). *Diamond Industry. T* **126** *and similar design. Imperf. (backing paper rou 20). Self-adhesive, backed with paper bearing advertisements.*

(a) Postage.

545	**126**	2 c. multicoloured ..	5	
546	,,	3½ c. multicoloured ..	8	
547	,,	10 c. multicoloured ..	15	1
548	,,	12½ c. multicoloured ..	20	2
549	,,	40 c. multicoloured ..	55	6
550	,,	1 l. multicoloured ..	1·75	1·7

(b) Air.

551	–	7½ c. multicoloured ..	12	1
552	–	9½ c. multicoloured ..	15	1
553	–	15 c. multicoloured ..	25	2
554	–	25 c. multicoloured ..	40	4
555	–	75 c. multicoloured ..	1·40	1·4
556	–	2 l. multicoloured ..	5·50	5·0
545/556	..	.. *Set of* 12	9·50	9·0

Design: *Horiz.* (63 × 61 *mm.*)–Nos. 551/ Diamond and Curtain.

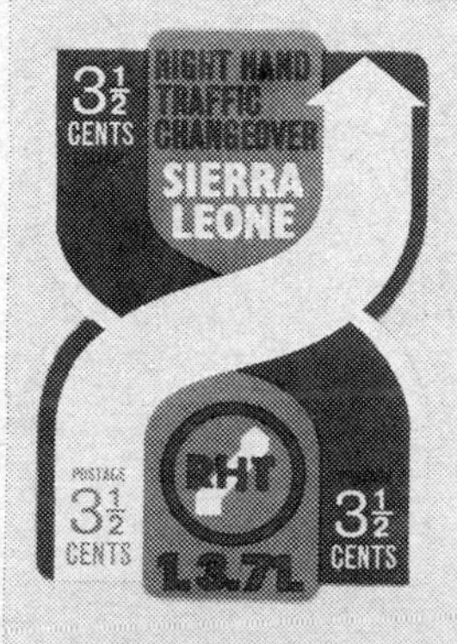

127. " Traffic Changeover ".

1971 (1 Mar.). *Changeover to Driving on the Right of the Road. Imperf. (backing paper roul. 20). Self-adhesive, backed with paper bearing advertisements.*

557	127	3½ c. yell.-orange, ultram. and black (postage)	8	8
558	,,	9½ c. ultram., yell.-orange and black (air) ..	20	20

10c
AIRMAIL
(128)

1971 (1 Mar.). *Air Various stamps surch. as T* **128**, *in red (No.* 559), *blue (Nos.* 560 *and* 562) *or black (others).*

559	48	10 c. on 2d. (No. 226) ..	15	15
560	45	20 c. on 1s. (No. 230) ..	30	30
561	59	50 c. on 1d. (No. 243) ..	70	70
562	–	70 c. on 30 c. (No. 476) ..	1·10	1·25
563	–	1 l. on 30 c. (No. 476) ..	1·50	1·75
559/63		.. .. *Set of* 5	3·25	3·75

III. REPUBLIC.

129. Flag and Lion's Head.

(Manufactured by Walsall Security Printers Ltd.)

1971 (27 Apr.). *Tenth Anniv. of Independence. T* **129** *and similar design. Imperf. Self-adhesive, backed with paper bearing advertisements.*

(a) Postage.

564	129	2 c. multicoloured ..	5	5
565	,,	3½ c. multicoloured ..	8	8
566	,,	10 c. multicoloured ..	15	15
567	,,	12½ c. multicoloured ..	20	20
568	,,	40 c. multicoloured ..	50	50
569	,,	1 l. multicoloured ..	1·10	1·25

(b) Air.

570	–	7½ c. multicoloured ..	12	12
571	–	9½ c. multicoloured ..	15	15
572	–	15 c. multicoloured ..	25	25
573	–	25 c. multicoloured ..	35	35
574	–	75 c. multicoloured ..	90	95
575	–	2 l. multicoloured ..	2·50	2·75
564/75		.. .. *Set of* 12	5·50	6·00

Design: "*Map*" *shaped as T* **129**—Nos. 570/5 Bugles and lion's head.

130. Siaka Stevens.

(Litho. D.L.R.)

1972. *Multicoloured; colour of background given. P* 13.

576	130	1 c. light rose-lilac ..	5	5
577	,,	2 c. lavender (*shades*) ..	5	5
578	,,	4 c. cobalt ..	5	5
579	,,	5 c. light cinnamon ..	5	5
580	,,	7 c. light rose ..	8	8
581	,,	10 c. olive-bistre ..	10	12
582	,,	15 c. pale yellow-green ..	15	20
583	,,	18 c. yellow-ochre ..	20	20
584	,,	20 c. pale greenish blue ..	20	25
585	,,	25 c. orange-ochre ..	25	30
586	,,	50 c. light turquoise-green	55	65
587	,,	1 l. bright reddish mauve	1·00	1·10
588	,,	2 l. orange-salmon ..	2·10	2·25
589	,,	5 l. light stone ..	5·25	5·50
576/89		.. .. *Set of* 14	8·50	9·50

131. Guma Valley Dam and Bank Emblem.

(Litho. D.L.R.)

1975 (14 Jan.). *Tenth Anniv. of African Development Bank* (1974). *P* 13½ × 13.

(a) Postage.

590	131	4 c. multicoloured ..	20·00	20·00

(b) Air.

591	131	15 c. multicoloured ..	60	60

132. Opening Ceremony.

(Litho. D.L.R.)

1975 (25 Aug.). *Opening of New Congo Bridge and President Stevens' 70th Birthday. P* 12½ × 13.

(a) Postage.

592	132	5 c. multicoloured ..	4·50	4·50

(b) Air.

593	132	20 c. multicoloured ..	50	50

133. Presidents Tolbert and Stevens, and Handclasp.

(Litho. D.L.R.)

1975 (3 Oct.). *Mano River Union. P* 12½ × 13.

(a) Postage.

594	133	4 c. multicoloured ..	75	75

(b) Air.

595	133	15 c. multicoloured ..	25	25

SINGAPORE

A Crown Colony until the end of 1957. From August 1st, 1958, an internally self-governing territory designated the State of Singapore. From Sept. 16th, 1963, part of the Malaysian Federation until 9th August, 1965, when it became an independent republic within the Commonwealth.

1948–52. *As T* **58** *of Straits Settlements, but inscr.* "SINGAPORE" *at foot. Wmk. Mult. Script CA. Chalk-surfaced paper. (a) P* 14.

1	1 c. black	5	5
2	2 c. orange	5	5
3	3 c. green	5	5
4	4 c. brown	5	5
5	6 c. grey	8	8
6	8 c. scarlet	8	8
7	10 c. purple	8	8
8	15 c. ultramarine	8	8
9	20 c. black and green ..	10	8
10	25 c. purple and orange ..	10	8
11	40 c. red and purple	45	60
12	50 c. black and blue	40	8
13	$1 blue and purple ..	65	8
14	$2 green and scarlet ..	1·40	80
15	$5 green and brown ..	3·25	1·10
1/15	.. .. *Set of* 15	6·00	3·00

Dates of issue: 1948—1 Sept., 1 c. to 6 c., and 10 c.; 1 Oct., 8 c., 15 c. to $1 and $5; 25 Oct., $2.

(b) P 17½ × 18.

16	1 c. black	8	8
17	2 c. orange	8	8
19	4 c. brown	8	8
19*a*	5 c. bright purple	8	8
21	6 c. grey	8	8
21*a*	8 c. green	20	10
22	10 c. purple	8	8
22*a*	12 c. scarlet	8	25
23	15 c. ultramarine	8	8
24	20 c. black and green ..	25	20
24*a*	20 c. bright blue	12	8
25	25 c. purple and orange ..	12	8
25*a*	35 c. scarlet and purple ..	40	20
26	40 c. red and purple	65	70
27	50 c. black and blue	40	8
28	$1 blue and purple ..	70	20
	a. Error. St. Edward's Crown ..	£170	
29	$2 green and scarlet ..	1·10	65
	a. Error. St. Edward's Crown ..	£170	
30	$5 green and brown ..	3·25	90
16/30	.. .. *Set of* 18	7·00	3·50

Dates of issue: 1949—1 July, 4 c., 31 Oct., 2 c., 20 c. blk. & grn. and $1: 1950—9 Feb., 10 c., 15 c., 25 c. and 50 c.; 1951—24 May, 40 c. and $2; 19 Dec., $5: 1952—21 May, 1 c.; 1 Sept., 5 c., 8 c., 12 c., 20 c. blue and 35 c.; 10 Dec., 6 c.

Nos. 28a and 29a occur on rows in the watermark in which the crowns and letters "C A" alternate.

1948 (25 Oct.). *Royal Silver Wedding. As Nos.* 30/1 *of Aden.*

31	10 c. violet	8	8
32	$5 brown	4·00	4·00

1949 (10 Oct.). *75th Anniv. of Universal Postal Union. As Nos.* 114/7 *of Antigua.*

33	10 c. purple	8	8
34	15 c. deep blue	12	20
35	25 c. orange	20	35
36	50 c. blue-black	40	55

1953 (2 June). *Coronation. As No.* 47 *of Aden.*

37	10 c. black and reddish purple	12	8

1. Chinese Sampan.

2. Malay Kolek.
3. Twa-Kow.
4. Lombok Sloop.
5. Trengganu Pinas.
6. Palari.
7. Timber Tongkong.
8. Hainan Trader.
9. Cocos-Keeling Schooner.
10. *Argonaut* Aircraft.
11. Oil Tanker.
12. M.S. *Chusan*.
(*Types* **2/12** *are horiz. as T* **1**.)

13. Raffles Statue.

14. Singapore River.

15. Arms of Singapore.

(Des. Dr. C. A. Gibson-Hill, except 25 c., 30 c., 50 c. and $5 (from photographs, etc.). Photo. Harrison (T **1/12**). Recess (centre typo. on $5). B.W. (others).)

1955 (4 Sept.). *Wmk. Mult. Script CA. P* 13½ × 14½ (*T* **1/12**) *or* 14 (T **13/15**).

38	**1**	1 c. black	5	5
39	**2**	2 c. yellow-orange ..	5	5
40	**3**	4 c. brown	5	5
41	**4**	5 c. bright purple	5	5
42	**5**	6 c. deep grey-blue ..	5	5
43	**6**	8 c. turquoise-blue ..	8	10
44	**7**	10 c. deep lilac	8	5
45	**8**	12 c. rose-carmine	15	20
46	**9**	20 c. ultramarine (*shades*) ..	20	8
47	**10**	25 c. orange-red and bluish violet (*shades*) ..	15	5
48	**11**	30 c. violet & brown-purple	15	5
49	**12**	50 c. blue and black ..	30	8
50	**13**	$1 blue and deep purple ..	75	12
51	**14**	$2 blue-green and scarlet	1·75	40
52	**15**	$5 yellow, red, brown and slate-black	4·00	1·00
38/52		.. .. *Set of* 15	7·00	2·00

Plates 2A and 2B of the 10 c. (12 Apr. 1960) and the blue " 3A " and " 3B " plates of the 50 c. " 3A–2A ", " 3B–2B " (part of the 24 Jan. 1961 issue and later printings) were printed with a finer screen (250 dots per inch, instead of the normal 200). (*Price* 10 *c.*, 65*p un. or us.*; 50 *c.*, 15*p un. or us.*)

16. The Singapore Lion.

(Photo. Harrison.)

1959 (1 June). *New Constitution. W* w.**12**. *P* 11½ × 12.

53	**16**	4 c. yell., sepia & rose-red	8	8
54	,,	10 c. yellow, sepia & reddish purple	12	12
55	,,	20 c. yell., sepia & brt. blue	25	25
56	,,	25 c. yellow, sepia and green	40	40
57	,,	30 c. yellow, sepia & violet	50	50
58	,,	50 c. yell., sepia & dp. slate	85	85
53/58		.. .. *Set of* 6	1·90	2·00

17. State Flag.

(Litho. J. Enschedé.)

1960 (3 June). *National Day. W* w.**12** (*sideways*). *P* 13½.

59	**17**	4 c. red, yellow and blue ..	12	8
60	,,	10 c. red, yellow and grey ..	15	10

18. Clasped Hands.

(Photo. Enschedé.)

1961 (3 June). *National Day. W* w.**12**. *P* 13½.

61	**18**	4 c. blk., brn. & pale yell.	12	8
62	,,	10 c. black, deep green and pale yellow	15	10

19. *Arachnis* " *Maggie Oei* " (orchid).

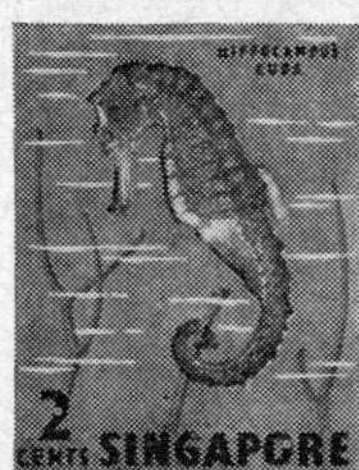

20. Sea-Horse.

21. Six-banded Barb.

22. Clown Fish.

23. Archer Fish.

24. *Vanda* " *Tan Cha Yan* " (orchid).

25. Harlequin.

26. *Grammaphotyllum speciosum* (orchid).

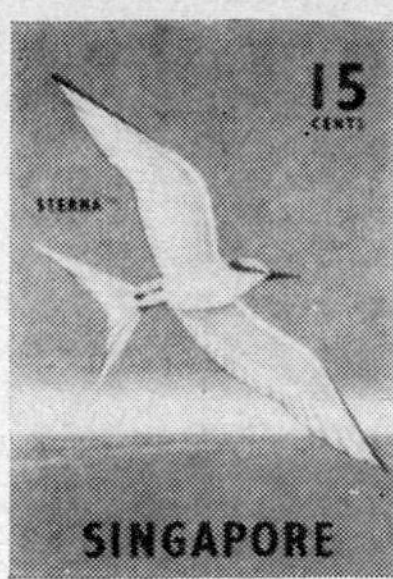

26*a*. Black-naped Tern.

27. Butterfly Fish.

29. *Vanda " Miss Joaquim "* (orchid).

28. Two-spot Gourami.

30. White-rumped Shama.

31. White-throated Kingfisher.

32. Yellow-breasted Sunbird.

33. White-bellied Sea Eagle.

(Photo. Harrison (orchids, fish and 15 c. bird), D.L.R. (birds, except 15 c.).)

1962 (31 Mar.)–**66.** *Orchid and bird designs multi-coloured; background colours given. W* w.**12.** *P* $12\frac{1}{2}$ (i), $14\frac{1}{2}\times13\frac{1}{2}$ (ii), $13\frac{1}{2}\times14\frac{1}{2}$ (iii), $13\frac{1}{2}\times13$ (iv) *or* $13\times13\frac{1}{2}$ (v).

63	**19**	1 c. mauve (i) (10.3.63) ..	5	5
64	**20**	2 c. brown and green (ii) ..	5	5
65	**21**	4 c. black & orange-red (iii)	5	5
		a. Black omitted	40·00	
66	**22**	5 c. red and black (iii) ..	5	5
		a. Red omitted	40·00	
67	**23**	6 c. black & grnish yell. (ii)	5	5
68	**24**	8 c. pale turq.-bl. (i)(10.3.63)	5	5
69	**25**	10 c. red-orange & blk. (iii)	5	5
		a. Red-orange omitted ..	35·00	
70	**26**	12 c. salmon (i) (10.3.63) ..	8	10
70*a*	**26***a*	15 c. bright bl. (i) (9.11.66)	8	5
71	**27**	20 c. orange and blue (ii)	12	8
		a. Orange omitted	45·00	
72	**28**	25 c. black and orange (iii)	12	8
73	**29**	30 c. stone (i) (10.3.63) ..	20	8
74	**30**	50 c. apple-green (iv) (10.3.63)	30	10
75	**31**	$1 yellow (iv) (10.3.63) ..	75	12
76	**32**	$2 grey-blue (iv) (10.3.63)	1·50	50
77	**33**	$5 cobalt (v) (10.3.63) ..	4·00	1·25
63/77		.. .. *Set of* 16	6·50	2·50

The 15 c., 30 c., $2 and $5 exist with PVA gum as well as gum arabic.

See also Nos. 83/88.

34. " The Role of Labour in Nation-Building ".

(Photo. Courvoisier.)

1962 (3 June). *National Day. P* $11\frac{1}{2}\times12$.

78	**34**	4 c. yellow, rose-carmine and black	12	5
79	,,	10 c. yellow, blue and black	15	10

35. Blocks of Flats, Singapore.

(Photo. Harrison.)

1963 (3 June). *National Day. W* w.**12.** *P* $12\frac{1}{2}$.

80	**35**	4 c. orange-red, blk., blue and turquoise-blue ..	12	5
81	,,	10 c. orge.-red, blk., yellow-olive & turquoise-blue	15	10

36. Dancers in National Costume.

(Photo. Harrison.)

1963 (8 Aug.). *South East Asia Cultural Festival. W* w.**12.** *P* $14\times14\frac{1}{2}$.

82	**36**	5 c. yellow, black, blue-green and turquoise-blue ..	8	8

1966 (9 June)–**67.** *As Nos.* 63, *etc. but W* w.**12** (*sideways*). *Orchid and bird designs multi-coloured; background colours given.*

83	**19**	1 c. mauve (22.2.67) ..	5	5
84	**22**	5 c. red and black (30.5.67)	5	5
85	**25**	10 c. red-orange and black (30.5.67)	8	8
86	**28**	25 c. black and orange (9.66*)	15	15
87	**30**	50 c. apple-green	35	30
88	**31**	$1 yellow (18.5.67) ..	75	75
83/88		.. .. *Set of* 6	1·25	1·10

* No. 86 was not released in London until 30.5.67 but it is known used in Singapore as early as Sept. 1966.

The 1 c. and 25 c. exist with PVA gum as well as gum arabic.

37. Workers.

(Photo. D.L.R.)

1966 (9 Aug.). *First Anniv. of Republic. W* w.**12** (30 *c.*) *or no wmk.* (*others*). *P* $12\frac{1}{2}\times13$.

89	**37**	15 c. multicoloured ..	10	8
90	,,	20 c. multicoloured ..	12	15
91	,,	30 c. multicoloured ..	20	20

38. Flag Procession.

(Photo. De La Rue.)

1967 (9 Aug.). *National Day. P* 14 × 14½.

92	**38**	6 c. rosine, brown & slate	8	8
93	,,	15 c. reddish purple, brown and slate	12	10
94	,,	50 c. bright blue, brown and slate	45	40

Nos. 92/4 are respectively inscribed "Build a Vigorous Singapore" in Chinese, Malay and Tamil in addition to the English inscription.

39. Skyscrapers and Afro-Asian Map.

(Photo. De La Rue.)

1967 (7 Oct.). *2nd Afro-Asian Housing Congress. P* 14 × 13.

95	**39**	10 c. multicoloured ..	8	8
		a. Opt. omitted		
96	,,	25 c. multicoloured ..	20	15
97	,,	50 c. multicoloured ..	40	40

The above were originally scheduled for release in 1966, and when finally issued were overprinted with the new date and a black oblong obliterating the old date.

40. Symbolical Figure wielding Hammer, and Industrial Outline of Singapore.

(Photo. Harrison.)

1968 (9 Aug.). *National Day. Inscription at top in Chinese* (6 *c.*), *Malay* (15 *c.*) *or Tamil* (50 *c.*). *P* 13½ × 14.

98	**40**	6 c. orge.-red, blk. & gold	8	8
99	,,	15 c. apple-grn., blk. & gold	12	12
100	,,	50 c. greenish blue, black and goid	40	40

41. Half check Pattern.

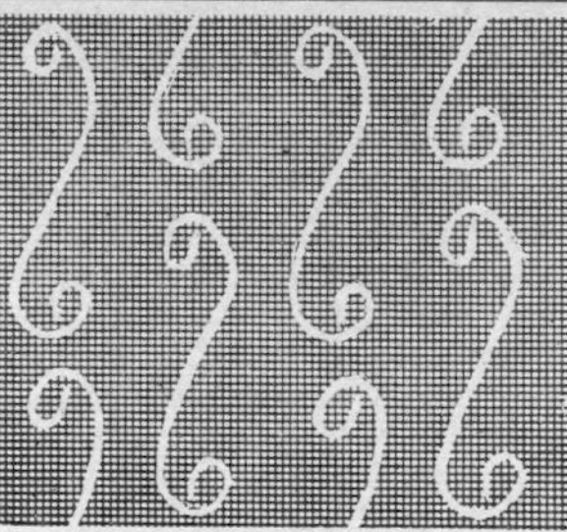

42. Scrolled "S" multiple.

43. Mirudhangam.

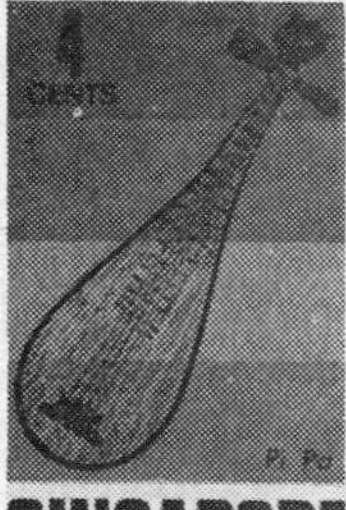

44. Pi Pa.

45. Sword Dance.

46. Lion Dance.

47. Bharatha Natyam.

48. Tari Payong.

49. Kathak Kali.

50. Lu Chih Shen and Lin Chung.

52. Tari Lilin.

51. Dragon Dance.

53. Tarian Kuda Kepang.

54. Yao Chi.

55. Rebab.

57. Ta Ku.

56. Vina.

(Photo. De La Rue (5 c. to $1), Govt. Printing Bureau, Tokyo (others).)

1968–73. 5 *c. to* $1: *Chalk-surfaced paper; W* **41**; *P* 14. *Others: Ordinary paper; W* **42** *upright* (1 *c.*, $5) *or sideways* (4 *c.*, $2, $10); *P* 13½.

101	**43**	1 c. mult. (10.11.69) ..	5	5
102	**44**	4 c. mult. (10.11.69) ..	5	5
103	**45**	5 c. mult. (29.12.68) ..	5	5
		a. Glazed unsurfaced paper (16.12.70)	10	10
		b. Chalky paper. Perf. 13 (27.6.73)	8	8
104	**46**	6 c. black, lemon and orange (1.12.68) ..	5	5

No.	Type	Description	Unused	Used
105	**47**	10 c. mult. (29.12.68) ..	5	5
		a. Glazed unsurfaced paper (1 .12.70)	15	15
		b. Chalky paper. Perf. 13 (12.9.73)	10	10
106	**48**	15 c. mult. (29.12.68) ..	10	8
107	**49**	20 c. mult. (1.12.68) ..	12	8
		a. Perf. 13 (12.9.73) ..	20	20
108	**50**	25 c. mult. (29.12.68) ..	15	12
		a. Perf. 13 (27.6.73) ..	25	25
109	**51**	30 c. mult. (1.12.68) ..	20	15
		a. Perf. 13 (12.9.73) ..	30	30
110	**52**	50 c. blk., orge.-red & light yellow-brn. (1.12.68)	30	30
		a. Perf. 13 (12.9.73) ..	50	50
111	**53**	75 c. mult. (1.12.68) ..	40	35
112	**54**	$1 mult. (29.12.68) ..	50	45
		a. Perf. 13 (12.9.73) ..	90	90
113	**55**	$2 mult. (10.11.69) ..	1·10	90
114	**56**	$5 mult. (10.11.69) ..	2·50	2·25
115	**57**	$10 mult. (6.12.69) ..	5·00	4·50
101/115		.. .. *Set of* 15	9·50	8·50
103b/112a		.. .. *Set of* 7	2·00	2·00

58. E.C.A.F.E. Emblem.

(Des. Eng. Siak Loy. Photo. Govt. Ptg. Bureau, Tokyo.)

1969 (15 APR.). *25th Plenary Session of the U.N. Economic Commission for Asia and the Far East. P* 13.

No.	Type	Description	Unused	Used
116	**58**	15 c. blk., silver & pale bl.	10	10
117	,,	30 c. black, silver and red	25	25
118	,,	75 c. blk., silver & vio.-bl.	60	60

59. " 100000 " and Slogan as Block of Flats.

(Des. Tay Siew Chiah. Litho. Bradbury, Wilkinson.)

1969 (20 JULY). *Completion of " 100,000 Homes for the People " Project. P* 13½.

No.	Type	Description	Unused	Used
119	**59**	25 c. black and emerald ..	20	20
120	,,	50 c. black and deep blue ..	35	35

60. Aircraft over Silhouette of Singapore Docks.

(Des. Eng. Siak Loy and Han Kuan Cheng. Litho. Bradbury, Wilkinson.)

1969 (9 AUG.). *150th Anniv. of Founding of Singapore. Type* **60** *and similar vert. designs. P* 14 × 14½.

No.	Description	Unused	Used
121	15 c. black, vermilion & yell.	8	8
122	30 c. black, blue & new blue	20	20
123	75 c. multicoloured	50	50
124	$1 black and vermilion ..	80	80
125	$5 vermilion and black ..	3·50	3·50
126	$10 black and bright green	6·50	6·50
121/6	.. .. *Set of* 6	10·00	10·00
MS127	120 × 120 mm. Nos. 121/6 Perf. 13½	20·00	20·00

Designs:—30 c. U.N. emblem and outline of Singapore; 75 c. Flags and outlines of Malaysian Federation; $1 Uplifted hands holding crescent and stars; $5 Tail of Japanese aircraft and searchlight beams; $10 Bust from statue of Sir Stamford Raffles.

61. Sea Shells.

(Des. Tay Siew Chiah (15 c.), Eng. Siak Loy (others). Litho. Rosenbaum Bros.)

1970 (15 MAR.). *World Fair, Osaka. Type* **61** *and similar vert. designs. Multicoloured. P* 13½.

No.	Description	Unused	Used
128	15 c. Type **61**	10	8
129	30 c. Tropical fish	20	20
130	75 c. Flamingo and hornbill	45	45
131	$1 Orchid	75	75
MS132	94 × 154 mm. Nos. 128/31	1·50	1·50

62. " Kindergarten ".

(Des. Choy Weng Yang. Litho. B.W.)

1970 (1 JULY). *Tenth Anniv. of People's Association. T* **62** *and similar square designs. P* 13½.

No.	Description	Unused	Used
133	15 c. agate and bright orange	10	8
134	50 c. ultramarine & yell. orge.	35	35
135	75 c. bright purple & black	45	45

Designs:—50 c. " Sport "; 75 c. " Culture ".

63. Soldier charging.

(Des. Choy Weng Yang. Litho. Rosenbaum Bros., Vienna.)

1970 (9 AUG.). *National Day. T* **63** *and similar vert. designs. Multicoloured. P* 13½.

No.	Description	Unused	Used
136	15 c. Type **63**	10	8
137	50 c. Soldier on assault course	35	35
138	$1 Soldier jumping ..	70	70

64. Sprinters.

(Des. Choy Weng Yang. Photo. Japanese Govt. Ptg. Bureau, Tokyo.)

1970 (23 AUG.). *Festival of Sports. T* **64** *and similar horiz. designs. P* 13 × 13½.

No.	Description	Unused	Used
139	10 c. magenta, black and ultramarine	5	5
140	15 c. black, ultramarine and red-orange	10	10
141	25 c. black, red-orange and bright green	20	20
142	50 c. black, bright green and magenta	40	40

Designs:—15 c. Swimmers; 25 c. Tennis-players; 50 c. Racing-cars.

Nos. 139/42 were issued together *se-tenant* in horizontal strips of four within the sheet.

65. Ship of Neptune Oriental Lines.

(*Illustration reduced. Actual size* 56 × 25 *mm.*)

(Des. W. Lee. Litho. Rosenbaum Bros., Vienna.)

1970 (1 NOV.). *Singapore Shipping. T* **65** *and similar horiz. designs. P* 12.

No.	Description	Unused	Used
143	15 c. multicoloured	10	10
144	30 c. yellow-ochre & ultram.	30	30
145	75 c. yellow-ochre & verm.	75	75

Designs:—30 c. Container berth; 75 c. Ship-building.

66. Country Names forming Circle.

(Des. W. Lee. Litho. D.L.R.)

1971 (1 Jan.). *Commonwealth Heads of Government Meeting, Singapore. T* **66** *and similar horiz. designs. Multicoloured. P* 14 ($1) *or* 15×14½ *(others).*

146	15 c. Type **66**	10	10
147	30 c. Flags in circle	20	20
148	75 c. Commonwealth flags ..	45	45
149	$1 Commonwealth flags linked to Singapore ..	60	60

The $1 is larger, 63×61 mm.

67. Bicycle Rickshaws.

(Des. Eng. Siak Loy (15, 20 and 30 c.), W. Lee (others). Litho. B.W.)

1971 (4 Apr.). *Visit ASEAN Year (ASEAN= Association of South East Asian Nations). T* **67** *and similar designs. P* 13×13½ (50, 75 *c.) or* 11½ *(others).*

150	15 c. black, deep bluish violet and orange	10	10
151	20 c. indigo, orge. & turq.-bl.	15	15
152	30 c. vermilion & dp. maroon	20	20
153	50 c. multicoloured	35	35
154	75 c. multicoloured	45	45
150/4	.. .. *Set of* 5	1·10	1·10

Designs: *As T* **67**—20 c. Houseboat "village" and boats; 30 c. Bazaar. *Horiz.* (68×18 *mm.*)—50 c. Modern harbour skyline; 75 c. Religious buildings.

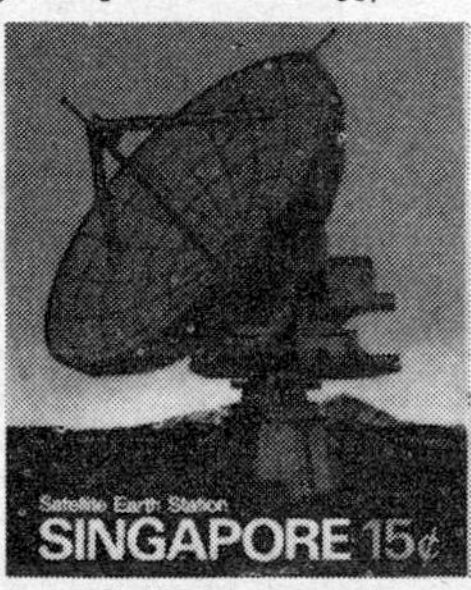

68. Chinese New Year.

(Des. W. Lee. Litho. Rosenbaum Bros., Vienna.)

1971 (9 Aug.). *Singapore Festivals. T* **68** *and similar vert. designs. Multicoloured. P* 14.

155	15 c. Type **68**	10	10
156	30 c. Hari Raya	20	20
157	50 c. Deepavali	35	35
158	75 c. Christmas	50	50
MS159	150×125 mm. Nos. 155/8	1·25	1·25

69. "Dish" Aerial.

(Des. W. Lee. Litho. B.W.)

1971 (23 Oct.). *Opening of Satellite Earth Station. P* 13½.

160 **69**	15 c. multicoloured ..	10	10
161 –	30 c. multicoloured ..	30	30
162 –	30 c. multicoloured ..	30	30
163 –	30 c. multicoloured ..	30	30
164 –	30 c. multicoloured ..	30	30
160/4	.. .. *Set of* 5	1·10	1·10

Designs:—Nos. 161/4 were printed in *se-tenant* blocks of four throughout the sheet, the four stamps forming a composite design similar to T **69.** They can be identified by the colour of the face value which is: yellow (No. 161), green (No. 162), magenta (No. 163) or orange (No. 164).

70. "Singapore River and Fort Canning, 1843–7" (Lieut. E. A. Porcher).

(Illustration reduced. Actual size 53×46 *mm.)*

(Des. W. Lee. Litho. B.W.)

1971 (5 Dec.). *Art. T* **70** *and similar horiz. designs. Multicoloured. P* 12½×13 (50 *c. and* $1 *or* 13 *(others).*

165	10 c. Type **70**	10	10
166	15 c. "The Padang, 1851" (J. T. Thomson) ..	12	12
167	20 c. "Singapore Waterfront, 1848–9"	15	15
168	35 c. "View from Fort Canning, 1846" (J. T. Thomson)	30	30
169	50 c. "View from Mt. Wallich, 1857" (P. Carpenter) ..	60	60
170	$1 "Singapore Waterfront, 1861" (W. Gray) ..	1·40	1·40
165/70	.. .. *Set of* 6	2·40	2·40

The 50 c. and $1 are larger, 69×47 mm.

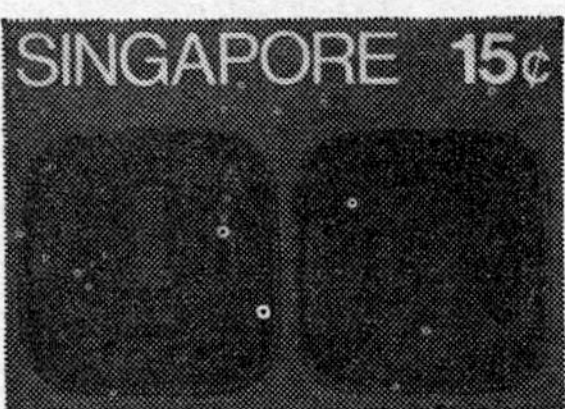

71. One-cent Coin of George V.

(Des. W. Lee. Litho. B.W.)

1972 (4 June). *Coins. T* **71** *and similar horiz. designs. P* 13½.

171	15 c. orange, black & deep green	10	10
172	35 c. black and vermilion	25	25
173	$1 yellow, black & bright blue	60	60

Designs:—35 c. One dollar of 1969; $1 One hundred and fifty dollar gold coin of 1969.

72. "Moon Festival" (Seah Kim Joo).

(Des. W. Lee. Litho. State Bank Not Printing Works, Helsinki.)

1972 (9 July). *Contemporary Art. T* **72** *an similar multicoloured designs. P* 12½.

174	15 c. Type **72**	10	1
175	35 c. "Complementary Force" (Thomas Yeo)	30	3
176	50 c. "Rhythm in Blue" (Yusman Aman) ..	40	4
177	$1 "Gibbons" (Chen Wen Hsi)	70	7

The 35 and 50 c. are 36×54 mm.

73. Lanterns and Fish.

(Des. Eng. Siak Loy. Litho. State Bank No Printing Works, Helsinki.)

1972 (9 Aug.). *National Day. T* **73** *and simil vert. designs symbolising Festivals. Mult coloured. P* 12½.

178	15 c. Type **73**	10
179	35 c. Altar and candles ..	25
180	50 c. Jug, bowl and gifts ..	40
181	75 c. Candle	50

74. Student Welding.

(Des. Eng. Siak Loy. Photo. Kultura, Budapest.)

1972 (1 Oct.). *Youth. T* **74** *and similar hori designs. P* 12.

182	15 c. multicoloured ..	10
183	35 c. multicoloured ..	25
184	$1 red-orange, blue-violet and yellowish green ..	60

Designs:—35 c. Sport; $1 Dancing.

75. *Maria Rickmers.*

(Des. Choy Weng Yang (Nos. 185/7), Eng Siak Loy (**MS**188). Litho. Harrison.)

1972 (17 Dec.). *Shipping. T* **75** *and similar multicoloured designs. P* 14 × 14½.

185	15 c. *Neptune Ruby* (42 × 29 *mm.*)	10	10
186	75 c. Type **75**	50	50
187	$1 Chinese junk	60	60
MS188	152 × 84 mm. Nos. 185/7 ..	2·00	2·00

76. P.Q.R. Slogan.

(Des. W. Lee. Litho. B.W.)

1973 (25 Feb.). *"Prosperity through Quality and Reliability" Campaign. T* **76** *and similar vert. designs. P* 14.

189	**76**	15 c. multicoloured ..	10	10
190	–	35 c. multicoloured ..	25	25
191	–	75 c. multicoloured ..	40	40
192	–	$1 multicoloured ..	55	55

Nos. 190/2 show various P.Q.R. emblems.

77. Jurong Bird Park.

(Des. H. K. Cheng. Litho. Harrison.)

1973 (29 Apr.). *Singapore Landmarks. T* **77** *and similar vert. designs. P* 12½.

193	15 c. black and red-orange ..	10	10
194	35 c. black and myrtle-green	25	25
195	50 c. black and red-brown ..	35	35
196	$1 black and purple ..	60	60

Designs:—35 c. National Theatre; 50 c. City Hall; $1 Fullerton Building and Singapore River.

78. Aircraft Tail-fins.

(Des. W. Lee. Litho. B.W.)

1973 (24 June). *Aviation. T* **78** *and similar horiz. designs. Multicoloured. P* 13½ × 13.

197	10 c. Type **78**	8	8
198	35 c. Emblem of Singapore Airlines and destinations	25	25
199	75 c. Emblem on tail-fin ..	40	40
200	$1 Emblems encircling the globe	55	55

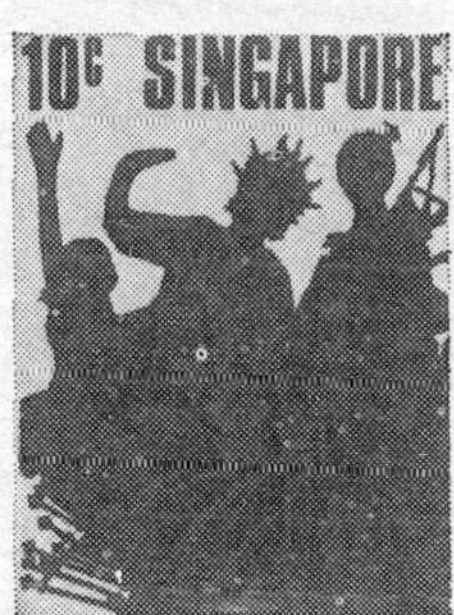

79. " Culture ".

(Des. Eng Siak Loy. Litho. Harrison.)

1973 (9 Aug.). *National Day. T* **79** *and similar vert. designs. P* 13½.

201	**79**	10 c. orange and black ..	8	8
202	–	35 c. orange and black ..	25	25
203	–	50 c. orange and black ..	35	35
204	–	75 c. orange and black ..	45	45

Nos. 201/4 were printed in *se-tenant* blocks of four within the sheet, and form a composite design representing Singapore's culture.

80. Athletics, Judo and Boxing.

(Des. C. Lim. Photo. Heraclio Fournier.)

1973 (1 Sept.). *Seventh S.E.A.P.* Games. T* **80** *and similar designs. P* 14 (10 *to* 35 *c.*) *or* 13 × 14 (*others*).

205	10 c. gold, silver and indigo ..	8	8
206	15 c. gold and grey-black ..	10	10
207	25 c. gold, silver and black ..	15	15
208	35 c. gold, silver and deep blue	25	25
209	50 c. multicoloured	30	30
210	$1 silver, Royal blue and yellow-green	60	60
205/10	.. .. *Set of* 6	1·25	1·25
MS211	130 × 111 mm. Nos. 205/10. *P* 13 × 14	1·50	1·50

Designs: *As T* **80**—15 c. Cycling, weight-lifting, pistol-shooting and sailing; 25 c. Footballs; 35 c. Table-tennis bat, shuttlecock, tennis ball and hockey stick. *Horiz.* (41 × 25 *mm.*):—50 c. Swimmers; $1 Stadium.

*S.E.A.P. = South East Asian Peninsula.

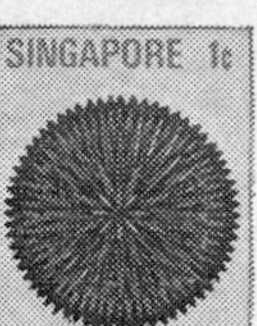

81. Agave.

82. Mangosteen.

(Des. W. Lee (1 c. to 75 c.), E. Siak Loy (others). Photo. Heraclio Fournier.)

1973 *Various multicoloured designs as T* **81/2**. *With fluorescent security markings.*

(*a*) *Stylized flowers and plants, size as T* **81**. *P* 13 (30.9.73).

212	1 c. Type **81**	5	5
213	5 c. *Coleus blumei*	5	5
	a. Booklet pane. Nos. 213 × 4, 214 × 4, 216 × 2 *se-tenant* ..	40	
214	10 c. *Vinca rosea*	5	5
215	15 c. *Helianthus angustifolius*	5	5
216	20 c. *Licuala grandis* ..	8	8
217	25 c. *Wedelia trilobula* ..	10	10
218	35 c. *Chrysanthemum frutescens*	12	15
219	50 c. *Costus malortieanus* ..	20	20
220	75 c. *Gerbera jamesonii* ..	30	35

(*b*) *Fruits, size as T* **82**. *P* 12½ × 13 (1.11.73).

221	$1 Type **82**	40	45
222	$2 Jackfruit	75	90
223	$5 Coconut	1·90	2·00
224	$10 Pineapple	3·75	4·00
212/24	.. .. *Set of* 13	6·50	7·00

83. Tiger and Orang-utans.

(Des. E. Siak Loy. Litho. B.W.)

1973 (16 Dec.). *Singapore Zoo. T* **83** *and similar vert. designs. Multicoloured. P* 13.

225	5 c. Type **83**	5	5
226	10 c. Leopard and gazelles ..	8	8
227	35 c. Panther and deer ..	25	25
228	75 c. Horse and lion	45	45

84. Multicolour Guppy.

(Des. Eng Siak Loy. Photo. Heraclio Fournier.)

1974 (21 Apr.). *Tropical Fish. T* **84** *and similar vert. designs. Multicoloured. P* 14.

229	5 c. Type **84**	5	5
230	10 c. Half Black Guppy ..	8	8
231	35 c. Multicolour Guppy (*different*)	20	20
232	$1 Black Guppy	55	55

85. Scout Badge within "9".

(Des. W. Lee. Litho. Harrison.)

1974 (9 June). *Ninth Asia-Pacific Scout Conference.* P 13½ × 14½.
233 **85** 10 c. multicoloured .. 8 8
234 „ 75 c. multicoloured .. 35 40

86. U.P.U. Emblem and Multiple "Centenary".

(Des. W. Lee. Litho. Harrison.)

1974 (7 July). *Centenary of Universal Postal Union.* T **86** *and similar vert. designs.* P 14 × 13½.
235 **86** 10 c. orange-brown, purple-brown and gold .. 8 8
236 – 35 c. new blue, deep blue and gold 20 20
237 – 75 c. multicoloured .. 40 40

Designs:—35 c. U.P.U. emblem and multiple U.N. symbols; 75 c. U.P.U. emblem and multiple peace doves.

87. Family Emblem.

(Des. Eng Siak Loy. Litho. B.W.)

1974 (9 Aug.). *World Population Year.* T **87** *and similar horiz. designs. Multicoloured.* P 12½ × 13½.
238 10 c. Type **87** 8 8
239 35 c. Male and female symbols 20 20
a. Emerald (male symbol) omitted 50·00
240 75 c. World population map .. 40 40

88. "Tree and Sun" (Chia Keng San).

(Des. Eng Siak Loy. Photo. Heraclio Fournier.)

1974 (1 Oct.). *Universal Children's Day.* T **88** *and similar vert. designs showing children's paintings. Multicoloured.* P 13½.
241 5 c. Type **88** 5 5
242 10 c. "My Daddy and Mummy" (Angeline Ang) 8 8
243 35 c. "A Dump Truck" (Si-Hoe Yeen Joong) 20 20
244 50 c. "My Aunt" (Raymond Teo) 30 30
MS245 138 × 100 mm. Nos. 241/4. P 13 .. .. .. 65 65

89. Street Scene.

(Des. Loy Chin. Litho. Secura, Singapore.)

1975 (26 Jan.). *Singapore Views.* T **89** *and similar horiz. designs. Multicoloured.* P 13½.
246 15 c. Type **89** 10 10
247 20 c. Singapore River .. 12 12
248 $1 " Kelong " (fish-trap) .. 50 50

90. Emblem and Lighters' Prows.

(Des. Choy Weng Yang. Litho. Secura, Singapore.)

1975 (10 Mar.). *Ninth Biennial Conference of International Association of Ports and Harbours, Singapore.* T **90** *and similar horiz. designs. Multicoloured.* P 14.
249 5 c. Type **90** 5 5
250 25 c. Freighter and ship's wheel 15 15
251 50 c. Oil-tanker and flags .. 25 25
252 $1 Container-ship and propellers 45 45

91. Satellite Earth Station, Sentosa.

(Des. Sim Tong Khern. Photo. Heraclio Fournier.)

1975 (29 June). "*Science and Industry*". T **91** *and similar multicoloured designs.* P 13½.
253 10 c. Type **91** 8 8
254 35 c. Oil refineries (*vert.*) .. 20 20
255 75 c. " Medical Sciences " .. 35 35

92. " Homes and Gardens ".

93. Crowned Cranes.

(Des. Tay Siew Chiah. Litho. Secura, Singapore.)

1975 (9 Aug.). *Tenth National Day.* T **92** *and similar square designs. Multicoloured.* P 13½.
256 10 c. Type **92** 5 5
257 35 c. " Shipping and Shipbuilding " 20 20
258 75 c. " Communications and Technology " 35 35
259 $1 " Trade, Commerce and Industry " 45 45

(Des. Eng Siak Loy. Litho. Harrison.)

1975 (5 Oct.). *Birds.* T **93** *and similar vert. designs. Multicoloured.* P 14½ × 13½.
260 5 c. Type **93** 5 5
261 10 c. Great Hornbill 5 5
262 35 c. Kingfishers 20 20
263 $1 Greater Sulphur-crested Cockatoo and Blue and Yellow Macaw 45 45

94. " Equality ".

(Des. Tay Siew Chiah. Litho. Secura, Singapore.)

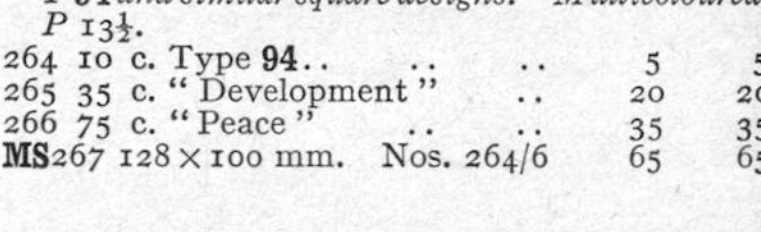

1975 (7 Dec.). *International Women's Year.* T **94** *and similar square designs. Multicoloured.* P 13½.
264 10 c. Type **94** 5 5
265 35 c. " Development " .. 20 20
266 75 c. " Peace " 35 35
MS267 128 × 100 mm. Nos. 264/6 65 65

95. Yellow Flame.

96. *Arachnis hookeriana* × *Vanda* Hilo Blue.

(Des. Tay Siew Chiah. Litho. Secura, Singapore.)

1976 (18 Apr.). *Wayside Trees. T* **95** *and similar vert. designs. Multicoloured. P* 13½.

268	10 c. Type **95**	5	5
269	35 c. Cabbage Tree	15	20
270	50 c. Rose of India	25	25
271	75 c. Variegated Coral Tree	35	35

(Des. Eng. Siak Loy. Litho. Secura, Singapore.)

1976 (20 June). *Singapore Orchids. T* **96** *and similar vert. designs. Multicoloured. P* 13½.

272	10 c. Type **96**	5	5
273	35 c. *Arachnis Maggie Oei* × *Vanda insignis* ..	15	20
274	50 c. *Arachnis Maggie Oei* × *Vanda* Rodman ..	20	25
275	75 c. *Arachnis hookeriana* × *Vanda* Dawn Nishimura	30	35

97. Festival Symbol and Band.

(Des. Han Kuan Cheng. Litho. Harrison.)

1976 (9 Aug.). *Tenth Anniv. of Singapore Youth Festival. Horiz. designs showing festival symbol as T* **97**. *Multicoloured. P* 12½.

276	10 c. Type **97**	5	5
277	35 c. Athletes	15	20
278	75 c. Dancers	30	35

98. " Queen Elizabeth Walk ".

(Des. H. Weepaul. Litho. Secura, Singapore.)

1976 (14 Nov.). *Paintings of Old Singapore, c.* 1905–10. *T* **98** *and similar horiz. designs. Multicoloured. With fluorescent security markings. P* 14.

279	10 c. Type **98**	5	5
280	50 c. " The Padang " ..	20	25
281	$1 " Raffles Place " ..	45	50
MS282	164 × 91 mm. Nos. 279/81. P 13½	75	

99. Chinese Costume.

(Des. Margaret Heng. Litho. Harrison.)

1976 (19 Dec.). *Bridal Costumes. T* **99** *and similar vert. designs. Multicoloured. P* 14.

283	10 c. Type **99**	5	5
284	35 c. Indian costume ..	15	20
285	75 c. Malay costume ..	30	35

POSTAGE DUE STAMPS.

The postage due stamps of Malayan Postal Union were in use in Singapore until replaced by the following issue.

D 1

(Litho. Bradbury, Wilkinson.)

1968 (1 Feb.). *W* w.**12**. *P* 9.

D1	D **1**	1 c. green	5	5
D2	"	2 c. red	5	5
D3	"	4 c. yellow-orange ..	5	5
D4	"	8 c. chocolate	5	8
D5	"	10 c. magenta	10	12
D6	"	12 c. slate-violet	8	10
D7	"	20 c. new blue	10	12
D8	"	50 c. drab	35	40
D1/8		.. .. *Set of* 8	70	80

The 10, 12 and 20 c. exist on both white and toned paper; the rest on toned paper only.

1973. *White paper. W* w.**12**. *P* 13 × 13½.

D13	D **1**	10 c. brt. magenta (27.4)	5	8
D16	"	50 c. sage-green (24.8) ..	20	25

SOLOMON ISLANDS.

(Formerly British Solomon Islands.)

I. BRITISH PROTECTORATE.

1

(Des. C. M. Woodford. Litho. W. E. Smith & Co., Sydney.)

1907 (14 Feb.). *No wmk. P* 11.

1	**1**	½d. ultramarine	5·50	8·50
2	"	1d. rose-carmine	11·00	12·00
3	"	2d. indigo	11·00	12·00
		a. Imperf. between (horiz. pair) ..	£2250	
4	"	2½d. orange-yellow	12·00	14·00
		a. Imperf. between (vert. pair) ..	£1200	
		b. Imperf. between (horiz. pair) ..	£1200	£1100
5	"	5d. emerald-green	22·00	28·00
6	"	6d. chocolate	28·00	28·00
		a. Imperf. between (vert. pair) ..	£650	
7	"	1s. bright purple	35·00	38·00
1/7		.. .. *Set of* 7	£110	£120

Three types exist of the ½d. and 2½d., and six each of the other values, differing in minor details.

2

(Recess. D.L.R.)

1908 (1 Nov.)–**11**. *Wmk. Mult. Crown CA (sideways). P* 14.

8	**2**	½d. green	40	65
9	"	1d. red	85	1·10
10	"	2d. greyish slate	1·25	1·40
11	"	2½d. ultramarine	1·40	2·00
11*a*	"	4d. red/*yellow* (3.11) ..	2·50	3·50
12	"	5d. olive	6·00	4·50
13	"	6d. claret	5·50	4·50
14	"	1s. black/*green*	7·00	7·00
15	"	2s. purple/*blue* (Mar., 1910)	17·00	18·00
16	"	2s. 6d. red/*blue* (Mar., 1910)	28·00	35·00
17	"	5s. green/*yell.* (Mar., 1910)	50·00	55·00
8/17		.. .. *Set of* 11	£110	£120
8/17 Optd. " Specimen "		*Set of* 11	£100	

The ½d. and 1d. were issued in 1913 on rather thinner paper and with brownish gum.

3

4

(T **3** and **4**. Typo. De La Rue & Co.)

1913. *Inscribed* " POSTAGE " " POSTAGE ". *Wmk. Mult. Crown CA. P* 14.

No.	Type	Description	Unused	Used
18	**3**	½d. green (1 April) ..	90	1·40
19	,,	1d. red (1 April)	1·00	4·00
20	,,	3d. purple/*yell.* (27 Feb.) ..	1·40	3·50
		a. On orange-buff	1·75	7·50
21	,,	11d. dull pur. & scar. (27 Feb.)	4·50	6·00
18/21		Optd. " Specimen " *Set of* 4	20·00	

1914–23. *Inscribed* " POSTAGE " " REVENUE ". *Wmk. Mult. Crown CA. P* 14.

No.	Type	Description	Unused	Used
22	**4**	½d. green, O	50	1·40
23	,,	½d. yellow-green, O (1917)	60	1·40
24	,,	1d. carmine-red, O ..	60	90
25	,,	1d. scarlet, O (1917) ..	1·10	2·50
26	,,	2d. grey, O	1·10	3·50
27	,,	2½d. ultramarine, O ..	1·25	3·00
28	,,	3d. purple/*p. yell.*, C (1.23)	8·00	14·00
29	,,	4d. black & red/*yellow*, C	4·00	3·75
30	,,	5d. dull pur. & olive-grn., C	6·00	7·50
31	,,	5d. brn.-pur. & olive-grn., C	6·00	8·00
32	,,	6d. dull & bright purple, C	2·75	7·50
33	,,	1s. black/*green*, C.. ..	5·00	7·50
		a. On blue-green, olive back ..	5·00	7·50
34	,,	2s. purple & blue/*blue*, C	7·50	11·00
35	,,	2s. 6d. black & red/*blue*, C	9·00	11·00
36	,,	5s. green & red/*yellow*, C	18·00	22·00
		a. On orange-buff (1920) ..	18·00	26·00
37	,,	10s. green and red/*green*, C	55·00	70·00
38	,,	£1 purple and black/*red*, C	£100	£120
22/38		.. .. *Set of* 14	£200	£250
22/38		Opt. " Specimen " *Set of* 14	£140	

Variations in the coloured papers are mostly due to climate and do not indicate separate printings.

1922–31. *Wmk. Mult. Script CA. P* 14.

No.	Type	Description	Unused	Used
39	**4**	½d. green, O (10.22) ..	30	50
40	,,	1d. scarlet, O (8.23) ..	3·25	3·25
41	,,	1d. dull violet, O (1927) ..	70	1·25
42	**3**	1½d. bright scarlet, O ('24)	90	30
43	**4**	2d. slate-grey, O (4.23) ..	65	1·40
44	,,	3d. p. ultram., O (11.23) ..	60	1·60
45	,,	4d. blk. & red/*yell.*, C ('27)	1·10	2·75
45*a*	,,	4½d. red-brown, O (1931) ..	2·75	3·50
46	,,	5d. dull pur. & olive-grn., C	1·60	3·50
47	,,	6d. dull & bright purple, C	1·60	2·75
48	,,	1s. black/*emerald*, C ..	2·25	4·00
49	,,	2s. pur. & blue/*blue*, C ('27)	7·50	11·00
50	,,	2s. 6d. black & red/*blue*, C	9·00	13·00
51	,,	5s. grn. & red/*pale yell.*, C	14·00	18·00
52	,,	10s. grn. & red/*emer.*, C ('25)	75·00	85·00
39/52		.. .. *Set of* 15	£110	£140
39/52		Optd./Perf. " Specimen " *Set of* 15	80·00	

1935 (6 MAY). *Silver Jubilee. As Nos.* 91/4 *of Antigua. P* 13½×14.

No.	Description	Unused	Used
53	1½d. deep blue and carmine ..	45	55
54	3d. brown and deep blue ..	1·60	2·25
55	6d. light blue and olive green	2·00	3·50
56	1s. slate and purple	3·50	5·00
53/6	Perf. " Specimen " *Set of* 4	17·00	

1937 (13 MAY). *Coronation Issue. As Nos.* 13/15 *of Aden but ptd. by B. W. P* 11×11½.

No.	Description	Unused	Used
57	1d. violet	30	30
58	1½d. carmine	30	30
59	3d. blue	50	45
57/9	Perf. " Specimen " *Set of* 3	13·00	

MINIMUM PRICE

The minimum price quoted is 5p which represents a handling charge rather than a basis for valuing common stamps. For further notes about prices see introductory pages.

5. Spears and Shield.

6. Native Constable and Chief.

7. Artificial Island, Malaita.

8. Canoe House.

9. Roviana Canoe.

10. Roviana Canoes.

11. Native House, Reef Islands.

13. Breadfruit.

12. Coconut Plantation.

14. Tinakula Volcano.

15. Megapodes.

16. Malaita Canoe.

(Recess. D.L.R. (2d., 3d., 2s. and 2s. 6d.). Waterlow (others).)

1939 (1 FEB.)–**1951.** *Wmk. Mult. Script CA. P* 13½ *(2d., 3d., 2s. and 2s. 6d.) or* 12½ *(others).*

No.	Type	Description	Unused	Used
60	**5**	½d. blue and blue-green ..	10	25
61	**6**	1d. brown and deep violet	15	25
62	**7**	1½d. blue-green and carmine	25	25
63	**8**	2d. orange-brown and black	30	30
		a. Perf. 12 (7.11.51) ..	20	25
64	**9**	2½d. magenta & sage-green	70	60
		a. Imperf. between (vert. pair)	£2250	
65	**10**	3d. black and ultramarine	60	60
		a. Perf. 12 (29.11.51) ..	20	85
66	**11**	4½d. green and chocolate ..	3·25	4·50
67	**12**	6d. deep vio. & reddish pur.	60	65
68	**13**	1s. green and black ..	85	1·00
69	**14**	2s. black and orange ..	2·75	2·75
70	**15**	2s. 6d. black and violet ..	6·00	7·50
71	**16**	5s. emerald-green & scarlet	4·50	5·50
72	**11**	10s. sage-green & magenta (27.4.42)	6·50	8·50
60/72		.. .. *Set of* 13	23·00	30·00
60/72		Perf. " Specimen " *Set of* 13	55·00	

1946 (15 OCT.). *Victory. As Nos.* 28/9 *of Aden.*

No.	Description	Unused	Used
73	1½d. carmine	12	12
74	3d. blue	15	15
73/4	Perf. " Specimen " *Set of* 2	14·00	

1949 (14 MAR.). *Royal Silver Wedding. As Nos* 30/1 *of Aden.*

No.	Description	Unused	Used
75	2d. black	15	1
76	10s. magenta	5·00	7·0

1949 (10 OCT.). *75th Anniv. of Universal Posta Union. As Nos.* 114/17 *of Antigua.*

No.	Description	Unused	Used
77	2d. red-brown	20	3
78	3d. deep blue	25	4
79	5d. deep blue-green	45	5
80	1s. blue-black	70	8

1953 (2 JUNE). *Coronation. As No.* 47 *of Aden*

No.	Description	Unused	Used
81	2d. black and grey-black ..	35	4

17. Ysabel Canoe.

18. Roviana Canoes. (*As T* **10.**)
19. Artificial Island, Malaita. (*As T* **7.**)
20. Canoe House. (*As T* **8.**)

21. Roviana Canoe.

30. Native Constable and Chief.

22. Malaita Canoe. (*As T* **16**).

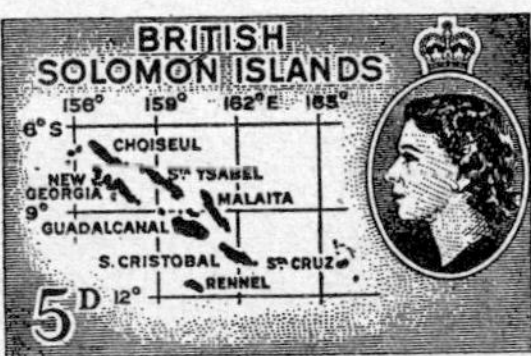

23. Map.

24. Trading Schooner.

25. Henderson Airfield, Guadalcanal.

26. Voyage of H.M.S. *Swallow*, 1767.

27. Tinakula Volcano. (*As T* **14**).

28. Native House, Reef Islands. (*As T* **11**.)

29. Mendaña and Ship.

31. Arms of the Protectorate.

(Des. Miss I. R. Stinson (½d.), R. Bailey (2½d.) R. A. Sweet (5d., 1s., 1s. 3d.), Capt. J. Brett Hilder (6d., 8d., 9d., 5s.). Recess. Bradbury, Wilkinson (½d., 2½d., 5d., 6d., 8d., 9d., 1s., 1s. 3d., 5s.), De La Rue & Co. (1d., 2d., 2s.), Waterlow & Sons (1½d., 3d., 2s. 6d., 10s., £1), until 1962, then De La Rue.)

1956 (1 Mar.)–**60.** *Wmk. Mult. Script CA.* *P* 12 (1*d.*, 2*d.*, 2*s.*), 13 (1½*d.*, 3*d.*, 2*s.* 6*d.*, 10*s.*, £1) *or* 11½ (*others*).

No.	Type	Description	Unused	Used
82	**17**	½d. orange and purple ..	5	5
83	**18**	1d. yell.-grn. & red-brown	5	5
84	**19**	1½d. slate-green and carmine-red (*shades*)	5	5
85	**20**	2d. deep brn. & dull green	8	10
86	**21**	2½d. black and blue ..	10	10
87	**22**	3d. blue-green and red ..	12	12
88	**23**	5d. black and blue ..	35	35
89	**24**	6d. black & turq.-green ..	15	20
90	**25**	8d. bright blue and black ..	35	35
90*a*	,,	9d. emerald & blk. (28.1.60)	30	30
91	**26**	1s. slate and yellow-brown (*shades*)	35	35
91*a*	**23**	1s. 3d. black and blue (*shades*) (28.1.60) ..	35	35
92	**27**	2s. black and carmine ..	70	70
93	**28**	2s. 6d. emerald and bright purple (*shades*) ..	85	1·25
94	**29**	5s. red-brown	2·50	3·50
95	**30**	10s. sepia	5·50	7·00
96	**31**	£1 black and blue (5.11.58)	9·50	11·00
82/96		.. .. *Set of* 17	19·00	23·00

II. LEGISLATIVE COUNCIL.

32. Frigate Bird.

(Litho. J. Enschedé & Sons.)

1961 (19 Jan.). *New Constitution,* 1960. *W* **w.12** (*sideways*). *P* 13 × 12½.

No.	Type	Description	Unused	Used
97	**32**	2d. black and turq.-green ..	8	10
98	,,	3d. black and rose-carmine	12	15
99	,,	9d. black and reddish purple	30	40

1963 (4 June). *Freedom from Hunger. As No.* 76 *of Aden.*

No.	Description	Unused	Used
100	1s. 3d. ultramarine	1·50	1·50

1963 (2 Sept.). *Red Cross Centenary. As Nos.* 147/8 *of Antigua.*

No.	Description	Unused	Used
101	2d. red and black	20	25
102	9d. red and blue	1·25	1·40

1963–64. *As Nos.* 83, *etc., but wmk.* **w.12.**

No.	Type	Description	Unused	Used
103	**18**	1d. yellow-green and red-brown (9.7.64) ..	10	10
104	**19**	1½d. slate-green and red (9.7.64)	10	10
105	**20**	2d. deep brown and dull green (9.7.64) ..	10	10
106	**22**	3d. light bl.-grn. & scar. (*shades*) (16.11.63) ..	20	20
107	**24**	6d. black & turq. (7.7.64)	40	50
108	**25**	9d. emer. & black (7.7.64)	50	60
109	**23**	1s. 3d. blk. & blue (7.7.64)	1·25	1·50
110	**27**	2s. blk. & carm. (9.7.64)	1·25	1·50
111	**28**	2s. 6d. emerald and reddish purple (9.7.64) ..	3·00	3·50
103/111		.. .. *Set of* 9	6·00	7·00

33. Makira Food Bowl.

34. *Dendrobium veratrifolium* (orchid).
35. Scorpion Shell.
36. Hornbill.
37. Ysabel Shield.
38. Rennellese Club.
39. Moorish Idol.
40. Frigate Bird.
41. *Dendrobium macrophyllum* (orchid).
42. *Dendrobium spectabilis* (orchid).
43. Sanford's Eagle.
44. Malaita Belt.
45. *Ornithoptera victoreae* (butterfly).
46. White Cockatoo.
47. Western Canoe Figurehead.

(Des. M. C. Farrar Bell. Litho. De La Rue.)

1965 (24 May). *W* **w.12.** *P* 13 × 12½.

No.	Type	Description	Unused	Used
112	**33**	½d. black, deep slate-blue and light blue ..	5	5
113	**34**	1d. black, orange & yellow	5	5
114	**35**	1½d. black, blue and yellow-green	5	5
115	**36**	2d. black, ultramarine and light blue ..	5	8
116	**37**	2½d. black, lt. brown and pale yellow-brown ..	8	8
117	**38**	3d. black, green and light green	10	10
118	**39**	6d. black, magenta and yellow-orange ..	12	12
119	**40**	9d. brn'sh blk., dp. bluish green and pale yellow	20	20
120	**41**	1s. black, chocolate and magenta	25	25
121	**42**	1s. 3d. black & rose-red	25	30
122	**43**	2s. black, bright purple and lilac	65	85
123	**44**	2s. 6d. black, olive-brown and light brown ..	80	1·25
124	**45**	5s. black, ultramarine and violet	1·50	2·00
125	**46**	10s. black, olive-green and yellow	2·50	3·00
126	**47**	£1 black, deep reddish violet and pink ..	5·00	6·00
112/126		.. .. *Set of* 15	10·00	13·00

1965 (28 June). *I.T.U. Centenary. As Nos.* 166/7 *of Antigua.*

No.	Description	Unused	Used
127	2d. orge.-red and turq.-blue	12	15
128	3d. turq.-blue & olive-brown	25	25

1965 (25 Oct.). *International Co-operation Year. As Nos.* 168/9 *of Antigua.*

No.	Description	Unused	Used
129	1d. reddish purple and turquoise-green	5	5
130	2s. 6d. deep bluish green and lavender	50	55

1966 (24 Jan.). *Churchill Commemoration. As Nos.* 170/3 *of Antigua.*

No.	Description	Unused	Used
131	2d. new blue	8	8
132	9d. deep green	20	25
133	1s. 3d. brown	30	35
134	2s. 6d. bluish violet	55	60

(100 cents = $1 Australian.)

2 c

(48)

1966–67. *Decimal Currency. Nos. 112 26 variously surch. as T* **48** *by De La Rue. A. Wmk. upright. B. Wmk. sideways.*

		A.		B.	
135	1 c. on ½d. ..	5	5	5	5
136	2 c. on 1d. ..	5	5	5	5
137	3 c. on 1½d. (*shades*)	5	5	5	8
138	4 c. on 2d. ..	8	10	8	8
139	5 c. on 6d. ..	10	12	8	10
140	6 c. on 2½d. ..	12	15	10	12
141	7 c. on 3d. (*shades*)	20	20	12	15
142	8 c. on 9d. ..	20	25	12	15
	a. Inverted "8"	6·00	7·00	†	
143	10 c. on 1s. (*shades*)	25	25	20	25
144	12 c. on 1s. 3d. ..	†		20	25
145	13 c. on 1s. 3d. ..	35	35	30	35
146	14 c. on 3d. ..	†		25	30
147	20 c. on 2s. ..	50	45	30	35
148	25 c. on 2s. 6d. ..	60	70	50	60
149	35 c. on 2d. ..	†		60	75
	a. Surch. omitted (horiz. pair with normal) ..	†		—	—
150	50 c. on 5s. (R.) ..	1·10	1·40	1·00	1·25
151	$1 on 10s. ..	1·75	2·00	2·00	2·25
152	$2 on £1 ..	3·25	3·50	4·00	4·50
135A/152A	*Set of* 15	8·00	9·00		
135B/152B	*Set of* 18 ..	..		9·00	11·00

Dates of issue: 1967—1 Mar., 12 c., 14 c., 35 c. 1966—14 Feb. All watermark upright. 1966—All other watermark sideways.

The positions of the bars in the surcharge vary considerably from stamp to stamp within the sheets.

The stamps with sideways watermark are all from new printings and in some instances there are marked shade variations from Nos. 112/26 which were used for making Nos. 135A/152A.

1966 (1 July). *World Cup Football Championships. As Nos. 176/7 of Antigua.*

153	8 c. violet, yellow-green, lake and yellow-brown ..	15	20
154	35 c. chocolate, blue-green, lake and yellow-brown	55	60

1966 (20 Sept.). *Inauguration of W.H.O. Headquarters, Geneva. As Nos. 178/9 of Antigua.*

155	3 c. black, yellow-green and light blue	8	8
156	50 c. black, light purple and yellow-brown	85	90

1966 (1 Dec.). *20th Anniv. of U.N.E.S.C.O. As Nos. 196/8 of Antigua.*

157	3 c. slate-violet, red, yellow and orange	8	8
158	25 c. orange-yellow, violet and deep olive	40	45
159	$1 black, bright purple and orange	1·40	1·60

49. Henderson Field.

50. Red Beach Landings.

(Des. V. Whiteley. Photo. Harrison.)

1967 (28 Aug.). *25th Anniv. of Guadalcanal Campaign (Pacific War). W* w.**12**. *P* 14×14½.

160	**49**	8 c. multicoloured ..	15	20
161	**50**	35 c. multicoloured ..	50	55

51. Mendaña off Point Cruz.

52. Arrival of Missionaries.

53. Pacific Campaign, World War II.

54. Proclamation of the Protectorate.

(Des. V. Whiteley. Photo. Harrison.)

1968 (7 Feb.). *Quater-centenary of the Discovery of the Solomon Islands. W* w.**12**. *P* 14.

162	**51**	3 c. multicoloured ..	8	8
163	**52**	8 c. multicoloured ..	10	12
164	**53**	35 c. multicoloured ..	50	55
165	**54**	$1 multicoloured ..	1·50	1·75

55. Vine Fishing.

56. Kite Fishing.

57. Platform Fishing.

58. Net Fishing.

59. Gold Lip Shell Diving.

60. Night Fishing.

61. Boat Building.

62. Cocoa.

63. Road building.

64. Geological Survey.

65. Hauling Timber.

66. Copra.

67. Harvesting Rice.

68. Honiara Port.

69. Internal Air Service.

(Des. R. Granger Barrett. Photo. Harrison.)

1968 (20 May)—**71**. *Chalk-surfaced paper. W* w.**12** (*inverted on No.* 167*a*). *P* 14½.

166	**55**	1 c. turq.-blue, blk. & brn.	5	5
		a. Glazed, ord. paper (9.8.71)	5	5
167	**56**	2 c. apple-grn., blk. & brn.	5	5
		a. Glazed, ord. paper (9.8.71)	8	8
168	**57**	3 c. green, myrtle-green and black	8	8
		a. Glazed, ord. paper (9.8.71)	8	8
169	**58**	4 c. brt. pur., blk. & brn.	8	8
		a. Glazed, ord. paper (9.8.71)	10	10
170	**59**	6 c. multicoloured ..	10	10
171	**60**	8 c. multicoloured ..	15	20
		a. Glazed, ord. paper (9.8.71)	20	20
172	**61**	12 c. yellow-ochre, brown-red and black ..	25	25
		a. Glazed, ord. paper (9.8.71)	30	30
173	**62**	14 c. orange-red, chocolate and black ..	30	30
174	**63**	15 c. multicoloured ..	30	30
		a. Glazed, ord. paper (9.8.71)	35	40
175	**64**	20 c. brt. blue, red & black	35	35
		a. Glazed, ord. paper (9.8.71)	45	55
176	**65**	24 c. rose-red, blk. & yell.	40	45
177	**66**	35 c. multicoloured ..	1·25	1·50
178	**67**	45 c. multicoloured ..	1·50	2·00
179	**68**	$1 violet-blue, light green and black	2·50	3·00
180	**69**	$2 multicoloured ..	5·00	6·00
166/80		.. .. *Set of* 15	11·00	13·00
166a/75a		.. .. *Set of* 8	1·40	1·50

The stamps on Glazed, ordinary paper exist with PVA gum only. The 1 c. to 12 c. and 20 c. on Chalk-surfaced paper exist with PVA gum as well as gum arabic, but the others exist with gum arabic only.

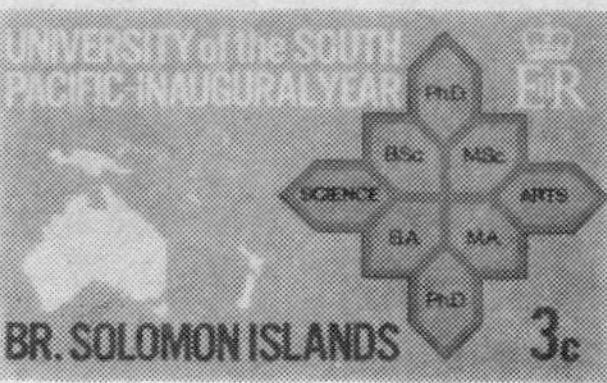

70. Map of Australasia and Diagram.

(Des. R. Gates. Litho. Enschedé.)

1969 (10 Feb.). *Inaugural Year of the South Pacific University. P* 12½×12.

181	**70**	3 c. multicoloured ..	8	8
182	,,	12 c. multicoloured ..	25	30
183	,,	35 c. multicoloured ..	55	60

71. Basketball Player.

72. Footballer.

73. Sprinter.

74. Rugby Player.

(Des. J. E. Cooter. Photo. Harrison.)

1969 (13 Aug.). *Third South Pacific Games, Port Moresby. W* w.**12** (*sideways*). *P* 14½×14.

184	**71**	3 c. multicoloured ..	8	8
185	**72**	8 c. multicoloured ..	15	20
186	**73**	14 c. multicoloured ..	25	25
187	**74**	45 c. multicoloured ..	70	75
MS188		126×120 mm. Nos. 184/7	1·25	1·40

Stamps from the miniature sheets differ slightly from those in the ordinary sheets, particularly the 14 c. value, which has a shadow below the feet on the runner. The footballer and rugby player on the 8 c. and 45 c. values also have shadows below their feet, but these are more pronounced than on the stamps from the ordinary sheets.

75. South Sea Island with Star of Bethlehem.

76. Southern Cross, "PAX" and Frigate-bird (stained glass window).

(Des. L. D. Curtis. Photo. Harrison.)

1969 (21 Nov.). *Christmas. W* w.**12** (*sideways*). *P* 14½×14.

189	**75**	8 c. blk., vio. & turq.-grn.	20	20
190	**76**	35 c. multicoloured ..	60	60

77. "Paid" Stamp and Tuiagi postmark, 1906–07 and 1896–1906 2d. Stamp of New South Wales.

78. 2d. Stamp, 1906–07 and C. M. Woodford.
79. 5s. Stamp, 1910–14 and Tulagi Postmark, 1913.
80. New G.P.O., Honiara.

(Des. G. Drummond. Litho. B.W.)

1970 (15 Apr.). *Inauguration of New G.P.O. Honiara.* *W* **w.12** *(sideways).* *P* 13.

191	**77**	7 c. light magenta, deep blue and black ..	15	15
192	**78**	14 c. sage-green, deep blue and black	25	25
193	**79**	18 c. multicoloured ..	35	35
194	**80**	23 c. multicoloured ..	40	40

81. Coat-of-Arms.

82. Map. (*Horiz.*)

(Des. V. Whiteley. Photo. Harrison.)

1970 (15 June). *New Constitution.* *W* **w.12** *(sideways on* 18 *c.).* *P* 14½×14 (18 *c.*) *or* 14×14½ (35 *c.*).

195	**81**	18 c multicoloured ..	30	35
196	**82**	35 c. pale apple-green, deep blue and ochre ..	70	70

83. British Red Cross H.Q., Honiara.

84. Wheelchair and Map. (*Vert.*).

(Des. L. D. Curtis. Litho. Questa.)

1970 (17 Aug.). *Centenary of British Red Cross.* *W* **w.12** *(sideways).* *P* 14×14½.

197	**83**	3 c. multicoloured ..	8	8
198	**84**	35 c. blue, vermilion and black	60	65

85. Carved Angel. (*Vert.*)

86. Reredos (Altar Screen).

(Des. L. D. Curtis. Litho. J.W.)

1970 (19 Oct.). *Christmas.* *W* **w.12** *(sideways on* 45 *c.).* *P* 14×13½ (8 *c.*) *or* 13½×14 (45 *c.*).

199	**85**	8 c. ochre and bluish violet	15	15
200	**86**	45 c. chestnut, yellow-orange and blackish brown ..	75	80

87. La Perouse and *La Boussole.*

(Des. J. Waddington Ltd. Litho. Questa.)

1971 (28 Jan.). *Ships and Navigators (First Series).* *T* **87** *and similar horiz. designs. Multicoloured.* *W* **w.12** *(sideways).* *P* 14.

201	3 c. Type **87**	8	8
202	4 c. Astrolabe and Polynesian Reed Map ..	10	10
203	12 c. Abel Tasman and the *Heemskerk*	30	30
204	35 c. Te puki Canoe	1·00	1·10

See also Nos. 215/18, 236/9, 254/7 and 272/5.

88. J. Atkin, Bishop Patteson and S. Taroaniara.

(Des. J. Waddington Ltd. Litho. Questa.)

1971 (5 April). *Death Centenary of Bishop Patteson.* *T* **88** *and similar multicoloured designs.* *W* **w.12** *(sideways on* 2 *c.,* 4 *c.).* *P* 14½×14 (2 *c.,* 4 *c.*) *or* 14×14½ *(others).*

205	2 c. Type **88**	5	8
206	4 c. Last Landing at Nukapu (*horiz.*)	10	10
207	14 c. Memorial Cross and Nukapu (*vert.*) ..	30	30
208	45 c. Knotted Leaf and Canoe (*vert.*)	75	80

89. Torch Emblem and Boxers.

(Des. C. Debenham. Litho. Questa.)

1971 (9 Aug.). *Fourth South Pacific Games, Tahiti.* *T* **89** *and similar horiz. designs. Multicoloured.* *W* **w.12** *(sideways).* *P* 14.

209	3 c. Type **89**	8	8
210	8 c. Emblem and footballers	15	15
211	12 c. Emblem and runner ..	30	30
212	35 c. Emblem and skin-diver	65	70

90. Melanesian Lectern.

(Des. C. Abbott. Litho. A. & M.)

1971 (15 Nov.). *Christmas.* *T* **90** *and similar vert. design. Multicoloured.* *W* **w.12.** *P* 13½.

213	9 c. Type **90**	20	20
214	45 c. "United we Stand" (Margarita Bara) ..	75	80

(Des. J.W. Ltd. Litho. Questa.)

1972 (1 Feb.). *Ships and Navigators (Second Series). Horiz. designs as* *T* **87.** *Multicoloured.* *W* **w.12** *(sideways).* *P* 14.

215	4 c. Bougainville and *La Boudeuse*	8	8
216	9 c. Horizontal planisphere and ivory backstaff ..	20	25
217	15 c. Philip Carteret and H.M.S. *Swallow* ..	35	35
218	45 c. Malaita canoe	95	1·00

91. *Cupha woodfordi.*

(Des. R. Granger Barrett. Litho. Questa.)

1972 (3 July)–**73.** *T* **91** *and similar horiz. designs. Multicoloured.* *W* **w.12** *(upright on* $5, *sideways on others).* *P* 14.

219	1 c. Type **91**	5	5
220	2 c. *Ornithoptera priamus urvillanus*	5	5
221	3 c. *Vindula sapor*	8	8
222	4 c. *Papilio ulysses orsippus*	8	8
223	5 c. Great Trevally	10	10
224	8 c. Little Bonito	12	12
225	9 c. Sapphire Demoiselle ..	15	15
226	12 c. *Costus speciosus* ..	20	20
227	15 c. Orange Anemone Fish	20	25
228	20 c. *Spathoglottis plicata* ..	30	35
229	25 c. *Ephemerantha comata*	35	40
230	35 c. *Dendrobium cuthbertsonii*	50	55
231	45 c. *Heliconia salomonica* ..	65	70
232	$1 Blue Finned Triggerfish	1·40	1·40
233	$2 *Ornithoptera allotti* ..	2·75	3·00
233*a*	$5 Great Frigate Bird (2.7.73)	6·50	7·00
219/33	*Set of* 16	12·00	13·00

The 1 to 4 c. and $2 are butterflies; the 5 to 9 c., 15 c. and $1 are fishes; and the 12 c. and 20 to 45 c. are flowers.

92. Greetings and Message Drum.

(Des. (from photograph by D. Groves) and photo. Harrison.)

1972 (20 Nov.). *Royal Silver Wedding. Multi-coloured; background colour given.* W **w.12.** *P* 14×14½.
234 **92** 8 c. rose-carmine .. 15 15
235 „ 45 c. deep yellow-olive .. 65 75

(Des. J.W. Ltd. Litho. Questa.)

1973 (9 Mar.). *Ships and Navigators (Third Series). Horiz. designs as T* **87**. *Multi-coloured.* W **w.12.** *P* 14.
236 4 c. D'Entrecasteaux and the *Recherche* 8 8
237 9 c. Ship's hour-glass and chronometer 20 20
238 15 c. Lt. Shortland and the *Alexander* 40 40
239 35 c. Tomoko (war canoe) .. 80 80

93. Pan Pipes.

(Des. and litho. J.W.)

1973 (1 Oct.). *Musical Instruments. T* **93** *and similar horiz. designs. Multicoloured.* W **w.12.** *P* 13½.
240 4 c. Type **93** 8 8
241 9 c. Castanets 20 20
242 15 c. Bamboo flute 25 30
243 35 c. Bauro gongs 55 60
244 45 c. Bamboo band 70 75
240/4 .. .. *Set of* 5 1·60 1·75

1973 (14 Nov.). *Royal Wedding. As Nos.* 165/6 *of Anguilla. Centre multicoloured.* W **w.12** *(sideways). P* 13½.
245 4 c. deep grey-blue .. 8 8
246 35 c. bright blue 45 50

94. " Adoration of the Kings " (Jan Brueghel).

(Des. PAD Studio. Litho. Questa.)

1973 (26 Nov.). *Christmas. T* **94** *and similar designs showing "Adoration of the Kings" by the artists listed. Multicoloured.* W **w.12** *(sideways on* 22 *c.). P* 13½ *(*45 *c.) or* 14 *(others).*
247 8 c. Type **94** 20 20
248 22 c. Pieter Brueghel *(vert.)* .. 40 45
249 45 c. Botticelli (48×35 *mm.)* 90 90

95. Queen Elizabeth II and Map.

(Des. G. Drummond. Litho. Questa.)

1974 (18 Feb.). *Royal Visit.* W **w.12.** *P* 13½.
250 **95** 4 c. multicoloured .. 8 8
251 „ 9 c. multicoloured .. 20 20
252 „ 15 c. multicoloured .. 30 35
253 „ 35 c. multicoloured .. 70 75

(Des. and litho. J.W.)

1974 (15 May). *Ships and Navigators (Fourth Series). Horiz. designs as T* **87**. *Multicoloured.* W **w.12** *(sideways). P* 14.
254 4 c. Commissioner landing from *S.S. Titus* .. 8 8
255 9 c. Radar scanner .. 20 20
256 15 c. Natives being transported to a "Blackbirder" 25 30
257 45 c. Lieut. John F. Kennedy's P.T. 109 .. 75 85

96. "Postman".

(Des. Jennifer Toombs. Litho. Questa.)

1974 (29 Aug.). *Centenary of Universal Postal Union. T* **96** *and similar designs showing Origami figures.* W **w.12** *(sideways on* 9 *and* 45 *c.). P* 14.
258 4 c. light yellow-green, deep green and black .. 8 8
259 9 c. light olive-bistre, lake-brown and black .. 20 20
260 15 c. mauve, purple and black 25 30
261 45 c. cobalt, dull ultramarine and black 60 65

Designs: *Horiz.*—9 c. Carrier-pigeon; 45 c. Pegasus. *Vert.*—15 c. St. Gabriel.

97. " New Constitution " Stamp of 1970.

(Des. R. Granger Barrett. Litho. Questa.)

1974 (16 Dec.). *New Constitution. T* **97** *and similar horiz. design.* W **w. 14** *(sideways). P* 14.
262 **97** 4 c. multicoloured .. 8 8
263 – 9 c. dull rose-red, black and light yellow-ochre 20 20
264 – 15 c. dull rose-red, blk. & lt. greenish yellow .. 25 30
265 **97** 35 c. multicoloured .. 55 60
MS266 134×84 mm. Nos. 262/5 1·10 1·25

Design:—9 c., 15 c. " New Constitution " stamp of 1961 (inscr. " 1960 ").

98. Golden Whistler.

(Des. G. Drummond. Litho. Questa.)

1975 (7 Apr.). *Birds. T* **98** *and similar horiz. designs. Multicoloured.* W **w. 12.** *P* 14.
267 1 c. Type **98** 5 5
268 2 c. River Kingfisher .. 5 5
269 3 c. Red-throated Fruit Dove 5 5
270 4 c. Button-quail 8 8
271 $2 Duchess Lorikeet .. 2·75 3·00
267/71 *Set of* 5 2·75 3·00

See also Nos. 305/20.

(Des. and litho. J.W.)

1975 (29 May). *Ships and Navigators (5th series). Horiz. designs as T* **87**. *Multi-coloured.* W **w.12.** *P* 13½.
272 4 c. M.V. *Walande* 8 8
273 9 c. M.V. *Melanesian* .. 15 15
274 15 c. M.V. *Marsina* 25 25
275 45 c. S.S. *Himalaya* 65 70

99. 800-Metres Race.

(Des. PAD Studio. Litho. Walsall.)

1975 (4 Aug.). *Fifth South Pacific Games, Guam. T* **99** *and similar horiz. designs. Multicoloured.* W **w.14** *(sideways). P* 13½.
276 4 c. Type **99** 8 8
277 9 c. Long-jump 15 15
278 15 c. Javelin-throwing .. 25 25
279 45 c. Football 65 70
MS280 130×95 mm. Nos. 276/9 1·00

100. Christmas Scene and Candles.

(Des. G. L. Vasarhelyi. Litho. Questa.)

1975 (13 Oct.). *Christmas. T* **100** *and similar horiz. designs. Multicoloured. W* w.**12** *(sideways). P* 14.

281 15 c. Type **100** 25 25
282 35 c. Shepherds, angels and candles 45 45
283 45 c. The Magi and candles.. 65 70
MS284 140×130 mm. Nos 281/3 1·40 1·50

(101)

1975 (12 Nov.). *Nos.* 267/70, 223/32, 271 *and* 233*a with obliterating bar as T* **101** *over* "BRITISH".

285 1 c. Type **98** 5 5
286 2 c. River Kingfisher .. 5 5
287 3 c. Red-throated Fruit Dove 5 5
288 4 c. Button-quail 8 8
289 5 c. Great Trevally 10 10
290 8 c. Little Bonito 12 12
291 9 c. Sapphire Demoiselle .. 15 15
292 12 c. *Costus speciosus* 15 20
293 15 c. Orange Anemone Fish .. 20 25
294 20 c. *Spathoglottis plicata* .. 25 30
295 25 c. *Ephemerantha comata* .. 30 35
296 35 c. *Dendrobium cuthbertsonii* 40 45
297 45 c. *Heliconia salomonica* .. 50 60
298 $1 Blue Finned Triggerfish 1·25 1·40
299 $2 Duchess Lorikeet .. 2·75 3·00
300 $5 Great Frigate Bird .. 6·50 7·00
285/300 *Set of* 16 12·00 13·00

III. SELF-GOVERNMENT.

2 January 1976

102. Ceremonial Food-bowl.

(Des. J. E. Cooter. Litho. Questa.)

1976 (12 Jan.). *Artifacts. T* **102** *and similar multicoloured designs. W* w.**12** *(upright on* 35 c.; *sideways on others. P* 14.

301 4 c. Type **102** 8 8
302 15 c. Chieftains' money .. 20 25
303 35 c. Nguzu-nguzu (canoe protector spirit) (*vert.*) 45 45
304 45 c. Nguzu-nguzu canoe prow 60 65

103. Golden Whistler.

(Des. G. Drummond. Litho. Questa.)

1976 (8 Mar.–6 Dec.). *Nos.* 267/71 *with new country inscr. (omitting* "BRITISH") *as T* **103**, *and new values. Multicoloured. W* w.**14** *(sideways). P* 14.

305 1 c. Type **103** 5 5
306 2 c. River Kingfisher 5 5
307 3 c. Red-throated Fruit Dove 5 5
308 4 c. Button Quail 5 5
309 5 c. Willie Wagtail 5 5
310 6 c. Golden Cowrie 5 8
311 10 c. Glory of the Sea Cone .. 10 12
312 12 c. Coconut Lory 12 15
313 15 c. Pearly Nautilus.. .. 15 20
314 20 c. Venus Comb Murex .. 20 25
315 25 c. Commercial Trochus .. 25 30
316 35 c. Melon or Baler Shell .. 35 40
317 45 c. Orange Spider Conch .. 45 50
318 $1 Pacific Triton .. 1·10 1·25
319 $2 Duchess Lorikeet .. 2·10 2·25
320 $5 Great Frigate Bird (6.12) 5·50 6·00
305/20 .. .. *Set of* 16 8·50 9·50

104. Coastwatchers, 1942.

(Des. J. E. Cooter. Litho. Walsall.)

1976 (24 May). *Bicentenary of American Revolution. T* **105** *and similar horiz. designs. Multicoloured. W* w.**12** *(sideways). P* 14.

321 6 c. Type **104** 10 10
322 20 c. *Amagiri* ramming PT109 and Lt. J. F. Kennedy.. 25 30
323 35 c. Henderson Airfield .. 45 50
324 45 c. Map of Guadalcanal .. 60 70
MS325 95×115 mm. Nos. 321/4 1·50

105. Alexander Graham Bell.

(Des. P. B. Powell. Litho. Harrison.)

1976 (26 July). *Telephone Centenary. T* **105** *and similar vert. designs. W* w.**14** *(sideways). P* 14½×14.

326 6 c. multicoloured 10 10
327 20 c. multicoloured 25 30
328 35 c. brown-orange, light orge. and light vermilion .. 45 50
329 45 c. multicoloured 60 70

Designs:—20 c. Radio telephone via satellite; 35 c. Ericson's magneto telephone; 45 c. Stick telephone and first telephone.

106. B.A.C. "1–11".

(Des. and litho. Walsall.)

1976 (13 Sept.). *50th Anniv. of First Flight to Solomon Is. T* **106** *and similar horiz. designs. Multicoloured. W* w.**14** *(sideways). P* 14.

330 6 c. Type **106** 8 8
331 20 c. Britten-Norman "Islander" 25 30
332 35 c. "Dakota DC3" .. 40 45
333 45 c. De Havilland "DH50A" 55 65

107. The Communion Plate.

(Des. Jennifer Toombs. Litho. Questa.)

1977 (7 Feb.). *Silver Jubilee. T* **107** *and similar vert. designs. Multicoloured. W* w.**14**. P 13½.

334 6 c. Queen's visit, 1974 .. 8 8
335 35 c. Type **107** .. 40 45
336 45 c. The Communion .. 55 65

POSTAGE DUE STAMPS.

D 1

(Typo. B.W.)

1940 (1 Sept.). *Wmk. Mult. Script CA. P* 12.

D1 D **1** 1d. emerald-green .. 30 45
D2 ,, 2d. scarlet 50 75
D3 ,, 3d. brown 75 85
D4 ,, 4d. blue .. .. .. 90 1·10
D5 ,, 5d. grey-green .. .. 1·00 1·25
D6 ,, 6d. purple .. .. .. 1·60 2·50
D7 ,, 1s. violet .. .. .. 2·50 4·00
D8 ,, 1s. 6d. turquoise-green .. 6·50 8·00
D1/8 .. .. *Set of* 8 12·00 17·00
D1/8 Perf. "Specimen" *Set of* 8 35·00

SOMALILAND PROTECTORATE.

(BRITISH SOMALILAND)

BRITISH
SOMALILAND
(1)

1903. *Stamps of India (Queen Victoria) optd. with T* **1**, *at top of stamp.*

1 **23** ½ a. yellow-green 35 75
a. "BRIT SH" .. .. 25·00
2 **25** 1 a. carmine 50 80
a. "BRIT SH" .. .. 25·00
3 **27** 2 a. pale violet 40 40
a. "BRIT SH" .. .. 45·00
b. Opt. double £130
4 **36** 2½ a. ultramarine .. .. 75 2·00
a. "BRIT SH" .. .. 85·00
5 **28** 3 a. brown-orange .. .. 80 1·50
a. "BRIT SH" .. .. 80·00
6 **29** 4 a. slate-green .. .. 1·00 2·00
7 **21** 6 a. olive-bistre .. .. 1·25 2·50
8 **31** 8 a. dull mauve .. .. 1·50 3·00
9 **32** 12 a. purple/*red* .. .. 2·25 3·50
10 **37** 1 r. green and carmine .. 3·00 5·00
11 **38** 2 r. carm. & yellow-brown 7·00 10·00
12 ,, 3 r. brown and green .. 8·00 11·00
13 ,, 5 r. ultramarine and violet 9·00 13·00
1/13 .. .. *Set of* 13 32·00 50·00

1903. *Stamps of India (Queen Victoria) optd. with T* **1**, *at bottom of stamp.*

18 **36** 2½ a. ultramarine .. .. 1·25 2·50
19 **21** 6 a. olive-bistre .. .. 75 1·50
20 **32** 12 a. purple/*red* .. .. 3·00 4·00
21 **37** 1 r. green and carmine .. 4·00 5·00
22 **38** 2 r. carm. & yellow-brown 16·00 20·00
23 ,, 3 r. brown and green .. 17·00 22·00
a. Opt. double (one albino), both inverted £140
24 ,, 5 r. ultramarine and violet 14·00 18·00
18/24 .. .. *Set of* 7 50·00 65·00

1903. *Stamps of India (King Edward VII) optd. with T* **1**.

25 **42** ½ a. green 30 50
a. "BRIT SH" .. .. 70·00
26 **43** 1 a. carmine 30 30
a. "BRITS H" .. .. 50·00
27 **44** 2 a. violet .. .. 1·00 1·50
a. "BRIT SH" £200
28 **46** 3 a. orange-brown .. 1·25 2·00
29 **47** 4 a. olive .. .. 1·25 2·00
30 **49** 8 a. mauve .. .. 1·50 2·50
25/30 .. .. *Set of* 6 5·00 8·00

2

3

(Typo. D.L.R.)

1904. *Wmk. Crown CA. P* 14.

32 **2** ½ a. dull green and green .. 30 1·25
33 ,, 1 a. grey-black and red .. 30 1·50
34 ,, 2 a. dull and bright purple 1·00 1·25
35 ,, 2½ a. bright blue .. .. 1·25 2·50
36 ,, 3 a. chocolate & grey-green 1·25 2·50
37 ,, 4 a. green and black .. 1·75 2·50
38 ,, 6 a. green and violet .. 3·00 3·50
39 ,, 8 a. grey-black & pale blue 3·00 4·00
40 ,, 12 a. grey-blk. & orange-buff 5·00 6·00

Wmk. Crown CC. P 14.

41 **3** 1 r. green .. .. 6·00 8·00
42 ,, 2 r. dull and bright purple .. 12·00 14·00
43 ,, 3 r. green and black .. .. 15·00 20·00
44 ,, 5 r. grey-black and red .. 15·00 20·00
32/44 .. .. *Set of* 13 55·00 80·00
32/44 Optd. "Specimen" *Set of* 13 60·00

1905–6. *Wmk. Mult. Crown CA. P* 14.

45 **2** ½ a. dull green and green, O 30 1·00
46 ,, 1 a. grey-black & red, OC 30 75
47 ,, 2 a. dull & brt. purple, OC 1·50 2·00
48 ,, 2½ a. bright blue, O .. 2·50 3·00
49 ,, 3 a. choc. & grey-green, OC 1·50 3·00
50 ,, 4 a. green and black, OC 1·50 3·00
51 ,, 6 a. green and violet, OC 1·50 3·00
52 ,, 8 a. grey-blk. & p. blue, O 2·50 3·50
a. Black and blue, C .. 6·00 8·00
53 ,, 12 a. grey-black and orange-buff, O.. .. 2·50 3·50
a. Black and orange-brown, C 6·00 8·00

1909. *Wmk. Mult. Crown CA. P* 14.

58 **2** ½ a. bluish green, O.. .. 1·50 2·00
59 ,, 1 a. red, O (Optd. S. £5) .. 1·50 1·50
45/59 .. .. *Set of* 11 15·00 24·00

4

5

(Typo. D.L.R.)

1912 (DEC.)–**19.** *Wmk. Mult. Crown CA. P* 14.

60 **4** ½ a. green, O 15 40
61 ,, 1 a. red, O 50 75
a. Scarlet, O (1917).. .. 1·00 1·25
62 ,, 2 a. dull & brt. purple, C 2·50 3·00
a. Dull purple and violet-purple, C (1919) .. .. 2·50 3·00
63 ,, 2½ a. bright blue, O .. 65 1·50
64 ,, 3 a. choc. & grey-green, C 65 1·50
65 ,, 4 a. green & black, C ('13) 75 1·50
66 ,, 6 a. green and violet, C .. 75 2·50
67 ,, 8 a. grey-blk. & pale blue, C 1·25 3·00
68 ,, 12 a. grey-black and orange-buff, C .. .. 1·25 3·00
69 **5** 1 r. green, C .. .. 1·75 3·00
70 ,, 2 r. dull pur. & pur., C ('19) 5·00 8·00
71 ,, 3 r. green & black, C ('19) 8·00 12·00
72 ,, 5 r. black & scar., C ('19) 13·00 20·00
60/72 .. .. *Set of* 13 32·00 55·00
60/72 Optd. "Specimen" *Set of* 13 70·00

1921. *Wmk. Mult. Script CA. P* 14.

73 **4** ½ a. blue-green, O .. 5 30
74 ,, 1 a. carmine-red, O .. 5 30
75 ,, 2 a. dull & bright purple, C 40 75
76 ,, 2½ a. bright blue, O .. 50 1·00
77 ,, 3 a. chocolate and green, C 90 1·50
78 ,, 4 a. green and black, C .. 90 1·50
79 ,, 6 a. green and violet, C .. 75 2·00
80 ,, 8 a. grey-blk. & pale blue, C 1·25 2·00
81 ,, 12 a. grey-blk. & orge.-buff, C 2·50 4·00
82 **5** 1 r. dull green, C .. 3·00 4·00
83 ,, 2 r. dull purple & purple, C 6·00 8·00
84 ,, 3 r. dull green and black, C 8·00 12·00
85 ,, 5 r. black and scarlet, C .. 16·00 24·00
73/85 .. .. *Set of* 13 35·00 55·00
73/85 Optd. "Specimen" *Set of* 13 70·00

1935 (6 MAY). *Silver Jubilee. As Nos.* 91/4 *of Antigua but ptd. by Waterlow. P* 11×12.

86 1 a. deep blue and scarlet .. 50 60
87 2 a. ultramarine and grey .. 75 1·25
88 3 a. brown and deep blue .. 1·00 2·00
89 1 r. slate and purple .. .. 2·50 4·00
86/9 Perf. "Specimen" *Set of* 4 15·00

1937 (13 MAY). *Coronation. As Nos.* 13/15 *of Aden. P* 14.

90 1 a. scarlet 5 10
91 2 a. grey-black 5 12
92 3 a. bright blue 20 50
90/2 Perf. "Specimen" *Set of* 3 10·00

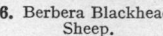

6. Berbera Blackhead Sheep.

7. Greater Kudu Antelope.

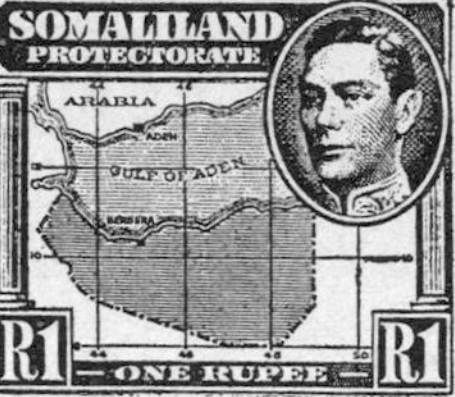

8. Somaliland Protectorate.

(Des. H. W. Claxton. Recess. Waterlow.)

1938 (10 MAY). *Portrait to left. Wmk. Mult. Script CA. P* 12½.

93 **6** ½ a. green 20 45
94 ,, 1 a. scarlet 20 45
95 ,, 2 a. maroon 15 50
96 ,, 3 a. bright blue .. .. 1·00 1·50
97 **7** 4 a. sepia .. .. 1·00 1·50
98 ,, 6 a. violet .. .. 60 1·00
99 ,, 8 a. grey .. .. .. 1·00 2·00
100 ,, 12 a. red-orange .. .. 1·10 2·25
101 **8** 1 r. green .. .. .. 3·00 6·00
102 ,, 2 r. purple .. .. 3·00 6·00
103 ,, 3 r. bright blue .. .. 2·50 5·50
104 ,, 5 r. black .. .. .. 3·50 5·50
a. Imperf. btwn. (horiz. pr.) £1100
93/104 .. .. *Set of* 12 15·00 30·00
93/104 Perf. "Specimen" *Set of* 12 35·00

9. Berbera Blackhead Sheep.

(Recess. Waterlow.)

1942 (27 APR.). *As T* **6/8** *but with full-face portrai of King George VI, as in T* **9**. *Wmk. Mult Script CA. P* 12½.

105 **9** ½ a. green 5 8
106 ,, 1 a. scarlet 5 8
107 ,, 2 a. maroon 30 25
108 ,, 3 a. bright blue 5 20
109 **7** 4 a. sepia 5 20
110 ,, 6 a. violet 10 20
111 ,, 8 a. grey 12 20
112 ,, 12 a. red-orange 20 30
113 **8** 1 r. green 50 60
114 ,, 2 r. purple .. .. 1·00 1·50
115 ,, 3 r. bright blue .. .. 1·00 1·75
116 ,, 5 r. black .. .. .. 1·75 2·00
105/116 .. .. *Set of* 12 5·00 6·00
105/16 Perf. "Specimen" *Set of* 12 45·00

1946 (15 OCT.). *Victory. As Nos.* 28/9 *of Aden P* 13½×14.

117 1 a. carmine 5 5
a. Perf. 13½ .. .. .. 30 2·25
118 3 a. blue 5 5
117/18 Perf. "Specimen" *Set of* 2 10·00

1949 (28 JAN.). *Royal Silver Wedding. As Nos* 30/1 *of Aden.*

119 1 a. scarlet 5 5
120 5 r. black .. .. .. 2·00 2·50

1949 (10 Oct.). *75th Anniv. of U.P.U. As Nos. 114/17 of Antigua surch. with new values.*

121	1 a. on 10 c. carmine ..	8	10
122	3 a. on 30 c. deep blue (R.)	15	20
123	6 a. on 50 c. purple	25	35
124	12 a. on 1s. red-orange ..	45	50

5 Cents (10) 1 Shilling (11)

1951 (2 Apr.). *1942 issue surch. as T* **10/11.**

125	5 c. on ½ a. green	5	5
126	10 c. on 2 a. maroon ..	5	5
127	15 c. on 3 a. bright blue ..	5	8
128	20 c. on 4 a. sepia	5	8
129	30 c. on 6 a. violet	10	15
130	50 c. on 8 a. grey	12	12
131	70 c. on 12 a. red-orange ..	15	20
132	1s. on 1 r. green ..	20	25
133	2s. on 2 r. purple	45	70
134	2s. on 3 r. bright blue ..	60	70
135	5s. on 5 r. black (R.) ..	1·25	1·60
125/35	.. .. *Set of* 11	2·75	3·50

1953 (2 June). *Coronation. As No.* 47 *of Aden.*

136	15 c. black and green ..	20	25

12. Camel and Gurgi.

13. Askari.

14. Somali Rock Pigeon.

15. Martial Eagle.

16. Berbera Blackhead Sheep.

17. Sheikh Isaaq's Tomb, Mait.

18. Taleh Fort.

(Recess. B.W.)

1953 (15 Sept.)–**58.** *Wmk. Mult. Script CA. P* 12½.

137	**12**	5 c. slate-black	5	5
138	**13**	10 c. red-orange (*shades*) ..	8	8
139	**12**	15 c. blue-green	12	15
140	,,	20 c. scarlet	15	15
141	**13**	30 c. reddish brown ..	25	25
142	**14**	35 c. blue	25	30
143	**15**	50 c. brown & rose-carmine	30	30
144	**16**	1s. light blue	35	35
145	**17**	1s. 30 c. ultramarine and black (1.9.58) ..	55	65
146	**14**	2s. brown & bluish violet	95	95
147	**15**	5s. red-brown & emerald	3·00	3·00
148	**18**	10s. brn. & reddish violet	4·00	6·50
137/148		.. .. *Set of* 12	9·00	11·00

OPENING OF THE LEGISLATIVE COUNCIL 1957 (19)

LEGISLATIVE COUNCIL UNOFFICIAL MAJORITY, 1960 (20)

1957 (21 May). *Opening of Legislative Council. Nos.* 140 *and* 144 *optd. with T* **19.**

149	**12**	20 c. scarlet	15	20
150	**16**	1s. light blue	35	40

1960 (5 Apr.). *Legislative Council's Unofficial Majority. Nos.* 140 *and* 145 *optd. as T* **20.**

151	**12**	20 c. scarlet	25	35
152	**17**	1s. 30, ultram. & black	35	40

OFFICIAL STAMPS.

BRITISH SOMALILAND (O 1)

SERVICE BRITISH SOMALILAND (O 2)

1903. *Stamps of India overprinted.*

(i) *Official stamps of* 1883–1900, *Queen Victoria, with Type* O **1** (*wider spaced on* 1 *r.*) (1 June).

O 1	**23**	½ a. yellow-green	3·00	10·00
O 2	**25**	1 a. carmine	3·50	4·00
O 3	**26**	2 a. pale violet	4·00	13·00
O 4	**31**	8 a. dull mauve ..	9·00	£120
O 5	**37**	1 r. green and carmine ..	9·00	90·00

Varieties exist on all values in which "BRITISH" measures 11 mm., and the 8 a. is known without stop after "M" in "H.M.S."

(ii) *Postage stamps of* 1902, *King Edward VII, with Type* O **2.**

O 6	**42**	½ a. green	60	
		a. "BRIT SH"	25·00	
O 7	**43**	1 a. carmine	60	
		a. "BRIT SH"	25·00	
O 8	**44**	2 a. violet	90	
		a. "BRIT SH"	40·00	
O 9	**49**	8 a. mauve	9·00	
		a. "BRIT SH"	£400	

Other varieties exist in which the second "E" of "SERVICE" is out of alignment, and also in which the word is in a different fount, measuring 11½ mm.

Prices for "BRIT SH" varieties are for examples showing the "I" completely omitted. Examples showing traces of it are worth less.

It is doubtful if Nos. O6/9 were issued. The 1 r. Queen's head in green and carmine also exists overprinted with Type O **2** but this was definitely not issued. (*Price* £9 *un., with* "BRIT SH" *variety,* £400 *un.*).

O.H.M.S.
(O 3)

1904. *Optd. with Type* O **3.** *P* 14.

(*a*) *Wmk. Crown CA.*

O10	**2**	½ a. dull green and green ..	2·50	15·00
		a. No stop after "M" ..	£120	
O11	,,	1 a. grey-black and carmine	4·00	5·00
		a. No stop after "M" ..	£120	£120
O12	,,	2 a. dull and bright purple	40·00	20·00
		a. No stop after "M" ..	£400	£200
O13	,,	8 a. grey-black & pale blue	25·00	45·00
		a. No stop after "M" ..	£120	

(*b*) *Wmk. Mult. Crown CA.*

O14	,,	2 a. dull & bright purple, O	25·00	£140
		a. No stop after "M" ..	£200	

Wmk. Crown CC.

O15	**3**	1 r. green	60·00	£150
O10/13, O15		Optd. "Specimen" *Set of* 5	80·00	

Prices quoted for no stop varieties are for examples with no trace of the stop. Stamps showing a slight impression of the stop are worth very much less.

The no stop varieties also exist with "Specimen" overprint.

All Somaliland Protectorate stamps were withdrawn from sale on 25 June, 1960 and until the unification on 1 July, issues of Italian Somalia together with Nos. 353/5 of Somalia Republic were used. Later issues will be found listed in Vol. 4 of the Stanley Gibbons Foreign Overseas Catalogue.

SOUTH AFRICA.

The following territories combined to form the Union of South Africa in 1910 (of which they became provinces) and their issues are listed in alphabetical order in this Catalogue:—

CAPE OF GOOD HOPE (incl. Griqualand West)

NATAL (incl. New Republic and Zululand)

ORANGE FREE STATE

TRANSVAAL

I. UNION OF SOUTH AFRICA.

Although South Africa is now a republic, outside the British Commonwealth, all its stamp issues are listed together here, purely as a matter of convenience to collectors.

1

(Des. H. S. Wilkinson. Recess. De La Rue & Co.)

1910 (4 Nov.). *Inscribed bilingually. Wmk. Multiple Rosettes. P 14.*

1	**1**	2½d. deep blue (H/S. S £175)	6·00	4·50
2	,,	2½d. blue	4·00	2·00

The deep blue shade is generally accompanied by a blueing of the paper.

The price quoted for the "Specimen" handstamp is for the small italic type with capital and lower case letters.

2 3

4. Springbok's Head.

(Typo. D.L.R.)

1913 (1 Sept.)–22. *Inscribed bilingually. W* **4**.

(a) P 14.

3	**2**	½d. green	12	8
		a. Stamp doubly printed ..	£5000	
		b. Blue-green	60	10
		c. Yellow-green	75	10
4	,,	1d. rose-red (*shades*) ..	25	8
		a. Carmine-red	50	8
		b. Scarlet (shades)	25	10
5	,,	1½d. chest. (*shades*) (23.8.20)	35	8
		a. Tête-bêche (pair)	1·25	1·00
6	**3**	2d. dull purple	75	8
		a. Deep purple	1·25	8
7	,,	2½d. bright blue	1·25	75
		a. Deep blue	2·50	1·50
8	,,	3d. black and orange-red ..	1·00	15
		a. Black and dull orange-red ..	2·50	50
9	,,	3d. ultram. (*shades*) (10.22)	1·00	1·00
10	,,	4d. orange-yell. & olive-grn.	3·50	30
		a. Orange-yellow & sage-green	2·50	20
11	,,	6d. black and violet ..	2·50	10
		a. Black and bright violet ..	3·00	10
12	**3**	1s. orange	8·00	25
		a. Orange-yellow	10·00	25
13	,,	1s. 3d. vio. (*shades*) (1.10.20)	12·00	7·00
14	,,	2s. 6d. purple and green ..	35·00	2·50
15	,,	5s. purple and blue ..	90·00	15·00
		a. Reddish purple & light blue ..	90·00	18·00
16	,,	10s. deep blue & olive-green	£200	20·00
17	,,	£1 green and red (7.16) ..	£500	£200
		a. Pale olive-green and red ..	£550	£600
3/17		.. .. *Set of* 15	£800	£250
3/17		(*excl.* 9) Optd./Perf. "Specimen" *Set of* 14	£750	

(b) Coil Stamps. P 14 × imperf.

18	**2**	½d. green	1·75	35
19	,,	1d. rose-red (13.2.14) ..	2·50	1·00
		a. Scarlet	3·00	1·50
20	,,	1½d. chestnut (15.11.20) ..	3·00	1·50
21	**3**	2d. dull purple (7.10.21) ..	2·00	75

The 6d. exists with "z" of "ZUID" wholly or partly missing due to wear of plate. (*Price wholly missing, £30 un., £15, us.*)

5

(Eng. A. J. Cooper. Offset-litho. *Cape Times Ltd.*)

1925 (25 Feb.). *Air. Inscr. bilingually. P 12.*

26	**5**	1d. carmine	4·00	6·00
27	,,	3d. ultramarine	6·00	7·00
28	,,	6d. magenta	12·00	15·00
29	,,	9d. green	25·00	30·00

Beware of forgeries of all values.

INSCRIPTIONS. From 1926 until 1951 (also Nos. 167 and 262/5), most issues were inscribed in English and Afrikaans alternately throughout the sheets.

As we only stock these in *se-tenant* pairs, unused and used, we no longer quote for single used copies and they must be considered to be worth very much less than half the prices quoted for pairs. Prices are for horizontal pairs, vertical pairs being worth about 50% less.

Similarly, the War Effort bantam stamps, Nos. (96/103), and Nos. 124 and D30/3 are priced for units of two or three as the case may be.

It is, therefore, necessary to watch the headings given at the top of the price columns or for individual issues to check whether prices are for pairs or singles.

6. Springbok.

7. Van Riebeeck's Ship.

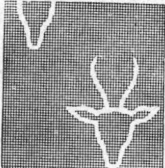

8. Orange Tree.

9

(Typo. first by Waterlow, later by Govt. Printer, Pretoria.)

1926. *W* **9**. *P* 14½ × 14.

			Un. pair	*Us. pair*
30	**6**	½d. black and green ..	80	80
		a. Missing "1" in "½" ..	£400	
		b. Perf. 13½ × 14	35·00	13·00
		ba. Tête-bêche (pair)	£400	
31	**7**	1d. black and carmine ..	1·25	75
		a. Perf. 13½ × 14	30·00	15·00
		aa. Tête-bêche (pair)	£400	
32	**8**	6d. green and orange ..	8·00	5·00

No. 30a exists in Afrikaans only. Nos. 30b and 31a are from booklets of Pretoria-printed stamps.

For ½d. with pale grey centre, see No. 126.

For rotogravure printing see Nos. 42, etc.

10. "Hope".

(Recess. B.W.)

1926. *T* **10**. *Inscribed in English* (E.) *or Afrikaans* (A.). *W* **9**. *Imperf.*

		Single stamps E.		A.	
33	4d. grey-bl. (*shades*)	75	75	75	75

In this value the English and Afrikaans inscriptions are on separate sheets.

This stamp is known with private perforations or roulettes.

11. Union Buildings, Pretoria.

12. Groot Schuur.

12a. A Native Kraal.

13. Gnus.

14. Ox-wagon inspanned.

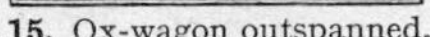

15. Ox-wagon outspanned.

16. Cape Town and Table Bay.

17. D.H. " Moth ".

(Recess. B.W.)

1927–28. *W* **9.** *P* 14 (*early ptgs.*) *or* 14×13½ (*from* 1930 *onwards*).

			Un. pair	Us. pair
34	**11**	2d. grey and maroon ..	15·00	15·00
35	**12**	3d. black and red ..	18·00	18·00
35*a*	**12*a***	4d. brown	25·00	25·00
36	**13**	1s. brown and deep blue	30·00	30·00
37	**14**	2s. 6d. green and brown	75·00	75·00
38	**15**	5s. black and green ..	£120	£120
39	**16**	10s. bright blue & brown	£120	£120
34/39		.. .. *Set of* 7	£350	£350
34/39	H/S	" Specimen " *Set of* 7	£600	

Typo. Govt. Ptg. Wks., Pretoria.)

1929 (16 AUG.). *Air. Inscribed bilingually. No wmk. P* 14×13½.

			Un. single	Us. single
40	**17**	4d. green	2·00	2·00
41	,,	1s. orange	15·00	12·00

PRINTER. All the following issues, except No. 126, are printed by rotogravure (the design having either plain lines or a dotted screen) by the Government Printer, Pretoria.

I II

The two types of the 1d. differ in the spacing of the horizontal lines in the side panels:—Type I close; Type II wide. The Afrikaans had the spacing of the words POSSEEL-INKOMSTE close in Type I and more widely spaced in Type II.

1930–45. *Types* **6** *to* **8** *and* **11** *to* **14** *redrawn,* " SUIDAFRIKA " (*in one word*) *on Afrikaans stamps. W* **9.** *P* 15×14 (½*d.*, 1*d.*, *and* 6*d.*) *or* 14.

			Un. pair	Us. pair
42		½d. black and green	50	75
		a. Two English or two Afrikaans stamps *se tenant* (vert. pair)..	15·00	
		b. Tête bêche	£400	
43		1d. black and carmine (I) ..	1·25	40
		a. Tête bêche	£400	
43*c*		1d. black and carmine (II)..	5·00	1·00
44		2d. slate-grey and lilac (Apr. '31)	4·00	1·00
		aa. Tête-bêche	£450	
44*b*		2d. blue and violet ('38) ..	60·00	20·00
45		3d. black and red	15·00	12·00
45*a*		3d. blue (Oct. '33)	4·00	1·75
46		4d. brown	10·00	7·00
46*a*		4d. brown (*shades*) ('36) (*again redrawn*)	3·00	2·00
47		6d. green and orange ..	10·00	1·50
48		1s. brn. & deep bl. (14.9.32)	25·00	12·00
49		2s. 6d. green & brn. (24.12.32)	60·00	40·00
49*a*		2s. 6d. blue and brown ('45)	12·00	8·00
42/49*a*		.. .. *Set of* 13	£175	£100

Variety: Frame omitted.

		Un. single
43*b*	1d. black (and carmine) ..	£150
44*a*	2d. slate-grey (and lilac) ..	£150

For similar designs with " SUID-AFRIKA " hyphenated, see Nos. 54 etc. and Nos. 114 etc.

The 1d. (Type I) exists without watermark from a trial printing (*Price* £40 *un.*).

The Rotogravure printings may be distinguished from the preceding Typographed and Recess printed issues by the following tests:—

TYPO. ROTO.

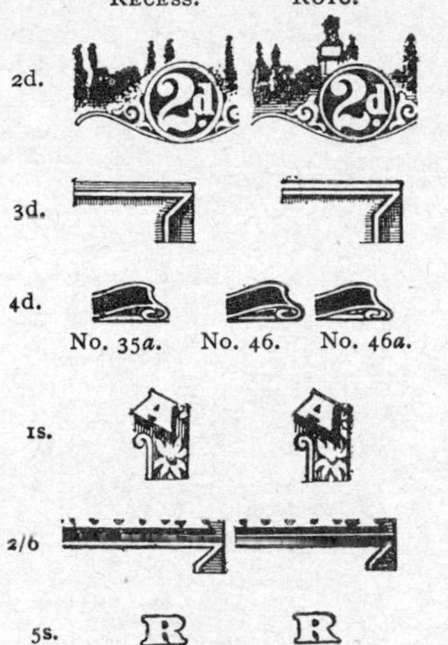

ROTOGRAVURE:

½d., 1d. & 6d. Leg of " R " in " AFR " ends squarely on the bottom line.

2d. The newly built War Memorial appears to the left of the value.

3d. Two fine lines have been removed from the top part of the frame.

4d. No. 46. The scroll is in solid colour. No. 46*a*. The scroll is white with a crooked line running through it. (No. 35*a*. The scroll is shaded by diagonal lines.)

1s. The shading of the last " A " partly covers the flower beneath.

2s. 6d. The top line of the centre frame is thick and leaves only one white line through it and the name.

5s. (Nos. 64/*a*). The leg of the " R " is straight.

Rotogravure impressions are generally coarser.

18. Church of the Vow.

19. "The Great Trek".

20. A Voortrekker.

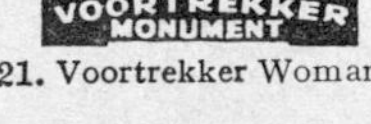

21. Voortrekker Woman.

1933–36. *Voortrekker Memorial Fund. W* **9.** P14.

			Un. pair	Us. pair
50	**18**	½d.+½d. black and green (15.1.36)	1·00	1·25
51	**19**	1d.+½d. grey-black & pink	1·50	1·50
52	**20**	2d.+1d. grey-green & pur.	3·00	3·00
53	**21**	3d.+1½d. grey-grn. & blue	6·00	6·00

22. Gold Mine.

22*a*. Groot Schuur.

I II II

6d.

23. Groot Constantia.

1933–48. " SUID-AFRIKA " (*hyphenated*) *on Afrikaans stamps. W* **9.** *P* 15×14 (½*d.*, 1*d.* *and* 6*d.*) *or* 14.

54	**6**	½d. grey and green ..	1·50	70
		a. Coil stamp. Perf. 13½×14	8·00	8·00
56	**7**	1d. grey and carmine (*shades*)	40	15
		a. Grey and brt. rose-carmine	20	30
		b. Coil stamp. Perf. 13½×14	8·00	8·00
57	**22**	1½d. green & bright gold	2·00	75
		a. Blue-green and dull gold ..	3·00	1·00
58	**11**	2d. blue and violet ..	20·00	12·00
58*a*	,,	2d. grey and dull purple	2·00	2·00
59	**22*a***	3d. ultramarine	1·50	40
61	**8**	6d. green & vermilion (I)	20·00	5·00
61*a*	,,	6d. green & vermilion (II)	3·00	2·50
61*b*	,,	6d. grn. & red-orange (III)	3·00	2·50
62	**13**	1s. brown & chalky blue	4·00	1·50
64	**15**	5s. black and green ..	25·00	12·00
		a. Black and blue-green ..	12·00	6·00
64*b*	**23**	10s. blue and sepia ..	25·00	12·00
		ba. Blue and blackish brown..	18·00	4·00
54/64*ba*		(*only* 1 6*d.*) *Set of* 10	40·00	30·00

The ½d. and 1d. coil stamps may be found in blocks emanating from the residue of the large rolls which were cut into sheets and distributed to Post Offices.

Varieties: (*a*) *Shading completely missing from mine dump* (*in pair with normal*).

57*aa* **22** 1½d. green & bright gold 35·00

(*b*) *Frame omitted.*

			Un. Single
56*c*	**7**	1d. grey (and carmine) ..	35·00
62*a*	**13**	1s. brown (& chalky blue)	

Dates of issue:—3.7.33, No. 64.19.4.34, No. 56. 25.9.35 No. 54. 12.11.36, No. 57. 1937, No. 61. 1938, Nos. 58, 61*a*. 1939, Nos. 62 and 64*b*. 1.3.40, No. 59. –1940, No. 57*a*. 1941, No. 58*a*. 1945, No. 64*ba*. 1946, No. 61*b*. 1948, No. 56*a*.

1d. Is printed from Type II. Frames of different sizes exist due to reductions made from time to time for the purpose of providing more space for the perforations.

3d. In No. 59 the frame is unscreened and composed of solid lines. Centre is diagonally screened. Scrolls above " 3d. " are clear lined, light in the middle and dark at sides.

6d. Die I. Green background lines faint. " SUID-AFRIKA " 16½ mm. long.
Die II. Green background lines heavy. " SUID-AFRIKA " 17 mm. long, " S " near end of tablet. Scroll open.
Die III. Scroll closed up and design smaller (18 × 22 mm.).

Single specimens of the 1930 issue inscribed in English may be distinguished from those listed above as follows:—

½d. and 1d. Centres in varying intensities of black instead of grey.

2d. The letters of " SOUTH AFRICA " are wider and thicker.
3d. The trees are shorter and the sky is lined.
6d. The frame is pale orange.
1s. The frame is greenish blue.

For similar designs, but printed in screened rotogravure, see Nos. 114 to 122*a*.

24

1937–40. *W* **9.** *P* 15 × 14.

			Un. pair	Us. pair
64*c*	**24**	½d. grey and green ..	1·50	75
		d. Grey and blue-green ('40) ..	25	15

The lines in shading in T **24** are all horizontal and thicker than in T **6.** In Nos. 64*c* and 64*d* the design is composed of solid lines. For stamps with designs composed of dotted lines, see No. 114. Later printings of No. 64*d* have a smaller design.

24*a*

1935 (1 MAY). *Silver Jubilee. Inscr. bilingually. W* **9.** *P* 15 × 14.

65	**24*a***	½d. black and blue-green ..	75	75
66	,,	1d. black and carmine ..	75	75
67	,,	3d. blue	12·00	12·00
68	,,	6d. green and orange ..	18·00	18·00

In stamps with English at top the ½d., 3d. and 6d. have " SILWER JUBILEUM " to left of portrait, and " POSTAGE REVENUE " or " POSTAGE " (3d. and 6d.) in left value tablet. In the 1d., " SILVER JUBILEE " is to the left of portrait. In alternate stamps the positions of English and Afrikaans inscriptions are reversed.

25

JIPEX

1936
(24*b*)

1936 (2 NOV.). *Johannesburg International Philatelic Exhibition. Optd. with T* **24*b*.**

			Un. sheet	Us. sheet
MS 69	**6**	½d. grey & green (No. 54)	2·00	5·00
MS 70	**7**	1d. grey & carm. (No. 56)	1·50	4·00

Issued each in miniature sheet of six stamps with marginal advertisements.

1937 (12 MAY). *Coronation. W* **9** *sideways. P* 14.

			Un. pair	Us. pair
71	**25**	½d. grey-black & blue-grn.	10	10
72	,,	1d. grey-black and carmine	12	10
73	,,	1½d. orange & greenish blue	12	15
74	,,	3d. ultramarine	15	20
75	,,	1s. red-brown & turq.-blue	75	75
71/75		.. .. *Set of* 5	1·10	1·10

26. Voortrekker Ploughing.

27. Wagon crossing Drakensberg.

28. Signing of Dingaan-Retief Treaty.

29. Voortrekker Monument.

1938 (14 DEC.). *Voortrekker Centenary Memorial Fund. W* **9.** *P* 14 (*Nos.* 76/7) *or* 15 × 14.

76	**26**	½d. + ½d. blue and green ..	1·00	1·00
77	**27**	1d. + 1d. blue and carmine	1·50	1·50
78	**28**	1½d. + 1½d. choc. & blue-grn.	4·00	4·00
79	**29**	3d. + 3d. bright blue ..	5·00	5·00

30. Wagon Wheel.

31. Voortrekker Family.

(Des. W. H. Coetzer.)

1938 (14 DEC.). *Voortrekker Commemoration. W* **9.** *P* 15 × 14.

			Un. pair	Us. pair
80	**30**	1d. blue and carmine ..	1·00	1·00
81	**31**	1½d. greenish blue & brown	1·00	1·00

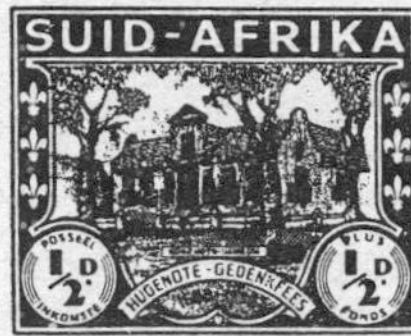

32. Old Vicarage, Paarl, now a museum.

33. Symbol of the Reformation.

34. Huguenot Dwelling, Drakenstein Mountain Valley.

1939 (17 JULY). *250th Anniv. of Huguenot Landing in S. Africa and Huguenot Commemoration Fund. W* **9.** *P* 14 (*Nos.* 82/3) *or* 15 × 14.

82	**32**	½d. + ½d. brown and green	1·25	1·25
83	**33**	1d. + 1d. green & carmine	1·50	1·50
84	**34**	1½d. + 1½d. blue-green and purple	3·00	4·00

34*a*. Gold Mine.

1941 (AUG.). *W* **9** *sideways. P* 14 × 15.

87	**34*a***	1½d. blue-green and yellow-buff (*shades*)	10	10
		a. Yellow-buff centre omitted	£300	

35. Infantry.

36. Nurse and Ambulance.

37. Airman.

38. Sailor, Destroyer and Lifebelts.

39. Women's Auxiliary Services.

40. Artillery.

41. Electric Welding.

42. Tank Corps.

1941–42. *War Effort. W* **9** *sideways, perf.* 14 (2*d.*, 4*d.*, 6*d.*) *or upright, perf.* 15×14 (*others*).

(*a*) *Inscr. alternately.*

			Un. pair	*Us. pair*
8	**35**	½d. green (19.11.41) ..	20	15
		a. Blue-green	50	50
9	**36**	1d. carmine (3.10.41) ..	10	12
0	**37**	1½d. myrtle-green (12.1.42)	10	10
1	**39**	3d. blue (1.8.41)	50	75
2	**40**	4d. orange-brown (20.8.41)	1·25	1·00
		a. Red-brown	6·00	5·00
3	**41**	6d. red-orange (3.9.41) ..	1·00	1·50

(*b*) *Inscr. bilingually.*

			Un. single	*Us. single*
4	**38**	2d. violet (15.9.41) ..	20	5
5	**42**	1s. brown (27.10.41) ..	1·50	70
8/95		.. .. *Set of 8 pairs and singles*	10·00	9·00

43. Infantry.

44. Nurse.

45. Airman.

46. Sailor.

47. Women's Auxiliary Services.

48. Electric Welding.

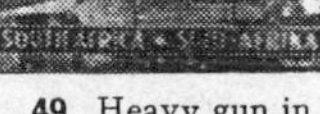
49. Heavy gun in concrete turret.

50. Tank Corps.

Unit (*pair*)

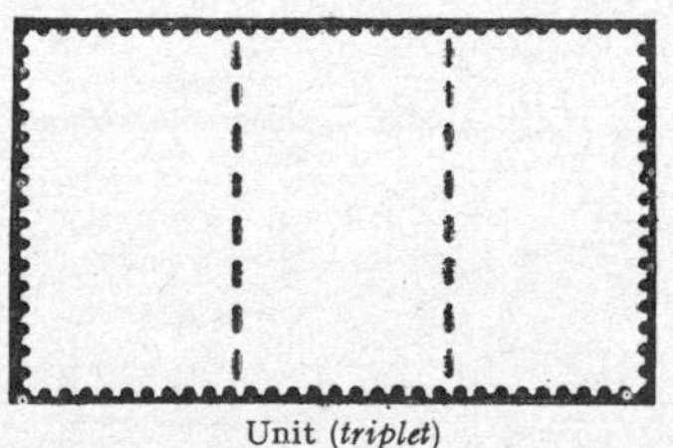
Unit (*triplet*)

1942–44. *War Effort. Reduced sizes. In pairs perf.* 14 (P) *or strips of three, perf.* 15×14 (T), *subdivided by roulette* 6½. *W* **9** (*sideways on* 3*d.*, 4*d. and* 1*s.*). (*a*) *Inscr. alternately.*

			Un. unit	*Us. unit*
96	**43**	½d. blue-green (T) (10.42)	20	10
		a. Green ('43)	80	45
		b. Greenish blue ('44) ..	50	45
		c. Roulette omitted ..	75·00	
97	**44**	1d. carmine-red (T) (5.1.43)	20	10
		a. Bright carmine	20	10
		b. Roulette omitted ..	75·00	
98	**45**	1½d. red-brown (P) (8.42) ..	12	12
		a. Roul. 13 instead of 6½ ..	1·00	1·00
		b. Roulette omitted ..	75·00	
99	**46**	2d. reddish violet (P) (2.43)	40	30
		a. Violet	15	20
		b. Roulette omitted ..	£100	
100	**47**	3d. blue (T) (10.42) ..	60	70
101	**48**	6d. red-orange (P) (10.42)	60	60
		(*b*) *Inscr. bilingually.*		
102	**49**	4d. slate-green (T) (10.42)	40	45
103	**50**	1s. brown (P) (11.42) ..	90	90
96/103		.. .. *Set of* 8	2·50	2·50

51. Signaller.

1943 (2 JAN.). *W* **9.** *P* 15×14.

			Un. pair	*Us. pair*
104	**51**	1s. 3d. olive-brown ..	1·50	2·00
		a. Blackish brown ..	1·00	1·00

52

53

1943. *Coil stamps. Redrawn. In single colours with plain background. W* **9.** *P* 15×14.

105	**52**	½d. blue-green (Mar.) ..	20	40
106	**53**	1d. carmine	30	35

54. Union Buildings, Pretoria.

1945–46. *Redrawn. W* 9. *P* 14.

107	**54**	2d. slate and violet ..	1·00	1·50
		a. Slate and brt. violet (shades)	75	1·25

In Nos. 107 and 107*a* the Union Buildings are shown at a different angle from Nos. 58 and 58*a*. Only the centre is screened i.e., composed of very small square dots of colour arranged in straight diagonal lines. For whole design screened and colours changed, see No. 116. No. 107*a* also shows "2" of "2d." clear of white circle at top.

55. "Victory".

6 "Peace".

57. " Hope ".

1945 (3 DEC.). *Victory.* *W* **9.** *P* 14.

No.	Type	Description	*Un. pair*	*Us. pair*
108	**55**	1d. brown and carmine ..	5	5
109	**56**	2d. slate-blue and violet ..	10	10
110	**57**	3d. deep blue and blue ..	10	15

58. King George VI.

59. King George VI and Queen Elizabeth.

60. Queen Elizabeth II as Princess, and Princess Margaret.

1947 (17 FEB.). *Royal Visit.* *W* **9.** *P* 15×14.

No.	Type	Description	Un.	Us.
111	**58**	1d. black and carmine ..	5	5
112	**59**	2d. violet	5	8
113	**60**	3d. blue	5	8

5s.

1947–54. "SUID-AFRIKA" *hyphenated on Afrikaans stamps. Printed from new cylinders with design in screened rotogravure.* *W* **9.** *P* 15×14 (½d., 1d. *and* 6d.), 14 (*others*).

No.	Type	Description	Un.	Us.
114	**24**	½d. grey and green	12	12
115	**7**	1d. grey and carmine ..	12	15
116	**54**	2d. slate-blue and purple	15	25
117	**22a**	3d. dull blue	30	35
117*a*	,,	3d. blue	20	35
		b. Deep blue	16·00	11·00
118	**12a**	4d. brown	25	25
119	**8**	6d. grn. & red-orange (III)	45	45
		a. Green & brn.-orange (III)	60	60
120	**13**	1s. brown & chalky blue	1·50	1·00
		a. Blackish brown and deep ultramarine ..	8·00	6·00
121	**14**	2s. 6d. green and brown	5·00	5·00
122	**15**	5s. black and pale blue-green (I)	10·00	7·00
122*a*	,,	5s. black and deep yellow-green (II)	12·00	12·00
114/122*a*	..	.. *Set of* 9	20·00	20·00

Dates of issue:—1947, No. 114; 4.49, No. 117; 8.49, No. 121; 9.49, No. 122; 1950, No. 116; 1.50, Nos. 119/*a*, 120; 1.9.50, No. 115; 3.51, No. 117*a*; 1952, No. 120*a*; 8.52, No. 118; 1954, No. 117*b*; 1.54, No. 122*a*.

In screened rotogravure the design is composed of very small squares of colour arranged in straight diagonal lines.

½d. Size 17¾×21¾ mm. Early printings have only the frame screened.

1d. Size 18×22 mm. For smaller, redrawn design, see No. 135.

2d. For earlier issue with centre only screened, and in different colours, see Nos. 107/*a*.

3d. No. 117. Whole stamp screened with irregular grain. Scrolls above " 3d. " solid and toneless. Printed from two cylinders.

No. 117*a*/*b*. Whole stamp diagonally screened, Printed from one cylinder. Clouds more pronounced.

4d. Two groups of white leaves below name tablet and a clear white line down left and right sides of stamp.

61. Gold Mine.

1948. *W* **9.** *In pair, perf.* 14, *subdivided by roulette* 6½.

No.	Type	Description	*Un. unit of* 4	*Us. unit*
124	**61**	1½d. blue-grn. & yellow-buff	10	20

62. King George VI and Queen Elizabeth.

1948 (26 APR.). *Silver Wedding.* *W* **9.** *P* 14.

No.	Type	Description	*Un. pair*	*Us. pair*
125	**62**	3d. blue and silver ..	5	8

(Typo. Government Printer, Pretoria.)

1948 *W* **9.** *P* 14½×14.

No.	Type	Description	Un.	Us.
126	**6**	½d. pale grey & blue-green	20	30

This was an economy printing made from the old plates of the 1926 issue for the purpose of using up a stock of cut paper. For the original printing in black and green, see No. 30.

63. *Wanderer* entering Durban.

1949 (2 MAY). *Centenary of Arrival of British Settlers in Natal.* *W* **9.** *P* 15×14.

No.	Type	Description	Un.	Us.
127	**63**	1½d. claret	10	10

64. Hermes.

1949 (1 OCT.). *75th Anniv. of Universal Posta[l] Union. As T* **64** *inscr.* " UNIVERSAL POSTA[L] UNION " *and* " WERELDPOSUNIE " *alternatel[y]* *W* **9** (*sideways*). *P* 14×15.

No.	Type	Description	*Un. pair*	*U[s. pair]*
128	**64**	½d. blue-green	5	
129	,,	1½d. brown-red	10	
130	,,	3d. bright blue	10	

65. Wagons Approaching Bingham's Berg.

66. Voortrekker Monument, Pretoria.

67. Bible, Candle and Voortrekkers.

(Des. W. H. Coetzer.)

1949 (1 DEC.). *Inauguration of Voortrekk[er] Monument, Pretoria.* *W* **9.** *P* 15×14.

No.	Type	Description	*Un. single*	*Us[.] sing[le]*
131	**65**	1d. magenta	5	
132	**66**	1½d. blue-green	5	
133	**67**	3d. blue	5	

68. Union Buildings, Pretoria.

1950 (APR.). *W* **9** (*sideways*). *P* 14×15.

No.	Type	Description	*Un. pair*	*U[s.] pa[ir]*
134	**68**	2d. blue and violet ..	10	

1951 (22 FEB.). *As No.* 115, *but redrawn w[ith] the horizon clearly defined. Size reduced [to] 17½×21¼ mm.*

No.	Type	Description	Un.	Us.
135	**7**	1d. grey and carmine ..	12	

INSCRIPTIONS. All later issues except No[s]. 167 and 262/5 are inscribed bilingually and pric[es] are for single copies, unused and used.

69. Seal and Monogram.

70. Maria de la Quellerie.

72. Jan van Riebeeck.

71. Arrival of Van Riebeeck's Ships.

73. Landing at the Cape.

1952 (14 MAR.). *Tercentenary of Landing of Van Riebeeck. W* **9** *(sideways on* 1d. *and* 4½d.*). P* 14 × 15 *(*1d. *and* 4½d.*) or* 15 × 14 *(others).*

			Un. single	*Used single*
136	**69**	½d. brown-purple & ol.-grey	5	5
137	**70**	1d. deep blue-green ..	5	5
138	**71**	2d. deep violet	8	5
139	**72**	4½d. blue	10	10
140	**73**	1s. brown	20	20
136/140		.. .. *Set of* 5	40	40

SATISE (74) **SADIPU** (75)

1952 (26 MAR.). *South African Tercentenary International Stamp Exhibition. No.* 137 *optd. with T* **74** *and No.* 138 *with T* **75.**

141	**70**	1d. deep blue-green ..	5	8
142	**71**	2d. deep violet	5	12

76. Queen Elizabeth II.

1953 (2 JUNE). *Coronation. W* **9** *(sideways). P* 14 × 15.

143	**76**	2d. deep violet-blue ..	8	5
		a. Ultramarine	8	5

77.

78. " Cape Triangular ".

1953 (1 SEPT.). *Centenary of First Cape of Good Hope Stamp. W* **9.** *P* 15 × 14.

144	**77**	1d. sepia and vermilion ..	5	5
145	**78**	4d. deep blue & light blue	10	10

79. Merino Ram.

80. Springbok.

81. Aloes.

1953. (1 OCT.). *W* **9.** *P* 14.

146	**79**	4½d. slate-purple & yellow	12	15
147	**80**	1s. 3d. chocolate ..	60	10
148	**81**	1s. 6d. vermilion & deep blue-green ..	50	15

82. Arms of Orange Free State and Scroll.

1954 (23 FEB.). *Centenary of Orange Free State. W* **9.** *P* 15 × 14.

149	**82**	2d. sepia & pale vermilion	8	5
150	,,	4½d. purple and slate ..	15	15

83. Warthog.

84. Gnu.

85. Leopard.

86. Zebra.

87. Rhinoceros.

88. Elephant.

89. Hippopotamus.

90. Lion.

91. Kudu.

92. Springbok.

93. Gemsbok.

94. Nyala.

95. Giraffe.

96. Sable Antelope.

1954 (14 Oct.). *W* **9** *(sideways on large vert. designs). P* 15×14 (½*d. to* 2*d.*), 14 *(others)*.

151 **83** ½d. deep blue-green .. 5 5
152 **84** 1d. brown-lake 5 5
153 **85** 1½d. sepia 8 5
154 **86** 2d. plum 8 5
155 **87** 3d. chocolate & turq.-blue 8 5
156 **88** 4d. indigo and emerald .. 8 5
157 **89** 4½d. blue-black & grey-blue 75 35
158 **90** 6d. sepia and orange .. 30 5
159 **91** 1s. dp. brn. & p. choc. 40 5
160 **92** 1s. 3d. brn. & bluish grn. 60 5
161 **93** 1s. 6d. brown and rose .. 1·00 30
162 **94** 2s. 6d. brown-black and apple-green .. .. 1·50 30
163 **95** 5s. black-brown and yellow-orange .. .. 5·00 75
164 **96** 10s. black and cobalt .. 10·00 2·00
151/164 .. .. *Set of* 14 15·00 3·00

See also Nos. 170/7.

97. President Kruger.

98. President Pretorius.

1955 (21 Oct.). *Centenary of Pretoria. W* **9** *(sideways). P* 14×15.

165 **97** 3d. slate-green 8 5
166 **98** 6d. maroon 12 10

99. A. Pretorius, Church of the Vow and Flag.

1955 (1 Dec.). *Voortrekker Covenant Celebrations, Pietermaritzburg. W* **9**. *P* 14.

		Un. pair	*Us. pair*
167 **99**	2d. blue and magenta ..	12	20

100. Settlers' Block-wagon and House.

1958 (1 July). *Centenary of Arrival of German Settlers in South Africa. W* **9**. *P* 14.

		Un. single	*Us. single*
168 **100**	2d. choc. and pale purple	10	12

101. Arms of the Academy.

1959 (1 May). *50th Anniv. of the South African Academy of Science and Art, Pretoria. W* **9**. *P* 15×14.

169 **101** 3d. dp. blue & turq.-blue 8 5
a. All deep blue ptg. omitted £450

102. Union Coat-of-Arms. I. II.

1959–61. *As Nos.* 151 *etc., but W* **102**.

170 **83** ½d. dp. greenish blue (12.60) 12 8
171 **84** 1d. brown-lake (I) (10.59) 8 5
a. Redrawn. Type II (10.60).. 20 10
172 **87** 3d. chocolate & turquoise-blue (9.59) 15 5
173 **88** 4d. indigo & emer. (1.60).. 40 20
174 **90** 6d. sepia & orange (2.60).. 25 10
175 **91** 1s. deep brown and pale chocolate (11.59) .. 1·00 30
176 **94** 2s. 6d. brown-black and apple-green (12.59) .. 3·00 1·50
177 **95** 5s. black-brown & yellow-orange (10.60).. .. 7·00 5·00
170/177 .. .. *Set of* 8 11·00 7·00

Nos. 171/a. In Type II "1d. Posgeld Postage" is more to the left in relation to "South Africa", with "1" almost central over "S" instead of to right as in Type I.

103. Globe and Antarctic Scene.

1959 (16 Nov.). *South African National Antarctic Expedition. W* **102**. *P* 14×15.

178 **103** 3d. blue-green & orange 8 5

104. Union Flag.

105. Union Arms.

106. "Wheel of Progress".

107. Union Festival Emblem.

1960 (2 May). *50th Anniv. of Union of Sout Africa. W* **102** *(sideways on* 4*d. and* 6*d.) P* 14×15 (4*d.*, 6*d.*) *or* 15×14 *(others)*.

179 **104** 4d. orange-red and blue 8
180 **105** 6d. red, brown & lt. green 8
181 **106** 1s. deep blue & lt. yellow 40 1
182 **107** 1s. 6d. black & lt. blue .. 1·00 7

See also Nos. 190, 192/3.

108. Locomotives of 1860 and 1960.

1960 (2 May). *Centenary of South African Rai ways. W* **102**. *P* 15×14.

183 **108** 1s. 3d. deep blue.. .. 1·50 1·(

109. Prime Ministers Botha, Smuts, Hertzo Malan, Strijdom and Verwoerd.

1960 (31 May). *Union Day. W* **102**. *P* 15×1

184 **109** 3d. brown and pale brown 8
a. Pale brown omitted* .. £250

*This is due to a rectangular piece of pape adhering to the background cylinder, resultin in R.2/1 missing the colour completely and si adjoining stamps having it partially omitted The item in block of eight is probably unique.

Currency changed. 100 cents = 1 rand.

1961 (14 Feb.). *Values in cents and rand. W* **1**(*(sideways on* 3½ *c.,* 7½ *c.,* 20 *c.,* 50 *c.,* 1 *r. P* 15×14 (½ *c. to* 2½ *c.,* 10 *c.*), 14×15 (3½ *c.* 7½ *c.) or* 14 *(others)*.

185 **83** ½ c. deep bluish green .. 5
186 **84** 1 c. brown-lake .. 5
187 **85** 1½ c. sepia 8
188 **86** 2 c. plum 8
189 **109** 2½ c. brown 8
190 **104** 3½ c. orge.-red and blue 12
191 **90** 5 c. sepia and orange .. 12
192 **105** 7½ c. red, brn., & lt. green 30
193 **106** 10 c. dp. blue & lt. yellow 30
194 **92** 12½ c. brn. & bluish green 50
195 **93** 20 c. brown and rose .. 75
196 **95** 50 c. blk.-brn. & orge.-yell. 3·00 3·(
197 **96** 1 r. black and cobalt .. 10·00 10·(
185/197 .. .. *Set of* 13 14·00 14·(

II. REPUBLIC.

31st May 1961.

1961–74

Key to designs, perfs., watermarks, papers and phosphors.

Value	Type	Perf.	W 102 Ordinary	No wmk. Ordinary	W 127 Chalky
½ c.	110	14×15	198	—	—
		14	198a	—	—
1 c.	111 (I)	15×14	199	211	—
	(II)		199a	211a	227
1½ c.	112	14×15	200	—	228
2 c.	113	14	201	212	229
2½ c.	114 (I)	14	202	—	—
	(II)		202a	213	230/*a*
3 c.	115	14	203	214	—
5 c.	116	14	204	215	231
7½ c.	117	14	205	216	232
10 c.	118	14	206	217	233
12½ c.	119	14	207	—	—
20 c.	120	14	208	218	234/*a*
50 c.	121	14	209	219	235
1 r.	122	14	210	—	236

Redrawn Designs

Value	Type	Perf.	W 127 Upright Plain or phosphorised	W 127 Tête-bêche Phos. frame	No wmk. Phosphorised Glossy	No wmk. Phosphorised Chalky
½ c.	130	14	237	—	—	—
		14×15	237c	—	—	—
1 c.	131	15×14	238	—	—	—
		13½×14	238a	—	—	—
1½ c.	132	14×15	239	286	—	—
		14×13½	239c	—	—	—
2 c.	133	14	240	287	315a	—
		12½	—	—	315	315b
2½ c.	134	14	241	288	—	—
3 c.	135	14	242	289	—	—
		12½	—	—	316	316a
4 c.	134	14	242*b*	290	—	—
5 c.	136	14	243	291	318a	—
		12½	—	—	318	318b
6 c.	137	14	—	292	—	—
		12½	—	—	—	319
7½ c.	137	14	244	293	—	—
9 c.	139	14	244*a*	294	—	—
		12½	—	—	320	—
10 c.	138	14	245	295	321a	—
		12½	—	—	321	321b
12½ c.	139	14	246/*a*	296	—	—
15 c.	140	14	247	297	—	—
20 c.	141	14	248	298	—	—
		12½	—	—	323	323a
50 c.	142	14	249	—	—	—
		12½	—	—	324	324a
1 r.	143	14	250	—	—	—
		12½	—	—	325	—

New Designs

Value	Type	Perf.	W 127 Tête-bêche Plain	W 127 Tête-bêche Phos. frame	No wmk. Phosphorised Glossy	No wmk. Phosphorised Chalky
½ c.	168	14×13½	276	284	—	—
		14×14½	276a	—	313	—
		14×15	—	284a	—	—
1 c.	169	13½×14	277	285	—	—
		14	—	—	314	—
4 c.	182	14	310/*a*	—	—	—
		12½	—	—	317/*b*	317c
15 c.	182*a*	14	311	—	—	—
		12½	—	—	—	322

110. Natal Kingfisher.

111. Kafferboom Flower.

112. Afrikaner Bull.

113. Pouring Gold.

114. Groot Constantia

115. Crimson-breasted Shrike.

116. Baobab Tree.

117. Maize.

118. Capetown Castle Entrance.

119. Protea.

120. Secretary Bird.

121. Capetown Harbour.

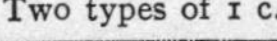
Two types of 1 c.

122. Strelitzia.

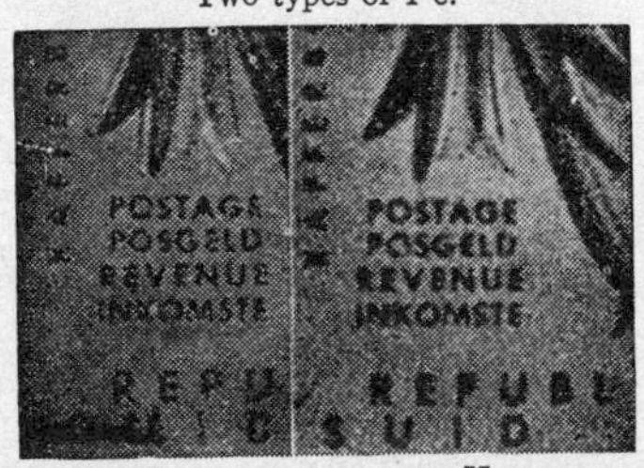

I II

Type I. Lowest point of flower between "OS" of "POSTAGE".

Type II. Flower has moved fractionally to the right so that lowest point is over "S" of "POSTAGE".

Two types of 2½ c.

In Type I the lines of the building are quite faint. In Type II all lines of the building have been strengthened by re-engraving.

(Des. Mrs. T. Campbell (½ c., 3 c., 1 r.); Miss N. Desmond (1 c.); De La Rue (2½ c., 5 c., 12½ c.); H. L. Prager (50 c.); Govt. Ptg. Dept. artist (others).)

1961 (31 MAY)–**63.** *Unsurfaced paper.* *W* **102** *(sideways on ½ c., 1½ c., 2½ c., 5 c. to 20 c.).* *P* 14×15 *(½ c., 1½ c.),* 15×14 *(1 c.) or* 14 *(others).*

No.	Type			
198	**110**	½ c. bright blue, carmine and brown ..	5	5
		a. Perf. 14 (3.63) ..	5	5
199	**111**	1 c. red & olive-grey (I)	5	5
		a. Type II (1.62) ..	5	5
200	**112**	1½ c. brn.-lake & lt. pur.	5	5
201	**113**	2 c. ultram. & yellow..	8	5
202	**114**	2½ c. violet and green (I)	15	5
		a. Type II. *Dp. violet and green* (9.61)	20	5
203	**115**	3 c. red and deep blue	12	5
204	**116**	5 c. yell. & grnish. blue	12	8
205	**117**	7½ c. yell.-brn. & lt. grn.	15	8
206	**118**	10 c. sepia and green ..	20	10
207	**119**	12½ c. red, yellow & black-green	25	12
208	**120**	20 c. turq.-blue, carmine and brown-orange	40	15
209	**121**	50 c. black & brt. blue	1·75	60
210	**122**	1 r. orange, olive-green and light blue ..	2·75	1·00
198/210		.. .. *Set of* 13	5·50	2·00

No. 198 was issued in coils on 18.5.63 with the spurs of the branch strengthened.

1961 (AUG.)–**63.** *As Nos.* 199, 201/6 *and* 208/9 *but without wmk.*

No.	Type			
211	**111**	1 c. red & olive-grey (I)	15	5
		a. Type II (9.62).. ..	8	5
212	**113**	2 c. ultram. & yell. (8.63)	12	5
213	**114**	2½ c. violet and green (II) (*shades*)	8	5
214	**115**	3 c. red and deep blue (10.61)	8	5
215	**116**	5 c. yell. & grnish. blue (12.61)	15	5
216	**117**	7½ c. yellow-brown and light green (3.62) ..	20	8
217	**118**	10 c. sepia & grn. (*shades*) (11.61)	35	8
218	**120**	20 c. turq.-blue, carmine & brn.-orge. (4.63) ..	65	15
219	**121**	50 c. black and bright blue (8.62)	1·60	45
211/219		.. .. *Set of* 9	3·00	75

See also Nos. 227/36, 237/50, 276/7, 284/98 and 313/25.

123. Blériot Monoplane and Boeing 707 Airliner over Table Mountain.

124. Folk-dancers.

1961 (1 DEC.). *50th Anniv. of First South African Aerial Post.* *W* **102** *(sideways).* *P* 14×15.

220	**123**	3 c. blue and red.. ..	8	5

(Des. K. Esterhuysen.)

1962 (1 MAR.). *50th Anniv. of Volkspele (Folk-dancing) in South Africa.* *W* **102** *(sideways).* *P* 14×15.

221	**124**	2½ c. orange-red & brown	8	5

125. The *Chapman.*

1962 (20 AUG.). *Unveiling of Precinct Stone, British Settlers Monument, Grahamstown.* *W* **102.** *P* 15×14.

222	**125**	2½ c. turq.-grn. & purple	8	5
223	,,	12½ c. blue and dp. choc.	25	15

126. Red Disa (orchid), Castle Rock and Gardens.

(Des. M. F. Stern.)

1963 (14 MAR.). *50th Anniv. of Kirstenbosch Botanic Gardens, Cape Town.* *P* 13½×14.

224	**126**	2½ c. multicoloured ..	8	5
		a. Red (orchid, etc.) omitted		

127 (normal version).

128. Centenary Emblem and Nurse.

129. Centenary Emblem and Globe.

1963 (30 AUG.). *Centenary of Red Cross. Chalk-surfaced paper.* *Wmk.* **127** *(sideways on* 2½ *c.).* *P* 14×13½ *(2½ c.) or* 15×14 *(12½ c.).*

225	**128**	2½ c. red, black, & reddish purple ..	8	5
226	**129**	12½ c. red and indigo ..	25	15
		a. Red cross omitted ..	£500	

1963–67. *As* 1961–3 *but chalk-surfaced paper and W* **127** *(sideways on* 1½ *c.,* 2½ *c.,* 5 *c.,* 7½ *c.,* 10 *c.,* 20 *c.).* *P* 15×14 *(1 c.),* 14×15 *(1½ c.), or* 14 *(others).*

No.	Type			
227	**111**	1 c. red and olive-grey (II) (9.63)	5	5
228	**112**	1½ c. brown-lake & light purple (1.67) ..	8	5
229	**113**	2 c. ultramarine and yellow (11.64) ..	8	5
230	**114**	2½ c. violet and green (II) (10.63)	8	5
		a. *Bright reddish violet and emerald* (II) (3.66) ..	15	5
231	**116**	5 c. yellow and greenish blue (9.66)	10	5
232	**117**	7½ c. yellow-brown and brt. green (23.2.66)	15	5
233	**118**	10 c. sepia-brown and light emerald (*shades*) (9.64)	20	15
234	**120**	20 c. turq.-blue, carmine & brn.-orange (7.64)		15
		a. *Deep turquoise-blue, carmine and flesh* (20.7.65)	40	10
235	**121**	50 c. black and ultramarine (4.66)	2·00	1·50
236	**122**	1 r. orange, light green and pale blue (7.64)	12·00	10·00
227/36		.. .. *Set of* 10	14·00	11·00

In the 2½ c. (No. 230*a*), 5 c., 7½ c., 10 c. (Jan. '67 printing only) and 50 c. the watermark is indistinct but can easily be distinguished from the stamps without watermark by their shades and the chalk-surfaced paper which is appreciably thicker and whiter.

130. Natal Kingfisher.

131. Kafferboom Flower.

132. Afrikaner Bull.

133. Pouring Gold.

134. Groot Constantia.

135. Crimson-breasted Shrike.

136. Baobab Tree.

137. Maize.

138. Capetown Castle Entrance.

139. Protea.

140. Industry.

141. Secretary Bird.

142. Capetown Harbour.

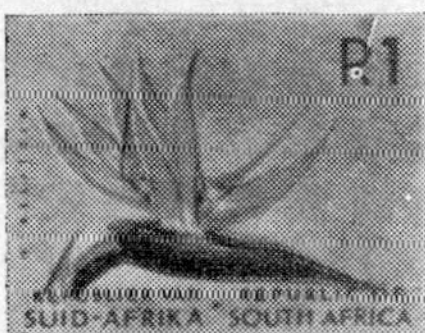

143. Strelitzia.

(15 c. des. C. E. F. Skotnes.)

Redrawn types.

½ c. "½C" larger and "REPUBLIEK VAN REPUBLIC OF" smaller.

3 c. and 12½ c. Inscriptions and figures of value larger.

Others. "SOUTH AFRICA" and "SUID-AFRIKA" larger and bolder. The differences vary in each design but are easy to see by comparing the position of the letters of the country name with "REPUBLIC OF" and "REPUBLIEK VAN".

1964–72. *As* 1961–63 *but designs redrawn and new values* (4 *c.*, 9 *c. and* 15 *c.*). *Chalk-surfaced paper and W* **127** (*sideways on all values to* 20 *c. except* 1 *and* 3 *c.*). *P* 14 × 15 (1½ *c.*), 15 × 14 (1 *c.*) *or* 14 (*others*).

237 **130** ½ c. bright blue, carmine and brown (*shades*) (21.5.64) 5 5
 a. Imperf. (pair) ..
 c. Perf. 14 × 15. *Bright blue, carmine & yellow-brown* (*shades*) (6.7.67) 5 5
238 **131** 1 c. red and olive-grey (9.3.67) 5 5
 a. Perf. 13½ × 14 (7.68).. 5 5
239 **132** 1½ c. dull red-brown and light purple (*shades*) (21.9.67) 5 5
 c. Perf. 14 × 13½. *Red-brown and light purple* (14.8.69) 5 5
240 **133** 2 c. ultram. & yellow (*shades*) (8.1.68) .. 5 5
241 **134** 2½ c. violet and green (*shades*) (19.4.67).. 8 5
242 **135** 3 c. red and deep blue (*shades*) (11.64) .. 8 5
242*b* **134** 4 c. violet and green (10.71) 8 5
243 **136** 5 c. yellow and greenish blue (*shades*) (14.2.68) 10 8
244 **137** 7½ c. yellow-brown and brt. green (26.7.67) 12 5
244*a* **139** 9 c. red, yellow and slate-green (2.72).. 12 8
245 **138** 10 c. sepia and green (*shades*) (10.6.68) .. 12 5
246 **139** 12½ c. red, yellow and black-green (3.64) 20 8
 a. Red, pale yellow and blue-green (2.2.66) .. 25 8
247 **140** 15 c. black, light olive-yellow and red-orange (1.3.67) .. 30 25
248 **141** 20 c. turquoise-blue, carmine and brown-orange (*shades*) (2.68) 50 40
249 **142** 50 c. black and bright blue (17.6.68) .. 1·50 1·50
250 **143** 1 r. orange, light green & light blue (6.65) 3·00 3·50
237/50 .. .. *Set of* 16 5·50 5·50

WATERMARK. Two forms of the watermark Type **127** exist in the above issue: the normal Type **127** (sometimes indistinct), and a very faint *tête-bêche* watermark. i.e. alternately facing up and down, which was introduced in mid-1967. As it is extremely difficult to distinguish these on single stamps we do not list it.

The ½ (both perfs.), 1, 2, 2½, 3 and 15 c. and 1 r. are known in both forms, the 1½, 4, 5, 7½, 9, 10, 20 and 50 c. only in the *tête-bêche* form, and the 12½ c. Type **127** only.

GUM. The 2, 3, 5, 20 and 50 c. and 1 r. exist with PVA gum as well as gum arabic.

PHOSPHORISED PAPER. From October 1971 onwards phosphor bands (see Nos. 284/98) gave way to phosphorised paper which cannot be distinguished from non-phosphor stamps without the aid of a lamp. For this reason we do not distinguish these printings in the above issue, but some are in slightly different shades which are listed in the *Elizabethan Catalogue* and all have PVA gum.

The 4 c. and 9 c. are on phosphorised paper only and differ from Nos. 290 and 294 by the lack of phosphor bands.

See also Nos. 284/98 and 313, etc.

144. Assembly Building, Umtata.

1963 (11 DEC.). *First Meeting of Transkei Legislative Assembly. Chalk-surfaced paper. W* **127**. *P* 15 × 14.

251 **144** 2½ c. sepia & light green.. 8 5

145. "Springbok" Badge of Rugby Board.

147. Calvin.

146. Rugby Footballer.

1964 (8 MAY). *75th Anniv. of South African Rugby Board. Chalk-surfaced paper. W* **127** (*sideways on* 2½ *c.*). *P* 14 × 15 (2½ *c.*) *or* 15 × 14 (12½ *c.*).

252 **145** 2½ c. yell.-brn. & dp. grn. 8 5
253 **146** 12½ c. blk. & lt. yell.-grn. 35 25

1964 (10 JULY). *400th Anniv. of Death of Calvin (Protestant Reformer). Chalk-surfaced paper. W* **127** (*sideways*). *P* 14 × 13½.

254 **147** 2½ c. cerise, violet & brn. 8 5

148. Nurse's Lamp.

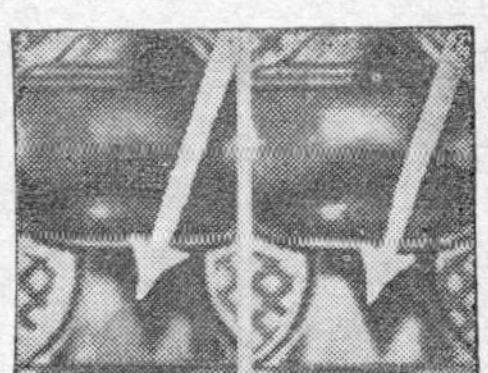
I. Screened base to lamp. II. Clear base to lamp.

149. Nurse holding Lamp.

1964 (12 OCT.). *50th Anniv. of South African Nursing Association. Chalk-surfaced paper. W* **127** (*sideways on* 2½ *c.*). *P* 14 × 15 (2½ *c.*) *or* 15 × 14 (12½ *c.*).

255 **148** 2½ c. ultramarine & dull gold (Type I) .. 8 5
256 ,, 2½ c. bright blue & yellow-gold (Type II) 15 10
 a. Ultram. & dull gold .. 8 5
257 **149** 12½ c. bright blue & gold 30 20
 a. Gold omitted ..

150. I.T.U. Emblem and Satellites.

151. I.T.U. Emblem and Symbols.

1965 (17 MAY). *I.T.U. Centenary. Chalk-surfaced paper. W* **127**. *P* 15 × 14.

258 **150** 2½ c. orange and blue .. 8 8
259 **151** 12½ c. brown-purple & grn. 25 25

152. Pulpit in Groote Kerk, Cape Town.

153. Church Emblem.

1965 (21 Oct.). *Tercentenary of Nederduites Gereformeerde Kerk (Dutch Reformed Church) in South Africa. Chalk-surfaced paper. W* **127** *(sideways on* $2\frac{1}{2}$ *c., inverted on* $12\frac{1}{2}$*c). P* 14×15 *(*$2\frac{1}{2}$ *c.) or* 15×14 *(*$12\frac{1}{2}$ *c.).*

260 **152** $2\frac{1}{2}$ c. brown & lt. yellow 8 8
261 **153** $12\frac{1}{2}$ c. blk., lt. orge. & bl. 25 25

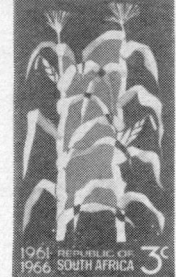

154. Diamond. **156.** Maize Plants.

155. Bird in flight.

157. Mountain Landscape. *(Horiz.)*

(Des. C. E. F. Skotnes.)

1966 (31 May). *Fifth Anniv. of Republic. Chalk-surfaced paper. W* **127** *(sideways on* 1 *c.,* 3 *c.). P* $14\times13\frac{1}{2}$ *(*1 *c.),* $13\frac{1}{2}\times14$ *(*$2\frac{1}{2}$ *c.),* 14×15 *(*3 *c.) or* 15×14 *(*$7\frac{1}{2}$ *c.).*

			Un. pair	*Us. pair*
262	**154**	1 c. black, bluish, green and olive-yellow ..	5	5
263	**155**	$2\frac{1}{2}$ c. blue, deep blue and yellow-green ..	10	12
264	**156**	3 c. red, greenish yellow and red-brown ..	12	15
265	**157**	$7\frac{1}{2}$ c. bl., ultram. & yell.	30	35

Nos. 262/5 exist on Swiss-made paper with *tête-bêche* watermark from a special printing made for use in presentation albums for delegates to the U.P.U. Congress in Tokyo in 1969, as supplies of the original Harrison paper were by then exhausted.

158. Verwoerd and Union Buildings, Pretoria.

159. Dr. H. F. Verwoerd. *(Vert.)*

160. Verwoerd and Map of South Africa. *(Horiz).*

(Des. from portrait by Dr. Henkel.)

1966 (6 Dec.). *Verwoerd Commemoration. Chalk-surfaced paper. W* **127** *(sideways on* 3 *c.). P* 14×15 *(*3 *c.) or* 15×14 *(others).*

			Un. single	*Us. single*
266	**158**	$2\frac{1}{2}$ c. blackish brown and turquoise	5	5
267	**159**	3 c. blackish brown and yellow-green ..	8	5
268	**160**	$12\frac{1}{2}$ c. blackish brown and greenish blue ..	30	30

161. Martin Luther. **162.** Wittenburg Church Door.

1967 (31 Oct.). *450th Anniv. of Reformation. W* **127** *(sideways), normal on* $2\frac{1}{2}$ *c., tête-bêche on* $12\frac{1}{2}$ *c.). P* 14×15.

269 **161** $2\frac{1}{2}$ c. black and rose-red 5 5
270 **162** $12\frac{1}{2}$ c. black & yell.-orge. 30 25

163. Profile of Pres. Fouché. **164.** Portrait of Pres. Fouché.

1968 (10 Apr.). *Inauguration of President Fouché. W* **127** *(sideways). P* 14×15.

271 **163** $2\frac{1}{2}$ c. choc. & pale choc. 5 5
272 **164** $12\frac{1}{2}$ c. deep blue & lt. blue 35 30

No. 272 also exists with the watermark *tête-bêche.*

165. Hertzog in 1902.

166. Hertzog in 1924. *(Horiz.)*

167. Hertzog Monument. *(Vert.)*

1968 (21 Sept.). *Inauguration of General Hertzog Monument, Bloemfontein. W* **127** *(tête-bêche on* $2\frac{1}{2}$ *c., inverted on* 3 *c., sideways on* $12\frac{1}{2}$ *c.). P* $14\times13\frac{1}{2}$ *(*$12\frac{1}{2}$ *c.) or* $13\frac{1}{2}\times14$ *(others).*

273 **165** $2\frac{1}{2}$ c. black, brown and olive-yellow .. 5 5
274 **166** 3 c. black, red-brown, red-orange & yell. 5 5
275 **167** $12\frac{1}{2}$ c. black, red and yellow-orange .. 35 30

168. Natal Kingfisher. **169.** Kafferboom Flower.

1969. *W* **127** *(tête-bêche, sideways on* $\frac{1}{2}$ *c.). P* $14\times13\frac{1}{2}$ *(*$\frac{1}{2}$ *c.) or* $13\frac{1}{2}\times14$ *(*1 *c.).*

276 **168** $\frac{1}{2}$ c. new blue, carm.-red., & yellow-ochre (1.69) 5 5
a. Coil. Perf. $14\times14\frac{1}{2}$ (5.69) 5 5
277 **169** 1 c. rose-red and olive-brown (1.69) .. 8 10

See also Nos. 284/5 and 313/4.

170. Springbok and Olympic Torch.

1969 (15 Mar.). *South African Games, Bloemfontein. W* **127** *(tête-bêche, sideways). P* $14\times13\frac{1}{2}$

278 **170** $2\frac{1}{2}$ c. black, blue-black, red and sage-green 5
279 „ $12\frac{1}{2}$ c. black, blue-black, red and cinnamon 25 3

171. Professor Barnard and Groote Schuur Hospital.

172. Hands holding Heart.

1969 (7 July). *World's First Heart Transplant and 47th South African Medical Association Congress. W* **127** *(tête-bêche). P* $13\frac{1}{2}\times14$ *(*$2\frac{1}{2}$ *c.) or* 15×14 *(*$12\frac{1}{2}$ *c.).*

280 **171** $2\frac{1}{2}$ c. plum and rose-red 5
281 **172** $12\frac{1}{2}$ c. carmine-red and Royal blue .. 25 2

173. Mail Coach.

174. Transvaal Stamp of 1869.

1969 (6 Oct.). *Centenary of First Stamps of South African Republic (Transvaal). Phosphor bands on all four sides* (2½ *c.*). *W* **127** (*tête-bêche, sideways on* 12½ *c.*). *P* 13½×14 (2½ *c.*) *or* 14×13½ (12½ *c.*).

282 **173** 2½ c. yellow, indigo and yellow-brown .. 10 10
283 **174** 12½ c. emerald, gold and yellow-brown .. 35 35

1969–71. *As* 1964–72 *issue and Nos.* 276/7, *and new value* (6 *c.*), *but with phosphor bands printed horizontally and vertically between the stamp designs, over the perforations, thus producing a frame effect. W* **127** *arranged tête-bêche* (*upright on* 1, 2 *and* 3 *c., sideways on others*). *P* 14×13½ (½ *c.*), 13½×14 (1 *c.*), 14×15 (1½ *c.*) *or* 14 (*others*).

284 **168** ½ c. new blue, carmine-red & yellow ochre (1.70) 5 5
a. Coil. P 14×15 (2.71) 10 5
285 **169** 1 c. rose-red and olive-brown (12.69) .. 5 5
286 **132** 1½ c. red-brown & light purple (12.69) .. 5 5
287 **133** 2 c. ultram. & yellow (*shades*) (11.69) .. 5 5
288 **134** 2½ c. violet and green (*shades*) (1.70) 8 5
289 **135** 3 c. red and deep blue (30.9.69) 8 5
290 **134** 4 c. vio. & grn. (1.3.71) 8 8
291 **136** 5 c. yellow & greenish blue (17.11.69) .. 10 10
292 **137** 6 c. yellow-brown and brt. green (3.5.71) 12 12
293 „ 7½ c. yellow-brown and brt. grn. (17.11.69) 15 15
294 **139** 9 c. red, yellow and black-grn. (17.5.71) 20 20
295 **138** 10 c. brown and pale green (1.70) .. 20 20
296 **139** 12½ c. red, yell. & black-green (2.5.70) .. 25 25
297 **140** 15 c. blk., lt. olive-yell. & red orge. (1.70) 30 30
298 **141** 20 c. turq.-bl., carm. & brn.-orge. (*shades*) (18.2.70) .. 50 50
284/98 .. .. *Set of* 15 2·00 1·90

No. 288 exists on normal RSA wmk. as well as RSA *tête-bêche* wmk.

The 1, 2, 2½, 3, 10, 15 and 20 c. exist with PVA gum as well as gum arabic, but the 4, 6 and 9 c. exist with PVA gum only.

For stamps without wmk., see Nos. 313, etc.

PHOSPHOR FRAME. Nos. 299/306 have phosphor applied on all four sides as a frame.

175. "Water 70" Emblem.

177. "The Sower".

176. Symbolic Waves. (*Horiz.*)

1970 (14 Feb.). *Water 70 Campaign. W* **127** (*tête-bêche* (*sideways on* 2½ *c.*)). *P* 14×13½ (2½ *c.*) *or* 13½×14 (3 *c.*).

299 **175** 2½ c. green, bright blue and chocolate .. 5 5
300 **176** 3 c. Prussian blue, Royal blue and buff .. 8 8

1970 (24 Aug.). 150*th Anniv. of Bible Society of South Africa. T* **177** *and similar horiz. design* (*gold die stamped on* 12½ *c.*). *W* **127** (*tête-bêche, sideways on* 2½ *c.*). *P* 14×13½ (2½ *c.*) *or* 13½×14 (12½ *c.*).

301 2½ c. multicoloured .. 5 5
302 12½ c. gold, black and blue .. 25 25

Design:—12½ c. "Biblia" and Open Book.

178. J. G. Strijdom and Strijdom Tower.

1971 (22 May). "*Interstex*" *Stamp Exhibition, Cape Town. P* 14×13½.
A. *W* **127** (*sideways tête-bêche*). B. *W* **102** (*sideways*).

		A.		B.	
303 **178** 5 c. lt. greenish blue, black & p. yellow		8	8	20	15

179. Map and Antarctic Landscape.

1971 (22 May). *Tenth Anniv. of Antarctic Treaty. W* **127** (*tête-bêche*). *P* 13½×14.

304 **179** 12½ c. blue-blk., greenish blue & orange-red 20 15

180. Landing of British Settlers, 1820.

1971 (31 May). *Tenth Anniv. of the Republic of South Africa. T* **180** *and similar design. W* **127** (*tête-bêche sideways on* 4 *c.*). *P* 13½×14 (2 *c.*) *or* 14×13½ (4 *c.*).

305 2 c. pale flesh and brown-red 5 5
306 4 c. green and black .. 8 8

Design: *Vert.*—4 c. Presidents Steyn and Kruger and Treaty of Vereeniging Monument.

No. 306 exists with PVA gum as well as gum arabic.

PHOSPHORISED PAPER. All issues from here are on phosphorised paper *unless otherwise stated.*

181. View of Dam.

(Des. C. Bridgeford (4 c.), C. Lindsay (others).)

1972 (4 Mar.). *Opening of Hendrik Verwoerd Dam. T* **181** *and similar horiz. designs. Multicoloured. W* **127** (*tête-bêche*). *P* 13½×14.

307 4 c. Type **181** 8 5
308 5 c. Aerial view of Dam .. 8 5
309 10 c. Dam and surrounding country (58×21 *mm.*) 20 20

182. Sheep.

182a. Lamb.

183. Black and Siamese Cats.

(Des. K. Esterhuysen (4 c.), H. Botha (15 c.).)

1972 (15 May–Oct.). *W* **127** (*tête-bêche*). *P* 14.

310 **182** 4 c. olive-brown, yellow, pale blue and slate-blue 8 5
a. Grey-olive, yellow, bright blue and slate-blue (10.72) 8 5
311 **182a** 15 c. pale stone, deep blue and dull blue .. 30 20

Other shades exist of the 4c.

See also Nos. 317 and 322.

1972 (19 Sept.). *Centenary of Societies for the Prevention of Cruelty to Animals. W* **127** (*sideways tête-bêche*). *P* 14×13½.

312 **183** 5 c. multicoloured .. 8 8

1972–74. *As Nos.* 310 *and* 284 *etc., but no wmk. P* 14 (1 *c.*) *or* 12½ (*others*). *Phosphorised, glossy paper.*

313 **168** ½ c. brt. bl., scar. & yell.-ochre, *p.* 14 × 14½ (*coil*) (6.73) .. 5 5
314 **169** 1 c. rose-red and olive-brown (1.74) .. 5 5
315 **133** 2 c. blue & orange-yellow (11.72) 5 5
 a. Perf. 14. *Dp. ultram. & orge.-yell.* (coil) (7.73) .. 5 5
 b. Chalky paper (17.7.74) 5 5
316 **135** 3 c. scar. & dp. bl. (8.5.73) 5 5
 a. Chalky paper (18.2.74) 5 5
317 **182** 4 c. grey-blue, yellow, bl. & bluish slate* (1.10.73) 5 5
 a. *Olive-sepia, yellow, azure and slate-blue* (18.2.74) 5 5
 b. *Lavender-brown, pale yellow, blue & bluish slate** (26.7.74) .. 5 5
 c. Chalky paper* (22.8.74) 5 5
318 **136** 5 c. orange-yellow and greenish blue (4.10.73) 10 8
 a. Perf. 14. *Yell. & lt. greenish blue* (coil) (7.73) .. 10 8
 b. Chalky paper (5.74) .. 5 5
319 **137** 6 c. yellow-brown and brt. grn. (*chalky paper*) (22.7.74) .. 10 8
320 **139** 9 c. red, yell. & grn.-blk. (*shades*) (6.73) .. 15 10
321 **138** 10 c. reddish brown and bright green (8.5.73) 15 10
 a. Perf. 14 (coil) (6.73) .. 20 15
 b. Chalky paper (17.7.74) .. 12 12
322 **182*a*** 15 c. pale stone, dp. blue & dull blue (*chalky paper*) (4.9.74) .. 20 15
323 **141** 20 c. turq.-bl., rose-carm. & orge-buff (8.5.73) 25 20
 a. Chalky paper (5.74) .. 25 20
324 **142** 50 c. black & brt. bl. (6.73) 70 50
 a. Chalky paper (22.7.74) .. 70 50
325 **143** 1 r. orge., lt. grn. & lt. blue (8.10.73) .. 1·40 1·00
 a. Orange omitted ..
313/325 .. .. *Set of* 13 2·75 2·25

* On these stamps the colours are known to vary within the sheet.

No. 314 also differs in that the central design has been moved down about 1 mm.

No. 317 also differs from No. 310 by measuring 26¼ × 21 mm. instead of 27¼ × 21¾ mm.

184. Transport and Industry.

(Des. J. Hoekstra (4 c.), M. Barnett (others).)

1973 (1 Feb.). 50*th Anniv. of ESCOM* (*Electricity Supply Commission*). *T* **184** *and similar vert. designs. Multicoloured. P* 12 × 12½ (4 *c.*) *or* 12½ (*others*).

326 4 c. Type **184** 8 5
327 5 c. Pylon (21 × 28 *mm*). 8 8
328 15 c. Cooling Towers (21 × 28 *mm.*) 20 20

185. University Coat-of-arms.

187. C. J. Langenhoven.

186. Rescuing Sailors.

(Des. P. de Wet (15 c.), H. Meiring (others).)

1973 (2 Apr.). *Centenary of University of South Africa. T* **185** *and similar designs. W* **127** *tête-bêche* (5 *c.*) *or no wmk.* (*others*). *P* 12 × 12½ (5 *c.*) *or* 12½ (*others*).

329 4 c. multicoloured 5 5
330 5 c. multicoloured 8 8
331 15 c. black and gold 20 20

Designs: *Horiz.* (37 × 21 *mm.*)—5 c. University Complex, Pretoria. *Vert.* (*As T* **185**)—15 c. Old University Building, Cape Town.

WATERMARK. All issues from this date are on unwatermarked paper.

(Des. M. Barnett.)

1973 (2 June). *Bicentenary of Rescue by Wolraad Woltemade. T* **186** *and similar horiz. designs. P* 11½ × 12½.

332 4 c. light red-brown, lt. yell.-green and black 8 8
333 5 c. yellow-olive, light yellow-green and black 8 8
334 15 c. red-brown, light yellow-green and black 20 20

Designs:—5 c. *De Jong Thomas* foundering; 15 c. *De Jong Thomas* breaking up and sailors drowning.

(Des. J. Mostert.)

1973 (1 Aug.). *Birth Centenary of C. J. Langenhoven* (*politician and composer of national anthem. T* **187** *and similar designs. P* 12½ (4 *and* 5 *c.*) *or* 11½ × 12½ (15 *c.*).

335 **187** 4 c. multicoloured .. 8 8
336 – 5 c. multicoloured .. 8 8
337 – 15 c. multicoloured .. 20 20

Nos. 336/7 are as T **187** but with motifs rearranged. The 5 c. is vert., 21 × 38 mm., and the 15 c. is horiz., 38 × 21 mm.

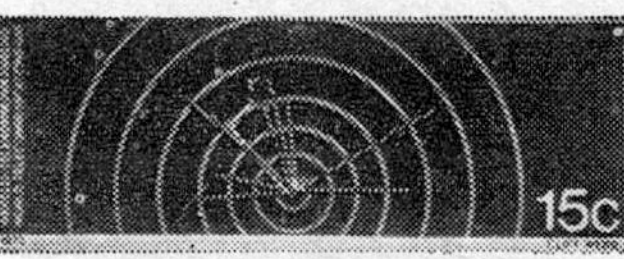

188. Communications Map.

(*Illustration reduced. Actual size* 52½ × 20 *mm.*)

(Des. C. Webb.)

1973 (1 Oct.). *World Communications Day. P* 12½. (*a*) *No wmk. Glossy paper.*

338 **188** 15 c. multicoloured .. 20 25

(*b*) *W* **127** (*tête-bêche*). *Chalky paper.*

339 **188** 15 c. multicoloured .. 40 40

189. Restored Buildings.

(Des. W. Jordaan.)

1974 (14 Mar.). *Restoration of Tulbagh. T* **189** *and similar multicoloured design. P* 12½.

340 4 c. Type **189** 8 8
341 5 c. Restored Church Street (58 × 21 *mm.*) 8 8

190. Burgerspond (Obverse and Reverse).

191. Dr. Malan.

(Des. P. de Wet. Litho.)

1974 (6 Apr.). *Centenary of the Burgerspond* (*coin*). *P* 12½ × 12.

342 **190** 9 c. brown, orange-red and pale yellow-olive .. 15 15

(Des. I. Henkel.)

1974 (22 May). *Birth Centenary of Dr. D. F. Malan* (*Prime Minister*). *P* 12½ × 12.

343 **191** 4 c. blue and light blue .. 5 5

192. Congress Emblem.

(Des. Ingrid Paul.)

1974 (13 June). 15*th World Sugar Congress, Durban. P* 12 × 12½.

344 **192** 15 c. deep ultramarine and silver 20 20

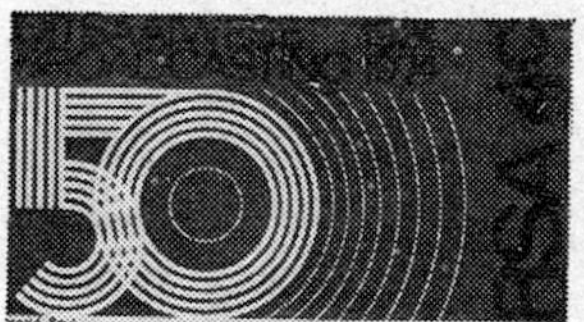
193. "50" and Radio Waves.

(Des. Ingrid Paul.)

1974 (13 July). 50*th Anniv. of Broadcasting in South Africa. P* 12 × 12½.

345 **193** 4 c. red and black .. 8 8

194. Monument Building.

(Des. G. Cunningham.)

1974 (13 July). *Inauguration of British Settlers' Monument, Grahamstown. P* 12 × 12½.

346 **194** 5 c. red and black .. 8 8

195. Stamps of the South African Provinces.

Illustration reduced. Actual size 57 × 21 *mm.*)

(Des. K. Esterhuysen.)

.**974** (9 Oct.). *Centenary of Universal Postal Union. P* 12½.
:47 **195** 15 c. multicoloured .. 20 25

196. Iris.

197. Bokmakieries.

(Des. E. de Jong. Recess and photo.)

.**974** (20 Nov.)–**75.** *Multicoloured. Glossy paper* (2, 3, 4, 6, 7, 30 *c. and* 1 *r.*) *or chalky paper* (*others*). *P* 12½ (1 *to* 25 *c.*) *or* 12 × 12½ (*others*).

(*a*) *Vert. designs as T* **196** *showing flowers, or horiz. designs showing birds or fish.*

48 1 c. Type **196** 5 5
49 2 c. Wild Heath 5 5
a. Chalk-surfaced paper (2.75) 5 5
50 3 c. Geranium 5 5
a. Chalk-surfaced paper (*shades*) (6.75) 5 5
ab. Imperf. (pair) £200
51 4 c. Arum Lily 5 5
a. Chalk-surfaced paper (2.75) 5 5
52 5 c. Cape Gannet 5 5
53 6 c. Galjoen (fish) 8 8
54 7 c. Zebra Fish 8 10
55 9 c. Angel Fish 10 12
56 10 c. Moorish Idol 12 12
57 14 c. Roman (fish) 15 20
58 15 c. Greater Double-coloured Sunbird 20 20
59 20 c. Yellow-billed Hornbill .. 25 25
60 25 c. Baberton Daisy .. 30 35

(*b*) *Horiz. designs as T* **197.**

61 30 c. Type **197** 35 40
62 50 c. Blue Cranes 60 70
63 1 r. Bateleur Eagles .. .. 1·25 1·40
48/63 .. .. *Set of* 16 3·25 3·75

A used block of 4 of No. 351 has been seen with he yellow omitted.

974 (20 Nov.)–**76.** *Coil stamps. As Nos.* 348/9, 352 *and* 356 *but photo., colours changed. Glossy paper. P* 12½.

70 1 c. reddish violet and pink .. 5 5
a. P 14. Chalk-surfaced paper (12.75) 5 5
71 2 c. bronze-grn. & yell.-ochre 5 5
a. Chalk-surfaced paper (7.75) .. 5 5
72 5 c. black and lt. slate-blue 5 5
73 10 c. deep violet-blue & lt. blue 12 15
a. P 14. Chalk-surfaced paper (4.76) 12 12

198. Voortrekker Monument and Encampment.

(*Illustration reduced. Actual size* 57 × 20 *mm.*)

(Des. J. Hoekstra.)

1974 (6 Dec.). 25*th. Anniv. of Voortrekker Monument, Pretoria. P* 12½.
374 **198** 4 c. multicoloured 8 8

199. SASOL Complex.

(Des. C. Webb.)

1975 (26 Feb.). 25*th Anniv. of SASOL* (*South African Coal, Oil and Gas Corporation Ltd.*). *P* 11½ × 12½.
375 **199** 15 c. multicoloured .. 20 25

200. President Diederichs. **201.** Jan Smuts.

(Des. J. L. Booysen. Recess (4 c.) or photo. (15 c.).)

1975 (19 Apr.). *Inauguration of the State President. P* 12½ × 11½.
376 **200** 4 c. agate and gold .. 8 8
377 ,, 15 c. royal blue 20 25

(Des. J. Hoekstra. Recess and photo.)

1975 (24 May). *Jan Smuts Commemoration. P* 12½ × 11½.
378 **201** 4 c. black & olive-black 8 8

202. Dutch East Indiaman, Table Bay.

(Des. J. Hoekstra. Photo. (Nos. 379/82) or litho. (**MS**383).)

1975 (18 June). *Death Centenary of Thomas Baines* (*painter*). *T* **202** *and similar horiz. designs. Multicoloured. P* 11½ × 12½.
379 5 c. Type **202** 8 8
380 9 c. Cradock, 1848 .. .. 12 12
381 15 c. Thirsty Flat, 1848 .. 20 20
382 30 c. Pretoria, 1874 .. .. 35 40
MS383 120 × 95 mm. Nos. 379/82 80 80

203. Gideon Malherbe's House, Paarl.

(Des. P. de Wet. Recess and photo.)

1975 (14 Aug.). *Centenary of Genootskap van Regte Afrikaners* (*Afrikaner Language Movement*). *P* 12½.
384 **203** 4 c. multicoloured .. 5 5

204. "Automatic Sorting". **205.** Title Page of *Die Afrikaanse Patriot.*

(Des. J. Sampson.)

1975 (11 Sept.). *Postal Mechanisation. P* 12½ × 11½.
385 **204** 4 c. multicoloured .. 5 5

(Des. K. Esterhuysen. Recess and photo. (4 c.). Des. P. de Wet. Litho (5 c.).)

1975 (10 Oct.). *Inauguration of the Language Monument, Paarl. T* **205** *and similar vert. design. P* 12½ × 11½.
386 4 c. black, pale stone and bright orange 5 5
387 5 c. multicoloured 5 5
Design:—5 c. "Afrikaanse Taalmonument".

206. Table Mountain.

(*Illustration reduced. Actual size* 57 × 20 *mm.*)

(Des. P. Bosman and J. Hoekstra. Litho.)

1975 (13 Nov.). *Tourism. T* **206** *and similar horiz. designs. Multicoloured. P* 12½.
388 15 c. Type **206** 20 20
389 15 c. Johannesburg 20 20
390 15 c. Cape Vineyards 20 20
391 15 c. Lions in Kruger National Park 20 20

Nos. 388/91 were printed together, in *se-tenant* blocks of 4 within the sheet.

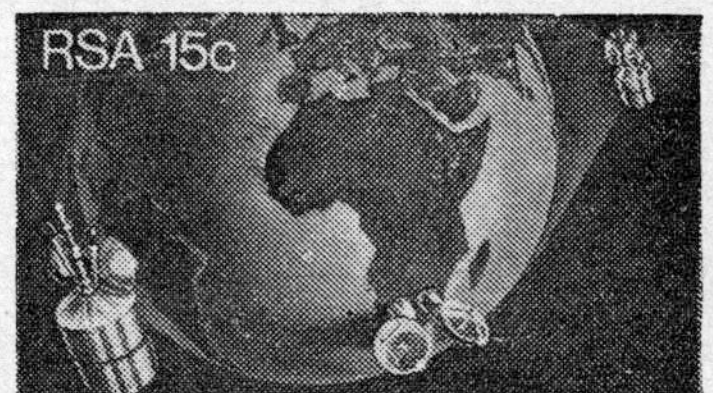

207. Globe and Satellites.

(Des. J. Hoekstra. Litho.)

1975 (3 Dec.). *Satellite Communication. P* 12½.
392 **207** 15 c. multicoloured .. 20 20

208. Bowls. (209)

(Des. J. Maskew. Litho.)

1976. *Sporting Commemorations. T* **208** *and similar vert. designs. P* 12½ × 11½.

393	15 c. blk. & lt. sage-grn. (18.2)	20	20
394	15 c. blk. & brt. yell.-grn. (15.3)	20	20
395	15 c. blk. & pale yell.-ol. (16.8)	20	20
396	15 c. blk. & apple-green (2.12)	20	20
MS397	161 × 109 mm. Nos. 393/6 (2.12)	90	

Designs: No. 393, Type **208** (World Bowls Championships, Johannesburg); No. 394, Batsman (Centenary of Organised Cricket in South Africa); No. 395, Polo player; No. 396, Gary Player (golfer).

1976 (6 Apr.). *South Africa's Victory in World Bowls Championships. No.* 393 *optd. with T* **209** *in gold.*

398 **208**	15 c. black & lt. sage-grn.	20	25

210. Hut and Baobab Tree.

(Des. J. Hoekstra. Photo. (4 c.) or litho. (others and **MS**403).)

1976 (20 Apr.). *Birth Centenary of Erich Mayer (painter). T* **210** *and similar horiz. designs. Multicoloured. P* 11½ × 12½.

399	4 c. Type **210**	5	5
	a. Imperf. (pair)		
400	10 c. Ox wagons	12	15
401	15 c. Harbeespoort Dam ..	15	20
402	20 c. Street scene, Doornfontein	25	25
MS403	121 × 95 mm. Nos. 396/9	60	

211. Cheetah.

(Des. P. Bosman. Photo. (3 c.) or litho. (others).)

1976 (5 June). *World Environmental Day. T* **211** *and similar horiz. designs. Multicoloured. P* 11½ × 12½.

404	3 c. Type **211**	5	5
405	10 c. Black Rhino	12	15
406	15 c. Bontebok	15	20
407	20 c. Mountain Zebra	25	25

212. Emily Hobhouse. 214. Family with Globe.

213. Early Mailship.

(Des. J. Hoekstra.)

1976 (8 June). *50th Death Anniv. of Emily Hobhouse (welfare worker). P* 12½ × 11½.

408 **212**	4 c. multicoloured ..	5	5

(Des. K. Esterhuysen. Litho.)

1976 (5 Oct.). *Ocean Mail Service Centenary. P* 11½ × 12½.

409 **213**	10 c. multicoloured ..	12	15
	a. Imperf. (horiz. pair) ..		

(Des. I. Ross.)

1976 (6 Nov.). *Family Planning and Child Welfare. P* 12½ × 11½.

410 **214**	4 c. chestnut & lt. salmon	5	5

215. Glasses of Wine. 216. Dr. Jacob du Toit.

(Des. H. Botha. Litho.)

1977 (14 Feb.). *International Wine Symposium, Cape Town. P* 12½ × 11½.

411 **215**	15 c. multicoloured ..	20	25

(Des. J. Hoekstra.)

1977 (21 Feb.). *Birth Centenary of J. D. du Toit (theologian and poet). P* 12½ × 11½.

412 **216**	4 c. multicoloured ..	5	5

POSTAGE DUE STAMPS.

D 1

UNION OF SOUTH AFRICA (A.)

UNION OF SOUTH AFRICA (B.)

(Typo. De La Rue.)

1914–22. *Type* **D 1.** *Inscribed bilingually. Lettering as* A. *W* **4.** *P* 14.

		Un. single	*Used single*
D1	½d. black and green (19.3.15)	15	30
D2	1d. black and scarlet (19.3.15)	10	10
D3	2d. blk. & reddish vio. (12.12.14)	35	15
	a. Black and bright violet ('22)	45	15
D4	3d. blk. & bright blue (2.2.15)	15	20
D5	5d. black and sepia (19.3.15)	1·10	1·75
D6	6d. black and slate (19.3.15) ..	2·25	3·00
D7	1s. red and black (19.3.15) ..	20·00	25·00

There are interesting minor varieties in some of the above values, e.g. ½d. to 3d., thick downstroke to "d"; 1d., short serif to "1"; raised "d"; 2d., forward point of "2" blunted; 3d., raised "d"; very thick "d".

(Litho. Govt. Printer, Pretoria.)

1922. *Type* D **1.** *Lettering as* A. *No wmk. Rouletted.*

D 8	½d. black & brt. grn. (6.6.22)	12	40
D 9	1d. black & rose-red (3.10.22)	20	40
D10	1½d. black & yell.-brn. (3.6.22)	35	70

(Litho. Govt. Printer, Pretoria.)

1922–26. *Type* D **1** *redrawn. Lettering as* B. *P* 14.

D11	½d. black and green (1.11.22)	5	12
D12	1d. black and rose (16.5.23)	5	5
D13	1½d. black & yell.-brn. (12.1.24)	8	15
D14	2d. black & pale vio. (16.5.23)	8	15
	a. Imperf. (pair)	50·00	
	b. Black and deep violet ..	1·00	30
D15	3d. black and blue (3.7.26) ..	1·50	1·00
D16	6d. black & slate (Sept. '23)	1·50	1·00

The locally printed stamps, perf. 14, differ both in border design and in figures of value from the rouletted stamps. All values except the 3d. and 6d. are known with closed "G" in "POSTAGE" usually referred to as the "POSTADE" variety. This was corrected in later printings.

D 2 D 3

(Typo. Pretoria.)

1927–28. *As Type* D **2.** *Inscribed bilingually. No wmk. P* 13½ × 14.

D17	½d. black and green ..	5	12
D18	1d. black and carmine ..	5	8
D19	2d. black and mauve ..	8	15
	a. Black and purple	75	75
D20	3d. black and blue	1·00	1·00
D21	6d. black and slate	1·50	1·2

1932–42. *Type* D **2** *redrawn. W* **9.** *P* 15 × 14.

(*a*) *Frame roto., value typo.*

D22	½d. blk. & blue-grn. (–.–.34)	5	1
D23	2d. blk. & dp. pur. (10.4.33)	20	1

(*b*) *Whole stamp roto.*

D25	1d. black & carm. (–.3.34) ..	5	5
D26	2d. blk. & dp. pur. ('40) ..	5	5
	a. Thick (double) "2d." ..	5·00	5·00
D27	3d. black & Prussian blue (3.8.32)	1·25	4

D28 3d. deep blue and blue ('35) 12 10
a. Indigo and milky blue ('42) 15 10
D29 6d. grn. & brn.-ochre (7.6.33) 2·00 75
a. Green and bright orange ('38) 40 20

In No. D26 the value, when magnified, has the meshed appearance of a photogravure screen, whereas in No. D23 the black of the value is solid.

1943–47. *Inscr. bilingually. Roto. W.9. In units of three, perf.* 15 × 14 *subdivided by roulette* 6½.

		Un. unit	Us. unit
D30 D 3	½d. blue-green ('47) ..	20	25
D31 „	1d. carmine	8	25
D32 „	2d. dull violet	10	30
	a. Bright violet	20	50
D33 „	3d. indigo ('45)	20	50

D 4

D 5

1948–49. *New figure of value and capital* "D". *Whole stamp roto. W* 9. *P* 15 × 14.

		Un. single	Us. single
D34 D 4	½d. black and blue-green	5	12
D35 „	1d. black and carmine ..	8	12
D36 „	2d. black and violet ('49)	5	12
	a. Thick (double) "2D." ..	3·00	3·00
D37 „	3d. deep blue and blue ..	10	20
D38 „	6d. green & bright orange	15	20

1950–58. *As Type* D 4, *but* "SUID-AFRIKA" *hyphenated. Whole stamp roto. W* 9. *P* 15 × 14.

D39	1d. black and carmine ..	5	8
D40	2d. black and violet (*shades*)	5	5
	a. Thick (double) "2D" ..	3·00	3·00
D41	3d. deep blue and blue ..	12	8
D42	4d. dp. myrtle-grn. & emer.	15	12
D43	6d. green and bright orange	50	25
D44	1s. blk.-brn. & purple-brown	1·00	1·00

Dates of issue:— -.5.50, Nos. D39 and D41; -.4.51, No. D40; 1952, No. D43; 1958, Nos. D42, D44.

1961 (14 FEB.). *Values in cents as Type D* 5. *Whole stamp roto. W* 102. *P* 15 × 14.

D45	1 c. black and carmine ..	5	10
D46	2 c. black and violet ..	5	10
D47	4 c. dp. myrtle-grn. & emer.	15	30
D48	5 c. deep blue and blue ..	50	40
D49	6 c. green and orange-red ..	75	1·00
D50	10 c. sepia and brown-lake ..	1·25	1·50
D45/D50	.. .. *Set of* 6	2·50	3·00

REPUBLIC.

D 6. Afrikaans at top.

D 7. English at top.

1961 (31 MAY)–**69.** *Roto. W* 102. *P* 15 × 14.

D51 D 6	1 c. black and carmine	10	15
D52 D 7	1 c. blk. & carm. (6.62)	5	5
D53 „	2 c. black and deep reddish violet ..	5	5
D54 D 6	4 c. deep myrtle-green and light emerald	8	8
D54a D 7	4 c. dp. myrtle-grn. & lt. emerald (6.69)	8	8
D55 „	5 c. dp. blue & grey-bl.	30	35
D56 „	5 c. black and grey-blue (6.62) ..	15	20
D57 D 6	6 c. dp. grn. & red-orge.	20	25
D58 D 7	10 c. sepia & purple-brn.	25	30
D51/58	.. .. *Set of* 9	1·10	1·25

1967 (DEC.)–**71.** *Roto. W* 127 (*tête-bêche*) *P* 15 × 14.

D59 D 6	1 c. black and carmine	5	5
D60 D 7	1 c. black and carmine	5	5
D61 D 6	2 c. black and deep reddish violet	5	5
	a. Perf. 14	12	12
D62 D 7	2 c. black and deep reddish violet	5	5
	a. Perf. 14	12	12
D62b „	4 c. deep myrtle-grn. & light emer. (6.69)*	75	75
D62c D 6	4 c. deep myrtle-grn. & light emer. (6.69)*		
D63 „	4 c. blk. & p. grn. (4.71)	8	5
	a. Perf. 14	35	35
D64 D 7	4 c. blk. & p. grn. (4.71)	8	5
	a. Perf. 14	35	35
D65 D 6	5 c. black & deep blue	8	8
D66 D 7	5 c. black & deep blue	8	8
D67 D 6	6 c. green and orange-red ('68)	8	8
D68 D 7	6 c. green and orange-red ('68)	8	8
D69 D 6	10 c. black & purp.-brn.	20	20
	a. Blk. & brown-lake (12.69)	15	15
D70 D 7	10 c. black & purp.-brn.	20	20
	a. Blk. & brown-lake (12.69)	15	15
D59/70a *except* D62b/c	*Set of* 12	85	85

Nos. D59/70 are printed in two panes, one with inscriptions as Type D 6 and the other as Type D 7.

* Nos. D62b/c were part of a printing of No. D54a. Most were printed on paper with the Arms watermark, but some were printed on RSA paper with the watermark upright and faint. Most of these were spoiled but a few sheets were issued in Types D 7 and D 6, the latter being very scarce.

D 8

1972 (22 MAR.). *English at right* (1, 4 *and* 8 *c.*) *or at left* (*others*). *W* 127 (*sideways tête-bêche*). *Phosphorised paper. P* 14 × 13½.

D71 D 8	1 c. deep olive	5	5
D72 „	2 c. bright orange ..	5	5
D73 „	4 c. plum	5	5
D74 „	6 c. chrome-yellow ..	8	8
	a. Phosphorised glossy paper	20	25
D75 „	8 c. ultramarine ..	10	12
D76 „	10 c. bright scarlet ..	12	12
D71/6	.. .. *Set of* 6	40	40

The 6 c. also exists on non-phosphor glossy paper.

OFFICIAL STAMPS.

OFFICIAL. OFFISIEEL.

(O 1)

(Approximate measurements between lines of opt. are shown in mm. in brackets.)

1926 (1 DEC.). *Optd. vertically upwards, with stops, as Type* O 1.

		Un. single	Us. single
	(*a*) *On* 1913 *issue*		
O1 3	2d. Nos. 6/6a (12½)	4·00	1·00
		Un. pair	**Us. pair**
	(*b*) *On* 1926 *issue*		
O2 6	½d. No. 30 (12½)	1·25	1·50
O3 7	1d. No. 31 (12½)	60	75
O4 8	6d. No. 32 (12½)	£125	15·00

This overprint is found on the ½d., 1d. and 6d. values of both the London and Pretoria printings. The London printings of the ½d. and 1d. stamps are considerably scarcer than the Pretoria, but the 6d. Pretoria printing is scarcer still.

1928–29. *Optd. vertically upwards, as Type* O 1. *but without stops.*

O5 11	2d. No. 34 (17½)	40	70
O6 „	2d. No. 34 (19) ('29) ..	40	70
O7 8	6d. No. 32 (11½)	2·50	3·00

OFFISIEEL OFFICIAL

(O 2)

OFFICIAL OFFISIEEL

(O 3)

Overprinted vertically downwards as Type O 2.

1929. *Typographed stamps optd. with Type* O 2.

		Un. pair	Us pair
O 8 6	½d. No. 30 (13½)	15	15
	a. Stop after "OFFISIEEL" on English stamp ..	3·00	2·00
	b. Do. On Afrikaans stamp..	4·00	2·00
O 9 7	1d. No. 31 (13½)	25	30
O10 8	6d. No. 32 (13½)	75	1·00
	a. Stop after "OFFISIEEL" on English stamp ..	5·00	5·00
	b. Do. On Afrikaans stamp..	6·00	6·00

1930–47. *Rotogravure stamps* ("SUIDAFRIKA" *in one word*) *optd. with Type* O 2.

O11 6	½d. No. 42 (9½–12) ..	25	25
	a. Stop after "OFFISIEEL" on English stamp ..	3·00	3·00
	b. Do. On Afrikaans stamp ..	2·50	2·50
O12 „	½d. No. 42 (12½)	25	25
O13 7	1d. No. 43 (12½ and 13½) ..	25	25
	a. Stop after "OFFISIEEL" on English stamp	2·00	2·00
	b. Do. On Afrikaans stamp..	3·00	3·00
	c. Opt. double	75·00	
O14 „	1d. No. 43c (12½) ..	40	40
O15 11	2d. No. 44 (21) ..	50	60
O15a „	2d. No. 44b (20½)	6·00	7·00
O16 8	6d. No. 47 (12½) ..	1·50	1·25
	a. Stop after "OFFISIEEL" on English stamp	4·00	5·00
	b. Do. On Afrikaans stamp ..	3·00	3·00
O17 13	1s. No. 48 (19)	5·00	6·00
O18 „	1s. No. 48 (21)	4·00	3·00
O19 14	2s. 6d. No. 49 (18) ..	7·00	7·00
O20 „	2s. 6d. No. 49 (21) ..	7·00	7·00
O20a „	2s. 6d. No. 49a (19½–20)	6·00	6·00
	ab. Diaeresis on second "E"	£175	

Nos. O8a/b, O10a/b, O11a/b, O13a/b and O16a/b. The pairs include one stamp with variety and the other normal. In No. O20ab the variety occurs on both the English and Afrikaans stamps.

Dates of issue:—1930, Nos. O13, O16; 1931, Nos. O11, O15; 1932, Nos. O12, O14, O17; 1933, No. O19; 1938, No. O18; 1939, Nos. O15a, O20; 1946, No. O20a; 1947, No. O20ab.

Nos. O17 to O20 were actually issued after Nos. O21 and O22, but are placed before them, in this list for convenience of reference.

1932–33. *Recess-printed stamps optd. with Type* O 2.

O21 13	1s. No. 36 (17½, 18 and 20½)	3·00	4·00
	a. Stop after "OFFICIAL" on Afrikaans stamp.. ..	20·00	20·00
O22 14	2s. 6d. No. 37 (17½ and 18)	4·00	6·00
	a. Stop after "OFFICIAL" on Afrikaans stamp.. ..	25·00	25·00

Nos. O21a and O22a. The pairs include one stamp with variety and the other normal.

1935–51. *Rotogravure stamps* ("SUID-AFRIKA" *hyphenated*). (*a*) *Optd. with Type* O 2 ("OFFICIAL" *at right*).

O23 6	½d. No. 54 (12½) ..	30	30
O24 24	½d. No. 64c (11 and 12½)	30	20
O24a „	½d. No. 64d (12) ..	20	20
O24b „	½d. No. 114 (11) ..	15	15
O25 7	1d. No. 56 (11½–13) ..	15	15
O26 22	1½d. No. 57 (20)	75	50
O26a „	1½d. No. 57a (20) ..	50	30
O26b 34a	1½d. No. 87 (14½) ..	15	15
	ba. Diaeresis on second "E"	10·00	7·00

				Un.	Us.
O26c	34a	1½d. No. 87 (16)	..	50	70
O27	11	2d. No. 58 (20) ..	..	1·00	1·00
O27a	54	2d. No. 107 (20)	..	20	30
		ab. Diaeresis on second "E"		25·00	15·00
O27b	,,	2d. No. 107a (20)	..	30	30
O28	8	6d. No 61 (12 and 13)	..	12·00	7·00
O28a	,,	6d. No. 61a (11½–13)	..	75	80
O28b	,,	6d. No. 61b (12)	..	60	55
O29	13	1s. No. 62 (20) ..	..	60	70
		aa. Diaeresis on second "E"			
O29a	,,	1s. No. 120 (17½–18½)	..	70	1·00
O29b	15	5s. No. 64a (20)	..	4·00	4·00
O29c	23	10s. No. 64b (19½)	..	13·00	12·00

(b) *Optd. with Type* O **3** (" OFFICIAL " *at left*).

O30	15	5s. No. 64a (18)..	..	5·00	5·00
O31	23	10s. No. 64b (19) ..	..	10·00	10·00

Dates of issue:—1935, O25; 1937, O23, O26; 1938, O24, O27, O28; 1940, O28a, O29, O30, O31; 1942, O26a; 1946?, O26ba, O29aa; 1947, O26b, O27a, O27ab, O28b; 1948, O24a; 1949, O24b, O27b; 1950, O26c, O29a, O29c; 1951, O29b.

The pairs of Nos. O26ba, O27ab and O29aa include one stamp with variety and one normal.

OFFICIAL OFFISIEEL (O 4)

OFFISIEEL OFFICIAL (O 5)

1944. *Optd. with Type* O **4** *reading up and down and with diæresis over the second* "E" *of* "OFFISIEEL".

				Un. pair	Us. pair
O32	24	½d. No. 64d (10) ..	..	15	15

1944. *Optd. with Type* O **5** *reading upwards* ("OFFICIAL" *at right*).

O33	11	2d. No. 58a (18½) ..	..	15	15

OFFICIAL OFFISIEEL (O 6)

OFFISIEEL OFFICIAL (O 7)

1949–50. *Optd. with Type* O **6** *reading upwards* (" OFFICIAL " *at left*).

O34	34a	1½d. No. 87 (16) ..	..	45	45
O35	68	2d. No. 134 ((16) ('50)	..	80·00	

1950–54. *Optd. as Type* O **7.**

O35a	24	½d. No. 64d (10)	..	5	8
O35b	,,	½d. No. 114 (10)	..	5	8
O36	7	1d. No. 56a (10)	..	8	8
O36a	,,	1d. No. 115 (10)	..	5	8
O36b	,,	1d. No. 135 (10)	..	8	8
O37	34a	1½d. No. 87 (14½)	..	8	8
O38	68	2d. No. 134 (14½)	..	8	8
O39	8	6d. No. 119 (10)	..	15	15
O39a	,,	6d. No. 119a (10)	..	15	15
O40	13	1s. No. 120 (19)	..	35	30
O40a	,,	1s. No. 120a (19)	..	35·00	10·00
O41	14	2s. 6d. No. 121 (19)	..	1·50	1·00
O41a	15	5s. No. 64a (19)	..	4·00	4·00
O41b	,,	5s. No. 122 (19)	..	5·00	5·00
O41c	,,	5s. No. 122a (19)	..	5·00	7·00
O42	23	10s. No. 64ba (19)	..	8·00	7·00

Dates of issue:—1950, Nos. O36, O38/9 and O40/2; 1951, Nos. O35a, O36a, O37, O39a and O41a; 1952, No. O36b; 1953, Nos. O35b, O40a and O41b; 1954, No. O41c.

On No. O36a the overprint is thicker.

The use of official stamps ceased in January 1955.

SOUTH ARABIA.

The stamps of the Aden States surcharged in fils and dinars and with the word " ADEN " obliterated and replaced by " SOUTH ARABIA " (or commemorative inscription also) are listed under the Aden States.

SOUTH ARABIAN FEDERATION.

Comprising Aden and most of the territories of the former Western Aden Protectorate plus one from the Eastern Aden Protectorate.

Currency. 100 cents = 1 shilling.

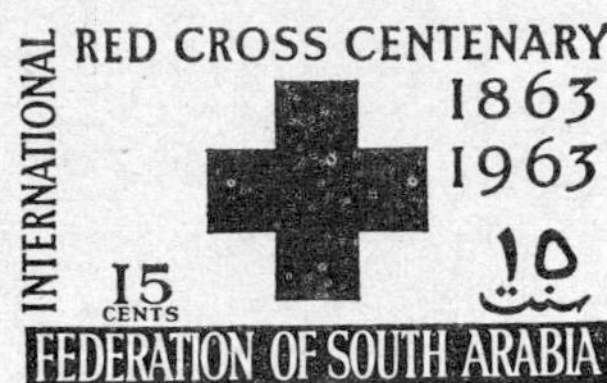

1. Red Cross Emblem.

1963 (25 Nov.). *Red Cross Centenary.* *W* w.12. *P* 13½.

1	**1**	15 c. red and black	12	15
2	,,	1s. 25, red and blue	30	45

(New currency. 1,000 fils = 1 dinar.)

2. Federal Crest.

3. Federal Flag.

(Des. V. Whiteley. Photo. Harrison.)

1965 (1 Apr.). *P* 14½×14 (*T* **1**) *or* 14½ (*T* **2**).

3	**2**	5 f. blue	5	5
4	,,	10 f. violet-blue	5	5
5	,,	15 f. turquoise-green ..	5	5
6	,,	20 f. green	5	5
7	,,	25 f. yellow-brown	8	5
8	,,	30 f. yellow-bistre	8	5
9	,,	35 f. chestnut	10	8
10	,,	50 f. red	12	12
11	,,	65 f. yellow-green	25	35
12	,,	75 f. crimson	25	45
13	**3**	100 f. multicoloured.. ..	25	25
14	,,	250 f. multicoloured.. ..	55	55
15	,,	500 f. multicoloured.. ..	1·50	1·40
16	,,	1 d. multicoloured.. ..	2·50	2·00
3/16		.. .. *Set of* 14	5·00	5·00

4. I.C.Y. Emblem.

(Des. V. Whiteley. Litho. Harrison.)

1965 (24 Oct.). *International Co-operation Year.* *W* w.12. *P* 14½.

17	**4**	5 f. reddish purple and turquoise-green	5	5
18	,,	65 f. dp. bluish green. & lav.	25	25

5. Sir Winston Churchill and St. Paul's Cathedral in Wartime.

(Des. Jennifer Toombs. Photo. Harrison.)

1966 (24 Jan.). *Churchill Commemoration. No wmk.* *P* 14.

19	**5**	5 f. black, cerise, gold and new blue	5	5
20	,,	10 f. black, cerise, gold and deep green	5	5
21	,,	65 f. black, cerise, gold and brown	20	30
22	,,	125 f. black, cerise, gold and bluish violet	50	60

6. Footballer's Legs, Ball and Jules Rimet Cup.

(Des. V. Whiteley. Litho. Harrison.)

1966 (1 July). *World Cup Football Championships. No wmk.* *P* 14.

23	**6**	10 f. violet, yellow-green, lake and yellow-brown ..	5	5
24	,,	50 f. chocolate, blue-grn., lake and yellow-brown ..	15	15

7. W.H.O. Building.

(Des. M. Goaman. Litho. Harrison.)

1966 (20 Sept.). *Inauguration of W.H.O. Headquarters, Geneva. No wmk.* *P* 14.

25	**7**	10 f. black, yellow-green and light blue	5	5
26	,,	75 f. black, light purple and yellow-brown	20	25

8. " Education ".

9. " Science ".

10. " Culture ".

(Des. Jennifer Toombs. Litho. Harrison.)

1966 (15 Dec.). *20th Anniv. of U.N.E.S.C.O. No wmk.* *P* 14.

27	**8**	10 f. slate-violet, red, yellow and orange ..	5	5
28	**9**	65 f. orange-yellow, violet and deep olive ..	20	40
29	**10**	125 f. black, bright purple and orange	40	80

The South Arabian Federation became fully independent on 30th November 1967. Later issues for this area will be found listed in Vol. 4 of the Stanley Gibbons Foreign Overseas Catalogue, under Yemen, People's Democratic Republic.

MINIMUM PRICE

The minimum price quoted is 5p which represents a handling charge rather than a basis for valuing common stamps. For further notes about prices see introductory pages.

SOUTH AUSTRALIA.

1

2. Large Star.

(Eng. Wm. Humphrys. Recess. Perkins, Bacon.)

1855. *Printed in London.* W 2. *Imperf.*
1 1 1d. dark green (26.10.55) .. £950 £130
2 ,, 2d. rose-carm. (*shades*) (1.1.55) £375 55·00
3 ,, 6d. deep blue (26.10.55) .. £750 60·00

NOTE.—Proofs of the 1d. and 6d. without wmk. exist, and these are found with forged star watermarks added, and are sometimes offered as originals.

For reprints of the above and later issues, see note after No. 194.

Prepared and sent to the Colony, but not issued.
4 1 1s. violet £1500

A printing of 500,000 of these 1s. stamps was made and delivered, but as the colour was liable to be confused with that of the 6d. stamp, the stock was destroyed on 5th June, 1857.

1856–58. *Printed by Govt. Ptr., Adelaide, from Perkins, Bacon plates.* W 2. *Imperf.*
5 1 1d. dp. yellow-green (15.6.58) £1500 £225
6 ,, 1d. yellow-green (11.10.58) .. — £250
7 ,, 2d. orange-red (23.4.56) .. — 55·00
8 ,, 2d. blood-red (14.11.56) .. £400 50·00
a. printed on both sides ..
9 ,, 2d. red (*shades*) (29.10.57) .. £225 23·00
a. printed on both sides .. — £275
10 ,, 6d. slate-blue (July, '57) .. £675 £110
11 ,, 1s. red-orange (8.7.57) .. — £250
12 ,, 1s. orange (11.6.58) £1100 £225

1858–59. W 2. *Rouletted.* (*This first rouletted issue has the same colours as the local imperf. issue.*)
13 1 1d. yellow-green (8.1.59) .. £150 19·00
14 ,, 1d. light yellow-grn. (18.3.59) £150 22·00
a. Imperf. between (pair) ..
15 ,, 2d. red (17.2.59) .. .. 40·00 6·50
a. Printed on both sides ..
17 ,, 6d. slate-blue (12.12.58) .. £110 11·00
18 ,, 1s. orange (18.3.59) .. .. £275 13·00
a. Printed on both sides .. — £350

3

4

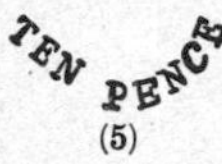

(5)

1860–69. *Second rouletted issue, printed in colours only found rouletted or perforated. Surch. with* T 5 (*Nos.* 35/7). W 2.
19 1 1d. brt. yellow-grn. (22.4.61) 22·00 7·50
20 ,, 1d. dull blue-grn. (17.12.63) 18·00 7·00
21 ,, 1d. sage-green .. .. 24·00 7·50
22 ,, 1d. pale sage-grn. (27.5.65) 18·00
23 ,, 1d. deep green (1864) .. 80·00 24·00
24 ,, 1d. deep yellow-grn. (1869) 38·00
24*a* ,, 2d. pale red .. .. .. 20·00 1·75
b. Printed on both sides .. — £120
25 ,, 2d. pale vermilion (3.2.63) .. 18·00 1·75
26 1 2d. bright verm. (19.8.64) 13·00 1·00
a. Imperf. between (horiz. pair) — £110
27 3 4d. dull violet (24.1.67) .. 20·00 7·00
28 1 6d. violet-blue (19.3.60) .. 55·00 2·75
29 ,, 6d. greenish blue (11.2.63) 20·00 1·75
30 ,, 6d. dull ultram. (25.4.64) .. 19·00 1·75
a. Imperf. between (horiz. pair) — £110
31 ,, 6d. violet-ultram. (11.4.68) 55·00 2·75
32 ,, 6d. dull blue (26.8.65) .. 35·00 3·00
a. Imperf. between (pair) .. — £200
33 ,, 6d. Prussian blue (7.9.69) .. £190 14·00
33*a* ,, 6d. indigo .. .. ..
34 4 9d. grey-lilac (24.12.60) .. 18·00 3·50
a. Imperf. between (horiz. pair)
35 ,, 10d. on 9d. orange-red (B.) (20.7.66) .. .. 35·00 7·00
36 ,, 10d. on 9d. yellow (B.) (29.7.67) .. .. 50·00 6·00
37 ,, 10d. on 9d. yellow (Bk.) (14.8.69) .. .. £550 10·00
a. Surch. inverted at the top .. — £1000
b. Printed on both sides .. — £275
38 1 1s. yellow (25.10.61) .. £130 10·00
a. Imperf. between (vert. pair)
39 ,, 1s. grey-brown (10.4.63) .. 60·00 7·00
40 ,, 1s. dark grey-brn. (26.5.63) 50·00 7·00
41 ,, 1s. chestnut (25.8.63) .. 50·00 5·00
42 ,, 1s. lake-brown (27.3.65) .. 42·00 5·00
a. Imperf. between (horiz. pair) — £130
43 3 2s. rose-carmine (24.1.67) 50·00 7·00
a. Imperf. between (vert. pair) — £225

1868–71. *Remainders of old stock subsequently perforated by the* 11½–12½ *machine.*

(*a*) *Imperf. stamps.* P 11½–12½.
44 1 2d. pale verm. (Feb. 1868) — £475
45 ,, 2d. vermilion (18.3.68) .. — £475

(*b*) *Rouletted stamps.* P 11½–12½.
46 1 1d. bright green (9.11.69) .. — £130
47 ,, 2d. pale vermilion (15.8.68) — £160
48 ,, 6d. Prussian blue (8.11.69) — 75·00
aa. Horiz. pair perf. all round, roul. between .. ..
48*a* ,, 6d. indigo .. .. ..
49 4 9d. grey-lilac (29.3.71) .. £350 65·00
a. Perf. × roulette .. .. — 60·00
49*b* 1 1s. lake-brown (23.5.70) ..

1867–70. W 2. P 11½–12½ × *roulette.*
50 1 1d. pale brt. grn. (2.11.67) 60·00 5·00
51 ,, 1d. bright green (1868) .. 48·00 5·00
52 ,, 1d. grey-green (26.1.70) .. 60·00 9·00
a. Imperf. between (horiz. pair)
53 ,, 1d. blue-green (29.11.67) .. 75·00 10·00
54 3 4d. dull violet (July, 1868) £475 50·00
55 ,, 4d. dull purple (1869) .. — 35·00
56 1 6d. brt. pale blue (29.5.67) £160 7·00
57 ,, 6d. Prussian blue (30.7.67) £130 7·00
a. Printed on both sides ..
58 ,, 6d. indigo (1.8.69) .. £160 10·00
59 4 10d. on 9d. yell. (B.) (2.2.69) £180 10·00
a. Printed on both sides .. — £200
60 1 1s. chestnut (April, 1868) 95·00 7·00
61 ,, 1s. lake-brown (3.3.69) .. 95·00 7·00

NOTE.—The stamps perf. 11½, 12½, or compound of the two, are here combined in one list, as both perforations are on the one machine, and all the varieties *may* be found in each sheet of stamps. This method of classifying the perforations by the machines is by far the most simple and convenient.

3-PENCE
(6)

1868–79. *Surch. with* T 6 (*Nos.* 66/8). W 2. P 11½–12½.
62 1 1d. pale brt. green (8.2.68) 60·00 6·00
63 ,, 1d. grey-green (18.2.68) .. 48·00 13·00
64 ,, 1d. dark green (20.3.68) .. 20·00 5·00
a. Printed on both sides ..
65 ,, 1d. deep yell.-grn. (28.6.72) 18·00 7·50
66 3 3d. on 4d. Prussian blue (Bk.) (7.2.71) .. .. — £200
67 ,, 3d. on 4d. sky-blue (Bk.) (12.8.70) .. .. 75·00 3·00
a. Imperf. .. .. ..
b. Rouletted .. .. — £150
68 ,, 3d. on 4d. deep ultram. (Bk.) (9.72) .. 18·00 2·50
a. Surch. double (10.9.74) .. — £1200
b. Additional surch. on back .. — £750
69 ,, 4d. deep ultramarine (error, T 3 omitted) (26.4.79) £2500 £2000
70 3 4d. dull purple (1.2.68) .. 20·00 6·0
a. Imperf. between (horiz. pair)
71 ,, 4d. dull violet (1868) .. 18·00 2·5
72 1 6d. brt. pale blue (23.2.68) £100 5·0
73 ,, 6d. Prussian blue (29.9.69) 35·00 2·2
a. P 11½ × imperf. (horiz. pr.)
74 ,, 6d. indigo (1869) .. .. 42·00 5·5
75 4 9d. claret (7.72) .. 42·00 3·0
76 ,, 9d. bright mauve (1.11.72) 42·00 3·0
a. Printed on both sides .. — £10
77 ,, 9d. red-purple (15.1.74) .. 17·00 2·7
78 ,, 10d. on 9d. yell. (B.) (15.8.68) £350 9·0
a. Error. Wmk. Crown and S A (1868) .. .. .. — £35
79 ,, 10d. on 9d. yellow (Bk.) (13.9.69) .. .. 70·00 10·0
80 1 1s. lake-brown (9.68) .. 60·00 5·0
81 ,, 1s. chestnut (8.10.72) .. 42·00 7·0
82 ,, 1s. dark red-brown .. 35·00 5·0
83 ,, 1s. red-brown (6.1.69) .. 42·00 5·0
84 3 2s. pale rose-pink (10.10.69) £300 55·0
85 ,, 2s. deep rose-pink (8.69) .. — 35·0
86 ,, 2s. crim.-carm. (16.10.69) 20·00 5·0
87 ,, 2s. carmine (1869) .. 18·00 3·2
a. Printed on both sides .. — 90·0

1870–71. W 2. P 10.
88 1 1d. grey-green (6.70) .. 48·00 7·0
89 ,, 1d. pale brt. green (9.8.70) 48·00 6·5
90 ,, 1d. bright green (1871) .. 35·00 6·5
91 3 3d. on 4d. dull ultram. (R.) (6.8.70) .. .. 90·00 14·0
92 ,, 3d. on 4d. pale ultram. (Bk.) (14.2.71) .. .. 70·00 5·0
93 ,, 3d. on 4d. ultramarine (Bk.) (14.8.71) .. .. 25·00 7·0
93*a* ,, 3d. on 4d. Prussian blue (Bk.) (16.12.71) ..
94 ,, 4d. dull lilac (1870) .. 42·00 5·0
95 ,, 4d. dull purple (1871) .. 35·00 5·0
96 1 6d. bright blue (19.6.70) .. 70·00 7·0
97 ,, 6d. indigo (11.10.71) .. 70·00 7·0
98 ,, 1s. chestnut (4.1.71) .. 60·00 7·0

1870–73. W 2. P 10 × 11½–12½, 11½–12½ × 10 *or compound.*
99 1 1d. pale bright green (11.10.70) .. .. 60·00 7·0
a. Printed on both sides ..
100 ,, 1d. grey-green .. 55·00 7·0
101 ,, 1d. deep green (19.6.71) .. 35·00 5·0
102 3 3d. on 4d. pale ultram. (Bk.) (9.11.70) .. .. 70·00 13·0
103 ,, 4d. dull lilac (11.5.72) .. — 4·5
104 ,, 4d. slate-lilac (5.3.73) .. 50·00 4·5
105 1 6d. Prussian blue (2.3.70) 42·00 3·0
106 ,, 6d. bright Prussian blue (26.10.70) .. 55·00 3·5
107 4 10d. on 9d. yell. (Bk.) (1.70) 40·00 5·0
108 1 1s. chestnut (17.6.71) .. — 10·0
109 3 2s. rose-pink (24.4.71) .. — 75·0
110 ,, 2s. carmine (2.3.72) .. 48·00 7·5

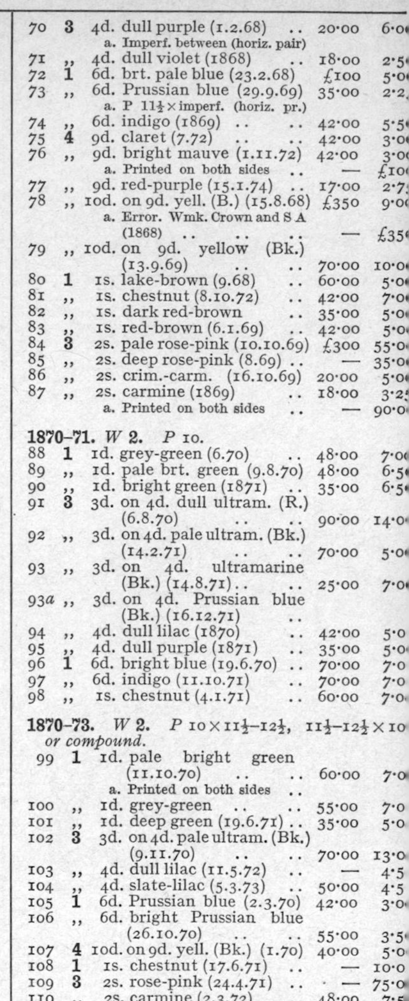

7 (=Victoria W 20.)

1871 (17 July). W 7. P 10.
111 3 4d. dull lilac .. .. £400 70·0
a. Printed on both sides ..

8. Broad Star.

8 PENCE
(9)

1876–1900. W 8. *Surch. with* T 9 (*Nos.* 118/21)
(*a*) P 11½–12½.
112 3 3d. on 4d. ultramarine (1.6.79) 13·00 5·0
a. Surch. double .. .. — £50

13 **3** 4d. violet-slate (15.3.79) .. 40·00 5·00
14 „ 4d. plum (16.4.80) .. 18·00 2·75
15 „ 4d. deep mauve (8.6.82) .. 17·00 1·75
16 **1** 6d. indigo (2.12.76) .. 30·00 1·50
a. Imperf. between (horiz. pr.)
17 „ 6d. Prussian blue (7.78) .. 17·00 1·25
18 **4** 8d. on 9d. brn.-orge. (7.76) 14·00 1·00
19 „ 8d. on 9d. burnt umber ('80) 18·00 70
20 „ 8d. on 9d. brown (9.3.80).. 17·00 80
a. Imperf. between (vert. pr.) £100
21 „ 8d. on 9d., grey-brn. (10.5.81) 14·00 1·10
a. Surch. double .. .. — £100
22 „ 9d. purple (9.3.80) .. .. 13·00 2·75
a. Printed on both sides .. — 75·00
23 „ 9d. rose-lilac (21.8.80) .. 3·25 70
24 „ 9d. rose-lilac (*large holes*) (26.5.00) .. .. 3·25 1·00
25 **1** 1s. red-brown (3.11.77) .. 14·00 1·10
a. Imperf. between (horiz. pr.) — 90·00
26 „ 1s. reddish lake-brn. ('80).. 15·00 1·40
27 „ 1s. lake-brown (9.1.83) .. 17·00 1·25
28 „ 1s. Vandyke brown (1891) 20·00 3·50
29 „ 1s. dull brown (1891) .. 13·00 1·25
30 „ 1s. choc. (*large holes*) (6.5.97) 7·00 1·10
a. Imperf. vert. (horiz. pair)
31 „ 1s. sepia (*large holes*) (22.5.00) 7·00 1·25
a. Imperf. between (vert. pair) 50·00
32 **3** 2s. carmine (15.2.77) .. 7·00 1·25
a. Imperf. between (horiz. pr.)
b. Imperf. (pair) .. ..
33 „ 2s. rose-carmine (1885) .. 9·00 2·75
34 „ 2s. rose-carmine (*large holes*) (6.12.98) .. .. 9·00 2·25

The perforation with larger, clean-cut holes resulted from the fitting of the machine with new pins.

(*b*) *P* 10.

35 **1** 6d. Prussian blue (11.11.79) 35·00 6·00
36 „ 6d. bright blue (1879) .. 42·00 5·00
36*a* „ 1s. reddish lake-brown .. 35·00

(*c*) *P* 10×11½–12½, 11½×12×10, *or compound.*

37 **3** 4d. violet-slate (21.5.79) .. 42·00 4·50
38 „ 4d. dull purple (4.10.79) .. 10·00 1·00
39 **1** 6d. Prussian blue (29.12.77) 13·00 1·00
40 „ 6d. bright blue .. .. 20·00 2·25
41 „ 6d. bright ultramarine .. 13·00 60
42 „ 1s. reddish lake-brn. (9.2.85) 26·00 2·75
43 „ 1s. dull brown (29.6.86) .. 35·00 3·00
44 **3** 2s. carmine (27.12.77) .. 13·00 1·25
45 „ 2s. rose-carmine (1887) .. 13·00 1·00
a. Imperf. between (horiz. pr.) — £130

10

201–2. *Wmk. Crown SA (wide), T* **10.** *P* 11½–12½, *large holes*).

6 **4** 9d. claret (1.2.02) .. .. 3·50 3·50
7 **1** 1s. dull brown (12.6.01) .. 5·00 3·00
8 „ 1s. dark reddish brn. ('02) 5·00 3·50
a. Imperf. between (vert. pr.)
9 „ 1s. red-brown (aniline) (18.7.02) .. .. 5·00 3·50
0 **3** 2s. crimson (29.8.01) .. 7·00 4·00
1 „ 2s. carmine .. .. 4·50 2·75

(Plates and electrotypes by De La Rue & Co. Printed in Adelaide.)

11

12

1868–76. *W* **10.** (*a*) *Rouletted.*

152 **12** 2d. deep brick-red (8.68).. 16·00 1·10
153 „ 2d. pale orge.-red (5.10.68) 16·00 1·00
a. Printed on both sides .. — 75·00
b. Imperf. between (horiz. pr.) — 75·00

(*b*) *P* 11½–12½.

154 **11** 1d. blue-green (10.1.75) .. 24·00 5·00
155 **12** 2d. pale orge.-red (5.5.69) £275 65·00

(*c*) *P* 11½–12½ × *roulette.*

156 **12** 2d. pale orge.-red (20.8.69) — 40·00

(*d*) *P* 10 × *roulette.*

157 **12** 2d. pale orge.-red (7.5.70) 75·00 6·50

(*e*) *P* 10.

158 **11** 1d. blue-green (4.75) .. 7·00 1·10
159 **12** 2d. brick-red (4.70) .. 3·25 10
160 „ 2d. orange-red (1.7.70) .. 3·25 10
a. Printed on both sides .. — 48·00

(*f*) *P* 10×11½–12½, 11½–12½×10, *or compound.*

161 **11** 1d. blue-green (27.8.75) .. 13·00 4·50
162 **12** 2d. brick-red (19.1.71) .. £120 3·25
163 „ 2d. orange red (3.2.71) .. — 4·00
a. Imperf. (8.76) .. ..

1869. *Wmk. Large Star, T* **2.**

(*a*) *Rouletted.*

164 **12** 2d. orange-red (13.3.69) .. 16·00 3·25

(*b*) *P* 11½–12½ × *roulette.*

165 **12** 2d. orange-red (1.8.69) .. — 32·00

(*c*) *P* 11½–12½.

165*a* **12** 2d. orange-red (7.69) ..

1871 (15 July). *Wmk. V and Crown, T* **7.** *P* 10.

166 **12** 2d. brick-red .. .. 16·00 4·00

13

HALF-

PENNY

(14)

1876–85. *Wmk. Crown SA (close), T* **13.** (*a*) *P* 10.

167 **11** 1d. blue-green (9.2.76) .. 65 8
168 „ 1d. yellowish green (11.78) 80 8
169 „ 1d. deep green (11.79) .. 1·00 8
a. Imperf. between (horiz. pr.)
170 **12** 2d. orange-red (8.76) .. 80 8
171 „ 2d. dull brick-red (21.5.77) 80 8
172 „ 2d. blood-red (31.10.79) .. 40·00 1·10
173 „ 2d. pale red (4.85) .. 80 8

(*b*) *P* 10×11½–12½, *or* 11½–12½×10, *or compound.*

174 **11** 1d. deep green (11.2.80) 6·50 45
175 „ 1d. blue-green (2.3.80) .. 2·25 25
176 **12** 2d. orange-red (4.9.77) .. 45·00 1·50
177 „ 2d. brick-red (6.80) .. 45·00 1·50

(*c*) *P* 11½–12½.

178 **11** 1d. blue-green (2.84) .. — 40·00
179 **12** 2d. orange-red (14.9.77) .. — 40·00
180 „ 2d. blood-red (1.4.80) .. — 40·00

For stamps perf. 15, see Nos. 238/40.

1882 (1 Jan.). *Surch. with T* **14.** *W* **13.** *P* 10.

181 **11** ½d. on 1d. green 30 25

15

16

17

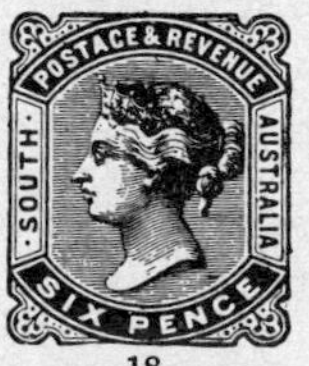

18

1883–95. *W* **13.** (*a*) *P* 10.

182 **15** ½d. chocolate (1.3.83) .. 30 12
a. Imperf. between (horiz. pr.)
183 „ ½d. Venetian red (4.4.89).. 25 8
184 „ ½d. brown (1895) .. 30 8
185 **16** 3d. sage-green (12.86) .. 2·75 45
186 „ 3d. olive-green (6.6.90) .. 2·75 65
187 „ 3d. deep green (12.4.93) .. 1·00 25
188 **17** 4d. pale violet (3.90) .. 1·25 40
189 „ 4d. aniline violet (3.1.93) 2·00 45
190 **18** 6d. pale blue (4.87) .. 1·25 25
191 „ 6d. blue (5.5.87) .. 1·75 20

(*b*) *P* 10×11½–12½, 11½–12½×10, *or compound.*

192 **15** ½d. pale brown (25.9.91) .. 4·00 45
193 „ ½d. dark brown (9.9.92) .. 1·10 35
a. Imperf. between (horiz. pr.)

(*c*) *P* 11½–12½.

194 **15** ½d. Venetian red (12.10.90) 1·75 25

In 1884, and in later years, reprints on paper wmkd. Crown SA, T **10**, were made of Nos. 1, 2, 3, 4, 12, 13, 14, 15, 19, 24, 27, 28, 32, 33, 34, 35, 36, 37, 38, 40, 43, 44, 49*a*, 53, 65, 67, 67 with surch. in red, 70, 71, 72, 73, 78, 79, 81, 83, 86, 90, 118, 119, 120, 121, 122, 155, 158, 159, 164, 181, 182. They are optd. with the word "REPRINT".

For stamps perf. 15, see Nos. 236/7 and 242/4.

19

(20) (21)

(Plates and electrotypes by D.L.R. Printed in Adelaide.)

1886–96. *T* **19** (*inscr.* "POSTAGE & REVENUE"). *W* **13.** *Parts of two or more wmks. on each stamp, sometimes sideways.* A. *Perf.* 10. B. *Perf.* 11½–12½ (*small or large holes*).

		A.		B.	
195	2s. 6d. mauve ..	3·50	1·75	†	
	a. Dull violet ..	†		3·00	1·25
	b. Bright aniline vio.	†		3·50	1·75
196	5s. rose-pink ..	7·00	3·50	4·50	3·50
	a. Rose-carmine ..	†		5·00	4·50
197	10s. green.. ..	13·00	5·00	7·00	5·00
198	15s. brownish yell.	26·00	—	50·00	20·00
199	£1 blue	55·00	12·00	35·00	10·00
200	£2 Venetian red	£160	60·00	£160	50·00
201	50s. dull pink ..	£275	65·00	£275	—
202	£3 sage green ..	£350	—	£300	—
203	£4 lemon ..	£375	—	£350	—
204	£5 grey	£750	—	£700	—
205	£5 brown (1896)	†		£700	—
206	£10 bronze	£850	£400	£800	£350
207	£15 silver.. ..	£2200	—	£2000	—
208	£20 claret ..	£3000	—	£3000	—

Variations exist in the length of the words and shape of the letters of the value inscription.

The 2s. 6d. dull violet, 5s. rose-pink, 10s., £1 and £5 brown exist perf. 11½–12½ with either large or small holes; the 2s. 6d. aniline, 5s. rose-carmine, 15s., £2 and 50s. with large holes only and the remainder only with small holes.

Stamps perforated 11½–12½ small holes, are, generally speaking, rather rarer than those with the 1895 (large holes) gauge.

Stamps perf. 10 were issued on 20 Dec., 1886. Stamps perf. 11½–12½ (small holes) are known with earliest dates covering the period from June, 1890 to Feb. 1896. Earliest dates of stamps with large holes range from July 1896 to May 1902.

1891 (1 Jan.). *Colours changed and surch. with T* **20/21.** *W* **13.**

(*a*) *P* 10.

229 **17** 2½d. on 4d. pale green (Br.) 45 55
a. Fraction bar omitted .. 22·00 22·00

230 **17** 2½d. on 4d. deep green (Br.) 55 8
a. "2" and "½" closer together 4·00 4·00
b. Fraction bar omitted ..
c. Imperf. between (horiz. pr.)
d. Imperf. between (vert. pr.) — 95·00
231 **18** 5d. on 6d. pale brown (C.) 1·25 55
232 „ 5d. on 6d. dark brown (C.) 1·40 60
a. No stop after "5D" .. 38·00

(*b*) *P* 10 × 11½–12½ *or* 11½–12½ × 10.

233 **17** 2½d. on 4d. pale green (Br.) 60 25
234 „ 2½d. on 4d. deep green (Br.) 60 25

(*c*) *P* 11½–12½.

235 **17** 2½d. on 4d. green (Br.) .. 5·00

1893–4. *Surch. with T* **20** (*No.* 241). *W* **13.** *P* 15.

236 **15** ½d. pale brown (1.93) .. 45 8
237 „ ½d. dark brown 45 8
a. Perf. 12½ between, p. 15 all round, pair .. .. 40·00 11·00
b. Imperf. between (horiz. pr.) 23·00
238 **11** 1d. green (8.5.93) .. 25 8
239 **12** 2d. pale orange (9.2.93) 80 8
240 „ 2d. orange-red 95 8
a. Imperf. between (vert. pr.) 55·00
241 **17** 2½d. on 4d. green (14.10.93) 95 30
a. "2" and "½" closer 6·50 5·00
b. No bar in fraction ..
242 „ 4d. purple (1.1.94) .. 1·50 55
243 „ 4d. slate-violet .. .. 1·50 45
244 **18** 6d. blue (20.11.93) .. 5·00 1·10

22

23

(Des. Tannenberg, Melbourne; plates by D.L.R. Typo. Sands and McDougall, Adelaide.)

1894 (1 MAR.). *W* **13.** *P* 15.

245 **22** 2½d. violet-blue .. .. 2·00 25
246 **23** 5d. brown-purple .. 1·50 30

1895–99. *W* **13.** *P* 13.

247 **15** ½d. pale brown (9.95) .. 45 8
248 „ ½d. deep brown (19.3.97) 45 8
249 **11** 1d. pale green (11.1.95) 40 8
250 „ 1d. green 45 8
a. Imperf. between (vert. pr.)
251 **12** 2d. pale orange (19.1.95) 25 8
252 „ 2d. orange-red (9.5.95) .. 25 8
253 **22** 2½d. violet-blue (11.2.95) .. 55 8
254 **16** 3d. pale ol.-grn. (26.7.97) 80 10
255 „ 3d. dark ol.-grn. (27.11.99) 80 8
256 **17** 4d. violet (21.1.96) .. 45 8
257 **23** 5d. brown-purple (1.96) .. 45 12
258 „ 5d. purple 45 10
259 **18** 6d. pale blue (3.96) .. 80 8
260 „ 6d. blue 55 8

The 1d. in pale green, formerly listed under No. 261 as redrawn with slightly thicker lettering, is now accepted as resulting from a printing from a worn plate.

24. G.P.O., Adelaide.

(½d. Typo. De La Rue & Co.)

1898–1906. *W* **13.**
A. *Perf.* 13 (1898–1900) *except* 264A/Aa.
B. *Perf.* 12 × 11½ (*comb.*) (1904–6).

			A.		B.	
262 **24**	½d. yell.-grn.	25	8	30	8
263 **11**	1d. rosine ..	30	8	1·40	8
264 „	1d. scarlet ..	80	8	95	8
	a. Deep red ..	55	8		†
265 **12**	2d. brt. violet	30	8	95	8
266 **22**	2½d. indigo ..	95	8	1·10	8
267 **23**	5d. dull purple	†		55	30

Earliest dates: Perf. 13. ½d., 27 Dec. 1899; 1d. rosine, 8 Aug. 1899; 1d. scarlet, 23 Dec. 1903; 2d. 10 Oct. 1899; 2½d. 25 Mar. 1898.

Perf. 12 × 11½. ½d. July, 1905; 1d. rosine, 2 Feb. 1904; 1d. scarlet, 25 July, 1904; 2d. 11 Oct. 1904; 2½d. 4 July, 1906; 5d. Jan. 1905.

25

The measurements given indicate the length of the value inscription in the bottom label. The dates are those of the earliest known postmarks.

1902–4. *As T* **19**, *but top tablet as T* **25** (*thin* "POSTAGE"). *W* **13.**

(*a*) *P* 11½–12½.

268 3d. ol.-grn. (18½ mm.) (1.8.02) 35 8
269 4d. red-orange (17 mm.) (29.11.02) 80 25
270 6d. blue-grn. (16–16½ mm.) (29.11.02) 70 25
271 8d. ultram. (19 mm. (25.4.02) 80 35
272 8d. ultram. (16½ mm.) (22.3.04) 80 30
a. Error. "EIGNT" £275 £225
273 9d. rosy lake (19.9.02) .. 45 25
a. Imperf. between (vert. pair) .. 75·00
b. Imperf. between (horiz. pair)
274 10d. dull yellow (29.11.02) .. 80 35
275 1s. brown (18.8.02) 90 30
a. Imperf. between (horiz. pair) ..
b. Imperf. between (vert. pair) ..
c. "POSTAGE" and value in red-brown .. .. .. 12·00 7·00
276 2s. 6d. pale violet (19.9.02) .. 5·00
a. Bright violet (2.2.03) .. .. 2·75 1·10
277 5s. rose (17.10.02) .. .. 10·00 4·50
278 10s. green (1.11.02) .. .. 16·00 12·00
279 £1 blue (1.11.02) .. .. 45·00 12·00

(*b*) *P* 12.

280 3d. ol.-grn. (20 mm.) (15.4.04) 80 25
a. "POSTAGE" omitted; value below "AUSTRALIA" .. 95·00
281 4d. orange-red (17½–18 mm.) (18.2.03) 80 30
282 6d. blue-green (15 mm.) (14.11.03) .. .. 3·00 95
283 9d. rosy lake (2.12.03) .. 4·00 1·00

26

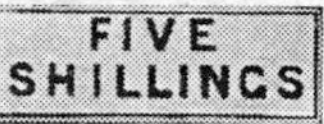

V X

In Type X the letters in the bottom line are slightly larger than in Type V, especially the "A", "S" and "P".

FIVE SHILLINGS FIVE SHILLINGS
Y Z

In Type Z the letters "S" and "G" are more open than in Type Y.

Nos. 196/*a* and 277 are similar to Type Y with all letters thick and regular and the last "S" has the top curve rounded instead of being slightly flattened.

1904–11. *As T* **19**, *but top tablet as T* **26** (*thick* "POSTAGE"). *W* **13.** *P* 12.

284 6d. blue-green (27.4.04) 40 25
285 8d. bright ultram. (4.7.05) .. 95 25
a. Value closer (15¼ mm.) .. 2·25
b. Dull ultramarine (2.4.08) .. 1·40 50
ba. Do. Value closer (15¼ mm.) .. 4·50
286 9d. rosy lake (17–17¼ mm.) (18.7.04) 55 2
a. Value 16½–16¾ mm. (2.06) .. 2·00 8
b. Brown-lake. Perf. 12½ small holes (6.6.11) 95
287 10d. dull yellow (8.07) .. 2·25 8
a. Imperf. between (horiz. pair) — 55·0
b. Imperf. between (vert. pair) ..
288 1s. brown (12.4.04) 55 2
a. Imperf. between (vert. pair) 45·00
b. Imperf. between (horiz. pair)
289 2s. 6d. bright violet (V) (14.7.05) .. .. .. 7·50 1·
a. Dull violet (X) (8.06) .. 7·50 1·
290 5s. rose-scarlet (Y) (8.04) .. 7·00 3·0
a. Scarlet (Z) (8.06) .. .. 7·00 3·0
b. Pale rose. Perf. 12½ (small holes) (Z) (7.10) .. .. 11·00 4·
291 10s. green (26.8.08) .. .. 26·00
292 £1 blue (29.12.04) .. .. 40·00
a. Perf. 12½ (small holes) (7.10) 38·00

The "value closer" variety on the 8d. occu six times in the sheet of 60. The value normal measures 16½ mm. but in the variety it is 15¼ mr

The 9d., 5s. and £1, perf. 12½ (small holes), a late printings made in 1910–11 to use up t Crown SA paper.

No. 286b has the value as Type C of the 9 on Crown A paper.

27

1905–11. *W* **27.** *P* 12 × 11½ (*new comb machin*

293 **24** ½d. pale green (4.07) .. 25
a. Yellow-green 35
294 **11** 1d. rosine (2.12.05) .. 30
a. Scarlet (4.11) 25
295 **12** 2d. bright violet (2.2.06) 45
aa. Imperf. between (pair) ..
a. Mauve (4.08) 25
296 **22** 2½d. indigo-blue (14.9.10) 1·50
297 **23** 5d. brown-pur. (11.3.08) 95

Three types of the 9d., perf. 12½, distinguis able by the distance between "NINE" a "PENCE".

A. Distance 1⅜ mm. B. Distance 2¼ mm.
C. Distance 2½ mm.

1906–12. *T* **19** ("POSTAGE" *thick as T* **2** *W* **27.** *P* 12 *or* 12½ (*small holes*).

298 3d. sage-green (19 mm.) (26.6.06) 95
a. Imperf. between (horiz. pair)..
b. Perf. 12½. *Sage-green* (17 mm.) (9.12.09) .. .. .. 1·10
c. Perf. 12½. *Deep olive* (20 mm.) (7.10) .. .. .. 5·00 1·
d. Perf. 12½. *Yellow-olive* (16.12.11) .. .. .. 2·00
da. Perf. 12½. *Bright olive-green* (19–19¾ mm.) (5.12).. .. 1·50
e. Perf. 11 (17 mm.) (10.7.11) .. 60·00
299 4d. orange-red (10.9.06) .. 1·25
a. Orange .. .. .. 1·90
b. Perf. 12½. *Orange* (27.10.09).. 1·25
300 6d. blue-green (1.9.06) .. 1·25
a. Perf. 12½ (21.4.10) .. 60
ab. Perf. 12½. Imperf. between (vert. pair) .. .. .. — 80
301 8d. bright ultramarine (*P* 12½) (8.09) .. .. .. 2·00
a. Value closer (8.09) .. 8·00 6
302 9d. brown-lake (3.2.06) .. 1·50
a. Imperf. between (vert. pair) .. 60·00
aa. Imperf. between (horiz. pair).. 70·00
b. Deep lake (9.5.08) .. .. 5·50
c. Perf. 12½. *Lake* (A) (5.9.09).. 2·00
d. Perf. 12½. *Lake* (B) (7.09) .. 2·25
e. Perf. 12½. *Brown-lake* (C) .. 5·50 1·
ea. Perf. 12½. *Deep lake.* Thin paper (C) .. .. .. 1·50
f. Perf. 11 (1909) .. ..

03 1s. brown (30.5.06) .. .. 1·40 35
a. Imperf. between (horiz. pair).. 42·00
b. Perf. 12½ (10.3.10) 55 8
304 2s. 6d. brt. vio. (X) (10.6.09) 3·00 1·10
a. Perf. 12½. *Pale violet* (X)(6.10) 3·25 1·25
ab. Perf. 12½. *Dp. pur.* (X)(5.11.12) 6·00 1·60
305 5s. brt. rose (*P* 12½) (Z) (24.4.11) .. .. 9·50

The " value closer " variety of the 8d. occurred 1 times in the sheet of 60 in the later printing nly. On No. 301 the value measures 16½ mm. while on No. 301a it is 15¼ mm.

The 1s. brown, perf. compound of 11½ and 2½, formerly listed is now omitted, as it must ave been perforated by the 12 machine, which n places varied from 11½ to 13.

OFFICIAL STAMPS.

A. *Departmental.*

868–74.

The following is a list of initials which are ound on the stamps of the above period, in *ed, blue,* and *black.* Selections can be submitted when in stock.

A. Architect; A.G. Attorney-General; A.O. udit Office; B.D. Barracks Department; B.G. otanic Gardens; B.M. Bench of Magistrates Licensing Bench); C. Customs; C.D. Convict Department; C.L. Crown Lands; C.O. Commissariat Officer; C.P. Commissioner of Police; .S. Chief Secretary; C.Sgn. Colonial Surgeon; D.B. Destitute Board; D.R. Deeds Registration; E. Engineer; E.B. Education Board; .F. Gold Fields; G.P. Government Printer; .S. Government Storekeeper; G.T. Goolwa ramway; H. Hospital; H.A. House of ssembly; I.A. Immigration Agent; I.E. ntestate Estates; I.S. Inspector of Sheep; .A. Lunatic Asylum; L.C. Legislative-Council; .L. Legislative Librarian; L.T. Lands Titles; I. Military; M.B. Marine Board; M.R. Manager of Railways; M.R.G. Main Roads, ambeirton; N.T. Northern Territory; O.A. fficial Assignee; P. Police; P.A. Protector of borigines; P.O. Post Office; P.S. Private ecretary; P.W. Public Works; R.B. Road Board; R.G. Registrar-General; S. Sheriff; .C. Supreme Court; S.G. Surveyor-General; .M. Stipendiary Magistrate; S.T. Superintendent of Telegraphs; T. Treasurer; T.R. Titles Registration; V. Volunteers; V.A. Valuator nd Auctioneer; Vn. Vaccination; W. Waterworks.

B. *General.*

O.S. (O 1) O.S. (O 2)

Contemporary stamps overprinted with Type **O 1.**

1874–77. *W* **2.** (*a*) *P* 10.
O 1 **3** 4d. dull purple (18.2.74) .. £250 60·00

(*b*) *P* 11½–12½ × 10.
O 2 **1** 1d. green (2.1.74) .. — 24·00
O 3 **3** 4d. dull violet (12.2.75) .. 9·50 1·40
O 4 **1** 6d. Prussian bl. (20.10.75) — 2·75
O 4a **3** 2s. rose-pink ..
O 5 „ 2s. carmine (3.12.76) .. — 24·00

(*c*) *P* 11½–12½.
O 6 **1** 1d. deep yell.-grn. (30.1.74) — 5·50
a. Printed on both sides ..
O 7 **3** 3d. on 4d. ultram. (26.6.77) — 42·00
a. No stop after " S " .. — 60·00
O 8 „ 4d. dull violet (13.7.74) .. 3·50 1·40
a. No stop after " S " .. — 4·00
O 9 **1** 6d. bright blue (31.8.75) .. 9·50 4·00
a. " O.S." double .. — 6·00
O10 „ 6d. Prussian bl. (27.3.74) 5·00 1·40
a. No stop after " S " .. — 4·00
O11 **4** 9d. red-purple (22.3.76) .. 32·00 6·00
a. No stop after " S " .. 40·00
O12 **1** 1s. red-brown (5.8.74) .. 9·50 1·40
a. " O.S." double .. — 4·00
b. No stop after " S " .. 9·50 4·00
O13 **3** 2s. crim.-carm. (13.7.75) 11·00 2·00
a. No stop after " S " ..
b. No stops .. .. — 4·00
c. Stops at top of letters ..

1876–85. *W* **8.** (*a*) *P* 10.
O14 **1** 6d. bright blue (1879) .. 13·00 2·00

(*b*) *P* 10 × 11½–12½, 11½–12½ × 10, *or compound.*
O15 **3** 4d. violet-slate (24.1.78) .. 13·00 2·00
O16 „ 4d. plum (29.11.81) .. 3·50 55
O17 „ 4d. deep mauve 95 35
a. No stop after " S " .. — 2·75
b. No stop after " O " ..
c. " O.S." double ..
d. " O.S." inverted ..
O18 **1** 6d. bright blue (1877) .. 2·00 25
a. " O.S." inverted ..
b. No stop after " O " ..
O19 „ 6d. brt. ultram (27.3.85) 1·75 10
a. " O.S." inverted ..
b. " O.S." double ..
c. " O.S." double, one invtd.
d. No stop after " S " ..
e. No stops after " O " & " S "
O20 „ 1s. red-brown (27.3.83) .. 5·00 85
a. " O.S." inverted
b. No stop after " O " ..
c. No stop after " S " ..
O21 **3** 2s. carmine (16.3.81) .. 2·75 70
a. " O.S." inverted ..
b. No stop after " S " ..

(*c*) *P* 11½–12½.
O22 **3** 3d. on 4d. ultramarine ..
O23 „ 4d. violet-slate (14.3.76) .. 32·00 1·75
O24 „ 4d. deep mauve (19.8.79) 7·00 40
a. " O.S." inverted ..
b. " O.S." double, one invrtd.
c. No stop after " S " ..
O25 **1** 6d. Prussian blue (6.77) .. 2·75 45
a. " O.S." double .. — 5·00
b. " O.S." inverted ..
O26 **4** 8d. on 9d. brown (9.11.76) 95·00 15·00
a. " O.S." double .. £130
b. " O " only .. — 25·00
O26*c* „ 9d. purple £160
O27 **1** 1s. red-brown (12.2.78) .. 2·75 60
a. " O.S." inverted .. 32·00 16·00
b. No stop after " S " .. 48·00
O28 „ 1s. lake-brown (8.11.83) .. 2·00 40
O29 **3** 2s. rose-carmine (12.8.85) 4·00 65
a. " O.S." double .. — 12·00
b. " O.S." inverted .. — 13·00
c. No stop after " S " .. — 4·00

1891–1903. *Contemporary stamps optd. with Type* **O 2.**

(*a*) *W* **8.** *P* 11½–12½.
O30 **1** 1s. lake-brown (18.4.91) .. 2·75 2·75
O31 „ 1s. Vandyke brown .. 4·00 1·40
O32 „ 1s. dull brown (2.7.96) .. 2·75 55
a. No stop after " S " ..
O33 „ 1s. sepia (*large holes*) (4.1.02) .. 1·40 25
a. " O.S." double ..
b. No stop after " S " ..
O34 **3** 2s. carmine (20.6.00) .. 5·00 1·40
a. No stop after " S " ..

(*b*) *W* **8.** *P* 10 × 11½–12½.
O35 **3** 2s. rose-carmine (9.11.95) 1·40 40
a. No stop after " S " .. 7·50
b. " O.S." double ..

(*c*) *W* **10.** *P* 11½–12½.
O36 **1** 1s. dull brown (7.3.03) .. 3·00 30

Contemporary stamps overprinted with Type **O 1.**

1874–76. *W* **10.** (*a*) *P* 10.
O37 **11** 1d. blue-green (30.9.75) .. 16·00 4·00
a. " O.S." inverted ..
b. No stop after " S " ..
O38 **12** 2d. orange-red (18.2.74) .. 2·00 10
a. No stop after " S " ..
b. " O.S." double ..

(*b*) *P* 10 × 11½–12½, 11½–12½ × 10, *or compound.*
O39 **11** 1d. blue-green (16.9.75) ..
a. No stop after " S " ..
O40 **12** 2d. orange-red (27.9.76) .. — 1·40

(*c*) *P* 11½–12½.
O41 **11** 1d. blue-green (13.8.75) .. — 3·00
a. " O.S." inverted ..
b. No stop after " S " ..
O42 **12** 2d. orange-red (20.5.74) .. — 25·00

1876–80. *W* **13.** (*a*) *P* 10.
O43 **11** 1d. blue-green (2.10.76) .. 35 8
a. " O.S." inverted .. — 8·00
b. " O.S." double .. 7·50 7·00
c. " O.S." double, one invtd.
d. No stops .. — 3·25
e. No stop after " S " .. — 1·75
f. No stop after " O " ..
O44 „ 1d. deep green .. 80 8
a. " O.S." double .. — 7·00
O45 **12** 2d. orange-red (21.9.77) .. 40 8
a. " O.S." double .. 8·00 4·00
b. " O.S." inverted — 3·25
c. " O.S." double, both invtd. — 18·00
d. " O.S." double, one invtd.
e. No stop after " O " .. — 2·75
f. No stop after " S " ..
g. No stops after " O " & " S "
O46 „ 2d. brick-red .. 6·50 25

(*b*) *P* 10 × 11½–12½, 11½–12½ × 10, *or compound.*
O47 **11** 1d. deep green (14.8.80) .. — 6·00
a. " O.S." double ..
O48 **12** 2d. orange-red (6.4.78) .. 11·00 2·75
a. " O.S." inverted ..
b. No stop after " S " ..

(*c*) *P* 11½–12½.
O49 **12** 2d. orange-red (15.7.80) .. — 20·00

1882 (20 Feb.). *Surch. with T* **14.** *W* **13.** *P* **10.**
O50 **11** ½d. on 1d. blue-green .. 70 10
a. " O.S." inverted ..

1888–91. *W* **13.** *P* 10.
O51 **17** 4d. violet (24.1.91) .. 1·25 25
O52 **18** 6d. blue (15.11.88) .. 70 8
a. " O.S." double ..
b. No stop after " S " ..

1891. *Surch. with T* **20.** *W* **13.** (*a*) *P* 10.
O53 **17** 2½d. on 4d. green (1.8.91) 2·00 85
a. " 2 " and " ½ " closer .. — 10·00
b. No stop after " S " ..
c. " O.S." omitted (in pair with normal) ..
d. " O.S." inverted ..
e. " O.S." double ..

(*b*) *P* 10 × 11½–12½, 11½–12½ × 10, *or compound.*
O54 **17** 2½d. on 4d. grn. (1.10.91) 5·00 2·50

(*c*) *Perf.* 11½–12½.
O54*a* **17** 2½d. on 4d. grn. (1.6.91)

Contemporary stamps overprinted with Type **O 2.**

1891–95. *W* **13.** (*a*) *P* 10.
O55 **15** ½d. brown (2.5.94) .. 95 25
a. No stop after " S " ..
O56 **11** 1d. green (22.4.91) .. 80 8
a. " O.S." double .. 9·50
b. No stop after " S " .. — 1·75
c. " O.S." in blackish blue 27·00 1·00
d. " O.S." double, one invtd.
O57 **12** 2d. orange-red (22.4.91) 55 8
a. No stop after " S " .. — 80·00
b. " O.S." double ..
O58 **17** 2½d. on 4d. green (18.8.94) 55 10
a. No stop after " S " .. — 2·75
b. " O.S." inverted .. 25·00
c. " 2 " and " ½ " closer .. 6·00 3·75
d. Fraction bar omitted ..
O59 „ 4d. pale violet (13.2.91) .. 95 10
a. " O " only .. — 9·50
b. " O.S." double ..
c. No stop after " S " ..
O60 „ 4d. aniline violet (31.8.93) 1·40 8
a. No stop after " S " ..
b. " O.S." double ..
O61 **18** 5d. on 6d. brn. (2.12.91) 55 25
a. No stop after " S " .. 7·50 2·75
b. No stop after " 5D " .. 27·00
O62 „ 6d. blue (4.4.93) .. 80 8
a. No stop after " S " ..
b. " O.S." in blackish blue..

(*b*) *P* 10 × 11½–12½.
O63 **15** ½d. pale brown (26.3.95) 70 25
O64 **17** 2½d. on 4d. green (17.9.95) — 8·00
a. " O.S." double ..

(*c*) *P* 11½–12½.
O65 **15** ½d. Venetian red (13.6.91) 3·00 40

1893–1901. *W* **13.** *P* 15.
O66 **15** ½d. pale brown (8.6.95) 40 8
O67 **11** 1d. green (8.9.94) .. 10 8
a. No stop after " S " ..
b. " O.S." double ..
O68 **12** 2d. orange-red (16.6.94) 55 8
a. " O.S." double .. — 3·50
b. " O.S." inverted .. — 2·75
O68*c* **22** 2½d. violet-blue .. 3·50 25
O69 **17** 4d. slate-violet (4.4.95) 2·00 25
a. " O.S." double .. — 3·50
O70 **23** 5d. purple (29.3.01) 2·00 45
O71 **18** 6d. blue (20.9.93) 45 8

1895–1901. *W* **13.** *P* 13.
O72 **15** ½d. brown (17.5.98) .. 55 8
a. Opt. triple, twice sideways

O73 **11** 1d. green (20.5.95) .. 40 8
a. No stop after "S" .. 3·50 1·90
O74 **12** 2d. orange (11.2.96) .. 35 8
a. No stop after "S" .. — 1·90
b. "O.S." double .. ..
O75 **22** 2½d. violet-blue (5.7.97) 2·75 10
a. No stop after "S" ..
O76 **17** 4d. violet (12.96) .. 55 8
a. No stop after "S" .. 3·50 1·90
b. "O.S." double .. .. 2·75 2·75
O77 **23** 5d. purple (29.9.01) .. 1·00 45
a. No stop after "S" ..
O78 **18** 6d. blue (13.9.99) .. 80 10
a. No stop after "S" .. 2·75

1898. *On the redrawn design, No.* 261. *W* **13.** *P* 13.

O79 **11** 1d. green (9.2.98) .. 40 8
a. No stop after "S" .. 1·50

O. S.

(O 3)

1899–1901. *Optd. with Type* O **3.** *W* **13.** *P* 13.

O80 **24** ½d. yellow-green (12.2.00) 10 8
a. No stop after "S" ..
b. "O.S." inverted ..
O81 **11** 1d. rosine (22.9.99) 10 8
a. "O.S" inverted ..
b. "O.S." double.. ..
c. No stop after "S" .. — 2·75
O82 **12** 2d. bright violet (1.6.00) 10 8
a. "O.S." inverted .. 3·50
b. "O.S." double.. ..
c. No stop after "S" .. 3·50
O83 **22** 2½d. indigo (2.10.01) 65 8
a. "O.S." inverted .. — 3·50
b. No stop after "S" .. 7·00
O84 **17** 4d. violet (18.11.00) 35 8
a. "O.S." inverted .. 15·00
b. No stop after "S" .. 3·50
O85 **18** 6d. blue (8.10.00) 55 8
a. No stop after "S" .. 3·50

1891 (MAY). *Optd. as Type* O **3** *but wider.* *W* **13.** *P* 10.

O86 **19** 2s. 6d. pale violet.. .. £350 £350
O87 ,, 5s. pale rose £350 £350

Only one sheet (60) of each of these stamps was printed.

South Australia now uses the stamps of AUSTRALIA.

SOUTH GEORGIA.

As South Georgia is still a dependency of the Falkland Islands the stamps are listed under FALKLAND ISLANDS DEPENDENCIES.

SOUTH WEST AFRICA.

(FORMERLY GERMAN S.W. AFRICA.)

INSCRIPTIONS. Most of the postage stamps up to No. 140 are inscribed alternately in English and Afrikaans throughout the sheets and the same applies to all the Official stamps and to Nos. D30/33.

The notes after No. 29 of South Africa apply to these and the prices quoted, both unused and used, are for pairs or units. Please refer to the headings at the top of the price columns.

South West **Zuid-West**

Africa. **Afrika.**

(1) (2)

1923. *Stamps of South Africa, T* **2** *and* **3**, *optd. typographically with T* **1** *and* **2** *alternately.*

I. 14 *mm. between lines of overprint.* (2 JAN.).

		Un. pair	Us. pair
1	½d. green	30	50
	a. "Wes" for "West".. ..	40·00	
2	1d. rose-red	45	55
	a. Opt. inverted	£275	
	b. "Wes" for "West".. ..	90·00	
	c. "Af.rica" for "Africa" ..	80·00	
	d. Opt. double	£225	
3	2d. dull purple	55	90
	a. Opt. inverted	£225	
4	3d. ultramarine	1·75	2·75
5	4d. orange-yell. & sage-green	2·75	3·50
6	6d. black and violet	4·00	6·00
7	1s. orange-yellow	9·00	10·00
8	1s. 3d. pale violet	13·00	15·00
	a. Opt. inverted	75·00	
9	2s. 6d. purple and green ..	55·00	70·00
10	5s. purple and blue	£130	£140
11	10s. blue and olive-green ..	£1000	£1100
12	£1 green and red	£600	£700
1/12	.. .. *Set of* 12	£1600	£1700
1/12	Optd. "Specimen" *Set of* 12 *singles*	£700	

Minor varieties, due to wear of type including broken "t" in "West," may be found. Varieties showing one line of overprint only, or lower line above upper line, due to misplacement, may also be found. All values may be found with faint stop after "Afrika," and the ½d., 1d., 2d. and 3d. occasionally without stop.

IA. 14 *mm. between lines, but opt. lithographed in shiny ink.*

12a	½d. green	1·75	2·75
12b	4d. orange-yell. & sage-green	11·00	13·00
12c	6d. black and violet	13·00	18·00
12d	1s. orange-yellow	18·00	27·00
12e	1s. 3d. pale violet	27·00	35·00
12f	2s. 6d. purple and green ..	90·00	£120
12a/12f	.. .. *Set of* 6	£150	£190

II. 10 *mm. between lines of overprint.* (MAY, 1923.)

13	5s. purple and blue	£130	£120
	a. "Afrika" without stop ..	£600	
14	10s. blue and olive-green ..	£400	£225
	a. "Afrika" without stop ..	£1000	£1000
15	£1 green and red	£500	£400
	a. "Afrika" without stop ..	£2000	

Zuidwest **South West**

Afrika. **Africa.**

(3) (4)

1923–24. *Stamps of South Africa, T* **2** *and* **3**, *optd. as T* **3** ("Zuidwest" *in one word, without hyphen) and* **4** *alternately.*

III. "South West" 14 *mm. long;* "Zuidwest" 11 *mm. long;* 14 *mm. between lines of opt.* (AUG.–SEPT., 1923).

16	½d. green (Sept. 1924) ..	90	1·10
	a. "outh" for "South" ..	£350	
17	1d. rose red	90	1·10
	a. "outh" for "South" ..	£400	
18	2d. dull purple	1·10	1·40
	a. Opt. double	£275	
19	3d. ultramarine	1·40	1·75
20	4d. orange-yellow & sage-green	2·25	2·75
21	6d. black and violet	3·25	4·75
22	1s. orange-yellow	4·25	5·50
23	1s. 3d. pale violet	9·00	11·00
24	2s. 6d. purple and green ..	32·00	40·00
25	5s. purple and blue	55·00	70·00
26	10s. blue and olive-green ..	90·00	£130
27	£1 green and red	£180	£225
16/27	.. .. *Set of* 12	£325	£425

Two sets may be made with this overprint, one with bold lettering, and the other with thinner lettering and smaller stops.

IV. "South West" 16 *mm. long;* "Zuidwest" 12 *mm. long;* 14 *mm. between lines of opt.* (JULY), 1924).

28	2s. 6d. purple and green ..	75·00	90·00

VI. "South West" 16 *mm. long;* * "Zuidwest" 12 *mm. long;* 9½ *mm. between lines of opt.* (DEC., 1924).

		Un. pair	Us. pair
29	½d. green	90	1·75
30	1d. rose-red	75	1·10
31	2d. dull purple	1·40	1·75
32	3d. ultramarine	1·75	2·75
	a. Deep bright blue	23·00	27·00
33	4d. orange-yellow & sage-green	2·75	3·2
34	6d. black and violet	3·25	3·7
35	1s. orange-yellow	4·75	5·5
36	1s. 3d. pale violet	4·75	7·5
37	2s. 6d. purple and green ..	17·00	23·0
38	5s. purple and blue	27·00	38·0
39	10s. blue and olive-green ..	45·00	55·0
40	£1 green and red	£130	£14
40a	£1 pale olive-green and red ..	£170	£18
29/40a	.. .. *Set of* 12	£225	£25
35, 39/40	Optd. "Specimen" *Set of* 3	£300	

* Two sets with this overprint may be mad one with "South West" 16 mm. long, and th other 16½ mm. the difference occurring in th spacing between the words. No. 40a only exis with the latter spacing.

Suidwes **Afrika.** **South West** **Africa.**

(5) (6)

1926. *Pictorial types of S. Africa optd. with T* (*on stamps inscr. in Afrikaans) and* **6** (*on stam inscr. in English) sideways, alternately in blac*

41	½d. black and green	70	9
42	1d. black and carmine ..	70	9
43	6d. green and orange	11·00	9·0

SOUTH WEST AFRICA (7) **SUIDWES-AFRIKA** (8)

Triangular stamps of S. Africa, imperf., op with T **7** (E.) *or T* **8** (A.).

Single stamps.

		E.		A.	
44 **10**	4d. grey-blue ..	1·00	1·00	1·00	1·
44	Optd. "Specimen"	65·00		65·00	

1927. *As Nos.* 41/3, *but Afrikaans opt. on stam inscr. in English and vice versa.*

		Un. pair	Us. pa
45	½d. black and green	70	9
	a. "Africa" without stop ..	60·00	
46	1d. black and carmine ..	70	9
	a. "Africa" without stop ..	60·00	
47	6d. green and orange	5·00	6·
	a. "Africa" without stop ..	60·00	

SOUTH WEST AFRICA

(9)

1927. *As No.* 44E, *but overprint T* **9.**

Single stam

48 4d. grey-blue (Optd. S. £50) .. 2·75 3·

1927. *Pictorial stamps of South Africa op alternately as T* **5** *and* **6**, *in blue, but w lines of overprint spaced* 16 *mm.*

		Un. pair	U pa
49	2d. grey and purple	2·25	3·
50	3d. black and red	3·75	4·
51	1s. brown and blue	6·50	9·
52	2s. 6d. green and brown ..	23·00	27·
53	5s. black and green	55·00	65·
54	10s. blue and bistre-brown ..	65·00	80·
49/54	.. .. *Set of* 6	£150	£1
49/54	Optd. "Specimen" *Set of* 6	£450	

A variety of Nos. 49, 50, 51, and 54, w spacing 16½ mm. between lines of overpri occurs in one vertical row of each sheet.

1927. *As No.* 44, *but perf.* 11½ *by John Meine Ltd., Windhoek.*

Single stamps.

		E.		A.	
55	4d. grey-blue ..	1·40	1·40	1·40	1·
	a. Imp. btwn. (pair)	10·00	—	10·00	

S.W.A.
(10)

927-30. *Optd. with* **T 10.**

(*a*) *T* **3** *of South Africa.*

		Single stamps.	
5	1s. 3d. pale vio. (Optd. S. £75)	2·75	3·75
	a. Without stop after "A"	90·00	
7	£1 pale olive-green and red	75·00	55·00
	a. Without stop after "A"	£600	£700

(*b*) *Pictorial stamps of South Africa.*

		Un. pair	*Us. pair*
8	½d. black and green	70	80
	a. Without stop after "A"	23·00	
	b. "S.W.A." opt. above value	3·50	5·00
	c. As b in vert. pair, top stamp without opt.		
9	1d. black and carmine	70	75
	a. Without stop after "A"	23·00	
	b. "S.W.A." opt. at top (30 4.30)	3·00	5·00
	c. As b in vert. pair, top stamp without opt.		
0	2d. grey and purple	1·75	2·25
	a. Without stop after "A"	40·00	
	b. Opt. double one inverted	£225	£225
1	3d. black and red	2·75	2·25
	a. Without stop after "A"	65·00	
2	4d. brown (1928)	3·25	3·75
	a. Without stop after "A"	65·00	
3	6d. green and orange	10·00	4·50
	a. Without stop after "A"	65·00	

		Un. pair	*Us. pair*
64	1s. brown and blue	5·50	9·00
	a. Without stop after "A"	£500	
65	2s. 6d. green and brown	17·00	13·00
	a. Without stop after "A"	£110	
66	5s. black and green	32·00	27·00
	a. Without stop after "A"	£130	
67	10s. blue and bistre-brown	75·00	65·00
	a. Without stop after "A"	£130	
58/67	*Set of* 10	£150	£120
58/67	Optd. "Specimen" *Set of* 10	£500	

The overprint is normally found at the base of the ½d., 1d., 6d., 1s. 3d. and £1 values and at the top of the remainder.

1930. *Nos.* 42 *and* 43 *of South Africa* (*rotogravure printing*), *optd. with* **T 10.**

68	½d. black and green	1·25	2·75
69	1d. black and carmine	1·25	2·75

1930 (27 Nov.). *Air.* **T 17** *of South Africa optd.* (*a*) *As* **T 10.**

		Un. single	*Us. single*
70	4d. green (*first printing*)	5·50	10·00
	a. No stop after "A" of "S.W.A."	45·00	50·00
	b. Later printings	2·75	4·50
71	1s. orange (*first printing*)	17·00	23·00
	a. No stop after "A" of "S.W.A."	£200	£250
	b. Later printings	9·00	11·00

First printing: Thick letters, blurred impression. Stops with rounded corners.
Later printings: Thinner letters, clear impression. Clean cut, square stops.

S.W.A.
(11)

(*b*) *As* **T 11** (12.30).

72	4d. green	2·25	2·75
	a. Opt. double	50·00	
	b. Opt. inverted	45·00	
73	1s. orange	4·50	5·50

(Recess. B.W.)

1931 (5 Mar.). *T* **12** *to* **25** (*inscr. alternately in English and Afrikaans*). *W* **9** *of South Africa. P* 14×13½. (*a*) *Postage.*

		Un. pair	*Us. pair*
74	½d. black and emerald	25	25
75	1d. indigo and scarlet	25	25
76	2d. blue and brown	25	25
77	3d. grey-blue and blue	35	35
78	4d. green and purple	45	55
79	6d. blue and brown	55	90
80	1s. chocolate and blue	1·40	1·10
81	1s. 3d. violet and yellow	2·25	3·25
82	2s. 6d. carmine and grey	4·50	5·50
83	5s. sage-green and red-brown	9·00	11·00
84	10s. red-brown and emerald	17·00	23·00
85	20s. lake and blue-green	35·00	45·00
	(*b*) *Air.*		
86	3d. brown and blue	6·50	9·00
87	10d. black and purple-brown	12·00	17·00
74/87	*Set of* 14	£100	£130

(Recess. Bradbury, Wilkinson.)

1935 (1 May). *Silver Jubilee. Inscr. bilingually. W* **9** *of South Africa. P* 14×13½.

			Un. single	*Us. single*
88	**26**	1d. black and scarlet	15	25
89	„	2d. black and sepia	25	35
90	„	3d. black and blue	4·50	5·50
91	„	6d. black and purple	3·75	3·75

1935-36. *Voortrekker Memorial Fund.* **T 18** *to* **21** *of South Africa optd. with* **T 10.**

		Un. pair	*Us. pair*
92	½d.+½d. olive-green and green	25	35
	a. Opt. inverted	75·00	
93	1d.+½d. grey-black and pink	45	1·00
94	2d.+1d. grey-green and purple	1·40	1·90
	a. Without stop after "A"	75·00	
	b. Opt. double	65·00	
95	3d.+1½d. grey-green and blue	2·75	3·25
	a. Without stop after "A"	75·00	

12. Gom-pauw.

13. Cape Cross.

14. Bogenfels.

15. Windhoek.

16. Waterberg.

17. Luderitz Bay.

18. Bush Scene.

19. Elands.

20. Zebra and Gnus.

21. Herero huts.

22. The Welwitschia plant.

23. Okuwahaken Falls.

Monoplane over Windhoek.

25. Biplane over Windhoek.

26

27. Mail transport.

28

(Recess. Bradbury, Wilkinson.)

1937 (1 Mar.). *W* **9** *of S. Africa. P* 14×13½.

96	**27**	1½d. purple-brown	35	25

(Recess. Bradbury, Wilkinson & Co., Ltd.)

1937 (12 May). *Coronation. W* **9** *of South Africa. P* 13½×14.

97	**28**	½d. black and emerald	10	15
98	„	1d. black and scarlet	10	15
99	„	1½d. black and orange	10	15
100	„	2d. black and brown	15	25
101	„	3d. black and blue	20	25
102	„	4d. black and purple	30	35
103	„	6d. black and yellow	35	45
104	„	1s. black	75	85
97/104		*Set of* 8	2·25	2·75

1938 (14 Dec.). *Voortrekker Centenary Memorial. Nos. 76 to 79 of South Africa optd. as T* **11.**

		Un. pair	Us. pair
105	½d.+½d. blue and green ..	20	30
106	1d.+1d. blue and carmine ..	30	40
107	1½d.+1½d. chocolate & bl.-grn.	75	1·00
108	3d.+3d. bright blue	1·50	2·00

1938 (14 Dec.). *Voortrekker Commemoration. Nos. 80/1 of South Africa optd. as T* **11.**

109	1d. blue and carmine ..	25	30
110	1½d. greenish blue and brown	60	70

1939 (17 July). *250th Anniv. of Landing of Huguenots in South Africa and Huguenot Commemoration Fund. Nos. 82/4 of South Africa optd. as T* **11.**

111	½d.+½d. brown and green ..	25	50
112	1d.+1d. green and carmine ..	50	75
113	1½d.+1½d. blue-green & pur.	1·25	2·00

SWA (29) **SWA** (30) **SWA** (31)

1941–42. *War Effort. Nos. 88/95 of South Africa optd. with T* **29** *or* **30** *(3d. and 1s.).*

(*a*) *Inscr. alternately.*

114	½d. green	5	10
	a. Blue-green ('42) ..	5	8
115	1d. carmine	5	8
116	1½d. myrtle-green ('42) ..	10	15
117	3d. blue	15	25
118	4d. orange-brown	30	45
	a. Red-brown	50	90
119	6d. red-orange	30	50

(*b*) *Inscr. bilingually.*

		Un. single	Us. single
120	2d. violet	8	8
121	1s. brown	40	30
114/121	*Set of* 8 *pairs and singles*	1·25	1·60

1943–44. *War Effort (reduced sizes). Nos. 96 to 103 of South Africa, optd. with T* **29** *(1½d. and 1s., No. 129), or T* **31** *(others).*

(*a*) *Inscr. alternately.*

		Un. unit	Us. unit
122	½d. blue-green (T)	8	8
	a. Green	12	12
	b. Greenish blue	8	8
123	1d. carmine-red (T)	10	15
	a. Bright carmine	5	10
124	1½d. red-brown (P)	10	12
125	2d. reddish violet (P) ..	20	20
	a. Violet	12	20
126	3d. blue (T)	15	25
127	6d. red-orange (P)	30	45
	a. Opt. inverted	£200	

(*b*) *Inscr. bilingually.*

128	4d. slate-green (T)	25	30
	a. Opt. inverted	£125	
129	1s. brown (opt. *T* **29**) (P) ..	75	1·00
	a. Opt. inverted	£125	
	b. Opt. *T* 31 ('44)	50	55
	c. Opt. *T* 31 inverted	£150	£100
122/129	.. .. *Set of* 8	1·40	2·00

The "units" referred to above consist of pairs (P) or triplets (T).

No. 127 exists with another type of opt. as Type **31**, but with broader "s", narrower "w" and more space between the letters.

1943 (15 Jan.). *No. 104 of South Africa, optd. with T* **29.**

		Un. pair	Us. pair
130	1s. 3d. olive-brown	1·00	1·00

1945. *Victory. Nos. 108 to 110 of South Africa optd. with T* **30.**

131	1d. brown and carmine ..	5	8
	a. Opt. inverted	75·00	
132	2d. slate-blue and violet ..	5	10
133	3d. deep blue and blue ..	8	12

1947 (17 Feb.). *Royal Visit. Nos. 111/3 of South Africa optd. as T* **31**, *but* 8½ × 2 *mm.*

134	1d. black and carmine ..	5	5
135	2d. violet	5	5
136	3d. blue	8	8

1948 (26 Apr.). *Royal Silver Wedding. No. 125 of South Africa, optd. as T* **31**, *but* 4 × 2 *mm.*

137	3d. blue and silver ..	5	5

1949 (1 Oct.). *75th Anniv. of U.P.U. Nos. 128/30 of South Africa optd. as T* **30**, *but* 13 × 4 *mm.*

		Un. pair	Us. pair
138	½d. blue-green	5	8
139	1½d. brown-red	5	8
140	3d. bright-blue	10	12

S W A (32)

1949 (1 Dec.). *Inauguration of Voortrekker Monument, Pretoria. Nos. 131/3 of South Africa optd. with T* **32.**

		Un. single	Us. single
141	1d. magenta	5	8
142	1½d. blue-green	5	8
143	3d. blue	5	8

1952 (14 Mar.). *Tercentenary of Landing of Van Riebeeck. Nos. 136/40 of South Africa optd. as T* **30**, *but* 8 × 3½ *mm. (1d., 4½d.) or* 11 × 4 *mm. (others).*

144	½d. brn.-purple & olive-grey	5	5
145	1d. deep blue-green ..	5	8
146	2d. deep violet	5	8
147	4½d. blue	12	20
148	1s. brown	25	50
144/148	.. *Set of* 5	45	80

PRINTERS. All the following stamps were rotogravure-printed by the Government Printer, Pretoria, *except where otherwise stated.*

33. Queen Elizabeth II and *Catophracies Alexandri.*

1953 (2 June). *Coronation. As T* **33** *(Queen and various indigenous flowers). P* 14.

149	1d. bright carmine	12	12
150	2d. deep bluish green ..	12	15
151	4d. magenta	30	35
152	6d. dull ultramarine	35	40
153	1s. deep orange-brown ..	50	60
149/153	.. .. *Set of* 5	1·25	1·40

Designs:—2d. *Bauhinia Macrantha*, 4d. *Caralluma Nebrownii*, 6d. *Gloriosa Virescens*, 1s. *Rhigozum Tricholotum.*

34. " Two Bucks " (rock painting).

36. " Rhinoceros Hunt " (rock painting).

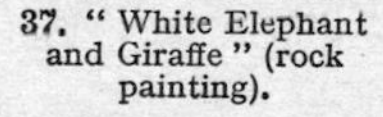

37. " White Elephant and Giraffe " (rock painting).

35. " White Lady " (rock painting).

38. Karakul Lamb.

39. Ovambo Woman blowing Horn.

40. Ovambo Woman.

41. Herero Woman.

42. Ovambo Girl.

43. Lioness.

44. Gemsbok.

45. Elephant.

(Des. O. Schroeder (1d. to 4d.), M. Vandensch (4½d. to 10s.).)

1954 (15 Nov.). *W* **9** *of South Africa (sidewa on vert. designs). P* 14.

154	**34**	1d. brown-red	5	
155	**35**	2d. deep brown	5	
156	**36**	3d. dull purple	12	
157	**37**	4d. blackish olive ..	12	
158	**38**	4½d. deep blue	20	
159	**39**	6d. myrtle-green ..	15	
160	**40**	1s. deep mauve	25	
161	**41**	1s. 3d. cerise	25	
162	**42**	1s. 6d. purple	50	
163	**43**	2s. 6d. bistre-brown ..	1·00	1·
164	**44**	5s. deep bright blue ..	2·00	2·
165	**45**	10s. deep myrtle-green ..	7·00	7·
154/165		.. .. *Set of* 12	10·00	10·

1960. *W* **102** *of South Africa (sideways on ve designs). P* 14.

166	**34**	1d. brown-red	5	
167	**35**	2d. deep brown	10	
168	**36**	3d. dull purple	12	
169	**37**	4d. blackish olive	35	
170	**42**	1s. 6d. purple	2·00	2·
166/170		.. .. *Set of* 5	2·25	2·

(Currency changed. 100 cents = 1 rand.)

46. G.P.O., Windhoek. **47.** Finger Rock.

48. Mounted Soldier Monument. **49.** Quivertree.

50. S.W.A. House, Windhoek. **50a.** Flamingoes and Swakopmund Lighthouse.

51. Fishing Industry. **52.** Flamingo.

53. German Lutheran Church, Windhoek. **54.** Diamond.

55. Fort Namutoni.

55a. Hardap Dam. **56.** Topaz.

57. Tourmaline. **58.** Heliodor.

1961 (14 FEB.)–**63.** *Unsurfaced paper.* W **102** *of South Africa (sideways on vert. designs).* P 14.

171	**46**	½ c. brown and pale blue	5	5
172	**47**	1 c. sepia & reddish lilac	5	5
173	**48**	1½ c. slate-violet & salmon	5	5
174	**49**	2 c. dp. grn. and yellow	8	5
175	**50**	2½ c. red-brown & lt. blue	8	5
176	**50a**	3 c. ultramarine and rose-red (1.10.62)	8	8
177	**51**	3½ c. indigo & blue-green	12	12
178	**52**	5 c. scarlet and grey-blue	12	12
179	**53**	7½ c. sepia and pale lemon	15	12
180	**54**	10 c. blue and grnish. yell.	20	20
181	**55**	12½ c. indigo and lemon ..	25	25
182	**55a**	15 c. chocolate & light blue (16.3.63)	50	50
183	**56**	20 c. brown & red-orange	60	60
184	**57**	50 c. dp. bluish green and yellow-orange ..	2·00	2·00
185	**58**	1 r. yell., maroon & blue	4·00	4·00
171/185		.. .. *Set of* 15	6·00	6·00

1962–66. *As No.* 171, *etc., but without watermark.*

186	**46**	½ c. brn. & pale bl. (8.62)	5	5
187	**48**	1½ c. slate-vio. & sal. (9.62)	5	5
188	**49**	2 c. dp. grn. & yell. (5. 62)	5	5
189	**50**	2½ c. red-brown and light blue ('64)	8	8
190	**51**	3½ c. indigo & bl.-grn. ('66)	10	10
191	**52**	5 c. scar. & grey-bl. (9.62)	12	10
186/191		.. .. *Set of* 6	40	35

See also Nos. 202/16, 224/6 and 240.

59. "Agricultural Development".

1963 (16 MAR.). *Opening of Hardap Dam.* W **102** *of South Africa (sideways).* P 14.

192	**59**	3 c. chocolate & lt. green	8	8

60. Centenary Emblem and Map. **61.** Centenary Emblem and part of Globe.

1963 (30 AUG.). *Centenary of Red Cross.* P 14.

193	**60**	7½ c. red, blk. and lt. blue	12	12
194	**61**	15 c. red, blk. & orge.-brn.	25	25

62. Interior of Assembly Hall. **63.** Calvin.

1964 (14 MAY). *Opening of Legislative Assembly Hall, Windhoek.* W **102** *of South Africa.* P 14.

195	**62**	3 c. ultramarine & salmon	8	5

1964 (1 OCT.). 400*th Anniv. of Death of Calvin (Protestant Reformer).* P 14.

196	**63**	2½ c. brown-purple & gold	5	5
197	,,	15 c. deep bluish green and gold	25	35

64. Mail Runner of 1890. **65.** Kurt von François (founder).

(Des. D. Aschenborn.)

1965 (18 OCT.). 75*th Anniv. of Windhoek. Chalk-surfaced paper.* W **127** *of South Africa (sideways).* P 14.

198	**64**	3 c. sepia and scarlet ..	8	8
199	**65**	15 c. red-brn. & blue-grn.	30	30

66. Dr. H. Vedder.

1966 (4 JULY). 90*th Birth Anniv. of Dr. H. Vedder (philosopher and writer). Chalk-surfaced paper.* W **127** *of South Africa (sideways).* P 14.

200	**66**	3 c. blackish grn. & salmon	8	8
201	,,	15 c. deep sepia & lt. blue	30	30

Nos. 200/1 exist on Swiss-made paper with *tête-bêche* watermark from a special printing made for use in presentation albums for delegates to the U.P.U. Congress in Tokyo in 1969, as supplies of the original Harrison paper were by then exhausted.

1966–72. *As 1961–66 but chalk-surfaced paper and W* **127** *of South Africa* (sideways on vert. designs).*

202 **46** ½ c. brn. & pale bl. ('67) 5 5
203 **47** 1 c. sepia and light reddish lilac (*shades*) ('67) .. 5 5
204 **48** 1½ c. slate-violet and salmon ('68) .. 5 5
205 **49** 2 c. deep bluish green and yellow .. 8 5
206 **50** 2½ c. deep red-brown & lt. turq.-bl. (*shades*) 8 5
207 **50a** 3 c. ultramarine and rose-red ('70) .. 5 5
208 **51** 3½ c. indigo and blue-green ('67) .. 8 5
209 **50** 4 c. deep red-brown & lt. turq.-bl. (1.4.71) 10 8
210 **52** 5 c. scar. & grey-bl. ('68) 10 8
211 **53** 6 c. sepia and greenish yellow (31.8.71) .. 10 8
212 „ 7½ c. sepia and pale lemon ('67) .. 20 20
213 **55** 9 c. indigo and greenish yellow (1.7.71) .. 20 20
214 **54** 10 c. bright blue and greenish yell. (6.70) 25 25
a. Whiter background† (9.72) 20 20
215 **55a** 15 c. chocolate and light blue (1.72) .. 30 30
216 **56** 20 c. brn. & red orge. ('68) 45 45
202/16 .. .. *Set of* 15 1·75 1·75

*** The watermark in this issue is indistinct but the stamps can be distinguished from the stamps without watermark by their shades and the chalk-surfaced paper which is appreciably thicker and whiter.** The 1, 1½, 3, 4, 5, 6, 9, 10 and 15 c. are known only with the watermark *tête-bêche* but the ½ c., 2½ c. and 20 c. exist with both forms, the remainder being as illustrated (*W* **127**).

† No. 214a, printed from sheets, has a much whiter background around the value and behind "SOUTH WEST AFRICA" compared with No. 214, which was issued in coils only.

See also Nos. 224/6 and 240.

67. Camelthorn Tree.

68. Waves breaking against rock. (*Vert.*)

69. Dr. H. F. Verwoerd. (*Vert.*)

Des. D. Aschenborn (2½ c., 3 c.), Govt. Printer, Pretoria (15 c.).)

1967 (6 Jan.). *Verwoerd Commemoration. Chalk-surfaced paper. W* **127** *of South Africa (sideways on vert. designs). P* 14.

217 **67** 2½ c. black & emerald-grn. 5 5
218 **68** 3 c. brown and new blue 8 5
219 **69** 15 c. blackish brown and reddish purple .. 25 25

70. President Swart. **71.** President and Mrs. Swart.

1968 (2 Jan.). *Swart Commemoration. Chalk-surfaced paper. W* **127** *of South Africa (tête-bêche, sideways). P* 14 × 15.

220 **70** 3 c. orange-red, black and turquoise-blue
G. Inscr. in German .. 8 8
A. Inscr. in Afrikaans .. 8 8
E. Inscr. in English .. 8 8
221 **71** 15 c. red, blackish olive & dull green (*shades*)
G. Inscr. in German .. 75 75
A. Inscr. in Afrikaans .. 75 75
E. Inscr. in English .. 75 75
220/1 · *Set of* 6 *in strips of three* 3·00 3·00

The three languages appear *se-tenant*, both horizontally and vertically, throughout the sheet.

1970 (14 Feb.). *Water 70 Campaign. As T* **175/6** *of South Africa, but without phosphor band and inscr.* "SWA".

222 2½ c. green, bright blue and chocolate 8 8
223 3 c. Prussian blue, Royal blue and buff 8 8

72. G.P.O., Windhoek.

1970–71. *As Nos.* 202 *and* 204/5 *but* "POSGELD INKOMSTE" *omitted and larger figure of value as in T* **72**. *W* **127** *of South Africa (tête-bêche, sideways on* 1½ *and* 2 *c.).*

224 **72** ½ c. brn. and pale bl. (6.70) 5 5
225 – 1½ c. slate-violet & salmon (1.6.71) 5 5
226 – 2 c. deep bluish green and lemon (11.70) .. 5 5

1970 (24 Aug.). *150th Anniv. of Bible Society of South Africa. As Nos.* 301/2 *of South Africa, but inscr.* "SWA".

228 2½ c. multicoloured .. 5 5
229 12½ c. gold, black and blue.. 20 20

No. 228 has a phosphor frame, probably added in error.

1971 (31 May). "*Interstex*" *Stamp Exhibition, Cape Town. As No.* 303A *of South Africa, but without phosphor frame and inscr.* "SWA".

230 5 c. light greenish blue, black and pale yellow.. 8 8

1971 (31 May). *Tenth Anniv. of Antarctic Treaty. As No.* 304 *of South Africa, but without phosphor frame, and inscr.* "SWA".

231 12½ c. blue-blk., greenish blue and orange-red 20 20

1971 (31 May). *Tenth Anniv. of the South African Republic. As Nos.* 305/6 *of South Africa, but without phosphor frame, and inscr.* "SWA".

232 2 c. pale flesh and brown-red 5 8
233 4 c. green and black 8 8

1972 (19 Sept.). *Centenary of S.P.C.A. As No.* 312 *of South Africa, but inscr.* "SWA".

234 5 c. multicoloured 10 10

WATERMARK. All issues from this date are on unwatermarked paper.

74. *Sarcocaulon rigidum.*

75. *Euphorbia virosa.*

(Des. Dick Findlay. Litho.)

1973 (1 May). *Scenery. T* **73** *and similar multi-coloured designs showing paintings by Adolph Jentsch. P* 11½ × 12½ (12 *and* 15 *c.) or* 12½ × 11½ (*others*).

235 2 c. Type **73** 5 5
236 4 c. Early morning scene .. 8
237 5 c. Hills 8
238 10 c. Schaap River (*vert.*) .. 15 1
239 15 c. Namib Desert (*vert.*) .. 20 2
235/9 .. .. .. *Set of* 5 40 5

1973 (28 May). *As No.* 207 *but without wmk Phosphorised paper.*

240 **50a** 3 c. ultram. & rose-red.. 20 2

No. 240 is also distinguishable in that th lettering of "SOUTH WEST AFRICA" is whiter.

73. Sand-dunes.

(Lettering by E. de Jong. Litho.)

1973 (1 Sept.). *Succulents. Various mult coloured designs as T* **74/5**. *Phosphorise glossy paper.*

(*a*) *As T* **74**. *P* 12½.

241 1 c. Type **74** 5
242 2 c. *Lapidaria margaretae* .. 5
243 3 c. *Titanopsis schwantesii* .. 5
244 4 c. *Lithops karasmontana* .. 5
245 5 c. *Caralluma lugardii* .. 5
a. Black (face value, etc.) omitted £100
246 6 c. *Dinteranthus microspermus* 8
247 7 c. *Conophytum gratum* .. 8 1
248 9 c. *Huernia oculata* .. 10 1
249 10 c. *Gasteria pillansii* .. 12 1
250 14 c. *Stapelia pedunculata* .. 15
251 15 c. *Fenestraria aurantiaca* .. 20
252 20 c. *Decabelone grandiflora* .. 25
253 25 c. *Hoodia bainii* 30 3

(*b*) *As T* **75**. *P* 11½ × 12½ (30 *c.*, 1 *r.*) *or* 12½ × 11½ (50 *c.*).

254 30 c. Type **75** 35 4
255 50 c. *Pachypodium namaquanum* (*vert.*) 60 7
256 1 r. *Welwitschia bainesii* .. 1·25 1·
241/56 .. .. *Set of* 16 3·25 3·

1973 (1 Sept.)–**76**. *Coil stamps. As Nos.* 241 *and* 245 *but photo., colours changed and perf.* 1

257 1 c. black and light mauve .. 5
a. Chalky paper (7.76?) .. 5
258 2 c. black and yellow .. 5
a. Chalky paper (7.76?) .. 5
259 5 c. black and light rose-red 5

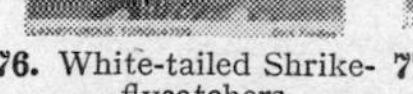

76. White-tailed Shrike-flycatchers. **77.** Giraffe, Antelope and Spoor.

(Des. D. Findlay. Litho.)

974 (13 Feb.). *Rare Birds.* *T* **76** *and similar vert. designs. Multicoloured.* *P* 12½×11½.
60 4 c. Type **76** 8 8
61 5 c. Rosy-faced Lovebirds 8 8
62 10 c. Damara Rock-jumper 15 15
63 15 c. Rüppell's Parrots .. 25 25

(Des. O. Schröder. Litho.)

974 (10 Apr.). *Twyfelfontein Rock-engravings.* *T* **77** *and similar multicoloured designs.* *P* 11½×12½ (15 *c.*) *or* 12½ (*others*).
64 4 c. Type **77** 8 5
65 5 c. Elephant, hyena, antelope and spoor .. 8 8
a. Black (value and "SWA") omitted .. .. ..
66 15 c. Kudu Cow (38×21 *mm.*) 25 25

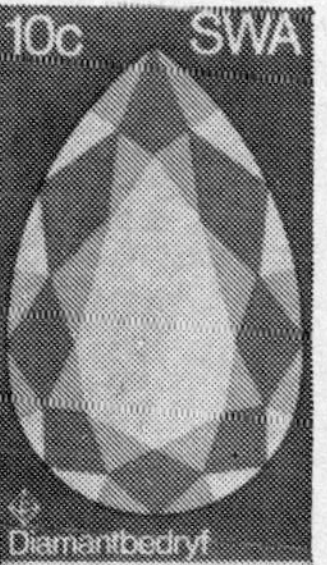

78. Cut Diamond.

80. Peregrine Falcon.

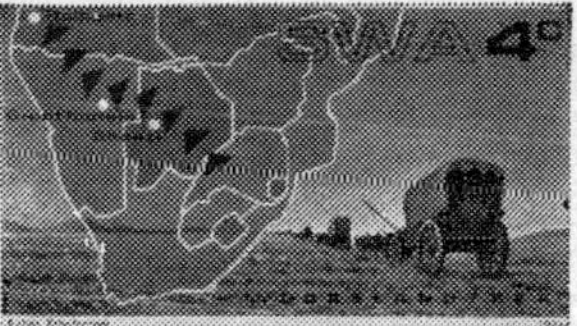

79. Wagons and Map of the Trek.

(Des. M. Barnett.)

974 (30 Sept.). *Diamond Mining.* *T* **78** *and similar vert. design. Multicoloured.* *P* 12½×11½.
57 10 c. Type **78** 12 15
58 15 c. Diagram of shore workings 20 25

(Des. K. Esterhuysen. Litho.)

974 (13 Nov.). *Centenary of Thirstland Trek.* *P* 11½×12½.
59 **79** 4 c. multicoloured 8 8

(Des. Dick Findlay. Litho.)

975 (19 Mar.). *Protected Birds of Prey.* *T* **80** *and similar vert. designs. Multicoloured.* *P* 12½×11½.
70 4 c. Type **80** 8 8
71 5 c. Black Eagle 8 8
72 10 c. Martial Eagle 12 15
73 15 c. Egyptian Vulture .. 20 25

81. Kolmannskop (ghost town).

(Des. A. H. Barrett. Litho.)

1975 (23 July). *Historic Monuments.* *T* **81** *and similar horiz. designs. Multicoloured.* *P* 11½×12½.
274 5 c. Type **81** 8 5
275 9 c. "Martin Luther" (steam tractor) 10 12
276 15 c. Kurt von Francois and Old Fort, Windhoek .. 20 20

82. "View of Swakopmund".

(Des. J. Hoekstra. Litho.)

1975 (15 Oct.). *Otto Schröder.* *T* **82** *and similar horiz. designs showing his paintings. Multicoloured.* *P* 11½×12½.
277 15 c. Type **82** 20 20
278 15 c. "View of Lüderitz" .. 20 20
279 15 c. "Harbour Scene" .. 20 20
280 15 c. "Quayside, Walvis Bay" 20 20
MS281 122×96 mm. Nos. 277/80 85

Nos. 277/80 were printed together, in *se-tenant* blocks of four within the sheet.

83. Elephants.

(Des. H. Pager. Litho.)

1976 (31 Mar.). *Prehistoric Rock Paintings.* *T* **83** *and similar horiz. designs. Multicoloured.* *P* 11½×12½.
282 4 c. Type **83** 5 5
283 10 c. Rhinoceros 12 12
284 15 c. Antelope 20 20
285 20 c. Man with bow and arrow 25 25
MS286 121×95 mm. Nos. 282/5 60

84. Schwerinsburg.

(Des. H. Pager. Litho.)

1976 (14 May). *Castles.* *T* **84** *and similar horiz. designs. Multicoloured.* *P* 11½×12½.
287 10 c. Type **84** 10 12
288 15 c. Schloss Duwisib 15 15
289 20 c. Heynitzburg 20 25

85. Dassie.

(Des. Dick Findlay. Litho.)

1976 (16 July). *Fauna Conservation.* *T* **85** *and similar horiz. designs. Multicoloured.* *P* 11½×12½.
290 4 c. Type **85** 10 12
291 10 c. Dik-Dik 15 15
292 15 c. Tree Squirrel 20 25

86. The Augustineum, Windhoek.

(Des. H. Pager. Litho.)

1976 (17 Sept.). *Modern Buildings.* *T* **86** *and similar horiz. design.* *P* 11½×12½.
293 15 c. black and yellow .. 20 25
294 20 c. black and light yellow .. 25 30
Design:—20 c. Katutura Hospital, Windhoek.

87. Ovambo Water Canal System.

(Des. A. Barrett. Litho.)

1976 (19 Nov.). *Water and Electricity Supply.* *T* **87** *and similar horiz. design. Multicoloured.* *P* 11½×12½.
295 15 c. Type **87** 20 25
296 20 c. Ruacana Falls Power Station 25 30

POSTAGE DUE STAMPS.

Postage Due stamps of Transvaal or South Africa overprinted.

1923. *Optd. with T* **1** *and* **2** *alternately.*

I. *14 mm. between lines of overprint.*

(*a*) *On stamps of Transvaal.*

		Un. pair	*Us. pair*
D1	5d. black and violet	75	3·00
	a. "Wes" for "West" ..	35·00	
	b. "Afrika" (no stop)	20·00	
D2	6d. black and red-brown ..	1·50	4·00
	a. "Wes" for "West" ..		
	b. "Afrika" (no stop)	25·00	

(*b*) *On S. African stamps* (*De La Rue printing*).

D3	2d. black and violet	1·50	2·00
	a. "Wes" for "West" ..	30·00	30·00
	b. "Afrika" (no stop)	35·00	
D4	3d. black and blue	75	1·50
	a. "Wes" for "West" ..	25·00	
D5	6d. black and slate	1·25	3·50
	a. "Wes" for "West" ..	20·00	

(*c*) *On S. African stamps* (*Pretoria printing*).

(i) *Type* D **1** (A). *Rouletted.*

D6	1d. black and rose	25	40
	a. "Wes" for "West" ..	20·00	
	b. "Afrika" (no stop)	20·00	
	c. Unrouletted between (pair) ..	£175	
D7	1½d. black and yellow-brown ..	15	30
	a. "Wes" for "West" ..	20·00	
	b. "Afrika" (no stop)	15·00	

(ii) *Type* D **1** (B). *P* 14.

D8	½d. black and green	10	15
	a. Opt. inverted	75·00	
	b. Opt. double		
	c. "Wes" for "West" ..	15·00	
	d. "Afrika" (no stop)	15·00	
D9	2d. black and violet	15	50
	a. "Wes" for "West" ..	20·00	
	b. "Afrika" (no stop)	20·00	

The "Wes" variety occurs in the English overprint only, in some printings.

A variety of Nos. D1, D4 D5 and D9 with spacing 15 mm. between lines of overprint occurs on four stamps in each pane of certain printings of this setting.

Nos. D1, D4, D6, D7 and D9 exist with 2 mm. spacing between "South" and "West," and also with 2½ mm.; Nos. D2, D3 and D8 only with 2 mm. spacing; and No. D5 only with 2½ mm.

II. *10 mm. between lines of overprint.*

(*a*) *On stamp of Transvaal.*

		Un. pair	*Us. pair*
D10	5d. black and violet ..	15·00	20·00

(*b*) *On S. African stamps* (*De La Rue printing*).

D11	2d. black and violet ..	1·00	1·50
	a. "Afrika" (no stop) ..	25·00	
D12	3d. black and blue	75	1·25
	a. "Afrika" (no stop) ..	20·00	

(*c*) *On S. African stamp* (*Pretoria printing*). *Type* D **1** (A), *rouletted.*

D13	1d. black & rose (July 1923)	£600	

1923–27. *Optd. as T* **3** ("Zuidwest" *in one word without hyphen*) *and* **4**.

III. "South West" *14 mm. long;* "Zuidwest" *11 mm. long; 14 mm. between lines of overprint* (Sept., 1923).

(*a*) *On stamp of Transvaal.*

D14	6d. black and red-brown ..	3·00	5·00

(*b*) *On S. African stamps* (*Pretoria printing*). *Type* D **1** (A). (i) *Rouletted.*

D15	1d. black and rose ..	20	65
	(ii) *P* 14.		
D16	½d. black and green ..	40	70
D17	1d. black and rose	40	80

IV. "South West" *16 mm. long;* "Zuidwest" *12 mm. long; 14 mm. between lines of overprint.*

(*a*) *On stamp of Transvaal.*

D17*a*	5d. black and violet ..	£100	£120

(*b*) *On S. African stamps* (*Pretoria printing*). *Type* D **1** (B). *P* 14.

D18	½d. black and green	20	30
D19	1d. black and rose	50	70
D20	6d. black and slate	30	70
	a. "Africa" (no stop) ..	50·00	

V. *As* IV, *but 12 mm. between lines of overprint.*

(*a*) *On stamp of Transvaal.*

D21	5d. black and violet	75	1·25

(*b*) *On S. African stamp* (*De La Rue printing*).

D22	3d. black and blue	75	1·75

(*c*) *On S. African stamps* (*Pretoria printing*). *Type* D **1** (B). *P* 14.

D23	½d. black and green ..	15	40
D24	1½d. black and yellow-brown	15	40

VI. *As* IV, *but 9½ mm. between lines of overprint.*

(*a*) *On stamp of Transvaal.*

D25	5d. black and violet ..	15	45
	a. "Africa" (no stop) ..	20·00	

(*b*) *On S. African stamp* (*De La Rue printing*).

D26	3d. black and blue	50	75

(*c*) *On S. African stamps* (*Pretoria printing*). *Type* D **1** (B). *P* 14.

D27	½d. black and green ..	20	30
D28	1d. black and rose	10	20
	a. "Africa" (no stop) ..	25·00	
D29	1½d. black and yellow-brown	15	20
	a. "Africa" (no stop) ..	20·00	
D30	2d. black and violet ..	15	30
	a. "Africa" (no stop) ..	20·00	
D31	3d. black and blue	10	20
	a. "Africa" (no stop) ..	20·00	
D32	6d. black and slate	50	90
	a. "Africa" (no stop) ..	25·00	

In Nos. D18/25, D29, D31 and D32, "South West" is 16 mm. long, and in Nos. D26 and D27, 16½ mm. long. Nos. D28 and D30 exist in both 16 mm. and 16½ mm. varieties. (*See note after* No. 40*a*.) In Nos. D20, D29, D31 and D32 a variety with "South West" 16½ mm. long occurs once only in each sheet of 120 stamps (in certain printings only, in the case of D20), and similarly Nos. D28 and D30 occur with the two measurements on the same sheet of certain printings.

Suidwes **South West**

Afrika. **Africa.**

(D 1) (D 2)

1927. *Optd. as Types* D **1** *and* D **2**, *alternately. 12 mm. between lines of overprint.*

(*a*) *On stamp of Transvaal.*

		Un. pair	*Us. pair*
D33	5d. black and violet	90	1·50

(*b*) *On S. African stamps* (*Pretoria printing*). *Type* D **1**, *redrawn.* *P* 14.

D34	1½d. black and yellow-brown	10	25
	a. "Africa" (no stop) ..	15·00	
D35	2d. black and pale violet ..	12	25
	a. "Africa" (no stop) ..	15·00	
D36	2d. black and deep violet ..	20	35
	a. "Africa" (no stop) ..	15·00	
D37	3d. black and blue	60	1·00
	a. "Africa" (no stop) ..	20·00	
D38	6d. black and slate	80	1·50
	a. "Africa" (no stop) ..	30·00	

(*c*) *On S. African stamp* (*Pretoria printing*). *Type* D **2**. *P* 14.

D39	1d. black and carmine ..	10	20
	a. "Africa" (no stop) ..	1·50	

1928–29. *Optd. with T* **10**. *On S. African stamps* (*Pretoria printing*). *P* 14.

(*a*) *Type* D **1**, *redrawn.*

		Un. single	*Us. single*
D40	3d. black and blue	15	25
	a. Without stop after "A" ..	10·00	
D41	6d. black and slate	40	6
	(*b*) *Type* D **2**.		
D42	½d. black and green ..	8	1
D43	1d. black and carmine ..	8	1
	a. Without stop after "A" ..		
D44	2d. black and mauve ..	8	1
D45	2d. black and blue	15	25
D46	6d. black and slate	20	3
	a. Without stop after "A" ..	4·50	

D 3

D 4

(Litho. Bradbury, Wilkinson.)

1931 (23 Feb.). *Inscribed bilingually. W* **9** *o South Africa. P* 12.

D47	D **3** ½d. black and green ..	8	1
D48	,, 1d. black and scarlet ..	8	1
D49	,, 2d. black and violet ..	8	1
D50	,, 3d. black and blue ..	12	1
D51	,, 6d. black and slate ..	30	3
D47/51	.. .. *Set of* 5	60	6

(The following issues have been printed by the S.A. Government printer, Pretoria.)

1959 (18 May). *Centre typo; frame roto. W of South Africa. P* 15×14.

D52	D **4** 1d. black and scarlet ..	10	1
D53	,, 2d. black & reddish vio.	20	2
D54	,, 3d. black and blue ..	30	3

1960 (Dec.). *As Nos.* D52 *and* D54 *but W* **102** *o South Africa.*

D55	1d. black and scarlet ..	1·00	1·0
D56	3d. black and blue	1·00	1·0

1961 (14 Feb.). *As Nos.* D52 *etc., but whole stam roto, and value in cents. W* **102** *of South Africa*

D57	1 c. black and blue-green ..	5	
D58	2 c. black and scarlet ..	5	
D59	4 c. black and reddish violet	5	
D60	5 c. black and light blue ..	8	
D61	6 c. black and green ..	8	1
D62	10 c. black and yellow ..	12	1
D57/62	.. .. *Set of* 6	35	4

D 5

1972 (22 Mar.). *W* **127** (*sideways tête-bêche*) *Phosphorised chalk-surfaced paper. P* 14×13

D63	D **5** 1 c. deep olive	5	
D67	,, 8 c. ultramarine ..	10	1

OFFICIAL STAMPS.

OFFICIAL OFFISIEEL

South West Africa. Suidwes Afrika.

(O 1) (O 2)

1926 (DEC.). *Nos.* 30, 31, 6 *and* 32 *of South Africa optd. with Type* O 1 *on English stamp and* O 2 *on Afrikaans stamp alternately.*

		Un. pair	Us. pair
O1	½d. black and green	20·00	25·00
O2	1d. black and carmine ..	20·00	25·00
O3	2d. dull purple	30·00	35·00
O4	6d. green and orange ..	20·00	25·00

OFFICIAL OFFISIEEL

S.W.A. S.W.A.

(O 3) (O 4)

1929 (MAY). *Nos.* 30, 31, 32 *and* 34 *of South Africa optd. with Type* O 3 *on English stamp and* O 4 *on Afrikaans stamp.*

O5	½d. black and green	30	20
O6	1d. black and carmine ..	15	30
O7	2d. grey and purple	35	70
	a. Pair, stamp without stop after "OFFICIAL"	2·00	2·50
	b. Pair, stamp without stop after "OFFISIEEL"	2·00	2·50
	c. Pair comprising a and b ..	3·00	4·50
O8	6d. green and orange ..	80	1·25

Types O 3 and O 4 are normally spaced 17 mm. between lines on all except the 2d. value, which is spaced 13 mm.

Except on No. O7, the words "OFFICIAL" or "OFFISIEEL" normally have no stops after them.

OFFICIAL S.W.A. OFFISIEEL S.W.A.

(O 5) (O 6)

OFFICIAL. S.W.A. OFFISIEEL. S.W.A.

(O 7) (O 8)

1929 (AUG.). *Nos.* 30, 31 *and* 32 *of South Africa optd. with Types* O 5 *and* O 6, *and No.* 34 *with Types* O 7 *and* O 8, *languages to correspond.*

O 9	½d. black and green ..	15	15
O10	1d. black and carmine ..	20	25
O11	2d. grey and purple ..	30	50
	a. Pair, one stamp without stop after "OFFICIAL" ..	2·00	
	b. Pair, one stamp without stop after "OFFISIEEL" ..	1·50	
	c. Pair consisting of a and b	3·00	
O12	6d. green and orange ..	35	90

OFFICIAL OFFISIEEL

(O 9) (O 10)

1931. *English stamp optd. with Type* O 9 *and Afrikaans stamp with Type* O 10 *in red.*

			Un. pair	Us. pair
O13	12	½d. black and emerald ..	5	12
O14	13	1d. indigo and scarlet ..	8	12
O15	14	2d. blue and brown ..	10	20
O16	17	6d. blue and brown ..	25	40

OFFICIAL OFFISIEEL

(O 11) (O 12)

1938 (1 JULY). *English stamp optd. with Type* O 11 *and Afrikaans with Type* O 12 *in red.*

O17	27	1½d. purple-brown ..	80	90

OFFICIAL OFFISIEEL

(O 13) (O 14)

1945–50. *English stamp optd. with Type* O 13, *and Afrikaans stamp with Type* O 14 *in red.*

O18	12	½d. black and emerald ..	8	15
O19	13	1d. indigo & scarlet ('50)	8	20
O20	27	1½d. purple-brown ..	15	25
O21	14	2d. blue & brown ('47?)	£150	£200
O22	17	6d. blue and brown ..	25	40

OFFICIAL OFFISIEEL

(O 15) (O 16)

1951 (16 NOV.)–**52.** *English stamp optd. with Type* O 15 *and Afrikaans stamp with Type* O 16, *in red.*

O23	12	½d. black & emerald ('52)	10	15
O24	13	1d. indigo and scarlet ..	10	15
		a. Opts. transposed ..	2·25	4·00
O25	27	1½d. purple-brown ..	20	30
		a. Opts. transposed ..	1·75	2·50
O26	14	2d. blue and brown ..	25	40
		a. Opts. transposed ..	1·75	2·50
O27	17	6d. blue and brown ..	45	60
		a. Opts. transposed ..	2·25	3·50

The above errors refer to stamps with the English overprint on Afrikaans stamp and *vice versa.*

The use of official stamps ceased in January 1955.

SOUTHERN CAMEROONS.

The following issue, although ordered by the Southern Cameroons authorities, was also on sale in Northern Cameroons, until the latter joined Nigeria. The stamps therefore can be found with Nigerian postmarks.

CAMEROONS
U.K.T.T.
(1)

1960 (1 Oct.)–**61**. *Stamps of Nigeria optd. with T* 1, *in red (on Waterlow ptgs. or De La Rue, Nos.* 2a, 4a, 7a *only).*

1 **18** ½d. black and orange .. 5 8
2 **19** 1d. black & bronze-green .. 5 8
a. Grey-black and dull bronze-green (19.9.61) 10 20
3 **20** 1½d. blue-green 8 10
4 **21** 2d. grey 8 10
aa. Violet-grey .. .. 12·00 12·00
a. Pale grey (19.9.61) 10 20
5 **22** 3d. black and deep lilac .. 8 8
6 **23** 4d. black and blue 10 15
7 **24** 6d. chestnut & black (*p.* 14) 10 15
a. Perf. 13×13½ (19.9.61) .. 20 40
8 **25** 1s. black and maroon .. 20 40
9 **26** 2s. 6d. black and green .. 50 1·25
10 **27** 5s. black and red-orange .. 85 2·00
11 **28** 10s. black and red-brown .. 2·00 5·00
12 **29** £1 black and violet .. 4·50 12·00
1/12 .. .. *Set of* 12 8·00 19·00

Nos. 2, 4 and 4*aa* were overprinted on stamps printed by Waterlows' subsidiary, Imprimerie Belge de Securité.

The above stamps were withdrawn on September 30th, 1961, when Southern Cameroons became part of the independent republic of Cameroons.

SOUTHERN NIGERIA.

For earlier issues, see under Lagos.

PRINTERS. All issues of Southern Nigeria were typographed by De La Rue & Co.

1

2

1901 (Mar.)–**02**. *Wmk. Crown CA. P* 14.

1 **1** ½d. black and pale green .. 25 25
a. Black and green (1902) .. 20 20
2 ,, 1d. black and carmine .. 25 30
3 ,, 2d. black and red-brown .. 1·00 90
4 ,, 4d. black and sage green .. 1·25 1·40
5 ,, 6d. black and purple .. 1·25 1·60
6 ,, 1s. green and black .. 2·75 3·00
7 ,, 2s. 6d. black and brown .. 7·50 8·50
8 ,, 5s. black & orange-yellow 20·00 20·00
9 ,, 10s. black and purple/*yellow* 38·00 45·00
1/9 .. .. *Set of* 9 55·00 70·00
1/9 Optd. "Specimen" *Set of* 9 45·00

1903 (Mar.)–**04**. *Wmk. Crown CA. P* 14.

10 **2** ½d. grey-black & pale green 25 20
11 ,, 1d. grey-black and carmine 40 20
12 ,, 2d. grey-black & chestnut 50 65
13 ,, 2½d. grey-black & blue ('04) 1·50 1·00
14 ,, 4d. grey-black & olive-grn. 1·00 1·10
15 ,, 6d. grey-black & purple .. 3·50 5·00
16 ,, 1s. green and black .. 4·00 3·50
17 ,, 2s. 6d. grey-black & brn. 5·00 6·00
a. Grey and yellow-brown .. 30·00 40·00
18 ,, 5s. grey-black and yellow 20·00 22·00
19 ,, 10s. grey-blk. & pur./*yellow* 22·00 22·00
20 ,, £1 green and violet .. £100 £110
10/20 .. .. *Set of* 11 £140 £150
10/20 Optd. "Specimen" *Set of* 11 70·00

1904 (June)–**08**. *Wmk. Mult. Crown CA. P* 14.

21 **2** ½d. grey-blk. & pale grn., OC 12 12
22 ,, 1d. grey-black & carm., OC 15 15
23 ,, 2d. grey-blk. & chestnut, O 40 40
a. Pale grey & chestnut ('07) .. 50 35
24 ,, 2½d. grey-black and bright blue, O (1905) .. 60 65
25 ,, 3d. orange-brown and bright pur., C (1907) (Optd. S.£7) 2·25 1·25
26 ,, 4d. grey-black and olive-green, OC (1905) .. 2·50 1·50
a. Grey-black and pale olive-green, C (1907) .. .. .. 1·75 3·50
27 ,, 6d. grey-blk. & brt. pur., OC 1·25 1·10
28 ,, 1s. grey-green & black, OC 1·00 1·00
29 ,, 2s. 6d. grey-black & brown, OC (1905) .. .. 6·00 5·00
30 ,, 5s. grey-black and yellow, OC (1905) .. .. 9·00 8·50
31 ,, 10s. grey-black and purple/*yellow*, C (1908) .. 50·00 60·00
32 ,, £1 green & violet, OC ('05) 55·00 70·00
21/32 *Set of* 12 .. .. .. £110 £130

I.

II.

Die I. Thick "1"; small "d".
Die II. Thinner "1"; larger "d".

1907–11. *Colours changed. Ordinary paper* (½*d. to* 2½*d.*) *or chalk-surfaced paper* (*others*). *Wmk. Mult. Crown CA. P* 14.

33 **2** ½d. pale green 35 15
a. Blue-green (1910) 15 15
34 ,, 1d. carmine (I) 50 25
a. Die II. *Carmine-red* ('10) .. 15 15
35 ,, 2d. greyish slate (1909) .. 70 50
36 ,, 2½d. blue (1909) .. .. 70 1·25
37 ,, 3d. purple/*yellow* (1909) .. 60 45
38 ,, 4d. black & red/*yellow* ('09) 70 70
39 ,, 6d. dull pur. and pur. (1909) 1·60 1·10
a. Dull pur. & bright pur. ('11) .. 2·25 1·10
40 ,, 1s. black/*green* (1909) .. 1·75 85
41 ,, 2s. 6d. black & red/*blue* ('09) 2·50 1·10
42 ,, 5s. green & red/*yellow* (1909) 15·00 16·00
43 ,, 10s. green & red/*green* (1909) 20·00 22·00
44 ,, £1 purple & black/*red* ('09) 50·00 60·00
33/44 *Set of* 12 80·00 90·00
33/44 Optd. "Specimen" *Set of* 12 90·00

It was formerly believed that the plate used for printing the head was retouched in 1907 but the fact that the 1d. Die II, which did not appear until 1910, only exists in the first state of the head threw some doubts on this theory. Specialists now recognise that two dies of the head existed and that plates from both were used in Southern Nigeria.

The differences are very small and we refrain from listing them until more research is done, both in this country and in others where they may have been used. The differences are illustrated below:—

A

B

In Head A the fifth line of shading on the king's cheek shows as a line of dots and the lines of shading up to the king's hair are broken in places. In Head B the lines of shading are more regular, especially the fifth line.

The following stamps are known:—

Original colours: 21 ordinary and chalky, A; 22 ordinary and chalky, A; 23, A; 23*a*, B; 24, A; 25, B; 26 ordinary and chalky, A; 27 ordinary, A; 27 chalky, B; 28 ordinary, A; 28 chalky, B; 29 ordinary, A; 29 chalky, A and B; 30 ordinary, A; 30 chalky, B; 31, B; 32 ordinary, A; 32 chalky, B.

New colours: 33, A and B; 33*a*, B; 34, A and B; 34a, A; 35/44, B.

3

1912. *Wmk. Mult. Crown CA. P* 14.

45 **3** ½d. green 20 2
46 ,, 1d. red 35 1
47 ,, 2d. grey 50 5
48 ,, 2½d. bright blue 65 8
49 ,, 3d. purple/*yellow* 40 3
50 ,, 4d. black and red/*yellow* .. 90 1·0
51 ,, 6d. dull and bright purple 1·00 5
52 ,, 1s. black/*green* .. .. 1·10 6
53 ,, 2s. 6d. black and red/*blue* 4·00 4·5
54 ,, 5s. green and red/*yellow* .. 8·00 8·5
55 ,, 10s. green and red/*green* .. 22·00 25·0
56 ,, £1 purple and black/*red* .. 48·00 55·0
45/56 .. .. *Set of* 12 80·00 90·0
45/56 Optd. "Specimen" *Set of* 12 95·00

Since 1914 Southern Nigeria has used th stamps of Nigeria.

SOUTHERN RHODESIA.

SELF-GOVERNMENT.

1

(Recess. Waterlow.)

1924 (1 Apr.)–**29**. *P* 14.

1 **1** ½d. blue-green 15 1
a. Imperf. between (horiz. pair) £140 £14
b. Imperf. between (vert. pair) £150 £15
c. Imperf. vert. (horiz. pair) .. £140
2 ,, 1d. bright rose 15 1
a. Imperf. between (horiz. pair) £160 £15
b. Imperf. between (vert. pair) .. £150
c. Perf. 12½ (coil) (1929) .. 4·00 9·0
3 ,, 1½d. bistre-brown 25 1
a. Imperf. between (horiz. pair) £450
b. Imperf. between (vert. pair) £500
4 ,, 2d. black and purple-grey .. 40 3
a. Imperf. between (horiz. pair) £700
5 ,, 3d. blue .. .. .. 1·00 8
6 ,, 4d. black and orange-red 1·00 1·2
7 ,, 6d. black and mauve .. 1·00 7
a. Imperf. between (horiz. pair) £800
8 ,, 8d. purple and pale green .. 4·00 4·5
9 ,, 10d. blue and rose .. .. 4·00 4·5
10 ,, 1s. black and light blue .. 1·50 1·5
11 ,, 1s. 6d. black and yellow .. 5·00 6·0
12 ,, 2s. black and brown .. 6·50 6·5
13 ,, 2s. 6d. blue and sepia .. 12·00 14·0
14 ,, 5s. blue and blue-green .. 22·00 22·0
a. Error. Blue and light blue .. £1000
1/14 .. .. *Set of* 14 55·00 55·0

Prices for "imperf. between" varieties are f adjacent stamps from the same pane and not f those separated by wide gutter margins betwee vertical or horizontal pairs, which come from t junction of two panes.

Collectors are warned against dangerous fak of No. 14a, chemically produced.

2. King George V.

3. Victoria Falls.

(T 2 recess. by Bradbury, Wilkinson ; T 3 typo. by Waterlow.)

.931 (1 April)–**37.** *T* **2** (*line perf.* 12 *unless otherwise stated*) *and* **3** (*comb. perf.* 15×14). (*The* 11½ *perf. is comb*).

5	2	½d. green	12	15
		a. Perf. 11½ ('33)	12	10
		b. Perf. 14 ('35)	12	10
.6	,,	1d. scarlet	20	12
		a. Perf. 11½ ('33)	30	10
		b. Perf. 14 ('35)	15	10
6c	,,	1½d. chocolate ('33) ..	9·00	10·00
		d. Perf. 11½ (1.4.32)	35	20
7	3	2d. black and sepia ..	1·50	1·40
8	,,	3d. deep ultramarine ..	3·00	3·50
9	2	4d. black and vermilion ..	90	30
		a. Perf. 11½ ('35)	4·00	1·50
		b. Perf. 14 (10.37)	7·50	7·50
o	,,	6d. black and magenta ..	1·10	30
		a. Perf. 11½ ('33)	2·75	30
		b. Perf. 14 ('36)	4·50	50
ɪ	,,	8d. violet and olive-green	1·50	2·00
		a. Perf. 11½ ('34)	4·50	5·00
ɪb	,,	9d. verm. & ol.-grn. (1.9.34)	3·75	3·75
2	,,	10d. blue and scarlet ..	2·75	2·00
		a. Perf. 11½ ('33)	2·75	3·00
3	,,	1s. black & greenish blue	2·50	75
		a. Perf. 11½ ('36)	5·00	4·00
		b. Perf. 14 (10.37)	30·00	20·00
4	,,	1s. 6d. blk. & orange-yell.	4·50	5·00
		a. Perf. 11½ ('36)	12·00	12·00
5	,,	2s. black and brown ..	3·50	4·00
		a. Perf. 11½ ('33)	12·00	8·00
6	,,	2s. 6d. blue and drab ..	7·50	7·50
		a. Perf. 11½ ('33)	12·00	7·50
7	,,	5s. blue and blue-green ..	12·00	12·00
		a. Printed on gummed side ..	£650	
5/27		.. .. *Set of* 15	40·00	40·00

No. 16*c* was issued in booklets only.

PRINTERS. All stamps from Types **4** to **29** vere recess-printed by Waterlow except where tated.

4

932 (1 May). *P* 12½.

9	4	2d. green and chocolate ..	30	12
o	,,	3d. deep ultramarine ..	1·50	50
		a. Imperf. between (vert. pair) ..	£1100	£1200

5. Victoria Falls.

1935 (6 May). *Silver Jubilee. P* 11×12.

31	5	1d. olive and rose-carmine ..	15	15
32	,,	2d. emerald and sepia ..	40	60
33	,,	3d. violet and deep blue ..	1·50	1·75
34	,,	6d. black and purple ..	1·60	1·75

1935–41. *Inscr.* "POSTAGE AND REVENUE".

35	4	2d. green & chocolate (*p.* 12½)	85	85
		a. Perf. 14 (1941)	8	5
35*b*	,,	3d. deep blue (*p.* 14) (1938)	25	15

6. Victoria Falls and Railway Bridge.

1937 (12 May). *Coronation. P* 12½.

36	6	1d. olive and rose-carmine ..	15	12
37	,,	2d. emerald and sepia ..	15	15
38	,,	3d. violet and blue	75	1·00
39	,,	6d. black and purple ..	50	40

7. King George VI.

1937 (25 Nov.). *P* 14.

40	7	½d. green	5	5
41	,,	1d. scarlet	5	5
42	,,	1½d. red-brown	5	8
43	,,	4d. red-orange	8	5
44	,,	6d. grey-black	12	5
45	,,	8d. emerald-green	35	20
46	,,	9d. pale blue	25	15
47	,,	10d. purple	30	65
48	,,	1s. black and blue-green ..	20	8
		a. Double print of frame ..	75·00	
49	,,	1s. 6d. black & orange-yell.	65	45
50	,,	2s. black and brown ..	70	25
51	,,	2s. 6d. ultramarine & purple	1·00	40
52	,,	5s. blue and blue-green ..	2·10	60
40/52		.. .. *Set of* 13	5·00	2·75

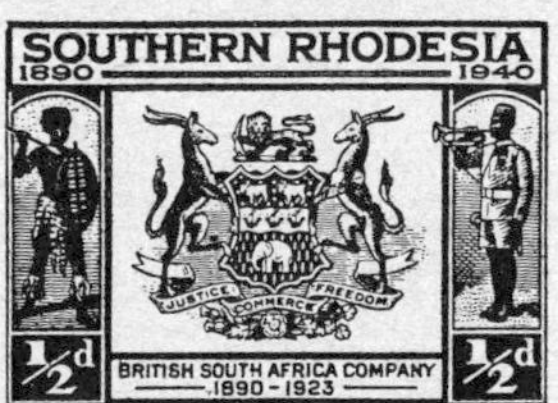

8. British South Africa Co's Arms.

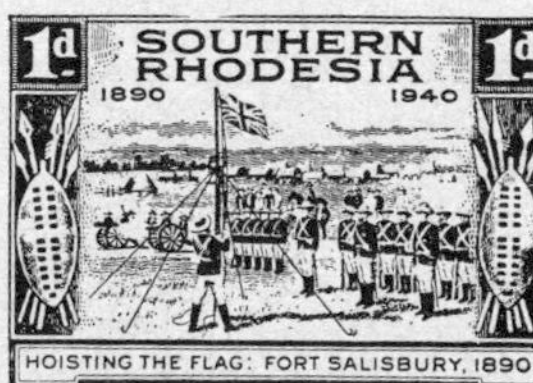

9. Fort Salisbury, 1890.

10. Cecil John Rhodes (after S. P. Kendrick).

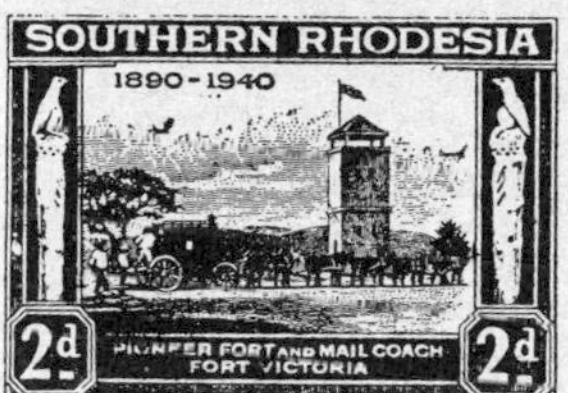

11. Fort Victoria.

12. Rhodes makes peace.

13. Victoria Falls Bridge.

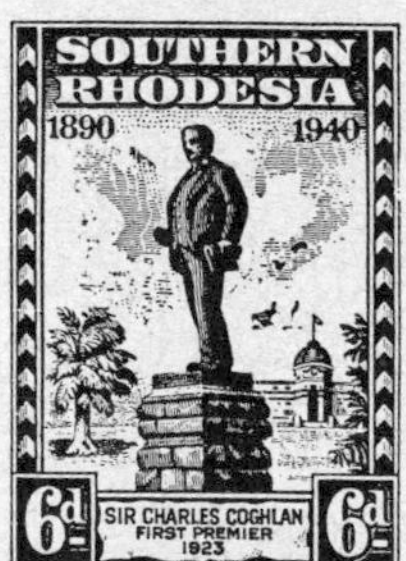

14. Statue of Sir Charles Coghlan.

15. Lobengula's Kraal and Govt. House, Salisbury.

(Des. Mrs. L. E. Curtis (½d., 1d., 1½d., 3d.), Mrs. I. Mount (others).)

1940 (3 JUNE). *British South Africa Company's Golden Jubilee. P 14.*

53	**8**	½d. slate-violet and green	8	5
54	**9**	1d. violet-blue and scarlet	8	5
55	**10**	1½d. black and red-brown ..	8	8
56	**11**	2d. green and bright violet	8	8
57	**12**	3d. black and blue ..	10	10
58	**13**	4d. green and brown ..	20	35
59	**14**	6d. chocolate and green ..	30	50
60	**15**	1s. blue and green ..	40	60
53/60		.. .. *Set of* 8	1·10	1·60

16. Mounted Pioneer.

(Roto. Union Govt. Stamp Ptrs., Pretoria.)

1943 (1 NOV.). *50th Anniv. of Occupation of Matabeleland. W 9 of South Africa (Mult. Springbok) sideways. P 14.*

61	**16**	2d. brown and green ..	5	5

17. Queen Elizabeth II when Princess and Princess Margaret.

18. King George VI and Queen Elizabeth.

1947 (1 APR.). *Royal Visit. P 14.*

62	**17**	½d. black and green	5	5
63	**18**	1d. black and scarlet ..	5	5

19. Queen Elizabeth. **20.** King George VI.

21. Queen Elizabeth II when Princess. **22.** Princess Margaret.

1947 (8 MAY). *Victory. P 14.*

64	**19**	1d. carmine	5	5
65	**20**	2d. slate	5	5
66	**21**	3d. blue	8	8
67	**22**	6d. orange	10	10

(Recess. Bradbury, Wilkinson & Co.)

1949 (10 OCT.). *75th Anniv. of Universal Postal Union. As Nos. 115/6 of Antigua.*

68	2d. slate-green	8	8
69	3d. blue	15	20

23. Queen Victoria, Arms and King George VI.

1950 (12 SEPT.). *Diamond Jubilee of Southern Rhodesia. P 14.*

70	**23**	2d. green and brown ..	8	5

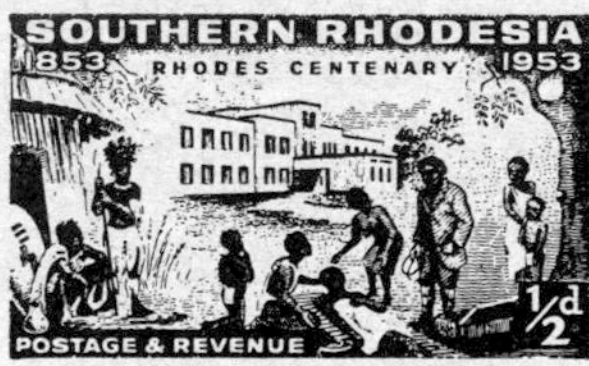

24. " Medical Services ".

25. " Agriculture ".

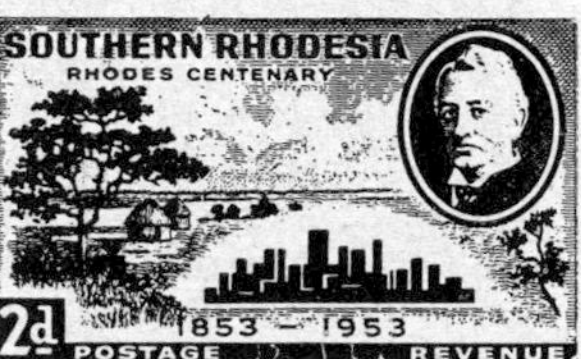

26. " Building ".

27. " Water Supplies ".

28. "Transport".

(Des. A. R. Winter (2d.), Mrs. J. M. Enali (others).)

1953 (15 APR.). *Centenary of Birth of Cec Rhodes. P 14.*

71	**24**	½d. pale blue and sepia ..	8	2
72	**25**	1d. chestnut & blue-green	10	
73	**26**	2d. grey-green and violet ..	10	1
74	**27**	4½d. dp bl.-grn. & dp. ultra.	40	8
75	**28**	1s. black and red-brown ..	40	5
71/75		.. .. *Set of* 5	90	1·4

No. 74 also commemorates the Diamon Jubilee of Matabeleland.

1953 (30 MAY). *Rhodes Centenary Exhibitio Bulawayo. As No. 59 of Northern Rhodes but without watermark.*

76	6d. violet	30	4

30. Queen Elizabeth II.

(Recess. De La Rue.)

1953 (1 JUNE). *Coronation. P 12×12½.*

77	**30**	2s. 6d. carmine	75	1·

31. Sable Antelope. **32.** Tobacco Plante

33. Rhodes's Grave. **34.** Farm Worker.

35. Flame Lily.

36. Victoria Falls.

37. Baobab Tree. **38.** Lion.

39. Zimbabwe Ruins.

40. Birchenough Bridge.

41. Kariba Gorge. **42.** Basket Maker.

43. Balancing Rocks.

MINIMUM PRICE

The minimum price quoted is 5p which represents a handling charge rather than a basis for valuing common stamps. For further notes about prices see introductory pages.

44. Coat-of-Arms.

(Recess; centre typo. (4d.). Bradbury, Wilkinson.)

1953 (31 AUG.). *P* 13½×14 (*2d., 6d., 5s.*), 14 (*10s., £1*) *or* 14×13½ (*others*).

78	**31**	½d.	grey-green and claret	5	5
79	**32**	1d.	green and brown ..	5	5
80	**33**	2d.	deep chestnut and reddish violet	8	5
81	**34**	3d.	chocolate and rose-red	8	10
82	**35**	4d.	red, green and indigo ..	12	8
83	**36**	4½d.	black & deep brt. blue	20	25
84	**37**	6d.	brown-olive and deep turquoise-green ..	15	10
85	**38**	9d.	dp. blue & reddish brn.	25	30
86	**39**	1s.	reddish vio. & light blue	30	20
87	**40**	2s.	purple and scarlet ..	1·10	1·40
88	**41**	2s.	6d. yellow-olive and orange-brown	1·50	2·00
89	**42**	5s.	yellow-brn. & dp. green	3·00	4·00
90	**43**	10s.	red-brown and olive ..	5·50	7·00
91	**44**	£1	rose-red and black ..	11·00	13·00
78/91			.. .. *Set of* 14	20·00	26·00

For issues from 1954 to 1963 see under RHODESIA AND NYASALAND.

45. Maize.

46. Buffalo.

47. Tobacco.

48. Kudu.

49. Citrus.

50. Flame Lily.

51. Ansellia Orchid.

52. Emeralds.

53. Aloe.

54. Lake Kyle.

55. Tiger Fish.

56. Cattle.

57. Guineafowl.

58. Coat-of-Arms.

(Des. V. Whiteley. Photo. Harrison.)

1964 (19 FEB.). *P* 14½ (½*d. to* 4*d.*), 13½×13 (6*d. to* 2*s.* 6*d.*) *or* 14½×14.

92	**45**	½d. yellow, yellow-green and light blue ..	5	5
93	**46**	1d. reddish violet & yellow-ochre	5	5
		a. Reddish violet omitted ..	£350	
94	**47**	2d. yellow & deep violet	5	5
95	**48**	3d. chocolate & pale blue	5	5
96	**49**	4d. yell.-orge. & dp. grn.	5	5
97	**50**	6d. carmine-red, yellow and deep dull green ..	8	8
98	**51**	9d. red-brown, yellow and olive-green	15	12
99	**52**	1s. blue-green and ochre	15	12
		a. Green ptg. (Queen and emeralds) omitted ..	£400	
100	**53**	1s. 3d. red, violet and yellow-green	30	20
101	**54**	2s. blue and ochre ..	40	40
102	**55**	2s. 6d. ultram. and verm.	45	30
		a. Vermilion omitted ..	£150	
103	**56**	5s. lt. brown, bistre-yellow and light blue ..	1·10	1·25
104	**57**	10s. black, yellow-ochre, lt. bl. & carmine-red	2·25	2·50
105	**58**	£1 brown, yellow-green, buff and salmon-pink	5·00	5·50
92/105		.. .. *Set of* 14	9·00	9·50

POSTAGE DUE STAMPS.

SOUTHERN

RHODESIA

(D 1)

1951–52? *Postage Due stamps of Great Britain optd. with Type* D **1**.

D1	D **1**	½d. emerald (No. D27) ..	8	12
D2	,,	1d. violet-blue (No. D36)	10	15
D3	,,	2d. agate (No. D29) ..	15	20
D4	,,	3d. violet (No. D30) ..	15	25
D5	,,	4d. blue (No. D38) ..	20	30
D6	,,	4d. dull grey-green (No. D31) ('52?)	12·00	15·00
D7	,,	1s. deep blue (No. D33) ..	35	50
D1/5, 7		.. .. *Set of* 6	90	1·25

In October 1964 Southern Rhodesia was renamed Rhodesia. Issues after this date will be found listed under RHODESIA.

SRI LANKA.

(Formerly CEYLON.)

REPUBLIC.

208. National Flower and Mountain of the Illustrious Foot.

(Des. L. D. P. Jayawardena. Litho. D.L.R.)

1972 (22 MAY). *Inauguration of the Republic of Sri Lanka. P* 13.

591 **208** 15 c. multicoloured .. 5 5

209. Map of World with Buddhist Flag.

(Des. L. D .P. Jayawardena. Litho. Harrison).

1972 (26 MAY). *Tenth Conference of the World Fellowship of Buddhists. P* 14×13.

592 **209** 5 c. multicoloured .. 5 5

This stamp was scheduled for release in May 1971, and when finally released had the year "1972" additionally overprinted in red. Sheets are known without this overprint but their status has not been established.

210. Book Year Emblem.

(Des. L. D. P. Jayawardena. Photo. Pakistan Security Printing Corp.)

1972 (8 SEPT.). *International Book Year. P* 13.

593 **210** 20 c. light yellow-orange and lake-brown .. 5 5

211. Imperial Angelfish.

(Des. G. D. Kariyawasam. Litho. Rosenbaum Bros., Vienna.)

1972 (12 OCT.). *T* **211** *and similar horiz. designs showing fish. Multicoloured. P* 13×13½.

594	2 c. Type **211**	5	5
	a. Plum colour omitted ..		
595	3 c. Green Chromide ..	5	5
596	30 c. Skipjack	5	5
597	2 r. Black Ruby Barb ..	25	30

On No. 594a the stripes of the fish are in green instead of plum.

212. Memorial Hall.

(Des. R. B. Nawilmada. Litho. D.L.R.)

1973 (17 MAY). *Opening of Bandaranaike Memorial Hall. P* 14.

598 **212** 15 c. light cobalt & deep grey-blue 5 5

213. King Vessantara Giving Away His Childre

(Des. P. Wanigatunga. Litho. D.L.R.)

1973 (3 SEPT.). *Rock and Temple Painting T* **213** *and similar vert. designs. Multicoloure P* 13½×14.

599	35 c. Type **213**	5	
600	50 c. The Prince and the Grave-digger	8	
601	90 c. Bearded old man ..	12	1
602	1 r. 55, Two female figures ..	25	3
MS603	115×141 mm. Nos. 599/602	45	

214. Bandaranaike Memorial Conference Hall.

(Des. and litho. Harrison.)

1974 (6 SEPT.). *20th Commonwealth Parli mentary Conference, Colombo. P* 14½.

604 **214** 85 c. multicoloured .. 10

215. Prime Minister Bandaranaike.

(Des. and photo. Harrison.)

1974 (25 SEPT.). *P* 14½.

605 **215** 15 c. multicoloured .. 5

a. Red (face value) omitted 15·00

b. Pale blue (background) omitted .. ..

216. "UPU" and "100".

(Des. P. Jayatilleke. Litho. German Bankno Ptg. Co., Leipzig.)

1974 (9 OCT.). *Centenary of Universal Pos Union. P* 13½×13.

606 **216** 50 c. multicoloured .. 8

217. Sri Lanka Parliament Building.

(Litho. Toppan Printing Co. Ltd., Japan.)

975 (1 Apr.). *Inter-Parliamentary Meeting. P* 13.
77 **217** 1 r. multicoloured .. 12 15

18. Sir Ponnambalam Ramanathan (politician).

Des. A. Rasiah. Litho. Toppan Ptg. Co., Japan.)

975 (4 Sept.). *Ramanathan Commemoration. P* 13.
98 **218** 75 c. multicoloured .. 10 10

219. D. J. Wimalasurendra (engineer).

Des. A. Dharmasiri. Litho. Toppan Ptg. Co., Japan.)

975 (17 Sept.). *Wimalasurendra Commemoration. P* 13.
99 **219** 75 c. blue-blk. & new blue 10 10

220. Mrs. Bandaranaike, Map and Dove.

Des. B. U. Ananda Somatilaka. Litho. Toppan Ptg. Co., Japan.)

75 (22 Dec.). *International Women's Year. P* 13.
o **220** 1 r. 15, multicoloured .. 15 20

221. Ma-ratmal.

(Des. and litho. Toppan Ptg. Co., Japan.)

1976 (1 Jan.). *Indigenous Flora. T* **221** *and similar vert. designs. Multicoloured. P* 13.

611	25 c. Type **221**	5	5
	a. Imperf. (pair)		
612	50 c. Binara	5	8
613	75 c. Daffodil orchid ..	8	10
614	10 r. Diyapara	1·10	1·25
MS615	153×153 mm. Nos. 611/14	1·25	

222. Mahaweli Dam.

(Des. R. B. Mawilmada. Litho. German Bank Note Ptg. Co., Leipzig.)

1976 (8 Jan.). *Diversion of the Mahaweli River. P* 13×12½.
616 **222** 85 c. turquoise, violet-blue and azure 10 10

223. Dish Aerial.

(Des. P. A. Miththapala. Litho. German Bank Note Ptg. Co., Leipzig.)

1976 (6 May). *Opening of Satellite Earth Station, Padukka. P* 14×13½.
617 **223** 1 r. multicoloured .. 12 15

224. Conception of the Buddha.

(Des. P. Wanigatunga. Litho. Toppan Ptg. Co., Japan.)

1976 (7 May). *Vesak. T* **224** *and similar horiz. designs showing paintings from the Danbava Temple. Multicoloured. P* 13.

618	5 c. Type **224**	5	5
619	10 c. King Suddhodana and the astrologers	5	5
620	1 r. 50, The astrologers being entertained	20	25
621	2 r. The Queen in a palanquin	25	30
622	2 r. 25, Royal procession ..	30	35
623	5 r. Birth of the Buddha ..	65	75
618/23	.. .. *Set of* 6	1·40	1·60
MS624	161×95 mm. Nos. 618/23	1·50	

225. Blue Sapphire.

(Des. State Gem Corporation. Litho. Toppan Ptg. Co., Japan.)

1976 (16 June). *Gems of Sri Lanka. T* **225** *and similar horiz. designs. Multicoloured. P* 12×12½.

625	60 c. Type **225**	8	8
626	1 r. 15, Cat's Eye	15	15
627	2 r. Star sapphire	25	30
628	5 r. Ruby	55	60
MS629	152×152 mm. Nos. 625/8	1·10	

226. President Mrs. S. Bandaranaike.

(Photo. Harrison.)

1976 (3 Aug.). *Non-aligned Summit Conference, Colombo. P* 14×14½.
630 **226** 1 r. 15, multicoloured .. 15 15
631 ,, 2 r. multicoloured .. 30 35

227. Statue of Liberty.

(Des. Ananda Harischandra. Litho. German Bank Note Ptg. Co., Leipzig.)

1976 (29 Nov.). *Bicentenary of American Revolution. P* 13½.
632 **227** 2 r. 25, cobalt and indigo 30 35

228. Bell, Early Telephone and Telephone Lines.

229. Maitreya (pre-carnate Buddha).

(Des. Ananda Harischandra. Litho. German Bank Note Ptg. Co., Leipzig.)

1976 (21 Dec.). *Telephone Centenary. P* 13.

633	**228**	1 r. multicoloured ..	15	15

(Des. P. Wanigatunga. Litho. German Bank Note Ptg. Co., Leipzig.)

1977 (1 Jan.). *Centenary of Colombo Museum. T* **229** *and similar vert. designs showing statues. Multicoloured. P* 12½.

634	50 c. Type **229**	8	8
635	1 r. Sundara Murti Swami (Tamil psalmist)	15	15
636	5 r. Tara (goddess)	70	80

STELLALAND.

Stellaland was annexed by Great Britain in 1884.

1. Arms of the Republic.

(Litho. by Van der Sandt, de Villiers & Co., Cape Town.)

1884 (Feb.). *P* 12.

1	**1**	1d. red	60·00
		a. Imperf. between (pair) ..	£400
2	,,	3d. orange	6·00
		a. Imperf. between (pair) ..	£120
3	,,	4d. blue	6·00
		a. Imperf. between (pair) ..	£120
4	,,	6d. lilac-mauve	6·00
		a. Imperf. between (pair) ..	£250
5	,,	1s. green	10·00

1885 (Oct.). *Surch.* "Twee" *in violet-lake.*

6	**1**	2d. on 4d. blue	£500

No date stamps were employed in Stellaland, the stamps being pen-cancelled with the initials of the postal official and date, but a date stamp was used on arrival at Barkly West or Kimberley.

Stellaland, with surrounding territory, was proclaimed the British Bechuanaland Colony on 30 September 1885. Its stamps were withdrawn and superseded by British Bechuanaland stamps on 2 December 1885. It is now part of South Africa.

SUDAN.

(Anglo-Egyptian Condominium)

السودان
SOUDAN

(1)

1897 (1 Mar.). 1884, 1888 *and* 1893 *issues o[f] Egypt (Sphinx and Pyramid) optd. as T* **1.**

1	1 m. pale brown	40	5
	a. Opt. inverted	£130	
2	1 m. deep brown	60	8
3	2 m. green	70	8
4	3 m. orange-yellow	70	7
5	5 m. rose-carmine	1·25	1·2
	a. Opt. inverted	£130	
6	1 p. ultramarine	2·50	2·5
7	2 p. orange-brown	11·00	8·5
8	5 p. slate	12·00	8·5
	a. Opt. double		
9	10 p. mauve	11·00	10·0
1/9	.. .. *Set of* 8	35·00	30·0

Numerous forgeries exist including some whic[h] show the characteristics of the varieties men[-] tioned below.

There are six varieties of the overprint on eac[h] value most of which can be supplied in vertica[l] strips at double the catalogue price.

In some printings the large dot is omitted fro[m] the left-hand Arabic character on some stamp[s] in the sheet.

The overprint was frequently misplaced, an[d] pairs may be found with and without it, and als[o] with the overprint diagonal.

PRINTERS. All stamps of Sudan wer[e] printed by De La Rue & Co. *except where other[-] wise stated.*

2. Arab Postman.

3

(Des. Col. E. A. Stanton, C.M.G. Typo.).

1898 (1 Mar.). *W* **3.** *P* 14.

10	**2**	1 m. brown and pink ..	20	1
11	,,	2 m. green and brown ..	60	7
12	,,	3 m. mauve and green ..	60	7
13	,,	5 m. carmine and black ..	25	1
14	,,	1 p. blue and brown ..	1·40	9
15	,,	2 p. black and blue ..	3·25	1·4
16	,,	5 p. brown and green ..	4·00	2·7
17	,,	10 p. black and mauve ..	5·50	2·5
10/17		.. .. *Set of* 8	14·00	8·0

HAVE YOU READ THE NOTES AT THE BEGINNING OF THIS CATALOGUE?

These often provide answers to the enquiries we receive

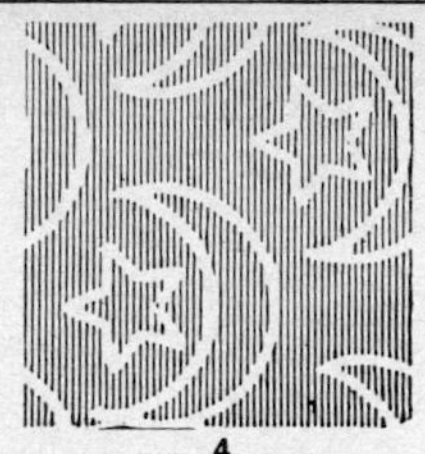

4

.902–21. *W* **4.** *P* 14.

8 **2** 1 m. brown & carmine (5.05) 8 8
9 ,, 2 m. green & brown (11.02) 15 12
0 ,, 3 m. mauve & green (7.03) 35 15
1 ,, 4 m. blue & bistre (20.1.07) 30 70
2 ,, 4 m. verm. & brown (10.07) 70 70
3 ,, 5 m. scarlet & black (12.03) 50 8
4 ,, 1 p. blue and brown (12.03) 80 15
5 ,, 2 p. black and blue (2.08) .. 3·00 90
6 ,, 2 p. purple and orange-yellow, C (22.12.21) .. 80 60
7 ,, 5 p. brown & grn. OC (2.08) 2·25 45
8 ,, 10 p. blk. & mve. OC (2.11) 5·50 70
8/28 .. .. *Set of* 11 13·00 4·00

5 Milliemes

(5)

903 (Sept.). *No.* 16 *surch. at Khartoum with T* **5**, *in blocks of* 30.

9 5 m. on 5 pi. brown and green 1·10 1·90
a. Surch. inverted .. .. 90·00 £110

6

7

921–22. *Chalk-surfaced paper. Typo. W* **4.** *P* 14.

0 **6** 1 m. black & orange (4.2.22) 25 30
1 ,, 2 m. yell.-orge. & choc. ('22) 1·00 65
a. Yellow and chocolate .. 1·25 85
2 ,, 3 m. mauve & grn. (25.1.22) 70 70
3 ,, 4 m. grn. & choc. (21.3.22) 75 70
4 ,, 5 m. ol.-brn. & blk. (4.2.22) 50 8
5 ,, 10 m. carmine & blk. (1922) 70 10
6 ,, 15 m. bright blue & chestnut (14.12.21) .. .. 1·10 75
0/36 .. .. *Set of* 7 4·50 3·00

927–40. *W* 7. *P* 14.

7 **6** 1 m. black & orange, CO 5 5
8 ,, 2 m. orange & choc., CO 5 5
9 ,, 3 m. mauve & green, CO 5 5
0 ,, 4 m. green and choc., CO 5 5
1 ,, 5 m. olive-brn. & blk., CO 5 5
2 ,, 10 m. carmine & black, CO 8 5
3 ,, 15 m. brt. bl. & chest., CO 8 5
4 **2** 2 p. pur. & orge.-yell., CO 10 5
4*a* ,, 3 p. red-brown & bl., CO 20 10
4*b* ,, 4 p. ultram. & black, C 20 8
5 ,, 5 p. chestnut & green, CO 25 8
5*a* ,, 6 p. grn'ish bl. & blk., CO 60 15
5*b* ,, 8 p. emerald & black, CO 65 25
6 ,, 10 p. black and violet, CO 50 15
6*a* ,, 20 p. pale blue & blue, CO 90 30
7/46*a* .. .. *Set of* 15 3·50 1·25

The ordinary paper of this issue is thick, mooth and opaque and is a wartime substitute or chalk-surfaced paper.

Dates of issue: 1927 (all except the following) –17.10.35, 20 p; 2.11.36, 4 p., 6 p. and 8 p.; .1.40, 3 p.

For similar stamps, but with different Arabic scriptions, see Nos. 96/111.

AIR MAIL

(8)

AIR MAIL

(9)

1931 (15 Feb.–1 Mar.). *Air. Stamps of* 1927 *optd. with T* **8** *or* **9** (2 *p.*).

47 5 m. olive-brown & blk. (1.3) 70 1·00
48 10 m. carmine and black .. 70 1·25
49 2 p. purple & orange-yellow .. 1·00 1·60

10. Statue of Gen. Gordon.

1931 (1 Sept.)–**37.** *Air. Recess. W* **7** (*sideways*). *P* 14.

49*a* **10** 3 m. green & sepia (1.1.33) 1·50 2·00
50 ,, 5 m. black and green .. 75 75
51 ,, 10 m. black and carmine .. 1·00 1·00
52 ,, 15 m. red-brown and sepia 50 50
a. Perf. 11½×12½ ('37) .. 75 40
53 ,, 2 p. black and orange .. 30 35
a. Perf. 11½×12½ ('37) .. 5·00 5·50
53*b* ,, 2½ p. mag. & blue (1.1.33) 1·00 50
c. Perf. 11½×12½ ('36) .. 70 70
54 ,, 3 p. black and grey .. 70 70
a. Perf. 11½×12½ ('37) .. 2·00 1·50
55 ,, 3½ p. black and violet .. 1·25 1·25
a. Perf. 11½×12½ ('37) .. 3·75 4·00
56 ,, 4½ p. red-brown and grey 5·00 6·00
57 ,, 5 p. black & ultramarine 1·60 1·60
a. Perf. 11½×12½ ('37) .. 1·25 1·25
57*b* ,, 7½ p. green and emerald (17.10.35) .. .. 2·50 2·75
c. Perf. 11½×12½ ('37) .. 2·50 2·50
57*d* ,, 10 p. brown and greenish blue (17.10.35) .. 3·75 2·00
e. Perf. 11½×12½ ('37) .. 2·75 3·00
49*a*/57*d* .. .. *Set of* 12 17·00 17·00

2½ 2½

AIR MAIL

٢½ ٢½

(11)

1932 (18 July). *Air. No.* 44 *surch. with T* **11.**

58 2½ p. on 2 p. pur. & orge.-yell. 3·50 4·00

12. Gen. Gordon.

13. Gordon Memorial College, Khartoum.

14. Gordon Memorial Service, Khartoum.

1935 (1 Jan.). 50*th Anniv. of Death of General Gordon. Recess. W* **7.** *P* 14.

59 **12** 5 m. green 35 30
60 ,, 10 m. yellow-brown .. 45 45
61 ,, 13 m. ultramarine .. .. 1·00 2·25
62 ,, 15 m. scarlet 65 75
63 **13** 2 p. blue 70 70
64 ,, 5 p. orange-vermilion .. 1·10 1·10
65 ,, 10 p. purple .. .. 3·25 3·00
66 **14** 20 p. black .. .. .. 14·00 16·00
67 ,, 50 p. red-brown .. .. 30·00 30·00
59/67 .. .. *Set of* 9 45·00 50·00

7½ PIASTRES

٧ ½ قروش

(15)

5 MILLIEMES

٥ مليمات

(16)

1935. *Air. Surch. as T* **15.**

68 **10** 15 m. on 10 m. black and carmine (Apr.) .. 60 65
a. Surch. double £250 £250
69 ,, 2½ p. on 3 m. green and sepia (Apr.) .. .. 1·25 2·00
a. Second Arabic letter from left missing .. .. 32·00 32·00
b. Small "½" .. .. 4·50 5·50
70 ,, 2½ p. on 5 m. black and green (Apr.) .. .. 70 1·00
a. Second Arabic letter from left missing .. .. 32·00 32·00
b. Small "½" .. .. 3·50 4·00
c. Surch. inverted £350 £375
d. Ditto. with variety a. ..
e. Ditto, with variety b. ..
71 ,, 3 p. on 4½ p. red-brown and grey (Apr.) .. 2·00 3·50
72 ,, 7½ p. on 4½ p. red-brown and grey (Mar.) .. 4·50 5·50
73 ,, 10 p. on 4½ p. red-brown and grey (Mar.) .. 3·75 5·50
68/73 .. .. *Set of* 6 12·00 16·00

The 7½ p. on 4½ p. exists but is from a proof sheet.

1938 (1 July). *Air. Surch. as T* **16.**

74 **10** 5 m. on 2½ p. (*p.* 11½×12½) 20 30
75 ,, 3 p. on 3½ p. (*p.* 14) .. 3·25 4·00
a. Perf. 11½×12½ £130 £130
76 ,, 3 p. on 7½ p. (*p.* 14) .. 70 1·10
a. Perf. 11½×12½ £130 £130
77 ,, 5 p. on 10 p. (*p.* 14) .. 90 1·25
a. Perf. 11½×12½ £130 £140

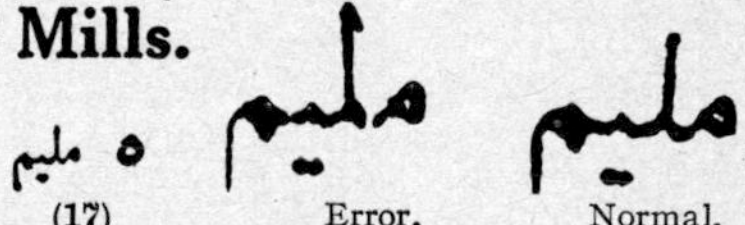

(17) Error. Normal.

In the error a wrong Arabic character was used so that it reads "Malmime" instead of "malime".

1940 (25 Feb.). *Surch. as T* **17.**

78 **6** 5 m. on 10 m. carm. & black 10 20
a. Error. "Malmime" .. 2·50 2·75
b. Two dots omitted .. 5·00 6·00

A variety known as "Inserted 5" occurs in the bottom right-hand pane, Row 4, No. 5. It may be a different fount, or it could be a damaged piece of type. There is also a dot over the right-hand end of the horizontal stroke, and another on the down stroke, which may be remnants of the original faulty figure. The "Inserted 5" is usually dropped and it is believed that it only occurred on a few sheets.

4½ PIASTRES (18)

4½ Piastres ٤ ١/٢ قرش (19)

1940–1. *Surch. as T* **18** *or* **19.**

No.	Type	Description	Unused	Used
79	**6**	4½ p. on 5 m. olive-brown and black (9.2.41) ..	3·50	2·50
80	**2**	4½ p. on 8 p. emerald and black (12.12.40) ..	3·50	2·50

20. Tuti Is., R. Nile, near Khartoum.

21. Tuti Is., R. Nile, near Khartoum.

(Des. Miss H. M. Hebbert. Litho. Security Printing Press, Nasik, India.)

1941 (MAR.–AUG.). *P* 14×13½ (*T* **20**) *or P* 13½×14 (*T* **21**).

No.	Type	Description	Unused	Used
81	**20**	1 m. slate and orange ..	8	25
82	,,	2 m. orange and chocolate	15	25
83	,,	3 m. mauve and green ..	10	10
84	,,	4 m. green and chocolate	8	15
85	,,	5 m. olive-brown and black	8	8
86	,,	10 m. carmine and black ..	1·50	1·25
87	,,	15 m. bright blue & chestnut	8	8
88	**21**	2 p. purple & orge.-yellow	2·00	1·40
89	,,	3 p. red-brown and blue ..	45	12
90	,,	4 p. ultramarine and black	40	20
91	,,	5 p. chestnut and green ..	2·50	2·50
92	,,	6 p. greenish blue & black	3·50	1·25
93	,,	8 p. emerald and black ..	3·50	1·40
94	,,	10 p. slate and purple ..	6·50	3·25
95	,,	20 p. pale blue and blue ..	11·00	9·00
81/95		.. .. *Set of* 15	29·00	19·00

Dates of issue: 15 m., 3 pi. and 4 pi. 25.3.41; others 10.8.41.

22 23

1948 (1 JAN.). *Arabic inscriptions below camel altered. Typo. W* **7.** *P* 14.

No.	Type	Description	Unused	Used
96	**22**	1 m. black and orange, C	5	8
97	,,	2 m. orange & choc., C ..	5	5
98	,,	3 m. mauve and green, C	5	5
99	,,	4 m. dp. grn. & choc., C	5	5
100	,,	5 m. olive-brn. & blk., C	5	5
101	,,	10 m. rose-red & black, C	5	5
		a. Centre inverted		
102	,,	15 m. ultra. & chestnut, C	8	5
103	**23**	2 p. pur. & orge.-yell., C	20	10
104	,,	3 p. red-brn. & dp. bl., C	20	12
105	**23**	4 p. ultram. & black, C	25	20
106	,,	5 p. brn.-orge. & dp. grn., C	45	25
107	,,	6 p. grnsh. blue & blk., C	35	40
108	,,	8 p. bluish grn. & blk., O	40	60
109	,,	10 p. black & mauve, OC	60	60
110	,,	20 p. pale bl. & dp. blue, O	1·50	65
		a. Perf. 13, O ..	7·00	
111	,,	50 p. carm. & ultram., C	2·00	1·40
96/111		.. .. *Set of* 16	5·50	4·25

For similar stamps, but with different Arabic inscriptions, see Nos. 37/46*a*.

24

1948 (OCT.). *Golden Jubilee of "Camel Postman" design. Chalk-surfaced paper. Typo. W* **7.** *P* 13.

No.	Type	Description	Unused	Used
112	**24**	2 p. black and light blue ..	20	20

25

1948 (DEC.). *Opening of Legislative Assembly. Chalk-surfaced paper. Typo. W* **7.** *P* 13.

No.	Type	Description	Unused	Used
113	**25**	10 m. rose-red and black ..	15	8
114	,,	5 p. brn.-orge. & dp. grn.	30	20

26. Blue Nile Bridge, Khartoum.

27. Kassala Jebel.
28. Sagia (Water Wheel).
29. Port Sudan.
30. Gordon Memorial College.
31. Nile Post Boat.
32. Suakin.
33. G.P.O., Khartoum.

(Des. Col. W. L. Atkinson (2½ p., 6 p.), G. R. Wilson (3 p.), others from photographs. Recess.)

1950 (1 JULY). *Air. W* **7.** *P* 12.

No.	Type	Description	Unused	Used
115	**26**	2 p. black and blue-grn.	20	10
116	**27**	2½ p. light blue & red-orge.	20	15
117	**28**	3 p. reddish purple & blue	25	10
118	**29**	3½ p. pur.-brn. & yell.-brn.	30	40
119	**30**	4 p. brown and light blue	30	35
120	**31**	4½ p. black and ultram. ..	35	40
121	**32**	6 p. black and carmine ..	30	30
122	**33**	20 p. black and purple ..	1·00	90
115/122		.. .. *Set of* 8	2·50	2·40

34. Ibex.

Designs as T **34**:—
35. Shoebill.
36. Giraffe.
37. Baggara Girl.
38. Shilluk Warrior.
39. Hadendowa.
40. Policeman.

41. Cotton Picking.

Designs as T **41**:—
42. Ambatch Canoe. **43.** Nuba Wrestlers.
44. Weaving. **45.** Saluka Farming.
46. Gum Tapping. **47.** Darfur Chief.
48. Stack Laboratory. **49.** Nile Lechwe.
50. Camel Postman.

T **42/9** are horiz. and T **50** is a vert. desigr

(Des. Col. W. L. Atkinson (1 m., 2 m., 4 m., 5 m 10 m., 3 p., 3½ p., 20 p.), Col. E. A. Stantc (50 p.), others from photographs. Typo.)

1951 (1 SEPT.). *Chalk-surfaced paper. W* **7.** *P* 1 (*millieme values*) *or* 13 (*piastre values*).

No.	Type	Description	Unused	Used
123	**34**	1 m. black and orange ..	5	
124	**35**	2 m. black & bright blue	5	
125	**36**	3 m. black and green ..	12	1
126	**37**	4 m. black & yell.-green	5	
127	**38**	5 m. blk. & pur. (*shades*)	5	
128	**39**	10 m. black and pale blue	5	
129	**40**	15 m. blk. & chest. (*shades*)	5	
130	**41**	2 p. deep blue and pale blue (*shades*) ..	8	
131	**42**	3 p. brown and pale ultramarine (*shades*)	10	
132	**43**	3½ p. bright green and red-brown (*shades*) ..	10	
133	**44**	4 p. blue & blk. (*shades*)	10	
134	**45**	5 p. orge.-brn. & yell.-grn.	10	
135	**46**	6 p. blue & blk. (*shades*)	12	
136	**47**	8 p. blue & brn. (*shades*)	25	1
137	**48**	10 p. black and green ..	25	1
138	**49**	20 p. blue-grn. and black	40	2
139	**50**	50 p. carmine and black ..	1·00	5
123/139		.. .. *Set of* 17	2·75	1·7

SELF-GOVERNMENT, 1954.

51. Camel Postman.

1054 (9 JAN.). *Self-Government. Chalk-surface paper. Typo. W* **7.** *P* 13.

No.	Type	Description	Unused	Used
140	**51**	15 m. orge.-brn. & brt. grn.	10	1
141	,,	3 p. blue and indigo ..	20	2
142	,,	5 p. blk. & reddish purple	25	2

Stamps as Type **51**, but dated "1953" were eleased in error at the Sudan Agency in London. They had no postal validity. (*Price per set, 8 un.*)

Later issues of Sudan as an Independent Republic will be found in Vol. 4 of the Stanley Gibbons Foreign Overseas Catalogue.

POSTAGE DUE STAMPS.

897 (1 MAR.). *Type* **D 28** *of Egypt (numeral type), optd. with T* **1**. *Wmk. Star and Crescent. P 14.*

D1 2 m. green 50 45
D2 4 m. maroon 50 55
a. Bisected (2m.) (on cover) ..
D3 1 pi. ultramarine 80 90
D4 2 pi. orange .. .. .. 1·50 1·75
a. Bisected (1 pi.) (on cover) ..

Varieties are known with the large dot omitted in the first Arabic character on left.

D 1. Gunboat *Zafir*. D 2.

901 (1 JAN.). *Typo. W* **4**. *P 14.*

5 **D 1** 2 m. black & brown, OC 10 10
6 „ 4 m. brown & green, OC 12 10
7 „ 10 m. grn. & mauve, OC 20 20
8 „ 20 m. ultram. & carm., C 55 40

927–30. *W* **7**. *P 14.*

9 **D 1** 2 m. blk. & brn., C ('30) 8 8
10 „ 4 m. brown & green, C 10 10
11 „ 10 m. grn. & mauve, CO 15 15

948 (1 JAN.). *Arabic inscriptions at foot altered. Chalk-surfaced paper. Typo. W* **7**. *P 14.*

12 **D 2** 2 m. black and brown .. 12 12
13 „ 4 m. brown and green .. 12 12
14 „ 10 m. green and mauve .. 12 12
15 „ 20 m. ultram. & carmine 15 15

OFFICIAL STAMPS.

900 (8 FEB.). *5 mils. of 1897 punctured* "S G" *by hand. The* "S" *has 14 and the* "G" *12 holes.*

1 5 m. rose-carmine .. .. 18·00 9·00

901 (JAN.). *1 m. wmk. Quatrefoil, punctured as No. O1.*

2 1 m. brown and pink .. 15·00 12·00

O.S.G.S **O.S.G.S**

(O 1) ("On Sudan Government Service".) (O 2)

902. *No. 10 optd. at Khartoum as Type* **O 1** *in groups of 30 stamps.*

3 **2** 1 m. brown and pink .. 90 1·10
a. Oval "O" (No. 19) .. 30·00
b. Round stops. (Nos. 25 to 30).. 4·00 5·00
c. Opt. inverted £100
d. Do. and oval "O" .. £850
e. Do. and round stops .. £200
f. Opt. double £120
g. Do. and round stops .. £275
h. Do. and oval "O" ..

903–12. *T* **2** *optd. as Type* **O 2**, *by D.L.R. in sheets of 120 stamps.*

(i) *Wmk. Quatrefoil* (3.06).

4 10 pi. black and mauve .. 2·00 2·00

(ii) *Wmk. Mult. Star and Crescent.*

5 1 m. brown & carmine (9.04) 15 12
a. Opt. double
6 3 m. mauve & green (2.04) .. 30 15
a. Opt. double .. ..
7 5 m. scarlet & black (1.1.03) 30 8
8 1 pi. blue and brown (1.1.03) 60 10
9 2 pi. black and blue (1.1.03) 1·00 20
10 5 pi. brown & green (1.1.03) 80 40
11 10 pi. black and mauve (9.12) 1·25 2·00
/11 .. .. Set of 8 5·50 4·50

S.G. (O 3) **S.G.** (O 4) Thick. **S.G.** (O 5) Thin.

1936–46. *Nos. 37/43 optd. with Type* **O 3**, *and 44/46a with Type* **O 4**. *W* **7**. *P 14.*

O12 **6** 1 m. black and orange, O 8 8
O13 „ 2 m. orange and choc., O 8 8
O14 „ 3 m. mauve and green, C 8 8
O15 „ 4 m. green and choc., C.. 8 8
O16 „ 5 m. olive-brn. & blk., CO 8 8
O17 „ 10 m. carmine & black, C 15 5
O18 „ 15 m. brt. bl. & chest., CO 12 10
O19 **2** 2 p. pur. & orge.-yell., CO 20 15
O19*a* „ 3 p. red-brn. & blue, O.. 30 35
O19*b* „ 4 p. ultram. & black, CO 30 20
O20 „ 5 p. chest. & green, CO 30 20
O20*a* „ 6 p. grnish. blue & blk., O 70 40
O20*b* „ 8 p. emerald & black, O 70 60
O21 „ 10 p. black and violet, CO 80 70
O22 „ 20 p. pale blue & blue, O 1·75 2·00
O12/22 .. .. Set of 15 5·00 4·50

Dates of issue:—19.9.36, 4 m. and 5 p.; Jan., '37, 3 m.; Apr., '37, 2 p.; 21.6.37, 15 m.; Oct., '37, 10 p.; Mar., '40, 5 m.; Apr. '45, 2 m., Apr., '46, 3 p., 4 p., 6 p., 8 p.; June, '46, 10 m., 20 p.; 22.11.46, 1 m.

1948 (1 JAN.). *Nos. 96/102 optd. with Type* **O 3**, *and 103/111 with Type* **O 4**.

O23 **22** 1 m. black and orange .. 5 5
O24 „ 2 m. orange & chocolate 5 5
O25 „ 3 m. mauve and green .. 8 5
O26 „ 4 m. deep-green & choc. 5 8
O27 „ 5 m. olive-brown & black 5 5
O28 „ 10 m. rose-red and black.. 8 5
O29 „ 15 m. ultram. and chestnut 8 8
O30 **23** 2 p. purple & orge-yell. 8 8
O31 „ 3 p. red-brn. & deep blue 12 8
O32 „ 4 p. ultram. and black.. 20 10
a. Perf. 13 .. .. 2·50 2·75
O33 „ 5 p. brn.-orge. & dp. grn. 25 15
O34 „ 6 p. greenish blue & black 30 15
O35 „ 8 p. bluish green & black 35 15
O36 „ 10 p. black and mauve .. 50 30
O37 „ 20 p. pale blue & dp. blue 1·00 45
O38 „ 50 p. carmine and ultram. 2·50 1·50
O23/38 .. .. Set of 16 5·00 2·75

1950 (1 JULY). *Air. Optd. with Type* **O 4**.

O39 **26** 2 p. blk. & blue-grn. (R.) 15 12
O40 **27** 2½ p. light blue and red-orange 15 15
O41 **28** 3 p. reddish pur. & blue 15 12
O42 **29** 3½ p. purple-brown and yellow-brown 20 20
O43 **30** 4 p. brown & lt. blue .. 25 30
O44 **31** 4½ p. black & ultram. (R.) 35 40
O45 **32** 6 p. black & carm. (R.) 30 45
O46 **33** 20 p. black & purple (R.) 1·00 1·10
O39/46 .. .. Set of 8 2·25 2·50

1951 (1 SEPT.)–**58.** *Nos. 123/9 optd. with Type* **O 3** *and 130/9 with Type* **O 4**.

O47 **34** 1 m. black & orange (R.) 5 5
O48 **35** 2 m. blk. & brt. blue (R.) 5 5
O49 **36** 3 m. black & green (R.).. 10 12
O50 **37** 4 m. blk. & yell.-grn. (R.) 5 5
O51 **38** 5 m. black & purple (R.) 5 5
O52 **39** 10 m. blk. & pale bl. (R.) 5 5
O53 **40** 15 m. blk. & chestnut (R.) 5 5
O54 **41** 2 p. deep blue and pale blue (*shades*) .. 5 5
a. Opt. inverted £225
O55 **42** 3 p. brown and deep ultramarine (*shades*) 12 5
O56 **43** 3½ p. bright green and red-brown (*shades*) 15 10
O57 **44** 4 p. blue & blk. (*shades*) 15
O58 **45** 5 p. orange-brown and yellow-green .. 15 8
O59 **46** 6 p. blue & blk. (*shades*) 20 10
O60 **47** 8 p. blue & brn. (*shades*) 25 12
O61 **48** 10 p. black & green (R.).. 40 15
O61*a* „ 10 p. blk. & grn. (Bk.) ('58) 40 15
O62 **49** 20 p. blue-green & black 70 25
a. Opt. inverted .. — £200
O63 **50** 50 p. carmine and black.. 1·75 75
O47/63 .. Set of 18 3·75 1·75

1962 (?). *Nos. 127, 128 and 129 optd. with Type* **O 5**, *in red.*

O63*a* **38** 5 m. blk. & reddish pur. 5 5
O63*b* **39** 10 m. black and pale blue 5 5
O63*c* **40** 15 m. black & brn.-orge. 5 5

ARMY SERVICE.

ARMY (A 1) **OFFICIAL ARMY** (A 2) **Army OFFICIAL Service** (A 3)

1905 (JAN.). *T* **2** *optd. at Khartoum as Type* **A 1** *and* **A 2**. *Wmk. Mult. Star and Crescent.*

(i) "ARMY" *reading up.*

A1 1 m. brown & carmine (A 1) 1·00 55
a. "!" for "I" .. .. 8·00 5·50
b. Opt. Type A 2 .. .. 6·00 3·25

(ii) *Overprint horizontal.*

A2 1 m. brown & carmine (A 1).. 90·00
a. "!" for "I" £1000
b. Opt. Type A 2 .. .. £600

The horizontal overprint exists with either "ARMY" or "OFFICIAL" reading the right way up. It did not fit the stamps, resulting in misplacements where more than one whole overprint appears, or when the two words are transposed.

(iii) "ARMY" *reading down.*

A3 1 m. brown & carmine (A 1) .. 10·00 10·00
a. "!" for "I" £200 £200
b. Opt. Type A 2 .. .. £140 £140

1905 (NOV.). *As No. A 1, but wmk. Quatrefoil.*

A4 1 m. brown and pink (A 1) .. 40·00 35·00
a. "!" for "I" .. .. — £700
b. Opt. Type A 2 .. .. £600

The 29th stamp in each setting of 30 (Nos. A1–A4) has an exclamation mark for first "I" in "OFFICIAL" while the 6th and 12th stamps are Type A 2.

Two varieties of the 1 mil.
A. 1st Ptg. 14 mm. between lines of opt.
B. Later Ptgs. 12 mm. between lines.
All other values are Type B.

1906 (JAN.)–**11.** *T* **2** *optd. as Type* **A 3**.

(i) *Wmk. Mult. Star and Crescent, T* **4**.

A 5 1 m. brown & carm. (Type A) 60·00 50·00
A 6 1 m. brown & carm. (Type B) 1·00 20
a. Opt. double .. .. — £200
b. Opt. inverted £130 £130
c. Pair, with and without opt.
d. "Service" omitted .. .. — £1500
A 7 2 m. green and brown .. 2·00 80
a. Pair, with and without opt. £700
b. "Army" omitted .. £850
A 8 3 m. mauve and green .. 1·75 40
a. Opt. inverted .. £850
A 9 5 m. scarlet and black .. 80 15
a. Opt. double.. .. £100 £100
b. Opt. inverted .. — 85·00
c. Error. "Amry" .. .. — £850
d. "A" for "A" in "Army" — 70·00
e. Opt. double, one inverted .. £250 £120
A10 1 pi. blue and brown .. 1·00 15
a. "Army" omitted .. £850 £850
A11 2 pi. black and blue (1.09) .. 4·00 3·00
A12 5 pi. brown and green (5.08) 17·00 6·00
A13 10 pi. black and mauve (5.11) £140 £140
A6/10 Optd. "Specimen" Set of 5 £130

There are a number of printings of these Army Service stamps; the earlier are as Type A 3; the 1908 printing has a narrower "A" in "Army" and the 1910–11 printings have the tail of the "y" in "Army" much shorter.

(ii) *Wmk. Quatrefoil, T* **3**.

A14 2 pi. black and blue .. 6·00 3·00
A15 5 pi. brown and green .. 22·00 22·00
A16 10 pi. black and mauve .. 28·00 28·00
A14/16 Optd. "Specimen" Set of 3 £140

Since 1913 a number of stamps have been issued punctured "S.G." (Sudan Government) or "AS" (Army Service), but we no longer list such varieties.

SWAZILAND.

I. PROVISIONAL GOVERNMENT.

Under the joint protection of Great Britain and the South African Republic (Transvaal).

Swazieland

(1)

1889 (18–20 Oct.). *Stamps of the South African Republic (Transvaal) optd. with T* **1**, *in black.*

(*a*) *P* 12½ × 12.

No.	Type	Description	Un.	Us.
1	**18**	1d. carmine	6·00	7·00
		a. Opt. inverted	£110	£130
2	,,	2d. olive-bistre	25·00	6·00
		a. Opt. inverted	—	£250
		b. "Swazielan"	£250	£160
3	,,	1s. green	4·50	5·00
		a. Opt. inverted	90·00	£100

(*b*) *P* 12½.

No.	Type	Description	Un.	Us.
4	**18**	½d. grey	4·50	5·00
		a. Opt. inverted	95·00	£100
		b. "Swazielan"	£200	£160
		c. "Swazielan" inverted ..	—	£450
5	,,	2d. olive-bistre	6·00	6·00
		a. Opt. inverted	£100	£120
		b. "Swazielan"	£100	£110
		c. "Swazielan" inverted ..	£325	£325
6	,,	6d. blue	6·00	8·00
7	,,	2s. 6d. buff (20 Oct.) ..	42·00	55·00
8	,,	5s. slate-blue (20 Oct.) ..	42·00	55·00
		a. Opt. inverted	£400	£400
		b. "Swazielan"	£1000	
		c. "Swazielan" inverted ..		
9	,,	10s. fawn (20 Oct.)	£450	£500

The variety without "d" occurs on the left-hand bottom corner stamp in each sheet of certain printings.

1892 (Aug.). *Optd. in carmine.* *P* 12½.

No.	Type	Description	Un.	Us.
10	**18**	½d. grey	4·00	5·00
		a. Opt. inverted	95·00	
		b. Opt. double	£110	£110
		c. Pair, one without opt. ..	—	£130

A printing of the above with stop after "Swazieland" was made in July 1894 but these were not issued.

In 1894 the South African Republic was, under a convention, given powers of protection and administration over Swaziland, but it was not incorporated. On 7 Nov. of that year the stamps were withdrawn from use. On 5 June 1903, authority over Swaziland was conferred on the Governor of the Transvaal, and on 1 Dec. 1906, this authority was transferred to a High Commissioner, Swaziland being considered as a British Protectorate. In 1933 stamps were again issued.

II. BRITISH PROTECTORATE.

2. King George V.

3. King George VI.

(Des. Rev. C. C. Tugman. Recess. D.L.R.)

1933 (2 Jan.). *Wmk. Mult. Script CA.* *P* 14.

No.	Type	Description	Un.	Us.
11	**2**	½d. green	10	20
12	,,	1d. carmine	12	10
13	,,	2d. brown	20	20
14	,,	3d. blue	20	40
15	,,	4d. orange	40	80
16	,,	6d. bright purple	65	1·00
17	,,	1s. olive	1·10	2·25
18	,,	2s. 6d. bright violet ..	3·50	6·50
19	,,	5s. grey	8·00	11·00
20	,,	10s. sepia	15·00	20·00
11/20		.. .. *Set of* 10	26·00	38·00
11/20		Perf. "Specimen" *Set of* 10	40·00	

The ½d., 1d., 2d. and 6d. values exist overprinted "OFFICIAL", but authority for their use was withdrawn before any were actually used. However, some stamps had already been issued to the Secretariat staff before instructions were received to invalidate their use. (*Price £3250 per set un.*)

1935 (4 May). *Silver Jubilee. As Nos.* 91/4 *of Antigua, but ptd. by B. W.* *P* 11 × 12.

No.	Description	Un.	Us.
21	1d. deep blue and scarlet ..	15	20
	a. Extra flagstaff	12·00	
22	2d. ultram. and grey-black ..	25	40
	a. Extra flagstaff	15·00	
23	3d. brown and deep blue ..	55	70
	a. Extra flagstaff	10·00	
24	6d. slate and purple	65	1·10
	a. Extra flagstaff	15·00	
21/4	Perf. "Specimen" *Set of* 4	16·00	

For illustration of "extra flagstaff" variety see Bechuanaland.

1937 (12 May). *Coronation. As Nos.* 13/15 *of Aden, but ptd. by B. W.* *P* 11 × 11½.

No.	Description	Un.	Us.
25	1d. carmine	10	10
26	2d. yellow-brown	12	12
27	3d. blue	15	15
25/7	Perf. "Specimen" *Set of* 3	10·00	

(Recess. D.L.R.)

1938 (1 Apr.)–**54** *Wmk. Mult. Script CA.* *P* 13½ × 13.

No.	Type	Description	Un.	Us.
28	**3**	½d. green	8	10
		a. Perf. 13½ × 14 (1.43) ..	8	12
		b. P. 13½ × 14. *Bronze-grn.* (2.50)	8	10
29	,,	1d. rose-red	10	12
		a. Perf. 13½ × 14 (1.43) ..	8	10
30	,,	1½d. light blue	25	20
		a. Perf. 14 (1941) ..	10	25
		b. Perf. 13½ × 14 (1.43)	10	12
31	,,	2d. yellow-brown	20	25
		a. Perf. 13½ × 14 (1.43) ..	8	8
32	,,	3d. ultramarine	25	35
		a. *Deep blue* (10.38) ..	25	35
		b. Perf. 13½ × 14. *Ultram.* (1.43)	20	25
		c. Perf. 13½ × 14. *Lt. ultram.* (10.46)	20	25
		d. Perf. 13½ × 14. *Dp. blue* (10.47)	10	20
33	,,	4d. orange	25	35
		a. Perf. 13½ × 14 (1.43) ..	15	25
34	,,	6d. deep magenta	30	30
		a. Perf. 13½ × 14 (1.43) ..	20	60
		b. Perf. 13½ × 14. *Reddish purple (shades)* (7.44)	10	12
		c. Perf. 13½ × 14. *Claret* (13.10.54)	15	30
35	,,	1s. brown-olive	70	35
		a. Perf. 13½ × 14 (1.43)	25	15
36	,,	2s. 6d. bright violet ..	90	1·25
		a. Perf. 13½ × 14. *Violet* (1.43) ..	50	55
		b. Perf. 13½ × 14. *Reddish violet* (10.47)	90	1·10
37	,,	5s. grey	2·25	2·25
		a. Perf. 13½ × 14. *Slate* (1.43) ..	5·00	7·00
		b. Perf. 13½ × 14. *Grey* (5.44) ..	1·50	1·10
38	,,	10s. sepia	4·00	3·00
		a. Perf. 13½ × 14 (1.43) ..	2·00	2·50
28a/38a		.. .. *Set of* 11	4·50	4·75
28/38		Perf. "Specimen" *Set of* 11	35·00	

The above perforations vary slightly from stamp to stamp, but the average measurements are respectively: 13.3 × 23.2 comb (13½ × 13), 14.2 line (14) and 13.3 × 13.8 comb (13½ × 14).

Swaziland

(4)

1945 (3 Dec.). *Victory. Nos.* 108/10 *of South Africa optd. with T* **4**.

No.	Description	Un. pair	Us. pair
39	1d. brown and carmine ..	10	15
40	2d. slate-blue & violet ..	12	15
41	3d. deep blue and blue ..	15	20

1947 (17 Feb.). *Royal Visit. As Nos.* 32/5 *of Basutoland.*

No.	Description	Un.	Us.
42	1d. scarlet	5	5
43	2d. green	5	5
44	3d. ultramarine	12	8
45	1s. mauve	20	20
42/5	Perf. "Specimen" *Set of* 4	30·00	

1948 (1 Dec.). *Royal Silver Wedding. As Nos.* 30/1 *of Aden.*

No.	Description	Un.	Us.
46	1½d. ultramarine	8	8
47	10s. purple-brown	3·50	4·00

1949 (10 Oct.). *75th Anniv. of Universal Postal Union. As Nos.* 114/7 *of Antigua.*

No.	Description	Un.	Us.
48	1½d. blue	8	8
49	3d. deep blue..	15	20
50	6d. magenta	20	30
51	1s. olive	40	45

1953 (3 June). *Coronation. As No.* 47 *of Aden*

No.	Description	Un.	Us.
52	2d. black and yellow-brown	15	2

5. Havelock Asbestos Mine.

6. A Highveld View.

7. Swazi Married Woman.

8. Swazi Courting Couple.

9. Swazi Warrior.

10. Greater Kudu Antelope.

(Recess. B.W.)

1956 (2 July). *Wmk. Mult. Script CA* *P* 13 × 13½ (*horiz.*) *or* 13½ × 13 (*vert.*).

No.	Type	Description	Un.	Us.
53	**5**	½d. black and orange ..	5	
54	**6**	1d. black and emerald ..	5	
55	**7**	2d. black and brown ..	5	
56	**8**	3d. black and rose-red ..	8	
57	**9**	4½d. black & dp. brt. blue..	12	2
58	**10**	6d. black and magenta ..	12	1
59	**5**	1s. black and deep olive..	25	2
60	**8**	1s. 3d. black and sepia ..	35	3
61	**6**	2s. 6d. emer. & carm.-red	60	8
62	**9**	5s. dp. lilac & slate-black	1·50	1·7
63	**7**	10s. black and deep lilac..	3·00	3·5
64	**10**	£1 black & turquoise-blue	6·50	9·0
53/64		.. .. *Set of* 12	12·00	15·0

Currency changed. 100 cents = 1 rand.

½c (11) **1c** (12) **2c** (13) **3½c** (14)

2½c (I) **2½c** (II) **4c** (I) **4c** (II)

5c 5c 25c 25c
(I) (II) (I) (II)

50c 50c 50c
(I) (II) (III)

R1 R1 R1 R2 R2
(I) (II) (III) (I) (II)

961 (14 Feb.). *T* **5** *to* **10** *surch. as T* **11** *to* **14**.

No.	Type	Description	Unused	Used
5	**11**	½ c. on ½d.	1·00	1·00
		a. Surch. inverted	£150	
6	**12**	1 c. on 1d.	8	8
		a. Surch. double	£200	
7	**13**	2 c. on 2d.	10	10
8	,,	2½ c. on 2d.	10	10
9	,,	2½ c. on 3d. (Type I)	30	30
		a. Type II	45	60
o	**14**	3½ c. on 2d. (May) ..	10	10
1	**13**	4 c. on 4½d. (Type I)	15	20
		a. Type II	15	15
2	,,	5 c. on 6d. (Type I)	20	20
		a. Type II	20	20
3	,,	10 c. on 1s.	3·00	4·00
		a. Surch. double (vert. pr.)* ..	£180	
4	,,	25 c. on 2s. 6d. (Type I) ..	60	90
		a. Type II (central) ..	60	1·00
		b. Type II (bottom left) ..	60·00	
5	,,	50 c. on 5s. (Type I) ..	1·00	1·25
		a. Type II	4·00	4·00
		b. Type III	£100	£150
6	,,	1 r. on 10s. (Type I) ..	2·00	2·25
		a. Type II	4·00	4·50
		b. Type III	20·00	25·00
7	,,	2 r. on £1 (Type I) ..	7·00	8·00
		a. Type II (middle left) ..	3·50	4·00
		b. Type II (bottom) ..	22·00	24·00
5/77a		.. .. *Set of* 13	11·00	13·00

*No. 73a is best collected as a vertical pair, ue to the fall of the second surcharge.

No. 74b has the thin Type II surcharge at ottom left, in similar position to the thicker ype I, No. 74, with which it should not be onfused.

No. 77b has the surcharge centrally placed at ottom. No. 77a has it at middle left, above KUDU".

No. 66 with surcharge central (instead of ottom left) and No. 75a bottom left (instead of iddle left) are believed to be from trial sheets leased with the normal stocks. They do not present separate printings. (No. 66 *price* £12 n.)

(Recess. B.W.)

961. *Values in cents. Wmk. Mult. Script CA. P* 13×13½ (*horiz.*) *or* 13½×13 (*vert.*).

No.	Type	Description	Unused	Used
8	**5**	½ c. black & orange (14.2)	5	5
9	**6**	1 c. black & emerald (14.2)	5	5
o	**7**	2 c. black & brown (10.9)	8	10
1	**8**	2½ c. black & rose-red (14.2)	15	15
2	**9**	4 c. blk. & dp. brt. bl. (10.9)	20	25
3	**10**	5 c. black & magenta (10.9)	20	20
4	**5**	10 c. blk. & dp. olive (14.2)	30	30
5	**8**	12½ c. black and sepia (14.2)	35	40
6	**6**	25 c. emer. & carm.-red (1.8)	80	80
7	**9**	50 c. d.lilac & slate-blk.(10.9)	1·50	1·75
8	**7**	1 r. black & dp. lilac (10.9)	2·50	2·75
9	**10**	2 r. blk. & turq.-blue (1.8)	6·50	7·00
8/89		.. .. *Set of* 12	11·00	12·00

15. Swazi Shields.

16. Battle Axe.

(Des. Mrs. C. Hughes. Photo. Enschedé.)

1962 (24 Apr.). *Various designs as T* **15/16**. *W* **w.12**. *P* 14×13 (*horiz.*) *or* 13×14 (*vert.*).

No.	Description	Unused	Used
90	½ c. black, brown and yellow-brown	5	5
91	1 c. yellow-orange & black	5	5
92	2 c. deep bluish green, black and yellow-olive ..	5	5
93	2½ c. black and vermilion (*shades*)	5	5
94	3½ c. yell.-grn. & deep grey ..	8	5
95	4 c. black & turquoise-green (*shades*)	8	10
96	5 c. black, red & orange-red	10	10
97	7½ c. deep brown and buff (*shades*)	12	15
98	10 c. black and light blue ..	15	20
99	12½ c. carmine & grey-olive ..	45	50
100	15 c. black & bright purple ..	45	50
101	20 c. black and green ..	45	50
102	25 c. black and bright blue ..	45	50
103	50 c. black and rose-red ..	1·75	2·00
104	1 r. emerald and ochre ..	2·25	2·75
105	2 r. carmine-red & ultram.	4·50	5·00
90/105	.. .. *Set of* 16	10·00	11·00

Designs: *Vert.*—2 c. Forestry; 2½ c. Ceremonial head-dress; 3½ c. Musical instrument; 4 c. Irrigation; 5 c. Widow Bird; 7½ c. Rock paintings; 10 c. Secretary Bird; 12½ c. Pink Arum; 15 c. Swazi married woman; 20 c. Malaria control; 25 c. Swazi warrior; 1 r. Aloes. *Horiz.*—50 c. Ground Hornbill; 2 r. Msinsi in flower.

1963 (4 June). *Freedom from Hunger. As No.* 76 *of Aden.*

No.	Description	Unused	Used
106	15 c. reddish violet	40	35

1963 (2 Sept.). *Red Cross Centenary. As Nos.* 147/8 *of Antigua.*

No.	Description	Unused	Used
107	2½ c. red and black	10	12
108	15 c. red and blue	40	40

31. Train and Map.

(Des. R. A. H. Street. Recess. Bradbury, Wilkinson.)

1964 (5 Nov.). *Opening of Swaziland Railway. W* **w.12**. *P* 11½.

No.	Type	Description	Unused	Used
109	**31**	2½ c. emer.-grn. & purple	8	8
110	,,	3½ c. turquoise-blue and deep yellow-olive ..	15	15
111	,,	15 c. red-orange and deep chocolate	30	35
112	,,	25 c. olive-yellow and deep ultramarine	40	45

1965 (17 May). *I.T.U. Centenary. As Nos.* 166/7 *of Antigua.*

No.	Description	Unused	Used
113	2½ c. light blue and bistre ..	8	8
114	15 c. bright purple and rose	30	30

1965 (25 Oct.). *International Co-operation Year. As Nos.* 168/9 *of Antigua.*

No.	Description	Unused	Used
115	½ c. reddish pur.&turq.-grn.	5	5
116	15 c. dp. bluish green & lav.	30	35

1966 (24 Jan.). *Churchill Commemoration. As Nos.* 170/3 *of Antigua.*

No.	Description	Unused	Used
117	½ c. new blue	5	5
118	2½ c. deep green	8	8
119	15 c. brown	30	35
120	25 c. bluish violet	45	50

1966 (1 Dec.). *20th Anniv. of U.N.E.S.C.O. As Nos.* 196/8 *of Antigua.*

No.	Description	Unused	Used
121	2½ c. slate-violet, red, yellow and orange	8	8
122	7½ c. orange-yellow, violet & deep olive	15	20
123	15 c. black, bright purple and orange	30	30

III. PROTECTED STATE.

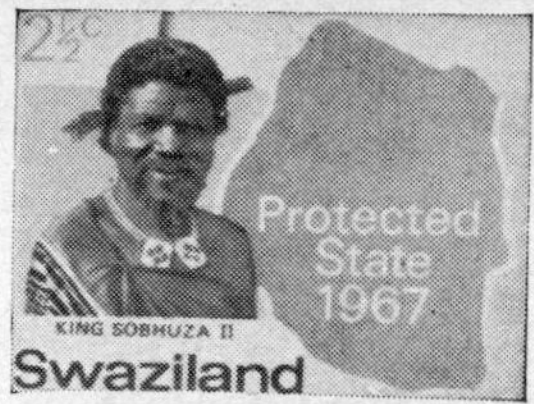

32. King Sobhuza II and Map.

33. King Sobhuza II.

(Des. and photo. Harrison.)

1967 (25 Apr.). *Protected State. W* **w.12** (*sideways on horiz. designs*). *P* 14½.

No.	Type	Description	Unused	Used
124	**32**	2½ c. multicoloured ..	5	5
125	**33**	7½ c. multicoloured ..	12	12
126	**32**	15 c. multicoloured ..	25	30
127	**33**	25 c. multicoloured ..	35	40

34. Students and University.

(Des. V. Whiteley. Photo. Harrison.)

1967 (7 Sept.). *First Conferment of University Degrees. P* 14×14½.

No.	Type	Description	Unused	Used
128	**34**	2½ c. sepia, ultramarine and light yellow-orange ..	5	5
129	,,	7½ c. sepia, ultramarine & light greenish blue ..	12	12
130	,,	15 c. sepia, ultram. & rose	25	25
131	,,	25 c. sepia, ultramarine & light violet	35	35

35. Incwala Ceremony.

36. Reed Dance.

3c

(37)

(Des. Mrs. G. Ellison. Photo. Harrison.)

1968 (5 Jan.). *Traditional Customs.* P 14.

132	**35**	3 c. silver, verm. & black	5	5
133	**36**	10 c. silver, light brown, orange and black ..	20	20
134	**35**	15 c. gold, verm. & black	30	30
135	**36**	25 c. gold, light brown, orange and black ..	50	50

1968 (1 May). *No.* 96 *surch. with T* **37.**

136	3 c. on 5 c. black, red and orange-red	8	10

IV. INDEPENDENCE.

38. Cattle Ploughing.

39. Overhead Cable carrying Asbestos.
40. Cutting Sugar Cane.
41. Iron Ore Mining and Railway Map.

(Des. Mrs. G. Ellison. Photo. Enschedé.)

1968 (6 Sept.). *Independence. W* w.**12** (*sideways*). *P* 14×12½.

137	**38**	3 c. multicoloured ..	5	5
138	**39**	4½ c. multicoloured ..	10	12
139	**40**	17½ c. yell., grn, blk. & gold	35	40
140	**41**	25 c. slate, black and gold	50	60
MS141		Sheet of 20	8·00	8·00

Nos. 137/40 were printed in sheets of 50, but also in sheets of 20 (4×5) containing *se-tenant* strips of each value.

INDEPENDENCE
1968

(42)

1968 (6 Sept.). *Nos.* 90/105 *optd. as T* **42**, *and No.* 93 *additionally surch.* 3 *c.*, *by Enschedé.*

(*a*) *Wmk. upright.*

142	½ c. black, brn. & yell.-brn.	5	5
143	1 c. yellow-orange & black	5	5
144	2 c. deep bluish green, black and yellow-olive ..	5	5
145	2½ c. black and vermilion (*shades*)	5	5
146	3 c. on 2½ c. black and vermilion (*shades*)	5	5
147	3½ c. yellow-green & dp. grey	8	8
148	4 c. black and turquoise-green (*shades*)	8	10
149	5 c. black, red & orange-red	10	10
150	7½ c. deep brown and buff ..	12	15
151	10 c. black and light blue ..	15	15
152	12½ c. carm. and grey-olive ..	25	30
153	15 c. black and bright purple	25	30
154	20 c. black and green	40	50
155	25 c. black and bright blue ..	45	50
156	50 c. black and rose-red ..	90	1·10
157	1 r. emerald and ochre ..	1·75	2·00
158	2 r. carmine-red & ultram.	3·25	4·00

(*b*) *Wmk. sideways.*

159	50 c. black and rose-red ..	80	90
160	2 r. carmine-red & ultram.	3·25	4·00
142/60	.. .. *Set of* 19	11·00	13·00

The 2½ c., 3½ c., 5 c., 12½ c., 50 c. (No. 156) and 2 r. (No. 158) exist with gum arabic only, the 1 c., 2 c., 3 c., 4 c. and 15 c. with both gum arabic and PVA gum and the remainder with PVA gum only.

43. Porcupine.

(Des. and litho. De La Rue.)

1969 (1 Aug.)–**75.** *T* **43** *and similar designs showing animals. Multicoloured. W* w.**12** (*sideways on* 3 *c.*, 3½ *c.*, 1 *r.*, 2 *r.*). *P* 13×13½ (3 *c.*, 3½*c.*), 12½×13 (1 *r.*, 2 *r.*) *or* 13×12½ (*others*).

161	½ c. Caracal. (African Lynx)	5	5
162	1 c. Type **43**	5	5
163	2 c. Crocodile	5	5
	a. Perf. 12½×12 (29.9.75) ..	10	10
164	3 c. Lion	5	5
165	3½ c. African Elephant ..	5	5
166	5 c. Bush pig	8	8
167	7½ c. Impala	10	10
168	10 c. Chacma Baboon ..	12	15
169	12½ c. Ratel (Honey Badger)	30	35
170	15 c. Leopard	25	25
171	20 c. Blue Wildebeest ..	30	35
172	25 c. White Rhinoceros ..	40	75
173	50 c. Burchell's Zebra ..	75	85
174	1 r. Waterbuck (*vert.*) ..	1·50	1·50
175	2 r. Giraffe (*vert.*)	3·00	3·25
161/75	.. .. *Set of* 15	6·00	7·00

Nos. 161/73 are horizontal designs as Type **43** but the 3 c. and 3½ c. are larger, 35×24½ *mm.*

No. 163a was printed by the D.L.R. works in Bogotá, Colombia.

See also Nos. 219/20 and 229.

44. King Sobhuza II and Flags.

45. King Sobhuza II, U.N. Building and Emblem.

(Des. De La Rue. Litho. P.B.)

1969 (24 Sept.). *Admission of Swaziland to the United Nations. W* w.**12** (*sideways*). *P* 13½.

176	**44**	3 c. multicoloured ..	5	5
177	**45**	7½ c. multicoloured ..	15	15
178	**44**	12½ c. multicoloured ..	25	25
179	**45**	25 c. multicoloured ..	50	50

46. Athlete, Shield and Spears.

(Des. L. D. Curtis. Litho. Format.)

1970 (16 July). *Ninth Commonwealth Games Edinburgh. T* **46** *and similar vert. designs Multicoloured. W* w.**12.** *P* 14.

180	3 c. Type **46**	5	
181	7½ c. Runner	12	1
182	12½ c. Hurdler	20	2
183	25 c. Procession of Swaziland Competitors	50	5

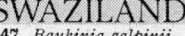

47. *Bauhinia galpinii.* **48.** King Sobhuza I in Ceremonial Dress

(Des. L. D. Curtis from "Wild Flowers of Natal by Dr. W. G. Wright. Litho. Questa.)

1971 (1 Feb.). *Flowers. T* **47** *and similar ver designs. Multicoloured. W* w.**12.** *P* 14½.

184	3 c. Type **47**	5	
185	10 c. *Crocosmia aurea* ..	20	
186	15 c. *Gloriosa superba* ..	30	3
187	25 c. *Watsonia densiflora* ..	50	5

(Des. L. D. Curtis. Litho. Format.)

1971 (22 Dec.). *Golden Jubilee of Accession King Sobhuza II. T* **48** *and similar ver designs. Multicoloured. W* w.**12.** *P* 14.

188	3 c. Type **48**	5	
189	3½ c. Sobhuza II in medallion	8	
190	7½ c. Sobhuza II attending Incwala Ceremony ..	15	
191	25 c. Sobhuza II and aides at opening of Parliament	50	

49. UNICEF Emblem.

(Des. Mrs. S. Goaman. Litho. J.W.)

1972 (17 Apr.). *25th Anniv. of UNICE W* w.**12** (*sideways*). *P* 13½.

192	**49**	15 c. black and bright lilac	30	3
193	–	25 c. black & yellow-olive	50	5

Design:—25 c. as T **49**, but inscription r arranged.

50. Local Dancers.

(Des. G. Drummond. Litho. Questa.)

972 (11 SEPT.). *Tourism. T* **50** *and similar horiz. designs. Multicoloured. W* **w.12.** *P* 13½×14.

4 3½ c. Type **50** 8 8
5 7½ c. Swazi beehive hut .. 15 15
6 15 c. Ezulwini Valley .. 30 30
7 25 c. Fishing, Usutu River .. 50 50

51. Spraying Mosquitoes.

(Des. PAD Studio. Litho. Questa.)

73 (21 MAY). *25th Anniv. of W.H.O. T* **51** *and similar horiz. design. Multicoloured. W* **w.12.** *P* 14.

8 3½ c. Type **51** 8 8
9 7½ c. Anti-malaria vaccination 15 15

52. Mining.

(Des. G. Drummond. Litho. Questa.)

73 (21 JUNE). *Natural Resources. T* **52** *and similar horiz. designs. Multicoloured. W* **w.12.** *P* 13½.

0 3½ c. Type **52** 8 8
1 7½ c. Cattle 12 12
2 15 c. Water 20 25
3 25 c. Rice 35 40

53. Coat-of-arms.

(Des. J.W. Ltd. Litho. Walsall Security Ptrs., Ltd.)

73 (7 SEPT.). *Fifth Anniv. of Independence. T* **53** *and similar horiz. designs. Multicoloured (except* 3 *c.). W* **w.12.** *P* 14.

4 3 c. Type **53** (salmon & blk.) 5 8
5 10 c. King Sobhuza II saluting 15 15
6 15 c. Parliament Buildings .. 20 25
7 25 c. National Somhlolo Stadium 35 40

54. Flags and Mortar-board.

(Des. P. B. Powell. Litho. Format.)

1974 (29 MAR.). *Tenth Anniv. of University of Botswana, Lesotho and Swaziland. T* **54** *and similar vert. designs. Multicoloured. W* **w.12** *(sideways). P* 14.

208 7½ c. Type **54** 12 12
209 12½ c. University campus .. 20 20
210 15 c. Map of Southern Africa 25 25
211 25 c. University badge .. 35 35

55. King Sobhuza as College Student.

(Des. Mary Nelson; adapted PAD Studio. Litho. Enschedé.)

1974 (22 JULY). *75th Birthday of King Sobhuza II. T* **55** *and similar vert. designs. Multicoloured. W* **w.12.** *P* 13×10½.

212 3 c. Type **55** 5 5
213 9 c. King Sobhuza in middle-age 12 15
214 50 c. King Sobhuza at 75 years of age 65 70

56. New Post Office, Lobamba.

(Des. R. Granger Barrett. Litho. Questa.)

1974 (9 OCT.). *Centenary of Universal Postal Union. T* **56** *and similar horiz. designs. Multicoloured. W* **w.12** *(sideways). P* 14.

215 4 c. Type **56** 8 8
216 10 c. Mbabane Temporary Post Office, 1902 .. .. 15 15
217 15 c. Carrying mail by cableway 20 25
218 25 c. Mule-drawn mail-coach .. 35 40

(New currency. 100 cents = 1 emalangeni.)

1975 (2 JAN.). *New currency. As Nos.* 174/5 *but inscr. in emalangeni. W* **w.12** *(upright). P* 12½×13.

219 1 e. Waterbuck .. .. 1·25 1·40
220 2 e. Giraffe .. .. .. 2·50 3·00

57. Umcwasho Ceremony.

(Des. PAD Studio. Litho. Kynoch Press.)

1975 (20 MAR.). *Swazi Youth. T* **57** *and similar multicoloured designs. W* **w.12** *(sideways on* 3, 10 *and* 25 *c.). P* 14.

221 3 c. Type **57** 5 5
222 10 c. Butimba (hunting party) 12 15
223 15 c. Lusekwane (sacred shrub) *(horiz.)* 20 20
224 25 c. Gcina Regiment .. 30 35

58. Control Tower, Matsapa Airport.

(Des. V. Whiteley Studio. Litho. Questa.)

1975 (18 AUG.). *Tenth Anniv. of Internal Air Service. T* **58** *and similar horiz. designs. Multicoloured. W* **w.14** *(sideways). P* 14.

225 4 c. Type **58** 8 8
226 5 c. Fire engine 8 8
227 15 c. Douglas "Dakota" .. 20 20
228 25 c. Hawker Siddeley "748" 30 30

(Litho. De La Rue, Bogotá, Colombia.)

1975 (29 SEPT.). *As No.* 164 *but W* **w.12** *upright.*

229 3 c. Lion 10 10

3c

(59)

1975 (15 NOV.). *Nos.* 167 *and* 169 *surch. as T* **59.**

230 3 c. on 7½ c. Impala .. 5 5
231 6 c. on 12½ c. Ratel 10 10

60. Elephant Symbol.

(Des. Mary-Jane Rostami. Litho. Questa.)

1975 (22 Dec.). *International Women's Year. T* **60** *and similar designs. W* w.**14** *(sideways on* 4 *and* 5 *c.). P* 14.

232 4 c. lt. bluish grey, black and light bright blue 5 5
233 5 c. multicoloured 8 8
234 15 c. multicoloured 20 20
235 25 c. multicoloured 30 30

Designs: *Horiz.*—5 c. Queen Labotsibeni. *Vert.*—15 c. Craftswoman; 25 c. "Women in Service".

61. Black-headed Oriole.

(Des. C. Abbott. Litho. Questa.)

1976 (2 Jan.). *Birds. T* **61** *and similar multicoloured designs. W* w.**14** *(sideways on* 1 *c.,* 3 *c.,* 2 *e.). P* 14.

236 1 c. Type **61** 5 5
237 2 c. Green Pigeon (*vert.*) .. 5 5
238 3 c. Melba Finch 5 5
239 4 c. Plum-coloured Starling (*vert.*) 5 5
240 5 c. Black-headed Heron (*vert.*) 5 5
241 6 c. Stonechat (*vert.*) 8 8
242 7 c. Chorister Robin (*vert.*) .. 10 10
243 10 c. Gorgeous Bush-shrike (*vert.*) 12 12
244 15 c. Black-collared Barbet (*vert.*) 20 20
245 20 c. Grey Heron (*vert.*) .. 25 25
246 25 c. Giant Kingfisher (*vert.*) 30 35
247 30 c. Black Eagle (*vert.*) .. 35 40
248 50 c. Red Bishop (*vert.*) .. 60 70
249 1 e. Pin-tailed Whydah (*vert.*) 1·25 1·40
250 2 e. Lilac-breasted Roller 2·50 2·75
236/50 .. .. *Set of* 15 5·50 6·00

62. Blindness from Malnutrition.

(Des. Jennifer Toombs. Litho. Questa.)

1976 (15 June). *Prevention of Blindness. T* **62** *and similar horiz. designs. Multicoloured. W* w.**14** *(sideways). P* 14.

251 5 c. Type **62** 5 8
252 10 c. Infected retina 12 15
253 20 c. Blindness from trachoma 25 30
254 25 c. Medicines 30 35

63. Marathon.

(Des. PAD Studio. Litho. Walsall.)

1976 (17 July). *Olympic Games, Montreal. T* **63** *and similar vert. designs. Multicoloured. W* w.**14** *(inverted). P* 14.

255 5 c. Type **63** 5 8
256 6 c. Boxing 8 10
257 20 c. Football 25 30
258 25 c. Olympic torch and flame 30 35

64. Footballer Shooting.

(Des. J.W. Ltd. Litho. Questa.)

1976 (13 Sept.). *F.I.F.A. Membership. T* **64** *and similar vert. designs. Multicoloured. W* w.**14.** *P* 14.

259 4 c. Type **64** 5 8
260 6 c. Heading 8 10
261 20 c. Goalkeeping 25 30
262 25 c. Player about to shoot .. 30 35

65. Alexander Graham Bell and Telephone.

(Des. J.W. Ltd. Litho. Walsall.)

1976 (22 Nov.). *Telephone Centenary. T* **65** *and similar horiz. designs. W* w.**14** *(sideways). P* 14.

263 **65** 4 c. multicoloured .. 5 5
264 – 5 c. multicoloured .. 5 8
265 – 10 c. multicoloured .. 12 15
266 – 15 c. multicoloured .. 20 25
267 – 20 c. multicoloured .. 25 30
263/7 .. .. *Set of* 5 55 65

Nos. 264/7 are as T **65**, but show different telephones.

66. Queen Elizabeth II and King Sobhuza II.

(Des. Walsall. Litho. Questa.)

1977 (7 Feb.). *Silver Jubilee. T* **66** *and similar horiz. designs. Multicoloured. W* w.**14** *(sideways). P* 13½.

268 20 c. Type **66** 25 30
269 25 c. Coronation Coach at Admiralty Arch 35 40
270 50 c. Queen in coach 70 80

POSTAGE DUE STAMPS.

D 1

Postage Due
2d

(D 2)

(Typo. D.L.R.)

1933 (2 Jan.)–**57.** *Wmk. Mult. Script CA. P* 1

D1 D **1** 1d. carmine, O 15
a. *Deep carmine*, C (24.10.51) 8
ac. Error. St. Edward's Crown, W9b, C .. .. .. 20·00
D2 „ 2d. pale violet, O .. 60
a. Chalky paper (22.5.57) .. 10
D1/2 Perf. "Specimen" *Set of* 2 15·00

1961 (8 Feb.). *No.* 55 *surch. with Type* D **2.**

D3 **7** 2d. on 2d. .. .. .. 2·50 3·

Another 2d. on 2d. Postage Due, with sm surcharge as Type D **5**, was produced *after t currency change*, to meet the philatelic deman (*Price* 35*p unused.*)

Currency changed. 100 cents = 1 rand.

D 3

Postage Du
1c

(D 4)

Postage Due
1c

(D 5)

(Typo. D.L.R.)

1961 (14 Feb.). *Chalk-surfaced paper. Wm Mult. Script CA. P* 14.

D4 D **3** 1 c. carmine 5
D5 „ 2 c. violet 8
D6 „ 5 c. green 10

1961. *No.* 55 *surcharged.*

A. (14 Feb.). *As Type* D **4.**

D7 **7** 1 c. on 2d. 45
D8 „ 2 c. on 2d. 45
D9 „ 5 c. on 2d. 45

B. (Date ?) *As Type* D **5.**

D10 **7** 1 c. on 2d. .. .. .. 75 1·
D11 „ 2 c. on 2d. 40
D12 „ 5 c. on 2d. .. .. .. 75 1·

D 6

(Des. and litho. Bradbury, Wilkinson & C

1971 (1 Feb.). *W* w.**12.** *P* 11½.

D13 D **6** 1 c. bright rose-red .. 5
D14 „ 2 c. purple 5
D15 „ 5 c. dull green 8

1977 (17 Jan.). *W* w.**14** *(sideways). P* 11

D16 D **6** 1 c. rose-red 5
D17 „ 2 c. purple 5
D18 „ 5 c. dull green 5

TANGANYIKA (TANZANIA).

(Formerly German East Africa.)

I. BRITISH OCCUPATION OF MAFIA ISLAND.

Mafia Island was captured by the British from e Germans in December 1914. Letters were st sent out unstamped, then with stamps hand-amped with Type M **1**. Later the military were pplied with handstamps by the post office in nzibar. These were used to produce Nos. 11/52.

G.R.

MAFIA

(M 1)

15 (Jan.). *German East Africa Yacht types, handstamped. Wmk. Lozenges, or no wmk.* (1 *r.*, 2 *r.*).

A. *In Black.* B. *In Violet.*

		A.	B.
1	2½ h. brown	70·00	50·00
2	4 h. green	70·00	60·00
3	7½ h. carmine ..	70·00	50·00
	a. Pair, one without handstamp ..	†	£180
4	15 h. ultramarine ..	80·00	60·00
	a. Pair, one without handstamp ..	†	£180
5	20 h. black & red/*yell.*	80·00	60·00
6	30 h. black & carmine	£110	60·00
	a. Pair, one without handstamp ..	†	£180
7	45 h. black & mauve	£110	80·00
8	1 r. carmine ..	£300	£225
9	2 r. green	£300	£225
10	3 r. blue-black & red	£450	£350

A few contemporary Zanzibar stamps (1, 3, and 15 c.) are known with the above handstamp.

15 (July). *German East Africa Yacht types with handstamped four-line surcharge* "G.R.—POST—6 CENTS—MAFIA" *in black, green or violet. Wmk. Lozenges or no wmk.* (1 *r.*, 2 *r.*).

11	6 c. on 2½ h. brown.. ..	£110	£120
12	6 c. on 4 h. green	£110	£120
13	6 c. on 7½ h. carmine ..	£110	£120
14	6 c. on 15 h. ultramarine ..	£120	£130
15	6 c. on 20 h. blk. & red/*yell.*	£110	£120
16	6 c. on 30 h. blk. & carmine	£150	£160
17	6 c. on 45 h. black & mve.	£150	£170
18	6 c. on 1 r. carmine ..		
	a. Surch. double	£450	
19	6 c. on 2 r. green ..		
20	6 c. on 3 r. blue-blk. & red		

The 5, 20 and 40 pesa values of the 1900 acht issue are also known with the above rcharge as are the contemporary 1 c. and 6 s. nzibar stamps.

M 3

15 (Sept.). *German East African fiscal stamps.* "Statistik des Waaren-Verkehrs" (*Trade Statistical Charge*) *overprinted in bluish green,* "O.H.B.M.S. Mafia" *in a circle, as Type* M **3**.

21	24 pesa, vermilion/*buff* ..	35·00	40·00
22	12½ heller, drab	35·00	40·00
23	25 heller, dull green ..	35·00	40·00
24	50 heller, slate	35·00	40·00
25	1 rupee, lilac	35·00	40·00
21/25	.. .. *Set of* 5	£150	£180

rman East African "Ubersetzungs-Gebühren" (*Translation fee*) *stamp, overprinted as before.*

26	25 heller, grey	70·00	75·00

G. R
POST
MAFIA
(M 4)

G. R.
Post
MAFIA.
(M 5)

Stamps as above, but with further opt. as Type M **4**, *in green.*

M27	24 pesa, vermilion/*buff* ..	35·00	40·00
M28	12½ heller, drab	35·00	40·00
M29	25 heller, dull green ..	35·00	40·00
M30	50 heller, slate	35·00	40·00
M31	1 rupee, lilac	35·00	40·00
M32	25 heller, grey (No. M26) ..	35·00	
M27/31	.. .. *Set of* 5	£150	£180

1915 (Sept.). *Stamps of India,* 1911–13, *optd.* "I.E.F." *in black, with a further opt. Type* M **4** *handstruck in green, greenish black or dull blue.*

M33	**55**	3 p. grey	1·75	2·00
		a. Pair, one stamp without opt.	—	27·00
M34	**56**	½ a. green	2·25	2·50
M35	**57**	1 a. carmine	2·75	3·00
M36	**59**	2 a. mauve	3·75	4·50
M37	**61**	2½ s. ultramarine	4·00	5·00
M38	**62**	3 a. orange-brown ..	4·00	4·00
M39	**63**	4 a. olive..	6·00	7·00
M40	**65**	8 a. purple	10·00	12·00
M41	**66**	12 a. dull claret	20·00	25·00
M42	**67**	1 r. brown and green ..	23·00	27·00
M33/M42		.. .. *Set of* 10	70·00	80·00

All values exist with the overprint inverted, and several are known with overprint double or sideways.

1916 (Oct.). *Stamps of India,* 1911–13, *optd.* "I.E.F." *in black with further opt. Type* M **5** *handstruck in green, greenish black or dull blue.*

M43	**55**	3 p. grey	11·00	11·00
M44	**56**	½ a. green	11·00	11·00
M45	**57**	1 a. carmine	12·00	12·00
M46	**59**	2 a. mauve	12·00	12·00
M47	**61**	2½ a. ultramarine	13·00	13·00
M48	**62**	3 a. orange-brown ..	14·00	14·00
M49	**63**	4 a. olive..	14·00	14·00
M50	**65**	8 a. purple	15·00	15·00
M51	**66**	12 a. dull claret	18·00	18·00
M52	**67**	1 r. brown and green ..	20·00	20·00

Stamps with handstamp inverted are known.

II. FOR USE OF NYASA-RHODESIAN FORCE.

N. F.

(D)

1916. *T* **15** *of Nyasaland optd. with Type* D *by Govt. Printer, Zomba.*

33	**15**	½d. green	45	80
34	„	1d. scarlet	35	70
35	„	3d. purple/*yellow*	1·25	2·50
		a. Opt. double	£1800	£2000
36	„	4d. black and red/*yellow* ..	6·00	7·00
37	„	1s. black/*green*	5·50	6·00
33/37		.. .. *Set of* 5	12·00	15·00
33/37		Optd. "Specimen" *Set of* 5	£110	

This issue was sanctioned for use by the Nyasa-Rhodesian Force in conquered territory in German East Africa.

Of No. 35a only six copies were printed, these being the bottom row on one pane issued at M'bamba Bay F.P.O., German East Africa.

This overprint was applied in a setting of 60 (10 rows of 6) and the following minor varieties occur on all values: small stop after "N" (No. 1); broken "F" (No. 21); very small stop after "F" (No. 35); no serifs at top left and bottom of "N" (No. 55).

III. BRITISH OCCUPATION OF GERMAN EAST AFRICA.

G.E.A. (1) G. E. A. (2) G.E.A. (3)

1917–21. *Stamps of Kenya optd. with* T **1** *and* **2**. *Wmk. Mult. Crown CA. Ordinary paper* (1 *c. to* 15 *c.*) *or chalk-surfaced paper* (*others*).

38	**3**	1 c. black (R.)	10	15
39	„	1 c. black (Verm.)	4·50	4·50
40	„	3 c. green	10	15
41	„	6 c. scarlet	10	15
42	„	10 c. orange	10	15
43	„	12 c. slate-grey	15	40
44	„	15 c. bright blue	15	35
45	„	25 c. black and red/*yellow* ..	30	50
		a. *On pale yellow* (1921) (Optd. S. £16)	30	50
46	„	50 c. black and lilac ..	45	90
47	„	75 c. black/*blue-green, olive-back* (R.)	60	1·40
		a. *On emerald back* (Optd. S. £16)	1·00	2·00
48	**4**	1 r. black/*green* (R.) ..	90	1·75
		a. *On emerald back* ..	1·25	2·25
49	„	2 r. red and black/*blue* ..	2·00	3·50
50	„	3 r. violet and green ..	3·00	4·00
51	„	4 r. red and green/*yellow* ..	4·00	5·50
52	„	5 r. blue and dull purple ..	5·50	7·50
53	„	10 r. red and green/*green* ..	20·00	26·00
		a. *On emerald back* ..	22·00	26·00
54	„	20 r. black and purple/*red* ..	50·00	55·00
55	„	50 r. carmine & grn. (S. £90)	£275	£300
38/53		.. .. *Set of* 15	32·00	48·00
38/54		Optd. "Specimen" *Set of* 16	£130	

Early printings of the rupee values exist with very large stop after the "E" in "G.E.A." (R. 5/3). There are round stops after "E" varieties, which in one position of later printings became a small stop.

1921. *As* 1917–22 *but wmk. Mult. Script CA.*

60	**3**	12 c. slate-grey, O	50	70
61	„	15 c. bright blue, O ..	10	25
63	„	50 c. black & dull purple, C	2·75	4·25
66	**4**	2 r. red and black/*blue*, C	15·00	22·00
67	„	3 r. violet and green, C	16·00	24·00
68	„	5 r. blue and dull purple, C	18·00	26·00
60/68		.. .. *Set of* 6	48·00	70·00
60/8		Optd. "Specimen" *Set of* 6	70·00	

1922. *T* **3** *of Kenya optd. by the Government printer at Dar-es-Salaam with T* **3**. *Wmk. Mult. Script CA.*

72		1 c. black (R.)	10	25
73		10 c. orange-yellow ..	12	50

IV. BRITISH MANDATE.

4

5

(Recess. B.W.)

1922. *T* **4** (5 *to* 75 *c.*) *and* **5**. *Head in black. Wmk. Mult. Script CA.*

(*a*) *P* 15 × 14.

74	5 c. slate-purple	25	20
75	10 c. green	15	20
76	15 c. carmine-red	40	8
77	20 c. orange	30	8
78	25 c. black	2·40	3·00
79	30 c. blue	1·00	1·00
80	40 c. yellow-brown	1·10	1·50
81	50 c. slate-grey	1·10	1·50
82	75 c. yellow-bistre	2·40	2·75

(*b*) *P* 14. A. *Wmk. sideways.* B. *Wmk. upright.*

		A.		B.	
83	1s. green ..	1·40	2·00	1·40	2·00
84	2s. purple ..	3·25	3·75	2·75	3·75
85	3s. black ..	3·25	4·25	†	
86	5s. scarlet ..	5·00	7·00	5·50	7·00
87	10s. deep blue ..	25·00	30·00	25·00	25·00
88	£1 yellow-orge.	60·00	60·00	48·00	48·00
74/88	*Set of* 15 (*incl.* 85A)			90·00	90·00
74/88	Optd. "Specimen" *Set of* 15			£130	

In the £1 stamp the words of value are on a curved scroll running across the stamp above the words "POSTAGE AND REVENUE".

1925. *As 1922. Frame colours changed.*

No.	Type	Description	Unused	Used
89	4	5 c. green	25	35
90	,,	10 c. orange-yellow	60	55
91	,,	25 c. blue	2·75	2·50
92	,,	30 c. purple	75	1·50
89/92		Optd. "Specimen" *Set of* 4	28·00	

6

7

(Typo. D.L.R.)

1927–31. *Head in black. Wmk. Mult. Script. CA. P 14.*

No.	Type	Description	Unused	Used
93	6	5 c. green	8	5
94	,,	10 c. yellow	8	5
95	,,	15 c. carmine-red	8	5
96	,,	20 c. orange-buff	15	8
97	,,	25 c. bright blue	35	30
98	,,	30 c. dull purple	45	40
98*a*	,,	30 c. bright blue ('31) ..	3·00	60
99	,,	40 c. yellow-brown	50	75
100	,,	50 c. grey	30	20
101	,,	75 c. olive-green	1·40	1·75
102	7	1s. green, O	75	50
103	,,	2s. deep purple, O ..	2·00	1·00
104	,,	3s. black, O	3·50	3·75
105	,,	5s. carmine-red, C ..	3·50	3·25
106	,,	10s. deep blue, C ..	11·00	12·00
107	,,	£1 brown-orange, C ..	27·00	27·00
93/107		.. .. *Set of* 16	50·00	48·00
93/107		Optd./Perf. "Specimen" *Set of* 16	70·00	

For issues between 1935 and 1961 see KENYA, UGANDA AND TANGANYIKA.

V. INDEPENDENT STATE.

8. Teacher and Pupils.

9. District Nurse and Child.

10. Coffee-picking.

11. Harvesting Maize.

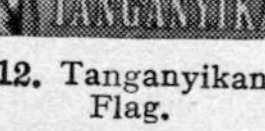

12. Tanganyikan Flag.

13. Serengeti Lions.

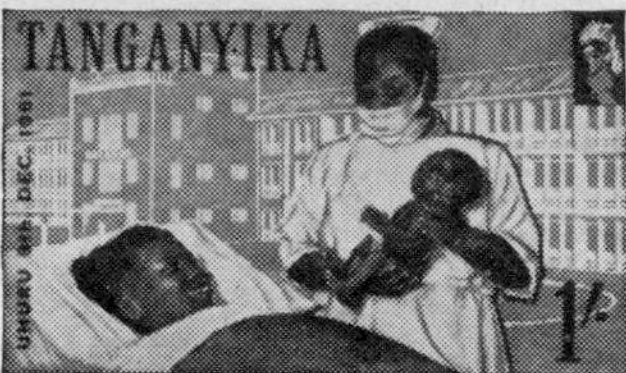

14. "Maternity".

15. Freedom Torch over Mt. Kilimanjaro.

16. Dar-es-Salaam Waterfront.

17. Land Tillage. (*As T* **16.**)

18. Diamond and Mine. (*As T* **16.**)

(Des. V. Whiteley. Photo. Harrison & Sons.)

1961 (9 DEC.). *Independence. P* 14 × 15 (5 *c.*, 30 *c.*), 15 × 14 (10 *c.*, 15 *c.*, 20 *c.*, 50 *c.*) *or* 14½ (*others*).

No.	Type	Description	Unused	Used
108	8	5 c. sepia & lt. apple-grn.	5	5
109	9	10 c. deep bluish green ..	5	5
110	10	15 c. sepia and blue ..	5	5
		a. Blue omitted	£130	
111	11	20 c. orange-brown ..	5	5
112	12	30 c. blk., emerald & yell.	8	5
		a. Inscr. "UHURU 196" ..	£300	£200
113	13	50 c. black and yellow ..	8	8
114	14	1s. brn., blue & olive-yell.	15	10
115	15	1s. 30, red, yellow, black, brown & blue (*shades*)	35	20
116	16	2s. blue, yellow, green and brown	35	20
117	17	5s. deep bluish green and orange-red	85	50
118	18	10s. black, reddish purple and light blue ..	1·75	1·75
		a. Reddish purple (diamond) omitted	60·00	
119	15	20s. red, yellow, black, brown and green ..	5·00	5·00
108/19		.. .. *Set of* 12	8·00	7·50

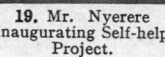

19. Mr. Nyerere inaugurating Self-help Project.

20. Hoisting Flag on Mt. Kilimanjaro.

21. Presidential Emblem.

22. Independence Monument.

(Photo. Harrison & Sons.)

1962 (9 DEC.). *Inauguration of Republic. P* 14½

No.	Type	Description	Unused	Used
120	19	30 c. emerald	8	
121	20	50 c. yellow, black, green, red and blue ..	10	
122	21	1s. 30, multicoloured ..	20	
123	22	2s. 50, black, red & blue	35	

23. Map of Republic.

24. Torch and Spear Emblem.

(Des. M. Goaman. Photo. Harrison.)

1964 (7 JULY). *United Republic of Tanganyika and Zanzibar Commemoration. P* 14 × 14½.

No.	Type	Description	Unused	Used
124	23	20 c. yellow-grn. & lt. blue	5	5
125	24	30 c. blue and sepia ..	5	5
126	,,	1s. 30, orange-brown and ultramarine	20	25
127	23	2s. 50, purple & ultram.	35	35

Despite the inscription on the stamps the above issue was only on sale in Tanganyika and had no validity in Zanzibar.

VI. TANZANIA.

(RENAMED.)

A. **For use in Tanzania and also valid for use in Kenya and Uganda, until 1976.**

25. Hale Hydro-Electric Scheme.

26. Tanzanian Flag.

27. National Servicemen.

28. Road-building.

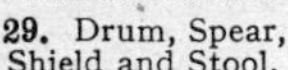

29. Drum, Spear, Shield and Stool.

30. Giraffes, Mikumi National Park.

31. Zebras, Manyara National Park.

32. Mt. Kilimanjaro.

33. Dar-es-Salaam Harbour.

34. Skull of Zinjanthropus and Excavations, Olduvai Gorge.

35. Fishing.

36. Sisal Industry.

37. State House, Dar-es-Salaam.

38. Arms of Tanzania.

(Des. V. Whiteley. Photo. Harrison.)

1965 (9 Dec.). *P* 14×14½ (5 *c.*, 10 *c.*, 20 *c.*, 50 *c.*, 65 *c.*), 14½×14 (15 *c.*, 30 *c.*, 40 *c.*), *or* 14 (*others*).

128 **25** 5 c. ultram. & yell.-orge. .. 5 5
129 **26** 10 c. black, greenish yellow, green and blue .. 5 5
130 **27** 15 c. multicoloured .. 5 5
131 **28** 20 c. sepia, grey-green and greenish blue .. 5 5
132 **29** 30 c. black and red-brown 8 5
133 **30** 40 c. multicoloured .. 8 5
134 **31** 50 c. multicoloured .. 10 5
135 **32** 65 c. grn., red-brn. & blue 12 15
136 **33** 1s. multicoloured .. 15 8
137 **34** 1s. 30, multicoloured .. 20 12
138 **35** 2s. 50, blue & orge.-brn. 55 45
139 **36** 5s. lake-brown, yellow-green and blue .. 1·00 75
140 **37** 10s. olive-yellow, olive-green and blue .. 1·40 1·40
141 **38** 20s. multicoloured .. 3·25 4·50
128/141 .. .. *Set of* 14 6·50 7·00

39. Cardinal. **40.** Mud Skipper.

41. White Spotted Puffer. **42.** Sea Horses.
43. Bat Fish. **44.** Sweetlips.
45. Blue Club-nosed Wrasse. **46.** Bennett's Butterfly.
46a. Striped Grouper.

(T **41**/**46a** *are as T* **39**/**40**).

47. Scorpion Fish.

48. Powder Blue Surgeon. **50.** Moorish Idol.
51. Picasso Fish.
48a. Fusilier. **52.** Squirrel Fish.
49. Red Snapper.

(*T* **48**/**52** are *as T* **47**.)

(Des. Mrs. R. M. Fennessy. Photo. Harrison.)

1967 (9 Dec.)–**73.** *Chalk-surfaced paper. P* 14×15 (5 *c. to* 70 *c.*) *or* 14½ (*others*).

142 **39** 5 c. magenta, yellow-olive and black .. 5 5
a. Glazed, ordinary paper (22.1.71) 5 5
143 **40** 10 c. brown and bistre .. 5 5
a. Glazed, ordinary paper (27.9.72) 5 5

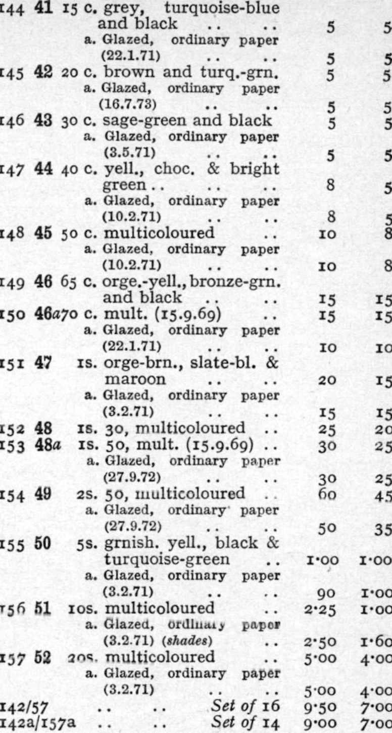

144 **41** 15 c. grey, turquoise-blue and black 5 5
a. Glazed, ordinary paper (22.1.71) 5 5
145 **42** 20 c. brown and turq.-grn. 5 5
a. Glazed, ordinary paper (16.7.73) 5 5
146 **43** 30 c. sage-green and black 5 5
a. Glazed, ordinary paper (3.5.71) 5 5
147 **44** 40 c. yell., choc. & bright green 8 5
a. Glazed, ordinary paper (10.2.71) 8 5
148 **45** 50 c. multicoloured .. 10 8
a. Glazed, ordinary paper (10.2.71) 10 8
149 **46** 65 c. orge.-yell., bronze-grn. and black 15 15
150 **46a** 70 c. mult. (15.9.69) .. 15 15
a. Glazed, ordinary paper (22.1.71) 10 10
151 **47** 1s. orge-brn., slate-bl. & maroon 20 15
a. Glazed, ordinary paper (3.2.71) 15 15
152 **48** 1s. 30, multicoloured .. 25 20
153 **48a** 1s. 50, mult. (15.9.69) .. 30 25
a. Glazed, ordinary paper (27.9.72) 30 25
154 **49** 2s. 50, multicoloured .. 60 45
a. Glazed, ordinary paper (27.9.72) 50 35
155 **50** 5s. grnish. yell., black & turquoise-green .. 1·00 1·00
a. Glazed, ordinary paper (3.2.71) .. .. 90 1·00
156 **51** 10s. multicoloured .. 2·25 1·00
a. Glazed, ordinary paper (3.2.71) (*shades*) .. 2·50 1·60
157 **52** 20s. multicoloured .. 5·00 4·00
a. Glazed, ordinary paper (3.2.71) .. .. 5·00 4·00
142/57 .. .. *Set of* 16 9·50 7·00
142a/157a .. .. *Set of* 14 9·00 7·00

On Chalk-surfaced paper all values except the 30 c., exist with PVA gum as well as gum arabic, but the 70 c. and 1s. 50 exist with PVA gum only. Stamps on Glazed, ordinary paper come only with PVA gum.

53. *Papilio hornimani.* **54.** *Euphaedra neophron.*

(Des. Mrs. R. Fennessy. Photo. Harrison.)

1973 (10 Dec.). *Various vert. designs as T* **53**/**4**.

(*a*) *Size as T* **53**. *P* 14½×14.

158 5 c. light yellow-olive, light violet-blue and black .. 5 5
159 10 c. multicoloured 5 5
160 15 c. light violet-blue & black 5 5
161 20 c. reddish cinnamon, orange-yellow and black .. 5 5
162 30 c. yellow, orange & black 5 5
163 40 c. multicoloured 5 5
164 50 c. multicoloured 5 5
165 60 c. light grey-brown, lemon and reddish brown .. 8 8
166 70 c. turquoise-green, pale orange and black .. 8 8

(*b*) *Size as T* **54**. *P* 14.

167 1s. multicoloured 10 12
168 1s. 50, multicoloured .. 15 20
169 2s. 50, multicoloured .. 25 30
170 5s. multicoloured 50 60
171 10s. multicoloured .. .. 1·00 1·25
172 20s. multicoloured .. .. 2·10 2·40
158/72 .. .. *Set of* 15 4·00 4·50

Butterflies:—10 c. *Colotis ione*; 15 c. *Amauris makuyuensis*; 20 c. *Libythea laius*; 30 c. *Danaus chrysippus*; 40 c. *Sallya rosa*; 50 c. *Axiocerses styx*; 60 c. *Eurema hecabe*; 70 c. *Acraea insignis*; 1 s. *Euphaedra neophron*; 1 s. 50 *Precis octavia*; 2 s. 50 *Charaxes eupale*; 5 s. *Charaxes pollux*; 10 s. *Salamis parhassus*; 20 s. *Papilio ophidicephalus*.

=

80c

(55)

1975 (17 Nov.). *Nos.* 165, 168/9 *and* 172 *surch. as T* **55**.
173 80 c. on 60 c. *Eurema hecabe* 15 15
174 2s. on 1s. 50, *Precis octavia* 40 40
175 3s. on 2s. 50, *Charaxes eupale* 10·00 10·00
176 40s. on 20s. *Papilio ophidicephalus* .. .. 5·00 5·25

NOTE. For commemorative stamps issued between 1964 and 1976, inscribed "UGANDA KENYA TANGANYIKA & ZANZIBAR" (or "TANZANIA UGANDA KENYA") see under EAST AFRICA.

B. For use in Tanzania only.

1976 (15 APR.). *Telecommunications Development. Designs as Nos.* 260/3 *of Kenya.*
177 50 c. Microwave Tower .. 5 8
178 1s. Cordless switchboard .. 12 15
179 2s. Telephones 25 30
180 3s. Message Switching Centre 35 40
MS181 120×120 mm. Nos. 177/80. Imperf. 80

1976 (5 JULY). *Olympic Games, Montreal. As Nos.* 265/8 *of Kenya.*
182 50 c. Akii Bua, Ugandan hurdler 5 8
183 1s. Filbert Bayi, Tanzanian runner 12 15
184 2s. Steve Muchoki, Kenyan boxer 25 30
185 3s. Flags and Olympic flame 35 40
MS186 129×154 mm. Nos. 182/5 80

1976 (4 OCT.). *Railway Transport. As Nos.* 269/72 *of Kenya.*
187 50 c. Tanzania–Zambia Railway 5 8
188 1s. Nile Bridge, Uganda .. 12 15
189 2s. Nakuru Station, Kenya .. 25 30
190 3s. Class A loco, 1896 .. 35 40
MS191 154×103 mm. Nos. 187/90 80

OFFICIAL STAMPS.

OFFICIAL (O 1) **OFFICIAL** (O 2) (3½ mm. tall.)

1961 (9 DEC.). *Optd. with Type* O **1** (10 *c.*, 15 *c.*, 20 *c.*, 50 *c.*) *or larger and measuring* 17 *mm.* (5 *c.*, 30 *c.*) *or with Type* O **2** (1*s.*) *or measuring* 22 *mm.* (5*s.*).
O1 **8** 5 c. sepia & lt. apple-grn. 5 5
O2 **9** 10 c. deep bluish green .. 5 5
O3 **10** 15 c. sepia and blue .. 5 5
O4 **11** 20 c. orange-brown .. 5 5
O5 **12** 30 c. blk., emerald & yell. 8 10
O6 **13** 50 c. black and yellow .. 10 12
O7 **14** 1s. brn., bl. & olive-yell. 20 25
O8 **17** 5s. deep bluish green and orange-red .. .. 85 1·00
O1/O8 .. .. *Set of* 8 1·25 1·40

1965 (9 DEC.). *Nos.* 128, *etc. optd. as Types* O **1** (15 *c.*, 30 *c.*) *or larger,* (*measuring* 17 *mm.* 5 *c.*, 10 *c.*, 20 *c.*, 50 *c.*), *or* O **2** (1*s.*, 5.*s.*)
O9 **25** 5 c. ultram. & yell.-orge. 5 8
O10 **26** 10 c. black, greenish yellow, green and blue .. 5 5
O11 **27** 15 c. multicoloured .. 5 5
O12 **28** 20 c. sepia, grey-green and greenish blue .. 5 5
O13 **29** 30 c. black and red-brown 5 5
O14 **31** 50 c. multicoloured .. 10 10
O15 **33** 1s. multicoloured .. 25 25
O16 **36** 5s. lake-brown, yellow-green and blue .. 1·00 1·00
O9/O16 .. .. *Set of* 8 1·25 1·25

OFFICIAL
(O 3) (3 mm. tall.)

1967 (Nov.?). 50 *c., optd. as on No.* O14, *others with Type* O **3**.
O17 **31** 50 c. multicoloured ..
O18 **33** 1s. multicoloured .. 5·00 2·00
O19 **36** 5s. lake-brown, yellow-green and blue .. 6·00 3·00

Nos. O9/16 were overprinted by Harrison in photogravure and Nos. O17/19 have litho. overprints by the Government Printer, Dar-es-Salaam. On No. O17 the overprint is the same size (17 mm. long) as on No. O14.

1967–71. *Optd. as Type* O **1**, *but larger* (*measuring* 17 *mm.*) (5 *c. to* 50 *c.*) *or as Type* O **2** (1*s. and* 5*s.*). *Chalk-surfaced paper.*
O20 **39** 5 c. magenta, yellow-olive and black 5 5
a. Glazed, ordinary paper .. 5 5
O21 **40** 10 c. brown and bistre .. 5 5
O22 **41** 15 c. grey, turq.-bl. & blk. 5 5
a. Glazed, ordinary paper .. 5 5
O23 **42** 20 c. brown & turq.-grn. 5 5
O24 **43** 30 c. sage-green and black 5 5
O25 **45** 50 c. multicoloured .. 10 5
a. Glazed, ordinary paper .. 10 8
O26 **47** 1s. orge-brn., slate-bl. & maroon 25 25
a. Glazed ordinary paper .. 15 10
O27 **50** 5s. grnish. yell., blk. & turquoise-green .. 1·00 1·00
a. Glazed, ordinary paper .. 65 55
O20/27 .. .. *Set of* 8 1·25 1·25
O20a/27a .. .. *Set of* 5 90 75

Dates of issue: 9.12.67, stamps on chalk-surfaced paper; 22.1.71, O20a, O22a, O25a; 3.2.71, O26a, O27a.

The Chalk-surfaced paper exists with both PVA gum and gum arabic, but the Glazed, ordinary paper exists PVA gum only.

1970 (10 DEC.)–**73**. *Stamps of* 1967–73 *optd. locally by letterpress as Type* O **1** *or Type* O **2**, *but measuring* 28 *mm.* (1*s.*) *or* 17½ *mm. in length.*

(*a*) *Chalk-surfaced paper.*
O28 **39** 5 c. magenta, yellow-olive and black 5 5
a. "OFFCIAL" (R.7/6) ..
O29 **40** 10 c. brown and bistre .. 5 5
a. "OFFCIAL" (R.7/6) ..
O30 **42** 20 c. brown and turquoise-green 10 8
O31 **43** 30 c. sage-green and black 15 12

(*b*) *Glazed, ordinary paper* (1973).
O32 **39** 5 c. magenta, yellow-olive and black .. ..
a. "OFFCIAL" (R.7/6) ..
O33 **40** 10 c. brown and bistre
a. "OFFCIAL" (R.7/6) ..
O34 **41** 15 c. grey, turq.-bl. and blk.
a. "OFFCIAL" (R.7/6) ..
O35 **42** 20 c. brown and turq.-grn.
O36 **44** 40 c. yellow, chocolate and bright green ..
a. Opt. double ..
b. "OFFICIA" .. ..
O37 **45** 50 c. multicoloured ..
a. "OFFCIAL" (R.7/6) ..
O38 **47** 1s. orange-brown, slate-blue and maroon ..
a. Opt. double ..
O39 **50** 5s. greenish yellow-black and turquoise-green

The letterpress overprint can be distinguished from the photogravure by its absence of screening dots and the overprint showing through to the reverse, apart from the difference in length.

OFFICIAL (O 4) **OFFICIAL** (O 5)

1973 (10 DEC.). *Nos.* 158 *etc. optd. with Type* O **4** (5 *to* 70 *c.*) *or Type* O **5** (*others*).
O40 5 c. light yellow-olive, light violet-blue and black .. 5 5
O41 10 c. multicoloured 5 5
O42 20 c. reddish cinnamon, orange-yellow and black 5 5
O43 40 c. multicoloured 8 8
O44 50 c. multicoloured 8 8
O45 70 c. turquoise-green, pale orange and black .. 10 10
O46 1s. multicoloured 12 12
O47 1s. 50, multicoloured .. 20 20
a. Pair, one without opt. .. † —
O48 2s. 50, multicoloured .. 30 30
O49 5s. multicoloured 55 60
O40/49 .. .. *Set of* 10 1·40 1·40

No. O47a is due to a paper fold and comes from a sheet used at Kigoma in 1974.

POSTAGE DUE STAMPS.

Postage Due stamps of Kenya and Uganda were issued for provisional use as such in Tanganyika on 1 July, 1933. The postmark is the only means of identification.

The Postage Due stamps of Kenya, Uganda and Tanganyika were used in Tanganyika until January 2nd, 1967.

D 1

(Litho. D.L.R.)

1967 (3 JAN.). *P* 14×13½.
D1 D **1** 5 c. scarlet 5 5
D2 ,, 10 c. green 5 5
D3 ,, 20 c. deep blue 8 8
D4 ,, 30 c. red-brown 10 10
D5 ,, 40 c. bright purple .. 12 12
D6 ,, 1s. orange 25 25
D1/6 .. .. *Set of* 6 55 55

1969–71. *As Nos.* D1/6, *but perf.* 14×15.
A. *Chalk-surfaced paper* (19.12.69).
B. *Glazed, ordinary paper* (13.7.71).

			A.		B.	
D 7 D **1**	5 c. scarlet		5	5	5	5
D 8 ,,	10 c. green (*shades*)		5	5	5	5
D 9 ,,	20 c. dp. blue		8	8	5	5
D10 ,,	30 c. red-brn. (*shades*)		10	10	5	8
D11 ,,	40 c. brt. pur.		10	10	10	10
D12 ,,	1s. orange		†		15	15
D7A/11A	*Set of* 5		25	25		
D7B/12B	*Set of* 6				35	40

The stamps on chalk-surfaced paper exist only with gum arabic, but the stamps on glazed paper exist only with PVA gum.

1973 (12 DEC.). *Glazed, ordinary paper.* *P* 15
D13 D **1** 5 c. scarlet 5 5
D14 ,, 10 c. emerald 5 5
D15 ,, 20 c. deep blue .. 5 5
D16 ,, 30 c. red-brown 5 8
D17 ,, 40 c. bright mauve .. 8 8
D18 ,, 1s. bright orange .. 12 15
D13/18 .. .. *Set of* 5 30 35

C. For use in Zanzibar only.

Z 1. Pres. Nyerere and First Vice-Pres. Karume within Bowl of Flame.

Z 2. Hands supporting Bowl of Flame.

(Des. J. O. Ahmed (Type Z 1), G. L. Vasarhelyi (Type Z 2). Photo. Enschedé.)

1966 (26 APR.). *2nd Anniv. of United Republic. P* 14×13.

Z1	Z 1	30 c. multicoloured	..	5	5
Z2	Z 2	50 c. multicoloured	..	8	8
Z3	,,	1s. 30, multicoloured	..	20	25
Z4	Z 1	2s. 50, multicoloured	..	40	45

The above are listed here instead of under Zanzibar because Type Z 1 is only inscribed "TANZANIA".

TASMANIA.

1

2

(Eng. C. W. Coard. Recess. H. and C. Best at the office of the *Courier* Newspaper.)

1853 (1 Nov.). *No wmk. Imperf. Twenty-four varieties in four rows of six each.* (*a*) *Medium soft yellowish paper with all lines clear and distinct.*

1 **1** 1d. pale blue £1300 £300
2 ,, 1d. blue £1300 £300

(*b*) *Thin hard white paper with lines of the engraving blurred and worn.*

3 **1** 1d. pale blue £1200 £275
4 ,, 1d. blue £1200 £275

1853–54. *No wmk. Imperf. In each plate there are twenty-four varieties in four rows of six each.*

1853. *Plate I. Finely engraved. All lines in network and background thin, clear, and well defined.*

(*a*) *First state of the plate, brilliant colours.*

5 **2** 4d. bright red-orange £1000 £200
a. Double impression .. ..
6 ,, 4d. bright brownish orange .. — £275

(*b*) *Second state of plate, with blurred lines and worn condition of the central background.*

7 **2** 4d. red-orange £700 £140
8 ,, 4d. orange £700 £140
9 ,, 4d. pale orange .. .. — £140

1854. *Plate II. Coarse engraving, lines in network and background thicker and blurred.*

10 **2** 4d. orange £600 £120
a. Double print, one albino ..
11 ,, 4d. dull orange £600 £120
12 ,, 4d. yellowish orange .. £600 £120

Variety. Laid paper, with wide vertical lines.

13 4d. red-orange £1600

No. 13 is from a proof sheet and is only known unused.

In the 4d. Plate I, the outer frame-line is thin all round. In Plate II it is, by comparison with other parts, thicker in the lower left angle.

In 1879 reprints were made of the 1d. in blue and the 4d., Plate I, in brownish yellow, on thin, tough, white wove paper, and perforated 11½. In 1887, a reprint from the other plate of the 4d. was made in reddish brown and in black, and in 1889 of the 1d. in blue and in black, and of the 4d. (both plates) in yellow and in black on white card, imperforate. The three plates having been defaced after the issue was superseded by new types, all these reprints show two thick strokes across the Queen's Head.

3

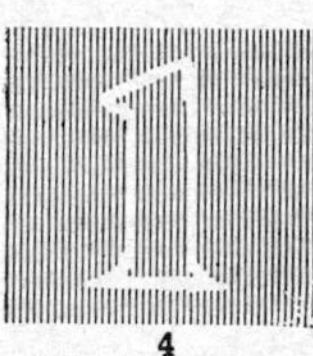
4

(Eng. W. Humphrys after water-colour sketch by E. Corbould. Recess. Perkins, Bacon & Co.)

1855 (Aug.). *Wmk. Large Star, Type* w.1. *Imperf.*

14 **3** 1d. carmine £2000 £350
15 ,, 2d. deep green £700 £250
16 ,, 2d. green £700 £250
17 ,, 4d. deep blue .. .. .. £650 28·00
18 ,, 4d. blue .. .. .. £600 30·00

There is a proof of the 1d. on thick, no wmk., paper that is sometimes sold as the issued stamp.

(Printed by H. and C. Best, of Hobart.)

1856–57. *No. wmk. Imperf.*

19 **3** 1d. pale brick-red. (4.56) .. £1900 £225
20 ,, 2d. dull emerald-green (1.57) £2500 £250
21 ,, 4d. deep blue (5.57) .. .. £275 28·00
22 ,, 4d. blue .. .. .. £250 28·00
23 ,, 4d. pale blue .. .. .. — 45·00

Pelure paper.

24 **3** 1d. deep red-brown (11.56) .. £1000 £200

1857 (Aug.)–**60.** *Wmk. double-lined numerals* "**1**", "**2**" *or* "**4**" *as T* **4.** *Imperf.*

25 **3** 1d. deep red-brown .. .. £140 7·50
26 ,, 1d. pale red-brown .. .. 90·00 5·50
27 ,, 1d. brick-red .. .. .. 50·00 5·50
28 ,, 1d. dull vermilion .. .. 30·00 5·50
29 ,, 1d. carmine .. .. .. 30·00 5·50
a. Double print .. .. — 35·00
30 ,, 2d. dull emerald-green .. — 17·00
31 ,, 2d deep green .. .. 65·00 14·00
32 ,, 2d. green .. .. .. — 13·00
a. Double print .. .. — 48·00
33 ,, 2d. yellow-green .. .. 80·00 17·00
34 ,, 2d. sage-green .. .. 45·00 17·00
35 ,, 4d. blue .. .. .. 35·00 5·50
a. Double print .. .. — 45·00
36 ,, 4d. pale blue .. .. 35·00 5·50
37 ,, 4d. bright blue .. .. 35·00 5·50
a. Printed on both sides ..
b. Double print .. .. — 38·00
38 ,, 4d. very deep blue .. .. — 16·00
a. Double print .. .. — 50·00
39 ,, 4d. cobalt-blue .. .. — 11·00

CANCELLATIONS. Beware of early Tasmanian stamps with pen-cancellations cleaned off and faked postmarks applied.

7

8

(Recess. Perkins, Bacon & Co.)

1858 (Jan.). *Wmk. double-lined numerals* "**6**" *or* "**12**". *Imperf.*

40 **7** 6d. dull lilac .. .. £225 11·00
41 **8** 1s. bright vermilion .. .. £100 11·00
42 ,, 1s. dull vermilion .. .. — 11·00

Prepared for use, but not issued.
Wmk. Large Star. Imperf.

43 **7** 6d. lilac £100

(Plates by Perkins, Bacon. Typo. in the Colony.)

1860–67. *Wmk. double-lined* "**6**". *Imperf.*

44 **7** 6d. dull slate-grey (3.60) .. 70·00 11·00
45 ,, 6d. grey .. .. .. — 11·00
46 ,, 6d. grey-violet (4.63) .. 35·00 11·00
a. Double print .. .. — 18·00
47 ,, 6d. dull bluish (2.65) .. 42·00 11·00
48 ,, 6d. bluish purple .. .. 70·00 12·00
49 ,, 6d. reddish mauve (1867) .. £225 55·00

In 1871 reprints were made of the 6d. (in mauve) and the 1s. on white wove paper, and perforated 11½. They are found with or without "REPRINT." In 1889 they were again reprinted on white card, imperforate and perforated 12. These later impressions are also found with or without "REPRINT."

1864–70. *Double-line numeral watermarks. Various local roulettes and perforations.*

(*a*) **1864.** *Roughly punctured roulette about* 8, *by J. Walch, at Hobart.*

50 **3** 1d. brick-red .. .. .. — 45·00
51 ,, 1d. carmine .. .. .. 65·00 28·00
52 ,, 4d. pale blue .. .. .. — 45·00
53 **7** 6d. dull lilac .. .. .. — 55·00
54 **8** 1s. vermilion .. .. .. — £200

(*b*) **1867** (March). *Pin-perf.* 5½ *to* 9½ *at Longford, near Launceston.*

55 **3** 1d. carmine .. .. .. 85·00 22·00
56 ,, 4d. bright blue .. .. — 60·00
57 **7** 6d. grey-violet .. .. .. — 45·00
58 ,, 6d. reddish mauve .. .. — £125
59 **8** 1s. vermilion .. .. ..

(*c*) **1867** (?). *Pin-perf.* 13½ *to* 14½.

60 **3** 1d. brick-red .. .. .. — 60·00
61 ,, 1d. dull vermilion .. .. — 60·00
62 ,, 1d. carmine .. .. ..
63 ,, 2d. yellow-green .. .. — 90·00
64 ,, 4d. pale blue .. .. .. — 60·00
65 **7** 6d. grey-violet .. .. — £110
66 **8** 1s. vermilion .. .. ..

(*d*) **1866** (?). *Oblique roulette* 10, 10½.

67 **3** 1d. brick-red .. .. — £110
68 ,, 1d. carmine £250 £100
69 ,, 2d. yellow-green .. .. — £160
70 ,, 4d. bright blue .. .. — £140
71 **7** 6d. grey-violet .. .. — £200

(*e*) **1867** (?). *Oblique roulette* 14 *to* 15, *used at Deloraine.*

72 **3** 1d. brick-red .. .. .. — £110
73 ,, 1d. dull vermilion .. .. — £110
74 ,, 1d. carmine .. .. .. — £110
75 ,, 2d. yellow-green .. .. — £140
76 ,, 4d. pale blue .. .. — £110
77 **7** 6d. grey-violet .. .. — £200
78 **8** 1s. vermilion .. .. .. — £250

(*f*) **1868–69.** *Serrated perf.* 19.

79 **3** 1d. carmine (*pen.-canc.* £3·50) 60·00 30·00
80 ,, 2d. yellow-green .. .. — 60·00
81 ,, 4d. deep blue .. .. .. £190 40·00
82 ,, 4d. cobalt-blue .. .. — 40·00
83 **7** 6d. bluish purple .. .. — £120

1864–80. *Double-line numeral watermarks.*

I. *Perforated by J. Walch and Sons, Hobart.*

(*a*) *P* 10.

84 **3** 1d. brick-red .. .. 12·00 4·00
85 ,, 1d. vermilion .. .. 12·00 4·00
86 ,, 1d. deep carmine .. 10·00 4·00
87 ,, 1d. pale carmine .. .. 12·00 4·00
88 ,, 2d. sage-green .. .. 55·00 32·00
89 ,, 2d. yellow-green .. .. 42·00 18·00
90 ,, 4d. blue .. .. .. 28·00 4·00
91 ,, 4d. pale blue .. .. 28·00 4·00
a. Double print .. .. — 25·00
92 **7** 6d. grey-violet .. .. 42·00 5·5
93 ,, 6d. dull bluish .. .. 28·00 4·00
94 ,, 6d. bluish purple .. — 6·00
95 ,, 6d. reddish mauve .. 95·00 16·00
96 **8** 1s. vermilion .. .. 28·00 4·00

(*b*) *P* 11½ *to* 12.

96*a* **3** 1d. vermilion .. .. 12·00
97 ,, 1d. deep carmine .. 8·50 3·00
98 ,, 1d. pale carmine .. .. 10·00 3·00
99 ,, 2d. pale yellow-green .. 42·00 12·0
100 ,, 2d. deep yellow-green .. 28·00 12·0
101 ,, 4d. blue .. .. .. 28·00 5·5
102 ,, 4d. deep blue .. .. 28·00 3·00
103 ,, 4d. cobalt-blue .. .. — 9·00
104 **7** 6d. bluish purple .. 42·00 5·5
105 ,, 6d. reddish mauve .. 28·00 8·00
106 **8** 1s. vermilion .. .. 32·00 5·5
a. Double print .. .. — 50·00

(*c*) *Perf. compound* 10 × 11½, 12.

107 **3** 1d. deep carmine .. £400
108 ,, 4d. blue .. .. .. — £25

Error. Wmk. double-lined "**2**". *P* 12½–1 (Nov. 1869).

109 **3** 1d. carm. (*pen.-canc.* £20) — £30

II. *Perforated by R. Harris, Launceston.*
P 12½, 12.

110 **3** 1d. brick-red .. .. 12·00 6·5
111 ,, 1d. vermilion .. .. 10·00 5·5
112 ,, 1d. deep carmine .. 6·00 3·0
113 ,, 2d. sage-green .. .. 55·00 25·0
114 ,, 2d· yellow-green .. .. 60·00 25·0
115 ,, 4d. bright blue .. .. 45·00 11·0
116 ,, 4d. blue .. .. .. 45·00 11·0
117 **7** 6d. dull bluish .. .. 50·00 11·0
118 ,, 6d. bluish purple .. 60·00 11·0
119 ,, 6d. reddish mauve .. £110 25·0
120 **8** 1s. vermilion .. .. 55·00 20·0

III. *Perforated by the Government at Hobart.*
(*a*) *P* 11, 11½. (1871–80.)

121 **7** 6d. dull mauve .. .. 28·00 8·0
122 ,, 6d. bright mauve .. 24·00 8·0
a. Imperf. between (pair) .. — £12
123 ,, 6d. dull purple (3.75) .. 24·00 5·5
a. Imperf. (pair) .. .. — £10
124 ,, 6d. bright purple .. 24·00 5·5
a. Double print .. .. — 25·0
b. Imperf. between (horiz. pr.) £175
125 ,, 6d. lilac-purple .. .. 28·00 8·0
126 **8** 1s. dull vermilion .. 28·00 8·0
a. Imperf. between (horiz. pr.)
127 ,, 1s. brownish vermilion .. 24·00 8·0

(*b*) *P* 12.

28 **7** 6d. bright purple .. 32·00 6·00
29 ,, 6d. dull claret .. .. 8·00 4·50

All stamps perforated by the "Walch" nachine gauge over 11½ and under 12, while hose of the Government machine gauge 11½ or nder.

11

12

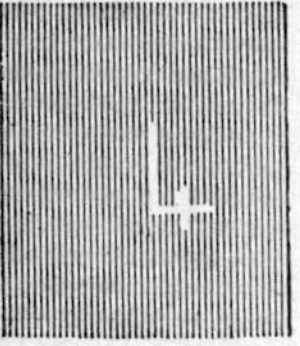
13

14

(Plates by D.L.R., Typo. in the Colony.)

870–71. *Wmk. single lined numerals T* **12, 13,** *or* **14.** (*a*) *P* 12.

30 **11** 1d. rose red (10) .. .. 10·00 3·50
31 ,, 1d. deep rose-red (10) .. 16·00 2·50
32 ,, 1d. rose-red (4) .. .. 14·00 3·50
33 ,, 2d. yellow-green (2) .. 14·00 1·75
34 ,, 2d. blue-green (2) .. 16·00 1·75
35 ,, 4d. blue (4) .. .. 40·00 40·00
36 ,, 10d. black (10) .. .. 1·25 1·25

(*b*) *P* 11½.

37 **11** 1d. rose-red (10) .. .. 70·00
38 ,, 2d. yellow-green (2) .. 27·00 2·75
39 ,, 2d. blue-green (2) .. 11·00 1·25
a. Double print .. ..
40 ,, 10d. black (10) .. .. 4·50 2·50

(*c*) *Imperf.* (*pairs*).

41 **11** 1d. rose-red (4) .. .. — 60·00
42 ,, 1d. rose-red (10) .. .. 65·00 70·00
43 ,, 2d. green (2) .. ..
44 ,, 10d. black (10) .. .. 30·00

The above were printed on paper borrowed rom New South Wales.

15

16

871–79. *W* **15.** (*a*) *P* 12.

45 **11** 1d. rose .. .. .. 16·00 2·25
46 ,, 1d. carmine .. .. 18·00 3·00
47 ,, 2d. green (11.72) .. 90·00 30·00
48 ,, 3d. red-brown .. .. 16·00 5·50
49 ,, 3d. deep red-brown .. 16·00 5·50
50 ,, 4d. buff (8.8.76) .. 42·00 3·00
51 ,, 9d. pale blue .. .. 8·00
52 ,, 5s. purple .. .. 30·00
53 ,, 5s. mauve .. .. 14·00

(*b*) *P* 11½.

54 **11** 1d. rose 80 20
55 ,, 1d. bright rose 80 20
56 ,, 1d. vermilion (4.73) .. 40·00 18·00
57 ,, 1d. carmine .. .. 1·25 20
58 ,, 1d. pink .. .. .. 1·25 20
59 ,, 2d. deep green (11.72) .. 3·00 20
60 ,, 2d. yellow-green (12.75) 35·00 20
61 ,, 2d. blue-green .. .. 7·50 20
62 ,, 3d. pale red-brown .. 8·00 1·10
63 ,, 3d. deep red-brown .. 8·00 1·25
a. Imperf. between (pair)

164 **11** 3d. purple-brown (1.78) 8·00 1·00
165 ,, 3d. brownish purple .. 8·00 1·00
166 ,, 4d. ochre .. .. 11·00 1·10
167 ,, 4d. buff (8.8.76) .. 8·00 1·50
168 ,, 4d. pale yellow .. .. 8·00 1·10
169 ,, 9d. blue .. .. .. 3·50 1·75
170 ,, 5s. pur. (*pen. canc.* 55p.) 11·00 4·00
171 ,, 5s. mauve .. .. 8·00 4·00

(*c*) *Imperf.* (*pairs*).

172 **11** 1d. rose (*pen. canc.* £10)
173 ,, 2d. green .. .. — 45·00
174 ,, 3d. pale red-brown .. 35·00
175 ,, 3d. purple-brown .. — 85·00
176 ,, 9d. blue .. .. .. 35·00
176*a* ,, 5s. purple .. ..

See also Nos. 209/15.

(Typo. D.L.R.)

1878 (28 Oct.). *W* **16.** *P* 14.

177 **11** 1d. carmine 50 15
178 ,, 1d. rose-carmine 50 15
179 ,, 1d. scarlet 40 15
180 ,, 2d. pale green 55 15
181 ,, 2d. green 55 15
182 ,, 8d. dull purple-brown .. 1·00 75

In 1871 the 1d., 2d., 3d., 4d. blue, 9d., 10d. and 5s., *T* **11** were reprinted on soft white wove, and perforated 11½; and in 1879 the 4d. yellow and 8d. were reprinted on thin, tough, white wove. All nine varieties are found with and without "REPRINT". In 1889 the 4d. blue was also reprinted on white card imperforate, and perforated 12. The 5s. has been reprinted in *mauve* on white card, perforated 12. These later impressions, like those of 1871 and 1879, are found with or without "REPRINT".

1880–91. *Colonial print.* *W* **16.**

(*a*) *P* 12.

183 **11** ½d. orange (1889) 60 35
184 ,, ½d. deep orange 50 30
185 ,, 1d. pink (1889) .. .. 4·00 90
a. Imperf. (pair) .. .. 25·00 30·00
186 ,, 1d. rosine .. .. .. 1·25 65
187 ,, 1d. dull rosine .. .. 2·00 90
a. Imperf. (pair) .. .. 25·00
188 ,, 3d. red-brown (1880) .. 65 35
a. Imperf. (pair) .. .. 25·00
b. Imperf. between (pair) .. £125
189 ,, 4d. deep yellow (1883) .. 11·00 3·00
190 ,, 4d. chrome-yellow .. 15·00 3·00
a. Printed both sides .. 35·00

(*b*) *P* 11½.

192 **11** ½d. orange (8.3.89) .. 45 10
193 ,, ½d. deep orange 45 15
194 ,, 1d. dull red (14.2.89) .. 90 30
195 ,, 1d. vermilion-red (4.80) .. 45 30
196 ,, 3d. red-brown (1.83) .. 1·25 80
197 ,, 4d. deep yellow (1.83) .. 6·00 95
198 ,, 4d. chrome-yellow .. 6·00 1·10
199 ,, 4d. olive-yellow .. .. 17·00 4·00
200 ,, 4d. buff .. .. .. 6·00 1·25

Halfpenny (**17**)

d. **2½** (**18**) (2¼ mm. between "d", and "2".)

d. **2½** (**19**) (3½ mm. between "d." and "2".)

1889–91. *W* **16.** (*a*) *Surch. locally with T* **17.** *P* 14.

201 **11** ½d. on 1d. scarlet (1.1.89) 40 30
a. "al" in "Half" reading down £175 £100

A minor variety has broken "p" in "Halfpenny".

(*b*) *Surch. locally with T* **18.** *P* 11½.

204 **11** 2½d. on 9d. pale blue .. 80 80
a. Imperf. (pair) .. .. 35·00
b. Surch. double, one inverted 35·00 35·00
205 ,, 2½d. on 9d. deep blue .. 1·00 1·10

(*c*) *Surch. locally with T* **19.** *P* 12.

207 **11** 2½d. on 9d. pale blue .. 60 80
a. Blue surch. .. ..

There is a reprint on the 2½d. on 9d. on stout white wove paper, perf. 12, overprinted "REPRINT".

1891. *Colonial print.* *Reissue with W* **15.**

(*a*) *P* 12.

209 **11** ½d. orange .. .. .. 5·00 2·50
a. Imperf. (pair) .. .. 20·00
210 ,, 1d. dull rosine .. .. 6·00 2·50
211 ,, 1d. rosine .. .. .. 9·50 4·50
212 ,, 4d. bistre .. .. .. 1·75 65

(*b*) *P* 11½.

213 **11** ½d. orange .. .. .. 5·00 1·40
214 ,, ½d. brown-orange .. .. 3·75 1·25
215 ,, 1d. rosine .. .. .. 3·00 1·40

20

21

21*a*

(Typo. D.L.R.)

1892–99. *W* **16.** *P* 14.

216 **20** ½d. orange and mauve .. 40 8
217 **21** 2½d. purple 75 15
218 **20** 5d. pale blue and brown 1·50 60
219 ,, 6d. violet and black .. 1·75 70
220 **21*a*** 10d. pur.-lake & dp. grn. 2·00 90
221 **20** 1s. rose and green .. 2·00 70
222 ,, 2s. 6d. brown and blue .. 5·00 2·00
223 ,, 5s. lilac and red .. .. 7·00 4·00
224 ,, 10s. mauve and brown .. 18·00 12·00
225 ,, £1 green and yellow .. 60·00 45·00
216/225 .. .. *Set of* 10 85·00 50·00
216/225 Optd. "Specimen" *Set of* 10 80·00

1896. *Colonial print.* *W* **16.** *P* 12.

226 **11** 4d. pale bistre .. .. 1·50 90
227 ,, 9d. pale blue .. .. 1·00 55
a. Blue .. .. .. 1·40 1·25

22. Lake Marion.

23. Mount Wellington.

24. Hobart.

25. Tasman's Arch.

26. Spring River, Port Davey.

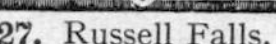
27. Russell Falls.

28. Mount Gould, Lake St. Clair.

29. Dilston Falls.

30

1899–1912.

PICTORIAL DESIGNS.

A. Recess-printed by De La Rue, London.

1899 (DEC.)–**1900.** *W* **30.** *P* 14.

229	**22**	½d. deep green	20	8
230	**23**	1d. bright lake	20	8
231	**24**	2d. deep violet	40	8
232	**25**	2½d. indigo	75	40
233	**26**	3d. sepia	1·40	35
234	**27**	4d. deep orange-buff ..	1·75	40
235	**28**	5d. bright blue	2·00	60
236	**29**	6d. lake	3·00	60
229/36		Optd. "Specimen" *Set of* 8	75·00	

B. Printed at the Government Printing Office, Melbourne, Victoria.

I. *Wmk. V over Crown, Type* w.**10.**

1902–3. LITHOGRAPHED. *Transfers from London plates. Wmk. upright on* 1d. *P* 12½.

237	**22**	½d. green (1903)	20	8
		a. Perf. 11	1·40	10
		b. Perf. comp. of 12½ and 11	12·00	10·00
238	**23**	1d. carmine-red	25	8
239	**24**	2d. violet	25	8
		a. Perf. 11	25	8
		b. Perf. comp. of 12½ and 11	15·00	10·00
		c. Purple	25	8
		ca. Purple. Perf. 11 ..	80	8
237/9		Optd. "Specimen" *Set of* 3	28·00	

As the V and Crown paper was originally prepared for stamps of smaller size, portions of two or more watermarks appear on each stamp.

The ½d. and 2d. may be found with wmk. upright, the normal position in these values being sideways.

We only list the main groups of shades in this and the following issues. There are variations of shade in all values, particularly in the 2d. where there is a wide range, also in the 1d. in some issues.

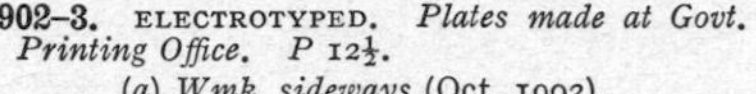

1902–3. ELECTROTYPED. *Plates made at Govt. Printing Office. P* 12½.

(*a*) *Wmk. sideways* (Oct. 1902).

240	**23**	1d. pale red (to rose) ..	30	8
		a. Perf. 11	2·75	8
		b. Perf. 12½ comp. with 11 ..	28·00	8·00

Stamps from this printing with wmk. upright, are scarce, especially perf. 11.

(*b*) *Wmk. upright* (April, 1903).

241	**23**	1d. rose-red	20	8
		a. Perf. 11	1·75	8
		b. Perf. comp. of 12½ and 11..	28·00	8·00
		c. Deep carmine-red. ..	12·00	25
		ca. Deep carmine-red. Perf. 11	—	4·00
		cb. Deep carmine-red. Perf. comp. of 12½ and 11 ..		

II. *Wmk. Crown over A. Type* w. **11** (*sideways on oblong stamps*).

1905 (SEPT.)–**1912.** LITHOGRAPHED. *Transfers from London plates. P* 12½.

242	**24**	2d. purple	85	8
		a. Perf. 11	1·25	8
		b. Perf. comp. of 12½ and 11..	4·00	1·00
		c. Perf. comp. of 12½ and 12..	—	12·00
		d. Perf. comp. of 11 and 12 ..		
		e. Dull purple	60	
		ea. Dull purple. Perf. 11 ..	2·25	10
243	**26**	3d. brown	1·50	15
		a. Perf. 11	2·00	30
		b. Perf. comp. of 12½ and 11..	13·00	
244	**27**	4d. orange-buff (1907) ..	1·25	30
		a. Perf. 11	95	20
		b. Perf. comp. of 12½ and 11..	35·00	
		c. Brown-ochre (wmk. sideways). Perf. 11 (1907) ..	6·00	1·50
		d. Orange-yellow (1912) ..	3·50	70
		da. Orange-yellow. Perf. 11 ('12)	2·50	
245	**29**	6d. lake	5·00	1·25
		a. Perf. 11	6·50	1·50
		b. Perf. comp. of 12½ and 11..	30·00	

Stamps with perf. compound of 12½ and 12 or 11 and 12 are found on sheets which were sent from Melbourne incompletely perforated. The line of perforation gauging 12 was done at the Government Printing Office, Hobart.

1905–11. ELECTROTYPED. *Plates made at Govt. Printing Office. P* 12½.

246	**22**	½d. yellow-green (1909) ..	20	8
		a. Perf. 11 (1908) ..	20	8
		b. Perf. comp. of 12½ and 11..	7·00	
		c. Perf. comp. of 11 and 12 ..		
247	**23**	1d. rose-red	20	8
		a. Perf. 11	20	8
		b. Perf. comp. of 12½ and 11..	60	40
		c. Perf. comp. of 12½ and 12..	7·00	2·00
		d. Perf. comp. of 11 and 12 ..	10·00	
		e. Bright rose	—	8
		ea. Bright rose. Perf. 11 ..	65	
		f. Crimson (1910)		
		fa. Crimson. Perf. 11 ..		
		fb. Crimson. Perf. comp. of 12½ and 12		
248	**24**	2d. purple	65	
		a. Perf. 11	75	
		b. Dull violet	65	
		ba. Dull violet. Perf. 11 ..	65	
		bb. Dull violet. Perf. comp. of 12½ and 11	3·00	1·5
		bc. Dull violet. Perf. comp. of 12½ and 11		
		bd. Dull violet. Perf. comp. of 11 and 12	18·00	10·0
		c. Bright violet (1910) ..	2·50	1
		ca. Bright violet. Perf 11 ..	2·50	1
249	**26**	3d. brown (1909) ..	1·00	3
		a. Perf. 11	1·40	5
		b. Perf. comp. of 12½ and 11	25·00	
250	**29**	6d. dull lake (1911) ..	2·00	1·0
		a. Perf. 11	2·00	7
		b. Perf. comp. of 12½ and 11..	25·00	

The note after No. 245 *re* perfs. compoun with perf. 12 also applies here.

The ½d. and 2d. are found with wmk. uprigh and the 1d. with wmk. sideways, each perf. 12 or 11.

Stamps showing blotchy or defective impre sion often with shading appearing as solid colou are from worn electro typed plates, with th exception of Nos. 244*d* and 244*da*.

1911. *Electrotyped from new plate. P* 12½.

251	**24**	2d. bright violet	40	
		a. Perf. 11	45	1
		b. Perf comp. of 12½ and 11 ..	18·00	

Stamps from this plate differ from Nos. 248 and 248*ca* in the width of the design (33 to 33 mm., against just over 32 mm.), in the talle bolder letters of "TASMANIA", in the slope o the mountain in the left background, which clearly outlined in white, and in the outer vertic frame-line at left, which appears "wavy" Compare Nos. 252, etc., which are always fro this plate.

ONE PENNY
(31)

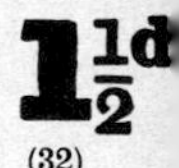

(32)

1912 (OCT.). *No.* 251 *surch. with T* **31.** *P* 12½

252	**24**	1d. on 2d. brt. violet (R.)	35	
		a. Perf. 11	55	
		b. Perf. comp. of 12½ and 11	—	30·0

1912 (DEC.). *Thin paper, white gum* (*as Vi toria*, 1912). *P* 12½.

253	**23**	1d. crimson	1·10	
		a. Perf. 11	1·50	
		b. Perf. comp. of 12½ and 11		
254	**26**	3d. brown	5·00	5·0

DIFFERENCES BETWEEN LITHOGRAPHED AND ELECTROTYPED ISSUES.

LITHOGRAPHED.	ELECTROTYPED.
General appearance fine.	*Comparatively cruc and coarse appearanc*
½d. All "V over Crown" wmk.	All "Crown over A wmk.
1d. The shading on the path on the right bank of the river consists of very fine dots. In printings from worn stones the dots hardly show.	The shading on th path is coarser, consis ing of large dots an small patches of colou
The shading on the white mountain is fine (or almost absent in many stamps).	The shading on th mountain is coarse, an clearly defined.
2d. Three rows of windows in large building on shore, at extreme left, against inner frame.	Two rows of wir dows.
3d. Clouds very white.	Clouds dark.
Stars in corner ornaments have long points.	Stars have sho points.
Shading of corner ornaments is defined by a coloured outer line.	Shading of ornament terminates agains white background.

4d. Lithographed only.	—
6d. No coloured dots at base of waterfall.	Coloured dots at base of waterfall.
Outer frame of value tablets is formed by outer line of design.	Thick line of colour between value tablets and outer line.
	Small break in inner frame below second "A" of "TASMANIA".

1903–5. *Wmk. V over Crown, Type* w. **10.** *P* 12½.

255 **11** 9d. blue .. .. .. 2·00 1·25
a. Perf. 11 .. .. .. 2·50 1·50
b. Perf. comp. of 12½ and 11 .. — £100
c. *Pale blue* .. .. .. 2·50 1·50
d. *Bright blue* .. .. .. 2·50 1·75
e. *Ultramarine* .. .. 80·00
f. *Indigo* .. .. .. 40·00
256 **20** 1s. rose and green .. 2·50 1·40
a. Perf. 11 .. .. .. 6·50
255/256 Optd. "Specimen" *Set of* 2 28·00

1904 (29 Dec.). *No.* 218 (*W* **16**) *surch. with T* **32.**

257 **20** 1½d. on 5d. pale blue and brown (optd. S. £14) 45 30

Stamps with inverted surcharge or without surcharge *se-tenant* with stamps with normal surcharge were obtained irregularly and were not issued for postal use.

1906–13. *Wmk. Crown over A, Type* w. **11.** *P* 12½.

258 **11** 8d. purple-brown (1907) 1·75 90
a. Perf. 11 .. .. 1·75 75
259 „ 9d. blue (1907) .. .. 1·75 90
a. Perf. 11 .. .. .. 1·75 90
b. Perf. comp. of 12½ and 11 (1909) .. .. .. 14·00
c. Perf. comp. of 12½ and 12 (1909) .. .. .. 25·00
d. Perf. comp. of 11 and 12 .. 60·00
260 **20** 1s. rose and green (1907) 1·75 55
a. Perf. 11 (1907) .. .. 1·75 1·00
b. Perf comp. of 12½ and 11 3·75
c. Perf. comp. of 12½ and 12 11·00
261 „ 10s. mauve & brn. (1906) 15·00 12·00
a. Perf. 11 .. .. .. 25·00
b. Perf. comp. of 12½ and 12 22·00

The note after No. 245 *re* perfs. compound with perf. 12, also applies here.

POSTAL FISCALS.

Authorized for use in 1882.

CLEANED STAMPS. Beware of postal fiscal stamps with pen-cancellations removed.

F 1 F 2

F 3 F 4

(Recess. Alfred Bock, Hobart.)

1863. *Wmk. double-lined* "1", *T* **4.** *Imperf.*

F1 **F 1** 3d. green .. .. 12·00
F2 **F 2** 2s. 6d. carmine .. 14·00
F3 **F 3** 5s. sage-green .. .. 4·00
F4 „ 5s. brown .. .. 12·00 15·00
F5 **F 4** 10s. salmon .. .. 3·50
F6 „ 10s. orange .. .. 5·50 8·00

1864. *Wmk. double-lined* "1", *T* **4.** (*a*) *P* 10.

F 7 F 1 3d. green .. .. 4·00 5·50
F 8 F 2 2s. 6d. carmine .. 4·50
F 9 F 3 5s. brown .. .. 4·50
F10 F 4 10s. orange .. .. 8·00

(*b*) *P* 12.

F11 **F 1** 3d. green .. .. 5·00 7·00
F12 **F 2** 2s. 6d. carmine .. 5·00 7·00
F13 **F 3** 5s. sage-green .. .. 4·00 7·00
F14 „ 5s. brown .. .. 9·00
F15 **F 4** 10s. salmon .. .. 6·50 8·00
F16 „ 10s. orange-brown .. 9·00 10·00

(*c*) *P* 12½, 13.

F17 **F 1** 3d. green .. .. 10·00
F18 **F 2** 2s. 6d. carmine .. 10·00
F19 **F 3** 5s. brown .. .. 10·00
F20 **F 4** 10s. orange-brown .. 11·00

(*d*) *P* 11½.

F21 **F 1** 3d. green .. ..
F22 **F 2** 2s. 6d. lake .. .. 5·00 7·00
F23 **F 3** 5s. sage-green .. .. 4·50 6·50
F24 **F 4** 10s. salmon .. .. 10·00 11·00

In 1879, the 3d., 2s. 6d., 5s. (brown), and 10s. (orange) were reprinted on thin, tough, white paper, and are found with or without "REPRINT". In 1889 another reprint was made on white card, imperforate and perforated 12. These are also found with or without "REPRINT".

W **16.** *P* 11½, 12.

F25 **F 2** 2s. 6d. lake .. .. 1·50 2·00
a. Imperf. between (horiz. pr.) £125

F 5. Duck-billed Platypus.

REVENUE

(F 6)

(Typo. D.L.R.)

1880. *W* **16.** *P* 14.

F26 **F 5** 1d. slate .. .. .. 1·50 1·00
F27 „ 3d. chestnut .. .. 1·40 40
F28 „ 6d. mauve .. .. 4·50 1·00
F29 „ 1s. rose-pink .. .. 7·00 2·00

All values are known imperf., but not used.

Reprints are known of the 1d. in *deep blue* and the 6d. in lilac. The former is on yellowish white, the latter on white card. Both values also exist on wove paper, perf. 12, with the word "REPRINT".

1900 (Nov.). *Optd. with* F **6.**

A. *Types* F **2** *and* F **4.** *W* **16.**

F30 2s. 6d. carmine (*imperf.*) .. 40·00
a. "REVFNUE" .. ..
F31 2s. 6d. carmine (*perf.* 12) .. 35·00 35·00
a. "REVFNUE" .. ..
b. Opt. inverted .. ..
c. "REVFNUE" inverted ..
F32 10s. salmon (*perf.* 12) ..
a. "REVFNUE" .. ..
F33 10s. salmon (*W* **4**, *perf.* 12) ..
a. "REVFNUE" .. ..

B. *Type* F **5.** *W* **16.** *P* 14.

F34 3d. chestnut .. .. .. 2·50 2·25
a. Double opt. one vertical ..

C. *Type* F **5.** *Lithographed.* *P* 12.

(*a*) *Thin transparent paper.* *W* **15.**

F35 1d. blue .. .. .. 14·00

(*b*) *Thick paper.* *W* **16.**

F36 1d. blue .. .. .. 2·50 2·50
a. Imperf. between (horiz. pair) £100
b. "REVENUE" inverted .. 25·00
c. "REVENUE" double .. 85·00
d. *Pale blue* .. .. .. 2·50 2·50
F37 2d. chestnut .. .. .. 2·50
a. Value omitted .. .. 50·00
b. Value double .. .. 65·00
F38 6d. mauve .. .. .. 8·00
a. Double print .. .. 40·00
F39 1s. pink .. .. .. 15·00 15·00

It is doubtful if Nos. F35 to F39 were authorized for postage, though some are known duly postmarked. No. F37 is somewhat different in design from Type F **5.**

D. *T* **20.** *W* **16.** *P* 14.

F40 £1 green and yellow .. .. 55·00 60·00
a. Opt. double, one vertical .. 75·00 80·00

Tasmania now uses the stamps of AUSTRALIA.

TOBAGO.

For GREAT BRITAIN stamps used in Tobago with "A 14" obliteration, see index to Great Britain Stamps Used Abroad list.

CANCELLATIONS. Beware of early stamps of Tobago with fiscal endorsements removed and forged wide "A 14" postmarks added.

1 2

(T **1** and **2.** Typo. D.L.R.)

1879 (1 Aug.). *Fiscal stamps issued provisionally pending the arrival of stamps inscr.* "POSTAGE". *Wmk. Crown CC.* *P* 14.

1 **1** 1d. rose .. .. .. 11·00 12·00
2 „ 3d. blue .. .. .. 13·00 12·00
3 „ 6d. orange .. .. .. 11·00 11·00
4 „ 1s. green .. .. .. £140 22·00
a. Bisected (6d.) (on cover) ..
5 „ 5s. slate £300 £250
6 „ £1 mauve £2000

Stamps of T **1**, watermark Crown CA, are fiscals which were never admitted to postal use.

1880 (Nov.). *No.* 3 *bisected vertically and surch. with pen and ink.*

7 **1** 1d. on half of 6d. orange .. — £225

1880 (20 Dec.). *Wmk. Crown CC.* *P* 14.

8 **2** ½d. purple-brown .. .. 7·00 8·00
9 „ 1d. Venetian red .. .. 10·00 7·00
a. Bisected (½d.) (on cover) .. † £500
10 „ 4d. yellow-green .. .. 65·00 9·00
a. Bisected (2d.) (on cover) .. † £500
b. Malformed "CE" in "PENCE" £300 £275
11 „ 6d. stone .. .. .. 70·00 45·00
12 „ 1s. yellow-ochre .. .. 10·00 11·00

2½ PENCE

(3)

1883 (Apr.). *No.* 11 *surch. with T* **3.**

13 **2** 2½d. on 6d. stone .. .. 5·00 2·25
a. Surch. double .. ..
b. Large "2" with long tail .. 20·00 20·00

1882–4. *Wmk. Crown CA.* *P* 14.

14 **2** ½d. purple-brown (1882) .. 1·10 7·00
15 „ 1d. Venetian red (5.82) .. 1·25 1·25
a. Bisected diag. (½d.) (on cover)
16 „ 2½d. dull blue (1883) .. 1·50 1·40
a. *Bright blue* 60 80
b. *Ultramarine* (1883) .. 60 60
18 „ 4d. yellow-green (8.84) .. 80·00 65·00
a. Malformed "CE" in "PENCE" £275
19 „ 6d. stone (8.84) £200 £180

1885–96. *Colours changed and new value.* *Wmk. Crown CA.* *P* 14.

20 **2** ½d. dull green (8.86) .. 12 12
21 „ 1d. carmine (1.86) .. 15 12
22 „ 4d. grey (4.85) 35 40
a. Malformed "CE" in "PENCE" 18·00
b. Imperf. (pair) £650
23 „ 6d. orange-brown (11.86) .. 90 1·75
24 „ 1s. olive-yellow (1894) .. 1·40 3·25
a. *Pale olive-yellow* (1894) ..
b. Error. Orange-brown (1896) 2·50
20, 21 and 23 Optd. "Specimen" *Set of* 3 55·00

½ PENNY 2½ PENCE

(4) (5)

1886–89. *Nos.* 16, 19 *and* 23 *surch. as T* **4.**

26 ½d. on 2½d. dull blue (Apr. '86) 1·25 2·50
a. Figure farther from word .. 7·00 8·00
b. Surch. double £425
c. Surch. omitted. Vert. pair with No. 26 .. .. .. £2000
d. Ditto, with No. 26a £3500
27 ½d. on 6d. stone (Jan. '86) .. 2·00 3·25
a. Figure farther from word .. 15·00 18·00
b. Surch. inverted £300
c. Surch. double £350
28 ½d. on 6d. orge.-brn. (Oct. '89) 14·00 15·00
a. Figure farther from word .. 80·00 90·00
b. Surch. double .. .. — £400
29 1d. on 2½d. dull blue (Jy. '89) 5·00 7·00
a. Figure farther from word .. 22·00 25·00

The surcharge is in a setting of 12 (two rows of 6) repeated five times in the pane. Nos. 7, 9 and 10 in the setting have a raised "P" in "PENNY", and No. 10 also shows the wider spacing between figure and word.

1891–2. *No.* 22 *surch. with T* **4** *or* **5.**

30 ½d. on 4d. grey (1892) .. 5·00 8·00
a. Malformed "CE" in "PENCE" £140
b. Surch. double £650
31 2½d. on 4d. grey .. .. 3·50 5·00
a. Malformed "CE" in "PENCE" £110
b. Surch. double £650

½d

POSTAGE

(6)

1896. *Fiscal stamps* (*T* **1**, *value in second colour, wmk. Crown CA, P* 14), *surch. with T* **6.**

33 ½d. on 4d. lilac and carmine .. 3·00 4·00
a. Space between "½" and "d" .. 5·50 8·00

From 1896 until 1913 Trinidad stamps were used in Tobago.

For issues from 1913 see TRINIDAD AND TOBAGO.

TOGO.

ANGLO-FRENCH OCCUPATION.

TOGO
Anglo-French
Occupation
(1)

Half penny
(2)

I. WIDE SETTING. LINES 3 MM. APART.

Stamps of German Colonial issue Types A *and* B 1900 *and* 1909–14 (5 *pf. and* 10 *pf.*).

1914 (28 SEPT.). *Optd. with T* **1.**

1 3 pf. brown .. .. .. 65·00 45·00
2 5 pf. green .. .. .. 65·00 45·00
3 10 pf. carm. (Wmk. Lozenges) 80·00 55·00
a. Opt. inverted .. .. — £2100
b. Opt. tête-bêche in vert. pair — £2500
c. Error. No wmk. .. .. — £1800
4 20 pf. ultramarine .. .. 15·00 10·00
5 25 pf. black and red/*yellow* .. 15·00 12·00
6 30 pf. black and orange/*buff* .. 15·00 12·00
7 40 pf. black and carmine .. £140 £100
8 50 pf. black and purple/*buff* .. £3000 £2500
9 80 pf. black and carmine/*rose* £140 £100
10 1 m. carmine £2000 £1200
11 2 m. blue £2700 £2200
a. "Occupation" double .. £3500 £3500
b. Opt. inverted £5000

1914 (1 OCT.). *Nos.* 1 *and* 2 *surch. as T* **2.**

12 ½d. on 3 pf. brown £200 £120
a. Thin "y" in "penny" .. £300 £200
13 1d. on 5 pf. green £200 £120
a. Thin "y" in "penny" .. £300 £200

TOGO
Anglo-French
Occupation
(3)

TOGO
Anglo-French
Occupation
Half penny
(4)

II. NARROW SETTING. LINES 2 MM. APART.

1914 (Mid-OCT.). *Optd. with T* **3.**

14 3 pf. brown £300 £275
a. "Occupation" omitted .. £900
15 5 pf. green £300 £275
16 10 pf. carmine £650 £650
17 20 pf. ultramarine .. .. 7·00 6·00
a. Error. "TOG" £2000 £2000
18 25 pf. black and red/*yellow* .. 9·00 9·00
a. Error. "TOG" £4500
19 30 pf. black and orange/*buff* .. 9·00 9·00
20 40 pf. black and carmine .. £300 £350
21 50 pf. black and purple/*buff* .. £3500 £2500
22 80 pf. black and carmine/*rose* £300 £350
23 1 m. carmine £3000 £2100
24 2 m. blue £3000 £2800
25 3 m. violet-black £6000
26 5 m. lake and black £6000

Narrow setting, but including value, as T **4.**

27 ½d. on 3 pf. brown .. .. 12·00 9·00
a. Error. "TOG" .. .. £180 90·00
b. Thin "y" in "penny" .. 26·00 17·00
28 1d. on 5 pf. green .. .. 3·25 3·00
a. Error. "TOG" .. .. 65·00 30·00
b. Thin "y" in "penny" .. 7·00 7·00

Wide setting, 3 mm. apart.

The overprint on the 3 pf. to 80 pf. was set up in five rows of 10, repeated twice on each sheet. There are many minor varieties.

The *tête-bêche* opt. in the 10 pf. is due to the sheet being turned round after the upper 50 stamps had been overprinted so that vertical pairs fron the two middle rows have the opt. *tête-bêche.*

In the 20 pf. one half of a sheet was overprinted with the wide setting (3 mm.), and the other half with the narrow setting (2 mm.), so that vertical pairs from the middle of the sheet show the two varieties of the overprint.

Narrow setting, 2 mm. apart.

In the ½d. on 3 pf. brown, the 1d. on 5 pf. green, and the 20 pf. blue stamp No. 37 in each setting has the error "TOG".

The ½d. on 3 pf. and 1d. on 5 pf. have the following variety in each of setting of 50:—

Thin dropped "y" with small serifs on Nos. 1, 2, 11, 21, 31, 41, and 42.

TOGO
Anglo-French
Occupation
(6)

1915 (7 JAN.). *Optd. as T* **6.** *The words* "Anglo-French" *measure* 15 *mm. instead of* 16 *mm. as in T* **3.**

29 3 pf. brown £2000 £1000
30 5 pf. green .. .. .. £110 60·00
31 10 pf. carmine .. .. £110 60·00
a. Error. No wmk. .. ..
32 20 pf. ultramarine £700 £200
33 50 pf. black and purple/*buff* .. £3000 £2000

This printing was made on another lot of German Togo stamps, found at Sansane-Mangu.

The setting is in groups of 25 (5 × 5), repeated four times on a sheet.

The fifth stamp in each setting has a broken second "O" in "TOGO", resembling a badly formed "U".

The German Colonial stamps optd. "Togo Occupation franco-anglaise" will be found in Vol. 4 of the Stanley Gibbons Foreign Overseas Catalogue.

TOGO
ANGLO-FRENCH
OCCUPATION
(7)

TOGO
ANGLO-FRENCH
OCCUPATION
(8)

1915 (MAY). *Stamps of Gold Coast, optd. locally with* T **7** ("OCCUPATION" 14½ *mm. long*).

34 **9** ½d. green 8 8
g. Opt. double .. .. 10·00 12·00
35 **10** 1d. red 8 8
g. Opt. double .. .. 12·00 13·00
h. Opt. inverted .. .. 9·00 10·00
ha. Ditto. "TOGO" omitted
36 **11** 2d. greyish slate 10 12
37 **9** 2½d. bright blue 15 15
38 **11** 3d. purple/*yellow* 25 25
a. *White back* .. .. 1·00 1·50
40 ,, 6d. dull and bright purple 25 50
41 **9** 1s. black/*green* 45 75
g. Opt. double .. .. 18·00
42 ,, 2s. purple and blue/*blue* .. 1·00 2·00
43 **11** 2s. 6d. black and red/*blue* 1·40 1·75
44 **9** 5s. green and red/*yellow* (*white back*) .. .. 2·00 3·25
45 ,, 10s. green and red/*green* 4·50 5·50
46 ,, 20s. purple and black/*red* .. 12·00 15·00
34/46 .. .. *Set of* 12 20·00 25·00

Varieties (*Nos. indicate positions in pane*).
A. *Small* "F" *in* "FRENCH" (25, 58, *and* 59).
B. *Thin* "G" *in* "TOGO" (24).
C. *No hyphen after* "ANGLO" (5).
D. *Two hyphens after* "ANGLO" (5).
E. "CUPATION" *for* "OCCUPATION" (33).
F. "CCUPATION" *for* "OCCUPATION" (57).

Prices are for unused. Used are worth more.

		A.	B.	C.	D.	E.	F.
34	½d. ..	50	1·00	60	†	20·00	11·00
35	1d. ..	60	1·40	90	†	†	12·00
	h. Inv.	65·00	65·00	55·00	†	†	†
36	2d. ..	60	2·10	16·00	6·00	†	11·00
37	2½d. ..	90	2·40	7·50	9·00	†	11·00
38	3d. ..	90	2·40	11·00	†	†	12·00
	g. W.b.	5·00	14·00	†	†	†	†
40	6d. ..	1·40	2·10	†	†	†	21·00
41	1s. ..	1·40	2·75	†	†	†	11·00
42	2s. ..	5·00	5·50	11·00	†	†	21·00
43	2s. 6d.	5·00	8·00	13·00	†	†	80·00
44	5s. ..	5·50	10·00	17·00	†	†	15·00
45	10s. ..	12·00	20·00	†	†	†	27·00
46	20s. ..	18·00	27·00	†	†	†	27·00

1916 (APR.). *London opt. T* **8** ("OCCUPATION" 15 *mm. long*). *Heavy type and thicker letters showing through on back.*

47 **9** ½d. green 8 8
48 **10** 1d. red 8 8
49 **11** 2d. greyish slate 15 15
50 **9** 2½d. bright blue .. .. 20 2[illegible]
51 **11** 3d. purple/*yellow* .. .. 25 3[illegible]
52 ,, 6d. dull and bright purple 25 3[illegible]
53 **9** 1s. black/*green* .. .. 60 6[illegible]
a. *On blue-green, olive back* .. 1·40 1·75
b. *On emerald back* .. .. 15·00
54 ,, 2s. purple and blue/*blue* .. 1·00 1·2[illegible]
55 **11** 2s. 6d. black and red/*blue* 1·10 1·4[illegible]
56 **9** 5s. green and red/*yellow* .. 2·00 2·2[illegible]
a. *On orange buff* .. .. 1·75 2·5[illegible]
57 ,, 10s. green and red/*green* .. 4·25 4·7[illegible]
a. *On blue-green, olive back* .. 3·50 4·0[illegible]
58 ,, 20s. purple and black/*red* .. 10·00 12·0[illegible]
47/58 .. .. *Set of* 12 17·00 20·0[illegible]
47/58 Optd. "Specimen" *Set of* 12 £180

TOKELAU ISLANDS.

(*See* after NEW ZEALAND.)

TONGA.

PROTECTORATE KINGDOM.

King George I, 1845–93.

1. King George I.

2

(Eng. Bock and Cousins. Plates made and typo. Govt. Ptg. Office, Wellington.)

1886–88. *W* 2. *P* 12½ (*line*) *or* 12×11½ (*comb*)*.
1 1 1d. carmine, *p.* 12½ (27.8.86) 30·00 8·00
a. Perf. 12½×10
b. Perf. 12×11½ (15.7.87) 4·00 4·50
ba. Pale carmine (p. 12×11½) 8·00 7·00
2 „ 2d. pale vio., *p.* 12½ (27.8.86) 9·00 6·00
a. Bright violet 14·00 6·00
b. Perf. 12×11½ (15.7.87) 9·00 5·00
ba. Bright violet (p. 12×11½) 10·00 6·00
3 „ 6d. blue, *p.* 12½ (9.10.86) 6·00 3·00
a. Perf. 12×11½ (15.10.88) 9·00 3·00
ab. Dull blue (p. 12×11½) 6·50 3·50
4 „ 1s. pale grn., *p.* 12½ (9.10.86) 16·00 4·00
a. Deep green, p. 12½ 20·00 4·00
b. Perf. 12×11½ (15.10.88) 9·00 6·00
ba. Deep green (p. 12×11½) 9·00 3·75

*See note after New Zealand, No. 186.

FOUR PENCE. (3) EIGHT PENCE. (4)

(Surch. Messrs. Wilson & Horton, Auckland, N.Z.)

1891 (10 Nov.). *Nos.* 1*b* and 2*b* *surch.*
5 3 4d. on 1d. carmine 2·00 4·50
a. No stop after "PENCE" 19·00 30·00
6 4 8d. on 2d. violet 14·00 16·00
a. Short "T" in "EIGHT" 22·00 30·00

1891 (23 Nov.). *Optd. with stars in upper right and lower left corners.* *P* 12½.
7 1 1d. carmine 18·00 18·00
a. Three stars 45·00
b. Four stars 70·00
c. Five stars £120
d. Perf. 12×11½ 50·00
da. Three stars 95·00
db. Four stars £110
dc. Five stars £250
8 „ 2d. violet 17·00 17·00
a. Perf. 12×11½ 50·00

1892 (15 Aug.). *W* 2. *P* 12×11½.
9 1 6d. yellow-orange 6·00 8·00

5. Arms of Tonga.

6. King George I.

(Des. eng. A. E. Cousins. Typo. at Govt. Printing Office, Wellington, N.Z.)

1892 (10 Nov.). *W* 2. *P* 12×11½.
10 5 1d. pale rose 7·00 9·00
a. Bright rose 6·00 9·00
b. Bisected diag. (½d.) (on cover) — £250
11 6 2d. olive 4·50 7·00
12 5 4d. chestnut 10·00 13·00
13 6 8d. bright mauve 20·00 22·00
14 „ 1s. brown 18·00 18·00
10/14 *Set of* 5 50·00 60·00

½d. (7) 2½d. (8)

FIVE PENCE. (9) 7½d. (10)

1893. *Printed in new colours and surch. with T* **7/10.** (*a*) *In carmine.* *P* 12½ (21 Aug.).
15 5 ½d. on 1d. bright ultram. 13·00 13·00
a. Surch. omitted
16 6 2½d. on 2d. green 7·00 6·00
17 5 5d. on 4d. orange 6·00 7·00
18 6 7½d. on 8d. carmine 19·00 19·00

(*b*) *In black.* *P* 12×11½ (Nov.).
19 5 ½d. on 1d. dull blue 16·00 19·00
20 6 2½d. on 2d. green 8·00 10·00
a. Surch. double £225

SURCHARGE. HALF-PENNY (11) SURCHARGE, 2½d. (12)

(Surch. at the "Star" Office, Auckland, N.Z.)

1894 (June). *Surch. with T* **11** *or* **12**.
21 5 ½d. on 4d. chestnut (B.) 2·00 5·00
a. "SURCHARCE" 3·50 6·00
22 6 ½d. on 1s. brown 2·00 6·00
a. "SURCHARCE" 5·00 6·00
b. Surch. double £140
c. Surch. double with "SURCHARCE"
23 „ 2½d. on 8d. brt. mauve 2·00 6·00
a. No stop after "SURCHARGE" 9·00 10·00
24 „ 2½d. on 1s. green (No. 4*a*) 10·00 12·00
a. No stop after "SURCHARGE" 26·00
b. Perf. 12×11½ 8·00 10·00
ba. No stop after "SURCHARGE" 17·00

(Design resembling No. 11 litho. and surch. at "Star" Office, Auckland, N.Z.)

1895 (May). *As T* **6** *surch. as T* **11** *and* **12**. *No wmk.* *P* 12.
25 11 1d. on 2d. pale blue (C.) 10·00 12·00
26 12 1½d. on 2d. pale blue (C.) 12·00 14·00
a. Perf. 12×11 11·00 12·00
27 „ 2½d. on 2d. pale blue (C.)* 14·00 16·00
a. No stop after "SURCHARGE" 85·00
28 „ 7½d. on 2d. pale blue (C.) 65·00
a. Perf. 12×11 25·00 25·00

*The 2½d. on 2d. is the only value which normally has a stop after the word "SURCHARGE".

King George II, 1893–1918.

13. King George II.

(Litho. "Star" Office, Auckland, N.Z.)

1895 (16 Aug.). *No. wmk.* *P* 12.
29 13 1d. olive-green 7·00 8·00
a. Bisected diagonally (½d.) (on cover) — £160
b. Imperf. between (pair) — £2700
30 13 2½d. rose 12·00 14·00
a. Stop (flaw) after "POSTAGE" 25·00 25·00
31 „ 5d. blue 6·00 7·00
a. Perf. 12×11 7·00 8·00
b. Perf. 11 £180
32 „ 7½d. orange-yellow 6·00 10·00
a. Yellow 6·00 10·00

1895 (Sept.). *T* **13** *redrawn and surch.* *No wmk.* *P* 12.
33 11 ½d. on 2½d. vermilion 12·00 15·00
a. "SURCHARCE" 25·00
b. stop after "POSTAGE" 40·00
34 „ 1d. of 2½d. vermilion 8·00 12·00
a. Stop after "POSTAGE" 18·00
35 12 7½d. on 2½d. vermilion 22·00 25·00
a. Stop after "POSTAGE" 40·00

In the ½d. surcharge there is a stop after "SURCHARGE" and not after "PENNY". In the 1d. and 7½d. the stop is after the value only.

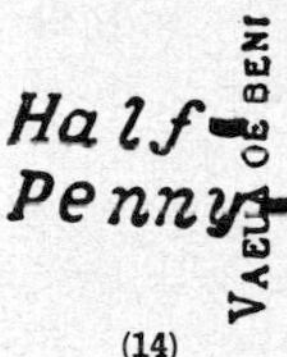

(14)

1896 (May). *Nos.* 26*a* *and* 28*a* *with typewritten surcharge* "Half Penny-" *in violet, and Tongan surcharge in black.*

(A) *Tongan surch. reading downwards.*

(B) *Tongan surch. reading upwards.*

	A.		B.	
36 6 ½d. on 1½d. on 2d.	55·00	—	75·00	—
a. Perf. 12	60·00	—	75·00	60·00
ab. "Haalf" (p. 12)	†		£250	—
37 6 ½d. on 7½d. on 2d.	7·00	9·00	7·00	10·00
a. "Hafl" for "Half"	£180	—	†	
b. "Hafl" ("Penny" omitted)	£180	—	†	
c. "PPenny"	90·00	—	†	
d. Stops instead of hyphens	90·00	—	†	
e. "Halyf"	—	—	†	
f. "Half-Penny-" inverted	£350	—	†	
g. No hyphen after "Penny"	—	—	†	
h. "Hwlf"	†		—	—
j. "Penny" double	†		—	—
k. "Penny" twice, with "Half" on top of upper "Penny"	†		—	—
l. Capital "P" over small "p"	—	—	†	
m. Perf. 12	—	—	—	—
ma. No hyphen after "Half" (p. 12)	—	—	†	

There are variations in the relative positions of the words "Half" and "Penny", both vertically and horizontally.

MINIMUM PRICE

The minimum price quoted is 5p which represents a handling charge rather than a basis for valuing common stamps. For further notes about prices see introductory pages.

15. Arms.

16. Ovava tree, Kana-Kubolu.

17. King George II.

18. Prehistoric Trilith at Haamonga.

19. Bread fruit.

20. Coral.

21. View of Haapai.

22. Parrot.

23. View of Vavau Harbour.

I. No sword hilt.

II. Top of hilt showing.

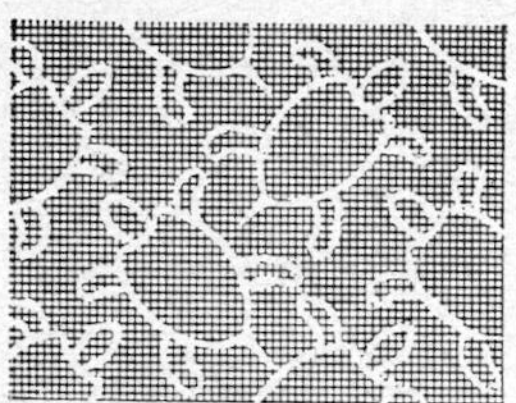
24. Tortoises.

(Recess. D.L.R.)

1897 (June). *W* **24.** *P* 14.

38	**15**	½d. indigo	20	30
39	**16**	1d. black and scarlet ..	30	20
40	**17**	2d. sepia and bistre (I) ..	1·10	1·25
41	,,	2d. sepia and bistre (II) ..	6·50	2·75
42	,,	2d. grey and bistre (II) ..	70	1·00
43	,,	2½d. black and blue ..	80	1·00
		a. No fraction bar in "½" ..	40·00	40·00
44	**18**	3d. black and yellow-green	60	1·00
45	**19**	4d. green and purple ..	3·00	3·50
46	**17**	5d. black and orange ..	2·75	3·50
47	**20**	6d. red	2·25	1·75
48	**17**	7½d. black and green ..	2·50	5·50
		a. Centre inverted	£1000	
49	,,	10d. black and lake ..	5·00	6·00
50	,,	1s. black and red-brown ..	3·50	4·50
		a. No hyphen before "TAHA"	65·00	
51	**21**	2s. black and ultramarine	7·00	9·00
52	**22**	2s. 6d. deep purple ..	10·00	11·00
53	**23**	5s. black and brown-red ..	9·00	10·00
38/53		.. .. *Set of* 14	42·00	50·00

The 1d., 3d. and 4d. are known bisected and used for half their value.

T - L

1 June, 1899.

(25)

26. Queen Salote.

1899 (1 June). *Royal Wedding. Optd. with T* **25** *at* "Star" *Office, Auckland, N.Z.*

54	**16**	1d. black and scarlet ..	12·00	17·00
		a. "1889" for "1899" ..	£150	£150

The Letters "T L" stand for Taufa'ahau, the King's family name, and Lavinia, the bride.

Die I.

Die II.

(Recess. D.L.R.)

1920–37. *W* **24.** *P* 14.

55	**15**	½d. yellow-green ('34) ..	10	3
56	**26**	1½d. grey-black ('35) ..	20	6
57	,,	2d. slate-purple and violet	1·25	1·7
57*a*	,,	2d. black and dull purple (Die I) ('24)	80	9
		b. Die II ('37)	1·00	1·5
58	,,	2½d. black and blue ..	1·40	3·0
59	,,	2½d. bright ultramarine ('34)	30	7
60	,,	5d. black & orange-verm.	2·00	2·7
61	,,	7½d. black & yellow-green	80	1·4
62	,,	10d. black and lake ..	2·00	2·7
63	,,	1s. black and red-brown ..	1·40	2·2
55/63		.. .. *Set of* 10	9·00	15·0
55/63		Optd./Perf. "Specimen" *Set of* 9	40·00	

In Die II the ball of the "2" is larger and th word "PENI-E-UA" is re-engraved and slightl shorter; the "U" has a spur on the left side.

TWO PENCE

TWO PENC

PENI-E-UA
(27)

PENI-E-UA
(28)

1923 (20 Oct.)–**24.** *Nos.* 46 *and* 48 *to* 53 *surc as T* **27** (*vert. stamps*) *or* **28** (*horiz. stamps*).

64	2d. on 5d. black & orange (B.)	80	1·0
65	2d. on 7½d. black & green (B.)	8·00	10·0
66	2d. on 10d. black & lake (B.)	7·00	8·5
67	2d. on 1s. blk. & red-brn. (B.)	10·00	12·0
	a. No hyphen before "TAHA" ..	£140	
68	2d. on 2s. blk. & ultram. (R.)	2·00	4·0
69	2d. on 2s. 6d. dp. purple (R.)	2·25	3·2
70	2d. on 5s. blk. & brn.-red (R.)	1·75	2·5
64/70	.. .. *Set of* 7	29·00	38·0

29. Queen Salote.

(Recess. De La Rue.)

1938 (12 Oct.). *20th Anniv. of Queen Salote' Accession. Tablet at foot dated* "1918–1938" *W* **24.** *P* 14.

71	**29**	1d. black and scarlet ..	30	7
72	,,	2d. black and purple ..	1·50	1·4
73	,,	2½d. black and ultramarine	1·50	2·2
71/3		Perf. "Specimen" *Set of* 3	30·00	

For Silver Jubilee issue in a similar desig see Nos. 83/87.

Die III.

(Recess. D.L.R.)

1942–49. *Wmk. Mult. Script CA (sideways on 5s.). P* 14.

74	**15**	½d. yellow-green ..	8	12
75	**16**	1d. black and scarlet ..	15	30
76	**26**	2d. black & purple (Die II)	10	20
		a. Die III (4.49)	2·00	2·25
77	,,	2½d. bright ultramarine ..	12	25
78	**18**	3d. black and yellow-green	15	20
79	**20**	6d. red	30	50
80	**26**	1s. black and red-brown	30	65
81	**22**	2s. 6d. deep purple ..	2·10	2·75
82	**23**	5s. black and brown-red..	1·60	2·25
74/82		.. .. *Set of* 9	4·25	6·50
74/82		Perf. "Specimen" *Set of* 9	38·00	

In Die III the foot of the "2" is longer than in Die II and extends towards the right beyond the curve of the loop; the letters of "PENI-E-UA" are taller and differently shaped.

HANIMA TA'U 'O E PULE 'A 'ENE 'AFIO 1918-1943

30

(Recess. De La Rue.)

1944 (25 Jan.). *Silver Jubilee of Queen Salote's Accession. As T* **29**, *but inscr.* "1918–1943" *at foot, as T* **30**. *Wmk. Mult. Script CA. P* 14.

83	1d. black and carmine ..	10	15
84	2d. black and purple	12	20
85	3d. black and green ..	15	25
86	6d. black and orange ..	25	35
87	1s. black and brown	30	45
83/87	.. .. *Set of* 5	80	1·10
83/7	Perf. "Specimen" *Set of* 5	30·00	

1949 (10 Oct.). *75th Anniv. of Universal Postal Union. As Nos.* 114/7 *of Antigua.*

88	2½d. ultramarine	12	10
89	3d. olive	20	25
90	6d. carmine-red	25	25
91	1s. red-brown	30	35

31. Queen Salote. **33.**

32. Queen Salote.

(Photo. Waterlow.)

1950 (1 Nov.). *Queen Salote's Fiftieth Birthday. Wmk. Mult. Script CA. P* 12½.

92	**31**	1d. carmine	15	25
93	**32**	5d. green	40	45
94	**33**	1s. violet	50	60

34. Map.

37. H.M.N.Z.S. *Bellona.*

35. Palace, Nuku'alofa.

36. Beach Scene.

38. Flag.

39. Arms of Tonga and G.B.

(Recess. Waterlow.)

1951 (2 July). *50th Anniv. of Treaty of Friendship between Great Britain and Tonga. Wmk. Mult. Script CA. P* 12½ (3*d.*), 13 × 13½ (½*d.*), 13½ × 13 (*others*).

95	**34**	½d. green	20	25
96	**35**	1d. black and carmine ..	30	30
97	**36**	2½d. green and brown ..	40	50
98	**37**	3d. yellow & bright blue	70	75
99	**38**	5d. carmine and green ..	70	90
100	**39**	1s. yellow-orge. & violet	1·10	1·40
95/100		.. .. *Set of* 6	3·00	3·75

40. Royal Palace, Nuku'alofa.

41. Shore Fishing with Throw-Net.

42. Ketches and Canoe.

43. Swallows' Cave, Vava'u.

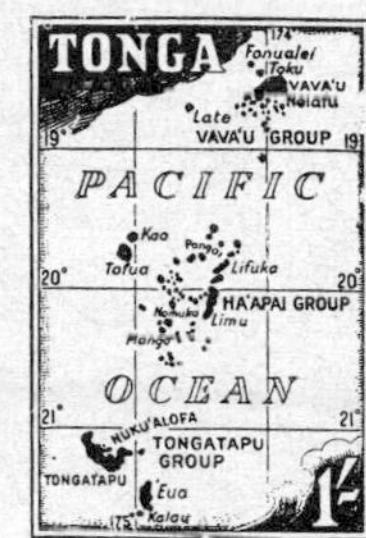

49. Map of Tonga Islands.

44. Map of Tongatapu.

45. Vava'u Harbour.

46. Post Office, Nuku'alofa.

47. Aerodrome, Fua'amotu.

48. Nuku'alofa Wharf.

50. Lifuka, Ha'apai.

51. Mutiny of the *Bounty*.

52. Queen Salote. **53.** Arms of Tonga.

(Des. J. Berry. Centre litho., frame recess (£1) recess (others). B.W.)

1953 (1 July). *W* **24**. *P* 11×11½ (*vert.*) *or* 11½×11 (*horiz.*).

101	**40**	1d. black and red-brown	5	5
102	**41**	1½d. blue and emerald ..	5	5
103	**42**	2d. dp. turq.-green & blk.	5	5
104	**43**	3d. blue & dp. bluish green	5	5
105	**44**	3½d. yellow & carmine-red	5	5
106	**45**	4d. yell. & dp. rose-carm.	8	8
107	**46**	5d. blue and red-brown ..	8	8
108	**47**	6d. black and deep blue ..	8	8
109	**48**	8d. emerald and deep reddish violet ..	10	10
110	**49**	1s. blue and black ..	12	12
111	**50**	2s. sage-green and brown	25	30
112	**51**	5s. orange-yellow and slate-lilac ..	70	1·25
113	**52**	10s. yellow and black ..	1·50	1·50
114	**53**	£1 yellow, scar., ultram. and deep bright blue	2·50	2·75
101/104		.. .. *Set of* 14	5·00	5·50

54. Stamp of 1886.

55. Whaler and Longboat.

56. Queen Salote and Post Office, Nuku'alofa.
57. Mail Steamer.
58. Mailplane over Tongatapu.

(Des. D. M. Bakeley. Photo. Harrison.)

1961 (1 Dec.). *75th Anniv. of Tongan Postal Service. W* **24**. *P* 14½×13½.

115	**54**	1d. carmine & brown-orange	10	10
116	**55**	2d. ultramarine	10	12
117	**56**	4d. blue-green	15	15
118	**57**	5d. violet	15	20
119	**58**	1s. red-brown	35	40
115/119		.. .. *Set of* 5	75	90

1862
TAU'ATAINA
EMANCIPATION
1962
(**59**)

1962 (7 Feb.). *Centenary of Emancipation. Various stamps optd. with T* **59** (*No.* 126 *surch. also*), *in red, by R. S. Wallbank, Govt. Printer.*

120	**40**	1d. black and red-brown	12	12
121	**56**	4d. blue-green	20	20
122	**46**	5d. blue and red-brown ..	20	20
123	**47**	6d. black and deep blue ..	25	25
124	**48**	8d. emer. & dp. redd. vio.	25	25
125	**49**	1s. blue and black ..	30	30
		a. Opt. inverted	£450	£275
126	**43**	2s. on 3d. blue and deep bluish green ..	50	75
		a. Missing fraction-bar in surch.	10·00	
127	**51**	5s. orge.-yell. & slate-lilac	1·25	1·50
		a. Opt. inverted	£200	
120/127		.. .. *Set of* 8	2·75	3·00

60. "Protein Foods".

(Des. M. Goaman. Photo. Harrison.)

1963 (4 June). *Freedom from Hunger. W* **24**. *P* 14×14½.

128	**60**	11d. ultramarine	25	30

61. Coat-of-Arms.

62. Queen Salote.

63. Queen Salote.

(Des. Ida West. Walsall Lithographic Co. Ltd.)

1963 (15 July). *First Polynesian Gold Coinage Commemoration. Circular designs. Embossed on gold foil, backed with paper, inscr. overall* "TONGA THE FRIENDLY ISLANDS". *Imperf.*

(*a*) *Postage.* ¼ *koula coin. Diameter* 1⅝ *in.*

129	**61**	1d. carmine	5	5
130	**62**	2d. deep blue	8	8
131	**61**	6d. blue-green	12	12
132	**62**	9d. bright purple ..	15	15
133	**61**	1s. 6d. violet	30	35
134	**62**	2s. light emerald ..	40	45

(*b*) *Air.* (*i*) ½ *koula coin. Diam.* 2⅛ *in.*

135	**63**	10d. carmine	20	20
136	**61**	11d. blue-green	25	25
137	**63**	1s. 1d. deep blue	25	30

(*ii*) 1 *koula coin. Diam.* 3⅛ *in.*

138	**63**	2s. 1d. bright purple ..	45	50
139	**61**	2s. 4d. light emerald ..	50	55
140	**63**	2s. 9d. violet	60	70
129/140 and O17		.. *Set of* 13	6·00	6·50

INTERNATIONAL RED CROSS CENTENARY 1863 1963 2d TONGA

64. Red Cross Emblem.

(Des. V. Whiteley. Litho. B.W.)

1963 (7 Oct.). *Red Cross Centenary.* *W* **24.** *P* 13½.

141	**64**	2d. red and black	8	8
142	,,	11d. red and blue	25	35

65. Queen Salote.

66. Map of Tongatapu.

(Illustrations reduced to approx. ¾ actual size.)

(Des. M. Meers. Walsall Lithographic Co. Ltd.)

1964 (19 Oct.). *Pan-Pacific South-East Asia Women's Association Meeting, Nuku'alofa. Embossed on gold foil, backed with paper inscr. overall* "TONGA THE FRIENDLY ISLANDS". *Imperf.* (a) *Postage.*

143	**65**	3d. pink	5	5
144	,,	9d. light blue	10	12
145	,,	2s. yellow-green	25	30
146	,,	5s. lilac	60	70
		(b) *Air.*		
147	**66**	10d. blue-green	12	12
148	,,	1s. 2d. black	15	20
149	,,	3s. 6d. cerise	40	50
150	,,	6s. 6d. violet	70	80
143/150		.. .. *Set of* 8	2·00	2·50

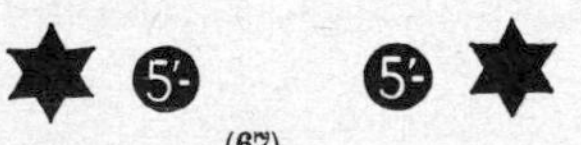

(67)

1965 (18 Mar.). *"Gold Coin" stamps of* 1963 *surch. as T* **67** *by Walsall Lithographic Co. New figures of value in gold; oblit. colours shown in brackets.* (a) *Postage.*

151	**61**	1s. 3d. on 1s. 6d. violet (R.)	15	15
152	**62**	1s. 9d. on 9d. brt. pur. (W.)	20	20
153	**61**	2s. 6d. on 6d. blue-grn. (R.)	30	35
154	,,	5s. on 1d. carmine ..	10·00	11·00
155	**62**	5s. on 2d. deep blue ..	2·50	2·75
156	,,	5s. on 2s. light emerald ..	1·00	1·25
		(b) *Air.*		
157	**63**	2s. 3d. on 10d. carmine ..	25	30
158	**61**	2s. 9d. on 11d. blue-grn. (W.)	30	35
159	**63**	4s. 6d. on 2s. 1d. brt. pur. (R.)	10·00	10·00
160	**61**	4s. 6d. on 2s. 4d. lt. emer. (R.)	10·00	10·00
161	**63**	4s. 6d. on 2s. 9d. violet (R.)	10·00	10·00
151/161 *and* O18		.. *Set of* 12	45·00	45·00

King Taufa'ahau IV, 16 December, 1965.

1866-1966
TUPOU COLLEGE
& SECONDARY
EDUCATION

(68)

AIRMAIL
1866 CENTENARY 1966
TUPOU COLLEGE
&
SECONDARY EDUCATION
10d XX

(69)

1966 (18 June). *Centenary of Tupou College and Secondary Education. Nos.* 115/6 *and* 118/9 *optd. or surch.*

		(a) *Postage. As T* **68.**		
162	**54**	1d. carmine and brown-orange (P.)	5	5
163	,,	3d. on 1d. carmine and brown-orange (P.) ..	8	8
164	**55**	6d. on 2d. ultram. (R.) ..	10	10
165	,,	1s. 2d. on 2d. ultram. (R.)	15	15
166	,,	2s. on 2d. ultram. (R.) ..	25	30
167	,,	3s. on 2d. ultram. (R.) ..	35	40
		(b) *Air. As T* **69.**		
168	**57**	5d. violet	5	5
169	**54**	10d. on 1d. carmine and brown-orange ..	12	12
170	**58**	1s. red brown	15	15
171	**55**	2s. 9d. on 2d. ultram. ..	35	40
		a. Sideways "X"	8·00	
172	**57**	3s. 6d. on 5d. violet ..	40	45
		a. Sideways "X"	8·00	
173	**58**	4s. 6d. on 1s. red-brown	50	60
		a. Sideways "X"	8·00	
162/173 *and* O19/20		.. *Set of* 14	5·00	5·50

(70)

(71)

1966 (16 Dec.). *Queen Salote Commemoration. "Women's Association" stamps of* 1964 *optd. as T* **70/1**, *or surch. also, by Walsall Lithographic Co. Inscriptions and new figures of value in first colour and obliterating shapes in second colour given.*

		(a) *Postage. Optd. as T* **70.**		
174	**65**	3d. (silver & ultramarine)	5	5
175	,,	5d. on 9d. (silver & black)	5	5
176	,,	9d. (silver and black) ..	10	10
177	,,	1s. 7d. on 3d. (silver and ultramarine) ..	20	20
178	,,	3s. 6d. on 9d. (silver and black)	40	45
179	,,	6s. 6d. on 3d. (silver and ultramarine) ..	70	80
		(b) *Air. Optd. as T* **71.**		
180	**66**	10d. (silver and black) ..	12	12
181	,,	1s. 2d. (black and gold) ..	15	15
182	,,	4s. on 10d. (silver & black)	45	50
183	,,	5s. 6d. on 1s. 2d. (black and gold) ..	60	70
184	,,	10s. 6d. on 1s. 2d. (gold and black)	1·25	1·40
174/184		.. .. *Set of* 11	3·50	4·00

(New currency. 100 seniti = 1 pa'anga.)

1 SENITI 1

(72)

10
Seniti
10

(73)

1967 (25 Mar.). *Decimal currency. Various stamps surch. as T* **72/3.**

185	1 s. on 1d. (No. 101) ..	5	5
186	2 s. on 4d. (No. 106) ..	5	5
187	3 s. on 5d. (No. 107) ..	5	5
188	4 s. on 5d. (No. 107) ..	5	5
189	5 s. on 3½d. (No. 105) ..	5	5
190	6 s. on 8d. (No. 109) ..	8	8
191	7 s. on 1½d. (No. 102) ..	10	10
192	8 s. on 6d. (No. 108) ..	10	10
193	9 s. on 3d. (No. 104) ..	12	12
194	10 s. on 1s. (No. 110) ..	12	12
195	11 s. on 3d. on 1d. (No. 163) ..	15	15
196	21 s. on 3s. on 2d. (No. 167) ..	25	30
197	23 s. on 1d. (No. 101) ..	30	30
198	30 s. on 2s. (No. 111) (R.) ..	50	55
199	30 s. on 2s. (No. 111) (R.) ..	50	55
200	50 s. on 6d. (No. 108) (R.) ..	65	70
201	60 s. on 2d. (No. 103) (R.) ..	80	90
185/201 *and* O21	.. *Set of* 18	4·75	5·00

The above surcharges come in a variety of types and sizes. No. 198 has the surcharged value expressed horizontally; No. 199 has the figures "30" above and below "SENITI".

74. Coat-of-Arms (reverse).

75. King Taufa'ahau IV (obverse).

(Die-cut. Walsall Security Printers Ltd.)

1967 (4 July). *Coronation of King Taufa'ahau IV. Circular designs. Embossed on palladium foil, backed with paper inscr. overall* "The Friendly Islands Tonga", *etc. Imperf.*

Sizes.

(*a*) *Diameter* $1\frac{3}{10}$ *in.* (*d*) *Diameter* $2\frac{3}{10}$ *in.*
(*b*) *Diameter* $1\frac{7}{10}$ *in.* (*e*) *Diameter* $2\frac{7}{10}$ *in.*
(*c*) *Diameter 2 in.* (*f*) *Diameter* $2\frac{9}{10}$ *in.*

(*a*) *Postage*

202 **74** 1 s. orange and greenish blue (*b*) 5 5
203 **75** 2 s. greenish blue and deep magenta (*c*) 5 5
204 **74** 4 s. emerald and bright purple (*d*) 8 8
205 **75** 15 s. turquoise & violet (*e*) 20 25
206 **74** 28 s. black and bright purple (*a*) 40 45
207 **75** 50 s. carmine-red and ultramarine (*c*) 65 75
208 **74** 1 p. blue and carmine (*f*) 1·25 1·50

(*b*) *Air.*

209 **75** 7 s. carm.-red & blk. (*b*) 10 10
210 **74** 9 s. brn.pur. & emer. (*c*) 12 12
211 **75** 11 s. greenish blue and orange (*d*) 15 15
212 **74** 21 s. black & emerald (*e*) 25 30
213 **75** 23 s. bright purple and lt. emerald (*a*) 35 35
214 **74** 29 s. ultram. & emerald (*c*) 40 45
215 **75** 2 p. brt. purple & orge. (*f*) 2·50 2·75
202/15 .. .. *Set of* 14 6·00 6·50

The commemorative coins depicted in reverse (Type **74**) are inscribed in various denominations as follows: 1 s.—"20 SENITI"; 4 s.—"PA'ANGA"; 9 s.—"50 SENITI"; 21 s.—"TWO PA'ANGA"; 28 s.—"QUARTER HAU"; 29 s.—"HALF HAU"; 1 p. "HAU".

The
Friendly Islands
welcome the
United States
Peace Corps

S

(**76**)

1967 (15 Dec.). *Arrival of U.S. Peace Corps in Tonga. As Nos.* 101/14, *but imperf., in different colours and surch. as T* **76**. (*a*) *Postage.*

216 **40** 1 s. on 1d. black and orange-yellow .. 5 5
217 **42** 2 s. on 2d. ultramarine and carmine-red .. 5 5
218 **43** 3 s. on 3d. chestnut and yellow 5 5
219 **45** 4 s. on 4d. reddish violet and yellow 8 8
220 **46** 5 s. on 5d. grn. & yellow 10 10
221 **49** 10 s. on 1s. carmine-red and yellow 15 15
222 **50** 20 s. on 2s. claret & new bl. 25 30
223 **51** 50 s. on 5s. sepia and orange-yellow .. 65 75
224 **52** 1 p. on 10s. orange-yellow 1·25 1·50

(*b*) *Air.*

225 **44** 11 s. on $3\frac{1}{2}$d. ultram. (R.) 15 15
226 **41** 21 s. on $1\frac{1}{2}$d. emerald .. 25 30
227 **44** 23 s. on $3\frac{1}{2}$d. ultramarine 30 30
216/27 *and* O26/8 .. *Set of* 15 5·75 6·50

On Nos. 219 and 224 the opt. is smaller, and in four lines instead of five. On Nos. 216/20 the surcharge takes the form of an alteration to the currency name as in T **76**.

2 SENITI 2

(**77**)

10
SENITI
10

(**78**)

1968 (6 Apr.). *Various stamps surch. as T* **77/8**.

(*a*) *Postage.*

228 **40** 1 s. on 1d. (No. 101) (R.) 5 5
229 **45** 2 s. on 4d. (No. 106) .. 5 5
230 **43** 3 s. on 3d. (No. 104) (B.) 5 5
231 **46** 4 s. on 5d. (No. 107) (R.) 5 5
232 **42** 5 s. on 2d. (No. 103) (R.) 5 5
233 **47** 6 s. on 6d. (No. 108) (R.) 8 8
234 **41** 7 s. on $1\frac{1}{2}$d. (No. 102) (R.) 10 10
235 **48** 8 s. on 8d. (No. 109) (R.) 10 12
236 **44** 9 s. on $3\frac{1}{2}$d. (No. 105) .. 12 12
237 **49** 10 s. on 1s. (No. 110) (R.) 15 15
238 **51** 20 s. on 5s. (No. 112) (R.) 25 30
239 **50** 2 p. on 2s. (No. 111) (R.) 2·50 2·75

(*b*) *Air. Surch. as T* **78** *with* "AIRMAIL" *added.*

240 **52** 11 s. on 10s. (No. 113) (R.) 15 15
241 „ 21 s. on 10s. (No. 113) (R.) 30 30
242 „ 23 s. on 10s. (No. 113) (R.) 35 35
228/42 *and* O22/5 .. *Set of* 19 8·50 9·50

(**79**)

1968 (4 July). *50th Birthday of King Taufa'ahua IV. Nos.* 202/15 *optd. as T* **79**.

(*a*) *Postage.*

243 **74** 1 s. orange and greenish blue (*b*) (R.) 5 5
244 **75** 2 s. greenish blue and deep magenta (*b*) (B.) .. 5 5
245 **74** 4 s. emerald and bright purple (*d*) (R.) .. 8 8
246 **75** 15 s. turquoise and violet (*e*) (B.) .. 20 25
247 **74** 28 s. black and bright purple (*a*) (R.) 35 40
248 **75** 50 s. carmine-red and ultramarine (*c*) (B.) .. 65 75
249 **74** 1 p. blue & carmine (*f*) (R.) 1·25 1·40

(*b*) *Air.*

250 **75** 7 s. carmine-red and black (*b*) (B.) 10 10
251 **74** 9 s. brown - purple and emerald (*c*) (R.) .. 12 12
252 **75** 11 s. greenish blue and orange (*d*) (B.) .. 15 15
253 **74** 21 s. black & emer. (*e*) (R.) 25 30
254 **75** 23 s. bright purple and light emerald (*a*) (B.) .. 30 30
255 **74** 29 s. ultramarine and emerald (*c*) (R.) 40 45
256 **75** 2 p. bright purple and orange (*f*) (B.) .. 2·50 2·75
243/56 *and* O29/32 .. *Set of* 18 10·00 11·00

The overprints vary in size, but are all crescent-shaped as Type **79** and inscribed "H.M's BIRTHDAY 4 JULY 1968" (Type **79**) or "HIS MAJESTY'S 50th BIRTHDAY" (others).

Friendly Islands
Field & Track Trials
South Pacific Games
Port Moresby
1969

S

(**80**)

1968 (19 Dec.). *South Pacific Games Field and Track Trials, Port Moresby, New Guinea. Nos.* 101/14, *but imperf., in different colours and surch. as T* **80**. (*a*) *Postage.*

257 **46** 5 s. on 5d. grn. & yell. (R.) 8 8
258 **49** 10 s. on 1s. carmine-red & yellow 12 15
259 **50** 15 s. on 2s. claret & new bl. 20 25
260 **42** 25 s. on 2d. ultramarine & carmine-red 30 35
261 **40** 50 s. on 1d. black & orange-yellow 65 75
262 **52** 75 s. on 10s. orge.-yell. (G.) 95 1·10

(*b*) *Air.*

263 **47** 6 s. on 6d. blk. & yellow* 8 8
264 **45** 7 s. on 4d. reddish violet and yellow 8 10
265 **48** 8 s. on 8d. blk. & greenish yellow 10 12
a. Surch. $11\frac{1}{2}$ mm. as on 6d † 65·00
266 **41** 9 s. on $1\frac{1}{2}$d. emerald .. 12 12
267 **43** 11 s. on 3d. chestnut & yell. 12 15
268 **44** 21 s. on $3\frac{1}{2}$d. ultramarine .. 25 30
269 **51** 38 s. on 5s. sepia & orange yellow 50 60
270 **52** 1 p. on 10s. orange-yellow 1·25 1·40
257/70 *and* O33/4 .. *Set of* 16 6·00 6·50

* On No. 263 the surcharge is smaller ($11\frac{1}{2}$ mm. wide).

1s

(**81**)

1s

(**82**)

1969. *Emergency Provisionals. Various stamps (Nos. 273/6 are imperf. and in different colours) surch. as T* **81** *or* **82**. (*a*) *Postage.*

271 **55** 1 s. on 1s. 2d. on 2d. ultramarine (No. 165) 10 12
272 „ 1 s. on 2s. on 2d. ultramarine (No. 166) .. 10 12
273 **47** 1 s. on 6d. black & yellow 5 5
274 **44** 2 s. on $3\frac{1}{2}$d. ultramarine .. 5 5
275 **41** 3 s. on $1\frac{1}{2}$d. emerald .. 5 5
276 **48** 4 s. on 8d. black and greenish yellow 8 8

(*b*) *Air. Nos.* 171/3 *surch. with T* **82**.

277 **55** 1 s. on 2s. 9d. on 2d. ultramarine .. .. .. 10 1[illegible]
a. Sideways "X" .. 5·00
278 **57** 1 s. on 3s. 6d. on 5d. violet 10 1[illegible]
a. Sideways "X" .. 5·00
279 **58** 1 s. on 4s. 6d. on 1s. red-brown .. .. .. 10 1[illegible]
a. Sideways 'X' .. 5·00
271/9 .. .. *Set of* 9 60 7[illegible]

83. Banana.

(Manufactured by Walsall Security Printers Ltd.)

1969 (21 Apr.). *Imperf.* (*backing paper roul.* 1[illegible] *horiz.*). *Self-adhesive.*

280 **83** 1 s. scarlet, black and greenish yellow .. 5
281 „ 2 s. bright green, black and greenish yellow .. 5
282 „ 3 s. violet, black and greenish yellow 8
283 „ 4 s. ultramarine, black and greenish yellow .. 10 1[illegible]
284 „ 5 s. bronze-green, black and greenish yellow .. 12 1[illegible]
280/4 .. .. *Set of* 5 30 3[illegible]

Nos. 280/4 were printed in rolls of 200, havin[g] alternate even numbers applied on the fron[t] of the backing paper, and the reverse is contin[u]ously printed with the words "*TONGA wher[e] time begins*" in blue.

See also Nos. 325/9 and 413/17.

84. Putting the Shot.

85. Boxing.

1969 (13 Aug.). *Third South Pacific Games, Port Moresby. Imperf. (backing paper roul. 10). Self-adhesive. (a) Postage.*

285	**84**	1 s. black, red and buff ..	5	5
286	,,	3 s. bright green, red and buff	8	8
287	,,	6 s. green, red and buff ..	10	10
288	,,	10s. bluish vio., red & buff	15	15
289	,,	30 s. blue, red and buff ..	45	45
		(b) Air.		
290	**85**	9 s. black, violet & orge.	15	15
291	,,	11 s. black, ultramarine and orange	15	15
292	,,	20 s. black, bright green and orange	30	30
293	,,	60 s. black, cerise & orge.	1·00	1·00
294	,,	1 p. blk., bl.-grn. & orge.	1·60	1·60
285/94 *and* O35/6 ..		*Set of* 12	5·50	5·50

SELF-ADHESIVE ISSUES. The above stamps and all subsequent self-adhesive issues are manufactured by Walsall Security Printers Ltd. and have the words "*TONGA where time begins*" printed continuously on the reverse of the backing paper, in various colours, the backing paper being separated by roulette. This also applies to the relative Official stamps.

86. Oil Derrick and Map.

1969 (23 Dec.). *First Oil Search in Tonga.* T **86** *and similar vert. design.* (a) *Postage.*

295	**86**	3 s. multicoloured ..	5	5
296	,,	7 s. multicoloured ..	12	12
297	,,	20 s. multicoloured ..	40	40
298	,,	25 s. multicoloured ..	50	50
299	,,	35 s. multicoloured ..	65	65
		(b) Air.		
300	–	9 s. multicoloured ..	20	20
301	–	10 s. multicoloured ..	20	20
302	–	24 s. multicoloured ..	45	45
303	–	29 s. multicoloured ..	60	60
304	–	38 s. multicoloured ..	80	80
295/304 *and* O37/8 ..		*Set of* 12	7·50	7·50

Design:—Nos. 300/4, Oil Derrick and Island of Tongatapu.

87. Members of the British and Tongan Royal Families.

88. Queen Elizabeth II and King Taufu'ahau Tupou IV.

1970 (7 Mar.). *Royal Visit. (a) Postage.*

305	**87**	3 s. bright bl., gold & blk.	5	5
306	,,	5 s. brt. emer., gold & blk.	10	10
307	,,	10 s. orange, gold & black	20	20
308	,,	25 s. brt. purple, gold & blk.	50	50
309	,,	50 s. rosine, gold & black	1·00	1·00
		(b) Air.		
310	**88**	7 s. multicoloured ..	15	15
311	,,	9 s. multicoloured ..	20	20
312	,,	24 s. multicoloured ..	50	50
313	,,	29 s. multicoloured ..	60	60
314	,,	38 s. multicoloured ..	80	80
305/14 *and* O39/41 ..		*Set of* 13	9·00	9·00

89. Book, Tongan Rulers and Flag.

(Illustration reduced. Actual size 69×38 *mm.)*

1970 (4 June). *Entry into British Commonwealth.* T **89** *and similar design.*

		(a) Postage.		
315	**89**	3 s. multicoloured ..	5	5
316	,,	7 s. multicoloured ..	15	15
317	,,	15 s. multicoloured ..	30	30
318	,,	25 s. multicoloured ..	50	50
319	,,	50 s. multicoloured ..	1·00	1·00
		(b) Air.		
320	–	9 s. turquoise-blue, gold and scarlet ..	15	15
321	–	10 s. bright purple, gold and greenish blue ..	20	20
322	–	24 s. olive-yellow, gold and green	50	50
323	–	29 s. new blue, gold and orange-red	60	60
324	–	38 s. dark orange-yellow, gold and brt. emerald	80	80
315/24 *and* O42/4 ..		*Set of* 13	9·00	9·00

Design: "*Star*" *shaped* (44×51 *mm.*)—Nos. 320/4, King Taufa'ahua Tupou IV.

90. Coconut.

1970 (9 June). (a) *As* T **83** *but colours changed.*

325	**83**	1 s. greenish yellow, bright purple and black ..	5	5
326	,,	2 s. greenish yellow, ultramarine and black ..	5	5
327	,,	3 s. greenish yellow, chocolate and black ..	5	5
328	,,	4 s. greenish yellow, emerald and black ..	5	5
329	,,	5 s. greenish yellow, orange-red and black ..	8	8
		(b) *Type* **90.** *Multicoloured; colour of face value given.*		
330	**90**	6 s. rose-carmine	10	10
331	,,	7 s. bright purple ..	12	12
332	,,	8 s. bluish violet ..	12	12
333	,,	9 s. turquoise	15	15
334	,,	10 s. pale orange	15	15
325/34		*Set of* 10	80	80

Nos. 325/34 were produced in rolls of 200, each even stamp having a number applied to the front of the backing paper, with the usual inscription on the reverse.

See also Nos. 413/22.

91. "Red Cross".

(Litho. (postage) or litho. & die-stamped (air).)

1970 (17 Oct.). *Centenary of British Red Cross.* T **91** *and similar "cross" shaped design.*

		(a) Postage.		
335	**91**	3 s. verm., blk. & lt. grn.	5	5
336	,,	7 s. verm., blk. & ultram.	15	15
337	,,	15 s. verm., blk. & brt. pur.	30	30
338	,,	25 s. verm., blk. & turq.-bl.	50	50
339	,,	75 s. vermilion, black and deep red-brown ..	1·50	1·50
		(b) Air.		
340	–	9 s. vermilion and silver	20	20
341	–	10 s. vermilion & brt. pur.	20	20
342	–	18 s. vermilion and green	35	35
343	–	38 s. vermilion and ultram.	80	80
344	–	1 p. vermilion and silver	2·00	2·00
335/44 *and* O55/57		*Set of* 13	9·00	9·00

Design: *As Type* **91**—Nos. 340/4 as Nos. 335/9 but with inscription rearranged and coat-of-arms omitted.

(92)

(93)

1971 (30 JAN.). *Fifth Death Anniv. of Queen Salote. Nos.* 174/84 *surch. as T* **92/3**. *Obliterating shapes in black; inscriptions and figures of value in colour given.*

(*a*) *Postage. Surch. as T* **92**.

No.	Type	Description	Unused	Used
345	**65**	2 s. on 5d. on 9d. (silver)	5	5
346	,,	3 s. on 9d. (orange-red) ..	8	8
347	,,	5 s. on 3d. (bright green)	10	10
348	,,	15 s. on 3s. 6d. on 9d. (orange-brown) ..	30	30
		a. Surch. double		
349	,,	25 s. on 6s. 6d. on 3d. (pur.)	50	50
350	,,	50 s. on 1s 7d. on 3d. (gold)	1·00	1·00

(*b*) *Air. Surch. as T* **93**.

No.	Type	Description	Unused	Used
351	**66**	9 s. on 10d. (silver) ..	20	20
352	,,	24 s. on 4s. on 10d. (orange-brown)	50	50
353	,,	29 s. on 5s. 6d. on 1s. 2d. (orange-red)	60	60
354	,,	38 s. on 10s. 6d. on 1s. 2d. (bright green) ..	80	80
345/54 *and* O58/61		*Set of* 14	8·00	8·00

3s

PHILATOKYO '71

(94)

HONOURING JAPANESE POSTAL CENTENARY 1871-1971

15s

(95)

1971 (17 APR.). *"Philatokyo '71" Stamp Exhibition. As Nos.* 101 *etc., but imperf., colours changed and surch. as T* **94** (*Nos.* 355/6, 358/61 *and* 363), *as T* **95** (*Nos.* 357, 362) *or with similar surcharge to T* **95** *in four lines* (*No.* 364).

(*a*) *Postage.*

No.	Type	Description	Unused	Used
355	**48**	3 s. on 8d. blk.& greenish yellow (Blk. and R.)	5	5
356	**45**	7 s. on 4d. reddish vio. & yellow (Blk. and R.)	15	15
357	**49**	15 s. on 1s. carm, red & yell.	30	30
358	**40**	25 s. on 1d. black and orge.-yellow (Blk. and R.)	50	50
359	**50**	75 s. on 2s. claret and new blue (Blk. and R.) ..	1·50	1·50

(*b*) *Air. Additionally surch.* "AIRMAIL".

No.	Type	Description	Unused	Used
360	**41**	9 s. on $1\frac{1}{2}$d. emerald (Blk. & R.)	20	20
361	**45**	10 s. on 4d. reddish vio. & yellow (Blk. and R.)	20	20
362	**49**	18 s. on 1s. carmine-red and yellow (V.)	35	35
363	**40**	38 s. on 1d. black & orge.-yellow (Blk. & R.) ..	80	80
364	**50**	1 p. on 2s. claret & new bl.	2·00	2·00
355/64 *and* O62/4 ..		*Set of* 13	9·00	9·00

96. Wristwatch.

1971 (20 JULY)–**72**. *Air. Backed with paper bearing advertisements.*

No.	Type	Description	Unused	Used
365	**96**	14 s. multicoloured ..	20	25
365*a*	,,	17 s. multicoloured (20.7.72)	30	30
366	,,	21 s. multicoloured ..	35	35
366*a*	,,	38 s. multicoloured (20.7.72)	55	55
365/6*a and* O65/6*a*		*Set of* 8	2·50	2·50

See also Nos. O65/6*a*.

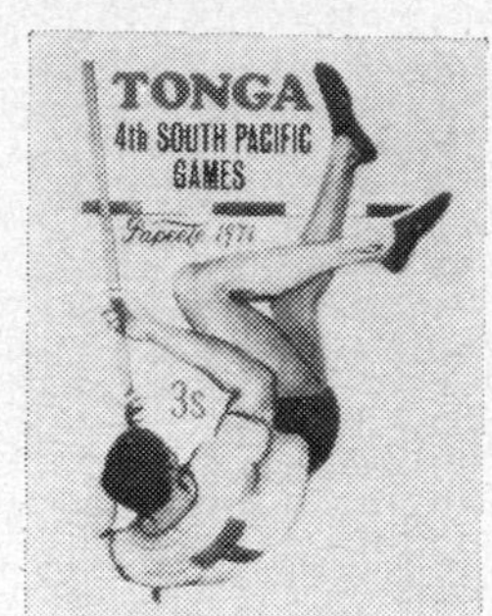

97. Pole-vaulter.

1971 (20 JULY). *Fourth South Pacific Games, Tahiti. T* **97** *and similar design.*

(*a*) *Postage.*

No.	Type	Description	Unused	Used
367	**97**	3 s. multicoloured ..	5	5
368	,,	7 s. multicoloured ..	10	10
369	,,	15 s. multicoloured ..	20	25
370	,,	25 s. multicoloured ..	30	35
371	,,	50 s. multicoloured ..	65	75

(*b*) *Air.*

No.	Type	Description	Unused	Used
372	–	9 s. multicoloured ..	12	12
373	–	10 s. multicoloured ..	12	15
374	–	24 s. multicoloured ..	30	35
375	–	29 s. multicoloured ..	40	45
376	–	38 s. multicoloured ..	50	60
367/76 *and* O67/9 ..		*Set of* 13	5·50	6·50

Design: *Horiz.*—Nos. 372/6, High-jumper.

98. Medal of Merit (reverse).

1971 (30 OCT.). *Investiture of Royal Tongan Medal of Merit. T* **98** *and similar "medal" shaped design. Multicoloured; colour of medal given.*

(*a*) *Postage.*

No.	Type	Description	Unused	Used
377	**98**	3 s. gold	5	5
378	,,	24 s. silver	30	35
379	–	38 s. brown	50	55

(*b*) *Air.*

No.	Type	Description	Unused	Used
380	–	10 s. gold	12	15
381	–	75 s. silver	95	1·10
382	**98**	1 p. brown	1·25	1·50
377/82 *and* O70/2 ..		*Set of* 9	5·50	6·50

Design: *As T* **98**—Nos. 379/81, Obverse of the Medal of Merit.

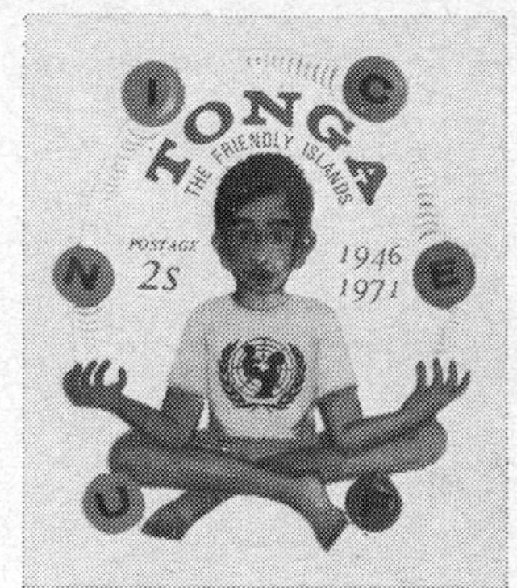

99. Child.

1971 (31 DEC.). *25th Anniv. of UNICEF. T* **99** *and similar design.*

(*a*) *Postage.*

No.	Type	Description	Unused	Used
383	**99**	2 s. multicoloured ..	5	5
384	,,	4 s. multicoloured ..	5	5
385	,,	8 s. multicoloured ..	10	12
386	,,	16 s. multicoloured ..	20	25
387	,,	30 s. multicoloured ..	40	45

(*b*) *Air.*

No.	Type	Description	Unused	Used
388	–	10 s. multicoloured ..	12	15
389	–	15 s. multicoloured ..	20	25
390	–	25 s. multicoloured ..	30	37
391	–	50 s. multicoloured ..	65	55
392	–	1 p. multicoloured ..	1·25	1·50
383/92 *and* O73/5 ..		*Set of* 13	5·50	6·50

Design: *Vert.* (21×42 *mm.*)—Nos. 388/92, Woman.

100. Map of South Pacific, and *Olovaha.*

(Illustration reduced. Actual size 53×47 *mm.)*

1972 (14 Apr.). *Merchant Marine Routes. T* **100** *and similar design. (a) Postage.*

No.	Type	Description	Unused	Used
393	**100**	2 s. multicoloured	5	5
394	,,	10 s. multicoloured	12	15
395	,,	17 s. multicoloured	20	25
396	,,	21 s. multicoloured	25	30
397	,,	60 s. multicoloured	65	70

(b) Air.

No.	Type	Description	Unused	Used
398	–	9 s. multicoloured	12	12
399	–	12 s. multicoloured	15	15
400	–	14 s. multicoloured	20	20
401	–	75 s. multicoloured	80	90
402	–	90 s. multicoloured	1·00	1·10
393/402 *and* O76/8		*Set of* 13	5·50	6·00

Design:—Nos. 398/402, Map of South Pacific, and *Niuvakai.*

101. ¼ Hau Coronation Coin.

(Illustration reduced. Actual size 60×40 *mm.)*

1972 (15 July). *Fifth Anniv. of Coronation. T* **101** *and similar design. (a) Postage.*

No.	Type	Description	Unused	Used
403	**101**	5 s. multicoloured	5	5
404	,,	7 s. multicoloured	8	8
405	,,	10 s. multicoloured	10	12
406	,,	17 s. multicoloured	15	20
407	,,	60 s. multicoloured	60	70

(b) Air.

No.	Type	Description	Unused	Used
408	–	9 s. multicoloured	10	10
409	–	12 s. multicoloured	12	12
410	–	14 s. multicoloured	15	20
411	–	21 s. multicoloured	20	25
412	–	75 s. multicoloured	75	85
403/12 *and* O79/81		*Set of* 13	4·50	4·75

Design (47×41 mm.):—Nos. 408/12, As *T* **101**, but with coins above inscription instead of beneath it.

102. Water Melon.

1972 (30 Sept.). *(a) As T* **83**, *but inscription altered, omitting "Best in the Pacific", and colours changed.*

No.	Type	Description	Unused	Used
413	**83**	1 s. light yellow, scarlet and black	5	5
414	,,	2 s. light yellow, ultram. and black	5	5
415	,,	3 s. light yellow, yellow-green and black	5	5
416	,,	4 s. light yellow, Royal blue and black	5	5
417	,,	5 s. light yellow, reddish brown and black	5	5

(b) As T **90** *but colours changed. Colour of face-value given.*

No.	Type	Description	Unused	Used
418	**90**	6 s. dull orange	8	8
419	,,	7 s. ultramarine	8	8
420	,,	8 s. bright magenta	10	10
421	,,	9 s. brown-orange	12	12
422	,,	10 s. light new blue	12	12

(c) Type **102.** *Colour of face-value given.*

No.	Type	Description	Unused	Used
423	**102**	15 s. new blue	20	20
424	,,	20 s. reddish orange	25	25
425	,,	25 s. chocolate	30	30
426	,,	40 s. yellow-orange	50	50
427	,,	50 s. lemon	65	65
413/27		*Set of* 15	2·25	2·25

Nos. 413/27 were produced in rolls, each even stamp having a number applied to the front of the backing paper, with the usual inscription on the reverse.

NOVEMBER 1972
INAUGURAL
Internal Airmail
Nuku'alofa — Vava'u

(**103**)

1972 (2 Nov.). *Inaugural Internal Airmail. No.* 398 *surch. with T* **103.**

No.	Type	Description	Unused	Used
428	–	7 s. on 9 s. multicoloured	35	35

104. Hoisting Tongan Flag.

(Illustration reduced. Actual size 60×41 *mm.)*

1972 (9 Dec.). *Proclamation of Sovereignty over Minerva Reefs. T* **104** *and similar design. (a) Postage.*

No.	Type	Description	Unused	Used
429	**104**	5 s. multicoloured	8	8
430	,,	7 s. multicoloured	8	10
431	,,	10 s. multicoloured	12	15
432	,,	15 s. multicoloured	20	25
433	,,	40 s. multicoloured	50	65

(b) Air.

No.	Type	Description	Unused	Used
434	–	9 s. multicoloured	12	12
435	–	12 s. multicoloured	15	20
436	–	14 s. multicoloured	20	25
437	–	38 s. multicoloured	50	55
438	–	1 p. multicoloured	1·25	1·50
429/38 *and* O97/9		*Set of* 13	5·50	6·00

Design: *Spherical* (52 *mm. diameter*)—Nos. 434/8, Proclamation in Govt. Gazette.

105. Coins around Bank.

(Illustration reduced. Actual size 53×48 *mm.)*

1973 (30 Mar.). *Foundation of Bank of Tonga. T* **105** *and similar design. (a) Postage.*

No.	Type	Description	Unused	Used
439	**105**	5 s. multicoloured	8	8
440	,,	7 s. multicoloured	10	10
441	,,	10 s. multicoloured	12	12
442	,,	20 s. multicoloured	25	25
443	,,	30 s. multicoloured	35	35

(b) Air.

No.	Type	Description	Unused	Used
444	–	9 s. multicoloured	12	12
445	–	12 s. multicoloured	15	15
446	–	17 s. multicoloured	25	25
447	–	50 s. multicoloured	55	60
448	–	90 s. multicoloured	1·00	1·10
439/48 *and* O100/2		*Set of* 13	5·00	5·50

Design: *Horiz.* (64×52 *mm.*)—Nos. 444/8, Bank and banknotes.

106. Handshake and Scout in Canoe.

(Illustration reduced. Actual size 61×43 *mm.)*

1973 (29 June). *Silver Jubilee of Scouting in Tonga. T* **106** *and similar design.*

(a) Postage.

No.	Type	Description	Unused	Used
449	**106**	5 s. multicoloured	8	8
450	,,	7 s. multicoloured	12	12
451	,,	15 s. multicoloured	25	25
452	,,	21 s. multicoloured	35	35
453	,,	50 s. multicoloured	80	80

(*b*) *Airmail.*

No.	Type	Description		Unused	Used
454	–	9 s. multicoloured	..	15	15
455	–	12 s. multicoloured	..	20	20
456	–	14 s. multicoloured	..	25	25
457	–	17 s. multicoloured	..	30	30
458	–	1 p. multicoloured	..	2·25	2·25
449/58 *and* O103/5 ..			*Set of* 13	14·00	14·00

Design: *Square* (53 × 53 *mm.*)—Nos. 454/8, Scout badge.

107. Excerpt from Cook's Log-book.

(*Illustration reduced. Actual size* 69 × 38 *mm.*)

1973 (2 Oct.). *Bicentenary of Capt. Cook's Visit to Tonga.* *T* **107** *and similar design.*

(*a*) *Postage.*

No.	Type	Description		Unused	Used
459	**107**	6 s. multicoloured	..	8	8
460	,,	8 s. multicoloured	..	10	10
461	,,	11 s. multicoloured	..	15	15
462	,,	35 s. multicoloured	..	40	45
463	,,	40 s. multicoloured	..	50	55

(*b*) *Air.*

No.	Type	Description		Unused	Used
464	–	9 s. multicoloured	..	12	12
465	–	14 s. multicoloured	..	20	20
466	–	29 s. multicoloured	..	35	40
467	–	38 s. multicoloured	..	50	55
468	–	75 s. multicoloured	..	90	1·00
459/68 *and* O106/8 ..			*Set of* 13	5·50	6·00

Design: *Vert.*—Nos. 464/8, The *Resolution.*

(108)

1973 (19 Dec.). *Commonwealth Games, Christchurch, New Zealand. Various stamps optd. as T* **108** (*No.* 474 *optd.* "AIRMAIL" *in addition*). (*a*) *Postage.*

No.	Description	Unused	Used
469	5 s. on 50 s. (No. 371) (Blk. and Gold)	8	8
470	12 s. on 38 s. (No. 379) (Red and Silver)	15	20
471	14 s. on 75 s. (No. 381) (Red and Gold)	20	20
472	20 s. on 1 p. (No. 382) (Black and Gold)	25	30
473	50 s. on 24 s. (No. 378) (Black and Silver)	60	65

(*b*) *Air.*

No.	Description	Unused	Used
474	7 s. on 25 s. (No. 370) (Black and Silver)	10	10
475	9 s. on 38 s. (No. 376) (V.)	12	12
476	24 s. (No. 374)	30	30
477	29 s. on 9 s. (No. 454) (B.) ..	35	40
478	40 s. on 14 s. (No. 456) ..	50	55
469/78 *and* O109/11 *Set of* 13		5·50	6·00

109. Parrot.

1974 (20 Mar.). *Air.*

No.	Type	Description		Unused	Used
479	**109**	7 s. multicoloured	..	8	8
480	,,	9 s. multicoloured	..	12	12
481	,,	12 s. multicoloured	..	15	15
482	,,	14 s. multicoloured	..	15	15
483	,,	17 s. multicoloured	..	20	20
484	,,	29 s. multicoloured	..	35	35
485	,,	38 s. multicoloured	..	45	45
486	,,	50 s. multicoloured	..	60	60
487	,,	75 s. multicoloured	..	90	90
479/87		.. ..	*Set of* 9	2·75	2·75

Nos. 479/87 were produced in rolls, each stamp having a number applied to the front of the backing paper, with the usual inscription on the reverse.

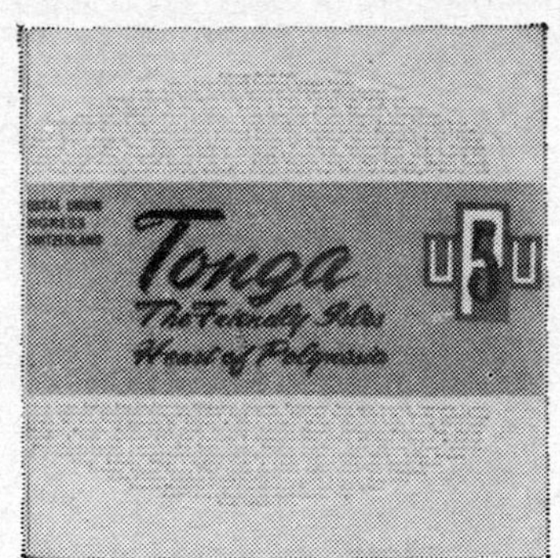

110. "Stamped Letter".

1974 (20 June). *Centenary of Universal Postal Union.* *T* **110** *and similar design.*

(*a*) *Postage.*

No.	Type	Description		Unused	Used
488	**110**	5 s. multicoloured	..	8	8
489	,,	10 s. multicoloured	..	15	15
490	,,	15 s. multicoloured	..	20	20
491	,,	20 s. multicoloured	..	30	30
492	,,	50 s. multicoloured	..	1·00	1·00

(*b*) *Air.*

No.	Type	Description		Unused	Used
493	–	14 s. multicoloured	..	20	20
494	–	21 s. multicoloured	..	35	35
495	–	60 s. multicoloured	..	1·10	1·10
496	–	75 s. multicoloured	..	1·40	1·40
497	–	1 p. multicoloured	..	2·00	2·00
488/97 *and* O121/3			*Set of* 13	8·00	8·00

Design: *Horiz.*—Nos. 493/7, Carrier pigeon scattering letters over Tonga.

111. Girl Guide Badges.

1974 (11 Sept.). *Tongan Girl Guides.* *T* **111** *and similar design.* (*a*) *Postage.*

No.	Type	Description		Unused	Used
498	**111**	5 s. multicoloured	..	8	8
499	,,	10 s. multicoloured	..	12	12
500	,,	20 s. multicoloured	..	25	25
501	,,	40 s. multicoloured	..	45	50
502	,,	60 s. multicoloured	..	70	75

(*b*) *Air.*

No.	Type	Description		Unused	Used
503	–	14 s. multicoloured	..	20	20
504	–	16 s. multicoloured	..	20	20
505	–	29 s. multicoloured	..	35	40
506	–	31 s. multicoloured	..	40	40
507	–	75 s. multicoloured	..	85	95
498/507 *and* O124/6			*Set of* 13	5·00	5·50

Design: *Vert.*—Nos. 503/7, Girl Guide leaders.

112. Sailing Ship.

1974 (11 Dec.). *Establishment of Royal Marine Institute.* *T* **112** *and similar design.*

(*a*) *Postage.*

No.	Type	Description		Unused	Used
508	**112**	5 s. multicoloured	..	8	8
509	,,	10 s. multicoloured	..	12	12
510	,,	25 s. multicoloured	..	30	35
511	,,	50 s. multicoloured	..	55	65
512	,,	75 s. multicoloured	..	85	90

(*b*) *Air.*

No.	Type	Description		Unused	Used
513	–	9 s. multicoloured	..	12	12
514	–	14 s. multicoloured	..	20	20
515	–	17 s. multicoloured	..	20	20
516	–	60 s. multicoloured	..	70	75
517	–	90 s. multicoloured	..	1·00	1·10
508/17 *and* O127/9 ..			*Set of* 13	5·00	5·50

Design: *Horiz.* (51 × 46 *mm.*)—Nos. 513/17, Tongan Freighter, *James Cook.*

113. Dateline Hotel, Nuku'alofa.

(Illustration reduced. Actual size 60 × 38 mm.)

1975 (11 Mar.). *South Pacific Forum and Tourism. T* **113** *and similar vert. designs.*

(a) Postage.

518 **113** 5 s. multicoloured .. 8 8
519 ,, 10 s. multicoloured .. 12 12
520 ,, 15 s. multicoloured .. 20 20
521 ,, 30 s. multicoloured .. 35 45
522 ,, 1 p. multicoloured .. 1·10 1·25

(b) Air.

523 – 9 s. multicoloured .. 12 12
524 – 12 s. multicoloured .. 15 15
525 – 14 s. multicoloured .. 20 20
526 – 17 s. multicoloured .. 20 20
527 – 38 s. multicoloured .. 45 50
518/27 *and* O130/2 *Set of* 13 5·00 5·50

Designs (46 × 60 *mm.*):—9, 12, 14 s. Beach; 17, 38 s. Surf and sea.

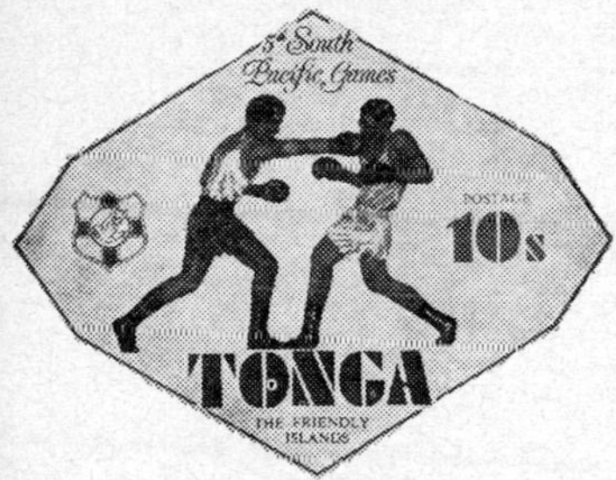

114. Boxing.

(Illustration reduced. Actual size 60 × 47 mm.)

1975 (11 June). *Fifth South Pacific Games, Guam. T* **114** *and similar " star "-shaped design. (a) Postage.*

528 **114** 5 s. multicoloured .. 8 8
529 ,, 10 s. multicoloured .. 12 12
530 ,, 20 s. multicoloured .. 25 25
531 ,, 25 s. multicoloured .. 30 30
532 ,, 65 s. multicoloured .. 75 75

(b) Air.

533 – 9 s. multicoloured .. 12 12
534 – 12 s. multicoloured .. 15 15
535 – 14 s. multicoloured .. 20 20
536 – 17 s. multicoloured .. 20 25
537 – 90 s. multicoloured .. 1·00 1·00
528/37 *and* O133/5 *Set of* 13 5·00 5·50

Design (37 × 43 *mm.*) :—Nos. 533/7, Throwing the Discus.

115. Commemorative Coin.

1975 (3 Sept.). *F.A.O. Commemoration. T* **115** *and similar designs. (a) Postage.*

538 5 s. multicoloured 5 5
539 20 s. multicoloured 20 25
540 50 s. new blue, black & silver 55 65
541 1 p. ultramarine, blk. & silver 1·10 1·25
542 2 p. black and silver .. .. 2·25 2·50

(b) Air.

543 12 s. multicoloured 12 15
544 14 s. multicoloured 15 15
545 25 s. vermilion, black and silver 25 30
546 50 s. brt. mag., black and silver 55 65
547 1 p. black and silver .. .. 1·10 1·25
538/47 .. .. *Set of* 10 5·75 6·25

Nos. 539/47 are as T **115** but show different coins. Nos. 542 and 544 are horiz., size 75 × 42 mm.

116. Commemorative Coin.

(Illustration reduced. Actual size 58 × 58 mm.)

1975 (4 Nov.). *Centenary of Tongan Constitution. T* **116** *and similar designs showing coinage. Multicoloured. (a) Postage.*

548 5 s. Type **116** 5 5
549 10 s. King George I .. 10 12
550 20 s. King Taufa'ahau IV .. 20 25
551 50 s. King George II 55 60
552 75 s. Tongan arms 60 70

(b) Air.

553 9 s. King Taufa'ahau IV .. 10 10
554 12 s. Queen Salote 12 15
555 14 s. Tongan arms 15 15
556 38 s. King Taufa'ahau IV .. 40 45
557 1 p. Four monarchs .. .. 1·10 1·25
548/57 *and* O136/8 .. *Set of* 13 4·75 5·25

Sizes:—60 × 40 mm., Nos. 549 and 551; 76 × 76 mm., Nos. 552 and 557; 57 × 56 mm., others.

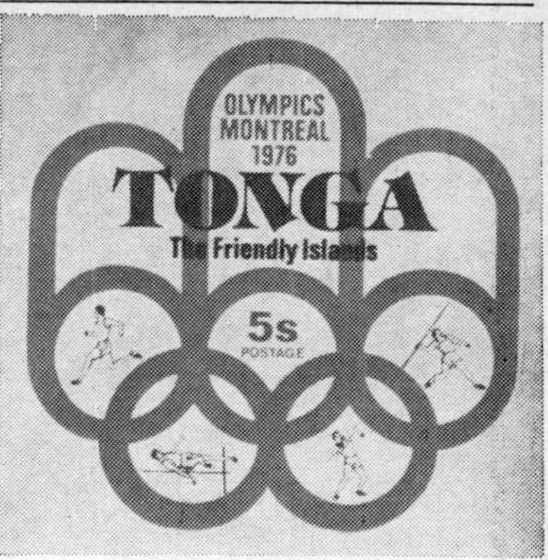

117. Montreal Logo.

1976 (24 Feb.). *First Participation in Olympic Games. (a) Postage.*

558 **117** 5 s. verm., black & blue 5 5
559 ,, 10 s. verm., blk. & emer. 10 12
560 ,, 25 s. verm., blk. & bistre 25 30
561 ,, 35 s. verm., blk. & mauve 40 45
562 ,, 70 s. vermilion, black and olive-yellow .. 75 85

(b) Air. Montreal logo optd. on Girl Guide stamps (Nos. 500 etc.).

563 **111** 12 s. on 20 s. multicoloured 12 15
564 – 14 s. on 16 s. multicoloured 15 20
565 – 16 s. multicoloured .. 20 20
566 **111** 38 s. on 40 s. multicoloured 40 45
567 – 75 s. multicoloured .. 75 85
558/67 *and* O139/41 *Set of* 13 4·75 5·25

118. Signatories of Declaration of Independence.

1976 (26 May). *Bicentenary of American Revolution. T* **118** *and similar horiz. designs showing signatories to the Declaration of Independence. (a) Postage.*

568 **118** 9 s. multicoloured .. 10 10
569 – 10 s. multicoloured .. 10 12
570 – 15 s. multicoloured .. 15 20
571 – 25 s. multicoloured .. 25 30
572 – 75 s. multicoloured .. 80 90

(b) Air.

573 – 12 s. multicoloured .. 12 15
574 – 14 s. multicoloured .. 15 20
575 – 17 s. multicoloured .. 20 20
576 – 38 s. multicoloured .. 40 45
577 – 1 p. multicoloured .. 1·10 1·25
568/77 *and* O142/4 .. *Set of* 13 4·75 5·25

The reverse of the backing paper shows the Declaration of Independence in full.

119. Nathaniel Turner and John Thomas (Methodist missionaries).

1976 (25 Aug.). *150th Anniv. of Christianity in Tonga. T* **119** *and similar design.* (a) *Postage.*

578 **119** 5 s. multicoloured .. 5 5
579 ,, 10 s. multicoloured .. 10 12
580 ,, 20 s. multicoloured .. 20 25
581 ,, 25 s. multicoloured .. 25 30
582 ,, 85 s. multicoloured .. 90 1·00

(b) *Air. Design showing Missionary Ship "Triton" (45×59 mm.).*

583 – 9 s. multicoloured .. 10 10
584 – 12 s. multicoloured .. 12 15
585 – 14 s. multicoloured .. 15 20
586 – 17 s. multicoloured .. 20 20
587 – 38 s. multicoloured .. 40 45
578/87 *and* O145/7 .. *Set of* 13 4·75 5·25

The reverse of the backing paper shows extracts from the diaries of John Thomas.

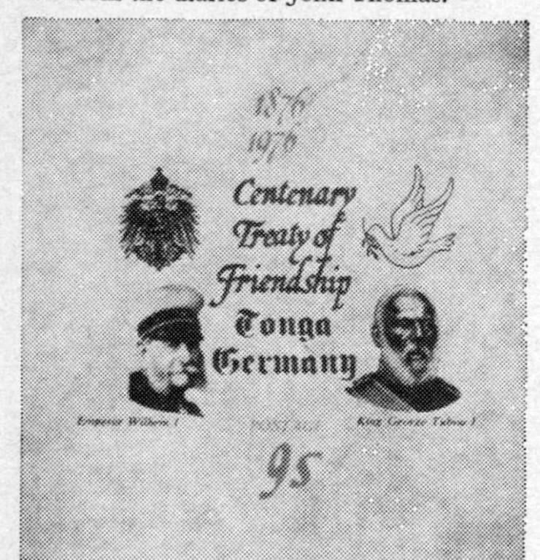

120. Emperor Wilhelm I and King George Toupo I.

1976 (1 Nov.). *Centenary of Treaty of Friendship with Germany.* (a) *Postage.*

588 **120** 9 s. multicoloured .. 10 10
589 ,, 15 s. multicoloured .. 15 20
590 ,, 22 s. multicoloured .. 25 25
591 ,, 50 s. multicoloured .. 50 55
592 ,, 73 s. multicoloured .. 75 85

(b) *Air. Circular design (52 mm. diameter) showing Treaty Signing.*

593 – 11 s. multicoloured .. 12 15
594 – 17 s. multicoloured .. 20 20
595 – 18 s. multicoloured .. 20 25
596 – 31 s. multicoloured .. 30 35
597 – 39 s. multicoloured .. 40 45
588/97 *and* O148/50 *Set of* 13 4·00 4·25

The treaty document is shown on the reverse of the backing paper.

OFFICIAL STAMPS.

G.F.B. (O 1) 1D/2 (O 2)

(G.F.B.=Gaue Faka Buleaga=On Government Service.)

1893 (13 Feb.). *Optd. with Type* O **1**. *W* **2**. *P* 12×11½.

O1 **5** 1d. ultramarine (C.) .. .. 3·00 7·00
a. Bisected diagonally (½d.) (on cover) .. .. ..
O2 **6** 2d. ultramarine (C.) .. .. 6·00 11·00
O3 **5** 4d. ultramarine (C.) .. .. 18·00 28·00
O4 **6** 8d. ultramarine (C.) .. .. 35·00 48·00
O5 ,, 1s. ultramarine (C.) .. .. 42·00 55·00

Above prices are for stamps in good condition and colour. Faded and stained stamps from the remainders are worth much less.

1893 (Dec.). *Nos.* O1 *to* O5 *variously surch. with new value, sideways as Type* O **2**.

O 6 **5** ½d. on 1d. ultramarine .. 3·00 7·00
O 7 **6** 2½d. on 2d. ultramarine .. 3·00 7·00
O 8 **5** 5d. on 4d. ultramarine .. 2·50 7·00
O 9 **6** 7½d. on 8d. ultramarine .. 3·50 12·00
a. "D" of "7½D." omitted
b. Surch. double .. £300
O10 ,, 10d. on 1s. ultramarine .. 3·50 12·00

OFFICIAL AIR MAIL 1862 TAU'ATAINA EMANCIPATION 1962 (O 3)

OFFICIAL AIRMAIL 40 SENITI (O 4)

1962 (7 Feb.). *Air. Centenary of Emancipation. Various stamps optd. with Type* O **3** *in red by R. S. Wallbank, Govt. Printer.*

O11 **55** 2d. ultramarine .. .. — 5·00
a. Error. "OFFICIAI" .. — 9·00
b. Error. "MAII" .. — 9·00
O12 **57** 5d. violet .. .. .. — 6·00
a. Error. "OFFICIAI" .. — 12·00
b. Error. "MAII" .. — 12·00
O13 **58** 1s. red-brown .. .. — 3·50
a. Error. "OFFICIAI" .. — 9·00
b. Error. "MAII" .. — 9·00
O14 **51** 5s. orge.-yell. & slate-lilac — 45·00
a. Error. "MAII" .. — 50·00
O15 **52** 10s. yellow and black .. — 18·00
a. Error. "MAII" ..
O16 **53** £1 yellow, scarlet, ultram. and deep bright blue — 25·00
a. Error. "MAII" ..
O11/O16 .. .. *Set of* 6 £150 £100

1963 (15 July). *Air. First Polynesian Gold Coinage Commemoration. As T* **63** *but inscr.* "OFFICIAL AIRMAIL". 1 *koula coin (diam.* 3⅛ *in.). Imperf.*

O17 **63** 15s. black .. .. 3·50 4·00

For complete set price see below No. 140.

1965 (18 Mar.). *No.* O17 *surch. as T* **67**.

O18 **63** 30s. on 15s. black .. .. 3·00 3·50

For complete set price see below No. 161.

1966 (18 June). *Air. Centenary of Tupou College and Secondary Education. No.* 117 *surch. with* "OFFICIAL AIRMAIL" *and new value, with commemorative inscription as in T* **69** *but in italic capital letters.*

O19 **56** 10s. on 4d. blue-green .. 1·10 1·25
a. Surch. inverted .. — £120
O20 ,, 20s. on 4d. blue-green .. 2·25 2·40

For complete set price see after No. 173.

1967 (25 Mar.). *Air. Decimal currency. No.* 112 *surch.* "OFFICIAL AIRMAIL ONE PA'ANGA" *in three lines, in red.*

O21 **51** 1 p. on 5s. .. .. 1·25 1·25
a. "AIRMAIL" above "OFFICIAL" .. 85·00

No. O21a occurred once in a number of sheets until it was corrected.

For complete set price see after No. 201.

1967 (4 July). *Air. No.* 114 *surch. in various denominations as Type* O **4**.

O22 **53** 40 s. on £1 .. .. 50 60
O23 ,, 60 s. on £1 .. .. 80 90
O24 ,, 1 p. on £1 .. .. 1·25 1·50
O25 ,, 2 p. on £1 .. .. 2·50 2·75

For complete set price see after No. 242.

Nos. O22/5 were first used on 4th July 1967, but supplies of unused stamps were not made available until April 1968.

The Friendly Islands welcome the United States Peace Corps Official Airmail 30s (O 5)

Friendly Islands Trials Field & Track South Pacific Games Port Moresby 1969 T$1·00 OFFICIAL AIRMAIL (O 6)

1967 (15 Dec.). *Air. Arrival of U.S. Peace Corps in Tonga. As No.* 114, *but imperf., and background colour changed, and surch. as Type* O **5**.

O26 **53** 30 s. on £1 yellow, scarlet, ultram. & emer.-grn. 40 45
O27 ,, 70 s. on £1 yellow, scarlet, ultram. & emer.-grn. 80 90
O28 ,, 1 p. 50, on £1 yell., scar., ultram. & emer.-grn. 1·90 2·10

For complete set price, see below No. 227.

1968 (4 July). *50th Birthday of King Taufa'ahua IV. No.* 207 *surch.* "HIS MAJESTY'S 50th BIRTHDAY" *(as T* **79**), "OFFICIAL AIRMAIL" *and new value.*

O29 **75** 40 s. on 50 s. (Turq.) .. 50 55
O30 ,, 60 s. on 50 s. (G.) .. 75 80
O31 ,, 1 p. on 50 s. (V.) .. 1·25 1·50
O32 ,, 2 p. on 50 s. (P.) .. 2·50 2·75

For complete set price see below No. 256.

1968 (19 Dec.). *Air. South Pacific Games Field and Track Trials, Port Moresby, New Guinea. As No.* 114, *but imperf., background colour changed and surch. as Type* O **6**.

O33 **53** 20 s. on £1 yell., scarlet, ultram. & emer.-grn. 30 35
O34 **53** 1 p. on £1 yell., scarlet, ultram. & emer.-grn. 1·50 1·75

For complete set price see after No. 270.

1969 (13 Aug.). *Air. Third South Pacific Games, Port Moresby. As Nos.* 290/4.

O35 **85** 70 s. carmine-red, bright green and turquoise 1·10 1·10
O36 ,, 80 s. carmine-red, orange and turquoise .. 1·25 1·25

For complete set price, see below No. 294.

OFFICIAL AIRMAIL 1969 OIL SEARCH 90s (O 7)

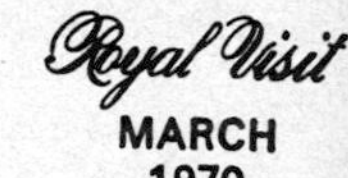

MARCH 1970 OFFICIAL AIRMAIL T$1·25 (O 8)

1969 (23 Dec.). *Air. First Oil Search in Tonga. As No.* 114 *but imperf., background colour changed to emerald-green, and surch. as Type* O **7**.

O37 **53** 90 s. on £1 mult. .. 2·00 2·00
a. "1966" for "1969" ..
O38 ,, 1 p. 10 on £1 multicoloured (R.) .. .. 2·25 2·25
a. "1966" for "1969" ..

For complete set price see after No. 304.

No. O38 is surch. as Type O 7, but without "OFFICIAL AIRMAIL".

1970 (7 Mar.). *Royal Visit. As No.* 110 *but imperf., colours changed, and surch. as Type* O **8.**

O39 **49** 75 s. on 1s. carmine-red and yellow .. .. 1·50 1·50
O40 „ 1 p. on 1s. carmine-red and yellow (B.) .. 2·00 2·00
O41 „ 1 p. 25 on 1s. carmine-red and yellow (G.) .. 2·50 2·50

For complete set price see after No. **314.**

OFFICIAL Commonwealth Member JUNE 1970 50s AIRMAIL

(O **9**)

1970 (4 June). *Entry into British Commonwealth. As No.* 112 *but imperf., background colour changed, and surch. as Type* O **9.**

O42 **51** 50 s. on 5s. orange-yellow and sepia .. .. 1·00 1·00
O43 „ 90 s. on 5s. orange-yellow and sepia (R.) .. 1·75 1·75
O44 „ 1 p. 50 on 5s. orange-yellow and sepia (G.) .. 3·00 3·00

For complete set price see after No. 324.

1970 (4 June). *As Nos.* 325/34, *but inscr.* " OFFICIAL POST ". *Colour of* " TONGA " *given for* 6 *to* 10 *s.*

O45 **83** 1 s. greenish yellow, bright purple & black 5 5
O46 „ 2 s. greenish yellow, ultramarine and black .. 5 5
O47 „ 3 s. greenish yellow, chocolate and black 5 5
O48 „ 4 s. greenish yellow, emerald and black .. 5 5
O49 „ 5 s. greenish yellow, orange-red & black 8 8
O50 **90** 6 s. ultramarine .. 8 8
O51 „ 7 s. deep mauve .. 10 10
O52 „ 8 s. gold 10 10
O53 „ 9 s. bright carmine .. 12 12
O54 „ 10 s. silver 12 12
O45/54 .. .. *Set of* 10 70 70

The note after No. 334 also applies here.
See also Nos. O82/91.

Centenary British Red Cross 1870-1970

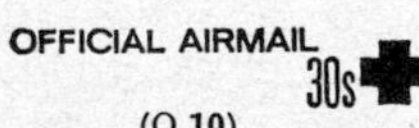

(O 10)

1970 (17 Oct.). *Centenary of British Red Cross. As Nos.* 102 *and* 112 *but imperf., colours changed and surch. as Type* O **10.**

O55 **41** 30 s. on 1½d. emerald (Blk. & R.) 60 60
O56 **51** 80 s. on 5s. orange-yellow and sepia (B. & R.) 1·60 1·60
O57 „ 90 s. on 5s. orange-yellow and sepia (B. & R.) 1·75 1·75

For complete set price see after No. 344.

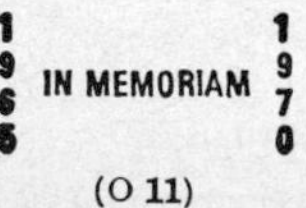

(O **11**)

(O **12**)

1971 (30 Jan.). *Air. Fifth Death Anniv. of Queen Salote. As No.* 113, *but imperf., colours changed and optd. as Type* O **11.**

O58 **52** 20 s. on 10s. orge.-yellow 40 40
O59 „ 30 s. on 10s. orge.-yellow 60 60
O60 „ 50 s. on 10s. orge.-yellow 1·00 1·00
O61 „ 2 p. on 10s. orge.-yellow 4·00 4·00

For complete set price see after No. 354.

1971 (17 Apr.). *Air.* " *Philatokyo '71* " *Stamp Exhibition. Unissued Red Cross surcharges on No.* 107, *but imperf., colours changed and additionally surch. as Type* O **12.**

O62 **46** 30 s. on 5d. green and yellow (B. & R.) 60 60
O63 „ 80 s. on 5d. green and yellow (Blk. & R.) .. 1·60 1·60
O64 „ 90 s. on 5d. green and yellow (P. & R.) .. 1·75 1·75

For complete set price see after No. 364.

1971 (20 July)–72. *Air. As Nos.* 365/6*a*, *but inscr.* " OFFICIAL AIRMAIL ".

O65 **96** 14 s. multicoloured .. 20 20
O65*a* „ 17 s. multicoloured (20.7.72) 30 30
O66 „ 21 s. multicoloured .. 35 35
O66*a* „ 38 s. multicoloured (20.7.72) 55 55

For complete set price see after No. 366*a*.

TONGA 4th SOUTH PACIFIC GAMES OFFICIAL AIRMAIL 50s

O **13.** Football.

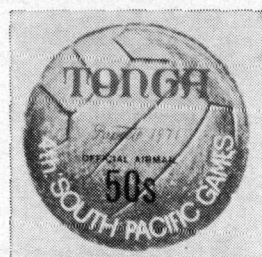

1971 (20 July). *Air. Fourth South Pacific Games, Tahiti.*

O67 O **13** 50 s. multicoloured .. 65 75
O68 „ 90 s. multicoloured .. 1·10 1·25
O69 „ 1 p. 50, multicoloured 1·90 2·00

For complete set price see after No. 376.

INVESTITURE 1971 OFFICIAL 60s AIRMAIL

(O **14**)

(*Illustration reduced. Actual size* 61 × 13 *mm.*)

1971 (30 Oct.). *Air. Investiture of Royal Tongan Medal of Merit. Nos.* 315, 318 *and* 316 *surch. as Type* O **14.**

O70 **89** 60 s. on 3 s. multicoloured 70 80
O71 „ 80 s. on 25 s. mult. .. 1·00 1·10
O72 „ 1 p. 10 on 7 s. mult. .. 1·40 1·60

For complete set price see after No. 382.

O **15.** " UNICEF " and Emblem.

1971 (31 Dec.). *Air. 25th Anniv. of UNICEF.*

O73 O **15** 70 s. multicoloured .. 90 1·00
O74 „ 80 s. multicoloured .. 1·00 1·10
O75 „ 90 s. multicoloured .. 1·10 1·25

For complete set price see after No. 392.

1972 (14 Apr.). *Air. Merchant Marine Routes. Design similar to T* **100,** *but inscr.* " OFFICIAL AIRMAIL ".

O76 20 s. multicoloured .. 25 30
O77 50 s. multicoloured .. 65 75
O78 1 p. 20, multicoloured .. 1·50 1·75

Design:—Nos. O76/8, Map of South Pacific, and *Aoniu*.

For complete set price see after No. 402.

1972 (15 July). *Air. Fifth Anniv. of Coronation. Design similar to T* **101,** *but inscr.* " OFFICIAL AIRMAIL ".

O79 50 s. multicoloured .. 60 65
O80 70 s. multicoloured .. 75 85
O81 1 p. 50, multicoloured .. 1·60 1·75

Design (47 × 57 mm):—Nos. O79/81, As T **101**, but with different background.

For complete set price see after No. 412.

1972 (30 Sept.). *As Nos.* 413/27, *but inscr.* " OFFICIAL POST ".

(*a*) *As Nos.* 413/17.

O82 **83** 1 s. light yellow, scarlet and black 5 5
O83 „ 2 s. light yellow, deep blue-green and black 5 5
O84 „ 3 s. light yellow, yellow-green and black .. 5 5
O85 „ 4 s. light yellow and blk. 5 5
O86 „ 5 s. light yellow and blk. 8 8

(*b*) *As Nos.* O50/4, *but colours changed. Colour of* " TONGA " *given.*

O87 **90** 6 s. light green 8 8
O88 „ 7 s. light green 8 8
O89 „ 8 s. light green 10 10
O90 „ 9 s. light green 12 12
O91 „ 10 s. light green 12 12

(*c*) *As Nos.* 423/7. *Colour of face value given.*

O92 **102** 15 s. new blue 20 20
O93 „ 20 s. reddish orange .. 25 25
O94 „ 25 s. chocolate .. 30 30
O95 „ 40 s. yellow-orange .. 50 50
O96 „ 50 s. Royal blue 65 65
O82/96 .. .. *Set of* 15 2·40 2·40

The note after No. 427 also applies here.

1972 (9 Dec.). *Air. Proclamation of Sovereignty over Minerva Reefs. Design similar to T* **104**, *but inscr.* " OFFICIAL AIRMAIL ".

O97 25 s. multicoloured .. 30 35
O98 75 s. multicoloured .. 85 90
O99 1 p. 50, multicoloured .. 1·60 1·75

Design: *Horiz.* (64 × 39 *mm.*)—Nos. O97/9, Flags and map.

For complete set price, see after No. 438.

TONGA 1973 ESTABLISHMENT BANK OF TONGA 40s OFFICIAL AIRMAIL

(O **16**)

1973 (30 Mar.). *Air. Foundation of Bank of Tonga. No.* 396 *surch. as Type* O **16.**

O100 **100** 40 s. on 21 s. multicoloured (Blk. & G.) 45 50
O101 „ 85 s. on 21 s. multicoloured (B. & G.) 90 1·00
O102 „ 1 p. 25 on 21 s. multicoloured (Br.) .. 1·40 1·50

For complete set price, see after No. 448.

SILVER JUBILEE
TONGAN SCOUTING
1948 - 1973

(O 17)

1973 (29 JUNE). *Silver Jubilee of Scouting in Tonga. Nos.* O76, O74 *and* 319 *variously optd. in silver* (*Nos.* O103/4) *or silver and gold* (*No.* O105).

O103	–	30 s. on 20 s. mult. ..	1·25	1·25
O104	O **15**	80 s. multicoloured ..	4·00	4·00
O105	**89**	1 p. 40 on 50 s. mult.	6·00	6·00

For complete set price see after No. 458.

1973 (2 OCT.). *Air. Bicentenary of Capt. Cook's Visit. Design similar to T* **107**, *but inscr.* "OFFICIAL AIRMAIL".

O106	25 s. multicoloured ..	35	35
O107	80 s. multicoloured ..	95	1·10
O108	1 p. 30, multicoloured ..	1·60	1·75

Design: *Horiz.* (52×45 *mm.*)—Nos. O106/8, Bulk Tanker *James Cook.*

For complete set price see after No. 468.

1974
Commonwealth
Games
Christchurch
OFFICIAL AIRMAIL
50s

(O 18)

1973 (19 DEC.). *Air. Commonwealth Games. Nos.* O67/9 *optd. with Type* O **18**, *in blue.*

O109	O **13**	50 s. multicoloured ..	60	65
O110	,,	90 s. multicoloured ..	1·10	1·25
O111	,,	1 p. 50, multicoloured	1·90	2·00

For complete set price see after No. 478.

O **19**. Dove of Peace.

(Des. M. Meers.)

1974 (20 MAR.). *Air.*

O112	O **19**	7 s. turq.-grn., reddish vio. and orange-red	8	8
O113	,,	9 s. turq.-grn., reddish vio. and red-brown	12	12
O114	,,	12 s. turq.-grn., reddish vio. and yellow-orange	15	15
O115	,,	14 s. turq.-grn., reddish vio. and bistre-yellow	15	15
O116	O **19**	17 s. multicoloured ..	20	20
O117	,,	29 s. multicoloured ..	35	35
O118	,,	38 s. multicoloured ..	45	45
O119	,,	50 s. multicoloured ..	60	60
O120	,,	75 s. multicoloured ..	90	90
O112/120		*Set of* 9	2·75	2·75

The note below No. 487 also applies here.

1974 (20 JUNE). *Air. Centenary of Universal Postal Union. Design similar to T* **110**, *but inscr.* "OFFICIAL AIRMAIL".

O121	25 s. deep red-orange, light yellow-green and black	50	50
O122	35 s. lemon, magenta & blk.	65	65
O123	70 s. deep orange, bright blue and black ..	1·40	1·40

Design: *Square* (40 *mm* × 40 *mm.*)—Letters "UPU".
For complete set price see after No. 497.

1974 (11 SEPT.). *Air. Tongan Girl Guides. Design similar to T* **111**, *but inscr.* "OFFICIAL AIRMAIL".

O124	45 s. multicoloured	50	55
O125	55 s. multicoloured	60	65
O126	1 p. multicoloured	1·10	1·25

Design: *Oval* (35×52 *mm.*)—Lady Baden-Powell.
For complete set price see after No. 507.

1974 (11 DEC.). *Air. Establishment of Royal Marine Institute. Designs similar to T* **112** *but inscr.* " Official Airmail ".

O127	30 s. multicoloured ..	35	40
O128	35 s. multicoloured ..	40	45
O129	80 s. multicoloured	90	1·00

Designs: *Horiz.* (61×43 *mm.*)—30 s., 35 s. Badge and handclasp. *Horiz.* 64×55 *mm.*)—80 s. Badge and Tongan banknotes.
For complete set price see after No. 517.

1975 (11 MAR.). *Air. South Pacific Forum and Tourism. Designs similar to T* **113** *but inscr.* "OFFICIAL AIRMAIL".

O130	50 s. multicoloured	55	65
O131	75 s. multicoloured	85	95
O132	1 p. 25, multicoloured ..	1·25	1·50

Designs (49×43 *mm.*):—50 s. Jungle arch; others, sunset scene.
For complete set price see after No. 527.

1975 (11 JUNE). *Air. Fifth South Pacific Games. Design similar to T* **114** *but inscr.* "OFFICIAL AIRMAIL".

O133	38 s. multicoloured	40	50
O134	75 s. multicoloured	75	80
O135	1 p. 20, multicoloured ..	1·25	1·50

Design: *Oval* (51×27 *mm.*):—Runners on track.
For complete set price see after No. 537.

O **20**. Tongan Monarchs.

(*Illustration reduced. Actual size* 69×39 *mm.*)

1975 (4 NOV.). *Air. Centenary of Tongan Constitution.*

O136	O **20**	17 s. multicoloured ..	20	20
O137	,,	60 s. multicoloured ..	65	75
O138	,,	90 s. multicoloured ..	1·00	1·10

For complete set price see after No. 557.

1976 (24 FEB.). *Air. First Participation in Olympic Games. Design similar to T* **117** *bu[t] inscr.* "OFFICIAL AIRMAIL".

O139	45 s. multicoloured	50	55
O140	55 s. multicoloured	55	65
O141	1 p. multicoloured	1·10	1·25

Design: Oval (36×53 *mm.*)—Montreal logo.

For complete set price see after No. 567.

1976 (26 MAY). *Air. Bicentenary of American Revolution. Designs as T* **118** *showing signatories to the Declaration of Independence. Inscr.* "OFFICIAL AIRMAIL".

O142	20 s. multicoloured	20	25
O143	50 s. multicoloured	55	65
O144	1 p. 15, multicoloured ..	1·10	1·25

For complete set price see after No. 577.

1976 (25 AUG.). *Air. 150th Anniv. of Christianity in Tonga. Hexagonal design* (65×52 *mm.*) *showing Lifuka Chapel.*

O145	65 s. multicoloured	65	75
O146	85 s. multicoloured	90	1·00
O147	1 p. 15, multicoloured ..	1·10	1·25

For complete set price see after No. 587.

1976 (1 NOV.). *Air. Centenary of Treaty of Friendship with Germany. Rectangular design* (51×47 *mm.*) *showing text.*

O148	30 s. multicoloured	35	40
O149	60 s. multicoloured	60	70
O150	1 p. 25, multicoloured ..	1·40	1·5[0]

The reverse of the backing paper shows the Declaration of American Independence.

For complete set price see after No. 597.

TRANSJORDAN.

This will be found listed under JORDAN in Vol. 2 of Stanley Gibbons Foreign Overseas Catalogue.

TRANSVAAL.

(Formerly SOUTH AFRICAN REPUBLIC.)

I. FIRST REPUBLIC.

NOTE.—For the 1d., 3d., 6d. and 1s. stamps, T 1 and 2, two plates of each value were made, each plate consisting of forty stamp blocks, arranged in five rows of eight in a row.

The two plates of a value were sometimes, but not always, used together, producing a sheet of eighty stamps in two panes of forty each.

One block was inverted in the original left-hand plate of the 6d. and also of the 1s. In the panes of the printed stamps this was No. 25 on the right-hand pane in the 6d. and No. 1 on the right pane of the 1s. From this cause arose the *tête-bêche* varieties of these two values in some of the printings; and later, when these stamps were overprinted, an inverted surcharge is found whenever these panes were so treated. In addition to this in the case of the 1d., 3d., 6d., and 1s. stamps it is known that at least one sheet of each of these values must have been printed with the whole surcharge inverted.

Many unauthorised imitations of these three values were made in Germany, but, with the exception of certain impressions of the 1s. value, in yellow-green on soft medium paper, they all differ from the originals in some parts of the design, particularly in the eagle and the ribbon bearing the motto under the coat-of-arms. To this class belong forgeries of the 1d., in red or black, in which the numerals in the top corners are enclosed in a white frame.

The exception—the 1s., in yellow-green, above mentioned—was once regarded as genuine and catalogued, but it has been proved by Mr. J. N. Luff (see his articles, "Otto's Printings," in Vols. XXXIII and XXXIV of the *Philatelic Record;* it is his "surreptitious printing J") that these were printed from an unauthorised small plate of four subjects, on each of which were certain flaws that can be easily identified in the impressions. They somewhat resemble the 1s. stamps of 1876–7, but the paper is smoother and firmer and the printing clearer.

1

2

(Typo. Adolph Otto in Gustrow, Mecklenburg-Schwerin.)

1869. *Thin paper, clear and distinct impressions.*

(*a*) *Imperf.*

No.	Type	Description	Unused	Used
1	1	1d. brown-lake	85·00	
		a. Orange-red	95·00	
2	„	6d. bright ultramarine	55·00	
		a. Pale ultramarine	45·00	48·00
3	„	1s. deep green	£180	
		a. Tête-bêche (pair)	£3500	

(*b*) *Fine roulette,* 15½ *to* 16.

No.	Type	Description	Unused	Used
4	1	1d. brown-lake	28·00	
		a. Brick-red	25·00	
		b. Orange-red	25·00	
		c. Vermilion	25·00	
5	„	6d. bright ultramarine	25·00	
		a. Pale ultramarine	25·00	
6	„	1s. deep green	30·00	
		a. Yellow-green	28·00	
		b. Emerald-green	28·00	

Stamps of this issue, genuinely used for postal purposes, are scarce.

These stamps were printed from two sets of plates, one with the stamps spaced 1¼ to 1½ mm. apart, the other with the stamps spaced 2¼ to 3½ mm. apart. The former are rouletted close to the design of all the four sides, and on the 1d. of that printing the outer frame-lines do not join at the right lower corner.

(Typo. as last, in Germany.)

1871 (July). *Thin paper, clear and distinct impressions.*

Fine roulette, 15½ to 16.

7 **2** 3d. pale reddish lilac .. .. 25·00 25·00
a. Deep lilac .. .. .. 26·00 25·00

These fine rouletted stamps and all subsequent printings are from the plates which were subsequently sent to South Africa.

Imperf. specimens of the 3d. pale reddish lilac were sent out to South Africa, but there is no evidence that they were issued for postal use. They are without the small dot on the left leg of the eagle which is always found in the issued stamps. They also exist *tête-bêche* (*price for un. pair* £1400).

(Typo. M. J. Viljoen at Pretoria.)

1870 (4 April). *Thin gummed paper from Germany. Impressions coarse and defective.*

(*a*) *Imperf.*

8 **1** 1d. dull rose-red .. .. 25·00
a. Reddish pink .. .. 25·00
b. Carmine-red .. .. 22·00
9 „ 6d. dull ultramarine .. .. 75·00
a. Tête-bêche (pair) £2700

(*b*) *Fine roulettes, 15½ to 16.*

10 **1** 1d. carmine-red .. .. £300 85·00
11 „ 6d. dull ultramarine .. .. 80·00 40·00

(*c*) *Wide roulette, 6½.*

12 **1** 1d. carmine-red .. .. — £400

1870. *Thick, hard paper, yellow streaky gum.*

(*a*) *Imperf.* (26 April).

13 **1** 1d. pale rose-red .. .. 22·00
a. Carmine-red .. .. 25·00 27·00
14 „ 1s. yellow-green .. .. 28·00 27·00
a. Tête-bêche (pair) £3500

(*b*) *Fine roulette.* 15½ to 16 (10 May).

15 **1** 6d. ultramarine .. .. 27·00 27·00
a. Tête-bêche (pair) £3000 £2700
16 „ 1s. yellow-green £225 £225

1870 (24 May). *Third hard paper, thin yellow smooth gum. Fine roulette, 15½ to 16.*

17 **1** 1d. carmine-red .. .. 30·00

1870 (4 July). *Medium paper, blotchy heavy printing and whitish gum. Fine roulette, 15½ to 16.*

18 **1** 1d. rose-red .. .. .. 16·00 16·00
a. Carmine-red .. .. 16·00 16·00
b. *Crimson.* From over-inked plate 45·00
19 „ 6d. ultramarine .. .. 27·00 27·00
a. Tête-bêche (pair) .. ..
b. *Dp. ultram.* From over-inked pl. £150 65·00
20 „ 1s. deep green .. .. 30·00 27·00
a. From over-inked plate .. £150 65·00

Nos. 18b, 19b and 20a were printed from over-inked plates, giving heavy, blobby impressions.

(Typo. J. P. Borrius, at Potchefstroom.)

1870 (Sept.).

I. *Stout paper, but with colour often showing through, whitish gum.*

(*a*) *Imperf.*

21 **1** 1d. black .. .. .. 45·00 45·00

(*b*) *Fine roulette, 15½ to 16.*

22 **1** 1d. black .. .. .. 5·00 6·00
a. Grey-black .. .. .. 5·00 6·00
23 „ 6d. blackish blue .. .. 40·00 18·00
a. Dull blue .. .. .. 28·00 16·00

II. *Thin transparent paper.*

Fine roulette, 15½ to 16.

24 **1** 1d. bright carmine .. .. 55·00 22·00
25 „ 1d. black .. .. .. 60·00 £225
26 „ 6d. ultramarine .. .. 28·00 16·00
27 „ 1s. green .. .. .. 27·00 16·00

1872 (Dec.).

I. *Thinnish opaque paper, clear printing.*

Fine roulette, 15½ to 16.

28 **1** 1d. reddish pink .. .. 25·00 15·00
a. Carmine-red .. .. 25·00 15·00
29 **2** 3d. grey-lilac .. .. 32·00 15·00
30 **1** 6d. ultramarine .. .. 22·00 11·00
a. Pale ultramarine .. .. 25·00 11·00
31 „ 1s. yellow-green .. .. 25·00 11·00
a. Green .. .. .. 25·00 11·00
aa. Bisected (6d.) (on cover) ..

II. *Thickish wove paper.*

(*a*) *Fine roulette, 15½ to 16.*

32 **1** 1d. dull rose .. .. £150 27·00
a. Brownish rose .. .. £200 38·00
b. Printed on both sides ..
33 „ 6d. milky blue .. .. 55·00 15·00
a. Deep dull blue .. .. 32·00 14·00
aa. Imperf. (pair) £250

(*b*) *Wide roulette, 6½.*

34 **1** 6d. dull blue .. ..

III. *Very thick dense paper.*

Fine roulette, 15½ to 16.

35 „ 1d. dull rose .. .. £200 45·00
a. Brownish rose .. .. — 38·00
36 „ 6d. dull ultramarine .. .. 75·00 25·00
a. Bright ultramarine .. .. 80·00 25·00
37 „ 1s. yellow-green £275 £250

3

(Typo. in Germany from a new plate made by A. Otto at Gustrow.)

1874 (30 Sept.). *Thin smooth paper, clearly printed. Fine roulette, 15½ to 16.*

38 **3** 6d. bright ultramarine .. 22·00 9·00
a. Bisected (3d.) (on cover) ..

Reprints of this stamp, both unused and with forged postmarks, are in a *duller* shade of colour than the originals, and the paper is rather thicker. Reprints also exist in fancy colours.

(Typo. P. Davis & Son, Pietermaritzburg.)

1874 (Sept.). *T* **1.** *P* 12½.

(*a*) *Thin transparent paper.*

39 **1** 1d. pale brick-red .. .. 27·00 15·00
a. Brownish red .. .. 28·00 15·00
40 „ 6d. deep blue .. .. 38·00 15·00

(*b*) *Thicker opaque paper.*

41 **1** 1d. pale red .. .. 45·00 27·00
42 „ 6d. blue .. .. 35·00 18·00
a. Imperf. between (pair) ..
b. Deep blue .. .. 35·00 18·00

(Typo. "The Stamp Commission" at Pretoria.)

I. **1875** (29 April). *Very thin soft opaque paper (semi-pelure).*

(*a*) *Imperf.*

43 **1** 1d. orange-red .. .. 45·00 18·00
a. Pin-perf. .. .. ..
44 **2** 3d. lilac .. .. 32·00 18·00
45 **1** 6d. blue .. .. 30·00 15·00
a. Milky blue .. .. 45·00 15·00
aa. Tête-bêche (pair) £2700
ab. Pin-perf. .. ..

(*b*) *Fine roulette, 15½ to 16.*

46 **1** 1d. orange-red .. .. £140 50·00
47 **2** 3d. lilac .. .. £150 55·00
48 **1** 6d. blue .. .. £140 48·00

(*c*) *Wide roulette, 6½.*

49 **1** 1d. orange-red .. .. — 60·00
50 **2** 3d. lilac .. .. — 85·00
51 **1** 6d. blue .. .. — 45·00
a. Bright blue .. .. — 45·00
b. Milky blue .. ..

II. **1876** (?). *Very thin hard transparent paper (pelure).* (*a*) *Imperf.*

52 **1** 1d. brownish red .. .. 18·00 8·00
a. Orange-red .. .. 15·00 8·00
b. Dull red .. .. 15·00 15·00
53 **2** 3d. lilac .. .. 18·00 15·00
a. Deep lilac .. .. 22·00 15·00
54 **1** 6d. pale blue .. .. 15·00 15·00
a. Blue .. .. 15·00 8·00
aa. Tête-bêche (pair) .. .. — £2100
b. Deep blue .. .. 15·00 8·00

(*b*) *Fine roulette, 15½ to 16.*

55 **1** 1d. orange-red .. .. £110 48·00
a. Brown-red .. .. £110 48·00
56 **2** 3d. lilac .. .. £120 45·00
57 **1** 6d. blue .. .. 65·00 40·00
a. Deep blue .. .. 65·00 45·00

(*c*) *Wide roulette, 6½.*

58 **1** 1d. orange-red .. .. £275 60·00
a. Bright red .. .. — 55·00
59 **2** 3d. lilac .. .. — 80·00
60 **1** 6d. deep blue .. .. £275 38·00

(*d*) *Pin-perf.*

61 **1** 1d. dull red .. .. £160 90·00
62 **2** 3d. lilac .. .. — 90·00
63 **1** 6d. blue .. .. — 85·00

1876. *Stout hard-surfaced paper.*

I. *Smooth, nearly white, gum.*

(*a*) *Imperf.*

64 **1** 1d. bright red .. .. 8·50 5·50
65 **2** 3d. lilac .. ..
66 **1** 6d. bright blue .. .. 30·00 7·00
a. Tête-bêche (pair) .. .. — £2100
b. Pale blue .. .. 30·00 8·50

(*b*) *Fine roulette, 15½ to 16.*

67 **1** 1d. bright red .. .. £150 60·00
68 **2** 3d. lilac .. .. 90·00
69 **1** 6d. bright blue .. .. — 60·00

(*c*) *Wide roulette, 6½.*

70 **1** 1d. bright red .. .. £160 60·00
71 „ 6d. pale blue .. .. — 85·00

II. *Deep brown gum, staining the paper.*

72 **1** 6d. deep blue (*imperf.*) .. 18·00 6·50
a. Tête-bêche (pair) .. .. — £1400
73 „ 6d. deep blue (*fine roulette*) — £150
74 „ 6d. deep blue (*wide roulette*) .. £200 90·00

1876–7.

I. *Coarse soft white paper, printed in the colours that were overprinted in July, 1877.*

(*a*) *Imperf.*

75 **1** 1d. brick-red .. .. 32·00 18·00
76 „ 6d. deep blue .. .. 55·00 18·00
a. Milky blue .. .. £110 30·00
77 „ 1s. yellow-green .. .. 80·00 32·00

(*b*) *Fine roulette, 15½ to 16.*

78 **1** 1d. brick-red .. .. — £110
79 „ 6d. deep blue .. .. — 55·00
80 „ 1s. yellow-green .. £250 £100

(*c*) *Wide roulette, 6½.*

81 **1** 1d. brick-red .. .. — £120
81*a* „ 6d. deep blue .. ..
82 „ 1s. yellow-green .. ..

(*d*) *Fine × wide roulette.*

83 **1** 1d. brick-red £250 £120

II. *Hard thick coarse yellowish paper.*

84 **1** 1d. brick-red (*imperf.*) ..
85 „ 1d. brick-red (*wide roulette*)

See also Nos. 171/4.

II. FIRST BRITISH OCCUPATION.

V. R. V. R.

TRANSVAAL. TRANSVAAL.

(4) (5)

T **4** is the normal overprint, but in some printings No. 11 on the pane has a wider-spaced overprint, as T **5.**

T **1** *and* **2** (*3d.*) *optd. with T* **4.**

1877 (July). *Optd. in red.*

(*a*) *Imperf.*

86 3d. lilac (*semi-pelure*) .. .. £500 90·00
a. Opt. Type 5 .. ..

87 3d. lilac (*pelure*) .. .. £500 60·00
a. Opt. Type 5 .. .. .. £2000
b. Opt. on back £1200
c. Opt. double, in red and in black £2000
88 6d. blue .. .. .. £550 70·00
a. Opt. inverted or tête-bêche pair — £2000
b. Opt. double £1500
c. Opt. Type 5 .. .. .. £2000
d. Deep blue .. .. .. — £100
89 1s. yellow-green .. .. £200 55·00
a. Bisected (6d.) (on cover) .. — £550
b. Opt. inverted or tête-bêche pair — £1200
c. Opt. Type 5 .. .. .. £1200

(*b*) *Fine roulette*, 15½ *to* 16.

90 3d. lilac (*pelure*) .. .. — £500
91 6d. blue .. .. .. — £500
92 1s. yellow-green £450 £200
a. Opt. Type 5 .. .. ..

(*c*) *Wide roulette*, 6½.

93 3d. lilac (*pelure*) .. .. — £500
a. Opt. Type 5 .. .. ..
94 6d. blue .. .. .. — £500
a. Opt. Type 5 .. .. ..
95 1s. yellow-green £1000 £450
a. Opt. inverted or tête-bêche pair — £1000

In the above, the stamps overprinted are the 3d. of the issues of April 1875 and 1876 and the 6d. and 1s. of 1876–77.

1877. *Opt. with T* **4** *in black.*

I. *Pelure paper.*

96 1d. orange-red (*imperf.*) .. 75·00 40·00
97 1d. orange-red (*fine roulette*) .. — £450

II. *Hard-surfaced paper.*

98 1d. bright red (*imperf.*) .. 7·00 7·00
a. Opt. inverted £175 £150
b. Opt. Type 5 .. .. £300 £350
99 1d. bright red (*fine roulette*) 55·00 20·00
a. Opt. inverted .. ..
b. Opt. double .. .. ..
100 1d. bright red (*wide roulette*) .. £200 65·00

III. *Coarse soft paper.*

(*a*) *Imperf.*

101 1d. brick-red (5.77) .. .. 7·00 7·00
a. Opt. double .. .. .. — £400
b. Opt. Type 5 .. .. ..
102 3d. lilac .. .. .. 27·00 12·00
a. Opt. inverted .. ..
b. Deep lilac .. .. .. 55·00 30·00
103 6d. dull blue .. .. .. 32·00 12·00
a. Opt. double £1000
b. Opt. inverted .. .. £550 60·00
c. Tête-bêche (pair) .. — £1200
d. Opt. Type 5 .. .. — £500
da. Opt. Type 5, inverted
e. Blue (bright to deep) .. 60·00 9·00
ea. Bright blue, opt. inverted — £200
f. Pin-perf. .. .. .. — £150
104 1s. yellow-green .. .. 30·00 15·00
a. Opt. inverted .. .. £400 60·00
b. Tête-bêche (pair) .. — £1200
c. Opt. Type 5 .. .. £1000 £400
d. Bisected (on cover) .. — £400

(*b*) *Fine roulette*, 15½ *to* 16.

105 1d. brick-red .. .. 27·00 27·00
106 3d. lilac .. .. .. 55·00 25·00
107 6d. dull blue .. .. .. 60·00 16·00
a. Opt. inverted .. .. — £250
b. Opt. Type 5 .. .. £1500
108 1s. yellow-green .. .. 65·00 35·00
a. Opt. inverted £350 £140
b. Opt. Type 5 .. .. — £800

(*c*) *Wide roulette*, 6½.

109 1d. brick red .. .. £250 55·00
a. Opt. Type 5 .. ..
110 3d. lilac .. .. .. — £200
111 6d. dull blue .. .. .. — £500
a. Opt. inverted .. .. — £1200
112 1s. yellow-green .. .. £125 42·00
a. Opt. inverted £500 £200

1877 (31 Aug.). *T* **1** *optd. with T* **4** *in black.*

113 6d. blue/*rose* (*imperf.*) .. 22·00 14·00
a. Bisected (3d.) (on cover) ..
b. Opt. inverted .. .. 22·00 14·00
c. Tête-bêche (pair) £800
d. Opt. omitted £1000
114 6d. blue/*rose* (*fine roulette*) .. 65·00 25·00
a. Opt. inverted .. .. £160 22·00
b. Tête-bêche (pair) .. ..
c. Opt. omitted .. .. ..
115 6d. blue/*rose* (*wide roulette*)
a. Opt. inverted .. ..
b. Opt. omitted .. ..

V. R. V. R.

Transvaal (6) Transvaal (7)

1877 (July). *T* **1** *and* **2** (3*d.*) *optd. with T* **6** *in black.*

(*a*) *Imperf.*

116 1d. red/*blue* .. .. .. 18·00 9·00
a. "Transvral" .. .. — £800
b. Opt. double £1200
c. Opt. inverted £275 £120
d. Opt. omitted .. ..
117 1d. red/*orange* .. .. 4·00 4·50
a. Pin-perf. .. .. ..
b. Printed both sides .. ..
118 3d. mauve/*buff* .. .. 9·00 9·00
a. Opt. inverted .. .. — £250
b. Pin-perf. .. .. ..
119 6d. blue/*green* .. .. 28·00 12·00
a. Deep blue/green .. .. 35·00 14·00
b. Broken "Y" for "V" in "V.R." .... ..
c. Small "V" in "Transvaal" ..
d. Stop in front of "R" (=V..R) — £250
e. Tête-bêche (pair) .. — £1200
f. Opt. inverted .. .. — £300
g. Pin-perf. .. .. ..
120 6d. blue/*blue* .. .. 18·00 9·00
a. Tête-bêche (pair) .. — £1000
b. Opt. inverted .. .. — £300
c. Opt. omitted .. .. — £750
d. Opt. double .. .. — £850
e. Pin-perf. .. .. ..
f. Bisected (3d.) (on cover) — £175

(*b*) *Fine roulette*, 15½ *to* 16.

121 1d. red/*blue* .. .. .. 28·00 14·00
a. "Transvral" .. .. — £1000
122 1d. red/*orange* .. .. 10·00 9·00
a. Imperf. between (pair)
123 3d. mauve/*buff* .. .. 35·00 9·00
a. Imperf. between (pair)
b. Opt. inverted .. .. — £800
124 6d. blue/*green* .. .. 27·00 7·00
a. Bisected (3d.) (on cover) — £175
b. Tête-bêche (pair) .. ..
c. Opt. inverted .. .. — £200
d. Opt. omitted .. .. — £1100
e. Stop in front of "R" (=V..R) — £500
125 6d. blue/*blue* .. .. 75·00 18·00
a. Bisected (3d.) (on cover) — £175
b. Imperf. between (pair)
c. Opt. inverted .. .. — £400
d. Opt. omitted .. .. — £850

(*c*) *Wide roulette*, 6½.

126 1d. red/*orange* .. .. 80·00 40·00
127 3d. mauve/*buff* .. .. — 40·00
128 6d. blue/*green* .. .. — £350
129 6d. blue/*blue* .. .. — 85·00
a. Opt. inverted .. ..

T **1** *and* **2** (3*d.*) *optd. with T* **7** *in black.*

(*a*) *Imperf.*

130 1d. red/*orange* .. .. 15·00 12·00
131 3d. mauve/*buff* .. .. 15·00 11·00
a. Pin-perf. about 9 .. — £250
132 6d. blue/*blue* .. .. 35·00 9·00
a. Tête-bêche (pair) .. £3500
b. Opt. inverted .. .. — £110

(*b*) *Fine roulette*, 15½ *to* 16.

133 1d. red/*orange* .. .. — 45·00
134 3d. mauve/*buff* .. .. 50·00 38·00
a. Imperf. between (pair)
135 6d. blue/*blue* .. .. — 38·00
a. Opt. inverted .. .. — £350

(*c*) *Wide roulette*, 6½.

136 1d. red/*orange* .. .. — 85·00
137 3d. mauve/*buff* .. .. — £110
138 6d. blue/*blue* .. .. — £110
a. Opt. inverted .. ..

1879 (18 April). *T* **2**.

(*a*) *Imperf.* (*b*) *Fine roulette.* (*c*) *Wide roulette.*

I. *Optd. with T* **6** *in black.*

139 3d. mauve/*green* (*a*) .. .. 50·00 11·00
a. Pin-perf. .. .. ..
b. Opt. inverted .. .. — £700
c. Opt. double .. ..
140 3d. mauve/*green* (*b*) .. .. £225 60·00
141 3d. mauve/*green* (*c*) .. .. — £100

II. *Optd. with T* **7** *in black.*

142 3d. mauve/*green* (*a*) .. .. 32·00 8·00
a. Opt. inverted .. .. — £700
b. Opt. omitted .. .. — £1000
c. Printed both sides .. ..
143 3d. mauve/*green* (*b*) .. .. £200 65·00
144 3d. mauve/*green* (*c*) .. .. — £110

V. R. V. R.

Transvaal (8) Transvaal (8*a*)

1879 (Aug.–Sept.). *T* **1** *and* **2** (3*d.*) *optd. with T* **8** *in black.*

(*a*) *Imperf.*

145 1d. red/*yellow* .. .. 15·00 14·00
a. Small "T", Type 8*a* .. 80·00 65·00
b. Red/orange .. .. 14·00 10·00
ba. Small "T", Type 8*a* .. 70·00 65·00
146 3d. mauve/*green* .. .. £100 8·00
a. Small "T", Type 8*a* .. £110 65·00
147 3d. mauve/*blue* .. .. 15·00 10·00
a. Small "T", Type 8*a* .. 75·00 32·00

(*b*) *Fine roulette*, 15½ *to* 16.

148 1d. red/*yellow* .. .. — 85·00
a. Small "T", Type 8*a* .. £300 £200
b. Red/orange .. .. — £140
ba. Small "T", Type 8*a* ..
149 3d. mauve/*green* £275 £100
a. Small "T", Type 8*a* ..
150 3d. mauve/*blue* .. .. — 65·00
a. Small "T", Type 8*a* .. — £250

(*c*) *Wide roulette*, 6½.

151 1d. red/*yellow* .. .. — £300
a. Small "T", Type 8*a* ..
b. Red/orange .. ..
152 3d. mauve/*green* .. ..
a. Small "T", Type 8*a* ..
153 3d. mauve/*blue* .. ..

(*d*) *Pin-perf.*, *about* 17.

154 1d. red/*yellow* .. .. — £200
a. Small "T", Type 8*a* ..
155 3d. mauve/*blue* .. ..

9

(Recess. B.W.)

1878 (26 Aug.)–**80**. *P* 14, 14½.

156 **9** ½d. vermilion (1880) .. 8·00 12·00
157 ,, 1d. pale red-brown .. .. 2·50 1·75
a. Brown-red .. .. 1·75 1·25
158 ,, 3d. dull rose .. .. 2·50 1·25
a. Claret .. .. 4·00 2·50
159 ,, 4d. sage-green .. .. 5·00 2·75
160 ,, 6d. olive-black .. .. 2·50 1·75
a. Black-brown .. .. 3·25 1·25
161 ,, 1s. green .. .. 25·00 15·00
162 ,, 2s. blue .. .. 30·00 24·00

The above prices are for specimens perforated on all four sides. Stamps from margins of sheets, with perforations absent on one or two sides, can be supplied for about 30% less.

1 Penny

(10)

1 Penny
(11)

1 Penny
(12)

1 Penny
(13)

1 Penny
(14)

1 PENNY
(15)

1 Penny
(16)

1879 (22 April). *No.* 160a *surch. with T* **10** *to* **16**

A. *In black.* B. *In red.*

			A.		B.	
163 **10**	1d. on 6d.	..	55·00	22·00	£140	65·00
164 **11**	1d. on 6d.	..	25·00	16·00	50·00	45·00
165 **12**	1d. on 6d.	..	55·00	22·00	£130	65·00
166 **13**	1d. on 6d.	..	28·00	22·00	65·00	45·00
167 **14**	1d. on 6d.	..	£140	50·00	—	—
168 **15**	1d. on 6d.	..	16·00	11·00	32·00	25·00
169 **16**	1d. on 6d.	..	60·00	30·00	£140	70·00

III. SECOND REPUBLIC.

Een Penny
(17)

1882. *No.* 159 *surch. with T* **17.**

170 **9** 1d. on 4d. sage-green	..	1·75	1·10
a. Surch. inverted ..	..	£125	

1883. *Re-issue of T* **1** *and* **2.** *P* 12.

171 **1** 1d. grey (to black) ..	..	70	40
172 **2** 3d. grey-blk. (to blk.)/*rose*		3·50	1·40
a. Bisected (1d.) (on cover) ..		—	£175
173 ,, 3d. pale red ..	..	1·75	60
a. Bisected (1d.) (on cover) ..			
b. Chestnut ..	..	8·00	1·25
c. Vermilion ..	..	7·00	1·40
174 **1** 1s. green (to deep) ..	..	4·00	90
a. Bisected (6d.) (on cover) ..		—	90·00
b. Tête-bêche (pair) ..	..	90·00	25·00

Reprints are known of Nos. 172, 173, 173*b* and 173*c*. The paper of the first is *bright rose* in place of *dull rose*, and the impression is brownish black in place of grey-black to deep black. The reprints on white paper have the paper thinner than the originals, and the gum yellowish instead of white. The colour is a dull deep orange-red.

18

(Des. J. Vurtheim. Typo. Enschedé & Son, Haarlem.)

REPRINTS. Reprints of the general issues 1885–93, 1894–95, 1895–96 and 1896–97 exist in large quantities. They cannot readily be distinguished from genuine originals except by comparison with used stamps, but the following general characteristics may be noted. The reprints are all perf. 12½, large holes; the paper is whiter than that usually employed for the originals and their colours lack the lustre of those of the genuine stamps.

Forged surcharges have been made on these reprints.

1885 (13 Mar.)–**1893.** *P* 12½.

175 **18** ½d. grey ..	..	5	5
a. Perf. 13½ ..	..	1·10	35
b. Perf. 12½ × 12 ..	..	55	5
ba. Var. Perf. 11½ × 12	..		
176 ,, 1d. carmine ..	..	5	5
a. Perf. 12½ × 12 ..	..	20	5
aa. Var. Perf. 11½ × 12	..	2·25	1·40
b. Rose ..	..	5	5
ba. Perf. 12½ × 12 ..	..	5	5
177 **18** 2d. brn.-pur. (*p.* 12½ × 12)		12	5
178 ,, 2d. olive-bistre (1887)	..	12	5
a. Perf. 12½ × 12 ..	..	1·00	5
179 ,, 2½d. mauve (to bright) ('93)		35	5
180 ,, 3d. mauve (to bright)	..	35	15
a. Perf. 12½ × 12 ..	..	2·00	35
aa. Var. Perf. 11½ × 12	..	7·00	5·00
181 ,, 4d. bronze-green ..	..	60	15
a. Perf. 13½ ..	..	1·25	35
b. Perf. 12½ × 12 ..	..	4·00	35
ba. Var. Perf. 11½ × 12	..	55·00	22·00
182 ,, 6d. pale dull blue	..	35	5
a. Perf. 13½ ..	..	1·40	35
b. Perf. 12½ × 12 ..	..	2·00	10
ba. Var. Perf. 11½ × 12	..		
183 ,, 1s. yellow-green	..	90	20
a. Perf. 13½ ..	..	4·00	2·00
b. Perf. 12½ × 12 ..	..	2·25	10
184 ,, 2s. 6d. orge.-buff (to buff)		1·40	70
a. Perf. 12½ × 12 ..	..	2·50	1·75
185 ,, 5s. slate ..	..	2·00	90
a. Perf. 12½ × 12 ..	..	2·50	80
186 ,, 10s. fawn ..	..	7·00	90
187 ,, £5 deep green (1892)*	..	£1000	85·00

The variety, perf. 11½ × 12 in the 1d., 3d., 4d. and 6d. is from sheets perforated with the 12½ × 12 machine. (See note after Netherlands No. 109.)

*Most examples of No. 187 on the market are either forgeries or reprints.

A horizontal strip of four on cover is known of No. 175 imperf. at top and bottom. It is not known if there are any vertical pairs imperf. horizontally.

HALVE PENNY
(19)

HALVE PENNY
(20)

1885. *Surch. with T* **19** *or* **20** (½*d. on* 3*d. mauve*).

A. *Reading down.* B. *Reading up.*

		A.		B.	
188 **2** ½d. on 3d. (No. 173)		55	55	55	55
189 **18** ½d. on 3d. (No. 180a)		55	55	†	
a. "PRNNY"		12·00	—	†	
b. 2nd "N" inverted		25·00	—	†	
c. Var. Perf. 11½ × 12		2·00	—	†	
190 **1** ½d. on 1s. (No. 174)		2·00	2·25	2·00	2·25
a. Tête-bêche (pair) ..		†		—	55·00

No. 188 was issued on May 22, No. 189 on Sept. 28 and No. 190 in August.

In sheets of Nos. 188 and 190 one half-sheet had the surch. reading upwards and the other half-sheet downwards.

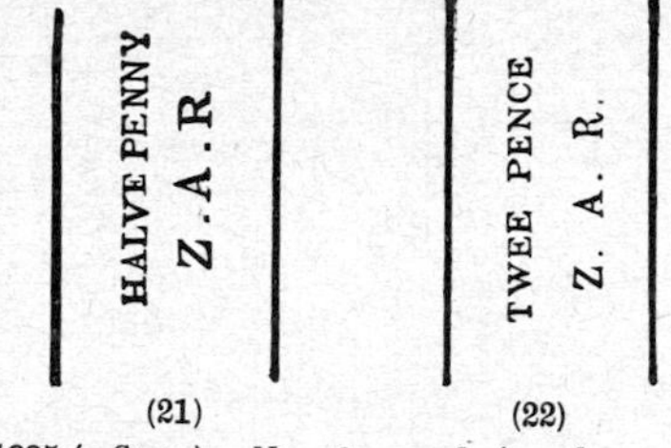

(21) (22)

1885 (1 Sept.). *No.* 160a *surch. in red.*

191 **21** ½d. on 6d. black-brown	..	3·50	4·00
192 **22** 2d. on 6d. black-brown	..	65	65

2d
(23)

2d
(24)

1887 (15 Jan.). *T* **18** *surch.* *P* 12½ × 12.

193 **23** 2d. on 3d. mauve	..	1·00	1·00
a. Surch. double ..	..	—	70·00
b. Var. Perf. 11½ × 12	..	1·75	1·75
194 **24** 2d. on 3d. mauve	..	30	30
a. Surch. double ..	..	—	80·00
b. Var. Perf. 11½ × 12	..	1·25	1·25

Halve Penny
(25)

1 Penny
(26)

2½ Pence
(27)

2½ Pence
(28)

Two varieties of surcharge:
A. Vertical distance between bars 12½ mm.
B. Distance 13½ mm.

1893. *T* **18** *surch.* *P* 12½.

(*a*) *In red.*

195 **25** ½d. on 2d. olive-bistre (A) (27 May)	..	30	35
a. Surch. inverted (A)	..	80	80
b. Variety B ..	..	60	60
ba. Variety B, inverted	..	2·00	

(*b*) *In black.*

196 **25** ½d. on 2d. olive-bistre (A) (2 July)	..	30	30
a. Surch. inverted (A)	..	1·75	1·75
b. Extra surch. on back inverted (A) ..	..	55·00	
c. Variety B ..	..	45	45
ca. Variety B, inverted	..	—	5·00
cb. Extra surch. on back inverted (B) ..	..		
197 **26** 1d. on 6d. bl. (A) (26 Jan.)		5	5
a. Surch. double (A)	..	20·00	18·00
b. Surch. inverted (A)	..	60	70
c. Variety B ..	..	20	20
ca. Variety B inverted	..	1·75	1·75
cb. Variety B double	..	—	25·00
d. Pair, with and without sur.		40·00	
198 **27** 2½d. on 1s. grn. (A) (2 Jan.)		25	30
a. "2/½" for "2½"	..	9·00	9·00
b. Surch. inverted (A)	..	70	80
ba. Surch inverted and "2/½" for "2½" ..	..	60·00	
c. Extra surch. on back inverted (A) ..	..		
d. Variety B ..	..	50	60
da. Variety B, inverted	..	2·50	3·00
199 **28** 2½d. on 1s. green (A) (24 June)	..	65	60
a. Surch. double (A)	..	14·00	14·00
b. Surch. inverted (A)	..	2·50	2·50
c. Variety B ..	..	2·25	2·25
ca. Variety B, double	..		
cb. Variety B, inverted	..		

29

30

1894–95. *Waggon with shafts.* *P* 12½.

200 **29** ½d. grey ..	..	5	5
201 ,, 1d. carmine ..	..	5	5
202 ,, 2d. olive-bistre ..	..	5	5
203 ,, 6d. pale dull blue	..	30	25
204 ,, 1s. yellow-green	..	1·50	1·75

For note *re* reprints, see below *T* **18.**

1895–96. *Waggon with pole.* *P* 12½.

205 **30** ½d. pearl-grey ..	..	5	5
a. Lilac-grey ..	..	5	5
206 ,, 1d. rose-red ..	..	5	5
207 ,, 2d. olive-bistre ..	..	5	5
208 ,, 3d. mauve ..	..	10	5
209 ,, 4d. olive-black ..	..	40	35
210 ,, 6d. pale dull blue	..	25	8
211 ,, 1s. yellow-green	..	45	40
212 ,, 5s. slate ..	..	1·75	2·00
212a ,, 10s. pale chestnut	..	2·00	85

For note *re* reprints, see below *T* **18.**

Halve Penny

(31)

1d. **1d.**

(32—Round dot.) (32*a*—Square dot.)

1895 (JULY-AUG.). *Nos.* 211 *and* 179 *surch.*

213 **31** ½d. on 1s. green (R.) .. 5 5
a. Surch. spaced 35 40
b. "Pennij" for "Penny" .. 18·00
c. Surch. inverted .. .. 2·00 1·75
d. Surch. double .. .. 20·00
214 **32** 1d. on 2½d. brt. mauve (G.) 5 5
a. Surch. inverted .. .. 7·00 5·00
b. Surch. double .. ..
c. Surch. on back only ..
d. Type 32*a* 65 65
da. Type 32*a* inverted .. 20·00

The normal surcharge on No. 213 is spaced 3 mm. between "Penny" and the bars; on No. 213a 4 mm. approx. Copies may be found in which one or both of the bars have failed to print.

33

1895 (JULY). *Fiscal stamp optd.* "POSTZEGEL". *P* 11½.

215 **33** 6d. bright rose (G.) .. 25 35
a. Imperf. between (pair) ..

1896–97. *P* 12½.

216 **30** ½d. green 5 5
217 „ 1d. rose-red and green .. 5 5
218 „ 2d. brown and green .. 5 5
219 „ 2½d. dull blue and green 5 5
220 „ 3d. purple and green .. 5 5
221 „ 4d. sage-green and green 5 5
222 „ 6d. lilac and green .. 5 5
223 „ 1s. ochre and green 12 5
224 „ 2s. 6d. dull violet & green 30 30

For note *re* reprints, see below T **18**.

34

(Litho. Printing Press and Publishing Co., Pretoria.)

1895 (6 SEPT.). *Introduction of Penny Postage. P* 11.

225 **34** 1d. red (pale to deep) .. 20 10
a. Imperf. between (pair) .. 7·00 5·00

IV. SECOND BRITISH OCCUPATION.

V. R. I.

(35)

FORGERIES. The forgeries of the "V.R.I." and "E.R.I." overprints most often met with can be recognised by the fact that the type used is perfect and the three stops are always in alignment with the bottom of the letters. In the genuine overprints, which were made from old type, it is impossible to find all three letters perfect and all three stops perfect and in exact alignment with the bottom of the letters.

1900 (18 JUNE). *Optd. with T* **35**.

226 **30** ½d. green 5 5
f. "V.I.R." £180
227 „ 1d. rose-red and green .. 5 5
f. No stop after "R" and "I" 22·00 22·00
228 „ 2d. brown and green .. 5 5
f. "V.I.R." £180
229 „ 2½d. dull blue and green .. 5 5
230 „ 3d. purple and green .. 5 5
231 „ 4d. sage-green and green 25 12
f. "V.I.R." £180
232 „ 6d. lilac and green .. 30 12
233 „ 1s. ochre and green .. 35 25
234 „ 2s. 6d. dull violet & grn. 75 60
235 „ 5s. slate .. .. 1·25 1·25
236 „ 10s. pale chestnut .. 2·50 2·50
237 **18** £5 green* .. ..

The error "V.I.R." occurred on stamp No. 34 in the first batch of stamps to be overprinted—a few sheets of the ½d., 2d. and 4d. The error was then corrected and stamps showing it are very rare.

*Most examples of No. 237 on the market are forgeries.

Varieties.

A. No stop after "V". B. No stop after "R". C. No stop after "I". D. Overprint inverted. E. Overprint double.

		A	B	C	D	E
226	½d. ..	4·00	2·50	1·50	1·50	—
227	1d. ..	4·00	2·50	90	1·50	15·00
228	2d. ..	5·50	†	7·00	2·50	—
229	2½d. ..	5·00	—	3·75	1·40	†
230	3d. ..	6·00	9·50	6·00	15·00	†
231	4d. ..	9·50	12·00	5·00	5·00	†
232	6d. ..	3·75	6·00	4·00	4·00	†
233	1s. ..	3·75	—	6·00	5·00	15·00
234	2s. 6d. ..	5·00	14·00	†	†	†
235	5s. ..	—	†	†	†	†
236	10s. ..	14·00	†	14·00	†	†
237	£5 ..	—	†	†	†	†

The above prices are for unused. Used are worth the same, or rather more in some cases.

E. R. I. (36) **E. R. I. Half Penny** (37)

FORGERIES. See note below T **35**.

1901–2. *Optd. with T* **36**.

238 **30** ½d. green (7.01) 5 5
239 „ 1d. rose-red & grn. (20.3.01) 5 5
a. "E" of opt. omitted .. 22·00
240 „ 3d. purple & green (6.02) 35 35
241 „ 4d. sage-grn. & grn. (6.02) 35 40
242 „ 2s. 6d. dull violet & green (10.02) .. .. 2·00 2·25

1901 (JULY). *Surch. with T* **37**.

243 **30** ½d. on 2d. brown & green 5 5
a. No stop after "E" .. 20·00

38 (POSTAGE REVENUE). **39** (POSTAGE POSTAGE).

(Typo. D.L.R.)

1902 (1 APRIL)–**1903.** *Wmk. Crown CA. P* 14.

244 **38** ½d. black & bluish green 5 5
245 „ 1d. black and carmine .. 5 5
246 „ 2d. black and purple .. 20 5
247 „ 2½d. black and blue .. 35 30
248 „ 3d. black & sage-grn. ('03) 40 12
249 „ 4d. black and brown ('03) 60 30
250 „ 6d. black & orange-brown 40 20
251 „ 1s. black and sage-green 1·40 75
252 **38** 2s. black and brown .. 5·00 4·00
253 **39** 2s. 6d. magenta & black 2·00 1·75
254 „ 5s. black & purple/*yellow* 2·75 3·00
255 „ 10s. black and purple/*red* 7·00 5·50
244/255 .. .. *Set of* 12 17·00 14·00
244/55 Optd. "Specimen" *Set of* 12 95·00

The colour of the "black" centres varies from brownish grey or grey to black.

1903. *Wmk. Crown CA. P* 14.

256 **39** 1s. grey-black & red-brn. 80 50
257 „ 2s. grey-black and yellow 2·50 2·00
258 „ £1 green and violet .. 22·00 18·00
259 „ £5 orange-brown & violet £600 £225
256/9 Optd. "Specimen" *Set of* 4 £160

1904–9. *Wmk. Mult. Crown CA. P* 14.

260 **38** ½d. blk. & bluish grn., O 40 5
261 „ 1d. black & carmine, O 35 5
262 „ 2d. blk. & purple, C ('06) 45 5
263 „ 2½d. black & blue, C O ('05) 45 20
264 „ 3d. black and sage-green, C ('06) 35 5
265 „ 4d. black & brown, C ('06) 40 5
266 „ 6d. black & orge., O ('05) 50 5
a. *Black and brown-orange*, C 45 5
267 **39** 1s. blk. and red-brn., O ('05) 50 5
268 „ 2s. blk. & yellow, O ('06) 1·75 70
269 „ 2s. 6d. mag. & blk., O ('09) 2·50 70
270 „ 5s. blk. & pur./*yellow*, O 4·00 80
271 „ 10s. blk. & pur./*red*, O ('07) 9·00 1·40
272 „ £1 grn. & vio., OC ('08) 20·00 2·50
260/272 .. .. *Set of* 13 35·00 5·00

There is considerable variation in the "black" centres as in the previous issue.

1905–9. *Wmk. Mult. Crown CA. P* 14.

273 **38** ½d. yellow-green .. 5 5
a. *Deep green* (1908) .. 5 5
274 „ 1d. scarlet 5 5
a. Error. Wmk. Cabled Anchor, T 13 of Cape of Good Hope — £450
275 „ 2d. purple (1909) .. 35 5
276 „ 2½d. bright blue (1909) .. 1·75 80
273/6 Optd. "Specimen" *Set of* 4 35·00

A 2d. grey, T **38**, was prepared for use but not issued. It exists overprinted "Specimen", *price* £120.

The monocoloured ½d. and 1d. are printed from new combined plates. These show a slight alteration in that the frame does not touch the crown.

Many of the King's Head stamps are found overprinted or perforated "C.S.A.R.", for use by the Central South African Railways.

FISCALS WITH POSTAL CANCELLATIONS.

Various fiscal stamps are found apparently postally used, but these were used on telegrams not on postal matter.

POSTAGE DUE STAMPS.

D 1

(Typo. D.L.R.)

1907. *Wmk. Mult. Crown CA. P* 14.

D1 **D 1** ½d. black and blue-green 30 30
D2 „ 1d. black and scarlet .. 30 12
D3 „ 2d. brown-orange .. 30 20
D4 „ 3d. black and blue .. 1·00 40
D5 „ 5d. black and violet .. 80 85
D6 „ 6d. black and red-brown.. 1·50 85
D7 „ 1s. scarlet and black 1·50 1·10

Transvaal now uses the stamps of SOUTH AFRICA.

PIETERSBURG.

Authorised by President Kruger and in use until 9th April 1901, when British troops entered the town.

PRICES. Genuinely used copies are very rare. Stamps cancelled by favour exist and are worth the same as the unused prices quoted.

The issued stamps are initialled by the Controller but three sheets of the ½d. were stuck together and this resulted in some being issued without initials. Other stamps without initials must be regarded as proofs and are worth about £4 each.

(i)

(ii)

(iii)

(Type-set. Office of *De Zoutpansberg Wachter*, Pietersburg.)

Printed in sheets of 24 (4 rows of 6).
(i) Large " P " in " POSTZEGEL " and large date (Rows 1 and 2).
(ii) Large " P " in " POSTZEGEL " and small date (Row 3).
(iii) Small " P " in " POSTZEGEL " and small date (Row 4).

1901 (20 MAR., 1d.; 3 APR., others). *T* (i) *to* (iii).

A. *Imperf.*

(*a*) *Controller's initials in black.*

1 ½d. black/*green* (i) .. .. 9·00
a. No stop after right " AFR " (No. 2) 42·00
b. " ⅓ " at top left, no bar over lower right " ½ " (No. 3) .. .. 42·00
c. No stop after date (No. 6) ..
d. " BEP " at left, no stop after date (No. 11) .. .. .. 42·00
e. Controller's initials omitted .. 50·00

2 ½d. black/*green* (ii) .. .. 27·00
a. " AFB " at left (No. 15) .. 42·00
b. " POSTZEGEI " (No. 16) .. 42·00
c. No bar over lower right " ½ " (No. 18) .. .. 42·00
d. Controller's initials omitted .. 50·00

3 ½d. black/*green* (iii) .. .. 27·00
a. No stop after right " AFR " (No. 19) .. .. 42·00
b. No stop after left " Z ", no bar under top right " ½ " (No. 22) .. 42·00
c. " POSTZECEL, AER " at left (No. 23) .. .. 42·00
d. Controller's initials omitted .. 50·00

4 1d. black/*red* (i) .. .. 2·10
a. Inverted " 1 " at lower left, first " 1 " of date dropped (No. 2) .. 27·00
b. No bar under top left " 1 " (No. 3) 27·00
c. No bar over lower right " 1 " (No. 4) .. .. 27·00
d. " POSTZFGEL " (No. 5) .. 27·00
e. " AFB " at right (No. 6) .. 27·00
f. " REB " at left (No. 7) .. 27·00
g. " BEP " at left (No. 8) .. .. 27·00
h. " POSTZEOEL " (No. 9) .. 27·00
i. " AER " at right (No. 10) .. 27·00
j. No stop after date (No. 11) .. 27·00
k. No stop after " PENNY " (No. 12) 27·00
l. First " 1 " in date dropped (No. 27·00

5 1d. black/*red* (ii) .. .. 3·75
a. Right spray inverted (No. 14) .. 27·00
b. No bar over lower left " 1 " (No. 15) .. .. 27·00
c. No stop after left " Z " (No. 16) .. 27·00
d. " POSTZEGFL ", no stop after right " AFR " (No. 18) .. .. 27·00
e. No stop after right " AFR " (No. 18) .. .. 27·00

6 1d. black/*red* (iii) .. .. 4·50
a. No stop after right " AFR " (No. 19) .. .. 27·00
b. Left spray inverted (Nos. 20 and 24) .. .. 17·00
c. " POSTZEGEI " (No. 21) .. 27·00
d. No bar under top right " 1 " (No. 22) .. .. 27·00
e. Dropped " P " in "PENNY" (No. 23) .. .. 27·00

Nos. 4l, 5e and 6e come from the corrected printing.

7 2d. black/*orange* (i) .. .. 4·00
a. " 1 " at lower right (No. 1) .. 35·00
b. No stop after left " AFR " (No. 2) 60·00
c. No bar over lower right " 2 " (No. 3) 60·00
d. " PENNY " for " PENCE " (No. 3) .. .. 35·00
e. " POSTZFGEL " (No. 5) .. 35·00
f. " AFB " at right (No. 6) .. 35·00
g. " REB " at left (No. 7) .. 35·00
h. " AFB " at left (No. 8) .. .. 35·00
i. " POSTZEOEL " (No. 9) .. 35·00
j. " AER " at right (No. 10) .. 35·00
k. No stop after date (No. 11) .. 35·00
l. No stop after date, vertical line after " POSTZEGEL " (No. 12) 35·00
m. First " 1 " in date dropped (No. 2) 35·00
n. No stop after left " REP " (No. 7) 35·00

8 2d. black/*orange* (ii) .. .. 8·00
a. Right spray inverted (No. 14) .. 35·00
b. No bar over lower left " 2 " (No. 15) 35·00
c. Centre " 2 " inverted, no stop after left " Z " (No. 16) .. .. 35·00
d. " POSTZEGFL ", no stop after right " AFR " (No. 18) .. .. 35·00
e. No stop after left " Z " (No. 16) .. 35·00
f. No stop after right " AFR " (No. 18) .. .. 35·00

9 2d. black/*orange* (iii) .. .. 14·00
a. Centre " 2 " wider, no stop after right " AFR " (No. 19) .. .. 35·00
b. Centre " 2 " wider, left spray inverted (No. 20) .. .. 35·00
c. " POSTZEGEI " (No. 21) .. 35·00
d. No bar under top right " 2 " (No. 22) .. .. 35·00
e. " 1 " at lower left, " P " in " PENCE " dropped (No. 23) .. 35·00
f. Left spray inverted (No. 24) .. 35·00
g. Centre " 2 " wider (No. 20) .. 35·00
h. " P " in " PENCE " dropped (No. 23) .. .. 35·00

Nos. 7b/c come only from a small part of the first printing. Nos. 7m/n, 8e/f and 9g/h come from the corrected printing and No. 9a exists in both printings.

10 4d. black/*blue* (i) .. .. 3·50
a. No stop after left " AFR " (No. 2) 35·00
b. No bar over lower right " 4 " (No. 3) .. .. 35·00
c. " PENNY " for " PENCE " (No. 3) 60·00
d. " POSTZFGEL " (No. 5) .. 35·00
e. " AFB " at right (No. 6) .. 35·00
f. " REB " at left (No. 7) .. 35·00
g. " AFB " at left (No. 8) .. .. 35·00
h. " POSTZEOEL " (No. 9) .. 35·00
i. " AER " at right (No. 10) .. 35·00
j. No stop after date (No. 11) .. 35·00
k. Left inner frame too high (No. 7) 35·00

11 4d. black/*blue* (ii) .. .. 6·50
a. Right spray inverted (No. 14) .. 35·00
b. No bar over lower left " 4 " (No. 15) .. .. 60·00
c. No stop after left " Z " (No. 16) .. 35·00
d. " POSTZEGFL " (No. 18) .. 35·00

12 4d. black/*blue* (iii) .. .. 20·00
a. Centre " 4 " wider, no stop after right " AFR " (No. 19) .. .. 35·00
b. Centre " 4 " wider, left spray inverted (No. 20) .. .. 35·00
c. " POSTZEGEI " (No. 21) .. 35·00
d. No bar under top right " 4 " (No. 22) .. .. 35·00
e. "AER" at left, "P" in "PENCE" dropped (No. 23) .. .. 35·00
f. Left spray inverted (No. 24) .. 35·00
g. Centre " 4 " wider (Nos. 19 and 20) 25·00
h. " P " in " PENCE " dropped (No. 23) .. .. 35·00

Nos. 10c and 11b come only from a small part of the first printing. Nos. 10k and 12g/h come from the corrected printing.

13 6d. black/*green* (i) .. .. 6·50
a. No stop after left " AFR " (No. 2) 40·00
b. No bar over lower right "6" (No. 3) 50·00
c. " PENNY " for " PENCE " (No. 3) 60·00
d. " POSTZFGEL " (No. 5) .. 40·00
e. " AFB " at right (No. 6) .. 40·00
f. " REB " at left (No. 7) .. 40·00
g. " AFB " at left (No. 8) .. 40·00
h. " POSTZEOEL " (No. 9) .. 40·00
i. " AER " at right (No. 10) .. 40·00
j. No stop after date (No. 11) .. 40·00
k. Left inner frame too high, no stop after left " REP " (No. 7) .. 40·00

14 6d. black/*green* (ii) .. .. 9·00
a. Right spray inverted (No. 14) .. 40·00
b. Centre " 6 " inverted, no stop after left " Z " (No. 16) .. .. 60·00
c. No stop after left " Z " (No. 16) .. 50·00
d. " POSTZEGFL " (No. 18) .. 40·00

15 6d. black/*green* (iii) .. .. 25·00
a. Centre " 6 " wider, no stop after right " AFR " (No. 19) .. .. 40·00
b. Centre " 6 " wider, left spray inverted (No. 20) .. .. 40·00
c. " POSTZEGEI " (No. 21) .. 40·00
d. No bar under top right " 6 " (No. 22) .. .. 40·00
e. "AER" at left, "P" in "PENCE" dropped (No. 23) .. .. 40·00
f. Left spray inverted (No. 24) .. 40·00
g. Centre " 6 " wider (Nos. 19 and 20) 32·00
h. " P " in " PENCE " dropped (No. 23) .. ..

Nos. 13c and 14b come only from a small part of the first printing. Nos. 13k and 15g/h come from the corrected printing.

16 1s. black/*yellow* (i) .. .. 5·00
a. No stop after left " AFR " (No. 2) 32·00
b. No bar over lower right " 1 " (No. 3) .. .. 32·00
c. No stop after date (No. 11) .. 32·00

17 1s. black/*yellow* (ii) .. .. 8·50
a. " POSTZEGEI ", no stop after left " Z " (No. 16) .. .. 32·00

18 1s. black/*yellow* (iii) .. .. 15·00
a. No stop after right " AFR " (No. 19) .. .. 32·00
b. No bar under top right " 1 " (No. 22) .. .. 32·00
c. " AER " at left (No. 23) .. 32·00

(b) Controller's initials in red.

19 ½d. black/*green* (i) .. .. 9·00
a. No stop after right "AFR" (No. 4) 48·00
b. Left side of inner frame too high (No. 7) .. .. .. 48·00
c. Top left "½" inverted, no stop after right "AFR" (Nos. 1 and 4) 50·00
d. Top right "½" inverted (No. 2) .. 60·00
e. "½" at lower right (No. 3) .. 60·00
f. "POSTZFGEL" (No. 5) .. 60·00
g. Left spray inverted, "AFB" at right (No. 6) .. .. .. 60·00
h. "REB" at left, left side of inner frame too high (No. 7) .. .. 60·00
i. "BEP" at left (No. 8).. .. 60·00
j. "POSTZEOEL" (No. 9) .. 60·00
k. "AER" at right (No. 10) .. 60·00
l. No stop after date (No. 11)

20 ½d. black/*green* (ii) .. 22·00
a. Centre figures "½" level (No. 17) 40·00
b. No stop after right "AFR" (No. 18) .. .. .. 40·00
c. "½" at top left, "PE" of "PENNY" spaced (No. 13) .. 60·00
d. Right spray inverted (No. 14) .. 60·00
e. Top left "½" inverted (No. 15) .. 60·00

21 ½d. black/*green* (iii) .. 25·00
a. Hyphen between right "AFR" and "REP" (No. 24) .. .. 40·00
b. "½" at top right (No. 21) .. 60·00
c. Lower left "½" inverted (No 22) 60·00
d. "½" at top left (No. 23) .. 60·00

Nos. 19a/b, 20a/b and 21a come from the corrected printing and the remainder from a very small third printing.

B. *P* 11½.

(a) Controller's initials in red.

22 ½d. black/*green* (i) .. .. 3·50
a. No stop after right "AFR" (No. 4) .. .. 32·00
b. Left side of inner frame too high (No. 7) .. .. .. 32·00
c. Imperf. vert. (horiz. pair) .. 50·00

23 ½d. black/*green* (ii) .. .. 9·50
a. Centre figures "½" level (No. 17).. 32·00
b. No stop after right "AFR" (No. 18) .. .. .. 32·00
c. Imperf. vert. (horiz. pair) .. 60·00

24 ½d. black/*green* (iii) .. 7·50
a. Hyphen between right "AFR" and "REP" (No. 24) .. .. 32·00
b. Imperf. vert. (horiz. pair) .. 60·00

(b) Controller's initials in black.

25 1d. black/*red* (i) .. .. 1·25
a. Lower left "1" inverted, first "1" in date dropped (No. 2) .. 17·00
b. No bar under top left "1" (No. 3) 17·00
c. No bar over lower right "1" (No. 4) .. ..
d. "POSTZFGEL" (No. 5) .. 17·00
e. "AFB" at right (No. 6) .. 17·00
f. "REB" at left (No. 7) .. 17·00
g. "BEP" at left (No. 8) .. 17·00
h. "POSTZEOEL" (No. 9) .. 17·00
i. "AER" at left (No. 10) .. 17·00
j. No stop after date (No. 11) .. 17·00
k. No stop after "PENNY" (No. 12) 17·00
l. First "1" in date dropped (No. 2) 17·00
m. Imperf. vert. (horiz. pair) .. 32·00

26 1d. black/*red* (ii) .. .. 1·75
a. Right spray inverted (No. 14) .. 17·00
b. No bar over lower left "1" (No. 15) .. .. 17·00
c. No stop after left "Z" (No. 16) 17·00
d. "POSTZEGFL", no stop after right "AFR" (No. 18).. .. 17·00
e. No stop after right "AFR" (No. 18) .. .. 17·00
f. Imperf. vert. (horiz. pair) .. 45·00

27 1d. black/*red* (iii) .. .. 2·50
a. No stop after right "AFR" (No. 19) .. .. .. 17·00
b. Left spray inverted (Nos. 20 and 24) .. .. 10·00
c. "POSTZEGEI" (No. 21) .. 17·00
d. No bar under top right "1" (No. 22) .. .. 17·00
e. "P" in "PENNY" dropped (No. 23) .. .. 17·00
f. Imperf. vert. (horiz. pair) .. 45·00

Nos. 25l, 26e and 27e are from the corrected printing.

28 2d. black/*orange* (i) .. .. 3·00
a. First "1" in date dropped (No. 2) 25·00
b. No stop after left "REP" (No. 7) 25·00

29 2d. black/*orange* (ii) .. 5·00
a. No stop after right "AFR" (No. 18) .. .. 25·00

30 2d. black/*orange* (iii) .. .. 8·50
a. Centre "2" wider, no stop after right "AFR" (No. 19).. .. 25·00
b. Centre "2" wider (No. 20) .. 25·00
c. "P" in "PENCE" dropped (No. 23) .. .. 25·00

LOCAL ISSUES DURING THE WAR 1900-2

Stamps of the Transvaal Republic, unless otherwise stated, variously overprinted or surcharged.

LYDENBURG.

V.R.I.
3d.
(L 1)

1900 (Sept.). *No. 217 surch. with Type* L **1**, *others optd.* "V.R.I." *only.*

1 **30** ½d. green .. .. .. 25·00 22·00
2 ,, 1d. rose-red and green .. 22·00 20·00
3 ,, 2d. brown and green .. £180 £150
4 ,, 2½d. blue and green .. .. — £150
5 ,, 3d. on 1d. rose-red & green 22·00 20·00
6 ,, 3d. purple and green ..
7 ,, 4d. sage green and green .. £400
8 ,, 6d. lilac and green .. £350 £140
9 ,, 1s. ochre and green .. £600

Only one genuine copy of No. 6 (unused) is known.

Type **34** surcharged "V.R.I. 1d." is now considered by experts to be bogus.

RUSTENBURG.

1900 (23 June). *Handstamped* **V.R.** *in violet.*

1 **30** ½d. green .. .. 25·00 24·00
2 ,, 1d. rose-red and green .. 22·00 20·00
3 ,, 2d. brown and green .. 35·00 25·00
4 ,, 2½d. blue and green .. .. 25·00 24·00
5 ,, 3d. purple and green .. 32·00 25·00
6 ,, 6d. lilac and green .. .. 85·00 80·00
7 ,, 1s. ochre and green .. £160 £140
8 ,, 2s. 6d. dull violet & green.. — £800

SCHWEIZER RENECKE.

BESIEGED
(SR 1)

1900 (Aug.). *Handstamped with Type* SR **1** *in black, reading vert. up or down.*

(a) On Stamps of Transvaal.

1 **30** ½d. green .. .. .. † 65·00
2 ,, 1d. rose-red and green .. † 65·00
3 ,, 2d. brown and green .. † 80·00
4 ,, 6d. lilac and green .. .. † £140

(b) On stamps of Cape of Good Hope.

5 **17** ½d. green .. .. .. † £100
6 ,, 1d. carmine .. .. .. † £100

This was a siege issue, authorised by the commander of the British troops in the town shortly after 19th August and exhausted by the end of September 1900. All stamps were cancelled with the dated circular town postmark ("Schweizer Reneke, Z.A.R."), usually after having been stuck on paper before use. Unused, without the postmark, do not exist.

VOLKSRUST.

1902 (Mar.). *Optd.* "V.R.I.", *T* **35**. *P* 12.

1 **33** 1d. pale blue .. .. 20·00 16·00
2 ,, 6d. dull carmine .. .. 22·00 18·00
3 ,, 1s. olive-bistre .. .. 22·00 24·00
4 ,, 1s. 6d. brown .. .. 38·00 25·00
5 ,, 2s. 6d. dull purple .. 40·00 25·00

These are the normal Transvaal Revenue stamps of the period, authorised for postal use in Volksrust.

WOLMARANSSTAD.

Cancelled V-R-I. (L 3)   Cancelled V-R-I. (L 4)

1900 (June). *Optd. with Type* L **3**.

1 **30** ½d. green (B.) .. .. 45·00
a. Opt. inverted .. ..
2 ,, 1d. rose-red and green (B.) 40·00
3 ,, 2d. brown and green (B.)
4 ,, 2½d. blue and green (R.) £200
a. Opt. in blue .. ..
5 ,, 3d. purple and green (B.) £350
6 ,, 4d. sage-green & green (B.) £400
7 ,, 6d. lilac and green (B.) .. £400
8 ,, 1s. ochre and green (B.) ..

1900 (July). *Optd. with Type* L **4**.

9 **34** 1d. red (B.) .. .. .. 45·00 40·00

TRINIDAD.

I. CROWN COLONY.

1

2. Britannia.

1847 (24 Apr.). *Litho. Imperf.*
1 **1** (5 c.) blue £6000 £3000

The "Lady McLeod" stamps were issued in April, 1847, by David Bryce, owner of the s.s. *Lady McLeod*, and sold at five cents each for the prepayment of the carriage of letters by his vessel between Port of Spain and San Fernando.

Used examples are pen-cancelled or have a corner skimmed off.

(Recess. Perkins, Bacon & Co.)

1851 (14 Aug.)–**1856**. *No value expressed. Imperf. Blued paper.*
2 **2** (1d.) purple-brown (1851) .. 4·00 22·00
3 ,, (1d.) blue *to* deep blue (1851) 3·50 16·00
4 ,, (1d.) deep blue (1853)* .. 60·00 40·00
5 ,, (1d.) grey (1851) .. .. 15·00 18·00
6 ,, (1d.) brownish grey (1853) .. 12·00 20·00
7 ,, (1d.) brownish red (1853) .. £110 25·00
8 ,, (1d.) brick-red (1856) .. .. 45·00 25·00

*No. 4 shows the paper deeply and evenly blued, especially on the back. It has more the appearance of having been printed on blue paper rather than on white paper that has become blued.

1854–57. *Imperf. White paper.*
9 **2** (1d.) deep purple (1854) .. 7·00 20·00
10 ,, (1d.) dark grey (1854) .. 10·00 28·00
11 ,, (1d.) blue (? date) .. ..
12 ,, (1d.) rose-red (1857) .. .. £450 25·00

PRICES. Prices quoted for the unused of most of the above issues and Nos. 25 and 29 are for "remainders" with original gum, found in London. Old colours that have been out to Trinidad are of much greater value.

1852–60. THE LITHOGRAPHS.

3.

Britannia. 4.

The following provisional issues were lithographed in the Colony (from die engraved by Charles Petit), and brought into use to meet shortages of the Perkins Bacon stamps during the following periods:

(1) *Sept. '52–May '53*; (2) *March '55–June '55*; (3) *Dec. '56–Jan. '57*; (4) *Oct. '58–Jan. '59*; (5) *March '60–June '60*.

No value expressed. Imperf.

A. *First Issue* (Sept. **1852**). *Yellowish paper. Fine impression; lines of background clear and distinct.*
13 **3** (1d.) blue .. .. .. — £1000

As last, but on bluish cartridge paper (Feb. **1853**)
14 **3** (1d.) blue .. .. .. — £1100

B. *Second issue* (March **1855**.). *Thinner paper. Impression less distinct than before.*
15 **3** (1d.) pale blue *to* greenish blue — £500

C. *Third issue* (December **1856**). *Background often of solid colour, but with clear lines in places.*
16 **3** (1d.) brt blue *to* deep blue .. — £550

D. *Fourth issue* (October **1858**). *Impression less distinct, and rarely showing more than traces of background lines.*
17 **3** (1d.) very deep greenish blue — £300
18 ,, (1d.) slate-blue .. .. — £300

E. *Fifth issue* (March **1860**). *Impression shows no (or hardly any) background lines.*
19 **3** (1d.) grey *to* bluish grey .. — £200
20 ,, (1d.) red (*shades*) .. .. 7·00 £175

In the worn impression of the fourth and fifth issues, the impression varies according to the position on the stone. Generally speaking, stamps of the fifth issue have a flatter appearance and cancellations are often less well defined. The paper of both these issues is thin or very thin. In all issues except 1853 (Feb.) the gum tends to give the paper a toned appearance.

Stamps in the slate-blue shade (No. 18) also occur in the Fifth Issue, but are not readily distinguishable.

(Recess. Perkins, Bacon.)

1859 (9 May). *Imperf.*
25 **4** 4d. grey-lilac .. .. 28·00 £100
28 ,, 6d. deep green .. .. — £200
29 ,, 1s. indigo .. .. .. 32·00 £110
30 ,, 1s. purple-slate .. ..

No. 30 may be of unissued status.

1859 (Sept.). (*a*) *Pin perf.* 12½.
31 **2** (1d.) rose-red .. .. .. £150 15·00
32 ,, (1d.) carmine-lake .. .. £150 15·00
33 **4** 4d. dull lilac .. .. .. — £250
34 ,, 4d. dull purple .. .. — £250
35 ,, 6d. yellow-green .. .. £700 70·00
36 ,, 6d. deep green .. .. £700 65·00
37 ,, 1s. purple-slate £1200 £350

(*b*) *Pin-perf.* 13½–14.
38 **2** (1d.) rose-red .. .. .. 35·00 9·00
39 ,, (1d.) carmine-lake .. .. 55·00 8·00
40 **4** 4d. dull lilac .. .. .. £250 32·00
40*a* ,, 4d. brownish purple .. 28·00 42·00
41 ,, 4d. dull purple .. .. 85·00 42·00
42 ,, 6d. yellow-green .. .. £110 32·00
43 ,, 6d. deep green .. .. £100 28·00
43*a* ,, 6d. bright yellow-green .. 30·00 40·00
b. Imperf. between (vert. pair) £1200
44 ,, 1s. purple-slate .. .. — £200

(*c*) *Compound pin-perf.* 13½–14 × 12½.
45 **2** (1d.) carmine-lake .. ..

PRICES. The Pin-perf. stamps are very scarce with perforations on all sides and the prices quoted above are for good average specimens.

The note after No. 12 also applies to Nos. 38, 40*a*, 43*a*, 46, 47 and 50.

1860 (Aug.). *Clean-cut perf.* 14–16½.
46 **2** (1d.) rose-red .. .. .. 32·00 12·00
b. Imperf. between (vert. pair) £250
47 **4** 4d. brownish lilac .. .. 40·00 24·00
48 ,, 4d. lilac .. .. .. — 85·00
49 ,, 6d. bright yellow-green .. 55·00 40·00
50 ,, 6d. deep green .. .. 75·00 60·00

1861 (June). *Rough perf.* 14–16½.
52 **2** (1d.) rose-red .. .. .. 25·00 8·00
53 ,, (1d.) rose .. .. .. 25·00 7·50
54 **4** 4d. brownish lilac .. .. 60·00 12·00
55 ,, 4d. lilac .. .. .. £120 12·00
a. Imperf. .. .. ..
56 ,, 6d. yellow-green .. .. 60·00 22·00
57 ,, 6d. deep green .. .. £120 16·00
58 ,, 1s. indigo .. .. .. £225 55·00
59 ,, 1s. deep bluish purple .. £300 95·00

(Recess. De La Rue.)

1862–63. *Thick paper.* (*a*) *P* 11½, 12.
60 **2** (1d.) crimson-lake .. .. 25·00 7·00
61 **4** 4d. deep purple .. .. 25·00 14·00
62 ,, 6d. deep green .. .. £180 14·00
63 ,, 1s. bluish slate .. .. £225 38·00

(*b*) *P* 11½, 12, *compound with* 11.
63*a* **2** (1d.) crimson-lake .. .. — £125
63*b* **4** 6d. deep green .. .. — £1800

(*c*) *P* 13 (1863).
64 **2** (1d.) lake .. .. .. 10·00 9·00
65 **4** 6d. emerald-green .. .. £100 20·00
67 ,, 1s. bright mauve £900 £100

(*d*) *P* 12½ (1863).
68 **2** (1d.) lake .. .. .. 6·00 6·50

1863–75. *Wmk. Crown CC. P* 12½.
69 **2** (1d.) lake .. .. .. 7·50 2·50
a. Wmk. sideways .. .. 25·00 4·25
70 ,, (1d.) rose .. .. .. 7·00 1·25
a. Imperf. (pair) .. ..
71 ,, (1d.) scarlet .. .. .. 6·50 1·00
72 ,, (1d.) carmine .. .. .. 7·50 1·10
73 **4** 4d. bright violet .. .. 22·00 4·25
74 ,, 4d. pale mauve .. .. 50·00 4·50
75 ,, 4d. dull lilac .. .. 9·00 5·00
77 ,, 6d. emerald-green .. .. 12·00 6·00
78 ,, 6d. deep green .. .. 85·00 5·50
80 ,, 6d. yellow-green .. .. 10·00 3·00
81 ,, 6d. apple-green .. .. 9·00 3·25
82 ,, 6d. blue-green .. .. 14·00 3·00
83 ,, 1s. bright deep mauve .. 50·00 4·00
84 ,, 1s. lilac-rose .. .. 28·00 3·50
85 ,, 1s. mauve (aniline) .. 22·00 4·00

The 1s. in a purple-slate shade is a colour changeling.

5

(Typo. De La Rue.)

1869. *Wmk. Crown CC. P* 12½.
87 **5** 5s. rose-lake .. .. .. 20·00 18·00

1872. *Colours changed. Wmk. Crown CC. P* 12½.
88 **4** 4d. grey .. .. .. 16·00 2·50
89 ,, 4d. bluish grey .. .. 16·00 2·75
90 ,, 1s. chrome-yellow .. .. 28·00 1·75

1876. *Wmk. Crown CC.* (*a*) *P* 14.
91 **2** (1d.) lake .. .. .. 1·75 55
a. Bisected (½d.) (on cover) .. † £100
92 ,, (1d.) rose-carmine .. .. 2·25 75
93 ,, (1d.) scarlet .. .. 10·00 75
94 **4** 4d. bluish grey .. .. 11·00 1·40
95 ,, 6d. bright yellow-green .. 11·00 1·25
96 ,, 6d. deep yellow-green .. 12·00 1·10
97 ,, 1s. chrome-yellow .. .. 12·00 3·25

(*b*) *P* 14 × 12½.
97*a* **4** 6d. yellow-green .. .. — £1800

HALFPENNY (6) **ONE PENNY** (7)

1879–82. *Surch. with T* **6** *or* **7**. *P* 14.
(*a*) *Wmk. Crown CC.* (June 1879.)
98 **2** ½d. lilac .. .. .. 3·50 4·00
99 ,, ½d. mauve .. .. .. 4·00 4·00
a. Wmk. sideways .. .. 7·00 8·00

(*b*) *Wmk. Crown CA.* (1882.)
100 **2** ½d. lilac .. .. .. £100 16·00
101 ,, 1d. rosy carmine .. .. 5·00 65
a. Bisected (½d.) (on cover) .. † 90·00

1882. *Wmk. Crown CA. P* 14.
102 **4** 4d. bluish grey .. .. 22·00 3·50

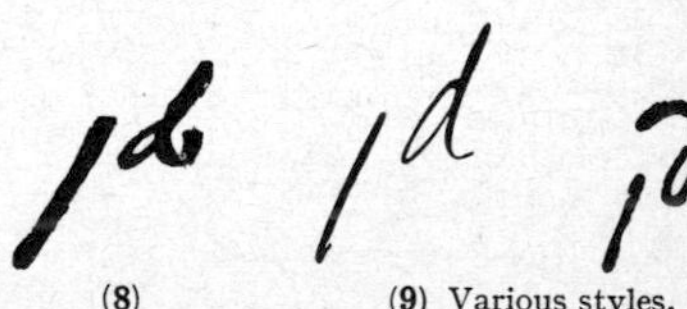
(8) (9) Various styles.

1882 (9 May). *Surch. by hand in red or black ink and the original value obliterated by a thick or thin bar or bars, of the same colour.*
103 **8** 1d. on 6d. (No. 95) (Bk.) .. — £275
104 **9** 1d. on 6d. (No. 95) (R.) .. 2·50 2·00
105 ,, 1d. on 6d. (No. 96) (R.) .. 2·50 2·50
a. Bisected (½d.) (on cover) .. † 80·00

10

(Typo. D.L.R.)

.883–94. *P* 14. (*a*) *Wmk. Crown CA.*

.06 **10** ½d. dull green 25 15

'07 ,, 1d. carmine 40 15

a. Bisected (½d.) (on cover) .. † 60·00

08 ,, 2½d. bright blue .. .. 1·00 15

10 ,, 4d. grey .. .. 1·00 30

11 ,, 6d. olive-black (1884) .. 1·25 1·50

12 ,, 1s. orange-brown (1884) 2·25 1·50

(*b*) *Wmk. Crown CC.*

13 **5** 5s. maroon (1894) .. 4·25 6·50

06/113 .. .. *Set of* 7 9·00 9·00

06/112 Optd. "Specimen" *Set of* 6 70·00

11. Britannia. **12.** Britannia.

ONE PENNY (I) (round "o") ONE PENNY (II) (oval "o")

(Typo. De La Rue & Co.)

896 (17 Aug.)–1900. *P* 14. (*a*) *Wmk. Crown CA.*

14 **11** ½d. dull purple and green 12 10

15 ,, 1d. dull purple & rose (I) 20 10

16 ,, 1d. dull purple & rose (II) (1900).. .. .. 30·00 1·00

17 ,, 2½d. dull purple and blue 40 30

18 ,, 4d. dull purple & orange 1·25 2·00

19 ,, 5d. dull purple and mauve 1·50 2·50

20 ,, 6d. dull purple and black 1·50 1·50

21 ,, 1s. green and brown .. 2·25 3·25

14/121 .. .. *Set of* 7 6·50 9·00

(*b*) *Wmk. CA over Crown.*

22 **12** 5s. green and brown, O .. 13·00 16·00

23 ,, 10s. green & ultramarine, O 80·00 70·00

24 ,, £1 green & carmine, OC 80·00 70·00

14/124 Optd. "Specimen" *Set of* 10 65·00

No. 119, surcharged "3d." was prepared for use but not issued. It exists overprinted "Specimen", *price* £50.

Collectors are warned against apparently postally used copies of this issue which bear "REGISTRAR-GENERAL" obliterations and are of very little value.

13. Landing of Columbus.

(Recess. De La Rue & Co.)

1898. *Discovery of Trinidad Commemoration. Wmk. Crown CC. P* 14.

125 **13** 2d. brown and dull violet 1·25 70

125 Optd. "Specimen" .. .. 30·00

1901–06. *Colours changed. Wmk. Crown CA or CA over Crown* (5s.). *P* 14.

126 **11** ½d. grey-green, O (1902) 15 10

127 ,, 1d. black/*red*, O (II) .. 20 8

a. Value omitted £2500

128 ,, 2½d. purple and blue/*blue*, O (1902) .. .. 1·10 50

129 ,, 4d. green & blue/*buff*, OC (1902).. .. 80 1·00

130 ,, 1s. black and blue/*yellow*, O (1903) .. .. 2·25 2·10

131 **12** 5s. lilac and mauve, O.. 8·50 9·50

a. Deep purple and mauve, OC (1906) .. .. 8·50 9·50

126/131 .. .. *Set of* 6 12·00 12·00

126/31 Optd. "Specimen" *Set of* 6 45·00

A pane of sixty of No. 127*a* was found in a post office in Trinidad but not more than nine copies are believed to have been sold, and the rest withdrawn.

1904–09. *Wmk. Mult. Crown CA. P* 14.

132 **11** ½d. grey-green, OC .. 35 20

133 ,, ½d. blue-green, O (1906) 90 40

134 ,, 1d. black/*red*, OC (II) .. 30 10

135 ,, 1d. rose-red, O (1907) .. 25 10

136 ,, 2½d. purple & blue/*blue*, C 4·00 1·25

137 ,, 2½d. blue, O (1906) 40 15

138 ,, 4d. grey and red/*yellow*, C (1906).. .. .. 1·10 2·00

a. Black and red/yellow, C .. 3·25 3·25

139 ,, 6d. dull purple and black, C (1905) .. .. 3·50 2·10

140 ,, 6d. dull and bright purple, 2·00 2·10 C (1906) .. ..

141 ,, 1s. black & blue/*yellow*, C 3·50 3·50

142 ,, 1s. purple and blue/*golden yellow*, C .. .. 4·00 4·00

143 ,, 1s. black/*green*, C (1906) 1·00 1·25

144 **12** 5s. deep purple & mauve C (1907) .. .. 12·00 14·00

145 ,, £1 green & carm., C ('07) 60·00 50·00

132/145 .. .. *Set of* 14 80·00 70·00

135/143 Optd. "Specimen" *Set of* 6 35·00

No. 135 is from a new die, the letters of "ONE PENNY" being short and thick, while the point of Britannia's spear breaks the uppermost horizontal line of shading in the background.

14

15

16

(Typo. De La Rue & Co.)

1909. *Wmk. Mult. Crown CA. P* 14.

146 **14** ½d. green, O 15 10

147 **15** 1d. rose-red, O .. 15 8

148 **16** 2½d. blue, O .. .. 1·00 1·10

146/8 Optd. "Specimen" *Set of* 3 25·00

TRINIDAD AND TOBAGO.

17

18

(Typo. De La Rue.)

1913–23. *Wmk. Mult. Crown CA. P* 14.

149 **17** ½d. green, O 12 10

a. Yellow-green (1915) .. 30 25

b. Blue-green (*thick paper*) (1917) 25 20

c. Blue-green/bluish (3.18) .. 4·00 4·00

150 ,, 1d. bright red, O .. 25 20

a. Red (*thick paper*) (1916) .. 10 5

b. Pink (1918) .. .. 2·00 40

c. Carmine-red (5.18) .. 10 5

151 ,, 2½d. ultramarine, O .. 1·10 40

a. Bright blue (*thick paper*) (1916) 90 50

b. Bright blue (*thin paper*) (1918) .. .. 1·75 80

152 ,, 4d. blk. & red/*yellow*, OC 70 1·00

a. White back (12.13) (Optd. S. £7) .. .. .. 2·00 2·25

b. On lemon (1917) .. .. 6·50

c. On pale yellow (1923) .. 1·75 2·50

153 ,, 6d. dull & reddish pur., C 2·50 1·50

a. Dull and deep purple ('18) 1·50 1·50

b. Dull purple & mauve (2.18) 1·60 2·00

154 ,, 1s. black/*green*, O .. 1·40 1·75

a. White back (Optd. S. £5) 90 1·75

b. On blue-green, olive back.. 1·40 1·50

c. On emerald back 1·40 1·10

155 **18** 5s. dull purple & mauve, C (1914) .. .. 6·50 8·00

a. Deep purple & mauve ('18) 7·00 8·00

b. Lilac and violet 9·50 10·00

c. Dull purple and violet .. 11·00 14·00

d. Brown-purple and violet .. 7·50 10·00

156 ,, £1 grey-green & carmine, C (1914) .. .. 45·00 50·00

a. Deep yellow-green & carm. (1918) .. .. 45·00 50·00

149/156 .. .. *Set of* 8 50·00 55·00

149/56 Optd. "Specimen" *Set of* 8 65·00

No. 156*a* is from a plate showing background lines very worn.

18*a*

1914 (18 Sept.). *Red Cross Label authorised for use as* ½*d. stamp. Typo. P* 11–12.

157 **18a** (½d.) Red .. .. .. 5·50 80·00

The above was authorised for internal use on one day only, to raise funds for the Red Cross. The used price is for stamp on cover.

19. 10. 16.

21. 10. 15.

(19)

(19*c*)

1915 (21 Oct.). *Optd. with T* **19.** *Cross in deep red with outline and date in black.*

174 **17** 1d. red 20 30
 a. Cross 2 mm. to right .. 5·50 5·50
 b. "1" of "15" forked foot 2·50 3·50
 c. Broken "0" in "10" .. 3·75 4·00

The varieties occur in the following positions on the *pane* of 60: a. No. 11. b. No. 42. c. No. 45. Variety a. is only found on the right-hand pane.

1916 (19 Oct.). *Optd. with T* **19a.** *Cross in scarlet with outline and date in black.*

175 **17** 1d. scarlet 12 25
 a. No stop after "16" .. 2·00 2·50
 b. "19.10.16" omitted ..

No. 175a appears on stamp No. 36 on the right-hand pane only.

FORGERIES. Beware of forgeries of the "War Tax" errors listed below. There are also other unlisted errors which are purely fakes.

WAR TAX (19*b*) — WAR TAX (20) — WAR TAX (21) — WAR TAX (22)

1917 (2 Apr.). *Optd. with T* **19b.**

176 **17** 1d. red 10 12
 a. Opt. inverted .. .. 50·00
 b. Scarlet 12 15

1917 (May.). *Optd. with T* **20.**

177 **17** ½d. green 8 8
 a. Pair, one without opt. .. 50·00
178 ,, 1d. red 8 10
 a. Pair, one without opt. .. 50·00
 b. Scarlet 12 8
 ba. Opt. double .. .. 27·00

The varieties without overprint were caused by the latter being shifted over towards the left so that one stamp in the lowest row of each pane escaped.

1917 (21 June). *Optd. with T* **21.**

179 **17** ½d. yellow-green .. 30 25
 a. Pale green 25 25
 b. Deep green 30 30
180 ,, 1d. red 8 8

Pairs are known of the 1d. stamps, one stamp without the overprint. This was caused by a shifting of the type to the left-hand side, but only a few stamps on the right-hand vertical row escaped the overprint and such pairs are very rare.

1917 (21 July–Sept.). *Optd. with T* **22.**

181 **17** ½d. yellow-green .. 60 80
 a. Deep green 8 12
182 ,, 1d. red (Sept.) 8 8

WAR TAX (23) — WAR TAX (24) — WAR TAX (25) — War Tax (26)

1917 (1 Sept.). *Optd. with T* **23** (*closer spacing between lines of opt.*).

183 **17** ½d. deep green .. 10 12
 a. Pale yellow-green ..
184 ,, 1d. red .. .. .. 3·00 4·00

1917 (31 Oct.). *Optd. with T* **24.**

185 **17** 1d. scarlet 8 8
 a. Opt. inverted .. .. 25·00

1918 (7 Jan.). *Optd. with T* **25.**

186 **17** 1d. scarlet 8 8
 a. Opt. double .. .. 40·00
 b. Opt. inverted .. .. 25·00

1918 (13 Feb.–May). *Optd. with T* **26.**

187 **17** ½d. bluish-green .. 8 8
 a. Pair, one without opt. .. 90·00
188 ,, 1d. scarlet 8 8
 a. Opt. double .. .. 26·00
 b. Rose-red (1.5.18) .. 12 12

1918 (14 Sept.). *New printing as T* **26**, *but* 19 *stamps on each sheet have the letters of the word* "Tax" *wider spaced, the* "x" *being to the right of* "r" *of* "War" *instead of under it. Thick bluish paper.*

189 **17** 1d. scar. ("Tax" spaced) 30 30
 a. Opt. double .. .. 45·00

1921–22. *Wmk. Mult. Script CA. P* 14.

206 **17** ½d. green, O 15 12
207 ,, 1d. scarlet, O 10 12
208 ,, 1d. brown, O (1922) .. 12 10
209 ,, 2d. grey, O (1922) .. 1·00 1·00
210 ,, 2½d. bright blue, O .. 50 1·00
211 ,, 3d. bright blue, O (1922) 90 1·00
212 ,, 6d. dull & brt. purple, C 90 1·00
213 **18** 5s. dull pur. & pur., C ('21) 11·00 13·00
214 ,, 5s. dp. pur. & pur., C ('22) 11·00 13·00
215 ,, £1 green and carmine, C 48·00 50·00
206/215 .. .. *Set of* 9 55·00 60·00
206/15 Optd. "Specimen" *Set of* 9 60·00

27

(Typo. D.L.R.)

1922–28. *P* 14. (*a*) *Wmk. Mult. Crown CA.*

216 **27** 4d. black & red/*pale yell.*, C 40 5[illegible]
217 ,, 1s. black/*emerald*, C .. 1·25 1·7[illegible]

(*b*) *Wmk. Mult. Script CA.*

218 **27** ½d. green, O .. .. 8 [illegible]
219 ,, 1d. brown, O .. .. 10 [illegible]
220 ,, 1½d. bright rose, O .. 30 1[illegible]
 a. Scarlet .. .. 15 1[illegible]
222 ,, 2d. grey, O .. .. 25 1[illegible]
223 ,, 3d. blue, O .. .. 65 2[illegible]
224 ,, 4d. black and red/*pale yellow*, C ('28) .. 1·25 1·4[illegible]
225 ,, 6d. dull purple & bright magenta, C .. .. 3·00 5·0[illegible]
226 ,, 6d. green & red/*emerald*, C ('24) .. .. 1·25 6[illegible]
227 ,, 1s. black/*emerald*, C .. 1·25 7[illegible]
228 ,, 5s. dull pur. & mauve, C 8·50 9·5[illegible]
229 ,, £1 green & bright rose, C 45·00 48·0[illegible]
216/229 .. .. *Set of* 13 55·00 60·0[illegible]
216/29 Optd. "Specimen" *Set of* 13 70·00

New currency. 100 cents = $1.

28. First Boca.

29. Imperial College of Tropical Agriculture.

30. Mt. Irvine Bay, Tobago

31. Discovery of Lake Asphalt.

32. Queen's Park, Savannah.

33. Town Hall, San Fernando

34. Government House.

35. Memorial Park.

36. Blue Basin.

(Recess. B.W.)

1935 (1 Feb.)–**37.** *Wmk. Mult. Script CA, sideways. P* 12.

230 **28** 1 c. blue and green .. 30 10
 a. Perf. 12½ ('36) 5 5
231 **29** 2 c. ultram. & yellow-brn. 40 20
 a. Perf. 12½ ('36) 8 8
232 **30** 3 c. black and scarlet .. 10 10
 a. Perf. 12½ ('36) 10 10
233 **31** 6 c. sepia and blue .. 20 20
 a. Perf. 12½ ('37) 20 30
234 **32** 8 c. sage-green & verm... 35 30
235 **33** 12 c. black and violet .. 30 40
 a. Perf. 12½ ('37) 45 80
236 **34** 24 c. black and olive-green 80 80
 a. Perf. 12½ ('37) .. .. 1·25 1·40
237 **35** 48 c. deep green .. .. 3·00 4·00
238 **36** 72 c. myrtle-green & carm. 6·50 7·50
230/238 .. .. *Set of* 9 10·00 12·00
230/8 Perf. "Specimen" *Set of* 9 30·00

1935 (6 May). *Silver Jubilee. As Nos.* 91/4 *of Antigua but ptd. by B. W. P* 11 × 12.

239 2 c. ultramarine & grey-black 8 8
 a. Extra flagstaff .. .. 10·00
240 3 c. deep blue and scarlet .. 10 15
 a. Extra flagstaff .. .. 15·00
241 6 c. brown and deep blue .. 35 5[illegible]
 a. Extra flagstaff .. .. 25·00
242 24 c. slate and purple .. 1·25 1·4[illegible]
 a. Extra flagstaff .. .. 22·00
239/42 Perf. "Specimen" *Set of* 4 14·00

For illustration of "Extra flagstaff" variety see Bechuanaland.

1937 (12 May). *Coronation. As Nos.* 13/1[illegible] *of Aden. P* 14.

243 1 c. green .. .. .. 5 [illegible]
244 2 c. yellow-brown .. .. 12 1[illegible]
245 8 c. orange .. .. .. 25 2[illegible]
243/5 Perf. "Specimen" *Set of* 3 10·00

37. First Boca.

38. Imperial College of Tropical Agriculture.

39. Mt. Irvine Bay, Tobago.

40. Memorial Park.

41. G.P.O. and Treasury.

42. Discovery of Lake Asphalt.

43. Queen's Park, Savannah.

44. Town Hall, San Fernando.

45 Government House.

46. Blue Basin.

47. King George VI.

(Recess. B.W.)

1938 (2 May)–**44.** *Wmk. Mult. Script CA sideways.* (*a*) *P* 11½×11.
246 **37** 1 c. blue and green .. 5 5
247 **38** 2 c. blue & yellow-brn. 5 5
248 **39** 3 c. black and scarlet .. 2·75 35
248*a* ,, 3 c. grn. & pur.-brn. ('41) 5 5
249 **40** 4 c. chocolate .. .. 1·25 70
249*a* ,, 4 c. scarlet ('41) .. 15 12
249*b* **41** 5 c. magenta (1.5.41) .. 8 5
250 **42** 6 c. sepia and blue .. 10 5
251 **43** 8 c. sage-green & verm. 10 8
252 **44** 12 c. black and purple .. 1·25 65
a. Black and slate-pur. ('44) 40 8
253 **45** 24 c. black & olive-green 35 15
254 **46** 60 c. myrtle-grn. & carm. 80 60

(*b*) *P* 12.
255 **47** $1.20, blue-green (1.40) .. 1·10 50
256 ,, $4.80, rose-carmine (1.40) 6·00 3·00
246/256 .. .. *Set of* 14 12·00 5·00
246/256 *Exc.* 249*b* Perf. "Specimen" *Set of* 13 40·00

1946 (1 Oct.). *Victory. As Nos.* 28/9 *of Aden.*
257 3 c. chocolate 5 5
258 6 c. blue 5 5
257/8 Perf. "Specimen" *Set of* 2 10·00

1948 (22 Nov.). *Silver Wedding. As Nos.* 30/1 *of Aden* (*recess* $4.80).
259 3 c. red-brown 5 5
260 $4.80, carmine .. .. 6·50 7·50

1949 (10 Oct.). *75th Anniv. of Universal Postal Union. As Nos.* 114/17 *of Antigua.*
261 5 c. bright reddish purple .. 8 8
262 6 c. deep blue 12 20
263 12 c. violet 25 25
264 24 c. olive 40 40

1951 (16 Feb.). *University College of B.W.I. As Nos.* 118/9 *of Antigua.*
265 3 c. green and red-brown 12 8
266 12 c. black & reddish violet 35 30

48. First Boca.

49. Mt. Irvine Bay, Tobago.

(Recess. B.W.)

1953 (20 Apr.)–**55.** *As T* **37/47**, *but with portrait of Queen Elizabeth II in place of King George VI as in T* **48** (*1 c., 2 c., 12 c.*) *or* **49** (*other values*). *Wmk. Mult. Script CA. P* 12 (*dollar values*) *or* 11½×11 (*others*).
267 **48** 1 c. blue & green (*shades*) 5 5
268 **38** 2 c. indigo & orge.-brown 5 5
269 **49** 3 c. dp. emer. & pur.-brn. 5 5
270 **40** 4 c. scarlet 8 8
271 **41** 5 c. magenta 10 10
272 **42** 6 c. brn. & greenish blue 12 10
273 **43** 8 c. deep yellow-green & orange-red 12 10
274 **44** 12 c. black and purple .. 15 10
275 **45** 24 c. black & yellow-olive (*shades*) 30 20
276 **46** 60 c. blackish green & carm. 60 30
277 **47** $1.20 bluish green .. 1·00 80
a. Perf. 11½ (19.1.55) .. 90 45
278 ,, $4.80 cerise .. .. 5·00 5·00
a. Perf. 11½ (16.11.55) .. 5·00 4·00
267/278a .. .. *Set of* 12 7·00 5·00

1953 (3 June). *Coronation. As No.* 47 *of Aden.*
279 3 c. black and green.. .. 8 8

ONE CENT

(50)

1956 (20 Dec.). *No.* 268 *surch. with T* **50.**
280 1 c. on 2 c. ind. & orge-brn. 60 85

1958 (22 Apr.). *Inauguration of British Caribbean Federation. As Nos.* 135/7 *of Antigua.*
281 5 c. deep green 10 10
282 6 c. blue 12 12
283 12 c. scarlet 25 25

PRINTERS. Nos. 284 to 354 were printed in photogravure by Harrison & Sons *unless otherwise stated.*

51. Cipriani Memorial. **52.** Queen's Hall.

53. Whitehall. **54.** Treasury Building.
55. Governor-General's House. **56.** General Hospital, San Fernando.
57. Oil Refinery. **58.** Crest.
58*a*. Coat-of-Arms. **59.** Scarlet Ibis.
60. Pitch Lake. **61.** Mohammed Jinnah Mosque.
62. Anthurium Lilies.

(*T* **53/61** *are horiz. and T* **62** *is vert. as T* **51/52.**)

63. Humming-Bird.

64. Map of Trinidad and Tobago.

(Des. V. Whiteley (1, 2, 12, 35, 60 c., $4.80), J. Matthews (5 c.), H. Baxter (6, 8, 10, 15 c.), M. Goaman (25 c., 50 c., $1.20).)

1960 (24 Sept.)–**65.** *W* w.**12** (*upright*). *P* 13½×14½ (*1 c., 60 c., $1.20, $4.80*) *or* 14½×13½ (*others*).

284 **51** 1 c. stone and black .. 5 5
285 **52** 2 c. bright blue (*shades*) 5 5
286 **53** 5 c. chalky blue .. 5 5
287 **54** 6 c. red-brown (*shades*) .. 5 5
288 **55** 8 c. yellow-green 8 5
289 **56** 10 c. deep lilac 8 5
290 **57** 12 c. vermilion 8 5
291 **58** 15 c. orange 45 45
291*a* **58*a*** 15 c. orange (15.9.64) .. 35 25
292 **59** 25 c. rose-carm. & dp. blue 25 20
293 **60** 35 c. emerald and black 25 15
294 **61** 50 c. yellow, grey & blue 35 20
295 **62** 60 c. vermilion, yellow-grn. and indigo .. 45 30
a. Perf. 14½ (2.65*) .. 35·00 5·00
296 **63** $1.20, multicoloured .. 1·25 60
297 **64** $4.80, apple-grn. & pale blue 4·00 3·00
284/297 .. .. *Set of* 15 7·00 5·00

*This is the earliest date reported to us. It comes from an unannounced printing which was despatched to Trinidad on 3 December 1964.

The 2, 5, 6, 12 and 25 c. exist with PVA gum as well as gum arabic.

See also No. 317.

65. Scouts and Gold Wolf Badge.

1961 (4 Apr.). *Second Caribbean Scout Jamboree. Design multicoloured; background colours below. W* w.**12.** *P* 13½×14½.

298 **65** 8 c. light green 15 20
299 ,, 25 c. light blue 35 35

II. INDEPENDENT

66. Underwater Scene after painting by Carlisle Chang.

67. Piarco Air Terminal.

68. Hilton Hotel, Port-of-Spain.

69. Bird of Paradise and Map.

70. Scarlet Ibis and Map.

1962 (31 Aug.). *Independence. W* w.**12.** *P* 14½.

300 **66** 5 c. bluish green .. 8 8
301 **67** 8 c. grey 12 12
302 **68** 25 c. reddish violet .. 25 25
303 **69** 35 c. brown, yellow, green and black 25 25
304 **70** 60 c. red, black and blue .. 50 50
300/304 .. .. *Set of* 5 1·10 1·10

71. " Protein Foods ".

(Des. M. Goaman.)

1963 (4 June). *Freedom from Hunger. W* w.**12.** *P* 14×13½.

305 **71** 5 c. brown-red 8 5
306 ,, 8 c. yellow-bistre .. 10 10
307 ,, 25 c. violet-blue 25 25

72. Jubilee Emblem.

1964 (15 Sept.). *Golden Jubilee of Trinidad and Tobago Girl Guides' Association. W* w.**12.** *P* 14½×14.

308 **72** 6 c. yellow, ultramarine and rose-red 8 8
309 ,, 25 c. yellow, ultramarine and bright blue .. 30 30
310 ,, 35 c. yellow, ultramarine and emerald-green .. 40 45

73. I.C.Y. Emblem.

(Litho. State Ptg. Wks., Vienna.)

1965 (15 Nov.). *International Co-operation Year. P* 12.

311 **73** 35 c. red-brown, deep green and ochre-yellow .. 30 30

74. Eleanor Roosevelt, Flag and U.N. Emblem.

1965 (10 Dec.). *Eleanor Roosevelt Memorial Foundation. W* w.**12.** *P* 13½×14.

312 **74** 25 c. black, red & ultram. 20 20

75. Parliament Building.

1966 (8 Feb.). *Royal Visit. T* **75** *and similar horiz. designs. Multicoloured. W* w.**12** (*sideways*). *P* 13½×14½.

313 5 c. Type **75** 5 5
314 8 c. Map, H.M. Yacht *Britannia* and Arms 8 8
315 25 c. Map and flag 15 20
316 35 c. Flag and panorama .. 30 30

1966 (15 Nov.). *As No.* 284 *but wmk.* w.**12** *sideways.*

317 **51** 1 c. stone and black .. 5 5

No. 317 exists with PVA gum as well as gum arabic.

FIFTH YEAR OF
INDEPENDENCE
31st AUGUST 1967
(79)

1967 (31 Aug.). *Fifth Year of Independence. Nos.* 288/9, 291*a and* 295 *optd. as T* **79.**

318 **55** 8 c. yellow-green .. 8 8
319 **56** 10 c. deep lilac 8 8
320 **58*a*** 15 c. orange 10 10
321 **62** 60 c. vermilion, yellow-green and indigo .. 35 40

On No. 321 the overprint is in five lines.

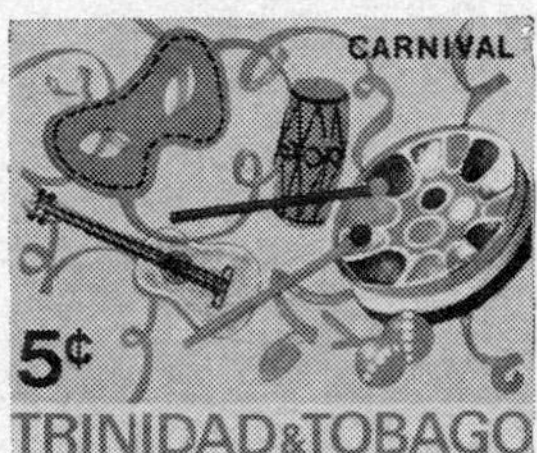

80. Musical Instruments.

81. Calypso King.

82. Steel Band. (*As T* **80.**)

83. Carnival Procession. (*As T* **80.**)

84. Carnival King. (*As T* **81.**)

85. Carnival Queen. (*As T* **81.**)

(Litho. De La Rue.)

1968 (Feb.). *Trinidad Carnival.* *P* 12.

322	**80**	5 c. multicoloured ..	5	5
323	**81**	10 c. multicoloured ..	8	8
324	**82**	15 c. multicoloured ..	10	8
325	**83**	25 c. multicoloured ..	12	12
326	**84**	35 c. multicoloured ..	20	20
327	**85**	60 c. multicoloured ..	35	35
322/7		.. .. *Set of* 6	75	75

86. Doctor giving Eye-Test.

1968 (7 May). *20th Anniv. of World Health Organization.* *W* **w.12** (*sideways*). *P* 14.

328	**86**	5 c. red, blackish brown and gold ..	5	5
329	,,	25 c. orange, blackish brn. and gold	15	15
330	,,	35 c. brt. blue, blk. & gold	20	20

87. Peoples of the World and Emblem.

1968 (5 Aug.). *Human Rights Year.* *W* **w.12** (*sideways*). *P* $13\frac{1}{2} \times 14$.

331	**87**	5 c. cerise, black and greenish yellow ..	5	5
332	,,	10 c. new blue, black and greenish yellow ..	8	8
333	,,	25 c. apple-green, black and greenish yellow	20	25

88. Cycling.

(Des. G. L. Vasarhelyi. Islands additionally die-stamped in gold (5 c. to 35 c.).)

1968 (Oct.). *Olympic Games, Mexico.* *T* **88** *and similar horiz. designs. Multicoloured.* *W* **w.12.** *P* 14.

334	5 c. Type **88**	5	5
335	15 c. Weightlifting	10	10
336	25 c. Relay-racing	15	15
337	35 c. Sprinting	20	20
338	$1.20, Maps of Mexico and Trinidad	75	90
334/8	.. .. *Set of* 5	1·10	1·25

93. Cocoa Beans.

94. Sugar Refinery. (*Horiz.*)

95. Cocrico (Red-tailed Guan). (*Horiz.*)

96. Oil Refinery. (*Horiz.*)

97. Fertilizer Plant. (*Horiz.*)

98. Green Hermit (Humming-bird).

99. Citrus Fruit. (*Vert.*)

100. Arms of Trinidad and Tobago. (*Vert.*)

101. Flag and Outline of Trinidad and Tobago. (*Vert.*)

102. Chaconia Plant. (*Vert.*)

103. Scarlet Ibis. (*Horiz.*)

104. Maracas Bay. (*Horiz.*)

105. Poui Tree. (*Vert.*)

106. Fishing. (*Horiz.*)

107. Red House. (*Horiz.*)

(*The* 40 *c.*, 50 *c. and* $5 *have name of country at left.*)

(Des. G. L. Vasarhelyi. Queen's profile die-stamped in gold (G.) or silver (S.), also the Islands on T **101.**)

1969–72. *W* **w.12** (*sideways on* 1 *to* 8 *c.*, 40 *c.*, 50 *c.*). *P* 14.

A. *Chalk-surfaced paper* (1.4.69)
B. *Glazed, ordinary paper* (24.3.72*)

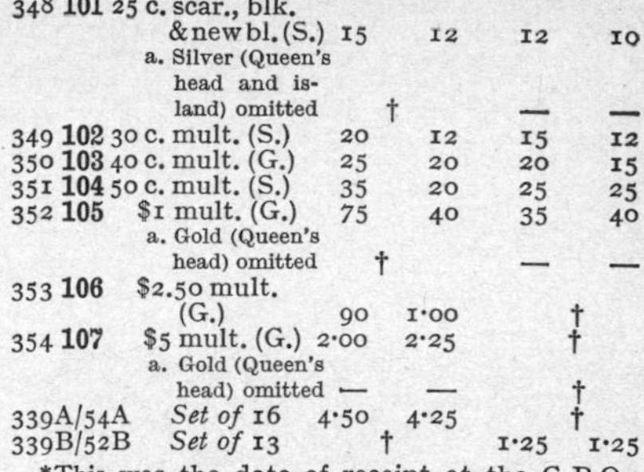

			A.		B.	
339	**93**	1 c. mult. (S.)	5	5	5	5
		a. Queen's head omitted	35·00	—	†	
340	**94**	3 c. mult. (G.)	5	5	5	5
341	**95**	5 c. mult. .. (*shades*) (G.)	5	5	5	5
		a. Queen's head omitted ..	†		—	—
		b. Imperf. (pair)	†		—	—
		ba. Do. and Queen's head omitted	†		—	—
342	**96**	6 c. mult. (G.)	5	5	5	5
		a. Queen's head omitted ..	—	—	†	
		b. Imperf. (pair)	—	—	†	
343	**97**	8 c. mult. (S.)	5	5	†	
344	**98**	10 c. mult. (G.)	10	8	8	5
345	**99**	12 c. mult. .. (*shades*) (S.)	8	5	8	8
346	**100**	15 c. mult. (S.)	10	5	8	8
		a. Queen's head omitted	£250	—	†	
347	**101**	20 c. scar., blk. & grey (G.)	15	10	10	8
348	**101**	25 c. scar., blk. & new bl. (S.)	15	12	12	10
		a. Silver (Queen's head and island) omitted	†		—	—
349	**102**	30 c. mult. (S.)	20	12	15	12
350	**103**	40 c. mult. (G.)	25	20	20	15
351	**104**	50 c. mult. (S.)	35	20	25	25
352	**105**	$1 mult. (G.)	75	40	35	40
		a. Gold (Queen's head) omitted	†		—	—
353	**106**	$2.50 mult. (G.)	90	1·00	†	
354	**107**	$5 mult. (G.)	2·00	2·25	†	
		a. Gold (Queen's head) omitted	—	—	†	
339A/54A		*Set of* 16	4·50	4·25	†	
339B/52B		*Set of* 13	†		1·25	1·25

*This was the date of receipt at the G.P.O.; the dates of issue are not known.

The listed missing die-stamped heads have the heads completely omitted and, except for No. 352a which results from a shift, show a blind impression of the die. They should not be confused with stamps from sheets containing a row of partially missing heads progressing down to mere specks of foil. The 20 c. value also exists with the gold omitted from the map only. We have also seen stamps with an additional "blind" profile cutting into the rear of the head but without a second die-stamped impression. Varieties of this nature are outside the scope of this catalogue.

See also Nos. 432/4 and 473.

108. Captain A. A. Cipriani (labour leader) and Entrance to Woodford Square.

109. Arms of Industrial Court and Entrance to Woodford Square.

(Photo. State Ptg. Works, Vienna.)

1969 (1 May). *50th Anniv. of International Labour Organization.* *P* 12.

355	**108**	6 c. black, gold and carmine-red	5	5
356	**109**	15 c. black, gold and new blue	12	20

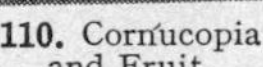

110. Cornucopia and Fruit.

111. Map showing "CARIFTA" Countries.

(Des. and photo. State Ptg. Works, Vienna.)

1969 (1 Aug.). *First Anniv. of CARIFTA (Caribbean Free Trade Area). T* **110/1** *and similar designs inscr.* " CARIFTA ". *P* 13½.

357 **110** 6 c. multicoloured .. 5 5
358 — 10 c. multicoloured .. 8 8
359 **111** 30 c. multicoloured .. 25 25
360 — 40 c. multicoloured .. 35 35

Designs: *Horiz.*—10 c. Flags of Britain and member-nations; 40 c. Boeing " 727 " in flight.

114. Space Module landing on Moon.

115. Space Module and Astronauts on Moon's Surface. (*Vert.*)

116. Astronauts seen from inside Space Module. (*Horiz.*)

(Des. G. L. Vasarhelyi. Litho. De La Rue.)

1969 (2 Sept.). *First Man on the Moon. P* 14.

361 **114** 6 c. multicoloured .. 5 5
362 **115** 40 c. multicoloured .. 25 30
363 **116** $1 multicoloured .. 65 75

The above were released by the Philatelic Agency in the U.S.A. on the 1st September, but not sold locally until the 2nd September.

117. Parliamentary Chamber, Flags and Emblems.

1969 (23 Oct.*). *15th Commonwealth Parliamentary Association Conference, Port of Spain. T* **117** *and similar horiz. designs. Multicoloured. W* w.**12**. *P* 14½ × 13½.

364 10 c. Type **117** 8 8
365 15 c. J. F. Kennedy College .. 10 10
366 30 c. Parliamentary maces .. 25 25
367 40 c. Cannon at Fort St. George 35 35

*This was the local release date; the Philatelic Agency in New York released the stamps ten days earlier.

121. Congress Emblem.

123. Emblem, Palm Trees and Ruin.

122. Emblem and Islands at Daybreak.

(Photo. Rosenbaum Bros., Vienna.)

1969 (3 Nov.). *International Congress of the Junior Chamber of Commerce. P* 13½.

368 **121** 6 c. black, red and gold 5 5
369 **122** 30 c. gold, lake & light bl. 20 25
370 **123** 40 c. blk., gold & ultram. 25 30

The above were released by the Philatelic Agency in the U.S.A. on 2nd November, but not sold locally until the 3rd.

124. " Man in the Moon ".

125. " City beneath the Sea ". (*Vert.*)

126. " Antelope " God Bamibara. (*Vert.*)

127. " Chanticleer " Pheasant Queen of Malaya (*Vert.*)

128. Steel-band of the Year. (*Horiz.*)

(Des. V. Whiteley. Litho. Questa Colour Security Printers Ltd.)

1970 (6 Feb.). *Carnival Winners. Multicoloured; background colours given. W* w.**12** *(sideways on* 40 *c.). P* 14.

371 **124** 5 c. sepia 5 5
372 **125** 6 c. deep blackish blue .. 5 5
373 **126** 15 c. violet-blue 10 10
374 **127** 30 c. slate-green 15 15
375 **128** 40 c. deep yellow-green .. 25 25
371/375 .. .. *Set of* 5 50 50

The above were released by the Philatelic Agency in the U.S.A. on 2nd February, but not sold locally until 6th February.

129. Statue of Gandhi.

130. Head of Gandhi and Flag of India. (*Horiz.*)

(Photo. State Printing Works, Vienna.)

1970 (2 Mar.). *Gandhi Centenary Year* (1969). *Multicoloured; background colours given. P* 12.

376 **129** 10 c. light ultramarine .. 8 8
377 **130** 30 c. rose-red 20 25

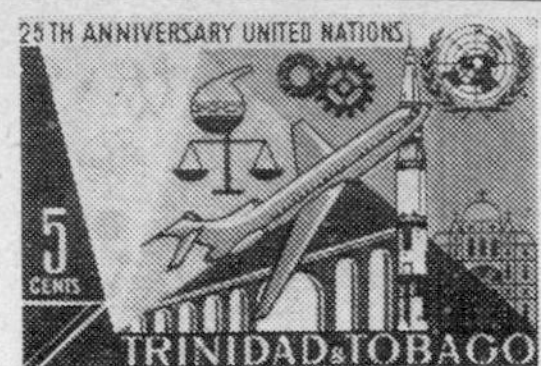

131. Symbols of Culture, Science, Arts and Technology.

132. New U.P.U. H.Q. Building.

(Des. G. Lee. Photo. State Printing Works, Vienna.)

1970 (26 June). *25th Anniv. of United Nations. T* **131/2** *and similar horiz. designs. Multicoloured. P* 12 (30 *c.*), 13½ × 14 (10 *c.*) *or* 13½ (*others*).

378 5 c. Type **131** 5 5
379 10 c. Children of different races, Map and Flag .. 5 5
380 20 c. Noah's Ark, Rainbow and Dove 15 15
381 30 c. Type **132** 25 25

The 10 c. is 34 × 25 mm. and the 20 c. is the same size as T **131**.

NATIONAL
COMMERCIAL
BANK
ESTABLISHED
1.7.70

(133)

1970 (1 July). *Inauguration of National Commercial Bank. No.* 341A *optd. with T* **133**.

382 **95** 5 c. multicoloured .. 8 8

134. " East Indian Immigrants ".

(Des. from paintings by Cazabon. Litho. Questa.)

1970 (Oct.). *125th Anniv. of San Fernando. T* **134** *and similar designs. W* w.**12** *(sideways on* 5 *c. and* 40 *c.). P* 13½.

383 3 c. multicoloured .. 5 5
384 5 c. black, blue and yellow-ochre 5 5
385 40 c. black, blue and yellow-ochre 30 40

Designs: *Horiz.*—5 c. " San Fernando Town Hall "; 40 c. " San Fernando Harbour ".

135. " The Adoration of the Shepherds " (detail, School of Seville).

(Des. G. Drummond. Litho. Format.)

970 (8 Dec.). *Christmas.* T **135** *and similar vert. designs.* P 13½.

86 3 c. multicoloured 5 5
87 5 c. multicoloured 5 5
88 30 c. multicoloured 20 20
89 40 c. multicoloured 25 25
90 $1 multicoloured 60 60
IS391 114×153 mm. Nos. 386/9 80 80
86/90 .. .. *Set of* 5 1·00 1·00

Designs:—5 c. " Madonna and Child with aints " (detail, Titian); 30 c. " The Adoration f the Shepherds " (detail, Le Nain); 40 c. " The irgin and Child, St. John and an Angel " Morando); $1 " The Adoration of the Magi " letail, Veronese).

136. Brocket Deer.

Des. State Printing Works, Vienna. Litho. Questa.)

971 (9 Aug.). *Trinidad Wildlife.* T **136** *and similar horiz. designs. Multicoloured.* W **w.12** *(sideways).* P 13½.

92 3 c. Type **136** 5 5
93 5 c. Quenk (pig) 5 5
94 6 c. Lappe (rodent) .. 5 5
95 30 c. Agouti (rodent) 20 20
96 40 c. Ocelot 30 30
92/6 .. .. *Set of* 5 55 55

137. A. A. Cipriani.

138. " Virgin and Child with St. Joan " (detail, Bartolommeo).

(Litho. D.L.R.)

1971 (30 Aug.*). *Ninth Anniv. of Independence.* T **137** *and similar vert. design. Multicoloured.* W **w.12.** P 14.

397 5 c. Type **137** 5 5
398 30 c. Chaconia medal .. 20 20

* This was the local release date, but the New York agency issued the stamps on 25th August.

(Litho. Harrison.)

1971 (25 Oct.). *Christmas.* T **138** *and similar vert. designs.* W **w.12** *(sideways on* 10 *c.,* 15 *c.).* P 14×14½.

399 **138** 3 c. multicoloured .. 5 5
400 – 5 c. multicoloured .. 5 5
401 – 10 c. multicoloured .. 10 10
402 – 15 c. multicoloured .. 15 15

Designs:—5 c. Local crèche; 10 c. " Virgin and Child with Saints Jerome and Dominic " (detail, Lippi); 15 c. " Virgin and Child with St. Anne " (detail, Gerolamo dai Libri).

139. Satellite Earth Station, Matura.

(Litho. Harrison.)

1971 (18 Nov.). *Satellite Earth Station.* T **139** *and similar vert. designs. Multicoloured.* W **w.12** *(sideways on* 10 *c. and* **MS**406). P 14 (10 *c.*) *or* 14×13½ *(others).*

403 10 c. Type **139** 8 8
404 30 c. Dish antennae .. 20 20
405 40 c. Satellite and the earth 25 25
MS406 140×76 mm. Nos. 403/5. Imperf. 60 60

140. Morpho Hybrid.

(Des. G. Drummond. Photo. Harrison.)

1972 (18 Feb.). *Butterflies.* T **140** *and similar horiz. designs. Multicoloured.* W **w.12** *(sideways on* 5 *c.).* P 14.

407 3 c. Type **140** 5 5
408 5 c. Purple Mort Bleu .. 5 5
409 6 c. Jaune d'Abricot .. 5 5
410 10 c. Purple King Shoemaker 8 8
411 20 c. Southern White Page .. 15 15
412 30 c. Little Jaune 25 25
407/12 .. .. *Set of* 6 50 50

141. S.S. *Lady McLeod* and McLeod Stamp.

(Des. J. E. Cooter. Litho. Harrison.)

1972 (24 Apr.*). *125th Anniv. of First Trinidad Postage Stamp.* T **141** *and similar horiz. designs.* W **w.12.** P 14.

413 5 c. multicoloured 8 8
414 10 c. multicoloured 10 10
415 30 c. greenish blue, reddish chestnut and black .. 25 25
MS416 83×140 mm. Nos. 413/5 40 40
a. Wmk. sideways .. 14·00 14·00

Designs:—10 c. Map and Lady McLeod stamp; 30 c. Lady McLeod stamp and inscription.

*This was the local release date, but the New York Agency issued the stamps on 12 April.

142. Trinity Cross.

(Des. G. Drummond. Photo. Enschedé.)

1972 (28 Aug.). *Tenth Anniv. of Independence.* T **142** *and similar vert. designs. Multicoloured.* W **w.12.** P 13½×13.

417 5 c. Type **142** 5 5
418 10 c. Chaconia medal .. 8 8
419 20 c. Humming-bird medal .. 15 15
420 30 c. Medal of Merit .. 25 25
MS421 93×121 mm. Nos. 417/20 60 60

One example of **MS**421 has been seen with the blue (background and frame) omitted from the 10 c. Another example has been seen with carmine (background and frame) omitted from the 30 c.

See also Nos. 440/**MS**444.

143. Bronze Medal, 1964 Relay.

(Des. G. Drummond. Litho. Questa.)

1972 (7 Sept.). *Munich Olympics.* T **143** *and similar horiz. designs. Multicoloured.* W **w.12.** P 14.

422 10 c. Type **143** 8 8
423 20 c. Bronze, 1964 200 metres 12 12
424 30 c. Silver, 1952 weight-lifting 20 20
425 40 c. Silver, 1964 400 metres 25 25
426 50 c. Silver, 1948 weight-lifting 30 30
422/6 .. .. *Set of* 5 85 85
MS427 153×82 mm. Nos. 422/6 .. 1·00 1·00

144. " Adoration of the Kings " (detail, Dosso).

(Des. G. Drummond. Photo. J.W.)

1972 (9 Nov.). *Christmas.* T **144** *and similar horiz. design. Multicoloured.* W **w.12.** P 14.

428 3 c. Type **144** 5 5
429 5 c. " The Holy Family " (Titian) 8 8
430 30 c. As 5 c. 25 25
MS431 73×99 mm. Nos. 428/30 .. 40 40

1973–74. *As No.* 339 *etc., but W* **w.12** *upright. Glazed, ordinary paper.*

432 **94** 3 c. multicoloured (9.74?) .. 10 10
433 **95** 5 c. multicoloured (1973) .. 1·00 75
a. Yellow (background) omitted 90·00
434 **96** 6 c. multicoloured (1974) .. 5 5

145. E.C.L.A. Building, Chile.

(Des. G. Drummond. Litho. Questa.)

1973 (15 Aug.). *Anniversaries. Events described on stamps. T* **145** *and similar horiz. designs. Multicoloured. W* **w.12.** *P* 14.

435 10 c. Type **145** 8 8
436 20 c. Interpol emblem .. 12 12
437 30 c. W.M.O. emblem .. 15 20
438 40 c. University of the West Indies 20 20
MS439 155×92 mm. Nos. 435/8 .. 60 65

(Des. J. E. Cooter. Litho. Harrison.)

1973 (30 Aug.). *Eleventh Anniv. of Independence. Vert. designs as T* **142.** *Multicoloured. W* **w.12.** *P* 14½×14.

440 10 c. Trinity Cross 8 8
441 20 c. Medal of Merit 12 12
442 30 c. Chaconia Medal .. 15 15
443 40 c. Hummingbird Medal .. 20 20
MS444 75×122 mm. Nos. 440/3. P 14 .. .. 60 60

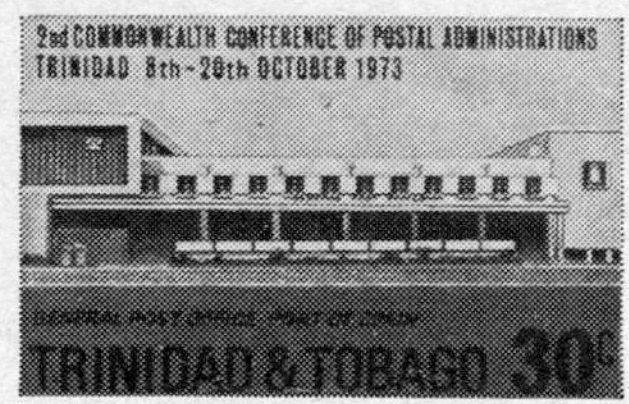

146. G.P.O., Port of Spain.

(Des. J. E. Cooter. Photo. J.W.)

1973 (8 Oct.). *Second Commonwealth Conference of Postal Administrations, Trinidad. T* **146** *and similar horiz. design. Multicoloured. W* **w.12** *(sideways). P* 14.

445 30 c. Type **146** 15 15
446 40 c. Conference Hall, Chaguaramas* 20 20
MS447 115×115 mm. Nos. 445/6 40 40

*Wrongly inscr. "CHAGARAMAS" on stamp.

147. "Virgin and Child" (Murillo).

(Des. PAD Studio. Photo. Harrison.)

1973 (22 Oct.). *Christmas. W* **w.12** *(sideways on* **MS**450). *P* 14½×14.

448 **147** 5 c. multicoloured .. 5 5
449 „ $1 multicoloured .. 50 50
MS450 94×88 mm. Nos. 448/9. P 14 .. .. 60 60

148. Berne H.Q. within U.P.U. Emblem.

(Des. PAD Studio. Photo. Harrison.)

1974 (18 Nov.). *Centenary of Universal Postal Union. T* **148** *and similar horiz. design. Multicoloured. W* **w.12** *(sideways). P* 13×14.

451 40 c. Type **148** 20 20
452 50 c. Map within emblem .. 25 25
MS453 117×104 mm. Nos. 451/2. P 13×14½ .. .. .. 15·00

149. *Humming Bird I* crossing Atlantic Ocean (1960).

(Des. and photo. Harrison.)

1974 (2 Dec.). *First Anniv. of World Voyage by H. and K. La Borde. T* **149** *and similar horiz. design. Multicoloured. W* **w.12** *(sideways on Nos.* 454/5, *upright on* **MS**456). *P* 14.

454 40 c. Type **149** 20 20
455 50 c. *Humming Bird II* crossing globe 25 25
MS456 109×84 mm. Nos. 454/5 1·25 1·25

150. "Sex Equality".

(Des. Hetty J. Mejias de Grannes; adapted V. Whiteley. Litho. Harrison.)

1975 (23 June). *International Women's Year. W* **w.14** *(sideways). P* 14.

457 **150** 15 c. multicoloured .. 5 8
458 „ 30 c. multicoloured .. 12 15

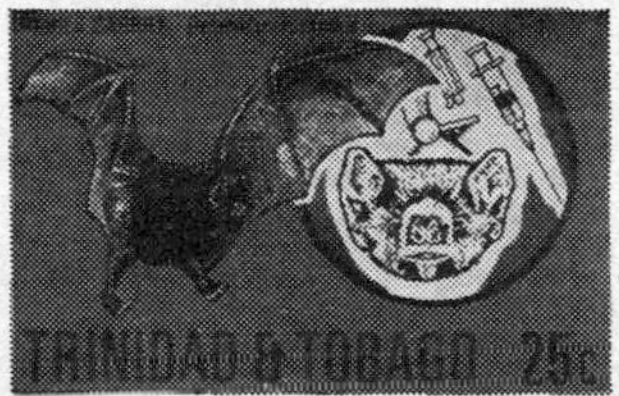

151. Vampire Bat, Microscope and Syringe.

(Des. PAD Studio. Photo. Harrison.)

1975 (23 Sept.). *Isolation of Rabies Virus. T* **151** *and similar horiz. designs. Multicoloured. W* **w.14.** *P* 14×14½.

459 25 c. Type **151** 12 12
460 30 c. Dr. Pawan, instruments and book 12 1

152. Route-map and Tail of Boeing "707".

(Des. C. Abbott. Litho. Walsall Security Ptrs.)

1975 (27 Nov.). *35th Anniv. of British West Indian Airways. T* **152** *and similar horiz. designs. W* **w.14** *(sideways). P* 14.

461 20 c. Type **152** 8 1
462 30 c. "707" on ground .. 12 1
463 40 c. "707" in flight 15 2
MS464 119×110 mm. Nos. 461/3 40 4

153. "From the Land of the Humming Bird".

(Des. and photo. Harrison.)

1976 (12 Jan.). *Carnival. 1974 Prizewinning Costumes. T* **153** *and similar horiz. designs. Multicoloured. W* **w.14** *(sideways). P* 14.

465 30 c. Type **153** 15 2
466 $1 "The Little Carib" .. 45 5
MS467 83×108 mm. Nos. 465/6 60 6

154. Angostura Building, Port of Spain.

(Des. Jennifer Toombs. Litho. J.W.)

1976 (14 July). *150th Anniv. of Angostura Bitters. T* **154** *and similar horiz. designs. Multicoloured. W* **w.14** *(sideways). P* 13.

468 5 c. Type **154** 5
469 35 c. Medal, New Orleans 1885/6 .. .. .. 15 1
470 45 c. Medal, Sydney 1879 .. 20 2
471 50 c. Medal, Brussels 1897 .. 20 2
MS472 119×112 mm. Nos. 468/71. P 14. .. .. 65 6

1976 (2 Aug.). *As No.* 344B *but W* **w.14.**

473 **98** 10 c. multicoloured .. 5

1976 (4 Oct.). *West Indian Victory in World Cricket Cup. As Nos.* 559/60 *of Barbados.*

474 35 c. Caribbean map 15 2
475 45 c. Prudential Cup 20 2
MS476 80×80 mm. Nos. 474/5 .. 40 4

155. "Columbus Sailing Through the Bocas" (Campins).

(Des. J.W. Ltd. Litho. Questa.)

1976 (1 Nov.). *Paintings. T* **155** *and similar horiz. designs. Multicoloured. W* w.**14**. *P* 14.

477	5 c. Type **155**	5	5
478	10 c. "Old View" (Cazabon)	5	5
479	20 c. "Trinidad Landscape" (Cazabon)	8	10
480	35 c. "Los Gallos Point" (Cazabon)	15	15
481	45 c. "Corbeaux Town" (Cazabon)	20	20
477/81	.. .. *Set of* 5	40	45
MS482	171×100 mm. Nos. 477/81. W w.**14** (sideways)	50	50

Nos. 483/99 have been reserved for further additions to this definitive set.

156. Hasely Crawford and Olympic Gold Medal.

(Des. J.W. Ltd. Litho. D.L.R.)

1977 (4 Jan.). *Hasely Crawford Commemoration. W* w.**14** (*sideways*). *P* 12×12½.

500 **156**	25 c. multicoloured ..	12	15
MS501	93×70 mm. No. 500 ..	15	

POSTAGE DUE STAMPS.

D 1

(Typo. De La Rue.)

1885 (1 Jan.). *Wmk. Crown CA.* *P* 14.

D1 **D 1** ½d. slate-black .. .. 6·00 65
D2 „ 1d. slate-black 25 15
D3 „ 2d. slate-black .. .. 2·00 20
D4 „ 3d. slate-black .. .. 2·50 40
D5 „ 4d. slate-black .. .. 3·25 1·10
D6 „ 5d. slate-black .. .. 3·25 45
D7 „ 6d. slate-black .. .. 4·50 1·60
D8 „ 8d. slate-black .. .. 4·50 1·60
D9 „ 1s. slate-black .. .. 4·50 3·25
D1/9 .. .. *Set of* 9 27·00 8·50

1905–6. *Wmk. Mult. Crown CA.* *P* 14.

D10 **D 1** 1d. slate-black 15 15
D11 „ 2d. slate-black 20 15
D12 „ 3d. slate-black 25 20
D13 „ 4d. slate-black 40 45
D14 „ 5d. slate-black 90 70
D15 „ 6d. slate-black .. .. 1·25 90
D16 „ 8d. slate-black .. .. 1·25 90
D17 „ 1s. slate-black .. .. 2·75 2·00
D10/17 .. .. *Set of* 8 6·50 5·00

1923–45. *Wmk. Mult. Script CA.* *P* 14.

D18 **D 1** 1d. black ('23) 20 25
D19 „ 2d. black ('23) 20 20
D20 „ 3d. black ('25) 25 25
D21 „ 4d. black ('29) 70 90
D22 „ 5d. black ('44) .. .. 80 1·00
D23 „ 6d. black ('45) .. .. 1·00 1·60
D24 „ 8d. black ('45) .. .. 1·25 2·25
D25 „ 1s. black ('45) .. .. 4·50 4·50
D18/25 .. .. *Set of* 8 8·00
D18/25 Optd./Perf. " Specimen " *Set of* 8 55·00

1947 (1 Sept.)–**61.** *Value in cents. Wmk. Mult. Script CA.* *P* 14.

D26 **D 1** 2 c. black, O 10 8
aa. Chalky paper (20.1.53) .. 10 8
a. Error. Crown missing. W9a, C .. .. 20·00
b. Error. St. Edward's Crown. W9b, C .. 12·00
D27 „ 4 c. black, O 8 8
a. Chalky paper (10.8.55) .. 8 8
D28 „ 6 c. black, O 8 8
aa. Chalky paper (20.1.53) 8 8
a. Error. Crown missing. W9a, C .. .. 20·00
b. Error. St. Edward's Crown. W9b, C .. 12·00
D29 „ 8 c. black, O 10 15
a. Chalky paper (10.9.58) 8 10
D30 „ 10 c. black, O 15 25
a. Chalky paper (10.8.55) .. 12 12
D31 „ 12 c. black, O 15 25
aa. Chalky paper (20.1.53) .. 10 10
a. Error. Crown missing. W9a, C .. .. 23·00
b. Error. St. Edward's Crown. W9b, C .. 14·00
D32 „ 16 c. black, O 20 40
a. Chalky paper (22.8.61) .. 15 15
D33 „ 24 c. black, O 25 30
a. Chalky paper (10.8.55).. 25 25
D26/33a .. .. *Set of* 8 85 85
D26/33 Perf. " Specimen " *Set of* 8 55·00

D 2

(Litho. Bradbury, Wilkinson.)

1969–70. *Size* 19×24 *mm.* *P* 14×13½.

D34 **D 2** 2 c. pale blue-green .. 5 5
D35 „ 4 c. magenta 5 8
D36 „ 6 c. brown 5 5
D37 „ 8 c. reddish violet .. 5 5
D38 „ 10 c. red 5 5
D39 „ 12 c. orange-yellow .. 10 12
D40 „ 16 c. bright apple green 5 8
D41 „ 24 c. grey 10 12
D42 „ 50 c. grey-blue 20 25
D43 „ 60 c. sage-green 25 30
D34/43 .. .. *Set of* 10 85 1·00

Dates of issue:—2 c. 25.11.69; others, 1970.

(Litho. Questa.)

1976 (3 May*). *Redrawn in smaller design* (17×21 *mm.*). *P* 13½×14.

D44 **D 2** 4 c. light claret .. 5 5
D48 „ 12 c. pale orange .. 5 5

*This is the local date of issue; the Crown Agents released the stamps on 19 March.

"TOO LATE" STAMPS.

A handstamp with the words " TOO LATE " was used upon letters on which a too-late fee had been paid, and was sometimes used for cancelling the stamps on such letters.

OFFICIAL STAMPS.

O S (O 1) OFFICIAL (O 2)

1894. *Optd. with Type* O **1.** *Wmk. Crown CA.* *P* 14.

O1 **10** ½d. dull green .. .. 7·00 7·00
O2 „ 1d. carmine .. .. 8·50 8·50
O3 „ 2½d. ultramarine .. .. 9·50 9·50
O4 „ 4d. grey .. .. 11·00 11·00
O5 „ 6d. olive-black .. .. 11·00 11·00
O6 „ 1s. orange-brown.. .. 17·00 17·00

Wmk. Crown CC. *P* 12½.

O7 **5** 5s. rose-lake .. .. 30·00 32·00

1909. *Optd. with Type* O **2.** *Wmk. Mult. Crown CA.* *P* 14.

O8 **11** ½d. green, O 25 25
O9 „ 1d. rose-red, O 12 12
a. Opt. double .. .. — 48·00
b. Opt. vertical .. .. 11·00
c. Opt. inverted .. .. — 45·00

1910. *Optd. with Type* O **2.** *Wmk. Mult. Crown CA.* *P* 14.

O10 **14** ½d. green, O 10 10

OFFICIAL (O 3) OFFICIAL (O 4)

1913. *Optd. with Type* O **3.**

O11 **17** ½d. green, O 10 10
a. Overprint vertical ..

1914. *Optd. with Type* O **4.**

O12 **17** ½d. green, O 40 50

OFFICIAL (O 5) OFFICIAL (O 6)

1914–17. *Optd. with Type* O **5** (*without stop*)

O13 **17** ½d. green 25 2
a. *Blue-green (thick paper)* (1917) 25 2

1916. *Optd. with Type* O **5** (*with stop*).

O14 **17** ½d. yellow-green, O .. 15 1
a. Overprint double .. 6·00

1917 (22 Aug.). *Optd. with Type* O **6.**

O15 **17** ½d. green, O 15 1
a. *Yellow-green* 25 4
b. *Blue-green (thick paper)* .. 12 1

TRISTAN DA CUNHA.

TRISTAN DA CUNHA (1)

1952 (1 Jan.). *Stamps of St. Helena, optd. wi T* **1.**

1 **31** ½d. violet 20 3
2 „ 1d. black and green .. 20 4
3 „ 1½d. black and carmine .. 20 7
4 „ 2d. black and scarlet .. 20 8
5 „ 3d. grey 40 9
6 „ 4d. ultramarine .. .. 55 1·1
7 „ 6d. light blue .. .. 90 1·1
8 „ 8d. sage-green .. .. 1·10 2·2
9 „ 1s. sepia .. .. .. 1·10 3·2
10 „ 2s. 6d. maroon .. .. 6·50 7·5
11 „ 5s. chocolate .. .. 10·00 12·0
12 „ 10s. purple .. .. 21·00 24·0
1/12 .. .. *Set of* 12 38·00 50·0

1953 (2 June). *Coronation. As No.* 47 *of Ade*

13 3d. black and grey-green .. 1·75 3·0

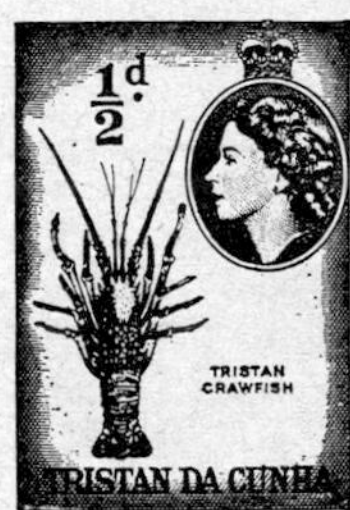

2. Tristan Crawfish.

3. Carting Flax for Thatching.

5. Big Beach Factory.

4. Rockhopper Penguin.

6. Mollymauk (sea-birds).

7. Island Boat.

8. Tristan from the South-West.

9. Girls on Donkeys.

10. Inaccessible Island from Tristan.

11. Nightingale Island.

12. St. Mary's Church.

3. Elephant Seal at Gough Is.

14. Flightless Rail.

15. Island Spinning Wheel.

(Recess. D.L.R.)

954 (2 Jan.). *Wmk. Mult. Script CA. P* 12½×13 (*horiz.*) *or* 13×12½ (*vert.*).

4	**2**	½d. red and deep brown ..	15	20
5	**3**	1d. sepia and bluish green	20	25
6	**4**	1½d. black & reddish purple	30	35
7	**5**	2d. grey-violet & brn.-orge.	30	30
8	**6**	2½d. black and carmine-red..	30	35
9	**7**	3d. ultram. & olive-green	30	35
0	**8**	4d. turq.-blue & deep blue	35	40
1	**9**	5d. emerald and black ..	40	45
2	**10**	6d. deep green and violet	40	45
3	**11**	9d. reddish violet and Venetian red	55	70
4	**12**	1s. dp. yellow-green & sepia	80	90
5	**13**	2s. 6d. dp. brn. & lt. blue	4·00	5·00
6	**14**	5s. black and red-orange..	11·00	13·00
7	**15**	10s. brown-orange & purple	18·00	19·00
4/27		.. .. *Set of* 14	32·00	38·00

16. Starfish.

17. Concha Fish.

18. Klip Fish.
19. Heron Fish.
20. Swordfish.
21. Tristan Crawfish.
22. Soldier Fish.
23. " Five Finger " Fish.
24. Mackerel.
25. Stumpnose Fish.
26. Blue Fish.
27. Snoek.
28. Shark.
29. Atlantic Right Whale.

(Des. Mr. and Mrs. G. F. Harris. Recess. Waterlow.)

1960 (1 Feb.). *W* w. **12**. *P* 13.

28	**16**	½d. black and orange ..	20	25
29	**17**	1d. black & bright purple	30	35
30	**18**	1½d. black & light turq.-blue	30	35
31	**19**	2d. black and bluish green	30	35
32	**20**	2½d. black and sepia ..	40	45
33	**21**	3d. black and brown-red..	40	45
34	**22**	4d. black and yellow-olive	45	50
35	**23**	5d. black & orange-yellow	55	65
36	**24**	6d. black and blue ..	60	80
37	**25**	9d. black & rose-carmine	85	1·10
38	**26**	1s. black and light brown	90	1·50
39	**27**	2s. 6d. black and ultram.	3·50	4·00
40	**28**	5s. black and light emerald	8·00	9·00
41	**29**	10s. black and violet ..	18·00	19·00
28/41		.. .. *Set of* 14	30·00	35·00

1961 (15 Apr.). *As T* **16/29** *but values in South African decimal currency.*

42	**16**	½ c. black and orange ..	10	12
43	**17**	1 c. black & bright purple	10	15
44	**18**	1½ c. black & lt. turq.-blue	15	25
45	**20**	2 c. black and sepia ..	20	30
46	**21**	2½ c. black and brown-red	25	30
47	**22**	3 c. black and yellow-olive	30	40
48	**23**	4 c. black & orange-yellow	40	50
49	**24**	5 c. black and blue ..	40	45
50	**25**	7½ c. black & rose-carmine	45	70
51	**26**	10 c. black and light brown	80	1·00
52	**27**	25 c. black and ultramarine	3·00	4·00
53	**28**	50 c. black and lt. emerald	8·00	9·00
54	**29**	1 r. black and violet ..	16·00	19·00
42/54		.. .. *Set of* 13	27·00	32·00

Following a volcanic eruption the island was evacuated on October 10th, 1961, but resettled in 1963.

TRISTAN DA CUNHA
RESETTLEMENT
1963

(30)

1963 (12 Apr.). *Tristan Resettlement. Types of St. Helena optd. with T* **30**. *Wmk. Mult. Script CA (sideways on* 1d., 2d., 7d., 10d., 2s. 6d., 10s.).

55	**50**	1d. bright blue, dull violet, yellow and carmine ..	5	5
56	**51**	1½d. yellow, green, black and light drab	5	5
57	**52**	2d. scarlet and grey ..	8	8
58	**53**	3d. light blue, black, pink and deep blue ..	10	10
59	**54**	4½d. yellow-green, green, brown and grey ..	10	12
60	**55**	6d. red, sep. & lt. yell.-ol.	15	20
61	**56**	7d. red-brn., blk. & violet	20	25
62	**57**	10d. brown-purple & lt. blue	25	30
63	**58**	1s. greenish yellow, bluish green and brown ..	30	35
64	**59**	1s. 6d. grey, blk. & ol. blue	55	60
65	**60**	2s. 6d. red, pl. yell. & turq.	1·50	1·75
66	**61**	5s. yellow, brown & green	2·50	2·75
67	**62**	10s. orge.-red, black & blue	4·50	5·00
55/67		.. .. *Set of* 13	9·00	10·00

1963 (1 Oct.). *Freedom from Hunger. As No.* 76 *of Aden.*

68	1s. 6d. carmine	2·00	2·25

1964 (1 Feb.). *Red Cross Centenary. As Nos.* 147/8 *of Antigua.*

69	3d. red and black	25	25
70	1s. 6d. red and blue	2·00	2·25

31. South Atlantic Map.

32. Flagship of Tristão D'Acunha. (wrongly inscr. " Tristão da Cunha " on stamp.)
33. *Heemstede.*
34. New England Whaler.
35. *Shenandoah.*
35*a*. H.M.S. *Challenger.*
36. H.M.S. *Galatea.*
37. H.M.S. *Cilicia.*
38. H.M. Yacht *Britannia.*
39. H.M.S. *Leopard.*
40. M.V. *Tjisadane.*
41. M.V. *Tristania.*
42. M.V. *Boissevain.*
43. M.S. *Bornholm.*

44. Queen Elizabeth II.

44*a*. Research Vessel *R.S.A.*

(*T* **33/43** *and* **44*a*** *are horiz. as T* **32.**)

(Queen's portrait by Anthony Buckley. Des. and eng. Bradbury, Wilkinson. Recess.)

1965 (17 Feb.)–**67.** *W* w.**12** (*sideways on* £1). *P* $11\frac{1}{2}\times11$ (*vert.*) *or* $11\times11\frac{1}{2}$ (*horiz.*).

71	**31**	$\frac{1}{2}$d. black and ultramarine	5	5
72	**32**	1d. black & emerald-green	5	5
73	**33**	$1\frac{1}{2}$d. black and blue ..	5	5
74	**34**	2d. black and purple ..	5	5
75	**35**	3d. black and turq.-blue ..	8	8
75*a*	**35*a***	4d. black & orange (1.9.67)	15	20
76	**36**	$4\frac{1}{2}$d. black and brown ..	12	15
77	**37**	6d. black and green ..	10	12
78	**38**	7d. black and rose-red ..	15	15
79	**39**	10d. black and chocolate ..	20	25
80	**40**	1s. black and carmine ..	20	25
81	**41**	1s. 6d. black & yell.-olive	40	45
82	**42**	2s. 6d. blk. & orge.-brown	80	90
83	**43**	5s. black and violet ..	1·25	1·50
84	**44**	10s. deep blue and carmine	3·50	3·50
84*a*	**44*a***	10s. black and deep turquoise-blue (1.9.67) ..	6·50	6·50
84*b*	**44**	£1 deep blue and orange-brown (1.9.67) ..	6·50	6·50
71/84*b*		.. .. *Set of* 17	18·00	18·00

1965 (11 May). *I.T.U. Centenary. As Nos.* 166/7 *of Antigua.*

85	3d. orange-red and grey ..	30	30
86	6d. reddish violet and yellow-orange	60	60

1965 (25 Oct.). *International Co-operation Year. As Nos.* 168/9 *of Antigua.*

87	1d. reddish pur. & turq.-grn.	15	15
88	6d. deep bluish green & lav..	90	90

1966 (24 Jan.). *Churchill Commemoration. As Nos.* 170/3 *of Antigua.*

89	1d. new blue	5	5
90	3d. deep green	25	20
91	6d. brown	1·00	1·25
92	1s. 6d. bluish violet	2·25	2·00

45. Ship at Tristan and Soldier of 1816.

(Des. V. Whiteley. Litho. Harrison.)

1966 (15 Aug.). *150th Anniv. of Tristan Garrison. W* w.**12** (*sideways*). *P* $14\frac{1}{2}$.

93	**45**	3d. multicoloured	12	12
94	,,	6d. multicoloured	30	25
95	,,	1s. 6d. multicoloured ..	85	60
96	,,	2s. 6d. multicoloured ..	1·10	85

1966 (1 Oct.*). *World Cup Football Championships. As Nos.* 176/7 *of Antigua.*

97	3d. violet, yellow-green, lake and yellow-brown ..	15	15
98	2s. 6d. chocolate, blue-green, lake and yellow-brown ..	1·10	1·00

*Released in St. Helena on 1.7.66 in error.

1966 (1 Oct.). *Inauguration of W.H.O. Headquarters, Geneva. As Nos.* 178/9 *of Antigua.*

99	6d. black, yellow-green and light blue	25	25
100	5s. black, light purple and yellow-brown	1·75	1·75

1966 (1 Dec.). *20th Anniv. of U.N.E.S.C.O. As Nos.* 196/8 *of Antigua.*

101	10d. slate-violet, red, yellow and orange	25	25
102	1s. 6d. orange-yellow, violet and deep olive	60	60
103	2s. 6d. black, bright purple and orange	85	85

46. Calshot Harbour.

(Des. V. Whiteley. Litho. D.L.R.)

1967 (2 Jan.). *Opening of Calshot Harbour. P* $14\times14\frac{1}{2}$.

104	**46**	6d. multicoloured ..	12	12
105	,,	10d. multicoloured ..	20	20
106	,,	1s. 6d. multicoloured ..	35	35
107	,,	2s. 6d. multicoloured ..	60	60

4d

(47)

48. Prince Alfred, First Duke of Edinburgh.

1967 (10 May). *No.* 76 *surch. with T* **47.**

108	**36**	4d. on $4\frac{1}{2}$d. black & brown	10	12

(Des. M. Goaman. Litho. Harrison.)

1967 (10 July). *Centenary of First Duke of Edinburgh's Visit to Tristan. W* w. **12.** *P* $14\frac{1}{2}$.

109	**48**	3d. multicoloured ..	10	10
110	,,	6d. multicoloured ..	15	15
111	,,	1s. 6d. multicoloured ..	30	30
112	,,	2s. 6d. multicoloured ..	55	55

49. Wandering Albatross.

50. Big-billed Bunting.

51. Tristan Thrush.

52. Great Shearwater.

(Des. V. Whiteley. Photo. Harrison.)

1968 (15 May). *Birds. W* w.**12.** *P* 14×14

113	**49**	4d. multicoloured ..	12	
114	**50**	1s. multicoloured ..	30	
115	**51**	1s. 6d. multicoloured ..	60	
116	**52**	2s. 6d. multicoloured ..	85	

53. Union Jack and Dependency Flag.

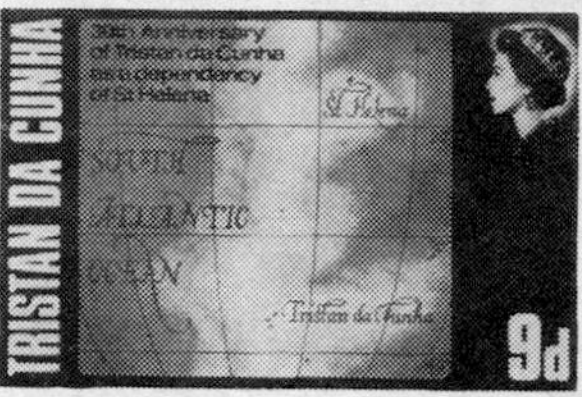

54. St. Helena and Tristan on Chart.

(Des. Jennifer Toombs. Litho. De La Rue

1968 (1 Nov.). *30th Anniv. of Tristan da Cun as a Dependency of St. Helena. W* w.**12** (*sid ways*). *P*14.

117	**53**	6d. multicoloured ..	12	
118	**54**	9d. sepia, blue and turquoise-blue	25	
119	**53**	1s. 6d. multicoloured ..	45	
120	**54**	2s. 6d. carmine, blue and turquoise-blue ..	75	

55. Frigate.

(Des. and recess. Bradbury, Wilkinson.)

1969 (1 June). *Clipper Ships. T* **55** *and simil horiz. designs. W* w.**12.** *P* $11\times11\frac{1}{2}$.

121	4d. new blue	10	
122	1s. carmine (Cape Horner) ..	30	
123	1s. 6d. blue-green (Barque) ..	45	
124	2s. 6d. chocolate (Tea Clipper)	70	

59. Sailing Ship off Tristan da Cunha.

60. Islanders going to first Gospel Service.

61. Landing of the First Minister.

62. Procession outside St. Mary's Church.

(Des. Jennifer Toombs. Litho. Format International.)

1969 (1 Nov.). *United Society for the Propagati of the Gospel. W* w.**12** (*sideways*). *P* $14\frac{1}{2}$× 1

125	**59**	4d. multicoloured	10	
126	**60**	9d. multicoloured	25	
127	**61**	1s. 6d. multicoloured ..	45	
128	**62**	2s. 6d. multicoloured ..	75	

63. Globe and Red Cross Emblem.

es. and litho. Bradbury, Wilkinson & Co.)

70 (1 June). *Centenary of British Red Cross. T* **63** *and similar design. W* w.**12** *(sideways on vert. designs.) P* 13.

9 **63** 4d. light emerald, scarlet and deep bluish green .. 10 10
o ,, 9d. bistre, scarlet and deep bluish green 25 25
1 – 1s. 9d. light drab, scarlet and ultramarine .. 45 45
2 – 2s. 6d. reddish purple, scarlet and ultramarine .. 70 70

Design: *Vert.*—1s. 9d., 2s. 6d., "Union Jack" d Red Cross Flag.

64. Crawfish and Fishing Boat.

(Des. Harrison & Sons. Litho. Enschedé.)

70 (1 Nov.). *Crawfish Industry. T* **64** *and similar horiz. design. Multicoloured. W* w.**12.** *P* 12½ × 13.

3 4d. Type **64** 10 10
4 10d. Packing and Storing Crawfish 25 25
5 1s. 6d. Type **64** 45 45
6 2s. 6d. As 10d. 70 70

(65)

71 (14 Feb.).* *Decimal Currency. As Nos. 71/84a surch. as T* **65**, *by B.W. in typo. Glazed paper.*

7 **32** ½p. on 1d. black and emerald-green .. 5 5
8 **34** 1p. on 2d. black and purple 5 5
9 **35a** 1½p. on 4d. black & orge. 8 8
o **37** 2½p. on 6d. black & grn. 10 10
1 **38** 3p. on 7d. black & rose-red 15 15
2 **39** 4p. on 10d. black and chocolate 20 20
3 **40** 5p. on 1s. blk. & carm. 25 25
4 **41** 7½p. on 1s. 6d. black and yellow-olive .. 40 40
5 **42** 12½p. on 2s. 6d. black and orange-brown .. 70 70
6 **33** 15p. on 1½d. black and blue 85 85
7 **43** 25p. on 5s. blk. & violet 1·75 1·75
8 **44a** 50p. on 10s. black and dp. turquoise-blue 3·50 3·50
7/48 .. .. *Set of* 12 7·00 7·00

* This was the local release date, but the own Agents issued the stamps one day later.

66. *Quest.*

(Des. V. Whiteley. Litho. J.W.)

1971 (1 June). *50th Anniv. of Shackleton–Rowett Expedition. T* **66** *and similar designs. W* w.**12** *(sideways). P* 13½ × 14.

149 1½p. multicoloured 8 10
150 4p. sepia, pale green and apple-green 25 25
151 7½p. blk., brt. pur. & pale grn. 50 50
152 12½p. multicoloured 70 75

Designs: *Horiz.*—4p. Presentation of Scout Troop flag; 7½p. Cachet on pair of 6d. G.B. stamps; 12½p. Shackleton, postmarks and boat taking mail to the *Quest.*

67. H.M.S. *Victory* at Trafalgar and Thomas Swain catching Nelson.

(Des. R. Granger Barrett. Litho. Questa.)

1971 (1 Nov.). *Island Families. T* **67** *and similar horiz. designs showing ships and the names of families associated with them. Multicoloured. W* w.**12** *(sideways). P* 13½.

153 1½p. Type **67** 12 12
154 2½p. *Emily of Stonington* (P. W. Green) 30 30
155 4p. *Italia* (Lavarello and Repetto) 45 45
156 7½p. H.M.S. *Falmouth* (William Glass) .. 1·25 1·25
157 12½p. American Whaler (Rogers and Hagan) .. 1·75 1·75
153/7 .. .. *Set of* 5 3·50 3·50

68. Cow Pudding.

(Des. M. and S. Goaman. Recess and litho. B.W. (50p., £1); Litho. A. & M. (others).)

1972 (29 Feb.). *T* **68** *and similar multicoloured designs showing flowering plants. W* w.**12** *(sideways on horiz. designs). P* 13.

158 ½p. Type **68** 5 5
159 1p. Peak Berry 5 5
160 1½p. Sand Flower (*horiz.*) .. 5 5
161 2½p. N.Z. Flax (*horiz.*) .. 5 5
162 3p. Island Tree 5 5
163 4p. Bog Fern 8 10
164 5p. Dog Catcher 8 10
165 7½p. Celery 12 15
166 12½p. Pepper Tree 20 25
167 25p. Foul Berry (*horiz.*) .. 45 50
168 50p. Tussock 85 90
169 £1 Tussac (*horiz.*) .. 1·75 1·90
158/69 .. .. *Set of* 12 3·50 3·75

69. Launching.

(Des. R. Svensson. Litho. Walsall Security Printers Ltd.)

1972 (1 June). *Tristan Longboats. T* **69** *and similar multicoloured designs. W* w.**12** *(sideways on 2½ and 4p.). P* 14.

170 2½p. Type **69** 12 12
171 4p. Under oars 20 20
172 7½p. Coxswain (*vert.*) .. 40 40
173 12½p. Under sail (*vert.*) .. 65 70

70. Tristan Thrushes and Wandering Albatrosses.

(Des. (from photographs by D. Groves) and photo. Harrison.)

1972 (20 Nov.). *Royal Silver Wedding. Multicoloured; background colours given. W* w.**12.** *P* 14 × 14½.

174 **70** 2½p. red-brown 35 45
175 ,, 7½p. dull ultramarine .. 1·25 1·40

71. Church Altar.

(Des. J. E. Cooter. Litho. Questa.)

1973 (8 July). *Golden Jubilee of St. Mary's Church. W* w.**12.** *P* 13½.

176 **71** 25p. multicoloured .. 85 85

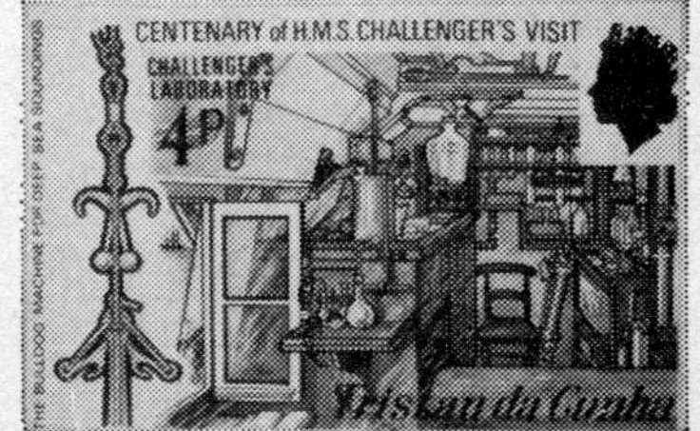

72. H.M.S. *Challenger*'s Laboratory.

(Des. V. Whiteley Studio. Litho. Questa.)

1973 (15 Oct.). *Centenary of H.M.S. Challenger's Visit.* *T* **72** *and similar horiz. designs. Multicoloured.* *W* w.**12**. *P* 13½.

177	4p. Type **72**	12	12
178	5p. H.M.S. *Challenger* off Tristan	15	15
179	7½p. *Challenger's* pinnace off Nightingale Is.	25	30
180	12½p. Survey route	45	50
MS181	145×96 mm. Nos. 177/80	2·00	2·00

73. Approaching English Port.

(Des. Jennifer Toombs. Litho. Questa.)

1973 (10 Nov.). *Tenth Anniv. of Return to Tristan da Cunha.* *T* **73** *and similar horiz. designs. Multicoloured (except 4p.).* *W* w.**12**. *P* 14.

182	4p. Type **73** (reddish brown, lemon and gold) ..	12	15
183	5p. Survey party	20	20
184	7½p. Embarking on *Bornholm*	30	30
185	12½p. Approaching Tristan ..	50	55

1973 (14 Nov.). *Royal Wedding. As Nos.* 165/6 *of Anguilla. Centre multicoloured.* *W* w.**12** (*sideways*). *P* 13½.

186	7½p. bright blue	20	20
187	12½p. light turquoise-green ..	35	35

74. Rockhopper and Egg.

(Des. R. Granger Barrett. Litho. Questa.)

1974 (1 May). *Penguins.* *T* **74** *and similar horiz. designs.* *W* w.**12**. *P* 14.

188	2½p. Type **74**	10	10
189	5p. Rockhopper Colony, Inaccessible Island	20	20
190	7½p. Rockhoppers fishing ..	25	25
191	25p. Adult and fledgling ..	75	75

75. Map with Penguin and Albatross.

(Des. J.W. Ltd. Litho. Questa.)

1974 (1 Oct.). *"The Lonely Island". Sheet* 154×104 *mm.* *W* w.**12** (*sideways*). *P* 13½.

MS192	**75** 35p. multicoloured ..	85	95

76. Blenheim Palace.

(Des. Sylvia Goaman. Litho. Questa.)

1974 (30 Nov.). *Birth Centenary of Sir Winston Churchill.* *T* **76** *and similar horiz. design.* *W* w.**14** *sideways* (*Nos.* 193/4) *or* *W* w.**12** *sideways* (**MS**195). *P* 14.

193	7½p. pale yellow and black ..	25	25
194	25p. black, sepia and grey ..	60	65
MS195	93×93 mm. Nos. 193/4	90	95

Design:—25p. Churchill with Queen Elizabeth II.

77. *Plocamium fuscorubrum.*

(Des. Sylvia Goaman. Litho. Harrison.)

1975 (16 Apr.). *Sea Plants.* *T* **77** *and similar horiz. designs.* *W* w.**12** (*sideways*). *P* 13×13½.

196	4p. rose-carm., lt. lilac & blk.	12	12
197	5p. apple-green, light violet-blue & dp. bluish green ..	15	15
198	10p. red-orange, stone and brown-purple	30	35
199	20p. multicoloured	50	55

Designs:—5p. *Ulva lactua*; 10p. *Epymenia flabellata*; 20p. *Macrocystis pyrifera.*

78. Killer Whale.

(Des. G. Drummond. Litho. Walsall.)

1975 (1 Nov.). *Whales.* *T* **78** *and similar horiz. designs. Multicoloured.* *W* w.**12** (*sideways*). *P* 13½.

200	2p. Type **78**	8	8
201	3p. Rough-toothed Dolphin	8	10
202	5p. Atlantic Right Whale ..	12	15
203	20p. Finback Whale	45	50

79. ½d. Stamp of 1952.

(Des. C. Abbott. Litho. J.W.)

1976 (4 May). *Festival of Stamps, London* *T* **79** *and similar designs.* *W* w.**14** (*sideway on* 5 *and* 25*p.*). *P* 13½.

204	5p. black, violet & light lilac	12	1
205	9p. black, deep green & turq.	20	2
206	25p. multicoloured	50	6

Designs: *Vert.*—9p. 1953 Coronation stamp *Horiz.*—25p. Mail carrier *Tristania II.*

For Miniature Sheet containing No. 206 see No **MS**218 of Ascension.

80. Island Cottage.

(Des. C. Abbott. Litho. Questa.)

1976 (4 Oct.). *Paintings by Roland Svensson* *T* **80** *and similar multicoloured design* *W* w.**14** (*sideways on* 5*p.*, 10*p. and* **MS**211 *P* 14.

207	3p. Type **80**	5	
208	5p. The potato patches (*horiz.*)	10	1
209	10p. Edinburgh from the sea (*horiz.*)	20	2
210	20p. Huts, Nightingale Island	40	4
MS211	110×100 mm. Nos. 207/10	75	

81. The Royal Standard.

(Des. and litho. J.W.)

1977 (7 Feb.). *Silver Jubilee.* *T* **81** *and simil horiz. designs. Multicoloured.* *W* w.**14** (*sid ways*). *P* 13.

212	10p. Royal Yacht *Britannia* ..	20	2
213	15p. Type **81**	30	3
214	25p. Royal Family	50	

POSTAGE DUE STAMPS

D 1

D 2

(Typo. D.L.R.)

1957 (1 Feb.). *Chalk-surfaced paper. Wmk. Mult. Script CA. P* 14.

No.	Type	Description	Unused	Used
D1	D 1	1d. scarlet..	25	70
D2	,,	2d. orange-yellow ..	45	1·10
D3	,,	3d. green	60	2·25
D4	,,	4d. ultramarine	90	3·25
D5	,,	5d. lake	1·40	5·00
D1/D5		.. .. *Set of* 5	3·25	11·00

(Des. J.W. Ltd. Litho. Questa.)

1976 (31 May). *W* w.**12** (*sideways*). *P* 13½×14.

No.	Type	Description	Unused	Used
D 6	D 2	1p. magenta	30	30
D 7	,,	2p. dull emerald ..	35	35
D 8	,,	4p. bluish violet ..	40	40
D 9	,,	5p. new blue	50	50
D10	,,	10p. chestnut	2·00	2·00
D6/10		.. .. *Set of* 5	3·25	3·25

1976 (3 Sept.). *W* w.**14** (*sideways*). *P* 13½×14.

No.	Type	Description	Unused	Used
D11	D 2	1p. magenta	5	5
D12	,,	2p. dull emerald ..	5	5
D13	,,	4p. bluish violet ..	8	8
D14	,,	5p. new blue	8	10
D15	,,	10p. chestnut	20	20
D11/15		.. .. *Set of* 5	35	40

POSTAL FISCAL STAMPS.

NATIONAL
SAVINGS
(F 1)

2½ P
(F 2)

1970 (15 May). *No.* 77 *optd. with Type* F **1** *in red.*

No.	Type	Description	Unused	Used
F1	**37**	6d. black and green ..	25	30

No. F1 was originally intended as a National Savings Stamp, but also retained postal validity.

(Handstamped locally by rubber handstamp, individually on each stamp.)

1971 (Feb.). *Decimal Currency. No.* F1 *handstamped with Type* F**2**, *in violet.*

No.	Type	Description	Unused	Used
F2	**37**	2½p. on 6d. black & green	15·00	17·00
		a. Pair, one without handstamp	£160	£170

Beware of forgeries of this handstamp.

TRUCIAL STATES.

The Trucial States consisted of Abu Dhabi, Ajman (with Manama), Dubai, Fujeira, Ras al Khaima, Sharjah and Umm al Qiwain. However the following issue of stamps was only put into use in Dubai, despite the inscription "TRUCIAL STATES".

Dubai had an Indian postal administration from 1909 using unoverprinted Indian stamps and a Pakistani administration using Pakistani stamps from October 1947 to March 1948. The subsequent British postal administration operated from 1st April 1948 and the stamps of the British Postal Agencies in Eastern Arabia were at first used.

1. Palms.

2. Dhow.

(Des. M. Goaman. Photo. Harrison (T 1). Des. M. C. Farrar-Bell. Recess. D.L.R. (T 2).)

1961 (7 Jan.). *P* 15×14 (*T* **1**) *or* 13×12½ (*T* **2**).

No.	Type	Description		Unused	Used
1	1	5 n.p. green ..	.. ..	5	5
2	,,	15 n.p. red-brown	.. ..	8	8
3	,,	20 n.p. bright blue	.. ..	10	12
4	,,	30 n.p. orange-red	.. ..	15	20
5	,,	40 n.p. reddish violet	..	15	20
6	,,	50 n.p. bistre ..	.. ..	20	25
7	,,	75 n.p. grey	.. ..	30	30
8	2	1 r. green ..	.. ..	45	45
9	,,	2 r. black ..	.. ..	85	85
10	,,	5 r. carmine-red ..	..	1·60	2·00
11	,,	10 r. deep ultramarine	..	3·75	4·50
1/11		.. .. *Set of* 11		7·00	8·00

The Dubai Post Department took over the postal services on 14th June 1963. Later issues for Dubai will be found in Vol. 2 of the Stanley Gibbons Foreign Overseas Catalogue.

MINIMUM PRICE

The minimum price quoted is 5p which represents a handling charge rather than a basis for valuing common stamps. For further notes about prices see introductory pages.

TURKS ISLANDS.

I. DEPENDENCY OF JAMAICA.

1

(Recess. Perkins, Bacon.)

1867 (4 April). *No wmk. P* 11–12.

No.	Type	Description		Unused	Used
1	1	1d. dull rose ..	.. ..	12·00	15·00
2	,,	6d. black ..	.. ..	20·00	20·00
3	,,	1s. dull blue ..	.. ..	18·00	18·00

1878–79. *Wmk. Small Star. Type* w.**2** (*sideways on Nos.* 5 *and* 6). *P* 11–12×14½–15½.

No.	Type	Description		Unused	Used
4	1	1d. dull rose-lake (7.73)	..	15·00	15·00
		a. Wmk. sideways	..		
5	,,	1d. dull red (1.79)	..	20·00	20·00
		a. Imperf. between (pair)	..	£1500	
		c. Wmk. upright	..		
6	,,	1s. lilac (1.79) ..	..	£1500	£700

1881 (1 Jan.). *Stamps of the preceding issues surcharged locally, in black.*

There are twelve different settings of the ½d., nine settings of the 2½d., and six settings of the 4d.

The halfpenny provisionals.

(2) (3)

Setting 1. *T* **2**. *Long fraction bar. Two varieties repeated fifteen times in the sheet.*

No.	Description		Unused	Used
7	½ on 6d. black ..	.. ..	22·00	25·00

Setting 2. *T* **3**. *Short fraction bar. Three varieties in a vertical strip repeated ten times in sheet.*

Setting 3. *Similar to setting* 2, *but the middle stamp of the three varieties has a longer bar.*

No.	Description		Unused	Used
8	½ on 6d. black (*setting* 2 *only*)	..	18·00	
9	½ on 1s. dull blue		20·00	25·00
	a. Surch. double	.. ..	£750	

(4) (5) (6)

Three varieties in a vertical strip repeated ten times in sheet.

Setting 4. *Types* **4, 5, 6.**
Setting 5. *Types* **4** (*without bar*), **5, 6.**
Setting 6. *Types* **4, 5, 6** (*without bar*).
Setting 7. *Types* **4** (*shorter thick bar*), **6, 6.**

No.	Description		Unused	Used
10	½ on 1d. dull red (*S.* 7 *only*) (T **6**)		£400	
	a. T 4 (shorter thick bar)	..	£750	
11	½ on 1s. dull blue (*S.* 6 *and* 7) (T **4**)		£200	
	a. T 4 (shorter thick bar)	..	£200	
	b. T 5	..	£200	
	c. T 6	..	£125	
	d. T 6 (without bar)..	..	£200	
	e. Surch. double (T 6 without bar)			
12	½ on 1s. lilac (T 4)	.. ..	£100	£100
	a. Without bar	..	£200	
	b. With short thick bar	..	£200	
13	½ on 1s. lilac (T 5)	.. ..	60·00	60·00
14	½ on 1s. lilac (T 6)	.. ..	50·00	
	a. Without bar	.. ..	£200	

(7) (8) (9) (10)

Setting 8. *T* **7**. *Three varieties in a vertical stri[p]. All have a very short bar.*

No.	Description		Unused	Used
15	½d. on 1d. dull red ..	..	15·00	

Setting 9. *T* **8**. *Three varieties in a vertical stri[p]. Bars long and thick and* "**1**" *leaning a little left.*

No.	Description		Unused	Used
16	½d. on 1d. dull red ..	..	22·00	
	a. Surch. double ..	..		

Setting 10. *T* **9** *and* **10**. *Fifteen varieti[es] repeated twice on a sheet. Ten are of T* **9**, *fi[ve] of T* **10**.

No.	Description		Unused	Used
17	½ on 1d. dull red (T **9**)	..	12·00	12·
	a. Surch. double ..	..		
18	½ on 1d. dull red (T **10**)	..	15·00	20·
19	½ on 1s. lilac (T **9**) ..	..	25·00	25·
20	½ on 1s. lilac (T **10**) ..	..	60·00	65·
20*a*	½ on 1s. dull blue (T **9**)	..		

Types **9** and **11**. The difference is in t[he] position of the "**2**" in relation to the "**1**". In setting 10 the "**2**" is to left of the "**1**" except on No. 10 and in setting 11 it is to t[he] right except on No. 2.

(11) (12) (13) (14)

Setting 11. *T* **11** *to* **14**. *Fifteen varieties repeat[ed] twice in a sheet. Ten of T* **11**, *three of T* **1**[**2**] *and one each of T* **13** *and* **14**.

Setting 12. *Similar to last, but T* **13** *replaced [by] another T* **12**.

No.	Description		Unused	Used
21	½ on 1d. dull red (T **11**)	..	20·00	
22	½ on 1d. dull red (T **12**)	..	35·00	
23	½ on 1d. dull red (T **13**)	..	£275	
24	½ on 1d. dull red (T **14**)	..	£125	
24*a*	½ on 1s. dull blue (T **11**)	..	£2000	

The twopence-halfpenny provisionals.

(15)

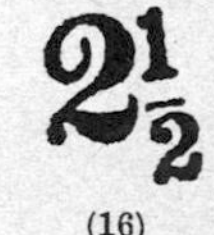
(16)

Setting 1. *T* **15**. *Fraction in very small ty[pe].*

No.	Description		Unused	Used
25	2½ on 6d. black	.. ..	£2000	

Setting 2. *T* **16**. *Large* "**2**" *on level with top [of] the* "**1**", *long thin bar.*

No.	Description		Unused	Used
26	2½ on 6d. black	.. ..	£110	
	a. Imperf. between (pair)	..		
	b. Double surch.	.. ..	£1200	

(17) (18) (19)

Setting 3. *T* **17**. *As T* **16**, *but large* "**2**" *[not] so high up.*

No.	Description		Unused	Used
27	2½ on 1s. lilac ..	.. ..	£400	

Setting 4. *T* **18**. *Three varieties in a verti[cal] strip repeated ten times in sheet. Large* "**2**" *placed lower and small bar.*

No.	Description		Unused	Used
28	2½ on 6d. black	.. ..	60·00	60
	a. Surch. double	..		

Setting 5. *T* **19**. *Three varieties in a verti[cal] strip repeated ten times in sheet.* "**2**" *furt[her] from* "½", *small fraction bar.*

No.	Description		Unused	Used
29	2½ on 1s. lilac ..	.. ..	£200	£

2½ 2½

(20) (21)

etting 6. *T* 20 *and* 21. *Fifteen varieties. Ten of T* 20 *and five of T* 21.

2½ on 1s. lilac (T 20) £1750
2½ on 1s. lilac (T 21) .. ..

2½ 2½ 2½

(22) (23) (24)

etting 7. *T* 22. *Three varieties in a vertical strip.*

2½ on 6d. black £1750
2½ on 1s. dull blue £1750

etting 8. *T* 23 *and* 24. *Fifteen varieties. Ten of T* 23 *and five of T* 24.

2½ on 1d. dull red (T 23) .. 75·00
2½ on 1d. dull red (T 24) .. £140
2½ on 1s. lilac (T 23) £200
a. Surch. "½" double .. £600
2½ on 1s. lilac (T 24) £450

2½ 2½ 2½

(25) (26) (27)

etting 9. *T* 25, 26, *and* 27. *Fifteen varieties. Ten of T* 25, *three of T* 26, *one of T* 26 *without bar, and one of T* 27.

2½ on 1s. dull blue (T 25) .. £140
2½ on 1s. dull blue (T 26) .. £450
2½ on 1s. dull blue (T 26) (without bar) £1750
2½ on 1s. dull blue (T 27) .. £1750

The fourpenny provisionals.

4 4 4

(28) (29) (30)

etting 1. *T* 28. "4" 8 *mm. high, pointed top.*

4 on 6d. black .. .. 65·00 65·00

etting 2. *T* 29 *and* 30.

4 on 6d. black (T 29) .. 14·00
4 on 6d. black (T 30) .. £140 £140
4 on 1s. lilac (T 29) .. £150
a. Surch. double .. ..
4 on 1s. lilac (T 30) .. £850
a. Surch. double .. ..
4 on 1d. dull red (T 29) .. £130 £130
4 on 1d. dull red (T 28) .. £150 £150

There are five other settings which can only be stinguished when in blocks. Particulars are ven in the handbook by Sir Edward Bacon.

31

One Penny

(32)

(Typo. De La Rue.)

881. *Wmk. Crown CC sideways; upright on 4d. P* 14.

1 1d. brown-red (Oct.) .. 10·00 10·00

50 31 4d. ultram., Die I (Aug.). 18·00 18·00
51 1 6d. olive-black (Oct.) .. 30·00 30·00
52 ,, 1s. slate-green (Oct.) .. 35·00 35·00

1882–84. *Wmk. Crown CA. P* 14.

53 31 ½d. blue-grn., Die I (2.82) 3·25 6·00
a. Pale green (1884) .. 75 1·50
55 1 1d. orange-brown (10.83) 10·00 15·00
a. Bisected (½d.) (on cover) .. — £300
56 31 2½d. red-brn., Die I (2.82) 6·00 8·00
57 ,, 4d. grey, Die I (10.84) 2·50 3·00
a. Bisected (2d.) (on cover) .. — £275

1887 (July). *Wmk. Crown CA.* (*a*) *P* 12.

58 1 1d. crimson-lake .. 3·00 3·50
a. Imperf. between (pair) ..

(*b*) *P* 14.

59 1 6d. yellow-brown .. 3·00 3·00
60 ,, 1s. sepia .. .. 1·50 2·50
59/60 Optd. "Specimen" *Set of* 2 25·00

1889 (May). *Surch. at Grand Turk with T* 32.

61 31 1d. on 2½d. red-brown .. 2·25 3·25

1889–93. *Wmk. Crown CA. P* 14.

62 1 1d. crimson-lake (7.89) .. 90 1·75
63 ,, 1d. lake .. .. 75 1·75
64 ,, 1d. pale rosy lake .. 70 2·50
65 31 2½d. ultramarine, Die II (4.93) (Optd. S. £20) .. 1·00 95

1d. / 2

(33)

34

1893 (June). *No.* 57, *surch. at Grand Turk with T* 33.

Setting 1. *Bars between* "1d." *and* "2" *separate, instead of continuous across the rows of stamps.*

66 ½d. on 4d. grey .. 65·00 45·00

Setting 2. *Continuous bars. Thin and thick bar* 10¾ *mm. apart.* "2" *under the* "1".

67 ½d. on 4d. grey .. .. 30·00 28·00

Setting 3. *As last, but bars* 11¾ *mm. apart.*

68 ½d. on 4d. grey .. .. 30·00 30·00

Setting 4. *Bars* 11 *mm. apart. Five out of the six varieties in the strip have the* "2" *below the space between the* "1" *and* "d".

69 ½d. on 4d. grey .. .. 30·00

There is a fifth setting, but the variation is slight.

(Typo. D.L.R.)

1894–95. *Wmk. Crown CA. P* 14.

70 31 ½d. dull green, Die II (1894) 25 35
71 ,, 4d. dull purple & ultramarine, Die II (5.95) 1·00 3·50
72 34 5d. olive-grn. & carm. (6.94) 1·00 3·50
a. Bisected (2½d.) (on cover) — £600
71/72 Optd. "Specimen" *Set of* 2 35·00

TURKS AND CAICOS ISLANDS.

35. Salt raking. 36.

The dates on the stamps have reference to the political separation from Bahamas.

(Recess. D.L.R.)

1900. *Wmk. Crown CA* (½*d. to* 1*s.*) *or Wmk. Crown CC* (2*s.*, 3*s.*). *P* 14.

101 35 ½d. green .. .. 1·10 1·75
102 ,, 1d. red .. .. 1·10 1·00
103 35 2d. sepia .. .. .. 1·25 1·25
104 ,, 2½d. blue .. .. 2·50 4·50
a. Greyish blue .. .. 1·25 1·75
105 ,, 4d. orange .. .. 2·25 2·75
106 ,, 6d. dull mauve .. .. 1·60 3·00
107 ,, 1s. purple-brown .. 1·40 3·00
108 36 2s. purple .. .. 25·00 30·00
109 ,, 3s. lake .. .. 25·00 28·00
101/109 .. .. *Set of* 9 55·00 65·00
101/9 Optd. "Specimen" *Set of* 9 90·00

1905–08. *Wmk. Mult. Crown CA. P* 14.

110 35 ½d. green 45 40
111 ,, 1d. red .. .. 3·00 1·50
112 ,, 3d. purple/*yellow* (1908) (Optd. S. £20) .. 1·40 3·00

37. Turk's-head Cactus. **38**

(Recess. D.L.R.)

1909 (Sept.)–**10.** *Wmk. Mult. Crown CA. P* 14.

115 37 ¼d. rosy mauve (1910) .. 25 25
116 ,, ¼d. red (1910) 12 15
117 38 ½d. yellow-green .. 12 12
118 ,, 1d. red 15 20
119 ,, 2d. greyish slate .. 1·75 2·50
120 ,, 2½d. blue .. .. 1·10 1·75
121 ,, 3d. purple/*yellow* .. 1·40 2·25
122 ,, 4d. red/*yellow* .. 2·50 2·50
123 ,, 6d. purple .. .. 4·00 3·50
124 ,, 1s. black/*green* .. 3·00 3·50
125 ,, 2s. red/*green* .. 14·00 17·00
126 ,, 3s. black/*red* .. 17·00 19·00
115/126 .. .. *Set of* 12 42·00 48·00
115/26 Optd. "Specimen" *Set of* 12 95·00

See also Nos. 154 and 162.

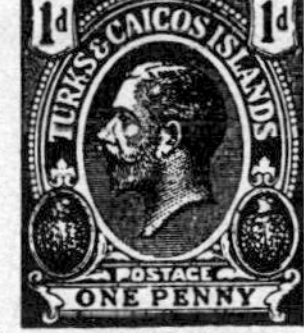

39

WAR TAX

(40)

1913–18. *Wmk. Mult. Crown CA. P* 14.

129 39 ½d. green 15 25
130 ,, 1d. red 75 60
a. Bright scarlet 75 75
b. Rose-carmine (1918) .. 70 70
131 ,, 2d. greyish slate .. 45 60
132 ,, 2½d. ultramarine .. 1·75 2·00
a. Bright blue (1918) .. 1·75 2·25
133 ,, 3d. purple/*yellow* .. 1·40 2·50
a. On lemon .. .. 6·00
b. On yellow-buff .. .. 1·75 2·00
c. On orange-buff .. .. 1·40
d. On pale yellow .. .. 2·00 1·40
134 ,, 4d. red/*yellow* .. .. 2·00 2·50
a. On orange-buff (Optd. S. £17) 1·40 2·50
b. Carmine on pale yellow .. 1·40 2·50
135 ,, 5d. pale olive-green (1916) 2·50 4·00
136 ,, 6d. dull purple .. .. 3·00 3·75
137 ,, 1s. brown-orange .. 1·40 2·50
138 ,, 2s. red/*blue-green* .. 5·00 6·00
a. On greenish white .. 15·00 20·00
b. On emerald (Optd. S. £17) 6·00 7·00
139 ,, 3s. black/*red* .. .. 11·00 15·00
129/139 .. .. *Set of* 11 26·00 35·00
129/39 Optd. "Specimen" *Set of* 11 75·00

1917 (3 Jan.). *Optd. with T* 40 *at bottom of stamp.*

140 39 1d. red 12 35
a. Overprint double .. 50·00
b. "TAX" omitted .. ..
c. "WAR TAX" omitted in vert. pair with normal ..
d. Opt. inverted at top .. 38·00
e. Opt. double, one inverted ..
f. Opt. inverted only, in pair with var. e .. ..

141 **39** 3d. purple/*yellow-buff* .. 25 45
a. Opt. double .. .. 14·00
142 ,, 3d. purple/*lemon* .. 40 45
a. Opt. double .. .. 13·00
b. Opt. double, one inverted

In Nos. 440e/f the inverted overprint is at foot and reads "TAX WAR" owing to displacement. No. 440e also exists with "WAR" omitted from the inverted overprint.

In both values of the first printings the stamp in the bottom left-hand corner of the sheet has a long "T" in "TAX", and on the first stamp of the sixth row the "X" is damaged and looks like an inverted "K".

1917 (Oct.). *Second printing with overprint at top or in middle of stamp.*
143 **39** 1d. red 12 20
a. Inverted opt. at bottom or centre .. .. .. 9·00
c. Overprint omitted, in pair with normal .. .. 50·00
d. Double overprint, one at top, one at bottom .. .. 13·00
e. As d., but additional overprint in top margin .. 35·00
f. Vertical pair, one as d., the other normal .. .. 65·00
g. Pair, one overprint inverted, one normal .. .. 80·00
h. Double overprint at top (in pair with normal) .. 65·00
l. Overprint double .. .. 14·00 14·00
144 ,, 3d. purple/*yellow* 25 40
a. Double .. .. .. 7·50
b. Double, one inverted .. 10·00
144c ,, 3d. purple/*lemon* .. ..

1918. *Overprinted with T* **40**.
145 **39** 3d. purple/*yellow* (R.) .. 1·10 1·60
a. Opt. double . ..

WAR

WAR
TAX
(41)

WAR
TAX
(42)

TAX
(43)

1918. *Optd. with T* **41**.
146 **39** 1d. rose-carmine 30 45
a. *Bright rose-scarlet* 12 20
147 ,, 3d. purple/*yellow* 15 30
146/7 Optd. "Specimen" *Set of* 2 35·00

1919. *Optd. with T* **41**.
148 **39** 3d. pur./*orange-buff* (R.) 25 30
148 Optd. "Specimen" .. .. 20·00

1919. *Local overprint, T* **40**, *in violet.*
149 **39** 1d. bright rose-scarlet .. 20 25
a. "WAR" omitted .. 35·00
b. Opt. double .. .. 6·00
c. Opt. double in pair with normal .. .. 35·00
d. *Rose-carmine* .. .. 1·60 2·00
da. Opt. double .. ..

1919. *Optd. with T* **42**.
150 **39** 1d. scarlet 12 20
a. Opt. double .. .. 35·00 35·00
151 ,, 3d. purple/*orange-buff* .. 50 65

1919 (17 Dec.). *Optd. with T* **43**.
152 **39** 1d. scarlet 15 20
a. Opt. inverted .. ..
153 ,, 3d. purple/*orange-buff* .. 15 25

The two bottom rows of this setting have the words "WAR" and "TAX" about 1 mm. further apart.

1921 (23 April). *Wmk. Mult. Script CA. P* 14.
154 **37** ½d. rose-red 12 25
155 **39** ½d. green 35 45
156 ,, 1d. carmine-red 35 45
157 ,, 2d. slate-grey .. .. 60 1·10
158 ,, 2½d. bright blue .. 1·00 2·25
159 ,, 5d. sage-green .. 2·25 3·50
160 ,, 6d. purple .. 3·25 5·50
161 **39** 1s. brown-orange .. 6·50 12·00
154/161 .. .. *Set of* 8 13·00 23·00
154/61 Optd. "Specimen" *Set of* 8 75·00

44

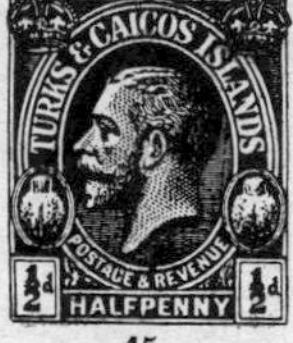

45

(Recess. D.L.R.)

1922–26. *P* 14. (*a*) *Wmk. Mult. Script CA.*
162 **37** ½d. black (1926) .. 10 15
163 **44** ½d. yellow-green .. 15 25
a. *Bright green* 30 40
b. *Apple-green* 70 75
164 ,, 1d. brown 50 65
165 ,, 1½d. scarlet (1925) .. 80 85
166 ,, 2d. slate 65 85
167 ,, 2½d. purple/*pale yellow* 15 40
168 ,, 3d. bright blue 80 90
169 ,, 4d. red/*pale yellow* .. 90 1·10
a. *Carmine/pale yellow* .. 1·40 2·25
170 ,, 5d. sage-green .. .. 80 1·50
171 ,, 6d. purple .. .. 1·00 1·50
172 ,, 1s. brown-orange .. 1·10 2·25
173 ,, 2s. red/*emerald* (1925) 3·50 4·50
(*b*) *Wmk. Mult. Crown CA.*
174 **44** 2s. red/*emerald* .. 7·00 8·00
175 ,, 3s. black/*red* .. 4·00 5·50
162/175 .. .. *Set of* 14 19·00 26·00
162/75 Optd. "Specimen" *Set of* 14 90·00

1928. *Inscr.* "POSTAGE & REVENUE". *Wmk. Mult. Script CA. P* 14.
176 **45** ½d. green 12 12
177 ,, 1d. brown 12 20
178 ,, 1½d. scarlet 20 40
179 ,, 2d. grey 25 20
180 ,, 2½d. purple/*yellow* 40 50
181 ,, 3d. bright blue 40 70
182 ,, 6d. purple 60 80
183 ,, 1s. brown-orange .. 1·00 1·50
184 ,, 2s. red/*emerald* .. 4·00 5·50
185 ,, 5s. green/*yellow* .. 16·00 20·00
186 ,, 10s. purple/*blue* .. 22·00 25·00
176/186 .. .. *Set of* 11 40·00 50·00
176/86 Optd. "Specimen" *Set of* 11 80·00

1935 (6 May). *Silver Jubilee. As Nos.* 91/4 *of Antigua, but ptd. by Waterlow. P* 11×12.
187 ½d. black and green 10 15
188 3d. brown and deep blue .. 55 70
189 6d. light blue and olive-grn. 80 90
190 1s. slate and purple .. .. 2·25 2·75
187/90 Perf. "Specimen" *Set of* 4 17·00

1937 (12 May). *Coronation. As Nos.* 13/15 *of Aden.*
191 ½d. green 8 8
192 2d. grey black 12 15
193 3d. bright blue 20 25
191/3 Perf. "Specimen" *Set of* 3 12·00

46. Raking Salt.

47. Salt Industry.

(Recess. Waterlow.)

1938 (18 June)–**45.** *Wmk. Mult. Script C P* 12½.
194 **46** ½d. black 8
195 ,, ½d. yellowish green .. 15
a. *Deep green* (6.11.44) .. 8
196 ,, 1d. red-brown 8
197 ,, 1½d. scarlet 8
198 ,, 2d. grey 8
199 ,, 2½d. yellow-orange .. 15
a. *Orange* (6.11.44) .. 8
200 ,, 3d. bright blue 8
201 ,, 6d. mauve .. .. 1·50 1·
201a ,, 6d. sepia (9.2.45) .. 20
202 ,, 1s. yellow-bistre .. 1·00 2·
202a ,, 1s. grey-olive (9.2.45) .. 45
203 **47** 2s. deep rose-carmine .. 1·00 1·
a. *Bright rose-carm.* (6.11.44) 80 1·
204 ,, 5s. yellowish green .. 2·25 3·
a. *Deep green* (6.11.44) .. 2·25 2·
205 ,, 10s. bright violet .. 3·00 3·
194/205 .. .. *Set of* 14 8·50 11·
194/205 Perf. "Specimen" *Set of* 14 60·00

1946 (4 Nov.). *Victory. As Nos.* 28/9 *of Ade*
206 2d. black 8
207 3d. blue 10
206/7 Perf. "Specimen" *Set of* 2 14·00

1948 (13 Sept.). *Royal Silver Wedding. As N* 30/1 *of Aden.*
208 1d. red-brown 8
209 10s. mauve .. .. .. 3·75 6·

50. Badge of the Islands.

51. Blue Ensign bearing Islands' Badge.

52. Turks and Caicos Islands.

53. Queen Victoria and King George VI.

(Recess. Waterlow.)

1948 (14 Dec.). *Centenary of Separation fr Bahamas. Wmk. Mult. Script CA. P* 1
210 **50** ½d. blue-green 10
211 ,, 2d. carmine 25
212 **51** 3d. blue 30
213 **52** 6d. violet 40

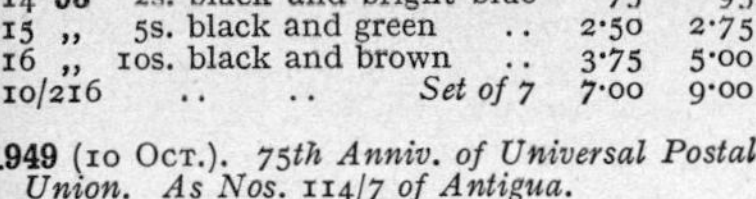

214	53	2s. black and bright blue	75	95
215	,,	5s. black and green ..	2·50	2·75
216	,,	10s. black and brown ..	3·75	5·00
210/216		.. .. *Set of* 7	7·00	9·00

1949 (10 Oct.). *75th Anniv. of Universal Postal Union. As Nos.* 114/7 *of Antigua.*

217	2½d. red-orange	10	20
218	3d. deep blue	25	35
219	6d. brown	40	50
220	1s. olive	65	80

54. Bulk Salt Loading.

66. Dependency's Badge.

(Recess. Waterlow.)

1950 (2 Aug.). *Wmk. Mult. Script CA.* T **54** *and similar horiz. designs and* T **66.** P 12½.

221	½d. green	12	12
222	1d. red-brown	12	20
223	1½d. deep carmine	15	25
224	2d. red-orange	12	25
225	2½d. grey-olive	15	35
226	3d. bright blue	15	35
227	4d. black and rose	50	60
228	6d. black and blue	70	75
229	1s. black and blue-green ..	60	75
230	1s. 6d. black and scarlet ..	90	1·10
231	2s. emerald and ultram. ..	1·25	2·00
232	5s. blue and black	3·00	3·75
233	10s. black and violet ..	5·00	6·00
221/233	.. .. *Set of* 13	12·00	15·00

Designs:—1d. Salt Cay; 1½d. Caicos mail; 2d. Grand Turk; 2½d. Sponge diving; 3d. South Creek; 4d. Map; 6d. Grand Turk Light; 1s. Government House; 1s. 6d. Cockburn Harbour; 2s. Government Offices; 5s. Loading salt.

1953 (2 June). *Coronation. As No.* 47 *of Aden, but ptd. by B.W. & Co.*

234	2d. black and orange-red ..	25	40

67. M.V. *Kirksons.*

68. Flamingoes in Flight.

(Recess. Waterlow.)

1955 (1 Feb.). *Wmk. Mult. Script CA.* P 12½.

235	**67**	5d. black and bright green	30	40
236	**68**	8d. black and brown ..	50	60

69. Queen Elizabeth II (after Annigoni).

70. Bonefish.

71. Red Grouper.

72. Spiny Lobster.

73. Albacore.

74. Muttonfish Snapper.

75. Permit.

76. Conch.

77. Flamingoes.

78. Spanish Mackerel.

79. Salt Cay.

80. Caicos Sloop.

81. Cable Office.

82. Dependency's Badge.

(Recess. B.W.)

1957 (25 Nov.). *W* w.**12**. *P* 13½×14 (1d.), 14 (10s.) *or* 13½ (*others*).

No.	Type	Description	Unused	Used
237	**69**	1d. deep blue & carmine	5	5
238	**70**	1½d. grey-green and orange	5	5
239	**71**	2d. red-brown and olive	5	5
240	**72**	2½d. carmine and green ..	8	8
241	**73**	3d. turquoise-blue & pur.	8	8
242	**74**	4d. lake and black ..	10	10
243	**75**	5d. slate-green & brown	12	12
244	**76**	6d. carmine-rose and blue	12	12
245	**77**	8d. vermilion and black	15	15
246	**78**	1s. deep blue and black	25	25
247	**79**	1s. 6d. sepia & dp. ultra.	60	70
248	**80**	2s. deep ultram. & brown	80	90
249	**81**	5s. black and carmine ..	1·75	2·00
250	**82**	10s. black and purple ..	3·50	4·00
237/250 *and* 253		.. *Set of* 15	14·00	16·00

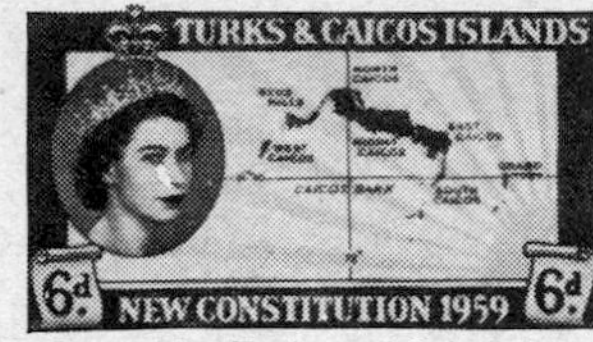

83. Map of the Turks and Caicos Islands.

(Photo. D.L.R.)

1959 (4 July). *New Constitution. Wmk. Mult. Script CA. P* 13½×14.

No.	Type	Description	Unused	Used
251	**83**	6d. dp. olive and lt. orange	40	50
252	,,	8d. violet and light orange	45	60

84. Pelican.

(Des. Mrs. S. Hurd. Photo. Harrison.)

1960 (1 Nov.). *W* w.**12**. *P* 14×14½.

No.	Type	Description	Unused	Used
253	**84**	£1 sepia and deep red ..	8·00	9·00

II. CROWN COLONY.

1963 (4 June). *Freedom from Hunger. As No.* 76 *of Aden.*

No.	Description	Unused	Used
254	8d. carmine	50	60

1963 (2 Sept.). *Red Cross Centenary. As Nos.* 147/8 *of Antigua.*

No.	Description	Unused	Used
255	2d. red and black	12	12
256	8d. red and blue	70	70

1964 (23 April). *400th Birth Anniv. of William Shakespeare. As No.* 164 *of Antigua.*

No.	Description	Unused	Used
257	8d. green	20	25

1965 (17 May). *I.T.U. Centenary. As Nos.* 166/7 *of Antigua.*

No.	Description	Unused	Used
258	1d. vermilion and brown ..	8	8
259	2s. lt. emerald & turq.-blue	60	65

1965 (25 Oct.). *International Co-operation Year. As Nos.* 168/9 *of Antigua.*

No.	Description	Unused	Used
260	1d. reddish pur. & turq.-grn.	5	5
261	8d. deep bluish green & lav.	30	35

1966 (24 Jan.). *Churchill Commemoration. As Nos.* 170/3 *of Antigua.*

No.	Description	Unused	Used
262	1d. new blue	5	5
263	2d. deep green	8	8
264	8d. brown	30	30
	a. Gold ptg double	£140	
265	1s. 6d. bluish violet	60	65

1966 (4 Feb.). *Royal Visit. As Nos.* 174/5 *of Antigua.*

No.	Description	Unused	Used
266	8d. black and ultramarine ..	25	30
267	1s. 6d. black and magenta ..	40	45

85. Andrew Symmer going ashore.

86. Andrew Symmer and Royal Warrant.

87. Arms and Royal Cypher.

(Des. V. Whiteley. Photo. De La Rue.)

1966 (1 Oct.). *Bicentenary of "Ties with Britain". P* 13½.

No.	Type	Description	Unused	Used
268	**85**	1d. deep blue and orange ..	5	5
269	**86**	8d. red, blue & orge.-yell.	20	20
270	**87**	1s. 6d. multicoloured ..	30	35

1966 (1 Dec.). *20th Anniv. of U.N.E.S.C.O. As Nos.* 196/8 *of Antigua.*

No.	Description	Unused	Used
271	1d. slate-violet, red, yellow and orange	5	5
272	8d. orange-yellow, violet and deep olive	25	30
273	1s. 6d. black, bright purple and orange	40	45

88. Turk's-head Cactus.

89. Boat-building.

90. Donkey Cart. (*Vert.*)
91. Sisal Industry. (*Vert.*)
92. Conch Industry. (*Horiz.*)
93. Salt Industry. (*Vert.*)
94. Skin-diving. (*Vert.*)
95. Fishing. (*Horiz.*)
96. Water-skiing. (*Vert.*)
97. Crawfish Industry. (*Horiz.*)
98. Map of Turks and Caicos Islands and (*inse* West Indies. (*Horiz.*)
99. Fishing Industry. (*Horiz.*)

100. Arms of Turks and Caicos Islands.

101. Queen Elizabeth II.

(Des. V. Whiteley. Photo. Harrison.)

1967 (1 Feb.). *W* w.**12**. *P* 14½×14 (*vert.*) 14×14½ (*horiz.*).

No.	Type	Description	Unused	Used
274	**88**	1d. olive-yellow, verm. & bright bluish violet	5	
275	**89**	1½d. brown & orge.-yellow	5	
276	**90**	2d. deep slate and deep orange-yellow ..	5	
277	**91**	3d. agate and dull green	5	
278	**92**	4d. bright mauve, black and turquoise ..	8	
279	**93**	6d. sepia and new blue ..	10	
280	**94**	8d. yellow, turquoise-blue and deep blue ..	12	
281	**95**	1s. maroon & turquoise	20	
282	**96**	1s. 6d. orange-yellow, lake-brown and deep turquoise-blue ..	40	
283	**97**	2s. multicoloured ..	40	
284	**98**	3s. maroon & turq.-blue	40	
285	**99**	5s. ochre, blue & new bl.	90	
286	**100**	10s. multicoloured ..	2·00	2·
287	**101**	£1 Prussian blue, silver and crimson ..	4·00	4·
274/287		.. .. *Set of* 14	8·00	9·

102. Turks Islands 1d. Stamp of 1867.

03. Queen Elizabeth "Stamp" and Turks Islands 6d. Stamp of 1867.

Des. R. Granger Barrett. Photo. Harrison.)

967 (1 May). *Stamp Centenary.* W **w.12.** P 14½.

88	**102**	1d. black & light magenta	5	5
39	**103**	6d. black and bluish grey	15	20
90	–	1s. black & turquoise-blue	30	30

The design of No. 290 is almost identical to 'ype **102**, but shows the 1s. stamp of 1867 in lace of the 1d.

104. Human Rights Emblem and Charter.

Des. R. Granger Barrett. Photo. Harrison.)

968 (1 Apr.). *Human Rights Year.* W **w.12.** P 14×14½.

91	**104**	1d. multicoloured ..	5	5
92	,,	8d. multicoloured ..	15	15
93	,,	1s. 6d. multicoloured ..	30	30

105. Dr. Martin Luther King and "Freedom March".

(Des. V. Whiteley. Photo. Harrison.)

968 (1 Oct.). *Martin Luther King Commemoration.* W **w.12.** P 14×14½.

94	**105**	2d. yellow-brown, blackish brown & deep blue	5	5
95	,,	8d. yellow-brown, blackish brown and lake ..	15	15
96	,,	1s. 6d. yell.-brn., blackish brown and violet	30	30

(New currency. 100 cents=1 dollar.)

1c

(**106**)

969 (8 Sept.). *Decimal Currency. Nos. 274/87 surch. as T* **106** *by Harrison & Sons, and new value in old design (¼ c.).*

97	**100**	¼ c. mult. (*shades*) ..	5	5
98	**88**	1 c. on 1d. ..	5	5
		a. Wmk. sideways ..	5	5
299	**90**	2 c. on 2d.	5	5
		a. Wmk. sideways ..	5	5
300	**91**	3 c. on 3d.	5	5
		a. Wmk. sideways ..	5	5
301	**92**	4 c. on 4d.	8	8
302	**93**	5 c. on 6d.	10	10
		a. Wmk. sideways ..	10	10
303	**94**	7 c. on 8d.	12	12
		a. Wmk. sideways ..	12	12
304	**89**	8 c. on 1½d.	12	15
305	**95**	10 c. on 1s.	20	20
306	**96**	15 c. on 1s. 6d.	30	35
		a. Wmk. sideways ..	25	30
307	**97**	20 c. on 2s.	30	35
308	**98**	30 c. on 3s.	45	50
309	**99**	50 c. on 5s.	75	85
310	**100**	$1 on 10s.	1·75	2·00
311	**101**	$2 on £1	7·00	8·00
		a. Wmk. sideways ..	3·00	4·00
297/311*a*		.. .. *Set of* 15	6·50	8·00

The 4, 8, 10, 20, 30, 50 c., and $1 exist with PVA gum as well as gum arabic.

No. 311 was only on sale through the Crown Agents.

107. "The Nativity with John the Baptist".

108. "The Flight into Egypt".

(Des. adapted by V. Whiteley. Litho. De La Rue.)

1969 (20 Oct.). *Christmas.* W **w.12.** P 13×12½.

312	**107**	1 c. multicoloured ..	5	5
313	**108**	3 c. multicoloured ..	5	5
314	**107**	15 c. multicoloured ..	30	30
315	**108**	30 c. multicoloured ..	45	50

109. Coat-of-Arms.

(Des. L. D. Curtis. Litho. Bradbury, Wilkinson.)

1970 (2 Feb.). *New Constitution. Multicoloured; background colours given.* W **w.12** (*sideways*). P 13×12½.

316	**109**	7 c. brown	15	15
317	,,	35 c. deep violet-blue ..	55	60

110. "Christ bearing the Cross" (Dürer).

111. "Christ on the Cross" (Dürer).

112. "The Lamentation for Christ" (Dürer).

(Des., recess and litho. Enschedé.)

1970 (17 Mar.). *Easter.* W **w.12** (*sideways*). P 13×13½.

318	**110**	5 c. olive-grey and blue	8	8
319	**111**	7 c. olive-grey & verm.	12	12
320	**112**	50 c. olive-grey & red-brn.	80	85

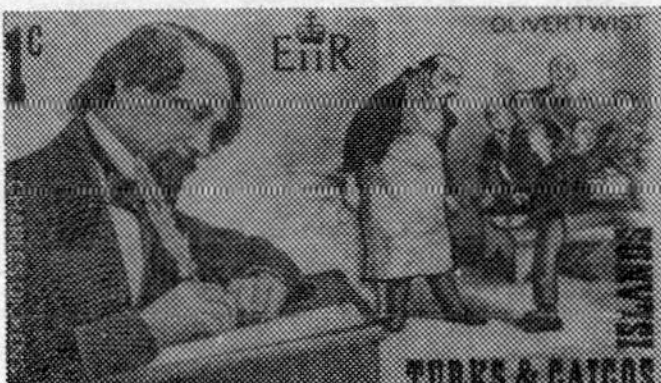

113. Dickens and Scene from "Oliver Twist".

(Des. Sylvia Goaman. Recess and litho. D.L.R.)

1970 (17 June). *Death Centenary of Charles Dickens. T* **113** *and similar horiz. designs.* W **w.12** (*sideways*). P 13.

321	1 c. black and yellow-brown/*yellow*	5	5
322	3 c. black and Prussian blue/*flesh*	8	8
323	15 c. black & grey-blue/*flesh*	30	35
324	30 c. black and drab/*blue* ..	50	60

Designs (each incorporating portrait of Dickens as in T **113**, and a scene from one of his novels):—3 c. "A Christmas Carol"; 15 c. "Pickwick Papers"; 30 c. "The Old Curiosity Shop".

114. Ambulance—1870.

(Des. Harrison. Litho. B.W.)

1970 (4 Aug.). *Centenary of British Red Cross. T* **114** *and similar horiz. design. Multicoloured.* W **w.12.** P 13½×14.

325	1 c. Type **114**	5	5
326	5 c. Ambulance—1970 ..	8	8
	a. Wmk. sideways	8	8
327	15 c. Type **114**	20	30
	a. Wmk. sideways	20	30
328	30 c. As 5 c.	40	45
	a. Wmk. sideways	40	45

No. 326a is known with grey omitted.

115. Duke of Albemarle and Coat-of-Arms.

(Des. V. Whiteley. Litho. Enschedé.)

1970 (1 DEC.). *Tercentenary of Issue of Letters Patent. T* **115** *and similar horiz. design. Multicoloured. W* w.**12**. *P* $12\frac{1}{2} \times 13\frac{1}{2}$.

329	1 c. Type **115**	5	5
330	8 c. Arms of Charles II and Elizabeth II	15	15
331	10 c. Type **115**	20	25
332	35 c. As 8 c.	55	60

116. Boat-building.

1971 (2 FEB.). *Decimal Currency. Designs as T* **88** *etc., but inscr. in decimal currency as in T* **116**. *W* w.**12** (*sideways on* 1 *c.,* 2 *c.,* 3 *c.,* 5 *c.,* 7 *c.,* 15 *c. and* $2).

333	**88**	1 c. olive-yellow, vermilion and bright bluish violet ..	5	5
334	**90**	2 c. deep slate and deep orange-yellow ..	5	5
335	**91**	3 c. agate and dull green	5	5
336	**92**	4 c. bright mauve, black and turquoise ..	5	5
337	**93**	5 c. sepia and new blue	8	8
338	**94**	7 c. yellow, turquoise-blue and deep blue..	10	10
339	**116**	8 c. brown & orange-yell.	10	10
340	**95**	10 c. maroon and turq...	12	15
341	**96**	15 c. orange-yellow, lake-brown and deep turquoise-blue ..	20	25
342	**97**	20 c. multicoloured ..	20	25
343	**98**	30 c. maroon & turq.-blue	40	45
344	**99**	50 c. ochre, blue and new blue	75	85
345	**100**	$1 multicoloured ..	1·50	1·75
346	**101**	$2 Prussian blue, silver and crimson ..	3·00	3·50
333/46		.. .. *Set of* 14	6·00	7·00

The $\frac{1}{4}$ c. value was also re-issued, but it can only be distinguished from No. 297 by its revised sheet format of 25 instead of 60.

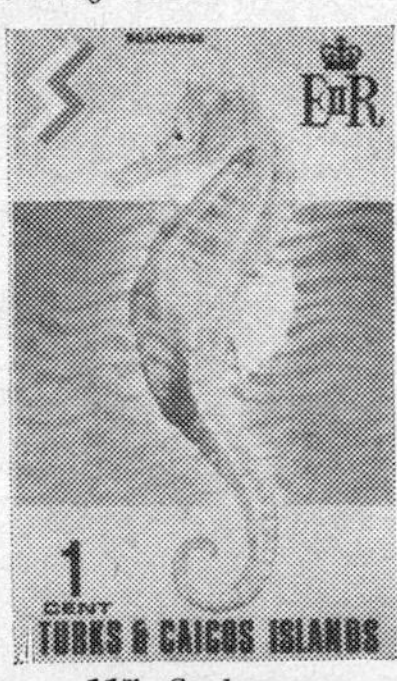

117. Seahorse.

(Des. G. L. Vasarhelyi. Litho. J.W.)

1971 (4 MAY). *Tourist Development. T* **117** *and similar multicoloured designs. W* w.**12** (*sideways on Nos.* 348/50). *P* $14 \times 14\frac{1}{2}$ (1 *c.*) *or* $14\frac{1}{2} \times 14$ (*others*).

347	1 c. Type **117**	5	5
348	3 c. Queen Conch Shell ..	5	5
349	15 c. Common Oyster Catcher	25	25
350	30 c. Blue Marlin	50	50

The 3, 15 and 30 c. are horizontal designs.

118. Pirate Sloop.

(Des. and litho. J.W.)

1971 (27 JULY). *Pirates. T* **118** *and similar horiz. designs. Multicoloured. W* w.**12** (*sideways*). *P* 14.

351	2 c. Type **118**	5	5
352	3 c. Pirate treasure ..	8	8
353	15 c. Marooned sailor ..	25	30
354	30 c. Buccaneers	50	55

119. The Wilton Diptych (Left Wing).

(Des. J. W. Ltd. Litho. Questa.)

1971 (12 OCT.). *Christmas. T* **119** *and similar vert. design. Multicoloured. W* w.**12**. *P* $13\frac{1}{2}$.

355	2 c. Type **119**	5	5
356	2 c. The Wilton Diptych (Right Wing)	5	5
357	8 c. Type **119**	12	15
358	8 c. As No. 356	12	15
359	15 c. Type **119**	25	25
360	15 c. As No. 356	25	25
355/60	.. .. *Set of* 6	75	80

The two stamps of each denomination were printed in horizontal *se-tenant* pairs throughout the sheet.

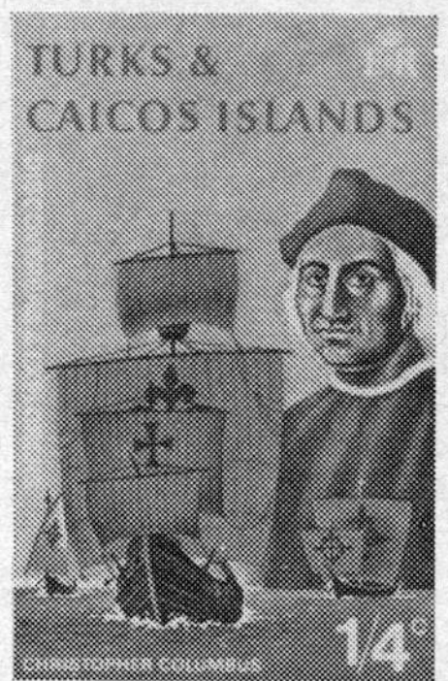

122. Christopher Columbus.

123. Turk's-head Cactus and Spiny Lobster.

120. Cape Kennedy Launching Area.

(Des. V. Whiteley. Litho. A. & M.)

1972 (21 FEB.). *Tenth Anniv. of Colonel Glenn's Splashdown. T* **120** *and similar multicoloured designs. W* w.**12** (*sideways on* 5, 10 *and* 15 *c.*). *P* $13\frac{1}{2}$.

361	5 c. Type **120**	8	8
362	10 c. "Friendship 7" space capsule	15	15
363	15 c. Map of Islands and splashdown	25	25
364	20 c. N.A.S.A. Space Medal (*vert.*)	35	35

121. "Christ before Pilate" (Rembrandt).

(Des. and litho. J.W.)

1972 (21 MAR.). *Easter. T* **121** *and simila designs. W* w.**12** (*sideways on* 15 *c.*). *P* $13\frac{1}{2}$.

365	2 c. black and lilac.. ..	5	
366	15 c. black and rose-pink ..	25	2
367	30 c. black and greenish yell.	45	5

Designs: *Horiz.*—15 c. "The Three Crosses" (Rembrandt). *Vert.*—30 c. "The Descent fror the Cross" (Rembrandt).

(Des. P. B. Powell. Litho. J.W.)

1972 (28 JULY*). *Discoverers and Explorer T* **122** *and similar multicoloured design W* w.**12** (*sideways on* 8 *and* 30 *c.*). *P* $13\frac{1}{2}$.

368	$\frac{1}{4}$ c. Type **122**	5	
369	8 c. Sir Richard Grenville (*horiz.*)	15	1
370	10 c. Capt. John Smith ..	20	2
371	30 c. Juan Ponce de Leon (*horiz.*)	60	6

*This was the local date of issue; the Crow Agents released the stamps on 4 July.

)es. (from photograph by D. Groves) and photo. Harrison.)

72 (20 Nov.). *Royal Silver Wedding. Multi-coloured; background colour given.* W w.**12**. P 14×14½.

2 **123**	10 c. dull ultramarine ..	20	20
3 ,,	20 c. myrtle-green ..	40	40

124. Treasure Hunting, *c.* 1700.

(Des. C. Abbott. Litho. Questa.)

73 (18 Jan.). *Treasure.* T **124** *and similar vert. designs.* W w.**12** (*sideways*). P 14×14½.

4	3 c. multicoloured	8	8
5	5 c. reddish purple, silver & black	10	10
6	10 c. magenta, silver & black	20	20
7	30 c. multicoloured	60	60
S378	127×108 mm. Nos. 374/7	1·10	1·10

Designs:—5 c. Silver Bank medallion (obverse); c. Silver Bank medallion (reverse); 30 c. Treasure hunting, 1973.

5. Arms of Jamaica and Turks & Caicos Islands.

)es. PAD Studio. Litho. Walsall Security Printers Ltd.)

73 (16 Apr.). *Centenary of Annexation to Jamaica.* W w.**12** (*sideways*). P 13½×14.

9 **125**	15 c. multicoloured ..	25	25
0 ,,	35 c. multicoloured ..	45	50

126. Sooty Tern.

(Des. R. Granger Barrett. Litho. Questa.)

73 (1 Aug.). T **126** *and similar vert. designs.* W w.**12** (*sideways*). P 14.

1	¼ c. Type **126**	5	5
2	1 c. Magnificent Frigate-bird	5	5
3	2 c. Noddy Tern	5	5
384	3 c. Blue-grey Gnatcatcher	8	8
385	4 c. Blue Heron	5	5
386	5 c. Catbird	5	5
387	7 c. Black Whiskered Vireo	5	8
388	8 c. Osprey	8	10
389	10 c. Flamingo	10	12
390	15 c. Brown Pelican	20	20
391	20 c. Parula Warbler ..	25	25
392	30 c. Mockingbird	35	40
393	50 c. Ruby-throated Humming-bird	50	60
394	$1 Bahama Bananaquit ..	1·10	1·25
395	$2 Cedar Waxwing	2·10	2·40
381/95	.. .. *Set of* 15	4·00	4·50

See also Nos. 412/21 and 454, etc.

127. Bermuda Sloop.

(Des. R. Granger Barrett. Litho. Questa.)

1973 (14 Aug.). *Vessels.* T **127** *and similar horiz. designs. Multicoloured.* W w.**12**. P 13½.

396	2 c. Type **127**	5	5
397	5 c. H.M.S. *Blanche* ..	8	8
398	8 c. U.S. privateer *Grand Turk* and P.O. packet *Hinchinbrooke*	12	12
399	10 c. H.M.S. *Endymion* ..	15	15
400	15 c. R.M.S. *Medina*	25	25
401	20 c. H.M.S. *Daring*	30	30
396/401	*Set of* 6	85	85
MS402	198×101 mm. Nos. 396/401	1·00	1·00

1973 (14 Nov.). *Royal Wedding. As Nos.* 165/6 *of Anguilla. Centre multicoloured.* W w.**12** (*sideways*). P 13½.

403	12 c. light turquoise-blue ..	20	20
404	18 c. dull indigo	30	30

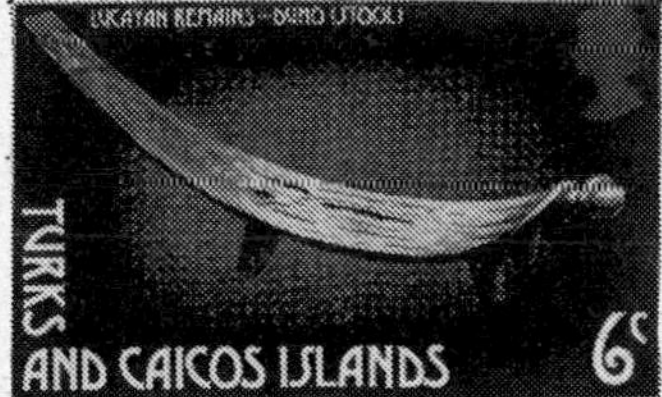

128. Duho (stool).

(Des. Jennifer Toombs. Litho. Questa.)

1974 (17 July). *Lucayan Remains.* T **128** *and similar horiz. designs. Multicoloured.* W w.**12** (*sideways*). P 14½×14.

405	6 c. Type **128**	8	8
406	10 c. Broken wood bowl ..	12	12
407	12 c. Greenstone axe	15	15
408	18 c. Wood bowl	20	25
409	35 c. Fragment of duho ..	40	45
405/9	.. .. *Set of* 5	85	95
MS410	240×90 mm. Nos. 405/9	95	1·00

1974–75. *As Nos.* 381 *etc. but* W w.**12** *upright.*

412	1 c. Magnificent Frigate Bird (11.6.75)	5	5
413	2 c. Noddy Tern (27.9.74) ..	5	5
414	3 c. Blue-grey Gnatcatcher (19.3.75)	8	8
421	20 c. Parula Warbler (11.6.75)	25	30

Nos. 411/25 have been reserved for any further additions to this issue.

129. G.P.O., Grand Turk.

(Des. G. Drummond. Litho. Questa.)

1974 (9 Oct.). *Centenary of Universal Postal Union.* T **129** *and similar horiz. designs. Multicoloured.* W w.**12**. P 14.

426	4 c. Type **129**	8	8
427	12 c. Sloop and island-map ..	15	15
428	18 c. "UPU" and globe ..	20	25
429	55 c. Posthorn and emblem ..	60	65

130. Churchill and Roosevelt.

(Des. V. Whiteley. Litho. Questa.)

1974 (30 Nov.). *Birth Centenary of Sir Winston Churchill.* T **130** *and similar horiz. design. Multicoloured.* W w.**14** (*sideways*). P 14.

430	12 c. Type **130**	15	15
431	18 c. Churchill and vapour-trails	25	25
MS432	85×85 mm. Nos. 430/1	45	50

131. Spanish Captain, *c.* 1492.

(Des. J.W. Ltd. Litho. Questa.)

1975 (26 Mar.). *Military Uniforms.* T **131** *and similar vert. designs. Multicoloured.* W w.**14**. P 14.

433	5 c. Type **131**	8	8
434	20 c. Officer, Royal Artillery, 1783	25	25
435	25 c. Officer, 67th Foot, 1798	30	30
436	35 c. Private, 1st West India Regt., 1833	40	45
MS437	145×88 mm. Nos. 433/6	1·10	1·25

132. Ancient Windmill, Salt Cay.

(Des. P. B. Powell. Litho. Questa.)

1975 (16 Oct.). *Salt-raking Industry. T* **132** *and similar multicoloured designs. W* w.**12** *(sideways on* 10 *and* 20 *c.). P* 14.

438	6 c. Type **132**	10	10
439	10 c. Salt pans drying in sun (*horiz.*)	12	12
440	20 c. Salt-raking (*horiz.*) ..	25	25
441	25 c. Unprocessed salt heaps	30	35

133. Star Coral.

(Des. C. Abbott. Litho. Questa.)

1975 (4 Dec.). *Island Coral. T* **133** *and similar horiz. designs. Multicoloured. W* w.**14** *(sideways). P* 14.

442	6 c. Type **133**	8	8
443	10 c. Elkhorn Coral	12	12
444	20 c. Brain Coral	25	25
445	25 c. Staghorn Coral	30	35

134. American Schooner.

(Des. J.W. Ltd. Litho. Questa.)

1976 (28 May). *Bicentenary of American Revolution. T* **134** *and similar vert. designs. Multicoloured. W* w.**14.** *P* 13½.

446	6 c. Type **134**	8	8
447	20 c. British ship of the line ..	20	25
448	25 c. American frigate *Grand Turk*	25	30
449	55 c. British ketch	55	65
MS450	95×151 mm. Nos. 446/9	1·10	1·40

Each value depicts, at the top, the engagement between the *Grand Turk* and the P.O. Packet *Hinchinbrooke*, as in T **134**.

1976. *As Nos.* 384 *and* 391 *but W* w.**14** *(upright). New value* ($5).

454	3 c. Blue-grey Gnatcatcher (14.5.76)	5	5
461	20 c. Parula Warbler (30.11.76)	20	25
465	$5 Painted Bunting (24.11.76)	5·50	5·75

Nos. 451/64 have been reserved for any further additions to this issue.

135. 1s. 6d. Royal Visit Stamp of 1966.

(Des. V. Whiteley Studio. Litho. Walsall.)

1976 (14 July). *Tenth Anniv. of Royal Visit. T* **135** *and similar horiz. design. Multicoloured. W* w.**14** *(sideways). P* 14½×14.

466	20 c. Type **135**	20	25
467	25 c. 8d. Royal Visit stamp ..	25	30

136. " Virgin and Child " (Dolci).

(Des. G. Drummond. Litho. Questa.)

1976 (10 Nov.). *Christmas. T* **136** *and similar vert. designs. Multicoloured. W* w.**14.** *P* 13½.

468	6 c. Type **136**	5	8
469	10 c. " Virgin and Child " (Studio of Botticelli) ..	12	15
470	20 c. " Adoration of the Magi " (Mestre do Paraiso) ..	25	25
471	25 c. " Adoration of the Magi " (French miniature) ..	30	35

137. Balcony Scene, Buckingham Palace.

(Des. C. Abbott. Litho. Questa.)

1977 (7 Feb.). *Silver Jubilee. T* **137** *and similar vert. designs. Multicoloured. W* w.**14.** *P* 13½.

472	6 c. Queen presenting O.B.E. to E. T. Wood	5	8
473	25 c. The Queen with regalia ..	30	35
474	55 c. Type **137**	65	75

TUVALU.

Formerly known as the Ellice Islands and shar ing a joint administration with the Gilbert grour On 1st January 1976 the two island-group separated and the Ellice Is. were rename Tuvalu.

1. Gilbertese and Tuvaluan.

(Des. Iakopo Nivatui; adapted J. E. Coote: Litho. Questa.)

1976 (1 Jan.). *Separation of the Islands. T and similar multicoloured designs. W* w.1 *(sideways on* 4 *and* 35 *c.). P* 13½.

1	4 c. Type **1**	5	
2	10 c. Map of the islands (*vert.*) ..	12	1
3	35 c. Canoes	45	5

TUVALU

(2)

1976 (1 Jan.). *Nos.* 173 *etc. of Gilbert & Elli Is. optd. as T* **2** *in silver* (35 *c.*) *or blue (others).*

(*a*) *W* w.**12** (*upright*).

4	2 c. Lagoon fishing	45·00	25·(
5	5 c. Gilbertese canoe	10	1
6	8 c. Weaving pandanus fronds	12	1
7	10 c. Weaving a basket ..	15	2
8	50 c. Local handicrafts	12·00	9·(
9	$1 Weaving coconut screen	20·00	

(*b*) *W* w.**12** (*sideways*).

10	2 c. Lagoon fishing	20·00	20·(
11	3 c. Cleaning pandanus leaves	10	1
12	5 c. Gilbertese canoe	30	3
13	25 c. Loading copra	35	4

(*c*) *W* w.**14** (*inverted*).

14	1 c. Cutting toddy	5	
15	6 c. De-husking coconuts ..	10	1
16	15 c. Tiger shark	25	2
17	50 c. Local handicrafts	75	8
18	$1 Weaving coconut screen ..	1·50	1·7
19	$2 Coat-of-arms	3·00	3·2

(*d*) *W* w.**14** (*sideways*).

20	2 c. Lagoon fishing	5	
21	3 c. Cleaning pandanus leaves	5	
22	4 c. Casting nets	8	
23	20 c. Beating a rolled pandanus leaf	30	3
24	25 c. Loading copra	35	4
25	35 c. Fishing at night	55	6
5/7 *and* 14/25	.. *Set of* 15	6·50	7·(

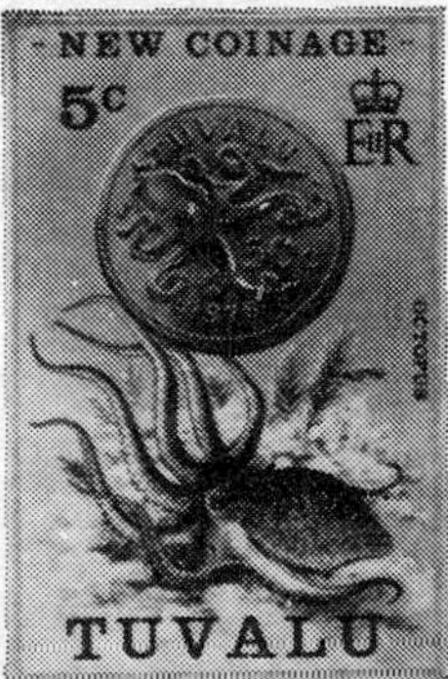

3. 50 c. Coin and Octopus.

(Des. G. Drummond. Litho. Questa.)

976 (21 Apr.). *New Coinage. Vert. designs, each showing coin as in T* **3**. *Multicoloured. W* w.**14** (*inverted*). *P* $13\frac{1}{2}$.

6	5 c. Type **3**	8	10
7	10 c. Red-eyed Crab	15	20
8	20 c. Flying Fish	30	35
9	$1 Green Turtle	1·50	1·75

4. Niulakita and Leathery Turtle.

(Des. J. E. Cooter. Litho. Questa.)

976 (1 July–1 Sept.). *Vert. designs showing maps (1 to 25 c.) or horiz. designs showing scenes (others). Multicoloured. W* w.**14** (*sideways on* 35 *c. to* $5). *P* $13\frac{1}{2}$.

0	1 c. Type **4**	5	5
1	2 c. Nukuulaelae and sleeping mat	5	5
2	4 c. Nui and talo (vegetable) ..	5	8
3	5 c. Nanumanga and grass skirt	8	8
4	6 c. Nukufetau and Coconut Crab	8	10
5	8 c. Funafuti and Banana tree	10	12
6	10 c. Map of Tuvalu	12	15
7	15 c. Niutao and Flying fish ..	20	25
8	20 c. Vaitupu and Maneapa (house)	25	30
9	25 c. Nanumea and fish-hook ..	35	35
0	35 c. Te Ano (game)	45	50
1	50 c. Canoe pole fishing ..	65	75
2	$1 Reef fishing by flare ..	1·25	1·40
3	$2 Living house	2·50	2·75
4	$5 M.V. *Nivanga* (1.9.76) ..	6·50	7·00
0/44	.. .. .. *Set of* 15	11·00	12·00

5. Title page of New Testament.

(Des. G. Drummond. Litho. Harrison.)

976 (6 Oct.). *Christmas. T* **5** *and similar horiz. designs. Multicoloured. W* w.**14**. *P* $14 \times 14\frac{1}{2}$.

5	5 c. Type **5**	5	8
6	20 c. Lotolelei Church	25	30
7	25 c. Kelupi Church	30	35
8	30 c. Mataloa o Tuvalu Church	35	40
9	35 c. Palatasio o Keliso Church ..	45	50
5/9	.. .. .. *Set of* 5	1·25	1·40

6. Queen Elizabeth and Prince Phillip.

(Des. G. L. Vasarhelyi. Litho. Format.)

1977 (9 Feb.). *Silver Jubilee. T* **6** *and similar horiz. designs. Multicoloured. P* $13\frac{1}{2}$.

50	15 c. Type **6**	20	20
51	35 c. Prince Phillip carried ashore at Vaitupu ..	45	50
52	50 c. Queen and attendants ..	60	70

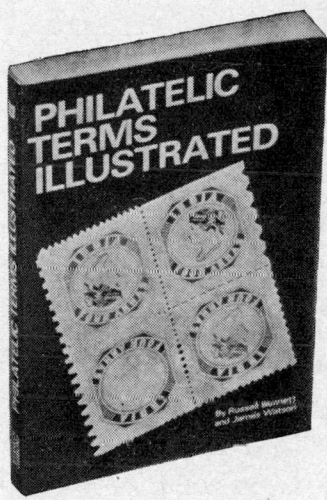

UGANDA.

I. BRITISH PROTECTORATE.

1

Type-written by Rev. E. Millar at Mengo. Wide letters. Thin laid paper. Imperf.

1895 (20 Mar.). A. *Wide stamps, 20 to 26 mm. wide.*

No.	Type	Description		Unused	Used
1	1	5 (cowries), black	..	£650	
2	,,	10 (cowries), black	..	£325	
3	,,	15 (cowries), black	..		
4	,,	20 (cowries), black		—	£275
5	,,	25 (cowries), black	..		
6	,,	30 (cowries), black	..	£275	£275
7	,,	40 (cowries), black	..	£325	
8	,,	50 (cowries), black	..	£225	£225
9	,,	60 (cowries), black	..	£325	

A strip of three of No. 2 is known on cover of which one copy has the value "10" altered to "5" in manuscript and initialled.

1895 (May). *Wide stamps with pen-written surcharges, in black.*

No.	Type	Description		Unused	Used
10	1	10 on 50 (c.) black	..	—	£650
11	,,	15 on 10 (c.) black	..	—	£650
12	,,	15 on 20 (c.) black	..	—	£1000
13	,,	15 on 40 (c.) black	..	—	£700
14	,,	15 on 50 (c.) black	..	—	£1100
15	,,	25 on 50 (c.) black	..	—	£1000
16	,,	50 on 60 (c.) black	..	—	£1000

1895 (April). B. *Narrow stamps, 16 to 18 mm. wide.*

No.	Type	Description		Unused	Used
17	1	5 (c.) black	.. ..	—	£225
18	,,	10 (c.) black	.. ..	£225	£250
19	,,	15 (c.) black	.. ..	£200	£160
20	,,	20 (c.) black	.. ..	£150	£160
21	,,	25 (c.) black	.. ..	£200	£200
22	,,	30 (c.) black	.. ..	£275	£275
23	,,	40 (c.) black	.. ..	£275	
24	,,	50 (c.) black	.. ..	£300	
25	,,	60 (c.) black	.. ..	£325	

2 3

1895. *Narrow letters. Narrow stamp, 16 to 18 mm. wide.* (May.)

No.	Type	Description		Unused	Used
26	2	5 (c.) black ..	.. ..	90·00	
27	,,	10 (c.) black ..	.. ..	90·00	
28	,,	15 (c.) black ..	.. ..	£120	
29	,,	20 (c.) black ..	.. ..	70·00	
30	,,	25 (c.) black ..	.. ..	£100	
31	,,	30 (c.) black ..	.. ..	£120	
32	,,	40 (c.) black ..	.. ..	90·00	
33	,,	50 (c.) black ..	.. ..	90·00	
34	,,	60 (c.) black ..	.. ..	£100	

Change of colour. (End of 1895.)

No.	Type	Description		Unused	Used
35	2	5 (c.) violet ..	.. ..	90·00	90·00
36	,,	10 (c.) violet ..	.. ..	90·00	90·00
37	,,	15 (c.) violet ..	.. ..	90·00	90·00
38	,,	20 (c.) violet ..	.. ..	90·00	90·00
		a. "G U" for "U G"	..		
39	,,	25 (c.) violet ..	.. ..	£110	
40	,,	30 (c.) violet ..	.. ..	£110	
41	,,	40 (c.) violet ..	.. ..	£110	
42	,,	50 (c.) violet ..	.. ..	£110	
43	,,	100 (c.) violet ..	.. ..	£1000	

Stamps of 35 (c.) and 45 (c.) have been chronicled in both colours. They were never prepared for postal use, and did not represent a postal rate, but were type-written to oblige a local collector.

1896 (June). *Type-written.*

No.	Type	Description		Unused	Used
44	3	5 (c). violet ..	.. ..	50·00	50·00
45	,,	10 (c.) violet ..	.. ..	50·00	50·00
46	,,	15 (c.) violet ..	.. ..	50·00	50·00
47	,,	20 (c.) violet ..	.. ..	50·00	50·00
48	,,	25 (c.) violet ..	.. ..	80·00	
49	,,	30 (c.) violet ..	.. ..	80·00	
50	,,	40 (c.) violet ..	.. ..	80·00	
51	,,	50 (c). violet ..	.. ..	80·00	
52	,,	60 (c.) violet ..	.. ..	£200	
53	,,	100 (c.) violet ..	.. ..	£225	£250

Many of the values of the above were made *se-tenant* in sheets.

4. (Thin "1".) 5. (Thick "1".)

6 7

In the 2 a. and 3 a. the dagger points upwards; the stars in the 2 a. are level with the top of "VR". The 8 a. is as T 6 but with left star at top and right star at foot. The 1 r. has three stars at foot. The 5 r. has central star raised and the others at foot.

(Printed by the Rev. F. Rowling at Lubwa's, in Usoga.)

1896 (7 Nov.).
A. *Normal.* B. *Small "o" in "POSTAGE".*

No.	Type	Description		A. Unused	A. Used	B. Unused	B. Used
54	4	1 a. black	..	7·00	9·00	26·00	26·00
55	5	1 a. black	..	2·75	3·25	7·00	7·00
56	6	2 a. black	..	3·25	4·25	6·50	6·50
57	,,	3 a. black	..	3·25	4·25	8·00	8·00
58	,,	4 a. black	..	3·25	4·25	8·00	8·00
59	,,	8 a. black	..	4·25	5·50	12·00	12·00
60	,,	1 r. black	..	9·00	11·00	55·00	55·00
61	,,	5 r. black	..	35·00	60·00	70·00	70·00

Optd. "L", in black as in T 7 for local use, by a postal official at Kampala.

No.	Type	Description		A. Unused	A. Used	B. Unused	B. Used
70	4	1 a. black	..	8·00	15·00	£120	—
71	6	2 a. black	..	8·00	15·00	19·00	24·00
72	,,	3 a. black	..	11·00	24·00	£150	—
73	,,	4 a. black	..	11·00	24·00	24·00	—
74	,,	8 a. black	..	24·00	26·00	55·00	—
75	,,	1 r. black	..	40·00	55·00	£110	—
76	,,	5 r. black	..	—	£600	—	—

Tête-bêche pairs of all values may be found owing to the settings being printed side by side or above one another. They are worth a premium.

8

9

(Recess. D.L.R.)

1898–1902. *P* 14. (*a*) *Wmk. Crown CA.*

No.	Type	Description		Unused	Used
84	8	1 a. scarlet ..	.. ..	10	1
		a. Carmine-rose (1902)	..	20	2
86	,,	2 a. red-brown	.. ..	20	4
87	,,	3 a. pale grey	.. ..	75	8
		a. Bluish grey	.. ..	50	7
88	,,	4 a. deep green	.. ..	60	8
89	,,	8 a. pale olive	.. ..	1·00	2·0
		a. Grey-green	.. ..	1·00	2·0
		(*b*) *Wmk. Crown CC.*			
90	9	1 r. dull blue	.. ..	3·00	3·5
		a. Bright blue	.. ..	5·50	6·0
91	,,	5 r. brown ..	.. ..	11·00	13·0
84/91		.. ..	*Set of 7*	15·00	18·0
84/91		Optd. "Specimen"	*Set of 7*	60·00	

UGANDA
(10)

1902. *T* **11** *of British East Africa optd. with T* **1**[0]

No.	Description		Unused	Used
92	½ a. yellow-green	.. ..	20	2
	a. Opt. omitted (pair) ..	..	£350	
	b. Opt. inverted (at foot)	..	£140	
	c. Opt. double..	.. ..	£250	
93	2½ a. deep blue (R.)	.. ..	30	4
	a. Opt. double..	.. ..	£250	

For issues between 1903 and 1962 see Kenya Uganda and Tanganyika.

II. SELF-GOVERNMENT.

11. Ripon Falls and Speke Memorial.

(Des. S. Scott. Recess. B.W.)

1962 (28 July). *Centenary of Speke's Discover*[y] *of Source of the Nile. W* w.**12**. *P* 14.

No.	Type	Description		Unused	Used
95	11	30 c. black and red	..	8	
96	,,	50 c. black and slate-violet		12	1
97	,,	1s. 30, black and green	..	20	2
98	,,	2s. 50, black and blue	..	45	5

III. INDEPENDENT.

12. Murchison Falls.

13. Tobacco-Growing.

14. Mulago Hospital.

(Des. V. Whiteley. Photo. Harrison.)

1962 (9 Oct.). *Independence. Various desig*[ns] *as T* **12/14.** *P* 15 × 14 (*5 c. to 50 c.*) *or* 14 (*others*).

No.	Description		Unused
99	5 c. deep bluish green	..	5
100	10 c. reddish brown (*shades*)		5
101	15 c. black, red and green		5
102	20 c. plum and buff	..	5

103 30 c. blue 8 5
104 50 c. black & turq.-green 8 5
105 1s. sepia, red & turq.-grn. 12 8
106 1s. 30, yell.-orge. & vio. 20 8
107 2s. blk., carm. & lt. blue 25 12
108 5s. vermilion & dp. green 75 55
109 10s. slate and chestnut .. 1·50 1·50
110 20s. brown and blue .. 5·00 5·00
99/110 .. .. *Set of* 12 7·50 7·00

Designs: *As T* **12/13**—10 c. Tobacco growing; 15 c. Coffee growing; 20 c. Ankole cattle; 30 c. Cotton; 50 c. Mountains of the Moon. *As T* **14**—1s. 30, Cathedrals and Mosque; 2s. Makerere College; 5s. Copper mining; 10s. Cement industry; 20s. Parliament Buildings.

15. Crowned Crane.

(Photo. Harrison.)

1965 (20 Feb.). *International Trade Fair, Kampala. P* 14½ × 14.
111 **15** 30 c. multicoloured .. 8 8
112 ,, 1s. 30, multicoloured .. 25 25

16. Black Bee-eater.

17. African Jacana.

18. Ruwenzori Turaco.

(Des. Mrs. R. M. Fennessy. Photo. Harrison.)

1965 (9 Oct.). *Birds. Various designs as T* **16/18**. *P* 15 × 14 (5 *c.*, 15 *c.*, 20 *c.*, 40 *c.*, 50 *c.*), 14 × 15 (10 *c.*, 30 *c.*, 65 *c.*) *or* 14½ (*others*).
113 5 c. multicoloured .. 5 5
114 10 c. chestnut, black & lt. blue 5 5
115 15 c. yellow and sepia 5 5
116 20 c. multicoloured 5 5
117 30 c. black and brown-red .. 5 5
118 40 c. multicoloured 8 5
119 50 c. grey-blue & reddish vio. 8 5
a. White bird (grey-blue omitted) .. .. ..
120 65 c. orange-red, blk. & lt. grey 15 15
121 1s. multicoloured 20 10
122 1s. 30, chestnut, blk. & yell. 20 8
123 2s. 50, multicoloured .. 40 35
124 5s. multicoloured 80 60
125 10s. multicoloured .. .. 1·50 1·25
126 20s. multicoloured .. .. 3·00 4·50
113/126 .. .. *Set of* 14 6·00 6·50

Designs: *Vert. as T* **16**—15 c. Orange Weaver; 20 c. Narina Trogon; 40 c. Blue-breasted Kingfisher; 50 c. Whale-headed Stork. *Horiz. as T* **17**—30 c. Sacred Ibis; 65 c. Black-winged Red Bishop. *As T* **18**—1s. 30, African Fish Eagle (*vert.*); 2s. 50, Great Blue Turaco; 5s. Lilac-breasted Roller (*vert.*); 10s. Black-collared Lovebird; 20s. Crowned Crane.

The 15 c., 40 c., 65 c. and 1s. exist with PVA gum as well as gum arabic.

19. Carved Screen.

(Des. Mrs. R. Fennessy. Photo. Harrison.)

1967 (26 Oct.). *13th Commonwealth Parliamentary Association Conference. T* **19** *and similar horiz. designs. Multicoloured. P* 14.
127 30 c. Type **19** 5 5
128 50 c. Arms of Uganda .. 8 8
129 1s. 30, Parliamentary Building 25 30
130 2s. 50, Conference Chamber 35 45

20. *Cordia abyssinica.*

21. *Acacia drepanolobium.*

(Des. Mrs. R. M. Fennessy. Photo. Harrison.)

1969 (9 Oct.)–**73**. *Flowers. Various designs as T* **20/1**. *Chalk-surfaced paper. P* 14½ × 14 (5 *c. to* 70 *c.*) *or* 14 (*others*).
131 5 c. brown, green and light olive-yellow 5 5
a. Glazed, ordinary paper (11.4.73) 5 5
132 10 c. multicoloured 5 5
a. Glazed, ordinary paper (27.9.72) 5 5
133 15 c. multicoloured 5 5
134 20 c. bluish violet, yellow-olive and pale sage-green .. 5 5
a. Glazed, ordinary paper (27.9.72) 5 5
135 30 c. multicoloured 5 5
136 40 c. reddish violet, yellow-green and pale olive-grey 8 5
137 50 c. multicoloured 8 8
138 60 c. multicoloured 15 15
a. Glazed, ordinary paper (9.5.73) 10 10
139 70 c. multicoloured 15 15
a. Glazed, ordinary paper (27.9.72) 12 10
140 1s. multicoloured 15 15
a. Glazed, ordinary paper (22.1.71) 20 15
141 1s. 50, multicoloured (*shades*) 25 25
a. Glazed, ordinary paper (3.2.71) 25 20
142 2s. 50, multicoloured .. 50 50
a. Glazed, ordinary paper (3.2.71) 35 35
143 5s. multicoloured .. .. 1·00 1·00
a. Glazed, ordinary paper (3.2.71) 60 70
144 10s. multicoloured .. .. 2·00 2·00
a. Glazed, ordinary paper (3.2.71) .. .. .. 1·50 1·40
145 20s. multicoloured .. .. 4·00 4·00
a. Glazed, ordinary paper (22.1.71) .. .. .. 2·75 2·75
131/145 .. .. *Set of* 15 8·00 8·00
131a/145a .. .. *Set of* 11 5·50 5·50

Designs: *As T* **20**—10 c. *Grewia similis*; 15 c. *Cassia didymobotrya*; 20 c. *Coleus barbatus*; 30 c. *Ockna ovata*; 40 c. *Ipomoea spathulata*; 50 c. *Spathodea nilotica*; 60 c. *Oncoba spinosa*; 70 c. *Carissa edulis*. *As T* **21**—1s. 50, *Clerodendrum myricoides*; 2s. 50, *Acanthus arboreus*; 5s. *Kigelia aethiopium*; 10s. *Erythrina abyssinica*; 20s. *Monodora myristica*.

(22)

1975 (29 Sept.). *Nos.* 141/2 *and* 145a *surch. as T* **22**.
146 2s. on 1s. 50, multicoloured 45 45
147 3s. on 2s. 50, multicoloured 10·00 10·00
148 40s. on 20s. multicoloured .. 5·00 5·50

23. Millet.

24. Maize.

(Des. Mrs. R. M. Fennessy. Photo. Harrison.)

1975 (9 Oct.). *Ugandan Crops. T* **23/4** *and similar horiz. designs. P* 14 × 14½ (10 *to* 80 *c.*) *or* 14 (*others*).
149 10 c. black, apple-green and yellow-brown 5 5
150 20 c. multicoloured 5 5
151 30 c. multicoloured 5 5
152 40 c. multicoloured 5 5
153 50 c. multicoloured 5 5
154 70 c. black, apple-green and light blue-green 8 8
155 80 c. multicoloured 8 10
156 1s. multicoloured 10 12
157 2s. multicoloured 20 25
158 3s. multicoloured 30 35
159 5s. multicoloured 50 60
160 10s. multicoloured .. .. 1·00 1·25
161 20s. apple-green, black and bright purple .. .. 2·10 2·40
162 40s. apple-green, black and yellow-orange .. .. 4·25 4·75
149/62 .. .. *Set of* 14 8·00 9·00

Designs: *As T* **23**—20 c. Sugar; 30 c. Tobacco; 40 c. Onions; 50 c. Tomatoes; 70 c. Tea; 80 c. Bananas. *As T* **24**—2s. Pineapples; 3s. Coffee; 5s. Oranges; 10s. Groundnuts; 20s. Cotton; 40s. Runner Beans.

NOTE. For commemorative stamps, issued between 1964 and 1976, inscribed "UGANDA KENYA TANGANYIKA & ZANZIBAR" (or "TANZANIA UGANDA KENYA") see under East Africa.

1976 (15 APR.). *Telecommunications Development. As Nos. 260/3 of Kenya.*

163	50 c. Microwave tower ..	8	8
164	1s. Cordless switchboard ..	15	15
165	2s. Telephones	25	30
166	3s. Message Switching Centre	35	40
MS167	120×120 mm. Nos. 163/6. Imperf.	80	

1976 (5 JULY). *Olympic Games, Montreal. As Nos. 265/8 of Kenya. P* 14½.

168	50c. Akii Bua, hurdler ..	5	8
169	1s. Filbert Bayi, runner ..	12	15
170	2s. Steve Muchoki, boxer ..	25	30
171	3s. East African flags ..	35	40
MS172	129×154 mm. Nos. 168/71. P 13	80	

1976 (4 OCT.). *Railway Transport. As Nos. 270/3 of Kenya. P* 14½.

173	50 c. Tanzania–Zambia railway	5	8
174	1s. Nile Bridge, Uganda ..	12	15
175	2s. Nakuru Station, Kenya ..	25	30
176	3s. Class A loco, 1896 ..	35	40
MS177	154×103 mm. Nos. 173/6. P 13	80	

POSTAGE DUE STAMPS.

The Postage Due stamps of Kenya, Uganda and Tanganyika were used in Uganda until 2nd January, 1967.

D 1

(Litho. D.L.R.)

1967 (3 JAN.). *Chalk-surfaced paper. P* 14×13½.

D1	D 1	5 c. scarlet	5	5
D2	,,	10 c. green	5	5
D3	,,	20 c. deep blue	5	8
D4	,,	30 c. red-brown	8	10
D5	,,	40 c. bright purple ..	10	12
D6	,,	1s. orange	25	35
D1/D6		.. .. *Set of* 6	40	60

1970 (31 MAR.). *As Nos.* D1/6, *but on glazed ordinary paper, perf.* 14×15.

D 7	D 1	5 c. scarlet	5	5
D 8	,,	10 c. green (*shades*) ..	5	5
D 9	,,	20 c. deep blue ..	5	8
D10	,,	30 c. red-brown (*shades*)	8	10
D11	,,	40 c. bright purple ..	10	12
D7/D11		.. .. *Set of* 5	25	30

1973 (12 DEC.). *Glazed, ordinary paper. P* 15.

D12	D 1	5 c. scarlet	5	5
D13	,,	10 c. emerald	5	5
D14	,,	20 c. deep blue ..	5	5
D15	,,	30 c. red-brown ..	5	5
D16	,,	40 c. bright mauve ..	5	5
D17	,,	1s. bright orange ..	10	12
D12/17		.. .. *Set of* 6	20	25

UNION OF SOUTH AFRICA.
See SOUTH AFRICA.

VICTORIA.

Unlike many British colonies, Victoria, with three exceptions only, produced her own dies, plates and stamps. The exceptions were the 1d. and 6d. "Queen-on-Throne" (the dies and plates for which were produced and the stamps printed by Perkins, Bacon) and the 2d. of 1870 for which though it was printed throughout in Victoria, the die and plates were produced by **De La Rue.** Being the products of local endeavour in a remote country, the stamps of Victoria possess great technical interest for students although its issues are too complicated for many collectors. The present list is an attempt alike to demonstrate their interest and to clarify their complications, particularly by the inclusion of carefully written notes on various aspects of their production.

I. THE PRIVATE CONTRACT PERIOD, 1850–59. (Ham, Campbell & Co., Campbell and Fergusson, Calvert, Robinson.)

1. Queen Victoria ("Half Length").

(Dies engraved on a single piece of steel by Thomas Ham, Melbourne.)

(Lithographed by Thomas Ham, Melbourne.

1850 (3 Jan.). *T* **1.** *Imperf. except groups* (9) *and* (10).

1d. Thin line at top.

2d. Fine border and background.

3d. White area to left of orb.

(1) Original state of dies: 1*d.* (*tops of letters of* "VICTORIA" *reach to top of stamp*); 2*d.* (*fine border and background*); 3*d.* (*thicker white outline around left of orb, central band of orb does not protrude at left*). *No frame-lines on dies.*

No.	Description		Unused	Used
1	1d. orange-vermilion		—	£400
	a. Orange-brown		—	£225
	b. Dull chocolate-brown (shades) ..		—	£225
2	2d. lilac-mauve (*shades*) ..		—	£130
3	2d. brown-lilac (*shades*) ..		£800	£120
	a. Grey-lilac		—	£120
4	3d. bright blue (*shades*) ..		—	£120
	a. *Blue (shades)*		—	80·00
	ab. Retouched (Nos. 10 & 11 in transfer-group only)		—	£130

Periods of use: 1d., 2d. and 3d. No. 4, (January 1850); 3d. No. 4*a*, (March 1850 to October, 1851).

Note on Group (1). With the exception of No. 4*a* all the above were printed from a small stone of 30 (5×6), laid down without the use of an Intermediate stone. The 3d. No. 4*a* was the first 'Half Length' to appear in sheets of 120, which was the case for all subsequent Ham printings. It was produced from an Intermediate stone of 15 (5×3). The 2d. No. 2 was the first printing (from Stone 'A') and Nos. 3 and 3*a* the second (from Stone 'B'). Impressions clear and fine.

Note on margins found in the Ham printings: These stamps divide into two groups—Nos. 1 to 7—which were from 5-wide groups (or sheets) and Nos. 8 to 17—which were from 6-wide groups. The spacing between stamps horizontally is greater for Nos. 1 to 7 than Nos. 8 to 17 (and see later notes).

1d. Thick line at top.

2d. Coarse background.

3d. White area small and band protruding to left of orb.

(2) Second state of dies: 1*d.* (*more colour over top of letters of* "VICTORIA"); 2*d. fine border as* (1) *but with coarse background*); 3*d.* (*thinner white outline around left of orb, central band of orb protrudes at left*).

No.	Description	Unused	Used
5	1d. red-brown (*shades*)	£1100	£130
	a. Pale dull red-brown	—	£130
6	2d. grey-lilac (*shades*)	£225	40·00
	a. Dull grey	—	40·00
7	3d. blue (*shades*)	—	55·00
	a. Retouched (22 varieties) *from*	—	£100

Periods of use: 1d. (Feb.-Sept. 1850); 2d. (Jan.-April 1850); 3d. (Oct. 1851 to Dec. 1852).

Note on Group (2). These were all printed in sheets of 120 (10×12), the Printing stones for the 1d. and 2d. being produced from an Intermediate stone of 30 (5×6), and that for the 3d. from one of 10 (5×2). Impressions are clear and fine.

Frame-lines added.

(3) Third state of dies: *As in* (2) *but with frame-lines added, very close up, on all four sides.*

No.	Description	Unused	Used
8	1d. dull orange-vermilion ..	—	60·00
	a. Dull red (shades)	—	60·00
9	1d. deep red-brown	—	£225
	a. Brownish red (shades)	—	50·00
	b. Dull rose (shades)	—	50·00
10	2d. grey (*shades*)	—	60·00
	a. Olive-grey (shades)	—	60·00
11	3d. blue (*shades*)	—	26·00
	a. Deep blue (shades)	—	26·00
	b. Pale greenish blue (shades) ..	—	40·00

Periods of use: 1d. No. 8 (Oct. 1850 to April 1851); 1d. No. 9 (April 1851 to March 1854): 2d. (Aug.-Oct. 1850); 3d. (Dec. 1852 to April 1854).

Note on Group (3). Although the above were all printed in sheets of 120 the format was 12×10—and continued so—and not 10×12 as in Group (2). For No. 8 (i.e. third 1d. printing) an Intermediate stone of 30 (6×5) was used, but for all the others (i.e. fourth printings) one of 12 (6×2) was employed. These stamps (and those under Group (4) following) are very closely spaced as compared with the (1) and (2) groups. Group (3) represented the last state of the 1d. and 3d. dies but not of the 2d. Impressions vary from medium to fine.

White veil.

(4) *As* (3) *but altered to give, for the* 1*d. and* 3*d., the so-called* "*white veils*", *and for the* 2*d., the effect of vertical drapes to the veil.*

No.	Description	Unused	Used
12	1d. reddish brown	—	50·00
	a. Bright pinky red (shades) ..	£150	50·00
13	2d. drab	—	55·00
	a. Grey-drab	—	55·00
	b. Lilac-drab	—	55·00
	c. Red-lilac	—	£275
	d. Void S.W. corner	—	£425
14	3d. blue (*shades*)	—	24·00
	a. Deep blue (shades)	—	24·00
	b. Greenish blue (shades)	—	24·00
	c. Retouched (9 varieties) ..	—	55·00

Periods of use: 1d. (April 1851–March 1854); 2d. (Aug.–Oct. 1850); 3d. (April–June 1854).

Note on Group (4): The alterations to the veils were made to each of the 12 impressions on the Intermediate Stones used for Group (3), and there are therefore 12 varieties of the veil in each value. Impressions are relatively coarse, particularly of the 2d. (save for No. 13*c*). Spacing of stamps is very close as in (3). In the 1d. and 2d. the shades found in Group (4) differ considerably from those met in (3).

2d. Coarse border and background.

(5) Fourth state of die. 2d. value only: *Coarse border and background. Veil details as in original die.*

No.	Description	Unused	Used
15	2d. red-lilac (*shades*)	—	80·00
	a. Lilac	—	80·00
	b. Grey	—	£130
	c. Dull brownish lilac	—	50·00
	d. Retouched lower label—value omitted. (Nos. 15 to 15*c*) ..	—	£800
	e. Other retouches (Nos. 15 to 15*c*) (17 varieties) *from*	—	£100

Period of use: May–August 1850.

Note on Group (5): This comprised the sixth printing of this value and was printed from Stone "A". For it (and also for Groups (6) and (7) below) Ham utilized an Intermediate Stone of 30 (6×5). This was the only printing of the 2d. value in which retouches were made to the printing stone. Impressions (save for No. 15*a*) are generally good, sometimes fine.

No. 15*b* can generally, and No. 15*c* can always be readily distinguished as they are on *thin* wove paper of good quality, not found elsewhere.

(6) 2d. only: *As* (5) *but with veils altered to give effect of vertical drapes.*

No.	Description	Unused	Used
16	2d. lilac-grey	—	60·00
	a. Deep grey	—	60·00
	b. Brown-lilac (shades)	—	32·00
17	2d. cinnamon (*shades*)	£110	50·00
	a. Drab (shades)	—	24·00
	b. Pale dull brown (shades) ..	—	32·00
	c. Greenish grey	—	32·00
	d. Olive-drab (shades)	—	60·00
	e. Buff	—	60·00

Periods of use: No. 16 etc. (Nov. 1850–March 1851), No. 17 etc. (March 1851–Dec. 1852).

Note on Group (6): The 2d. Stone "B" (No. 16, etc.) and Stone "C" (No. 17, etc.) constituted Ham's seventh and eighth printings respectively. Two shades in the Stone "B" printings do not differ greatly from shades in the Stone "A" printings, but all those listed under No. 17 are entirely and peculiarly distinctive.

The veil alterations were again made to each of the impressions on the Intermediate Stones so that there are 30 varieties of these.

General note on Ham printings. Ham's contract was completed in May 1850 but his 1d. and 3d. stamps remained in use up till March and June 1854 respectively. The 2d. 'Half Length' design was, however, as the result of an injury to the die, superseded by Ham's 'Queen-on-Throne' design in December 1852. In all Ham made five printings of each of the 1d. and 3d. and eight of the 2d. The paper employed by the three contractors was distinctive. For instance, for the whole of the Campbell and Fergusson printings (1d. and 3d. only) a coarse wove paper of poor quality, easily thinned and with a marked "mesh" (horizontal or vertical) was used. This paper is nothing like any paper used for the Ham or Campbell printings, and affords the best preliminary test for all 1d. and 3d. 'Half Lengths'.

II. Lithographed by J. S. Campbell & Co., Melbourne.

(7) *Wide settings. Stamps 2½–3 mm. apart* (1d.) *or 1½–2 mm. apart* (3d.).

18 1d. orange-red (*shades*) .. £130 55·00
a. Rose .. .. .. — £160
19 3d. blue (*shades*) .. £110 17·00
a. Retouched (No. 17 in group) .. — 60·00

Periods of use: 1d. (Mar. 1854–Jan. 1855); 3d. (June, 1854–April 1855, also 1858/9).

Note on Group (7): The Campbell 1d. was printed from a stone of 192 impressions (96×2), and the 3d. from a stone of 320 (160×2). For each value an intermediate stone of 24 (6×4) was used. Impressions are generally good.

III. Lithographed by Campbell and Fergusson, Melbourne.

(8) *Wide settings, as* (7). *Impressions medium to poor, depending on state of printing stones. Paper used is distinctive (see final note after Ham printings).*

(*a*) *Same intermediate stones as had been employed for Group* (7).

20 1d. brown (*shades*) .. .. £110 50·00
a. Brick-red (shades) .. .. — 40·00
b. Dull red (shades) .. .. — 40·00
21 1d. orange-brown (*shades*) .. — 55·00
a. Dull rose-red (shades) .. .. — 32·00
b. Bright rose-pink .. .. — 55·00
c. Retouched (4 varieties) .. — £200
22 1d. pink (*shades*) .. .. £100 16·00
a. Rose (shades) .. .. £100 16·00
b. Lilac-rose (shades) .. .. — 16·00
c. Dull brown-red (shades) .. .. — 55·00
d. Retouched (9 varieties) .. — £150
23 3d. bright blue (*shades*) .. £110 26·00
a. Greenish blue (shades) .. £100 20·00
b. Retouched (No. 17 in group) .. — 50·00
24 3d. Prussian blue (*shades*) .. — 36·00
a. Milky blue .. .. .. — 60·00
b. Retouched (No. 17 in group) .. — £110

Periods of use: 1d. No. 20, etc. (Stone 2, July 1854 and December 1855–May 1856): 1d. No. 21, etc. (Stone 3, Aug.–Nov. 1855); 1d. No. 22, etc. (Stones, 4, 5, Feb.–Aug. 1855 and May–Oct., 1856); 3d. No. 23, etc. (Stone "B", July 1857–Dec. 1858); 3d. No. 24 etc. (Stone "C". Nov. 1856–June 1857).

(*b*) *New intermediate stone of similar size* (6×4) *and spacing 2½–3 mm. apart horizontally.* (*Stone* "D").

25 3d. steel-blue (*shades*) .. .. — 24·00
a. Greenish blue (shades) .. .. 90·00 15·00
b. Blue (shades) .. .. .. 90·00 15·00
c. Deep blue (shades) .. .. 90·00 15·00
d. Indigo (shades) .. .. .. — 20·00

Period of use: May 1855 to November 1856. Impressions generally heavier than previous 3d.

Note on Group (8): All printing stones were of 400 impressions, consisting of an upper and lower pane of 200 (20×10) save in two cases, viz.: the 3d. No. 23 which was of 320 (160×2) and No. 24 which was probably of 200 (20×10) impressions. The 3d. No. 24, etc., presents a considerably worn appearance. No. 25 (steel-blue) comprised the earlier part of the printing and is, comparatively, of good appearance and impression.

No. 21*b* is only found with barred oval cancellations as these were not used after the end of 1855 and are thus of assistance in identification.

IV. 3d. stamps rouletted and perforated in 1857 and 1859 respectively.

(9) *Rouletted 7 to 8½ at G.P.O., Melbourne (see later notes).*

(*a*) *Campbell printing* (*No.* 19).

26 3d. blue (*shades*) .. .. — 70·00
a. Retouched. (No. 17 in group) ..

(*b*) *Campbell & Fergusson printing* (*No.* 23).

27 3d. bright blue (*shades*) .. — 80·00
a. Greenish blue (shades) .. .. — 70·00
b. Retouched. (No. 17 in group) ..

Period of use: Sept.–Dec., 1858.

(10) *Perforated 12 by Robinson.*

(*a*) *Campbell printing* (*No.* 19).

28 3d. blue (*shades*) .. .. — 55·00
a. Retouched. (No. 17 in group) .. — £120

(*b*) *Campbell & Fergusson printing* (*No.* 23).

29 3d. greenish blue (*shades*) .. — £130
a. Retouched. (No. 17 in group) ..

Period of use: Jan. 1859 to Jan. 1860.

Note on Groups (9) *and* (10)*:* The roulettes are seldom found on all four sides. The great majority of the perforated stamps are badly off-centre.

Lithographic Reprints of the three values (the 2d. die then being in a defaced condition) were made in 1891, on paper wmk. V over Crown (Type *V* **2**) *W* **23**, perf. 12½. The 1891 Reprints of all issues were the direct result of Victoria, in that year, joining the Universal Postal Union. As a member she was expected to supply specimens of her old issues to other members. None of these being available and most of the old plates having been destroyed she was, in the majority of cases, compelled to make new plates for which, fortunately, all the original dies (save the "Emblems" (3) and the "Woodblocks" (4) were available.

FURTHER INFORMATION on these interesting issues, including the details of the numbers printed, the plating of the Transfer Groups, the papers used, the retouches, creased transfers, "abnormal" combinations, "stitch" watermarks, etc., etc., will be found in "The Half-Lengths of Victoria", the work by J. R. W. Purves, F.R.P.S.L., on which the above list is based.

2. Queen on Throne.

1852–54. *T* **2**. *Imperf.*

Corner letters: Each of the fifty subjects of the original plate show different letter combinations of A to Z, except J.

I. Dec. 1852. *Recess-printed by Thomas Ham from a steel plate of* 50 (10×5) *impressions, engraved by him by hand.*

30 2d. reddish brown .. .. 36·00 13·00
a. Chestnut .. .. .. — 55·00
b. Purple-brown .. .. .. 36·00 13·00

Reprints were made in 1891 (and later) using the original plate, on paper wmk. V over Crown Type V **2**, both imperf. and perf. 12½.

II. Dec. 1853–May 1854. *Lithographed by Campbell & Co., transfers for the stones being taken from Ham's steel plate. Period of issue: Dec.* 1853–*April* 1855 *and May* 1856–*May* 1857. *On various types of good quality paper, hand-made and machine-wove.*

(i) *Early printings: full impression, detail around back of throne generally complete. Impressions fine and clear; colours rich.*

31 2d. brownish purple .. .. 60·00 11·00
a. Grey-brown .. .. .. — 11·00
b. Purple-black .. .. .. — 11·00
c. Dull lilac-brown (spotty print on toned) .. .. .. — 13·00

Papers: The papers used for (i) and (ii) were, save in the two cases indicated, distinguished by their *whiteness,* as compared with the toned (yellowish) character of all that follow. Thi toning is due in part to the type of gum used bu also to the larger proportion of wood pulp use in manufacture. The *hand-made* paper, which i always *white,* is found in (i) and (ii) only.

(ii) *Intermediate printings. Impressions nc so full or sharp, background round top c throne not so fully defined.*

32 2d. violet-black .. .. .. — 11·0
a. Grey-black .. .. .. — 13·0
b. Grey-lilac .. .. .. — 13·0
c. Dull brown (on toned) .. .. — 13·0
d. Substituted transfer (in pair) .. — £130

(iii) *Later printings, on toned paper onl Background round top of throne generall whiter. Stamps lack the detail of* (i) *an* (ii) *although impression is reasonably gooc*

33 2d. grey-black .. .. .. 36·00 9·0
a. Purple-black .. .. .. 36·00 9·0

(iv) *Last printing; on toned paper onl Background generally full as* (i) *but im pression is singularly flat, and lacking i fineness and sharpness. Normal colour i distinctive.*

34 2d. grey-drab (*shades*) .. .. — 9·0
a. Black .. .. — 32·0

Notes on the Campbell & Co. Printings.

(*a*) *Stones:* In all, 2,000,000 stamps wer printed (and issued) under this contract. The were not printed on the one occasion but o several. A total of 22 transfers were taken fron the steel plate, *nine* printing stones being used Of these the first eight were of 100 impression (one "fifty" over another "fifty") and th ninth was of 300 impressions (three "fifties" over three "fifties"). Only three of thes stones were used to a point where they showe wear and in those cases the wear was nothin like that found in the Campbell & Fergusso printings. Whiteness in the background aroun the throne, where it occurs, is more often th result of weak pressure in the taking of th transfers.

(*b*) *Shades:* These should be readily distin guishable from the C. & F. printings, with th possible exception of No. 32*b* which has a pinkis element.

(*c*) *Papers:* At least *six* varieties, all of goo quality (comprising both hand and machin made papers) were used but they were all s different (and of so much better quality) to tha employed for the C. & F. contract that, once C. & F. stamp is acquired, no difficulty shoul be encountered in identifying a Campbell.

(*d*) *Vertical pairs* (they are rare) have been me from four of the Campbell stones, with *wid* distances (up to 19 mm.) between the stamp In such cases the top stamp is from the lowe row of a top transfer of fifty and the bottor stamp from the top row of a similar lowe transfer.

(*e*) "*Substituted Transfers*". These (a bloc of four in the S.W. corner of a sheet) occurred o one out of the 22 transfers on printing ston 5. The horizontal pairs read WA-HN and GM SX respectively and the vertical pairs VZ ove VZ and WA over WA respectively. They ar all of the greatest rarity.

(*f*) No "*Creased Transfer*" varieties are to b met in the Campbell printings where the metho followed for laying down the printing stone differed from that employed for the Campbell & Fergussons. The same is true of the "Half Lengths" printed by these two contractors.

Some instances of *retouching* (they are rare may be met. One stone only was affected.

III. June 1854. ***Lithographed by Campbell & Fergusson; transfers for the stones again bein taken from Ham's steel plate. Period of Issue March 1855–May 1856. Printed, like th Campbell & Fergusson Half-Lengths, on machine-wove paper of poor quality (easil thinned and torn). This factor alone provides a unfailing guide for distinguishing the products c the two contractors.***

(i) *Printings from stones which were not over used; background around top of thron generally full and detail good.*

35 2d. lilac (*shades*) .. .. 40·00 9·0
a. Purple (shades) .. .. — 9·0
b. Variety "TVO" .. .. — £25

(ii) *Early printings from stones which were over-used. Similar characteristics to (i) above, though detail is not quite so full. Distinctive shades.*

36 2d. brown .. .. .. — 36·00
a. Brown-purple .. .. .. 60·00 11·00
b. Warm purple .. .. .. — 11·00
c. Rose-lilac .. .. .. — 11·00
d. Substituted transfer (pair) .. — £400

(iii) *Later printings from the same stones used for (ii) when in a worn condition. Impressions heavy, coarse and overcoloured; details blurred; generally white background around top of throne.*

37 2d. dull lilac-mauve .. .. 36·00 11·00
a. Dull mauve .. .. .. 36·00 11·00
b. Grey-violet .. .. .. — 11·00
c. Red-lilac .. .. .. — 13·00
d. Substituted transfer (pair) .. — £400

(iv) *Printings from a stone giving (from the start) blotchy and unpleasing results, with poor definition. Mainly shows in extra colour patches found on most stamps.*

38 2d. dull purple .. .. .. — 11·00
a. Dull grey-lilac .. .. 60·00 11·00
b. On thick card paper .. .. — £250

Notes on the Campbell & Fergusson Printings.

(*a*) *Stones:* 3,000,000 stamps in all were printed under this contract, of which, however, 1,500,000 (deemed to be in excess of requirements) were destroyed. A total of four printing stones (comprising 16 transfers from the steel plate) were used. The greater size of the printing and the smaller number taken of transfers of fifty (and hence of printing impressions) explains the *over-use* of certain stones, and the badly-worn prints (with filled-in colour, finer details missing, etc.) that are often met.

(*b*) *Shades:* At least 95 per cent of these printings, whatever their actual shade names, have—by comparison with the Campbell stamps—a *pink* quality. Only about 2 per cent of the Campbells, a proportion of the stamps printed from one stone only, have such a quality, but in that case the paper used was wholly different.

(*c*) *Paper* is invariably of vertical mesh. *Both* horizontal and vertical meshes are found in the Campbells.

(*d*) *Vertical pairs* with *wide* spacing have been found. They are rare: See note above on similar Campbell pairs.

(*e*) "*Substituted Transfers*": Here the entire *five* impressions comprising the left vertical row of a sheet were affected. The *horizontal* pairs (starting at the top and going down) are as follows: UY-BF, TX-MQ, DI-WA, SW-GM and CH-RW. The *vertical* pairs are UY over TX and DI over SW. They occur in various shades and stages of wear.

(*f*) "*Creased Transfer*" varieties. As in the C. & F. "Half-Length" printings, various major instances are met, including the "TVO" variety. At least two transfer groups of 50 were affected.

No retouching has been met in any printing.

3

(Die engraved and stamps lithographed by Campbell & Fergusson.)

1854–65. *T* **3**. (*a*) *Imperf.*

39 1s. blue (*shades*) (6.7.54) .. 32·00 11·00
a. Greenish blue .. .. .. 36·00 11·00
b. Indigo-blue .. .. .. — 55·00

(*b*) *Rouletted 7–7½ at G.P.O., Melbourne (see later notes).*

40 1s. greenish blue (27.8.57) .. — 40·00
a. Blue .. .. — 40·00

(*c*) *Perf. 12 by Robinson, early in* 1859.

41 1s. blue (*shades*) (13.4.59) .. 20·00 7·00
a. Greenish blue .. .. .. 17·00 5·50
b. Indigo-blue .. .. .. — 11·00

For this stamp four printing stones, each of 400 impressions (in four panes of 100), were used. These were built up from an "intermediate" stone of 40 (8×5) impressions. Retouches and "creased transfer" varieties also exist. At least two classes of paper were used.

This stamp was reprinted (by lithography) in 1891, wmk. V over Crown, Type V **2**, perf. 12½. The transfers were taken from the original die.

4. Queen on Throne.

(Recess. Perkins, Bacon & Co.)

1856–58. *T* **4**. *Wmk. Large Star, Type* **w. 1**.

(*a*) *Imperf.*

42 1d. yellow-green (23.10.56) .. 20·00 9·00

(*b*) *Rouletted 5½–6½ by F. W. Robinson, in Melbourne.*

43 6d. bright blue (1.11.58) .. 13·00 5·50
a. Light blue .. .. .. 40·00 13·00

The gumming for the 6d. was deemed unsatisfactory and it was not used until the exhaustion of Nos. 44–48. The stock was imperf. and was rouletted by Robinson before issue. It only exists imperf., obliterated "CANCELLED" in London, in 1861.

Re-entries and re-cuts occur in both values.

These two stamps were reprinted in 1891, Wmk. V over Crown, Type V **2**, Imperf., using the original steel plates. The 1d. is found in two colours—a dull yellow-green and a bright blue-green. The 6d. has an indigo quality and can be found in two shades.

5

6

7

1854–59. *T* **5** *to* **7** (*the* "*Woodblocks*"). *Typo.*

I. *T* **5**. *6d.: Printed in sheets of 100 stamps, representing two impressions from a plate of 50 woodblocks (in two panes of 25—5×5), engraved individually by S. Calvert. These all differ but are of two main types:—*

A. *Small white mark after* "VICTORIA" *like an apostrophe.*

B. *No white mark after* "VICTORIA".

(*a*) *Imperf.*

44 6d. reddish brown (13.9.54) .. 24·00 7·00
a. Dull orange .. .. .. 20·00 5·50
b. Orange-yellow .. .. .. 20·00 6·00

(*b*) *Rouletted 7–9.*

45 6d. reddish brown (12.8.57) .. — 20·00
a. Dull orange (3.12.57) .. .. — 15·00
b. Orange-yellow .. .. .. — 20·00

These stamps may be met rouletted on two sides only, and also (with finer points) on all four sides. The first class emanates from some "rouletters" used by the window-clerks at the G.P.O., Melbourne (see note after No. 62). The latter class were "perforated" by Calvert, and this gauge was also used for the Rouletted "Emblems" of early 1858.

(*c*) *Serpentine Roulette* 10½.

46 6d. orange-yellow (5.12.57) .. — 24·00

(*d*) *Serrated 18–19×serpentine 10½; also serrated compound on one side with serpentine.*

47 6d. orange-yellow (19.10.57) .. — 24·00

(*e*) *Serrated 18–19.*

48 6d. orange-yellow .. .. — 24·00

Part of (*b*) and all of (*c*), (*d*) and (*e*) were "perforated" by Calvert under his contract of 14.10.57, a total of 163,000 stamps being so treated. The "pin-perf. about 10" variety previously listed belongs to 1856 and is clearly not of official origin.

II. *T* **5**. *2s.: For this value Calvert employed a plate of 25 (5×5) separately engraved woodblocks, two impressions of which made up the sheet of* 50.

(*a*) *Imperf.*

49 2s. dull bluish green (1.9.54) .. £250 60·00

(*b*) *Rouletted 7–7½.*

50 2s. dull bluish green .. .. — £160

(*c*) *Perf. 12 (by Robinson)*, 1859.

51 2s. dull bluish green .. .. 90·00 16·00
a. Pale bluish green .. .. 90·00 20·00

Nos. 49–51 were printed on a printed *yellow* background which is usually faint. For the blue-on-green printings of 1864–81 see Nos. 127, 130, 140 and 147. These latter were printed in sheets of 30, in two panes of 15 (3×5). The plate comprised 18 of the original woodblocks and 12 electros.

III. *T* **6**. REGISTRATION *stamp*.

(*a*) *Imperf.*

52 1s. rose-pink and blue (1.12.54) £250 26·00

(*b*) *Rouletted 7–7½.*

53 1s. rose-pink and blue .. £900 90·00

IV. *T* **7**. "TOO LATE" *stamp. Imperf.*

54 6d. lilac and green (1.1.55) .. £110 55·00

The *same* main plate of 25 woodblock impressions (5×5 printed four times make up a sheet of 100) was originally used for both the "Registered" and "Too Late" stamps. For the portions printed in blue and green respectively separate stereotype plates were used of each stamp.

A second woodblock plate of 25 (5×5) impressions from a different model was used (with the first plate) for later printings of the "Registered" only. Die 2 is distinguished by the longer head 'R' of "VICTORIA" and the absence of the small white letters "V" and "R" etc. The "Registered" stamp ceased to be so used from 5.1.58 although Postmasters were then instructed to use up remaining stocks for normal postal purposes. The "Too Late" stamp was withdrawn from issue as from 1.7.57. A very few used multiples of both these stamps are known. They all represent abnormal usage.

8

1857–60. *T* **8** ("*Emblems*"). *Typo.*

For these stamps the dies were "woodblocks" engraved by Calvert, and the "plates" consisted of 120 individual electrotypes clamped together. In all, six settings were employed for the 4d. value and three each for the 1d. and 2d. values.

I. 1857. Printed by Calvert.

(i) *Wmk. Large Star, Type* **w. 1**.

(*a*) *Imperf.*

55 1d. yellow-green (18.2.57) .. 13·00 7·00
a. Deep green .. .. .. 22·00 15·00
b. Printed on both sides .. .. — £325

56 4d. vermilion (26.1.57) .. .. 65·00 4·00
a. Brown-vermilion .. .. 60·00 4·00
b. Printed on both sides .. .. — £275

57 4d. dull red (20.7.57) .. .. 50·00 4·00
58 4d. dull rose (6.9.57) .. .. 50·00 4·00

(b) *Rouletted* 7–9 (*often on two sides only*).

59 1d. yellow-green .. .. £110 33·00
60 4d. vermilion .. .. — 40·00
61 4d. dull red (1.8.57) .. .. — 20·00
62 4d. dull rose .. .. — 13·00

Nos. 59–62 were not rouletted by Calvert, but by one or other of three "rouletters" used by the clerks at the selling windows of the G.P.O., Melbourne. One of these "rouletters" gauged 6½–7½ and another 7½–9. The most effective of them was purchased from one Raymond early in August, 1857.

(c) *P* 12.

63 1d. yellow-green .. .. — £130

This stamp and Nos. 66, 66*a*, 72 and 77 were the result of the perforating (by Robinson), probably in 1860, of a few sheets of old stock.

(ii) *No wmk. On good quality medium-wove paper.*

(a) *Imperf.*

64 2d. pale lilac (25.5.57) .. .. 55·00 5·50
a. Grey-lilac .. .. .. 55·00 5·50

(b) *Rouletted* 7–9 (*often on two sides only*).

65 2d. pale lilac .. .. .. — 13·00
a. Grey-lilac .. .. .. — 13·00

See note following No. 62.

(c) *P* 12.

66 2d. pale lilac .. .. .. — £100
a. Grey-lilac .. .. .. — £100

See note following No. 63.

(d) *Serrated* 18–19.

67 2d. grey-lilac £150 £130

This variety is probably the result of an experiment by Calvert. Most of the copies seen are unused.

II. 1858: Printed by Calvert on white wove paper of good quality.

(a) *Rouletted all round* 8–9 (*usually fine points*).

68 1d. pale emerald (19.1.58) .. 55·00 7·00
a. Emerald-green .. .. 55·00 8·00
b. Roul. horiz. only .. .. — £150
69 4d. rose-pink (10.1.58) .. .. 70·00 2·50
a. Bright rose .. .. 70·00 2·50
b. Reddish pink .. .. — 5·50
c. Roul. horiz. only .. .. — £120
d. Roul. vert. only .. .. — £120

(b) *Imperf.* (April 1858).

70 1d. pale emerald .. .. 55·00 5·50
a. Emerald-green .. .. — 7·00
71 4d. rose-pink .. .. 90·00 13·00
a. Bright rose .. .. — 13·00
b. Reddish pink .. .. — 17·00

The imperf. varieties above were stamps which *should* have been rouletted by Calvert. On the cancellation of his contract they were taken over from him but since supplies were urgently required (and Robinson not having then commenced his contract) were put into use as they were. They *follow* and do not precede the roulettes.

(c) *P* 12.

72 1d. emerald-green .. .. — £130
a. Imperf. between (horiz. pr.) ..

III. 1858–9: Printed under contract by F. W. Robinson, first outside and later (1859) inside the Post Office Establishment.

(i) *On wove paper of a somewhat poorer quality than Calvert's. Imperf.*

73 4d. dull rose (5.58) .. .. — 33·00

(ii) *On smooth vertically laid paper of good quality.*

(a) *Imperf.*

74 4d. dull rose (8.5.58) .. .. — 13·00
a. Dull rose-red .. .. — 13·00
b. Dull rose-red (normal ink) .. £150 8·00

The imperforate stamps Nos. 73, 74, and 74*a* can be easily distinguished by their distinctive *heavy, coarse* impression and the *oily* nature of the ink employed. They were the *first* stamps printed by Robinson and because of the demand were rushed into circulation without being rouletted, as also was No. 74*b* which was the first stamp printed by him using a more satisfactory quality of ink.

(b) *Rouletted* 5½–6½.

75 2d. brown-lilac (*shades*) (9.58) .. 55·00 5·00
76 4d. pale dull rose (5.58) .. — 1·25
a. Dull rose-red .. .. 24·00 1·25
b. Rose-red .. .. 24·00 1·10

(c) *P* 12.

77 4d. dull rose .. .. — £130

See note following No. 63.

(d) *Serrated* 19.

78 4d. rose-red .. .. .. — £130

(iii) *On smooth horizontally laid paper of same quality as* (ii) *above.*

(a) *Rouletted* 5½–6½.

79 2d. brown-lilac (*shades*) (7.58) .. 15·00 3·25
a. Violet (shades) (27.11.58) .. 24·00 3·25
b. Dull violet .. .. — 9·00
80 4d. pale dull rose .. .. — £300

(iv) *On good quality wove paper.*

(a) *Rouletted* 5½–6½.

81 1d. yellow-green (25.12.58) .. £110 13·00
82 4d. dull rose .. .. .. — £160

(b) *Perf.* 12 (*the first perforated stamps to be issued in Victoria*).

83 1d. yell.-grn. (*shades*) (11.1.59) 55·00 7·00
a. Imperf. × perf. (vert. pair) .. — £130
84 4d. dull rose (16.2.59) .. .. 36·00 1·75

Note: No. 83 is found on two classes of paper.

(v) *P* 12. *On poorer quality wove paper of coarser mesh.*

85 1d. dull green (7.59) .. .. 36·00 4·00
a. Green (11.59) .. .. 36·00 4·00
86 4d. dull rose (19.4.59) .. .. — 2·00
a. Rose-carmine (6.59) .. .. 36·00 2·00
b. Rose-pink (12.59) .. .. — 4·00

Save in the rouletted 1d. (where a second paper of ***vertical*** mesh was also employed) all the paper used for (iv) above was of ***horizontal*** mesh, whereas under (v) except for No. 86*b* (which was printed on a tough, thick, handmade paper) it is always of ***vertical*** mesh. In two printings of the 1d. ***both*** wove and laid papers were included.

(vi) *P* 12. ***On horizontally laid papers, of coarser quality and not so smooth as those previously employed by Robinson.***

(a) ***Laid lines closer together.***

87 1d. dull green (July 59) .. — 8·00
88 4d. rose-pink (23.12.59) .. — 3·25

(b) ***Laid lines farther apart.***

89 1d. green (*shades*) (Oct. 59) .. 40·00 5·00
90 4d. rose-pink (*shades*) (Jan. 60) 24·00 3·00

(vii) *P* 12. ***On thin glazed paper, emanating from Bordeaux.***

91 1d. deep yell.-grn. (July 1859) — 50·00

This stamp must have been printed *before* the "dull greens" of July 1859.

PLATES: 1857–68

The plates prepared for use between January 1857 and December 1867 (with one exception, see note after No. 51 on 2s. value) consisted of a number of individual electros (usually 120) clamped together in a "forme" and spaced and arranged to fit the pattern of the watermarked paper. Five such schemes are to be found, viz.: (*a*) from 1857 to Sept. '63 when (save for the 2d. of May 1857) the forme comprised 4 blocks of 30 (6 × 5) electros; (*b*) for the 2d. of May 1857 only, the sheet consisted of 20 blocks of 6 (2 × 3); (*c*) from Sept. 63 to Feb. 1866 when *three* separate arrangements, constant for any one value, are found. These were based on the face value of the stamps in the unit group and were as follows :—(i) For the 1d., 2d. and 4d. values the forme was composed of 8 blocks of 15 (3 × 5) separated by "gutters"; (ii) for the 3d., 6d. and 1s. values of 6 blocks (or 3, in the case of the 1s.) of 20 (4 × 5) separated by "gutters" and (iii) in the case of the 10d. of 20 blocks of 6 (3 × 2) separated by "gutters"; (*d*) over and following the period Jan.–July 1866, in anticipation of the introduction of the V over Crown watermarked paper, the old formes (with the exception of the 10d.) were reset and the new formes (e.g. 3d. and 6d.) arranged to give one block of 120 (12 × 10) evenly spaced units without "gutters". For various values, therefore, two "settings" were employed of the same electrotypes. Those interested in this subject should consult an article in *Philately from Australia* for March 1954. From 1869 to 1874 new printing plates consisted of 4 electrotypes each of 30 impressions (6 × 5) clamped together. These were produced via one (or two) "master" electrotypes of the same size. From 1875 (with four exceptions in the 1885 issues) all new printing plates consisted of a continuous surface electrotype of 120 (12 × 10) impressions. The foregoing remarks apply to normal size stamps only and require modification for other sizes.

II. GOVERNMENT STAMP PRINTING. THE FIRST PERIOD, 1860–1884.

Robinson was employed, in April 1858, to finish Calvert's uncompleted Contracts of 1857. Subsequently, under further Contracts, he printed more stamps. The work being satisfactory the Government (on 12.4.59) undertook to continue his employment and at the same time purchased the whole of his equipment, paper stocks, etc. As from 1.1.60 a Government Stamp Printing Branch was set up, Robinson was appointed its Chief Officer and there was no more Stamp Printing in terms of Private Contract. He was succeeded in 1867 by James Atkinson, and from 1883 to 1906 the same work was performed by William Bond. In December 1885 printing operations were transferred from the Post Office to the Government Printing Office and the Stamp Printer then joined the staff of the Government Printer. The Stamp Printers after Bond were J. Kemp and J. B. Cooke (1909–12), the latter being also appointed the first Commonwealth Stamp Printer.

Note: **All issues of this period, 1860–84, were printed by typography from electrotypes.**

9

10

11

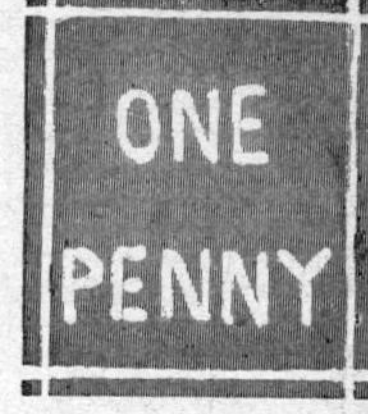

12

(Dies for 3d., 4d. and 6d. (T **9**) designed and engraved by Frederick Grosse. The die for the 6d. T **11** consisted of a frame die engraved by Grosse into which was plugged a head portion, cut out of his die for the 6d. T **9**. The design, die and plate for the 1d. T **10** were all supplied by Messrs. De Gruchy and Leigh of Melbourne.)

1860–66. *T* **5, 8, 9, 10** *and* **11.** *P* 12.

(i) *No wmk. On horizontally laid paper* (*lines further apart, as* (vi) (*b*) *above*).

92 **9** 3d. deep blue (31.1.60) .. 90·00 11·00
a. Light blue .. .. .. £400 50·00

(ii) *No wmk. On thin glazed paper emanating from Bordeaux* (*see also under* (vii) *above*).

93 **8** 1d. bright green (25.5.60) .. — 12·00
94 **9** 4d. rose (21.4.60) .. .. £110 5·50
a. Rose-pink .. .. .. — 2·75

(iii) *No wmk. On a thicker, coarser paper.*

95 ,, 4d. rose-pink (July 60) .. £110 2·75

(iv) 1860–66: ***Watermarked with the appropriate words of value as T 12. The paper, which was hand-made, was supplied by T. H. Saunders of London.***

96 **8** 1d. pale yellowish green .. (8.7.60) .. .. 13·00 2·25
a. Yellow-green .. .. 15·00 2·50
b. Var. Wmk. "FOUR PENCE" — £600
97 **10** 1d. pale green (1.10.61) .. 19·00 2·25
a. Olive-green .. .. — 2·50
b. Pale green (deep brown gum) (Feb. '63) .. .. 19·00 2·50
98 **8** 2d. brown-lilac (7.7.61) .. — 8·00
99 ,, 2d. bluish slate (Aug. 61, June 62) .. .. 21·00 1·75
a. Greyish lilac (Sept. 61) .. 24·00 1·75
b. Slate-grey (Jan. 62) .. — 1·75

100 **9** 3d. pale blue (Jan. '61) .. 15·00 2·50
a. Bright blue (Aug. '61) .. 15·00 3·25
b. Blue (dp. brn. gum) (Feb. '63) 17·00 2·00
ba. Error "TRREE" for "THREE" in wmk. ..
c. Deep blue (1864) .. .. 17·00 2·00
101 ,, 3d. maroon (13.2.66) .. 15·00 7·50
a. Perf. 13 .. .. 20·00 9·00
102 ,, 4d. rose-pink (1.8.60) .. — 1·25
a. Rose-red (shades) (Sept. '60) 15·00 55
b. Rose-carmine (Dec. '60) .. — 3·00
c. Dull rose (shades) (1861) .. 15·00 55
103 ,, 6d. orange (18.10.60) .. £400 90·00
104 **5** 6d. black (22.6.61) .. 32·00 9·00
105 **9** 6d. black (20.8.61) .. 32·00 1·75
a. Grey-black .. .. 32·00 1·75
106 **11** 6d. grey (26.4.62) .. 15·00 1·25
a. Grey-black .. 15·00 1·75
b. Jet black (deep brown gum) (Mar. '63) .. .. 20·00 2·50

Reprints on paper wmkd. V over Crown (T **23**), perf. $12\frac{1}{2}$, were made in 1891 of the 1d. Type **10**, 3d. and 4d. Type **9** and 6d. Type **11**. In all cases new plates were used, and certain "die flaws" are found on the "Reprints" which are not met on the originals.

13

14

1862–63. *Emergency printings owing to supplies of the appropriate paper not being available.*

(*a*) *On paper wmkd.* "FIVE SHILLINGS", *T* **13**.
107 **9** 4d. dull rose-pink (11.9.62) £200 9·00
a. Dull rose .. .. .. — 9·00

(*b*) *On paper wmkd.* "THREE PENCE", *T* **12**.
108 **8** 2d. pale slate (27.12.62) .. 30·00 5·00
a. Bluish grey (deep brown gum) (Feb. 63) .. .. .. 32·00 5·50

Note: Certain stamps are to be met on the "words of value" papers with wmk. *reversed* under Nos. 99, 100, 102, also 173 and 176. *Inverted* wmks. may also be found in several cases. All these wmk. varieties are scarce to rare.

(v) 1862–64: *Same types as before but wmkd. with the appropriate single-lined numeral of value, as T* **14**, *the paper being supplied by De La Rue. P 12 unless otherwise described.*
109 **10** 1d. olive-green (1.2.63) .. 11·00 1·75
a. Pale green (9.63) .. .. 11·00 1·75
b. Apple-green (4.64) .. — 1·75
110 **8** 2d. dull reddish-lilac (21.4.63) .. .. 32·00 3·00
111 ,, 2d. grey-lilac (10.63) .. 40·00 5·00
a. Var: Wmk. '6' (10.63) .. — £2000
b. Grey-violet (shades) (11.63) .. — 4·00
c. Slate (12.63) .. .. 40·00 8·00
112 **9** 4d. dull rose-pink (9.10.62) 22·00 1·10
a. Dull rose (deep brown gum) (2.63) .. .. .. 24·00 1·25
b. Rose-red .. .. .. — 1·10
113 **11** 6d. grey (18.6.63) .. .. 13·00 1·00
a. Grey-black (2.64.) .. 13·00 1·10
b. Intense black .. .. — 1·50
114 ,, 6d. jet-black, *p.* 13 (12.64) 15·00 1·25
a. Grey-black .. .. 15·00 1·50

July-Aug. 1863: *Varieties due to a temporary break-down of the perforating machine.*
115 **9** 4d. dull rose-pink (*imperf.*) — 24·00
116 ,, 4d. dull rose-pink (*roul.*) .. — 50·00

Notes on plate varieties found on stamps printed from plates made by Robinson.

The electros prepared by Robinson over the period 1860–66 (many, e.g. the 4d., which lasted until 1881, remaining in use for a long time after) furnish perhaps the most interesting varieties found in typographed stamps. Since the lead moulds for these were struck by hand, on semi-fused metal, and without the aid of a "collar", the stamps present us with certain constant abnormalities, viz. *partial strikes, double strikes* and *internal distortion* varieties of a nature and extent not found in any other issues, as well as also providing all the more usual types of flaw found in typographed stamps. The whole to the Robinson "Beaded Ovals" and "Laureates" are plateable since the process used made it *impossible* for any stamp to be a perfect reproduction of the die. The 6d. black (Type **11**) is the most interesting of all since the die here was in two parts. This meant the adherence of lead along the line of junction, etc., and gave rise to yet further classes of plate variety. For information on this stamp see various articles in the *London Philatelist*.

Notes on the two single-line numeral watermark papers.

Two different English firms supplied the single-line numeral wmk. papers used from October 1862 onwards. The two classes of paper supplied are so distinct that they have now been given separate listing. Their characteristics are as follows:—

1. *De La Rue papers* (several consignments). Comprised *white* paper wmkd. "1", "2", "4", "6" and "8" respectively, *blue* paper wmkd. "1" and *green* paper wmkd. "2". In certain printings particularly in the 1d., 2d. and 4d. Laureates and the 6d. black (1863–65) on this paper, a *pelure* type—thin, hard and semi-transparent—may be found. This variety has not been separately listed but is worthy of the specialist's attention. Generally the quality of these De La Rue papers varied considerably among the different consignments.

2. *T. H. Saunders papers* (one consignment only). Comprised *white* paper wmkd. "1", "4" and "6" respectively, *blue* paper wmkd. "1", *green* paper wmkd. "2", and *pink* paper wmkd. "10". It was first used in December 1865 and the white papers were exhausted by August 1867. The paper was (apart from the *blue* variety, which was rather thinner than the rest) of even quality throughout and was smoother, thicker, more brittle and (in the white variety) not so white as the De La Rue product. It will be noted that the "2" and "8" papers were supplied by De La Rue only, whereas the "10" paper (pink) was supplied by Saunders only. Comparison of these should assist collectors in accurate classification. The *coloured* papers lasted much longer than the white, as will be seen from the listings. The *blue* lasted until 1875, and the *green* and *pink* until 1879.

In both papers, in practically all cases, *reversed* and/or *inverted* wmks. may be met. *Sideways* wmks. have been found under Nos. 113, 124 and 200. Stamps showing little or no wmk. are from the left or right sides of badly cut sheets.

15

16

17

18

19

(The "*Laureated*" series: Dies engraved by Frederick Grosse. Printing plates (see previous note) made by F. W. Robinson until late in 1867.)

Note. **Since various printings of the 2s. Calvert (Type 5) were also made between 1864 and 1881 these have been included where appropriate.**

1863–80.

(i) 1863–64. *Early printings. Wmk. with appropriate single-lined numeral as T* **14**, *on paper supplied by De La Rue. P* 12.
117 **15** 1d. pale green (8.9.64) .. 8·00 2·75
118 ,, 2d. violet (late April '64) .. 8·00 1·10
a. Dull violet (10.64) .. .. 9·00 1·25
119 ,, 4d. deep rose (4.9.63) .. — 1·25
a. Doubly printed .. .. — £200
b. Rose-pink (9.63) .. .. 9·00 65
c. Pink (4.64) .. .. 9·00 65

Emergency printings on Perkins, Bacon paper wmkd. double-lined numerals "**1**" *and* "**4**" *respectively, supplied by Tasmania. P* 12.
120 **10** 1d. yellow-green (10.12.63) 32·00 3·25
a. Dull green (4.64) .. .. — 3·25
b. Imperf. between (pair) ..
121 **15** 4d. deep rose (7.1.64) .. 20 00 1·10
a. Pale rose .. .. .. — 1·10

Like the 1d. and 4d. Perkins, Bacon types of Van Diemen's Land most of the Victorian stamps printed on the above two papers may occasionally be found with wmk. *inverted*. This applies both to the 1d. and 4d. above and also to the various "Laureates" of the 1867–68 printings. Instances are also known where the work is *reversed* and one (in No. 132) where it is *sideways*. Most of these varieties are rare.

(ii) *Printings of Oct.* 1864 *onwards. As* (i) *but P* 13.
122 **15** 1d. pale green (10.10.64) .. 4·75 1·10
a. Bluish green (12.64) .. 4·00 80
aa. Doubly printed .. .. — £225
b. Green (shades) (8.65) .. 4·00 1·10
c. Deep green (12.65) .. — 1·00
123 ,, 2d. dull violet (10.64) .. 5·50 80
a. Dull lilac (shades) (4.65) .. 5·50 65
b. Reddish mauve (11.65) .. 7·50 70
124 ,, 4d. dull rose (10.64) .. 8·00 65
a. Dull rose-red (2.65) .. 7·50 65
125 ,, 8d. orange (22.2.65) .. 24·00 10·00
126 **18** 1s. blue/*blue* (10.4.65) .. 20·00 1·25
127 **5** 2s. lt. blue/*grn.* (22.11.64) 20·00 2·50
a. Deep blue/green (1865) .. 20·00 2·50

The above 1s. stamp can be immediately identified by the white patches (comprising an *albino* impression) due to the lack of a *make-ready* which are found on all stamps. The 8d. was withdrawn from issue on 11.6.69.

(iii) July–August 1865. *As before but P* 12 *or* 12×13 *from repaired state of* 12 *machine, with larger holes and sharper teeth than previously.*

(*a*) *Perf.* 12.
128 **15** 1d. green (*shades*) .. .. 7·00 1·00
a. Deep green .. .. 7·00 1·00
129 ,, 4d. dull rose-red (8.65) .. 26·00 3·50
130 **5** 2s. dark blue/*green* .. 32·00 4·75

(*b*) *Perf.* 12×13.
131 **15** 1d. deep green .. .. — 2·50

August and December 1865. *Emergency printings* (2) *on Perkins, Bacon paper wmkd. double-lined* "**4**" *supplied by Tasmania.*
132 **15** 4d. dull reddish rose, *p.* 13 (11.8.65) .. .. 22·00 1·00
a. Perf. 12 .. .. — 1·25
b. Perf. 12×13 .. .. — 5·50
133 ,, 4d. red, *p.* 13 (6.12.65) .. 26·00 1·00

Oct. 1865. *Emergency printing on De La Rue paper wmkd. single-lined* "8", *no* "10" *paper having arrived. Perf.* 13.
134 **17** 10d. grey (21.10.65) .. 32·00 13·00
a. Grey-black .. .. 32·00 13·00

(iv) Dec. 1865–66 *printings. These, in general, were of finer impression than the previous* 1865 *printings.*

A. On Saunders paper, wmkd. with the appropriate single-line numerals as T **14**.
135 **15** 1d. dp. yellow-green, *p.* 13 (1.66) .. .. .. 4·00 90
a. Perf. 12 .. .. — 2·75
b. Perf. 12×13 .. .. — 2·50
136 ,, 4d. rose-red, *p.* 13 (12.12.65) 7·50 80
a. Perf. 12 .. .. — 1·75
b. Perf. 12×13 .. .. — 1·50

137 **17** 6d. blue, *p.* 13 (13.2.66) 5·50 55
a. Perf. 12 .. .. .. 8·00 1·25
b. Perf. 12×13 .. .. 5·50 60
c. Imperf. between (pair) .. — £200
138 ,, 10d. dull purple/*pink*, p. 13 (22.3.66) .. .. 7·00 70
a. Perf. 12×13 .. .. 8·00 1·10
b. Blackish brn./pink, p. 13 ('69) 9·00 1·10
139 **18** 1s. indigo-blue/*blue*, *p.* 13 (70) .. .. .. 8·00 1·10
a. Perf. 12 (1873) .. .. — 2·00
b. Brt. blue/blue, p. 13 (1.71) .. 8·00 75
ba. Perf. 12 .. .. — 1·10
c. Pale dull blue/blue, p. 13 (1.75) — 3·25
ca. Perf. 12 .. .. .. — 1·10
140 **5** 2s. dark blue/*green* (12.67) 30·00 3·00
a. Perf. 12 (1875) .. .. 38·00 3·00
b. Blue/green (1872, '78) .. 30·00 2·00
c. Greenish blue/green, p. 12 .. ('75) .. .. .. 38·00 3·00
d. Deep greenish blue/green, p. 12½ (80) .. .. 30·00 4·00

The 1s. on Saunders paper was issued later than 1866 but it and the 2s. printing are included here for the sake of convenience. The Saunders green paper is distinctly *deeper* in shade and more apparently *green* than the De La Rue variety.

B. On De La Rue paper wmkd. with the appropriate single-line numerals as T **14.** *P* 13.

141 **15** 1d. brt. yellow-grn. (1.67) — 8·00
142 ,, 2d. rosy lilac (1.66) .. 5·50 1·10
a. Perf. 12×13 .. .. 8·00 1·10
143 ,, 2d. dull lilac (6.66) .. — 1·10
a. Perf. 12 .. .. .. — 2·00
b. Perf. 12×13 .. .. — 3·00
144 ,, 2d. grey (25.7.66) .. 5·50 55
a. Perf. 12 .. .. .. 20·00 2·00
145 **17** 6d. blue (13.2.66) .. 8·00 1·10
a. Perf. 12 .. .. .. 8·00 2·00
b. Perf. 12×13 .. .. 5·50 65
146 **18** 1s. blue/*blue* (66, 69) .. 8·00 1·10
a. Perf. 12×13 (66) .. .. 8·00 1·25
b. Bright blue/blue, p. 13 ('67, '71) — 1·10
ba. Perf. 12 (1871) .. .. — 1·25
c. Indigo/blue, p. 13 .. .. — 1·00
d. Dull blue/blue, p. 12 (1874) .. — 1·25
e. Imperf. btwn. vert. pr. (12×13) — £200
147 **5** 2s. blue/*green* (68) .. 15·00 2·00
a. Greenish blue/green (1873) .. 15·00 2·00
aa. Perf. 12 .. .. .. 30·00 2·50
b. Dark blue/grn., p. 12½ (1880) 15·00 2·00

The 1d. of 1867 on De La Rue, distinguishable only by its shade, was presumably the result of the discovery of a small quantity of old stock. The 2d. and 4d. of 1866 may also be found 13×12 but are rare in *this* condition. The 10d. was withdrawn from issue on 21.6.71. There were, between 1864 and 1881, no less than 21 different printings of the 2s. blue on green. Only the main schools of colour have been listed.

1866 (Sept.)–**67.** *Various Emergency printings, all the results of the non-arrival of the first shipment of* " *V over Crown* " *paper.*

1. *Printings on De La Rue paper wmkd. single-lined* " **8** ". *P* 13.

148 **15** 1d. bt. yell-grn. (27.12.66) 35·00 4·25
149 ,, 2d. grey (18.1.67) .. .. 30·00 1·00
150 **16** 3d. lilac (29.9.66) .. .. 11·00 5·50
151 **15** 4d. rose-red (? date) ..

Only one copy of the 4d. has been recorded and that is understood to have been lost, although its authenticity seems to have been established.

2. *Printings on Saunders paper wmkd. single-lined* " **4** ". *P* 13.

152 **15** 1d. bt. yellow-grn. (6.3.67) 11·00 2·50
153 ,, 2d. grey (21.2.67) .. .. 15·00 1·25

3. *Printings on paper wmkd. single-lined* " **6** " *P* 13.

(*a*) *On De La Rue paper.*

154 **15** 1d. bt. yellow-green (6.67) — 7·00

(*b*) *On Saunders paper.*

155 **15** 1d. bt. yellow-green (6.67) 30·00 5·50
156 ,, 2d. grey (13.5.67) .. .. 38·00 2·00

20 (*V*1)

WATERMARKS. *Many stamps watermarked V and Crown may be found with watermark inverted or sideways. We do not list these as separate varieties, but copies can be supplied if in stock.*

1867–68. *Printings on first consignment of paper wmkd.* "*V over Crown*", *T* **20**, *received in July* 1867. *P* 13.

157 **15** 1d. bt. yellow-grn. (10.8.67) 11·00 1·10
158 ,, 2d. slate-grey (*shades*) (26.8.67) .. .. 13·00 65
a. Grey-lilac (1.68) .. .. — 1·25
159 **16** 3d. lilac (8.67) .. .. 10·00 7·50
a. Grey-lilac (8.68) .. .. 13·00 8·00
160 **15** 4d. dull rose (11.67) .. 8·00 1·75
161 **17** 6d. dark blue (12.67) .. — 1·25
162 **19** 5s. blue/*yellow* (26.12.67) 55·00 65·00
a. Wmk. reversed .. .. — £150

The above shades (there are also paper differences) are sufficiently distinctive to enable separation of the five lower values from *later* " V over Crown " printings. The 5s. was printed from the first electros prepared by Atkinson. There were two printings, both in sheets of 25 (5×5). The first (1,200) was from a single vertical column of 5 electros clamped together. The second (2,000) was from a plate of 25 impressions, comprising a different " 5 vertical ", repeated 5 times (i.e. giving 5 types). The reversed wmk. variety belongs to the first printing and was created *deliberately* to avoid the appearance of the " page number " on the front of one stamp in every four sheets of 25.

1867 (Sept.)–**68** and **1870.** *Various Emergency printings due first to the* 1867 *shipment of white* "*V over Crown*" *paper being so small, later to its exhaustion and the non-arrival of the second shipment ordered, later still* (1870) *to a further shortage of this paper.*

1. *Printings on the Perkins, Bacon paper wmkd. double-lined* " 1 " *received from Tasmania in* 1863. *P* 13.

163 **15** 1d. pale yellowish green (24.9.67) .. .. 4·25 1·10
a. Deep yellow-green (6.68) .. — 1·10
164 ,, 2d. slate (5.68) .. .. 32·00 1·75
a. Mauve (30.6.68) .. .. 32·00 2·00
165 **16** 3d. grey-lilac (8.68) .. 35·00 13·00
166 **17** 6d. blue (28.7.68) .. .. 25·00 1·75

2. *Printings on the Perkins, Bacon paper wmkd. double-lined* " 4 " *received from Tasmania in* 1863. *P* 13.

167 **15** 1d. pale yell.-grn. (27.5.68) £325 35·00
168 ,, 2d. grey-lilac (3.2.68) .. 26·00 70
a. Slate (28.3.68) .. .. 26·00 65
b. Mauve (3.7.68) .. .. — 1·00
169 ,, 4d. dull rose-red (5.68) .. 24·00 1·00
170 **17** 6d. blue (20.6.68) .. .. 70·00 5·50
a. Indigo-blue .. .. — 7·50

3. *Printing on Saunders paper wmkd.* " six pence " *as T* **12**. *P* 13.

171 **15** 1d. pale yellow-grn. (5.6.68) £120 7·50
172 ,, 2d. slate-grey .. .. — £400
173 **17** 6d. blue (23.5.68) .. .. 70·00 5·00
a. Indigo-blue .. .. — 7·00

Only one copy is apparently known of No. 172. From its shade it would appear to belong to an 1867–68 printing. No. 171 is known with the wmk. *sideways.*

4. *Printings on lilac paper wmkd. V over Crown from* 1867 *consignment. P* 13.

174 **15** 2d. mauve/*lilac* (12.8.68) .. 5·00 2·00
a. Lilac/lilac .. .. 5·00 1·75

5. 1870: 6d. *value only. Printings on various wmkd. papers as indicated. P* 13.

175 **17** 6d. dull blue (three pence) (23.4.70) .. .. 50·00 2·75
a. Deep blue .. .. — 3·25
176 ,, 6d. dull blue (four pence) (18.6.70) .. .. £110 10·00
a. Deep blue .. .. — 11·00
177 ,, 6d. dull bl. (" 4 ") (21.5.70) — £250
178 ,, 6d. dull blue (" 2 ") (1870) — £250

Of the six or seven copies known of No. 17[illegible] all but one have the watermark reversed.

1868 (Aug.)–**71.** *Printings on second an[illegible] later consignments of V over Crown paper W* **20**. *P* 13 *only.*

(i) *Printed from Robinson plates.*

179 **15** 2d. lilac (26.8.68) .. .. 2·75 5[illegible]
a. Dull mauve (*shades*) (10.68) 2·75 5[illegible]
b. Lilac-grey (1.69) .. .. — 7[illegible]
c. Lilac-rose (2.69) .. .. — 1·1[illegible]
180 **16** 3d. yellow-orange (12.6.69) 4·00 1·1[illegible]
181 **15** 4d. pale red (*anil.*) (21.4.69) — 2·5[illegible]
a. Deep red (*anil.*) (16.7.69) .. — 2·5[illegible]
b. Rose-pink (2.70) .. .. — 1·7[illegible]
182 **17** 6d. blue (*shades*) .. .. 2·50 3[illegible]
a. Indigo-blue (1869) .. .. 2·50 3[illegible]
183 **19** 5s. indigo-blue & carmine (I) (8.10.68) .. .. 24·00 5·0[illegible]
a. Blue and carmine (1869) .. 20·00 2·7[illegible]

Nos. 179*b*/*c* were printed from badly wor[illegible] plates.

For the frame-plate of the 5s. (I) the electro of the 1867 plate, with the Crown, " victoria [illegible] and " five shillings " cut out, were employed A new plate, also produced via cut-out portion[illegible] of the 1867 plate, was brought into use for th[illegible] red portion.

(ii) *Printed from new plates made by Atkinson.*

184 **15** 1d. bt. yellow-grn. (10.68) 2·75 7[illegible]
a. Bright olive-green (1.69) .. — 6·5[illegible]
b. Dull yellow-green (4.69) .. — 5[illegible]
c. Dull green (3.70) .. .. 2·75 5[illegible]
d. Very pale green (10.70) .. — 5[illegible]
185 ,, 2d. lilac-grey (15.1.69) .. — 8[illegible]
a. Lilac-rose (*shades*) (24.2.69) 5·50 8[illegible]
b. Mauve (20.4.69) .. .. — 5[illegible]
c. Red-lilac (*shades*) (5.69) .. 5·00 3[illegible]
d. Dull lilac (*shades*) 6.69) .. 5·00 2[illegible]
e. Silver-grey (2.9.69) .. 30·00 2·5[illegible]

The Atkinson plates, produced by an improve[illegible] technique, do not show the *double* and *partia[illegible] strikes* and *internal distortion* varieties met on [illegible] large proportion of the stamps from the Robinso[illegible] plates. Further, the later printings from the 2d and 6d. Robinson plates show obvious signs o[illegible] wear. These factors and the differing shade should make classification relatively easy. Fo[illegible] the first two printings of the 2d. in 1869 the firs[illegible] of the new Atkinson plates was used in conjunc[illegible] tion with the old Robinson plate, following whic[illegible] the latter was replaced by a second Atkinso[illegible] plate. The dates of introduction of the Atkinso[illegible] plates were 1d., Oct. 1868; 2d., Jan. 1869 an[illegible] 6d., Dec. 1875.

9 9

NINEPENCE

(21)

1871. *Provisional. Surch. with T* **21**, *in blu[illegible] On Saunders paper wmkd. single-lined* " 10 [illegible] *P* 13.

186 **17** 9d. on 10d. purple-brown/*pink* (22.4.71) .. .. 20·00 3·0[illegible]
a. Blackish brown/pink .. — 4·0[illegible]
b. Surch. double .. .. — £30[illegible]

Perforations (to 1883).

The perforations of Victoria, particularly thos[illegible] of the period Oct. 1864–80, form a comple[illegible] study for specialists. We have adopted in th[illegible] listing a simplified classification based on *thre[illegible]* descriptions—Perf. 12, Perf. 13 and Perf. 12 respectively, the latter being substituted f[illegible] Perf. 13 for the period 1881 on. The position ca[illegible] be concisely put as follows:—

A. " *Perf.* 12 "; Here the gauge is *neve[illegible]* quite 12 and nearer 11½. It is not found afte[illegible] 1883. There were two machines (both singl[illegible] line), the first introduced by Robinson in Ja[illegible] 1859 and the second purchased in 1871. N[illegible] " perf. 12 " are found in the period mid 1866 mid 1871. At various periods, more particularl[illegible] in 1865 and 1880, one or both of the machin[illegible] was repaired, to give larger holes and sharp[illegible] teeth over a succeeding period.

B. " *Perf.* 13 ": Here the gauge is invariably over 12 and with a sole exception (covering a section of the pins on one machine over the period 1876–80) invariably *under* 13. Generally speaking up to the end of 1880, these machines gauged 12½ to 12¾. Two classes of machine are found:

(i) *Single-line* machines. These were three in number—purchased in Oct. 1864, 1866 and 1873 respectively. Two of them were converted into combs in 1873. The other was repaired on several occasions, particularly in 1879–80, to give larger holes and sharper teeth.

(ii) *Comb* machines. First introduced in 1873 (see above). Over the period of use they gave various gauges, depending on the machine and its state of repair. They were all *vertical* combs adapted only for normal size stamps of either dimension as likewise (until 1913) were all other comb-machines used in Victoria for perforating stamps.

C. " *Perf.* 12½ ": Found from late 1876 onwards, in both single-line (used mainly for the larger-size stamps) and vertical comb machines. Gradually superseded the A and B gauges. Certain stamps of the 1879–80 period are found in both B and C gauges but these are no longer differentiated as separate varieties, being only listed under the one or the other gauge. This applies also to the Postal Fiscal section.

" *Compound* " *perforations*: In previous editions certain 12 × 13 perforations were listed which were not true compounds of A and B but simply the product of one or other of the *comb* machines. Such varieties have now been eliminated. The " Compounds " now listed are all true compounds (or " mixeds ") of A and B. They generally fall into two categories: (i) those of the 1865–66 period where the two machines were both used for the original perforating, one in the one direction (top and bottom) and the other in the other (sides); (ii) isolated examples, better termed " mixed " perfs., from 1873 on, where one gauge machine was used to correct off-centre perforating done by the other gauge machine. Such cases are almost invariably associated with " mends ", viz. the pasting of gummed strips down the back of the faulty line of perforation.

1871–84 Printings.

These are listed separately from the 1868–71 printings because of the perforation changes made in the period, viz. the reintroduction of the 12 gauge (1871), the introduction of comb machines (1873), the repairs of various 12 and 13 machines (1879), and the introduction of the 12½ gauge (1879–80). Many stamps issued in the latter period are found both perf. 13 and 12½ but no distinction is made. The 13 gauge disappears in 1880–81.

Papers: All printings on white paper made after April 1878 and also the last 8d. printing were on the " *glazed* " variety of paper and this furnishes another means of identification. Some shades, e.g. 6d. blue of 1878–79 are found on both papers.

Shades are different from those found in the 1868–71 printings.

1871–84.

(i) *Printed from Robinson plates; W* **20**; *P* 13, 12½ *unless otherwise described.*

187 **16** 3d. dull orange (1871) .. 2·75 65
a. Perf. 12 (1872) .. 2·75 10·00
b. Orange (1874) .. .. — 80
ba. Perf. 12 .. .. — 70
c. Bright orange .. .. — 1·00
ca. Perf. 12 .. .. — 1·10
188 „ 3d. orange-brown (late '78) 7·00 2·75
189 „ 3d. dull orange-yellow ('81) 8·00 1·00
a. Perf. 12
190 **15** 4d. rose (*shades*) (1871–78) 8·00 80
a. Perf. 12 .. .. 7·00 80
b. Dull rose (5.3.79) .. — 80
ba. Perf. 12 .. .. — 80
c. Dull rose red (23.12.79) .. — 80
ca. Perf. 12.. .. .. — 80
d. Bt. lilac-rose (anil.) (3.3.80) 8·00 1·25
da. Perf. 12 .. .. — 2·50
191 „ 4d. rosine (*anil.*) (22.9.80) 50·00 2·00
a. Perf. 12 .. .. 15·00 1·50
b. Compound p. 12 with 12½ .. — £160
192 **17** 6d. Prussian blue ('72, '74) 2·00 20
a. Perf. 12 .. .. 2·75 35
b. Indigo (1873) .. .. 2·75 40
ba. Perf. 12 .. .. 4·00 65
c. Dull blue (worn plate) .. — 20
193 **15** 8d. lilac-brown/*pink* (24.1.77) .. .. 5·50 1·50
a. Purple-brown/pink (21.3.78) 7·00 1·50
b. Chocolate/pink (6.8.78) 9·00 1·25
bb. Compound p. 13 × 12 .. — £150
194 „ 8d. red-brn./*pink* (20.5.78) 7·50 1·25
195 „ 8d. dark red-brn./*pink*, p. 12 (*glazed*) (30.11.80) .. 7·00 1·50
a. Perf. 12½ .. ..
196 **18** 1s. light blue/*blue* (May '75) 20·00 2·75
a. Perf. 12 .. .. — 2·75
197 **19** 5s. pale bt. blue & carmine (I) (July '77) .. .. — 5·00
a. Grey-blue & carm. (Aug. '78) 26·00 3·75
b. Deep lavender-blue & carmine (May '80) .. .. 26·00 3·75
198 „ 5s. bright blue and red (II) (12.5.81) .. .. 20·00 3·00
a. Perf. 12 .. .. 11·00 3·75
b. Indigo-blue and red .. — 5·00
ba. Perf. 12 .. .. — 5·50
c. Second " I " in " SHILLINGS " short at foot .. — 50·00

The 4d. " pink " previously listed is a *faded* rosine. For the 5s. (Type II) new dies were made for *each* portion of the design. All Type I stamps have a blue line under the Crown, which is missing in Type II. The latter were printed in sheets of 100 (10 × 10), as compared with 25 (5 × 5) for Type I.

No. 197*b* has the watermark sideways.

1877–79. *Printings of the 8d. value on Saunders paper wmkd. single-lined* " 10 ". Perf. 13, 12½ unless otherwise stated.

199 **15** 8d. lilac-brn./*pink* Dec. '77) — £150
a. Purple-brown/pink (20.2.'78) 20·00 2·00
200 „ 8d. red-brown/*pink* (8.8.79) 10·00 1·40
a. Perf. 12 .. .. — 3·00

The 8d. printings (save that of 1880) were *mixed* and comprised stamps on *both* V over Crown and " 10 " papers.

½ ½

HALF

(22)

(ii) *Printed from plates made by Atkinson. The* ½d. *made by surch. with T* **22**, *in red.*

201 **15** ½d. on 1d. green (25.6.73) 2·75 1·50
a. Perf. 12 .. .. 5·00 2·50
b. Grass-green .. .. 4·00 1·50
ba. Perf. 12 .. .. 5·00 2·50
c. Short " 1 " at right .. — 30·00
202 „ 1d. pale green (1871) .. 2·75 55
a. Perf. 12 (Oct. '71) .. 7·50 70
b. Green (shades) .. 3·25 50
ba. Perf. 12 .. .. 5·00 50
c. Grass-green .. .. — 60
ca. Perf. 12 .. .. — 70
d. Bluish green (shades) .. 5·50 60
da. Perf. 12 .. .. — 70
203 **17** 6d. dull ultram. (2.12.75) 5·00 40
a. Lt. Prussian blue (29.12.75) — 35
b. Dull violet blue (Apr. '78) .. — 2·50
c. Blue (13.5.78) .. .. 5·50 12
ca. Perf. 12 .. .. — 12
d. Dull milky blue (7.3.79) .. 5·00 35
da. Perf. 12 .. .. — 35
e. Blue (light ink) (Aug. '80) .. — 20
f. Light blue (10.5.81) .. 5·50 35
fa. Perf. 12 .. .. — 80
g. Deep blue (15.1.82) .. 5·00 20

23 (*V2*)

The *V2* watermarks are much easier to see than the *V1* watermarks.

The type of V over Crown watermark (1867–1912).

In all, *five* types were employed.

The first two types (*V1* and *V2*) belong to the contracts made with De La Rue to supply postage stamp paper. That firm lost the contract in 1895 to Waterlow and Sons, who held it until 1912. The third and fourth types are therefore products of the Waterlow contracts. The fifth type (found only in 1912) was supplied by James Spicer & Sons. The change in the pattern from *V1* to *V2* is explained by the dandy-roll (which was the property of De La Rue) requiring replacement. Since *all* the changes in pattern are also associated with changes in the nature and texture of the paper supplied, little difficulty should be encountered, with the new descriptions, in identifying the various types. Each pattern (save in a few cases of " left over " stock) succeeded the previous pattern.

Types *V1* and *V2* are mainly to be distinguished from one another by the four " points " around the top of the Crown which are found in *V1* but not in *V2*. Also, as compared with *V2*, the shapes of the top ornaments in *V1* resemble diamonds, and not ovals. It must be remembered that *V1 coloured* papers continued in use long after the exhaustion of the *V1* white paper, the earliest date met for the *V2* white paper being 15.8.82. The first *V2* coloured papers (blue and green) were not used until February 1890. In general the papers supplied by De La Rue were whiter than their successors. The quality found with the *V1* wmk. varied greatly both with and without a pronounced mesh. The quality of the *V2* papers on the other hand varied little. It is generally more " loaded " and opaque than any of the *V1* papers and the wmk. clearer when held to the light.

(iii) 1882–4. *As* (ii) *above but on paper wmkd. V over Crown* (*V2*), *W* **23**. *P* 12½.

204 **16** 3d. yellow-orange (13.4.83) 5·00 2·00
a. Dull brownish orange .. 7·50 3·00
205 **17** 6d. dull vio.-blue (10.11.82) 1·50 20
a. Indigo-blue (Nov. 83) .. 1·50 35
b. Light ultramarine (Sept. 84) 1·50 45

The above 3d. was printed from two new plates made by Atkinson. For the 6d. the same Atkinson plates introduced in Dec. 1875 were employed.

Reprints were made, in 1891, on V over Crown paper, Type 23, perf. 12½, of the 1d., 2d., 3d., 4d., 6d., 8d., 10d., 1s. and 5s. " Laureates ". The shades are distinctive and a number of values show " die flaws " not found in the originals. The 3d. was printed in yellow, the 8d. in orange-yellow, the 10d. in greenish-slate and the 5s. in blue and red.

24

(Printed in Melbourne from a double electrotyped plate of 240 subjects supplied by De La Rue.)

1870 (28 Jan.). *Wmk. V over Crown* (*V1*), *W* **20**. *P* 13.

206 **24** 2d. brown-lilac .. .. 5·50 40
a. Dull lilac-mauve (Sept. '70) 2·75 15
aa. Perf. 12 (1871) .. .. 5·50 40
b. Mauve (worn plate, Mar. '73) 2·75 35
ba. Perf. 12 .. .. 5·50 20

25

26

27 (28) 29 30 31 (Die I) 32 (Die II)

(Des. and dies eng. by William Bell and stamps printed from electrotyped plates.)

1873–84. *Two dies of 2d.: I, single-lined outer oval; II, double-lined outer oval. The 8d. is made by surch. with T* **28** *in blue. P* 13 *unless otherwise described.*

(*a*) *On Saunders paper, wmkd. single-lined* " 10 ".

207 **29** 9d. pale brn./*pink* (25.3.73) 10·00 1·50
 a. Perf. 12 .. .. 11·00 3·25
 b. Red-brown/pink (Aug. '74) 8·00 1·75

(*b*) *Wmk. V over Crown* (*V*1), *W* **20.**

208 **25** ½d. rose-red (10.2.74) .. 1·00 20
 a. Perf. 12 .. .. 1·25 35
 b. Lilac-rose '74 on) .. 1·25 35
 ba. Perf. 12 .. .. 1·00 35
 c. Rosine (shades) (Dec. '80) 65 20
 ca. Perf. 12 .. .. 1·00 12
 d. Pale red ('82) .. .. 1·00 12
 da. Perf. 12 .. .. 1·00 15
 e. Mixed p. 13 and 12 .. — 50·00
209 **26** 1d. dull bluish green (14.12.75) .. .. 1·50 20
 a. Perf. 12 .. .. 2·75 20
 b. Green (shades) ('77 on) .. 1·50 15
 ba. Perf. 12 .. .. 2·00 2·00
 c. Yellow-green ('78 and '80) 1·50 12
 ca. Perf. 12 .. .. — 70
210 **27** 2d. deep lilac-mauve, Die I (1.10.73) .. .. 1·50 5
 a. Perf. 12 .. .. — 75
 b. Dull violet-mauve .. 1·50 5
 ba. Perf. 12 .. .. — 70
 c. Dull mauve .. .. 1·50 5
 ca. Perf. 12 .. .. 2·75 12
 d. *Pale mauve (worn plate)* (Jan. '79) .. .. 2·00 12
 da. Perf. 12 .. .. — 20
 e. Mixed p. 13 and 12 .. 50·00 48·00
211 „ 2d. lilac-mauve, Die II (17.12.78) 35 5
 a. Perf. 12 .. .. 2·00 5
 b. Grey-mauve (Jan. '80) .. — 10
 ba. Perf. 12 .. .. — 35
 c. Pale mauve (June 80) .. — 10
 ca. Perf. 12 .. .. — 60
 d. Imperf. (pair) .. .. — £200
 e. Imperf. between (pair) .. — £200
212 **29** 8d. on 9d. lilac-brown/*pink*, *p.* 12 (1.7.76) .. 18·00 4·00
 a. "F.IGHT" (broken "E") — 55·00
213 „ 9d. lilac-brown/*pink*, *p.* 12 (1.12.75) .. .. 13·00 3·25
214 **30** 1s. indigo-bl./*blue* (16.8.76) 3·25 60
 a. Deep blue/blue (1877) .. 3·25 60
 aa. Perf. 12 (Oct. '80) .. — 2·00
 b. Blue/blue (1878) .. .. 3·25 60
 ba. Perf. 12 .. .. — 2·00
 c. Ultramarine/blue (1879) .. 10·00 2·00
 d. *Bright blue/blue* (Nov. '83) 8·00 1·00

(*c*) 18 Feb.–April 1878. *Emergency printings on various coloured papers, due to the exhaustion of white V*1 *paper. W* **20.** (*V*1), *P* 13 *only.*

215 **25** ½d. rose-red/*pink* (1.3.78) .. 2·00 1·00
216 **26** 1d. yell.-grn./*yell.* (25.2.78) 5·00 2·00
217 „ 1d. yellow-green/*drab* (4.78) 8·00 7·50
218 **27** 2d. vio.-mve./*grn.* (18.2.78) 7·50 1·00
219 „ 2d. vio.-mve./*lilac* (21.2.78) — 65·00
220 „ 2d. vio.-mve./*brn.* (21.3.78) 7·50 1·50

Two shades of yellow paper, termed *pale canary* and *deep canary* respectively, are found.

All supplies of *V*1 paper received in Victoria after 15.3.78 were, as compared with previous supplies, highly surfaced on the printing side. An experimental printing was made on the new paper in July 1877 (1d., 2d., 6d. and 5s.) and all printings on white *V*1 paper from April 1878 on were made on this glazed paper. The glazed *V*1 coloured papers, with few exceptions, made their appearance later.

(*d*) 1882–83. *On white paper wmkd. V over Crown* (*V*2) *W* **23.** *P* 13.

221 **25** ½d. rosine (April '83) .. 1·25 35
 a. Perf. 12 .. .. .. — 7·00
222 **26** 1d. yellow-green (Sept. '82) 2·00 35
 a. Perf. 12 .. .. ..

Reprints: The ½d., 1d., 2d. (Die 2), 9d. and 1s. values were reprinted in 1891, perf. 12½, the first four from new plates, made from Dies containing *die flaws* not found in the originals. The 9d. was on *V*1 and the others on *V*2 paper.

33

34

35

(Des. and eng. by Charles Naish (T **33** & **34**) and William Bell (T **35**). Typo. from electrotyped plates.)

1880–84. *P* 12½ *unless otherwise described, this description including the P* 13 *varieties found in* 1880.

(*a*) *W* **20** (*V*1).

223 **33** 2d. sepia (3.11.80) .. 2·25 5
 a. Perf. 12 .. .. .. — 20·00
 b. Sepia-brown (Feb. '81) .. 1·10 5
 ba. Perf. 12 .. .. .. 50·00 20·00
 c. Brown (anil.) (May '81) .. 2·25 5
 ca. Perf. 12 .. .. .. — 20·00
 d. Dull black-brown (Oct. '81) — 5
 e. Dull grey-brown (Mar. '82) 70 5
 f. Mixed p. 13 and 12 .. — 90·00
224 „ 2d. mauve (*worn plate*) (Feb. '84) .. .. — 2·25
225 **34** 4d. rose-carmine (Oct. '81) 2·25 80
 a. Rosine (Aug. '82) .. 2·25 70
226 **35** 2s. dark blue (*shades*)/*green* (8.7.81) .. .. 8·00 2·50
 a. Light blue/green (wmk. sideways) (Aug. '83) .. 7·50 5·00
 b. Ultramarine/green (July '84) — 8·00
 ba. Wmk. sideways .. .. — 16·00

(*b*) *W* **23** (*V*2).

227 **33** 2d. dull grey-brn. (15.8.82) 65 5
228 „ 2d. chocolate (Mar. '83) .. 65 5
 a. Perf. 12 .. .. .. — 8·00
229 „ 2d. mauve (20.12.83) .. 1·50 5
 a. Worn plate .. .. 2·00 5
 b. Perf. 12 .. .. .. — 80·00
 c. Mixed perfs. 12½ and 12 .. — 80·00
230 **34** 4d. rose-red (Mar. '83) .. 2·50 90

For the scarce perf. 12 stamps listed above the holes are large and the teeth sharp. See also the note about perf. 12 stamps after No. 186b.

The first printings of the 2d. in mauve were from the two plates used for the browns. Later printings were from two new plates. Reprints were made in 1891 of the 2d. (brown), 4d. (in pale red) and 2s., all on *V*2 paper.

36

(Des. and die eng. Charles Naish. Typo.)

1883 (29 Oct)–**84.** *P* 12½.

(*a*) *W* **20** (*V*1).

231 **36** 1d. green (2.84) .. .. 32·00 2·00

(*b*) *W* **23** (*V*2).

232 **36** 1d. yellow-green (29.10.83) 1·50 10
 a. Green .. .. .. 1·50 10
 b. Pale green (5.84) .. .. 1·50 10

Nos. 224 and 231 represent a printing on old stocks of paper.

III. THE "POSTAGE AND REVENUE" PERIOD, 1884–1901.

Under the provisions of the Postage Act 1883 the stamps of the three series then in use (Postage, Duty, Fee) became, as from 1.1.84, mutually interchangeable. It was, at the same time decided to issue (as soon as possible) the *one* stamp only, for any value, to serve *all* purposes. Since these were available many more dies (and plates) inscribed "Stamp Duty" than there were of either the "Postage" or "Fee" (Stamp Statute) series it was agreed that all values should be inscribed "Stamp Duty" by the beginning of 1885. All stamps *printed* after 1.1.84 are therefore true "Postage and Revenue" stamps whereas all Stamp Duty and Fee stamps printed before that date are Postal Fiscals, since they were originally printed solely for fiscal purposes. These principles have been strictly adhered to in our listing. Little difficulty should however be met in distinguishing between the printings of the one stamp found respectively in the main list and in the "Postal Fiscal" section since there are many major differences of printing, watermark perforation and shade. On 1.1.84 there were no "Stamp Duty" designs for the ½d., 2d., 4d., 8d. and 2s. 6d. values. Also the existing "Stamp Duty" designs for the 1d., 6d., 1s. and 2s. were deemed to be too large to be convenient for general and extensive use. For all these values it was therefore necessary to produce new and smaller designs inscribed "Stamp Duty". Pending the preparation of new dies and plates printings were made in 1884 (for the ½d., 1d., 2d. 4d., 6d., 1s. and 2s. values) from the existing "Postage" plates. These printings are also "Postage and Revenue" stamps but have naturally been included, for the sake of convenience, in the previous period. By the beginning of 1885 printings were available, in the new designs of all values save the 1s. and 2s., and these latter appeared later.

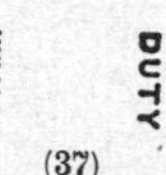

(37)

A. **1885.** *Postage Stamps optd. with T* **37.** *The* 1s. *and* 2s. *appeared in February* 1885, 3d. *and* 4d. *in November* 1885. *P* 12½.

(*a*) *W* **20** (*V*1).

233 **16** 3d. dull or.-yell. (Pl. 1) (B.) — 40·00
234 **30** 1s. ultramarine/*blue* .. 7·50 4·00
 a. Dull blue/blue .. .. — 5·50
235 „ 1s. deep. ultram./*blue* (B.) (F.C. £8) .. .. — £180
236 **35** 2s. ultramarine/*blue* .. 5·50 2·50
 a. Wmk. sideways .. .. 11·00 4·50

(*b*) *W* **23** (*V*2).

237 **16** 3d. yellow-orange Pl. 2 (B.) 5·00 2·00
a. Dull brownish-orange (B.) 5·50 2·50

238 **34** 4d. rose-carmine (B.) .. 5·00 2·00

The overprinted 1s. was replaced by the 1s. Type **44** on lemon. Collectors should beware of faded black overprints purporting to be the "blue". In genuine examples the blue of the overprint is difficult to distinguish in the blue of the stamp.

Reprints of the 4d. and 1s. (with and without overprint) were made in 1895–6. The 1s. is wmkd. *V*2 and the 4d. (from a new plate) is a pale red. Examples of the latter genuinely postally used are sometimes met.

38

39

40

41

42

43

(Typo. Dies for ½d., 2d., 3d., 4d., 8d. and 2s. 6d. eng. by Charles Naish, the other values being derived from these.)

B. 1884–95. *New designs inscr.* "*STAMP DUTY*". *P* 12½. (*a*) *W* **20** (*V*1).

239 **42** 8d. rose/*pink* (*shades*) (1.1.85) .. .. 1·50 65
a. Rose-red/pink .. .. 2·00 65

240 **40** 1s. deep dull blue/*lemon* (Nov. '85) .. .. 3·25 1·00
a. Dull blue/yellow (June '86) .. 3·25 1·10

241 **42** 2s. olive/*bluish grn.* (*shades*) (May '86) .. .. 2·00 65

(*b*) *W* **23** (*V*2).

243 **38** ½d. pale rosine (1.1.85) .. 65 12
a. Deep rosine (July '85) .. 70 35
b. Salmon (Sept. '85) .. .. 1·10 55

244 **39** 1d. yellowish green (*shades*) (1.1.85) 70 10
a. Dull pea-green (Feb. '85) .. 2·50 80

245 **40** 2d. lilac (*shades*) (1.1.85) .. 80 5
a. Mauve (Jan. '86) .. .. 1·00 5
b. Rosy-mauve (June '86) .. 2·00 20

246 **39** 3d. yellowish brown (1.1.85) 1·10 10
a. Pale ochre (Nov. '86) .. 1·00 12
b. Bistre-yellow (Dec. '92) .. 1·10 12

247 **41** 4d. magenta (1.1.85) .. 2·50 80
a. Bright mauve-rose (Jan. '87) 2·75 1·00

248 ,, 4d. dull lilac (*error*) (Dec. '86) £800 £175

249 **39** 6d. chalky blue (1.1.85) .. 5·00 80
a. Bright blue (Feb. '85) .. 2·75 65
b. Cobalt (Sept. '85) .. .. 2·75 65

250 **42** 8d. bright scarlet/*pink* ('92) 2·50 2·00

251 ,, 2s. olive-green/*pale green* (*shades*) (Mar. '90) .. 2·00 65

252 ,, 2s. apple-green (12.8.95) .. 2·00 1·50

253 ,, 2s. blue-green (29.10.95) .. 1·50 1·00

254 **43** 2s. 6d. brown-orange (23.4.84) .. .. 2·50 1·50
a. Yellow ('85) .. .. 2·00 1·10
b. Lemon-yellow (Jan. '93) .. 2·00 90

In each of the 1d., 6d., 1s. and 2s. values six types are to be found differing, *inter alia*, in the engraving of the words of value.

In the 2d. two die states are found: the *original* (1) which occurs on all but seven stamps in the Plate I sheet and the *damaged* (1a) which occurs on seven stamps in the Plate 1 sheet and on all 120 stamps in the Plate 2 sheet. The damage consists of a clear break in the top frame just in from the top right corner.

4d. "*error*": This comprised a printing of 6,000 stamps, in 1886, in a *dull lilac* shade. It is true that only some seven unused specimens are known but it is not true (as previously stated) that it is unknown used, since a leading authority has himself seen upwards of 30 undoubted used copies, all of which have certain characteristics which distinguish them from certain colour changelings, accidental or deliberate. The records show that the whole printing of 6,000 was issued which confirms the finding of so many used copies.

The 8d. value was withdrawn from sale on 24.8.95.

Reprints were made in 1891, using one of the original plates in each case, of the ½d., 1d., 2d., 4d., 6d. and 1s. values. In the three lower values the shades are fairly distinctive. The 1s. was wmkd. *V*1. In all cases the wmk. is equally common normal and inverted and this applies to *all* the Reprints made in 1891 or later.

44 45 46 47

48 49 50 51

52 53 54 55

56 57 58

(The above illustrations are ⅔ size.)

C. 1884–96. *New printings, all typographed from electrotypes, of* "*STAMP DUTY*" *designs first issued in* 1879. (*Des. Charles Jackson and Ludwig Lang. Dies eng. by Charles Jackson, Arthur Williams, Charles Evans and possibly others, supplied* (1879) *by Messrs. Sands and McDougall of Melbourne.*) *Perf.* 12½. *Wmk. sideways save where shown as upright* (U).

NOTE.—Stamps of the above designs printed by lithography or line-engraving, or similar designs not found in the following list should be looked for among the Postal Fiscals.

(*a*) *W* **20** (*V*1).

255 **44** 1s. ultram./*blue* (Nov. '84) 5·50 1·50

256 ,, 1s. chalky blue/*lemon* (3.3.85) .. .. 2·75 65

257 **46** 3s. maroon/*blue* (Aug. '84) 4·00 2·00

258 **48** 5s. reddish pur./*lemon* (June '87) .. .. 2·00 90
a. Brown-red/yellow (Jan. '94) 20·00 5·00

259 **52** £1 orge./*yellow* (Sept. '84) — 6·00
a. Reddish orge./yell. (Dec. '90) 11·00 5·50

(*b*) *W* **23** (*V*2).

260 **45** 1s. 6d. pink (Feb. 1885) .. 7·50 2·00
a. Bright rose-carm. (May '86) 5·50 1·50

261 **46** 3s. drab (Nov. '85) .. 2·50 1·10
a. Olive-drab (Oct. '93) .. 2·25 1·10

262 **47** 4s. red-orange (27.5.86) .. 2·00 1·00
a. Yellow-orange (8, U) .. 4·00 1·10

263 **48** 5s. rosine (8.5.96) .. 2·25 1·10

264 **49** 6s. pea-green (12.11.91) .. 5·00 2·50
a. Apple-green (U) (Apr. '96) 5·50 2·50

265 **50** 10s. dull bluish green (Oct. '85) .. .. 8·00 2·50
a. Grey-green (Sept. '87) .. 7·50 2·25

266 **51** 15s. purple-brn. (Dec. '85) 14·00 8·00

267 ,, 15s. brown (U) (May '95) .. 35·00 16·00

268 **53** £1 5s. pink† (U) (6.8.90) 35·00 7·00

269 **54** £1 10s. pale olive† (Oct. '88) .. .. 40·00 8·00

270 **55** £2 blue† (Aug. '88) .. 40·00 11·00

271 **56** 45s. lilac† (15.8.90) .. — 11·00

272 **57** £5 pink (Oct. '85) .. — 20·00

273 **58** £10 lilac (July '85) .. — 20·00
a. Mauve† (July '93) .. — 16·00

† Both here and later indicates that prices quoted are for stamps postmarked to order by the Victorian postal authorities for sale in sets.

59

(Illustration ⅔ size.)

D. 1896–1900. *Type* **59** *and similar types. W* **23** (*V*2) *sideways* (S) *or upright* (U). *The line-engraved stamps were all printed singly direct from the dies and both the lithographed and typographed stamps were in sheets of* 10 (2×5).

(i) *Lithographed. Printings of* 1886 *to* 1889.

274 £25 dull yellowish-green (S, U) (Jan. 86) F.C. 24·00
a. Dull blue-green (U) (Oct. 88) F.C. 24·00

275 £50 bright violet (U) (Feb. 86) F.C. 30·00
a. Dull purple (U) (Oct. 87) .. F.C. 30·00

276 £100 rosine (S, U) (Jan. 86) .. F.C. 35·00

(ii) *Recess-printed. Printings of Nov.* 1890 *to April* 1897.

277 £25 bright blue-green (S, U) (Nov. 90) .. .. F.C. 24·00

278 £50 black-violet (S) (Nov. 90) F.C. 30·00

279 £100 crimson (aniline) (S, U) (Nov. 90) .. .. F.C. 30·00
a. Scarlet-red† (1897) .. .. — 32·00

For earlier recess-printed printings, see under "POSTAL FISCALS".

(iii) *Typographed from Electrotyped plates. Printings of Nov.* 1897 *on.*

280 £25 dull blue-green† (U) .. — 15·00

281 £50 bright mauve† (U) .. — 24·00

282 £100 pink-red† (U) (Oct. 1900) — 24·00

Collectors should beware of stamps with cleaned fiscal markings particularly in the higher values. Some of these bear forged cancellations but others, in fraud of the revenue, did genuine postal service.

60

61

62

63

64

65

66

67

(Typo. Previous 2d. and 4d. dies "lined" by Charles Naish; 1s. 6d. des. and eng. Charles Naish; rest des. Philip Astley, probably eng. Samuel Reading and supplied by Fergusson and Mitchell.)

1886–96. *W* **23** (*V*2) *upright save in ½d., 1s. and high values (excepting the £6) where it is sideways. P 12½.*

283 **60** ½d. lilac-grey (20.8.86) .. 75 35
a. Grey-black .. .. — 13·00
284 ,, ½d. pink (15.2.87) .. 70 10
a. Rosine (aniline) (Dec. '89).. 60 10
b. Rose-red (May '91) .. 55 5
c. Vermilion (Mar. '96) .. 60 15
285 **61** 1d. green (26.7.86) .. 70 5
a. Yellow-green (July '87) .. 70 5
286 **62** 2d. pale lilac (17.12.86) .. 70 5
a. Pale mauve ('87) .. 55 5
b. Deep lilac ('88, '92) .. 55 5
c. Purple (May '94).. .. 70 12
d. Violet (May '95) 55 5
e. Imperforate ('90) .. — £325
287 **63** 4d. rose-red (1.4.87) .. 1·25 12
a. Red ('93) .. .. 1·10 8
288 **64** 6d. bright ultram. (27.8.86) 1·10 8
a. Pale ultramarine (Oct. '87) 1·00 5
b. Dull blue (Feb. '91) .. 60 5
289 **65** 1s. dull pur.-brn. (14.3.87) 2·75 55
a. Lake (Feb. '90) .. .. 3·00 55
b. Carmine-lake (May '92) .. 2·00 12
c. Brownish red (Jan. '96) .. 2·50 15
290 **66** 1s. 6d. pale blue (June '88) 8·00 5·00
291 ,, 1s. 6d. orange (18.9.89) .. 1·50 1·00
a. Red-orange .. .. 1·75 1·10
292 **67** £5 pale blue & maroon† (7.2.88) .. .. 50·00 6·50
293 ,, £6 yellow & pale blue† (1.10.87) .. .. 55·00 8·00
294 ,, £7 rosine & blk.† (17.10.89) 60·00 11·00
295 ,, £8 mauve & brn.-orange† (U) (2.8.90) .. .. 90·00 13·00
296 ,, £9 apple-green & rosine† (21.8.88) .. .. £110 14·00

Reprints of the ½d. grey and 1s. 6d. blue were made in 1894–5. They differ from the originals in shade. A £10 (*T* **67**) was prepared for use but not issued.

An imperforate sheet of the 2d. was on sale at the Mortlake Post Office in 1890 and a pair was noted in 1902.

68

69

70

(1d. die supplied, des. and eng. by Samuel Reading; 2½d. and 5d. des. by M. Tannenberg; 9d. first printed from the new Reprint plate of 1891. Typo.)

1890–96. *New designs and values. P 12½.*

(*a*) *W* **20** (*V*1).

297 **68** 1d. orge.-brn./*pnk.* (16.6.91) 20 5

This was an emergency printing, caused by a temporary shortage of white *V*2 paper.

(*b*) *W* **23** (*V*2).

298 **68** 1d. dull chestnut (1.1.90) 35 5
a. Deep red-brown (Jan. '90) 40 12
b. Orange-brown (Apr. '90) .. 35 5
c. Yellow-brown (1891) .. 12 5
d. Brown-red ('90, '92) .. 12 5
e. Brt. yell.-orange (Jan. '94) 4·00 12
f. Brownish orange (Aug. '94) 12 5
299 **69** 2½d. red-brown/*lemon* .. (18.12.90) .. 70 5
300 ,, 2½d. brown-red/*yellow* ('92) 55 5
a. Red/yellow (1893) 55 5
301 **70** 5d. purple-brown .. 90 12
a. Pale reddish brown (1892) 70 8
302 **29** 9d. apple-green (18.10.92) 2·75 1·00
303 ,, 9d. carm.-rose (18.10.95) 1·50 70
a. Rosine (aniline) (1896) .. 2·00 75

The yellow papers used for the 2½d. value differed considerably in tint.

71

72 (*V*3)

(Eng. A. Williams (1½d.).)

1896 (June)–**1899** (Aug.). *W* **72** (*V*3). *Paper supplied by Waterlow and Sons. This paper differs noticeably from the previous De La Rue products. It is less white, softer and generally thicker, and has a coarser grain or mesh than any previous V over Crown paper. It will be noted that some coloured V2 papers of earlier manufacture were utilised during this period. Types* **60, 65, 71** *and the larger size stamps have the wmk. sideways unless marked* U (*upright*). *P 12½.*

304 **60** ½d. light scarlet (1.7.96) .. 12 5
a. Carmine-rose (Nov. '97) .. 20 5
b. Deep carmine-red (coarse impression '99) .. .. — 35
305 **68** 1d. brown-red (13.6.96) .. 20 5
a. Brownish orange ('99) .. 12 5
306 **71** 1½d. apple-green (8.10.97) 25 20
307 **62** 2d. violet (*shades*) (12.6.96) 35 5
308 **39** 3d. ochre (Nov. '96) .. 1·10 10
a. Buff (Feb. '98) .. .. 1·00 5
309 **63** 4d. red (June '97) .. 70 5
310 **70** 5d. red-brown (July '97) 1·10 5
311 **64** 6d. dull blue (Sept. '96) 60 5
312 **29** 9d. rosine (Oct. '96) .. 2·75 40
a. Rose-carmine (Apr. '98) — 40
b. Dull rose (June '98) .. 1·25 40
313 **65** 1s. brownish red (Mar.'97) 1·10 20
314 **66** 1s. 6d. brown-orange (Aug. '98) .. .. 5·00 2·25
315 **42** 2s. blue-green (Apr. '97) 4·00 1·50
316 **43** 2s. 6d. yellow (Sept. '96) 4·00 2·00
a. Yellow (U) (Sept. '98) .. 5·00 2·00
317 **46** 3s. olive-drab (Dec. '96) 3·75 2·50
a. Olive-drab (U) (Oct. '98) .. 4·00 2·00
318 **47** 4s. orange (Sept. '97) .. 3·75 1·00
319 **48** 5s. rosine (Feb. '97) .... 3·75 1·25
a. Rose-carmine (Nov. '97) .. 3·00 1·10
b. Rosine (U) (Mar. '99) .. 5·50 1·50
320 **49** 6s. p. yell.-grn.† (Apr. '99) 3·75 1·25
321 **50** 10s. grey-green (Apr. '97) 9·00 2·75
a. Blue-green (July '98) .. 9·00 3·00
322 **51** 15s. brown† (Apr. '97) .. 10·00 2·00
323 **59** £25 dull bluish green† (U) ('99) .. .. .. — 35·00
324 ,, £50 dull pur.† (U) (Nov. '97) — 32·00

73

74

(*Illustrations reduced. Actual size* 31½ × 38½ *mm.*)

(Des. M. Tannenberg. Eng. R. R. Mitchelhill.)

1897 (7 Oct.). *Charity. W* **72** (*V*3) *sideways. P 12½.*

325 **73** 1d. (1s.) blue .. .. 5·00 5·00
326 **74** 2½d. (2s. 6d.) red-brown .. 18·00 18·00
325/326 Optd. "Specimen" *Set of* 2 45·00

These stamps, sold at 1s. and 2s. 6d. respectively, paid postage of 1d. and 2½d. only, the difference being given to a Hospital Fund.

1899 (1 Aug.)–**1900.** *Colours changed for ½d., 1d., 1½d. and 2½d. P 12½.*

(*a*) *W* **23** (*V*2).

327 **71** 1½d. brn.-red/*yell.* (1.8.99) 20 20

(*b*) *W* **72** (*V*3).

328 **60** ½d. emerald (Aug. '99) .. 40 5
329 **69** 2½d. blue (1.8.99) 35 10

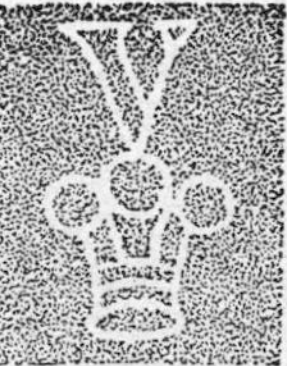
75 (*V*4)

(c) W **75** (V4).

This wmk. and paper, like V3, was supplied by Waterlow and Sons and it continued in use until 1905. It was the result of an amended specification. Like the V3 paper it has a marked mesh but is whiter, smoother and harder. The 1s. and the four higher values have the wmk. sideways, the ½d. being found with both positions.

330	**60**	½d. emerald (1.8.99) ..	12	5
		a. Deep blue-green	35	5
331	**68**	1d. rosine (1.8.99) ..	12	5
		a. Rose-red (1900)	12	5
332	**62**	2d. violet (*shades*) (1.8.99)	40	5
333	**69**	2½d. blue (Feb. 1900) ..	20	5
334	**39**	3d. bistre-yell. (Sept. '99)	40	10
335	**63**	4d. rose-red (Dec. '99) ..	65	10
336	**70**	5d. red-brown (Oct. '99) ..	40	5
337	**64**	6d. dull ultram. (Feb. '00)	65	5
338	**29**	9d. rose-red (Aug. '99) ..	65	20
339	**65**	1s. brown-red (May 1900)	80	35
340	**66**	1s. 6d. orange (Dec. '99)	1·10	1·00
341	**42**	2s. blue-green (June 1900)	1·25	1·00
342	**43**	2s. 6d. yellow (Jan. 1900)	2·50	65
343	**46**	3s. pale olive† (May 1900)	5·00	80
344	**48**	5s. rose-red (April 1900)	5·00	1·10
345	**50**	10s. green† (Mar. 1900) ..	7·00	1·25

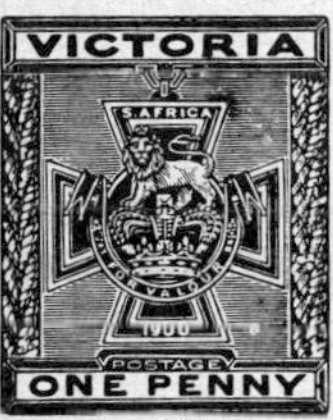

76

77

(*Illustrations reduced. Actual size* 33×39 *mm.*)

(Eng. S. Reading.)

1900 (MAY). *Charity.* W **75** (V4) *sideways. P* 12½.

346	**76**	1d. (1s.) olive-brown ..	12·00	12·00
347	**77**	2d. (2s.) emerald-green ..	30·00	35·00

These stamps were sold for a Boer War Patriotic Fund, on a similar basis to the issue of 1897.

V Over Crown Wmks.: A Note on "Abnormal" Watermark Positions.

It should always be remembered that the block of 120 wmks. (12×10) in the sheet was designed to fit the normal size stamp in an upright position. *Other* sizes, larger and smaller, were printed, at various times, with the wmk. *both* upright and sideways. The following note concerns only varieties as they are found on stamps of normal size.

Inverted Wmks.: This description also embraces cases of wmks. lying sideways with V at right found on stamps of Type **60** etc. which are of the same dimensions (but reversed) as the usual size stamp. In printings before 1882 all inverted wmks. may be regarded as "abnormals". In this period all sheets of 240 wmks. were, where necessary, cut into two before printing. From 1882 to mid-1896 the *only* inverted "abnormals" are found in certain of the common values where the area of the printing surface (i.e. 2 plates of 120) more or less equalled the area of the complete sheet of watermarked paper as it was supplied by De La Rue's. This was of 240 wmks., consisting of one pane of 120 wmks. over another pane of 120. In this period the sheet of 240 wmks. was not cut up before printing from single plates as had been done previously. Where only one plate was employed the sheet was fed in in one direction, removed, dried, and fed in the other direction, giving in the result 120 normal and 120 inverted wmks. (This fact is of assistance when distinguishing certain Reprints.) From 1896 the same principle applied save that the complete sheets supplied were of 480 wmks. so that the only "abnormal" inverteds found are in those cases, e.g. 1d. and 2d. where the stamps were printed from a block of similar size viz. of 4 plates of 120 impressions clamped together.

However, in 1901 to 1912, following a change in postal rates resulting in a smaller demand for the 2d. value, this was again printed from two plates so that inverted watermarks in this period are always normal.

Sideways Wmks.: This description includes upright wmks. on stamps of the dimensions of Type **60** etc. They usually arose through the suppliers placing the paper in the wrong direction in the bound books (and later unbound reams) of paper supplied. *Three* periods concern us in this regard.

(i) 1867–1882: Before 1867 paper was supplied in single sheets of 120 wmks. and from 1867 in double sheets of 240 wmks. From 1867 to 1882 wherever it was necessary (i.e. where only one plate was used) the double sheets were cut into half before printing. The variety may be found under the following numbers. All are extremely rare—viz. 174, 180, 190, 192, 193, 202, 214, 225.

(ii) 1882–1896. In this period no "abnormal" sideways wmks. are met since the paper supplied was not cut up before printing and since the complete sheet supplied was rectangular and *not square* in shape.

(iii) 1896–1912: Here the wmkd. paper supplied was of 480 (120×4) wmks. and such sheets were practically square. One meets "abnormals" under the following numbers, many of these being extremely rare—viz. 304, 305, 307, 308, 312, 313, 328, 330, 331, 332, 334, 338, 356, 357, 359, 366, 367, 368, 371, 373, 386, 400, 405, 407, 414, 417, 445, 447, 451.

Reversed Wmks.: These involved a printing on the wrong side of the paper. Since the side which should have been printed was usually 'surfaced' to some degree these varieties almost invariably show the impression of the stamp coarser than normally and the back of the stamp smoother and glossier. From 1878 to 1896 the back of the paper supplied by De La Rue was treated with a special preparation to prevent the gum soaking through to the front. This preparation was susceptible to moisture and when printed upon and subsequently exposed to moisture occasionally shed portions of the design, so that in this period such varieties often bear the superficial appearance of having been printed on the gum, whereas in fact, up to July 1912, all gumming was done after printing. Reversed wmks., many of them very rare, have been found under the following Nos.—158, 162, 179, 181, 183, 184, 185, 187, 190, 192, 193, 197, 198, 206, 210, 211, 214, 228, 243, 244, 245, 263, 283, 284, 285, 286, 287, 288, 289, 298, 305, 307, 310, 331, 332, 356, 357, 366, 373, 400, 401, 403, 406, 407, 408, 447, 448—also in certain of the £25, £50 and £100 stamps (in both sections) and in various items in the Postal Fiscal list. In the reversed V over Crown cases—looking through the front of the stamp in a normal upright position—the double side of the 'V' will appear on the *right* and not on the left as it should do.

IV. THE COMMONWEALTH PERIOD, 1901–12.

All postage stamps issued by the States in this period were in reality COMMONWEALTH stamps. This viewpoint has now received official endorsement ("Commonwealth of Australia Philatelic Bulletin" No. 2, Oct. 1953). Prior to the actual coming into being of the Commonwealth it had been agreed between the States that the Postal Services were to be the concern of the Commonwealth and that the postal revenue was to go to it. This decision meant, for Victoria, the separation of the Postage and the Fiscal systems. So long, however, as the Commonwealth lacked printing facilities and a Postal administration of its own the work had to be done by each State on its behalf. Separate series of Postage stamps (for which the State was obliged to account to the Commonwealth) and of Duty stamps (which were to continue as a State concern) therefore became necessary. The first Kangaroo stamps were not issued by the Commonwealth until Jan. 1913, but in the intervening period a long chain of philatelic events had contributed to make this issue possible. From the beginning of 1902 all the stamps of Tasmania and Western Australia were printed in Melbourne, on Victorian paper. Later Papua (1907) and later again South Australia (1909) were added to these. In the same year (1902) the first Commonwealth Postage Dues, printed in Sydney on New South Wales paper, appeared. In 1903 a 9d. stamp of the same "Commonwealth" design was issued in New South Wales and Queensland. In 1905 all States commenced using one or other of four types of Crown over A paper, marginally wmkd. "COMMONWEALTH OF AUSTRALIA". In 1909, printed in Melbourne, appeared new bi-coloured Postage Dues, the first stamps to be inscribed "AUSTRALIA". This followed the appointment of J. B. Cooke, the South Australian stamp printer, as Commonwealth Stamp Printer. As from 13.10.10 the stamps of any State could legally be used in any other State, and in April 1911 the first Commonwealth Postal Stationery was issued. In short, in the period 1901 to 1912, although certain States printed and issued postage stamps, this was a privilege, subject at all times to Commonwealth control and direction and conducted, in respect of the nett revenue received, solely for the Commonwealth's benefit.

The Commonwealth was proclaimed as from 1st January 1901. In only three cases in the first issue, viz. the 1d., 2½d. and 5d. values was there sufficient time to alter the dies and produce new plates. In all the other cases the same plates were used as had been employed to produce the 1891 Reprints.

1901 (29 JAN.)–**1905.** *P* 12½ *or* 12×12½. (*a*) *Without the word "POSTAGE" in the design.*

(i) W **72** (V3).

348	**35**	2s. blue/*pink*	1·50	1·25

(ii) W **75** (V4).

349	**25**	½d. bluish green	12	5
		a. Var. "VICTCRIA" ..	7·50	7·00
350	**33**	2d. reddish violet	12	5
351	**16**	3d. dull orange	40	10
352	**34**	4d. bistre-yellow	55	20
353	**17**	6d. emerald	55	35
354	**30**	1s. yellow	70	40
355	**19**	5s. pale red and deep blue	7·00	3·00

78

79

80

(*b*) *With the word "POSTAGE" in the design* W **75** (V4).

356	**78**	1d. rose (Die I)	12	5
		a. Dull red (Dec. '01) ..	12	5
357	,,	1d. rose (Die II) (2.4.'01)	12	5
		a. Dull red (Dec. '01) ..	12	5
358	,,	1d. pale rose-red (Die III) (3.5.'05)	55	5
359	**79**	2½d. dull blue (1901) ..	20	5
		a. Deep blue (1902) ..	20	5
360	**80**	5d. reddish brown ..	55	5
		a. Purple-brown (1903) ..	40	5

I.

II.

III.

I and II.

III.

Three dies of the 1d.: Principal differences are:

I. Horizontal lines over Queen's head fill oval surround under "VICTORIA". Found in two plates employed Jan. 1901–Feb. 1903.

II. Practically all the lines of shading to the left of and on top of the head have been "thinned", giving a lighter appearance. Some lines at the top have been cut away, leaving small white patches, particularly under the "OR". Found in ten plates in use between April 1901 and April 1905.

III. As II but with stop at lower left clearly separated from circle line at its right; spot of colour in shading between "O" and "R"; two lines of shading meet in lower left portion of "P" of "PENNY". Found in twelve plates in use between May 1905 and the end of 1912.

1901 (JUNE). *W* **75** (*V4*). *P* 12×12½.

361	**68**	1d. olive (6.6.'01)	80	65
362	**39**	3d. slate-green (20.6.'01) ..	1·25	1·10

These stamps were available for postal purposes to 30.6.01, afterwards for fiscal purposes only.

81

82

83

84

85

86

87

88

Type A
"POSTAGE" 6 mm.

89

Type B
"POSTAGE" 7 mm.

90

91

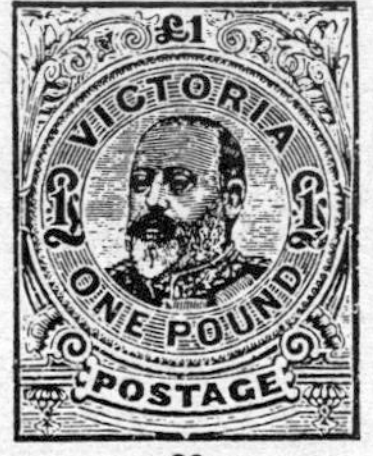

92

93

1901 (JUNE)–**10.** *Similar to former types but "POSTAGE" inserted in design.* *W* **75** (*V4*).

(*a*) *P* 12½ *or* 12×12½.

363	**81**	½d. blue-green (*shades*) (Die I) (26.6.01) ..	20	5
		a. Blue-green (U)	20	5
364	,,	½d. pale blue-grn. (Die II) (June, 04)	35	5
365	,,	½d. pale bluish green (Die III) (June, 05) ..	1·00	20
366	**82**	1½d. maroon/*yellow* (9.7.'01)	65	10
		a. Brown-red/yellow (1901) ..	20	5
		b. Dull red/yellow (1906) ..	20	5
367	**83**	2d. lilac (16.7.'01) ..	20	5
		a. Reddish violet (1902) ..	20	5
		b. Violet (1904)	75	5
		c. Bright purple (1905) ..	75	8
368	**84**	3d. dull orge.-brn. (2.7.'01)	80	5
		a. Chestnut (1901)	80	5
		b. Yellowish brown (1903) ..	80	5
369	**85**	4d. bistre-yellow (26.6.'01)	55	5
		a. Brownish bistre (1905) ..	80	10
370	**86**	6d. emerald (5.7.'01) ..	60	5
		a. Dull green (1904) ..	1·10	20
371	**87**	9d. dull rose-red (5.7.'01)	1·00	12
		a. Pale red (1901)	1·10	10
		b. Dull brownish red (1905) ..	1·25	40
372	**88**	1s. yellow-orge. (Type A) (5.7.'01)	1·00	35
		a. Yellow (1902)	1·25	20
373	**89**	1s. yellow (Type B) (April 1903)	1·25	55
		a. Yellow-orange (1903) ..	1·25	30
374	**90**	2s. blue/*rose* (5.7.'01) ..	1·00	12

375	**91**	5s. rose-red and pale blue (5.7.'01)	5·50	2·50
		a. Scarlet and deep blue (1902)	5·00	1·50
		b. Rosine and blue (1905) ..	5·00	1·50
376	**92**	£1 carm.-rose (18.11.'01)	75·00	60·00
377	**93**	£2 deep blue (2.6.'02) ..	£110	£100
		(*b*) *Perf.* 11.		
378	**81**	½d. blue-green (Die I) (Sept. '02)	1·00	35
		a. Blue-green (U)	60	8
379	,,	½d. blue-green (Die II) ..	60	10
380	,,	½d. bluish green (Die III)	80	20
381	**78**	1d. dull red (Die I) ..	—	10·00
382	,,	1d. dull red (Die II) ..	—	7·50
		a. Pale red (anil.) (*Mar.* '03)	70	40
		b. Pale rose (aniline) (1904)	—	1·50
383	,,	1d. pale rose-red (Die III)	11·00	10·00
384	**82**	1½d. dull red/*yellow* (1910)	11·00	12·00
385	**83**	2d. violet (1904)	—	60·00
		a. Bright purple (1905) ..	—	60·00
386	**84**	3d. orange-brown (1903)	1·25	1·25
387	**86**	6d. emerald (1903) ..	1·40	1·40
		a. Dull green (1905) ..	80·00	75·00
388	**92**	£1 carmine-red (1905) ..	80·00	80·00
389	**93**	£2 deep blue (1905) ..	£325	£325
		(*c*) *Compound or mixed perf.* 12½ *and* 11.		
390	**81**	½d. blue-green (Die I) ..	—	1·50
		a. Blue-green (U) (1903) ..	—	1·50
391	,,	½d. blue-green (Die II) (1904)	5·50	5·00
392	**78**	1d. dull red (Die I) ..	—	75·00
393	,,	1d. dull red (Die II) ..	—	50·00
394	**82**	1½d. dull red/*yellow* ..	—	80·00
395	**83**	2d. reddish violet ..	—	£110
396	**84**	3d. orange-brown ..	—	80·00
397	**86**	6d. emerald	—	80·00
398	**91**	5s. rose and blue ..	£250	

I.

II.

III.

Three dies of the ½d.: Principal differences are:

I. Outer of two vertical lines of colour to left of "V" is continuous save for a marked break opposite top of "V". Found in two plates in use 1901–May 1904.

II. Outer vertical line to left of "V" is broken in three places; the triangular space S.W. of "V", has also been "opened up" and shows more white lines than in I. Found in two plates in use June 1904–June 1905.

III. As II but the thin vertical coloured line to right of the "A" of "VICTORIA" (previously broken in the middle) is now broken in four or five places. The triangular ornament to S.E. of the same "A" has also been "opened up", the white cross-hatching now being stronger than in I and II. Found in two plates introduced in June 1905 and in two subsequent plates introduced late in 1909.

The paper used for the 1½d. value for two printings in 1908–9 was yellow-buff in colour but in used copies the difference is not so marked as to warrant separate description.

There were two main states of the 2d. Die, the original showing the S.E. corner correctly squared and the later showing it damaged and blunter. There are other differences. The original state is found in all printings before April 1904 but not after, and the later state to a small extent (5 per cent) in the printings before April 1904 and *solely* in the printings from that date.

For the 1s. Type A the same plate was used as for the 1s. "No Postage" of 1901, the words "POSTAGE" being separately punched on. For Type B two new plates, prepared via an etched line-block, were introduced.

Certain *unlisted shades* (due to their being unsatisfactory) are found *only* punctured O.S. Marked instances of this are found in the 2d., 3d. and 4d. values.

1905–13. *Wmk. Crown over A Type* **W 11.** *A Medium paper, supplied, like the V 4 paper, by Waterlow & Sons.*

(*a*) *P* 12½ *or* 12×12½.

399 **81** ½d. blue-green (21.10.05) 12 5
 a. Light bluish green .. 12 5
400 **78** 1d. rose-red (*shades*) (16.7.05) 12 5
 a. Pale rose (1907) .. 12 5
 b. Rose-carmine (Sept. '11) .. 55 5
401 **83** 2d. dull mauve (13.9.05) 55 5
 a. Bright mauve (1906) .. 55 5
 b. Reddish violet (1907) .. 55 5
 c. Lilac (1910) .. 35 5
402 **79** 2½d. blue (*shades*) (4.08) .. 35 8
 a. Indigo (1909) 35 8
403 **84** 3d. orange-brn. (11.11.05) 55 5
 a. Yellow-orange (1908) .. 65 8
 b. Dull orange-buff (1909) .. 55 8
 c. Ochre (1912) 55 8
404 **85** 4d. yell.-bistre (15.1.06) 65 5
 a. Bistre (1908) 70 5
 b. Yellow-olive (1912) .. 70 8
405 **80** 5d. chocolate (14.8.06) .. 80 20
 a. Dull reddish brown (1908) 80 10
406 **86** 6d. dull green (25.10.05) 80 8
 a. Dull yellow-green (1907) .. 60 5
 b. Emerald (1909) 70 8
 c. Yellowish green (1911) .. 70 5
407 **87** 9d. rose-red (11.12.05) .. 80 12
 a. Pale salmon-red (1906) .. 80 10
 b. Brown-red (1908) .. 1·10 12
 c. Pale dull rose (worn pl.) .. 2·00 65
 d. Rose-carmine (new pl.) (Dec. '09) .. 75 12
408 **80** 1s. yellow-orge. (13.2.06) 75 8
 a. Yellow (1906) 75 8
 b. Lemon (1908) 90 8
409 **91** 5s. rose-red and ultram. (U) (Nov. '07) .. 10·00 3·00
 a. Rose-red & blue (U) (1912) 11·00 3·00
 b. Rose-red and blue (S) .. 13·00 4·00
410 **92** £1 salmon (Feb. 1907) .. 75·00 65·00
411 „ £1 dull rose (1910) .. 75·00 75·00
 a. Deep dull rose (U) (1912) .. 75·00 75·00
412 **93** £2 dull blue (1906) .. £130 £110

Perforations of period 1901–12.

In general, up to 1910, five machines were available at any one time—three single-line (two "11" and one "12½") and two vertical combs (12×12½). Only single-line machines were used for the 5s., £1 and £2 values. The "12½" single line was used on many occasions for the ½d. and occasionally for other values. The "11" machines were primarily employed for larger size stamps, e.g. Victorian Duty Stamps, Tasmanian Pictorials and Papua, and their use for the normal size Victorian postage stamps was in the main restricted to emergencies. At certain periods, e.g. 1909–10 one encounters the true "compounds" i.e. the products of two single-line machines, 12½ and 11 respectively. For the ½d. the vertical comb 12×12½ was also used, particularly in the earlier period, on the sheet turned sideways. In the result the alternate vertical margins between stamps were left imperforate and a single-line machine (either 12½ or 11) was often used to complete the perforating, in the latter case (11) giving us a variety for separate listing. "Mixed" perforations in this period are, like their predecessors of the '70s, the result of the correction—with another machine—of faultily centred lines of perforation (either single-line or comb), the back of these faulty lines being usually pasted over with gummed strips to assist in tearing down the corrected lines.

The rotary-comb machines gauging 11½×12¼ were brought over from South Australia by J. B. Cooke when he moved to Melbourne in 1909.

The ½d. perf. 11 and the 2½d. and 5s. first printings (all perforated with single line machines) may be met with *full imperforate base margins.* Likewise in the Crown over A issues the ½d. perf. 12½ and the 5s. perf. 12½ (1912) have been similarly found. Such varieties are, of course, rare.

(*b*) *Perf.* 11.

413 **81** ½d. light bluish green .. 12 5
 a. Blue-green 12 5
414 **78** 1d. rose-red (1905) .. 20 40
 a. Pale rose (1907) .. 35 40
 b. Rose-carmine (1911) .. 1·00 1·25
415 **83** 2d. mauve (1906) .. — 75·00
 a. Reddish violet (1908) .. 24·00 6·00
 b. Lilac (1910) .. .. 7·00 3·00
416 **79** 2½d. blue (1909) .. 6·00 2·75
 a. Indigo (1909) .. .. 1·50 1·00
417 **84** 3d. brown (1908) .. 2·00 1·50
 a. Orange-buff (1909) .. 4·00 3·00
 b. Dull orange-yellow (1911) — 40·00
 c. Ochre (1912) .. .. 1·00 60
418 **85** 4d. yellow-bistre (1908) .. 1·50
 a. Yellow-olive (1912) .. 1·25 1·00
419 **80** 5d. reddish brown .. — £130
420 **86** 6d. emerald (1910) .. 80 70
 a. Yellowish green (1911 .. 2·00 70
421 **87** 9d. rose-carmine .. .. — £130
422 **89** 1s. yellow-orange .. £100
 a. Yellow .. .. .. — 90·00
423 **91** 5s. rose-red and ultram. 6·50 2·00
424 **92** £1 salmon (1907) .. 80·00 70·00
425 **93** £2 dull blue (1906) .. £120 £110

(*c*) *Compound or mixed perfs.* 12½ *and* 11.

426 **81** ½d. light bluish green (6.09) 7·00 7·00
427 **78** 1d. rose-red .. .. 13·00 14·00
428 **83** 2d. mauve .. .. .. — 80·00
429 **84** 3d. brown (1908) .. 55·00 90·00
 a. Ochre (1912) .. .. — 75·00
430 **85** 4d. bistre .. .. .. — £110
431 **86** 6d. yellowish green .. — £110
432 **87** 9d. dull rose-red .. .. — £150
433 **89** 1s. yellow-orange .. — £150

(*d*) *Rotary comb perf.* 11½×12¼.

434 **78** 1d. pale scarlet-red (2.10) 90 8
 a. Rose-red (C.10) 65 20
435 **83** 2d. lilac (*shades*) 90 20

B: *On thinner paper, ready gummed with white gum.* (July–Nov. 1912).

(*a*) *P* 12½ *or* 12×12½.

436 **81** ½d. blue-green 70 10
437 **78** 1d. rose-red .. .. 1·50 10
438 **83** 2d. lilac .. .. .. 2·75 1·00
439 **80** 5d. brown .. .. 1·25 65
440 **86** 6d. emerald .. .. 1·25 65
441 **89** 1s. dull yellow (11.12) .. 3·25 1·00
 a. Pale orange (1.13) .. 3·25 1·00

(*b*) *P* 11.

442 **81** ½d. blue-green .. .. 5·00 2·75
443 **78** 1d. rose-red .. .. 2·00 1·00

(*c*) *P* 11×12½.

444 **81** ½d. blue-green .. .. 40·00 35·00

(*d*) *Rotary comb perf.* 11½×12¼.

445 **78** 1d. rose-carmine (2.7.12) .. 55 5
 a. Rose-red (10.12) 65 5

Two qualities of the "thin" paper were supplied, the first supply (earliest date 2.7.12) being thicker and with a less obvious mesh than the second (earliest date 2.10.12). The ½d. and 1d. are found on both classes of paper, the 2d. on the first only, and the 5d., 6d. and 1s. on the second only. There was a shortage pending the arrival of the second supply, and this gap was filled by the use of the "Stamp Duty" paper next described and the ONE PENNY overprint of 1.7.12. The 5d. perforated O.S. on the thin paper may be met in *dull red-brown.*

94 (*V*5)

ONE PENNY

(95)

C: *Printed on* "*Stamp Duty*" *paper,* W **94** (*V*5). *This paper is rather softer and of a more pronounced mesh than the V*4 *paper.* (Aug.–Oct. 1912.)

(*a*) *P* 12½ *or* 12×12½.

446 **81** ½d. bluish green 55 10
447 **78** 1d. rose-carmine (7.8.12) .. 60 8
448 **83** 2d. reddish violet 65 10
 a. Lilac .. .. .. 1·10 55
449 **87** 9d. carmine-red .. .. 1·00 55

(*b*) *P* 11.

450 **81** ½d. bluish green .. .. 5·00 3·00
451 **78** 1d. rose-carmine (8.12) .. 8·50 2·75
452 **87** 9d. carmine-red .. .. 2·50 1·00

(*c*) *Compound perf.* 11 *with* 12½.

453 **87** 9d. carmine-red .. .. — £160

This paper was supplied by Spicer Bros. at the beginning of 1911 and continued to be used for many years in the production of Duty Stamps for this State.

1912 (1 July). *Surch. with T* **95** *in red. Wmk. Crown over A. P* 11½×12¼.

454 **83** 1d. on 2d. lilac 10 8

Late in June 1912 the first consignment of "thin" paper was exhausted and the second had not arrived. A further supply of the 1d. value was urgently required, and the expedient of overprinting current 2d. stock was employed to fill the gap. The same reason also produced the 1d. on 2d. overprints of Tasmania and Western Australia, respectively.

POSTAL FISCALS.

This section embraces those printings of Duty and Fee stamps made before 1.1.84. These were made available for postal purposes as from 1.1.84. The two series were in concurrent use between December 1879 and 1884.

A. The "STAMP STATUTE" series.

This series was first issued on 26th April 1871 and it was in the main used to record the payment of various Court fees. The issue of the series ceased in April 1884.

F 1 F 2 F 3

F 4

(Illustrations ⅔ size.)

1870–83. *Large rectangular stamps of various designs as Types* F **1** *to* F **4**. *All save the* 3d. *and* 2s. 6d. (*eng. by James Turner*) *have the Queen's head included in the design* (*eng. by William Bell*). *Typo. at the Stamp Printing Office, Melbourne.*

(*a*) *Wmk. single-lined numerals* (1, 2, *and* 10) *as used for Postage Stamps* (1863–67). *On Saunders paper unless otherwise noted. Both sideways and upright wmks. are found in certain cases.*

F 1 1s. blue/*blue*, *p.* 13 .. 2·50 2·75
 a. Perf. 12 .. .. .. 5·00
F 2 2s. blue/*grn.* (D.L.R.), *p.* 13 5·00 5·50
 a. Perf. 12 .. .. .. 5·00 5·50
F 3 2s. deep blue/*green* (S), *p.* 13 6·00
 a. Perf. 12 .. .. .. — 6·50
F 4 10s. brown-olive/*pink*, *p.* 13 (June '71) .. ..
F 5 10s. red-brown/*pink*, *p.* 13 (1879) .. .. .. 24·00 7·50
 a. Perf. 12 .. .. ..

(*b*) *Wmk. V over Crown Type* **20** (*V*1).

The wmk. is usually *sideways* but in certain cases the whole of a printing was *upright*. One also meets "abnormal" upright wmks.

F 7 ½d. on 1d. pale grn. (R.), *p.* 13 1·10 1·10
F 8 1d. pale green, *p.* 13 .. 80 60
a. Green, p. 12½ (U) ('80) 1·25 1·50
F 9 3d. mauve, *p.* 13 (Sept. '79) 8·00 5·50
F10 4d. rose, *p.* 13 .. .. 2·25 2·00
F11 6d. blue, *p.* 13 ('71) .. .. 2·75 2·25
a. Dull ultramarine, p. 13 ('76) .. 80 70
aa. Perf. 12 .. .. — 1·00
F12 1s. blue/*blue*, *p.* 13 (June '76) 2·50
a. Perf. 12 .. .. — 2·00
b. Ultram./blue, p. 12½ ('82) .. — 2·00
ba. Perf. 12 .. .. — 2·00
c. Deep blue/blue, p. 12½ ('83) .. 2·75 2·00
ca. Perf. 12 .. .. — 2·00
F13 2s. blue/*grn.*, *p.* 13 (July '76) 8·00 5·00
a. Perf. 12 .. ..
b. Deep blue/blue-green, p. 13 ('83) 7·00 3·00
ba. Perf. 12 .. .. 7·50 3·50
F15 2s. 6d. orge., *p.* 13 (July '76) — 6·50
a. Perf. 12 .. ..
b. Yellow, p. 13 (Nov. '78) .. 7·50
ba. Perf. 12 .. .. 7·50 7·00
c. Orange-yellow, p. 12½ ('82) ..
ca. Perf. 12 .. ..
F16 5s. blue/*yellow*, *p.* 13 .. 10·00 5·00
a. Perf. 12 .. ..
b. Ultram./lemon, p. 12½ ('81) .. 10·00 5·00
F17 10s. brown/*pink*, *p.* 13 (Aug. '76) .. .. 24·00
a. Purple-brown/pink, p. 12½ ('82) 24·00
aa. Perf. 12 .. ..
F18 £1 slate-violet/*yellow* (S, U) *p.* 13 ('71) .. .. 24·00
a. Perf. 12 (1880) .. 24·00
b. Mauve/yellow, p. 13 ('73) ..
ba. Perf. 12 ('81) .. 24·00
bb. Perf. 12½ ('82) ..
F19 £5 black and yellow-green *p.* 12 (Nov. '71) .. ..
a. Perf. 13 .. ..
b. Perf. 12½ (U) .. ..

(*c*) 1882–3: *Wmk. V over Crown Type* **23** (*V*2).

F20 1d. yellowish green, *p.* 12½ 2·00 2·00
F21 2s. 6d. pale orange-yellow, *p.* 12½ .. .. 7·00
F22 £5 black & yellow-grn., *p.* 12

Reversed watermarks, all rare, have been found under Nos. F12, F15, F18 and F19.

All the values of the "Stamp Statute" series were reprinted in 1891 on paper wmkd. V1 (5s., 10s. and £1) and V2 (the rest). The colours used, in all cases, differed radically from the originals. Except for the £5, for which the old electrotypes were used, new plates were made for the Reprints, from dies which showed "die flaws" not to be found on the originals. In 1877 a 12s. 6d. value was prepared for use but although it was placed on sale at the Law Courts and was available there for some months not a single copy was sold, and it was withdrawn. Proofs are known.

B. The "STAMP DUTY" Series.

This series was used mainly to record the payment of duties on the sale of land, receipts and numerous other documents.

F 5 F 6 F 7 F 8

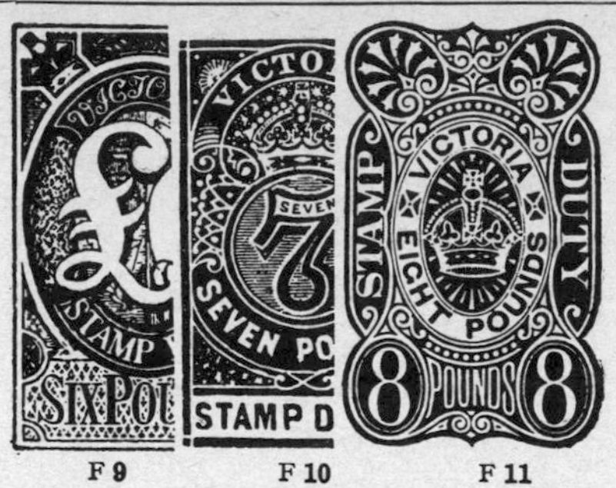

F 9 F 10 F 11

(Illustrations ⅔ size.)

(Dies for these issues (except 1d. of 1880) supplied by Messrs. Sands and McDougall. Des. Charles Jackson and Ludwig Lang. Eng. Charles Jackson, Arthur Williams and others (See previously). The 1d. of 1880 was eng. by Charles Naish.)

1879 (Dec.)–**1883** (Dec.). I. *December* 1879. *Litho. Stamp Printing Office, Melbourne. Wmk. V over Crown, Type* **20** (*V*1). *Sideways unless otherwise indicated* (*U*).

F23 F **5** 1d. blue-green, *p.* 13 .. 75 75
a. Perf. 12 .. .. 1·25 75
F24 **45** 1s. 6d. rosine, *p.* 13 .. 1·25 1·25
a. Perf. 12 .. ..
F25 **46** 3s. purple/*blue*, *p.* 13 .. 2·75 2·00
a. Perf. 12 .. .. — 3·50
F26 **47** 4s. orange-red, *p.* 13 .. 2·75 1·00
a. Perf. 12 .. .. 2·75 1·00
F27 **40** 6s. apple-grn., *p.* 13 (U) 3·00 1·00
a. Perf. 12 (U) .. ..
F28 **50** 10s. brown/*rose* *p.* 13 (S, U) .. .. 11·00 5·00
a. Perf. 12 (S, U) ..
F29 **51** 15s. mauve, *p.* 13 .. — 8·00
F30 **52** £1 red-orange, *p.* 13 .. — 8·00
F31 **53** £1 5s. dull rose, *p.* 13 (U) .. .. — 11·00
F32 **54** £1 10s. deep grey-olive, *p.* 13 (S, U) .. — 6·50
F33 35s. grey-violet, *p.* 13 (U) F.C. £18
F34 **55** £2 blue, *p.* 13 .. — 14·00
F35 **56** 45s. dull brown-lilac, *p.* 13 (U) .. — 14·00
F36 **57** £5 rose-red, *p.* 13 (U) .. — 20·00
F37 F **9** £6 blue/*pink*, *p.* 13 (U) — 50·00
F38 F **10** £7 violet/*blue*, *p.* 13 (U) — 50·00
F39 F **11** £8 brnish-red/*yellow*, *p.* 13 (U) .. — 50·00
F40 – £9 yellow-green/*green*, *p.* 13 (U) F.C. £10

Apart from the "Half-Lengths", the 2d. Queen-on-Throne, the first 1s. Octagonal and the £25, £50 and £100 of 1886–89 these were the only stamps of Victoria to be printed by lithography and its adoption on this occasion was dictated by the necessity for speed of production. *All* the Lithographed stamps can be distinguished from the typographed stamps of the same design by their colours which are highly distinctive. Other differences, of wmk. & perf., will be found. Some values, e.g. the 6s., 25s. and 30s. (1884–91) were available for postage over a considerable period.

No. F32 occurs with *reversed* watermark (rare).

II. Dec. 1879–1882: *Typographed from electrotypes at Stamp Printing Office, Melbourne.*

(i) *Wmk. V over Crown, Type* **20** (V1).

F41 F **5** 1d. yellowish green, *p.* 13 (Dec. '79) 65 40
a. Perf. 12 .. .. 75 65
F42 F **6** 1d. pale bistre, *p.* 12½ (June '80) 20 8
a. Perf. 12 .. .. 55 12
F43 F **7** 6d. dull blue, *p.* 13 (Dec. '79) 80 40
a. Perf. 12 .. ..
F44 **44** 1s. deep blue/*blue*, *p.* 13 (Dec. '79) 70 10
a. Perf. 12 .. .. 80 35
b. Bright bl./bl., p. 12½ ('82) 80 20
ba. Perf. 12 .. .. — 40
F45 F **8** 2s. deep blue/*green*, *p.* 13 (Dec. '79) .. .. 1·00 65
a. Perf. 12 .. .. — 70
b. Indigo/green .. .. 7·50 4·00
ba. Perf. 12 .. .. 7·50 4·00
F46 **48** 5s. claret/*yellow*, *p.* 13 (Dec. '79) .. .. 2·00 65
a. Perf. 12 .. .. — 1·00
b. Pale claret/yellow, p. 12½ (1880) .. .. 3·00 65
ba. Perf. 12 .. .. 3·50 1·00
F47 **50** 10s. chocolate/*rose*, *p.* 13 (S, U) (Dec. '79) .. — 7·50
a. Perf. 12 (S, U) ..
F48 **52** £1 yellow-orange/*yellow* *p.* 12 (1882)
F49 **55** £2 deep blue, *p.* 12½ (1881) .. .. — 7·50
F50 **58** £10 dull mauve, *p.* 12 (1879)
a. Deep red-lilac (1882) .. — 20·00

(ii) 1882–3: *Wmk. V over Crown, Type* **23** (*V*2).

F51 F **6** 1d. ochre (*shades*), *p.* 12½ 20 8
a. Perf. 12 .. .. 40 10
F52 F **7** 6d. ultramarine, *p.* 12½ 75 40
a. Perf. 12 .. .. 70 40
F53 **55** £2 blue, *p.* 12 .. .. — 10·00
F54 **57** £5 rose-pink, *p.* 12 .. — 20·00

III. 1879–80: *Recess-printed direct from the die.*

(i) *Wmk. V over Crown, Type* **20** (*V*1) *p.* 13.

F55 **59** £25 yellow-green (1879) F.C. £15
a. Deep grn. (1880) F.C. £15
F56 ,, £50 bright mauve (1879) F.C. £24
F57 ,, £100 crimson-lake (1879) F.C. £24

(ii) 1882–3: *Wmk. V over Crown, Type* **23** (*V*2). *p.* 12½.

F58 **59** £50 dull lilac-mauve F.C. £30
F59 ,, £100 crimson .. F.C. £32
a. Perf. 12 .. F.C. £32

Nos. F44 and F45 occur with *reversed* watermark (both rare).

Reprints of Stamp Duty Series: The only stamps in this series to be reprinted in 1891 (on wmk. *V*2) were the two types of 1d. which by then had become obsolete. Again the colours are distinctive from the originals.

In 1879 certain other values inscribed "STAMP DUTY" (of varying heraldic designs) viz.; **7s., 8s., 9s., 11s., 12s., 13s., 14s., 16s., 17s., 18s. and 19s. were prepared for use but were not issued. Proofs are known.**

POSTAGE DUE STAMPS.

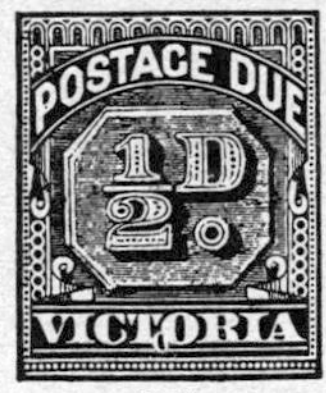

D 1

(Dies eng. Arthur Williams (values) and John McWilliams (frame). Typo.)

1890–1908. *Type* D **1**. A. *Wmk. V over Crown, Type* **23** (*V*2). *P* 12 × 12½.

(i) 1st. Nov. 1890 (½*d.*, 24.12.90)

D 1 ½d. dull blue & brown-lake 35 35
D 2 1d. dull blue & brown-lake 35 40
D 3 2d. dull blue & brown-lake 40 40
D 4 4d. dull blue & brown-lake 55 35
D 5 5d. dull blue & brown-lake 65 35
D 6 6d. dull blue & brown-lake 40 20
D 7 10d. dull blue & brown-lake 3·50 2·00
D 8 1s. dull blue & brown-lake 1·25 1·00
D 9 2s. dull blue & brown-lake 24·00 20·00
D10 5s. dull blue & brown-lake 40·00 24·00

The blue shades vary considerably.

(ii) 1890–94.

D11 ½d. dull blue and deep claret (1890) 20 20
D12 1d. dull blue and brownish red (20.1.93) 20 12

No.	Description	Unused	Used
D13	2d. dull blue and brownish red (28.3.93)	55	20
D14	4d. dull blue and pale claret (28.5.94)	80	55

Nos. D1 and D11 were separate printings, both made in December 1890.

(iii) 17th Jan. 1895. *Colours changed.*

No.	Description	Unused	Used
D15	½d. rosine and bluish green	40	20
D16	1d. rosine and bluish green	15	10
D17	2d. rosine and bluish green	10	5
D18	4d. rosine and bluish green	35	35
D19	5d. rosine and bluish green	75	55
D20	6d. rosine and bluish green	40	20
D21	10d. rosine and bluish green	80	75
D22	1s. rosine and bluish green	80	90

(iv) 28th March 1895.

No.	Description	Unused	Used
D23	2s. p. red & yellowish green	7·00	6·50
D24	5s. p. red & yellowish green	12·00	14·00

(v) March 1896 on.

No.	Description	Unused	Used
D25	½d. p. scarlet & yellow-green	35	12
D26	1d. p. scarlet & yellow-green	20	5
D27	2d. p. scarlet & yellow-green	20	5
D28	4d. p. scarlet & yellow-green	35	12
D29	5d. p. scarlet & yellow green	40	20

B. *W* **72** (*V*3). *P* 12½ *or* 12×12½.

(i) July 1897 on.

No.	Description	Unused	Used
D30	1d. p. scarlet & yellow-green	5	5
D31	2d. p. scarlet & yellow-green	8	5
D32	4d. p. scarlet & yellow-green	12	8
D33	5d. p. scarlet & yellow-green	65	40
D34	6d. p. scarlet & yellow-green	35	20

(ii) July–Sept. 1899.

No.	Description	Unused	Used
D35	1d. dull red & bluish green	35	5
D36	2d. dull red & bluish green	20	8
D37	4d. dull red & bluish green	40	8

C. *W* **75** (*V*4). *P* 12½ *or* 12×12½.

(i) 1900–1.

No.	Description	Unused	Used
D38	½d. rose-red and pale green	5	5
D39	1d. rose-red and pale green	8	8
D40	2d. rose-red and pale green	12	5
D41	4d. rose-red and pale green	40	35

(ii) 1901–2.

No.	Description	Unused	Used
D42	½d. pale red and deep green	8	8
D43	1d. pale red and deep green	10	5
D44	2d. pale red and deep green	20	8
D45	4d. pale red and deep green	40	20

(iii) 1902–3.

No.	Description	Unused	Used
D45*a*	½d. scarlet and deep green ..		
D46	1d. scarlet and deep green ..	10	5
D47	2d. scarlet and deep green ..	35	5
D48	4d. scarlet and deep green ..	40	10
D49	5d. scarlet and deep green ..	65	30
D50	1s. scarlet and deep green ..	1·10	60
D51	2s. scarlet and deep green ..	20·00	11·00
D52	5s. scarlet and deep green ..	24·00	14·00

The deep green of Nos. D46–52 has more "yellow" than that of D42–45.

(iv) 1904.

No.	Description	Unused	Used
D53	½d. rosine (*aniline*) and green	35	10
D54	1d. rosine (*aniline*) and green	10	5
D55	2d. rosine (*aniline*) and green	20	8
D56	4d. rosine (*aniline*) and green	40	12

D. *Wmk. Crown over A* (*Type W* **11**). *P* 12½ *or* 12×12½.

(i) Jan. 1906.

No.	Description	Unused	Used
D57	½d. rosine (*aniline*) & p. green	80	80
D58	1d. rosine (*aniline*) and green	7·00	80

(ii) Mar. 1906.

No.	Description	Unused	Used
D59	½d. scarlet & p. yellow-green	10	12
D60	1d. scarlet & p. yellow-green	20	5

(iii) Dec. 1906.

No.	Description	Unused	Used
D61	1d. scarlet (*aniline*) and deep yellow-green	20	5
D62	2d. scarlet (*aniline*) and deep yellow-green	55	8

(iv) 1907–8.

No.	Description	Unused	Used
D63	½d. dull scarlet & pea-green	8	8
D64	1d. dull scarlet & pea-green	35	5
D65	2d. dull scarlet & pea-green	55	8
D66	4d. dull scarlet & pea-green	1·25	1·10

Perf. compound 12×12½ *with* 11.

No.	Description	Unused	Used
D67	½d. dull scarlet & pea-green	7·00	7·00

In D59 and D60 the centre is more clearly printed than in the later printings. A 5d. value was prepared and printed on Crown over A paper but was not issued. A few copies are known postmarked to order from presentation sets.

Victoria now uses the stamps of Australia.

VIRGIN ISLANDS.

BRITISH VIRGIN ISLANDS.

Apart from the 1951 Legislative Council issue, the word "BRITISH" first appeared regularly on the stamps in 1968 to avoid confusion with the nearby Virgin Islands of the United States (the former Danish West Indies). However, as no special stamps are issued by the U.S. Virgin Is., we have not altered the position of this country in the catalogue.

For GREAT BRITAIN stamps used in Tortola with "A 13" obliteration, see index to Great Britain Stamps Used Abroad list.

CROWN COLONY.

1 St. Ursula. 2

(Litho. Nissen & Parker. Original dies by Waterlow & Sons.)

1866. *No wmk.* *P* 12.

(*a*) *White wove paper.*

No.	Type	Description	Unused	Used
1	**1**	1d. green	17·00	22·00
2	„	1d. deep green	17·00	22·00
3	**2**	6d. rose	35·00	42·00
4	„	6d. deep rose	50·00	60·00
		a. Large "V" in "VIRGIN" ..	£140	£160

(*b*) *Toned paper.*

No.	Type	Description	Unused	Used
5	**1**	1d. green	17·00	22·00
6	„	1d. deep green	35·00	48·00
7	**2**	6d. rose-red	25·00	35·00
		a. Large "V" in "VIRGIN" ..	£120	£140

Error. P 15×12.

No.	Type	Description	Unused	Used
7*b*	**1**	1d. green	£1300	£2000

The above were printed in sheets of 25.

6d. stamps showing part of the papermaker's watermark ("A. Cowan & Sons Extra Superfine A. C. & S.") are worth 50% more.

Beware of fakes of No. 7*b* made from perf. 12 stamps.

3

4

Normal Variety

1s. Long-tailed "s" in "ISLANDS".

1867–70. *No Wmk.* *P* 15. 1*s. with double-lined frame.*

(*a*) *White wove paper.*

No.	Type	Description	Unused	Used
8	**1**	1d. blue-green ('70) ..	25·00	28·00
9	„	1d. yellow-green ('68) ..	30·00	32·00
10	**2**	6d. pale rose	£130	£130
11	**4**	1s. black and rose-carmine	90·00	£100
		a. Long-tailed "S"	£200	£225

(*b*) *Toned paper.*

No.	Type	Description	Unused	Used
12	**1**	1d. yellow-green ('68) ..	30·00	32·00
13	**2**	6d. dull rose ('68)	90·00	£100
14	**4**	1s. black and rose-carmine (*blued*)	90·00	£100
		aa. Long-tailed "S"	£200	£225
14*a*	„	1s. black and rose-carmine	£100	£120
		b. Long-tailed "S"	£225	£250

(*c*) *Pale rose paper.*

No.	Type	Description	Unused	Used
15	**3**	4d. lake-red	17·00	24·00

(*d*) *Buff paper.*

No.	Type	Description	Unused	Used
16	**3**	4d. lake-red	17·00	24·00
17	„	4d. lake-brown	17·00	24·00

The thin lines of the frame on the 1s. are close together and sometimes merge into one.

The 1d. was originally in sheets of 20, but from 1870 was in sheets of 12; the 4d. was in sheets of 25; the 6d. and 1s. were in sheets of 20.

As last, but with crimson frames superimposed with bands extending through margins.

No.	Type	Description	Unused	Used
18	**4**	1s. black and rose-carmine (*white* paper)	18·00	25·00
		a. Long-tailed "S"	38·00	45·00
19	„	1s. black and rose-carmine (*toned* paper)	18·00	25·00
		a. Long-tailed "S"	38·00	45·00
20	„	1s. black and rose-carmine (*blued* paper)	£250	£275
		aa. Long-tailed "S"	£550	£600

Error. Figure of Virgin missing.

No.	Type	Description	Unused	Used
20*a*	**4**	1s. rose-carmine ..	£30000	

Nos. 11 and 14a with frame lines retouched so as to make them single lines. Margins remain white.

No.	Type	Description	Unused	Used
21	**4**	1s. black and rose-carmine (*white* paper) ('68) ..	50·00	65·00
		aa. Long-tailed "S"	£110	£130
21*a*	„	1s. black and rose-carmine (*toned* paper) ('68) ..	50·00	65·00
		b. Long-tailed "S"	£110	£130

(Litho. De La Rue.)

1878. *Wmk. Crown CC* (*sideways*). *P* 14.

No.	Type	Description	Unused	Used
22	**1**	1d. green	25·00	28·00
		a. Yellow-green	50·00	48·00
		b. Wmk. upright	28·00	35·00

6 (Die I)

(Typo. De La Rue.)

1880. *Wmk. Crown CC.* *P* 14.

No.	Type	Description	Unused	Used
24	**6**	1d. emerald-green	14·00	20·00
25	„	2½d. red-brown	20·00	25·00

1883–84. *Wmk. Crown CA.* *P* 14.

No.	Type	Description	Unused	Used
26	**6**	½d. yellow-buff	18·00	23·00
27	„	½d. yellow-green	1·75	3·50
28	„	½d. dull bluish green ..	3·50	5·50
29	„	1d. pale rose	6·50	7·50
30	„	1d. deep rose	14·00	18·00
31	„	2½d. ultramarine (1884) ..	2·25	3·50

Nos. 25, 27 and 31 exist imperf. but it is not known whether they were issued (*Price* £500 *in pairs, each*).

(Litho. De La Rue.)

1887–89. *Wmk. Crown CA.* *P* 14.

No.	Type	Description	Unused	Used
32	**1**	1d. red	2·50	2·75
33	„	1d. rose-red	2·50	2·75
34	„	1d. rose	2·50	5·50
35	**3**	4d. chestnut	9·00	11·00
36	„	4d. pale chestnut	9·00	11·00
37	„	4d. brown-red	11·00	13·00
38	**2**	6d. dull violet	9·00	13·00
39	„	6d. deep violet	9·00	13·00
40	**4**	1s. sepia	17·00	22·00
41	„	1s. brown (light *to* deep) ..	14·00	17·00
41*a*	„	1s. very light brown ..	£180	
33/41		Optd. "Specimen" *Set of* 4	65·00	

The De La Rue transfers of T **1** to **4** are new transfers and differ from those of Messrs. Nissen and Parker, particularly T **4**.

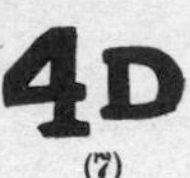

(7)

8

1888 (JULY). *No. 19 surch. with T* **7**, *in violet.*

42 **4** 4d. on 1s. black and rose-carmine/*toned* .. .. 35·00 50·00
a. Surch. double £2250
b. Surch. inverted (in pair with normal) £9000
c. Long-tailed "S" .. .. 80·00 £110

The special issues for Virgin Islands were superseded on 31 October 1890, by the general issue for Leeward Islands. In 1899, however, a new special issue (given below) appeared; it did not supersede the general issue for Leeward Islands, but was used concurrently, as were all subsequent issues, until 1 July 1956, when the general Leeward Islands stamps were withdrawn.

(Recess. D.L.R.)

1899. *Wmk. Crown CA.* *P* 14.

43 **8** ½d. yellow-green 40 80
a. Error. "HALFPFNNY" .. 26·00 32·00
b. Error. "HALFPENNY" .. 26·00 32·00
c. Imp. between (horiz. pair) .. £2250
44 „ 1d. brick-red .. .. 1·75 1·75
45 „ 2½d. ultramarine .. .. 5·50 6·00
46 „ 4d. brown .. .. 5·50 7·00
a. Error. "FOURPENCF" .. £500 £500
47 „ 6d. dull violet .. .. 4·00 5·00
48 „ 7d. deep green .. .. 5·50 5·50
49 „ 1s. brown-yellow .. .. 9·00 9·00
50 „ 5s. indigo .. .. .. 30·00 35·00
43/50 .. .. *Set of* 8 55·00 65·00
43/50 Optd. "Specimen" *Set of* 8 75·00

9

10

(Typo. D.L.R.)

1904 (1 JUNE). *Wmk. Mult. Crown CA.* *P* 14.

54 **9** ½d. dull purple and green 35 40
55 „ 1d. dull purple and scarlet 60 65
56 **10** 2d. dull purple and ochre 2·75 4·50
57 **9** 2½d. dull purple and ultram. 2·00 3·00
58 **10** 3d. dull purple and black 2·50 3·50
59 **9** 6d. dull purple and brown 3·00 4·00
60 **10** 1s. green and scarlet .. 4·50 6·00
61 „ 2s. 6d. green and black .. 15·00 18·00
62 **9** 5s. green and blue .. 27·00 32·00
54/62 .. .. *Set of* 9 50·00 65·00
54/62 Optd. "Specimen" *Set of* 9 80·00

11

12

(Typo. D.L.R.)

1913–19. *Wmk. Mult. Crown CA.* *P* 14.

63 **11** ½d. green, O 35 50
64 „ ½d. yellow-green, O ('16) 55 75
65 „ ½d. blue-green and deep green, O ('19) .. 35 55
66 „ 1d. deep red, O .. .. 2·75 3·50
67 „ 1d. deep red & carmine, O 2·50 3·50
68 „ 1d. scarlet, O ('17) .. 1·40 1·75
69 „ 1d. carmine-red, O ('19) .. 10·00 3·50
70 **12** 2d. grey, O .. .. 1·40 3·00
71 „ 2d. slate-grey, O ('19) .. 2·00 3·00
72 **11** 2½d. bright blue, O .. 1·40 2·50
73 **12** 3d. purple/*yellow*, C .. 90 2·50
74 **11** 6d. dull & bright purple, C 1·40 2·75
75 **12** 1s. black/*green*, C .. 2·50 3·50
76 „ 2s. 6d. blk. & red/*blue*, C 11·00 13·00
77 **11** 5s. green & red/*yellow*, C 24·00 27·00
63/77 .. .. *Set of* 9 40·00 50·00
63/77 Optd. "Specimen" *Set of* 9 80·00

WAR STAMP

(13)

14

1917. *Optd. with T* **13**.

78 **11** 1d. carmine .. .. .. 85 1·40
a. Pale red/bluish 15 35
b. Scarlet 20 70
79 **12** 3d. purple/*yellow* 25 80
a. Purple/lemon .. .. 1·60 2·25
b. Purple/pale yellow .. .. 1·00 1·50
78/9 Optd. "Specimen" *Set of* 2 32·00

1921. *As* 1913–19, *but wmk. Mult. Script CA.*

80 **11** ½d. green, O 25 55
81 „ 1d. scarlet & dp. carmine, O 70 85
80/1 Optd. "Specimen" *Set of* 2 26·00

(Typo. D.L.R.)

1922–29. *T* **14**. *P* 14.

(*a*) *Wmk. Mult. Crown CA.*

82 3d. purple/*pale yellow*, C .. 25 75
83 1s. black/*emerald*, C .. 85 2·50
84 2s. 6d. black and red/*blue*, C 2·75 4·00
85 5s. green & red/*pale yellow*, C 17·00 22·00
82/5 Optd. "Specimen" *Set of* 4 35·00

(*b*) *Wmk. Mult. Script CA.*

86 ½d. dull green, O 10 15
87 1d. rose-carmine, O .. 12 35
88 1d. bright violet, O (1927) 70 1·10
89 1d. scarlet, O (1929) .. 70 80
90 1½d. carmine-red, O (1927) .. 1·25 1·50
91 1½d. Venetian red, O (1928) 1·50 1·50
92 2d. grey, O 55 70
93 2½d. pale bright blue, O .. 1·40 2·75
94 2½d. dull orange, O (1923) .. 1·00 65
95 2½d. bright blue, O (1927) .. 1·50 2·50
96 3d. purple/*pale yell.*, O ('28) 60 1·00
97 5d. dull purple and olive, C 3·75 7·00
98 6d. dull and bright purple, C 85 1·75
99 1s. black/*emerald*, C (1928) 1·40 2·00
100 2s. 6d. blk. & red/*bl.*, C ('28) 4·50 6·50
101 5s. green & red/*yell.*, C ('23) 11·00 13·00
86/101 .. .. *Set of* 14 26·00 35·00
86/101 Optd./Perf. "Specimen" *Set of* 16 £120

In the 1½d. stamps the value is in colour on a white ground.

1935 (6 MAY). *Silver Jubilee. As Nos.* 91/4 *of Antigua but ptd. by Waterlow.* *P* 11×12.

103 1d. deep blue and scarlet .. 10 15
104 1½d. ultramarine and grey .. 12 25
105 2½d. brown and deep blue .. 35 45
106 1s. slate and purple .. 1·50 2·00
103/6 Perf. "Specimen" *Set of* 4 17·00

1937 (12 MAY). *Coronation. As T* **2** *of Aden. Recess. B.W. Wmk. Mult. Script CA. P* 11×11½.

107 1d. carmine 8 8
108 1½d. yellow-brown 20 15
109 2½d. blue 25 30
107/9 Perf. "Specimen" *Set of* 3 12·00

15. King George VI and Badge of Colony.

(Photo. Harrison.)

1938 (1 AUG.)–**47.** *Wmk. Mult. Script. CA.* *P* 14.

110 **15** ½d. green, C O 8 8
111 „ 1d. scarlet, C O .. 8 8
112 „ 1½d. red-brown, C O .. 8 8
113 „ 2d. grey, C O 8 8
114 „ 2½d. ultramarine, C O .. 12 10
115 „ 3d. orange, C O 12 12
116 „ 6d. mauve, C O 20 20
117 „ 1s. olive-brown, C O .. 35 35
118 „ 2s. 6d. sepia, C O .. 1·40 1·25
119 „ 5s. carmine, C O .. 1·75 1·75
120 „ 10s. blue, C (1.12.47) .. 3·50 4·00
121 „ £1 black, C (1.12.47) .. 7·50 8·50
110/121 .. .. *Set of* 12 14·00 15·00
110/21 Perf. "Specimen" *Set of* 12 55·00

In substitution for the original chalky paper, the ordinary paper of Nos. 110/19 is thick, smooth and opaque and first appeared in August 1942 (1s. to 5s.) and in October 1943 (pence values).

1946 (1 NOV.). *Victory. As Nos.* 28/9 *of Aden.*

122 1½d. lake-brown 8 8
123 3d. orange 8 8
122/3 Perf. "Specimen" *Set of* 2 14·00

1949 (3 JAN.). *Royal Silver Wedding. As Nos.* 30/1 *of Aden.*

124 2½d. ultramarine 8 8
125 £1 black .. .. .. 5·50 8·00

1949 (10 OCT.). *75th Anniv. of U.P.U. As Nos.* 114/17 *of Antigua.*

126 2½d. ultramarine 15 12
127 3d. orange 25 20
128 6d. magenta 40 35
129 1s. olive 75 80

(New currency. 100 cents = 1 B.W.I. dollar.)

1951. *Inauguration of B.W.I. University College. As Nos.* 118/9 *of Antigua.*

130 3 c. blk. & brown-red (10.4) 12 10
131 12 c. blk. & reddish viol. (16.2) 40 40

16. Map.

(Recess. Waterlow.)

1951 (2 APR.). *Restoration of Legislative Council. Wmk. Mult. Script CA.* *P* 14½×14.

132 **16** 6 c. orange 15 25
133 „ 12 c. purple 15 40
134 „ 24 c. olive 40 65
135 „ $1.20 carmine .. .. 2·00 2·75

18. Map of Jost Van Dyke.

17. Sombrero Lighthouse.

19. Sheep Industry.

20. Map of Anegada.

21. Cattle Industry.

22. Map of Virgin Gorda.

23. Map of Tortola.

24. Badge of the Presidency.

25. Dead Man's Chest.

26. Sir Francis Drake Channel.

27. Road Town.

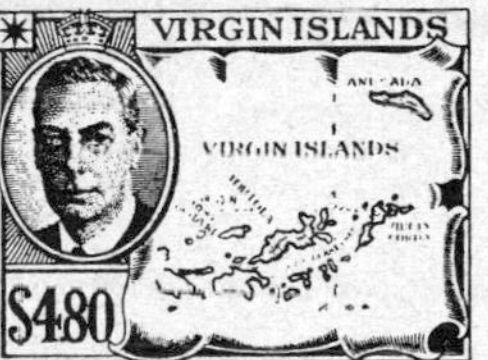

28. Map of Virgin Islands.

(Recess. D.L.R.)

1952 (15 Apr.). *Wmk. Mult. Script CA. P* $12\frac{1}{2} \times 13$ *(vert.) or* $13 \times 12\frac{1}{2}$ *(horiz.).*

No.	Type	Description	Unused	Used
136	**17**	1 c. black	12	15
137	**18**	2 c. deep green	25	15
138	**19**	3 c. black and brown ..	15	20
139	**20**	4 c. carmine-red	25	30
140	**21**	5 c. claret and black ..	40	50
141	**22**	8 c. bright blue	20	25
142	**23**	12 c. dull violet	25	40
143	**24**	24 c. deep brown	30	45
144	**25**	60 c. yellow-green and blue	60	1·00
145	**26**	$1.20 black & bright blue	2·00	2·50
146	**27**	$2.40 yellowish green and red-brown ..	3·00	3·50
147	**28**	$4.80 brt. blue & carmine	5·50	7·00
136/147		.. .. *Set of* 12	12·00	15·00

1953 (2 June). *Coronation. As No.* 47 *of Aden.*

No.	Description	Unused	Used
148	2 c. black and green ..	25	25

29. Map of Tortola.

30. Virgin Islands Sloop.
31. Nelthrop Red Poll Bull.
32. Road Harbour.
33. Mountain Travel.
34. Badge of the Presidency.
35. Beach Scene.
36. Boat Launching.
37. White Cedar Tree.
38. Bonito.
39. Treasury Square.

(*T* **30/39** *are horiz. as T* **29.**)

40. Brown Pelican.

41. Man-o'-War Bird. (*As T* **40.**)

(Recess. D.L.R.)

1956 (1 Nov.). *Wmk. Mult. Script CA. P* $13 \times 12\frac{1}{2}$ ($\frac{1}{2}$ *c. to* $1.20) *or* $12 \times 11\frac{1}{2}$ ($2.40 *and* $4.80).

No.	Type	Description	Unused	Used
149	**29**	$\frac{1}{2}$ c. black & reddish purple (*shades*)	5	5
150	**30**	1 c. turquoise-blue and slate (*shades*) ..	5	5
151	**31**	2 c. vermilion and black	5	8
152	**32**	3 c. blue and deep olive ..	8	8
153	**33**	4 c. deep brown & turquoise-green ..	10	10
154	**34**	5 c. grey-black	10	10
155	**35**	8 c. yellow-orange and deep blue	10	12
156	**36**	12 c. ultram. & rose-red ..	12	15
157	**37**	24 c. myrtle-green and brown-orange ..	30	30
158	**38**	60 c. indigo & yell.-orange	1·10	1·40
159	**39**	$1.20, deep yellow-green and carmine-red ..	2·00	2·50
160	**40**	$2.40, lemon & dp. dull pur.	3·75	4·50
161	**41**	$4.80, blackish brown and turquoise-blue ..	7·50	9·00
149/161		.. .. *Set of* 13	14·00	17·00

(New currency. 100 cents = 1 U.S. dollar.)

≡ 1¢

(42)

1962 (10 Dec.). *T* **29/41** *surch. in U.S. currency as T* **42** *by D. L. R. W* w.**12.**

No.	Type	Description	Unused	Used
162	**29**	1 c. on $\frac{1}{2}$ c. black and deep reddish purple ..	5	5
163	**30**	2 c. on 1 c. turquoise and slate-violet	5	5
164	**31**	3 c. on 2 c. verm. & black	5	8
165	**32**	4 c. on 3 c. bl. & dp. olive	10	10
166	**33**	5 c. on 4 c. dp. brown and turquoise-green ..	10	12
167	**35**	8 c. on 8 c. yellow-orange and deep blue ..	15	15
168	**36**	10 c. on 12 c. ultramarine and rose-red ..	20	25
169	**37**	12 c. on 24 c. myrtle-green and brown-orange ..	20	25
170	**38**	25 c. on 60 c. indigo and yellow-orange ..	40	45
171	**39**	70 c. on $1.20, dp. yell.-green and carmine-red	1·50	1·75
		a. Stop to right (In pair with normal)	3·25	4·50
172	**40**	$1.40 on $2.40, lemon and deep dull purple ..	2·50	3·00
173	**41**	$2.80 on $4.80, blackish brown & turq.-blue	5·50	6·00
162/173		.. .. *Set of* 12	9·50	11·00

1963 (4 June). *Freedom from Hunger. As No.* 76 *of Aden.*

No.	Description	Unused	Used
174	25 c. reddish violet	50	50

1963 (2 Sept.). *Red Cross Centenary. As Nos.* 147/8 *of Antigua.*

No.	Description	Unused	Used
175	2 c. red and black ..	10	12
176	25 c. red and blue ..	55	60

1964 (23 April). 400*th Anniv. of Birth of William Shakespeare. As No.* 164 *of Antigua.*

No.	Description	Unused	Used
177	10 c. bright blue	20	25

43. Bonito.

44. Soper's Hole.
45. Brown Pelican.
46. Dead Man's Chest.
47. Road Harbour.
48. Fallen Jerusalem.
49. The Baths, Virgin Gorda.
50. Map of Virgin Islands.
51. Tortola–St. Thomas Ferry.

52. The Towers, Tortola.
53. Beef Island Airfield.
(*T* **44/53** *are horiz.*)

54. Map of Tortola.

55. Virgin Gorda.
56. Yachts at Anchor.
(*T* **55/56** *are vert.*)

57. Badge of the Colony.

(Recess. D.L.R.)

1964 (2 Nov.). *W* w.**12**. *P* 11½×12 ($2.80), 13×13½ (70 c., $1, $1.40), *or* 13×12½ (*others*).

178	**43**	1 c. blue and olive-green	5	5
179	**44**	2 c. yellow-olive & rose-red	5	5
180	**45**	3 c. sepia & turquoise-blue	5	5
181	**46**	4 c. black & carmine-red	5	8
182	**47**	5 c. black & dp. bluish grn.	8	10
183	**48**	6 c. black & brown-orange	10	12
184	**49**	8 c. black and magenta	12	15
185	**50**	10 c. lake and deep lilac (*shades*)	20	25
186	**51**	12 c. deep bluish green and deep violet-blue	20	25
187	**52**	15 c. yell.-grn. & grey-blk.	25	30
188	**53**	25 c. green and purple ..	30	35
189	**54**	70 c. black & yellow-brn.	1·00	1·10
190	**55**	$1 yellow-green & chest.	1·75	2·00
191	**56**	$1.40, light blue and rose	2·50	3·00
192	**57**	$2.80, black & brt. purple	5·00	6·00
178/192		.. .. *Set of* 15	11·00	13·00

1965 (17 May). *I.T.U. Centenary. As Nos.* 166/7 *of Antigua*

193	4 c. yellow and turquoise ..	10	10
194	25 c. lt. blue and orange buff	40	50

1965 (25 Oct.). *International Co-operation Year. As Nos.* 168/9 *of Antigua.*

195	1 c. reddish pur. & turq.-grn.	5	5
196	25 c. dp. bluish green & lav.	40	45

1966 (24 Jan.). *Churchill Commemoration. As Nos.* 170/3 *of Antigua.*

197	1 c. new blue	5	5
198	2 c. deep green	8	8
199	10 c. brown	30	30
200	25 c. bluish violet	55	60

1966 (22 Feb.). *Royal Visit. As Nos.* 174/5 *of Antigua.*

201	4 c. black and ultramarine ..	10	10
202	70 c. black and magenta ..	90	1·00

58. R.M.S. *Atrato*, 1866.

59. 1d. and 6d. Stamps of 1866.

60. Air Mail Transport, Beef Island, and 6d. Stamp of 1866.

61. Landing Mail at Roadtown, 1866, and 1d. Stamp of 1866. (*As T* **60.**)

(Des. R. Granger Barrett. Litho. B.W.)

1966 (25 Apr.). *Stamp Centenary. W* w.**12** (*sideways*). *P* 13.

203	**58**	5 c. black, red, yellow & emerald	10	10
204	**59**	10 c. black, green and rose-red/*cream*	15	20
205	**60**	25 c. black, rose-red and blue/*pale green* ..	35	40
206	**61**	60 c. black, red and green/*pale blue*	85	90

50c.

(**62**)

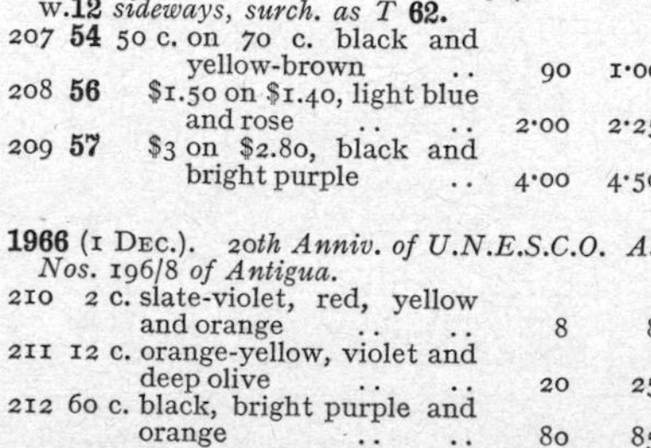

1966 (15 Sept.). *As Nos.* 189 *and* 191/2 *but wmk.* w.**12** *sideways, surch. as T* **62.**

207	**54**	50 c. on 70 c. black and yellow-brown ..	90	1·00
208	**56**	$1.50 on $1.40, light blue and rose	2·00	2·25
209	**57**	$3 on $2.80, black and bright purple ..	4·00	4·50

1966 (1 Dec.). *20th Anniv. of U.N.E.S.C.O. As Nos.* 196/8 *of Antigua.*

210	2 c. slate-violet, red, yellow and orange ..	8	8
211	12 c. orange-yellow, violet and deep olive	20	25
212	60 c. black, bright purple and orange	80	85

63. Map of Virgin Islands.

(Des. G. L. Vaserhelyi. Photo. Harrison.)

1967 (18 Apr.). *New Constitution. W* w.**12**. *P* 14½.

213	**63**	2 c. multicoloured ..	5	5
214	,,	10 c. multicoloured ..	20	20
215	,,	25 c. multicoloured ..	40	40
216	,,	$1 multicoloured ..	1·25	1·40

64. Cable Ship and Bermuda–Tortola Link.

65. Chalwell Telecommunications Station.
66. Cable Ship *Mercury*.

(Des. G. Drummond. Photo. Harrison.)

1967 (14 Sept.). *Inauguration of Bermuda-Tortola Telephone Service. W* w.**12**. *P* 14½.

217	**64**	4 c. multicoloured ..	8	8
218	**65**	10 c. multicoloured ..	15	20
219	**66**	50 c. multicoloured ..	60	65

67. Blue Marlin.

68. Cobia.
69. Wahoo.
70. Fishing Launch and Map.

(Des. V. Whiteley. Photo. Enschedé.)

1968 (2 Jan.). *Game Fishing. W* w.**12** (*sideways*). *P* 12½×12.

220	**67**	2 c. multicoloured ..	5	5
221	**68**	10 c. multicoloured ..	15	20
222	**69**	25 c. blk., blue & brt. vio.	35	40
223	**70**	40 c. multicoloured ..	55	60

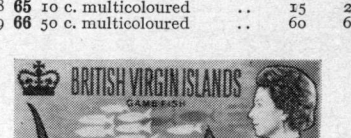

1968
INTERNATIONAL
YEAR FOR
HUMAN RIGHTS
(**71**)

1968 (29 July). *Human Rights Year. Nos.* 185 *and* 188 *optd. with T* **71.**

224	**50**	10 c. lake and deep lilac ..	15	20
225	**53**	25 c. green and purple ..	35	40

29 July was the date of issue in the islands. The Crown Agents supplies went on sale in London on 1 July, the local consignment being delayed in transit.

72. Dr. Martin Luther King, Bible, Sword and Armour Gauntlet.

(Des. V. Whiteley. Litho. Format.)

1968 (15 Oct.). *Martin Luther King Commemoration. W* **w.12** *(sideways). P* 14.

226 **72** 4 c. multicoloured .. 8 8
227 ,, 25 c. multicoloured .. 35 40

73. DHC-6 Twin Otter.
74. HS 748 Airliner.
75. HS Heron.
76. Royal Engineers Cap Badge.

(Des. R. Granger Barrett. Litho. Format International.)

1968 (16 Dec.). *Opening of Beef Island Airport Extension. P* 14.

228 **73** 2 c. multicoloured .. 5 5
229 **74** 10 c. multicoloured .. 15 20
230 **75** 25 c. multicoloured .. 35 40
231 **76** $1 multicoloured .. 1·25 1·40

77. Long John Silver and Jim Hawkins. **79.** The Fight with Israel Hands.

78. Jim Hawkins escaping from the Pirates.
80. Treasure Trove. (*Horiz.*)

(Des. Jennifer Toombs. Photo. Enschedé.)

1969 (18 Mar.). *75th Death Anniv. of Robert Louis Stevenson. W* **w.12** *(sideways on* 10 c., $1). *P* 13½ × 13 *(*4 c., 40 c.*) or* 13 × 13½ *(others).*

232 **77** 4 c. indigo, pale yellow and carmine-red .. 8 8
233 **78** 10 c. multicoloured .. 15 20
234 **79** 40 c. brown, black & blue 55 60
235 **80** $1 multicoloured .. 1·40 1·75

81. Tourist and Rock Grouper (fish). (*Vert.*)

82. Yachts in Road Harbour, Tortola.
83. Sun-bathing at Virgin Gorda National Park. (*Horiz.*)
84. Tourist and Pipe Organ Cactus, at Virgin Gorda. (*Vert.*)

(Des. J. E. Cooter. Litho. Perkins, Bacon.)

1969 (20 Oct.). *Tourism. W* **w.12** *(sideways on* 2 c., $1). *P* 12½.

236 **81** 2 c. multicoloured .. 5 5
237 **82** 10 c. multicoloured .. 15 20
238 **83** 20 c. multicoloured .. 25 30
239 **84** $1 multicoloured .. 1·25 1·50

85. Carib Canoe.
86. *Santamariagallante* (Columbus' Flagship).
87. *Elizabeth Bonaventure* (Drake's Flagship).
88. Dutch Buccaneer, *c.* 1660.
89. *Thetis*, 1827 (after etching by E. W. Cooke).
90. Henry Morgan's Ship (17th-cent.).
91. H.M. Frigate *Boreas* (Capt. Nelson, 1784).
92. H.M. Schooner *Eclair*, 1804.
93. H.M.S. *Formidable*, 1782.
94. H.M. Sloop *Nymph*, 1778.
95. *Windsor Castle*, Post Office Packet, 1807.
96. H.M. Frigate *Astrea*, 1808.
97. Wreck of R.M.S. *Rhone*, 1860.
98. Tortola Sloop.
99. H.M. Cruiser *Frobisher*.
100 Merchant Tanker *Booker Viking*, 1967.
101. Hydrofoil *Sun Arrow*.

(Des. and litho. J. Waddington Ltd.)

1970 (16 Feb.)–**74**. *Wmk.* **w.12** *(sideways). P* 14.

240 **85** ½ c. buff, red-brn. & sepia 5 5
241 **86** 1 c. new blue, apple-green & chalky blue 5 5
a. Perf. 13½ (12.11.74) .. 5 5
242 **87** 2 c. yellow-orange, red-brown and slate .. 8 8
243 **88** 3 c. orange-red, cobalt and sepia 10 10
244 **89** 4 c. greenish blue, chalky blue & bistre-brown 10 10
245 **90** 5 c. emerald, pink & blk. 10 10
246 **91** 6 c. reddish violet, mauve and myrtle-green .. 10 10
247 **92** 8 c. apple-green, greenish yellow and sepia 12 12
248 **93** 10 c. greenish blue, yellbrown & red-brown 20 20
a. Perf. 13½ (12.11.74) .. 15 20
249 **94** 12 c. yell., crimson & brn. 25 25
a. Perf. 13½ (12.11.74) .. 20 25
250 **95** 15 c. turq.-green, orange and bistre-brown .. 25 25
a. Perf. 13½ (12.11.74) .. 25 25
251 **96** 25 c. grey-green, steel-blue and plum 30 35
252 **97** 50 c. magenta, dull green and purple-brown .. 60 70
253 **98** $1 salmon, olive-green and red-brown .. 1·10 1·25
254 **99** $2 buff, slate and grey 2·25 2·50
255 **100** $3 ochre, deep blue and sepia .. .. 3·25 4·00
256 **101** $5 violet and grey .. 5·50 6·00
240/256 .. .. *Set of* 17 13·00 14·00

See also Nos. 295/300.

102. " A Tale of Two Cities ".

(Des. W. G. Brown. Litho. D.L.R.)

1970 (4 May). *Death Centenary of Charles Dickens. T* **120** *and similar horiz. designs. W* **w.12** *(sideways). P* 14.

257 5 c. black, light rose & grey 10 10
258 10 c. black, light blue and pale green 25 30
259 25 c. black, light green and pale yellow 60 65

Designs:—10 c. " Oliver Twist "; 25 c. " Great Expectations ".

103. Hospital Visit.

(Des. R. Granger Barrett. Litho. Questa.)

1970 (10 Aug.). *Centenary of British Red Cross. T* **103** *and similar horiz. designs. Multicoloured. W* **w.12** *(sideways). P* 14.

260 4 c. Type **103** 8 8
261 10 c. First Aid Class .. 20 20
262 25 c. Red Cross and Coat of Arms 40 40

104. Mary Read.

(Des. and litho. John Waddington Ltd.)

1970 (16 Nov.). *Pirates. T* **104** *and similar vert. designs. Multicoloured. W* **w.12**. *P* 14 × 14½.

263 ½ c. Type **104** 5 5
264 10 c. George Lowther .. 15 20
265 30 c. Edward Teach (Blackbeard) 40 45
266 60 c. Henry Morgan .. 80 85

105. Children and " UNICEF ".

(Des. L. D. Curtis. Litho. Format.)

1971 (13 Dec.). *25th Anniv. of UNICEF. W* **w.12** *(sideways). P* 13½×14.

267 **105** 15 c. multicoloured .. 25 30
268 „ 30 c. multicoloured .. 40 45

VISIT OF
H.R.H.
THE
PRINCESS MARGARET

1972 1972

(106)

1972 (7 Mar.). *Royal Visit of Princess Margaret. Nos.* 244 *and* 251 *optd. with T* **106**.

269 **89** 4 c. greenish blue, chalky blue and bistre-brown 10 10
270 **96** 25 c. grey-green, steel-blue and plum 45 45

107. Seaman of 1800.

(Des. J. W. Ltd. Litho. Questa.)

1972 (17 Mar.). *"Interpex" Stamp Exhibition, New York. T* **107** *and similar vert. designs showing Naval Uniforms. Multicoloured. W* **w.12** *(sideways). P* 13½.

271 ½ c. Type **107** 5 5
272 10 c. Boatswain, 1787–1807 15 15
273 30 c. Captain, 1795–1812 .. 40 40
274 60 c. Admiral, 1787–95 .. 75 75

108. Sailfish and the Yacht *Sir Winston Churchill.*

(Des. (from photograph by D. Groves) and photo. Harrison.)

1972 (24 Nov.). *Royal Silver Wedding. Multicoloured; background colour given. W* **w.12**. *P* 14×14½.

275 **108** 15 c. bright blue 20 25
276 „ 25 c. turquoise-blue .. 35 40
a. Blue omitted* ..

*The omission of the blue colour results in the Duke's suit appearing sepia instead of deep blue.

109. Blue Marlin.

(Des. G. Drummond. Litho. Questa.)

1972 (12 Dec.). *Game Fish. T* **109** *and similar horiz. designs. Multicoloured. W* **w.12**. *P* 13½.

277 ½ c. Type **109** 5 5
278 ½ c. Wahoo 5 5
279 15 c. Allison Tuna 25 30
280 25 c. White Marlin 40 50
281 50 c. Sailfish 70 90
282 $1 Dolphin .. .. 1·40 1·60
277/82 .. .. *Set of* 6 2·50 3·25
MS283 194×158 mm. Nos. 277/82 3·50 4·00

Nos. 277/8 were printed horizontally and vertically *se-tenant* within the sheet.

110. J. C. Lettsom.

(Des. J. E. Cooter. Litho. Questa.)

1973 (9 Mar.). *"Interpex 1973" (Quakers). T* **110** *and similar multicoloured designs. W* **w.12** *(sideways on* ½ *c. and* 15 *c.). P* 13½.

284 ½ c. Type **110** 5 5
285 10 c. Lettsom House *(horiz.)* 15 20
286 15 c. Dr. W. Thornton .. 25 30
287 30 c. Dr. Thornton and Capitol, Washington *(horiz.)* 40 45
288 $1 William Penn *(horiz.)* .. 1·25 1·40
284/8 .. .. *Set of* 5 1·90 2·25

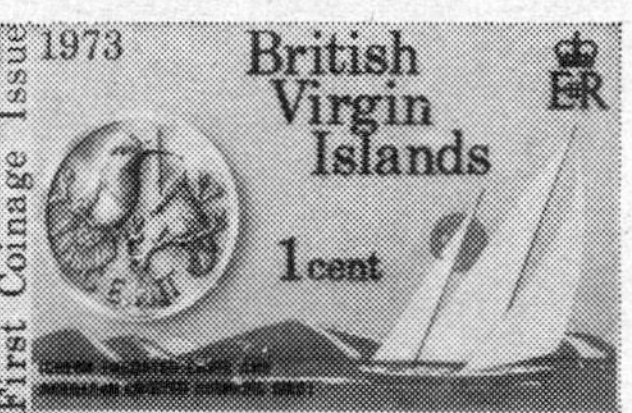

111. Green-throated Carib and Antillean Crested Hummingbird.

(Des. G. Drummond. Litho. Questa.)

1973 (30 June). *First Issue of Coinage. T* **111** *and similar horiz. designs showing coins and local scenery. Multicoloured. W* **w.12**. *P* 14.

289 1 c. Type **111** 5 5
290 5 c. Zenaida Dove 10 10
291 10 c. Ringed Kingfisher .. 12 15
292 25 c. Mangrove Cuckoo .. 30 35
293 50 c. Brown Pelican 60 65
294 $1 Magnificent Frigate-bird .. .. .. 1·25 1·40
289/94 .. .. *Set of* 6 2·25 2·40

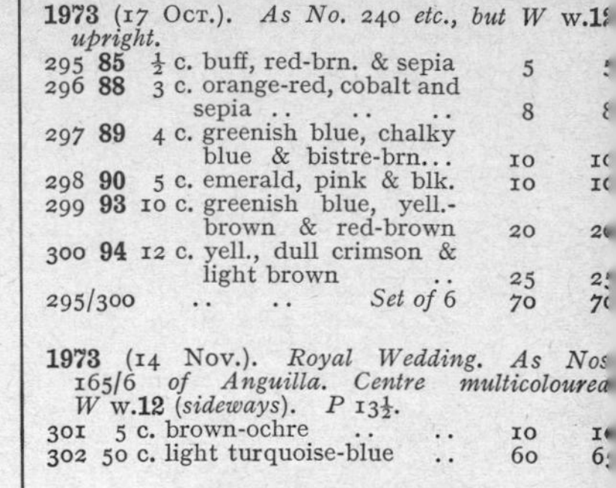

1973 (17 Oct.). *As No.* 240 *etc., but W* **w.1**[2] *upright.*

295 **85** ½ c. buff, red-brn. & sepia 5 5
296 **88** 3 c. orange-red, cobalt and sepia 8 8
297 **89** 4 c. greenish blue, chalky blue & bistre-brn... 10 10
298 **90** 5 c. emerald, pink & blk. 10 10
299 **93** 10 c. greenish blue, yell.-brown & red-brown 20 20
300 **94** 12 c. yell., dull crimson & light brown .. 25 25
295/300 .. .. *Set of* 6 70 70

1973 (14 Nov.). *Royal Wedding. As Nos* 165/6 *of Anguilla. Centre multicoloured W* **w.12** *(sideways). P* 13½.

301 5 c. brown-ochre 10 1
302 50 c. light turquoise-blue .. 60 6

112. "Virgin and Child" (Pintoricchio).

(Des. G. Drummond. Litho. Questa.)

1973 (7 Dec.). *Christmas. T* **112** *and simila vert. designs. Multicoloured. W* **w.12**.

303 ½ c. Type **112** 5
304 3 c. "Virgin and Child" (Lorenzo di Credi) .. 8
305 25 c. "Virgin and Child" (Crivelli) 30 3
306 50 c. "Virgin and Child with St. John" (Luini) .. 60 6

113. Crest of the *Canopus* (French).

(Des. G. Drummond. Litho. Questa.)

1974 (22 Mar.). *"Interpex 1974" (Naval Crests T* **113** *and similar vert. designs. Multicoloure W* **w.12**. *P* 14.

307 5 c. Type **113** 10 1
308 18 c. U.S.S. *Saginaw* .. 25 3
309 25 c. H.M.S. *Rothesay* .. 30 3
310 50 c. H.M.C.S. *Ottawa* .. 60
MS311 196×128 mm. Nos. 307/10 1·40 1·

114. Christopher Columbus.

(Des. J.W. Ltd. Litho. Format.)

1974 (19 Aug.). *Historical Figures. T* **114** *and similar vert. designs. W* w.**12**. *P* 14.

312	5 c. orange and black ..	10	10
313	10 c. greenish blue and black ..	15	15
314	25 c. reddish violet and black ..	30	35
315	40 c. yellow-brown and sepia ..	45	50
MS316	84×119 mm. Nos. 312/15	1·25	

Portraits:—10 c. Sir Walter Raleigh; 25 c. Sir Martin Frobisher; 40 c. Sir Francis Drake.

115. Trumpet Triton.

(Des. G. Drummond. Litho. Harrison.)

1974 (30 Sept.). *Seashells. T* **115** *and similar horiz. designs. Multicoloured. W* w.**12**. *P* 13×13½.

317	5 c. Type **115**	10	10
	a. Wmk. T 53 of Lesotho (sideways)	70·00	
318	18 c. West Indian Murex ..	25	30
319	25 c. Bleeding Tooth	30	35
320	75 c. Virgin Islands Latirus ..	85	90
MS321	146×95 mm. Nos. 317/20	1·50	1·75

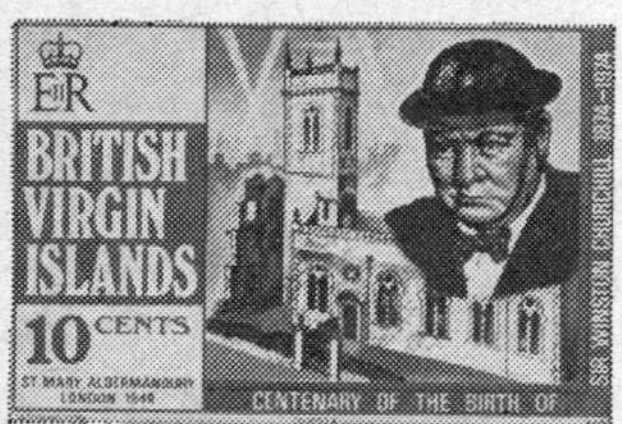

116. Churchill and St. Mary, Aldermanbury, London.

(Des. J.W. Ltd. Litho. Questa.)

1974 (30 Nov.). *Birth Centenary of Sir Winston Churchill. T* **116** *and similar horiz. design. Multicoloured. W* w.**14** *(sideways). P* 14.

322	10 c. Type **116**	15	15
323	50 c. St. Mary, Fulton, Missouri	60	65
MS324	141×108 mm. Nos. 322/3	75	80

117. H.M.S. *Boreas.*

(Des. J. E. Cooter. Litho. J.W.)

1975 (14 Mar.). *"Interpex 1975" Stamp Exhibition, New York. Ships Figureheads. T* **117** *and similar vert. designs. Multicoloured. W* w.**12**. *P* 13.

325	5 c. Type **117**	25	25
326	18 c. *Golden Hind*	40	40
327	40 c. H.M.S. *Superb*	45	50
328	85 c. H.M.S. *Formidable* ..	1·00	1·25
MS329	192×127 mm. Nos. 325/8. W w. **12** *(inverted)*. P 14 ..	2·25	2·50

118. Rock Beauty.

(Des. C. Abbott. Litho. Questa.)

1975 (16 June–15 Aug.). *Fishes. T* **118** *and similar horiz. designs. Multicoloured. W* w.**14** *(sideways). P* 14.

330	½ c. Type **118**	5	5
331	1 c. Squirrelfish	5	5
332	3 c. Queen Triggerfish ..	5	5
333	5 c. Blue Angelfish ..	5	5
334	8 c. Stoplight Parrotfish ..	8	10
335	10 c. Queen Angelfish	10	12
336	12 c. Nassau Grouper	12	15
337	13 c. Blue Tang	12	15
338	15 c. Sergeant Major	15	20
339	18 c. Jewfish	20	20
340	20 c. Bluehead Wrasse ..	20	25
341	25 c. Grey Angelfish	25	30
342	60 c. Glasseye Snapper ..	65	75
343	$1 Blue Chromis	1·10	1·25
344	$2.50, French Angelfish ..	2·50	2·75
345	$3 Queen Parrotfish ..	3·25	3·50
346	$5 Four-eye Butterfly Fish (15.8)	5·50	6·00
330/46	.. .. *Set of* 17	12·00	13·00

119. St. George's Parish School (First meeting-place, 1950).

(Des. R. Granger Barrett. Litho. Questa.)

1975 (27 Nov.). *25th Anniv. of Restoration of Legislative Council. T* **119** *and similar horiz. designs. Multicoloured. W* w.**14** *(sideways). P* 14.

347	5 c. Type **119**	8	8
348	25 c. Legislative Council Building	30	35
349	40 c. Mace and gavel	25	50
350	75 c. Commemorative scroll ..	75	80

120. Copper Mine Point.

(Des. PAD Studio. Litho. Walsall Security Ptrs. Ltd.)

1976 (12 Mar.). *Historic Sites. T* **120** *and similar horiz. designs. Multicoloured. W* w.**14** *(sideways). P* 14½.

351	5 c. Type **120**	8	8
352	18 c. Pleasant Valley	20	20
353	50 c. Callwood Distillery ..	50	55
354	75 c. The Dungeon	70	75

121. Massachusetts Brig *Hazard.*

(Des. J.W. Ltd. Litho. Questa.)

1976 (29 May). *Bicentenary of American Revolution. T* **121** *and similar horiz. designs. Multicoloured. W* w.**14** *(sideways). P* 14.

355	8 c. Type **121**	10	10
356	22 c. American Privateer *Spy*	25	30
357	40 c. Continental Navy frigate *Raleigh*	45	50
358	75 c. Frigate *Alliance* and H.M.S. *Trepasy* ..	80	90
MS359	114×89 mm. Nos. 355/8	1·60	

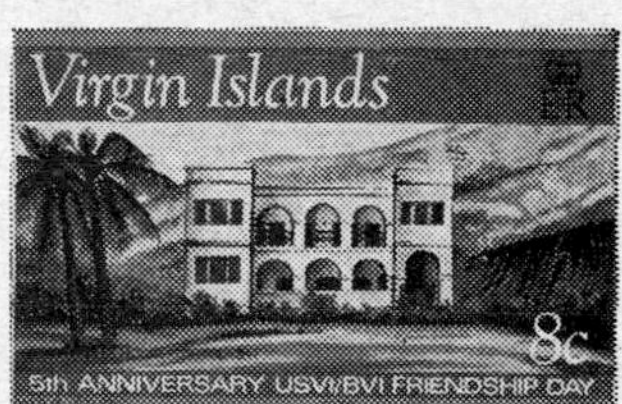

122. Government House, Tortola.

(Des. Walsall. Litho. Questa.)

1976 (29 Oct.). *Fifth Anniv. of Friendship Day with U.S. Virgin Is. T* **122** *and similar multicoloured designs. W* w.**14** *(sideways on 8 and 75 c.). P* 14.

360	8 c. Type **122**	10	12
361	15 c. Government House, St. Croix *(vert.)*	20	20
362	30 c. Flags *(vert.)*	35	40
363	75 c. Government seals ..	90	1·00

123. Royal Visit, 1966.

(Des. J. E. Cooter. Litho. Walsall.)

1977 (7 Feb.). *Silver Jubilee.* T **123** *and similar vert. designs. Multicoloured.* W w.**14.** P 13½.

364	8 c. Type **123**	10	12
365	30 c. The Holy Bible	35	40
366	60 c. Presentation of Holy Bible	75	85

WESTERN AUSTRALIA.

1

2

3

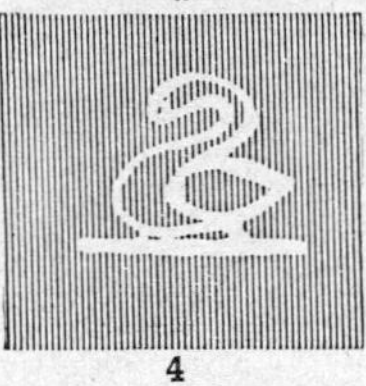
4

(Recess. Perkins, Bacon & Co.)

1854 (1 Aug.). *W* **4** (*sideways*). *Imperf.*

No.	Type	Description	Unused	Used
1	**1**	1d. black	£500	80·00

(Litho. H. Samson, Govt. Lithographer.)

1854. *W* **4** (*sideways*).

(*a*) *Imperf.*

No.	Type	Description	Unused	Used
2	**2**	4d. pale blue	80·00	42·00
3	,,	4d. blue	80·00	42·00
3*a*	,,	4d. deep dull blue	£500	£200
4	,,	4d. slate-blue	£500	£200
5	**3**	1s. pale brown	£110	80·00
6	,,	1s. grey brown	£130	£100
7	,,	1s. deep red-brown	£200	£120
8	,,	1s. salmon	—	£550

Transfer varieties of the 4d. blue.

Variety	Unused	Used
3aa. Frame inverted	—	£20000
b. Top of letters of "AUSTRALIA" cut off so that they are barely 1 mm. in height	—	£3000
ba. "PEICE" instead of "PENCE"	—	£2500
bb. "CE" of "PENCE" close together	—	£2250
c. "WEST" in squeezed-down letters and "F" of "FOUR" has pointed foot (No. 37)	£300	£300
d. "ESTERN" in squeezed-down letters and "U" of "FOUR" squeezed up (No. 57)	£500	£500
e. Small "S" in "POSTAGE" (No. 77)	£300	£300
f. "EN" of "PENCE" shorter (No. 104)	£250	£250
g. "N" of "PENCE" has the first downstroke thinner and the letter slants to the right (No. 116)	£225	£225
h. The water and part of swan damaged above "ENCE" (No. 120)	£275	£275
ha. Tilted border (Nos. 124, 129, 134 and 139)	£250	£250
i. "T" of "POSTAGE" shaved off to a point at foot (No. 125)	£250	£250
j. "F" of "FOUR" slanting to left (No. 137)	£250	£250
k. Coloured line above "AGE" of "POSTAGE" (No. 146)	£250	£250
l. No outer line above "GE" of "POSTAGE" and a coloured line under "FOU" of "FOUR" (No. 151)	£250	£250
m. "WESTERN" in squeezed-down letters, only 1½ mm. in height (No. 157)	£300	£300
n. "P" of "PENCE" small head (No. 175)	£250	£250
o. "RALIA" in squeezed-down letters only 1½ mm. in height (No. 176)	£300	£300
p. "PE" of "PENCE" close together (No. 195)	£250	£250
q. "N" of "PENCE" narrow (No. 196)	£250	£250
r. Part of the right cross-stroke and down-stroke of "T" of "POSTAGE" is cut off (No. 215)	£250	£250
s. Defective "A" in "POSTAGE" the right limb being very thin (No. 216)	£225	£225

Nos. 3aa/bb occur only on the original blue shade printed from Stone I of which there were about 36,000. Nos. 3c/s come from Stone II of which there were about 360,000; they occur on all shades of blue and are rare on the slate-blue shade. They can also be found on the rouletted stamps.

(*b*) *Rouletted* 8 *to* 14 *and compound.*

No.	Type	Description	Unused	Used
10	**1**	1d. black	£300	£120
11	**2**	4d. pale blue	£300	£120
12	,,	4d. blue	—	£120
12*a*	,,	4d. slate-blue	—	£250
13	**3**	1s. pale brown	£550	£200
14	,,	1s. grey-brown	£600	£200

The above are hardly ever seen with gum and unused prices are for stamps without gum.

5

(Litho. A. Hillman, Government Lithographer.)

1857. *W* **4** (*sideways*). (*a*) *Imperf.*

No.	Type	Description	Unused	Used
15	**5**	2d. brown-black/*red*	£700	£225
		a. Printed both sides	£750	£300
16	,,	2d. brn.-blk./*Indian red*	—	£350
		a. Printed both sides	£700	£350
17	,,	6d. black-bronze	£600	£275
18	,,	6d. grey-black	£600	£275
19	,,	6d. golden bronze	£900	£550

(*b*) *Rouletted* 9 *to* 14 *and compound.*

No.	Type	Description	Unused	Used
20	**5**	2d. brown-black/*red*	£800	£375
		a. Printed both sides		
21	,,	2d. brown-black/*Indian red*	—	£450
22	,,	6d. black-bronze	£750	£250
23	,,	6d. grey-black	—	£300

The 1d., 2d., 6d., and 1s. are known pin-perf.

(Printed in the colony from Messrs. Perkins, Bacon & Co.'s plates.)

1860. *W* **4** (*sideways*). (*a*) *Imperf.*

No.	Type	Description	Unused	Used
24	**1**	2d. pale orange	27·00	27·00
25	,,	2d. orange-vermilion	27·00	27·00
25*a*	,,	2d. deep vermilion	£100	£140
26	,,	4d. blue	70·00	£180
27	,,	4d. deep blue	70·00	£200
28	,,	6d. sage-green	£400	£180
28*a*	,,	6d. deep sage-green	—	£200

(*b*) *Rouletted* 7½ *to* 14.

No.	Type	Description	Unused	Used
29	**1**	2d. pale orange	£150	55·00
30	,,	2d. orange-vermilion	£175	55·00
31	,,	4d. deep blue	£800	
32	,,	6d. sage-green	—	£175

(Printed by Perkins, Bacon & Co.)

1861. *W* **4.** (*a*) *Perf. clean-cut* 14–16.

No.	Type	Description	Unused	Used
33	**1**	2d. blue	30·00	11·00
		a. Imperf. between (pair)		
34	,,	6d. purple-brown	55·00	13·00
35	,,	1s. yellow-green	85·00	17·00

(*b*) *Intermediate perf.* 14–16.

No.	Type	Description	Unused	Used
36	**1**	1d. rose	£100	30·00
37	,,	2d. blue	45·00	18·00
38	,,	4d. vermilion	£110	70·00
39	,,	6d. purple-brown	£110	25·00
40	,,	1s. yellow-green	£140	40·00

(*c*) *P* 14–16 *very rough* (July).

No.	Type	Description	Unused	Used
41	**1**	1d. rose-carmine	70·00	12·00
42	,,	6d. purple/*blue*	£200	45·00
43	,,	1s. deep green	£375	75·00

(*d*) *P* 14.

No.	Type	Description	Unused	Used
44	**1**	1d. rose	50·00	17·00
45	,,	2d. blue	20·00	12·00
46	,,	4d. vermilion	55·00	38·00

The 6d. purple-brown and 1s. yellow-green are known, perf. 14, with "SPECIMEN" overprint.

(Printed by De La Rue & Co.)

1864. *T* **1.** *No wmk. P* 13.

No.	Description	Unused	Used
49	1d. carmine-rose	12·00	4·00
50	1d. lake	12·00	3·00
51	6d. deep lilac	32·00	11·00
51*a*	6d. dull violet	35·00	13·00

Both values exist on thin and on thick papers, the former being the scarcer.

Several varieties, both with wmk. (Swan) and without wmk. are to be found *imperf.*, but the majority of these were probably never issued.

1865. *Wmk. Crown CC. P* 12½.

No.	Type	Description	Unused	Used
52	**1**	1d. bistre	10·00	65
53	,,	1d. yellow-ochre	14·00	1·75
54	,,	2d. chrome-yellow	11·00	15
55	,,	2d. yellow	11·00	15
56	,,	4d. carmine	8·00	1·50
		a. Doubly printed	£2250	
57	,,	6d. lilac	35·00	2·25
58	,,	6d. mauve	28·00	2·25
59	,,	6d. violet	18·00	2·25
		a. Doubly printed		
60	,,	6d. indigo-violet	80·00	12·00
61	,,	1s. bright green (H/S S. £35)	18·00	4·00
62	,,	1s. sage-green	75·00	6·00

Error of colour.

No.	Type	Description	Unused	Used
65	**1**	2d. mauve (1879)	£2000	£1100

Beware of fakes of No. 65 made by altering the value tablet of the 6d.

ONE PENNY

(7)

8

1875 (Feb.). *No.* 55 *surch. with T* **7.**

No.	Type	Description	Unused	Used
67	**1**	1d. on 2d. yellow (G.)	12·00	8·00
		a. Pair, one without surch.		
		b. Surch. three times	—	£250
		c. "O" of "ONE" omitted		

Forged surcharges of T 7 are known on stamps wmk. Crown CC. perf. 14, and on Crown CA, perf. 12 and 14.

1872–78. *Wmk. Crown CC. P* 14.

No.	Type	Description	Unused	Used
68	**1**	1d. bistre	13·00	70
69	,,	1d. ochre	13·00	12
70	,,	1d. yellow-ochre	12·00	12
71	,,	2d. chrome-yellow	12·00	12
72	**8**	3d. pale brown (H/S S. £30)	6·00	1·25
73	,,	3d. cinnamon	4·00	85
74	**1**	4d. carmine	50·00	20·00
75	,,	6d. lilac	30·00	1·00
75*a*	,,	6d. reddish lilac	30·00	1·25

1882–90. *Wmk. Crown CA.* (*a*) *P* 12.

No.	Type	Description	Unused	Used
76	**1**	1d. yellow-ochre	18·00	25
77	,,	2d. chrome-yellow	22·00	20
		a. Imperf. between (pair)		
78	,,	4d. carmine	40·00	10·00
79	,,	6d. lilac	55·00	8·00

(*b*) *P* 14.

No.	Type	Description	Unused	Used
81	**1**	1d. yellow-ochre	3·00	8
82	,,	2d. chrome-yellow	3·50	8
83	**8**	3d. pale brown	2·25	12
84	,,	3d. red-brown	2·50	8
85	**1**	4d. carmine	12·00	3·00
86	,,	6d. lilac (H/S S. £30)	14·00	70
87	,,	6d. reddish lilac	14·00	60

(*c*) *P* 12 × 14.

No.	Type	Description	Unused	Used
88	**1**	1d. yellow-ochre (1883)	£400	35·00

The 3d. sage-green, wmk. Crown CA, perf. 12, is known unused, but was never issued.

½ (9) 1d. (10) 1d. (11)

1884. *T* **1** *surch. with T* **9**, *in red.*

No.	Description	Unused	Used
89	½ on 1d. yellow-ochre (No. 76)	2·75	1·00
	a. Thin bar	12·00	10·00
90	½ on 1d. yellow-ochre (No. 81)	4·00	3·00
	a. Thin bar	18·00	11·00

Inverted or double surcharges are forgeries made in London about 1886.

1885. *T* **8** *surch. in green. Wmk. Crown CC. P* 14.

(*a*) *Thick* " **1** " *with slanting top, T* **10.**

91 1d. on 3d. pale brown .. .. 8·00 2·50
92 1d. on 3d. cinnamon .. .. 4·00 2·00

(*b*) *Thin* " **1** " *with straight top, T* **11.**

93 1d. on 3d. pale brown .. .. 13·00 2·50
94 1d. on 3d. cinnamon .. .. 6·00 3·00

1888. *Wmk. Crown CA. P* 14.

95 **1** 1d. carmine-pink .. .. 2·50 15
96 „ 2d. grey .. .. .. 3·00 45
97 „ 4d. red-brown .. .. 35·00 5·00
95/7 H/S " Specimen " *Set of* 3 25·00

12 13

14 15

1885–93. *Wmk. Crown CA* (*sideways*). *P* 14.

98 **12** ½d. yellow-green 15 5
98*a* „ ½d. green 15 5
99 **13** 1d. carmine 20 5
100 **14** 2d. bluish grey 50 5
100*a* „ 2d. grey 40 5
101 **15** 2½d. deep blue .. .. 1·75 5
101*a* „ 2½d. blue .. .. 2·00 5
102 „ 4d. chestnut .. .. 2·25 5
103 „ 5d. bistre .. .. 2·25 20
104 „ 6d. bright violet .. .. 2·25 15
105 „ 1s. pale olive-green .. 3·00 20
106 „ 1s. olive-green .. .. 2·25 20
98, 99, 100*a*, 101*a*/3, 106 Optd./ H.S. " Specimen " *Set of* 7 45·00

ONE PENNY (16) **Half-penny** (17)

1893. *T* **8** *surch. with T* **16**, *in green.*

107 1d. on 3d. pale brown (No. 72) 2·50 80
108 1d. on 3d. cinnamon (No. 73) 2·50 1·00
a. Double surcharge £150
109 1d. on 3d. brown (No. 83) .. 8·00 1·75

1895. *T* **8** *surch. with T* **17**, *in green.*

110 ½d. on 3d. pale brown (No. 72) 2·50 80
110*a* ½d. on 3d. cinnamon (No. 73) 1·25 60
b. Double surcharge £150

Variety. Surch. in red and in green.

111 ½d. on 3d. cinnamon (No. 73) 25·00

The double surcharge is also found on the 3d. Crown CA, but this was printed off specially to supply a local philatelic (!) demand, and is therefore a reprint.

18 19

1899–1900. *Wmk. W Crown A, T* **18.** *P* 14.

112 **13** 1d. carmine 35 8
a. Imperf. .. ..
113 **14** 2d. bright yellow .. 45 8
a. Imperf. .. ..
114 **19** 2½d. blue (1900) 90 8

19*a* 20

(Printed in Melbourne.)

1902–11. *Wmk. V and Crown, T* **30.**

(*a*) *P* 12½ *or* 12½ × 12 (*horiz.*), 12 × 12½ (*vert.*)

115 **19*a*** 1d. carmine-rose 25 8
116 **20** 2d. yellow 55 8
117 **21** 4d. chestnut .. .. 1·25 20
118 **15** 5d. bistre (1905) .. 14·00 5·00
119 **22** 8d. apple-green .. .. 3·25 85
120 **23** 9d. yellow-orange (1906) 3·75 1·00
a. Red-orange .. .. 3·50 1·40
121 **24** 10d. red .. .. .. 7·50 1·10
122 **25** 2s. red/*yellow* .. .. 8·00 2·75
a. Orange/yellow .. .. 8·00 2·25
123 **26** 2s. 6d. deep blue/*rose* .. 9·00 2·50
124 **27** 5s. emerald-green .. 11·00 7·00
125 **28** 10s. deep mauve .. 32·00 10·00
a. Bright purple (1911) .. 35·00 18·00
126 **29** £1 orange-brown .. 55·00 32·00
a. Orange (1911) .. .. £120 60·00

(*b*) *P* 11.

127 **19*a*** 1d. carmine-rose .. .. 14·00 1·75
128 **20** 2d. yellow .. .. 16·00 1·75
129 **21** 4d. chestnut .. .. 60·00 20·00
130 **15** 5d. bistre (1905) .. .. 9·00 3·25
131 **23** 9d. orange (1906) .. 14·00 6·00
132 **25** 2s. red/*yellow* .. .. 16·00 9·00

(*c*) *Perf. compound of* 12½ *or* 12 *and* 11.

133 **19*a*** 1d. carmine-rose .. .. — 25·00
134 **20** 2d. yellow .. .. — 30·00

Type **19*a*** is similar to Type **13** but larger.

The wmk. is generally sideways, except on the 2s. 6d., and 10s., which have the wmk. upright. It is known upright on the 1d., 2d., 4d., and 9d., perf. 12½, and on the 2d., perf. 11. On the 2s. perf. 12½, the upright wmk. is the commoner.

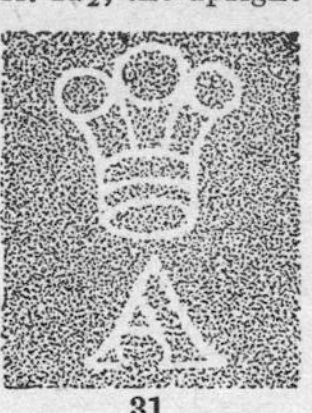

31

32

1905–12. *Wmk. Crown and A, T* **31** (*sideways*).

(*a*) *P* 12½ *or* 12½ × 12 (*horiz.*), 12 × 12½ (*vert.*).

138 **12** ½d. green (1910) .. 30 10
139 **19*a*** 1d. rose-pink 35 10
a. Carmine (1910) .. 35 10
b. Carmine-red (1912) .. 30 10
c. Wmk. upright 30 10
140 **20** 2d. yellow 30 10
a. Wmk. upright 30 10
141 **8** 3d. brown 90 12
142 **21** 4d. bistre-brown .. 1·40 20
a. Pale chestnut .. .. 3·00 12
b. Bright brown-red .. 2·25 15
143 **15** 5d. pale olive-green .. 2·25 20
a. Olive-bistre .. .. 2·25 25
144 **22** 8d. apple-green (1912) .. 2·25 1·10
145 **23** 9d. orange .. .. 2·25 50
a. Red-orange .. .. 4·00 55
b. Wmk. upright .. .. 3·50 55
146 **24** 10d. rose-orange .. .. 5·00 2·00
148 **27** 5s. emerald-green .. 20·00 11·00

(*b*) *P* 11.

151 **19*a*** 1d. rose-pink .. .. 1·10 25
a. Carmine-red .. .. 1·10 20
b. Wmk. upright .. .. 1·10 20
152 **20** 2d. yellow .. .. 2·25 55
153 **8** 3d. brown .. .. 2·25 55
154 **21** 4d. yellow-brown .. 90·00 25·00
155 **15** 5d. olive .. .. .. 7·00 2·00
a. Pale greenish yellow .. 10·00 6·00
b. Olive-bistre .. .. 2·75 70
157 **23** 9d. orange .. .. 18·00 20·00
a. Red-orange .. .. — 15·00

(*c*) *Perf. compound of* 12½ *or* 12 *and* 11.

161 **19*a*** 1d. rose-pink .. .. 30·00 18·00
162 **20** 2d. yellow .. .. 35·00 20·00
163 **8** 3d. brown .. .. 40·00 20·00

33 34

(Typo. D.L.R.)

1906–7. *Wmk. W Crown A, T* **18.** *P* 14.

164 **33** 6d. bright violet .. .. 3·50 20
165 **34** 1s. olive-green .. .. 6·00 1·10

1912. *Wmk. Crown and A, T* **32.** *P* 11½ × 12.

168 **33** 6d. bright violet .. .. 3·50 50
169 **34** 1s. sage-green .. .. 6·00 1·00
a. Perf. 12½ (single line) ..

ONE PENNY

(**35**)

1912. *Nos.* 140 *and* 162 *surch. with T* **35.**

(*a*) *P* 12½ *or* 12 × 12½.

170 **20** 1d. on 2d. yellow 30 8
a. Wmk. upright 25 8

(*b*) *Perf. compound of* 12½ *and* 11.

171 **20** 1d. on 2d. yellow .. .. 75·00

1912. *W* **31** (*sideways*). *Thin paper and white gum* (*as Victoria*).

172 **8** 3d. brown (*perf.* 12½) .. 6·00 5·00
a. Wmk. upright .. .. 6·00 5·00
173 „ 3d. brown (*perf.* 11) .. 35·00 40·00
a. Wmk. upright .. .. 35·00 40·00

POSTAL FISCAL STAMPS.

F 1

I. R.

TWO PENCE

(F 2)

(F 3)

1893. *Wmk. CA over Crown.* *P* 14.

F1	**F 1**	1d. dull purple	1·00	20
F2	,,	2d. dull purple	3·50	1·40
F3	,,	3d. dull purple	3·75	45
F4	,,	6d. dull purple	5·00	1·00
F5	,,	1s. dull purple	7·00	1·00
F6	,,	2s. 6d. dull purple	25·00	18·00
F7	,,	3s. dull purple	75·00	35·00
F8	,,	5s. dull purple	30·00	18·00

Surch. as Type F 2. *Wmk. Crown CC.*

F 9	**8**	1d. on 3d. lilac	35·00	25·00
F10	,,	2d. on 3d. lilac	2·50	1·00
F11	,,	3d. on 3d. lilac	5·00	2·50
F12	,,	6d. on 3d. lilac	35·00	32·00
F13	,,	1s. on 3d. lilac	£100	65·00

1899. *Wmk. W Crown A, T* **13.** *P* 14.

F14	**F 1**	1d. dull purple	80	20
F15	,,	3d. dull purple	1·40	25
F16	,,	6d. dull purple	3·50	50
F17	,,	1s. dull purple	4·00	90
F18	,,	2s. 6d. dull purple ..	18·00	15·00
F19	,,	3s. dull purple	32·00	30·00
F20	,,	5s. dull purple	70·00	60·00

Various stamps are known with the overprint Type F **3**, most of which are forgeries, although the 1d. and 2d., wmk. Crown CC, perf. 14, were so overprinted, but purely for fiscal purposes.

TELEGRAPH STAMPS USED FOR POSTAGE.

T 1

1886. *Wmk. Crown CC.*

T1	**T 1**	1d. bistre (*perf.* 12½) ..	3·00	1·00
		a. Imperf.		
T2	,,	1d. bistre (*perf.* 14) ..	3·50	1·75
T3	,,	6d. lilac (*perf.* 14) ..	5·50	3·75

OFFICIAL STAMPS.

Stamps of the various issues from 1854–85 are found with a circular hole punched out, the earlier size being about 3 mm. in diameter and the later 4 mm. These were used on official correspondence. This system of punching ceased in 1886. Any in stock will be supplied at the same price as similar stamps without the hole. Stamps from No. 98 onward exist punctured " O S ".

Western Australia now uses the stamps of AUSTRALIA.

WESTERN SAMOA.

(*See* SAMOA.)

ZAMBIA.

(FORMERLY NORTHERN RHODESIA.)

INDEPENDENT.

11. Pres. Kaunda and Victoria Falls.

13. Barotse Dancer.

12. College of Further Education, Lusaka.

(Des. M. Goaman (3d., 6d.), Mrs. G. Ellison (1s. 3d.). Photo. Harrison.)

1964 (24 OCT.). *Independence.* *P* 13½×14½ (*6d.*) *or* 14½×13½ (*others*).

91	**11**	3d. sepia, yell.-grn. & blue	5	5
92	**12**	6d. deep violet and yellow	10	10
93	**13**	1s. 3d. red, black, sepia and orange	20	20

14. Maize-Farmer and Silo.

15. Health—Radiographer.

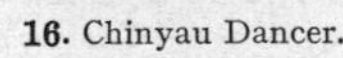
16. Chinyau Dancer.

18. Angoni Bull.

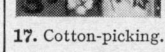

17. Cotton-picking.

19. Communications, Old and New.

20. Zambezi Sawmills and Redwood Flower.

21. Fishing at Mpulungu.

22. Tobacco Worker.

23. Tonga Basket-making.

24. Luangwa Game Reserve.

25. Education—Student.

26. Copper Mining.

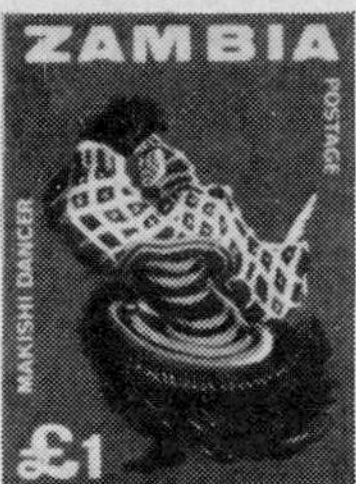

27. Makishi Dancer.

(Des. Mrs. G. Ellison. Photo. Harrison.)

1964 (24 Oct.). *P* 14½ (½*d. to* 4*d.*), 14½×13½ (1*s.* 3*d.*, 2*s. and* £1) *or* 13½×14½ (*others*).

No.	Type	Description	Unused	Used
94	**14**	½d. red, black & yell.-grn.	5	5
95	**15**	1d. brn., blk. & brt. blue	5	5
96	**16**	2d. red, dp. brn. & orange	5	5
97	**17**	3d. black and red ..	5	5
98	**18**	4d. black, brown & orange	5	5
99	**19**	6d. orange, deep brown & deep bluish green ..	8	5
100	**20**	9d. carmine, black and bright blue	12	10
101	**21**	1s. black, yellow-bistre and blue	20	10
102	**22**	1s. 3d. light red, yellow, black and blue ..	25	15
103	**23**	2s. bright blue, black, deep brown and orange ..	30	25
104	**24**	2s. 6d. black & orge.-yell.	40	35
105	**25**	5s. black, yellow & green	70	65
106	**26**	10s. black and orange ..	2·00	1·25
107	**27**	£1 blk., brn., yell. & red	3·50	3·50
94/107		.. .. *Set of* 14	7·00	6·00

28. I.T.U. Emblem and Symbols.

(Photo. Harrison.)

1965 (26 July). *I.T.U. Centenary.* *P* 14×14½.

No.	Type	Description	Unused	Used
108	**28**	6d. lt. reddish violet & gold	10	10
109	,,	2s. 6d. brownish grey & gold	30	35

29. I.C.Y. Emblem.

(Photo. Harrison.)

1965 (26 July). *International Co-operation Year.* *P* 14½.

No.	Type	Description	Unused	Used
110	**29**	3d. turquoise and gold ..	8	8
111	,,	1s. 3d. ultram. and gold ..	20	25

30. State House, Lusaka.

31. Fireworks, Independence Stadium. (*Horiz.*)
32. Clematopsis. (*Vert.*)
33. *Tithonia diversifolia.* (*Vert.*)

(Des. Mrs. G. Ellison. Photo. Harrison.)

1965 (18 Oct.). *First Anniv. of Independence. No wmk.* *P* 13½×14½ (3*d.*), 14×13½ (6*d.*) *or* 13½×14 (*others*).

No.	Type	Description	Unused	Used
112	**30**	3d. multicoloured	5	5
113	**31**	6d. multicoloured	8	8
114	**32**	1s. 3d. multicoloured ..	20	25
115	**33**	2s. 6d. multicoloured ..	35	45

34. W.H.O. Building and U.N. Flag.

(Des. M. Goaman. Photo. Harrison.)

1966 (18 May). *Inauguration of W.H.O. Headquarters, Geneva.* *P* 14½.

No.	Type	Description	Unused	Used
116	**34**	3d. lake-brown, gold and new blue	5	5
		a. Gold omitted		
117	,,	1s. 3d. gold, new blue & deep bluish violet. ..	25	25

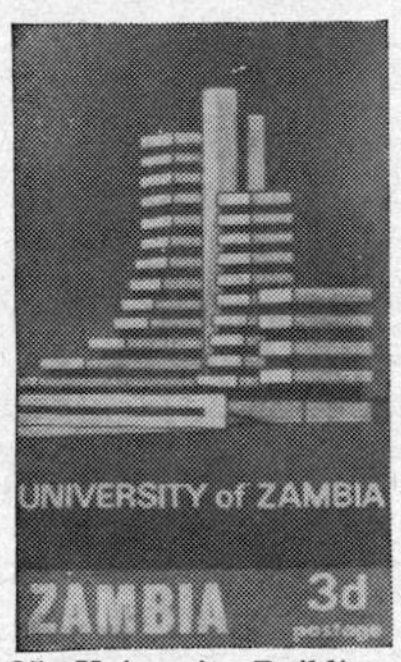

35. University Building.

(Des. Mrs. G. Ellison. Photo. Harrison.)

1966 (12 July). *Opening of Zambia University.* *P* 14½.

No.	Type	Description	Unused	Used
118	**35**	3d. blue-green and copper-bronze	5	5
119	**35**	1s. 3d. reddish violet and copper-bronze	20	20

36. National Assembly Building.

(Des. Mrs. G. Ellison. Photo. Harrison.)

1967 (2 May). *Inauguration of National Assembly Building.* *P* 14½.

No.	Type	Description	Unused	Used
120	**36**	3d. black and gold ..	5	5
121	,,	6d. olive-green and gold ..	8	8

37. Airport Scene.

(Des. Mrs. G. Ellison. Photo. Harrison.)

1967 (2 Oct.). *Opening of Lusaka International Airport.* *P* 13½×14½.

No.	Type	Description	Unused	Used
122	**37**	6d. violet-blue and copper-bronze	8	8
123	,,	2s. 6d. brown and copper-bronze	40	40

38. Youth Service Badge.

39. "Co-operative Farming".

40. "Communications". **41.** Coalfields.

42. Road Link with Tanzania.

(Des. Mrs. G. Ellison. Photo. Harrison.)

1967 (23 Oct.). *National Development.* P $13\frac{1}{2}\times14\frac{1}{2}$ (*6d., 1s. 6d.*) or $14\frac{1}{2}\times13\frac{1}{2}$ (*others*).

124	**38**	4d. black, red and gold ..	5	5
125	**39**	6d. black, gold & vio.-blue	8	10
126	**40**	9d. black, grey-blue & silver	12	15
127	**41**	1s. multicoloured ..	15	20
128	**42**	1s. 6d. multicoloured ..	25	30
124/8		.. .. *Set of* 5	55	75

(New currency. 100 ngwee = 1 kwacha.)

43. Lusaka Cathedral.

44. Baobab Tree.

46. National Museum, Livingstone.

45. Zambia Airways Jetliner.

47. Vimbuza Dancer.

48. Tobacco Picking.

49. *Nudaurelia zambesina.*

50. Crowned Cranes.

51. Angoni Warrior.

52. Chokwe Dancer.

53. Kafue Railway Bridge.

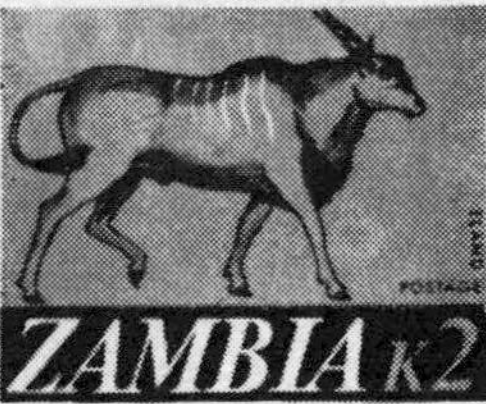

54. Eland.

(Des. Mrs. G. Ellison. Photo. Harrison.)

1968 (16 Jan.). *Decimal Currency.* P $13\frac{1}{2}\times14\frac{1}{2}$ (*1, 3, 15, 50 n.*) or $14\frac{1}{2}\times13\frac{1}{2}$ (*others*).

129	**43**	1 n. multicoloured ..	5	5
		a. Copper-bronze (incl. value) omitted ..	20·00	
130	**44**	2 n. multicoloured ..	5	5
131	**45**	3 n. multicoloured ..	8	8
132	**46**	5 n. bistre-brn. & copper-bronze	10	10
133	**47**	8 n. multicoloured ..	15	15
134	**48**	10 n. multicoloured ..	20	15
135	**49**	15 n. multicoloured ..	25	25
136	**50**	20 n. multicoloured ..	35	30
137	**51**	25 n. multicoloured ..	40	35
138	**52**	50 n. chocolate, red-orange and copper-bronze ..	85	75
139	**53**	1 k. Royal blue and copper-bronze ..	1·75	1·50
140	**54**	2 k. black and copper-bronze	3·25	3·00
129/40		.. .. *Set of* 12	6·50	6·00

All values exist with PVA gum as well as gum arabic.

55. Ndola on Outline of Zambia.

(Des. Mrs. G. Ellison. Photo. Harrison.)

1968 (29 June). *Trade Fair, Ndola.* P 14.

141	**55**	15 n. green and gold ..	25	30

56. Human Rights Emblem and Heads.

(Des. Mrs. G. Ellison. Photo. Gold (emblem) die-stamped. Harrison.)

1968 (23 Oct.). *Human Rights Year.* P 14.

142	**56**	3 n. deep blue, pale violet and gold	12	12

57. W.H.O. Emblem.

(Des. Mrs. G. Ellison. Photo. Gold (Staff and "20") die-stamped. Harrison.)

1968 (23 Oct.). *20th Anniv. of World Health Organization.* P 14.

143	**57**	10 n. gold and bluish violet	20	20

58. Group of Children.

(Des. Mrs. G. Ellison. Photo. Gold (children) die-stamped. Harrison.)

1968 (23 Oct.). *21st Anniv. of U.N.I.C.E.F.* P 14.

144	**58**	25 n. black, gold & ultram.	45	55

59. Copper Miner.

60. Poling a Furnace. (*Horiz.*)

(Des. Mrs. G. Ellison. Photo. Harrison.)

1969 (18 June). *50th Anniv. of International Labour Organization. P* 14½×13½ (3 *n.*) *or* 13½×14½ (25 *n.*).

145 **59** 3 n. gold and deep violet .. 8 8
146 **60** 25 n. pale yellow, gold and blackish brown .. 45 50

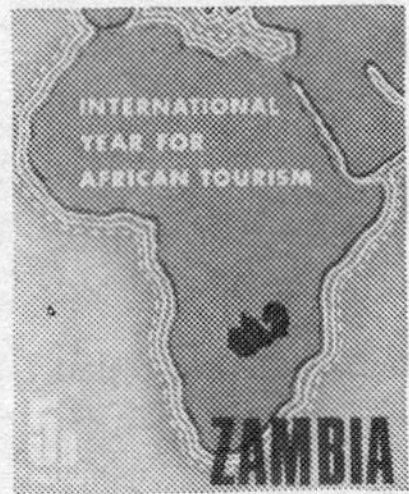

61. Zambia outlined on Map of Africa.

62. Defassa Waterbuck. (*Horiz.*)
63. Golden Perch. (*Horiz.*)
64. Carmine Bee-eater. (*Vert.*)

(Des. Mrs. G. Ellison. Photo. Harrison.)

1969 (23 Oct.). *International African Tourist Year. P* 14×14½ (5 *n.*, 25 *n.*) *or* 14½×14 (*others*).

147 **61** 5 n. multicoloured .. 10 10
148 **62** 10 n. multicoloured .. 15 15
149 **63** 15 n. multicoloured .. 25 25
150 **64** 25 n. multicoloured .. 45 45

65. Satellite "Nimbus 3" orbiting the Earth.

(Des. Mrs. G. Ellison. Litho. Enschedé.)

1970 (23 Mar.). *World Meteorological Day. P* 13×10½.

151 **65** 15 n. multicoloured .. 25 30

66. Woman collecting Water from Well.

(Des. V. Whiteley (from local designs). Litho. B.W.)

1970 (4 July). *Preventive Medicine. T* **66** *and similar vert. designs. P* 13½×12.

152 3 n. multicoloured 8 8
153 15 n. multicoloured 25 25
154 25 n. greenish blue, rosine and sepia 45 45

Designs:—15 n. Child on scales; 25 n. Child being Immunized.

67. Mural (Gabriel Ellison).

(Des. Mrs. G. Ellison. Litho. Harrison.)

1970 (8 Sept.). *Conference of Non-Aligned Nations. P* 14×14½.

155 **67** 15 n. multicoloured .. 25 30

68. Ceremonial Axe.

(Des. Mrs. G. Ellison. Litho. D.L.R.)

1970 (30 Nov.). *Traditional Crafts. T* **68** *and similar multicoloured designs. P* 13½ (15 *n.*), 12½ (25 *n.*) *or* 14 (*others*).

156 3 n. Type **68** 8 8
157 5 n. Clay Smoking-Pipe Bowl (*horiz.*) 10 10
158 15 n. Makishi Mask (*vert.*) .. 25 30
159 25 n. Kuomboka Ceremony (*horiz.*). 45 45
MS160 133×83 mm. Nos. 156/9 Imperf. 95 95

Sizes:—5 n. as T **68**; 15 n. 30×47 mm.; 25 n. 72×19 mm.

69. Dag Hammarskjöld and U.N. General Assembly.

(Des. J.W. Ltd. Litho. Questa.)

1971 (18 Sept.). *Tenth Death Anniv. of Dag Hammarskjöld. T* **69** *and similar horiz. designs, each with portrait of Hammarskjöld. Multicoloured. P* 13½.

161 4 n. Type **69** 8 8
162 10 n. Tail of aircraft .. 15 15
163 15 n. Dove of Peace 25 25
164 25 n. Memorial tablet .. 45 45

70. Red-breasted Bream.

(Des. G. Drummond. Litho. J.W.)

1971 (10 Dec.). *Fish. T* **70** *and similar horiz. designs. Multicoloured. P* 13½.

165 4 n. Type **70** 8 8
166 10 n. Green-headed Bream .. 15 20
167 15 n. Tiger fish 25 30

71. Porcupine.

(Des. and litho. J.W.)

1972 (15 Mar.). *Conservation Year* (*1st issue*). *T* **71** *and similar multicoloured designs. P* 13½.

168 4 n. Cheetah (58×21 *mm.*) 8 8
169 10 n. Lechwe (58×21 *mm.*) 15 20
170 15 n. Type **71** 25 25
171 25 n. Elephant 40 45

(Des. and litho. J.W.)

1972 (30 June). *Conservation Year* (*2nd issue*). *Designs similar to T* **71**. *Multicoloured. P* 13½.

172 4 n. Soil conservation .. 8 8
173 10 n. Forestry 20 20
174 15 n. Water (58×21 *mm.*) .. 25 30
175 25 n. Maize (58×21 *mm.*) .. 45 45

72. Giraffe and Zebra.

1972 (30 JUNE). *National Parks. Sheet* 114 × 140 *mm. containing T* **72** *and similar vert. designs. Multicoloured. P* 13½.

MS176	10 n. (×4) giraffe and zebra; rhino; hippo and deer; lion	85	90

Each design includes part of a map showing Zambian National Parks, the four forming a composite design.

73. Zambian Flowers.

(Des. and litho. J.W.)

1972 (22 SEPT.). *Conservation Year* (3*rd issue*). *T* **73** *and similar horiz. designs. Multicoloured. P* 13½.

177	4 n. Type **73**	8	8
178	10 n. Citrus Swallowtail Butterfly	20	20
179	15 n. Bees	25	25
180	25 n. Red Locusts	45	45

74. Mary and Joseph.

(Des. V. Whiteley. Litho. Questa.)

1972 (1 DEC.). *Christmas. T* **74** *and similar horiz. designs. Multicoloured. P* 14.

181	4 n. Type **74**	8	8
182	9 n. Mary, Joseph and Jesus	15	15
183	15 n. Mary, Jesus and the shepherds	25	25
184	25 n. The Three Wise Men ..	45	45

75. *Oudenodon* and *Rubidgea*.

(Des. Mrs. G. Ellison; adapted J.W. Ltd. Litho. Questa.)

1973 (1 FEB.). *Zambian Prehistoric Animals. T* **75** *and similar horiz. designs. Multicoloured. P* 14 × 13½ (4 *n.*) *or* 13½ × 14 (*others*).

185	4 n. Type **75**	10	10
186	9 n. Broken Hill Man ..	15	15
187	10 n. *Zambiasaurus*	20	25
188	15 n. *Luangwa drysdalli* ..	35	35
189	25 n. *Glossopteris*	50	55
185/9	.. .. *Set of* 5	1·10	1·25

Nos. 186/9 are smaller (38 × 21 mm.) and show fossils.

76. "Dr. Livingstone, I Presume".

(Des. J.W. Ltd. Litho. Format.)

1973 (1 MAY). *Death Centenary of Dr. Livingstone. T* **76** *and similar horiz. designs. Multicoloured. P* 13½.

190	3 n. Type **76**	8	8
191	4 n. Scripture Lesson ..	8	8
192	9 n. Victoria Falls ..	15	15
193	10 n. Scattering slavers ..	20	20
194	15 n. Healing the sick ..	30	30
195	25 n. Burial place of Livingstone's heart	45	50
190/5	.. .. *Set of* 6	1·10	1·10

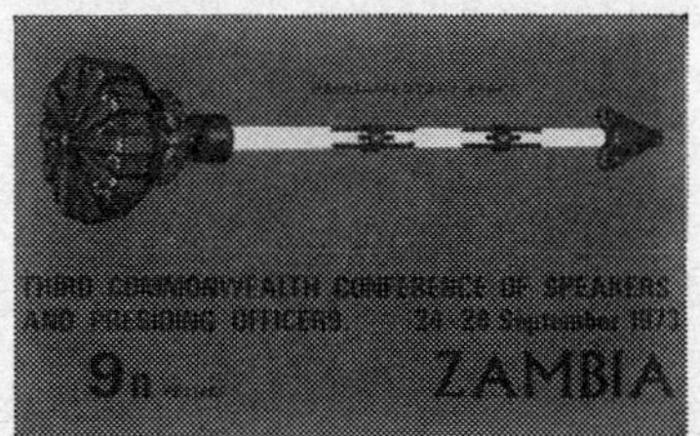

77. Parliamentary Mace.

(Des. Mrs. G. Ellison. Litho. Questa.)

1973 (24 SEPT.). *Third Commonwealth Conference of Speakers and Presiding Officers, Lusaka. P* 13½.

196	**77**	9 n. multicoloured ..	15	15
197	,,	15 n. multicoloured ..	25	30
198	,,	25 n. multicoloured ..	45	50

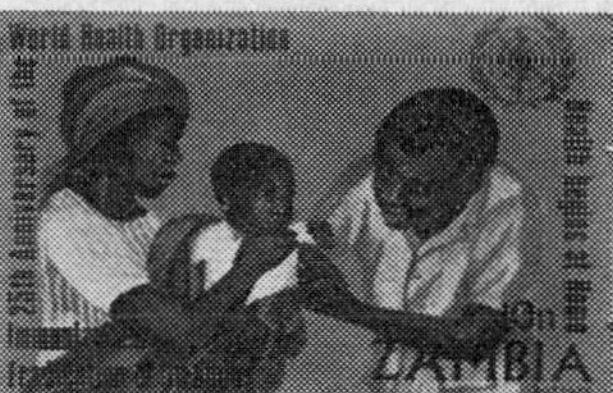

78. Inoculation.

(Des. Mrs. G. Ellison. Litho. Questa.)

1973 (16 OCT.). 25*th Anniv. of W.H.O. T* **78** *and similar multicoloured designs. P* 14.

199	4 n. Mother washing baby	3·50	1·25
200	9 n. Nurse weighing baby	20	20
201	10 n. Type **78**	25	25
202	15 n. Child eating meal ..	30	35

The 4 and 9 n. are vert. designs: the others are horiz.

Only a small quantity of No. 199 was produced, and most of them were issued to post offices for local use.

79. U.N.I.P. Flag.

(Des. Mrs. G. Ellison. Litho. Questa.)

1973 (13 DEC.). *"Birth of 2nd Republic". T* **79** *and similar vert. designs inscr. "13.12.72". Multicoloured. P* 14 × 13½.

203	4 n. Type **79**	2·00	1·10
204	9 n. Freedom House	20	20
205	10 n. Army band ..	20	20
206	15 n. "Celebrations" (dancers)	30	35
207	25 n. Presidential chair ..	45	50
203/7	.. .. *Set of* 5	2·75	2·00

80. President Kaunda at Mulungushi.

(Des. Mrs. G. Ellison. Litho. Harrison.)

1974 (28 APR.). *President Kaunda's 50th Birthday. T* **80** *and similar horiz. designs. Multicoloured. P* 14½ × 14 (4 *n.*) *or* 14 × 14½ (*others*).

208	4 n. Type **80**	8	8
209	9 n. President's former residence	15	15
210	15 n. President holding Independence flame	25	30

81. Nakambala Sugar Estate.

(Des. G. L. Vasarhelyi. Litho. Questa.)

1974 (23 Oct.). *Tenth Anniv. of Independence. T* **81** *and similar horiz. designs. Multicoloured. P* 13½.

211	3 n. Type **81**	8	8
212	4 n. Local market	8	8
213	9 n. Kapiri glass factory ..	15	15
214	10 n. Kafue hydro-electric scheme	20	20
215	15 n. Kafue hook bridge ..	25	30
216	25 n. Non-aligned Conference, Lusaka, 1970	40	45
211/16	.. .. *Set of* 6	1·00	1·10
MS217	141×105 mm. 15 n. (×4) Academic Education; Teacher Training College; Technical Education; Zambia University ..	1·00	1·10

82. Mobile Post-van.

(Des. Mrs. G. Ellison. Litho. Format.)

1974 (15 Nov.). *Centenary of Universal Postal Union. T* **82** *and similar horiz. designs. Multicoloured. P* 13½.

218	4 n. Type **82**	8	8
219	9 n. Aeroplane on tarmac ..	15	15
220	10 n. Chipata Post Office ..	20	20
221	15 n. Modern training centre ..	25	30

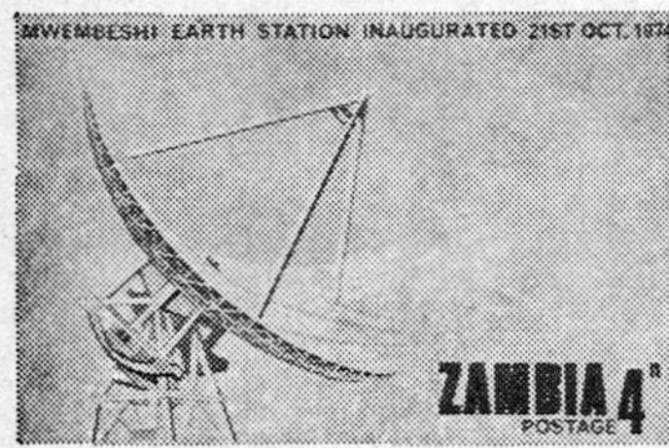

83. Dish Aerial.

(Des. Mrs. G. Ellison. Litho. Questa.)

1974 (15 Dec.). *Opening of Mwembeshi Earth Station (21st October). T* **83** *and similar horiz. designs. Multicoloured. P* 13½.

222	4 n. Type **83**	8	8
223	9 n. View at dawn	15	15
224	15 n. View at dusk	25	30
225	25 n. Aerial view	40	45

84. Rhinoceros and Calf.

85. Independence Monument.

(Des. Mrs. G. Ellison. Litho. J.W.)

1975 (2 Jan.). *T* **84** *and similar horiz. designs. Multicoloured.*

(*a*) *Size as T* **84**. *P* 13½×14.

226	1 n. Type **84**	5	5
227	2 n. Guinea-fowl	5	5
228	3 n. National Dancing Troupe	5	5
229	4 n. Fish Eagle	5	5
230	5 n. Knife-edge Bridge ..	8	8
231	8 n. Sitatunga (antelope) ..	10	12
232	9 n. Elephant, Kasaba Bay ..	12	12
233	10 n. Giant Pangolin	12	15

(*b*) *Size as T* **85**. *P* 13.

234	15 n. Type **85**	20	25
235	20 n. Harvesting groundnuts	25	30
236	25 n. Tobacco-growing ..	35	40
237	50 n. Flying-Doctor service ..	60	70
238	1 k. Lady Ross's Turaco ..	1·25	1·50
239	2 k. Village scene	2·75	3·00
226/39	.. .. *Set of* 14	5·50	6·00

86. Map of Namibia.

(Des. PAD Studio. Litho. Questa.)

1975 (26 Aug.). *Namibia Day. P* 13½.

240	**86**	4 n. grn. & lt. yell.-grn.	8	8
241	,,	9 n. steel-blue and light turquoise-green ..	15	15
242	,,	15 n. orange-yellow and greenish yellow ..	25	25
243	,,	25 n. orange & light orange	40	45

87. Erection of Sprinkler Irrigation.

(Des. and Litho. J.W. Ltd.)

1975 (16 Dec.). *Silver Jubilee of the International Commission on Irrigation and Drainage. T* **87** *and similar horiz. designs. Multicoloured. P* 13.

244	4 n. Type **87**	8	8
245	9 n. Sprinkler irrigation (*different*)	15	15
246	15 n. Furrow irrigation ..	40	45

88. Mutondo.

(Des. A. Chimfwembe. Litho. J.W.)

1976 (22 Mar.). *World Forestry Day. T* **88** *and similar horiz. designs showing trees. Multicoloured. P* 13.

247	3 n. Type **88**	8	8
248	4 n. Mukunyu	8	8
249	9 n. Mukusi	15	15
250	10 n. Mopane	20	20
251	15 n. Musuku	25	25
252	25 n. Mukwa	40	45
247/52	.. .. *Set of* 6	1·00	1·10

89. Passenger Train.

(Des. A. Chimfwembe. Litho. J.W.)

1976 (10 Dec.). *Opening of Tanzania–Zambia Railway. T* **89** *and similar horiz. designs. Multicoloured. P* 13½ (**MS**257) *or* 13 (*others*).

253	4 n. Type **89**	8	8
254	9 n. Copper exports	15	20
255	15 n. Machinery imports ..	25	30
256	25 n. Goods train	40	45
MS257	140×106 mm. 10 n. Clearing bush; 15 n. Laying track; 20 n. Railway workers; 25 n. Completed track	1·10	

90. Kayowe Dance.

(Des. BG Studio. Litho. Questa.)

1977 (18 Jan.). *Second World Black and African Festival of Arts and Culture, Nigeria. T* **90** *and similar horiz. designs. Multicoloured. P* 13½.

258	4 n. Type **90**	8	8
259	9 n. Lilombola dance ..	15	20
260	15 n. Initiation ceremony ..	25	30
261	25 n. Munkhwele dance ..	40	45

MINIMUM PRICE

The minimum price quoted is 5p which represents a handling charge rather than a basis for valuing common stamps. For further notes about prices see introductory pages.

POSTAGE DUE STAMPS

D 3

(Des. D. Smith. Litho. Govt. Printer, Lusaka.)

1964 (24 Oct.). *P* 12½.

D11	**D 3**	1d. orange	5	8
D12	„	2d. deep blue	5	8
D13	„	3d. lake	5	8
D14	„	4d. ultramarine	8	10
D15	„	6d. purple	12	15
D16	„	1s. light emerald ..	25	35
D11/D16		.. .. *Set of* 6	50	70

In all values the left-hand vertical row of the sheet is imperf. at left and the bottom horizontal row is imperf. at bottom. The above were crudely perforated, resulting in variations in the sizes of the stamps.

The above were withdrawn on 15 January 1968 and thereafter decimal currency postage stamps were used for postage due purposes with appropriate cancellations.

HAVE YOU READ THE NOTES AT THE BEGINNING OF THIS CATALOGUE?

These often provide answers to the enquiries we receive.

ZANZIBAR.

I. BRITISH PROTECTORATE.

Zanzibar
(1)

1895 (10 Nov.). *Contemporary stamps of India optd. with T* **1**.

(a) In blue.

1 **23** ½ a. blue-green £500 £170
2 **25** 1 a. plum £225 £100
j. "Zanzidar" .. .. — £1500

(b) In black.

3 **23** ½ a. blue-green .. .. 90 1·25
j. "Zanzidar" .. .. 80·00 50·00
k. "Zanibar" .. .. 85·00 65·00
l. Diaeresis over last "a" .. 50·00
4 **25** 1 a. plum .. .. .. 1·00 1·10
j. "Zanzidar" .. .. 85·00 55·00
k. "Zanibar" .. .. 90·00 65·00
5 **26** 1 a. 6 p. sepia 90 90
j. "Zanzidar" £130 £100
k. "Zanibar" .. .. £100 90·00
l. "Zanizbar" £130
m. Diaeresis over last "a" 50·00
6 **27** 2 a. pale blue 75 75
7 „ 2 a. blue .. .. .. 1·10 1·10
j. "Zanzidar" £170 £130
k. "Zanibar" .. .. £100 80·00
l. Diaeresis over last "a" 55·00
m. Opt. double .. .. 45·00
8 **36** 2½ a. yellow-green .. .. 1·25 1·00
j. "Zanzidar" .. .. £130 80·00
k. "Zanibar" .. .. 50·00 60·00
l. "Zapzibar" .. ..
m. "Zanzipar" £130
n. Diaeresis over last "a" 60·00
o. Second "z" italic .. 8·50
9 **28** 3 a. orange .. .. .. 2·00 2·50
10 „ 3 a. brown-orange .. 1·40 2·50
j. "Zanzidar" .. .. 65·00 65·00
k. "Zanizbar" £275 £275
11 **29** 4 a. olive-green .. .. 2·75 2·75
12 „ 4 a. slate-green .. .. 2·25 2·75
j. "Zanzidar" £225 £140
13 **21** 6 a. pale brown .. .. 2·50 3·00
j. "Zanzidar" £150 £150
k. "Zanibar" £110 £110
l. "Zanzibarr" £225 £225
m. Opt. double .. ..
14 **31** 8 a. dull mauve .. .. 4·00 4·00
j. "Zanzidar" £250 £250
15 „ 8 a. magenta .. .. 3·00 3·50
16 **32** 12 a. purple/*red* .. .. 3·00 3·50
j. "Zanzidar" £250 £250
17 **33** 1 r. slate .. .. .. 20·00 24·00
j. "Zanzidar" £400 £400
18 **37** 1 r. green and carmine .. 3·50 4·00
j. Opt. vert. downwards .. 60·00
19 **38** 2 r. carmine & yell.-brown 7·00 8·00
j. "r" omitted £450
k. "r" inverted £140 £150
20 „ 3 r. brown and green .. 7·00 7·50
j. "r" omitted £450
k. "r" inverted £130 £140
21 „ 5 r. ultramarine and violet 7·00 7·50
j. "r" omitted £450
k. "r" inverted £140 £150
l. Opt. double, one invtd. .. 80·00
3/21 .. .. *Set of* 15 65·00 75·00

Many forgeries of this overprint exist and also bogus errors.

Minor Varieties of the Type.

A. First "Z" antique.
B. Broken "p" for "n".
C. Tall second "z".
D. Small second "z".
E. Small second "z" and inverted "q" for "b".
F. Second "z" Gothic.
G. No dot over "i".
H. Inverted "q" for "b".
I. Arabic "2" for "r".

		A.		B.		C.		D. or E.		F.		G.		H.		I.	
						(a) Blue overprint											
1	½ a. blue-green	£600	£350	£700	£500	£600	£250	£600	£250	†		£600	£350	£600	£300	†	
2	1 a. plum	£300	£170	£350	£250	£300	£130	£300	£130	†		£325	£170	£325	£180	†	
						(b) Black overprint											
3	½ a. blue-green	3·00	3·25	4·75	4·75	2·50	2·50	1·50	1·50	3·25	3·25	3·25	3·50	3·25	3·50	3·25	3·50
4	1 a. plum	3·25	3·50	4·75	4·75	2·50	2·50	1·50	1·50	3·25	3·25	3·25	3·50	3·25	3·50	3·25	3·50
5	1 a. 6 p. sepia	3·00	3·00	4·75	4·75	2·50	2·50	1·50	1·50	3·00	3·00	3·00	3·00	3·00	3·00	3·00	3·00
6	2 a. pale blue..	3·00	3·00	4·75	4·75	2·50	2·50	1·50	1·50	3·00	3·00	3·00	3·25	3·00	3·00	3·00	3·25
7	2 a. blue	3·50	3·50	6·00	6·00	3·00	2·50	1·75	1·75	3·25	3·25	3·50	3·50	3·50	3·50	3·50	3·50
8	2½ a. yellow-green	3·00	2·75	6·00	6·00	3·25	2·75	1·75	1·75	3·25	3·25	3·50	3·50	3·00	2·75	3·50	3·50
9	3 a. orange	4·25	5·00	8·50	8·50	3·50	3·75	2·50	3·00	3·75	3·75	5·00	6·00	4·25	5·00	5·00	6·00
10	3 a. brown-orange	3·00	4·00	8·50	8·50	2·75	4·00	2·25	2·75	3·50	3·50	3·50	6·00	3·00	4·25	3·50	6·00
11	4 a. olive-green	4·25	4·25	11·00	11·00	4·25	4·25	3·25	3·25	3·50	4·00	6·00	6·00	4·25	4·25	6·00	6·00
12	4 a. slate-green	3·75	4·50	9·50	9·50	3·50	4·25	2·75	3·50	3·50	3·50	5·50	6·00	3·75	4·50	5·00	6·00
13	6 a. pale brown	5·00	6·00	11·00	11·00	4·25	5·00	3·00	3·25	3·75	3·75	6·00	8·50	5·00	6·00	6·00	8·50
14	8 a. dull mauve	8·50	8·50	18·00	18·00	6·00	6·00	5·00	5·00	8·50	8·50	9·50	9·50	9·00	9·00	9·50	9·50
15	8 a. magenta	6·00	6·50	17·00	17·00	4·50	6·00	3·50	4·00	8·50	8·50	8·50	9·50	9·00	9·00	8·50	9·50
16	12 a. purple/*red*	5·50	8·50	17·00	17·00	5·50	6·00	3·50	5·00	8·50	9·50	8·50	9·50	9·00	9·00	8·50	9·50
17	1 r. slate	32·00	32·00	£110	£110	35·00	38·00	27·00	29·00	†		48·00	55·00	32·00	32·00	48·00	55·00
18	1 r. green and carmine ..	8·50	8·50	15·00	15·00	6·50	6·50	4·25	5·00	9·50	9·50	9·50	1100	9·00	9·00	9·50	11·00
19	2 r. carm. & yellow-brown ..	9·00	9·00	†		15·00	15·00	9·00	9·00	†		†		†		†	
20	3 r. brown and green ..	9·00	9·50	†		15·00	15·00	9·00	9·50	†		†		†		†	
21	5 r. ultramarine and violet ..	9·00	9·50	†		15·00	15·00	9·00	9·50	†		†		†		†	

1895–98. PROVISIONALS.

I. *Stamps used for postal purposes.*

(2)

1895 (Dec.). *No.* 5 *surch. with T* **2** *in red.*

22 2½ on 1½ a. sepia .. .. 5·00 5·00
j. "Zanzidar" £160 £160
k. "Zanizbar" £200 £200
l. Inverted "1" in "½" .. £130 £130

(3) (4) (5)

1896 (11 May). *No.* 4 *surch. in black.*

23 **3** 2½ on 1 a. plum .. .. 20·00 14·00
24 **4** 2½ on 1 a. plum .. .. 40·00 28·00
j. Inverted "1" in "½" .. £250
25 **5** 2½ on 1 a. plum .. .. 20·00 14·00

(6) (7) (8)

1896 (15 Aug.). *No.* 6 *surch. in red.*

26 **6** 2½ on 2 a. pale blue .. .. 6·50 6·50
j. Inverted "1" in "½" .. 35·00 35·00
k. Roman "I" in "½" .. 60·00 60·00
27 **7** 2½ on 2 a. pale blue .. .. 20·00 14·00
j. "2¼" for "2½" .. £225
k. "2²" for "2½" .. £225
l. "2⅜" for "2½" .. £225 £225
28 **8** 2½ on 2 a. pale blue £140 £140

No. 28 only exists with small "2".

1896 (15 Nov.). *No.* 5 *surch. in red.*

29 **6** 2½ on 1½ a. sepia .. .. 20·00 14·00
j. Inverted "1" in "½" .. £110 £110
k. Roman "I" in "½" .. £110 £110
30 **7** 2½ on 1½ a. sepia .. .. 48·00
31 **8** 2½ on 1½ a. sepia £325

No. 31 only exists with small "2".

II. *Stamps prepared for official purposes.*

1898 (Jan.). *Nos.* 4, 5, *and* 7 *surch. as before in red.*

32 **3** 2½ on 1 a. plum .. .. 42·00 42·00
33 **4** 2½ on 1 a. plum .. .. 50·00 50·00
34 **5** 2½ on 1 a. plum .. .. 32·00 38·00
35 **3** 2½ on 1½ a. sepia .. .. 14·00 17·00
j. Diaeresis over last "a" .. £120 £120
36 **4** 2½ on 1½ a. sepia .. .. 20·00 24·00
37 **5** 2½ on 1½ a. sepia .. .. 18·00 18·00
38 **3** 2½ on 2 a. dull blue .. .. 12·00 12·00
39 **4** 2½ on 2 a. dull blue .. .. 23·00 23·00
40 **5** 2½ on 2 a. dull blue .. .. 16·00 16·00

It is doubtful whether Nos. 32/40 were issued to the public.

1896. *Stamps of British East Africa, T* **11** *optd. with T* **1**.

41 ½ a. yellow-green (1 June) .. 7·00 6·50
42 1 a. carmine-rose (1 June) .. 7·00 6·50
j. Opt. double .. .. 70·00 55·00
43 2½ a. deep blue (R.) (1 June) .. 16·00 13·00
44 4½ a. orange-yellow (12 Aug.) .. 6·50 6·50
45 5 a. olive-bistre (12 Aug.) .. 7·00 7·00
46 7½ a. mauve (12 Aug.) .. 7·50 7·50
41/46 .. .. *Set of* 6 45·00 42·00

Minor Varieties of the Type

A. First " Z " antique.
B. Broken " p " for " n ".
C. Tall second " z ".
D. Small second " z ".
E. Small second " z " and inverted " q " for " b ".
F. Second " z " Gothic.
G. No dot over " i ".
H. Inverted " q " for " b ".
I. Arabic " 2 " for " r ".

No.		A.	B.	C.	D. or E.	F.	G.	H.	I.
	(a) On Provisionals of 1895–98.								
22	**2** 2½ on 1½ a. (R.)	†	17·00 17·00	8·50 8·50	6·00 6·00	8·50 8·50	†	8·50 8·50	†
23	**3** 2½ on 1 a. (Bk.)	32·00 30·00	†	†	23·00 17·00	†	†	†	†
24	**4** 2½ on 1 a. (Bk.)	†	†	†	42·00 30·00	†	†	†	†
25	**5** 2½ on 1 a. (Bk.)	†	†	— —	23·00 17·00	38·00 32·00	38·00 32·00	†	†
26	**6** 2½ on 2 a. (R.)	†	19·00 19·00	— —	8·50 8·50	14·00 14·00	19·00 19·00	†	14·00 14·00
27	**7** 2½ on 2 a. (R.)	38·00 30·00	†	†	22·00 18·00	†	†	†	†
28	**8** 2½ on 2 a. (R.)	†	†	†	£170 £170	†	†	†	†
29	**6** 2½ on 1½ a. (R.)	†	50·00 42·00	†	22·00 18·00	32·00 24·00	50·00 42·00	†	†
30	**7** 2½ on 1½ a. (R.)	65·00 —	£170 —	†	55·00 —	†	†	†	†
31	**8** 2½ on 1½ a. (R.)	†	†	†	£325 —	†	†	†	†
32	**3** 2½ on 1 a. (R.)	†	— —	†	48·00 —	†	†	†	†
33	**4** 2½ on 1 a. (R.)	†	£120 £120	†	60·00 60·00	†	†	†	†
34	**5** 2½ on 1 a. (R.)	†	†	†	35·00 42·00	†	†	†	†
35	**3** 2½ on 1½ a. (R.)	24·00 26·00	†	†	17·00 19·00	†	38·00 42·00	†	24·00 26·00
36	**4** 2½ on 1½ a. (R.)	†	70·00 70·00	— —	24·00 29·00	†	†	†	†
37	**5** 2½ on 1½ a. (R.)	†	†	†	22·00 22·00	†	55·00 55·00	†	†
38	**3** 2½ on 2 a. (R.)	23·00 23·00	†	†	13·00 13·00	†	32·00 32·00	†	22·00 22·00
39	**4** 2½ on 2 a. (R.)	†	65·00 65·00	†	27·00 27·00	†	†	†	†
40	**5** 2½ on 2 a. (T.)	†	†	— —	18·00 18·00	†	48·00 48·00	†	†
	On British East Africa stamps of 1896.								
41	½ a. yellow-green	17·00 16·00	†	24·00 23·00	8·50 8·00	15·00 14·00	15·00 14·00	*	17·00 16·00
42	1 a. carmine-rose	17·00 16·00	†	24·00 23·00	8·50 8·00	15·00 14·00	15·00 14·00	*	17·00 16·00
43	2½ a. deep blue (R.) ..	32·00 30·00	†	42·00 35·00	18·00 15·00	32·00 29·00	32·00 29·00	*	32·00 29·00
44	4½ a. orange-yellow.. ..	14·00 15·00	20·00 22·00	21·00 22·00	7·00 7·00	13·00 14·00	13·00 14·00	*	13·00 14·00
45	5 a. olive-bistre	17·00 18·00	24·00 26·00	24·00 26·00	8·50 8·50	17·00 18·00	17·00 18·00	*	17·00 18·00
46	7½ a. mauve..	17·00 18·00	24·00 26·00	24·00 26·00	9·00 9·00	17·00 18·00	17·00 18·00	*	17·00 18·00

*On Nos. 41/46 variety H appears on the same stamp that shows variety C.

PRINTERS. All Zanzibar stamps up to Type **37** were printed by De La Rue & Co.

12

13

14. Sultan Seyyid Hamed-bin-Thwain.

18

1896 (20 Sept.). *Recess.* W **12.** P 14. *Flags in red on all values.*

156 **13** ½ a. yellow-green 12 12
157 ,, 1 a. indigo 25 25
158 ,, 1 a. violet-blue 40 25
159 ,, 2 a. red-brown 25 35
160 ,, 2½ a. bright blue 30 25
161 ,, 2½ a. pale blue 40 30
162 ,, 3 a. grey 55 55
163 ,, 3 a. bluish grey 75 75
164 ,, 4 a. myrtle-green .. 60 70
165 ,, 4½ a. orange 65 75
166 ,, 5 a. bistre 75 75
a. Bisected (2½ a.) (on cover) — 90·00
167 ,, 7½ a. mauve 75 75
168 ,, 8 a. grey-olive 65 65
169 **14** 1 r. blue .. .. .. 2·50 3·00
170 ,, 1 r. deep blue .. .. 3·00 3·00
171 ,, 2 r. green .. .. 3·00 3·00
172 **14** 3 r. dull purple .. .. 6·50 5·00
173 ,, 4 r. lake .. .. 6·50 5·50
174 ,, 5 r. sepia .. .. .. 10·00 7·00
156/174 .. .. *Set of* 15 35·00 30·00
156/74 Optd. " Specimen " *Set of* 15 70·00

The ½, 1, 2, 2½ and 8 a. are known without wmk., these being from edges of the sheets.

1897 (5 Jan.). *No. 164 surch. as before, in red.*

175 **3** 2½ on 4 a. myrtle-green .. 6·50 6·50
176 **4** 2½ on 4 a. myrtle-green .. 14·00 14·00
177 **5** 2½ on 4 a. myrtle-green .. 6·50 6·50

1898 (May). *Recess.* W **18.** P 14.

178 **13** ½ a. yellow-green .. 15 15
179 ,, 1 a. indigo 25 15
a. *Greenish black* .. 45 25
180 ,, 2 a. red-brown 30 35
a. *Deep brown* 35 40
181 ,, 2½ a. bright blue .. 30 25
182 ,, 3 a. grey.. .. .. 45 45
183 ,, 4 a. myrtle-green .. 45 50
184 ,, 4½ a. orange 70 40
185 ,, 5 a. bistre 85 70
a. *Pale bistre* .. .. 1·10 80
186 ,, 7½ a. mauve .. .. 1·10 1·10
187 ,, 8 a. grey-olive .. .. 1·25 1·00
178/187 .. .. *Set of* 10 5·00 4·50

19

20. Sultan Seyyid Hamoud-bin-Mahommed bin Said.

1899 (Sept.)–**1901.** *Flags in red.* *Recess.* W **18.** P 14.

188 **19** ½ a. yellow-green .. 12 15
189 ,, 1 a. indigo 30 15
190 ,, 1 a. carmine (1901) .. 25 12
191 ,, 2 a. red-brown 30 20
192 ,, 2½ a. bright blue 30 25
193 ,, 3 a. grey 50 70
194 ,, 4 a. myrtle-green .. 45 65
195 ,, 4½ a. orange .. .. 1·10 1·10
196 ,, 4½ a. blue-black (1901) .. 1·25 1·40
197 ,, 5 a. bistre 80 90
198 ,, 7½ a. mauve .. .. 1·10 1·60
199 ,, 8 a. grey-olive .. .. 95 1·60

W **12.** P 14.

200 **20** 1 r. blue .. .. .. 6·50 6·50
201 ,, 2 r. green .. .. .. 6·50 6·50
202 ,, 3 r. dull purple .. .. 6·50 6·50
203 ,, 4 r. lake .. .. .. 10·00 10·00
204 ,, 5 r. sepia .. .. .. 12·00 12·00
188/204 .. .. *Set of* 17 45·00 45·00
188/204 Optd. "Specimen" *Set of* 17 65·00

One	Two & Half	Two & Half	Two & Half
(21)	(22)	(22a)	(22b)

1904. *Stamps of 1899/1901 surch. as T* **21** *and* **22**, *in black or lake* (L.).

205 **19** 1 on 4½ a. orange .. 70 1·00
206 ,, 1 on 4½ a. blue-black (L.) 2·00 2·50

No.	Type	Description	Unused	Used
207	**19**	2 on 4 a. myrtle-grn. (L.)	6·50	6·50
208	,,	2½ on 7½ a. mauve ..	6·00	6·50
209	,,	2½ on 8 a. grey-olive ..	7·00	8·00
205/209		.. .. *Set of* 5	20·00	22·00

Varieties. Thin, open " w ", *as in T* **22a**.

No.	Description	Unused	Used
209a	2½ on 7½ a. mauve ..	26·00	26·00
	b. Serif to foot of " f " (T 22b) ..	26·00	26·00
	c. " Hlaf " for " Half " ..		
209d	2½ on 8 a. grey-olive ..	35·00	35·00
	e. Serif to foot of " f " (T 22b) ..	35·00	35·00
	f. " Hlaf " for " Half " ..		

23

24

Monogram of Sultan Seyyid Ali bin Hamoud bin Naherud.

1904 (8 June). *Typo.* *W* **18**. *P* 14. *Background of centre in second colour.*

No.	Type	Description	Unused	Used
210	**23**	½ a. green	15	10
211	,,	1 a. rose-red	15	8
212	,,	2 a. brown	40	35
213	,,	2½ a. blue	40	25
214	,,	3 a. grey	50	55
215	,,	4 a. deep green	70	65
216	,,	4½ a. black	1·00	1·00
217	,,	5 a. yellow-brown ..	1·10	1·10
218	,,	7½ a. purple	1·75	1·75
219	,,	8 a. olive-green	1·25	1·25
220	**24**	1 r. blue and red ..	4·00	3·00
221	,,	2 r. green and red ..	5·50	6·00
222	,,	3 r. violet and red ..	13·00	13·00
223	,,	4 r. claret and red ..	15·00	15·00
224	,,	5 r. olive-brown and red	18·00	20·00
210/224		.. .. *Set of* 15	55·00	55·00
210/24 Optd. " Specimen "		*Set of* 15	60·00	

25

26

27. Sultan Ali bin Hamoud.

28. View of Port.

1908 (May)–**09**. *Recess.* *W* **18**. *P* 14.

No.	Type	Description	Unused	Used
225	**25**	1 c. pearl-grey (10.09)	8	8
226	,,	3 c. yellow-green	10	8
227	,,	6 c. rose-carmine ..	15	8
228	,,	10 c. brown (10.09) ..	60	85
229	,,	12 c. violet	50	25
230	**26**	15 c. ultramarine	55	45
231	,,	25 c. sepia	1·00	65
232	,,	50 c. blue-green	1·60	1·40
233	,,	75 c. grey-black (10.09) ..	2·25	2·25
234	**27**	1 r. yellow-green ..	2·75	2·40
235	,,	2 r. violet	6·00	6·00
236	,,	3 r. orange-bistre ..	9·50	9·50
237	,,	4 r. vermilion	13·00	13·00
238	,,	5 r. Antwerp blue ..	15·00	15·00
239	**28**	10 r. bl.-grn. & brn. (S. £15)	45·00	45·00
240	,,	20 r. black & yellow-green (S. £22)	£100	£100
241	,,	30 r. blk. & sepia (S. £30)	£180	£170
242	,,	40 r. black & orange-brown (S. £42)	£450	
243	,,	50 r. blk. & mve. (S. £55)	£400	
244	,,	100 r. black & Antwerp blue (S. £85)	£600	
245	,,	200 r. brown & greenish blue (S. £150)	£950	
225/238		.. .. *Set of* 14	48·00	48·00
225/38 Optd. " Specimen "		*Set of* 14	65·00	

Specimen copies of Nos. 239/45 are all overprinted.

29. Sultan Kalif bin Harub.

30. Native Craft.

31

1913. *Recess.* *W* **18** (*sideways on* 75 *c. and T* **31**). *P* 14.

No.	Type	Description	Unused	Used
246	**29**	1 c. grey	8	8
247	,,	3 c. yellow-green	8	8
248	,,	6 c. rose-carmine ..	8	8
249	,,	10 c. brown	25	25
250	,,	12 c. violet	12	10
251	,,	15 c. blue	25	25
252	,,	25 c. sepia	30	25
253	,,	50 c. blue-green	1·10	85
254	,,	75 c. grey-black	55	50
255	**30**	1 r. yellow-green ..	1·10	1·10
256	,,	2 r. violet	3·50	4·00
257	,,	3 r. orange-bistre ..	5·50	6·00
258	,,	4 r. scarlet	6·00	7·00
259	,,	5 r. Antwerp blue ..	9·50	9·00
260	**31**	10 r. green and brown ..	20·00	17·00
260a	,,	20 r. black & green (S. £14)	55·00	40·00
260b	,,	30 r. black & brown (S. £22)	90·00	80·00
260c	,,	40 r. black & verm. (S. £38)	£180	£170
260d	,,	50 r. black & purple (S. £45)	£190	£180
260e	,,	100 r. black & blue (S. £75)	£300	£225
260f	,,	200 r. brown & black (S. £110)	£650	£550
246/260		.. .. *Set of* 15	45·00	45·00
246/60 Optd. "Specimen"		*Set of* 15	60·00	

Specimen copies of Nos. 260a/f are all overprinted.

1914–22. *Wmk. Mult. Crown CA.* *P* 14.

No.	Type	Description	Unused	Used
261	**29**	1 c. grey	8	10
262	,,	3 c. yellow-green	10	8
		a. *Dull green*	12	8
263	,,	6 c. deep carmine ..	12	8
		a. *Bright rose-carmine* ..	8	8
264	,,	8 c. purple/*pale yell.* ('22)	25	30
265	,,	10 c. myrtle/*pale yell.* ('22)	30	15
266	,,	15 c. deep ultramarine ..	20	40
268	,,	50 c. blue-green	1·60	1·60
269	,,	75 c. grey-black	90	95
270	**30**	1 r. yellow-green	1·25	80
271	,,	2 r. violet	1·60	2·25
272	,,	3 r. orange-bistre ..	3·00	4·00
273	,,	4 r. scarlet	6·50	6·50
274	,,	5 r. Antwerp blue ..	8·00	9·00
275	**31**	10 r. green and brown ..	22·00	22·00
261/275		.. .. *Set of* 14	42·00	45·00
261/75 Optd. " Specimen "		*Set of* 14	65·00	

1921–29. *Wmk. Mult. Script CA.* *P* 14.

No.	Type	Description	Unused	Used
276	**29**	1 c. slate-grey	8	12
277	,,	3 c. yellow-green	10	12
278	,,	3 c. yellow (1922) ..	8	8
279	,,	4 c. green (1922)	20	25
280	,,	6 c. carmine-red	15	15
281	,,	6 c. purple/*blue* (1922) ..	15	8
282	,,	10 c. brown	40	45
283	,,	12 c. violet	20	25
284	,,	12 c. carmine-red (1922) ..	30	20
285	,,	15 c. blue	35	40
286	,,	20 c. indigo (1922) ..	50	30
287	,,	25 c. sepia	50	60
288	,,	50 c. myrtle-green ..	50	55
289	,,	75 c. slate	75	70
290	**30**	1 r. yellow-green	70	80
291	,,	2 r. deep violet	80	1·25
292	,,	3 r. orange-bistre ..	1·50	2·00
293	,,	4 r. scarlet	3·25	4·00
294	,,	5 r. Prussian blue ..	5·00	6·00
295	**31**	10 r. green and brown ..	9·00	9·00
296	,,	20 r. black and green (Optd. S. £22)	65·00	65·00
297	,,	30 r. black and brown ('29) (Perf. S. £24)	95·00	95·00
276/295		.. .. *Set of* 20	22·00	24·00
276/95 Optd. " Specimen "		*Set of* 20	70·00	

32. Sultan Kalif bin Harub. **33.**

1926–27. *T* **32** (" CENTS " *in seriffed capitals*) *Recess.* *Wmk. Mult. Script. CA.* *P* 14.

No.	Type	Description	Unused	Used
299	**32**	1 c. brown	8	8
300	,,	3 c. yellow-orange ..	8	8
301	,,	4 c. deep dull green ..	10	12
302	,,	6 c. violet	8	8
303	,,	8 c. slate	45	60
304	,,	10 c. olive-green	35	12
305	,,	12 c. carmine-red	35	10
306	,,	20 c. bright blue	15	10
307	,,	25 c. purple/*yellow* ('27) ..	60	30
308	,,	50 c. claret	45	35
309	,,	75 c. sepia ('27)	45	1·10
299/309		.. .. *Set of* 11	3·00	2·75
299/309 Optd. "Specimen"		*Set of* 11	50·00	

(*New currency.* 100 *cents* = 1 *shilling.*)

1936 (1 Jan.). *T* **33** (" CENTS " *in sans-serif capitals*), *and T* **30/1**, *but values in shillings* *Recess.* *Wmk. Mult. Script CA.* *P* 14 × 13½–14

No.	Type	Description	Unused	Used
310	**33**	5 c. green	5	5
311	,,	10 c. black	5	5
312	,,	15 c. carmine-red	5	12
313	,,	20 c. orange	5	5
314	,,	25 c. purple/*yellow* ..	5	10
315	,,	30 c. ultramarine	5	8
316	,,	40 c. sepia	8	15
317	,,	50 c. claret	8	5
318	**30**	1s. yellow-green ..	15	12
319	,,	2s. slate-violet	30	3[illegible]
320	,,	5s. scarlet	1·75	1·60
321	,,	7s. 50 light blue ..	3·00	3·25
322	**31**	10s. green and brown ..	2·50	2·50
310/322		.. .. *Set of* 13	7·00	7·50
310/22 Perf. " Specimen "		*Set of* 13	25·00	

36. Sultan Kalif bin Harub.

1936 (9 Dec.). *Silver Jubilee of Sultan.* Recess. *Wmk. Mult. Script CA.* P 14.

No.	Type	Description	Unused	Used
323	**36**	10 c. black and olive-green	20	30
324	,,	20 c. black & bright purple	20	25
325	,,	30 c. black & deep ultram.	20	25
326	,,	50 c. black & orange-verm.	15	30
323/6		Perf. "Specimen" *Set of* 4	24·00	

37. Native Craft.

VICTORY ISSUE
8TH JUNE 1946
(38)

1944 (20 Nov.). *Bicentenary of Al Busaid Dynasty. Recess. Wmk. Mult. Script CA.* P 14.

No.	Type	Description	Unused	Used
327	**37**	10 c. ultramarine	10	12
328	,,	20 c. red	10	12
329	,,	50 c. blue-green	8	10
330	,,	1s. dull purple	10	12
327/30		Perf. "Specimen" *Set of* 4	40·00	

1946 (11 Nov.). *Victory. Optd. with T* **38.**

No.	Type	Description	Unused	Used
331	**33**	10 c. black (R.)	8	8
332	,,	30 c. ultramarine (R.) ..	8	8
331/2		Perf. "Specimen" *Set of* 2	26·00	

1949 (10 Jan.). *Royal Silver Wedding. As Nos.* 30/1 *of Aden.*

No.	Description	Unused	Used
333	20 c. orange	8	10
334	10s. brown	2·00	2·50

1949 (10 Oct.). *75th Anniv. of U.P.U. As Nos.* 114/7 *of Antigua.*

No.	Description	Unused	Used
335	20 c. red-orange	10	12
336	30 c. deep blue	10	15
337	50 c. magenta	12	20
338	1s. blue-green	15	30

39. Sultan Kalif bin Harub.

40. Seyyid Khalifa Schools, Beit-el-Ras.

(Recess. D.L.R.)

1952 (26 Aug.). *Wmk. Mult. Script CA.* P 12½ (*cent values*) *or* 13 (*shilling values*).

No.	Type	Description	Unused	Used
339	**39**	5 c. black	5	5
340	,,	10 c. red-orange	5	5
341	,,	15 c. green (*shades*) ..	5	5
342	,,	20 c. carmine-red ..	5	5
343	,,	25 c. reddish purple ..	5	5
344	,,	30 c. dp. bluish grn. (*shades*)	8	10
345	,,	35 c. bright blue	10	12
346	,,	40 c. deep brown (*shades*)	20	30
347	,,	50 c. violet (*shades*) ..	12	12
348	**40**	1s. dp. green & dp. brown	20	25
349	,,	2s. bt. blue & dp. purple	35	45
350	,,	5s. black & carmine-red	85	1·00
351	,,	7s. 50 c. grey-blk. & emer.	1·75	3·00
352	,,	10s. carmine-red & black	1·90	2·40
399/352		.. .. *Set of* 14	5·00	7·00

41. Sultan Kalif bin Harub.

(Photo. Harrison & Sons.)

1954 (26 Aug.). *Sultan's 75th Birthday. Wmk. Mult. Script CA. Chalk-surfaced paper.* P 13×12.

No.	Type	Description	Unused	Used
353	**41**	15 c. deep green	10	10
354	,,	20 c. rose-red	12	12
355	,,	30 c. bright blue	15	20
356	,,	50 c. purple	25	25
357	,,	1s. 25 c. orange-red ..	50	70
353/357		.. .. *Set of* 5	1·00	1·25

42. Cloves.

43. Dhows.

44. Sultan's Barge. **46.** Minaret Mosque.

45. Map of East African Coast. **47.** Dimbani Mosque.

48. Kibweni Palace. **49.** Sultan Seyyid Sir Abdulla bin Khalifa.

(Des. W. J. Jennings (T **42**), A. Farhan (T **43**), Mrs. M. Broadbent (T **44**, **46**), R. A. Sweet (T **45**), A. S. B. New (T **47**), B. J. Woolley (T **48**). Recess. Bradbury, Wilkinson & Co.)

1957 (26 Aug.). *W* **w.12.** P 11½ (5 *c.*, 10 *c.*), 11×11½ (15 *c.*, 30 *c.*, 1*s.* 25), 14×13½ (20 *c.*, 25 *c.*, 35 *c.*, 50 *c.*), 13½×14 (40 *c.*, 1*s.*, 2*s.*) *or* 13×13½ (5*s.*, 7*s.* 50, 10*s.*).

No.	Type	Description	Unused	Used
358	**42**	5 c. orange & deep green	5	5
359	,,	10 c. emerald & carm.-red	5	5
360	**43**	15 c. green and sepia ..	5	5
361	**44**	20 c. ultramarine	5	5
362	**45**	25 c. orange-brn. & black	5	5
363	**43**	30 c. carmine-red & black	8	5
364	**45**	35 c. slate and emerald ..	8	8
365	**46**	40 c. brown and black ..	12	12
366	**45**	50 c. blue and grey-green ..	12	10
367	**47**	1s. carmine and black ..	20	15
368	**43**	1s. 25, slate and carmine	25	20
369	**47**	2s. orange & deep green	35	30
370	**48**	5s. deep bright blue ..	70	75
371	,,	7s. 50, green	1·25	1·60
372	,,	10s. carmine	1·60	1·40
358/372		.. .. *Set of* 15	4·50	4·50

(Recess. Bradbury, Wilkinson.)

1961 (17 Oct.). *As T* **42/8** *but with portrait of Sultan Sir Abdulla as in T* **49.** *W* **w.12.** P 13×13½ (20*s.*), *others as before.*

No.	Type	Description	Unused	Used
373	**49**	5 c. orange & deep green	5	5
374	,,	10 c. emer. & carmine-red	5	5
375	**43**	15 c. green and sepia ..	5	5
376	**44**	20 c. ultramarine	5	5
377	**45**	25 c. orge.-brown & black	5	5
378	**43**	30 c. carmine-red & black	8	8
379	**45**	35 c. slate and emerald ..	8	8
380	**46**	40 c. brown and black ..	10	8
381	**45**	50 c. blue and grey-green	12	10
382	**47**	1s. carmine and black ..	20	15
383	**43**	1s. 25, slate and carmine	25	20
384	**47**	2s. orange & deep green	35	30
385	**48**	5s. deep bright blue ..	70	55
386	,,	7s. 50, green	1·40	1·60
387	,,	10s. carmine	1·50	1·75
388	,,	20s. sepia	3·50	3·75
373/388		.. .. *Set of* 16	8·00	8·00

50. "Protein Foods".

(Des. M. Goaman. Photo. Harrison.)

1963 (4 June). *Freedom from Hunger.* *W* w.**12**. *P* 14×14½.

389	**50**	1s. 30, sepia	25	30

II. INDEPENDENT.

51. Zanzibar Clove.

52. " To Prosperity " (Zanzibar doorway).

53. " Religious Tolerance " (mosques and churches).

54. " Towards the Light " (Mangapwani Cave).

(Photo. Harrison.)

1963 (10 Dec.). *Independence. Portrait of Sultan Seyyid Jamshid bin Abdulla.* *P* 12½.

390	**51**	30 c. multicoloured ..	5	5
391	**52**	50 c. multicoloured ..	10	10
392	**53**	1s. 30, multicoloured ..	15	30
393	**54**	2s. 50, multicoloured ..	35	60

III. REPUBLIC.

When the Post Office opened on 14 Jan. 1964, after the revolution deposing the Sultan, the stamps on sale had the portrait cancelled by a manuscript cross. Stamps thus cancelled on cover or piece used between Jan. 14 and 17 are therefore of interest.

JAMHURI 1964

(**55**=" Republic ".)

1964 (17 Jan.). *Locally handstamped as T* **55** *in black.* (*i*) *Nos.* 373/88.

394	**49**	5 c. orange & deep green	5	5
395	„	10 c. emer. & carmine-red	5	5
396	**43**	15 c. green and sepia ..	5	5
397	**44**	20 c. ultramarine	8	8
398	**45**	25 c. orange-brown & black	8	8
399	**43**	30 c. carmine-red & black	10	10
400	**45**	35 c. slate and emerald ..	12	12
401	**46**	40 c. brown and black ..	12	12
402	**45**	50 c. blue and grey-green ..	12	12
403	**47**	1s. carmine and black ..	15	15
404	**43**	1s. 25, slate and carmine	20	15
405	**47**	2s. orange & deep green	30	30
406	**48**	5s. deep bright blue ..	60	70
407	„	7s. 50, green	90	1·00
408	„	10s. carmine	1·25	1·40
409	„	20s. sepia	2·40	2·50
		(*ii*) *Nos.* 390/3 (*Independence*).		
410	**51**	30 c. multicoloured ..	8	8
411	**52**	50 c. multicoloured ..	12	12
412	**53**	1s. 30, multicoloured ..	20	20
413	**54**	2s. 50, multicoloured ..	30	35
394/413		.. .. *Set of* 20	6·50	7·00

T **55** occurs in various positions—diagonally, horizontally or vertically.

NOTE. Nos. 394 to 413 are the only stamps officially authorised to receive the handstamp, but it has also been seen on No. 389 and the Postage Dues. There are numerous errors but it is impossible to distinguish between cases of genuine oversight and those made deliberately at the request of purchasers.

JAMHURI 1964 (**56**)

JAMHURI 1964 (**57**)

1964 (28 Feb.). *Optd. by Bradbury, Wilkinson.* (i) *As T* **56** *on Nos.* 373/88.

414	**49**	5 c. orange & deep green	5	5
415	„	10 c. emerald & carm.-red	5	5
416	**43**	15 c. green and sepia ..	5	5
417	**44**	20 c. ultramarine ..	5	5
418	**45**	25 c. orange-brown & black	8	8
419	**43**	30 c. carmine-red & black	8	8
420	**45**	35 c. slate and emerald ..	8	8
421	**46**	40 c. brown and black ..	10	12
422	**45**	50 c. blue and grey-green ..	10	10
423	**47**	1s. carmine and black ..	12	15
424	**43**	1s. 25, slate and carmine	15	15
425	**47**	2s. orange and dp. green	25	30
426	**48**	5s. deep bright blue ..	60	70
427	„	7s. 50, green	90	1·00
428	„	10s. carmine	1·25	1·40
429	„	20s. sepia	2·40	2·50

The opt. T **56** is set in two lines on Types **46/8**.

(ii) *As T* **57** *on Nos.* 390/3 (*Independence*).

430	**51**	30 c. multicoloured ..	5	8
431	**52**	50 c. multicoloured ..	8	10
432	**53**	1s. 30, multicoloured ..	15	20
433	**54**	2s. 50, multicoloured ..	30	35
414/433		.. .. *Set of* 20	6·00	7·00

The opt. T **57** is set in one line on No. 432.

For the set inscribed " UNITED REPUBLIC OF TANGANYIKA & ZANZIBAR " see Nos. 124/7 of Tanganyika.

58. Axe, Spear and dagger. **59.** Zanzibari with Rifle.

(Litho. German Bank Note Ptg. Co., Leipzig.)

1964 (21 June). *T* **58/9** *and similar design inscr.* " JAMHURI ZANZIBAR 1964 ". *Multi coloured.* *P* 13×13½ (*vert.*) *or* 13½×13 (*horiz.*)

434	5 c. Type **58**	5	
435	10 c. Bow and arrow breaking chains	5	
436	15 c. Type **58**	5	
437	20 c. As 10 c.	5	
438	25 c. Type **59**	8	
439	30 c. Zanzibari breaking manacles	8	
440	40 c. Type **59**	10	1
441	50 c. As 30 c.	12	1
442	1s. Zanzibari, flag and Sun	15	1
443	1s. 30, Hands breaking chains (*horiz.*)	20	2
444	2s. Hand waving flag (*horiz.*)	25	3
445	5s. Map of Zanzibar and Pemba on flag (*horiz.*) ..	60	7
446	10s. Flag on map	1·25	1·4
447	20s. National flag (*horiz.*) ..	2·40	2·5
434/447	.. .. *Set of* 14	5·00	5·2

68. Soldier and Maps.

69. Building Construction.

(Litho. German Bank Note Ptg. Co., Leipzig

1965 (12 Jan.). *First Anniv. of Revolution* *P* 13×13½ (*vert.*) *or* 13½×13 (*horiz.*).

448	**68**	20 c. apple-grn. & dp. grn.	5	
449	**69**	30 c. chocolate and yellow-orange	5	
450	**68**	1s. 30, light blue and ultramarine	15	2
451	**69**	2s. 50, reddish violet and rose	30	3

70. Planting Rice.

71. Hands holding Rice.

(Litho. German Bank Note Ptg. Co., Leipzig.)

1965 (17 Oct.). *Agricultural Development. P* 13×12½.

No.	Type	Description	Unused	Used
452	**70**	20 c. sepia and blue ..	5	5
453	**71**	30 c. sepia and magenta ..	5	5
454	,,	1s. 30, sepia & yell.-orge	15	20
455	**70**	2s. 50, sepia and emerald	30	35

72. Ship, Tractor, Factory, and Open Book and Torch.

73. Soldier.

(Litho. German Bank Note Ptg. Co., Leipzig.)

1966 (12 Jan.). *2nd Anniv. of Revolution. P* 12½×13.

No.	Type	Description	Unused	Used
456	**72**	20 c. multicoloured ..	5	5
457	**73**	50 c. multicoloured ..	8	8
458	**72**	1s. 30, multicoloured	15	20
459	**73**	2s. 50, multicoloured ..	30	35

For stamps with similar inscription or inscribed "TANZANIA" only, and with commemorative date 26th April, 1966, see Nos. Z1/4 of TANZANIA.

74. Tree-felling.

75. Clove Cultivation. (*Horiz.*)

76. Chair-making. (*Horiz.*)

77. Lumumba College. (*Horiz.*)

78. Agriculture (*Horiz.*)

79. Agricultural Workers. (*Horiz.*)

80. Zanzibar Street.

(Litho. German Bank Note Ptg. Co., Leipzig.)

1966 (5 June). *P* 12½×13 (50 *c.*, 10*s.*) *or* 13×12½ (*others*).

No.	Type	Description	Unused	Used
460	**74**	5 c. maroon & yell.-olive	5	5
461	**75**	10 c. brown-purple and bright emerald ..	5	5
462	**76**	15 c. brn.-pur. & lt. blue	5	5
463	**77**	20 c. ultram. & lt. orange	5	5
464	**78**	25 c. maroon & orge.-yell.	5	5
465	**79**	30 c. maroon & ochre-yell.	5	5
466	**76**	40 c. purple-brown & rose-pink	5	5
467	**80**	50 c. green & pale greenish yellow	8	8
468	**75**	1s. maroon and brt. blue	12	15
469	**78**	1s. 30, maroon and turq.	15	20
470	**79**	2s. brown purple & light blue-green	25	30
471	**77**	5s. rose-red and pale blue	60	70
472	**80**	10s. crimson and pale yell.	1·25	1·40
473	**74**	20s. deep purple-brown & magenta	2·40	2·50
460/473		.. .. *Set of* 14	4·50	4·75

81. " Education ".

(Litho. De La Rue.)

1966 (25 Sept.). *Introduction of Free Education. P* 13½×13.

No.	Type	Description	Unused	Used
474	**81**	50 c. black, light blue and orange	8	8
475	,,	1s. 30, black, light blue and yellow-green ..	15	25
476	,,	2s. 50, black, light blue and pink	30	50

82. A.S.P. Flag.

83. Vice-President M. A. Karume of Tanzania, Flag and Crowd. (*Vert.*)

(Litho. De La Rue.)

1967 (5 Feb.). *Tenth Anniv. of Afro-Shirazi Party* (*A.S.P.*). *P* 14.

No.	Type	Description	Unused	Used
477	**82**	30 c. multicoloured	5	5
478	**83**	50 c. multicoloured	8	8
479	,,	1s. 30, multicoloured ..	20	30
480	**82**	2s. 50, multicoloured ..	35	45

84. Workers.

(Photo. Delrieu.)

1967 (20 Aug.). *Voluntary Workers Brigade. P* 12½×12.

No.	Type	Description	Unused	Used
481	**84**	1s. 30, multicoloured ..	15	20
482	,,	2s. 50, multicoloured ..	30	35

NOTE. Stamps inscribed "UGANDA KENYA TANGANYIKA & ZANZIBAR (or TANZANIA UGANDA KENYA ") will be found listed under East Africa.

POSTAGE DUE STAMPS.

Insufficiently prepaid.
Postage due.
1 cent.

D 1

(Types **D 1** and **D 2** typo. by the Government Printer.)

1930–33.

(*a*) *Rouletted* 10, *with imperf. sheet edges. No gum.*

No.	Type	Description	Unused	Used
D 1	**D 1**	1 c. black/*orange* ..	60	
D 2	,,	2 c. black/*orange* ..	60	
D 3	,,	3 c. black/*orange* ..	60	
		a. " cent.s " for " cents." ..	3·50	
D 4	,,	6 c. black/*orange* ..		
		a. " cent.s " for " cents." ..		
D 5	,,	9 c. black/*orange* ..	60	
		a. " cent.s " for " cents." ..	3·50	4·00
D 6	,,	12 c. black/*orange* ..		
		a. " cent.s " for " cents." ..		
D 7	,,	12 c. black/*green*	25·00	14·00
		a. " cent.s " for " cents."	£225	£100
D 8	,,	15 c. black/*orange* ..	60	70
		a. " cent.s " for " cents." ..	3·50	4·00
D 9	,,	18 c. black/*salmon* ..	2·50	2·75
		a. " cent.s " for " cents." ..	14·00	19·00
D10	,,	18 c. black/*orange* ..	1·00	1·40
		a. " cent.s " for " cents." ..	7·00	8·00
D11	,,	20 c. black/*orange* ..	1·00	1·40
		a. " cent.s " for " cents." ..	7·00	9·00
D12	,,	21 c. black/*orange* ..	1·00	1·40
		a. " cent.s " for " cents." ..	7·00	8·00
D13	,,	25 c. black/*magenta* ..	£150	£150
		a. " cent.s " for " cents." ..		
D14	,,	25 c. black/*orange* ..		
D15	,,	31 c. black/*orange* ..	2·25	
		a. " cent.s " for " cents."	12·00	
D16	,,	50 c. black/*orange* ..	6·00	
		a. " cent.s " for " cents." ..	20·00	
D17	,,	75 c. black/*orange* ..	12·00	
		a " cent.s " for " cents." ..	40·00	

Sheets of the first printings of all values except the 1 c. and 2 c. contained one stamp showing the error " cent.s " for " cents."

Insufficiently prepaid
Postage due.
6 cents.

D 2

(*b*) *Rouletted* 5. *No gum.*

No.	Type	Description	Unused	Used
D18	**D 2**	2 c. black/*salmon* ..	50	1·00
D19	,,	3 c. black/*rose*	60	1·25
D21	,,	6 c. black/*yellow* ..	70	1·50
D22	,,	12 c. black/*blue*	95	1·50
D23	,,	25 c. black/*rose*	2·50	3·00
D24	,,	25 c. black/*lilac*	1·50	3·00

D 3

(Typo. De La Rue & Co.)

1936 (1 Jan.)–**62.** *Wmk. Mult. Script CA. P* 14.

No.	Type	Description	Unused	Used
D25	**D 3**	5 c. violet, O	12	12
		a. Chalky paper (18.7.56)	12	12
D26	,,	10 c. scarlet, O ..	12	12
		a Chalky paper (6.3.62) ..	12	12
D27	,,	20 c. green, O	12	12
		a. Chalky paper (6.3.62) ..	12	12
D28	,,	30 c. brown, O ..	20	20
		a. Chalky paper (18.7.56)	12	12

D29 D **3** 40 c. ultramarine, O .. 20 25
a. Chalky paper (18.7.56).. 12 12
D30 ,, 1s. grey, O 35 45
a. Chalky paper (18.7.56) .. 30 30
D25a/D30a .. *Set of* 6 80 80
D25/30 Perf. "Specimen" *Set of* 6 20·00

See footnote after No. 413.

All Zanzibar issues were withdrawn on 1 January 1968 and replaced by Tanzania issues. Zanzibar stamps remained valid for postage in Zanzibar for a limited period.

ZULULAND.

ZULULAND (1) **ZULULAND.** (2)

1888–93. *Stamps of Great Britain optd. with T* **1**.
1 **71** ½d. vermilion .. .. 2·00 2·50
2 **57** 1d. deep purple .. .. 5·00 5·00
3 **73** 2d. green and carmine .. 7·00 8·00
4 **74** 2½d. purple/*blue* .. .. 8·00 9·00
5 **75** 3d. purple/*yellow* .. .. 10·00 12·00
6 **76** 4d. green and brown .. 11·00 13·00
7 **78** 5d. dull purple & blue ('93) 25·00 25·00
8 **79** 6d. purple/*rose-red* .. 14·00 14·00
9 **80** 9d. dull purple and blue .. 35·00 35·00
10 **82** 1s. green .. .. .. 50·00 55·00
11 **59** 5s. rose £130 £140
1/11 .. .. *Set of* 11 £275 £300
1 and 3/11 H/S "Specimen"
Set of 10 £200

No. 97a of Natal optd. with T **2**.
12 **23** ½d. green .. .. .. 9·00 11·00
a. Opt. double £350
b. Opt. inverted £400
c. Without stop .. .. 20·00 24·00
d. Opt. omtd. (pr. with normal) £900 £950

1894 (Jan.). *No. 103 of Natal optd. with T* **1**.
16 **15** 6d. mauve .. .. .. 22·00 22·00

3

4

(Typo. D.L.R.)

1894–96. *Wmk. Crown CA. P* 14.
20 **3** ½d. dull mauve and green .. 1·25 1·2
21 ,, 1d. dull mauve and carmine 3·50 1·0
22 ,, 2½d. dull mauve and ultram. 6·00 6·0
23 ,, 3d. dull mauve & olive-brn. 8·00 3·5
24 **4** 6d. dull mauve and black .. 8·00 9·0
25 ,, 1s. green .. .. .. 11·00 13·0
26 ,, 2s. 6d. green and black .. 30·00 30·0
27 ,, 4s. green and carmine .. 40·00 50·0
28 ,, £1 purple/*red* £160 £18
29 ,, £5 purple & blk./*red* (Optd. S. £100) £1500 £55
20/28 .. .. *Set of* 9 £250 £27
20/8 Optd. "Specimen" *Set of* 9 £100

Dangerous forgeries exist of the £1 and £5.

FISCAL STAMPS USED FOR POSTAGE.

Fiscal stamps of Natal (*Type F* **1**, *name and valu in second colour, wmk. Crown CA, P* 14) *optd with T* **1**.
F1 1d. dull mauve (Optd. S. £40) 2·00 3·0
F2 1s. mauve and carmine .. 80·00 £10
F3 5s. mauve and carmine .. £140 £17
F4 9s. mauve and carmine .. £190 £25
F5 £1 green £400 £37
F6 £5 green and red £2500 £150
F7 £20 green and black £4500

The issue of Zululand stamps ceased on 3 June, 1898, the territory having been annexe to Natal on 31 December, 1897.

SET PRICES FOR BRITISH COMMONWEALTH OMNIBUS ISSUES.

The composition of these sets is in accordance with the table on the following page. Perforation varieties and miniature sheets are excluded but where Great Britain stamps exist ordinary and phosphor, both are included

Stamps issued in connection with any of the events by countries which are no longer in the British Commonwealth and which are not listed in the British Commonwealth Catalogue are excluded.

			No. of stamps	Price Un.	Used
1935	Silver Jubilee	Complete	250	£275	£300
1937	Coronation	Complete	202	26·00	28·00
1945–46	Victory..	Complete	164	11·00	12·00
1948–49	Silver Wedding	Complete	138	£300	£400
1949	U.P.U.	Complete	314	80·00	£100
1951	B.W.I. University College	Complete	28	4·50	4·50
1953	Coronation	Complete	106	32·00	42·00
1953–54	Royal Visit	Complete	13	2·25	2·50
1958	Caribbean Fed.	Complete	30	4·50	5·00
1963	Freedom from Hunger	Complete	76	65·00	60·00
1963	Red Cross	Complete	106	90·00	90·00
1964	Shakespeare	Complete	25	30·00	28·00
1965	I.T.U.	Complete	110	42·00	42·00
1965	I.C.Y.	Complete	100	26·00	26·00
1965–67	Churchill	Complete	172	65·00	70·00
1966	Royal Visit	Complete	34	7·00	7·50
1966	Football Cup	Complete	66	15·00	15·00
1966	W.H.O...	Complete	56	14·00	15·00
1966–67	U.N.E.S.C.O.	Complete	101	32·00	35·00
1972	Silver Wedding	Complete	78	34·00	40·00
1973	Royal Wedding. 72 stamps and 6 miniature sheets for Antigua, Cook Is., Aitutaki, Dominica, Grenada and Grenadines of Grenada	Complete	76	40·00	44·00

OMNIBUS ISSUES

Issuing Countries	1935 Silver Jubilee	1937 Coronation	1945–46 Victory	1948 Silver Wedding	1949 U.P.U.	1951 B.W.I. Univ.	1953 Coronation	1953–54 Royal Visit	1958 Caribbean Fed.	1963 F.F.H.	1963 Red Cross	1964 Shakespeare	1965 I.T.U.	1965 I.C.Y.	1965–66 Churchill	1966 Royal Visit	1966 Football Cup	1966 W.H.O.	1966–67 UNESCO	1972 Silver Wedding	1973 Royal Wedding
Great Britain	4	1	2	2	4	..	4	..	..	2+2	3+3	5+4	2+2	2+2	2+2	..	3+3	..	..	2	2
Guernsey & Jersey	..	..	..	..	..	..	..	..	..	..	..	..	..	..	..	..	..	..	..	4+4	1+2
Isle of Man	..	..	..	..	..	..	..	..	..	..	..	..	..	..	..	..	..	..	..	..	1
Aden/S. Arabian Fed.	..	3	2	2	4	..	1	1	..	1	2	..	..	2	4	..	2	2	3	..	..
Seiyun	..	..	2	2	4	..	1	..	..	..	..	..	7	..	1	..	7	..	..	..	..
Shihr & Mukalla	..	..	2	2	4	..	1	..	..	..	..	..	..	8	3	..	8	..	..	..	..
Anguilla	..	..	..	..	..	..	..	..	..	..	..	..	..	..	..	..	..	..	..	2	2
Antigua	4	3	2	2	4	2	1	..	3	1	2	1	2	2	4	2	2	2	3	2	2
Barbuda	..	..	..	..	..	..	..	..	..	..	..	..	..	..	..	..	..	..	..	..	2
Ascension	4	3	2	2	4	..	1	..	..	1	2	..	2	2	4	..	2	2	3	2	2
Australia	3	..	3	..	1	..	3	3	..	..	1	..	1	1	1	..	..	..	..	..	..
Bahamas	4	3	2	2	4	..	1	..	..	1	2	1	2	2	4	2	2	2	3	2	..
Bahrain	..	..	..	2	4	..	4	..	..	..	..	..	..	..	..	..	..	..	..	..	..
Barbados	4	3	2	2	4	2	1	..	3	..	..	..	2	..	4	2	..	..	3	..	..
Basutoland/Lesotho	4	3	3×2	2	4	..	1	..	..	1	2	..	2	2	4	..	..	..	4	..	..
Bechuanaland	4	3	3×2	2	4	..	1	..	..	1	2	1	2	2	4	..	..	..	..	..	..
Bermuda	4	3	2	2	4	..	1	1	..	1	2	..	2	2	4	..	2	..	3	2	2
Br. Antarctic Terr.	..	..	..	..	..	..	..	..	..	..	..	..	..	..	4	..	..	..	..	2	2
Br. Forces in Egypt	1	..	..	..	..	..	..	..	..	..	..	..	..	..	..	..	..	..	..	..	..
Br. Guiana	4	3	2	2	4	2	1	..	..	1	2	..	2	2	2	2	..	..	..	..	..
Br. Honduras/Belize	4	3	2	2	4	2	1	..	..	1	2	..	2	2	4	..	..	..	..	2	2
B.I.O.T.	..	..	..	..	..	..	..	..	..	..	..	..	..	..	..	..	..	..	..	2	..
Br. P.A's in E. Arabia	..	..	..	2	4	..	4	..	..	..	..	..	..	..	..	..	..	..	..	..	..
Br. Solomon Is.	4	3	2	2	4	..	1	..	..	1	2	..	2	2	4	..	2	2	3	2	2
Brunei	..	..	..	..	4	..	..	..	..	1	..	..	2	2	4	..	2	2	3	2	2
Burma	..	..	4	..	..	..	..	..	..	..	..	..	..	..	..	..	..	..	..	..	..
Canada	6	1	..	..	..	..	1	..	..	..	..	..	..	1	1	..	..	..	..	..	..
Cayman Is.	4	3	2	2	4	..	1	..	..	1	2	1	2	2	4	2	2	2	3	2	2
Ceylon/Sri Lanka	4	3	2	..	3	..	1	1	..	2	..	..	2	2	..	..	..	2	2	..	..
Cook Is.	3	3	4	..	..	..	2	..	..	..	..	..	..	..	6	..	..	..	..	4	3
Aitutaki	..	..	..	..	..	..	..	..	..	..	..	..	..	..	..	..	..	..	..	2	2
Penrhyn Is.	..	..	..	..	..	..	..	..	..	..	..	..	..	..	..	..	..	..	..	..	3
Cyprus	4	3	2	2	4	..	1	..	..	2	2	4	3	2	..	..	..	..	1	..	..
Dominica	4	3	2	2	4	2	1	..	3	1	2	1	2	2	4	2	2	2	3	2	2
Falkland Islands	4	3	2	2	4	..	1	..	..	1	2	1	2	2	4	..	..	..	..	2	2
Falkland Is. Dep.	..	..	2	2	4	..	1	..	..	..	..	..	..	..	..	..	..	..	..	..	..
South Georgia	..	..	..	..	..	..	..	..	..	..	..	..	..	..	..	..	..	..	..	2	2
Fiji	4	3	2	2	4	..	1	1	..	1	2	..	2	2	4	..	2	2	..	2	..
Gambia	4	3	2	2	4	..	1	..	..	1	2	1	2	..	3	..	..	..	..	..	..
Gibraltar	4	3	2	2	4	..	1	1	..	1	2	1	2	2	4	..	2	2	3	2	2
Gilbert & Ellice Is.	4	3	2	2	4	..	1	..	..	1	2	..	2	2	4	..	2	2	3	2	2
Gold Coast/Ghana	4	3	2	2	4	..	1	..	..	3	4	..	4	4	..	..	5	4	5	..	..
Grenada	4	3	2	2	4	2	1	..	3	1	2	..	2	2	4	2	2	2	3	2	2
Grenadines	..	..	..	..	..	..	..	..	..	..	..	..	..	..	..	..	..	..	..	..	2
Hong Kong	4	3	2	2	4	..	1	..	..	1	2	..	2	2	4	..	..	2	3	2	2
India	7	..	4	..	4	..	..	..	..	1	1	..	1	1	..	..	..	..	..	..	..
Hyderabad	..	..	1	..	..	..	..	..	..	..	..	..	..	..	..	..	..	..	..	..	..
Ireland	..	..	..	..	..	..	..	..	..	2	2	..	2	2	..	..	..	..	..	..	..
Jamaica	4	3	2	2	4	2	1	1	3	2	2	..	1	..	2	4	..	..	..	..	..
K.U.T./East Africa	4	3	2	2	4	..	1	1	..	4	2	..	4	4	..	..	..	..	4	..	..
Kuwait	..	..	..	2	4	..	4	..	..	..	..	..	..	..	..	..	..	..	..	..	..
Leeward Is.	4	3	2	2	4	2	1	..	..	..	..	..	..	..	..	..	..	..	..	..	..
Malayan States, etc.	4	3	..	22	44	..	11	..	..	3	..	..	3	..	..	..	..	..	..	..	..
Maldive Is.	..	..	..	..	..	..	..	..	..	7	5	..	..	..	..	..	..	..	..	..	..
Malta	4	3	2	2	4	..	1	1	..	1	2	..	..	..	4	..	..	..	..	..	..
Mauritius	4	3	2	2	4	..	1	..	..	1	2	..	2	2	4	..	..	..	3	..	..
Montserrat	4	3	2	2	4	2	1	..	3	1	2	1	2	2	4	2	..	2	3	2	2
Morocco/Tangier	15	3	2	4	4	..	4	..	..	..	..	..	..	..	..	..	..	..	..	..	..
Nauru	4	4	..	..	..	..	..	..	..	..	..	..	..	..	..	..	..	..	..	..	..
Newfoundland	4	14	..	..	..	..	..	..	..	..	..	..	..	..	..	..	..	..	..	..	..
New Guinea	2	4	..	..	..	..	..	..	..	..	..	..	..	..	..	..	..	..	..	..	..
New Hebrides	..	..	..	..	4	..	1	..	..	1	2	..	2	2	4	..	2	2	3	2	..
New Zealand	3	3	11	..	..	..	5	2	..	..	..	..	1	1	1	..	..	..	..	..	..
Niue	3	3	4	..	..	..	2	..	..	..	..	..	..	..	..	..	..	..	..	..	..
Tokelau Is.	..	..	..	..	..	..	1	..	..	..	..	..	..	..	..	..	..	..	..	..	..
Nigeria	4	3	2	2	4	..	1	..	..	2	3	..	3	3	..	..	..	..	3	..	..
North Borneo	..	..	..	2	4	..	1	..	..	1	..	..	..	..	..	..	..	..	..	..	..
N. Rhodesia/Zambia	4	3	2	2	4	..	1	..	..	..	..	..	2	2	..	..	..	2	..	..	..
Nyasaland	4	3	2	2	4	..	1	..	..	..	..	..	..	..	..	..	..	..	..	..	..
Pakistan	..	..	..	..	..	..	..	..	..	2	1	..	1	2	..	..	..	..	1	..	..
Bahawalpur Post.	..	..	..	..	4+4	..	..	..	..	..	..	..	..	..	..	..	..	..	..	..	..
,, Official	..	..	1	..	4+4	..	..	..	..	..	..	..	..	..	..	..	..	..	..	..	..
Papua/P.N.G.	4	4	..	..	..	..	..	..	..	..	1	..	..	..	..	..	..	..	..	..	..
Pitcairn Is.	..	..	2	2	4	..	1	..	..	1	2	..	2	2	4	..	2	2	3	2	2
St. Christopher, etc.	4	3	2	2	4	2	1	..	3	..	2	..	2	2	4	2	2	2	3	2	2
St. Helena	4	3	2	2	4	..	1	..	..	1	2	..	2	2	4	..	2	2	3	2	2
St. Lucia	4	3	2	2	4	2	1	..	3	1	2	1	2	2	4	2	2	2	3	2	2
St. Vincent	4	3	2	2	4	2	1	..	3	1	2	..	2	..	4	2	..	2	3	2	2
Grenadines	..	..	..	..	..	..	..	..	..	..	..	..	..	..	..	..	..	..	..	..	2
Samoa	3	..	4	..	..	..	2	..	..	..	..	..	..	..	..	..	..	4	..	..	..
Sarawak	..	..	..	2	4	..	1	..	..	1	..	..	..	..	..	..	..	..	..	..	..
Seychelles	4	3	2	2	4	..	1	..	..	1	2	..	2	2	4	..	2	2	3	2	2
Sierra Leone	4	3	2	2	4	..	1	..	..	2	3	..	..	..	11	..	..	..	..	..	..
Singapore	..	..	..	2	4	..	1	..	..	..	..	..	..	..	..	..	..	..	..	..	..
Somaliland Prot.	4	3	2	2	4	..	1	..	..	..	..	..	..	..	..	..	..	..	..	..	..
South Africa	4×2	5×2	3×2	1×2	3×2	..	1	..	..	..	2	..	2	..	..	..	..	..	..	..	..
South West Africa	4	8×2	3×2	1×2	3×2	..	5	..	..	..	2	..	..	..	..	..	..	..	..	..	..
S. Rhodesia/Rhodesia	4	4	4	..	2	..	1	..	..	..	1	..	3	..	1	..	..	..	..	..	..
Swaziland	4	3	3×2	2	4	..	1	..	..	1	2	..	2	2	4	..	..	..	3	..	..
Tonga	..	..	..	..	4	..	..	..	..	1	2	..	..	..	..	..	..	..	..	..	..
Trinidad & Tobago	4	3	2	2	4	2	1	..	3	3	..	..	..	1	..	4	..	..	..	..	..
Tristan da Cunha	..	..	..	..	..	..	1	..	..	1	2	..	2	2	4	..	2	2	3	2	2
Turks & Caicos Is.	4	3	2	2	4	..	1	..	..	1	2	1	2	2	4	2	..	..	3	2	2
Virgin Is.	4	3	2	2	4	2	1	..	..	1	2	1	2	2	4	2	..	..	3	2	2
Zanzibar	..	..	2	2	4	..	..	..	..	1	..	..	..	..	..	..	..	..	..	..	..
Total number of stamps	250	202	164	138	314	28	106	13	30	76	106	25	110	100	172	34	66	56	101	76	72

APPENDIX.

In accordance with our policy of not stocking the commemorative issues of certain countries which issue an excessive number of stamps in relation to their postal needs, we give below the particulars of stamps issued under the authority of the rulers of the Aden States up to the time when their territories were occupied by the National Liberation Front.

We do not quote selling prices but instead give in brackets the sterling equivalent of the face value at the time of issue.

ADEN.

KATHIRI STATE OF SEIYUN.

1967. *Hunting.* 20 f. (*Face value* 5p.).
1967. *Olympic Games, Grenoble.* *Postage* 10, 25, 35, 50, 75 f.; *Air* 100, 200 f. (55p.).
1967. *Scout Jamboree, Idaho.* *Air.* 150 f. (15p.).
1967. *Paintings—Renoir.* *Postage* 10, 35, 50, 65, 75 f.; *Air* 100, 200, 250 f. (80p.).
1967. *Paintings—Toulouse-Lautrec.* *Postage* 10, 35, 50, 65, 75 f.; *Air* 100, 200, 250 f. (80p.).

Stated to have been occupied by the N.L.F. on 1st October, 1967.

QU'AITI STATE IN HADHRAMAUT.

1967. *Stampex, London.* *Postage* 5, 10, 15, 20, 25 f. *Air* 50, 65 f. (20p.).
1967. *Amphilex, Amsterdam.* *Air* 75 f. (8p.).
1967. *Olympic Games, Mexico* (1968). 75 f. (8p.).
1967. *Famous Paintings.* *Postage* 5, 10, 15, 20, 25 f.; *Air* 50, 65 f. (20p.).
1967. *Scout Jamboree, Idaho.* *Air* 35 f. (5p.).
1967. *Space Research.* *Postage* 10, 25, 35, 50, 75 f.; *Air* 100, 250 f. (55p.).

Stated to have been occupied by the N.L.F. on 17th September, 1967.

MAHRA SULTANATE OF QISHN AND SOCOTRA.

1967. *Scout Jamboree, Idaho.* 15, 75, 100, 150 f. (35p.).
1967. *Kennedy.* *Postage* 10, 15, 25, 50, 75, 100, 150 f.: *Air* 250, 500 f. (1·40).
1967. *Olympic Games, Mexico* (1968). *Postage* 10, 25, 50 f.; *Air* 250, 500 f. (85p.).

Stated to have been occupied by the N.L.F. on 1st October, 1967.

Although the British Government did not officially relinquish control over Eastern Aden Protectorate (which comprises the above states) until 30th November, 1967 to the National Liberation Front (later the People's Republic of Southern Yemen) that Government claimed that the N.L.F. were in control of them on the dates given above and repudiated the contract under which the former rulers authorised some further new issues which were placed on the market. However, despite this claim there is some uncertainty as to whether any of these later issues were delivered and actually used for postal purposes.

ADDENDA AND CORRIGENDA

GREAT BRITAIN.

513. Queen Elizabeth II and Decorated Initials. (*Horiz.*—38 × 29 mm.)

(Des. Prof. R. Guyatt.)

1977 (11 May). *Silver Jubilee.* *"All-over" phosphor.* *P* 15 × 14.

1033	**513**	8½p. multicoloured ..	15	20
1035	–	10p. multicoloured ..	20	20
1036	–	11p. multicoloured ..	20	20
1037	–	13p. multicoloured ..	25	30

Nos. 1034/7 each have different decorations in the initials "E R".

ANGUILLA.

59. French Ships approaching Anguilla.

(Des. J. Lister Ltd. Litho. Questa.)

1976 (8 Nov.). *Battle for Anguilla,* 1796. *T* **59** *and similar horiz. designs.* *Multicoloured.* *P* 13½.

255	1 c. Type **59** ..	5	5
256	3 c. Sailing boat leaving Anguilla ..	5	5
257	15 c. Naval engagement ..	5	8
258	25 c. *La Vaillante* forced aground ..	10	12
259	$1 H.M.S. *Lapwing* ..	40	45
260	$1.50, *Le Desius* burning ..	60	70
255/60	*Set of* 6	1·10	1·25
MS261	205 × 103 mm. Nos. 255/60	1·25	

Nos. 256/60 are *se-tenant* within one sheet.

60. "Christmas Carnival" (A. Richardson).

(Litho. Questa.)

1976 (22 Nov.). *Christmas.* *T* **60** *and similar horiz. designs showing children's paintings.* *Multicoloured.* *P* 13½.

262	1 c. Type **60** ..	5	5
263	3 c. "Dreams of Christmas Gifts" (J. Connor) ..	5	8
264	15 c. "Carolling" (P. Richardson) ..	5	8
265	25 c. "Candle-light Procession" (A. Mussington) ..	10	12
266	$1 "Going to Church" (B. Franklin) ..	40	45
267	$1.50, "Coming Home for Christmas" (E. Gumbs) ..	60	70
262/7	*Set of* 6	1·10	1·25
MS268	232 × 147 mm. Nos. 262/7	1·25	

Nos. 263/7 are *se-tenant* within one sheet.

61. Prince Charles and H.M.S. *Minerva.*

(Des. J. Lister Ltd. Litho. Questa.)

1977 (9 Feb.). *Silver Jubilee.* *T* **61** *and similar horiz. designs.* *Multicoloured.* *P* 13½.

269	25 c. Type **61** ..	10	12
270	40 c. Prince Philip landing at Road Bay, 1964 ..	15	20
271	$1.20, Coronation scene ..	50	60
272	$2.50, Coronation regalia and map of Anguilla ..	1·00	1·10
MS273	145 × 96 mm. Nos. 269/72	1·75	

ANTIGUA.

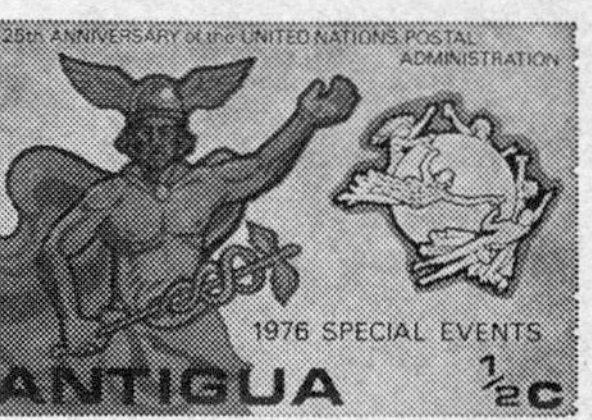

129. Mercury and U.P.U. Emblem.

(Des. BG Studio. Litho. Questa.)

1976 (28 Dec.). *Special Events,* 1976. *T* **129** *and similar horiz. designs.* *Multicoloured.* *P* 14.

519	½ c. Type **129** ..	5	5
520	1 c. Alfred Nobel ..	5	5
521	10 c. Space satellite ..	5	5
522	50 c. Viv Richards and Andy Roberts ..	20	25
523	$1 Bell and telephones ..	40	45
524	$2 Yacht *Freelance* ..	80	90
519/24	*Set of* 6	1·40	1·50
MS525	127 × 101 mm. Nos. 521/4	1·40	

Events:—½ c. 25th Anniv. of U.N. Postal Administration; 1 c. 75th Anniv. of Nobel Prize; 10 c. *Viking* Space Mission; 50 c. Cricketing achievements; $1 Telephone Centenary; $2 "Operation Sail", U.S. Bicentennial.

130. Royal Family.

(Des. J.W. Ltd. Litho. Questa.)

1977 (7 FEB.). *Silver Jubilee.* *T* **130** *and similar vert. designs. Multicoloured.* *P* 13½×14.

526	10 c. Type **130**	5	5
527	30 c. Queen Elizabeth and Prince Philip in car	12	15
528	50 c. The Queen enthroned	20	25
529	90 c. The Queen after Coronation	35	40
530	$2.50, Queen and Prince Charles	1·00	1·10
526/30	*Set of* 5	1·50	1·60
MS531	116×78 mm. $5 Queen and Prince Philip	2·00	

BARBUDA.

BARBUDA (53)	**BARBUDA** (54)

1976 (2 DEC.). *Christmas.* *Nos.* 514/18 *of Antigua optd. with T* **53**.

281	8 c. The Annunciation	5	5
282	10 c. The Holy Family	5	5
283	15 c. The Magi	5	8
284	50 c. The Shepherds	20	25
285	$1 Epiphany scene	40	45
281/5	*Set of* 5	65	75

1976 (28 DEC.). *Olympic Games, Montreal. Nos.* 495/501 *of Antigua optd. with T* **54**. *P* 14½.

286	½ c. High-jump	5	5
287	1 c. Boxing	5	5
288	2 c. Pole-vault	5	5
289	15 c. Swimming	8	10
290	30 c. Running	15	20
291	$1 Cycling	50	55
292	$2 Shot put	90	1·00
286/92	*Set of* 7	1·60	1·75
MS293	88×138 mm. Nos. 289/92. P 13½	1·75	

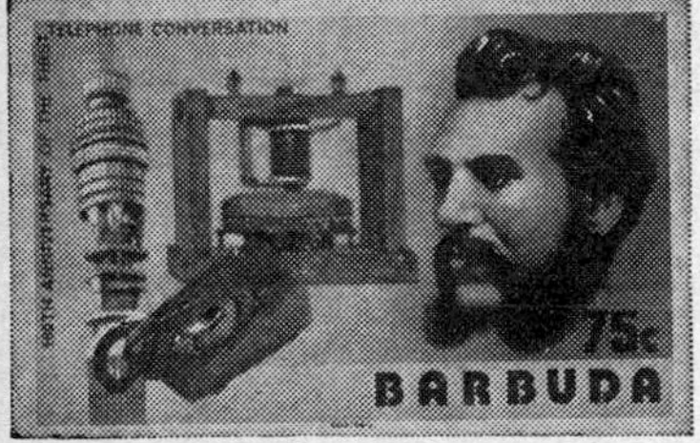

55. Post Office Tower, Telephones and Alexander Graham Bell.

(Des. G. L. Vasarhelyi. Litho. Format.)

1977 (31 JAN.). *Telephone Centenary* (1976). *T* **55** *and similar horiz. designs. Multicoloured.* *P* 13½.

294	75 c. Type **55**	30	35
295	$1.25, Dish aerial and television	50	55
296	$2 Globe and satellites	80	90
MS297	96×144 mm. Nos. 294/6. P 15	1·75	

56. St. Margaret's Church, Westminster.

(Litho.)

1977 (7 FEB.). *Silver Jubilee.* *T* **56** *and similar horiz. designs. Multicoloured.* *P* 13½×13.

298	75 c. Type **56**	30	35
299	75 c. Entrance, Westminster Abbey	30	35
300	75 c. Westminster Abbey	30	35
301	$1.25, Household Cavalry	50	55
302	$1.25, Coronation Coach	50	55
303	$1.25, Team of Horses	50	55
298/303	*Set of* 6	2·25	2·40
MS304	148×83 mm. Nos. 298/303. P 15	2·40	

Nos. 298/300 and 301/3 were printed horizontally *se-tenant*, forming composite designs.

ASCENSION.

65. Royal Visit, 1957.

(Des. J. E. Cooter. Litho. Walsall.)

1977 (7 FEB.). *Silver Jubilee.* *T* **65** *and similar horiz. designs. Multicoloured.* *W* w.**14** (*sideways on* 12 *and* 25*p.*). *P* 13½.

222	8p. Type **65**	15	20
223	12p. The Queen leaving Buckingham Palace	25	30
224	25p. Coronation Coach	50	60

AUSTRALIA.

CORRECTION: The 45 c. 1976 Christmas stamp is No. 636 and not 646.

324. "Music". **325.** Queen Elizabeth II.

(Des. Wendy Tamlyn.)

1977 (19 JAN.). *Performing Arts.* *T* **324** *and similar vert. designs. Multicoloured.* *P* 14×14½.

641	20 c. Type **324**	25	30
642	30 c. Drama	45	50
643	40 c. Dance	50	55
644	60 c. Opera	75	85

(Des. Post Office Graphic Design Section. Litho. Govt. Printer, Canberra.)

1977 (2 FEB.). *Silver Jubilee.* *T* **325** *and similar vert. design. Multicoloured.* *P* 14×14½.

645	18 c. Type **325**	20	25
646	45 c. The Queen and Prince Philip	55	65

326. Fielder and Wicket Keeper.

(Des. B. Weatherhead.)

1977 (9 MAR.). *Australia–England Test Cricket Centenary.* *T* **326** *and similar vert. designs. Multicoloured.* *P* 13½×13.

647	18 c. Type **326**	20	25
648	18 c. Umpire, batsman and scoreboard	20	25
649	18 c. Fielders	20	25
650	18 c. Batsman and umpire	20	25
651	18 c. Bowler and fielder	20	25
652	45 c. Batsman awaiting delivery	55	65
647/52	*Set of* 6	1·40	1·60

Nos. 647/51 were printed horizontally *se-tenant* within the sheet to form a composite design of a cricket match.

BAHAMAS.

CORRECTION: Change Nos. 482/**MS**486 to 483/**MS**487.

Add to Nos. 460/74:—

467	16 c. Hibiscus (9.76?)	15	20
468	21 c. As 2 c. (9.76?)	20	25
469	25 c. Hawksbill turtle (9.76?)	25	30
470	40 c. As 10 c. (9.76?)	45	50

Add to Nos. 478/81:—

MS482	100×126 mm. Nos. 478/81	1·00	

119. Queen beneath Cloth of Gold Canopy.

(46×30 *mm*)

(Des. G. L. Vasarhelyi. Litho. Cartor S.A., France.)

1977 (7 FEB.). *Silver Jubilee.* *T* **119** *and similar horiz. designs. Multicoloured.* *P* 12.

488	8 c. Type **119**	10	12
489	16 c. The Crowning	20	20
490	21 c. Taking the Oath	25	25
491	40 c. Queen with sceptre and orb	50	55
MS492	122×90 mm. Nos. 488/91	1·10	

BANGLADESH.

Add to Nos. 49/50:

50*a*	5 t. grey-blue (1975)	50	55

Add to Nos. 63/72:

68	60 p. greenish slate (1976)	5	5
69	75 p. yellow-orange (1976)	8	8
70	90 p. orange-brown (1976)	8	10

23. Hurdling (32×43 *mm.*)

(Litho. Asher & Co., Melbourne.)

1976 (Nov.). *Olympic Games, Montreal.* *T* **23** *and similar multicoloured designs.* *P* 14½.

86	25 p. Type **23**	5	5
87	30 p. Running (*horiz.*)	5	5
88	1 t. Pole vault	10	12
89	2 t. 25, Swimming (*horiz.*) ..	25	25
90	3 t. 50, Gymnastics	35	40
91	5 t. Football	55	60
86/91	.. .. .. *Set of* 6	1·10	1·25

OFFICIAL STAMPS

SERVICE

(O 1)

1973 (30 Apr.). *Nos.* 22 *etc. optd. with Type* O **1**.

O 1	**7**	2 p. black (R.)	5	5
O 2	–	3 p. blue-green	5	5
O 3	–	5 p. light brown	5	5
O 4	–	10 p. slate-black (R.) ..	5	5
O 5	–	20 p. yellow-green	5	5
O 6	–	25 p. brt. reddish mauve ..	8	8
O 7	–	60 p. greenish slate (R.) ..	8	8
O 8	–	75 p. yellow-orange ..	10	10
O 9	**8**	1 t. light violet	12	15
O10	–	5 t. grey-blue	60	65
O1/10		.. .. *Set of* 10	1·10	1·25

1974–75. *Nos.* 49/51a *optd. with Type* O **1**.

O11	**14**	1 t. light violet	12	15
O12	–	2 t. olive	15	20
O13	–	5 t. grey-blue (1975) ..	60	65

SERVICE (O 2) **SERVICE** (O 3)

1976. *Nos.* 63/7 *optd. with Type* O **2** *and No.* 71 *optd. with Type* O **3**.

O14	5 p. dp. yellow-grn. (11.2.76)	5	5
O15	10 p. slate-black (R.) (28.4.76)	5	5
O16	20 p. yellow-green (1.76)	5	5
O17	25 p. brt. reddish mve. (1.76)	8	10
O18	50 p. light purple (8.6.76) ..	10	12
O19	1 t. ultramarine (1.76) ..	12	15
O14/19	.. .. *Set of* 6	40	45

BELIZE.

Add to No. 403:—

407	4 c. *Battus belus* (7.3.77) ..	5	5
408	5 c. *Callicore patelina* (11.2.77)	5	5
409	10 c. *Callicore astala* (11.2.77)	5	5

Add to Nos. 426 *etc.*:—

428	25 c. *Papilio thoas* (7.3.77) ..	12	15
429	50 c. *Thecla bathildis* (7.3.77)	25	30

91. Queen and Bishops.

(Des. R. Granger Barrett. Litho. Enschedé.)

1977 (7 Feb.). *Silver Jubilee.* *T* **91** *and similar horiz. designs. Multicoloured.* *W* w.**14** (*sideways*). *P* 13×13½.

448	10 c. Royal Visit, 1975 ..	5	8
449	35 c. Queen and Rose window	20	25
450	$2 Type **91**	1·25	1·40

1977. *No.* 426 *surch.* "5 c" *and bar.*

451	5 c. on 15 c. *Nessaea aglaura*	5	5

BERMUDA.

101. Royal Visit, 1975.

(Des. Harrison. Litho. Walsall.)

1977 (7 Feb.). *Silver Jubilee.* *T* **101** *and similar vert. designs. Multicoloured.* *W* w.**14**. *P* 13½.

371	5 c. Type **101**	5	8
372	20 c. St. Edward Crown ..	25	30
373	$1 Queen in Chair of Estate	1·25	1·40

BOTSWANA.

108. Coronation Coach.

(Des. M. F. Bryan and G. L. Vasarhelyi. Litho. Cartor S.A., France.)

1977 (7 Feb.). *Silver Jubilee.* *T* **108** *and similar horiz. designs. Multicoloured.* *P* 12.

391	4 t. Queen and Sir Seretse Khama	5	5
392	25 t. Type **108**	35	40
393	40 t. The Recognition ..	55	65

BRITISH ANTARCTIC TERRITORY.

23. Sperm Whale.

(*Illustration reduced. Actual size* 59×22 *mm.*)

(Des. J. E. Cooter. Litho. Questa.)

1977 (4 Jan.). *Whale Conservation.* *T* **23** *and similar horiz. designs.* *W* w.**14** (*sideways*). *P* 13½.

79	2p. brownish black, slate and bright blue	5	5
80	8p. grey, brownish blk. & rosine	15	20
81	11p. multicoloured	20	25
82	25p. grey-blue, brownish black and light blue-green ..	50	55

Designs:—8p. Fin Whale; 11p. Humpback Whale; 25p. Blue Whale.

24. The Queen Before Taking the Oath.

(Des. J.W. Ltd. Litho. Questa.)

1977 (7 Feb.). *Silver Jubilee.* *T* **24** *and similar horiz. designs. Multicoloured.* *W* w.**14** (*sideways*). *P* 13½.

83	6p. Prince Philip's visit, 1956/7	12	15
84	11p. Coronation Oath	25	25
85	33p. Type **24**	65	75

CANADA.

Add to No. 700:—

a. Perf. 13	8	10

398. *Northcote.*

(Des. T. Bjarnason. Recess & litho. C.B.N.)

1976 (19 Nov.). *Inland Vessels.* *T* **398** *and similar horiz. designs.* *P* 12×12½.

851	10 c. ochre, chestnut and black	12	15
852	10 c. bright blue and black ..	12	15
853	10 c. violet-blue and black ..	12	15
854	10 c. apple-green, olive-green and black	12	15

Designs:—No. 851, Type **398**; No. 852, *Chicora*; No. 853, *Passport*; No. 854, *Athabasca*.

Nos. 851/4 were printed in *se-tenant* combinations throughout a sheet of 50, giving 10 blocks of 4 and 10 single stamps.

399. Queen Elizabeth II. **400.** Queen Elizabeth II.

(Des. K. Rodmell from photograph by P. Grugeon. Photo. Ashton-Potter.)

1977 (4 Feb.). *Silver Jubilee.* *P* 12½×12.

855	**399**	25 c. multicoloured ..	30	35

(Des. Heather Cooper from bas-relief by J. Huta. Photo. and recess. B.A.B.N.)

1977 (1 Mar.). *P* 13.

862	**400**	12 c. lt. vio.-bl., grey & blk.	12	15

No. 862 is the first of a new definitive series to which Nos. 856/75 have been allocated.

CAYMAN ISLANDS.

119. Queen and Westminster Abbey.

(Des. BG Studio. Litho. Questa.)

1977 (7 FEB.). *Silver Jubilee. T* **119** *and similar multicoloured designs. W* w.**14** (*sideways on* 50 c.). *P* 13$\frac{1}{2}$.

227	8 c. Prince of Wales' visit, 1973	12	15
228	30 c. Type **119**	45	50
229	50 c. Preparation for the Anointing (*horiz.*)	75	85

COOK ISLANDS.

158. Mangaia Kingfisher on $5 Coin.

1976 (15 Nov.). *Wildlife Conservation. P* 13.

563 **158**	$1 multicoloured	1·00	1·10

159. Imperial State Crown.

1977 (7 FEB.). *Silver Jubilee. T* **159** *and similar vert. designs. Multicoloured. P* 13.

564	25 c. Type **159**	25	30
565	25 c. Queen with regalia	25	30
566	50 c. Westminster Abbey	55	65
567	50 c. Coronation Coach	55	65
568	$1 Queen and Prince Philip	1·10	1·25
569	$1 Investiture of Sir Albert Henry	1·10	1·25
564/9	*Set of* 6	3·50	3·75
MS570	130 × 136 mm. Nos. 564/9	3·75	

AITUTAKI.

CORRECTION: Nos. 209/16 are all surcharged "+1c.", and not "+2c." as listed. Stamps from **MS**217, however, do have a "+2c." surcharge.

32. Alexander Graham Bell and First Telephone.

1977 (3 MAR.). *Telephone Centenary* (1976). *T* **32** *and similar horiz. design. P* 13.

218	25 c. blk., gold and dull scarlet	25	30
219	70 c. black, gold and lilac	75	85
MS220	116 × 59 mm. Nos. 218/19	1·10	

Design:—70 c. Earth Station and satellite.

CYPRUS.

188. "Cyprus 74" (wood-engraving by A. Tassos.)

1977 (10 JAN.). *Obligatory Tax. Refugee Fund. W* **58**. *P* 12$\frac{1}{2}$ × 12.

481 **188**	10 m. grey-black	5	5

DOMINICA.

147. Island Craft Co-operative.

(Des. G. Drummond. Litho. Questa.)

1976 (Nov.). *National Day. T* **147** *and similar horiz. designs. Multicoloured. P* 13$\frac{1}{2}$.

550	10 c. Type **147**	5	5
551	50 c. Harvesting bananas	20	25
552	$1 Boxing plant	40	45
MS553	96 × 122 mm. Nos. 550/2	70	

148. Common Sundial.

(Des. J.W. Ltd. Litho. Questa.)

1976 (DEC.). *Shells. T* **148** *and similar vert. designs. Multicoloured. P* 14.

554	$\frac{1}{2}$ c. Type **148**	5	5
555	1 c. Flame Helmet	5	5
556	2 c. Mouse Cone	5	5
557	20 c. Caribbean Vase	8	10
558	40 c. West Indian Fighting Conch	15	20
559	50 c. Short Coral Shell	20	25
560	$3 Apple Murex	1·25	1·40
554/60	*Set of* 7	1·50	1·75
MS561	101 × 55 mm. $2 Long-spined Star Shell	80	

149. The Queen Crowned and Enthroned.

(Des. J.W. Ltd. Litho. Questa.)

1977 (7 FEB.). *Silver Jubilee. T* **149** *and similar horiz. designs. Multicoloured. P* 14 × 13$\frac{1}{2}$.

562	$\frac{1}{2}$ c. Type **149**	5	5
563	1 c. Imperial State Crown	5	5
564	45 c. Queen Elizabeth and Princess Anne	20	20
565	$2 Coronation Ring	80	90
566	$2.50, Ampulla and Spoon	1·00	1·10
562/6	*Set of* 5	1·90	2·10
MS567	104 × 79 mm. $5 Queen Elizabeth and Prince Philip	2·00	

FIJI.

160. Map of the World.

(Des. J.W. Ltd. Litho. Walsall.)

1977 (12 APR.). *E.E.C./A.C.P.* Council of Ministers Conference, Fiji. T* **160** *and similar horiz. design. Multicoloured. W* w.**14** (*sideways*). *P* 14.

539	4 c. Type **160**	5	5
540	30 c. Map of Fiji group	40	45

*A.C.P. = African, Caribbean Pacific Group.

GAMBIA.

94. Stone Circles, Kuntaur.

(Des. J.W. Ltd. Litho. Questa.)

1977 (18 Feb.). *Tourism.* T **94** *and similar horiz. designs. Multicoloured.* P 14.

368	25 b. Type **94**	12	15
369	50 b. Ruined fort, James Is.	25	30
370	1 d. 25, Mungo Park Monument	60	70

GHANA.

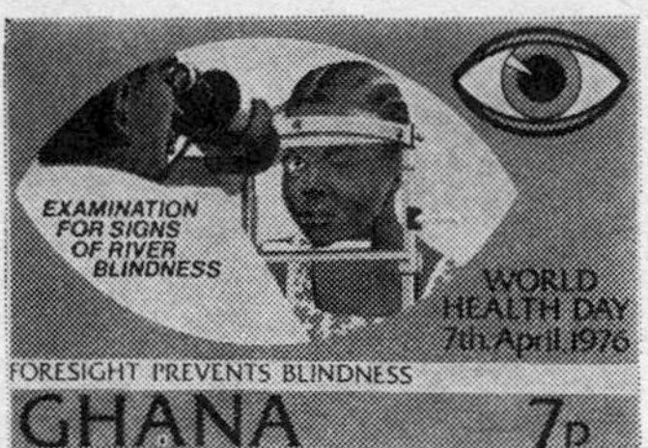

353. Examination for River Blindness.

(Des. and litho. D.L.R.)

1976 (28 Oct.). *Prevention of Blindness.* T **353** *and similar horiz. designs. Multicoloured.* P 14 × 13½.

782	7 p. Type **353**	5	5
783	30 p. Entomologist	25	30
784	60 p. Normal vision	50	55
785	1 c. Blackfly eradication	85	95

354. Alexander Graham Bell and "Gallows Frame" Telephone.

(Des. A. S. Larkins. Litho. Format.)

1976 (Oct.). *Telephone Centenary. Horiz. designs each with Bell's portrait, as in* T **354.** *Multicoloured.* P 13.

786	8 p. Type **354**	5	8
787	30 p. 1895 telephone	25	30
788	60 p. 1929 telephone	50	55
789	1 c. 1976 telephone	85	95
MS790	125 × 91 mm. 15, 40, 65 and 80 p. as Nos. 786/9	1·60	

355. Fireworks Party, Christmas Eve.

(Des. A. Adom & A. S. Larkins. Litho. D.L.R.)

1976 (15 Dec.). *Christmas.* T **355** *and similar horiz. designs. Multicoloured.* P 13.

791	6 p. Type **355**	5	5
792	8 p. Children and gifts	5	8
793	30 p. Christmas feast	25	30
794	1 c. As 8 p.	85	95
MS795	122 × 98 mm. 15, 40, 65 and 80 p. as Nos. 791/4	1·60	

1977 (22 Feb.). *Olympic Winners. Nos. 773/6 optd. with the name of the country given.* P 13½.

796	7 p. East Germany	5	5
797	30 p. East Germany	25	30
798	60 p. U.S.S.R.	50	55
799	1 c. U.S.A.	85	95
MS800	103 × 135 mm. 15, 40, 65 and 80 p. as Nos. 796/9	1·75	

GIBRALTAR.

111. Toothed Orchid.

(Des. A. G. Ryman. Litho. Questa.)

1977 (1 Apr.). *Various multicoloured designs as* T **111.** W w.**14** *(sideways on horiz. designs).* P 14.

374	½p. Type **111**	5	5
375	1p. Red Mullet	5	5
376	2p. Large Blue butterfly	5	5
377	2½p. Sardinian Warbler	5	5
378	3p. Giant Squill	5	5
379	4p. Grey Wrasse	8	8
380	5p. Red Admiral butterfly	8	10
381	6p. Black Kite	10	12
382	9p. Shrubby Scorpion-vetch	15	20
383	10p. John Dory (fish)	20	20
384	12p. Clouded Yellow butterfly	20	25
385	20p. Adouin's Gull	40	45
386	25p. Barbary Nut (iris)	45	50
387	50p. Swordfish	85	95
388	£1 Swallow-tail butterfly	1·75	2·00
389	£2 Hoopoe	3·50	4·00
374/89	*Set of* 16	7·00	8·00

The 1, 2, 4, 5, 10, 12, 50p. and £1 are horizontal designs.

GRENADA.

227. "Altarpiece of San Barbara" (Botticelli).

(Des. PAD Studio. Litho. Questa.)

1976 (8 Dec.). *Christmas.* T **227** *and similar horiz. designs. Multicoloured.* P 14.

841	½ c. Type **227**	5	5
842	1 c. "Annunciation" (Botticelli)	5	5
843	2 c. "Madonna with Chancellor Rolin" (van Eyck)	5	5
844	35 c. "Annunciation" (Fra Filippo Lippi)	15	15
845	50 c. "Madonna of the Magnificat" (Botticelli)	20	25
846	75 c. "Madonna of the Pomegranate" (Botticelli)	30	35
847	$3 "Madonna with St. Cosmas and Other Saints" (Botticelli)	1·25	1·40
841/7	*Set of* 7	1·75	2·00
MS848	71 × 57 mm. $2 "Gypsy Madonna" (Titian)	80	

228. Alexander Graham Bell and Telephones.

(Des. G. L. Vasarhelyi. Litho. Questa.)

1976 (17 Dec.). *Telephone Centenary.* T **228** *and similar horiz. designs. Multicoloured.* P 14.

849	½ c. Type **228**	5	5
850	1 c. Telephone-users within globe	5	5
851	2 c. Telephone satellite	5	5
852	18 c. Telephone viewer and console	8	10
853	40 c. Satellite and tracking stations	15	20
854	$1 Satellite transmitting to ships	40	45
855	$2 Dish aerial and modern telephone	80	90
849/55	*Set of* 7	1·40	1·60
MS856	107 × 80 mm. $5 Globe encircled by flags	1·75	

229. Coronation Scene.

(Des. J.W. Ltd. Litho. Questa.)

1977 (8 Feb.). *Silver Jubilee.* T **229** *and similar vert. designs. Multicoloured.*

(*a*) P 13½ × 14.

857	½ c. Type **229**	5	5
858	1 c. Sceptre and Orb	5	5
859	35 c. Queen on horseback	15	15
860	$2 Spoon and Ampulla	80	90
861	$2.50, Queen and Prince Philip	1·00	1·10
857/61	*Set of* 5	1·75	1·90
MS862	103 × 79 mm. $5 Royal Visit to Grenada	2·00	

(*b*) *From booklets. Self-adhesive. Imperf.* × *roul.*

863	35 c. As No. 861	15	15
864	50 c. As No. 860	20	25
	a. Booklet pane. Nos. 864/6 *se-tenant*	2·00	
865	$1 As No. 858	40	45
866	$3 As No. 859	1·25	1·40

GRENADINES OF GRENADA.

18. Bell and First Telephone.

(Des. G. L. Vasarhelyi. Litho. Questa.)

1977 (Jan.). *Telephone Centenary* (1976). *Horiz. designs each showing Alexander Graham Bell as T* **18**. *Multicoloured. P* 14.

207	½ c. Type **18**	5	5
208	1 c. Telephone, 1895	5	5
209	2 c. Telephone, 1900	5	5
210	35 c. Telephone, 1915	15	15
211	75 c. Telephone, 1920	30	35
212	$1 Telephone, 1929	40	45
213	$2 Telephone, 1963	80	90
207/213	.. .. *Set of* 7	1·60	1·75
MS214	107×78 mm. $3 Telephone, 1976	65	

19. Coronation Coach.

(Des. Jennifer Toombs. Litho. & embossed. Walsall.)

1977 (8 Feb.). *Silver Jubilee. T* **19** *and similar horiz. designs. Multicoloured. P* 13½.

215	35 c. Type **19**	15	15
216	$2 Queen entering Abbey ..	80	90
217	$4 The Queen crowned ..	1·75	2·00
MS218	100×70 mm. $5 The Mall on Coronation Night ..	2·00	

GUYANA.

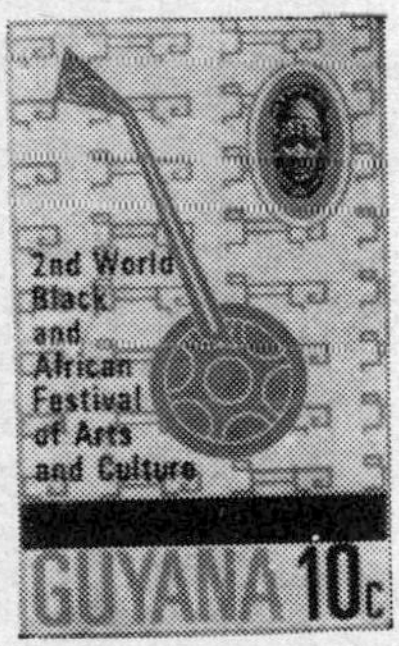

159. Festival Emblem and "Musical Instrument".

(Des. C. Henriques. Litho. Questa.)

1977 (1 Feb.). *Second World Black and African Festival of Arts and Culture, Nigeria. W* **106**. *P* 14.

666	**159**	10 c. dull red, black & gold	5	8
667	,,	35 c. dp. violet, blk. & gold	15	20
668	,,	50 c. ultram., blk. & gold	20	25
669	,,	$1 blue-grn., blk. & gold	45	50
MS670		90×157 mm. Nos. 666/9	90	

The above were scheduled for release in 1975, and when finally issued had the original inscription obliterated and a new one applied by overprinting.

INDIA.

Add to No. 521:—

520*a*	**461**	2 p. red-brown (1975) ..	5	5

721. Swamp Deer.

(Des. from photos by Rajesh Bedi.)

1976 (1 Oct.). *Wildlife. T* **721** *and similar multicoloured designs. P* 14×14½ (25, 50 *p.*) *or* 14½×14 (*others*).

825	25 p. Type **721**	5	5
826	50 p. Lion	5	5
827	1 r. Leopard (*horiz.*)	10	12
828	2 r. Caracal (*horiz.*)	20	25

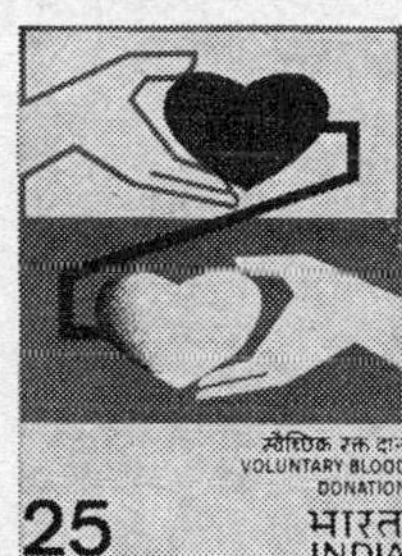

722. Hands holding Hearts.

(Des. B. G. Varma.)

1976 (1 Oct.). *Voluntary Blood Donation. P* 13.

829	**722**	25p. yellow-ochre, scarlet and black	5	5

723. Suryakant Tripathi ("Nirala").

1976 (15 Oct.). *80th Birth Anniv. of "Nirala" (poet and novelist). P* 13.

830	**723**	25p. deep blue	5	5

724. Painting of Folk-tale (H. D. Bhatia).

1976 (14 Nov.). *Children's Day. P* 13½×14.

831	**724**	25 p. multicoloured ..	5	5

725. Hiralal Shastri (politician).

1976 (24 Nov.). *Shastri Commemoration. P* 13.

832	**725**	25 p. sepia	5	5

726. Dr. Hari Singh Gour (lawyer).

1976 (26 Nov.). *Dr. Gour Commemoration. P* 13.

833	**726**	25 p. deep reddish purple	5	5

727. A300 B2 Airbus.

1976 (1 Dec.). *Inauguration of Indian Airlines' Airbus. P* 14½×14.

834	**727**	2 r. multicoloured ..	20	25

728. Hybrid Coconut Palm.

1976 (27 Dec.). *50th Anniv. of Coconut Research. P* 13.

835	**728**	25 p. multicoloured ..	5	5

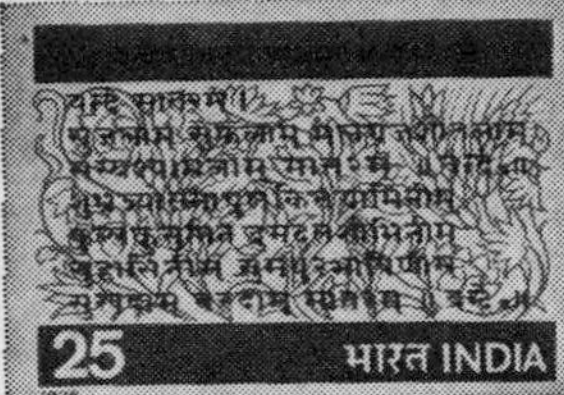

729. First Stanza of *Vande Mataram* (patriotic song by B. C. Chatterjee).

1976 (30 Dec.). *"Vande Mataram" Commemoration.* *P* 13.

836	**729**	25 p. multicoloured ..	5	5

730. Globe and Film Strip.

1977 (3 Jan.). *Sixth International Film Festival of India, New Delhi.* *P* 13.

837	**730**	2 r. multicoloured ..	20	20

731. Seismograph and Crack in Earth's Crust.

1977 (10 Jan.). *Sixth World Conference on Earthquake Engineering, New Delhi.* *P* 13.

838	**731**	2 r. deep plum	20	20

JAMAICA.

(Des L. D. Curtis. Litho. J.W.)

1977 (28 Feb.). *17th Century Maps of Jamaica. Designs as T* **186**. *W* **111** (*sideways*). *P* 13.

425	9 c. multicoloured	12	15
426	10 c. multicoloured	12	15
427	25 c. grey-black, pale and bright blue	30	35
428	40 c. grey-black, light turquoise and grey-blue ..	50	55

Designs:—9 c. Hickeringill map, 1661; 10 c. Ogilby map, 1671; 25 c. Visscher map, 1680; 40 c. Thornton map, 1689.

KENYA.

59. Nile Perch.

(Des. A. Kennaway. Litho. Format.)

1977 (10 Jan.). *Game Fish of East Africa. T* **59** *and similar vert. designs. Multicoloured. P* 14.

275	50 c. Type **59**	5	8
276	1s. Tilapia	12	15
277	3s. Sailfish	35	40
278	5s. Black Marlin	60	70

60. Maasai Manyatta (animal slaughter), Kenya.

(Des. Mrs. R. Fennessy. Litho. Questa.)

1977 (15 Jan.). *Second World Black and African Festival of Arts and Culture, Nigeria. T* **60** *and similar horiz. designs. Multicoloured. P* 13½.

279	50 c. Type **60**	5	8
280	1s. "Heartbeat of Africa" (Ugandan dancers) ..	12	15
281	2s. Makonde sculpture, Tanzania	25	30
282	3s. "Early Man and Technology" (skinning animal)	35	40
MS283	132 × 109 mm. Nos. 279/82	80	

LESOTHO.

103. "Rising Sun".

(Des. L. D. Curtis. Litho. Questa.)

1976 (4 Oct.). *Tenth Anniv. of Independence. T* **103** *and similar vert. designs. Multicoloured. W* **53**. *P* 14.

314	4 c. Type **103**	5	5
315	10 c. Open gates	12	15
316	15 c. Broken chains	20	20
317	25 c. Aeroplane over hotel ..	30	35

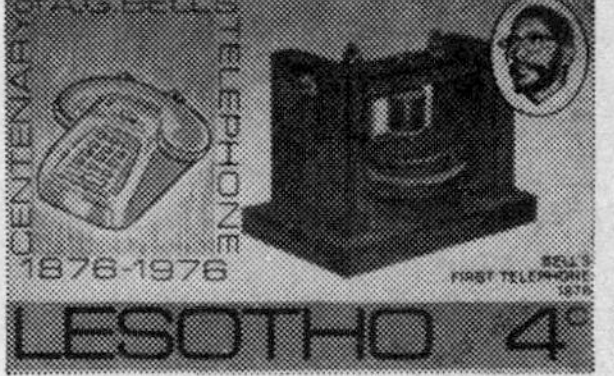

104. Telephones, 1876 and 1976.

(Des. and litho. J.W.)

1976 (6 Dec.). *Telephone Centenary. T* **104** *and similar horiz. designs. Multicoloured. W* **53** (*sideways*). *P* 13.

318	4 c. Type **104**	5	5
319	10 c. Early handset and telephone-user, 1976 ..	12	15
320	15 c. Wall telephone and telephone exchange	20	25
321	25 c. Stick telephone and Alexander Graham Bell	35	40

105. *Aloe striatula.*

(Des. Dick Findlay. Litho. Walsall.)

1977 (14 Feb.). *Aloes and Succulents. T* **105** *and similar vert. designs. Multicoloured. W* **53**. *P* 14.

322	3 c. Type **105**	5	5
323	4 c. *Aloe aristata*	5	5
324	5 c. *Kniphofia caulescens* ..	5	8
325	10 c. *Euphorbia pulvinata* ..	12	15
326	15 c. *Aloe saponaria*	20	25
327	20 c. *Caralluma lutea*	25	30
328	25 c. *Aloe polyphylla*	35	40
322/8	.. .. *Set of* 7	1·00	1·10

106. Rock Rabbit.

(Des. Dick Findlay. Litho. Questa.)

1977 (25 Apr.). *Animals. T* **106** *and similar horiz. designs. Multicoloured. W* **53** *(sideways). P* 14.

329	4 c. Type **106**		5	5
330	5 c. Porcupine		5	8
331	10 c. Polecat		12	15
332	15 c. Klipspringer		20	25
333	25 c. Baboon		35	40
329/33		*Set of* 5	70	80

MALAWI.

Add to Nos. 537/40:—
MS541 135 × 95 mm. Nos. 537/40 1·00

MALTA.

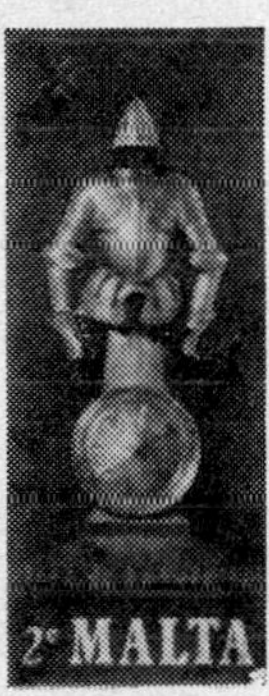

237. Jean de la Valette's Armour.

(Des. J. Briffa.)

1977 (20 Jan.). *Suits of Armour. T* **237** *and similar vert. designs. Multicoloured. W* **105.** *P* 13½.

572	2 c. Type **237**	5	8
573	7 c. Aloph de Wignacourt's armour	20	25
574	11 c. Jean Jacques de Verdelin's armour	30	30

MAURITIUS.

162. The Queen with Sceptre and Rod.

(Des. L. D. Curtis. Litho. Harrison.)

1977 (7 Feb.). *Silver Jubilee. T* **162** *and similar vert. designs. Multicoloured. W* w.**14** *(sideways). P* 14½ × 14.

516	50 c. The Queen at Mauritius Legislative Assembly, 1972	8	10
517	75 c. Type **162**	12	12
518	5 r. Presentation of Sceptre and Rod	75	85

NEW HEBRIDES.

80. Royal Visit, 1974.

(Des. BG Studio. Litho. Walsall.)

1977 (7 Feb.). *Silver Jubilee. T* **80** *and similar vert. designs. Multicoloured. W* w.**14.** *P* 13½.

217	35 c. Type **80**	15	15
218	70 c. Imperial State Crown	30	35
219	2 f. The Blessing	80	90

NEW ZEALAND.

359. Arms of Hamilton.

(Des. P. L. Blackie. Litho. Harrison.)

1977 (19 Jan.). *Anniversaries. T* **359** *and similar vert. designs. Multicoloured. P* 13 × 13½.

1132	8 c. Type **359**	8	10
1133	8 c. Arms of Gisbourne	8	10
1134	8 c. Arms of Masterton	8	10
1135	10 c. A.A. emblem	10	12
1136	10 c. Arms of the College of Surgeons	10	12
1132/6	*Set of* 5	40	50

Events:—Nos. 1132/4 City Centenaries; No. 1135, 75th Anniv. of the Automobile Association in New Zealand; No. 1136, 50th Anniv. of Royal Australasian College of Surgeons.

PAKISTAN.

The following illustration goes with the listing on page 716:—

252. Dancing-girl, Ruins and King Priest.

(*Illustration reduced. Actual size* 65 × 22 *mm.*)

257. Children Reading.

(Des. M. Ahmed.)

1976 (15 Dec.). *Children's Literature. P* 13.
435 **257** 20 p. multicoloured 5 5

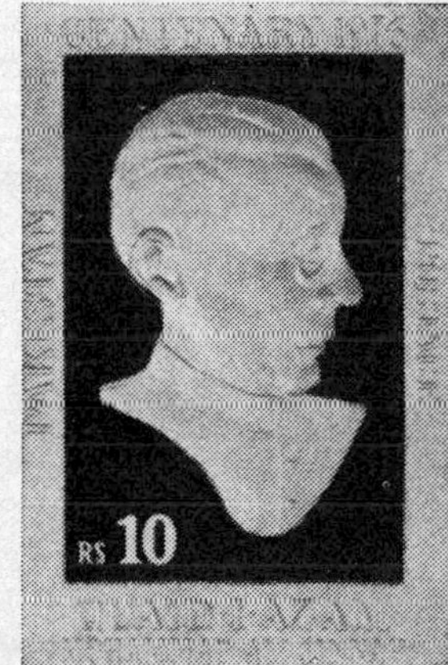

258. Mahomed Ali Jinnah.

(Litho. and embossed. Cartor SA, France.)

1976 (25 Dec.). *Birth Centenary of Mahomed Ali Jinnah (2nd issue). P* 12½.
436 **258** 10 r. emerald and gold 1·00 1·10

PAPUA NEW GUINEA.

202. National Flag and Queen Elizabeth II.

(Des. and photo. Harrison.)

1977 (16 Mar.). *Silver Jubilee. Horiz. designs showing Queen Elizabeth as T* **202.** *Multicoloured. P* 14½ × 14.

320	7 t. Type **202**	12	15
321	15 t. National emblem	25	30
322	35 t. Map of P.N.G.	55	65

ST. LUCIA.

102. Queen Elizabeth II.

(Des. Daphne Padden. Litho. Questa.)

977 (7 Feb.). *Silver Jubilee. W* w.**14** (*sideways*). *P* 14.

43 **102** 10 c. multicoloured .. 5 5
44 ,, 20 c. multicoloured .. 8 10
45 ,, 40 c. multicoloured .. 15 20
46 ,, $2 multicoloured .. 80 90
IS447 128×95 mm. Nos. 443/6 1·10

ST. VINCENT.

he following illustration goes with the listing on age 786:—

88. St. Mary's Church, Kingstown.

SEYCHELLES.

Idd to Nos. 369/72. B. *Chalky paper* (7.3.77):—

69B 20 c. Type **98** 5 5
70B 1 r. 25, Seychelles Sunbird 20 25
71B 1 r. 50, Seychelles White-eye 25 30
72B 5 r. Seychelles Black Parrot 75 80

The original stamps were on ordinary paper.

SINGAPORE.

100. Radar, Missile and Soldiers.

(Des. Eng. Siak Loy. Litho. Harrison.)

977 (12 Mar.). *Tenth Anniv. of National Service. T* **100** *and similar vert. designs. Multicoloured. P* 14.

86 10 c. Type **100** 5 5
87 50 c. Tank and soldiers .. 20 25
88 75 c. Soldiers, wireless operators, pilot and aircraft .. 30 35

SOUTH AFRICA.

Add to Nos. 370 *etc.*:—

(371) b. P 14. Chalk-surfaced paper (11.76?) 5 5

SRI LANKA.

230. Kandyan Crown.

(Des. R. B. Mawilmada. Litho. Toppan Ptg. Co., Japan.)

1977 (18 Jan.). *Regalia of the Kings of Kandy. T* **230** *and similar vert. design. Multicoloured. P* 13.

637 1 r. Type **230** 15 15
638 2 r. Throne and footstool .. 30 30

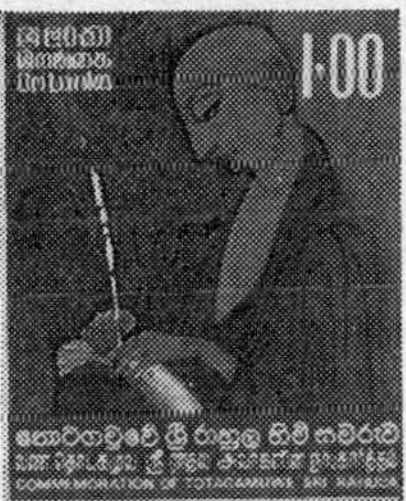

231. Sri Rahula Thero (poet).

(Des. S. Dissanayaka. Litho. Toppan Ptg. Co., Japan.)

1977 (23 Feb.). *Sri Rahula Commemoration. P* 13.

639 **231** 1 r. multicoloured .. 30 30

232. Sir Ponnambalam Arunachalam (social reformer).

(Litho. Toppan Ptg. Co., Japan.)

1977 (10 Mar.). *Ponnambalam Arunachalam Commemoration. P* 13.

640 **232** 1 r. multicoloured .. 30 30

SWAZILAND.

67. Matsapa College.

(Des. J. E. Cooter. Litho. Questa.)

1977 (2 May). *50th Anniv. of Police Training. T* **67** *and similar multicoloured designs. W* w.**14** (*upright on* 20 c., *sideways on others*). *P* 14.

271 5 c. Type **67** 5 8
272 10 c. Uniformed police and land rover 12 15
273 20 c. Police badge (*vert.*) .. 25 30
274 25 c. Dog handling 35 40

TANZANIA.

1977 (10 Jan.). *Game Fish of East Africa. As Nos.* 275/8 *of Kenya.*

192 50 c. Nile Perch 5 8
193 1s. Tilapia 12 15
194 3s. Sailfish 35 40
195 5s. Black Marlin 60 70

1977 (15 Jan.). *Second World Black and African Festival of Arts and Culture, Nigeria. As Nos.* 279/82 *of Kenya.*

196 50 c. Maasai Manyatta (animal slaughter) 5 8
197 1s. "Heartbeat of Africa" (Ugandan dancers) .. 12 15
198 2s. Makonde sculpture .. 25 30
199 3s. "Early Man and Technology" (skinning animal) 35 40
MS200 132×109 mm. Nos. 196/9 80

UGANDA.

1977 (10 Jan.). *Game Fish of East Africa. As Nos.* 275/8 *of Kenya.*

178 50 c. Nile Perch 5 8
179 1s. Tilapia 12 15
180 3s. Sailfish 35 40
181 5s. Black Marlin 60 70

1977 (15 Jan.). *Second World Black and African Festival of Arts and Culture, Nigeria. As Nos.* 279/82 *of Kenya.*

182 50 c. Maasai Manyatta (animal slaughter) 5 8
183 1s. "Heartbeat of Africa" (Ugandan dancers) .. 12 15
184 2s. Makonde sculpture .. 25 30
185 3s. "Early Man and Technology" (skinning animal) 35 40
MS186 132×109 mm. Nos. 182/5 80

NOTE. The first Supplement recording new stamps not in this Catalogue or the Addenda, appeared in the June, 1977 number of *Stamp Monthly*.